PETERSON'S®
GRADUATE PROGRAMS
IN BUSINESS, EDUCATION,
INFORMATION STUDIES,
LAW & SOCIAL WORK

2019

About Peterson's

Peterson's® has been your trusted educational publisher for over 50 years. It's a milestone we're quite proud of, as we continue to offer the most accurate, dependable, high-quality educational content in the field, providing you with everything you need to succeed. No matter where you are on your academic or professional path, you can rely on Peterson's for its books, online information, expert test-prep tools, the most up-to-date education exploration data, and the highest quality career success resources—everything you need to achieve your education goals. For our complete line of products, visit **www.petersons.com**.

For more information about Peterson's range of educational products, contact Peterson's, 8740 Lucent Blvd., Suite 400 Highlands Ranch, CO 80129, or find us online at **www.petersons.com**.

CONTENTS

ACADEMIC AND PROFESSIONAL PROGRAMS IN LAW

ACADEMIC AND PROFESSIONAL PROGRAMS IN LIBRARY AND INFORMATION STUDIES

ACADEMIC AND PROFESSIONAL PROGRAMS IN PHYSICAL EDUCATION, SPORTS, AND RECREATION

ACADEMIC AND PROFESSIONAL PROGRAMS IN SOCIAL WORK

APPENDIXES

INDEXES

A Note from the Peterson's Editors

The six volumes of Peterson's *Graduate and Professional Programs*, the only annually updated reference work of its kind, provide wide-ranging information on the graduate and professional programs offered by accredited colleges and universities in the United States, U.S. territories, and Canada and by those institutions outside the United States that are accredited by U.S. accrediting bodies. More than 44,000 individual academic and professional programs at nearly 2,300 institutions are listed. Peterson's *Graduate and Professional Programs* have been used for more than fifty years by prospective graduate and professional students, placement counselors, faculty advisers, and all others interested in postbaccalaureate education.

Graduate & Professional Programs: An Overview contains information on institutions as a whole, while the other books in the series are devoted to specific academic and professional fields:

- *Graduate Programs in the Biological/Biomedical Sciences & Health-Related Medical Professions*

- *Graduate Programs in Business, Education, Information Studies, Law & Social Work*

- *Graduate Programs in Engineering & Applied Sciences*

- *Graduate Programs in the Humanities, Arts & Social Sciences*

- *Graduate Programs in the Physical Sciences, Mathematics, Agricultural Sciences, the Environment & Natural Resources*

The books may be used individually or as a set. For example, if you have chosen a field of study but do not know what institution you want to attend or if you have a college or university in mind but have not chosen an academic field of study, it is best to begin with the Overview guide.

Graduate & Professional Programs: An Overview presents several directories to help you identify programs of study that might interest you; you can then research those programs further in the other books in the series by using the Directory of Graduate and Professional Programs by Field, which lists 500 fields and gives the names of those institutions that offer graduate degree programs in each.

For geographical or financial reasons, you may be interested in attending a particular institution and will want to know what it has to offer. You should turn to the Directory of Institutions and Their Offerings, which lists the degree programs available at each institution. As in the Directory of Graduate and Professional Programs by Field, the level of degrees offered is also indicated.

All books in the series include advice on graduate education, including topics such as admissions tests, financial aid, and accreditation. **The Graduate Adviser** includes two essays and information about accreditation. The first essay, "The Admissions Process," discusses general admission requirements, admission tests, factors to consider when selecting a graduate school or program, when and how to apply, and how admission decisions are made. Special information for international students and tips for minority students are also included. The second essay, "Financial Support," is an overview of the broad range of support available at the graduate level. Fellowships, scholarships, and grants; assistantships and internships; federal and private loan programs, as well as Federal Work-Study; and the GI bill are detailed. This essay concludes with advice on applying for need-based financial aid. "Accreditation and Accrediting Agencies" gives information on accreditation and its purpose and lists institutional accrediting agencies first and then specialized accrediting agencies relevant to each volume's specific fields of study.

With information on more than 40,000 graduate programs in more than 500 disciplines, Peterson's *Graduate and Professional Programs* give you all the information you need about the programs that are of interest to you in three formats: **Profiles** (capsule summaries of basic information), **Displays** (information that an institution or program wants to emphasize), and **Close-Ups** (written by administrators, with more expansive information than the **Profiles**, emphasizing different aspects of the programs). By using these various formats of program information, coupled with **Appendixes** and **Indexes** covering directories and subject areas for all six books, you will find that these guides provide the most comprehensive, accurate, and up-to-date graduate study information available.

Peterson's publishes a full line of resources with information you need to guide you through the graduate admissions process. Peterson's publications can be found at college libraries and career centers and your local bookstore or library—or visit us on the Web at www.petersons.com.

Colleges and universities will be pleased to know that Peterson's helped you in your selection. Admissions staff members are more than happy to answer questions, address specific problems, and help in any way they can. The editors at Peterson's wish you great success in your graduate program search!

THE GRADUATE ADVISER

THE GRADUATE ADVISER

The Admissions Process

Generalizations about graduate admissions practices are not always helpful because each institution has its own set of guidelines and procedures. Nevertheless, some broad statements can be made about the admissions process that may help you plan your strategy.

Factors Involved in Selecting a Graduate School or Program

Selecting a graduate school and a specific program of study is a complex matter. Quality of the faculty; program and course offerings; the nature, size, and location of the institution; admission requirements; cost; and the availability of financial assistance are among the many factors that affect one's choice of institution. Other considerations are job placement and achievements of the program's graduates and the institution's resources, such as libraries, laboratories, and computer facilities. If you are to make the best possible choice, you need to learn as much as you can about the schools and programs you are considering before you apply.

The following steps may help you narrow your choices.

- Talk to alumni of the programs or institutions you are considering to get their impressions of how well they were prepared for work in their fields of study.
- Remember that graduate school requirements change, so be sure to get the most up-to-date information possible.
- Talk to department faculty members and the graduate adviser at your undergraduate institution. They often have information about programs of study at other institutions.
- Visit the websites of the graduate schools in which you are interested to request a graduate catalog. Contact the department chair in your chosen field of study for additional information about the department and the field.
- Visit as many campuses as possible. Call ahead for an appointment with the graduate adviser in your field of interest and be sure to check out the facilities and talk to students.

General Requirements

Graduate schools and departments have requirements that applicants for admission must meet. Typically, these requirements include undergraduate transcripts (which provide information about undergraduate grade point average and course work applied toward a major), admission test scores, and letters of recommendation. Most graduate programs also ask for an essay or personal statement that describes your personal reasons for seeking graduate study. In some fields, such as art and music, portfolios or auditions may be required in addition to other evidence of talent. Some institutions require that the applicant have an undergraduate degree in the same subject as the intended graduate major.

Most institutions evaluate each applicant on the basis of the applicant's total record, and the weight accorded any given factor varies widely from institution to institution and from program to program.

The Application Process

You should begin the application process at least one year before you expect to begin your graduate study. Find out the application deadline for each institution (many are provided in the **Profile** section of this guide). Go to the institution's website and find out if you can apply online. If not, request a paper application form. Fill out this form thoroughly and neatly. Assume that the school needs all the information it is requesting and that the admissions officer will be sensitive to the neatness and overall quality of what you submit. Do not supply more information than the school requires.

The institution may ask at least one question that will require a three- or four-paragraph answer. Compose your response on the assumption that the admissions officer is interested in both what you think and how you express yourself. Keep your statement brief and to the point, but, at the same time, include all pertinent information about your past experiences and your educational goals. Individual statements vary greatly in style and content, which helps admissions officers differentiate among applicants. Many graduate departments give considerable weight to the statement in making their admissions decisions, so be sure to take the time to prepare a thoughtful and concise statement.

If recommendations are a part of the admissions requirements, carefully choose the individuals you ask to write them. It is generally best to ask current or former professors to write the recommendations, provided they are able to attest to your intellectual ability and motivation for doing the work required of a graduate student. It is advisable to provide stamped, preaddressed envelopes to people being asked to submit recommendations on your behalf.

Completed applications, including references, transcripts, and admission test scores, should be received at the institution by the specified date.

Be advised that institutions do not usually make admissions decisions until all materials have been received. Enclose a self-addressed postcard with your application, requesting confirmation of receipt. Allow at least ten days for the return of the postcard before making further inquiries.

If you plan to apply for financial support, it is imperative that you file your application early.

ADMISSION TESTS

The major testing program used in graduate admissions is the Graduate Record Examinations (GRE®) testing program, sponsored by the GRE Board and administered by Educational Testing Service, Princeton, New Jersey.

The Graduate Record Examinations testing program consists of a General Test and six Subject Tests. The General Test measures critical thinking, verbal reasoning, quantitative reasoning, and analytical writing skills. It is offered as an Internet-based test (iBT) in the United States, Canada, and many other countries.

The GRE® revised General Test's questions were designed to reflect the kind of thinking that students need to do in graduate or business school and demonstrate that students are indeed ready for graduate-level work.

- **Verbal Reasoning**—Measures ability to analyze and evaluate written material and synthesize information obtained from it, analyze relationships among component parts of sentences, and recognize relationships among words and concepts.
- **Quantitative Reasoning**—Measures problem-solving ability, focusing on basic concepts of arithmetic, algebra, geometry, and data analysis.
- **Analytical Writing**—Measures critical thinking and analytical writing skills, specifically the ability to articulate and support complex ideas clearly and effectively.

The computer-delivered GRE® revised General Test is offered year-round at Prometric™ test centers and on specific dates at testing locations outside of the Prometric test center network. Appointments are scheduled on a first-come, first-served basis. The GRE® revised General Test is also offered as a paper-based test three times a year in areas where computer-based testing is not available.

You can take the computer-delivered GRE® revised General Test once every twenty-one days, up to five times within any continuous rolling twelve-month period (365 days)—even if you canceled your scores on a previously taken test. You may take the paper-based GRE® revised General Test as often as it is offered.

Three scores are reported on the revised General Test:

1. A **Verbal Reasoning score** is reported on a 130–170 score scale, in 1-point increments.

2. A **Quantitative Reasoning score** is reported on a 130–170 score scale, in 1-point increments.

3. An **Analytical Writing score** is reported on a 0–6 score level, in half-point increments.

The GRE® Subject Tests measure achievement and assume undergraduate majors or extensive background in the following six disciplines:

- Biology
- Chemistry
- Literature in English
- Mathematics
- Physics
- Psychology

The Subject Tests are available three times per year as paper-based administrations around the world. Testing time is approximately 2 hours and 50 minutes. You can obtain more information about the GRE® by visiting the ETS website at **www.ets.org** or consulting the *GRE® Information Bulletin*. The *Bulletin* can be obtained at many undergraduate colleges. You can also download it from the ETS website or obtain it by contacting Graduate Record Examinations, Educational Testing Service, P.O. Box 6000, Princeton, NJ 08541-6000; phone: 609-771-7670 or 866-473-4373.

If you expect to apply for admission to a program that requires any of the GRE® tests, you should select a test date well in advance of the application deadline. Scores on the computer-based General Test are reported within ten to fifteen days; scores on the paper-based Subject Tests are reported within six weeks.

Another testing program, the Miller Analogies Test® (MAT®), is administered at more than 500 Controlled Testing Centers in the United States, Canada, and other countries. The MAT® computer-based test is now available. Testing time is 60 minutes. The test consists of 120 partial analogies. You can obtain the *Candidate Information Booklet*, which contains a list of test centers and instructions for taking the test, from **www.milleranalogies.com** or by calling 800-328-5999 (toll-free).

Check the specific requirements of the programs to which you are applying.

How Admission Decisions Are Made

The program you apply to is directly involved in the admissions process. Although the final decision is usually made by the graduate dean (or an associate) or the faculty admissions committee, recommendations from faculty members in your intended field are important. At some institutions, an interview is incorporated into the decision process.

A Special Note for International Students

In addition to the steps already described, there are some special considerations for international students who intend to apply for graduate study in the United States. All graduate schools require an indication of competence in English. The purpose of the Test of English as a Foreign Language (TOEFL®) is to evaluate the English proficiency of people who are nonnative speakers of English and want to study at colleges and universities where English is the language of instruction. The TOEFL® is administered by Educational Testing Service (ETS) under the general direction of a policy board established by the College Board and the Graduate Record Examinations Board.

The TOEFL iBT® assesses four basic language skills: listening, reading, writing, and speaking. The Internet-based test is administered at secure, official test centers. The testing time is approximately 4 hours.

The TOEFL® is also offered in a paper-based format in areas of the world where internet-based testing is not available. In 2017, ETS launched a revised TOEFL® paper-based Test, that more closely aligned to the TOEFL iBT® test. This revised paper-based test consists of three sections—listening, reading, and writing. The testing time is approximately 3 hours.

You can obtain more information for both versions of the TOEFL® by visiting the ETS website at **www.ets.org/toefl**. Information can also be obtained by contacting TOEFL® Services, Educational Testing Service, P.O. Box 6151, Princeton, NJ 08541-6151. Phone: 609-771-7100 or 877-863-3546 (toll free).

International students should apply especially early because of the number of steps required to complete the admissions process. Furthermore, many United States graduate schools have a limited number of spaces for international students, and many more students apply than the schools can accommodate.

International students may find financial assistance from institutions very limited. The U.S. government requires international applicants to submit a certification of support, which is a statement attesting to the applicant's financial resources. In addition, international students *must* have health insurance coverage.

Tips for Minority Students

Indicators of a university's values in terms of diversity are found both in its recruitment programs and its resources directed to student success. Important questions: Does the institution vigorously recruit minorities for its graduate programs? Is there funding available to help with the costs associated with visiting the school? Are minorities represented in the institution's brochures or website or on its faculty rolls? What campus-based resources or services (including assistance in locating housing or career counseling and placement) are available? Is funding available to members of underrepresented groups?

At the program level, it is particularly important for minority students to investigate the "climate" of a program under consideration. How many minority students are enrolled and how many have graduated? What opportunities are there to work with diverse faculty and mentors whose research interests match yours? How are conflicts resolved or concerns addressed? How interested are faculty in building strong and supportive relations with students? "Climate" concerns should be addressed by posing questions to various individuals, including faculty members, current students, and alumni.

Information is also available through various organizations, such as the Hispanic Association of Colleges & Universities (HACU), and publications such as *Diverse Issues in Higher Education* and *Hispanic Outlook* magazine. There are also books devoted to this topic, such as *The Multicultural Student's Guide to Colleges* by Robert Mitchell.

Financial Support

The range of financial support at the graduate level is very broad. The following descriptions will give you a general idea of what you might expect and what will be expected of you as a financial support recipient.

Fellowships, Scholarships, and Grants

These are usually outright awards of a few hundred to many thousands of dollars with no service to the institution required in return. Fellowships and scholarships are usually awarded on the basis of merit and are highly competitive. Grants are made on the basis of financial need or special talent in a field of study. Many fellowships, scholarships, and grants not only cover tuition, fees, and supplies but also include stipends for living expenses with allowances for dependents. However, the terms of each should be examined because some do not permit recipients to supplement their income with outside work. Fellowships, scholarships, and grants may vary in the number of years for which they are awarded.

In addition to the availability of these funds at the university or program level, many excellent fellowship programs are available at the national level and may be applied for before and during enrollment in a graduate program. A listing of many of these programs can be found at the Council of Graduate Schools' website, **https://cgsnet.org/**. There is a wealth of information in the "Programs" and "Awards" sections.

Assistantships and Internships

Many graduate students receive financial support through assistantships, particularly involving teaching or research duties. It is important to recognize that such appointments should not be viewed simply as employment relationships but rather should constitute an integral and important part of a student's graduate education. As such, the appointments should be accompanied by strong faculty mentoring and increasingly responsible apprenticeship experiences. The specific nature of these appointments in a given program should be considered in selecting that graduate program.

TEACHING ASSISTANTSHIPS

These usually provide a salary and full or partial tuition remission and may also provide health benefits. Unlike fellowships, scholarships, and grants, which require no service to the institution, teaching assistantships require recipients to provide the institution with a specific amount of undergraduate teaching, ideally related to the student's field of study. Some teaching assistants are limited to grading papers, compiling bibliographies, taking notes, or monitoring laboratories. At some graduate schools, teaching assistants must carry lighter course loads than regular full-time students.

RESEARCH ASSISTANTSHIPS

These are very similar to teaching assistantships in the manner in which financial assistance is provided. The difference is that recipients are given basic research assignments in their disciplines rather than teaching responsibilities. The work required is normally related to the student's field of study; in most instances, the assistantship supports the student's thesis or dissertation research.

ADMINISTRATIVE INTERNSHIPS

These are similar to assistantships in application of financial assistance funds, but the student is given an assignment on a part-time basis, usually as a special assistant with one of the university's administrative offices. The assignment may not necessarily be directly related to the recipient's discipline.

RESIDENCE HALL AND COUNSELING ASSISTANTSHIPS

These assistantships are frequently assigned to graduate students in psychology, counseling, and social work, but they may be offered to students in other disciplines, especially if the student has worked in this capacity during his or her undergraduate years. Duties can vary from being available in a dean's office for a specific number of hours for consultation with undergraduates to living in campus residences and being responsible for both counseling and administrative tasks or advising student activity groups. Residence hall assistantships often include a room and board allowance and, in some cases, tuition assistance and stipends. Contact the Housing and Student Life Office for more information.

Health Insurance

The availability and affordability of health insurance is an important issue and one that should be considered in an applicant's choice of institution and program. While often included with assistantships and fellowships, this is not always the case and, even if provided, the benefits may be limited. It is important to note that the U.S. government requires international students to have health insurance.

The GI Bill

This provides financial assistance for students who are veterans of the United States armed forces. If you are a veteran, contact your local Veterans Administration office to determine your eligibility and to get full details about benefits. There are a number of programs that offer educational benefits to current military enlistees. Some states have tuition assistance programs for members of the National Guard. Contact the VA office at the college for more information.

Federal Work-Study Program (FWS)

Employment is another way some students finance their graduate studies. The federally funded Federal Work-Study Program provides eligible students with employment opportunities, usually in public and private nonprofit organizations. Federal funds pay up to 75 percent of the wages, with the remainder paid by the employing agency. FWS is available to graduate students who demonstrate financial need. Not all schools have these funds, and some only award them to undergraduates. Each school sets its application deadline and workstudy earnings limits. Wages vary and are related to the type of work done. You must file the Free Application for Federal Student Aid (FAFSA) to be eligible for this program.

Loans

Many graduate students borrow to finance their graduate programs when other sources of assistance (which do not have to be repaid) prove insufficient. You should always read and understand the terms of any loan program before submitting your application.

FEDERAL DIRECT LOANS

Federal Direct Loans. The Federal Direct Loan Program offers a variable-fixed interest rate loan to graduate students with the Department of Education acting as the lender. Students receive a new rate with each new loan, but that rate is fixed for the life of the loan. Beginning with loans made on or after July 1, 2013, the interest rate for loans made each July 1st to June 30th period are determined based on the last 10-year Treasury note auction prior to June 1st of that year, plus an added percentage. The interest rate can be no higher than 9.5%.

Beginning July 1, 2012, the Federal Direct Loan for graduate students is an unsubsidized loan. Under the *unsubsidized* program, the grad borrower pays the interest on the loan from the day proceeds are issued and is responsible for paying interest during all periods. If the borrower chooses not to pay the interest while in school, or during the grace periods, deferment, or forbearance, the interest accrues and will be capitalized.

Graduate students may borrow up to $20,500 per year through the Direct Loan Program, up to a cumulative maximum of $138,500, including undergraduate borrowing. No more than $65,500 of the $138,500 can be from subsidized loans, including loans the grad borrower may have received for periods of enrollment that began before July 1, 2012, or for prior undergraduate borrowing. You may borrow up to the cost of attendance at the school in which you are enrolled or will attend, minus estimated financial assistance from other federal, state, and private sources, up to a maximum of $20,500. Grad borrowers who reach the aggregate loan limit over the course of their education cannot receive additional loans; however, if they repay some of their loans to bring the outstanding balance below the aggregate limit, they could be eligible to borrow again, up to that limit.

Under the *subsidized* Federal Direct Loan Program, repayment begins six months after your last date of enrollment on at least a half-time basis. Under the *unsubsidized* program, repayment of interest begins within thirty days from disbursement of the loan proceeds, and repayment of the principal begins six months after your last enrollment on at least a half-time basis. Some borrowers may choose to defer interest payments while they are in school. The accrued interest is added to the loan balance when the borrower begins repayment. There are several repayment options.

Federal Perkins Loans. The Federal Perkins Loan is available to students demonstrating financial need and is administered directly by the school. Not all schools have these funds, and some may award them to undergraduates only. Eligibility is determined from the information you provide on the FAFSA. The school will notify you of your eligibility.

Eligible graduate students may borrow up to $8,000 per year, up to a maximum of $60,000, including undergraduate borrowing (even if your previous Perkins Loans have been repaid). The interest rate for Federal Perkins Loans is 5 percent, and no interest accrues while you remain in school at least half-time. Students who are attending less than half-time need to check with their school to determine the length of their grace period. There are no guarantee, loan, or disbursement fees. Repayment begins nine months after your last date of enrollment on at least a half-time basis and may extend over a maximum of ten years with no prepayment penalty.

Federal Direct Graduate PLUS Loans. Effective July 1, 2006, graduate and professional students are eligible for Graduate PLUS loans. This program allows students to borrow up to the cost of attendance, less any other aid received. These loans have a fixed interest rate (7.6% for loans first disbursed on or after July 1, 2018, and before July 1, 2019) and interest begins to accrue at the time of disbursement. Beginning with loans made on or after July 1, 2013, the interest rate for loans made each July 1st to June 30th period are determined based on the last 10-year Treasury note auction prior to June 1st of that year. The interest rate can be no higher than 10.5%. The PLUS loans do involve a credit check; a PLUS borrower may obtain a loan with a cosigner if his or her credit is not good enough. Grad PLUS loans may be deferred while a student is in school and for the six months following a drop below half-time enrollment. For more information, you should contact a representative in your college's financial aid office.

Deferring Your Federal Loan Repayments. If you borrowed under the Federal Direct Loan Program, Federal Direct PLUS Loan Program, or the Federal Perkins Loan Program for previous undergraduate or graduate study, your payments may be deferred when you return to graduate school, depending on when you borrowed and under which program.

There are other deferment options available if you are temporarily unable to repay your loan. Information about these deferments is provided at your entrance and exit interviews. If you believe you are eligible for a deferment of your loan payments, you must contact your lender or loan servicer to request a deferment. The deferment must be filed prior to the time your payment is due, and it must be re-filed when it expires if you remain eligible for deferment at that time.

SUPPLEMENTAL (PRIVATE) LOANS

Many lending institutions offer supplemental loan programs and other financing plans, such as the ones described here, to students seeking additional assistance in meeting their education expenses. Some loan programs target all types of graduate students; others are designed specifically for business, law, or medical students. In addition, you can use private loans not specifically designed for education to help finance your graduate degree.

If you are considering borrowing through a supplemental or private loan program, you should carefully consider the terms and be sure to read the fine print. Check with the program sponsor for the most current terms that will be applicable to the amounts you intend to borrow for graduate study. Most supplemental loan programs for graduate study offer unsubsidized, credit-based loans. In general, a credit-ready borrower is one who has a satisfactory credit history or no credit history at all. A creditworthy borrower generally must pass a credit test to be eligible to borrow or act as a cosigner for the loan funds.

Many supplemental loan programs have minimum and maximum annual loan limits. Some offer amounts equal to the cost of attendance minus any other aid you will receive for graduate study. If you are planning to borrow for several years of graduate study, consider whether there is a cumulative or aggregate limit on the amount you may borrow. Often this cumulative or aggregate limit will include any amounts you borrowed and have not repaid for undergraduate or previous graduate study.

The combination of the annual interest rate, loan fees, and the repayment terms you choose will determine how much you will repay over time. Compare these features in combination before you decide which loan program to use. Some loans offer interest rates that are adjusted monthly, quarterly, or annually. Some offer interest rates that are lower during the in-school, grace, and deferment periods and then increase when you begin repayment. Some programs include a loan origination fee, which is usually deducted from the principal amount you receive when the loan is disbursed and must be repaid along with the interest and other principal when you graduate, withdraw from school, or drop below half-time study. Sometimes the loan fees are reduced if you borrow with a qualified cosigner. Some programs allow you to defer interest and/or principal payments while you are enrolled in graduate school. Many programs allow you to capitalize your interest payments; the interest due on your loan is added to the outstanding balance of your loan, so you don't have to repay immediately, but this increases the amount you owe. Other programs allow you to pay the interest as you go, which reduces the amount you later have to repay. The private loan market is very competitive, and your financial aid office can help you evaluate these programs.

Applying for Need-Based Financial Aid

Schools that award federal and institutional financial assistance based on need will require you to complete the FAFSA and, in some cases, an institutional financial aid application.

If you are applying for federal student assistance, you **must** complete the FAFSA. A service of the U.S. Department of Education, the FAFSA is free to all applicants. Most applicants apply online at **www.fafsa.ed.gov**. Paper applications are available at the financial aid office of your local college.

After your FAFSA information has been processed, you will receive a Student Aid Report (SAR). If you provided an e-mail address on the FAFSA, this will be sent to you electronically; otherwise, it will be mailed to your home address.

Follow the instructions on the SAR if you need to correct information reported on your original application. If your situation changes after you file your FAFSA, contact your financial aid officer to discuss amending your information. You can also appeal your financial aid award if you have extenuating circumstances.

If you would like more information on federal student financial aid, visit the FAFSA website or download the most recent version of *Do You Need Money for College* at www.studentaid.ed.gov/sa/sites/default/files/2018-19-do-you-need-money.pdf. This guide is also available in Spanish.

The U.S. Department of Education also has a toll-free number for questions concerning federal student aid programs. The number is 1-800-4-FED AID (1-800-433-3243). If you are hearing impaired, call toll-free, 1-800-730-8913.

Summary

Remember that these are generalized statements about financial assistance at the graduate level. Because each institution allots its aid differently, you should communicate directly with the school and the specific department of interest to you. It is not unusual, for example, to find that an endowment vested within a specific department supports one or more fellowships. You may fit its requirements and specifications precisely.

Accreditation and Accrediting Agencies

Colleges and universities in the United States, and their individual academic and professional programs, are accredited by nongovernmental agencies concerned with monitoring the quality of education in this country. Agencies with both regional and national jurisdictions grant accreditation to institutions as a whole, while specialized bodies acting on a nationwide basis—often national professional associations—grant accreditation to departments and programs in specific fields.

Institutional and specialized accrediting agencies share the same basic concerns: the purpose an academic unit—whether university or program—has set for itself and how well it fulfills that purpose, the adequacy of its financial and other resources, the quality of its academic offerings, and the level of services it provides. Agencies that grant institutional accreditation take a broader view, of course, and examine university-wide or college-wide services with which a specialized agency may not concern itself.

Both types of agencies follow the same general procedures when considering an application for accreditation. The academic unit prepares a self-evaluation, focusing on the concerns mentioned above and usually including an assessment of both its strengths and weaknesses; a team of representatives of the accrediting body reviews this evaluation, visits the campus, and makes its own report; and finally, the accrediting body makes a decision on the application. Often, even when accreditation is granted, the agency makes a recommendation regarding how the institution or program can improve. All institutions and programs are also reviewed every few years to determine whether they continue to meet established standards; if they do not, they may lose their accreditation.

Accrediting agencies themselves are reviewed and evaluated periodically by the U.S. Department of Education and the Council for Higher Education Accreditation (CHEA). Recognized agencies adhere to certain standards and practices, and their authority in matters of accreditation is widely accepted in the educational community.

This does not mean, however, that accreditation is a simple matter, either for schools wishing to become accredited or for students deciding where to apply. Indeed, in certain fields the very meaning and methods of accreditation are the subject of a good deal of debate. For their part, those applying to graduate school should be aware of the safeguards provided by regional accreditation, especially in terms of degree acceptance and institutional longevity. Beyond this, applicants should understand the role that specialized accreditation plays in their field, as this varies considerably from one discipline to another. In certain professional fields, it is necessary to have graduated from a program that is accredited in order to be eligible for a license to practice, and in some fields the federal government also makes this a hiring requirement. In other disciplines, however, accreditation is not as essential, and there can be excellent programs that are not accredited. In fact, some programs choose not to seek accreditation, although most do.

Institutions and programs that present themselves for accreditation are sometimes granted the status of candidate for accreditation, or what is known as "preaccreditation." This may happen, for example, when an academic unit is too new to have met all the requirements for accreditation. Such status signifies initial recognition and indicates that the school or program in question is working to fulfill all requirements; it does not, however, guarantee that accreditation will be granted.

Institutional Accrediting Agencies—Regional

MIDDLE STATES COMMISSION ON HIGHER EDUCATION

Accredits institutions in Delaware, District of Columbia, Maryland, New Jersey, New York, Pennsylvania, Puerto Rico, and the Virgin Islands.

Dr. Elizabeth Sibolski, President
Middle States Commission on Higher Education
3624 Market Street, Second Floor West
Philadelphia, Pennsylvania 19104
Phone: 267-284-5000
Fax: 215-662-5501
E-mail: info@msche.org
Website: www.msche.org

NEW ENGLAND ASSOCIATION OF SCHOOLS AND COLLEGES

Accredits institutions in Connecticut, Maine, Massachusetts, New Hampshire, Rhode Island, and Vermont.

Dr. Barbara E. Brittingham, President/Director
Commission on Institutions of Higher Education
3 Burlington Woods Drive, Suite 100
Burlington, Massachusetts 01803-4531
Phone: 855-886-3272 or 781-425-7714
Fax: 781-425-1001
E-mail: cihe@neasc.org
Website: https://cihe.neasc.org

THE HIGHER LEARNING COMMISSION

Accredits institutions in Arizona, Arkansas, Colorado, Illinois, Indiana, Iowa, Kansas, Michigan, Minnesota, Missouri, Nebraska, New Mexico, North Dakota, Ohio, Oklahoma, South Dakota, West Virginia, Wisconsin, and Wyoming.

Dr. Barbara Gellman-Danley, President
The Higher Learning Commission
230 South LaSalle Street, Suite 7-500
Chicago, Illinois 60604-1413
Phone: 800-621-7440 or 312-263-0456
Fax: 312-263-7462
E-mail: info@hlcommission.org
Website: www.hlcommission.org

NORTHWEST COMMISSION ON COLLEGES AND UNIVERSITIES

Accredits institutions in Alaska, Idaho, Montana, Nevada, Oregon, Utah, and Washington.

Dr. Sandra E. Elman, President
8060 165th Avenue, NE, Suite 100
Redmond, Washington 98052
Phone: 425-558-4224
Fax: 425-376-0596
E-mail: selman@nwccu.org
Website: www.nwccu.org

SOUTHERN ASSOCIATION OF COLLEGES AND SCHOOLS

Accredits institutions in Alabama, Florida, Georgia, Kentucky, Louisiana, Mississippi, North Carolina, South Carolina, Tennessee, Texas, and Virginia.

Dr. Belle S. Wheelan, President
Commission on Colleges
1866 Southern Lane
Decatur, Georgia 30033-4097
Phone: 404-679-4500 Ext. 4504
Fax: 404-679-4558
E-mail: questions@sacscoc.org
Website: www.sacscoc.org

WESTERN ASSOCIATION OF SCHOOLS AND COLLEGES

Accredits institutions in California, Guam, and Hawaii.

Jamienne S. Studley, President
WASC Senior College and University Commission
985 Atlantic Avenue, Suite 100
Alameda, California 94501
Phone: 510-748-9001
Fax: 510-748-9797
E-mail: wasc@wscuc.org
Website: https://www.wscuc.org/

Institutional Accrediting Agencies—Other

ACCREDITING COUNCIL FOR INDEPENDENT COLLEGES AND SCHOOLS
Michelle Edwards, President
750 First Street NE, Suite 980
Washington, DC 20002-4223
Phone: 202-336-6780
Fax: 202-842-2593
E-mail: info@acics.org
Website: www.acics.org

DISTANCE EDUCATION ACCREDITING COMMISSION (DEAC)
Leah Matthews, Executive Director
1101 17th Street NW, Suite 808
Washington, DC 20036-4704
Phone: 202-234-5100
Fax: 202-332-1386
E-mail: info@deac.org
Website: www.deac.org

Specialized Accrediting Agencies

ACUPUNCTURE AND ORIENTAL MEDICINE
Mark S. McKenzie, LAc MsOM DiplOM, Executive Director
Accreditation Commission for Acupuncture and Oriental Medicine
8941 Aztec Drive, Suite 2
Eden Prairie, Minnesota 55347
Phone: 952-212-2434
Fax: 301-313-0912
E-mail: info@acaom.org
Website: www.acaom.org

ALLIED HEALTH
Kathleen Megivern, Executive Director
Commission on Accreditation of Allied Health Education Programs (CAAHEP)
25400 US Hwy 19 North, Suite 158
Clearwater, Florida 33763
Phone: 727-210-2350
Fax: 727-210-2354
E-mail: mail@caahep.org
Website: www.caahep.org

ART AND DESIGN
Karen P. Moynahan, Executive Director
National Association of Schools of Art and Design (NASAD)
Commission on Accreditation
11250 Roger Bacon Drive, Suite 21
Reston, Virginia 20190-5248
Phone: 703-437-0700
Fax: 703-437-6312
E-mail: info@arts-accredit.org
Website: http://nasad.arts-accredit.org

ATHLETIC TRAINING EDUCATION
Pamela Hansen, CAATE Director of Accreditation
Commission on Accreditation of Athletic Training Education (CAATE)
6850 Austin Center Blvd., Suite 100
Austin, Texas 78731-3184
Phone: 512-733-9700
E-mail: pamela@caate.net
Website: www.caate.net

AUDIOLOGY EDUCATION
Meggan Olek, Director
Accreditation Commission for Audiology Education (ACAE)
11480 Commerce Park Drive, Suite 220
Reston, Virginia 20191
Phone: 202-986-9500
Fax: 202-986-9550
E-mail: info@acaeaccred.org
Website: https://acaeaccred.org/

AVIATION
Dr. Gary J. Northam, President
Aviation Accreditation Board International (AABI)
3410 Skyway Drive
Auburn, Alabama 36830
Phone: 334-844-2431
Fax: 334-844-2432
E-mail: gary.northam@auburn.edu
Website: www.aabi.aero

BUSINESS
Stephanie Bryant, Executive Vice President and Chief Accreditation Officer
AACSB International—The Association to Advance Collegiate Schools of Business
777 South Harbour Island Boulevard, Suite 750
Tampa, Florida 33602
Phone: 813-769-6500
Fax: 813-769-6559
E-mail: stephanie.bryant@aacsb.edu
Website: www.aacsb.edu

BUSINESS EDUCATION
Dr. Phyllis Okrepkie, President
International Assembly for Collegiate Business Education (IACBE)
11374 Strang Line Road
Lenexa, Kansas 66215
Phone: 913-631-3009
Fax: 913-631-9154
E-mail: iacbe@iacbe.org
Website: www.iacbe.org

CHIROPRACTIC
Dr. Craig S. Little, President
Council on Chiropractic Education (CCE)
Commission on Accreditation
8049 North 85th Way
Scottsdale, Arizona 85258-4321
Phone: 480-443-8877 or 888-443-3506
Fax: 480-483-7333
E-mail: cce@cce-usa.org
Website: www.cce-usa.org

CLINICAL LABORATORY SCIENCES
Dianne M. Cearlock, Ph.D., Chief Executive Officer
National Accrediting Agency for Clinical Laboratory Sciences
5600 North River Road, Suite 720
Rosemont, Illinois 60018-5119
Phone: 773-714-8880 or 847-939-3597
Fax: 773-714-8886
E-mail: info@naacls.org
Website: www.naacls.org

CLINICAL PASTORAL EDUCATION
Trace Haythorn, Ph.D., Executive Director/CEO
Association for Clinical Pastoral Education, Inc.
One West Court Square, Suite 325
Decatur, Georgia 30030-2576
Phone: 678-363-6226
Fax: 404-320-0849
E-mail: acpe@acpe.edu
Website: www.acpe.edu

DANCE
Karen P. Moynahan, Executive Director
National Association of Schools of Dance (NASD)
Commission on Accreditation
11250 Roger Bacon Drive, Suite 21
Reston, Virginia 20190-5248
Phone: 703-437-0700
Fax: 703-437-6312
E-mail: info@arts-accredit.org
Website: http://nasd.arts-accredit.org

DENTISTRY
Dr. Kathleen T. O'Loughlin, Executive Director

Commission on Dental Accreditation
American Dental Association
211 East Chicago Avenue
Chicago, Illinois 60611
Phone: 312-440-2500
E-mail: accreditation@ada.org
Website: www.ada.org

DIETETICS AND NUTRITION
Mary B. Gregoire, Ph.D., Executive Director; RD, FADA, FAND
Academy of Nutrition and Dietetics
Accreditation Council for Education in Nutrition and Dietetics (ACEND)
120 South Riverside Plaza
Chicago, Illinois 60606-6995
Phone: 800-877-1600 or 312-899-0040
E-mail: acend@eatright.org
Website: www.eatright.org/cade

EDUCATION PREPARATION
Christopher Koch, President
Council for the Accreditation of Educator Preparation (CAEP)
1140 19th Street NW, Suite 400
Washington, DC 20036
Phone: 202-223-0077
Fax: 202-296-6620
E-mail: caep@caepnet.org
Website: www.caepnet.org

ENGINEERING
Michael Milligan, Ph.D., PE, Executive Director
Accreditation Board for Engineering and Technology, Inc. (ABET)
415 North Charles Street
Baltimore, Maryland 21201
Phone: 410-347-7700
E-mail: accreditation@abet.org
Website: www.abet.org

FORENSIC SCIENCES
Nancy J. Jackson, Director of Development and Accreditation
American Academy of Forensic Sciences (AAFS)
Forensic Science Education Program Accreditation Commission (FEPAC)
410 North 21st Street
Colorado Springs, Colorado 80904
Phone: 719-636-1100
Fax: 719-636-1993
E-mail: njackson@aafs.org
Website: www.fepac-edu.org

FORESTRY
Carol L. Redelsheimer
Director of Science and Education
Society of American Foresters
10100 Laureate Way
Bethesda, Maryland 20814-2198
Phone: 301-897-8720 or 866-897-8720
Fax: 301-897-3690
E-mail: membership@safnet.org
Website: www.eforester.com

HEALTHCARE MANAGEMENT
Commission on Accreditation of Healthcare Management Education (CAHME)
Anthony Stanowski, President and CEO
6110 Executive Boulevard, Suite 614
Rockville, Maryland 20852
Phone: 301-298-1820
E-mail: info@cahme.org
Website: www.cahme.org

HEALTH INFORMATICS AND HEALTH MANAGEMENT
Angela Kennedy, EdD, MBA, RHIA, Chief Executive Officer
Commission on Accreditation for Health Informatics and Information Management Education (CAHIIM)
233 North Michigan Avenue, 21st Floor
Chicago, Illinois 60601-5800

Phone: 312-233-1134
Fax: 312-233-1948
E-mail: info@cahiim.org
Website: www.cahiim.org

HUMAN SERVICE EDUCATION
Dr. Elaine Green, President
Council for Standards in Human Service Education (CSHSE)
3337 Duke Street
Alexandria, Virginia 22314
Phone: 571-257-3959
E-mail: info@cshse.org
Website: www.cshse.org

INTERIOR DESIGN
Holly Mattson, Executive Director
Council for Interior Design Accreditation
206 Grandview Avenue, Suite 350
Grand Rapids, Michigan 49503-4014
Phone: 616-458-0400
Fax: 616-458-0460
E-mail: info@accredit-id.org
Website: www.accredit-id.org

JOURNALISM AND MASS COMMUNICATIONS
Patricia Thompson, Executive Director
Accrediting Council on Education in Journalism and Mass Communications (ACEJMC)
201 Bishop Hall
P.O. Box 1848
University, MS 38677-1848
Phone: 662-915-5504
E-mail: pthomps1@olemiss.edu
Website: www.acejmc.org

LANDSCAPE ARCHITECTURE
Nancy Somerville, Executive Vice President, CEO
American Society of Landscape Architects (ASLA)
636 Eye Street, NW
Washington, DC 20001-3736
Phone: 202-898-2444
Fax: 202-898-1185
E-mail: info@asla.org
Website: www.asla.org

LAW
Barry Currier, Managing Director of Accreditation & Legal Education
American Bar Association
321 North Clark Street, 21st Floor
Chicago, Illinois 60654
Phone: 312-988-6738
Fax: 312-988-5681
E-mail: legaled@americanbar.org
Website: https://www.americanbar.org/groups/legal_education/accreditation.html

LIBRARY
Karen O'Brien, Director
Office for Accreditation
American Library Association
50 East Huron Street
Chicago, Illinois 60611-2795
Phone: 800-545-2433, ext. 2432 or 312-280-2432
Fax: 312-280-2433
E-mail: accred@ala.org
Website: http://www.ala.org/aboutala/offices/accreditation/

MARRIAGE AND FAMILY THERAPY
Tanya A. Tamarkin, Director of Educational Affairs
Commission on Accreditation for Marriage and Family Therapy Education (COAMFTE)
American Association for Marriage and Family Therapy
112 South Alfred Street
Alexandria, Virginia 22314-3061

Phone: 703-838-9808
Fax: 703-838-9805
E-mail: coa@aamft.org
Website: www.aamft.org

MEDICAL ILLUSTRATION
Kathleen Megivern, Executive Director
Commission on Accreditation of Allied Health Education Programs
    (CAAHEP)
25400 US Highway 19 North, Suite 158
Clearwater, Florida 33756
Phone: 727-210-2350
Fax: 727-210-2354
E-mail: mail@caahep.org
Website: www.caahep.org

MEDICINE
Liaison Committee on Medical Education (LCME)
Robert B. Hash, M.D., LCME Secretary
American Medical Association
Council on Medical Education
330 North Wabash Avenue, Suite 39300
Chicago, Illinois 60611-5885
Phone: 312-464-4933
E-mail: lcme@aamc.org
Website: www.ama-assn.org

Liaison Committee on Medical Education (LCME)
Heather Lent, M.A., Director
Accreditation Services
Association of American Medical Colleges
655 K Street, NW
Washington, DC 20001-2399
Phone: 202-828-0596
E-mail: lcme@aamc.org
Website: www.lcme.org

MUSIC
Karen P. Moynahan, Executive Director
National Association of Schools of Music (NASM)
Commission on Accreditation
11250 Roger Bacon Drive, Suite 21
Reston, Virginia 20190-5248
Phone: 703-437-0700
Fax: 703-437-6312
E-mail: info@arts-accredit.org
Website: http://nasm.arts-accredit.org/

NATUROPATHIC MEDICINE
Daniel Seitz, J.D., Ed.D., Executive Director
Council on Naturopathic Medical Education
P.O. Box 178
Great Barrington, Massachusetts 01230
Phone: 413-528-8877
E-mail: https://cnme.org/contact-us/
Website: www.cnme.org

NURSE ANESTHESIA
Francis R.Gerbasi, Ph.D., CRNA, COA Executive Director
Council on Accreditation of Nurse Anesthesia Educational Programs
    (CoA-NAEP)
American Association of Nurse Anesthetists
222 South Prospect Avenue
Park Ridge, Illinois 60068-4001
Phone: 847-655-1160
Fax: 847-692-7137
E-mail: accreditation@coa.us.com
Website: http://www.coacrna.org

NURSE EDUCATION
Jennifer L. Butlin, Executive Director
Commission on Collegiate Nursing Education (CCNE)
One Dupont Circle, NW, Suite 530
Washington, DC 20036-1120
Phone: 202-887-6791
Fax: 202-887-8476
E-mail: jbutlin@aacn.nche.edu
Website: www.aacn.nche.edu/accreditation

Marsal P. Stoll, Chief Executive Officer
Accreditation Commission for Education in Nursing (ACEN)
3343 Peachtree Road, NE, Suite 850
Atlanta, Georgia 30326
Phone: 404-975-5000
Fax: 404-975-5020
E-mail: mstoll@acenursing.org
Website: www.acenursing.org

NURSE MIDWIFERY
Heather L. Maurer, M.A., Executive Director
Accreditation Commission for Midwifery Education (ACME)
American College of Nurse-Midwives
8403 Colesville Road, Suite 1550
Silver Spring, Maryland 20910
Phone: 240-485-1800
Fax: 240-485-1818
E-mail: info@acnm.org
Website: www.midwife.org/Program-Accreditation

NURSE PRACTITIONER
Gay Johnson, CEO
National Association of Nurse Practitioners in Women's Health
Council on Accreditation
505 C Street, NE
Washington, DC 20002
Phone: 202-543-9693 Ext. 1
Fax: 202-543-9858
E-mail: info@npwh.org
Website: www.npwh.org

NURSING
Marsal P. Stoll, Chief Executive Director
Accreditation Commission for Education in Nursing (ACEN)
3343 Peachtree Road, NE, Suite 850
Atlanta, Georgia 30326
Phone: 404-975-5000
Fax: 404-975-5020
E-mail: info@acenursing.org
Website: www.acenursing.org

OCCUPATIONAL THERAPY
Heather Stagliano, DHSc, OTR/L, Executive Director
The American Occupational Therapy Association, Inc.
4720 Montgomery Lane, Suite 200
Bethesda, Maryland 20814-3449
Phone: 301-652-6611 Ext. 2682
TDD: 800-377-8555
Fax: 240-762-5150
E-mail: accred@aota.org
Website: www.aoteonline.org

OPTOMETRY
Joyce L. Urbeck, Administrative Director
Accreditation Council on Optometric Education (ACOE)
American Optometric Association
243 North Lindbergh Boulevard
St. Louis, Missouri 63141-7881
Phone: 314-991-4100, Ext. 4246
Fax: 314-991-4101
E-mail: accredit@aoa.org
Website: www.theacoe.org

OSTEOPATHIC MEDICINE
Director, Department of Accreditation
Commission on Osteopathic College Accreditation (COCA)
American Osteopathic Association
142 East Ontario Street
Chicago, Illinois 60611
Phone: 312-202-8048
Fax: 312-202-8202
E-mail: predoc@osteopathic.org
Website: www.aoacoca.org

PHARMACY
Peter H. Vlasses, PharmD, Executive Director
Accreditation Council for Pharmacy Education
135 South LaSalle Street, Suite 4100
Chicago, Illinois 60603-4810
Phone: 312-664-3575
Fax: 312-664-4652
E-mail: csinfo@acpe-accredit.org
Website: www.acpe-accredit.org

PHYSICAL THERAPY
Sandra Wise, Senior Director
Commission on Accreditation in Physical Therapy Education (CAPTE)
American Physical Therapy Association (APTA)
1111 North Fairfax Street
Alexandria, Virginia 22314-1488
Phone: 703-706-3245
Fax: 703-706-3387
E-mail: accreditation@apta.org
Website: www.capteonline.org

PHYSICIAN ASSISTANT STUDIES
Sharon L. Luke, Executive Director
Accredittion Review Commission on Education for the Physician
   Assistant, Inc. (ARC-PA)
12000 Findley Road, Suite 275
Johns Creek, Georgia 30097
Phone: 770-476-1224
Fax: 770-476-1738
E-mail: arc-pa@arc-pa.org
Website: www.arc-pa.org

PLANNING
Jesmarie Soto Johnson, Executive Director
American Institute of Certified Planners/Association of Collegiate
   Schools of Planning/American Planning Association
Planning Accreditation Board (PAB)
2334 West Lawrence Avenue, Suite 209
Chicago, Illinois 60625
Phone: 773-334-7200
E-mail: smerits@planningaccreditationboard.org
Website: www.planningaccreditationboard.org

PODIATRIC MEDICINE
Heather Stagliano, OTR/L, DHSc, Executive Director
Council on Podiatric Medical Education (CPME)
American Podiatric Medical Association (APMA)
9312 Old Georgetown Road
Bethesda, Maryland 20814-1621
Phone: 301-581-9200
Fax: 301-571-4903
Website: www.cpme.org

PSYCHOLOGY AND COUNSELING
Jacqueline Remondet, Associate Executive Director, CEO of the
Accrediting Unit,
Office of Program Consultation and Accreditation
American Psychological Association
750 First Street, NE
Washington, DC 20002-4202
Phone: 202-336-5979 or 800-374-2721
TDD/TTY: 202-336-6123
Fax: 202-336-5978
E-mail: apaaccred@apa.org
Website: www.apa.org/ed/accreditation

Kelly Coker, Executive Director
Council for Accreditation of Counseling and Related Educational
   Programs (CACREP)
1001 North Fairfax Street, Suite 510
Alexandria, Virginia 22314
Phone: 703-535-5990
Fax: 703-739-6209
E-mail: cacrep@cacrep.org
Website: www.cacrep.org

Richard M. McFall, Executive Director
Psychological Clinical Science Accreditation System (PCSAS)
1101 East Tenth Street
IU Psychology Building
Bloomington, Indiana 47405-7007
Phone: 812-856-2570
Fax: 812-322-5545
E-mail: rmmcfall@pcsas.org
Website: www.pcsas.org

PUBLIC HEALTH
Laura Rasar King, M.PH., MCHES, Executive Director
Council on Education for Public Health
1010 Wayne Avenue, Suite 220
Silver Spring, Maryland 20910
Phone: 202-789-1050
Fax: 202-789-1895
E-mail: Lking@ceph.org
Website: www.ceph.org

PUBLIC POLICY, AFFAIRS AND ADMINISTRATION
Crystal Calarusse, Chief Accreditation Officer
Commission on Peer Review and Accreditation
Network of Schools of Public Policy, Affairs, and Administration
(NASPAA-COPRA)
1029 Vermont Avenue, NW, Suite 1100
Washington, DC 20005
Phone: 202-628-8965
Fax: 202-626-4978
E-mail: copra@naspaa.org
Website: accreditation.naspaa.org

RADIOLOGIC TECHNOLOGY
Leslie Winter, Chief Executive Officer Joint Review Committee on
Education in Radiologic Technology (JRCERT)
20 North Wacker Drive, Suite 2850
Chicago, Illinois 60606-3182
Phone: 312-704-5300
Fax: 312-704-5304
E-mail: mail@jrcert.org
Website: www.jrcert.org

REHABILITATION EDUCATION
Frank Lane, Ph.D., Executive Director
Council for Accreditation of Counseling and Related Educational
   Programs (CACREP)
1001 North Fairfax Street, Suite 510
Alexandria, Virginia 22314
Phone: 703-535-5990
Fax: 703-739-6209
E-mail: cacrep@cacrep.org
Website: www.cacrep.org

RESPIRATORY CARE
Thomas Smalling, Executive Director
Commission on Accreditation for Respiratory Care (CoARC)
1248 Harwood Road
Bedford, Texas 76021-4244
Phone: 817-283-2835
Fax: 817-354-8519
E-mail: tom@coarc.com
Website: www.coarc.com

SOCIAL WORK
Dr. Stacey Borasky, Director of Accreditation
Office of Social Work Accreditation
Council on Social Work Education
1701 Duke Street, Suite 200
Alexandria, Virginia 22314
Phone: 703-683-8080
Fax: 703-519-2078
E-mail: info@cswe.org
Website: www.cswe.org

SPEECH-LANGUAGE PATHOLOGY AND AUDIOLOGY
Kimberlee Moore, Accreditation Executive Director
American Speech-Language-Hearing Association
Council on Academic Accreditation in Audiology and Speech-Language
    Pathology
2200 Research Boulevard #310
Rockville, Maryland 20850-3289
Phone: 301-296-5700
Fax: 301-296-8750
E-mail: accreditation@asha.org
Website: http://caa.asha.org

TEACHER EDUCATION
Christopher A. Koch, President
National Council for Accreditation of Teacher Education (NCATE)
Teacher Education Accreditation Council (TEAC)
1140 19th Street, Suite 400
Washington, DC 20036
Phone: 202-223-0077
Fax: 202-296-6620
E-mail: caep@caepnet.org
Website: www.ncate.org

TECHNOLOGY
Michale S. McComis, Ed.D., Executive Director
Accrediting Commission of Career Schools and Colleges
2101 Wilson Boulevard, Suite 302
Arlington, Virginia 22201
Phone: 703-247-4212
Fax: 703-247-4533
E-mail: mccomis@accsc.org
Website: www.accsc.org

TECHNOLOGY, MANAGEMENT, AND APPLIED ENGINEERING
Kelly Schild, Director of Accreditation
The Association of Technology, Management, and Applied Engineering
(ATMAE)
275 N. York Street, Suite 401
Elmhurst, Illinois 60126
Phone: 630-433-4514
Fax: 630-563-9181
E-mail: Kelly@atmae.org
Website: www.atmae.org

THEATER
Karen P. Moynahan, Executive Director
National Association of Schools of Theatre Commission on
    Accreditation
11250 Roger Bacon Drive, Suite 21
Reston, Virginia 20190
Phone: 703-437-0700
Fax: 703-437-6312
E-mail: info@arts-accredit.org
Website: http://nast.arts-accredit.org/

THEOLOGY
Dr. Bernard Fryshman, Executive VP
Emeritus and Interim Executive Director
Association of Advanced Rabbinical and Talmudic Schools (AARTS)
Accreditation Commission
11 Broadway, Suite 405
New York, New York 10004
Phone: 212-363-1991
Fax: 212-533-5335
E-mail: k.sharfman.aarts@gmail.com

Frank Yamada, Executive Director
Association of Theological Schools in the United States and Canada
    (ATS)
Commission on Accrediting
10 Summit Park Drive
Pittsburgh, Pennsylvania 15275
Phone: 412-788-6505
Fax: 412-788-6510
E-mail: ats@ats.edu
Website: www.ats.edu

Dr. Timothy Eaton, President
Transnational Association of Christian Colleges and Schools (TRACS)
Accreditation Commission
15935 Forest Road
Forest, Virginia 24551
Phone: 434-525-9539
Fax: 434-525-9538
E-mail: info@tracs.org
Website: www.tracs.org

VETERINARY MEDICINE
Dr. Karen Brandt, Director of Education and Research
American Veterinary Medical Association (AVMA)
Council on Education
1931 North Meacham Road, Suite 100
Schaumburg, Illinois 60173-4360
Phone: 847-925-8070 Ext. 6674
Fax: 847-285-5732
E-mail: info@avma.org
Website: www.avma.org

How to Use These Guides

As you identify the particular programs and institutions that interest you, you can use both the *Graduate & Professional Programs: An Overview* volume and the specialized volumes in the series to obtain detailed information.

- *Graduate Programs in the Biological/Biomedical Sciences & Health-Related Professions*
- *Graduate Programs in Business, Education, Information Studies, Law & Social Work*
- *Graduate Programs in Engineering & Applied Sciences*
- *Graduate Programs the Humanities, Arts & Social Sciences*
- *Graduate Programs in the Physical Sciences, Mathematics, Agricultural Sciences, the Environment & Natural Resources*

Each of the specialized volumes in the series is divided into sections that contain one or more directories devoted to programs in a particular field. If you do not find a directory devoted to your field of interest in a specific volume, consult "Directories and Subject Areas" (located at the end of each volume). After you have identified the correct volume, consult the "Directories and Subject Areas in This Book" index, which shows (as does the more general directory) what directories cover subjects not specifically named in a directory or section title.

Each of the specialized volumes in the series has a number of general directories. These directories have entries for the largest unit at an institution granting graduate degrees in that field. For example, the general Engineering and Applied Sciences directory in the *Graduate Programs in Engineering & Applied Sciences* volume consists of Profiles for colleges, schools, and departments of engineering and applied sciences.

General directories are followed by other directories, or sections, that give more detailed information about programs in particular areas of the general field that has been covered. The general Engineering and Applied Sciences directory, in the previous example, is followed by nineteen sections with directories in specific areas of engineering, such as Chemical Engineering, Industrial/Management Engineering, and Mechanical Engineering.

Because of the broad nature of many fields, any system of organization is bound to involve a certain amount of overlap. Environmental studies, for example, is a field whose various aspects are studied in several types of departments and schools. Readers interested in such studies will find information on relevant programs in the *Graduate Programs in the Biological/Biomedical Sciences & Health-Related Professions* volume under Ecology and Environmental Biology and Environmental and Occupational Health; in the *Graduate Programs in the Physical Sciences, Mathematics, Agricultural Sciences, the Environment & Natural Resources* volume under Environmental Management and Policy and Natural Resources; and in the *Graduate Programs in Engineering & Applied Sciences* volume under Energy Management and Policy and Environmental Engineering. To help you find all of the programs of interest to you, the introduction to each section within the specialized volumes includes, if applicable, a paragraph suggesting other sections and directories with information on related areas of study.

Directory of Institutions with Programs in the Physical Sciences, Mathematics, Agricultural Sciences, the Environment & Natural Resources

This directory lists institutions in alphabetical order and includes beneath each name the academic fields in which each institution offers graduate programs. The degree level in each field is also indicated, provided that the institution has supplied that information in response to

Peterson's Annual Survey of Graduate and Professional Institutions.

An M indicates that a master's degree program is offered; a D indicates that a doctoral degree program is offered; an O signifies that other advanced degrees (e.g., certificates or specialist degrees) are offered; and an * (asterisk) indicates that a **Close-Up** and/or **Display** is located in this volume. See the index, "Close-Ups and Displays," for the specific page number.

Profiles of Academic and Professional Programs in the Specialized Volumes

Each section of **Profiles** has a table of contents that lists the Program Directories, **Displays**, and **Close-Ups**. Program Directories consist of the **Profiles** of programs in the relevant fields, with **Displays** following if programs have chosen to include them. **Close-Ups,** which are more individualized statements, are also listed for those graduate schools or programs that have chosen to submit them.

The **Profiles** found in the 500 directories in the specialized volumes provide basic data about the graduate units in capsule form for quick reference. To make these directories as useful as possible, **Profiles** are generally listed for an institution's smallest academic unit within a subject area. In other words, if an institution has a College of Liberal Arts that administers many related programs, the **Profile** for the individual program (e.g., Program in History), not the entire College, appears in the directory.

There are some programs that do not fit into any current directory and are not given individual **Profiles**. The directory structure is reviewed annually in order to keep this number to a minimum and to accommodate major trends in graduate education.

The following outline describes the **Profile** information found in the guides and explains how best to use that information. Any item that does not apply to or was not provided by a graduate unit is omitted from its listing. The format of the **Profiles** is constant, making it easy to compare one institution with another and one program with another.

A ★ graphic next to the school's name indicates the institution has additional detailed information in a "Premium Profile" on Petersons.com. After reading their information here, you can learn more about the school by visiting www.petersons.com and searching for that particular college or university's graduate program.

Identifying Information. The institution's name, in boldface type, is followed by a complete listing of the administrative structure for that field of study. (For example, University of Akron, Buchtel College of Arts and Sciences, Department of Theoretical and Applied Mathematics, Program in Mathematics.) The last unit listed is the one to which all information in the **Profile** pertains. The institution's city, state, and ZIP code follow.

Offerings. Each field of study offered by the unit is listed with all postbaccalaureate degrees awarded. Degrees that are not preceded by a specific concentration are awarded in the general field listed in the unit name. Frequently, fields of study are broken down into subspecializations, and those appear following the degrees awarded; for example, "Offerings in secondary education (M.Ed.), including English education, mathematics education, science education." Students enrolled in the M.Ed. program would be able to specialize in any of the three fields mentioned.

Professional Accreditation. Some **Profiles** indicate whether a program is professionally accredited. Because it is possible for a program to receive or lose professional accreditation at any time, students entering fields in which accreditation is important to a career should verify the status of programs by contacting either the chairperson or the appropriate accrediting association.

Jointly Offered Degrees. Explanatory statements concerning programs that are offered in cooperation with other institutions are included in the list of degrees offered. This occurs most commonly on a regional basis (for example, two state universities offering a cooperative Ph.D. in special education) or where the specialized nature of the institutions encourages joint efforts (a J.D./M.B.A. offered by a law school at an institution with no formal business programs and an institution with a business school but lacking a law school). Only programs that are truly cooperative are listed; those involving only limited course work at another institution are not. Interested students should contact the heads of such units for further information.

Program Availability. This may include the following: part-time, evening/weekend, online only, 100% online, blended/hybrid learning, and/or minimal on-campus study. When information regarding the availability of part-time or evening/weekend study appears in the **Profile**, it means that students are able to earn a degree exclusively through such study. Blended/hybrid learning describes those courses in which some traditional in-class time has been replaced by online learning activities. Hybrid courses take advantage of the best features of both face-to-face and online learning.

Faculty. Figures on the number of faculty members actively involved with graduate students through teaching or research are separated into full- and part-time as well as men and women whenever the information has been supplied.

Students. Figures for the number of students enrolled in graduate and professional programs pertain to the semester of highest enrollment from the 2017–18 academic year. These figures are broken down into full- and part-time and men and women whenever the data have been supplied. Information on the number of matriculated students enrolled in the unit who are members of a minority group or are international students appears here. The average age of the matriculated students is followed by the number of applicants, the percentage accepted, and the number enrolled for fall 2017.

Degrees Awarded. The number of degrees awarded in the calendar year is listed. Many doctoral programs offer a terminal master's degree if students leave the program after completing only part of the requirements for a doctoral degree; that is indicated here. All degrees are classified into one of four types: master's, doctoral, first professional, and other advanced degrees. A unit may award one or several degrees at a given level; however, the data are only collected by type and may therefore represent several different degree programs.

Degree Requirements. The information in this section is also broken down by type of degree, and all information for a degree level pertains to all degrees of that type unless otherwise specified. Degree requirements are collected in a simplified form to provide some very basic information on the nature of the program and on foreign language, thesis or dissertation, comprehensive exam, and registration requirements. Many units also provide a short list of additional requirements, such as fieldwork or an internship. For complete information on graduation requirements, contact the graduate school or program directly.

Entrance Requirements. Entrance requirements are broken down into the four degree levels of master's, doctoral, first professional, and other advanced degrees. Within each level, information may be provided in two basic categories: entrance exams and other requirements. The entrance exams are identified by the standard acronyms used by the testing agencies, unless they are not well known. Other entrance requirements are quite varied, but they often contain an undergraduate or graduate grade point average (GPA). Unless otherwise stated, the GPA is calculated on a 4.0 scale and is listed as a minimum required for admission. Additional exam requirements/recommendations for international students may be listed here. Application deadlines for domestic and international students, the application fee, and whether electronic applications are accepted may be listed here. Note that the deadline should be used for reference only; these dates are subject to change, and students interested in applying should always contact the graduate unit directly about application procedures and deadlines.

Expenses. The typical cost of study for the 2018–2019 academic year (2017–18 if 2018–19 figures were not available) is given in two basic categories: tuition and fees. Cost of study may be quite complex at a graduate institution. There are often sliding scales for part-time study, a different cost for first-year students, and other variables that make it impossible to completely cover the cost of study for each graduate program. To provide the most usable information, figures are given for full-time study for a full year where available and for part-time study in terms of a per-unit rate (per credit, per semester hour, etc.). Occasionally, variances may be noted in tuition and fees for reasons such as the type of program, whether courses are taken during the day or evening, whether courses are at the master's or doctoral level, or other institution-specific reasons. Respondents were also given the opportunity to provide more specific and detailed tuition and fees information at the unit level. When provided, this information will appear in place of any typical costs entered elsewhere on the university-level survey. Expenses are usually subject to change; for exact costs at any given time, contact your chosen schools and programs directly. Keep in mind that the tuition of Canadian institutions is usually given in Canadian dollars.

Financial Support. This section contains data on the number of awards administered by the institution and given to graduate students during the 2017–18 academic year. The first figure given represents the total number of students receiving financial support enrolled in that unit. If the unit has provided information on graduate appointments, these are broken down into three major categories: fellowships give money to graduate students to cover the cost of study and living expenses and are not based on a work obligation or research commitment, research assistantships provide stipends to graduate students for assistance in a formal research project with a faculty member, and teaching assistantships provide stipends to graduate students for teaching or for assisting faculty members in teaching undergraduate classes. Within each category, figures are given for the total number of awards, the average yearly amount per award, and whether full or partial tuition reimbursements are awarded. In addition to graduate appointments, the availability of several other financial aid sources is covered in this section. Tuition waivers are routinely part of a graduate appointment, but units sometimes waive part or all of a student's tuition even if a graduate appointment is not available. Federal Work Study is made available to students who demonstrate need and meet the federal guidelines; this form of aid normally includes 10 or more hours of work per week in an office of the institution. Institutionally sponsored loans are low-interest loans available to graduate students to cover both educational and living expenses. Career-related internships or fieldwork offer money to students who are participating in a formal off-campus research project or practicum. Grants, scholarships, traineeships, unspecified assistantships, and other awards may also be noted. The availability of financial support to part-time students is also indicated here.

Some programs list the financial aid application deadline and the forms that need to be completed for students to be eligible for financial awards. There are two forms: FAFSA, the Free Application for Federal Student Aid, which is required for federal aid, and the CSS PROFILE®.

Faculty Research. Each unit has the opportunity to list several keyword phrases describing the current research involving faculty members and graduate students. Space limitations prevent the unit from listing complete information on all research programs. The total expenditure for funded research from the previous academic year may also be included.

Unit Head and Application Contact. The head of the graduate program for each unit may be listed with academic title, phone and fax numbers, and e-mail address. In addition to the unit head's contact information, many graduate programs also list a separate contact for application and admission information, followed by the graduate school, program, or department's website. If no unit head or application contact is given, you should contact the overall institution for information on graduate admissions.

Displays and Close-Ups

The **Displays** and **Close-Ups** are supplementary insertions submitted by deans, chairs, and other administrators who wish to offer an additional, more individualized statement to readers. A number of graduate school and program administrators have attached a **Display** ad near the **Profile** listing. Here you will find information that an institution or program wants to emphasize. The **Close-Ups** are by their very nature more expansive and flexible than the **Profiles**, and the administrators who have written them may emphasize different aspects of their programs. All of the **Close-Ups** are organized in the same way (with the exception of a few that describe research and training opportunities instead of degree programs), and in each one you will find information on the same basic topics, such as programs of study, research facilities, tuition and fees, financial aid, and application procedures. If an institution or program has submitted a **Close-Up**, a boldface cross-reference appears below its **Profile**. As with the **Displays**, all of the **Close-Ups** in the guides have been submitted by choice; the absence of a **Display** or **Close-Up** does not reflect any type of editorial judgment on the part of Peterson's, and their presence in the guides should not be taken as an indication of status, quality, or approval. Statements regarding a university's objectives and accomplishments are a reflection of its own beliefs and are not the opinions of the Peterson's editors.

Appendixes

This section contains two appendixes. The first, "Institutional Changes Since the 2018 Edition," lists institutions that have closed, merged, or changed their name or status since the last edition of the guides. The second, "Abbreviations Used in the Guides," gives abbreviations of degree names, along with what those abbreviations stand for. These appendixes are identical in all six volumes of *Peterson's Graduate and Professional Programs*.

Indexes

There are three indexes presented here. The first index, "Close-Ups and Displays," gives page references for all programs that have chosen to place **Close-Ups** and **Displays** in this volume. It is arranged alphabetically by institution; within institutions, the arrangement is alphabetical by subject area. It is not an index to all programs in the book's directories of **Profiles**; readers must refer to the directories themselves for **Profile** information on programs that have not submitted the additional, more individualized statements. The second index, "Directories and Subject Areas in Other Books in This Series", gives book references for the directories in the specialized volumes and also includes cross-references for subject area names not used in the directory structure, for example, "Computing Technology (see Computer Science)." The third index, "Directories and Subject Areas in This Book," gives page references for the directories in this volume and cross-references for subject area names not used in this volume's directory structure.

Data Collection Procedures

The information published in the directories and Profiles of all the books is collected through Peterson's Annual Survey of Graduate and Professional Institutions. The survey is sent each spring to nearly 2,300 institutions offering postbaccalaureate degree programs, including accredited institutions in the United States, U.S. territories, and Canada and those institutions outside the United States that are accredited by U.S. accrediting bodies. Deans and other administrators complete these surveys, providing information on programs in the 500 academic and professional fields covered in the guides as well as overall institutional information. While every effort has been made to ensure the accuracy and completeness of the data, information is sometimes unavailable or changes occur after publication deadlines. All usable information received in time for publication has been included. The omission of any particular item from a directory or Profile signifies either that the item is not applicable to the institution or program or that information was not available. Profiles of programs scheduled to begin during the 2018–19 academic year cannot, obviously, include statistics on enrollment or, in many cases, the number of faculty members. If no usable data were submitted by an institution, its name, address, and program name appear in order to indicate the availability of graduate work.

Criteria for Inclusion in This Guide

To be included in this guide, an institution must have full accreditation or be a candidate for accreditation (preaccreditation) status by an institutional or specialized accrediting body recognized by the U.S. Department of Education or the Council for Higher Education Accreditation (CHEA). Institutional accrediting bodies, which review each institution as a whole, include the six regional associations of schools and colleges (Middle States, New England, North Central, Northwest, Southern, and Western), each of which is responsible for a specified portion of the United States and its territories. Other institutional accrediting bodies are national in scope and accredit specific kinds of institutions (e.g., Bible colleges, independent colleges, and rabbinical and Talmudic schools). Program registration by the New York State Board of Regents is considered to be the equivalent of institutional accreditation, since the board requires that all programs offered by an institution meet its standards before recognition is granted. A Canadian institution must be chartered and authorized to grant degrees by the provincial government, affiliated with a chartered institution, or accredited by a recognized U.S. accrediting body. This guide also includes institutions outside the United States that are accredited by these U.S. accrediting bodies. There are recognized specialized or professional accrediting bodies in more than fifty different fields, each of which is authorized to accredit institutions or specific programs in its particular field. For specialized institutions that offer programs in one field only, we designate this to be the equivalent of institutional accreditation. A full explanation of the accrediting process and complete information on recognized institutional (regional and national) and specialized accrediting bodies can be found online at **www.chea.org** or at **www.ed.gov/admins/finaid/accred/index.html**.

DIRECTORY OF INSTITUTIONS AND THEIR OFFERINGS

ABILENE CHRISTIAN UNIVERSITY

Accounting	M
Business Administration and Management—General	M
Business Analytics	M
Education—General	M,O
Educational Leadership and Administration	M,D,O
Finance and Banking	M
Higher Education	M
Human Resources Development	M
Human Resources Management	M
Human Services	M,O
International Business	M
Marketing	M
Nonprofit Management	M
Reading Education	M
Social Work	M
Supply Chain Management	M

ABRAHAM LINCOLN UNIVERSITY SCHOOL OF LAW

Law	D

ACACIA UNIVERSITY

Education—General	M
Educational Leadership and Administration	M
Elementary Education	M
English as a Second Language	M
Secondary Education	M
Special Education	M

ACADEMY OF ART UNIVERSITY

Advertising and Public Relations	M
Art Education	M

ACADIA UNIVERSITY

Counselor Education	M
Curriculum and Instruction	M
Education—General	M,D
Educational Leadership and Administration	M
Music Education	M
Recreation and Park Management	M
Special Education	M

ADAMS STATE UNIVERSITY

Business Administration and Management—General	M
Counselor Education	M,D
Curriculum and Instruction	M
Education—General	M
Educational Leadership and Administration	M
Exercise and Sports Science	M
Mathematics Education	M
Music Education	M
Physical Education	M
Science Education	M
Sports Management	M

ADELPHI UNIVERSITY

Accounting	M
Art Education	M
Business Administration and Management—General	M
Education—General	M,D,O
Educational Media/Instructional Technology	M
Elementary Education	M
English as a Second Language	M,O
Finance and Banking	M
Health Education	M,O
Human Resources Management	M,O
Management Information Systems	M
Marketing	M
Physical Education	M
Reading Education	M
Secondary Education	M
Social Work	M,D
Special Education	M,O
Sports Management	M
Supply Chain Management	M

ADLER GRADUATE SCHOOL

Counselor Education	M

ADLER UNIVERSITY

Counselor Education	D
Nonprofit Management	M
Student Affairs	M
Sustainability Management	M

ADRIAN COLLEGE

Accounting	M
Athletic Training and Sports Medicine	M

AIR FORCE INSTITUTE OF TECHNOLOGY

Logistics	M,D
Management Information Systems	M

ALABAMA AGRICULTURAL AND MECHANICAL UNIVERSITY

Art Education	M
Business Administration and Management—General	M
Business Education	M,O
Counselor Education	M,O
Early Childhood Education	M,D,O
Education—General	M,D,O
Educational Media/Instructional Technology	M,O
Elementary Education	M,D,O
English Education	M,O
Home Economics Education	M,O
Hospitality Management	M
Kinesiology and Movement Studies	M
Mathematics Education	M,O
Music Education	M
Physical Education	M
Reading Education	M,D,O
Science Education	M,O
Secondary Education	M,O
Social Sciences Education	M,O

Social Work	M,O
Special Education	M,D,O

ALABAMA STATE UNIVERSITY

Accounting	M
Business Administration and Management—General	M
Counselor Education	M,D,O
Early Childhood Education	M,O
Education—General	M,D,O
Educational Leadership and Administration	M,D,O
Educational Media/Instructional Technology	M,D,O
Educational Policy	M,D,O
Elementary Education	M,O
English Education	M,O
Health Education	M
Mathematics Education	M,O
Music Education	M,O
Physical Education	M
Reading Education	M,O
Science Education	M,O
Secondary Education	M,O
Social Sciences Education	M,O
Social Work	M
Special Education	M,O

ALASKA PACIFIC UNIVERSITY

Business Administration and Management—General	M
Education—General	M
Elementary Education	M
Environmental Education	M
Investment Management	M
Middle School Education	M

ALBANY LAW SCHOOL

Law	M,D

ALBANY STATE UNIVERSITY

Accounting	M
Business Administration and Management—General	M
Counselor Education	M,O
Early Childhood Education	M,O
Education—General	M,O
Educational Leadership and Administration	M,O
English Education	M
Health Education	M,O
Human Resources Management	M
Logistics	M
Middle School Education	M,O
Physical Education	M,O
Social Work	M
Special Education	M,O
Supply Chain Management	M

ALBERTUS MAGNUS COLLEGE

Accounting	M
Business Administration and Management—General	M
Education—General	M
Human Resources Management	M
Human Services	M
Organizational Management	M
Project Management	M

ALBRIGHT COLLEGE

Early Childhood Education	M
Education—General	M
Elementary Education	M
English as a Second Language	M
Special Education	M

ALCORN STATE UNIVERSITY

Agricultural Education	M,O
Business Administration and Management—General	M
Counselor Education	M,O
Education—General	M,O
Elementary Education	M,O
Health Education	M,O
Physical Education	M,O
Secondary Education	M,O
Special Education	M,O
Vocational and Technical Education	M,O

ALFRED UNIVERSITY

Accounting	M
Business Administration and Management—General	M
Counselor Education	M,D,O
Education—General	M
Reading Education	M
Student Affairs	M

ALLEN COLLEGE

Health Education	M,D

ALLIANT INTERNATIONAL UNIVERSITY–IRVINE

Educational Psychology	M,D,O

ALLIANT INTERNATIONAL UNIVERSITY–LOS ANGELES

Business Administration and Management—General	D
Education—General	M,O
Educational Psychology	M,D,O
Student Affairs	M,D,O

ALLIANT INTERNATIONAL UNIVERSITY–SACRAMENTO

Education—General	M,O

ALLIANT INTERNATIONAL UNIVERSITY–SAN DIEGO

Business Administration and Management—General	M
Education—General	M,O
Educational Leadership and Administration	M,O
Educational Psychology	M,D,O
English as a Second Language	M,D,O
Higher Education	M,D,O
Student Affairs	M,D,O

ALLIANT INTERNATIONAL UNIVERSITY–SAN FRANCISCO

Counselor Education	M
Education—General	M,O
Educational Leadership and Administration	M,D,O
Educational Psychology	M,D,O
English as a Second Language	M,O
Higher Education	M,D,O
Law	D
Multilingual and Multicultural Education	M,O
Special Education	M,O

ALVERNIA UNIVERSITY

Business Administration and Management—General	M
Education—General	M
Organizational Management	D
Urban Education	M

ALVERNO COLLEGE

Adult Education	M
Business Administration and Management—General	M
Education—General	M
Educational Leadership and Administration	M
Educational Media/Instructional Technology	M
Reading Education	M
Science Education	M
Special Education	M

AMBERTON UNIVERSITY

Business Administration and Management—General	M
Counselor Education	M
Human Resources Development	M
Human Resources Management	M
International Business	M
Management Strategy and Policy	M
Project Management	M

AMERICAN BUSINESS & TECHNOLOGY UNIVERSITY

Accounting	M
Business Administration and Management—General	M
Finance and Banking	M
International Business	M
Management Information Systems	M
Marketing	M
Project Management	M

AMERICAN COLLEGE DUBLIN

Business Administration and Management—General	M
International Business	M

AMERICAN COLLEGE OF EDUCATION

Curriculum and Instruction	M
Education—General	M
Educational Leadership and Administration	M
Educational Media/Instructional Technology	M
English as a Second Language	M
Multilingual and Multicultural Education	M

THE AMERICAN COLLEGE OF FINANCIAL SERVICES

Business Administration and Management—General	M
Finance and Banking	M
Organizational Management	M

AMERICAN COLLEGE OF THESSALONIKI

Business Administration and Management—General	M,O
Entrepreneurship	M,O
Finance and Banking	M,O
Marketing	M,O

AMERICAN GRADUATE UNIVERSITY

Business Administration and Management—General	M,O
Supply Chain Management	M,O

AMERICAN INTERCONTINENTAL UNIVERSITY ATLANTA

International Business	M
Management Information Systems	M

AMERICAN INTERCONTINENTAL UNIVERSITY HOUSTON

Business Administration and Management—General	M

AMERICAN INTERCONTINENTAL UNIVERSITY ONLINE

Accounting	M
Business Administration and Management—General	M
Curriculum and Instruction	M
Education—General	M
Educational Leadership and Administration	M
Educational Measurement and Evaluation	M
Educational Media/Instructional Technology	M
Finance and Banking	M
Human Resources Management	M
Industrial and Manufacturing Management	M
International Business	M
Marketing	M
Project Management	M

AMERICAN INTERNATIONAL COLLEGE

Accounting	M,D,O
Business Administration and Management—General	M,D,O
Counselor Education	M,D,O

ALLIANT INTERNATIONAL UNIVERSITY–SAN FRANCISCO

(continued)

Early Childhood Education	M,D,O
Education—General	M,D
Educational Leadership and Administration	M,D
Educational Psychology	M,D,O
Elementary Education	M,D,O
Exercise and Sports Science	M,D,O
Hospitality Management	M,D,O
Middle School Education	M,D,O
Reading Education	M,D,O
Secondary Education	M,D,O
Special Education	M,D,O
Taxation	M,D,O

AMERICAN JEWISH UNIVERSITY

Business Administration and Management—General	M
Education—General	M
Nonprofit Management	M
Social Work	M

AMERICAN NATIONAL UNIVERSITY

Business Administration and Management—General	M

AMERICAN PUBLIC UNIVERSITY SYSTEM

Accounting	M,D
Business Administration and Management—General	M,D
Business Analytics	M,D
Educational Leadership and Administration	M,D
Logistics	M,D
Secondary Education	M,D
Sports Management	M,D
Transportation Management	M,D

AMERICAN SENTINEL UNIVERSITY

Business Administration and Management—General	M
Management Information Systems	M

AMERICAN UNIVERSITY

Accounting	M,O
Business Administration and Management—General	M,O
Education—General	M,O
Educational Measurement and Evaluation	M,O
Educational Media/Instructional Technology	M,O
English as a Second Language	M,O
Entrepreneurship	M,D,O
Finance and Banking	M,O
Health Education	M,O
Human Resources Management	M,O
Law	M,O
Management Information Systems	M,D,O
Marketing	M,O
Nonprofit Management	M,D,O
Organizational Management	M,D,O
Project Management	M,O
Real Estate	M,O
Sports Management	M,O
Sustainability Management	M,O
Taxation	M,O

AMERICAN UNIVERSITY IN BULGARIA

Business Administration and Management—General	M

THE AMERICAN UNIVERSITY IN CAIRO

Business Administration and Management—General	M,O
Education—General	M
Educational Leadership and Administration	M
English as a Second Language	M,O
Finance and Banking	M,O
International and Comparative Education	M
Law	M,O

THE AMERICAN UNIVERSITY IN DUBAI

Business Administration and Management—General	M
Education—General	M
Finance and Banking	M
International Business	M
Marketing	M

AMERICAN UNIVERSITY OF ARMENIA

Business Administration and Management—General	M
English as a Second Language	M
Law	M
Management Information Systems	M

AMERICAN UNIVERSITY OF BEIRUT

Business Administration and Management—General	M
Education—General	M,D
Educational Leadership and Administration	M,D
Educational Policy	M,D
Elementary Education	M,D
English as a Second Language	M,D
Finance and Banking	M,D
Human Resources Management	M
Mathematics Education	M,D
Science Education	M,D

THE AMERICAN UNIVERSITY OF PARIS

Business Administration and Management—General	M
International Business	M
Law	M

AMERICAN UNIVERSITY OF PUERTO RICO

Art Education	M
Education—General	M
Elementary Education	M
Physical Education	M
Science Education	M
Special Education	M

AMERICAN UNIVERSITY OF SHARJAH
Accounting — M,D
Business Administration and
   Management—General — M,D
English as a Second Language — M,D

AMRIDGE UNIVERSITY
Counselor Education — M,D
Human Services — M,D

ANAHEIM UNIVERSITY
Business Administration and
   Management—General — M,D,O
English as a Second Language — M,D,O
Entrepreneurship — M,D,O
International Business — M,D,O
Sustainability Management — M,D,O

ANDERSON UNIVERSITY (IN)
Accounting — M,D
Business Administration and
   Management—General — M,D
Education—General — M

ANDERSON UNIVERSITY (SC)
Business Administration and
   Management—General — M
Education—General — M
Educational Leadership and
   Administration — M
Elementary Education — M
Human Resources Management — M
Marketing — M
Music Education — M
Organizational Management — M
Supply Chain Management — M

ANDREWS UNIVERSITY
Accounting — M
Curriculum and Instruction — M,D,O
Education—General — M,D,O
Educational Leadership and
   Administration — M,D,O
Educational Psychology — M,D
Elementary Education — M
English as a Second Language — M,D,O
English Education — M,D,O
Finance and Banking — M
Foreign Languages Education — M,D,O
Higher Education — M,D,O
International and Comparative
   Education — M
Religious Education — M,D,O
Science Education — M,D,O
Secondary Education — M,D,O
Social Sciences Education — M,D,O
Social Work — M
Special Education — M

ANGELO STATE UNIVERSITY
Accounting — M
Business Administration and
   Management—General — M
Counselor Education — M
Curriculum and Instruction — M
Educational Leadership and
   Administration — M
English as a Second Language — M
Higher Education — M
Sports Management — M

ANNA MARIA COLLEGE
Business Administration and
   Management—General — M,O
Early Childhood Education — M,O
Education—General — M,O
Elementary Education — M,O
English Education — M,O
Social Work — M

ANTIOCH UNIVERSITY LOS ANGELES
Business Administration and
   Management—General — M
Education—General — M
Human Resources Development — M
Organizational Management — M

ANTIOCH UNIVERSITY NEW ENGLAND
Business Administration and
   Management—General — M
Early Childhood Education — M
Education—General — M,O
Educational Leadership and
   Administration — M,O
Educational Media/Instructional
   Technology — M,O
Elementary Education — M,O
Environmental Education — M
Foundations and Philosophy of
   Education — M,O
Science Education — M
Special Education — M,O
Sustainability Management — M

ANTIOCH UNIVERSITY SANTA BARBARA
Business Administration and
   Management—General — M
Education—General — M
Management Strategy and Policy — M
Nonprofit Management — M

ANTIOCH UNIVERSITY SEATTLE
Adult Education — M
Counselor Education — M,D
Education—General — M

APOLLOS UNIVERSITY
Business Administration and
   Management—General — M,D
Organizational Management — M,D

APPALACHIAN SCHOOL OF LAW
Law — D

APPALACHIAN STATE UNIVERSITY
Accounting — M
Business Administration and
   Management—General — M
Counselor Education — M
Curriculum and Instruction — M
Educational Leadership and
   Administration — M,O
Educational Media/Instructional
   Technology — M,O
Elementary Education — M
English Education — M
Exercise and Sports Science — M
Foreign Languages Education — M
Higher Education — M,O
Library Science — M
Mathematics Education — M
Middle School Education — M
Reading Education — M
Science Education — M
Social Sciences Education — M
Social Work — M
Special Education — M
Student Affairs — M
Taxation — M
Vocational and Technical Education — M

AQUINAS COLLEGE (MI)
Business Administration and
   Management—General — M
Education—General — M
Marketing — M
Organizational Management — M
Sustainability Management — M

AQUINAS COLLEGE (TN)
Education—General — M
Elementary Education — M
Secondary Education — M

ARCADIA UNIVERSITY
Advertising and Public Relations — M
Art Education — M,D,O
Business Administration and
   Management—General — M
Computer Education — M,D,O
Curriculum and Instruction — M,D,O
Early Childhood Education — M,D,O
Education—General — M,D,O
Educational Leadership and
   Administration — M,D,O
Educational Media/Instructional
   Technology — M,D,O
Elementary Education — M,D,O
English Education — M,D,O
Environmental Education — M
Health Education — M
Mathematics Education — M,D,O
Music Education — M,D,O
Reading Education — M,D,O
Science Education — M,D,O
Secondary Education — M,D,O
Special Education — M,D,O

ARGOSY UNIVERSITY, ATLANTA
Accounting — M,D
Business Administration and
   Management—General — M,D
Counselor Education — M,D,O
Education—General — M,D,O
Educational Leadership and
   Administration — M,D,O
Educational Media/Instructional
   Technology — M,D
Elementary Education — M
Finance and Banking — M,D
Higher Education — M,D,O
International Business — M,D
Management Information Systems — M,D
Marketing — M,D
Secondary Education — M,D,O

ARGOSY UNIVERSITY, CHICAGO
Accounting — M,D
Adult Education — M,D,O
Business Administration and
   Management—General — M,D
Community College Education — D
Counselor Education — M,D,O
Education—General — M
Educational Leadership and
   Administration — M,D,O
Elementary Education — M,D,O
Finance and Banking — M,D
Higher Education — M,D
International Business — M,D
Management Information Systems — M,D
Marketing — M,D
Organizational Behavior — D
Organizational Management — D
Secondary Education — M,D,O
Sustainability Management — M,D

ARGOSY UNIVERSITY, HAWAI'I
Accounting — M,D,O
Adult Education — M,D
Business Administration and
   Management—General — M,D,O
Education—General — M,D
Educational Leadership and
   Administration — M,D
Elementary Education — M,D,O
Finance and Banking — M,D,O
Higher Education — M,D,O
International Business — M,D,O
Management Information Systems — M,D,O
Marketing — M,D,O
Organizational Management — D
Secondary Education — M,D
Sustainability Management — M,D

ARGOSY UNIVERSITY, LOS ANGELES
Accounting — M,D

ARGOSY UNIVERSITY, NORTHERN VIRGINIA
Accounting — M,D,O
Business Administration and
   Management—General — M,D,O
Community College Education — M,D,O
Counselor Education — M,D
Education—General — M,D,O
Educational Leadership and
   Administration — M,D,O
Elementary Education — M,D,O
Finance and Banking — M,D,O
Higher Education — M,D,O
International Business — M,D,O
Management Information Systems — M,D,O
Marketing — M,D,O
Organizational Management — M,D
Secondary Education — M,D,O
Sustainability Management — M,D,O

ARGOSY UNIVERSITY, ORANGE COUNTY
Accounting — M,D,O
Business Administration and
   Management—General — M,D,O
Community College Education — M,D
Education—General — M,D
Educational Leadership and
   Administration — M,D
Educational Media/Instructional
   Technology — M,D
Elementary Education — M,D,O
Finance and Banking — M,D,O
Higher Education — M,D,O
International Business — M,D,O
Management Information Systems — M,D,O
Marketing — M,D,O
Organizational Management — D
Secondary Education — M,D
Sustainability Management — M,D,O

ARGOSY UNIVERSITY, PHOENIX
Accounting — M,D
Adult Education — M,D,O
Business Administration and
   Management—General — M,D,O
Community College Education — M,D,O
Education—General — M,D,O
Educational Leadership and
   Administration — M,D,O
Educational Media/Instructional
   Technology — M,D,O
Elementary Education — M,D,O
Finance and Banking — M,D,O
Higher Education — M,D,O
International Business — M,D
Management Information Systems — M,D
Marketing — M,D
Secondary Education — M,D,O
Sustainability Management — M,D

ARGOSY UNIVERSITY, SEATTLE
Accounting — M,D
Adult Education — M,D
Business Administration and
   Management—General — M,D
Community College Education — M,D
Education—General — M,D
Educational Leadership and
   Administration — M,D
Educational Media/Instructional
   Technology — M,D
Elementary Education — M,D
Finance and Banking — M,D
Higher Education — M,D
International Business — M,D
Management Information Systems — M,D
Marketing — M,D
Organizational Management — M,D
Secondary Education — M,D
Sustainability Management — M,D

ARGOSY UNIVERSITY, TAMPA
Accounting — M,D
Business Administration and
   Management—General — M,D
Community College Education — M,D,O
Counselor Education — M,D,O
Education—General — M,D
Educational Leadership and
   Administration — M,D,O
Elementary Education — M,D,O
Finance and Banking — M,D,O
Higher Education — M,D,O
International Business — M,D
Management Information Systems — M,D
Marketing — M,D
Organizational Management — M,D,O
Secondary Education — M,D,O
Sustainability Management — M,D

ARGOSY UNIVERSITY, TWIN CITIES
Accounting — M,D
Business Administration and
   Management—General — M,D
Education—General — M,D,O

ARIZONA STATE UNIVERSITY AT THE TEMPE CAMPUS
Educational Leadership and
   Administration — M,D,O
Educational Media/Instructional
   Technology — M,D,O
Elementary Education — M,D
Finance and Banking — M,D
Higher Education — M,D,O
International Business — M,D
Management Information Systems — M,D
Marketing — M,D
Organizational Management — M,D
Secondary Education — M,D,O
Sustainability Management — M,D

ARIZONA STATE UNIVERSITY AT THE TEMPE CAMPUS
Accounting — M,D
Art Education — M
Aviation Management — M
Business Administration and
   Management—General — M,D
Counselor Education — M
Curriculum and Instruction — M
Education—General — M,D,O
Educational Leadership and
   Administration — M,D
Educational Measurement and
   Evaluation — D
Educational Media/Instructional
   Technology — M,O
Educational Policy — D
Elementary Education — M
English as a Second Language — M,D,O
Entrepreneurship — M,D
Exercise and Sports Science — M,D
Finance and Banking — M,D
Foreign Languages Education — D
Health Education — M
Higher Education — M,D
International Business — M,D
Law — M,D
Legal and Justice Studies — M,D,O
Management Information Systems — M,D
Management Strategy and Policy — M,D
Marketing — M,D
Mathematics Education — M,D,O
Music Education — M,D
Nonprofit Management — M,D,O
Organizational Behavior — M,D
Physical Education — M
Real Estate — M,D
Secondary Education — M
Social Work — M,D,O
Special Education — M,O
Sports and Entertainment Law — M,D
Supply Chain Management — M,D
Travel and Tourism — M,D,O

ARIZONA SUMMIT LAW SCHOOL
Law — D

ARKANSAS STATE UNIVERSITY
Accounting — M
Agricultural Education — M,O
Business Administration and
   Management—General — M
Business Education — O
Community College Education — M,D,O
Counselor Education — M,O
Early Childhood Education — M,D,O
Education of the Gifted — M,D,O
Education—General — M,D,O
Educational Leadership and
   Administration — M,D,O
Elementary Education — M,D,O
English Education — M,O
Exercise and Sports Science — M,O
Foundations and Philosophy of
   Education — M,D,O
Health Education — M,D,O
Management Information Systems — O
Mathematics Education — M
Middle School Education — M,D,O
Music Education — M,O
Physical Education — M,D,O
Reading Education — M,O
Science Education — M,D,O
Social Sciences Education — M,D,O
Social Work — M,O
Special Education — M,D,O
Sports Management — M,O
Student Affairs — M,O

ARKANSAS TECH UNIVERSITY
Business Administration and
   Management—General — M
Counselor Education — M,D,O
Education—General — M,D,O
Educational Leadership and
   Administration — M,D,O
Educational Media/Instructional
   Technology — M,D,O
Elementary Education — M,D,O
English as a Second Language — M
English Education — M
Special Education — M,D,O
Student Affairs — M,D,O

ARLINGTON BAPTIST UNIVERSITY
Curriculum and Instruction — M
Education—General — M
Educational Leadership and
   Administration — M

ART ACADEMY OF CINCINNATI
Art Education — M

ASBURY THEOLOGICAL SEMINARY
Religious Education — M,D,O

ASBURY UNIVERSITY
Educational Leadership and
   Administration — M

---

*M—masters degree; D—doctorate; O—other advanced degree; *—Close-Up and/or Display*

English as a Second Language	M
Mathematics Education	M
Reading Education	M
Science Education	M
Social Sciences Education	M
Social Work	M
Special Education	M

ASHLAND THEOLOGICAL SEMINARY

Counselor Education	M,D

ASHLAND UNIVERSITY

Accounting	M
Business Administration and Management—General	M
Business Analytics	M
Education—General	M,D
Educational Leadership and Administration	M,D
Entrepreneurship	M
Exercise and Sports Science	M
Finance and Banking	M
Human Resources Management	M
International Business	M
Management Information Systems	M
Project Management	M
Sports Management	M
Supply Chain Management	M

ASHWORTH COLLEGE

Business Administration and Management—General	M
Human Resources Management	M
International Business	M
Marketing	M

ASPEN UNIVERSITY

Business Administration and Management—General	M,O
Finance and Banking	M,O
Management Information Systems	M,O
Project Management	M,O

ASSUMPTION COLLEGE

Accounting	M,O
Business Administration and Management—General	M,O
Finance and Banking	M,O
Human Resources Management	M,O
International Business	M,O
Marketing	M,O
Nonprofit Management	M,O
Special Education	M,O

ATHABASCA UNIVERSITY

Adult Education	M,O
Business Administration and Management—General	M,D,O
Counselor Education	M,O
Distance Education Development	M,D,O
Education—General	M,D,O
Organizational Management	M,O
Project Management	M,D,O
Science Education	M,O

ATHENS STATE UNIVERSITY

Logistics	M
Supply Chain Management	M
Vocational and Technical Education	M

ATLANTA'S JOHN MARSHALL LAW SCHOOL

Law	M,D

ATLANTIC UNIVERSITY

Organizational Management	M,O

ATLANTIS UNIVERSITY

Business Administration and Management—General	M,D

A.T. STILL UNIVERSITY

Athletic Training and Sports Medicine	M,D,O
Kinesiology and Movement Studies	M,D,O
Organizational Behavior	M,D,O

AUBURN UNIVERSITY

Accounting	M
Adult Education	M,D,O
Business Administration and Management—General	M,D
Curriculum and Instruction	M,D,O
Education—General	M,D,O
Educational Leadership and Administration	M,D,O
Educational Media/Instructional Technology	M,D,O
Exercise and Sports Science	M,D,O
Finance and Banking	M
Health Education	M,D,O
Higher Education	M,D,O
Physical Education	M,D,O
Real Estate	M
Special Education	M,D

AUBURN UNIVERSITY AT MONTGOMERY

Accounting	M
Business Administration and Management—General	M
Counselor Education	M,O
Early Childhood Education	M,O
Education—General	M
Educational Leadership and Administration	M,O
Educational Media/Instructional Technology	M,O
Elementary Education	M,O
Exercise and Sports Science	M,O
Legal and Justice Studies	M
Management Information Systems	M
Organizational Management	M
Physical Education	M,O
Secondary Education	M,O
Special Education	M,O
Sports Management	M,O

AUGSBURG UNIVERSITY

Business Administration and Management—General	M
Education—General	M
Organizational Management	M
Social Work	M

AUGUSTANA UNIVERSITY

Accounting	M
Education—General	M
Educational Media/Instructional Technology	M
Reading Education	M
Science Education	M
Special Education	M
Sports Management	M

AUGUSTA UNIVERSITY

Business Administration and Management—General	M
Counselor Education	M,O
Curriculum and Instruction	M,O
Education—General	M,D,O
Educational Leadership and Administration	M,O
Educational Media/Instructional Technology	D
Elementary Education	M,O
Foreign Languages Education	M,O
Middle School Education	M,O
Music Education	M,O
Secondary Education	M,O
Special Education	M,O

AURORA UNIVERSITY

Accounting	M
Adult Education	M,D
Business Administration and Management—General	M
Curriculum and Instruction	M,D
Education—General	M,D
Educational Leadership and Administration	M,D
Educational Media/Instructional Technology	M,D
English as a Second Language	M,D
Mathematics Education	M,D
Reading Education	M,D
Science Education	M
Social Work	M,D
Special Education	M,D

AUSTIN COLLEGE

Education—General	M

AUSTIN PEAY STATE UNIVERSITY

Business Administration and Management—General	M
Counselor Education	M,O
Curriculum and Instruction	M,O
Education—General	M,O
Educational Leadership and Administration	M,O
Elementary Education	M,O
Exercise and Sports Science	M
Health Education	M
Mathematics Education	M
Music Education	M
Organizational Management	M
Reading Education	M,O
Science Education	M
Secondary Education	M,O
Social Work	M
Sports Management	M

AVE MARIA SCHOOL OF LAW

Law	D

AVERETT UNIVERSITY

Accounting	M
Business Administration and Management—General	M
Curriculum and Instruction	M
Education—General	M
Educational Leadership and Administration	M
Human Resources Management	M
Marketing	M
Special Education	M

AVILA UNIVERSITY

Accounting	M
Art Education	M,O
Business Administration and Management—General	M
Early Childhood Education	M,O
Education—General	M,O
Educational Media/Instructional Technology	M
Elementary Education	M,O
English as a Second Language	M,O
Finance and Banking	M
Human Resources Management	M
International Business	M
Management Information Systems	M
Marketing	M
Middle School Education	M,O
Nonprofit Management	M
Organizational Management	M
Physical Education	M,O
Project Management	M
Reading Education	M,O
Secondary Education	M,O
Special Education	M,O

AZUSA PACIFIC UNIVERSITY

Accounting	M
Athletic Training and Sports Medicine	M
Business Administration and Management—General	M
Counselor Education	M
Curriculum and Instruction	M
Education—General	M,D
Educational Leadership and Administration	M,D

Educational Media/Instructional Technology	M
English as a Second Language	M
Entrepreneurship	M
Finance and Banking	M
Higher Education	M,D
International Business	M
Kinesiology and Movement Studies	M
Marketing	M
Music Education	M
Organizational Management	M
Social Work	M
Special Education	M
Sports Management	M

BABSON COLLEGE

Accounting	M,O
Business Administration and Management—General	M,O
Business Analytics	M,O
Entrepreneurship	M,O
Finance and Banking	M,O

BAKER COLLEGE CENTER FOR GRADUATE STUDIES—ONLINE

Accounting	M,D
Business Administration and Management—General	M,D
Finance and Banking	M,D
Human Resources Management	M,D
Management Information Systems	M,D
Marketing	M,D

BAKER UNIVERSITY

Business Administration and Management—General	M
Education—General	M
Organizational Management	M

BAKKE GRADUATE UNIVERSITY

Business Administration and Management—General	M,D
Entrepreneurship	M,D
Urban Education	M,D

BALDWIN WALLACE UNIVERSITY

Accounting	M
Business Administration and Management—General	M
Business Analytics	M
Education—General	M
Educational Leadership and Administration	M
Educational Media/Instructional Technology	M
Health Education	M
Human Resources Management	M
International Business	M
Marketing Research	M
Reading Education	M
Special Education	M

BALL STATE UNIVERSITY

Accounting	M
Actuarial Science	M
Adult Education	M,D
Advertising and Public Relations	M
Business Administration and Management—General	M,O
Business Education	M,O
Computer Science	M,D,O
Counselor Education	M,D
Curriculum and Instruction	M,D
Education of the Gifted	M,D,O
Education—General	M,D,O
Educational Leadership and Administration	M,D,O
Educational Measurement and Evaluation	M,D,O
Educational Media/Instructional Technology	M,D
Educational Policy	D
Educational Psychology	M,D
Elementary Education	M
English as a Second Language	M
Environmental Education	M
Exercise and Sports Science	M,D
Foundations and Philosophy of Education	D
Higher Education	M,D
Kinesiology and Movement Studies	M,D,O
Management Information Systems	M,O
Mathematics Education	M
Middle School Education	M,O
Music Education	M,D,O
Physical Education	M
Reading Education	M,D,O
Secondary Education	M
Special Education	M
Sports Management	M

BANK STREET COLLEGE OF EDUCATION

Early Childhood Education	M
Education—General	M
Educational Leadership and Administration	M
Elementary Education	M
Foundations and Philosophy of Education	M
Mathematics Education	M
Multilingual and Multicultural Education	M
Museum Education	M
Reading Education	M
Special Education	M

BAPTIST THEOLOGICAL SEMINARY AT RICHMOND

Religious Education	M,D,O

BARD COLLEGE

Education—General	M
Mathematics Education	M
Science Education	M
Secondary Education	M
Sustainability Management	M,O

BARRY UNIVERSITY

Accounting	M
Athletic Training and Sports Medicine	M
Business Administration and Management—General	M,O
Counselor Education	M,D,O
Curriculum and Instruction	D,O
Distance Education Development	O
Early Childhood Education	M,D,O
Education of the Gifted	M,D,O
Education—General	M,D,O
Educational Leadership and Administration	M,D,O
Educational Media/Instructional Technology	M,D,O
Elementary Education	M,D,O
English as a Second Language	M,D,O
Exercise and Sports Science	M
Finance and Banking	O
Higher Education	M,D
Human Resources Development	M,D
Human Resources Management	O
International Business	O
Kinesiology and Movement Studies	M
Law	D
Management Information Systems	O
Marketing	O
Reading Education	M,D,O
Social Work	M,D
Special Education	M,D,O
Sports Management	M

BARTON COLLEGE

Elementary Education	M

BARUCH COLLEGE OF THE CITY UNIVERSITY OF NEW YORK

Accounting	M,D
Business Administration and Management—General	M,D,O
Educational Leadership and Administration	M,O
Entrepreneurship	M,D
Finance and Banking	M,D
Higher Education	M
Human Resources Management	M,D
Industrial and Manufacturing Management	M,D
International Business	M,D
Management Information Systems	M,D
Marketing	M,D
Nonprofit Management	M,D
Organizational Behavior	M,D
Quantitative Analysis	M
Real Estate	M
Sustainability Management	M,D
Taxation	M

BAYAMÓN CENTRAL UNIVERSITY

Accounting	M
Business Administration and Management—General	M
Counselor Education	M,O
Early Childhood Education	M,O
Education—General	M,O
Educational Leadership and Administration	M,O
Elementary Education	M,O
Finance and Banking	M
Marketing	M
Special Education	M,O

BAYLOR UNIVERSITY

Accounting	M
Athletic Training and Sports Medicine	M,D
Business Administration and Management—General	M,D
Curriculum and Instruction	M,D
Education—General	M,D,O
Educational Leadership and Administration	M,O
Educational Psychology	M,D,O
Entrepreneurship	D
Exercise and Sports Science	M,D
Health Education	M,D
Kinesiology and Movement Studies	M,D
Law	D
Management Information Systems	M,D
Physical Education	M,D
Social Work	M,D
Special Education	M,D,O

BAY PATH UNIVERSITY

Accounting	M
Curriculum and Instruction	M
Educational Leadership and Administration	M
Educational Media/Instructional Technology	M
Entrepreneurship	M
Higher Education	M
Management Information Systems	M
Management Strategy and Policy	M
Nonprofit Management	M
Special Education	M

BECKER COLLEGE

Counselor Education	M

BELHAVEN UNIVERSITY (MS)

Business Administration and Management—General	M
Education—General	M,D,O
Educational Leadership and Administration	M,D,O
Human Resources Management	M,D,O
Reading Education	M,D,O
Sports Management	M

BELLARMINE UNIVERSITY

Athletic Training and Sports Medicine	M,D
Business Administration and Management—General	M
Education—General	M,D,O

Educational Leadership and
   Administration — M,D,O
Elementary Education — M,D,O
Higher Education — M,D,O
Middle School Education — M,D,O
Reading Education — M,D,O
Secondary Education — M,D,O

BELLEVUE UNIVERSITY
Business Administration and
   Management—General — M,D
Counselor Education — M
Educational Media/Instructional
   Technology — M,D
Finance and Banking — M,D
Human Resources Management — M,D
Human Services — M
Management Information Systems — M
Organizational Management — M
Project Management — M

BELMONT UNIVERSITY
Accounting — M
Business Administration—General — M
Law — D

BEMIDJI STATE UNIVERSITY
Education—General — M
Mathematics Education — M
Special Education — M

BENEDICTINE COLLEGE
Business Administration and
   Management—General — M
Education—General — M
Educational Leadership and
   Administration — M

BENEDICTINE UNIVERSITY
Accounting — M
Business Administration and
   Management—General — M,D
Curriculum and Instruction — M
Education—General — M
Educational Leadership and
   Administration — M,D
Elementary Education — M
Entrepreneurship — M
Exercise and Sports Science — M
Finance and Banking — M
Health Education — D
Higher Education — M
Human Resources Management — M
International Business — M
Logistics — M
Management Information Systems — M
Marketing — M
Organizational Behavior — M,D
Organizational Management — M,D
Reading Education — M
Science Education — M
Secondary Education — M
Special Education — M

BENTLEY UNIVERSITY
Accounting — M,D
Business Administration and
   Management—General — M,D,O
Business Analytics — M,O
Finance and Banking — M
Marketing — M
Taxation — M

BERKELEY COLLEGE–WOODLAND PARK CAMPUS
Business Administration and
   Management—General — M

BERKLEE COLLEGE OF MUSIC
Entertainment Management — M

BERRY COLLEGE
Business Administration and
   Management—General — M
Curriculum and Instruction — M,O
Early Childhood Education — M
Education—General — M,O
Educational Leadership and
   Administration — O
Middle School Education — M
Reading Education — M
Secondary Education — M

BETHANY COLLEGE
Education—General — M

BETHEL COLLEGE
Business Administration and
   Management—General — M
Education—General — M

BETHEL UNIVERSITY (MN)
Business Administration and
   Management—General — M,D,O
Education—General — M,D,O
Educational Leadership and
   Administration — M,D,O
Elementary Education — M,D,O
Organizational Management — M,D,O
Secondary Education — M,D,O
Special Education — M,D,O

BETHEL UNIVERSITY (TN)
Business Administration and
   Management—General — M
Educational Leadership and
   Administration — M

BINGHAMTON UNIVERSITY, STATE UNIVERSITY OF NEW YORK
Accounting — M
Business Administration and
   Management—General — M,D
Early Childhood Education — M
Education—General — M,D,O

Educational Leadership and
   Administration — M,D,O
English as a Second Language — M
English Education — M
Finance and Banking — D
Foreign Languages Education — M
Foundations and Philosophy of
   Education — D
Legal and Justice Studies — M,D
Management Information Systems — D
Marketing — D
Mathematics Education — M
Organizational Management — D
Reading Education — M
Science Education — M
Secondary Education — M
Social Sciences Education — M
Social Work — M
Special Education — M
Student Affairs — M
Supply Chain Management — D

BIOLA UNIVERSITY
Business Administration and
   Management—General — M
Curriculum and Instruction — M,O
Early Childhood Education — M,O
Education—General — M,O
English as a Second Language — M,D,O
Religious Education — M,D,O
Science Education — M,O
Special Education — M,O

BISHOP'S UNIVERSITY
Education—General — M,O
English as a Second Language — M,O

BLACK HILLS STATE UNIVERSITY
Business Administration and
   Management—General — M
Curriculum and Instruction — M
Management Strategy and Policy — M

BLOOMFIELD COLLEGE
Accounting — M

BLOOMSBURG UNIVERSITY OF PENNSYLVANIA
Accounting — M
Athletic Training and Sports
   Medicine — M
Business Administration and
   Management—General — M,O
Business Education — M
Counselor Education — M
Curriculum and Instruction — M,O
Early Childhood Education — M
Education—General — M,O
Educational Leadership and
   Administration — M
Educational Media/Instructional
   Technology — M,O
English Education — M
Exercise and Sports Science — M
Mathematics Education — M
Middle School Education — M
Reading Education — M
Science Education — M
Social Sciences Education — M
Special Education — M,O
Student Affairs — M

BLUEFIELD COLLEGE
Education—General — M

BLUE MOUNTAIN COLLEGE
Elementary Education — M
Reading Education — M
Science Education — M
Secondary Education — M

BLUFFTON UNIVERSITY
Accounting — M
Business Administration and
   Management—General — M
Curriculum and Instruction — M
Education—General — M
Educational Leadership and
   Administration — M
Finance and Banking — M
Industrial and Manufacturing
   Management — M
Reading Education — M
Special Education — M
Sustainability Management — M

BOB JONES UNIVERSITY
Accounting — M,D,O
Business Administration and
   Management—General — M,D,O
Counselor Education — M,D,O
Curriculum and Instruction — M,D,O
Educational Leadership and
   Administration — M,D,O
Elementary Education — M,D,O
English Education — M,D,O
Mathematics Education — M,D,O
Music Education — M,D,O
Secondary Education — M,D,O
Social Sciences Education — M,D,O
Special Education — M,D,O
Student Affairs — M

BOISE STATE UNIVERSITY
Accounting — M
Business Administration and
   Management—General — M
Counselor Education — M,D,O
Curriculum and Instruction — M,D,O
Distance Education Development — M
Early Childhood Education — M
Education—General — M,D,O
Educational Leadership and
   Administration — M,D,O

Educational Media/Instructional
   Technology — M,D,O
English as a Second Language — M
English Education — M
Kinesiology and Movement Studies — M
Mathematics Education — M
Multilingual and Multicultural
   Education — M
Music Education — M
Organizational Management — M,O
Reading Education — M
Social Work — M
Special Education — M
Sports Management — M
Taxation — M

BORICUA COLLEGE
English as a Second Language — M
Human Services — M

BOSTON COLLEGE
Accounting — M
Business Administration and
   Management—General — M
Curriculum and Instruction — M,D,O
Early Childhood Education — M
Education—General — M,D,O
Educational Leadership and
   Administration — M,D,O
Educational Measurement and
   Evaluation — M,D
Educational Psychology — M,D
Elementary Education — M
Finance and Banking — M,D
Higher Education — M,D
International and Comparative
   Education — M
Law — D
Organizational Behavior — D
Organizational Management — D
Reading Education — M,O
Religious Education — M,D,O
Science Education — M,D
Secondary Education — M
Social Work — M,D
Special Education — M,O

BOSTON UNIVERSITY
Actuarial Science — M
Advertising and Public Relations — M
Art Education — M
Athletic Training and Sports
   Medicine — M,D
Business Administration and
   Management—General — M,D
Business Analytics — M
Education—General — M,D,O
Finance and Banking — M
Health Education — M
Health Law — M,D
Hospitality Management — M
International Business — M
Law — M
Management Information Systems — M,O
Management Strategy and Policy — M,O
Music Education — M,D
Organizational Management — M
Project Management — M
Religious Education — M,D
Risk Management — M
Social Work — M,D
Supply Chain Management — M
Travel and Tourism — M

BOWIE STATE UNIVERSITY
Business Administration and
   Management—General — M
Counselor Education — M
Education—General — M
Educational Leadership and
   Administration — M,D
Elementary Education — M
Human Resources Development — M
Management Information Systems — M,O
Reading Education — M
Secondary Education — M
Special Education — M

BOWLING GREEN STATE UNIVERSITY
Accounting — M
Art Education — M
Business Administration and
   Management—General — M
Business Education — M
Counselor Education — M
Curriculum and Instruction — M
Educational Leadership and
   Administration — M,D,O
Educational Media/Instructional
   Technology — D
Higher Education — D
International and Comparative
   Education — M
Kinesiology and Movement Studies — M
Leisure Studies — M
Mathematics Education — M,D
Music Education — M,D
Organizational Management — M
Reading Education — M,O
Recreation and Park Management — M
Science Education — M
Special Education — M
Sports Management — M
Student Affairs — M
Vocational and Technical Education — M

BRADLEY UNIVERSITY
Accounting — M
Business Administration and
   Management—General — M
Counselor Education — M
Curriculum and Instruction — M
Education—General — M,D,O

Educational Leadership and
   Administration — M
Nonprofit Management — M

BRANDEIS UNIVERSITY
Business Administration and
   Management—General — M
Distance Education Development — M
Educational Leadership and
   Administration — M,O
Educational Measurement and
   Evaluation — O
Elementary Education — M,O
Entrepreneurship — M
Finance and Banking — M,D
Foreign Languages Education — D
Health Education — M
Human Services — M
International Business — M,D
Management Information Systems — M
Management Strategy and Policy — M
Marketing — M
Nonprofit Management — M
Project Management — M
Real Estate — M
Religious Education — M,O
Risk Management — M
Secondary Education — M

BRANDMAN UNIVERSITY
Accounting — M
Business Administration and
   Management—General — M
Counselor Education — M,D
Curriculum and Instruction — M,D
Early Childhood Education — M,D
Education—General — M,D
Educational Leadership and
   Administration — M,D
Educational Media/Instructional
   Technology — M,D
Elementary Education — M,D
Entrepreneurship — M
Finance and Banking — M
Human Resources Management — M
International Business — M
Marketing — M
Organizational Management — M
Secondary Education — M,D
Social Work — M
Special Education — M,D

BRANDON UNIVERSITY
Counselor Education — M,O
Curriculum and Instruction — M,O
Education—General — M,O
Educational Leadership and
   Administration — M,O
Music Education — M
Special Education — M,O

BRENAU UNIVERSITY
Accounting — M
Business Administration and
   Management—General — M
Early Childhood Education — M,O
Education—General — M,O
Middle School Education — M,O
Organizational Management — M
Project Management — M
Secondary Education — M,O
Special Education — M,O

BRESCIA UNIVERSITY
Business Administration and
   Management—General — M
Curriculum and Instruction — M
Social Work — M

BRIDGEWATER COLLEGE
Athletic Training and Sports
   Medicine — M

BRIDGEWATER STATE UNIVERSITY
Accounting — M
Art Education — M
Business Administration and
   Management—General — M
Counselor Education — M,O
Early Childhood Education — M
Education—General — M,O
Educational Leadership and
   Administration — M,O
Educational Media/Instructional
   Technology — M
Elementary Education — M
Finance and Banking — M
Mathematics Education — M
Physical Education — M
Reading Education — M,O
Science Education — M
Secondary Education — M
Social Sciences Education — M
Social Work — M
Special Education — M

BRIERCREST SEMINARY
Business Administration and
   Management—General — M
Organizational Management — M

BRIGHAM YOUNG UNIVERSITY
Art Education — M
Athletic Training and Sports
   Medicine — M,D
Business Administration and
   Management—General — M
Education—General — M,D,O
Educational Leadership and
   Administration — M,D
Educational Measurement and
   Evaluation — D
Educational Media/Instructional
   Technology — M,D

---

*M—masters degree; D—doctorate; O—other advanced degree; *—Close-Up and/or Display*

Brigham Young University (continued)

Educational Policy	M,D
Educational Psychology	M,D
English as a Second Language	M
Entrepreneurship	M
Exercise and Sports Science	M,D
Finance and Banking	M
Foreign Languages Education	M
Foundations and Philosophy of Education	M,D
Human Resources Management	M
Law	M,D
Marketing	M
Mathematics Education	M
Music Education	M
Nonprofit Management	M
Religious Education	M
Science Education	M,D
Social Work	M
Special Education	M,D,O
Supply Chain Management	M

BROADVIEW UNIVERSITY–WEST JORDAN
Business Administration and Management—General	M
Management Information Systems	M

BROCK UNIVERSITY
Accounting	M
Business Administration and Management—General	M
Education—General	M,D
English as a Second Language	M
Legal and Justice Studies	M

BROOKLYN COLLEGE OF THE CITY UNIVERSITY OF NEW YORK
Accounting	M
Art Education	M
Business Administration and Management—General	M
Counselor Education	M
Early Childhood Education	M,O
Education—General	M,O
Educational Leadership and Administration	M
Elementary Education	M,O
English Education	M
Environmental Education	M
Exercise and Sports Science	M
Finance and Banking	M
Foreign Languages Education	M
International Business	M
Kinesiology and Movement Studies	M
Mathematics Education	M
Middle School Education	M,O
Multilingual and Multicultural Education	M
Music Education	M
Organizational Behavior	M,D
Physical Education	M
Science Education	M
Secondary Education	M
Social Sciences Education	M
Special Education	M,O
Sports Management	M

BROOKLYN LAW SCHOOL
Law	M,D

BROWN UNIVERSITY
Education—General	M
Elementary Education	M
English as a Second Language	M,D
English Education	M
Multilingual and Multicultural Education	M,D
Science Education	M
Secondary Education	M
Social Sciences Education	M
Urban Education	M

BRYAN COLLEGE
Business Administration and Management—General	M
Human Resources Management	M
Marketing	M
Sports Management	M

BRYANT UNIVERSITY
Accounting	M
Business Administration and Management—General	M
Business Analytics	M
Finance and Banking	M
International Business	M
Supply Chain Management	M
Taxation	M

BRYAN UNIVERSITY
Business Administration and Management—General	M

BRYN MAWR COLLEGE
Social Work	M,D

BUCKNELL UNIVERSITY
Education—General	M
Student Affairs	M

BUENA VISTA UNIVERSITY
Counselor Education	M
Curriculum and Instruction	M
Education—General	M
English as a Second Language	M

BUFFALO STATE COLLEGE, STATE UNIVERSITY OF NEW YORK
Adult Education	M,O
Art Education	M
Business Education	M
Early Childhood Education	M
Educational Leadership and Administration	O
Educational Media/Instructional Technology	M
Elementary Education	M
English Education	M

Human Resources Management	M
Mathematics Education	M
Multilingual and Multicultural Education	M
Reading Education	M
Science Education	M
Social Sciences Education	M
Special Education	M
Student Affairs	M
Vocational and Technical Education	M

BUTLER UNIVERSITY
Accounting	M
Business Administration and Management—General	M
Counselor Education	M,O
Education—General	M,O
Educational Leadership and Administration	M,O
Entrepreneurship	M
Finance and Banking	M
International Business	M
Marketing	M
Music Education	M
Sports Management	M,O

CABRINI UNIVERSITY
Accounting	M,D
Curriculum and Instruction	M,D
Early Childhood Education	M,D
Educational Leadership and Administration	M,D
Elementary Education	M,D
English as a Second Language	M,D
Middle School Education	M,D
Organizational Management	M,D
Reading Education	M,D
Secondary Education	M,D
Special Education	M,D

CAIRN UNIVERSITY
Accounting	M,O
Business Administration and Management—General	M,O
Education—General	M,O
Educational Leadership and Administration	M,O
Entrepreneurship	M,O
Nonprofit Management	M,O
Organizational Management	M,O

CALDWELL UNIVERSITY
Accounting	M
Business Administration and Management—General	M
Counselor Education	M,O
Curriculum and Instruction	M,D,O
Education—General	M,D,O
Educational Leadership and Administration	M,D,O
Reading Education	M,D,O
Special Education	M,D,O

CALIFORNIA BAPTIST UNIVERSITY
Accounting	M
Adult Education	M
Advertising and Public Relations	M
Athletic Training and Sports Medicine	M
Business Administration and Management—General	M
Counselor Education	M
Curriculum and Instruction	M
Distance Education Development	M
Education—General	M
Educational Leadership and Administration	M
Educational Media/Instructional Technology	M
English as a Second Language	M
English Education	M
Exercise and Sports Science	M
Health Education	M
Higher Education	M
International and Comparative Education	M
Music Education	M
Nonprofit Management	M
Organizational Management	M
Physical Education	M
Reading Education	M
Science Education	M
Social Work	M
Special Education	M
Sports Management	M
Vocational and Technical Education	M

CALIFORNIA COAST UNIVERSITY
Business Administration and Management—General	M
Curriculum and Instruction	M,D
Education—General	M,D
Educational Leadership and Administration	M,D
Educational Psychology	M,D
Human Resources Management	M,D
Marketing	M
Organizational Management	M,D

CALIFORNIA COLLEGE OF THE ARTS
Finance and Banking	M
Organizational Management	M

CALIFORNIA INSTITUTE OF ADVANCED MANAGEMENT
Business Administration and Management—General	M
Entrepreneurship	M

CALIFORNIA INTERCONTINENTAL UNIVERSITY
Business Administration and Management—General	M,D
Entertainment Management	M,D
Entrepreneurship	M,D
Finance and Banking	M,D
Human Resources Management	M,D

International Business	M,D
Management Information Systems	M,D
Marketing	M
Organizational Management	M,D
Project Management	M,D
Quality Management	M,D

CALIFORNIA INTERNATIONAL BUSINESS UNIVERSITY
Business Administration and Management—General	M,D

CALIFORNIA LUTHERAN UNIVERSITY
Business Administration and Management—General	M,O
Counselor Education	M,D
Education—General	M,D
Educational Leadership and Administration	M,D
Elementary Education	M
Entrepreneurship	M,O
Finance and Banking	M,O
Higher Education	M,O
International Business	M,O
Management Information Systems	M,O
Marketing	M,O
Middle School Education	M,D
Special Education	M,D

CALIFORNIA MIRAMAR UNIVERSITY
Business Administration and Management—General	M
Management Strategy and Policy	M
Taxation	M

CALIFORNIA POLYTECHNIC STATE UNIVERSITY, SAN LUIS OBISPO
Accounting	M
Agricultural Education	M
Business Administration and Management—General	M
Business Analytics	M
Education—General	M
Supply Chain Management	M
Taxation	M

CALIFORNIA STATE POLYTECHNIC UNIVERSITY, POMONA
Accounting	M
Business Administration and Management—General	M
Curriculum and Instruction	M
Educational Leadership and Administration	D
Hospitality Management	M
Kinesiology and Movement Studies	M
Management Information Systems	M
Reading Education	M

CALIFORNIA STATE UNIVERSITY, BAKERSFIELD
Business Administration and Management—General	M
Counselor Education	M
Education—General	M,D
Educational Leadership and Administration	M,D
Mathematics Education	M
Middle School Education	M
Science Education	M
Secondary Education	M
Social Work	M
Special Education	M
Student Affairs	M

CALIFORNIA STATE UNIVERSITY CHANNEL ISLANDS
Business Administration and Management—General	M

CALIFORNIA STATE UNIVERSITY, CHICO
Agricultural Education	M
Business Administration and Management—General	M
Curriculum and Instruction	M
Kinesiology and Movement Studies	M
Mathematics Education	M
Recreation and Park Management	M
Social Work	M
Special Education	M
Travel and Tourism	M

CALIFORNIA STATE UNIVERSITY, DOMINGUEZ HILLS
Business Administration and Management—General	M
Counselor Education	M
Early Childhood Education	M
Education—General	M
English as a Second Language	M,O
International and Comparative Education	M
Quality Management	M
Social Work	M
Special Education	M

CALIFORNIA STATE UNIVERSITY, EAST BAY
Accounting	M
Actuarial Science	M
Business Administration and Management—General	M
Counselor Education	M
Early Childhood Education	M
Education—General	M
Educational Leadership and Administration	M,D
Educational Media/Instructional Technology	M
English as a Second Language	M
Finance and Banking	M
Human Resources Management	M
Industrial and Manufacturing Management	M
Management Strategy and Policy	M

Marketing	M
Mathematics Education	M
Organizational Behavior	M
Physical Education	M
Reading Education	M
Recreation and Park Management	M
Social Sciences Education	M
Social Work	M
Special Education	M
Supply Chain Management	M
Travel and Tourism	M

CALIFORNIA STATE UNIVERSITY, FRESNO
Business Administration and Management—General	M
Counselor Education	M
Curriculum and Instruction	M
Early Childhood Education	M
Education—General	M,D
Educational Leadership and Administration	M,D
English as a Second Language	M
Exercise and Sports Science	M
Kinesiology and Movement Studies	M
Mathematics Education	M
Music Education	M
Reading Education	M
Social Sciences Education	M
Social Work	M
Special Education	M
Sports Management	M
Student Affairs	M

CALIFORNIA STATE UNIVERSITY, FULLERTON
Accounting	M
Business Administration and Management—General	M
Business Analytics	M
Counselor Education	M
Educational Leadership and Administration	M,D
Educational Media/Instructional Technology	M
Electronic Commerce	M
Elementary Education	M
Finance and Banking	M
Insurance	M
International Business	M
Management Information Systems	M
Mathematics Education	M
Multilingual and Multicultural Education	M
Music Education	M
Organizational Management	M
Physical Education	M
Reading Education	M
Risk Management	M
Secondary Education	M
Social Work	M
Special Education	M
Taxation	M
Travel and Tourism	M

CALIFORNIA STATE UNIVERSITY, LONG BEACH
Art Education	M
Athletic Training and Sports Medicine	M
Business Administration and Management—General	M
Counselor Education	M,D
Education—General	M,D
Educational Leadership and Administration	M,D
Educational Psychology	M,D
Elementary Education	M
English as a Second Language	M,O
Exercise and Sports Science	M
Health Education	M
Higher Education	M
Kinesiology and Movement Studies	M
Leisure Studies	M
Mathematics Education	M
Physical Education	M
Recreation and Park Management	M
Science Education	M
Secondary Education	M
Social Work	M
Special Education	M,D
Sports Management	M
Student Affairs	M,D

CALIFORNIA STATE UNIVERSITY, LOS ANGELES
Accounting	M
Art Education	M
Business Administration and Management—General	M,O
Counselor Education	M,D
Curriculum and Instruction	M
Education—General	M,D,O
Elementary Education	M
Finance and Banking	M
International Business	M
Kinesiology and Movement Studies	M,O
Management Information Systems	M
Marketing	M
Music Education	M
Physical Education	M,O
Social Work	M
Special Education	M,D

CALIFORNIA STATE UNIVERSITY MARITIME ACADEMY
Transportation Management	M

CALIFORNIA STATE UNIVERSITY, MONTEREY BAY
Business Administration and Management—General	M
Education—General	M
Management Information Systems	M
Social Work	M

CALIFORNIA STATE UNIVERSITY, NORTHRIDGE

Art Education	M
Business Administration and Management—General	M
Counselor Education	M
Curriculum and Instruction	M
Early Childhood Education	M
Education—General	M,D
Educational Leadership and Administration	M,D
Educational Media/Instructional Technology	M
Educational Psychology	M
Elementary Education	M
English Education	M
Entertainment Management	M,O
Health Education	M,O
Hospitality Management	M,O
Kinesiology and Movement Studies	M
Mathematics Education	M
Multilingual and Multicultural Education	M
Music Education	O
Nonprofit Management	M
Reading Education	M
Recreation and Park Management	M,O
Science Education	M
Secondary Education	M
Social Work	M,O
Special Education	M,O
Taxation	M
Travel and Tourism	M

CALIFORNIA STATE UNIVERSITY, SACRAMENTO

Accounting	M
Business Administration and Management—General	M
Counselor Education	M,D,O
Curriculum and Instruction	M,D,O
Early Childhood Education	M,D,O
Education—General	M,D,O
Educational Leadership and Administration	M,D,O
Educational Media/Instructional Technology	M,D,O
Educational Policy	M,D,O
Elementary Education	M,D,O
English as a Second Language	M
Exercise and Sports Science	M
Foreign Languages Education	M,D,O
Higher Education	M
Human Resources Development	M
Human Resources Management	M
Human Services	M
Multilingual and Multicultural Education	M,D,O
Physical Education	M
Reading Education	M,D,O
Real Estate	M
Recreation and Park Management	M
Social Work	M
Special Education	M,D,O

CALIFORNIA STATE UNIVERSITY, SAN BERNARDINO

Accounting	M
Business Administration and Management—General	M
Community College Education	M
Counselor Education	M
Education—General	M
Educational Leadership and Administration	M,D
Entrepreneurship	M
Finance and Banking	M
International Business	M
Management Information Systems	M
Marketing	M
Mathematics Education	M
Social Work	M
Supply Chain Management	M

CALIFORNIA STATE UNIVERSITY, SAN MARCOS

Business Administration and Management—General	M
Education—General	M,D
Educational Leadership and Administration	M,D
Health Education	M,D
Reading Education	M,D
Social Work	M
Special Education	M,D

CALIFORNIA STATE UNIVERSITY, STANISLAUS

Business Administration and Management—General	M
Community College Education	D
Counselor Education	M
Curriculum and Instruction	M
Education—General	M,D
Educational Leadership and Administration	M,D
Educational Media/Instructional Technology	M
Elementary Education	M
English as a Second Language	M,O
Multilingual and Multicultural Education	M
Physical Education	M
Reading Education	M
Secondary Education	M
Social Work	M
Special Education	M

CALIFORNIA UNIVERSITY OF MANAGEMENT AND SCIENCES

Business Administration and Management—General	M,D

CALIFORNIA UNIVERSITY OF PENNSYLVANIA

Athletic Training and Sports Medicine	M
Business Administration and Management—General	M
Business Analytics	M
Counselor Education	M
Early Childhood Education	M
Education—General	M,D
Educational Leadership and Administration	M,D
Elementary Education	M
Entrepreneurship	M
Exercise and Sports Science	M
Legal and Justice Studies	M
Mathematics Education	M
Reading Education	M
Science Education	M
Secondary Education	M
Social Work	M
Special Education	M
Sports Management	M
Vocational and Technical Education	M

CALIFORNIA WESTERN SCHOOL OF LAW

Accounting	M,D
Law	M,D

CALUMET COLLEGE OF SAINT JOSEPH

Educational Leadership and Administration	M
Quality Management	M

CALVARY UNIVERSITY

Curriculum and Instruction	M
Education—General	M
Educational Leadership and Administration	M
Elementary Education	M
Organizational Management	M
Religious Education	M

CALVIN COLLEGE

Accounting	M
Curriculum and Instruction	M
Education—General	M

CALVIN THEOLOGICAL SEMINARY

Religious Education	M,D

CAMBRIDGE COLLEGE

Business Administration and Management—General	M
Counselor Education	M,D,O
Curriculum and Instruction	M,D,O
Early Childhood Education	M,D,O
Education—General	M,D,O
Educational Leadership and Administration	M,D,O
Educational Measurement and Evaluation	M
Educational Media/Instructional Technology	M,D,O
Elementary Education	M,D,O
English as a Second Language	M,D,O
Entrepreneurship	M
Health Education	M,D,O
Home Economics Education	M,D,O
Mathematics Education	M,D,O
Middle School Education	M,D,O
Nonprofit Management	M
Organizational Management	M
Reading Education	M,D,O
Science Education	M,D,O
Social Sciences Education	M,D,O
Special Education	M,D,O

CAMERON UNIVERSITY

Business Administration and Management—General	M
Education—General	M
Educational Leadership and Administration	M
Entrepreneurship	M

CAMPBELLSVILLE UNIVERSITY

Business Administration and Management—General	M,D
Education—General	M
Educational Leadership and Administration	M
English Education	M
Legal and Justice Studies	M
Music Education	M
Science Education	M
Social Work	M
Special Education	M
Sports Management	M

CAMPBELL UNIVERSITY

Business Administration and Management—General	M
Counselor Education	M
Education—General	M
Educational Leadership and Administration	M
Elementary Education	M
Law	D
Middle School Education	M
Physical Education	M
Secondary Education	M

CANISIUS COLLEGE

Accounting	M
Business Administration and Management—General	M
Business Education	M,O
Counselor Education	M

Early Childhood Education (right column continued)

Early Childhood Education	M
Education of the Gifted	M,O
Education—General	M,O
Educational Leadership and Administration	M,O
Educational Media/Instructional Technology	M,O
Elementary Education	M,O
English as a Second Language	M,O
International Business	M
Kinesiology and Movement Studies	M
Middle School Education	M
Physical Education	M
Reading Education	M,O
Secondary Education	M,O
Special Education	M
Sports Management	M
Student Affairs	M,O

CAPE BRETON UNIVERSITY

Business Administration and Management—General	M

CAPELLA UNIVERSITY

Accounting	M,D
Adult Education	M,D
Business Administration and Management—General	M,D
Business Education	D
Counselor Education	M,D
Curriculum and Instruction	M
Distance Education Development	M,D
Early Childhood Education	M
Education—General	M,D
Educational Leadership and Administration	M,D
Educational Media/Instructional Technology	M,D
Educational Psychology	M,D
Elementary Education	M,D
Entrepreneurship	M,D
Finance and Banking	M,D
Higher Education	M,D
Human Resources Management	M,D
Human Services	M,D
Management Information Systems	M,D
Management Strategy and Policy	M,D
Marketing	M,D
Middle School Education	M
Nonprofit Management	D
Organizational Management	M
Project Management	M,D
Reading Education	D
Social Work	M,D
Special Education	M,D
Supply Chain Management	M,D
Vocational and Technical Education	D

CAPITAL UNIVERSITY

Business Administration and Management—General	M
Law	M,D
Legal and Justice Studies	M
Music Education	M
Taxation	M

CAPITOL TECHNOLOGY UNIVERSITY

Business Administration and Management—General	M
Management Information Systems	M

CARDINAL STRITCH UNIVERSITY

Business Administration and Management—General	M
Education—General	M,D
Educational Leadership and Administration	M,D
Higher Education	M
Marketing	M
Reading Education	M,D
Special Education	M,D
Sports Management	M,D
Student Affairs	M,D
Urban Education	M,D

CARIBBEAN UNIVERSITY

Curriculum and Instruction	M,D
Early Childhood Education	M,D
Education—General	M,D
Educational Leadership and Administration	M,D
Educational Media/Instructional Technology	M,D
Elementary Education	M,D
English Education	M,D
Foreign Languages Education	M,D
Human Resources Management	M,D
Mathematics Education	M,D
Physical Education	M,D
Science Education	M,D
Social Sciences Education	M,D
Special Education	M,D

CARLETON UNIVERSITY

Business Administration and Management—General	M,D
Legal and Justice Studies	M,O
Social Work	M

CARLOS ALBIZU UNIVERSITY, MIAMI CAMPUS

Business Administration and Management—General	M,D
Education of the Gifted	M,D
English as a Second Language	M,D
Entrepreneurship	M,D
Human Services	M,D
Nonprofit Management	M,D
Organizational Management	M,D
Special Education	M,D

CARLOW UNIVERSITY

Business Administration and Management—General	M

Curriculum and Instruction (right column)

Curriculum and Instruction	M
Distance Education Development	M,O
Early Childhood Education	M,O
Education—General	M,O
Human Resources Management	M
Organizational Management	M,D,O
Project Management	M
Science Education	M
Social Work	M
Special Education	M
Student Affairs	M

CARNEGIE MELLON UNIVERSITY

Accounting	D
Business Administration and Management—General	M,D
Entertainment Management	M
Entrepreneurship	M
Finance and Banking	D
Industrial and Manufacturing Management	M,D
Management Information Systems	M,D
Marketing	D
Music Education	M
Organizational Behavior	D

CAROLINA CHRISTIAN COLLEGE

Religious Education	M

CARROLL UNIVERSITY

Adult Education	M
Business Administration and Management—General	M
Early Childhood Education	M
Education—General	M
Educational Leadership and Administration	M
Elementary Education	M
Exercise and Sports Science	M
Secondary Education	M

CARSON-NEWMAN UNIVERSITY

Business Administration and Management—General	M
Counselor Education	M
Curriculum and Instruction	M
Education—General	M
Educational Leadership and Administration	M
Elementary Education	M
English as a Second Language	M
Organizational Management	M
Secondary Education	M

CARTHAGE COLLEGE

Art Education	M,O
Counselor Education	M,O
Education of the Gifted	M,O
Education—General	M,O
Educational Leadership and Administration	M,O
English Education	M,O
Reading Education	M,O
Science Education	M,O
Social Sciences Education	M,O

CASE WESTERN RESERVE UNIVERSITY

Accounting	M,D
Art Education	M
Business Administration and Management—General	M,D
Business Analytics	M
Finance and Banking	M
Health Law	M,D
Industrial and Manufacturing Management	M,D
Intellectual Property Law	M,D
Law	M,D
Legal and Justice Studies	M,D
Logistics	M,D
Music Education	M,D
Nonprofit Management	M,D,O
Organizational Behavior	M,D
Social Work	M,D
Supply Chain Management	M,D
Sustainability Management	D

CASTLETON UNIVERSITY

Curriculum and Instruction	M
Education—General	M,O
Educational Leadership and Administration	M,O
Reading Education	M,O
Special Education	M,O

CATAWBA COLLEGE

Elementary Education	M
Science Education	M

THE CATHOLIC UNIVERSITY OF AMERICA

Accounting	M
Business Administration and Management—General	M
Early Childhood Education	M,O
Education—General	M,O
Educational Leadership and Administration	M,O
Human Resources Management	M
Information Studies	M
Law	M,D
Legal and Justice Studies	M,D,O
Library Science	M
Management Information Systems	M,O
Music Education	M,D,O
Project Management	M,O
Secondary Education	M,O
Social Work	M,O
Special Education	M,O

CEDAR CREST COLLEGE

Business Administration and Management—General	M
Education—General	M

---

*M—masters degree; D—doctorate; O—other advanced degree; *—Close-Up and/or Display*

CEDARVILLE UNIVERSITY
Business Administration and Management—General	M,D
Industrial and Manufacturing Management	M,D

CENTENARY COLLEGE OF LOUISIANA
Business Administration and Management—General	M
Education—General	M
Elementary Education	M
Secondary Education	M

CENTENARY UNIVERSITY
Accounting	M
Business Administration and Management—General	M
Education—General	M,D
Educational Leadership and Administration	M,D
Reading Education	M,D
Special Education	M,D

CENTRAL CONNECTICUT STATE UNIVERSITY
Accounting	M
Actuarial Science	M,O
Advertising and Public Relations	M,O
Art Education	M,O
Business Administration and Management—General	M
Counselor Education	M,O
Early Childhood Education	M,O
Education—General	M,D,O
Educational Leadership and Administration	M,D,O
Elementary Education	M,O
English as a Second Language	M,O
English Education	M,O
Exercise and Sports Science	M,O
Foreign Languages Education	M,O
Industrial and Manufacturing Management	M,O
Information Studies	M
Logistics	M,O
Music Education	M,O
Physical Education	M,O
Reading Education	M,O
Science Education	M,O
Secondary Education	M,O
Special Education	M,O
Supply Chain Management	M,O
Vocational and Technical Education	M

CENTRAL EUROPEAN UNIVERSITY
Business Administration and Management—General	M,D
Business Analytics	M,D
Finance and Banking	M,D
International Business	M,D
Law	M,D
Legal and Justice Studies	M,D

CENTRAL METHODIST UNIVERSITY
Counselor Education	M
Education—General	M
Music Education	M

CENTRAL MICHIGAN UNIVERSITY
Accounting	M,O
Business Administration and Management—General	M,O
Community College Education	M,D,O
Counselor Education	M
Curriculum and Instruction	M,D,O
Early Childhood Education	M,O
Education—General	M,D,O
Educational Leadership and Administration	M,D,O
Educational Media/Instructional Technology	M,D,O
Elementary Education	M,D,O
English as a Second Language	M
Exercise and Sports Science	M,D
Finance and Banking	M
Higher Education	M,D,O
Human Resources Management	M,O
Industrial and Manufacturing Management	M
International Business	M,O
Logistics	M,O
Management Information Systems	M,O
Marketing	M,O
Mathematics Education	M,D
Music Education	M
Nonprofit Management	M,O
Reading Education	M,D,O
Recreation and Park Management	M,O
Science Education	M
Secondary Education	M,D,O
Special Education	M,O
Sports Management	M,O
Student Affairs	M,D,O

CENTRAL PENN COLLEGE
Management Information Systems	M
Organizational Management	M

CENTRAL WASHINGTON UNIVERSITY
Curriculum and Instruction	M
Education—General	M
Educational Leadership and Administration	M
English as a Second Language	M
Health Education	M
Higher Education	M
Home Economics Education	M
Music Education	M
Physical Education	M
Reading Education	M
Sports Management	M
Vocational and Technical Education	M

CHADRON STATE COLLEGE
Business Administration and Management—General	M
Business Education	M,O

CHAMINADE UNIVERSITY OF HONOLULU
Accounting	M
Business Administration and Management—General	M
Early Childhood Education	M
Education—General	M
Educational Leadership and Administration	M
Elementary Education	M
Nonprofit Management	M
Secondary Education	M
Special Education	M

CHAMPLAIN COLLEGE
Business Administration and Management—General	M
Early Childhood Education	M
Law	M

CHAPMAN UNIVERSITY
Accounting	M
Athletic Training and Sports Medicine	M
Business Administration and Management—General	M
Counselor Education	M,D,O
Curriculum and Instruction	M,D,O
Education—General	M,D,O
Educational Leadership and Administration	M,D,O
Educational Psychology	M,D,O
Elementary Education	M,D,O
Environmental Law	M
Law	M,D
Secondary Education	M,D,O
Special Education	M,D,O
Sports and Entertainment Law	M,D
Taxation	M,D

CHARLESTON SCHOOL OF LAW
Law	D

CHARLESTON SOUTHERN UNIVERSITY
Accounting	M
Business Administration and Management—General	M
Education—General	M
Educational Leadership and Administration	M
Elementary Education	M
Finance and Banking	M
Human Resources Management	M
Management Information Systems	M
Organizational Management	M

CHARTER COLLEGE
Business Administration and Management—General	M

CHARTER OAK STATE COLLEGE
Organizational Management	M

CHATHAM UNIVERSITY
Accounting	M
Art Education	M
Business Administration and Management—General	M
Early Childhood Education	M
Education—General	M
Elementary Education	M
English Education	M
Environmental Education	M
Mathematics Education	M
Science Education	M
Secondary Education	M
Social Sciences Education	M
Special Education	M
Sustainability Management	M

CHESTNUT HILL COLLEGE
Early Childhood Education	M
Education—General	M
Educational Leadership and Administration	M
Educational Media/Instructional Technology	M,O
Elementary Education	M
Human Services	M,O
Middle School Education	M
Reading Education	M
Secondary Education	M
Special Education	M,O

CHEYNEY UNIVERSITY OF PENNSYLVANIA
Education—General	M,O
Educational Leadership and Administration	M,O
Elementary Education	M
Special Education	M
Urban Education	M

THE CHICAGO SCHOOL OF PROFESSIONAL PSYCHOLOGY
Organizational Management	M,D

CHICAGO STATE UNIVERSITY
Adult Education	M
Counselor Education	M
Early Childhood Education	M
Education—General	M,D
Educational Leadership and Administration	M,D
Elementary Education	M
Foundations and Philosophy of Education	M
Higher Education	M,D
Library Science	M

CHOWAN UNIVERSITY
Education—General	M

CHRISTIAN BROTHERS UNIVERSITY
Accounting	M,O
Business Administration and Management—General	M,O
Education—General	M
Educational Leadership and Administration	M
International Business	M,O
Project Management	M,O

CHRISTOPHER NEWPORT UNIVERSITY
Education—General	M

THE CITADEL, THE MILITARY COLLEGE OF SOUTH CAROLINA
Business Administration and Management—General	M
Counselor Education	M,O
Early Childhood Education	M,O
Education—General	M,O
Educational Leadership and Administration	M,O
English Education	M,O
Exercise and Sports Science	M,O
Mathematics Education	M,O
Middle School Education	M,O
Physical Education	M,O
Project Management	M,O
Reading Education	M,O
Science Education	M,O
Secondary Education	M,O
Social Sciences Education	M,O
Sports Management	M,O
Student Affairs	M,O

CITY COLLEGE OF THE CITY UNIVERSITY OF NEW YORK
Business Administration and Management—General	M
Early Childhood Education	M
Education—General	M,O
Educational Leadership and Administration	M,O
English as a Second Language	M
English Education	M
Foreign Languages Education	M
Management Information Systems	M,D
Marketing	M
Mathematics Education	M
Middle School Education	M,O
Multilingual and Multicultural Education	M
Reading Education	M
Science Education	M
Secondary Education	M
Social Sciences Education	M,O
Special Education	M,O

CITY UNIVERSITY OF NEW YORK SCHOOL OF LAW
Law	D

CITY UNIVERSITY OF SEATTLE
Accounting	M,O
Business Administration and Management—General	M,O
Counselor Education	M,O
Curriculum and Instruction	M,O
Education—General	M,O
Educational Leadership and Administration	M,D,O
Elementary Education	M,O
Finance and Banking	M,O
Human Resources Management	M,O
International Business	M,O
Management Information Systems	M,O
Marketing	M,O
Organizational Management	M,O
Project Management	M,O
Reading Education	M,O
Special Education	M,O
Sustainability Management	M,O

CITY VISION UNIVERSITY
Entrepreneurship	M

CLAFLIN UNIVERSITY
Business Administration and Management—General	M

CLAREMONT GRADUATE UNIVERSITY
Archives/Archival Administration	M,D,O
Business Administration and Management—General	M,D,O
Education—General	M,D,O
Educational Leadership and Administration	M,D,O
Educational Measurement and Evaluation	M,D,O
Electronic Commerce	M,D,O
Higher Education	M,D,O
Human Resources Development	M,D,O
Human Resources Management	M
Management Information Systems	M,D,O
Management Strategy and Policy	M,D,O
Special Education	M,D,O
Student Affairs	M,D,O
Urban Education	M,D,O

CLAREMONT SCHOOL OF THEOLOGY
Religious Education	M,D

CLARION UNIVERSITY OF PENNSYLVANIA
Accounting	M

CLARION UNIVERSITY OF PENNSYLVANIA (continued)
Advertising and Public Relations	O
Business Administration and Management—General	M
Curriculum and Instruction	M
Early Childhood Education	M
Education—General	M
Educational Media/Instructional Technology	M
Entrepreneurship	M
Finance and Banking	M
Library Science	M,O
Mathematics Education	M
Reading Education	M
Science Education	M
Special Education	M
Vocational and Technical Education	M

CLARK ATLANTA UNIVERSITY
Accounting	M
Business Administration and Management—General	M
Counselor Education	M
Curriculum and Instruction	M
Education—General	M,D,O
Educational Leadership and Administration	M,D,O
Educational Psychology	M
Mathematics Education	M
Science Education	M
Social Work	M,D
Special Education	M

CLARKE UNIVERSITY
Business Administration and Management—General	M
Education—General	M
Educational Leadership and Administration	M
Social Work	M

CLARKSON UNIVERSITY
Business Administration and Management—General	O
Early Childhood Education	M
Education—General	M
English as a Second Language	M
Human Resources Management	O
International Business	O
Middle School Education	M
Secondary Education	M
Supply Chain Management	O
Vocational and Technical Education	M

CLARKS SUMMIT UNIVERSITY
Counselor Education	M
Curriculum and Instruction	M
Educational Leadership and Administration	M
Organizational Management	M,D
Religious Education	M,D

CLARK UNIVERSITY
Accounting	M
Business Administration and Management—General	M
Business Analytics	M
Education—General	M,D
Finance and Banking	M
Health Education	M
Management Information Systems	M
Marketing	M
Sustainability Management	M

CLAYTON STATE UNIVERSITY
Accounting	M
Archives/Archival Administration	M
Business Administration and Management—General	M
Education—General	M
English Education	M
Human Resources Management	M
International Business	M
Mathematics Education	M
Sports Management	M
Supply Chain Management	M

CLEARY UNIVERSITY
Business Administration and Management—General	M,O
Business Analytics	M,O
Finance and Banking	M,O
Management Strategy and Policy	M,O

CLEMSON UNIVERSITY
Accounting	M
Agricultural Education	M,D
Business Administration and Management—General	M,D
Business Analytics	M
Business Education	M,D
Counselor Education	M,D,O
Curriculum and Instruction	M,D,O
Distance Education Development	M,D,O
Early Childhood Education	M,D,O
Education—General	M,D,O
Educational Leadership and Administration	M,D,O
Educational Measurement and Evaluation	M,D,O
Elementary Education	M,D,O
Entrepreneurship	M,D
Higher Education	M,D,O
Human Resources Development	M,D,O
Management Information Systems	M,D
Marketing	M
Mathematics Education	M,D,O
Middle School Education	M,D,O
Organizational Behavior	M,D
Reading Education	M,D,O
Real Estate	M
Recreation and Park Management	M,D,O
Science Education	D,O
Secondary Education	M,D,O
Special Education	M,D,O
Sports Management	M,D,O
Student Affairs	M,D,O
Supply Chain Management	M,D

Travel and Tourism · M,D,O

CLEVELAND STATE UNIVERSITY
Accounting · M
Adult Education · M,D,O
Art Education · M
Business Administration and
Management—General · M,D
Counselor Education · M,D,O
Early Childhood Education · M
Education of Students with
Severe/Multiple Disabilities · M
Education—General · M,D,O
Educational Leadership and
Administration · M,D,O
Educational Media/Instructional
Technology · D
Educational Policy · D
English as a Second Language · M
Foreign Languages Education · M
Health Education · M
Higher Education · D
Human Resources Management · M,D,O
Law · D
Management Information Systems · D
Marketing · M
Mathematics Education · M
Music Education · M
Nonprofit Management · M,O
Physical Education · M
Real Estate · M,O
Science Education · M
Social Work · M
Special Education · M
Urban Education · D

CLEVELAND UNIVERSITY–KANSAS CITY
Health Education · M

COASTAL CAROLINA UNIVERSITY
Accounting · M,O
Business Administration and
Management—General · M,O
Distance Education Development · M,O
Education—General · M,O
Educational Leadership and
Administration · M,O
Educational Media/Instructional
Technology · M,O
English as a Second Language · M,O
Management Information Systems · M,D,O
Reading Education · M,O
Special Education · M,D,O
Sports Management · M,O

COGSWELL POLYTECHNICAL COLLEGE
Entrepreneurship · M

COKER COLLEGE
Business Administration and
Management—General · M
Curriculum and Instruction · M
Educational Media/Instructional
Technology · M
Reading Education · M
Sports Management · M

COLGATE UNIVERSITY
Secondary Education · M

THE COLLEGE AT BROCKPORT, STATE UNIVERSITY OF NEW YORK
Accounting · M,O
Counselor Education · M,O
Curriculum and Instruction · M
Early Childhood Education · M
Education—General · M,O
Educational Leadership and
Administration · M,O
English Education · M,O
Health Education · M
Mathematics Education · M,O
Middle School Education · M
Multilingual and Multicultural
Education · M,O
Nonprofit Management · M,O
Physical Education · M,O
Reading Education · M,O
Science Education · M,O
Social Sciences Education · M,O
Social Work · M,O
Sports Management · M,O

COLLEGE FOR FINANCIAL PLANNING
Finance and Banking · M

COLLEGE OF CHARLESTON
Accounting · M
Business Administration and
Management—General · M
Early Childhood Education · M
Education—General · M,O
Elementary Education · M
English as a Second Language · O
Foreign Languages Education · M
Management Information Systems · M
Mathematics Education · M
Music Education · M
Science Education · M
Special Education · M

THE COLLEGE OF IDAHO
Curriculum and Instruction · M
Education—General · M

COLLEGE OF MOUNT SAINT VINCENT
Education—General · M,O
Educational Media/Instructional
Technology · M,O
English as a Second Language · M,O
Middle School Education · M,O

Multilingual and Multicultural
Education · M,O
Urban Education · M,O

THE COLLEGE OF NEW JERSEY
Counselor Education · M
Early Childhood Education · M
Education—General · M,O
Educational Leadership and
Administration · M
Elementary Education · M
English as a Second Language · M,O
International and Comparative
Education · M,O
Reading Education · M,O
Secondary Education · M
Special Education · M,O

THE COLLEGE OF NEW ROCHELLE
Art Education · M
Early Childhood Education · M
Education of the Gifted · O
Education—General · M,O
Educational Leadership and
Administration · M,O
Elementary Education · M
English as a Second Language · M,O
Human Resources Development · M,O
Multilingual and Multicultural
Education · M,O
Reading Education · M
Special Education · M

COLLEGE OF SAINT ELIZABETH
Business Administration and
Management—General · M
Distance Education Development · M,O
Early Childhood Education · M,O
Education—General · M,O
Educational Leadership and
Administration · M,D,O
Elementary Education · M
English as a Second Language · M,O
Higher Education · M,D,O
Human Resources Management · M
Middle School Education · M,O
Organizational Management · M
Special Education · M,O

COLLEGE OF ST. JOSEPH
Business Administration and
Management—General · M
Counselor Education · M
Education—General · M
Elementary Education · M
English Education · M
Reading Education · M
Secondary Education · M
Social Sciences Education · M
Special Education · M

COLLEGE OF SAINT MARY
Education—General · M
Educational Leadership and
Administration · M
Educational Measurement and
Evaluation · M
English as a Second Language · M
Health Education · D
Organizational Management · M

THE COLLEGE OF SAINT ROSE
Accounting · M
Business Administration and
Management—General · M
Business Analytics · M,O
Counselor Education · M,O
Curriculum and Instruction · M,O
Early Childhood Education · M,O
Education—General · M,O
Educational Leadership and
Administration · M,O
Educational Psychology · M,O
Finance and Banking · O
Higher Education · M,O
Middle School Education · M,O
Organizational Management · O
Reading Education · M,O
Secondary Education · M,O
Social Work · M
Special Education · M
Student Affairs · M

THE COLLEGE OF ST. SCHOLASTICA
Athletic Training and Sports
Medicine · M
Business Administration and
Management—General · M,O
Education—General · M,O
Exercise and Sports Science · M
Management Information Systems · M,O
Social Work · M

COLLEGE OF STATEN ISLAND OF THE CITY UNIVERSITY OF NEW YORK
Accounting · M
Business Administration and
Management—General · M
Early Childhood Education · M
Education—General · M,O
Educational Leadership and
Administration · O
Elementary Education · M
English as a Second Language · M,O
English Education · M
Management Strategy and Policy · M
Mathematics Education · M
Middle School Education · M
Multilingual and Multicultural
Education · O
Secondary Education · M
Social Work · M
Special Education · M,O

THE COLLEGE OF WILLIAM AND MARY
Accounting · M
Business Administration and
Management—General · M
Business Analytics · M
Counselor Education · M,D
Curriculum and Instruction · M,D
Education of the Gifted · M
Education—General · M,D,O*
Educational Leadership and
Administration · M,D
Educational Media/Instructional
Technology · M,D
Educational Policy · M,D
Elementary Education · M
English as a Second Language · M
Foreign Languages Education · M
Law · M,D
Mathematics Education · M
Multilingual and Multicultural
Education · M
Reading Education · M
Science Education · M
Secondary Education · M
Special Education · M

COLORADO CHRISTIAN UNIVERSITY
Business Administration and
Management—General · M
Business Education · M
Curriculum and Instruction · M
Distance Education Development · M
Early Childhood Education · M
Education—General · M
Educational Media/Instructional
Technology · M
Elementary Education · M
Project Management · M
Special Education · M

THE COLORADO COLLEGE
Art Education · M
Education—General · M
Elementary Education · M
English Education · M
Foreign Languages Education · M
Mathematics Education · M
Music Education · M
Science Education · M
Secondary Education · M
Social Sciences Education · M

COLORADO MESA UNIVERSITY
Business Administration and
Management—General · M
Education of the Gifted · M,O
Education—General · M,O
Educational Leadership and
Administration · M
English as a Second Language · M,O
Special Education · M,O

COLORADO STATE UNIVERSITY
Accounting · M
Adult Education · M,D
Advertising and Public Relations · M,D
Agricultural Education · M
Business Administration and
Management—General · M
Counselor Education · M,D
Education—General · M,D
Educational Leadership and
Administration · M,D
Exercise and Sports Science · M
Finance and Banking · M
Higher Education · M,D
Management Information Systems · M
Recreation and Park Management · M,D
Social Work · M,D
Student Affairs · M,D
Sustainability Management · M
Travel and Tourism · M,D

COLORADO STATE UNIVERSITY–GLOBAL CAMPUS
Accounting · M
Business Administration and
Management—General · M
Education—General · M
Educational Leadership and
Administration · M
Finance and Banking · M
Human Resources Management · M
International Business · M
Management Information Systems · M
Organizational Management · M
Project Management · M

COLORADO STATE UNIVERSITY–PUEBLO
Art Education · M
Business Administration and
Management—General · M
Education—General · M
Educational Media/Instructional
Technology · M
Foreign Languages Education · M
Health Education · M
Music Education · M
Physical Education · M
Special Education · M

COLORADO TECHNICAL UNIVERSITY AURORA
Accounting · M
Business Administration and
Management—General · M
Finance and Banking · M
Human Resources Management · M
Industrial and Manufacturing
Management · M
Marketing · M
Project Management · M

COLORADO TECHNICAL UNIVERSITY COLORADO SPRINGS
Accounting · M,D
Business Administration and
Management—General · M,D
Finance and Banking · M,D
Human Resources Management · M,D
Industrial and Manufacturing
Management · M,D
Logistics · M,D
Marketing · M,D
Project Management · M,D

COLUMBIA COLLEGE (MO)
Accounting · M
Business Administration and
Management—General · M
Education—General · M
Educational Leadership and
Administration · M
Human Resources Management · M

COLUMBIA COLLEGE (SC)
Education—General · M
Educational Leadership and
Administration · M
Elementary Education · M
Higher Education · M
Organizational Management · M

COLUMBIA COLLEGE CHICAGO
Business Administration and
Management—General · M
Entertainment Management · M

COLUMBIA INTERNATIONAL UNIVERSITY
Counselor Education · M,D,O
Curriculum and Instruction · M,D,O
Early Childhood Education · M,D,O
Education—General · M,D,O
Educational Leadership and
Administration · M,D,O
Elementary Education · M,D,O
English as a Second Language · M,D,O
Multilingual and Multicultural
Education · M,D,O
Religious Education · M,D,O

COLUMBIA SOUTHERN UNIVERSITY
Business Administration and
Management—General · M,D
Finance and Banking · M
Human Resources Management · M
Marketing · M
Organizational Management · M

COLUMBIA UNIVERSITY
Accounting · M,D
Actuarial Science · M
Archives/Archival Administration · M
Business Administration and
Management—General · M,D
Entrepreneurship · M
Finance and Banking · M,D
Foreign Languages Education · M,D
Foundations and Philosophy of
Education · M,D
Human Resources Management · M
Information Studies · M
International Business · M
Kinesiology and Movement Studies · M,D
Law · M,D
Legal and Justice Studies · M,D
Marketing · M
Nonprofit Management · M
Quantitative Analysis · M,D
Real Estate · M
Science Education · M,D,O
Social Work · M,D
Sports Management · M
Sustainability Management · M

COLUMBUS STATE UNIVERSITY
Art Education · M
Business Administration and
Management—General · M,O
Counselor Education · M,D,O
Curriculum and Instruction · M,O
Early Childhood Education · M,D,O
Education—General · M,D,O
Educational Leadership and
Administration · M,D,O
English as a Second Language · O
English Education · M,O
Exercise and Sports Science · M
Health Education · M
Higher Education · M,D,O
Human Resources Management · M,O
Mathematics Education · M,O
Middle School Education · M,O
Music Education · M,O
Organizational Management · M,O
Physical Education · M,O
Science Education · M,O
Secondary Education · M,O
Social Sciences Education · M,O
Special Education · M,O

CONCORDIA COLLEGE
Education—General · M
Foreign Languages Education · M

CONCORDIA COLLEGE–NEW YORK
Organizational Management · M
Special Education · M

CONCORDIA UNIVERSITY (CANADA)
Adult Education · M
Art Education · M,D
Business Administration and
Management—General · M,D,O
Education—General · M,O

*M—masters degree; D—doctorate; O—other advanced degree; *—Close-Up and/or Display*

Educational Media/Instructional
Technology — M,O
English as a Second Language — M,O
Exercise and Sports Science — M
Finance and Banking — M,D,O
Marketing — M,D,O
Mathematics Education — M,D
Organizational Management — M,O
Supply Chain Management — M,O

CONCORDIA UNIVERSITY (UNITED STATES)
Business Administration and
Management—General — M
Curriculum and Instruction — M,D
Early Childhood Education — M,D
Education—General — M,D
Educational Leadership and
Administration — M,D
Educational Media/Instructional
Technology — M,D
Elementary Education — M,D
English as a Second Language — M,D
Environmental Education — M,D
Law — D
Mathematics Education — M,D
Reading Education — M,D
Science Education — M,D
Secondary Education — M,D
Special Education — M,D
Vocational and Technical Education — M,D

CONCORDIA UNIVERSITY ANN ARBOR
Curriculum and Instruction — M
Educational Leadership and
Administration — M
Organizational Management — M

CONCORDIA UNIVERSITY CHICAGO
Business Administration and
Management—General — M
Counselor Education — M,O
Curriculum and Instruction — M
Early Childhood Education — M,D
Education—General — M
Educational Leadership and
Administration — M,D,O
Educational Media/Instructional
Technology — M
Elementary Education — M
Exercise and Sports Science — M
Human Services — M
Reading Education — M
Religious Education — M
Secondary Education — M

CONCORDIA UNIVERSITY IRVINE
Business Administration and
Management—General — M
Counselor Education — M
Curriculum and Instruction — M
Education—General — M
Educational Leadership and
Administration — M
Educational Media/Instructional
Technology — M
Physical Education — M
Sports Management — M

CONCORDIA UNIVERSITY, NEBRASKA
Early Childhood Education — M
Education—General — M
Educational Leadership and
Administration — M
Elementary Education — M
Reading Education — M
Religious Education — M
Secondary Education — M

CONCORDIA UNIVERSITY, ST. PAUL
Business Administration and
Management—General — M
Curriculum and Instruction — M,D,O
Early Childhood Education — M,D,O
Education—General — M,D,O
Educational Leadership and
Administration — M,D,O
Educational Media/Instructional
Technology — M,D,O
Exercise and Sports Science — M,D
Human Resources Management — M
Organizational Management — M
Reading Education — M,D,O
Special Education — M,D,O
Sports Management — M,D

CONCORDIA UNIVERSITY TEXAS
Education—General — M

CONCORDIA UNIVERSITY WISCONSIN
Art Education — M
Business Administration and
Management—General — M
Counselor Education — M
Early Childhood Education — M
Education—General — M
Educational Leadership and
Administration — M
Environmental Education — M
Finance and Banking — M
Health Education — M,D
Human Resources Management — M
International Business — M
Management Information Systems — M
Marketing — M
Organizational Management — M
Reading Education — M
Risk Management — M
Special Education — M

CONCORD LAW SCHOOL
Law — D

CONCORD UNIVERSITY
Education—General — M
Educational Leadership and
Administration — M

Reading Education — M
Social Work — M
Special Education — M

CONSERVATORIO DE MUSICA DE PUERTO RICO
Music Education — M

CONVERSE COLLEGE
Art Education — M
Education of the Gifted — M
Educational Leadership and
Administration — M,O
Elementary Education — M
English Education — M
Mathematics Education — M
Middle School Education — M
Music Education — M
Reading Education — O
Science Education — M
Secondary Education — M
Social Sciences Education — M
Special Education — M

COPENHAGEN BUSINESS SCHOOL
Business Administration and
Management—General — M,D
International Business — M,D
Logistics — M,D
Management Information Systems — M,D

COPPIN STATE UNIVERSITY
Adult Education — M
Curriculum and Instruction — M
Education—General — M
Human Services — M
Reading Education — M
Special Education — M

CORBAN UNIVERSITY
Business Administration and
Management—General — M
Education—General — M
Nonprofit Management — M

CORNELL UNIVERSITY
Accounting — M,D
Adult Education — M,D
Agricultural Education — M,D
Business Administration and
Management—General — M,D
Curriculum and Instruction — M,D
Education—General — M,D
Educational Policy — M,D
Facilities Management — M
Finance and Banking — D
Foreign Languages Education — M,D
Hospitality Management — M,D
Human Resources Management — M,D
Information Studies — D
Law — M,D
Marketing — D
Mathematics Education — M,D
Organizational Behavior — M,D
Real Estate — M
Secondary Education — M,D
Social Work — M,D

CORNERSTONE UNIVERSITY
Business Administration and
Management—General — M,O
Education—General — M,O
English as a Second Language — M,O

COVENANT COLLEGE
Education—General — M

CRANDALL UNIVERSITY
Education—General — M
Organizational Management — M
Reading Education — M

CREIGHTON UNIVERSITY
Accounting — M,D
Business Administration and
Management—General — M,D
Business Analytics — M,D
Counselor Education — M
Education—General — M
Educational Leadership and
Administration — M,D
Elementary Education — M
Finance and Banking — M,D
Investment Management — M,D
Law — M,D,O
Organizational Management — M
Secondary Education — M

CULVER-STOCKTON COLLEGE
Accounting — M
Business Administration and
Management—General — M
Finance and Banking — M

CUMBERLAND UNIVERSITY
Business Administration and
Management—General — M
Education—General — M

CURRY COLLEGE
Business Administration and
Management—General — M,O
Education—General — M,O
Elementary Education — M,O
Finance and Banking — M,O
Foundations and Philosophy of
Education — M,O
Reading Education — M,O
Special Education — M,O

DAEMEN COLLEGE
Accounting — M
Business Administration and
Management—General — M
Early Childhood Education — M
Education—General — M
Health Education — M
International Business — M
Management Information Systems — M

Marketing — M
Middle School Education — M
Nonprofit Management — M
Social Work — M
Special Education — M

DAKOTA STATE UNIVERSITY
Business Administration and
Management—General — M,D,O
Business Analytics — M,D,O
Education—General — M
Educational Media/Instructional
Technology — M
Management Information Systems — M,D,O

DAKOTA WESLEYAN UNIVERSITY
Curriculum and Instruction — M
Education—General — M
Educational Leadership and
Administration — M
Secondary Education — M

DALHOUSIE UNIVERSITY
Business Administration and
Management—General — M,O
Electronic Commerce — M,D
Finance and Banking — M
Health Education — M
Information Studies — M
Kinesiology and Movement Studies — M,D
Law — M,D
Leisure Studies — M
Library Science — M
Management Information Systems — M
Social Work — M

DALLAS BAPTIST UNIVERSITY
Accounting — M
Business Administration and
Management—General — M
Counselor Education — M
Curriculum and Instruction — M
Distance Education Development — M
Early Childhood Education — M,D
Education—General — M
Educational Leadership and
Administration — M,D
Educational Media/Instructional
Technology — M
Elementary Education — M
English as a Second Language — M
Entrepreneurship — M
Finance and Banking — M
Higher Education — M,D
Human Resources Management — M
International Business — M
Kinesiology and Movement Studies — M
Management Information Systems — M
Marketing — M
Multilingual and Multicultural
Education — M
Nonprofit Management — M
Organizational Management — M,D
Project Management — M
Reading Education — M
Religious Education — M
Secondary Education — M
Special Education — M
Sports Management — M
Student Affairs — M

DALLAS THEOLOGICAL SEMINARY
Adult Education — M,D,O
Educational Leadership and
Administration — M,D,O
Religious Education — M,D,O

DARTMOUTH COLLEGE
Business Administration and
Management—General — M
Entrepreneurship — D

DAVENPORT UNIVERSITY
Accounting — M
Business Administration and
Management—General — M
Finance and Banking — M
Human Resources Management — M
Management Strategy and Policy — M

DEFIANCE COLLEGE
Business Administration and
Management—General — M
Education—General — M
Management Strategy and Policy — M

DELAWARE STATE UNIVERSITY
Adult Education — M
Art Education — M
Business Administration and
Management—General — M
Curriculum and Instruction — M
Education—General — M,D
Educational Leadership and
Administration — M,D
Exercise and Sports Science — M
Foreign Languages Education — M
Mathematics Education — M
Reading Education — M
Science Education — M,D
Social Work — M
Special Education — M

DELAWARE VALLEY UNIVERSITY
Accounting — M
Business Administration and
Management—General — M
Curriculum and Instruction — M
Educational Leadership and
Administration — M
Educational Media/Instructional
Technology — M
Entrepreneurship — M
Finance and Banking — M
Human Resources Management — M
International Business — M
Supply Chain Management — M

DELTA STATE UNIVERSITY
Accounting — M
Aviation Management — M
Business Administration and
Management—General — M
Counselor Education — M,D,O
Education—General — M,D,O
Educational Leadership and
Administration — M,D,O
Elementary Education — M,D,O
English Education — M
Exercise and Sports Science — M
Health Education — D
Higher Education — M
Physical Education — M
Recreation and Park Management — M
Secondary Education — M,D,O
Social Sciences Education — M
Special Education — M

DEPAUL UNIVERSITY
Accounting — M,D
Adult Education — M
Advertising and Public Relations — M
Business Administration and
Management—General — M,D
Business Analytics — M,D
Counselor Education — M,D
Curriculum and Instruction — M,D
Early Childhood Education — M,D
Education—General — M,D
Educational Leadership and
Administration — M,D
Electronic Commerce — M,D
Elementary Education — M,D
Entrepreneurship — M,D
Finance and Banking — M,D
Foreign Languages Education — M,D
Foundations and Philosophy of
Education — M,D
Health Law — M,D
Higher Education — M,D
Hospitality Management — M,D
Human Resources Management — M,D
Intellectual Property Law — M,D
International Business — M,D
Law — M,D
Management Information Systems — M,D
Management Strategy and Policy — M,D
Marketing — M,D
Mathematics Education — M,D
Middle School Education — M,D
Multilingual and Multicultural
Education — M,D
Music Education — M
Nonprofit Management — M
Physical Education — M,D
Reading Education — M,D
Real Estate — M,D
Risk Management — M,D
Science Education — M,D
Secondary Education — M,D
Social Work — M
Special Education — M,D
Student Affairs — M,D
Supply Chain Management — M,D
Sustainability Management — M,D
Taxation — M,D

DEREE - THE AMERICAN COLLEGE OF GREECE
Marketing — M

DESALES UNIVERSITY
Accounting — M
Business Administration and
Management—General — M
Education—General — M,O
Educational Media/Instructional
Technology — M,O
English as a Second Language — M,O
Finance and Banking — M
Human Resources Management — M
Management Information Systems — M,O
Marketing — M
Project Management — M,O
Secondary Education — M,O
Special Education — M,O
Supply Chain Management — M

DEVRY COLLEGE OF NEW YORK–MIDTOWN MANHATTAN CAMPUS
Business Administration and
Management—General — M

DEVRY UNIVERSITY–ALPHARETTA CAMPUS
Business Administration and
Management—General — M

DEVRY UNIVERSITY–ARLINGTON CAMPUS
Business Administration and
Management—General — M

DEVRY UNIVERSITY–CHARLOTTE CAMPUS
Business Administration and
Management—General — M

DEVRY UNIVERSITY–CHESAPEAKE CAMPUS
Business Administration and
Management—General — M

DEVRY UNIVERSITY–CHICAGO CAMPUS
Business Administration and
Management—General — M

DEVRY UNIVERSITY–CHICAGO LOOP CAMPUS
Business Administration and
Management—General — M

DEVRY UNIVERSITY–CINCINNATI CAMPUS
Business Administration and
  Management—General ... M

DEVRY UNIVERSITY–COLUMBUS CAMPUS
Business Administration and
  Management—General ... M

DEVRY UNIVERSITY–DECATUR CAMPUS
Business Administration and
  Management—General ... M

DEVRY UNIVERSITY–FOLSOM CAMPUS
Accounting ... M
Business Administration and
  Management—General ... M
Curriculum and Instruction ... M
Educational Leadership and
  Administration ... M
Educational Media/Instructional
  Technology ... M
Finance and Banking ... M
Higher Education ... M
Human Resources Management ... M
Management Information Systems ... M
Project Management ... M

DEVRY UNIVERSITY–FREMONT CAMPUS
Business Administration and
  Management—General ... M

DEVRY UNIVERSITY–FT. WASHINGTON CAMPUS
Business Administration and
  Management—General ... M

DEVRY UNIVERSITY–HENDERSON CAMPUS
Business Administration and
  Management—General ... M

DEVRY UNIVERSITY–IRVING CAMPUS
Business Administration and
  Management—General ... M

DEVRY UNIVERSITY–JACKSONVILLE CAMPUS
Business Administration and
  Management—General ... M

DEVRY UNIVERSITY–LONG BEACH CAMPUS
Business Administration and
  Management—General ... M

DEVRY UNIVERSITY–MIRAMAR CAMPUS
Business Administration and
  Management—General ... M

DEVRY UNIVERSITY–MORRISVILLE CAMPUS
Business Administration and
  Management—General ... M

DEVRY UNIVERSITY–NASHVILLE CAMPUS
Business Administration and
  Management—General ... M

DEVRY UNIVERSITY–NORTH BRUNSWICK CAMPUS
Business Administration and
  Management—General ... M

DEVRY UNIVERSITY ONLINE
Business Administration and
  Management—General ... M

DEVRY UNIVERSITY–ORLANDO CAMPUS
Business Administration and
  Management—General ... M

DEVRY UNIVERSITY–PHOENIX CAMPUS
Business Administration and
  Management—General ... M

DEVRY UNIVERSITY–POMONA CAMPUS
Business Administration and
  Management—General ... M

DEVRY UNIVERSITY–SAN DIEGO CAMPUS
Business Administration and
  Management—General ... M,O

DEVRY UNIVERSITY–SEVEN HILLS CAMPUS
Business Administration and
  Management—General ... M,O

DEVRY UNIVERSITY–TINLEY PARK CAMPUS
Business Administration and
  Management—General ... M

DOANE UNIVERSITY
Business Administration and
  Management—General ... M
Counselor Education ... M
Curriculum and Instruction ... M,D,O
Education—General ... M,D,O
Educational Leadership and
  Administration ... M,D,O

DOMINICAN COLLEGE
Accounting ... M
Business Administration and
  Management—General ... M
Education—General ... M
Elementary Education ... M
Special Education ... M

DOMINICAN UNIVERSITY
Accounting ... M
Business Administration and
  Management—General ... M
Early Childhood Education ... M
Education—General ... M
Elementary Education ... M
English as a Second Language ... M,D,O
Information Studies ... M,D,O
Management Information Systems ... M,D,O
Reading Education ... M
Secondary Education ... M
Social Work ... M
Special Education ... M

DOMINICAN UNIVERSITY OF CALIFORNIA
Business Administration and
  Management—General ... M
Education—General ... M
Special Education ... M

DORDT COLLEGE
Education—General ... M

DRAKE UNIVERSITY
Accounting ... M
Athletic Training and Sports
  Medicine ... M,D
Business Administration and
  Management—General ... M
Counselor Education ... M,D,O
Education—General ... M,D,O
Educational Leadership and
  Administration ... M,D,O
Law ... M,D
Mathematics Education ... M,D,O
Reading Education ... M,D,O
Science Education ... M,D,O
Special Education ... M,D,O

DREW UNIVERSITY
Community College Education ... M,D,O
Education—General ... M,D,O
Elementary Education ... M,D,O
Finance and Banking ... M,D,O
Health Education ... M,D,O
Secondary Education ... M,D,O
Special Education ... M,D,O

DREXEL UNIVERSITY
Accounting ... M,D,O
Archives/Archival Administration ... M
Business Administration and
  Management—General ... M,D,O
Curriculum and Instruction ... M,D
Education—General ... M,D*
Educational Leadership and
  Administration ... M,D
Educational Media/Instructional
  Technology ... M,D
Entrepreneurship ... M
Finance and Banking ... M,D,O
Health Law ... M,D
Higher Education ... M,D
Hospitality Management ... M
Human Resources Development ... M,D
Intellectual Property Law ... M,D
International and Comparative
  Education ... M,D
Law ... M,D
Library Science ... M,D,O
Management Information Systems ... M,D,O
Management Strategy and Policy ... M,D,O
Marketing ... M,D,O
Organizational Behavior ... M,D,O
Project Management ... M
Quantitative Analysis ... M,D,O
Real Estate ... M
Special Education ... M,D
Sports and Entertainment Law ... M,D
Sports Management ... M

DRURY UNIVERSITY
Business Administration and
  Management—General ... M
Curriculum and Instruction ... M
Distance Education Development ... M
Education of the Gifted ... M
Education—General ... M
Educational Leadership and
  Administration ... M
Educational Media/Instructional
  Technology ... M
Elementary Education ... M
Middle School Education ... M
Nonprofit Management ... M
Organizational Management ... M
Reading Education ... M
Secondary Education ... M
Special Education ... M

DUKE UNIVERSITY
Accounting ... D
Business Administration and
  Management—General ... M,D,O
Business Analytics ... M
Education—General ... M
Entrepreneurship ... M,O
Finance and Banking ... M,D,O
Industrial and Manufacturing
  Management ... M,D,O
International Business ... M,O
Law ... M,D
Management Strategy and Policy ... M,D,O
Marketing ... M,D,O
Organizational Management ... M,D,O
Quantitative Analysis ... M,D,O

DUNLAP-STONE UNIVERSITY
Law ... M

DUQUESNE UNIVERSITY
Accounting ... M

Business Administration and
  Management—General ... M
Counselor Education ... M,D,O
Curriculum and Instruction ... M,O
Early Childhood Education ... M
Education—General ... M,D,O
Educational Leadership and
  Administration ... M,D,O
Educational Measurement and
  Evaluation ... M
Educational Media/Instructional
  Technology ... M,D,O
Elementary Education ... M
English as a Second Language ... M
English Education ... M
Finance and Banking ... M
Foreign Languages Education ... M
Foundations and Philosophy of
  Education ... M
Law ... M,D
Management Information Systems ... M
Marketing ... M
Mathematics Education ... M
Middle School Education ... M
Music Education ... M,O
Organizational Management ... M
Reading Education ... M
Science Education ... M
Secondary Education ... M
Social Sciences Education ... M
Special Education ... M,D
Sports Management ... M
Supply Chain Management ... M
Sustainability Management ... M

D'YOUVILLE COLLEGE
Business Administration and
  Management—General ... M
Education—General ... M,D
Educational Leadership and
  Administration ... M,D
Elementary Education ... M,D
International Business ... M
Secondary Education ... M,D
Special Education ... M,D

EARLHAM COLLEGE
Education—General ... M

EAST CAROLINA UNIVERSITY
Accounting ... M
Adult Education ... M,O
Art Education ... M
Business Administration and
  Management—General ... M,D,O
Business Education ... M,O
Community College Education ... M,D,O
Counselor Education ... M,D,O
Curriculum and Instruction ... M,O
Distance Education Development ... M,O
Early Childhood Education ... M
Education—General ... M,D,O
Educational Leadership and
  Administration ... M,D,O
Educational Media/Instructional
  Technology ... M,O
Elementary Education ... M,O
English as a Second Language ... M,D,O
English Education ... M,D,O
Exercise and Sports Science ... M,D,O
Health Education ... M
Higher Education ... M,O
Hospitality Management ... M,O
Industrial and Manufacturing
  Management ... M,D,O
International and Comparative
  Education ... M,O
Kinesiology and Movement Studies ... M,D,O
Leisure Studies ... M,O
Library Science ... M,O
Logistics ... M,D,O
Management Information Systems ... M,D,O
Mathematics Education ... M,O
Middle School Education ... M
Music Education ... M
Physical Education ... M,D,O
Reading Education ... M
Recreation and Park Management ... M,O
Science Education ... M,O
Social Sciences Education ... M
Social Work ... M,O
Special Education ... M,O
Sports Management ... M,D,O
Vocational and Technical Education ... M,O

EAST CENTRAL UNIVERSITY
Education—General ... M
Human Resources Management ... M

EASTERN CONNECTICUT STATE UNIVERSITY
Accounting ... M
Early Childhood Education ... M
Education—General ... M
Educational Media/Instructional
  Technology ... M
Elementary Education ... M
Organizational Management ... M
Secondary Education ... M

EASTERN ILLINOIS UNIVERSITY
Accounting ... M
Art Education ... M
Business Administration and
  Management—General ... M
Counselor Education ... M
Curriculum and Instruction ... M
Early Childhood Education ... M
Education—General ... M,O
Educational Leadership and
  Administration ... M,O
Elementary Education ... M
Exercise and Sports Science ... M

Human Services ... M
Kinesiology and Movement Studies ... M
Mathematics Education ... M
Middle School Education ... M
Music Education ... M
Secondary Education ... M
Special Education ... M
Student Affairs ... M

EASTERN KENTUCKY UNIVERSITY
Agricultural Education ... M
Art Education ... M
Business Administration and
  Management—General ... M
Business Education ... M
Counselor Education ... M
Curriculum and Instruction ... M
Education—General ... M
Educational Leadership and
  Administration ... M
Elementary Education ... M
English Education ... M
Exercise and Sports Science ... M
Health Education ... M
Higher Education ... M
Home Economics Education ... M
Library Science ... M
Mathematics Education ... M
Music Education ... M
Physical Education ... M
Recreation and Park Management ... M
Science Education ... M
Secondary Education ... M
Social Sciences Education ... M
Special Education ... M
Sports Management ... M
Vocational and Technical Education ... M

EASTERN MENNONITE UNIVERSITY
Business Administration and
  Management—General ... M
Counselor Education ... M
Curriculum and Instruction ... M
Education—General ... M
Nonprofit Management ... M
Organizational Management ... M
Reading Education ... M
Special Education ... M

EASTERN MICHIGAN UNIVERSITY
Accounting ... M
Art Education ... M
Athletic Training and Sports
  Medicine ... M,O
Business Administration and
  Management—General ... M,O
Community College Education ... M,D,O
Counselor Education ... M,O
Curriculum and Instruction ... M,O
Distance Education Development ... M,O
Early Childhood Education ... M
Education—General ... M,D,O
Educational Leadership and
  Administration ... M,D,O
Educational Measurement and
  Evaluation ... M,O
Educational Media/Instructional
  Technology ... M
Educational Policy ... M
Educational Psychology ... M,O
Electronic Commerce ... M,O
English as a Second Language ... M,O
English Education ... M
Entrepreneurship ... M
Exercise and Sports Science ... M
Finance and Banking ... M,O
Foreign Languages Education ... M,O
Foundations and Philosophy of
  Education ... M
Health Education ... M,O
Higher Education ... M,D,O
Hospitality Management ... O
Human Resources Management ... M,O
Human Services ... O
International Business ... M
Kinesiology and Movement Studies ... M
Management Information Systems ... M,O
Marketing ... M,O
Middle School Education ... O
Museum Education ... M
Nonprofit Management ... M,O
Organizational Management ... M,O
Physical Education ... M
Quality Management ... M,O
Reading Education ... M,O
Science Education ... M
Secondary Education ... M
Social Work ... M,O
Special Education ... M,O
Sports Management ... M
Student Affairs ... M,D,O
Supply Chain Management ... M,O
Urban Education ... M,O

EASTERN NAZARENE COLLEGE
Business Administration and
  Management—General ... M
Early Childhood Education ... M,O
Education—General ... M,O
Educational Leadership and
  Administration ... M,O
Elementary Education ... M,O
English as a Second Language ... M,O
Middle School Education ... M,O
Reading Education ... M,O
Secondary Education ... M,O
Special Education ... M,O

EASTERN NEW MEXICO UNIVERSITY
Business Administration and
  Management—General ... M
Counselor Education ... M

M—masters degree; D—doctorate; O—other advanced degree; *—Close-Up and/or Display

Curriculum and Instruction M
Early Childhood Education M
Education of the Gifted M
Education—General M
Educational Leadership and
  Administration M
Educational Media/Instructional
  Technology M
Elementary Education M
English as a Second Language M
Exercise and Sports Science M
Multilingual and Multicultural
  Education M
Physical Education M
Reading Education M
Secondary Education M
Special Education M
Sports Management M
Vocational and Technical Education M

EASTERN OREGON UNIVERSITY
Business Administration and
  Management—General M
Education—General M
Elementary Education M
Secondary Education M

EASTERN UNIVERSITY
Business Administration and
  Management—General M,D,O
Early Childhood Education M,O
Educational Leadership and
  Administration M,D,O
Elementary Education M,O
English as a Second Language M,O
English Education M,O
Foreign Languages Education M,O
Health Education M,O
Mathematics Education M,O
Middle School Education M,O
Multilingual and Multicultural
  Education M,O
Nonprofit Management D,O
Organizational Management M,D,O
Physical Education M,O
Reading Education M,O
Science Education M,O
Secondary Education M,O
Social Sciences Education M,O
Special Education M,O

EASTERN WASHINGTON UNIVERSITY
Accounting M
Adult Education M
Business Administration and
  Management—General M
Computer Education M
Counselor Education M
Curriculum and Instruction M
Early Childhood Education M
Education—General M
Educational Leadership and
  Administration M
Elementary Education M
English as a Second Language M
Exercise and Sports Science M
Foundations and Philosophy of
  Education M
Music Education M
Physical Education M
Reading Education M
Recreation and Park Management M
Social Work M
Sports Management M

EAST STROUDSBURG UNIVERSITY OF PENNSYLVANIA
Athletic Training and Sports
  Medicine M
Early Childhood Education M
Education—General M,D
Educational Media/Instructional
  Technology M
Elementary Education M
Health Education M
Physical Education M
Reading Education M
Secondary Education M,D
Special Education M
Sports Management M

EAST TENNESSEE STATE UNIVERSITY
Accounting M
Archives/Archival Administration M,O
Business Administration and
  Management—General M,O
Counselor Education M
Curriculum and Instruction M,O
Developmental Education M,O
Early Childhood Education M,D,O
Education—General M,D,O
Educational Leadership and
  Administration M,D,O
Educational Media/Instructional
  Technology M,O
Elementary Education M,O
English as a Second Language M,O
Entrepreneurship M,O
Exercise and Sports Science M,D
Human Services M
Kinesiology and Movement Studies M,D
Library Science M,O
Management Strategy and Policy M,O
Marketing M,O
Middle School Education M,O
Nonprofit Management M,O
Reading Education M,O
Secondary Education M,O
Social Work M
Special Education M,O
Sports Management M,D

EAST TEXAS BAPTIST UNIVERSITY
Business Administration and
  Management—General M
Education—General M

Kinesiology and Movement Studies M

ECOLE HÔTELIÈRE DE LAUSANNE
Hospitality Management M

EDGEWOOD COLLEGE
Accounting M
Adult Education M,D,O
Business Administration and
  Management—General M
Education—General M,D,O
Educational Leadership and
  Administration M,D,O
Special Education M,D,O
Sustainability Management M

EDINBORO UNIVERSITY OF PENNSYLVANIA
Art Education M
Counselor Education M
Early Childhood Education M,O
Educational Leadership and
  Administration M
Educational Psychology M
Middle School Education M
Reading Education M
Secondary Education M
Social Work M
Special Education M,O

ELIZABETH CITY STATE UNIVERSITY
Community College Education M
Education—General M
Educational Leadership and
  Administration M
Elementary Education M
Mathematics Education M
Science Education M

ELMHURST COLLEGE
Business Administration and
  Management—General M
Educational Leadership and
  Administration M
Management Information Systems M
Project Management M
Special Education M
Supply Chain Management M

ELMS COLLEGE
Accounting M,O
Business Administration and
  Management—General M,O
Early Childhood Education M,O
Education—General M,O
Elementary Education M,O
English as a Second Language M,O
English Education M,O
Entrepreneurship M,O
Finance and Banking M,O
Foreign Languages Education M,O
Reading Education M,O
Science Education M,O
Secondary Education M,O
Special Education M,O

ELON UNIVERSITY
Business Administration and
  Management—General M
Education of the Gifted M
Education—General M
Elementary Education M
Law D
Special Education M

EMBRY-RIDDLE AERONAUTICAL UNIVERSITY–DAYTONA
Business Administration and
  Management—General M
Finance and Banking M
Human Resources Management M

EMBRY-RIDDLE AERONAUTICAL UNIVERSITY–WORLDWIDE
Aviation Management M
Business Administration and
  Management—General M
Education—General M
Entrepreneurship M
Finance and Banking M
Human Resources Management M
Industrial and Manufacturing
  Management M
International Business M
Logistics M
Management Information Systems M
Organizational Management M
Project Management M
Supply Chain Management M

EMMANUEL COLLEGE (UNITED STATES)
Business Administration and
  Management—General M,O
Education—General M,O
Human Resources Management M,O
Special Education M,O
Urban Education M,O

EMORY & HENRY COLLEGE
Education—General M,D
Organizational Management M,D
Reading Education M,D

EMORY UNIVERSITY
Accounting M,D
Business Administration and
  Management—General M,D
Education—General M,D
Entrepreneurship M
Finance and Banking M,D
Health Education M,D
Industrial and Manufacturing
  Management M
International Business M
Law M,D,O
Management Information Systems M,D
Marketing M,D

Middle School Education M,D
Organizational Management M,D
Real Estate M
Secondary Education M,D

EMPIRE COLLEGE
Law M,D

EMPORIA STATE UNIVERSITY
Accounting M
Business Administration and
  Management—General M
Counselor Education M
Curriculum and Instruction M
Distance Education Development M,O
Early Childhood Education M
Education of the Gifted M
Education—General M
Educational Leadership and
  Administration M
Educational Media/Instructional
  Technology M,O
Elementary Education M
English as a Second Language M,O
Library Science M,D,O
Physical Education M
Reading Education M
Special Education M

ENDICOTT COLLEGE
Business Administration and
  Management—General M
Distance Education Development M
Early Childhood Education M
Educational Leadership and
  Administration M,D
Elementary Education M
Management Information Systems M
Organizational Management M
Reading Education M
Secondary Education M
Special Education M,D,O
Sports Management M

ERIKSON INSTITUTE
Early Childhood Education M,D
English as a Second Language M,O

ESSEC BUSINESS SCHOOL
Business Administration and
  Management—General M,D
Hospitality Management M,D
International Business M,D

EVANGEL UNIVERSITY
Counselor Education M
Curriculum and Instruction M,D
Education—General M
Educational Leadership and
  Administration M,D
Organizational Management M
Reading Education M
Secondary Education M

EVERGLADES UNIVERSITY
Accounting M
Business Administration and
  Management—General M
Entrepreneurship M
Human Resources Management M
Industrial and Manufacturing
  Management M
Project Management M

THE EVERGREEN STATE COLLEGE
Education—General M

EXCELSIOR COLLEGE
Business Administration and
  Management—General M,O
Health Education M
Human Resources Management M,O
Organizational Management M

FAIRFIELD UNIVERSITY
Accounting M,O
Business Administration and
  Management—General M,O
Business Analytics M,O
Counselor Education M,O
Education—General M,O
Educational Media/Instructional
  Technology M,O
Elementary Education M,O
English as a Second Language M,O
Finance and Banking M,O
Foundations and Philosophy of
  Education M,O
Health Education M,D
Management Information Systems M,O
Marketing M,O
Multilingual and Multicultural
  Education M,O
Secondary Education M,O
Special Education M,O
Taxation M,O

FAIRLEIGH DICKINSON UNIVERSITY, FLORHAM CAMPUS
Accounting M
Business Administration and
  Management—General M,O
Early Childhood Education M,O
Education—General M,O
Educational Leadership and
  Administration M
Educational Media/Instructional
  Technology M,O
Entrepreneurship M,O
Finance and Banking M,O
Hospitality Management M
Human Resources Management M,O
International Business M,O
Marketing M,O
Organizational Behavior M,O
Organizational Management M,O
Reading Education M,O
Sports Management M

Supply Chain Management M
Sustainability Management O
Taxation M

FAIRLEIGH DICKINSON UNIVERSITY, METROPOLITAN CAMPUS
Accounting M,O
Business Administration and
  Management—General M,O
Curriculum and Instruction M,O
Early Childhood Education M
Education—General M,O
Educational Leadership and
  Administration M
Educational Media/Instructional
  Technology M,O
Electronic Commerce M
Entrepreneurship M,O
Finance and Banking M,O
Foundations and Philosophy of
  Education M
Hospitality Management M
Human Resources Management M,O
International Business M
Management Information Systems M,O
Marketing M,O
Multilingual and Multicultural
  Education M
Nonprofit Management M,O
Reading Education M,O
Science Education M
Special Education M
Sports Management M
Taxation M

FAIRMONT STATE UNIVERSITY
Business Administration and
  Management—General M
Education—General M
Educational Media/Instructional
  Technology M
Exercise and Sports Science M
Reading Education M
Special Education M

FASHION INSTITUTE OF TECHNOLOGY
Business Administration and
  Management—General M
Marketing M

FAULKNER UNIVERSITY
Business Administration and
  Management—General M
Counselor Education M
Curriculum and Instruction M
Education—General M
Elementary Education M
Law D

FAYETTEVILLE STATE UNIVERSITY
Business Administration and
  Management—General M
Educational Leadership and
  Administration M,D
Elementary Education M
Middle School Education M
Secondary Education M
Social Sciences Education M
Social Work M

FELICIAN UNIVERSITY
Business Administration and
  Management—General M,D
Education—General M,O
Educational Leadership and
  Administration M,O
Entrepreneurship M,D
Religious Education M,O

FERRIS STATE UNIVERSITY
Art Education M
Business Administration and
  Management—General M
Community College Education D
Curriculum and Instruction M
Developmental Education M
Education—General M
Educational Leadership and
  Administration M,D
Human Services M
Management Information Systems M
Project Management M
Social Work M
Special Education M
Supply Chain Management M

FIELDING GRADUATE UNIVERSITY
Early Childhood Education M,D,O
Education—General M,D
Organizational Management O

FISHER COLLEGE
Business Administration and
  Management—General M
Management Strategy and Policy M

FITCHBURG STATE UNIVERSITY
Accounting M
Art Education M,O
Business Administration and
  Management—General M,O
Counselor Education M,O
Curriculum and Instruction M
Early Childhood Education M
Educational Leadership and
  Administration M,O
Elementary Education M,O
English Education M,O
Higher Education M,O
Human Resources Management M
Mathematics Education M
Middle School Education M,O
Reading Education M,O
Science Education M
Social Sciences Education M
Special Education M,O
Vocational and Technical Education M

FIVE TOWNS COLLEGE
Early Childhood Education — M,D
Music Education — M,D

FLAGLER COLLEGE
Special Education — M

FLORIDA AGRICULTURAL AND MECHANICAL UNIVERSITY
Accounting — M
Adult Education — M,D
Business Administration and
  Management—General — M
Business Education — M
Counselor Education — M,D
Education—General — M,D
Educational Leadership and
  Administration — M,D
Elementary Education — M
English Education — M
Finance and Banking — M
Law — D
Management Information Systems — M
Marketing — M
Mathematics Education — M
Physical Education — M
Science Education — M
Secondary Education — M
Social Sciences Education — M
Social Work — M
Sports Management — M
Vocational and Technical Education — M

FLORIDA ATLANTIC UNIVERSITY
Accounting — M
Adult Education — M,D,O
Art Education — M
Business Administration and
  Management—General — M
Counselor Education — M,D
Curriculum and Instruction — M,D,O
Early Childhood Education — M,D,O
Education—General — M
Educational Leadership and
  Administration — M,D,O
Educational Media/Instructional
  Technology — M
Educational Psychology — M
Elementary Education — M
English as a Second Language — M,D,O
English Education — M
Entrepreneurship — M
Environmental Education — M
Exercise and Sports Science — M
Foundations and Philosophy of
  Education — M
Higher Education — M,D,O
International Business — M
Management Information Systems — M
Mathematics Education — M
Multilingual and Multicultural
  Education — M
Music Education — M
Nonprofit Management — M,D
Reading Education — M
Science Education — M,D
Social Sciences Education — M,D
Social Work — M,D
Special Education — M,D
Sports Management — M

FLORIDA COASTAL SCHOOL OF LAW
Law — D

FLORIDA GULF COAST UNIVERSITY
Accounting — M
Business Administration and
  Management—General — M
Curriculum and Instruction — M
Education of the Gifted — M
Education—General — M
Educational Leadership and
  Administration — M
Elementary Education — M
English as a Second Language — M
English Education — M
Management Information Systems — M
Mathematics Education — M
Middle School Education — M
Reading Education — M
Science Education — M
Social Sciences Education — M
Social Work — M
Special Education — M
Taxation — M

FLORIDA INSTITUTE OF TECHNOLOGY
Aviation Management — M
Business Administration and
  Management—General — M,D
Computer Education — M
Education—General — M
Educational Media/Instructional
  Technology — M
Electronic Commerce — M,D
Elementary Education — M
Entrepreneurship — M
Environmental Education — M,D
Human Resources Management — M
Logistics — M,D
Management Information Systems — M,D
Mathematics Education — M,D,O
Organizational Behavior — M
Organizational Management — M
Project Management — M,D
Quality Management — M,D
Science Education — M,D,O
Supply Chain Management — M,D
Transportation Management — M,D

FLORIDA INTERNATIONAL UNIVERSITY
Accounting — M
Adult Education — M,D,O

Art Education — M,D,O
Athletic Training and Sports
  Medicine — M
Counselor Education — M,D,O
Curriculum and Instruction — M,D,O
Early Childhood Education — M,D,O
Educational Leadership and
  Administration — M,D,O
Educational Media/Instructional
  Technology — M,D,O
Elementary Education — M,D,O
English as a Second Language — M,D,O
English Education — M,D,O
Finance and Banking — M
Foreign Languages Education — M,D,O
Higher Education — M,D,O
Hospitality Management — M
Human Resources Development — M,D,O
Human Resources Management — M,D
International and Comparative
  Education — M,D
International Business — M,D
Law — M,D
Management Information Systems — M,D
Marketing — M
Mathematics Education — M,D,O
Multilingual and Multicultural
  Education — M,D,O
Music Education — M
Physical Education — M,D,O
Reading Education — M,D,O
Real Estate — M
Recreation and Park Management — M,D,O
Science Education — M,D,O
Social Sciences Education — M,D,O
Social Work — M,D
Special Education — M,D,O
Sports Management — M,D,O
Urban Education — M,D,O

FLORIDA MEMORIAL UNIVERSITY
Business Administration and
  Management—General — M
Education—General — M
Elementary Education — M
Reading Education — M
Special Education — M

FLORIDA NATIONAL UNIVERSITY
Accounting — M
Business Administration and
  Management—General — M
Finance and Banking — M
Marketing — M

FLORIDA SOUTHERN COLLEGE
Accounting — M
Business Administration and
  Management—General — M
Education—General — M,D
Educational Leadership and
  Administration — M,D

FLORIDA STATE UNIVERSITY
Accounting — M,D
Actuarial Science — M,D
Art Education — M,D
Business Administration and
  Management—General — M,D
Curriculum and Instruction — M,D,O
Early Childhood Education — M,D,O
Education—General — M,D,O
Educational Leadership and
  Administration — M,D,O
Educational Measurement and
  Evaluation — M,D,O
Educational Media/Instructional
  Technology — M,D,O
Educational Policy — M,D,O
Educational Psychology — M,D,O
Elementary Education — M,D,O
English as a Second Language — M,D,O
English Education — M,D,O
Environmental Law — M,D
Exercise and Sports Science — M,D
Finance and Banking — M,D
Foreign Languages Education — M,D,O
Foundations and Philosophy of
  Education — M,D,O
Health Education — M,D
Health Law — M,D
Higher Education — M,D,O
Human Resources Management — M,D
Information Studies — M,D,O
Insurance — M,D
International and Comparative
  Education — M,D,O
International Business — M
Law — M,D
Library Science — M,D,O
Management Information Systems — M,D,O
Management Strategy and Policy — M,D
Marketing — M,D
Mathematics Education — M,D,O
Organizational Behavior — M,D
Reading Education — M,D,O
Risk Management — M,D
Science Education — M,D,O
Social Sciences Education — M,D,O
Social Work — M,D,O
Special Education — M,D,O
Sports Management — M,D
Taxation — M,D

FONTBONNE UNIVERSITY
Accounting — M
Art Education — M
Business Administration and
  Management—General — M
Curriculum and Instruction — M
Early Childhood Education — M
Education—General — M

Educational Media/Instructional
  Technology — M
Elementary Education — M
Middle School Education — M
Reading Education — M
Secondary Education — M
Special Education — M
Supply Chain Management — M

FORDHAM UNIVERSITY
Accounting — M,D
Business Administration and
  Management—General — M,D
Counselor Education — M,D
Curriculum and Instruction — M,O
Early Childhood Education — M,O
Education—General — M,D,O
Educational Leadership and
  Administration — M,D,O
Educational Psychology — M,D
Electronic Commerce — M,D
Elementary Education — M,O
English as a Second Language — M,O
Entrepreneurship — M,D
Finance and Banking — M,D
Intellectual Property Law — M,D
Investment Management — M,D
Law — M,D
Management Information Systems — M,D
Marketing — M,D
Nonprofit Management — M,D
Quantitative Analysis — M,D
Religious Education — M,D
Social Work — M,D
Special Education — M,O
Taxation — M,D

FORT HAYS STATE UNIVERSITY
Business Administration and
  Management—General — M
Counselor Education — M
Education—General — M,O
Educational Leadership and
  Administration — M,O
Educational Media/Instructional
  Technology — M
Health Education — M
Physical Education — M
Special Education — M

FORT LEWIS COLLEGE
Educational Leadership and
  Administration — M,O

FORT VALLEY STATE UNIVERSITY
Counselor Education — M,O

FRAMINGHAM STATE UNIVERSITY
Art Education — M
Business Administration and
  Management—General — M
Curriculum and Instruction — M
Early Childhood Education — M
Educational Leadership and
  Administration — M
Educational Media/Instructional
  Technology — M
Elementary Education — M
English as a Second Language — M,O
Human Resources Management — M
Mathematics Education — M
Reading Education — M
Special Education — M

FRANCISCAN UNIVERSITY OF STEUBENVILLE
Business Administration and
  Management—General — M
Curriculum and Instruction — M
Education—General — M
Educational Leadership and
  Administration — M

FRANCIS MARION UNIVERSITY
Business Administration and
  Management—General — M
Education—General — M
Special Education — M

FRANKLIN COLLEGE
Athletic Training and Sports
  Medicine — M

FRANKLIN PIERCE UNIVERSITY
Business Administration and
  Management—General — M,D,O
Curriculum and Instruction — M,D,O
Elementary Education — M,D,O
Human Resources Management — M,D,O
Management Information Systems — M,D,O
Special Education — M,D,O
Sports Management — M,D,O
Sustainability Management — M,D,O

FRANKLIN UNIVERSITY
Accounting — M
Business Administration and
  Management—General — M
Educational Media/Instructional
  Technology — M
Marketing — M

FRANKLIN UNIVERSITY SWITZERLAND
International Business — M

FREED-HARDEMAN UNIVERSITY
Accounting — M
Business Administration and
  Management—General — M
Counselor Education — M,O
Curriculum and Instruction — M,O
Education—General — M,O
Educational Leadership and
  Administration — M,O
Management Strategy and Policy — M

Educational Media/Instructional
  Technology — M
Elementary Education — M
Middle School Education — M
Reading Education — M
Secondary Education — M
Special Education — M
Supply Chain Management — M

FRESNO PACIFIC UNIVERSITY
Business Administration and
  Management—General — M
Counselor Education — M
Curriculum and Instruction — M
Education—General — M,O
Educational Leadership and
  Administration — M
Educational Media/Instructional
  Technology — M
English as a Second Language — M
Kinesiology and Movement Studies — M
Mathematics Education — M
Reading Education — M
Science Education — M
Special Education — M
Student Affairs — M,O

FRIENDS UNIVERSITY
Accounting — M
Law — M
Logistics — M
Management Information Systems — M
Management Strategy and Policy — M
Supply Chain Management — M

FROSTBURG STATE UNIVERSITY
Business Administration and
  Management—General — M
Counselor Education — M
Curriculum and Instruction — M,D
Education—General — M,D
Educational Leadership and
  Administration — M,D
Educational Media/Instructional
  Technology — M,D
Elementary Education — M,D
Reading Education — M,D
Recreation and Park Management — M
Secondary Education — M,D
Special Education — M

FULL SAIL UNIVERSITY
Business Administration and
  Management—General — M
Educational Media/Instructional
  Technology — M
Entertainment Management — M
Marketing — M

FURMAN UNIVERSITY
Curriculum and Instruction — M,O
Early Childhood Education — M,O
Education—General — M,O
Educational Leadership and
  Administration — M,O
English as a Second Language — M,O
Reading Education — M,O
Special Education — M,O

GALLAUDET UNIVERSITY
Counselor Education — M,D,O
Early Childhood Education — M,D,O
Education—General — M,D,O
Elementary Education — M,D,O
International and Comparative
  Education — M,D,O
Multilingual and Multicultural
  Education — M,D,O
Secondary Education — M,D,O
Social Work — M,D,O
Special Education — M,D,O

GANNON UNIVERSITY
Athletic Training and Sports
  Medicine — M
Business Administration and
  Management—General — M
Curriculum and Instruction — M,O
Education—General — M,O
Educational Leadership and
  Administration — D,O
English as a Second Language — O
Exercise and Sports Science — M
Finance and Banking — M
Human Resources Management — M
Marketing — M
Organizational Management — D
Reading Education — M,O

GARDNER-WEBB UNIVERSITY
Business Administration and
  Management—General — M
Curriculum and Instruction — M,D,O
Education—General — M,D,O
Educational Leadership and
  Administration — M,D,O
English Education — M
Exercise and Sports Science — M
Organizational Management — M,D,O
Physical Education — M
Religious Education — M,D

GARRETT-EVANGELICAL THEOLOGICAL SEMINARY
Religious Education — M,D

GATEWAY SEMINARY
Early Childhood Education — M,D,O
Educational Leadership and
  Administration — M,D,O

GENEVA COLLEGE
Business Administration and
  Management—General — M
Counselor Education — M
Education—General — M
Educational Leadership and
  Administration — M
Finance and Banking — M
Higher Education — M
Marketing — M
Nonprofit Management — M

---

*M—masters degree; D—doctorate; O—other advanced degree; *—Close-Up and/or Display*

Organizational Management M
Project Management M

GEORGE FOX UNIVERSITY
Accounting M,D
Business Administration and
   Management—General M,D
Counselor Education M,O
Education—General M,D,O
Educational Leadership and
   Administration M,O
English as a Second Language M
Finance and Banking M,D
Human Resources Management M
Marketing M,D
Organizational Management M,D
Reading Education M,O
Social Work M
Special Education M,O

GEORGE MASON UNIVERSITY
Accounting M
Art Education M
Athletic Training and Sports
   Medicine M,O
Business Administration and
   Management—General M
Counselor Education M
Curriculum and Instruction M
Early Childhood Education M
Education of the Gifted M
Education—General M,D,O
Educational Leadership and
   Administration M,O
Educational Media/Instructional
   Technology M
Educational Psychology M,O
Elementary Education M
English as a Second Language M
English Education M,D,O
Exercise and Sports Science M,O
Foreign Languages Education M
Higher Education M,D,O
Human Resources Management M
International Business M,O
Law M,D
Logistics M
Management Information Systems M
Mathematics Education M
Multilingual and Multicultural
   Education M
Music Education M
Organizational Management M
Physical Education M
Project Management M,D
Reading Education M
Science Education M
Secondary Education M
Social Sciences Education M
Social Work M
Special Education M,O
Sports Management M,O
Student Affairs M,O
Transportation Management M

GEORGETOWN COLLEGE
Education—General M
Reading Education M
Special Education M

GEORGETOWN UNIVERSITY
Advertising and Public Relations M
Business Administration and
   Management—General M
Educational Measurement and
   Evaluation M
Environmental Law M,D
Finance and Banking M,D
Health Law M,D
Hospitality Management M,D
Human Resources Management M,D
Industrial and Manufacturing
   Management D
International Business M,D
Law M,D
Real Estate M,D
Sports Management M,D
Taxation M,D

THE GEORGE WASHINGTON UNIVERSITY
Accounting M
Adult Education O
Art Education M
Business Administration and
   Management—General M,D,O
Business Analytics M,O
Counselor Education M,D,O
Curriculum and Instruction M,D,O
Distance Education Development O
Early Childhood Education M
Education—General M,D,O
Educational Leadership and
   Administration M,D,O
Educational Media/Instructional
   Technology M,O
Educational Policy M,D,O
Elementary Education M
Exercise and Sports Science M
Finance and Banking M,D
Foreign Languages Education M
Higher Education M,D,O
Hospitality Management M,O
Human Resources Development M,D,O
Human Resources Management M,O
International and Comparative
   Education M,D,O
International Business M,D
Investment Management M,D
Law M,D
Legal and Justice Studies M,D,O
Management Information Systems M,D
Management Strategy and Policy M,D,O
Marketing M,D

Mathematics Education M
Multilingual and Multicultural
   Education M,D,O
Museum Education M
Nonprofit Management M,O
Organizational Management M
Project Management M,D,O
Real Estate O
Science Education M
Secondary Education M
Special Education M,D,O
Sports Management M
Student Affairs M,O
Travel and Tourism M,O
Vocational and Technical Education O

GEORGIA COLLEGE & STATE UNIVERSITY
Accounting M
Business Administration and
   Management—General M
Curriculum and Instruction M
Early Childhood Education M
Education—General M
Educational Leadership and
   Administration M,O
Educational Media/Instructional
   Technology M
Exercise and Sports Science M
Health Education M
Kinesiology and Movement Studies M
Logistics M
Management Information Systems M
Middle School Education M
Music Education M
Physical Education M
Secondary Education M
Special Education M

GEORGIA INSTITUTE OF TECHNOLOGY
Business Administration and
   Management—General M,D
International Business M
Logistics M
Management Information Systems M

GEORGIAN COURT UNIVERSITY
Business Administration and
   Management—General M,O
Counselor Education M,O
Education—General M,O
Educational Leadership and
   Administration M,O
Educational Media/Instructional
   Technology M,O
Legal and Justice Studies M,O
Nonprofit Management M,O
Special Education M,O

GEORGIA SOUTHERN UNIVERSITY
Accounting M
Business Administration and
   Management—General M
Counselor Education M
Curriculum and Instruction M,D
Early Childhood Education M,O
Education—General M,D,O
Educational Leadership and
   Administration M,D,O
Educational Measurement and
   Evaluation M,D,O
Educational Media/Instructional
   Technology M,O
English Education M
Foreign Languages Education M
Health Education M,D
Higher Education M,D
Kinesiology and Movement Studies M
Logistics D
Management Information Systems M,O
Middle School Education M,O
Multilingual and Multicultural
   Education D
Music Education M
Nonprofit Management O
Reading Education M,O
Secondary Education M,O
Special Education M,O
Sports Management M
Supply Chain Management D

GEORGIA SOUTHERN UNIVERSITY–ARMSTRONG CAMPUS
Adult Education M,O
Athletic Training and Sports
   Medicine M,O
Business Administration and
   Management—General M,O
Curriculum and Instruction M,O
Early Childhood Education M,O
Education—General M,O
Exercise and Sports Science M,O
Physical Education M,O
Reading Education M,O
Secondary Education M,O
Special Education M,O

GEORGIA SOUTHWESTERN STATE UNIVERSITY
Business Administration and
   Management—General M,O
Early Childhood Education M,O
Education—General M,O
English Education M,O
Management Information Systems M,O
Mathematics Education M,O
Middle School Education M,O
Special Education M,O

GEORGIA STATE UNIVERSITY
Accounting M
Actuarial Science M
Art Education M
Athletic Training and Sports
   Medicine M

Business Administration and
   Management—General M,D
Counselor Education M,O
Curriculum and Instruction M,D
Early Childhood Education M,D,O
Education of Students with
   Severe/Multiple Disabilities M
Education—General M,D,O
Educational Leadership and
   Administration M,D,O
Educational Measurement and
   Evaluation M,D
Educational Media/Instructional
   Technology M,D
Educational Policy M,D,O
Educational Psychology M,D
Elementary Education M,D,O
English Education M,D
Entrepreneurship M,D
Exercise and Sports Science M
Finance and Banking M,D,O
Foreign Languages Education M,O
Foundations and Philosophy of
   Education M,D
Health Education M
Human Resources Management M,D
Human Services M,O
Insurance M,D,O
International Business M
Kinesiology and Movement Studies D
Law D
Management Information Systems M,D,O
Management Strategy and Policy M,D
Marketing M,D
Mathematics Education M,D,O
Middle School Education M,D
Music Education M,D,O
Nonprofit Management M,D,O
Organizational Management M,D
Physical Education M
Reading Education M,D
Real Estate M,D,O
Risk Management M,D,O
Science Education M,D
Secondary Education M,D
Social Sciences Education M,D
Social Work M,O
Special Education M,D
Sports Management M
Taxation M
Urban Education M,D,O

GLION INSTITUTE OF HIGHER EDUCATION
Hospitality Management M

GLOBAL UNIVERSITY
Religious Education M,D

GODDARD COLLEGE
Business Administration and
   Management—General M
Education—General M
Sustainability Management M

GOLDEN GATE UNIVERSITY
Accounting M,D,O
Business Administration and
   Management—General M,D,O
Business Analytics M,D,O
Entrepreneurship M,D,O
Environmental Law M,D
Finance and Banking M,D,O
Human Resources Management M,D,O
Intellectual Property Law M,D
International Business M,D,O
Law M,D
Legal and Justice Studies M,D
Management Information Systems M,D,O
Marketing M,D,O
Project Management M,D,O
Supply Chain Management M,D,O
Taxation M,D,O

GOLDEY-BEACOM COLLEGE
Business Administration and
   Management—General M
Finance and Banking M
Human Resources Management M
International Business M
Management Information Systems M
Marketing M
Taxation M

GONZAGA UNIVERSITY
Accounting M
Business Administration and
   Management—General M
Education—General M
Educational Leadership and
   Administration M,D
Elementary Education M
English as a Second Language M
Law D
Organizational Management M,D
Secondary Education M,D
Special Education M,D
Sports Management M,D
Taxation M

GORDON COLLEGE
Early Childhood Education M,O
Education—General M,O
Educational Leadership and
   Administration M,O
Elementary Education M,O
English as a Second Language M,O
Finance and Banking M
Mathematics Education M,O
Middle School Education M,O
Music Education M,O
Reading Education M,O
Secondary Education M,O
Special Education M,O

GOSHEN COLLEGE
Environmental Education M

GOUCHER COLLEGE
Education—General M,O
Educational Leadership and
   Administration M,O
Educational Media/Instructional
   Technology M,O
Elementary Education M,O
Middle School Education M,O
Physical Education M,O
Reading Education M,O
Secondary Education M,O
Special Education M,O

GOVERNORS STATE UNIVERSITY
Accounting M
Actuarial Science M
Business Administration and
   Management—General M
Early Childhood Education M
Education—General M
Educational Leadership and
   Administration M,D
Human Services M,D
Legal and Justice Studies M
Management Information Systems M
Reading Education M
Social Work M
Special Education M

GRACELAND UNIVERSITY (IA)
Curriculum and Instruction M
Education—General M
Educational Leadership and
   Administration M
Educational Media/Instructional
   Technology M
Organizational Management M,D,O
Reading Education M
Special Education M

THE GRADUATE CENTER, CITY UNIVERSITY OF NEW YORK
Accounting D
Business Administration and
   Management—General D
Educational Psychology D
Finance and Banking D
Management Information Systems D
Organizational Behavior D
Social Work D
Urban Education D

GRADUATE INSTITUTE OF APPLIED LINGUISTICS
Multilingual and Multicultural
   Education M,O

GRAMBLING STATE UNIVERSITY
Counselor Education M,D,O
Curriculum and Instruction M,D,O
Developmental Education M,D,O
Education—General M,D,O
Educational Leadership and
   Administration M,D,O
Educational Media/Instructional
   Technology M,D,O
Higher Education M,D,O
Human Resources Management M
Mathematics Education M,D,O
Reading Education M,D,O
Science Education M,D,O
Social Sciences Education M
Social Work M
Special Education M
Sports Management M
Student Affairs M,D,O

GRAND CANYON UNIVERSITY
Accounting M
Business Administration and
   Management—General M,D
Business Analytics M
Curriculum and Instruction M,D,O
Early Childhood Education M,D,O
Education of the Gifted M,D,O
Education—General M,D,O
Educational Leadership and
   Administration M,D,O
Educational Media/Instructional
   Technology M,D,O
Elementary Education M,D,O
English as a Second Language M,D,O
Entrepreneurship M
Finance and Banking M
Human Resources Management M
Marketing M,D
Organizational Management M,D
Project Management M
Reading Education M,D,O
Science Education M,D,O
Secondary Education M,D,O
Special Education M,D,O
Sports Management M

GRAND VALLEY STATE UNIVERSITY
Accounting M
Adult Education M
Business Administration and
   Management—General M
Curriculum and Instruction M
Early Childhood Education M
Education—General M
Educational Leadership and
   Administration M,O
Educational Media/Instructional
   Technology M
Elementary Education M
English as a Second Language M
English Education M
Higher Education M
Management Information Systems M
Middle School Education M
Nonprofit Management M
Reading Education M
Secondary Education M
Social Work M

Special Education — M
Taxation — M

GRAND VIEW UNIVERSITY
Athletic Training and Sports Medicine — M
Educational Leadership and Administration — M,O
Organizational Management — M,O
Sports Management — M
Urban Education — M,O

GRANITE STATE COLLEGE
Business Administration and Management—General — M
Organizational Management — M
Project Management — M

GRANTHAM UNIVERSITY
Business Administration and Management—General — M,O
Human Resources Development — M,O
Human Resources Management — M,O
Management Information Systems — M,O
Management Strategy and Policy — M,O
Project Management — M,O

GRATZ COLLEGE
Education—General — M
Educational Leadership and Administration — M,D
Nonprofit Management — M
Religious Education — M,D
Social Work — M,O

GREEN MOUNTAIN COLLEGE
Business Administration and Management—General — M

GREENSBORO COLLEGE
Education—General — M
Elementary Education — M
English as a Second Language — M
Special Education — M

GREENVILLE UNIVERSITY
Education—General — M
Elementary Education — M
Secondary Education — M

GWYNEDD MERCY UNIVERSITY
Business Administration and Management—General — M
Counselor Education — M,D
Education—General — M,D
Educational Leadership and Administration — M,D
Management Strategy and Policy — M
Special Education — M,D

HALLMARK UNIVERSITY
Business Administration and Management—General — M
International Business — M

HAMLINE UNIVERSITY
Business Administration and Management—General — M,D
Education—General — M,D
English as a Second Language — M,D
Environmental Education — M,D
Nonprofit Management — M,D
Reading Education — M,D
Science Education — M,D

HAMPTON UNIVERSITY
Business Administration and Management—General — M,D
Counselor Education — M,D,O
Early Childhood Education — M
Education—General — M,D,O
Educational Leadership and Administration — M,D
English Education — M
Mathematics Education — M
Middle School Education — M
Music Education — M
Organizational Behavior — M
Science Education — M
Sports Management — M
Student Affairs — M,D,O

HANNIBAL-LAGRANGE UNIVERSITY
Education—General — M
Reading Education — M

HARDING UNIVERSITY
Art Education — M,O
Business Administration and Management—General — M
Counselor Education — M,O
Early Childhood Education — M,O
Education—General — M,O
Educational Leadership and Administration — M,O
Elementary Education — M,O
English as a Second Language — M,O
English Education — M,O
Foreign Languages Education — M,O
Health Education — M,O
International Business — M
Mathematics Education — M,O
Organizational Management — M
Reading Education — M,O
Secondary Education — M,O
Social Sciences Education — M,O
Special Education — M,O

HARDIN-SIMMONS UNIVERSITY
Business Administration and Management—General — M
Counselor Education — M
Education of the Gifted — M
Education—General — M,D
Educational Leadership and Administration — D

Higher Education — D
Kinesiology and Movement Studies — M
Music Education — M
Reading Education — M
Recreation and Park Management — M
Science Education — M,D
Sports Management — M

HARRISBURG UNIVERSITY OF SCIENCE AND TECHNOLOGY
Educational Media/Instructional Technology — M
Entrepreneurship — M
Management Information Systems — M
Management Strategy and Policy — M
Project Management — M

HARRISON MIDDLETON UNIVERSITY
Education—General — M,D
Legal and Justice Studies — M,D
Science Education — M,D

HARVARD UNIVERSITY
Accounting — D
Art Education — M
Business Administration and Management—General — M,D,O
Curriculum and Instruction — M
Education—General — M,D
Educational Leadership and Administration — M,D
Educational Media/Instructional Technology — M,O
Educational Policy — M
Educational Psychology — M
Foundations and Philosophy of Education — M,O
Industrial and Manufacturing Management — D
International and Comparative Education — M
Law — M,D
Legal and Justice Studies — D
Management Strategy and Policy — D
Marketing — D
Mathematics Education — M,O
Organizational Behavior — D
Quantitative Analysis — M,D
Reading Education — M

HASTINGS COLLEGE
Education—General — M

HAWAI'I PACIFIC UNIVERSITY
Business Administration and Management—General — M
Educational Leadership and Administration — M
Elementary Education — M
English as a Second Language — M
Finance and Banking — M
Human Resources Management — M
International Business — M
Management Information Systems — M
Marketing — M
Organizational Management — M
Secondary Education — M
Social Work — M

HEBREW COLLEGE
Early Childhood Education — M,O
Education—General — M,O
Middle School Education — M,O
Music Education — M,O
Religious Education — M,O
Special Education — M,O

HEBREW UNION COLLEGE–JEWISH INSTITUTE OF RELIGION (NY)
Education—General — M
Nonprofit Management — M
Religious Education — M

HEC MONTREAL
Accounting — M,D,O
Business Administration and Management—General — M,D,O
Business Analytics — M
Electronic Commerce — M,O
Entrepreneurship — M,O
Finance and Banking — M,D,O
Human Resources Development — O
Human Resources Management — M,D,O
Industrial and Manufacturing Management — M
International Business — M,D
Logistics — M
Management Information Systems — M
Management Strategy and Policy — M
Marketing — M,D
Organizational Management — M
Supply Chain Management — M,O
Taxation — M,O

HEIDELBERG UNIVERSITY
Business Administration and Management—General — M
Education—General — M
Music Education — M

HENDERSON STATE UNIVERSITY
Business Administration and Management—General — M
Counselor Education — M,O
Curriculum and Instruction — M,O
Early Childhood Education — M,O
Education—General — M,O
Educational Leadership and Administration — M,O
English as a Second Language — M,O
Middle School Education — M
Physical Education — M
Special Education — M,O
Sports Management — M

HENDRIX COLLEGE
Accounting — M

HERITAGE UNIVERSITY
Counselor Education — M
Education—General — M
Educational Leadership and Administration — M
English as a Second Language — M
Multilingual and Multicultural Education — M
Reading Education — M
Science Education — M
Special Education — M

HERZING UNIVERSITY ONLINE
Accounting — M
Business Administration and Management—General — M
Human Resources Management — M
Marketing — M
Project Management — M

HIGH POINT UNIVERSITY
Athletic Training and Sports Medicine — M,D
Business Administration and Management—General — M,D
Educational Leadership and Administration — M,D
Elementary Education — M,D
Mathematics Education — M,D
Secondary Education — M,D
Special Education — M,D

HIGH TECH HIGH GRADUATE SCHOOL OF EDUCATION
Educational Leadership and Administration — M

HODGES UNIVERSITY
Accounting — M
Business Administration and Management—General — M
Legal and Justice Studies — M
Management Information Systems — M

HOFSTRA UNIVERSITY
Accounting — M,O
Advertising and Public Relations — M
Art Education — M,D,O
Business Administration and Management—General — M,O
Business Education — M,O
Counselor Education — M,O
Early Childhood Education — M,D,O
Education of the Gifted — M,O
Education—General — M,D,O
Educational Leadership and Administration — M,O
Educational Media/Instructional Technology — M,D,O
Elementary Education — M,D,O
English as a Second Language — M,D,O
English Education — M,O
Entertainment Management — M,O
Exercise and Sports Science — M,O
Finance and Banking — M,O
Foreign Languages Education — M,D,O
Health Education — M,D,O
Health Law — M,O
Higher Education — M,D,O
Human Resources Management — M,O
Intellectual Property Law — M,O
International Business — M,O
Investment Management — M,O
Law — M,D,O
Legal and Justice Studies — M,D,O
Management Information Systems — M,O
Management Strategy and Policy — M,O
Marketing Research — M,O
Marketing — M,O
Mathematics Education — M,D,O
Middle School Education — M,D,O
Multilingual and Multicultural Education — M,D,O
Music Education — M,D,O
Physical Education — M,O
Quality Management — M,O
Quantitative Analysis — M,O
Reading Education — M,D,O
Science Education — M,D,O
Secondary Education — M,D,O
Social Sciences Education — M,D,O
Special Education — M,D,O
Sports Management — M,O
Taxation — M,O

HOLLINS UNIVERSITY
Education—General — M

HOLY FAMILY UNIVERSITY
Accounting — M
Business Administration and Management—General — M
Early Childhood Education — M
Education—General — M,D
Educational Leadership and Administration — M,D
Elementary Education — M
English as a Second Language — M
Finance and Banking — M
Human Resources Management — M
Management Information Systems — M
Reading Education — M
Special Education — M

HOLY NAMES UNIVERSITY
Business Administration and Management—General — M
Education—General — M,O
Educational Psychology — M,O
Finance and Banking — M
Marketing — M

Music Education — M,O
Special Education — M,O
Urban Education — M,O

HOOD COLLEGE
Accounting — M,O
Business Administration and Management—General — M,O
Curriculum and Instruction — M,O
Education—General — M,O
Educational Leadership and Administration — M,O
Elementary Education — M,O
Finance and Banking — M,O
Human Resources Management — M,O
Management Information Systems — M,O
Marketing — M,O
Mathematics Education — M,O
Middle School Education — M,O
Organizational Management — M,D,O
Reading Education — M,O
Science Education — M,O
Secondary Education — M,O
Special Education — M,O

HOPE INTERNATIONAL UNIVERSITY
Education—General — M
Educational Leadership and Administration — M
Elementary Education — M
International Business — M
Marketing — M
Nonprofit Management — M
Secondary Education — M

HOUSTON BAPTIST UNIVERSITY
Business Administration and Management—General — M,D
Counselor Education — M,D
Curriculum and Instruction — M,D
Education—General — M,D
Educational Leadership and Administration — M,D
Educational Measurement and Evaluation — M,D
Educational Media/Instructional Technology — M,D
Elementary Education — M,D
English as a Second Language — M,D
English Education — M,D
Higher Education — M,D
Human Resources Management — M
International Business — M
Kinesiology and Movement Studies — M
Middle School Education — M
Multilingual and Multicultural Education — M,D
Reading Education — M,D
Religious Education — M,D
Science Education — M,D
Special Education — M,D
Sports Management — M

HOWARD PAYNE UNIVERSITY
Business Administration and Management—General — M
Educational Leadership and Administration — M
Sports Management — M

HOWARD UNIVERSITY
Accounting — M
Business Administration and Management—General — M
Counselor Education — M
Education—General — M,D,O
Educational Leadership and Administration — M,D,O
Educational Policy — M,D,O
Educational Psychology — D
Elementary Education — M
Exercise and Sports Science — M
Finance and Banking — M
Health Education — M
Human Resources Management — M
International Business — M
Law — M,D
Leisure Studies — M
Management Information Systems — M
Marketing — M
Multilingual and Multicultural Education — M,D
Music Education — M
Physical Education — M
Secondary Education — M
Social Work — M,D
Special Education — M
Sports Management — M
Supply Chain Management — M

HULT INTERNATIONAL BUSINESS SCHOOL (UNITED STATES)
Business Administration and Management—General — M
Business Analytics — M
Entrepreneurship — M
Finance and Banking — M
International Business — M
Marketing — M
Project Management — M

HUMBOLDT STATE UNIVERSITY
Business Administration and Management—General — M
Education—General — M
English as a Second Language — M
Kinesiology and Movement Studies — M
Social Work — M

HUMPHREYS UNIVERSITY
Law — D

---

*M—masters degree; D—doctorate; O—other advanced degree; *—Close-Up and/or Display*

HUNTER COLLEGE OF THE CITY UNIVERSITY OF NEW YORK

Accounting	M
Counselor Education	M
Early Childhood Education	M,D,O
Education of Students with Severe/Multiple Disabilities	M
Education—General	M,D,O
Educational Leadership and Administration	D,O
Elementary Education	M
English as a Second Language	M
English Education	M
Foreign Languages Education	M
Mathematics Education	M
Multilingual and Multicultural Education	M
Music Education	M
Science Education	M
Secondary Education	M
Social Sciences Education	M
Social Work	M
Special Education	M

HUNTINGTON UNIVERSITY

Business Administration and Management—General	M,D
Elementary Education	M,D
English as a Second Language	M,D
Middle School Education	M,D
Organizational Management	M,D

HUSSON UNIVERSITY

Business Administration and Management—General	M
Counselor Education	M
Educational Leadership and Administration	M,O
Hospitality Management	M
Organizational Management	M
Risk Management	M
Sports Management	M

HUSTON-TILLOTSON UNIVERSITY

Educational Leadership and Administration	M

IDAHO STATE UNIVERSITY

Athletic Training and Sports Medicine	M
Business Administration and Management—General	M,O
Counselor Education	M,D,O
Education—General	M,D,O
Educational Leadership and Administration	M,D,O
Educational Media/Instructional Technology	M,D
Elementary Education	M
English as a Second Language	M,D,O
Health Education	M
Human Resources Management	M,D
Management Information Systems	M,O
Mathematics Education	M,D
Music Education	M
Physical Education	M
Reading Education	M
Secondary Education	M
Special Education	M
Sports Management	M

IGLOBAL UNIVERSITY

Accounting	M
Business Administration and Management—General	M
Entrepreneurship	M
Finance and Banking	M
Hospitality Management	M
Human Resources Management	M
International Business	M
Management Information Systems	M
Project Management	M
Travel and Tourism	M

ILLINOIS COLLEGE

Education—General	M

ILLINOIS INSTITUTE OF TECHNOLOGY

Business Administration and Management—General	M,D
Computer Education	M
Entrepreneurship	M
Finance and Banking	M,D
Human Resources Development	M,D
Industrial and Manufacturing Management	M
Law	M,D
Legal and Justice Studies	M,D
Management Information Systems	M,D
Marketing	M
Mathematics Education	M,D
Science Education	M,D
Sustainability Management	M
Taxation	M,D

ILLINOIS STATE UNIVERSITY

Accounting	M
Business Administration and Management—General	M
Curriculum and Instruction	M,D
Education—General	M,D,O
Educational Leadership and Administration	M,D
Educational Policy	M,D
Health Education	M
Higher Education	M,D
Management Information Systems	M
Mathematics Education	M,D
Physical Education	M
Reading Education	M
Social Work	M
Special Education	M,D,O
Student Affairs	M

IMCA–INTERNATIONAL MANAGEMENT CENTRES ASSOCIATION

Business Administration and Management—General	M

IMMACULATA UNIVERSITY

Educational Leadership and Administration	M,D,O
Educational Psychology	M,D,O
English as a Second Language	M
Multilingual and Multicultural Education	M
Organizational Management	M
Secondary Education	M,D,O
Special Education	M,D,O

INDEPENDENCE UNIVERSITY

Business Administration and Management—General	M

INDIANA STATE UNIVERSITY

Athletic Training and Sports Medicine	M,D
Business Administration and Management—General	M
Counselor Education	M,D,O
Curriculum and Instruction	M,D
Education—General	M,D
Educational Leadership and Administration	M,D
Educational Media/Instructional Technology	M,D
English as a Second Language	M,D,O
Foreign Languages Education	M,D,O
Health Education	M,D
Higher Education	M,D,O
Human Resources Development	M
Multilingual and Multicultural Education	M,D,O
Music Education	M
Physical Education	M
Recreation and Park Management	M,D
Science Education	M,D
Social Work	M
Sports Management	M,D
Student Affairs	M,D,O
Vocational and Technical Education	M

INDIANA TECH

Accounting	M
Business Administration and Management—General	M
Human Resources Development	M
Human Resources Management	M
International Business	D
Marketing	M
Organizational Management	M

INDIANA UNIVERSITY BLOOMINGTON

Art Education	M,D,O
Athletic Training and Sports Medicine	M,D
Business Administration and Management—General	M,D
Counselor Education	M,D,O
Curriculum and Instruction	M,D,O
Education—General	M,D,O
Educational Leadership and Administration	M,D,O
Educational Measurement and Evaluation	M,D,O
Educational Media/Instructional Technology	M,D
Educational Policy	M,D,O
Educational Psychology	M,D,O
Elementary Education	M,D,O
English as a Second Language	M,D
Exercise and Sports Science	M,D,O
Finance and Banking	M,D,O
Foreign Languages Education	M,D
Foundations and Philosophy of Education	M,D,O
Health Education	M,D
Higher Education	M,D,O
International and Comparative Education	M,D,O
Kinesiology and Movement Studies	M,D
Law	M,D,O
Leisure Studies	M,D
Library Science	M,D,O
Management Information Systems	M,D,O
Mathematics Education	M,D,O
Multilingual and Multicultural Education	M,D
Nonprofit Management	M,D,O
Organizational Management	M,D,O
Physical Education	M,D,O
Reading Education	M,D,O
Recreation and Park Management	M,D
Science Education	M,D,O
Secondary Education	M,D,O
Social Sciences Education	M,D,O
Special Education	M,D,O
Sports Management	M,D
Student Affairs	M,D,O
Sustainability Management	M,D,O
Travel and Tourism	M,D

INDIANA UNIVERSITY EAST

Education—General	M
Social Work	M

INDIANA UNIVERSITY KOKOMO

Accounting	M,O
Business Administration and Management—General	M,O

INDIANA UNIVERSITY NORTHWEST

Accounting	M,O
Business Administration and Management—General	M,O
Education—General	M,O
Educational Leadership and Administration	M,O
Elementary Education	M,O
Management Information Systems	M,O

Nonprofit Management	M,O
Secondary Education	M,O
Social Work	M

INDIANA UNIVERSITY OF PENNSYLVANIA

Adult Education	M
Business Administration and Management—General	M
Business Education	M
Counselor Education	M
Curriculum and Instruction	D
Education—General	M,D,O
Educational Leadership and Administration	D,O
Educational Psychology	M,O
English as a Second Language	M,D
English Education	M,D
Exercise and Sports Science	M
Foreign Languages Education	M
Health Education	M
Higher Education	M
Human Resources Development	M
Mathematics Education	M
Music Education	M
Nonprofit Management	D
Physical Education	M
Reading Education	M
Special Education	M
Sports Management	M
Student Affairs	M
Vocational and Technical Education	M

INDIANA UNIVERSITY–PURDUE UNIVERSITY FORT WAYNE

Business Administration and Management—General	M
Counselor Education	M,O
Education—General	M,O
Educational Leadership and Administration	M,O
Elementary Education	M,O
English as a Second Language	M,O
English Education	M,O
Facilities Management	M
Mathematics Education	M,O
Organizational Management	M,O
Secondary Education	M
Special Education	M,O

INDIANA UNIVERSITY–PURDUE UNIVERSITY INDIANAPOLIS

Accounting	M
Business Administration and Management—General	M
Counselor Education	M,O
Curriculum and Instruction	M,O
Early Childhood Education	M,O
Education—General	M,O
Educational Leadership and Administration	M,O
English as a Second Language	M,O
Entrepreneurship	M
Finance and Banking	M
Foreign Languages Education	M,O
Health Education	M,D
Health Law	M,D,O
Intellectual Property Law	M,D,O
Kinesiology and Movement Studies	M,O
Law	M,D,O
Library Science	M,O
Marketing	M
Mathematics Education	M,D
Nonprofit Management	M,O
Organizational Management	M,O
Physical Education	M,O
Reading Education	M,O
Social Work	M,D,O
Special Education	M,O
Supply Chain Management	M

INDIANA UNIVERSITY SOUTH BEND

Accounting	M,O
Business Administration and Management—General	M,O
Counselor Education	M,O
Education—General	M,O
Educational Leadership and Administration	M,O
Educational Media/Instructional Technology	M,O
Elementary Education	M,O
Finance and Banking	M,O
Human Resources Management	M,O
Legal and Justice Studies	M,O
Marketing	M,O
Nonprofit Management	M,O
Secondary Education	M,O
Social Work	M
Special Education	M,O

INDIANA UNIVERSITY SOUTHEAST

Business Administration and Management—General	M
Counselor Education	M
Education—General	M
Elementary Education	M
Finance and Banking	M
Secondary Education	M

INDIANA WESLEYAN UNIVERSITY

Accounting	M,O
Business Administration and Management—General	M,O
Counselor Education	M
Educational Leadership and Administration	M
Higher Education	M
Human Resources Management	M,O
Organizational Management	M,D,O

INSTITUTE FOR CHRISTIAN STUDIES

Education—General	M,D

INSTITUTE FOR CLINICAL SOCIAL WORK

Social Work	D

INSTITUTO CENTROAMERICANO DE ADMINISTRACIÓN DE EMPRESAS

Business Administration and Management—General	M
Finance and Banking	M
Real Estate	M

INSTITUTO TECNOLOGICO DE SANTO DOMINGO

Accounting	M,O
Adult Education	M,O
Business Administration and Management—General	M,O
Education—General	M,O
Educational Leadership and Administration	M,O
Educational Psychology	M,O
Environmental Education	M,D,O
Finance and Banking	M,O
Human Resources Management	M,O
Industrial and Manufacturing Management	M,O
International Business	M,O
Marketing	M,O
Organizational Management	M,O
Quality Management	M,O
Quantitative Analysis	M,O
Secondary Education	M,O
Social Sciences Education	M,O
Taxation	M,O
Transportation Management	M,O

INSTITUTO TECNOLÓGICO Y DE ESTUDIOS SUPERIORES DE MONTERREY, CAMPUS CENTRAL DE VERACRUZ

Business Administration and Management—General	M
Education—General	M
Educational Leadership and Administration	M
Educational Media/Instructional Technology	M
Electronic Commerce	M
Finance and Banking	M
International Business	M
Management Information Systems	M
Marketing	M

INSTITUTO TECNOLÓGICO Y DE ESTUDIOS SUPERIORES DE MONTERREY, CAMPUS CHIHUAHUA

International Business	M,O

INSTITUTO TECNOLÓGICO Y DE ESTUDIOS SUPERIORES DE MONTERREY, CAMPUS CIUDAD DE MÉXICO

Business Administration and Management—General	M,D
Education—General	M,D
Educational Media/Instructional Technology	M,D
Finance and Banking	M,D
International Business	M,D
Law	O
Management Information Systems	M,D
Quality Management	M,D

INSTITUTO TECNOLÓGICO Y DE ESTUDIOS SUPERIORES DE MONTERREY, CAMPUS CIUDAD JUÁREZ

Business Administration and Management—General	M
Education—General	M
Educational Leadership and Administration	M
Educational Media/Instructional Technology	M,D
Electronic Commerce	M
Management Information Systems	M
Quality Management	M

INSTITUTO TECNOLÓGICO Y DE ESTUDIOS SUPERIORES DE MONTERREY, CAMPUS CIUDAD OBREGÓN

Business Administration and Management—General	M
Developmental Education	M
Education—General	M
Finance and Banking	M
Management Information Systems	M
Marketing	M
Mathematics Education	M

INSTITUTO TECNOLÓGICO Y DE ESTUDIOS SUPERIORES DE MONTERREY, CAMPUS CUERNAVACA

Business Administration and Management—General	M
Finance and Banking	M
Human Resources Management	M
International Business	M
Marketing	M

INSTITUTO TECNOLÓGICO Y DE ESTUDIOS SUPERIORES DE MONTERREY, CAMPUS ESTADO DE MÉXICO

Business Administration and Management—General	M,D
Education—General	M,D
Educational Leadership and Administration	M,D
Educational Media/Instructional Technology	M,D
Electronic Commerce	M,D
Finance and Banking	M,D

Industrial and Manufacturing
  Management

Management Information Systems	M,D
Marketing	M,D
Quality Management	M,D

INSTITUTO TECNOLÓGICO Y DE ESTUDIOS SUPERIORES DE MONTERREY, CAMPUS GUADALAJARA

Business Administration and Management—General	M
Finance and Banking	M

INSTITUTO TECNOLÓGICO Y DE ESTUDIOS SUPERIORES DE MONTERREY, CAMPUS IRAPUATO

Business Administration and Management—General	M,D
Education—General	M,D
Educational Leadership and Administration	M,D
Educational Media/Instructional Technology	M,D
Electronic Commerce	M,D
Finance and Banking	M,D
Industrial and Manufacturing Management	M,D
International Business	M,D
Library Science	M,D
Management Information Systems	M,D
Marketing Research	M,D
Quality Management	M,D

INSTITUTO TECNOLÓGICO Y DE ESTUDIOS SUPERIORES DE MONTERREY, CAMPUS LAGUNA

Business Administration and Management—General	M
Management Information Systems	M

INSTITUTO TECNOLÓGICO Y DE ESTUDIOS SUPERIORES DE MONTERREY, CAMPUS LEÓN

Business Administration and Management—General	M

INSTITUTO TECNOLÓGICO Y DE ESTUDIOS SUPERIORES DE MONTERREY, CAMPUS MONTERREY

Business Administration and Management—General	M,D
Finance and Banking	M
International Business	M
Marketing	M
Science Education	M,D

INSTITUTO TECNOLÓGICO Y DE ESTUDIOS SUPERIORES DE MONTERREY, CAMPUS QUERÉTARO

Business Administration and Management—General	M

INSTITUTO TECNOLÓGICO Y DE ESTUDIOS SUPERIORES DE MONTERREY, CAMPUS SONORA NORTE

Business Administration and Management—General	M
Education—General	M

INSTITUTO TECNOLÓGICO Y DE ESTUDIOS SUPERIORES DE MONTERREY, CAMPUS TOLUCA

Business Administration and Management—General	M

INTER AMERICAN UNIVERSITY OF PUERTO RICO, AGUADILLA CAMPUS

Accounting	M
Business Administration and Management—General	M
Educational Leadership and Administration	M
Elementary Education	M
Finance and Banking	M
Human Resources Management	M
Management Information Systems	M
Marketing	M

INTER AMERICAN UNIVERSITY OF PUERTO RICO, ARECIBO CAMPUS

Accounting	M
Business Administration and Management—General	M
Counselor Education	M
Curriculum and Instruction	M
Education—General	M
Educational Leadership and Administration	M
Elementary Education	M
English as a Second Language	M
Finance and Banking	M
Foreign Languages Education	M
Human Resources Management	M
Mathematics Education	M
Science Education	M
Social Sciences Education	M

INTER AMERICAN UNIVERSITY OF PUERTO RICO, BARRANQUITAS CAMPUS

Accounting	M
Business Administration and Management—General	M
Curriculum and Instruction	M
Education—General	M
Educational Leadership and Administration	M
Elementary Education	M
English as a Second Language	M
Foreign Languages Education	M
Human Resources Management	M
Library Science	M

SPECIAL EDUCATION

Special Education	M

INTER AMERICAN UNIVERSITY OF PUERTO RICO, BAYAMÓN CAMPUS

Human Resources Management	M

INTER AMERICAN UNIVERSITY OF PUERTO RICO, FAJARDO CAMPUS

Business Administration and Management—General	M
Educational Leadership and Administration	M
Human Resources Management	M
Management Information Systems	M
Marketing	M
Special Education	M

INTER AMERICAN UNIVERSITY OF PUERTO RICO, GUAYAMA CAMPUS

Business Administration and Management—General	M
Early Childhood Education	M
Elementary Education	M
Marketing	M

INTER AMERICAN UNIVERSITY OF PUERTO RICO, METROPOLITAN CAMPUS

Accounting	M
Athletic Training and Sports Medicine	M
Business Administration and Management—General	M
Business Education	M
Counselor Education	M,D
Curriculum and Instruction	M,D
Education—General	M,D
Educational Leadership and Administration	M,D
Educational Media/Instructional Technology	M
Elementary Education	M
English as a Second Language	M
Exercise and Sports Science	M
Finance and Banking	M
Foreign Languages Education	M
Health Education	M
Higher Education	M
Human Resources Development	M
Human Resources Management	M
Industrial and Manufacturing Management	M
International Business	M,D
Management Information Systems	M
Marketing	M
Mathematics Education	M
Music Education	M
Physical Education	M
Religious Education	D
Science Education	M
Social Sciences Education	M
Social Work	M
Special Education	M
Vocational and Technical Education	M

INTER AMERICAN UNIVERSITY OF PUERTO RICO, PONCE CAMPUS

Accounting	M
Elementary Education	M
English as a Second Language	M
Finance and Banking	M
Human Resources Management	M
Marketing	M
Mathematics Education	M
Science Education	M
Social Sciences Education	M

INTER AMERICAN UNIVERSITY OF PUERTO RICO, SAN GERMÁN CAMPUS

Accounting	M,D
Business Administration and Management—General	M,D
Business Education	M
Counselor Education	M,D
Curriculum and Instruction	D
Elementary Education	M
English as a Second Language	M
Finance and Banking	M,D
Health Education	M
Human Resources Development	M
Human Resources Management	M,D
Industrial and Manufacturing Management	M,D
International Business	M,D
Kinesiology and Movement Studies	M
Library Science	M
Management Information Systems	M,D
Marketing	M
Mathematics Education	M
Music Education	M
Physical Education	M
Science Education	M
Special Education	M

INTER AMERICAN UNIVERSITY OF PUERTO RICO SCHOOL OF LAW

Law	D

INTERDENOMINATIONAL THEOLOGICAL CENTER

Religious Education	M,D

INTERNATIONAL BAPTIST COLLEGE AND SEMINARY

Education—General	M

INTERNATIONAL INSTITUTE FOR RESTORATIVE PRACTICES

Organizational Behavior	M,O

INTERNATIONAL TECHNOLOGICAL UNIVERSITY

Business Administration and Management—General	M,D

INTERNATIONAL UNIVERSITY IN GENEVA

Business Administration and Management—General	M,D
Entrepreneurship	M,D
International Business	M,D
Marketing	M,D

THE INTERNATIONAL UNIVERSITY OF MONACO

Business Administration and Management—General	M
Entrepreneurship	M
Finance and Banking	M
International Business	M
Marketing	M

IONA COLLEGE

Accounting	M,O
Advertising and Public Relations	M,O
Business Administration and Management—General	M,O
Early Childhood Education	M
Education—General	M
Educational Leadership and Administration	M
English Education	M,O
Finance and Banking	M,O
Foreign Languages Education	M,O
Human Resources Management	M,O
International Business	M,O
Management Information Systems	M,O
Marketing	M,O
Mathematics Education	M,O
Nonprofit Management	M,O
Project Management	M,O
Recreation and Park Management	M,O
Risk Management	M,O
Science Education	M
Social Sciences Education	M
Special Education	M
Sports Management	M,O

IOWA STATE UNIVERSITY OF SCIENCE AND TECHNOLOGY

Accounting	M
Agricultural Education	M,D
Business Administration and Management—General	M
Business Analytics	M
Counselor Education	M,D
Curriculum and Instruction	M,D
Education—General	M,D
Educational Leadership and Administration	M,D
Educational Measurement and Evaluation	M,D
Educational Media/Instructional Technology	M,D
Elementary Education	M,D
English as a Second Language	M
Exercise and Sports Science	M
Finance and Banking	M
Foundations and Philosophy of Education	M,D
Higher Education	M,D
Human Resources Development	M,D
Kinesiology and Movement Studies	M,D
Management Information Systems	M,D
Mathematics Education	M,D
Science Education	M,D
Special Education	M,D
Student Affairs	M,D
Transportation Management	M
Vocational and Technical Education	M,D

ITHACA COLLEGE

Accounting	M
Agricultural Education	M
Business Administration and Management—General	M
Elementary Education	M
English Education	M
Exercise and Sports Science	M
Health Education	M
Music Education	M
Physical Education	M
Secondary Education	M
Sports Management	M

JACKSON STATE UNIVERSITY

Accounting	M
Business Administration and Management—General	M,D
Counselor Education	M
Early Childhood Education	M,D,O
Education—General	M,D,O
Educational Leadership and Administration	M,D,O
Elementary Education	M,D,O
English Education	M
Health Education	M
Higher Education	M,D,O
Mathematics Education	M
Music Education	M
Physical Education	M
Reading Education	M,D,O
Science Education	M
Social Work	M,D
Special Education	M,O
Sports Management	M
Vocational and Technical Education	M,D

JACKSONVILLE STATE UNIVERSITY

Business Administration and Management—General	M
Counselor Education	M
Early Childhood Education	M
Education—General	M,O
Educational Leadership and Administration	M,O

Educational Media/Instructional Technology

Educational Media/Instructional Technology	M
Elementary Education	M
Physical Education	M,O
Reading Education	M
Secondary Education	M
Special Education	M

JACKSONVILLE UNIVERSITY

Accounting	M
Business Administration and Management—General	M,D*
Educational Leadership and Administration	M
Finance and Banking	M
Kinesiology and Movement Studies	M
Marketing	M
Organizational Management	M
Sports Management	M

JAMES MADISON UNIVERSITY

Accounting	M
Art Education	M
Business Administration and Management—General	M
Early Childhood Education	M
Education of the Gifted	M
Educational Leadership and Administration	M
Educational Measurement and Evaluation	M,D
Educational Media/Instructional Technology	M
Elementary Education	M
English as a Second Language	M
Entrepreneurship	M
Exercise and Sports Science	M
Foreign Languages Education	M
Health Education	M
Higher Education	M
Human Resources Management	M
Kinesiology and Movement Studies	M
Management Information Systems	M
Management Strategy and Policy	D
Mathematics Education	M
Middle School Education	M
Multilingual and Multicultural Education	M
Music Education	M
Nonprofit Management	M,D
Organizational Management	D
Physical Education	M
Reading Education	M
Secondary Education	M
Special Education	M
Sustainability Management	M
Taxation	M
Vocational and Technical Education	M

THE JEWISH THEOLOGICAL SEMINARY

Religious Education	M,D

JOHN BROWN UNIVERSITY

Business Administration and Management—General	M
Counselor Education	M,O
Curriculum and Instruction	M
Education—General	M
International Business	M
Secondary Education	M

JOHN CARROLL UNIVERSITY

Accounting	M
Business Administration and Management—General	M
Counselor Education	M,O
Education—General	M
Educational Psychology	M,O
Nonprofit Management	M

JOHN F. KENNEDY UNIVERSITY

Business Administration and Management—General	M,O
Education—General	M
Health Education	M
Human Resources Development	M,O
Law	D
Organizational Management	M,O

JOHN JAY COLLEGE OF CRIMINAL JUSTICE OF THE CITY UNIVERSITY OF NEW YORK

Legal and Justice Studies	M,D
Organizational Behavior	M,D

THE JOHN MARSHALL LAW SCHOOL

Law	M,D

JOHNS HOPKINS UNIVERSITY

Business Administration and Management—General	M,O
Business Analytics	M
Counselor Education	M,O
Early Childhood Education	M
Education of the Gifted	M,O
Education—General	M,D,O
Educational Leadership and Administration	M,D,O
Educational Media/Instructional Technology	M
Educational Policy	D
Elementary Education	M
Finance and Banking	M,D,O
Health Education	M,D
Investment Management	M,O
Management Information Systems	M,O
Marketing	M
Nonprofit Management	M,O
Organizational Management	M
Reading Education	M
Real Estate	M
Risk Management	M
Secondary Education	M
Social Sciences Education	M

---

*M—masters degree; D—doctorate; O—other advanced degree; *—Close-Up and/or Display*

Special Education — M,O
Urban Education — O

JOHNSON & WALES UNIVERSITY
Accounting — M
Business Administration and Management—General — M
Business Education — M
Education—General — M
Educational Leadership and Administration — D
Elementary Education — M
Finance and Banking — M
Hospitality Management — M
Human Resources Management — M
Management Information Systems — M
Nonprofit Management — M
Organizational Management — M
Secondary Education — M
Special Education — M
Sports Management — M
Supply Chain Management — M
Travel and Tourism — M

JOHNSON C. SMITH UNIVERSITY
Social Work — M

JOHNSON UNIVERSITY
Counselor Education — M,D,O
Education—General — M,D,O
Educational Media/Instructional Technology — M,D,O
Higher Education — M,D,O
Nonprofit Management — M,D,O

JOSE MARIA VARGAS UNIVERSITY
Early Childhood Education — M

THE JUDGE ADVOCATE GENERAL'S SCHOOL, U.S. ARMY
Law — M

JUDSON UNIVERSITY
Business Administration and Management—General — M
Human Services — M
Organizational Management — M
Reading Education — M,D

JUNIATA COLLEGE
Accounting — M

KANSAS STATE UNIVERSITY
Accounting — M
Adult Education — M,D,O
Advertising and Public Relations — M
Agricultural Education — M
Business Administration and Management—General — M,O
Counselor Education — M,D,O
Curriculum and Instruction — M,D,O
Distance Education Development — M,D,O
Early Childhood Education — M,D,O
Education—General — M,D,O
Educational Leadership and Administration — M,D,O
Educational Media/Instructional Technology — M,D,O
Elementary Education — M,D,O
English as a Second Language — M,D,O
English Education — M,D,O
Entrepreneurship — M,O
Finance and Banking — M,D,O
Health Education — M,D
Hospitality Management — M,D
Human Services — M,D,O
Kinesiology and Movement Studies — M,D
Marketing — M,O
Middle School Education — M,D,O
Reading Education — M,D,O
Special Education — M,D,O
Student Affairs — M,D,O

KANSAS WESLEYAN UNIVERSITY
Business Administration and Management—General — M
Sports Management — M

KEAN UNIVERSITY
Accounting — M
Art Education — M
Business Administration and Management—General — M
Counselor Education — M
Curriculum and Instruction — M
Early Childhood Education — M
Education—General — M
Educational Leadership and Administration — M,D
English as a Second Language — M
Exercise and Sports Science — M
Foreign Languages Education — M
International Business — M
Management Information Systems — M
Multilingual and Multicultural Education — M
Nonprofit Management — M
Social Work — M
Special Education — M

KEENE STATE COLLEGE
Counselor Education — M,O
Curriculum and Instruction — M,O
Education—General — M,O
Educational Leadership and Administration — M,O
Special Education — M,O

KEISER UNIVERSITY
Accounting — M
Business Administration and Management—General — M,D
Distance Education Development — M
Education—General — M
Educational Leadership and Administration — M,D,O
Educational Media/Instructional Technology — D,O

Health Education — M
International Business — M,D
Management Information Systems — M
Marketing — M,D
Organizational Management — M

KENNESAW STATE UNIVERSITY
Accounting — M
Art Education — M
Business Administration and Management—General — M,D
Early Childhood Education — M
Education—General — M,D,O
Educational Leadership and Administration — M,D,O
Educational Media/Instructional Technology — M
Elementary Education — M
English as a Second Language — M
English Education — M
Exercise and Sports Science — M
Foreign Languages Education — M
Mathematics Education — M
Middle School Education — M
Reading Education — M
Secondary Education — M
Social Work — M
Special Education — M

KENT STATE UNIVERSITY
Accounting — M
Advertising and Public Relations — M
Art Education — M
Athletic Training and Sports Medicine — M,D
Business Administration and Management—General — M
Computer Education — M,D
Counselor Education — M,D,O
Curriculum and Instruction — M,D,O
Early Childhood Education — M,D,O
Education of the Gifted — M,D,O
Education—General — M,D,O
Educational Leadership and Administration — M,D,O
Educational Measurement and Evaluation — M,D
Educational Media/Instructional Technology — M,D
Educational Psychology — M
English as a Second Language — M,D
English Education — M,D
Exercise and Sports Science — M,D
Finance and Banking — D
Foundations and Philosophy of Education — M
Health Education — M,D
Higher Education — M,D,O
Hospitality Management — M
Human Services — M,D,O
Library Science — M
Management Information Systems — D
Marketing — D
Mathematics Education — M,D
Middle School Education — M
Music Education — M,D
Reading Education — M
Recreation and Park Management — M
Secondary Education — M,D
Social Sciences Education — M,D
Special Education — M,D,O
Sports Management — M
Student Affairs — M
Travel and Tourism — M
Vocational and Technical Education — M

KENT STATE UNIVERSITY AT STARK
Business Administration and Management—General — M
Curriculum and Instruction — M
Education—General — M

KENTUCKY STATE UNIVERSITY
Business Administration and Management—General — M
Human Resources Development — M,D
Special Education — M,D

KETTERING UNIVERSITY
Business Administration and Management—General — M

KEUKA COLLEGE
Business Administration and Management—General — M
Early Childhood Education — M
Elementary Education — M
Secondary Education — M
Social Work — M

KEYSTONE COLLEGE
Accounting — M
Business Administration and Management—General — M
Early Childhood Education — M
Educational Leadership and Administration — M
Sports Management — M

KING'S COLLEGE
Education—General — M

KING UNIVERSITY
Accounting — M
Business Administration and Management—General — M
Finance and Banking — M
Human Resources Management — M
Marketing — M
Project Management — M

KUTZTOWN UNIVERSITY OF PENNSYLVANIA
Art Education — M
Business Administration and Management—General — M
Counselor Education — M

Curriculum and Instruction — M,D
Education—General — M,D
Educational Leadership and Administration — M
Educational Media/Instructional Technology — M
Elementary Education — M
English Education — M,D
Library Science — M,D
Middle School Education — M,D
Reading Education — M,D
Secondary Education — M,D
Social Sciences Education — M,D
Social Work — M,D

LAGRANGE COLLEGE
Curriculum and Instruction — M,O
Education—General — M,O
Middle School Education — M,O
Organizational Management — M,O
Secondary Education — M,O

LAKE ERIE COLLEGE
Business Administration and Management—General — M
Education—General — M
Management Information Systems — M

LAKE ERIE COLLEGE OF OSTEOPATHIC MEDICINE
Health Education — M,D,O

LAKE FOREST COLLEGE
Art Education — M
Education—General — M
Elementary Education — M
English Education — M
Mathematics Education — M
Music Education — M
Science Education — M
Secondary Education — M
Social Sciences Education — M

LAKE FOREST GRADUATE SCHOOL OF MANAGEMENT
Business Administration and Management—General — M
Finance and Banking — M
International Business — M
Marketing — M
Organizational Behavior — M

LAKEHEAD UNIVERSITY
Education—General — M,D
Exercise and Sports Science — M
Kinesiology and Movement Studies — M
Social Work — M

LAKELAND UNIVERSITY
Accounting — M
Business Administration and Management—General — M
Counselor Education — M
Education—General — M
Finance and Banking — M
Project Management — M

LAMAR UNIVERSITY
Accounting — M
Business Administration and Management—General — M
Counselor Education — M
Education—General — M,D,O
Educational Leadership and Administration — M,D
Educational Media/Instructional Technology — M,D
Entrepreneurship — M
Foreign Languages Education — M
Kinesiology and Movement Studies — M
Special Education — M,D

LANCASTER BIBLE COLLEGE
Counselor Education — M,D
Elementary Education — M,D
Secondary Education — M,D
Special Education — M,D

LANCASTER THEOLOGICAL SEMINARY
Religious Education — M,D,O

LANDER UNIVERSITY
Early Childhood Education — M
Education—General — M

LANGSTON UNIVERSITY
Education—General — M
Elementary Education — M
English as a Second Language — M
Multilingual and Multicultural Education — M
Urban Education — M

LA ROCHE COLLEGE
Accounting — M
Human Resources Management — M,O

LA SALLE UNIVERSITY
Accounting — M,O
Advertising and Public Relations — M,O
Business Administration and Management—General — M,O
Business Analytics — M,O
Early Childhood Education — M,O
Education—General — M,O
Educational Leadership and Administration — M,O
Educational Media/Instructional Technology — M,O
English as a Second Language — M,O
Finance and Banking — M,O
Human Resources Development — M,O
Human Resources Management — M,O
International Business — M,O
Marketing — M,O
Middle School Education — M,O
Multilingual and Multicultural Education — M,O
Nonprofit Management — M

Reading Education — M,O
Secondary Education — M,O
Social Sciences Education — M,O
Special Education — M,O

LASELL COLLEGE
Advertising and Public Relations — M,O
Business Administration and Management—General — M,O
Curriculum and Instruction — M,O
Education—General — M,O
Educational Leadership and Administration — M,O
Elementary Education — M,O
English as a Second Language — M,O
Hospitality Management — M,O
Human Resources Management — M,O
Marketing — M,O
Project Management — M,O
Recreation and Park Management — M,O
Special Education — M,O
Sports Management — M,O
Travel and Tourism — M,O

LA SIERRA UNIVERSITY
Accounting — M,O
Advertising and Public Relations — M
Business Administration and Management—General — M,O
Counselor Education — M,O
Curriculum and Instruction — M,D,O
Education—General — M,D,O
Educational Leadership and Administration — M,D,O
Educational Psychology — M,O
Finance and Banking — M,O
Human Resources Management — M,O
Marketing — M,O
Religious Education — M

LAURENTIAN UNIVERSITY
Business Administration and Management—General — M
Science Education — O
Social Work — M

LAWRENCE TECHNOLOGICAL UNIVERSITY
Business Administration and Management—General — M,D,O
Educational Media/Instructional Technology — M,D,O
Finance and Banking — M,D,O
Human Resources Development — M,O
Industrial and Manufacturing Management — M,D
Management Strategy and Policy — M,D,O
Marketing — M,D,O
Nonprofit Management — M,D,O
Project Management — M,D,O
Science Education — M,O

LEBANESE AMERICAN UNIVERSITY
Business Administration and Management—General — M

LEBANON VALLEY COLLEGE
Athletic Training and Sports Medicine — M
Business Administration and Management—General — M
Human Resources Management — M
Mathematics Education — M
Music Education — M
Project Management — M
Science Education — M,O
Social Sciences Education — M,O

LEE UNIVERSITY
Business Administration and Management—General — M
Counselor Education — M
Curriculum and Instruction — M,O
Early Childhood Education — M,O
Education—General — M,O
Educational Leadership and Administration — M,O
Elementary Education — M,O
English as a Second Language — M,O
Higher Education — M,O
Mathematics Education — M,O
Middle School Education — M,O
Music Education — M
Secondary Education — M
Social Sciences Education — M,O
Special Education — M,O

LEHIGH UNIVERSITY
Accounting — M
Business Administration and Management—General — M
Counselor Education — M,D,O
Curriculum and Instruction — M,D,O
Early Childhood Education — M,D,O
Education—General — M,D,O
Educational Leadership and Administration — M,D,O
Educational Media/Instructional Technology — M,D
Elementary Education — M
Entrepreneurship — M
Environmental Law — M,O
Finance and Banking — M
Human Services — M,D,O
Project Management — M
Quantitative Analysis — M
Special Education — M,D

LEHMAN COLLEGE OF THE CITY UNIVERSITY OF NEW YORK
Accounting — M
Business Education — M
Counselor Education — M
Early Childhood Education — M
Education—General — M
Elementary Education — M
English as a Second Language — M

English Education	M
Health Education	M
Mathematics Education	M
Multilingual and Multicultural Education	M
Music Education	M
Reading Education	M
Recreation and Park Management	M
Science Education	M
Social Sciences Education	M
Special Education	M

LE MOYNE COLLEGE

Business Administration and Management—General	M
Early Childhood Education	M,O
Education—General	M,O
Educational Leadership and Administration	M,O
Elementary Education	M,O
English as a Second Language	M,O
English Education	M,O
Foreign Languages Education	M
Management Information Systems	M
Middle School Education	M,O
Reading Education	M,O
Secondary Education	M,O
Social Sciences Education	M,O
Special Education	M,O

LENOIR-RHYNE UNIVERSITY

Accounting	M
Athletic Training and Sports Medicine	M
Business Administration and Management—General	M
Business Analytics	M
Community College Education	M
Counselor Education	M
Distance Education Development	M
Education—General	M
Educational Leadership and Administration	M
Educational Media/Instructional Technology	M
Entrepreneurship	M
Human Services	M
International Business	M
Management Information Systems	M
Management Strategy and Policy	M
Organizational Management	M
Secondary Education	M

LESLEY UNIVERSITY

Adult Education	M,D,O
Art Education	M,D,O
Computer Education	M,D,O
Curriculum and Instruction	M,D,O
Distance Education Development	M,D,O
Early Childhood Education	M
Education—General	M,D,O
Educational Leadership and Administration	M,D,O
Educational Media/Instructional Technology	M,D,O
Elementary Education	M,D,O
English as a Second Language	M,D,O
Mathematics Education	M,D,O
Middle School Education	M,D,O
Reading Education	M,D,O
Science Education	M,D,O
Secondary Education	M,D,O
Special Education	M,D,O

LES ROCHES INTERNATIONAL SCHOOL OF HOTEL MANAGEMENT

Hospitality Management	M

LETOURNEAU UNIVERSITY

Business Administration and Management—General	M
Curriculum and Instruction	M
Educational Leadership and Administration	M
Management Strategy and Policy	M

LEWIS & CLARK COLLEGE

Curriculum and Instruction	M
Educational Leadership and Administration	M,D,O
Elementary Education	M
Environmental Law	M,D
Law	M
Secondary Education	M
Special Education	M
Student Affairs	M,D,O

LEWIS UNIVERSITY

Accounting	M
Aviation Management	M
Business Administration and Management—General	
Business Analytics	M
Counselor Education	M
Curriculum and Instruction	M
Early Childhood Education	M
Education—General	M,D
Educational Leadership and Administration	M,D
Educational Media/Instructional Technology	M
Electronic Commerce	M
Elementary Education	M
English as a Second Language	M
English Education	M
Finance and Banking	M
Foreign Languages Education	M
Higher Education	M
Human Resources Management	M
International Business	M
Management Information Systems	M
Marketing	M
Mathematics Education	M

Middle School Education	M
Nonprofit Management	M
Organizational Management	M
Project Management	M
Reading Education	M
Science Education	M
Secondary Education	M
Social Sciences Education	M
Social Work	M
Special Education	M
Sports Management	M
Student Affairs	M

LIBERTY UNIVERSITY

Accounting	M,D
Advertising and Public Relations	M,D
Business Administration and Management—General	M,D
Counselor Education	M,D,O
Curriculum and Instruction	M,D,O
Education of the Gifted	M,D,O
Education—General	M,D,O
Educational Leadership and Administration	M,D,O
Elementary Education	M,D,O
Exercise and Sports Science	M,D
Facilities Management	M,D
Finance and Banking	M,D
Human Services	M,D,O
International Business	M,D
Law	M
Legal and Justice Studies	M
Management Information Systems	M,D
Marketing	M,D,O
Mathematics Education	M,D,O
Middle School Education	M,D,O
Music Education	M,D
Nonprofit Management	M
Project Management	M,D
Reading Education	M,D
Religious Education	M,D
Secondary Education	M,D,O
Special Education	M,D,O
Sports Management	M,D,O
Taxation	M,D
Travel and Tourism	M,D,O

LIFE UNIVERSITY

Athletic Training and Sports Medicine	M
Exercise and Sports Science	M

LIM COLLEGE

Business Administration and Management—General	M
Marketing	M

LIMESTONE COLLEGE

Business Administration and Management—General	M

LINCOLN CHRISTIAN SEMINARY

Religious Education	M,D

LINCOLN CHRISTIAN UNIVERSITY

Organizational Management	M

LINCOLN MEMORIAL UNIVERSITY

Business Administration and Management—General	M
Counselor Education	M,D,O
Curriculum and Instruction	M,D,O
Education—General	M,D,O
Educational Leadership and Administration	M,D,O
English Education	M,D,O
Higher Education	M,D,O
Human Resources Development	M,D,O
Law	D

LINCOLN UNIVERSITY (CA)

Business Administration and Management—General	M,D
Finance and Banking	M,D
Human Resources Management	M,D
International Business	M,D
Investment Management	M,D
Management Information Systems	M,D

LINCOLN UNIVERSITY (MO)

Accounting	M
Business Administration and Management—General	M
Counselor Education	M
Elementary Education	M
Higher Education	M
Management Information Systems	M
Middle School Education	M
Secondary Education	M

LINCOLN UNIVERSITY (PA)

Early Childhood Education	M
Educational Leadership and Administration	M
Finance and Banking	M
Human Resources Management	M
Human Services	M
Special Education	M

LINDENWOOD UNIVERSITY

Accounting	M
Advertising and Public Relations	M
Business Administration and Management—General	M,O
Education of the Gifted	M,D,O
Education—General	M,D,O
Educational Leadership and Administration	M,D,O
Educational Media/Instructional Technology	M,D,O
English as a Second Language	M,D,O
Entrepreneurship	M
Finance and Banking	M
Human Resources Management	M,O
International Business	M

Management Information Systems	M,O
Marketing	M,O
Nonprofit Management	M
Project Management	M,O
Sports Management	M
Supply Chain Management	M

LINDENWOOD UNIVERSITY–BELLEVILLE

Business Administration and Management—General	M
Counselor Education	M
Education—General	M
Educational Leadership and Administration	M
Human Resources Management	M

LINDSEY WILSON COLLEGE

Counselor Education	M,D
Educational Leadership and Administration	M

LIPSCOMB UNIVERSITY

Accounting	M,O
Business Administration and Management—General	
Education—General	M,D,O
Educational Leadership and Administration	M,D,O
Educational Media/Instructional Technology	M,D,O
English Education	M
Exercise and Sports Science	M
Finance and Banking	M,O
Management Information Systems	M,O
Management Strategy and Policy	M,O
Nonprofit Management	M,O
Organizational Management	M,O
Reading Education	M,O
Special Education	M,D,O
Taxation	M,O

LOCK HAVEN UNIVERSITY OF PENNSYLVANIA

Actuarial Science	M
Athletic Training and Sports Medicine	M
Business Education	M
Education—General	M
Educational Leadership and Administration	M
Elementary Education	M
Health Education	M
Human Services	M
Information Studies	M
Sports Management	M

LOGAN UNIVERSITY

Exercise and Sports Science	M,D
Health Education	M,D

LOMA LINDA UNIVERSITY

Counselor Education	M,D,O
Health Education	M,D
Social Work	M,D

LONDON METROPOLITAN UNIVERSITY

Athletic Training and Sports Medicine	M,D
Early Childhood Education	M,D
Education—General	M,D
English Education	M,D
Foreign Languages Education	M,D
Higher Education	M,D
Human Resources Management	M,D
Law	M,D
Management Information Systems	M,D
Social Work	M,D
Special Education	M,D
Sports and Entertainment Law	M,D

LONG ISLAND UNIVERSITY–BRENTWOOD CAMPUS

Counselor Education	M,O
Early Childhood Education	M,O
Educational Leadership and Administration	M,O
Elementary Education	M,O
Library Science	M,O
Reading Education	M,O
Social Work	M,O
Special Education	M,O

LONG ISLAND UNIVERSITY–HUDSON

Counselor Education	M,O
Early Childhood Education	M,O
Educational Leadership and Administration	M,O
Elementary Education	M,O
English as a Second Language	M,O
Middle School Education	M,O
Multilingual and Multicultural Education	M,O
Reading Education	M,O
Special Education	M,O

LONG ISLAND UNIVERSITY–LIU BROOKLYN

Accounting	M,O
Athletic Training and Sports Medicine	M,D,O
Business Administration and Management—General	M,O
Counselor Education	M,O
Early Childhood Education	M,O
Education—General	M,O
Educational Leadership and Administration	M,O
English as a Second Language	M,O
Exercise and Sports Science	M,O
Human Resources Management	M,O
Multilingual and Multicultural Education	M,O
Nonprofit Management	M,O

Social Sciences Education	M,D,O
Social Work	M,D,O
Special Education	M,O
Taxation	M,O
Urban Education	M,O

LONG ISLAND UNIVERSITY–LIU POST

Accounting	M,D,O
Art Education	M
Business Administration and Management—General	M
Early Childhood Education	M,D,O
Education—General	M,D,O
Educational Leadership and Administration	M,D,O
Educational Media/Instructional Technology	M,D,O
English as a Second Language	M
Finance and Banking	M
International Business	M
Library Science	M,D,O
Management Information Systems	M
Marketing	M
Middle School Education	M,D,O
Music Education	M
Nonprofit Management	M,O
Reading Education	M,D,O
Secondary Education	M,D,O
Social Work	M
Special Education	M,D,O
Taxation	M

LONG ISLAND UNIVERSITY–RIVERHEAD

Early Childhood Education	M,O
Elementary Education	M,O
English as a Second Language	M,O
Reading Education	M,O
Special Education	M,O

LONGWOOD UNIVERSITY

Business Administration and Management—General	M
Counselor Education	M
Education—General	M
Educational Media/Instructional Technology	M
Elementary Education	M
Health Education	M
Mathematics Education	M
Middle School Education	M
Physical Education	M
Reading Education	M
Real Estate	M
Special Education	M

LORAS COLLEGE

Educational Leadership and Administration	M
Special Education	M

LOUISIANA COLLEGE

Education—General	M

LOUISIANA STATE UNIVERSITY AND AGRICULTURAL & MECHANICAL COLLEGE

Accounting	M,D
Agricultural Education	M,D
Business Administration and Management—General	M,D
Business Education	M,D
Counselor Education	M,D,O
Education—General	M,D,O
Educational Leadership and Administration	M,D,O
Educational Measurement and Evaluation	M,D,O
Educational Media/Instructional Technology	M,D,O
Elementary Education	M,D,O
Finance and Banking	M,D
Higher Education	M,D,O
Home Economics Education	M,D
Human Resources Development	M,D
Information Studies	M
International and Comparative Education	M,D
Kinesiology and Movement Studies	M,D
Law	M,D
Library Science	M,D
Management Information Systems	M,D
Music Education	M,D,O
Secondary Education	M,D,O
Social Work	M,D
Vocational and Technical Education	M,D

LOUISIANA STATE UNIVERSITY IN SHREVEPORT

Business Administration and Management—General	M
Counselor Education	M
Curriculum and Instruction	M,D
Education—General	M,D
Educational Leadership and Administration	M,D
Nonprofit Management	M

LOUISIANA TECH UNIVERSITY

Accounting	M,D
Business Administration and Management—General	M,D,O
Curriculum and Instruction	M,D,O
Early Childhood Education	M,D,O
Education—General	M,D,O
Educational Leadership and Administration	M,D,O
Elementary Education	M,D,O
Finance and Banking	M,D
Higher Education	M,D,O
Human Services	M
Kinesiology and Movement Studies	M,D,O
Management Information Systems	M,D

---

*M—masters degree; D—doctorate; O—other advanced degree; *—Close-Up and/or Display*

Marketing — M,D
Middle School Education — M,D,O
Secondary Education — M,D,O
Special Education — M,D,O

LOURDES UNIVERSITY
Business Administration and
Management—General — M
Curriculum and Instruction — M
Educational Leadership and
Administration — M
Organizational Management — M
Reading Education — M

LOYOLA MARYMOUNT UNIVERSITY
Accounting — M
Business Administration and
Management—General — M
Counselor Education — M
Education—General — M,D
Educational Leadership and
Administration — M,D
Elementary Education — M
Higher Education — M
Law — M,D
Mathematics Education — M
Multilingual and Multicultural
Education — M
Reading Education — M
Recreation and Park Management — M
Secondary Education — M
Special Education — M
Urban Education — M

LOYOLA UNIVERSITY CHICAGO
Accounting — M
Business Administration and
Management—General — M,O
Business Analytics — M,O
Counselor Education — M,O
Curriculum and Instruction — M,D
Education—General — M,D,O
Educational Leadership and
Administration — M,D,O
Educational Measurement and
Evaluation — M,D,O
Educational Policy — M,D
Elementary Education — M
Entrepreneurship — M
Finance and Banking — M
Health Law — M,D,O
Higher Education — M,D
Human Resources Management — M
International and Comparative
Education — M,D
International Business — M
Law — M,D,O
Legal and Justice Studies — M,O
Management Information Systems — M
Marketing — M
Religious Education — M,O
Risk Management — M
Secondary Education — M
Social Work — M,D,O
Special Education — M
Supply Chain Management — M,O
Taxation — M,D,O

LOYOLA UNIVERSITY MARYLAND
Business Administration and
Management—General — M
Counselor Education — M,O
Curriculum and Instruction — M
Early Childhood Education — M,O
Education—General — M,O
Educational Leadership and
Administration — M,O
Educational Media/Instructional
Technology — M,O
Elementary Education — M,O
Finance and Banking — M
Investment Management — M
Management Information Systems — M
Marketing — M
Music Education — M
Reading Education — M
Secondary Education — M

LOYOLA UNIVERSITY NEW ORLEANS
Business Administration and
Management—General — M
Education—General — M
Law — M,D
Organizational Management — M
Secondary Education — M

LYNN UNIVERSITY
Aviation Management — M
Business Administration and
Management—General — M
Early Childhood Education — M,D
Education of the Gifted — M,D
Education—General — M,D
Educational Leadership and
Administration — M,D
Entrepreneurship — M
Hospitality Management — M
Human Resources Management — M
International Business — M
Investment Management — M
Marketing — M
Middle School Education — M,D
Special Education — M,D
Sports Management — M

MAASTRICHT SCHOOL OF MANAGEMENT
Business Administration and
Management—General — M,D
Facilities Management — M,D
Sustainability Management — M,D

MADONNA UNIVERSITY
Business Administration and
Management—General — M
Education—General — M

Educational Leadership and
Administration — M
English as a Second Language — M
International Business — M
Quality Management — M
Reading Education — M
Special Education — M

MAHARISHI UNIVERSITY OF MANAGEMENT
Accounting — M,D
Business Administration and
Management—General — M,D
Sustainability Management — M,D

MAINE MARITIME ACADEMY
International Business — M
Supply Chain Management — M
Transportation Management — M

MALONE UNIVERSITY
Business Administration and
Management—General — M
Counselor Education — M
Curriculum and Instruction — M
Education—General — M
Educational Leadership and
Administration — M
Organizational Management — M
Special Education — M

MANCHESTER UNIVERSITY
Athletic Training and Sports
Medicine — M

MANHATTAN COLLEGE
Business Administration and
Management—General — M,O
Counselor Education — M,O
Early Childhood Education — M,O
Education—General — M,O
Educational Leadership and
Administration — M,O
Educational Media/Instructional
Technology — M
Elementary Education — M,O
Multilingual and Multicultural
Education — M,O
Organizational Management — M,O
Special Education — M,O
Student Affairs — M,O

MANHATTANVILLE COLLEGE
Accounting — M,O
Art Education — M,O
Business Education — M,O
Early Childhood Education — M,O
Education—General — M,D,O
Educational Leadership and
Administration — M,D,O
Elementary Education — M,O
English as a Second Language — M,O
English Education — M,O
Entertainment Management — M,O
Entrepreneurship — M
Exercise and Sports Science — M,O
Finance and Banking — M,O
Foreign Languages Education — M,O
Human Resources Management — M,O
International Business — M,O
Investment Management — M,O
Management Strategy and Policy — M,O
Marketing — M,O
Mathematics Education — M,O
Middle School Education — M,O
Multilingual and Multicultural
Education — M,O
Music Education — M,O
Organizational Management — M,O
Reading Education — M,O
Science Education — M,O
Secondary Education — M,O
Social Sciences Education — M,O
Special Education — M,O
Sports Management — M,O
Urban Education — M,O

MANSFIELD UNIVERSITY OF PENNSYLVANIA
Art Education — M
Education—General — M
Elementary Education — M
Information Studies — M
Library Science — M
Organizational Management — M
Secondary Education — M
Special Education — M

MAPLE SPRINGS BAPTIST BIBLE COLLEGE AND SEMINARY
Religious Education — M,D,O

MARANATHA BAPTIST UNIVERSITY
Education—General — M
Organizational Management — M

MARCONI INTERNATIONAL UNIVERSITY
Business Administration and
Management—General — M,D
Educational Leadership and
Administration — M,D
Educational Media/Instructional
Technology — M,D
International Business — M,D

MARIAN UNIVERSITY (IN)
Counselor Education — M
Education—General — M

MARIAN UNIVERSITY (WI)
Business Administration and
Management—General — M
Curriculum and Instruction — M,D
Education—General — M,D
Educational Leadership and
Administration — M,D
Educational Media/Instructional
Technology — M,D

Organizational Management — M
Special Education — M,D

MARIST COLLEGE
Business Administration and
Management—General — M,O
Education—General — M,O
Management Information Systems — M,O
Marketing — M

MARLBORO COLLEGE
Business Administration and
Management—General — M
Educational Media/Instructional
Technology — M,O
English as a Second Language — M
Entrepreneurship — M
Legal and Justice Studies — M
Organizational Management — M
Project Management — M

MARQUETTE UNIVERSITY
Accounting — M
Advertising and Public Relations — M,O
Business Administration and
Management—General — M,O
Counselor Education — M,D
Curriculum and Instruction — M,D,O
Education—General — M,D,O
Educational Leadership and
Administration — M,D,O
Educational Policy — M,D,O
Elementary Education — M,O
Entrepreneurship — M,O
Finance and Banking — M,O
Foreign Languages Education — M
Foundations and Philosophy of
Education — M,D,O
Human Resources Development — M,O
Human Resources Management — M,O
Industrial and Manufacturing
Management — M,O
International Business — M,O
Law — D
Management Information Systems — M,O
Marketing Research — M
Marketing — M,O
Mathematics Education — M,D
Reading Education — M,D,O
Real Estate — M
Secondary Education — M,O
Sports Management — M
Student Affairs — M,D,O
Supply Chain Management — M,O

MARSHALL UNIVERSITY
Accounting — M
Adult Education — M
Advertising and Public Relations — M,O
Athletic Training and Sports
Medicine — M
Business Administration and
Management—General — M,O
Counselor Education — M
Education—General — M,D,O
Educational Leadership and
Administration — M
Exercise and Sports Science — M
Health Education — M
Human Resources Management — M
Reading Education — M
Social Work — M
Special Education — M
Sports Management — M

MARS HILL UNIVERSITY
Elementary Education — M

MARTIN LUTHER COLLEGE
Curriculum and Instruction — M
Early Childhood Education — M
Education—General — M
Educational Leadership and
Administration — M
Educational Media/Instructional
Technology — M
Special Education — M

MARY BALDWIN UNIVERSITY
Education—General — M
Elementary Education — M
Middle School Education — M

MARYGROVE COLLEGE
Curriculum and Instruction — M,O
Early Childhood Education — M,O
Educational Leadership and
Administration — M,O
Educational Media/Instructional
Technology — M,O
Elementary Education — M,O
Human Resources Management — M,O
Legal and Justice Studies — M,O
Middle School Education — M,O
Reading Education — M,O
Special Education — M,O

MARYLAND INSTITUTE COLLEGE OF ART
Art Education — M
Business Administration and
Management—General — M

MARYMOUNT CALIFORNIA UNIVERSITY
Business Administration and
Management—General — M

MARYMOUNT UNIVERSITY
Business Administration and
Management—General — M,O
Community College Education — M,O
Counselor Education — M
Curriculum and Instruction — M
Education—General — M
Elementary Education — M
English Education — M
Health Education — M
Human Resources Management — O

Management Information Systems — M,O
Nonprofit Management — M,O
Project Management — M,O
Secondary Education — M
Special Education — M

MARYVILLE UNIVERSITY OF SAINT LOUIS
Accounting — M,O
Actuarial Science — M
Business Administration and
Management—General — M,O
Business Education — M,O
Early Childhood Education — M,D
Education—General — M,D
Educational Leadership and
Administration — M,D
Elementary Education — M,D
Finance and Banking — M,O
Higher Education — M,D
Human Resources Management — M,O
Logistics — M,O
Marketing — M,O
Middle School Education — M,D
Project Management — M,O
Reading Education — M,D
Secondary Education — M,O
Sports Management — M,O
Supply Chain Management — M,O

MARYWOOD UNIVERSITY
Art Education — M
Business Administration and
Management—General — M
Counselor Education — M
Early Childhood Education — M
Education—General — M
Educational Leadership and
Administration — M,D
Elementary Education — M
Exercise and Sports Science — M
Finance and Banking — M
Health Education — D
Higher Education — M,D
Investment Management — M
Management Information Systems — M
Music Education — M
Reading Education — M
Secondary Education — M
Social Work — M,D
Special Education — M

MASSACHUSETTS COLLEGE OF ART AND DESIGN
Art Education — M,O

MASSACHUSETTS COLLEGE OF LIBERAL ARTS
Business Administration and
Management—General — M,O
Curriculum and Instruction — M,O
Education—General — M,O
Educational Leadership and
Administration — M,O
Educational Media/Instructional
Technology — M,O
Health Education — M,O
Physical Education — M,O
Reading Education — M,O
Special Education — M,O

MASSACHUSETTS INSTITUTE OF TECHNOLOGY
Business Administration and
Management—General — M,D
Logistics — M
Real Estate — M

MASSACHUSETTS MARITIME ACADEMY
Facilities Management — M

MASSACHUSETTS SCHOOL OF LAW AT ANDOVER
Law — D

MCDANIEL COLLEGE
Counselor Education — M
Curriculum and Instruction — M
Educational Leadership and
Administration — M
Educational Media/Instructional
Technology — M
Elementary Education — M,O
English as a Second Language — M
Human Resources Development — M
Human Services — M
Kinesiology and Movement Studies — M
Library Science — M
Mathematics Education — M,O
Reading Education — M
Science Education — M,O
Secondary Education — M,O
Special Education — M

MCGILL UNIVERSITY
Accounting — M,D,O
Business Administration and
Management—General — M,D,O
Curriculum and Instruction — M,D,O
Education—General — M,D,O
Educational Leadership and
Administration — M,D,O
Educational Psychology — M,D,O
Entrepreneurship — M,D,O
Finance and Banking — M,D,O
Foreign Languages Education — M,D,O
Foundations and Philosophy of
Education — M,D,O
Industrial and Manufacturing
Management — M,D,O
Information Studies — M,D,O
International Business — M,D,O
Kinesiology and Movement Studies — M,D,O
Law — M,D,O
Library Science — M,D,O
Management Information Systems — M,D,O
Management Strategy and Policy — M,D,O

Marketing — M,D,O
Music Education — M,D
Physical Education — M,D,O
Social Work — M,D,O
Transportation Management — M,D

MCKENDREE UNIVERSITY
Business Administration and
  Management—General — M
Curriculum and Instruction — M,D,O
Education—General — M,D,O
Educational Leadership and
  Administration — M,D,O
Higher Education — M,D,O
Human Resources Management — M
International Business — M
Music Education — M,D,O
Reading Education — M,D,O
Special Education — M,D,O

MCMASTER UNIVERSITY
Business Administration and
  Management—General — M,D
Human Resources Management — M,D
Kinesiology and Movement Studies — M,D
Management Information Systems — D
Social Work — M

MCNEESE STATE UNIVERSITY
Art Education — O
Business Administration and
  Management—General — M
Counselor Education — M
Curriculum and Instruction — M
Early Childhood Education — O
Education of the Gifted — M
Education—General — O
Educational Leadership and
  Administration — M,O
Educational Measurement and
  Evaluation — M,O
Educational Media/Instructional
  Technology — M,O
Elementary Education — M,O
Exercise and Sports Science — O
Health Education — O
Library Science — O
Mathematics Education — O
Middle School Education — O
Music Education — O
Physical Education — M
Reading Education — O
Science Education — O
Secondary Education — M,O
Special Education — M,O

MCPHERSON COLLEGE
Education—General — M

MEDAILLE COLLEGE
Business Administration and
  Management—General — M
Curriculum and Instruction — M
Education—General — M
Elementary Education — M
Organizational Management — M
Reading Education — M
Secondary Education — M
Special Education — M

MELBOURNE BUSINESS SCHOOL
Business Administration and
  Management—General — M,D,O
Marketing — M,D,O

MEMORIAL UNIVERSITY OF NEWFOUNDLAND
Adult Education — M,D,O
Business Administration and
  Management—General — M
Curriculum and Instruction — M,D,O
Education—General — M,D,O
Educational Leadership and
  Administration — M,D,O
Educational Media/Instructional
  Technology — M,D,O
Educational Psychology — M,D,O
Exercise and Sports Science — M
Kinesiology and Movement Studies — M
Physical Education — M
Social Work — M,D

MERCER UNIVERSITY
Accounting — M
Athletic Training and Sports
  Medicine — M,D
Business Administration and
  Management—General — M
Counselor Education — M,D
Curriculum and Instruction — M,D,O
Early Childhood Education — M,D,O
Education—General — M
Educational Leadership and
  Administration — M,D,O
Entrepreneurship — M
Higher Education — M,D,O
Human Services — M,D
Law — D
Middle School Education — M,D,O
Nonprofit Management — M,D
Organizational Management — M
Science Education — M,D,O
Secondary Education — M,D,O

MERCY COLLEGE
Accounting — M
Business Administration and
  Management—General — M
Counselor Education — M,O
Early Childhood Education — M
Education—General — M,O
Educational Leadership and
  Administration — M,O
Elementary Education — M

English as a Second Language — M,O
Human Resources Management — M
Middle School Education — M,O
Organizational Management — M
Reading Education — M,O
Secondary Education — M

MERCYHURST UNIVERSITY
Accounting — M,O
Educational Leadership and
  Administration — M,O
Entrepreneurship — M,O
Higher Education — M,O
Human Resources Management — M,O
Management Strategy and Policy — M,O
Organizational Management — M,O
Secondary Education — M
Special Education — M
Sports Management — M,O

MEREDITH COLLEGE
Business Administration and
  Management—General — M
Education of the Gifted — M,O
Education—General — M,O
Elementary Education — M,O
English as a Second Language — M,O
Entrepreneurship — M
Health Education — M,O
Human Resources Management — M
Physical Education — M,O
Project Management — M
Reading Education — M,O
Special Education — M,O

MERRIMACK COLLEGE
Accounting — M
Adult Education — M,O
Athletic Training and Sports
  Medicine — M
Business Administration and
  Management—General — M
Business Analytics — M
Curriculum and Instruction — M,O
Early Childhood Education — M,O
Education—General — M,O
Educational Leadership and
  Administration — M,O
Elementary Education — M,O
English as a Second Language — M,O
Exercise and Sports Science — M
Health Education — M
Higher Education — M,O
Middle School Education — M,O
Secondary Education — M,O
Special Education — M,O
Student Affairs — M,O

MESSIAH COLLEGE
Business Administration and
  Management—General — M,O
Counselor Education — M,O
Curriculum and Instruction — M
English as a Second Language — M
Higher Education — M
Management Strategy and Policy — M,O
Organizational Management — M,O
Special Education — M
Sports Management — M
Student Affairs — M

METHODIST UNIVERSITY
Business Administration and
  Management—General — M

METROPOLITAN COLLEGE OF NEW YORK
Business Administration and
  Management—General — M
Elementary Education — M
Finance and Banking — M
Risk Management — M
Special Education — M

METROPOLITAN STATE UNIVERSITY
Business Administration and
  Management—General — M,D,O
Business Analytics — M,D,O
Information Studies — M,D,O
Management Information Systems — M,D,O
Project Management — M,D,O
Supply Chain Management — M,D,O

METROPOLITAN STATE UNIVERSITY OF DENVER
Accounting — M
Education—General — M
Elementary Education — M
Social Work — M
Special Education — M
Taxation — M

MGH INSTITUTE OF HEALTH PROFESSIONS
Reading Education — M,O

MIAMI UNIVERSITY
Accounting — M
Art Education — M
Business Administration and
  Management—General — M
Education—General — M,D,O
Educational Leadership and
  Administration — M,D
Educational Psychology — M,O
Exercise and Sports Science — M
Mathematics Education — M
Music Education — M
Student Affairs — M,D

MICHIGAN SCHOOL OF PROFESSIONAL PSYCHOLOGY
Educational Psychology — M,D

MICHIGAN STATE UNIVERSITY
Accounting — M,D
Adult Education — M,D,O
Advertising and Public Relations — M,D
Business Administration and
  Management—General — M,D
Business Analytics — M
Counselor Education — M,D,O
Curriculum and Instruction — M,D,O
Education—General — M,D,O
Educational Leadership and
  Administration — M,D,O
Educational Measurement and
  Evaluation — M,D,O
Educational Media/Instructional
  Technology — M,D,O
Educational Policy — D
Educational Psychology — M,D,O
English as a Second Language — M,D
Finance and Banking — M,D
Foreign Languages Education — D
Higher Education — M,D,O
Hospitality Management — M
Human Resources Management — M,D
Kinesiology and Movement Studies — M,D
Logistics — M,D
Management Information Systems — M,D
Management Strategy and Policy — M,D
Marketing Research — M,D
Marketing — M,D
Mathematics Education — M,D
Music Education — M
Reading Education — M
Recreation and Park Management — M,D
Science Education — M,D
Social Sciences Education — M,D
Social Work — M,D
Special Education — M,D,O
Supply Chain Management — M,D
Taxation — M,D

MICHIGAN STATE UNIVERSITY COLLEGE OF LAW
Intellectual Property Law — M,D
Law — M,D
Legal and Justice Studies — M,D

MICHIGAN TECHNOLOGICAL UNIVERSITY
Accounting — M
Business Administration and
  Management—General — M
Kinesiology and Movement Studies — M,D
Science Education — M,D,O
Sustainability Management — M,D,O

MID-AMERICA CHRISTIAN UNIVERSITY
Business Administration and
  Management—General — M
Organizational Management — M

MIDAMERICA NAZARENE UNIVERSITY
Business Administration and
  Management—General — M
Education—General — M
Educational Media/Instructional
  Technology — M
English as a Second Language — M
Reading Education — M

MIDDLEBURY INSTITUTE OF INTERNATIONAL STUDIES AT MONTEREY
English as a Second Language — M
Foreign Languages Education — M
International and Comparative
  Education — M

MIDDLE GEORGIA STATE UNIVERSITY
Management Information Systems — M

MIDDLE TENNESSEE STATE UNIVERSITY
Accounting — M
Actuarial Science — M
Archives/Archival Administration — M,D,O
Aviation Management — M
Business Administration and
  Management—General — M
Business Education — M
Counselor Education — M
Curriculum and Instruction — M,O
Early Childhood Education — M,O
Education—General — M,D,O
Educational Leadership and
  Administration — M,O
Educational Media/Instructional
  Technology — M,O
Elementary Education — M,O
English as a Second Language — M,O
Exercise and Sports Science — M,D
Foreign Languages Education — M
Health Education — M
Human Resources Management — M
Management Information Systems — M
Management Strategy and Policy — M
Mathematics Education — M,D
Middle School Education — M,O
Physical Education — M
Reading Education — M
Recreation and Park Management — M
Science Education — M
Secondary Education — M,O
Social Work — M
Special Education — M
Vocational and Technical Education — M

MIDWAY UNIVERSITY
Business Administration and
  Management—General — M
Education—General — M
Organizational Management — M

MIDWESTERN BAPTIST THEOLOGICAL SEMINARY
Religious Education — M,D,O

MIDWESTERN STATE UNIVERSITY
Business Administration and
  Management—General — M
Counselor Education — M
Curriculum and Instruction — M
Education—General — M
Educational Leadership and
  Administration — M
Educational Media/Instructional
  Technology — M
Exercise and Sports Science — M
Human Resources Development — M
Reading Education — M
Special Education — M
Sports Management — M

MILLENNIA ATLANTIC UNIVERSITY
Accounting — M
Business Administration and
  Management—General — M
Human Resources Management — M

MILLERSVILLE UNIVERSITY OF PENNSYLVANIA
Art Education — M
Distance Education Development — M
Early Childhood Education — M
Education of the Gifted — M
Education—General — M,D,O
Educational Leadership and
  Administration — M,D
English as a Second Language — M
English Education — M
Mathematics Education — M
Physical Education — M,O
Reading Education — M,D
Science Education — M,D
Social Work — M,D
Special Education — M
Sports Management — M,O
Vocational and Technical Education — M

MILLIGAN COLLEGE
Business Administration and
  Management—General — M,O
Counselor Education — M,O
Early Childhood Education — M
Education—General — M,D,O
Educational Leadership and
  Administration — M,D,O
Elementary Education — M,D,O
Industrial and Manufacturing
  Management — M,D,O
Middle School Education — M,D,O
Religious Education — M,D,O
Secondary Education — M,D,O
Special Education — M,D,O

MILLIKIN UNIVERSITY
Business Administration and
  Management—General — M

MILLSAPS COLLEGE
Accounting — M
Business Administration and
  Management—General — M

MILLS COLLEGE
Business Administration and
  Management—General — M
Early Childhood Education — M
Education—General — M,D,O
Educational Leadership and
  Administration — M

MILWAUKEE SCHOOL OF ENGINEERING
Business Administration and
  Management—General — M
Business Education — M
Industrial and Manufacturing
  Management — M
International Business — M
Marketing — M

MINNESOTA STATE UNIVERSITY MANKATO
Accounting — M
Art Education — M
Business Administration and
  Management—General — M
Counselor Education — M,D
Education—General — M,D,O
Educational Leadership and
  Administration — M,O
English as a Second Language — M,O
Foreign Languages Education — M
Health Education — M,O
Higher Education — M
Human Services — M
Mathematics Education — M
Music Education — M
Nonprofit Management — M,O
Physical Education — M
Science Education — M
Social Sciences Education — M
Social Work — M
Special Education — M,O
Student Affairs — M,D

MINNESOTA STATE UNIVERSITY MOORHEAD
Accounting — M
Business Administration and
  Management—General — M
Counselor Education — M,D,O
Curriculum and Instruction — M,D,O
Education—General — M,D,O
Educational Leadership and
  Administration — M,D,O

English as a Second Language — M
Finance and Banking — M
Special Education — M,D,O

MINOT STATE UNIVERSITY
Business Administration and
   Management—General — M
Elementary Education — M
Management Information Systems — M
Mathematics Education — M
Middle School Education — M
Science Education — M
Special Education — M

MISERICORDIA UNIVERSITY
Accounting — M
Business Administration and
   Management—General — M
Curriculum and Instruction — M
Education—General — M
Educational Media/Instructional
   Technology — M
Human Resources Management — M
Organizational Management — M
Reading Education — M
Special Education — M
Sports Management — M

MISSISSIPPI COLLEGE
Accounting — M,O
Advertising and Public Relations — M
Art Education — M,D,O
Business Administration and
   Management—General — M,O
Business Education — M,D,O
Computer Education — M,D,O
Counselor Education — M,O
Curriculum and Instruction — M,D,O
Education—General — M,D,O
Educational Leadership and
   Administration — M,D,O
Elementary Education — M,D,O
English as a Second Language — M
English Education — M,D,O
Finance and Banking — M,O
Higher Education — M,D,O
Kinesiology and Movement Studies — M
Law — D,O
Legal and Justice Studies — M,O
Mathematics Education — M,D,O
Music Education — M
Science Education — M,D,O
Secondary Education — M,D,O
Social Sciences Education — M,D,O
Special Education — M,D,O

MISSISSIPPI STATE UNIVERSITY
Accounting — M
Agricultural Education — M,D
Business Administration and
   Management—General — M,D
Community College Education — M,D,O
Counselor Education — M,D,O
Curriculum and Instruction — M,D,O
Early Childhood Education — M,D,O
Education—General — M,D,O
Educational Leadership and
   Administration — M,D,O
Educational Media/Instructional
   Technology — M,D,O
Educational Psychology — M,D,O
Elementary Education — M,D,O
Exercise and Sports Science — M,D
Finance and Banking — M,D
Foreign Languages Education — M
Higher Education — M,D,O
Human Resources Development — M,D,O
Industrial and Manufacturing
   Management — M,D
Kinesiology and Movement Studies — M,D
Management Information Systems — M,D
Marketing — D
Middle School Education — M,D,O
Physical Education — M,D
Project Management — M,D
Reading Education — M,D,O
Secondary Education — M,D,O
Special Education — M,D,O
Sports Management — M,D
Student Affairs — M,D,O
Taxation — M
Vocational and Technical Education — M,D,O

MISSISSIPPI UNIVERSITY FOR WOMEN
Curriculum and Instruction — M
Education of the Gifted — M
Education—General — M
Educational Leadership and
   Administration — M
Health Education — M,D,O
Reading Education — M

MISSISSIPPI VALLEY STATE UNIVERSITY
Education—General — M

MISSOURI BAPTIST UNIVERSITY
Business Administration and
   Management—General — M,O
Counselor Education — M,O
Education—General — M,O
Educational Leadership and
   Administration — M,O

MISSOURI SOUTHERN STATE UNIVERSITY
Business Administration and
   Management—General — M
Early Childhood Education — M
Education—General — M
Educational Media/Instructional
   Technology — M

MISSOURI STATE UNIVERSITY
Accounting — M
Athletic Training and Sports
   Medicine — M

Business Administration and
   Management—General — M
Counselor Education — M
Early Childhood Education — M
Educational Leadership and
   Administration — M,O
Educational Measurement and
   Evaluation — O
Educational Media/Instructional
   Technology — M,O
Elementary Education — M,O
English as a Second Language — M,O
English Education — M,O
Higher Education — M
Kinesiology and Movement Studies — M
Mathematics Education — M
Physical Education — M
Project Management — M
Reading Education — M
Science Education — M,O
Secondary Education — M,O
Social Sciences Education — M,O
Social Work — M
Special Education — M
Sports Management — M
Student Affairs — M

MISSOURI UNIVERSITY OF SCIENCE AND TECHNOLOGY
Business Administration and
   Management—General — M
Mathematics Education — M,D

MISSOURI WESTERN STATE UNIVERSITY
Accounting — M
Business Administration and
   Management—General — M
Early Childhood Education — M,O
Educational Measurement and
   Evaluation — M,O
English as a Second Language — M,O
Information Studies — M
Special Education — M,O
Sports Management — M

MITCHELL HAMLINE SCHOOL OF LAW
Law — M,D

MOLLOY COLLEGE
Accounting — M,O
Business Administration and
   Management—General — M,O
Early Childhood Education — M,O
Education—General — M,O
Educational Media/Instructional
   Technology — M,O
English as a Second Language — M,O
English Education — M,O
Finance and Banking — M,O
Foreign Languages Education — M,O
Marketing — M,O
Mathematics Education — M,O
Multilingual and Multicultural
   Education — M,O
Science Education — M,O
Social Sciences Education — M,O
Special Education — M,O

MONMOUTH UNIVERSITY
Accounting — M
Advertising and Public Relations — M,O
Business Administration and
   Management—General — M,O*
Early Childhood Education — M,D,O
Education—General — M,D,O
Educational Leadership and
   Administration — M,D,O
Elementary Education — M,D,O
English as a Second Language — M,D,O
Finance and Banking — M,O
Human Resources Management — M,O
Information Studies — M
Marketing — M,O
Reading Education — M,D,O
Real Estate — M,O
Secondary Education — M,D,O
Social Work — M,O
Special Education — M,D,O
Student Affairs — M,D,O

MONROE COLLEGE
Accounting — M
Business Administration and
   Management—General — M
Entrepreneurship — M
Finance and Banking — M
Hospitality Management — M
Human Resources Management — M
Marketing — M

MONTANA STATE UNIVERSITY
Accounting — M
Adult Education — M,D,O
Agricultural Education — M
Curriculum and Instruction — M,D,O
Education—General — M,D,O
Educational Leadership and
   Administration — M,D,O
Health Education — M
Higher Education — M,D,O
Home Economics Education — M
Mathematics Education — M,D
Vocational and Technical Education — M,D,O

MONTANA STATE UNIVERSITY BILLINGS
Advertising and Public Relations — M
Athletic Training and Sports
   Medicine — M
Counselor Education — M
Curriculum and Instruction — M
Education—General — M,O
Educational Media/Instructional
   Technology — M
Elementary Education — M
Reading Education — M

Secondary Education — M
Special Education — M

MONTANA STATE UNIVERSITY– NORTHERN
Counselor Education — M
Education—General — M

MONTANA TECH OF THE UNIVERSITY OF MONTANA
Project Management — M

MONTCLAIR STATE UNIVERSITY
Accounting — M,O
Advertising and Public Relations — M
Archives/Archival Administration — M
Art Education — M
Business Administration and
   Management—General — M,O
Counselor Education — M,D
Curriculum and Instruction — M
Education—General — M,D,O
Educational Leadership and
   Administration — M,D
Educational Measurement and
   Evaluation — O
English as a Second Language — M
English Education — M,O
Environmental Education — M
Environmental Law — O
Exercise and Sports Science — M,O
Health Education — M
Intellectual Property Law — M,O
Law — M,O
Legal and Justice Studies — O
Mathematics Education — M,D,O
Music Education — M
Physical Education — M
Reading Education — M
Science Education — M
Special Education — M
Sports Management — M

MOODY THEOLOGICAL SEMINARY– MICHIGAN
Religious Education — M,O

MOORE COLLEGE OF ART & DESIGN
Art Education — M

MORAVIAN COLLEGE
Accounting — M
Athletic Training and Sports
   Medicine — M,D
Business Administration and
   Management—General — M
Business Analytics — M
Curriculum and Instruction — M
Education—General — M
Human Resources Development — M
Human Resources Management — M
Supply Chain Management — M

MOREHEAD STATE UNIVERSITY
Adult Education — M,O
Art Education — M
Business Administration and
   Management—General — M
Business Education — M,O
Counselor Education — M,O
Curriculum and Instruction — M,O
Education of the Gifted — M,O
Education—General — M,O
Educational Leadership and
   Administration — M,O
Educational Media/Instructional
   Technology — M,O
Elementary Education — M,O
English Education — M,O
Exercise and Sports Science — M
Foreign Languages Education — M
Health Education — M
Higher Education — M,O
International and Comparative
   Education — M,O
Management Information Systems — M
Mathematics Education — M
Middle School Education — M,O
Music Education — M
Physical Education — M
Reading Education — M,O
Science Education — M,O
Secondary Education — M,O
Social Sciences Education — M,O
Special Education — M
Sports Management — M
Vocational and Technical Education — M

MORGAN STATE UNIVERSITY
Accounting — M,D
Business Administration and
   Management—General — M,D
Community College Education — D
Education—General — M,D
Educational Leadership and
   Administration — M,D
Elementary Education — M
Higher Education — M,D
Hospitality Management — M
Management Information Systems — D
Marketing — M
Mathematics Education — M,D
Project Management — M
Science Education — M,D
Social Work — M
Student Affairs — M,D
Urban Education — D

MORNINGSIDE COLLEGE
Education—General — M
Special Education — M

MOUNT ALOYSIUS COLLEGE
Accounting — M
Business Administration and
   Management—General — M
Nonprofit Management — M

Project Management — M

MOUNT HOLYOKE COLLEGE
Educational Leadership and
   Administration — M
Mathematics Education — M

MOUNT MARTY COLLEGE
Business Administration and
   Management—General — M

MOUNT MARY UNIVERSITY
Business Administration and
   Management—General — M
Counselor Education — M,O
Education—General — M

MOUNT MERCY UNIVERSITY
Business Administration and
   Management—General — M
Education—General — M
Educational Leadership and
   Administration — M
Human Resources Management — M
Management Strategy and Policy — M
Quality Management — M
Reading Education — M
Special Education — M

MOUNT ST. JOSEPH UNIVERSITY
Business Administration and
   Management—General — M
Early Childhood Education — M,O
Education—General — M,O
Middle School Education — M,O
Multilingual and Multicultural
   Education — M,O
Organizational Management — M
Reading Education — M,O
Secondary Education — M,O
Special Education — M,O

MOUNT SAINT MARY COLLEGE
Business Administration and
   Management—General — M
Education—General — M
Finance and Banking — M
Middle School Education — M,O
Reading Education — M,O
Special Education — M,O

MOUNT SAINT MARY'S UNIVERSITY (CA)
Business Administration and
   Management—General — M,D,O
Education—General — M,D,O

MOUNT ST. MARY'S UNIVERSITY (MD)
Business Administration and
   Management—General — M
Education—General — M
Sports Management — M

MOUNT SAINT VINCENT UNIVERSITY
Adult Education — M
Curriculum and Instruction — M
Education—General — M
Educational Psychology — M
Elementary Education — M
English as a Second Language — M
Foundations and Philosophy of
   Education — M
Middle School Education — M
Reading Education — M
Special Education — M

MOUNT VERNON NAZARENE UNIVERSITY
Business Administration and
   Management—General — M
Education—General — M

MULTNOMAH UNIVERSITY
Education—General — M
English as a Second Language — M

MURRAY STATE UNIVERSITY
Accounting — M
Advertising and Public Relations — M
Agricultural Education — M,O
Business Administration and
   Management—General — M
Counselor Education — M,D,O
Early Childhood Education — M,O
Education—General — M,D,O
Educational Leadership and
   Administration — M,D,O
Educational Media/Instructional
   Technology — M,D,O
Elementary Education — M,O
English as a Second Language — M,D,O
English Education — M,D,O
Finance and Banking — M
Human Resources Management — M
Human Services — M
Management Information Systems — M
Marketing — M
Mathematics Education — M
Middle School Education — M,D,O
Music Education — M
Nonprofit Management — M,O
Secondary Education — M,D,O
Special Education — M,O
Vocational and Technical Education — M,O

MUSKINGUM UNIVERSITY
Education—General — M

NAROPA UNIVERSITY
Counselor Education — M
Recreation and Park Management — M
Sustainability Management — M

NATIONAL AMERICAN UNIVERSITY (TX)
Accounting — M,D
Aviation Management — M,D
Business Administration and
   Management—General — M,D
Community College Education — M,D

Educational Leadership and
  Administration — M,D
Higher Education — M,D
Human Resources Management — M,D
International Business — M,D
Management Information Systems — M,D
Marketing — M,D
Project Management — M,D

THE NATIONAL GRADUATE SCHOOL OF QUALITY MANAGEMENT
Quality Management — M,D

NATIONAL LOUIS UNIVERSITY
Adult Education — M,D,O
Business Administration and
  Management—General — M
Counselor Education — M,D,O
Curriculum and Instruction — M,D,O
Developmental Education — M,D,O
Early Childhood Education — M,D,O
Education—General — M,D,O
Educational Leadership and
  Administration — M,D,O
Educational Media/Instructional
  Technology — M,D,O
Educational Psychology — M,D,O
Elementary Education — M,D,O
English Education — M,D,O
Human Resources Development — M
Human Resources Management — M
Human Services — M,D,O
Mathematics Education — M,D,O
Middle School Education — M,D,O
Reading Education — M,D,O
Science Education — M,D,O
Secondary Education — M,D,O
Special Education — M,D,O

NATIONAL PARALEGAL COLLEGE
Legal and Justice Studies — M
Taxation — M

NATIONAL UNIVERSITY
Accounting — M,O
Business Administration and
  Management—General — M,O
Business Analytics — M,O
Counselor Education — M,O
Distance Education Development — M,O
Education—General — M,O
Educational Leadership and
  Administration — M,O
Educational Media/Instructional
  Technology — M,O
Higher Education — M,O
Human Resources Management — M,O
International Business — M,O
Legal and Justice Studies — M
Management Information Systems — M,O
Marketing — M,O
Mathematics Education — M,O
Organizational Management — M,O
Special Education — M,O
Sustainability Management — M

NATIONAL UNIVERSITY COLLEGE
Business Administration and
  Management—General — M
Marketing — M
Special Education — M

NAVAL POSTGRADUATE SCHOOL
Business Administration and
  Management—General — M
Finance and Banking — M
Logistics — M
Management Information Systems — M,D,O
Supply Chain Management — M
Transportation Management — M

NAZARETH COLLEGE OF ROCHESTER
Art Education — M
Business Administration and
  Management—General — M
Early Childhood Education — M
Education—General — M
Educational Media/Instructional
  Technology — M
Elementary Education — M
English as a Second Language — M
Human Resources Management — M
Middle School Education — M
Music Education — M
Reading Education — M
Social Work — M

NEUMANN UNIVERSITY
Accounting — M
Business Administration and
  Management—General — M
Education—General — M
Educational Leadership and
  Administration — M,D
Elementary Education — M
Management Strategy and Policy — M
Organizational Management — M
Secondary Education — M
Special Education — M
Sports Management — M

NEW CHARTER UNIVERSITY
Business Administration and
  Management—General — M
Finance and Banking — M

NEW ENGLAND COLLEGE
Accounting — M
Business Administration and
  Management—General — M
Education—General — M,D
Educational Leadership and
  Administration — M,D
Higher Education — M,D

Human Services — M
Management Strategy and Policy — M
Marketing — M
Nonprofit Management — M
Project Management — M
Recreation and Park Management — M
Special Education — M,D
Sports Management — M

NEW ENGLAND COLLEGE OF BUSINESS AND FINANCE
Finance and Banking — M

NEW ENGLAND INSTITUTE OF TECHNOLOGY
Management Information Systems — M

NEW ENGLAND LAW–BOSTON
Law — M,D

NEW HAMPSHIRE INSTITUTE OF ART
Art Education — M

NEW JERSEY CITY UNIVERSITY
Accounting — M,O
Art Education — M
Business Administration and
  Management—General — M,O
Counselor Education — M
Early Childhood Education — M,D
Education—General — M
Educational Leadership and
  Administration — M
Educational Media/Instructional
  Technology — M,D
Elementary Education — M
English as a Second Language — M
Finance and Banking — M,O
Health Education — M
Marketing — M
Mathematics Education — M
Multilingual and Multicultural
  Education — M
Music Education — M
Organizational Management — M
Secondary Education — M
Special Education — M
Urban Education — M

NEW JERSEY INSTITUTE OF TECHNOLOGY
Business Administration and
  Management—General — M,D,O
Management Information Systems — M,D,O
Transportation Management — M,D

NEWMAN THEOLOGICAL COLLEGE
Religious Education — M,O

NEWMAN UNIVERSITY
Business Administration and
  Management—General — M
Curriculum and Instruction — M
Education—General — M
Educational Leadership and
  Administration — M
English as a Second Language — M
Finance and Banking — M
International Business — M
Management Information Systems — M
Organizational Management — M
Reading Education — M
Social Work — M

NEW MEXICO HIGHLANDS UNIVERSITY
Business Administration and
  Management—General — M
Counselor Education — M
Curriculum and Instruction — M
Education—General — M
Educational Leadership and
  Administration — M
Exercise and Sports Science — M
Health Education — M
Human Resources Management — M
International Business — M
Social Work — M
Special Education — M
Sports Management — M

NEW MEXICO INSTITUTE OF MINING AND TECHNOLOGY
Science Education — M

NEW MEXICO STATE UNIVERSITY
Accounting — M
Agricultural Education — M
Business Administration and
  Management—General — M,D
Counselor Education — M,D,O
Curriculum and Instruction — M,D,O
Distance Education Development — O
Early Childhood Education — M,D,O
Education—General — M,D,O
Educational Leadership and
  Administration — M,D
Educational Measurement and
  Evaluation — M,D,O
English as a Second Language — M,D,O
English Education — M,D
Finance and Banking — M,O
Foreign Languages Education — M,D,O
Higher Education — M
Kinesiology and Movement Studies — D
Management Information Systems — M
Marketing — D
Multilingual and Multicultural
  Education — M,D,O
Music Education — M
Reading Education — M,D,O
Social Work — M
Special Education — M,D,O
Travel and Tourism — M

NEW ORLEANS BAPTIST THEOLOGICAL SEMINARY
Religious Education — M,D

THE NEW SCHOOL
English as a Second Language — M
Finance and Banking — M,D
Management Strategy and Policy — M,O
Nonprofit Management — M
Organizational Management — M,O
Sustainability Management — M

NEW YORK INSTITUTE OF TECHNOLOGY
Business Administration and
  Management—General — M
Counselor Education — M,O
Early Childhood Education — M
Education—General — M,O
Educational Leadership and
  Administration — O
Educational Media/Instructional
  Technology — M
Elementary Education — M
English Education — M
Finance and Banking — M
Human Resources Management — M,O
Marketing — M
Mathematics Education — M
Middle School Education — M
Science Education — M,O
Secondary Education — M
Social Sciences Education — M
Supply Chain Management — M

NEW YORK LAW SCHOOL
Law — M,D

NEW YORK MEDICAL COLLEGE
Business Administration and
  Management—General — M,D,O
Health Education — M,D,O

NEW YORK UNIVERSITY
Accounting — M,D
Advertising and Public Relations — M
Archives/Archival Administration — M,D,O
Art Education — M,O
Business Administration and
  Management—General — M,D,O
Business Education — M,O
Counselor Education — M,D,O
Early Childhood Education — M
Education—General — M,D,O
Educational Leadership and
  Administration — M,D,O
Educational Media/Instructional
  Technology — M,D,O
Educational Policy — M,D
Educational Psychology — M,D
Elementary Education — M
English as a Second Language — M,D,O
English Education — M,D,O
Entrepreneurship — M
Environmental Education — M
Finance and Banking — M,D
Foreign Languages Education — M,D,O
Foundations and Philosophy of
  Education — M,D
Higher Education — M,D
Hospitality Management — M,D
Human Resources Development — M
Human Resources Management — M
International and Comparative
  Education — M,D,O
International Business — M,D
Investment Management — M
Kinesiology and Movement Studies — M,D,O
Law — M,D,O
Legal and Justice Studies — M,D
Management Information Systems — M,D
Management Strategy and Policy — M,D
Marketing — M,D
Mathematics Education — M
Middle School Education — M,D,O
Multilingual and Multicultural
  Education — M,D,O
Music Education — M,D,O
Nonprofit Management — M,D,O
Organizational Behavior — M,D
Organizational Management — M,D
Project Management — M
Reading Education — M
Real Estate — M
Risk Management — M
Science Education — M,D,O
Secondary Education — M,D,O
Social Sciences Education — M,D,O
Social Work — M,D
Special Education — M
Sports and Entertainment Law — M
Student Affairs — M,D
Taxation — M,D,O
Transportation Management — M
Travel and Tourism — M

NIAGARA UNIVERSITY
Accounting — M
Business Administration and
  Management—General — M
Counselor Education — M,O
Early Childhood Education — M,O
Education—General — M,D,O
Educational Leadership and
  Administration — M,D,O
Educational Policy — M,O
Elementary Education — M,O
English as a Second Language — M,O
Finance and Banking — M
Human Resources Management — M
International Business — M
Management Strategy and Policy — M
Marketing — M

Middle School Education — M,O
Reading Education — M
Secondary Education — M,O
Special Education — M,O
Supply Chain Management — M

NICHOLLS STATE UNIVERSITY
Business Administration and
  Management—General — M
Counselor Education — M,O
Curriculum and Instruction — M
Education—General — M
Educational Leadership and
  Administration — M
Elementary Education — M
Health Education — M
Middle School Education — M
Secondary Education — M

NICHOLS COLLEGE
Business Administration and
  Management—General — M
Organizational Management — M

NIPISSING UNIVERSITY
Education—General — M,O

NORFOLK STATE UNIVERSITY
Early Childhood Education — M
Education of Students with
  Severe/Multiple Disabilities — M
Education—General — M
Educational Leadership and
  Administration — M
Music Education — M
Secondary Education — M
Social Work — M,D
Special Education — M
Urban Education — M

NORTH AMERICAN UNIVERSITY
Educational Leadership and
  Administration — M

NORTH CAROLINA AGRICULTURAL AND TECHNICAL STATE UNIVERSITY
Accounting — M
Adult Education — M
Agricultural Education — M
Business Administration and
  Management—General — M
Business Education — M
Counselor Education — M
Early Childhood Education — M
Education—General — M
Educational Leadership and
  Administration — M
Educational Media/Instructional
  Technology — M
Elementary Education — M
English Education — M
Health Education — M
Human Resources Management — M
Management Information Systems — M
Physical Education — M
Reading Education — M
Science Education — M
Secondary Education — M
Social Work — M
Supply Chain Management — M
Vocational and Technical Education — M

NORTH CAROLINA CENTRAL UNIVERSITY
Business Administration and
  Management—General — M
Counselor Education — M
Education—General — M
Educational Leadership and
  Administration — M
Educational Media/Instructional
  Technology — M
Information Studies — M
Law — D
Library Science — M
Physical Education — M
Recreation and Park Management — M
Special Education — M

NORTH CAROLINA STATE UNIVERSITY
Accounting — M
Adult Education — M,D
Agricultural Education — M,O
Business Administration and
  Management—General — M
Business Education — M,D
Community College Education — M,D
Counselor Education — M,D
Curriculum and Instruction — M,D
Developmental Education — M,D,O
Education—General — M,D,O
Educational Leadership and
  Administration — M,D
Educational Measurement and
  Evaluation — D
Educational Media/Instructional
  Technology — M,D
Elementary Education — M
English Education — M
Entrepreneurship — M
Higher Education — M,D
Human Resources Development — M
Mathematics Education — M,D
Middle School Education — M
Nonprofit Management — M,D,O
Recreation and Park Management — M,D
Science Education — M,D
Secondary Education — M
Social Sciences Education — M
Social Work — M
Special Education — M
Sports Management — M,D
Supply Chain Management — M

Travel and Tourism — M,D

NORTH CENTRAL COLLEGE
Business Administration and Management—General — M
Education—General — M
Educational Leadership and Administration — M
Finance and Banking — M
Human Resources Management — M
Management Strategy and Policy — M

NORTHCENTRAL UNIVERSITY
Business Administration and Management—General — M,D,O
Education—General — M,D,O

NORTH DAKOTA STATE UNIVERSITY
Accounting — M
Adult Education — M,D,O
Agricultural Education — M
Athletic Training and Sports Medicine — M,D
Business Administration and Management—General — M*
Counselor Education — M
Curriculum and Instruction — M
Education—General — M,D,O
Educational Leadership and Administration — M,O
Exercise and Sports Science — M,D
Higher Education — O
Logistics — M,D
Mathematics Education — M,D,O
Music Education — M,D,O
Science Education — M,D,O
Social Sciences Education — M,D,O
Transportation Management — M
Vocational and Technical Education — M,D,O

NORTHEASTERN ILLINOIS UNIVERSITY
Accounting — M
Business Administration and Management—General — M
Counselor Education — M
Early Childhood Education — M
Education of the Gifted — M
Education—General — M
Educational Leadership and Administration — M
Elementary Education — M
English as a Second Language — M
English Education — M
Exercise and Sports Science — M
Human Resources Development — M
Mathematics Education — M
Music Education — M
Reading Education — M
Science Education — M
Secondary Education — M
Social Sciences Education — M
Special Education — M
Urban Education — M

NORTHEASTERN STATE UNIVERSITY
Accounting — M
Business Administration and Management—General — M
Early Childhood Education — M
Education—General — M
Educational Leadership and Administration — M
Educational Media/Instructional Technology — M
Finance and Banking — M
Health Education — M
Kinesiology and Movement Studies — M
Mathematics Education — M
Reading Education — M
Science Education — M
Special Education — M

NORTHEASTERN UNIVERSITY
Accounting — M
Business Administration and Management—General — M,D,O
Educational Leadership and Administration — M
Elementary Education — M
Entrepreneurship — M
Exercise and Sports Science — M,D,O
Finance and Banking — M
Higher Education — M
Human Services — M
International Business — M
Law — M,D
Legal and Justice Studies — M,D
Management Information Systems — M,D,O
Nonprofit Management — M
Project Management — M
Special Education — M
Sports Management — M
Taxation — M

NORTHERN ARIZONA UNIVERSITY
Business Administration and Management—General — M,O
Community College Education — M,D,O
Counselor Education — M,D,O
Curriculum and Instruction — M,D
Early Childhood Education — M,D,O
Education—General — M,D,O
Educational Leadership and Administration — M,D,O
Educational Media/Instructional Technology — M,O
Educational Psychology — M,D,O
Elementary Education — M,D
English as a Second Language — M,D,O
Foreign Languages Education — M
Foundations and Philosophy of Education — M,D,O
Higher Education — M,D,O
International Business — M
Mathematics Education — M,O

Multilingual and Multicultural Education — M,O
Organizational Management — M
Recreation and Park Management — M,O
Science Education — M
Secondary Education — M,D,O
Special Education — M,O
Student Affairs — M,D,O
Vocational and Technical Education — M,O

NORTHERN ILLINOIS UNIVERSITY
Accounting — M
Adult Education — M,D
Business Administration and Management—General — M
Counselor Education — M,D
Curriculum and Instruction — M
Early Childhood Education — M
Education—General — M,D,O
Educational Leadership and Administration — M,D,O
Educational Media/Instructional Technology — M,D
Educational Psychology — M,D,O
Elementary Education — M
Foundations and Philosophy of Education — M,D,O
Higher Education — M,D
Industrial and Manufacturing Management — M
Law — D
Management Information Systems — M
Physical Education — M
Special Education — M
Taxation — M

NORTHERN KENTUCKY UNIVERSITY
Accounting — M,O
Advertising and Public Relations — M,O
Business Administration and Management—General — M,O
Counselor Education — M
Education—General — M,D,O
Educational Leadership and Administration — M,D,O
Law — D
Nonprofit Management — M
Organizational Management — M
Social Work — M
Special Education — M,O
Taxation — M,O

NORTHERN MICHIGAN UNIVERSITY
Business Administration and Management—General — M
Curriculum and Instruction — M
Education—General — M
Educational Leadership and Administration — M
English as a Second Language — M,O
Exercise and Sports Science — M
Reading Education — M
Science Education — M
Special Education — M

NORTHERN STATE UNIVERSITY
Counselor Education — M
Curriculum and Instruction — M
Education—General — M
Educational Leadership and Administration — M
Educational Media/Instructional Technology — M
Finance and Banking — M
Music Education — M
Sports Management — M

NORTHERN VERMONT UNIVERSITY–JOHNSON
Counselor Education — M
Curriculum and Instruction — M
Education—General — M
Foundations and Philosophy of Education — M
Special Education — M

NORTHERN VERMONT UNIVERSITY–LYNDON
Counselor Education — M
Curriculum and Instruction — M
Education—General — M
Reading Education — M
Science Education — M
Special Education — M

NORTH GREENVILLE UNIVERSITY
Education—General — M,D
Finance and Banking — M,D
Human Resources Management — M,D

NORTH PARK UNIVERSITY
Business Administration and Management—General — M
Education—General — M
Nonprofit Management — M

NORTHWEST CHRISTIAN UNIVERSITY
Accounting — M
Business Administration and Management—General — M
Counselor Education — M
Education—General — M
Elementary Education — M
English as a Second Language — M
Secondary Education — M
Special Education — M

NORTHWESTERN COLLEGE
Early Childhood Education — M,O
Education—General — M,O
Educational Leadership and Administration — M,O

NORTHWESTERN OKLAHOMA STATE UNIVERSITY
Adult Education — M
Counselor Education — M
Curriculum and Instruction — M

Education—General — M
Educational Leadership and Administration — M
Elementary Education — M
Reading Education — M
Secondary Education — M

NORTHWESTERN POLYTECHNIC UNIVERSITY
Business Administration and Management—General — M,D

NORTHWESTERN STATE UNIVERSITY OF LOUISIANA
Adult Education — M
Counselor Education — M,O
Curriculum and Instruction — M
Early Childhood Education — M
Education—General — M,O
Educational Leadership and Administration — M,O
Educational Media/Instructional Technology — M,O
Elementary Education — M,O
Health Education — M
Middle School Education — M
Reading Education — M,O
Secondary Education — M,O
Special Education — M,O
Student Affairs — M

NORTHWESTERN UNIVERSITY
Accounting — M,D
Business Administration and Management—General — M,D
Business Analytics — M,D
Education—General — M,D
Educational Leadership and Administration — M
Educational Media/Instructional Technology — M,D
Electronic Commerce — M
Elementary Education — M
Entrepreneurship — M,D
Finance and Banking — M,D
Human Resources Management — M,D
Industrial and Manufacturing Management — M,D
International Business — M
Kinesiology and Movement Studies — D
Law — M,D
Management Information Systems — M,D
Management Strategy and Policy — M,D
Marketing — M,D
Music Education — M,D
Organizational Behavior — M
Organizational Management — M,D
Project Management — M
Quality Management — M
Real Estate — M,D
Secondary Education — M
Sports Management — M
Taxation — M,D

NORTHWEST MISSOURI STATE UNIVERSITY
Agricultural Education — M
Business Administration and Management—General — M
Business Analytics — M
Early Childhood Education — M,D,O
Education—General — M,D,O
Educational Leadership and Administration — M,D,O
Educational Media/Instructional Technology — M,D,O
Educational Policy — M,D,O
Elementary Education — M,D,O
English as a Second Language — M,D,O
English Education — M,O
Exercise and Sports Science — M,O
Health Education — M,O
Higher Education — M,D,O
Human Resources Management — M
Management Information Systems — M
Marketing — M
Mathematics Education — M,D,O
Middle School Education — M,D,O
Physical Education — M
Reading Education — M,D,O
Recreation and Park Management — M,O
Science Education — M,O
Social Sciences Education — M,O
Special Education — M,D,O

NORTHWEST NAZARENE UNIVERSITY
Business Administration and Management—General — M
Counselor Education — M,D,O
Curriculum and Instruction — M,D,O
Education—General — M,D,O
Educational Leadership and Administration — M,D,O
Social Work — M
Special Education — M,D,O

NORTHWEST UNIVERSITY
Business Administration and Management—General — M
Education—General — M
International Business — M
Organizational Management — M
Project Management — M

NORTHWOOD UNIVERSITY, MICHIGAN CAMPUS
Business Administration and Management—General — M

NORWICH UNIVERSITY
Business Administration and Management—General — M
Finance and Banking — M
Human Resources Management — M
International Business — M
Logistics — M

Management Strategy and Policy — M
Nonprofit Management — M
Organizational Management — M
Project Management — M
Supply Chain Management — M

NOTRE DAME COLLEGE (OH)
Reading Education — M,O
Special Education — M,O

NOTRE DAME DE NAMUR UNIVERSITY
Business Administration and Management—General — M
Curriculum and Instruction — M
Education—General — M
Educational Leadership and Administration — M
Finance and Banking — M
Human Resources Management — M
Marketing — M
Special Education — M

NOTRE DAME OF MARYLAND UNIVERSITY
Business Administration and Management—General — M
Education—General — M
Educational Leadership and Administration — M,D
English as a Second Language — M
Nonprofit Management — M

NOVA SOUTHEASTERN UNIVERSITY
Accounting — M
Business Administration and Management—General — M
Business Analytics — M
Business Education — M
Counselor Education — M,D,O
Distance Education Development — M,D,O
Education—General — M,D,O
Educational Media/Instructional Technology — M,D,O
Entrepreneurship — M
Finance and Banking — M
Health Education — M,D,O
Health Law — M,D
Human Resources Management — M
International Business — M
Law — M,D
Legal and Justice Studies — M,D
Management Information Systems — M,D
Management Strategy and Policy — M
Marketing — M
Student Affairs — M,D,O
Supply Chain Management — M

NYACK COLLEGE
Business Administration and Management—General — M
Counselor Education — M
Elementary Education — M
English as a Second Language — M
Organizational Management — M
Social Work — M
Special Education — M

OAKLAND CITY UNIVERSITY
Business Administration and Management—General — M
Education—General — M,D
Educational Leadership and Administration — M,D

OAKLAND UNIVERSITY
Accounting — M,O
Business Administration and Management—General — M,O
Early Childhood Education — M,D,O
Education—General — M,D,O
Educational Leadership and Administration — M,D,O
Elementary Education — M,O
English as a Second Language — M,O
Entrepreneurship — M,O
Exercise and Sports Science — M,D,O
Finance and Banking — M,O
Higher Education — M,D,O
Human Resources Management — M,O
Industrial and Manufacturing Management — M,O
International Business — M,O
Management Information Systems — M,D,O
Marketing — M,O
Music Education — M,D
Nonprofit Management — M,O
Organizational Management — M,D,O
Reading Education — M,D,O
Secondary Education — M,O
Special Education — M,O

OGLALA LAKOTA COLLEGE
Business Administration and Management—General — M
Educational Leadership and Administration — M

OHIO CHRISTIAN UNIVERSITY
Accounting — M
Business Administration and Management—General — M
Finance and Banking — M
Human Resources Management — M
Marketing — M
Organizational Management — M

OHIO DOMINICAN UNIVERSITY
Accounting — M
Business Administration and Management—General — M
Curriculum and Instruction — M
Education—General — M
Educational Leadership and Administration — M
English as a Second Language — M
Finance and Banking — M
Management Strategy and Policy — M

Risk Management — M
Sports Management — M

OHIO NORTHERN UNIVERSITY
Accounting — M
Law — M,D

THE OHIO STATE UNIVERSITY
Accounting — M
Actuarial Science — M,D
Agricultural Education — M
Art Education — M,D
Business Administration and Management—General — M,D
Education—General — M,D,O
Educational Leadership and Administration — M,D,O
Educational Policy — M,D,O
Finance and Banking — M
Human Resources Management — M,D
Kinesiology and Movement Studies — M,D
Law — M,D
Logistics — M,D
Management Information Systems — M,D
Mathematics Education — M,D
Physical Education — M,D
Social Work — M,D
Special Education — D

THE OHIO STATE UNIVERSITY AT LIMA
Social Work — M

THE OHIO STATE UNIVERSITY AT MANSFIELD
Education—General — M
Social Work — M

THE OHIO STATE UNIVERSITY AT MARION
Education—General — M

THE OHIO STATE UNIVERSITY AT NEWARK
Education—General — M
Social Work — M

OHIO UNIVERSITY
Athletic Training and Sports Medicine — M
Business Administration and Management—General — M
Computer Education — M,D
Counselor Education — M,D
Curriculum and Instruction — M,D
Education—General — M,D
Educational Leadership and Administration — M,D
Educational Measurement and Evaluation — M,D
Educational Media/Instructional Technology — M,D
Exercise and Sports Science — M,D
Finance and Banking — M
Higher Education — M,D
Middle School Education — M,D
Music Education — M
Physical Education — M
Reading Education — M
Recreation and Park Management — M
Secondary Education — M
Social Work — M
Special Education — M
Sports Management — M
Student Affairs — M,D

OHIO VALLEY UNIVERSITY
Curriculum and Instruction — M
Education—General — M

OKLAHOMA BAPTIST UNIVERSITY
Business Administration and Management—General — M

OKLAHOMA CHRISTIAN UNIVERSITY
Accounting — M
Business Administration and Management—General — M
Finance and Banking — M
Human Resources Management — M
International Business — M
Marketing — M
Nonprofit Management — M
Organizational Management — M
Project Management — M

OKLAHOMA CITY UNIVERSITY
Business Administration and Management—General — M
Counselor Education — M
Early Childhood Education — M
Elementary Education — M
English as a Second Language — M
Law — M,D

OKLAHOMA STATE UNIVERSITY
Accounting — M,D
Agricultural Education — M,D
Business Administration and Management—General — M,D
Curriculum and Instruction — M
Education—General — M,D,O
Educational Leadership and Administration — M,D
Educational Psychology — M,D,O
Entrepreneurship — M
Finance and Banking — M
Health Education — M,D,O
Higher Education — M,D
Hospitality Management — M,D
International Business — M,D
Management Information Systems — M,D
Marketing — M
Music Education — M
Nonprofit Management — M,D,O
Sustainability Management — M,D,O

OKLAHOMA WESLEYAN UNIVERSITY
Management Strategy and Policy — M

OLD DOMINION UNIVERSITY
Accounting — M
Athletic Training and Sports Medicine — M
Business Administration and Management—General — M,D
Business Education — M,D
Community College Education — M
Counselor Education — M,D,O
Curriculum and Instruction — M,D
Early Childhood Education — M,D
Education—General — M,D,O
Educational Leadership and Administration — M,D,O
Educational Measurement and Evaluation — D
Educational Media/Instructional Technology — M,D,O
Educational Psychology — M,O
Elementary Education — M
English as a Second Language — M
Entrepreneurship — M,O
Exercise and Sports Science — M
Finance and Banking — D
Health Education — M,D,O
Higher Education — M,D,O
International Business — M
Kinesiology and Movement Studies — M,D
Library Science — M,O
Management Information Systems — M,D
Marketing — M,D
Middle School Education — M,O
Music Education — M
Physical Education — M,D
Reading Education — M,D
Secondary Education — M,D
Special Education — M,D
Sports Management — M
Supply Chain Management — M
Vocational and Technical Education — M,D

OLIVET COLLEGE
Insurance — M

OLIVET NAZARENE UNIVERSITY
Business Administration and Management—General — M
Curriculum and Instruction — M
Education—General — M
Educational Leadership and Administration — M
Elementary Education — M
Library Science — M
Organizational Management — M
Reading Education — M
Secondary Education — M

OPEN UNIVERSITY
Business Administration and Management—General — M
Education—General — M

ORAL ROBERTS UNIVERSITY
Accounting — M
Business Administration and Management—General — M
Curriculum and Instruction — M,D
Education—General — M,D
Educational Leadership and Administration — M,D
Entrepreneurship — M
Finance and Banking — M
Higher Education — M,D
International Business — M
Marketing — M
Nonprofit Management — M
Religious Education — M,D

OREGON STATE UNIVERSITY
Accounting — M,D
Actuarial Science — M,D
Adult Education — M,D
Agricultural Education — M,D
Athletic Training and Sports Medicine — M
Business Administration and Management—General — M,D
Counselor Education — M,D
Education—General — M,D
Educational Leadership and Administration — M,D
Educational Policy — M,D
Elementary Education — M
English Education — M
Environmental Education — M,D
Finance and Banking — M,D
Higher Education — M,D
Kinesiology and Movement Studies — M,D
Mathematics Education — M,D
Music Education — M,D
Science Education — M,D
Social Sciences Education — M,D
Student Affairs — M
Sustainability Management — M,D

OREGON STATE UNIVERSITY–CASCADES
Education—General — M

OTTAWA UNIVERSITY
Business Administration and Management—General — M
Counselor Education — M
Curriculum and Instruction — M
Early Childhood Education — M
Education—General — M
Educational Leadership and Administration — M
Educational Media/Instructional Technology — M

Elementary Education — M
Finance and Banking — M
Human Resources Development — M
Human Resources Management — M
Marketing — M
Special Education — M

OTTERBEIN UNIVERSITY
Business Administration and Management—General — M
Education—General — M

OUR LADY OF THE LAKE UNIVERSITY
Accounting — M
Business Administration and Management—General — M
Counselor Education — M
Curriculum and Instruction — M
Finance and Banking — M
Management Information Systems — M
Nonprofit Management — M
Organizational Management — M,D
Science Education — M
Social Work — M

OXFORD GRADUATE SCHOOL
Organizational Management — M,D

PACE UNIVERSITY
Accounting — M,O
Business Administration and Management—General — M,D,O
Early Childhood Education — M,O
Education—General — M,O
Educational Media/Instructional Technology — M,O
Electronic Commerce — O
Elementary Education — M,O
Entrepreneurship — M
Environmental Law — M,D
Finance and Banking — M,D,O
Foreign Languages Education — M,O
Human Resources Management — M
International Business — M
Investment Management — M
Law — M,D
Legal and Justice Studies — M
Management Information Systems — M,D,O
Management Strategy and Policy — M
Marketing — M,D,O
Nonprofit Management — M,O
Reading Education — M,O
Risk Management — M
Social Sciences Education — M,O
Special Education — M,O
Taxation — M

PACIFIC LUTHERAN UNIVERSITY
Accounting — M
Business Administration and Management—General — M
Curriculum and Instruction — M
Education—General — M
Finance and Banking — M
Marketing Research — M

PACIFIC OAKS COLLEGE
Early Childhood Education — M
Education—General — M
Special Education — M

PACIFIC STATES UNIVERSITY
Accounting — M,O
Business Administration and Management—General — M,O
Finance and Banking — M,O
International Business — M,O
Management Information Systems — M,O
Project Management — M,O
Real Estate — M,O

PACIFIC UNION COLLEGE
Education—General — M
Elementary Education — M
Secondary Education — M

PACIFIC UNIVERSITY
Athletic Training and Sports Medicine — M,D
Business Administration and Management—General — M
Early Childhood Education — M
Education of the Gifted — M
Education—General — M
Elementary Education — M
English as a Second Language — M
Finance and Banking — M
Middle School Education — M
Science Education — M
Secondary Education — M
Social Work — M
Special Education — M

PALM BEACH ATLANTIC UNIVERSITY
Business Administration and Management—General — M
Counselor Education — M
Education—General — M
Organizational Management — M
Religious Education — M

PARK UNIVERSITY
Business Administration and Management—General — M,O
Curriculum and Instruction — M,O
Education—General — M,O
Educational Leadership and Administration — M,O
Finance and Banking — M,O
International Business — M,O
Management Information Systems — M,O
Nonprofit Management — M,O
Reading Education — M,O
Social Work — M,O

PEIRCE COLLEGE
Organizational Management — M

PENN STATE ERIE, THE BEHREND COLLEGE
Accounting — M
Business Administration and Management—General — M
Industrial and Manufacturing Management — M
Quality Management — M

PENN STATE GREAT VALLEY
Business Administration and Management—General — M,O
Entrepreneurship — M,O
Finance and Banking — M,O
Human Resources Development — M,O
Human Resources Management — M,O
Sustainability Management — M,O

PENN STATE HARRISBURG
Accounting — M,O
Adult Education — M,D,O
Business Administration and Management—General — M,O
Curriculum and Instruction — M,D,O
Developmental Education — M,D,O
Education—General — M,D,O
English as a Second Language — M,D,O
Finance and Banking — M,D,O
Health Education — M,D,O
Human Resources Management — M,D,O
Management Information Systems — M,D,O
Nonprofit Management — M,D,O
Reading Education — M,D,O
Supply Chain Management — M,O

PENN STATE UNIVERSITY–DICKINSON LAW
Law — M,D

PENN STATE UNIVERSITY PARK
Accounting — M,D
Adult Education — M,D,O
Agricultural Education — M,D,O
Art Education — M,D,O
Business Administration and Management—General — M,D
Counselor Education — M,D,O
Curriculum and Instruction — M,D,O
Education—General — M,D,O
Educational Leadership and Administration — M,D,O
Educational Media/Instructional Technology — M,D,O
Educational Policy — M,D,O
Educational Psychology — M,D,O
English as a Second Language — M,D
Entrepreneurship — M
Foundations and Philosophy of Education — M,D,O
Higher Education — M,D,O
Hospitality Management — M,D
Human Resources Development — M
Human Resources Management — M
Kinesiology and Movement Studies — M,D,O
Law — M,D
Leisure Studies — M,D
Management Information Systems — M,D
Music Education — M,D,O
Organizational Management — M,D
Recreation and Park Management — M,D
Special Education — M,D
Travel and Tourism — M,D
Vocational and Technical Education — M,D,O

PENN STATE YORK
Curriculum and Instruction — M,O
Education—General — M,O
English as a Second Language — M,O

PENNSYLVANIA COLLEGE OF HEALTH SCIENCES
Health Education — M

PENSACOLA CHRISTIAN COLLEGE
Business Administration and Management—General — M,D,O
Curriculum and Instruction — M,D,O
Educational Leadership and Administration — M,D,O

PEPPERDINE UNIVERSITY
Accounting — M
Business Administration and Management—General — M
Business Education — M
Educational Leadership and Administration — M,D
Educational Media/Instructional Technology — M
Finance and Banking — M
Human Resources Management — M
International Business — M
Law — M,D
Organizational Management — M,D
Science Education — M,D
Sports and Entertainment Law — M

PERU STATE COLLEGE
Curriculum and Instruction — M
Education—General — M
Entrepreneurship — M
Organizational Management — M

PFEIFFER UNIVERSITY
Business Administration and Management—General — M
Elementary Education — M
Organizational Management — M
Religious Education — M

---

*M—masters degree; D—doctorate; O—other advanced degree; *—Close-Up and/or Display*

PHILADELPHIA COLLEGE OF OSTEOPATHIC MEDICINE
Educational Psychology — M,D,O

PHILLIPS GRADUATE UNIVERSITY
Counselor Education — M
Organizational Behavior — D

PHILLIPS THEOLOGICAL SEMINARY
Business Administration and
  Management—General — M,D
Higher Education — M,D
Religious Education — M,D
Social Work — M,D

PIEDMONT COLLEGE
Art Education — M,D,O
Business Administration and
  Management—General — M
Curriculum and Instruction — M,D,O
Early Childhood Education — M,D,O
Education—General — M,D,O
Educational Media/Instructional
  Technology — M,D,O
Middle School Education — M,D,O
Music Education — M,D,O
Secondary Education — M,D,O
Special Education — M,D,O

PIEDMONT INTERNATIONAL UNIVERSITY
Curriculum and Instruction — M,D
Educational Leadership and
  Administration — M,D

PITTSBURG STATE UNIVERSITY
Accounting — M
Business Administration and
  Management—General — M
Counselor Education — M
Education—General — M,O
Educational Leadership and
  Administration — M,O
Educational Media/Instructional
  Technology — M
English as a Second Language — M,O
Exercise and Sports Science — M
Health Education — M
Human Resources Development — M
International Business — M
Music Education — M
Physical Education — M
Secondary Education — M,O
Special Education — M
Sports Management — M
Vocational and Technical Education — M,O

PLYMOUTH STATE UNIVERSITY
Adult Education — D
Art Education — M
Athletic Training and Sports
  Medicine — M
Business Administration and
  Management—General — M
Counselor Education — M
Curriculum and Instruction — M
Education—General — O
Educational Leadership and
  Administration — M,O
Educational Media/Instructional
  Technology — M
Elementary Education — M
English Education — M
Foreign Languages Education — M
Health Education — M
Higher Education — D,O
Mathematics Education — M
Music Education — M
Physical Education — M
Reading Education — M
Science Education — M
Secondary Education — M
Social Sciences Education — M
Special Education — M

POINT LOMA NAZARENE UNIVERSITY
Business Administration and
  Management—General — M
Counselor Education — M
Education—General — M
Educational Leadership and
  Administration — M
Entrepreneurship — M
Exercise and Sports Science — M
Kinesiology and Movement Studies — M
Organizational Management — M
Project Management — M
Special Education — M
Sports Management — M

POINT PARK UNIVERSITY
Adult Education — M,D
Business Administration and
  Management—General — M
Business Analytics — M
Curriculum and Instruction — M,D
Education—General — M,D
Educational Leadership and
  Administration — M,D
Elementary Education — M,D
Entertainment Management — M
International Business — M
Management Information Systems — M
Middle School Education — M,D
Organizational Management — M
Secondary Education — M,D
Special Education — M,D
Sports Management — M

POINT UNIVERSITY
Business Administration and
  Management—General — M

POLYTECHNIC UNIVERSITY OF PUERTO RICO
Business Administration and
  Management—General — M

Industrial and Manufacturing
  Management — M
International Business — M
Management Information Systems — M

POLYTECHNIC UNIVERSITY OF PUERTO RICO, MIAMI CAMPUS
Accounting — M
Business Administration and
  Management—General — M
Finance and Banking — M
Human Resources Management — M
Industrial and Manufacturing
  Management — M
International Business — M
Logistics — M
Marketing — M
Project Management — M
Supply Chain Management — M

POLYTECHNIC UNIVERSITY OF PUERTO RICO, ORLANDO CAMPUS
Accounting — M
Business Administration and
  Management—General — M
Finance and Banking — M
Human Resources Management — M
Industrial and Manufacturing
  Management — M
International Business — M

PONTIFICAL CATHOLIC UNIVERSITY OF PUERTO RICO
Accounting — M,O
Business Administration and
  Management—General — M,D,O
Business Education — M,D
Counselor Education — M
Curriculum and Instruction — M,D
Education—General — M,D
Educational Leadership and
  Administration — D
Educational Psychology — M
English as a Second Language — M
Finance and Banking — M
Human Resources Management — M,O
Human Services — M,D
International Business — M
Law — D,O
Logistics — O
Management Information Systems — M,O
Marketing — M
Religious Education — M
Social Work — M
Transportation Management — O

PONTIFICIA UNIVERSIDAD CATOLICA MADRE Y MAESTRA
Business Administration and
  Management—General — M
Early Childhood Education — M
Entrepreneurship — M
Finance and Banking — M
Hospitality Management — M
Human Resources Management — M
Insurance — M
International Business — M
Law — M
Logistics — M
Management Strategy and Policy — M
Marketing — M
Real Estate — M
Travel and Tourism — M

PORTLAND STATE UNIVERSITY
Business Administration and
  Management—General — M,D,O
Education—General — M,D
English as a Second Language — M,O
Finance and Banking — M
Foreign Languages Education — M
Human Resources Management — M,D,O
International Business — M
Mathematics Education — M,D,O
Middle School Education — M,D,O
Nonprofit Management — M,D,O
Real Estate — M,D,O
Science Education — M,D,O
Social Sciences Education — M
Social Work — M,D
Supply Chain Management — M

POST UNIVERSITY
Accounting — M
Business Administration and
  Management—General — M
Curriculum and Instruction — M
Distance Education Development — M
Education—General — M
Educational Leadership and
  Administration — M
Educational Media/Instructional
  Technology — M
English as a Second Language — M
Finance and Banking — M
Human Services — M
Marketing — M
Nonprofit Management — M
Project Management — M

PRAIRIE VIEW A&M UNIVERSITY
Accounting — M
Business Administration and
  Management—General — M
Counselor Education — M,D
Curriculum and Instruction — M
Education—General — M,D
Educational Leadership and
  Administration — M,D
Health Education — M
Kinesiology and Movement Studies — M
Legal and Justice Studies — M,D
Management Information Systems — M,D

PRATT INSTITUTE
Art Education — M,O

Facilities Management — M
Information Studies — M,O*
Library Science — M,O
Real Estate — M

PRESCOTT COLLEGE
Counselor Education — M,D
Early Childhood Education — M,D
Education—General — M,D
Educational Leadership and
  Administration — M,D
Elementary Education — M,D
Environmental Education — M,D
Legal and Justice Studies — M
Leisure Studies — M
Secondary Education — M,D
Special Education — M,D

PRESIDIO GRADUATE SCHOOL (CA)
Business Administration and
  Management—General — M,O
Sustainability Management — M,O

PRINCETON UNIVERSITY
Finance and Banking — M

PROVIDENCE COLLEGE
Accounting — M
Business Administration and
  Management—General — M
Counselor Education — M
Educational Leadership and
  Administration — M
Elementary Education — M
Finance and Banking — M
International Business — M
Marketing — M
Mathematics Education — M
Reading Education — M
Secondary Education — M
Special Education — M
Urban Education — M

PROVIDENCE UNIVERSITY COLLEGE & THEOLOGICAL SEMINARY
English as a Second Language — M,D,O
Religious Education — M,D,O
Student Affairs — M,D,O

PURCHASE COLLEGE, STATE UNIVERSITY OF NEW YORK
Entrepreneurship — M

PURDUE UNIVERSITY
Agricultural Education — M,D,O
Art Education — M,D,O
Aviation Management — M
Business Administration and
  Management—General — M,D
Counselor Education — M,D,O
Curriculum and Instruction — M,D,O
Education of the Gifted — M,D,O
Education—General — M,D,O
Educational Leadership and
  Administration — M,D,O
Educational Media/Instructional
  Technology — M,D,O
Educational Psychology — M,D,O
Elementary Education — M,D,O
English Education — M,D,O
Exercise and Sports Science — M,D
Finance and Banking — M
Foreign Languages Education — M,D,O
Foundations and Philosophy of
  Education — M,D,O
Health Education — M,D
Higher Education — M,D,O
Home Economics Education — M,D,O
Hospitality Management — M,D
Human Resources Management — M,D
International Business — M
Kinesiology and Movement Studies — M,D
Management Information Systems — M
Mathematics Education — M,D,O
Organizational Behavior — D
Physical Education — M,D
Reading Education — M,D,O
Recreation and Park Management — M,D
Science Education — M,D,O
Social Sciences Education — M,D,O
Special Education — M,D,O
Sports Management — M,D
Travel and Tourism — M
Vocational and Technical Education — M,D,O

PURDUE UNIVERSITY GLOBAL
Business Administration and
  Management—General — M
Education—General — M
Educational Leadership and
  Administration — M
Educational Media/Instructional
  Technology — M
Entrepreneurship — M
Finance and Banking — M
Higher Education — M
Human Resources Management — M
International Business — M
Law — M
Legal and Justice Studies — M,O
Logistics — M
Management Information Systems — M
Marketing — M
Mathematics Education — M
Organizational Management — M
Project Management — M
Reading Education — M
Science Education — M
Secondary Education — M
Special Education — M
Student Affairs — M
Supply Chain Management — M

PURDUE UNIVERSITY NORTHWEST
Accounting — M
Business Administration and
  Management—General — M

Counselor Education — M
Education—General — M
Educational Leadership and
  Administration — M
Educational Media/Instructional
  Technology — M
Human Services — M
Mathematics Education — M
Science Education — M
Special Education — M

QUEENS COLLEGE OF THE CITY UNIVERSITY OF NEW YORK
Accounting — M
Archives/Archival Administration — M,O
Art Education — M,O
Counselor Education — M,O
Early Childhood Education — M,O
Education—General — M,O
Educational Leadership and
  Administration — M,O
Elementary Education — M,O
English as a Second Language — M,O
English Education — M,O
Exercise and Sports Science — M,O
Finance and Banking — M
Foreign Languages Education — M,O
Information Studies — M,O
Library Science — M,O
Mathematics Education — M,O
Middle School Education — M,O
Multilingual and Multicultural
  Education — M,O
Music Education — M,O
Physical Education — M,O
Reading Education — M,O
Risk Management — M
Science Education — M,O
Secondary Education — M,O
Social Sciences Education — M,O
Special Education — M,O

QUEEN'S UNIVERSITY AT KINGSTON
Business Administration and
  Management—General — M
Education—General — M,D
Entrepreneurship — M
Exercise and Sports Science — M,D
Finance and Banking — M
Information Studies — M,D
Law — M,D
Legal and Justice Studies — M,D
Marketing — M
Project Management — M

QUEENS UNIVERSITY OF CHARLOTTE
Business Administration and
  Management—General — M
Education—General — M
Educational Leadership and
  Administration — M
Elementary Education — M
Organizational Management — M
Reading Education — M

QUINCY UNIVERSITY
Business Administration and
  Management—General — M
Counselor Education — M
Curriculum and Instruction — M
Education—General — M
Educational Leadership and
  Administration — M
English as a Second Language — M
Multilingual and Multicultural
  Education — M
Reading Education — M
Student Affairs — M

QUINNIPIAC UNIVERSITY
Accounting — M
Advertising and Public Relations — M
Business Administration and
  Management—General — M
Education—General — M,O
Educational Leadership and
  Administration — M,O
Educational Media/Instructional
  Technology — M
Elementary Education — M
English Education — M
Finance and Banking — M
Foreign Languages Education — M
Law — M,D
Mathematics Education — M
Organizational Management — M
Science Education — M
Secondary Education — M
Social Sciences Education — M
Social Work — M
Supply Chain Management — M

RADFORD UNIVERSITY
Business Administration and
  Management—General — M
Counselor Education — M
Early Childhood Education — M
Educational Leadership and
  Administration — M
Management Information Systems — M
Mathematics Education — M
Reading Education — M
Social Work — M
Special Education — M,O

RAMAPO COLLEGE OF NEW JERSEY
Accounting — M
Business Administration and
  Management—General — M
Educational Leadership and
  Administration — M
Educational Media/Instructional
  Technology — M
Social Work — M
Special Education — M

RANDOLPH COLLEGE
Curriculum and Instruction	M
Education—General	M
Special Education	M

REFORMED THEOLOGICAL SEMINARY–JACKSON CAMPUS
Religious Education	M,D,O

REGENT'S UNIVERSITY LONDON
Business Administration and Management—General	M
Finance and Banking	M
Human Resources Management	M
International Business	M
Management Information Systems	M
Marketing	M

REGENT UNIVERSITY
Accounting	M,D,O
Adult Education	M,D,O
Business Administration and Management—General	M,D,O
Business Analytics	M,D,O
Counselor Education	M,D,O
Curriculum and Instruction	M,D,O
Distance Education Development	M,D,O
Early Childhood Education	M,D,O
Education of the Gifted	M,D,O
Education—General	M,D,O
Educational Leadership and Administration	M,D,O
Educational Media/Instructional Technology	M,D,O
Educational Psychology	M,D,O
Elementary Education	M,D,O
English as a Second Language	M,D,O
Entrepreneurship	M,D,O
Finance and Banking	M,D,O
Higher Education	M,D,O
Human Resources Development	M,D,O
Human Resources Management	M,D,O
Human Services	M,D,O
Investment Management	M,D,O
Law	M,D
Legal and Justice Studies	M,D,O
Management Strategy and Policy	M,D,O
Marketing	M,D,O
Nonprofit Management	M,D,O
Organizational Management	M,D,O
Reading Education	M,D,O
Religious Education	M,D,O
Science Education	M,D,O
Special Education	M,D,O
Student Affairs	M,D,O

REGIS COLLEGE (MA)
Education—General	M,D
Educational Leadership and Administration	M,D
Elementary Education	M,D
Higher Education	M,D
Quality Management	M
Special Education	M,D

REGIS UNIVERSITY
Accounting	M,O
Business Education	M,O
Counselor Education	M,D,O
Curriculum and Instruction	M,O
Education—General	M
Educational Leadership and Administration	M,O
Elementary Education	M,O
Finance and Banking	M,O
Human Resources Management	M,O
Industrial and Manufacturing Management	M,O
Management Information Systems	M,O
Management Strategy and Policy	M,O
Marketing	M,O
Nonprofit Management	M,O
Organizational Management	M,O
Project Management	M,O
Reading Education	M,O
Secondary Education	M,O
Special Education	M,O

REINHARDT UNIVERSITY
Business Administration and Management—General	M
Early Childhood Education	M
Education—General	M

RELAY GRADUATE SCHOOL OF EDUCATION
Education—General	M

RENSSELAER AT HARTFORD
Business Administration and Management—General	M

RENSSELAER POLYTECHNIC INSTITUTE
Business Administration and Management—General	M,D
Business Analytics	M
Entrepreneurship	M
Supply Chain Management	M

RHODE ISLAND COLLEGE
Accounting	M,O
Art Education	M
Counselor Education	M,O
Early Childhood Education	M
Education—General	D
Educational Leadership and Administration	M,O
Elementary Education	M
English as a Second Language	M
English Education	M
Finance and Banking	M,O
Foreign Languages Education	M
Health Education	M
Legal and Justice Studies	M
Mathematics Education	M
Music Education	M
Physical Education	M,O
Reading Education	M
Secondary Education	M
Social Sciences Education	M
Social Work	M
Special Education	M,O

RHODE ISLAND SCHOOL OF DESIGN
Art Education	M

RHODES COLLEGE
Accounting	M

RICE UNIVERSITY
Business Administration and Management—General	M
Education—General	M
Science Education	M,D

RICHMONT GRADUATE UNIVERSITY
Counselor Education	M

RIDER UNIVERSITY
Accounting	M
Business Administration and Management—General	M
Business Education	O
Counselor Education	M
Education—General	M,O
Educational Leadership and Administration	O
Elementary Education	O
English as a Second Language	O
English Education	O
Finance and Banking	M
Foreign Languages Education	O
Mathematics Education	O
Multilingual and Multicultural Education	O
Music Education	M
Organizational Management	M
Reading Education	M,O
Science Education	O
Secondary Education	O
Social Sciences Education	O
Special Education	M,O

RIVIER UNIVERSITY
Business Administration and Management—General	M
Counselor Education	M,D,O
Curriculum and Instruction	M,D,O
Early Childhood Education	M,D,O
Education—General	M,D,O
Educational Leadership and Administration	M,D,O
Elementary Education	M,D,O
Foreign Languages Education	M,D,O
Management Information Systems	M
Reading Education	M
Social Sciences Education	M
Special Education	M,D,O

ROBERT MORRIS UNIVERSITY
Business Administration and Management—General	M
Business Education	M,D,O
Education—General	M,D,O
Educational Leadership and Administration	M,D,O
Higher Education	M,D,O
Human Resources Management	M
Management Information Systems	M,D
Organizational Management	M
Project Management	M,D
Reading Education	M,D,O
Special Education	M,D,O
Taxation	M

ROBERT MORRIS UNIVERSITY ILLINOIS
Accounting	M
Business Administration and Management—General	M
Business Analytics	M
Educational Leadership and Administration	M
Finance and Banking	M
Higher Education	M
Human Resources Management	M
Management Information Systems	M
Sports Management	M

ROBERTS WESLEYAN COLLEGE
Business Administration and Management—General	M
Counselor Education	M,D
Early Childhood Education	M
Education—General	M
Human Services	M
Management Strategy and Policy	M
Marketing	M
Middle School Education	M
Reading Education	M
Secondary Education	M
Social Work	M
Special Education	M

ROCHESTER COLLEGE
Religious Education	M

ROCHESTER INSTITUTE OF TECHNOLOGY
Accounting	M
Art Education	M
Business Administration and Management—General	M
Entrepreneurship	M
Finance and Banking	M
Hospitality Management	M
Human Resources Development	M
Industrial and Manufacturing Management	M

International Business	M
Management Information Systems	O
Organizational Management	O
Project Management	O
Secondary Education	M
Special Education	M
Sustainability Management	M,D
Travel and Tourism	M

ROCKFORD UNIVERSITY
Business Administration and Management—General	M
Early Childhood Education	M
Education—General	M
Educational Media/Instructional Technology	M
Elementary Education	M
Reading Education	M
Secondary Education	M
Special Education	M

ROCKHURST UNIVERSITY
Accounting	M,O
Business Administration and Management—General	M,O
Business Analytics	M,O
Education—General	M
Entrepreneurship	M,O
Finance and Banking	M,O
Human Resources Development	M,O
International Business	M,O
Management Strategy and Policy	M,O
Nonprofit Management	M,O

ROCKY MOUNTAIN COLLEGE
Accounting	M
Educational Leadership and Administration	M

ROCKY MOUNTAIN COLLEGE OF ART + DESIGN
Art Education	M

ROGERS STATE UNIVERSITY
Business Administration and Management—General	M

ROGER WILLIAMS UNIVERSITY
Business Administration and Management—General	M
Education—General	M,O
Law	M,D
Middle School Education	M,O
Reading Education	M,O

ROLLINS COLLEGE
Business Administration and Management—General	M
Counselor Education	M
Education—General	M
Elementary Education	M
Entrepreneurship	M
Finance and Banking	M
Human Resources Development	M
Human Resources Management	M
International Business	M

ROOSEVELT UNIVERSITY
Accounting	M
Actuarial Science	M
Business Administration and Management—General	M
Early Childhood Education	M
Education—General	M
Educational Leadership and Administration	M
Elementary Education	M
Hospitality Management	M
Human Resources Development	M
Human Resources Management	M
Marketing	M
Organizational Management	M
Reading Education	M
Real Estate	M
Secondary Education	M
Special Education	M

ROSALIND FRANKLIN UNIVERSITY OF MEDICINE AND SCIENCE
Health Administration	M

ROSE-HULMAN INSTITUTE OF TECHNOLOGY
Management Information Systems	M

ROSEMAN UNIVERSITY OF HEALTH SCIENCES
Business Administration and Management—General	M,O

ROSEMONT COLLEGE
Business Administration and Management—General	M
Counselor Education	M
Education—General	M
Elementary Education	M
Human Services	M

ROWAN UNIVERSITY
Advertising and Public Relations	M
Business Administration and Management—General	M,O
Counselor Education	M
Education—General	M,D,O
Educational Leadership and Administration	M,D,O
Educational Media/Instructional Technology	M,O
English as a Second Language	O
English Education	O
Exercise and Sports Science	M
Higher Education	M
Library Science	M,D,O
Marketing	O
Mathematics Education	M

Middle School Education	O
Reading Education	M,O
Science Education	M,O
Special Education	M,O

ROYAL MILITARY COLLEGE OF CANADA
Business Administration and Management—General	M

ROYAL ROADS UNIVERSITY
Environmental Education	M,O
Legal and Justice Studies	M,O
Sustainability Management	M,O
Travel and Tourism	M,O

RUTGERS UNIVERSITY–CAMDEN
Business Administration and Management—General	M
Educational Leadership and Administration	M
Educational Policy	M
Law	D
Mathematics Education	M

RUTGERS UNIVERSITY–NEWARK
Accounting	M,D
Business Administration and Management—General	M,D
Finance and Banking	M,D
Health Education	M,D
Human Resources Management	M,D
International Business	D
Law	D
Logistics	M
Management Information Systems	M,D
Marketing	D
Organizational Management	D
Quantitative Analysis	M,O
Real Estate	M
Supply Chain Management	D

RUTGERS UNIVERSITY–NEW BRUNSWICK
Counselor Education	M
Developmental Education	M
Early Childhood Education	M,D
Education—General	M,D
Educational Leadership and Administration	M,D
Educational Measurement and Evaluation	M
Educational Policy	D
Educational Psychology	M,D
Elementary Education	M,D
English as a Second Language	M
English Education	M
Foreign Languages Education	M,D
Foundations and Philosophy of Education	M
Health Education	M,D,O
Human Resources Management	M
Information Studies	M,D
Legal and Justice Studies	M,D
Library Science	D
Mathematics Education	M,D
Multilingual and Multicultural Education	M,D
Music Education	M,D,O
Quality Management	M,D
Reading Education	M,D
Science Education	M,D
Social Sciences Education	M,D
Social Work	M,D
Special Education	M,D
Student Affairs	M

RYERSON UNIVERSITY
Business Administration and Management—General	M

SACRED HEART UNIVERSITY
Accounting	M,O
Business Administration and Management—General	M,O
Education—General	M,O
Educational Leadership and Administration	O
Exercise and Sports Science	M
Finance and Banking	M,D,O
Human Resources Management	M,O
Investment Management	M,D,O
Marketing	M,O
Reading Education	O
Social Work	M

SAGE GRADUATE SCHOOL
Business Administration and Management—General	M
Counselor Education	M,O
Education—General	M,D,O
Educational Leadership and Administration	D
Elementary Education	M
Health Education	M
Organizational Management	M
Reading Education	M
Special Education	M

SAGINAW VALLEY STATE UNIVERSITY
Business Administration and Management—General	M
Early Childhood Education	M
Education—General	M,O
Educational Leadership and Administration	M,O
Educational Media/Instructional Technology	M
Foreign Languages Education	M
Reading Education	M
Social Work	M
Special Education	M

---

*M—masters degree; D—doctorate; O—other advanced degree; *—Close-Up and/or Display*

ST. AMBROSE UNIVERSITY

Accounting	M
Business Administration and Management—General	M,D
Early Childhood Education	M
Education—General	M
Educational Leadership and Administration	M
Exercise and Sports Science	M
Human Resources Management	M,D
Organizational Management	M
Social Work	M

ST. AUGUSTINE'S SEMINARY OF TORONTO

Religious Education	M,O

ST. BONAVENTURE UNIVERSITY

Accounting	M
Business Administration and Management—General	M
Counselor Education	M,O
Early Childhood Education	M
Education of the Gifted	M,O
Education—General	M,O
Educational Leadership and Administration	M,O
Marketing	M
Middle School Education	M
Reading Education	M
Secondary Education	M
Special Education	M,O

ST. CATHERINE UNIVERSITY

Business Administration and Management—General	M
Curriculum and Instruction	M
Early Childhood Education	M
Education—General	M,O
Information Studies	M
Library Science	M
Marketing	M
Organizational Management	M
Social Work	M

ST. CLOUD STATE UNIVERSITY

Business Administration and Management—General	M
Counselor Education	M
Curriculum and Instruction	M
Education—General	M,D
Educational Leadership and Administration	M,D
Educational Media/Instructional Technology	M
English as a Second Language	M
Exercise and Sports Science	M
Higher Education	M,D
Music Education	M
Nonprofit Management	M
Social Work	M
Special Education	M
Sports Management	M
Student Affairs	M

ST. EDWARD'S UNIVERSITY

Accounting	M
Education—General	M,O
Organizational Management	M
Student Affairs	M

ST. FRANCIS COLLEGE

Accounting	M

SAINT FRANCIS UNIVERSITY

Business Administration and Management—General	M
Education—General	M
Educational Leadership and Administration	M
Health Education	M
Human Resources Management	M
Reading Education	M

ST. FRANCIS XAVIER UNIVERSITY

Adult Education	M
Curriculum and Instruction	M
Education—General	M
Educational Leadership and Administration	M

ST. JOHN FISHER COLLEGE

Business Administration and Management—General	M
Education—General	M,D,O
Educational Leadership and Administration	M,D
Educational Media/Instructional Technology	M
Elementary Education	M,O
English Education	M
Foreign Languages Education	M
Mathematics Education	M
Middle School Education	M
Reading Education	M
Science Education	M
Social Sciences Education	M
Special Education	M,O

ST. JOHN'S UNIVERSITY (NY)

Accounting	M
Actuarial Science	M
Business Administration and Management—General	M
Business Analytics	M
Counselor Education	M,O
Curriculum and Instruction	D
Early Childhood Education	M,D,O
Education of the Gifted	D,O
Education—General	M,D,O
Educational Leadership and Administration	M,D,O
Elementary Education	M
English as a Second Language	M,O
Finance and Banking	M
Information Studies	M,O
Insurance	M

International and Comparative Education	D
International Business	M
Law	D
Legal and Justice Studies	M
Library Science	M,O
Management Information Systems	M
Management Strategy and Policy	M
Marketing	M
Mathematics Education	D
Multilingual and Multicultural Education	M,O
Reading Education	M,D,O
Risk Management	M
Science Education	D
Secondary Education	M
Special Education	M,O
Sports Management	M
Taxation	M

ST. JOSEPH'S COLLEGE, LONG ISLAND CAMPUS

Accounting	M
Business Administration and Management—General	M
Early Childhood Education	M
Educational Leadership and Administration	M
Human Resources Management	M
Human Services	M
Mathematics Education	M
Organizational Management	M
Reading Education	M
Special Education	M

ST. JOSEPH'S COLLEGE, NEW YORK

Accounting	M
Business Administration and Management—General	M
Education—General	M
Educational Leadership and Administration	M
Human Resources Management	M
Human Services	M
Organizational Management	M
Reading Education	M
Special Education	M

SAINT JOSEPH'S COLLEGE OF MAINE

Accounting	M
Adult Education	M
Business Administration and Management—General	M
Education—General	M
Educational Leadership and Administration	M
Health Education	M

SAINT JOSEPH'S UNIVERSITY

Accounting	M,O
Business Administration and Management—General	M,O*
Business Analytics	M*
Curriculum and Instruction	M,D,O
Early Childhood Education	M,D,O
Education—General	M,D,O
Educational Leadership and Administration	M,D,O
Elementary Education	M,D,O
Finance and Banking	M,O*
Human Resources Management	M,O
International Business	M,O
Law	M,O
Marketing	M,O*
Middle School Education	M,D,O
Reading Education	M,D,O
Secondary Education	M,D,O
Special Education	M,D,O

ST. LAWRENCE UNIVERSITY

Counselor Education	M,O
Education—General	M,O
Educational Leadership and Administration	M,O

SAINT LEO UNIVERSITY

Accounting	M,D
Agricultural Education	M
Business Administration and Management—General	M,D
Education of the Gifted	M,O
Education—General	M,O
Educational Leadership and Administration	M,O
Educational Media/Instructional Technology	M,O
Human Resources Management	M,D
Human Services	M
International Business	M,D
Legal and Justice Studies	M
Marketing Research	M,D
Marketing	M,D
Project Management	M,D
Reading Education	M,O
Social Work	M
Supply Chain Management	M,D

SAINT LOUIS UNIVERSITY

Accounting	M
Athletic Training and Sports Medicine	M,D
Business Administration and Management—General	M
Curriculum and Instruction	M,D
Education—General	M,D
Educational Leadership and Administration	M,D,O
Finance and Banking	M
Foundations and Philosophy of Education	M,D
Higher Education	M,D,O
International Business	M,D
Law	M,D
Social Work	M,D
Special Education	M,D
Student Affairs	M,D,O

SAINT MARTIN'S UNIVERSITY

Business Administration and Management—General	M
Education—General	M

SAINT MARY-OF-THE-WOODS COLLEGE

Management Strategy and Policy	M
Nonprofit Management	M
Organizational Management	M

SAINT MARY'S COLLEGE OF CALIFORNIA

Accounting	M
Business Administration and Management—General	M
Business Analytics	M
Counselor Education	M,O
Early Childhood Education	M
Education—General	M,D,O
Educational Leadership and Administration	M,D,O
Exercise and Sports Science	M
Finance and Banking	M
Investment Management	M
Kinesiology and Movement Studies	M
Organizational Management	M
Special Education	M
Sports Management	M

ST. MARY'S COLLEGE OF MARYLAND

Education—General	M

SAINT MARY'S UNIVERSITY (CANADA)

Business Administration and Management—General	M,D

ST. MARY'S UNIVERSITY (UNITED STATES)

Business Administration and Management—General	M
Counselor Education	D
Education—General	M
Educational Leadership and Administration	M
Environmental Law	M
Health Law	M
Law	M,D
Legal and Justice Studies	M

SAINT MARY'S UNIVERSITY OF MINNESOTA

Accounting	M
Business Administration and Management—General	M,D
Education of the Gifted	M,O
Education—General	M,O
Educational Leadership and Administration	M,D,O
Educational Media/Instructional Technology	M
Elementary Education	M
Human Resources Management	M
Multilingual and Multicultural Education	M,O
Organizational Management	M
Project Management	M,O
Reading Education	M,O
Religious Education	M
Secondary Education	M
Special Education	M,O

SAINT MICHAEL'S COLLEGE

Art Education	M,O
Education—General	M,O
Educational Leadership and Administration	M,O
English as a Second Language	M,O
Reading Education	M,O
Special Education	M,O

ST. NORBERT COLLEGE

Business Administration and Management—General	M
Supply Chain Management	M

SAINT PETER'S UNIVERSITY

Accounting	M
Business Administration and Management—General	M
Counselor Education	M,O
Education—General	M,D,O
Educational Leadership and Administration	M,D
Elementary Education	M,O
Finance and Banking	M
Higher Education	D
Human Resources Management	M
International Business	M
Management Information Systems	M
Marketing	M
Mathematics Education	M,D,O
Middle School Education	M,O
Reading Education	M,O
Risk Management	M
Secondary Education	M,O
Special Education	M,O

SAINTS CYRIL AND METHODIUS SEMINARY

Religious Education	M,O

ST. THOMAS AQUINAS COLLEGE

Business Administration and Management—General	M
Education—General	M,O
Educational Leadership and Administration	M,O
Elementary Education	M,O
Finance and Banking	M
Marketing	M
Middle School Education	M,O
Reading Education	M,O
Secondary Education	M,O
Special Education	M,O

ST. THOMAS UNIVERSITY

Accounting	M,O

SAINT VINCENT COLLEGE

Business Administration and Management—General	M,O
Counselor Education	M,O
Education of the Gifted	M,D,O
Education—General	M,D,O
Educational Leadership and Administration	M,D,O
Educational Media/Instructional Technology	M,D,O
Elementary Education	M,D,O
English as a Second Language	M,D,O
Human Resources Management	M,O
International Business	M,O
Law	M,D
Reading Education	M,D,O
Special Education	M,D,O
Sports Management	M,O
Taxation	M,D

SAINT VINCENT COLLEGE

SAINT XAVIER UNIVERSITY

Business Administration and Management—General	M,O
Counselor Education	M
Curriculum and Instruction	M
Early Childhood Education	M
Education—General	M
Educational Leadership and Administration	M
Educational Media/Instructional Technology	M
Elementary Education	M
English as a Second Language	M
Finance and Banking	M,O
Foreign Languages Education	M
Marketing	M,O
Music Education	M
Project Management	M,O
Reading Education	M
Science Education	M
Secondary Education	M
Special Education	M

SALEM COLLEGE

Art Education	M
Counselor Education	M
Education—General	M
Elementary Education	M
English as a Second Language	M
Middle School Education	M
Reading Education	M
Secondary Education	M
Special Education	M

SALEM INTERNATIONAL UNIVERSITY

Business Administration and Management—General	M
Curriculum and Instruction	M
Education—General	M
Educational Leadership and Administration	M
International Business	M

SALEM STATE UNIVERSITY

Art Education	M
Business Administration and Management—General	M
Counselor Education	M
Early Childhood Education	M
Educational Leadership and Administration	M
Educational Media/Instructional Technology	M
Elementary Education	M
English as a Second Language	M
Higher Education	M
Mathematics Education	M
Middle School Education	M
Physical Education	M
Reading Education	M
Science Education	M
Secondary Education	M
Social Work	M
Special Education	M

SALISBURY UNIVERSITY

Athletic Training and Sports Medicine	M
Business Administration and Management—General	M
Curriculum and Instruction	M
Educational Leadership and Administration	M
English as a Second Language	M
Mathematics Education	M
Middle School Education	M
Reading Education	M,D
Secondary Education	M
Social Work	M

SALUS UNIVERSITY

Special Education	M,O

SALVE REGINA UNIVERSITY

Business Administration and Management—General	M,O
Business Education	M,O
Educational Leadership and Administration	O
Entrepreneurship	M
Human Resources Management	M,O
Management Strategy and Policy	M,O
Nonprofit Management	M,O
Organizational Management	M,O

SAMFORD UNIVERSITY

Accounting	M

Athletic Training and Sports
  Medicine — M,D
Business Administration and
  Management—General — M
Education of the Gifted — M,D,O
Education—General — M,D,O
Educational Leadership and
  Administration — M,D,O
Educational Media/Instructional
  Technology — M,D,O
Elementary Education — M,D,O
Entrepreneurship — M
Finance and Banking — M
Law — M,D
Marketing — M
Music Education — M
Secondary Education — M,D,O
Social Work — M
Special Education — M

SAM HOUSTON STATE UNIVERSITY
Accounting — M
Business Administration and
  Management—General — M
Counselor Education — M,D
Curriculum and Instruction — M,D
Developmental Education — M,D
Education—General — M,D
Educational Leadership and
  Administration — M,D
Finance and Banking — M
Higher Education — M,D
Kinesiology and Movement Studies — M
Library Science — M
Project Management — M
Reading Education — M,D
Special Education — M,D
Sports Management — M

SAN DIEGO CHRISTIAN COLLEGE
Education—General — M
Organizational Management — M

SAN DIEGO STATE UNIVERSITY
Accounting — M
Advertising and Public Relations — M
Business Administration and
  Management—General — M
Counselor Education — M
Curriculum and Instruction — M
Education—General — M,D
Educational Leadership and
  Administration — M
Educational Media/Instructional
  Technology — M,D
Elementary Education — M
English as a Second Language — M,O
Entrepreneurship — M
Exercise and Sports Science — M
Finance and Banking — M
Higher Education — M
Human Resources Management — M
Kinesiology and Movement Studies — M
Management Information Systems — M
Marketing — M
Mathematics Education — M,D
Multilingual and Multicultural
  Education — M,D
Music Education — M
Reading Education — M
Science Education — M,D
Secondary Education — M
Social Work — M
Special Education — M
Sports Management — M

SAN FRANCISCO CONSERVATORY OF MUSIC
Music Education — M,O

SAN FRANCISCO STATE UNIVERSITY
Accounting — M
Adult Education — M
Business Administration and
  Management—General — M
Early Childhood Education — M,D,O
Education—General — M,D,O
Educational Leadership and
  Administration — M,D,O
Educational Media/Instructional
  Technology — M
Elementary Education — M
English as a Second Language — M
English Education — M
Entrepreneurship — M
Finance and Banking — M
Health Education — M
Hospitality Management — M
Industrial and Manufacturing
  Management — M
International Business — M
Kinesiology and Movement Studies — M
Legal and Justice Studies — M
Leisure Studies — M
Management Information Systems — M
Marketing — M
Mathematics Education — M,O
Music Education — M
Nonprofit Management — M
Quantitative Analysis — M
Reading Education — M,O
Recreation and Park Management — M
Secondary Education — M,O
Social Work — M
Special Education — M,D,O
Sustainability Management — M
Travel and Tourism — M

SAN IGNACIO UNIVERSITY
Business Administration and
  Management—General — M
Early Childhood Education — M

Education—General — M
Educational Leadership and
  Administration — M
Hospitality Management — M
Human Resources Management — M
International Business — M
Marketing — M
Special Education — M
Travel and Tourism — M

SAN JOAQUIN COLLEGE OF LAW
Law — D

SAN JOSE STATE UNIVERSITY
Accounting — M
Athletic Training and Sports
  Medicine — M
Business Administration and
  Management—General — M
Counselor Education — M,D
Curriculum and Instruction — M
Education—General — M,D
Educational Leadership and
  Administration — M,D
Elementary Education — M
English as a Second Language — M
Exercise and Sports Science — M
Kinesiology and Movement Studies — M
Legal and Justice Studies — M
Library Science — M
Mathematics Education — M
Music Education — M
Social Work — M
Sports Management — M
Taxation — M
Transportation Management — M

THE SANTA BARBARA AND VENTURA COLLEGES OF LAW–SANTA BARBARA
Law — M,D
Legal and Justice Studies — M,D

THE SANTA BARBARA AND VENTURA COLLEGES OF LAW–VENTURA
Law — M,D
Legal and Justice Studies — M,D

SANTA CLARA UNIVERSITY
Business Administration and
  Management—General — M
Business Analytics — M
Counselor Education — M,O
Education—General — M,O
Educational Leadership and
  Administration — M,O
Finance and Banking — M
Intellectual Property Law — M,D,O
Law — M,D,O
Management Information Systems — M
Supply Chain Management — M

SARAH LAWRENCE COLLEGE
Education—General — M
Kinesiology and Movement Studies — M

SAVANNAH COLLEGE OF ART AND DESIGN
Advertising and Public Relations — M
Travel and Tourism — M

SAVANNAH LAW SCHOOL
Law — D

SAVANNAH STATE UNIVERSITY
Business Administration and
  Management—General — M
Human Resources Management — M
Social Work — M

SAYBROOK UNIVERSITY
Organizational Behavior — M,D
Organizational Management — M,D

SCHILLER INTERNATIONAL UNIVERSITY (GERMANY)
Business Administration and
  Management—General — M
International Business — M
Management Information Systems — M

SCHILLER INTERNATIONAL UNIVERSITY
Business Administration and
  Management—General — M
International Business — M

SCHILLER INTERNATIONAL UNIVERSITY (SPAIN)
Business Administration and
  Management—General — M
International Business — M

SCHILLER INTERNATIONAL UNIVERSITY (UNITED STATES)
Business Administration and
  Management—General — M
Finance and Banking — M
Hospitality Management — M
International Business — M
Management Information Systems — M
Travel and Tourism — M

SCHOOL OF THE ART INSTITUTE OF CHICAGO
Art Education — M

SCHOOL OF VISUAL ARTS (NY)
Art Education — M

SCHREINER UNIVERSITY
Business Administration and
  Management—General — M
Education—General — M,O
Educational Leadership and
  Administration — M,O

SEATTLE PACIFIC UNIVERSITY
Business Administration and
  Management—General — M
Counselor Education — M,D,O
Education—General — D
Educational Leadership and
  Administration — M,D,O
Educational Media/Instructional
  Technology — M
English as a Second Language — M
Human Resources Management — M
Management Information Systems — M
Mathematics Education — M
Reading Education — M
Science Education — M
Secondary Education — M
Sustainability Management — M

SEATTLE UNIVERSITY
Accounting — M
Adult Education — M,O
Business Administration and
  Management—General — M,O
Counselor Education — M,O
Education—General — M,D,O
Educational Leadership and
  Administration — M,D,O
English as a Second Language — M,O
Finance and Banking — M,O
Health Law — M,D
Law — M,D
Organizational Management — M,O
Social Work — M
Special Education — M,O
Sports Management — M

SELMA UNIVERSITY
Religious Education — M

SETON HALL UNIVERSITY
Accounting — M,O
Advertising and Public Relations — M
Athletic Training and Sports
  Medicine — M
Business Administration and
  Management—General — M,O
Counselor Education — M,D
Education—General — M,D,O
Educational Leadership and
  Administration — D,O
Educational Measurement and
  Evaluation — M,D,O
Educational Media/Instructional
  Technology — M
Entrepreneurship — M,O
Finance and Banking — M,O
Health Law — M,D
Higher Education — D
International Business — M,O
Law — M,D
Marketing — M,O
Nonprofit Management — M
Social Work — M
Special Education — M
Sports Management — M,O
Student Affairs — M,O
Supply Chain Management — O
Taxation — O

SETON HILL UNIVERSITY
Accounting — M
Business Administration and
  Management—General — M
Educational Media/Instructional
  Technology — M
Elementary Education — M
Entrepreneurship — M
Middle School Education — M
Special Education — M

SHASTA BIBLE COLLEGE
Educational Leadership and
  Administration — M
Religious Education — M

SHAWNEE STATE UNIVERSITY
Curriculum and Instruction — M
Education—General — M

SHAW UNIVERSITY
Curriculum and Instruction — M
Early Childhood Education — M

SHENANDOAH UNIVERSITY
Athletic Training and Sports
  Medicine — M,D,O
Business Administration and
  Management—General — M,O
Early Childhood Education — M,D,O
Education—General — M,D,O
Educational Leadership and
  Administration — M,D,O
Elementary Education — M,D,O
Health Education — M,D,O
Middle School Education — M,D,O
Music Education — M,D,O
Physical Education — M,D,O
Reading Education — M,D,O
Secondary Education — M,D,O
Special Education — M,D,O

SHEPHERD UNIVERSITY (WV)
Curriculum and Instruction — M

SHIPPENSBURG UNIVERSITY OF PENNSYLVANIA
Business Administration and
  Management—General — M,D,O
Business Analytics — M,D
Counselor Education — M,D
Curriculum and Instruction — M
Early Childhood Education — M
Education—General — M,D

Educational Leadership and
  Administration — M,D
Elementary Education — M
Finance and Banking — M,D,O
Foreign Languages Education — M
Higher Education — M
Logistics — M,D,O
Management Information Systems — M,D,O
Mathematics Education — M
Middle School Education — M
Organizational Management — M
Reading Education — M
Science Education — M
Social Work — M
Special Education — M,D
Student Affairs — M,D
Supply Chain Management — M,D,O

SHORTER UNIVERSITY
Accounting — M
Business Administration and
  Management—General — M

SIENA COLLEGE
Accounting — M
Business Administration and
  Management—General — M

SIENA HEIGHTS UNIVERSITY
Early Childhood Education — M,O
Education—General — M,O
Educational Leadership and
  Administration — M,O
Elementary Education — M,O
Higher Education — M,O
Organizational Management — M,O
Reading Education — M,O
Secondary Education — M,O
Special Education — M,O

SIERRA NEVADA COLLEGE
Education—General — M
Educational Leadership and
  Administration — M
Elementary Education — M
Secondary Education — M

SILVER LAKE COLLEGE OF THE HOLY FAMILY
Business Administration and
  Management—General — M
Education—General — M
Educational Leadership and
  Administration — M

SIMMONS COLLEGE
Business Administration and
  Management—General — M
Education—General — M,D,O
Elementary Education — M,D,O
Health Education — M,D,O
Library Science — M,D,O
Nonprofit Management — M
Reading Education — M,D,O
Social Work — M,D,O
Special Education — M,D,O

SIMON FRASER UNIVERSITY
Actuarial Science — M,D
Art Education — M,D
Business Administration and
  Management—General — M,D,O
Counselor Education — M
Curriculum and Instruction — M,D
Education—General — M,D
Educational Leadership and
  Administration — M,D
Educational Media/Instructional
  Technology — M,D
Educational Psychology — M,D
English as a Second Language — M
English Education — M,D
Finance and Banking — M,D,O
Foundations and Philosophy of
  Education — M,D
Kinesiology and Movement Studies — M,D
Legal and Justice Studies — M,D
Mathematics Education — M,D
Reading Education — D

SIMPSON COLLEGE
Education—General — M
Secondary Education — M

SIMPSON UNIVERSITY
Curriculum and Instruction — M
Education—General — M
Educational Leadership and
  Administration — M
Organizational Management — M

SINTE GLESKA UNIVERSITY
Education—General — M
Elementary Education — M

SIT GRADUATE INSTITUTE
Business Administration and
  Management—General — M
Educational Leadership and
  Administration — M
English as a Second Language — M
Entrepreneurship — M
International and Comparative
  Education — M
International Business — M
Organizational Management — M
Sustainability Management — M

SITTING BULL COLLEGE
Curriculum and Instruction — M

SLIPPERY ROCK UNIVERSITY OF PENNSYLVANIA
Accounting — M

---

*M—masters degree; D—doctorate; O—other advanced degree; *—Close-Up and/or Display*

Peterson's Graduate Programs in Business, Education,
Information Studies, Law & Social Work 2019

Business Administration and
Management—General — M
Counselor Education — M
Education—General — M,D
Educational Leadership and
Administration — M,D
Educational Media/Instructional
Technology — M,D
Elementary Education — M
English as a Second Language — M
English Education — M
Environmental Education — M
Finance and Banking — M
Marketing — M
Mathematics Education — M
Physical Education — M
Reading Education — M
Recreation and Park Management — M
Science Education — M
Secondary Education — M
Social Sciences Education — M
Special Education — M,D
Student Affairs — M

SMITH COLLEGE
Education—General — M
Elementary Education — M
English Education — M
Exercise and Sports Science — M
Mathematics Education — M
Middle School Education — M
Science Education — M
Secondary Education — M
Social Sciences Education — M
Social Work — M,D

SOKA UNIVERSITY OF AMERICA
Educational Leadership and
Administration — M*

SONOMA STATE UNIVERSITY
Business Administration and
Management—General — M
Curriculum and Instruction — M,O
Early Childhood Education — M,O
Education—General — M,O
Educational Leadership and
Administration — M,O
Exercise and Sports Science — M
Kinesiology and Movement Studies — M
Reading Education — M,O
Special Education — M,O
Sports Management — M

SOUTH CAROLINA STATE UNIVERSITY
Business Administration and
Management—General — M
Business Education — M
Counselor Education — M
Early Childhood Education — M
Education—General — M
Educational Leadership and
Administration — D,O
Elementary Education — M
English Education — M
Entrepreneurship — M
Home Economics Education — M
Human Services — M
Mathematics Education — M
Science Education — M
Secondary Education — M
Social Sciences Education — M
Special Education — M
Vocational and Technical Education — M

SOUTH DAKOTA STATE UNIVERSITY
Agricultural Education — M
Athletic Training and Sports
Medicine — M,D
Counselor Education — M
Curriculum and Instruction — M
Education—General — M,D
Educational Leadership and
Administration — M
Exercise and Sports Science — M,D
Human Resources Development — M
Recreation and Park Management — M,D

SOUTHEASTERN BAPTIST THEOLOGICAL SEMINARY
Religious Education — M,D

SOUTHEASTERN LOUISIANA UNIVERSITY
Advertising and Public Relations — M
Business Administration and
Management—General — M
Counselor Education — M
Curriculum and Instruction — M
Education—General — M,D
Educational Leadership and
Administration — M,D
Elementary Education — M
English Education — M
Health Education — M
Kinesiology and Movement Studies — M
Marketing — M
Reading Education — M
Special Education — M
Sustainability Management — M

SOUTHEASTERN OKLAHOMA STATE UNIVERSITY
Aviation Management — M
Business Administration and
Management—General — M
Counselor Education — M
Education—General — M
Educational Leadership and
Administration — M
Management Information Systems — M
Mathematics Education — M
Reading Education — M

SOUTHEASTERN UNIVERSITY (FL)
Business Administration and
Management—General — M,D

Counselor Education — M
Curriculum and Instruction — M,D
Education of the Gifted — M,D
Education—General — M,D
Educational Leadership and
Administration — M,D
Elementary Education — M,D
English as a Second Language — M,D
Entrepreneurship — M,D
Human Services — M
International Business — M
Kinesiology and Movement Studies — M,D
Management Strategy and Policy — M,D
Organizational Management — M
Reading Education — M,D
Social Work — M
Sports Management — M,D

SOUTHEAST MISSOURI STATE UNIVERSITY
Accounting — M
Business Administration and
Management—General — M
Counselor Education — M,O
Educational Leadership and
Administration — M,D,O
Elementary Education — M,D,O
English as a Second Language — M
Entrepreneurship — M
Exercise and Sports Science — M
Finance and Banking — M
Higher Education — M,D,O
Leisure Studies — M
Middle School Education — M
Secondary Education — M,D,O
Special Education — M
Sports Management — M

SOUTHERN ADVENTIST UNIVERSITY
Accounting — M
Business Administration and
Management—General — M
Counselor Education — M
Education—General — M
Educational Leadership and
Administration — M
Finance and Banking — M
Marketing — M
Reading Education — M
Religious Education — M
Social Work — M

SOUTHERN ARKANSAS UNIVERSITY–MAGNOLIA
Adult Education — M
Business Administration and
Management—General — M
Counselor Education — M
Curriculum and Instruction — M
Education of the Gifted — M
Education—General — M
Educational Leadership and
Administration — M
Higher Education — M
Kinesiology and Movement Studies — M
Library Science — M
Organizational Management — M
Student Affairs — M
Supply Chain Management — M

SOUTHERN CONNECTICUT STATE UNIVERSITY
Art Education — M
Business Administration and
Management—General — M
Counselor Education — M,O
Education—General — M,D,O
Educational Leadership and
Administration — M,D,O
Educational Measurement and
Evaluation — M,D,O
Elementary Education — M,O
English as a Second Language — M
Environmental Education — M,O
Exercise and Sports Science — M
Foreign Languages Education — M
Health Education — M
Information Studies — M,O
Leisure Studies — M
Library Science — M,O
Multilingual and Multicultural
Education — M
Physical Education — M
Reading Education — M,O
Recreation and Park Management — M
Science Education — M,O
Social Work — M
Special Education — M

SOUTHERN EVANGELICAL SEMINARY
Religious Education — M,D,O

SOUTHERN ILLINOIS UNIVERSITY CARBONDALE
Accounting — M,D
Business Administration and
Management—General — M,D
Curriculum and Instruction — M
Education—General — M,D
Educational Leadership and
Administration — M,D
Educational Psychology — M,D
English as a Second Language — M
Health Education — M
Health Law — M
Higher Education — M
Kinesiology and Movement Studies — M
Law — M
Legal and Justice Studies — M
Physical Education — M
Recreation and Park Management — M
Social Work — M
Special Education — M,D
Vocational and Technical Education — M,D

SOUTHERN ILLINOIS UNIVERSITY EDWARDSVILLE
Accounting — M
Advertising and Public Relations — M
Business Administration and
Management—General — M
Business Analytics — M
Curriculum and Instruction — M
Education—General — M,D,O
Educational Leadership and
Administration — M,D,O
Educational Media/Instructional
Technology — M,O
English as a Second Language — M,O
English Education — M,O
Exercise and Sports Science — M
Finance and Banking — M
Foundations and Philosophy of
Education — M
Health Education — M,D,O
Higher Education — M
Kinesiology and Movement Studies — M
Management Information Systems — M
Marketing Research — M
Mathematics Education — M
Music Education — M,O
Physical Education — M
Project Management — M
Reading Education — M,O
Social Work — M
Special Education — M,O
Student Affairs — M
Taxation — M

SOUTHERN METHODIST UNIVERSITY
Accounting — M
Advertising and Public Relations — M
Business Administration and
Management—General — M
Counselor Education — M
Education of the Gifted — M,D
Education—General — M,D
Entrepreneurship — M
Finance and Banking — M
Law — M,D
Management Information Systems — M
Management Strategy and Policy — M
Marketing — M
Multilingual and Multicultural
Education — M,D
Music Education — M
Reading Education — M,D
Real Estate — M
Special Education — M
Sports Management — M
Taxation — M,D

SOUTHERN NAZARENE UNIVERSITY
Business Administration and
Management—General — M
Sports Management — M

SOUTHERN NEW HAMPSHIRE UNIVERSITY
Accounting — M,D,O
Advertising and Public Relations — M
Business Administration and
Management—General — M,D,O
Business Analytics — M,D,O
Curriculum and Instruction — M,D,O
Early Childhood Education — M,D,O
Education—General — M,D,O
Educational Leadership and
Administration — M,D,O
Educational Media/Instructional
Technology — M,D,O
Elementary Education — M,D,O
English as a Second Language — M,D,O
Entertainment Management — M,D,O
Entrepreneurship — M,D,O
Finance and Banking — M,D,O
Higher Education — M,D,O
Human Resources Management — M,D,O
Industrial and Manufacturing
Management — M,D,O
International Business — M,D,O
Investment Management — M,D,O
Legal and Justice Studies — M,D,O
Management Information Systems — M,D,O
Marketing — M,D,O
Nonprofit Management — M,D,O
Organizational Management — M,D,O
Project Management — M,D,O
Quality Management — M,D,O
Quantitative Analysis — M,D,O
Reading Education — M,D,O
Special Education — M,D,O
Sports Management — M,D,O
Supply Chain Management — M,D,O
Sustainability Management — M,D,O
Taxation — M,D,O

SOUTHERN OREGON UNIVERSITY
Accounting — M,O
Business Administration and
Management—General — M,O
Early Childhood Education — M
Education—General — M
Educational Leadership and
Administration — M
Elementary Education — M
Environmental Education — M
Foreign Languages Education — M
International Business — M,O
Reading Education — M
Secondary Education — M
Special Education — M

SOUTHERN UNIVERSITY AND AGRICULTURAL AND MECHANICAL COLLEGE
Business Administration and
Management—General — M
Counselor Education — M
Education—General — M,D

SOUTHERN ILLINOIS UNIVERSITY EDWARDSVILLE
Educational Leadership and
Administration — M
Educational Media/Instructional
Technology — M
Elementary Education — M
Law — D
Mathematics Education — D
Recreation and Park Management — M
Science Education — D
Secondary Education — D
Special Education — M,D

SOUTHERN UNIVERSITY AT NEW ORLEANS
Management Information Systems — M
Social Work — M

SOUTHERN UTAH UNIVERSITY
Accounting — M
Business Administration and
Management—General — M
Education—General — M,O
Exercise and Sports Science — M

SOUTHERN WESLEYAN UNIVERSITY
Business Administration and
Management—General — M
Education—General — M

SOUTH TEXAS COLLEGE OF LAW HOUSTON
Law — D

SOUTH UNIVERSITY (AL)
Business Administration and
Management—General — M
Management Information Systems — M

SOUTH UNIVERSITY
Business Administration and
Management—General — M
Management Information Systems — M

SOUTH UNIVERSITY
Business Administration and
Management—General — M
Management Information Systems — M

SOUTH UNIVERSITY (GA)
Business Administration and
Management—General — M
Entrepreneurship — M
Hospitality Management — M
Organizational Management — M
Sustainability Management — M

SOUTH UNIVERSITY (SC)
Business Administration and
Management—General — M
Organizational Management — M

SOUTH UNIVERSITY (TX)
Business Administration and
Management—General — M
Management Information Systems — M

SOUTH UNIVERSITY
Business Administration and
Management—General — M

SOUTH UNIVERSITY
Business Administration and
Management—General — M
Management Information Systems — M
Organizational Management — M

SOUTHWEST BAPTIST UNIVERSITY
Business Administration and
Management—General — M
Education—General — M,O
Educational Leadership and
Administration — M,O

SOUTHWESTERN ADVENTIST UNIVERSITY
Accounting — M
Business Administration and
Management—General — M
Curriculum and Instruction — M
Education—General — M
Educational Leadership and
Administration — M
Finance and Banking — M
Reading Education — M

SOUTHWESTERN ASSEMBLIES OF GOD UNIVERSITY
Curriculum and Instruction — M
Education—General — M
Educational Leadership and
Administration — M
Religious Education — M
Secondary Education — M

SOUTHWESTERN BAPTIST THEOLOGICAL SEMINARY
Religious Education — M

SOUTHWESTERN COLLEGE (KS)
Business Administration and
Management—General — M
Curriculum and Instruction — M,D
Early Childhood Education — M,D
Education—General — M,D
Educational Leadership and
Administration — M,D
Elementary Education — M,D
Higher Education — M,D
Special Education — M,D

SOUTHWESTERN LAW SCHOOL
Law — M,D*

SOUTHWESTERN OKLAHOMA STATE UNIVERSITY
Art Education — M
Business Administration and
Management—General — M
Counselor Education — M
Early Childhood Education — M

Education—General M
Educational Leadership and
   Administration M
Educational Measurement and
   Evaluation M
Elementary Education M
English Education M
Kinesiology and Movement Studies M
Mathematics Education M
Music Education M
Recreation and Park Management M
Science Education M
Secondary Education M
Social Sciences Education M
Special Education M

SOUTHWEST MINNESOTA STATE UNIVERSITY
Business Administration and
   Management—General M
Early Childhood Education M
Education—General M
Educational Leadership and
   Administration M
English as a Second Language M
Marketing M
Mathematics Education M
Reading Education M
Special Education M

SOUTHWEST UNIVERSITY
Business Administration and
   Management—General M
Organizational Management M

SPALDING UNIVERSITY
Art Education M
Athletic Training and Sports
   Medicine M
Business Education M
Counselor Education M
Education—General M,D
Educational Leadership and
   Administration M,D
Elementary Education M
Foreign Languages Education M
Middle School Education M
Secondary Education M
Social Work M
Special Education M

SPRING ARBOR UNIVERSITY
Business Administration and
   Management—General M
Education—General M
Reading Education M
Special Education M

SPRINGFIELD COLLEGE
Athletic Training and Sports
   Medicine M
Business Administration and
   Management—General M
Counselor Education M,D,O
Early Childhood Education M,O
Education—General M,O
Educational Leadership and
   Administration M,D,O
Elementary Education M,O
Exercise and Sports Science M,D,O
Higher Education M,D,O
Human Services M
Organizational Management M
Physical Education M
Recreation and Park Management M
Secondary Education M,O
Social Work M
Special Education M,O
Sports Management M,D,O
Student Affairs M,D,O

SPRING HILL COLLEGE
Business Administration and
   Management—General M
Early Childhood Education M
Education—General M
Elementary Education M
Foundations and Philosophy of
   Education M
Secondary Education M

STANFORD UNIVERSITY
Business Administration and
   Management—General M,D
Curriculum and Instruction M
Education—General M,D
Educational Leadership and
   Administration M
Educational Media/Instructional
   Technology M
Educational Policy M
Elementary Education M
Environmental Law M,D
International and Comparative
   Education M,D
Law M,D
Legal and Justice Studies M,D
Secondary Education M

STATE UNIVERSITY OF NEW YORK AT FREDONIA
Curriculum and Instruction M
Early Childhood Education M
Education—General M
English as a Second Language M
English Education M
Mathematics Education M,O
Middle School Education M,O
Music Education M
Reading Education M
Secondary Education M

STATE UNIVERSITY OF NEW YORK AT NEW PALTZ
Accounting M
Art Education M
Business Administration and
   Management—General M
Counselor Education M,O
Early Childhood Education M,O
Education—General M,O
Educational Leadership and
   Administration M,O
Elementary Education M
English as a Second Language M,O
English Education M,O
Multilingual and Multicultural
   Education M,O
Reading Education M
Science Education M,O
Secondary Education M
Social Sciences Education M
Special Education M

STATE UNIVERSITY OF NEW YORK AT OSWEGO
Agricultural Education M
Art Education M
Business Administration and
   Management—General M
Business Education M
Curriculum and Instruction M
Early Childhood Education M
Education—General M,O
Educational Leadership and
   Administration O
Elementary Education M
Middle School Education M
Reading Education M
Secondary Education M
Special Education M
Vocational and Technical Education M

STATE UNIVERSITY OF NEW YORK AT PLATTSBURGH
Counselor Education M,O
Curriculum and Instruction M
Early Childhood Education O
Educational Leadership and
   Administration O
Elementary Education M,O
English Education M
Foreign Languages Education M
Mathematics Education M
Reading Education M
Science Education M
Secondary Education M
Social Sciences Education M
Special Education M
Student Affairs M,O

STATE UNIVERSITY OF NEW YORK COLLEGE AT CORTLAND
Early Childhood Education M
Education—General M,O
Educational Leadership and
   Administration O
English as a Second Language M
English Education M
Environmental Education M
Health Education M
Mathematics Education M
Physical Education M
Reading Education M
Recreation and Park Management M
Science Education M
Secondary Education M
Special Education M
Sports Management M

STATE UNIVERSITY OF NEW YORK COLLEGE AT GENESEO
Accounting M
Business Administration and
   Management—General M
Education—General M
English Education M
Multilingual and Multicultural
   Education M
Reading Education M
Secondary Education M
Social Sciences Education M

STATE UNIVERSITY OF NEW YORK COLLEGE AT OLD WESTBURY
Accounting M
Business Administration and
   Management—General M
Education—General M
English Education M
Foreign Languages Education M
Mathematics Education M
Science Education M
Social Sciences Education M
Taxation M

STATE UNIVERSITY OF NEW YORK COLLEGE AT ONEONTA
Counselor Education M,O
Education—General M,O
Educational Psychology M,O
Elementary Education M
Reading Education M
Special Education M,O

STATE UNIVERSITY OF NEW YORK COLLEGE AT POTSDAM
Curriculum and Instruction M
Early Childhood Education M
Educational Media/Instructional
   Technology M
Elementary Education M
English Education M
Mathematics Education M

Middle School Education M
Music Education M
Organizational Management M
Reading Education M
Science Education M
Secondary Education M
Social Sciences Education M
Special Education M

STATE UNIVERSITY OF NEW YORK COLLEGE OF ENVIRONMENTAL SCIENCE AND FORESTRY
Sustainability Management M,D,O

STATE UNIVERSITY OF NEW YORK EMPIRE STATE COLLEGE
Adult Education M
Business Administration and
   Management—General M
Education—General M
Educational Media/Instructional
   Technology M
International Business M

STATE UNIVERSITY OF NEW YORK MARITIME COLLEGE
Transportation Management M

STATE UNIVERSITY OF NEW YORK POLYTECHNIC INSTITUTE
Accounting M
Business Administration and
   Management—General M
Finance and Banking M
Human Resources Management M
Marketing M

STEPHEN F. AUSTIN STATE UNIVERSITY
Accounting M
Agricultural Education M
Athletic Training and Sports
   Medicine M
Business Administration and
   Management—General M
Counselor Education M
Early Childhood Education M
Education—General M,D
Educational Leadership and
   Administration M,D
Elementary Education M
Kinesiology and Movement Studies M
Marketing M
Mathematics Education M
Secondary Education M,D
Social Work M
Special Education M

STEPHENS COLLEGE
Counselor Education M,O

STETSON UNIVERSITY
Accounting M
Business Administration and
   Management—General M
Counselor Education M
Education—General M
Educational Leadership and
   Administration M
Law M,D

STEVENS INSTITUTE OF TECHNOLOGY
Business Administration and
   Management—General M,O
Business Analytics M,O
Electronic Commerce M,O
Entrepreneurship M,O
Finance and Banking M,O
Human Resources Management M
Industrial and Manufacturing
   Management M
International Business M
Logistics O
Management Information Systems M,D,O
Management Strategy and Policy M
Marketing M,O
Project Management M,O
Quality Management M,O

STEVENSON UNIVERSITY
Education—General M
Educational Leadership and
   Administration M
Mathematics Education M
Project Management M
Quality Management M
Science Education M

STOCKTON UNIVERSITY
Business Administration and
   Management—General M
Education—General M
Educational Media/Instructional
   Technology M
Management Strategy and Policy M
Organizational Management D
Quantitative Analysis M
Social Work M

STONY BROOK UNIVERSITY, STATE UNIVERSITY OF NEW YORK
Accounting M,O
Business Administration and
   Management—General M,O
Computer Education M
Educational Leadership and
   Administration M,O
Educational Media/Instructional
   Technology M,O
English as a Second Language M
English Education M,D,O
Entrepreneurship M,O
Finance and Banking M,O
Foreign Languages Education M,O
Health Education M,O

Middle School Education M
Music Education M
Organizational Management M
Reading Education M
Science Education M
Secondary Education M
Social Sciences Education M
Special Education M

STRATFORD UNIVERSITY (MD)
Hospitality Management M

STRATFORD UNIVERSITY (VA)
Accounting M,D
Business Administration and
   Management—General M,D
Management Information Systems M,D

STRAYER UNIVERSITY
Accounting M
Business Administration and
   Management—General M
Education—General M
Educational Media/Instructional
   Technology M
Finance and Banking M
Hospitality Management M
Human Resources Management M
Management Information Systems M
Marketing M
Supply Chain Management M
Taxation M
Travel and Tourism M

SUFFOLK UNIVERSITY
Accounting M,O
Advertising and Public Relations M
Business Administration and
   Management—General M,D,O
Counselor Education M,D,O
Educational Leadership and
   Administration M,O
Entrepreneurship M
Finance and Banking M
Health Law M,D
Intellectual Property Law M,D
International Business M
Law M,D
Management Information Systems M
Management Strategy and Policy M
Marketing M
Nonprofit Management M
Organizational Behavior M
Supply Chain Management M
Taxation M,O

SULLIVAN UNIVERSITY
Business Administration and
   Management—General M,D

SUL ROSS STATE UNIVERSITY
Art Education M
Business Administration and
   Management—General M
Counselor Education M
Education—General M,O
Educational Leadership and
   Administration M
Educational Measurement and
   Evaluation M,O
Elementary Education M
Multilingual and Multicultural
   Education M
Physical Education M
Reading Education M,O
Secondary Education M

SWEET BRIAR COLLEGE
Education—General M

SYRACUSE UNIVERSITY
Accounting M
Advertising and Public Relations M
Art Education M
Business Administration and
   Management—General M,D
Business Analytics M
Counselor Education M,D
Curriculum and Instruction M,D,O
Early Childhood Education M
Education of Students with
   Severe/Multiple Disabilities M
Education—General M,D,O
Educational Leadership and
   Administration M,D,O
Educational Measurement and
   Evaluation M,D,O
Educational Media/Instructional
   Technology M,O
English as a Second Language M,O
English Education M
Entertainment Management M
Entrepreneurship M
Exercise and Sports Science M
Finance and Banking M,D
Foundations and Philosophy of
   Education M,D,O
Higher Education M,D,O
Hospitality Management M,O
Information Studies M
Kinesiology and Movement Studies M,D,O
Law M,D
Library Science M*
Management Information Systems M
Marketing M
Mathematics Education M,D
Music Education M,O
Organizational Management O
Reading Education M,D
Real Estate M
Science Education M,D
Social Sciences Education M
Social Work M

*M—masters degree; D—doctorate; O—other advanced degree; *—Close-Up and/or Display*

Special Education — M,D
Sports Management — M
Student Affairs — M
Supply Chain Management — M
Sustainability Management — O
Travel and Tourism — M

TABOR COLLEGE
Accounting — M
Business Administration and Management—General — M

TAFT UNIVERSITY SYSTEM
Education—General — M
Law — M,D
Legal and Justice Studies — M,D
Taxation — M,D

TARLETON STATE UNIVERSITY
Accounting — M
Athletic Training and Sports Medicine — M
Business Administration and Management—General — M
Curriculum and Instruction — M
Education—General — M,D,O
Educational Leadership and Administration — M,D,O
Educational Media/Instructional Technology — M
Elementary Education — M
Human Resources Management — M
Kinesiology and Movement Studies — M
Management Information Systems — M
Marketing — M
Music Education — M
Secondary Education — M
Social Work — M
Special Education — M

TAYLOR COLLEGE AND SEMINARY
English as a Second Language — M,O

TAYLOR UNIVERSITY
Higher Education — M

TEACHERS COLLEGE, COLUMBIA UNIVERSITY
Adult Education — M,D
Art Education — M,D,O
Computer Education — M,D
Curriculum and Instruction — M,D
Early Childhood Education — M,D
Education of Students with Severe/Multiple Disabilities — M,D,O
Education—General — M,D
Educational Leadership and Administration — M,D
Educational Measurement and Evaluation — M,D
Educational Media/Instructional Technology — M,D
Educational Policy — M,D
Educational Psychology — M,D,O
Elementary Education — M,D
English as a Second Language — M,D,O
English Education — M,D,O
Foundations and Philosophy of Education — M,D,O
Health Education — M,D,O
Higher Education — M,D
International and Comparative Education — M,D
Kinesiology and Movement Studies — M,D
Mathematics Education — M,D
Multilingual and Multicultural Education — M,D,O
Music Education — M,D,O
Physical Education — M,D
Reading Education — M,D,O
Science Education — M,D
Secondary Education — M,D
Social Sciences Education — M,D,O
Special Education — M,D,O
Urban Education — M,D

TEACHERS COLLEGE OF SAN JOAQUIN
Early Childhood Education — M
Education—General — M
Educational Leadership and Administration — M
Educational Measurement and Evaluation — M
Mathematics Education — M
Science Education — M
Special Education — M

TÉLÉ-UNIVERSITÉ
Distance Education Development — M,D
Finance and Banking — M,D

TEMPLE UNIVERSITY
Accounting — M,D
Actuarial Science — M
Art Education — M
Athletic Training and Sports Medicine — M,D
Business Administration and Management—General — M,D
Business Education — M
Education—General — M,D,O
Educational Leadership and Administration — M,D
Educational Psychology — M,D,O
English as a Second Language — M
English Education — M
Entrepreneurship — M,D
Finance and Banking — M,D
Hospitality Management — M,D
Human Resources Management — M
Insurance — D
International Business — M,D
Investment Management — M,O
Kinesiology and Movement Studies — M
Law — M,D,O
Legal and Justice Studies — M,D

Management Information Systems — M,D
Management Strategy and Policy — D
Marketing — M,D
Mathematics Education — M
Middle School Education — M
Music Education — M,D
Physical Education — M
Recreation and Park Management — M,D
Risk Management — D
Science Education — M
Secondary Education — M
Social Sciences Education — M
Social Work — M
Sports Management — M,D
Taxation — M
Transportation Management — M,O
Travel and Tourism — M,D
Urban Education — M
Vocational and Technical Education — M

TENNESSEE STATE UNIVERSITY
Agricultural Education — M,D
Business Administration and Management—General — M
Curriculum and Instruction — M,D
Education—General — M,D,O
Elementary Education — M,D
Exercise and Sports Science — M
Human Resources Management — M,D
Management Strategy and Policy — M
Physical Education — M
Social Work — M
Special Education — M,D
Sports Management — M

TENNESSEE TECHNOLOGICAL UNIVERSITY
Accounting — M
Business Administration and Management—General — M
Curriculum and Instruction — M,O
Early Childhood Education — M,O
Education of the Gifted — D
Education—General — M,D,O
Educational Leadership and Administration — M,O
Educational Measurement and Evaluation — D
Educational Media/Instructional Technology — M,O
Educational Psychology — M,O
Elementary Education — M,O
English as a Second Language — M
Finance and Banking — M
Health Education — M
Human Resources Management — M
International Business — M
Kinesiology and Movement Studies — M
Library Science — M,O
Management Information Systems — M
Management Strategy and Policy — M
Mathematics Education — M,O
Middle School Education — M
Music Education — M
Physical Education — M
Reading Education — M,D,O
Science Education — M,O
Secondary Education — M,O
Special Education — M,O
Sports Management — M

TENNESSEE WESLEYAN UNIVERSITY
Accounting — M
Business Administration and Management—General — M

TEXAS A&M INTERNATIONAL UNIVERSITY
Accounting — M
Business Administration and Management—General — M,D
Counselor Education — M
Curriculum and Instruction — M
Education—General — M
Educational Leadership and Administration — M
Finance and Banking — M
Foreign Languages Education — M,D
International Business — M,D
Management Information Systems — M,D
Special Education — M

TEXAS A&M UNIVERSITY
Accounting — M
Agricultural Education — M,D
Athletic Training and Sports Medicine — M,D
Business Administration and Management—General — M
Curriculum and Instruction — M,D
Education—General — M,D
Educational Leadership and Administration — M,D
Educational Media/Instructional Technology — M,D
Educational Psychology — M,D
Entrepreneurship — M
Finance and Banking — M
Health Education — M,D
Human Resources Development — M
Human Resources Management — M
Intellectual Property Law — M
Kinesiology and Movement Studies — M,D
Law — M,D
Management Information Systems — M
Marketing — M
Multilingual and Multicultural Education — M,D
Nonprofit Management — M,O
Real Estate — M
Recreation and Park Management — M,D
Special Education — M,D
Sports Management — M,D
Transportation Management — M

TEXAS A&M UNIVERSITY–CENTRAL TEXAS
Accounting — M,O
Business Administration and Management—General — M,O
Counselor Education — M,O
Curriculum and Instruction — M,O
Educational Leadership and Administration — M,O
Educational Psychology — M,O
Human Resources Management — M,O
Management Information Systems — M,O

TEXAS A&M UNIVERSITY–COMMERCE
Accounting — M
Business Administration and Management—General — M
Business Analytics — M
Counselor Education — M,D,O
Curriculum and Instruction — M,D,O
Early Childhood Education — M,D,O
Education—General — M,D,O
Educational Leadership and Administration — M,D,O
Educational Media/Instructional Technology — M,D,O
Educational Psychology — M,D,O
Elementary Education — M,D,O
English as a Second Language — M,D,O
Exercise and Sports Science — M,D,O
Finance and Banking — M
Higher Education — M,D,O
Kinesiology and Movement Studies — M,D,O
Library Science — M,D,O
Marketing — M
Music Education — M,D,O
Reading Education — M,D,O
Secondary Education — M,D,O
Social Work — M,D,O
Special Education — M,D,O

TEXAS A&M UNIVERSITY–CORPUS CHRISTI
Accounting — M
Business Administration and Management—General — M
Counselor Education — M,D
Curriculum and Instruction — M,D
Early Childhood Education — M,D
Education—General — M,D
Educational Leadership and Administration — M,D
Educational Media/Instructional Technology — M,D
Elementary Education — M
Finance and Banking — M
International Business — M
Kinesiology and Movement Studies — M,D
Reading Education — M
Secondary Education — M
Special Education — M

TEXAS A&M UNIVERSITY–KINGSVILLE
Adult Education — M
Business Administration and Management—General — M
Counselor Education — M
Early Childhood Education — M
Education—General — M,D,O
Educational Leadership and Administration — M,D
Educational Media/Instructional Technology — M
English as a Second Language — M,D
Foreign Languages Education — M
Health Education — M
Industrial and Manufacturing Management — M
Kinesiology and Movement Studies — M
Multilingual and Multicultural Education — M,D
Music Education — M
Reading Education — M
Science Education — M
Special Education — M

TEXAS A&M UNIVERSITY–SAN ANTONIO
Accounting — M
Business Administration and Management—General — M
Counselor Education — M
Early Childhood Education — M
Education—General — M
Educational Leadership and Administration — M
Educational Measurement and Evaluation — M
Kinesiology and Movement Studies — M
Multilingual and Multicultural Education — M
Reading Education — M
Special Education — M

TEXAS A&M UNIVERSITY–TEXARKANA
Accounting — M
Adult Education — M
Business Administration and Management—General — M
Curriculum and Instruction — M
Education—General — M
Educational Leadership and Administration — M
Educational Media/Instructional Technology — M
Special Education — M

TEXAS CHRISTIAN UNIVERSITY
Accounting — M
Business Administration and Management—General — M
Counselor Education — M,D
Curriculum and Instruction — M,D
Education—General — M,D
Educational Leadership and Administration — M,D

Kinesiology and Movement Studies — M
Mathematics Education — M
Music Education — M,D
Reading Education — M
Science Education — M,D
Social Work — M
Special Education — M
Taxation — M

TEXAS HEALTH AND SCIENCE UNIVERSITY
Business Administration and Management—General — M,D

TEXAS LUTHERAN UNIVERSITY
Accounting — M

TEXAS SOUTHERN UNIVERSITY
Business Administration and Management—General — M
Counselor Education — M,D
Curriculum and Instruction — M,D
Education—General — M,D
Educational Leadership and Administration — M,D
Health Education — M
Higher Education — M,D
Human Services — M
Law — D
Management Information Systems — M
Multilingual and Multicultural Education — M,D
Physical Education — M
Secondary Education — M,D
Transportation Management — M

TEXAS STATE UNIVERSITY
Accounting — M
Adult Education — M,D
Agricultural Education — M
Athletic Training and Sports Medicine — M
Business Administration and Management—General — M
Counselor Education — M
Developmental Education — M,D
Early Childhood Education — M
Education—General — M,D,O
Educational Leadership and Administration — M,D
Educational Media/Instructional Technology — M
Elementary Education — M
Health Education — M
Higher Education — M
Human Resources Management — M
Legal and Justice Studies — M
Leisure Studies — M
Management Information Systems — M
Mathematics Education — M,D
Multilingual and Multicultural Education — M
Music Education — M
Physical Education — M
Reading Education — M
Recreation and Park Management — M
Secondary Education — M
Social Work — M
Special Education — M
Student Affairs — M
Vocational and Technical Education — M

TEXAS TECH UNIVERSITY
Accounting — M,D
Agricultural Education — M,D
Art Education — M
Business Administration and Management—General — M,D
Counselor Education — M,D
Curriculum and Instruction — M,D
Education—General — M,D
Educational Leadership and Administration — M,D
Educational Media/Instructional Technology — M,D
Educational Psychology — M,D
Elementary Education — M,D
Exercise and Sports Science — M,D
Finance and Banking — M,D
Higher Education — M,D
Home Economics Education — M,D
Hospitality Management — M,D
Kinesiology and Movement Studies — M,D
Law — M,D
Legal and Justice Studies — M,D
Management Information Systems — M,D
Marketing — M,D
Multilingual and Multicultural Education — M,D
Music Education — M,D
Reading Education — M,D
Science Education — M,D
Secondary Education — M,D
Social Sciences Education — M,D
Social Work — M,D
Special Education — M,D
Sports Management — M,D
Taxation — M,D

TEXAS TECH UNIVERSITY HEALTH SCIENCES CENTER
Athletic Training and Sports Medicine — M

TEXAS WESLEYAN UNIVERSITY
Business Administration and Management—General — M
Education—General — M,D

TEXAS WOMAN'S UNIVERSITY
Accounting — M
Art Education — M
Business Administration and Management—General — M
Business Analytics — M
Counselor Education — M,D
Curriculum and Instruction — M,D

Early Childhood Education	M,D
Education—General	M,D,O
Educational Leadership and Administration	M,D
English Education	M,D
Exercise and Sports Science	M,D
Health Education	M,D
Human Resources Management	M
Kinesiology and Movement Studies	M
Library Science	M
Mathematics Education	M
Music Education	M
Physical Education	M,D
Reading Education	M,D,O
Special Education	M,D
Sports Management	M,D

THEOLOGICAL UNIVERSITY OF THE CARIBBEAN
Early Childhood Education	M,D
Middle School Education	M,D

THOMAS COLLEGE
Business Administration and Management—General	M
Business Education	M
Computer Education	M
Human Resources Management	M

THOMAS EDISON STATE UNIVERSITY
Accounting	M
Business Administration and Management—General	M
Distance Education Development	M,O
Educational Leadership and Administration	M,O
Educational Media/Instructional Technology	M,O
Finance and Banking	M
Hospitality Management	M
Human Resources Management	M
International Business	M
Nonprofit Management	M
Organizational Management	M
Project Management	M

THOMAS JEFFERSON SCHOOL OF LAW
Law	D

THOMAS JEFFERSON UNIVERSITY
Athletic Training and Sports Medicine	M
Business Administration and Management—General	M
Business Analytics	M
Health Education	M,D,O
Management Strategy and Policy	M,D
Marketing	M
Real Estate	M
Taxation	M

THOMAS MORE COLLEGE
Business Administration and Management—General	M
Education—General	M
Educational Leadership and Administration	M

THOMAS UNIVERSITY
Business Administration and Management—General	M
Education—General	M
Human Services	M

THOMPSON RIVERS UNIVERSITY
Business Administration and Management—General	M
Education—General	M
Social Work	M

TIFFIN UNIVERSITY
Business Administration and Management—General	M
Education—General	M
Educational Leadership and Administration	M
Educational Media/Instructional Technology	M
Finance and Banking	M
Higher Education	M
Human Resources Management	M
International Business	M
Marketing	M
Nonprofit Management	M
Sports Management	M

TOURO COLLEGE
Education—General	M
Educational Leadership and Administration	M
Educational Media/Instructional Technology	M
English as a Second Language	M
Law	M,D
Legal and Justice Studies	M,D
Management Information Systems	M
Mathematics Education	M
Reading Education	M
Social Work	M
Special Education	M

TOURO UNIVERSITY CALIFORNIA
Education—General	M,D

TOWSON UNIVERSITY
Accounting	M
Art Education	M,O
Early Childhood Education	M,O
Education—General	M
Educational Leadership and Administration	M,O
Educational Media/Instructional Technology	M,O
Electronic Commerce	M,O
Elementary Education	

Human Resources Development	M
Human Resources Management	M
Marketing Research	M
Mathematics Education	M
Music Education	M
Reading Education	M
Secondary Education	M
Special Education	M,O
Supply Chain Management	M

TREVECCA NAZARENE UNIVERSITY
Business Administration and Management—General	M
Counselor Education	M,D
Curriculum and Instruction	M,O
Education—General	M,O
Educational Leadership and Administration	M,D,O
Educational Media/Instructional Technology	M
Elementary Education	M,O
English as a Second Language	M,O
Library Science	M,O
Organizational Management	M,D
Secondary Education	M,O
Special Education	M,O

TRIDENT UNIVERSITY INTERNATIONAL
Adult Education	M
Business Administration and Management—General	M,D
Early Childhood Education	M
Education—General	M,D
Educational Leadership and Administration	M,D
Educational Media/Instructional Technology	M,D
Finance and Banking	M,D,O
Health Education	M,D
Higher Education	M,D
Human Resources Management	M,D
International Business	M,D
Legal and Justice Studies	M,D,O
Logistics	M,D
Management Information Systems	M,D,O
Marketing	M,D
Project Management	M,D
Quality Management	M,D,O
Reading Education	M

TRINITY BAPTIST COLLEGE
Curriculum and Instruction	M
Educational Leadership and Administration	M
Special Education	M

TRINITY CHRISTIAN COLLEGE
Special Education	M

TRINITY INTERNATIONAL UNIVERSITY
Athletic Training and Sports Medicine	M
Business Administration and Management—General	M,D,O
Education—General	M
Human Resources Management	M,D
Law	M,D
Religious Education	M,D,O

TRINITY LUTHERAN SEMINARY
Religious Education	M

TRINITY UNIVERSITY
Accounting	M
Business Administration and Management—General	M
Education—General	M
Educational Leadership and Administration	M

TRINITY WASHINGTON UNIVERSITY
Business Administration and Management—General	M
Counselor Education	M
Curriculum and Instruction	M
Early Childhood Education	M
Education—General	M
Educational Leadership and Administration	M
Elementary Education	M
English Education	M
Human Resources Management	M
Nonprofit Management	M
Organizational Management	M
Reading Education	M
Secondary Education	M
Social Sciences Education	M
Special Education	M

TRINITY WESTERN UNIVERSITY
Business Administration and Management—General	M
Educational Leadership and Administration	M,O
English as a Second Language	M
International Business	M
Nonprofit Management	M,O
Organizational Management	M,O

TROPICAL AGRICULTURE RESEARCH AND HIGHER EDUCATION CENTER
Travel and Tourism	M,D

TROY UNIVERSITY
Accounting	M
Adult Education	M
Business Administration and Management—General	M
Counselor Education	M,O
Early Childhood Education	M,O
Education—General	M,O
Educational Leadership and Administration	M,O
Elementary Education	M
English as a Second Language	M

Finance and Banking	M
Human Resources Management	M
Management Information Systems	M
Secondary Education	M
Social Work	M
Sports Management	M,D

TRUETT MCCONNELL UNIVERSITY
Business Administration and Management—General	M

TRUMAN STATE UNIVERSITY
Accounting	M
Education—General	M

TUFTS UNIVERSITY
Art Education	M,D,O
Education—General	M,D,O
Elementary Education	M,D
Entrepreneurship	M
International Business	M,D
Law	M,D
Management Strategy and Policy	O
Mathematics Education	M,D
Middle School Education	M,D
Museum Education	M
Nonprofit Management	O
Organizational Management	M,D
Science Education	M,D
Secondary Education	M,D

TULANE UNIVERSITY
Accounting	M,D
Business Administration and Management—General	M,D
Business Analytics	M,D
Entrepreneurship	M,D
Finance and Banking	M,D
International Business	M,D
Law	M,D
Management Information Systems	M,D
Management Strategy and Policy	M,D
Social Work	M,D

TUSCULUM COLLEGE
Business Administration and Management—General	M
Curriculum and Instruction	M
Education—General	M
Human Resources Development	M
Special Education	M

TUSKEGEE UNIVERSITY
Management Information Systems	M

UNIFICATION THEOLOGICAL SEMINARY
Religious Education	M,D

UNION COLLEGE (KY)
Education—General	M
Educational Leadership and Administration	M
Elementary Education	M
Health Education	M
Middle School Education	M
Music Education	M
Physical Education	M
Reading Education	M
Secondary Education	M
Special Education	M

UNION INSTITUTE & UNIVERSITY
Education—General	D
Organizational Management	M

UNION PRESBYTERIAN SEMINARY
Religious Education	M,D

UNION UNIVERSITY
Accounting	M
Business Administration and Management—General	M
Education—General	M,D,O
Educational Leadership and Administration	M,D,O
Higher Education	M,D,O
Social Work	M

UNITED STATES INTERNATIONAL UNIVERSITY–AFRICA
Business Administration and Management—General	M
Entrepreneurship	M
Finance and Banking	M
Human Resources Management	M
International Business	M
Management Information Systems	M
Management Strategy and Policy	M
Marketing	M
Organizational Management	M

UNITED STATES SPORTS ACADEMY
Exercise and Sports Science	M
Physical Education	M
Recreation and Park Management	M
Sports Management	M,D

UNIVERSIDAD ADVENTISTA DE LAS ANTILLAS
Curriculum and Instruction	M
Educational Leadership and Administration	M

UNIVERSIDAD AUTONOMA DE GUADALAJARA
Advertising and Public Relations	M,D
Business Administration and Management—General	M,D
Education—General	M,D
Entertainment Management	M,D
International Business	M,D
Law	M,D
Legal and Justice Studies	M,D
Marketing Research	M,D
Mathematics Education	M,D

UNIVERSIDAD CENTRAL DEL ESTE
Finance and Banking	M
Higher Education	M
Human Resources Development	M
Law	D

UNIVERSIDAD DE IBEROAMERICA
Educational Psychology	M

UNIVERSIDAD DE LAS AMERICAS, A.C.
Business Administration and Management—General	M
Education—General	M
Finance and Banking	M
Marketing Research	M
Organizational Behavior	M
Quality Management	M

UNIVERSIDAD DE LAS AMÉRICAS PUEBLA
Business Administration and Management—General	M
Education—General	M
Finance and Banking	M
Industrial and Manufacturing Management	M

UNIVERSIDAD DEL ESTE
Accounting	M
Adult Education	M
Business Administration and Management—General	M
Electronic Commerce	M
Elementary Education	M
English as a Second Language	M
Foreign Languages Education	M
Human Resources Management	M
Management Information Systems	M
Management Strategy and Policy	M
Social Work	M
Special Education	M

UNIVERSIDAD DEL TURABO
Accounting	M
Athletic Training and Sports Medicine	M
Business Administration and Management—General	M,D
Counselor Education	M,D
Curriculum and Instruction	M
Early Childhood Education	M,D
Education—General	M,D
Educational Leadership and Administration	M,D
English as a Second Language	M
Human Resources Management	M
Human Services	M
Information Studies	M
Library Science	M
Logistics	D
Management Information Systems	M
Marketing	M
Physical Education	M
Project Management	M
Quality Management	M
Special Education	M

UNIVERSIDAD IBEROAMERICANA
Business Administration and Management—General	M,D
Educational Leadership and Administration	M,D
Human Resources Development	M,D
Law	M,D
Marketing	M,D
Real Estate	M,D
Special Education	M,D

UNIVERSIDAD METROPOLITANA
Accounting	M
Adult Education	M
Business Administration and Management—General	M
Curriculum and Instruction	M
Education—General	M
Educational Leadership and Administration	M,D
Elementary Education	M,D
Finance and Banking	M
Human Resources Management	M
International Business	M
Leisure Studies	M
Management Information Systems	M
Marketing	M
Physical Education	M
Recreation and Park Management	M
Secondary Education	M
Special Education	M

UNIVERSIDAD NACIONAL PEDRO HENRIQUEZ URENA
Project Management	M
Science Education	M

UNIVERSITÉ DE MONCTON
Business Administration and Management—General	M
Counselor Education	M
Education—General	M
Educational Leadership and Administration	M
Educational Psychology	M
Social Work	M

UNIVERSITÉ DE MONTRÉAL
Curriculum and Instruction	M,D,O
Education—General	M,D,O
Educational Leadership and Administration	M,D,O
Educational Psychology	M,D,O
Electronic Commerce	D
Human Services	M,D
Information Studies	M,D
Kinesiology and Movement Studies	M,D,O

*M—masters degree; D—doctorate; O—other advanced degree; *—Close-Up and/or Display*

Law	M,D,O
Library Science	M,D
Physical Education	M,D,O
Social Work	O
Taxation	M,D,O

UNIVERSITÉ DE SAINT-BONIFACE

Education—General	M

UNIVERSITÉ DE SHERBROOKE

Accounting	M
Business Administration and Management—General	M,D
Education—General	M,O
Educational Leadership and Administration	M
Electronic Commerce	M
Elementary Education	M,O
Finance and Banking	M
Health Law	M,D,O
Higher Education	M
International Business	M
Kinesiology and Movement Studies	M,D,O
Law	M,D,O
Management Information Systems	M,O
Marketing	M
Organizational Behavior	M
Physical Education	M,O
Social Work	M
Special Education	M
Taxation	M

UNIVERSITÉ DU QUÉBEC À CHICOUTIMI

Business Administration and Management—General	M
Education—General	M,D
Project Management	M

UNIVERSITÉ DU QUÉBEC À MONTRÉAL

Accounting	M,O
Actuarial Science	O
Business Administration and Management—General	M,D,O
Education—General	M,D,O
Environmental Education	M,O
Finance and Banking	O
Kinesiology and Movement Studies	M,O
Law	O
Management Information Systems	M
Project Management	M,O
Social Work	M

UNIVERSITÉ DU QUÉBEC À RIMOUSKI

Business Administration and Management—General	M,O
Education—General	M,D,O
Project Management	M,O

UNIVERSITÉ DU QUÉBEC À TROIS-RIVIÈRES

Accounting	M
Business Administration and Management—General	M,D
Education—General	M,D
Educational Leadership and Administration	O
Educational Psychology	M,D
Finance and Banking	O
Leisure Studies	M,O
Physical Education	M
Travel and Tourism	M,O

UNIVERSITÉ DU QUÉBEC, ÉCOLE NATIONALE D'ADMINISTRATION PUBLIQUE

International Business	M,O

UNIVERSITÉ DU QUÉBEC EN ABITIBI-TÉMISCAMINGUE

Business Administration and Management—General	M
Education—General	M,D,O
Project Management	M,O
Social Work	M

UNIVERSITÉ DU QUÉBEC EN OUTAOUAIS

Accounting	M,O
Education—General	M
Educational Psychology	M
Finance and Banking	M,O
Foreign Languages Education	O
Project Management	M,O
Social Work	M

UNIVERSITÉ LAVAL

Accounting	M,O
Advertising and Public Relations	O
Business Administration and Management—General	M,D,O
Counselor Education	M,D
Curriculum and Instruction	M,D
Education—General	M,D,O
Educational Leadership and Administration	M,D,O
Educational Measurement and Evaluation	M,D,O
Educational Media/Instructional Technology	M,D
Educational Psychology	M,D
Electronic Commerce	M,O
Entrepreneurship	M,O
Facilities Management	M,O
Finance and Banking	M,O
International Business	M,O
Kinesiology and Movement Studies	M,D
Law	M,D,O
Legal and Justice Studies	O
Management Information Systems	M,O
Marketing	M,D
Music Education	M,D
Organizational Management	M,D
Social Work	M,D

UNIVERSITÉ SAINTE-ANNE

Education—General	M

UNIVERSITY AT ALBANY, STATE UNIVERSITY OF NEW YORK

Business Administration and Management—General	M
Business Analytics	M
Curriculum and Instruction	M,D,O
Education—General	M,D,O
Educational Leadership and Administration	M,D,O
Educational Media/Instructional Technology	M,D,O
Educational Policy	M,D,O
Entrepreneurship	M
Finance and Banking	M,D,O
Higher Education	M,D,O
Human Resources Management	M,D,O
International and Comparative Education	M,D,O
Management Information Systems	M,D,O
Marketing	M
Nonprofit Management	M,D,O
Organizational Behavior	M,D,O
Reading Education	M,D,O
Social Work	M

UNIVERSITY AT BUFFALO, THE STATE UNIVERSITY OF NEW YORK

Accounting	M,D
Business Administration and Management—General	M,D
Business Analytics	M,D
Counselor Education	M,D,O
Curriculum and Instruction	M,D,O
Distance Education Development	M,D,O
Early Childhood Education	M,D,O
Education of the Gifted	M,D,O
Education—General	M,D,O
Educational Leadership and Administration	M,D,O
Educational Media/Instructional Technology	M,D,O
Educational Psychology	M,D,O
Electronic Commerce	M,D,O
Elementary Education	M,D,O
English as a Second Language	M,D,O
English Education	M,D,O
Environmental Law	M,D
Exercise and Sports Science	M,D
Finance and Banking	M,D
Foreign Languages Education	M,D,O
Foundations and Philosophy of Education	M,D,O
Higher Education	M,D,O
Human Resources Management	M,D,O
Information Studies	M,D
International Business	M,D
Law	M,D
Legal and Justice Studies	M,D
Library Science	M,O
Logistics	M,D
Management Information Systems	M,D,O
Marketing	M,D
Mathematics Education	M,D,O
Multilingual and Multicultural Education	M,D,O
Music Education	M,D
Quantitative Analysis	M,D
Reading Education	M,D,O
Real Estate	M,D
Science Education	M,D,O
Social Sciences Education	M,D,O
Social Work	M,D
Special Education	M,D,O
Supply Chain Management	M,D
Transportation Management	M

THE UNIVERSITY OF AKRON

Accounting	M
Art Education	M
Business Administration and Management—General	M
Counselor Education	M,D
Curriculum and Instruction	M
Education—General	M
Educational Leadership and Administration	M
Educational Measurement and Evaluation	M,O
Educational Media/Instructional Technology	M
Elementary Education	M
English Education	M
Exercise and Sports Science	M
Finance and Banking	M
Higher Education	M
International Business	M
Law	M,D
Management Information Systems	M
Marketing	M
Mathematics Education	M
Music Education	M
Physical Education	M
Reading Education	M
Science Education	M
Secondary Education	M
Social Sciences Education	M
Social Work	M
Special Education	M
Supply Chain Management	M
Taxation	M

THE UNIVERSITY OF ALABAMA

Accounting	M,D
Business Administration and Management—General	M,D
Counselor Education	M,D,O
Education of the Gifted	M,D,O
Educational Leadership and Administration	M,D,O
Elementary Education	M,D,O
English as a Second Language	M,D
Exercise and Sports Science	M,D
Finance and Banking	M,D
Health Education	M,D
Higher Education	M,D

Hospitality Management	M
Industrial and Manufacturing Management	M,D
Information Studies	M,D
Kinesiology and Movement Studies	M,D
Law	M,D
Library Science	M,D
Marketing	M,D
Music Education	M,D,O
Physical Education	M,D
Quality Management	M
Secondary Education	M,D,O
Social Work	M,D
Special Education	M,D,O
Sports Management	M,D
Taxation	M,D

THE UNIVERSITY OF ALABAMA AT BIRMINGHAM

Accounting	M
Art Education	M
Business Administration and Management—General	M
Counselor Education	M
Curriculum and Instruction	O
Early Childhood Education	M,D
Education—General	M,D,O
Educational Leadership and Administration	M,D,O
Elementary Education	M
English as a Second Language	M,O
Finance and Banking	M
Health Education	D
Management Information Systems	M
Marketing	M
Quantitative Analysis	M,D
Reading Education	M
Secondary Education	M
Special Education	M

THE UNIVERSITY OF ALABAMA IN HUNTSVILLE

Accounting	M,O
Business Administration and Management—General	M,O
Business Analytics	M,O
Education—General	M,O
English as a Second Language	M,O
English Education	M,O
Entrepreneurship	M,O
Finance and Banking	M,O
Human Resources Management	M,O
Logistics	M,O
Management Information Systems	M,O
Marketing	M,O
Mathematics Education	M,D,O
Project Management	M,O
Reading Education	M,O
Science Education	M,D,O
Secondary Education	M,O
Social Sciences Education	M,O
Special Education	M,O
Supply Chain Management	M,O
Taxation	M

UNIVERSITY OF ALASKA ANCHORAGE

Business Administration and Management—General	M
Counselor Education	M
Early Childhood Education	M,O
Education—General	M,O
Educational Leadership and Administration	M,O
Logistics	M,O
Project Management	M
Social Work	M,O
Special Education	M,O

UNIVERSITY OF ALASKA FAIRBANKS

Business Administration and Management—General	M
Counselor Education	M,O
Education—General	M,O
Finance and Banking	M
Multilingual and Multicultural Education	M
Special Education	M

UNIVERSITY OF ALASKA SOUTHEAST

Education—General	M
Educational Leadership and Administration	M
Educational Media/Instructional Technology	M
Elementary Education	M
Mathematics Education	M
Reading Education	M
Secondary Education	M
Special Education	M

UNIVERSITY OF ALBERTA

Accounting	D
Adult Education	M,D,O
Business Administration and Management—General	M,D
Counselor Education	M,D
Educational Leadership and Administration	M,D,O
Educational Media/Instructional Technology	M,D
Educational Policy	M,D,O
Educational Psychology	M,D
Elementary Education	M,D
English as a Second Language	M,D
Exercise and Sports Science	M,D
Finance and Banking	M
Information Studies	M
International Business	M,D
Law	M,D
Library Science	M,D
Marketing	D
Multilingual and Multicultural Education	M
Organizational Management	D
Physical Education	M,D
Recreation and Park Management	M,D

Secondary Education	M,D
Special Education	M,D
Sports Management	M

UNIVERSITY OF ANTELOPE VALLEY

Business Administration and Management—General	M

THE UNIVERSITY OF ARIZONA

Accounting	M
Agricultural Education	M,O
Art Education	M,D
Business Administration and Management—General	M,D,O
Counselor Education	M
Education—General	M,D,O
Educational Leadership and Administration	M,D,O
Educational Psychology	M,D,O
Elementary Education	M,D
English as a Second Language	M,D
English Education	M,D
Finance and Banking	M
Higher Education	M,D
Information Studies	M,D
Law	M,D
Library Science	M,D
Management Information Systems	M,D
Management Strategy and Policy	M
Marketing	M,D
Mathematics Education	M,D
Music Education	M,D
Organizational Management	M,D
Reading Education	M,D,O
Secondary Education	M,D
Special Education	M,D

UNIVERSITY OF ARKANSAS

Accounting	M
Adult Education	M,D
Agricultural Education	M
Athletic Training and Sports Medicine	M
Business Administration and Management—General	M,D
Counselor Education	M,D
Curriculum and Instruction	M,D,O
Early Childhood Education	M
Education—General	M,D,O
Educational Leadership and Administration	M,D,O
Educational Measurement and Evaluation	M,D
Educational Media/Instructional Technology	M
Educational Policy	D
Health Education	M,D
Higher Education	M,D,O
Human Resources Development	M,D,O
Industrial and Manufacturing Management	M
Kinesiology and Movement Studies	M,D
Law	M
Management Information Systems	M
Mathematics Education	M
Middle School Education	M,D,O
Physical Education	M
Recreation and Park Management	M,D
Secondary Education	M,O
Social Work	M
Special Education	M,O
Sports Management	M,D
Vocational and Technical Education	M,D,O

UNIVERSITY OF ARKANSAS AT LITTLE ROCK

Adult Education	M
Art Education	M
Business Administration and Management—General	M,O
Community College Education	M,D
Counselor Education	M
Curriculum and Instruction	M
Education of the Gifted	M,O
Education—General	M,D,O
Educational Leadership and Administration	M,D,O
Educational Media/Instructional Technology	M
English as a Second Language	M
Entrepreneurship	O
Exercise and Sports Science	M
Foreign Languages Education	M
Health Education	M,D
Higher Education	M,D
Law	D
Management Information Systems	M,O
Middle School Education	M
Nonprofit Management	O
Reading Education	M,D,O
Secondary Education	M
Social Work	M
Special Education	M,O
Sports Management	M
Student Affairs	M,D

UNIVERSITY OF ARKANSAS AT MONTICELLO

Education—General	M
Educational Leadership and Administration	M

UNIVERSITY OF ARKANSAS AT PINE BLUFF

Education—General	M
Elementary Education	M
English Education	M
Mathematics Education	M
Science Education	M
Secondary Education	M
Social Sciences Education	M

UNIVERSITY OF ARKANSAS FOR MEDICAL SCIENCES

Health Education	M,D,O

UNIVERSITY OF BALTIMORE

Accounting	M,O
Business Administration and Management—General	M,O
Entrepreneurship	M
Finance and Banking	M
Human Services	M
Intellectual Property Law	M,D
International Business	M,D
Law	M
Legal and Justice Studies	M,O
Management Information Systems	M,O
Marketing	M
Taxation	M,D

UNIVERSITY OF BRIDGEPORT

Accounting	M
Business Administration and Management—General	M
Computer Education	M,D,O
Early Childhood Education	M,D,O
Education—General	M,D,O
Educational Leadership and Administration	M,D,O
Elementary Education	M,D,O
Entrepreneurship	M
Finance and Banking	M
Human Resources Development	M
Human Resources Management	M
Human Services	M
Industrial and Manufacturing Management	M
International and Comparative Education	M,D,O
International Business	M
Management Information Systems	M
Marketing	M
Middle School Education	M,D,O
Music Education	M,D,O
Reading Education	M,D,O
Secondary Education	M,D,O
Student Affairs	M

THE UNIVERSITY OF BRITISH COLUMBIA

Accounting	D
Adult Education	M,D
Archives/Archival Administration	M,D
Art Education	M,D
Business Administration and Management—General	M,D
Business Analytics	M
Curriculum and Instruction	M,D
Education—General	M,D,O
Educational Leadership and Administration	M,D
Educational Measurement and Evaluation	M,D,O
Educational Policy	M,D
English as a Second Language	M,D
Finance and Banking	D
Foundations and Philosophy of Education	M,D
Higher Education	M,D
Home Economics Education	M,D
Information Studies	M,D
Kinesiology and Movement Studies	M,D
Law	M,D
Library Science	M,D
Management Information Systems	D
Management Strategy and Policy	D
Marketing	D
Mathematics Education	M,D
Music Education	M,D
Organizational Behavior	D
Physical Education	M,D
Quantitative Analysis	M,D
Reading Education	M,D
Science Education	M,D
Social Sciences Education	M,D
Social Work	M,D
Special Education	M,D,O
Sustainability Management	M,D
Taxation	D
Transportation Management	D
Vocational and Technical Education	M,D

UNIVERSITY OF CALGARY

Adult Education	M,D
Business Administration and Management—General	M,D
Curriculum and Instruction	M,D
Educational Leadership and Administration	M,D
Educational Measurement and Evaluation	M,D
Environmental Law	M,O
Kinesiology and Movement Studies	M,D
Law	M,D,O
Legal and Justice Studies	M,O
Management Strategy and Policy	M,D
Multilingual and Multicultural Education	M,D
Project Management	M
Social Work	M,D,O

UNIVERSITY OF CALIFORNIA, BERKELEY

Accounting	D,O
Business Administration and Management—General	M,D,O
Education—General	M,D,O
Educational Leadership and Administration	M,D
English as a Second Language	O
Facilities Management	O
Finance and Banking	D,O
Human Resources Management	O
Information Studies	M,D
International Business	O
Law	M,D
Legal and Justice Studies	D

UNIVERSITY OF CALIFORNIA, DAVIS

Accounting	M
Business Administration and Management—General	M
Business Analytics	M,D
Curriculum and Instruction	M,D
Education—General	M,D
Educational Psychology	M,D
Entrepreneurship	M
Exercise and Sports Science	M
Finance and Banking	M
Law	M,D
Management Strategy and Policy	M
Marketing	M
Organizational Behavior	M
Transportation Management	M,D

UNIVERSITY OF CALIFORNIA, HASTINGS COLLEGE OF THE LAW

Law	M

UNIVERSITY OF CALIFORNIA, IRVINE

Accounting	M
Business Administration and Management—General	M,D
Education—General	M,D
Educational Leadership and Administration	M,D
Elementary Education	M,D
Foreign Languages Education	M,D
Law	D
Secondary Education	M,D

UNIVERSITY OF CALIFORNIA, LOS ANGELES

Accounting	M,D
Archives/Archival Administration	M,D,O
Business Administration and Management—General	M,D
Business Analytics	M,D
Education—General	M,D
Educational Leadership and Administration	D
English as a Second Language	M,D,O
Finance and Banking	M,D
Information Studies	M,D,O
Law	M,D
Library Science	M,D,O
Management Strategy and Policy	M,D
Marketing	M,D
Social Work	M,D
Special Education	D

UNIVERSITY OF CALIFORNIA, MERCED

Entrepreneurship	M
Sustainability Management	M,D

UNIVERSITY OF CALIFORNIA, RIVERSIDE

Accounting	M,D
Archives/Archival Administration	M,D
Business Administration and Management—General	M,D
Education—General	M,D,O
Educational Leadership and Administration	M,D
Educational Measurement and Evaluation	M,D,O
Educational Policy	M,D,O
Educational Psychology	M,D,O
English as a Second Language	M,D,O
Finance and Banking	M,D
Foundations and Philosophy of Education	M,D,O
Higher Education	M,D,O
Multilingual and Multicultural Education	M,D,O
Special Education	M,D,O

UNIVERSITY OF CALIFORNIA, SAN DIEGO

Business Administration and Management—General	M,D
Business Analytics	M,D
Curriculum and Instruction	M,D
Education—General	M,D
Educational Leadership and Administration	M,D
Finance and Banking	M,D
International Business	M
Mathematics Education	D
Multilingual and Multicultural Education	M,D
Nonprofit Management	M
Science Education	D

UNIVERSITY OF CALIFORNIA, SAN FRANCISCO

Health Law	M

UNIVERSITY OF CALIFORNIA, SANTA BARBARA

Education—General	M,D,O
Finance and Banking	M,D
Quantitative Analysis	M,D
Transportation Management	M,D

UNIVERSITY OF CALIFORNIA, SANTA CRUZ

Education—General	M,D
Finance and Banking	M
Management Information Systems	D
Social Sciences Education	M

UNIVERSITY OF CENTRAL ARKANSAS

Accounting	M,O
Adult Education	M,O
Business Administration and Management—General	M
Counselor Education	M
Curriculum and Instruction	M,O
Education of the Gifted	M,O
Education—General	M,O
Educational Leadership and Administration	M,O
Educational Media/Instructional Technology	M
Foreign Languages Education	M
Health Education	M
Kinesiology and Movement Studies	M
Library Science	M
Mathematics Education	M
Music Education	M
Organizational Management	D
Reading Education	M
Special Education	M,O
Student Affairs	M

UNIVERSITY OF CENTRAL FLORIDA

Accounting	M
Art Education	M
Business Administration and Management—General	M,D,O
Community College Education	M,O
Counselor Education	M,D,O
Curriculum and Instruction	M,D,O
Early Childhood Education	D
Educational Leadership and Administration	M,D,O
Educational Media/Instructional Technology	M,D,O
Elementary Education	M,D
English as a Second Language	M,D,O
English Education	M,D
Entrepreneurship	M,O
Exercise and Sports Science	M,D
Foreign Languages Education	M,O
Higher Education	M,D,O
Hospitality Management	M,D,O
Mathematics Education	M
Middle School Education	M
Nonprofit Management	M,O
Quality Management	M,D,O
Reading Education	M,D,O
Real Estate	M
Science Education	M,D,O
Social Sciences Education	M,D
Social Work	M,O
Special Education	M,O
Sports Management	M
Student Affairs	M,O
Travel and Tourism	M,D,O
Vocational and Technical Education	M,D,O

UNIVERSITY OF CENTRAL MISSOURI

Accounting	M,D,O
Business Administration and Management—General	M,D,O
Counselor Education	M,D,O
Early Childhood Education	M,D,O
Education—General	M,D,O
Educational Leadership and Administration	M,D,O
Educational Media/Instructional Technology	M,D,O
Elementary Education	M,D,O
English as a Second Language	M,D,O
Finance and Banking	M,D,O
Human Services	M,D,O
Industrial and Manufacturing Management	M,D,O
Kinesiology and Movement Studies	M,D,O
Library Science	M,D,O
Management Information Systems	M,D,O
Marketing	M,D,O
Reading Education	M,D,O
Special Education	M,D,O
Student Affairs	M,D,O
Vocational and Technical Education	M,D,O

UNIVERSITY OF CENTRAL OKLAHOMA

Adult Education	M
Athletic Training and Sports Medicine	M
Business Analytics	M
Counselor Education	M
Early Childhood Education	M
Education—General	M
Educational Leadership and Administration	M
Educational Media/Instructional Technology	M
Elementary Education	M
English as a Second Language	M
Exercise and Sports Science	M
Foundations and Philosophy of Education	M
Library Science	M
Music Education	M
Nonprofit Management	M
Reading Education	M
Secondary Education	M
Special Education	M
Student Affairs	M

UNIVERSITY OF CHARLESTON

Accounting	M
Business Administration and Management—General	M
Legal and Justice Studies	M
Management Strategy and Policy	M
Organizational Management	D

UNIVERSITY OF CHICAGO

Accounting	M,O

UNIVERSITY OF CINCINNATI (continued)

Business Administration and Management—General	M,D,O
Entrepreneurship	M,O
Finance and Banking	M,O
Industrial and Manufacturing Management	M,O
International Business	M,O
Law	M,D
Management Strategy and Policy	M,O
Marketing	M,O
Organizational Behavior	M,O
Science Education	D
Social Work	M,D
Urban Education	M

UNIVERSITY OF CINCINNATI

Accounting	M,D
Art Education	M
Business Administration and Management—General	M,D
Business Analytics	M,D
Counselor Education	M,D,O
Curriculum and Instruction	M,D
Education—General	M,D,O
Educational Leadership and Administration	M,D,O
English as a Second Language	M,D
Finance and Banking	M,D
Foundations and Philosophy of Education	M,D
Health Education	M,D
Human Resources Management	M
Industrial and Manufacturing Management	D
Law	M,D
Management Information Systems	M,D
Marketing	M,D
Mathematics Education	M,D
Music Education	M
Organizational Management	M
Reading Education	M
Social Work	M
Special Education	M
Sports Management	M
Taxation	M

UNIVERSITY OF COLORADO BOULDER

Advertising and Public Relations	M,D
Business Administration and Management—General	M,D
Curriculum and Instruction	M,D
Education—General	M,D
Educational Measurement and Evaluation	D
Educational Policy	M,D
Educational Psychology	M,D
Kinesiology and Movement Studies	M,D
Law	D
Multilingual and Multicultural Education	M,D
Music Education	M,D
Organizational Management	

UNIVERSITY OF COLORADO COLORADO SPRINGS

Business Administration and Management—General	M
Counselor Education	M,D
Curriculum and Instruction	M,D
Education—General	M,D
Educational Leadership and Administration	M,D
English as a Second Language	M,D
Human Services	M,D
Special Education	M,D

UNIVERSITY OF COLORADO DENVER

Accounting	M
Adult Education	M
Business Administration and Management—General	M
Counselor Education	M
Distance Education Development	M
Early Childhood Education	M
Education—General	M,D,O
Educational Leadership and Administration	M,D,O
Educational Measurement and Evaluation	M,D,O
Educational Media/Instructional Technology	M
Educational Policy	D
Educational Psychology	M,D,O
Elementary Education	M
English Education	M
Entertainment Management	M
Entrepreneurship	M
Environmental Education	M
Environmental Law	M,D
Finance and Banking	M
Health Education	M
Human Resources Management	M
Insurance	M
International Business	M
Investment Management	M
Management Information Systems	M,D
Management Strategy and Policy	M
Marketing Research	M
Marketing	M
Mathematics Education	M,D
Multilingual and Multicultural Education	M
Nonprofit Management	M
Quantitative Analysis	M
Reading Education	M
Risk Management	M
Science Education	M,D
Secondary Education	M
Special Education	M,D
Sports Management	M
Sustainability Management	M
Taxation	M

*M—masters degree; D—doctorate; O—other advanced degree; *—Close-Up and/or Display*

UNIVERSITY OF CONNECTICUT

Accounting	M
Adult Education	M,O
Agricultural Education	M,D
Business Administration and Management—General	M,D*
Counselor Education	M,D
Curriculum and Instruction	M,D
Education of the Gifted	O
Education—General	M,D
Educational Leadership and Administration	M
Educational Media/Instructional Technology	M,D
Educational Psychology	M,D,O
Elementary Education	M,D
English Education	M,D
Exercise and Sports Science	M,D
Finance and Banking	M,D,O
Foreign Languages Education	M,D
Higher Education	M
Human Resources Management	M
Law	D
Marketing	M,D
Mathematics Education	M,D
Multilingual and Multicultural Education	M,D
Music Education	M,D
Nonprofit Management	M,O
Quantitative Analysis	M,O
Reading Education	M,D
Science Education	M,D
Secondary Education	M,D
Social Sciences Education	M,D
Social Work	M,D
Sports Management	M

UNIVERSITY OF DALLAS

Accounting	M,D
Business Administration and Management—General	M,D
Business Analytics	M,D
Entertainment Management	M,D
Finance and Banking	M,D
Human Resources Management	M,D
International Business	M,D
Logistics	M,D
Management Information Systems	M,D
Management Strategy and Policy	M,D
Marketing	M,D
Organizational Management	M,D
Project Management	M,D
Sports Management	M,D
Supply Chain Management	M,D

UNIVERSITY OF DAYTON

Accounting	M
Business Administration and Management—General	M
Counselor Education	M,O
Early Childhood Education	M
Educational Leadership and Administration	M,D,O
Educational Media/Instructional Technology	M
Elementary Education	M
English as a Second Language	M
Exercise and Sports Science	M
Finance and Banking	M
Foreign Languages Education	M
Law	M,D
Marketing	M
Mathematics Education	M
Middle School Education	M
Music Education	M
Physical Education	M
Reading Education	M
Secondary Education	M
Student Affairs	M,O

UNIVERSITY OF DELAWARE

Accounting	M
Agricultural Education	M
Business Administration and Management—General	M,D
Business Education	M,D
Curriculum and Instruction	M,D,O
Education—General	M,D,O
Educational Leadership and Administration	M,D,O
English as a Second Language	M,D,O
Entrepreneurship	M
Finance and Banking	M
Foreign Languages Education	M
Higher Education	M,D,O
Hospitality Management	M
Kinesiology and Movement Studies	M,D
Management Information Systems	M,D
Multilingual and Multicultural Education	M,D,O
Music Education	M

UNIVERSITY OF DENVER

Accounting	M
Art Education	M,O
Business Administration and Management—General	M
Curriculum and Instruction	M,D,O
Early Childhood Education	M,D,O
Education—General	M,D,O
Educational Leadership and Administration	M,D,O
Educational Measurement and Evaluation	M,D,O
Educational Policy	M,D,O
Finance and Banking	M
Higher Education	M,D,O
Human Resources Management	M,O
Law	M,O
Legal and Justice Studies	M,O
Library Science	M,D,O
Marketing	M
Music Education	M,O
Organizational Management	M,O
Project Management	M,O

Real Estate	M
Social Work	M,D,O
Special Education	M,D,O
Taxation	M

UNIVERSITY OF DETROIT MERCY

Accounting	M,O
Business Administration and Management—General	M,O
Curriculum and Instruction	M,D,O
Educational Leadership and Administration	M,D,O
Finance and Banking	M,D,O
Law	D
Management Information Systems	M,O
Management Strategy and Policy	M,O
Mathematics Education	M,O
Religious Education	M,D,O
Special Education	M,D,O

UNIVERSITY OF DUBUQUE

Business Administration and Management—General	M

UNIVERSITY OF EVANSVILLE

Athletic Training and Sports Medicine	M

THE UNIVERSITY OF FINDLAY

Accounting	M,D
Athletic Training and Sports Medicine	M,D
Business Administration and Management—General	M,D
Education—General	M,D
Educational Leadership and Administration	M,D
Educational Media/Instructional Technology	M,D
English as a Second Language	M,D
Hospitality Management	M,D
Reading Education	M,D
Science Education	M,D

UNIVERSITY OF FLORIDA

Accounting	M,D
Advertising and Public Relations	M,D
Agricultural Education	M,D
Art Education	M,D
Athletic Training and Sports Medicine	M,D
Business Administration and Management—General	M,D
Counselor Education	M,D,O
Curriculum and Instruction	M,D,O
Early Childhood Education	M,D,O
Education—General	M,D,O
Educational Leadership and Administration	M,D,O
Educational Measurement and Evaluation	M,D,O
Educational Policy	M,D,O
Elementary Education	M,D,O
English as a Second Language	M,D,O
English Education	M,D,O
Entrepreneurship	M,D,O
Environmental Education	M,D,O
Environmental Law	M,D
Exercise and Sports Science	M,D
Finance and Banking	M,D
Foreign Languages Education	M,D
Health Education	M,D,O
Higher Education	M,D,O
Human Resources Management	M,D
Insurance	M,D,O
International Business	M,D
Kinesiology and Movement Studies	M,D
Law	M,D
Management Information Systems	M,D,O
Marketing	M,D
Mathematics Education	M,D,O
Music Education	M,D
Nonprofit Management	M
Physical Education	M,D
Quantitative Analysis	M,D,O
Reading Education	M,D,O
Real Estate	M,D
Recreation and Park Management	M,D
Science Education	M,D,O
Social Sciences Education	M,D,O
Special Education	M,D,O
Sports Management	M,D
Student Affairs	M,D
Supply Chain Management	M,D,O
Taxation	M,D
Travel and Tourism	M,D

UNIVERSITY OF GEORGIA

Accounting	M
Adult Education	D,O
Business Administration and Management—General	M
Business Education	M,D,O
Counselor Education	M,D,O
Education—General	M,D,O
Educational Leadership and Administration	D,O
Educational Media/Instructional Technology	M,D,O
Educational Policy	D,O
Educational Psychology	O
English Education	M,D
Health Education	M,D
Higher Education	M,D
Kinesiology and Movement Studies	M,D
Law	M,D
Mathematics Education	M,D,O
Music Education	M,D,O
Nonprofit Management	M,D,O
Physical Education	M,D
Reading Education	M,D
Science Education	M,D,O
Social Work	M,D,O
Special Education	M,D,O
Student Affairs	M
Vocational and Technical Education	M,D,O

UNIVERSITY OF GUAM

Business Administration and Management—General	M
Counselor Education	M
Education—General	M
Educational Leadership and Administration	M
English as a Second Language	M
Reading Education	M
Secondary Education	M
Social Work	M
Special Education	M

UNIVERSITY OF GUELPH

Business Administration and Management—General	M,D
Hospitality Management	M
Organizational Management	M

UNIVERSITY OF HARTFORD

Accounting	M,O
Business Administration and Management—General	M
Counselor Education	M,O
Early Childhood Education	M
Education—General	M,D,O
Educational Leadership and Administration	D,O
Educational Media/Instructional Technology	M
Elementary Education	M
Music Education	M,D,O
Organizational Behavior	M
Taxation	M

UNIVERSITY OF HAWAII AT HILO

Education—General	M
Foreign Languages Education	M

UNIVERSITY OF HAWAII AT MANOA

Accounting	M,D
Business Administration and Management—General	M
Curriculum and Instruction	M,D
Early Childhood Education	M
Education—General	M,D,O
Educational Leadership and Administration	M,D
Educational Media/Instructional Technology	M,D
Educational Policy	D
Educational Psychology	M,D
English as a Second Language	M,D
Entrepreneurship	M,O
Finance and Banking	M,D
Foreign Languages Education	M,D,O
Foundations and Philosophy of Education	M,D
Human Resources Management	M
Information Studies	M,O
International Business	M,D
Kinesiology and Movement Studies	M,D
Law	M,D,O
Library Science	M
Management Information Systems	M,D,O
Marketing	M
Organizational Behavior	M,D
Organizational Management	M,D
Real Estate	M
Social Work	M,D
Special Education	M,D
Taxation	M
Transportation Management	M,D,O
Travel and Tourism	M

UNIVERSITY OF HOLY CROSS

Business Administration and Management—General	M,D
Counselor Education	M,D
Education—General	M,D
Educational Leadership and Administration	M,D

UNIVERSITY OF HOUSTON

Accounting	M,D
Advertising and Public Relations	M
Business Administration and Management—General	M,D
Curriculum and Instruction	M,D
Education—General	M,D
Educational Leadership and Administration	M,D
Educational Psychology	M,D
Environmental Law	M,D
Exercise and Sports Science	M,D
Finance and Banking	M
Foundations and Philosophy of Education	M,D
Health Education	M,D
Health Law	M,D
Higher Education	M,D
Hospitality Management	M
Human Resources Development	M
Intellectual Property Law	M,D
Kinesiology and Movement Studies	M,D
Law	M,D
Logistics	M
Marketing	D
Music Education	M,D
Physical Education	M,D
Project Management	M
Social Work	M,D
Special Education	M,D
Supply Chain Management	M,D
Taxation	M,D

UNIVERSITY OF HOUSTON—CLEAR LAKE

Accounting	M
Business Administration and Management—General	M
Counselor Education	M
Curriculum and Instruction	M
Early Childhood Education	M
Education—General	M,D

Educational Leadership and Administration	M,D
Educational Media/Instructional Technology	M
Exercise and Sports Science	M
Finance and Banking	M
Foundations and Philosophy of Education	M
Human Resources Management	M
Library Science	M
Management Information Systems	M
Multilingual and Multicultural Education	M
Reading Education	M

UNIVERSITY OF HOUSTON–DOWNTOWN

Accounting	M
Business Administration and Management—General	M
Curriculum and Instruction	M
Finance and Banking	M
Human Resources Management	M
International Business	M
Investment Management	M
Nonprofit Management	M
Project Management	M
Social Work	M
Supply Chain Management	M
Urban Education	M

UNIVERSITY OF HOUSTON–VICTORIA

Accounting	M
Adult Education	M,O
Business Administration and Management—General	M
Counselor Education	M,O
Curriculum and Instruction	M,O
Education—General	M,O
Educational Leadership and Administration	M,O
Educational Media/Instructional Technology	M,O
Entrepreneurship	M
Finance and Banking	M
Higher Education	M,O
International Business	M
Management Information Systems	M
Marketing	M
Reading Education	M,O
Special Education	M,O

UNIVERSITY OF IDAHO

Accounting	M
Athletic Training and Sports Medicine	M,D
Business Administration and Management—General	M
Counselor Education	M,O
Curriculum and Instruction	M,O
Education—General	M,D,O
Educational Leadership and Administration	M,O
Exercise and Sports Science	M,D
Human Services	M,D
Kinesiology and Movement Studies	M,D
Law	M,D
Physical Education	M,D
Special Education	M,O
Sports Management	M,D
Travel and Tourism	M,D
Vocational and Technical Education	M,O

UNIVERSITY OF ILLINOIS AT CHICAGO

Accounting	M
Business Administration and Management—General	M,D
Computer Education	D
Curriculum and Instruction	M,D
Early Childhood Education	M,D
Education—General	M,D
Educational Leadership and Administration	M,D
Educational Measurement and Evaluation	M,D
Educational Policy	M,D
Educational Psychology	M,D
Elementary Education	M,D
English as a Second Language	M,D
Finance and Banking	M
Foreign Languages Education	M,D
Health Education	M,D
Kinesiology and Movement Studies	M,D
Management Information Systems	M,D
Mathematics Education	M,D
Real Estate	M
Science Education	D
Secondary Education	M,D
Social Sciences Education	D
Social Work	M,D,O
Special Education	M,D
Urban Education	M,D

UNIVERSITY OF ILLINOIS AT SPRINGFIELD

Accounting	M
Business Administration and Management—General	M
Distance Education Development	M,O
Education—General	M,O
Educational Leadership and Administration	M,O
Educational Media/Instructional Technology	M,O
English as a Second Language	M,O
English Education	M,O
Health Education	M,O
Higher Education	M,O
Human Services	M,O
Legal and Justice Studies	M
Management Information Systems	M

UNIVERSITY OF ILLINOIS AT URBANA–CHAMPAIGN

Accounting	M,D
Actuarial Science	M,D

Advertising and Public Relations — M
Agricultural Education — M
Art Education — M,D
Business Administration and
  Management—General — M,D
Counselor Education — M,D
Curriculum and Instruction — M,D,O
Education of Students with
  Severe/Multiple Disabilities — M,D,O
Education—General — M,D,O
Educational Leadership and
  Administration — M,D,O
Educational Policy — M,D,O
Educational Psychology — M,D,O
English as a Second Language — M,D
Finance and Banking — M,D
Foreign Languages Education — M,D
Human Resources Management — M,D
Human Services — M,D
Information Studies — M,D,O
Kinesiology and Movement Studies — M,D
Law — M,D
Leisure Studies — M,D
Library Science — M,D,O
Management Information Systems — M,D,O
Management Strategy and Policy — M,D,O
Mathematics Education — M,D
Music Education — M,D
Science Education — M,D
Social Work — M,D
Special Education — M,D,O

UNIVERSITY OF INDIANAPOLIS
Art Education — M
Business Administration and
  Management—General — M,O
Curriculum and Instruction — M
Education—General — M
Educational Leadership and
  Administration — M
Elementary Education — M
English Education — M
Foreign Languages Education — M
Mathematics Education — M
Physical Education — M
Science Education — M
Secondary Education — M
Social Sciences Education — M
Sports Management — M

THE UNIVERSITY OF IOWA
Accounting — M,D
Actuarial Science — M,D
Art Education — M,D
Athletic Training and Sports
  Medicine — M,D
Business Administration and
  Management—General — M,D
Business Analytics — M
Counselor Education — M,D
Developmental Education — M,D
Education—General — M,D,O
Educational Leadership and
  Administration — M,D,O
Educational Measurement and
  Evaluation — M,D,O
Educational Policy — M,D,O
Educational Psychology — M,D,O
Elementary Education — M,D
English as a Second Language — M,D
English Education — M,D
Exercise and Sports Science — M,D
Finance and Banking — M,D
Foreign Languages Education — M,D
Foundations and Philosophy of
  Education — M,D,O
Higher Education — M,D
Information Studies — M,D
Law — M,D
Leisure Studies — M,D
Library Science — M,D
Marketing — M,D
Mathematics Education — M,D
Music Education — M,D
Quantitative Analysis — M,D,O
Recreation and Park Management — M,D
Science Education — M,D
Secondary Education — M,D
Social Sciences Education — M,D
Social Work — M,D
Special Education — M,D
Sports Management — M,D
Student Affairs — M,D

UNIVERSITY OF JAMESTOWN
Curriculum and Instruction — M
Education—General — M

THE UNIVERSITY OF KANSAS
Accounting — M
Art Education — M
Business Administration and
  Management—General — M,D
Curriculum and Instruction — M,D
Early Childhood Education — M,D,O
Education—General — M,D,O
Educational Leadership and
  Administration — M,D
Educational Measurement and
  Evaluation — M,D
Educational Media/Instructional
  Technology — M,D
Educational Policy — M,D
Educational Psychology — M,D
Exercise and Sports Science — M,D
Finance and Banking — M,D
Health Education — M,D,O
Higher Education — M,D
Human Resources Management — M,D
Law — D
Logistics — M,D
Management Information Systems — M

Management Strategy and Policy — M,D
Marketing — M,D
Music Education — M,D
Organizational Behavior — M,D
Organizational Management — M,D,O
Physical Education — M,D
Project Management — M
Social Work — M,D
Special Education — M,D,O
Sports Management — M,D
Supply Chain Management — M,D

UNIVERSITY OF KENTUCKY
Accounting — M
Art Education — M
Athletic Training and Sports
  Medicine — M
Business Administration and
  Management—General — M,D
Curriculum and Instruction — M,D
Early Childhood Education — M,D
Education—General — M,D,O
Educational Leadership and
  Administration — M,D,O
Educational Measurement and
  Evaluation — M,D
Educational Media/Instructional
  Technology — M,D
Educational Policy — M,D
Educational Psychology — M,D,O
Elementary Education — M,D
Exercise and Sports Science — M,D
Foreign Languages Education — M
Higher Education — M
Hospitality Management — M
International Business — M
Kinesiology and Movement Studies — M,D
Law — D
Library Science — M
Middle School Education — M,D
Music Education — M,D
Physical Education — M,D
Reading Education — M,D
Secondary Education — M,D
Social Work — M,D
Special Education — M,D

UNIVERSITY OF LA VERNE
Accounting — M
Business Administration and
  Management—General — M,D,O
Counselor Education — M,D,O
Education—General — M,O
Educational Leadership and
  Administration — M,D,O
Elementary Education — M
Finance and Banking — M
Higher Education — M
Human Resources Management — M,O
International Business — M
Law — D
Management Information Systems — M
Marketing — M
Nonprofit Management — M,O
Organizational Management — M,D,O
Reading Education — M,O
Secondary Education — M,D,O
Special Education — M,D,O
Student Affairs — M
Supply Chain Management — M

UNIVERSITY OF LETHBRIDGE
Accounting — M,D
Business Administration and
  Management—General — M,D
Counselor Education — M,D
Education—General — M,D
Educational Leadership and
  Administration — M,D
Exercise and Sports Science — M,D
Finance and Banking — M,D
Human Resources Management — M,D
International Business — M,D
Kinesiology and Movement Studies — M,D
Management Information Systems — M,D
Management Strategy and Policy — M,D
Marketing — M,D

UNIVERSITY OF LOUISIANA AT LAFAYETTE
Business Administration and
  Management—General — M
Counselor Education — M
Curriculum and Instruction — M
Education of the Gifted — M
Education—General — M,D
Educational Leadership and
  Administration — M,D
Music Education — M

UNIVERSITY OF LOUISIANA AT MONROE
Business Administration and
  Management—General — M,O
Counselor Education — M
Curriculum and Instruction — M,D
Education—General — M,D
Elementary Education — M
Exercise and Sports Science — M
Recreation and Park Management — M
Secondary Education — M
Special Education — M
Sports Management — M

UNIVERSITY OF LOUISVILLE
Accounting — M
Art Education — M,D,O
Business Administration and
  Management—General — M
Counselor Education — M
Curriculum and Instruction — M,D,O
Early Childhood Education — M,D,O
Education—General — M,D,O

Educational Leadership and
  Administration — M,D,O
Educational Measurement and
  Evaluation — M,D
Educational Psychology — M,D
Elementary Education — M,D
Entrepreneurship — M,D
Exercise and Sports Science — M,D,O
Health Education — M,D,O
Higher Education — M,D,O
Human Resources Development — M,D,O
Human Resources Management — M,D,O
International Business — M
Law — D
Logistics — M,D,O
Middle School Education — M,D,O
Music Education — M,D
Nonprofit Management — M,D
Physical Education — M,D,O
Secondary Education — M,D,O
Social Work — M,D,O
Special Education — M,D,O
Sports Management — M,D,O
Student Affairs — M,D
Supply Chain Management — M,D,O
Sustainability Management — M,D

UNIVERSITY OF LYNCHBURG
Athletic Training and Sports
  Medicine — M
Business Administration and
  Management—General — M
Counselor Education — M
Curriculum and Instruction — M
Educational Leadership and
  Administration — M,D
Higher Education — M
Nonprofit Management — M
Reading Education — M
Science Education — M
Special Education — M

UNIVERSITY OF MAINE
Business Administration and
  Management—General — M,O
Early Childhood Education — M,D,O
Education—General — M,D,O
Educational Leadership and
  Administration — M,D,O
Educational Media/Instructional
  Technology — M,D,O
Exercise and Sports Science — M,D,O
Finance and Banking — M
Foreign Languages Education — M
Higher Education — M,D,O
Kinesiology and Movement Studies — M,D,O
Law — D
Physical Education — M,D,O
Reading Education — M,D,O
Social Sciences Education — M,D,O
Social Work — M,O
Special Education — M,D,O

UNIVERSITY OF MAINE AT FARMINGTON
Early Childhood Education — M
Education—General — M
Educational Leadership and
  Administration — M
Educational Media/Instructional
  Technology — M

UNIVERSITY OF MANAGEMENT AND TECHNOLOGY
Business Administration and
  Management—General — M,D,O
Management Information Systems — M,O
Project Management — M,D,O

THE UNIVERSITY OF MANCHESTER
Accounting — M
Actuarial Science — M,D
Business Administration and
  Management—General — M
Business Analytics — M
Education—General — M,D
Educational Psychology — M,D
English as a Second Language — M,D
Entrepreneurship — M
Finance and Banking — M
Health Law — M
Human Resources Management — M
Industrial and Manufacturing
  Management — M,D
International Business — M,D
Law — M,D
Management Strategy and Policy — M,D
Marketing — M
Project Management — M
Social Work — M,D
Supply Chain Management — M

UNIVERSITY OF MANITOBA
Adult Education — M
Archives/Archival Administration — M,D
Business Administration and
  Management—General — M
Counselor Education — M
Curriculum and Instruction — M
Education—General — M,D
Educational Leadership and
  Administration — M
Educational Psychology — M
English as a Second Language — M
English Education — M
Foundations and Philosophy of
  Education — M
Higher Education — M
Kinesiology and Movement Studies — M
Law — M
Physical Education — M
Recreation and Park Management — M
Social Work — M

Special Education — M

UNIVERSITY OF MARY
Business Administration and
  Management—General — M
Curriculum and Instruction — M
Education—General — M,D
Educational Leadership and
  Administration — M,D
Exercise and Sports Science — M
Human Resources Management — M
Kinesiology and Movement Studies — M
Physical Education — M
Project Management — M,D
Reading Education — M,D
Special Education — M,D
Sports Management — M

UNIVERSITY OF MARY HARDIN-BAYLOR
Accounting — M
Business Administration and
  Management—General — M
Counselor Education — M,D
Curriculum and Instruction — M,D
Education—General — M,D
Educational Leadership and
  Administration — M,D
Elementary Education — M,D
Exercise and Sports Science — M
Higher Education — M,D
International Business — M
Management Information Systems — M
Secondary Education — M
Sports Management — M

UNIVERSITY OF MARYLAND, BALTIMORE
Law — M,D
Social Work — M,D

UNIVERSITY OF MARYLAND, BALTIMORE COUNTY
Art Education — M
Distance Education Development — M,O
Early Childhood Education — M
Education—General — M,O
Educational Media/Instructional
  Technology — M,O
Educational Policy — M,D
Elementary Education — M
English as a Second Language — M,O
English Education — M
Foreign Languages Education — M
Human Services — M,D
Mathematics Education — M
Multilingual and Multicultural
  Education — M,D
Music Education — M
Nonprofit Management — M,O
Science Education — M
Social Sciences Education — M

UNIVERSITY OF MARYLAND, COLLEGE PARK
Advertising and Public Relations — M,D
Business Administration and
  Management—General — M,D
Counselor Education — M,D,O
Curriculum and Instruction — M,D,O
Education—General — M,D,O
Educational Leadership and
  Administration — M,D,O
Educational Measurement and
  Evaluation — M,D
Educational Media/Instructional
  Technology — M,D,O
English as a Second Language — M,D,O
Foreign Languages Education — D
Foundations and Philosophy of
  Education — M,D,O
Health Education — M,D
Information Studies — M,D
Kinesiology and Movement Studies — M,D
Law
Library Science
Music Education — M,D
Quantitative Analysis — M,D
Reading Education — M,D,O
Real Estate — M
Secondary Education — M,D,O
Social Work
Student Affairs — M,D,O

UNIVERSITY OF MARYLAND EASTERN SHORE
Counselor Education — M
Education—General — M
Educational Leadership and
  Administration — D
Organizational Management — D
Special Education — M
Vocational and Technical Education — M

UNIVERSITY OF MARYLAND UNIVERSITY COLLEGE
Accounting — M
Business Administration and
  Management—General — M,D,O
Distance Education Development — M
Education—General — M
Educational Media/Instructional
  Technology — M
Finance and Banking — M

UNIVERSITY OF MARY WASHINGTON
Business Administration and
  Management—General — M
Education—General — M
Elementary Education — M

UNIVERSITY OF MASSACHUSETTS AMHERST
Accounting — M,D

---

*M—masters degree; D—doctorate; O—other advanced degree; *—Close-Up and/or Display*

Art Education — M
Business Administration and Management—General — M,D
Counselor Education — M,D,O
Early Childhood Education — M,D,O
Education—General — M,D,O
Educational Leadership and Administration — M,D,O
Educational Measurement and Evaluation — M,D,O
Educational Media/Instructional Technology — M,D,O
Educational Policy — M,D,O
Elementary Education — M,D,O
English as a Second Language — M,D,O
Entertainment Management
Entrepreneurship — M,D
Finance and Banking — M,D
Foreign Languages Education — M
Health Education — M,D
Higher Education — M,D,O
Hospitality Management — M,D
International and Comparative Education — M,D,O
Kinesiology and Movement Studies — M,D
Management Strategy and Policy — M,D
Marketing — M,D
Multilingual and Multicultural Education — M,D,O
Music Education — M,D
Organizational Management — M,D
Reading Education — M,D,O
Science Education — M,D,O
Secondary Education — M,D,O
Special Education — M,D,O
Sports Management — M,D
Travel and Tourism — M,D

UNIVERSITY OF MASSACHUSETTS BOSTON

Accounting — M
Archives/Archival Administration — M
Business Administration and Management—General — M
Business Analytics — M
Counselor Education — M
Early Childhood Education — D
Education—General — M,D,O
Educational Leadership and Administration — M,D,O
Educational Media/Instructional Technology — M,O
Educational Policy — D
Exercise and Sports Science — M,D
Finance and Banking — M
Higher Education — D
Human Services — M
International Business — M
Management Information Systems — M
Quality Management — M,O
Special Education — M
Urban Education — D

UNIVERSITY OF MASSACHUSETTS DARTMOUTH

Accounting — M,O
Art Education — M
Business Administration and Management—General — M,O
Education—General — M,D,O
Educational Leadership and Administration — D
Educational Policy — M,D,O
English as a Second Language — M,D,O
Finance and Banking — M,O
Law — D
Mathematics Education — M,D,O
Middle School Education — M,D,O
Science Education — M,D,O
Secondary Education — M,D,O
Special Education — M,O

UNIVERSITY OF MASSACHUSETTS LOWELL

Business Administration and Management—General — M,D
Curriculum and Instruction — M
Education—General — M
Entrepreneurship — M,D
Legal and Justice Studies — M
Music Education — M

UNIVERSITY OF MEMPHIS

Accounting — M,D
Adult Education — M,D,O
Business Administration and Management—General — M,D
Community College Education — M,D,O
Counselor Education — M,D
Curriculum and Instruction — M,D,O
Early Childhood Education — M,D,O
Education—General — M,D,O
Educational Leadership and Administration — M,D,O
Educational Measurement and Evaluation — M,D
Educational Media/Instructional Technology — M,D,O
Educational Psychology — M,D
Elementary Education — M,D,O
English as a Second Language — M,D,O
Exercise and Sports Science — M,O
Finance and Banking — M,D
Higher Education — M,D,O
Hospitality Management — M,O
Human Resources Management — M,O
Law — D
Management Information Systems — M,D,O
Management Strategy and Policy — M,O
Marketing — M,D
Mathematics Education — M,D
Music Education — M,D
Nonprofit Management — M,O
Physical Education — M,O
Reading Education — M,D,O

Real Estate — M,D
Science Education — M,D,O
Secondary Education — M,D,O
Social Work — M
Special Education — M,D,O
Supply Chain Management — M,D
Urban Education — M,D,O

UNIVERSITY OF MIAMI

Advertising and Public Relations — M,D
Athletic Training and Sports Medicine — M,D
Business Administration and Management—General — M,D
Counselor Education — M,O
Early Childhood Education — M,O
Education—General — M,D,O
Educational Measurement and Evaluation — M,D
Exercise and Sports Science — M,D
Higher Education — M,D,O
Law — M,D*
Mathematics Education — D
Multilingual and Multicultural Education — D
Music Education — M,D,O
Reading Education — M,D
Real Estate — M,D
Science Education — D
Special Education — M,D,O
Sports and Entertainment Law — M,D
Sports Management — M
Taxation — M,D

UNIVERSITY OF MICHIGAN

Accounting — M,D
Business Administration and Management—General — M,D
Education—General — D
English Education — D
Foreign Languages Education — M,D
Health Education — M,D
Information Studies — M,D
Kinesiology and Movement Studies — M,D
Law — M,D
Music Education — M,D,O
Quantitative Analysis — M,D
Risk Management — M,D
Social Work — M
Sports Management — M,D
Supply Chain Management — M
Taxation — M,D

UNIVERSITY OF MICHIGAN–DEARBORN

Accounting — M
Business Administration and Management—General — M
Curriculum and Instruction — D,O
Early Childhood Education — M
Education—General — M
Educational Leadership and Administration — M,D,O
Educational Measurement and Evaluation — M
Educational Media/Instructional Technology — M
Finance and Banking — M
Management Information Systems — M
Project Management — M
Science Education — M
Special Education — M
Supply Chain Management — M
Urban Education — M,D

UNIVERSITY OF MICHIGAN–FLINT

Accounting — M,O
Business Administration and Management—General — M,O
Curriculum and Instruction — M,D,O
Early Childhood Education — M,D,O
Education—General — M,D,O
Educational Leadership and Administration — M,D,O
Educational Media/Instructional Technology — M,D,O
Finance and Banking — M,O
Health Education — M
Industrial and Manufacturing Management — M,O
International Business — M,O
Management Information Systems — M,O
Marketing — M,O
Nonprofit Management — M
Organizational Management — M,O
Reading Education — M,D,O
Secondary Education — M,D,O

UNIVERSITY OF MINNESOTA, DULUTH

Business Administration and Management—General — M
Education—General — M,D
Music Education — M
Social Work — M

UNIVERSITY OF MINNESOTA ROCHESTER

Business Administration and Management—General — M,D

UNIVERSITY OF MINNESOTA, TWIN CITIES CAMPUS

Accounting — M,D
Adult Education — M,D,O
Art Education — M
Business Administration and Management—General — M,D
Counselor Education — M
Curriculum and Instruction — M,D
Early Childhood Education — M,D,O
Education of the Gifted — M,D,O
Education—General — M,D,O
Educational Leadership and Administration — M,D
Educational Measurement and Evaluation — M,D

Educational Media/Instructional Technology — M,D,O
Educational Policy — M,D
Educational Psychology — M,D,O
Elementary Education — M
English as a Second Language — M,D,O
English Education — M
Entrepreneurship — D
Exercise and Sports Science — M,D
Finance and Banking — M,D
Foreign Languages Education — M
Foundations and Philosophy of Education — M,D
Higher Education — M,D
Human Resources Development — M,D,O
Human Resources Management — M
International and Comparative Education — M,D
Kinesiology and Movement Studies — M,D
Law — M,D
Management Information Systems — M,D
Management Strategy and Policy — D
Marketing — M,D
Mathematics Education — M,D,O
Multilingual and Multicultural Education — M,D
Quantitative Analysis — M,D
Reading Education — M,D,O
Science Education — M
Social Sciences Education — M
Social Work — M,D
Special Education — M,D
Sports Management — M,D
Student Affairs — M
Supply Chain Management — M,D
Taxation — M
Travel and Tourism — M,D
Vocational and Technical Education — M,D,O

UNIVERSITY OF MISSISSIPPI

Accounting — M,D
Business Administration and Management—General — M,D
Counselor Education — M,D,O
Early Childhood Education — M,D,O
Education—General — M,D,O
Educational Leadership and Administration — M,D,O
Elementary Education — M,D,O
Exercise and Sports Science — M,D
Finance and Banking — M,D
Foreign Languages Education — M,D
Higher Education — M,D,O
Hospitality Management — M,D
Kinesiology and Movement Studies — M,D
Law — M,D
Management Information Systems — M,D
Marketing — M,D
Mathematics Education — M,D,O
Reading Education — M,D,O
Recreation and Park Management — M,D
Secondary Education — M,D,O
Social Work — M,D
Special Education — M,D,O
Taxation — M,D

UNIVERSITY OF MISSOURI

Accounting — M,D,O
Adult Education — M,D,O
Agricultural Education — M,D,O
Art Education — M,D,O
Business Administration and Management—General — M,D
Business Education — M,D
Curriculum and Instruction — M,D,O
Early Childhood Education — M,D
Education of the Gifted — M,D
Education—General — M,D,O
Educational Leadership and Administration — M,D,O
Educational Media/Instructional Technology — M,D,O
Educational Psychology — M,D,O
Elementary Education — M,D,O
English Education — M,D,O
Finance and Banking — M,D
Foreign Languages Education — M,D,O
Health Education — M,D,O
Higher Education — M,D,O
Hospitality Management — M,D
Information Studies — M,D
Law — M,D
Library Science — M,D,O
Marketing — M,D
Mathematics Education — M,D,O
Music Education — M,D,O
Nonprofit Management — M,D,O
Organizational Management — M,D,O
Reading Education — M,D,O
Science Education — M,D,O
Social Sciences Education — M,D,O
Social Work — M,D,O
Special Education — M,D
Taxation — M,D
Vocational and Technical Education — M,D,O

UNIVERSITY OF MISSOURI–KANSAS CITY

Accounting — M,D
Business Administration and Management—General — M,D
Counselor Education — M,D,O
Curriculum and Instruction — M,D,O
Education—General — M,D,O
Educational Leadership and Administration — M,D
Finance and Banking — M,D
Health Education — M,D
Higher Education — M,D
Law — M,D
Music Education — M,D
Reading Education — M,D,O
Social Work — M
Special Education — M,D,O

UNIVERSITY OF MISSOURI–ST. LOUIS

Accounting — M,D,O
Adult Education — M,O
Business Administration and Management—General — M,D,O
Counselor Education — D
Curriculum and Instruction — M
Early Childhood Education — M
Education—General — M,D,O
Educational Leadership and Administration — D
Educational Measurement and Evaluation — M,O
Educational Policy — D
Educational Psychology — D
Elementary Education — M
English as a Second Language — M
Higher Education — M,O
Human Resources Management — M,D,O
Logistics — M,D,O
Management Information Systems — M,D,O
Marketing Research — M,D,O
Marketing — M,D,O
Middle School Education — M
Nonprofit Management — M,O
Reading Education — M
Secondary Education — M
Social Sciences Education — M,O
Social Work — M
Special Education — M
Supply Chain Management — M,D,O

UNIVERSITY OF MOBILE

Business Administration and Management—General — M
Education—General — M
Educational Leadership and Administration — M
Educational Policy — M

UNIVERSITY OF MONTANA

Accounting — M
Art Education — M
Business Administration and Management—General — M
Counselor Education — M,D,O
Curriculum and Instruction — M,D
Early Childhood Education — M,D
Education—General — M,D,O
Educational Leadership and Administration — M,D,O
English Education — M
Exercise and Sports Science — M
Health Education — M
Law — D
Legal and Justice Studies — M
Mathematics Education — M,D
Physical Education — M
Recreation and Park Management — M,D
Social Work — M

UNIVERSITY OF MONTEVALLO

Business Administration and Management—General — M
Counselor Education — M
Education—General — M,O
Educational Leadership and Administration — M,O
Elementary Education — M
Secondary Education — M

UNIVERSITY OF MOUNT OLIVE

Business Administration and Management—General — M

UNIVERSITY OF MOUNT UNION

Educational Leadership and Administration — M

UNIVERSITY OF NEBRASKA AT KEARNEY

Accounting — M
Art Education — M
Business Administration and Management—General — M
Counselor Education — M,O
Curriculum and Instruction — M
Early Childhood Education — M
Education of the Gifted — M
Education—General — M,O
Educational Leadership and Administration — M,O
Educational Media/Instructional Technology — M
Elementary Education — M
English as a Second Language — M
Exercise and Sports Science — M
Foreign Languages Education — M
Human Resources Management — M
Human Services — M
Leisure Studies — M
Library Science — M
Management Information Systems — M
Marketing — M
Mathematics Education — M
Music Education — M
Physical Education — M
Reading Education — M
Recreation and Park Management — M
Science Education — M
Secondary Education — M
Special Education — M,O
Sports Management — M
Student Affairs — M,O

UNIVERSITY OF NEBRASKA AT OMAHA

Accounting — M
Athletic Training and Sports Medicine — M,D
Business Administration and Management—General — M,O
Counselor Education — M
Education—General — M,D,O
Educational Leadership and Administration — M,D,O
Elementary Education — M

English as a Second Language	M,O
Exercise and Sports Science	M,D
Foreign Languages Education	M
Health Education	M,D
Human Resources Development	M,D,O
Kinesiology and Movement Studies	M,D
Management Information Systems	M,D,O
Organizational Management	M
Project Management	M,D,O
Science Education	M,O
Secondary Education	M,O
Social Work	M
Special Education	M
Urban Education	M,O

UNIVERSITY OF NEBRASKA–LINCOLN

Accounting	M,D
Actuarial Science	M
Adult Education	M,D,O
Advertising and Public Relations	M,D
Agricultural Education	M
Business Administration and Management—General	M,D
Curriculum and Instruction	M,D,O
Early Childhood Education	M,D
Educational Leadership and Administration	M,D,O
Educational Measurement and Evaluation	M,D,O
Educational Psychology	M,D,O
Exercise and Sports Science	M,D
Finance and Banking	M,D
Home Economics Education	M,D
Law	M,D
Legal and Justice Studies	M
Management Information Systems	M,D
Marketing	M,D
Music Education	M,D
Special Education	M,D,O
Vocational and Technical Education	M,D

UNIVERSITY OF NEVADA, LAS VEGAS

Accounting	M,O
Business Administration and Management—General	M,O
Counselor Education	M,D,O
Curriculum and Instruction	M,D,O
Distance Education Development	M,D,O
Early Childhood Education	M,D,O
Education—General	M,D,O
Educational Leadership and Administration	M,D,O
Educational Media/Instructional Technology	M,D,O
Elementary Education	M,D,O
English as a Second Language	M,D,O
Exercise and Sports Science	M,D
Higher Education	M,D,O
Hospitality Management	M,D
Kinesiology and Movement Studies	M,D
Law	M,O
Management Information Systems	M,O
Nonprofit Management	M,D,O
Secondary Education	M,D,O
Social Work	M
Special Education	M,D,O

UNIVERSITY OF NEVADA, RENO

Accounting	M
Business Administration and Management—General	M
Counselor Education	M,D,O
Curriculum and Instruction	D
Education—General	M,D,O
Educational Leadership and Administration	M,D,O
Educational Psychology	M,D,O
Elementary Education	M
English as a Second Language	M
Finance and Banking	M
Foreign Languages Education	M
Legal and Justice Studies	M
Management Information Systems	M
Mathematics Education	M,D
Reading Education	M,D
Secondary Education	M
Social Work	M
Special Education	M,D

UNIVERSITY OF NEW BRUNSWICK FREDERICTON

Business Administration and Management—General	M
Education—General	M,D
Entrepreneurship	M
Exercise and Sports Science	M
Marketing	M,D
Physical Education	M
Recreation and Park Management	M
Sports Management	M

UNIVERSITY OF NEW BRUNSWICK SAINT JOHN

Business Administration and Management—General	M
Electronic Commerce	M
International Business	M

UNIVERSITY OF NEW ENGLAND

Curriculum and Instruction	M,D,O
Early Childhood Education	M,D,O
Education—General	M,D,O
Educational Leadership and Administration	M,D,O
Reading Education	M,D,O
Social Work	M
Vocational and Technical Education	M,D,O

UNIVERSITY OF NEW HAMPSHIRE

Accounting	M
Business Administration and Management—General	M,O
Curriculum and Instruction	D,O

Early Childhood Education	M
Education—General	M,D,O
Educational Leadership and Administration	M,O
Educational Media/Instructional Technology	M,O
Elementary Education	M,O
Higher Education	O
Intellectual Property Law	M,D,O
Kinesiology and Movement Studies	M,O
Law	M,D,O
Legal and Justice Studies	M,D,O
Management Information Systems	M,O
Mathematics Education	M,D,O
Physical Education	M,O
Quantitative Analysis	M
Recreation and Park Management	M
Science Education	M,O
Secondary Education	M,O
Social Work	M,O
Special Education	M,O
Sports and Entertainment Law	M,D,O
Sustainability Management	M,O

UNIVERSITY OF NEW HAVEN

Accounting	M,O
Business Administration and Management—General	M*
Facilities Management	M,O
Finance and Banking	M,O
Human Resources Management	M,O
Industrial and Manufacturing Management	M,O
International Business	M
Management Strategy and Policy	M
Marketing	M
Nonprofit Management	M,O
Organizational Management	M,O
Sports Management	M,O
Taxation	M,O

UNIVERSITY OF NEW MEXICO

Accounting	M
Art Education	M
Business Administration and Management—General	M
Counselor Education	M
Early Childhood Education	D
Education—General	M,D,O
Educational Leadership and Administration	M,D,O
Educational Media/Instructional Technology	M,D,O
Educational Psychology	M,D
Elementary Education	M
English as a Second Language	M,D
English Education	M,D
Entrepreneurship	M
Exercise and Sports Science	D
Finance and Banking	M
Foundations and Philosophy of Education	M,D
Health Education	M
Higher Education	O
Human Resources Management	M
International Business	M
Law	D
Management Information Systems	M
Management Strategy and Policy	M
Marketing	M
Multilingual and Multicultural Education	M,D
Music Education	M
Organizational Behavior	M
Organizational Management	D
Physical Education	D
Quantitative Analysis	D
Reading Education	M
Science Education	O
Secondary Education	M
Special Education	M,D,O
Sports Management	D
Taxation	M

UNIVERSITY OF NEW ORLEANS

Accounting	M
Business Administration and Management—General	M
Counselor Education	M,D
Curriculum and Instruction	M,D
Education—General	M,D
Educational Leadership and Administration	M,D
Finance and Banking	M,D
Hospitality Management	M
Special Education	M,D
Taxation	M
Transportation Management	M
Travel and Tourism	M

UNIVERSITY OF NORTH ALABAMA

Accounting	M
Business Administration and Management—General	M
Counselor Education	M
Education—General	M,O
Educational Leadership and Administration	M,O
Elementary Education	M,O
Exercise and Sports Science	M
Finance and Banking	M
International Business	M
Kinesiology and Movement Studies	M
Law	M
Management Information Systems	M
Physical Education	M
Project Management	M
Secondary Education	M
Special Education	M

THE UNIVERSITY OF NORTH CAROLINA AT CHAPEL HILL

Accounting	M,D
Athletic Training and Sports Medicine	M
Business Administration and Management—General	M,D
Counselor Education	M
Curriculum and Instruction	M,D
Early Childhood Education	M,D
Education—General	M,D
Educational Leadership and Administration	M,D
Educational Measurement and Evaluation	M,D
Educational Psychology	M,D
English as a Second Language	M
English Education	M
Exercise and Sports Science	D
Finance and Banking	D
Foreign Languages Education	M
Information Studies	M,D,O
Kinesiology and Movement Studies	D
Law	M,D
Library Science	M,D,O
Management Information Systems	D
Management Strategy and Policy	D
Marketing	D
Mathematics Education	M
Music Education	M
Organizational Behavior	D
Physical Education	M
Reading Education	M,D
Science Education	M
Secondary Education	M
Social Sciences Education	M
Social Work	M,D
Sports Management	M

THE UNIVERSITY OF NORTH CAROLINA AT CHARLOTTE

Accounting	M
Art Education	M,D,O
Business Administration and Management—General	M,D,O
Business Analytics	M,D,O
Business Education	D
Counselor Education	M,D,O
Curriculum and Instruction	M,D,O
Early Childhood Education	M,D,O
Education of the Gifted	M
Education—General	M,D,O
Educational Leadership and Administration	M,D,O
Educational Media/Instructional Technology	M,D,O
Elementary Education	M,O
English as a Second Language	M,D,O
Facilities Management	M,O
Finance and Banking	M,O
Foreign Languages Education	M,D,O
Industrial and Manufacturing Management	M,D,O
Kinesiology and Movement Studies	M
Logistics	M,O
Management Information Systems	M,O
Middle School Education	M,D,O
Nonprofit Management	M,O
Reading Education	M,O
Real Estate	M,O
Secondary Education	M,D,O
Social Work	M
Special Education	M,D,O
Supply Chain Management	M,O

THE UNIVERSITY OF NORTH CAROLINA AT GREENSBORO

Accounting	M,O
Adult Education	M,D,O
Athletic Training and Sports Medicine	M,D
Business Administration and Management—General	M,O
Counselor Education	M,D,O
Curriculum and Instruction	M,D,O
Early Childhood Education	M,D,O
Education—General	M,D,O
Educational Leadership and Administration	M,D,O
Educational Measurement and Evaluation	D
Educational Media/Instructional Technology	M,D,O
Elementary Education	D
English as a Second Language	M,D,O
English Education	M,D
Finance and Banking	M,O
Foreign Languages Education	M,D,O
Higher Education	D
Information Studies	M
Kinesiology and Movement Studies	M,D
Library Science	M
Management Information Systems	M
Marketing	M,D
Mathematics Education	M,D,O
Middle School Education	M,D,O
Multilingual and Multicultural Education	M,D,O
Music Education	M,D
Nonprofit Management	M,O
Reading Education	M,D,O
Recreation and Park Management	M,O
Science Education	M,D,O
Social Sciences Education	M,D,O
Social Work	M
Special Education	M,D,O
Supply Chain Management	M,D,O

THE UNIVERSITY OF NORTH CAROLINA AT PEMBROKE

Art Education	M

Business Administration and Management—General	M
Counselor Education	M
Education—General	M
Educational Leadership and Administration	M
Elementary Education	M
English Education	M
Exercise and Sports Science	M
Health Education	M
Mathematics Education	M
Physical Education	M
Reading Education	M
Science Education	M
Social Sciences Education	M
Social Work	M
Sports Management	M

THE UNIVERSITY OF NORTH CAROLINA WILMINGTON

Accounting	M
Business Administration and Management—General	M
Curriculum and Instruction	M,D
Early Childhood Education	M,D
Education—General	M,D
Educational Leadership and Administration	M,D
Educational Media/Instructional Technology	M
Educational Policy	M
Elementary Education	M
English as a Second Language	M
Higher Education	M
International Business	M
Management Information Systems	M
Middle School Education	M
Reading Education	M
Secondary Education	M
Social Work	M
Special Education	M

UNIVERSITY OF NORTH DAKOTA

Business Administration and Management—General	M
Early Childhood Education	M
Education—General	M,D,O
Educational Leadership and Administration	M,D,O
Educational Media/Instructional Technology	M
Elementary Education	M
Kinesiology and Movement Studies	M
Law	D
Music Education	M,D
Reading Education	M
Social Work	M
Special Education	M

UNIVERSITY OF NORTHERN BRITISH COLUMBIA

Education—General	M,D,O
Social Work	M,D,O

UNIVERSITY OF NORTHERN COLORADO

Accounting	M
Art Education	M
Business Administration and Management—General	M
Counselor Education	M,D
Curriculum and Instruction	M,D
Education of the Gifted	M,D
Education—General	M,D,O
Educational Leadership and Administration	M,D,O
Educational Measurement and Evaluation	M,D
Educational Policy	M,D,O
Educational Psychology	M,D
Elementary Education	M,D
English as a Second Language	M,D
English Education	M,D
Exercise and Sports Science	M,D
Foreign Languages Education	M,D
Health Education	M
Higher Education	M
Human Resources Management	M
Mathematics Education	M,D
Multilingual and Multicultural Education	M,D
Music Education	M,D
Physical Education	M,D
Reading Education	M,D
Science Education	M,D
Special Education	M,D
Sports Management	M,D
Student Affairs	M,D

UNIVERSITY OF NORTHERN IOWA

Accounting	M
Art Education	M
Athletic Training and Sports Medicine	M
Business Administration and Management—General	M
Community College Education	M
Counselor Education	M
Curriculum and Instruction	D
Early Childhood Education	M
Education—General	M,D,O
Educational Leadership and Administration	M,D
Educational Measurement and Evaluation	M
Educational Media/Instructional Technology	M
Educational Psychology	M
Elementary Education	M
English as a Second Language	M
English Education	M
Foreign Languages Education	M

M—masters degree; D—doctorate; O—other advanced degree; *—Close-Up and/or Display

Health Education — M
Higher Education — M
Human Services — M
Kinesiology and Movement Studies — M
Mathematics Education — M
Middle School Education — M
Music Education — M
Nonprofit Management — M
Physical Education — M
Reading Education — M
Science Education — M
Secondary Education — M
Social Work — M
Special Education — M
Sports Management — M
Student Affairs — M
Vocational and Technical Education — M

UNIVERSITY OF NORTH FLORIDA
Accounting — M
Adult Education — M
Business Administration and Management—General — M
Counselor Education — M,D
Education—General — M,D
Educational Leadership and Administration — M
Educational Media/Instructional Technology — M,D
Electronic Commerce — M
Elementary Education — M
English as a Second Language — M
Exercise and Sports Science — M,D
Finance and Banking — M
Human Resources Management — M
International Business — M
Logistics — M
Management Information Systems — M
Nonprofit Management — M,O
Reading Education — M
Secondary Education — M
Special Education — M
Sports Management — M,D

UNIVERSITY OF NORTH GEORGIA
Athletic Training and Sports Medicine — M
Business Administration and Management—General — M
Curriculum and Instruction — M
Early Childhood Education — M
Education—General — M
Educational Leadership and Administration — D,O
English Education — M
Higher Education — D
Human Services — M
Kinesiology and Movement Studies — M
Mathematics Education — M
Middle School Education — M
Physical Education — M
Science Education — M
Secondary Education — M
Social Sciences Education — M

UNIVERSITY OF NORTH TEXAS
Accounting — M,D,O
Advertising and Public Relations — M,D,O
Art Education — M,D,O
Business Administration and Management—General — M,D,O
Counselor Education — M,D,O
Curriculum and Instruction — M,D,O
Early Childhood Education — M,D,O
Education of the Gifted — M,D,O
Education—General — M,D,O
Educational Leadership and Administration — M,D,O
Educational Measurement and Evaluation — M,D,O
Educational Psychology — M,D,O
English as a Second Language — M,D,O
Finance and Banking — M,D,O
Higher Education — M,D,O
Hospitality Management — M,D,O
Human Resources Management — M,D,O
Industrial and Manufacturing Management — M,D,O
Kinesiology and Movement Studies — M,D,O
Logistics — M,D,O
Management Information Systems — M,D,O
Management Strategy and Policy — M,D,O
Marketing — M,D,O
Music Education — M,D,O
Nonprofit Management — M,D,O
Quantitative Analysis — M,D,O
Special Education — M,D,O
Supply Chain Management — M,D,O
Travel and Tourism — M,D,O
Vocational and Technical Education — M

UNIVERSITY OF NORTH TEXAS AT DALLAS
Accounting — M
Business Administration and Management—General — M
Counselor Education — M
Curriculum and Instruction — M
Educational Leadership and Administration — M
Human Resources Management — M
Law — D
Management Strategy and Policy — M
Organizational Behavior — M

UNIVERSITY OF NORTHWESTERN OHIO
Business Administration and Management—General — M

UNIVERSITY OF NORTHWESTERN–ST. PAUL
Business Administration and Management—General — M
Education—General — M
Human Services — M
Organizational Management — M

UNIVERSITY OF NOTRE DAME
Accounting — M
Business Administration and Management—General — M
Business Analytics — M
Education—General — M
Entrepreneurship — M
Finance and Banking — M
Investment Management — M
Law — M,D
Marketing — M
Nonprofit Management — M
Taxation — M

UNIVERSITY OF OKLAHOMA
Accounting — M,D
Adult Education — M,D
Archives/Archival Administration — M,D,O
Business Administration and Management—General — M,D
Business Analytics — M,O
Curriculum and Instruction — M,D
Early Childhood Education — M,D
Education—General — M,D,O
Educational Leadership and Administration — M,D
Educational Media/Instructional Technology — M,D,O
Educational Psychology — M,D
Elementary Education — M,D
English Education — M,D
Entrepreneurship — M,D
Exercise and Sports Science — M,D
Finance and Banking — M,D
Foreign Languages Education — M,D
Higher Education — M,D
Human Resources Management — M,O
Human Services — M,O
Information Studies — M,D,O
International Business — M,D
Law — M,D
Library Science — M,D,O
Management Information Systems — M,D,O
Marketing — M,D
Mathematics Education — M,D
Music Education — M,D,O
Nonprofit Management — M,O
Organizational Behavior — M,O
Organizational Management — M,O
Project Management — M,O
Reading Education — M,O
Science Education — M,D
Social Sciences Education — M,D
Social Work — M
Special Education — M,D
Student Affairs — M,D
Supply Chain Management — M,D

UNIVERSITY OF OKLAHOMA HEALTH SCIENCES CENTER
Health Education — D
Reading Education — M,D,O
Special Education — M,D,O

UNIVERSITY OF OREGON
Accounting — M,D
Business Administration and Management—General — M,D
Curriculum and Instruction — M,D
Education—General — M,D
Educational Leadership and Administration — M,D
Finance and Banking — D
Law — M,D
Management Information Systems — M
Marketing — D
Music Education — M,D
Nonprofit Management — M,O
Quantitative Analysis — M
Special Education — M,D
Sports Management — M

UNIVERSITY OF OTTAWA
Business Administration and Management—General — M
Education—General — M,D,O
Electronic Commerce — M,D,O
Finance and Banking — D,O
Kinesiology and Movement Studies — M
Law — M,D
Music Education — M,O
Project Management — M,O
Social Work — M

UNIVERSITY OF PENNSYLVANIA
Accounting — M,D
Business Administration and Management—General — M,D
Counselor Education — M
Education—General — M,D,O*
Educational Leadership and Administration — M,D
Educational Measurement and Evaluation — M,D
Educational Media/Instructional Technology — M
Educational Policy — M,D
Elementary Education — M
English as a Second Language — M
English Education — M,D
Entrepreneurship — M
Finance and Banking — M,D
Foundations and Philosophy of Education — M,D
Higher Education — M,D
Insurance — M,D
International and Comparative Education — M
International Business — M
Law — M,D
Legal and Justice Studies — M,D
Management Information Systems — M,D
Marketing — M,D
Multilingual and Multicultural Education — M
Nonprofit Management — M,O

Organizational Management — M,O
Reading Education — M
Real Estate — M,D
Risk Management — M,D
Science Education — M,O
Secondary Education — M
Social Work — M,D
Urban Education — M

UNIVERSITY OF PHOENIX–BAY AREA CAMPUS
Accounting — M,D
Adult Education — M,D,O
Business Administration and Management—General — M,D
Early Childhood Education — M,D,O
Education—General — M,D,O
Educational Leadership and Administration — M,D,O
Elementary Education — M,D,O
Higher Education — M,D,O
Human Resources Management — M,D
International Business — M,D
Management Information Systems — M,D
Marketing — M,D
Organizational Management — M,D
Project Management — M,D
Secondary Education — M,D,O
Special Education — M,D,O

UNIVERSITY OF PHOENIX–CENTRAL VALLEY CAMPUS
Accounting — M
Business Administration and Management—General — M
Computer Education — M
Curriculum and Instruction — M
Education—General — M
Elementary Education — M
Human Resources Management — M
International Business — M
Management Information Systems — M
Marketing — M
Secondary Education — M

UNIVERSITY OF PHOENIX–DALLAS CAMPUS
Accounting — M
Business Administration and Management—General — M
Curriculum and Instruction — M
Education—General — M
Electronic Commerce — M
Human Resources Management — M
International Business — M
Management Information Systems — M
Marketing — M

UNIVERSITY OF PHOENIX–HAWAII CAMPUS
Accounting — M
Business Administration and Management—General — M
Curriculum and Instruction — M
Education—General — M
Educational Leadership and Administration — M
Elementary Education — M
Human Resources Management — M
International Business — M
Management Information Systems — M
Marketing — M
Secondary Education — M
Special Education — M

UNIVERSITY OF PHOENIX–HOUSTON CAMPUS
Accounting — M
Business Administration and Management—General — M
Curriculum and Instruction — M
Education—General — M
Electronic Commerce — M
Human Resources Management — M
International Business — M
Management Information Systems — M
Marketing — M

UNIVERSITY OF PHOENIX–LAS VEGAS CAMPUS
Accounting — M
Business Administration and Management—General — M
Counselor Education — M
Curriculum and Instruction — M
Education—General — M
Educational Leadership and Administration — M
Elementary Education — M
Human Resources Management — M
International Business — M
Management Information Systems — M
Marketing — M

UNIVERSITY OF PHOENIX–ONLINE CAMPUS
Accounting — M,O
Adult Education — M,O
Business Administration and Management—General — M,D,O
Computer Education — M,O
Curriculum and Instruction — M,D,O
Early Childhood Education — M,O
Education—General — M,O
Educational Leadership and Administration — M,D,O
Educational Media/Instructional Technology — D,O
Elementary Education — M,O
English as a Second Language — M,O
English Education — M,O
Health Education — M,O
Higher Education — D,O
Human Resources Management — M,O
International Business — M,O
Management Information Systems — M

Marketing — M,O
Mathematics Education — M,O
Middle School Education — M,O
Organizational Management — D,O
Project Management — M,O
Reading Education — M,O
Science Education — M,O
Secondary Education — M,O
Special Education — M,O

UNIVERSITY OF PHOENIX–PHOENIX CAMPUS
Accounting — M,O
Adult Education — M
Business Administration and Management—General — M,O
Counselor Education — M
Curriculum and Instruction — M
Early Childhood Education — M
Education—General — M
Educational Leadership and Administration — M
Elementary Education — M
Human Resources Management — M,O
International Business — M
Marketing — M,O
Project Management — M,O
Reading Education — M
Secondary Education — M
Special Education — M
Vocational and Technical Education — M

UNIVERSITY OF PHOENIX–SACRAMENTO VALLEY CAMPUS
Accounting — M
Adult Education — M,O
Business Administration and Management—General — M
Curriculum and Instruction — M,O
Education—General — M,O
Elementary Education — M,O
Human Resources Management — M
International Business — M
Management Information Systems — M
Marketing — M
Secondary Education — M,O

UNIVERSITY OF PHOENIX–SAN ANTONIO CAMPUS
Accounting — M
Business Administration and Management—General — M
Curriculum and Instruction — M
Electronic Commerce — M
Human Resources Management — M
International Business — M
Management Information Systems — M
Marketing — M

UNIVERSITY OF PHOENIX–SAN DIEGO CAMPUS
Accounting — M
Business Administration and Management—General — M
Computer Education — M
Curriculum and Instruction — M
Education—General — M
Elementary Education — M
English as a Second Language — M
Human Resources Management — M
International Business — M
Management Information Systems — M
Marketing — M
Secondary Education — M

UNIVERSITY OF PIKEVILLE
Business Administration and Management—General — M
Education—General — M
Educational Leadership and Administration — M
Entrepreneurship — M

UNIVERSITY OF PITTSBURGH
Accounting — M,D
Athletic Training and Sports Medicine — M
Business Administration and Management—General — M,D*
Business Analytics — D
Early Childhood Education — M
Education—General — M,D*
Educational Leadership and Administration — M,D
Educational Measurement and Evaluation — M,D
Educational Policy — D
Elementary Education — M
English as a Second Language — D,O
English Education — M,D
Environmental Law — M
Exercise and Sports Science — M,D
Finance and Banking — M,D
Foreign Languages Education — M,D
Foundations and Philosophy of Education — M,D
Health Education — M,D
Health Law — M
Higher Education — M,D
Human Resources Management — M,D
Industrial and Manufacturing Management — M
Intellectual Property Law — M
International and Comparative Education — M,D
International Business — O
Law — M
Legal and Justice Studies — M
Library Science — M,D
Management Information Systems — M,D
Management Strategy and Policy — M,D
Marketing — M,D
Mathematics Education — M,D
Nonprofit Management — M,D
Organizational Behavior — M,D
Reading Education — M,D

Science Education	M,D
Secondary Education	M,D
Social Sciences Education	M,D
Social Work	M,D,O
Special Education	M,D
Supply Chain Management	M

UNIVERSITY OF PORTLAND

Business Administration and Management—General	M
Education—General	M,D
Educational Leadership and Administration	M,D
English as a Second Language	M,D
Entrepreneurship	M
Finance and Banking	M
Industrial and Manufacturing Management	M
Marketing	M
Nonprofit Management	M
Organizational Management	M,D
Reading Education	M,D
Special Education	M,D
Sustainability Management	M

UNIVERSITY OF PRINCE EDWARD ISLAND

Education—General	M,D
Educational Leadership and Administration	M,D

UNIVERSITY OF PROVIDENCE

Human Services	M

UNIVERSITY OF PUERTO RICO–MAYAGÜEZ

Agricultural Education	M
Business Administration and Management—General	M
English Education	M
Exercise and Sports Science	M
Finance and Banking	M
Higher Education	M
Human Resources Management	M
Industrial and Manufacturing Management	M
Kinesiology and Movement Studies	M
Mathematics Education	M

UNIVERSITY OF PUERTO RICO–MEDICAL SCIENCES CAMPUS

Health Education	M
Special Education	O

UNIVERSITY OF PUERTO RICO–RÍO PIEDRAS

Accounting	M,D
Business Administration and Management—General	M,D
Counselor Education	M,D
Curriculum and Instruction	M,D
Early Childhood Education	M
Education—General	M,D
Educational Leadership and Administration	M,D
Educational Measurement and Evaluation	M
English as a Second Language	M
Exercise and Sports Science	M
Finance and Banking	M,D
Foreign Languages Education	M,D
Human Resources Management	M,D
Industrial and Manufacturing Management	M,D
Information Studies	M,O
International Business	M,D
Law	M,D
Library Science	M,O
Marketing	M,D
Mathematics Education	M,D
Quantitative Analysis	M,D
Science Education	M,D
Social Sciences Education	M,D
Social Work	M,D
Special Education	M

UNIVERSITY OF PUGET SOUND

Counselor Education	M
Education—General	M
Elementary Education	M
Secondary Education	M

UNIVERSITY OF REDLANDS

Business Administration and Management—General	M
Education—General	M,D,O
Management Information Systems	M

UNIVERSITY OF REGINA

Adult Education	M
Business Administration and Management—General	M,O
Curriculum and Instruction	M
Education—General	M,D,O
Educational Leadership and Administration	M
Educational Psychology	M
Human Resources Development	M
Human Resources Management	M,O
International Business	M,O
Kinesiology and Movement Studies	M,D
Organizational Management	M,O
Project Management	M,O
Social Work	M,D

UNIVERSITY OF RHODE ISLAND

Accounting	M
Business Administration and Management—General	M,D*
Education—General	M,D
Entrepreneurship	M,D,O
Exercise and Sports Science	M,D
Finance and Banking	M,D
Health Education	M

Human Resources Management	M,O
Information Studies	M
Library Science	M
Management Strategy and Policy	M,D,O
Marketing	M
Music Education	M
Physical Education	M
Reading Education	M,D
Recreation and Park Management	M
Special Education	M,D
Student Affairs	M
Supply Chain Management	M,D

UNIVERSITY OF RICHMOND

Business Administration and Management—General	M
Law	D

UNIVERSITY OF RIO GRANDE

Art Education	M
Education—General	M
Educational Leadership and Administration	M
Physical Education	M
Special Education	M

UNIVERSITY OF ROCHESTER

Accounting	M,D
Archives/Archival Administration	M
Business Administration and Management—General	M,D
Counselor Education	M,D
Curriculum and Instruction	M,D
Education—General	M,D
Educational Leadership and Administration	M,D
Educational Policy	M,D
Entrepreneurship	M
Finance and Banking	M,D
Foundations and Philosophy of Education	D
Higher Education	M,D
Industrial and Manufacturing Management	D
Management Information Systems	M,D
Management Strategy and Policy	M
Marketing Research	M
Marketing	M,D
Music Education	M,D
Student Affairs	M

UNIVERSITY OF ST. AUGUSTINE FOR HEALTH SCIENCES

Athletic Training and Sports Medicine	M
Health Education	M,D

UNIVERSITY OF ST. FRANCIS (IL)

Art Education	M,D,O
Curriculum and Instruction	M,D,O
Education—General	M,D,O
Educational Leadership and Administration	M,D,O
Elementary Education	M,D,O
English as a Second Language	M,D,O
English Education	M,D,O
Mathematics Education	M,D,O
Reading Education	M,D,O
Science Education	M,D,O
Secondary Education	M,D,O
Social Sciences Education	M,D,O
Social Work	M,O
Special Education	M,D,O

UNIVERSITY OF SAINT FRANCIS (IN)

Business Administration and Management—General	M
Counselor Education	M,O
Education—General	M
Organizational Management	M
Secondary Education	M
Special Education	M
Sustainability Management	M

UNIVERSITY OF SAINT JOSEPH

Business Administration and Management—General	M
Counselor Education	M
Curriculum and Instruction	M
Education—General	M
Educational Media/Instructional Technology	M
Elementary Education	M
English as a Second Language	M
Reading Education	M
Secondary Education	M
Special Education	M,O

UNIVERSITY OF SAINT MARY

Advertising and Public Relations	M
Business Administration and Management—General	M
Education—General	M
Elementary Education	M
Finance and Banking	M
Human Resources Management	M
Marketing	M
Risk Management	M
Special Education	M

UNIVERSITY OF ST. MICHAEL'S COLLEGE

Religious Education	M,D,O

UNIVERSITY OF ST. THOMAS (MN)

Accounting	M
Business Administration and Management—General	M,D,O
Education—General	M,D,O
Educational Leadership and Administration	M,D,O
Higher Education	M,O
Law	M,D
Music Education	M,D

Organizational Management	D
Religious Education	M
Social Work	M
Special Education	M,O
Student Affairs	M,D,O

UNIVERSITY OF ST. THOMAS (TX)

Accounting	M
Business Administration and Management—General	M
Counselor Education	M,D
Curriculum and Instruction	M,D
Education—General	M,D
Educational Leadership and Administration	M,D
Educational Measurement and Evaluation	M,D
Elementary Education	M,D
English as a Second Language	M,D
Finance and Banking	M
International Business	M
Multilingual and Multicultural Education	M,D
Reading Education	M,D
Religious Education	M,D
Secondary Education	M,D
Special Education	M,D

UNIVERSITY OF SAN DIEGO

Accounting	M
Business Administration and Management—General	M
Counselor Education	M
Curriculum and Instruction	M
Education—General	M,D,O
Educational Leadership and Administration	M,D,O
English as a Second Language	M
Finance and Banking	M
Higher Education	M,D,O
International Business	M
Law	M,D,O
Legal and Justice Studies	M,D,O
Nonprofit Management	M
Reading Education	M
Real Estate	M
Science Education	M
Special Education	M
Supply Chain Management	M
Taxation	M,D,O

UNIVERSITY OF SAN FRANCISCO

Business Administration and Management—General	M
Counselor Education	M
Curriculum and Instruction	M,D
Education—General	M,D
Educational Leadership and Administration	M,D
Educational Media/Instructional Technology	M
Entrepreneurship	M
Finance and Banking	M
Intellectual Property Law	M
International and Comparative Education	M,D
International Business	M
Law	D
Management Information Systems	M
Marketing	M
Multilingual and Multicultural Education	M
Nonprofit Management	M
Organizational Management	M
Reading Education	M,D
Religious Education	M,D
Special Education	M,D
Sports Management	M
Urban Education	M

UNIVERSITY OF SASKATCHEWAN

Accounting	M
Business Administration and Management—General	M,D
Curriculum and Instruction	M,D,O
Education—General	M,D,O
Educational Leadership and Administration	M,D,O
Educational Psychology	M,D,O
Finance and Banking	M
Foundations and Philosophy of Education	M,D,O
International Business	M,D
Kinesiology and Movement Studies	M,D,O
Law	M,D
Marketing	M
Special Education	M,D,O
Sustainability Management	M

THE UNIVERSITY OF SCRANTON

Accounting	M
Business Administration and Management—General	M
Counselor Education	M
Curriculum and Instruction	M
Education—General	M
Educational Leadership and Administration	M
Finance and Banking	M
Human Resources Development	M
International Business	M
Management Information Systems	M
Marketing	M
Reading Education	M
Secondary Education	M
Special Education	M

UNIVERSITY OF SIOUX FALLS

Business Administration and Management—General	M
Education—General	M,O
Educational Leadership and Administration	M,O

Educational Media/Instructional Technology	M,O
Entrepreneurship	M
Marketing	M
Reading Education	M,O

UNIVERSITY OF SOUTH AFRICA

Accounting	M,D
Adult Education	M,D
Business Administration and Management—General	M,D
Counselor Education	M,D
Curriculum and Instruction	M,D
Education—General	M,D
Educational Leadership and Administration	M,D
Educational Media/Instructional Technology	M,D
Educational Psychology	M,D
English as a Second Language	M,D
Environmental Education	M,D
Foundations and Philosophy of Education	M,D
Health Education	M,D
Human Resources Development	M,D
International and Comparative Education	M,D
Law	M,D
Logistics	M,D
Management Information Systems	M,D
Marketing	M,D
Mathematics Education	M,D
Quantitative Analysis	M,D
Real Estate	M,D
Science Education	M,D
Social Work	M,D
Travel and Tourism	M,D
Vocational and Technical Education	M,D

UNIVERSITY OF SOUTH ALABAMA

Accounting	M
Art Education	M,D
Business Administration and Management—General	M,D
Counselor Education	M,D,O
Early Childhood Education	M
Education—General	M,D,O
Educational Leadership and Administration	M,D
Educational Media/Instructional Technology	M,D,O
Elementary Education	M,D
Exercise and Sports Science	M
Health Education	M
Kinesiology and Movement Studies	M
Management Information Systems	M,D
Marketing	M,D
Music Education	M
Physical Education	M
Reading Education	M,D
Science Education	M,D
Secondary Education	M,D
Special Education	M,D
Sports Management	M

UNIVERSITY OF SOUTH CAROLINA

Accounting	M
Archives/Archival Administration	M,O
Art Education	M,D
Business Administration and Management—General	M,D
Business Education	M,D
Counselor Education	D,O
Curriculum and Instruction	D
Early Childhood Education	M,D
Education—General	M,D,O
Educational Leadership and Administration	M,D,O
Educational Measurement and Evaluation	M,D
Educational Media/Instructional Technology	M
Educational Psychology	M,D
Elementary Education	M,D
English as a Second Language	M,D,O
English Education	M,D
Entertainment Management	M
Exercise and Sports Science	M,D
Foreign Languages Education	M,D
Foundations and Philosophy of Education	D
Health Education	M,D,O
Higher Education	M,D
Hospitality Management	M
Human Resources Management	M
Information Studies	M,D,O
International Business	M
Law	D
Library Science	M,D,O
Mathematics Education	M,D
Music Education	M,D,O
Physical Education	M,D
Reading Education	M,D
Science Education	M,D
Secondary Education	M,D
Social Sciences Education	M,D
Social Work	M,D
Special Education	M,D
Sports Management	M
Student Affairs	M
Travel and Tourism	M

UNIVERSITY OF SOUTH CAROLINA AIKEN

Business Administration and Management—General	M
Educational Media/Instructional Technology	M

UNIVERSITY OF SOUTH CAROLINA UPSTATE

Early Childhood Education	M

---

*M—masters degree; D—doctorate; O—other advanced degree; *—Close-Up and/or Display*

Education—General M
Elementary Education M
Special Education M

UNIVERSITY OF SOUTH DAKOTA

Accounting M
Adult Education M,D,O
Art Education M
Business Administration and
  Management—General M,D
Business Analytics M,O
Counselor Education M,D,O
Curriculum and Instruction M,D,O
Early Childhood Education M,D,O
Education—General M,D,O
Educational Leadership and
  Administration M,D,O
Educational Media/Instructional
  Technology M
Educational Psychology M,D,O
Elementary Education M
English as a Second Language M
Exercise and Sports Science M
Higher Education M,D,O
Human Resources Management M
Kinesiology and Movement Studies M
Law D
Marketing M,O
Mathematics Education M
Music Education M
Organizational Management M
Reading Education M
Science Education M
Secondary Education M
Social Work M
Special Education M,D,O
Supply Chain Management M,O

UNIVERSITY OF SOUTHERN CALIFORNIA

Accounting M
Advertising and Public Relations M
Business Administration and
  Management—General M,D
Counselor Education M
Education—General M,D
Educational Leadership and
  Administration D
Educational Policy D
Educational Psychology D
English as a Second Language M
Entrepreneurship M
Health Education M
Higher Education D
Kinesiology and Movement Studies M,D
Law M,D
Multilingual and Multicultural
  Education D
Music Education M,D,O
Nonprofit Management M,O
Organizational Management M
Quantitative Analysis M,D
Real Estate M
Social Work M,D
Student Affairs M
Supply Chain Management M,D,O
Taxation M
Urban Education D

UNIVERSITY OF SOUTHERN INDIANA

Accounting M
Business Administration and
  Management—General M
Education—General M,D
Educational Leadership and
  Administration M,D
Elementary Education M
English as a Second Language M
Human Resources Management M
Industrial and Manufacturing
  Management M
Mathematics Education M
Nonprofit Management M
Secondary Education M
Social Work M
Sports Management M

UNIVERSITY OF SOUTHERN MAINE

Accounting M
Adult Education M,O
Business Administration and
  Management—General M,O
Counselor Education M,O
Education of the Gifted M,O
Education—General M,D,O
Educational Leadership and
  Administration M,O
Educational Psychology M,O
English as a Second Language M,O
Finance and Banking M,O
Higher Education M,O
Music Education M
Reading Education M,O
Social Work M
Special Education M,O
Sustainability Management M

UNIVERSITY OF SOUTHERN MISSISSIPPI

Accounting M
Business Administration and
  Management—General M
Curriculum and Instruction M,D
Education—General M,D,O
Educational Leadership and
  Administration M,D,O
Educational Measurement and
  Evaluation M,D,O
Educational Media/Instructional
  Technology M,D
Elementary Education M,D
English Education M,D
Foreign Languages Education M
Higher Education M,D,O
Library Science M,O
Music Education M,D

Physical Education M,D
Secondary Education M,D
Social Work M
Special Education M,D
Student Affairs M,D,O

UNIVERSITY OF SOUTH FLORIDA

Accounting M,D
Adult Education M,D,O
Athletic Training and Sports
  Medicine M,D
Business Administration and
  Management—General M
Community College Education M,D,O
Counselor Education M,D,O
Distance Education Development O
Early Childhood Education M,D,O
Education—General M,D,O
Educational Leadership and
  Administration M,D,O
Educational Measurement and
  Evaluation O
Educational Media/Instructional
  Technology O
Educational Psychology M,D,O
Elementary Education M,D,O
English as a Second Language M,D,O
Entrepreneurship M,O
Finance and Banking M,D
Foreign Languages Education O
Health Education M
Higher Education M,D,O
Human Resources Development M
Human Resources Management M
Information Studies O
Legal and Justice Studies O
Library Science M
Management Information Systems M,D,O
Management Strategy and Policy M,D,O
Marketing M,D
Music Education M,D
Nonprofit Management M
Reading Education M,D,O
Real Estate M
Secondary Education O
Social Sciences Education M,D,O
Social Work M,D,O
Special Education O
Sports Management M,D
Student Affairs M,D
Sustainability Management M,O
Taxation M,O
Travel and Tourism M,O
Vocational and Technical Education M,D,O

UNIVERSITY OF SOUTH FLORIDA, ST. PETERSBURG

Business Administration and
  Management—General M
Education—General M
Educational Leadership and
  Administration M
Elementary Education M
English Education M
Mathematics Education M
Middle School Education M
Reading Education M
Science Education M

UNIVERSITY OF SOUTH FLORIDA SARASOTA-MANATEE

Business Administration and
  Management—General M
Curriculum and Instruction M
Educational Leadership and
  Administration M
Elementary Education M
English Education M
Hospitality Management M
Social Work M

THE UNIVERSITY OF TAMPA

Accounting M,O
Business Administration and
  Management—General M,O
Business Analytics M,O
Curriculum and Instruction M
Education—General M
Educational Leadership and
  Administration M
Educational Media/Instructional
  Technology M
Entrepreneurship M,O
Exercise and Sports Science M
Finance and Banking M,O
International Business M,O
Management Information Systems M,O
Marketing M,O
Nonprofit Management M,O

THE UNIVERSITY OF TENNESSEE

Accounting M,D
Adult Education M,D
Advertising and Public Relations M,D
Agricultural Education M
Art Education M,D,O
Athletic Training and Sports
  Medicine M,D
Business Administration and
  Management—General M,D
Counselor Education M,D,O
Curriculum and Instruction M,D,O
Early Childhood Education M,D,O
Education—General M,D,O
Educational Leadership and
  Administration M,D,O
Educational Measurement and
  Evaluation M,D,O
Educational Media/Instructional
  Technology M,D,O
Educational Psychology M,D,O
Elementary Education M,D,O
English as a Second Language M,D,O
English Education M,D,O
Exercise and Sports Science M,D
Finance and Banking M,D

Foreign Languages Education M,D,O
Foundations and Philosophy of
  Education M,D,O
Health Education M
Hospitality Management M
Human Resources Development M
Industrial and Manufacturing
  Management M,D
Kinesiology and Movement Studies M,D
Law D
Leisure Studies M,D
Logistics M,D
Marketing M,D
Mathematics Education M,D,O
Multilingual and Multicultural
  Education M,D,O
Music Education M
Reading Education M,D,O
Recreation and Park Management M,D
Science Education M,D
Secondary Education M,D,O
Social Sciences Education M,D,O
Social Work M,D,O
Special Education M,D,O
Sports Management M,D
Student Affairs M
Transportation Management M,D
Travel and Tourism M,D

THE UNIVERSITY OF TENNESSEE AT CHATTANOOGA

Accounting M
Athletic Training and Sports
  Medicine M
Business Administration and
  Management—General M
Counselor Education M,D,O
Education—General M,D,O
Educational Leadership and
  Administration M,D,O
Elementary Education M,D,O
Logistics M,O
Mathematics Education M
Music Education M
Nonprofit Management M,O
Physical Education M
Project Management M,O
Quality Management M,O
Secondary Education M,D,O
Social Work M
Special Education M,O
Supply Chain Management M,O

THE UNIVERSITY OF TENNESSEE AT MARTIN

Business Administration and
  Management—General M
Counselor Education M
Curriculum and Instruction M
Education—General M
Educational Leadership and
  Administration M
Elementary Education M
Finance and Banking M
Physical Education M
Secondary Education M
Special Education M
Student Affairs M

THE UNIVERSITY OF TEXAS AT ARLINGTON

Accounting M,D
Athletic Training and Sports
  Medicine M,D
Curriculum and Instruction M
Education—General M,D
Educational Leadership and
  Administration M,D
Educational Policy M,D
English as a Second Language M
Exercise and Sports Science M,D
Finance and Banking M,D
Higher Education M,D
Human Resources Management M
Kinesiology and Movement Studies M,D
Logistics M
Management Information Systems M,D
Marketing Research M
Marketing M
Mathematics Education M,D
Music Education M
Quantitative Analysis M,D
Reading Education M
Real Estate M
Science Education M
Social Work M,D
Taxation M,D

THE UNIVERSITY OF TEXAS AT AUSTIN

Accounting M,D
Actuarial Science M,D
Advertising and Public Relations M,D
Art Education M
Business Administration and
  Management—General M,D
Counselor Education M,D
Curriculum and Instruction M,D
Early Childhood Education M,D
Education—General M,D
Educational Leadership and
  Administration M,D
Educational Media/Instructional
  Technology M,D
Educational Psychology M,D
Entrepreneurship M,D
Exercise and Sports Science M,D
Finance and Banking M,D
Health Education M,D
Industrial and Manufacturing
  Management M,D
Information Studies M,D
Kinesiology and Movement Studies M,D
Law M,D
Management Information Systems M,D
Marketing M,D

Multilingual and Multicultural
  Education M,D
Music Education M,D
Organizational Behavior M
Physical Education M,D
Quantitative Analysis M,D
Reading Education M,D
Risk Management M,D
Social Work M,D
Special Education M,D
Supply Chain Management M,D

THE UNIVERSITY OF TEXAS AT DALLAS

Accounting M
Actuarial Science M
Business Administration and
  Management—General M,D
Entrepreneurship M,D
Finance and Banking M
Industrial and Manufacturing
  Management M,D
International Business M,D
Law M
Management Information Systems M
Management Strategy and Policy M
Marketing M
Mathematics Education M
Nonprofit Management M,D
Project Management M,D
Real Estate M
Science Education M
Supply Chain Management M

THE UNIVERSITY OF TEXAS AT EL PASO

Accounting M
Art Education M
Business Administration and
  Management—General M,D,O
Counselor Education M
Curriculum and Instruction M,D
Education—General M,D
Educational Leadership and
  Administration M,D
Educational Measurement and
  Evaluation M
Educational Psychology M
English as a Second Language M,O
English Education M,D,O
International Business M,D,O
Kinesiology and Movement Studies M
Mathematics Education M
Multilingual and Multicultural
  Education M,D,O
Music Education M
Reading Education M,D
Science Education M
Social Work M
Special Education M

THE UNIVERSITY OF TEXAS AT SAN ANTONIO

Accounting M,D
Business Administration and
  Management—General M,D,O
Counselor Education M,D
Curriculum and Instruction M,D
Early Childhood Education M,D
Educational Leadership and
  Administration M,D
Educational Measurement and
  Evaluation M,O
Educational Media/Instructional
  Technology M,D
Educational Psychology M,O
English as a Second Language M,D,O
Finance and Banking M,D
Health Education M
Higher Education M,D
Kinesiology and Movement Studies M
Marketing M,D
Mathematics Education M
Multilingual and Multicultural
  Education M,D
Organizational Management D
Reading Education M,D
Social Work M
Special Education M

THE UNIVERSITY OF TEXAS AT TYLER

Accounting M
Business Administration and
  Management—General M
Early Childhood Education M
Educational Leadership and
  Administration M
Health Education M
Human Resources Development M,D
Industrial and Manufacturing
  Management M
Kinesiology and Movement Studies M
Marketing M
Organizational Management M
Quality Management M
Reading Education M
Special Education M

THE UNIVERSITY OF TEXAS HEALTH SCIENCE CENTER AT HOUSTON

Quantitative Analysis M,D

THE UNIVERSITY OF TEXAS HEALTH SCIENCE CENTER AT SAN ANTONIO

Special Education M,D

THE UNIVERSITY OF TEXAS OF THE PERMIAN BASIN

Accounting M
Business Administration and
  Management—General M
Counselor Education M
Early Childhood Education M
Education—General M
Educational Leadership and
  Administration M
English as a Second Language M

Foundations and Philosophy of Education	M
Kinesiology and Movement Studies	M
Reading Education	M
Special Education	M

THE UNIVERSITY OF TEXAS RIO GRANDE VALLEY

Accounting	M
Business Administration and Management—General	M,D
Counselor Education	M
Curriculum and Instruction	M,D
Early Childhood Education	M
Education—General	M,D
Educational Leadership and Administration	M,D
Educational Media/Instructional Technology	M,D
Educational Psychology	M
Elementary Education	M
English as a Second Language	M
Exercise and Sports Science	M
Finance and Banking	M,D
Kinesiology and Movement Studies	M
Management Information Systems	M
Marketing	M,D
Multilingual and Multicultural Education	M
Reading Education	M
Secondary Education	M,D
Social Work	M
Special Education	M

THE UNIVERSITY OF THE ARTS

Art Education	M
Museum Education	M
Music Education	M

UNIVERSITY OF THE CUMBERLANDS

Accounting	M
Business Administration and Management—General	M
Business Education	M,D,O
Counselor Education	M,D,O
Education—General	M,D,O
Educational Leadership and Administration	M,D,O
Elementary Education	M,D,O
Marketing	M,D,O
Middle School Education	M,D,O
Reading Education	M,D,O
Secondary Education	M,D,O
Special Education	M,D,O
Student Affairs	M,D,O

UNIVERSITY OF THE DISTRICT OF COLUMBIA

Adult Education	O
Business Administration and Management—General	M
Early Childhood Education	M
Elementary Education	M
English Education	M
Law	M,D
Legal and Justice Studies	M,D
Mathematics Education	M
Middle School Education	M
Secondary Education	M
Social Sciences Education	M

UNIVERSITY OF THE FRASER VALLEY

Social Work	M

UNIVERSITY OF THE INCARNATE WORD

Business Administration and Management—General	M,D
Education—General	M,D
Kinesiology and Movement Studies	M,D
Mathematics Education	M
Organizational Management	M
Sports Management	M,D

UNIVERSITY OF THE PACIFIC

Business Administration and Management—General	M
Curriculum and Instruction	M,D,O
Education—General	M,D,O
Educational Leadership and Administration	M,D,O
Educational Psychology	M,D,O
Exercise and Sports Science	M
Hospitality Management	M
Law	M,D
Music Education	M
Special Education	M,D,O

UNIVERSITY OF THE PEOPLE

Business Administration and Management—General	M

UNIVERSITY OF THE POTOMAC

Business Administration and Management—General	M

UNIVERSITY OF THE SACRED HEART

Accounting	M,O
Advertising and Public Relations	M
Business Administration and Management—General	M,O
Early Childhood Education	M,O
Education—General	M,O
Educational Media/Instructional Technology	M
English Education	M,O
Foreign Languages Education	M,O
Human Resources Management	M
Legal and Justice Studies	M
Management Information Systems	M
Marketing	M,O
Mathematics Education	M,O
Nonprofit Management	M
Taxation	M

UNIVERSITY OF THE SOUTHWEST

Business Administration and Management—General	M
Counselor Education	M
Curriculum and Instruction	M
Early Childhood Education	M
Education—General	M
Educational Leadership and Administration	M
English as a Second Language	M
Multilingual and Multicultural Education	M
Special Education	M
Sports Management	M

UNIVERSITY OF THE VIRGIN ISLANDS

Business Administration and Management—General	M,D,O
Education—General	M,D,O
Educational Leadership and Administration	M,D,O
Mathematics Education	M
Secondary Education	M

UNIVERSITY OF THE WEST

Business Administration and Management—General	M
Finance and Banking	M
International Business	M
Management Information Systems	M
Nonprofit Management	M

THE UNIVERSITY OF TOLEDO

Accounting	M
Art Education	M,D,O
Athletic Training and Sports Medicine	M,D
Business Administration and Management—General	M,D,O
Business Education	M,D,O
Counselor Education	M,D,O
Curriculum and Instruction	M,D,O
Early Childhood Education	M,D,O
Education of the Gifted	M,D,O
Education—General	M,D,O
Educational Leadership and Administration	M,D,O
Educational Measurement and Evaluation	M,D,O
Educational Media/Instructional Technology	M,D,O
Educational Psychology	M,D,O
Elementary Education	M,D,O
English as a Second Language	M,D,O
English Education	M,D,O
Exercise and Sports Science	M,D
Finance and Banking	M
Foreign Languages Education	M,D,O
Foundations and Philosophy of Education	M,D,O
Health Education	M,D,O
Higher Education	M,D,O
International Business	M
Law	M,D,O
Leisure Studies	M,D
Marketing	M
Mathematics Education	M,D,O
Middle School Education	M,D,O
Music Education	M,O
Nonprofit Management	M,O
Physical Education	M
Recreation and Park Management	M,D
Science Education	M,D,O
Secondary Education	M,D,O
Social Sciences Education	M,O
Social Work	M,D,O
Special Education	M,D,O
Vocational and Technical Education	M,D,O

UNIVERSITY OF TORONTO

Business Administration and Management—General	M,D
Education—General	M,D
Finance and Banking	M
Human Resources Management	M,D
Information Studies	M,D
Kinesiology and Movement Studies	M,D
Law	M,D
Music Education	M,D
Physical Education	M,D
Social Work	M,D

THE UNIVERSITY OF TULSA

Accounting	M
Business Administration and Management—General	M
Business Analytics	M
Education—General	M
English Education	M
Environmental Law	M,D,O
Finance and Banking	M
Health Law	M,D,O
Kinesiology and Movement Studies	M
Law	M,D,O
Mathematics Education	M
Risk Management	M
Science Education	M

UNIVERSITY OF UTAH

Accounting	M,D
Art Education	M
Business Administration and Management—General	M,D,O
Counselor Education	M,D,O
Early Childhood Education	M,D
Education—General	M,D,O
Educational Leadership and Administration	M,D
Educational Media/Instructional Technology	M,D,O
Educational Policy	M,D
Educational Psychology	M,D,O
Elementary Education	M,D,O
Finance and Banking	M,D
Foundations and Philosophy of Education	M,D
Health Education	M,D
Higher Education	M,D
Industrial and Manufacturing Management	M,D,O
Kinesiology and Movement Studies	M,D
Law	M,D
Leisure Studies	M,D
Management Information Systems	M,D,O
Management Strategy and Policy	M,D,O
Marketing	M,D
Mathematics Education	M,D
Music Education	M,D
Organizational Behavior	M,D
Reading Education	M,D,O
Real Estate	M
Recreation and Park Management	M,D
Science Education	M,D
Secondary Education	M,D
Social Work	M,D
Special Education	M,D
Student Affairs	M,D

UNIVERSITY OF VERMONT

Accounting	M
Business Administration and Management—General	M
Counselor Education	M
Curriculum and Instruction	M
Early Childhood Education	M
Education—General	M,D
Educational Leadership and Administration	M,D
Educational Policy	D
Elementary Education	M
Foreign Languages Education	M,O
Higher Education	M
Middle School Education	M
Science Education	M,D
Secondary Education	M
Social Work	M
Special Education	M
Sustainability Management	M

UNIVERSITY OF VICTORIA

Art Education	M,D
Business Administration and Management—General	M
Counselor Education	M,D
Curriculum and Instruction	M,D
Early Childhood Education	M,D
Education—General	M,D
Educational Leadership and Administration	M,D
Educational Measurement and Evaluation	M,D
Educational Psychology	M,D
English Education	M,D
Environmental Education	M,D
Foreign Languages Education	M
Foundations and Philosophy of Education	M,D
Kinesiology and Movement Studies	M
Law	M,D
Leisure Studies	M
Mathematics Education	M,D
Music Education	M,D
Physical Education	M
Reading Education	M,D
Science Education	M,D
Social Sciences Education	M,D
Social Work	M
Special Education	M,D
Vocational and Technical Education	M,D

UNIVERSITY OF VIRGINIA

Accounting	M
Business Administration and Management—General	M,D,O
Counselor Education	M,D,O
Curriculum and Instruction	M,D,O
Early Childhood Education	M,D
Education of the Gifted	M,D,O
Education—General	M,D,O
Educational Leadership and Administration	M,D,O
Educational Measurement and Evaluation	M,D,O
Educational Media/Instructional Technology	M,D,O
Educational Policy	D
Educational Psychology	M,D,O
Elementary Education	M,D,O
English Education	M,D,O
Finance and Banking	M
Foreign Languages Education	M,D,O
Higher Education	M,D,O
International Business	M,O
Kinesiology and Movement Studies	M,D
Law	M,D,O
Management Strategy and Policy	M,O
Marketing	M
Mathematics Education	M,D,O
Physical Education	M,D
Reading Education	M,D
Science Education	M,D,O
Social Sciences Education	M,D,O
Special Education	M,D,O
Student Affairs	M,D,O

UNIVERSITY OF WASHINGTON

Accounting	M,D
Business Administration and Management—General	M,D
Curriculum and Instruction	M,D
Education—General	M,D
Educational Leadership and Administration	M,D
Educational Measurement and Evaluation	M,D

Educational Media/Instructional Technology	M,D
Educational Policy	M,D
Educational Psychology	M,D
English as a Second Language	M,D
English Education	M,D
Entrepreneurship	M,D
Foundations and Philosophy of Education	M,D
Higher Education	M,D
Intellectual Property Law	M,D
International Business	M,D,O
Law	M,D
Legal and Justice Studies	M,D
Library Science	M,D
Logistics	O
Management Information Systems	M,D
Mathematics Education	M,D
Multilingual and Multicultural Education	M,D
Music Education	M,D
Physical Education	M,D
Reading Education	M,D
Science Education	M,D
Social Sciences Education	M,D
Social Work	M,D
Special Education	M,D
Supply Chain Management	M,D
Taxation	M,D
Transportation Management	O

UNIVERSITY OF WASHINGTON, BOTHELL

Business Administration and Management—General	M
Education—General	M
Educational Leadership and Administration	M
Middle School Education	M
Secondary Education	M

UNIVERSITY OF WASHINGTON, TACOMA

Accounting	M
Business Administration and Management—General	M
Education—General	M
Educational Leadership and Administration	M
Elementary Education	M
Finance and Banking	M
Mathematics Education	M
Science Education	M
Social Work	M
Special Education	M

UNIVERSITY OF WATERLOO

Accounting	M,D
Actuarial Science	M,D
Business Administration and Management—General	M
Entrepreneurship	M
Finance and Banking	M,D
Health Education	M,D
Kinesiology and Movement Studies	M,D
Leisure Studies	M,D
Recreation and Park Management	M,D
Taxation	M

THE UNIVERSITY OF WEST ALABAMA

Adult Education	M
Business Administration and Management—General	M,O
Counselor Education	M,O
Early Childhood Education	M,O
Education—General	M,O
Educational Leadership and Administration	M,O
Educational Media/Instructional Technology	M,O
Elementary Education	M,O
English Education	M
Finance and Banking	M
Higher Education	M
Mathematics Education	M
Physical Education	M
Science Education	M
Secondary Education	M
Social Sciences Education	M
Special Education	M
Student Affairs	M

THE UNIVERSITY OF WESTERN ONTARIO

Business Administration and Management—General	M,D
Curriculum and Instruction	M
Education—General	M
Educational Policy	M
Educational Psychology	M
Entrepreneurship	M,D
Finance and Banking	M,D
Information Studies	M,D
International Business	M,D
Kinesiology and Movement Studies	M,D
Law	M,D,O
Library Science	M,D
Management Strategy and Policy	M,D
Marketing	M,D
Special Education	M

UNIVERSITY OF WEST FLORIDA

Accounting	M
Business Administration and Management—General	M
Curriculum and Instruction	M,O
Educational Leadership and Administration	M,D
Educational Media/Instructional Technology	M,D
Elementary Education	M
Exercise and Sports Science	M
Leisure Studies	M

*M—masters degree; D—doctorate; O—other advanced degree; *—Close-Up and/or Display*

Middle School Education M
Physical Education M,D
Reading Education M
Secondary Education M
Social Work M
Special Education M
Student Affairs M

UNIVERSITY OF WEST GEORGIA
Accounting M
Business Administration and
  Management—General M
Business Education M,D,O
Counselor Education M,D,O
Early Childhood Education M,D,O
Education—General M,D,O
Educational Leadership and
  Administration M,D,O
Educational Media/Instructional
  Technology M,D,O
Music Education M,O
Nonprofit Management M,D,O
Reading Education M
Secondary Education M,D,O
Special Education M,D,O

UNIVERSITY OF WINDSOR
Business Administration and
  Management—General M
Education—General M,D
Kinesiology and Movement Studies M
Legal and Justice Studies M
Social Work M

UNIVERSITY OF WISCONSIN–EAU CLAIRE
Business Administration and
  Management—General M
Education—General M
Library Science M
Reading Education M
Secondary Education M
Special Education M

UNIVERSITY OF WISCONSIN–GREEN BAY
Business Administration and
  Management—General M
Education—General M
Social Work M
Sustainability Management M

UNIVERSITY OF WISCONSIN–LA CROSSE
Athletic Training and Sports
  Medicine M
Education—General M,O
English Education M,O
Exercise and Sports Science M
Health Education M
Higher Education M,D
Physical Education M
Reading Education M,O
Recreation and Park Management M
Special Education M,O
Student Affairs M,D

UNIVERSITY OF WISCONSIN–MADISON
Accounting M,D
Actuarial Science D
Business Administration and
  Management—General M
Counselor Education M
Curriculum and Instruction M,D
Education—General M,D,O
Educational Leadership and
  Administration M,D,O
Educational Policy M,D,O
Educational Psychology M,D
English as a Second Language M,D
Finance and Banking M,D
Higher Education M,D,O
Human Resources Management M,D
Information Studies M,D
Insurance M,D
International and Comparative
  Education M,D,O
Investment Management D
Kinesiology and Movement Studies M,D
Law M,D
Library Science M,D
Management Information Systems D
Management Strategy and Policy M,D
Marketing Research M
Marketing D
Music Education M,D
Real Estate M,D
Risk Management M,D
Social Work M,D
Special Education M,D
Supply Chain Management M
Taxation M

UNIVERSITY OF WISCONSIN–MILWAUKEE
Actuarial Science M,D
Adult Education M,D,O
Art Education M,D,O
Athletic Training and Sports
  Medicine M,D
Business Administration and
  Management—General M,D,O
Business Analytics M,O
Curriculum and Instruction M,D,O
Early Childhood Education M
Education—General M,D,O
Educational Leadership and
  Administration M,D,O
Educational Measurement and
  Evaluation M,D,O
Educational Media/Instructional
  Technology M,O
Educational Policy M,O
Educational Psychology M,D,O
Elementary Education M
English as a Second Language M,D,O

English Education M,D
Entrepreneurship M,D,O
Exercise and Sports Science M
Foreign Languages Education M,O
Foundations and Philosophy of
  Education M,D,O
Higher Education M,D,O
Human Resources Management M
Information Studies M,D,O
Investment Management M,O
Kinesiology and Movement Studies M,D
Library Science M,D,O
Management Strategy and Policy M,D,O
Mathematics Education M,D,O
Middle School Education M
Multilingual and Multicultural
  Education M,D,O
Nonprofit Management M,D,O
Reading Education M
Recreation and Park Management M
Science Education M
Secondary Education M,D
Social Sciences Education M
Social Work M,D,O
Special Education M
Taxation M,O
Urban Education M,D,O

UNIVERSITY OF WISCONSIN–OSHKOSH
Business Administration and
  Management—General M
Counselor Education M
Curriculum and Instruction M
Early Childhood Education M
Education—General M
Educational Leadership and
  Administration M
International Business M
Mathematics Education M
Reading Education M
Social Work M
Special Education M

UNIVERSITY OF WISCONSIN–PARKSIDE
Business Administration and
  Management—General M
Sports Management M
Sustainability Management M

UNIVERSITY OF WISCONSIN–PLATTEVILLE
Adult Education M
Education—General M
Human Resources Management M
Organizational Management M
Project Management M
Supply Chain Management M

UNIVERSITY OF WISCONSIN–RIVER FALLS
Agricultural Education M
Business Administration and
  Management—General M
Counselor Education M,O
Education—General M
Elementary Education M
English as a Second Language M
Mathematics Education M
Reading Education M
Science Education M
Social Sciences Education M

UNIVERSITY OF WISCONSIN–STEVENS POINT
Advertising and Public Relations M
Business Administration and
  Management—General M
Counselor Education M
Education—General M,D
Educational Leadership and
  Administration M
Elementary Education M
Music Education M
Reading Education M
Science Education M
Secondary Education M
Special Education M

UNIVERSITY OF WISCONSIN–STOUT
Education—General M,D,O
Human Resources Development M
Project Management M
Quality Management M
Supply Chain Management M
Sustainability Management M
Vocational and Technical Education M,D,O

UNIVERSITY OF WISCONSIN–SUPERIOR
Art Education M
Counselor Education M
Curriculum and Instruction M
Education—General M
Educational Leadership and
  Administration M,O
Reading Education M
Special Education M
Sustainability Management M

UNIVERSITY OF WISCONSIN–WHITEWATER
Accounting M
Business Administration and
  Management—General M
Business Education M
Education—General M,O
Educational Leadership and
  Administration M
Finance and Banking M
Marketing M
Special Education M,O

UNIVERSITY OF WYOMING
Accounting M
Business Administration and
  Management—General M
Counselor Education M,D
Curriculum and Instruction M,D

Educational Leadership and
  Administration M,D,O
Educational Media/Instructional
  Technology M,D
Exercise and Sports Science M
Finance and Banking M
Health Education M
Kinesiology and Movement Studies M
Law D
Mathematics Education M,D
Music Education M
Physical Education M
Science Education M
Social Work M
Special Education M,D,O
Student Affairs M,D

UPPER IOWA UNIVERSITY
Accounting M
Business Administration and
  Management—General M
Early Childhood Education M
Education—General M
Educational Leadership and
  Administration M
English as a Second Language M
Finance and Banking M
Higher Education M
Human Resources Management M
Human Services M
Nonprofit Management M
Organizational Management M
Reading Education M
Sports Management M

URBANA UNIVERSITY–A BRANCH CAMPUS OF FRANKLIN UNIVERSITY
Business Administration and
  Management—General M
Education—General M

URSULINE COLLEGE
Accounting M
Business Administration and
  Management—General M
Early Childhood Education M
Educational Leadership and
  Administration M
Entrepreneurship M
Finance and Banking M
Marketing M
Middle School Education M
Secondary Education M
Special Education M

UTAH STATE UNIVERSITY
Accounting M
Agricultural Education M
Business Administration and
  Management—General M
Business Education D
Counselor Education M
Curriculum and Instruction D
Education—General M,D,O
Educational Measurement and
  Evaluation M,D
Educational Media/Instructional
  Technology M,D,O
Elementary Education M
Finance and Banking M
Health Education M,D
Home Economics Education M
Human Resources Management M
Kinesiology and Movement Studies M,D
Management Information Systems M
Multilingual and Multicultural
  Education M
Music Education M
Physical Education M,D
Recreation and Park Management M,D
Secondary Education M
Social Work M,D
Special Education M,D,O
Vocational and Technical Education D

UTAH VALLEY UNIVERSITY
Accounting M
Business Administration and
  Management—General M
Education—General M
Educational Leadership and
  Administration M
Educational Media/Instructional
  Technology M
Elementary Education M
English as a Second Language M
Mathematics Education M
Reading Education M

UTICA COLLEGE
Accounting M
Education—General M,O

VALDOSTA STATE UNIVERSITY
Accounting M
Business Administration and
  Management—General M
Counselor Education M,O
Educational Leadership and
  Administration M,D,O
Elementary Education M
English Education M
Exercise and Sports Science M
Information Studies M
Library Science M
Social Work M
Special Education M,D,O

VALLEY CITY STATE UNIVERSITY
Education—General M
Educational Media/Instructional
  Technology M
Elementary Education M
English as a Second Language M
English Education M
Library Science M
Vocational and Technical Education M

VALPARAISO UNIVERSITY
Business Administration and
  Management—General M,O
Education—General M,O
Educational Leadership and
  Administration M,O
Elementary Education M,O
English as a Second Language M,O
Entertainment Management M
Finance and Banking M,O
Law M,D
Management Information Systems M
Management Strategy and Policy M
Secondary Education M,O
Sports Management M

VANCOUVER ISLAND UNIVERSITY
Business Administration and
  Management—General M
Finance and Banking M
International Business M
Marketing M

VANCOUVER SCHOOL OF THEOLOGY
Religious Education M,O

VANDERBILT UNIVERSITY
Accounting M
Business Administration and
  Management—General M
Counselor Education M
Education—General M,D*
Educational Leadership and
  Administration M
Educational Policy M,D
Elementary Education M
English Education M
Finance and Banking M
Foreign Languages Education M,D
Higher Education M,D
International and Comparative
  Education M,D
Law M,D
Management Strategy and Policy M
Marketing M
Multilingual and Multicultural
  Education M,D
Organizational Management M,D
Quantitative Analysis M
Reading Education M
Science Education M,D
Secondary Education M
Special Education M,D
Urban Education M

VANDERCOOK COLLEGE OF MUSIC
Music Education M

VANGUARD UNIVERSITY OF SOUTHERN CALIFORNIA
Education—General M

VAUGHN COLLEGE OF AERONAUTICS AND TECHNOLOGY
Aviation Management M

VERMONT COLLEGE OF FINE ARTS
Art Education M

VERMONT LAW SCHOOL
Environmental Law M
Law D
Legal and Justice Studies M

VILLANOVA UNIVERSITY
Accounting M
Business Administration and
  Management—General M
Counselor Education M
Education—General M
Educational Leadership and
  Administration M
Finance and Banking M
Human Resources Development M
International Business M
Law D
Management Strategy and Policy M
Marketing M
Nonprofit Management M,O
Real Estate M
Taxation M

VIRGINIA COMMONWEALTH UNIVERSITY
Accounting M
Adult Education M
Advertising and Public Relations M
Art Education M,D
Business Administration and
  Management—General M,D
Counselor Education M,D
Curriculum and Instruction D
Early Childhood Education M
Education—General M,D,O
Educational Leadership and
  Administration M,D
Educational Measurement and
  Evaluation D
Educational Media/Instructional
  Technology M
Educational Psychology D
Elementary Education M
Exercise and Sports Science M
Finance and Banking M
Human Resources Development M
Human Resources Management M
Management Information Systems M
Music Education M
Nonprofit Management O
Reading Education M,O
Real Estate M
Recreation and Park Management M
Social Work M,D
Special Education M,D
Student Affairs M
Urban Education D

VIRGINIA INTERNATIONAL UNIVERSITY

Accounting	M,O
Advertising and Public Relations	M,O
Business Administration and Management—General	M,O
Education—General	M
English as a Second Language	M
Entrepreneurship	M,O
Finance and Banking	M,O
Hospitality Management	M,O
Human Resources Management	M,O
International Business	M,O
Logistics	M,O
Management Information Systems	M,O
Marketing	M,O
Project Management	M,O

VIRGINIA POLYTECHNIC INSTITUTE AND STATE UNIVERSITY

Accounting	M,D
Business Administration and Management—General	M,D
Business Analytics	M,D
Counselor Education	M,D,O
Curriculum and Instruction	M,D,O
Distance Education Development	M,O
Education—General	M,O
Educational Leadership and Administration	M,D,O
Educational Measurement and Evaluation	M,D,O
Educational Media/Instructional Technology	M,O
Educational Policy	M,D,O
Exercise and Sports Science	M,D
Finance and Banking	M,O
Management Information Systems	M,D,O
Marketing	M,D
Nonprofit Management	M,O
Quantitative Analysis	M,O
Social Sciences Education	M,D,O
Vocational and Technical Education	M,D,O

VIRGINIA STATE UNIVERSITY

Counselor Education	M
Education—General	M,D
Educational Leadership and Administration	M,D
Health Education	M,D
Mathematics Education	M

VIRGINIA THEOLOGICAL SEMINARY

Educational Leadership and Administration	M,D

VIRGINIA UNION UNIVERSITY

Curriculum and Instruction	M
Education—General	M

VIRGINIA WESLEYAN UNIVERSITY

Business Administration and Management—General	M
Education—General	M
Secondary Education	M

VITERBO UNIVERSITY

Business Administration and Management—General	M,O
Early Childhood Education	M,O
Education of the Gifted	M,O
Education—General	M,O
Educational Leadership and Administration	M,O
International Business	M
Organizational Management	M,O
Project Management	M
Reading Education	M,O
Special Education	M,O

WAGNER COLLEGE

Accounting	M
Business Administration and Management—General	M
Early Childhood Education	M
Education—General	M
Elementary Education	M
English Education	M
Finance and Banking	M
Foreign Languages Education	M
Higher Education	M
Marketing	M
Mathematics Education	M
Middle School Education	M
Science Education	M
Secondary Education	M
Social Sciences Education	M
Special Education	M

WAKE FOREST UNIVERSITY

Accounting	M
Business Administration and Management—General	M
Business Analytics	M
Counselor Education	M
Education—General	M
Exercise and Sports Science	M
Law	M
Secondary Education	M
Taxation	M

WALDEN UNIVERSITY

Accounting	M,D,O
Adult Education	M,D,O
Business Administration and Management—General	M,D,O
Counselor Education	M,D
Curriculum and Instruction	M,D,O
Developmental Education	M,D,O
Distance Education Development	M,D,O
Early Childhood Education	M,D,O
Education—General	M,D,O
Educational Leadership and Administration	M,D,O

Educational Measurement and Evaluation	M,D,O
Educational Media/Instructional Technology	M,D,O
Educational Psychology	M,D,O
Elementary Education	M,D,O
English as a Second Language	M,D,O
Entrepreneurship	M,D,O
Finance and Banking	M,D,O
Health Education	M,D,O
Higher Education	M,D,O
Human Resources Management	M,D,O
Human Services	M,D
International and Comparative Education	M,D,O
International Business	M,D,O
Law	M,D,O
Management Information Systems	M,D,O
Marketing	M,D,O
Mathematics Education	M,D,O
Multilingual and Multicultural Education	M,D,O
Nonprofit Management	M,O
Organizational Management	M,D,O
Project Management	M,D,O
Reading Education	M,D,O
Science Education	M,D,O
Social Work	M,D
Special Education	M,D,O
Supply Chain Management	M,D,O

WALDORF UNIVERSITY

Educational Leadership and Administration	M
Human Resources Development	M
Organizational Management	M
Sports Management	M

WALLA WALLA UNIVERSITY

Curriculum and Instruction	M
Education—General	M
Educational Leadership and Administration	M
Reading Education	M
Social Work	M
Special Education	M

WALSH COLLEGE OF ACCOUNTANCY AND BUSINESS ADMINISTRATION

Accounting	M
Business Administration and Management—General	M
Business Analytics	M
Finance and Banking	M
Human Resources Management	M
International Business	M
Investment Management	M
Management Information Systems	M
Management Strategy and Policy	M
Marketing	M
Project Management	M
Taxation	M

WALSH UNIVERSITY

Business Administration and Management—General	M
Counselor Education	M
Education—General	M
Higher Education	M
Marketing	M
Reading Education	M
Religious Education	M
Student Affairs	M

WARNER PACIFIC UNIVERSITY

Education—General	M
Human Services	M
Nonprofit Management	M
Organizational Management	M

WARNER UNIVERSITY

Accounting	M
Business Administration and Management—General	M
Curriculum and Instruction	M
Education—General	M
Educational Media/Instructional Technology	M
Elementary Education	M
Human Resources Management	M
International Business	M
Science Education	M

WASHBURN UNIVERSITY

Accounting	M
Business Administration and Management—General	M
Curriculum and Instruction	M
Education—General	M
Educational Leadership and Administration	M
Health Education	M
Human Services	M
Law	M,D
Legal and Justice Studies	M,D
Reading Education	M
Social Work	M
Special Education	M

WASHINGTON ADVENTIST UNIVERSITY

Business Administration and Management—General	M

WASHINGTON & JEFFERSON COLLEGE

Accounting	M,O

WASHINGTON AND LEE UNIVERSITY

Law	D

WASHINGTON STATE UNIVERSITY

Accounting	M
Business Administration and Management—General	M,D
Business Education	M,D
Curriculum and Instruction	M,D

Education—General	M,D
Educational Leadership and Administration	M,D
Educational Psychology	M,D
Elementary Education	M,D
English as a Second Language	M,D
Exercise and Sports Science	M
Foreign Languages Education	M
Mathematics Education	M,D
Reading Education	M,D
Secondary Education	M,D
Special Education	M,D
Sports Management	M,D
Vocational and Technical Education	M,D

WASHINGTON UNIVERSITY IN ST. LOUIS

Accounting	M
Business Administration and Management—General	M,D
Education—General	M,D
Educational Measurement and Evaluation	D
Elementary Education	M
Entrepreneurship	M,D
Finance and Banking	M,D
Kinesiology and Movement Studies	D
Law	M,D
Organizational Management	M
Secondary Education	M
Social Work	M,D
Special Education	M
Supply Chain Management	M

WAYLAND BAPTIST UNIVERSITY

Accounting	M,D
Business Administration and Management—General	M,D
Education—General	M
Educational Leadership and Administration	M
Educational Measurement and Evaluation	M
Educational Media/Instructional Technology	M
Elementary Education	M
English as a Second Language	M
English Education	M
Higher Education	M
Human Resources Management	M,D
International Business	M,D
Management Information Systems	M,D
Organizational Management	M,D
Project Management	M,D
Science Education	M
Secondary Education	M
Social Sciences Education	M
Special Education	M
Sports Management	M

WAYNESBURG UNIVERSITY

Business Administration and Management—General	M,D
Counselor Education	M,D
Curriculum and Instruction	M,D
Distance Education Development	M,D
Educational Leadership and Administration	M,D
Educational Media/Instructional Technology	M,D
Finance and Banking	M,D
Human Resources Management	M,D
Organizational Management	M,D
Special Education	M,D

WAYNE STATE COLLEGE

Business Administration and Management—General	M
Business Education	M
Counselor Education	M
Curriculum and Instruction	M
Early Childhood Education	M
Education—General	M,O
Educational Leadership and Administration	M,O
Elementary Education	M
English as a Second Language	M
English Education	M
Exercise and Sports Science	M
Home Economics Education	M
Mathematics Education	M
Music Education	M
Organizational Management	M
Physical Education	M
Science Education	M
Social Sciences Education	M
Special Education	M
Sports Management	M
Vocational and Technical Education	M

WAYNE STATE UNIVERSITY

Accounting	M,D,O
Advertising and Public Relations	M,D,O
Archives/Archival Administration	M,O
Art Education	M,D,O
Athletic Training and Sports Medicine	M,D
Business Administration and Management—General	M,D,O
Counselor Education	M,D,O
Curriculum and Instruction	M,D,O
Distance Education Development	M,D,O
Early Childhood Education	M,D,O
Education—General	M,D,O
Educational Leadership and Administration	M,D,O
Educational Measurement and Evaluation	M,D,O
Educational Media/Instructional Technology	M,D,O
Educational Policy	M,D,O
Educational Psychology	M,D,O

Elementary Education	M,D,O
English as a Second Language	M,D,O
English Education	M,D,O
Entrepreneurship	M,D,O
Exercise and Sports Science	M,D
Finance and Banking	M,D,O
Foreign Languages Education	M,D,O
Foundations and Philosophy of Education	M,D,O
Health Education	M,D,O
Human Resources Management	M,D
Industrial and Manufacturing Management	M,D
Information Studies	M,D
Kinesiology and Movement Studies	M,D
Law	M,D
Library Science	M,O
Management Information Systems	M,D,O
Management Strategy and Policy	M,D,O
Mathematics Education	M,D,O
Multilingual and Multicultural Education	M,D,O
Music Education	M,O
Nonprofit Management	M,D
Organizational Behavior	M,D
Organizational Management	M,O
Physical Education	M,D
Reading Education	M,D,O
Science Education	M,D,O
Secondary Education	M,D,O
Social Sciences Education	M,D,O
Social Work	M,D,O
Special Education	M,D,O
Sports Management	M,D
Taxation	M,O

WEBBER INTERNATIONAL UNIVERSITY

Accounting	M
Business Administration and Management—General	M
International Business	M
Sports Management	M

WEBER STATE UNIVERSITY

Accounting	M
Athletic Training and Sports Medicine	M
Business Administration and Management—General	M,O
Curriculum and Instruction	M
Education—General	M
Legal and Justice Studies	M
Taxation	M

WEBSTER UNIVERSITY

Accounting	M
Advertising and Public Relations	M
Business Administration and Management—General	M,D,O
Early Childhood Education	M,O
Education—General	M,O
Educational Media/Instructional Technology	M,O
Educational Psychology	M,O
Elementary Education	M,O
English as a Second Language	M,O
Finance and Banking	M
Human Resources Development	M,D,O
Human Resources Management	M,D,O
Human Services	M
International Business	M
Legal and Justice Studies	M
Management Information Systems	M,D,O
Marketing	M,O
Mathematics Education	M,O
Middle School Education	M
Music Education	M
Nonprofit Management	M,O
Reading Education	M,O
Secondary Education	M,O
Special Education	M,O

WENTWORTH INSTITUTE OF TECHNOLOGY

Facilities Management	M

WESLEYAN COLLEGE

Business Administration and Management—General	M
Early Childhood Education	M
Education—General	M

WESLEY BIBLICAL SEMINARY

Religious Education	M

WESLEY COLLEGE

Business Administration and Management—General	M
Education—General	M

WEST CHESTER UNIVERSITY OF PENNSYLVANIA

Athletic Training and Sports Medicine	M,O
Business Administration and Management—General	M,O
Business Analytics	M,O
Business Education	M,O
Counselor Education	M,O
Early Childhood Education	M,O
Education—General	M,D,O
Educational Leadership and Administration	M,D,O
Educational Media/Instructional Technology	M,O
Educational Policy	M,D,O
English as a Second Language	M,O
English Education	M,O
Exercise and Sports Science	M,O
Foreign Languages Education	M,O
Foundations and Philosophy of Education	M,O
Higher Education	M,O

Peterson's Graduate Programs in Business, Education, Information Studies, Law & Social Work 2019

Program	
Human Resources Management	M,O
Kinesiology and Movement Studies	M,O
Management Information Systems	M,O
Mathematics Education	M,O
Music Education	M,O
Nonprofit Management	M,O
Physical Education	M,O
Reading Education	M,O
Science Education	M,O
Social Work	M,O
Special Education	M,O
Sports Management	M,O
Student Affairs	M,O

WESTERN CAROLINA UNIVERSITY

Accounting	M
Business Administration and Management—General	M
Education—General	M
English as a Second Language	M,O
Entrepreneurship	M
Project Management	M,O
Social Work	M

WESTERN CONNECTICUT STATE UNIVERSITY

Accounting	M
Business Administration and Management—General	M
Counselor Education	M
Curriculum and Instruction	M
Education—General	M,D
Educational Leadership and Administration	D
Educational Media/Instructional Technology	M
Music Education	M
Reading Education	M
Special Education	M

WESTERN GOVERNORS UNIVERSITY

Business Administration and Management—General	M
Education—General	M,O
Educational Leadership and Administration	M,O
Educational Measurement and Evaluation	M,O
Educational Media/Instructional Technology	M,O
Elementary Education	M,O
English Education	M,O
Higher Education	M,O
Management Information Systems	M
Management Strategy and Policy	M
Mathematics Education	M,O
Science Education	M,O
Social Sciences Education	M,O
Special Education	M,O

WESTERN ILLINOIS UNIVERSITY

Accounting	M
Business Administration and Management—General	M,O
Counselor Education	M
Curriculum and Instruction	M
Distance Education Development	M,O
Education—General	M,D,O
Educational Leadership and Administration	M,D,O
Educational Media/Instructional Technology	M,O
English as a Second Language	M,O
Foundations and Philosophy of Education	M,O
Health Education	M
Higher Education	M
Kinesiology and Movement Studies	M
Reading Education	M
Recreation and Park Management	M
Social Work	M
Special Education	M
Sports Management	M
Student Affairs	M
Supply Chain Management	M,O
Travel and Tourism	M

WESTERN KENTUCKY UNIVERSITY

Adult Education	M,D,O
Art Education	M
Business Administration and Management—General	M
Counselor Education	M
Early Childhood Education	M,O
Educational Leadership and Administration	M,D,O
Educational Media/Instructional Technology	M,O
Elementary Education	M,O
English as a Second Language	M
English Education	M
Foreign Languages Education	M
Higher Education	M
Middle School Education	M,O
Music Education	M
Physical Education	M
Reading Education	M,O
Recreation and Park Management	M
Secondary Education	M,O
Social Work	M,O
Special Education	M,O
Sports Management	M
Student Affairs	M

WESTERN MICHIGAN UNIVERSITY

Accounting	M
Art Education	M
Athletic Training and Sports Medicine	M
Business Administration and Management—General	M
Counselor Education	M,D
Education—General	M,D,O
Educational Leadership and Administration	M,D,O

Educational Measurement and Evaluation	M,D,O
Educational Media/Instructional Technology	M,D,O
English Education	M,D
Exercise and Sports Science	M
Health Education	D,O
Higher Education	M
Human Services	D,O
Mathematics Education	M,D
Music Education	M,D
Nonprofit Management	M,D,O
Physical Education	M
Reading Education	M,D
Science Education	M,D,O
Social Work	M
Special Education	M
Sports Management	M
Vocational and Technical Education	M

WESTERN MICHIGAN UNIVERSITY THOMAS M. COOLEY LAW SCHOOL

Environmental Law	M,D
Finance and Banking	M,D
Insurance	M,D
Intellectual Property Law	M,D
Law	M,D
Legal and Justice Studies	M,D
Taxation	M,D

WESTERN NEW ENGLAND UNIVERSITY

Accounting	M
Advertising and Public Relations	M
Business Administration and Management—General	M
Curriculum and Instruction	M
English Education	M
Law	M,D
Mathematics Education	M
Organizational Management	M
Sports Management	M

WESTERN NEW MEXICO UNIVERSITY

Business Administration and Management—General	M
Education—General	M
Educational Leadership and Administration	M
Elementary Education	M
English as a Second Language	M
Multilingual and Multicultural Education	M
Reading Education	M
Secondary Education	M
Social Work	M
Special Education	M

WESTERN OREGON UNIVERSITY

Early Childhood Education	M
Education—General	M
Educational Media/Instructional Technology	M
Health Education	M
Mathematics Education	M
Multilingual and Multicultural Education	M
Science Education	M
Secondary Education	M
Social Sciences Education	M
Special Education	M

WESTERN SEMINARY

Human Resources Development	M

WESTERN STATE COLLEGE OF LAW AT ARGOSY UNIVERSITY

Law	D

WESTERN STATE COLORADO UNIVERSITY

Education—General	M
Educational Leadership and Administration	M
Reading Education	M

WESTERN UNIVERSITY OF HEALTH SCIENCES

Health Education	M

WESTERN WASHINGTON UNIVERSITY

Adult Education	M
Business Administration and Management—General	M
Counselor Education	M
Education of the Gifted	M
Education—General	M
Educational Leadership and Administration	M
Elementary Education	M
Environmental Education	M
Exercise and Sports Science	M
Higher Education	M
Physical Education	M
Science Education	M
Secondary Education	M

WESTFIELD STATE UNIVERSITY

Accounting	M
Counselor Education	M
Early Childhood Education	M
Education—General	M
Elementary Education	M
Mathematics Education	M
Nonprofit Management	M
Physical Education	M
Reading Education	M
Science Education	M
Secondary Education	M
Social Sciences Education	M
Social Work	M
Special Education	M
Vocational and Technical Education	M

WEST LIBERTY UNIVERSITY

Education of Students with Severe/Multiple Disabilities	M
Education—General	M

Educational Leadership and Administration	M
Organizational Management	M
Physical Education	M
Reading Education	M
Special Education	M
Sports Management	M

WESTMINSTER COLLEGE (PA)

Counselor Education	M
Early Childhood Education	M
Educational Leadership and Administration	M
Reading Education	M
Special Education	M

WESTMINSTER COLLEGE (UT)

Accounting	M,O
Business Administration and Management—General	M,O
Education—General	M

WEST TEXAS A&M UNIVERSITY

Accounting	M
Business Administration and Management—General	M
Counselor Education	M
Curriculum and Instruction	M
Education—General	M
Educational Leadership and Administration	M
Educational Measurement and Evaluation	M
Educational Media/Instructional Technology	M
Exercise and Sports Science	M
Finance and Banking	M
Reading Education	M
Social Work	M
Sports Management	M

WEST VIRGINIA UNIVERSITY

Accounting	M,D,O
Agricultural Education	M,D
Art Education	M,D
Athletic Training and Sports Medicine	M,D
Business Administration and Management—General	M,D,O
Business Analytics	M,D,O
Counselor Education	M,D
Curriculum and Instruction	M,D
Early Childhood Education	M,D
Education of the Gifted	M,D
Education—General	M,D
Educational Leadership and Administration	M,D
Educational Media/Instructional Technology	M,D
Educational Psychology	M,D
Elementary Education	M,D
English Education	M,D
Exercise and Sports Science	M,D
Finance and Banking	M,D,O
Higher Education	M,D
Human Services	M,D
Law	M,D
Legal and Justice Studies	M,D
Marketing	M,D,O
Music Education	M,D
Physical Education	M,D
Reading Education	M,D
Recreation and Park Management	M,D
Secondary Education	M,D
Social Work	M
Special Education	M,D
Sports Management	M,D
Travel and Tourism	M,D

WEST VIRGINIA WESLEYAN COLLEGE

Athletic Training and Sports Medicine	M
Business Administration and Management—General	M
Education—General	M

WHEATON COLLEGE

Education—General	M
Elementary Education	M
English as a Second Language	M,O
Religious Education	M
Secondary Education	M

WHEELING JESUIT UNIVERSITY

Accounting	M
Business Administration and Management—General	M
Educational Leadership and Administration	M
Organizational Management	M

WHITTIER COLLEGE

Education—General	M
Educational Leadership and Administration	M
Elementary Education	M
Secondary Education	M

WHITWORTH UNIVERSITY

Business Administration and Management—General	M
Counselor Education	M
Education of the Gifted	M
Education—General	M
Educational Leadership and Administration	M
Elementary Education	M
Secondary Education	M
Special Education	M

WHU - OTTO BEISHEIM SCHOOL OF MANAGEMENT

Business Administration and Management—General	M

WICHITA STATE UNIVERSITY

Accounting	M

Business Administration and Management—General	M
Counselor Education	M,D,O
Curriculum and Instruction	M
Early Childhood Education	M
Education of the Gifted	M
Education—General	M,D,O
Educational Leadership and Administration	M,D,O
Educational Psychology	M,D,O
Entrepreneurship	M
Exercise and Sports Science	M
Human Services	M
Management Information Systems	M
Middle School Education	M
Music Education	M
Secondary Education	M
Social Work	M
Special Education	M
Sports Management	M
Supply Chain Management	M
Taxation	M

WIDENER UNIVERSITY

Adult Education	M,D
Business Administration and Management—General	M
Counselor Education	M,D
Early Childhood Education	M,D
Education—General	M,D
Educational Leadership and Administration	M,D
Educational Media/Instructional Technology	M,D
Educational Psychology	M,D
Elementary Education	M,D
English Education	M,D
Foundations and Philosophy of Education	M,D
Health Education	M,D
Health Law	M,D
Law	M,D
Mathematics Education	M,D
Middle School Education	M,D
Reading Education	M,D
Science Education	M,D
Social Sciences Education	M,D
Social Work	M,D
Special Education	M,D
Taxation	M

WILFRID LAURIER UNIVERSITY

Accounting	M,D
Business Administration and Management—General	M,D
Finance and Banking	M,D
Human Resources Management	M,D
Kinesiology and Movement Studies	M
Legal and Justice Studies	D
Marketing	M,D
Organizational Behavior	M,D
Organizational Management	M,D
Physical Education	M
Social Work	M,D
Supply Chain Management	M,D

WILKES UNIVERSITY

Accounting	M
Business Administration and Management—General	M
Distance Education Development	M,D
Education—General	M,D
Educational Leadership and Administration	M,D
Educational Measurement and Evaluation	M,D
Educational Media/Instructional Technology	M,D
English as a Second Language	M
Entrepreneurship	M
Finance and Banking	M
Human Resources Management	M
Industrial and Manufacturing Management	M
International and Comparative Education	M,D
International Business	M
Middle School Education	M,D
Organizational Management	M
Reading Education	M,D
Special Education	M,D

WILLAMETTE UNIVERSITY

Business Administration and Management—General	M
Law	M,D

WILLIAM CAREY UNIVERSITY

Art Education	M,O
Business Administration and Management—General	M
Education of the Gifted	M,O
Education—General	M,O
Elementary Education	M,O
English Education	M,O
Secondary Education	M,O
Social Sciences Education	M,O
Special Education	M,O

WILLIAM JAMES COLLEGE

Student Affairs	M,D,O

WILLIAM JESSUP UNIVERSITY

Education—General	M
English Education	M
Mathematics Education	M

WILLIAM JEWELL COLLEGE

Education—General	M

WILLIAM PATERSON UNIVERSITY OF NEW JERSEY

Business Administration and Management—General	M,O
Business Analytics	M,O
Counselor Education	M,O
Early Childhood Education	M,O

Education—General | M,O
Educational Leadership and Administration | M,O
Educational Media/Instructional Technology | M,O
Elementary Education | M,O
English as a Second Language | M,D,O
Exercise and Sports Science | M,D,O
Foundations and Philosophy of Education | M,D,O
Higher Education | M,O
Middle School Education | M,O
Multilingual and Multicultural Education | M,D,O
Reading Education | M,O
Secondary Education | M,O
Special Education | M,O

WILLIAM PENN UNIVERSITY
Organizational Management | M

WILLIAMS BAPTIST COLLEGE
Education—General | M

WILLIAMSON COLLEGE
Organizational Management | M

WILLIAM WOODS UNIVERSITY
Advertising and Public Relations | M,D,O
Business Administration and Management—General | M,D,O
Curriculum and Instruction | M,D,O
Educational Leadership and Administration | M,D,O
Educational Media/Instructional Technology | M,D,O
Human Resources Development | M,D,O
Marketing | M,D,O
Physical Education | M,D,O

WILMINGTON COLLEGE
Education—General | M
Reading Education | M
Special Education | M

WILMINGTON UNIVERSITY
Accounting | M,D
Business Administration and Management—General | M,D
Counselor Education | M,D
Education of the Gifted | M,D
Education—General | M,D
Educational Leadership and Administration | M,D
Educational Media/Instructional Technology | M,D
Elementary Education | M,D
English as a Second Language | M,D
Finance and Banking | M,D
Higher Education | M,D
Human Resources Management | M,D
Human Services | M,D
Management Information Systems | M,D
Marketing | M,D
Organizational Management | M,D
Project Management | M
Reading Education | M,D
Secondary Education | M,D
Special Education | M,D
Vocational and Technical Education | M,D

WILSON COLLEGE
Accounting | M
Business Administration and Management—General | M
Education—General | M

Educational Media/Instructional Technology | M
Elementary Education | M
Secondary Education | M
Special Education | M

WINGATE UNIVERSITY
Accounting | M
Business Administration and Management—General | M
Community College Education | M,D,O
Education—General | M,D,O
Educational Leadership and Administration | M,D,O
Elementary Education | M,D,O
Entrepreneurship | M
Finance and Banking | M
Marketing | M
Project Management | M
Sports Management | M

WINONA STATE UNIVERSITY
Counselor Education | M,O
Education—General | O
Educational Leadership and Administration | M,O
English as a Second Language | M
Human Services | M,O
Multilingual and Multicultural Education | O
Organizational Management | M,D,O
Special Education | M
Sports Management | M,O

WINSTON-SALEM STATE UNIVERSITY
Business Administration and Management—General | M
Education—General | M
Management Information Systems | M
Middle School Education | M
Special Education | M

WINTHROP UNIVERSITY
Art Education | M
Business Administration and Management—General | M
Counselor Education | M
Education—General | M
Educational Leadership and Administration | M
Music Education | M
Physical Education | M
Secondary Education | M
Social Work | M
Special Education | M

WISCONSIN LUTHERAN COLLEGE
Curriculum and Instruction | M
Educational Leadership and Administration | M
Educational Media/Instructional Technology | M
Science Education | M

WITTENBERG UNIVERSITY
Education—General | M

WOODBURY UNIVERSITY
Business Administration and Management—General | M
Organizational Management | M

WORCESTER POLYTECHNIC INSTITUTE
Business Administration and Management—General | M,D,O
Educational Media/Instructional Technology | M,D

Management Information Systems | M,D,O
Marketing | M,D,O
Organizational Management | M,D,O
Supply Chain Management | M,D,O

WORCESTER STATE UNIVERSITY
Accounting | M
Business Administration and Management—General | M
Curriculum and Instruction | M,O
Early Childhood Education | M,O
Education—General | M,O
Educational Leadership and Administration | M,O
Elementary Education | M,O
English as a Second Language | M,O
English Education | M
Foreign Languages Education | M
Health Education | M
Marketing | M
Middle School Education | M,O
Nonprofit Management | M
Organizational Management | M
Reading Education | M,O
Secondary Education | M,O
Social Sciences Education | M
Special Education | M,O

WRIGHT STATE UNIVERSITY
Accounting | M
Business Administration and Management—General | M
Counselor Education | M
Curriculum and Instruction | O
Education—General | M,O
Educational Leadership and Administration | O
Elementary Education | M
Health Education | M
Logistics | M
Management Information Systems | M
Mathematics Education | D
Music Education | M
Science Education | M,D
Secondary Education | M
Special Education | M
Supply Chain Management | M

XAVIER UNIVERSITY
Accounting | M
Athletic Training and Sports Medicine | M
Business Administration and Management—General | M
Counselor Education | M
Early Childhood Education | M
Education—General | M,D
Educational Leadership and Administration | M,D
Elementary Education | M
Finance and Banking | M
Human Resources Development | M,D
International Business | M
Management Strategy and Policy | M
Marketing | M
Multilingual and Multicultural Education | M
Reading Education | M
Religious Education | M
Secondary Education | M
Special Education | M
Sports Management | M

XAVIER UNIVERSITY OF LOUISIANA
Counselor Education | M
Curriculum and Instruction | M

Education—General | M
Educational Leadership and Administration | M

YALE UNIVERSITY
Accounting | D
Business Administration and Management—General | M,D
Finance and Banking | D
Law | M,D
Marketing | D
Organizational Management | D

YESHIVA UNIVERSITY
Accounting | M
Business Administration and Management—General | M
Educational Leadership and Administration | M,D,O
Intellectual Property Law | M,D
Law | M,D
Marketing | M
Religious Education | M,D,O
Risk Management | M
Social Work | M,D
Taxation | M

YORK COLLEGE OF PENNSYLVANIA
Accounting | M
Business Administration and Management—General | M
Education—General | M
Educational Leadership and Administration | M
Educational Media/Instructional Technology | M
Finance and Banking | M
Marketing | M
Reading Education | M

YORK UNIVERSITY
Accounting | M,D
Business Administration and Management—General | M,D
Business Analytics | M,D
Education—General | M,D
Finance and Banking | M,D
Human Resources Management | M,D
International Business | M,D
Kinesiology and Movement Studies | M,D
Law | M,D
Social Work | M,D

YOUNGSTOWN STATE UNIVERSITY
Accounting | M
Business Administration and Management—General | M,O
Counselor Education | M
Curriculum and Instruction | M
Early Childhood Education | M
Education of the Gifted | M
Education—General | M,D
Educational Leadership and Administration | M,D
Educational Media/Instructional Technology | M
Finance and Banking | M
Human Services | M
Marketing | M
Mathematics Education | M
Middle School Education | M
Music Education | M
Reading Education | M
Science Education | M
Secondary Education | M
Special Education | M

*M—masters degree; D—doctorate; O—other advanced degree; *—Close-Up and/or Display*

ACADEMIC AND PROFESSIONAL
PROGRAMS IN BUSINESS

Section 1
Business Administration and Management

This section contains a directory of institutions offering graduate work in business administration and management, followed by in-depth entries submitted by institutions that chose to prepare detailed program descriptions. Additional information about programs listed in the directory but not augmented by an in-depth entry may be obtained by writing directly to the dean of a graduate school or chair of a department at the address given in the directory.

For programs offering related work, see also in this book Sections 2–18, Education (Business Education), and Sports Management. In the other guides in this series:

Graduate Programs in the Humanities, Arts & Social Sciences

See *Art and Art History (Arts Administration), Economics, Family and Consumer Sciences (Consumer Economics), Political Science and International Affairs, Psychology (Industrial and Organizational Psychology),* and *Public, Regional, and Industrial Affairs (Industrial and Labor Relations)*

Graduate Programs in the Biological/Biomedical Sciences & Health-Related Medical Professions

See *Health Services and Nursing (Nursing and Healthcare Administration)*

Graduate Programs in the Physical Sciences, Mathematics, Agricultural Sciences, the Environment & Natural Resources

See *Environmental Sciences and Management (Environmental Management and Policy)* and *Mathematical Sciences*

Graduate Programs in Engineering & Applied Sciences

See *Computer Science and Information Technology, Civil and Environmental Engineering (Construction Engineering and Management), Industrial Engineering,* and *Management of Engineering and Technology*

CONTENTS

Program Directory

Featured Schools: Displays and Close-Ups

Business Administration and Management— General

Abilene Christian University, College of Graduate and Professional Studies, Program in Business Administration, Addison, TX 75001. Offers business analytics (MBA); corporate finance (MBA); general management (MBA); healthcare administration (MBA); human resource management (MBA); international business (MBA); management: business analytics (MS); management: healthcare administration (MS); management: international business (MS); management: marketing (MS); management: operations and supply chain management (MS); marketing (MBA); nonprofit leadership (MBA); operations and supply chain management (MBA). *Program availability:* Part-time, online only, 100% online. *Faculty:* 2 full-time (0 women), 6 part-time/adjunct (2 women). *Students:* 109 full-time (47 women), 51 part-time (22 women); includes 42 minority (33 Black or African American, non-Hispanic/Latino; 1 American Indian or Alaska Native, non-Hispanic/Latino; 2 Asian, non-Hispanic/Latino; 6 Hispanic/Latino). 125 applicants, 65% accepted, 58 enrolled. *Entrance requirements:* Additional exam requirements/recommendations for international students: Required—TOEFL (minimum score 80 iBT), IELTS (minimum score 6). *Application deadline:* For fall admission, 8/14 priority date for domestic students; for winter admission, 10/1 priority date for domestic students; for spring admission, 12/15 priority date for domestic students; for summer admission, 4/15 priority date for domestic students. Applications are processed on a rolling basis. Application fee: $50. Electronic applications accepted. *Expenses:* $700 per hour. *Financial support:* In 2017–18, 2 students received support. Application deadline: 4/1; applicants required to submit FAFSA. *Faculty research:* Organizational structure, financial management, cost accounting, unit analysis management. *Unit head:* Phil Vardiman, Program Director, 325-674-2153, E-mail: pxv02b@acu.edu. *Application contact:* Graduate Advisor, 817-219-7300, E-mail: gradonline@acu.edu.
Website: http://www.acu.edu/online/academics/mba-business-administration.html

Adams State University, Office of Graduate Studies, School of Business, Alamosa, CO 81101. Offers MBA. *Expenses:* Tuition, state resident: full-time $4800; part-time $2400 per credit. Tuition, nonresident: full-time $7100; part-time $3550 per credit. *Required fees:* $213; $106 per credit. One-time fee: $100. Tuition and fees vary according to campus/location and program.

Adelphi University, Robert B. Willumstad School of Business, MBA Program, Garden City, NY 11530-0701. Offers accounting (MBA); finance (MBA); health services administration (MBA); human resource management (MBA); management (MBA); management information systems (MBA); marketing (MBA); sport management (MBA). *Accreditation:* AACSB. *Program availability:* Part-time, evening/weekend. *Students:* 257 full-time (110 women), 78 part-time (38 women); includes 56 minority (18 Black or African American, non-Hispanic/Latino; 16 Asian, non-Hispanic/Latino; 19 Hispanic/Latino; 3 Two or more races, non-Hispanic/Latino), 181 international. Average age 28. 435 applicants, 61% accepted, 205 enrolled. In 2017, 130 master's awarded. *Degree requirements:* For master's, capstone course. *Entrance requirements:* For master's, GMAT, 2 letters of recommendation. Additional exam requirements/recommendations for international students: Required—TOEFL (minimum score 550 paper-based; 80 iBT), IELTS (minimum score 6.5). *Application deadline:* For fall admission, 4/1 for international students; for spring admission, 11/1 for international students. Applications are processed on a rolling basis. Application fee: $50. Electronic applications accepted. *Expenses:* Contact institution. *Financial support:* Research assistantships with partial tuition reimbursements, career-related internships or fieldwork, Federal Work-Study, institutionally sponsored loans, scholarships/grants, tuition waivers (partial), and unspecified assistantships available. Financial award application deadline: 3/1; financial award applicants required to submit FAFSA. *Faculty research:* Supply chain management, distribution channels, productivity benchmark analysis, data envelopment analysis, financial portfolio analysis. *Unit head:* Dr. Rakesh Gupta, Associate Dean, 516-877-4629. *Application contact:* E-mail: graduateadmissions@adelphi.edu.
Website: http://business.adelphi.edu/degree-programs/graduate-degree-programs/m-b-a/

Alabama Agricultural and Mechanical University, School of Graduate Studies, College of Business and Public Affairs, Huntsville, AL 35811. Offers MBA. *Program availability:* Part-time, evening/weekend. *Degree requirements:* For master's, comprehensive exam. *Entrance requirements:* For master's, minimum undergraduate GPA of 2.5. Additional exam requirements/recommendations for international students: Required—TOEFL (minimum score 500 paper-based; 61 iBT). Electronic applications accepted. *Faculty research:* Consumer behavior of blacks, small business marketing, economics of education.

Alabama State University, College of Business Administration, Montgomery, AL 36101-0271. Offers M Acc. *Accreditation:* ACBSP. *Program availability:* Part-time. *Faculty:* 4 full-time (1 woman), 1 part-time/adjunct (0 women). *Students:* 18 full-time (12 women), 6 part-time (4 women); includes 17 minority (15 Black or African American, non-Hispanic/Latino; 2 Hispanic/Latino), 5 international. Average age 22. 16 applicants, 63% accepted, 8 enrolled. In 2017, 8 master's awarded. *Degree requirements:* For master's, comprehensive exam. *Entrance requirements:* For master's, minimum GPA of 2.75 (undergraduate), 3.0 (graduate); bachelor's degree or its equivalent from accredited college or university. Additional exam requirements/recommendations for international students: Required—TOEFL (minimum score 500 paper-based). *Application deadline:* For fall admission, 4/15 for domestic and international students; for spring admission, 11/15 for domestic students, 11/1 for international students; for summer admission, 3/15 for domestic and international students. Application fee: $25. Electronic applications accepted. *Expenses:* Tuition, state resident: part-time $412 per credit hour. Tuition, nonresident: part-time $824 per credit hour. *Required fees:* $685 per semester. *Financial support:* Fellowships and unspecified assistantships available. Financial award application deadline: 6/30; financial award applicants required to submit FAFSA. *Unit head:* Dr. Dave Thompson, Director, Master of Accountancy, 334-229-6809, E-mail: dthompson@alasu.edu. *Application contact:* Dr. William Person, Dean of Graduate Studies, 334-229-4274, Fax: 334-229-4928, E-mail: wperson@alasu.edu.
Website: http://www.alasu.edu/academics/colleges—departments/college-of-business-administration/index.aspx

Alaska Pacific University, Graduate Programs, Business Administration Department, Program in Business Administration, Anchorage, AK 99508-4672. Offers business administration (MBA); health services administration (MBA). *Program availability:* Part-time, evening/weekend. *Degree requirements:* For master's, capstone course. *Entrance requirements:* For master's, GMAT or GRE General Test, minimum GPA of 3.0.

Albany State University, College of Business, Albany, GA 31705-2717. Offers accounting (MBA); general business administration (MBA); healthcare (MBA); public administration (MBA); supply chain and logistics (MBA). *Accreditation:* ACBSP. *Program availability:* Part-time, evening/weekend. *Degree requirements:* For master's, comprehensive exam, internship, 3 hours of physical education. *Entrance requirements:* For master's, GMAT (minimum score of 450)/GRE (minimum score of 800) for those without earned master's degree or higher, minimum undergraduate GPA of 2.5, 2 letters of reference, official transcript, pre-entrance medical record and certificate of immunization. Electronic applications accepted. *Faculty research:* Diversity issues, ancestry, understanding finance through use of technology.

Albertus Magnus College, Master of Arts in Leadership Program, New Haven, CT 06511-1189. Offers MA. *Program availability:* Part-time, evening/weekend, blended/hybrid learning. *Degree requirements:* For master's, thesis optional. *Entrance requirements:* For master's, interview, minimum GPA of 2.7. Additional exam requirements/recommendations for international students: Required—TWE; Recommended—TOEFL (minimum score 550 paper-based). *Application deadline:* Applications are processed on a rolling basis. Application fee: $50. Electronic applications accepted. *Expenses:* Contact institution. *Financial support:* Federal Work-Study and unspecified assistantships available. Support available to part-time students. Financial award applicants required to submit FAFSA. *Faculty research:* Leadership, quality management, employee motivation. *Unit head:* Dr. Howard Fero, Director, 203-773-4424, E-mail: hfero@albertus.edu. *Application contact:* Anthony Reich, Director of Admission, Division of Professional and Graduate Studies, 203-773-5032, Fax: 203-773-5257, E-mail: leadership@albertus.edu.
Website: http://www.albertus.edu/leadership/ms/

Albertus Magnus College, Master of Business Administration Program, New Haven, CT 06511-1189. Offers accounting (MBA); general management (MBA); health care management (MBA); human resource management (MBA); leadership (MBA); project management (MBA). Program also offered in East Hartford, CT. *Program availability:* Part-time, evening/weekend, 100% online, blended/hybrid learning. *Degree requirements:* For master's, thesis, capstone project, business plan, minimum cumulative GPA of 3.0, completion of all requirements within seven years of matriculation. *Entrance requirements:* For master's, 3 years of management or related experience, minimum GPA of 2.5, 2 letters of recommendation, official transcripts. Additional exam requirements/recommendations for international students: Recommended—TOEFL (minimum score 550 paper-based; 80 iBT). *Application deadline:* Applications are processed on a rolling basis. Application fee: $50. Electronic applications accepted. *Expenses:* Contact institution. *Financial support:* Federal Work-Study and unspecified assistantships available. Support available to part-time students. Financial award applicants required to submit FAFSA. *Faculty research:* Finance, project management, accounting, business administration, generalist. *Unit head:* Dr. Wayne Gineo, Director, 203-672-6670, E-mail: wgineo@albertus.edu. *Application contact:* Anthony Reich, Director of Admission, Division of Professional and Graduate Studies, 203-773-5302, E-mail: arreich@albertus.edu.
Website: http://www.albertus.edu/business-administration/ms/

Alcorn State University, School of Graduate Studies, School of Business, Lorman, MS 39096-7500. Offers MBA. *Accreditation:* ACBSP.

Alfred University, Graduate School, School of Business, Alfred, NY 14802-1205. Offers accounting (MBA); business administration (MBA). *Accreditation:* AACSB. *Program availability:* Part-time. *Entrance requirements:* For master's, GMAT. Additional exam requirements/recommendations for international students: Required—TOEFL (minimum score 590 paper-based; 90 iBT), IELTS (minimum score 6.5). Electronic applications accepted.

Alliant International University–Los Angeles, Marshall Goldsmith School of Management, Business Division, Alhambra, CA 91803. Offers DBA.

Alliant International University–San Diego, Alliant School of Management, Business and Management Division, San Diego, CA 92131. Offers business administration (MBA); MBA/MA; MBA/PhD. *Program availability:* Part-time, evening/weekend. *Entrance requirements:* For master's, GMAT or GRE, minimum GPA of 2.75. Additional exam requirements/recommendations for international students: Required—TOEFL (minimum score 550 paper-based; 80 iBT), TWE (minimum score 5). Electronic applications accepted. *Faculty research:* Financial and commodity markets, market micro-structures, risk measurement, virtual teams, sustainable work environments.

Alvernia University, School of Graduate Studies, Department of Business, Reading, PA 19607-1799. Offers MBA. *Accreditation:* ACBSP. *Program availability:* Part-time, evening/weekend. *Degree requirements:* For master's, thesis optional. *Entrance requirements:* For master's, GMAT, GRE, or MAT. Electronic applications accepted.

Alverno College, School of Professional Studies - Business Division, Milwaukee, WI 53234-3922. Offers MBA. *Program availability:* Part-time, evening/weekend. *Faculty:* 4 full-time (3 women), 3 part-time/adjunct (0 women). *Students:* 53 full-time (45 women), 4 part-time (3 women); includes 24 minority (12 Black or African American, non-Hispanic/Latino; 3 Asian, non-Hispanic/Latino; 5 Hispanic/Latino; 4 Two or more races, non-Hispanic/Latino). Average age 34. 33 applicants, 100% accepted, 23 enrolled. In 2017, 24 master's awarded. *Entrance requirements:* For master's, 3 or more years of relevant work experience. Additional exam requirements/recommendations for international students: Required—TOEFL. *Application deadline:* For fall admission, 7/15 priority date for domestic and international students; for spring admission, 12/15 priority date for domestic and international students. Applications are processed on a rolling basis. Application fee: $0. Electronic applications accepted. *Expenses:* Contact institution. *Financial support:* Federal Work-Study and scholarships/grants available. Support available to part-time students. Financial award applicants required to submit FAFSA. *Unit head:* Dr. Patricia Luebke, Dean, School of Professional Studies, 414-382-6368, E-mail: patricia.luebke@alverno.edu. *Application contact:* Janet Stikel, Associate Director of Adult and Graduate Admissions, 414-382-6112, Fax: 414-382-6354, E-mail: janet.stikel@alverno.edu.

Amberton University, Graduate School, Department of Business Administration, Garland, TX 75041-5595. Offers agile project management (MS); general business (MBA); international business (MBA); management (MBA); project management (MBA); strategic leadership (MBA). *Program availability:* Part-time, evening/weekend. *Entrance requirements:* For master's, minimum GPA of 3.0. *Application deadline:* Applications are processed on a rolling basis. Application fee: $0. *Expenses:* Tuition: Part-time $795 per course. *Unit head:* Dr. Don Hebbard, Academic Dean, 972-635-8641 Ext. 157, Fax: 972-279-9773, E-mail: dhebbard@amberton.edu. *Application contact:* Adviser, 972-279-6511 Ext. 180, Fax: 972-279-9773, E-mail: advisor@amberton.edu.

Amberton University, Graduate School, Program in Managerial Science, Garland, TX 75041-5595. Offers MS. Application fee: $0. *Expenses: Tuition:* Part-time $795 per course. *Unit head:* Academic Dean, 972-279-6511 Ext. 153, Fax: 972-279-9773. *Application contact:* Adviser, 972-279-6511 Ext. 180, Fax: 972-279-9773, E-mail: advisor@amberton.edu.
Website: http://www.amberton.edu/programs-and-courses/masters-degree-programs/managerial-science/index.html

American Business & Technology University, Programs in Business Administration, Saint Joseph, MO 64506. Offers business administration (MBA); financial management (MBA); global business management (MBA); information systems management (MBA); marketing and social media (MBA); project and operations management (MBA); public accounting (MBA). *Program availability:* Online learning.

American College Dublin, Graduate Programs, Dublin, Ireland. Offers business administration (MBA); creative writing (MFA); international business (MBA); oil and gas management (MBA); performance (MFA).

The American College of Financial Services, Graduate Programs, Bryn Mawr, PA 19010-2105. Offers financial services (MSFS); leadership (MSM). *Program availability:* Part-time, evening/weekend, online learning. Electronic applications accepted. *Faculty research:* Retirement counseling, social security, aging, family composition, inflation.

American College of Thessaloniki, Department of Business Administration, Pylea, Greece. Offers banking and finance (MBA); entrepreneurship (MBA, Certificate); finance (Certificate); management (MBA, Certificate); marketing (MBA, Certificate). *Program availability:* Part-time, evening/weekend. *Degree requirements:* For master's, thesis. *Entrance requirements:* For master's, bachelor's degree. Additional exam requirements/recommendations for international students: Recommended—TOEFL. Electronic applications accepted.

American Graduate University, Program in Acquisition Management, Covina, CA 91724. Offers MAM, Certificate. *Program availability:* Part-time, online learning. *Degree requirements:* For master's, thesis (for some programs), comprehensive exam or project. *Entrance requirements:* For master's, undergraduate degree from institution accredited by accrediting agency recognized by the U.S. Department of Education. Additional exam requirements/recommendations for international students: Required—TOEFL. Electronic applications accepted.

American Graduate University, Program in Business Administration, Covina, CA 91724. Offers acquisition and contracting (MBA); supply chain management (MBA). *Program availability:* Part-time, online learning. *Degree requirements:* For master's, thesis. *Entrance requirements:* For master's, undergraduate degree from institution accredited by accrediting agency recognized by the U.S. Department of Education. Additional exam requirements/recommendations for international students: Required—TOEFL. Electronic applications accepted.

American Graduate University, Program in Contract Management, Covina, CA 91724. Offers MCM, Certificate. *Program availability:* Part-time, online learning. *Degree requirements:* For master's, comprehensive exam (for some programs), thesis (for some programs), comprehensive exam or project. *Entrance requirements:* For master's, undergraduate degree from institution accredited by accrediting agency recognized by the U.S. Department of Education. Additional exam requirements/recommendations for international students: Required—TOEFL. Electronic applications accepted.

American InterContinental University Houston, School of Business, Houston, TX 77042. Offers management (MBA).

American InterContinental University Online, Program in Business Administration, Schaumburg, IL 60173. Offers accounting and finance (MBA); finance (MBA); healthcare management (MBA); human resource management (MBA); international business (MBA); management (MBA); marketing (MBA); operations management (MBA); organizational psychology and development (MBA); project management (MBA). *Accreditation:* ACBSP. *Program availability:* Evening/weekend, online learning. *Entrance requirements:* Additional exam requirements/recommendations for international students: Required—TOEFL (minimum score 550 paper-based). Electronic applications accepted.

American International College, School of Business, Arts and Sciences, Springfield, MA 01109-3189. Offers accounting and taxation (MS); business administration (MBA); clinical psychology (MA); educational psychology (Ed D); forensic psychology (MS); general psychology (MA, CAGS); management (CAGS); resort and casino management (MBA, CAGS). *Program availability:* Part-time, evening/weekend. *Faculty:* 4 full-time (2 women), 25 part-time/adjunct (13 women). *Students:* 178 full-time (120 women), 24 part-time (20 women); includes 94 minority (42 Black or African American, non-Hispanic/Latino; 1 American Indian or Alaska Native, non-Hispanic/Latino; 4 Asian, non-Hispanic/Latino; 39 Hispanic/Latino; 8 Two or more races, non-Hispanic/Latino), 13 international. Average age 28. 155 applicants, 83% accepted, 71 enrolled. In 2017, 87 master's, 3 doctorates awarded. *Degree requirements:* For master's, practicum; for doctorate, comprehensive exam, thesis/dissertation, practicum. *Entrance requirements:* For master's, BS or BA, minimum undergraduate GPA of 2.75, 2 letters of recommendation, official transcripts, personal goal statement or essay; for doctorate, 3 letters of recommendation; BS or BA, minimum undergraduate GPA of 3.0 (3.25 recommended); official transcripts; personal goal statement or essay. Additional exam requirements/recommendations for international students: Required—TOEFL (minimum score 550 paper-based; 80 iBT). *Application deadline:* For fall admission, 8/15 for domestic and international students; for spring admission, 12/15 for domestic and international students. Applications are processed on a rolling basis. Application fee: $50. *Expenses:* Contact institution. *Financial support:* In 2017–18, 6 students received support, including 6 research assistantships with full tuition reimbursements available (averaging $1,500 per year). Financial award application deadline: 4/1; financial award applicants required to submit FAFSA. *Faculty research:* Substance abuse, forensic psychology, special education. *Unit head:* Dr. Susanne Swanker, Dean, 413-205-3216, Fax: 413-205-3943, E-mail: susanne.swanker@aic.edu. *Application contact:* Kerry Barnes, Dean of Graduate Admissions, 413-205-3703, Fax: 413-205-3051, E-mail: kerry.barnes@aic.edu.
Website: http://www.aic.edu/school-of-business-arts-and-sciences/

American Jewish University, Graduate School of Nonprofit Management, Program in Business Administration, Bel Air, CA 90077-1599. Offers general nonprofit administration (MBA); Jewish nonprofit administration (MBA). *Program availability:* Part-time, evening/weekend. *Degree requirements:* For master's, thesis, internship. *Entrance requirements:* For master's, GMAT or GRE General Test, interview, minimum undergraduate GPA of 3.0. Additional exam requirements/recommendations for international students: Required—TOEFL (minimum score 550 paper-based).

American National University, Program in Business Administration, Salem, VA 24153. Offers MBA.

American Public University System, AMU/APU Graduate Programs, Charles Town, WV 25414. Offers accounting (MS); applied business analytics (MS); business administration (MBA); criminal justice (MA); cybersecurity studies (MS); educational leadership (M Ed); environmental policy and management (MS); global security (DGS); health information management (MS); history (MA), including American military history, American Revolution, civil war, war since 1945, World War II; information technology

(MS); international relations and conflict resolution (MA), including American politics and government, comparative government and development, general, international relations, public policy; national security studies (MA); nursing (MSN); political science (MA); public policy (MPP); reverse logistics management (MA), including comparative and security issues, conflict resolution, international and transnational security issues, peacekeeping; space studies (MS); sports management (MS); strategic intelligence (DSI); teaching (M Ed), including secondary social studies; transportation and logistics management (MA). *Program availability:* Part-time, evening, online only, 100% online. *Students:* 455 full-time (227 women), 7,939 part-time (3,353 women); includes 2,793 minority (1,429 Black or African American, non-Hispanic/Latino; 48 American Indian or Alaska Native, non-Hispanic/Latino; 205 Asian, non-Hispanic/Latino; 766 Hispanic/Latino; 62 Native Hawaiian or other Pacific Islander, non-Hispanic/Latino; 283 Two or more races, non-Hispanic/Latino), 101 international. Average age 37. In 2017, 2,977 master's awarded. *Degree requirements:* For master's, comprehensive exam or practicum. *Entrance requirements:* For master's, official transcript showing earned bachelor's degree from institution accredited by recognized accrediting body. Additional exam requirements/recommendations for international students: Required—TOEFL (minimum score 550 paper-based), IELTS (minimum score 6.5). *Application deadline:* Applications are processed on a rolling basis. Application fee: $0. Electronic applications accepted. *Expenses: Tuition:* Full-time $6300; part-time $350 per credit. *Required fees:* $300; $50 per course. *Financial support:* Scholarships/grants available. Financial award applicants required to submit FAFSA. *Unit head:* Dr. Wallace Boston, President, 877-468-6268, Fax: 304-728-2348, E-mail: president@apus.edu. *Application contact:* Yoci Deal, Associate Vice President, Graduate and International Admissions, 877-468-6268, Fax: 304-724-3764, E-mail: info@apus.edu.
Website: http://www.apus.edu

American Sentinel University, Graduate Programs, Aurora, CO 80014. Offers business administration (MBA); business intelligence (MS); computer science (MSCS); health information management (MS); healthcare (MBA); information systems (MSIS); nursing (MSN). *Program availability:* Part-time, evening/weekend, online learning. *Entrance requirements:* Additional exam requirements/recommendations for international students: Required—TOEFL (minimum score 600 paper-based). Electronic applications accepted.

American University, Kogod School of Business, MBA Program, Washington, DC 20016-8044. Offers MBA, Certificate, MBA/JD, MBA/LL M, MBA/MA, MBA/MS. *Program availability:* Part-time, evening/weekend, 100% online. *Students:* 262 full-time (124 women), 218 part-time (102 women); includes 245 minority (133 Black or African American, non-Hispanic/Latino; 1 American Indian or Alaska Native, non-Hispanic/Latino; 36 Asian, non-Hispanic/Latino; 53 Hispanic/Latino; 2 Native Hawaiian or other Pacific Islander, non-Hispanic/Latino; 20 Two or more races, non-Hispanic/Latino), 16 international. Average age 31. 509 applicants, 74% accepted, 177 enrolled. In 2017, 71 master's awarded. *Entrance requirements:* For master's, GMAT/GRE, resume, personal statement, interview, 2 letters of recommendation, transcripts. Additional exam requirements/recommendations for international students: Required—TOEFL (minimum score 100 iBT). *Application deadline:* For fall admission, 10/2 priority date for domestic students. Applications are processed on a rolling basis. Application fee: $100. *Expenses:* Contact institution. *Financial support:* Application deadline: 2/1; applicants required to submit FAFSA. *Faculty research:* Information technology, decision-aiding methodology, negotiation. *Unit head:* Dr. Parthiban David, Department Chair, Management, 202-885-2080, E-mail: parthiban.david@american.edu. *Application contact:* Jason Garner, Associate Director, Admissions, 202-885-1922, E-mail: jgarner@american.edu.
Website: http://www.american.edu/kogod/mba/

American University in Bulgaria, Executive MBA Program, Blagoevgrad, Bulgaria. Offers EMBA. *Entrance requirements:* For master's, two essays, two professional recommendations, resume or professional curriculum vitae. Additional exam requirements/recommendations for international students: Required—TOEFL.

The American University in Cairo, School of Business, Cairo, Egypt. Offers business administration (MBA); economics (MA); economics in international development (MA, Diploma); finance (MS). *Program availability:* Part-time, evening/weekend. *Faculty:* 30 full-time (10 women), 8 part-time/adjunct (3 women). *Students:* 49 full-time (25 women), 67 part-time (38 women), 5 international. Average age 29. 112 applicants, 35% accepted, 26 enrolled. In 2017, 51 master's awarded. *Degree requirements:* For master's, comprehensive exam (for some programs), thesis (for some programs). *Entrance requirements:* For master's, GMAT, GRE. Additional exam requirements/recommendations for international students: Required—TOEFL (minimum score 450 paper-based; 45 iBT), IELTS (minimum score 5). *Application deadline:* For fall admission, 2/1 priority date for domestic and international students; for spring admission, 10/15 priority date for domestic and international students. Applications are processed on a rolling basis. Application fee: $85. Electronic applications accepted. *Expenses:* Contact institution. *Financial support:* Fellowships with partial tuition reimbursements, scholarships/grants, tuition waivers (partial), and unspecified assistantships available. Financial award application deadline: 3/10. *Faculty research:* Marketing and quality management, banking operations management, economics, finance. *Unit head:* Dr. Sherif Kamel, Dean, 20-2-2615-2118, E-mail: skamel@aucegypt.edu. *Application contact:* Maha Hegazi, Director of Graduate Admissions, 20-2-2615-1462, E-mail: mahahegazi@aucegypt.edu.
Website: http://www.aucegypt.edu/Business/Pages/default.aspx

The American University in Dubai, Graduate Programs, Dubai, United Arab Emirates. Offers construction management (MS); education (M Ed); finance (MBA); generalist (MBA); marketing (MBA). *Program availability:* Part-time, evening/weekend. *Degree requirements:* For master's, thesis optional. *Entrance requirements:* For master's, GMAT (for MBA); GRE (for M Ed and MS), minimum undergraduate GPA of 3.0, official transcripts, two reference forms, curriculum vitae/resume, statement of career objectives, work experience. Additional exam requirements/recommendations for international students: Required—TOEFL (minimum score 550 paper-based; 79 iBT). Electronic applications accepted.

American University of Armenia, Graduate Programs, Yerevan, Armenia. Offers business administration (MBA); computer and information science (MS), including business management, design and manufacturing, energy (ME, MS), industrial engineering and systems management; economics (MS); industrial engineering and systems management (ME), including business, computer aided design/manufacturing, energy (ME, MS), information technology; law (LL M); political science and international affairs (MPSIA); public health (MPH); teaching English as a foreign language (MA). *Program availability:* Part-time, evening/weekend. *Degree requirements:* For master's, thesis (for some programs), capstone/project. *Entrance requirements:* For master's, GRE, GMAT, or LSAT. Additional exam requirements/recommendations for international students: Recommended—TOEFL (minimum score 79 iBT), IELTS (minimum score 6.5). *Faculty research:* Microfinance, finance (rural/development, international, corporate), firm life cycle theory, TESOL, language proficiency testing, public policy, administrative law, economic development, cryptography, artificial intelligence, energy efficiency/renewable energy, computer-aided design/manufacturing, health financing, tuberculosis control, mother/child health, preventive ophthalmology, post-earthquake psychopathological investigations, tobacco control, environmental health risk assessments.

Business Administration and Management—General

American University of Beirut, Graduate Programs, Suliman S. Olayan School of Business, MBA Program, 1107 2020, Lebanon. Offers MBA. *Faculty:* 10 full-time (3 women), 2 part-time/adjunct (0 women). *Students:* 3 full-time (0 women), 3 part-time (2 women). Average age 27. 59 applicants, 27% accepted, 6 enrolled. In 2017, 16 master's awarded. *Degree requirements:* For master's, thesis. *Entrance requirements:* Additional exam requirements/recommendations for international students: Required—TOEFL (minimum score 583 paper-based; 97 iBT), IELTS (minimum score 7). *Application deadline:* For fall admission, 2/8 for domestic students; for spring admission, 4/4 for domestic students. Application fee: $50. Electronic applications accepted. *Expenses: Tuition:* Full-time $17,244; part-time $958 per credit. *Required fees:* $740. Tuition and fees vary according to course load and program. *Financial support:* In 2017–18, 10 research assistantships with full tuition reimbursements (averaging $21,000 per year) were awarded; fellowships, teaching assistantships, scholarships/grants, health care benefits, tuition waivers, and unspecified assistantships also available. Financial award application deadline: 4/4. *Unit head:* Maya Naim El-Helou, Director of Graduate Programs, 961-1-352700 Ext. 3955, Fax: 961-1-750214, E-mail: helou@aub.edu.lb. *Application contact:* Maya Naim El-Helou, Director of Graduate Programs, 961-1-352700 Ext. 3955, Fax: 961-1-750214, E-mail: helou@aub.edu.lb.
Website: http://www.aub.edu.lb/osb/osb_home/program/MBA/Pages/index.aspx

The American University of Paris, Graduate Programs, Paris, France. Offers cross-cultural and sustainable business management (MA); cultural translation (MA); global communications (MA); global communications and civil society (MA); international affairs (MA); international affairs, conflict resolution and civil society development (MA); Middle East and Islamic studies (MA); Middle East and Islamic studies and international affairs (MA); public policy and international affairs (MA); public policy and international law (MA). *Degree requirements:* For master's, thesis (for some programs). *Entrance requirements:* For master's, minimum undergraduate GPA of 3.0. Additional exam requirements/recommendations for international students: Recommended—TOEFL, IELTS. Electronic applications accepted.

American University of Sharjah, Graduate Programs, 26666, United Arab Emirates. Offers accounting (MS); biomedical engineering (MSBME); business administration (MBA); chemical engineering (MS Ch E); civil engineering (MSCE); computer engineering (MS); electrical engineering (MSEE); engineering systems management (MS, PhD); mathematics (MS); mechanical engineering (MSME); mechatronics engineering (MS); teaching English to speakers of other languages (MA); translation and interpreting (MA); urban planning (MUP). *Program availability:* Part-time, evening/weekend. *Students:* 108 full-time (73 women), 287 part-time (207 women). Average age 27. 203 applicants, 83% accepted, 121 enrolled. In 2017, 114 master's awarded. *Degree requirements:* For master's, thesis (for some programs). *Entrance requirements:* For master's, GMAT (for MBA). Additional exam requirements/recommendations for international students: Required—TOEFL (minimum score 550 paper-based; 80 iBT), TWE (minimum score 5); Recommended—IELTS (minimum score 6.5). *Application deadline:* For fall admission, 8/5 priority date for domestic students, 7/1 priority date for international students; for spring admission, 12/30 priority date for domestic students, 12/9 for international students; for summer admission, 5/21 for domestic and international students. Applications are processed on a rolling basis. Application fee: $110. Electronic applications accepted. *Expenses: Tuition:* Full-time $20,000; part-time $1350 per credit. Tuition and fees vary according to degree level and program. *Financial support:* In 2017–18, 82 students received support, including 54 research assistantships, 54 teaching assistantships; scholarships/grants also available. Financial award application deadline: 6/3. *Faculty research:* Water pollution, management and waste water treatment, energy and sustainability, air pollution, Islamic finance, family business and small and medium enterprises. *Unit head:* Salwa Mohammed, Office of Graduate Studies, 971-6515-2934, E-mail: ogs@aus.edu. *Application contact:* Salwa H. Mohammed, Office of Graduate Studies, 971-65152934, E-mail: ogs@aus.edu.
Website: https://www.aus.edu/masters-degrees

Anaheim University, Programs in Business Administration, Anaheim, CA 92806-5150. Offers entrepreneurship (ME, DBA); global sustainable management (MBA); international business (MBA, DBA, Certificate, Diploma); management (DBA); sustainable management (DBA, Certificate, Diploma). *Program availability:* Part-time, evening/weekend, online only, 100% online. Electronic applications accepted.

Anderson University, College of Business, Anderson, SC 29621-4035. Offers business administration (MBA); healthcare leadership (MBA); human resources (MBA); marketing (MBA); organizational leadership (MOL); supply chain management (MBA). *Accreditation:* ACBSP. *Expenses:* Contact institution. *Financial support:* Tuition waivers available. Financial award application deadline: 3/1; financial award applicants required to submit FAFSA. *Unit head:* Steve Nail, Dean, 864-MBA-6000. *Application contact:* Mallory Knight, Graduate Admission Counselor, 864-231-2182, Fax: 864-231-2115, E-mail: malloryknight@andersonuniversity.edu.
Website: http://www.andersonuniversity.edu/business

Anderson University, Falls School of Business, Anderson, IN 46012-3495. Offers accountancy (MA); business administration (MBA, DBA). *Accreditation:* ACBSP.

Angelo State University, College of Graduate Studies and Research, College of Business, Department of Management and Marketing, San Angelo, TX 76909. Offers business administration (MBA). *Accreditation:* ACBSP. *Program availability:* Part-time, evening/weekend. *Students:* 65 full-time (26 women), 66 part-time (24 women); includes 43 minority (9 Black or African American, non-Hispanic/Latino; 1 Asian, non-Hispanic/Latino; 32 Hispanic/Latino; 1 Two or more races, non-Hispanic/Latino), 8 international. Average age 30. *Entrance requirements:* For master's, GMAT or GRE, essay, resume. *Application deadline:* Applications are processed on a rolling basis. Application fee: $40 ($50 for international students). Electronic applications accepted. *Expenses:* Tuition, state resident: full-time $3856. Tuition, nonresident: full-time $11,324. *Required fees:* $2650. *Financial support:* Career-related internships or fieldwork, Federal Work-Study, and scholarships/grants available. Support available to part-time students. Financial award application deadline: 3/1; financial award applicants required to submit FAFSA. *Unit head:* Dr. Brian W. Kulik, Chair, 325-942-2383, Fax: 325-942-2384, E-mail: brian.kulik@angelo.edu. *Application contact:* Dr. Sharynn Tomlin, MBA Director, 325-486-6635, E-mail: sharynn.tomlin@angelo.edu.
Website: http://www.angelo.edu/dept/management_marketing/

Anna Maria College, Graduate Division, Program in Business Administration, Paxton, MA 01612. Offers MBA, AC. *Program availability:* Part-time, evening/weekend. *Degree requirements:* For master's, capstone project. *Entrance requirements:* For master's, minimum GPA of 2.7. Additional exam requirements/recommendations for international students: Required—TOEFL (minimum score 500 paper-based). Electronic applications accepted. *Faculty research:* Management organization.

Antioch University Los Angeles, Program in Leadership, Management and Business, Culver City, CA 90230. Offers human resource development (MA); leadership (MA); organizational development (MA). *Program availability:* Part-time, evening/weekend. *Faculty:* 7. *Students:* 25 full-time (20 women); includes 16 minority (5 Black or African American, non-Hispanic/Latino; 2 Asian, non-Hispanic/Latino; 7 Hispanic/Latino; 2 Two or more races, non-Hispanic/Latino), 1 international. Average age 33. In 2017, 8 master's awarded. *Entrance requirements:* For master's, interview. Additional exam

requirements/recommendations for international students: Required—TOEFL. *Application deadline:* For fall admission, 8/4 for domestic students; for winter admission, 11/3 for domestic students; for spring admission, 2/2 for domestic students. *Financial support:* In 2017–18, 23 students received support. Career-related internships or fieldwork, Federal Work-Study, and scholarships/grants available. Support available to part-time students. Financial award application deadline: 3/24; financial award applicants required to submit CSS PROFILE or FAFSA. *Faculty research:* Systems thinking and chaos theory, technology and organizational structure, nonprofit management, power and empowerment. *Unit head:* Dr. Susan Nero, Chair, 310-578-1080 Ext. 226, Fax: 310-882-4824, E-mail: susan_nero@antiochla.edu. *Application contact:* Information Contact, 310-578-1090, Fax: 310-822-4824, E-mail: admissions@antiochla.edu.
Website: http://www.antiochla.edu

Antioch University New England, Graduate School, Department of Management, Program in Sustainability (Green MBA), Keene, NH 03431-3552. Offers MBA. *Program availability:* Part-time. *Entrance requirements:* For master's, GRE, resume, 3 letters of recommendation. Additional exam requirements/recommendations for international students: Required—TOEFL (minimum score 600 paper-based).

Antioch University Santa Barbara, Program in Business Administration, Santa Barbara, CA 93101-1581. Offers non-profit management (MBA); social business (MBA); strategic leadership (MBA).

Apollos University, School of Business and Management, Great Falls, MT 59401. Offers business administration (MBA, DBA); organizational management (MS).

Appalachian State University, Cratis D. Williams Graduate School, Program in Business Administration, Boone, NC 28608. Offers general management (MBA). *Accreditation:* AACSB. *Program availability:* Part-time, online learning. *Degree requirements:* For master's, comprehensive exam. *Entrance requirements:* For master's, GMAT, 3 letters of recommendation. Additional exam requirements/recommendations for international students: Required—TOEFL (minimum score 550 paper-based; 79 iBT), IELTS (minimum score 6.5). Electronic applications accepted.

Aquinas College, School of Management, Grand Rapids, MI 49506. Offers marketing management (MM); organizational leadership (MM); sustainable business (MM). *Program availability:* Part-time, evening/weekend. *Students:* 11 full-time (6 women), 30 part-time (20 women); includes 7 minority (2 Black or African American, non-Hispanic/Latino; 1 Asian, non-Hispanic/Latino; 4 Hispanic/Latino). *Entrance requirements:* For master's, GMAT, minimum undergraduate GPA of 2.75, 2 years of work experience. Additional exam requirements/recommendations for international students: Required—TOEFL (minimum score 550 paper-based). *Application deadline:* Applications are processed on a rolling basis. Application fee: $0. *Expenses:* Contact institution. *Financial support:* Scholarships/grants available. Support available to part-time students. Financial award application deadline: 3/15; financial award applicants required to submit FAFSA. *Unit head:* Cynthia G. VanGelderen, Interim Director, 616-632-2922, Fax: 616-732-4489. *Application contact:* Lynn Atkins-Rykert, Program Coordinator, 616-632-2925, Fax: 616-732-4489, E-mail: atkinlyn@aquinas.edu.

Arcadia University, Program in Business Administration, Glenside, PA 19038-3295. Offers MBA. *Accreditation:* ACBSP. *Entrance requirements:* Additional exam requirements/recommendations for international students: Required—TOEFL. *Expenses:* Contact institution.

Argosy University, Atlanta, College of Business, Atlanta, GA 30328. Offers accounting (DBA); corporate compliance (MBA); customized professional concentration (MBA, DBA); finance (MBA); healthcare administration (MBA); information systems (DBA); information systems management (MBA); international business (MBA, DBA); management (MBA, MSM, DBA); marketing (MBA, DBA). *Accreditation:* ACBSP.

Argosy University, Chicago, College of Business, Chicago, IL 60601. Offers accounting (DBA); customized professional concentration (MBA, DBA); finance (DBA); fraud examination (MBA); global business sustainability (DBA); healthcare administration (MBA); information systems (DBA); information systems management (MBA); international business (MBA, DBA); management (MBA, MSM, DBA); marketing (MBA, DBA); organizational leadership (Ed D); public administration (MBA); sustainable management (MBA). *Accreditation:* ACBSP. *Program availability:* Online learning.

Argosy University, Hawai`i, College of Business, Honolulu, HI 96813. Offers accounting (DBA); corporate compliance (MBA); customized professional concentration (MBA, DBA); finance (MBA, Certificate); fraud examination (MBA); global business sustainability (DBA); healthcare administration (MBA, Certificate); information systems (DBA); information systems management (MBA, Certificate); international business (MBA, DBA, Certificate); management (MBA, MSM, DBA); marketing (MBA, DBA, Certificate); organizational leadership (Ed D); public administration (MBA); sustainable management (MBA).

Argosy University, Los Angeles, College of Business, Los Angeles, CA 90045. Offers accounting (DBA); corporate compliance (MBA); customized professional concentration (MBA, DBA); finance (MBA); fraud examination (MBA); global business sustainability (DBA); healthcare administration (MBA); information systems (DBA); information systems management (MBA); international business (MBA, DBA); management (MBA, MSM, DBA); marketing (MBA, DBA); organizational leadership (Ed D); public administration (MBA); sustainable management (MBA).

Argosy University, Northern Virginia, College of Business, Arlington, VA 22209. Offers accounting (DBA); customized professional concentration (MBA, DBA); finance (MBA); fraud examination (MBA); global business sustainability (DBA); healthcare administration (MBA); information systems (DBA); information systems management (MBA); international business (MBA, DBA, Certificate); management (MBA, MSM, DBA); marketing (MBA, DBA, Certificate); organizational leadership (Ed D); public administration (MBA); sustainable management (MBA).

Argosy University, Orange County, College of Business, Orange, CA 92868. Offers accounting (DBA, Adv C); corporate compliance (MBA); customized professional concentration (MBA, DBA); finance (MBA, Certificate); fraud examination (MBA); global business sustainability (DBA); healthcare administration (MBA, Certificate); information systems (DBA, Adv C, Certificate); information systems management (MBA); international business (MBA, DBA, Adv C, Certificate); management (MBA, MSM, DBA, Adv C); marketing (MBA, DBA, Adv C, Certificate); organizational leadership (Ed D); public administration (MBA, Certificate); sustainable management (MBA).

Argosy University, Phoenix, College of Business, Phoenix, AZ 85021. Offers accounting (DBA); corporate compliance (MBA); customized professional concentration (MBA, DBA); finance (MBA); fraud examination (MBA); global business sustainability (DBA); healthcare administration (MBA); information systems (DBA); information systems management (MBA); international business (MBA, DBA); management (MBA, DBA); marketing (MBA, DBA); public administration (MBA); sustainable management (MBA).

Argosy University, Seattle, College of Business, Seattle, WA 98121. Offers accounting (DBA); corporate compliance (MBA); customized professional concentration (MBA, DBA); finance (MBA); fraud examination (MBA); global business sustainability (DBA);

healthcare administration (MBA); information systems (DBA); information systems management (MBA); international business (MBA, DBA); management (MBA, MSM, DBA); marketing (MBA, DBA); organizational leadership (Ed D); public administration (MBA); sustainable management (MBA).

Argosy University, Tampa, College of Business, Tampa, FL 33607. Offers accounting (DBA); corporate compliance (MBA); customized professional concentration (MBA, DBA); finance (MBA); fraud examination (MBA); global business sustainability (DBA); healthcare administration (MBA); information systems (DBA); information systems management (MBA); international business (MBA, DBA); management (MBA, MSM, DBA); marketing (MBA, DBA); organizational leadership (Ed D); public administration (MBA); sustainable management (MBA).

Argosy University, Twin Cities, College of Business, Eagan, MN 55121. Offers accounting (DBA); customized professional concentration (MBA, DBA); finance (MBA); fraud examination (MBA); global business sustainability (DBA); healthcare administration (MBA); information systems (DBA); information systems management (MBA); international business (MBA, DBA); management (MBA, MSM, DBA); marketing (MBA, DBA); organizational leadership (Ed D); public administration (MBA); sustainable management (MBA).

Arizona State University at the Tempe campus, Thunderbird School of Global Management, Tempe, AZ 85287. Offers global affairs and management (MA); global management (MGM). *Accreditation:* AACSB. *Program availability:* Online learning. *Degree requirements:* For master's, one foreign language. *Entrance requirements:* For master's, GMAT. Additional exam requirements/recommendations for international students: Required—TOEFL.

Arizona State University at the Tempe campus, W. P. Carey School of Business, Program in Business Administration, Tempe, AZ 85287-4906. Offers entrepreneurship (MBA); finance (MBA); health sector management (MBA); international business (MBA); leadership (MBA); marketing (MBA); organizational behavior (PhD); strategic management (PhD); supply chain management (MBA, PhD); JD/MBA; MBA/M Acc; MBA/M Arch. *Accreditation:* AACSB. *Program availability:* Part-time, evening/weekend, online learning. Terminal master's awarded for partial completion of doctoral program. *Degree requirements:* For master's, thesis or alternative, internship, interactive Program of Study (iPOS) submitted before completing 50 percent of required credit hours; for doctorate, comprehensive exam, thesis/dissertation, interactive Program of Study (iPOS) submitted before completing 50 percent of required credit hours. *Entrance requirements:* For master's, GMAT, minimum GPA of 3.0 in last 2 years of work leading to bachelor's degree, 2 letters of recommendation, professional resume, official transcripts, 3 essays; for doctorate, GMAT or GRE, minimum GPA of 3.0 in last 2 years of work leading to bachelor's degree, 3 letters of recommendation, resume, personal statement/essay. Additional exam requirements/recommendations for international students: Required—TOEFL (minimum score 550 paper-based; 80 iBT), IELTS (minimum score 6.5). Electronic applications accepted. *Expenses:* Contact institution.

Arkansas State University, Graduate School, College of Business, Department of Economics and Finance, State University, AR 72467. Offers business administration (MBA). *Accreditation:* AACSB. *Program availability:* Part-time. *Degree requirements:* For master's, comprehensive exam, thesis or alternative. *Entrance requirements:* For master's, GMAT, appropriate bachelor's degree, letters of reference, official transcripts, immunization records. Additional exam requirements/recommendations for international students: Required—TOEFL (minimum score 550 paper-based; 79 iBT), IELTS (minimum score 6), PTE (minimum score 56). Electronic applications accepted. *Expenses:* Contact institution.

Arkansas Tech University, College of Business, Russellville, AR 72801. Offers MBA. *Accreditation:* AACSB. *Program availability:* Part-time, evening/weekend, 100% online, blended/hybrid learning. *Students:* 2 full-time (0 women), 44 part-time (30 women); includes 4 minority (2 Black or African American, non-Hispanic/Latino; 2 Two or more races, non-Hispanic/Latino). Average age 31. In 2017, 15 master's awarded. *Degree requirements:* For master's, completion of all required coursework with minimum cumulative GPA of 3.0 within six years. *Entrance requirements:* Additional exam requirements/recommendations for international students: Required—TOEFL (minimum score 550 paper-based; 79 iBT), IELTS (minimum score 6.5), PTE (minimum score 58). *Application deadline:* For fall admission, 3/1 priority date for domestic students, 5/1 priority date for international students; for spring admission, 10/1 priority date for domestic and international students. Applications are processed on a rolling basis. Application fee: $40 ($90 for international students). Electronic applications accepted. *Expenses:* Tuition, state resident: full-time $6816; part-time $284 per credit hour. Tuition, nonresident: full-time $13,632; part-time $568 per credit hour. *Required fees:* $420 per semester. Tuition and fees vary according to course load. *Financial support:* In 2017–18, research assistantships with full and partial tuition reimbursements (averaging $4,800 per year), teaching assistantships with full and partial tuition reimbursements (averaging $4,800 per year) were awarded; career-related internships or fieldwork, Federal Work-Study, scholarships/grants, health care benefits, and unspecified assistantships also available. Support available to part-time students. Financial award application deadline: 4/15; financial award applicants required to submit FAFSA. *Unit head:* Dr. Jeff Robertson, Dean, 479-968-0498, E-mail: jrobertson@atu.edu. *Application contact:* Dr. Mary B. Gunter, Dean of Graduate College, 479-968-0398, Fax: 479-964-0542, E-mail: gradcollege@atu.edu.
Website: http://www.atu.edu/business/

Ashland University, Dauch College of Business and Economics, Ashland, OH 44805-3702. Offers accounting (MBA); business analytics (MBA); entrepreneurship (MBA); financial management (MBA); global management (MBA); health care management and leadership (MBA); human resource management (MBA); human resources (MBA); management information systems (MBA); project management (MBA); sport management (MBA); supply chain management (MBA). *Accreditation:* ACBSP. *Program availability:* Part-time, evening/weekend, 100% online, blended/hybrid learning. *Faculty:* 20 full-time (8 women), 13 part-time/adjunct (2 women). *Students:* 458 full-time (210 women), 144 part-time (52 women); includes 88 minority (63 Black or African American, non-Hispanic/Latino; 1 American Indian or Alaska Native, non-Hispanic/Latino; 10 Asian, non-Hispanic/Latino; 14 Hispanic/Latino), 202 international. Average age 31. 216 applicants, 74% accepted, 115 enrolled. In 2017, 184 master's awarded. Terminal master's awarded for partial completion of doctoral program. *Degree requirements:* For master's, thesis optional, capstone course. *Entrance requirements:* For master's, 2 years of full-time work experience. Additional exam requirements/recommendations for international students: Required—TOEFL (minimum score 550 paper-based; 78 iBT) *Application deadline:* For fall admission, 8/1 priority date for domestic students; for spring admission, 12/1 priority date for domestic students. Applications are processed on a rolling basis. Application fee: $30. Electronic applications accepted. *Expenses:* $815 per credit hour, $15 technology fee for online sections. *Financial support:* Scholarships/grants, tuition waivers (partial), and unspecified assistantships available. Financial award application deadline: 4/15; financial award applicants required to submit FAFSA. *Faculty research:* Relationship marketing strategy, executive compensation and company performance, online marketplaces in electronic commerce, diversity training in campus recreation departments, entrepreneurship in developing and emerging economies. *Unit head:* Dr. Elad Granot, Dean, 419-289-5932, E-mail: egranot@

ashland.edu. *Application contact:* Stephen W. Krispinsky, Executive Director of MBA Program, 419-289-5236, Fax: 419-289-5910, E-mail: skrispin@ashland.edu.
Website: http://www.mba.ashland.edu

Ashworth College, Graduate Programs, Norcross, GA 30092. Offers business administration (MBA); criminal justice (MS); health care administration (MBA, MS); human resource management (MBA, MS); international business (MBA); management (MS); marketing (MBA, MS).

Aspen University, Program in Business Administration, Denver, CO 80246-1930. Offers business administration (MBA); finance (MBA); information management (MBA); project management (MBA, Certificate). *Program availability:* Part-time, evening/weekend, online learning. *Entrance requirements:* Additional exam requirements/recommendations for international students: Required—TOEFL (minimum score 530 paper-based). Electronic applications accepted.

Assumption College, Business Studies Program, Worcester, MA 01609-1296. Offers accounting (MBA); business studies (CAGS); finance/economics (MBA); human resources (MBA); international business (MBA); management (MBA); marketing (MBA); nonprofit leadership (MBA). *Program availability:* Part-time, evening/weekend. *Faculty:* 5 full-time (1 woman), 21 part-time/adjunct (6 women). *Students:* 29 full-time (13 women), 87 part-time (50 women); includes 15 minority (1 Black or African American, non-Hispanic/Latino; 4 Asian, non-Hispanic/Latino; 8 Hispanic/Latino; 2 Two or more races, non-Hispanic/Latino), 4 international. Average age 29. 34 applicants, 100% accepted, 26 enrolled. In 2017, 81 master's, 2 other advanced degrees awarded. *Degree requirements:* For master's, capstone. *Entrance requirements:* For master's, bachelor's degree, three letters of recommendation, official transcripts, personal statement, current resume; for CAGS, MBA or equivalent degree in a closely related field, three letters of recommendation, official transcripts, personal statement, current resume. Additional exam requirements/recommendations for international students: Required—TOEFL (minimum score 540 paper-based; 76 iBT), IELTS (minimum score 6). *Application deadline:* For fall admission, 8/10 priority date for domestic and international students; for spring admission, 1/4 priority date for domestic and international students; for summer admission, 5/10 priority date for domestic and international students. Application fee: $30. Electronic applications accepted. *Expenses: Tuition:* Full-time $11,952; part-time $664 per credit. *Required fees:* $70 per term. *Financial support:* In 2017–18, 19 students received support. Tuition waivers (full and partial), unspecified assistantships, and institutional discounts available. Financial award applicants required to submit FAFSA. *Faculty research:* Workplace diversity, dynamics of team interaction, utilization of leased employees, experiential learning project on due diligence market for prostheses. *Unit head:* Dr. Robin Frkal, Director, 508-767-7622, E-mail: ra.frkal@assumption.edu. *Application contact:* Karen Stoyanoff, Director of Recruitment for Graduate Enrollment, 508-767-7442, Fax: 508-799-4412, E-mail: graduate@assumption.edu.
Website: http://graduate.assumption.edu/mba/assumption-mba

Athabasca University, Faculty of Business, Edmonton, AB T5L 4W1, Canada. Offers business administration (MBA); information technology management (MBA), including policing concentration; innovative management (DBA); management (GDM); project management (MBA, GDM). *Program availability:* Part-time, evening/weekend, online learning. *Degree requirements:* For master's, thesis or alternative, applied project. *Entrance requirements:* For master's, 3-8 years of managerial experience, 3 years with undergraduate degree, 5 years' managerial experience with professional designation, 8-10 years' management experience (on exception). Electronic applications accepted. *Expenses:* Contact institution. *Faculty research:* Human resources, project management, operations research, information technology management, corporate stewardship, energy management.

Atlantis University, School of Business, Miami, FL 33132. Offers MBA, DBA.

Auburn University, Graduate School, College of Business, Department of Management, Auburn University, AL 36849. Offers management (PhD). *Accreditation:* AACSB. *Program availability:* Part-time. *Faculty:* 47 full-time (13 women), 9 part-time/adjunct (4 women). *Students:* 191 full-time (58 women), 414 part-time (112 women); includes 113 minority (41 Black or African American, non-Hispanic/Latino; 2 American Indian or Alaska Native, non-Hispanic/Latino; 25 Asian, non-Hispanic/Latino; 36 Hispanic/Latino; 9 Two or more races, non-Hispanic/Latino), 32 international. Average age 33. 443 applicants, 56% accepted, 165 enrolled. In 2017, 218 master's, 2 doctorates awarded. *Degree requirements:* For master's, thesis (for some programs); for doctorate, thesis/dissertation. *Entrance requirements:* For master's, GMAT, GRE General Test (for MS); for doctorate, GMAT, GRE General Test. Additional exam requirements/recommendations for international students: Required—TOEFL. *Application deadline:* Applications are processed on a rolling basis. Application fee: $50 ($60 for international students). Electronic applications accepted. *Expenses:* Tuition, state resident: full-time $10,974; part-time $519 per credit hour. Tuition, nonresident: full-time $29,658; part-time $1557 per credit hour. *Required fees:* $816 per semester. Tuition and fees vary according to degree level and program. *Financial support:* Teaching assistantships and Federal Work-Study available. Support available to part-time students. Financial award application deadline: 3/15; financial award applicants required to submit FAFSA. *Unit head:* Kevin Mossholder, Department Chair, 334-844-9565. *Application contact:* Dr. George Flowers, Dean of the Graduate School, 334-844-2125.
Website: http://business.auburn.edu/academics/departments/department-of-management/

Auburn University, Graduate School, College of Business, Program in Business Administration, Auburn University, AL 36849. Offers MBA. *Accreditation:* AACSB. *Program availability:* Part-time. *Faculty:* 47 full-time (13 women), 9 part-time/adjunct (4 women). *Students:* 163 full-time (51 women), 370 part-time (101 women); includes 102 minority (35 Black or African American, non-Hispanic/Latino; 2 American Indian or Alaska Native, non-Hispanic/Latino; 21 Asian, non-Hispanic/Latino; 35 Hispanic/Latino; 9 Two or more races, non-Hispanic/Latino), 13 international. Average age 33. 342 applicants, 60% accepted, 153 enrolled. In 2017, 189 master's awarded. *Entrance requirements:* For master's, GMAT. *Application deadline:* Applications are processed on a rolling basis. Application fee: $50 ($60 for international students). Electronic applications accepted. *Expenses:* Tuition, state resident: full-time $10,974; part-time $519 per credit hour. Tuition, nonresident: full-time $29,658; part-time $1557 per credit hour. *Required fees:* $816 per semester. Tuition and fees vary according to degree level and program. *Financial support:* Federal Work-Study available. Support available to part-time students. Financial award application deadline: 3/15; financial award applicants required to submit FAFSA. *Unit head:* Stan Harris, Associate Dean, 334-844-4060. *Application contact:* Dr. George Flowers, Dean of the Graduate School, 334-844-2125.
Website: http://www.auburn.edu/business/mbaprog.html

Auburn University at Montgomery, College of Business, Department of Business Administration, Montgomery, AL 36124-4023. Offers business and management (MBA). *Accreditation:* AACSB. *Faculty:* 8 full-time (2 women). *Students:* 35 full-time (12 women), 39 part-time (24 women); includes 16 minority (12 Black or African American, non-Hispanic/Latino; 3 Asian, non-Hispanic/Latino; 1 Hispanic/Latino), 13 international.

Business Administration and Management—General

Average age 35. 64 applicants, 75% accepted, 34 enrolled. In 2017, 46 master's awarded. *Entrance requirements:* For master's, GMAT. Additional exam requirements/recommendations for international students: Required—TOEFL (minimum score 500 paper-based; 61 iBT), IELTS (minimum score 5.5), PTE (minimum score 44). *Application deadline:* Applications are processed on a rolling basis. Application fee: $25 ($0 for international students). Electronic applications accepted. *Expenses:* Tuition, state resident: full-time $6930; part-time $385 per credit hour. Tuition, nonresident: full-time $15,588; part-time $866 per credit hour. *Required fees:* $640. *Financial support:* Application deadline: 3/1; applicants required to submit FAFSA. *Unit head:* Dr. Kevin Banning, Department Head, 334-244-3485, E-mail: kbanning@aum.edu. *Application contact:* Jennifer Taylor, Assistant Director of Graduate Programs, 334-244-3587, Fax: 334-244-3137, E-mail: jtaylor5@aum.edu.
Website: http://business.aum.edu/academic-departments/business-administration

Augsburg University, Program in Business Administration, Minneapolis, MN 55454-1351. Offers MBA. *Program availability:* Evening/weekend. Electronic applications accepted.

Augusta University, Hull College of Business, Augusta, GA 30912. Offers business administration (MBA); information security management (MS). *Accreditation:* AACSB. *Program availability:* Part-time, evening/weekend. *Entrance requirements:* For master's, GMAT.

Aurora University, Dunham School of Business and Public Policy, Aurora, IL 60506-4892. Offers accountancy (MS); business (MBA). *Program availability:* Part-time, evening/weekend, 100% online. *Faculty:* 4 full-time (0 women), 22 part-time/adjunct (9 women). *Students:* 193 full-time (106 women), 34 part-time (20 women); includes 83 minority (31 Black or African American, non-Hispanic/Latino; 6 Asian, non-Hispanic/Latino; 36 Hispanic/Latino; 1 Native Hawaiian or other Pacific Islander, non-Hispanic/Latino; 9 Two or more races, non-Hispanic/Latino), 2 international. Average age 33. 135 applicants, 100% accepted, 52 enrolled. In 2017, 122 master's awarded. *Entrance requirements:* For master's, minimum GPA of 3.0, 2 years of work experience, resume. Additional exam requirements/recommendations for international students: Required—TOEFL (minimum score 550 paper-based; 79 iBT). *Application deadline:* For fall admission, 6/1 for international students; for spring admission, 10/1 for international students. Applications are processed on a rolling basis. Application fee: $0. Electronic applications accepted. *Expenses:* Contact institution. *Financial support:* In 2017–18, 58 students received support. Federal Work-Study, scholarships/grants, and unspecified assistantships available. Support available to part-time students. Financial award applicants required to submit FAFSA. *Unit head:* Dr. Toby Arquette, Dean, School of Business and Policy, 630-844-5614, E-mail: tarquett@aurora.edu. *Application contact:* Tom Gergits, Recruiter for Graduate Programs, 630-947-8945, E-mail: tgergits@aurora.edu.

Austin Peay State University, College of Graduate Studies, College of Business, Clarksville, TN 37044. Offers management (MS). *Program availability:* Part-time, evening/weekend, online learning. *Faculty:* 6 full-time (2 women). *Students:* 17 full-time (9 women), 46 part-time (26 women); includes 14 minority (5 Black or African American, non-Hispanic/Latino; 2 Asian, non-Hispanic/Latino; 2 Hispanic/Latino; 5 Two or more races, non-Hispanic/Latino). Average age 35. 44 applicants, 73% accepted, 16 enrolled. In 2017, 32 master's awarded. *Degree requirements:* For master's, comprehensive exam. *Entrance requirements:* For master's, GMAT, minimum undergraduate GPA of 2.5. Additional exam requirements/recommendations for international students: Required—TOEFL (minimum score 500 paper-based). *Application deadline:* For fall admission, 8/8 priority date for domestic students. Applications are processed on a rolling basis. Application fee: $45 ($55 for international students). Electronic applications accepted. *Expenses:* Tuition, state resident: full-time $7686; part-time $427 per credit hour. Tuition, nonresident: full-time $20,268; part-time $1126 per credit hour. *Required fees:* $1529; $76.45 per credit hour. *Financial support:* Research assistantships with full tuition reimbursements, career-related internships or fieldwork, Federal Work-Study, institutionally sponsored loans, scholarships/grants, and unspecified assistantships available. Support available to part-time students. Financial award application deadline: 4/1; financial award applicants required to submit FAFSA. *Unit head:* Dr. Mickey Hepner, Dean, 931-221-7675, Fax: 931-221-7355, E-mail: hepnerm@apsu.edu. *Application contact:* Megan Mitchell, Coordinator of Graduate Admissions, 931-221-6189, Fax: 931-221-7641, E-mail: mitchellm@apsu.edu.
Website: http://www.apsu.edu/business/index.php

Averett University, Master of Business Administration Program, Danville, VA 24541. Offers business administration (MBA); human resources management (MBA); leadership (MBA); marketing (MBA). *Program availability:* Part-time, evening/weekend, 100% online, blended/hybrid learning. *Faculty:* 7 full-time (0 women), 12 part-time/adjunct (4 women). *Students:* 53 full-time (28 women), 129 part-time (83 women); includes 82 minority (65 Black or African American, non-Hispanic/Latino; 1 American Indian or Alaska Native, non-Hispanic/Latino; 5 Asian, non-Hispanic/Latino; 4 Hispanic/Latino; 7 Two or more races, non-Hispanic/Latino). Average age 38. 88 applicants, 81% accepted, 65 enrolled. In 2017, 129 master's awarded. *Degree requirements:* For master's, 41-credit core curriculum, minimum GPA of 3.0 throughout program, no more than 2 grades of C, completion of degree requirements within six years from start of program. *Entrance requirements:* For master's, minimum cumulative GPA of 3.0 over the last 60 semester hours of undergraduate study toward a baccalaureate degree, official transcripts, three years of full-time work experience, three letters of recommendation, current resume. Additional exam requirements/recommendations for international students: Required—TOEFL (minimum score 600 paper-based; 100 iBT). *Application deadline:* Applications are processed on a rolling basis. Electronic applications accepted. *Expenses:* $11,790. *Financial support:* Application deadline: 3/1; applicants required to submit FAFSA. *Unit head:* Dr. Peggy C. Wright, Chair, Business Department, 434-791-7118, E-mail: pwright@averett.edu. *Application contact:* Melissa Anderson, Director of Admissions, Graduate and Professional Studies, 804-729-8285, E-mail: manderson@averett.edu.
Website: http://gps.averett.edu/programs/master-degrees/

Avila University, School of Business, Kansas City, MO 64145-1698. Offers accounting (MBA); finance (MBA); health care administration (MBA); international business (MBA); management (MBA); management information systems (MBA); marketing (MBA). *Program availability:* Part-time, evening/weekend. *Faculty:* 6 full-time (2 women), 6 part-time/adjunct (2 women). *Students:* 49 full-time (19 women), 29 part-time (14 women); includes 16 minority (12 Black or African American, non-Hispanic/Latino; 1 Asian, non-Hispanic/Latino; 3 Hispanic/Latino), 19 international. Average age 32. 51 applicants, 47% accepted, 20 enrolled. In 2017, 31 master's awarded. *Degree requirements:* For master's, comprehensive exam, capstone course. *Entrance requirements:* For master's, GMAT (minimum score 420), minimum GPA of 3.0, interview. Additional exam requirements/recommendations for international students: Required—TOEFL (minimum score 550 paper-based). *Application deadline:* For fall admission, 7/30 priority date for domestic and international students; for winter admission, 11/30 priority date for domestic and international students; for spring admission, 2/28 priority date for domestic and international students; for summer admission, 6/1 priority date for domestic and international students. Applications are processed on a rolling basis. Application fee: $0. Electronic applications accepted. *Expenses:* Contact institution. *Financial support:* In

2017–18, 18 students received support. Career-related internships or fieldwork and scholarships/grants available. Support available to part-time students. Financial award applicants required to submit FAFSA. *Faculty research:* Leadership characteristics, financial hedging, group dynamics. *Unit head:* Dr. Wendy L. Acker, Interim Dean, 816-501-3720, Fax: 816-501-2463, E-mail: wendy.acker@avila.edu. *Application contact:* Brandon Black, MBA Admission Advisor, 816-501-3601, Fax: 816-501-2463, E-mail: brandon.black@avila.edu.
Website: https://www.avila.edu/mrk/mba

Avila University, School of Professional Studies, Kansas City, MO 64145-1698. Offers executive leadership (MS); fundraising (MA); instructional design and technology (MA, MS); leadership coaching (MS); project management (MA); strategic human resources (MS). *Program availability:* Part-time-only, evening/weekend, 100% online, blended/hybrid learning. *Faculty:* 14 part-time/adjunct (8 women). *Students:* 85 full-time (61 women), 45 part-time (33 women); includes 42 minority (35 Black or African American, non-Hispanic/Latino; 2 Asian, non-Hispanic/Latino; 4 Hispanic/Latino; 1 Two or more races, non-Hispanic/Latino), 3 international. Average age 37. 63 applicants, 60% accepted, 29 enrolled. In 2017, 39 master's awarded. *Degree requirements:* For master's, thesis optional. *Entrance requirements:* For master's, 2 letters of recommendation, minimum GPA of 3.0 during last 60 hours, resume, statement of intent. Additional exam requirements/recommendations for international students: Required—TOEFL (minimum score 550 paper-based; 79 iBT). *Application deadline:* Applications are processed on a rolling basis. Application fee: $0. Electronic applications accepted. *Expenses:* Contact institution. *Financial support:* In 2017–18, 14 students received support. Unspecified assistantships available. Support available to part-time students. Financial award applicants required to submit FAFSA. *Unit head:* Kari Clevenger, Associate Dean/Director, 816-501-3675, Fax: 816-941-4650, E-mail: advantage@avila.edu. *Application contact:* Jessica Burson, Graduate Admission Advisor, 816-501-2482, Fax: 816-941-4650, E-mail: advantage@avila.edu.
Website: https://www.avila.edu/mrk/advantage-3

Azusa Pacific University, School of Business and Management, Azusa, CA 91702-7000. Offers accounting (MBA); business administration (MBA); entrepreneurship (MBA); finance (MBA); international business (MBA); marketing (MBA); organizational science (MBA); professional accountancy (M Acc); sport management (MBA). *Program availability:* Part-time, evening/weekend. *Degree requirements:* For master's, thesis (for some programs), final project. *Entrance requirements:* For master's, GMAT, minimum GPA of 3.0. Additional exam requirements/recommendations for international students: Required—TOEFL (minimum score 600 paper-based). *Expenses:* Contact institution. *Faculty research:* Gender issues, financial risk, leadership and ethics, marketing strategy.

Babson College, F. W. Olin Graduate School of Business, Babson Park, MA 02457-0310. Offers accounting (MSA); advanced management (Certificate); business administration (MBA); business analytics (MS); finance (MS); global entrepreneurship (MS); technological entrepreneurship (MS). *Accreditation:* AACSB. *Program availability:* Part-time, evening/weekend, online learning. *Entrance requirements:* For master's, GMAT, 2 years of work experience, resume, letters of recommendation. Additional exam requirements/recommendations for international students: Required—TOEFL (minimum score 100 iBT), IELTS (minimum score 6.5). Electronic applications accepted. *Faculty research:* Entrepreneurship, sustainability, global markets, process of innovation, social media and advertising.

Baker College Center for Graduate Studies–Online, Graduate Programs, Flint, MI 48507. Offers accounting (MBA); business administration (DBA); finance (MBA); general business (MBA); health care management (MBA); human resources management (MBA); information management (MBA); leadership studies (MBA); management information systems (MSIS); marketing (MBA). *Program availability:* Part-time, evening/weekend, online learning. *Degree requirements:* For master's, portfolio. *Entrance requirements:* For master's, 3 years of work experience, minimum undergraduate GPA of 2.5, writing sample, 3 letters of recommendation; for doctorate, MBA or acceptable related master's degree from accredited association, 5 years work experience, minimum graduate GPA of 3.25, writing sample, 3 professional references. Additional exam requirements/recommendations for international students: Required—TOEFL (minimum score 550 paper-based). Electronic applications accepted.

Baker University, School of Professional and Graduate Studies, Programs in Business, Baldwin City, KS 66006-0065. Offers MAOL, MBA, MSM, MSSM. Programs also offered in Overland Park, KS; Topeka, KS; and Wichita, KS. *Program availability:* Part-time, evening/weekend, online learning. *Students:* 23 full-time (14 women), 346 part-time (160 women); includes 106 minority (40 Black or African American, non-Hispanic/Latino; 19 American Indian or Alaska Native, non-Hispanic/Latino; 10 Asian, non-Hispanic/Latino; 24 Hispanic/Latino; 13 Two or more races, non-Hispanic/Latino), 1 international. Average age 34. In 2017, 192 master's awarded. *Entrance requirements:* For master's, 2 years of full-time work experience. Additional exam requirements/recommendations for international students: Required—TOEFL (minimum score 600 paper-based; 100 iBT). *Application deadline:* Applications are processed on a rolling basis. *Financial support:* Applicants required to submit FAFSA. *Unit head:* Dr. Emily Ford, Interim Dean of the School of Professional and Graduate Studies, 785-594-8475, E-mail: emily.ford@bakeru.edu. *Application contact:* Kelly Belk, Vice President of Enrollment Management, 913-491-4432, E-mail: kelly.belk@learn.bakeru.edu.
Website: https://www.bakeru.edu/spgs/

Bakke Graduate University, Programs in Pastoral Ministry and Business, Dallas, TX 75243-7039. Offers business administration (MBA); church and ministry multiplication (D Min); global urban leadership (MA); leadership (D Min); ministry in complex contexts (D Min); social and civic entrepreneurship (MA); theology of work (D Min); theology reflection (D Min); transformational leadership (DTL); urban youth ministry (D Min). *Program availability:* Part-time, online learning. *Faculty:* 5 full-time (3 women), 27 part-time/adjunct (12 women). *Students:* 120 full-time (48 women), 54 part-time (24 women). *Degree requirements:* For master's, thesis; for doctorate, thesis/dissertation. *Entrance requirements:* For master's, 2 years of ministry experience, BA in Biblical studies or theology; for doctorate, 3 years of ministry experience, M Div. Additional exam requirements/recommendations for international students: Required—TOEFL. *Application deadline:* For fall admission, 7/1 priority date for domestic students; for winter admission, 12/1 for domestic students; for spring admission, 3/15 for domestic students. Applications are processed on a rolling basis. Application fee: $50. Electronic applications accepted. *Expenses:* Tuition: Full-time $6120; part-time $3000 per credit. *Required fees:* $50 per course. $50 per quarter. *Financial support:* Scholarships/grants and tuition waivers (partial) available. Financial award applicants required to submit FAFSA. *Faculty research:* Theological systems, church management, worship. *Unit head:* Dr. Gwen Dewey, Senior Vice President of International Partnerships, 214-329-4447 Ext. 119, E-mail: gwen.dewey@bgu.edu. *Application contact:* Traci Tucker, Director of Admissions, 214-329-4447 Ext. 122, Fax: 214-347-9367, E-mail: traci.tucker@bgu.edu.
Website: http://www.bgu.edu/

Baldwin Wallace University, Graduate Programs, School of Business, Master's in Management Program, Berea, OH 44017-2088. Offers MAM. *Students:* 12 applicants, 42% accepted. *Entrance requirements:* Additional exam requirements/recommendations for international students: Required—TOEFL. *Expenses:* Contact institution. *Financial support:* Applicants required to submit FAFSA. *Unit head:* Ann Conrad, Director of One-Year MBA and MA in Management Program, 440-826-2390, Fax: 440-826-3868, E-mail: aconrad@bw.edu. *Application contact:* Laura Spencer, Graduate Application Specialist, 440-826-2191, Fax: 440-826-3868, E-mail: lspencer@bw.edu. Website: http://www.bw.edu/academics/master-management/

Baldwin Wallace University, Graduate Programs, School of Business, MBA in Management - Hybrid Program, Berea, OH 44017-2088. Offers MBA. *Program availability:* Part-time, evening/weekend, blended/hybrid learning. *Students:* 23 full-time (12 women); includes 4 minority (2 Black or African American, non-Hispanic/Latino; 1 Asian, non-Hispanic/Latino; 1 Two or more races, non-Hispanic/Latino). Average age 32. 7 applicants, 71% accepted, 4 enrolled. In 2017, 14 master's awarded. *Entrance requirements:* For master's, GMAT or minimum undergraduate GPA of 3.0, bachelor's degree in any field, work experience. Additional exam requirements/recommendations for international students: Required—TOEFL (minimum score 79 iBT). *Application deadline:* For fall admission, 7/31 for domestic students; for summer admission, 4/15 for domestic students. Applications are processed on a rolling basis. Electronic applications accepted. *Expenses:* $948 per credit hour. *Financial support:* Applicants required to submit FAFSA. *Unit head:* Dale Kramer, Program Director, 440-826-3331, Fax: 440-826-3868, E-mail: dkramer@bw.edu. *Application contact:* Laura Spencer, Graduate Application Specialist, 440-826-2191, Fax: 440-826-3868, E-mail: lspencer@bw.edu. Website: http://www.bw.edu/graduate/business/mba/

Baldwin Wallace University, Graduate Programs, School of Business, Program in Management, Berea, OH 44017-2088. Offers MBA. *Program availability:* Part-time, evening/weekend. *Students:* 66 full-time (28 women), 40 part-time (15 women); includes 22 minority (9 Black or African American, non-Hispanic/Latino; 6 Asian, non-Hispanic/Latino; 5 Hispanic/Latino; 2 Two or more races, non-Hispanic/Latino), 1 international. Average age 28. 47 applicants, 79% accepted, 24 enrolled. In 2017, 33 master's awarded. *Degree requirements:* For master's, minimum overall GPA of 3.0. *Entrance requirements:* For master's, GMAT or minimum GPA of 3.0, bachelor's degree in any field, work experience. Additional exam requirements/recommendations for international students: Required—TOEFL (minimum score 550 paper-based; 79 iBT). *Application deadline:* For fall admission, 7/25 priority date for domestic students, 4/30 priority date for international students; for spring admission, 12/15 priority date for domestic students, 9/30 priority date for international students; for summer admission, 4/15 priority date for domestic students. Applications are processed on a rolling basis. Application fee: $25. Electronic applications accepted. Application fee is waived when completed online. *Expenses:* $948 per credit hour. *Financial support:* Applicants required to submit FAFSA. *Unit head:* Dale Kramer, MBA/EMBA Director, 440-826-2392, Fax: 440-826-3868, E-mail: dkramer@bw.edu. *Application contact:* Laura Spencer, Graduate Application Specialist, 440-826-2191, Fax: 440-826-3868, E-mail: lspencer@bw.edu. Website: http://www.bw.edu/graduate/business/mba/

Ball State University, Graduate School, Miller College of Business, Interdepartmental Program in Business Administration, Muncie, IN 47306. Offers business administration (MBA); business essentials (Graduate Certificate); community and economic development (Certificate). *Accreditation:* AACSB. *Program availability:* Part-time, 100% online, blended/hybrid learning. *Students:* 33 full-time (15 women), 221 part-time (78 women); includes 20 minority (5 Black or African American, non-Hispanic/Latino; 8 Asian, non-Hispanic/Latino; 4 Hispanic/Latino; 1 Native Hawaiian or other Pacific Islander, non-Hispanic/Latino; 2 Two or more races, non-Hispanic/Latino), 8 international. Average age 31. 203 applicants, 41% accepted, 58 enrolled. In 2017, 70 master's awarded. *Entrance requirements:* For master's, GMAT or GRE, minimum baccalaureate GPA of 2.75 or 3.0 in latter half of baccalaureate, resume or curriculum vitae, four professional letters of recommendation. Additional exam requirements/recommendations for international students: Required—TOEFL (minimum score 550 paper-based; 79 iBT), IELTS (minimum score 6.5). *Application deadline:* For fall admission, 7/1 for domestic students; for spring admission, 12/1 for domestic students; for summer admission, 4/1 for domestic students. Applications are processed on a rolling basis. Application fee: $60. Electronic applications accepted. *Expenses:* Contact institution. *Financial support:* Research assistantships with partial tuition reimbursements, teaching assistantships with partial tuition reimbursements, and unspecified assistantships available. Financial award application deadline: 3/1; financial award applicants required to submit FAFSA. *Unit head:* Jason Webber, Director, 765-285-1931, Fax: 765-285-8818, E-mail: jjwebber@bsu.edu. Website: http://www.bsu.edu/mba

Barry University, Andreas School of Business, Graduate Certificate Programs, Miami Shores, FL 33161-6695. Offers finance (Certificate); health services administration (Certificate); international business (Certificate); management (Certificate); management information systems (Certificate); marketing (Certificate).

Barry University, Andreas School of Business, Program in Business Administration, Miami Shores, FL 33161-6695. Offers MBA, DPM/MBA, MBA/MS, MBA/MSN. *Accreditation:* AACSB.

Barry University, School of Adult and Continuing Education, Division of Nursing and Andreas School of Business, Program in Nursing Administration and Business Administration, Miami Shores, FL 33161-6695. Offers MSN/MBA. *Accreditation:* AACN. *Program availability:* Part-time, evening/weekend. Electronic applications accepted. *Faculty research:* Power/empowerment, health delivery systems, managed care, employee health well-being.

Barry University, School of Adult and Continuing Education, Program in Administrative Studies, Miami Shores, FL 33161-6695. Offers MA. *Program availability:* Part-time, evening/weekend. *Entrance requirements:* For master's, GMAT, GRE or MAT, recommendations. Electronic applications accepted.

Barry University, School of Human Performance and Leisure Sciences and Andreas School of Business, Program in Sport Management and Business Administration, Miami Shores, FL 33161-6695. Offers MS/MBA. *Program availability:* Part-time, evening/weekend. Electronic applications accepted. *Faculty research:* Economic impact of professional sports, sport marketing.

Barry University, School of Podiatric Medicine, Podiatric Medicine and Surgery Program and Andreas School of Business, Podiatric Medicine/Business Administration Option, Miami Shores, FL 33161-6695. Offers DPM/MBA.

Baruch College of the City University of New York, Zicklin School of Business, New York, NY 10010-5585. Offers MBA, MS, PhD, Certificate, JD/MBA. JD/MBA offered jointly with Brooklyn Law School and New York Law School. *Accreditation:* AACSB. *Program availability:* Part-time, evening/weekend. *Degree requirements:* For doctorate, comprehensive exam, thesis/dissertation. *Entrance requirements:* For master's, GMAT or GRE, 2 letters of recommendation, resume, 2 years of work experience; for doctorate, GMAT or GRE. Additional exam requirements/recommendations for international students: Required—TOEFL (minimum iBT score of 102) or PTE. Electronic applications accepted.

Baruch College of the City University of New York, Zicklin School of Business, Zicklin Executive Programs, Executive MBA Program, New York, NY 10010-5585. Offers MBA. *Accreditation:* AACSB. *Entrance requirements:* For master's, 5 years of management-level work experience, personal interview. Additional exam requirements/recommendations for international students: Required—TOEFL. *Expenses:* Contact institution. *Faculty research:* Entrepreneurship, corporate governance, international finance, mergers and acquisitions.

Bayamón Central University, Graduate Programs, Program in Business Administration, Bayamón, PR 00960-1725. Offers accounting (MBA); finance (MBA); general business (MBA); management (MBA); marketing (MBA). *Program availability:* Part-time, evening/weekend. *Degree requirements:* For master's, comprehensive exam (for some programs). *Entrance requirements:* For master's, EXADEP, bachelor's degree in business or related field.

Baylor University, Graduate School, Hankamer School of Business, Program in Business Administration, Waco, TX 76798. Offers MBA, JD/MBA, MBA/MSIS. *Accreditation:* AACSB. *Program availability:* Part-time. *Students:* 163 full-time (51 women), 15 part-time (3 women); includes 59 minority (14 Black or African American, non-Hispanic/Latino; 15 Asian, non-Hispanic/Latino; 19 Hispanic/Latino; 1 Native Hawaiian or other Pacific Islander, non-Hispanic/Latino; 10 Two or more races, non-Hispanic/Latino), 6 international. 240 applicants, 52% accepted, 83 enrolled. In 2017, 198 master's awarded. *Entrance requirements:* For master's, GMAT, minimum AACSB index of 1050. *Application deadline:* Applications are processed on a rolling basis. Application fee: $0. *Expenses:* Contact institution. *Financial support:* Research assistantships, teaching assistantships, career-related internships or fieldwork, Federal Work-Study, and institutionally sponsored loans available. *Unit head:* Dr. Gary Carini, Associate Dean, 254-710-3718, Fax: 254-710-1092, E-mail: gary_carini@baylor.edu. *Application contact:* Laurie Wilson, Director, Graduate Business Programs, 254-710-4163, Fax: 254-710-1066, E-mail: laurie_wilson@baylor.edu.

Belhaven University, School of Business, Jackson, MS 39202-1789. Offers business administration (MBA); health administration (MBA, MHA); human resources (MBA, MSL); leadership (MBA); public administration (MPA); sports administration (MBA, MSA). *Program availability:* Part-time, evening/weekend, 100% online. *Faculty:* 11 full-time (4 women), 93 part-time/adjunct (39 women). *Students:* 20 full-time (12 women), 1,441 part-time (1,061 women); includes 1,168 minority (1,100 Black or African American, non-Hispanic/Latino; 22 American Indian or Alaska Native, non-Hispanic/Latino; 2 Asian, non-Hispanic/Latino; 23 Hispanic/Latino; 1 Native Hawaiian or other Pacific Islander, non-Hispanic/Latino; 20 Two or more races, non-Hispanic/Latino), 21 international. Average age 35. 501 applicants, 74% accepted, 261 enrolled. In 2017, 326 master's awarded. *Degree requirements:* For master's, comprehensive exam (for some programs), thesis or alternative. *Entrance requirements:* For master's, minimum GPA of 2.8 (for MBA and MHA), 2.5 (for MSL, MPA and MSA). *Application deadline:* Applications are processed on a rolling basis. Application fee: $25. Electronic applications accepted. *Expenses:* Contact institution. *Financial support:* Applicants required to submit FAFSA. *Unit head:* Dr. Ralph Mason, Dean, 601-968-8949, Fax: 601-968-8951, E-mail: cmason@belhaven.edu. *Application contact:* Dr. Audrey Kelleher, Vice President of Adult and Graduate Marketing and Development, 407-804-1424, Fax: 407-620-5210, E-mail: akelleher@belhaven.edu. Website: http://www.belhaven.edu/campuses/index.htm

Bellarmine University, W. Fielding Rubel School of Business, Louisville, KY 40205. Offers MBA. *Accreditation:* AACSB. *Program availability:* Part-time, evening/weekend. *Faculty:* 15 full-time (5 women), 1 part-time/adjunct (0 women). *Students:* 54 full-time (22 women), 42 part-time (13 women); includes 17 minority (6 Black or African American, non-Hispanic/Latino; 6 Asian, non-Hispanic/Latino; 3 Hispanic/Latino; 2 Two or more races, non-Hispanic/Latino), 2 international. Average age 30. In 2017, 54 master's awarded. *Entrance requirements:* For master's, GMAT or GRE, letters of recommendation; resume; essay. Additional exam requirements/recommendations for international students: Required—TOEFL (minimum score of 80), IELTS (minimum score 6), or Michigan English Language Assessment Battery (78). *Application deadline:* Applications are processed on a rolling basis. Application fee: $40. Electronic applications accepted. *Expenses:* Contact institution. *Financial support:* Career-related internships or fieldwork, scholarships/grants, and unspecified assistantships available. Support available to part-time students. Financial award applicants required to submit FAFSA. *Faculty research:* Marketing, management, small business and entrepreneurship, finance, economics. *Unit head:* Dr. Sharon Kerrick, Dean, 800-272-8249, Fax: 502-272-7443, E-mail: skerrick@bellarmine.edu. *Application contact:* Dr. Sara Pettingill, Dean of Graduate Admission, 800-274-4723 Ext. 8258, Fax: 502-272-8002, E-mail: spettingill@bellarmine.edu. Website: http://www.bellarmine.edu/business.aspx

Bellevue University, Graduate School, College of Business, Bellevue, NE 68005-3098. Offers acquisition and contract management (MS); business administration (MBA); finance (MS); human capital management (PhD); management (MSM).

Belmont University, Jack C. Massey Graduate School of Business, Nashville, TN 37212. Offers accounting (M Acc); business (AMBA, PMBA); healthcare (MBA). *Accreditation:* AACSB. *Program availability:* Part-time, evening/weekend. *Faculty:* 29 full-time (9 women), 7 part-time/adjunct (3 women). *Students:* 163 full-time (72 women), 42 part-time (19 women); includes 36 minority (13 Black or African American, non-Hispanic/Latino; 9 Asian, non-Hispanic/Latino; 5 Hispanic/Latino; 9 Two or more races, non-Hispanic/Latino), 10 international. Average age 30. 135 applicants, 96% accepted, 102 enrolled. In 2017, 110 master's awarded. *Entrance requirements:* For master's, GMAT, 2 years of work experience (MBA). Additional exam requirements/recommendations for international students: Required—TOEFL (minimum score 550 paper-based). *Application deadline:* For fall admission, 7/1 for domestic and international students; for spring admission, 11/1 for domestic and international students. Applications are processed on a rolling basis. Application fee: $50. Electronic applications accepted. *Expenses:* Contact institution. *Financial support:* In 2017–18, 86 students received support. Scholarships/grants, tuition waivers (partial), and unspecified assistantships available. Financial award application deadline: 7/1; financial award applicants required to submit FAFSA. *Faculty research:* Music business, strategy, ethics, finance, accounting systems. *Unit head:* Dr. Patrick Raines, Dean, 615-460-6480, Fax: 615-460-6455, E-mail: pat.raines@belmont.edu. *Application contact:* 615-460-6480, E-mail: masseyadmissions@belmont.edu.

Benedictine College, Master of Business Administration Program, Atchison, KS 66002. Offers MBA. *Program availability:* Part-time, evening/weekend. *Faculty:* 6 part-time/adjunct (0 women). *Students:* 44 full-time (9 women), 4 part-time (2 women); includes 8 minority (4 Black or African American, non-Hispanic/Latino; 1 Asian, non-Hispanic/Latino; 3 Hispanic/Latino), 3 international. Average age 28. In 2017, 12 master's awarded. *Entrance requirements:* For master's, GMAT. Additional exam requirements/recommendations for international students: Recommended—TOEFL, IELTS. *Application deadline:* Applications are processed on a rolling basis. Application fee: $50. Electronic applications accepted. Application fee is waived when completed online. *Expenses:* Contact institution. *Financial support:* Unspecified assistantships available. Financial award application deadline: 3/15; financial award applicants required to submit FAFSA. *Faculty research:* Banking, strategic planning, ethics, leadership and entrepreneurship. *Unit head:* Michael King, Chair, School of Business, 913-360-7160, E-mail: mking@benedictine.edu. Website: http://www.benedictine.edu/mba

Business Administration and Management—General

Benedictine University, Graduate Programs, Program in Business Administration, Lisle, IL 60532. Offers accounting (MBA); entrepreneurship and managing innovation (MBA); financial management (MBA); health administration (MBA); human resource management (MBA); information systems security (MBA); international business (MBA); management consulting (MBA); management information systems (MBA); marketing management (MBA); operations management and logistics (MBA); organizational leadership (MBA). *Program availability:* Part-time, evening/weekend, online learning. *Entrance requirements:* For master's, GMAT. Additional exam requirements/recommendations for international students: Required—TOEFL (minimum score 550 paper-based). Electronic applications accepted. *Faculty research:* Strategic leadership in professional organizations, sociology of professions, organizational change, social identity theory, applications to change management.

Benedictine University, Graduate Programs, Program in Management and Organizational Behavior, Lisle, IL 60532. Offers MS, PhD, MBA/MS, MPH/MS. *Program availability:* Part-time, evening/weekend. *Entrance requirements:* For master's, GMAT. Additional exam requirements/recommendations for international students: Required—TOEFL (minimum score 550 paper-based). Electronic applications accepted. *Faculty research:* Organizational change, transformation, development, learning organizations, career transitions for academics.

Bentley University, McCallum Graduate School of Business, Accelerated Online MBA Program, Waltham, MA 02452-4705. Offers MBA. *Program availability:* Part-time-only, evening/weekend, 100% online. *Application deadline:* Applications are processed on a rolling basis. Electronic applications accepted. *Expenses: Tuition:* Part-time $4445 per course. *Required fees:* $170 per unit. *Unit head:* Dr. Roy A. Wiggins, III, Acting Co-Provost, Dean of Business, 781-891-3166. *Application contact:* Sharon Hill, Assistant Dean/Director of Graduate Admissions, 781-891-2108, Fax: 781-891-2464, E-mail: bentleygraduateadmissions@bentley.edu.

Bentley University, McCallum Graduate School of Business, Bentley MBA Program, Waltham, MA 02452-4705. Offers MBA. *Faculty:* 71 full-time (25 women), 33 part-time/adjunct (15 women). *Students:* 29 full-time (20 women); includes 6 minority (4 Black or African American, non-Hispanic/Latino; 2 Hispanic/Latino), 23 international. Average age 33. 88 applicants, 55% accepted, 29 enrolled. In 2017, 25 master's awarded. *Entrance requirements:* For master's, GMAT or GRE General Test, current resume; two letters of recommendation; official copies of all university-level transcripts; in-person interview. Additional exam requirements/recommendations for international students: Required—TOEFL (minimum score 600 paper-based; 100 iBT), IELTS (minimum score 7), or PTE. *Application deadline:* For fall admission, 12/1 for domestic and international students. Applications are processed on a rolling basis. Application fee: $50. Electronic applications accepted. *Expenses: Tuition:* Part-time $4445 per course. *Required fees:* $170 per unit. *Financial support:* In 2017–18, 29 students received support. Scholarships/grants available. Financial award application deadline: 6/1; financial award applicants required to submit FAFSA. *Faculty research:* Strategy and innovation; personal and group creativity; stakeholder analysis; corporate social responsibility; organizational change and leadership. *Unit head:* Dr. David Schwarzkopf, Director, 781-891-2783, E-mail: dschwarzkopf@bentley.edu. *Application contact:* Sharon Hill, Assistant Dean/Director of Graduate Admissions, 781-891-2108, Fax: 781-891-2464, E-mail: bentleygraduateadmissions@bentley.edu.
Website: http://www.bentley.edu/graduate/mba-programs/bentley-mba

Bentley University, McCallum Graduate School of Business, Full-time MBA Program, Waltham, MA 02452-4705. Offers MBA. *Accreditation:* AACSB. *Faculty:* 71 full-time (25 women), 33 part-time/adjunct (15 women). *Students:* 92 full-time (41 women), 5 part-time (2 women); includes 6 minority (1 Black or African American, non-Hispanic/Latino; 3 Asian, non-Hispanic/Latino; 1 Hispanic/Latino; 1 Two or more races, non-Hispanic/Latino), 61 international. Average age 24. 117 applicants, 91% accepted, 58 enrolled. In 2017, 61 master's awarded. *Entrance requirements:* For master's, GMAT or GRE General Test, interview, current resume, two letters of recommendation, official copies of all university-level transcripts, 2 essays. Additional exam requirements/recommendations for international students: Required—TOEFL (minimum score 100) or IELTS (minimum score 7). *Application deadline:* Applications are processed on a rolling basis. Application fee: $75. Electronic applications accepted. *Expenses:* Contact institution. *Financial support:* In 2017–18, 72 students received support. Scholarships/grants, tuition waivers (partial), and unspecified assistantships available. Financial award application deadline: 6/1; financial award applicants required to submit FAFSA. *Faculty research:* Strategy and innovation, business process management, corporate social responsibility, organizational change and leadership, digital innovation. *Unit head:* Dr. David Schwarzkopf, Associate Professor/MBA Director, 781-891-2783, Fax: 781-891-2464, E-mail: dschwarzkopf@bentley.edu. *Application contact:* Graduate Admissions, 781-891-2108, Fax: 781-891-2464, E-mail: applygrad@bentley.edu.
Website: https://admissions.bentley.edu/graduate/mba

Bentley University, McCallum Graduate School of Business, Graduate Business Certificate Program, Waltham, MA 02452-4705. Offers accounting (GBC); business analytics (GBC); business ethics (GBC); financial planning (GBC); fraud and forensic accounting (GBC); marketing analytics (GBC); taxation (GBC). *Accreditation:* AACSB. *Program availability:* Part-time, evening/weekend. *Faculty:* 71 full-time (25 women), 33 part-time/adjunct (15 women). *Students:* 7 part-time (3 women); includes 2 minority (1 Black or African American, non-Hispanic/Latino; 1 Asian, non-Hispanic/Latino). Average age 42. 9 applicants, 100% accepted, 6 enrolled. In 2017, 58 GBCs awarded. *Entrance requirements:* For degree, GMAT or GRE General Test, current resume; two letters of recommendation; official copies of all university-level transcripts; 2 essays. Additional exam requirements/recommendations for international students: Required—TOEFL (minimum score 100) or IELTS (minimum score 7). *Application deadline:* Applications are processed on a rolling basis. Application fee: $75. Electronic applications accepted. *Expenses:* Contact institution. *Financial support:* Application deadline: 6/1; applicants required to submit FAFSA. *Unit head:* Dr. Roy A. Wiggins, III, Acting Co-Provost, Dean of Business, 781-891-3166. *Application contact:* Graduate Admissions, 781-891-2108, Fax: 781-891-2464, E-mail: applygrad@bentley.edu.
Website: https://www.bentley.edu/current-graduate-students/programs-certificates#certificates

Bentley University, McCallum Graduate School of Business, MS+MBA Program, Waltham, MA 02452-4705. Offers MS/MBA. *Accreditation:* AACSB. *Faculty:* 71 full-time (25 women), 33 part-time/adjunct (15 women). *Students:* 6 full-time (1 woman), 1 part-time (0 women), 5 international. Average age 25. 7 applicants, 71% accepted. *Entrance requirements:* Additional exam requirements/recommendations for international students: Required—TOEFL (minimum score 600 paper-based; 100 iBT), IELTS (minimum score 7), or PTE. *Application deadline:* Applications are processed on a rolling basis. Application fee: $50. Electronic applications accepted. *Expenses:* Contact institution. *Financial support:* In 2017–18, 5 students received support. Scholarships/grants and unspecified assistantships available. Financial award application deadline: 6/1; financial award applicants required to submit FAFSA. *Faculty research:* Strategy and innovation, business process management, corporate social responsibility, IT strategy, organizational change and leadership. *Unit head:* Dr. David Schwarzkopf, Associate Professor, 781-891-2783, Fax: 781-891-2464, E-mail: dschwarzkopf@bentley.edu. *Application contact:* Sharon Hill, Associate Dean/Director of Graduate Admissions, 781-

891-2108, Fax: 781-891-2464, E-mail: bentleygraduateadmissions@bentley.edu.
Website: http://www.bentley.edu/graduate/mba-programs/elmba/ms-mba

Bentley University, McCallum Graduate School of Business, Part-time MBA Program, Waltham, MA 02452-4705. Offers MBA. *Accreditation:* AACSB. *Program availability:* Part-time, evening/weekend. *Faculty:* 71 full-time (25 women), 33 part-time/adjunct (15 women). *Students:* 15 full-time (6 women), 209 part-time (98 women); includes 41 minority (16 Black or African American, non-Hispanic/Latino; 18 Asian, non-Hispanic/Latino; 3 Hispanic/Latino; 4 Two or more races, non-Hispanic/Latino), 9 international. Average age 33. 96 applicants, 92% accepted, 69 enrolled. In 2017, 77 master's awarded. *Entrance requirements:* For master's, GMAT or GRE General Test, current resume; two letters of recommendation; official copies of all university-level transcripts; 2 essays; interview. Additional exam requirements/recommendations for international students: Required—TOEFL (minimum score 100) or IELTS (minimum score 7). *Application deadline:* Applications are processed on a rolling basis. Application fee: $75. Electronic applications accepted. *Expenses: Tuition:* Part-time $4445 per course. *Required fees:* $170 per unit. *Financial support:* In 2017–18, 75 students received support. Scholarships/grants available. Financial award application deadline: 6/1; financial award applicants required to submit FAFSA. *Faculty research:* Strategy and innovation, corporate social responsibility, business process management, organizational change and leadership, digital innovation. *Unit head:* Dr. David Schwarzkopf, Associate Professor/MBA Director, 781-891-2783, Fax: 781-891-2464, E-mail: dschwarzkopf@bentley.edu. *Application contact:* Graduate Admissions, 781-891-2108, Fax: 781-891-2464, E-mail: applygrad@bentley.edu.
Website: https://admissions.bentley.edu/graduate/mba

Bentley University, McCallum Graduate School of Business, PhD Program in Business, Waltham, MA 02452-4705. Offers PhD. *Faculty:* 33 full-time (17 women). *Students:* 22 full-time (11 women), 1 (woman) part-time, 16 international. Average age 32. 88 applicants, 7% accepted, 6 enrolled. In 2017, 1 doctorate awarded. *Degree requirements:* For doctorate, comprehensive exam, thesis/dissertation. *Entrance requirements:* For doctorate, GMAT or GRE General Test, master's degree; official copies of transcripts; research paper; personal statement; 3 letters of recommendation; curriculum vitae; interview. Additional exam requirements/recommendations for international students: Required—TOEFL. *Application deadline:* For fall admission, 1/15 for domestic and international students. Electronic applications accepted. *Expenses: Tuition:* Part-time $4445 per course. *Required fees:* $170 per unit. *Financial support:* In 2017–18, 17 students received support. Scholarships/grants available. Financial award application deadline: 6/1; financial award applicants required to submit FAFSA. *Faculty research:* Management (including: strategy; corporate governance; organization behavior; entrepreneurship; ethics; CSR); business analytics; information systems; marketing. *Unit head:* Patricia A. Caffrey, Administrative Director of PhD Programs, 781-891-2541, Fax: 781-891-3121, E-mail: pacaffrey@bentley.edu. *Application contact:* PhD Program Office, 781-891-2404, E-mail: phd@bentley.edu.
Website: https://www.bentley.edu/offices/phd/phd-business

Berkeley College–Woodland Park Campus, MBA Program, Woodland Park, NJ 07424. Offers management (MBA).

Berry College, Graduate Programs, Campbell School of Business, Mount Berry, GA 30149-0159. Offers MBA. *Accreditation:* AACSB. *Program availability:* Part-time, evening/weekend. *Faculty:* 4 part-time/adjunct (1 woman). *Students:* 1 full-time (0 women), 29 part-time (10 women); includes 3 minority (all Black or African American, non-Hispanic/Latino). Average age 32. In 2017, 10 master's awarded. *Degree requirements:* For master's, thesis. *Entrance requirements:* For master's, GMAT or GRE, minimum GPA of 3.0, essay/goals statement. Additional exam requirements/recommendations for international students: Required—TOEFL (minimum score 550 paper-based). *Application deadline:* For fall admission, 7/20 for domestic students; for spring admission, 12/1 for domestic students. Applications are processed on a rolling basis. Application fee: $25 ($30 for international students). Electronic applications accepted. *Expenses: Tuition:* Full-time $11,430; part-time $635 per credit hour. *Required fees:* $176. Tuition and fees vary according to program. *Financial support:* In 2017–18, 21 students received support, including 10 research assistantships with full tuition reimbursements available (averaging $6,096 per year); scholarships/grants, tuition waivers (partial), and unspecified assistantships also available. Support available to part-time students. Financial award application deadline: 3/1; financial award applicants required to submit FAFSA. *Faculty research:* Sports economics, human resource management, public choice, applied microeconomics, labor. *Total annual research expenditures:* $6,800. *Unit head:* Dr. Joyce Heames, Dean, 706-236-2233, Fax: 706-802-6728, E-mail: jheames@berry.edu. *Application contact:* Brett Kennedy, Assistant Vice President of Enrollment Management, 706-236-2215, Fax: 706-290-2178, E-mail: admissions@berry.edu.
Website: http://www.berry.edu/mba/

Bethel College, Adult and Graduate Programs, Program in Business Administration, Mishawaka, IN 46545-5591. Offers MBA. *Program availability:* Part-time, evening/weekend, 100% online, blended/hybrid learning. *Faculty:* 7 part-time/adjunct (0 women). *Students:* 23 full-time (14 women), 68 part-time (38 women); includes 25 minority (16 Black or African American, non-Hispanic/Latino; 5 Hispanic/Latino; 4 Two or more races, non-Hispanic/Latino), 3 international. Average age 37. 76 applicants, 55% accepted, 38 enrolled. In 2017, 24 master's awarded. *Entrance requirements:* For master's, GMAT. Additional exam requirements/recommendations for international students: Required—TOEFL (minimum score 540 paper-based). *Application deadline:* For fall admission, 5/1 for international students; for spring admission, 10/1 for international students. Applications are processed on a rolling basis. Application fee: $0. Electronic applications accepted. Tuition and fees vary according to program. *Financial support:* Career-related internships or fieldwork available. Financial award applicants required to submit FAFSA. *Faculty research:* Marketing. *Unit head:* Dale Gadd, Coordinator of Instruction, 574-807-7322, E-mail: dale.gadd@bethelcollege.edu.
Website: http://www.bethelcollege.edu/academics/graduate/mba/

Bethel University, Graduate Programs, McKenzie, TN 38201. Offers administration and supervision (MA Ed); business administration (MBA); conflict resolution (MA); physician assistant studies (MS). *Program availability:* Part-time, evening/weekend. *Degree requirements:* For master's, thesis (for some programs). *Entrance requirements:* For master's, GRE General Test or MAT, minimum undergraduate GPA of 2.5.

Bethel University, Graduate School, St. Paul, MN 55112-6999. Offers business administration (MBA); classroom management (Certificate); counseling (MA); K-12 education (MA); leadership (Ed D); leadership foundations (Certificate); nurse educator (MS, Certificate); nurse-midwifery (MS); physician assistant (MS); special education (MA); strategic leadership (MA); teaching (MA); teaching and learning (Certificate). *Program availability:* Part-time, evening/weekend, 100% online, blended/hybrid learning. *Faculty:* 22 full-time (16 women), 70 part-time/adjunct (44 women). *Students:* 611 full-time (431 women), 393 part-time (249 women); includes 176 minority (82 Black or African American, non-Hispanic/Latino; 4 American Indian or Alaska Native, non-Hispanic/Latino; 31 Asian, non-Hispanic/Latino; 39 Hispanic/Latino; 2 Native Hawaiian or other Pacific Islander, non-Hispanic/Latino; 18 Two or more races, non-Hispanic/Latino), 9 international. Average age 36. 668 applicants, 42% accepted, 223 enrolled. In 2017, 287 master's, 30 doctorates, 172 other advanced degrees awarded. *Degree* *requirements:* For master's, comprehensive exam (for some programs), thesis (for some programs); for doctorate, comprehensive exam, thesis/dissertation. *Entrance requirements:* Additional exam requirements/recommendations for international students: Required—TOEFL (minimum score 550 paper-based, 80 iBT) or IELTS. *Application deadline:* Applications are processed on a rolling basis. Application fee: $0. Electronic applications accepted. *Expenses:* Contact institution. *Financial support:* Teaching assistantships, career-related internships or fieldwork, and scholarships/grants available. Support available to part-time students. Financial award applicants required to submit FAFSA. *Unit head:* Dr. Randy Bergen, Associate Provost, 651-635-8000, Fax: 651-635-8004, E-mail: r-bergen@bethel.edu. *Application contact:* Director of Admissions, 651-635-8000, Fax: 651-635-8004, E-mail: gs@bethel.edu. Website: https://www.bethel.edu/graduate/

Binghamton University, State University of New York, Graduate School, School of Management, Program in Business Administration, Binghamton, NY 13902-6000. Offers business administration (MBA); corporate executive (MBA); executive business administration (MBA); health care professional executive (MBA); professional business administration (MBA). Executive and Professional MBA programs offered in Manhattan. *Accreditation:* AACSB. *Program availability:* Part-time. *Students:* 120 full-time (37 women), 6 part-time (5 women); includes 23 minority (2 Black or African American, non-Hispanic/Latino; 11 Asian, non-Hispanic/Latino; 6 Hispanic/Latino; 4 Two or more races, non-Hispanic/Latino), 25 international. Average age 24. 209 applicants, 72% accepted, 99 enrolled. In 2017, 101 master's awarded. *Entrance requirements:* For master's, GMAT. Additional exam requirements/recommendations for international students: Required—TOEFL (minimum score 96 iBT). *Application deadline:* Applications are processed on a rolling basis. Application fee: $75. Electronic applications accepted. *Expenses:* Contact institution. *Financial support:* In 2017–18, 12 students received support, including 10 teaching assistantships with full tuition reimbursements available (averaging $17,000 per year); career-related internships or fieldwork, Federal Work-Study, institutionally sponsored loans, scholarships/grants, health care benefits, tuition waivers (full and partial), and unspecified assistantships also available. Financial award applicants required to submit FAFSA. *Unit head:* Dr. Upinder Dhillon, Dean, 607-777-2314, E-mail: dhillon@binghamton.edu. *Application contact:* Ben Balkaya, Assistant Dean and Director, 607-777-2151, Fax: 607-777-2501, E-mail: balkaya@binghamton.edu.

Binghamton University, State University of New York, Graduate School, School of Management, Program in Management, Binghamton, NY 13902-6000. Offers finance (PhD); management information systems (PhD); marketing (PhD); organizational studies (PhD); supply chain management (PhD). *Students:* 8 full-time (5 women), 12 part-time (5 women), 19 international. Average age 30. 57 applicants, 21% accepted, 7 enrolled. In 2017, 3 doctorates awarded. *Degree requirements:* For doctorate, thesis/dissertation. *Entrance requirements:* For doctorate, GMAT. *Application deadline:* For fall admission, 2/1 for domestic students. *Financial support:* In 2017–18, 18 students received support. *Unit head:* Dr. Upinder Dhillon, Dean, 607-777-2314, E-mail: dhillon@binghamton.edu. *Application contact:* Marianne Ferry, Administrative Assistant, Executive Education and PhD Programs, 607-777-2342, E-mail: mferry@binghamton.edu.

Biola University, Crowell School of Business, La Mirada, CA 90639-0001. Offers MBA, MP Acc. *Accreditation:* ACBSP. *Program availability:* Part-time, evening/weekend. *Faculty:* 11. *Students:* 36 full-time (19 women), 40 part-time (18 women); includes 27 minority (5 Black or African American, non-Hispanic/Latino; 13 Asian, non-Hispanic/Latino; 9 Hispanic/Latino), 1 international. In 2017, 10 master's awarded. *Entrance requirements:* For master's, GMAT. Additional exam requirements/recommendations for international students: Required—TOEFL (minimum score 600 paper-based; 100 iBT). *Application deadline:* For fall admission, 4/15 priority date for domestic and international students; for spring admission, 12/1 for domestic students. Applications are processed on a rolling basis. Application fee: $65. Electronic applications accepted. *Financial support:* Scholarships/grants available. Support available to part-time students. Financial award applicants required to submit FAFSA. *Faculty research:* Integration of theology with business and accounting principles. *Unit head:* Dr. Gary Lindblad, Dean, 562-777-4015, Fax: 562-906-4545, E-mail: mba@biola.edu. *Application contact:* Christina Gramenz, MBA Coordinator, 562-777-4015, E-mail: mba@biola.edu. Website: http://crowell.biola.edu

Black Hills State University, Graduate Studies, Program in Business Administration, Spearfish, SD 57799. Offers MBA. *Accreditation:* AACSB. *Program availability:* Evening/weekend. *Entrance requirements:* Additional exam requirements/recommendations for international students: Required—TOEFL (minimum score 500 paper-based; 60 iBT).

Bloomsburg University of Pennsylvania, School of Graduate Studies, Zeigler College of Business, Program in Business Administration, Bloomsburg, PA 17815-1301. Offers business administration (MBA); management (Certificate). *Accreditation:* AACSB. *Program availability:* Part-time, evening/weekend. *Degree requirements:* For master's, minimum QPA of 3.0, practicum. *Entrance requirements:* For master's, GMAT, resume, 3 letters of recommendation, personal statement. Additional exam requirements/recommendations for international students: Required—TOEFL (minimum score 550 paper-based; 79 iBT), IELTS (minimum score 7.5). Electronic applications accepted. *Expenses:* Tuition, state resident: full-time $10,000; part-time $500 per credit hour. Tuition, nonresident: full-time $15,000; part-time $750 per credit hour. *Required fees:* $2484; $110.75 per credit hour. $75 per term. Tuition and fees vary according to program.

Bluffton University, Programs in Business, Bluffton, OH 45817. Offers accounting and financial management (MBA); health care management (MBA); leadership (MAOM, MBA); production and operations management (MBA); sustainability management (MBA). *Program availability:* Evening/weekend, blended/hybrid learning, videoconference. *Faculty:* 5 full-time (2 women), 8 part-time/adjunct (2 women). *Students:* 48 full-time (31 women); includes 11 minority (5 Black or African American, non-Hispanic/Latino; 1 Asian, non-Hispanic/Latino; 3 Hispanic/Latino; 2 Two or more races, non-Hispanic/Latino), 1 international. Average age 33. 44 applicants, 70% accepted, 26 enrolled. In 2017, 41 master's awarded. *Degree requirements:* For master's, integrated research project (for some programs). *Entrance requirements:* For master's, current resume, official transcript, bachelor's degree, minimum GPA of 3.0, personal essay. Additional exam requirements/recommendations for international students: Recommended—TOEFL (minimum score 550 paper-based). *Application deadline:* For fall admission, 7/31 priority date for domestic and international students. Applications are processed on a rolling basis. Application fee: $0. Electronic applications accepted. *Expenses:* $550 per credit hour, $150 per semester technology fee, $25 per semester payment plan fee. *Financial support:* Unspecified assistantships and faculty/staff grants available. Financial award applicants required to submit FAFSA. *Unit head:* Dr. Melissa Green, Director of Graduate Programs in Business, 419-358-3447, E-mail: greenm@bluffton.edu. *Application contact:* Carrie Mast, Administrative Assistant, Graduate Programs in Business, 419-358-3065, E-mail: mastc@bluffton.edu. Website: http://www.bluffton.edu/grad/

Bob Jones University, Graduate Programs, Greenville, SC 29614. Offers accountancy (MS); Bible (MA); Bible translation (MA); Biblical studies (Certificate); broadcast management (MS); business administration (MBA); church history (MA, PhD); church ministries (MA); church music (MM); cinema and video production (MA); counseling (MS); curriculum and instruction (Ed D); divinity (M Div); dramatic production (MA); educational leadership (MS, Ed D, Ed S); elementary education (M Ed, MAT); English (M Ed, MA, MAT); fine arts (MA); graphic design (MA); history (M Ed, MA); illustration (MA); interpretative speech (MA); mathematics (M Ed, MAT); medical missions (Certificate); ministry (MM, D Min); multi-categorical special education (M Ed, MAT); music (M Ed); New Testament interpretation (PhD); Old Testament interpretation (PhD); orchestral instrument performance (MM); organ performance (MM); pastoral studies (MA); personnel services (MS, Ed S); piano pedagogy (MM); piano performance (MM); platform arts (MA); radio and television broadcasting (MS); rhetoric and public address (MA); secondary education (M Ed); studio art (MA); teaching Bible (MA); theology (MA, PhD); voice performance (MM); youth ministries (MA); M Div/MM.

Boise State University, College of Business and Economics, Program in Business Administration, Boise, ID 83725-0399. Offers MBA. *Accreditation:* AACSB. *Program availability:* Part-time, 100% online. *Faculty:* 6. *Students:* 128 full-time (44 women), 159 part-time (46 women); includes 28 minority (3 Black or African American, non-Hispanic/Latino; 1 American Indian or Alaska Native, non-Hispanic/Latino; 6 Asian, non-Hispanic/Latino; 13 Hispanic/Latino; 5 Two or more races, non-Hispanic/Latino), 11 international. Average age 33. 207 applicants, 62% accepted, 104 enrolled. In 2017, 98 master's awarded. *Entrance requirements:* For master's, GMAT, minimum GPA of 3.0. Additional exam requirements/recommendations for international students: Required—TOEFL (minimum score 587 paper-based; 95 iBT), IELTS (minimum score 6.5). *Application deadline:* For fall admission, 4/15 for domestic and international students. Applications are processed on a rolling basis. Application fee: $65 ($95 for international students). Electronic applications accepted. *Expenses:* Tuition, state resident: full-time $6471; part-time $390 per credit. Tuition, nonresident: full-time $21,787; part-time $685 per credit. *Required fees:* $2283; $100 per term. Part-time tuition and fees vary according to course load and program. *Financial support:* Scholarships/grants and unspecified assistantships available. Financial award application deadline: 2/15; financial award applicants required to submit FAFSA. *Unit head:* Dr. Kirk Smith, Associate Dean, Graduate Studies, 208-426-3180. *Application contact:* Trisha Stevens-Lamb, Director, Career Start MBA, 208-426-1120, E-mail: trishastevenslamb@boisestate.edu. Website: https://cobe.boisestate.edu/graduate-programs-overview/

Boston College, Carroll School of Management, Business Administration Program, Chestnut Hill, MA 02467-3800. Offers MBA, JD/MBA, MBA/MA, MBA/MS, MBA/MSA, MBA/MSF, MBA/MSW, MBA/PhD. *Accreditation:* AACSB. *Program availability:* Part-time, evening/weekend. *Entrance requirements:* For master's, GMAT, GRE, 2 letters of recommendation, resume, transcript. Additional exam requirements/recommendations for international students: Required—TOEFL (minimum score 600 paper-based, 100 iBT), IELTS (minimum score 7.5), or PTE (minimum score 68). Electronic applications accepted. *Faculty research:* Investments, corporate finance, management of financial services, strategic management.

Boston University, Metropolitan College, Department of Administrative Sciences, Boston, MA 02215. Offers applied business analytics (MS); economic development and tourism management (MSAS); enterprise risk management (MS); financial management (MS); global marketing management (MS); innovation and technology (MSAS); insurance management (MS); project management (MS); supply chain management (MS). *Accreditation:* AACSB. *Program availability:* Part-time, evening/weekend, 100% online, blended/hybrid learning. *Faculty:* 21 full-time (5 women), 34 part-time/adjunct (5 women). *Students:* 297 full-time (156 women), 597 part-time (298 women); includes 183 minority (58 Black or African American, non-Hispanic/Latino; 2 American Indian or Alaska Native, non-Hispanic/Latino; 56 Asian, non-Hispanic/Latino; 51 Hispanic/Latino; 2 Native Hawaiian or other Pacific Islander, non-Hispanic/Latino; 14 Two or more races, non-Hispanic/Latino), 391 international. Average age 30. 963 applicants, 64% accepted, 209 enrolled. In 2017, 372 master's awarded. *Degree requirements:* For master's, thesis optional. *Entrance requirements:* For master's, 1 year of work experience, minimum GPA of 3.0. Additional exam requirements/recommendations for international students: Required—TOEFL (minimum score 84 iBT). *Application deadline:* Applications are processed on a rolling basis. Application fee: $85. Electronic applications accepted. *Expenses:* Contact institution. *Financial support:* In 2017–18, 15 students received support, including 18 research assistantships (averaging $8,400 per year), 12 teaching assistantships (averaging $2,700 per year); career-related internships or fieldwork, Federal Work-Study, and unspecified assistantships also available. Financial award applicants required to submit FAFSA. *Faculty research:* International business, innovative process. *Unit head:* Dr. John Sullivan, Chair, 617-353-3016, E-mail: adminsc@bu.edu. *Application contact:* Fiona Niven, Administrative Sciences Department, 617-353-3016, E-mail: adminsc@bu.edu. Website: http://www.bu.edu/met/academic-community/departments/administrative-sciences/

Boston University, Questrom School of Business, Boston, MA 02215. Offers business (EMBA); digital innovation (MS); management (PhD); management studies (MSMS); mathematical finance (MS, PhD); JD/MBA; MBA/MA; MBA/MPH; MBA/MS; MD/MBA. *Accreditation:* AACSB. *Program availability:* Part-time, evening/weekend. *Faculty:* 85 full-time (23 women), 28 part-time/adjunct (10 women). *Students:* 690 full-time (320 women), 650 part-time (278 women); includes 241 minority (41 Black or African American, non-Hispanic/Latino; 1 American Indian or Alaska Native, non-Hispanic/Latino; 119 Asian, non-Hispanic/Latino; 58 Hispanic/Latino; 22 Two or more races, non-Hispanic/Latino), 427 international. Average age 27. 1,069 applicants, 40% accepted, 164 enrolled. In 2017, 496 master's, 15 doctorates awarded. *Degree requirements:* For doctorate, comprehensive exam, thesis/dissertation. *Entrance requirements:* For master's, GMAT or GRE (for MBA and MS in mathematical finance programs), essay, resume, 2 letters of recommendation, official transcripts; for doctorate, GMAT or GRE, personal statement, resume, 3 letters of recommendation, official transcripts. Additional exam requirements/recommendations for international students: Required—TOEFL (minimum score 600 paper-based, 90 iBT), IELTS (6.5), or PTE. *Application deadline:* For fall admission, 3/18 for domestic and international students; for spring admission, 11/7 for domestic and international students. Application fee: $125. Electronic applications accepted. *Expenses:* Contact institution. *Financial support:* Career-related internships or fieldwork, Federal Work-Study, institutionally sponsored loans, scholarships/grants, and tuition waivers (partial) available. Support available to part-time students. Financial award applicants required to submit FAFSA. *Faculty research:* Digital innovation, sustainable energy, corporate social responsibility, finance, marketing. *Unit head:* Kenneth W. Freeman, Professor/Dean, 617-353-9720, Fax: 617-353-5581, E-mail: kfreeman@bu.edu. *Application contact:* Meredith C. Siegel, Assistant Dean, Graduate Admissions Office, 617-353-2670, Fax: 617-353-7368, E-mail: mba@bu.edu. Website: http://www.bu.edu/questrom/

Bowie State University, Graduate Programs, Program in Business Administration, Bowie, MD 20715-9465. Offers MBA. *Accreditation:* ACBSP. *Program availability:* Part-time, evening/weekend. *Faculty:* 4 full-time (0 women), 3 part-time/adjunct (1 woman). *Students:* 18 full-time (10 women), 8 part-time (3 women); includes 23 minority (20 Black or African American, non-Hispanic/Latino; 1 Hispanic/Latino; 2 Two or more races, non-Hispanic/Latino), 1 international. Average age 32. 35 applicants, 86% accepted, 20

Business Administration and Management—General

enrolled. In 2017, 19 master's awarded. *Degree requirements:* For master's, comprehensive exam. *Entrance requirements:* For master's, GMAT, minimum undergraduate GPA of 2.5. *Application deadline:* For fall admission, 4/1 priority date for domestic and international students; for spring admission, 11/1 priority date for domestic and international students. Applications are processed on a rolling basis. Application fee: $40. Electronic applications accepted. *Unit head:* Dr. Falih Alsaaty, Program Coordinator, 301-860-3644, E-mail: falsaaty@bowiestate.edu. *Application contact:* Angela Issac, Information Contact, 301-860-4000.

Bowling Green State University, Graduate College, College of Business, Master of Business Administration Program, Bowling Green, OH 43403. Offers MBA. *Accreditation:* AACSB. *Program availability:* Part-time, evening/weekend. *Degree requirements:* For master's, thesis or alternative, research project. *Entrance requirements:* For master's, GMAT. Additional exam requirements/recommendations for international students: Required—TOEFL. Electronic applications accepted. *Faculty research:* Management of change processes, supply chain management, impacts of money on society, corporate financing strategies, macro-marketing/management of sales staff and services.

Bradley University, The Graduate School, Foster College of Business, Business Administration Program, Peoria, IL 61625-0002. Offers MBA. *Accreditation:* AACSB. *Program availability:* Part-time, evening/weekend. *Degree requirements:* For master's, comprehensive exam. *Entrance requirements:* For master's, GMAT or GRE, minimum undergraduate GPA of 2.75 in major, 2 letters of recommendation. Additional exam requirements/recommendations for international students: Required—TOEFL (minimum score 550 paper-based; 79 iBT), IELTS (minimum score 6.5). Electronic applications accepted.

Bradley University, The Graduate School, Foster College of Business, Theresa S. Falcon Executive MBA Program, Peoria, IL 61625-0002. Offers MBA. *Accreditation:* AACSB. *Program availability:* Evening/weekend. *Entrance requirements:* For master's, company sponsorship, 7 years of managerial experience, letters of recommendation. Additional exam requirements/recommendations for international students: Required—TOEFL (minimum score 550 paper-based; 79 iBT), IELTS (minimum score 6.5). Electronic applications accepted. *Expenses:* Contact institution.

Brandeis University, The Heller School for Social Policy and Management, Program in Nonprofit Management, Waltham, MA 02454-9110. Offers child, youth, and family management (MBA); health care management (MBA); social impact management (MBA); social policy and management (MBA); sustainable development (MBA); MBA/MA; MBA/MD. MBA/MD program offered in conjunction with Tufts University School of Medicine. *Accreditation:* AACSB. *Program availability:* Part-time. *Degree requirements:* For master's, team consulting project. *Entrance requirements:* For master's, GMAT (preferred) or GRE, 2 letters of recommendation, problem statement analysis, 3-5 years of professional experience. Additional exam requirements/recommendations for international students: Required—TOEFL (minimum score 600 paper-based; 100 iBT). Electronic applications accepted. *Expenses:* Contact institution. *Faculty research:* Health care; children and families; elder and disabled services; social impact management; organizations in the non-profit, for-profit, or public sector.

Brandman University, School of Business and Professional Studies, Irvine, CA 92618. Offers accounting (MBA); business administration (MBA); business intelligence and data analytics (MBA); e-business strategic management (MBA); entrepreneurship (MBA); finance (MBA); health administration (MBA); human resources (MBA, MS); international business (MBA); marketing (MBA); organizational leadership (MA, MBA, MPA); public administration (MPA). *Expenses:* Tuition: Part-time $640 per credit hour. Tuition and fees vary according to degree level and program. *Unit head:* Dr. Glenn Worthington, Dean, 253-861-1024, E-mail: gworthin@brandman.edu. *Application contact:* Dr. Glenn Worthington, Dean, 253-861-1024, E-mail: gworthin@brandman.edu. Website: https://www.brandman.edu/academic-programs/business-and-professional-studies

Brenau University, Sydney O. Smith Graduate School, College of Business and Mass Communication, Gainesville, GA 30501. Offers accounting (MBA); business administration (MBA); healthcare management (MBA); organizational leadership (MS); project management (MBA). *Accreditation:* ACBSP. *Program availability:* Part-time, evening/weekend, online learning. *Degree requirements:* For master's, comprehensive exam (for some programs). *Entrance requirements:* For master's, resume, minimum undergraduate GPA of 2.5. Additional exam requirements/recommendations for international students: Required—TOEFL (minimum score 500 paper-based; 61 iBT); Recommended—IELTS (minimum score 5). Electronic applications accepted. *Expenses:* Contact institution.

Brescia University, Program in Business Administration, Owensboro, KY 42301-3023. Offers MBA. *Program availability:* Part-time, evening/weekend. *Entrance requirements:* For master's, minimum cumulative GPA of 2.5. Additional exam requirements/recommendations for international students: Required—TOEFL (minimum score 100 iBT). Electronic applications accepted. Application fee is waived when completed online.

Brescia University, Program in Management, Owensboro, KY 42301-3023. Offers MSM. *Program availability:* Part-time, evening/weekend. *Entrance requirements:* For master's, minimum GPA of 2.5. Additional exam requirements/recommendations for international students: Required—TOEFL (minimum score 100 iBT).

Bridgewater State University, College of Graduate Studies, Ricciardi College of Business, Department of Management, Bridgewater, MA 02325. Offers MSM. *Entrance requirements:* For master's, GMAT.

Briercrest Seminary, Graduate Programs, Program in Leadership and Management, Caronport, SK S0H 0S0, Canada. Offers organizational leadership (MA). *Program availability:* Part-time. *Degree requirements:* For master's, comprehensive exam, thesis optional. *Entrance requirements:* Additional exam requirements/recommendations for international students: Required—TOEFL (minimum score 550 paper-based).

Brigham Young University, Graduate Studies, BYU Marriott School of Business, Executive Master of Business Administration Program, Provo, UT 84602. Offers MBA. *Accreditation:* AACSB. *Program availability:* Part-time-only, evening/weekend. *Faculty:* 134 full-time (15 women), 65 part-time/adjunct (16 women). *Students:* 140 part-time (23 women); includes 10 minority (2 Black or African American, non-Hispanic/Latino; 1 Asian, non-Hispanic/Latino; 4 Hispanic/Latino; 3 Native Hawaiian or other Pacific Islander, non-Hispanic/Latino), 9 international. Average age 39. 125 applicants, 63% accepted, 69 enrolled. In 2017, 65 master's awarded. *Entrance requirements:* For master's, GMAT (minimum score 560) or GRE, 5 years of management experience, commitment to BYU Honor Code. Additional exam requirements/recommendations for international students: Required—TOEFL (minimum score 590 paper-based; 100 iBT), IELTS (minimum score 7). *Application deadline:* For fall admission, 5/1 for domestic students, 1/15 for international students. Applications are processed on a rolling basis. Application fee: $50. Electronic applications accepted. *Expenses:* Contact institution. *Faculty research:* Finance, marketing, supply chain management, entrepreneurship, strategic human resources. *Unit head:* Dr. Grant McQueen, Director, 801-422-3500, Fax: 801-422-0513, E-mail: emba@byu.edu. *Application contact:* Yvette Anderson, MBA Program Admissions

Director, 801-422-3500, Fax: 801-422-0513, E-mail: mba@byu.edu. Website: http://emba.byu.edu

Brigham Young University, Graduate Studies, BYU Marriott School of Business, MBA Program, Provo, UT 84602. Offers entrepreneurship (MBA); finance (MBA); global supply chain management (MBA); marketing (MBA); strategic human resources (MBA); JD/MBA; MBA/MS. *Accreditation:* AACSB. *Faculty:* 134 full-time (15 women), 65 part-time/adjunct (16 women). *Students:* 303 full-time (65 women); includes 26 minority (3 American Indian or Alaska Native, non-Hispanic/Latino; 8 Asian, non-Hispanic/Latino; 11 Hispanic/Latino; 4 Native Hawaiian or other Pacific Islander, non-Hispanic/Latino), 58 international. Average age 30. 339 applicants, 52% accepted, 136 enrolled. In 2017, 163 master's awarded. *Entrance requirements:* For master's, GMAT or GRE, commitment to BYU Honor Code, undergraduate degree. Additional exam requirements/recommendations for international students: Required—TOEFL (minimum score 590 paper-based; 100 iBT), IELTS (minimum score 7). *Application deadline:* For fall admission, 5/1 for domestic students, 3/1 for international students. Applications are processed on a rolling basis. Application fee: $50. Electronic applications accepted. *Expenses:* Contact institution. *Financial support:* Research assistantships, teaching assistantships, career-related internships or fieldwork, institutionally sponsored loans, and scholarships/grants available. Financial award application deadline: 3/1; financial award applicants required to submit FAFSA. *Faculty research:* Finance, marketing, supply chain management, entrepreneurship, strategic human resources. *Unit head:* Dr. Grant McQueen, Director, 801-422-3500, E-mail: mba@byu.edu. *Application contact:* Yvette Anderson, MBA Program Admissions Director, 801-422-3500, Fax: 801-422-0513, E-mail: mba@byu.edu. Website: http://mba.byu.edu

Broadview University–West Jordan, Graduate Programs, West Jordan, UT 84088. Offers business administration (MBA); health care management (MSM); information technology (MSM); managerial leadership (MSM).

Brock University, Faculty of Graduate Studies, Faculty of Business, Program in Business Administration, St. Catharines, ON L2S 3A1, Canada. Offers MBA. *Degree requirements:* For master's, thesis or alternative. *Entrance requirements:* For master's, honours degree. Additional exam requirements/recommendations for international students: Required—TOEFL (minimum score 575 paper-based; 89 iBT), IELTS (minimum score 7), TWE (minimum score 4.5). Electronic applications accepted.

Brock University, Faculty of Graduate Studies, Faculty of Business, Program in Management, St. Catharines, ON L2S 3A1, Canada. Offers M Sc. *Program availability:* Part-time. *Degree requirements:* For master's, thesis. *Entrance requirements:* For master's, GMAT, honors degree. Additional exam requirements/recommendations for international students: Required—TOEFL (minimum score 600 paper-based; 100 iBT), IELTS (minimum score 7), TWE (minimum score 4.5). Electronic applications accepted.

Brooklyn College of the City University of New York, School of Business, Brooklyn, NY 11210-2889. Offers accounting (MS); business administration (MS), including economic analysis, general business, global business and finance. *Program availability:* Part-time, evening/weekend. *Degree requirements:* For master's, comprehensive exam, thesis or alternative. *Entrance requirements:* For master's, GMAT, 2 letters of recommendation. Additional exam requirements/recommendations for international students: Required—TOEFL (minimum score 550 paper-based; 79 iBT). Electronic applications accepted. *Faculty research:* Econometrics, environmental economics, microeconomics, macroeconomics, taxation.

Bryan College, MBA Program, Dayton, TN 37321. Offers business administration (MBA); healthcare administration (MBA); human resources (MBA); marketing (MBA); ministry (MBA); sports management (MBA). *Program availability:* Online only, 100% online. *Entrance requirements:* For master's, resume, 2 letters of recommendation. Additional exam requirements/recommendations for international students: Required—TOEFL. *Application deadline:* For fall admission, 7/1 for domestic and international students; for winter admission, 11/15 for domestic and international students; for spring admission, 12/1 for domestic and international students; for summer admission, 5/1 for domestic and international students. Applications are processed on a rolling basis. Application fee: $50. Electronic applications accepted. *Expenses:* Contact institution. *Financial support:* Scholarships/grants available. Financial award applicants required to submit FAFSA. *Unit head:* Dr. Adina Scruggs, Dean of Adult and Graduate Studies, 423-634-2057, E-mail: adina.scruggs@bryan.edu. *Application contact:* Mandi K Sullivan, Director of Academic Programs, 423-634-9880, E-mail: mandi.sullivan@bryan.edu. Website: http://www.bryan.edu/academics/adult-education/graduate/online-mba/

Bryant University, Graduate School of Business, Smithfield, RI 02917. Offers accounting (MPAC); business administration (MBA), including business analytics, general management, global finance, global supply chain management, international business; taxation (MST). *Program availability:* Part-time, 100% online. *Faculty:* 30 full-time (5 women), 7 part-time/adjunct (2 women). *Students:* 84 full-time (31 women), 91 part-time (35 women); includes 24 minority (4 Black or African American, non-Hispanic/Latino; 1 American Indian or Alaska Native, non-Hispanic/Latino; 6 Asian, non-Hispanic/Latino; 8 Hispanic/Latino; 5 Two or more races, non-Hispanic/Latino), 6 international. Average age 26. 215 applicants, 66% accepted, 96 enrolled. In 2017, 118 master's awarded. *Degree requirements:* For master's, comprehensive exam (for some programs). *Entrance requirements:* For master's, GMAT, resume, recommendation, college transcripts. Additional exam requirements/recommendations for international students: Required—TOEFL (minimum score 580 paper-based; 95 iBT). *Application deadline:* For fall admission, 7/15 for domestic and international students; for spring admission, 11/15 for domestic and international students; for summer admission, 4/15 for domestic and international students. Applications are processed on a rolling basis. Application fee: $80. Electronic applications accepted. *Expenses:* $45,102 total, $1,118 per credit hour, $1,500 study abroad fee (for full-time MBA); $40,248 total, $1,118 per credit hour (for part-time MBA); $30,280 total, $1,176 per credit hour (for MP Ac and MST); $13,146, $1,118 per credit hour (for CGS). *Financial support:* In 2017–18, 95 fellowships with full and partial tuition reimbursements (averaging $9,825 per year), 9 research assistantships with full and partial tuition reimbursements (averaging $7,100 per year) were awarded; scholarships/grants and unspecified assistantships also available. Support available to part-time students. Financial award application deadline: 2/15; financial award applicants required to submit FAFSA. *Faculty research:* International business, public sector auditing, taxation of partnerships, information systems security, financial markets microstructure. *Unit head:* Bjorn Carlsson, Graduate Program Director, 401-232-6707, E-mail: bcarlsson@bryant.edu. *Application contact:* Terri Rogers, Admissions Assistant, 401-232-6230, Fax: 401-232-6494, E-mail: graduateprograms@bryant.edu. Website: http://gradschool.bryant.edu/business/

Bryan University, Program in Business Administration, Springfield, MO 65804. Offers MBA. *Program availability:* Online learning.

Butler University, Lacy School of Business, Indianapolis, IN 46208-3485. Offers entrepreneurship and innovation (MBA); finance (MBA); international business (MBA); leadership (MBA); marketing (MBA); professional accounting (MP Acc). *Accreditation:* AACSB. *Program availability:* Part-time. *Faculty:* 14 full-time (4 women), 9 part-time/adjunct (2 women). *Students:* 35 full-time (16 women), 111 part-time (38 women); includes 15 minority (2 Black or African American, non-Hispanic/Latino; 5 Asian, non-

Hispanic/Latino; 8 Hispanic/Latino), 6 international. Average age 30. 149 applicants, 64% accepted, 43 enrolled. In 2017, 90 master's awarded. *Degree requirements:* For master's, comprehensive exam, thesis optional. *Entrance requirements:* For master's, GMAT, minimum AACSB index of 950, personal statement, two letters of recommendation, official transcripts, current resume. Additional exam requirements/ recommendations for international students: Required—TOEFL (minimum score 550 paper-based; 79 iBT), IELTS (minimum score 6), Michigan English Language Assessment Battery (minimum score of 80). *Application deadline:* For fall admission, 8/1 for domestic and international students; for spring admission, 12/1 for domestic and international students; for summer admission, 4/1 for domestic and international students. Applications are processed on a rolling basis. Application fee: $0. Electronic applications accepted. *Expenses:* $820 per credit. *Financial support:* In 2017–18, 22 students received support. Scholarships/grants, tuition waivers (full and partial), and unspecified assistantships available. Financial award application deadline: 7/15; financial award applicants required to submit FAFSA. *Faculty research:* Higher education and pedagogy; ecotourism; healthcare issues and marketing public policy; domestic public policy, international finance and banking, international and management entrepreneurship, organizational management. *Unit head:* Dr. Stephen Standifird, Dean, 317-940-6307. *Application contact:* Diane Dubord, Graduate Student Service Specialist, 317-940-8107, Fax: 317-940-8250, E-mail: ddubord@butler.edu.
Website: https://www.butler.edu/lacyschool

Cairn University, School of Business, Langhorne, PA 19047-2990. Offers accounting (MBA); business administration (MBA); international entrepreneurship (MBA); nonprofit leadership (MBA); organizational leadership (MSOL, Postbaccalaureate Certificate). *Program availability:* Part-time, evening/weekend, 100% online, blended/hybrid learning. *Entrance requirements:* Additional exam requirements/recommendations for international students: Required—TOEFL (minimum score 550 paper-based). Electronic applications accepted. Application fee is waived when completed online. *Expenses:* Contact institution.

Caldwell University, School of Business and CIS, Caldwell, NJ 07006-6195. Offers accounting (MS); business administration (MBA). *Accreditation:* ACBSP. *Program availability:* Part-time. *Faculty:* 8 full-time (4 women), 12 part-time/adjunct (2 women). *Students:* 23 full-time (14 women), 54 part-time (37 women); includes 25 minority (11 Black or African American, non-Hispanic/Latino; 2 Asian, non-Hispanic/Latino; 11 Hispanic/Latino; 1 Two or more races, non-Hispanic/Latino), 4 international. Average age 31. 39 applicants, 100% accepted, 23 enrolled. In 2017, 20 master's awarded. *Entrance requirements:* For master's, undergraduate accounting, marketing, economics, and finance; minimum three years' relevant experience. Additional exam requirements/ recommendations for international students: Required—TOEFL (minimum score 580 paper-based). *Application deadline:* Applications are processed on a rolling basis. Application fee: $50. Electronic applications accepted. *Expenses:* $975 per credit, $225 comprehensive fee per semester. *Financial support:* 1 general assistantship available. *Unit head:* Bernard O'Rourke, Associate Dean, 973-618-3409, Fax: 973-618-3355, E-mail: borourke@caldwell.edu. *Application contact:* Tom Disch, Senior Admissions Counselor, 973-618-3544, E-mail: graduate@caldwell.edu.

California Baptist University, Program in Business Administration, Riverside, CA 92504-3206. Offers accounting (MBA); construction management (MBA); healthcare management (MBA); management (MBA). *Accreditation:* ACBSP. *Program availability:* Part-time, evening/weekend, 100% online, blended/hybrid learning. *Faculty:* 19 full-time (7 women), 18 part-time/adjunct (6 women). *Students:* 123 full-time (64 women), 101 part-time (55 women); includes 108 minority (22 Black or African American, non-Hispanic/Latino; 15 Asian, non-Hispanic/Latino; 62 Hispanic/Latino; 1 Native Hawaiian or other Pacific Islander, non-Hispanic/Latino; 8 Two or more races, non-Hispanic/Latino), 29 international. Average age 30. 285 applicants, 62% accepted, 142 enrolled. In 2017, 147 master's awarded. *Degree requirements:* For master's, interdisciplinary capstone project. *Entrance requirements:* For master's, GMAT, minimum GPA of 2.5; two recommendations; comprehensive essay; resume; interview. Additional exam requirements/recommendations for international students: Required—TOEFL (minimum score 80 iBT). *Application deadline:* For fall admission, 8/1 priority date for domestic students, 7/1 for international students; for spring admission, 12/1 priority date for domestic students, 11/1 for international students. Applications are processed on a rolling basis. Application fee: $45. Electronic applications accepted. *Expenses:* Contact institution. *Financial support:* In 2017–18, 38 students received support. Federal Work-Study and scholarships/grants available. Financial award applicants required to submit CSS PROFILE or FAFSA. *Faculty research:* Behavioral economics, economic indicators, marketing ethics, international business, microfinance. *Unit head:* Dr. Andrea Scott, Dean, School of Business, 951-343-4701, Fax: 951-343-4361, E-mail: ascott@calbaptist.edu. *Application contact:* Deanna Meyer, Graduate Admissions Counselor, 951-343-4463, E-mail: dmeyer@calbaptist.edu.
Website: http://www.calbaptist.edu/mba/about/

California Coast University, School of Administration and Management, Santa Ana, CA 92701. Offers business marketing (MBA); health care management (MBA); human resource management (MBA); management (MBA, MS). *Program availability:* Online learning. Electronic applications accepted.

California Institute of Advanced Management, The MBA Program, El Monte, CA 91731. Offers executive management and entrepreneurship (MBA).

California Intercontinental University, School of Business, Irvine, CA 92614. Offers banking and finance (MBA); entrepreneurship and business management (DBA); global business leadership (DBA); international management and marketing (MBA); organizational management and human resource management (MBA).

California International Business University, Graduate Programs, San Diego, CA 92101. Offers MBA, MSIM, DBA.

California Lutheran University, Graduate Studies, School of Management, Thousand Oaks, CA 91360-2787. Offers business (IMBA); entrepreneurship (MBA, Certificate); finance (MBA, Certificate); financial planning (MBA, MS, Certificate); human capital management (MBA, Certificate); information technology (MS); information technology management (MBA, Certificate); international business (MBA, Certificate); marketing (MBA, Certificate); public policy and administration (MPPA); quantitative economics (MS). *Program availability:* Part-time, evening/weekend, 100% online, blended/hybrid learning. *Faculty:* 17 full-time (4 women), 40 part-time/adjunct (9 women). *Students:* 423 full-time (168 women), 153 part-time (72 women); includes 124 minority (11 Black or African American, non-Hispanic/Latino; 1 American Indian or Alaska Native, non-Hispanic/Latino; 21 Asian, non-Hispanic/Latino; 75 Hispanic/Latino; 16 Two or more races, non-Hispanic/Latino), 294 international. Average age 31. 467 applicants, 72% accepted, 108 enrolled. In 2017, 306 master's awarded. *Degree requirements:* For master's, comprehensive exam (for some programs). *Entrance requirements:* For master's, GMAT, interview, minimum GPA of 3.0. *Application deadline:* Applications are processed on a rolling basis. Application fee: $50. Electronic applications accepted. *Expenses:* Contact institution. *Unit head:* Dr. Gerhard Apfelthaler, Dean, 805-493-3360. *Application contact:* 805-493-3325, Fax: 805-493-3861, E-mail: clugrad@callutheran.edu.
Website: http://www.callutheran.edu/management/

California Miramar University, Program in Business Administration, San Diego, CA 92108. Offers MBA.

California Polytechnic State University, San Luis Obispo, Orfalea College of Business, Program in Business Administration, San Luis Obispo, CA 93407. Offers MBA. *Students:* 34 full-time (14 women), 12 part-time (6 women); includes 11 minority (2 Asian, non-Hispanic/Latino; 6 Hispanic/Latino; 3 Two or more races, non-Hispanic/ Latino), 2 international. Average age 26. In 2017, 29 master's awarded. *Degree requirements:* For master's, comprehensive exam (for some programs), thesis (for some programs). *Entrance requirements:* For master's, GMAT. Additional exam requirements/ recommendations for international students: Required—TOEFL (minimum score 80 iBT). *Application deadline:* Applications are processed on a rolling basis. Application fee: $55. Electronic applications accepted. *Expenses:* Tuition, state resident: full-time $7176; part-time $4164 per year. *Required fees:* $3690; $3219 per year. $1073 per trimester. *Financial support:* Fellowships, career-related internships or fieldwork, Federal Work-Study, institutionally sponsored loans, scholarships/grants, and unspecified assistantships available. Support available to part-time students. Financial award application deadline: 3/2; financial award applicants required to submit FAFSA. *Faculty research:* Management of high-tech firms, Pacific Rim, capital market structures, economics of environmental policy, marketing of services. *Unit head:* Dr. Scott Dawson, Dean, 805-756-2705, E-mail: scdawson@calpoly.edu. *Application contact:* Dr. Sanjiv Jaggia, Associate Dean, Graduate Programs, 805-756-7519, E-mail: sjaggia@calpoly.edu.
Website: http://www.cob.calpoly.edu/gradbusiness/degree-programs/mba/

California State Polytechnic University, Pomona, Master of Science in Business Administration Program, Pomona, CA 91768-2557. Offers information systems auditing (MS). *Accreditation:* AACSB. *Program availability:* Part-time, evening/weekend. *Students:* 5 part-time (2 women); includes 3 minority (1 Asian, non-Hispanic/Latino; 2 Hispanic/Latino), 1 international. Average age 28. 24 applicants, 38% accepted, 5 enrolled. In 2017, 4 master's awarded. *Entrance requirements:* Additional exam requirements/recommendations for international students: Required—TOEFL (minimum score 550 paper-based). *Application deadline:* Applications are processed on a rolling basis. Application fee: $55. Electronic applications accepted. *Expenses:* Contact institution. *Financial support:* Application deadline: 3/2; applicants required to submit FAFSA. *Unit head:* Dr. Tarique Hossain, Associate Professor/Director of Graduate Programs, 909-869-2362, Fax: 909-869-4559, E-mail: tmhossain@cpp.edu. *Application contact:* Deborah L. Brandon, Executive Director of Admissions and Enrollment Planning, 909-869-3427, Fax: 909-869-5315, E-mail: dlbrandon@cpp.edu.
Website: http://www.cpp.edu/~cba/graduate-business-programs/programs/MSBA.shtml

California State Polytechnic University, Pomona, MBA Program, Pomona, CA 91768-2557. Offers MBA. *Program availability:* Part-time, evening/weekend. *Students:* 45 part-time (18 women); includes 29 minority (2 Black or African American, non-Hispanic/Latino; 9 Asian, non-Hispanic/Latino; 18 Hispanic/Latino), 4 international. Average age 30. 73 applicants, 44% accepted, 21 enrolled. In 2017, 13 master's awarded. *Entrance requirements:* Additional exam requirements/recommendations for international students: Required—TOEFL (minimum score 580 paper-based). *Application deadline:* Applications are processed on a rolling basis. Application fee: $55. Electronic applications accepted. *Expenses:* $180 per unit. *Financial support:* Application deadline: 3/2; applicants required to submit FAFSA. *Unit head:* Dr. Tarique Hossain, Associate Professor/Director of Graduate Programs, 909-869-2362, Fax: 909-869-4559, E-mail: tmhossain@cpp.edu. *Application contact:* Deborah L. Brandon, Executive Director of Admissions and Enrollment Planning, 909-869-3427, Fax: 909-869-5315, E-mail: dlbrandon@cpp.edu.
Website: http://www.cpp.edu/~cba/graduate-business-programs/programs/MBA.shtml

California State University, Bakersfield, Division of Graduate Studies, Program in Administration, Bakersfield, CA 93311. Offers MSA. *Program availability:* Online learning. *Degree requirements:* For master's, capstone experience. *Entrance requirements:* For master's, official transcripts, three professional references, current resume, statement of purpose. *Application deadline:* For fall admission, 5/5 priority date for domestic students; for spring admission, 10/6 priority date for domestic students; for summer admission, 3/2 priority date for domestic students. Application fee: $75. *Expenses:* Contact institution. *Financial support:* Application deadline: 3/2; applicants required to submit FAFSA. *Unit head:* Dr. Chandra Commuri, Academic Coordinator, 661-654-6140, E-mail: ccommuri@csub.edu. *Application contact:* Raushel Salyards, Degree Programs Coordinator, 661-664-2441, Fax: 661-654-2447, E-mail: rsalyards@csub.edu.
Website: http://www.csub.edu/eud/degrees/msa/

California State University, Bakersfield, Division of Graduate Studies, School of Business and Public Administration, Program in Business Administration, Bakersfield, CA 93311. Offers MBA. *Accreditation:* AACSB. *Faculty:* 8 full-time (0 women), 2 part-time/adjunct (0 women). *Students:* 41 full-time (21 women), 23 part-time (14 women); includes 25 minority (5 Black or African American, non-Hispanic/Latino; 6 Asian, non-Hispanic/Latino; 14 Hispanic/Latino), 4 international. Average age 35. 72 applicants, 39% accepted, 25 enrolled. In 2017, 50 master's awarded. *Entrance requirements:* For master's, GMAT or GRE, baccalaureate degree, minimum undergraduate GPA of 2.75. *Application deadline:* Applications are processed on a rolling basis. Application fee: $55. *Expenses:* Tuition, state resident: full-time $7176; part-time $4164 per year. *Financial support:* In 2017–18, fellowships (averaging $1,850 per year) were awarded; Federal Work-Study, scholarships/grants, and tuition waivers (full and partial) also available. Financial award application deadline: 3/2; financial award applicants required to submit FAFSA. *Unit head:* Dr. Michael Way, Director, 661-654-2780, E-mail: mba@csub.edu. *Application contact:* Susan Rogers, Administrative Support Coordinator, 661-654-2780, E-mail: mba@csub.edu.
Website: http://www.csub.edu/mba/index.html

California State University Channel Islands, Extended University and International Programs, Master of Business Administration Program, Thousand Oaks, CA 91360. Offers MBA. *Program availability:* Part-time, evening/weekend. *Entrance requirements:* For master's, GMAT, 2 years of work experience. Additional exam requirements/ recommendations for international students: Required—TOEFL (minimum score 550 paper-based; 80 iBT), IELTS (minimum score 6). Electronic applications accepted. *Expenses:* Contact institution.

California State University, Chico, Office of Graduate Studies, College of Behavioral and Social Sciences, Department of Political Science and Criminal Justice, Program in Public Administration, Chico, CA 95929-0722. Offers health administration (MPA); local government management (MPA). *Accreditation:* NASPAA. *Program availability:* Part-time. *Degree requirements:* For master's, thesis or culminating practicum. *Entrance requirements:* For master's, 2 letters of recommendation. Additional exam requirements/ recommendations for international students: Required—TOEFL (minimum score 550 paper-based; 80 iBT), IELTS (minimum score 6.5), PTE. Electronic applications accepted.

California State University, Chico, Office of Graduate Studies, College of Business, Chico, CA 95929-0722. Offers MBA. *Program availability:* Part-time. *Degree requirements:* For master's, thesis, project, or comprehensive exam. *Entrance requirements:* For master's, GMAT or GRE, two letters of recommendation, statement of

Business Administration and Management—General

purpose, resume. Additional exam requirements/recommendations for international students: Required—TOEFL (minimum score 550 paper-based; 80 iBT), PTE Academic (minimum score 59) or IELTS (6.5). Electronic applications accepted. *Expenses:* Contact institution.

California State University, Dominguez Hills, College of Business Administration and Public Policy, Program in Business Administration, Carson, CA 90747-0001. Offers MBA. *Program availability:* Part-time, evening/weekend, online learning. *Entrance requirements:* For master's, GMAT, minimum GPA of 2.75. Additional exam requirements/recommendations for international students: Required—TOEFL (minimum score 570 paper-based; 88 iBT). *Faculty research:* Management.

California State University, East Bay, Office of Graduate Studies, College of Business and Economics, MBA Program, Hayward, CA 94542-3000. Offers finance (MBA); human resources and organizational behavior (MBA); marketing management (MBA); operations and supply chain management (MBA); strategy and innovation (MBA). *Accreditation:* AACSB. *Program availability:* Part-time, evening/weekend. *Students:* 109 full-time (53 women), 146 part-time (72 women); includes 118 minority (15 Black or African American, non-Hispanic/Latino; 75 Asian, non-Hispanic/Latino; 17 Hispanic/Latino; 3 Native Hawaiian or other Pacific Islander, non-Hispanic/Latino; 8 Two or more races, non-Hispanic/Latino), 91 international. Average age 33. 261 applicants, 53% accepted, 62 enrolled. In 2017, 158 master's awarded. *Degree requirements:* For master's, comprehensive exam or thesis. *Entrance requirements:* For master's, GMAT (minimum 20th percentile verbal and quantitative section), bachelor's degree, minimum GPA of 2.75. Additional exam requirements/recommendations for international students: Required—TOEFL (minimum score 550 paper-based; 79 iBT). *Application deadline:* For fall admission, 6/1 for domestic and international students. Applications are processed on a rolling basis. Application fee: $55. Electronic applications accepted. *Expenses:* Contact institution. *Financial support:* Career-related internships or fieldwork, Federal Work-Study, institutionally sponsored loans, and scholarships/grants available. Support available to part-time students. Financial award application deadline: 3/2; financial award applicants required to submit FAFSA. *Unit head:* Dr. Eric Fricke, Interim Associate Dean, 510-885-3290, E-mail: eric.fricke@csueastbay.edu. *Application contact:* Nancy Flinn, Graduate Programs Manager, 510-885-3912, E-mail: nancy.flinn@csueastbay.edu.
Website: http://www20.csueastbay.edu/ecat/graduate-chapters/g-buad.html#mba

California State University, Fresno, Division of Research and Graduate Studies, Craig School of Business, Fresno, CA 93740-8027. Offers MBA. *Program availability:* Part-time, blended/hybrid learning. *Degree requirements:* For master's, comprehensive exam, thesis or alternative. *Entrance requirements:* For master's, GMAT, minimum GPA of 2.5, official transcripts. Additional exam requirements/recommendations for international students: Required—TOEFL (minimum score 550 paper-based; 80 iBT), IELTS (minimum score 6.5). Electronic applications accepted. *Faculty research:* Conflict resolution, business marketing, business communication.

California State University, Fullerton, Graduate Studies, College of Business and Economics, Program in Business Administration, Fullerton, CA 92831-3599. Offers business administration (MBA); business analytics (MBA); international business (MBA); organizational leadership (MBA); risk management and insurance (MBA). *Accreditation:* AACSB. *Program availability:* Part-time. *Faculty:* 12 full-time (5 women), 1 part-time/adjunct (0 women). *Students:* 64 full-time (35 women), 103 part-time (46 women); includes 81 minority (40 Asian, non-Hispanic/Latino; 36 Hispanic/Latino; 5 Two or more races, non-Hispanic/Latino), 36 international. Average age 29. 254 applicants, 47% accepted, 62 enrolled. *Entrance requirements:* For master's, GMAT. Application fee: $55. *Financial support:* Career-related internships or fieldwork, Federal Work-Study, institutionally sponsored loans, and scholarships/grants available. Support available to part-time students. Financial award application deadline: 3/1; financial award applicants required to submit FAFSA. *Unit head:* Shaun Pichler, Director, 657-278-7373, E-mail: spichler@fullerton.edu. *Application contact:* Admissions/Applications, 657-278-2371.

California State University, Long Beach, Graduate Studies, College of Business Administration, Long Beach, CA 90840. Offers MS. *Accreditation:* AACSB. *Program availability:* Part-time, evening/weekend. *Entrance requirements:* For master's, GMAT. Electronic applications accepted. *Faculty research:* Attitude formation theory, consumer motivation, gift giving, derivative and synthetic securities, financial applications of artificial intelligence.

California State University, Los Angeles, Graduate Studies, College of Business and Economics, Department of Information Systems, Los Angeles, CA 90032-8530. Offers management (MS). *Program availability:* Part-time, evening/weekend. *Degree requirements:* For master's, comprehensive exam (MBA), thesis (MS). *Entrance requirements:* For master's, GMAT, minimum GPA of 2.5 during previous 2 years of course work. Additional exam requirements/recommendations for international students: Required—TOEFL (minimum score 550 paper-based). Electronic applications accepted.

California State University, Los Angeles, Graduate Studies, College of Business and Economics, Department of Management, Los Angeles, CA 90032-8530. Offers health care management (MS); management (MBA). *Accreditation:* AACSB. *Program availability:* Part-time, evening/weekend. *Entrance requirements:* For master's, GMAT, minimum GPA of 2.5 during previous 2 years of course work. Additional exam requirements/recommendations for international students: Required—TOEFL (minimum score 550 paper-based). Electronic applications accepted.

California State University, Monterey Bay, College of Business, Seaside, CA 93955-8001. Offers MBA. *Program availability:* Part-time, evening/weekend, online learning. *Entrance requirements:* For master's, recommendation, resume, work experience, bachelor's degree from accredited university. Additional exam requirements/recommendations for international students: Recommended—TOEFL (minimum score 550 paper-based; 79 iBT). Electronic applications accepted.

California State University, Northridge, Graduate Studies, David Nazarian College of Business and Economics, Northridge, CA 91330. Offers MBA. *Accreditation:* AACSB. *Program availability:* Part-time. *Students:* 61 full-time (27 women), 95 part-time (47 women); includes 58 minority (7 Black or African American, non-Hispanic/Latino; 25 Asian, non-Hispanic/Latino; 21 Hispanic/Latino; 5 Two or more races, non-Hispanic/Latino), 22 international. Average age 32. 374 applicants, 39% accepted, 64 enrolled. In 2017, 85 master's awarded. *Degree requirements:* For master's, thesis or alternative. *Entrance requirements:* For master's, GMAT, minimum GPA of 3.0 in last 60 units. Additional exam requirements/recommendations for international students: Required—TOEFL. *Application deadline:* For fall admission, 11/30 for domestic students. Application fee: $55. *Financial support:* Teaching assistantships and Federal Work-Study available. Support available to part-time students. Financial award application deadline: 3/1. *Unit head:* Dr. Kenneth Lord, Dean, 818-677-2455. *Application contact:* Dr. Deborah Heisley, Director of Graduate Programs, 818-677-2467.
Website: http://www.csun.edu/mba

California State University, Northridge, Graduate Studies, Tseng College, Program in Public Sector Management and Leadership, Northridge, CA 91330. Offers MPA. *Program availability:* Online learning. *Unit head:* Henrik Minassians, Director, 818-677-3332.
Website: http://tsengcollege.csun.edu/programs/MPA/online-PSML

California State University, Sacramento, College of Business Administration, Sacramento, CA 95819. Offers accountancy (MS); business administration (IMBA, MBA); human resources (MBA); urban land development (MBA). *Accreditation:* AACSB. *Program availability:* Part-time, evening/weekend, 100% online, blended/hybrid learning. *Students:* 122 full-time (62 women), 153 part-time (75 women); includes 114 minority (10 Black or African American, non-Hispanic/Latino; 2 American Indian or Alaska Native, non-Hispanic/Latino; 73 Asian, non-Hispanic/Latino; 25 Hispanic/Latino; 4 Native Hawaiian or other Pacific Islander, non-Hispanic/Latino), 6 international. Average age 34. 230 applicants, 75% accepted, 134 enrolled. In 2017, 123 master's awarded. *Degree requirements:* For master's, comprehensive exam, project, thesis, or writing proficiency exam. *Entrance requirements:* For master's, GMAT. Additional exam requirements/recommendations for international students: Required—TOEFL (minimum score 550 paper-based; 80 iBT). *Application deadline:* For fall admission, 2/1 for domestic students, 3/1 for international students; for spring admission, 9/15 for domestic students, 9/30 for international students. Applications are processed on a rolling basis. Application fee: $55. Electronic applications accepted. *Expenses:* Contact institution. *Financial support:* Teaching assistantships, career-related internships or fieldwork, Federal Work-Study, and scholarships/grants available. Support available to part-time students. Financial award application deadline: 3/1; financial award applicants required to submit FAFSA. *Unit head:* Dr. Pierre A. Balthazard, Dean, 916-278-6578, Fax: 916-278-5793, E-mail: cba@csus.edu. *Application contact:* Jose Martinez, Graduate Admissions Supervisor, 916-278-7871, E-mail: martinj@skymail.csus.edu.
Website: http://www.cba.csus.edu

California State University, San Bernardino, Graduate Studies, College of Business and Public Administration, Program in Business Administration, San Bernardino, CA 92407. Offers accounting (MBA); entrepreneurship (MBA); finance (MBA); global business (MBA); information management (MBA); information security (MBA); management (MBA); supply chain management (MBA). *Accreditation:* AACSB. *Program availability:* Part-time, evening/weekend, online learning. *Faculty:* 4 full-time (3 women), 6 part-time/adjunct (4 women). *Students:* 21 full-time (15 women), 122 part-time (30 women); includes 82 minority (15 Black or African American, non-Hispanic/Latino; 1 American Indian or Alaska Native, non-Hispanic/Latino; 19 Asian, non-Hispanic/Latino; 44 Hispanic/Latino; 3 Two or more races, non-Hispanic/Latino), 37 international. Average age 33. 258 applicants, 44% accepted, 50 enrolled. In 2017, 134 master's awarded. *Degree requirements:* For master's, comprehensive exam, thesis. *Entrance requirements:* Additional exam requirements/recommendations for international students: Required—TOEFL. *Application deadline:* For fall admission, 7/16 for domestic students, 7/20 for international students; for winter admission, 10/23 for domestic students, 10/20 for international students; for spring admission, 1/22 for domestic students, 1/20 for international students. Application fee: $55. *Expenses:* Contact institution. *Financial support:* Application deadline: 3/1. *Unit head:* Dr. Lawrence C. Rose, Dean, 909-537-3703, Fax: 909-537-7026, E-mail: lrose@csusb.edu. *Application contact:* Dr. Vipin Gupta, Associate Dean/MBA Director, 909-537-7380, Fax: 909-537-7026, E-mail: vgupta@csusb.edu.
Website: http://mba.csusb.edu/

California State University, San Marcos, College of Business Administration, San Marcos, CA 92096-0001. Offers MBA. *Program availability:* Evening/weekend. *Entrance requirements:* For master's, GMAT, minimum GPA of 3.0 in last 60 units, 3 years of full-time work experience. Additional exam requirements/recommendations for international students: Required—TOEFL (minimum score 550 paper-based). *Application deadline:* For fall admission, 4/30 priority date for domestic students. Applications are processed on a rolling basis. Application fee: $55. *Expenses:* Contact institution. *Financial support:* Applicants required to submit FAFSA. *Unit head:* Dr. Mohammad Oskoorouchi, Director of Graduate Programs, 760-750-4267, Fax: 760-750-4263, E-mail: mba@csusm.edu.
Website: http://www.csusm.edu/coba/

California State University, Stanislaus, College of Business Administration, Executive MBA Program, Turlock, CA 95382. Offers EMBA. *Accreditation:* AACSB. *Program availability:* Part-time, evening/weekend. *Degree requirements:* For master's, comprehensive exam, thesis or alternative. *Entrance requirements:* For master's, GMAT or GRE, minimum GPA of 2.5, 2 letters of reference, personal statement, interview. Additional exam requirements/recommendations for international students: Required—TOEFL (minimum score 550 paper-based). Electronic applications accepted. *Expenses:* Contact institution.

California State University, Stanislaus, College of Business Administration, Master of Business Administration Program, Turlock, CA 95382. Offers MBA. *Accreditation:* AACSB. *Program availability:* Part-time, evening/weekend. *Degree requirements:* For master's, comprehensive exam, thesis or alternative. *Entrance requirements:* For master's, GMAT or GRE, minimum GPA of 2.5, 3 letters of reference, personal statement. Additional exam requirements/recommendations for international students: Required—TOEFL (minimum score 550 paper-based). Electronic applications accepted. *Expenses:* Contact institution. *Faculty research:* Teaching creativity, graduate operations management, curricula data mining, foreign direct investment.

California University of Management and Sciences, Graduate Programs, Anaheim, CA 92801. Offers business administration (MBA, DBA); computer information systems (MS); economics (MS); international business (MS); sports management (MS).

California University of Pennsylvania, School of Graduate Studies and Research, Eberly College of Science and Technology, Program in Business Administration, California, PA 15419-1394. Offers business analytics (MBA); entrepreneurship (MBA); healthcare management (MBA). *Program availability:* Part-time, evening/weekend. *Degree requirements:* For master's, comprehensive exam. *Entrance requirements:* For master's, minimum GPA of 3.0, official transcripts. Additional exam requirements/recommendations for international students: Required—TOEFL (minimum score 550 paper-based). *Application deadline:* For fall admission, 8/1 priority date for domestic and international students; for winter admission, 12/1 priority date for domestic and international students; for spring admission, 5/1 priority date for domestic and international students. Applications are processed on a rolling basis. Application fee: $25. Electronic applications accepted. *Financial support:* Applicants required to submit FAFSA. *Faculty research:* Economics, applied economics, consumer behavior, technology and business, impact of technology. *Unit head:* Dr. Arshad Chawdhry, Graduate Coordinator, 724-938-5990, Fax: 724-938-5908, E-mail: chawdhry@cup.edu. *Application contact:* Suzanne C. Powers, Director of Graduate Admissions and Recruitment, 724-938-4029, Fax: 724-938-5712, E-mail: powers_s@cup.edu.

Cambridge College, School of Management, Boston, MA 02129. Offers business negotiation and conflict resolution (M Mgt); general business (M Mgt); health care informatics (M Mgt); health care management (M Mgt); leadership in human and organizational dynamics (M Mgt); non-profit and public organization management (M Mgt); small business development (M Mgt); technology management (M Mgt). *Program availability:* Part-time, evening/weekend. *Degree requirements:* For master's, thesis, seminars. *Entrance requirements:* For master's, resume, 2 professional references. Additional exam requirements/recommendations for international students: Required—TOEFL (minimum score 550 paper-based; 79 iBT), Michigan English Language Assessment Battery (minimum score 85); Recommended—IELTS (minimum score 6). Electronic applications accepted. *Expenses:* Contact institution. *Faculty* *research:* Negotiation, mediation and conflict resolution; leadership; management of diverse organizations; case studies and simulation methodologies for management education, digital as a second language: social networking for digital immigrants, non-profit and public management.

Cameron University, Office of Graduate Studies, Program in Business Administration, Lawton, OK 73505-6377. Offers MBA. *Accreditation:* ACBSP. *Program availability:* Part-time, evening/weekend, online learning. *Degree requirements:* For master's, comprehensive exam. *Entrance requirements:* Additional exam requirements/recommendations for international students: Required—TOEFL (minimum score 550 paper-based). Electronic applications accepted. *Faculty research:* Financial liberalization, right to work, recession, teaching evaluations, database management.

Campbellsville University, School of Business, Economics, and Technology, Campbellsville, KY 42718-2799. Offers business administration (MBA, Professional MBA); information technology management (MS); management (PhD); management and leadership (MML). *Program availability:* Part-time, evening/weekend, 100% online, blended/hybrid learning. *Faculty:* 20 full-time (4 women), 9 part-time/adjunct (3 women). *Students:* 74 full-time (16 women), 3,218 part-time (642 women); includes 28 minority (16 Black or African American, non-Hispanic/Latino; 9 Asian, non-Hispanic/Latino; 3 Hispanic/Latino), 3,164 international. Average age 27. 3,261 applicants, 95% accepted, 2220 enrolled. In 2017, 89 master's awarded. *Degree requirements:* For master's, comprehensive exam (for some programs), thesis optional; for doctorate, comprehensive exam, thesis/dissertation. *Entrance requirements:* For master's, GRE or GMAT, letters of recommendation, college transcripts; for doctorate, GMAT, resume, official transcripts, references, personal essay, interview, completion of course in statistics and research methods. Additional exam requirements/recommendations for international students: Required—TOEFL (minimum score 550 paper-based; 79 iBT); Recommended—IELTS (minimum score 6). *Application deadline:* Applications are processed on a rolling basis. Application fee: $25. Electronic applications accepted. Application fee is waived when completed online. *Expenses:* $479 per credit hour (for MBA and MML); $525 per credit hour (for MSITM and PMBA); $620 per credit hour (for PhD). *Financial support:* In 2017–18, 7 students received support. Unspecified assistantships and employee tuition waivers available. Financial award application deadline: 6/1; financial award applicants required to submit FAFSA. *Unit head:* Dr. Patricia H. Cowherd, Dean, 270-789-5553, Fax: 270-789-5066, E-mail: phcowherd@campbellsville.edu. *Application contact:* Monica Bamwine, Assistant Director of Graduate Admissions, 270-789-5221, Fax: 270-789-5071, E-mail: mkbamwine@campbellsville.edu.
Website: http://www.campbellsville.edu

Campbell University, Graduate and Professional Programs, Lundy-Fetterman School of Business, Buies Creek, NC 27506. Offers MBA, MTWM. *Accreditation:* ACBSP. *Program availability:* Part-time, evening/weekend. *Degree requirements:* For master's, comprehensive exam, thesis or alternative. *Entrance requirements:* For master's, GMAT or GRE, minimum GPA of 2.7, 3 letters of reference, resume. Additional exam requirements/recommendations for international students: Required—TOEFL (minimum score 550 paper-based). *Faculty research:* Agricultural economics, investments, leadership, marketing, law and economics.

Canisius College, Graduate Division, Richard J. Wehle School of Business, Department of Management, Buffalo, NY 14208-1098. Offers business administration (MBA); international business (MS). *Accreditation:* AACSB. *Program availability:* Part-time, evening/weekend. *Faculty:* 8 full-time (4 women), 1 (woman) part-time/adjunct. *Students:* 104 full-time (49 women), 113 part-time (43 women); includes 25 minority (8 Black or African American, non-Hispanic/Latino; 2 American Indian or Alaska Native, non-Hispanic/Latino; 4 Asian, non-Hispanic/Latino; 6 Hispanic/Latino; 3 Native Hawaiian or other Pacific Islander, non-Hispanic/Latino; 2 Two or more races, non-Hispanic/Latino), 31 international. Average age 28. 140 applicants, 82% accepted, 72 enrolled. In 2017, 103 master's awarded. *Entrance requirements:* For master's, GMAT, GRE, official transcript from colleges attended, current resume. Additional exam requirements/recommendations for international students: Required—TOEFL (minimum score 550 paper-based, 80 iBT), IELTS (minimum score 6.5), or CAEL (minimum score 70). *Application deadline:* For fall admission, 7/1 priority date for domestic students; for spring admission, 11/1 priority date for domestic students. Applications are processed on a rolling basis. Application fee: $0. Electronic applications accepted. *Expenses:* Tuition: Full-time $22,860; part-time $820 per credit. *Required fees:* $720; $25 per credit. $65 per semester. One-time fee: $425. *Financial support:* Career-related internships or fieldwork, Federal Work-Study, scholarships/grants, tuition waivers (partial), and unspecified assistantships available. Support available to part-time students. Financial award application deadline: 4/30; financial award applicants required to submit FAFSA. *Faculty research:* Global leadership effectiveness, global supply chain management, quality management. *Unit head:* Dr. Lynn A. Fish, Chair of Management, Entrepreneurship and International Business, 716-888-2634, E-mail: fishl@canisius.edu.
Website: http://www.canisius.edu/graduate/

Cape Breton University, Shannon School of Business, Sydney, NS B1P 6L2, Canada. Offers MBA. *Program availability:* Part-time. *Entrance requirements:* For master's, GMAT. Additional exam requirements/recommendations for international students: Required—TOEFL (minimum score 550 paper-based; 80 iBT), IELTS (minimum score 6.5). Electronic applications accepted.

Capella University, School of Business and Technology, Doctoral Programs in Business, Minneapolis, MN 55402. Offers accounting (DBA, PhD); business intelligence (DBA); finance (DBA, PhD); general business management (PhD); human resource management (DBA, PhD); leadership (DBA, PhD); management education (PhD); marketing (DBA, PhD); project management (DBA, PhD); strategy and innovation (DBA, PhD). *Accreditation:* ACBSP.

Capella University, School of Business and Technology, Master's Programs in Business, Minneapolis, MN 55402. Offers accounting (MBA); business analysis (MS); business intelligence (MBA); entrepreneurship (MBA); finance (MBA); general business administration (MBA); general human resource management (MS); general leadership (MS); health care management (MBA); human resource management (MBA); marketing (MBA); project management (MBA, MS). *Accreditation:* ACBSP.

Capital University, Law School, Program in Business Law and Taxation, Columbus, OH 43209-2394. Offers business (LL M); business and taxation (LL M); taxation (LL M); JD/LL M. *Program availability:* Part-time, evening/weekend. *Degree requirements:* For master's, thesis or alternative. *Entrance requirements:* For master's, previous course work in accounting, business law, and taxation. Additional exam requirements/recommendations for international students: Required—TOEFL (minimum score 600 paper-based). Electronic applications accepted.

Capital University, School of Management, Columbus, OH 43209-2394. Offers leadership (MBA); MBA/JD; MBA/MSN. *Accreditation:* ACBSP. *Program availability:* Part-time, evening/weekend. *Entrance requirements:* For master's, 2-3 years of professional work experience. Additional exam requirements/recommendations for international students: Required—TOEFL (minimum score 550 paper-based; 80 iBT); Recommended—IELTS (minimum score 6.5). Electronic applications accepted.

Application fee is waived when completed online. *Expenses:* Contact institution. *Faculty research:* Taxation, public policy, health care, management of non-profits.

Capitol Technology University, Graduate Programs, Laurel, MD 20708-9759. Offers business administration (MBA); computer science (MS); electrical engineering (MS); information and telecommunications systems management (MS); information architecture (MS); network security (MS). *Program availability:* Part-time, evening/weekend, online learning. *Entrance requirements:* For master's, minimum GPA of 3.0. Electronic applications accepted.

Cardinal Stritch University, College of Business and Management, Milwaukee, WI 53217-3985. Offers cyber security (MBA); healthcare management (MBA); justice administration (MBA); marketing (MBA). *Accreditation:* ACBSP. *Program availability:* Part-time, evening/weekend, 100% online, blended/hybrid learning. *Students:* 133 full-time (72 women), 98 part-time (54 women); includes 88 minority (64 Black or African American, non-Hispanic/Latino; 1 American Indian or Alaska Native, non-Hispanic/Latino; 12 Asian, non-Hispanic/Latino; 10 Hispanic/Latino; 1 Two or more races, non-Hispanic/Latino), 8 international. Average age 36. 144 applicants, 100% accepted, 57 enrolled. In 2017, 118 master's awarded. *Degree requirements:* For master's, thesis. *Entrance requirements:* For master's, 3 years of management or related experience, minimum GPA of 2.5. Additional exam requirements/recommendations for international students: Required—TOEFL (minimum score 79 iBT), IELTS (minimum score 6.5). *Application deadline:* Applications are processed on a rolling basis. Application fee: $0. Electronic applications accepted. *Expenses:* $665 per credit. *Financial support:* Career-related internships or fieldwork, Federal Work-Study, and scholarships/grants available. Financial award applicants required to submit FAFSA. *Unit head:* Janette Braverman, Dean, 414-410-4004, E-mail: jmbraverman1@stritch.edu. *Application contact:* Graduate Admissions, 414-410-4042, E-mail: admissions@stritch.edu.
Website: http://www.stritch.edu/cbm

Carleton University, Faculty of Graduate Studies, Faculty of Business, Sprott School of Business, Ottawa, ON K1S 5B6, Canada. Offers business administration (MBA); management (PhD). *Degree requirements:* For master's, thesis optional; for doctorate, comprehensive exam, thesis/dissertation. *Entrance requirements:* For master's, GMAT, honors degree; for doctorate, GMAT. Additional exam requirements/recommendations for international students: Required—TOEFL. *Faculty research:* Business information systems, finance, international business, marketing, production and operations.

Carlos Albizu University, Miami Campus, Graduate Programs, Miami, FL 33172-2209. Offers clinical psychology (PhD, Psy D); entrepreneurship (MBA); exceptional student education (MS); human services (PhD); industrial/organizational psychology (MS); marriage and family therapy (MS); mental health counseling (MS); nonprofit management (MBA); organizational management (MBA); psychology (MS); speech and language pathology (MS); teaching English for speakers of other languages (MS). *Accreditation:* APA. *Program availability:* Part-time, evening/weekend, 100% online, blended/hybrid learning. *Faculty:* 32 full-time (24 women), 27 part-time/adjunct (15 women). *Students:* 411 full-time (345 women), 248 part-time (215 women); includes 562 minority (53 Black or African American, non-Hispanic/Latino; 4 Asian, non-Hispanic/Latino; 498 Hispanic/Latino; 7 Two or more races, non-Hispanic/Latino), 23 international. Average age 34. 391 applicants, 42% accepted, 154 enrolled. In 2017, 96 master's, 54 doctorates awarded. Terminal master's awarded for partial completion of doctoral program. *Degree requirements:* For master's, comprehensive exam (for some programs), integrative project (for MBA); research project (for exceptional student education, teaching English as a second language); for doctorate, comprehensive examinations, internship, project/dissertation. *Entrance requirements:* For master's, GRE/EXADEP, bachelor's degree from accredited institution, minimum GPA of 3.0, 3 letters of recommendation, interview, resume, statement of purpose, official transcripts; for doctorate, GRE (for Psy D), 3 letters of recommendation, resume, interview, statement of purpose, official transcripts; bachelor's degree and minimum GPA of 3.25 (for Psy D); master's degree and minimum GPA of 3.0 (for PhD). Additional exam requirements/recommendations for international students: Required—Michigan Test of English Language Proficiency. *Application deadline:* For fall admission, 4/1 priority date for domestic students, 5/1 priority date for international students; for spring admission, 11/1 priority date for domestic students, 9/1 priority date for international students. Applications are processed on a rolling basis. Application fee: $50. Electronic applications accepted. Application fee is waived when completed online. *Expenses:* Contact institution. *Financial support:* In 2017–18, 145 students received support. Federal Work-Study, scholarships/grants, unspecified assistantships, and tuition discounts available. Financial award application deadline: 6/1; financial award applicants required to submit FAFSA. *Faculty research:* Psychotherapy, forensic psychology, neuropsychology, special education, speech-language pathology, criminal justice. *Unit head:* Dr. Etiony Aldarondo, Provost, 305-593-1223 Ext. 3138, Fax: 305-592-7930, E-mail: ealdarondo@albizu.edu. *Application contact:* Sonia Feliciano, Institutional Director of Student Recruitment, 305-593-1223 Ext. 3108, Fax: 305-477-8983, E-mail: sfeliciano@albizu.edu.

Carlow University, College of Health and Wellness, MSN-MBA Dual Degree Program, Pittsburgh, PA 15213-3165. Offers MSN/MBA. *Program availability:* Part-time, 100% online, blended/hybrid learning. *Students:* 31 full-time (24 women), 7 part-time (all women); includes 2 minority (both Black or African American, non-Hispanic/Latino). Average age 35. 9 applicants, 100% accepted, 7 enrolled. *Entrance requirements:* Additional exam requirements/recommendations for international students: Required—TOEFL (minimum score 550 paper-based). *Application deadline:* Applications are processed on a rolling basis. Electronic applications accepted. *Expenses: Tuition:* Full-time $12,103; part-time $825 per credit hour. Tuition and fees vary according to program. *Financial support:* Application deadline: 4/1; applicants required to submit FAFSA. *Unit head:* Dr. Renee Ingel, Program Director, 412-578-6103, E-mail: rmingel@carlow.edu. *Application contact:* E-mail: gradstudies@carlow.edu.
Website: http://www.carlow.edu/MSN-MBA_Dual_Degree.aspx

Carlow University, College of Leadership and Social Change, MBA Program, Pittsburgh, PA 15213-3165. Offers fraud and forensics (MBA); healthcare management (MBA); human resource management (MBA); leadership and management (MBA); project management (MBA). *Program availability:* Part-time, evening/weekend, 100% online, blended/hybrid learning. *Students:* 81 full-time (62 women), 28 part-time (18 women); includes 32 minority (26 Black or African American, non-Hispanic/Latino; 2 Asian, non-Hispanic/Latino; 1 Hispanic/Latino; 3 Two or more races, non-Hispanic/Latino). Average age 32. 46 applicants, 98% accepted, 32 enrolled. In 2017, 57 master's awarded. *Entrance requirements:* For master's, minimum undergraduate GPA of 3.0 (preferred); personal essay; resume; official transcripts; two professional recommendations. Additional exam requirements/recommendations for international students: Required—TOEFL (minimum score 550 paper-based). *Application deadline:* Applications are processed on a rolling basis. Electronic applications accepted. *Expenses: Tuition:* Full-time $12,103; part-time $825 per credit hour. Tuition and fees vary according to program. *Financial support:* Application deadline: 4/1; applicants required to submit FAFSA. *Unit head:* Dr. Howard Stern, Chair, MBA Program, 412-578-8828, E-mail: hastern@carlow.edu. *Application contact:* 412-578-6059, Fax: 412-578-6321, E-mail: gradstudies@carlow.edu.
Website: http://www.carlow.edu/Business_Administration.aspx

Business Administration and Management—General

Carnegie Mellon University, Heinz College, School of Public Policy and Management, Master of Entertainment Industry Management Program, Pittsburgh, PA 15213-3891. Offers MEIM. *Accreditation:* AACSB. *Entrance requirements:* For master's, GRE or GMAT, college-level course in advanced algebra/pre-calculus; college-level courses in economics and statistics (recommended). Additional exam requirements/ recommendations for international students: Required—TOEFL or IELTS.

Carnegie Mellon University, Heinz College, School of Public Policy and Management, Master of Science Program in Biotechnology and Management, Pittsburgh, PA 15213-3891. Offers MS. *Accreditation:* AACSB. *Entrance requirements:* For master's, GRE or GMAT, college-level course in advanced algebra/pre-calculus; college-level courses in economics and statistics (recommended). Additional exam requirements/ recommendations for international students: Required—TOEFL or IELTS.

Carnegie Mellon University, Tepper School of Business, Pittsburgh, PA 15213-3891. Offers accounting (PhD); business management and software engineering (MBMSE); business technologies (PhD); civil engineering and industrial management (MS); computational finance (MSCF); economics (PhD); environmental engineering and management (MEEM); financial economics (PhD); industrial administration (MBA), including administration and public management; marketing (PhD); mathematical finance (PhD); operations management (PhD); operations research (PhD); organizational behavior and theory (PhD); production and operations management (PhD); public policy and management (MS, MSED); software engineering and business management (MS); JD/MS; JD/MSIA; M Div/MS; MOM/MSIA; MSCF/MSIA. JD/MSIA offered jointly with University of Pittsburgh. *Program availability:* Part-time. Terminal master's awarded for partial completion of doctoral program. *Degree requirements:* For doctorate, thesis/dissertation. *Entrance requirements:* For master's, GMAT. *Expenses:* Contact institution.

Carroll University, Program in Business Administration, Waukesha, WI 53186-5593. Offers MBA. *Program availability:* Part-time. *Entrance requirements:* For master's, GRE or GMAT (waived if GPA is 2.75 or above), resume, transcripts. Additional exam requirements/recommendations for international students: Required—TOEFL. Electronic applications accepted.

Carson-Newman University, Program in Business Administration, Jefferson City, TN 37760. Offers MBA. *Program availability:* Part-time, evening/weekend, 100% online, blended/hybrid learning. *Faculty:* 4 full-time (2 women), 6 part-time/adjunct (1 woman). *Students:* 75 full-time (30 women), 33 part-time (13 women); includes 12 minority (10 Black or African American, non-Hispanic/Latino; 2 Hispanic/Latino), 21 international. Average age 29. 47 applicants, 100% accepted, 44 enrolled. In 2017, 34 master's awarded. *Entrance requirements:* Additional exam requirements/recommendations for international students: Recommended—TOEFL (minimum score 79 iBT), IELTS (minimum score 6.5), TSE (minimum score 53). *Application deadline:* For fall admission, 7/15 priority date for domestic students. Applications are processed on a rolling basis. Application fee: $50. *Expenses: Tuition:* Full-time $10,516; part-time $478 per credit hour. *Required fees:* $240; $120 per semester. One-time fee: $150. *Financial support:* Federal Work-Study and tuition waivers (full and partial) available. Financial award applicants required to submit FAFSA. *Unit head:* Dr. Kyle J. Kaplan, Director, 865-471-7124, E-mail: kkaplan@cn.edu. *Application contact:* Nilma Stewart, Graduate Admissions and Services Adviser, 865-471-3230, Fax: 865-471-3875, E-mail: adults@cn.edu.
Website: http://www.cn.edu/graduate-adult-studies/programs/business

Case Western Reserve University, Weatherhead School of Management, Executive Doctor of Management Program, Cleveland, OH 44106. Offers management (EDM). *Program availability:* Part-time, evening/weekend. *Degree requirements:* For doctorate, thesis/dissertation. *Entrance requirements:* For doctorate, GMAT. Electronic applications accepted. *Expenses:* Contact institution. *Faculty research:* Information technology and design, emotional intelligence and leadership, entrepreneurship, governing of NP organizations, social ethics.

Case Western Reserve University, Weatherhead School of Management, Executive MBA Program, Cleveland, OH 44106. Offers EMBA. *Accreditation:* AACSB. *Entrance requirements:* For master's, GMAT (if candidate does not have an undergraduate degree from an accredited institution), work experience, interview. Electronic applications accepted. *Expenses:* Contact institution.

Case Western Reserve University, Weatherhead School of Management, Full Time MBA Program, Cleveland, OH 44106. Offers MBA, MBA/JD, MBA/M Acc, MBA/MD, MBA/MIM, MBA/MNO, MBA/MSM, MBA/MSN, MBA/MSSA. *Accreditation:* AACSB. *Entrance requirements:* For master's, GMAT, letters of recommendation, interview, work experience. Additional exam requirements/recommendations for international students: Required—TOEFL (minimum score 600 paper-based). Electronic applications accepted. *Expenses: Tuition:* Full-time $43,854; part-time $1827 per credit hour. *Required fees:* $50; $50 per credit hour. Tuition and fees vary according to course load and program.

Case Western Reserve University, Weatherhead School of Management, Part-time MBA Program, Cleveland, OH 44106. Offers MBA, MBA/M Acc, MBA/MSM, MBA/MSSA. *Accreditation:* AACSB. *Program availability:* Part-time, evening/weekend. *Entrance requirements:* For master's, GMAT, interview, work experience. Additional exam requirements/recommendations for international students: Recommended—TOEFL (minimum score 600 paper-based). Electronic applications accepted. *Expenses: Tuition:* Full-time $43,854; part-time $1827 per credit hour. *Required fees:* $50; $50 per credit hour. Tuition and fees vary according to course load and program.

The Catholic University of America, Busch School of Business and Economics, Washington, DC 20064. Offers accounting (MS); business analysis (MSBA); integral economic development management (MA); integral economic development policy (MA); management (MS), including Federal contract management, human resource management, leadership and management, project management, sales management. *Program availability:* Part-time. *Faculty:* 27 full-time (6 women), 45 part-time/adjunct (12 women). *Students:* 74 full-time (50 women), 9 part-time (3 women); includes 26 minority (5 Black or African American, non-Hispanic/Latino; 1 American Indian or Alaska Native, non-Hispanic/Latino; 3 Asian, non-Hispanic/Latino; 9 Hispanic/Latino; 8 Two or more races, non-Hispanic/Latino, 18 international. Average age 31. 99 applicants, 86% accepted, 61 enrolled. In 2017, 46 master's awarded. *Degree requirements:* For master's, comprehensive exam (for some programs). *Entrance requirements:* For master's, GRE General Test, statement of purpose, official copies of academic transcripts, three letters of recommendation. Additional exam requirements/ recommendations for international students: Required—TOEFL (minimum score 550 paper-based; 80 iBT). *Application deadline:* For fall admission, 7/15 priority date for domestic students, 7/1 for international students; for spring admission, 11/15 priority date for domestic students, 11/1 for international students. Applications are processed on a rolling basis. Application fee: $55. Electronic applications accepted. *Expenses:* Contact institution. *Financial support:* Fellowships, research assistantships, teaching assistantships, Federal Work-Study, scholarships/grants, tuition waivers (full and partial), and unspecified assistantships available. Financial award application deadline: 2/1; financial award applicants required to submit FAFSA. *Faculty research:* Integrity of the marketing process, economics of energy and the environment, emerging markets,

social change, international finance and economic development. *Total annual research expenditures:* $31,390. *Unit head:* Dr. William Bowman, Dean, 202-319-5290, Fax: 202-319-4426, E-mail: otey@cua.edu. *Application contact:* Dr. Steven Brown, Director of Graduate Admissions, 202-319-5057, Fax: 202-319-6533, E-mail: cua-admissions@cua.edu.
Website: https://business.catholic.edu/

The Catholic University of America, Metropolitan School of Professional Studies, Washington, DC 20064. Offers emergency service administration (MS); health administration (MHA); social service administration (MS). *Program availability:* Part-time, evening/weekend, 100% online. *Faculty:* 20 part-time/adjunct (6 women). *Students:* 14 full-time (8 women), 36 part-time (20 women); includes 26 minority (16 Black or African American, non-Hispanic/Latino; 1 Asian, non-Hispanic/Latino; 4 Hispanic/Latino; 5 Two or more races, non-Hispanic/Latino), 3 international. Average age 36. 45 applicants, 80% accepted, 21 enrolled. In 2017, 100 master's awarded. *Degree requirements:* For master's, minimum GPA of 3.0, capstone course. *Entrance requirements:* For master's, statement of purpose, official copies of academic transcripts, three letters of recommendation, resume. Additional exam requirements/ recommendations for international students: Required—TOEFL (minimum score 550 paper-based; 80 iBT). *Application deadline:* For fall admission, 7/15 priority date for domestic students, 7/1 for international students; for spring admission, 11/15 priority date for domestic students, 11/1 for international students. Applications are processed on a rolling basis. Application fee: $55. Electronic applications accepted. *Expenses:* Contact institution. *Financial support:* Scholarships/grants available. Financial award application deadline: 3/15; financial award applicants required to submit FAFSA. *Unit head:* Dr. Vince Kiernan, Dean, 202-319-5256, Fax: 202-319-6260, E-mail: kiernan@cua.edu. *Application contact:* Dr. Steven Brown, Director of Graduate Admissions, 202-319-5057, Fax: 202-319-6533, E-mail: cua-admissions@cua.edu.
Website: https://metro.catholic.edu/

Cedar Crest College, Program in Business Administration, Allentown, PA 18104-6196. Offers MBA. *Program availability:* Part-time, evening/weekend, blended/hybrid learning. *Faculty:* 2 full-time (1 woman), 9 part-time/adjunct (4 women). *Students:* 22 full-time (15 women), 13 part-time (10 women); includes 10 minority (3 Black or African American, non-Hispanic/Latino; 2 Asian, non-Hispanic/Latino; 5 Hispanic/Latino), 1 international. Average age 36. In 2017, 21 master's awarded. *Entrance requirements:* For master's, GRE or GMAT, two letters of recommendation, copy of current resume, official transcripts. *Application deadline:* Applications are processed on a rolling basis. Electronic applications accepted. *Expenses:* Contact institution. *Unit head:* Stephanie Colbry, Chair, 610-437-4471 Ext. 4453, E-mail: slcolbry@cedarcrest.edu. *Application contact:* Nancy Wunderly, Director of School of Adult and Graduate Education, 610-437-4471, E-mail: sage@cedarcrest.edu.
Website: http://mba.cedarcrest.edu/

Cedarville University, Graduate Programs, Cedarville, OH 45314. Offers business administration (MBA); family nurse practitioner (MSN); global ministry (M Div); global public health nursing (MSN); healthcare administration (MBA); ministry (M Min); nurse educator (MSN); operations management (MBA); pharmacy (Pharm D). *Program availability:* Part-time, evening/weekend, 100% online, blended/hybrid learning. *Faculty:* 23 full-time (9 women), 48 part-time/adjunct (21 women). *Students:* 202 full-time (123 women), 146 part-time (96 women); includes 63 minority (39 Black or African American, non-Hispanic/Latino; 3 American Indian or Alaska Native, non-Hispanic/Latino; 15 Asian, non-Hispanic/Latino; 2 Hispanic/Latino; 1 Native Hawaiian or other Pacific Islander, non-Hispanic/Latino; 3 Two or more races, non-Hispanic/Latino), 3 international. Average age 24. 345 applicants, 37% accepted, 91 enrolled. In 2017, 53 master's, 47 doctorates awarded. *Degree requirements:* For master's, portfolio; for doctorate, comprehensive exam. *Entrance requirements:* For master's, GRE, 2 professional recommendations; for doctorate, PCAT, professional recommendation from a practicing pharmacist or current employer/supervisor, resume, essay, interview. Additional exam requirements/recommendations for international students: Required—TOEFL (minimum score 550 paper-based; 80 iBT). *Application deadline:* For fall admission, 5/1 priority date for domestic and international students; for spring admission, 11/1 priority date for domestic and international students. Applications are processed on a rolling basis. Application fee: $0. Electronic applications accepted. *Expenses: Tuition:* Full-time $12,594; part-time $566 per credit. One-time fee: $100 full-time. Tuition and fees vary according to degree level and program. *Financial support:* Scholarships/grants and unspecified assistantships available. Support available to part-time students. Financial award application deadline: 1/30; financial award applicants required to submit FAFSA. *Faculty research:* Establishing competencies of clinical reasoning for nursing students in Taiwan, social determinants of health in pediatric primary care, meeting needs of palliative care populations, natural product utility in cancer, monoclonal antibodies directed at angiogenesis regulation. *Total annual research expenditures:* $3,800. *Unit head:* Dr. Janice Supplee, Dean of Graduate Studies, 937-766-7700, E-mail: suppleej@cedarville.edu. *Application contact:* Jim Amstutz, Director of Graduate Admissions, 937-766-7878, Fax: 937-766-7575, E-mail: amstutzj@cedarville.edu.
Website: https://www.cedarville.edu/Admissions/Graduate/Graduate-Programs.aspx

Centenary College of Louisiana, Graduate Programs, Frost School of Business, Shreveport, LA 71104. Offers MBA. *Program availability:* Part-time, evening/weekend. *Degree requirements:* For master's, thesis. *Entrance requirements:* For master's, GMAT, minimum 5 years of professional/managerial experience. *Expenses:* Contact institution. *Faculty research:* Leadership, organizational change strategy, market behavior, executive compensation.

Centenary University, Program in Business Administration, Hackettstown, NJ 07840-2100. Offers MBA. *Program availability:* Part-time, evening/weekend, online learning. *Entrance requirements:* For master's, GMAT.

Central Connecticut State University, School of Graduate Studies, School of Business, Program in Business Administration, New Britain, CT 06050-4010. Offers MBA. *Program availability:* Part-time, evening/weekend. *Faculty:* 9 full-time (4 women), 1 part-time/adjunct (0 women). *Students:* 4 full-time (1 woman), 195 part-time (87 women); includes 65 minority (37 Black or African American, non-Hispanic/Latino; 10 Asian, non-Hispanic/Latino; 16 Hispanic/Latino; 2 Two or more races, non-Hispanic/Latino), 2 international. Average age 31. 137 applicants, 81% accepted, 71 enrolled. In 2017, 43 master's awarded. *Degree requirements:* For master's, thesis or alternative. *Entrance requirements:* For master's, GMAT or GRE, minimum undergraduate GPA of 2.7, resume. Additional exam requirements/recommendations for international students: Required—TOEFL (minimum score 550 paper-based; 79 iBT); Recommended—IELTS (minimum score 6.5). *Application deadline:* For fall admission, 8/1 for domestic students, 5/1 for international students; for spring admission, 11/1 for domestic and international students. Applications are processed on a rolling basis. Application fee: $50. Electronic applications accepted. *Expenses: Tuition, area resident:* Full-time $6757. Tuition, state resident: full-time $9750; part-time $374 per credit. Tuition, nonresident: full-time $18,102; part-time $374 per credit. *Required fees:* $4635; $255 per credit. *Financial support:* In 2017–18, 14 students received support. Career-related internships or fieldwork, Federal Work-Study, and scholarships/grants available. Support available to part-time students. Financial award application deadline: 3/1; financial award applicants

required to submit FAFSA. *Unit head:* Dr. Mark Cistulli, Director, 860-832-3247, E-mail: mark.cistulli@ccsu.edu. *Application contact:* Patricia Gardner, Associate Director of Graduate Admissions, 860-832-2350, Fax: 860-832-2362.
Website: http://www.ccsu.edu/mba/

Central European University, Department of Economics, 1051, Hungary. Offers business administration (PhD); business analytics (M Sc); economic policy in global markets (MA); economics (MA, PhD); finance (MS); global economic relations (MA); technology management and innovation (MS). *Program availability:* Part-time. *Faculty:* 23 full-time (2 women), 25 part-time/adjunct (4 women). *Students:* 177 full-time (77 women), 125 part-time (39 women). Average age 31. 530 applicants, 49% accepted, 144 enrolled. In 2017, 150 master's, 6 doctorates awarded. *Degree requirements:* For master's, one foreign language, thesis; for doctorate, one foreign language, comprehensive exam, thesis/dissertation. *Entrance requirements:* For master's and doctorate, interview. Additional exam requirements/recommendations for international students: Required—TOEFL (minimum score 570 paper-based); Recommended—IELTS (minimum score 6.5). *Application deadline:* For fall admission, 2/4 for domestic and international students. Application fee: $30. Electronic applications accepted. *Expenses: Tuition:* Full-time 12,000 euros. *Required fees:* 230 euros. One-time fee: 30 euros full-time. Tuition and fees vary according to course level, course load, degree level and program. *Financial support:* Fellowships, teaching assistantships, career-related internships or fieldwork, institutionally sponsored loans, scholarships/grants, health care benefits, and tuition waivers (full and partial) available. *Faculty research:* Economic theory (microeconomics and macroeconomics) and econometrics, as well as study of many applied fields, including labor economics, health economics and economics of education, industrial organization, monetary economics, international economics, law and economics, comparative institutional economics, corporate governance, and economics of transition. *Unit head:* Miklos Koren, Head of Department, 36 1 327-3000 Ext. 2212, E-mail: econbusi@ceu.edu. *Application contact:* Zsuzsanna Jaszberenyi, Admissions Officer, 361-324-3009, Fax: 367-327-3211, E-mail: admissions@ceu.edu. Website: http://economics.ceu.edu/

Central Michigan University, Central Michigan University Global Campus, Program in Business Administration, Mount Pleasant, MI 48859. Offers enterprise resource planning (MBA, Certificate); human resource management (MBA); logistics management (MBA, Certificate); marketing (MBA); value-driven organization (MBA). *Program availability:* Part-time, evening/weekend. *Entrance requirements:* For master's, GMAT.

Central Michigan University, College of Graduate Studies, College of Business Administration, MBA Program, Mount Pleasant, MI 48859. Offers accounting (MBA); business economics (MBA); consulting (MBA); finance (MBA); general business (MBA); human resource management (MBA); information systems (MBA); international business (MBA); logistics management (MBA); marketing (MBA); value-driven organization (MBA). *Program availability:* Part-time, evening/weekend, online learning. Electronic applications accepted. *Faculty research:* Accounting, consulting, international business, marketing, information systems.

Central Michigan University, College of Graduate Studies, Interdisciplinary Administration Programs, Mount Pleasant, MI 48859. Offers acquisitions administration (MSA, Graduate Certificate); general administration (MSA, Graduate Certificate); health services administration (MSA, Graduate Certificate); human resource administration (Graduate Certificate); human resources administration (MSA); information resource management (MSA, Graduate Certificate); international administration (MSA, Graduate Certificate); leadership (MSA, Graduate Certificate); public administration (MSA, Graduate Certificate); research administration (Graduate Certificate); sport administration (MSA). *Accreditation:* AACSB. *Program availability:* Part-time, evening/weekend, online learning. *Degree requirements:* For master's, thesis or alternative. *Entrance requirements:* For master's, bachelor's degree with minimum GPA of 2.7. Electronic applications accepted. *Faculty research:* Interdisciplinary studies in acquisitions administration, health services administration, sport administration, recreation and park administration, and international administration.

Chadron State College, School of Professional and Graduate Studies, Department of Business and Economics, Chadron, NE 69337. Offers MBA. *Accreditation:* ACBSP. *Program availability:* Part-time, evening/weekend, online learning. *Degree requirements:* For master's, thesis optional. *Entrance requirements:* For master's, GMAT, minimum GPA of 2.75 or 12 graduate hours at CSC with minimum GPA of 3.25. Additional exam requirements/recommendations for international students: Required—TOEFL. Electronic applications accepted.

Chaminade University of Honolulu, Office of Professional and Continuing Education, Program in Business Administration, Honolulu, HI 96816-1578. Offers accounting (MBA); business (MBA); island business (MBA); not-for-profit (MBA). *Program availability:* Part-time, evening/weekend, 100% online, blended/hybrid learning. *Faculty:* 5 full-time (2 women), 8 part-time/adjunct (2 women). *Students:* 80 full-time (44 women), 54 part-time (37 women); includes 95 minority (6 Black or African American, non-Hispanic/Latino; 2 American Indian or Alaska Native, non-Hispanic/Latino; 42 Asian, non-Hispanic/Latino; 8 Hispanic/Latino; 34 Native Hawaiian or other Pacific Islander, non-Hispanic/Latino; 3 Two or more races, non-Hispanic/Latino), 5 international. Average age 32. 36 applicants, 94% accepted, 24 enrolled. In 2017, 39 master's awarded. *Entrance requirements:* For master's, minimum GPA of 3.0, resume, two years or more of work experience. Additional exam requirements/recommendations for international students: Required—TOEFL (minimum score 550 paper-based; 79 iBT). *Application deadline:* Applications are processed on a rolling basis. Application fee: $40. Electronic applications accepted. *Expenses:* $900 per credit hour with $93 fee per online course. *Financial support:* Applicants required to submit FAFSA. *Unit head:* Dr. Scott J. Schroeder, Dean, 808-739-4612, Fax: 808-735-4734, E-mail: mba@chaminade.edu. *Application contact:* 808-735-4755, E-mail: gradserv@chaminade.edu. Website: https://pace.chaminade.edu/graduate-programs/mba-program/

Champlain College, Graduate Studies, Burlington, VT 05402-0670. Offers business (MBA); digital forensic science (MS); early childhood education (M Ed); emergent media (MFA, MS); executive leadership (MS); health care administration (MS); information security operations (MS); law (MS); mediation and applied conflict studies (MS). MS in emergent media program held in Shanghai. *Program availability:* Part-time, online learning. *Degree requirements:* For master's, capstone project. *Entrance requirements:* Additional exam requirements/recommendations for international students: Required—TOEFL (minimum score 550 paper-based; 80 iBT). Electronic applications accepted.

Chapman University, The George L. Argyros School of Business and Economics, Orange, CA 92866. Offers accounting (MS); behavioral and computational economics (MS); business administration (Exec MBA, MBA). *Accreditation:* AACSB. *Program availability:* Part-time, evening/weekend. *Faculty:* 60 full-time (16 women), 46 part-time/adjunct (8 women). *Students:* 180 full-time (87 women), 100 part-time (45 women); includes 86 minority (4 Black or African American, non-Hispanic/Latino; 1 American Indian or Alaska Native, non-Hispanic/Latino; 39 Asian, non-Hispanic/Latino; 28 Hispanic/Latino; 1 Native Hawaiian or other Pacific Islander, non-Hispanic/Latino; 13 Two or more races, non-Hispanic/Latino), 89 international. Average age 28. 250 applicants, 75% accepted, 94 enrolled. In 2017, 119 master's awarded. Application fee: $60. Electronic applications accepted. *Expenses:* Contact institution. *Financial support:*

Fellowships, Federal Work-Study, and scholarships/grants available. Financial award applicants required to submit FAFSA. *Unit head:* Thomas Turk, Interim Dean, 714-997-6819, E-mail: turk@chapman.edu. *Application contact:* Debra Gonda, Associate Dean, 714-997-6894, E-mail: gonda@chapman.edu.
Website: https://www.chapman.edu/business/index.aspx

Charleston Southern University, College of Business, Charleston, SC 29423-8087. Offers accounting (MBA); finance (MBA); general management (MBA); human resource management (MS); leadership (MBA); management information systems (MBA); organizational leadership (MA). *Program availability:* Part-time, evening/weekend. *Degree requirements:* For master's, thesis optional. *Entrance requirements:* For master's, GMAT. Additional exam requirements/recommendations for international students: Required—TOEFL (minimum score 550 paper-based; 79 iBT). *Application deadline:* Applications are processed on a rolling basis. Application fee: $40. Electronic applications accepted. *Expenses: Tuition:* Part-time $500 per credit hour. One-time fee: $30. Tuition and fees vary according to program. *Financial support:* Research assistantships with full tuition reimbursements available. Financial award application deadline: 4/15; financial award applicants required to submit FAFSA. *Unit head:* Dr. David Palmer, Dean, 843-863-7025, Fax: 843-863-7922, E-mail: dpalmer@csuniv.edu. *Application contact:* Dr. Darin L. Gerdes, Associate Professor of Management, 843-863-7814, Fax: 843-863-7922, E-mail: dgerdes@csuniv.edu.
Website: http://www.csuniv.edu/business/

Charter College, Program in Business Administration, Vancouver, WA 98683. Offers MBA. *Program availability:* Online learning. *Entrance requirements:* For master's, bachelor's degree in business-related field, official transcripts with minimum GPA of 2.5, three letters of recommendation, current copy of resume or curriculum vitae.

Chatham University, Program in Business Administration, Pittsburgh, PA 15232-2826. Offers business administration (MBA); healthcare management (MBA); sustainability (MBA); women's leadership (MBA). *Program availability:* Part-time, evening/weekend. *Faculty:* 6 part-time/adjunct (2 women). *Students:* 19 full-time (12 women), 36 part-time (20 women); includes 8 minority (4 Black or African American, non-Hispanic/Latino; 3 Asian, non-Hispanic/Latino; 1 Hispanic/Latino), 5 international. Average age 31. 57 applicants, 56% accepted, 24 enrolled. In 2017, 20 master's awarded. *Entrance requirements:* For master's, minimum GPA of 3.0, letters of recommendation. Additional exam requirements/recommendations for international students: Required—TOEFL (minimum score 600 paper-based; 100 iBT), IELTS (minimum score 7), TWE. *Application deadline:* For fall admission, 4/1 for domestic and international students; for spring admission, 11/1 for domestic students, 10/1 for international students. Applications are processed on a rolling basis. Application fee: $45. Electronic applications accepted. Application fee is waived when completed online. *Expenses:* Contact institution. *Financial support:* Applicants required to submit FAFSA. *Unit head:* Dr. Rachel Chung, Director of Business and Entrepreneurship Program, 412-365-2433. *Application contact:* Katie Noel, Assistant Director of Graduate Admission, 412-365-2758, Fax: 412-365-1609, E-mail: gradadmissions@chatham.edu.
Website: http://www.chatham.edu/mba

Christian Brothers University, School of Business, Memphis, TN 38104-5581. Offers accountancy (M Acc); business (MBA); international business (MIB); project management (Certificate); MBA/MIB. *Program availability:* Part-time, evening/weekend. *Entrance requirements:* For master's, GMAT, GRE. Additional exam requirements/recommendations for international students: Required—TOEFL.

The Citadel, The Military College of South Carolina, Citadel Graduate College, Tommy and Victoria Baker School of Business, Charleston, SC 29409. Offers MBA. *Accreditation:* AACSB. *Program availability:* Part-time, evening/weekend, 100% online, blended/hybrid learning. *Entrance requirements:* For master's, GMAT or GRE (5 years old or less), 2 letters of recommendation from professor, supervisor, military official, or someone familiar with applicant's academic or professional work; resume detailing professional work experience. Additional exam requirements/recommendations for international students: Required—TOEFL (minimum score 550 paper-based; 79 iBT). Electronic applications accepted. *Expenses:* Tuition, state resident: part-time $587 per credit hour. Tuition, nonresident: part-time $988 per credit hour. *Required fees:* $90 per term.

City College of the City University of New York, Graduate School, Colin Powell School for Civic and Global Leadership, Department of Economics and Business, New York, NY 10031-9198. Offers economics (MA). *Program availability:* Part-time. *Degree requirements:* For master's, comprehensive exam, proficiency in a foreign language or advanced statistics. *Entrance requirements:* Additional exam requirements/recommendations for international students: Required—TOEFL (minimum score 550 paper-based; 79 iBT). Electronic applications accepted. *Faculty research:* International economics, health, banking.

City University of Seattle, Graduate Division, School of Management, Seattle, WA 98121. Offers accounting (Certificate); change leadership (MBA, Certificate); computer systems (MS); finance (Certificate); financial management (MBA); general management (MBA); general management-Europe (MBA); global marketing (MBA); human resources management (Certificate); individualized study (MBA); information security (MS); information systems (MBA); leadership (MA); marketing (MBA, Certificate); project management (MBA, MS, Certificate); sustainable business (Certificate); technology management (MBA, Certificate). *Program availability:* Part-time, evening/weekend, online learning. *Degree requirements:* For master's, comprehensive exam (for some programs), thesis (for some programs). *Entrance requirements:* For master's, baccalaureate degree or equivalent from an accredited or otherwise recognized institution. Additional exam requirements/recommendations for international students: Required—TOEFL (minimum score 567 paper-based; 87 iBT); Recommended—IELTS. Electronic applications accepted.

Claflin University, Graduate Programs, Orangeburg, SC 29115. Offers biotechnology (MS); business administration (MBA). *Program availability:* Part-time. *Degree requirements:* For master's, comprehensive exam, thesis. *Entrance requirements:* For master's, GRE, GMAT, baccalaureate degree, 3 letters of recommendation, resume, statement of purpose. Additional exam requirements/recommendations for international students: Recommended—TOEFL (minimum score 550 paper-based).

Claremont Graduate University, Graduate Programs, Peter F. Drucker and Masatoshi Ito Graduate School of Management, Claremont, CA 91711-6160. Offers EMBA, MA, MBA, MS, PhD, Certificate, MBA/MA, MBA/PhD, MS/MBA. *Program availability:* Part-time. *Entrance requirements:* For doctorate, GMAT or GRE General Test. Additional exam requirements/recommendations for international students: Required—TOEFL (minimum score 75 iBT). Electronic applications accepted. *Expenses:* Contact institution. *Faculty research:* Strategy and leadership, brand management, cost management and control, organizational transformation, general management.

Claremont Graduate University, Graduate Programs, School of Social Science, Policy and Evaluation, Program in Politics, Economics, and Business, Claremont, CA 91711-6160. Offers MA. *Program availability:* Part-time. *Entrance requirements:* For master's, GRE General Test. Additional exam requirements/recommendations for international students: Required—TOEFL (minimum score 75 iBT). Electronic applications accepted.

Business Administration and Management—General

Clarion University of Pennsylvania, College of Business Administration and Information Sciences, Master of Business Administration Program, Clarion, PA 16214. Offers accounting (MBA); finance (MBA); health care administration (MBA); innovation and entrepreneurship (MBA); non-profit business (MBA). *Accreditation:* AACSB. *Program availability:* Part-time, evening/weekend, 100% online. *Faculty:* 4 full-time (1 woman), 3 part-time/adjunct (0 women). *Students:* 19 full-time (7 women), 66 part-time (34 women); includes 10 minority (6 Black or African American, non-Hispanic/Latino; 1 Asian, non-Hispanic/Latino; 3 Hispanic/Latino), 2 international. Average age 31. 86 applicants, 63% accepted, 21 enrolled. In 2017, 33 master's awarded. *Degree requirements:* For master's, portfolio. *Entrance requirements:* For master's, GMAT, minimum QPA of 2.75. Additional exam requirements/recommendations for international students: Required—TOEFL (minimum score 550 paper-based, 80 iBT) or IELTS (7). *Application deadline:* For fall admission, 8/1 priority date for domestic students, 4/15 priority date for international students; for spring admission, 12/1 priority date for domestic students, 9/15 priority date for international students. Applications are processed on a rolling basis. Application fee: $40. Electronic applications accepted. *Expenses:* $655.05 per credit. *Financial support:* Unspecified assistantships available. Support available to part-time students. Financial award application deadline: 3/1; financial award applicants required to submit FAFSA. *Unit head:* Juanice Vega, Assistant to the Dean, 814-393-2600, Fax: 814-393-1910, E-mail: mba@clarion.edu. *Application contact:* Dana Bearer, Assistant Director, Graduate Programs, 814-393-2337, Fax: 814-393-2722, E-mail: gradstudies@clarion.edu. Website: http://www.clarion.edu/admissions/graduate/index.html

Clark Atlanta University, School of Business Administration, Department of Business Administration, Atlanta, GA 30314. Offers MBA. *Accreditation:* AACSB. *Program availability:* Part-time. *Faculty:* 10 full-time (5 women), 2 part-time/adjunct (both women). *Students:* 36 full-time (22 women), 4 part-time (1 woman); includes 28 minority (27 Black or African American, non-Hispanic/Latino; 1 Hispanic/Latino), 6 international. Average age 26. 50 applicants, 62% accepted, 16 enrolled. In 2017, 31 master's awarded. *Degree requirements:* For master's, thesis (for some programs). *Entrance requirements:* For master's, GMAT. Additional exam requirements/recommendations for international students: Required—TOEFL (minimum score 500 paper-based; 61 iBT). *Application deadline:* For fall admission, 4/1 for domestic and international students; for spring admission, 11/1 for domestic and international students. Applications are processed on a rolling basis. Application fee: $40 ($55 for international students). Electronic applications accepted. *Financial support:* Career-related internships or fieldwork, Federal Work-Study, scholarships/grants, and unspecified assistantships available. Support available to part-time students. Financial award application deadline: 4/30; financial award applicants required to submit FAFSA. *Unit head:* Dr. Raphael Boyd, Chairperson, 404-880-6050, E-mail: rboyd@cau.edu.

Clarke University, Graduate Business Programs, Dubuque, IA 52001-3198. Offers MBA, MOL. *Program availability:* Part-time, evening/weekend, blended/hybrid learning. *Faculty:* 4 full-time (2 women), 3 part-time/adjunct (1 woman). *Students:* 13 full-time (9 women), 26 part-time (16 women); includes 5 minority (2 Black or African American, non-Hispanic/Latino; 1 Asian, non-Hispanic/Latino; 2 Hispanic/Latino), 1 international. Average age 33. 19 applicants, 100% accepted, 13 enrolled. In 2017, 19 master's awarded. *Entrance requirements:* For master's, GMAT if GPA under 3.0, minimum GPA of 2.8, previous undergraduate course work in business, two recommendations, resume, essay, interview. Additional exam requirements/recommendations for international students: Required—TOEFL (minimum score 550 paper-based; 80 iBT), IELTS (minimum score 6.5). *Application deadline:* Applications are processed on a rolling basis. Application fee: $35. Electronic applications accepted. *Expenses:* Contact institution. *Financial support:* Applicants required to submit FAFSA. *Unit head:* Jody Wolfe, Director of Graduate Business Studies, 563-588-8143, E-mail: jody.wolfe@clarke.edu. *Application contact:* Kimberly Roush, Director of Admission, Graduate and Adult Programs, 563-588-6539, Fax: 563-552-7994, E-mail: graduate@clarke.edu. Website: https://www.clarke.edu/academics/#graduate

Clarkson University, David D. Reh School of Business, Master's Program in Business Administration, Potsdam, NY 13699. Offers business fundamentals (Advanced Certificate); global supply chain management (Advanced Certificate); human resource management (Advanced Certificate); management and leadership (Advanced Certificate). *Accreditation:* AACSB. *Program availability:* Part-time, evening/weekend, 100% online, blended/hybrid learning. *Faculty:* 55 full-time (14 women), 38 part-time/adjunct (10 women). *Students:* 92 full-time (31 women), 50 part-time (24 women); includes 20 minority (5 Black or African American, non-Hispanic/Latino; 1 American Indian or Alaska Native, non-Hispanic/Latino; 8 Asian, non-Hispanic/Latino; 5 Hispanic/Latino; 1 Two or more races, non-Hispanic/Latino), 11 international. 174 applicants, 55% accepted, 67 enrolled. In 2017, 1 Advanced Certificate awarded. *Entrance requirements:* Additional exam requirements/recommendations for international students: Required—TOEFL (minimum score 550 paper-based, 80 iBT) or IELTS (6.5). *Application deadline:* Applications are processed on a rolling basis. Application fee: $50. Electronic applications accepted. *Expenses: Tuition:* Full-time $24,210; part-time $1345 per credit hour. Tuition and fees vary according to campus/location and program. *Financial support:* Scholarships/grants available. *Unit head:* Dr. Alan Bowman, Senior Associate Dean of Graduate Business Programs, 518-631-9887, E-mail: abowman@clarkson.edu. *Application contact:* Dan Capogna, Director of Graduate Admissions, 518-631-9910, E-mail: graduate@clarkson.edu. Website: https://www.clarkson.edu/academics/graduate

Clark University, Graduate School, Graduate School of Management, Business Administration Program, Worcester, MA 01610-1477. Offers accounting (MBA); finance (MBA); information management and business analytics (MBA); management (MBA); marketing (MBA); social change (MBA); sustainability (MBA). *Accreditation:* AACSB. *Program availability:* Part-time, evening/weekend. *Students:* 87 full-time (41 women), 41 part-time (26 women); includes 19 minority (10 Black or African American, non-Hispanic/Latino; 4 Asian, non-Hispanic/Latino; 4 Hispanic/Latino; 1 Two or more races, non-Hispanic/Latino), 40 international. Average age 30. 242 applicants, 50% accepted, 54 enrolled. In 2017, 102 master's awarded. *Degree requirements:* For master's, thesis optional. *Entrance requirements:* For master's, GMAT or GRE, 2 references, resume or curriculum vitae, personal statement. Additional exam requirements/recommendations for international students: Required—TOEFL (minimum score 575 paper-based; 90 iBT), IELTS (minimum score 6.5). *Application deadline:* For fall admission, 4/15 priority date for domestic and international students; for spring admission, 12/1 priority date for domestic and international students. Application fee: $75. Electronic applications accepted. *Expenses:* $4,490 tuition per 14-week course, $2,245 per half-unit (7-week course); $40 activity fee (full-time students only); $80 miscellaneous one-time fee; $1,750 student services fee. *Financial support:* Fellowships, research assistantships, teaching assistantships, career-related internships or fieldwork, Federal Work-Study, institutionally sponsored loans, and tuition waivers (partial) available. Support available to part-time students. Financial award application deadline: 5/31. *Faculty research:* Marketing, accounting, human resource management, management information systems, business finance. *Unit head:* Dr. Priscilla Elsass, Dean, 508-793-7543, Fax: 508-793-8822, E-mail: pelsass@clarku.edu. *Application contact:* Yingying Chen, Assistant Director of Graduate Admissions, 508-793-7373, Fax: 508-798-4386, E-mail: graduateadmissions@clarku.edu. Website: http://www.clarku.edu/programs/masters-business-administration

Clark University, Graduate School, Graduate School of Management, Program in Management, Worcester, MA 01610-1477. Offers MSM. *Program availability:* Part-time, evening/weekend. *Students:* 4 part-time (3 women); includes 1 minority (Black or African American, non-Hispanic/Latino). Average age 37. 61 applicants, 36% accepted, 4 enrolled. *Entrance requirements:* For master's, GMAT or GRE, 2 references, resume or curriculum vitae, personal statement. Additional exam requirements/recommendations for international students: Required—TOEFL (minimum score 575 paper-based; 90 iBT), IELTS (minimum score 6.5). *Application deadline:* For fall admission, 4/15 for domestic and international students; for spring admission, 12/1 for domestic and international students. Application fee: $75. Electronic applications accepted. *Expenses:* $4,920 tuition per 14-week course, $2,460 per half-unit (7-week course); $40 activity fee (full-time students only); $80 miscellaneous one-time fee; $1,800 student services fee. *Unit head:* Dr. Priscilla Elsass, Dean, 508-793-8822, Fax: 508-793-8822, E-mail: pelsass@clarku.edu. *Application contact:* Yingying Chen, Assistant Director of Graduate Admissions, 508-793-7373, Fax: 508-798-4386, E-mail: graduateadmissions@clarku.edu. Website: http://www.clarku.edu/programs/masters-management

Clayton State University, School of Graduate Studies, College of Business, Program in Business Administration, Morrow, GA 30260-0285. Offers accounting (MBA); human resource leadership (MBA); international business (MBA); sports and entertainment management (MBA); supply chain management (MBA). *Accreditation:* AACSB. *Program availability:* Part-time, evening/weekend. *Degree requirements:* For master's, thesis. *Entrance requirements:* For master's, GMAT, 3 letters of recommendation; statement of purpose; 2 official transcripts. Additional exam requirements/recommendations for international students: Required—TOEFL (minimum score 550 paper-based; 80 iBT). Electronic applications accepted. *Expenses:* Contact institution.

Cleary University, Online Program in Business Administration, Howell, MI 48843. Offers analytics, technology, and innovation (MBA, Graduate Certificate); financial planning (Graduate Certificate); global leadership (MBA, Graduate Certificate); health care leadership (MBA, Graduate Certificate). *Program availability:* Part-time, evening/weekend, online learning. *Degree requirements:* For master's, thesis. *Entrance requirements:* For master's, bachelor's degree; minimum GPA of 2.5; professional resume indicating minimum of 2 years of management or related experience; undergraduate degree from accredited college or university with at least 18 quarter hours (or 12 semester hours) of accounting study (for MBA in accounting). Additional exam requirements/recommendations for international students: Required—TOEFL (minimum score 550 paper-based; 79 iBT), Michigan English Language Assessment Battery (minimum score 75). Electronic applications accepted.

Clemson University, Graduate School, College of Business, Department of Management, Clemson, SC 29634. Offers business administration (PhD), including management information systems, strategy, entrepreneurship and organizational behavior, supply chain and operations management; management (MS). *Accreditation:* AACSB. *Faculty:* 34 full-time (12 women), 1 part-time/adjunct (0 women). *Students:* 14 full-time (3 women), 1 part-time (0 women), 9 international. Average age 33. 30 applicants, 13% accepted. In 2017, 4 master's, 4 doctorates awarded. Terminal master's awarded for partial completion of doctoral program. *Degree requirements:* For master's, comprehensive exam, thesis optional; for doctorate, comprehensive exam, thesis/dissertation. *Entrance requirements:* For master's and doctorate, GMAT or GRE General Test, unofficial transcripts, two letters of reference, curriculum vitae. Additional exam requirements/recommendations for international students: Required—TOEFL (minimum score 94 iBT), IELTS (minimum score 7), PTE (minimum score 64). *Application deadline:* For fall admission, 1/15 priority date for domestic and international students. Application fee: $80 ($90 for international students). Electronic applications accepted. *Expenses:* $6,564 per semester full-time resident, $12,538 per semester full-time non-resident, $743 per credit hour part-time resident, $1,486 per credit hour part-time non-resident, $1,203 per credit hour online, other fees may apply per session. *Financial support:* In 2017–18, 10 students received support, including 1 fellowship with partial tuition reimbursement available (averaging $1,000 per year), 1 research assistantship with partial tuition reimbursement available (averaging $12,000 per year), 2 teaching assistantships with partial tuition reimbursements available (averaging $18,770 per year); unspecified assistantships also available. Financial award application deadline: 1/15. *Faculty research:* Effective use of information technology in business, manufacturing and service operations strategy, lean operations and quality management, healthcare operations, behavioral market design. *Total annual research expenditures:* $89,179. *Unit head:* Dr. V. Sridharan, Department Chair, 864-656-2624, E-mail: suhas@clemson.edu. *Application contact:* Dr. Janis Miller, Graduate Program Coordinator, 864-656-3757, E-mail: janism@clemson.edu. Website: https://www.clemson.edu/business/departments/management/

Clemson University, Graduate School, College of Business, Master of Business Administration Program, Greenville, SC 29634. Offers business administration (MBA); business analytics (MBA); entrepreneurship and innovation (MBA). *Accreditation:* AACSB. *Program availability:* Part-time, evening/weekend. *Faculty:* 2 full-time (1 woman), 8 part-time/adjunct (1 woman). *Students:* 242 full-time (96 women), 736 part-time (222 women); includes 81 minority (46 Black or African American, non-Hispanic/Latino; 13 Asian, non-Hispanic/Latino; 17 Hispanic/Latino; 1 Native Hawaiian or other Pacific Islander, non-Hispanic/Latino; 4 Two or more races, non-Hispanic/Latino), 35 international. Average age 31. 413 applicants, 82% accepted, 233 enrolled. In 2017, 364 master's awarded. *Entrance requirements:* For master's, GMAT, resume, unofficial transcripts, personal statement, letters of recommendation. Additional exam requirements/recommendations for international students: Required—TOEFL (minimum score 80 iBT), IELTS (minimum score 6.5), PTE (minimum score 54). *Application deadline:* For fall admission, 7/15 for domestic students, 4/15 for international students; for spring admission, 12/1 for domestic students. Applications are processed on a rolling basis. Application fee: $80 ($90 for international students). Electronic applications accepted. *Expenses:* Contact institution. *Unit head:* Dr. Gregory Pickett, Senior Associate Dean, 864-656-3975, E-mail: pgregor@clemson.edu. *Application contact:* Laura Fischman, Assistant Director of Admissions, 864-365-0604, E-mail: ann6@clemson.edu. Website: https://www.clemson.edu/business/departments/mba/

Cleveland State University, College of Graduate Studies, Monte Ahuja College of Business, Doctor of Business Administration Program, Cleveland, OH 44115. Offers information systems (DBA); marketing (DBA). *Accreditation:* AACSB. *Program availability:* Part-time, evening/weekend. *Faculty:* 50 full-time (11 women). *Students:* 3 full-time (2 women), 16 part-time (8 women); includes 6 minority (3 Black or African American, non-Hispanic/Latino; 3 Asian, non-Hispanic/Latino), 2 international. Average age 40. In 2017, 7 doctorates awarded. *Degree requirements:* For doctorate, comprehensive exam, thesis/dissertation, oral dissertation defense. *Entrance requirements:* For doctorate, GMAT, MBA or equivalent. Additional exam requirements/recommendations for international students: Required—TOEFL (minimum score 550 paper-based; 78 iBT). *Application deadline:* For fall admission, 2/1 for domestic and international students. Application fee: $40. Electronic applications accepted. *Financial support:* In 2017–18, 5 research assistantships with full tuition reimbursements (averaging $12,700 per year), 4 teaching assistantships with full tuition reimbursements

(averaging $12,700 per year) were awarded; tuition waivers (full) and unspecified assistantships also available. *Faculty research:* Supply chain management, international business, strategic management, risk analysis, consumer behavior. *Unit head:* Dr. Raj Shekhar G. Javalgi, Director, 216-687-3786, Fax: 216-687-9354, E-mail: r.javalgi@csuohio.edu. *Application contact:* Melinda J. Arnold, Administrative Secretary, 216-687-6952, Fax: 216-687-9257, E-mail: m.arnold@csuohio.edu.
Website: http://www.csuohio.edu/business/academics/mbajuris-doctor

Cleveland State University, College of Graduate Studies, Monte Ahuja College of Business, MBA Programs, Cleveland, OH 44115. Offers AMBA, EMBA, MBA, JD/MBA, MSN/MBA. Programs also offered at Progressive Insurance Corporation, The Cleveland Clinic, and Metro Health Medical Center. *Accreditation:* AACSB. *Program availability:* Part-time, evening/weekend, online learning. *Faculty:* 33 full-time (9 women), 16 part-time/adjunct (2 women). *Students:* 198 full-time (105 women), 333 part-time (146 women); includes 112 minority (60 Black or African American, non-Hispanic/Latino; 28 Asian, non-Hispanic/Latino; 18 Hispanic/Latino; 6 Two or more races, non-Hispanic/Latino), 49 international. Average age 29. 674 applicants, 48% accepted, 126 enrolled. In 2017, 214 master's awarded. *Degree requirements:* For master's, variable foreign language requirement, comprehensive exam (for some programs), thesis (for some programs). *Entrance requirements:* For master's, GMAT or GRE, minimum cumulative GPA of 2.75 from bachelor's degree; resume, statement of purpose and two letters of reference (for health care administration MBA). Additional exam requirements/recommendations for international students: Required—TOEFL (minimum score 550 paper-based; 78 iBT). *Application deadline:* For fall admission, 6/1 priority date for domestic students, 6/1 for international students; for spring admission, 11/1 priority date for domestic students, 11/1 for international students. Applications are processed on a rolling basis. Application fee: $40. Electronic applications accepted. *Financial support:* In 2017–18, 594 students received support, including 45 research assistantships with tuition reimbursements available (averaging $6,960 per year), 1 teaching assistantship with tuition reimbursement available (averaging $7,800 per year); tuition waivers (full) and unspecified assistantships also available. Financial award application deadline: 5/15; financial award applicants required to submit FAFSA. *Faculty research:* Accounting and finance, management and organizational behavior, marketing, computer information systems, international business. *Total annual research expenditures:* $70,000. *Unit head:* Ronald John Mickler, Jr., Acting Assistant Director, Graduate Programs, 216-687-3730, Fax: 216-687-5311, E-mail: cbacsu@csuohio.edu. *Application contact:* Kenneth Dippong, Director, Student Services, 216-523-7545, Fax: 216-687-9354, E-mail: k.dippong@csuohio.edu.
Website: http://www.csuohio.edu/cba/

Coastal Carolina University, E. Craig Wall, Sr. College of Business Administration, Conway, SC 29528-6054. Offers accounting (M Acc); business administration (MBA); business foundations (Certificate); fraud examination (Certificate). *Accreditation:* AACSB. *Program availability:* Part-time, evening/weekend, 100% online, blended/hybrid learning. *Faculty:* 11 full-time (5 women), 2 part-time/adjunct (0 women). *Students:* 58 full-time (31 women), 34 part-time (16 women); includes 26 minority (19 Black or African American, non-Hispanic/Latino; 2 Asian, non-Hispanic/Latino; 1 Hispanic/Latino; 1 Native Hawaiian or other Pacific Islander, non-Hispanic/Latino; 3 Two or more races, non-Hispanic/Latino), 9 international. Average age 27. 103 applicants, 74% accepted, 54 enrolled. In 2017, 68 master's awarded. *Entrance requirements:* For master's, GMAT, official transcripts, 2 letters of recommendation, resume, baccalaureate degree, statement of purpose, minimum cumulative GPA of 3.0 overall from completed undergraduate and graduate coursework; for Certificate, GMAT, official transcripts; 2 letters of recommendation; baccalaureate degree or evidence of receiving a CPA certificate, law degree, or admittance to an accredited law school. Additional exam requirements/recommendations for international students: Required—TOEFL (minimum score 550 paper-based; 79 iBT), IELTS (minimum score 6.5). *Application deadline:* For fall admission, 6/15 priority date for domestic and international students; for spring admission, 11/15 priority date for domestic and international students; for summer admission, 4/15 priority date for domestic and international students. Applications are processed on a rolling basis. Application fee: $45. Electronic applications accepted. *Expenses:* Tuition, state resident: full-time $5184; part-time $576 per credit hour. Tuition, nonresident: full-time $9369; part-time $1041 per credit hour. *Required fees:* $90; $5 per credit hour. *Financial support:* Fellowships, research assistantships, teaching assistantships, and tuition waivers available. Financial award application deadline: 3/1; financial award applicants required to submit FAFSA. *Unit head:* Dr. Mark Mitchell, Associate Dean/Professor/Director of Graduate Programs and Executive Education, 843-349-2392, Fax: 843-349-2455, E-mail: mmitchel@coastal.edu. *Application contact:* Dr. James O. Luken, Associate Provost for Graduate Program/Interim Vice-Dean of the Coastal Environment, 843-349-2235, Fax: 843-349-6444, E-mail: joluken@coastal.edu.
Website: http://www.coastal.edu/business/

Coker College, Graduate Programs, Hartsville, SC 29550. Offers college athletic administration (MS); criminal and social justice policy (MS); curriculum and instructional technology (M Ed); literacy studies (M Ed); management and leadership (MS). *Program availability:* Part-time, 100% online. *Faculty:* 9 full-time (4 women), 3 part-time/adjunct (2 women). *Students:* 77 full-time (47 women), 9 part-time (4 women); includes 21 minority (15 Black or African American, non-Hispanic/Latino; 1 American Indian or Alaska Native, non-Hispanic/Latino; 1 Hispanic/Latino; 4 Two or more races, non-Hispanic/Latino), 1 international. Average age 30. *Degree requirements:* For master's, comprehensive exam, portfolio. *Entrance requirements:* For master's, GRE or GMAT, minimum overall GPA of 2.85 in bachelor's program, official transcripts, resume, three letters of recommendation, teacher licensure. *Application deadline:* Applications are processed on a rolling basis. Application fee: $25. Electronic applications accepted. *Expenses: Tuition:* Full-time $14,424; part-time $601 per credit hour. *Required fees:* $176; $176 per credit hour. Tuition and fees vary according to course load and program. *Financial support:* Unspecified assistantships available. Financial award application deadline: 6/30; financial award applicants required to submit FAFSA. *Application contact:* Lacey Rice-Serafin, Director of Graduate Programs, 843-857-4128, E-mail: lriceserafin@coker.edu.

College of Charleston, Graduate School, School of Business, Program in Business Administration, Charleston, SC 29424-0001. Offers MBA. *Entrance requirements:* For master's, GMAT or GRE, transcripts, recommendations, goal statement, bachelor's degree. Additional exam requirements/recommendations for international students: Required—TOEFL (minimum score 81 iBT), IELTS. Electronic applications accepted.

College of Saint Elizabeth, Department of Business Administration and Management, Morristown, NJ 07960-6989. Offers human resource management (MS); organizational change (MS). *Program availability:* Part-time. *Faculty:* 1 (woman) full-time, 5 part-time/adjunct (3 women). *Students:* 5 full-time (all women), 19 part-time (14 women); includes 8 minority (4 Black or African American, non-Hispanic/Latino; 1 Asian, non-Hispanic/Latino; 2 Hispanic/Latino; 1 Two or more races, non-Hispanic/Latino), 3 international. Average age 37. 11 applicants, 100% accepted, 5 enrolled. In 2017, 5 master's awarded. *Degree requirements:* For master's, thesis. *Entrance requirements:* Additional exam requirements/recommendations for international students: Required—TOEFL (minimum score 550 paper-based; 79 iBT), IELTS (minimum score 6.5). *Application deadline:* For fall admission, 5/1 for international students. Applications are processed on a rolling basis. Application fee: $35. Electronic applications accepted. Application fee is waived when completed online. *Financial support:* Career-related internships or fieldwork, scholarships/grants, tuition waivers (partial), and unspecified assistantships available. Financial award applicants required to submit FAFSA. *Unit head:* Dr. Regina Riccioni, Program Chair and Director, 973-290-4271, E-mail: rriccioni@cse.edu. *Application contact:* Lori J. Fragoso, Director of Graduate and Continuing Studies Admissions, 973-290-4413, Fax: 973-290-4710, E-mail: apply@cse.edu.
Website: http://www.cse.edu/academics/prof-studies/

College of St. Joseph, Graduate Programs, Division of Business, Program in Business Administration, Rutland, VT 05701-3899. Offers MBA. *Program availability:* Part-time, evening/weekend. *Entrance requirements:* For master's, two letters of reference from academic or professional sources; official transcripts of all graduate and undergraduate study; access to computer; computer literacy. Additional exam requirements/recommendations for international students: Required—TOEFL (minimum score 550 paper-based). Electronic applications accepted. *Expenses:* Contact institution.

The College of Saint Rose, Graduate Studies, Huether School of Business, Program in Business Administration, Albany, NY 12203-1419. Offers MBA, JD/MBA. JD/MBA offered jointly with Albany Law School. *Accreditation:* ACBSP. *Program availability:* Part-time, evening/weekend. *Students:* 34 full-time (10 women), 44 part-time (25 women); includes 8 minority (7 Black or African American, non-Hispanic/Latino; 1 Two or more races, non-Hispanic/Latino), 9 international. Average age 26. 48 applicants, 88% accepted, 28 enrolled. In 2017, 46 master's awarded. *Entrance requirements:* For master's, GMAT, graduate degree, or minimum undergraduate GPA of 3.0. Additional exam requirements/recommendations for international students: Required—TOEFL (minimum score 550 paper-based; 80 iBT), IELTS (minimum score 6), PTE (minimum score 56). *Application deadline:* For fall admission, 4/1 priority date for domestic students, 4/1 for international students; for spring admission, 10/15 priority date for domestic students, 10/15 for international students; for summer admission, 3/15 priority date for domestic and international students. Applications are processed on a rolling basis. Application fee: $40. Electronic applications accepted. *Expenses: Tuition:* Full-time $7191; part-time $799 per credit hour. *Required fees:* $924; $462 per credit hour. Tuition and fees vary according to course load. *Financial support:* Career-related internships or fieldwork, scholarships/grants, tuition waivers (partial), and unspecified assistantships available. Support available to part-time students. Financial award application deadline: 4/15. *Unit head:* John F. Dion, Program Coordinator, 518-458-5488, E-mail: dionj@strose.edu. *Application contact:* Cris Murray, Assistant Vice President for Graduate Recruitment and Enrollment, 518-485-3390, Fax: 518-458-5479, E-mail: grad@strose.edu.
Website: https://www.strose.edu/mba/

The College of St. Scholastica, Graduate Studies, Department of Management, Duluth, MN 55811-4199. Offers MA, Certificate. *Program availability:* Part-time, evening/weekend, online learning. *Degree requirements:* For master's, thesis. *Entrance requirements:* Additional exam requirements/recommendations for international students: Required—TOEFL (minimum score 550 paper-based; 79 iBT). Electronic applications accepted. *Expenses:* Contact institution. *Faculty research:* Violence in higher education and workplace, screening and selection procedures in law enforcement, Internet use in criminal justice, stress management in law enforcement.

College of Staten Island of the City University of New York, Graduate Programs, School of Business, Program in Business Management, Staten Island, NY 10314-6600. Offers large scale data analysis (MS); strategic management (MS). *Program availability:* Part-time, evening/weekend. *Faculty:* 2 full-time (0 women), 2 part-time/adjunct (0 women). *Students:* 25. 57 applicants, 35% accepted, 15 enrolled. In 2017, 11 master's awarded. *Degree requirements:* For master's, 30 credit hours, or ten courses at three credits each. *Entrance requirements:* For master's, GMAT or GRE, baccalaureate degree in business or related field; minimum overall GPA of 3.0; letter of intent; two letters of recommendation; 2 courses each in accounting, economics, and quantitative methods; 1 course each in communications, computer fundamentals, management, and marketing. Additional exam requirements/recommendations for international students: Required—TOEFL (minimum score 550 paper-based; 79 iBT), IELTS (minimum score 6.5). *Application deadline:* For fall admission, 6/30 priority date for domestic and international students. Applications are processed on a rolling basis. Application fee: $125. Electronic applications accepted. *Expenses:* Tuition, state resident: full-time $10,450; part-time $440 per credit. Tuition, nonresident: full-time $19,320; part-time $440 per credit. *Required fees:* $181.10 per semester. Tuition and fees vary according to program. *Faculty research:* Knowledge integration, management innovation, organizational decision-making, strategic alliances. *Unit head:* Dr. Heidi Bertels, 718-982-2924, E-mail: heidi.bertels@csi.cuny.edu. *Application contact:* Sasha Spence, Associate Director for Graduate Admissions, 718-982-2019, Fax: 718-982-2500, E-mail: sasha.spence@csi.cuny.edu.
Website: https://www.csi.cuny.edu/sites/default/files/pdf/admissions/grad/pdf/Business%20Management%20Fact%20Sheet.pdf

The College of William and Mary, Raymond A. Mason School of Business, Williamsburg, VA 23185. Offers EMBA, M Acc, MBA, MS, JD/MBA, MBA/MPP. *Accreditation:* AACSB. *Program availability:* Part-time, evening/weekend, 100% online. *Faculty:* 61 full-time (22 women), 13 part-time/adjunct (2 women). *Students:* 458 full-time (171 women), 402 part-time (127 women); includes 210 minority (81 Black or African American, non-Hispanic/Latino; 2 American Indian or Alaska Native, non-Hispanic/Latino; 47 Asian, non-Hispanic/Latino; 50 Hispanic/Latino; 2 Native Hawaiian or other Pacific Islander, non-Hispanic/Latino; 28 Two or more races, non-Hispanic/Latino), 131 international. Average age 29. 1,323 applicants, 56% accepted, 447 enrolled. In 2017, 345 master's awarded. *Degree requirements:* For master's, three international residencies and two international trips (EMBA). *Entrance requirements:* For master's, GMAT or GRE. Additional exam requirements/recommendations for international students: Required—TOEFL (minimum score 600 paper-based; 100 iBT), IELTS (minimum score 6.5), PTE. *Application deadline:* For fall admission, 11/16 for domestic and international students; for winter admission, 1/18 for domestic and international students; for spring admission, 5/16 for domestic and international students; for summer admission, 7/15 for domestic students. Application fee: $100. Electronic applications accepted. *Expenses:* Contact institution. *Financial support:* Scholarships/grants and unspecified assistantships available. Financial award applicants required to submit FAFSA. *Faculty research:* Saving and asset allocation decisions in retirement accounts, design strategy and consumer needs, virtual and networked organizations, healthcare informatics, reporting of non-GAAP metrics in financial disclosure. *Total annual research expenditures:* $57,823. *Unit head:* Dr. Lawrence Pulley, Dean, 757-221-2891, Fax: 757-221-2937, E-mail: larry.pulley@mason.wm.edu. *Application contact:* Amanda K. Barth, Director, Full-time MBA Admissions, 757-221-2944, Fax: 757-221-2958, E-mail: amanda.barth@mason.wm.edu.
Website: http://mason.wm.edu/

Colorado Christian University, Program in Business Administration, Lakewood, CO 80226. Offers corporate training (MBA); information security (MA); leadership (MBA); project management (MBA). *Program availability:* Part-time, evening/weekend, online learning. *Degree requirements:* For master's, thesis optional. *Entrance requirements:* For master's, GMAT, 2 letters of recommendation, resume. Additional exam requirements/recommendations for international students: Required—TOEFL. Electronic applications accepted. *Expenses:* Contact institution.

Business Administration and Management—General

Colorado Mesa University, Department of Business, Grand Junction, CO 81501-3122. Offers MBA. *Program availability:* Part-time, evening/weekend. *Degree requirements:* For master's, thesis or research practicum, written comprehensive exams. *Entrance requirements:* For master's, GMAT, MAT, or GRE, minimum GPA of 3.0 for last 60 undergraduate hours, 2 letters of recommendation. Additional exam requirements/recommendations for international students: Required—TOEFL (minimum score 550 paper-based). Electronic applications accepted. *Expenses:* Contact institution.

Colorado State University, College of Business, College of Business, Fort Collins, CO 80523-1201. Offers MBA, MS, MBA/DVM. *Accreditation:* AACSB. *Program availability:* Part-time, evening/weekend, 100% online, blended/hybrid learning. *Students:* 126 full-time (60 women), 686 part-time (263 women); includes 159 minority (17 Black or African American, non-Hispanic/Latino; 4 American Indian or Alaska Native, non-Hispanic/Latino; 40 Asian, non-Hispanic/Latino; 72 Hispanic/Latino; 1 Native Hawaiian or other Pacific Islander, non-Hispanic/Latino; 25 Two or more races, non-Hispanic/Latino), 44 international. Average age 35. 408 applicants, 80% accepted, 224 enrolled. In 2017, 305 master's awarded. *Entrance requirements:* For master's, GMAT or GRE (for Global Social and Sustainable Enterprise MBA), minimum undergraduate GPA of 3.0, official transcripts, three professional recommendations, statement of purpose, resume, professional work experience. Additional exam requirements/recommendations for international students: Required—TOEFL (minimum score 86 iBT), IELTS (minimum score 6.5), PTE (minimum score 58). *Application deadline:* Applications are processed on a rolling basis. Application fee: $60 ($70 for international students). Electronic applications accepted. *Expenses:* $438 per credit hour (for global social and sustainable enterprise MBA program); $313 per credit hour (for all other MBA programs); $974 per credit hour (for online MBA program). *Financial support:* In 2017–18, 3 fellowships (averaging $7,128 per year) were awarded; scholarships/grants and unspecified assistantships also available. *Total annual research expenditures:* $252,871. *Unit head:* Dr. Sanjay Ramchander, Associate Dean of Academic Programs, 970-491-5027, E-mail: cobgradinfo@colostate.edu. *Application contact:* Graduate Program Admissions, 970-491-5027, E-Mail: gradadmissions@business.colostate.edu.
Website: https://biz.colostate.edu/Academics/Graduate-Programs/Master-of-Business-Administration/Professional-MBA

Colorado State University–Global Campus, Graduate Programs, Greenwood Village, CO 80111. Offers criminal justice and law enforcement administration (MS); education leadership (MS); finance (MS); healthcare administration and management (MS); human resource management (MHRM); information technology management (MITM); international management (MS); management (MS); organizational leadership (MS); professional accounting (MPA); project management (MS); teaching and learning (MS). *Accreditation:* ACBSP. *Program availability:* Online learning.

Colorado State University–Pueblo, Malik and Seeme Hasan School of Business, Pueblo, CO 81001-4901. Offers MBA. *Accreditation:* AACSB. *Program availability:* Part-time, evening/weekend. *Degree requirements:* For master's, thesis optional. *Entrance requirements:* For master's, GMAT, minimum GPA of 3.0. Additional exam requirements/recommendations for international students: Required—TOEFL (minimum score 550 paper-based). *Faculty research:* Total quality management, leadership, small business studies, case research and writing.

Colorado Technical University Aurora, Programs in Business Administration and Management, Aurora, CO 80014. Offers accounting (MBA); business administration (MBA); business administration and management (EMBA); finance (MBA); human resource management (MBA); marketing (MBA); mediation and dispute resolution (MBA); operations management (MBA); project management (MBA); technology management (MBA). *Program availability:* Part-time, evening/weekend. *Degree requirements:* For master's, thesis or alternative. *Entrance requirements:* For master's, minimum undergraduate GPA of 3.0, resume.

Colorado Technical University Colorado Springs, Graduate Studies, Program in Management, Colorado Springs, CO 80907. Offers accounting (MBA, MSA); business administration (MBA); finance (MBA); human resources management (MBA); logistics/supply chain management (MBA); management (DM); marketing (MBA); mediation and dispute resolution (MBA); operations management (MBA); project management (MBA); technology management (MBA). *Accreditation:* ACBSP. *Program availability:* Part-time, evening/weekend, online learning. *Degree requirements:* For master's, thesis or alternative; for doctorate, thesis/dissertation. *Entrance requirements:* For doctorate, minimum graduate GPA of 3.0, 5 years of related work experience. *Faculty research:* Sexual harassment, performance evaluation, critical thinking.

Columbia College, Master of Business Administration Program, Columbia, MO 65216-0002. Offers accounting (MBA); business administration (MBA); human resources (MBA). *Program availability:* Part-time, evening/weekend, 100% online, blended/hybrid learning. *Faculty:* 7 full-time (0 women), 76 part-time/adjunct (26 women). *Students:* 53 full-time (37 women), 389 part-time (241 women); includes 114 minority (60 Black or African American, non-Hispanic/Latino; 2 American Indian or Alaska Native, non-Hispanic/Latino; 7 Asian, non-Hispanic/Latino; 28 Hispanic/Latino; 1 Native Hawaiian or other Pacific Islander, non-Hispanic/Latino; 16 Two or more races, non-Hispanic/Latino), 22 international. Average age 37. 368 applicants, 99% accepted, 111 enrolled. In 2017, 209 master's awarded. *Entrance requirements:* For master's, 3 letters of recommendation, minimum cumulative undergraduate GPA of 3.0, resume, goal statement. Additional exam requirements/recommendations for international students: Required—TOEFL (minimum score 550 paper-based; 79 iBT). *Application deadline:* For fall admission, 8/9 priority date for domestic and international students; for spring admission, 12/27 priority date for domestic and international students. Applications are processed on a rolling basis. Application fee: $55. Electronic applications accepted. *Expenses:* Contact institution. *Financial support:* In 2017–18, 27 students received support. Federal Work-Study and scholarships/grants available. Financial award application deadline: 3/1; financial award applicants required to submit FAFSA. *Unit head:* Dr. Shanda Davis, Dean, School of Business Administration, 573-875-7561, Fax: 573-876-4493, E-mail: sdavis19@ccis.edu. *Application contact:* Stephanie Johnson, Director of Admissions, 573-875-7352, Fax: 573-875-7506, E-mail: sjohnson@ccis.edu. Website: http://www.ccis.edu/graduate/academics/degrees.asp?MBA

Columbia College Chicago, School of Graduate Studies, Business and Entrepreneurship Department, Chicago, IL 60605-1996. Offers arts, entertainment and media management (MAM). *Students:* 40 full-time (30 women); includes 7 minority (4 Black or African American, non-Hispanic/Latino; 1 Asian, non-Hispanic/Latino; 2 Hispanic/Latino), 17 international. 82 applicants, 54% accepted, 20 enrolled. *Entrance requirements:* For master's, self-assessment essay, resume, letters of recommendation, transcripts. Additional exam requirements/recommendations for international students: Required—TOEFL, IELTS. *Application deadline:* For fall admission, 1/15 priority date for domestic and international students. Applications are processed on a rolling basis. Application fee: $55 ($100 for international students). Electronic applications accepted. *Expenses:* Contact institution. *Financial support:* In 2017–18, 16 students received support. Federal Work-Study, scholarships/grants, and unspecified assistantships available. Financial award application deadline: 1/15. *Unit head:* Mary Filice, Chair, 312-369-7882, E-mail: mfilice@colum.edu. *Application contact:* Emily Schmidt, Graduate Admissions, 312-369-7298, E-mail: eschmidt@colum.edu.

Website: https://www.colum.edu/academics/fine-and-performing-arts/business-and-entrepreneurship/index.html

Columbia Southern University, DBA Program, Orange Beach, AL 36561. Offers DBA. *Program availability:* Part-time, evening/weekend, online learning. *Entrance requirements:* For doctorate, 2 years professional experience, relevant academic experience. Electronic applications accepted.

Columbia Southern University, MBA Program, Orange Beach, AL 36561. Offers finance (MBA); health care management (MBA); human resource management (MBA); marketing (MBA); project management (MBA); public administration (MBA). *Program availability:* Part-time, evening/weekend, online learning. *Entrance requirements:* For master's, bachelor's degree from accredited/approved institution. Additional exam requirements/recommendations for international students: Required—TOEFL. Electronic applications accepted.

Columbia University, Graduate School of Business, Berkeley-Columbia Executive MBA Program, New York, NY 10027. Offers EMBA. Offered jointly with University of California, Berkeley. *Program availability:* Part-time. *Entrance requirements:* For master's, GMAT, 2 letters of reference, interview, minimum 5 years of work experience, transcripts, resume, employee support, personal essays. Additional exam requirements/recommendations for international students: Required—TOEFL (minimum score 570 paper-based; 68 iBT). Electronic applications accepted. *Expenses:* Contact institution.

Columbia University, Graduate School of Business, Doctoral Program in Business, New York, NY 10027. Offers business (PhD), including accounting, decision, risk, and operations, finance and economics, management, marketing. *Accreditation:* AACSB. *Degree requirements:* For doctorate, comprehensive exam, thesis/dissertation, major field exam, research paper, thesis proposal. *Entrance requirements:* For doctorate, GMAT or GRE (finance), 2 letters of reference, resume. Additional exam requirements/recommendations for international students: Required—TOEFL. Electronic applications accepted. *Expenses:* Contact institution. *Faculty research:* Human decision making and behavioral research; real estate market and mortgage defaults; financial crisis and corporate governance; international business; security analysis and accounting.

Columbia University, Graduate School of Business, Executive MBA Global Program, New York, NY 10027. Offers EMBA. Program offered jointly with London Business School. *Entrance requirements:* For master's, GMAT, 2 letters of reference, interview, minimum 5 years of work experience, curriculum vitae or resume, employer support. Additional exam requirements/recommendations for international students: Recommended—TOEFL, IELTS. Electronic applications accepted. *Expenses:* Contact institution.

Columbia University, Graduate School of Business, Executive MBA Program, New York, NY 10027. Offers EMBA. *Entrance requirements:* For master's, GMAT, minimum 5 years of work experience, 2 letters of reference, interview, company sponsorship. Additional exam requirements/recommendations for international students: Recommended—TOEFL. Electronic applications accepted. *Expenses:* Contact institution. *Faculty research:* Human decision making and behavioral research; real estate market and mortgage defaults; financial crisis and corporate governance; and security analysis and accounting.

Columbia University, Graduate School of Business, MBA Program, New York, NY 10027. Offers accounting (MBA); decision, risk, and operations (MBA); entrepreneurship (MBA); finance and economics (MBA); healthcare and pharmaceutical management (MBA); human resource management (MBA); international business (MBA); leadership and ethics (MBA); management (MBA); marketing (MBA); media (MBA); private equity (MBA); real estate (MBA); social enterprise (MBA); value investing (MBA); DDS/MBA; JD/MBA; MBA/MIA; MBA/MPH; MBA/MS; MD/MBA. *Entrance requirements:* For master's, GMAT, 2 letters of recommendation. Additional exam requirements/recommendations for international students: Required—TOEFL. Electronic applications accepted. *Expenses:* Contact institution. *Faculty research:* Human decision making and behavioral research; real estate market and mortgage defaults; financial crisis and corporate governance; international business; security analysis and accounting.

Columbus State University, Graduate Studies, Turner College of Business, Columbus, GA 31907-5645. Offers applied computer science (MS), including informational assurance, modeling and simulation, software development; business administration (MBA); cyber security (MS); human resource management (Certificate); information systems security (Certificate); modeling and simulation (Certificate); organizational leadership (MS), including human resource management, leader development, servant leadership; servant leadership (Certificate). *Accreditation:* AACSB. *Program availability:* Part-time, evening/weekend, 100% online, blended/hybrid learning. *Faculty:* 20 full-time (5 women), 1 (woman) part-time/adjunct. *Students:* 70 full-time (20 women), 134 part-time (44 women); includes 76 minority (34 Black or African American, non-Hispanic/Latino; 2 American Indian or Alaska Native, non-Hispanic/Latino; 11 Asian, non-Hispanic/Latino; 20 Hispanic/Latino; 9 Two or more races, non-Hispanic/Latino), 30 international. Average age 30. 218 applicants, 56% accepted, 73 enrolled. In 2017, 110 master's, 1 other advanced degree awarded. *Entrance requirements:* For master's, GMAT, GRE, minimum undergraduate GPA of 2.75, letters of recommendation. Additional exam requirements/recommendations for international students: Required—TOEFL (minimum score 550 paper-based; 79 iBT). *Application deadline:* For fall admission, 6/30 for domestic students, 5/1 for international students; for spring admission, 11/1 for domestic and international students; for summer admission, 3/1 for domestic and international students. Applications are processed on a rolling basis. Application fee: $50. Electronic applications accepted. *Expenses:* Contact institution. *Financial support:* In 2017–18, 20 students received support, including 18 research assistantships (averaging $3,000 per year); Federal Work-Study also available. Financial award application deadline: 5/1; financial award applicants required to submit FAFSA. *Unit head:* Dr. Linda U. Hadley, Dean, 706-507-8153, Fax: 706-568-2184, E-mail: hadley_linda@columbusstate.edu. *Application contact:* Catrina Smith-Edmond, Assistant Director for Graduate and Global Admission, 706-507-8824, Fax: 706-568-5091, E-mail: smithedmond_catrina@columbusstate.edu.
Website: http://turner.columbusstate.edu/

Concordia University, School of Graduate Studies, John Molson School of Business, Montreal, QC H3H 0A1, Canada. Offers administration (M Sc), including finance, management, marketing; business administration (MBA, PhD, Certificate, Diploma); executive business administration (EMBA); supply chain management (MSCM). PhD program offered jointly with HEC Montreal, McGill University, and Université du Québec à Montréal. *Program availability:* Part-time, evening/weekend. *Degree requirements:* For master's, one foreign language, thesis (for some programs), research project; for doctorate, one foreign language, thesis/dissertation; for other advanced degree, one foreign language. *Entrance requirements:* For master's, GMAT, minimum 2 years of work experience (for MBA); letters of recommendation, bachelor's degree from recognized university with minimum GPA of 3.0, curriculum vitae; for doctorate, GMAT (minimum score of 600), official transcripts, curriculum vitae, 3 letters of reference, statement of purpose; for other advanced degree, minimum GPA of 2.7, 2 letters of reference, statement of purpose, resume. Additional exam requirements/recommendations for international students: Required—TOEFL (minimum score 90 iBT), IELTS (minimum score 7). Electronic applications accepted. *Expenses:* Contact institution. *Faculty research:* General business, capital markets, international business.

Concordia University, School of Management, Portland, OR 97211-6099. Offers MBA. *Accreditation:* ACBSP. *Program availability:* Evening/weekend. *Degree requirements:* For master's, thesis optional. *Entrance requirements:* For master's, GMAT or professional portfolio, minimum GPA of 3.0, 2 letters of recommendation, 5 years of work experience, resume. Additional exam requirements/recommendations for international students: Required—TOEFL (minimum score 525 paper-based). *Faculty research:* Leadership characteristics in internships, marketing of MBA programs, entrepreneurship.

Concordia University Chicago, College of Graduate and Innovative Programs, Program in Business Administration, River Forest, IL 60305-1499. Offers MBA.

Concordia University Irvine, School of Business, Irvine, CA 92612-3299. Offers business administration (MBA). *Program availability:* Part-time, evening/weekend. *Degree requirements:* For master's, capstone project or thesis. *Entrance requirements:* For master's, official college transcript(s), signed statement of intent, resume, two references, interview (MBA); passport photo, photocopies of valid U.S. passport, and college diploma (MAIS). Additional exam requirements/recommendations for international students: Required—TOEFL. Electronic applications accepted. *Expenses:* Contact institution.

Concordia University, St. Paul, College of Business and Technology, St. Paul, MN 55104-5494. Offers business administration (MBA), including cyber-security leadership; health care management (MBA); human resource management (MA); information technology (MBA); leadership and management (MA); strategic communication management (MA). *Accreditation:* ACBSP. *Program availability:* Part-time, evening/weekend, 100% online, blended/hybrid learning. *Faculty:* 12 full-time (5 women), 33 part-time/adjunct (16 women). *Students:* 475 full-time (293 women), 35 part-time (17 women); includes 122 minority (57 Black or African American, non-Hispanic/Latino; 1 American Indian or Alaska Native, non-Hispanic/Latino; 34 Asian, non-Hispanic/Latino; 12 Hispanic/Latino; 1 Native Hawaiian or other Pacific Islander, non-Hispanic/Latino; 17 Two or more races, non-Hispanic/Latino), 47 international. Average age 33. 203 applicants, 70% accepted, 136 enrolled. In 2017, 172 master's awarded. *Degree requirements:* For master's, thesis (for some programs). *Entrance requirements:* For master's, official transcripts from regionally-accredited institution stating the conferral of a bachelor's degree with minimum cumulative GPA of 3.0; personal statement; professional resume. Additional exam requirements/recommendations for international students: Recommended—TOEFL (minimum score 547 paper-based; 78 iBT), IELTS (minimum score 6). *Application deadline:* For fall admission, 8/1 for domestic and international students; for spring admission, 12/1 for domestic and international students; for summer admission, 5/1 for domestic and international students. Applications are processed on a rolling basis. Application fee: $0. Electronic applications accepted. *Expenses:* $625 per credit (for MBA); $475 per credit (for MA). *Financial support:* In 2017–18, 292 students received support. Scholarships/grants and unspecified assistantships available. Financial award applicants required to submit FAFSA. *Faculty research:* Alternative dispute resolution, franchising, entrepreneurship, applied business ethics, strategic leadership development. *Unit head:* Dr. Kevin Hall, Dean, 651-603-6165, Fax: 651-641-8807, E-mail: khall@csp.edu. *Application contact:* Amber Faletti, Director of Enrollment Management, 651-641-8838, Fax: 651-603-6320, E-mail: faletti@csp.edu.

Concordia University Wisconsin, Graduate Programs, School of Business Administration, Mequon, WI 53097-2402. Offers MBA, MS.

Copenhagen Business School, Graduate Programs, Copenhagen, Denmark. Offers business administration (Exec MBA, MBA, PhD); business administration and information systems (M Sc); business, language and culture (M Sc); economics and business administration (M Sc); health management (MHM); international business and politics (M Sc); public administration (MPA); shipping and logistics (Exec MBA); technology, market and organization (MBA).

Corban University, Graduate School, The Corban MBA, Salem, OR 97301-9392. Offers management (MBA); non-profit management (MBA). *Program availability:* Online learning.

Cornell University, Graduate School, Graduate Field of Management, Ithaca, NY 14853. Offers accounting (PhD); finance (PhD); marketing (PhD); organizational behavior (PhD); production and operations management (PhD). *Accreditation:* AACSB. *Degree requirements:* For doctorate, comprehensive exam, thesis/dissertation. *Entrance requirements:* For doctorate, GMAT or GRE General Test. Additional exam requirements/recommendations for international students: Required—TOEFL (minimum score 600 paper-based; 77 iBT). Electronic applications accepted. *Expenses:* Contact institution. *Faculty research:* Operations and manufacturing.

Cornell University, Samuel Curtis Johnson Graduate School of Management, Ithaca, NY 14853. Offers business administration (Exec MBA); management (MBA, PhD); management - accounting (MPS); JD/MBA; M Eng/MBA; MBA/MD; MBA/MHA; MBA/MILR; MBA/MPS. *Accreditation:* AACSB. *Faculty:* 65 full-time (17 women). *Students:* 573 full-time (165 women); includes 72 minority (11 Black or African American, non-Hispanic/Latino; 1 American Indian or Alaska Native, non-Hispanic/Latino; 36 Asian, non-Hispanic/Latino; 16 Hispanic/Latino; 8 Two or more races, non-Hispanic/Latino), 189 international. Average age 28. 1,653 applicants, 30% accepted, 277 enrolled. In 2017, 283 master's awarded. *Entrance requirements:* For master's, GMAT or GRE, resume, two essays, two recommendations. Additional exam requirements/recommendations for international students: Required—TOEFL. *Application deadline:* For fall admission, 10/5 for domestic and international students; for winter admission, 11/15 for domestic and international students; for spring admission, 1/10 for domestic and international students; for summer admission, 4/5 for domestic and international students. Application fee: $200. Electronic applications accepted. *Expenses:* $66,894 per year. *Financial support:* Fellowships, institutionally sponsored loans, and scholarships/grants available. Financial award applicants required to submit FAFSA. *Faculty research:* Wholesale prices and revenue sharing contracts in markets with imperfect competition; differential access to information among traders in financial markets and how it impacts price efficiency; how corporate governance mechanisms matter for corporate financial policy choices and performance outcomes; conflict resolution in teams by conflict type, conflict management strategies, and team outcomes; information and incentive problems in operations and supply-chain management. *Unit head:* Dr. Mark Nelson, Dean, 607-255-6418, E-mail: dean@johnson.cornell.edu. *Application contact:* Admissions Office, 800-847-2082, Fax: 607-255-0065, E-mail: mba@johnson.cornell.edu.
Website: http://www.johnson.cornell.edu

Cornerstone University, Graduate Programs, Grand Rapids, MI 49525-5897. Offers business administration (MBA); education (MA Ed); management (MSM); teaching English to speakers of other languages (MA, Graduate Certificate). Programs also offered at Holland, Kalamazoo, and Troy, MI campuses. *Program availability:* Part-time, online learning. *Degree requirements:* For master's, comprehensive exam (for some programs), thesis (for some programs). *Entrance requirements:* For master's, minimum GPA of 2.5, 2 letters of reference. Additional exam requirements/recommendations for international students: Required—TOEFL (minimum score 575 paper-based). Electronic applications accepted.

Creighton University, Graduate School, Heider College of Business, Omaha, NE 68178-0001. Offers accounting (MAC); business administration (MBA, DBA); business intelligence and analytics (MS); finance (M Fin); investment management and financial analysis (MIMFA); JD/MBA; MBA/MIMFA; MD/MBA; Pharm D/MBA. *Accreditation:* AACSB. *Program availability:* Part-time, evening/weekend, 100% online, blended/hybrid learning. *Faculty:* 33 full-time (10 women), 22 part-time/adjunct (3 women). *Students:* 60 full-time (24 women), 308 part-time (95 women); includes 31 minority (14 Black or African American, non-Hispanic/Latino; 1 American Indian or Alaska Native, non-Hispanic/Latino; 9 Asian, non-Hispanic/Latino; 3 Hispanic/Latino; 2 Native Hawaiian or other Pacific Islander, non-Hispanic/Latino; 2 Two or more races, non-Hispanic/Latino), 28 international. Average age 32. 253 applicants, 74% accepted, 123 enrolled. In 2017, 139 master's awarded. *Degree requirements:* For master's, thesis optional; for doctorate, thesis/dissertation optional. *Entrance requirements:* For master's, GMAT, resume, 2 letters of recommendation. Additional exam requirements/recommendations for international students: Required—TOEFL (minimum score 90 iBT). *Application deadline:* For fall admission, 7/1 priority date for domestic students, 3/1 for international students; for winter admission, 10/1 priority date for domestic students, 7/1 for international students; for spring admission, 4/1 priority date for domestic students, 10/1 for international students; for summer admission, 5/1 for domestic and international students. Applications are processed on a rolling basis. Application fee: $50. Electronic applications accepted. *Expenses:* Contact institution. *Financial support:* In 2017–18, 10 fellowships with partial tuition reimbursements (averaging $8,448 per year) were awarded; career-related internships or fieldwork, tuition waivers (partial), and unspecified assistantships also available. Financial award application deadline: 3/1. *Faculty research:* Small business issues, economics, business analytics. *Unit head:* Dr. Deborah Wells, Associate Dean for Graduate Programs, 402-280-2841, E-mail: deborahwells@creighton.edu. *Application contact:* Chris Karasek, Assistant Dean, 402-280-2829, Fax: 402-280-2172, E-mail: chriskarasek@creighton.edu.
Website: http://business.creighton.edu

Culver-Stockton College, MBA Program, Canton, MO 63435-1299. Offers accounting and finance (MBA).

Cumberland University, Program in Business Administration, Lebanon, TN 37087. Offers MBA. *Accreditation:* ACBSP. *Program availability:* Part-time, evening/weekend. *Degree requirements:* For master's, comprehensive exam. *Entrance requirements:* For master's, GMAT or GRE General Test, 3 letters of recommendation. Additional exam requirements/recommendations for international students: Required—TOEFL (minimum score 500 paper-based). *Expenses:* Contact institution.

Curry College, Graduate Studies, Program in Business Administration, Milton, MA 02186-9984. Offers business administration (MBA); finance (Certificate). *Program availability:* Part-time, evening/weekend. *Degree requirements:* For master's, capstone applied project. *Entrance requirements:* For master's, resume, recommendations, interview, written statement. Additional exam requirements/recommendations for international students: Required—TOEFL (minimum score 550 paper-based; 80 iBT). *Expenses:* Contact institution.

Daemen College, Program in Executive Leadership and Change, Amherst, NY 14226-3592. Offers business (MS); health professions (MS); not-for-profit organizations (MS). *Program availability:* Part-time, evening/weekend. *Degree requirements:* For master's, thesis, cohort learning sequence (2 years for weekend cohort; 3 years for weeknight cohort). *Entrance requirements:* For master's, 2 letters of recommendation, interview, goal statement, official transcripts, resume. Additional exam requirements/recommendations for international students: Required—TOEFL (minimum score 500 paper-based; 63 iBT), IELTS (minimum score 5.5). Electronic applications accepted.

Dakota State University, College of Business and Information Systems, Madison, SD 57042-1799. Offers analytics (MSA); business analytics (Graduate Certificate); general management (MBA); health informatics (MSHI); information systems (MSIS, D Sc IS); information technology (Graduate Certificate). *Accreditation:* ACBSP. *Program availability:* Part-time, evening/weekend, 100% online, blended/hybrid learning. *Faculty:* 22 full-time (6 women), 1 (woman) part-time/adjunct. *Students:* 37 full-time (9 women), 168 part-time (52 women); includes 60 minority (29 Black or African American, non-Hispanic/Latino; 3 American Indian or Alaska Native, non-Hispanic/Latino; 15 Asian, non-Hispanic/Latino; 10 Hispanic/Latino; 1 Native Hawaiian or other Pacific Islander, non-Hispanic/Latino; 2 Two or more races, non-Hispanic/Latino), 40 international. Average age 38. 179 applicants, 57% accepted, 59 enrolled. In 2017, 49 master's, 8 doctorates, 5 other advanced degrees awarded. *Degree requirements:* For master's, comprehensive exam, thesis optional, integrative project; for doctorate, comprehensive exam, thesis/dissertation, portfolio. *Entrance requirements:* For master's, GRE General Test, demonstration of information systems skills, minimum GPA of 2.7; for doctorate, GRE General Test, demonstration of information systems skills; for Graduate Certificate, GMAT. Additional exam requirements/recommendations for international students: Required—TOEFL (minimum score 550 paper-based, 76 iBT) or IELTS (6.0). *Application deadline:* For fall admission, 6/15 for domestic students, 4/15 priority date for international students; for spring admission, 11/15 for domestic students, 10/15 priority date for international students; for summer admission, 4/15 for domestic students. Applications are processed on a rolling basis. Application fee: $35. Electronic applications accepted. *Expenses:* Tuition, state resident: full-time $5749. Tuition, nonresident: full-time $10,733. *Required fees:* $715. Tuition and fees vary according to campus/location and reciprocity agreements. *Financial support:* Research assistantships with partial tuition reimbursements, teaching assistantships with partial tuition reimbursements, and unspecified assistantships available. Financial award applicants required to submit FAFSA. *Faculty research:* Data mining and analytics, biometrics and information assurance, decision support systems, health informatics, STEM education for K-12 teachers/students and underrepresented populations. *Unit head:* Dr. Dorine Bennett, Dean of College of Business and Information Systems, 605-256-5165, E-mail: dorine.bennett@dsu.edu. *Application contact:* Erin Blankespoor, Senior Secretary, Office of Graduate Studies and Research, 605-256-5799, E-mail: erin.blankespoor@dsu.edu.
Website: http://dsu.edu/academics/colleges/college-of-business-and-information-systems

Dalhousie University, Faculty of Management, Centre for Advanced Management Education, Halifax, NS B3H 3J5, Canada. Offers financial services (MBA); information management (MIM); management (MPA); natural resources (MBA). *Program availability:* Part-time, online learning. *Entrance requirements:* For master's, GMAT, minimum GPA of 3.0, resume. Additional exam requirements/recommendations for international students: Required—TOEFL, IELTS, CANTEST, CAEL, or Michigan English Language Assessment Battery. Electronic applications accepted.

Dalhousie University, Faculty of Management, Rowe School of Business, Halifax, NS B3H 3J5, Canada. Offers business administration (MBA); financial services (MBA); LL B/MBA; MBA; MBA/MLIS. *Program availability:* Part-time. *Entrance requirements:* For master's, GMAT, letter of non-financial guarantee for non-Canadian students, resume, Corporate Residency Preference Form. Additional exam requirements/recommendations for international students: Required—TOEFL, IELTS, CANTEST, CAEL, or Michigan English Language Assessment Battery. Electronic applications accepted. *Faculty research:* International business, quantitative methods, operations research, MIS, marketing, finance.

Business Administration and Management—General

Dalhousie University, Faculty of Management, School of Public Administration, Halifax, NS B3H 3J5, Canada. Offers management (MPA); public administration (MPA, GDPA); LL B/MPA; MLIS/MPA. *Program availability:* Part-time. *Entrance requirements:* For master's, GMAT. Additional exam requirements/recommendations for international students: Required—TOEFL, IELTS, CANTEST, CAEL, or Michigan English Language Assessment Battery. Electronic applications accepted. *Expenses:* Contact institution. *Faculty research:* Municipal management, policy and program management, environmental policy, economic and social policy, business and government.

Dallas Baptist University, College of Business, Management Program, Dallas, TX 75211-9299. Offers conflict resolution management (MA); general management (MA, MS); health care management (MA); human resource management (MA); organizational communication (MA); performance management (MA); professional sales and management optimization (MA). *Program availability:* Part-time, evening/weekend, online learning. *Application deadline:* Applications are processed on a rolling basis. Application fee: $25. Electronic applications accepted. Application fee is waived when completed online. *Expenses: Tuition:* Full-time $16,308; part-time $906 per credit hour. *Required fees:* $900; $450 per semester. Tuition and fees vary according to course load and degree level. *Unit head:* Dr. Sandra Reid, Chair, Graduate School of Business, 214-333-6860, E-mail: sandra@dbu.edu. *Application contact:* Richard Nassar, Director, 214-333-6801, E-mail: richardn@dbu.edu.
Website: http://www.dbu.edu/gsb/ma-in-management

Dallas Baptist University, College of Business, Master of Business Administration Program, Dallas, TX 75211-9299. Offers accounting (MBA); business communication (MBA); conflict resolution management (MBA); entrepreneurship (MBA); finance (MBA); health care management (MBA); international business (MBA); leading the non-profit organization (MBA); management (MBA); management information systems (MBA); marketing (MBA); project management (MBA); technology and engineering management (MBA). *Accreditation:* ACBSP. *Program availability:* Part-time, evening/weekend, 100% online, blended/hybrid learning. *Application deadline:* Applications are processed on a rolling basis. Application fee: $25. Electronic applications accepted. Application fee is waived when completed online. *Expenses: Tuition:* Full-time $16,308; part-time $906 per credit hour. *Required fees:* $900; $450 per semester. Tuition and fees vary according to course load and degree level. *Unit head:* Dr. Sandra Reid, Chair of Graduate Business Programs, 214-333-5280, E-mail: sandra@dbu.edu. *Application contact:* Bobby Soto, Director of Admissions, 214-333-5242, E-mail: graduate@dbu.edu.
Website: http://www.dbu.edu/gsb/mba

Dallas Baptist University, Gary Cook School of Leadership, Program in Leadership Studies, Dallas, TX 75211-9299. Offers leadership studies (PhD), including business, general leadership, higher education, ministry. *Program availability:* Part-time. *Degree requirements:* For doctorate, thesis/dissertation. *Application deadline:* Applications are processed on a rolling basis. Application fee: $25. Electronic applications accepted. Application fee is waived when completed online. *Expenses: Tuition:* Full-time $16,308; part-time $906 per credit hour. *Required fees:* $900; $450 per semester. Tuition and fees vary according to course load and degree level. *Unit head:* Dr. Jack Goodyear, Director, 214-333-5595, Fax: 214-333-6809, E-mail: jackg@dbu.edu. *Application contact:* Dr. Mary Nelson, Program Director, 214-333-5396, E-mail: maryn@dbu.edu.
Website: http://www4.dbu.edu/leadership/phdleadership

Dallas Baptist University, Professional Development Program, Dallas, TX 75211-9299. Offers accounting (MA); church leadership (MA); communication (MA); counseling (MA); criminal justice (MA); English as a second language (MA); finance (MA); higher education (MA); leadership studies (MA); management (MA). *Program availability:* Part-time, evening/weekend. *Application deadline:* Applications are processed on a rolling basis. Application fee: $25. Electronic applications accepted. Application fee is waived when completed online. *Expenses: Tuition:* Full-time $16,308; part-time $906 per credit hour. *Required fees:* $900; $450 per semester. Tuition and fees vary according to course load and degree level. *Unit head:* Jared Ingram, Program Director, 214-333-5584, E-mail: jaredi@dbu.edu. *Application contact:* Bobby Soto, Director of Admissions, 214-333-5242, E-mail: bobby@dbu.edu.
Website: http://www3.dbu.edu/graduate/mapd.asp

Dartmouth College, Tuck School of Business at Dartmouth, Hanover, NH 03755-9000. Offers MBA. *Accreditation:* AACSB. *Faculty:* 53 full-time (11 women). *Students:* 582 full-time (259 women); includes 118 minority (27 Black or African American, non-Hispanic/Latino; 1 American Indian or Alaska Native, non-Hispanic/Latino; 52 Asian, non-Hispanic/Latino; 30 Hispanic/Latino; 1 Native Hawaiian or other Pacific Islander, non-Hispanic/Latino; 7 Two or more races, non-Hispanic/Latino), 172 international. Average age 28. 2,610 applicants, 23% accepted, 293 enrolled. In 2017, 282 master's awarded. *Entrance requirements:* For master's, GMAT or GRE, 2 letters of recommendation, 2 essays, resume/curriculum vitae. Additional exam requirements/recommendations for international students: Required—TOEFL. *Application deadline:* For fall admission, 10/1 for domestic and international students; for winter admission, 1/1 for domestic and international students; for spring admission, 4/1 for domestic and international students. Application fee: $250. Electronic applications accepted. *Financial support:* Institutionally sponsored loans and scholarships/grants available. Financial award application deadline: 4/1; financial award applicants required to submit FAFSA. *Faculty research:* Global production sourcing, customer waitlist management, origin of great strategies, effects of shopping in warehouse club stores, impact of bank credit on productivity. *Unit head:* Matthew J. Slaughter, Dean, 603-646-2460, E-mail: tuck.public.relations@tuck.dartmouth.edu. *Application contact:* Luke Anthony Pena, Executive Director of Admissions and Financial Aid, 603-646-3162, Fax: 603-646-1441, E-mail: tuck.admissions@tuck.dartmouth.edu.
Website: http://www.tuck.dartmouth.edu

Davenport University, Sneden Graduate School, Grand Rapids, MI 49512. Offers accounting (MBA); business administration (EMBA); finance (MBA); health care management (MBA); human resources (MBA); information assurance (MS); public health (MPH); strategic management (MBA). *Program availability:* Evening/weekend. *Entrance requirements:* For master's, GMAT, minimum undergraduate GPA of 2.75. Additional exam requirements/recommendations for international students: Required—TOEFL. Electronic applications accepted. *Faculty research:* Leadership, management, marketing, organizational culture.

Defiance College, Program in Business Administration, Defiance, OH 43512-1610. Offers leadership (MBA). *Program availability:* Part-time, evening/weekend. *Degree requirements:* For master's, thesis. *Entrance requirements:* For master's, minimum GPA of 2.75. Additional exam requirements/recommendations for international students: Recommended—TOEFL. *Application deadline:* For fall admission, 8/1 for domestic and international students. Applications are processed on a rolling basis. Application fee: $25. Electronic applications accepted. *Unit head:* William Sholl, Assistant Professor, 419-783-2441, Fax: 419-784-0426, E-mail: wsholl@defiance.edu. *Application contact:* William Sholl, Assistant Professor, 419-783-2441, Fax: 419-784-0426, E-mail: wsholl@defiance.edu.
Website: http://www.defiance.edu/graduate-programs/mba-home.html

Delaware State University, Graduate Programs, College of Business, Program in Business Administration, Dover, DE 19901-2277. Offers MBA. *Accreditation:* AACSB. *Program availability:* Part-time, evening/weekend. *Degree requirements:* For master's, exit exam. *Entrance requirements:* For master's, GMAT (minimum score 400), minimum GPA of 3.0 in major, 2.75 overall. Additional exam requirements/recommendations for international students: Required—TOEFL (minimum score 550 paper-based). Electronic applications accepted. *Faculty research:* Managerial economics, strategic management, qualitative effort, finance.

Delaware Valley University, MBA Program, Doylestown, PA 18901-2697. Offers accounting (MBA); entrepreneurship (MBA); finance (MBA); food and agribusiness (MBA); general business (MBA); global executive leadership (MBA); human resource management (MBA); supply chain management (MBA). *Program availability:* Part-time, evening/weekend, online learning. *Entrance requirements:* For master's, minimum undergraduate GPA of 3.0. Electronic applications accepted. *Expenses:* Contact institution.

Delta State University, Graduate Programs, College of Business, Division of Management, Marketing, and Business Administration, Cleveland, MS 38733-0001. Offers business administration (MBA). *Accreditation:* ACBSP. *Program availability:* Part-time, evening/weekend. *Entrance requirements:* For master's, GMAT.

DePaul University, Kellstadt Graduate School of Business, Chicago, IL 60604. Offers accountancy (MBA, MSA); applied economics (MBA); audit and advisory services (MS); business administration (DBA); business analytics (MS); business strategy and decision-making (MBA); computational finance (MS); economics and policy analysis (MS); enterprise risk management (MS); entrepreneurship (MBA, MS); finance (MBA, MS); general business (MBA); hospitality leadership (MBA); hospitality leadership and operational performance (MS); human resources (MS); international business (MBA); management (MBA, MS); management information systems (MBA); marketing (MBA, MS); marketing analysis (MS); marketing strategy and planning (MBA); real estate (MS); real estate finance and investment (MBA); strategy, execution and valuation (MBA); supply chain management (MS); sustainable management (MS); taxation (MS); JD/MBA. *Accreditation:* AACSB. *Program availability:* Part-time, evening/weekend, online learning. *Entrance requirements:* For master's, GMAT/GRE, 2 letters of recommendation, resume, essay, official transcripts. Additional exam requirements/recommendations for international students: Required—TOEFL (minimum score 550 paper-based; 80 iBT). *Application deadline:* For fall admission, 7/1 for domestic students, 6/1 for international students; for winter admission, 10/1 for domestic students, 9/1 for international students; for spring admission, 2/1 for domestic students, 1/1 for international students. Applications are processed on a rolling basis. Application fee: $60. Electronic applications accepted. *Expenses:* Contact institution. *Financial support:* Application deadline: 4/1; applicants required to submit FAFSA. *Unit head:* Christa Hinton, Assistant Dean and Director, 312-362-8810, Fax: 312-362-6677, E-mail: chinton@depaul.edu. *Application contact:* Garry Cooke, Director of Recruitment and Admissions, 312-362-8810, Fax: 312-362-6677, E-mail: kgsb@depaul.edu.
Website: http://kellstadt.depaul.edu

DeSales University, Division of Business, Center Valley, PA 18034-9568. Offers accounting (MBA); computer information systems (MBA); finance (MBA); health care systems management (MBA); human resources management (MBA); management (MBA); marketing (MBA); project management (MBA); self-design (MBA); supply chain management (MBA); DNP/MBA; MSN/MBA. *Accreditation:* ACBSP. *Program availability:* Part-time, evening/weekend, 100% online, blended/hybrid learning. *Faculty:* 9 full-time (3 women), 32 part-time/adjunct (8 women). *Students:* 78 full-time (44 women), 323 part-time (164 women); includes 71 minority (22 Black or African American, non-Hispanic/Latino; 17 Asian, non-Hispanic/Latino; 24 Hispanic/Latino; 8 Two or more races, non-Hispanic/Latino), 1 international. Average age 34. 213 applicants, 40% accepted, 64 enrolled. In 2017, 123 master's awarded. *Entrance requirements:* For master's, GMAT (waived if undergraduate GPA is 3.0 or better), minimum GPA of 3.0 in undergraduate work, literacy in basic software, background or interest in the field of study, personal statement, 2 years of work experience. Additional exam requirements/recommendations for international students: Required—TOEFL. *Application deadline:* Applications are processed on a rolling basis. Application fee: $50. Electronic applications accepted. *Expenses:* Contact institution. *Financial support:* Applicants required to submit FAFSA. *Faculty research:* Quality improvement, executive development, productivity, cross-cultural managerial differences, leadership. *Unit head:* Dr. David M. Gilfoil, Director, MBA Program, 610-282-1100 Ext. 1828, Fax: 610-282-2869, E-mail: david.gilfoil@desales.edu. *Application contact:* Julia Ferraro, Director of Graduate Admissions, 610-282-1100 Ext. 1768, E-mail: gradadmissions@desales.edu.

DeVry College of New York–Midtown Manhattan Campus, Keller Graduate School of Management, New York, NY 10016. Offers M Acc, MAFM, MBA, MHRM, MISM, MNCM, MPA, MPM.

DeVry University–Alpharetta Campus, Keller Graduate School of Management, Alpharetta, GA 30009. Offers MAFM, MBA, MHRM, MISM, MNCM, MPA, MPM. *Accreditation:* ACBSP.

DeVry University–Arlington Campus, Keller Graduate School of Management, Arlington, VA 22202. Offers M Acc, MAFM, MBA, MHRM, MISM, MPM.

DeVry University–Charlotte Campus, Keller Graduate School of Management, Charlotte, NC 28273. Offers MAFM, MBA, MHRM, MISM, MNCM, MPA, MPM. *Accreditation:* ACBSP.

DeVry University–Chesapeake Campus, Keller Graduate School of Management, Chesapeake, VA 23320. Offers MAFM, MBA, MHRM, MISM, MNCM, MPA, MPM.

DeVry University–Chicago Campus, Keller Graduate School of Management, Chicago, IL 60618. Offers M Acc, MAFM, MBA, MHRM, MISM, MPM. *Accreditation:* ACBSP.

DeVry University–Chicago Loop Campus, Keller Graduate School of Management, Chicago, IL 60606. Offers MAFM, MBA, MHRM, MISM, MNCM, MPM. *Accreditation:* ACBSP.

DeVry University–Cincinnati Campus, Keller Graduate School of Management, Cincinnati, OH 45249. Offers MAFM, MBA, MHRM, MISM, MNCM, MPA, MPM. *Accreditation:* ACBSP.

DeVry University–Columbus Campus, Keller Graduate School of Management, Columbus, OH 43209. Offers MAFM, MBA, MHRM, MISM, MPM. *Accreditation:* ACBSP.

DeVry University–Decatur Campus, Keller Graduate School of Management, Decatur, GA 30030. Offers MAFM, MBA, MHRM, MISM, MNCM, MPA, MPM, MSA. *Accreditation:* ACBSP.

DeVry University–Folsom Campus, Graduate Programs, Folsom, CA 95630. Offers accounting (M Acc); accounting and financial management (MAFM); business administration (MBA); curriculum leadership (M Ed); educational leadership (M Ed); educational technology (M Ed); higher education leadership (M Ed); human resource management (MHRM); information systems management (MISM); network and communications management (MNCM); project management (MPM); public administration (MPA).

DeVry University–Fremont Campus, Keller Graduate School of Management, Fremont, CA 94555. Offers MAFM, MBA, MHRM, MISM, MNCM, MPA, MPM. *Accreditation:* ACBSP.

DeVry University–Ft. Washington Campus, Keller Graduate School of Management, Fort Washington, PA 19034. Offers MAFM, MBA, MHRM, MISM, MNCM, MPA, MPM. *Accreditation:* ACBSP.

DeVry University–Henderson Campus, Keller Graduate School of Management, Henderson, NV 89074. Offers MAFM, MBA, MHRM, MISM, MNCM, MPA, MPM.

DeVry University–Irving Campus, Keller Graduate School of Management, Irving, TX 75063. Offers M Acc, MAFM, MBA, MHRM, MISM, MPM.

DeVry University–Jacksonville Campus, Keller Graduate School of Management, Jacksonville, FL 32256. Offers MAFM, MBA, MHRM, MISM, MNCM, MPA, MPM. *Accreditation:* ACBSP.

DeVry University–Long Beach Campus, Keller Graduate School of Management, Long Beach, CA 90806. Offers MAFM, MBA, MHRM, MISM, MNCM, MPA, MPM. *Accreditation:* ACBSP.

DeVry University–Miramar Campus, Keller Graduate School of Management, Miramar, FL 33027. Offers MAFM, MBA, MHRM, MISM, MPM, MSA.

DeVry University–Morrisville Campus, Keller Graduate School of Management, Morrisville, NC 27560. Offers MBA, MHRM, MISM, MNCM, MPA, MPM.

DeVry University–Nashville Campus, Keller Graduate School of Management, Nashville, TN 37211. Offers MAFM, MBA, MHRM, MISM, MNCM, MPA, MPM. *Accreditation:* ACBSP.

DeVry University–North Brunswick Campus, Keller Graduate School of Management, North Brunswick, NJ 08902. Offers MBA. *Accreditation:* ACBSP.

DeVry University Online, Keller Graduate School of Management, Addison, IL 60101. Offers M Acc, MAFM, MBA, MHRM, MISM, MNCM, MPA, MPM.

DeVry University–Orlando Campus, Keller Graduate School of Management, Orlando, FL 32819. Offers MAFM, MBA, MHRM, MISM, MPA, MPM, MSA.

DeVry University–Phoenix Campus, Keller Graduate School of Management, Phoenix, AZ 85021. Offers MAFM, MBA, MISM, MPM, MSA.

DeVry University–Pomona Campus, Keller Graduate School of Management, Pomona, CA 91768. Offers MAFM, MBA, MHRM, MISM, MPM, MSA.

DeVry University–San Diego Campus, Keller Graduate School of Management, San Diego, CA 92108. Offers MAFM, MBA, MHRM, MISM, MNCM, MPA, MPM, Graduate Certificate. *Accreditation:* ACBSP.

DeVry University–Seven Hills Campus, Keller Graduate School of Management, Seven Hills, OH 44131. Offers MAFM, MBA, MHRM, MISM, MNCM, MPA, MPM, Graduate Certificate.

DeVry University–Tinley Park Campus, Keller Graduate School of Management, Tinley Park, IL 60477. Offers MAFM, MBA, MHRM, MISM, MNCM, MPA, MPM. *Accreditation:* ACBSP.

Doane University, Program in Management, Crete, NE 68333-2430. Offers MA, MBA. *Program availability:* Part-time, evening/weekend. *Faculty:* 3 full-time (2 women), 21 part-time/adjunct (9 women). *Students:* 109 full-time (68 women), 53 part-time (29 women); includes 26 minority (13 Black or African American, non-Hispanic/Latino; 1 American Indian or Alaska Native, non-Hispanic/Latino; 5 Asian, non-Hispanic/Latino; 5 Hispanic/Latino; 2 Two or more races, non-Hispanic/Latino), 6 international. Average age 36. In 2017, 54 master's awarded. *Degree requirements:* For master's, thesis. *Entrance requirements:* For master's, minimum GPA of 3.0. Additional exam requirements/recommendations for international students: Required—TOEFL. *Application deadline:* Applications are processed on a rolling basis. Application fee: $25. Electronic applications accepted. *Expenses:* Contact institution. *Financial support:* Application deadline: 6/1; applicants required to submit FAFSA. *Unit head:* Dr. Debora Sepich, Director of Graduate Business Program, 880-333-6263, E-mail: deb.sepich@doane.edu. *Application contact:* Cathy Dillon, Director of Academic Advising, 402-466-4774, Fax: 404-466-4228, E-mail: cathy.dillon@doane.edu.

Dominican College, MBA Program, Orangeburg, NY 10962-1210. Offers accounting (MBA); healthcare management (MBA); management (MBA). *Program availability:* Part-time, evening/weekend. *Faculty:* 1 full-time (0 women). *Students:* 1 (woman) full-time, 21 part-time (15 women); includes 11 minority (6 Black or African American, non-Hispanic/Latino; 1 Asian, non-Hispanic/Latino; 3 Hispanic/Latino; 1 Two or more races, non-Hispanic/Latino), 1 international. In 2017, 14 master's awarded. *Entrance requirements:* For master's, GMAT, 2 letters of recommendation. Additional exam requirements/recommendations for international students: Required—TOEFL (minimum score 550 paper-based; 90 iBT). *Application deadline:* Applications are processed on a rolling basis. Application fee: $50. Electronic applications accepted. *Expenses:* Contact institution. *Financial support:* Application deadline: 2/1; applicants required to submit FAFSA. *Unit head:* Ken Mias, MBA Director, 845-848-4102, E-mail: ken.mias@dc.edu. *Application contact:* Christina Lifshey, Assistant Director of Graduate Admissions, 845-848-7908, Fax: 845-365-3150, E-mail: admissions@dc.edu.

Dominican University, Brennan School of Business, River Forest, IL 60305-1099. Offers MBA, MSA, JD/MBA, MBA/MLIS, MBA/MSW. JD/MBA offered jointly with John Marshall Law School. *Accreditation:* AACSB. *Program availability:* Part-time, evening/weekend, 100% online, blended/hybrid learning. *Faculty:* 20 full-time (8 women), 17 part-time/adjunct (6 women). *Students:* 68 full-time (52 women), 79 part-time (48 women); includes 34 minority (10 Black or African American, non-Hispanic/Latino; 7 Asian, non-Hispanic/Latino; 14 Hispanic/Latino; 1 Native Hawaiian or other Pacific Islander, non-Hispanic/Latino; 2 Two or more races, non-Hispanic/Latino), 25 international. Average age 29. 80 applicants, 78% accepted, 40 enrolled. In 2017, 77 master's awarded. *Entrance requirements:* For master's, GMAT. Additional exam requirements/recommendations for international students: Required—TOEFL (minimum score 550 paper-based; 79 iBT); Recommended—IELTS (minimum score 6). *Application deadline:* Applications are processed on a rolling basis. Application fee: $25. Electronic applications accepted. *Expenses:* $22,824. *Financial support:* Research assistantships, career-related internships or fieldwork, scholarships/grants, tuition waivers (partial), and unspecified assistantships available. Financial award application deadline: 3/1; financial award applicants required to submit FAFSA. *Faculty research:* Entrepreneurship, small business finance, business ethics, marketing strategy. *Unit head:* Dr. Roberto Curci, Dean, 708-524-6321, Fax: 708-524-6939, E-mail: rcurci@dom.edu. *Application contact:* Dr. Kathleen Odell, Associate Dean, Brennan School of Business, 708-488-5394, Fax: 708-524-6939, E-mail: kodell@dom.edu. Website: http://business.dom.edu/

Dominican University of California, Barowsky School of Business, San Rafael, CA 94901-2298. Offers business (MBA); healthcare leadership (MBA). MBA in healthcare leadership offered jointly with School of Health and Natural Sciences. *Program availability:* Part-time, evening/weekend. *Faculty:* 9 full-time (2 women). *Students:* 14 full-time (7 women), 24 part-time (13 women); includes 19 minority (4 Black or African American, non-Hispanic/Latino; 5 Asian, non-Hispanic/Latino; 7 Hispanic/Latino; 1 Native Hawaiian or

other Pacific Islander, non-Hispanic/Latino; 2 Two or more races, non-Hispanic/Latino), 3 international. Average age 36. 35 applicants, 71% accepted, 15 enrolled. In 2017, 36 master's awarded. *Degree requirements:* For master's, thesis, capstone (for MBA). *Entrance requirements:* For master's, minimum GPA of 3.0. Additional exam requirements/recommendations for international students: Required—TOEFL (minimum score 550 paper-based; 80 iBT), IELTS (minimum score 6.5). *Application deadline:* For fall admission, 5/15 priority date for domestic and international students; for spring admission, 11/15 priority date for domestic and international students. Applications are processed on a rolling basis. Application fee: $0. Electronic applications accepted. *Expenses:* $1,010 per unit rate. *Financial support:* In 2017–18, 18 students received support. Scholarships/grants available. Support available to part-time students. Financial award application deadline: 3/2; financial award applicants required to submit FAFSA. *Unit head:* Dr. Sam Beldona, Dean, 415-458-3737, E-mail: sriam.beldona@dominican.edu. *Application contact:* Michael Lavigna, Assistant Director, Graduate Admissions, 415-485-3253, Fax: 415-485-3214, E-mail: gradmissions@dominican.edu. Website: https://bsb.dominican.edu/

Drake University, College of Business and Public Administration, Des Moines, IA 50311-4516. Offers accounting (M Acc); business administration (MBA); public administration (MPA); JD/MBA; JD/MPA; Pharm D/MBA; Pharm D/MPA. *Program availability:* Part-time, evening/weekend. *Degree requirements:* For master's, comprehensive exam (for some programs), thesis (for some programs), internships. *Entrance requirements:* For master's, GMAT, letters of recommendation, resume. Additional exam requirements/recommendations for international students: Required—TOEFL (minimum score 550 paper-based). *Application deadline:* For fall admission, 8/15 priority date for domestic students; for winter admission, 12/20 priority date for domestic students; for spring admission, 12/1 priority date for domestic students. Applications are processed on a rolling basis. Application fee: $25. Electronic applications accepted. *Expenses:* Contact institution. *Financial support:* Fellowships with tuition reimbursements, teaching assistantships, career-related internships or fieldwork, and institutionally sponsored loans available. Support available to part-time students. Financial award application deadline: 3/1; financial award applicants required to submit FAFSA. *Faculty research:* Venture capital, online commerce, professional ethics, process improvement, project management. *Unit head:* Dr. Daniel J. Connolly, Dean, 515-271-2872, Fax: 515-271-4518, E-mail: daniel.connolly@drake.edu. *Application contact:* Danette Kenne, Assistant Dean, 515-271-2188, Fax: 515-271-4518, E-mail: cbpa.gradprograms@drake.edu. Website: http://www.drake.edu/cbpa/

Drexel University, LeBow College of Business, Program in Business Administration, Philadelphia, PA 19104-2875. Offers business administration (MBA, PhD, APC), including accounting (MBA, PhD), decision sciences (PhD), economics (MBA, PhD), finance (MBA, PhD), legal studies (MBA), management (MBA), marketing (MBA, PhD), organizational sciences (PhD), quantitative methods (MBA), strategic management (PhD). *Accreditation:* AACSB. *Program availability:* Part-time, evening/weekend, online learning. Terminal master's awarded for partial completion of doctoral program. *Entrance requirements:* For master's, GMAT, minimum GPA of 2.75; for doctorate, GMAT. Additional exam requirements/recommendations for international students: Required—TOEFL. Electronic applications accepted. *Faculty research:* Decision support systems, individual and group behavior, operations research, techniques and strategy.

Drury University, Master of Business Administration Program, Springfield, MO 65802. Offers MBA. *Accreditation:* AACSB; ACBSP. *Program availability:* Part-time, evening/weekend. *Degree requirements:* For master's, international business trip. *Entrance requirements:* For master's, GMAT, bachelor's degree; minimum GPA of 3.0; prerequisite course requirements: financial accounting, managerial accounting, microeconomics, macroeconomics, marketing, management or organizational behavior, finance, and statistics. Additional exam requirements/recommendations for international students: Recommended—TOEFL (minimum score 80 iBT), IELTS (minimum score 6.5). Electronic applications accepted. *Expenses:* Contact institution. *Faculty research:* Cybersecurity leadership, health care management, cross cultural management, corporate finance, social entrepreneurship.

Duke University, The Fuqua School of Business, The Duke MBA-Daytime Program, Durham, NC 27708-0586. Offers academic excellence in finance (Certificate); business administration (MBA); decision sciences (MBA); energy and environment (MBA); energy finance (MBA); entrepreneurship and innovation (MBA); finance (MBA); financial analysis (MBA); health sector management (Certificate); leadership and ethics (MBA); management (MBA); management science and technology management (Certificate); marketing (MBA); operations management (MBA); social entrepreneurship (MBA); strategy (MBA). *Faculty:* 96 full-time (19 women), 48 part-time/adjunct (15 women). *Students:* 876 full-time (297 women); includes 180 minority (39 Black or African American, non-Hispanic/Latino; 2 American Indian or Alaska Native, non-Hispanic/Latino; 83 Asian, non-Hispanic/Latino; 50 Hispanic/Latino; 6 Two or more races, non-Hispanic/Latino), 321 international. Average age 29. In 2017, 445 master's awarded. *Entrance requirements:* For master's, GMAT or GRE, transcripts, essays, resume, recommendation letters, interview. *Application deadline:* For fall admission, 9/12 for domestic and international students; for winter admission, 10/10 for domestic and international students; for spring admission, 1/3 for domestic and international students; for summer admission, 3/20 for domestic and international students. Application fee: $225. Electronic applications accepted. *Expenses:* $69,342 first-year tuition and fees. *Financial support:* In 2017–18, 423 students received support. Scholarships/grants available. Financial award applicants required to submit FAFSA. *Unit head:* Steve Misuraca, Assistant Dean, Daytime MBA Program. *Application contact:* Shari Hubert, Associate Dean, Office of Admissions, 919-660-7705, Fax: 919-681-8026, E-mail: admissions-info@fuqua.duke.edu. Website: https://www.fuqua.duke.edu/programs/daytime-mba

Duke University, The Fuqua School of Business, The Duke MBA-Global Executive Program, Durham, NC 27708-0586. Offers business administration (MBA); energy and environment (MBA); entrepreneurship and innovation (MBA); finance (MBA); health sector management (Certificate); marketing (MBA); strategy (MBA). *Faculty:* 96 full-time (19 women), 48 part-time/adjunct (15 women). *Students:* 94 full-time (26 women); includes 34 minority (8 Black or African American, non-Hispanic/Latino; 21 Asian, non-Hispanic/Latino; 4 Hispanic/Latino; 1 Two or more races, non-Hispanic/Latino), 25 international. Average age 39. In 2017, 27 master's awarded. *Entrance requirements:* For master's, Executive Assessment, GMAT, or GRE, transcripts, essays, resume, recommendation letters, letter of company support, interview. *Application deadline:* For fall admission, 10/12 priority date for domestic and international students; for winter admission, 12/7 priority date for domestic and international students; for spring admission, 3/20 priority date for domestic and international students; for summer admission, 5/31 for domestic and international students. Applications are processed on a rolling basis. Application fee: $225. Electronic applications accepted. *Expenses:* Contact institution. *Financial support:* In 2017–18, 31 students received support. Scholarships/grants available. Financial award applicants required to submit FAFSA. *Unit head:* Karen Courtney, Associate Dean, Executive Programs. *Application contact:* Shari Hubert, Associate Dean, Office of Admissions, 919-660-7705, Fax: 919-681-8026, E-mail: admissions-info@fuqua.duke.edu. Website: https://www.fuqua.duke.edu/programs/global-executive-mba

Business Administration and Management—General

Duke University, The Fuqua School of Business, The Duke MBA-Weekend Executive Program, Durham, NC 27708-0586. Offers business administration (MBA); energy and environment (MBA); entrepreneurship and innovation (MBA); finance (MBA); health sector management (Certificate); marketing (MBA); strategy (MBA). *Faculty:* 96 full-time (19 women), 48 part-time/adjunct (15 women). *Students:* 219 full-time (59 women); includes 80 minority (13 Black or African American, non-Hispanic/Latino; 3 American Indian or Alaska Native, non-Hispanic/Latino; 45 Asian, non-Hispanic/Latino; 13 Hispanic/Latino; 6 Two or more races, non-Hispanic/Latino), 32 international. Average age 35. In 2017, 92 master's awarded. *Entrance requirements:* For master's, Executive Assessment, GMAT or GRE, transcripts, essays, resume, recommendation letters, letter of company support, interview. *Application deadline:* For fall admission, 10/12 priority date for domestic and international students; for winter admission, 12/7 priority date for domestic and international students; for spring admission, 2/7 priority date for domestic and international students; for summer admission, 3/20 for domestic and international students. Applications are processed on a rolling basis. Application fee: $225. Electronic applications accepted. *Expenses:* Contact institution. *Financial support:* In 2017–18, 44 students received support. Scholarships/grants available. Financial award applicants required to submit FAFSA. *Unit head:* Karen Courtney, Associate Dean, Executive Programs. *Application contact:* Shari Hubert, Associate Dean, Office of Admissions, 919-660-7705, Fax: 919-681-8026, E-mail: admissions-info@fuqua.duke.edu. Website: https://www.fuqua.duke.edu/programs/weekend-executive-mba

Duke University, The Fuqua School of Business, MMS: Foundations of Business Program, Durham, NC 27708-0586. Offers MMS. *Faculty:* 96 full-time (19 women), 48 part-time/adjunct (15 women). *Students:* 137 full-time (70 women); includes 33 minority (7 Black or African American, non-Hispanic/Latino; 17 Asian, non-Hispanic/Latino; 8 Hispanic/Latino; 1 Two or more races, non-Hispanic/Latino), 61 international. Average age 23. In 2017, 117 master's awarded. *Entrance requirements:* For master's, GMAT or GRE, transcripts, essays, resume, recommendation letters, interview. *Application deadline:* For fall admission, 9/21 for domestic and international students; for winter admission, 1/24 for domestic and international students; for spring admission, 3/7 for domestic and international students; for summer admission, 4/11 for domestic and international students. Application fee: $125. Electronic applications accepted. *Expenses:* $53,887 tuition and fees. *Financial support:* In 2017–18, 55 students received support. Scholarships/grants available. Financial award applicants required to submit FAFSA. *Unit head:* Jeremy Petranka, Associate Dean for the Master of Management Studies. *Application contact:* Shari Hubert, Associate Dean, Office of Admissions, 919-660-7705, Fax: 919-681-8026, E-mail: mms-fob-info@fuqua.duke.edu. Website: https://www.fuqua.duke.edu/programs/mms-foundations-business

Duke University, The Fuqua School of Business, PhD Program, Durham, NC 27708-0586. Offers accounting (PhD); decision sciences (PhD); finance (PhD); management and organizations (PhD); marketing (PhD); operations management (PhD); strategy (PhD). *Faculty:* 96 full-time (19 women). *Students:* 64 full-time (25 women); includes 1 minority (Hispanic/Latino), 41 international. Average age 27. 617 applicants, 5% accepted, 14 enrolled. In 2017, 15 doctorates awarded. *Degree requirements:* For doctorate, thesis/dissertation, major field requirement (exam or major paper, depending upon the area). *Entrance requirements:* For doctorate, GMAT or GRE, transcripts, essays, recommendation letters, statement of purpose. Additional exam requirements/recommendations for international students: Required—TOEFL (minimum score 577 paper-based; 108 iBT), IELTS (minimum score 8). *Application deadline:* For fall admission, 12/31 priority date for domestic and international students. Application fee: $85. Electronic applications accepted. *Expenses:* $52,253. *Financial support:* In 2017–18, 66 students received support, including 66 fellowships with full tuition reimbursements available (averaging $29,200 per year), 63 research assistantships with full tuition reimbursements available (averaging $7,000 per year), institutionally sponsored loans, scholarships/grants, and tuition waivers (full) also available. Financial award applicants required to submit FAFSA. *Unit head:* William Boulding, Dean. *Application contact:* Qi Chen, Director of Graduate Studies, 919-660-7753, Fax: 919-660-7971, E-mail: qc2@duke.edu.

Duke University, Graduate School, Department of Business Administration, Durham, NC 27708. Offers PhD. *Accreditation:* AACSB. *Degree requirements:* For doctorate, thesis/dissertation. *Entrance requirements:* For doctorate, GMAT or GRE General Test. Additional exam requirements/recommendations for international students: Required—TOEFL (minimum score 577 paper-based; 90 iBT) or IELTS (minimum score 7). Electronic applications accepted.

Duquesne University, Palumbo-Donahue School of Business, Pittsburgh, PA 15282-0001. Offers accounting (M Acc); finance (MBA); information systems management (MSISM); management (MBA, MS); marketing (MBA); sports business (MS); supply chain management (MS); sustainability (MBA); JD/MBA; MBA/M Acc; MBA/MA; MBA/MES; MBA/MHMS; MSISM/MBA; Pharm D/MBA. *Accreditation:* AACSB. *Program availability:* Part-time, evening/weekend, minimal on-campus study. *Faculty:* 59 full-time (23 women), 25 part-time/adjunct (6 women). *Students:* 232 full-time (83 women), 46 part-time (18 women); includes 28 minority (14 Black or African American, non-Hispanic/Latino; 8 Asian, non-Hispanic/Latino; 4 Hispanic/Latino; 2 Two or more races, non-Hispanic/Latino), 24 international. Average age 29. 220 applicants, 83% accepted, 121 enrolled. In 2017, 113 master's awarded. *Entrance requirements:* For master's, GMAT or GRE, undergraduate transcripts, 2 letters of recommendation, current resume, personal statement. Additional exam requirements/recommendations for international students: Required—TOEFL (minimum score 577 paper-based; 90 iBT), IELTS (minimum score 7). *Application deadline:* For fall admission, 7/1 priority date for domestic and international students; for spring admission, 12/1 for domestic and international students; for summer admission, 4/1 for domestic and international students. Applications are processed on a rolling basis. Application fee: $0. Electronic applications accepted. *Expenses:* $934 per credit (MS in management, sports business); $1,259 per credit (MBA, MS in accountancy, information systems management). *Financial support:* In 2017–18, 211 students received support, including 12 fellowships with partial tuition reimbursements available (averaging $14,200 per year), 20 research assistantships with partial tuition reimbursements available (averaging $22,662 per year); career-related internships or fieldwork, scholarships/grants, and unspecified assistantships also available. Support available to part-time students. Financial award application deadline: 7/1; financial award applicants required to submit FAFSA. *Faculty research:* Investment management, business ethics, technology management, supply chain management, entrepreneurship. *Unit head:* Dr. Karen Donovan, Associate Dean of Graduate Programs and Executive Education, 412-396-6276, Fax: 412-396-1726, E-mail: donovan6@duq.edu. *Application contact:* Jeff Jewett, Director of Admissions and Enrollment Management, 412-396-6244, Fax: 412-396-1726, E-mail: decrostam@duq.edu.
Website: http://www.duq.edu/business/grad

D'Youville College, Department of Business, Buffalo, NY 14201-1084. Offers business administration (MBA); international business (MS). *Program availability:* Part-time, evening/weekend. *Degree requirements:* For master's, one foreign language, project or thesis. *Entrance requirements:* For master's, minimum GPA of 3.0. Additional exam requirements/recommendations for international students: Required—TOEFL (minimum score 500 paper-based). Electronic applications accepted. *Faculty research:* Assessment, accreditation, supply chain, online learning, adult learning.

East Carolina University, Graduate School, College of Business, Program in Business Administration, Greenville, NC 27858-4353. Offers MBA, MD/MBA. *Program availability:* Part-time, evening/weekend, online learning. *Students:* 179 full-time (84 women), 590 part-time (275 women); includes 176 minority (106 Black or African American, non-Hispanic/Latino; 1 American Indian or Alaska Native, non-Hispanic/Latino; 23 Asian, non-Hispanic/Latino; 37 Hispanic/Latino; 9 Two or more races, non-Hispanic/Latino), 10 international. Average age 33. 342 applicants, 92% accepted, 249 enrolled. In 2017, 191 master's awarded. *Entrance requirements:* For master's, GMAT or GRE. Additional exam requirements/recommendations for international students: Recommended—TOEFL (minimum score 78 iBT), IELTS (minimum score 6.5). *Expenses:* Tuition, state resident: full-time $4749; part-time $297 per credit hour. Tuition, nonresident: full-time $17,898; part-time $1119 per credit hour. *Required fees:* $2691; $224 per credit hour. Part-time tuition and fees vary according to course load and program. *Unit head:* Dr. Michael Harris, Chair, 252-328-4353, E-mail: gradbus@ecu.edu.
Website: http://www.ecu.edu/cs-bus/grad/mba.cfm

East Carolina University, Graduate School, College of Engineering and Technology, Department of Technology Systems, Greenville, NC 27858-4353. Offers computer network professional (Certificate); cyber security professional (Certificate); information assurance (Certificate); Lean Six Sigma Black Belt (Certificate); network technology (MS), including computer networking management, digital communications technology, information security, Web technologies; occupational safety (MS); technology management (MS, PhD), including industrial distribution and logistics (MS); Website developer (Certificate). *Students:* 19 full-time (4 women), 158 part-time (35 women); includes 43 minority (28 Black or African American, non-Hispanic/Latino; 2 American Indian or Alaska Native, non-Hispanic/Latino; 3 Asian, non-Hispanic/Latino; 6 Hispanic/Latino; 4 Two or more races, non-Hispanic/Latino), 6 international. Average age 39. 44 applicants, 91% accepted, 37 enrolled. In 2017, 30 master's, 29 other advanced degrees awarded. *Entrance requirements:* For master's and Certificate, GRE General Test or MAT, minimum GPA of 2.5; for doctorate, GRE General Test, related work experience. Additional exam requirements/recommendations for international students: Recommended—TOEFL (minimum score 78 iBT), IELTS (minimum score 6.5). *Application deadline:* For fall admission, 6/1 priority date for domestic students. Applications are processed on a rolling basis. Application fee: $75. *Expenses:* Tuition, state resident: full-time $4749; part-time $297 per credit hour. Tuition, nonresident: full-time $17,898; part-time $1119 per credit hour. *Required fees:* $2691; $224 per credit hour. Part-time tuition and fees vary according to course load and program. *Financial support:* Application deadline: 6/1. *Unit head:* Dr. Tijjani Mohammed, Chair, 252-328-9668, E-mail: mohammedt@ecu.edu.
Website: http://www.ecu.edu/cs-cet/techsystems/index.cfm

Eastern Illinois University, Graduate School, Lumpkin College of Business and Technology, Program in Business Administration, Charleston, IL 61920. Offers accountancy (MBA); applied management (MBA); geographic information systems (MBA); research (MBA). *Accreditation:* AACSB. *Program availability:* Part-time, evening/weekend. *Entrance requirements:* For master's, GMAT or GRE. Additional exam requirements/recommendations for international students: Required—TOEFL (minimum score 500 paper-based; 61 iBT), IELTS (minimum score 6). *Application deadline:* For fall admission, 5/15 for domestic and international students; for spring admission, 10/15 for domestic and international students. Applications are processed on a rolling basis. Application fee: $30. Electronic applications accepted. *Financial support:* Research assistantships with full tuition reimbursements, teaching assistantships with full tuition reimbursements, career-related internships or fieldwork, Federal Work-Study, and unspecified assistantships available. Support available to part-time students. Financial award application deadline: 3/1; financial award applicants required to submit FAFSA. *Unit head:* Dr. Melody L. Wollan, Coordinator, 217-581-3028, Fax: 217-581-6642, E-mail: mlwollan@eiu.edu. *Application contact:* Dr. Melody L. Wollan, Coordinator, 217-581-3028, Fax: 217-581-6642, E-mail: mlwollan@eiu.edu.
Website: http://www.eiu.edu/mba/index.php

Eastern Kentucky University, The Graduate School, College of Business and Technology, Program in Business Administration, Richmond, KY 40475-3102. Offers MBA. *Accreditation:* AACSB.

Eastern Mennonite University, Program in Business Administration, Harrisonburg, VA 22802-2462. Offers general management (MBA); health services administration (MBA); non-profit leadership (MBA). *Program availability:* Part-time, evening/weekend. *Degree requirements:* For master's, final capstone course. *Entrance requirements:* For master's, GMAT, minimum GPA of 2.5, 2 years of work experience, 2 letters of reference. Additional exam requirements/recommendations for international students: Required—TOEFL (minimum score 500 paper-based). *Application deadline:* For fall admission, 3/1 priority date for domestic and international students. Applications are processed on a rolling basis. Application fee: $25. Electronic applications accepted. *Expenses:* Contact institution. *Financial support:* Application deadline: 6/30; applicants required to submit FAFSA. *Faculty research:* Information security, Anabaptist/Mennonite experiences and perspectives, limits of multi-cultural education, international development performance criteria. *Unit head:* Dr. James M. Leaman, Department Chair, 540-432-4152, Fax: 540-432-4071, E-mail: james.leaman@emu.edu. *Application contact:* Patricia S. Eckard, Administrative Coordinator, 540-432-4150, Fax: 540-432-4071, E-mail: eckardp@emu.edu.
Website: http://www.emu.edu/mba/

Eastern Michigan University, Graduate School, College of Business, Department of Management, Ypsilanti, MI 48197. Offers entrepreneurship (Postbaccalaureate Certificate); human resources management and organizational development (MSHROD). *Program availability:* Part-time, evening/weekend, online learning. *Faculty:* 21 full-time (11 women). *Students:* 10 full-time (4 women), 58 part-time (40 women); includes 19 minority (11 Black or African American, non-Hispanic/Latino; 2 Asian, non-Hispanic/Latino; 3 Hispanic/Latino; 3 Two or more races, non-Hispanic/Latino), 4 international. Average age 31. 41 applicants, 76% accepted, 18 enrolled. In 2017, 92 master's awarded. *Degree requirements:* For master's, thesis optional. *Entrance requirements:* For master's, GMAT. Additional exam requirements/recommendations for international students: Required—TOEFL. *Application deadline:* For fall admission, 5/15 priority date for domestic students, 2/15 priority date for international students; for winter admission, 10/15 priority date for domestic students, 9/1 priority date for international students; for summer admission, 3/15 priority date for domestic students, 3/1 priority date for international students. Applications are processed on a rolling basis. Application fee: $45. *Financial support:* Fellowships, research assistantships with full tuition reimbursements, teaching assistantships with full tuition reimbursements, career-related internships or fieldwork, Federal Work-Study, institutionally sponsored loans, scholarships/grants, tuition waivers (partial), and unspecified assistantships available. Support available to part-time students. Financial award applicants required to submit FAFSA. *Unit head:* Dr. Fraya Wagner-Marsh, Department Head, 734-487-3240, Fax: 734-487-4100, E-mail: fraya.wagner@emich.edu.

Eastern Michigan University, Graduate School, College of Business, Programs in Business Administration, Ypsilanti, MI 48197. Offers business administration (MBA, Graduate Certificate); computer information systems (Graduate Certificate); e-business (MBA, Graduate Certificate); enterprise business intelligence (MBA); entrepreneurship

(MBA, Graduate Certificate); finance (MBA, Graduate Certificate); human resources (MBA); human resources management (Graduate Certificate); information systems (MBA); internal auditing (MBA); international business (MBA, Graduate Certificate); marketing management (Graduate Certificate); nonprofit management (MBA); organizational development (Graduate Certificate); supply chain management (MBA, Graduate Certificate). *Accreditation:* AACSB. *Program availability:* Part-time, online learning. *Students:* 53 full-time (30 women), 297 part-time (170 women); includes 121 minority (72 Black or African American, non-Hispanic/Latino; 4 American Indian or Alaska Native, non-Hispanic/Latino; 15 Asian, non-Hispanic/Latino; 20 Hispanic/Latino; 10 Two or more races, non-Hispanic/Latino), 20 international. Average age 31. 247 applicants, 74% accepted, 94 enrolled. In 2017, 71 master's, 34 other advanced degrees awarded. *Entrance requirements:* For master's, GMAT (minimum score 450), minimum cumulative undergraduate GPA of 2.75. Additional exam requirements/recommendations for international students: Required—TOEFL. *Application deadline:* For fall admission, 5/15 priority date for domestic students, 2/15 priority date for international students; for winter admission, 10/15 priority date for domestic students, 9/1 priority date for international students; for summer admission, 3/15 priority date for domestic students, 3/1 priority date for international students. Applications are processed on a rolling basis. Application fee: $45. *Financial support:* Fellowships, research assistantships with full tuition reimbursements, teaching assistantships with full tuition reimbursements, career-related internships or fieldwork, Federal Work-Study, institutionally sponsored loans, scholarships/grants, tuition waivers (partial), and unspecified assistantships available. Support available to part-time students. Financial award applicants required to submit FAFSA. *Unit head:* K. Michelle Henry, Director, Graduate Business Programs, 734-487-4444, Fax: 734-483-1316, E-mail: cob.graduate@emich.edu.
Website: http://www.emich.edu/cob/mba/

Eastern Nazarene College, Adult and Graduate Studies, Program in Management, Quincy, MA 02170. Offers MSM.

Eastern New Mexico University, Graduate School, College of Business, Portales, NM 88130. Offers MBA. *Accreditation:* ACBSP. *Program availability:* Part-time, evening/weekend, online learning. *Degree requirements:* For master's, comprehensive exam, comprehensive integrative project and presentation. *Entrance requirements:* For master's, GMAT (minimum score 450), minimum undergraduate GPA of 3.0. Additional exam requirements/recommendations for international students: Required—TOEFL (minimum score 550 paper-based; 79 iBT), IELTS (minimum score 6). *Application deadline:* For fall admission, 7/20 priority date for domestic students, 6/20 priority date for international students; for spring admission, 12/15 priority date for domestic students, 11/15 priority date for international students. Applications are processed on a rolling basis. Application fee: $10. Electronic applications accepted. *Financial support:* Applicants required to submit FAFSA. *Unit head:* Dr. Pattarapong Burusnukul, Graduate Coordinator, 575-562-2366, E-mail: pattarapong.burusnukul@enmu.edu. *Application contact:* Gail Crozier, Receptionist/Records Clerk, 575-562-2147, Fax: 575-562-2500, E-mail: gail.crozier@enmu.edu.
Website: http://business.enmu.edu/

Eastern Oregon University, Program in Business Administration, La Grande, OR 97850-2899. Offers MBA. *Program availability:* Part-time, 100% online. *Faculty:* 6 full-time (2 women), 4 part-time/adjunct (1 woman). *Students:* 30 full-time (15 women), 59 part-time (33 women); includes 20 minority (2 Black or African American, non-Hispanic/Latino; 4 American Indian or Alaska Native, non-Hispanic/Latino; 3 Asian, non-Hispanic/Latino; 10 Hispanic/Latino; 1 Two or more races, non-Hispanic/Latino), 1 international. Average age 31. In 2017, 43 master's awarded. *Degree requirements:* For master's, thesis. *Entrance requirements:* For master's, baccalaureate degree in business or related fields (agribusiness, finance, accounting, economics, etc.) from accredited institution with minimum cumulative GPA of 3.0. *Application deadline:* For fall admission, 5/15 priority date for domestic students. Applications are processed on a rolling basis. Electronic applications accepted. *Expenses:* Contact institution. *Financial support:* In 2017–18, 7 students received support. Federal Work-Study, scholarships/grants, and tuition waivers (full and partial) available. Support available to part-time students. *Faculty research:* Good customer service as a global sustainable business practice; analysis and marketing of tribal business plans. *Unit head:* Les Mueller, Program Coordinator, 541-962-3225, E-mail: lmueller@eou.edu. *Application contact:* Kristin Johnson, MAT Advisor/Recruiter, 541-962-3529, Fax: 541-962-3701, E-mail: kristin.johnson@eou.edu.
Website: https://www.eou.edu/cobe/business/mba/

Eastern University, Graduate Programs in Business and Leadership, St. Davids, PA 19087-3696. Offers health administration (MBA); health services management (MS); management (MBA); organizational leadership (MA); social impact (MBA). *Program availability:* Part-time, evening/weekend, online learning. *Students:* 55 full-time (34 women), 195 part-time (126 women); includes 123 minority (93 Black or African American, non-Hispanic/Latino; 1 American Indian or Alaska Native, non-Hispanic/Latino; 12 Asian, non-Hispanic/Latino; 12 Hispanic/Latino; 5 Two or more races, non-Hispanic/Latino), 23 international. Average age 34. In 2017, 123 master's awarded. *Application deadline:* Applications are processed on a rolling basis. Application fee: $35. Electronic applications accepted. Application fee is waived when completed online. *Expenses:* Contact institution. *Financial support:* Applicants required to submit FAFSA. *Unit head:* Michael Dziedziak, Executive Director of Enrollment, 800-452-0996, E-mail: gpsadmissions@eastern.edu.
Website: https://www.eastern.edu/academics/programs/graduate-business

Eastern University, Program in Organizational Leadership, St. Davids, PA 19087-3696. Offers leadership studies (CAGS); organizational leadership (PhD), including business management, educational administration, public and nonprofit administration. *Students:* 98 full-time (60 women); includes 31 minority (26 Black or African American, non-Hispanic/Latino; 2 Asian, non-Hispanic/Latino; 2 Hispanic/Latino; 1 Two or more races, non-Hispanic/Latino), 4 international. Average age 47. In 2017, 8 doctorates, 10 other advanced degrees awarded. *Application deadline:* Applications are processed on a rolling basis. Application fee: $75. Electronic applications accepted. *Expenses:* Contact institution. *Unit head:* Michael Dziedziak, Executive Director of Enrollment, 800-452-0996, E-mail: gpsadmissions@eastern.edu.
Website: https://www.eastern.edu/academics/programs/phd-organizational-leadership/phd-organizational-leadership-0

Eastern Washington University, Graduate Studies, College of Business and Public Administration, Business Administration Program, Cheney, WA 99004-2431. Offers MBA, MBA/MPA. *Accreditation:* AACSB. *Students:* 35 full-time (15 women), 32 part-time (15 women); includes 5 minority (1 Black or African American, non-Hispanic/Latino; 1 American Indian or Alaska Native, non-Hispanic/Latino; 3 Hispanic/Latino), 9 international. Average age 31. 66 applicants, 56% accepted, 27 enrolled. In 2017, 38 master's awarded. *Degree requirements:* For master's, comprehensive exam, thesis optional. *Entrance requirements:* For master's, GMAT, minimum GPA of 3.0. Additional exam requirements/recommendations for international students: Required—TOEFL (minimum score 580 paper-based; 92 iBT), IELTS (minimum score 7), PTE (minimum score 63). *Application deadline:* For fall admission, 4/1 priority date for domestic students; for spring admission, 1/15 for domestic students. Applications are processed

on a rolling basis. Application fee: $75. Electronic applications accepted. *Expenses:* Tuition, state resident: full-time $11,191; part-time $373.06 per credit. Tuition, nonresident: full-time $25,995; part-time $866.52 per credit. *Financial support:* In 2017–18, 5 students received support. Teaching assistantships with partial tuition reimbursements available, career-related internships or fieldwork, Federal Work-Study, institutionally sponsored loans, scholarships/grants, health care benefits, tuition waivers (partial), and unspecified assistantships available. Support available to part-time students. Financial award application deadline: 2/1. *Unit head:* Lorene Winters, 509-828-1232, E-mail: mba@ewu.edu.
Website: http://www.ewu.edu/cbpa.xml

East Tennessee State University, School of Graduate Studies, College of Business and Technology, Department of Management and Marketing, Johnson City, TN 37614. Offers business administration (MBA, Postbaccalaureate Certificate); digital marketing (MS); entrepreneurial leadership (Postbaccalaureate Certificate); health care management (Postbaccalaureate Certificate). *Program availability:* Part-time, evening/weekend. *Degree requirements:* For master's, comprehensive exam, capstone. *Entrance requirements:* For master's, GMAT, minimum GPA of 2.5 (for MBA), 3.0 (for MS); current resume; three letters of recommendation; for Postbaccalaureate Certificate, minimum GPA of 2.5, undergraduate degree. Additional exam requirements/recommendations for international students: Required—TOEFL (minimum score 550 paper-based; 79 iBT). *Application deadline:* For fall admission, 6/1 for domestic students, 4/29 for international students; for spring admission, 11/1 for domestic students, 9/29 for international students. Application fee: $55 ($65 for international students). Electronic applications accepted. *Financial support:* Research assistantships with full tuition reimbursements, teaching assistantships with full tuition reimbursements, career-related internships or fieldwork, institutionally sponsored loans, scholarships/grants, and unspecified assistantships available. Financial award application deadline: 7/1; financial award applicants required to submit FAFSA. *Faculty research:* Sustainability, healthcare effectiveness, consumer behavior, merchandising trends, organizational management issues. *Unit head:* Charles Gorman, Chair, 423-439-4433, Fax: 423-439-5661, E-mail: gormanc@etsu.edu. *Application contact:* Charles Gorman, Chair, 423-439-4433, Fax: 423-439-5661, E-mail: gormanc@etsu.edu.
Website: http://www.etsu.edu/cbat/mgmtmkt/

East Texas Baptist University, Master of Business Administration Program, Marshall, TX 75670-1498. Offers MBA. *Program availability:* Part-time, evening/weekend, 100% online. *Faculty:* 2 full-time (1 woman), 2 part-time/adjunct (0 women). *Students:* 15 full-time (11 women), 12 part-time (7 women); includes 13 minority (10 Black or African American, non-Hispanic/Latino; 2 Hispanic/Latino; 1 Two or more races, non-Hispanic/Latino). Average age 26. 20 applicants, 65% accepted, 13 enrolled. In 2017, 16 master's awarded. *Entrance requirements:* Additional exam requirements/recommendations for international students: Recommended—TOEFL (minimum score 550 paper-based; 79 iBT). *Application deadline:* For fall admission, 8/13 for domestic students; for spring admission, 1/7 for domestic students; for summer admission, 5/10 for domestic students. Applications are processed on a rolling basis. Application fee: $50. Electronic applications accepted. *Expenses:* $700 per credit hour tuition, $150 per semester fees ($75 per semester if less than 6 hours). *Financial support:* In 2017–18, 16 students received support. Federal Work-Study, scholarships/grants, unspecified assistantships, and staff grants available. Financial award applicants required to submit FAFSA. *Unit head:* Den Murley, Director of Graduate Admissions, 903-923-2079, Fax: 903-934-8115, E-mail: dmurley@etbu.edu.
Website: https://www.etbu.edu/business/master-business-administration/

Edgewood College, Program in Business, Madison, WI 53711-1997. Offers accountancy (MS); sustainability leadership (MBA). *Accreditation:* ACBSP. *Program availability:* Part-time, evening/weekend. *Students:* 19 full-time (12 women), 107 part-time (63 women); includes 16 minority (3 Black or African American, non-Hispanic/Latino; 5 Asian, non-Hispanic/Latino; 4 Hispanic/Latino; 4 Two or more races, non-Hispanic/Latino), 13 international. Average age 34. In 2017, 47 master's awarded. *Entrance requirements:* For master's, GMAT (minimum score 430), minimum GPA of 2.75, 2 letters of recommendation. Additional exam requirements/recommendations for international students: Required—TOEFL. *Application deadline:* For fall admission, 8/15 for domestic students, 5/1 for international students; for spring admission, 1/8 for domestic students, 11/1 for international students. Applications are processed on a rolling basis. Application fee: $30. Electronic applications accepted. *Expenses: Tuition:* Part-time $930 per credit. *Financial support:* Career-related internships or fieldwork and scholarships/grants available. *Unit head:* Dr. Stevie Watson, Dean, 608-663-2224, Fax: 608-663-3291, E-mail: swatson@edgewood.edu. *Application contact:* Joann Eastman, Admissions Counselor, 608-663-3250, Fax: 608-663-2214, E-mail: gps@edgewood.edu.
Website: https://www.edgewood.edu/academics/schools/school-of-business

Elmhurst College, Graduate Programs, Program in Business Administration, Elmhurst, IL 60126-3296. Offers MBA. *Program availability:* Part-time, evening/weekend, 100% online. *Faculty:* 2 full-time (1 woman), 14 part-time/adjunct (3 women). *Students:* 5 full-time (2 women), 127 part-time (58 women); includes 35 minority (7 Black or African American, non-Hispanic/Latino; 8 Asian, non-Hispanic/Latino; 17 Hispanic/Latino; 1 Native Hawaiian or other Pacific Islander, non-Hispanic/Latino; 2 Two or more races, non-Hispanic/Latino), 1 international. Average age 30. 89 applicants, 73% accepted, 61 enrolled. In 2017, 47 master's awarded. *Entrance requirements:* For master's, 3 recommendations, resume, statement of purpose. Additional exam requirements/recommendations for international students: Required—TOEFL (minimum score 550 paper-based; 79 iBT). *Application deadline:* Applications are processed on a rolling basis. Application fee: $0. Electronic applications accepted. *Expenses:* Contact institution. *Financial support:* In 2017–18, 50 students received support. Scholarships/grants and unspecified assistantships available. Support available to part-time students. Financial award application deadline: 3/1; financial award applicants required to submit FAFSA. *Unit head:* Kelly Cunningham, Associate Professor, 630-617-3223, E-mail: mcunningham@elmhurst.edu. *Application contact:* Timothy J. Panfil, Director of Enrollment Management, 630-617-3300 Ext. 3256, Fax: 630-617-6471, E-mail: panfilt@elmhurst.edu.
Website: http://www.elmhurst.edu/mba

Elms College, Division of Business, Chicopee, MA 01013-2839. Offers accounting (MBA); accounting and finance (MS); financial planning (MBA, Certificate); healthcare leadership (MBA); lean entrepreneurship (MBA); management (MBA). *Program availability:* Part-time, evening/weekend. *Faculty:* 5 full-time (all women), 7 part-time/adjunct (4 women). *Students:* 51 part-time (30 women); includes 9 minority (4 Black or African American, non-Hispanic/Latino; 2 Asian, non-Hispanic/Latino; 3 Hispanic/Latino), 2 international. Average age 33. 14 applicants, 93% accepted, 10 enrolled. In 2017, 28 master's awarded. *Entrance requirements:* For master's, minimum GPA of 3.0. *Application deadline:* Applications are processed on a rolling basis. Application fee: $30. Electronic applications accepted. *Expenses: Tuition:* Full-time $13,860; part-time $770 per credit hour. *Required fees:* $200. Tuition and fees vary according to degree level and program. *Unit head:* Dr. David Kimball, Chair, Division of Business, 413-265-2300, E-mail: kimballd@elms.edu. *Application contact:* MBA Program Coordinator, 413-265-2592, E-mail: mba@elms.edu.

Business Administration and Management—General

Elon University, Program in Business Administration, Elon, NC 27244-2010. Offers business (MBA); management (M Sc). *Accreditation:* AACSB. *Program availability:* Part-time, evening/weekend. *Faculty:* 20 full-time (10 women), 7 part-time/adjunct (3 women). *Students:* 60 full-time (25 women), 68 part-time (30 women); includes 25 minority (13 Black or African American, non-Hispanic/Latino; 6 Asian, non-Hispanic/Latino; 4 Hispanic/Latino; 2 Two or more races, non-Hispanic/Latino). Average age 33. 126 applicants, 75% accepted, 73 enrolled. In 2017, 40 master's awarded. *Entrance requirements:* For master's, GMAT. Additional exam requirements/recommendations for international students: Required—TOEFL (minimum score 550 paper-based; 79 iBT). *Application deadline:* For fall admission, 8/15 priority date for domestic students; for spring admission, 2/15 priority date for domestic students. Applications are processed on a rolling basis. Application fee: $50. Electronic applications accepted. *Financial support:* Federal Work-Study and scholarships/grants available. Support available to part-time students. Financial award application deadline: 3/15; financial award applicants required to submit FAFSA. *Faculty research:* Business ethics, international business and global economics, sales force management, sustainable business practices, consumer behavior. *Unit head:* Dr. Jen Platania, Associate Dean of the Love School of Business/Associate Professor of Economics, 336-278-5938, E-mail: jplatania@elon.edu. *Application contact:* Art Fadde, Director of Graduate Admissions, 800-334-8448 Ext. 3, Fax: 336-278-7699, E-mail: afadde@elon.edu.
Website: http://www.elon.edu/mba/

Embry-Riddle Aeronautical University–Daytona, College of Business, Daytona Beach, FL 32114-3900. Offers airline management (MBA); airport management (MBA); aviation finance (MSAF); aviation human resources (MBA); aviation management (MBA-AM); aviation system management (MBA); finance (MBA). *Accreditation:* ACBSP. *Faculty:* 14 full-time (2 women). *Students:* 95 full-time (31 women), 19 part-time (8 women); includes 15 minority (5 Black or African American, non-Hispanic/Latino; 1 Asian, non-Hispanic/Latino; 1 Hispanic/Latino; 8 Two or more races, non-Hispanic/Latino), 65 international. Average age 27. 141 applicants, 38% accepted, 41 enrolled. In 2017, 49 master's awarded. *Degree requirements:* For master's, thesis (for some programs). *Entrance requirements:* For master's, GRE (for some programs). Additional exam requirements/recommendations for international students: Required—TOEFL (minimum score 550 paper-based, 79 iBT) or IELTS (6). *Application deadline:* For fall admission, 1/15 priority date for domestic students; for spring admission, 11/1 priority date for domestic students; for summer admission, 4/1 priority date for domestic students. Applications are processed on a rolling basis. Application fee: $50. Electronic applications accepted. *Expenses: Tuition:* Full-time $16,704; part-time $1392 per credit hour. *Required fees:* $1314; $657 per semester. Tuition and fees vary according to degree level. *Financial support:* Research assistantships, teaching assistantships, career-related internships or fieldwork, scholarships/grants, unspecified assistantships, and on-campus employment available. Financial award application deadline: 3/15; financial award applicants required to submit FAFSA. *Unit head:* Michael J. Williams, PhD, Dean of the College of Business and Professor of Information Systems, 386-226-6293, E-mail: michael.williams@erau.edu. *Application contact:* Graduate Admissions, 386-226-6176, E-mail: graduate.admissions@erau.edu.
Website: https://daytonabeach.erau.edu/college-business/index.html

Embry-Riddle Aeronautical University–Worldwide, Department of Business Administration, Daytona Beach, FL 32114-3900. Offers aviation (MBAA); MS/MBA. *Program availability:* Part-time, evening/weekend, online only, EagleVision Classroom (between classrooms), EagleVision Home (faculty and students at home), and a blend of Classroom or Home. *Faculty:* 12 full-time (5 women), 60 part-time/adjunct (18 women). *Students:* 374 full-time (77 women), 292 part-time (65 women); includes 163 minority (54 Black or African American, non-Hispanic/Latino; 3 American Indian or Alaska Native, non-Hispanic/Latino; 27 Asian, non-Hispanic/Latino; 43 Hispanic/Latino; 4 Native Hawaiian or other Pacific Islander, non-Hispanic/Latino; 32 Two or more races, non-Hispanic/Latino), 55 international. Average age 35. 166 applicants, 74% accepted, 115 enrolled. In 2017, 214 master's awarded. *Degree requirements:* For master's, comprehensive exam. *Entrance requirements:* Additional exam requirements/recommendations for international students: Required—TOEFL (minimum score 550 paper-based; 79 iBT), IELTS (minimum score 6). *Application deadline:* Applications are processed on a rolling basis. Application fee: $50. Electronic applications accepted. *Expenses:* Contact institution. *Financial support:* Career-related internships or fieldwork and scholarships/grants available. Financial award applicants required to submit FAFSA. *Unit head:* Ronald Mau, PhD, Department Chair, E-mail: ronald.mau@erau.edu. *Application contact:* Worldwide Campus, 800-522-6787, E-mail: worldwide@erau.edu.
Website: http://worldwide.erau.edu/degrees-programs/colleges/business/department-of-business-admin/index.html

Embry-Riddle Aeronautical University–Worldwide, Department of Decision Sciences, Daytona Beach, FL 32114-3900. Offers aviation and aerospace (MSPM); aviation/aerospace management (MSEM); financial management (MSEM, MSPM); general management (MSPM); global management (MSPM); human resources management (MSPM); information systems (MSPM); leadership (MSEM, MSPM); logistics and supply chain management (MSEM, MSLSCM, MSPM); management (MSEM, MSPM); project management (MSEM); systems engineering (MSEM, MSPM); technical management (MSPM). *Program availability:* Part-time, evening/weekend, EagleVision Classroom (between classrooms), EagleVision Home (faculty and students at home), and a blend of Classroom or Home. *Faculty:* 12 full-time (3 women), 53 part-time/adjunct (10 women). *Students:* 514 full-time (141 women), 476 part-time (111 women); includes 337 minority (136 Black or African American, non-Hispanic/Latino; 6 American Indian or Alaska Native, non-Hispanic/Latino; 39 Asian, non-Hispanic/Latino; 81 Hispanic/Latino; 4 Native Hawaiian or other Pacific Islander, non-Hispanic/Latino; 71 Two or more races, non-Hispanic/Latino), 21 international. Average age 36. 297 applicants, 72% accepted, 209 enrolled. In 2017, 292 master's awarded. *Degree requirements:* For master's, comprehensive exam (for some programs), thesis (for some programs). *Entrance requirements:* Additional exam requirements/recommendations for international students: Required—TOEFL (minimum score 550 paper-based; 79 iBT), IELTS (minimum score 6). *Application deadline:* Applications are processed on a rolling basis. Application fee: $50. Electronic applications accepted. *Expenses:* Contact institution. *Financial support:* Career-related internships or fieldwork and scholarships/grants available. Financial award applicants required to submit FAFSA. *Unit head:* Aman Gupta, PhD, Department Chair, E-mail: aman.gupta@erau.edu. *Application contact:* Worldwide Campus, 800-522-6787, E-mail: worldwide@erau.edu.

Embry-Riddle Aeronautical University–Worldwide, Department of Management, Daytona Beach, FL 32114-3900. Offers global management (MS); human resources management (MS); leadership (MS); operations management (MS); project management (MS). *Program availability:* Part-time, evening/weekend, EagleVision Classroom (between classrooms), EagleVision Home (faculty and students at home), and a blend of Classroom or Home. *Students:* 148 full-time (48 women), 192 part-time (52 women); includes 91 minority (46 Black or African American, non-Hispanic/Latino; 1 American Indian or Alaska Native, non-Hispanic/Latino; 11 Asian, non-Hispanic/Latino; 16 Hispanic/Latino; 17 Two or more races, non-Hispanic/Latino), 7 international. Average age 39. In 2017, 104 master's awarded. *Entrance requirements:* Additional

exam requirements/recommendations for international students: Required—TOEFL (minimum score 550 paper-based, 79 iBT) or IELTS (6). *Application deadline:* Applications are processed on a rolling basis. Application fee: $50. Electronic applications accepted. *Expenses:* Contact institution. *Financial support:* Career-related internships or fieldwork and scholarships/grants available. Financial award applicants required to submit FAFSA. *Unit head:* Thomas Henkel, PhD, Department Chair, E-mail: thomas.henkel@erau.edu. *Application contact:* Worldwide Campus, 800-522-6787, E-mail: worldwide@erau.edu.

Emmanuel College, Graduate and Professional Programs, Graduate Programs in Management, Boston, MA 02115. Offers management (MSM); management and leadership (Graduate Certificate); research administration (MSM, Graduate Certificate). *Program availability:* Part-time, evening/weekend, blended/hybrid learning. *Faculty:* 11 part-time/adjunct (3 women). *Students:* 1 full-time (0 women), 32 part-time (22 women); includes 12 minority (7 Black or African American, non-Hispanic/Latino; 4 Asian, non-Hispanic/Latino; 1 Hispanic/Latino). Average age 33. 25 applicants, 28% accepted, 5 enrolled. In 2017, 39 master's, 7 other advanced degrees awarded. *Degree requirements:* For master's, 36 credits. *Entrance requirements:* For master's and Graduate Certificate, transcripts from all regionally-accredited institutions attended (showing proof of bachelor's degree completion), 2 letters of recommendation, essay, resume. Additional exam requirements/recommendations for international students: Required—TOEFL. *Application deadline:* Applications are processed on a rolling basis. Electronic applications accepted. *Expenses:* $24,112 (for MSM); $13,152 (for Graduate Certificate). *Financial support:* Application deadline: 2/15; applicants required to submit FAFSA. *Unit head:* Cindy O'Callaghan, Dean of Academic Administration and Graduate and Professional Programs, 617-735-9700, E-mail: gpp@emmanuel.edu. *Application contact:* Helen Muterperl, Director of Graduate and Professional Programs, 617-735-9700, Fax: 617-507-0434, E-mail: gpp@emmanuel.edu.
Website: http://www.emmanuel.edu/graduate-professional-programs/academics/management.html

Emory University, Goizueta Business School, Doctoral Program in Business, Atlanta, GA 30322. Offers accounting (PhD); finance (PhD); information systems and operations management (PhD); marketing (PhD); organization and management (PhD). *Students:* 250 applicants, 5% accepted. *Degree requirements:* For doctorate, comprehensive exam, thesis/dissertation. *Entrance requirements:* For doctorate, GMAT, interview. Additional exam requirements/recommendations for international students: Required—TOEFL (minimum score 600 paper-based; 100 iBT). *Application deadline:* For fall admission, 1/3 priority date for domestic and international students. Applications are processed on a rolling basis. Application fee: $75. Electronic applications accepted. *Expenses:* Contact institution. *Financial support:* Fellowships, scholarships/grants, and health care benefits available. Financial award application deadline: 1/3. *Faculty research:* Financial and managerial accounting, asset pricing strategy and organizational behavior, information technology marketing analytics and consumer behavior. *Unit head:* Kathryn Kadous, Associate Dean, 404-727-2306, Fax: 404-727-5337, E-mail: kathryn.kadous@emory.edu. *Application contact:* Allison Gilmore, Director of Admissions and Student Services, 404-727-6353, Fax: 404-727-5337, E-mail: allison.gilmore@emory.edu.
Website: https://goizueta.emory.edu/degree/phd/index.html

Emory University, Goizueta Business School, Evening MBA Program, Atlanta, GA 30322. Offers MBA. *Program availability:* Part-time, evening/weekend. *Faculty:* 44 full-time (7 women), 14 part-time/adjunct (2 women). *Students:* 250 part-time (86 women); includes 69 minority (14 Black or African American, non-Hispanic/Latino; 31 Asian, non-Hispanic/Latino; 19 Hispanic/Latino; 5 Two or more races, non-Hispanic/Latino), 26 international. Average age 30. 209 applicants, 64% accepted, 90 enrolled. In 2017, 85 master's awarded. *Entrance requirements:* For master's, GMAT/GRE, undergraduate degree, interview, essays, recommendation letters, resume, work experience. Additional exam requirements/recommendations for international students: Required—TOEFL (minimum score 100 iBT), IELTS (minimum score 7), PTE (minimum score 68). *Application deadline:* For fall admission, 11/3 for domestic and international students; for winter admission, 2/16 for domestic and international students; for spring admission, 5/4 for domestic and international students; for summer admission, 6/22 for domestic and international students. Application fee: $150. Electronic applications accepted. *Expenses:* Contact institution. *Financial support:* Scholarships/grants available. Financial award application deadline: 6/22; financial award applicants required to submit FAFSA. *Faculty research:* Improving health care delivery systems; corporate-based valuation; marketing; finance interface, asset allocation and portfolio management; social media and network processes. *Unit head:* Wendy Tsung, Associate Dean, 404-727-1787, E-mail: wendy.tsung@emory.edu. *Application contact:* Kathleen Edwards, Director of MBA Admissions, 404-727-8124, Fax: 404-727-4612, E-mail: kathleen.edwards@emory.edu.
Website: http://www.goizueta.emory.edu/degree/eveningmba/index.html

Emory University, Goizueta Business School, Full Time MBA Program, Atlanta, GA 30322. Offers accounting (MBA); alternative investments (MBA); business process consulting (MBA); business technology management (MBA); capital markets (MBA); corporate finance (MBA); customer relationship management (MBA); decision analytics (MBA); entrepreneurship (MBA); finance (MBA); global management (MBA); investment banking (MBA); management consulting (MBA); marketing (MBA); marketing analytics (MBA); marketing consulting (MBA); operations management (MBA); organization and management (MBA); product and brand management (MBA); real estate (MBA); social enterprise (MBA); strategy consulting (MBA). *Accreditation:* AACSB. *Faculty:* 74 full-time (18 women), 18 part-time/adjunct (6 women). *Students:* 353 full-time (96 women); includes 80 minority (18 Black or African American, non-Hispanic/Latino; 2 American Indian or Alaska Native, non-Hispanic/Latino; 39 Asian, non-Hispanic/Latino; 16 Hispanic/Latino; 1 Native Hawaiian or other Pacific Islander, non-Hispanic/Latino; 4 Two or more races, non-Hispanic/Latino), 104 international. Average age 29. 1,380 applicants, 34% accepted, 172 enrolled. In 2017, 179 master's awarded. *Degree requirements:* For master's, 1 leadership course; 2 mid-semester module programs; 2 global components. *Entrance requirements:* For master's, GMAT/GRE, essays, recommendation letters; undergraduate degree; interview. Additional exam requirements/recommendations for international students: Required—TOEFL (minimum score 100 iBT), IELTS (minimum score 7), PTE (minimum score 68). *Application deadline:* For fall admission, 10/6 for domestic and international students; for winter admission, 11/17 for domestic and international students; for spring admission, 1/3 priority date for domestic and international students; for summer admission, 3/9 for domestic and international students. Application fee: $150. Electronic applications accepted. *Expenses:* $59,616. *Financial support:* In 2017–18, 273 students received support. Career-related internships or fieldwork, institutionally sponsored loans, and scholarships/grants available. Financial award application deadline: 4/1; financial award applicants required to submit FAFSA. *Faculty research:* Corporate finance, information systems, digital marketing, asset pricing, sports management. *Unit head:* Brian Mitchell, Associate Dean, 404-727-4824, Fax: 404-712-9648, E-mail: brian.mitchell@emory.edu. *Application contact:* Julie Barefoot, Associate Dean, 404-727-6311, Fax: 404-727-4612, E-mail: mbaadmissions@emory.edu.
Website: http://www.goizueta.emory.edu

Emory University, Goizueta Business School, Modular MBA for Executives Program, Atlanta, GA 30322. Offers MBA. *Program availability:* Part-time-only. *Faculty:* 19 full-time (2 women), 6 part-time/adjunct (1 woman). *Students:* 56 full-time (16 women); includes 21 minority (5 Black or African American, non-Hispanic/Latino; 9 Asian, non-Hispanic/Latino; 5 Hispanic/Latino; 2 Two or more races, non-Hispanic/Latino), 11 international. Average age 40. 84 applicants, 65% accepted, 24 enrolled. In 2017, 31 master's awarded. *Degree requirements:* For master's, minimum of 50 credit hours, which includes lock-step core coursework, two elective courses, experiential learning, and global business practices through week-long international colloquium. *Entrance requirements:* For master's, GMAT/GRE (or waiver), interview, essays, letters of recommendation, undergraduate degree, resume, work experience. Additional exam requirements/recommendations for international students: Required—TOEFL (minimum score 100 iBT), IELTS (minimum score 7), PTE (minimum score 68). *Application deadline:* For fall admission, 2/1 for domestic and international students; for winter admission, 3/30 for domestic and international students; for spring admission, 5/15 for domestic and international students; for summer admission, 7/1 for domestic and international students. Application fee: $150. Electronic applications accepted. *Expenses:* Contact institution. *Financial support:* Scholarships/grants available. Financial award application deadline: 8/10. *Faculty research:* Alternative investments, quality management and statistical methodology, entrepreneurial finance, effects of competition on marketing strategies, strategies for niche and specialized firms. *Unit head:* Wendy Tsung, Associate Dean, 404-727-1787, E-mail: wendy.tsung@emory.edu. *Application contact:* Caroline Grimes, Senior Associate Director of MBA Admissions, 404-727-9859, Fax: 404-727-4612, E-mail: caroline.grimes@emory.edu. Website: http://goizueta.emory.edu/degree/emba/memba

Emory University, Goizueta Business School, Weekend MBA for Executives Program, Atlanta, GA 30322. Offers MBA. *Program availability:* Part-time-only. *Faculty:* 24 full-time (2 women), 10 part-time/adjunct (2 women). *Students:* 103 full-time (35 women); includes 54 minority (19 Black or African American, non-Hispanic/Latino; 24 Asian, non-Hispanic/Latino; 10 Hispanic/Latino; 1 Two or more races, non-Hispanic/Latino), 7 international. Average age 37. 121 applicants, 68% accepted, 43 enrolled. In 2017, 48 master's awarded. *Degree requirements:* For master's, minimum of 51 credit hours. *Entrance requirements:* For master's, GMAT/GRE (or waiver), interview, essays, letters of recommendation, undergraduate degree, resume, work experience. Additional exam requirements/recommendations for international students: Required—TOEFL (minimum score 100 iBT), IELTS (minimum score 7), PTE (minimum score 68). *Application deadline:* For fall admission, 2/1 for domestic and international students; for winter admission, 3/30 for domestic and international students; for spring admission, 5/15 for domestic and international students; for summer admission, 7/1 for domestic and international students. Application fee: $150. Electronic applications accepted. *Expenses:* Contact institution. *Financial support:* Scholarships/grants available. Financial award application deadline: 8/10. *Faculty research:* Neuro-imaging, how technology and social forces create and sustain competitive advantage, entrepreneurial finance, alternative investments, digital commerce. *Unit head:* Wendy Tsung, Associate Dean, 404-727-1787, E-mail: wendy.tsung@emory.edu. *Application contact:* Caroline Grimes, Senior Associate Director of MBA Admissions, 404-727-9859, Fax: 404-727-4612, E-mail: caroline.grimes@emory.edu. Website: http://goizueta.emory.edu/degree/emba/wemba/

Emporia State University, Program in Business Administration, Emporia, KS 66801-5415. Offers MBA. *Accreditation:* AACSB. *Program availability:* Part-time, evening/weekend, blended/hybrid learning. *Faculty:* 29 full-time (8 women). *Students:* 49 full-time (18 women), 44 part-time (24 women); includes 11 minority (3 Black or African American, non-Hispanic/Latino; 1 American Indian or Alaska Native, non-Hispanic/Latino; 3 Asian, non-Hispanic/Latino; 2 Hispanic/Latino; 2 Two or more races, non-Hispanic/Latino), 29 international. 51 applicants, 63% accepted, 17 enrolled. In 2017, 45 master's awarded. *Entrance requirements:* For master's, GRE, 15 undergraduate credits in business, minimum undergraduate GPA of 2.7 in last 60 hours. Additional exam requirements/recommendations for international students: Required—TOEFL (minimum score 520 paper-based; 68 iBT). *Application deadline:* For fall admission, 8/15 for domestic students. Applications are processed on a rolling basis. Application fee: $30 ($75 for international students). Electronic applications accepted. *Expenses:* Tuition, state resident: full-time $6084; part-time $253.50 per credit hour. Tuition, nonresident: full-time $18,924; part-time $788.50 per credit hour. *Required fees:* $1943; $80.95 per credit hour. Tuition and fees vary according to campus/location. *Financial support:* In 2017–18, 1 research assistantship with full tuition reimbursement (averaging $7,344 per year), 9 teaching assistantships with full tuition reimbursements (averaging $4,488 per year) were awarded; career-related internships or fieldwork, health care benefits, and unspecified assistantships also available. Financial award applicants required to submit FAFSA. *Unit head:* James Willingham, Coordinator, Graduate and Career Services, 620-341-5456, E-mail: jwilling@emporia.edu. *Application contact:* Mary Sewell, Admissions Coordinator, 800-950-GRAD, Fax: 620-341-5909, E-mail: msewell@emporia.edu. Website: http://www.emporia.edu/business/programs/mba/

Endicott College, Van Loan School of Graduate and Professional Studies, Program in Business Administration, Beverly, MA 01915-2096. Offers business administration (MBA); organizational leadership (MBA). *Program availability:* Part-time, evening/weekend, 100% online, blended/hybrid learning. *Faculty:* 3 full-time (1 woman), 39 part-time/adjunct (11 women). *Students:* 149 full-time (66 women), 79 part-time (38 women); includes 39 minority (13 Black or African American, non-Hispanic/Latino; 7 Asian, non-Hispanic/Latino; 12 Hispanic/Latino; 7 Two or more races, non-Hispanic/Latino), 9 international. Average age 31. 98 applicants, 100% accepted, 82 enrolled. In 2017, 135 master's awarded. *Degree requirements:* For master's, thesis, project. *Entrance requirements:* For master's, two recommendations, undergraduate transcript, essay. Additional exam requirements/recommendations for international students: Required—TOEFL. *Application deadline:* Applications are processed on a rolling basis. Application fee: $50. Electronic applications accepted. *Expenses:* Tuition varies by track. *Financial support:* Scholarships/grants available. Financial award applicants required to submit FAFSA. *Faculty research:* Adult learning and development, supply chain management, marketing, ethics. *Unit head:* Richard Maybury, Dean, MBA Programs, 978-232-2764, Fax: 978-232-3000, E-mail: rmaybury@endicott.edu. *Application contact:* Ian Menchini, Director, Graduate Enrollment and Advising, 978-232-5292, Fax: 978-232-3000, E-mail: imenchin@endicott.edu. Website: https://vanloan.endicott.edu/programs-of-study/masters-programs/master-of-business-administration-mba-programs

ESSEC Business School, Graduate Programs, Paris, France. Offers business administration (PhD); executive business administration (MBA); global business administration (MBA); hospitality management (MBA); international luxury brand management (MBA); management (MSM).

Everglades University, Graduate Programs, Program in Aviation Science, Boca Raton, FL 33431. Offers aviation operations management (MSA); aviation security (MSA); business administration (MSA). *Program availability:* Part-time, evening/weekend, 100% online. *Entrance requirements:* For master's, GMAT (minimum score of 400) or GRE (minimum score of 290), bachelor's or graduate degree from college accredited by an

agency recognized by the U.S. Department of Education; minimum cumulative GPA of 2.0 at the baccalaureate level, 3.0 at the master's level. Additional exam requirements/recommendations for international students: Recommended—TOEFL (minimum score 500 paper-based). Electronic applications accepted. *Expenses:* Contact institution.

Everglades University, Graduate Programs, Program in Business Administration, Boca Raton, FL 33431. Offers accounting for managers (MBA); aviation management (MBA); human resource management (MBA); project management (MBA). *Program availability:* Part-time, evening/weekend, 100% online. *Entrance requirements:* For master's, GMAT (minimum score of 400) or GRE (minimum score of 290), bachelor's or graduate degree from college accredited by an agency recognized by the U.S. Department of Education; minimum cumulative GPA of 2.0 at the baccalaureate level, 3.0 at the master's level. Additional exam requirements/recommendations for international students: Recommended—TOEFL (minimum score 500 paper-based). Electronic applications accepted. *Expenses:* Contact institution.

Excelsior College, School of Business and Technology, Albany, NY 12203-5159. Offers business administration (MBA); cybersecurity - information assurance (MS); cybersecurity - medical data security (MS); cybersecurity - policy administration (MS); cybersecurity management (MBA, Graduate Certificate); general business management (MS); health care management (MBA); human performance technology (MBA); human resource management (MS); human resources management (MBA); leadership (MBA, MS); mediation and arbitration (MBA, MS); social media management (MBA); technology management (MBA). *Program availability:* Part-time, evening/weekend, online learning. *Faculty:* 30 part-time/adjunct (12 women). *Students:* 1,204 part-time (333 women); includes 560 minority (310 Black or African American, non-Hispanic/Latino; 7 American Indian or Alaska Native, non-Hispanic/Latino; 42 Asian, non-Hispanic/Latino; 140 Hispanic/Latino; 10 Native Hawaiian or other Pacific Islander, non-Hispanic/Latino; 51 Two or more races, non-Hispanic/Latino). Average age 40. In 2017, 294 master's awarded. *Application deadline:* Applications are processed on a rolling basis. Application fee: $50. Electronic applications accepted. *Expenses:* Tuition: Part-time $645 per credit. *Required fees:* $265 per credit. *Financial support:* Scholarships/grants available. *Unit head:* Dr. Lifang Shih, Dean, 888-647-2388. *Application contact:* Admissions, 888-647-2388 Ext. 133, Fax: 518-464-8777, E-mail: admissions@excelsior.edu.

Fairfield University, Dolan School of Business, Fairfield, CT 06824. Offers accounting (MBA, MS, CAS); business analytics (MS); finance (MBA, MS, CAS); information systems and business analytics (MBA); management (MBA, CAS); marketing (MBA, CAS); taxation (CAS). *Accreditation:* AACSB. *Program availability:* Part-time, evening/weekend. *Faculty:* 18 full-time (6 women), 6 part-time/adjunct (2 women). *Students:* 120 full-time (57 women), 67 part-time (27 women); includes 20 minority (3 Black or African American, non-Hispanic/Latino; 1 American Indian or Alaska Native, non-Hispanic/Latino; 3 Asian, non-Hispanic/Latino; 11 Hispanic/Latino; 2 Two or more races, non-Hispanic/Latino), 33 international. Average age 26. 195 applicants, 87% accepted, 112 enrolled. In 2017, 93 master's awarded. *Degree requirements:* For master's, capstone course. *Entrance requirements:* For master's, GMAT (minimum score 500), 2 letters of reference, resume, minimum GPA of 3.0. Additional exam requirements/recommendations for international students: Required—TOEFL (minimum score 550 paper-based; 80 iBT) or IELTS (minimum score 6.5). *Application deadline:* For fall admission, 5/15 for international students; for spring admission, 10/15 for international students. Applications are processed on a rolling basis. Application fee: $60. Electronic applications accepted. *Expenses:* $925 per credit hour. *Financial support:* In 2017–18, 31 students received support. Scholarships/grants and unspecified assistantships available. Financial award applicants required to submit FAFSA. *Faculty research:* International finance, leadership and careers, ethics in accounting, emotions in consumer behavior and organizations, data analytics. *Unit head:* Dr. Mark Ligas, Interim Dean, 203-254-4070, Fax: 203-254-4105, E-mail: mligas@fairfield.edu. *Application contact:* Marianne Gumpper, Director of Graduate and Continuing Studies Admission, 203-254-4184, Fax: 203-254-4073, E-mail: gradadmis@fairfield.edu. Website: http://fairfield.edu/mba

Fairleigh Dickinson University, Florham Campus, Anthony J. Petrocelli College of Continuing Studies, School of Administrative Science, Program in Administrative Science, Madison, NJ 07940-1099. Offers MAS.

Fairleigh Dickinson University, Florham Campus, Silberman College of Business, Madison, NJ 07940-1099. Offers EMBA, MBA, MS, Certificate, MA/MBA, MBA/MA. *Accreditation:* AACSB. *Program availability:* Part-time, evening/weekend.

Fairleigh Dickinson University, Florham Campus, Silberman College of Business, Departments of Management, Marketing, and Entrepreneurial Studies, Program in Management, Madison, NJ 07940-1099. Offers evolving technology (Certificate); management (MBA); MBA/MA.

Fairleigh Dickinson University, Florham Campus, Silberman College of Business, Executive MBA Programs, Executive MBA Program in Management, Madison, NJ 07940-1099. Offers EMBA.

Fairleigh Dickinson University, Metropolitan Campus, Anthony J. Petrocelli College of Continuing Studies, School of Administrative Science, Program in Administrative Science, Teaneck, NJ 07666-1914. Offers MAS, Certificate.

Fairleigh Dickinson University, Metropolitan Campus, Silberman College of Business, Teaneck, NJ 07666-1914. Offers EMBA, MBA, MS, Certificate, MBA/MA. *Accreditation:* AACSB. *Entrance requirements:* For master's, GMAT.

Fairleigh Dickinson University, Metropolitan Campus, Silberman College of Business, Departments of Management, Marketing, and Entrepreneurial Studies, Program in Management, Teaneck, NJ 07666-1914. Offers management (MBA); management information systems (Certificate). *Accreditation:* AACSB.

Fairmont State University, Program in Business Administration, Fairmont, WV 26554. Offers MBA. *Accreditation:* ACBSP. *Program availability:* Part-time, evening/weekend. *Entrance requirements:* For master's, GRE, MAT, or GMAT, minimum overall undergraduate GPA of 2.75 or 3.0 on the last 60 hours. Additional exam requirements/recommendations for international students: Required—TOEFL (minimum score 80 iBT), IELTS (minimum score 6.5). Electronic applications accepted.

Fashion Institute of Technology, School of Graduate Studies, Program in Global Fashion Management, New York, NY 10001-5992. Offers MPS. Offered in collaboration with Hong Kong Polytechnic University and Institute Francais de la Mode. *Degree requirements:* For master's, capstone seminar. *Entrance requirements:* Additional exam requirements/recommendations for international students: Required—TOEFL (minimum score 550 paper-based). Electronic applications accepted.

Faulkner University, Harris College of Business and Executive Education, Montgomery, AL 36109-3398. Offers business administration (MBA); management (MSM). *Program availability:* Part-time, evening/weekend, 100% online, blended/hybrid learning. *Faculty:* 4 full-time (1 woman), 1 part-time/adjunct (0 women). *Students:* 95 full-time (60 women), 8 part-time (7 women); includes 52 minority (47 Black or African American, non-Hispanic/Latino; 1 American Indian or Alaska Native, non-Hispanic/Latino; 1 Hispanic/Latino; 3 Two or more races, non-Hispanic/Latino), 2 international. Average age 36. 148 applicants, 59% accepted, 67 enrolled. In 2017, 61 master's

Business Administration and Management—General

awarded. *Degree requirements:* For master's, comprehensive exam (for MBA only). *Entrance requirements:* For master's, GMAT (no more than two years old), bachelor's degree from regionally-accredited college or university; official transcripts from all colleges and universities attended; minimum GPA of 2.5 on undergraduate degree; resume including education and at least 4 years of relevant work experience; course in statistics, quantitative business analysis, or operations research. Additional exam requirements/recommendations for international students: Required—TOEFL (minimum score 500 paper-based). *Application deadline:* For fall admission, 9/1 for domestic students; for spring admission, 1/15 for domestic students. Applications are processed on a rolling basis. Application fee: $35. Electronic applications accepted. *Expenses:* $550 per hour tuition (for MBA); $525 per hour tuition (for MSM); $220 per semester fees. *Financial support:* Applicants required to submit FAFSA. *Unit head:* Dr. Dave A. Khadanga, Dean, Harris College of Business, 334-386-7112, E-mail: dkhadanga@faulkner.edu. *Application contact:* Ralph W. Aisnworth, Director, MSM Program, 334-386-7571, Fax: 334-386-7569, E-mail: rainsworth@faulkner.edu.
Website: https://www.faulkner.edu/graduate/graduate-admissions-3/

Fayetteville State University, Graduate School, Program in Business Administration, Fayetteville, NC 28301. Offers MBA. *Accreditation:* AACSB. *Program availability:* Part-time, evening/weekend. *Faculty:* 9 full-time (4 women), 7 part-time/adjunct (3 women). *Students:* 157 full-time (86 women), 184 part-time (81 women); includes 177 minority (142 Black or African American, non-Hispanic/Latino; 2 American Indian or Alaska Native, non-Hispanic/Latino; 19 Asian, non-Hispanic/Latino; 13 Hispanic/Latino; 1 Native Hawaiian or other Pacific Islander, non-Hispanic/Latino), 7 international. Average age 33. 294 applicants, 76% accepted, 162 enrolled. In 2017, 40 master's awarded. *Entrance requirements:* For master's, GMAT. Additional exam requirements/recommendations for international students: Required—TOEFL. *Application deadline:* For fall admission, 4/15 for domestic students; for spring admission, 10/15 for domestic students. Application fee: $40. *Expenses:* Tuition, state resident: full-time $8604. Tuition, nonresident: full-time $19,669. *Financial support:* Application deadline: 3/1; applicants required to submit FAFSA. *Faculty research:* Business ethics, optimization and business simulation, consumer behavior, e-commerce and supply chain management, financial institutions. *Unit head:* Dr. Pamela Jackson, Dean, School of Business and Economics, 910-672-1267, Fax: 910-672-2046, E-mail: pjackson@uncfsu.edu. *Application contact:* John Scarsella, MBA Admission Director, 910-672-2910, Fax: 910-672-2046, E-mail: jscarse1@uncfsu.edu.

Felician University, Program in Business, Lodi, NJ 07644-2117. Offers business administration (DBA); innovation and entrepreneurial leadership (MBA). *Program availability:* Part-time-only, evening/weekend, online learning. *Faculty:* 5 full-time (0 women), 17 part-time/adjunct (3 women). *Students:* 17 full-time (11 women), 94 part-time (59 women); includes 59 minority (25 Black or African American, non-Hispanic/Latino; 10 Asian, non-Hispanic/Latino; 24 Hispanic/Latino), 5 international. Average age 34. 68 applicants, 81% accepted, 34 enrolled. In 2017, 20 master's awarded. Terminal master's awarded for partial completion of doctoral program. *Degree requirements:* For master's, comprehensive exam, thesis, presentation; for doctorate, thesis/dissertation, scholarly project. *Entrance requirements:* For master's and doctorate, GMAT, resume, personal statement, graduation from accredited baccalaureate program. Additional exam requirements/recommendations for international students: Required—TOEFL (minimum score 550 paper-based; 79 iBT), IELTS (minimum score 6.5), PTE (minimum score 56). *Application deadline:* Applications are processed on a rolling basis. Application fee: $40. Electronic applications accepted. Application fee is waived when completed online. *Expenses:* Contact institution. *Financial support:* Federal Work-Study and scholarships/grants available. Financial award applicants required to submit FAFSA. *Faculty research:* Social media, assessment, small business management, mission integration. *Unit head:* Dr. David M. Turi, Associate Dean/Associate Professor, School of Business, 201-559-3327, E-mail: turid@felician.edu. *Application contact:* Michael Szarek, Assistant Vice-President of Graduate Admissions, 201-355-1450, E-mail: szarekm@felician.edu.

Ferris State University, College of Business, Big Rapids, MI 49307. Offers business intelligence (MBA); design and innovation management (MBA); incident response (MBA); information security and intelligence (MS), including business intelligence, incident response, project management; lean systems and leadership (MBA); performance metrics (MBA); project management (MBA); supply chain management and lean logistics (MBA). *Accreditation:* ACBSP. *Program availability:* Part-time, evening/weekend, 100% online, blended/hybrid learning. *Faculty:* 18 full-time (7 women), 6 part-time/adjunct (3 women). *Students:* 19 full-time (10 women), 73 part-time (45 women); includes 8 minority (1 Black or African American, non-Hispanic/Latino; 2 Asian, non-Hispanic/Latino; 3 Hispanic/Latino; 2 Two or more races, non-Hispanic/Latino), 12 international. Average age 32. 52 applicants, 77% accepted, 16 enrolled. In 2017, 88 master's awarded. *Degree requirements:* For master's, comprehensive exam, thesis. *Entrance requirements:* For master's, GRE or GMAT, minimum GPA of 3.0 in junior-/senior-level classes and overall; statement of purpose; 3 letters of reference; resume; transcripts. Additional exam requirements/recommendations for international students: Required—TOEFL (minimum score 500 paper-based; 70 iBT), IELTS (minimum score 6.5). *Application deadline:* For fall admission, 7/1 priority date for domestic students, 6/15 for international students; for winter admission, 11/1 priority date for domestic students, 10/15 for international students; for spring admission, 3/1 priority date for domestic students, 2/15 for international students. Applications are processed on a rolling basis. Application fee: $0 ($30 for international students). Electronic applications accepted. *Expenses:* Contact institution. *Financial support:* Career-related internships or fieldwork, Federal Work-Study, scholarships/grants, and unspecified assistantships available. Support available to part-time students. Financial award application deadline: 3/15; financial award applicants required to submit FAFSA. *Faculty research:* Lifestyle medicine business models, lean systems value chain optimization, digital forensics/incident response, location-based services, passive data capture and analysis. *Unit head:* Dr. David Nicol, College of Business Dean, 231-591-2168, Fax: 231-591-3521, E-mail: davidnicol@ferris.edu. *Application contact:* Dr. Greg Gogolin, Professor, 231-591-3159, Fax: 231-591-3521, E-mail: greggogolin@ferris.edu.
Website: http://cbgp.ferris.edu

Fisher College, Master of Business Administration Program, Boston, MA 02116-1500. Offers strategic leadership (MBA). *Program availability:* Part-time, evening/weekend, online only, 100% online. *Faculty:* 5 full-time (1 woman), 6 part-time/adjunct (1 woman). *Students:* 12 full-time (6 women), 29 part-time (16 women); includes 13 minority (2 Black or African American, non-Hispanic/Latino; 1 Asian, non-Hispanic/Latino; 9 Hispanic/Latino; 1 Two or more races, non-Hispanic/Latino), 5 international. Average age 31. 57 applicants, 56% accepted, 19 enrolled. In 2017, 8 master's awarded. *Degree requirements:* For master's, comprehensive exam. *Entrance requirements:* Additional exam requirements/recommendations for international students: Required—TOEFL (minimum score 80 iBT), IELTS (minimum score 6.5). *Application deadline:* For fall admission, 8/1 for domestic and international students; for winter admission, 11/1 for domestic and international students. Applications are processed on a rolling basis. Electronic applications accepted. *Expenses:* Tuition: Full-time $28,512; part-time $14,256 per semester. *Required fees:* $4800. Tuition and fees vary according to class time. *Financial support:* In 2017-18, 2 students received support. Scholarships/grants and unspecified assistantships available. Financial award applicants required to submit FAFSA. *Faculty research:* Humanistic management, the role of human resources in employee engagement. *Unit head:* Neil Trotta, Assistant Dean, School of Graduate Studies/MBA Program Director, 617-236-8867, Fax: 617-236-5462, E-mail: ntrotta@fisher.edu.
Website: http://www.fisher.edu/mba

Fitchburg State University, Division of Graduate and Continuing Education, Program in Business Administration, Fitchburg, MA 01420-2697. Offers accounting (MBA); human resources management (MBA); management (MBA). *Program availability:* Part-time, evening/weekend, 100% online. *Faculty:* 7 full-time (2 women), 6 part-time/adjunct (2 women). *Students:* 356 full-time (179 women), 129 part-time (71 women); includes 132 minority (55 Black or African American, non-Hispanic/Latino; 1 American Indian or Alaska Native, non-Hispanic/Latino; 29 Asian, non-Hispanic/Latino; 42 Hispanic/Latino; 5 Two or more races, non-Hispanic/Latino). Average age 35. 332 applicants, 97% accepted, 259 enrolled. In 2017, 39 master's awarded. *Entrance requirements:* Additional exam requirements/recommendations for international students: Required—TOEFL (minimum score 550 paper-based; 79 iBT). *Application deadline:* For fall admission, 7/15 for international students; for spring admission, 12/1 for international students. Applications are processed on a rolling basis. Application fee: $50. Electronic applications accepted. *Expenses:* Contact institution. *Financial support:* In 2017-18, research assistantships with partial tuition reimbursements (averaging $5,500 per year) were awarded; Federal Work-Study, scholarships/grants, and unspecified assistantships also available. Support available to part-time students. Financial award application deadline: 3/1; financial award applicants required to submit FAFSA. *Unit head:* Joseph McAloon, Chair, 978-665-3745, Fax: 978-665-3658, E-mail: gce@fitchburgstate.edu. *Application contact:* Jinawa McNeil, Director of Admissions, 978-665-3140, Fax: 978-665-4540, E-mail: admissions@fitchburgstate.edu.
Website: http://www.fitchburgstate.edu

Florida Agricultural and Mechanical University, Division of Graduate Studies, Research, and Continuing Education, School of Business and Industry, Tallahassee, FL 32307-3200. Offers accounting (MBA); finance (MBA); management information systems (MBA); marketing (MBA). *Accreditation:* ACBSP. *Degree requirements:* For master's, residency. *Entrance requirements:* For master's, GMAT, minimum GPA of 3.0.

Florida Atlantic University, College of Business, Department of Management, Boca Raton, FL 33431-0991. Offers business administration (MBA); entrepreneurship (MBA); health administration (MBA); international business (MBA); sport management (MBA). *Faculty:* 4 full-time (1 woman). *Students:* 122 full-time (86 women), 81 part-time (67 women); includes 117 minority (61 Black or African American, non-Hispanic/Latino; 12 Asian, non-Hispanic/Latino; 44 Hispanic/Latino), 3 international. Average age 35. 124 applicants, 73% accepted, 75 enrolled. In 2017, 70 master's awarded. *Entrance requirements:* For master's, GMAT or GRE General Test, minimum GPA of 3.0 in last 60 hours of course work. Additional exam requirements/recommendations for international students: Required—TOEFL (minimum score 600 paper-based; 61 iBT), IELTS (minimum score 6). *Application deadline:* For fall admission, 7/25 for domestic students, 2/15 for international students; for spring admission, 12/10 for domestic students, 7/15 for international students. Applications are processed on a rolling basis. Application fee: $30. Electronic applications accepted. *Expenses:* Tuition, state resident: full-time $7400; part-time $369.82 per credit. Tuition, nonresident: full-time $20,496; part-time $1042.81 per credit. *Financial support:* Research assistantships with full tuition reimbursements, career-related internships or fieldwork, tuition waivers (partial), and unspecified assistantships available. *Faculty research:* Sports administration, healthcare, policy, finance, real estate, senior living. *Unit head:* Dr. Roland Kidwell, Chair, 561-297-5634, E-mail: kidwellr@fau.edu.
Website: http://business.fau.edu/departments/management/index.aspx

Florida Gulf Coast University, Lutgert College of Business, Master of Business Administration Program, Fort Myers, FL 33965-6565. Offers MBA. *Accreditation:* AACSB. *Program availability:* Part-time, evening/weekend. *Faculty:* 60 full-time (24 women), 31 part-time/adjunct (7 women). *Students:* 32 full-time (15 women), 77 part-time (36 women); includes 25 minority (4 Black or African American, non-Hispanic/Latino; 1 American Indian or Alaska Native, non-Hispanic/Latino; 4 Asian, non-Hispanic/Latino; 13 Hispanic/Latino; 3 Two or more races, non-Hispanic/Latino), 6 international. Average age 29. 85 applicants, 54% accepted, 36 enrolled. In 2017, 40 master's awarded. *Entrance requirements:* For master's, GMAT, minimum GPA of 3.0. Additional exam requirements/recommendations for international students: Required—TOEFL (minimum score 550 paper-based). *Application deadline:* For fall admission, 5/1 priority date for domestic students; for spring admission, 9/15 priority date for domestic students. Applications are processed on a rolling basis. Application fee: $30. Electronic applications accepted. *Expenses:* Tuition, state resident: part-time $290 per credit hour. Tuition, nonresident: part-time $1173 per credit hour. *Required fees:* $127 per credit hour. Tuition and fees vary according to course load. *Financial support:* In 2017-18, 13 students received support. Application deadline: 6/30; applicants required to submit FAFSA. *Faculty research:* Fraud in audits, production planning in cell manufacturing systems, collaborative learning in distance courses, characteristics of minority and women-owned businesses. *Unit head:* Robert Beatty, Dean, 239-590-7300, Fax: 239-590-7330, E-mail: rbeatty@fgcu.edu. *Application contact:* Marisa Ouverson, Director of Enrollment Management, 239-590-7403, Fax: 239-590-7330, E-mail: mouverso@fgcu.edu.

Florida Institute of Technology, Extended Studies Division, Melbourne, FL 32901-6975. Offers acquisition and contract management (MS); aerospace engineering (MS); business administration (MBA, DBA); computer information systems (MS); computer science (MS); electrical engineering (MS); engineering management (MS); human resources management (MS); logistics management (MS), including humanitarian and disaster relief logistics; management (MS), including acquisition and contract management, e-business, human resources management, information systems, logistics management, management, transportation management; material acquisition management (MS); mechanical engineering (MS); operations research (MS); project management (MS), including information systems, operations research; public administration (MPA); quality management (MS); software engineering (MS); space systems (MS); space systems management (MS); supply chain management (MS); systems management (MS), including information systems, operations research; technology management (MS). *Program availability:* Part-time, evening/weekend, online learning. *Students:* Average age 36. 962 applicants, 48% accepted, 323 enrolled. In 2017, 403 master's awarded. *Entrance requirements:* For master's, GMAT or resume showing 8 years of supervised experience, minimum GPA of 3.0, 2 letters of recommendation, resume. Additional exam requirements/recommendations for international students: Required—TOEFL (minimum score 550 paper-based; 79 iBT). *Application deadline:* For fall admission, 4/1 for international students; for spring admission, 9/30 for international students. Applications are processed on a rolling basis. Electronic applications accepted. *Expenses:* Contact institution. *Financial support:* Application deadline: 3/1; applicants required to submit FAFSA. *Unit head:* Dr. Theodore R. Richardson, III, Dean, 321-674-8123, Fax: 321-674-7597, E-mail: trichardson@fit.edu. *Application contact:* Carolyn Farrior, Director of Graduate Admissions, Online Learning and Off-Campus Programs, 321-674-7118, Fax: 321-674-8216, E-mail: cfarrior@fit.edu.
Website: http://es.fit.edu

Florida Institute of Technology, Nathan M. Bisk College of Business, Melbourne, FL 32901-6975. Offers MBA, MS. *Program availability:* Part-time, online learning. *Students:* Average age 33. 206 applicants, 40% accepted, 18 enrolled. In 2017, 192 master's awarded. *Degree requirements:* For master's, comprehensive exam (for some programs), thesis optional, capstone. *Entrance requirements:* For master's, GMAT, GRE or resume showing 8 years of supervised experience, minimum GPA of 3.0 (for MBA), 2 letters of recommendation, resume, statement of objectives. Additional exam requirements/recommendations for international students: Required—TOEFL (minimum score 550 paper-based; 79 iBT). *Application deadline:* For fall admission, 4/1 for international students; for spring admission, 9/30 for international students. Applications are processed on a rolling basis. Electronic applications accepted. *Expenses: Tuition:* Part-time $1241 per credit hour. Part-time tuition and fees vary according to campus/location. *Financial support:* Research assistantships with partial tuition reimbursements, career-related internships or fieldwork, institutionally sponsored loans, and unspecified assistantships available. Support available to part-time students. Financial award application deadline: 3/1; financial award applicants required to submit FAFSA. *Faculty research:* Investment analysis, marketing research, strategy analysis, ethics, small business. *Unit head:* Dr. Theodore R. Richardson, III, Dean, 321-674-8123, Fax: 321-674-7597, E-mail: trichardson@fit.edu. *Application contact:* Cheryl A. Brown, Associate Director of Graduate Admissions, 321-674-7581, Fax: 321-723-9468, E-mail: cbrown@fit.edu.
Website: http://cob.fit.edu

Florida Memorial University, School of Business, Miami-Dade, FL 33054. Offers MBA. *Accreditation:* ACBSP. *Program availability:* Part-time. *Entrance requirements:* For master's, GMAT, 3 letters of recommendation.

Florida National University, Program in Business Administration, Hialeah, FL 33012. Offers accounting (MBA); finance (MBA); general management (MBA); health services administration (MBA); marketing (MBA); public management and leadership (MBA). *Program availability:* Part-time, blended/hybrid learning. *Degree requirements:* For master's, capstone. *Entrance requirements:* For master's, writing assessment, bachelor's degree from accredited institution; official undergraduate transcripts; minimum undergraduate GPA of 2.5, GMAT (minimum score of 400), or GRE (minimum score of 900); two letters of recommendation; resume. Additional exam requirements/recommendations for international students: Required—TOEFL (minimum score 500 paper-based; 62 iBT), IELTS (minimum score 5.5). *Application deadline:* Applications are processed on a rolling basis. Electronic applications accepted. *Expenses:* Contact institution. *Financial support:* Federal Work-Study, institutionally sponsored loans, scholarships/grants, and tuition waivers available. Financial award applicants required to submit FAFSA. *Unit head:* Dr. Ernesto Gonzalez, Business and Economics Department Head, 305-821-3333 Ext. 1070, Fax: 305-362-0595, E-mail: egonzalez@fnu.edu.
Website: https://www.fnu.edu/prospective-students/our-programs/select-a-program/master-of-business-administration-mba-masters/

Florida Southern College, Program in Business Administration, Lakeland, FL 33801-5698. Offers MBA. *Accreditation:* AACSB. *Program availability:* Part-time, 100% online, blended/hybrid learning. *Faculty:* 7 full-time (3 women), 1 part-time/adjunct (0 women). *Students:* 73 full-time (41 women), 4 part-time (1 woman); includes 12 minority (4 Black or African American, non-Hispanic/Latino; 2 Asian, non-Hispanic/Latino; 6 Hispanic/Latino), 7 international. Average age 22, 26 applicants, 60% accepted, 37 enrolled. In 2017, 37 master's awarded. *Entrance requirements:* For master's, GMAT or GRE General Test, letter of reference, resume, personal statement. Additional exam requirements/recommendations for international students: Required—TOEFL (minimum score 550 paper-based; 79 iBT), IELTS (minimum score 6.5). *Application deadline:* For fall admission, 6/1 for domestic and international students; for spring admission, 10/1 for domestic and international students. Applications are processed on a rolling basis. Application fee: $30. Electronic applications accepted. *Expenses:* $775 per credit hour, $100 fees. *Financial support:* Scholarships/grants and unspecified assistantships available. Support available to part-time students. Financial award application deadline: 3/1; financial award applicants required to submit FAFSA. *Unit head:* Dr. Charles DuVal, Program Coordinator, 863-680-4280, Fax: 863-680-4355, E-mail: cduval@flsouthern.edu. *Application contact:* Kamalie Morales, Senior Assistant Director of Adult and Graduate Education, 863-680-4205, Fax: 863-680-3872, E-mail: kmorales@flsouthern.edu.
Website: http://www.flsouthern.edu/KCMS/Master-of-Business-Administration.aspx

Florida State University, The Graduate School, College of Business, Tallahassee, FL 32306-1110. Offers accounting (M Acc), including assurance and advisory services, generalist, taxation; business administration (MBA, PhD), including accounting (PhD), finance (PhD), management information systems (PhD), marketing (PhD), organizational behavior and human resources (PhD), risk management and insurance (PhD), strategy (PhD); finance (MS); management information systems (MS); risk management and insurance (MS); JD/MBA; MSW/MBA. *Accreditation:* AACSB. *Program availability:* Part-time, 100% online. *Faculty:* 93 full-time (23 women), 2 part-time/adjunct (1 woman). *Students:* 229 full-time (96 women), 423 part-time (154 women); includes 159 minority (44 Black or African American, non-Hispanic/Latino; 24 Asian, non-Hispanic/Latino; 75 Hispanic/Latino; 1 Native Hawaiian or other Pacific Islander, non-Hispanic/Latino; 15 Two or more races, non-Hispanic/Latino), 48 international. Average age 31. 300 applicants, 61% accepted, 133 enrolled. In 2017, 268 master's, 9 doctorates awarded. Terminal master's awarded for partial completion of doctoral program. *Degree requirements:* For doctorate, comprehensive exam, thesis/dissertation. *Entrance requirements:* For master's, GMAT, GRE (for all except MS in finance), work experience (MBA, MS); minimum GPA of 3.0, letters of recommendation; for doctorate, GMAT, GRE (for marketing, organizational behavior, risk management and insurance, management information systems, and human resources only), minimum graduate GPA of 3.5, letters of recommendation. Additional exam requirements/recommendations for international students: Required—TOEFL (minimum score 600 paper-based; 85 iBT); Recommended—IELTS (minimum score 6). *Application deadline:* For fall admission, 6/1 for domestic and international students; for spring admission, 10/1 for domestic and international students; for summer admission, 3/1 for domestic and international students. Applications are processed on a rolling basis. Application fee: $30. Electronic applications accepted. *Expenses:* Contact institution. *Financial support:* In 2017–18, 146 students received support, including 26 fellowships (averaging $1,500 per year), 77 research assistantships with full tuition reimbursements available (averaging $20,000 per year), 43 teaching assistantships with full tuition reimbursements available (averaging $20,000 per year); career-related internships or fieldwork, scholarships/grants, health care benefits, tuition waivers (full and partial), and unspecified assistantships also available. Support available to part-time students. Financial award application deadline: 1/1; financial award applicants required to submit FAFSA. *Faculty research:* Business strategy, marketing, finance, accounting, business analytics. *Total annual research expenditures:* $1.4 million. *Unit head:* Dr. Michael Hartline, Dean, 850-644-4405, Fax: 850-644-0915, E-mail: mhartline@business.fsu.edu. *Application contact:* Jennifer Clark, Director, 850-644-6458, E-mail: gradprograms@business.fsu.edu.
Website: http://business.fsu.edu/

Fontbonne University, Graduate Programs, St. Louis, MO 63105-3098. Offers accounting (MBA, MS); art (MA); art (K-12) (MAT); business (MBA); computer science (MS); deaf education (MA); early intervention in deaf education (MA); education (MA), including autism spectrum disorders, curriculum and instruction, diverse learners, early childhood education, reading, special education; elementary education (MAT); family and consumer sciences (MA), including multidisciplinary health communication studies; fine arts (MFA); instructional design and technology (MS); management and leadership (MM); middle school education (MAT); secondary education (MAT); special education (MAT); speech-language pathology (MS); supply chain management (MS); theatre (MA). *Program availability:* Part-time, evening/weekend, online learning. *Degree requirements:* For master's, comprehensive exam (for some programs), thesis (for some programs). *Entrance requirements:* Additional exam requirements/recommendations for international students: Required—TOEFL (minimum score 500 paper-based; 65 iBT). Electronic applications accepted.

Fordham University, Gabelli School of Business, New York, NY 10023. Offers accounting (MBA, MS); applied statistics and decision-making (MS); business economics (DPS); capital markets (DPS); communications and media management (MBA); electronic business (MBA); entrepreneurship (MBA); finance (MBA, PhD); global finance (MS); global sustainability (MBA); health administration (MS); healthcare management (MBA); information systems (MBA, MS); investor relations (MS); management (EMBA, MBA, MS, PhD); marketing (MBA); marketing intelligence (MS); media management (MS); nonprofit leadership (MS); quantitative finance (MS); strategy and decision-making (DPS); taxation (MS); JD/MBA; MS/MBA. *Accreditation:* AACSB. *Program availability:* Part-time, evening/weekend. *Faculty:* 130 full-time (46 women), 42 part-time/adjunct (5 women). *Students:* 1,051 full-time (570 women), 563 part-time (313 women); includes 190 minority (48 Black or African American, non-Hispanic/Latino; 72 Asian, non-Hispanic/Latino; 69 Hispanic/Latino; 1 Native Hawaiian or other Pacific Islander, non-Hispanic/Latino), 1,106 international. Average age 27. 4,577 applicants, 58% accepted, 794 enrolled. In 2017, 937 master's awarded. Terminal master's awarded for partial completion of doctoral program. *Degree requirements:* For master's, internships (for some degrees); for doctorate, comprehensive exam (for some programs), thesis/dissertation. *Entrance requirements:* For master's, GMAT/GRE, 2 letters of recommendation, resume, 2 essays, transcripts, interview. Additional exam requirements/recommendations for international students: Required—TOEFL (minimum score 100 iBT), IELTS (minimum score 7). *Application deadline:* For fall admission, 11/15 priority date for domestic and international students; for winter admission, 1/19 priority date for domestic students, 1/1 priority date for international students; for spring admission, 4/15 for domestic students, 3/1 for international students; for summer admission, 6/1 for domestic students. Application fee: $130. Electronic applications accepted. *Expenses:* $1,495 per credit. *Financial support:* Career-related internships or fieldwork, institutionally sponsored loans, scholarships/grants, and unspecified assistantships available. Support available to part-time students. Financial award application deadline: 6/30; financial award applicants required to submit FAFSA. *Unit head:* Dr. Donna Rapaccioli, Dean, 212-636-6165, Fax: 212-307-1779, E-mail: rapaccioli@fordham.edu. *Application contact:* Lawrence Murray, Senior Assistant Dean of Graduate Admissions and Advising, 212-636-6200, Fax: 212-636-7076, E-mail: admissionsgb@fordham.edu.
Website: http://www.fordham.edu/gabelli

Fort Hays State University, Graduate School, College of Business and Entrepreneurship, Department of Management, Hays, KS 67601-4099. Offers MBA. *Degree requirements:* For master's, thesis optional. *Entrance requirements:* For master's, GMAT. Additional exam requirements/recommendations for international students: Required—TOEFL (minimum score 550 paper-based). Electronic applications accepted. *Faculty research:* Organizational behavior and performance appraisal, data processing, international marketing.

Framingham State University, Graduate Studies, Program in Business Administration, Framingham, MA 01701-9101. Offers biotechnology operations (MBA); management (MBA). *Program availability:* Part-time, evening/weekend. *Entrance requirements:* For master's, GMAT, GRE, or MAT. *Unit head:* Dr. Steven Moysey, Director, E-mail: smoysey@framingham.edu. *Application contact:* 508-626-4550, Fax: 508-626-4030, E-mail: dgce@frc.mass.edu.
Website: http://www.framingham.edu/mba

Franciscan University of Steubenville, Graduate Programs, Department of Business, Steubenville, OH 43952-1763. Offers MBA. *Program availability:* Part-time, evening/weekend, 100% online, blended/hybrid learning. *Faculty:* 9 part-time/adjunct (3 women). *Students:* 9 full-time (2 women), 39 part-time (15 women); includes 7 minority (1 Asian, non-Hispanic/Latino; 5 Hispanic/Latino; 1 Two or more races, non-Hispanic/Latino), 1 international. Average age 32. 33 applicants, 76% accepted, 12 enrolled. In 2017, 14 master's awarded. *Degree requirements:* For master's, research paper. *Entrance requirements:* For master's, GMAT, minimum undergraduate GPA of 2.5. Additional exam requirements/recommendations for international students: Required—TOEFL (minimum score 550 paper-based; 80 iBT). *Application deadline:* For fall admission, 8/15 for domestic students, 5/31 for international students; for spring admission, 1/10 for domestic students, 9/30 for international students. Applications are processed on a rolling basis. Application fee: $0. Electronic applications accepted. *Expenses: Tuition:* Full-time $9000; part-time $500 per semester hour. *Required fees:* $16 per semester hour. Tuition and fees vary according to program. *Financial support:* Federal Work-Study and scholarships/grants available. Support available to part-time students. Financial award application deadline: 8/1; financial award applicants required to submit FAFSA. *Unit head:* Joseph Zoric, Program Director, 740-284-5801, E-mail: jzoric@franciscan.edu. *Application contact:* Ryan Welch, Online Enrollment Counselor, 740-284-5239, Fax: 740-284-5456, E-mail: rwelch@franciscan.edu.
Website: http://www.franciscan.edu/mba/

Francis Marion University, Graduate Programs, School of Business, Florence, SC 29502-0547. Offers business (MBA); health executive management (MBA). *Accreditation:* AACSB. *Program availability:* Part-time, evening/weekend. *Degree requirements:* For master's, comprehensive exam. *Entrance requirements:* For master's, GMAT or GRE, official transcripts, two letters of recommendation. Additional exam requirements/recommendations for international students: Required—TOEFL (minimum score 550 paper-based; 79 iBT). *Faculty research:* Ethics, directions of MBA, international business, regional economics, environmental issues.

Franklin Pierce University, Graduate and Professional Studies, Rindge, NH 03461-0060. Offers curriculum and instruction (M Ed); elementary education (MS Ed); emerging network technologies (Graduate Certificate); energy and sustainability studies (MBA, Graduate Certificate); health administration (MBA, Graduate Certificate); human resource management (MBA, Graduate Certificate); information technology (MBA); leadership (MBA); nursing education (MS); nursing leadership (MS); physical therapy (DPT); physician assistant studies (MPAS); special education (M Ed); sports management (MBA). *Accreditation:* APTA. *Program availability:* Part-time, 100% online, blended/hybrid learning. *Degree requirements:* For master's, concentrated original research projects; student teaching; fieldwork and/or internship; leadership project; PRAXIS I and II (for M Ed); for doctorate, concentrated original research projects, clinical fieldwork and/or internship, leadership project. *Entrance requirements:* For

Business Administration and Management—General

master's, minimum GPA of 2.5, 3 letters of recommendation; competencies in accounting, economics, statistics, and computer skills through life experience or undergraduate coursework (for MBA); certification/e-portfolio, minimum C grade in all education courses (for M Ed); license to practice as RN (for MS); for doctorate, GRE, 80 hours of observation/work in PT settings; completion of anatomy, chemistry, physics, and statistics; minimum GPA of 3.0. Additional exam requirements/recommendations for international students: Required—TOEFL (minimum score 550 paper-based; 61 iBT). Electronic applications accepted. *Faculty research:* Evidence-based practice in sports physical therapy, human resource management in economic crisis, leadership in nursing, innovation in sports facility management, differentiated learning and understanding by design.

Franklin University, MBA Program, Columbus, OH 43215-5399. Offers MBA. *Program availability:* Part-time, evening/weekend, online learning. *Entrance requirements:* For master's, minimum undergraduate GPA of 2.75. Additional exam requirements/ recommendations for international students: Required—TOEFL (minimum score 550 paper-based). Electronic applications accepted.

Freed-Hardeman University, Program in Business Administration, Henderson, TN 38340-2399. Offers accounting (MBA); corporate responsibility (MBA); leadership (MBA). *Accreditation:* ACBSP. *Program availability:* Part-time, evening/weekend, online learning. *Entrance requirements:* For master's, GMAT. Additional exam requirements/ recommendations for international students: Required—TOEFL (minimum score 500 paper-based).

Fresno Pacific University, Graduate Programs, MBA Program, Fresno, CA 93702-4709. Offers MBA. *Entrance requirements:* For master's, GMAT, GRE, or MAT, three references; resume; official transcripts verifying BA/BS; minimum GPA of 3.0; prerequisite courses in economics, statistics, and accounting. *Expenses:* Contact institution.

Fresno Pacific University, Graduate Programs, Program in Leadership and Organizational Studies, Fresno, CA 93702-4709. Offers MA. *Program availability:* Part-time, evening/weekend. *Degree requirements:* For master's, thesis. *Entrance requirements:* For master's, MAT, GRE or GMAT, interview, three references. Additional exam requirements/recommendations for international students: Required—TOEFL (minimum score 550 paper-based). Electronic applications accepted. *Expenses:* Contact institution. *Faculty research:* Ethics, servant leadership, communication, creative problem solving.

Frostburg State University, College of Business, Frostburg, MD 21532-1099. Offers MBA. *Accreditation:* AACSB. *Program availability:* Part-time, evening/weekend. *Faculty:* 12 full-time (5 women), 2 part-time/adjunct (1 woman). *Students:* 33 full-time (14 women), 143 part-time (77 women); includes 38 minority (20 Black or African American, non-Hispanic/Latino; 9 Asian, non-Hispanic/Latino; 6 Hispanic/Latino; 3 Two or more races, non-Hispanic/Latino), 3 international. Average age 34. 55 applicants, 60% accepted, 22 enrolled. In 2017, 75 master's awarded. *Entrance requirements:* For master's, GMAT. Additional exam requirements/recommendations for international students: Required—TOEFL. *Application deadline:* For fall admission, 7/15 priority date for domestic students. Applications are processed on a rolling basis. Application fee: $45. Electronic applications accepted. *Expenses:* Tuition, state resident: part-time $433 per credit hour. Tuition, nonresident: part-time $557 per credit hour. *Required fees:* $121 per credit hour. $27 per term. *Financial support:* In 2017–18, 3 research assistantships with full tuition reimbursements (averaging $5,000 per year) were awarded; career-related internships or fieldwork and Federal Work-Study also available. Financial award application deadline: 4/1; financial award applicants required to submit FAFSA. *Faculty research:* Cooperative teaching methods, strategic change processes, political marketing. *Unit head:* Dr. Sudhir Singh, Dean, 301-687-4019, E-mail: ssingh@frostburg.edu. *Application contact:* Vickie Mazer, Director, Graduate Services, 301-687-7053, Fax: 301-687-4597, E-mail: vmmazer@frostburg.edu.
Website: http://www.frostburg.edu/colleges/cob/

Full Sail University, Entertainment Business Master of Science Program - Online, Winter Park, FL 32792-7437. Offers MS. *Program availability:* Online learning. *Entrance requirements:* Additional exam requirements/recommendations for international students: Required—TOEFL (minimum score 550 paper-based; 79 iBT).

Gannon University, School of Graduate Studies, College of Engineering and Business, Dahlkemper School of Business, Program in Business Administration, Erie, PA 16541-0001. Offers business administration (MBA); finance (MBA); human resources management (MBA); marketing (MBA). *Accreditation:* ACBSP. *Program availability:* Part-time, evening/weekend, 100% online, blended/hybrid learning. *Entrance requirements:* For master's, GMAT, bachelor's degree in any discipline from any accredited college or university, resume, transcripts, 3 letters of recommendation. Additional exam requirements/recommendations for international students: Required—TOEFL (minimum score 79 iBT). Electronic applications accepted. Application fee is waived when completed online.

Gardner-Webb University, Graduate School of Business, Boiling Springs, NC 28017. Offers IMBA, M Acc, MBA. *Accreditation:* ACBSP. *Program availability:* Part-time, evening/weekend, online learning. *Faculty:* 11 full-time (3 women), 5 part-time/adjunct (1 woman). *Students:* 27 full-time (13 women), 236 part-time (126 women); includes 63 minority (45 Black or African American, non-Hispanic/Latino; 1 American Indian or Alaska Native, non-Hispanic/Latino; 3 Asian, non-Hispanic/Latino; 10 Hispanic/Latino; 4 Two or more races, non-Hispanic/Latino), 1 international. Average age 26. *Entrance requirements:* For master's, GMAT, GRE, 2 semesters of course work each in economics, statistics, and accounting. Additional exam requirements/recommendations for international students: Required—TOEFL (minimum score 500 paper-based; 61 iBT). *Application deadline:* For spring admission, 1/15 for domestic students. Applications are processed on a rolling basis. Electronic applications accepted. *Expenses:* Contact institution. *Financial support:* In 2017–18, 23 students received support. Unspecified assistantships available. Support available to part-time students. Financial award applicants required to submit FAFSA. *Unit head:* Mischia Taylor, Dean, 704-406-2324, E-mail: mtaylor@gardner-webb.edu.
Website: http://gardner-webb.edu/academic-programs-and-resources/colleges-and-schools/business/index

Geneva College, Program in Business Administration, Beaver Falls, PA 15010-3599. Offers business administration (MBA); finance (MBA); marketing (MBA); operations (MBA). *Accreditation:* ACBSP. *Program availability:* Part-time, evening/weekend. *Faculty:* 5 full-time (1 woman), 3 part-time/adjunct (0 women). *Students:* 33 full-time (13 women), 8 part-time (2 women); includes 6 minority (4 Black or African American, non-Hispanic/Latino; 1 American Indian or Alaska Native, non-Hispanic/Latino; 1 Asian, non-Hispanic/Latino). Average age 37. 25 applicants, 52% accepted, 10 enrolled. In 2017, 14 master's awarded. *Degree requirements:* For master's, 36 credit hours of course work (30 of which are required of all students). *Entrance requirements:* For master's, GMAT (if college GPA less than 2.5), undergraduate transcript, 2 letters of recommendation, resume, goals statement. Additional exam requirements/recommendations for international students: Required—TOEFL. *Application deadline:* For fall admission, 3/1 priority date for domestic students; for spring admission, 11/1 priority date for domestic students. Applications are processed on a rolling basis.

Electronic applications accepted. *Expenses:* $710 per credit. *Financial support:* In 2017–18, 1 student received support. Scholarships/grants available. Financial award application deadline: 8/1; financial award applicants required to submit FAFSA. *Unit head:* Dr. Gary Vander Plaats, Director of the MBA Program, 724-847-6619, E-mail: gpvander@geneva.edu. *Application contact:* Marina Frazier, Director of Graduate Enrollment, 724-847-6697, E-mail: mba@geneva.edu.
Website: http://www.geneva.edu/page/masters_business

George Fox University, College of Business, Newberg, OR 97132-2697. Offers accounting (DBA); finance (MBA); management (DBA); management and leadership (MBA); marketing (DBA); organizational strategy (MBA); strategic human resource management (MBA). MBA offered in Newberg, OR and in Portland, OR. *Accreditation:* ACBSP. *Program availability:* Part-time, evening/weekend, online learning. *Degree requirements:* For master's, capstone project; for doctorate, credit-applied research project. *Entrance requirements:* For master's, resume (5 years of professional experience); 3 professional references; interview; financial e-learning course; official transcripts; for doctorate, GRE or GMAT, resume; personal mission statement; academic research writing sample; official transcript from each college/university attended; three professional references. Additional exam requirements/ recommendations for international students: Required—TOEFL (minimum score 577 paper-based; 90 iBT) or IELTS (minimum score 7). Electronic applications accepted. *Expenses:* Contact institution.

George Mason University, School of Business, Program in Business Administration, Fairfax, VA 22030. Offers MBA. *Accreditation:* AACSB. *Program availability:* Part-time. *Faculty:* 97 full-time (36 women), 47 part-time/adjunct (12 women). *Students:* 253 full-time (104 women), 30 part-time (12 women); includes 99 minority (34 Black or African American, non-Hispanic/Latino; 36 Asian, non-Hispanic/Latino; 24 Hispanic/Latino; 3 Native Hawaiian or other Pacific Islander, non-Hispanic/Latino; 3 Two or more races, non-Hispanic/Latino), 21 international. Average age 32. 309 applicants, 80% accepted, 119 enrolled. In 2017, 123 master's awarded. *Entrance requirements:* For master's, GMAT/GRE, resume; 2 official copies of transcripts; 2 professional letters of recommendation; personal career goals statement; professional essay; interview. Additional exam requirements/recommendations for international students: Required—TOEFL (minimum score 575 paper-based; 93 iBT), IELTS (minimum score 7), PTE (minimum score 59). *Application deadline:* For fall admission, 2/1 for domestic and international students. Application fee: $75 ($80 for international students). Electronic applications accepted. *Expenses:* $1,645.83 per credit tuition (Executive MBA); $950 per credit in-state, $1,751.50 out-of-state (for MBA). *Financial support:* In 2017–18, 4 students received support, including 2 research assistantships, 3 teaching assistantships with tuition reimbursements (averaging $2,952 per year); career-related internships or fieldwork, Federal Work-Study, scholarships/grants, unspecified assistantships, and health care benefits (for full-time research or teaching assistantship recipients) also available. Support available to part-time students. Financial award application deadline: 3/1; financial award applicants required to submit FAFSA. *Faculty research:* Electronic commerce, marketing information systems, group decision-making, corporate governance, risk management. *Unit head:* Victoria Grady, Director, 703-993-8711, Fax: 703-993-1870, E-mail: vgrady3@gmu.edu. *Application contact:* Rebecca Diemer, Director, Graduate Academic Services, 703-993-2216, Fax: 703-993-1778, E-mail: rdiemer@gmu.edu.
Website: http://business.gmu.edu/mba-programs/

George Mason University, School of Business, Program in Management, Fairfax, VA 22030. Offers MS. *Program availability:* Evening/weekend, 100% online, blended/hybrid learning. *Faculty:* 20 full-time (7 women), 10 part-time/adjunct (4 women). *Students:* 55 full-time (34 women), 2 part-time (1 woman); includes 16 minority (7 Black or African American, non-Hispanic/Latino; 4 Asian, non-Hispanic/Latino; 5 Hispanic/Latino), 28 international. Average age 24. 68 applicants, 71% accepted, 30 enrolled. In 2017, 31 master's awarded. *Degree requirements:* For master's, thesis optional, professional experience. *Entrance requirements:* For master's, GMAT or GRE. Additional exam requirements/recommendations for international students: Required—TOEFL (minimum score 575 paper-based; 88 iBT), IELTS (minimum score 6.5), PTE (minimum score 59). Application fee: $75 ($80 for international students). *Expenses:* $965 per credit in-state tuition, $1,778.25 out-of-state. *Financial support:* In 2017–18, 2 students received support, including 2 research assistantships. *Unit head:* Anne Magro, Interim Dean, 703-993-1765, Fax: 703-993-2472, E-mail: amagro@gmu.edu. *Application contact:* Paige Wolf, Senior Assistant Dean of Graduate Programs, 703-993-1758, Fax: 703-993-1870, E-mail: pwolf1@gmu.edu.
Website: http://business.gmu.edu/masters-in-management/

Georgetown University, Graduate School of Arts and Sciences, McDonough School of Business, Washington, DC 20057. Offers business administration (EMBA, GEMBA, MBA); finance (MS); leadership (EML). *Accreditation:* AACSB. *Entrance requirements:* For master's, GMAT. Additional exam requirements/recommendations for international students: Required—TOEFL. *Expenses:* Contact institution.

The George Washington University, School of Business, Washington, DC 20052. Offers M Accy, MBA, MS, MSF, MSIST, MTA, PMBA, PhD, Certificate, Professional Certificate, JD/MBA, MBA/MA. PMBA also offered in Alexandria and Ashburn, VA. *Program availability:* Part-time, evening/weekend, online learning. *Faculty:* 126 full-time (35 women), 65 part-time/adjunct (15 women). *Students:* 930 full-time (458 women), 850 part-time (436 women); includes 525 minority (212 Black or African American, non-Hispanic/Latino; 4 American Indian or Alaska Native, non-Hispanic/Latino; 164 Asian, non-Hispanic/Latino; 103 Hispanic/Latino; 4 Native Hawaiian or other Pacific Islander, non-Hispanic/Latino; 38 Two or more races, non-Hispanic/Latino), 686 international. Average age 32. 4,247 applicants, 49% accepted, 665 enrolled. In 2017, 817 master's, 3 doctorates, 94 other advanced degrees awarded. *Entrance requirements:* For doctorate, GMAT or GRE. Additional exam requirements/recommendations for international students: Required—TOEFL. *Application deadline:* For fall admission, 4/1 priority date for domestic students; for spring admission, 10/1 for domestic students. Applications are processed on a rolling basis. Application fee: $75. Electronic applications accepted. *Expenses:* Tuition: Full-time $28,800; part-time $1655 per credit hour. *Required fees:* $45; $2.75 per credit hour. *Financial support:* In 2017–18, 194 students received support. Fellowships, teaching assistantships, career-related internships or fieldwork, Federal Work-Study, institutionally sponsored loans, and tuition waivers (partial) available. Financial award application deadline: 4/1. *Unit head:* Dr. Vivek Choudhury, Dean, 202-994-6380, E-mail: vchoudhury@gwu.edu. *Application contact:* Christopher Storer, Executive Director, Graduate Admissions, 202-994-1212, E-mail: gwmba@gwu.edu.
Website: http://business.gwu.edu/grad

Georgia College & State University, Graduate School, The J. Whitney Bunting School of Business, Program in Business Administration, Milledgeville, GA 31061. Offers MBA. *Accreditation:* AACSB. *Program availability:* Part-time, evening/weekend, online only, 100% online. *Students:* 67 part-time (31 women); includes 23 minority (13 Black or African American, non-Hispanic/Latino; 5 Asian, non-Hispanic/Latino; 2 Hispanic/Latino; 3 Two or more races, non-Hispanic/Latino). Average age 35. 28 applicants, 75% accepted, 13 enrolled. In 2017, 42 master's awarded. *Degree requirements:* For master's, minimum GPA of 3.0 on all business courses taken in the program, complete

program within 7 years of start date. *Entrance requirements:* For master's, GRE or GMAT (not required for students who earned a business degree at an AACSB accredited business school and maintained an overall undergraduate GPA of 3.15), transcript, certificate of immunization, two years of documented related work experience. *Application deadline:* For fall admission, 7/1 priority date for domestic students; for spring admission, 11/1 priority date for domestic students; for summer admission, 4/1 priority date for domestic students. Applications are processed on a rolling basis. Application fee: $40. Electronic applications accepted. *Expenses:* $8,868 tuition ($739 per credit hour); $686 fees per year. *Financial support:* In 2017–18, 2 students received support. Unspecified assistantships available. Financial award application deadline: 3/1; financial award applicants required to submit FAFSA. *Unit head:* Dr. Dale Young, Dean, School of Business, 478-445-5497, E-mail: dale.younge@gcsu.edu. *Application contact:* Lynn Hanson, Director of Graduate Programs, 478-445-5115, E-mail: lynn.hanson@gcsu.edu.
Website: http://gcsu.edu/business/gradbusiness/mba

Georgia Institute of Technology, Graduate Studies, Scheller College of Business, Program in Business Administration, Atlanta, GA 30332-0001. Offers business administration (MBA); global business (MBA); management of technology (MBA). *Accreditation:* AACSB. *Program availability:* Part-time, evening/weekend. *Entrance requirements:* For master's, GMAT, two essays, three letters of recommendation, transcript from each college/university attended. Additional exam requirements/recommendations for international students: Required—TOEFL (minimum score 600 paper-based; 100 iBT). Electronic applications accepted. *Expenses:* Contact institution.

Georgia Institute of Technology, Graduate Studies, Scheller College of Business, Program in Management, Atlanta, GA 30332-0001. Offers MS, PhD. *Accreditation:* AACSB. *Program availability:* Part-time. *Degree requirements:* For doctorate, comprehensive exam, thesis/dissertation, oral exams. *Entrance requirements:* For doctorate, GMAT, two essay questions, three letters of recommendation, transcripts from each college/university attended, copy of most recent resume. Additional exam requirements/recommendations for international students: Required—TOEFL (minimum score 600 paper-based; 100 iBT). Electronic applications accepted. *Faculty research:* Management information systems, management of technology, international business, entrepreneurship, operations management.

Georgian Court University, School of Business and Digital Media, Lakewood, NJ 08701-2697. Offers business (MBA); business essentials (Certificate); nonprofit management (Certificate). *Program availability:* Part-time, evening/weekend. *Faculty:* 6 full-time (3 women), 11 part-time/adjunct (3 women). *Students:* 29 full-time (19 women), 31 part-time (24 women); includes 17 minority (7 Black or African American, non-Hispanic/Latino; 3 Asian, non-Hispanic/Latino; 4 Hispanic/Latino; 3 Two or more races, non-Hispanic/Latino), 2 international. Average age 31. 54 applicants, 65% accepted, 21 enrolled. In 2017, 33 master's, 7 other advanced degrees awarded. *Entrance requirements:* For master's, GMAT or CPA exam, 3 letters of recommendation. Additional exam requirements/recommendations for international students: Required—TOEFL (minimum score 550 paper-based). *Application deadline:* For fall admission, 8/15 priority date for domestic students, 5/1 for international students; for spring admission, 1/15 priority date for domestic students, 10/1 for international students. Applications are processed on a rolling basis. Application fee: $40. Electronic applications accepted. *Expenses: Tuition:* Part-time $839 per credit. *Required fees:* $248 per semester. Tuition and fees vary according to campus/location and program. *Financial support:* Scholarships/grants, health care benefits, and unspecified assistantships available. Financial award application deadline: 4/15; financial award applicants required to submit FAFSA. *Unit head:* Dr. Cathleen McQuillen, Dean, 732-987-2623, Fax: 732-987-2024, E-mail: cmcquillen@georgian.edu. *Application contact:* Patrick Givens, Director of Graduate and Professional Studies Admissions, 732-987-2736, Fax: 732-987-2000, E-mail: gps@georgian.edu.
Website: http://georgian.edu/academics/school-of-business/

Georgia Southern University, Jack N. Averitt College of Graduate Studies, College of Business, The Georgia Web MBA, Statesboro, GA 30460. Offers MBA. *Program availability:* Part-time-only, evening/weekend, online only, 100% online. *Faculty:* 24 full-time (9 women), 1 part-time/adjunct (0 women). *Students:* 106 part-time (45 women); includes 37 minority (26 Black or African American, non-Hispanic/Latino; 1 American Indian or Alaska Native, non-Hispanic/Latino; 2 Asian, non-Hispanic/Latino; 8 Hispanic/Latino), 2 international. Average age 35. 69 applicants, 80% accepted, 41 enrolled. In 2017, 46 master's awarded. *Entrance requirements:* For master's, GMAT. Additional exam requirements/recommendations for international students: Required—TOEFL (minimum score 550 paper-based; 80 iBT), IELTS (minimum score 6). *Application deadline:* For fall admission, 8/1 for domestic students, 3/1 for international students; for spring admission, 12/1 for domestic students. Applications are processed on a rolling basis. Application fee: $50. Electronic applications accepted. *Expenses:* Contact institution. *Financial support:* In 2017–18, 5 students received support. Application deadline: 4/15; applicants required to submit FAFSA. *Faculty research:* International business, leadership, marketing, managerial finance, operations. *Unit head:* Dr. Lowell Mooney, MBA Director, 912-478-5217, Fax: 912-478-0292, E-mail: lmooney@georgiasouthern.edu. *Application contact:* Karen Wells, Coordinator for Graduate Student Recruitment, 912-478-5767, Fax: 912-478-0740, E-mail: kwells@georgiasouthern.edu.
Website: http://cob.georgiasouthern.edu/mba/online/

Georgia Southern University, Jack N. Averitt College of Graduate Studies, College of Business, Program in Business Administration, Statesboro, GA 30458. Offers MBA. *Accreditation:* AACSB. *Program availability:* Part-time, evening/weekend, online learning. *Faculty:* 1 full-time (0 women). *Students:* 43 full-time (13 women), 43 part-time (20 women); includes 21 minority (14 Black or African American, non-Hispanic/Latino; 4 Asian, non-Hispanic/Latino; 2 Hispanic/Latino; 1 Two or more races, non-Hispanic/Latino), 5 international. Average age 29. 71 applicants, 87% accepted, 42 enrolled. In 2017, 57 master's awarded. *Entrance requirements:* For master's, GMAT. Additional exam requirements/recommendations for international students: Required—TOEFL (minimum score 550 paper-based; 80 iBT), IELTS (minimum score 6). *Application deadline:* For fall admission, 3/1 priority date for domestic students, 6/1 for international students; for spring admission, 10/1 priority date for domestic students, 10/1 for international students. Applications are processed on a rolling basis. Application fee: $50. Electronic applications accepted. *Expenses:* Tuition, state resident: full-time $4986; part-time $3324 per year. Tuition, nonresident: full-time $21,982; part-time $15,352 per year. *Required fees:* $2092; $1802 per credit hour. $901 per semester. Tuition and fees vary according to course load, campus/location and program. *Financial support:* In 2017–18, 14 students received support, including research assistantships with partial tuition reimbursements available (averaging $7,200 per year), teaching assistantships with partial tuition reimbursements available (averaging $7,200 per year); career-related internships or fieldwork, Federal Work-Study, scholarships/grants, tuition waivers (partial), and unspecified assistantships also available. Support available to part-time students. Financial award application deadline: 4/15; financial award applicants required to submit FAFSA. *Unit head:* Gordon Smith, Graduate Program Director, 912-478-2357, Fax: 912-478-7480, E-mail: gsmith@georgiasouthern.edu. *Application contact:* Karen Wells, Coordinator for Graduate Student Recruitment, 912-

478-5767, Fax: 912-478-0740, E-mail: kwells@georgiasouthern.edu.
Website: http://coba.georgiasouthern.edu/mba/

Georgia Southern University–Armstrong Campus, College of Graduate Studies, Program in Professional Communication and Leadership, Savannah, GA 31419-1997. Offers MA, Certificate. *Program availability:* Part-time, evening/weekend. *Faculty:* 2 full-time (1 woman), 1 (woman) part-time/adjunct. *Students:* 26 full-time (16 women), 48 part-time (37 women); includes 46 minority (39 Black or African American, non-Hispanic/Latino; 7 Hispanic/Latino). Average age 35. 53 applicants, 53% accepted, 21 enrolled. In 2017, 29 master's awarded. *Degree requirements:* For master's, comprehensive exam, project. *Entrance requirements:* For master's, minimum GPA of 2.5, letters of recommendation, letter of intent, resume. Additional exam requirements/recommendations for international students: Required—TOEFL (minimum score 523 paper-based; 70 iBT). *Application deadline:* For fall admission, 6/1 priority date for domestic students, 5/1 priority date for international students; for spring admission, 11/15 priority date for domestic students, 9/15 priority date for international students; for summer admission, 4/15 for domestic students, 9/15 priority date for international students. Applications are processed on a rolling basis. Application fee: $30. Electronic applications accepted. *Expenses:* Tuition, state resident: part-time $211 per credit hour. Tuition, nonresident: part-time $782 per credit hour. *Required fees:* $737 per semester. Tuition and fees vary according to course load, degree level, campus/location and program. *Financial support:* In 2017–18, research assistantships with full tuition reimbursements (averaging $5,000 per year) were awarded; scholarships/grants and unspecified assistantships also available. Financial award application deadline: 3/15; financial award applicants required to submit FAFSA. *Faculty research:* Organizational communication, conflict resolution and mediation, language identity, brand identity and marketing, communication theory. *Unit head:* Dr. Kimberly Martin, Program Coordinator, 912-344-2698, E-mail: kimberly.martin@armstrong.edu. *Application contact:* McKenzie Peterman, Graduate Admissions Specialist, 912-478-5678, Fax: 912-478-0740, E-mail: mpeterman@georgiasouthern.edu.
Website: http://www.armstrong.edu/Majors/degree/
master_professional_communication_leadership

Georgia Southwestern State University, School of Business Administration, Americus, GA 31709-4693. Offers MBA. *Accreditation:* AACSB. *Program availability:* Part-time, online only, 100% online. *Faculty:* 12 full-time (5 women), 2 part-time/adjunct (both women). *Students:* 5 full-time (4 women), 62 part-time (41 women); includes 14 minority (all Black or African American, non-Hispanic/Latino). Average age 33. 43 applicants, 35% accepted, 9 enrolled. In 2017, 15 master's awarded. *Degree requirements:* For master's, minimum cumulative GPA of 3.0; requirements completed within 7 years. *Entrance requirements:* For master's, GMAT or GRE, baccalaureate degree from a regionally-accredited institution; minimum undergraduate overall GPA of 2.7 as reported on official final transcripts; letters of recommendation. *Application deadline:* For fall admission, 6/30 for domestic students; for spring admission, 11/30 for domestic students; for summer admission, 4/30 for domestic students. Applications are processed on a rolling basis. Application fee: $25. Electronic applications accepted. *Expenses:* $257 per credit hour for online courses plus fees which vary according to number of enrolled credit hours. *Financial support:* Application deadline: 6/1; applicants required to submit FAFSA. *Unit head:* Dr. Liz Wilson, Dean, 229-931-2090. *Application contact:* Whitney Ford, Admissions Specialist, Office of Graduate Admissions, 800-338-0082, Fax: 229-931-2983, E-mail: graduateadmissions@gsw.edu.
Website: https://gsw.edu/academics/schools-and-departments/school-of-business-administration/mba-program

Georgia State University, J. Mack Robinson College of Business, Department of Managerial Sciences, Atlanta, GA 30302-3083. Offers business analysis (MBA, MS); entrepreneurship (MBA); human resources management (MBA, MS); operations management (MBA, MS); organization behavior/human resource management (PhD); organization management (MBA); organizational change (MS); strategic management (PhD). *Accreditation:* AACSB. *Program availability:* Part-time, evening/weekend. *Faculty:* 25 full-time (11 women). *Students:* 20 full-time (12 women); includes 7 minority (4 Black or African American, non-Hispanic/Latino; 2 Hispanic/Latino; 1 Two or more races, non-Hispanic/Latino), 6 international. Average age 33. 77 applicants, 18% accepted, 10 enrolled. In 2017, 25 master's, 1 doctorate awarded. *Entrance requirements:* For master's, GRE or GMAT, transcripts from all institutions attended, resume, essays; for doctorate, GMAT, three letters of recommendation, personal statement, transcripts from all institutions attended, resume. Additional exam requirements/recommendations for international students: Required—TOEFL (minimum score 610 paper-based; 101 iBT), IELTS (minimum score 7). *Application deadline:* For fall admission, 5/1 priority date for domestic students, 2/1 priority date for international students; for spring admission, 9/15 priority date for domestic students, 4/1 priority date for international students. Applications are processed on a rolling basis. Application fee: $50. Electronic applications accepted. *Expenses:* Tuition, state resident: full-time $7020. Tuition, nonresident: full-time $22,518. *Required fees:* $2128. Tuition and fees vary according to degree level and program. *Financial support:* Research assistantships, teaching assistantships, scholarships/grants, tuition waivers, and unspecified assistantships available. Financial award applicants required to submit FAFSA. *Faculty research:* Entrepreneurship and innovation; strategy process; workplace interactions, relationships, and processes; leadership and culture; supply chain management. *Unit head:* Dr. Pamela S. Barr, Interim Chair, 404-413-7525, Fax: 404-413-7571. *Application contact:* Toby McChesney, Assistant Dean for Graduate Recruiting and Student Services, 404-413-7167, Fax: 404-413-7162, E-mail: rcbgradadmissions@gsu.edu.
Website: http://mgmt.robinson.gsu.edu/

Georgia State University, J. Mack Robinson College of Business, Executive Doctorate in Business Program, Atlanta, GA 30302-3083. Offers EDB. *Accreditation:* AACSB. *Program availability:* Part-time, evening/weekend. *Entrance requirements:* Additional exam requirements/recommendations for international students: Required—TOEFL (minimum score 610 paper-based; 101 iBT), IELTS (minimum score 7). *Application deadline:* Applications are processed on a rolling basis. Application fee: $100. Electronic applications accepted. *Expenses:* Tuition, state resident: full-time $7020. Tuition, nonresident: full-time $22,518. *Required fees:* $2128. Tuition and fees vary according to degree level and program. *Financial support:* Scholarships/grants available. *Unit head:* Maury C. Kalnitz, Director of the Executive Doctorate in Business, 404-413-7178. *Application contact:* Heather Jacobs, Assistant Director of the Executive Doctorate in Business, 404-413-7178, E-mail: hjacob3@gsu.edu.
Website: http://robinson.gsu.edu/execdoctorate/index.html

Georgia State University, J. Mack Robinson College of Business, Program in General Business Administration, Atlanta, GA 30302-3083. Offers business administration (MBA); executive business administration (EMBA); global business administration (GMBA); professional business administration (PMBA); PMBA/MHA. *Accreditation:* AACSB. *Program availability:* Part-time, evening/weekend. *Entrance requirements:* For master's, GRE or GMAT, transcripts from all institutions attended, resume, essays. Additional exam requirements/recommendations for international students: Required—TOEFL (minimum score 610 paper-based; 101 iBT), IELTS (minimum score 7). *Application deadline:* Applications are processed on a rolling basis. Application fee: $50.

Business Administration and Management—General

Electronic applications accepted. *Expenses:* Tuition, state resident: full-time $7020. Tuition, nonresident: full-time $22,518. *Required fees:* $2128. Tuition and fees vary according to degree level and program. *Financial support:* Research assistantships, scholarships/grants, tuition waivers, and unspecified assistantships available. Financial award application deadline: 5/1. *Unit head:* Dr. Richard D. Phillips, Associate Dean for Academic Initiatives and Innovation, 404-413-7000, Fax: 404-413-7035. *Application contact:* Toby McChesney, Assistant Dean for Graduate Recruiting and Student Services, 404-413-7167, Fax: 404-413-7162, E-mail: rcbgradadmissions@gsu.edu. Website: http://robinson.gsu.edu/mba/index.html

Goddard College, Graduate Division, Master of Arts in Social Innovation and Sustainability Program, Plainfield, VT 05667-9432. Offers MA. *Program availability:* Part-time, online learning. *Degree requirements:* For master's, thesis. *Entrance requirements:* For master's, 3 letters of recommendation, relevant prior training or experience, interview. Electronic applications accepted.

Golden Gate University, Ageno School of Business, San Francisco, CA 94105-2968. Offers accounting (MBA); adaptive leadership (MBA); advanced financial planning (MS); business administration (EMBA, MBA, DBA); business analytics (MBA, MS); entrepreneurship (MBA); finance (MBA, MS, Certificate); financial life planning (Certificate); financial planning (MS, Certificate); global supply chain management (MBA, Certificate); human resource management (MBA, MS, Certificate); information technology management (MBA, MS, Certificate); international business (MBA); marketing (MBA, MS, Certificate); project management (MBA, MS, Certificate); psychology (MA, Certificate); public administration (EMPA, MBA); public administration leadership (Certificate); JD/MBA. *Program availability:* Part-time, evening/weekend. *Faculty:* 17 full-time (7 women), 280 part-time/adjunct (95 women). *Students:* 309 full-time (147 women), 527 part-time (266 women); includes 286 minority (56 Black or African American, non-Hispanic/Latino; 1 American Indian or Alaska Native, non-Hispanic/Latino; 131 Asian, non-Hispanic/Latino; 83 Hispanic/Latino; 4 Native Hawaiian or other Pacific Islander, non-Hispanic/Latino; 11 Two or more races, non-Hispanic/Latino), 209 international. Average age 35. 549 applicants, 66% accepted, 185 enrolled. *Degree requirements:* For doctorate, thesis/dissertation, qualifying examination. *Entrance requirements:* For master's, GMAT (for MBA), minimum GPA of 2.5 (MS). Additional exam requirements/recommendations for international students: Required—TOEFL (minimum score 550 paper-based; 79 iBT). *Application deadline:* For fall admission, 5/15 for domestic and international students; for winter admission, 1/15 for domestic and international students; for spring admission, 9/15 for domestic and international students. Applications are processed on a rolling basis. Application fee: $65 ($105 for international students). Electronic applications accepted. *Expenses:* $3,150 per 3-unit course. *Financial support:* Career-related internships or fieldwork, Federal Work-Study, institutionally sponsored loans, and scholarships/grants available. Support available to part-time students. Financial award applicants required to submit FAFSA. *Unit head:* Marianne Koch, Associate Dean, 415-442-6542, Fax: 415-442-6579, E-mail: mkoch@ggu.edu. *Application contact:* Angela Melero, Enrollment Services, 415-442-7800, Fax: 415-442-7807, E-mail: info@ggu.edu. Website: http://www.ggu.edu/programs/business-and-management

Goldey-Beacom College, Graduate Program, Wilmington, DE 19808-1999. Offers business administration (MBA); finance (MS); financial management (MBA); health care management (MBA); human resource management (MBA); information technology (MBA); international business management (MBA); major finance (MBA); major taxation (MBA); management (MM); marketing management (MBA); taxation (MBA, MS). *Accreditation:* ACBSP. *Program availability:* Part-time, evening/weekend. *Entrance requirements:* For master's, GMAT, MAT, GRE, minimum GPA of 3.0. Additional exam requirements/recommendations for international students: Required—TOEFL (minimum score 65 iBT); Recommended—IELTS (minimum score 6). Electronic applications accepted.

Gonzaga University, School of Business Administration, Spokane, WA 99258. Offers accountancy (M Acc); American Indian entrepreneurship (MBA); business administration (MBA); taxation (MS); JD/M Acc; JD/MBA. *Accreditation:* AACSB. *Program availability:* Part-time, evening/weekend. *Faculty:* 17 full-time (3 women), 11 part-time/adjunct (3 women). *Students:* 94 full-time (32 women), 118 part-time (64 women); includes 41 minority (2 Black or African American, non-Hispanic/Latino; 9 American Indian or Alaska Native, non-Hispanic/Latino; 8 Asian, non-Hispanic/Latino; 10 Hispanic/Latino; 1 Native Hawaiian or other Pacific Islander, non-Hispanic/Latino; 11 Two or more races, non-Hispanic/Latino), 11 international. Average age 29. 218 applicants, 75% accepted, 101 enrolled. In 2017, 96 master's awarded. *Degree requirements:* For master's, capstone course. *Entrance requirements:* For master's, GMAT or GRE, essay, two professional recommendations, resume/curriculum vitae, copy of official transcripts from all colleges attended, minimum GPA of 3.0. Additional exam requirements/recommendations for international students: Required—TOEFL (minimum score 570 paper-based, 89 iBT) or IELTS (minimum score 6.5). *Application deadline:* Applications are processed on a rolling basis. Application fee: $50. Electronic applications accepted. *Expenses:* Contact institution. *Financial support:* In 2017–18, 117 students received support. Scholarships/grants, tuition waivers, and unspecified assistantships available. Support available to part-time students. Financial award applicants required to submit FAFSA. *Unit head:* Dr. Ken Anderson, Dean, 509-313-5991, E-mail: anderson@gonzaga.edu. *Application contact:* Stacey Chatman, Assistant Director for Admissions, 509-313-4622, E-mail: chatman@gonzaga.edu. Website: https://www.gonzaga.edu/school-of-business-administration

Governors State University, College of Business, Program in Business Administration, University Park, IL 60484. Offers MBA. *Program availability:* Part-time. *Faculty:* 12 full-time (5 women), 19 part-time/adjunct (3 women). *Students:* 25 full-time (12 women), 76 part-time (54 women); includes 64 minority (49 Black or African American, non-Hispanic/Latino; 4 Asian, non-Hispanic/Latino; 6 Hispanic/Latino; 5 Two or more races, non-Hispanic/Latino), 3 international. Average age 36. 78 applicants, 47% accepted, 30 enrolled. In 2017, 17 master's awarded. *Application deadline:* For fall admission, 4/1 for domestic students. Applications are processed on a rolling basis. Application fee: $50. Electronic applications accepted. *Expenses:* Contact institution. *Financial support:* Application deadline: 5/1; applicants required to submit FAFSA. *Unit head:* Olumide Ijose, Chair, Division of Management, Marketing and Entrepreneurship, 708-534-5000 Ext. 4932, E-mail: oijose@govst.edu.

The Graduate Center, City University of New York, Graduate Studies, Program in Business, New York, NY 10016-4039. Offers accounting (PhD); behavioral science (PhD); finance (PhD); management planning systems (PhD). *Faculty:* 66 full-time (5 women). *Students:* 56 full-time (30 women); includes 6 minority (1 Black or African American, non-Hispanic/Latino; 1 American Indian or Alaska Native, non-Hispanic/Latino; 2 Asian, non-Hispanic/Latino; 2 Hispanic/Latino), 42 international. Average age 33. 177 applicants, 7% accepted, 10 enrolled. In 2017, 10 doctorates awarded. *Degree requirements:* For doctorate, thesis/dissertation. *Entrance requirements:* For doctorate, GMAT, writing sample (15 pages). Additional exam requirements/recommendations for international students: Required—TOEFL. *Application deadline:* For fall admission, 1/15 for domestic students. Application fee: $125. Electronic applications accepted. *Financial support:* In 2017–18, 50 students received support, including 54 fellowships, 5 teaching assistantships; research assistantships, career-related internships or fieldwork, Federal

Work-Study, institutionally sponsored loans, and tuition waivers (full and partial) also available. Financial award application deadline: 2/1; financial award applicants required to submit FAFSA. *Unit head:* Dr. Joseph Weintrop, Executive Officer, 646-312-3092, Fax: 646-312-3031. *Application contact:* Les Gribben, Director of Admissions, 212-817-7470, Fax: 212-817-1624, E-mail: lgribben@gc.cuny.edu.

Grand Canyon University, Colangelo College of Business, Phoenix, AZ 85017-1097. Offers accounting (MBA, MS); business analytics (MS); disaster preparedness and executive fire service leadership (MS); finance (MBA); general management (MBA); health systems management (MBA); information technology management (MS); leadership (MBA, MS); marketing (MBA); organizational leadership and entrepreneurship (MS); project management (MBA); sports business (MBA); strategic human resource management (MBA). *Accreditation:* ACBSP. *Program availability:* Part-time, evening/weekend, online learning. *Entrance requirements:* For master's, equivalent of two years' full-time professional work experience. Additional exam requirements/recommendations for international students: Required—TOEFL (minimum score 575 paper-based; 90 iBT), IELTS (minimum score 7). Electronic applications accepted.

Grand Canyon University, College of Doctoral Studies, Phoenix, AZ 85017-1097. Offers data analytics (DBA); general psychology (PhD), including cognition and instruction, industrial and organizational psychology, integrating technology, learning, and psychology, performance psychology; management (DBA); marketing (DBA); organizational leadership (Ed D), including behavioral health, Christian ministry, health care administration, organizational development. *Degree requirements:* For doctorate, comprehensive exam, thesis/dissertation. *Entrance requirements:* For doctorate, minimum GPA of 3.4 on earned advanced degree from regionally-accredited institution; transcripts; goals statement.

Grand Valley State University, Seidman College of Business, Program in Business Administration, Allendale, MI 49401-9403. Offers MBA. *Accreditation:* AACSB. *Program availability:* Part-time, evening/weekend. *Students:* 54 full-time (25 women), 122 part-time (45 women); includes 17 minority (2 Black or African American, non-Hispanic/Latino; 4 Asian, non-Hispanic/Latino; 7 Hispanic/Latino; 4 Two or more races, non-Hispanic/Latino), 9 international. Average age 32. 48 applicants, 81% accepted, 19 enrolled. In 2017, 71 master's awarded. *Degree requirements:* For master's, capstone course. *Entrance requirements:* For master's, GMAT, personal statement. Additional exam requirements/recommendations for international students: Required—TOEFL (minimum iBT score of 80), IELTS (6.5), or Michigan English Language Assessment Battery (77). *Application deadline:* For fall admission, 8/1 priority date for domestic students, 5/1 priority date for international students; for winter admission, 12/1 priority date for domestic students, 11/1 priority date for international students; for spring admission, 4/1 priority date for domestic students, 3/1 priority date for international students. Applications are processed on a rolling basis. Application fee: $30. Electronic applications accepted. *Expenses:* $686 per credit hour. *Financial support:* In 2017–18, 33 students received support, including 27 fellowships, 6 research assistantships with full and partial tuition reimbursements available (averaging $4,000 per year); institutionally sponsored loans and unspecified assistantships also available. Support available to part-time students. Financial award application deadline: 2/15. *Faculty research:* E-commerce, continuous improvement, currency futures, manufacturing flexibility. *Unit head:* Dr. Jaideep Motwani, Director, 616-331-7467, Fax: 616-331-7490, E-mail: motwanij@gvsu.edu. *Application contact:* Koleta Moore, Assistant Dean of Student Engagement, Graduate Program Operations, 616-331-7386, Fax: 616-331-7389, E-mail: moorekol@gvsu.edu. Website: http://www.gvsu.edu/business/

Granite State College, MS in Management Program, Concord, NH 03301. Offers MS. *Program availability:* Part-time, 100% online, blended/hybrid learning. *Faculty:* 1 (woman) full-time, 13 part-time/adjunct (3 women). *Students:* 1 full-time (0 women), 18 part-time (11 women); includes 2 minority (1 Hispanic/Latino; 1 Two or more races, non-Hispanic/Latino). Average age 38. 5 applicants, 60% accepted, 3 enrolled. In 2017, 4 master's awarded. *Degree requirements:* For master's, capstone. *Entrance requirements:* For master's, bachelor's degree with minimum GPA of 3.0 on last 60 credit hours, 500-1000 word statement of purpose, two letters of professional or academic reference, resume, official transcripts. Additional exam requirements/recommendations for international students: Required—TOEFL (minimum score 80 iBT), IELTS (minimum score 6.5). *Application deadline:* Applications are processed on a rolling basis. Application fee: $0. Electronic applications accepted. *Expenses:* Tuition, state resident: full-time $9450; part-time $525 per credit. Tuition, nonresident: full-time $10,080; part-time $560 per credit. *Financial support:* Federal Work-Study and National Guard course waivers available. Financial award applicants required to submit FAFSA. *Unit head:* Dr. Johnna Herrick-Phelps, Vice Provost of Academic Affairs, 855-228-3000, E-mail: johnna.herrick-phelps@granite.edu. *Application contact:* Ana Gonzalez, Administrative Assistant, Office of Graduate Studies, 603-822-5433, Fax: 603-513-1387, E-mail: gsc.graduatestudies@granite.edu. Website: http://www.granite.edu/academics/degrees/masters/management.php

Grantham University, Mark Skousen School of Business, Lenexa, KS 66219. Offers business administration (MBA); business intelligence (MS); human resources (Certificate); information management (MBA); performance improvement (MS); project management (MBA, Certificate). *Program availability:* Part-time, evening/weekend, online only, 100% online. *Faculty:* 1 full-time, 34 part-time/adjunct. *Students:* 610 full-time (231 women), 333 part-time (128 women); includes 466 minority (321 Black or African American, non-Hispanic/Latino; 12 American Indian or Alaska Native, non-Hispanic/Latino; 29 Asian, non-Hispanic/Latino; 71 Hispanic/Latino; 4 Native Hawaiian or other Pacific Islander, non-Hispanic/Latino; 29 Two or more races, non-Hispanic/Latino). Average age 40. 273 applicants, 87% accepted, 202 enrolled. In 2017, 362 master's awarded. *Degree requirements:* For master's, comprehensive exam (for some programs), PMP Prep Exams throughout the term (for MBA in project management); for Certificate, comprehensive exam (for some programs), PMP Prep Exam (for project management). *Entrance requirements:* For master's, baccalaureate or master's degree with minimum cumulative GPA of 2.5 from institution accredited by agency recognized by U.S. DOE or foreign equivalent; official transcripts showing proof of degree. Additional exam requirements/recommendations for international students: Required—TOEFL (minimum score 530 paper-based; 71 iBT), IELTS (minimum score 6.5), PTE (minimum score 50). *Application deadline:* Applications are processed on a rolling basis. Application fee: $0. Electronic applications accepted. *Expenses:* $325 per credit hour. *Financial support:* Scholarships/grants available. Financial award applicants required to submit FAFSA. *Faculty research:* How chronic diseases contribute to the rising costs of healthcare, marketing for entrepreneurs, managers' hiring practices of workers with disability, organizational structures, organizational change, online pedagogy, impact of instructor video tips in the online classroom, decision-making techniques. *Unit head:* Dr. David Marker, Dean of the Mark Skousen School of Business, 913-309-4747, Fax: 844-260-6287, E-mail: dmarker@grantham.edu. *Application contact:* Jared Parlette, Vice President of Student Enrollment, 800-955-2527 Ext. 803, Fax: 866-914-4557, E-mail: admissions@grantham.edu. Website: https://grantham.edu/school-of-business/

Green Mountain College, Program in Business Administration, Poultney, VT 05764-1199. Offers MBA. Distance learning only. *Program availability:* Online learning. *Entrance requirements:* For master's, GMAT or Quantitative Skills Assessment, 3 recommendations. Electronic applications accepted. *Faculty research:* Migrant farm workers and world systems theory ecosystem assessments.

Gwynedd Mercy University, School of Graduate and Professional Studies, Gwynedd Valley, PA 19437-0901. Offers health care administration (MBA); management (MSM); strategic management and leadership (MBA). *Program availability:* Part-time, evening/weekend. *Faculty:* 5 full-time (all women), 22 part-time/adjunct (8 women). *Students:* 63 full-time (37 women); includes 20 minority (16 Black or African American, non-Hispanic/Latino; 2 Asian, non-Hispanic/Latino; 2 Hispanic/Latino). Average age 39. In 2017, 56 master's awarded. *Degree requirements:* For master's, thesis. *Entrance requirements:* For master's, minimum GPA of 3.0. *Application deadline:* Applications are processed on a rolling basis. *Expenses:* $640 per credit, $17 per credit part-time fee, $165 graduation fee. *Financial support:* Career-related internships or fieldwork, Federal Work-Study, tuition waivers (full and partial), and unspecified assistantships available. Financial award application deadline: 8/31; financial award applicants required to submit FAFSA. *Unit head:* Dr. Mary Sortino, Dean, 215-646-7300, E-mail: sortino.m@gmercyu.edu. *Application contact:* Information Contact, 800-342-5462, Fax: 215-641-5556.

Hallmark University, School of Business, San Antonio, TX 78230. Offers global management (MBA). *Degree requirements:* For master's, thesis (for some programs). *Entrance requirements:* For master's, bachelor's degree; minimum undergraduate GPA of 2.5; completion of one course each in college-level statistics, quanitative methods, and calculus or pre-calculus; official undergraduate transcripts; professional resume; personal statement; two letters of recommendation; two 200-word typed essays. Additional exam requirements/recommendations for international students: Required—TOEFL (minimum score 450 paper-based; 45 iBT). *Expenses:* Contact institution.

Hamline University, School of Business, St. Paul, MN 55104-1284. Offers business administration (MBA); nonprofit management (MNM); public administration (MPA, DPA); MBA/MNM; MBA/MPA; MPA/MNM. *Program availability:* Part-time, evening/weekend, blended/hybrid learning. *Faculty:* 16 full-time (6 women), 15 part-time/adjunct (4 women). *Students:* 18 full-time (8 women), 309 part-time (165 women); includes 89 minority (43 Black or African American, non-Hispanic/Latino; 3 American Indian or Alaska Native, non-Hispanic/Latino; 22 Asian, non-Hispanic/Latino; 12 Hispanic/Latino; 9 Two or more races, non-Hispanic/Latino), 15 international. Average age 34. 174 applicants, 61% accepted, 68 enrolled. In 2017, 152 master's, 4 doctorates awarded. *Degree requirements:* For master's, thesis (for some programs); for doctorate, comprehensive exam, thesis/dissertation. *Entrance requirements:* For master's and doctorate, personal statement, official transcripts, resume or curriculum vitae, letters of recommendation, writing sample. Additional exam requirements/recommendations for international students: Required—TOEFL (minimum score 550 paper-based; 80 iBT), IELTS (minimum score 6.5). *Application deadline:* For fall admission, 6/1 for domestic and international students; for spring admission, 11/1 for domestic students, 10/1 for international students; for summer admission, 3/1 for domestic students, 2/1 for international students. Applications are processed on a rolling basis. Application fee: $0 ($100 for international students). Electronic applications accepted. *Expenses:* $530 per credit (for MPA), $495 per credit (for MNM), $775 per credit plus fees (for DPA). *Financial support:* Career-related internships or fieldwork, Federal Work-Study, scholarships/grants, and unspecified assistantships available. Support available to part-time students. Financial award application deadline: 4/20; financial award applicants required to submit FAFSA. *Faculty research:* Experiential learning, organizational process/politics, gender differences, social equity, pyramid schemes. *Unit head:* Dr. Anne McCarthy, Dean, 651-523-2284, Fax: 651-523-3098, E-mail: hsb@hamline.edu. *Application contact:* Shawn Skoog, Director of Graduate Recruitment and Admission, 651-523-2900, Fax: 651-523-3058, E-mail: gradprog@hamline.edu. Website: http://www.hamline.edu/business

Hampton University, Program in Business Administration, Hampton, VA 23668. Offers MBA, PhD. *Program availability:* Part-time, online learning. *Students:* 25 full-time (17 women), 18 part-time (15 women); includes 40 minority (39 Black or African American, non-Hispanic/Latino; 1 Hispanic/Latino), 1 international. Average age 30. 29 applicants, 21% accepted, 1 enrolled. In 2017, 29 master's, 4 doctorates awarded. *Degree requirements:* For master's, comprehensive exam (for some programs), thesis (for some programs); for doctorate, comprehensive exam (for some programs), thesis/dissertation, oral defense, qualifying exam, journal article. *Entrance requirements:* For master's, GMAT. Additional exam requirements/recommendations for international students: Required—TOEFL (minimum score 525 paper-based) or IELTS (6.5). *Application deadline:* For fall admission, 6/1 priority date for domestic students, 4/1 priority date for international students; for spring admission, 11/1 priority date for domestic students, 9/1 priority date for international students; for summer admission, 4/1 priority date for domestic students, 2/1 priority date for international students. Applications are processed on a rolling basis. Application fee: $35. Electronic applications accepted. *Expenses: Tuition:* Full-time $22,630; part-time $575 per semester hour. *Required fees:* $70. Tuition and fees vary according to program. *Financial support:* Teaching assistantships, career-related internships or fieldwork, Federal Work-Study, institutionally sponsored loans, scholarships/grants, unspecified assistantships, and stipends available. Support available to part-time students. Financial award application deadline: 6/30; financial award applicants required to submit FAFSA. *Unit head:* Dr. Ziette Hayes, Dean, School of Business, 757-727-5361.

Harding University, Paul R. Carter College of Business Administration, Searcy, AR 72149-0001. Offers international business (MBA); leadership and organizational management (MBA). *Accreditation:* ACBSP. *Program availability:* Part-time, evening/weekend, 100% online. *Faculty:* 26 part-time/adjunct (6 women). *Students:* 15 full-time (8 women), 90 part-time (36 women); includes 12 minority (8 Black or African American, non-Hispanic/Latino; 2 Asian, non-Hispanic/Latino; 2 Hispanic/Latino), 2 international. Average age 34. 15 applicants, 100% accepted, 15 enrolled. In 2017, 66 master's awarded. *Degree requirements:* For master's, portfolio. *Entrance requirements:* For master's, GMAT (minimum score of 500) or GRE (minimum score of 300), minimum GPA of 3.0, 2 letters of recommendation, resume, 3 essays, all official transcripts. Additional exam requirements/recommendations for international students: Required—TOEFL (minimum score 550 paper-based; 79 iBT). *Application deadline:* For fall admission, 8/1 priority date for domestic and international students; for spring admission, 12/1 priority date for domestic and international students. Applications are processed on a rolling basis. Application fee: $40. Tuition and fees vary according to course load, degree level, campus/location and program. *Financial support:* Unspecified assistantships available. Financial award application deadline: 7/30; financial award applicants required to submit FAFSA. *Unit head:* 501-279-5789, Fax: 501-279-4805, E-mail: mba@harding.edu. *Website:* www.harding.edu/mba

Hardin-Simmons University, Graduate School, Kelley College of Business, Abilene, TX 79698-0001. Offers business administration (MBA); information science (MS); sports management (MBA). *Accreditation:* ACBSP. *Program availability:* Part-time. *Faculty:* 6 full-time (3 women). *Students:* 17 full-time (7 women), 14 part-time (5 women); includes 5 minority (1 Black or African American, non-Hispanic/Latino; 4 Hispanic/Latino), 2

international. Average age 26. 25 applicants, 100% accepted, 15 enrolled. In 2017, 14 master's awarded. *Degree requirements:* For master's, thesis or alternative. *Entrance requirements:* For master's, GMAT, minimum GPA of 3.0 in upper-level course work, resume, interview. Additional exam requirements/recommendations for international students: Required—TOEFL (minimum score 550 paper-based; 75 iBT). *Application deadline:* For fall admission, 8/15 priority date for domestic students, 4/1 for international students; for spring admission, 1/5 priority date for domestic students, 9/1 for international students. Applications are processed on a rolling basis. Application fee: $50. Electronic applications accepted. *Expenses: Tuition:* Full-time $13,500; part-time $750 per semester hour. *Required fees:* $220 per term. One-time fee: $50. Tuition and fees vary according to course load, campus/location and program. *Financial support:* In 2017–18, 22 students received support. Fellowships and scholarships/grants available. Support available to part-time students. Financial award application deadline: 6/30; financial award applicants required to submit FAFSA. *Unit head:* Dr. Jennifer Plantier, Program Director, 325-671-2166, Fax: 325-670-1523, E-mail: jplantier@hsutx.edu. *Application contact:* Dr. Nancy Kucinski, Dean of Graduate Studies, 325-670-1298, Fax: 325-670-1564, E-mail: gradoff@hsutx.edu. Website: http://www.hsutx.edu/academics/kelley/graduate/

Harvard University, Extension School, Cambridge, MA 02138-3722. Offers applied sciences (CAS); biotechnology (ALM); educational technologies (ALM); educational technology (CET); English for graduate and professional studies (DGP); environmental management (ALM, CEM); information technology (ALM); journalism (ALM); liberal arts (ALM); management (ALM, CM); mathematics for teaching (ALM); museum studies (ALM); premedical studies (Diploma); publication and communication (CPC). *Program availability:* Part-time, evening/weekend. *Degree requirements:* For master's, thesis. *Entrance requirements:* For master's, 3 completed graduate courses with grade of B or higher. Additional exam requirements/recommendations for international students: Required—TOEFL (minimum score 600 paper-based), TWE (minimum score 5). *Expenses:* Contact institution.

Harvard University, Harvard Business School, Doctoral Programs in Management, Boston, MA 02163. Offers accounting and management (DBA); business economics (PhD); health policy management (PhD); management (DBA); marketing (DBA); organizational behavior (PhD); science, technology and management (PhD); strategy (DBA); technology and operations management (DBA). *Degree requirements:* For doctorate, comprehensive exam (for some programs), thesis/dissertation. *Entrance requirements:* For doctorate, GRE General Test or GMAT. Additional exam requirements/recommendations for international students: Required—TOEFL.

Harvard University, Harvard Business School, Master's Program in Business Administration, Boston, MA 02163. Offers MBA, JD/MBA. *Entrance requirements:* For master's, GMAT. Additional exam requirements/recommendations for international students: Required—TOEFL.

Hawai'i Pacific University, College of Business, Honolulu, HI 96813. Offers MA, MBA, MSIS. *Program availability:* Part-time, evening/weekend, 100% online, blended/hybrid learning. *Faculty:* 16 full-time (6 women), 6 part-time/adjunct (0 women). *Students:* 121 full-time (47 women), 51 part-time (27 women); includes 96 minority (10 Black or African American, non-Hispanic/Latino; 26 Asian, non-Hispanic/Latino; 22 Hispanic/Latino; 3 Native Hawaiian or other Pacific Islander, non-Hispanic/Latino; 35 Two or more races, non-Hispanic/Latino), 33 international. Average age 33. 118 applicants, 77% accepted, 61 enrolled. In 2017, 116 master's awarded. *Entrance requirements:* For master's, GMAT or GRE. Additional exam requirements/recommendations for international students: Recommended—TOEFL (minimum score 550 paper-based; 80 iBT), IELTS (minimum score 6), TWE (minimum score 5). *Application deadline:* For fall admission, 1/15 priority date for domestic students; for spring admission, 10/15 priority date for domestic students. Applications are processed on a rolling basis. Application fee: $50. Electronic applications accepted. *Expenses: Tuition:* Full-time $18,000; part-time $1000 per credit. *Required fees:* $200; $26 per credit. Tuition and fees vary according to course load and program. *Financial support:* In 2017–18, 29 students received support. Research assistantships, teaching assistantships, career-related internships or fieldwork, Federal Work-Study, scholarships/grants, tuition waivers (partial), and unspecified assistantships available. Financial award application deadline: 3/1; financial award applicants required to submit FAFSA. *Unit head:* Dr. William Rhey, Dean, 808-544-0275, E-mail: wrhey@hpu.edu. *Application contact:* Danny Lam, Assistant Director of Graduate Admissions, 808-544-1135, E-mail: graduate@hpu.edu. Website: https://www.hpu.edu/cob/index.html

HEC Montreal, School of Business Administration, Doctoral Program in Administration, Montréal, QC H3T 2A7, Canada. Offers accounting (PhD); applied economics (PhD); data science (PhD); finance (PhD); financial engineering (PhD); information technology (PhD); international business (PhD); logistics and operations management (PhD); management science (PhD); management, strategy and organizations (PhD); marketing (PhD); organizational behaviour and human resources (PhD). Program offered jointly with Concordia University, McGill University, and Universite du Quebec a Montreal. *Accreditation:* AACSB. *Students:* 114 full-time (47 women). 78 applicants, 42% accepted, 24 enrolled. In 2017, 23 doctorates awarded. *Entrance requirements:* For doctorate, TAGE MAGE, GMAT, or GRE, master's degree in administration or related field. *Application deadline:* For fall admission, 1/15 for domestic and international students. Application fee: $88 ($187 for international students). Electronic applications accepted. *Expenses:* Tuition, state resident: full-time $2869 Canadian dollars; part-time $79.70 Canadian dollars per credit. Tuition, nonresident: full-time $8883 Canadian dollars; part-time $246.76 Canadian dollars per credit. *International tuition:* $19,648 Canadian dollars full-time. *Required fees:* $41.20 Canadian dollars per credit. $67.94 Canadian dollars per term. Tuition and fees vary according to degree level and program. *Financial support:* Research assistantships, teaching assistantships, and scholarships/grants available. Financial award application deadline: 9/2. *Faculty research:* Art management, business policy, entrepreneurship, new technologies, transportation. *Unit head:* Jacques Robert, Director, 514-340-6853, E-mail: jacques.robert@hec.ca. *Application contact:* Julie Bilodeau, PhD Program Analyst, 514-340-6151, Fax: 514-340-6411, E-mail: analyste.phd@hec.ca. Website: http://www.hec.ca/en/programs/phd/index.html

HEC Montreal, School of Business Administration, Graduate Diploma Programs in Administration, Program in Management, Montréal, QC H3T 2A7, Canada. Offers Graduate Diploma. All courses are given in French. *Accreditation:* AACSB. *Students:* 60 full-time (33 women), 295 part-time (179 women). 266 applicants, 73% accepted, 138 enrolled. In 2017, 171 Graduate Diplomas awarded. *Entrance requirements:* For degree, bachelor's degree. *Application deadline:* For fall admission, 4/1 for domestic and international students; for winter admission, 9/15 for domestic and international students. Applications are processed on a rolling basis. Application fee: $88 Canadian dollars ($184 Canadian dollars for international students). Electronic applications accepted. *Expenses:* Tuition, state resident: full-time $2869 Canadian dollars; part-time $79.70 Canadian dollars per credit. Tuition, nonresident: full-time $8883 Canadian dollars; part-time $246.76 Canadian dollars per credit. *International tuition:* $19,648 Canadian dollars full-time. *Required fees:* $41.20 Canadian dollars per credit. $67.94 Canadian dollars per term. Tuition and fees vary according to degree level and program. *Financial support:* Research assistantships, teaching assistantships, and scholarships/

Business Administration and Management—General

grants available. Financial award application deadline: 9/2. *Unit head:* Renaud Lachance, Director, 514-340-7165, E-mail: renaud.lachance@hec.ca. *Application contact:* Anny Caron, Administrative Director, 514-340-6151, Fax: 514-340-6411, E-mail: aide@hec.ca.
Website: http://www.hec.ca/programmes/dess/dess-gestion-management/index.html

HEC Montreal, School of Business Administration, Graduate Diploma Programs in Administration, Program in Management and Sustainable Development, Montréal, QC H3T 2A7, Canada. Offers Graduate Diploma. All courses are given in French. *Students:* 15 full-time (7 women), 34 part-time (23 women). 36 applicants, 86% accepted, 24 enrolled. In 2017, 12 Graduate Diplomas awarded. *Entrance requirements:* For degree, bachelor's degree. *Application deadline:* For fall admission, 4/15 for domestic and international students; for winter admission, 9/15 for domestic and international students. Applications are processed on a rolling basis. Application fee: $88 ($184 for international students). Electronic applications accepted. *Expenses:* Tuition, state resident: full-time $2869 Canadian dollars; part-time $79.70 Canadian dollars per credit. Tuition, nonresident: full-time $8883 Canadian dollars; part-time $246.76 Canadian dollars per credit. *International tuition:* $19,648 Canadian dollars full-time. *Required fees:* $41.20 Canadian dollars per credit. $67.94 Canadian dollars per term. Tuition and fees vary according to degree level and program. *Financial support:* Research assistantships, teaching assistantships, and scholarships/grants available. Financial award application deadline: 9/2. *Unit head:* Renaud Lachance, Director, 514-340-7165, E-mail: renaud.lachance@hec.ca. *Application contact:* Anny Caron, Administrative Director, 514-340-6151, Fax: 514-340-6411, E-mail: aide@hec.ca.
Website: http://www.hec.ca/programmes/dess/dess-gestion-developpement-durable/index.html

HEC Montreal, School of Business Administration, Master of Science Programs in Administration, Program on Accounting, Management, Control, and Audit, Montréal, QC H3T 2A7, Canada. Offers M Sc. *Students:* 3 full-time (2 women), 7 part-time (3 women). 10 applicants, 100% accepted, 6 enrolled. In 2017, 15 master's awarded. *Entrance requirements:* For master's, short graduate program in public accounting from HEC Montreal, minimum GPA of 3.0 on 4.3 scale. Additional exam requirements/recommendations for international students: Required—TAGE MAGE (minimum recommended score of 283), GMAT (minimum recommended score of 630), or GRE. *Application deadline:* For fall admission, 3/15 for domestic and international students; for winter admission, 9/15 for domestic and international students. Application fee: $88 ($184 for international students). Electronic applications accepted. *Expenses:* Tuition, state resident: full-time $2869 Canadian dollars; part-time $79.70 Canadian dollars per credit. Tuition, nonresident: full-time $8883 Canadian dollars; part-time $246.76 Canadian dollars per credit. *International tuition:* $19,648 Canadian dollars full-time. *Required fees:* $41.20 Canadian dollars per credit. $67.94 Canadian dollars per term. Tuition and fees vary according to degree level and program. *Financial support:* Research assistantships, teaching assistantships, and scholarships/grants available. Financial award application deadline: 9/2. *Unit head:* Dr. Marie-Helene Jobin, Director, 514-340-6283, E-mail: marie-helene.jobin@hec.ca. *Application contact:* Marianne de Moura, Administrative Director, 514-340-6151, Fax: 514-340-6411, E-mail: aide@hec.ca.
Website: http://www.hec.ca/programmes/maitrises/maitrise-comptabilite-controle-audit/index.html

HEC Montreal, School of Business Administration, Master's Program in Business Administration and Management, Montréal, QC H3T 2A7, Canada. Offers MBA. *Accreditation:* AACSB. *Students:* 162 full-time (59 women), 149 part-time (47 women). 147 applicants, 63% accepted, 85 enrolled. In 2017, 148 master's awarded. *Entrance requirements:* For master's, GMAT, GRE, or TAGE MAGE, undergraduate degree. Additional exam requirements/recommendations for international students: Required—TOEFL (minimum score 94 iBT). *Application deadline:* For fall admission, 6/1 for domestic and international students; for summer admission, 1/15 for domestic students, 11/1 for international students. Application fee: $88 Canadian dollars ($184 Canadian dollars for international students). Electronic applications accepted. *Expenses:* Tuition, state resident: full-time $2869 Canadian dollars; part-time $79.70 Canadian dollars per credit. Tuition, nonresident: full-time $8883 Canadian dollars; part-time $246.76 Canadian dollars per credit. *International tuition:* $19,648 Canadian dollars full-time. *Required fees:* $41.20 Canadian dollars per credit. $67.94 Canadian dollars per term. Tuition and fees vary according to degree level and program. *Financial support:* Research assistantships, teaching assistantships, and scholarships/grants available. Financial award application deadline: 9/2. *Unit head:* Louis Hebert, Director, 514-340-6830, E-mail: louis.hebert@hec.ca. *Application contact:* Anik Low, Administrative Director, 514-340-6151, Fax: 514-340-7327, E-mail: aide@hec.ca.
Website: http://www.hec.ca/en/programs/mba/index.html

Heidelberg University, Master of Business Administration Program, Tiffin, OH 44883-2462. Offers MBA. *Accreditation:* ACBSP. *Program availability:* Part-time. *Students:* 34 full-time (13 women), 10 part-time (6 women). In 2017, 17 master's awarded. *Entrance requirements:* For master's, bachelor's degree with minimum GPA of 2.7; goal statement. Additional exam requirements/recommendations for international students: Required—TOEFL (minimum score 550 paper-based, 79 iBT) or IELTS (minimum score 6.5). *Application deadline:* Applications are processed on a rolling basis. Application fee: $0. Electronic applications accepted. *Expenses:* Contact institution. *Financial support:* Scholarships/grants and unspecified assistantships available. Financial award applicants required to submit FAFSA. *Unit head:* Dr. Haseeb Ahmed, Dean of the School of Business, 419-448-2284, E-mail: hahmed@heidelberg.edu. *Application contact:* Katie Zeyen, Graduate Admissions Coordinator, 419-448-2602, Fax: 419-448-2565, E-mail: kzeyen@heidelberg.edu.
Website: https://www.heidelberg.edu/academics/programs/master-of-business-administration

Henderson State University, Graduate Studies, School of Business, Arkadelphia, AR 71999-0001. Offers MBA. *Accreditation:* AACSB. *Program availability:* Part-time, 100% online. *Entrance requirements:* For master's, GMAT (minimum score 400), minimum AACSB index of 1000, minimum GPA of 2.7. Additional exam requirements/recommendations for international students: Required—TOEFL (minimum score 600 paper-based); Recommended—IELTS (minimum score 6.5).

Herzing University Online, Program in Business Administration, Menomonee Falls, WI 53051. Offers accounting (MBA); business administration (MBA); business management (MBA); healthcare management (MBA); human resources (MBA); marketing (MBA); project management (MBA); technology management (MBA). *Program availability:* Online learning.

High Point University, Norcross Graduate School, High Point, NC 27268. Offers athletic training (MSAT); business administration (MBA); educational leadership (M Ed, Ed D); elementary education (M Ed, MAT); pharmacy (Pharm D); physical therapy (DPT); physician assistant studies (MPAS); secondary mathematics (M Ed, MAT); special education (M Ed); strategic communication (MA). *Accreditation:* NCATE. *Program availability:* Part-time, evening/weekend. *Degree requirements:* For master's, comprehensive exam (for some programs), thesis (for some programs). *Entrance requirements:* For master's, GMAT (MBA), GRE, MAT, minimum GPA of 3.0. Additional

exam requirements/recommendations for international students: Required—TOEFL (minimum score 550 paper-based). Electronic applications accepted.

Hodges University, Graduate Programs, Naples, FL 34119. Offers accounting (M Acc); business administration (MBA); clinical mental health counseling (MS); health services administration (MS); information systems management (MIS); legal studies (MS); management (MSM). *Program availability:* Part-time, evening/weekend, 100% online, blended/hybrid learning. *Degree requirements:* For master's, comprehensive exam (for some programs), thesis (for some programs). *Entrance requirements:* For master's, essay. Additional exam requirements/recommendations for international students: Recommended—TOEFL. Electronic applications accepted.

Hofstra University, Frank G. Zarb School of Business, Executive Master's Program in Business Administration, Hempstead, NY 11549. Offers EMBA. *Program availability:* Evening/weekend, blended/hybrid learning. *Students:* 10 full-time (5 women), 12 part-time (4 women); includes 13 minority (7 Black or African American, non-Hispanic/Latino; 5 Asian, non-Hispanic/Latino; 1 Hispanic/Latino). Average age 37. 26 applicants, 62% accepted, 10 enrolled. In 2017, 9 master's awarded. *Entrance requirements:* For master's, 2 letters of recommendation, minimum 7 years of management experience, resume, essay, interview. Additional exam requirements/recommendations for international students: Required—TOEFL (minimum score 550 paper-based; 80 iBT); Recommended—IELTS (minimum score 6). *Application deadline:* Applications are processed on a rolling basis. Application fee: $75. Electronic applications accepted. *Expenses:* Contact institution. *Financial support:* In 2017–18, 10 students received support, including 9 fellowships with full and partial tuition reimbursements available (averaging $5,056 per year); research assistantships with full and partial tuition reimbursements available, career-related internships or fieldwork, Federal Work-Study, institutionally sponsored loans, scholarships/grants, tuition waivers (full and partial), and unspecified assistantships also available. Support available to part-time students. Financial award applicants required to submit FAFSA. *Faculty research:* Marketing strategy; consumer behavior. *Unit head:* Dr. Barry Berman, Director, 516-463-5711, Fax: 516-463-5268, E-mail: barry.berman@hofstra.edu. *Application contact:* Sunil Samuel, Assistant Vice President of Admissions, 516-463-4723, Fax: 516-463-4664, E-mail: graduateadmission@hofstra.edu.
Website: http://www.hofstra.edu/business/

Hofstra University, Frank G. Zarb School of Business, Programs in Accounting and Taxation, Hempstead, NY 11549. Offers accounting (MS, Advanced Certificate); business administration (MBA), including accounting, professional accountancy, taxation; taxation (MS, Advanced Certificate). *Program availability:* Part-time, evening/weekend, blended/hybrid learning. *Students:* 161 full-time (89 women), 35 part-time (16 women); includes 28 minority (2 Black or African American, non-Hispanic/Latino; 1 American Indian or Alaska Native, non-Hispanic/Latino; 9 Asian, non-Hispanic/Latino; 12 Hispanic/Latino; 2 Native Hawaiian or other Pacific Islander, non-Hispanic/Latino; 2 Two or more races, non-Hispanic/Latino), 87 international. Average age 25. 328 applicants, 77% accepted, 82 enrolled. In 2017, 129 master's awarded. *Degree requirements:* For master's, capstone course (for MBA), thesis (for MS), minimum GPA of 3.0. *Entrance requirements:* For master's, GMAT/GRE, 2 letters of recommendation, resume, essay. Additional exam requirements/recommendations for international students: Required—TOEFL (minimum score 550 paper-based; 80 iBT); Recommended—IELTS (minimum score 6). *Application deadline:* Applications are processed on a rolling basis. Application fee: $75. Electronic applications accepted. *Expenses:* $1,322 per credit. *Financial support:* In 2017–18, 63 students received support, including 54 fellowships with full and partial tuition reimbursements available (averaging $4,794 per year); research assistantships with full and partial tuition reimbursements available, career-related internships or fieldwork, Federal Work-Study, institutionally sponsored loans, scholarships/grants, tuition waivers (full and partial), and unspecified assistantships also available. Support available to part-time students. Financial award applicants required to submit FAFSA. *Faculty research:* Corporate compliance, international accounting and auditing, financial accounting fraud, tax reform legislation, accounting analytics. *Unit head:* Dr. Jacqueline Burke, Chairperson, 516-463-6987, E-mail: jacqueline.a.burke@hofstra.edu. *Application contact:* Sunil Samuel, Assistant Vice President of Admissions, 516-463-4723, Fax: 516-463-4664, E-mail: graduateadmission@hofstra.edu.
Website: http://www.hofstra.edu/business/

Hofstra University, Frank G. Zarb School of Business, Programs in Finance, Hempstead, NY 11549. Offers business administration (MBA), including finance; corporate finance (Advanced Certificate); finance (MS), including financial and risk management, investment analysis; investment management (Advanced Certificate); quantitative finance (MS). *Program availability:* Part-time, evening/weekend, blended/hybrid learning. *Students:* 157 full-time (55 women), 44 part-time (11 women); includes 23 minority (6 Black or African American, non-Hispanic/Latino; 1 American Indian or Alaska Native, non-Hispanic/Latino; 7 Asian, non-Hispanic/Latino; 8 Hispanic/Latino; 1 Two or more races, non-Hispanic/Latino), 134 international. Average age 25. 530 applicants, 75% accepted, 71 enrolled. In 2017, 103 master's awarded. *Degree requirements:* For master's, capstone course (for MBA), thesis (for MS), minimum GPA of 3.0. *Entrance requirements:* For master's, GMAT/GRE, 2 letters of recommendation, resume, essay. Additional exam requirements/recommendations for international students: Required—TOEFL (minimum score 550 paper-based; 80 iBT); Recommended—IELTS (minimum score 6). *Application deadline:* Applications are processed on a rolling basis. Application fee: $75. Electronic applications accepted. *Expenses:* $1,322 per credit. *Financial support:* In 2017–18, 57 students received support, including 51 fellowships with full and partial tuition reimbursements available (averaging $5,604 per year); research assistantships with full and partial tuition reimbursements available, career-related internships or fieldwork, Federal Work-Study, institutionally sponsored loans, scholarships/grants, tuition waivers (full and partial), and unspecified assistantships also available. Support available to part-time students. Financial award applicants required to submit FAFSA. *Faculty research:* Individual investors and financial crisis; short-sale constraints and futures trading; social media and sentiment in financial markets; external monitoring of firms; CEO inside debt and insider trading. *Unit head:* Dr. K. G. Viswanathan, Chairperson, 516-463-5699, Fax: 516-463-4834, E-mail: k.g.viswanathan@hofstra.edu. *Application contact:* Sunil Samuel, Assistant Vice President of Admissions, 516-463-4723, Fax: 516-463-4664, E-mail: graduateadmission@hofstra.edu.
Website: http://www.hofstra.edu/business/

Hofstra University, Frank G. Zarb School of Business, Programs in Management and General Business, Hempstead, NY 11549. Offers business administration (MBA), including health services management, management, sports and entertainment management, strategic business management, strategic healthcare management; general management (Advanced Certificate); human resource management (MS, Advanced Certificate). *Program availability:* Part-time, evening/weekend, blended/hybrid learning. *Students:* 131 full-time (58 women), 145 part-time (65 women); includes 102 minority (23 Black or African American, non-Hispanic/Latino; 39 Asian, non-Hispanic/Latino; 37 Hispanic/Latino; 3 Two or more races, non-Hispanic/Latino), 25 international. Average age 33. 327 applicants, 72% accepted, 104 enrolled. In 2017, 116 master's awarded. *Degree requirements:* For master's, thesis optional, capstone course (for

MBA), thesis (for MS), minimum GPA of 3.0. *Entrance requirements:* For master's, GMAT/GRE, 2 letters of recommendation, resume, essay. Additional exam requirements/recommendations for international students: Required—TOEFL (minimum score 550 paper-based; 80 iBT); Recommended—IELTS (minimum score 6). *Application deadline:* Applications are processed on a rolling basis. Application fee: $75. Electronic applications accepted. *Expenses:* $1,322 per credit. *Financial support:* In 2017–18, 78 students received support, including 75 fellowships with full and partial tuition reimbursements available (averaging $4,785 per year); research assistantships with full and partial tuition reimbursements available, career-related internships or fieldwork, Federal Work-Study, institutionally sponsored loans, scholarships/grants, tuition waivers (full and partial), and unspecified assistantships also available. Support available to part-time students. Financial award applicants required to submit FAFSA. *Faculty research:* Organizational change; sustainability; entrepreneurial spawning; family business; global supply chain strategies. *Unit head:* Dr. Kaushik Sengupta, Chairperson, 516-463-7825, Fax: 516-463-4834, E-mail: kaushik.sengupta@hofstra.edu. *Application contact:* Sunil Samuel, Assistant Vice President of Admissions, 516-463-4723, Fax: 516-463-4664, E-mail: graduateadmission@hofstra.edu.
Website: http://www.hofstra.edu/business/

Hofstra University, Frank G. Zarb School of Business, Programs in Marketing and International Business, Hempstead, NY 11549. Offers business administration (MBA), including international business, marketing; international business (Advanced Certificate); marketing (MS, Advanced Certificate); marketing research (MS). *Program availability:* Part-time, evening/weekend, blended/hybrid learning. *Students:* 72 full-time (40 women), 20 part-time (11 women); includes 11 minority (2 Black or African American, non-Hispanic/Latino; 6 Asian, non-Hispanic/Latino; 2 Hispanic/Latino; 1 Two or more races, non-Hispanic/Latino), 58 international. Average age 25. 227 applicants, 74% accepted, 35 enrolled. In 2017, 51 master's awarded. *Degree requirements:* For master's, capstone course (for MBA), thesis (for MS), minimum GPA of 3.0. *Entrance requirements:* For master's, GMAT/GRE, 2 letters of recommendation, resume, essay. Additional exam requirements/recommendations for international students: Required—TOEFL (minimum score 550 paper-based; 80 iBT); Recommended—IELTS (minimum score 6). *Application deadline:* Applications are processed on a rolling basis. Application fee: $75. Electronic applications accepted. *Expenses:* $1,322 per credit. *Financial support:* In 2017–18, 28 students received support, including 24 fellowships with full and partial tuition reimbursements available (averaging $5,002 per year), 2 research assistantships with full and partial tuition reimbursements available (averaging $7,390 per year); career-related internships or fieldwork, Federal Work-Study, institutionally sponsored loans, scholarships/grants, tuition waivers (full and partial), and unspecified assistantships also available. Support available to part-time students. Financial award applicants required to submit FAFSA. *Faculty research:* Cross-cultural consumer behavior; social, digital, global, and strategic issues in marketing; consumer health/well-being; ethnocentrism and animosity. *Unit head:* Dr. Anil Mathur, Chairperson, 516-463-5346, Fax: 516-463-4834, E-mail: anil.mathur@hofstra.edu. *Application contact:* Sunil Samuel, Assistant Vice President of Admissions, 516-463-4723, Fax: 516-463-4664, E-mail: graduateadmission@hofstra.edu.
Website: http://www.hofstra.edu/business/

Holy Family University, Graduate and Professional Programs, School of Business Administration, Philadelphia, PA 19114. Offers accountancy (MS); finance (MBA); health care administration (MBA); human resource management (MBA); information systems management (MBA). *Accreditation:* ACBSP. *Program availability:* Part-time, evening/weekend. *Degree requirements:* For master's, comprehensive exam, thesis optional. *Entrance requirements:* For master's, minimum GPA of 3.0, interview, essay/personal statement, current resume, official transcript of all college or university work. Additional exam requirements/recommendations for international students: Required—TOEFL (minimum score 550 paper-based; 79 iBT), IELTS (minimum score 6), PTE (minimum score 54). Electronic applications accepted. *Expenses: Tuition:* Full-time $13,518; part-time $9012 per credit hour. Tuition and fees vary according to degree level and program.

Holy Names University, Graduate Division, Department of Business, Oakland, CA 94619-1699. Offers finance (MBA); management and leadership (MBA); marketing (MBA). *Program availability:* Part-time, evening/weekend. *Entrance requirements:* For master's, minimum undergraduate GPA of 2.6 overall, 3.0 in major; two recommendations (letter or form) from previous professors or current or previous work supervisors; 1-3 page personal statement; resume. Additional exam requirements/recommendations for international students: Required—TOEFL (minimum score 550 paper-based; 79 iBT). Electronic applications accepted. Application fee is waived when completed online. *Expenses:* Contact institution. *Faculty research:* Business ethics, sustainable economics, accounting models, cross-cultural management, diversity in organizations.

Hood College, Graduate School, Department of Economics and Business Administration, Frederick, MD 21701-8575. Offers accounting (MBA, Certificate); finance (MBA); financial management (Certificate); human resource management (MBA); information systems (MBA); marketing (MBA); organizational management (Certificate); public management (MBA). *Accreditation:* ACBSP. *Program availability:* Part-time, evening/weekend. *Faculty:* 4 full-time (2 women), 7 part-time/adjunct (1 woman). *Students:* 21 full-time (12 women), 91 part-time (47 women); includes 19 minority (8 Black or African American, non-Hispanic/Latino; 3 Asian, non-Hispanic/Latino; 8 Hispanic/Latino), 15 international. Average age 31. 34 applicants, 97% accepted, 23 enrolled. In 2017, 42 master's awarded. *Degree requirements:* For master's, capstone/final research project. *Entrance requirements:* For master's, minimum GPA of 3.0 (or resume and two letters of recommendation), copy of official transcripts, essay. Additional exam requirements/recommendations for international students: Required—TOEFL (minimum score 575 paper-based; 89 iBT), IELTS (minimum score 6.5). *Application deadline:* For fall admission, 8/15 for domestic students, 8/5 for international students; for spring admission, 12/1 for domestic and international students; for summer admission, 5/1 for domestic students, 4/15 for international students. Applications are processed on a rolling basis. Application fee: $35. Electronic applications accepted. *Expenses:* $550 per credit hour plus $110 per semester comprehensive fee. *Financial support:* Tuition waivers (partial) and unspecified assistantships available. Financial award applicants required to submit FAFSA. *Faculty research:* Corporate strategy and sustainable competitive advantages, business ethics, entrepreneurship, investments management, economic development. *Unit head:* Dr. April M. Boulton, Dean of the Graduate School, 301-696-3600, Fax: 301-696-3597, E-mail: gofurther@hood.edu. *Application contact:* Jan Marcus, Assistant Director of Graduate Admissions, 301-696-3603, E-mail: gofurther@hood.edu.

Houston Baptist University, Archie W. Dunham College of Business, Program in Business Administration, Houston, TX 77074-3298. Offers MBA. *Program availability:* Part-time, evening/weekend. *Students:* 37 full-time (16 women), 52 part-time (33 women); includes 47 minority (23 Black or African American, non-Hispanic/Latino; 4 Asian, non-Hispanic/Latino; 16 Hispanic/Latino; 1 Native Hawaiian or other Pacific Islander, non-Hispanic/Latino; 3 Two or more races, non-Hispanic/Latino), 17 international. Average age 30. 204 applicants, 22% accepted, 18 enrolled. In 2017, 51 master's awarded. *Entrance requirements:* For master's, GMAT or GRE, minimum GPA of 2.5, essay/personal statement, resume, bachelor's degree conferred transcript.

Additional exam requirements/recommendations for international students: Required—TOEFL (minimum score 80 iBT), IELTS (minimum score 6.5). *Application deadline:* For fall admission, 8/1 for domestic students, 6/1 for international students; for spring admission, 1/1 for domestic students, 11/1 for international students; for summer admission, 5/1 for domestic students, 3/1 for international students. Applications are processed on a rolling basis. Application fee: $0 ($100 for international students). Electronic applications accepted. Application fee is waived when completed online. *Expenses:* Contact institution. *Financial support:* In 2017–18, 15 students received support. Career-related internships or fieldwork, Federal Work-Study, and scholarships/grants available. Support available to part-time students. Financial award application deadline: 4/1; financial award applicants required to submit FAFSA. *Unit head:* Dr. Michael Weeks, Dean, Archie W. Dunham College of Business, 281-649-3014, E-mail: mweeks@hbu.edu. *Application contact:* Laurel Motal, Graduate Student Services Coordinator, 281-649-3306, Fax: 281-649-3306, E-mail: lmotal@hbu.edu.
Website: http://www.hbu.edu/mba

Houston Baptist University, College of Education and Behavioral Sciences, Programs in Education, Houston, TX 77074-3298. Offers bilingual education (M Ed); counselor education (M Ed); curriculum and instruction (M Ed); curriculum and instruction (EC-6 bilingual) (M Ed); curriculum and instruction in all-level art, Spanish, music, or physical education (M Ed); curriculum and instruction in EC-6 and special education (EC-12) (M Ed); curriculum and instruction in instructional technology (M Ed); curriculum and instruction in mathematics, science, or social studies (4-8) (M Ed); curriculum and instruction with EC-6 generalist (M Ed); curriculum and instruction with English language arts and reading (4-8) (M Ed); educational administration (M Ed); educational diagnostician (M Ed); executive educational leadership (Ed D); higher education in business management (M Ed); higher education in Christian studies (M Ed); higher education in counseling (M Ed); higher education in educational technology (M Ed); reading (M Ed); special educational leadership (Ed D). *Program availability:* Part-time, evening/weekend, 100% online, blended/hybrid learning. *Students:* 83 full-time (65 women), 187 part-time (156 women); includes 189 minority (114 Black or African American, non-Hispanic/Latino; 2 American Indian or Alaska Native, non-Hispanic/Latino; 9 Asian, non-Hispanic/Latino; 58 Hispanic/Latino; 6 Two or more races, non-Hispanic/Latino), 7 international. Average age 36. 309 applicants, 31% accepted, 70 enrolled. In 2017, 92 master's awarded. *Degree requirements:* For master's, comprehensive exam; for doctorate, thesis/dissertation. *Entrance requirements:* For master's, minimum GPA of 2.75, two recommendations, resume, bachelor's degree conferred transcript; interview (for non-certified teachers); for doctorate, GRE, 5 letters of recommendation. Additional exam requirements/recommendations for international students: Required—TOEFL (minimum score 80 iBT), IELTS (minimum score 6.5). *Application deadline:* For fall admission, 8/1 for domestic students, 6/1 for international students; for spring admission, 1/1 for domestic students, 11/1 for international students; for summer admission, 5/1 for domestic students, 3/1 for international students. Applications are processed on a rolling basis. Application fee: $0 ($100 for international students). Electronic applications accepted. Application fee is waived when completed online. *Expenses:* $22,000 tuition; $4,500 fees (general, technology and parking). *Financial support:* In 2017–18, 59 students received support. Research assistantships, teaching assistantships, Federal Work-Study, and scholarships/grants available. Support available to part-time students. Financial award application deadline: 4/1; financial award applicants required to submit FAFSA. *Faculty research:* Autism and inclusion, integrating technology into instruction, school change and leadership trust. *Unit head:* Dr. Charlotte Fontenot, Director, Graduate Programs, 281-649-3078, Fax: 281-649-3361, E-mail: cfontenot@hbu.edu. *Application contact:* Kristy Wright, Administrative Assistant for Graduate Programs, 281-649-3094, Fax: 281-649-3361, E-mail: kwright@hbu.edu.
Website: http://www.hbu.edu/MED

Howard Payne University, Program in Business Administration, Brownwood, TX 76801-2715. Offers MBA. *Program availability:* Part-time, evening/weekend. *Degree requirements:* For master's, comprehensive exam, research project. *Entrance requirements:* For master's, minimum undergraduate GPA of 3.0, 3.3 in first 9 hours of coursework; business foundation classes (for those without undergraduate business degree and no business-related coursework). Additional exam requirements/recommendations for international students: Required—TOEFL (minimum score 79 iBT). Electronic applications accepted.

Howard University, School of Business, Graduate Programs in Business, Washington, DC 20059-0002. Offers accounting (MBA); entrepreneurship (MBA); finance (MBA); general management (MBA); human resources management (MBA); information systems (MBA); international business (MBA); marketing (MBA); supply chain management (MBA); JD/MBA. *Accreditation:* AACSB. *Program availability:* Part-time, evening/weekend, online learning. *Entrance requirements:* For master's, GMAT, minimum 1 year post undergraduate work experience, resume, 3 letters of recommendation, advanced college algebra. Additional exam requirements/recommendations for international students: Required—TOEFL. *Faculty research:* Marketing research in multi-ethnic populations, U.S. trade policies and international relations, risk management (finance).

Hult International Business School, Graduate Programs, Cambridge, MA 02141. Offers business administration (EMBA); business analytics (MBA, MIB); business statistics (MBS); disruptive innovation (MDI); entrepreneurship (MBA, MIB); family business (MBA, MIB); finance (MBA, MF, MIB); international marketing (MIM); marketing (MBA, MIB); project management (MBA, MIB). MDI and MBS offered in San Francisco; MBA also offered in Boston, San Francisco, Dubai, Shanghai, and New York. *Entrance requirements:* For master's, GMAT, 3 years of work experience. Additional exam requirements/recommendations for international students: Required—TOEFL. Electronic applications accepted. *Expenses:* Contact institution.

Humboldt State University, Academic Programs, College of Professional Studies, School of Business, Arcata, CA 95521-8299. Offers MBA. *Program availability:* Part-time, evening/weekend. *Degree requirements:* For master's, thesis or alternative. *Entrance requirements:* For master's, GMAT or GRE, minimum GPA of 2.5. Additional exam requirements/recommendations for international students: Required—TOEFL (minimum score 500 paper-based). *Expenses:* Contact institution. *Faculty research:* International business development, small town entrepreneurship, international trade: Pacific Rim.

Huntington University, Graduate School, Huntington, IN 46750-1299. Offers adolescent and young adult education (M Ed); business administration (MBA); counseling (MA), including licensed mental health counselor; early adolescent education (M Ed); elementary education (M Ed); global youth ministry (MA); occupational therapy (OTD); organizational leadership (MA); pastoral leadership (MA); TESOL education (M Ed). *Program availability:* Part-time, online learning. *Faculty:* 17 full-time (10 women), 14 part-time/adjunct (4 women). *Students:* 221 full-time (163 women), 22 part-time (13 women). *Degree requirements:* For master's, comprehensive exam (for some programs), thesis (for some programs). *Entrance requirements:* For master's, GRE (for counseling and education students only); for doctorate, GRE (for occupational therapy students). Additional exam requirements/recommendations for international students: Required—TOEFL (minimum score 85 iBT), IELTS (minimum score 6.5). *Application*

Business Administration and Management—General

deadline: For fall admission, 7/1 for domestic students, 5/1 for international students; for winter admission, 10/1 for domestic students, 9/1 for international students; for spring admission, 11/30 for domestic students, 10/30 for international students. Applications are processed on a rolling basis. Application fee: $30. Electronic applications accepted. *Expenses:* Contact institution. *Financial support:* Scholarships/grants and unspecified assistantships available. Support available to part-time students. Financial award application deadline: 8/1; financial award applicants required to submit FAFSA. *Faculty research:* Leadership, educational technology trends, evangelism, youth ministry, mental health. *Unit head:* Michael Wanous, Vice President for Academic Affairs, 260-359-4008, Fax: 260-359-4126, E-mail: mwanous@huntington.edu. *Application contact:* Evan Bennett, Assistant Director of Graduate Admissions, 260-359-4111, Fax: 260-359-4126, E-mail: graduate@huntington.edu.
Website: http://www.huntington.edu/graduate

Husson University, Master of Business Administration Program, Bangor, ME 04401-2999. Offers athletic administration (MBA); biotechnology and innovation (MBA); general business administration (MBA); healthcare management (MBA); hospitality and tourism management (MBA); organizational management (MBA); risk management (MBA). *Program availability:* Part-time, evening/weekend, 100% online, blended/hybrid learning. *Faculty:* 11 full-time (5 women), 19 part-time/adjunct (4 women). *Students:* 83 full-time (44 women), 287 part-time (176 women); includes 25 minority (7 Black or African American, non-Hispanic/Latino; 11 Asian, non-Hispanic/Latino; 4 Hispanic/Latino; 3 Two or more races, non-Hispanic/Latino), 16 international. Average age 35. 158 applicants, 77% accepted, 49 enrolled. In 2017, 120 master's awarded. *Degree requirements:* For master's, comprehensive exam (for some programs), thesis optional. *Entrance requirements:* For master's, minimum GPA of 3.0, letter of recommendation. Additional exam requirements/recommendations for international students: Required—TOEFL (minimum score 550 paper-based; 80 iBT), IELTS (minimum score 6.5). *Application deadline:* Applications are processed on a rolling basis. Application fee: $50. Electronic applications accepted. *Expenses:* $464 per credit. *Financial support:* In 2017–18, 13 students received support. Career-related internships or fieldwork, Federal Work-Study, scholarships/grants, and unspecified assistantships available. Financial award application deadline: 4/15; financial award applicants required to submit FAFSA. *Unit head:* Prof. Stephanie Shayne, Director, Graduate and Online Programs, 207-404-5632, Fax: 207-992-4987, E-mail: shaynes@husson.edu. *Application contact:* Kristen Card, Director of Graduate Admissions, 207-404-5660, Fax: 207-941-7935, E-mail: cardk@husson.edu.
Website: http://www.husson.edu/college-of-business/school-of-business-and-management/master-of-business-administration-mba/

Idaho State University, Office of Graduate Studies, College of Business, Pocatello, ID 83209-8020. Offers business administration (MBA, Postbaccalaureate Certificate); computer information systems (MS, Postbaccalaureate Certificate). *Accreditation:* AACSB. *Program availability:* Part-time. *Degree requirements:* For master's, comprehensive exam, thesis (for some programs), oral exam; for Postbaccalaureate Certificate, comprehensive exam, thesis (for some programs), 6 hours of clerkship. *Entrance requirements:* For master's, GMAT, GRE General Test, minimum GPA of 3.0, resume outlining work experience, 2 letters of reference; for Postbaccalaureate Certificate, GMAT, GRE General Test, minimum upper-level GPA of 3.0, resume of work experience. Additional exam requirements/recommendations for international students: Required—TOEFL (minimum score 550 paper-based; 80 iBT). Electronic applications accepted. *Faculty research:* Information assurance, computer information technology, finance management, marketing.

IGlobal University, Graduate Programs, Vienna, VA 22182. Offers accounting (MBA); data management and analytics (MSIT); entrepreneurship (MBA); finance (MBA); global business management (MBA); health care management (MBA); hospitality and tourism management (MBA); human resources management (MBA); information technology (MBA); information technology systems and management (MSIT); leadership and management (MBA); project management (MBA); public service and administration (MBA); software design and management (MSIT).

Illinois Institute of Technology, Stuart School of Business, Program in Business Administration, Chicago, IL 60661. Offers sustainability (MBA); JD/MBA; M Des/MBA; MBA/MS. *Accreditation:* AACSB. *Program availability:* Part-time, evening/weekend. *Entrance requirements:* For master's, GRE (minimum score 298) or GMAT (500). Additional exam requirements/recommendations for international students: Required—TOEFL (minimum score 600 paper-based; 85 iBT); Recommended—IELTS (minimum score 7). Electronic applications accepted. *Expenses:* Contact institution. *Faculty research:* Global management and marketing strategy, technological innovation, management science, financial management, knowledge management.

Illinois Institute of Technology, Stuart School of Business, Program in Management Science, Chicago, IL 60661. Offers PhD. *Accreditation:* AACSB. *Program availability:* Part-time. *Degree requirements:* For doctorate, comprehensive exam, thesis/dissertation. *Entrance requirements:* For doctorate, GRE (minimum score 316) or GMAT (minimum score 650). Additional exam requirements/recommendations for international students: Required—TOEFL (minimum score 600 paper-based; 85 iBT). Electronic applications accepted. *Expenses:* Contact institution. *Faculty research:* Scheduling systems, queuing systems, optimization, quality systems, foreign exchange, enterprise risk management, credit risk modeling.

Illinois State University, Graduate School, College of Business, Program in Business Administration, Normal, IL 61790. Offers MBA. *Accreditation:* AACSB. *Program availability:* Part-time. *Degree requirements:* For master's, thesis optional. *Entrance requirements:* For master's, GMAT, minimum GPA of 2.75 during previous 2 years of course work. Additional exam requirements/recommendations for international students: Required—TOEFL. *Faculty research:* McLean County small business development center.

IMCA–International Management Centres Association, Programs in Business Administration, Buckingham, United Kingdom. Offers M Mgt, M Phil, MBA, MS. *Program availability:* Online learning.

Independence University, Program in Business Administration, Salt Lake City, UT 84107. Offers MBA.

Indiana State University, College of Graduate and Professional Studies, Scott College of Business, Terre Haute, IN 47809. Offers MBA. *Accreditation:* AACSB. *Program availability:* Part-time, evening/weekend. *Degree requirements:* For master's, thesis optional. *Entrance requirements:* For master's, GMAT. Electronic applications accepted. *Faculty research:* Small business and entrepreneurial sciences, production and operations management.

Indiana Tech, Program in Business Administration, Fort Wayne, IN 46803-1297. Offers accounting (MBA); health care management (MBA); human resources (MBA); management (MBA); marketing (MBA). *Program availability:* Part-time, evening/weekend, online learning. *Entrance requirements:* For master's, GMAT, bachelor's degree from regionally-accredited university; minimum undergraduate GPA of 2.5; 2 years of significant work experience; 3 letters of recommendation. Electronic applications accepted.

Indiana Tech, Program in Management, Fort Wayne, IN 46803-1297. Offers MSM. *Program availability:* Part-time, evening/weekend, 100% online. *Entrance requirements:* For master's, bachelor's degree from regionally-accredited university; minimum undergraduate GPA of 2.5; 2 years of significant work experience; 3 letters of recommendation. Electronic applications accepted.

Indiana University Bloomington, Kelley School of Business, Bloomington, IN 47405-7000. Offers MBA, MPA, MS, DBA, PhD, DBA/MIS, JD/MBA, JD/MPA, MBA/MA, PhD/MIS. PhD offered through University Graduate School. *Accreditation:* AACSB. *Degree requirements:* For doctorate, comprehensive exam, thesis/dissertation. *Entrance requirements:* For master's, GMAT; for doctorate, GMAT, GRE General Test. Additional exam requirements/recommendations for international students: Required—TOEFL (minimum score 100 iBT). Electronic applications accepted. *Expenses:* Contact institution. *Faculty research:* Entrepreneurial ventures, technology-based innovation, on-line price competition, on-line shopping behavior.

Indiana University Kokomo, School of Business, Kokomo, IN 46904. Offers accounting (Postbaccalaureate Certificate); business administration (MBA); business fundamentals (Postbaccalaureate Certificate). *Accreditation:* AACSB. *Program availability:* Part-time, evening/weekend. *Degree requirements:* For master's, thesis optional, research project. *Entrance requirements:* For master's, GMAT. Additional exam requirements/recommendations for international students: Required—TOEFL (minimum score 550 paper-based; 73 iBT). Electronic applications accepted. *Expenses:* Contact institution. *Faculty research:* Investments, outsourcing, technology, adoption.

Indiana University Northwest, School of Business and Economics, Gary, IN 46408. Offers accounting (Graduate Certificate); management (Certificate); management and administrative studies (MBA). *Accreditation:* AACSB. *Program availability:* Part-time, evening/weekend. *Entrance requirements:* For master's, GMAT (not for Weekend MBA for Professionals), letter of recommendation. Electronic applications accepted. *Expenses:* Contact institution. *Faculty research:* International finance, employment law and testing, business ethics, taxation, financial institutions.

Indiana University of Pennsylvania, School of Graduate Studies and Research, Eberly College of Business and Information Technology, MBA Executive Track Program, Indiana, PA 15705. Offers MBA. *Program availability:* Part-time, evening/weekend. *Faculty:* 32 full-time (4 women), 1 part-time/adjunct (0 women). *Students:* 1 (woman) full-time, 112 part-time (44 women); includes 18 minority (6 Black or African American, non-Hispanic/Latino; 4 Asian, non-Hispanic/Latino; 4 Hispanic/Latino; 4 Two or more races, non-Hispanic/Latino), 49 international. Average age 35. 83 applicants, 92% accepted, 65 enrolled. In 2017, 32 master's awarded. *Entrance requirements:* Additional exam requirements/recommendations for international students: Required—TOEFL (minimum score 540 paper-based). *Application deadline:* Applications are processed on a rolling basis. Application fee: $50. Electronic applications accepted. *Expenses:* Contact institution. *Financial support:* Fellowships, research assistantships, career-related internships or fieldwork, Federal Work-Study, scholarships/grants, and unspecified assistantships available. Financial award application deadline: 4/15; financial award applicants required to submit FAFSA. *Unit head:* Dr. Krish Krishnan, Graduate Coordinator, 724-357-2522, E-mail: krishnan@iup.edu.
Website: http://www.iup.edu/mba/grad/executive-mba/

Indiana University of Pennsylvania, School of Graduate Studies and Research, Eberly College of Business and Information Technology, Program in Business Administration, Indiana, PA 15705. Offers MBA. *Accreditation:* AACSB. *Program availability:* Part-time. *Faculty:* 32 full-time (4 women), 1 part-time/adjunct (0 women). *Students:* 150 full-time (51 women), 10 part-time (6 women); includes 7 minority (4 Black or African American, non-Hispanic/Latino; 2 Asian, non-Hispanic/Latino; 1 Hispanic/Latino), 124 international. Average age 24. 160 applicants, 71% accepted, 66 enrolled. In 2017, 147 master's awarded. *Entrance requirements:* For master's, GMAT, 2 letters of recommendation. Additional exam requirements/recommendations for international students: Required—TOEFL (minimum score 540 paper-based). *Application deadline:* Applications are processed on a rolling basis. Application fee: $50. Electronic applications accepted. *Expenses:* Tuition, state resident: full-time $12,000; part-time $500 per credit. Tuition, nonresident: full-time $18,000; part-time $750 per credit. *Required fees:* $4073; $165.55 per credit. $64 per term. *Financial support:* Fellowships, research assistantships, career-related internships or fieldwork, Federal Work-Study, scholarships/grants, and unspecified assistantships available. Support available to part-time students. Financial award application deadline: 4/15; financial award applicants required to submit FAFSA. *Unit head:* Dr. Krish Krishnan, Graduate Coordinator, 724-357-2522, E-mail: krishnan@iup.edu.
Website: http://www.iup.edu/grad/mba/default.aspx

Indiana University–Purdue University Fort Wayne, Doermer School of Business, Fort Wayne, IN 46805-1499. Offers MBA. *Accreditation:* AACSB. *Program availability:* Part-time. *Entrance requirements:* For master's, GMAT, minimum GPA of 3.0, two letters of recommendation, essay, interview. Additional exam requirements/recommendations for international students: Required—TOEFL (minimum score 600 paper-based; 100 iBT). *Faculty research:* Buddhist ethics education framework, earth orbit pollution, information technology and business school graduates.

Indiana University–Purdue University Indianapolis, Kelley School of Business, Indianapolis, IN 46202-5151. Offers MBA, MSA, MBA/JD, MBA/MD, MBA/MHA, MBA/MS, MBA/MSA, MBA/MSE. *Accreditation:* AACSB.

Indiana University South Bend, Judd Leighton School of Business and Economics, South Bend, IN 46615. Offers accounting (MSA); business (Graduate Certificate); business administration (MBA), including finance, human resource management, marketing; MBA/MSA. *Program availability:* Part-time, evening/weekend. *Entrance requirements:* For master's, GMAT. Additional exam requirements/recommendations for international students: Required—TOEFL (minimum score 550 paper-based; 79 iBT). Electronic applications accepted. *Expenses:* Contact institution. *Faculty research:* Financial accounting, consumer research, capital budgeting research, business strategy research.

Indiana University Southeast, School of Business, New Albany, IN 47150-6405. Offers business administration (MBA); strategic finance (MS). *Accreditation:* AACSB. *Program availability:* Part-time. *Degree requirements:* For master's, community service. *Entrance requirements:* For master's, GMAT, work experience. Additional exam requirements/recommendations for international students: Required—TOEFL. Electronic applications accepted. *Expenses:* Contact institution.

Indiana Wesleyan University, College of Adult and Professional Studies, Graduate Studies in Business, Marion, IN 46953. Offers accounting (MBA, Graduate Certificate); applied management (MBA); business administration (MBA); health care (MBA, Graduate Certificate); human resources (MBA, Graduate Certificate); management (MS); organizational leadership (MA). *Program availability:* Part-time, evening/weekend, online learning. *Degree requirements:* For master's, applied business or management project. *Entrance requirements:* For master's, minimum GPA of 2.5, 2 years of related work experience. Additional exam requirements/recommendations for international students: Required—TOEFL (minimum score 550 paper-based). Electronic applications accepted.

Instituto Centroamericano de Administración de Empresas, Graduate Programs, La Garita, Costa Rica. Offers agribusiness management (MIAM); business administration (EMBA); finance (MBA); real estate management (MGREM); sustainable development (MBA); technology (MBA). *Degree requirements:* For master's, comprehensive exam, essay. *Entrance requirements:* For master's, GMAT or GRE General Test, fluency in Spanish, interview, letters of recommendation, minimum 1 year of work experience. Additional exam requirements/recommendations for international students: Recommended—TOEFL. Electronic applications accepted. *Faculty research:* Competitiveness, production.

Instituto Tecnologico de Santo Domingo, Graduate School, Area of Business, Santo Domingo, Dominican Republic. Offers banking and securities markets (M Mgmt); corporate finance (M Mgmt); human resources management (M Mgmt, Certificate); international trade management (M Mgmt); marketing (M Mgmt); organizational development (M Mgmt); quality and productivity management (Certificate); tax management and planning (M Mgmt); upper management (M Mgmt).

Instituto Tecnológico y de Estudios Superiores de Monterrey, Campus Central de Veracruz, Graduate Programs, Córdoba, Mexico. Offers administration (MA); administration of information technologies (MTI); computer sciences (MCC); education (MEE); educational institution administration (MAD); educational technology (MTE); electronic commerce (MCE); finance (MAF); humanistic studies (MEH); international business for Latin America (MNL); marketing (MMT); science (MCP). *Program availability:* Part-time, evening/weekend, online learning. *Degree requirements:* For master's, thesis (for some programs). *Entrance requirements:* For master's, PAEP College Board. Electronic applications accepted.

Instituto Tecnológico y de Estudios Superiores de Monterrey, Campus Ciudad de México, School of Business Administration, Ciudad de Mexico, Mexico. Offers business administration (EMBA, MBA, PhD); economy (MBA); finance (MBA). EMBA program offered jointly with The University of Texas at Austin. *Program availability:* Part-time, evening/weekend, online learning. *Entrance requirements:* For master's and doctorate, Instituto entrance exam. Additional exam requirements/recommendations for international students: Required—TOEFL.

Instituto Tecnológico y de Estudios Superiores de Monterrey, Campus Ciudad Juárez, Program in Business Administration, Ciudad Juárez, Mexico. Offers MBA. *Program availability:* Part-time, online learning. *Entrance requirements:* Additional exam requirements/recommendations for international students: Required—TOEFL (minimum score 500 paper-based).

Instituto Tecnológico y de Estudios Superiores de Monterrey, Campus Ciudad Obregón, Program in Administration, Ciudad Obregón, Mexico. Offers MA.

Instituto Tecnológico y de Estudios Superiores de Monterrey, Campus Cuernavaca, Programs in Business Administration, Temixco, Mexico. Offers finance (MA); human resources management (MA); international business (MA); marketing (MA).

Instituto Tecnológico y de Estudios Superiores de Monterrey, Campus Estado de México, Professional and Graduate Division, Estado de Mexico, Mexico. Offers administration of information technologies (MITA); architecture (M Arch); business administration (GMBA, MBA); computer sciences (MCS, PhD); education (M Ed); educational institution administration (MAD); educational technology and innovation (PhD); electronic commerce (MEC); environmental systems (MS); finance (MAF); humanistic studies (MHS); information sciences and knowledge management (MISKM); information systems (MS); manufacturing systems (MS); marketing (MEM); quality systems and productivity (MS); science and materials engineering (PhD); telecommunications management (MTM). *Program availability:* Part-time, online learning. *Degree requirements:* For master's, one foreign language, thesis (for some programs); for doctorate, one foreign language, thesis/dissertation. *Entrance requirements:* For master's, E-PAEP 500, interview; for doctorate, E-PAEP 500, research proposal. Additional exam requirements/recommendations for international students: Required—TOEFL (minimum score 550 paper-based). *Faculty research:* Surface treatments by plasmas, mechanical properties, robotics, graphical computing, mechatronics security protocols.

Instituto Tecnológico y de Estudios Superiores de Monterrey, Campus Guadalajara, Program in Business Administration, Zapopan, Mexico. Offers IEMBA, M Ad. *Program availability:* Part-time, evening/weekend, online learning. *Degree requirements:* For master's, one foreign language. *Entrance requirements:* For master's, ITESM admission test. *Faculty research:* Strategic alliances in small business, family business practice in Mexico, competitiveness under NAFTA for Mexican firms.

Instituto Tecnológico y de Estudios Superiores de Monterrey, Campus Irapuato, Graduate Programs, Irapuato, Mexico. Offers administration (MBA); administration of information technology (MAIT); administration of telecommunications (MAT); architecture (M Arch); computer science (MCS); education (M Ed); educational administration (MEA); educational innovation and technology (DEIT); educational technology (MET); electronic commerce (MBA); environmental administration and planning (MEAP); environmental systems (MES); finances (MBA); humanistic studies (MHS); international management for Latin American executives (MIMLAE); library and information science (MLIS); manufacturing quality management (MMQM); marketing research (MBA).

Instituto Tecnológico y de Estudios Superiores de Monterrey, Campus Laguna, Graduate School, Torreón, Mexico. Offers business administration (MBA); industrial engineering (MIE); management information systems (MS). *Program availability:* Part-time. *Entrance requirements:* For master's, GMAT. *Faculty research:* Computer communications from home to the university.

Instituto Tecnológico y de Estudios Superiores de Monterrey, Campus León, Program in Business Administration, León, Mexico. Offers MBA. *Program availability:* Part-time.

Instituto Tecnológico y de Estudios Superiores de Monterrey, Campus Monterrey, Graduate School of Business Administration and Leadership, Program in Business Administration, Monterrey, Mexico. Offers business administration (MA, MBA); finance (M Sc); international business (M Sc); marketing (M Sc). *Program availability:* Part-time. *Degree requirements:* For master's, one foreign language, thesis. *Entrance requirements:* For master's, GMAT. Additional exam requirements/recommendations for international students: Required—TOEFL. *Faculty research:* Technology management, quality management, organizational theory and behavior.

Instituto Tecnológico y de Estudios Superiores de Monterrey, Campus Monterrey, Graduate School of Business Administration and Leadership, Program in Management, Monterrey, Mexico. Offers PhD. *Accreditation:* AACSB. *Program availability:* Part-time. *Degree requirements:* For doctorate, one foreign language, thesis/dissertation. *Entrance requirements:* For doctorate, GMAT. Additional exam requirements/recommendations for international students: Required—TOEFL. *Faculty research:* Quality management, manufacturing and technology management, information systems, managerial economics, business policy.

Instituto Tecnológico y de Estudios Superiores de Monterrey, Campus Querétaro, School of Business, Santiago de Querétaro, Mexico. Offers MBA. *Entrance requirements:* For master's, GRE General Test. *Faculty research:* Organizational analysis, industrial marketing, international trade.

Instituto Tecnológico y de Estudios Superiores de Monterrey, Campus Sonora Norte, Program in Business, Hermosillo, Mexico. Offers MA. *Entrance requirements:* For master's, GMAT.

Instituto Tecnológico y de Estudios Superiores de Monterrey, Campus Toluca, Graduate Programs, Toluca, Mexico. Offers MBA. *Program availability:* Part-time, evening/weekend. *Degree requirements:* For master's, one foreign language. *Faculty research:* Management in the industrial valley of Toluca.

Inter American University of Puerto Rico, Aguadilla Campus, Graduate School, Aguadilla, PR 00605. Offers accounting (MBA); counseling psychology specializing in family (MS); criminal justice (MA); educative management and leadership (MA); elementary education (M Ed); finance (MBA); human resources (MBA); industrial management (MBA); management information systems (MBA); marketing (MBA). *Program availability:* Part-time, evening/weekend. *Degree requirements:* For master's, comprehensive exam. *Entrance requirements:* For master's, EXADEP, 2 letters of recommendation, minimum GPA of 2.5. Electronic applications accepted.

Inter American University of Puerto Rico, Arecibo Campus, Program in Business Administration, Arecibo, PR 00614-4050. Offers accounting (MBA); finance (MBA); human resources (MBA).

Inter American University of Puerto Rico, Barranquitas Campus, Business Administration Program, Barranquitas, PR 00794. Offers accounting (MBA); human resources (MBA); managerial information systems (MBA). *Program availability:* Part-time, evening/weekend. *Faculty:* 2 full-time (1 woman), 2 part-time/adjunct (both women). *Students:* 11 full-time (9 women), 1 (woman) part-time; all minorities (all Hispanic/Latino). Average age 31. 6 applicants, 83% accepted, 5 enrolled. In 2017, 3 master's awarded. *Degree requirements:* For master's, 2 foreign languages, comprehensive exam (for some programs), thesis or alternative, minimum GPA of 3.0. *Entrance requirements:* For master's, BBA or its equivalent from accredited institution, official academic transcript from institution that conferred bachelor's degree, minimum GPA of 2.5, interview (for some programs). *Application deadline:* Applications are processed on a rolling basis. Application fee: $31. Electronic applications accepted. *Expenses:* $3,392 full-time tuition plus $652 fees. *Financial support:* Applicants required to submit FAFSA. *Unit head:* Juan A. Negron-Berrios, PhD, Chancellor, 787-857-3600 Ext. 2002, Fax: 787-857-2125, E-mail: janegron@br.inter.edu. *Application contact:* Aramilda Cartagena-Santiago, Dean of Students, 787-857-3600 Ext. 2009, Fax: 787-857-2125, E-mail: aramildacartagena@br.inter.edu.

Inter American University of Puerto Rico, Fajardo Campus, Graduate Programs, Fajardo, PR 00738-7003. Offers computer science (MS); educational management and leadership (MA Ed); general business (MBA); human resources (MBA); management information systems (MBA); marketing (MBA); special education (MA Ed). *Program availability:* Online learning. *Faculty:* 1 full-time (0 women), 25 part-time/adjunct (13 women). *Students:* 1 (woman) full-time, 126 part-time (81 women).

Inter American University of Puerto Rico, Guayama Campus, Department of Business Administration, Guayama, PR 00785. Offers marketing (MBA).

Inter American University of Puerto Rico, Metropolitan Campus, Graduate Programs, Program in General Business, San Juan, PR 00919-1293. Offers MBA.

Inter American University of Puerto Rico, San Germán Campus, Graduate Studies Center, Program in Business Administration, San Germán, PR 00683-5008. Offers accounting (MBA); finance (MBA); general business administration (MBA); human resources (MBA, PhD); industrial relations (MBA); information systems (MBA); international and interregional business (PhD); management (MBA); marketing (MBA). *Program availability:* Part-time, evening/weekend. *Degree requirements:* For master's, comprehensive exam. *Entrance requirements:* For master's, GRE General Test or EXADEP, minimum GPA of 3.0.

International Technological University, Program in Business Administration, San Jose, CA 95134. Offers MBA, DBA. *Program availability:* Part-time, evening/weekend. Terminal master's awarded for partial completion of doctoral program. *Degree requirements:* For master's, thesis or alternative, capstone project; for doctorate, comprehensive exam, thesis/dissertation. *Entrance requirements:* Additional exam requirements/recommendations for international students: Required—TOEFL, IELTS. Electronic applications accepted.

International University in Geneva, Business Programs, Geneva, Switzerland. Offers business administration (MBA, DBA); entrepreneurship (MBA); international business (MIB); international trade (MIT); sales and marketing (MBA). *Accreditation:* ACBSP. *Program availability:* Part-time, evening/weekend. *Degree requirements:* For master's, comprehensive exam. *Entrance requirements:* For master's, GMAT. Additional exam requirements/recommendations for international students: Required—TOEFL. Electronic applications accepted.

The International University of Monaco, Graduate Programs, Monte Carlo, Monaco. Offers entrepreneurship (EMBA, MBA); financial engineering (M Sc); hedge fund and private equity (M Sc); international marketing (EMBA, MBA); international wealth management (M Sc); luxury goods and services (EMBA, M Sc, MBA); wealth and asset management (EMBA, MBA). *Program availability:* Part-time. *Degree requirements:* For master's, comprehensive exam (for some programs), applied research project. *Entrance requirements:* Additional exam requirements/recommendations for international students: Required—TOEFL (minimum score 550 paper-based), IELTS. Electronic applications accepted. *Faculty research:* Gaming, leadership, disintermediation.

Iona College, School of Business, New Rochelle, NY 10801-1890. Offers MBA, MS, AC, PMC. *Accreditation:* AACSB. *Program availability:* Part-time, evening/weekend, 100% online, blended/hybrid learning. *Faculty:* 33 full-time (6 women), 18 part-time/adjunct (6 women). *Students:* 163 full-time (83 women), 114 part-time (56 women); includes 93 minority (33 Black or African American, non-Hispanic/Latino; 2 American Indian or Alaska Native, non-Hispanic/Latino; 11 Asian, non-Hispanic/Latino; 45 Hispanic/Latino; 1 Native Hawaiian or other Pacific Islander, non-Hispanic/Latino; 1 Two or more races, non-Hispanic/Latino), 19 international. Average age 28. 115 applicants, 97% accepted, 65 enrolled. In 2017, 249 master's, 169 other advanced degrees awarded. *Entrance requirements:* For master's, letter of recommendation, all undergraduate and graduate transcripts, copy of current résumé; for other advanced degree, copy of current resume and all official undergraduate transcripts (for AC). Additional exam requirements/recommendations for international students: Required—TOEFL (minimum score 550 paper-based; 80 iBT), IELTS (minimum score 6.5). *Application deadline:* For fall admission, 8/15 priority date for domestic students, 8/1 priority date for international students; for winter admission, 11/15 priority date for domestic students, 11/1 priority date for international students; for spring admission, 2/15 priority date for domestic students, 2/1 priority date for international students; for summer admission, 5/15 priority date for domestic students, 5/1 priority date for international students. Applications are processed on a rolling basis. Application fee: $0. Electronic applications accepted. *Expenses:* $1,149 per credit tuition. *Financial support:*

Business Administration and Management—General

Scholarships/grants, tuition waivers (partial), and unspecified assistantships available. Support available to part-time students. Financial award application deadline: 4/15; financial award applicants required to submit FAFSA. *Faculty research:* Artificial intelligence, financial services, value-based management, public policy, business ethics. *Unit head:* Dr. William B. Lamb, Dean of the School of Business, 914-633-2254, E-mail: wlamb@iona.edu. *Application contact:* Katelyn Brunck, Director of Graduate Admissions, 914-633-2451, Fax: 914-633-2277, E-mail: kbrunck@iona.edu. Website: https://www.iona.edu/academics/school-of-business.aspx

Iowa State University of Science and Technology, Program in Business Administration, Ames, IA 50011. Offers MBA, M Arch/MBA, MBA/MCRP, MBA/MS. *Entrance requirements:* For master's, GMAT, resume. Additional exam requirements/recommendations for international students: Recommended—TOEFL (minimum score 600 paper-based; 100 iBT), IELTS (minimum score 7). Electronic applications accepted. *Expenses:* Contact institution.

Ithaca College, School of Business, Program in Business Administration, Ithaca, NY 14850. Offers sport management (MBA). *Accreditation:* AACSB. *Program availability:* Part-time. *Faculty:* 6 full-time (4 women). *Students:* 8 full-time (2 women), 2 part-time (1 woman). Average age 24. 18 applicants, 56% accepted, 8 enrolled. In 2017, 12 master's awarded. *Entrance requirements:* For master's, GMAT. Additional exam requirements/recommendations for international students: Required—TOEFL (minimum score 550 paper-based; 80 iBT). *Application deadline:* For fall admission, 5/15 for domestic and international students; for spring admission, 11/1 for domestic and international students. Applications are processed on a rolling basis. Application fee: $40. Electronic applications accepted. *Expenses:* Contact institution. *Financial support:* In 2017–18, 7 students received support, including 5 fellowships (averaging $7,600 per year); career-related internships or fieldwork, Federal Work-Study, and scholarships/grants also available. Support available to part-time students. Financial award application deadline: 3/1; financial award applicants required to submit FAFSA. *Unit head:* Dr. Rasoul Rezvanian, Associate Dean and Director, MBA Programs, 607-274-1762, Fax: 607-274-1263, E-mail: rrezvanian@ithaca.edu. *Application contact:* Nicole Eversley Bradwell, Director, Office of Admission, 607-274-3124, Fax: 607-274-1263, E-mail: admission@ithaca.edu.
Website: http://www.ithaca.edu/business/programs/busadmin

Jackson State University, Graduate School, College of Business, Department of Economics, Finance and General Business, Jackson, MS 39217. Offers business administration (MBA, PhD). *Accreditation:* AACSB. *Program availability:* Part-time, evening/weekend. *Degree requirements:* For master's, comprehensive exam, thesis. *Entrance requirements:* For master's, GRE General Test, GMAT. Additional exam requirements/recommendations for international students: Required—TOEFL.

Jacksonville State University, College of Graduate Studies and Continuing Education, College of Commerce and Business Administration, Jacksonville, AL 36265-1602. Offers MBA. *Accreditation:* AACSB. *Program availability:* Part-time, evening/weekend, 100% online, blended/hybrid learning. *Degree requirements:* For master's, comprehensive exam, thesis (for some programs). *Entrance requirements:* For master's, GMAT. Additional exam requirements/recommendations for international students: Required—TOEFL (minimum score 500 paper-based; 61 iBT). Electronic applications accepted.

Jacksonville University, Davis College of Business, Accelerated Day-time MBA Program, Jacksonville, FL 32211. Offers accounting and finance (MBA); business administration (MBA); consumer goods and services marketing (MBA); management (MBA); management accounting (MBA). *Faculty:* 5 full-time (2 women). *Students:* 43 full-time (17 women), 7 part-time (2 women); includes 9 minority (4 Black or African American, non-Hispanic/Latino; 4 Hispanic/Latino; 1 Two or more races, non-Hispanic/Latino), 18 international. Average age 26. 70 applicants, 90% accepted, 44 enrolled. In 2017, 42 master's awarded. *Entrance requirements:* For master's, GMAT or GRE, bachelor's degree from regionally-accredited institution, original transcripts of academic work, statement of intent, resume, 3 letters of recommendation; 3 years of work experience (recommended); interview with program advisor. Additional exam requirements/recommendations for international students: Required—TOEFL (minimum score 550 paper-based; 79 iBT), IELTS (minimum score 6), PTE (minimum score 53). *Application deadline:* For fall admission, 7/1 priority date for domestic students, 6/15 priority date for international students; for spring admission, 12/1 priority date for domestic students, 11/15 priority date for international students; for summer admission, 4/1 for domestic students, 3/15 for international students. Applications are processed on a rolling basis. Application fee: $50. Electronic applications accepted. *Expenses:* $793 per credit hour; $150-$250 books per course (estimated). *Financial support:* Scholarships/grants, health care benefits, and unspecified assistantships available. Financial award application deadline: 6/30; financial award applicants required to submit FAFSA. *Faculty research:* Behavioral finance, game theory, regional economic integration, information sabotage, public choice and public finance. *Unit head:* Dr. Douglas Johansen, Associate Dean and Graduate Programs Director, 904-256-7763, Fax: 904-256-7168, E-mail: djohans@ju.edu. *Application contact:* AnnaMaria Murphy, Assistant Director of Graduate Admissions, 904-256-7426, Fax: 904-256-7012, E-mail: mba@ju.edu.

See Display on the next page and Close-Up on page 175.

Jacksonville University, Davis College of Business, Doctor of Business Administration Program, Jacksonville, FL 32211. Offers DBA. *Program availability:* Evening/weekend. *Faculty:* 1 full-time (0 women), 1 part-time/adjunct (0 women). *Students:* 36 full-time (14 women), 18 part-time (9 women); includes 24 minority (18 Black or African American, non-Hispanic/Latino; 2 Asian, non-Hispanic/Latino; 4 Hispanic/Latino), 4 international. Average age 44. 62 applicants, 61% accepted, 16 enrolled. In 2017, 1 doctorate awarded. *Degree requirements:* For doctorate, comprehensive exam, thesis/dissertation, completion of program within six years of starting. *Entrance requirements:* For doctorate, MBA or master's degree from regionally-accredited institution or comparable foreign institution with minimum GPA of 3.25; curriculum vitae or resume with minimum of 7 years' professional experience in business management or not-for-profit administration; statement of purpose; 3 letters of recommendation. Additional exam requirements/recommendations for international students: Required—TOEFL (minimum score 550 paper-based; 79 iBT), IELTS (minimum score 6), PTE (minimum score 53). *Application deadline:* For fall admission, 5/1 priority date for domestic students, 4/15 for international students. Applications are processed on a rolling basis. Application fee: $50. Electronic applications accepted. *Expenses:* Contact institution. *Financial support:* Scholarships/grants, health care benefits, and unspecified assistantships available. Financial award application deadline: 6/30; financial award applicants required to submit FAFSA. *Faculty research:* Leadership of organizations and ethical business practices in a contemporary world; emphasize practical application of more advanced business analytics and evidence-based decision making. *Unit head:* Dr. Douglas Johansen, Associate Dean and Graduate Programs Director, 904-256-7763, Fax: 904-256-7168, E-mail: djohans@ju.edu. *Application contact:* AnnaMaria Murphy, Assistant Director of Graduate Admissions, 904-256-7426, Fax: 904-256-7012, E-mail: amurphy8@ju.edu.
Website: https://www.ju.edu/dcob/doctorate/

Jacksonville University, Davis College of Business, Executive Master of Business Administration Program, Jacksonville, FL 32211. Offers consumer goods and services marketing (MBA); leadership development (MBA). *Accreditation:* AACSB. *Program availability:* Evening/weekend. *Faculty:* 23 full-time (8 women), 4 part-time/adjunct (2 women). *Students:* 25 full-time (10 women), 13 part-time (7 women); includes 6 minority (5 Black or African American, non-Hispanic/Latino; 1 Two or more races, non-Hispanic/Latino). Average age 39. 43 applicants, 91% accepted, 32 enrolled. In 2017, 10 master's awarded. *Entrance requirements:* For master's, resume, 5-7 years of professional experience, 3 letters of recommendation, corporate letter of support, statement of purpose, interview. Additional exam requirements/recommendations for international students: Required—TOEFL (minimum score 550 paper-based; 79 iBT), IELTS (minimum score 6), PTE (minimum score 53). *Application deadline:* For fall admission, 7/1 priority date for domestic students, 6/15 priority date for international students; for spring admission, 12/1 priority date for domestic students, 11/15 for international students; for summer admission, 4/1 priority date for domestic students, 3/15 for international students. Applications are processed on a rolling basis. Application fee: $50. Electronic applications accepted. *Expenses:* $61,360 tuition (includes books, international trip, executive physical at Mayo Clinic, software, fees and meals while on campus). *Financial support:* In 2017–18, 2 students received support. Scholarships/grants, health care benefits, and unspecified assistantships available. Financial award application deadline: 6/30; financial award applicants required to submit FAFSA. *Faculty research:* Data analytics, emerging markets and economic development, high-performing teams, government deficit, learning from corporate failure. *Unit head:* Dr. Douglas Johansen, Associate Dean and Director of Graduate Studies, 904-256-7763, Fax: 904-256-7168, E-mail: djohans@ju.edu. *Application contact:* AnnaMaria Murphy, Assistant Director of Graduate Admissions, 904-256-7426, Fax: 904-256-7012, E-mail: mba@ju.edu.

See Display on the next page and Close-Up on page 175.

Jacksonville University, Davis College of Business, FLEX Master of Business Administration Program, Jacksonville, FL 32211. Offers accounting and finance (MBA); business management (MBA); consumer goods and services marketing (MBA); management (MBA); management accounting (MBA); JD/MBA; MBA/MPP; MSN/MBA. MBA/JD offered jointly with Florida School of Law; MSN/MBA offered jointly with JU's Keigwin School of Nursing; MBA/MPP offered jointly with JU's Public Policy Institute. *Accreditation:* AACSB. *Program availability:* Part-time, evening/weekend, blended/hybrid learning. *Faculty:* 23 full-time (8 women), 4 part-time/adjunct (2 women). *Students:* 32 full-time (7 women), 80 part-time (30 women); includes 34 minority (15 Black or African American, non-Hispanic/Latino; 1 American Indian or Alaska Native, non-Hispanic/Latino; 6 Asian, non-Hispanic/Latino; 10 Hispanic/Latino; 2 Two or more races, non-Hispanic/Latino), 2 international. Average age 33. 43 applicants, 91% accepted, 32 enrolled. In 2017, 56 master's awarded. *Entrance requirements:* For master's, GMAT or GRE, bachelor's degree from regionally-accredited institution, 3 years of full-time work experience (recommended), resume, statement of intent, 3 letters of recommendation, interview with program advisor. Additional exam requirements/recommendations for international students: Required—TOEFL (minimum score 550 paper-based; 79 iBT), IELTS (minimum score 6), PTE (minimum score 53). *Application deadline:* For fall admission, 7/1 priority date for domestic students, 6/15 priority date for international students; for spring admission, 12/1 priority date for domestic students, 11/15 priority date for international students; for summer admission, 4/1 priority date for domestic students, 3/15 priority date for international students. Applications are processed on a rolling basis. Application fee: $50. Electronic applications accepted. *Expenses:* $793 per credit hour; $150-$250 books per course (estimated). *Financial support:* Scholarships/grants and health care benefits available. Financial award application deadline: 6/30; financial award applicants required to submit FAFSA. *Faculty research:* Downsizing with integrity; impact of YouTube videos; game theory; analysis of effective tax rates; creativity innovation and change. *Unit head:* Dr. Douglas Johansen, Associate Dean and Director of Graduate Studies, 904-256-7763, Fax: 904-256-7168, E-mail: djohans@ju.edu. *Application contact:* AnnaMaria Murphy, Assistant Director of Graduate Admissions, 904-256-7426, Fax: 904-256-7012, E-mail: mba@ju.edu.

See Display on the next page and Close-Up on page 175.

James Madison University, The Graduate School, College of Business, Program in Business Administration, Harrisonburg, VA 22801. Offers business (MBA), including executive leadership, information security, innovation. *Accreditation:* AACSB. *Program availability:* Part-time, evening/weekend, blended/hybrid learning. *Students:* 34 full-time (12 women), 96 part-time (33 women); includes 29 minority (10 Black or African American, non-Hispanic/Latino; 9 Asian, non-Hispanic/Latino; 8 Hispanic/Latino; 2 Two or more races, non-Hispanic/Latino), 3 international. Average age 30. In 2017, 39 master's awarded. Application fee: $55. Electronic applications accepted. *Expenses:* Tuition, state resident: full-time $10,512; part-time $438 per credit hour. Tuition, nonresident: full-time $28,358; part-time $1162 per credit hour. *Required fees:* $1128. *Financial support:* In 2017–18, 1 student received support. Federal Work-Study and 1 assistantship (averaging $7911) available. Financial award application deadline: 3/1; financial award applicants required to submit FAFSA. *Unit head:* Dr. Matthew A. Rutherford, Department Head, 540-568-8777, E-mail: rutherma@jmu.edu. *Application contact:* Lynette D. Michael, Director of Graduate Admissions, 540-568-6131 Ext. 6395, Fax: 540-568-7860, E-mail: michaeld@jmu.edu.
Website: http://www.jmu.edu/cob/graduate/mba/index.shtml

John Brown University, Soderquist College of Business, Siloam Springs, AR 72761-2121. Offers international business (MBA); leadership and ethics (MBA, MS). *Accreditation:* ACBSP. *Program availability:* Part-time, evening/weekend, online only, 100% online, blended/hybrid learning. *Entrance requirements:* For master's, MAT, GMAT or GRE if undergraduate GPA is less than 3.0, recommendation forms from three people, 200-word essay describing professional plans and reason for seeking acceptance. Additional exam requirements/recommendations for international students: Required—TOEFL (minimum score 550 paper-based; 79 iBT). Electronic applications accepted. *Faculty research:* Ethical leadership.

John Carroll University, Graduate Studies, John M. and Mary Jo Boler School of Business, University Heights, OH 44118. Offers accountancy (MS); business (MBA); laboratory administration (MS). *Accreditation:* AACSB. *Program availability:* Part-time, evening/weekend. *Faculty:* 11 full-time (1 woman), 9 part-time/adjunct (3 women). *Students:* 63 full-time (21 women), 67 part-time (22 women); includes 18 minority (10 Black or African American, non-Hispanic/Latino; 4 Asian, non-Hispanic/Latino; 3 Hispanic/Latino; 1 Two or more races, non-Hispanic/Latino), 10 international. Average age 26. In 2017, 50 master's awarded. *Entrance requirements:* For master's, GMAT, minimum GPA of 2.5. Additional exam requirements/recommendations for international students: Required—TOEFL (minimum score 550 paper-based). *Application deadline:* Applications are processed on a rolling basis. Application fee: $25 ($35 for international students). Electronic applications accepted. *Expenses:* Contact institution. *Financial support:* Research assistantships with full tuition reimbursements, scholarships/grants, and unspecified assistantships available. Financial award application deadline: 3/15; financial award applicants required to submit FAFSA. *Faculty research:* Accounting, economics and finance, management, marketing and logistics. *Unit head:* Dr. Alan R.

Miciak, Dean, 216-397-4391, Fax: 216-397-1833. *Application contact:* Gayle T. Bruno-Gannon, Assistant to the Dean, 216-397-1970, Fax: 216-397-1728, E-mail: ggannon@jcu.edu.
Website: http://www.jcu.edu/boler/grads

John F. Kennedy University, School of Management, Program in Business Administration, Pleasant Hill, CA 94523-4817. Offers business administration (MBA); organizational leadership (Certificate). *Program availability:* Part-time, evening/weekend. *Degree requirements:* For master's, thesis or alternative. *Entrance requirements:* For master's, interview. Additional exam requirements/recommendations for international students: Required—TOEFL.

Johns Hopkins University, Carey Business School, Certificate Programs, Baltimore, MD 21218. Offers financial management (Certificate); investments (Certificate). *Program availability:* Part-time, evening/weekend. *Faculty:* 93 full-time (33 women), 45 part-time/adjunct (11 women). *Students:* 19 part-time (10 women); includes 7 minority (2 Black or African American, non-Hispanic/Latino; 2 Asian, non-Hispanic/Latino; 2 Hispanic/Latino; 1 Two or more races, non-Hispanic/Latino), 3 international. Average age 34. 12 applicants, 83% accepted, 3 enrolled. In 2017, 31 Certificates awarded. *Degree requirements:* For Certificate, 16 credits. *Entrance requirements:* Additional exam requirements/recommendations for international students: Required—TOEFL, IELTS. *Application deadline:* Applications are processed on a rolling basis. Application fee: $100. Electronic applications accepted. *Expenses:* Contact institution. *Unit head:* Dr. Kevin Frick, Vice Dean of Education, 410-234-9272, E-mail: kfrick@jhu.edu. *Application contact:* Office of Admissions, 410-234-9220, Fax: 443-234-1554, E-mail: carey.admissions@jhu.edu.
Website: http://carey.jhu.edu/academics/certificate-programs/

Johns Hopkins University, Carey Business School, MBA Full-time Programs, Baltimore, MD 21218. Offers MBA, MBA/MA. MBA/MA offered with Maryland Institute College of Art. *Faculty:* 93 full-time (33 women), 45 part-time/adjunct (11 women). *Students:* 210 full-time (93 women); includes 43 minority (4 Black or African American, non-Hispanic/Latino; 22 Asian, non-Hispanic/Latino; 12 Hispanic/Latino; 5 Two or more races, non-Hispanic/Latino), 88 international. Average age 27. 263 applicants, 66% accepted, 91 enrolled. In 2017, 126 master's awarded. *Degree requirements:* For master's, 54 credits. *Entrance requirements:* For master's, GMAT or GRE. Additional exam requirements/recommendations for international students: Required—TOEFL, IELTS. *Application deadline:* For fall admission, 5/1 for domestic and international students. Applications are processed on a rolling basis. Application fee: $100. Electronic applications accepted. *Expenses:* Contact institution. *Financial support:* In 2017–18, 82 students received support. Scholarships/grants available. Financial award application deadline: 4/15; financial award applicants required to submit FAFSA. *Unit head:* Dr. Kevin Frick, Vice Dean of Education, 410-234-9272, E-mail: kfrick@jhu.edu. *Application contact:* Office of Admissions, 410-234-9220, Fax: 443-529-1554, E-mail: carey.admissions@jhu.edu.
Website: http://carey.jhu.edu/academics/master-of-business-administration/

Johns Hopkins University, Carey Business School, MBA Part-time Program, Baltimore, MD 21218. Offers MBA, MBA/MA. MBA/MA offered through the Zanvyl Krieger School of Arts and Sciences. *Program availability:* Part-time, evening/weekend, blended/hybrid learning, on-site residency requirement. *Faculty:* 93 full-time (33 women), 45 part-time/adjunct (11 women). *Students:* 843 part-time (348 women); includes 316 minority (87 Black or African American, non-Hispanic/Latino; 148 Asian, non-Hispanic/Latino; 61 Hispanic/Latino; 20 Two or more races, non-Hispanic/Latino), 45 international. Average age 33. 311 applicants, 85% accepted, 180 enrolled. In 2017, 117 master's awarded. *Degree requirements:* For master's, 54 credits. *Entrance requirements:* For master's, GMAT or GRE. Additional exam requirements/

recommendations for international students: Required—TOEFL, IELTS. *Application deadline:* For fall admission, 5/1 for domestic and international students. Applications are processed on a rolling basis. Application fee: $100. Electronic applications accepted. *Expenses:* $1,330 per credit. *Financial support:* In 2017–18, 16 students received support. Scholarships/grants available. Support available to part-time students. Financial award application deadline: 4/15; financial award applicants required to submit FAFSA. *Unit head:* Dr. Kevin Frick, Vice Dean of Education, 410-234-9272, E-mail: kfrick@jhu.edu. *Application contact:* Office of Admissions, 410-234-9220, Fax: 443-529-1554, E-mail: carey.admissions@jhu.edu.
Website: http://carey.jhu.edu/academics/master-of-business-administration/flexible-mba

Johnson & Wales University, Graduate Studies, MBA Program, Providence, RI 02903-3703. Offers accounting (MBA); business administration (MBA); finance (MBA); global fashion merchandising and management (MBA); hospitality (MBA); human resource management (MBA); information security/assurance (MBA); information technology (MBA); nonprofit management (MBA); operations and supply chain management (MBA); organizational leadership (MBA); organizational psychology (MBA); sport leadership (MBA). Program also offered on Denver campus. *Program availability:* Part-time, online learning. *Entrance requirements:* For master's, minimum GPA of 2.75. Additional exam requirements/recommendations for international students: Required—TOEFL (minimum score 550 paper-based); Recommended—IELTS, TWE. *Application deadline:* For fall admission, 8/15 priority date for domestic students, 6/28 priority date for international students; for winter admission, 11/10 priority date for domestic students, 9/20 priority date for international students; for spring admission, 2/5 priority date for domestic students, 12/20 priority date for international students. Applications are processed on a rolling basis. *Expenses: Tuition:* Full-time $12,636; part-time $702 per credit hour. *Financial support:* Tuition waivers (partial) and unspecified assistantships available. Support available to part-time students. Financial award application deadline: 5/1. *Faculty research:* International banking, global economy, international trade, cultural differences. *Unit head:* Dr. Karen Silva, Director, 401-598-2849, Fax: 401-598-1125. *Application contact:* Graduate School Admissions, 401-598-1015, Fax: 401-598-1286, E-mail: gradadm@jwu.edu.

Judson University, Master of Business Administration Program, Elgin, IL 60123-1498. Offers MBA. *Program availability:* Evening/weekend, 100% online. *Faculty:* 8 full-time (3 women), 33 part-time/adjunct (13 women). *Students:* 41 full-time (17 women), 9 part-time (6 women); includes 19 minority (5 Black or African American, non-Hispanic/Latino; 1 Asian, non-Hispanic/Latino; 13 Hispanic/Latino). Average age 34. 20 applicants, 75% accepted, 14 enrolled. In 2017, 38 master's awarded. *Entrance requirements:* For master's, bachelor's degree; minimum overall undergraduate GPA of 3.0; two years of work experience; two letters of recommendation; resume; essay. *Application deadline:* Applications are processed on a rolling basis. Application fee: $35. Electronic applications accepted. *Expenses:* Contact institution. *Financial support:* In 2017–18, 6 teaching assistantships were awarded; tuition waivers (partial) also available. Financial award applicants required to submit FAFSA. *Faculty research:* Ethics. *Unit head:* John C. Boggs, Chair, 847-628-1041, E-mail: john.boggs@judsonu.edu. *Application contact:* Maria Aguirre, Student Academic Advisor, 847-628-1160, E-mail: maguirre@judsonu.edu.
Website: http://www.judsonu.edu/Graduate/Master_of_Business_Administration/Overview/

Kansas State University, Graduate School, College of Business, Program in Business Administration, Manhattan, KS 66506. Offers data analytics (MBA); finance (MBA); management (MBA); marketing (MBA); technology entrepreneurship (MBA). *Accreditation:* AACSB. *Program availability:* Part-time, 100% online. *Entrance requirements:* For master's, GMAT (minimum score of 500), minimum undergraduate GPA of 3.0. Additional exam requirements/recommendations for international students:

Business Administration and Management—General

Required—TOEFL (minimum score 550 paper-based; 79 iBT); Recommended—IELTS (minimum score 7). Electronic applications accepted. *Expenses:* Contact institution. *Faculty research:* Organizational citizenship behavior, service marketing, impression management, human resources management, lean manufacturing and supply chain management, financial market behavior and investment management, data analytics, corporate responsibility, technology entrepreneurship.

Kansas Wesleyan University, Program in Business Administration, Salina, KS 67401-6196. Offers business administration (MBA); sports management (MBA). *Program availability:* Part-time, evening/weekend. *Entrance requirements:* For master's, GMAT, minimum graduate GPA of 3.0 or undergraduate GPA of 3.25.

Kean University, Nathan Weiss Graduate College, Program in Educational Administration, Union, NJ 07083. Offers school business administrator (MA); supervisor and principal (MA); supervisors, principals, and school business administrators (MA). *Accreditation:* NCATE. *Program availability:* Part-time, 100% online. *Faculty:* 3 full-time (2 women). *Students:* 16 full-time (10 women), 82 part-time (50 women); includes 36 minority (21 Black or African American, non-Hispanic/Latino; 1 Asian, non-Hispanic/Latino; 13 Hispanic/Latino; 1 Two or more races, non-Hispanic/Latino). Average age 35. 33 applicants, 85% accepted, 23 enrolled. In 2017, 23 master's awarded. *Degree requirements:* For master's, comprehensive exam (for some programs), portfolio, field experience, research component, internship, teaching experience. *Entrance requirements:* For master's, GRE General Test or MAT, minimum GPA of 3.0; New Jersey or out-of-state Standard Instructional or Educational Services Certificate; one year of experience under the appropriate certificate; official transcripts from all institutions attended; two letters of recommendation; personal statement; professional resume/curriculum vitae. Additional exam requirements/recommendations for international students: Required—TOEFL (minimum score 550 paper-based; 79 iBT), IELTS (minimum score 6.5). *Application deadline:* For fall admission, 6/30 for domestic and international students; for spring admission, 12/1 for domestic and international students; for summer admission, 5/15 for domestic and international students. Applications are processed on a rolling basis. Application fee: $75. Electronic applications accepted. *Expenses:* Tuition, state resident: full-time $13,419; part-time $653 per credit. Tuition, nonresident: full-time $18,188; part-time $801 per credit. *Required fees:* $3382; $154 per credit. Tuition and fees vary according to course level, course load, degree level and program. *Financial support:* Scholarships/grants and unspecified assistantships available. Financial award applicants required to submit FAFSA. *Unit head:* Dr. Steven Locasio, Program Coordinator, 908-737-5977, E-mail: locascst@kean.edu. *Application contact:* Brittany Gerstenhaber, Admissions Counselor, 908-737-7100, E-mail: gradadmissions@kean.edu.
Website: http://grad.kean.edu/edleadership/ma-combined

Keiser University, Doctor of Business Administration Program, Fort Lauderdale, FL 33309. Offers global business (DBA); global management (DBA); marketing (DBA). Website: http://www.keiseruniversity.edu/graduateschool/business-administration-phd.php

Keiser University, Joint MS Ed/MBA Program, Fort Lauderdale, FL 33309. Offers MS Ed/MBA.
Website: http://www.keiseruniversity.edu/graduateschool/msed-mba.php

Keiser University, Master of Business Administration Program, Fort Lauderdale, FL 33309. Offers accounting (MBA); health services administration (MBA); international business (MBA); management (MBA); marketing (MBA); technology management (MBA). All concentrations except technology management also offered in Mandarin. *Program availability:* Part-time, online learning. *Unit head:* Yan Luo-Beitler, Department Chair.
Website: http://www.keiseruniversity.edu/graduateschool/mba.php#accounting

Kennesaw State University, Michael J. Coles College of Business, Doctor of Business Administration Program, Kennesaw, GA 30144. Offers DBA. *Accreditation:* AACSB. *Program availability:* Part-time. *Degree requirements:* For doctorate, thesis/dissertation. *Entrance requirements:* Additional exam requirements/recommendations for international students: Required—TOEFL (minimum score 550 paper-based; 80 iBT), IELTS (minimum score 6.5). Electronic applications accepted. *Expenses:* Contact institution.

Kennesaw State University, Michael J. Coles College of Business, Program in Business Administration, Kennesaw, GA 30144. Offers MBA. *Accreditation:* AACSB. *Program availability:* Part-time, evening/weekend, online learning. *Entrance requirements:* For master's, GMAT (minimum score 530), minimum GPA of 2.8, 1 year of work experience. Additional exam requirements/recommendations for international students: Required—TOEFL (minimum score 550 paper-based; 80 iBT), IELTS (minimum score 6.5). Electronic applications accepted.

Kent State University, College of Business Administration, Master's Program in Business Administration, Kent, OH 44240. Offers MBA. *Accreditation:* AACSB. *Program availability:* Part-time, evening/weekend, 100% online. *Faculty:* 69 full-time (27 women). *Students:* 57 full-time (24 women), 61 part-time (24 women); includes 5 minority (1 Asian, non-Hispanic/Latino; 4 Two or more races, non-Hispanic/Latino), 12 international. Average age 29. 106 applicants, 74% accepted, 45 enrolled. In 2017, 50 master's awarded. *Degree requirements:* For master's, 30-37 credit hours, minimum GPA of 3.0. *Entrance requirements:* For master's, GMAT or GRE, minimum GPA of 3.0. Additional exam requirements/recommendations for international students: Required—TOEFL (minimum score 550 paper-based; 79 iBT), IELTS (minimum score 6.5). *Application deadline:* For fall admission, 6/1 for domestic students, 3/15 for international students; for spring admission, 10/15 for domestic students; for summer admission, 5/1 for domestic students. Applications are processed on a rolling basis. Application fee: $45 ($70 for international students). Electronic applications accepted. *Expenses:* $515 per credit full-time residents, $928 non-residents, $1,200 per year fees; $830 per credit hour (online). *Financial support:* In 2017–18, 2 students received support, including 2 research assistantships with full tuition reimbursements available (averaging $8,000 per year); career-related internships or fieldwork and Federal Work-Study also available. Financial award application deadline: 3/15; financial award applicants required to submit FAFSA. *Unit head:* Louise M. Ditchey, Administrative Director, 330-672-2282, Fax: 330-672-7303, E-mail: gradbus@kent.edu. *Application contact:* Felecia A. Urbanek, Coordinator, Graduate Programs, 330-672-2282, Fax: 330-672-7303, E-mail: gradbus@kent.edu.
Website: http://www.kent.edu/business/degrees/masters-programs

Kent State University at Stark, Professional MBA Program, Canton, OH 44720-7599. Offers MBA.

Kentucky State University, College of Business and Computer Science, Frankfort, KY 40601. Offers business administration (MBA); computer science technology (MS). *Program availability:* Part-time, evening/weekend. *Faculty:* 12 full-time (1 woman). *Students:* 26 full-time (10 women), 22 part-time (8 women); includes 25 minority (16 Black or African American, non-Hispanic/Latino; 8 Asian, non-Hispanic/Latino; 1 Two or more races, non-Hispanic/Latino), 13 international. Average age 30. 28 applicants, 79% accepted, 18 enrolled. In 2017, 16 master's awarded. *Degree requirements:* For master's, comprehensive exam, thesis optional. *Entrance requirements:* For master's, GMAT, GRE, letters of recommendation, essay, transcript. Additional exam

requirements/recommendations for international students: Required—TOEFL (minimum score 525 paper-based, 41 iBT) or IELTS (minimum score 4). *Application deadline:* For fall admission, 7/1 for domestic students, 4/1 for international students; for spring admission, 11/15 for domestic students, 8/15 for international students; for summer admission, 5/1 for domestic students, 2/1 for international students. Applications are processed on a rolling basis. Application fee: $30 ($100 for international students). Electronic applications accepted. *Expenses:* Contact institution. *Financial support:* In 2017–18, 40 students received support, including 2 research assistantships (averaging $11,970 per year); scholarships/grants, tuition waivers (partial), and unspecified assistantships also available. Financial award application deadline: 4/15; financial award applicants required to submit FAFSA. *Faculty research:* Digital gaming, digital simulation, cyber security. *Total annual research expenditures:* $1.6 million. *Unit head:* Dr. Kristen Broady, Assistant Vice President and Dean of Graduate Programs, 502-597-6386, E-mail: kristen.broady@kysu.edu. *Application contact:* Dr. James Obielodan, Director of Graduate Studies, 502-597-4723, E-mail: james.obielodan@kysu.edu.
Website: http://kysu.edu/academics/college-of-business-and-computer-science/

Kettering University, Graduate School, Department of Business, Flint, MI 48504. Offers MBA, MS. *Accreditation:* ACBSP. *Program availability:* Part-time, evening/weekend, online learning. *Entrance requirements:* Additional exam requirements/recommendations for international students: Required—TOEFL (minimum score 550 paper-based; 79 iBT). Electronic applications accepted.

Keuka College, Program in Management, Keuka Park, NY 14478. Offers MS. *Program availability:* Part-time, evening/weekend, 100% online, blended/hybrid learning. *Degree requirements:* For master's, thesis, capstone/action research project. *Entrance requirements:* For master's, 2 letters of recommendation, minimum GPA of 3.0. Additional exam requirements/recommendations for international students: Required—TOEFL (minimum score 550 paper-based). *Expenses:* Contact institution. *Faculty research:* Inventory control and supply chain management; optimal order policies and supply chain coordination sustainability; using nature as an innovator and designing tool.

Keystone College, Program in Business Administration, La Plume, PA 18440. Offers MBA. *Program availability:* Part-time, online only, 100% online. *Students:* 5 full-time (2 women). 10 applicants, 100% accepted, 5 enrolled. *Entrance requirements:* For master's, official college transcripts. Additional exam requirements/recommendations for international students: Required—TOEFL (minimum score 80 iBT) or IELTS (minimum score 6.5). *Application deadline:* For fall admission, 8/1 for domestic students; for spring admission, 1/1 for domestic students; for summer admission, 5/1 for domestic students. Applications are processed on a rolling basis. Application fee: $0. Electronic applications accepted. *Expenses:* $575 per credit. *Financial support:* Unspecified assistantships available. Financial award applicants required to submit FAFSA. *Unit head:* Dr. Dana Harris, Associate Professor/Coordinator of MBA Program, 570-945-8421, E-mail: dana.harris@keystone.edu. *Application contact:* Sarah Louzon, Admissions Counselor, 570-945-8126, Fax: 570-945-7916, E-mail: sarah.louzon@keystone.edu.

King University, School of Business and Economics, Bristol, TN 37620-2699. Offers accounting (MBA); finance (MBA); healthcare management (MBA); human resources management (MBA); leadership (MBA); management (MBA); marketing (MBA); project management (MBA). *Program availability:* Part-time, evening/weekend, online learning. *Degree requirements:* For master's, comprehensive exam, thesis optional. *Entrance requirements:* For master's, GMAT, 2 years of work experience. Additional exam requirements/recommendations for international students: Required—TOEFL (minimum score 550 paper-based). Electronic applications accepted. *Faculty research:* International monetary policy.

Kutztown University of Pennsylvania, College of Business, Program in Business Administration, Kutztown, PA 19530-0730. Offers MBA. *Accreditation:* AACSB. *Program availability:* Part-time, evening/weekend, 100% online, blended/hybrid learning. *Faculty:* 6 full-time (3 women). *Students:* 14 full-time (5 women), 17 part-time (6 women); includes 5 minority (1 Black or African American, non-Hispanic/Latino; 1 Asian, non-Hispanic/Latino; 1 Hispanic/Latino; 2 Two or more races, non-Hispanic/Latino), 4 international. Average age 28. 38 applicants, 74% accepted, 11 enrolled. In 2017, 11 master's awarded. *Degree requirements:* For master's, comprehensive exam, thesis (for some programs). *Entrance requirements:* For master's, GMAT or GRE, 2 letters of recommendation, resume, goal statement. Additional exam requirements/recommendations for international students: Required—TOEFL (minimum score 550 paper-based, 79 iBT), IELTS (minimum score 6.5), or PTE (minimum score 53). *Application deadline:* For fall admission, 8/1 priority date for domestic and international students; for spring admission, 12/1 priority date for domestic and international students. Application fee: $35. Electronic applications accepted. *Expenses:* Tuition, state resident: part-time $500 per credit. Tuition, nonresident: part-time $750 per credit. *Required fees:* $115 per credit. One-time fee: $50 part-time. Tuition and fees vary according to degree level. *Financial support:* Career-related internships or fieldwork, Federal Work-Study, and unspecified assistantships available. Financial award application deadline: 3/1; financial award applicants required to submit FAFSA. *Unit head:* Dr. Anne Carroll, Dean, 610-683-4575, Fax: 610-683-4573, E-mail: acarroll@kutztown.edu. *Application contact:* E-mail: mba@kutztown.edu.
Website: http://www.kutztown.edu/MBA

Lake Erie College, School of Business, Painesville, OH 44077-3389. Offers general management (MBA); health care administration (MBA); information technology management (MBA). *Program availability:* Part-time, evening/weekend. *Entrance requirements:* For master's, GMAT or minimum GPA of 3.0, resume, personal statement. Additional exam requirements/recommendations for international students: Required—TOEFL (minimum score 550 paper-based; 79 iBT), IELTS (minimum score 6), STEP Eiken 1st and pre-1st grade level (for Japanese students). Electronic applications accepted. Application fee is waived when completed online. *Expenses:* Contact institution.

Lake Forest Graduate School of Management, The Leadership MBA Program, Lake Forest, IL 60045. Offers finance (MBA); global business (MBA); healthcare management (MBA); management (MBA); marketing (MBA); organizational behavior (MBA). *Program availability:* Part-time, evening/weekend. *Entrance requirements:* For master's, 4 years of work experience in field, interview, 2 letters of recommendation. Electronic applications accepted.

Lakeland University, Graduate Studies Division, Program in Business Administration, Plymouth, WI 53073. Offers accounting (MBA); finance (MBA); healthcare management (MBA); project management (MBA). *Entrance requirements:* For master's, GMAT. *Expenses:* Contact institution.

Lamar University, College of Graduate Studies, College of Business, Beaumont, TX 77701. Offers accounting (MBA); experiential business and entrepreneurship (MBA); healthcare administration (MBA); MSA/MBA. *Accreditation:* AACSB. *Program availability:* Part-time, evening/weekend. *Faculty:* 50 full-time (14 women), 6 part-time/adjunct (2 women). *Students:* 20 full-time (11 women), 228 part-time (118 women); includes 98 minority (58 Black or African American, non-Hispanic/Latino; 10 Asian, non-Hispanic/Latino; 26 Hispanic/Latino; 4 Two or more races, non-Hispanic/Latino), 32 international. Average age 32. 205 applicants, 92% accepted, 78 enrolled. In 2017, 69 master's awarded. *Degree requirements:* For master's, comprehensive exam (for some

programs), thesis optional. *Entrance requirements:* For master's, GMAT. Additional exam requirements/recommendations for international students: Required—TOEFL (minimum score 550 paper-based; 79 iBT), IELTS (minimum score 6.5). *Application deadline:* For fall admission, 8/10 for domestic students, 7/1 for international students; for spring admission, 1/5 for domestic students, 12/1 for international students. Applications are processed on a rolling basis. Application fee: $25 ($50 for international students). Electronic applications accepted. *Expenses:* Contact institution. *Financial support:* Fellowships with tuition reimbursements, research assistantships with partial tuition reimbursements, career-related internships or fieldwork, Federal Work-Study, institutionally sponsored loans, scholarships/grants, and tuition waivers (partial) available. Support available to part-time students. Financial award application deadline: 4/1; financial award applicants required to submit FAFSA. *Faculty research:* Marketing, finance, quantitative methods, management information systems, legal, environmental. *Unit head:* Dr. Enrique R. Venta, Dean, 409-880-8603, Fax: 409-880-8088, E-mail: henry.venta@lamar.edu. *Application contact:* Deidre Mayer, Interim Director, Admissions and Academic Services, 409-880-8888, Fax: 409-880-7419, E-mail: gradmissions@lamar.edu.
Website: http://business.lamar.edu

La Salle University, School of Business, Master of Business Administration Program, Philadelphia, PA 19141-1199. Offers accounting (MBA, Post-MBA Certificate); business systems and analytics (MBA, Post-MBA Certificate); finance (MBA, Post-MBA Certificate); general business administration (MBA, Post-MBA Certificate); human resource management (MBA, Post-MBA Certificate); management (MBA, Post-MBA Certificate); marketing (Post-MBA Certificate); MBA/MSN. Program also offered in Switzerland. *Accreditation:* AACSB. *Program availability:* Part-time, evening/weekend, online learning. *Faculty:* 22 full-time (10 women), 10 part-time/adjunct (3 women). *Students:* 59 full-time (25 women), 200 part-time (109 women); includes 66 minority (36 Black or African American, non-Hispanic/Latino; 21 Asian, non-Hispanic/Latino; 7 Hispanic/Latino; 2 Two or more races, non-Hispanic/Latino), 22 international. Average age 31. 216 applicants, 57% accepted, 74 enrolled. In 2017, 146 master's awarded. *Entrance requirements:* For master's, GMAT or GRE, two letters of reference; resume; for Post-MBA Certificate, MBA with minimum GPA of 3.0. Additional exam requirements/recommendations for international students: Required—TOEFL. *Application deadline:* For fall admission, 8/15 priority date for domestic students, 7/15 for international students; for spring admission, 12/15 priority date for domestic students, 11/15 for international students; for summer admission, 4/15 priority date for domestic students, 3/15 for international students. Applications are processed on a rolling basis. Application fee: $35. Electronic applications accepted. Application fee is waived when completed online. *Expenses:* Contact institution. *Financial support:* In 2017–18, 51 students received support. Scholarships/grants available. Support available to part-time students. Financial award application deadline: 8/31; financial award applicants required to submit FAFSA. *Unit head:* Dr. MarySheila McDonald, Interim Dean, 215-951-1040, Fax: 215-951-1886, E-mail: mcdonaldms@lasalle.edu. *Application contact:* Elizabeth Heenan, Director, Graduate and Adult Enrollment, 215-951-1100, Fax: 215-951-1462, E-mail: heenan@lasalle.edu.

Lasell College, Graduate and Professional Studies in Management, Newton, MA 02466-2709. Offers business administration (MBA); elder care management (MSM); hospitality and event management (MSM); human resources management (MSM, Graduate Certificate); management (MSM, Graduate Certificate); marketing (MS, Graduate Certificate); project management (MSM, Graduate Certificate). *Accreditation:* ACBSP. *Program availability:* Part-time, evening/weekend, 100% online, blended/hybrid learning. *Faculty:* 1 full-time (0 women), 15 part-time/adjunct (11 women). *Students:* 41 full-time (25 women), 102 part-time (70 women); includes 34 minority (19 Black or African American, non-Hispanic/Latino; 5 Asian, non-Hispanic/Latino; 8 Hispanic/Latino; 2 Two or more races, non-Hispanic/Latino), 29 international. Average age 32. 128 applicants, 46% accepted, 38 enrolled. In 2017, 66 master's, 3 other advanced degrees awarded. *Degree requirements:* For master's, minimum GPA of 3.0; internship or research paper (for MSM). *Entrance requirements:* For master's, one-page personal statement, 2 letters of recommendation, resume, bachelor's degree transcript; proof of microeconomics and statistics (for MBA); for Graduate Certificate, bachelor's degree transcript, 2 letters of recommendation, 1-page personal statement, resume. Additional exam requirements/recommendations for international students: Required—TOEFL (minimum score 550 paper-based, 79 iBT) or IELTS (minimum score 6). *Application deadline:* For fall admission, 8/31 priority date for domestic students, 6/30 priority date for international students; for spring admission, 12/31 priority date for domestic students, 10/31 priority date for international students. Applications are processed on a rolling basis. Electronic applications accepted. *Expenses:* $600 per credit. *Financial support:* Federal Work-Study, scholarships/grants, and tuition discounts available. Support available to part-time students. Financial award application deadline: 8/31; financial award applicants required to submit FAFSA. *Unit head:* Eric Turner, Vice President of Graduate and Professional Studies, 617-243-2071, Fax: 617-243-2450, E-mail: gradinfo@lasell.edu. *Application contact:* Adrienne Franciosi, Director of Graduate Enrollment, 617-243-2214, Fax: 617-243-2450, E-mail: gradinfo@lasell.edu.
Website: http://www.lasell.edu/academics/graduate-and-professional-studies/programs-of-study/master-of-science-in-management.html

La Sierra University, School of Business and Management, Riverside, CA 92505. Offers accounting (MBA); finance (MBA); general management (MBA); human resources management (MBA); leadership, values, and ethics for business and management (Certificate); marketing (MBA). *Degree requirements:* For master's, research project. *Entrance requirements:* For master's, GMAT, minimum GPA of 3.0. Additional exam requirements/recommendations for international students: Required—TOEFL. *Faculty research:* Financial econometrics, institutional assessment and strategic planning, legal issues in management, behavioral finance, content of financial reports.

Laurentian University, School of Graduate Studies and Research, School of Commerce and Administration, Sudbury, ON P3E 2C6, Canada. Offers MBA. *Program availability:* Part-time, evening/weekend. *Entrance requirements:* For master's, GMAT, 2 years of work experience. *Faculty research:* Small business and entrepreneurship development, mutual fund performance, donorship behavior, stress and organizations, quality programs.

Lawrence Technological University, College of Management, Southfield, MI 48075-1058. Offers business administration (MBA, DBA), including business analytics (MBA, MS), cybersecurity (MBA, MS), finance (MBA), information systems (MBA), information technology (MBA), marketing (MBA), project management (MBA, MS); cybersecurity (Graduate Certificate); health IT management (Graduate Certificate); information assurance management (Graduate Certificate); information systems (MS), including enterprise resource planning, enterprise security management, project management (MBA, MS); information technology (MS, DM), including business analytics (MBA, MS), cybersecurity (MBA, MS), information assurance (MS), project management (MBA, MS); management (PhD); nonprofit management and leadership (Graduate Certificate); operations management (MS), including manufacturing operations, service operations; project management (Graduate Certificate). *Accreditation:* ACBSP. *Program availability:* Part-time, evening/weekend, 100% online. *Faculty:* 13 full-time (6 women), 7 part-time/

adjunct (1 woman). *Students:* 8 full-time (3 women), 280 part-time (102 women); includes 70 minority (34 Black or African American, non-Hispanic/Latino; 2 American Indian or Alaska Native, non-Hispanic/Latino; 18 Asian, non-Hispanic/Latino; 11 Hispanic/Latino; 5 Two or more races, non-Hispanic/Latino), 73 international. Average age 34. 143 applicants, 50% accepted, 68 enrolled. In 2017, 114 master's, 7 doctorates, 10 other advanced degrees awarded. Terminal master's awarded for partial completion of doctoral program. *Degree requirements:* For master's, thesis (for some programs); for doctorate, comprehensive exam, thesis/dissertation. *Entrance requirements:* Additional exam requirements/recommendations for international students: Required—TOEFL (minimum score 550 paper-based; 79 iBT), IELTS (minimum score 6.5). *Application deadline:* For fall admission, 5/27 for international students; for spring admission, 10/8 for international students; for summer admission, 2/14 for international students. Applications are processed on a rolling basis. Application fee: $50. Electronic applications accepted. *Expenses:* Tuition: Full-time $15,274; part-time $1091 per credit. One-time fee: $150. *Financial support:* In 2017–18, 35 students received support, including 8 research assistantships with partial tuition reimbursements available (averaging $3,360 per year); career-related internships or fieldwork, unspecified assistantships, and corporate tuition incentives also available. Financial award application deadline: 4/1; financial award applicants required to submit FAFSA. *Faculty research:* Cybersecurity; risk management; IT governance; security controls and countermeasures; threat modeling cyber resilience; autonomous cars; natural language processing; text mining; machine learning; reflective leadership; emerging leadership theories and practice; motivational studies; teaching effectiveness strategies; teamwork; organization development; strategic planning; strengths-based and positive organizational scholarship; global leadership; globalization; corporate governance. *Unit head:* Dr. Bahman Mirshab, Dean, 248-204-3050, E-mail: mgtdean@ltu.edu. *Application contact:* Jane Rohrback, Director of Admissions, 248-204-3160, Fax: 248-204-2228, E-mail: admissions@ltu.edu.
Website: http://www.ltu.edu/management/index.asp

Lebanese American University, School of Business, Beirut, Lebanon. Offers MBA.

Lebanon Valley College, Program in Business Administration, Annville, PA 17003-1400. Offers business administration (MBA); healthcare management (MBA); human resources (MBA); leadership and ethics (MBA); project management (MBA). *Program availability:* Part-time, evening/weekend. *Faculty:* 7 full-time (1 woman), 8 part-time/adjunct (1 woman). *Students:* 11 full-time (5 women), 66 part-time (28 women); includes 11 minority (3 Black or African American, non-Hispanic/Latino; 4 Asian, non-Hispanic/Latino; 4 Hispanic/Latino), 3 international. Average age 34. 21 applicants, 81% accepted, 16 enrolled. In 2017, 32 master's awarded. *Degree requirements:* For master's, capstone course. *Entrance requirements:* For master's, GMAT, 3 years of work experience, resume, professional statement (application form, resume, personal statement, transcripts). Additional exam requirements/recommendations for international students: Required—TOEFL (minimum score 80 iBT), IELTS (minimum score 6.5) or STEP Eiken (grade 1). *Application deadline:* Applications are processed on a rolling basis. Application fee: $0. Electronic applications accepted. *Expenses:* $660 per credit hour. *Financial support:* Career-related internships or fieldwork and scholarships/grants available. Financial award application deadline: 3/1; financial award applicants required to submit FAFSA. *Faculty research:* Leadership, motivation, BI, information systems strategies, emerging market development, the role of informational business education, economic growth. *Unit head:* Dr. David Setley, Associate Professor/Chair of Business Administration/Director of the MBA Program, 717-867-6104, Fax: 717-867-6018, E-mail: setley@lvc.edu. *Application contact:* Christine M. Martin, Enrollment and Operations Specialist, 717-867-6486, Fax: 717-867-6013, E-mail: cmartin@lvc.edu.
Website: http://www.lvc.edu/mba

Lee University, MBA Program, Cleveland, TN 37320-3450. Offers MBA. *Program availability:* Part-time, evening/weekend, 100% online. *Faculty:* 6 full-time (2 women), 1 (woman) part-time/adjunct. *Students:* 15 full-time (5 women), 54 part-time (21 women); includes 10 minority (4 Black or African American, non-Hispanic/Latino; 2 American Indian or Alaska Native, non-Hispanic/Latino; 1 Asian, non-Hispanic/Latino; 3 Hispanic/Latino), 7 international. Average age 29. 35 applicants, 77% accepted, 23 enrolled. In 2017, 26 master's awarded. *Degree requirements:* For master's, variable foreign language requirement, comprehensive exam, thesis optional, practicum. *Entrance requirements:* For master's, GMAT (taken within last 5 years), minimum undergraduate cumulative GPA of 3.0. Additional exam requirements/recommendations for international students: Required—TOEFL (minimum score 61 iBT). *Application deadline:* For fall admission, 4/1 priority date for domestic and international students; for spring admission, 10/1 priority date for domestic and international students. Applications are processed on a rolling basis. Application fee: $25. Electronic applications accepted. *Expenses:* Tuition: Full-time $12,780; part-time $710 per credit hour. *Required fees:* $60; $60 per term. Tuition and fees vary according to program. *Financial support:* In 2017–18, 36 students received support. Scholarships/grants available. Financial award application deadline: 3/1; financial award applicants required to submit FAFSA. *Unit head:* Dr. Shane Griffith, Director, 423-614-8694, E-mail: mba@leeuniversity.edu.
Website: http://www.leeuniversity.edu/academics/graduate/mba/

Lehigh University, College of Business and Economics, Department of Management, Bethlehem, PA 18015. Offers business administration (MBA); project management (MBA); MBA/E; MBA/M Ed. *Accreditation:* AACSB. *Program availability:* Part-time, evening/weekend, synchronous with live class. *Faculty:* 11 full-time (2 women), 1 part-time/adjunct (0 women). *Students:* 42 full-time (20 women), 158 part-time (40 women); includes 35 minority (6 Black or African American, non-Hispanic/Latino; 15 Asian, non-Hispanic/Latino; 10 Hispanic/Latino; 4 Two or more races, non-Hispanic/Latino), 20 international. Average age 33. 194 applicants, 68% accepted, 40 enrolled. In 2017, 70 master's awarded. *Entrance requirements:* For master's, GMAT or GRE. Additional exam requirements/recommendations for international students: Required—TOEFL (minimum score 600 paper-based; 94 iBT), IELTS (minimum score 7). *Application deadline:* For fall admission, 7/15 for domestic students, 5/1 for international students; for spring admission, 12/1 for domestic students. Application fee: $75. Electronic applications accepted. *Financial support:* In 2017–18, 33 students received support, including 10 fellowships (averaging $5,250 per year); teaching assistantships, scholarships/grants, health care benefits, tuition waivers (partial), and unspecified assistantships also available. Support available to part-time students. Financial award application deadline: 1/15. *Faculty research:* Information systems, organizational behavior, supply chain management, strategic management, entrepreneurship. *Unit head:* Dr. Yuliang Yao, Department Chair, 610-758-6726, Fax: 610-758-6941, E-mail: yuy3@lehigh.edu. *Application contact:* Michael Tarantino, Director of Recruitment and Admissions, 610-758-3418, Fax: 610-758-5283, E-mail: mgt215@lehigh.edu.
Website: http://www4.lehigh.edu/business/academics/depts/management

Le Moyne College, Madden School of Business, Syracuse, NY 13214. Offers business administration (MBA); information systems (MS). *Accreditation:* AACSB. *Program availability:* Part-time, evening/weekend. *Faculty:* 13 full-time (4 women), 4 part-time/adjunct (2 women). *Students:* 55 full-time (19 women), 65 part-time (27 women); includes 11 minority (3 Black or African American, non-Hispanic/Latino; 1 American Indian or Alaska Native, non-Hispanic/Latino; 3 Asian, non-Hispanic/Latino; 4 Hispanic/

Business Administration and Management—General

Latino), 2 international. Average age 28. 75 applicants, 92% accepted, 66 enrolled. In 2017, 57 master's awarded. *Degree requirements:* For master's, capstone-level course. *Entrance requirements:* For master's, GMAT or GRE General Test, bachelor's degree with minimum GPA of 3.0, resume, 2 letters of recommendation, personal statement, transcripts, interview. Additional exam requirements/recommendations for international students: Required—TOEFL (minimum score 550 paper-based; 79 iBT); Recommended—IELTS (minimum score 6.5). *Application deadline:* For fall admission, 7/1 priority date for domestic and international students; for spring admission, 11/1 priority date for domestic and international students; for summer admission, 4/1 priority date for domestic and international students. Applications are processed on a rolling basis. Application fee: $0. Electronic applications accepted. *Expenses:* $797 per credit hour. *Financial support:* In 2017–18, 41 students received support. Career-related internships or fieldwork, scholarships/grants, health care benefits, and unspecified assistantships available. Support available to part-time students. Financial award applicants required to submit FAFSA. *Faculty research:* Performance evaluation outcomes assessment, technology outsourcing, international business, systems for Web-based information-seeking, non-profit business practices, business sustainability practices, management/leadership development, operations management optimization applications. *Unit head:* James Joseph, Dean of Madden School of Business, 315-445-4280, Fax: 315-445-4787, E-mail: josepjae@lemoyne.edu. *Application contact:* Kristen P. Richards, Senior Director of Enrollment Management, 315-445-5444, Fax: 315-445-6092, E-mail: trapaskp@lemoyne.edu.
Website: http://www.lemoyne.edu/madden

Lenoir-Rhyne University, Graduate Programs, Charles M. Snipes School of Business, Hickory, NC 28601. Offers accounting (MBA); business analytics and information technology (MBA); entrepreneurship (MBA); global business (MBA); healthcare administration (MBA); innovation and change management (MBA); leadership development (MBA). *Accreditation:* ACBSP. *Program availability:* Part-time, evening/weekend, online learning. *Degree requirements:* For master's, capstone course. *Entrance requirements:* For master's, GMAT, GRE, MAT, minimum undergraduate GPA of 2.7, graduate 3.0. Additional exam requirements/recommendations for international students: Required—TOEFL (minimum score 600 paper-based). Electronic applications accepted. *Expenses:* Contact institution.

LeTourneau University, Graduate Programs, Longview, TX 75607-7001. Offers business (MBA); counseling (MA), including licensed professional counselor, marriage and family therapy, school counseling; curriculum and instruction (M Ed); educational administration (M Ed); engineering (ME, MS); engineering management (MEM); health care administration (MS); marriage and family therapy (MA); psychology (MA); strategic leadership (MSL); teacher leadership (M Ed); teaching and learning (M Ed). *Program availability:* Part-time, 100% online, blended/hybrid learning. *Students:* 55 full-time (35 women), 337 part-time (266 women); includes 218 minority (140 Black or African American, non-Hispanic/Latino; 2 American Indian or Alaska Native, non-Hispanic/Latino; 5 Asian, non-Hispanic/Latino; 32 Hispanic/Latino; 39 Two or more races, non-Hispanic/Latino), 3 international. Average age 37. *Entrance requirements:* Additional exam requirements/recommendations for international students: Required—TOEFL. *Application deadline:* For fall admission, 8/22 for domestic students, 8/29 for international students; for winter admission, 10/10 for domestic students; for spring admission, 1/2 for domestic students, 1/10 for international students; for summer admission, 5/1 for domestic and international students. Applications are processed on a rolling basis. Electronic applications accepted. *Expenses:* Contact institution. *Financial support:* Research assistantships, institutionally sponsored loans, and unspecified assistantships available. Financial award applicants required to submit FAFSA.
Website: http://www.letu.edu

Lewis University, College of Nursing and Health Professions and College of Business, Program in Nursing/Business, Romeoville, IL 60446. Offers MSN/MBA. *Program availability:* Part-time, evening/weekend. *Students:* 3 full-time (all women), 27 part-time (23 women); includes 10 minority (4 Black or African American, non-Hispanic/Latino; 2 Asian, non-Hispanic/Latino; 4 Hispanic/Latino). Average age 38. *Entrance requirements:* Additional exam requirements/recommendations for international students: Required—TOEFL (minimum score 550 paper-based; 80 iBT). *Application deadline:* For fall admission, 4/2 priority date for domestic students, 5/1 priority date for international students; for spring admission, 11/15 priority date for international students. Applications are processed on a rolling basis. Electronic applications accepted. Tuition and fees vary according to program. *Financial support:* Scholarships/grants, tuition waivers (full and partial), and unspecified assistantships available. Financial award application deadline: 5/1; financial award applicants required to submit FAFSA. *Faculty research:* Cancer prevention, phenomenological methods, public policy analysis. *Total annual research expenditures:* $1,000. *Unit head:* Dr. Suling Li, Associate Dean and Director, Graduate Studies in Nursing, 815-838-0500 Ext. 5878, E-mail: lisu@lewisu.edu. *Application contact:* Nancy Wiksten, Adult Admission Counselor, 815-838-0500 Ext. 5628, Fax: 815-836-5578, E-mail: wikstena@lewisu.edu.

Liberty University, School of Business, Lynchburg, VA 24515. Offers accounting (MBA, MS), including audit and financial reporting (MS), business (MS), financial services (MS), forensic accounting (MS), leadership (MS), taxation (MS); criminal justice (MBA); cyber security (MS); executive leadership (MA); information systems (MS), including information assurance, technology management; international business (MBA, DBA); leadership (DBA); marketing (MBA, MS, DBA), including digital marketing and advertising (MS), project management (MS), public relations (MS), sports marketing and media (MS); project management (MBA, DBA); public administration (MBA); public relations (MBA). *Program availability:* Part-time, online learning. *Students:* 1,887 full-time (1,003 women), 4,223 part-time (1,950 women); includes 1,570 minority (1,133 Black or African American, non-Hispanic/Latino; 30 American Indian or Alaska Native, non-Hispanic/Latino; 118 Asian, non-Hispanic/Latino; 149 Hispanic/Latino; 13 Native Hawaiian or other Pacific Islander, non-Hispanic/Latino; 127 Two or more races, non-Hispanic/Latino), 109 international. Average age 35. 5,680 applicants, 51% accepted, 1510 enrolled. In 2017, 1,290 master's, 17 doctorates awarded. *Entrance requirements:* For master's, minimum undergraduate GPA of 3.0, 15 hours of upper-level business courses. Additional exam requirements/recommendations for international students: Required—TOEFL (minimum score 600 paper-based; 100 iBT). *Application deadline:* Applications are processed on a rolling basis. Application fee: $50. Electronic applications accepted. *Expenses:* Contact institution. *Financial support:* Applicants required to submit FAFSA. *Unit head:* Dr. Scott Hicks, Dean, 434-592-4808, Fax: 434-582-2366, E-mail: smhicks@liberty.edu. *Application contact:* Jay Bridge, Director of Graduate Admissions, 800-424-9595, Fax: 800-628-7977, E-mail: gradadmissions@liberty.edu.
Website: http://www.liberty.edu/academics/business/index.cfm?PID-149

Liberty University, School of Health Sciences, Lynchburg, VA 24515. Offers anatomy and cell biology (PhD); biomedical sciences (MS); epidemiology (MPH); exercise science (MS), including clinical, community physical activity, human performance, nutrition; global health (MPH); health promotion (MPH); medical sciences (MA), including biopsychology, business management, health informatics, molecular medicine, public health; nutrition (MPH). *Program availability:* Part-time, online learning. *Students:* 542 full-time (394 women), 696 part-time (541 women); includes 402 minority (286 Black

or African American, non-Hispanic/Latino; 10 American Indian or Alaska Native, non-Hispanic/Latino; 34 Asian, non-Hispanic/Latino; 46 Hispanic/Latino; 1 Native Hawaiian or other Pacific Islander, non-Hispanic/Latino; 25 Two or more races, non-Hispanic/Latino), 59 international. Average age 32. 1,592 applicants, 40% accepted, 297 enrolled. In 2017, 204 master's awarded. *Degree requirements:* For master's, thesis (for some programs); for doctorate, thesis/dissertation. *Entrance requirements:* For doctorate, MAT or GRE, minimum GPA of 3.25 in master's program, 2-3 recommendations, writing samples (for some programs), letter of intent, professional vitae. Additional exam requirements/recommendations for international students: Required—TOEFL (minimum score 600 paper-based; 100 iBT). Application fee: $50. *Financial support:* Applicants required to submit FAFSA. *Unit head:* Dr. Ralph Linstra, Dean. *Application contact:* Jay Bridge, Director of Admissions, 800-424-9595, Fax: 800-628-7977, E-mail: gradadmissions@liberty.edu.

LIM College, MPS Program, New York, NY 10022-5268. Offers business of fashion (MPS); fashion marketing (MPS); fashion merchandising and retail management (MPS); global fashion supply chain management (MPS). *Accreditation:* ACBSP. *Program availability:* Part-time, 100% online. *Faculty:* 1 full-time, 28 part-time/adjunct. *Students:* 113 full-time (111 women), 48 part-time (44 women). Average age 24. 285 applicants, 71% accepted, 114 enrolled. *Entrance requirements:* Additional exam requirements/recommendations for international students: Required—TOEFL (minimum score 550 paper-based), IELTS (minimum score 6.5), PTE (minimum score 55). *Application deadline:* Applications are processed on a rolling basis. Application fee: $40. Electronic applications accepted. *Expenses:* Tuition: Full-time $27,750; part-time $925 per credit. *Required fees:* $100 per term. *Unit head:* Dr. Susan Baxter, Dean of Graduate Studies, E-mail: graduatestudies@limcollege.edu. *Application contact:* Haley Drogus, Assistant Director of Graduate Admissions, 212-310-0639, E-mail: graduateadmissions@limcollege.edu.
Website: http://www.limcollege.edu/academics/graduate

Limestone College, MBA Program, Gaffney, SC 29340-3799. Offers MBA. *Program availability:* Part-time, evening/weekend, 100% online, but there are three 1-hour group dynamics classes offered during weekends between semesters. *Faculty:* 1 full-time (2 women), 1 (woman) part-time/adjunct. *Students:* 52 full-time (39 women), 12 part-time (0 women); includes 23 minority (21 Black or African American, non-Hispanic/Latino; 2 Asian, non-Hispanic/Latino), 1 international. Average age 40. 74 applicants, 33 enrolled. In 2017, 25 master's awarded. *Degree requirements:* For master's, comprehensive exam, three weekend residency seminars (on campus). *Entrance requirements:* For master's, GMAT/GRE, two letters of recommendation, official transcript(s). Additional exam requirements/recommendations for international students: Required—TOEFL (minimum score 500 paper-based; 90 iBT). *Application deadline:* For fall admission, 8/1 priority date for domestic and international students; for winter admission, 12/12 priority date for domestic and international students; for spring admission, 4/1 priority date for domestic and international students. Applications are processed on a rolling basis. Application fee: $25. Electronic applications accepted. Application fee is waived when completed online. *Expenses:* Contact institution. *Financial support:* Scholarships/grants available. Financial award application deadline: 6/15; financial award applicants required to submit FAFSA. *Faculty research:* Health care management. *Unit head:* Shannon Creighton, Director, MBA Program, 864-488-4371, Fax: 864-487-8706, E-mail: screighton@limestone.edu. *Application contact:* Adair Haynes, Administrative Assistant, MBA Program, 800-795-7151 Ext. 4370, Fax: 864-467-8706, E-mail: ahaynes@limestone.edu.
Website: http://www.limestone.edu/mba-program

Lincoln Memorial University, School of Business, Harrogate, TN 37752-1901. Offers MBA. *Accreditation:* ACBSP. *Program availability:* Part-time, evening/weekend. *Degree requirements:* For master's, comprehensive exam, thesis. *Entrance requirements:* For master's, GMAT, resume, letters of recommendation, interview. Additional exam requirements/recommendations for international students: Required—TOEFL (minimum score 500 paper-based).

Lincoln University, Graduate Studies, Oakland, CA 94612. Offers finance and investments (DBA); finance management (MS); finance management and investments (MBA); general business (MBA); human resource management (MBA, DBA); international business (MBA, MS); management information systems (MBA). *Program availability:* Part-time. *Faculty:* 14 full-time (2 women), 20 part-time/adjunct (6 women). *Students:* 606 full-time (222 women), 31 part-time (14 women); includes 10 minority (8 Asian, non-Hispanic/Latino; 1 Hispanic/Latino; 1 Two or more races, non-Hispanic/Latino), 623 international. Average age 26. *Degree requirements:* For master's, research project (thesis), internship report, or comprehensive exam; for doctorate, comprehensive exam, thesis/dissertation. *Entrance requirements:* For master's, minimum GPA of 2.7; for doctorate, GMAT (minimum score: 550), GRE (minimum score: 1000), or equivalent test results (waived for master's degree with minimum cumulative GPA of 3.3). Additional exam requirements/recommendations for international students: Required—TOEFL minimum score 525 paper-based; 71 iBT or IELTS minimum score 5.5 (for MBA); TOEFL minimum score 550 paper-based; 79 iBT or IELTS minimum score 6 (for MS and DBA). *Application deadline:* For fall admission, 8/7 for domestic students, 7/14 for international students; for spring admission, 11/30 for domestic students, 10/31 for international students; for summer admission, 5/29 for domestic students, 5/5 for international students. Applications are processed on a rolling basis. Application fee: $75. Electronic applications accepted. *Expenses:* Tuition: Full-time $8100; part-time $450 per unit. *Required fees:* $360; $180 per semester. Tuition and fees vary according to course level, course load, degree level and program. *Financial support:* Teaching assistantships, career-related internships or fieldwork, and scholarships/grants available. Financial award applicants required to submit FAFSA. *Unit head:* Dr. Marshall Burak, Provost, 510-628-8016, Fax: 510-628-8012, E-mail: mburak@lincolnuca.edu. *Application contact:* Reenu Shrestha, Assistant to the President, 510-628-8017, Fax: 510-208-2826, E-mail: sreenu@lincolnuca.edu.

Lincoln University, Graduate Studies, Jefferson City, MO 65101. Offers business administration (MBA), including accounting, management, management information systems, public administration/policy; elementary teaching (M Ed); environmental science (MS); guidance and counseling (M Ed), including community/agency counseling, elementary school, secondary school; higher education (MA); history (MA); integrated agricultural systems (MS); middle school (M Ed); natural sciences (MS); secondary teaching (M Ed); sociology (MA); sociology/criminal justice (MA). *Program availability:* Part-time, evening/weekend, 100% online, blended/hybrid learning. *Students:* 40 full-time (23 women), 64 part-time (32 women); includes 33 minority (30 Black or African American, non-Hispanic/Latino; 2 Hispanic/Latino; 1 Two or more races, non-Hispanic/Latino), 12 international. Average age 33. 48 applicants, 81% accepted, 22 enrolled. In 2017, 46 master's awarded. *Degree requirements:* For master's, comprehensive exam, thesis optional. *Entrance requirements:* For master's, GRE, MAT, or GMAT, minimum GPA of 2.75 overall, 3.0 in courses related to specialization; 3 letters of recommendation; minimum C average in English composition; personal statement of purpose. Additional exam requirements/recommendations for international students: Required—TOEFL (minimum score 500 paper-based; 61 iBT), IELTS (minimum score 5.5), Michigan English Language Assessment Battery (minimum score 80). *Application deadline:* For fall admission, 7/1 priority date for domestic students, 5/1

priority date for international students; for spring admission, 11/1 priority date for domestic students, 10/1 priority date for international students; for summer admission, 6/1 priority date for domestic students. Applications are processed on a rolling basis. Application fee: $30. Electronic applications accepted. *Expenses:* Tuition, state resident: part-time $291 per credit hour. Tuition, nonresident: part-time $541.50 per credit hour. *Financial support:* In 2017–18, 2 fellowships with tuition reimbursements, 3 research assistantships with tuition reimbursements were awarded; Federal Work-Study, scholarships/grants, and unspecified assistantships also available. Support available to part-time students. Financial award application deadline: 3/1; financial award applicants required to submit FAFSA. *Unit head:* Dr. Debra F. Greene, Interim Provost, 573-681-5247, Fax: 573-681-5106, E-mail: gradschool@lincolnu.edu. *Application contact:* Irasema Steck, Administrative Assistant, 573-681-5247, Fax: 573-681-5106, E-mail: gradschool@lincolnu.edu.
Website: http://www.lincolnu.edu/web/graduate-studies/graduate-studies

Lindenwood University, Graduate Programs, Plaster School of Business and Entrepreneurship, St. Charles, MO 63301-1695. Offers accountancy (M Acc); accounting (MBA); business administration (MBA); entrepreneurial studies (MBA); finance (MBA, MS); human resource management (MBA); international business (MBA); leadership (MA); management (MBA); marketing (MBA, MS); nonprofit administration (MA); public administration (MBA); sport management (MA); supply chain management (MBA). *Accreditation:* ACBSP. *Program availability:* Part-time, evening/weekend, 100% online. *Faculty:* 15 full-time (8 women), 26 part-time/adjunct (9 women). *Students:* 201 full-time (116 women), 253 part-time (153 women); includes 102 minority (80 Black or African American, non-Hispanic/Latino; 2 American Indian or Alaska Native, non-Hispanic/Latino; 6 Asian, non-Hispanic/Latino; 7 Hispanic/Latino; 7 Two or more races, non-Hispanic/Latino), 61 international. Average age 32. 370 applicants, 42% accepted, 134 enrolled. In 2017, 178 master's awarded. *Degree requirements:* For master's, comprehensive exam (for some programs), thesis (for some programs), minimum GPA of 3.0. *Entrance requirements:* For master's, interview, minimum undergraduate cumulative GPA of 3.0, letter of recommendation. Additional exam requirements/recommendations for international students: Required—TOEFL (minimum score 550 paper-based; 80 iBT); Recommended—IELTS (minimum score 6.5). *Application deadline:* For fall admission, 8/27 priority date for domestic and international students; for winter admission, 1/14 priority date for domestic and international students; for spring admission, 3/18 for domestic students, 3/18 priority date for international students; for summer admission, 6/3 priority date for domestic and international students. Applications are processed on a rolling basis. Application fee: $30 ($100 for international students). Electronic applications accepted. *Expenses:* Contact institution. *Financial support:* In 2017–18, 439 students received support. Career-related internships or fieldwork, Federal Work-Study, institutionally sponsored loans, scholarships/grants, tuition waivers (partial), and unspecified assistantships available. Financial award application deadline: 6/30; financial award applicants required to submit FAFSA. *Unit head:* Roger Ellis, Dean, School of Business and Entrepreneurship, 636-949-4839, E-mail: rellis@lindenwood.edu. *Application contact:* Kara Schilli, Director, Evening and Graduate Admissions, 636-949-4349, Fax: 636-949-4109, E-mail: adultadmissions@lindenwood.edu.
Website: http://www.lindenwood.edu/academics/academic-schools/robert-w-plaster-school-of-business-entrepreneurship/

Lindenwood University, Graduate Programs, School of Accelerated Degree Programs, St. Charles, MO 63301-1695. Offers administration (MSA), including management, marketing, project management; business administration (MBA); communications (MA), including digital and multimedia, media management, promotions, training and development; criminal justice and administration (MS); healthcare administration (MS); human resource management (MS); information technology (Certificate); managing information security (MS); managing information technology (MS); managing virtualization and cloud computing (MS); writing (MFA). *Program availability:* Part-time, evening/weekend, 100% online. *Faculty:* 12 full-time (5 women), 90 part-time/adjunct (37 women). *Students:* 597 full-time (383 women), 202 part-time (138 women); includes 248 minority (206 Black or African American, non-Hispanic/Latino; 3 American Indian or Alaska Native, non-Hispanic/Latino; 6 Asian, non-Hispanic/Latino; 21 Hispanic/Latino; 1 Native Hawaiian or other Pacific Islander, non-Hispanic/Latino; 11 Two or more races, non-Hispanic/Latino), 69 international. Average age 36. 526 applicants, 46% accepted, 204 enrolled. In 2017, 537 master's awarded. *Degree requirements:* For master's, thesis (for some programs), minimum cumulative GPA of 3.0; for Certificate, minimum cumulative GPA of 3.0. *Entrance requirements:* For master's, resume, personal statement, official undergraduate transcript, minimum undergraduate cumulative GPA of 3.0. Additional exam requirements/recommendations for international students: Required—TOEFL (minimum score 550 paper-based; 80 iBT); Recommended—IELTS (minimum score 6.5). *Application deadline:* For fall admission, 9/24 priority date for domestic and international students; for winter admission, 1/7 priority date for domestic and international students; for spring admission, 4/8 priority date for domestic and international students; for summer admission, 7/8 priority date for domestic and international students. Applications are processed on a rolling basis. Application fee: $30 ($100 for international students). Electronic applications accepted. *Expenses: Tuition:* Full-time $16,300; part-time $460 per credit. *Required fees:* $660; $330 per credit. Tuition and fees vary according to degree level and program. *Financial support:* In 2017–18, 738 students received support. Career-related internships or fieldwork, institutionally sponsored loans, scholarships/grants, tuition waivers (partial), and unspecified assistantships available. Financial award application deadline: 6/30; financial award applicants required to submit FAFSA. *Unit head:* Dr. Gina Ganahl, Dean, Accelerated Degree Programs, 636-949-4501, Fax: 636-949-4505, E-mail: gganahl@lindenwood.edu. *Application contact:* Kara Schilli, Director, Evening and Graduate Admissions, 636-949-4349, Fax: 636-949-4109, E-mail: adultadmissions@lindenwood.edu.
Website: http://www.lindenwood.edu/academics/academic-schools/school-of-accelerated-degree-programs/

Lindenwood University–Belleville, Graduate Programs, Belleville, IL 62226. Offers business administration (MBA); communications (MA), including digital and multimedia, media management, promotions, training and development; counseling (MA); criminal justice administration (MS); education (MA); healthcare administration (MS); human resource management (MS); school administration (MA); teaching (MAT).

Lipscomb University, College of Business, Nashville, TN 37204-3951. Offers accounting and finance (MBA); audit/accounting (M Acc); business (Certificate); business administration (MM); healthcare management (MBA); leadership (MBA); tax (M Acc); MBA/MS; Pharm D/MM. *Accreditation:* ACBSP. *Program availability:* Part-time, evening/weekend. *Faculty:* 14 full-time (2 women), 8 part-time/adjunct (1 woman). *Students:* 157 full-time (68 women), 9 part-time (6 women); includes 26 minority (9 Black or African American, non-Hispanic/Latino; 7 Asian, non-Hispanic/Latino; 8 Hispanic/Latino; 2 Two or more races, non-Hispanic/Latino), 9 international. Average age 30. 249 applicants, 49% accepted, 52 enrolled. In 2017, 130 master's awarded. *Entrance requirements:* For master's, GMAT, transcripts, interview, 2 references, resume. Additional exam requirements/recommendations for international students: Required—TOEFL (minimum score 570 paper-based). *Application deadline:* For fall admission, 6/15 for domestic students, 2/1 for international students; for winter admission, 6/1 for

international students; for spring admission, 11/15 for domestic students. Applications are processed on a rolling basis. Application fee: $50 ($75 for international students). Electronic applications accepted. *Expenses:* Contact institution. *Financial support:* Career-related internships or fieldwork, scholarships/grants, tuition waivers (partial), and unspecified assistantships available. Support available to part-time students. Financial award application deadline: 7/1; financial award applicants required to submit FAFSA. *Faculty research:* Impact of spirituality on organization commitment, women in corporate leadership, psychological empowerment, training. *Unit head:* Allison Duke, Associate Dean of Graduate Business Programs, 615-966-5732, Fax: 615-966-1818, E-mail: allison.duke@lipscomb.edu. *Application contact:* Karen Risley, Manager, Graduate Business Recruiting, 615-966-5145, E-mail: karen.risley@lipscomb.edu.
Website: http://www.lipscomb.edu/business/Graduate-Programs

Long Island University–LIU Brooklyn, School of Business, Public Administration and Information Sciences, Brooklyn, NY 11201-8423. Offers accounting (MBA); accounting (MS); business administration (MBA); computer science (MS); gerontology (Advanced Certificate); health administration (MPA); human resources management (MS); not-for-profit management (Advanced Certificate); public administration (MPA); taxation (MS). *Program availability:* Part-time, evening/weekend. *Faculty:* 18 full-time (7 women), 28 part-time/adjunct (8 women). *Students:* 226 full-time (140 women), 232 part-time (150 women); includes 272 minority (192 Black or African American, non-Hispanic/Latino; 2 American Indian or Alaska Native, non-Hispanic/Latino; 35 Asian, non-Hispanic/Latino; 40 Hispanic/Latino; 3 Two or more races, non-Hispanic/Latino), 88 international. Average age 32. 495 applicants, 64% accepted, 149 enrolled. In 2017, 189 master's, 13 other advanced degrees awarded. *Entrance requirements:* Additional exam requirements/recommendations for international students: Required—TOEFL (minimum score 550 paper-based; 75 iBT). *Application deadline:* Applications are processed on a rolling basis. Application fee: $50. Electronic applications accepted. *Expenses: Tuition:* Full-time $21,618; part-time $1201 per credit. *Required fees:* $1840; $920 per term. Tuition and fees vary according to course load. *Financial support:* In 2017–18, 78 students received support. Career-related internships or fieldwork, Federal Work-Study, scholarships/grants, and unspecified assistantships available. Support available to part-time students. Financial award application deadline: 2/15; financial award applicants required to submit FAFSA. *Faculty research:* Tax policy; public sector budgeting and gender inequities; technology and innovation; game theory; knowledge management. *Unit head:* Dr. Edward Rogoff, Dean, 718-488-1159, E-mail: edward.rogoff@liu.edu. *Application contact:* Luis Santiago, Dean of Enrollment, 718-488-1011, Fax: 718-780-6110, E-mail: bkln-admissions@liu.edu.
Website: http://liu.edu/Brooklyn/Academics/School-of-Business-Public-Administration-and-Information-Sciences

Long Island University–LIU Post, College of Management, Brookville, NY 11548-1300. Offers accountancy (MS); finance (MBA); information systems (MS); international business (MBA); management (MBA); management engineering (MS); marketing (MBA); taxation (MS); technical project management (MS); JD/MBA. *Accreditation:* AACSB. *Program availability:* Part-time, evening/weekend, blended/hybrid learning. *Faculty:* 23 full-time (7 women), 7 part-time/adjunct (1 woman). *Students:* 119 full-time (47 women), 62 part-time (23 women); includes 33 minority (11 Black or African American, non-Hispanic/Latino; 8 Asian, non-Hispanic/Latino; 13 Hispanic/Latino; 1 Two or more races, non-Hispanic/Latino), 56 international. Average age 28. 162 applicants, 62% accepted, 41 enrolled. In 2017, 91 master's awarded. *Entrance requirements:* For master's, GMAT, GRE, or LSAT. Additional exam requirements/recommendations for international students: Required—TOEFL (minimum score 550 paper-based, 75 iBT) or IELTS. *Application deadline:* Applications are processed on a rolling basis. Application fee: $50. Electronic applications accepted. *Expenses: Tuition:* Full-time $21,618; part-time $1201 per credit. *Required fees:* $1840; $920 per term. Tuition and fees vary according to course load. *Financial support:* In 2017–18, 47 students received support. Career-related internships or fieldwork, Federal Work-Study, and scholarships/grants available. Support available to part-time students. Financial award application deadline: 2/15; financial award applicants required to submit FAFSA. *Faculty research:* Innovation and property rights, knowledge sourcing, sustainability and firm performance, China and growth markets, corporate social responsibility, workforce compensation and issues. *Unit head:* Dr. Robert M. Valli, Dean, 516-299-3004, E-mail: rob.valli@liu.edu. *Application contact:* Rita Langdon, Graduate Admissions, 516-299-2900, Fax: 516-299-2137, E-mail: post-enroll@liu.edu.
Website: http://liu.edu/CWPost/Academics/Schools/COM

Longwood University, College of Graduate and Professional Studies, College of Business and Economics, Farmville, VA 23909. Offers general business (MBA); real estate (MBA); retail management (MBA). *Accreditation:* AACSB. *Program availability:* Part-time, online only, 100% online. *Degree requirements:* For master's, internship. *Entrance requirements:* For master's, GMAT or GRE, personal essay, 3 recommendations, official transcripts from all colleges and universities attended. Additional exam requirements/recommendations for international students: Required—TOEFL (minimum score 570 paper-based), IELTS (minimum score 6.5). Electronic applications accepted. *Expenses:* Contact institution.

Louisiana State University and Agricultural & Mechanical College, Graduate School, E. J. Ourso College of Business, Department of Finance, Baton Rouge, LA 70803. Offers business administration (PhD), including finance; finance (MS). *Faculty:* 12 full-time (2 women). *Students:* 20 full-time (5 women), 6 part-time (1 woman); includes 4 minority (1 Black or African American, non-Hispanic/Latino; 2 Hispanic/Latino; 1 Two or more races, non-Hispanic/Latino). Average age 26. 32 applicants, 72% accepted, 12 enrolled. In 2017, 18 master's awarded. *Financial support:* In 2017–18, 2 teaching assistantships (averaging $17,700 per year) were awarded. *Total annual research expenditures:* $18,685.

Louisiana State University and Agricultural & Mechanical College, Graduate School, E. J. Ourso College of Business, Flores MBA Program, Baton Rouge, LA 70803. Offers EMBA, MBA, PMBA, JD/IMBA. *Accreditation:* AACSB. *Students:* 240 full-time (96 women), 135 part-time (29 women); includes 75 minority (37 Black or African American, non-Hispanic/Latino; 7 Asian, non-Hispanic/Latino; 24 Hispanic/Latino; 7 Two or more races, non-Hispanic/Latino), 40 international. Average age 31. 354 applicants, 46% accepted, 124 enrolled. In 2017, 131 master's awarded. *Financial support:* In 2017–18, 37 research assistantships (averaging $27,291 per year), 62 teaching assistantships (averaging $16,002 per year) were awarded. *Total annual research expenditures:* $257,535.

Louisiana State University in Shreveport, College of Business, Education, and Human Development, Program in Business Administration, Shreveport, LA 71115-2399. Offers MBA. *Accreditation:* AACSB. *Program availability:* Part-time, evening/weekend. *Students:* 377 full-time (189 women), 1,812 part-time (848 women); includes 744 minority (485 Black or African American, non-Hispanic/Latino; 10 American Indian or Alaska Native, non-Hispanic/Latino; 61 Asian, non-Hispanic/Latino; 132 Hispanic/Latino; 1 Native Hawaiian or other Pacific Islander, non-Hispanic/Latino; 55 Two or more races, non-Hispanic/Latino), 81 international. Average age 34. 1,779 applicants, 94% accepted, 848 enrolled. In 2017, 321 master's awarded. *Degree requirements:* For master's, comprehensive exam. *Entrance requirements:* For master's, minimum undergraduate GPA of 2.5, 2.75 for last 60 credits. Additional exam requirements/

Business Administration and Management—General

recommendations for international students: Required—TOEFL (minimum score 550 paper-based; 61 iBT). *Application deadline:* For fall admission, 6/30 for domestic and international students; for spring admission, 11/30 for domestic and international students; for summer admission, 4/30 for domestic and international students. Applications are processed on a rolling basis. Application fee: $20 ($30 for international students). Electronic applications accepted. *Expenses:* Tuition, state resident: full-time $3098; part-time $344 per credit hour. Tuition, nonresident: full-time $9923; part-time $1103 per credit hour. *Required fees:* $384 per semester. Tuition and fees vary according to program. *Financial support:* In 2017–18, 5 research assistantships (averaging $5,000 per year) were awarded; scholarships/grants also available. *Unit head:* Dr. Tami Knotts, Program Director, 318-797-5268, Fax: 318-797-5176, E-mail: tami.knotts@lsus.edu. *Application contact:* Mary Catherine Harvison, Director, Admissions, 318-797-2400, Fax: 318-797-5286, E-mail: mary.harvison@lsus.edu.

Louisiana Tech University, Graduate School, College of Business, Ruston, LA 71272. Offers accounting (M Acc, DBA); computer information systems (DBA); finance (MBA, DBA); information assurance (MBA); innovation (MBA); management (DBA); marketing (MBA, DBA). *Accreditation:* AACSB. *Program availability:* Part-time, evening/weekend, 100% online, blended/hybrid learning. *Faculty:* 36 full-time (7 women), 8 part-time/adjunct (3 women). *Students:* 104 full-time (43 women), 40 part-time (16 women); includes 22 minority (13 Black or African American, non-Hispanic/Latino; 2 Asian, non-Hispanic/Latino; 7 Two or more races, non-Hispanic/Latino), 32 international. Average age 29. 104 applicants, 58% accepted, 25 enrolled. In 2017, 71 master's, 4 doctorates awarded. *Degree requirements:* For doctorate, thesis/dissertation. *Entrance requirements:* For master's and doctorate, GMAT, transcript with bachelor's degree awarded. Additional exam requirements/recommendations for international students: Required—TOEFL (minimum score 550 paper-based; 80 iBT), IELTS (minimum score 6.5). *Application deadline:* For fall admission, 8/1 priority date for domestic students, 6/1 for international students; for winter admission, 11/1 priority date for domestic students, 9/1 for international students; for spring admission, 2/1 priority date for domestic students, 12/1 for international students; for summer admission, 5/1 priority date for domestic students, 3/1 for international students. Application fee: $40. Electronic applications accepted. *Expenses:* Tuition, state resident: full-time $5146. Tuition, nonresident: full-time $10,147. *International tuition:* $10,267 full-time. *Required fees:* $2273. *Financial support:* In 2017–18, 24 students received support, including 17 research assistantships with partial tuition reimbursements available (averaging $12,500 per year), 7 teaching assistantships with partial tuition reimbursements available (averaging $12,500 per year); scholarships/grants and unspecified assistantships also available. Financial award application deadline: 2/1. *Faculty research:* Consumer environmental behavior; identifying and analyzing current issues and future concerns in real estate; information assurance and related areas in business for Northwest Louisiana and the United States (business continuity, disaster recovery, accounting controls, auditing, computer forensics, and security attribution); value creation driven by the consumer and employee interface within exchange environments. *Unit head:* Dr. Christopher D. Martin, Dean, 318-257-4526, Fax: 318-257-4253. *Application contact:* Samantha J. Bailey, Graduate Management Admissions Specialist, 318-257-2924, Fax: 318-257-4487, E-mail: samantha@latech.edu.
Website: http://www.business.latech.edu/

Louisiana Tech University, Graduate School, College of Education, Ruston, LA 71272. Offers counseling and guidance (MA), including clinical mental health counseling, human services, orientation and mobility; counseling psychology (PhD); curriculum and instruction (M Ed); cyber education (Graduate Certificate); dynamics of domestic and family violence (Graduate Certificate); early childhood education - PreK-3 (MAT); educational leadership (M Ed, Ed D); elementary education and special education mild/moderate grades 1-5 (MAT); higher education administration (Graduate Certificate); industrial/organizational psychology (MA, PhD); kinesiology (MS); middle school education (MAT), including mathematics; orientation and mobility (Graduate Certificate); rehabilitation teaching for the blind (Graduate Certificate); secondary education (MAT), including agriculture, biology, business, chemistry, English; special education: visually impaired (MAT); teacher leader education (Graduate Certificate); visual impairments - blind education (Graduate Certificate). *Accreditation:* NCATE. *Program availability:* Part-time. *Faculty:* 28 full-time (16 women), 23 part-time/adjunct (22 women). *Students:* 269 full-time (192 women), 194 part-time (150 women); includes 127 minority (94 Black or African American, non-Hispanic/Latino; 2 American Indian or Alaska Native, non-Hispanic/Latino; 6 Asian, non-Hispanic/Latino; 16 Hispanic/Latino; 1 Native Hawaiian or other Pacific Islander, non-Hispanic/Latino; 8 Two or more races, non-Hispanic/Latino), 8 international. Average age 34. 226 applicants, 74% accepted, 60 enrolled. In 2017, 5 master's, 2 doctorates, 1 other advanced degree awarded. *Degree requirements:* For master's, thesis; for doctorate, thesis/dissertation. *Entrance requirements:* For master's and doctorate, GRE General Test. Additional exam requirements/recommendations for international students: Required—TOEFL (minimum score 550 paper-based; 80 iBT), IELTS (minimum score 6.5). *Application deadline:* For fall admission, 9/1 priority date for domestic students, 6/1 for international students; for winter admission, 11/1 priority date for domestic students, 9/1 for international students; for spring admission, 2/1 priority date for domestic students, 12/1 for international students; for summer admission, 5/1 priority date for domestic students, 3/1 for international students. Application fee: $40. Electronic applications accepted. *Expenses:* Tuition, state resident: full-time $5146. Tuition, nonresident: full-time $10,147. *International tuition:* $10,267 full-time. *Required fees:* $2273. *Financial support:* In 2017–18, 40 students received support, including 23 research assistantships (averaging $10,346 per year), 15 teaching assistantships (averaging $6,887 per year); fellowships and career-related internships or fieldwork also available. Financial award application deadline: 2/1. *Faculty research:* Blindness and the best methods for increasing independence for individuals who are blind or visually impaired; educating and investigating factors contributing to improvements in human performance across the lifespan and a reduction in injury rates during training. *Total annual research expenditures:* $2.1 million. *Unit head:* Dr. Don Schillinger, Dean, 318-257-3712, E-mail: dschill@latech.edu. *Application contact:* Dr. Dawn Basinger, Associate Dean of Academic Affairs, 318-257-2977, Fax: 318-257-2379, E-mail: dbasing@latech.edu.
Website: http://education.latech.edu/

Lourdes University, Graduate School, Sylvania, OH 43560-2898. Offers business (MBA); leadership (M Ed); nurse anesthesia (MSN); nurse educator (MSN); nurse leader (MSN); organizational leadership (MOL); reading (M Ed); teaching and curriculum (M Ed); theology (MA). *Program availability:* Evening/weekend. *Entrance requirements:* Additional exam requirements/recommendations for international students: Required—TOEFL.

Loyola Marymount University, College of Business Administration, Los Angeles, CA 90045-2659. Offers MBA, MS, MBA/JD, MBA/MS. *Accreditation:* AACSB. *Program availability:* Part-time. *Faculty:* 33 full-time (9 women), 14 part-time/adjunct (3 women). *Students:* 135 full-time (57 women), 12 part-time (4 women); includes 57 minority (15 Black or African American, non-Hispanic/Latino; 1 American Indian or Alaska Native, non-Hispanic/Latino; 18 Asian, non-Hispanic/Latino; 23 Hispanic/Latino), 30 international. Average age 31. 205 applicants, 55% accepted, 61 enrolled. In 2017, 99 master's awarded. *Entrance requirements:* For master's, official transcripts, letters of recommendation. Additional exam requirements/recommendations for international

students: Required—TOEFL, IELTS. Application fee: $50. Electronic applications accepted. *Financial support:* Research assistantships, career-related internships or fieldwork, institutionally sponsored loans, scholarships/grants, and unspecified assistantships available. Support available to part-time students. Financial award applicants required to submit FAFSA. *Unit head:* Dr. Dennis W. Draper, Dean, College of Business Administration, 310-338-7504, E-mail: ddraper@lmu.edu. *Application contact:* Chake H. Kouyoumjian, Associate Dean of Graduate Studies, 310-338-2721, Fax: 310-338-6086, E-mail: graduateinfo@lmu.edu.
Website: http://cba.lmu.edu

Loyola University Chicago, Quinlan School of Business, Chicago, IL 60611. Offers MBA, MS, MSA, MSF, MSHR, MSSCM, Certificate. *Accreditation:* AACSB. *Program availability:* Part-time, evening/weekend. *Faculty:* 84 full-time (28 women), 131 part-time/adjunct (3 women). *Students:* 481 full-time (274 women), 131 part-time (57 women); includes 144 minority (43 Black or African American, non-Hispanic/Latino; 1 American Indian or Alaska Native, non-Hispanic/Latino; 46 Asian, non-Hispanic/Latino; 47 Hispanic/Latino; 7 Two or more races, non-Hispanic/Latino), 181 international. Average age 28. 999 applicants, 57% accepted, 196 enrolled. In 2017, 349 master's, 53 other advanced degrees awarded. *Entrance requirements:* For master's, GMAT or GRE, official transcripts, two letters of recommendation, statement of purpose, resume. Additional exam requirements/recommendations for international students: Required—TOEFL (minimum score 90 iBT), IELTS (minimum score 6.5). *Application deadline:* For fall admission, 7/15 for domestic and international students; for winter admission, 10/1 for domestic and international students; for spring admission, 1/15 for domestic and international students; for summer admission, 4/1 for domestic and international students. Applications are processed on a rolling basis. Application fee: $50. Electronic applications accepted. Application fee is waived when completed online. *Expenses:* $4,488 per course. *Financial support:* In 2017–18, 101 students received support. Research assistantships, career-related internships or fieldwork, Federal Work-Study, scholarships/grants, and health care benefits available. *Faculty research:* Social enterprise and responsibility, emerging markets, supply chain management, risk management. *Unit head:* Katherine Acles, Assistant Dean for Graduate Programs, 312-915-6124, Fax: 312-915-7207, E-mail: kacles@luc.edu.
Website: http://www.luc.edu/quinlan/mba/index.shtml

Loyola University Maryland, Graduate Programs, Sellinger School of Business, Emerging Leaders MBA Program, Baltimore, MD 21210-2699. Offers MBA. *Program availability:* Part-time. *Students:* 20 full-time (10 women); includes 9 minority (1 Black or African American, non-Hispanic/Latino; 2 Asian, non-Hispanic/Latino; 5 Hispanic/Latino; 1 Two or more races, non-Hispanic/Latino), 1 international. Average age 24. *Entrance requirements:* For master's, GMAT, essay, 2 letters of recommendation, resume, transcripts. Additional exam requirements/recommendations for international students: Required—TOEFL (minimum score 550 paper-based, 80 iBT) or IELTS (minimum score 7). *Application deadline:* For fall admission, 3/1 priority date for domestic students, 4/1 for international students. Applications are processed on a rolling basis. Application fee: $60. Electronic applications accepted. *Expenses:* Contact institution. *Financial support:* Fellowships, scholarships/grants, and traineeships available. Financial award application deadline: 4/15; financial award applicants required to submit FAFSA. *Unit head:* Kelly Fader, Director, Graduate Cohort Program, 410-617-1617, E-mail: kgfader@loyola.edu. *Application contact:* Office of Graduate Business Programs, 410-617-5067, E-mail: elmba@loyola.edu.
Website: https://www.loyola.edu/sellinger-business/academics/graduate/full-time-mba

Loyola University Maryland, Graduate Programs, Sellinger School of Business, Professional MBA Program, Baltimore, MD 21210-2699. Offers finance (MBA); information systems (MBA); investments and applied portfolio management (MBA); management (MBA); marketing (MBA). *Accreditation:* AACSB. *Program availability:* Part-time, evening/weekend. *Entrance requirements:* For master's, GMAT, resume, essay, official transcripts, professional letter of recommendation. Additional exam requirements/recommendations for international students: Required—TOEFL (minimum score 550 paper-based, 80 iBT) or IELTS (minimum score 7). *Application deadline:* For fall admission, 8/1 priority date for domestic students, 4/1 for international students; for spring admission, 12/1 priority date for domestic students, 9/1 for international students; for summer admission, 5/1 priority date for domestic students. Applications are processed on a rolling basis. Application fee: $60. Electronic applications accepted. *Expenses:* Contact institution. *Financial support:* In 2017–18, 26 students received support. Scholarships/grants available. Financial award application deadline: 4/15; financial award applicants required to submit FAFSA. *Unit head:* Kelly Fader, Director of Graduate Cohort Program, 410-617-1617, E-mail: kgfader@loyola.edu. *Application contact:* Office of Graduate Business Programs, 410-617-5067, E-mail: mba@loyola.edu.

Loyola University New Orleans, Joseph A. Butt, S.J., College of Business, Program in Business Administration, New Orleans, LA 70118-6195. Offers organizational performance excellence (MBA); JD/MBA; MBA/MPS. *Accreditation:* AACSB. *Program availability:* Part-time, evening/weekend, online learning. *Faculty:* 6 full-time (3 women), 7 part-time/adjunct (0 women). *Students:* 22 full-time (10 women), 61 part-time (36 women); includes 23 minority (13 Black or African American, non-Hispanic/Latino; 2 Asian, non-Hispanic/Latino; 8 Hispanic/Latino), 8 international. Average age 31. 51 applicants, 92% accepted, 37 enrolled. In 2017, 42 master's awarded. *Degree requirements:* For master's, capstone project. *Entrance requirements:* For master's, GMAT or GRE, minimum GPA of 3.0, transcript, resume, 2 letters of recommendation, work experience in field, personal statement. Additional exam requirements/recommendations for international students: Required—TOEFL (minimum score 580 paper-based; 92 iBT). *Application deadline:* For fall admission, 6/15 priority date for domestic students, 5/15 priority date for international students; for spring admission, 11/15 priority date for domestic students, 10/15 priority date for international students. Applications are processed on a rolling basis. Application fee: $50. Electronic applications accepted. *Expenses:* $1,005 per hour tuition; $733 per semester full-time fees, $376.50 part-time. *Financial support:* Research assistantships, scholarships/grants, tuition waivers (partial), and unspecified assistantships available. Financial award application deadline: 5/1; financial award applicants required to submit FAFSA. *Faculty research:* Ethics, international business, entrepreneurship, quality management, risk management. *Unit head:* Dr. J. Patrick O'Brien, Interim Dean, 504-864-7979, Fax: 504-864-7970, E-mail: mba@loyno.edu. *Application contact:* Ashley Francis, Director of Graduate Programs, 504-864-7979, Fax: 504-864-7970, E-mail: mba@loyno.edu.
Website: http://www.business.loyno.edu/mba/programs

Lynn University, College of Business and Management, Boca Raton, FL 33431-5598. Offers business administration (MBA), including aviation management, entrepreneurial management, financial valuation and investment management, hospitality management, human resource management, international business management, marketing, media management, social innovation management, sports management, Web development. *Program availability:* Part-time, evening/weekend, 100% online, blended/hybrid learning. *Faculty:* 29 full-time (11 women), 19 part-time/adjunct (7 women). *Students:* 287 full-time (124 women), 195 part-time (105 women); includes 110 minority (44 Black or African American, non-Hispanic/Latino; 2 American Indian or Alaska Native, non-Hispanic/Latino; 11 Asian, non-Hispanic/Latino; 47 Hispanic/Latino; 6 Two or more races, non-

Hispanic/Latino), 135 international. Average age 28. 293 applicants, 94% accepted, 192 enrolled. In 2017, 236 master's awarded. *Degree requirements:* For master's, thesis, minimum GPA of 3.0, strategic management seminar, written presentation reflecting the integration and application of theory to practice. *Entrance requirements:* For master's, bachelor's degree from accredited institution, minimum undergraduate GPA of 2.5, official undergraduate transcripts, resume, personal statement, letter of recommendation from academic or professional sources, writing sample demonstrating capacity to perform at graduate level. Additional exam requirements/recommendations for international students: Required—TOEFL (minimum score 550 paper-based; 80 iBT), IELTS (minimum score 6.5). *Application deadline:* For fall admission, 8/18 for domestic students, 8/4 for international students; for spring admission, 12/15 for domestic students, 12/1 for international students; for summer admission, 4/17 for domestic students, 4/3 for international students. Applications are processed on a rolling basis. Application fee: $45. Electronic applications accepted. *Expenses:* $740 per credit. *Financial support:* Career-related internships or fieldwork, Federal Work-Study, scholarships/grants, tuition waivers (full and partial), and unspecified assistantships available. Support available to part-time students. Financial award application deadline: 3/1; financial award applicants required to submit FAFSA. *Faculty research:* Knowledge economy, urban economy, U.S. manufacturing industries, leadership personality, stock market reactions to terrorism, personality psychology, industrial/organizational psychology. *Unit head:* Dr. RT Good, Dean of the College of Business and Management, 561-237-7458, E-mail: rgood@lynn.edu. *Application contact:* Steven Pruitt, Director of Graduate and Undergraduate Evening Admission, 561-237-7834, Fax: 561-237-7100, E-mail: spruitt@lynn.edu.
Website: http://www.lynn.edu/academics/colleges/business-and-management

Maastricht School of Management, Graduate Programs, Maastricht, Netherlands. Offers business administration (MBA, DBA, PhD); facility management (Exec MBA); management (M Sc); sustainability (Exec MBA).

Madonna University, School of Business, Livonia, MI 48150-1173. Offers business administration (MBA); international business (MSBA); leadership studies (MSBA); leadership studies in criminal justice (MSBA); quality and operations management (MSBA). *Program availability:* Part-time, evening/weekend, online learning. *Degree requirements:* For master's, thesis (for some programs), foreign language proficiency (international business). *Entrance requirements:* For master's, GMAT, GRE General Test, minimum GPA of 3.0. Electronic applications accepted. *Faculty research:* Management, women in management, future studies.

Maharishi University of Management, Graduate Studies, Program in Business Administration, Fairfield, IA 52557. Offers accounting (MBA); management (PhD); sustainability (MBA). *Program availability:* Evening/weekend, online learning. *Degree requirements:* For doctorate, thesis/dissertation. *Entrance requirements:* For master's, GMAT, minimum GPA of 3.0; for doctorate, minimum GPA of 3.0. Additional exam requirements/recommendations for international students: Required—TOEFL. *Faculty research:* Leadership, effects of the group dynamics of consciousness on the economy, innovation, employee development, cooperative strategy.

Malone University, Graduate Program in Business, Canton, OH 44709. Offers MBA. *Accreditation:* ACBSP. *Program availability:* Part-time, evening/weekend, online learning. *Entrance requirements:* For master's, minimum GPA of 3.0. Additional exam requirements/recommendations for international students: Required—TOEFL (minimum score 550 paper-based; 79 iBT). *Expenses:* Contact institution. *Faculty research:* Leadership, business ethics, sustainability, globalization, non-profit financial management.

Manhattan College, Graduate Programs, School of Business, Riverdale, NY 10471. Offers MBA. *Accreditation:* AACSB. *Program availability:* Part-time, 100% online, blended/hybrid learning. *Faculty:* 35 full-time (19 women), 2 part-time/adjunct (1 woman). *Students:* 43 full-time (23 women), 26 part-time (12 women). Average age 25. In 2017, 42 master's awarded. *Entrance requirements:* For master's, GMAT, minimum overall GPA of 3.0, official transcripts, current resume, 2 letters of recommendation. Additional exam requirements/recommendations for international students: Required—TOEFL, IELTS. *Application deadline:* For fall admission, 8/1 for domestic and international students; for spring admission, 1/1 for domestic and international students; for summer admission, 4/1 for domestic and international students. Applications are processed on a rolling basis. Application fee: $75. Electronic applications accepted. *Expenses: Tuition:* Part-time $1034 per credit. *Required fees:* $280 per term. One-time fee: $590 part-time. Tuition and fees vary according to program. *Financial support:* Research assistantships, career-related internships or fieldwork, scholarships/grants, and unspecified assistantships available. *Faculty research:* Supply chain networks, industrial/organizational psychology, emerging economies, financial modeling, business analytics. *Unit head:* Dr. Janet Rovenpor, Interim Dean, 718-862-7440, Fax: 718-862-8032, E-mail: janet.rovenpor@manhattan.edu. *Application contact:* Dr. Marc Waldman, MBA Program Director, 718-862-3856, E-mail: marc.waldman@manhattan.edu.
Website: https://manhattan.edu/academics/schools-and-departments/school-of-business/index.php

Marconi International University, Graduate Programs, Pembroke Pines, FL 33028. Offers business administration (DBA); education leadership (Ed D); education leadership, management and emerging technologies (M Ed); international business administration (IMBA).

Marian University, School of Business and Public Safety, Fond du Lac, WI 54935-4699. Offers organizational leadership (MS). *Program availability:* Part-time, evening/weekend. *Degree requirements:* For master's, comprehensive group project. *Entrance requirements:* For master's, 3 years of managerial experience, minimum GPA of 2.75, letters of professional reference. Additional exam requirements/recommendations for international students: Required—TOEFL (minimum score 525 paper-based; 70 iBT). Electronic applications accepted. *Expenses:* Contact institution. *Faculty research:* Organizational values, statistical decision-making, learning organization, quality planning, customer research.

Marist College, Graduate Programs, School of Management, Business Administration Program, Poughkeepsie, NY 12601-1387. Offers business administration (MBA); executive leadership (Adv C). *Accreditation:* AACSB. *Program availability:* Part-time, evening/weekend. *Entrance requirements:* For master's, GMAT, resume, 2 letters of recommendation. Additional exam requirements/recommendations for international students: Required—TOEFL (minimum score 550 paper-based; 80 iBT); Recommended—IELTS (minimum score 6.5). Electronic applications accepted. *Faculty research:* International trade law, process management, AIDS and the medical provider, mid-Hudson region economics, time quality management and organizational behavior.

Marist College, Graduate Programs, School of Management, Online MBA Program, Poughkeepsie, NY 12601-1387. Offers MBA. *Program availability:* Online learning.

Marlboro College, Graduate and Professional Studies, Program in Business Administration, Marlboro, VT 05344. Offers mission-driven organizations (MBA); project management (MBA); social innovation (MBA). *Program availability:* Part-time, evening/weekend, blended/hybrid learning. *Degree requirements:* For master's, 45 credits including a Master Workshop. *Entrance requirements:* For master's, letter of intent, essay, transcripts, 2 letters of recommendation. *Application deadline:* For fall admission, 7/1 priority date for domestic students; for winter admission, 11/1 priority date for

domestic students. Applications are processed on a rolling basis. Application fee: $0. Electronic applications accepted. *Expenses:* $794 per credit. *Financial support:* Scholarships/grants available. Financial award applicants required to submit FAFSA. *Unit head:* Tristan Toleno, Co-Chair, 802-258-9200, Fax: 802-258-9201, E-mail: tristant@gradschool.marlboro.edu. *Application contact:* Amanda Mehegan, Assistant Director of Graduate Admissions, 802-258-9209, Fax: 802-258-9201, E-mail: graduateadmissions@marlboro.edu.
Website: https://www.marlboro.edu/academics/graduate/management

Marlboro College, Graduate and Professional Studies, Program in Management, Marlboro, VT 05344. Offers mission-driven organizations (MS); project management (MS); social innovation (MS). *Program availability:* Part-time, evening/weekend, blended/hybrid learning. *Degree requirements:* For master's, capstone project. *Entrance requirements:* For master's, statement of intent, 2 letters of recommendation. Additional exam requirements/recommendations for international students: Recommended—TOEFL (minimum score 577 paper-based; 90 iBT), IELTS (minimum score 7). *Application deadline:* For fall admission, 8/5 for domestic students; for winter admission, 12/5 for domestic students; for spring admission, 4/5 for domestic students. Applications are processed on a rolling basis. Application fee: $0. Electronic applications accepted. *Expenses:* $794 per credit. *Financial support:* Scholarships/grants available. Financial award applicants required to submit FAFSA. *Unit head:* Tristan Toleno, Co-Chair, 802-258-9200, Fax: 802-258-9201, E-mail: tristant@gradschool.marlboro.edu. *Application contact:* Amanda Mehegan, Assistant Director of Graduate Admissions, 802-258-9209, Fax: 802-258-9201, E-mail: graduateadmissions@marlboro.edu.
Website: https://www.marlboro.edu/academics/graduate/management

Marquette University, Graduate School of Management, Executive MBA Program, Milwaukee, WI 53201-1881. Offers economics (MBA); finance (MBA); human resources (MBA); international business (MBA); management information systems (MBA); marketing (MBA); operations and supply chain management (MBA); sports business (MBA). *Accreditation:* AACSB. *Degree requirements:* For master's, international trip. *Entrance requirements:* For master's, GMAT or GRE, two letters of recommendation, official transcripts from current and previous colleges/universities. Additional exam requirements/recommendations for international students: Required—TOEFL (minimum score 550 paper-based; 88 iBT), IELTS (minimum score 6.5), PTE. Electronic applications accepted. *Expenses:* Contact institution. *Faculty research:* International trade and finance, customer relationship management, consumer satisfaction, customer service.

Marquette University, Graduate School of Management, Program in Business Administration, Milwaukee, WI 53201-1881. Offers business administration (MBA); economics (MBA); entrepreneurship (Certificate); finance (MBA); human resources (MBA); international business (MBA); management information systems (MBA); marketing (MBA); operations and supply chain management (MBA); sports business (MBA); JD/MBA; MBA/MA; MBA/MSN. *Accreditation:* AACSB. *Program availability:* Part-time, evening/weekend. *Degree requirements:* For Certificate, business plan. *Entrance requirements:* For master's, GMAT or GRE, letters of recommendation. Additional exam requirements/recommendations for international students: Required—TOEFL (minimum score 550 paper-based; 88 iBT), IELTS (minimum score 6.5), PTE. Electronic applications accepted. *Faculty research:* Ethics in the professions, services marketing, technology impact on decision-making, mentoring.

Marshall University, Academic Affairs Division, College of Business, Program in Business Administration, Huntington, WV 25755. Offers business administration (MBA); management foundations (Certificate). *Accreditation:* AACSB. *Program availability:* Part-time, evening/weekend. *Students:* 148 full-time (58 women), 53 part-time (23 women); includes 30 minority (13 Black or African American, non-Hispanic/Latino; 14 Asian, non-Hispanic/Latino; 1 Hispanic/Latino; 2 Two or more races, non-Hispanic/Latino). Average age 28. In 2017, 92 master's awarded. *Degree requirements:* For master's, comprehensive assessment. *Entrance requirements:* For master's, GMAT. *Application deadline:* Applications are processed on a rolling basis. Application fee: $40. *Financial support:* Tuition waivers (full) available. Support available to part-time students. Financial award applicants required to submit FAFSA. *Unit head:* Dr. Margie McInerney, Associate Dean, 304-696-2675, E-mail: mcinerney@marshall.edu. *Application contact:* Wesley Spradlin, Information Contact, 304-746-8964, Fax: 304-746-1902, E-mail: spradlin2@marshall.edu.

Maryland Institute College of Art, Graduate Studies, Design Leadership MBA/MA Program, Baltimore, MD 21201. Offers MBA/MA. Program offered in collaboration with The Johns Hopkins University. *Entrance requirements:* Additional exam requirements/recommendations for international students: Required—TOEFL (minimum score 100 iBT) or IELTS (minimum score 7). Electronic applications accepted. *Expenses:* Contact institution.

Maryland Institute College of Art, Graduate Studies, MPS Program in Business of Art and Design, Baltimore, MD 21201. Offers MPS. *Program availability:* Part-time. *Degree requirements:* For master's, business plan presentation. *Entrance requirements:* For master's, essay, resume. Additional exam requirements/recommendations for international students: Required—TOEFL (minimum score 550 paper-based; 80 iBT), IELTS (minimum score 6.5). Electronic applications accepted. *Expenses:* Contact institution.

Marymount California University, Program in Business Administration, Rancho Palos Verdes, CA 90275-6299. Offers MBA. *Degree requirements:* For master's, field project experience.

Marymount University, School of Business Administration, Program in Business Administration, Arlington, VA 22207-4299. Offers MBA, MBA/MA, MS/MBA. *Accreditation:* ACBSP. *Program availability:* Part-time, evening/weekend. *Faculty:* 11 full-time (8 women), 1 (woman) part-time/adjunct. *Students:* 23 full-time (14 women), 49 part-time (34 women); includes 34 minority (22 Black or African American, non-Hispanic/Latino; 8 Asian, non-Hispanic/Latino; 4 Hispanic/Latino), 11 international. Average age 30. 56 applicants, 91% accepted, 18 enrolled. In 2017, 39 master's awarded. *Degree requirements:* For master's, thesis or alternative. *Entrance requirements:* For master's, GMAT or GRE General Test, resume. Additional exam requirements/recommendations for international students: Required—TOEFL (minimum score 600 paper-based; 96 iBT), IELTS (minimum score 6.5). *Application deadline:* For fall admission, 7/16 priority date for domestic and international students; for spring admission, 11/16 priority date for domestic and international students; for summer admission, 4/16 for domestic and international students. Applications are processed on a rolling basis. Application fee: $40. Electronic applications accepted. *Expenses:* $990 per credit. *Financial support:* In 2017–18, 4 students received support, including 3 teaching assistantships with full and partial tuition reimbursements available (averaging $17,820 per year); research assistantships with full and partial tuition reimbursements available, career-related internships or fieldwork, Federal Work-Study, scholarships/grants, and unspecified assistantships also available. Support available to part-time students. Financial award application deadline: 3/1; financial award applicants required to submit FAFSA. *Unit head:* Dr. Linda Christie, MBA Director, 703-284-5918, E-mail: linda.christie@marymount.edu. *Application contact:* Francesca Reed, Director, Graduate Admissions, 703-284-5901, Fax: 703-527-3815, E-mail: grad.admissions@marymount.edu.
Website: http://www.marymount.edu/Academics/School-of-Business-Administration/Graduate-Programs/Business-Administration

Business Administration and Management—General

Marymount University, School of Business Administration, Program in Leadership and Management, Arlington, VA 22207-4299. Offers association and nonprofit management (Certificate); leadership and management (MS); management studies (Certificate). *Program availability:* Part-time, evening/weekend. *Faculty:* 2 full-time (1 woman). *Students:* 1 (woman) full-time, 13 part-time (8 women); includes 4 minority (3 Black or African American, non-Hispanic/Latino; 1 Two or more races, non-Hispanic/Latino). Average age 40. 5 applicants, 100% accepted, 2 enrolled. In 2017, 4 master's awarded. *Degree requirements:* For master's, thesis or alternative. *Entrance requirements:* For master's, GMAT or GRE General Test, resume, interview, at least 3 years of managerial experience, essay on a topic provided by School of Business Administration; for Certificate, resume, at least 3 years of managerial experience. Additional exam requirements/recommendations for international students: Required—TOEFL (minimum score 600 paper-based; 96 iBT), IELTS (minimum score 6.5). *Application deadline:* For fall admission, 7/16 priority date for domestic and international students; for spring admission, 11/16 priority date for domestic and international students; for summer admission, 4/16 for domestic and international students. Applications are processed on a rolling basis. Application fee: $40. Electronic applications accepted. *Expenses:* $990 per credit. *Financial support:* Career-related internships or fieldwork, Federal Work-Study, scholarships/grants, and unspecified assistantships available. Support available to part-time students. Financial award application deadline: 3/1; financial award applicants required to submit FAFSA. *Unit head:* Dr. Lorri Cooper, Chair, Management and Marketing/Director, 703-284-5950, Fax: 703-527-3830, E-mail: lorri.cooper@marymount.edu. *Application contact:* Francesca Reed, Director, Graduate Admissions, 703-284-5901, Fax: 703-527-3815, E-mail: grad.admissions@marymount.edu. Website: http://www.marymount.edu/Academics/School-of-Business-Administration/Graduate-Programs/Leadership-Management-(M-S)

Maryville University of Saint Louis, The John E. Simon School of Business, St. Louis, MO 63141-7299. Offers accounting (MBA, MS, Certificate); business studies (Certificate); cybersecurity (MBA, MS, Certificate); financial services (MBA, Certificate); healthcare practice management (MBA, Certificate); human resource management (MBA, Certificate); information technology (MBA, Certificate); management (MBA, Certificate); management and leadership (MA); marketing (MBA, Certificate); project management (MBA, Certificate); sport business management (MBA); supply chain management (Certificate); supply chain management/logistics (MBA). *Accreditation:* ACBSP. *Program availability:* Part-time, 100% online, blended/hybrid learning. *Faculty:* 5 full-time (3 women), 51 part-time/adjunct (16 women). *Students:* 222 full-time (96 women), 498 part-time (222 women); includes 185 minority (104 Black or African American, non-Hispanic/Latino; 5 American Indian or Alaska Native, non-Hispanic/Latino; 30 Asian, non-Hispanic/Latino; 37 Hispanic/Latino; 9 Two or more races, non-Hispanic/Latino), 26 international. Average age 33. In 2017, 106 master's awarded. *Degree requirements:* For master's, capstone course (for MBA). *Entrance requirements:* Additional exam requirements/recommendations for international students: Required—TOEFL (minimum score 563 paper-based; 85 iBT). *Application deadline:* Applications are processed on a rolling basis. Electronic applications accepted. *Expenses:* Contact institution. *Financial support:* Career-related internships or fieldwork, Federal Work-Study, tuition waivers (partial), and campus employment available. Financial award application deadline: 4/1; financial award applicants required to submit FAFSA. *Unit head:* Pam Horwitz, Interim Dean, 314-529-9680, Fax: 314-529-9975. *Application contact:* Dustin Loeffler, Director for Graduate Studies in Business, 314-529-9571, Fax: 314-529-9975, E-mail: dloeffler@maryville.edu. Website: http://www.maryville.edu/bu/business-administration-masters/

Marywood University, Academic Affairs, Munley College of Liberal Arts and Sciences, School of Business and Global Innovation, Scranton, PA 18509-1598. Offers finance/investment (MBA); general management (MBA); management information systems (MBA, MS). *Accreditation:* ACBSP. *Program availability:* Part-time, online learning. Electronic applications accepted. *Faculty research:* Problem formulation in ill-structured situations, corporate tax structures.

Massachusetts College of Liberal Arts, Graduate Programs, North Adams, MA 01247-4100. Offers business (MBA); educational administration (M Ed); educational leadership (CAGS); instruction and curriculum (M Ed); instructional technology (M Ed); physical education and health (M Ed); reading (M Ed); special education (M Ed). *Program availability:* Part-time, evening/weekend. *Degree requirements:* For master's, thesis. *Entrance requirements:* For master's, writing sample.

Massachusetts Institute of Technology, MIT Sloan School of Management, Cambridge, MA 02142. Offers M Fin, MBA, MS, SM, PhD. *Accreditation:* AACSB. *Degree requirements:* For master's, thesis (for some programs); for doctorate, thesis/dissertation, exams. Electronic applications accepted. *Expenses:* Contact institution.

McGill University, Faculty of Graduate and Postdoctoral Studies, Desautels Faculty of Management, Montréal, QC H3A 2T5, Canada. Offers administration (PhD); entrepreneurial studies (MBA); finance (MBA); general management (Post Master's Certificate); information systems (MBA); international business (MBA); international practicing management (MM); management (MBA); management for development (MBA); manufacturing management (MMM); marketing (MBA); operations management (MBA); public accountancy (Diploma); strategic management (MBA); MBA/LL B; MD/MBA. MMM offered jointly with Faculty of Engineering; PhD with Concordia University, HEC Montreal, Université de Montréal, Université du Québec à Montréal.

McKendree University, Graduate Programs, Master of Business Administration Program, Lebanon, IL 62254-1299. Offers business administration (MBA); human resource management (MBA); international business (MBA). *Program availability:* Part-time, evening/weekend, online learning. *Entrance requirements:* For master's, official transcripts from all institutions attended, essay, minimum GPA of 3.0, three references, resume. Additional exam requirements/recommendations for international students: Required—TOEFL. Electronic applications accepted.

McMaster University, School of Graduate Studies, DeGroote School of Business, Hamilton, ON L8S 4M2, Canada. Offers MBA, PhD. *Program availability:* Part-time. *Degree requirements:* For doctorate, comprehensive exam, thesis/dissertation. *Entrance requirements:* For master's, GMAT; for doctorate, GMAT or GRE, master's degree. Additional exam requirements/recommendations for international students: Required—TOEFL (minimum score 580 paper-based). *Faculty research:* Mergers, acquisitions, and restructuring; business investment; capital structure and dividend policy; employee pay/reward systems; pay and employment equity.

McNeese State University, Doré School of Graduate Studies, College of Business, Master of Business Administration Program, Lake Charles, LA 70609. Offers MBA. *Accreditation:* AACSB. *Program availability:* Evening/weekend. *Entrance requirements:* For master's, GMAT. *Application deadline:* For fall admission, 5/15 priority date for domestic and international students; for spring admission, 10/15 priority date for domestic and international students. Applications are processed on a rolling basis. Application fee: $20 ($30 for international students). *Financial support:* Application deadline: 5/1. *Faculty research:* Management development, integrating technology into the work force, union/management relations, economic development. *Unit head:* Dr. Akm Rahman, MBA Director, 337-475-5576, Fax: 337-475-5986, E-mail: mrahman@

mcneese.edu. *Application contact:* Dr. Akm Rahman, MBA Director, 337-475-5576, Fax: 337-475-5986, E-mail: mrahman@mcneese.edu.

Medaille College, Program in Business Administration - Amherst, Amherst, NY 14221. Offers business administration (MBA); organizational leadership (MA). *Program availability:* Evening/weekend. *Degree requirements:* For master's, thesis or alternative. *Entrance requirements:* For master's, GMAT, minimum undergraduate GPA of 2.7, 3 years of work experience. Additional exam requirements/recommendations for international students: Required—TOEFL (minimum score 550 paper-based). Electronic applications accepted. *Expenses:* Contact institution.

Medaille College, Program in Business Administration - Rochester, Rochester, NY 14623. Offers business administration (MBA); organizational leadership (MA). *Program availability:* Evening/weekend. *Degree requirements:* For master's, thesis or alternative. *Entrance requirements:* For master's, GMAT, 3 years of work experience, minimum undergraduate GPA of 2.7. Additional exam requirements/recommendations for international students: Required—TOEFL (minimum score 550 paper-based). *Expenses:* Contact institution.

Melbourne Business School, Graduate Programs, Carlton, Australia. Offers business administration (Exec MBA, MBA); management (PhD); management science (PhD); marketing (PhD); social impact (Graduate Certificate); JD/MBA.

Memorial University of Newfoundland, School of Graduate Studies, Faculty of Business Administration, St. John's, NL A1C 5S7, Canada. Offers MBA. *Program availability:* Part-time. *Degree requirements:* For master's, thesis (for some programs). *Entrance requirements:* For master's, GMAT. Electronic applications accepted. *Faculty research:* International business, marketing, organizational theory and behavior, management science and information systems, small business.

Mercer University, Graduate Studies, Cecil B. Day Campus, Eugene W. Stetson School of Business and Economics (Atlanta), Atlanta, GA 30341. Offers accounting (M Acc); innovation (PMBA), including entrepreneurship; international business (MBA); DPT/MBA; M Div/MBA; MBA/M Acc; Pharm D/MBA. *Accreditation:* AACSB. *Program availability:* Part-time, evening/weekend, 100% online, blended/hybrid learning. *Faculty:* 22 full-time (8 women), 7 part-time/adjunct (3 women). *Students:* 222 full-time (130 women), 138 part-time (72 women); includes 154 minority (114 Black or African American, non-Hispanic/Latino; 1 American Indian or Alaska Native, non-Hispanic/Latino; 27 Asian, non-Hispanic/Latino; 8 Hispanic/Latino; 4 Two or more races, non-Hispanic/Latino), 76 international. Average age 31. 207 applicants, 77% accepted, 110 enrolled. In 2017, 124 master's awarded. *Entrance requirements:* For master's, GMAT or GRE. Additional exam requirements/recommendations for international students: Required—TOEFL (minimum score 550 paper-based, 80 iBT) or IELTS. *Application deadline:* For fall admission, 6/15 priority date for domestic and international students; for spring admission, 11/1 priority date for domestic and international students; for summer admission, 3/15 priority date for domestic and international students. Applications are processed on a rolling basis. Application fee: $100 (for international students). Electronic applications accepted. *Expenses:* $740 per credit (for evening, online and 2-year MBA); $818 per credit (for full-time MBA); $42,500 per degree (for PMBA); $727 per credit (for MSBA and M Acc). *Financial support:* In 2017–18, 25 students received support. Federal Work-Study and tuition discounts available. Financial award application deadline: 5/1; financial award applicants required to submit FAFSA. *Faculty research:* Entrepreneurship, market studies, international business strategy, financial analysis. *Unit head:* Dr. Susan P. Gilbert, Dean, 678-547-6438, Fax: 678-547-6337, E-mail: gilbert_sp@mercer.edu. *Application contact:* Lael Whiteside, Director of Admissions, 678-547-6300, Fax: 678-547-6160, E-mail: whiteside_l@mercer.edu. Website: http://business.mercer.edu

Mercer University, Graduate Studies, Macon Campus, Eugene W. Stetson School of Business and Economics (Macon), Macon, GA 31207. Offers business and economics (MBA); health care (MBA); innovation (MBA). *Accreditation:* AACSB. *Program availability:* Part-time, evening/weekend. *Faculty:* 4 full-time (1 woman), 4 part-time/adjunct (2 women). *Students:* 43 full-time (16 women), 27 part-time (11 women); includes 28 minority (20 Black or African American, non-Hispanic/Latino; 1 American Indian or Alaska Native, non-Hispanic/Latino; 3 Asian, non-Hispanic/Latino; 3 Hispanic/Latino; 1 Two or more races, non-Hispanic/Latino), 2 international. Average age 29. 69 applicants, 78% accepted, 27 enrolled. In 2017, 47 master's awarded. *Entrance requirements:* For master's, GMAT/GRE. Additional exam requirements/recommendations for international students: Required—TOEFL (minimum score 550 paper-based). *Application deadline:* For fall admission, 8/1 for domestic students; for spring admission, 12/1 for domestic students; for summer admission, 5/1 for domestic students. Applications are processed on a rolling basis. Application fee: $50 ($100 for international students). Electronic applications accepted. *Expenses:* $740 per credit hour with $17 per credit hour fee, capped at $150 per semester. *Financial support:* Unspecified assistantships and employee tuition waivers available. *Faculty research:* Federal Reserve system, management of nurses, sales promotion, systems for common stock selection, interest rate premiums. *Unit head:* Dr. Susan P. Gilbert, Dean, 478-301-6438, E-mail: gilbert_sp@mercer.edu. *Application contact:* Carl Collins, Director of Graduate Admissions and Academic Advising Services, 478-301-2835, Fax: 478-301-2635, E-mail: collins_rc@mercer.edu. Website: https://business.mercer.edu/programs/macon-mba/

Mercy College, School of Business, Program in Business Administration, Dobbs Ferry, NY 10522-1189. Offers MBA. *Program availability:* Part-time, evening/weekend, 100% online, blended/hybrid learning. *Students:* 314 full-time (184 women), 66 part-time (39 women); includes 260 minority (117 Black or African American, non-Hispanic/Latino; 32 Asian, non-Hispanic/Latino; 105 Hispanic/Latino; 1 Native Hawaiian or other Pacific Islander, non-Hispanic/Latino; 5 Two or more races, non-Hispanic/Latino), 29 international. Average age 32. 337 applicants, 71% accepted, 143 enrolled. In 2017, 160 master's awarded. *Degree requirements:* For master's, thesis or alternative. *Entrance requirements:* For master's, interview, two letters of recommendation, undergraduate transcripts. Additional exam requirements/recommendations for international students: Required—TOEFL (minimum score 600 paper-based; 100 iBT), IELTS (minimum score 8). *Application deadline:* For fall admission, 8/1 for international students. Applications are processed on a rolling basis. Application fee: $40. Electronic applications accepted. *Expenses:* Contact institution. *Financial support:* Career-related internships or fieldwork, Federal Work-Study, scholarships/grants, and unspecified assistantships available. Support available to part-time students. Financial award applicants required to submit FAFSA. *Unit head:* Ed Weis, Dean, School of Business, 914-674-7490, E-mail: eweis@mercy.edu. *Application contact:* Allison Gurdineer, Senior Director of Admissions, 877-637-2946, Fax: 914-674-7382, E-mail: admissions@mercy.edu. Website: https://www.mercy.edu/degrees-programs/mba-business-administration

Meredith College, School of Business, Raleigh, NC 27607-5298. Offers entrepreneurship and family business (MBA); human resource management (MBA); project management (MBA). *Accreditation:* AACSB. *Program availability:* Part-time, evening/weekend. *Students:* 5 full-time (all women), 88 part-time (73 women); includes 33 minority (24 Black or African American, non-Hispanic/Latino; 1 Asian, non-Hispanic/Latino; 6 Hispanic/Latino; 2 Two or more races, non-Hispanic/Latino), 4 international. Average age 34. 62 applicants, 63% accepted, 29 enrolled. In 2017, 18 master's awarded. *Degree requirements:* For master's, thesis optional. *Entrance requirements:* For master's, GMAT, interview, minimum GPA of 2.5, letters of recommendation. Additional exam requirements/recommendations for international students: Required—TOEFL. *Application deadline:* For fall admission, 7/1 priority date for domestic and international students; for spring admission, 11/1 priority date for domestic and international students. Applications are processed on a rolling basis. Application fee: $50. Electronic applications accepted. *Expenses:* Contact institution. *Financial support:* Career-related internships or fieldwork, institutionally sponsored loans, scholarships/grants, and tuition waivers (partial) available. Support available to part-time students. Financial award application deadline: 2/15; financial award applicants required to submit FAFSA. *Unit head:* Kristie Ogilvie, Dean, 919-760-8432, Fax: 919-760-8470. Website: https://www.meredith.edu/school-of-business

Merrimack College, Girard School of Business, North Andover, MA 01845-5800. Offers accounting (MS); business analytics (MS); management (MS). *Program availability:* Part-time, evening/weekend, 100% online. *Faculty:* 13 full-time, 19 part-time/adjunct. *Students:* 86 full-time (33 women), 31 part-time (11 women); includes 10 minority (2 Black or African American, non-Hispanic/Latino; 2 Asian, non-Hispanic/Latino; 6 Hispanic/Latino), 34 international. Average age 27. 139 applicants, 78% accepted, 61 enrolled. In 2017, 74 master's awarded. *Degree requirements:* For master's, comprehensive exam (for some programs), thesis optional, capstone. *Entrance requirements:* For master's, official college transcripts, resume, personal statement, 2 recommendations. Additional exam requirements/recommendations for international students: Required—TOEFL (minimum score 84 iBT), IELTS (minimum score 6.5), PTE (minimum score 56). *Application deadline:* For fall admission, 8/24 for domestic students, 7/30 for international students; for spring admission, 1/10 for domestic and international students; for summer admission, 5/10 for domestic students, 4/10 for international students. Applications are processed on a rolling basis. Application fee: $0. Electronic applications accepted. *Expenses:* Contact institution. *Financial support:* Career-related internships or fieldwork, scholarships/grants, health care benefits, and unspecified assistantships available. Support available to part-time students. Financial award application deadline: 5/1; financial award applicants required to submit FAFSA. *Application contact:* Jennifer Greenwood, Graduate Admission Counselor, 978-837-3563, E-mail: graduate@merrimack.edu. Website: http://www.merrimack.edu/academics/graduate/

Messiah College, Program in Business and Leadership, Mechanicsburg, PA 17055. Offers leadership (MBA, Certificate); management (Certificate); strategic leadership (MA). *Program availability:* Online learning.

Methodist University, School of Graduate Studies, Professional Master of Business Administration Program, Fayetteville, NC 28311. Offers MBA. *Accreditation:* ACBSP. *Program availability:* Part-time, evening/weekend. *Degree requirements:* For master's, thesis. *Entrance requirements:* For master's, GMAT or MAT. Additional exam requirements/recommendations for international students: Required—TOEFL (minimum score 500 paper-based; 60 iBT). Electronic applications accepted. Application fee is waived when completed online. *Faculty research:* Governmental accounting, public economics, systems modeling, organizational culture.

Metropolitan College of New York, Program in Business Administration, New York, NY 10006. Offers financial services (MBA); general management (MBA); healthcare systems and risk management (MBA); media management (MBA). *Accreditation:* ACBSP. *Program availability:* Evening/weekend. *Students:* 164 full-time (106 women), 37 part-time (31 women); includes 153 minority (112 Black or African American, non-Hispanic/Latino; 3 American Indian or Alaska Native, non-Hispanic/Latino; 10 Asian, non-Hispanic/Latino; 24 Hispanic/Latino; 1 Native Hawaiian or other Pacific Islander, non-Hispanic/Latino; 3 Two or more races, non-Hispanic/Latino), 31 international. Average age 37. 133 applicants, 62% accepted, 66 enrolled. In 2017, 100 master's awarded. *Degree requirements:* For master's, thesis, 10-day study abroad. *Entrance requirements:* For master's, GMAT. Additional exam requirements/recommendations for international students: Required—TOEFL (minimum score 600 paper-based). *Application deadline:* For fall admission, 7/15 priority date for domestic students; for winter admission, 11/15 priority date for domestic students; for spring admission, 3/30 priority date for domestic students. Applications are processed on a rolling basis. Application fee: $45. Electronic applications accepted. *Expenses:* $926 per credit, $395 fee per semester. *Financial support:* Scholarships/grants available. Financial award application deadline: 8/15; financial award applicants required to submit FAFSA. *Unit head:* Dr. Tilokie Depoo, Dean and Professor, School for Business, 212-343-1234 Ext. 2204. *Application contact:* Steebo Varghese, Assistant Director of Admissions, 212-343-1234 Ext. 2708, Fax: 212-343-8470.

Metropolitan State University, College of Management, St. Paul, MN 55106-5000. Offers business administration (MBA, DBA); business analytics (Graduate Certificate); database administration (Graduate Certificate); global supply chain management (Graduate Certificate); information assurance security (Graduate Certificate); management information systems (MMIS); MIS generalist (Graduate Certificate); MIS systems analysis and design (Graduate Certificate); project management (Graduate Certificate). *Program availability:* Part-time, evening/weekend. *Degree requirements:* For master's, thesis optional, computer language (MMIS). *Entrance requirements:* For master's, GMAT (for MBA), resume. Additional exam requirements/recommendations for international students: Required—TOEFL (minimum score 550 paper-based). *Application deadline:* For fall admission, 7/15 for international students; for winter admission, 11/15 for international students; for spring admission, 3/15 for international students. Applications are processed on a rolling basis. Application fee: $20. Electronic applications accepted. *Expenses:* Tuition, state resident: part-time $388.55 per credit. Tuition, nonresident: part-time $777.11 per credit. *Required fees:* $35.11 per credit. Part-time tuition and fees vary according to campus/location and program. *Financial support:* Research assistantships with partial tuition reimbursements, career-related internships or fieldwork, and Federal Work-Study available. Support available to part-time students. Financial award applicants required to submit FAFSA. *Faculty research:* Yugoslav economic system, workers' cooperatives, participative management and job enrichment, global business systems. *Unit head:* Allen Bellas, Interim Dean, 612-659-7272, Fax: 612-659-7268, E-mail: allen.bellas@metrostate.edu. *Application contact:* Allen Bellas, Interim Dean, 612-659-7272, Fax: 612-659-7268, E-mail: allen.bellas@metrostate.edu. Website: https://www.metrostate.edu/academics/management

Miami University, Farmer School of Business, Oxford, OH 45056. Offers M Acc, MA, MBA. *Accreditation:* AACSB. *Expenses:* Tuition, state resident: full-time $13,812; part-time $575 per credit hour. Tuition, nonresident: full-time $30,860; part-time $1286 per credit hour. *Unit head:* Dr. Marc Rubin, Dean/Chair in Business Leadership, 513-529-3381, E-mail: deanofbusiness@miamioh.edu. *Application contact:* Admission Coordinator, 513-529-3734, E-mail: applygrad@miamioh.edu. Website: http://www.fsb.miamioh.edu/

Michigan State University, The Graduate School, Eli Broad College of Business, Department of Management, East Lansing, MI 48224. Offers management (PhD); management, strategy, and leadership (MS). *Program availability:* Part-time, online learning. *Degree requirements:* For doctorate, comprehensive exam, thesis/dissertation. *Entrance requirements:* For master's, full-time managerial experience in a supervisory

role; for doctorate, GMAT or GRE, letters of recommendation, experience in teaching and conducting research, work experience in business contexts, personal essay. Additional exam requirements/recommendations for international students: Required—TOEFL (minimum score 600 paper-based). Electronic applications accepted.

Michigan State University, The Graduate School, Eli Broad College of Business, Program in Business Administration, East Lansing, MI 48224. Offers finance (MBA); human resource management (MBA); integrative management (MBA); marketing (MBA); supply chain management (MBA). MBA in integrative management is through Weekend MBA Program; other 4 concentrations are through Full-Time MBA Program. *Program availability:* Evening/weekend. *Degree requirements:* For master's, enrichment experience. *Entrance requirements:* For master's, GMAT or GRE, 4-year bachelor's degree; resume; work experience (minimum of 5 years for Weekend MBA); 2-3 personal essays; 2 letters of recommendation; personal interview. Additional exam requirements/recommendations for international students: Required—PTE (minimum score 70), TOEFL (minimum score 100 iBT) or IELTS (minimum score 7) for full-time MBA applicants. Electronic applications accepted. *Expenses:* Contact institution.

Michigan Technological University, Graduate School, School of Business and Economics, Houghton, MI 49931. Offers accounting (MS); applied natural resource economics (MS); business administration (MBA). *Accreditation:* AACSB. *Program availability:* Part-time, evening/weekend. *Faculty:* 24 full-time (6 women), 1 part-time/adjunct. *Students:* 25 full-time (12 women), 21 part-time (13 women); includes 1 minority (Two or more races, non-Hispanic/Latino), 14 international. Average age 27. 165 applicants, 23% accepted, 22 enrolled. In 2017, 24 master's awarded. *Degree requirements:* For master's, thesis (for some programs). *Entrance requirements:* For master's, GMAT/GRE (recommended minimum score in the 55th percentile), statement of purpose, personal statement, official transcripts, 2 letters of recommendation, resume/curriculum vitae. Additional exam requirements/recommendations for international students: Required—TOEFL (recommended minimum score 95 iBT) or IELTS (minimum score 7). *Application deadline:* For fall admission, 7/1 for domestic and international students; for spring admission, 12/1 for domestic and international students. Applications are processed on a rolling basis. Electronic applications accepted. *Expenses:* Tuition, state resident: full-time $17,100; part-time $950 per credit. Tuition, nonresident: full-time $17,100; part-time $950 per credit. *Required fees:* $248; $124 per term. Tuition and fees vary according to course load and program. *Financial support:* In 2017–18, 22 students received support. Health care benefits and unspecified assistantships available. Financial award application deadline: 2/1; financial award applicants required to submit FAFSA. *Faculty research:* Natural resource and mineral economics, entrepreneurship, management of technology and innovation, engineering management, management information systems. *Total annual research expenditures:* $5,749. *Unit head:* Dr. Dean Johnson, Dean, 906-487-2668, Fax: 906-487-1863, E-mail: dean@mtu.edu. *Application contact:* Carol T. Wingerson, Administrative Aide, 906-487-2328, Fax: 906-487-2284, E-mail: gradadms@mtu.edu. Website: http://www.mtu.edu/business/

Mid-America Christian University, Program in Business Administration, Oklahoma City, OK 73170-4504. Offers MBA. *Entrance requirements:* For master's, bachelor's degree from regionally-accredited college or university, minimum overall cumulative GPA of 2.75 on undergraduate course work. Additional exam requirements/recommendations for international students: Required—TOEFL (minimum score 550 paper-based).

MidAmerica Nazarene University, School of Business, Olathe, KS 66062-1899. Offers management (MBA, MSM). *Program availability:* Part-time, evening/weekend, 100% online, blended/hybrid learning. Terminal master's awarded for partial completion of doctoral program. *Entrance requirements:* For master's, official transcript for bachelor's degree from regionally-accredited college or university; minimum GPA of 3.0 in last 60 hours of undergraduate coursework; completion of college algebra, statistics, or other higher level math with minimum grade of B-. Additional exam requirements/recommendations for international students: Required—TOEFL (minimum score 81 iBT), IELTS (minimum score 6). Electronic applications accepted. *Expenses:* Contact institution. *Faculty research:* Project management, global business, entrepreneurship, experience learning.

Middle Tennessee State University, College of Graduate Studies, Jennings A. Jones College of Business, Department of Management and Marketing, Murfreesboro, TN 37132. Offers business administration (MBA); management (MS). *Accreditation:* AACSB. *Program availability:* Part-time, evening/weekend, online learning. *Degree requirements:* For master's, comprehensive exam. *Entrance requirements:* For master's, GMAT (minimum score of 400). Additional exam requirements/recommendations for international students: Required—TOEFL (minimum score 525 paper-based; 71 iBT) or IELTS (minimum score 6). Electronic applications accepted.

Midway University, Graduate Programs, Midway, KY 40347-1120. Offers education (MAT); leadership (MBA). *Degree requirements:* For master's, capstone course. *Entrance requirements:* For master's, GMAT (for MBA); GRE or PRAXIS I (for MAT), bachelor's degree; interview; minimum GPA of 3.0 (for MBA), 2.75 (for MAT); 3 years of professional work experience (for MBA). Additional exam requirements/recommendations for international students: Required—TOEFL (minimum score 550 paper-based; 80 iBT).

Midwestern State University, Billie Doris McAda Graduate School, Dillard College of Business Administration, Wichita Falls, TX 76308. Offers MBA. *Accreditation:* AACSB. *Program availability:* Part-time, evening/weekend. *Degree requirements:* For master's, comprehensive exam, thesis optional. *Entrance requirements:* For master's, GMAT. Additional exam requirements/recommendations for international students: Required—TOEFL (minimum score 550 paper-based). Electronic applications accepted. *Faculty research:* Citizenship behavior, software solutions, mediations, sales force training, stock trading volume.

Millennia Atlantic University, Graduate Programs, Doral, FL 33178. Offers accounting (MBA); business administration (MBA); health information management (MS); human resource management (MA). *Program availability:* Online learning.

Milligan College, Area of Business Administration, Milligan College, TN 37682. Offers health sector management (MBA, Graduate Certificate); leadership (MBA, Graduate Certificate); operations management (MBA, Graduate Certificate). *Program availability:* 100% online, blended/hybrid learning. *Faculty:* 4 full-time (1 woman), 3 part-time/adjunct (2 women). *Students:* 30 full-time (16 women), 1 international. Average age 38. 30 applicants, 83% accepted, 24 enrolled. In 2017, 27 master's awarded. *Degree requirements:* For master's, thesis or alternative. *Entrance requirements:* For master's, GMAT if undergraduate GPA less than 3.0, undergraduate degree and supporting transcripts, relevant full-time work experience, essay/personal statement, professional recommendations. Additional exam requirements/recommendations for international students: Required—TOEFL (minimum score 550 paper-based, 79 iBT) or IELTS (6.5). *Application deadline:* For fall admission, 8/1 for domestic students, 6/1 for international students; for spring admission, 1/15 for domestic students, 12/1 for international students. Applications are processed on a rolling basis. Application fee: $30. Electronic applications accepted. *Expenses:* Contact institution. *Financial support:* Scholarships/grants available. Financial award application deadline: 12/1; financial award applicants

required to submit FAFSA. *Faculty research:* International microfinance; economic development in Appalachia; job satisfaction; business ethics; internal migration. *Unit head:* Dr. David Campbell, Area Chair of Business, 423-461-8674, Fax: 423-461-8677, E-mail: dacampbell@milligan.edu. *Application contact:* Rebecca Banton, Graduate Admissions Recruiter, Business Area, 423-461-8662, Fax: 423-461-8789, E-mail: rbbanton@milligan.edu.
Website: http://www.milligan.edu/GPS

Millikin University, Tabor School of Business, Decatur, IL 62522-2084. Offers MBA. *Accreditation:* ACBSP. *Program availability:* Evening/weekend. *Faculty:* 7 full-time (2 women), 7 part-time/adjunct (2 women). *Students:* 22 full-time (7 women), 4 part-time (2 women); includes 5 minority (4 Black or African American, non-Hispanic/Latino; 1 Hispanic/Latino). Average age 34. 106 applicants, 50% accepted, 25 enrolled. In 2017, 32 master's awarded. *Degree requirements:* For master's, comprehensive exam. *Entrance requirements:* For master's, GMAT or GRE, resume, 3 reference letters, interview, statement of purpose, transcripts. Additional exam requirements/recommendations for international students: Required—TOEFL (minimum score 550 paper-based; 79 iBT), IELTS (minimum score 6.5). *Application deadline:* For fall admission, 6/1 priority date for domestic students, 5/1 priority date for international students; for spring admission, 11/1 priority date for domestic students, 8/1 priority date for international students. Applications are processed on a rolling basis. Application fee: $0. Electronic applications accepted. *Expenses:* $832 per credit hour. *Financial support:* In 2017–18, 10 students received support, including 1 research assistantship with partial tuition reimbursement available (averaging $6,000 per year), 3 teaching assistantships with partial tuition reimbursements available (averaging $6,000 per year); tuition waivers also available. Financial award applicants required to submit FAFSA. *Faculty research:* E-commerce, international marketing, pedagogy, total quality management, auditing. *Unit head:* Dr. Anthony Liberatore, MBA Director/Associate Professor, 217-424-6338, E-mail: aliberatore@millikin.edu.
Website: http://www.millikin.edu/mba

Millsaps College, Else School of Management, Jackson, MS 39210-0001. Offers accounting (M Acc); business administration (MBA). *Accreditation:* AACSB. *Program availability:* Part-time. *Entrance requirements:* For master's, GMAT. Additional exam requirements/recommendations for international students: Required—TOEFL. Electronic applications accepted. *Faculty research:* Ethics, audit independence, satisfaction with assurance services, political business cycles, economic development, commercialization of new products.

Mills College, Graduate Studies, Joint MBA/MPP Program, Oakland, CA 94613-1000. Offers MBA/MPP. *Faculty:* 5 full-time (3 women), 14 part-time/adjunct (10 women). *Students:* 16 full-time (13 women), 4 part-time (all women); includes 10 minority (5 Black or African American, non-Hispanic/Latino; 4 Hispanic/Latino; 1 Two or more races, non-Hispanic/Latino). Average age 34. 13 applicants, 69% accepted, 6 enrolled. *Entrance requirements:* Additional exam requirements/recommendations for international students: Required—TOEFL (minimum score 550 paper-based; 80 iBT) or IELTS (minimum score 6). *Application deadline:* For winter admission, 2/1 priority date for domestic students, 12/15 priority date for international students. Application fee: $50. Electronic applications accepted. *Expenses:* Contact institution. *Financial support:* In 2017–18, 19 students received support, including 19 fellowships (averaging $8,957 per year). Financial award application deadline: 2/1; financial award applicants required to submit FAFSA. *Faculty research:* Diversity and inclusion, applied econometrics, non-profit management, business communication and effective public speaking, social media, Internet marketing, organizational and cultural chance, economics of the family, urbanization and land conservation, gender and science, comparative race and ethnic relations. *Unit head:* Dr. Lorien Rice, Professor of Public Policy, 510-430-3113, Fax: 510-430-2159, E-mail: lrice@mills.edu. *Application contact:* Robynne Lofton, Director of Admissions, 510-430-3295, Fax: 510-430-2159, E-mail: grad-admission@mills.edu.
Website: http://www.mills.edu/academics/graduate/ppol/program/joint_MPPMBA.php

Mills College, Graduate Studies, Lorry I. Lokey Graduate School of Business, Oakland, CA 94613-1000. Offers applied economics (MA); management (MBA, MM). *Program availability:* Part-time. *Faculty:* 4 full-time (3 women), 8 part-time/adjunct (5 women). *Students:* 31 full-time (24 women), 23 part-time (22 women); includes 33 minority (13 Black or African American, non-Hispanic/Latino; 2 American Indian or Alaska Native, non-Hispanic/Latino; 1 Asian, non-Hispanic/Latino; 10 Hispanic/Latino; 7 Two or more races, non-Hispanic/Latino), 1 international. Average age 33. 49 applicants, 84% accepted, 20 enrolled. In 2017, 31 master's awarded. *Entrance requirements:* For master's, GRE, SAT, or ACT, 3 letters of recommendation, 2 transcripts. Additional exam requirements/recommendations for international students: Required—TOEFL (minimum score 550 paper-based; 80 iBT) or IELTS (minimum score 6). *Application deadline:* For fall admission, 2/1 priority date for domestic students, 12/15 for international students; for spring admission, 10/1 for domestic students. Applications are processed on a rolling basis. Application fee: $50. *Expenses:* Contact institution. *Financial support:* In 2017–18, 59 students received support, including 59 fellowships with tuition reimbursements available (averaging $6,398 per year), 19 teaching assistantships with tuition reimbursements available; scholarships/grants and unspecified assistantships also available. Support available to part-time students. Financial award application deadline: 2/1; financial award applicants required to submit FAFSA. *Faculty research:* Diversity and inclusion, applied econometrics, non-profit management, business communication and effective public speaking, social media and Internet marketing. *Unit head:* Dr. Kate Karniouchina, Dean, Lorry I. Lokey School of Business and Public Policy, 510-430-3345, Fax: 510-430-2159, E-mail: kkarniouchina@mills.edu. *Application contact:* Robynne Lofton, Director of Admissions, 510-430-3295, Fax: 510-430-2159, E-mail: grad-admission@mills.edu.
Website: http://www.mills.edu/mba

Milwaukee School of Engineering, Program in Business Administration, Milwaukee, WI 53202-3109. Offers MBA. *Program availability:* Part-time, evening/weekend, 100% online, blended/hybrid learning. *Students:* 17 full-time (9 women), 48 part-time (16 women); includes 13 minority (4 Black or African American, non-Hispanic/Latino; 3 Asian, non-Hispanic/Latino; 3 Hispanic/Latino; 3 Two or more races, non-Hispanic/Latino), 2 international. Average age 29. 27 applicants, 81% accepted, 19 enrolled. In 2017, 19 master's awarded. *Degree requirements:* For master's, thesis or alternative. *Entrance requirements:* For master's, GRE General Test or GMAT if undergraduate GPA less than 2.8, bachelor's degree from accredited university; 2 letters of recommendation; work experience (strongly recommended). Additional exam requirements/recommendations for international students: Required—TOEFL (minimum score 90 iBT), IELTS (minimum score 7). *Application deadline:* Applications are processed on a rolling basis. Application fee: $0. Electronic applications accepted. *Expenses:* Tuition: Part-time $814 per credit hour. *Required fees:* $12.50 per credit hour. *Financial support:* In 2017–18, 30 students received support. Fellowships, career-related internships or fieldwork, scholarships/grants, and tuition waivers (partial) available. Financial award application deadline: 3/15; financial award applicants required to submit FAFSA. *Unit head:* David Schmitz, Program Director, 414-277-2487, Fax: 414-277-7479, E-mail: schmitz@msoe.edu. *Application contact:* Brian Rutz, Graduate Admission Counselor, 414-277-7200, E-mail: rutz@msoe.edu.
Website: https://www.msoe.edu/academics/graduate-degrees/business/msoe-mba/

Minnesota State University Mankato, College of Graduate Studies and Research, College of Business, Mankato, MN 56001. Offers accounting (MSA); business (MBA). *Accreditation:* AACSB. *Entrance requirements:* For master's, GMAT, 2 letters of reference, resume. Additional exam requirements/recommendations for international students: Required—TOEFL. Electronic applications accepted.

Minnesota State University Moorhead, Graduate Studies, College of Business and Innovation, Moorhead, MN 56563. Offers accounting and finance (MS); business administration (MBA); health care management (MBA). *Accreditation:* AACSB. *Program availability:* Part-time. *Faculty:* 13. *Students:* 17 full-time (5 women), 26 part-time (17 women). Average age 29. 21 applicants, 81% accepted. In 2017, 13 master's awarded. *Degree requirements:* For master's, comprehensive exam (for some programs), thesis, final oral defense. *Entrance requirements:* For master's, GMAT, minimum GPA of 3.0. Additional exam requirements/recommendations for international students: Required—TOEFL (minimum score 550 paper-based); Recommended—IELTS (minimum score 6.5). *Application deadline:* For fall admission, 3/15 for domestic students; for spring admission, 10/15 for domestic students. Applications are processed on a rolling basis. Application fee: $20. Electronic applications accepted. *Expenses:* Tuition, state resident: full-time $9000; part-time $374 per credit. Tuition, nonresident: full-time $18,000; part-time $748 per credit. *Required fees:* $1055; $43.96 per credit. Tuition and fees vary according to degree level, program and reciprocity agreements. *Financial support:* Federal Work-Study and unspecified assistantships available. Financial award application deadline: 10/1; financial award applicants required to submit FAFSA. *Faculty research:* Union decertification, small business development, business innovation, pedagogy, curriculum design. *Unit head:* Denise Gorsline, Interim Dean, 218-477-4623, E-mail: gorsline@mnstate.edu. *Application contact:* Karla Wenger, Coordinator, 218-477-2344, E-mail: wengerk@mnstate.edu.
Website: http://www.mnstate.edu/cbi/

Minot State University, Graduate School, Program in Management, Minot, ND 58707-0002. Offers MSM. *Program availability:* Part-time. *Degree requirements:* For master's, comprehensive exam (for some programs), thesis optional. *Entrance requirements:* For master's, GRE, minimum GPA 2.75. Additional exam requirements/recommendations for international students: Required—TOEFL (minimum score 79 iBT), IELTS (minimum score 6).

Misericordia University, College of Business, Master of Business Administration Program, Dallas, PA 18612-1098. Offers accounting (MBA); healthcare management (MBA); human resource management (MBA); management (MBA); sport management (MBA). *Program availability:* Part-time, evening/weekend, online learning. *Entrance requirements:* For master's, GMAT, MAT, GRE (50th percentile or higher), or minimum undergraduate GPA of 3.0, interview. Additional exam requirements/recommendations for international students: Required—TOEFL. Electronic applications accepted. Application fee is waived when completed online. *Expenses:* Contact institution.

Misericordia University, College of Business, Program in Organizational Management, Dallas, PA 18612-1098. Offers healthcare management (MS); human resource management (MS); management (MS). *Program availability:* Part-time, evening/weekend, online learning. *Entrance requirements:* For master's, GRE General Test, MAT (35th percentile or higher), or minimum undergraduate GPA of 3.0. Additional exam requirements/recommendations for international students: Required—TOEFL. Electronic applications accepted. Application fee is waived when completed online. *Expenses:* Contact institution.

Mississippi College, Graduate School, School of Business, Clinton, MS 39058. Offers accounting (Certificate); business administration (MBA), including accounting; business education (M Ed); finance (MBA, Certificate); JD/MBA. *Accreditation:* ACBSP. *Program availability:* Part-time, evening/weekend. *Degree requirements:* For master's, comprehensive exam, thesis optional. *Entrance requirements:* For master's, GMAT, minimum GPA of 2.5, 24 hours of undergraduate course work in business. Additional exam requirements/recommendations for international students: Recommended—TOEFL, IELTS. Electronic applications accepted.

Mississippi State University, College of Business, Department of Management and Information Systems, Mississippi State, MS 39762. Offers business administration (MBA); information systems (MSIS, PhD); management (PhD); project management (MBA). *Program availability:* Part-time. *Faculty:* 19 full-time (5 women). *Students:* 63 full-time (21 women), 194 part-time (44 women); includes 21 minority (5 Black or African American, non-Hispanic/Latino; 4 Asian, non-Hispanic/Latino; 9 Hispanic/Latino; 3 Two or more races, non-Hispanic/Latino), 16 international. Average age 30. 163 applicants, 48% accepted, 63 enrolled. In 2017, 96 master's, 4 doctorates awarded. *Degree requirements:* For master's, comprehensive exam; for doctorate, comprehensive exam, thesis/dissertation. *Entrance requirements:* For master's, GMAT, minimum GPA of 3.0 in last 60 hours of undergraduate course work; for doctorate, GMAT (minimum score of 550), minimum GPA of 3.25 on all graduate work; BS with minimum GPA of 3.0 cumulative and last 60 hours. Additional exam requirements/recommendations for international students: Required—TOEFL (minimum score 575 paper-based; 84 iBT); Recommended—IELTS (minimum score 7). *Application deadline:* For fall admission, 7/1 for domestic students, 5/1 for international students; for spring admission, 11/1 for domestic students, 9/1 for international students. Applications are processed on a rolling basis. Application fee: $60 ($80 for international students). Electronic applications accepted. *Expenses:* Tuition, state resident: full-time $8318; part-time $462.12 per credit hour. Tuition, nonresident: full-time $22,358; part-time $1242.12 per credit hour. *Required fees:* $110; $12.24 per credit hour. $6.12 per semester. *Financial support:* Career-related internships or fieldwork, Federal Work-Study, institutionally sponsored loans, scholarships/grants, and unspecified assistantships available. Financial award applicants required to submit FAFSA. *Faculty research:* Electronic commerce, management of information technology. *Total annual research expenditures:* $1.3 million. *Unit head:* Dr. James J. Chrisman, Professor and Head, 662-325-1991, Fax: 662-325-8651, E-mail: jchrisman@business.msstate.edu. *Application contact:* Lakan Drinker, Admissions and Enrollment Assistant, 662-325-8951, E-mail: ldrinker@grad.msstate.edu.
Website: http://www.business.msstate.edu/programs/mis/index.php

Missouri Baptist University, Graduate Programs, St. Louis, MO 63141-8660. Offers business administration (MBA); Christian ministries (MACM); counseling (MAC); education (MSE); education administration (MEA); educational leadership (MSE, Ed S); teaching (MAT).

Missouri Southern State University, Program in Business Administration, Joplin, MO 64801-1595. Offers MBA. Program offered jointly with Northwest Missouri State University. *Program availability:* Online learning. *Degree requirements:* For master's, capstone seminar.

Missouri State University, Graduate College, College of Business, Business Administration Program, Springfield, MO 65897. Offers MBA. *Accreditation:* AACSB. *Program availability:* Part-time, evening/weekend. *Faculty:* 17 full-time (5 women). *Students:* 249 full-time (143 women), 281 part-time (110 women); includes 41 minority (8 Black or African American, non-Hispanic/Latino; 2 American Indian or Alaska Native, non-Hispanic/Latino; 7 Asian, non-Hispanic/Latino; 17 Hispanic/Latino; 7 Two or more races, non-Hispanic/Latino), 204 international. Average age 23. 291 applicants, 64%

accepted, 158 enrolled. In 2017, 302 master's awarded. *Degree requirements:* For master's, thesis optional. *Entrance requirements:* For master's, GMAT or GRE, minimum GPA of 2.75. Additional exam requirements/recommendations for international students: Required—TOEFL (minimum score 550 paper-based; 79 iBT), IELTS (minimum score 6). *Application deadline:* For fall admission, 7/20 priority date for domestic students, 5/1 for international students; for spring admission, 12/20 priority date for domestic students, 9/1 for international students; for summer admission, 5/20 priority date for domestic students. Applications are processed on a rolling basis. Application fee: $35 ($50 for international students). Electronic applications accepted. *Expenses:* Tuition, state resident: full-time $2915; part-time $2021 per credit hour. Tuition, nonresident: full-time $5354; part-time $3647 per credit hour. *International tuition:* $11,992 full-time. *Required fees:* $173; $173 per credit hour. Tuition and fees vary according to class time, course level, course load, degree level, campus/location and program. *Financial support:* Federal Work-Study, institutionally sponsored loans, scholarships/grants, and unspecified assistantships available. Support available to part-time students. Financial award application deadline: 3/31; financial award applicants required to submit FAFSA. *Unit head:* Dr. Elizabeth Rozell, MBA Program Director, 417-836-5616, Fax: 417-836-4407, E-mail: mbaprogram@missouristate.edu. *Application contact:* Stephanie Praschan, Director, Graduate Enrollment Management, 417-836-5330, Fax: 417-836-6200, E-mail: stephaniepraschan@missouristate.edu.
Website: http://mba.missouristate.edu

Missouri University of Science and Technology, Department of Business and Information Technology, Rolla, MO 65401. Offers business administration (MBA); information science and technology (MS). *Faculty:* 356 full-time (90 women), 51 part-time/adjunct (6 women). *Students:* 65 full-time (26 women), 69 part-time (22 women); includes 17 minority (9 Black or African American, non-Hispanic/Latino; 5 Asian, non-Hispanic/Latino; 2 Hispanic/Latino; 1 Two or more races, non-Hispanic/Latino), 65 international. Average age 29. 146 applicants, 85% accepted, 41 enrolled. In 2017, 18 master's awarded. *Degree requirements:* For master's, thesis or alternative. *Entrance requirements:* Additional exam requirements/recommendations for international students: Required—TOEFL (minimum score 600 paper-based); Recommended—IELTS. Application fee: $55 ($75 for international students). Electronic applications accepted. *Expenses:* Tuition, state resident: full-time $7391; part-time $3696 per year. Tuition, nonresident: full-time $21,712; part-time $10,857 per year. *Required fees:* $728; $564 per unit. Tuition and fees vary according to course load. *Financial support:* In 2017–18, 5 research assistantships (averaging $1,792 per year), 6 teaching assistantships (averaging $1,814 per year) were awarded. Financial award applicants required to submit FAFSA. *Total annual research expenditures:* $750,846. *Unit head:* Keng Siau, Chair, 573-341-4528, Fax: 573-341-4812, E-mail: siauk@mst.edu. *Application contact:* Debbie Schwertz, Admissions Coordinator, 573-341-6013, Fax: 573-341-6271, E-mail: schwertz@mst.edu.
Website: http://www.bit.mst.edu

Missouri Western State University, Program in Applied Science, St. Joseph, MO 64507-2294. Offers engineering technology management (MAS); industrial life science (MAS); sport and fitness management (MAS). *Accreditation:* AACSB. *Program availability:* Part-time. *Students:* 37 full-time (16 women), 20 part-time (9 women); includes 8 minority (6 Black or African American, non-Hispanic/Latino; 1 Asian, non-Hispanic/Latino; 1 Two or more races, non-Hispanic/Latino), 10 international. Average age 27. 28 applicants, 86% accepted, 16 enrolled. In 2017, 32 master's awarded. *Entrance requirements:* Additional exam requirements/recommendations for international students: Recommended—TOEFL (minimum score 79 iBT), IELTS (minimum score 6). *Application deadline:* For fall admission, 7/15 for domestic and international students; for spring admission, 10/1 for domestic and international students; for summer admission, 3/15 for domestic students. Applications are processed on a rolling basis. Application fee: $45 ($50 for international students). Electronic applications accepted. *Expenses:* Tuition, state resident: full-time $6391; part-time $336 per credit hour. Tuition, nonresident: full-time $11,483; part-time $604 per credit hour. *Required fees:* $542; $99 per credit hour. $176 per semester. One-time fee: $45. Tuition and fees vary according to course load and program. *Financial support:* Scholarships/grants and unspecified assistantships available. Support available to part-time students. *Unit head:* Dr. Benjamin D. Caldwell, Dean of the Graduate School, 816-271-4394, Fax: 816-271-4525, E-mail: graduate@missouriwestern.edu.

Missouri Western State University, Program in Business Administration, St. Joseph, MO 64507-2294. Offers animal and life sciences (MBA); enterprise resource planning (MBA); forensic accounting (MBA); general business (MBA). *Program availability:* Part-time. *Students:* 4 full-time (3 women), 24 part-time (8 women); includes 5 minority (3 Black or African American, non-Hispanic/Latino; 1 Asian, non-Hispanic/Latino; 1 Two or more races, non-Hispanic/Latino). Average age 35. 30 applicants, 93% accepted, 18 enrolled. *Entrance requirements:* Additional exam requirements/recommendations for international students: Recommended—TOEFL (minimum score 79 iBT), IELTS (minimum score 6). *Application deadline:* For fall admission, 7/15 for domestic and international students; for spring admission, 10/1 for domestic and international students; for summer admission, 3/15 for domestic students. Applications are processed on a rolling basis. Application fee: $45 ($50 for international students). Electronic applications accepted. *Expenses:* Tuition, state resident: full-time $6391; part-time $336 per credit hour. Tuition, nonresident: full-time $11,483; part-time $604 per credit hour. *Required fees:* $542; $99 per credit hour. $176 per semester. One-time fee: $45. Tuition and fees vary according to course load and program. *Financial support:* Scholarships/grants and unspecified assistantships available. Support available to part-time students. *Unit head:* Dr. Logan Jones, Director, 816-271-4351, E-mail: jjones81@missouriwestern.edu. *Application contact:* Dr. Benjamin D. Caldwell, Dean of the Graduate School, 816-271-4394, Fax: 816-271-4525, E-mail: graduate@missouriwestern.edu.
Website: http://www.missouriwestern.edu/mba/

Molloy College, Graduate Business Program, Rockville Centre, NY 11571-5002. Offers accounting (MBA); finance (MBA, Post-Master's Certificate, Postbaccalaureate Certificate); healthcare (MBA, Post-Master's Certificate, Postbaccalaureate Certificate); management (MBA); marketing (MBA, Post-Master's Certificate, Postbaccalaureate Certificate); personal financial planning (MBA). *Program availability:* Part-time, evening/weekend. *Faculty:* 8 full-time (3 women), 7 part-time/adjunct (2 women). *Students:* 53 full-time (29 women), 175 part-time (89 women); includes 88 minority (38 Black or African American, non-Hispanic/Latino; 18 Asian, non-Hispanic/Latino; 30 Hispanic/Latino; 2 Two or more races, non-Hispanic/Latino), 3 international. Average age 39. 128 applicants, 68% accepted, 81 enrolled. In 2017, 125 master's awarded. *Entrance requirements:* Additional exam requirements/recommendations for international students: Required—TOEFL (minimum score 550 paper-based; 79 iBT). *Application deadline:* Applications are processed on a rolling basis. Application fee: $60. Electronic applications accepted. *Expenses:* Tuition: Full-time $19,980; part-time $1110 per credit. *Required fees:* $1040. Tuition and fees vary according to course load and degree level. *Financial support:* Application deadline: 3/1; applicants required to submit FAFSA. *Faculty research:* Graduate education - pedagogy and the capstone experience; Freedom of Speech in the workplace; employer liability for sexual harassment in the workplace; educational economics and industrial organization; corporate governance and distressed debt analysis; social network analysis; market segmentation. *Unit head:*

Dr. Maureen Mackenzie, Dean, Division of Business/Director of Graduate Programs, 516-323-3080, E-mail: mmackenzie@molloy.edu. *Application contact:* Jaclyn Machowicz, Assistant Director for Admissions, 516-323-4010, E-mail: jmachowicz@molloy.edu.
Website: http://www.molloy.edu/academics/graduate-programs/graduate-business

Monmouth University, Graduate Studies, Leon Hess Business School, West Long Branch, NJ 07764-1898. Offers accounting (MBA, Certificate); business administration (MBA); finance (MBA); management (MBA); marketing (MBA); real estate (MBA). *Accreditation:* AACSB. *Program availability:* Part-time, evening/weekend. *Faculty:* 20 full-time (4 women), 8 part-time/adjunct (0 women). *Students:* 101 full-time (55 women), 107 part-time (44 women); includes 19 minority (3 Black or African American, non-Hispanic/Latino; 6 Asian, non-Hispanic/Latino; 6 Hispanic/Latino; 1 Native Hawaiian or other Pacific Islander, non-Hispanic/Latino; 3 Two or more races, non-Hispanic/Latino), 13 international. Average age 30. In 2017, 61 master's, 1 other advanced degree awarded. *Degree requirements:* For master's, capstone course. *Entrance requirements:* For master's, GMAT or GRE, current resume; essay (500 words or less). Additional exam requirements/recommendations for international students: Required—TOEFL (minimum score 550 paper-based; 79 iBT), IELTS (minimum score 6), Michigan English Language Assessment Battery (minimum score 77) or Certificate of Advanced English (minimum score 160). *Application deadline:* For fall admission, 7/15 priority date for domestic students, 6/1 for international students; for spring admission, 12/1 priority date for domestic students, 11/1 for international students; for summer admission, 5/1 for domestic students. Applications are processed on a rolling basis. Application fee: $50. Electronic applications accepted. *Expenses:* Tuition: Full-time $21,366; part-time $7122 per credit. *Required fees:* $700; $175 per term. *Financial support:* In 2017–18, 42 students received support. Institutionally sponsored loans, scholarships/grants, and unspecified assistantships available. Support available to part-time students. Financial award applicants required to submit FAFSA. *Faculty research:* Information technology and marketing, behavioral research in accounting, human resources, management of technology. *Unit head:* Dr. Susan Gupta, MBA Program Director, 732-571-3639, Fax: 732-263-5517, E-mail: sgupta@monmouth.edu. *Application contact:* Laurie Kuhn, Associate Director of Graduate Admission, 732-571-3452, Fax: 732-263-5123, E-mail: gradadm@monmouth.edu.
Website: https://www.monmouth.edu/business-school/leon-hess-business-school.aspx

See Display on the next page and Close-Up on page 177.

Monroe College, King Graduate School, Bronx, NY 10468. Offers accounting (MS); business administration (MBA), including entrepreneurship, finance, general business administration, healthcare management, human resources, information technology, marketing; computer science (MS); criminal justice (MS); hospitality management (MS); public health (MPH), including biostatistics and epidemiology, community health, health administration and leadership. *Program availability:* Online learning. Application fee: $50.
Website: https://www.monroecollege.edu/Degrees/King-Graduate-School/

Montclair State University, The Graduate School, College of Humanities and Social Sciences, MA Program in Law and Governance, Montclair, NJ 07043-1624. Offers conflict management and peace studies (MA); governance, compliance and regulation (MA); intellectual property (MA); law and governance (MA); legal management (MA). *Program availability:* Part-time, evening/weekend. *Degree requirements:* For master's, thesis or comprehensive exam. *Entrance requirements:* For master's, GRE General Test, minimum cumulative GPA of 2.75 for undergraduate work, 2 letters of recommendation, essay. Additional exam requirements/recommendations for international students: Required—TOEFL (minimum score 83 iBT) or IELTS (minimum score 6.5). Electronic applications accepted.

Montclair State University, The Graduate School, Feliciano School of Business, General MBA Program, Montclair, NJ 07043-1624. Offers MBA. *Program availability:* Part-time, evening/weekend. *Degree requirements:* For master's, culminating experience. *Entrance requirements:* For master's, GMAT or GRE General Test, 2 letters of recommendation, resume, essay. Additional exam requirements/recommendations for international students: Required—TOEFL (minimum score 83 iBT), IELTS (minimum score 6.5). Electronic applications accepted. *Faculty research:* Accounting, management, marketing.

Moravian College, Graduate and Continuing Studies, Business and Management Programs, Bethlehem, PA 18018-6650. Offers accounting (MBA); business analytics (MBA); business management (MBA); health administration (MHA); healthcare management (MBA); HR leadership (MSHRM); human resource management (MBA); learning and performance management (MSHRM); supply chain management (MBA). *Program availability:* Part-time, evening/weekend. *Faculty:* 5 full-time (2 women), 9 part-time/adjunct (3 women). *Students:* 13 full-time (10 women), 80 part-time (45 women); includes 13 minority (6 Black or African American, non-Hispanic/Latino; 6 Hispanic/Latino; 1 Two or more races, non-Hispanic/Latino). Average age 31. 55 applicants, 91% accepted, 31 enrolled. In 2017, 29 master's awarded. *Entrance requirements:* For master's, current resume, official transcripts, 2 letters of recommendation. Additional exam requirements/recommendations for international students: Required—TOEFL (minimum score 550 paper-based), IELTS (minimum score 6.5). *Application deadline:* For fall admission, 8/1 priority date for domestic and international students; for spring admission, 1/1 priority date for domestic and international students; for summer admission, 5/1 priority date for domestic and international students. Applications are processed on a rolling basis. Electronic applications accepted. *Expenses:* Tuition: Full-time $15,714; part-time $2619 per course. *Required fees:* $45 per semester. Tuition and fees vary according to program. *Financial support:* In 2017–18, 3 students received support, including 2 research assistantships with full tuition reimbursements available. Financial award applicants required to submit FAFSA. *Faculty research:* Leadership, change management, human resources. *Unit head:* Dr. Liz Kleintop, Associate Chair of Graduate Business, 610-861-1400, Fax: 610-861-1466, E-mail: graduate@moravian.edu. *Application contact:* Sean Rossi, Student Experience Mentor, 610-861-1400, Fax: 610-861-1466, E-mail: graduate@moravian.edu.
Website: https://www.moravian.edu/graduate

Morehead State University, Graduate Programs, College of Business and Public Affairs, Morehead, KY 40351. Offers MA, MBA, MPA, MSIS. *Accreditation:* AACSB. *Program availability:* Part-time, evening/weekend, online learning. *Entrance requirements:* For master's, GMAT, GRE General Test, minimum GPA of 2.5 on undergraduate work. Additional exam requirements/recommendations for international students: Required—TOEFL (minimum score 525 paper-based). Electronic applications accepted. *Faculty research:* Regional economic development, accounting systems, banking market structures, macroeconomics, distance learning.

Morgan State University, School of Graduate Studies, Earl G. Graves School of Business and Management, Master of Business Administration Program, Baltimore, MD 21251. Offers MBA. *Accreditation:* AACSB. *Program availability:* Part-time, evening/weekend. *Entrance requirements:* For master's, GMAT. Additional exam requirements/recommendations for international students: Required—TOEFL (minimum score 550 paper-based). *Application deadline:* For fall admission, 2/1 priority date for domestic students; for spring admission, 10/1 priority date for domestic students. Applications are processed on a rolling basis. Application fee: $0. *Expenses:* Tuition, state resident: part-time $433 per credit. Tuition, nonresident: part-time $851 per credit. *Required fees:* $81.50 per credit. *Financial support:* Application deadline: 2/1. *Faculty research:* Total quality management, disaster management, impact of globalization, marketing of services. *Unit head:* Dr. Augustus Abbey, Department Chair, 443-885-3285, E-mail: augustus.abbey@morgan.edu. *Application contact:* Dr. Dean Campbell, Graduate Recruitment Specialist, 443-885-3185, Fax: 443-885-8226, E-mail: dean.campbell@morgan.edu.

Morgan State University, School of Graduate Studies, Earl G. Graves School of Business and Management, PhD Program in Business Administration, Baltimore, MD 21251. Offers business administration (PhD), including accounting, information systems, management and marketing. *Accreditation:* AACSB. *Entrance requirements:* For doctorate, GMAT. Additional exam requirements/recommendations for international students: Required—TOEFL (minimum score 550 paper-based). *Application deadline:* For fall admission, 2/1 priority date for domestic students; for spring admission, 10/1 priority date for domestic students. Applications are processed on a rolling basis. Application fee: $0. *Expenses:* Tuition, state resident: part-time $433 per credit. Tuition, nonresident: part-time $851 per credit. *Required fees:* $81.50 per credit. *Financial support:* Application deadline: 2/1. *Unit head:* Dr. Augustus Abbey, Department Chair, 443-885-3285, E-mail: augustus.abbey@morgan.edu. *Application contact:* Dr. Dean Campbell, Graduate Recruitment Specialist, 443-885-3185, Fax: 443-885-8226, E-mail: dean.campbell@morgan.edu.

Mount Aloysius College, Program in Business Administration, Cresson, PA 16630. Offers accounting (MBA); health and human services administration (MBA); non-profit management (MBA); project management (MBA). *Program availability:* Part-time, evening/weekend. *Entrance requirements:* Additional exam requirements/recommendations for international students: Required—IELTS (minimum score 5.5); Recommended—TOEFL. *Application deadline:* For fall admission, 8/1 for domestic students; for spring admission, 12/1 for domestic students. Applications are processed on a rolling basis. Application fee: $30. Electronic applications accepted. Application fee is waived when completed online. *Expenses: Tuition:* Full-time $14,000; part-time $790 per credit hour. *Financial support:* Unspecified assistantships available. Financial award applicants required to submit FAFSA. *Application contact:* Matthew P. Bodenschatz, Director of Graduate and Continuing Education Admissions, 814-886-6556, Fax: 814-886-6441, E-mail: mbodenschatz@mtaloy.edu.
Website: http://www.mtaloy.edu

Mount Marty College, Graduate Studies Division, Yankton, SD 57078-3724. Offers business administration (MBA); nurse anesthesia (MS); nursing (MSN); pastoral ministries (MPM). *Accreditation:* AANA/CANAEP (one or more programs are accredited). *Degree requirements:* For master's, thesis or alternative. *Entrance requirements:* For master's, GRE General Test, minimum GPA of 3.0. Electronic applications accepted. *Faculty research:* Clinical anesthesia, professional characteristics, motivations of applicants.

Mount Mary University, Graduate Programs, Program in Business Administration, Milwaukee, WI 53222-4597. Offers general management (MBA); health systems leadership (MBA). *Program availability:* Part-time, evening/weekend. *Degree requirements:* For master's, terminal project. *Entrance requirements:* For master's, minimum GPA of 2.75. Additional exam requirements/recommendations for international students: Required—TOEFL (minimum score 550 paper-based; 80 iBT); Recommended—IELTS (minimum score 6.5). Electronic applications accepted. *Expenses:* Contact institution. *Faculty research:* Economics, quantitative analysis, accounting, finance.

Mount Mercy University, Program in Business Administration, Cedar Rapids, IA 52402-4797. Offers human resource (MBA); quality management (MBA). *Program availability:* Evening/weekend. *Entrance requirements:* For master's, minimum cumulative GPA of 3.0, 2 letters of recommendation, resume. Additional exam requirements/recommendations for international students: Required—TOEFL (minimum score 570 paper-based; 88 iBT). Electronic applications accepted.

Mount St. Joseph University, Master of Business Administration Program, Cincinnati, OH 45233-1670. Offers MBA. *Program availability:* Part-time, evening/weekend. *Faculty:* 6 full-time (2 women), 4 part-time/adjunct (1 woman). *Students:* 22 full-time (6 women), 30 part-time (14 women); includes 7 minority (5 Black or African American, non-Hispanic/Latino; 1 Hispanic/Latino; 1 Two or more races, non-Hispanic/Latino), 1 international. Average age 32. In 2017, 24 master's awarded. *Degree requirements:* For master's, 15 hours of foundational course work, 36 hours of MBA coursework, minimum GPA of 3.0, integrative project. *Entrance requirements:* For master's, official undergraduate transcript with minimum cumulative GPA of 3.0; MBA Required Foundational Course form; two references; one-page personal statement; interview with MBA program director or designee. Additional exam requirements/recommendations for international students: Required—TOEFL (minimum score 560 paper-based; 83 iBT). *Application deadline:* Applications are processed on a rolling basis. Application fee: $50. Electronic applications accepted. *Expenses:* $600 per credit hour (for MBA 4+1 degree); $635 per credit hour (for MBA Saturday degree). *Financial support:* In 2017–18, 2 students received support. Scholarships/grants available. Financial award applicants required to submit FAFSA. *Faculty research:* Gender and cultural effects on management education, group identity formation, leadership skill development, methods for improving instructional effectiveness, technology-based productivity improvement. *Unit head:* Dr. Anna Goldhahn, Assistant Dean/Director of Graduate Programs, 513-244-4924, Fax: 513-244-4270, E-mail: anna.goldhahn@msj.edu. *Application contact:* Amy Wolf, Senior Admissions Counselor for Graduate Studies, 513-244-4204, Fax: 513-745-4629, E-mail: amy.wolf@msj.edu.
Website: http://www.msj.edu/academics/graduate-programs/master-of-business-administration/

Mount Saint Mary College, School of Business, Newburgh, NY 12550-3494. Offers business (MBA); financial planning (MBA); health care management (MBA). *Program availability:* Part-time, evening/weekend. *Faculty:* 4 full-time (1 woman), 8 part-time/adjunct (4 women). *Students:* 48 full-time (21 women), 30 part-time (21 women); includes 20 minority (6 Black or African American, non-Hispanic/Latino; 1 Asian, non-Hispanic/Latino; 12 Hispanic/Latino; 1 Two or more races, non-Hispanic/Latino). Average age 32. 17 applicants, 65% accepted, 6 enrolled. In 2017, 41 master's awarded. *Degree requirements:* For master's, thesis or alternative. *Entrance requirements:* For master's, GMAT or minimum undergraduate GPA of 2.7. Additional exam requirements/recommendations for international students: Required—TOEFL (minimum score 80 iBT). *Application deadline:* Applications are processed on a rolling basis. Application fee: $45. Electronic applications accepted. Application fee is waived when completed online. *Expenses: Tuition:* Full-time $14,454; part-time $803 per credit. *Required fees:* $172; $86 per semester. *Financial support:* In 2017–18, 18 students received support. Unspecified assistantships available. Financial award application deadline: 4/15; financial award applicants required to submit FAFSA. *Faculty research:* Financial reform, entrepreneurship and small business development, global business relations, technology's impact on business decision-making, college-assisted business education. *Unit head:* Dr. Moira Tolan, Graduate Coordinator, 845-569-3121, Fax: 845-562-6762, E-mail: moira.tolan@msmc.edu. *Application contact:* Lisa Alvarez, Director of

Admissions for Graduate Programs and Adult Degree Completion, 845-569-3166, Fax: 845-569-3450, E-mail: lisa.gallina@msmc.edu. Website: http://www.msmc.edu/Academics/Graduate_Programs/master_of_business_administration.be

Mount Saint Mary's University, Graduate Division, Los Angeles, CA 90049. Offers business administration (MBA); counseling psychology (MS); creative writing (MFA); education (MS, Certificate); film and television (MFA); health policy and management (MS); humanities (MA); nursing (MSN, Certificate); physical therapy (DPT); religious studies (MA). *Program availability:* Part-time, evening/weekend. *Faculty:* 50 full-time (35 women), 116 part-time/adjunct (81 women). *Students:* 670 full-time (518 women), 147 part-time (116 women); includes 414 minority (73 Black or African American, non-Hispanic/Latino; 4 American Indian or Alaska Native, non-Hispanic/Latino; 60 Asian, non-Hispanic/Latino; 259 Hispanic/Latino; 7 Native Hawaiian or other Pacific Islander, non-Hispanic/Latino; 11 Two or more races, non-Hispanic/Latino), 4 international. Average age 32. 1,398 applicants, 21% accepted, 242 enrolled. In 2017, 170 master's, 28 doctorates, 35 other advanced degrees awarded. *Entrance requirements:* Additional exam requirements/recommendations for international students: Required—TOEFL. *Application deadline:* For fall admission, 6/30 priority date for domestic and international students; for spring admission, 10/30 priority date for domestic and international students; for summer admission, 3/30 priority date for domestic and international students. Applications are processed on a rolling basis. Application fee: $50. Electronic applications accepted. *Expenses: Tuition:* Part-time $905 per unit. One-time fee: $155 part-time. Tuition and fees vary according to degree level and program. *Financial support:* Career-related internships or fieldwork, Federal Work-Study, institutionally sponsored loans, and tuition waivers (full and partial) available. Support available to part-time students. Financial award application deadline: 3/15; financial award applicants required to submit FAFSA. *Unit head:* Albert Ramos, Director of Graduate Admissions, 213-477-2800, E-mail: gradprograms@msmu.edu. *Application contact:* Shawn Peters, Graduate Admission Counselor, 213-477-2676, E-mail: gradprograms@msmu.edu. Website: http://www.msmu.edu/graduate-programs/

Mount St. Mary's University, Program in Business Administration, Emmitsburg, MD 21727-7799. Offers MBA. *Program availability:* Part-time, evening/weekend. *Degree requirements:* For master's, thesis. *Entrance requirements:* For master's, minimum undergraduate GPA of 2.75, 5 years' relevant professional business experience, or GMAT (minimum score of 500). Additional exam requirements/recommendations for international students: Required—TOEFL (minimum score 550 paper-based; 83 iBT). Electronic applications accepted. *Expenses:* Contact institution.

Mount Vernon Nazarene University, Program in Management, Mount Vernon, OH 43050-9500. Offers MSM. *Accreditation:* ACBSP. *Program availability:* Part-time, evening/weekend.

Murray State University, Arthur J. Bauernfeind College of Business, MBA Program, Murray, KY 42071. Offers accounting (MBA); finance (MBA); global communications (MBA); human resource management (MBA); marketing (MBA). *Accreditation:* AACSB. *Program availability:* Part-time, evening/weekend, 100% online, blended/hybrid learning. *Faculty:* 49 full-time (18 women), 3 part-time/adjunct (0 women). *Students:* 54 full-time (22 women), 79 part-time (37 women); includes 13 minority (6 Black or African American, non-Hispanic/Latino; 1 American Indian or Alaska Native, non-Hispanic/Latino; 2 Asian, non-Hispanic/Latino; 2 Hispanic/Latino; 2 Two or more races, non-Hispanic/Latino), 30 international. Average age 29. 70 applicants, 81% accepted, 34 enrolled. In 2017, 61 master's awarded. *Entrance requirements:* For master's, GRE or GMAT, minimum university GPA of 2.75. Additional exam requirements/recommendations for international students: Required—TOEFL (minimum score 527 paper-based; 71 iBT). *Application deadline:* Applications are processed on a rolling basis. Application fee: $40 ($50 for international students). *Expenses:* Tuition, state resident: full-time $9504. Tuition, nonresident: full-time $26,811. *International tuition:* $14,400 full-time. Tuition and fees vary according to course load, degree level and reciprocity agreements. *Financial support:* In 2017–18, 5 research assistantships, 5 teaching assistantships were awarded; Federal Work-Study also available. Financial award applicants required to submit FAFSA. *Faculty research:* Human resource management, e-commerce, supply-chain management, investment management, accounting. *Unit head:* Dr. Joy Humphreys, Assistant Dean and MBA Director, 270-809-4259, Fax: 270-809-3482, E-mail: jumphreys4@murraystate.edu. *Application contact:* Kaitlyn Burzynski, Interim Assistant Director for Graduate Admission and Records, 270-809-5732, Fax: 270-809-3780, E-mail: msu.graduateadmissions@murraystate.edu. Website: http://www.murraystate.edu/academics/CollegesDepartments/CollegeOfBusiness/Programs/mba/index.aspx

National American University, Roueche Graduate Center, Austin, TX 78731. Offers accounting (MBA); aviation management (MBA, MM); care coordination (MSN); community college leadership (Ed D); criminal justice (MM); e-marketing (MBA, MM); health care administration (MBA, MM); higher education (MM); human resources management (MBA, MM); information technology management (MBA, MM); international business (MBA); leadership (EMBA); management (MBA); nursing administration (MSN); nursing education (MSN); nursing informatics (MSN); operations and configuration management (MBA, MM); project and process management (MBA, MM). Master's programs offered online through the Harold D. Buckingham Graduate School. *Program availability:* Part-time, evening/weekend, online learning. *Entrance requirements:* For master's, minimum undergraduate GPA of 2.75. Additional exam requirements/recommendations for international students: Required—TOEFL, TWE. Electronic applications accepted. *Faculty research:* Tourism, finance, marketing.

National Louis University, College of Management and Business, Chicago, IL 60603. Offers business administration (MBA); human resource management and development (MS); management (MS). *Program availability:* Part-time, evening/weekend. *Entrance requirements:* For master's, college-administered critical thinking and writing skills test, minimum GPA of 3.0, resume, 3 references. Additional exam requirements/recommendations for international students: Required—TOEFL (minimum score 550 paper-based; 79 iBT).

National University, Academic Affairs, School of Business and Management, La Jolla, CA 92037-1011. Offers accountancy (M Acc, Certificate); business administration (GMBA, MBA); business analytics (MS); cause leadership (MA); global management (MGM); human resource management (MA); management information systems (MS); marketing (MS); organizational leadership (MS). GMBA offered in Spanish. *Program availability:* Part-time, evening/weekend, 100% online, blended/hybrid learning. *Degree requirements:* For master's, thesis (for some programs). *Entrance requirements:* For master's, interview, minimum GPA of 2.5. Additional exam requirements/recommendations for international students: Required—TOEFL (minimum score 550 paper-based; 79 iBT), IELTS (minimum score 6). *Application deadline:* Applications are processed on a rolling basis. Application fee: $60 ($65 for international students). Electronic applications accepted. *Expenses: Tuition:* Part-time $430 per quarter hour. *Financial support:* Career-related internships or fieldwork, scholarships/grants, and tuition waivers (partial) available. Support available to part-time students. Financial award application deadline: 6/30; financial award applicants required to submit FAFSA. *Unit head:* Dr. Alfred Ntoko, Dean, 858-642-8400, Fax: 858-642-8719, E-mail: sobm@nu.edu. *Application contact:* Brandon Jouganatos, Vice President for Enrollment Services, 800-628-8648, E-mail: advisor@nu.edu. Website: http://www.nu.edu/OurPrograms/SchoolOfBusinessAndManagement.html

National University College, Graduate Programs, Bayamón, PR 00960. Offers digital marketing (MBA); general business (MBA); special education (M Ed).

Naval Postgraduate School, Departments and Academic Groups, Graduate School of Business and Public Policy, Monterey, CA 93943. Offers acquisition and contract management (MBA); business administration (EMBA, MBA); contract management (MS); defense business management (MBA); defense systems analysis (MS), including management; defense systems management (international) (MBA); financial management (MBA); information management (MBA); manpower systems analysis (MS); material logistics support management (MBA); program management (MS); resource planning and management for international defense (MBA); supply chain management (MBA); systems acquisition management (MBA); transportation management (MBA). Program only open to commissioned officers of the United States and friendly nations and selected United States federal civilian employees. *Accreditation:* AACSB; NASPAA. *Program availability:* Part-time, online learning. *Degree requirements:* For master's, thesis (for some programs), terminal project/capstone (for some programs). *Faculty research:* U.S. and European public procurement policies for small and medium-sized enterprises, examining external validity criticisms in the choice of students as subjects in accounting experiment studies, assurance of learning in contract management education, contracting for cloud computing: opportunities and risks, NPS, Apple App Store as a business model supporting U.S. Navy requirements.

Nazareth College of Rochester, Graduate Studies, Department of Business, Program in Management, Rochester, NY 14618. Offers MS. *Program availability:* Part-time, evening/weekend. *Entrance requirements:* For master's, minimum GPA of 3.0. Additional exam requirements/recommendations for international students: Required—TOEFL (minimum score 550 paper-based, 79 iBT) or IELTS (6.5).

Neumann University, Graduate Programs in Business and Information Management, Aston, PA 19014-1298. Offers accounting (MS), including forensic and fraud detection; sport business (MS). *Program availability:* Part-time, evening/weekend. *Faculty:* 2 full-time (both women), 4 part-time/adjunct (1 woman). *Students:* 7 full-time (1 woman), 29 part-time (14 women); includes 12 minority (10 Black or African American, non-Hispanic/Latino; 1 Asian, non-Hispanic/Latino; 1 Hispanic/Latino). Average age 30. 35 applicants, 37% accepted, 7 enrolled. In 2017, 16 master's awarded. *Degree requirements:* For master's, thesis (for some programs). *Entrance requirements:* For master's, official transcripts from all institutions attended, resume, letter of intent, 2-3 letters of recommendation. Additional exam requirements/recommendations for international students: Required—TOEFL (minimum score 70 iBT). *Application deadline:* Applications are processed on a rolling basis. Application fee: $0. Electronic applications accepted. *Expenses:* $600 per credit hour (for accounting program); $495 per credit hour (for sport business program). *Financial support:* Scholarships/grants and health care benefits available. Support available to part-time students. Financial award application deadline: 3/15; financial award applicants required to submit FAFSA. *Unit head:* Dr. Eric R. Wellington, Dean of Business and Information Management, 610-558-5596, Fax: 610-558-5574, E-mail: wellinge@neumann.edu. *Application contact:* Dr. Erika K. Davis, Director of Adult and Graduate Admissions, 800-9-NEUMANN Ext. 5208, Fax: 610-361-2548, E-mail: gradadultadmiss@neumann.edu.

New Charter University, College of Business, Salt Lake City, UT 84101. Offers finance (MBA); health care management (MBA); management (MBA). *Program availability:* Part-time, evening/weekend, online learning. *Entrance requirements:* For master's, course work in calculus, statistics, macroeconomics. Additional exam requirements/recommendations for international students: Required—TOEFL (minimum score 550 paper-based). Electronic applications accepted.

New England College, Program in Management, Henniker, NH 03242-3293. Offers accounting (MSA); healthcare administration (MS); international relations (MA); marketing management (MS); nonprofit leadership (MS); project management (MS); strategic leadership (MS). *Program availability:* Part-time, evening/weekend. *Degree requirements:* For master's, independent research project. Electronic applications accepted.

New Jersey City University, School of Business, Jersey City, NJ 07305-1597. Offers MBA, MS, Graduate Certificate. *Accreditation:* ACBSP. *Program availability:* Part-time, evening/weekend. *Entrance requirements:* Additional exam requirements/recommendations for international students: Required—TOEFL (minimum score 79 iBT).

New Jersey Institute of Technology, Martin Tuchman School of Management, Newark, NJ 07102. Offers business administration (MBA); business data science (PhD); finance for managers (Certificate); management (MS); management essentials (Certificate); management of technology (Certificate). *Accreditation:* AACSB. *Program availability:* Part-time, evening/weekend. *Students:* Average age 31. 385 applicants, 52% accepted, 80 enrolled. In 2017, 81 master's, 11 other advanced degrees awarded. Terminal master's awarded for partial completion of doctoral program. *Degree requirements:* For master's, thesis optional. *Entrance requirements:* For doctorate, GRE General Test, minimum graduate GPA of 3.5. Additional exam requirements/recommendations for international students: Required—TOEFL (minimum score 550 paper-based; 79 iBT). *Application deadline:* For fall admission, 6/1 priority date for domestic students, 5/1 priority date for international students; for spring admission, 11/15 priority date for domestic and international students. Applications are processed on a rolling basis. Application fee: $75. Electronic applications accepted. *Expenses:* Contact institution. *Financial support:* In 2017–18, 7 students received support, including 1 fellowship (averaging $900 per year), 3 research assistantships (averaging $13,701 per year), 10 teaching assistantships (averaging $25,653 per year); career-related internships or fieldwork, Federal Work-Study, institutionally sponsored loans, and unspecified assistantships also available. Financial award application deadline: 1/15. *Faculty research:* Manufacturing systems analysis, earnings management, knowledge-based view of the firm, data envelopment analysis, human factors in human/machine systems. *Unit head:* Dr. Reggie Caudill, Interim Dean, 973-596-5856, Fax: 973-596-3074, E-mail: reggie.j.caudill@njit.edu. *Application contact:* Stephen Eck, Director of Admissions, 973-596-3300, Fax: 973-596-3461, E-mail: admissions@njit.edu. Website: http://management.njit.edu

New Jersey Institute of Technology, Ying Wu College of Computing, Newark, NJ 07102. Offers big data management and mining (Certificate); business and information systems (Certificate); computer science (MS, PhD), including bioinformatics (MS), computer science, computing and business (MS), cyber security and privacy (MS), software engineering (MS); data mining (Certificate); information security (Certificate); information systems (MS, PhD), including business and information systems (MS), emergency management and business continuity (MS), information systems; information technology administration and security (MS); IT administration (Certificate); network security and information assurance (Certificate); software engineering analysis/design (Certificate); Web systems development (Certificate). *Program availability:* Part-time, evening/weekend. *Faculty:* 64 full-time (10 women), 38 part-time/adjunct (4

Business Administration and Management—General

women). *Students:* 818 full-time (241 women), 225 part-time (53 women); includes 162 minority (35 Black or African American, non-Hispanic/Latino; 77 Asian, non-Hispanic/Latino; 41 Hispanic/Latino; 9 Two or more races, non-Hispanic/Latino), 772 international. Average age 27. 2,666 applicants, 51% accepted, 377 enrolled. In 2017, 398 master's, 10 doctorates, 9 other advanced degrees awarded. Terminal master's awarded for partial completion of doctoral program. *Degree requirements:* For master's, thesis optional; for doctorate, thesis/dissertation. *Entrance requirements:* For master's, GRE General Test; for doctorate, GRE General Test, minimum graduate GPA of 3.5. Additional exam requirements/recommendations for international students: Required—TOEFL (minimum score 550 paper-based; 79 iBT). *Application deadline:* For fall admission, 6/1 priority date for domestic students, 5/1 priority date for international students; for spring admission, 11/15 priority date for domestic and international students. Applications are processed on a rolling basis. Application fee: $75. Electronic applications accepted. *Expenses:* Contact institution. *Financial support:* In 2017–18, 57 students received support, including 2 fellowships (averaging $23,254 per year), 47 research assistantships (averaging $24,412 per year), 44 teaching assistantships (averaging $23,528 per year); career-related internships or fieldwork, Federal Work-Study, institutionally sponsored loans, and unspecified assistantships also available. Financial award application deadline: 1/15. *Faculty research:* Computer systems, communications and networking, artificial intelligence, database engineering, systems analysis, analytics and optimization in crowdsourcing. *Total annual research expenditures:* $3 million. *Unit head:* Dr. Craig Gotsman, Dean, 973-542-5488, Fax: 973-596-5777, E-mail: marek.rusinkiewicz@njit.edu. *Application contact:* Stephen Eck, Director of Admissions, 973-596-3300, Fax: 973-596-3461, E-mail: admissions@njit.edu.
Website: http://computing.njit.edu/

Newman University, MBA Program, Wichita, KS 67213-2097. Offers finance (MBA); international business (MBA); leadership (MBA); management (MBA); management information technology (MBA). *Program availability:* Part-time. *Degree requirements:* For master's, thesis optional. *Entrance requirements:* For master's, minimum GPA of 3.0; 2 letters of recommendation; course work in algebra, statistics, macroeconomics, and financial accounting. Additional exam requirements/recommendations for international students: Required—TOEFL (minimum score 600 paper-based; 100 iBT). Electronic applications accepted. *Expenses:* Contact institution.

New Mexico Highlands University, Graduate Studies, School of Business, Media and Technology, Las Vegas, NM 87701. Offers business administration (MBA), including human resource management, international business, management; media arts and technology (MA), including media arts and computer science. *Accreditation:* ACBSP. *Degree requirements:* For master's, comprehensive exam, thesis or alternative. *Entrance requirements:* For master's, minimum undergraduate GPA of 3.0. Additional exam requirements/recommendations for international students: Required—TOEFL (minimum score 540 paper-based). *Faculty research:* Real estate valuation, studying expert judgments in complex accounting, decision environments, green marketing, environmentalism, marketing research methodology.

New Mexico State University, College of Business, Department of Management, Las Cruces, NM 88003. Offers PhD. *Faculty:* 8 full-time (2 women). *Students:* 8 full-time (6 women), 2 part-time (1 woman); includes 5 minority (1 American Indian or Alaska Native, non-Hispanic/Latino; 2 Asian, non-Hispanic/Latino; 2 Hispanic/Latino), 2 international. Average age 39. 19 applicants, 100% accepted. In 2017, 5 doctorates awarded. *Entrance requirements:* For doctorate, GMAT (preferred) or GRE. Additional exam requirements/recommendations for international students: Required—TOEFL (minimum score 550 paper-based; 79 iBT), IELTS (minimum score 6.5). *Application deadline:* For fall admission, 2/15 for domestic and international students. Application fee: $40 ($50 for international students). Electronic applications accepted. *Expenses:* Tuition, state resident: full-time $4390. Tuition, nonresident: full-time $15,309. *Required fees:* $853. *Financial support:* In 2017–18, 8 students received support, including 3 fellowships (averaging $4,390 per year), 7 teaching assistantships (averaging $23,234 per year); career-related internships or fieldwork, Federal Work-Study, scholarships/grants, traineeships, health care benefits, and unspecified assistantships also available. Support available to part-time students. Financial award application deadline: 3/1. *Faculty research:* Supply chain management and integration; enterprise systems; organizational behavior; production/operations; human resource management; entrepreneurship; operations management; electronic commerce; policy and strategy; information systems; governance mechanisms; partnerships and collaborative networks; compensation and staffing; employee safety and attachment; research methodology; critical postmodern studies; storytelling, ethnography, content analysis, deconstruction, and rhetorical analysis. *Unit head:* Dr. Harikumar Sankaran, Interim Department Head, 575-646-1201, Fax: 575-646-1372, E-mail: sankaran@nmsu.edu. *Application contact:* Dr. William L. Smith, Director, Management PhD Program, 575-646-1422, Fax: 575-646-1372, E-mail: smith@nmsu.edu.
Website: http://business.nmsu.edu/departments/mgt

New Mexico State University, College of Business, Department of Marketing, Las Cruces, NM 88003. Offers business administration (PhD), including marketing. *Program availability:* Part-time. *Faculty:* 5 full-time (1 woman). *Students:* 9 full-time (6 women), 3 part-time (2 women); includes 3 minority (2 Hispanic/Latino; 1 Two or more races, non-Hispanic/Latino), 6 international. Average age 35. 18 applicants, 44% accepted, 4 enrolled. In 2017, 1 doctorate awarded. *Entrance requirements:* For doctorate, GMAT or GRE, graduate degree, work experience. Additional exam requirements/recommendations for international students: Required—TOEFL (minimum score 550 paper-based; 79 iBT), IELTS (minimum score 6.5). *Application deadline:* For fall admission, 2/1 for domestic and international students. Application fee: $40 ($50 for international students). Electronic applications accepted. *Expenses:* Tuition, state resident: full-time $4390. Tuition, nonresident: full-time $15,309. *Required fees:* $853. *Financial support:* In 2017–18, 9 students received support, including 2 fellowships (averaging $4,390 per year), 8 teaching assistantships (averaging $21,775 per year); career-related internships or fieldwork, Federal Work-Study, scholarships/grants, traineeships, health care benefits, and unspecified assistantships also available. Support available to part-time students. Financial award application deadline: 3/1. *Faculty research:* Consumer behavior, social media marketing, ethics in marketing, advertising, public policy. *Unit head:* Dr. Nancy Oretskin, Interim Department Head, 575-646-3341, Fax: 575-646-1498, E-mail: noretski@nmsu.edu.
Website: http://business.nmsu.edu/departments/marketing

New Mexico State University, College of Business, MBA Program, Las Cruces, NM 88003. Offers agribusiness (MBA); finance (MBA); information systems (MBA). *Accreditation:* AACSB. *Program availability:* Part-time-only, evening/weekend, online with required 2-3 day orientation and 2-3 day concluding session in Las Cruces. *Students:* 47 full-time (24 women), 123 part-time (74 women); includes 98 minority (2 Black or African American, non-Hispanic/Latino; 3 American Indian or Alaska Native, non-Hispanic/Latino; 4 Asian, non-Hispanic/Latino; 85 Hispanic/Latino; 1 Native Hawaiian or other Pacific Islander, non-Hispanic/Latino; 3 Two or more races, non-Hispanic/Latino), 6 international. Average age 33. 166 applicants, 82% accepted, 19 enrolled. In 2017, 79 master's awarded. *Entrance requirements:* For master's, GMAT or GRE (depending upon undergraduate or graduate degree institution and GPA),

minimum GPA of 3.5 from AACSB international or ACBSP-accredited institution or graduate degree from regionally-accredited U.S. university (without GMAT or GRE). Additional exam requirements/recommendations for international students: Required—TOEFL (minimum score 550 paper-based; 79 iBT), IELTS (minimum score 6.5). *Application deadline:* For fall admission, 7/15 priority date for domestic students, 4/15 priority date for international students; for spring admission, 4/15 priority date for domestic students, 9/15 priority date for international students; for summer admission, 4/15 for domestic students, 1/15 for international students. Applications are processed on a rolling basis. Application fee: $40 ($50 for international students). Electronic applications accepted. *Expenses:* Tuition, state resident: full-time $4390. Tuition, nonresident: full-time $15,309. *Required fees:* $853. *Financial support:* In 2017–18, 29 students received support. Fellowships, Federal Work-Study, institutionally sponsored loans, scholarships/grants, health care benefits, and unspecified assistantships available. Financial award application deadline: 3/1. *Unit head:* Dr. Kathy Brook, Associate Dean, 575-646-8003, Fax: 575-646-7977, E-mail: kbrook@nmsu.edu. *Application contact:* John Shonk, MBA Advisor, 575-646-8003, Fax: 575-646-7977, E-mail: mbaprog@nmsu.edu.
Website: http://business.nmsu.edu/mba

New York Institute of Technology, School of Management, Department of Business Administration, Old Westbury, NY 11568-8000. Offers executive management (MBA), including finance, marketing, operations and supply chain management. *Accreditation:* AACSB. *Program availability:* Part-time. *Faculty:* 25 full-time (4 women), 20 part-time/adjunct (6 women). *Students:* 398 full-time (187 women), 138 part-time (63 women); includes 43 minority (9 Black or African American, non-Hispanic/Latino; 1 American Indian or Alaska Native, non-Hispanic/Latino; 22 Asian, non-Hispanic/Latino; 9 Hispanic/Latino; 2 Two or more races, non-Hispanic/Latino), 432 international. Average age 26. 635 applicants, 75% accepted, 196 enrolled. In 2017, 230 master's awarded. *Entrance requirements:* For master's, bachelor's degree; minimum undergraduate GPA of 3.0. Additional exam requirements/recommendations for international students: Required—TOEFL (minimum score 79 iBT), IELTS (minimum score 6). *Application deadline:* Applications are processed on a rolling basis. Application fee: $50. Electronic applications accepted. *Expenses:* $1,285 per credit plus fees. *Financial support:* Career-related internships or fieldwork, Federal Work-Study, scholarships/grants, tuition waivers (full and partial), and unspecified assistantships available. Support available to part-time students. Financial award application deadline: 2/15; financial award applicants required to submit FAFSA. *Faculty research:* Accounting, economics, finance, management, marketing. *Unit head:* Dr. Jess Boronico, Dean, 516-686-7838, E-mail: som@nyit.edu. *Application contact:* Alice Dolitsky, Director, Graduate Admissions, 516-686-7520, Fax: 516-686-1116, E-mail: nyitgrad@nyit.edu.
Website: http://www.nyit.edu/degrees/management_mba

New York Medical College, School of Health Sciences and Practice, Valhalla, NY 10595. Offers behavioral sciences and health promotion (MPH); biostatistics (MS); children with special health care (Graduate Certificate); emergency preparedness (Graduate Certificate); environmental health science (MPH); epidemiology (MPH, MS); global health (Graduate Certificate); health education (Graduate Certificate); health policy and management (MPH, Dr PH); industrial hygiene (Graduate Certificate); pediatric dysphagia (Post-Graduate Certificate); physical therapy (DPT); public health (Graduate Certificate); speech-language pathology (MS). *Accreditation:* CEPH. *Program availability:* Part-time, evening/weekend, 100% online, blended/hybrid learning. *Faculty:* 48 full-time (33 women), 235 part-time/adjunct (141 women). *Students:* 221 full-time (153 women), 270 part-time (194 women); includes 202 minority (83 Black or African American, non-Hispanic/Latino; 2 American Indian or Alaska Native, non-Hispanic/Latino; 64 Asian, non-Hispanic/Latino; 47 Hispanic/Latino; 1 Native Hawaiian or other Pacific Islander, non-Hispanic/Latino; 5 Two or more races, non-Hispanic/Latino), 19 international. Average age 29. 1,118 applicants, 38% accepted, 169 enrolled. In 2017, 110 master's, 41 doctorates awarded. *Degree requirements:* For master's, comprehensive exam (for some programs), thesis (for some programs); for doctorate, thesis/dissertation. *Entrance requirements:* For master's, GRE (for MS in speech-language pathology); for doctorate, GRE. Additional exam requirements/recommendations for international students: Required—TOEFL, IELTS. *Application deadline:* For fall admission, 8/1 for domestic students, 4/15 for international students; for spring admission, 12/1 for domestic students; for summer admission, 5/1 for domestic students, 4/15 for international students. Application fee: $125. Electronic applications accepted. *Expenses:* $1,125 per credit, $245 fees. *Financial support:* In 2017–18, 10,000 students received support. Scholarships/grants and unspecified assistantships available. Financial award application deadline: 4/30; financial award applicants required to submit FAFSA. *Unit head:* Ben Watson, PhD, Vice Dean, 914-594-4531, E-mail: ben_watson@nymc.edu. *Application contact:* Irene Bundziak, Assistant to Director of Admissions, 914-594-4905, E-mail: irene_bundziak@nymc.edu.
Website: http://www.nymc.edu/school-of-health-sciences-and-practice-shsp/

New York University, Leonard N. Stern School of Business, Department of Marketing, New York, NY 10012-1019. Offers entertainment, media and technology (MBA); general marketing (MBA); marketing (PhD); product management (MBA). *Expenses:* Tuition: Full-time $41,352; part-time $19,968 per year. *Required fees:* $2496; $1628 per unit. $814 per term. Tuition and fees vary according to course load and program.

New York University, School of Law, New York, NY 10012-1019. Offers law (LL M, JD, JSD); law and business (Advanced Certificate); taxation (MSL, Advanced Certificate); JD/LL M; JD/MA; JD/MBA; JD/MPA; JD/MPP; JD/MSW; JD/MUP; JD/PhD. *Accreditation:* ABA. *Program availability:* Part-time, blended/hybrid learning. *Faculty:* 158 full-time (51 women), 204 part-time/adjunct (55 women). *Students:* 1,364 full-time (728 women); includes 394 minority (72 Black or African American, non-Hispanic/Latino; 147 Asian, non-Hispanic/Latino; 124 Hispanic/Latino; 51 Two or more races, non-Hispanic/Latino), 127 international. 6,534 applicants, 427 enrolled. In 2017, 516 master's, 484 doctorates awarded. *Entrance requirements:* For doctorate, LSAT (for JD). *Application deadline:* For fall admission, 2/15 for domestic students. Applications are processed on a rolling basis. Application fee: $85. Electronic applications accepted. *Expenses:* Contact institution. *Financial support:* Fellowships, research assistantships, teaching assistantships, career-related internships or fieldwork, Federal Work-Study, scholarships/grants, and loan repayment assistance available. Financial award application deadline: 4/15; financial award applicants required to submit FAFSA. *Faculty research:* International law, environmental law, corporate law, globalization of law, philosophy of law. *Unit head:* Trevor Morrison, Dean, 212-998-6000, Fax: 212-995-3150. *Application contact:* Cassandra Williams, Assistant Dean for Admissions, 212-998-6060, Fax: 212-995-4527.
Website: http://www.law.nyu.edu/

New York University, Tandon School of Engineering, Department of Technology Management, New York, NY 10012-1019. Offers industrial engineering (MS); management (MS); management of technology (MS); manufacturing engineering (MS); organizational behavior (MS); technology management (MBA, PhD). *Program availability:* Part-time, evening/weekend. *Faculty:* 10 full-time (2 women), 38 part-time/adjunct (4 women). *Students:* 313 full-time (132 women), 118 part-time (41 women); includes 58 minority (13 Black or African American, non-Hispanic/Latino; 25 Asian, non-Hispanic/Latino; 19 Hispanic/Latino; 1 Two or more races, non-Hispanic/Latino), 338

international. Average age 26. 976 applicants, 44% accepted, 104 enrolled. In 2017, 287 master's, 1 doctorate awarded. *Entrance requirements:* For master's, GMAT, minimum B average in undergraduate course work. Additional exam requirements/recommendations for international students: Required—TOEFL (minimum score 550 paper-based; 90 iBT); Recommended—IELTS (minimum score 7). *Application deadline:* For fall admission, 2/15 priority date for domestic and international students; for spring admission, 11/1 priority date for domestic and international students. Applications are processed on a rolling basis. Application fee: $75. Electronic applications accepted. *Expenses:* $1,720 per credit tuition plus $89 per credit fees. *Financial support:* In 2017–18, 1 fellowship (averaging $26,400 per year) was awarded; research assistantships, teaching assistantships, institutionally sponsored loans, scholarships/grants, and unspecified assistantships also available. Support available to part-time students. Financial award applicants required to submit FAFSA. *Faculty research:* Global innovation and research and development strategy, managing emerging technologies, technology and development, service design and innovation, tech entrepreneurship and commercialization, sustainable and clean-tech innovation, impacts of information technology upon individuals, organizations and society. *Total annual research expenditures:* $2.9 million. *Unit head:* Dr. Bharadwaj Rao, Head, 646-997-3617, E-mail: bharat.rao@nyu.edu. *Application contact:* Elizabeth Ensweiler, Senior Director of Graduate Enrollment and Graduate Admissions, 646-997-3182, E-mail: elizabeth.ensweiler@nyu.edu.
Website: http://www.poly.edu/academics/departments/technology/

Niagara University, Graduate Division of Business Administration, Niagara University, NY 14109. Offers accounting (MBA); business administration (MBA); finance (MBA, MS); financial planning (MBA); healthcare administration (MBA, MHA); human resources (MBA); international business (MBA); marketing (MBA); professional accountancy (MBA); strategic management (MBA); supply chain management (MBA). *Accreditation:* AACSB. *Program availability:* Part-time, evening/weekend. *Faculty:* 17 full-time, 11 part-time/adjunct. *Students:* 173 full-time (92 women), 77 part-time (39 women); includes 38 minority (8 Black or African American, non-Hispanic/Latino; 3 American Indian or Alaska Native, non-Hispanic/Latino; 8 Asian, non-Hispanic/Latino; 8 Hispanic/Latino; 11 Two or more races, non-Hispanic/Latino), 46 international. Average age 27. In 2017, 139 master's awarded. *Entrance requirements:* For master's, GMAT. Additional exam requirements/recommendations for international students: Required—TOEFL (minimum score 550 paper-based; 79 iBT), IELTS (minimum score 6). *Application deadline:* For fall admission, 8/1 for domestic students; for spring admission, 11/1 for domestic students. Applications are processed on a rolling basis. Electronic applications accepted. *Expenses:* Contact institution. *Financial support:* Fellowships, research assistantships, career-related internships or fieldwork, and Federal Work-Study available. Support available to part-time students. Financial award application deadline: 4/15; financial award applicants required to submit FAFSA. *Faculty research:* Capital flows, Federal Reserve policy, human resource management, public policy, issues in marketing, auctions, economics of information, risk and capital markets, management strategy, consumer behavior, Internet and social media marketing. *Unit head:* Dr. Paul Richardson, MBA Director/Chair of the Marketing Department, 716-286-8169, Fax: 716-286-8206, E-mail: psr@niagara.edu. *Application contact:* Evan Pierce, Associate Director for Graduate Recruitment, 716-286-8769, Fax: 716-286-8170, E-mail: epierce@niagara.edu.
Website: http://mba.niagara.edu

Nicholls State University, Graduate Studies, College of Business Administration, Thibodaux, LA 70310. Offers MBA. *Accreditation:* AACSB. *Program availability:* Part-time, evening/weekend. *Degree requirements:* For master's, thesis optional. *Entrance requirements:* For master's, GMAT. Additional exam requirements/recommendations for international students: Required—TOEFL (minimum score 550 paper-based). Electronic applications accepted.

Nichols College, Graduate and Professional Studies, Dudley, MA 01571-5000. Offers business administration (MBA); counterterrorism (MS); organizational leadership (MSOL). *Program availability:* Part-time, evening/weekend, online learning. *Degree requirements:* For master's, project (for MOL). *Entrance requirements:* For master's, 2 letters of recommendation, current resume, official transcripts, 800-word personal statement. Additional exam requirements/recommendations for international students: Required—TOEFL (minimum score 500 paper-based). Electronic applications accepted.

North Carolina Agricultural and Technical State University, School of Graduate Studies, School of Business and Economics, Greensboro, NC 27411. Offers accounting (MBA); business education (MAT); human resources management (MBA); supply chain systems (MBA).

North Carolina Central University, School of Business, Durham, NC 27707-3129. Offers MBA. *Accreditation:* AACSB. *Program availability:* Part-time, evening/weekend. *Entrance requirements:* For master's, GMAT. Additional exam requirements/recommendations for international students: Required—TOEFL. *Application deadline:* For fall admission, 8/1 for domestic students. Application fee: $30. *Expenses:* Tuition, state resident: full-time $2770; part-time $692.50 per credit hour. Tuition, nonresident: full-time $9247; part-time $2311.75 per credit hour. *Financial support:* Teaching assistantships, Federal Work-Study, institutionally sponsored loans, and unspecified assistantships available. Support available to part-time students. Financial award application deadline: 5/1; financial award applicants required to submit FAFSA. *Unit head:* Sharon D. White, Graduate Program Director, 919-530-6404, Fax: 919-530-6163, E-mail: sharon.white@nccu.edu. *Application contact:* Sharon D. White, Graduate Program Director, 919-530-6404, Fax: 919-530-6163, E-mail: sharon.white@nccu.edu.
Website: http://www.nccu.edu/business

North Carolina State University, Graduate School, Poole College of Management, Program in Business Administration, Raleigh, NC 27695. Offers biosciences management (MBA); entrepreneurship and technology commercialization (MBA); financial management (MBA); innovation management (MBA); marketing management (MBA); services management (MBA); supply chain management (MBA). *Accreditation:* AACSB. *Program availability:* Part-time. *Degree requirements:* For master's, thesis optional. *Entrance requirements:* For master's, GMAT, interview, 3 letters of recommendation. Additional exam requirements/recommendations for international students: Required—TOEFL (minimum score 600 paper-based; 100 iBT). Electronic applications accepted. *Faculty research:* Manufacturing strategy, information systems, technology commercialization, managing research and development, historical stock returns.

North Central College, School of Graduate and Professional Studies, Program in Business Administration, Naperville, IL 60566-7063. Offers change management (MBA); finance (MBA); human resource management (MBA); management (MBA). *Program availability:* Part-time, evening/weekend. *Degree requirements:* For master's, thesis optional, project. *Entrance requirements:* For master's, interview. Additional exam requirements/recommendations for international students: Required—TOEFL (minimum score 550 paper-based; 80 iBT), IELTS (minimum score 6.5). Electronic applications accepted. Application fee is waived when completed online. *Expenses:* Contact institution.

North Central College, School of Graduate and Professional Studies, Program in Leadership Studies, Naperville, IL 60566-7063. Offers MLD. *Program availability:* Part-time, evening/weekend. *Degree requirements:* For master's, thesis optional, project. *Entrance requirements:* For master's, interview. Additional exam requirements/recommendations for international students: Required—TOEFL (minimum score 550 paper-based; 80 iBT), IELTS (minimum score 6.5). Electronic applications accepted. Application fee is waived when completed online. *Expenses:* Contact institution.

Northcentral University, Graduate Studies, San Diego, CA 92106. Offers business (MBA, DBA, PhD, Postbaccalaureate Certificate); education (M Ed, Ed D, PhD, Ed S, Post-Master's Certificate, Postbaccalaureate Certificate); marriage and family therapy (MA, DMFT, PhD, Post-Master's Certificate, Postbaccalaureate Certificate); psychology (MA, PhD, Post-Master's Certificate, Postbaccalaureate Certificate); technology (MS, PhD), including computer science, cybersecurity (MS), data science, technology and innovation management (PhD). *Program availability:* Part-time, evening/weekend, online only, 100% online. *Faculty:* 98 full-time (63 women), 385 part-time/adjunct (203 women). *Students:* 5,036 full-time (3,291 women), 5,747 part-time (3,977 women); includes 3,777 minority (2,550 Black or African American, non-Hispanic/Latino; 76 American Indian or Alaska Native, non-Hispanic/Latino; 192 Asian, non-Hispanic/Latino; 603 Hispanic/Latino; 39 Native Hawaiian or other Pacific Islander, non-Hispanic/Latino; 317 Two or more races, non-Hispanic/Latino). Average age 45. In 2017, 929 master's, 782 doctorates, 278 other advanced degrees awarded. *Degree requirements:* For doctorate, comprehensive exam, thesis/dissertation. *Entrance requirements:* For master's, bachelor's degree from regionally- or nationally-accredited institution, current resume or curriculum vitae, statement of intent, interview, and background check (for marriage and family therapy); for doctorate, post-baccalaureate master's degree and/or doctoral degree from nationally- or regionally-accredited academic institution; for other advanced degree, bachelor's-level or higher degree from accredited institution or university (for Post-Baccalaureate Certificate); master's and/or doctoral degree from regionally- or nationally-accredited academic institution (for Post-Master's Certificate). Additional exam requirements/recommendations for international students: Required—TOEFL (minimum score 550 paper-based; 79 iBT), IELTS (minimum score 6.5), PTE (minimum score 53). *Application deadline:* Applications are processed on a rolling basis. Application fee: $0. Electronic applications accepted. Tuition and fees vary according to program. *Financial support:* Scholarships/grants available. *Faculty research:* Business management, curriculum and instruction, educational leadership, health psychology, organizational behavior. *Unit head:* Dr. David Harpool, Acting Provost, 888-327-2877 Ext. 8181, E-mail: provost@ncu.edu. *Application contact:* Ken Boutelle, Vice President, Enrollment Services, 888-628-4979, E-mail: enrollmentservices@ncu.edu.

★ **North Dakota State University,** College of Graduate and Interdisciplinary Studies, College of Business, Fargo, ND 58102. Offers accountancy (M Acc); business administration (MBA). *Accreditation:* AACSB. *Program availability:* Part-time, evening/weekend. *Entrance requirements:* For master's, GMAT. Additional exam requirements/recommendations for international students: Required—TOEFL (minimum score 550 paper-based; 79 iBT). Electronic applications accepted. *Faculty research:* Labor management, operations, international finance, agency, Internet marketing.

See Display on the next page and Close-Up on page 179.

Northeastern Illinois University, College of Graduate Studies and Research, College of Business and Management, MBA Program, Chicago, IL 60625. Offers MBA. *Expenses:* Tuition, state resident: full-time $7274; part-time $404.11 per credit hour. Tuition, nonresident: full-time $14,548; part-time $808.23 per credit hour. *Required fees:* $1284. *Unit head:* Dr. Jian Li, Coordinator/Advisor, 773-442-6129, E-mail: j-li3@neiu.edu. *Application contact:* Martha Narvaez, Graduate Admission Representative, 773-442-6006, E-mail: m-narvaez@neiu.edu.

Northeastern State University, College of Business and Technology, Master of Business Administration Program, Tahlequah, OK 74464-2399. Offers MBA. *Accreditation:* ACBSP. *Program availability:* Part-time, evening/weekend. *Faculty:* 6 full-time (1 woman), 1 part-time/adjunct (0 women). *Students:* 22 full-time (11 women), 32 part-time (17 women); includes 28 minority (4 Black or African American, non-Hispanic/Latino; 12 American Indian or Alaska Native, non-Hispanic/Latino; 2 Asian, non-Hispanic/Latino; 3 Hispanic/Latino; 7 Two or more races, non-Hispanic/Latino), 2 international. Average age 32. In 2017, 47 master's awarded. *Degree requirements:* For master's, comprehensive exam, thesis, business plan, oral exam. *Entrance requirements:* For master's, GMAT, minimum GPA of 2.5. Additional exam requirements/recommendations for international students: Required—TOEFL. *Application deadline:* For fall admission, 6/1 priority date for domestic students. Applications are processed on a rolling basis. Application fee: $25. Electronic applications accepted. *Expenses:* Tuition, state resident: part-time $222 per credit hour. Tuition, nonresident: part-time $501.75 per credit hour. *Required fees:* $37.40 per credit hour. Tuition and fees vary according to degree level. *Financial support:* Teaching assistantships and Federal Work-Study available. Financial award application deadline: 3/1. *Unit head:* Dr. Sandra Edwards, Director, Business and Technology Graduate Studies, 918-449-6542, E-mail: edwar001@nsuok.edu. *Application contact:* Josh McCollum, Graduate Coordinator, 918-444-2093, E-mail: mccolluj@nsuok.edu.
Website: http://academics.nsuok.edu/businesstechnology/Graduate/MBA.aspx

Northeastern State University, College of Business and Technology, Professional Master of Business Administration Program, Tahlequah, OK 74464-2399. Offers PMBA. *Program availability:* Part-time. *Faculty:* 4 full-time (1 woman). *Students:* 2 full-time (0 women), 20 part-time (9 women); includes 8 minority (1 Black or African American, non-Hispanic/Latino; 4 American Indian or Alaska Native, non-Hispanic/Latino; 3 Hispanic/Latino), 1 international. Average age 34. In 2017, 6 master's awarded. *Degree requirements:* For master's, integrative project or research. *Application deadline:* Applications are processed on a rolling basis. Application fee: $25. Electronic applications accepted. *Expenses:* Tuition, state resident: part-time $222 per credit hour. Tuition, nonresident: part-time $501.75 per credit hour. *Required fees:* $37.40 per credit hour. Tuition and fees vary according to degree level. *Unit head:* Dr. Sandra Edwards, Director, Business and Technology Graduate Studies, 918-449-6542, E-mail: edwar001@nsuok.edu. *Application contact:* Josh McCollum, Graduate Coordinator, 918-444-2093, E-mail: mccolluj@nsuok.edu.
Website: http://academics.nsuok.edu/businesstechnology/Graduate/PMBA.aspx

Northeastern University, Bouvé College of Health Sciences, Boston, MA 02115-5096. Offers applied behavior analysis (MS); audiology (Au D); counseling psychology (MS, PhD, CAGS); exercise science (MS); nursing (MS, PhD, CAGS), including administration (MS), adult-gerontology acute care nurse practitioner (MS, CAGS), adult-gerontology primary care nurse practitioner (MS, CAGS), anesthesia (MS), family nurse practitioner (MS, CAGS), neonatal nurse practitioner (MS, CAGS), pediatric nurse practitioner (MS, CAGS), psychiatric mental health nurse practitioner (MS, CAGS); nursing practice (DNP); pharmaceutical sciences (MS, PhD), including interdisciplinary concentration, pharmaceutics and drug delivery systems; pharmacology (MS); pharmacy (Pharm D); school psychology (PhD); speech-language pathology (MS); urban health (MPH); MS/MBA. *Accreditation:* ACPE (one or more programs are accredited). *Program availability:* Part-time, evening/weekend, online learning. *Faculty:*

Business Administration and Management—General

192 full-time. *Students:* 1,685. In 2017, 352 master's, 312 doctorates, 25 other advanced degrees awarded. *Degree requirements:* For doctorate, thesis/dissertation (for some programs); for CAGS, comprehensive exam. Application fee: $75. Electronic applications accepted. *Expenses:* Contact institution. *Financial support:* Fellowships, research assistantships, teaching assistantships, career-related internships or fieldwork, scholarships/grants, health care benefits, tuition waivers, and unspecified assistantships available. Support available to part-time students. Financial award applicants required to submit FAFSA. *Unit head:* Susan L. Parish, Dean, Bouve College of Health Sciences, 617-373-3321, Fax: 617-373-3030, E-mail: s.parish@northeastern.edu. *Application contact:* 617-373-2708, Fax: 617-373-4701, E-mail: bouvegrad@northeastern.edu.
Website: https://www.northeastern.edu/bouve/

Northeastern University, D'Amore-McKim School of Business, Boston, MA 02115-5096. Offers accounting (MS); business administration (EMBA, MBA); finance (MS); innovation (MS); international business (MS); international management (MS); taxation (MS); technological entrepreneurship (MS); JD/MBA; LL M/MBA; MBA/MSN; MS/MBA. *Accreditation:* AACSB. *Program availability:* Part-time, evening/weekend, online learning. *Faculty:* 184. *Students:* 1,489. In 2017, 800 master's awarded. *Entrance requirements:* For master's, GMAT or GRE. Application fee: $75. Electronic applications accepted. *Expenses:* Contact institution. *Financial support:* Scholarships/grants available. Financial award applicants required to submit FAFSA. *Unit head:* Dr. Raj Echambadi, Dean, D'Amore-McKim School of Business, 617-373-3232, Fax: 617-373-2056. *Application contact:* Evelyn Tate, Director, Graduate Recruitment and Admissions, 617-373-3258, E-mail: e.tate@northeastern.edu.
Website: http://damore-mckim.northeastern.edu/

Northern Arizona University, The W. A. Franke College of Business, Flagstaff, AZ 86011. Offers business administration (MBA); business foundations (Graduate Certificate). *Accreditation:* AACSB. *Program availability:* Part-time, 100% online, blended/hybrid learning. *Faculty:* 88 full-time (33 women), 21 part-time/adjunct (9 women). *Students:* 26 full-time (13 women), 1 (woman) part-time; includes 8 minority (1 Black or African American, non-Hispanic/Latino; 1 Asian, non-Hispanic/Latino; 2 Hispanic/Latino; 1 Native Hawaiian or other Pacific Islander, non-Hispanic/Latino; 3 Two or more races, non-Hispanic/Latino), 2 international. Average age 23. 77 applicants, 45% accepted, 35 enrolled. In 2017, 31 master's awarded. *Degree requirements:* For master's, variable foreign language requirement, comprehensive exam (for some programs), thesis (for some programs); for Graduate Certificate, comprehensive exam (for some programs). *Entrance requirements:* For master's, GMAT/GRE. Additional exam requirements/recommendations for international students: Required—TOEFL (minimum score 83 iBT). *Application deadline:* For fall admission, 5/1 for domestic students, 3/1 for international students. Application fee: $65. Electronic applications accepted. *Expenses:* Contact institution. *Financial support:* In 2017–18, 11 students received support, including 11 research assistantships with partial tuition reimbursements available (averaging $4,500 per year); institutionally sponsored loans and tuition waivers (partial) also available. Financial award application deadline: 2/1; financial award applicants required to submit FAFSA. *Faculty research:* Data processing applications for business situations and problems, accounting fraud, effects of sales tactics, self-efficacy and performance. *Unit head:* Dr. Daniel Goebel, Dean, 928-523-3657, Fax: 928-523-7331, E-mail: daniel.goebel@nau.edu. *Application contact:* Michelle Brown, Assistant to the Dean, 928-523-7345, Fax: 928-523-6559, E-mail: michelle.brown@nau.edu.
Website: http://franke.nau.edu/

Northern Illinois University, Graduate School, College of Business, MBA Program, De Kalb, IL 60115-2854. Offers MBA. *Accreditation:* AACSB. *Program availability:* Part-time, evening/weekend. *Faculty:* 53 full-time (17 women), 3 part-time/adjunct (0 women). *Students:* 94 full-time (27 women), 297 part-time (83 women); includes 131 minority (20 Black or African American, non-Hispanic/Latino; 1 American Indian or Alaska Native, non-Hispanic/Latino; 55 Asian, non-Hispanic/Latino; 41 Hispanic/Latino; 14 Two or more races, non-Hispanic/Latino), 18 international. Average age 34. 143 applicants, 84% accepted, 79 enrolled. In 2017, 215 master's awarded. *Degree requirements:* For master's, thesis optional, seminar. *Entrance requirements:* For master's, GMAT, minimum GPA of 2.75. Additional exam requirements/recommendations for international students: Required—TOEFL (minimum score 550 paper-based). *Application deadline:* For fall admission, 6/1 for domestic students, 5/1 for international students; for spring admission, 11/1 for domestic students, 10/1 for international students. Applications are processed on a rolling basis. Application fee: $40. Electronic applications accepted. *Financial support:* In 2017–18, 8 research assistantships with full tuition reimbursements, 3 teaching assistantships with full tuition reimbursements were awarded; fellowships with full tuition reimbursements, career-related internships or fieldwork, Federal Work-Study, scholarships/grants, tuition waivers (full), and unspecified assistantships also available. Support available to part-time students. Financial award applicants required to submit FAFSA. *Unit head:* Mona Salmon, Director, 815-753-1245, E-mail: mba@niu.edu. *Application contact:* Office of Graduate Studies in Business, 815-753-6301.
Website: http://www.cob.niu.edu/mbaprograms/

Northern Kentucky University, Office of Graduate Programs, College of Business, Program in Business Administration, Highland Heights, KY 41099. Offers MBA, Certificate, JD/MBA. *Accreditation:* AACSB. *Program availability:* Part-time, evening/weekend. *Degree requirements:* For master's, thesis optional, capstone course. *Entrance requirements:* For master's, GMAT, 3 years of work experience; undergraduate transcripts; 3 letters of recommendation; resume; essay explaining how MBA will benefit student in life and career. Additional exam requirements/recommendations for international students: Required—TOEFL (minimum score 79 iBT); Recommended—IELTS (minimum score 6.5). Electronic applications accepted. *Expenses:* Contact institution. *Faculty research:* Influence, diversity, organizational culture, ethics, corporate governance, corporate scandals, market research methods, consumer privacy, mergers and acquisitions of financial institutions, sustainability.

Northern Kentucky University, Office of Graduate Programs, College of Business, Program in Executive Leadership and Organizational Change, Highland Heights, KY 41099. Offers MS. *Program availability:* Part-time, evening/weekend. *Entrance requirements:* For master's, resume, current career essay, future career objectives essay, personal statement, 3 letters of recommendation with cover forms, transcripts. Additional exam requirements/recommendations for international students: Required—TOEFL (minimum score 79 iBT); Recommended—IELTS (minimum score 6.5). Electronic applications accepted. *Expenses:* Contact institution. *Faculty research:* Leadership assessment and development, teams and conflict management, organizational strategy development and systems thinking, organizational consultation.

Northern Michigan University, Office of Graduate Education and Research, College of Business, Marquette, MI 49855-5301. Offers MBA. *Accreditation:* AACSB. *Program availability:* Part-time. *Degree requirements:* For master's, strategic analysis research project and report in capstone course. *Entrance requirements:* For master's, GMAT, bachelor's degree; minimum undergraduate GPA of 3.0; statement of purpose; resume. Additional exam requirements/recommendations for international students: Required—TOEFL (minimum score 550 paper-based; 79 iBT), IELTS (minimum score 6.5). *Application deadline:* For fall admission, 7/1 for domestic students; for winter admission, 11/15 for domestic students. Applications are processed on a rolling basis. Application fee: $50. Electronic applications accepted. *Expenses:* Tuition, state resident: full-time $9417; part-time $542 per credit hour. Tuition, nonresident: full-time $12,873; part-time $758 per credit hour. Tuition and fees vary according to course load, degree level and program. *Financial support:* Research assistantships with full tuition reimbursements,

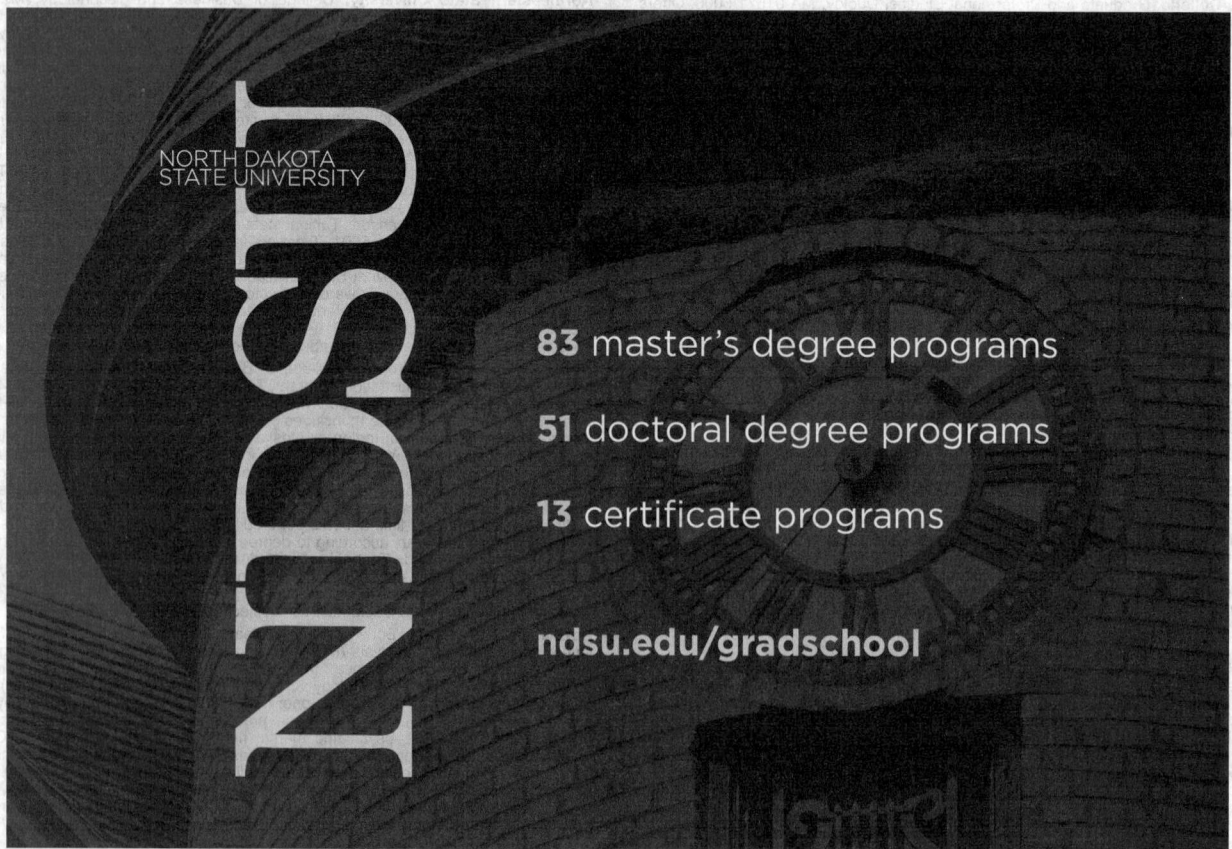

Federal Work-Study, institutionally sponsored loans, scholarships/grants, and unspecified assistantships available. Support available to part-time students. Financial award applicants required to submit FAFSA. *Unit head:* Carol W. Johnson, Interim Dean, 906-227-2947, E-mail: business@nmu.edu. *Application contact:* Carol W. Johnson, Interim Dean, 906-227-2947, E-mail: business@nmu.edu.
Website: http://www.nmu.edu/business/

North Park University, School of Business and Nonprofit Management, Chicago, IL 60625-4895. Offers MBA, MHEA, MHRM, MM, MNA. *Program availability:* Part-time, evening/weekend, online learning. *Entrance requirements:* For master's, GMAT, GRE. Additional exam requirements/recommendations for international students: Required—TOEFL. *Expenses:* Contact institution.

Northwest Christian University, School of Business and Management, Eugene, OR 97401-3745. Offers accounting (MBA); management (MBA). *Program availability:* Part-time, evening/weekend, online only, 100% online. *Faculty:* 6 full-time (1 woman), 8 part-time/adjunct (3 women). *Students:* 61 full-time (30 women), 10 part-time (4 women); includes 21 minority (2 Black or African American, non-Hispanic/Latino; 1 American Indian or Alaska Native, non-Hispanic/Latino; 4 Asian, non-Hispanic/Latino; 8 Hispanic/Latino; 1 Native Hawaiian or other Pacific Islander, non-Hispanic/Latino; 5 Two or more races, non-Hispanic/Latino). Average age 33. In 2017, 36 master's awarded. *Entrance requirements:* For master's, GMAT, GRE, MAT, minimum undergraduate GPA of 3.0, 500-word essay, resume. Additional exam requirements/recommendations for international students: Required—TOEFL (minimum score 550 paper-based; 80 iBT). *Application deadline:* Applications are processed on a rolling basis. Electronic applications accepted. *Expenses:* $630 per credit. *Unit head:* Dr. Peter Diffenderfer, Assistant Dean, 541-684-7441, Fax: 541-684-7336, E-mail: pdiffenderfer@nwcu.edu. *Application contact:* Billy Dorsch, Admission Counselor for Graduate Studies, 541-684-7279, Fax: 541-349-5281, E-mail: wdorsch@nwcu.edu.

Northwestern Polytechnic University, School of Business and Information Technology, Fremont, CA 94539-7482. Offers MBA, DBA. *Program availability:* Part-time, evening/weekend. *Degree requirements:* For master's, thesis optional; for doctorate, thesis/dissertation. *Entrance requirements:* For master's, GMAT, minimum GPA of 3.0. Additional exam requirements/recommendations for international students: Required—TOEFL (minimum score 550 paper-based; 79 iBT). *Expenses:* Contact institution. *Faculty research:* Entrepreneurship, accounting, information technology.

Northwestern University, The Graduate School, Kellogg School of Management, Management Programs, Evanston, IL 60208. Offers accounting information and management (MBA, PhD); analytical finance (MBA); business administration (MBA); decision sciences (MBA); entrepreneurship and innovation (MBA); finance (MBA, PhD); health enterprise management (MBA); human resources management (MBA); international business (MBA); management and organizations (MBA, PhD); management and organizations and sociology (PhD); management and strategy (MBA); management studies (MS); managerial analytics (MBA); managerial economics (MBA); managerial economics and strategy (PhD); marketing (MBA, PhD); marketing management (MBA); media management (MBA); operations management (MBA, PhD); real estate (MBA); social enterprise at Kellogg (MBA); JD/MBA. *Program availability:* Part-time, evening/weekend. Terminal master's awarded for partial completion of doctoral program. *Degree requirements:* For doctorate, thesis/dissertation, 2 years of coursework, qualifying (field) exam and candidacy, summer research papers and presentations to faculty, proposal defense, final exam/defense. *Entrance requirements:* For master's, GMAT, GRE, interview, 2 letters of recommendation, college transcripts, resume, essays, Kellogg honor code; for doctorate, GMAT, GRE, statement of purpose, transcripts, 2 letters of recommendation, resume, interview. Additional exam requirements/recommendations for international students: Required—TOEFL, IELTS. Electronic applications accepted. *Expenses:* Contact institution. *Faculty research:* Business cycles and international finance, health policy, networks, non-market strategy, consumer psychology.

Northwestern University, McCormick School of Engineering and Applied Science, MMM Program, Evanston, IL 60208. Offers design innovation (MBA, MS). *Entrance requirements:* For master's, GMAT or GRE, transcripts, two letters of recommendation, resume, evaluative interview report, work experience, two core essays, interest essay, video essay. Additional exam requirements/recommendations for international students: Required—TOEFL, IELTS. *Expenses:* Contact institution.

Northwest Missouri State University, Graduate School, Melvin and Valorie Booth College of Business and Professional Studies, Maryville, MO 64468-6001. Offers agricultural economics (MBA); business decision and analytics (MBA); general management (MBA); human resource management (MBA); marketing (MBA). *Program availability:* Part-time. *Faculty:* 17 full-time (6 women). *Students:* 40 full-time (13 women), 95 part-time (48 women); includes 16 minority (8 Black or African American, non-Hispanic/Latino; 1 American Indian or Alaska Native, non-Hispanic/Latino; 2 Asian, non-Hispanic/Latino; 3 Hispanic/Latino; 2 Two or more races, non-Hispanic/Latino), 15 international. Average age 31. 142 applicants, 66% accepted, 70 enrolled. In 2017, 53 master's awarded. *Degree requirements:* For master's, comprehensive exam. *Entrance requirements:* For master's, GMAT, GRE, minimum GPA of 2.5. Additional exam requirements/recommendations for international students: Required—TOEFL (minimum score 550 paper-based). *Application deadline:* For fall admission, 7/1 for domestic and international students; for spring admission, 11/15 for domestic and international students; for summer admission, 4/1 for domestic and international students. Applications are processed on a rolling basis. Application fee: $0 ($50 for international students). Electronic applications accepted. *Expenses:* $389.11 per credit in-state tuition; $641.97 per credit out-of-state tuition. *Financial support:* Research assistantships with full tuition reimbursements, teaching assistantships with full tuition reimbursements, career-related internships or fieldwork, and administrative assistantships, tutorial assistantships available. Financial award application deadline: 4/1; financial award applicants required to submit FAFSA. *Unit head:* Dr. Steve Ludwig, Director of the Melvin And Valorie Booth School of Business, 660-562-1749, Fax: 660-562-1096, E-mail: sludwig@nwmissouri.edu.
Website: https://www.nwmissouri.edu/business/index.htm

Northwest Nazarene University, Program in Business Administration, Nampa, ID 83686-5897. Offers business administration (MBA). *Accreditation:* ACBSP. *Program availability:* Part-time, evening/weekend, 100% online, blended/hybrid learning. *Students:* Average age 34. 26 applicants, 62% accepted, 11 enrolled. In 2017, 41 master's awarded. *Degree requirements:* For master's, comprehensive exam, thesis or alternative. *Entrance requirements:* For master's, minimum GPA of 3.0. Additional exam requirements/recommendations for international students: Required—TOEFL (minimum score 82 iBT). *Application deadline:* Applications are processed on a rolling basis. Application fee: $50. Electronic applications accepted. *Expenses:* Contact institution. *Faculty research:* Leadership, international business, economic sustainability, teaching pedagogy, teaching abroad. *Unit head:* Dr. Brenda Johnson, Director, 208-467-8415, Fax: 208-467-8440, E-mail: mba@nnu.edu. *Application contact:* Heather Beam, MBA Program Coordinator, 208-467-8100, Fax: 208-467-8440, E-mail: nnu-mba@nnu.edu.
Website: http://nnu.edu/mba

Northwest University, College of Business, Kirkland, WA 98033. Offers business administration (MBA); international business (MBA); project management (MBA); social entrepreneurship (MBA). *Accreditation:* ACBSP. *Program availability:* Part-time, evening/weekend. *Degree requirements:* For master's, formalized research. *Entrance requirements:* For master's, GMAT. Additional exam requirements/recommendations for international students: Required—TOEFL (minimum score 550 paper-based; 75 iBT). Electronic applications accepted. *Expenses:* Contact institution.

Northwood University, Michigan Campus, DeVos Graduate School, Midland, MI 48640-2398. Offers MBA, MSOL. MBA also offered on Florida and Texas campuses; MSOL offered online only. *Program availability:* Part-time, evening/weekend, online learning. *Degree requirements:* For master's, capstone project. *Entrance requirements:* For master's, GMAT, interview, letters of recommendation, resume. Additional exam requirements/recommendations for international students: Required—TOEFL (minimum score 550 paper-based). Electronic applications accepted.

Norwich University, College of Graduate and Continuing Studies, Master of Business Administration Program, Northfield, VT 05663. Offers construction management (MBA); energy management (MBA); finance (MBA); logistics (MBA); organizational leadership (MBA); project management (MBA); supply chain management (MBA). *Accreditation:* ACBSP. *Program availability:* Evening/weekend, online only, mostly all online with a week-long residency requirement. *Degree requirements:* For master's, comprehensive exam. *Entrance requirements:* For master's, minimum undergraduate GPA of 2.75. Additional exam requirements/recommendations for international students: Required—TOEFL (minimum score 550 paper-based; 80 iBT), IELTS (minimum score 6.5). Electronic applications accepted. *Expenses:* Contact institution.

Notre Dame de Namur University, Division of Academic Affairs, School of Business and Management, Program in Business Administration, Belmont, CA 94002-1908. Offers finance (MBA); human resource management (MBA); marketing (MBA); media and promotion (MBA). *Accreditation:* ACBSP. *Program availability:* Part-time, evening/weekend. *Students:* 28 full-time (24 women), 93 part-time (56 women). Average age 35. *Entrance requirements:* For master's, minimum GPA of 2.5. Additional exam requirements/recommendations for international students: Required—TOEFL (minimum score 550 paper-based; 79 iBT). *Application deadline:* For fall admission, 8/1 priority date for domestic students; for spring admission, 12/1 priority date for domestic students. Applications are processed on a rolling basis. Application fee: $60. Electronic applications accepted. *Expenses:* Tuition: Full-time $16,128; part-time $8064 per credit hour. *Required fees:* $80; $80 per credit hour. $40 per semester. *Financial support:* Available to part-time students. Applicants required to submit FAFSA. *Unit head:* Jordan Holtzman, Program Director, Graduate Business Programs, 510-375-1348, E-mail: jholtzman@ndnu.edu.
Website: http://www.ndnu.edu/academics/schools-programs/school-business/

Notre Dame of Maryland University, Graduate Studies, Program in Management, Baltimore, MD 21210-2476. Offers MA. *Program availability:* Part-time, evening/weekend. *Degree requirements:* For master's, thesis optional. *Entrance requirements:* For master's, minimum GPA of 3.0. Additional exam requirements/recommendations for international students: Required—TOEFL (minimum score 500 paper-based; 61 iBT). Electronic applications accepted.

Nova Southeastern University, H. Wayne Huizenga College of Business and Entrepreneurship, Fort Lauderdale, FL 33314-7796. Offers accounting (M Acc); business (MBA); business intelligence/analytics (MBA); complex health systems (MBA); enterprise informatics (MBA); entrepreneurship (MBA); finance (MBA); human resource management (MBA); international business (MBA); management (MBA); marketing (MBA); process improvement (MBA); public administration (MPA); real estate development (MS); sport revenue generation (MBA); supply chain management (MBA). *Accreditation:* NASPAA. *Program availability:* Part-time, evening/weekend, 100% online, blended/hybrid learning. *Faculty:* 85 full-time (37 women), 59 part-time/adjunct (19 women). *Students:* 1,999 full-time (1,225 women), 335 part-time (210 women); includes 1,516 minority (597 Black or African American, non-Hispanic/Latino; 4 American Indian or Alaska Native, non-Hispanic/Latino; 92 Asian, non-Hispanic/Latino; 789 Hispanic/Latino; 3 Native Hawaiian or other Pacific Islander, non-Hispanic/Latino; 31 Two or more races, non-Hispanic/Latino), 291 international. Average age 34. 1,269 applicants, 59% accepted, 551 enrolled. In 2017, 1,055 master's awarded. *Entrance requirements:* For master's, GMAT or GRE (depending on undergraduate GPA), official transcripts from all schools attended while in pursuit of bachelor's degree; minimum GPA of 2.5 from regionally-accredited institution. Additional exam requirements/recommendations for international students: Required—TOEFL (minimum score 550 paper-based; 79 iBT), IELTS (minimum score 6), PTE (minimum score 54). *Application deadline:* For fall admission, 8/5 priority date for domestic students, 7/29 priority date for international students; for winter admission, 12/16 priority date for domestic students, 12/9 priority date for international students; for summer admission, 4/21 priority date for domestic and international students. Applications are processed on a rolling basis. Application fee: $50. Electronic applications accepted. *Expenses:* $37,785 (online), $35,640 (in-classroom). *Financial support:* In 2017–18, 325 students received support. Federal Work-Study and scholarships/grants available. Support available to part-time students. Financial award application deadline: 4/15; financial award applicants required to submit FAFSA. *Faculty research:* Entrepreneurship and venture capital, ethics and social responsibility, global commerce and cultures, business process management. *Unit head:* Dr. J. Preston Jones, Dean, 954-262-5127, E-mail: prestonj@nova.edu. *Application contact:* Zeida Rodriguez, Associate Director of Enrollment Services, 954-262-5163, Fax: 954-262-3822, E-mail: zeida@nova.edu.
Website: http://www.huizenga.nova.edu

Nyack College, School of Business and Leadership, Nyack, NY 10960. Offers business administration (MBA); organizational leadership (MS). *Program availability:* Part-time, evening/weekend, 100% online, blended/hybrid learning. *Students:* 33 full-time (22 women), 10 part-time (7 women); includes 31 minority (23 Black or African American, non-Hispanic/Latino; 7 Hispanic/Latino; 1 Two or more races, non-Hispanic/Latino), 3 international. Average age 38. In 2017, 33 master's awarded. *Degree requirements:* For master's, thesis (in some programs), capstone project (for MBA). *Entrance requirements:* For master's, transcripts, personal goals statement, recommendations, resume, interview. Additional exam requirements/recommendations for international students: Required—TOEFL (minimum score 550 paper-based; 80 iBT), IELTS (minimum score 6.5). *Application deadline:* Applications are processed on a rolling basis. Application fee: $50. Electronic applications accepted. *Expenses:* $725 per credit (for MS); $800 per credit (for MBA). *Financial support:* Scholarships/grants available. Financial award applicants required to submit FAFSA. *Unit head:* Dr. Anita Underwood, Dean, 845-675-4511. *Application contact:* Joseph M. Williams, Graduate Admissions Associate, 845-770-5711, E-mail: admissions.grad@nyack.edu.
Website: http://www.nyack.edu/sbl

Oakland City University, School of Adult and Extended Learning, Oakland City, IN 47660-1099. Offers MBA. *Program availability:* Part-time, evening/weekend. *Degree requirements:* For master's, thesis or alternative. *Entrance requirements:* For master's, GMAT, GRE, or MAT, appropriate bachelor's degree, computer literacy. Additional exam requirements/recommendations for international students: Required—TOEFL. *Faculty research:* Leadership and management styles, international business, new technologies.

Business Administration and Management—General

Oakland University, Graduate Study and Lifelong Learning, School of Business Administration, Rochester, MI 48309-4401. Offers EMBA, M Acc, MBA, MS, Certificate. *Accreditation:* AACSB. *Program availability:* Part-time, evening/weekend. *Entrance requirements:* For master's, GMAT, minimum GPA of 3.0. Additional exam requirements/recommendations for international students: Required—TOEFL (minimum score 550 paper-based). Electronic applications accepted. *Expenses:* Contact institution.

Oglala Lakota College, Graduate Studies, Program in Lakota Leadership and Management, Kyle, SD 57752-0490. Offers MA. *Program availability:* Part-time, evening/weekend. *Degree requirements:* For master's, thesis. *Entrance requirements:* For master's, minimum GPA of 2.5. *Faculty research:* Curriculum, values, retention of administrators, behavior, graduate follow-up.

Ohio Christian University, Graduate Programs, Circleville, OH 43113. Offers accounting (MBA); business administration (MBA); digital marketing (MBA); finance (MBA); healthcare management (MBA); human resources (MBA); management (MM); organizational leadership (MBA); pastoral care and counseling (MAM); practical theology (MAM).

Ohio Dominican University, Division of Business, Columbus, OH 43219-2099. Offers business administration (MBA), including accounting, data analytics, finance, leadership, risk management, sport management; healthcare administration (MS); sport management (MS). *Accreditation:* ACBSP. *Program availability:* Part-time, evening/weekend, 100% online, blended/hybrid learning. *Faculty:* 9 full-time (4 women), 14 part-time/adjunct (5 women). *Students:* 65 full-time (26 women), 130 part-time (57 women); includes 48 minority (30 Black or African American, non-Hispanic/Latino; 1 American Indian or Alaska Native, non-Hispanic/Latino; 6 Asian, non-Hispanic/Latino; 6 Hispanic/Latino; 5 Two or more races, non-Hispanic/Latino), 9 international. Average age 30. 148 applicants, 45% accepted, 53 enrolled. *Degree requirements:* For master's, thesis or alternative. *Entrance requirements:* Additional exam requirements/recommendations for international students: Required—TOEFL (minimum score 550 paper-based), IELTS (minimum score 6.5). *Application deadline:* For fall admission, 8/15 for domestic students, 6/10 for international students; for spring admission, 1/4 for domestic students, 11/2 for international students. Applications are processed on a rolling basis. Application fee: $25. Electronic applications accepted. *Financial support:* Applicants required to submit FAFSA. *Unit head:* Dr. Kenneth C. Fah, Chair, 614-251-4566, E-mail: fahk@ohiodominican.edu. *Application contact:* John W. Naughton, Director for Graduate Admissions, 614-251-4721, Fax: 614-251-6654, E-mail: grad@ohiodominican.edu. Website: http://www.ohiodominican.edu/academics/graduate/mba

The Ohio State University, Graduate School, Max M. Fisher College of Business, Program in Business Administration, Columbus, OH 43210. Offers MA, MBA, PhD. *Accreditation:* AACSB. *Students:* 316 full-time (95 women), 320 part-time (121 women); includes 128 minority (38 Black or African American, non-Hispanic/Latino; 2 American Indian or Alaska Native, non-Hispanic/Latino; 66 Asian, non-Hispanic/Latino; 17 Hispanic/Latino; 5 Two or more races, non-Hispanic/Latino), 105 international. Average age 32. In 2017, 300 master's, 11 doctorates awarded. *Degree requirements:* For doctorate, thesis/dissertation. *Entrance requirements:* For master's and doctorate, GMAT. Additional exam requirements/recommendations for international students: Required—TOEFL (minimum score 600 paper-based; 100 iBT), Michigan English Language Assessment Battery (minimum score 86); Recommended—IELTS (minimum score 7). *Application deadline:* For fall admission, 11/15 priority date for domestic and international students. Applications are processed on a rolling basis. Application fee: $60 ($70 for international students). Electronic applications accepted. *Financial support:* Fellowships, research assistantships, teaching assistantships, Federal Work-Study, institutionally sponsored loans, and unspecified assistantships available. Support available to part-time students. *Unit head:* Dr. Walter Zinn, Associate Dean for Students and Programs, 614-292-0797, E-mail: zinn.13@osu.edu. *Application contact:* Graduate and Professional Admissions, 614-292-9444, Fax: 614-292-3895, E-mail: gpadmissions@osu.edu.
Website: http://fisher.osu.edu/

The Ohio State University, Graduate School, Max M. Fisher College of Business, Program in Business Logistics Engineering, Columbus, OH 43210. Offers MBLE. *Students:* 48 (25 women). Average age 23. In 2017, 38 master's awarded. *Entrance requirements:* For master's, GRE or GMAT. Additional exam requirements/recommendations for international students: Required—TOEFL (minimum score 550 paper-based; 79 iBT), Michigan English Language Assessment Battery (minimum score 82); Recommended—IELTS (minimum score 7). *Application deadline:* For fall admission, 12/13 priority date for domestic students, 11/30 priority date for international students. Applications are processed on a rolling basis. Application fee: $60 ($70 for international students). Electronic applications accepted. *Financial support:* Scholarships/grants available. *Unit head:* Steve Denunzio, Program Director, 614-769-3155, E-mail: dununzio.4@osu.edu. *Application contact:* Graduate and Professional Admissions, 614-292-9444, Fax: 614-292-3895, E-mail: gpadmissions@osu.edu.
Website: http://fisher.osu.edu/mble

Ohio University, Graduate College, College of Business, Program in Business Administration, Athens, OH 45701-2979. Offers executive management (MBA); MBA/MSA. *Accreditation:* AACSB. *Program availability:* Part-time, evening/weekend, online learning. *Entrance requirements:* For master's, minimum GPA of 3.0. Additional exam requirements/recommendations for international students: Required—TOEFL (minimum score 600 paper-based). Electronic applications accepted. *Expenses:* Contact institution.

Oklahoma Baptist University, Program in Business Administration, Shawnee, OK 74804. Offers business administration (MBA); energy management (MBA). *Accreditation:* ACBSP. *Program availability:* Online learning.

Oklahoma Christian University, Graduate School of Business, Oklahoma City, OK 73136-1100. Offers accounting (M Acc, MBA); financial services (MBA); general business (MBA); health services management (MBA); human resources (MBA); international business (MBA); leadership and organizational development (MBA); marketing (MBA); nonprofit management (MBA); project management (MBA). *Accreditation:* ACBSP. *Program availability:* Part-time, 100% online. *Entrance requirements:* For master's, bachelor's degree. Additional exam requirements/recommendations for international students: Required—TOEFL (minimum score 550 paper-based). Electronic applications accepted. *Expenses:* Contact institution.

Oklahoma City University, Meinders School of Business, Oklahoma City, OK 73106-1402. Offers business (MBA, MSA); computer science (MS); energy legal studies (MS); energy management (MS); JD/MBA. *Program availability:* Part-time, evening/weekend, 100% online. *Faculty:* 18 full-time (4 women), 8 part-time/adjunct (3 women). *Students:* 121 full-time (49 women), 213 part-time (88 women); includes 85 minority (19 Black or African American, non-Hispanic/Latino; 6 American Indian or Alaska Native, non-Hispanic/Latino; 25 Asian, non-Hispanic/Latino; 21 Hispanic/Latino; 14 Two or more races, non-Hispanic/Latino), 58 international. Average age 33. 167 applicants, 79% accepted, 106 enrolled. In 2017, 184 master's awarded. *Degree requirements:* For master's, practicum/capstone. *Entrance requirements:* For master's, undergraduate degree from accredited institution, minimum GPA of 3.0, essay, letters of recommendation. Additional exam requirements/recommendations for international students: Required—TOEFL (minimum score 550 paper-based; 80 iBT). *Application deadline:* Applications are processed on a rolling basis. Application fee: $50. Electronic applications accepted. *Expenses:* $8,580. *Financial support:* In 2017–18, 252 students received support. Career-related internships or fieldwork, Federal Work-Study, institutionally sponsored loans, scholarships/grants, and tuition waivers (full and partial) available. Support available to part-time students. Financial award application deadline: 6/1; financial award applicants required to submit FAFSA. *Faculty research:* Group support systems, leadership, decision models in accounting. *Unit head:* Dr. Steve Agee, Dean, 405-208-5275, Fax: 405-208-5008, E-mail: sagee@okcu.edu. *Application contact:* Michael Harrington, Director of Graduate Admission, 800-633-7242, Fax: 405-208-5916, E-mail: gadmissions@okcu.edu.
Website: http://msb.okcu.edu

Oklahoma City University, Petree College of Arts and Sciences, Oklahoma City, OK 73106-1402. Offers applied behavioral studies (M Ed); applied sociology: nonprofit leadership (MA); creative writing (MFA); criminology (MS); early childhood education (M Ed); elementary education (M Ed); general studies (MLA); leadership/management (MLA); moving image arts (MFA); professional counseling (M Ed); teaching (MA); teaching English to speakers of other languages (MA). *Program availability:* Part-time, evening/weekend. *Faculty:* 6 full-time (2 women), 16 part-time/adjunct (10 women). *Students:* 84 full-time (61 women), 32 part-time (23 women); includes 31 minority (13 Black or African American, non-Hispanic/Latino; 3 American Indian or Alaska Native, non-Hispanic/Latino; 1 Asian, non-Hispanic/Latino; 9 Hispanic/Latino; 5 Two or more races, non-Hispanic/Latino), 30 international. Average age 34. 192 applicants, 67% accepted, 57 enrolled. In 2017, 65 master's awarded. *Degree requirements:* For master's, capstone/practicum. *Entrance requirements:* For master's, bachelor's degree from accredited institution with minimum GPA of 3.0, essay, recommendation letters. Additional exam requirements/recommendations for international students: Required—TOEFL (minimum score 550 paper-based; 80 iBT). *Application deadline:* Applications are processed on a rolling basis. Application fee: $50. Electronic applications accepted. *Expenses:* $8,580. *Financial support:* In 2017–18, 19 students received support. Federal Work-Study, institutionally sponsored loans, scholarships/grants, and tuition waivers (full and partial) available. Support available to part-time students. Financial award application deadline: 6/1; financial award applicants required to submit FAFSA. *Unit head:* Dr. Amy Cataldi, Dean, 405-208-5446, Fax: 405-208-5447, E-mail: acataldi@okcu.edu. *Application contact:* Michael Harrington, Director of Graduate Admissions, 800-633-7242, Fax: 405-208-5356, E-mail: gadmissions@okcu.edu.
Website: https://www.okcu.edu/artsci/home

Oklahoma State University, Spears School of Business, Department of Management, Stillwater, OK 74078. Offers MBA, MS, PhD. *Program availability:* Part-time. *Faculty:* 27 full-time (10 women), 15 part-time/adjunct (5 women). *Students:* 5 full-time (2 women), 1 (woman) part-time; includes 1 minority (Black or African American, non-Hispanic/Latino), 2 international. Average age 33. 2 applicants, 100% accepted, 2 enrolled. In 2017, 3 doctorates awarded. *Entrance requirements:* For master's and doctorate, GRE or GMAT. Additional exam requirements/recommendations for international students: Required—TOEFL (minimum score 550 paper-based; 79 iBT). *Application deadline:* For fall admission, 3/1 priority date for international students; for spring admission, 8/1 priority date for international students. Applications are processed on a rolling basis. Application fee: $40 ($75 for international students). Electronic applications accepted. *Expenses:* Tuition, state resident: full-time $4019; part-time $2679.60 per year. Tuition, nonresident: full-time $15,286; part-time $10,190.40 per year. *Required fees:* $2129; $1419 per unit. Tuition and fees vary according to program. *Financial support:* Research assistantships, teaching assistantships, career-related internships or fieldwork, Federal Work-Study, scholarships/grants, health care benefits, tuition waivers (partial), and unspecified assistantships available. Support available to part-time students. Financial award application deadline: 3/1; financial award applicants required to submit FAFSA. *Faculty research:* Telecommunications management, innovative decision support techniques, knowledge networking, organizational research methods, strategic planning. *Unit head:* Dr. James Pappas, Department Head, 405-744-5201, Fax: 405-744-5180, E-mail: james.pappas@okstate.edu. *Application contact:* Dr. Toby Joplin, PhD Coordinator, 405-744-5115, Fax: 405-744-5180, E-mail: toby.joplin@okstate.edu.
Website: https://business.okstate.edu/management/

Old Dominion University, Strome College of Business, Doctoral Program in Business Administration, Norfolk, VA 23529. Offers business administration (PhD), including finance, IT and supply chain management, marketing, strategic management. *Accreditation:* AACSB. *Faculty:* 35 full-time (6 women). *Students:* 27 full-time (8 women), 25 part-time (6 women); includes 1 minority (Asian, non-Hispanic/Latino), 41 international. Average age 35. 63 applicants, 30% accepted, 8 enrolled. In 2017, 9 doctorates awarded. *Degree requirements:* For doctorate, comprehensive exam, thesis/dissertation. *Entrance requirements:* For doctorate, GMAT or GRE. Additional exam requirements/recommendations for international students: Required—TOEFL (minimum score 550 paper-based; 79 iBT). *Application deadline:* For fall admission, 3/1 priority date for domestic and international students. Application fee: $50. Electronic applications accepted. *Expenses:* Tuition, state resident: full-time $8928; part-time $496 per credit. Tuition, nonresident: full-time $22,482; part-time $1249 per credit. *Required fees:* $66 per semester. *Financial support:* In 2017–18, 36 students received support, including 15 research assistantships with full tuition reimbursements available (averaging $18,500 per year), 13 teaching assistantships with full tuition reimbursements available (averaging $18,500 per year); unspecified assistantships and tuition grants (for fourth-year students) also available. Financial award application deadline: 3/1; financial award applicants required to submit FAFSA. *Faculty research:* International business, buyer behavior, financial markets, strategy, operations research. *Unit head:* Dr. John B. Ford, Graduate Program Director, 757-683-3587, Fax: 757-683-4076, E-mail: jbford@odu.edu. *Application contact:* Katrina Davenport, Program Coordinator, 757-683-5138, Fax: 757-683-4076, E-mail: kdavenpo@odu.edu.
Website: http://www.odu.edu/business/academics/graduate/scb-phd

Old Dominion University, Strome College of Business, MBA Program, Norfolk, VA 23529. Offers MBA. *Accreditation:* AACSB. *Program availability:* Part-time, evening/weekend, 100% online, blended/hybrid learning. *Faculty:* 83 full-time (20 women), 8 part-time/adjunct (3 women). *Students:* 15 full-time (8 women), 151 part-time (68 women); includes 31 minority (13 Black or African American, non-Hispanic/Latino; 5 Asian, non-Hispanic/Latino; 5 Hispanic/Latino; 8 Two or more races, non-Hispanic/Latino), 12 international. Average age 32. 70 applicants, 61% accepted, 33 enrolled. In 2017, 39 master's awarded. *Entrance requirements:* For master's, GMAT or GRE, letter of reference, resume, essay, official transcripts from all previously attended institutions. Additional exam requirements/recommendations for international students: Required—TOEFL or IELTS. *Application deadline:* For fall admission, 6/1 priority date for domestic students, 4/15 priority date for international students; for spring admission, 11/1 priority date for domestic students, 10/1 priority date for international students; for summer admission, 3/1 priority date for domestic students, 2/1 priority date for international students. Applications are processed on a rolling basis. Application fee: $50. Electronic applications accepted. *Expenses:* Tuition, state resident: full-time $8928; part-time $496 per credit. Tuition, nonresident: full-time $22,482; part-time $1249 per credit. *Required*

fees: $66 per semester. *Financial support:* In 2017–18, 51 students received support, including 48 research assistantships with partial tuition reimbursements available (averaging $8,900 per year); career-related internships or fieldwork, scholarships/grants, and unspecified assistantships also available. Support available to part-time students. Financial award application deadline: 2/15; financial award applicants required to submit FAFSA. *Faculty research:* International business, buyer behavior, financial markets, strategy, operations research, maritime and transportation economics. *Total annual research expenditures:* $248,316. *Unit head:* Dr. David Cook, Assistant Dean for Graduate Studies, 757-683-3585, Fax: 757-683-5750, E-mail: mbainfo@odu.edu. *Application contact:* Sandi Phillips, Assistant MBA Program Manager, 757-683-3585, Fax: 757-683-5750, E-mail: mbainfo@odu.edu.
Website: http://www.odu.edu/mba

Olivet Nazarene University, Graduate School, Department of Business, Bourbonnais, IL 60914. Offers business administration (MBA). *Program availability:* Evening/weekend. *Degree requirements:* For master's, thesis or alternative. *Expenses:* Contact institution.

Open University, Graduate Programs, Milton Keynes, United Kingdom. Offers business (MBA); education (M Ed); engineering (M Eng); history (MA); music (MA); philosophy (MA).

Oral Roberts University, School of Business, Tulsa, OK 74171. Offers accounting (MBA); entrepreneurship (MBA); finance (MBA); international business (MBA); management (MBA); marketing (MBA); not for profit management (MNM). *Accreditation:* ACBSP. *Program availability:* Part-time, online learning. *Faculty:* 7 full-time (0 women), 5 part-time/adjunct (4 women). *Students:* 71 applicants, 94% accepted, 56 enrolled. *Degree requirements:* For master's, thesis optional. *Entrance requirements:* For master's, minimum cumulative GPA of 3.0 from regionally-accredited institution. *Application deadline:* Applications are processed on a rolling basis. Application fee: $35. Electronic applications accepted. Application fee is waived when completed online. *Financial support:* In 2017–18, 39 students received support. Scholarships/grants and unspecified assistantships available. Financial award application deadline: 6/1. *Faculty research:* Social media, international business and marketing. *Unit head:* Dr. Marshal Wright, Chair of the Graduate School of Business, 918-495-6988, E-mail: mwright@oru.edu. *Application contact:* Sam Park, Enrollment Counselor, 918-495-7179, E-mail: sampark@oru.edu.
Website: http://www.oru.edu/university/departments/schools/bus

Oregon State University, College of Business, Program in Business Administration, Corvallis, OR 97331. Offers business administration (PhD), including accounting; corporate finance (MBA). *Program availability:* Part-time, blended/hybrid learning. *Entrance requirements:* For master's, GMAT. Additional exam requirements/recommendations for international students: Required—TOEFL (minimum score 91 iBT), IELTS (minimum score 7). *Application deadline:* For fall admission, 2/1 priority date for domestic and international students; for winter admission, 9/15 priority date for domestic and international students; for spring admission, 1/1 priority date for domestic and international students. Applications are processed on a rolling basis. Application fee: $75 ($85 for international students). *Expenses:* Contact institution. *Financial support:* Application deadline: 1/15. *Unit head:* Matt Alex, Associate Director, 541-737-5340, E-mail: matt.alex@oregonstate.edu. *Application contact:* Matt Alex, Associate Director, 541-737-5340, E-mail: matt.alex@oregonstate.edu.
Website: http://business.oregonstate.edu/graduate-programs

Ottawa University, Graduate Studies-Arizona, Programs in Business, Ottawa, KS 66067-3399. Offers business administration (MBA); finance (MBA); human resources (MA, MBA); leadership (MBA); marketing (MBA). Programs offered in Mesa, Phoenix, Tempe and West Valley, AZ. *Program availability:* Part-time, evening/weekend, online learning. *Degree requirements:* For master's, thesis or alternative. *Entrance requirements:* For master's, minimum undergraduate GPA of 3.0. Additional exam requirements/recommendations for international students: Required—TOEFL (minimum score 550 paper-based). Electronic applications accepted.

Ottawa University, Graduate Studies-International, Ottawa, KS 66067-3399. Offers business administration (MBA). *Program availability:* Online learning. *Degree requirements:* For master's, thesis or alternative. *Entrance requirements:* For master's, minimum undergraduate GPA of 3.0. Additional exam requirements/recommendations for international students: Required—TOEFL (minimum score 550 paper-based). Electronic applications accepted. *Expenses:* Contact institution.

Ottawa University, Graduate Studies-Kansas City, Overland Park, KS 66211. Offers business administration (MBA); human resources (MA). *Program availability:* Part-time, evening/weekend, online learning. *Degree requirements:* For master's, thesis or alternative. *Entrance requirements:* For master's, resume, 3 letters of recommendation. Additional exam requirements/recommendations for international students: Required—TOEFL (minimum score 550 paper-based). Electronic applications accepted. *Expenses:* Contact institution.

Ottawa University, Graduate Studies-Wisconsin, Brookfield, WI 53005. Offers business administration (MBA). *Program availability:* Part-time, evening/weekend, online learning. *Degree requirements:* For master's, thesis or alternative. *Entrance requirements:* For master's, resume, 3 letters of recommendation. Additional exam requirements/recommendations for international students: Required—TOEFL (minimum score 550 paper-based). Electronic applications accepted.

Otterbein University, Department of Business, Accounting and Economics, Westerville, OH 43081. Offers MBA. *Program availability:* Part-time, evening/weekend. *Degree requirements:* For master's, consulting project team. *Entrance requirements:* For master's, GMAT, 2 reference forms, resume. Additional exam requirements/recommendations for international students: Required—TOEFL (minimum score 550 paper-based; 79 iBT). *Expenses:* Contact institution. *Faculty research:* Organizational design, dispute resolution international trade, developing economies, marketing consumer goods, human resources development.

Our Lady of the Lake University, School of Business and Leadership, Program in Management, San Antonio, TX 78207-4689. Offers MBA. *Program availability:* Part-time, evening/weekend, 100% online, blended/hybrid learning. *Faculty:* 1 full-time (0 women), 6 part-time/adjunct (1 woman). *Students:* 83 full-time (46 women), 17 part-time (12 women); includes 65 minority (9 Black or African American, non-Hispanic/Latino; 56 Hispanic/Latino). Average age 35. 34 applicants, 71% accepted, 13 enrolled. In 2017, 52 master's awarded. *Entrance requirements:* For master's, official transcripts showing 6 hours of coursework in economics and 3 hours of coursework in each of the following ares: statistics, management, business law, and finance; résumé including detailed work history describing managerial or professional work experience. Additional exam requirements/recommendations for international students: Required—TOEFL. *Application deadline:* For fall admission, 6/15 for domestic and international students; for spring admission, 11/15 for domestic and international students; for summer admission, 4/15 for domestic and international students. Applications are processed on a rolling basis. Application fee: $40 ($50 for international students). Electronic applications accepted. Application fee is waived when completed online. *Expenses: Tuition:* Full-time $10,668; part-time $5334 per year. *Required fees:* $816; $816 per year. $408 per semester. *Financial support:* In 2017–18, 52 students received support. Federal Work-Study, scholarships/grants, unspecified assistantships, and tuition discounts available.

Support available to part-time students. Financial award application deadline: 5/1; financial award applicants required to submit FAFSA. *Unit head:* Dr. Ronald Crowe, E-mail: rcrowe@ollusa.edu. *Application contact:* Office of Graduate Admissions, 210-431-3995, Fax: 210-431-3945, E-mail: gradadm@ollusa.edu.
Website: http://www.ollusa.edu/s/1190/hybrid/default-hybrid-ollu.aspx?sid-1190&gid-1&pgid-7873

Pace University, Lubin School of Business, New York, NY 10038. Offers MBA, MS, DPS, APC. *Accreditation:* AACSB. *Program availability:* Part-time, evening/weekend, blended/hybrid learning. *Students:* 465 full-time (257 women), 351 part-time (181 women); includes 193 minority (50 Black or African American, non-Hispanic/Latino; 1 American Indian or Alaska Native, non-Hispanic/Latino; 80 Asian, non-Hispanic/Latino; 52 Hispanic/Latino; 1 Native Hawaiian or other Pacific Islander, non-Hispanic/Latino; 9 Two or more races, non-Hispanic/Latino; 368 international. Average age 30. 950 applicants, 63% accepted, 222 enrolled. In 2017, 363 master's, 4 doctorates awarded. *Degree requirements:* For doctorate, thesis/dissertation, oral and written exam. *Entrance requirements:* For master's, GMAT, GRE, undergraduate degree, transcripts from all accredited colleges/universities attended, two letters of recommendation, resume, personal statement; for doctorate and APC, MBA or similar master's degree, 10 years of experience in business, transcripts from all accredited colleges/universities attended, 4 letters of recommendation, interview. Additional exam requirements/recommendations for international students: Required—TOEFL (minimum score 90 iBT), IELTS (minimum score 7) or PTE (minimum score 61). *Application deadline:* For fall admission, 8/1 priority date for domestic students, 6/1 for international students; for spring admission, 12/1 priority date for domestic students, 10/1 for international students; for summer admission, 5/1 priority date for domestic students, 3/1 for international students. Applications are processed on a rolling basis. Application fee: $70. Electronic applications accepted. *Expenses:* Contact institution. *Financial support:* Research assistantships, career-related internships or fieldwork, Federal Work-Study, tuition waivers (full and partial), and unspecified assistantships available. Support available to part-time students. Financial award application deadline: 2/15; financial award applicants required to submit FAFSA. *Faculty research:* Accounting standards and reporting, financial markets and instruments, strategy and entrepreneurship, management learning, marketing and customers. *Total annual research expenditures:* $11,058. *Unit head:* Neil S. Braun, Dean, Lubin School of Business, 212-618-6600, Fax: 212-618-6603, E-mail: nbraun@pace.edu. *Application contact:* Susan Ford-Goldschein, Director of Graduate Admissions, 212-346-1531, Fax: 212-346-1585, E-mail: graduateadmission@pace.edu.
Website: http://www.pace.edu/lubin

Pacific Lutheran University, School of Business, MBA Program, Tacoma, WA 98447. Offers MBA. *Program availability:* Part-time, evening/weekend. *Entrance requirements:* For master's, GMAT or GRE, statement of professional goals, resume, two letters of recommendation. Additional exam requirements/recommendations for international students: Required—TOEFL (minimum score 88 iBT), IELTS (minimum score 6.5). Electronic applications accepted. *Expenses:* Contact institution.

Pacific States University, College of Business, Los Angeles, CA 90010. Offers accounting (MBA, Certificate); beauty management (MBA); finance (MBA); international business (MBA); management of information technology (MBA); project management (Certificate); real estate management (MBA). *Program availability:* Part-time, evening/weekend, online learning. *Entrance requirements:* For master's, minimum undergraduate GPA of 2.5 during last 90 quarter units of course work, bachelor's degree in business administration or economics. Additional exam requirements/recommendations for international students: Required—TOEFL (minimum score 500 paper-based; 61 iBT), IELTS (minimum score 5.5). *Application deadline:* For fall admission, 9/1 priority date for domestic students, 8/1 priority date for international students; for winter admission, 12/1 priority date for domestic students, 11/1 priority date for international students; for spring admission, 3/1 priority date for domestic students, 2/1 priority date for international students; for summer admission, 6/1 priority date for domestic students, 5/1 priority date for international students. Applications are processed on a rolling basis. Application fee: $100. *Expenses: Tuition:* Part-time $380 per unit. *Financial support:* Scholarships/grants available. Financial award applicants required to submit FAFSA. *Unit head:* Chase C. Rhee, MBA Program Administrator, 323-731-2383 Ext. 208, Fax: 323-731-7276, E-mail: ccrhee@psuca.edu. *Application contact:* Maawiya Ayeva, Director of Admissions, 323-731-2383 Ext. 204, Fax: 323-731-7276, E-mail: admissions@psuca.edu.

Pacific University, College of Business, Forest Grove, OR 97116-1797. Offers business administration (MBA); finance (MSF).

Palm Beach Atlantic University, Rinker School of Business, West Palm Beach, FL 33416-4708. Offers MACC, MBA. *Program availability:* Part-time, evening/weekend. *Entrance requirements:* For master's, minimum GPA of 3.0. Additional exam requirements/recommendations for international students: Required—TOEFL (minimum score 550 paper-based; 79 iBT). Electronic applications accepted. *Faculty research:* International business, finance, banking.

Park University, School of Graduate and Professional Studies, Kansas City, MO 54105. Offers adult education (M Ed); business and government leadership (Graduate Certificate); business, government, and global society (MPA); communication and leadership (MA); creative and life writing (Graduate Certificate); disaster and emergency management (MPA, Graduate Certificate); educational leadership (M Ed); finance (MBA, Graduate Certificate); general business (MBA); global business (Graduate Certificate); healthcare administration (MHA); healthcare services management and leadership (Graduate Certificate); international business (MBA); language and literacy (M Ed), including English for speakers of other languages, special reading teacher/literacy coach; leadership of international healthcare organizations (Graduate Certificate); management information systems (MBA, Graduate Certificate); music performance (ADP, Graduate Certificate), including cello (MM, ADP), piano (MM, ADP), viola (MM, ADP), violin (MM, ADP); nonprofit and community services management (MPA); nonprofit leadership (Graduate Certificate); performance (MM), including cello (MM, ADP), piano (MM, ADP), viola (MM, ADP), violin (MM, ADP); public management (MPA); social work (MSW); teacher leadership (M Ed), including curriculum and assessment, instructional leader. *Program availability:* Part-time, evening/weekend, online learning. *Degree requirements:* For master's, comprehensive exam (for some programs), thesis (for some programs), internship (for some programs); exam (for some programs). *Entrance requirements:* For master's, GRE or GMAT (for some programs), teacher certification (for some M Ed programs), letters of recommendation, essay, resume (for some programs). Additional exam requirements/recommendations for international students: Required—TOEFL (minimum score 550 paper-based; 79 iBT), IELTS (minimum score 6). Electronic applications accepted.

Penn State Erie, The Behrend College, Graduate School, Erie, PA 16563. Offers accounting (MPAC); applied clinical psychology (MA); business administration (MBA); quality and manufacturing management (MMM). *Accreditation:* AACSB. *Program availability:* Part-time. *Students:* 31 full-time (15 women), 126 part-time (39 women); includes 10 minority (4 Black or African American, non-Hispanic/Latino; 1 Hispanic/Latino; 5 Two or more races, non-Hispanic/Latino). Average age 31. 104 applicants, 75% accepted, 75 enrolled. In 2017, 72 master's awarded. *Entrance requirements:*

Business Administration and Management—General

Additional exam requirements/recommendations for international students: Required—TOEFL (minimum score 550 paper-based; 80 iBT), IELTS. *Application deadline:* Applications are processed on a rolling basis. Application fee: $65. Electronic applications accepted. *Financial support:* Federal Work-Study available. Financial award application deadline: 2/15; financial award applicants required to submit FAFSA. *Unit head:* Dr. Ralph M. Ford, Chancellor, 814-898-6160, Fax: 814-898-6461. *Application contact:* Ann M. Burbules, Assistant Director, Graduate Admissions, 866-374-3378, Fax: 814-898-6044, E-mail: behrend.admissions@psu.edu.
Website: http://behrend.psu.edu/

Penn State Great Valley, Graduate Studies, Management Division, Malvern, PA 19355-1488. Offers business administration (MBA); cyber security (Certificate); data analytics (MPS, MS, Certificate); distributed energy and grid modernization (Certificate); finance (M Fin); health sector management (Certificate); human resource management (Certificate); information science (MSIS); leadership development (MLD); new ventures and entrepreneurship (Certificate); sustainable management practices (Certificate). *Accreditation:* AACSB. *Unit head:* Dr. James A. Nemes, Chancellor, 610-648-3202, Fax: 610-725-5296. *Application contact:* JoAnn Kelly, Director of Admissions, 610-648-3315, Fax: 610-725-5296, E-mail: jek2@psu.edu.
Website: http://greatvalley.psu.edu/academics/masters-degrees/engineering-management

Penn State Harrisburg, Graduate School, School of Business Administration, Middletown, PA 17057. Offers accounting (MPAC, Certificate); business administration (MBA); information systems (MS); operations and supply chain management (Certificate). *Program availability:* Part-time, evening/weekend. *Unit head:* Dr. Mukund S. Kulkarni, Chancellor, 717-948-6105, Fax: 717-948-6452. *Application contact:* Robert W. Coffman, Jr., Director of Enrollment Management, Recruitment and Admissions, 717-948-6250, Fax: 717-948-6325, E-mail: hbgadmit@psu.edu.
Website: https://harrisburg.psu.edu/business-administration

Penn State University Park, Graduate School, Smeal College of Business, University Park, PA 16802. Offers accounting (M Acc); business administration (MBA, MS, PhD); management and organizational leadership (MPS). *Accreditation:* AACSB. *Program availability:* Part-time, evening/weekend. *Students:* 290 full-time (97 women), 7 part-time (2 women). Average age 29. 1,125 applicants, 27% accepted, 236 enrolled. In 2017, 235 master's, 10 doctorates awarded. *Entrance requirements:* Additional exam requirements/recommendations for international students: Required—TOEFL (minimum score 550 paper-based; 80 iBT), IELTS. *Application deadline:* Applications are processed on a rolling basis. Application fee: $65. Electronic applications accepted. *Expenses:* Contact institution. *Financial support:* Fellowships, research assistantships, teaching assistantships, career-related internships or fieldwork, Federal Work-Study, scholarships/grants, traineeships, health care benefits, and unspecified assistantships available. Support available to part-time students. Financial award application deadline: 2/15; financial award applicants required to submit FAFSA. *Unit head:* Dr. Charles H. Whiteman, Dean, 814-863-0448, Fax: 814-865-7064. *Application contact:* Lori Hawn, Director, Graduate Student Services, 814-865-1795, Fax: 814-863-4627, E-mail: l-gswww@lists.psu.edu.
Website: http://smeal.psu.edu/

Pensacola Christian College, Graduate Studies, Pensacola, FL 32503-2267. Offers business administration (MBA); curriculum and instruction (MS, Ed D, Ed S); dramatics (MFA); educational leadership (MS, Ed D, Ed S); graphic design (MA, MFA); music (MA); nursing (MSN); performance studies (MA); studio art (MA, MFA).

Pepperdine University, Graziadio Business School, Full-Time MBA Programs, Malibu, CA 90263. Offers business administration (MBA); international business administration (MBA); JD/MBA; MBA/MPP. *Unit head:* Dr. Deryck J. Rensburg, Dean, 310-568-5689, Fax: 310-568-5500, E-mail: deryck.rensburg@pepperdine.edu. *Application contact:* Morag Knapp, Assistant Director of Admission, Graziadio School of Business and Management, 310-568-5527, E-mail: morag.knapp@pepperdine.edu.
Website: https://bschool.pepperdine.edu/mba-programs/full-time-mba/

Pepperdine University, Graziadio Business School, Master of Science Programs, Malibu, CA 90263. Offers accounting (MS); applied analytics (MS); applied finance (MS); global business (MS); human resources (MS); management and leadership (MS); organization development (MS); real estate investment and finance (MS). *Accreditation:* AACSB. *Students:* 462 full-time (277 women), 104 part-time (68 women); includes 67 minority (23 Black or African American, non-Hispanic/Latino; 1 American Indian or Alaska Native, non-Hispanic/Latino; 41 Asian, non-Hispanic/Latino; 2 Hispanic/Latino), 380 international. Average age 27. 2,180 applicants, 63% accepted, 336 enrolled. In 2017, 291 master's awarded. *Entrance requirements:* For master's, GMAT or GRE, two letters of recommendation. Additional exam requirements/recommendations for international students: Required—TOEFL. *Application deadline:* For fall admission, 5/1 for domestic students, 4/1 for international students. Application fee: $75. Electronic applications accepted. *Financial support:* Applicants required to submit FAFSA. *Unit head:* Dr. Michael L. Williams, Associate Dean, 310-506-4112, Fax: 310-506-4126, E-mail: michael.williams@pepperdine.edu.
Website: http://bschool.pepperdine.edu/masters-degree/

Pepperdine University, Graziadio Business School, Part-Time MBA Programs, Malibu, CA 90263. Offers MBA. *Students:* 335 full-time (162 women), 549 part-time (258 women); includes 278 minority (71 Black or African American, non-Hispanic/Latino; 8 American Indian or Alaska Native, non-Hispanic/Latino; 166 Asian, non-Hispanic/Latino; 32 Hispanic/Latino; 1 Two or more races, non-Hispanic/Latino), 10 international. Average age 33. 403 applicants, 70% accepted, 159 enrolled. In 2017, 358 master's awarded. *Entrance requirements:* For master's, GMAT or GRE, two letters of recommendation. Additional exam requirements/recommendations for international students: Required—TOEFL. *Application deadline:* For fall admission, 1/10 for domestic students. Application fee: $75. *Financial support:* Scholarships/grants available. Financial award applicants required to submit FAFSA. *Unit head:* Annie Carr, Director of Program Advisement and Student Support, 310-568-5515, E-mail: annie.carr@pepperdine.edu.
Website: http://bschool.pepperdine.edu/masters-degree/

Pepperdine University, Seaver College, Malibu, CA 90263. Offers business (MS), including accounting; communication (MA, MFA), including cinematic media production (MFA), strategic communication (MA); humanities (MA, MFA), including American studies (MA), writing for screen and television (MFA); religion (M Div, MA, MS), including ministry (MS), religion (M Div, MA); JD/M Div. *Program availability:* Part-time, evening/weekend. *Students:* 22 full-time (11 women), 82 part-time (50 women); includes 25 minority (10 Black or African American, non-Hispanic/Latino; 1 American Indian or Alaska Native, non-Hispanic/Latino; 6 Asian, non-Hispanic/Latino; 6 Hispanic/Latino; 2 Two or more races, non-Hispanic/Latino), 6 international. Average age 30. 129 applicants, 31% accepted, 29 enrolled. In 2017, 24 master's awarded. *Entrance requirements:* For master's, GRE General Test. Additional exam requirements/recommendations for international students: Required—TOEFL. *Application deadline:* For fall admission, 2/1 priority date for domestic students. Applications are processed on a rolling basis. Application fee: $55. *Expenses:* Contact institution. *Financial support:* Fellowships, research assistantships, teaching assistantships, career-related

internships or fieldwork, Federal Work-Study, institutionally sponsored loans, scholarships/grants, and tuition waivers (partial) available. Support available to part-time students. Financial award application deadline: 2/15; financial award applicants required to submit FAFSA. *Unit head:* Dr. Dana Dudley, Assistant Dean, Special Academic and Graduate Programs for Seaver College, 310-506-6047, Fax: 310-506-4816, E-mail: dana.dudley@pepperdine.edu. *Application contact:* Joy Brown, Admission Counselor, 310-506-4392, E-mail: joy.brown@pepperdine.edu.
Website: http://seaver.pepperdine.edu/

Pfeiffer University, Program in Business Administration, Misenheimer, NC 28109-0960. Offers MBA, MBA/MHA. *Program availability:* Part-time, evening/weekend, online learning. *Entrance requirements:* For master's, GMAT, minimum GPA of 3.0.

Phillips Theological Seminary, Programs in Theology, Tulsa, OK 74116. Offers administration of church agencies (M Div); campus ministry (M Div); church-related social work (M Div); college and seminary teaching (M Div); global mission work (M Div); institutional chaplaincy (M Div); ministerial vocations in Christian education (M Div); ministry (D Min), including parish ministry, pastoral counseling, practices of ministry; ministry and culture (MAMC), including Christian education, congregational leadership, history and practice of Christian spirituality, theology, ethics, and culture; ministry of music (M Div); pastoral care and counseling (M Div); pastoral ministry (M Div); theological studies (MTS). *Accreditation:* ATS. *Program availability:* Part-time, online learning. *Degree requirements:* For master's, thesis (for some programs); for doctorate, thesis/dissertation. *Entrance requirements:* For master's, minimum GPA of 2.5; for doctorate, M Div, minimum GPA of 3.0. *Faculty research:* Biblical studies, historical studies, theology and culture, practical theology, theology and film.

Piedmont College, School of Business, Demorest, GA 30535. Offers MBA. *Accreditation:* ACBSP. *Program availability:* Part-time, evening/weekend. *Students:* 46 full-time (25 women), 11 part-time (4 women); includes 11 minority (8 Black or African American, non-Hispanic/Latino; 1 Asian, non-Hispanic/Latino; 1 Hispanic/Latino; 1 Native Hawaiian or other Pacific Islander, non-Hispanic/Latino). Average age 29. 32 applicants, 38% accepted, 10 enrolled. In 2017, 37 master's awarded. *Degree requirements:* For master's, capstone. *Entrance requirements:* For master's, GMAT, GRE. Additional exam requirements/recommendations for international students: Required—TOEFL (minimum score 550 paper-based). *Application deadline:* For fall admission, 7/15 for domestic students; for spring admission, 12/1 for domestic students. Applications are processed on a rolling basis. Electronic applications accepted. *Expenses: Tuition:* Full-time $9360; part-time $520 per credit hour. *Required fees:* $200; $200 per year. $100 per term. *Financial support:* Federal Work-Study and unspecified assistantships available. Financial award applicants required to submit FAFSA. *Unit head:* Dr. Edward Taylor, Dean, 706-778-3000, E-mail: etaylor@piedmont.edu. *Application contact:* Kathleen Carter, Director of Graduate Enrollment Management, 706-778-3000, E-mail: kcarter@piedmont.edu.
Website: http://www.piedmont.edu

Pittsburg State University, Graduate School, Kelce College of Business, Department of Management and Marketing, Pittsburg, KS 66762. Offers general administration (MBA); international business (MBA). *Accreditation:* AACSB. *Program availability:* Part-time. *Students:* 80 (30 women). In 2017, 35 master's awarded. *Degree requirements:* For master's, thesis or alternative. *Entrance requirements:* For master's, GMAT or GRE. Additional exam requirements/recommendations for international students: Required—TOEFL (minimum score 550 paper-based; 79 iBT), IELTS (minimum score 6.5), PTE (minimum score 53). *Application deadline:* For fall admission, 7/15 for domestic students, 6/1 for international students; for spring admission, 12/15 for domestic students, 10/15 for international students; for summer admission, 5/15 for domestic students, 4/1 for international students. Applications are processed on a rolling basis. Application fee: $35 ($60 for international students). Electronic applications accepted. *Expenses:* Contact institution. *Financial support:* In 2017–18, 10 teaching assistantships with full tuition reimbursements (averaging $5,500 per year) were awarded; research assistantships, career-related internships or fieldwork, Federal Work-Study, and unspecified assistantships also available. Financial award application deadline: 2/1; financial award applicants required to submit FAFSA. *Faculty research:* Consumer behavior, productions management, forecasting interest rate swaps, strategy management. *Unit head:* Dr. Bienvenido Cortes, MBA Coordinator, 620-235-4594, E-mail: bcortes@pittstate.edu. *Application contact:* Lisa Allen, Assistant Director of Graduate and Continuing Studies, 620-235-4218, Fax: 620-235-4219, E-mail: lallen@pittstate.edu.
Website: http://www.pittstate.edu/mgmkt/

Plymouth State University, College of Graduate Studies, Graduate Studies in Business, Plymouth, NH 03264-1595. Offers general management (MBA). *Accreditation:* ACBSP. *Program availability:* Part-time, evening/weekend, online learning. *Entrance requirements:* For master's, minimum GPA of 2.5. Additional exam requirements/recommendations for international students: Required—TOEFL (minimum score 550 paper-based). *Expenses:* Contact institution.

Point Loma Nazarene University, Fermanian School of Business, San Diego, CA 92106-2899. Offers general business (MBA); healthcare management (MBA); innovation and entrepreneurship (MBA); organizational leadership (MBA); project management (MBA). *Accreditation:* ACBSP. *Program availability:* Part-time, evening/weekend. *Faculty:* 7 full-time (0 women), 5 part-time/adjunct (3 women). *Students:* 27 full-time (8 women), 94 part-time (45 women); includes 52 minority (6 Black or African American, non-Hispanic/Latino; 1 American Indian or Alaska Native, non-Hispanic/Latino; 7 Asian, non-Hispanic/Latino; 33 Hispanic/Latino; 5 Two or more races, non-Hispanic/Latino), 11 international. Average age 31. 74 applicants, 99% accepted, 56 enrolled. In 2017, 45 master's awarded. *Entrance requirements:* For master's, GMAT, letters of recommendation, essay, interview. Additional exam requirements/recommendations for international students: Required—TOEFL. *Application deadline:* For fall admission, 7/26 priority date for domestic students; for spring admission, 11/29 priority date for domestic students; for summer admission, 4/2 priority date for domestic students. Applications are processed on a rolling basis. Application fee: $50. Electronic applications accepted. *Expenses:* Contact institution. *Financial support:* Applicants required to submit FAFSA. *Unit head:* Jamie McIlwaine, Associate Dean, Graduate Business, 619-849-2721, E-mail: jmcilwai@pointloma.edu. *Application contact:* Joanie Joy, Senior Director of Enrollment Management, 619-329-6785, E-mail: gradinfo@pointloma.edu.
Website: https://www.pointloma.edu/schools-departments-colleges/fermanian-school-business

Point Park University, Rowland School of Business, Program in Business Administration, Pittsburgh, PA 15222-1984. Offers business analytics (MBA); global management and administration (MBA); health systems management (MBA); international business (MBA); management (MBA); management information systems (MBA); sports, arts and entertainment management (MBA). *Program availability:* Evening/weekend, 100% online.

Point University, Graduate Programs, West Point, GA 31833. Offers business transformation (MBA); transformative ministry (MTM). *Program availability:* Part-time, 100% online, blended/hybrid learning. *Students:* 24 full-time (9 women), 2 part-time (both women); includes 7 minority (6 Black or African American, non-Hispanic/Latino; 1 Hispanic/Latino). Average age 36. *Application deadline:* Applications are processed on a rolling basis. Electronic applications accepted. *Expenses:* $515 per credit hour (for MBA); $450 per credit hour (for MTM).

Polytechnic University of Puerto Rico, Graduate School, Hato Rey, PR 00918. Offers business administration (MBA), including computer information systems, general management, management of information systems, management of international enterprises; civil engineering (ME, MS); computer engineering (ME, MS); computer science (MCS, MS); electrical engineering (ME, MS); engineering management (MEM); environmental management (MEM); landscape architecture (M Land Arch); manufacturing competitiveness (MMC, MS); manufacturing engineering (ME, MS); mechanical engineering (M Mech E). *Program availability:* Part-time, evening/weekend. *Entrance requirements:* For master's, 3 letters of recommendation.

Polytechnic University of Puerto Rico, Miami Campus, Graduate School, Miami, FL 33166. Offers accounting (MBA); business administration (MBA); construction management (MEM); environmental management (MEM); finance (MBA); human resources management (MBA); logistics and supply chain management (MBA); management of international enterprises (MBA); manufacturing management (MEM); marketing management (MBA); project management (MBA). *Program availability:* Part-time, evening/weekend, online learning. *Entrance requirements:* For master's, minimum GPA of 3.0. Electronic applications accepted.

Polytechnic University of Puerto Rico, Orlando Campus, Graduate School, Orlando, FL 32825. Offers accounting (MBA); business administration (MBA); construction management (MEM); engineering management (MEM); environmental management (MEM); finance (MBA); human resources management (MBA); management of international enterprises (MBA); management of technology (MBA); manufacturing management (MEM). *Program availability:* Part-time, evening/weekend, online learning. *Entrance requirements:* For master's, minimum GPA of 3.0. Additional exam requirements/recommendations for international students: Recommended—TOEFL. Electronic applications accepted.

Pontifical Catholic University of Puerto Rico, College of Business Administration, Ponce, PR 00717-0777. Offers MBA, DBA, PhD, Professional Certificate. *Program availability:* Part-time, evening/weekend. *Degree requirements:* For master's, thesis; for doctorate, comprehensive exam, thesis/dissertation. *Entrance requirements:* For master's, GRE, interview, minimum GPA of 2.75; for doctorate, 2 letters of recommendation, 2 years experience in a related field, interview.

Pontificia Universidad Catolica Madre y Maestra, Graduate School, Faculty of Social and Administrative Sciences, Santiago, Dominican Republic. Offers business administration (MBA), including business development, finance, international business, management skills (M Mgmt, MBA), marketing, operations, strategic cost management, strategy, tourist destination planning and management; law (LL M), including civil law, corporate business law, criminal law, international relations, real estate law; management (M Mgmt), including higher financial management, insurance program administration, management skills (M Mgmt, MBA); psychology (MA), including clinical child and adolescent psychology, forensic psychology; strategic human resources (EMBA).

Portland State University, Graduate Studies, College of Liberal Arts and Sciences, Systems Science Program, Portland, OR 97207-0751. Offers computational intelligence (Certificate); computer modeling and simulation (Certificate); systems science (MS); systems science/anthropology (PhD); systems science/business administration (PhD); systems science/civil engineering (PhD); systems science/economics (PhD); systems science/engineering management (PhD); systems science/general (PhD); systems science/mathematical sciences (PhD); systems science/mechanical engineering (PhD); systems science/psychology (PhD); systems science/sociology (PhD). *Faculty:* 2 full-time (0 women), 4 part-time/adjunct (0 women). *Students:* 12 full-time (4 women), 22 part-time (6 women); includes 6 minority (4 Hispanic/Latino; 2 Two or more races, non-Hispanic/Latino). Average age 37. 18 applicants, 94% accepted, 16 enrolled. In 2017, 6 master's awarded. *Degree requirements:* For master's, comprehensive exam (for some programs), thesis optional; for doctorate, variable foreign language requirement, comprehensive exam (for some programs), thesis/dissertation. *Entrance requirements:* For master's, GRE/GMAT (recommended), minimum GPA of 3.0 on undergraduate or graduate work, 2 letters of recommendation, statement of interest; for doctorate, GMAT, GRE General Test, minimum GPA of 3.0 undergraduate, 3.25 graduate; 3 letters of recommendation; statement of interest. Additional exam requirements/recommendations for international students: Required—TOEFL (minimum score 550 paper-based; 80 iBT). *Application deadline:* For fall admission, 1/15 for domestic and international students; for spring admission, 11/1 for domestic students. Application fee: $65. Electronic applications accepted. *Expenses:* Tuition, state resident: full-time $14,436; part-time $401 per credit. Tuition, nonresident: full-time $21,780; part-time $605 per credit. *Required fees:* $1380; $22 per credit. $119 per quarter. One-time fee: $325. Tuition and fees vary according to program. *Financial support:* In 2017–18, 1 teaching assistantship with full and partial tuition reimbursement (averaging $7,830 per year) was awarded; research assistantships, career-related internships or fieldwork, Federal Work-Study, scholarships/grants, and unspecified assistantships also available. Support available to part-time students. Financial award application deadline: 3/1; financial award applicants required to submit FAFSA. *Faculty research:* Systems theory and methodology, artificial intelligence neural networks, information theory, nonlinear dynamics/chaos, modeling and simulation. *Total annual research expenditures:* $169,034. *Unit head:* Dr. Wayne Wakeland, Chair, 503-725-4975, E-mail: wakeland@pdx.edu.
Website: http://www.pdx.edu/sysc/

Portland State University, Graduate Studies, The School of Business, Program in Business Administration, Portland, OR 97207-0751. Offers MBA. *Accreditation:* AACSB. *Program availability:* Part-time, evening/weekend. *Faculty:* 41 full-time (22 women), 72 part-time/adjunct (18 women). *Students:* 186 full-time (95 women), 97 part-time (40 women); includes 61 minority (11 Black or African American, non-Hispanic/Latino; 22 Asian, non-Hispanic/Latino; 18 Hispanic/Latino; 1 Native Hawaiian or other Pacific Islander, non-Hispanic/Latino; 9 Two or more races, non-Hispanic/Latino), 45 international. Average age 33. 306 applicants, 68% accepted, 155 enrolled. In 2017, 89 master's awarded. *Degree requirements:* For master's, one foreign language, project. *Entrance requirements:* For master's, GMAT or GRE, minimum GPA of 3.0 in upper-division course work, 2 recommendations, resume, interview. Additional exam requirements/recommendations for international students: Required—TOEFL (minimum score 550 paper-based). *Application deadline:* For fall admission, 2/1 priority date for domestic and international students. Applications are processed on a rolling basis. Application fee: $65. Electronic applications accepted. *Expenses:* Contact institution. *Financial support:* In 2017–18, 46 students received support, including 15 research assistantships with full and partial tuition reimbursements available (averaging $7,987 per year); career-related internships or fieldwork, Federal Work-Study, and scholarships/grants also available. Support available to part-time students. Financial award application deadline: 3/1; financial award applicants required to submit FAFSA. *Faculty research:* Quality management and organizational excellence, performance measurement, customer satisfaction, values, technology management and technology

transfer. *Total annual research expenditures:* $211,260. *Unit head:* Tichelle Sorensen, MBA Academic Director, 503-725-9936, Fax: 503-725-5850, E-mail: sorenset@pdx.edu.
Website: http://www.pdx.edu/sba/master-of-business-administration

Post University, Program in Business Administration, Waterbury, CT 06723-2540. Offers accounting (MSA); business administration (MBA); corporate finance (MBA); corporate innovation (MBA); healthcare systems leadership (MBA); leadership (MBA); marketing (MBA); project management (MBA, MS). *Accreditation:* ACBSP. *Program availability:* Online learning. *Entrance requirements:* For master's, resume. *Expenses:* Tuition: Part-time $730 per credit hour. Part-time tuition and fees vary according to degree level and program. *Application contact:* Veronica Montalvo, Vice President, Online Education Enrollment Management and Admissions, 203-596-6164, E-mail: vmontalvo@post.edu.

Prairie View A&M University, College of Business, Prairie View, TX 77446. Offers accounting (MS); business administration (MBA). *Accreditation:* AACSB. *Program availability:* Part-time, evening/weekend. *Faculty:* 18 full-time (3 women). *Students:* 82 full-time (48 women), 143 part-time (81 women); includes 192 minority (174 Black or African American, non-Hispanic/Latino; 10 Asian, non-Hispanic/Latino; 8 Hispanic/Latino), 17 international. Average age 29. 180 applicants, 84% accepted, 106 enrolled. In 2017, 98 master's awarded. *Degree requirements:* For master's, comprehensive exam, thesis optional. *Entrance requirements:* For master's, GMAT, GRE, minimum GPA of 2.45, essay. Additional exam requirements/recommendations for international students: Required—TOEFL (minimum score 550 paper-based; 79 iBT). *Application deadline:* For fall admission, 5/1 for domestic students, 5/1 priority date for international students; for spring admission, 10/1 for domestic students, 9/1 priority date for international students; for summer admission, 3/1 for domestic students, 2/1 for international students. Applications are processed on a rolling basis. Application fee: $50. Electronic applications accepted. *Expenses:* $1,167 per semester credit hour (for EMBA). *Financial support:* Research assistantships, teaching assistantships, scholarships/grants, and unspecified assistantships available. Financial award application deadline: 4/1; financial award applicants required to submit FAFSA. *Faculty research:* Accounting (energy, oil and gas); finance (international finance, personal finance, real estate markets and institutions); marketing management (supply chain, human resources, entrepreneurship, small business ownership, ethics); management information systems (cyber-security, managing social media during crises). *Unit head:* Dr. Munir Quddus, Dean, 936-261-9200, Fax: 936-261-9241, E-mail: cob@pvamu.edu. *Application contact:* Gabriel Crosby, Director, Graduate Programs in Business, 936-261-9217, Fax: 936-261-9232, E-mail: mba@pvamu.edu.
Website: http://www.pvamu.edu/business/

Presidio Graduate School, MBA Programs - Seattle, San Francisco, CA 94129. Offers cooperative management (Certificate); sustainable business (MBA); sustainable systems (MBA). *Program availability:* Part-time, evening/weekend, blended/hybrid learning. *Entrance requirements:* For master's and Certificate, Quantitative Assessment Summary, GRE, or GMAT, resume, two letters of recommendation, essay, transcripts. Additional exam requirements/recommendations for international students: Required—TOEFL (minimum score 90 iBT), IELTS (minimum score 6.5). *Application deadline:* For fall admission, 6/1 priority date for domestic and international students. Applications are processed on a rolling basis. Application fee: $75. Electronic applications accepted. *Financial support:* Scholarships/grants available. Financial award application deadline: 6/15; financial award applicants required to submit FAFSA. *Unit head:* Dariush Rafinejad, Provost, 415-651-6555, E-mail: info@presidio.edu. *Application contact:* Kari Dorth, Director of Admissions, 415-655-8912, E-mail: admissions@presidio.edu.
Website: https://www.presidio.edu/seattle-mba-overview/

Providence College, School of Business, Providence, RI 02918. Offers accounting (MBA); finance (MBA); international business (MBA); management (MBA); marketing (MBA). *Accreditation:* AACSB. *Program availability:* Part-time, evening/weekend. *Entrance requirements:* For master's, GMAT. Additional exam requirements/recommendations for international students: Required—TOEFL (minimum score 577 paper-based; 90 iBT). *Expenses:* Contact institution.

Purdue University, Graduate School, Krannert School of Management, Doctoral Program in Management, West Lafayette, IN 47907-2056. Offers PhD. *Students:* 59 full-time (19 women), 40 international. Average age 32. 340 applicants, 7% accepted, 13 enrolled. In 2017, 13 doctorates awarded. *Degree requirements:* For doctorate, comprehensive exam, thesis/dissertation, first-year summer paper, dissertation proposal, dissertation defense. *Entrance requirements:* For doctorate, GMAT or GRE. Additional exam requirements/recommendations for international students: Required—TOEFL (minimum score 575 paper-based); Recommended—TWE. *Application deadline:* For fall admission, 1/15 priority date for domestic and international students. Application fee: $60 ($75 for international students). Electronic applications accepted. *Financial support:* In 2017–18, fellowships with full tuition reimbursements (averaging $25,000 per year), research assistantships with partial tuition reimbursements (averaging $23,000 per year), teaching assistantships with full tuition reimbursements (averaging $23,000 per year) were awarded; institutionally sponsored loans, scholarships/grants, health care benefits, tuition waivers (full and partial), unspecified assistantships, and travel funds to present at a major conference also available. Financial award application deadline: 1/15. *Faculty research:* Accounting, finance, marketing, management information systems, supply chain and operations management, organizational behavior and human resource management, quantitative methods/management science, strategic management. *Unit head:* Dr. David Hummels, Dean/Professor, 765-494-4366. *Application contact:* Kelly Felty, Associate Director, Krannert PhD Programs, 765-494-4375, E-mail: krannertphd@purdue.edu.
Website: http://www.krannert.purdue.edu/programs/phd/

Purdue University, Graduate School, Krannert School of Management, Executive MBA Programs, West Lafayette, IN 47907. Offers MBA. *Faculty:* 17 full-time (5 women), 6 part-time/adjunct (0 women). *Students:* 55 part-time (11 women); includes 14 minority (1 Black or African American, non-Hispanic/Latino; 9 Asian, non-Hispanic/Latino; 4 Hispanic/Latino), 1 international. Average age 38. 41 applicants, 98% accepted, 28 enrolled. In 2017, 1 master's awarded. *Entrance requirements:* For master's, GMAT or GRE, two professional recommendations; essays; official transcripts and, in some instances, copy of diploma; current professional resume; in-person or virtual interview. Additional exam requirements/recommendations for international students: Required—TOEFL, IELTS. *Application deadline:* For fall admission, 8/1 for domestic and international students. Applications are processed on a rolling basis. Application fee: $60 ($75 for international students). Electronic applications accepted. *Expenses:* $48,000. *Financial support:* In 2017–18, 29 students received support. Scholarships/grants available. Financial award application deadline: 8/1; financial award applicants required to submit FAFSA. *Faculty research:* Trust in organizations, alliances, organizational change, negotiations, risk management. *Unit head:* Dr. Aldas P. Kriauciunas, Executive Director, 765-496-1860, Fax: 765-494-0862, E-mail: akriauci@purdue.edu. *Application contact:* Nancy Smigiel, Associate Director of Admissions, 765-494-4580, Fax: 765-494-0862, E-mail: nks@purdue.edu.
Website: http://www.krannert.purdue.edu/executive/home.php

Purdue University, Graduate School, Krannert School of Management, Master of Business Administration Program, West Lafayette, IN 47907. Offers MBA. *Accreditation:*

Business Administration and Management—General

AACSB. *Faculty:* 143 full-time (32 women), 6 part-time/adjunct (1 woman). *Students:* 120 full-time (39 women); includes 19 minority (6 Black or African American, non-Hispanic/Latino; 7 Asian, non-Hispanic/Latino; 1 Hispanic/Latino; 1 Native Hawaiian or other Pacific Islander, non-Hispanic/Latino; 4 Two or more races, non-Hispanic/Latino), 53 international. Average age 27. 332 applicants, 37% accepted, 45 enrolled. In 2017, 70 master's awarded. *Entrance requirements:* For master's, GMAT, four-year baccalaureate degree, minimum GPA of 3.0, essays, recommendation letters, work/internship experience. Additional exam requirements/recommendations for international students: Required—TOEFL (minimum score 600 paper-based; 93 iBT), IELTS (minimum score 7.5), or PTE (minimum score 70). *Application deadline:* For fall admission, 11/15 for domestic and international students; for winter admission, 1/15 for domestic and international students; for spring admission, 3/1 for domestic and international students; for summer admission, 5/1 for domestic students. Applications are processed on a rolling basis. Application fee: $60 ($75 for international students). Electronic applications accepted. *Expenses:* Contact institution. *Financial support:* In 2017–18, 34 students received support. Scholarships/grants and unspecified assistantships available. Financial award applicants required to submit FAFSA. *Faculty research:* Capital market imperfections and the sensitivity of investment to stock prices, identifying beneficial collaboration in decentralized logistics systems, performance periods and the dynamics of the performance-risk relationship, applications of global optimization to process and molecular design. *Unit head:* Dr. David Hummels, Dean/Professor of Economics, 765-494-4366, E-mail: krannertdean@purdue.edu. *Application contact:* Thomas Bates, Associate Director of Admissions, 765-494-0773, Fax: 765-494-9841, E-mail: krannertmasters@purdue.edu.
Website: http://www.krannert.purdue.edu/masters/mba/mba-fulltime/

Purdue University, Graduate School, Krannert School of Management, Weekend Master of Business Administration Program, West Lafayette, IN 47907. Offers MBA. *Program availability:* Part-time-only, evening/weekend. *Faculty:* 12 full-time (3 women), 1 part-time/adjunct (0 women). *Students:* 100 part-time (25 women); includes 15 minority (4 Black or African American, non-Hispanic/Latino; 7 Asian, non-Hispanic/Latino; 1 Hispanic/Latino; 3 Two or more races, non-Hispanic/Latino), 6 international. Average age 34. 77 applicants, 90% accepted, 57 enrolled. In 2017, 30 master's awarded. *Entrance requirements:* For master's, GMAT, minimum GPA of 3.0, four-year baccalaureate degree, essays, letters of recommendation. Additional exam requirements/recommendations for international students: Required—TOEFL (minimum score 600 paper-based; 93 iBT), IELTS (minimum score 7.5), PTE (minimum score 70). *Application deadline:* For fall admission, 11/1 for domestic students, 11/15 for international students; for winter admission, 1/15 for domestic and international students; for spring admission, 3/1 for domestic and international students; for summer admission, 5/1 for domestic and international students. Applications are processed on a rolling basis. Application fee: $60 ($75 for international students). Electronic applications accepted. *Expenses:* Contact institution. *Financial support:* In 2017–18, 41 students received support. Scholarships/grants available. Financial award application deadline: 7/18; financial award applicants required to submit FAFSA. *Unit head:* Dr. David Hummels, Dean/Professor of Economics, 765-494-4366, E-mail: krannertdean@purdue.edu. *Application contact:* Thomas Bates, Associate Director of Admissions, 765-494-0773, Fax: 765-494-9841, E-mail: krannertmasters@purdue.edu.
Website: http://www.krannert.purdue.edu/masters/mba/weekend-mba/

Purdue University Global, School of Business, Davenport, IA 52807. Offers business administration (MBA); change leadership (MS); entrepreneurship (MBA); finance (MBA); health care management (MBA, MS); human resource (MBA); international business (MBA); management (MS); marketing (MBA); project management (MBA, MS); supply chain management and logistics (MBA, MS). *Accreditation:* ACBSP. *Program availability:* Part-time, evening/weekend, online learning. *Entrance requirements:* Additional exam requirements/recommendations for international students: Required—TOEFL (minimum score 550 paper-based; 80 iBT). Electronic applications accepted.

Purdue University Northwest, Graduate Studies Office, School of Management, Hammond, IN 46323-2094. Offers accountancy (M Acc); business administration (MBA); business administration for executives (EMBA). *Accreditation:* AACSB. *Program availability:* Part-time, evening/weekend. *Entrance requirements:* For master's, GMAT. Additional exam requirements/recommendations for international students: Required—TOEFL. Electronic applications accepted.

Queen's University at Kingston, Queens School of Business, Program in Business Administration, Kingston, ON K7L 3N6, Canada. Offers consulting and project management (MBA); finance (MBA); innovation and entrepreneurship (MBA); marketing (MBA). *Degree requirements:* For master's, thesis optional, research project. *Entrance requirements:* For master's, GMAT, minimum B+ average. Additional exam requirements/recommendations for international students: Required—TOEFL. Electronic applications accepted. *Faculty research:* Management fundamentals, strategic thinking, global business, innovation and change, leadership.

Queens University of Charlotte, McColl School of Business, Charlotte, NC 28274-0002. Offers business administration (EMBA, MBA, PMBA); organization development (MSOD). *Accreditation:* AACSB. *Program availability:* Part-time, evening/weekend, online learning. *Degree requirements:* For master's, capstone course. *Entrance requirements:* For master's, GMAT, minimum GPA of 2.5. Additional exam requirements/recommendations for international students: Required—TOEFL. Electronic applications accepted. *Expenses:* Contact institution.

Quincy University, MBA Program, Quincy, IL 62301-2699. Offers MBA. *Program availability:* Part-time, evening/weekend, online learning. *Entrance requirements:* For master's, GMAT (if GPA less than 3.0), previous course work in accounting, economics, finance, management or marketing, and statistics. Additional exam requirements/recommendations for international students: Required—TOEFL (minimum score 550 paper-based; 79 iBT). *Application deadline:* Applications are processed on a rolling basis. Application fee: $25. Electronic applications accepted. *Expenses:* Contact institution. *Financial support:* Applicants required to submit FAFSA. *Faculty research:* Macroeconomic forecasting. *Unit head:* Dr. Cynthia Haliemun, Director, 217-228-5432 Ext. 3067, E-mail: haliecy@quincy.edu. *Application contact:* Office of Admissions, 217-228-5210, Fax: 217-228-5479, E-mail: admissions@quincy.edu.
Website: http://www.quincy.edu/academics/graduate-programs/master-of-business-administration/

Quinnipiac University, School of Business, Program in Business Administration, Hamden, CT 06518-1940. Offers finance (MBA); health care management (MBA); supply chain management (MBA); JD/MBA. *Accreditation:* AACSB. *Program availability:* Part-time, evening/weekend, 100% online, blended/hybrid learning. *Faculty:* 32 full-time (11 women), 8 part-time/adjunct (3 women). *Students:* 201 full-time (95 women), 215 part-time (95 women); includes 48 minority (9 Black or African American, non-Hispanic/Latino; 12 Asian, non-Hispanic/Latino; 20 Hispanic/Latino; 7 Two or more races, non-Hispanic/Latino), 19 international. 307 applicants, 79% accepted, 223 enrolled. In 2017, 264 master's awarded. *Entrance requirements:* For master's, GMAT or GRE, minimum GPA of 3.0. Additional exam requirements/recommendations for international students: Required—TOEFL (minimum score 575 paper-based; 90 iBT), IELTS (minimum score 6.5). *Application deadline:* For fall admission, 7/30 priority date for domestic students, 4/30 priority date for international students; for spring admission, 12/15 priority date for domestic students, 9/30 priority date for international students. Applications are processed on a rolling basis. Application fee: $45. Electronic applications accepted. *Expenses:* Contact institution. *Financial support:* Career-related internships or fieldwork, Federal Work-Study, scholarships/grants, and unspecified assistantships available. Financial award application deadline: 6/1; financial award applicants required to submit FAFSA. *Faculty research:* Financial markets and investments, international business, supply chain management, health care management, corporate governance. *Unit head:* Lisa Braiewa, Director of the MBA Program, 800-462-1944, Fax: 203-582-3443, E-mail: graduate@qu.edu. *Application contact:* Office of Graduate Admissions, 800-462-1944, Fax: 203-582-3443, E-mail: graduate@qu.edu.
Website: http://www.qu.edu/mba

Radford University, College of Graduate Studies and Research, Program in Business Administration, Radford, VA 24142. Offers MBA. *Accreditation:* AACSB. *Program availability:* Part-time, evening/weekend, online learning. *Faculty:* 6 full-time (1 woman). *Students:* 9 full-time (5 women), 32 part-time (11 women); includes 1 minority (Black or African American, non-Hispanic/Latino), 6 international. Average age 34. 31 applicants, 74% accepted, 12 enrolled. In 2017, 14 master's awarded. *Entrance requirements:* For master's, GMAT or GRE (waiver may be submitted based on work experience), minimum GPA of 2.75, 2 letters of reference, letter of intent, resume, official transcripts. Additional exam requirements/recommendations for international students: Required—TOEFL (minimum score 550 paper-based; 79 iBT), IELTS (minimum score 6.5). *Application deadline:* For fall admission, 7/15 priority date for domestic students, 12/1 for international students; for spring admission, 11/1 priority date for domestic students, 7/1 for international students. Applications are processed on a rolling basis. Application fee: $50. Electronic applications accepted. *Expenses:* Tuition, state resident: full-time $8336; part-time $347 per credit hour. Tuition, nonresident: full-time $16,862; part-time $702 per credit hour. *Required fees:* $3220; $135 per credit hour. Tuition and fees vary according to course load and program. *Financial support:* In 2017–18, 5 students received support, including 4 teaching assistantships (averaging $8,750 per year); scholarships/grants and unspecified assistantships also available. Support available to part-time students. Financial award application deadline: 12/1; financial award applicants required to submit FAFSA. *Unit head:* Dr. Gary Schirr, MBA Program Director, 540-831-6905, E-mail: radfordmba@radford.edu.
Website: http://www.radford.edu/content/cobe/home/programs/mba.html

Ramapo College of New Jersey, Master of Business Administration Program, Mahwah, NJ 07430-1680. Offers leadership (MBA). *Accreditation:* AACSB. *Program availability:* Part-time-only, evening/weekend. *Faculty:* 3 full-time (all women). *Students:* 63 part-time (30 women); includes 14 minority (2 Asian, non-Hispanic/Latino; 12 Hispanic/Latino). Average age 33. 95 applicants, 55% accepted, 33 enrolled. In 2017, 34 master's awarded. *Degree requirements:* For master's, capstone course. *Entrance requirements:* For master's, official transcript of baccalaureate degree from accredited institution with minimum recommended GPA of 3.0; personal statement; 2 letters of recommendation; resume. Additional exam requirements/recommendations for international students: Required—TOEFL (minimum score 550 paper-based; 79 iBT); Recommended—IELTS (minimum score 6). *Application deadline:* For fall admission, 5/1 for domestic and international students. Applications are processed on a rolling basis. Application fee: $65. Electronic applications accepted. *Expenses:* $961.35 per credit tuition, $56.95 per credit tuition-related fees, $83.00 per credit Immersion Trip fees. *Financial support:* In 2017–18, 2 students received support. Career-related internships or fieldwork and scholarships/grants available. Financial award application deadline: 3/1; financial award applicants required to submit FAFSA. *Faculty research:* Ethical implications of taxation on society, organizational governance, applied labor economics, empirical market microstructure, foreign direct investment. *Unit head:* Dr. Edward Petkus, Dean of the Anisfield School of Business, 201-684-7377, E-mail: epetkus@ramapo.edu. *Application contact:* Timothy Landers, Assistant Dean/Director of the MBA Program, 201-684-7771, E-mail: tlanders@ramapo.edu.
Website: http://www.ramapo.edu/mba/

Regent's University London, Webster Graduate School, London, United Kingdom. Offers business (MBA); finance (MS); human resources (MA); information technology management (MA); international business (MA); international non-governmental organizations (MA); international relations (MA); management and leadership (MA); marketing (MA). *Program availability:* Part-time.

Regent University, Graduate School, School of Business and Leadership, Virginia Beach, VA 23464-9800. Offers business administration (MBA), including accounting, economics, entrepreneurship, finance and investing, general management, healthcare management (MA, MBA), human resource management (MA, MBA), innovation management, leadership, marketing, not-for-profit management (MA, MBA); business analytics (MS); business and design management (MA); church leadership (MA); leadership (Certificate); organizational leadership (MA, PhD), including ecclesia leadership (DSL, PhD), entrepreneurial leadership (PhD), healthcare management (MA, MBA), human resource development (PhD), human resource management (MA, MBA), individualized studies (DSL, PhD), interdisciplinary studies (MA), leadership coaching and mentoring (MA), not-for-profit management (MA, MBA), organizational development consulting (MA), servant leadership (MA, DSL); strategic leadership (DSL), including ecclesial leadership (DSL, PhD), global consulting, healthcare leadership, individualized studies (DSL, PhD), leadership coaching, servant leadership (MA, DSL), strategic foresight. *Program availability:* Part-time, evening/weekend, 100% online, blended/hybrid learning. *Faculty:* 9 full-time (2 women), 38 part-time/adjunct (11 women). *Students:* 129 full-time (80 women), 1,152 part-time (598 women); includes 685 minority (546 Black or African American, non-Hispanic/Latino; 10 American Indian or Alaska Native, non-Hispanic/Latino; 29 Asian, non-Hispanic/Latino; 65 Hispanic/Latino; 6 Native Hawaiian or other Pacific Islander, non-Hispanic/Latino; 29 Two or more races, non-Hispanic/Latino), 62 international. Average age 41. 1,721 applicants, 48% accepted, 624 enrolled. In 2017, 125 master's, 69 doctorates awarded. *Degree requirements:* For master's, thesis or alternative, 3-credit hour culminating experience; for doctorate, thesis/dissertation. *Entrance requirements:* For master's, college transcripts, resume, essay; for doctorate, college transcripts, resume, essay, writing sample; for Certificate, writing sample, resume, transcripts. Additional exam requirements/recommendations for international students: Required—TOEFL (minimum score 577 paper-based). *Application deadline:* For fall admission, 5/1 priority date for domestic students; for spring admission, 10/1 priority date for domestic students. Applications are processed on a rolling basis. Application fee: $50. Electronic applications accepted. *Expenses:* $650 per credit (MA, MS, MBA); $995 per credit (PhD); $300 per semester technology fee. *Financial support:* In 2017–18, 829 students received support. Career-related internships or fieldwork, scholarships/grants, and unspecified assistantships available. Support available to part-time students. *Faculty research:* Servant leadership, global business, team effectiveness, technology utilization, leadership development. *Unit head:* Dr. Doris Gomez, Dean, 757-352-4686, Fax: 757-352-4634, E-mail: dorigom@regent.edu. *Application contact:* Heidi Cece, Assistant Vice President of Enrollment Management, 800-373-5504, Fax: 757-352-4381, E-mail: admissions@regent.edu.
Website: https://www.regent.edu/school-of-business-and-leadership/

Reinhardt University, McCamish School of Business, Waleska, GA 30183-2981. Offers MBA. Program offered at the Chattahoochee Technical College campus in downtown Woodstock, GA. *Program availability:* Part-time, evening/weekend. *Degree requirements:* For master's, comprehensive exam. *Entrance requirements:* For master's, GMAT (minimum score 500), bachelor's degree with minimum GPA of 2.75, current resume, interview, 3 professional references. Additional exam requirements/recommendations for international students: Required—TOEFL. Electronic applications accepted. *Expenses:* Contact institution.

Rensselaer at Hartford, Lally School of Management and Technology, Hartford, CT 06120-2991. Offers MBA, MS. *Program availability:* Part-time, evening/weekend, online learning. *Degree requirements:* For master's, capstone course. *Entrance requirements:* For master's, GMAT (MBA). Additional exam requirements/recommendations for international students: Required—TOEFL (minimum score 600 paper-based; 100 iBT). Electronic applications accepted.

Rensselaer Polytechnic Institute, Graduate School, Lally School of Management, Troy, NY 12180-3590. Offers MBA, MS, PhD, MS/MBA. *Accreditation:* AACSB. *Program availability:* Part-time, evening/weekend. *Faculty:* 36 full-time (9 women), 5 part-time/adjunct (0 women). *Students:* 154 full-time (64 women), 45 part-time (26 women); includes 26 minority (2 Black or African American, non-Hispanic/Latino; 10 Asian, non-Hispanic/Latino; 5 Hispanic/Latino; 9 Two or more races, non-Hispanic/Latino), 133 international. Average age 26. 1,250 applicants, 33% accepted, 79 enrolled. In 2017, 79 master's, 7 doctorates awarded. *Degree requirements:* For doctorate, thesis/dissertation. *Entrance requirements:* For master's and doctorate, GMAT or GRE. Additional exam requirements/recommendations for international students: Required—TOEFL (minimum score 570 paper-based; 88 iBT), IELTS (minimum score 6.5), PTE (minimum score 60). *Application deadline:* For fall admission, 1/1 priority date for domestic and international students; for spring admission, 8/15 priority date for domestic and international students. Applications are processed on a rolling basis. Application fee: $75. Electronic applications accepted. *Expenses:* Contact institution. *Financial support:* In 2017–18, 64 students received support. Scholarships/grants available. Financial award application deadline: 1/1; financial award applicants required to submit FAFSA. *Faculty research:* Business analytics, quantitative finance and risk analytics, management, supply chain management, technology commercialization and entrepreneurship. *Total annual research expenditures:* $314,757. *Unit head:* Dr. Chanaka Edirisinghe, Associate Dean, Lally School of Management, 518-276-3336, E-mail: edirin@rpi.edu.
Website: http://lallyschool.rpi.edu/

Rice University, Graduate Programs, Jesse H. Jones Graduate School of Business, Houston, TX 77251-1892. Offers business administration (EMBA, MBA, PMBA); MBA/M.Eng; MD/MBA. *Accreditation:* AACSB. *Program availability:* Evening/weekend. *Faculty:* 64 full-time, 68 part-time/adjunct. *Students:* 228 full-time (67 women); includes 66 minority (5 Black or African American, non-Hispanic/Latino; 3 American Indian or Alaska Native, non-Hispanic/Latino; 39 Asian, non-Hispanic/Latino; 19 Hispanic/Latino), 52 international. Average age 28. 813 applicants, 27% accepted, 118 enrolled. In 2017, 110 master's awarded. *Degree requirements:* For master's, one foreign language, comprehensive exam. *Entrance requirements:* For master's, GMAT or GRE. Additional exam requirements/recommendations for international students: Required—TOEFL (minimum score 600 paper-based). *Application deadline:* For fall admission, 10/5 priority date for domestic students; for winter admission, 1/9 priority date for domestic students; for spring admission, 4/7 priority date for domestic students. Applications are processed on a rolling basis. Application fee: $200. Electronic applications accepted. *Expenses:* Contact institution. *Financial support:* Fellowships, career-related internships or fieldwork, Federal Work-Study, institutionally sponsored loans, scholarships/grants, and tuition waivers (full and partial) available. Financial award applicants required to submit FAFSA. *Faculty research:* Marketing strategy, technology transfer initiatives, management accounting, leadership and change management, financial management. *Unit head:* Dr. Peter Rodriguez, Dean, 713-348-5928, E-mail: prod@rice.edu. *Application contact:* Sue Oldham, Executive Director of Recruiting and Admissions, 713-348-6153, E-mail: ricemba@rice.edu.
Website: https://business.rice.edu/

Rider University, College of Business Administration, Executive MBA Program, Lawrenceville, NJ 08648-3001. Offers EMBA. *Program availability:* Evening/weekend.

Rider University, College of Business Administration, MBA Program, Lawrenceville, NJ 08648-3001. Offers MBA. *Program availability:* Online learning.

Rivier University, School of Graduate Studies, Department of Business Administration, Nashua, NH 03060. Offers MBA. *Program availability:* Part-time, evening/weekend. *Entrance requirements:* Additional exam requirements/recommendations for international students: Recommended—TOEFL.

Robert Morris University, School of Business, Moon Township, PA 15108-1189. Offers business administration (MBA); human resource management (MS); taxation (MS); MBA/MS. *Accreditation:* AACSB. *Program availability:* Part-time-only, evening/weekend, 100% online. *Faculty:* 12 full-time (4 women), 3 part-time/adjunct (2 women). *Students:* 163 part-time (61 women); includes 13 minority (6 Black or African American, non-Hispanic/Latino; 6 Asian, non-Hispanic/Latino; 1 Two or more races, non-Hispanic/Latino), 8 international. Average age 30. 167 applicants, 40% accepted, 32 enrolled. In 2017, 87 master's awarded. *Entrance requirements:* For master's, GMAT, letters of recommendation. Additional exam requirements/recommendations for international students: Required—TOEFL (minimum score 550 paper-based; 79 iBT). *Application deadline:* For fall admission, 7/1 priority date for domestic and international students; for spring admission, 11/1 priority date for domestic and international students. Applications are processed on a rolling basis. Application fee: $35. Electronic applications accepted. Application fee is waived when completed online. *Expenses:* $955 tuition per credit plus fees of $80 per credit. *Financial support:* Institutionally sponsored loans available. Support available to part-time students. Financial award application deadline: 5/1; financial award applicants required to submit FAFSA. *Unit head:* Dr. Michelle L. Patrick, Dean, 412-397-5445, Fax: 412-397-2585, E-mail: patrick@rmu.edu. *Application contact:* E-mail: graduateadmissions@rmu.edu.
Website: http://sbus.rmu.edu

Robert Morris University Illinois, Morris Graduate School of Management, Chicago, IL 60605. Offers accounting (MBA); accounting/finance (MBA); business analytics (MIS); health care administration (MM); higher education administration (MM); human performance (MS); human resource management (MBA); information security (MIS); information systems management (MIS); law enforcement administration (MM); management (MBA); management/finance (MBA); management/human resource management (MBA); sports administration (MM). *Program availability:* Part-time, evening/weekend. *Faculty:* 2 full-time (0 women), 26 part-time/adjunct (8 women). *Students:* 186 full-time (108 women), 114 part-time (57 women); includes 167 minority (88 Black or African American, non-Hispanic/Latino; 15 Asian, non-Hispanic/Latino; 62 Hispanic/Latino; 1 Native Hawaiian or other Pacific Islander, non-Hispanic/Latino; 1 Two or more races, non-Hispanic/Latino), 18 international. Average age 32. 157 applicants, 78% accepted, 72 enrolled. In 2017, 191 master's awarded. *Entrance requirements:* For master's, official transcripts and letters of recommendation (for some programs); written

personal statement. Additional exam requirements/recommendations for international students: Required—TOEFL (minimum score 550 paper-based). *Application deadline:* Applications are processed on a rolling basis. Application fee: $20 ($100 for international students). Electronic applications accepted. *Expenses: Tuition:* Full-time $17,100; part-time $2850 per course. *Financial support:* In 2017–18, 381 students received support. Federal Work-Study, scholarships/grants, and unspecified assistantships available. Support available to part-time students. Financial award applicants required to submit FAFSA. *Unit head:* Kayed Akkawi, Dean, 312-935-6050, Fax: 312-935-6020, E-mail: kakkawi@robertmorris.edu. *Application contact:* Mark Daugherty, Director of Admissions, 312-935-4814, Fax: 312-935-6020, E-mail: mdaugherty@robertmorris.edu.

Roberts Wesleyan College, Graduate Business Programs, Rochester, NY 14624-1997. Offers strategic leadership (MS); strategic marketing (MS). *Program availability:* Evening/weekend. *Degree requirements:* For master's, thesis or alternative. *Entrance requirements:* For master's, GMAT, minimum GPA of 2.75, verifiable work experience. *Expenses:* Contact institution.

Rochester Institute of Technology, Graduate Enrollment Services, Saunders College of Business, Rochester, NY 14623-5608. Offers Exec MBA, MBA, MS. *Program availability:* Part-time, evening/weekend, 100% online, blended/hybrid learning. *Students:* 227 full-time (99 women), 105 part-time (51 women); includes 24 minority (8 Black or African American, non-Hispanic/Latino; 1 American Indian or Alaska Native, non-Hispanic/Latino; 5 Asian, non-Hispanic/Latino; 5 Hispanic/Latino; 5 Two or more races, non-Hispanic/Latino), 94 international. Average age 30. 588 applicants, 49% accepted, 138 enrolled. In 2017, 134 master's awarded. *Entrance requirements:* For master's, GMAT or GRE, minimum GPA of 3.0 (recommended). Additional exam requirements/recommendations for international students: Required—PTE (minimum score 58). *Application deadline:* Applications are processed on a rolling basis. Application fee: $65. Electronic applications accepted. *Expenses:* $1,815 per credit hour. *Financial support:* In 2017–18, 221 students received support. Research assistantships with partial tuition reimbursements available, teaching assistantships with partial tuition reimbursements available, career-related internships or fieldwork, Federal Work-Study, scholarships/grants, and unspecified assistantships available. Support available to part-time students. Financial award applicants required to submit FAFSA. *Faculty research:* Corporate environmental strategy and sustainability, lean manufacturing and environmental performance, entrepreneurship, data analytics, computational finance, technology and information management, marketing and digital marketing. *Unit head:* Dr. Jacqueline Mozrall, Dean, 585-475-6025, E-mail: gradbus@saunders.rit.edu. *Application contact:* Diane Ellison, Senior Associate Vice President, Graduate Enrollment Services, 585-475-2229, Fax: 585-475-7164, E-mail: gradinfo@rit.edu.
Website: http://saunders.rit.edu/

Rochester Institute of Technology, Graduate Enrollment Services, Saunders College of Business, Marketing and Management Department, MBA Executive Program - Online, Rochester, NY 14623. Offers MBA. *Program availability:* Part-time, evening/weekend, online only, 100% online. *Students:* 36 full-time (17 women); includes 1 minority (Black or African American, non-Hispanic/Latino), 1 international. Average age 39. 21 applicants, 71% accepted, 11 enrolled. In 2017, 9 master's awarded. *Entrance requirements:* For master's, minimum GPA of 3.0 (recommended), five years of work experience. Additional exam requirements/recommendations for international students: Required—PTE (minimum score 58). *Application deadline:* For fall admission, 6/1 priority date for domestic and international students. Applications are processed on a rolling basis. Application fee: $65. Electronic applications accepted. *Expenses:* $1,815 per credit hour. *Financial support:* In 2017–18, 42 students received support. Scholarships/grants available. Support available to part-time students. Financial award applicants required to submit FAFSA. *Faculty research:* Active learning pedagogy; consumer experience; relationship marketing; virtual ethnography; online learning; globalization of manufacturing R&D and engineering; competitive dynamics and internal vs. external network idea sourcing new products; creativity, cognitive learning style and innovation outcomes; R&D project management in resource-constrained business conditions; crowd sourcing vs. mergers and acquisitions as open innovation strategies; cultural impacts on technology adoption. *Unit head:* Amanda Williams, Admissions Officer, 585-475-2729, E-mail: awilliams@saunders.rit.edu. *Application contact:* Diane Ellison, Senior Associate Vice President, Graduate Enrollment Services, 585-475-2229, Fax: 585-475-7164, E-mail: gradinfo@rit.edu.
Website: http://executivembaonline.rit.edu/

Rochester Institute of Technology, Graduate Enrollment Services, Saunders College of Business, Marketing and Management Department, MBA Program, Rochester, NY 14623. Offers MBA. *Accreditation:* AACSB. *Program availability:* Part-time, evening/weekend. *Students:* 89 full-time (31 women), 49 part-time (21 women); includes 10 minority (3 Black or African American, non-Hispanic/Latino; 3 Asian, non-Hispanic/Latino; 2 Hispanic/Latino; 2 Two or more races, non-Hispanic/Latino), 52 international. Average age 27. 195 applicants, 50% accepted, 47 enrolled. In 2017, 65 master's awarded. *Entrance requirements:* For master's, GMAT or GRE, minimum GPA of 3.0 (recommended). Additional exam requirements/recommendations for international students: Required—TOEFL (minimum score 580 paper-based; 92 iBT), IELTS (minimum score 7), PTE (minimum score 63). *Application deadline:* Applications are processed on a rolling basis. Application fee: $65. Electronic applications accepted. *Expenses:* $1,815 per credit hour. *Financial support:* In 2017–18, 89 students received support. Research assistantships with partial tuition reimbursements available, teaching assistantships with partial tuition reimbursements available, career-related internships or fieldwork, scholarships/grants, and unspecified assistantships available. Support available to part-time students. Financial award applicants required to submit FAFSA. *Faculty research:* Health IT adoption; technology management, creativity, and innovation; social media and entrepreneurship; leadership; cybersecurity; and corporate social responsibility and business ethics. *Unit head:* Matt Cornwell, Assistant Director of Student Services and Outreach, 585-475-6916, E-mail: mcornwell@saunders.rit.edu. *Application contact:* Diane Ellison, Senior Associate Vice President, Graduate Enrollment Services, 585-475-2229, Fax: 585-475-7164, E-mail: gradinfo@rit.edu.
Website: http://saunders.rit.edu/programs/graduate/mba_main.php

Rochester Institute of Technology, Graduate Enrollment Services, Saunders College of Business, Marketing and Management Department, MBA Program–Executive Option, Rochester, NY 14623. Offers Exec MBA. *Accreditation:* AACSB. *Program availability:* Part-time-only, evening/weekend. *Students:* 31 full-time (14 women), 25 part-time (16 women); includes 3 minority (1 Black or African American, non-Hispanic/Latino; 1 American Indian or Alaska Native, non-Hispanic/Latino; 1 Hispanic/Latino). Average age 37. 26 applicants, 85% accepted, 19 enrolled. In 2017, 20 master's awarded. *Entrance requirements:* For master's, minimum of 6 years of work experience, minimum GPA of 3.0 (recommended). Additional exam requirements/recommendations for international students: Required—TOEFL, IELTS, PTE (minimum score 58). *Application deadline:* For fall admission, 6/30 priority date for domestic and international students. Applications are processed on a rolling basis. Application fee: $65. Electronic applications accepted. *Expenses:* $1,815 per credit hour. *Financial support:* In 2017–18, 31 students received support. Scholarships/grants available. Support available to part-time students. Financial award applicants required to submit FAFSA. *Faculty*

Business Administration and Management—General

research: Active learning pedagogy; consumer experience; relationship marketing; virtual ethnography; online learning; globalization of manufacturing R&D and engineering; competitive dynamics and internal vs. external network idea sourcing new products; creativity, cognitive learning style and innovation outcomes; R&D project management in resource-constrained business conditions; crowd sourcing vs. mergers and acquisitions as open innovation strategies; cultural impacts on technology adoption. *Unit head:* Amanda Williams, Admissions Officer, 585-475-2729, E-mail: awilliams@saunders.rit.edu. *Application contact:* Diane Ellison, Senior Associate Vice President, Graduate Enrollment Services, 585-475-2229, Fax: 585-475-7164, E-mail: gradinfo@rit.edu.
Website: https://www.rit.edu/emba/on-campus-emba-program

Rockford University, Graduate Studies, Program in Business Administration, Rockford, IL 61108-2393. Offers MBA. *Program availability:* Part-time, evening/weekend. *Entrance requirements:* For master's, GMAT, 3 letters of recommendation. Additional exam requirements/recommendations for international students: Required—TOEFL (minimum score 550 paper-based; 79 iBT). Electronic applications accepted. *Faculty research:* Entrepreneurship, leadership, international business, services marketing, project management.

Rockhurst University, Helzberg School of Management, Kansas City, MO 64110-2561. Offers accounting (MBA); business intelligence (MBA, Certificate); business intelligence and analytics (MS); data science (MBA, Certificate); entrepreneurship (MBA); finance (MBA); fundraising leadership (MBA, Certificate); healthcare management (MBA, Certificate); human capital (Certificate); international business (Certificate); management (MA, MBA, Certificate); nonprofit administration (Certificate); organizational development (Certificate); science leadership (Certificate). *Accreditation:* AACSB. *Program availability:* Part-time, evening/weekend. *Faculty:* 18 full-time (4 women), 20 part-time/adjunct (9 women). *Students:* 99 full-time (30 women), 355 part-time (132 women); includes 95 minority (30 Black or African American, non-Hispanic/Latino; 29 Asian, non-Hispanic/Latino; 25 Hispanic/Latino; 11 Two or more races, non-Hispanic/Latino), 8 international. Average age 32. 249 applicants, 81% accepted, 175 enrolled. In 2017, 145 master's, 17 other advanced degrees awarded. *Entrance requirements:* For master's, GMAT or GRE. Additional exam requirements/recommendations for international students: Required—TOEFL (minimum score 550 paper-based; 79 iBT). *Application deadline:* Applications are processed on a rolling basis. Application fee: $0. Electronic applications accepted. *Financial support:* Applicants required to submit FAFSA. *Faculty research:* Offshoring/outsourcing, systems analysis/synthesis, work teams, multilateral trade, path dependencies/creation. *Unit head:* Cheryl McConnell, Dean, 816-501-4201, Fax: 816-501-4650, E-mail: cheryl.mcconnell@rockhurst.edu. *Application contact:* Jonnae Hill, Director of Graduate Business Advising, 816-501-4823, E-mail: jonnae.hill@rockhurst.edu.
Website: https://www.rockhurst.edu/helzberg

Rogers State University, Program in Business Administration, Claremore, OK 74017-3252. Offers MBA.

Roger Williams University, Mario J. Gabelli School of Business, Bristol, RI 02809. Offers MBA. *Faculty:* 4 full-time (1 woman), 1 part-time/adjunct (0 women). *Students:* 8 full-time (6 women); includes 1 minority (Hispanic/Latino). Average age 22. 15 applicants, 87% accepted, 8 enrolled. *Degree requirements:* For master's, internship, international experience. *Entrance requirements:* For master's, GRE or GMAT, 2 letters of recommendation, letter of intent, official college transcripts. Additional exam requirements/recommendations for international students: Required—TOEFL (minimum score 85 iBT), IELTS (minimum score 6.5). *Application deadline:* For fall admission, 4/1 priority date for domestic students. Application fee: $50. Electronic applications accepted. *Expenses:* $860 per credit hour, $258 graduation fee (for MBA). *Financial support:* In 2017–18, 7 students received support. Scholarships/grants available. Financial award application deadline: 4/1; financial award applicants required to submit FAFSA. *Unit head:* Dr. Susan McTiernan, Dean, 401-254-3444, E-mail: smctiernan@rwu.edu. *Application contact:* Marcus Hanscom, Director of Graduate Admissions, 401-254-3345, Fax: 401-254-3557, E-mail: mhanscom@rwu.edu.
Website: https://www.rwu.edu/academics/schools-and-colleges/gsb

Rollins College, Crummer Graduate School of Business, Winter Park, FL 32789-4499. Offers entrepreneurship (MBA); finance (MBA); international business (MBA); management (MBA). *Accreditation:* AACSB. *Program availability:* Part-time, evening/weekend, online learning. *Faculty:* 20 full-time (4 women). *Students:* 261 full-time (119 women), 114 part-time (45 women); includes 86 minority (24 Black or African American, non-Hispanic/Latino; 13 Asian, non-Hispanic/Latino; 44 Hispanic/Latino; 5 Two or more races, non-Hispanic/Latino), 31 international. Average age 32. In 2017, 134 master's awarded. *Degree requirements:* For master's, minimum GPA of 2.85. *Entrance requirements:* For master's, GMAT or GRE, official transcripts, two letters of recommendation, essay, current resume/curriculum vitae, interview. Additional exam requirements/recommendations for international students: Required—TOEFL (minimum score 100 iBT) or IELTS (minimum score 7). *Application deadline:* Applications are processed on a rolling basis. Application fee: $50. Electronic applications accepted. *Expenses:* Contact institution. *Financial support:* Scholarships/grants available. Support available to part-time students. Financial award applicants required to submit FAFSA. *Faculty research:* Sustainability, world financial markets, international business, market research, strategic marketing. *Unit head:* Deborah Crown, Dean, 407-646-2249, Fax: 407-646-1550, E-mail: dcrown@rollins.edu. *Application contact:* Maralyn E. Graham, Admissions Coordinator, 407-646-2405, Fax: 407-646-1550, E-mail: mbaadmissions@rollins.edu.
Website: http://www.rollins.edu/mba/

Roosevelt University, Graduate Division, Walter E. Heller College of Business, Program in Business Administration, Chicago, IL 60605. Offers MBA. *Accreditation:* ACBSP. *Program availability:* Part-time, evening/weekend. *Students:* 85 full-time (41 women), 179 part-time (105 women); includes 130 minority (78 Black or African American, non-Hispanic/Latino; 19 Asian, non-Hispanic/Latino; 28 Hispanic/Latino; 5 Two or more races, non-Hispanic/Latino), 51 international. Average age 29. 143 applicants, 92% accepted, 49 enrolled. In 2017, 143 master's awarded. *Application deadline:* Applications are processed on a rolling basis. Application fee: $40. Electronic applications accepted. *Financial support:* Scholarships/grants and unspecified assistantships available. *Application contact:* Michael Conwell, Graduate Admission Counselor, 312-281-3250, E-mail: mconwell@roosevelt.edu.
Website: https://www.roosevelt.edu

Roseman University of Health Sciences, College of Dental Medicine - Henderson Campus, Henderson, NV 89014. Offers business administration (MBA); dental medicine (Post-Doctoral Certificate). *Faculty:* 6 full-time (2 women), 6 part-time/adjunct (1 woman). *Students:* 30 full-time (12 women); includes 19 minority (18 Asian, non-Hispanic/Latino; 1 Hispanic/Latino). Average age 30. 92 applicants, 16% accepted, 10 enrolled. In 2017, 12 other advanced degrees awarded. *Degree requirements:* For master's, comprehensive exam, thesis or alternative. *Entrance requirements:* For master's, National Board Dental Examination 1 and 2, graduation from U.S. or Canadian dental school, Nevada dental license. *Application deadline:* For fall admission, 1/31 for domestic and international students. Application fee: $50. *Expenses:* Contact institution. *Financial support:* In 2017–18, 10 students received support. Scholarships/grants available. Financial award application deadline: 6/15; financial award applicants required

to submit FAFSA. *Faculty research:* Oral cancer; CBCT (Cone Beam Computed Tomography) 3D scan data related projects; in-vitro biomaterial testing such as orthodontic bond strength studies using Instron; nanotechnology and orthodontic practice management research. *Unit head:* Dr. Prashanti Bollu, Program Director, 702-968-5690, Fax: 702-968-5277, E-mail: pbollu@roseman.edu. *Application contact:* Carol Shannon, Administrative Assistant to the Program Director, 702-968-1682, E-mail: cshannon@roseman.edu.
Website: http://www.roseman.edu

Roseman University of Health Sciences, MBA Program, Henderson, NV 89014. Offers MBA. *Program availability:* Part-time, evening/weekend. *Faculty:* 4 full-time (1 woman), 16 part-time/adjunct (5 women). *Students:* 18 part-time (11 women); includes 5 minority (2 Black or African American, non-Hispanic/Latino; 2 Asian, non-Hispanic/Latino; 1 Hispanic/Latino). Average age 42. 5 applicants, 100% accepted, 5 enrolled. In 2017, 41 master's awarded. *Degree requirements:* For master's, comprehensive exam, entrepreneurial project, summative assessment and capstone. *Entrance requirements:* For master's, GMAT or leveling course (for applicants whose overall GPA is below 3.0), bachelor's degree. Additional exam requirements/recommendations for international students: Required—TOEFL (minimum score 550 paper-based; 79 iBT). *Application deadline:* For fall admission, 5/15 for domestic and international students. Application fee: $100. *Financial support:* In 2017–18, 1 student received support. Federal Work-Study and scholarships/grants available. Financial award application deadline: 5/1; financial award applicants required to submit FAFSA. *Faculty research:* Using a cash flow-based Z-score to access the progressive solvency of the U.S. commercial banking system; identifying the causes and consequences associated with; groups and retirement preparedness; evaluating the performance of individual stocks relative to indexes. *Unit head:* Dr. Okeleke Nzeogwu, Program Director, 702-968-1659, Fax: 702-968-1685, E-mail: onzeogwu@roseman.edu.
Website: http://www.roseman.edu

Rosemont College, Schools of Graduate and Professional Studies, Business Administration and Leadership Programs, Rosemont, PA 19010-1699. Offers business administration (MBA); leadership (MS); management (MS). *Program availability:* Part-time, evening/weekend, online learning. *Degree requirements:* For master's, thesis (for some programs). *Entrance requirements:* For master's, minimum college GPA of 3.0, 3 letters of recommendation. Application fee is waived when completed online. *Expenses:* Contact institution.

Rowan University, Graduate School, Rohrer College of Business, Department of Business Administration, Glassboro, NJ 08028-1701. Offers MBA. *Accreditation:* AACSB. *Program availability:* Part-time, evening/weekend. *Degree requirements:* For master's, comprehensive exam, thesis. *Entrance requirements:* For master's, GRE General Test. Additional exam requirements/recommendations for international students: Required—TOEFL. Electronic applications accepted. *Expenses:* Tuition, state resident: full-time $15,020; part-time $751 per semester hour. Tuition, nonresident: full-time $15,020; part-time $751 per semester hour. *Required fees:* $3158; $157.90 per semester hour. Tuition and fees vary according to course load, campus/location and program.

Rowan University, Graduate School, Rohrer College of Business, Department of Marketing and Business Information Systems, Program in Business, Glassboro, NJ 08028-1701. Offers CGS. *Program availability:* Part-time, evening/weekend. *Entrance requirements:* Additional exam requirements/recommendations for international students: Required—TOEFL. Electronic applications accepted. *Expenses:* Tuition, state resident: full-time $15,020; part-time $751 per semester hour. Tuition, nonresident: full-time $15,020; part-time $751 per semester hour. *Required fees:* $3158; $157.90 per semester hour. Tuition and fees vary according to course load, campus/location and program.

Royal Military College of Canada, Division of Graduate Studies and Research, Continuing Studies, Department of Business Administration, Kingston, ON K7K 7B4, Canada. Offers MBA. *Degree requirements:* For master's, thesis. *Entrance requirements:* For master's, GMAT, honours degree with second-class standing. Electronic applications accepted.

Rutgers University–Camden, School of Business, Camden, NJ 08102-1401. Offers MBA, JD/MBA. *Accreditation:* AACSB. *Program availability:* Part-time, evening/weekend. *Entrance requirements:* For master's, GMAT, 2 letters of recommendation. Additional exam requirements/recommendations for international students: Required—TOEFL (minimum score 89 iBT). Electronic applications accepted. *Expenses:* Contact institution. *Faculty research:* Efficiency in utility industry, management information systems development, management/labor relations.

Rutgers University–Newark, Graduate School, Program in Management, Newark, NJ 07102. Offers accounting (PhD); accounting information systems (PhD); computer information systems (PhD); finance (PhD); information technology (PhD); international business (PhD); management science (PhD); marketing (PhD); organization management (PhD). Program offered jointly with New Jersey Institute of Technology. *Accreditation:* AACSB. *Degree requirements:* For doctorate, thesis/dissertation, cumulative exams. *Entrance requirements:* For doctorate, GMAT or GRE General Test, minimum undergraduate B average. Additional exam requirements/recommendations for international students: Required—TOEFL. Electronic applications accepted. *Faculty research:* Technology management, leadership and teams, consumer behavior, financial and markets, logistics.

Rutgers University–Newark, Rutgers Business School–Newark and New Brunswick, Program in Business Administration, Newark, NJ 07102. Offers MBA. *Entrance requirements:* For master's, GMAT. Additional exam requirements/recommendations for international students: Required—TOEFL.

Ryerson University, School of Graduate Studies, Ted Rogers School of Management, Toronto, ON M5B 2K3, Canada. Offers global business administration (MBA); management (MSM); management of technology and innovation (MBA).

Sacred Heart University, Graduate Programs, Jack Welch College of Business, Department of Management, Fairfield, CT 06825. Offers administration (MBA); human resource management (MS, Graduate Certificate); management (Graduate Certificate). *Program availability:* Part-time, evening/weekend. *Faculty:* 4 full-time (1 woman), 1 part-time/adjunct (0 women). *Students:* 72 full-time (38 women), 133 part-time (72 women); includes 44 minority (9 Black or African American, non-Hispanic/Latino; 1 American Indian or Alaska Native, non-Hispanic/Latino; 8 Asian, non-Hispanic/Latino; 24 Hispanic/Latino; 2 Two or more races, non-Hispanic/Latino), 45 international. Average age 31. 158 applicants, 89% accepted, 62 enrolled. In 2017, 85 master's awarded. *Degree requirements:* For master's, capstone project. *Entrance requirements:* For master's, GMAT/GRE, bachelor's degree. Additional exam requirements/recommendations for international students: Required—TOEFL (minimum score 570 paper-based, 80 iBT), TWE, or IELTS (6.5). *Application deadline:* Applications are processed on a rolling basis. Application fee: $75. Electronic applications accepted. *Expenses:* Contact institution. *Financial support:* Applicants required to submit FAFSA. *Unit head:* Nadene Koliopoulos, Director of Graduate Business Programs, 203-365-7660, E-mail: koliopoulosn@sacredheart.edu. *Application contact:* Pam Pillo, Executive Director of Graduate Admissions, 203-365-7619, E-mail: gradstudies@sacredheart.edu.

Business Administration and Management—General

Sage Graduate School, School of Management, Program in Business Administration, Troy, NY 12180-4115. Offers MBA. *Program availability:* Part-time, evening/weekend. *Faculty:* 5 full-time (3 women), 5 part-time/adjunct (1 woman). *Students:* 35 full-time (24 women), 51 part-time (36 women); includes 19 minority (10 Black or African American, non-Hispanic/Latino; 1 American Indian or Alaska Native, non-Hispanic/Latino; 3 Asian, non-Hispanic/Latino; 5 Hispanic/Latino), 2 international. Average age 31. 75 applicants, 48% accepted, 17 enrolled. In 2017, 30 master's awarded. *Entrance requirements:* For master's, minimum GPA of 2.75, resume, 2 letters of recommendation. Additional exam requirements/recommendations for international students: Required—TOEFL (minimum score 550 paper-based). *Application deadline:* Applications are processed on a rolling basis. Application fee: $30. Electronic applications accepted. Tuition and fees vary according to degree level and program. *Financial support:* Fellowships, research assistantships, and unspecified assistantships available. Financial award application deadline: 3/1; financial award applicants required to submit FAFSA. *Unit head:* Dr. Kimberly Fredericks, Dean, School of Management, 518-292-1782, Fax: 518-292-1964, E-mail: fredek1@sage.edu. *Application contact:* Wendy D. Diefendorf, Director of Graduate and Adult Admission, 518-244-2443, Fax: 518-244-6880, E-mail: diefew@sage.edu.

Saginaw Valley State University, College of Business and Management, Program in Business Administration, University Center, MI 48710. Offers MBA. *Accreditation:* AACSB. *Program availability:* Part-time, evening/weekend, online only, 100% online, blended/hybrid learning. *Faculty:* 12 full-time (4 women), 1 part-time/adjunct (0 women). *Students:* 29 full-time (13 women), 32 part-time (13 women); includes 8 minority (5 Black or African American, non-Hispanic/Latino; 1 Asian, non-Hispanic/Latino; 1 Hispanic/Latino; 1 Two or more races, non-Hispanic/Latino), 30 international. Average age 28. 42 applicants, 57% accepted, 11 enrolled. In 2017, 34 master's awarded. *Degree requirements:* For master's, thesis optional. *Entrance requirements:* For master's, GMAT. Additional exam requirements/recommendations for international students: Required—TOEFL (minimum score 550 paper-based; 79 iBT). *Application deadline:* For fall admission, 7/15 for international students; for winter admission, 11/15 for international students; for spring admission, 4/15 for international students. Applications are processed on a rolling basis. Application fee: $30 ($90 for international students). Electronic applications accepted. *Expenses:* Tuition, state resident: full-time $10,156; part-time $564.20 per credit hour. Tuition, nonresident: full-time $19,336; part-time $1074.20 per credit hour. *Required fees:* $263; $14.60 per credit hour. Tuition and fees vary according to degree level and program. *Financial support:* Federal Work-Study and scholarships/grants available. Support available to part-time students. Financial award application deadline: 4/15; financial award applicants required to submit FAFSA. *Unit head:* Dr. Mark McCartney, MBA Program Coordinator, 989-964-4064. *Application contact:* Jenna Briggs, Director, Graduate and International Admissions, 989-964-6096, Fax: 989-964-2788, E-mail: gradadm@svsu.edu.
Website: http://www.svsu.edu/mba/

St. Ambrose University, College of Business, Program in Business Administration, Davenport, IA 52803-2898. Offers business administration (DBA); health care (MBA); human resources (MBA). *Accreditation:* ACBSP. *Program availability:* Part-time, evening/weekend. *Degree requirements:* For master's, comprehensive exam (for some programs), thesis or alternative, capstone seminar; for doctorate, comprehensive exam, thesis/dissertation, oral and written exams. *Entrance requirements:* For master's, GMAT; for doctorate, GMAT, master's degree. Additional exam requirements/recommendations for international students: Required—TOEFL. Electronic applications accepted. *Expenses:* Contact institution.

St. Bonaventure University, School of Graduate Studies, School of Business, St. Bonaventure, NY 14778-2284. Offers general business (MBA); professional accountancy (MBA). *Accreditation:* AACSB. *Program availability:* Part-time, evening/weekend, 100% online. *Faculty:* 14 full-time (4 women), 4 part-time/adjunct (1 woman). *Students:* 81 full-time (33 women), 92 part-time (47 women); includes 16 minority (3 Black or African American, non-Hispanic/Latino; 1 American Indian or Alaska Native, non-Hispanic/Latino; 4 Asian, non-Hispanic/Latino; 5 Hispanic/Latino; 1 Native Hawaiian or other Pacific Islander, non-Hispanic/Latino; 2 Two or more races, non-Hispanic/Latino), 7 international. Average age 28. 104 applicants, 98% accepted, 79 enrolled. In 2017, 78 master's awarded. *Entrance requirements:* For master's, GMAT or GRE, undergraduate degree, transcripts, current resume. Additional exam requirements/recommendations for international students: Required—TOEFL (minimum score 550 paper-based; 79 iBT). *Application deadline:* For fall admission, 6/15 priority date for domestic students, 2/1 priority date for international students; for spring admission, 11/1 priority date for domestic students, 7/1 priority date for international students. Applications are processed on a rolling basis. Application fee: $0. Electronic applications accepted. *Expenses:* $733 per credit hour, $100 graduation fee. *Financial support:* Career-related internships or fieldwork, Federal Work-Study, scholarships/grants, health care benefits, and unspecified assistantships available. Support available to part-time students. Financial award application deadline: 4/15; financial award applicants required to submit FAFSA. *Faculty research:* High performance computing, sports economics, influence of crowd-sourcing from virtual brand communities on brand perception. *Unit head:* Dr. Matrecia James, Dean, 716-375-2200, Fax: 716-372-2191, E-mail: mjames@sbu.edu. *Application contact:* Bruce Campbell, Director of Graduate Admissions, 716-375-2429, Fax: 716-375-4015, E-mail: gradsch@sbu.edu.
Website: http://www.sbu.edu/academics/schools/business/graduate-degrees/master-of-business-administration-(mba)

St. Catherine University, Graduate Programs, Program in Business Administration, St. Paul, MN 55105. Offers healthcare (MBA); integrated marketing communications (MBA); management (MBA). *Program availability:* Part-time, evening/weekend. *Students:* 62 part-time (54 women); includes 8 minority (4 Black or African American, non-Hispanic/Latino; 2 Asian, non-Hispanic/Latino; 2 Two or more races, non-Hispanic/Latino), 1 international. Average age 33. 28 applicants, 71% accepted, 18 enrolled. In 2017, 34 master's awarded. *Entrance requirements:* For master's, GMAT (if undergraduate GPA is less than 3.0), 2+ years' work or volunteer experience in professional setting(s). Additional exam requirements/recommendations for international students: Required—TOEFL. *Application deadline:* For fall admission, 8/1 priority date for domestic students; for spring admission, 12/15 priority date for domestic students. Application fee: $35. *Expenses:* Contact institution. *Unit head:* Michelle Wieser, Director, 651-690-6355, E-mail: mawieser@stkate.edu.

St. Cloud State University, School of Graduate Studies, Herberger Business School, Program in Business Administration, St. Cloud, MN 56301-4498. Offers business administration (MBA); information assurance (MS). *Accreditation:* AACSB. *Program availability:* Part-time, evening/weekend. *Degree requirements:* For master's, thesis or alternative. *Entrance requirements:* For master's, GMAT, minimum GPA of 2.75. Additional exam requirements/recommendations for international students: Required—Michigan English Language Assessment Battery; Recommended—TOEFL (minimum score 550 paper-based), IELTS (minimum score 6.5).

Saint Francis University, School of Business, Loretto, PA 15940-0600. Offers business administration (MBA); human resource management (MHRM). *Program availability:* Part-time, evening/weekend. *Faculty:* 10 full-time (4 women), 13 part-time/adjunct (9 women). *Students:* 52 full-time (17 women), 76 part-time (44 women); includes 10 minority (8 Black or African American, non-Hispanic/Latino; 1 Native Hawaiian or other Pacific Islander, non-Hispanic/Latino; 1 Two or more races, non-Hispanic/Latino), 1 international. Average age 30. 65 applicants, 77% accepted, 45 enrolled. In 2017, 67 master's awarded. *Degree requirements:* For master's, comprehensive exam (for some programs), thesis (for some programs). *Entrance requirements:* For master's, GMAT (waived if undergraduate QPA is 3.3 or above), 2 letters of recommendation, minimum GPA of 2.75, two essays. Additional exam requirements/recommendations for international students: Required—TOEFL (minimum score 550 paper-based; 57 iBT). *Application deadline:* For fall admission, 8/15 priority date for domestic and international students; for spring admission, 12/1 priority date for domestic students, 12/1 for international students. Applications are processed on a rolling basis. Application fee: $30. Electronic applications accepted. *Expenses:* Contact institution. *Financial support:* Fellowships with partial tuition reimbursements, career-related internships or fieldwork, and unspecified assistantships available. Financial award application deadline: 8/15; financial award applicants required to submit FAFSA. *Total annual research expenditures:* $425,000. *Unit head:* Dr. Randy L. Frye, Director, Graduate Business Programs, 814-472-3041, Fax: 814-472-3174, E-mail: rfrye@francis.edu. *Application contact:* Nicole Marie Bauman, Coordinator, Graduate Business Programs, 814-472-3026, Fax: 814-472-3369, E-mail: nbauman@francis.edu.
Website: http://francis.edu/school-of-business/

St. John Fisher College, School of Business, MBA Program, Rochester, NY 14618-3597. Offers MBA. *Accreditation:* AACSB. *Program availability:* Part-time, evening/weekend. *Faculty:* 9 full-time (0 women), 6 part-time/adjunct (3 women). *Students:* 64 full-time (32 women), 75 part-time (34 women); includes 17 minority (6 Black or African American, non-Hispanic/Latino; 2 Asian, non-Hispanic/Latino; 9 Hispanic/Latino), 5 international. Average age 28. 114 applicants, 80% accepted, 63 enrolled. In 2017, 69 master's awarded. *Degree requirements:* For master's, capstone project. *Entrance requirements:* For master's, 2 letters of recommendation, personal statement, current resume, interview. Additional exam requirements/recommendations for international students: Required—TOEFL (minimum score 575 paper-based; 80 iBT). *Application deadline:* Applications are processed on a rolling basis. Application fee: $30. Electronic applications accepted. *Expenses:* Contact institution. *Financial support:* Scholarships/grants available. Financial award applicants required to submit FAFSA. *Faculty research:* Business strategy, consumer behavior, cross-cultural management practices, international finance, organizational trust. *Unit head:* Dr. David Kunsch, Program Director, 585-385-5245, E-mail: dkunsch@sjfc.edu. *Application contact:* Michelle Gosier, Director of Transfer and Graduate Admissions, 585-385-8064, E-mail: mgosier@sjfc.edu.
Website: https://www.sjfc.edu/graduate-programs/master-of-business-administration-mba/

St. John Fisher College, School of Business, MS in Management Program, Rochester, NY 14618-3597. Offers MS. *Program availability:* Evening/weekend. *Faculty:* 2 full-time (0 women), 2 part-time/adjunct (1 woman). *Students:* 12 full-time (5 women), 1 (woman) part-time; includes 2 minority (1 Black or African American, non-Hispanic/Latino; 1 Asian, non-Hispanic/Latino), 1 international. Average age 29. 31 applicants, 71% accepted, 12 enrolled. *Entrance requirements:* For master's, baccalaureate degree, official transcripts, two letters of recommendation, current resume, personal goals statement. Additional exam requirements/recommendations for international students: Required—TOEFL (minimum score 575 paper-based; 80 iBT). *Application deadline:* Applications are processed on a rolling basis. Application fee: $30. Electronic applications accepted. *Expenses:* Contact institution. *Financial support:* Scholarships/grants available. Financial award applicants required to submit FAFSA. *Unit head:* Dr. David Kunsch, Director, 585-385-5245, E-mail: dkunsch@sjfc.edu. *Application contact:* Michelle Gosier, Director of Transfer and Graduate Admissions, 585-385-8064, E-mail: mgosier@sjfc.edu.
Website: https://www.sjfc.edu/graduate-programs/ms-in-management/

St. John's University, The Peter J. Tobin College of Business, Department of Management, Queens, NY 11439. Offers business administration (MBA), including strategic management. *Faculty:* 15 full-time (5 women), 9 part-time/adjunct (4 women). *Students:* 31 full-time (13 women), 21 part-time (7 women); includes 24 minority (8 Black or African American, non-Hispanic/Latino; 3 Asian, non-Hispanic/Latino; 10 Hispanic/Latino; 1 Native Hawaiian or other Pacific Islander, non-Hispanic/Latino; 2 Two or more races, non-Hispanic/Latino), 2 international. Average age 26. 37 applicants, 86% accepted, 30 enrolled. In 2017, 17 master's awarded. *Entrance requirements:* For master's, GMAT or GRE, 2 letters of recommendation, essay, resume, unofficial transcripts. Additional exam requirements/recommendations for international students: Required—TOEFL (minimum score 80 iBT), IELTS (minimum score 6.5). *Application deadline:* For fall admission, 11/1 for domestic and international students; for winter admission, 3/1 for domestic and international students; for spring admission, 6/1 for domestic and international students. Applications are processed on a rolling basis. Application fee: $70. Electronic applications accepted. *Expenses:* $22,410 per year. *Financial support:* Research assistantships, teaching assistantships, scholarships/grants, and unspecified assistantships available. Support available to part-time students. Financial award application deadline: 2/1; financial award applicants required to submit FAFSA. *Total annual research expenditures:* $27,189. *Unit head:* Dr. John Angelidis, Chair, 718-990-6495, E-mail: angelidj@stjohns.edu. *Application contact:* Amber Steiger, Associate Director of Enrollment Management, 718-990-1345, E-mail: steigera@stjohns.edu.
Website: http://www.stjohns.edu/academics/schools-and-colleges/peter-j-tobin-college-business/management

St. John's University, The Peter J. Tobin College of Business, Department of Marketing, Queens, NY 11439. Offers business administration (MBA), including marketing management. *Faculty:* 12 full-time (5 women), 5 part-time/adjunct (1 woman). *Students:* 40 full-time (27 women), 17 part-time (10 women); includes 16 minority (7 Black or African American, non-Hispanic/Latino; 2 Asian, non-Hispanic/Latino; 5 Hispanic/Latino; 2 Two or more races, non-Hispanic/Latino), 14 international. Average age 25. 41 applicants, 88% accepted, 26 enrolled. In 2017, 22 master's awarded. *Entrance requirements:* For master's, GMAT or GRE, 2 letters of recommendation, essay, resume, unofficial transcripts. Additional exam requirements/recommendations for international students: Required—TOEFL (minimum score 80 iBT), IELTS (minimum score 6.5). *Application deadline:* For fall admission, 11/1 for domestic and international students; for winter admission, 3/1 for domestic students; for spring admission, 6/1 for domestic and international students. Applications are processed on a rolling basis. Application fee: $70. Electronic applications accepted. *Expenses:* $22,410 per year. *Financial support:* Research assistantships, teaching assistantships, scholarships/grants, and unspecified assistantships available. Support available to part-time students. Financial award application deadline: 2/1; financial award applicants required to submit FAFSA. *Unit head:* Dr. Iris Mohr, Chair, 718-990-7307, E-mail: mohri@stjohns.edu. *Application contact:* Amber Steiger, Associate Director of Enrollment Management, 718-990-1345, E-mail: steigera@stjohns.edu.
Website: http://www.stjohns.edu/academics/schools-and-colleges/peter-j-tobin-college-business/marketing

Business Administration and Management—General

St. John's University, The Peter J. Tobin College of Business, Program in International Business, Queens, NY 11439. Offers business administration (MBA), including international business. *Students:* 16 full-time (8 women), 6 part-time (2 women); includes 8 minority (3 Black or African American, non-Hispanic/Latino; 2 Asian, non-Hispanic/Latino; 3 Hispanic/Latino), 2 international. Average age 30. 21 applicants, 86% accepted, 15 enrolled. In 2017, 11 master's awarded. *Entrance requirements:* For master's, GMAT or GRE, 2 letters of recommendation, essay, resume, unofficial transcripts. Additional exam requirements/recommendations for international students: Required—TOEFL (minimum score 80 iBT), IELTS (minimum score 6.5). *Application deadline:* For fall admission, 11/1 for domestic and international students; for winter admission, 3/1 for domestic and international students; for spring admission, 6/1 for domestic and international students. Applications are processed on a rolling basis. Application fee: $70. Electronic applications accepted. *Expenses:* $22,410 per year. *Financial support:* Research assistantships, teaching assistantships, scholarships/grants, and unspecified assistantships available. Support available to part-time students. Financial award application deadline: 2/1; financial award applicants required to submit FAFSA. *Unit head:* Dr. John Angelidis, Chair, 718-990-6495, E-mail: angelidj@stjohns.edu. *Application contact:* Amber Steiger, Associate Director of Enrollment Management, 718-990-1345, E-mail: steigera@stjohns.edu.

St. John's University, The Peter J. Tobin College of Business, School of Risk Management, Insurance and Actuarial Science, Queens, NY 11439. Offers actuarial science (MS); business administration (MBA), including risk management and insurance; enterprise risk management (MBA, MS), including enterprise risk management (MS); risk management and insurance (MS). *Faculty:* 11 full-time (2 women), 7 part-time/adjunct (1 woman). *Students:* 51 full-time (24 women), 28 part-time (13 women); includes 15 minority (7 Black or African American, non-Hispanic/Latino; 4 Asian, non-Hispanic/Latino; 3 Hispanic/Latino; 1 Two or more races, non-Hispanic/Latino), 40 international. Average age 27. 58 applicants, 78% accepted, 27 enrolled. In 2017, 32 master's awarded. *Entrance requirements:* For master's, GMAT or GRE, 2 letters of recommendation, essay, resume, unofficial transcripts. Additional exam requirements/recommendations for international students: Required—TOEFL (minimum score 80 iBT), IELTS (minimum score 6.5). *Application deadline:* For fall admission, 11/1 for domestic and international students; for winter admission, 3/1 for domestic and international students; for spring admission, 6/1 for domestic and international students. Applications are processed on a rolling basis. Application fee: $70. Electronic applications accepted. *Expenses:* $22,410 per year. *Financial support:* Research assistantships, teaching assistantships, scholarships/grants, and unspecified assistantships available. Support available to part-time students. Financial award application deadline: 2/1; financial award applicants required to submit FAFSA. *Faculty research:* Insurance company operations and financial analysis, enterprise risk management, risk theory and modeling, credibility theory and actuarial price modeling, international insurance. *Unit head:* Dr. Mark J. Browne, Chair, 212-277-5175, E-mail: brownem1@stjohns.edu. *Application contact:* Amber Steiger, Associate Director of Enrollment Management, 718-990-1345, E-mail: steigera@stjohns.edu. Website: https://www.stjohns.edu/academics/schools-and-colleges/peter-j-tobin-college-business/school-risk-management-insurance-and-actuarial-science

St. Joseph's College, Long Island Campus, Programs in Business Management and Administration, Field in Business Administration, Patchogue, NY 11772-2399. Offers MBA. *Program availability:* Part-time, evening/weekend, 100% online, blended/hybrid learning. *Faculty:* 15 full-time (7 women), 22 part-time/adjunct (7 women). *Entrance requirements:* For master's, official college transcripts, two letters of recommendation, resume, verification of employment letter and form, 200-250 word essay or personal statement. Additional exam requirements/recommendations for international students: Recommended—TOEFL (minimum score 550 paper-based; 80 iBT). Application fee: $25. *Expenses:* Tuition: Full-time $17,550; part-time $975 per credit. *Required fees:* $362. *Unit head:* Mary A. Chance, Assistant Professor/Interim Director of Graduate Management Studies, 631-687-1297, E-mail: mchance@sjcny.edu.

St. Joseph's College, Long Island Campus, Programs in Business Management and Administration, Field of Executive Business Administration, Patchogue, NY 11772-2399. Offers EMBA. *Program availability:* Part-time, evening/weekend, 100% online, blended/hybrid learning. *Faculty:* 15 full-time (7 women), 22 part-time/adjunct (7 women). *Students:* 18 full-time (12 women), 72 part-time (43 women); includes 24 minority (11 Black or African American, non-Hispanic/Latino; 2 Asian, non-Hispanic/Latino; 10 Hispanic/Latino; 1 Two or more races, non-Hispanic/Latino). Average age 34. 54 applicants, 67% accepted, 24 enrolled. In 2017, 24 master's awarded. *Entrance requirements:* For master's, official college transcripts, two letters of recommendation, resume, verification of employment letter and form, 200-250 word essay or personal statement. Additional exam requirements/recommendations for international students: Recommended—TOEFL (minimum score 550 paper-based; 79 iBT), IELTS (minimum score 7). *Application deadline:* Applications are processed on a rolling basis. Application fee: $25. Electronic applications accepted. *Expenses:* Tuition: Full-time $17,550; part-time $975 per credit. *Required fees:* $362. *Financial support:* In 2017–18, 20 students received support. Federal Work-Study available. *Unit head:* Mary A. Chance, Assistant Professor/Interim Director of Graduate Management Studies, 631-687-1297, E-mail: mchance@sjcny.edu. Website: http://www.sjcny.edu

St. Joseph's College, Long Island Campus, Programs in Management, Patchogue, NY 11772-2399. Offers health care management (MS); human resources management (MS); human services leadership (MS); organizational management (MS). *Program availability:* Part-time, evening/weekend, 100% online, blended/hybrid learning. *Faculty:* 15 full-time (7 women), 22 part-time/adjunct (7 women). *Students:* 23 full-time (17 women), 120 part-time (94 women); includes 39 minority (19 Black or African American, non-Hispanic/Latino; 1 Asian, non-Hispanic/Latino; 17 Hispanic/Latino; 2 Two or more races, non-Hispanic/Latino). Average age 36. 133 applicants, 64% accepted, 55 enrolled. In 2017, 41 master's awarded. *Application deadline:* Applications are processed on a rolling basis. Application fee: $25. Electronic applications accepted. *Expenses:* Tuition: Full-time $17,550; part-time $975 per credit. *Required fees:* $362. *Financial support:* In 2017–18, 27 students received support. *Unit head:* Mary A. Chance, Assistant Professor/Interim Director of Graduate Management Studies, 631-687-1297, E-mail: mchance@sjcny.edu.

St. Joseph's College, New York, Programs in Business Management and Administration, Field of Business Administration, Brooklyn, NY 11205-3688. Offers MBA. *Program availability:* Part-time, evening/weekend, 100% online, blended/hybrid learning. *Faculty:* 1 full-time (0 women), 6 part-time/adjunct (4 women). *Entrance requirements:* For master's, two letters of recommendation, resume, 250-word essay, official college transcripts. Additional exam requirements/recommendations for international students: Required—TOEFL (minimum score 80 iBT). Application fee: $25. *Expenses:* Tuition: Full-time $17,550; part-time $975 per credit. *Required fees:* $362. *Unit head:* John Capela, Associate Chair, 718-940-5843, E-mail: jcapela@sjcny.edu. Website: https://www.sjcny.edu

St. Joseph's College, New York, Programs in Business Management and Administration, Field of Executive Business Administration, Brooklyn, NY 11205-3688. Offers EMBA. *Program availability:* Part-time, evening/weekend, 100% online, blended/

hybrid learning. *Faculty:* 1 full-time (0 women), 6 part-time/adjunct (4 women). *Students:* 3 full-time (1 woman), 29 part-time (20 women); includes 26 minority (12 Black or African American, non-Hispanic/Latino; 2 Asian, non-Hispanic/Latino; 8 Hispanic/Latino; 4 Two or more races, non-Hispanic/Latino). Average age 40. 11 applicants, 100% accepted, 11 enrolled. In 2017, 16 master's awarded. *Entrance requirements:* For master's, two letters of recommendation, resume, 250-word essay, official college transcripts. Additional exam requirements/recommendations for international students: Required—TOEFL (minimum score 80 iBT). *Application deadline:* Applications are processed on a rolling basis. Application fee: $25. Electronic applications accepted. *Expenses:* Tuition: Full-time $17,550; part-time $975 per credit. *Required fees:* $362. *Financial support:* In 2017–18, 6 students received support. *Unit head:* Sharon Didier, Co-Director of Graduate Management Studies/Assistant Professor, 718-940-5790, E-mail: sdidier@sjcny.edu. Website: http://www.sjcny.edu

Saint Joseph's College of Maine, Master of Business Administration in Leadership Program, Standish, ME 04084. Offers MBA. *Program availability:* Part-time, online learning. *Entrance requirements:* For master's, two years of work experience.

★ **Saint Joseph's University,** Erivan K. Haub School of Business, Philadelphia, PA 19131-1395. Offers MBA, MS, Post Master's Certificate, Postbaccalaureate Certificate, DO/MBA. *Accreditation:* AACSB. *Program availability:* Part-time-only, evening/weekend, 100% online. *Faculty:* 46 full-time (12 women), 51 part-time/adjunct (9 women). *Students:* 235 full-time (94 women), 859 part-time (371 women); includes 235 minority (109 Black or African American, non-Hispanic/Latino; 65 Asian, non-Hispanic/Latino; 45 Hispanic/Latino; 2 Native Hawaiian or other Pacific Islander, non-Hispanic/Latino; 14 Two or more races, non-Hispanic/Latino), 156 international. Average age 33. 712 applicants, 73% accepted, 281 enrolled. In 2017, 381 master's awarded. *Degree requirements:* For master's and other advanced degree, minimum GPA of 3.0. *Entrance requirements:* For master's, GMAT, MAT, GRE, letters of recommendation, resume, personal statement, official undergraduate and graduate transcripts; structured interview (for some programs); for other advanced degree, official master's-level transcripts. Additional exam requirements/recommendations for international students: Required—PTE, TOEFL, IELTS, or PTE. *Application deadline:* For fall admission, 7/15 priority date for domestic students, 5/15 priority date for international students; for spring admission, 11/15 priority date for domestic students, 10/15 priority date for international students; for summer admission, 4/15 priority date for domestic students, 2/15 priority date for international students. Applications are processed on a rolling basis. Application fee: $35. Electronic applications accepted. *Financial support:* Scholarships/grants and unspecified assistantships available. Financial award application deadline: 5/1; financial award applicants required to submit FAFSA. *Unit head:* Dr. Joseph A. DiAngelo, Dean, 610-660-1645, Fax: 610-660-1649, E-mail: jodiange@sju.edu. *Application contact:* Jeannine Lajeunesse, Director, MBA and MS Programs, 610-660-1626, Fax: 610-660-1599, E-mail: jlajeune@sju.edu. Website: https://www.sju.edu/majors-programs/graduate-business

See Display on the next page and Close-Up on page 181.

Saint Leo University, Graduate Studies in Business, Saint Leo, FL 33574-6665. Offers accounting (M Acc, MBA); cybersecurity (MS); cybersecurity management (MBA); data analytics (MBA); health care management (MBA); human resource management (MBA); international and experiential business administration (MBA); management (MBA, DBA); marketing (MBA); marketing research and social media analytics (MBA); project management (MBA); social media marketing (MBA); sport business (MBA); supply chain global integration management (MBA). *Accreditation:* ACBSP. *Program availability:* Part-time, evening/weekend, 100% online, blended/hybrid learning. *Faculty:* 54 full-time (18 women), 52 part-time/adjunct (18 women). *Students:* 9 full-time (3 women), 1,867 part-time (1,079 women); includes 861 minority (598 Black or African American, non-Hispanic/Latino; 3 American Indian or Alaska Native, non-Hispanic/Latino; 38 Asian, non-Hispanic/Latino; 186 Hispanic/Latino; 3 Native Hawaiian or other Pacific Islander, non-Hispanic/Latino; 33 Two or more races, non-Hispanic/Latino), 68 international. Average age 37. 868 applicants, 63% accepted, 537 enrolled. In 2017, 859 master's, 3 doctorates awarded. *Degree requirements:* For doctorate, comprehensive exam, thesis/dissertation. *Entrance requirements:* For master's, GMAT with minimum score 500 (for M Acc), official transcripts, current resume, 2 professional recommendations, personal statement, bachelor's degree from regionally-accredited university; undergraduate degree in accounting and minimum undergraduate GPA of 3.0 (for M Acc); minimum undergraduate GPA of 3.0 in final 2 years of undergraduate study and 2 years' work experience (for MBA); for doctorate, GMAT (minimum score of 550) if master's GPA is under 3.25, official transcripts, current resume, 2 professional recommendations, personal statement, master's degree from regionally-accredited university with minimum GPA of 3.25, 3 years' work experience, interview. Additional exam requirements/recommendations for international students: Required—TOEFL (minimum score 550 paper-based; 78 iBT). *Application deadline:* For fall admission, 7/1 priority date for domestic and international students; for spring admission, 11/12 priority date for domestic students, 11/1 for international students. Applications are processed on a rolling basis. Application fee: $80. Electronic applications accepted. *Expenses:* Contact institution. *Financial support:* In 2017–18, 106 students received support. Career-related internships or fieldwork, health care benefits, and tuition remission for Saint Leo employees and their dependents available. Financial award application deadline: 3/1; financial award applicants required to submit FAFSA. *Faculty research:* Servant leadership, work/life balance, emotional intelligence, pricing, marketing. *Unit head:* Dr. Charles Hale, Dean, School of Business, 352-588-8599, Fax: 352-588-8912, E-mail: mbaslu@saintleo.edu. *Application contact:* Mark Russum, Assistant Vice President, Enrollment, 800-707-8846, Fax: 352-588-7873, E-mail: grad.admissions@saintleo.edu. Website: https://www.saintleo.edu/school-of-business

Saint Louis University, Graduate Programs, John Cook School of Business, Program in Business Administration, St. Louis, MO 63103. Offers MBA. *Accreditation:* AACSB. *Program availability:* Part-time, evening/weekend. *Entrance requirements:* For master's, GMAT, letter of recommendation, resume. Additional exam requirements/recommendations for international students: Required—TOEFL (minimum score 570 paper-based; 88 iBT). Electronic applications accepted. *Expenses:* Contact institution.

Saint Martin's University, Office of Graduate Studies, School of Business, Lacey, WA 98503. Offers MBA. *Accreditation:* ACBSP. *Program availability:* Part-time, evening/weekend. *Faculty:* 3 full-time (1 woman), 11 part-time/adjunct (4 women). *Students:* 29 full-time (14 women), 33 part-time (10 women); includes 28 minority (8 Black or African American, non-Hispanic/Latino; 7 Asian, non-Hispanic/Latino; 8 Hispanic/Latino; 1 Native Hawaiian or other Pacific Islander, non-Hispanic/Latino; 4 Two or more races, non-Hispanic/Latino), 6 international. Average age 34. 16 applicants, 100% accepted, 14 enrolled. In 2017, 48 master's awarded. *Entrance requirements:* For master's, personal essay. Additional exam requirements/recommendations for international students: Required—TOEFL (minimum score 550 paper-based; 79 iBT); Recommended—IELTS (minimum score 6.5). *Application deadline:* For fall admission, 7/1 priority date for domestic and international students; for spring admission, 12/1 for domestic students, 12/1 priority date for international students. Applications are processed on a rolling basis. Application fee: $50. Electronic applications accepted.

Business Administration and Management—General

Expenses: Tuition: Full-time $21,420; part-time $1190 per credit. *Financial support:* Career-related internships or fieldwork and scholarships/grants available. Support available to part-time students. Financial award application deadline: 3/1; financial award applicants required to submit FAFSA. *Unit head:* Dr. Donald Conant, Director, MBA Program, 360-556-7359, E-mail: dconant@stmartin.edu. *Application contact:* Casey Caronna, Administrative Assistant, 360-412-6128, E-mail: ccaronna@stmartin.edu.
Website: https://www.stmartin.edu

Saint Mary's College of California, School of Economics and Business Administration, Executive MBA Program, Moraga, CA 94556. Offers MBA. *Accreditation:* AACSB. *Program availability:* Part-time, evening/weekend, blended/hybrid learning. *Entrance requirements:* For master's, 5 years of management experience. Additional exam requirements/recommendations for international students: Required—TOEFL. *Expenses:* Contact institution.

Saint Mary's College of California, School of Economics and Business Administration, MS in Management Program, Moraga, CA 94575. Offers MS.

Saint Mary's College of California, School of Economics and Business Administration, Professional MBA Program, Moraga, CA 94556. Offers MBA. *Accreditation:* AACSB. *Program availability:* Part-time, evening/weekend. *Degree requirements:* For master's, 4 half-day management practica. *Entrance requirements:* For master's, GMAT. Additional exam requirements/recommendations for international students: Required—TOEFL. *Expenses:* Contact institution.

St. Mary's University, Graduate Studies, Greehey School of Business, San Antonio, TX 78228. Offers business administration (MBA); JD/MBA. *Accreditation:* AACSB. *Program availability:* Part-time, evening/weekend. *Students:* 78 full-time (36 women), 28 part-time (15 women); includes 49 minority (4 Black or African American, non-Hispanic/Latino; 5 Asian, non-Hispanic/Latino; 39 Hispanic/Latino; 1 Native Hawaiian or other Pacific Islander, non-Hispanic/Latino), 16 international. Average age 32. 145 applicants, 36% accepted, 40 enrolled. In 2017, 28 master's awarded. *Degree requirements:* For master's, comprehensive exam. *Entrance requirements:* For master's, GMAT (minimum score of 525) or GRE (minimum score of 306), undergraduate degree from accredited institution, letters of reference, current resume. Additional exam requirements/recommendations for international students: Required—TOEFL (minimum score 570 paper-based; 87 iBT); Recommended—IELTS (minimum score 6.5), TSE. *Application deadline:* For fall admission, 7/1 for domestic students; for spring admission, 11/15 for domestic students; for summer admission, 4/1 for domestic students. Application fee: $0. Electronic applications accepted. *Expenses: Tuition:* Full-time $16,200; part-time $900 per credit hour. *Required fees:* $810; $405 per semester. *Financial support:* Research assistantships, institutionally sponsored loans, scholarships/grants, and unspecified assistantships available. Financial award application deadline: 3/31; financial award applicants required to submit FAFSA. *Faculty research:* Investment strategies, cross-culture marketing, organizational culture, supply chain management, small-firm internalization. *Unit head:* Jeremy Grace, Director, Master of Business Administration Programs, 210-431-2027, E-mail: jmgrace@stmarytx.edu.
Website: https://www.stmarytx.edu/academics/business/

Saint Mary's University, Sobey School of Business, Halifax, NS B3H 3C3, Canada. Offers MBA, MF, PhD. *Program availability:* Part-time, evening/weekend. *Degree requirements:* For master's, research project; for doctorate, thesis/dissertation. *Entrance requirements:* For master's, GMAT, minimum B average; for doctorate, GMAT or GRE, MBA or other master's-level degree, minimum B+ average. *Expenses:* Contact institution.

Saint Mary's University of Minnesota, Schools of Graduate and Professional Programs, Graduate School of Business and Technology, Business Administration Program, Winona, MN 55987-1399. Offers MBA, DBA. *Unit head:* Holly Tapper, Director, 612-238-4547, Fax: 612-728-5121, E-mail: htapper@smumn.edu. *Application contact:* James Callinan, Director of Admissions for Graduate and Professional Programs, 612-728-5158, Fax: 612-728-5121, E-mail: jcallina@smumn.edu.
Website: http://www.smumn.edu/graduate-home/areas-of-study/graduate-school-of-business-technology/master-of-business-administration-mba

Saint Mary's University of Minnesota, Schools of Graduate and Professional Programs, Graduate School of Business and Technology, Doctor of Business Administration Program, Winona, MN 55987-1399. Offers DBA. *Unit head:* Dr. Matt Nowakowski, Director, 612-728-5142, E-mail: mnowakow@smumn.edu. *Application contact:* James Callinan, Director of Admissions for Graduate and Professional Programs, 612-728-5158, Fax: 612-728-5121, E-mail: jcallina@smumn.edu.
Website: http://www.smumn.edu/academics/graduate/business-technology/programs/doctor-of-business-administration-dba

Saint Mary's University of Minnesota, Schools of Graduate and Professional Programs, Graduate School of Business and Technology, Management Program, Winona, MN 55987-1399. Offers MA. *Entrance requirements:* For master's, undergraduate degree from regionally-accredited institution with minimum overall GPA of 2.75, official transcripts, personal statement, two letters of recommendation, resume. Application fee: $25. Electronic applications accepted. *Unit head:* Paula Justich, Director, 612-728-5165, E-mail: pjustich@smumn.edu. *Application contact:* James Callinan, Director of Admissions for Graduate and Professional Programs, 612-728-5158, Fax: 612-728-5121, E-mail: jcallina@smumn.edu.
Website: http://www.smumn.edu/graduate-home/areas-of-study/graduate-school-of-business-technology/ma-in-management

St. Norbert College, Master of Business Administration Program, De Pere, WI 54115-2099. Offers business (MBA); health care (MBA); supply chain and manufacturing (MBA). *Program availability:* Part-time-only, evening/weekend. *Faculty:* 10 full-time (3 women), 8 part-time/adjunct (2 women). *Students:* 68 part-time (40 women); includes 5 minority (1 American Indian or Alaska Native, non-Hispanic/Latino; 1 Asian, non-Hispanic/Latino; 2 Hispanic/Latino; 1 Two or more races, non-Hispanic/Latino), 1 international. Average age 33. 15 applicants, 100% accepted, 14 enrolled. In 2017, 12 master's awarded. *Entrance requirements:* For master's, official transcripts, letters of recommendation, professional resume, essay. *Application deadline:* For fall admission, 8/4 for domestic students; for winter admission, 12/15 for domestic students; for spring admission, 3/2 for domestic students; for summer admission, 4/20 for domestic students. Applications are processed on a rolling basis. Application fee: $50. Electronic applications accepted. *Expenses:* $675 per credit tuition, $37.50 per course technology fee. *Financial support:* Federal Work-Study available. Financial award application deadline: 1/1; financial award applicants required to submit FAFSA. *Faculty research:* Urban segregation, religious identity, crisis decision-making, normative ethics, psychological effects of change on individuals and organizations. *Unit head:* Lisa Gray, Coordinator of MBA Program, 920-403-3449, E-mail: lisa.gray@snc.edu. *Application contact:* Brenda Busch, Associate Director of Graduate Recruitment, 920-403-3942, Fax: 920-403-4072, E-mail: brenda.busch@snc.edu.
Website: http://www.snc.edu/mba/

Saint Peter's University, Graduate Business Programs, MBA Program, Jersey City, NJ 07306-5997. Offers finance (MBA); health care administration (MBA); human resource management (MBA); international business (MBA); management (MBA); management

Business Administration and Management—General

information systems (MBA); marketing (MBA); risk management (MBA); MBA/MS. *Program availability:* Part-time, evening/weekend. *Entrance requirements:* Additional exam requirements/recommendations for international students: Required—TOEFL. Electronic applications accepted. *Faculty research:* Finance, health care management, human resource management, international business, management, management information systems, marketing, risk management.

St. Thomas Aquinas College, Division of Business Administration, Sparkill, NY 10976. Offers business administration (MBA); finance (MBA); management (MBA); marketing (MBA). *Program availability:* Part-time, evening/weekend. *Entrance requirements:* For master's, GMAT. Additional exam requirements/recommendations for international students: Required—TOEFL. Electronic applications accepted.

St. Thomas University, School of Business, Department of Business Administration, Miami Gardens, FL 33054-6459. Offers M Acc, MBA, Certificate. *Program availability:* Part-time, evening/weekend. *Degree requirements:* For master's, comprehensive exam. *Entrance requirements:* Additional exam requirements/recommendations for international students: Required—TOEFL (minimum score 550 paper-based; 79 iBT). Electronic applications accepted.

St. Thomas University, School of Business, Department of Management, Miami Gardens, FL 33054-6459. Offers accounting (MBA); general management (MSM, Certificate); health management (MBA, MSM, Certificate); human resource management (MBA, MSM, Certificate); international business (MBA, MIB, MSM, Certificate); justice administration (MSM, Certificate); management accounting (MSM, Certificate); public management (MSM, Certificate); sports administration (MS). *Program availability:* Part-time, evening/weekend. *Degree requirements:* For master's, comprehensive exam. *Entrance requirements:* For master's, interview, minimum GPA of 3.0 or GMAT. Additional exam requirements/recommendations for international students: Required—TOEFL (minimum score 550 paper-based; 79 iBT). Electronic applications accepted.

St. Thomas University, School of Leadership Studies, Program in Professional Studies, Miami Gardens, FL 33054-6459. Offers executive management (MPS). *Entrance requirements:* Additional exam requirements/recommendations for international students: Required—TOEFL (minimum score 550 paper-based; 79 iBT).

Saint Vincent College, Program in Business, Latrobe, PA 15650-2690. Offers MS. *Entrance requirements:* For master's, bachelor's degree, minimum overall GPA of 3.0, three recommendations, personal statement, curriculum vitae or resume. Additional exam requirements/recommendations for international students: Required—TOEFL (minimum score 91 iBT), IELTS (minimum score 6.5).

Saint Xavier University, Graduate Studies, Graham School of Management, Chicago, IL 60655-3105. Offers employee health benefits (Certificate); finance (MBA); financial fraud examination and management (MBA, Certificate); financial planning (MBA, Certificate); generalist/individualized (MBA); health administration (MBA); managed care (Certificate); management (MBA); marketing (MBA); project management (MBA, Certificate); MBA/MS. *Accreditation:* AACSB. *Program availability:* Part-time, evening/weekend. *Entrance requirements:* For master's, GMAT, minimum GPA of 3.0, 2 years of work experience. Electronic applications accepted. *Expenses:* Contact institution.

Salem International University, School of Business, Salem, WV 26426-0500. Offers information security (MBA); international business (MBA). *Program availability:* Part-time, online learning. *Entrance requirements:* For master's, minimum undergraduate GPA of 2.5, course work in business, resume. Additional exam requirements/recommendations for international students: Recommended—TOEFL (minimum score 550 paper-based), IELTS (minimum score 6.5). Electronic applications accepted. *Expenses:* Contact institution. *Faculty research:* Organizational behavior strategy, marketing services.

Salem State University, School of Graduate Studies, Program in Business Administration, Salem, MA 01970-5353. Offers MBA. *Program availability:* Part-time, evening/weekend. *Entrance requirements:* For master's, GMAT. Additional exam requirements/recommendations for international students: Required—TOEFL (minimum score 550 paper-based; 80 iBT) or IELTS (minimum score 5.5).

Salisbury University, Perdue School of Business, Salisbury, MD 21801. Offers business administration (MBA). *Accreditation:* AACSB. *Program availability:* Part-time, evening/weekend, 100% online, blended/hybrid learning. *Faculty:* 7 full-time (2 women). *Students:* 34 full-time (17 women), 25 part-time (12 women); includes 14 minority (7 Black or African American, non-Hispanic/Latino; 2 Asian, non-Hispanic/Latino; 5 Two or more races, non-Hispanic/Latino), 4 international. Average age 29. 72 applicants, 67% accepted, 41 enrolled. In 2017, 40 master's awarded. *Entrance requirements:* For master's, GMAT, three letters of recommendation; transcripts from all colleges or universities attended; essay; resume; minimum GPA of 2.5. Additional exam requirements/recommendations for international students: Required—TOEFL (minimum score 550 paper-based; 79 iBT), IELTS (minimum score 6.5). *Application deadline:* For fall admission, 3/1 priority date for domestic and international students. Applications are processed on a rolling basis. Application fee: $65. Electronic applications accepted. *Expenses:* $392 per credit hour resident; $703 per credit hour non-resident; $92 per credit hour fees; $750 per credit hour (online, no fees charge). *Financial support:* In 2017–18, 4 students received support, including 4 teaching assistantships with full tuition reimbursements available (averaging $8,500 per year); career-related internships or fieldwork and scholarships/grants also available. Support available to part-time students. Financial award application deadline: 3/1; financial award applicants required to submit FAFSA. *Faculty research:* Supply chain management; SAP (enterprise resource planning); shared entrepreneurship. *Unit head:* Yvonne Downie Hanley, Graduate Program Director, Business Administration, 410-548-3983, E-mail: yxdownie@salisbury.edu.
Website: http://www.salisbury.edu/gsr/gradstudies/MBApage.html

Salve Regina University, Program in Business Administration, Newport, RI 02840-4192. Offers cybersecurity issues in business (MBA); entrepreneurial enterprise (MBA); health care administration and management (MBA); nonprofit management (MBA); social ventures (MBA). *Program availability:* Part-time, evening/weekend, online learning. *Entrance requirements:* For master's, GMAT, GRE General Test, or MAT, 6 undergraduate credits each in accounting, economics, quantitative analysis and calculus or statistics. Additional exam requirements/recommendations for international students: Required—TOEFL (minimum score 600 paper-based; 100 iBT) or IELTS. Electronic applications accepted.

Salve Regina University, Program in Management, Newport, RI 02840-4192. Offers business studies (CGS); human resource management (CGS); innovation and strategic management (MS); management (CGS); nonprofit management (CGS); social entrepreneurship (CGS). *Program availability:* Part-time, evening/weekend, online learning. *Entrance requirements:* For master's, GMAT, GRE General Test, or MAT. Additional exam requirements/recommendations for international students: Required—TOEFL (minimum score 600 paper-based; 100 iBT). Electronic applications accepted.

Samford University, Brock School of Business, Birmingham, AL 35229. Offers accountancy (M Acc); entrepreneurship (MBA); finance (MBA); marketing (MBA); JD/M Acc; JD/MBA; MBA/M Acc; MBA/M Div; MBA/MSEM; MBA/Pharm D. Programs offered jointly with Cumberland School of Law, Beeson School of Divinity, Howard College of Arts and Sciences, and McWhorter School of Pharmacy. *Accreditation:* AACSB. *Program availability:* Part-time, 100% online, blended/hybrid learning. *Faculty:* 8 full-time (1 woman), 5 part-time/adjunct (0 women). *Students:* 79 full-time (31 women), 18 part-time (8 women); includes 7 minority (2 Black or African American, non-Hispanic/Latino; 1 Asian, non-Hispanic/Latino; 3 Hispanic/Latino; 1 Two or more races, non-Hispanic/Latino), 8 international. Average age 28. 46 applicants, 78% accepted, 16 enrolled. In 2017, 78 master's awarded. *Degree requirements:* For master's, capstone course. *Entrance requirements:* For master's, GMAT or GRE, resume, transcripts; essay (international applicants only). Additional exam requirements/recommendations for international students: Required—TOEFL (minimum score 90 iBT), IELTS (minimum score 6.5). *Application deadline:* For fall admission, 8/1 for domestic and international students; for spring admission, 12/1 for domestic and international students; for summer admission, 5/1 for domestic and international students. Applications are processed on a rolling basis. Application fee: $35. Electronic applications accepted. Application fee is waived when completed online. *Expenses:* $813 per credit hour tuition; $425 per semester fees. *Financial support:* In 2017–18, 59 students received support. Scholarships/grants available. Financial award application deadline: 2/15; financial award applicants required to submit FAFSA. *Unit head:* Dr. Barbara Cartledge, Assistant Dean, 205-726-2935, Fax: 205-726-2540, E-mail: bhcartle@samford.edu. *Application contact:* Elizabeth Anne Gambrell, Associate Director, 205-726-2040, Fax: 205-726-2540, E-mail: eagambre@samford.edu.
Website: http://www.samford.edu/business

Sam Houston State University, College of Business Administration, Department of General Business and Finance, Huntsville, TX 77341. Offers banking and financial institutions (EMBA); business administration (MBA). *Accreditation:* AACSB. *Program availability:* Part-time, evening/weekend, online learning. *Degree requirements:* For master's, comprehensive exam (for some programs). *Entrance requirements:* For master's, GMAT, interview (for EMBA); resume, transcript(s). Additional exam requirements/recommendations for international students: Required—TOEFL (minimum score 550 paper-based; 79 iBT), IELTS (minimum score 6.5). Electronic applications accepted.

San Diego State University, Graduate and Research Affairs, College of Business Administration, Department of Management, San Diego, CA 92182. Offers entrepreneurship (MS); human resources management (MS); management science (MS). *Program availability:* Part-time, evening/weekend. *Degree requirements:* For master's, thesis or alternative. *Entrance requirements:* For master's, GMAT, resume, letters of reference. Additional exam requirements/recommendations for international students: Required—TOEFL. Electronic applications accepted.

San Diego State University, Graduate and Research Affairs, College of Business Administration, Program in Business Administration, San Diego, CA 92182. Offers MBA. *Accreditation:* AACSB. *Program availability:* Part-time. *Degree requirements:* For master's, thesis or alternative. *Entrance requirements:* For master's, GMAT, resume, letters of reference. Additional exam requirements/recommendations for international students: Required—TOEFL. Electronic applications accepted.

San Francisco State University, Division of Graduate Studies, College of Business, San Francisco, CA 94132-1722. Offers EMBA, MA, MBA, MSA. *Unit head:* Linda Oubre, Dean, 415-338-1276, Fax: 415-338-6237, E-mail: loubre@sfsu.edu. *Application contact:* Dr. Yim-Yu Wong, Associate Dean, 415-338-1276, Fax: 415-338-6237, E-mail: yywong@sfsu.edu. Website: http://cob.sfsu.edu/

San Ignacio University, Graduate Programs, Doral, FL 33178. Offers business administration (MBA), including human resources management, international business, marketing management; education (M Ed), including early childhood education, educational leadership, special education; hospitality management (MA), including gastronomy and restaurant management, tourism management.

San Jose State University, Graduate Studies and Research, Lucas Graduate School of Business, San Jose, CA 95192-0065. Offers accountancy (MS); business administration (MBA); taxation (MS); transportation management (MS). *Program availability:* Part-time, evening/weekend, online learning. *Faculty:* 15 full-time (7 women), 6 part-time/adjunct (3 women). *Students:* 85 full-time (49 women), 51 part-time (28 women); includes 77 minority (2 Black or African American, non-Hispanic/Latino; 44 Asian, non-Hispanic/Latino; 16 Hispanic/Latino; 1 Native Hawaiian or other Pacific Islander, non-Hispanic/Latino; 14 Two or more races, non-Hispanic/Latino), 42 international. Average age 28. 328 applicants, 43% accepted, 88 enrolled. In 2017, 155 master's awarded. *Degree requirements:* For master's, graduate writing assessment, culminating project. *Entrance requirements:* Additional exam requirements/recommendations for international students: Required—TOEFL (minimum score 80 iBT), IELTS (minimum score 6.5), PTE (minimum score 53). *Application deadline:* For fall admission, 2/1 for domestic and international students. Applications are processed on a rolling basis. Application fee: $55. Electronic applications accepted. *Expenses:* Contact institution. *Financial support:* Fellowships, research assistantships, career-related internships or fieldwork, Federal Work-Study, institutionally sponsored loans, scholarships/grants, and unspecified assistantships available. Support available to part-time students. Financial award application deadline: 4/28; financial award applicants required to submit FAFSA. *Faculty research:* Financial effects of cyber-security breaches, health care analytics, innovation and teamwork, corporate bankruptcy prediction, multi-domain executive coaching. *Unit head:* Dr. Dan Moshavi, Dean, 408-924-3400, Fax: 408-924-3426, E-mail: dan.moshavi@sjsu.edu.
Website: http://www.sjsu.edu/lucasschool/

Santa Clara University, Leavey School of Business, Santa Clara, CA 95053. Offers business administration (MBA); business analytics (MS); finance (MS); information systems (MS); supply chain management and analytics (MS); JD/MBA. *Accreditation:* AACSB. *Program availability:* Part-time, evening/weekend, online curriculum with 2 on-campus intensives. *Faculty:* 100 full-time (30 women), 42 part-time/adjunct (16 women). *Students:* 413 full-time (226 women), 308 part-time (131 women); includes 246 minority (10 Black or African American, non-Hispanic/Latino; 175 Asian, non-Hispanic/Latino; 40 Hispanic/Latino; 2 Native Hawaiian or other Pacific Islander, non-Hispanic/Latino; 19 Two or more races, non-Hispanic/Latino), 256 international. Average age 31. 761 applicants, 63% accepted, 271 enrolled. In 2017, 267 master's awarded. *Entrance requirements:* For master's, GMAT, resume, essays, 2 letters of recommendation, 2 official transcripts. Additional exam requirements/recommendations for international students: Required—TOEFL (minimum score 100 iBT) or IELTS (7.0). Application fee: $100 ($150 for international students). Electronic applications accepted. *Expenses:* Contact institution. *Financial support:* In 2017–18, 192 students received support. Career-related internships or fieldwork, scholarships/grants, and unspecified assistantships available. Financial award applicants required to submit FAFSA. *Faculty research:* Digital marketing, database mining and retail, product innovation, industry disruption, entrepreneurship and cluster dynamics, innovation and temporary advantage, platform strategy, ethics and leadership, bank regulation, monetary policy, poverty alleviation, costs of financial crises, information technology and business intelligence, supply chain management, corporate social responsibility and institutional ownership, audits and financial reporting. *Unit head:* Caryn Beck-Dudley, Dean, 408-554-4523, E-mail: cbeckdudley@scu.edu. *Application contact:* Lenore Grant, Director, Graduate Business Recruitment and Admissions, 408-551-1633, E-mail: lgrant@scu.edu.
Website: http://www.scu.edu/business/

Savannah State University, Master of Business Administration Program, Savannah, GA 31404. Offers MBA. *Accreditation:* AACSB. *Program availability:* Part-time, evening/weekend. *Entrance requirements:* For master's, GMAT, GRE, or successful completion of pre-MBA program, BA/BS from an accredited institution, official transcripts, essay, 3 letters of recommendation, immunization certificate, current resume. Additional exam requirements/recommendations for international students: Required—TOEFL. Electronic applications accepted. *Expenses:* Contact institution.

Schiller International University, MBA Program, Madrid, Spain, Madrid, Spain. Offers international business (MBA). *Program availability:* Part-time. *Degree requirements:* For master's, comprehensive exam, thesis optional. *Entrance requirements:* Additional exam requirements/recommendations for international students: Required—TOEFL (minimum score 550 paper-based).

Schiller International University, MBA Program Paris, France, Paris, France. Offers international business (MBA). Bilingual French/English MBA available for native French speakers. *Program availability:* Part-time, evening/weekend, online learning. *Degree requirements:* For master's, comprehensive exam, thesis or alternative. *Entrance requirements:* Additional exam requirements/recommendations for international students: Required—TOEFL (minimum score 550 paper-based).

Schiller International University, MBA Programs, Florida, Largo, FL 33771. Offers financial planning (MBA); information technology (MBA); international business (MBA); international hotel and tourism management (MBA). *Program availability:* Part-time, evening/weekend, online learning. *Degree requirements:* For master's, thesis optional. *Entrance requirements:* Additional exam requirements/recommendations for international students: Required—TOEFL (minimum score 550 paper-based).

Schiller International University, MBA Programs, Heidelberg, Germany, Heidelberg, Germany. Offers international business (MBA, MIM); management of information technology (MBA). *Program availability:* Part-time, evening/weekend. *Degree requirements:* For master's, thesis optional. *Entrance requirements:* Additional exam requirements/recommendations for international students: Required—TOEFL (minimum score 550 paper-based). *Faculty research:* Leadership, international economy, foreign direct investment.

Schreiner University, MBA Program, Kerrville, TX 78028-5697. Offers ethical leadership (MBA). *Program availability:* Part-time, online learning. *Entrance requirements:* For master's, 3 recommendations; personal essay; transcripts; resume. Additional exam requirements/recommendations for international students: Required—TOEFL. Electronic applications accepted. *Expenses:* Contact institution.

Seattle Pacific University, Master of Arts in Management Program, Seattle, WA 98119-1997. Offers business intelligence and data analytics (MA); cybersecurity (MA); faith and business (MA); human resources (MA); social and sustainable management (MA). *Students:* 4 full-time (all women), 12 part-time (8 women), 4 international. Average age 28. 15 applicants, 60% accepted, 7 enrolled. In 2017, 18 master's awarded. *Entrance requirements:* For master's, GMAT or GRE (waived with cumulative GPA of 3.3 or above), bachelor's degree from accredited college or university, resume, essay, official transcript. *Application deadline:* For fall admission, 8/1 for domestic students, 6/1 for international students; for winter admission, 11/1 for domestic students, 9/1 for international students; for spring admission, 2/1 for domestic students, 12/1 for international students; for summer admission, 5/1 for domestic students. Application fee: $50. *Application contact:* E-mail: drj@spu.edu.
Website: http://spu.edu/academics/school-of-business-and-economics/graduate-programs/ma-management

Seattle Pacific University, Master of Business Administration Program, Seattle, WA 98119-1997. Offers business administration (MBA); social and sustainable enterprise (MBA). *Accreditation:* AACSB. *Program availability:* Part-time. *Students:* 3 full-time (1 woman), 25 part-time (16 women); includes 6 minority (1 Black or African American, non-Hispanic/Latino; 1 Asian, non-Hispanic/Latino; 3 Hispanic/Latino; 1 Two or more races, non-Hispanic/Latino), 4 international. Average age 34. 26 applicants, 38% accepted, 7 enrolled. In 2017, 12 master's awarded. *Entrance requirements:* For master's, GMAT (minimum preferred scores of 500; 25 verbal; 30 quantitative; 4.4 analytical writing), BA, resume as evidence of substantive work experience. Additional exam requirements/recommendations for international students: Required—TOEFL (minimum score 90 iBT), IELTS (minimum score 7). *Application deadline:* For fall admission, 8/1 for domestic and international students; for winter admission, 11/1 for domestic and international students; for spring admission, 2/1 for domestic and international students. Applications are processed on a rolling basis. Application fee: $50. Electronic applications accepted. *Financial support:* Scholarships/grants available. Financial award applicants required to submit FAFSA. *Unit head:* Gary Karns, Associate Dean for Graduate Studies, 206-281-2948, Fax: 206-281-2733. *Application contact:* 206-281-2091.
Website: http://spu.edu/academics/school-of-business-and-economics/graduate-programs/mba

Seattle University, Albers School of Business and Economics, Bridge MBA Program, Seattle, WA 98122-1090. Offers MBA. *Faculty:* 22 full-time (6 women), 10 part-time/adjunct (1 woman). *Students:* 23 full-time (12 women); includes 2 minority (1 Asian, non-Hispanic/Latino; 1 Hispanic/Latino), 7 international. Average age 23. 52 applicants, 54% accepted, 23 enrolled. In 2017, 24 master's awarded. *Entrance requirements:* For master's, GMAT. Additional exam requirements/recommendations for international students: Required—TOEFL or IELTS. *Application deadline:* For fall admission, 7/1 for domestic students. Applications are processed on a rolling basis. Application fee: $55. Electronic applications accepted. *Expenses:* Contact institution. *Financial support:* In 2017–18, 6 students received support. Scholarships/grants available. Financial award application deadline: 6/1. *Unit head:* John Merle, Director, 206-398-4628, E-mail: merlej@seattleu.edu. *Application contact:* Jeff Millard, Assistant Dean of Graduate Programs, 206-296-5700, E-mail: albersgrad@seattleu.edu.
Website: http://www.seattleu.edu/albers/bridgemba

Seattle University, Albers School of Business and Economics, Master of Business Administration Program, Seattle, WA 98122-1090. Offers MBA, Certificate, JD/MBA, MBA/MSBA, MBA/MSF. *Accreditation:* AACSB. *Program availability:* Part-time, evening/weekend. *Faculty:* 29 full-time (10 women), 10 part-time/adjunct (1 woman). *Students:* 78 full-time (39 women), 226 part-time (92 women); includes 91 minority (3 Black or African American, non-Hispanic/Latino; 1 American Indian or Alaska Native, non-Hispanic/Latino; 54 Asian, non-Hispanic/Latino; 18 Hispanic/Latino; 2 Native Hawaiian or other Pacific Islander, non-Hispanic/Latino; 13 Two or more races, non-Hispanic/Latino), 47 international. Average age 31. 137 applicants, 61% accepted, 43 enrolled. In 2017, 169 master's, 46 other advanced degrees awarded. *Entrance requirements:* For master's, GMAT, minimum GPA of 3.0, 2 years of related work experience. Additional exam requirements/recommendations for international students: Required—TOEFL (minimum score 580 paper-based; 92 iBT). *Application deadline:* For fall admission, 8/20 priority date for domestic students, 4/1 priority date for international students; for winter admission, 11/20 priority date for domestic students, 9/1 priority date for international students; for spring admission, 2/20 priority date for domestic students, 12/1 priority date for international students. Applications are processed on a rolling basis. Application fee: $55. Electronic applications accepted. *Expenses:* Contact institution. *Financial support:*

In 2017–18, 86 students received support. Career-related internships or fieldwork and Federal Work-Study available. Support available to part-time students. Financial award applicants required to submit FAFSA. *Unit head:* Dr. Greg Magnan, Director, 206-296-5700, Fax: 206-296-5795. E-mail: gmagnan@seattleu.edu. *Application contact:* Janet Shandley, Director of Graduate Admissions, 206-296-5900, Fax: 206-298-5656, E-mail: grad_admissions@seattleu.edu.
Website: http://www.seattleu.edu/albers/mba/

Seton Hall University, Stillman School of Business, South Orange, NJ 07079-2697. Offers MBA, MS, Certificate. *Accreditation:* AACSB. *Program availability:* Part-time, evening/weekend. *Faculty:* 29 full-time (4 women), 18 part-time/adjunct (0 women). *Students:* 140 full-time (58 women), 154 part-time (49 women); includes 66 minority (25 Black or African American, non-Hispanic/Latino; 14 Asian, non-Hispanic/Latino; 23 Hispanic/Latino; 4 Two or more races, non-Hispanic/Latino), 88 international. Average age 32. 416 applicants, 73% accepted, 100 enrolled. In 2017, 132 master's awarded. *Degree requirements:* For master's, 20 hours of community service (Social Responsibility Project). *Entrance requirements:* For master's, GMAT or GRE, MS in business discipline, professional degree or designation (MD, JD, PhD, DVM, DDS, CPA, etc.), minimum undergraduate GPA of 3.0. Additional exam requirements/recommendations for international students: Required—TOEFL (minimum score 607 paper-based; 80 iBT), IELTS (minimum score 6), PTE. *Application deadline:* For fall admission, 5/31 priority date for domestic students, 3/31 priority date for international students; for spring admission, 10/31 priority date for domestic students, 9/30 priority date for international students; for summer admission, 4/30 priority date for domestic students, 3/31 priority date for international students. Applications are processed on a rolling basis. Application fee: $75. Electronic applications accepted. Application fee is waived when completed online. *Expenses:* $1,305 per credit; $126 fees (fall and spring semester), $51 (summer semester). *Financial support:* In 2017–18, 41 students received support, including 41 research assistantships with full tuition reimbursements available (averaging $3,644 per year); career-related internships or fieldwork, scholarships/grants, and unspecified assistantships also available. Financial award application deadline: 6/30; financial award applicants required to submit FAFSA. *Faculty research:* Sport, hedge funds, executive compensation, social media, and legal issues. *Unit head:* Dr. Joyce Strawser, Dean, 973-761-9013, Fax: 973-275-2465, E-mail: joyce.strawser@shu.edu. *Application contact:* Alfred Ayoub, Director of Graduate Admissions, 973-761-9262, Fax: 973-761-9208, E-mail: alfred.ayoub@shu.edu.
Website: http://www.shu.edu/academics/business/

Seton Hill University, MBA Program, Greensburg, PA 15601. Offers entrepreneurship (MBA); forensic accounting and fraud examination (MBA); healthcare administration (MBA); management (MBA). *Program availability:* Part-time, evening/weekend. *Entrance requirements:* For master's, resume, 3 letters of recommendation, personal statement, transcripts. Additional exam requirements/recommendations for international students: Required—TOEFL (minimum score 600 paper-based; 100 iBT), IELTS (minimum score 6.5). *Application deadline:* Applications are processed on a rolling basis. Application fee: $0. Electronic applications accepted. *Expenses: Tuition:* Part-time $734 per credit. Tuition and fees vary according to class time, course level, course load and program. *Financial support:* Federal Work-Study, scholarships/grants, and tuition discounts available. Financial award application deadline: 8/15; financial award applicants required to submit FAFSA. *Unit head:* Dr. Douglas Nelson, Associate Professor, Business/MBA Program Director, E-mail: dnelson@setonhill.edu.
Website: http://www.setonhill.edu/academics/graduate_programs/mba

Shenandoah University, Harry F. Byrd, Jr. School of Business, Winchester, VA 22601-5195. Offers business administration (MBA); business administration essentials (Certificate); healthcare management (Certificate). *Accreditation:* AACSB. *Program availability:* Part-time, evening/weekend. *Faculty:* 16 full-time (8 women), 2 part-time/adjunct (0 women). *Students:* 53 full-time (18 women), 59 part-time (37 women); includes 26 minority (10 Black or African American, non-Hispanic/Latino; 1 American Indian or Alaska Native, non-Hispanic/Latino; 5 Asian, non-Hispanic/Latino; 8 Hispanic/Latino; 2 Two or more races, non-Hispanic/Latino), 28 international. Average age 32. 73 applicants, 93% accepted, 46 enrolled. In 2017, 35 master's awarded. *Entrance requirements:* For master's, transcripts from all institutions of higher learning; minimum GPA of 3.0 in appropriate undergraduate course work; 2 letters of recommendation; resume; interview; brief narrative essay (2-3 pages) of career, professional development and goals, as they relate to the completion of an MBA. Additional exam requirements/recommendations for international students: Required—TOEFL (minimum score 550 paper-based, 79 iBT) or IELTS (6.5). *Application deadline:* For fall admission, 5/1 for domestic students, 4/15 for international students; for spring admission, 11/15 for domestic students, 10/15 for international students; for summer admission, 6/15 for domestic students, 5/1 for international students. Application fee: $30. Electronic applications accepted. *Expenses:* $31,080 tuition, $1,297 fees (technology fee and student services fee). *Financial support:* In 2017–18, 27 students received support. Scholarships/grants and unspecified assistantships available. Financial award applicants required to submit FAFSA. *Faculty research:* Entrepreneurship, sports ethics, healthcare economics, leaderships, sustainability. *Unit head:* Bogdan Daraban, PhD, Associate Dean, School of Business, 540-542-6282, Fax: 540-665-5437, E-mail: bdaraban@su.edu. *Application contact:* Andrew Woodall, Executive Director of Recruitment and Admissions, 540-665-4581, Fax: 540-665-4627, E-mail: admit@su.edu.
Website: http://www.su.edu/business/

Shippensburg University of Pennsylvania, School of Graduate Studies, College of Arts and Sciences, Department of Sociology and Anthropology, Shippensburg, PA 17257-2299. Offers organizational development and leadership (MS), including business, higher education structure and policy, historical administration, leadership in society, management information systems, public organizations. *Program availability:* Part-time, evening/weekend. *Faculty:* 4 full-time (2 women). *Students:* 14 full-time (6 women), 19 part-time (11 women); includes 7 minority (4 Black or African American, non-Hispanic/Latino; 2 Hispanic/Latino; 1 Two or more races, non-Hispanic/Latino), 1 international. Average age 26. 31 applicants, 81% accepted, 15 enrolled. In 2017, 22 master's awarded. *Degree requirements:* For master's, capstone experience including internship. *Entrance requirements:* For master's, interview (if GPA less than 2.75), current resume, personal goals statement. Additional exam requirements/recommendations for international students: Required—TOEFL (minimum score 550 paper-based, 68 iBT) or IELTS (minimum score 6). *Application deadline:* For fall admission, 4/30 for international students; for spring admission, 9/30 for international students. Applications are processed on a rolling basis. Application fee: $45. Electronic applications accepted. *Expenses:* Tuition, state resident: part-time $500 per credit. Tuition, nonresident: part-time $750 per credit. *Required fees:* $145 per credit. *Financial support:* In 2017–18, 12 students received support. Career-related internships or fieldwork, scholarships/grants, unspecified assistantships, and resident hall director and student payroll positions available. Support available to part-time students. Financial award application deadline: 3/1; financial award applicants required to submit FAFSA. *Unit head:* Dr. Barbara J. Denison, Departmental Chair and Program Coordinator, 717-477-1735, Fax: 717-477-4011, E-mail: bjdeni@ship.edu. *Application contact:* Maya T. Mapp, Director of Admissions, 717-477-1231, Fax: 717-477-4016, E-mail: mtmapp@ship.edu.
Website: http://www.ship.edu/odl/

Business Administration and Management—General

Shippensburg University of Pennsylvania, School of Graduate Studies, John L. Grove College of Business, Shippensburg, PA 17257-2299. Offers advanced studies in business (Certificate); advanced supply chain and logistics management (Certificate); business administration (MBA, DBA), including business administration (MBA), business analytics (MBA), finance (MBA), healthcare management (MBA), management information systems (MBA), supply chain management (MBA); finance (Certificate); health care management (Certificate); management information systems (Certificate). *Accreditation:* AACSB. *Program availability:* Part-time, evening/weekend, 100% online, blended/hybrid learning. *Faculty:* 23 full-time (5 women), 1 part-time/adjunct (0 women). *Students:* 46 full-time (14 women), 201 part-time (71 women); includes 35 minority (12 Black or African American, non-Hispanic/Latino; 10 Asian, non-Hispanic/Latino; 11 Hispanic/Latino; 2 Two or more races, non-Hispanic/Latino), 22 international. Average age 32. 169 applicants, 65% accepted, 77 enrolled. In 2017, 105 master's, 82 other advanced degrees awarded. *Degree requirements:* For master's, thesis optional, practicum; for doctorate, comprehensive exam, thesis/dissertation. *Entrance requirements:* For master's, GMAT (minimum score 450 if less than 5 years of mid-level experience, including management experience), current resume; relevant work/classroom experience; 500-word statement of purpose; prerequisites of quantitative analysis, computer usage, and oral and written communications; laptop computer; for doctorate, GMAT (minimum score of 600 if less than 5 years of substantive professional or teaching experience), 2 letters of recommendation from professionals in academia or industry; 2-3 page personal and professional statement; interview; resume. Additional exam requirements/recommendations for international students: Required—TOEFL (minimum score 550 paper-based, 68 iBT) or IELTS (minimum score 6). *Application deadline:* For fall admission, 4/30 for international students; for spring admission, 9/30 for international students. Applications are processed on a rolling basis. Application fee: $45. Electronic applications accepted. *Expenses:* Tuition, state resident: part-time $500 per credit. Tuition, nonresident: part-time $750 per credit. *Required fees:* $145 per credit. *Financial support:* In 2017–18, 14 students received support. Career-related internships or fieldwork, scholarships/grants, unspecified assistantships, and resident hall director and student payroll positions available. Support available to part-time students. Financial award application deadline: 3/1; financial award applicants required to submit FAFSA. *Unit head:* Dr. John G. Kooti, Dean of the College of Business, 717-477-1435, Fax: 717-477-4003, E-mail: jgkooti@ship.edu. *Application contact:* Maya T. Mapp, Director of Admissions, 717-477-1231, Fax: 717-477-4016, E-mail: mtmapp@ship.edu.
Website: http://www.ship.edu/business

Shorter University, Professional Studies, Rome, GA 30165. Offers accountancy (MAC); business administration (MBA); management (MM). *Program availability:* Evening/weekend. *Degree requirements:* For master's, project. *Entrance requirements:* For master's, minimum undergraduate GPA of 2.75 in last 60 hours, 3 years of work experience. Additional exam requirements/recommendations for international students: Required—TOEFL (minimum score 550 paper-based; 79 iBT). Electronic applications accepted.

Siena College, School of Business, Loudonville, NY 12211-1462. Offers accounting (MS). *Program availability:* Evening/weekend. *Degree requirements:* For master's, internship.

Silver Lake College of the Holy Family, Graduate School, Graduate Business Program, Manitowoc, WI 54220-9319. Offers leadership and organizational development (MS). *Program availability:* Part-time, evening/weekend. *Degree requirements:* For master's, comprehensive exam (for some programs), thesis optional, capstone culminating project, thesis research, comprehensive portfolio, or public presentation of project. *Entrance requirements:* For master's, ACT (preferred) or SAT, minimum undergraduate GPA of 3.0. Additional exam requirements/recommendations for international students: Required—TOEFL (minimum score 550 paper-based; 89 iBT). Electronic applications accepted. *Expenses:* Contact institution. *Faculty research:* Leadership development; organizational change; organizational behavior.

Simmons College, School of Management, Boston, MA 02115. Offers business administration (MBA); health care (MBA); management (MS, MSM), including communications management (MS), non-profit management (MS); MBA/MSW; MS/MA. *Accreditation:* AACSB. *Program availability:* Part-time, evening/weekend, 100% online, blended/hybrid learning. *Faculty:* 23 full-time (15 women), 5 part-time/adjunct (all women). *Students:* 7 full-time (all women), 130 part-time (118 women); includes 34 minority (14 Black or African American, non-Hispanic/Latino; 8 Asian, non-Hispanic/Latino; 10 Hispanic/Latino; 2 Two or more races, non-Hispanic/Latino), 1 international. Average age 32. 53 applicants, 68% accepted, 19 enrolled. In 2017, 77 master's awarded. *Entrance requirements:* For master's, GMAT or GRE. Additional exam requirements/recommendations for international students: Required—TOEFL. *Application deadline:* For fall admission, 7/18 priority date for domestic students; for summer admission, 4/24 priority date for domestic students. Applications are processed on a rolling basis. Application fee: $75. Electronic applications accepted. *Expenses:* $1,295 per credit hour, $3,885 per course, $123 activity fee per semester. *Financial support:* Scholarships/grants and unspecified assistantships available. Financial award applicants required to submit FAFSA. *Faculty research:* Gender and organizations, leadership, health care management. *Unit head:* Patricia Deyton, Associate Dean for Graduate Programs, 617-521-3876.
Website: http://www.simmons.edu/som

Simon Fraser University, Office of Graduate Studies and Postdoctoral Fellows, Faculty of Business Administration, Vancouver, BC V6B 5K3, Canada. Offers business administration (EMBA, PhD, Graduate Diploma); finance (M Sc); management of technology (MBA); management of technology/biotechnology (MBA). *Program availability:* Online learning. *Degree requirements:* For master's, thesis (for some programs); for doctorate, comprehensive exam, thesis/dissertation. *Entrance requirements:* For master's, GMAT, minimum GPA of 3.0 (on scale of 4.33) or 3.33 based on last 60 credits of undergraduate courses; for doctorate, minimum GPA of 3.5 (on scale of 4.33); for Graduate Diploma, minimum GPA of 2.5 (on scale of 4.33) or 2.67 based on last 60 credits of undergraduate courses. Additional exam requirements/recommendations for international students: Recommended—TOEFL (minimum score 580 paper-based; 93 iBT), IELTS (minimum score 7), TWE (minimum score 5). *Expenses:* Contact institution. *Faculty research:* Accounting, management and organizational studies, technology and operations management, finance, international business.

SIT Graduate Institute, Graduate Programs, Master's Programs in Intercultural Service, Leadership, and Management, Brattleboro, VT 05302-0676. Offers intercultural service, leadership, and management (self-designed) (MA); international education (MA); peace and justice leadership (MA); sustainable development (MA). *Program availability:* Online learning. *Degree requirements:* For master's, one foreign language, thesis. *Entrance requirements:* For master's, 3 letters of reference. Additional exam requirements/recommendations for international students: Required—TOEFL, IELTS. *Faculty research:* Intercultural communication, conflict resolution, international education, world issues, international affairs.

Slippery Rock University of Pennsylvania, Graduate Studies (Recruitment), College of Business, School of Business, Slippery Rock, PA 16057-1383. Offers accounting/

finance (MBA); general (MBA); marketing/management (MBA). *Program availability:* Part-time, evening/weekend. *Degree requirements:* For master's, comprehensive exam (for some programs), thesis (for some programs). *Entrance requirements:* For master's, minimum cumulative GPA of 3.0, official transcripts, three references. Additional exam requirements/recommendations for international students: Required—TOEFL (minimum score 550 paper-based; 80 iBT). Electronic applications accepted. *Expenses:* Contact institution.

Sonoma State University, School of Business and Economics, Rohnert Park, CA 94928. Offers wine business (Exec MBA, MBA). *Accreditation:* AACSB. *Program availability:* Part-time, evening/weekend. *Degree requirements:* For master's, thesis or alternative. *Entrance requirements:* For master's, GMAT. Additional exam requirements/recommendations for international students: Required—TOEFL (minimum score 500 paper-based). *Application deadline:* For fall admission, 1/31 priority date for domestic students; for spring admission, 8/31 for domestic students. Applications are processed on a rolling basis. Application fee: $55. *Financial support:* Career-related internships or fieldwork, Federal Work-Study, institutionally sponsored loans, and scholarships/grants available. Support available to part-time students. Financial award application deadline: 3/2; financial award applicants required to submit FAFSA. *Unit head:* Karen Thompson, Dean, 707-664-2220. *Application contact:* John Stayton, Executive Director, Graduate and Executive Programs, 707-664-3954, E-mail: john.stayton@sonoma.edu.
Website: http://web.sonoma.edu/sbe/

South Carolina State University, College of Graduate and Professional Studies, School of Business, Orangeburg, SC 29117-0001. Offers agribusiness (MBA); entrepreneurship (MBA); general business administration (MBA); healthcare management (MBA). *Program availability:* Part-time, evening/weekend. *Faculty:* 7 full-time (3 women), 2 part-time/adjunct (0 women). *Students:* 20 full-time (10 women), 11 part-time (7 women); all minorities (all Black or African American, non-Hispanic/Latino). Average age 27. 12 applicants, 92% accepted, 11 enrolled. In 2017, 10 master's awarded. *Degree requirements:* For master's, comprehensive exam, business plan. *Entrance requirements:* For master's, GMAT, minimum GPA of 2.8. Additional exam requirements/recommendations for international students: Required—TOEFL. *Application deadline:* For fall admission, 6/15 for domestic and international students; for spring admission, 11/1 for domestic and international students. Application fee: $25. Electronic applications accepted. *Expenses:* Tuition, state resident: full-time $9388; part-time $607 per credit hour. Tuition, nonresident: full-time $19,968; part-time $1194 per credit hour. *Required fees:* $766; $766 per credit hour. *Financial support:* Fellowships, research assistantships, career-related internships or fieldwork, Federal Work-Study, scholarships/grants, and unspecified assistantships available. Financial award application deadline: 6/1. *Unit head:* Dr. David Jamison, Interim Chair, 803-536-8443, Fax: 803-536-8078, E-mail: djamison@scsu.edu. *Application contact:* Ellen R. Ricoma, MBA Program Director, 803-533-3777, Fax: 803-516-4651, E-mail: ericoma1@scsu.edu.

Southeastern Louisiana University, College of Business, Hammond, LA 70402. Offers MBA. *Accreditation:* AACSB. *Faculty:* 14 full-time (1 woman). *Students:* 77 full-time (39 women), 24 part-time (16 women); includes 14 minority (3 Black or African American, non-Hispanic/Latino; 1 Asian, non-Hispanic/Latino; 7 Hispanic/Latino; 3 Two or more races, non-Hispanic/Latino), 8 international. Average age 26. 62 applicants, 66% accepted, 31 enrolled. In 2017, 60 master's awarded. *Entrance requirements:* For master's, GRE/GMAT, minimum cumulative GPA of 2.75 for all undergraduate work attempted or 3.0 on all upper-division undergraduate course work attempted. Additional exam requirements/recommendations for international students: Required—TOEFL (minimum score 500 paper-based; 61 iBT). *Application deadline:* For fall admission, 7/15 priority date for domestic students, 6/1 priority date for international students; for spring admission, 12/1 priority date for domestic students, 10/1 priority date for international students. Applications are processed on a rolling basis. Application fee: $20 ($30 for international students). Electronic applications accepted. *Expenses:* Tuition, state resident: full-time $6684. Tuition, nonresident: full-time $19,162. *Required fees:* $2088. *Financial support:* In 2017–18, 39 students received support, including 31 teaching assistantships (averaging $8,523 per year); career-related internships or fieldwork, Federal Work-Study, institutionally sponsored loans, scholarships/grants, and unspecified assistantships also available. Support available to part-time students. Financial award application deadline: 5/1; financial award applicants required to submit FAFSA. *Faculty research:* Ethical decision-making in accounting, entrepreneurship and emerging information, leadership and organizational performance. *Unit head:* Dr. Antoinette Phillips, Dean, 985-549-2258, Fax: 985-549-5038, E-mail: business@southeastern.edu. *Application contact:* Amanda Harper, Graduate Admissions Analyst, 985-549-5620, Fax: 985-549-5882, E-mail: admissions@southeastern.edu.
Website: http://www.selu.edu/acad_research/colleges/bus/index.html

Southeastern Oklahoma State University, John Massey School of Business, Durant, OK 74701-0609. Offers MBA. *Accreditation:* AACSB. *Program availability:* Part-time, evening/weekend. *Degree requirements:* For master's, thesis optional. *Entrance requirements:* For master's, GMAT, minimum GPA of 3.0 in last 60 hours or 2.75 overall. Additional exam requirements/recommendations for international students: Required—TOEFL (minimum score 550 paper-based; 79 iBT). Electronic applications accepted.

Southeastern University, Jannetides College of Business and Entrepreneurial Leadership, Lakeland, FL 33801-6099. Offers executive leadership (MBA); global business administration (MBA); healthcare administration (MBA); missional leadership (MBA); organizational leadership (PhD); sport management (MBA); strategic leadership (DSL). *Accreditation:* ACBSP. *Program availability:* Evening/weekend, online learning. *Faculty:* 10 full-time (2 women), 8 part-time/adjunct (1 woman). *Students:* 80 full-time (38 women), 110 part-time (54 women); includes 51 minority (18 Black or African American, non-Hispanic/Latino; 5 Asian, non-Hispanic/Latino; 28 Hispanic/Latino), 7 international. Average age 31. *Entrance requirements:* For master's, GMAT, minimum cumulative GPA of 3.0, writing sample. Application fee: $50. Electronic applications accepted. *Unit head:* Lyle L. Bowlin, Dean, 863-667-5118, E-mail: llbowlin@seu.edu.
Website: http://www.seu.edu/business/

Southeast Missouri State University, School of Graduate Studies, Harrison College of Business, Cape Girardeau, MO 63701-4799. Offers accounting (MBA); entrepreneurship (MBA); financial management (MBA); sport management (MBA). *Accreditation:* AACSB. *Program availability:* Part-time, evening/weekend, 100% online. *Faculty:* 27 full-time (7 women), 1 (woman) part-time/adjunct. *Students:* 71 full-time (38 women), 68 part-time (31 women); includes 13 minority (7 Black or African American, non-Hispanic/Latino; 4 Asian, non-Hispanic/Latino; 2 Two or more races, non-Hispanic/Latino), 47 international. Average age 30. 51 applicants, 100% accepted, 51 enrolled. In 2017, 95 master's awarded. *Degree requirements:* For master's, variable foreign language requirement, comprehensive exam (for some programs), thesis or alternative. *Entrance requirements:* For master's, GMAT or GRE, minimum undergraduate GPA of 2.5, minimum grade of C in prerequisite courses. Additional exam requirements/recommendations for international students: Required—TOEFL (minimum score 550 paper-based; 79 iBT), IELTS (minimum score 6), PTE (minimum score 53). *Application deadline:* For fall admission, 8/1 for domestic students, 6/1 for international students; for spring admission, 11/21 for domestic students, 10/1 for international students; for summer admission, 5/15 for domestic students. Applications are processed on a rolling

basis. Application fee: $30 ($40 for international students). Electronic applications accepted. *Expenses:* $270.35 per credit hour in-state tuition, $33.40 per credit hour fees. *Financial support:* In 2017–18, 26 students received support. Career-related internships or fieldwork, Federal Work-Study, scholarships/grants, traineeships, tuition waivers (full), and unspecified assistantships available. Financial award application deadline: 6/30; financial award applicants required to submit FAFSA. *Faculty research:* Organizational justice, ethics, leadership, corporate finance, generational differences. *Unit head:* Dr. Judy A. Wiles, Interim Dean, Harrison College of Business, 573-651-2913, Fax: 573-651-5032, E-mail: jwiles@semo.edu.
Website: http://www.semo.edu/mba

Southern Adventist University, School of Business, Collegedale, TN 37315-0370. Offers accounting (MBA); finance (MBA); healthcare administration (MBA); management (MBA); marketing management (MBA). *Program availability:* Part-time, evening/weekend, 100% online. *Entrance requirements:* For master's, GMAT, minimum cumulative undergraduate GPA of 3.0. Additional exam requirements/recommendations for international students: Required—TOEFL (minimum score 600 paper-based; 100 iBT). *Application deadline:* For fall admission, 7/1 for domestic students, 5/1 for international students; for winter admission, 11/1 for domestic students, 9/1 for international students; for summer admission, 4/1 for domestic students, 2/1 for international students. Applications are processed on a rolling basis. Application fee: $40. Electronic applications accepted. *Expenses: Tuition:* Full-time $11,430; part-time $635 per credit hour. Tuition and fees vary according to degree level and program. *Financial support:* Scholarships/grants and unspecified assistantships available. Financial award application deadline: 9/1; financial award applicants required to submit FAFSA. *Unit head:* Dr. Stephanie Sheehan, Dean, 423-236-2659, Fax: 423-236-1527, E-mail: ssheehan@southern.edu. *Application contact:* Teshia Price, Graduate Studies Coordinator, 423-236-2751, Fax: 423-236-1527, E-mail: tprice@southern.edu.
Website: https://www.southern.edu/academics/business.html

Southern Arkansas University–Magnolia, School of Graduate Studies, Magnolia, AR 71753. Offers agriculture (MS); business administration (MBA), including agribusiness, social entrepreneurship, supply chain management; clinical and mental health counseling (MS); computer and information sciences (MS), including cyber security and privacy, data science, information technology; gifted and talented (M Ed), including curriculum and instruction, educational administration and supervision, gifted and talented P-8/7-12, instructional specialist P-4; higher, adult and lifelong education (M Ed); kinesiology (M Ed), including coaching; library media and information specialist (M Ed); public administration (MPA); school counseling K-12 (M Ed); student affairs and college counseling (M Ed); teaching (MAT). *Accreditation:* NCATE. *Program availability:* Part-time, 100% online, blended/hybrid learning. *Faculty:* 36 full-time (20 women), 31 part-time/adjunct (12 women). *Students:* 242 full-time (89 women), 889 part-time (459 women); includes 167 minority (143 Black or African American, non-Hispanic/Latino; 7 American Indian or Alaska Native, non-Hispanic/Latino; 7 Asian, non-Hispanic/Latino; 3 Hispanic/Latino; 7 Two or more races, non-Hispanic/Latino), 562 international. Average age 28. 400 applicants, 100% accepted, 239 enrolled. In 2017, 875 master's awarded. *Degree requirements:* For master's, comprehensive exam (for some programs), thesis optional. *Entrance requirements:* For master's, GRE, MAT or GMAT, minimum GPA of 2.5. Additional exam requirements/recommendations for international students: Required—TOEFL (minimum score 550 paper-based), IELTS (minimum score 6). *Application deadline:* For fall admission, 7/20 for domestic students, 7/10 for international students; for spring admission, 12/1 for domestic students, 11/15 for international students; for summer admission, 4/1 for domestic students, 5/1 for international students. Applications are processed on a rolling basis. Application fee: $25 ($50 for international students). Electronic applications accepted. *Expenses:* Tuition, state resident: full-time $6038. Tuition, nonresident: full-time $8558. *Required fees:* $804. One-time fee: $110 full-time. Tuition and fees vary according to course load. *Financial support:* Career-related internships or fieldwork, Federal Work-Study, scholarships/grants, tuition waivers (full), and unspecified assistantships available. Financial award applicants required to submit FAFSA. *Faculty research:* Alternative certification for teachers, supervision of instruction, instructional leadership, counseling. *Unit head:* Dr. Kim Bloss, Dean, School of Graduate Studies, 870-235-4150, Fax: 870-235-5227, E-mail: kkbloss@saumag.edu. *Application contact:* Shrijana Malakar, Admissions Specialist, 870-235-4150, Fax: 870-235-5227, E-mail: smalakar@saumag.edu.
Website: http://www.saumag.edu/graduate

Southern Connecticut State University, School of Graduate Studies, School of Business, Program in Business Administration, New Haven, CT 06515-1355. Offers MBA. *Program availability:* Part-time, evening/weekend. *Entrance requirements:* For master's, GMAT, interview. Electronic applications accepted.

Southern Illinois University Carbondale, Graduate School, College of Business and Administration, Department of Business Administration, Carbondale, IL 62901-4701. Offers MBA, PhD, JD/MBA, MBA/MA, MBA/MS. *Accreditation:* AACSB. *Degree requirements:* For doctorate, thesis/dissertation. *Entrance requirements:* For master's, GMAT, minimum GPA of 2.7; for doctorate, GMAT, minimum graduate GPA of 3.25. Additional exam requirements/recommendations for international students: Required—TOEFL (minimum score 550 paper-based; 80 iBT). Electronic applications accepted. *Faculty research:* Marketing, corporate finance, organizational behavior, accounting, management information systems, international business.

Southern Illinois University Edwardsville, Graduate School, School of Business, Program in Business Administration, Edwardsville, IL 62026. Offers business analytics (MBA); management information systems (MBA); project management (MBA). *Accreditation:* AACSB. *Program availability:* Part-time, evening/weekend. *Degree requirements:* For master's, comprehensive exam. *Entrance requirements:* For master's, GMAT. Additional exam requirements/recommendations for international students: Required—TOEFL (minimum score 550 paper-based; 79 iBT), IELTS (minimum score 6.5). Electronic applications accepted.

Southern Methodist University, Cox School of Business, Dallas, TX 75275. Offers accounting (MSA); business (Exec MBA); business administration (MBA), including accounting, finance, information technology and operations management, management, marketing, strategy and entrepreneurship; entrepreneurship (MS); finance (MSF); management (MSM); JD/MBA. *Accreditation:* AACSB. *Program availability:* Part-time, evening/weekend. *Entrance requirements:* For master's, GMAT. Additional exam requirements/recommendations for international students: Required—TOEFL, PTE. Electronic applications accepted. *Expenses:* Contact institution. *Faculty research:* Financial markets structure, international finance, accounting disclosure, corporate finance, leadership, change management, organizational behavior, entrepreneurship, strategic marketing, corporate strategy, product innovation, information systems, knowledge management, energy markets, customer relationship management.

Southern Nazarene University, College of Professional and Graduate Studies, School of Business, Bethany, OK 73008. Offers business administration (MBA); health care management (MBA); management (MS Mgt). *Accreditation:* ACBSP. *Program availability:* Part-time, evening/weekend, online learning. *Degree requirements:* For master's, thesis optional. *Entrance requirements:* For master's, resume. Additional exam requirements/recommendations for international students: Required—TOEFL (minimum score 550 paper-based; 80 iBT), IELTS (minimum score 7). Electronic applications accepted.

Southern New Hampshire University, School of Business, Manchester, NH 03106-1045. Offers accounting (MBA, Graduate Certificate); accounting finance (MS); accounting/auditing (MS); accounting/forensic accounting (MS); accounting/management accounting (MS); accounting/taxation (MS); applied economics (MS); athletic administration (MBA, Graduate Certificate); business administration (IMBA, Certificate), including business information systems (Certificate), human resource management (Certificate); business analytics (MBA); business intelligence (MBA); communication (MA), including new media and marketing, public relations; community economic development (MBA); criminal justice (MBA); data analytics (MS); economics (MBA); engineering management (MBA); entrepreneurship (MBA); finance (MBA, MS, Graduate Certificate); finance/corporate finance (MS); finance/investments (MS); forensic accounting (MBA); forensic accounting and fraud examination (Graduate Certificate); healthcare informatics (MBA); healthcare management (MBA); human resource management (MS); human resources (MBA); information technology (MS); information technology management (MBA); international business (PhD); Internet marketing (MBA); leadership (MBA); leadership of nonprofit organizations (Graduate Certificate); management (MS); marketing (MBA, MS, Graduate Certificate); music business (MBA); operations and project management (MS); operations and supply chain management (MBA, Graduate Certificate); organizational leadership (MS); project management (MBA, Graduate Certificate); public administration (MBA, Graduate Certificate); quantitative analysis (MBA); Six Sigma (Graduate Certificate); Six Sigma quality (MBA); social media marketing (MBA, Graduate Certificate); sport management (MBA, MS, Graduate Certificate); sustainability and environmental compliance (MBA); MBA/Certificate. *Accreditation:* ACBSP. *Program availability:* Part-time, evening/weekend, online learning. Terminal master's awarded for partial completion of doctoral program. *Degree requirements:* For master's, one foreign language, comprehensive exam (for some programs), thesis or alternative; for doctorate, one foreign language, comprehensive exam, thesis/dissertation. *Entrance requirements:* For master's, minimum GPA of 2.5; for doctorate, GMAT. Additional exam requirements/recommendations for international students: Required—TOEFL (minimum score 500 paper-based). *Application deadline:* Applications are processed on a rolling basis. Application fee: $40. Electronic applications accepted. *Expenses: Tuition:* Part-time $627 per credit hour. Part-time tuition and fees vary according to campus/location and program. *Financial support:* Career-related internships or fieldwork, Federal Work-Study, institutionally sponsored loans, scholarships/grants, tuition waivers (partial), and unspecified assistantships available. Support available to part-time students. Financial award applicants required to submit FAFSA. *Unit head:* Dr. Bill Lightfoot, Dean, 603-644-3102, Fax: 603-644-3144. *Application contact:* Office of Graduate Admission, 888-327-SNHU, Fax: 603-644-3144, E-mail: enroll@snhu.edu.

Southern Oregon University, Graduate Studies, School of Business, Ashland, OR 97520. Offers accounting (Postbaccalaureate Certificate); business administration (MBA); international management (MIM). *Accreditation:* ACBSP. *Program availability:* Part-time, evening/weekend, online learning. *Degree requirements:* For master's, comprehensive exam. *Entrance requirements:* For master's, GMAT, minimum cumulative GPA of 3.0 in the last 90 quarter credits (60 semester credits) of undergraduate coursework. Additional exam requirements/recommendations for international students: Required—TOEFL (minimum score 540 paper-based; 76 iBT), IELTS (minimum score 6), ELPT (minimum score 964) or ELS (minimum score 112). Electronic applications accepted.

Southern University and Agricultural and Mechanical College, College of Business, Baton Rouge, LA 70813. Offers MBA. *Accreditation:* AACSB. *Degree requirements:* For master's, comprehensive exam. *Entrance requirements:* For master's, GMAT. Additional exam requirements/recommendations for international students: Required—TOEFL (minimum score 525 paper-based). *Faculty research:* Accounting theory, auditing, governmental and non-profit accounting.

Southern Utah University, Master of Accountancy/MBA Dual Degree Program, Cedar City, UT 84720-2498. Offers MBA/M Acc. *Program availability:* Part-time, 100% online. *Students:* 3 full-time (1 woman), 1 (woman) part-time. Average age 26. 8 applicants, 75% accepted. *Entrance requirements:* Additional exam requirements/recommendations for international students: Required—TOEFL (minimum score 550 paper-based, 79 iBT) or IELTS (minimum score 6). *Application deadline:* For fall admission, 3/1 for domestic and international students; for spring admission, 10/1 for domestic and international students; for summer admission, 3/1 for domestic and international students. Applications are processed on a rolling basis. Application fee: $60 ($65 for international students). Electronic applications accepted. *Expenses:* Contact institution. *Financial support:* Unspecified assistantships available. *Application contact:* Patricia Palmer, Academic Advisor and Graduate Program Coordinator, 435-865-8167, Fax: 435-586-5493, E-mail: patriciapalmer@suu.edu.
Website: https://www.suu.edu/business/graduate/

Southern Utah University, Program in Business Administration, Cedar City, UT 84720-2498. Offers MBA. *Accreditation:* AACSB. *Program availability:* Part-time, evening/weekend, 100% online. *Faculty:* 8 full-time (0 women), 2 part-time/adjunct (0 women). *Students:* 25 full-time (4 women), 51 part-time (15 women); includes 6 minority (2 Black or African American, non-Hispanic/Latino; 1 Asian, non-Hispanic/Latino; 3 Hispanic/Latino), 9 international. Average age 30. 84 applicants, 40% accepted, 22 enrolled. In 2017, 22 master's awarded. *Entrance requirements:* For master's, GMAT or GRE. Additional exam requirements/recommendations for international students: Required—TOEFL (minimum score 550 paper-based, 79 iBT) or IELTS (minimum score 6). *Application deadline:* For fall admission, 3/1 for domestic and international students; for spring admission, 10/1 for domestic and international students; for summer admission, 3/1 for domestic students, 2/1 for international students. Applications are processed on a rolling basis. Application fee: $60 ($65 for international students). Electronic applications accepted. *Expenses:* Contact institution. *Financial support:* Unspecified assistantships available. *Unit head:* Dr. Kim Craft, Department Chair/MBA Program Director, 435-586-5414, Fax: 435-586-5493, E-mail: craft@suu.edu. *Application contact:* Patricia Palmer, Academic Advisor and Graduate Program Coordinator, 435-865-8167, Fax: 435-586-5493, E-mail: patriciapalmer@suu.edu.
Website: https://www.suu.edu/business/mgmt/mba.html

Southern Wesleyan University, Program in Business Administration, Central, SC 29630-1020. Offers MBA. *Program availability:* Evening/weekend. *Degree requirements:* For master's, comprehensive exam. *Entrance requirements:* For master's, GMAT, GRE, or MAT, minimum of 3 undergraduate semester credit hours each in accounting, economics, and statistics; minimum of 18 undergraduate semester credit hours in business administration; minimum of 2 years' significant work experience. Additional exam requirements/recommendations for international students: Required—TOEFL (minimum score 500 paper-based).

Southern Wesleyan University, Program in Management, Central, SC 29630-1020. Offers MSM. *Program availability:* Evening/weekend. *Entrance requirements:* For master's, GMAT, GRE, or MAT, minimum of 18 undergraduate semester credit hours in business administration; minimum of 2 years significant work experience. Additional exam requirements/recommendations for international students: Required—TOEFL (minimum score 500 paper-based). *Expenses:* Contact institution.

Business Administration and Management—General

South University, Graduate Programs, College of Business, Savannah, GA 31406. Offers corrections (MBA); entrepreneurship and small business (MBA); healthcare administration (MBA); hospitality management (MBA); leadership (MS); public administration (MPA); sustainability (MBA).

South University, Program in Business Administration, Royal Palm Beach, FL 33411. Offers business administration (MBA); healthcare administration (MBA).

South University, Program in Business Administration, Montgomery, AL 36116-1120. Offers MBA.

South University, Program in Business Administration, Columbia, SC 29203. Offers MBA.

South University, Program in Business Administration, Glen Allen, VA 23060. Offers MBA.

South University, Program in Business Administration, Virginia Beach, VA 23452. Offers MBA.

South University, Program in Business Administration, Round Rock, TX 78681. Offers MBA.

South University, Program in Business Administration, Tampa, FL 33614. Offers MBA.

Southwest Baptist University, Program in Business, Bolivar, MO 65613-2597. Offers business administration (MBA); health administration (MBA). *Accreditation:* ACBSP. *Program availability:* Part-time, online learning. *Degree requirements:* For master's, comprehensive exam. *Entrance requirements:* For master's, interviews, minimum GPA of 2.75. Additional exam requirements/recommendations for international students: Required—TOEFL (minimum score 550 paper-based).

Southwestern Adventist University, Business Administration Department, Keene, TX 76059. Offers accounting (MBA); finance (MBA); management/leadership (MBA). *Program availability:* Part-time, evening/weekend. *Degree requirements:* For master's, capstone course. *Entrance requirements:* For master's, GMAT, GRE General Test.

Southwestern College, Fifth-Year Graduate Programs, Winfield, KS 67156-2499. Offers management (MBA). *Program availability:* Part-time. *Faculty:* 4 full-time (2 women), 1 (woman) part-time/adjunct. *Students:* 7 full-time (1 woman), 14 part-time (8 women); includes 6 minority (4 Black or African American, non-Hispanic/Latino; 2 Hispanic/Latino), 5 international. Average age 24. 19 applicants, 100% accepted, 9 enrolled. In 2017, 25 master's awarded. *Entrance requirements:* For master's, baccalaureate degree, minimum GPA of 3.0. Additional exam requirements/recommendations for international students: Required—TOEFL (minimum score 550 paper-based; 80 iBT). *Application deadline:* For fall admission, 8/28 for domestic students; for spring admission, 1/23 for domestic students. Applications are processed on a rolling basis. Application fee: $25. Electronic applications accepted. *Expenses:* $698 per credit hour. *Financial support:* In 2017–18, 13 students received support, including 1 fellowship (averaging $25,128 per year); unspecified assistantships also available. Financial award applicants required to submit FAFSA. *Unit head:* Dr. Kurt Keiser, Professor/Division Chair, 620-229-6361, E-mail: kurt.keiser@sckans.edu. *Application contact:* Adam Jenkins, Vice President for Enrollment Management, 620-229-6091, E-mail: adam.jenkins@sckans.edu.
Website: http://www.sckans.edu/graduate

Southwestern College, Professional Studies Programs, Wichita, KS 67207. Offers business administration (MBA); leadership (MS); management (MS); security administration (MS); specialized ministries (MA). *Program availability:* Part-time, evening/weekend, online only, 100% online. *Faculty:* 15 part-time/adjunct (6 women). *Students:* 50 part-time (13 women); includes 11 minority (7 Black or African American, non-Hispanic/Latino; 1 American Indian or Alaska Native, non-Hispanic/Latino; 3 Hispanic/Latino). Average age 39. 57 applicants, 74% accepted, 11 enrolled. In 2017, 43 master's awarded. *Degree requirements:* For master's, thesis (for some programs), practicum/capstone project. *Entrance requirements:* For master's, baccalaureate degree; minimum GPA of 3.0. Additional exam requirements/recommendations for international students: Required—TOEFL (minimum score 550 paper-based; 80 iBT). *Application deadline:* Applications are processed on a rolling basis. Application fee: $40. Electronic applications accepted. *Expenses:* $662 per credit hour (for MBA); $599 per credit hour (for MSL, MSSA, MSM, and Graduate Certificates); $476 per credit hour (for MASM and MATS). *Financial support:* In 2017–18, 13 students received support. Unspecified assistantships available. Financial award applicants required to submit FAFSA. *Unit head:* Dennis Russell, Director of Admissions and Student Services, 888-684-5335 Ext. 3372, Fax: 316-688-5218, E-mail: dennis.russell@sckans.edu.
Website: http://www.southwesterncollege.org

Southwestern Oklahoma State University, College of Professional and Graduate Studies, School of Business and Technology, Weatherford, OK 73096-3098. Offers MBA. MBA distance learning degree program offered to Oklahoma residents only. *Program availability:* Part-time, evening/weekend, online learning. *Degree requirements:* For master's, comprehensive exam. *Entrance requirements:* For master's, GMAT, minimum GPA of 2.5. Additional exam requirements/recommendations for international students: Required—TOEFL.

Southwest Minnesota State University, Department of Business and Public Affairs, Marshall, MN 56258. Offers leadership (MBA); management (MBA); marketing (MBA). *Program availability:* Part-time, evening/weekend, online learning. *Degree requirements:* For master's, thesis. *Entrance requirements:* For master's, GMAT (minimum score: 450). Additional exam requirements/recommendations for international students: Recommended—TOEFL (minimum score 550 paper-based; 79 iBT), IELTS. Electronic applications accepted.

Southwest University, MBA Program, Kenner, LA 70062. Offers business administration (MBA); management (MBA); organizational management (MBA).

Southwest University, Program in Management, Kenner, LA 70062. Offers MA.

Spring Arbor University, Gainey School of Business, Spring Arbor, MI 49283-9799. Offers MBA. *Program availability:* Part-time, evening/weekend, online learning. *Degree requirements:* For master's, thesis. *Entrance requirements:* For master's, minimum overall GPA of 3.0 for all undergraduate coursework, bachelor's degree from regionally-accredited college or university, two recommendation forms from professional/academic individuals. Additional exam requirements/recommendations for international students: Required—TOEFL (minimum score 600 paper-based).

Springfield College, Graduate Programs, Program in Business Administration, Springfield, MA 01109-3797. Offers MBA. *Program availability:* Part-time, evening/weekend. *Faculty:* 4 full-time (1 woman), 4 part-time/adjunct (1 woman). *Students:* 18 full-time (3 women), 5 part-time (3 women). Average age 23. 20 applicants, 85% accepted, 10 enrolled. *Entrance requirements:* Additional exam requirements/recommendations for international students: Required—TOEFL (minimum score 90 iBT); Recommended—IELTS (minimum score 7). *Application deadline:* Applications are processed on a rolling basis. Electronic applications accepted. *Financial support:* Fellowships with partial tuition reimbursements, teaching assistantships, career-related internships or fieldwork, Federal Work-Study, scholarships/grants, and unspecified assistantships available. Financial award application deadline: 3/1; financial award applicants required to submit FAFSA. *Faculty research:* Marketing theory and practice,

measurement of attribution of leadership to entrepreneurial output, brand management. *Unit head:* Dr. Mike Musante, Director, 413-748-3203, E-mail: mmsuante@springfield.edu. *Application contact:* Anne Griffin, Director of Graduate Admissions, 413-748-3225, Fax: 413-748-3694, E-mail: agriffin2@springfield.edu.
Website: http://springfield.edu/mba

Spring Hill College, Graduate Programs, Program in Business Administration, Mobile, AL 36608-1791. Offers MBA. *Program availability:* Part-time, evening/weekend. *Faculty:* 4 full-time (1 woman). *Students:* 5 full-time (0 women), 32 part-time (10 women); includes 9 minority (8 Black or African American, non-Hispanic/Latino; 1 Native Hawaiian or other Pacific Islander, non-Hispanic/Latino). Average age 33. In 2017, 3 master's awarded. *Degree requirements:* For master's, comprehensive exam, capstone course, completion of program within 6 calendar years. *Entrance requirements:* For master's, GMAT, bachelor's degree. Additional exam requirements/recommendations for international students: Required—TOEFL (minimum score 550 paper-based; 80 iBT), IELTS (minimum score 6.5), CPE or CAE (minimum score C), Michigan English Language Assessment Battery (minimum score 90). *Application deadline:* For fall admission, 8/1 priority date for domestic and international students; for spring admission, 12/1 priority date for domestic and international students. Applications are processed on a rolling basis. Application fee: $25 ($35 for international students). Electronic applications accepted. *Expenses:* Contact institution. *Financial support:* Applicants required to submit FAFSA. *Unit head:* Dr. Sergio Castello, Director, 251-380-4123, Fax: 251-460-2178, E-mail: scastello@shc.edu. *Application contact:* Robert Stewart, Vice President of Enrollment, 251-380-3030, Fax: 251-460-2186, E-mail: rstewart@shc.edu.
Website: http://ug.shc.edu/graduate-degrees/master-business-administration/

Stanford University, Graduate School of Business, Stanford, CA 94305-2004. Offers MBA, PhD, JD/MBA, MBA/MS. *Accreditation:* AACSB. Terminal master's awarded for partial completion of doctoral program. *Degree requirements:* For doctorate, thesis/dissertation. *Entrance requirements:* For master's, GMAT; for doctorate, GMAT, GRE. Electronic applications accepted. *Expenses:* Contact institution.

State University of New York at New Paltz, Graduate and Extended Learning School, School of Business, New Paltz, NY 12561. Offers business administration (MBA); public accountancy (MBA). *Accreditation:* AACSB. *Program availability:* Part-time, evening/weekend. *Faculty:* 15 full-time (3 women), 2 part-time/adjunct (0 women). *Students:* 62 full-time (27 women), 36 part-time (24 women); includes 28 minority (8 Black or African American, non-Hispanic/Latino; 6 Asian, non-Hispanic/Latino; 11 Hispanic/Latino; 3 Two or more races, non-Hispanic/Latino), 12 international. 59 applicants, 68% accepted, 28 enrolled. In 2017, 43 master's awarded. *Entrance requirements:* For master's, GMAT or GRE, minimum GPA of 3.0. Additional exam requirements/recommendations for international students: Required—TOEFL (minimum score 550 paper-based; 80 iBT), IELTS (minimum score 6.5). *Application deadline:* Applications are processed on a rolling basis. Application fee: $50. Electronic applications accepted. *Expenses:* Contact institution. *Financial support:* In 2017–18, 6 research assistantships with partial tuition reimbursements (averaging $5,000 per year), 1 teaching assistantship with partial tuition reimbursement (averaging $5,000 per year) were awarded; scholarships/grants, traineeships, and unspecified assistantships also available. Financial award application deadline: 8/1. *Faculty research:* Cognitive styles in management education, supporting SME e-commerce migration through e-learning, earnings management and board activity, trading future spread portfolio, global equity market correlation and volatility. *Unit head:* Dr. Kristin Backhaus, Dean, 845-257-2930, E-mail: mba@newpaltz.edu. *Application contact:* Aaron Hines, Director of MBA Program, 845-257-2968, E-mail: mba@newpaltz.edu.
Website: http://mba.newpaltz.edu

State University of New York at Oswego, Graduate Studies, School of Business, Oswego, NY 13126. Offers MBA. *Program availability:* Part-time, evening/weekend. *Entrance requirements:* For master's, GMAT, minimum GPA of 2.6. Additional exam requirements/recommendations for international students: Required—TOEFL (minimum score 560 paper-based).

State University of New York College at Geneseo, Graduate Studies, School of Business, Geneseo, NY 14454. Offers accounting (MS). *Accreditation:* AACSB. *Faculty:* 3 full-time (1 woman), 2 part-time/adjunct (0 women). *Students:* 19 full-time (7 women); includes 2 minority (both Asian, non-Hispanic/Latino). Average age 22. 39 applicants, 59% accepted, 19 enrolled. In 2017, 17 master's awarded. *Degree requirements:* For master's, thesis. *Entrance requirements:* For master's, GMAT, bachelor's degree in accounting. Additional exam requirements/recommendations for international students: Required—TOEFL (minimum score 525 paper-based; 71 iBT), IELTS (minimum score 6.5), PTE, iTEP. *Application deadline:* For fall admission, 6/1 priority date for domestic students. Applications are processed on a rolling basis. Application fee: $50. Electronic applications accepted. *Expenses:* Contact institution. *Financial support:* In 2017–18, 9 students received support. Research assistantships with partial tuition reimbursements available and scholarships/grants available. Financial award application deadline: 4/1; financial award applicants required to submit FAFSA. *Unit head:* Dr. Michael Schinski, Dean of the School of Business, 585-245-5367, Fax: 585-245-5467, E-mail: schinski@geneseo.edu. *Application contact:* Michael R. George, Director of Graduate Admissions, 585-245-5148, Fax: 585-245-5550, E-mail: georgem@geneseo.edu.
Website: http://www.geneseo.edu/business/accounting_ms

State University of New York College at Old Westbury, School of Business, Old Westbury, NY 11568-0210. Offers accounting (MS); taxation (MS). *Program availability:* Part-time, evening/weekend. *Faculty:* 10 full-time (2 women), 1 part-time/adjunct (0 women). *Students:* 30 full-time (13 women), 47 part-time (15 women); includes 19 minority (3 Black or African American, non-Hispanic/Latino; 11 Asian, non-Hispanic/Latino; 5 Hispanic/Latino). Average age 31. 35 applicants, 91% accepted, 25 enrolled. In 2017, 25 master's awarded. *Entrance requirements:* For master's, GMAT, 2 letters of recommendation. Additional exam requirements/recommendations for international students: Required—TOEFL (minimum score 550 paper-based). *Application deadline:* For fall admission, 6/15 priority date for domestic students; for spring admission, 11/15 priority date for domestic students. Applications are processed on a rolling basis. Application fee: $50. Electronic applications accepted. *Financial support:* Applicants required to submit FAFSA. *Faculty research:* Corporate governance, asset pricing, corporate finance, hedge funds, taxation. *Unit head:* Rita Buttermilch, Director of Graduate Business Programs, 516-876-3900, E-mail: langec@oldwestbury.edu. *Application contact:* Philip D'Angelo, Graduate Admissions Office, 516-876-3073, E-mail: enroll@oldwestbury.edu.
Website: http://www.oldwestbury.edu/schools/business

State University of New York Empire State College, School for Graduate Studies, Program in Business Administration, Saratoga Springs, NY 12866-4391. Offers global leadership (MBA); management (MBA). *Program availability:* Part-time, online learning. *Degree requirements:* For master's, thesis or alternative. *Entrance requirements:* For master's, previous course work in statistics, macroeconomics, microeconomics, and accounting. Additional exam requirements/recommendations for international students: Required—TOEFL (minimum score 600 paper-based). Electronic applications accepted. *Expenses:* Contact institution. *Faculty research:* Corporate strategy, managerial competencies, decision analysis, economics in transition, organizational communication.

Peterson's Graduate Programs in Business, Education, Information Studies, Law & Social Work 2019

State University of New York Polytechnic Institute, MBA Program in Technology Management, Utica, NY 13502. Offers accounting and finance (MBA); business management (MBA); health informatics (MBA); human resource management (MBA); marketing management (MBA). *Program availability:* Part-time, online only, 100% online. *Faculty:* 8 full-time (2 women), 2 part-time/adjunct (1 woman). *Students:* 29 full-time (13 women), 85 part-time (41 women); includes 18 minority (4 Black or African American, non-Hispanic/Latino; 8 Asian, non-Hispanic/Latino; 6 Hispanic/Latino). Average age 32. 83 applicants, 55% accepted, 37 enrolled. In 2017, 41 master's awarded. *Degree requirements:* For master's, comprehensive exam, capstone project. *Entrance requirements:* For master's, GMAT, resume, letter of reference. Additional exam requirements/recommendations for international students: Required—TOEFL (minimum score 550 paper-based; 79 iBT), IELTS (minimum score 6.5). *Application deadline:* For fall admission, 7/1 priority date for domestic students, 7/1 for international students; for spring admission, 12/1 for domestic students, 11/1 for international students. Applications are processed on a rolling basis. Application fee: $60. Electronic applications accepted. *Expenses:* Contact institution. *Financial support:* Fellowships, research assistantships, and unspecified assistantships available. Financial award application deadline: 6/1; financial award applicants required to submit FAFSA. *Faculty research:* Economic development and design thinking, transfer of training, trade intensity and liquidity, enforcement and punishment, acculturation attitudes and consumption behavior. *Total annual research expenditures:* $20,000. *Unit head:* Dr. Rafael Romero, Program Coordinator, 315-792-7207, E-mail: rafael.romero@sunyit.edu. *Application contact:* Alicia Foster, Director of Graduate Admissions, E-mail: alicia.foster@sunyit.edu.
Website: https://sunypoly.edu/academics/majors-and-programs/technology-management.html

Stephen F. Austin State University, Graduate School, College of Business, Program in Business Administration, Nacogdoches, TX 75962. Offers business (MBA); management and marketing (MBA). *Accreditation:* AACSB. *Program availability:* Part-time, evening/weekend. *Degree requirements:* For master's, comprehensive exam. *Entrance requirements:* For master's, GMAT, minimum AACSB index of 1000. Additional exam requirements/recommendations for international students: Required—TOEFL (minimum score 550 paper-based). *Faculty research:* Strategic implications, information search, multinational firms, philosophical guidance.

Stetson University, School of Business Administration, Program in Business Administration, DeLand, FL 32723. Offers EMBA, MBA, JD/MBA, MBA/MS. *Accreditation:* AACSB. *Program availability:* Part-time, evening/weekend, online learning. *Faculty:* 16 full-time (4 women), 3 part-time/adjunct (1 woman). *Students:* 78 full-time (41 women), 19 part-time (14 women); includes 32 minority (7 Black or African American, non-Hispanic/Latino; 3 Asian, non-Hispanic/Latino; 13 Hispanic/Latino; 9 Two or more races, non-Hispanic/Latino), 7 international. Average age 32. 86 applicants, 77% accepted, 43 enrolled. In 2017, 65 master's awarded. *Entrance requirements:* For master's, GMAT, GRE, transcripts, resume, two letters of recommendation, personal statement. Additional exam requirements/recommendations for international students: Required—TOEFL (minimum score 90 iBT), IELTS (minimum score 7.5). *Application deadline:* For fall admission, 8/1 for domestic students; for spring admission, 1/1 for domestic students; for summer admission, 5/1 for domestic students. Applications are processed on a rolling basis. Application fee: $50. Electronic applications accepted. *Expenses:* Contact institution. *Financial support:* In 2017–18, 24 students received support. Career-related internships or fieldwork, Federal Work-Study, scholarships/grants, unspecified assistantships, and tuition waivers (for staff and dependents) available. Support available to part-time students. Financial award applicants required to submit FAFSA. *Unit head:* Yiorgos Bakamitsos, Associate Dean, 386-822-7410, E-mail: bakamitsos@stetson.edu. *Application contact:* Jamie Vanderlip, Director of Admissions for Graduate, Transfer and Adult Programs, 386-822-7100, Fax: 386-822-7112, E-mail: jlvander@stetson.edu.

Stevens Institute of Technology, Graduate School, School of Business, Program in Business Administration, Hoboken, NJ 07030. Offers business intelligence and analytics (MBA); engineering management (MBA); finance (MBA); information systems (MBA); innovation and entrepreneurship (MBA); marketing (MBA); pharmaceutical management (MBA); project management (MBA, Certificate); technology management (MBA); telecommunications management (MBA). *Accreditation:* AACSB. *Program availability:* Part-time, evening/weekend. *Students:* 46 full-time (19 women), 179 part-time (88 women); includes 46 minority (10 Black or African American, non-Hispanic/Latino; 2 American Indian or Alaska Native, non-Hispanic/Latino; 30 Asian, non-Hispanic/Latino; 4 Hispanic/Latino), 45 international. Average age 36. 218 applicants, 49% accepted, 53 enrolled. In 2017, 33 master's awarded. *Degree requirements:* For master's, thesis optional, minimum B average in major field and overall; for Certificate, minimum B average. *Entrance requirements:* Additional exam requirements/recommendations for international students: Required—TOEFL (minimum score 74 iBT), IELTS (minimum score 6). *Application deadline:* For fall admission, 7/1 for domestic students, 4/15 for international students; for spring admission, 12/1 for domestic and international students. Applications are processed on a rolling basis. Application fee: $60. Electronic applications accepted. *Expenses:* Tuition: Full-time $34,494; part-time $1554 per credit. *Required fees:* $291 per semester. *Financial support:* Fellowships, research assistantships, teaching assistantships, career-related internships or fieldwork, Federal Work-Study, scholarships/grants, and unspecified assistantships available. Financial award application deadline: 2/15; financial award applicants required to submit FAFSA. *Unit head:* Dr. Gregory Prastacos, Dean, 201-216-8366, E-mail: gprastac@stevens.edu. *Application contact:* Graduate Admissions, 888-783-8367, Fax: 888-511-1306, E-mail: graduate@stevens.edu.
Website: https://www.stevens.edu/school-business/masters-programs/mbaemba

Stevens Institute of Technology, Graduate School, School of Business, Program in Management, Hoboken, NJ 07030. Offers general management (MS); global innovation management (MS); human resource management (MS); information management (MS); project management (MS); technology commercialization (MS); technology management (MS). *Program availability:* Part-time, evening/weekend. *Students:* 56 full-time (18 women), 88 part-time (32 women); includes 18 minority (5 Black or African American, non-Hispanic/Latino; 12 Asian, non-Hispanic/Latino; 1 Hispanic/Latino), 87 international. Average age 30. 194 applicants, 78% accepted, 68 enrolled. In 2017, 87 master's awarded. *Degree requirements:* For master's, thesis optional, minimum B average in major field and overall. *Entrance requirements:* Additional exam requirements/recommendations for international students: Required—TOEFL (minimum score 74 iBT), IELTS (minimum score 6). *Application deadline:* For fall admission, 7/1 for domestic students, 4/15 for international students; for spring admission, 12/1 for domestic and international students. Applications are processed on a rolling basis. Application fee: $60. Electronic applications accepted. *Expenses:* Tuition: Full-time $34,494; part-time $1554 per credit. *Required fees:* $291 per semester. *Financial support:* Fellowships, research assistantships, teaching assistantships, career-related internships or fieldwork, Federal Work-Study, scholarships/grants, and unspecified assistantships available. Financial award application deadline: 2/15; financial award applicants required to submit FAFSA. *Unit head:* Brian Rothschild, Director, 201-216-3677, E-mail: brian.rothschild@stevens.edu. *Application contact:* Graduate Admissions,

888-783-8367, Fax: 888-511-1306, E-mail: graduate@stevens.edu.
Website: https://www.stevens.edu/school-business/masters-programs/management

Stockton University, Office of Graduate Studies, Program in Business Administration, Galloway, NJ 08205-9441. Offers MBA. *Accreditation:* AACSB. *Program availability:* Part-time, evening/weekend. *Faculty:* 9 full-time (2 women), 2 part-time/adjunct (0 women). *Students:* 22 full-time (14 women), 68 part-time (39 women); includes 26 minority (3 Black or African American, non-Hispanic/Latino; 4 Asian, non-Hispanic/Latino; 17 Hispanic/Latino; 2 Two or more races, non-Hispanic/Latino), 1 international. Average age 32. 42 applicants, 74% accepted, 27 enrolled. In 2017, 45 master's awarded. *Degree requirements:* For master's, project. *Entrance requirements:* For master's, GMAT. Additional exam requirements/recommendations for international students: Required—TOEFL (minimum score 550 paper-based; 80 iBT). *Application deadline:* For fall admission, 7/1 for domestic and international students; for spring admission, 12/1 for domestic and international students, 11/1 for international students. Applications are processed on a rolling basis. Application fee: $50. Electronic applications accepted. *Expenses:* Contact institution. *Financial support:* Fellowships, research assistantships with partial tuition reimbursements, career-related internships or fieldwork, Federal Work-Study, scholarships/grants, and unspecified assistantships available. Support available to part-time students. Financial award application deadline: 3/1; financial award applicants required to submit FAFSA. *Faculty research:* Business ethics, marketing channels development, event studies, total quality management. *Unit head:* Dr. Diane Holtzman, Graduate Program Director, 609-626-3640, E-mail: mba@stockton.edu. *Application contact:* Tara Williams, Assistant Director of Graduate Enrollment Management, 609-626-3640, Fax: 609-626-6050, E-mail: gradschool@stockton.edu.

Stony Brook University, State University of New York, Graduate School, College of Business, Program in Business Administration, Stony Brook, NY 11794. Offers accounting (MBA); business administration (MBA); finance (MBA, Certificate); health care management (MBA); human resources (MBA); innovation (MBA); management (MBA); marketing (MBA); operations management (MBA). *Faculty:* 39 full-time (13 women), 14 part-time/adjunct (5 women). *Students:* 181 full-time (98 women), 145 part-time (73 women); includes 68 minority (16 Black or African American, non-Hispanic/Latino; 1 American Indian or Alaska Native, non-Hispanic/Latino; 35 Asian, non-Hispanic/Latino; 11 Hispanic/Latino; 1 Native Hawaiian or other Pacific Islander, non-Hispanic/Latino; 4 Two or more races, non-Hispanic/Latino), 69 international. Average age 29. 154 applicants, 66% accepted, 58 enrolled. In 2017, 105 master's awarded. *Entrance requirements:* For master's, GMAT, 3 letters of recommendation from current or former employers or professors, transcripts, personal statement, resume. Additional exam requirements/recommendations for international students: Required—TOEFL (minimum score 550 paper-based; 90 iBT), IELTS (minimum score 6.5). *Application deadline:* For fall admission, 5/15 for domestic students, 3/15 for international students; for spring admission, 11/15 for domestic students, 10/15 for international students. Application fee: $100. *Expenses:* Contact institution. *Financial support:* Teaching assistantships available. *Total annual research expenditures:* $2,070. *Unit head:* Dr. Manuel London, Dean, 631-632-7159, E-mail: manuel.london@stonybrook.edu. *Application contact:* Dr. Dmytro Holod, Associate Dean for Academic Programs/Graduate Director, 631-632-7183, Fax: 631-632-8181, E-mail: dmytro.holod@stonybrook.edu.
Website: https://www.stonybrook.edu/commcms/business/

Stratford University, School of Graduate Studies, Falls Church, VA 22043. Offers accounting (MS); business administration (MBA, DBA); cyber security (MS); cyber security leadership and policy (MS); digital forensics (MS); healthcare administration (MS); information systems (MS); information technology (DIT); networking and telecommunications (MS); software engineering (MS). *Program availability:* Part-time, evening/weekend, 100% online, blended/hybrid learning. *Students:* 272 full-time (110 women), 204 part-time (89 women). *Degree requirements:* For master's, comprehensive exam, capstone project. *Entrance requirements:* For master's, GRE or GMAT, baccalaureate degree. Additional exam requirements/recommendations for international students: Required—TOEFL (minimum score 79 iBT), IELTS (minimum score 6.5), PTE (minimum score 5). *Application deadline:* Applications are processed on a rolling basis. Application fee: $50. Electronic applications accepted. *Expenses: Tuition:* Full-time $33,405; part-time $11,135 per credit hour. One-time fee: $385 full-time. Tuition and fees vary according to degree level and program. *Financial support:* Federal Work-Study and scholarships/grants available. Financial award applicants required to submit FAFSA. *Unit head:* Dr. Valarie Trimarchi, Campus President, 703-539-6890, Fax: 703-539-6960. *Application contact:* Lori Smith, Admissions, 214-649-7113, E-mail: lasmith@stratford.edu.

Strayer University, Graduate Studies, Washington, DC 20005-2603. Offers accounting (MS); acquisition (MBA); business administration (MBA); communications technology (MS); educational management (M Ed); finance (MBA); health services administration (MHSA); hospitality and tourism management (MBA); human resource management (MBA); information systems (MS), including computer security management, decision support system management, enterprise resource management, network management, software engineering management, systems development management; management (MBA); management information systems (MS); marketing (MBA); professional accounting (MS), including accounting information systems, controllership, taxation; public administration (MPA); supply chain management (MBA); technology in education (M Ed). Programs also offered at campus locations in Birmingham, AL; Chamblee, GA; Cobb County, GA; Morrow, GA; White Marsh, MD; Charleston, SC; Columbia, SC; Greensboro, NC; Greenville, SC; Lexington, KY; Louisville, KY; Nashville, TN; North Raleigh, NC; Washington, DC. *Accreditation:* ACBSP. *Program availability:* Part-time, evening/weekend, online learning. *Degree requirements:* For master's, thesis. *Entrance requirements:* For master's, GMAT, GRE General Test, bachelor's degree from an accredited college or university, minimum undergraduate GPA of 2.75. Electronic applications accepted.

Suffolk University, Sawyer Business School, Master of Business Administration Program, Boston, MA 02108-2770. Offers accounting (MBA); entrepreneurship (MBA); executive business administration (EMBA); finance (MBA); global business administration (GMBA); health administration (MBA); international business (MBA); marketing (MBA); nonprofit management (MBA); organizational behavior (MBA); strategic management (MBA); supply chain management (MBA); taxation (MBA); JD/MBA, MBA/MHA, MBA/MSA, MBA/MSF, MBA/MST. *Accreditation:* AACSB. *Program availability:* Part-time, evening/weekend, 100% online. *Faculty:* 16 full-time (6 women), 9 part-time/adjunct (1 woman). *Students:* 106 full-time (57 women), 236 part-time (135 women); includes 80 minority (23 Black or African American, non-Hispanic/Latino; 23 Asian, non-Hispanic/Latino; 28 Hispanic/Latino; 6 Two or more races, non-Hispanic/Latino), 41 international. Average age 30. 354 applicants, 69% accepted, 115 enrolled. In 2017, 170 master's awarded. *Entrance requirements:* For master's, GMAT, minimum undergraduate GPA of 2.75 (MBA), 5 years of managerial experience (EMBA). Additional exam requirements/recommendations for international students: Required—TOEFL (minimum score 550 paper-based; 80 iBT). *Application deadline:* For fall admission, 3/15 priority date for domestic students, 10/15 priority date for international students; for spring admission, 10/15 priority date for domestic and international

Business Administration and Management—General

students. Applications are processed on a rolling basis. Application fee: $50. Electronic applications accepted. *Expenses:* $43,980 per year full-time, $1,466 per credit part-time (for MBA); $1,794 per credit part-time (for Executive MBA). *Financial support:* In 2017–18, 198 students received support, including 1 fellowship (averaging $2,325 per year); career-related internships or fieldwork, Federal Work-Study, institutionally sponsored loans, and scholarships/grants also available. Support available to part-time students. Financial award application deadline: 4/1; financial award applicants required to submit FAFSA. *Faculty research:* Foreign investments; career strategies and boundaryless careers; corporate ethics codes; interest rates, inflation, and growth options; innovation and product development performance. *Unit head:* Jodi Detjen, Director of MBA Programs, 617-573-8306, E-mail: jdetjen@suffolk.edu. *Application contact:* Mara Marzocchi, Associate Director of Graduate Admissions, 617-573-8302, Fax: 617-305-1733, E-mail: grad.admission@suffolk.edu.
Website: http://www.suffolk.edu/mba

Sullivan University, School of Business, Louisville, KY 40205. Offers EMBA, MBA, MPM, MSCM, MSCS, MSHRL, MSM, MSMIT, PhD, Pharm D. *Program availability:* Part-time, online learning. *Degree requirements:* For doctorate, comprehensive exam, thesis/dissertation. *Entrance requirements:* Additional exam requirements/recommendations for international students: Required—TOEFL.

Sul Ross State University, College of Professional Studies, Department of Business Administration, Alpine, TX 79832. Offers EMBA, MBA. Two-year Executive MBA program in cooperation with La Universidad de Chihuahua, Mexico (UACH). *Program availability:* Part-time, evening/weekend. *Degree requirements:* For master's, thesis optional. *Entrance requirements:* For master's, GMAT or GRE General Test, minimum GPA of 2.5 in last 60 hours of undergraduate work. *Faculty research:* Cross-cultural comparisons, U.S.-Mexico management relations.

Sul Ross State University, Rio Grande College of Sul Ross State University, Alpine, TX 79832. Offers business administration (MBA); teacher education (M Ed), including bilingual education, counseling, educational diagnostics, elementary education, general education, reading, school administration, secondary education. *Program availability:* Part-time, evening/weekend, online learning. *Degree requirements:* For master's, comprehensive exam, thesis optional, minimum GPA of 3.0. *Entrance requirements:* For master's, GMAT or GRE General Test, minimum GPA of 2.5 in last 60 hours of undergraduate work. Additional exam requirements/recommendations for international students: Required—TOEFL.

Syracuse University, Martin J. Whitman School of Management, Syracuse, NY 13244. Offers MBA, MS, PhD, JD/MBA. *Accreditation:* AACSB. *Program availability:* Part-time, 100% online. *Faculty:* 73 full-time (27 women), 64 part-time/adjunct (19 women). *Students:* 318 full-time (154 women), 1,099 part-time (368 women); includes 446 minority (169 Black or African American, non-Hispanic/Latino; 3 American Indian or Alaska Native, non-Hispanic/Latino; 100 Asian, non-Hispanic/Latino; 132 Hispanic/Latino; 5 Native Hawaiian or other Pacific Islander, non-Hispanic/Latino; 37 Two or more races, non-Hispanic/Latino), 202 international. Average age 33. 1,363 applicants, 60% accepted, 333 enrolled. In 2017, 274 master's, 13 doctorates awarded. *Degree requirements:* For master's, comprehensive exam (for MS in business analytics); for doctorate, comprehensive exam, thesis/dissertation, summer research paper. *Entrance requirements:* For master's and doctorate, GMAT or GRE. Additional exam requirements/recommendations for international students: Required—PTE (minimum score 68), TOEFL (minimum iBT score of 100) or IELTS (7); GMAT; GRE. *Application deadline:* For fall admission, 11/30 for domestic and international students; for winter admission, 1/1 for domestic and international students; for spring admission, 2/15 for domestic and international students; for summer admission, 4/19 for domestic students. Application fee: $75. Electronic applications accepted. *Financial support:* In 2017–18, 45 students received support. Fellowships with full tuition reimbursements available, research assistantships with tuition reimbursements available, teaching assistantships with tuition reimbursements available, career-related internships or fieldwork, and scholarships/grants available. Financial award application deadline: 2/15. *Faculty research:* Marketing, supply chain management, management, finance, entrepreneurship. *Unit head:* Eugene Anderson, Dean, 315-443-9494, Fax: 315-443-9517, E-mail: genea@syr.edu. *Application contact:* Shri Ramakrishnan, Assistant Director, Graduate Recruitment, 315-443-3497, Fax: 315-443-9517, E-mail: sramak01@syr.edu.
Website: http://whitman.syr.edu

Tabor College, Graduate Program, Hillsboro, KS 67063. Offers accounting (MBA). Program offered at the Wichita campus only.

Tarleton State University, College of Graduate Studies, College of Business Administration, Master of Business Administration Program, Stephenville, TX 76402. Offers MBA. *Program availability:* Part-time, evening/weekend, 100% online, blended/hybrid learning. *Faculty:* 29 full-time (7 women), 4 part-time/adjunct (1 woman). *Students:* 29 full-time (20 women), 248 part-time (119 women); includes 68 minority (22 Black or African American, non-Hispanic/Latino; 1 American Indian or Alaska Native, non-Hispanic/Latino; 11 Asian, non-Hispanic/Latino; 26 Hispanic/Latino; 8 Two or more races, non-Hispanic/Latino), 1 international. Average age 32. 161 applicants, 86% accepted, 109 enrolled. In 2017, 51 master's awarded. *Degree requirements:* For master's, comprehensive exam, thesis (for some programs). *Entrance requirements:* For master's, GRE, minimum GPA of 3.0. Additional exam requirements/recommendations for international students: Required—TOEFL (minimum score 550 paper-based; 80 iBT), IELTS (minimum score 6). *Application deadline:* For fall admission, 8/15 for domestic students; for spring admission, 1/1 for domestic students. Applications are processed on a rolling basis. Application fee: $45 ($145 for international students). Electronic applications accepted. *Expenses:* Contact institution. *Financial support:* Applicants required to submit FAFSA. *Unit head:* Dr. Steve Steed, Dean, 254-968-9645, Fax: 254-968-9496, E-mail: ssteed@tarleton.edu. *Application contact:* Information Contact, 254-968-9104, E-mail: gradoffice@tarleton.edu.

Temple University, Fox School of Business, Doctoral Programs in Business, Philadelphia, PA 19122-6096. Offers accounting (PhD); entrepreneurship (PhD); finance (PhD); international business (PhD); management information systems (PhD); marketing (PhD); risk management and insurance (PhD); statistics (PhD); strategic management (PhD); tourism and sport (PhD). *Accreditation:* AACSB. *Degree requirements:* For doctorate, thesis/dissertation. *Entrance requirements:* For doctorate, GRE General Test, GMAT, minimum GPA of 3.0, master's degree. Additional exam requirements/recommendations for international students: Required—TOEFL (minimum score 600 paper-based; 100 iBT), IELTS (minimum score 7.5). Electronic applications accepted. *Expenses:* Tuition, state resident: full-time $16,164; part-time $898 per credit hour. Tuition, nonresident: full-time $22,158; part-time $1231 per credit hour. *Required fees:* $890; $445 per semester. Full-time tuition and fees vary according to course load, degree level, campus/location and program.

Temple University, Fox School of Business, MBA Programs, Philadelphia, PA 19122-6096. Offers accounting (MBA); business management (MBA); financial management (MBA); healthcare and life sciences innovation (MBA); human resource management (MBA); international business (IMBA); IT management (MBA); marketing management (MBA); pharmaceutical management (MBA); strategic management (EMBA, MBA).

EMBA offered in Philadelphia, PA and Tokyo, Japan. *Accreditation:* AACSB. *Program availability:* Part-time, evening/weekend, online learning. *Entrance requirements:* For master's, GMAT, minimum undergraduate GPA of 3.0. Additional exam requirements/recommendations for international students: Required—TOEFL (minimum score 600 paper-based; 100 iBT), IELTS (minimum score 7.5). *Expenses:* Tuition, state resident: full-time $16,164; part-time $898 per credit hour. Tuition, nonresident: full-time $22,158; part-time $1231 per credit hour. *Required fees:* $890; $445 per semester. Full-time tuition and fees vary according to course load, degree level, campus/location and program.

Temple University, Fox School of Business, Specialized Master's Programs, Philadelphia, PA 19122-6096. Offers accountancy (MS); actuarial science (MS); finance (MS); financial engineering (MS); human resource management (MS); innovation management and entrepreneurship (MS); marketing (MS); statistics (MS). MS in innovation management and entrepreneurship delivered jointly with College of Engineering. *Accreditation:* AACSB. *Program availability:* Part-time. *Entrance requirements:* For master's, GRE General Test or GMAT, minimum undergraduate GPA of 3.0. Additional exam requirements/recommendations for international students: Required—TOEFL (minimum score 600 paper-based; 100 iBT), IELTS (minimum score 7.5). *Expenses:* Tuition, state resident: full-time $16,164; part-time $898 per credit hour. Tuition, nonresident: full-time $22,158; part-time $1231 per credit hour. *Required fees:* $890; $445 per semester. Full-time tuition and fees vary according to course load, degree level, campus/location and program.

Tennessee State University, The School of Graduate Studies and Research, College of Business, Nashville, TN 37209-1561. Offers MBA. *Accreditation:* AACSB. *Program availability:* Part-time, evening/weekend, online learning. *Entrance requirements:* For master's, GMAT. Additional exam requirements/recommendations for international students: Required—TOEFL (minimum score 500 paper-based). Electronic applications accepted. *Faculty research:* Supply chain management, health economics, accounting, e-commerce, international business.

Tennessee Technological University, College of Graduate Studies, College of Business, MBA Program, Cookeville, TN 38505. Offers finance (MBA); human resource management (MBA); international business (MBA); management information systems (MBA). *Program availability:* Part-time, evening/weekend. In 2017, 77 master's awarded. *Entrance requirements:* For master's, GMAT or GRE. *Expenses:* Tuition, state resident: full-time $9925; part-time $565 per credit hour. Tuition, nonresident: full-time $22,993; part-time $1291 per credit hour. *Financial support:* In 2017–18, 2 research assistantships, 3 teaching assistantships were awarded; fellowships and unspecified assistantships also available. Financial award application deadline: 4/1; financial award applicants required to submit FAFSA. *Unit head:* Kate Nicewicz, Director, E-mail: knicewicz@tntech.edu. *Application contact:* Shelia K. Kendrick, Coordinator of Graduate Studies, 931-372-3808, Fax: 931-372-3497, E-mail: skendrick@tntech.edu.
Website: https://www.tntech.edu/cob/mba/

Tennessee Wesleyan University, Graduate Programs, Athens, TN 37303. Offers accounting (MBA); management (MBA). *Program availability:* Evening/weekend. *Faculty:* 4 full-time (1 woman), 1 (woman) part-time/adjunct. *Students:* 2 full-time (1 woman), 14 part-time (10 women). *Entrance requirements:* For master's, GMAT, official transcripts, three letters of recommendation, current curriculum vitae or resume. *Expenses: Tuition:* Part-time $500 per semester hour. *Application contact:* Mark Bucco, Adult and Graduate Admissions Counselor, 423-252-1114, Fax: 423-745-9335, E-mail: mbucco@tnwesleyan.edu.
Website: http://www.tnwesleyan.edu/academics/graduate-programs/

Texas A&M International University, Office of Graduate Studies and Research, A.R. Sanchez, Jr. School of Business, Laredo, TX 78041. Offers MBA, MP Acc, MSIS, PhD. *Accreditation:* AACSB. *Program availability:* Part-time, evening/weekend. *Degree requirements:* For master's, thesis (for some programs). *Entrance requirements:* For master's, GMAT or GRE General Test. Additional exam requirements/recommendations for international students: Required—TOEFL (minimum score 550 paper-based; 79 iBT), IELTS (minimum score 6.5).

Texas A&M University, Mays Business School, Department of Management, College Station, TX 77843. Offers entrepreneurial leadership (MS); human resource management (MS). *Faculty:* 32. *Students:* 90 full-time (63 women); includes 20 minority (3 Black or African American, non-Hispanic/Latino; 2 American Indian or Alaska Native, non-Hispanic/Latino; 2 Asian, non-Hispanic/Latino; 10 Hispanic/Latino; 3 Two or more races, non-Hispanic/Latino), 5 international. Average age 26. 163 applicants, 31% accepted, 40 enrolled. In 2017, 45 master's awarded. Terminal master's awarded for partial completion of doctoral program. *Degree requirements:* For master's, comprehensive exam. *Entrance requirements:* For master's, GMAT or GRE. Additional exam requirements/recommendations for international students: Required—TOEFL (minimum score 550 paper-based; 80 iBT), IELTS (minimum score 6), PTE (minimum score 53). *Application deadline:* For fall admission, 5/26 for domestic and international students. Applications are processed on a rolling basis. Application fee: $50 ($90 for international students). Electronic applications accepted. *Expenses:* Contact institution. *Financial support:* In 2017–18, 76 students received support, including 28 research assistantships with tuition reimbursements available (averaging $8,154 per year), 24 teaching assistantships with tuition reimbursements available (averaging $4,822 per year); career-related internships or fieldwork, institutionally sponsored loans, scholarships/grants, traineeships, health care benefits, tuition waivers (full and partial), and unspecified assistantships also available. Support available to part-time students. Financial award application deadline: 3/15; financial award applicants required to submit FAFSA. *Faculty research:* Strategic and human resource management, business and public policy, organizational behavior, organizational theory. *Unit head:* Dr. Wendy R. Boswell, Head, 979-845-4045, Fax: 979-845-9641, E-mail: wboswell@mays.tamu.edu. *Application contact:* Kristi R. Mora, Senior Academic Advisor II, 979-845-6127, Fax: 979-845-9641, E-mail: kmora@mays.tamu.edu.
Website: http://mays.tamu.edu/mgmt/

Texas A&M University–Central Texas, Graduate Studies and Research, Killeen, TX 76549. Offers accounting (MS); business administration (MBA); clinical mental health counseling (MS); criminal justice (MCJ); curriculum and instruction (M Ed); educational administration (M Ed); educational psychology - experimental psychology (MS); history (MA); human resource management (MS); information systems (MS); liberal studies (MS); management and leadership (MS); marriage and family therapy (MS); mathematics (MS); political science (MA); school counseling (M Ed); school psychology (Ed S).

Texas A&M University–Commerce, College of Business, Commerce, TX 75429. Offers accounting (MSA); business administration (MBA); business analytics (MS); finance (MSF); management (MS); marketing (MS). *Accreditation:* AACSB. *Program availability:* Part-time, evening/weekend, 100% online, blended/hybrid learning. *Faculty:* 50 full-time (19 women), 7 part-time/adjunct (0 women). *Students:* 479 full-time (248 women), 1,056 part-time (556 women); includes 660 minority (281 Black or African American, non-Hispanic/Latino; 4 American Indian or Alaska Native, non-Hispanic/Latino; 120 Asian, non-Hispanic/Latino; 222 Hispanic/Latino; 33 Two or more races, non-Hispanic/Latino), 224 international. Average age 33. 930 applicants, 61% accepted,

363 enrolled. In 2017, 686 master's awarded. *Degree requirements:* For master's, comprehensive exam. *Entrance requirements:* For master's, GRE General Test, GMAT, letter of recommendation. Additional exam requirements/recommendations for international students: Required—TOEFL (minimum score 550 paper-based; 79 iBT), IELTS (minimum score 6). *Application deadline:* For fall admission, 6/1 priority date for international students; for spring admission, 10/15 priority date for international students; for summer admission, 3/15 priority date for international students. Applications are processed on a rolling basis. Application fee: $50 ($75 for international students). Electronic applications accepted. *Expenses:* Contact institution. *Financial support:* In 2017–18, 46 students received support, including 20 research assistantships with partial tuition reimbursements available (averaging $8,000 per year); Federal Work-Study, institutionally sponsored loans, scholarships/grants, health care benefits, and unspecified assistantships also available. Financial award application deadline: 5/1; financial award applicants required to submit FAFSA. *Faculty research:* Applied economics with emphasis on industries that are important to the region including health, energy and agriculture; finance research on banking, investments, financial institutions and risk management; marketing and big data decisions of product choice behavior and channel behavior of consumers; strategic management and organizational behavior phenomena; international accounting in governmental sectors. *Total annual research expenditures:* $1,920. *Unit head:* Dr. Shanan Gwaltney Gibson, Dean of College of Business, 903-886-5191, Fax: 903-886-5650, E-mail: shanan.gibson@tamuc.edu. *Application contact:* Vicky Turner, Doctoral Degree and Special Programs Coordinator, 903-886-5167, E-mail: vicky.turner@tamuc.edu.
Website: http://www.tamuc.edu/academics/graduateSchool/programs/businessEntrepreneurship/default.aspx

Texas A&M University–Corpus Christi, College of Graduate Studies, College of Business, Corpus Christi, TX 78412. Offers accounting (M Acc); business (MBA); finance (MBA); health care administration (MBA); international business (MBA). *Accreditation:* AACSB. *Program availability:* Part-time, evening/weekend, 100% online, blended/hybrid learning. *Faculty:* 31 full-time (11 women), 2 part-time/adjunct (0 women). *Students:* 107 full-time (50 women), 583 part-time (283 women); includes 259 minority (80 Black or African American, non-Hispanic/Latino; 85 Asian, non-Hispanic/Latino; 83 Hispanic/Latino; 11 Two or more races, non-Hispanic/Latino; 77 international. Average age 34. 485 applicants, 57% accepted, 236 enrolled. In 2017, 310 master's awarded. *Degree requirements:* For master's, 30 to 42 hours (for MBA; varies by concentration area, delivery format, and necessity for foundational courses for students with nonbusiness degrees). *Entrance requirements:* For master's, GMAT, GRE. Additional exam requirements/recommendations for international students: Required—TOEFL (minimum score 550 paper-based; 79 iBT), IELTS (minimum score 6.5). *Application deadline:* For fall admission, 7/15 priority date for domestic students, 5/1 priority date for international students; for spring admission, 11/15 priority date for domestic students, 9/1 priority date for international students; for summer admission, 4/15 priority date for domestic and international students. Applications are processed on a rolling basis. Application fee: $50 ($70 for international students). Electronic applications accepted. *Expenses:* Tuition, state resident: full-time $3568; part-time $198.24 per credit hour. Tuition, nonresident: full-time $11,038; part-time $613.24 per credit hour. *Required fees:* $2129; $1422.58 per semester. Tuition and fees vary according to program. *Financial support:* Research assistantships, teaching assistantships, career-related internships or fieldwork, Federal Work-Study, institutionally sponsored loans, scholarships/grants, health care benefits, and unspecified assistantships available. Support available to part-time students. Financial award application deadline: 3/15; financial award applicants required to submit FAFSA. *Unit head:* Dr. John Gamble, Dean, 361-825-6045, Fax: 361-825-2725, E-mail: john.gamble@tamucc.edu. *Application contact:* Sharon Polansky, Director of Master's Programs, 361-825-3448, Fax: 361-825-2755, E-mail: gradweb@tamucc.edu.
Website: http://cob.tamucc.edu

Texas A&M University–Kingsville, College of Graduate Studies, College of Business Administration, Kingsville, TX 78363. Offers MBA. *Program availability:* Online only, 100% online, blended/hybrid learning. *Entrance requirements:* Additional exam requirements/recommendations for international students: Required—TOEFL (minimum score 550 paper-based; 79 iBT); Recommended—IELTS. Electronic applications accepted.

Texas A&M University–San Antonio, School of Business, San Antonio, TX 78224. Offers business administration (MBA); professional accounting (MPA). *Program availability:* Part-time, evening/weekend, online learning. *Faculty:* 19 full-time (7 women), 2 part-time/adjunct (1 woman). *Students:* 104 full-time (54 women), 391 part-time (200 women); includes 355 minority (43 Black or African American, non-Hispanic/Latino; 21 Asian, non-Hispanic/Latino; 280 Hispanic/Latino; 2 Native Hawaiian or other Pacific Islander, non-Hispanic/Latino; 9 Two or more races, non-Hispanic/Latino; 11 international. Average age 32. 365 applicants, 71% accepted, 160 enrolled. In 2017, 128 master's awarded. *Degree requirements:* For master's, comprehensive exam. *Entrance requirements:* For master's, GMAT. Additional exam requirements/recommendations for international students: Required—TOEFL (minimum score 550 paper-based; 79 iBT), IELTS (minimum score 6). *Application deadline:* For fall admission, 3/15 priority date for domestic and international students; for spring admission, 11/1 priority date for domestic and international students; for summer admission, 4/1 priority date for domestic and international students. Applications are processed on a rolling basis. Application fee: $35 ($50 for international students). Electronic applications accepted. *Expenses:* Tuition, state resident: full-time $3475; part-time $1930 per semester. Tuition, nonresident: full-time $10,945; part-time $6080 per semester. *Required fees:* $2148; $1412 per year. $706 per semester. Tuition and fees vary according to course load. *Financial support:* In 2017–18, 29 students received support. Federal Work-Study, scholarships/grants, and tuition waivers available. Financial award application deadline: 3/15; financial award applicants required to submit FAFSA. *Faculty research:* Culture and its effect on organizational processes; diversity and teams. *Unit head:* Dr. Tracy Hurley, Dean of the College of Business. *Application contact:* Caitie Garza, Graduate Admissions Coordinator, 210-784-1300, E-mail: beajaguar@tamusa.edu.
Website: http://www.tamusa.edu/collegeofbusiness/index.html

Texas A&M University–Texarkana, Graduate Studies and Research, College of Business, Texarkana, TX 75503. Offers accounting (MSA); business administration (MBA, MS). *Program availability:* Part-time, evening/weekend. *Degree requirements:* For master's, thesis or alternative. *Entrance requirements:* For master's, minimum GPA of 2.5 in last 60 hours of bachelor's degree. Additional exam requirements/recommendations for international students: Required—TOEFL. Electronic applications accepted.

Texas Christian University, Neeley School of Business, Executive MBA Program, Fort Worth, TX 76129. Offers MBA. *Program availability:* Evening/weekend. *Faculty:* 83 full-time (26 women), 14 part-time/adjunct (5 women). *Students:* 59 full-time (13 women); includes 13 minority (4 Black or African American, non-Hispanic/Latino; 1 Asian, non-Hispanic/Latino; 8 Hispanic/Latino), 1 international. Average age 39. 38 applicants, 95% accepted, 29 enrolled. In 2017, 30 master's awarded. *Entrance requirements:* Additional exam requirements/recommendations for international students: Recommended—TOEFL. *Application deadline:* For winter admission, 2/1 for domestic

and international students; for summer admission, 7/21 for domestic and international students. Applications are processed on a rolling basis. Application fee: $100. Electronic applications accepted. *Expenses:* $2,500 seat deposit, $20,300 per semester. *Financial support:* In 2017–18, 9 students received support. Scholarships/grants and tuition waivers (partial) available. Financial award application deadline: 8/15; financial award applicants required to submit FAFSA. *Unit head:* Dr. Suzanne M. Carter, EMBA Executive Director/Professor of Strategy Practice, 817-257-7543, E-mail: s.carter@tcu.edu. *Application contact:* Kevin T. Davis, Director, Executive MBA Recruiting and External Relations, 817-257-4681, Fax: 817-257-7719, E-mail: kevin.davis@tcu.edu.
Website: http://emba.tcu.edu

Texas Christian University, Neeley School of Business, Full-time Master's Program in Business Administration and Accelerated MBA, Fort Worth, TX 76109-1728. Offers MBA. *Accreditation:* AACSB. *Program availability:* Part-time, evening/weekend. *Faculty:* 83 full-time (26 women), 14 part-time/adjunct (5 women). *Students:* 93 full-time (26 women); includes 11 minority (3 Black or African American, non-Hispanic/Latino; 1 American Indian or Alaska Native, non-Hispanic/Latino; 1 Asian, non-Hispanic/Latino; 5 Hispanic/Latino; 1 Two or more races, non-Hispanic/Latino), 25 international. Average age 28. 170 applicants, 54% accepted, 48 enrolled. In 2017, 47 master's awarded. *Entrance requirements:* For master's, GMAT (preferred); GRE. Additional exam requirements/recommendations for international students: Required—TOEFL (minimum score 100 iBT); Recommended—IELTS (minimum score 7), TSE (minimum score 68). *Application deadline:* For fall admission, 3/1 for domestic and international students; for winter admission, 1/15 for domestic and international students; for spring admission, 11/1 for domestic and international students; for summer admission, 1/15 for domestic and international students. Applications are processed on a rolling basis. Application fee: $100. Electronic applications accepted. Application fee is waived when completed online. *Expenses:* $34,230 tuition, $7,200 fees. *Financial support:* In 2017–18, 94 students received support. Career-related internships or fieldwork, scholarships/grants, and unspecified assistantships available. Financial award application deadline: 4/1; financial award applicants required to submit FAFSA. *Faculty research:* Emerging financial markets, derivative trading activity, salesforce deployment, examining sales activity, litigation against tax practitioners. *Unit head:* Anne Rooney, Executive Director, Graduate Programs, 817-257-7991, Fax: 817-257-6431, E-mail: mbainfo@tcu.edu. *Application contact:* Peggy Conway, Director, Full-time MBA Admissions, 817-257-7989, Fax: 817-257-6431, E-mail: mbainfo@tcu.edu.
Website: http://www.neeley.tcu.edu/mba

Texas Christian University, Neeley School of Business, Professional MBA Program, Fort Worth, TX 76129. Offers MBA. *Program availability:* Part-time-only, evening/weekend. *Faculty:* 83 full-time (26 women), 14 part-time/adjunct (5 women). *Students:* 124 full-time (35 women), 23 part-time (6 women); includes 18 minority (4 Black or African American, non-Hispanic/Latino; 1 American Indian or Alaska Native, non-Hispanic/Latino; 5 Asian, non-Hispanic/Latino; 8 Hispanic/Latino), 1 international. Average age 30. 97 applicants, 97% accepted, 66 enrolled. In 2017, 59 master's awarded. *Entrance requirements:* For master's, GMAT (preferred) or GRE. *Application deadline:* For fall admission, 11/1 for domestic and international students; for winter admission, 1/15 for domestic and international students; for spring admission, 4/15 for domestic and international students. Applications are processed on a rolling basis. Application fee: $100. Electronic applications accepted. Application fee is waived when completed online. *Expenses:* Contact institution. *Financial support:* Application deadline: 5/1. *Unit head:* Kelli Kilpatrick, Director, Evening Graduate Programs, 817-257-5148, E-mail: k.kilpatrick@tcu.edu.
Website: http://www.neeley.tcu.edu/Professional_MBA.aspx

Texas Health and Science University, Graduate Programs, Austin, TX 78704. Offers acupuncture and Oriental medicine (MS, DAOM); business administration (MBA); healthcare management (MBA). *Accreditation:* ACAOM. *Faculty:* 8 full-time (3 women), 7 part-time/adjunct (5 women). *Students:* 102 full-time (64 women), 9 part-time (8 women); includes 43 minority (1 Black or African American, non-Hispanic/Latino; 1 American Indian or Alaska Native, non-Hispanic/Latino; 35 Asian, non-Hispanic/Latino; 6 Hispanic/Latino). Average age 34. *Entrance requirements:* For master's, 60 hours applicable to bachelor's degree. Additional exam requirements/recommendations for international students: Required—TOEFL (minimum score 500 paper-based), TWE. *Application deadline:* For fall admission, 8/25 priority date for domestic and international students; for spring admission, 12/22 priority date for domestic and international students. Applications are processed on a rolling basis. Application fee: $75 ($300 for international students). Electronic applications accepted. *Expenses:* Tuition: Full-time $11,460. *Required fees:* $600. Tuition and fees vary according to course load, degree level and program. *Financial support:* Teaching assistantships with partial tuition reimbursements, career-related internships or fieldwork, Federal Work-Study, institutionally sponsored loans, scholarships/grants, and tuition waivers (partial) available. Financial award applicants required to submit FAFSA. *Unit head:* Dr. David G. Vequist, IV, Vice President of Academic Affairs, 512-444-8082. *Application contact:* Caleb Li, Admissions Coordinator, 512-444-8082, Fax: 512-444-6345, E-mail: admissions@thsu.edu.

Texas Southern University, Jesse H. Jones School of Business, Program in Business Administration, Houston, TX 77004-4584. Offers MBA. *Accreditation:* AACSB. *Program availability:* Part-time, evening/weekend. *Degree requirements:* For master's, comprehensive exam. *Entrance requirements:* For master's, GMAT, minimum GPA of 2.5. Electronic applications accepted.

Texas State University, The Graduate College, Emmett and Miriam McCoy College of Business Administration, Program in Business Administration, San Marcos, TX 78666. Offers MBA. *Accreditation:* AACSB. *Program availability:* Part-time. *Faculty:* 31 full-time (11 women), 1 part-time/adjunct (0 women). *Students:* 75 full-time (32 women), 174 part-time (72 women); includes 70 minority (9 Black or African American, non-Hispanic/Latino; 1 American Indian or Alaska Native, non-Hispanic/Latino; 11 Asian, non-Hispanic/Latino; 43 Hispanic/Latino; 6 Two or more races, non-Hispanic/Latino), 11 international. Average age 30. 235 applicants, 47% accepted, 64 enrolled. In 2017, 104 master's awarded. *Degree requirements:* For master's, comprehensive exam, thesis optional. *Entrance requirements:* For master's, GMAT or GRE, baccalaureate degree from regionally-accredited university; two letters or forms of recommendation from persons best able to assess applicant's ability to succeed in graduate school; essay; detailed resume showing work experience, extracurricular and community activities, and honors and achievements. Additional exam requirements/recommendations for international students: Required—TOEFL (minimum score 550 paper-based; 78 iBT), IELTS (minimum score 6.5). *Application deadline:* For fall admission, 2/1 priority date for domestic and international students; for spring admission, 10/1 for domestic and international students. Application fee: $40 ($90 for international students). Electronic applications accepted. *Expenses:* Tuition, state resident: full-time $7868; part-time $3934 per semester. Tuition, nonresident: full-time $17,828; part-time $8914 per semester. *Required fees:* $2092; $1435 per semester. Tuition and fees vary according to course load. *Financial support:* In 2017–18, 104 students received support, including 11 teaching assistantships (averaging $12,218 per year); research assistantships, Federal Work-Study, institutionally sponsored loans, scholarships/grants, health care benefits, and unspecified assistantships also available. Support available to part-time

Business Administration and Management—General

students. Financial award application deadline: 3/1; financial award applicants required to submit FAFSA. *Unit head:* Dr. William Chittenden, Graduate Advisor, 512-245-3591, Fax: 512-245-7973, E-mail: wc10@txstate.edu. *Application contact:* Dr. Andrea Golato, Dean of Graduate School, 512-245-2581, Fax: 512-245-8365, E-mail: gradcollege@txstate.edu.
Website: http://graduate.mccoy.txstate.edu/

Texas Tech University, Rawls College of Business Administration, Lubbock, TX 79409-2101. Offers accounting (MSA, PhD), including audit/financial reporting (MSA); taxation (MSA); data science (MS); finance (PhD); general business (MBA); healthcare management (MS); information systems and operations management (PhD); management (PhD); marketing (PhD); STEM (MBA); JD/MBA; JD/MSA; MBA/M Arch; MBA/MD; MBA/MS; MBA/Pharm D. *Accreditation:* AACSB. *Program availability:* Evening/weekend, 100% online, blended/hybrid learning. *Faculty:* 89 full-time (22 women). *Students:* 660 full-time (252 women); includes 174 minority (30 Black or African American, non-Hispanic/Latino; 3 American Indian or Alaska Native, non-Hispanic/Latino; 20 Asian, non-Hispanic/Latino; 104 Hispanic/Latino; 17 Two or more races, non-Hispanic/Latino), 99 international. Average age 29. 492 applicants, 51% accepted, 148 enrolled. In 2017, 439 master's, 6 doctorates awarded. *Degree requirements:* For master's, thesis (for MS); capstone course; for doctorate, comprehensive exam, thesis/dissertation, qualifying exams. *Entrance requirements:* For master's, GMAT, GRE, MCAT, PCAT, LSAT, or DAT, holistic review of academic credentials, resume, essay, letters of recommendation; for doctorate, GMAT, GRE, holistic review of academic credentials, resume, statement of purpose, letters of recommendation. Additional exam requirements/recommendations for international students: Required—TOEFL (minimum score 550 paper-based; 79 iBT), IELTS (minimum score 6.5), PTE (minimum score 60). *Application deadline:* For fall admission, 7/1 priority date for domestic students, 1/15 for international students; for spring admission, 12/1 priority date for domestic students, 6/15 for international students; for summer admission, 5/1 for domestic students. Applications are processed on a rolling basis. Application fee: $60. Electronic applications accepted. *Expenses:* $5,167.50 full-time; $9,000 per semester (for hybrid MBA). *Financial support:* In 2017–18, 81 students received support, including 1 research assistantship with full tuition reimbursement available (averaging $22,725 per year), 63 teaching assistantships with full tuition reimbursements available (averaging $22,725 per year); career-related internships or fieldwork, Federal Work-Study, scholarships/grants, health care benefits, and unspecified assistantships also available. Financial award application deadline: 3/1; financial award applicants required to submit FAFSA. *Faculty research:* Governmental and nonprofit accounting, securities and options futures, statistical analysis and design, leadership, consumer behavior. *Total annual research expenditures:* $230,000. *Unit head:* Dr. Margaret Williams, Dean, 806-834-2839, Fax: 806-742-1092, E-mail: margaret.l.williams@ttu.edu. *Application contact:* Jennifer Yack, Applications Manager, Graduate and Professional Programs, 806-742-3184, E-mail: rawlsgrad@ttu.edu.
Website: http://www.depts.ttu.edu/rawlsbusiness/graduate/

Texas Wesleyan University, Graduate Programs, Graduate Business Programs, Fort Worth, TX 76105. Offers MBA. *Accreditation:* AACSB; ACBSP. *Program availability:* Part-time, online only, 100% online. *Faculty:* 16 full-time (8 women). *Students:* 35 full-time (20 women), 41 part-time (22 women); includes 20 minority (16 Black or African American, non-Hispanic/Latino; 4 Asian, non-Hispanic/Latino), 11 international. Average age 33. 154 applicants, 54% accepted, 60 enrolled. In 2017, 23 master's awarded. *Degree requirements:* For master's, capstone course. *Entrance requirements:* For master's, GMAT or GRE, bachelor's degree, minimum overall undergraduate GPA of 2.6, three letters of recommendation, written essay that shows objectives in pursuing an MBA. Additional exam requirements/recommendations for international students: Required—TOEFL (minimum score 550 paper-based; 79 iBT), IELTS (minimum score 6.5). *Application deadline:* Applications are processed on a rolling basis. Electronic applications accepted. *Expenses:* Contact institution. *Financial support:* In 2017–18, 6 students received support. Federal Work-Study and tuition waivers (full and partial) available. Support available to part-time students. Financial award application deadline: 3/15; financial award applicants required to submit FAFSA. *Unit head:* Dr. Hector Quintanilla, Dean, 817-531-6480, Fax: 817-531-6585. *Application contact:* Amy Orcutt, Interim Director of Graduate Admissions, 817-531-4288, E-mail: arorcutt@txwes.edu.
Website: https://txwes.edu/academics/business-administration/

Texas Woman's University, Graduate School, College of Business, Denton, TX 76204. Offers business administration (MBA), including accounting, business analytics, healthcare administration (MBA, MHA), human resources management, management; health systems management (MHSM); healthcare administration (MHA), including healthcare administration (MBA, MHA). *Accreditation:* ACBSP. *Program availability:* Part-time. *Faculty:* 32 full-time (12 women), 13 part-time/adjunct (9 women). *Students:* 373 full-time (312 women), 432 part-time (368 women); includes 569 minority (312 Black or African American, non-Hispanic/Latino; 1 American Indian or Alaska Native, non-Hispanic/Latino; 116 Asian, non-Hispanic/Latino; 118 Hispanic/Latino; 3 Native Hawaiian or other Pacific Islander, non-Hispanic/Latino; 19 Two or more races, non-Hispanic/Latino), 35 international. Average age 35. 314 applicants, 82% accepted, 184 enrolled. In 2017, 443 master's awarded. *Degree requirements:* For master's, thesis or alternative, capstone. *Entrance requirements:* For master's, minimum GPA of 3.0 in last 60 hours of undergraduate coursework and prior graduate coursework, 2 letters of reference, resume, 5 years of relevant experience (EMBA only). Additional exam requirements/recommendations for international students: Required—TOEFL (minimum score 550 paper-based; 79 iBT); Recommended—IELTS (minimum score 6.5), TSE (minimum score 53). *Application deadline:* For fall admission, 3/1 priority date for domestic students, 3/1 for international students; for spring admission, 11/1 priority date for domestic students, 7/1 for international students. Applications are processed on a rolling basis. Application fee: $50 ($75 for international students). Electronic applications accepted. *Expenses:* $7,520 per year full-time in-state; $16,820 per year full-time out-of-state. *Financial support:* In 2017–18, 198 students received support. Career-related internships or fieldwork, Federal Work-Study, institutionally sponsored loans, scholarships/grants, traineeships, health care benefits, and unspecified assistantships available. Support available to part-time students. Financial award application deadline: 3/1; financial award applicants required to submit FAFSA. *Faculty research:* Marketing and market research, economics, accounting, logistics and supply chain management, health systems. *Unit head:* Dr. Margaret A. Young, Director, 940-898-2458, Fax: 940-898-2120, E-mail: mba@twu.edu. *Application contact:* Korie Hawkins, Associate Director of Admissions, Graduate Recruitment, 940-898-3188, Fax: 940-898-3081, E-mail: admissions@twu.edu.
Website: http://www.twu.edu/business/

Thomas College, Graduate School, Programs in Business, Waterville, ME 04901-5097. Offers business (MBA); computer technology education (MS); education (MS); human resource management (MBA). *Program availability:* Part-time, evening/weekend. *Entrance requirements:* For master's, GMAT, GRE, MAT or minimum GPA of 3.3 in first 3 graduate-level courses. Additional exam requirements/recommendations for international students: Recommended—TOEFL.

Thomas Edison State University, School of Business and Management, MBA Program, Trenton, NJ 08608. Offers MBA. *Program availability:* Online learning. *Expenses:* Contact institution.

Thomas Edison State University, School of Business and Management, Program in Management, Trenton, NJ 08608. Offers accounting (MSM); organizational leadership (MSM); project management (MSM). *Program availability:* Part-time, 100% online. *Degree requirements:* For master's, final capstone project. *Entrance requirements:* For master's, bachelor's degree from a regionally-accredited college or university; minimum 2 letters of recommendation; 3-5 years of related working experience; current resume. Additional exam requirements/recommendations for international students: Required—TOEFL (minimum score 550 paper-based; 79 iBT). Electronic applications accepted.

Thomas Jefferson University, Kanbar College of Design, Engineering and Commerce, Innovation MBA Program, Philadelphia, PA 19107. Offers business analytics (MBA); general business (MBA); management (MBA); marketing (MBA); strategy and design thinking (MBA); MBA/MS. *Program availability:* Part-time, evening/weekend, online learning. *Entrance requirements:* For master's, GMAT. Additional exam requirements/recommendations for international students: Required—TOEFL (minimum score 550 paper-based; 79 iBT).

Thomas More College, Program in Business Administration, Crestview Hills, KY 41017-3495. Offers MBA. *Accreditation:* ACBSP. *Program availability:* Evening/weekend, 100% online. *Degree requirements:* For master's, comprehensive exam, final project. *Entrance requirements:* For master's, GMAT, minimum GPA of 2.7. Additional exam requirements/recommendations for international students: Required—TOEFL (minimum score 600 paper-based; 100 iBT). Electronic applications accepted. *Expenses:* Contact institution. *Faculty research:* Leadership, elder abuse and neglect, community health asset mapping, critical thinking in higher education, business communication, corporate social responsibility.

Thomas University, Department of Business Administration, Thomasville, GA 31792-7499. Offers MBA. *Program availability:* Part-time. *Entrance requirements:* For master's, resume, 3 professional or academic references. Additional exam requirements/recommendations for international students: Required—TOEFL (minimum score 600 paper-based). Electronic applications accepted.

Thompson Rivers University, Program in Business Administration, Kamloops, BC V2C 0C8, Canada. Offers MBA. *Program availability:* Part-time. *Entrance requirements:* For master's, GMAT, undergraduate degree with minimum B- average in last 60 credits, personal resume. Additional exam requirements/recommendations for international students: Required—TOEFL (570 paper-based, 88 iBT), IELTS (6.5), or CAEL (70).

Tiffin University, Program in Business Administration, Tiffin, OH 44883-2161. Offers finance (MBA); general management (MBA); healthcare administration (MBA); human resource management (MBA); international business (MBA); leadership (MBA); marketing (MBA); non-profit management (MBA); sports management (MBA). *Accreditation:* ACBSP. *Program availability:* Part-time, evening/weekend, online learning. *Entrance requirements:* For master's, minimum undergraduate GPA of 2.5, work experience. Additional exam requirements/recommendations for international students: Required—TOEFL (minimum score 550 paper-based; 79 iBT), IELTS. Electronic applications accepted. Application fee is waived when completed online. *Faculty research:* Small business, executive development operations, research and statistical analysis, market research, management information systems.

Trevecca Nazarene University, Graduate Business Programs, Nashville, TN 37210-2877. Offers business administration (MBA); health care leadership and innovation (MS); management (MSM). *Program availability:* Evening/weekend, online learning. *Faculty:* 12 full-time (1 woman), 15 part-time/adjunct (8 women). *Students:* 236 full-time (145 women), 50 part-time (29 women); includes 154 minority (128 Black or African American, non-Hispanic/Latino; 1 American Indian or Alaska Native, non-Hispanic/Latino; 4 Asian, non-Hispanic/Latino; 18 Hispanic/Latino; 3 Two or more races, non-Hispanic/Latino), 4 international. Average age 33. In 2017, 55 master's awarded. *Entrance requirements:* For master's, minimum GPA of 2.75, resume, official transcript from regionally accredited institution, minimum math grade of C, minimum English composition grade of C. Additional exam requirements/recommendations for international students: Required—TOEFL (minimum score 550 paper-based; 80 iBT). *Application deadline:* Applications are processed on a rolling basis. Application fee: $0. Electronic applications accepted. *Expenses:* $520 per credit hour. *Financial support:* Applicants required to submit FAFSA. *Unit head:* Dr. Rick Mann, Director of Graduate and Professional Programs for School of Business, 615-248-1529, E-mail: management@trevecca.edu. *Application contact:* 615-248-1529, E-mail: sgcsadmissions@trevecca.edu.
Website: http://www.trevecca.edu/mba

Trident University International, College of Business Administration, Program in Business Administration, Cypress, CA 90630. Offers business administration (PhD); conflict and negotiation management (MBA); criminal justice administration (MBA); entrepreneurship (MBA); finance (MBA); general management (MBA); government accounting (MBA); human resource management (MBA); information security and digital assurance management (MBA); information technology management (MBA); international business (MBA); logistics management (MBA); marketing (MBA); project management (MBA); public management (MBA); quality management (MBA); strategic leadership (MBA). *Program availability:* Part-time, evening/weekend, online learning. *Degree requirements:* For doctorate, comprehensive exam, thesis/dissertation, defense of dissertation. *Entrance requirements:* For master's, minimum GPA of 2.5 (students with GPA 3.0 or greater may transfer up to 30% of graduate level credits); for doctorate, minimum GPA of 3.4, curriculum vitae, course work in research methods or statistics. Additional exam requirements/recommendations for international students: Required—TOEFL. Electronic applications accepted.

Trinity International University, Trinity Evangelical Divinity School, Deerfield, IL 60015-1284. Offers academic ministry (M Div); Biblical and Near Eastern archaeology and languages (MA); chaplaincy and ministry care (MA); Christian studies (Certificate); church and parachurch ministry (M Div); church history (MA, Th M); counseling (Th M); educational ministries (MA); educational ministry (Th M); educational studies (PhD); intercultural studies (MA, PhD); leadership and management (D Min); mental health counseling (MA); military chaplaincy (D Min); ministry (MA); missions (Th M); missions and evangelism (D Min); New Testament (MA, Th M); Old Testament (Th M); Old Testament and Semitic languages (MA); pastoral ministry and care (D Min); pastoral theology (Th M); preaching and teaching (D Min); spiritual formation and education (D Min); systematic theology (MA, Th M); theological studies (MA, PhD); urban ministry (MA). *Program availability:* Part-time, online learning. *Degree requirements:* For master's, comprehensive exam, thesis, fieldwork; for doctorate, comprehensive exam (for some programs), thesis/dissertation; for Certificate, comprehensive exam, integrative papers. *Entrance requirements:* For master's, GRE, MAT, minimum cumulative undergraduate GPA of 3.0; for doctorate, GRE, minimum cumulative graduate GPA of 3.2; for Certificate, GRE, MAT, minimum undergraduate GPA of 2.5. Additional exam requirements/recommendations for international students: Required—TOEFL (minimum score 580 paper-based), TWE (minimum score 4). Electronic applications accepted.

Trinity University, School of Business, San Antonio, TX 78212-7200. Offers accounting (MS). *Accreditation:* AACSB. *Entrance requirements:* For master's, GMAT, minimum GPA of 3.0, course work in accounting and business law, letters of recommendation. *Application deadline:* For fall admission, 2/1 for domestic and international students. Electronic applications accepted. *Financial support:* Institutionally sponsored loans and scholarships/grants available. Financial award application deadline: 5/1; financial award applicants required to submit FAFSA. *Unit head:* Dr. Julie Persellin, Chair, Department of Accounting, 210-999-7230, E-mail: jpersell@trinity.edu. *Application contact:* Dr. Julie Persellin, Chair, Department of Accounting, 210-999-7230, E-mail: jpersell@trinity.edu. Website: https://new.trinity.edu/academics/departments/school-business/graduate-accounting-program

Trinity Washington University, School of Business and Graduate Studies, Washington, DC 20017-1094. Offers business administration (MBA); communication (MA); international security studies (MA); organizational management (MSA), including federal program management, human resource management, nonprofit management, organizational development, public and community health. *Program availability:* Part-time, evening/weekend. *Degree requirements:* For master's, thesis (for some programs), capstone project (MSA). *Entrance requirements:* For master's, minimum GPA of 2.5. Additional exam requirements/recommendations for international students: Required—TOEFL (minimum score 550 paper-based).

Trinity Western University, School of Graduate Studies, Program in Business Administration, Langley, BC V2Y 1Y1, Canada. Offers international business (MBA); management of the growing enterprise (MBA); non-profit and charitable organization management (MBA). *Program availability:* Part-time, online learning. *Degree requirements:* For master's, thesis or alternative, applied project. *Entrance requirements:* For master's, GMAT (minimum score of 550 recommended). Additional exam requirements/recommendations for international students: Required—TOEFL (minimum score 600 paper-based; 100 iBT), IELTS. Electronic applications accepted.

Troy University, Graduate School, College of Business, Program in Business Administration, Troy, AL 36082. Offers accounting (EMBA, MBA); criminal justice (EMBA); finance (MBA); general management (EMBA, MBA); healthcare management (EMBA); information systems (EMBA, MBA); international economic development (MBA). *Accreditation:* ACBSP. *Program availability:* Part-time, evening/weekend. *Faculty:* 6 full-time (2 women), 1 part-time/adjunct (0 women). *Students:* 43 full-time (22 women), 115 part-time (55 women); includes 50 minority (31 Black or African American, non-Hispanic/Latino; 12 Asian, non-Hispanic/Latino; 6 Hispanic/Latino; 1 Two or more races, non-Hispanic/Latino). Average age 30. 156 applicants, 76% accepted, 36 enrolled. In 2017, 95 master's awarded. *Degree requirements:* For master's, minimum GPA of 3.0, capstone course, research course. *Entrance requirements:* For master's, GMAT (minimum score 500) or GRE (minimum score 900 on old exam or 294 on new exam), bachelor's degree; minimum undergraduate GPA of 2.5 or 3.0 on last 30 semester hours, letter of recommendation. Additional exam requirements/recommendations for international students: Required—TOEFL (minimum score 523 paper-based; 70 iBT), IELTS (minimum score 6). *Application deadline:* Applications are processed on a rolling basis. Application fee: $50. Electronic applications accepted. *Expenses:* Tuition, state resident: part-time $417 per credit hour. Tuition, nonresident: part-time $834 per credit hour. *Required fees:* $42 per credit hour. $50 per semester. Tuition and fees vary according to campus/location. *Financial support:* Fellowships, career-related internships or fieldwork, and scholarships/grants available. Support available to part-time students. Financial award applicants required to submit FAFSA. *Unit head:* Dr. Phillip Mixon, MBA Director, 334-670-3140, Fax: 334-670-3708, E-mail: pamixon@troy.edu. *Application contact:* Jessica A. Kimbro, Director of Graduate Admissions, 334-670-3178, E-mail: jacord@troy.edu.

Troy University, Graduate School, College of Business, Program in Management, Troy, AL 36082. Offers MS, MSM. *Accreditation:* ACBSP. *Program availability:* Part-time, evening/weekend. *Faculty:* 15 full-time (4 women). *Students:* 53 full-time (25 women), 283 part-time (128 women); includes 87 minority (70 Black or African American, non-Hispanic/Latino; 4 American Indian or Alaska Native, non-Hispanic/Latino; 7 Hispanic/Latino; 6 Two or more races, non-Hispanic/Latino). Average age 36. 142 applicants, 96% accepted, 99 enrolled. In 2017, 188 master's awarded. *Degree requirements:* For master's, Graduate Educational Testing Service Major Field Test, capstone exam, minimum GPA of 3.0. *Entrance requirements:* For master's, GRE (minimum score of 900 on old exam or 294 on new exam) or GMAT (minimum score of 500), bachelor's degree; minimum undergraduate GPA of 2.5 or 3.0 on last 30 semester hours, letter of recommendation. Additional exam requirements/recommendations for international students: Required—TOEFL (minimum score 523 paper-based; 70 iBT), IELTS (minimum score 6). *Application deadline:* Applications are processed on a rolling basis. Application fee: $50. Electronic applications accepted. *Expenses:* Contact institution. *Financial support:* Fellowships, career-related internships or fieldwork, and scholarships/grants available. Support available to part-time students. *Unit head:* Dr. Bob Wheatley, Director, Graduate Business Programs, 334-670-3143, Fax: 334-670-3599, E-mail: rwheat@troy.edu. *Application contact:* Jessica A. Kimbro, Director of Graduate Admissions, 334-670-3178, E-mail: kimbro@troy.edu.

Truett McConnell University, Hans Hut School of Business, Cleveland, GA 30528. Offers MBA. *Program availability:* Part-time, evening/weekend, 100% online. *Faculty:* 2 full-time (both women). *Students:* 6 full-time (1 woman), 3 part-time (0 women). *Entrance requirements:* For master's, bachelor's degree from accredited institution, minimum GPA of 2.75. *Application deadline:* For fall admission, 8/1 for domestic students; for spring admission, 12/1 for domestic students; for summer admission, 5/1 for domestic students. Applications are processed on a rolling basis. Electronic applications accepted. *Expenses:* Tuition: Part-time $325 per credit hour. *Required fees:* $910 per year. $455 per semester. *Financial support:* Applicants required to submit FAFSA. *Unit head:* Dr. Janet Forney, Dean, 706-865-2134 Ext. 6501, E-mail: jforney@truett.edu. *Application contact:* Jim Dunnington, Coordinator of Online and Graduate Admissions, 706-865-2134 Ext. 2131, E-mail: jdunnington@truett.edu. Website: https://truett.edu/degrees/master-business-administration/

Tulane University, A. B. Freeman School of Business, New Orleans, LA 70118-5669. Offers accounting (M Acct); analytics (MBA); banking and financial services (M Fin); energy (M Fin, MBA); entrepreneurship (MBA); finance (MBA, PhD); financial accounting (PhD); international business (MBA); international management (MBA); strategic management and leadership (MBA); JD/M Acct; JD/MBA; MBA/M Acc; MBA/MA; MBA/MD; MBA/ME; MBA/MPH. *Accreditation:* AACSB. *Program availability:* Part-time, evening/weekend. *Faculty:* 51 full-time (15 women), 38 part-time/adjunct (3 women). *Students:* 561 full-time (287 women), 297 part-time (151 women); includes 112 minority (43 Black or African American, non-Hispanic/Latino; 2 American Indian or Alaska Native, non-Hispanic/Latino; 24 Asian, non-Hispanic/Latino; 38 Hispanic/Latino; 5 Two or more races, non-Hispanic/Latino), 515 international. Average age 27. 2,021 applicants, 74% accepted, 476 enrolled. In 2017, 632 master's, 9 doctorates awarded. Terminal master's awarded for partial completion of doctoral program. *Degree requirements:* For master's, one foreign language, comprehensive exam (for some programs); for doctorate, one foreign language, comprehensive exam, thesis/ dissertation. *Entrance requirements:* For master's and doctorate, GMAT or GRE, interview. Additional exam requirements/recommendations for international students:

Required—TOEFL or IELTS. *Application deadline:* For fall admission, 11/1 priority date for domestic and international students; for winter admission, 1/6 for domestic and international students; for spring admission, 3/1 priority date for domestic and international students; for summer admission, 5/5 for domestic students. Applications are processed on a rolling basis. Application fee: $125. Electronic applications accepted. *Expenses:* Contact institution. *Financial support:* In 2017–18, 176 students received support. Fellowships with tuition reimbursements available, research assistantships, teaching assistantships, career-related internships or fieldwork, Federal Work-Study, tuition waivers (full and partial), and unspecified assistantships available. Support available to part-time students. Financial award application deadline: 4/15; financial award applicants required to submit FAFSA. *Faculty research:* Corporate finance, managerial accounting and financial reporting, strategic management and leadership, consumer behavior and decision making, organizational behavior and human resource management. *Unit head:* Ira Solomon, PhD, Dean, 504-865-5407, Fax: 504-865-5491, E-mail: businessdean@tulane.edu. *Application contact:* Melissa Booth, Assistant Dean for Graduate Admissions, 800-223-5402, E-mail: freeman.admissions@tulane.edu. Website: http://www.freeman.tulane.edu

Tusculum College, Program in Business Administration, Greeneville, TN 37743-9997. Offers general management (MBA). *Program availability:* Evening/weekend. *Entrance requirements:* For master's, GMAT, GRE, 3 years of work experience, minimum GPA of 2.75. *Unit head:* Dr. Jacob Fait, Dean of the School of Business, 423-636-7300 Ext. 5022, E-mail: jfait@tusculum.edu. *Application contact:* Lindsey Seal, Director of Enrollment, 423-636-7300 Ext. 5006, E-mail: lseal@tusculum.edu. Website: http://home.tusculum.edu/gps/graduate-degrees/master-business-administration/

Union University, McAfee School of Business Administration, Jackson, TN 38305-3697. Offers accountancy (M Acc). Program also available at Germantown campus. *Program availability:* Evening/weekend, online learning. *Entrance requirements:* For master's, GMAT, minimum GPA of 2.5. Electronic applications accepted. *Expenses:* Contact institution. *Faculty research:* Personal financial management, strategy, accounting, marketing, economics.

United States International University–Africa, School of Business Administration, Nairobi, Kenya. Offers business administration (GEMBA); entrepreneurship (MBA); finance (MBA); human resource management (MBA); information technology management (MBA); integrated studies (MBA); international business administration (MBA); management and organizational development (MS); marketing (MBA); organizational development (EMS); strategic management (MBA). *Program availability:* Part-time, evening/weekend. *Degree requirements:* For master's, thesis. *Entrance requirements:* For master's, GMAT, 2 letters of reference, resume. Additional exam requirements/recommendations for international students: Required—TOEFL (minimum score 550 paper-based). *Faculty research:* Marketing in small business enterprises, total quality management in Kenya.

Universidad Autonoma de Guadalajara, Graduate Programs, Guadalajara, Mexico. Offers administrative law and justice (LL M); advertising and corporate communications (MA); architecture (M Arch); business (MBA); computational science (MCC); education (Ed M, Ed D); English-Spanish translation (MA); entrepreneurship and management (MBA); integrated management of digital animation (MA); international business (MIB); international corporate law (LL M); internet technologies (MS); manufacturing systems (MMS); occupational health (MS); philosophy (MA, PhD); power electronics (MS); quality systems (MQS); renewable energy (MS); social evaluation of projects (MBA); strategic market research (MBA); tax law (MA); teaching mathematics (MA).

Universidad de las Americas, A.C., Program in Business Administration, Mexico City, Mexico. Offers finance (MBA); marketing research (MBA); production and quality (MBA).

Universidad de las Américas Puebla, Division of Graduate Studies, School of Business and Economics, Puebla, Mexico. Offers business administration (MBA); finance (M Adm). *Program availability:* Part-time, evening/weekend. *Degree requirements:* For master's, one foreign language, thesis. *Entrance requirements:* Additional exam requirements/recommendations for international students: Required—TOEFL. *Faculty research:* System dynamics, information technology, marketing, international business, strategic planning, quality.

Universidad del Este, Graduate School, Carolina, PR 00984. Offers accounting (MBA); adult education (M Ed); agribusiness (MBA); criminal justice and criminology (MA); curriculum and instruction - early education (M Ed); curriculum and instruction - elementary (M Ed); curriculum and instruction - English (M Ed); curriculum and instruction - Spanish (M Ed); human resources (MBA); information security management (MBA); information technology and Web business development (MBA); management (MBA); public policy (MPA); social work (MA), including clinical social work; special education (M Ed); strategic leadership (MBA).

Universidad del Turabo, Graduate Programs, School of Business and Entrepreneurship, Program in Management, Gurabo, PR 00778-3030. Offers MBA, DBA. *Program availability:* Part-time, evening/weekend. *Entrance requirements:* For master's, GRE, EXADEP or GMAT, interview, essay, official transcript, recommendation letters; for doctorate, GRE, EXADEP or GMAT, official transcript, recommendation letters, essay, curriculum vitae, interview. Electronic applications accepted.

Universidad Iberoamericana, Graduate School, Santo Domingo D.N., Dominican Republic. Offers business administration (MBA, PMBA); constitutional law (LL M); dentistry (DMD); educational management (MA); integrated marketing communication (MA); psychopedagogical intervention (M Ed); real estate law (LL M); strategic management of human talent (MM).

Universidad Metropolitana, School of Business Administration, San Juan, PR 00928-1150. Offers accounting (MBA); finance (MBA); human resources management (MBA); international business (MBA); management (MBA); management information systems (MBA); marketing (MBA). *Program availability:* Part-time, evening/weekend. *Degree requirements:* For master's, thesis or alternative. Electronic applications accepted. *Faculty research:* Latin American trade, international investments, central city business development, Hispanic consumer research, Caribbean and Asian trade cooperation.

Université de Moncton, Faculty of Administration, Moncton, NB E1A 3E9, Canada. Offers MBA, JD/MBA. *Program availability:* Part-time, evening/weekend, 100% online. *Faculty:* 23 full-time (9 women), 24 part-time/adjunct (9 women). *Students:* 27 full-time (11 women), 16 international. Average age 26. 125 applicants, 41% accepted, 17 enrolled. In 2017, 20 master's awarded. *Degree requirements:* For master's, one foreign language, thesis. *Entrance requirements:* For master's, minimum undergraduate GPA of 3.0. *Application deadline:* For fall admission, 6/1 for domestic students, 2/1 for international students; for winter admission, 11/15 for domestic students, 9/1 for international students; for spring admission, 3/31 for domestic students, 1/1 for international students; for summer admission, 3/31 for domestic students, 1/1 for international students. Applications are processed on a rolling basis. Application fee: $60. Electronic applications accepted. *Expenses:* Contact institution. *Financial support:* In 2017–18, 7 fellowships (averaging $2,500 per year) were awarded; teaching assistantships and institutionally sponsored loans also available. Support available to part-time students. Financial award application deadline: 5/30. *Faculty research:* Service

Business Administration and Management—General

management, corporate reputation, financial management, accounting, supply chain. *Total annual research expenditures:* $150,000. *Unit head:* Jean-Pierre Booto Ekionea, Director, 506-858-4174, Fax: 506-858-4093, E-mail: jean-pierre.booto.ekionea@ umoncton.ca. *Application contact:* Natalie Allain, Admission Counselor, 506-858-4273, Fax: 506-858-4093, E-mail: natalie.allain@umoncton.ca.
Website: http://www.umoncton.ca/umcm-administration/

Université de Sherbrooke, Faculty of Administration, Doctoral Program in Business Administration, Sherbrooke, QC J1K 2R1, Canada. Offers DBA. *Degree requirements:* For doctorate, one foreign language, comprehensive exam, thesis/dissertation. *Entrance requirements:* For doctorate, 3 years of related work experience, interview, fluency in French, advanced English, good oral and written French comprehension (tested with an interview). Electronic applications accepted. *Faculty research:* Change management, international business and finance, work organization, information technology implementation and impact on organizations, strategic management.

Université de Sherbrooke, Faculty of Administration, Master of Business Administration Program, Sherbrooke, QC J1K 2R1, Canada. Offers executive business administration (EMBA); general management (MBA). *Program availability:* Part-time, evening/weekend. *Entrance requirements:* For master's, bachelor's degree, minimum GPA of 2.7 (on 4.3 scale), minimum of two years of work experience, letters of recommendation. Electronic applications accepted.

Université de Sherbrooke, Faculty of Law, Sherbrooke, QC J1K 2R1, Canada. Offers alternative dispute resolution (LL M, Diploma); business law (Diploma); common law (JD); criminal and penal law (Diploma); health law (LL M, Diploma); international law (LL M); law (LL D); legal management (Diploma); notarial law (Diploma); transnational law (Diploma). *Program availability:* Part-time, evening/weekend. *Degree requirements:* For master's, thesis; for Diploma, one foreign language. *Entrance requirements:* For master's and Diploma, LL B. Electronic applications accepted.

Université du Québec à Chicoutimi, Graduate Programs, Program in Small and Medium-Sized Organization Management, Chicoutimi, QC G7H 2B1, Canada. Offers M Sc. *Program availability:* Part-time. *Degree requirements:* For master's, thesis. *Entrance requirements:* For master's, appropriate bachelor's degree, proficiency in French.

Université du Québec à Montréal, Graduate Programs, PhD Program in Business Administration, Montréal, QC H3C 3P8, Canada. Offers PhD. *Program availability:* Part-time. *Degree requirements:* For doctorate, thesis/dissertation. *Entrance requirements:* For doctorate, appropriate master's degree or equivalent, proficiency in French.

Université du Québec à Montréal, Graduate Programs, Program in Business Administration (Professional), Montréal, QC H3C 3P8, Canada. Offers business administration (MBA); management consultant (Diploma). *Program availability:* Part-time. *Entrance requirements:* For master's and Diploma, appropriate bachelor's degree or equivalent, proficiency in French.

Université du Québec à Montréal, Graduate Programs, Program in Business Administration (Research), Montréal, QC H3C 3P8, Canada. Offers MBA. *Program availability:* Part-time. *Entrance requirements:* For master's, appropriate bachelor's degree or equivalent and proficiency in French.

Université du Québec à Rimouski, Graduate Programs, Program in Business Administration, Rimouski, QC G5L 3A1, Canada. Offers MBA.

Université du Québec à Rimouski, Graduate Programs, Program in Management of People in Working Situation, Rimouski, QC G5L 3A1, Canada. Offers M Sc, Diploma.

Université du Québec à Trois-Rivières, Graduate Programs, Program in Business Administration, Trois-Rivières, QC G9A 5H7, Canada. Offers MBA, DBA. DBA offered jointly with Université de Sherbrooke. *Degree requirements:* For doctorate, thesis/dissertation.

Université du Québec en Abitibi-Témiscamingue, Graduate Programs, Program in Business Administration, Rouyn-Noranda, QC J9X 5E4, Canada. Offers MBA.

Université du Québec en Abitibi-Témiscamingue, Graduate Programs, Program in Organization Management, Rouyn-Noranda, QC J9X 5E4, Canada. Offers M Sc. *Program availability:* Part-time. *Degree requirements:* For master's, thesis. *Entrance requirements:* For master's, appropriate bachelor's degree, proficiency in French.

Université Laval, Faculty of Administrative Sciences, Program in Organizations Management and Development, Québec, QC G1K 7P4, Canada. Offers Diploma. *Program availability:* Part-time. *Entrance requirements:* For degree, knowledge of French. Electronic applications accepted.

Université Laval, Faculty of Administrative Sciences, Programs in Administrative Studies, Québec, QC G1K 7P4, Canada. Offers administrative studies (M Sc, PhD); financial engineering (M Sc). *Accreditation:* AACSB. Terminal master's awarded for partial completion of doctoral program. *Degree requirements:* For master's, thesis (for some programs); for doctorate, comprehensive exam, thesis/dissertation. *Entrance requirements:* For master's and doctorate, knowledge of French and English. Electronic applications accepted.

Université Laval, Faculty of Administrative Sciences, Programs in Business Administration, Québec, QC G1K 7P4, Canada. Offers accounting (MBA); agri-food management (MBA); electronic business (MBA, Diploma); factory management and logistics (MBA); finance (MBA); firm management (MBA); geomatic management (MBA); information technology management (MBA); international management (MBA); management (MBA); management accounting (MBA, Diploma); marketing (MBA); modeling and organizational decision (MBA); occupational health and safety management (MBA); pharmacy management (MBA); social and environmental responsibility (MBA); technological entrepreneurship (Diploma). *Accreditation:* AACSB. *Program availability:* Part-time, evening/weekend, online learning. *Entrance requirements:* For master's and Diploma, knowledge of French and English. Electronic applications accepted.

University at Albany, State University of New York, School of Business, Albany, NY 12222-0001. Offers MBA, MS. *Accreditation:* AACSB. *Program availability:* Part-time, evening/weekend. *Faculty:* 45 full-time (17 women), 20 part-time/adjunct (7 women). *Students:* 265 full-time (105 women), 172 part-time (64 women); includes 101 minority (22 Black or African American, non-Hispanic/Latino; 1 American Indian or Alaska Native, non-Hispanic/Latino; 47 Asian, non-Hispanic/Latino; 22 Hispanic/Latino; 9 Two or more races, non-Hispanic/Latino), 45 international. 485 applicants, 63% accepted, 236 enrolled. In 2017, 221 master's awarded. Terminal master's awarded for partial completion of doctoral program. *Degree requirements:* For master's, project. *Entrance requirements:* For master's, GMAT. Additional exam requirements/recommendations for international students: Required—TOEFL (minimum score 550 paper-based). *Application deadline:* For fall admission, 3/1 for domestic students, 5/1 for international students. Applications are processed on a rolling basis. Application fee: $75. Electronic applications accepted. *Expenses:* $16,326 per year in-state tuition and fees; $26,306 per year out-of-state. *Financial support:* Fellowships, research assistantships, career-related internships or fieldwork, and Federal Work-Study available. *Unit head:* Hany Shawky, Dean, 518-956-8370, E-mail: hshawky@albany.edu. *Application contact:* Michael DeRensis, Director, Graduate Admissions, 518-442-3980, Fax: 518-442-3922,

E-mail: graduate@albany.edu.
Website: http://www.albany.edu/business

University at Buffalo, the State University of New York, Graduate School, School of Management, Buffalo, NY 14260. Offers accounting (MS); analytics (MBA); business administration (PMBA); consulting (MBA); finance (MBA, MS), including financial risk management (MS), quantitative finance (MS); healthcare (MBA); information assurance (MBA); information systems (MBA); international management (MBA); management (EMBA, PhD); management information systems (MS); marketing (MBA); supply chain and operations (MBA); supply chains and operations management (MS); Au D/MBA; DDS/MBA; JD/MBA; M Arch/MBA; MD/MBA; MPH/MBA; MSW/MBA; Pharm D/MBA. *Accreditation:* AACSB. *Program availability:* Part-time, evening/weekend. *Faculty:* 80 full-time (26 women), 45 part-time/adjunct (12 women). *Students:* 597 full-time (251 women); includes 83 minority (19 Black or African American, non-Hispanic/Latino; 59 Asian, non-Hispanic/Latino; 5 Hispanic/Latino), 306 international. Average age 25. 2,109 applicants, 46% accepted, 376 enrolled. In 2017, 371 master's, 13 doctorates awarded. *Degree requirements:* For master's, capstone courses or projects; for doctorate, comprehensive exam, thesis/dissertation. *Entrance requirements:* For master's, GMAT (for MS in accounting, finance); GRE or GMAT (for MBA, MS in management information systems, supply chains and operations management), essays, letters of recommendation; for doctorate, GMAT or GRE, essays, writing sample, letters of recommendation. Additional exam requirements/recommendations for international students: Required—TOEFL (minimum score 95 iBT) or IELTS (minimum score 6.5); Recommended—TSE (minimum score 73). *Application deadline:* For fall admission, 10/15 priority date for domestic and international students; for winter admission, 2/1 priority date for domestic and international students; for spring admission, 4/15 for domestic students; for summer admission, 5/15 for domestic students. Application fee: $100. Electronic applications accepted. *Expenses:* Varies by program. *Financial support:* Fellowships with full and partial tuition reimbursements, research assistantships with full and partial tuition reimbursements, teaching assistantships with full and partial tuition reimbursements, career-related internships or fieldwork, Federal Work-Study, institutionally sponsored loans, scholarships/grants, health care benefits, and unspecified assistantships available. Financial award application deadline: 2/15. *Faculty research:* Data analytics, accounting and law, rate finance, consumer behavior, supply chain logistics, leadership and team effectiveness. *Total annual research expenditures:* $968,376. *Unit head:* Erin K. O'Brien, Assistant Dean and Director of Graduate Programs, 716-645-3204, Fax: 716-645-2341, E-mail: ekobrien@buffalo.edu. *Application contact:* Meghan Felser, Director of Admissions and Recruiting, 716-645-3204, Fax: 716-645-2341, E-mail: mpwood@buffalo.edu.
Website: http://mgt.buffalo.edu/

The University of Akron, Graduate School, College of Business Administration, Department of Management, Program in Management, Akron, OH 44325. Offers MBA. *Students:* 16 full-time (5 women), 40 part-time (10 women); includes 5 minority (1 Black or African American, non-Hispanic/Latino; 1 Asian, non-Hispanic/Latino; 1 Hispanic/Latino; 2 Two or more races, non-Hispanic/Latino), 3 international. Average age 28. 17 applicants, 88% accepted, 12 enrolled. In 2017, 37 master's awarded. *Entrance requirements:* For master's, GMAT, GRE, MCAT, LSAT, PCAT, or CAT, minimum GPA of 3.0 (preferred), two letters of recommendation, resume, statement of purpose. Additional exam requirements/recommendations for international students: Required—TOEFL (minimum score 79 iBT), IELTS (minimum score 6.5). *Application deadline:* For fall admission, 7/15 for domestic and international students; for spring admission, 11/15 for domestic and international students; for summer admission, 4/15 for domestic and international students. Application fee: $45 ($75 for international students). Electronic applications accepted. *Unit head:* Dr. Steve Ash, Chair, 330-972-6429, E-mail: ash@uakron.edu. *Application contact:* Dr. William Hauser, Director of Graduate Business Programs, 330-972-7043, Fax: 330-972-6588, E-mail: whauser@uakron.edu.
Website: http://www.uakron.edu/cba/graduate/programs/msm/

The University of Alabama, Graduate School, Manderson Graduate School of Business, Department of Management, Tuscaloosa, AL 35487. Offers MA, MS, PhD. *Accreditation:* AACSB. *Program availability:* Part-time, evening/weekend, online learning. *Faculty:* 26 full-time (7 women). *Students:* 12 full-time (6 women), 50 part-time (16 women); includes 7 minority (4 Black or African American, non-Hispanic/Latino; 1 Asian, non-Hispanic/Latino; 1 Hispanic/Latino; 1 Two or more races, non-Hispanic/Latino), 7 international. Average age 32. 42 applicants, 45% accepted, 17 enrolled. In 2017, 19 master's, 1 doctorate awarded. Terminal master's awarded for partial completion of doctoral program. *Degree requirements:* For master's, comprehensive exam (for some programs), thesis (for some programs), formal project paper; for doctorate, comprehensive exam, thesis/dissertation. *Entrance requirements:* For master's and doctorate, GMAT or GRE, minimum GPA of 3.0. *Application deadline:* For fall admission, 6/30 priority date for domestic students, 1/31 for international students; for spring admission, 10/30 for domestic students. Applications are processed on a rolling basis. Application fee: $50 ($60 for international students). *Financial support:* In 2017–18, 23 students received support, including fellowships with full tuition reimbursements available (averaging $15,000 per year), research assistantships with full tuition reimbursements available (averaging $18,000 per year), teaching assistantships with tuition reimbursements available (averaging $18,000 per year); scholarships/grants, health care benefits, and unspecified assistantships also available. *Faculty research:* Leadership, entrepreneurship, health care management, organizational behavior, strategy. *Unit head:* Dr. William E. Jackson, III, Department Head, 205-348-6183, Fax: 205-348-6695, E-mail: wjackson@cba.ua.edu. *Application contact:* Courtney Cox, Office Associate II, 205-348-6183, Fax: 205-348-6695, E-mail: crhodes@cba.ua.edu.
Website: http://cba.ua.edu/mgt

The University of Alabama, Graduate School, Manderson Graduate School of Business, Program in General Commerce and Business, Tuscaloosa, AL 35487. Offers EMBA, MBA. *Accreditation:* AACSB. *Students:* 239 full-time (73 women), 2 part-time (0 women); includes 40 minority (17 Black or African American, non-Hispanic/Latino; 1 American Indian or Alaska Native, non-Hispanic/Latino; 5 Asian, non-Hispanic/Latino; 7 Hispanic/Latino; 10 Two or more races, non-Hispanic/Latino), 2 international. Average age 28. 289 applicants, 75% accepted, 73 enrolled. In 2017, 145 master's awarded. *Entrance requirements:* For master's, GMAT or GRE. Additional exam requirements/recommendations for international students: Required—TOEFL (minimum score 550 paper-based). *Application deadline:* For winter admission, 1/5 priority date for domestic and international students; for spring admission, 4/15 for domestic and international students. Applications are processed on a rolling basis. Application fee: $50 ($60 for international students). Electronic applications accepted. *Financial support:* In 2017–18, research assistantships with partial tuition reimbursements (averaging $6,800 per year) were awarded; teaching assistantships, scholarships/grants, health care benefits, and unspecified assistantships also available. Financial award application deadline: 4/15. *Unit head:* Dr. J. Brian Gray, Associate Dean, Manderson Graduate School of Business, 205-348-8912, Fax: 205-348-4504, E-mail: bgray@cba.ua.edu. *Application contact:* Patricia Wilson, Director of MBA Recruiting and Admissions, 205-348-9122, Fax: 205-348-4504, E-mail: pewilson@cba.ua.edu.

The University of Alabama at Birmingham, Collat School of Business, Birmingham, AL 35294. Offers M Acct, MBA, MS, MD/MBA. MD/MBA program offered in partnership with the School of Medicine. *Accreditation:* AACSB. *Program availability:* Part-time, evening/weekend, blended/hybrid learning. *Faculty:* 44 full-time (8 women), 11 part-time/adjunct (4 women). *Students:* 136 full-time (50 women), 508 part-time (227 women); includes 174 minority (110 Black or African American, non-Hispanic/Latino; 2 American Indian or Alaska Native, non-Hispanic/Latino; 32 Asian, non-Hispanic/Latino; 17 Hispanic/Latino; 13 Two or more races, non-Hispanic/Latino), 55 international. Average age 34. In 2017, 232 master's awarded. *Entrance requirements:* For master's, GMAT. Additional exam requirements/recommendations for international students: Required—TOEFL (minimum score 80 iBT), IELTS (minimum score 6.5). *Application deadline:* For fall admission, 8/1 for domestic and international students; for spring admission, 12/1 for domestic and international students; for summer admission, 5/1 for domestic and international students. Applications are processed on a rolling basis. Application fee: $60 ($75 for international students). Electronic applications accepted. *Financial support:* In 2017–18, 2 research assistantships (averaging $5,000 per year), 4 teaching assistantships (averaging $5,000 per year) were awarded; career-related internships or fieldwork and unspecified assistantships also available. Financial award applicants required to submit FAFSA. *Faculty research:* Open innovation, capital markets, business to business sales and marketing, healthcare management, workplace issues, global supply chain. *Total annual research expenditures:* $240,000. *Unit head:* Dr. Eric Jack, Dean, 205-934-8800, Fax: 205-934-8886, E-mail: ejack@uab.edu. *Application contact:* Susan Noblitt Banks, Director of Graduate School Operations, 205-934-8227, Fax: 205-934-8413, E-mail: gradschool@uab.edu.
Website: http://www.uab.edu/business/

The University of Alabama in Huntsville, School of Graduate Studies, College of Business Administration, Programs in Business and Management, Huntsville, AL 35899. Offers business analytics (MSMS); federal contracting and procurement management (Certificate); human resource management (MSM); management (MBA), including acquisition management, entrepreneurship, federal contract accounting, finance, human resource management, logistics and supply chain management, marketing, project management; supply chain management (Certificate); technology and innovation management (Certificate). *Accreditation:* AACSB. *Program availability:* Part-time, evening/weekend. *Degree requirements:* For master's, comprehensive exam, thesis or alternative. *Entrance requirements:* For master's, GMAT (minimum score 500), minimum AACSB index of 1080. Additional exam requirements/recommendations for international students: Required—TOEFL (minimum score 550 paper-based; 80 iBT), IELTS (minimum score 6.5). Electronic applications accepted. *Faculty research:* Supply chain management, management of research and development, international marketing and branding, organizational behavior and human resource management, social networks and computational economics.

University of Alaska Anchorage, College of Business and Public Policy, Program in Business Administration, Anchorage, AK 99508. Offers MBA. *Accreditation:* AACSB. *Program availability:* Part-time. *Degree requirements:* For master's, comprehensive exam, thesis (for some programs), capstone projects. *Entrance requirements:* Additional exam requirements/recommendations for international students: Required—TOEFL (minimum score 550 paper-based). *Faculty research:* Complex global environments.

University of Alaska Fairbanks, School of Management, Department of Business Administration, Fairbanks, AK 99775-6080. Offers capital markets (MBA); general management (MBA). *Accreditation:* AACSB. *Program availability:* Part-time, online only, 100% online. *Degree requirements:* For master's, comprehensive exam, thesis or alternative. *Entrance requirements:* For master's, GRE General Test, GMAT, bachelor's degree from accredited institution with minimum cumulative undergraduate and major GPA of 3.0. Additional exam requirements/recommendations for international students: Required—TOEFL (minimum score 550 paper-based; 79 iBT), IELTS (minimum score 6.5). Electronic applications accepted. *Expenses:* Contact institution. *Faculty research:* Consumer behavior, marketing, international finance and business, strategic risk, organization theory.

University of Alberta, Faculty of Graduate Studies and Research, Doctoral Program in Business, Edmonton, AB T6G 2E1, Canada. Offers accounting (PhD); finance (PhD); human resources/industrial relations (PhD); management science (PhD); marketing (PhD); organizational analysis (PhD); MBA/PhD. *Accreditation:* AACSB. *Program availability:* Part-time. *Degree requirements:* For doctorate, comprehensive exam, thesis/dissertation. *Entrance requirements:* For doctorate, GMAT. Additional exam requirements/recommendations for international students: Required—TOEFL (minimum score 550 paper-based). Electronic applications accepted. *Faculty research:* Accounting, capital markets and corporate finance, organizational change and human resource management, marketing, strategic management.

University of Alberta, Faculty of Graduate Studies and Research, Executive MBA Program, Edmonton, AB T6G 2E1, Canada. Offers Exec MBA. Program offered jointly with University of Calgary. *Accreditation:* AACSB. *Entrance requirements:* For master's, GMAT. Additional exam requirements/recommendations for international students: Required—TOEFL. Electronic applications accepted. *Expenses:* Contact institution.

University of Alberta, Faculty of Graduate Studies and Research, Program in Business Administration, Edmonton, AB T6G 2E1, Canada. Offers international business (MBA); leisure and sport management (MBA); natural resources and energy (MBA); technology commercialization (MBA); MBA/LL B; MBA/M Ag; MBA/M Eng; MBA/MF; MBA/PhD. *Accreditation:* AACSB. *Program availability:* Part-time, evening/weekend. *Degree requirements:* For master's, thesis or alternative. *Entrance requirements:* For master's, GMAT. Additional exam requirements/recommendations for international students: Required—TOEFL (minimum score 600 paper-based). Electronic applications accepted. *Faculty research:* Natural resources and energy/management and policy/family enterprise/international business/healthcare research management.

University of Antelope Valley, Program in Business Management, Lancaster, CA 93534. Offers MS. *Degree requirements:* For master's, capstone. *Entrance requirements:* For master's, official transcripts documenting earned bachelor's degree from nationally- or regionally-accredited institution with minimum cumulative GPA of 2.0.

The University of Arizona, Eller College of Management, Tucson, AZ 85721. Offers M Ac, MA, MBA, MS, PhD, Graduate Certificate, JD/MBA. *Accreditation:* AACSB. *Program availability:* Evening/weekend. *Degree requirements:* For doctorate, thesis/dissertation. *Entrance requirements:* Additional exam requirements/recommendations for international students: Required—TOEFL (minimum score 550 paper-based; 79 iBT). Electronic applications accepted. *Expenses:* Contact institution.

University of Arkansas, Graduate School, Sam M. Walton College of Business Administration, Program in Business Administration, Fayetteville, AR 72701. Offers MBA, PhD. *Accreditation:* AACSB. *Program availability:* Part-time, evening/weekend, online learning. In 2017, 105 master's, 5 doctorates awarded. *Degree requirements:* For doctorate, thesis/dissertation. *Entrance requirements:* For master's and doctorate, GMAT. *Application deadline:* For fall admission, 8/1 for domestic students, 4/1 for international students; for spring admission, 12/1 for domestic students, 10/1 for international students; for summer admission, 4/15 for domestic students, 3/1 for international students. Application fee: $60. Electronic applications accepted. *Expenses:*

Tuition, state resident: full-time $3782. Tuition, nonresident: full-time $10,238. *Financial support:* In 2017–18, 23 research assistantships were awarded; fellowships with tuition reimbursements, teaching assistantships, career-related internships or fieldwork, and Federal Work-Study also available. Support available to part-time students. Financial award application deadline: 4/1; financial award applicants required to submit FAFSA. *Unit head:* Dr. Raja Kali, Department Chair, 479-575-6219, E-mail: kali@walton.uark.edu. *Application contact:* Marion Dunagan, Assistant Director of Marketing and Recruiting, 479-575-2996, E-mail: gsb@walton.uark.edu.
Website: https://gsb.uark.edu/executive-mba/

University of Arkansas at Little Rock, Graduate School, College of Business, Little Rock, AR 72204-1099. Offers business administration (MBA); business information systems (MS, Graduate Certificate); management (Graduate Certificate). *Accreditation:* AACSB. *Program availability:* Part-time, evening/weekend. *Entrance requirements:* For master's, GMAT, minimum undergraduate GPA of 2.7. Additional exam requirements/recommendations for international students: Required—TOEFL (minimum score 525 paper-based).

University of Baltimore, Graduate School, Merrick School of Business, Baltimore, MD 21201-5779. Offers MBA, MS, Graduate Certificate, JD/MBA, MBA/MSN, MBA/Pharm D. *Accreditation:* AACSB. *Program availability:* Part-time, evening/weekend, online learning. *Entrance requirements:* For master's, GMAT. Additional exam requirements/recommendations for international students: Required—TOEFL (minimum score 550 paper-based). Electronic applications accepted. *Faculty research:* Finance, economics, accounting, health care, management information systems.

University of Baltimore, Joint University of Baltimore/Towson University (UB/Towson) MBA Program, Baltimore, MD 21201-5779. Offers MBA, JD/MBA, MBA/MSN, MBA/Pharm D. MBA/MSN, MBA/Pharm D offered jointly with University of Maryland, Baltimore. *Accreditation:* AACSB. *Program availability:* Part-time, evening/weekend, online learning. *Entrance requirements:* For master's, GMAT. Additional exam requirements/recommendations for international students: Required—TOEFL (minimum score 550 paper-based).

University of Bridgeport, School of Business, Bridgeport, CT 06604. Offers accounting (MBA); finance (MBA); general business (MBA); global financial services (MBA); human resource management (MBA); information systems and knowledge management (MBA); international business (MBA); management (MBA); marketing (MBA); operations management (MBA); small business and entrepreneurship (MBA); specialized business (MBA). *Accreditation:* ACBSP. *Program availability:* Part-time, evening/weekend. *Degree requirements:* For master's, thesis optional. *Entrance requirements:* For master's, GMAT. Additional exam requirements/recommendations for international students: Recommended—TOEFL (minimum score 550 paper-based; 80 iBT), IELTS (minimum score 6.5). Electronic applications accepted. *Expenses:* Contact institution.

The University of British Columbia, Sauder School of Business, Doctoral Program in Business Administration, Vancouver, BC V6T 1Z2, Canada. Offers accounting (PhD); finance (PhD); management information systems (PhD); management science (PhD); marketing (PhD); organizational behavior (PhD); strategy and business economics (PhD); transportation and logistics (PhD); urban land economics (PhD). *Degree requirements:* For doctorate, comprehensive exam, thesis/dissertation. *Entrance requirements:* For doctorate, GMAT or GRE. Additional exam requirements/recommendations for international students: Required—TOEFL (minimum score 600 paper-based; 100 iBT). Electronic applications accepted. *Expenses:* Contact institution.

The University of British Columbia, Sauder School of Business, MBA Program, Vancouver, BC V6T 1Z2, Canada. Offers IMBA, MBA. *Expenses:* Contact institution.

University of Calgary, Faculty of Graduate Studies, Haskayne School of Business, Alberta/Haskayne Executive MBA Program, Calgary, AB T2N 1N4, Canada. Offers EMBA. Program offered with School of Business at University of Alberta. *Accreditation:* AACSB. *Program availability:* Part-time. *Entrance requirements:* For master's, GMAT, minimum GPA of 3.0, minimum 7 years of work experience, 3 letters of reference. Additional exam requirements/recommendations for international students: Required—TOEFL (minimum score 600 paper-based; 100 iBT). *Expenses:* Contact institution. *Faculty research:* Accounting, data analysis and modeling, strategy, entrepreneurship, negotiations.

University of Calgary, Faculty of Graduate Studies, Haskayne School of Business, Program in Business Administration, Calgary, AB T2N 1N4, Canada. Offers MBA, MBA/LL B, MBA/MBT, MBA/MD, MBA/MSW. *Accreditation:* AACSB. *Program availability:* Part-time, evening/weekend. *Degree requirements:* For master's, comprehensive exam, thesis optional. *Entrance requirements:* For master's, GMAT (minimum score 550), minimum GPA of 3.0, resume, 3 years of work experience, 3 letters of reference, 4 year bachelor degree. Additional exam requirements/recommendations for international students: Required—TOEFL (minimum score 600 paper-based). Electronic applications accepted. *Expenses:* Contact institution. *Faculty research:* Entrepreneurship, ethics, strategy, finance energy management and sustainability.

University of Calgary, Faculty of Graduate Studies, Haskayne School of Business, Program in Management, Calgary, AB T2N 1N4, Canada. Offers MBA, PhD. *Accreditation:* AACSB. Terminal master's awarded for partial completion of doctoral program. *Degree requirements:* For master's, one foreign language, comprehensive exam, thesis; for doctorate, one foreign language, comprehensive exam, thesis/dissertation, written and oral exams. *Entrance requirements:* For master's, GMAT, GRE, minimum GPA of 3.3 in last 2 years of course work, 2 letters of reference; for doctorate, GMAT, GRE, minimum GPA of 3.5 in last 2 years of course work, 2 letters of reference. Additional exam requirements/recommendations for international students: Required—TOEFL (minimum score 600 paper-based; 100 iBT), IELTS (minimum score 7). Electronic applications accepted. *Faculty research:* Operations management, international business, management information systems, accounting, finance, sustainable development.

University of California, Berkeley, Graduate Division, Haas School of Business, The Berkeley MBA for Executives Program, Berkeley, CA 94720. Offers MBA. *Accreditation:* AACSB. *Program availability:* Part-time. *Students:* 139 part-time (45 women); includes 60 minority (4 Black or African American, non-Hispanic/Latino; 46 Asian, non-Hispanic/Latino; 4 Hispanic/Latino; 2 Native Hawaiian or other Pacific Islander, non-Hispanic/Latino; 4 Two or more races, non-Hispanic/Latino). Average age 36. In 2017, 69 master's awarded. *Entrance requirements:* For master's, GMAT or GRE, BA or BS. Additional exam requirements/recommendations for international students: Required—TOEFL (minimum score 570 paper-based, 90 iBT) or IELTS (minimum score 7). *Application deadline:* For fall admission, 12/6 for domestic students; for winter admission, 2/5 for domestic students; for spring admission, 2/8 for domestic students. Applications are processed on a rolling basis. Application fee: $200. Electronic applications accepted. *Expenses:* Contact institution. *Financial support:* Fellowships with partial tuition reimbursements, teaching assistantships with partial tuition reimbursements, institutionally sponsored loans, scholarships/grants, and tuition waivers available. Support available to part-time students. *Unit head:* Jamie Breen, Assistant Dean, Berkeley MBA for Executives, 415-990-9115, E-mail: jamiebreen@berkeley.edu. *Application contact:* Marjorie DeGraca, Assistant Dean of Admissions, MBA for Working Professionals, E-mail: mbaforexecs@haas.berkeley.edu.
Website: http://mbaforexecs.haas.berkeley.edu/

Business Administration and Management—General

University of California, Berkeley, Graduate Division, Haas School of Business and School of Law, Concurrent JD/MBA Program, Berkeley, CA 94720-1500. Offers JD/MBA. *Accreditation:* AACSB; ABA. *Students:* 2 full-time (1 woman). Average age 29. *Entrance requirements:* Additional exam requirements/recommendations for international students: Required—TOEFL (minimum score 570 paper-based; 90 iBT). *Application deadline:* For fall admission, 10/1 for domestic and international students; for winter admission, 1/7 for domestic and international students; for spring admission, 3/31 for domestic and international students. Application fee: $200. Electronic applications accepted. *Expenses:* Contact institution. *Financial support:* Fellowships, research assistantships with partial tuition reimbursements, teaching assistantships with partial tuition reimbursements, career-related internships or fieldwork, institutionally sponsored loans, scholarships/grants, and non-resident tuition waivers for some students, such as veterans available. Financial award applicants required to submit FAFSA. *Faculty research:* Accounting, business and public policy, economic analysis and public policy, entrepreneurship, finance, management of organizations, marketing, operations and information technology management, real estate. *Application contact:* Morgan Bernstein, Executive Director, Full-time MBA Admissions, 510-642-1405, Fax: 510-643-6659, E-mail: mbernstein@haas.berkeley.edu.
Website: http://mba.haas.berkeley.edu/academics/concurrentdegrees.html

University of California, Berkeley, Graduate Division, Haas School of Business and School of Public Health, Concurrent MBA/MPH Program, Berkeley, CA 94720-1500. Offers MBA/MPH. *Accreditation:* AACSB. *Students:* 45 full-time (23 women); includes 14 minority (1 Black or African American, non-Hispanic/Latino; 9 Asian, non-Hispanic/Latino; 2 Hispanic/Latino; 2 Two or more races, non-Hispanic/Latino). Average age 29. *Entrance requirements:* Additional exam requirements/recommendations for international students: Required—TOEFL (minimum score 570 paper-based; 90 iBT); Recommended—IELTS (minimum score 7). *Application deadline:* For fall admission, 10/1 for domestic and international students; for winter admission, 1/7 for domestic and international students; for spring admission, 3/31 for domestic students, 3/11 for international students. Application fee: $200. Electronic applications accepted. *Expenses:* Contact institution. *Financial support:* Fellowships, research assistantships with partial tuition reimbursements, teaching assistantships with partial tuition reimbursements, career-related internships or fieldwork, institutionally sponsored loans, scholarships/grants, and non-resident tuition waivers for some students, such as veterans available. *Faculty research:* Accounting, business and public policy, economic analysis and public policy, entrepreneurship, finance, management of organizations, marketing, operations and information technology management, real estate. *Unit head:* Prof. Kim MacPherson, Associate Director, Health Services Management Program, 510-642-9175, Fax: 510-643-6659, E-mail: kmacpherson@haas.berkeley.edu. *Application contact:* Morgan Bernstein, Executive Director of Admissions, 510-642-1405, Fax: 510-643-6659, E-mail: mbaadm@haas.berkeley.edu.
Website: http://www.haas.berkeley.edu/

University of California, Berkeley, Graduate Division, Haas School of Business, Evening and Weekend MBA Program, Berkeley, CA 94720-1500. Offers MBA. *Accreditation:* AACSB. *Program availability:* Part-time, evening/weekend. *Students:* 794 part-time (230 women); includes 419 minority (13 Black or African American, non-Hispanic/Latino; 350 Asian, non-Hispanic/Latino; 32 Hispanic/Latino; 1 Native Hawaiian or other Pacific Islander, non-Hispanic/Latino; 23 Two or more races, non-Hispanic/Latino; 1 international. Average age 33. *Degree requirements:* For master's, comprehensive exam, orientation, academic retreat, experiential learning course, 42 units of coursework. *Entrance requirements:* For master's, GMAT or GRE, BA or BS. Additional exam requirements/recommendations for international students: Required—TOEFL (minimum score 570 paper-based; 90 iBT); Recommended—IELTS (minimum score 7). *Application deadline:* For fall admission, 11/15 for domestic students; for winter admission, 1/16 for domestic students; for spring admission, 3/7 for domestic students; for summer admission, 4/18 for domestic students. Application fee: $200. Electronic applications accepted. *Expenses:* Contact institution. *Financial support:* Fellowships, research assistantships with partial tuition reimbursements, teaching assistantships with partial tuition reimbursements, career-related internships or fieldwork, institutionally sponsored loans, scholarships/grants, and non-resident tuition waivers for some students, such as veterans available. Support available to part-time students. Financial award applicants required to submit CSS PROFILE. *Faculty research:* Accounting, business and public policy, economic analysis and public policy, finance, management of organizations, marketing, operations and information technology management, real estate. *Unit head:* Jamie Breen, Assistant Dean, 510-643-0434, Fax: 510-643-5902, E-mail: ewmbaadm@haas.berkeley.edu. *Application contact:* Marjorie DeGraca, Evening and Weekend MBA Admissions Office, 510-642-0292, Fax: 510-643-5902, E-mail: ewmbaadm@haas.berkeley.edu.
Website: http://ewmba.haas.berkeley.edu/

University of California, Berkeley, Graduate Division, Haas School of Business, Full-Time MBA Program, Berkeley, CA 94720-1902. Offers MBA. *Accreditation:* AACSB. *Students:* 496 full-time (195 women); includes 97 minority (28 Black or African American, non-Hispanic/Latino; 1 American Indian or Alaska Native, non-Hispanic/Latino; 45 Asian, non-Hispanic/Latino; 14 Hispanic/Latino; 9 Two or more races, non-Hispanic/Latino), 180 international. Average age 29. 4,132 applicants, 282 enrolled. In 2017, 240 master's awarded. *Degree requirements:* For master's, 51 units, one experiential learning course. *Entrance requirements:* For master's, GMAT or GRE, four-year degree (BA/BS). Additional exam requirements/recommendations for international students: Required—TOEFL (minimum score 570 paper-based; 90 iBT) or IELTS (minimum score 7). *Application deadline:* For fall admission, 9/21 for domestic and international students; for winter admission, 1/4 for domestic and international students; for spring admission, 4/5 for domestic and international students. Application fee: $200. Electronic applications accepted. *Expenses:* Contact institution. *Financial support:* In 2017–18, 249 students received support, including 237 fellowships (averaging $27,259 per year), 110 teaching assistantships with partial tuition reimbursements available (averaging $11,699 per year); research assistantships with partial tuition reimbursements available, career-related internships or fieldwork, institutionally sponsored loans, scholarships/grants, and non-resident tuition waivers for some students, such as veterans also available. Financial award application deadline: 5/18. *Unit head:* Peter Johnson, Assistant Dean, Full-time MBA Program and Admissions, 510-642-1405, Fax: 510-643-6659, E-mail: pjohnson@haas.berkeley.edu. *Application contact:* Morgan Bernstein, Executive Director, Full-time MBA Admissions, 510-642-1405, Fax: 510-643-6659, E-mail: mbaadm@haas.berkeley.edu.
Website: http://mba.haas.berkeley.edu/

University of California, Berkeley, Graduate Division, Haas School of Business, PhD in Business Administration Program, Berkeley, CA 94720-1500. Offers accounting (PhD); business and public policy (PhD); finance (PhD); management of organizations (PhD); marketing (PhD); real estate (PhD). *Accreditation:* AACSB. *Students:* 72 full-time (20 women); includes 30 minority (26 Asian, non-Hispanic/Latino; 4 Hispanic/Latino). Average age 27. *Degree requirements:* For doctorate, comprehensive exam, thesis/dissertation, written preliminary exams, oral qualifying exam. *Entrance requirements:* For doctorate, GMAT or GRE, minimum GPA of 3.0 in undergraduate and graduate coursework. Additional exam requirements/recommendations for international students: Required—TOEFL (minimum score 570 paper-based; 70 iBT), IELTS (minimum score

7). *Application deadline:* For fall admission, 12/1 for domestic and international students. Application fee: $105 ($125 for international students). Electronic applications accepted. *Expenses:* Contact institution. *Financial support:* Fellowships with tuition reimbursements, research assistantships with tuition reimbursements, teaching assistantships with tuition reimbursements, scholarships/grants, health care benefits, tuition waivers (full), unspecified assistantships, and transit passes, travel grants available. Financial award application deadline: 12/1. *Faculty research:* Accounting, business and public policy, entrepreneurship, finance, management of organizations, marketing, operations and information technology management, real estate. *Unit head:* Dr. Nicolae Garleanu, Director, 510-643-6349, Fax: 510-643-4255. *Application contact:* Melissa Hacker, Director, Student Affairs, 510-642-3944, Fax: 510-643-4255, E-mail: melhacker@haas.berkeley.edu.
Website: http://www.haas.berkeley.edu/Phd/

University of California, Berkeley, UC Berkeley Extension, Certificate Programs in Business, Berkeley, CA 94720-1500. Offers accounting (Certificate); business administration (Certificate); finance (Certificate); human resource management (Certificate); management (Certificate); marketing (Certificate); project management (Certificate). *Accreditation:* AACSB. *Program availability:* Online learning.

University of California, Berkeley, UC Berkeley Extension, International Diploma Programs, Berkeley, CA 94720-1500. Offers business administration (Certificate); finance (Certificate); global business management (Certificate); marketing (Certificate); project management (Certificate). *Accreditation:* AACSB.

University of California, Davis, Graduate School of Management, Full-Time MBA Program, Davis, CA 95616. Offers business analytics and technologies (MBA); entrepreneurship and innovation (MBA); finance and accounting (MBA); general management (MBA); marketing (MBA); organizational behavior (MBA); public health management (MBA); strategy (MBA); technology management (MBA); DVM/MBA; JD/MBA; M Engr/MBA; MBA/MPH; MBA/MS; MD/MBA; MSN/MBA; PhD/MBA. *Faculty:* 52 full-time (15 women). *Students:* 96 full-time (42 women); includes 31 minority (1 Black or African American, non-Hispanic/Latino; 17 Asian, non-Hispanic/Latino; 5 Hispanic/Latino; 8 Two or more races, non-Hispanic/Latino), 36 international. Average age 29. 290 applicants, 37% accepted, 45 enrolled. In 2017, 44 master's awarded. *Degree requirements:* For master's, integrated management project. *Entrance requirements:* For master's, GMAT or GRE, letters of recommendation, resume, essays, equivalent of a 4-year U.S. undergraduate degree, transcript. Additional exam requirements/recommendations for international students: Required—TOEFL (minimum score 600 paper-based; 100 iBT), IELTS (minimum score 7). *Application deadline:* For fall admission, 5/18 priority date for domestic and international students. Application fee: $125. Electronic applications accepted. *Expenses:* Contact institution. *Financial support:* In 2017–18, 90 students received support. Fellowships, research assistantships, teaching assistantships with partial tuition reimbursements available, institutionally sponsored loans, scholarships/grants, health care benefits, tuition waivers (partial), and unspecified assistantships available. Financial award application deadline: 3/1; financial award applicants required to submit FAFSA. *Faculty research:* Finance, marketing, management, business analytics, accounting. *Unit head:* James Stevens, Senior Assistant Dean of Student Affairs, 530-752-7658, Fax: 530-754-9355, E-mail: admissions@gsm.ucdavis.edu. *Application contact:* Kristy Bird MaKieve, Interim Director of Admissions, 530-754-5476, Fax: 530-754-9355, E-mail: admissions@gsm.ucdavis.edu.
Website: http://gsm.ucdavis.edu/daytime-mba-program

University of California, Davis, Graduate School of Management, MBA Programs in Sacramento and San Francisco Bay Area, Davis, CA 95616. Offers business analytics and technologies (MBA); entrepreneurship and innovation (MBA); finance and accounting (MBA); general management (MBA); marketing (MBA); organizational behavior (MBA); public health management (MBA); strategy (MBA); technology management (MBA). *Program availability:* Part-time-only, evening/weekend. *Faculty:* 99 part-time/adjunct (30 women). *Students:* 323 part-time (133 women); includes 148 minority (7 Black or African American, non-Hispanic/Latino; 96 Asian, non-Hispanic/Latino; 26 Hispanic/Latino; 1 Native Hawaiian or other Pacific Islander, non-Hispanic/Latino; 18 Two or more races, non-Hispanic/Latino), 37 international. Average age 30. 202 applicants, 75% accepted, 111 enrolled. In 2017, 112 master's awarded. *Degree requirements:* For master's, integrated management project. *Entrance requirements:* For master's, GMAT or GRE, letters of recommendation, resume, equivalent of a 4-year undergraduate degree. Additional exam requirements/recommendations for international students: Required—TOEFL (minimum score 600 paper-based; 100 iBT), IELTS (minimum score 7). *Application deadline:* For fall admission, 5/18 priority date for domestic and international students. Application fee: $125. Electronic applications accepted. *Expenses:* Contact institution. *Financial support:* In 2017–18, 67 students received support. Fellowships, teaching assistantships with partial tuition reimbursements available, scholarships/grants, and unspecified assistantships available. Support available to part-time students. Financial award application deadline: 3/1; financial award applicants required to submit FAFSA. *Faculty research:* Accounting, finance, marketing, management, business analytics. *Unit head:* James Stevens, Senior Assistant Dean of Student Affairs, 530-752-7658, Fax: 530-754-9355, E-mail: admissions@gsm.ucdavis.edu. *Application contact:* Kristy Bird MaKieve, Interim Director of Admissions, 530-754-5476, Fax: 530-754-9355, E-mail: admissions@gsm.ucdavis.edu.
Website: http://gsm.ucdavis.edu/mba-programs

University of California, Irvine, The Paul Merage School of Business, Doctoral Program in Management, Irvine, CA 92697. Offers PhD. *Students:* 57 full-time (29 women); includes 10 minority (1 American Indian or Alaska Native, non-Hispanic/Latino; 7 Asian, non-Hispanic/Latino; 1 Hispanic/Latino; 1 Native Hawaiian or other Pacific Islander, non-Hispanic/Latino), 37 international. Average age 31. 264 applicants, 6% accepted, 15 enrolled. In 2017, 9 doctorates awarded. Application fee: $105 ($125 for international students). *Unit head:* Dr. Terry Shevlin, Director, 949-824-6149, E-mail: tshevlin@uci.edu. *Application contact:* Noel Negrete, Associate Director, 949-824-8318, Fax: 949-824-1592, E-mail: nnegrete@uci.edu.
Website: http://merage.uci.edu/PhD/Default.aspx

University of California, Irvine, The Paul Merage School of Business, Executive MBA Program, Irvine, CA 92697. Offers EMBA. *Students:* 71 full-time (26 women), 1 part-time (0 women); includes 46 minority (3 Black or African American, non-Hispanic/Latino; 4 American Indian or Alaska Native, non-Hispanic/Latino; 38 Asian, non-Hispanic/Latino; 1 Hispanic/Latino), 2 international. Average age 41. 62 applicants, 82% accepted, 33 enrolled. In 2017, 31 master's awarded. Application fee: $105 ($125 for international students). *Unit head:* Anthony Hansford, Senior Assistant Dean, 949-824-3801, E-mail: hansfora@uci.edu. *Application contact:* Jon Masciana, Senior Director, 949-824-8595, E-mail: jmascian@uci.edu.
Website: http://merage.uci.edu/ExecutiveMBA/

University of California, Irvine, The Paul Merage School of Business, Full-Time MBA Program, Irvine, CA 92697. Offers MBA. *Students:* 160 full-time (44 women), 7 part-time (4 women); includes 57 minority (2 Black or African American, non-Hispanic/Latino; 1 American Indian or Alaska Native, non-Hispanic/Latino; 52 Asian, non-Hispanic/Latino; 2 Hispanic/Latino), 80 international. Average age 30. 803 applicants, 23% accepted, 91

enrolled. In 2017, 93 master's awarded. Application fee: $105 ($125 for international students). *Unit head:* Jon Kaplan, Assistant Dean, 949-824-9654, E-mail: jbkaplan@uci.edu. *Application contact:* Courtney Watts, Director of Recruitment and Admissions, 949-824-0462, Fax: 949-824-2235, E-mail: courtney.elmes@uci.edu.
Website: http://merage.uci.edu/FullTimeMBA/default.aspx

University of California, Irvine, The Paul Merage School of Business, Fully Employed MBA Program, Irvine, CA 92697. *Program availability:* Part-time. *Students:* 124 full-time (47 women), 206 part-time (73 women); includes 168 minority (6 Black or African American, non-Hispanic/Latino; 15 American Indian or Alaska Native, non-Hispanic/Latino; 140 Asian, non-Hispanic/Latino; 7 Hispanic/Latino), 10 international. Average age 30. 198 applicants, 80% accepted, 100 enrolled. In 2017, 128 master's awarded. *Application deadline:* For fall admission, 7/11 for domestic students. Application fee: $105 ($125 for international students). *Unit head:* Anthony Hansford, Senior Assistant Dean, 949-824-3801, Fax: 949-824-2944, E-mail: hansfora@uci.edu. *Application contact:* Melanie Coburn, Senior Associate Director, Admissions, 949-824-7505, E-mail: mcoburn@uci.edu.
Website: http://merage.uci.edu/FullyEmployedMBA/default.aspx

University of California, Los Angeles, Graduate Division, UCLA Anderson School of Management, Los Angeles, CA 90095-1481. Offers accounting (PhD); behavioral decision making (PhD); business administration (EMBA, MBA); business analytics (MSBA); decisions, operations, and technology management (PhD); finance (PhD); financial engineering (MFE); global economics and management (PhD); management and organizations (PhD); marketing (PhD); strategy and policy (PhD); DDS/MBA; MBA/JD; MBA/MD; MBA/MLAS; MBA/MLIS; MBA/MN; MBA/MPH; MBA/MPP; MBA/MSCS; MBA/MURP. *Accreditation:* AACSB. *Program availability:* Part-time, evening/weekend. *Faculty:* 88 full-time (20 women), 107 part-time/adjunct (21 women). *Students:* 918 full-time (314 women), 1,269 part-time (399 women); includes 743 minority (38 Black or African American, non-Hispanic/Latino; 3 American Indian or Alaska Native, non-Hispanic/Latino; 531 Asian, non-Hispanic/Latino; 115 Hispanic/Latino; 4 Native Hawaiian or other Pacific Islander, non-Hispanic/Latino; 52 Two or more races, non-Hispanic/Latino), 544 international. Average age 31. 5,842 applicants, 29% accepted, 1015 enrolled. In 2017, 855 master's, 14 doctorates awarded. Terminal master's awarded for partial completion of doctoral program. *Degree requirements:* For master's, comprehensive exam, field consulting project (for MBA, FEMBA, EMBA and GEMBA); internship (for MBA only); thesis/dissertation (for MFE); 10 capstone (for MSBA); for doctorate, comprehensive exam, thesis/dissertation, oral and written qualifying exams. *Entrance requirements:* For master's, GMAT or GRE, 4-year bachelor's degree or equivalent; 2 letters of recommendation; interview (by invitation only); 2 essays; 4-8 years of full-time work experience (for FEMBA only); minimum eight years of work experience with at least three years at management level (for EMBA only); for doctorate, GMAT or GRE, bachelor's degree from college or university of fully-recognized standing, minimum B average during junior and senior undergraduate years, 3 letters of recommendation, statement of purpose. Additional exam requirements/recommendations for international students: Required—TOEFL (minimum score 560 paper-based; 87 iBT), IELTS (minimum score 7), TOEFL with minimum iBT score of 100 (for MSBA). *Application deadline:* For fall admission, 10/2 for domestic and international students; for winter admission, 1/8 for domestic and international students; for spring admission, 4/16 for domestic and international students. Applications are processed on a rolling basis. Application fee: $200. Electronic applications accepted. *Expenses:* Contact institution. *Financial support:* In 2017–18, 649 students received support, including 440 fellowships (averaging $29,273 per year); research assistantships with partial tuition reimbursements available, teaching assistantships with partial tuition reimbursements available, career-related internships or fieldwork, institutionally sponsored loans, and scholarships/grants also available. Support available to part-time students. *Faculty research:* Finance/global economics, entrepreneurship, accounting, human resources/organizational behavior, marketing and behavioral decision-making. *Total annual research expenditures:* $1.3 million. *Unit head:* Dean, 310-825-7982, Fax: 310-206-2073. *Application contact:* Alex Lawrence, Assistant Dean and Director of MBA Admissions, 310-825-6944, Fax: 310-825-8582, E-mail: mba.admissions@anderson.ucla.edu.
Website: http://www.anderson.ucla.edu/

University of California, Riverside, Graduate Division, The A. Gary Anderson Graduate School of Management, Riverside, CA 92521-0102. Offers accounting (MPAC); business administration (MBA, PhD); finance (M Fin). *Accreditation:* AACSB. *Program availability:* Part-time, evening/weekend. *Faculty:* 32 full-time (8 women), 38 part-time/adjunct (7 women). *Students:* 180 full-time (92 women), 114 part-time (48 women); includes 75 minority (13 Black or African American, non-Hispanic/Latino; 1 American Indian or Alaska Native, non-Hispanic/Latino; 33 Asian, non-Hispanic/Latino; 28 Hispanic/Latino), 187 international. Average age 27. 722 applicants, 63% accepted, 169 enrolled. In 2017, 133 master's, 1 doctorate awarded. Terminal master's awarded for partial completion of doctoral program. *Degree requirements:* For master's, thesis optional; for doctorate, comprehensive exam, thesis/dissertation. *Entrance requirements:* For master's and doctorate, GMAT or GRE. Additional exam requirements/recommendations for international students: Required—TOEFL (minimum score 550 paper-based; 80 iBT), IELTS (minimum score 7). *Application deadline:* For fall admission, 9/1 for domestic students, 5/1 for international students; for winter admission, 12/1 for domestic students, 9/1 for international students; for spring admission, 3/1 for domestic students, 10/1 for international students. Applications are processed on a rolling basis. Application fee: $100 ($125 for international students). Electronic applications accepted. *Expenses:* Contact institution. *Financial support:* Fellowships with partial tuition reimbursements, research assistantships with full tuition reimbursements, teaching assistantships with partial tuition reimbursements, career-related internships or fieldwork, institutionally sponsored loans, scholarships/grants, and tuition waivers (full) available. Financial award application deadline: 5/1; financial award applicants required to submit FAFSA. *Faculty research:* Finance, management, marketing, operations and supply chain management, accounting and information systems. *Unit head:* Yunzeng Wang, Dean, School of Business, 951-827-3704, E-mail: yunzeng.wang@ucr.edu. *Application contact:* Mark Estrada, Director of Graduate Admissions, 951-827-2915, E-mail: mark.estrada@ucr.edu.
Website: http://agsm.ucr.edu/

University of California, San Diego, Graduate Division, Rady School of Management, La Jolla, CA 92093. Offers business administration (MBA); business analytics (MS); finance (MF); management (PhD). *Accreditation:* AACSB. *Program availability:* Part-time, evening/weekend. *Faculty:* 28 full-time (5 women), 5 part-time/adjunct (1 woman). *Students:* 436 full-time (201 women), 119 part-time (60 women). 2,265 applicants, 33% accepted, 307 enrolled. In 2017, 193 master's, 2 doctorates awarded. *Degree requirements:* For master's, capstone project; for doctorate, comprehensive exam, thesis/dissertation. *Entrance requirements:* For master's, GMAT (for MBA); GMAT or GRE General Test (for MF); for doctorate, GMAT or GRE General Test. Additional exam requirements/recommendations for international students: Required—TOEFL (minimum score 550 paper-based; 80 iBT), IELTS (minimum score 7). *Application deadline:* Applications are processed on a rolling basis. Application fee: $200. Electronic applications accepted. *Expenses:* Contact institution. *Financial support:* Fellowships, teaching assistantships, and scholarships/grants available. Financial award applicants

required to submit FAFSA. *Faculty research:* Innovation technology, operations management, finance, behavioral economics, organizational strategy, marketing, business analytics. *Unit head:* Robert Sullivan, Dean, 858-822-0830, E-mail: rssullivan@ucsd.edu. *Application contact:* Jay Bryant, Director of Graduate Recruitment and Admissions, 858-534-0864, E-mail: radygradadmissions@ucsd.edu.
Website: http://rady.ucsd.edu/

University of Central Arkansas, Graduate School, College of Business Administration, Program in Business Administration, Conway, AR 72035-0001. Offers MBA. *Accreditation:* AACSB. *Program availability:* Part-time, evening/weekend. *Entrance requirements:* For master's, GMAT or GRE, minimum GPA of 2.7. Additional exam requirements/recommendations for international students: Required—TOEFL (minimum score 550 paper-based).

University of Central Florida, College of Business Administration, Department of Management, Orlando, FL 32816. Offers entrepreneurship (Graduate Certificate); management (MSM); technology ventures (Graduate Certificate). *Accreditation:* AACSB. *Program availability:* Part-time. *Students:* 73 part-time (38 women); includes 33 minority (10 Black or African American, non-Hispanic/Latino; 5 Asian, non-Hispanic/Latino; 15 Hispanic/Latino; 3 Two or more races, non-Hispanic/Latino). Average age 30. 68 applicants, 72% accepted, 39 enrolled. In 2017, 35 master's, 29 other advanced degrees awarded. *Degree requirements:* For master's, capstone course. *Entrance requirements:* For master's, GMAT, minimum GPA of 3.0 in last 60 hours, letters of recommendation, resume, goal statement. Additional exam requirements/recommendations for international students: Required—TOEFL. *Application deadline:* For fall admission, 6/15 for domestic students; for spring admission, 11/15 for domestic students. Application fee: $30. Electronic applications accepted. *Expenses:* Tuition, state resident: part-time $288.16 per credit hour. Tuition, nonresident: part-time $1073.31 per credit hour. Tuition and fees vary according to program. *Financial support:* Fellowships available. Financial award application deadline: 3/1; financial award applicants required to submit FAFSA. *Unit head:* Dr. Stephen Goodman, Chair, 407-823-2675, Fax: 407-823-3725, E-mail: sgoodman@ucf.edu. *Application contact:* Associate Director, Graduate Admissions, 407-823-2766, Fax: 407-823-6442, E-mail: gradadmissions@ucf.edu.
Website: http://business.ucf.edu/departments-schools/management/

University of Central Florida, College of Business Administration, Program in Business Administration, Orlando, FL 32816. Offers MBA, PhD. *Accreditation:* AACSB. *Program availability:* Part-time, evening/weekend. *Students:* 98 full-time (42 women), 500 part-time (240 women); includes 225 minority (51 Black or African American, non-Hispanic/Latino; 36 Asian, non-Hispanic/Latino; 130 Hispanic/Latino; 8 Two or more races, non-Hispanic/Latino), 25 international. Average age 31. 487 applicants, 56% accepted, 224 enrolled. In 2017, 182 master's, 10 doctorates awarded. *Degree requirements:* For master's, capstone course; for doctorate, comprehensive exam, thesis/dissertation, departmental candidacy exam. *Entrance requirements:* For master's and doctorate, GMAT, minimum GPA of 3.0 in last 60 hours, letters of recommendation, goal statement, resume. Additional exam requirements/recommendations for international students: Required—TOEFL. *Application deadline:* For fall admission, 7/1 for domestic students. Application fee: $30. Electronic applications accepted. *Expenses:* Tuition, state resident: part-time $288.16 per credit hour. Tuition, nonresident: part-time $1073.31 per credit hour. Tuition and fees vary according to program. *Financial support:* In 2017–18, 27 students received support, including 10 fellowships with partial tuition reimbursements available (averaging $4,540 per year), 1 research assistantship (averaging $946 per year), 35 teaching assistantships with partial tuition reimbursements available (averaging $13,525 per year); career-related internships or fieldwork, Federal Work-Study, institutionally sponsored loans, health care benefits, tuition waivers (partial), and unspecified assistantships also available. Financial award application deadline: 3/1; financial award applicants required to submit FAFSA. *Unit head:* Dr. Paul Jarley, Dean, 407-823-5113, E-mail: pjarley@bus.ucf.edu. *Application contact:* Associate Director, Graduate Admissions, 407-823-2766, Fax: 407-823-6442, E-mail: gradadmissions@bus.ucf.edu.
Website: http://www.bus.ucf.edu

University of Central Missouri, The Graduate School, Warrensburg, MO 64093. Offers accountancy (MA); accounting (MBA); applied mathematics (MS); aviation safety (MA); biology (MS); business administration (MBA); career and technical education leadership (MS); college student personnel administration (MS); communication (MA); computer science (MS); counseling (MS); criminal justice (MS); educational leadership (Ed D); educational technology (MS); elementary and early childhood education (MSE); English (MA); environmental studies (MA); finance (MBA); history (MA); human services/educational technology (Ed S); human services/learning resources (Ed S); human services/professional counseling (Ed S); industrial hygiene (MS); industrial management (MS); information systems (MBA); information technology (MS); kinesiology (MS); library science and information services (MS); literacy education (MSE); marketing (MBA); mathematics (MS); music (MA); occupational safety management (MS); psychology (MS); rural family nursing (MS); school administration (MSE); social gerontology (MS); sociology (MA); special education (MSE); speech language pathology (MS); superintendency (Ed S); teaching (MAT); teaching English as a second language (MA); technology (MS); technology management (PhD); theatre (MA). *Program availability:* Part-time, 100% online, blended/hybrid learning. *Faculty:* 337 full-time (145 women), 41 part-time/adjunct (28 women). *Students:* 785 full-time (398 women), 1,633 part-time (1,063 women); includes 231 minority (102 Black or African American, non-Hispanic/Latino; 4 American Indian or Alaska Native, non-Hispanic/Latino; 16 Asian, non-Hispanic/Latino; 52 Hispanic/Latino; 57 Two or more races, non-Hispanic/Latino), 692 international. Average age 30. In 2017, 2,605 master's, 122 other advanced degrees awarded. *Degree requirements:* For master's and Ed S, comprehensive exam (for some programs), thesis (for some programs). *Entrance requirements:* Additional exam requirements/recommendations for international students: Required—TOEFL (minimum score 550 paper-based; 79 iBT). *Application deadline:* For fall admission, 6/1 priority date for domestic and international students; for spring admission, 10/1 priority date for domestic and international students; for summer admission, 4/1 priority date for domestic and international students. Applications are processed on a rolling basis. Application fee: $30 ($75 for international students). Electronic applications accepted. *Expenses:* Tuition, state resident: full-time $8771; part-time $292.35 per credit hour. Tuition, nonresident: full-time $17,541; part-time $584.70 per credit hour. *Required fees:* $372; $24.78 per credit hour. *Financial support:* In 2017–18, 99 students received support. Research assistantships, teaching assistantships, career-related internships or fieldwork, Federal Work-Study, scholarships/grants, and administrative and laboratory assistantships available. Support available to part-time students. Financial award application deadline: 3/1; financial award applicants required to submit FAFSA. *Unit head:* Shellie Hewitt, Director of Graduate and International Student Services, 660-543-4621, Fax: 660-543-4778, E-mail: hewitt@ucmo.edu. *Application contact:* 660-543-4621, E-mail: admit_intl@ucmo.edu.
Website: http://www.ucmo.edu/graduate/

University of Charleston, Master of Business Administration Program, Charleston, WV 25304-1099. Offers MBA. *Program availability:* Part-time, evening/weekend. *Entrance requirements:* Additional exam requirements/recommendations for international students: Required—TOEFL, IELTS. Electronic applications accepted.

Business Administration and Management—General

University of Chicago, Booth School of Business, Doctoral Program in Business, Chicago, IL 60637-1513. Offers PhD. *Accreditation:* AACSB. *Students:* 137 full-time (38 women). In 2017, 22 doctorates awarded. *Entrance requirements:* For doctorate, GMAT or GRE (for most areas of study), transcripts, resume, two letters of reference, essays. Additional exam requirements/recommendations for international students: Required—TOEFL or IELTS. Electronic applications accepted. *Expenses:* Contact institution. *Application contact:* PhD Program Office, 773-702-7298, E-mail: phd@chicagobooth.edu.
Website: https://www.chicagobooth.edu/programs/phd

University of Chicago, Booth School of Business, Full-Time MBA Program, Chicago, IL 60637. Offers accounting (MBA); analytic finance (MBA); analytic management (MBA); econometrics and statistics (MBA); economics (MBA); entrepreneurship (MBA); finance (MBA); general management (MBA); health administration and policy (Certificate); international business (MBA); managerial and organizational behavior (MBA); marketing analytics (MBA); marketing management (MBA); operations management (MBA); strategic management (MBA); MBA/AM; MBA/JD; MBA/MA; MBA/MD; MBA/MPP. *Accreditation:* AACSB. *Faculty:* 154 full-time (26 women), 61 part-time/adjunct (12 women). *Students:* 1,176 full-time (481 women). In 2017, 586 master's awarded. *Entrance requirements:* For master's, GMAT or GRE, transcripts, resume, 2 letters of recommendation, essays, interview. Additional exam requirements/recommendations for international students: Required—TOEFL, IELTS, or PTE. *Application deadline:* For fall admission, 9/1 for domestic and international students; for winter admission, 1/1 for domestic and international students; for spring admission, 4/1 for domestic and international students. Application fee: $250. Electronic applications accepted. *Expenses:* Contact institution. *Unit head:* Stacey Kole, Deputy Dean for Alumni, Corporate Relations, and the Full-time MBA Program, 773-702-7121. *Application contact:* Kurt Ahlm, Associate Dean for Student Recruitment and Admissions, 773-702-7369, Fax: 773-702-9085, E-mail: admissions@chicagobooth.edu.
Website: https://www.chicagobooth.edu/programs/full-time

University of Chicago, Booth School of Business, Part-Time Evening and Weekend MBA Programs, Chicago, IL 60611. Offers MBA. *Accreditation:* AACSB. *Program availability:* Part-time-only, evening/weekend. *Students:* 1,377 part-time (361 women). In 2017, 439 master's awarded. *Entrance requirements:* For master's, GMAT or GRE, transcripts, resume, 2 letters of recommendation, essay, interview. Additional exam requirements/recommendations for international students: Required—TOEFL or IELTS. *Application deadline:* Applications are processed on a rolling basis. Electronic applications accepted. *Expenses:* Contact institution. *Unit head:* Glenn Sykes, Associate Dean for Evening and Weekend MBA Programs and Program Innovation, 312-464-8675. *Application contact:* Evening and Weekend MBA Programs Admissions, 312-464-8700, E-mail: eveningweekend-admissions@chicagobooth.edu.
Website: https://www.chicagobooth.edu/programs/part-time-mba

University of Cincinnati, Carl H. Lindner College of Business, MBA Program, Cincinnati, OH 45221. Offers MBA. *Accreditation:* AACSB. *Program availability:* Part-time, evening/weekend, 100% online, blended/hybrid learning. *Faculty:* 70 full-time (20 women), 23 part-time/adjunct (4 women). *Students:* 102 full-time (35 women), 222 part-time (91 women); includes 69 minority (25 Black or African American, non-Hispanic/Latino; 19 Asian, non-Hispanic/Latino; 12 Hispanic/Latino; 1 Native Hawaiian or other Pacific Islander, non-Hispanic/Latino; 12 Two or more races, non-Hispanic/Latino), 36 international. Average age 29. 357 applicants, 39% accepted, 122 enrolled. In 2017, 174 master's awarded. *Degree requirements:* For master's, capstone project. *Entrance requirements:* For master's, GMAT or GRE, resume, letters of recommendation, essays, official transcripts. Additional exam requirements/recommendations for international students: Required—TOEFL (minimum score 577 paper-based; 90 iBT), IELTS (minimum score 6.5). *Application deadline:* For fall admission, 6/30 priority date for domestic students, 3/15 for international students; for spring admission, 12/15 for domestic students, 9/15 for international students; for summer admission, 4/15 for domestic and international students. Applications are processed on a rolling basis. Application fee: $65 ($70 for international students). Electronic applications accepted. *Expenses:* Contact institution. *Financial support:* In 2017–18, 119 students received support. Scholarships/grants, tuition waivers (full and partial), and unspecified assistantships available. Financial award application deadline: 3/15; financial award applicants required to submit FAFSA. *Faculty research:* Business analytics, financial management, organizational behavior, financial accounting, consumer insights. *Total annual research expenditures:* $24,842. *Unit head:* Dr. David Szymanski, Dean, 513-556-7001, Fax: 513-556-4891, E-mail: david.szymanski@uc.edu. *Application contact:* Dona Clary, Executive Director, Graduate Programs, 513-556-3546, Fax: 513-558-7006, E-mail: dona.clary@uc.edu.
Website: http://business.uc.edu/graduate/mba.html

University of Cincinnati, Carl H. Lindner College of Business, PhD Programs, Cincinnati, OH 45221. Offers accounting (PhD); business analytics (PhD); economics (PhD); finance (PhD); information systems (PhD); management (PhD); marketing (PhD); operations and business analytics (PhD); operations research (PhD). *Faculty:* 37 full-time (13 women). *Students:* 29 full-time (12 women), 12 part-time (6 women); includes 5 minority (1 Black or African American, non-Hispanic/Latino; 4 Asian, non-Hispanic/Latino), 20 international. Average age 30. 123 applicants, 16% accepted, 11 enrolled. In 2017, 5 doctorates awarded. *Degree requirements:* For doctorate, comprehensive exam, thesis/dissertation. *Entrance requirements:* For doctorate, GMAT, GRE, transcripts, essays, resume, letters of recommendation. Additional exam requirements/recommendations for international students: Required—TOEFL (minimum score 600 paper-based; 100 iBT), IELTS (minimum score 7). *Application deadline:* For fall admission, 1/15 for domestic and international students. Application fee: $65 ($70 for international students). Electronic applications accepted. *Expenses:* $7,234 resident per term, $13,105 nonresident per term. *Financial support:* In 2017–18, 41 students received support, including 29 research assistantships with full tuition reimbursements available (averaging $23,250 per year); scholarships/grants, health care benefits, tuition waivers (full), and unspecified assistantships also available. Financial award application deadline: 1/15; financial award applicants required to submit FAFSA. *Faculty research:* Bayesian Prediction Theory, organizational fairness, consumer insight and market research, consumer insight and market research, density estimation from correlated data. *Unit head:* Dr. Suzanne Masterson, Director, 513-556-7125, Fax: 513-556-5499, E-mail: suzanne.masterson@uc.edu. *Application contact:* Angel Elvin, Assistant Director, 513-556-7190, Fax: 513-558-7006, E-mail: angel.elvin@uc.edu.
Website: http://business.uc.edu/graduate/phd.html

University of Colorado Boulder, Leeds School of Business, MBA Program, Boulder, CO 80309. Offers MBA. *Accreditation:* AACSB. *Students:* 351 full-time (122 women), 2 part-time (1 woman); includes 45 minority (5 Black or African American, non-Hispanic/Latino; 15 Asian, non-Hispanic/Latino; 22 Hispanic/Latino; 3 Two or more races, non-Hispanic/Latino), 43 international. Average age 30. 438 applicants, 73% accepted, 107 enrolled. In 2017, 150 master's awarded. *Entrance requirements:* For master's, GMAT, minimum undergraduate GPA of 2.75. *Application deadline:* For fall admission, 12/1 for domestic students; for spring admission, 12/1 for domestic students. Applications are processed on a rolling basis. Application fee: $60 ($80 for international students). Electronic applications accepted. Application fee is waived when completed online.

Financial support: In 2017–18, 357 students received support, including 273 fellowships (averaging $8,866 per year), 2 teaching assistantships with full and partial tuition reimbursements available (averaging $9,804 per year); institutionally sponsored loans, scholarships/grants, health care benefits, and unspecified assistantships also available. Financial award application deadline: 2/15; financial award applicants required to submit FAFSA. *Application contact:* E-mail: leedsmba@colorado.edu.
Website: http://www.colorado.edu/leedsmba/

University of Colorado Boulder, Leeds School of Business, MS and PhD Programs, Boulder, CO 80309. Offers MS, PhD. *Students:* 223 full-time (99 women); includes 39 minority (4 Black or African American, non-Hispanic/Latino; 13 Asian, non-Hispanic/Latino; 15 Hispanic/Latino; 7 Two or more races, non-Hispanic/Latino), 39 international. Average age 25. 359 applicants, 38% accepted, 63 enrolled. In 2017, 87 master's, 3 doctorates awarded. *Entrance requirements:* For master's, GMAT, minimum undergraduate GPA of 3.0. *Application deadline:* For fall admission, 12/1 for domestic and international students. Application fee: $60 ($80 for international students). Electronic applications accepted. Application fee is waived when completed online. *Financial support:* In 2017–18, 237 students received support, including 129 fellowships (averaging $5,358 per year), 35 teaching assistantships with full and partial tuition reimbursements available (averaging $24,613 per year); institutionally sponsored loans, scholarships/grants, health care benefits, and unspecified assistantships also available. Financial award application deadline: 2/15; financial award applicants required to submit FAFSA. *Application contact:* E-mail: leedsms@colorado.edu.
Website: https://www.colorado.edu/business/ms-programs

University of Colorado Colorado Springs, College of Business, Colorado Springs, CO 80918. Offers MBA, MSA. *Accreditation:* AACSB. *Program availability:* Part-time, evening/weekend, 100% online, blended/hybrid learning. *Faculty:* 40 full-time (14 women), 57 part-time/adjunct (19 women). *Students:* 65 full-time (18 women), 267 part-time (126 women); includes 73 minority (9 Black or African American, non-Hispanic/Latino; 17 Asian, non-Hispanic/Latino; 29 Hispanic/Latino; 18 Two or more races, non-Hispanic/Latino), 11 international. Average age 34. 161 applicants, 81% accepted, 92 enrolled. In 2017, 106 master's awarded. *Entrance requirements:* For master's, goal statement. Additional exam requirements/recommendations for international students: Recommended—TOEFL (minimum score 500 paper-based; 80 iBT). *Application deadline:* For fall admission, 6/1 priority date for domestic students, 6/1 for international students; for spring admission, 11/1 priority date for domestic students, 11/1 for international students; for summer admission, 4/1 priority date for domestic students, 4/1 for international students. Applications are processed on a rolling basis. Application fee: $60 ($100 for international students). Electronic applications accepted. *Expenses:* $12,691 per year resident tuition, $22,339 nonresident, $15,003 nonresident online; annual costs vary depending on program, course-load, and residency status. *Financial support:* In 2017–18, 35 students received support. Career-related internships or fieldwork, Federal Work-Study, and scholarships/grants available. Support available to part-time students. Financial award application deadline: 3/1; financial award applicants required to submit FAFSA. *Faculty research:* Management information systems, marketing science, organizational behavior and human decision processes, accounting. *Total annual research expenditures:* $18,962. *Unit head:* Dr. Eric Olson, Interim Dean, 719-255-3113, Fax: 719-255-3100, E-mail: eolson@uccs.edu. *Application contact:* Janice Dowsett, Director of Graduate Programs, 719-255-3070, E-mail: cobgrad@uccs.edu.
Website: http://www.uccs.edu/mba

University of Colorado Denver, Business School, Master of Business Administration Program, Denver, CO 80217. Offers bioinnovation and entrepreneurship (MBA); business intelligence (MBA); business strategy (MBA); business to business marketing (MBA); business to consumer marketing (MBA); change management (MBA); corporate financial management (MBA); enterprise technology management (MBA); entrepreneurship (MBA); health administration (MBA), including financial management, health administration, health information technologies, international health management and policy; human resources management (MBA); international business (MBA); investment management (MBA); managing for sustainability (MBA); sports and entertainment management (MBA). *Accreditation:* AACSB. *Program availability:* Part-time, evening/weekend, 100% online, blended/hybrid learning. *Degree requirements:* For master's, 48 semester hours, including 30 of core courses, 3 in international business, and 15 in electives from over 50 other business courses. *Entrance requirements:* For master's, GMAT, resume, official transcripts, essay, two letters of recommendation, financial statements (for international applicants). Additional exam requirements/recommendations for international students: Required—TOEFL (minimum score 560 paper-based; 83 iBT); Recommended—IELTS (minimum score 6.5). Electronic applications accepted. *Expenses:* Contact institution. *Faculty research:* Marketing, management, entrepreneurship, finance, health administration.

University of Colorado Denver, Business School, Program in Management and Organization, Denver, CO 80217. Offers business strategy (MS); change and innovation (MS); enterprise technology management (MS); entrepreneurship and innovation (MS); global management (MS); leadership (MS); managing for sustainability (MS); managing human resources (MS); sports and entertainment management (MS). *Accreditation:* AACSB. *Program availability:* Part-time, evening/weekend, online learning. *Degree requirements:* For master's, 30 semester hours (12 of required courses, 12 of management electives, and 6 of free electives). *Entrance requirements:* For master's, GMAT, resume, two letters of recommendation, essay, financial statements (for international applicants). Additional exam requirements/recommendations for international students: Required—TOEFL (minimum score 525 paper-based; 71 iBT); Recommended—IELTS (minimum score 6.5). Electronic applications accepted. *Expenses:* Contact institution. *Faculty research:* Human resource management, management of catastrophe, turnaround strategies.

★ **University of Connecticut,** Graduate School, School of Business, Storrs, CT 06269. Offers accounting (MS, PhD); business administration (MBA, PhD); finance (PhD); health care management and insurance studies (MBA); management (PhD); management consulting (MBA); marketing (PhD); marketing intelligence (MBA). *Accreditation:* AACSB. *Degree requirements:* For master's, comprehensive exam; for doctorate, thesis/dissertation. *Entrance requirements:* For master's and doctorate, GMAT. Additional exam requirements/recommendations for international students: Required—TOEFL (minimum score 550 paper-based). Electronic applications accepted.
See Display on the next page and Close-Up on page 183.

University of Dallas, Satish and Yasmin Gupta College of Business, Irving, TX 75062-4736. Offers accounting (MBA, MS); business administration (DBA); business analytics (MS); business management (MBA); corporate finance (MBA); cybersecurity (MS); finance (MS); financial services (MBA); global business (MBA, MS); health services management (MBA); human resource management (MBA); information and technology management (MS); information assurance (MBA); information technology (MBA); information technology service management (MBA); marketing management (MBA); organization development (MBA); project management (MBA); sports and entertainment management (MBA); strategic leadership (MBA); supply chain management (MBA).

Accreditation: AACSB. *Program availability:* Part-time, evening/weekend, online learning. *Entrance requirements:* Additional exam requirements/recommendations for international students: Required—TOEFL. *Application deadline:* Applications are processed on a rolling basis. Application fee: $50. Electronic applications accepted. *Expenses:* Contact institution. *Financial support:* Application deadline: 2/15; applicants required to submit FAFSA. *Unit head:* Brett J.L. Landry, Dean, 972-721-5356, E-mail: blandry@udallas.edu. *Application contact:* Dr. David Sweet, Dean, Braniff Graduate School, 972-721-5288, Fax: 972-721-5280, E-mail: dsweet@udallas.edu.
Website: http://www.udallas.edu/cob/

University of Dayton, School of Business Administration, Dayton, OH 45469. Offers accounting (MBA); cyber security (MBA); finance (MBA); marketing (MBA); JD/MBA. *Accreditation:* AACSB. *Program availability:* Part-time, evening/weekend, blended/hybrid learning. *Faculty:* 23 full-time (8 women), 12 part-time/adjunct (2 women). *Students:* 57 full-time (24 women), 82 part-time (32 women); includes 10 minority (5 Black or African American, non-Hispanic/Latino; 2 Asian, non-Hispanic/Latino; 3 Hispanic/Latino), 18 international. Average age 31. 269 applicants, 31% accepted. In 2017, 88 master's awarded. *Entrance requirements:* For master's, GMAT (minimum score of 500 total, 19 verbal); GRE (minimum score of 149 verbal, 146 quantitative), minimum GPA of 3.0, current resume. Additional exam requirements/recommendations for international students: Required—TOEFL (minimum score 550 paper-based; 80 iBT); Recommended—IELTS (minimum score 6.5). *Application deadline:* For fall admission, 5/1 for international students; for spring admission, 11/1 for international students. Applications are processed on a rolling basis. Application fee: $0 ($50 for international students). Electronic applications accepted. *Expenses:* Contact institution. *Financial support:* In 2017–18, 10 research assistantships with partial tuition reimbursements (averaging $9,295 per year) were awarded; teaching assistantships, career-related internships or fieldwork, institutionally sponsored loans, scholarships/grants, traineeships, tuition waivers, and unspecified assistantships also available. Financial award application deadline: 3/1; financial award applicants required to submit FAFSA. *Faculty research:* Management information systems, economics, finance, marketing, entrepreneurship, accounting, cyber security, analytics. *Unit head:* Scott MacDonald, Director, MBA Program, 937-229-3733, Fax: 937-229-3882, E-mail: smacdonald1@udayton.edu. *Application contact:* Mandy Bingaman, MBA Program Manager, 937-229-3733, Fax: 937-229-3882, E-mail: mbingaman1@udayton.edu.
Website: https://www.udayton.edu/business/academics/master_of_business_administration/index.php

University of Delaware, Alfred Lerner College of Business and Economics, Program in Business Administration, Newark, DE 19716. Offers MBA, MA/MBA, MBA/MIB, MBA/MS. *Accreditation:* AACSB. *Program availability:* Part-time, evening/weekend. *Entrance requirements:* For master's, GMAT, 2 letters of recommendation, resume. Additional exam requirements/recommendations for international students: Required—TOEFL (minimum score 600 paper-based; 79 iBT). Electronic applications accepted. *Expenses:* Contact institution. *Faculty research:* Finance, corporate governance, information systems, leadership, marketing.

University of Delaware, College of Agriculture and Natural Resources, Department of Entomology and Wildlife Ecology, Newark, DE 19716. Offers entomology and applied ecology (MS, PhD), including avian ecology, evolution and taxonomy, insect biological control, insect ecology and behavior (MS), insect genetics, pest management, plant-insect interactions, wildlife ecology and management. *Program availability:* Part-time. *Degree requirements:* For master's, comprehensive exam, thesis, oral exam, seminar; for doctorate, comprehensive exam, thesis/dissertation, qualifying exam, seminar. *Entrance requirements:* For master's, GRE General Test, minimum GPA of 3.0 in field, 2.8 overall; for doctorate, GRE General Test, GRE Subject Test (biology), minimum GPA of 3.0 in field, 2.8 overall. Additional exam requirements/recommendations for international students: Required—TOEFL. Electronic applications accepted. *Faculty research:* Ecology and evolution of plant-insect interactions, ecology of wildlife conservation management, habitat restoration, biological control, applied ecosystem management.

University of Denver, Daniels College of Business, Denver, CO 80208. Offers M Acc, MBA, MS. *Accreditation:* AACSB. *Program availability:* Part-time, evening/weekend. *Faculty:* 104 full-time (36 women), 48 part-time/adjunct (12 women). *Students:* 429 full-time (190 women), 212 part-time (104 women); includes 117 minority (16 Black or African American, non-Hispanic/Latino; 1 American Indian or Alaska Native, non-Hispanic/Latino; 24 Asian, non-Hispanic/Latino; 59 Hispanic/Latino; 17 Two or more races, non-Hispanic/Latino), 124 international. Average age 30. 1,032 applicants, 53% accepted. In 2017, 485 master's awarded. *Entrance requirements:* For master's, GRE General Test or GMAT, bachelor's degree, transcripts, essays, resume, two letters of recommendation, interview. Additional exam requirements/recommendations for international students: Required—TOEFL (minimum score 550 paper-based; 80 iBT). *Application deadline:* For fall admission, 11/15 priority date for domestic and international students; for spring admission, 10/1 priority date for domestic and international students. Applications are processed on a rolling basis. Application fee: $100. Electronic applications accepted. *Expenses:* $47,823 per year full-time; $1,320 per credit. *Financial support:* In 2017–18, 536 students received support, including 3 teaching assistantships with tuition reimbursements available (averaging $3,217 per year); career-related internships or fieldwork, Federal Work-Study, institutionally sponsored loans, scholarships/grants, and unspecified assistantships also available. Support available to part-time students. Financial award application deadline: 2/15; financial award applicants required to submit FAFSA. *Faculty research:* Corporate governance, decision making, emerging economies, ethics, leadership. *Unit head:* Dr. Brent Chrite, Dean, 303-871-4324, Fax: 303-871-2156, E-mail: brent.chrite@du.edu. *Application contact:* Information Contact, 303-871-3416, Fax: 303-871-4466, E-mail: daniels@du.edu.
Website: http://daniels.du.edu/

University of Detroit Mercy, College of Business Administration, Detroit, MI 48221. Offers business administration (MBA); business fundamentals (Certificate); business turnaround management (Certificate); ethical leadership and change management (Certificate); finance (Certificate); forensic accounting (Certificate); JD/MBA; MBA/MHSA. *Program availability:* Part-time, evening/weekend, 100% online, blended/hybrid learning. *Entrance requirements:* For master's, GMAT, resume, letter of recommendation, transcripts; for Certificate, resume, letter of recommendation, transcripts. Electronic applications accepted. Application fee is waived when completed online. *Expenses:* Contact institution. *Faculty research:* Ethics, international finance, trade policy, leadership, information technology.

University of Dubuque, Program in Business Administration, Dubuque, IA 52001-5099. Offers MBA. *Program availability:* Part-time, evening/weekend. *Entrance requirements:* For master's, 2 letters of recommendation. Electronic applications accepted.

The University of Findlay, Office of Graduate Admissions, Findlay, OH 45840. Offers applied security and analytics (MSAS); athletic training (MAT); business (MBA), including certified management accountant, certified public accountant, health care management, hospitality management; education (MA Ed, Ed D), including children's literature (MA Ed), curriculum and teaching (MA Ed), education (MA Ed), educational administration (MA Ed), human resource development (MA Ed), mathematics (MA Ed), reading (MA Ed), science education (MA Ed), superintendent (Ed D), teaching (Ed D), technology (MA Ed); environmental, safety, and health management (MSEM); health informatics (MS); occupational therapy (MOT); pharmacy (Pharm D); physical therapy (DPT); physician assistant (MPA); rhetoric and writing (MA); teaching English to

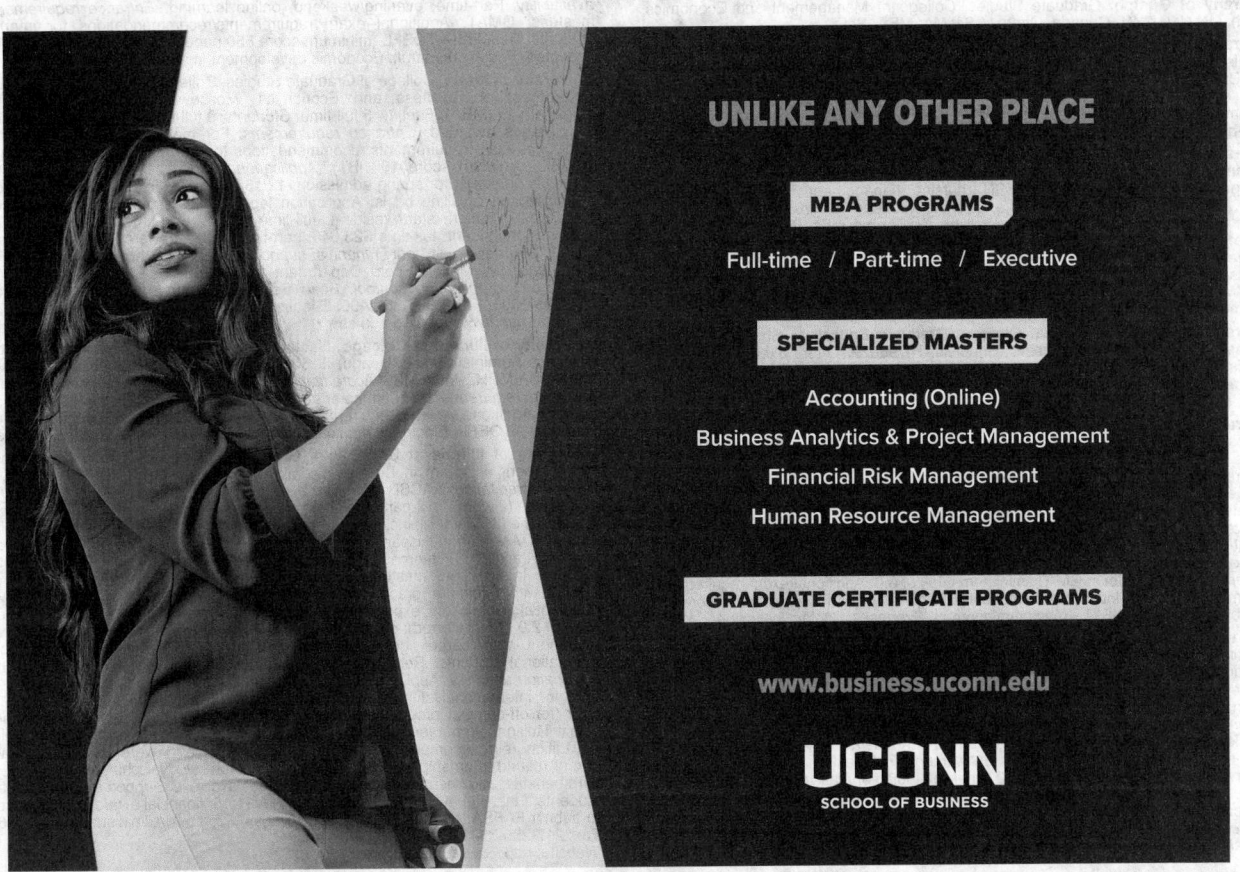

Business Administration and Management—General

speakers of other languages (TESOL) and applied linguistics (MA). *Program availability:* Part-time, evening/weekend, 100% online, blended/hybrid learning. *Students:* 688 full-time (430 women), 553 part-time (308 women), 170 international. Average age 28. In 2017, 366 master's, 137 doctorates awarded. *Degree requirements:* For master's, comprehensive exam (for some programs), thesis (for some programs), cumulative project, capstone project; for doctorate, thesis/dissertation (for some programs). *Entrance requirements:* For master's, GRE/GMAT, bachelor's degree from accredited institution, minimum undergraduate GPA of 2.5 in last 64 hours of course work; for doctorate, GRE, MAT, minimum cumulative GPA of 3.0. Additional exam requirements/recommendations for international students: Required—TOEFL (minimum score 79 iBT), IELTS (minimum score 7), PTE (minimum score 61). *Application deadline:* Applications are processed on a rolling basis. Electronic applications accepted. *Financial support:* In 2017–18, 10 research assistantships with partial tuition reimbursements (averaging $7,200 per year), 35 teaching assistantships with partial tuition reimbursements (averaging $7,200 per year) were awarded; Federal Work-Study, institutionally sponsored loans, and unspecified assistantships also available. Financial award applicants required to submit FAFSA. *Unit head:* Christopher M. Harris, Director of Admissions, 419-434-4347, E-mail: harrisc1@findlay.edu. *Application contact:* Madeline Fauser Brennan, Graduate Admissions Counselor, 419-434-4636, Fax: 419-434-4898, E-mail: fauserbrennan@findlay.edu.
Website: http://www.findlay.edu/admissions/graduate/Pages/default.aspx

University of Florida, Graduate School, Warrington College of Business Administration, Hough Graduate School of Business, Department of Management, Gainesville, FL 32611. Offers health care risk management (MS); international business (MA); management (MS, PhD). *Accreditation:* AACSB. *Program availability:* Online learning. *Degree requirements:* For master's, comprehensive exam, thesis. *Entrance requirements:* For master's, GMAT (minimum score of 465) or GRE General Test, minimum GPA of 3.0. Additional exam requirements/recommendations for international students: Required—TOEFL (minimum score 550 paper-based; 80 iBT), IELTS (minimum score 6). Electronic applications accepted. *Faculty research:* Job attitudes, personality and individual differences, organizational entry and exit, knowledge management, competitive dynamics.

University of Florida, Graduate School, Warrington College of Business Administration, Hough Graduate School of Business, Programs in Business Administration, Gainesville, FL 32611. Offers business administration (MA, MS, PhD); competitive strategy (MBA); finance (MBA); global management (MBA); Graham-Buffett security analysis (MBA); human resource management (MBA); information systems and operations management (MBA); international studies (MBA); management (MBA); real estate (MBA); JD/MBA; MBA/MS; MBA/PhD; MBA/Pharm D; MD/MBA. *Accreditation:* AACSB. *Program availability:* Part-time, evening/weekend, online learning. *Degree requirements:* For master's, capstone course. *Entrance requirements:* For master's and doctorate, GMAT (minimum score 465), minimum GPA of 3.0, interview. Additional exam requirements/recommendations for international students: Required—TOEFL (minimum score 550 paper-based; 80 iBT), IELTS (minimum score 6). Electronic applications accepted. *Faculty research:* Accounting, finance, insurance, management, real estate, urban analysis marketing.

University of Georgia, Terry College of Business, Program in Business Administration, Athens, GA 30602. Offers Exec MBA, MBA. *Accreditation:* AACSB. *Degree requirements:* For master's, thesis (MA). *Entrance requirements:* For master's, GMAT (for MBA), GRE General Test (for MA). Electronic applications accepted.

University of Guam, Office of Graduate Studies, School of Business and Public Administration, Business Administration Program, Mangilao, GU 96923. Offers PMBA. *Entrance requirements:* For master's, GMAT. Additional exam requirements/recommendations for international students: Required—TOEFL.

University of Guelph, Graduate Studies, College of Management and Economics, Guelph, ON N1G 2W1, Canada. Offers M Sc, MA, MBA, PhD.

University of Hartford, Barney School of Business, Program in Business Administration, West Hartford, CT 06117-1599. Offers MBA, MBA/M Eng. *Accreditation:* AACSB. *Program availability:* Part-time, evening/weekend. *Entrance requirements:* For master's, GMAT, 2 letters of recommendation, resume. Additional exam requirements/recommendations for international students: Required—TOEFL (minimum score 550 paper-based). Electronic applications accepted.

University of Hartford, College of Education, Nursing, and Health Professions, Program in Nursing, West Hartford, CT 06117-1599. Offers community/public health nursing (MSN); nursing education (MSN); nursing management (MSN). *Accreditation:* AACN. *Program availability:* Part-time, evening/weekend. *Degree requirements:* For master's, research project. *Entrance requirements:* For master's, BSN, Connecticut RN license. Additional exam requirements/recommendations for international students: Required—TOEFL (minimum score 550 paper-based). Electronic applications accepted. *Expenses:* Contact institution. *Faculty research:* Child development, women in doctoral study, applying feminist theory in teaching methods, near death experience, grandmothers as primary care providers.

University of Hawaii at Manoa, Office of Graduate Education, Shidler College of Business, Executive MBA Programs, Honolulu, HI 96822. Offers executive business administration (EMBA); Vietnam focused business administration (EMBA). *Accreditation:* AACSB. *Program availability:* Part-time. *Entrance requirements:* For master's, GMAT, minimum GPA of 3.0.

University of Hawaii at Manoa, Office of Graduate Education, Shidler College of Business, Program in Business Administration, Honolulu, HI 96822. Offers Asian business studies (MBA); Chinese business studies (MBA); decision sciences (MBA); entrepreneurship (MBA); finance (MBA); finance and banking (MBA); human resources management (MBA); information management (MBA); information technology (MBA); international business (MBA); Japanese business studies (MBA); marketing (MBA); organizational behavior (MBA); organizational management (MBA); real estate (MBA); student-designed track (MBA). *Accreditation:* AACSB. *Program availability:* Part-time, evening/weekend. *Degree requirements:* For master's, thesis optional. *Entrance requirements:* For master's, GMAT, minimum GPA of 3.0. Additional exam requirements/recommendations for international students: Required—TOEFL (minimum score 600 paper-based; 100 iBT), IELTS (minimum score 7). *Expenses:* Contact institution.

University of Holy Cross, Graduate Programs, New Orleans, LA 70131-7399. Offers biomedical sciences (MS); Catholic theology (MA); counseling (MA, PhD), including community counseling (MA), marriage and family counseling (MA), school counseling (MA); educational leadership (M Ed); executive leadership (Ed D); management (MS), including healthcare management, operations management; teaching and learning (M Ed). *Accreditation:* ACA; NCATE. *Program availability:* Part-time, evening/weekend, online learning. *Faculty:* 7 full-time (4 women), 8 part-time/adjunct (3 women). *Students:* 67 full-time (55 women), 69 part-time (55 women); includes 51 minority (46 Black or African American, non-Hispanic/Latino; 2 American Indian or Alaska Native, non-Hispanic/Latino; 1 Asian, non-Hispanic/Latino; 2 Hispanic/Latino). Average age 30. 20 applicants, 50% accepted. In 2017, 28 degrees awarded. *Degree requirements:* For master's, thesis. *Entrance requirements:* For master's, GRE General Test, minimum GPA of 2.7. *Application deadline:* For fall admission, 9/1 for domestic students. Application fee: $15.

Expenses: Tuition: Full-time $10,890; part-time $605 per credit hour. *Required fees:* $1624; $812 per semester. One-time fee: $50. *Financial support:* Federal Work-Study and tuition waivers (partial) available. Support available to part-time students. Financial award application deadline: 6/1. *Unit head:* Dr. Myles Seghers, Dean of Humanities, Education, and Counseling, 504-394-7744 Ext. 214, Fax: 504-391-2421, E-mail: mseghers@olhcc.edu. *Application contact:* Anne-Katherine Lene, Director of Student Enrollment, 504-394-7744 Ext. 110, Fax: 504-391-2421, E-mail: aklene@olhcc.edu.

University of Houston, Bauer College of Business, Houston, TX 77204. Offers MBA, MS, MS Accy, PhD. *Accreditation:* AACSB. *Program availability:* Part-time, evening/weekend. *Degree requirements:* For master's, 30 hours completed in residence, minimum cumulative GPA of 3.0 at UH, no more than 11 semester hours of 'C' grades or below in graduate courses taken at UH; for doctorate, comprehensive exam, thesis/dissertation, minimum GPA of 3.25, continuous full time enrollment, dissertation defense within 6 years of entering the program. *Entrance requirements:* For master's, GMAT or GRE (MBA), official transcripts from all higher education institutions attended, resume, letters of recommendation, self appraisal and goal statement (MBA); for doctorate, GMAT or GRE, letter of financial backing, statement of understanding, reference letters, statement of academic and research interests. Additional exam requirements/recommendations for international students: Required—TOEFL (minimum score 603 paper-based; 100 iBT), IELTS (minimum score 6.5), PTE (minimum score 70). Electronic applications accepted. *Faculty research:* Accountancy and taxation, finance, international business, management.

University of Houston–Clear Lake, School of Business, Program in Business Administration, Houston, TX 77058-1002. Offers MBA. *Accreditation:* AACSB. *Program availability:* Part-time, evening/weekend. *Degree requirements:* For master's, thesis optional. *Entrance requirements:* For master's, GMAT. Additional exam requirements/recommendations for international students: Required—TOEFL (minimum score 550 paper-based). Electronic applications accepted.

University of Houston–Downtown, Marilyn Davies College of Business, MBA Program, Houston, TX 77002. Offers accounting (MBA); finance (MBA); human resource management (MBA); international business (MBA); investment management (MBA); leadership (MBA); project management and process improvement (MBA); sales management and business development (MBA); supply chain management (MBA). *Accreditation:* AACSB. *Program availability:* Part-time, evening/weekend. *Faculty:* 36 full-time (13 women), 11 part-time/adjunct (6 women). *Students:* 4 full-time (2 women), 1,065 part-time (605 women); includes 821 minority (383 Black or African American, non-Hispanic/Latino; 3 American Indian or Alaska Native, non-Hispanic/Latino; 136 Asian, non-Hispanic/Latino; 299 Hispanic/Latino), 33 international. Average age 33. 418 applicants, 89% accepted, 308 enrolled. In 2017, 310 master's awarded. *Entrance requirements:* For master's, GMAT, two letters of recommendation from professional references, personal statement, resume. Additional exam requirements/recommendations for international students: Required—TOEFL (minimum score 81 iBT). *Application deadline:* For fall admission, 8/1 for domestic and international students. Application fee: $35 ($60 for international students). Electronic applications accepted. *Expenses:* $360 per credit resident; $725 per credit non-resident. *Financial support:* Federal Work-Study and scholarships/grants available. Financial award application deadline: 4/1; financial award applicants required to submit FAFSA. *Unit head:* Dr. Charles E. Gengler, Dean, 713-221-8179, Fax: 713-221-8675. *Application contact:* Ceshia Love, Director of Admissions, 713-221-8093, Fax: 713-223-7408, E-mail: gradadmissions@uhd.edu.
Website: http://mba.uhd.edu/

University of Houston–Victoria, School of Business Administration, Victoria, TX 77901-4450. Offers accounting (MBA); economic development and entrepreneurship (MS); finance (GMBA, MBA); general business (MBA); international business (MBA); management (GMBA, MBA); marketing (MBA). *Accreditation:* AACSB. *Program availability:* Part-time, evening/weekend, online learning. *Entrance requirements:* For master's, GMAT. Additional exam requirements/recommendations for international students: Required—TOEFL (minimum score 550 paper-based). Electronic applications accepted. *Faculty research:* Economic development, marketing, finance.

University of Idaho, College of Graduate Studies, College of Business and Economics, Department of Business and Economics, Moscow, ID 83844. Offers general management (MBA). *Faculty:* 5 full-time. *Students:* 9 full-time. Average age 43. In 2017, 14 master's awarded. *Entrance requirements:* For master's, minimum GPA of 3.0. Additional exam requirements/recommendations for international students: Required—TOEFL (minimum score 100 iBT). *Application deadline:* For fall admission, 8/1 for domestic students; for spring admission, 12/15 for domestic students. Applications are processed on a rolling basis. Application fee: $60. Electronic applications accepted. *Expenses:* Tuition, state resident: full-time $6722; part-time $430 per credit hour. Tuition, nonresident: full-time $23,046; part-time $1337 per credit hour. *Required fees:* $2142; $63 per credit hour. *Financial support:* Applicants required to submit FAFSA. *Unit head:* Dr. Metlen Scott, Department Head, 208-885-6295, E-mail: canthony@uidaho.edu. *Application contact:* Sean Scoggin, Graduate Recruitment Coordinator, 208-885-4001, Fax: 208-885-4406, E-mail: graduateadmissions@uidaho.edu.
Website: http://www.uidaho.edu/cbe

University of Illinois at Chicago, Liautaud Graduate School of Business, Program in Business Administration, Chicago, IL 60607-7128. Offers MBA, PhD, MBA/MA, MBA/MD, MBA/MPH, MBA/MS. *Accreditation:* AACSB. *Program availability:* Part-time. *Entrance requirements:* For master's, GMAT, minimum GPA of 2.75; for doctorate, GMAT. Additional exam requirements/recommendations for international students: Required—TOEFL. Electronic applications accepted. *Expenses:* Contact institution.

University of Illinois at Springfield, Graduate Programs, College of Business and Management, Program in Business Administration, Springfield, IL 62703-5407. Offers MBA. *Accreditation:* AACSB. *Program availability:* Part-time, evening/weekend. *Faculty:* 13 full-time (2 women), 2 part-time/adjunct (1 woman). *Students:* 46 full-time (23 women), 41 part-time (21 women); includes 11 minority (3 Black or African American, non-Hispanic/Latino; 6 Asian, non-Hispanic/Latino; 1 Hispanic/Latino; 1 Two or more races, non-Hispanic/Latino), 10 international. Average age 32. 99 applicants, 37% accepted, 31 enrolled. In 2017, 46 master's awarded. *Degree requirements:* For master's, closure course with minimum grade of B. *Entrance requirements:* For master's, GMAT or substantial supervisory experience and managerial responsibility, minimum cumulative GPA of 2.0 (2.5 preferred); current resume; 3 letters of reference; personal and academic statement with career goals. Additional exam requirements/recommendations for international students: Required—TOEFL (minimum score 550 paper-based; 61 iBT). *Application deadline:* Applications are processed on a rolling basis. Application fee: $60 ($75 for international students). Electronic applications accepted. *Expenses:* $280 per hour (for off-campus program). *Financial support:* In 2017–18, research assistantships with full tuition reimbursements (averaging $10,249 per year), teaching assistantships with full tuition reimbursements (averaging $10,303 per year) were awarded; fellowships, career-related internships or fieldwork, Federal Work-Study, scholarships/grants, health care benefits, and unspecified assistantships also available. Support available to part-time students. Financial award application deadline: 11/15; financial award applicants required to submit FAFSA. *Unit head:* Dr. Jorge Villegas, Program Administrator, 217-206-6780, Fax: 217-206-7541, E-mail: jvill2@uis.edu. *Application contact:* Dr. Jorge Villegas, Program Administrator, 217-206-6780, Fax: 217-206-7541, E-mail: jvill2@uis.edu.
Website: http://www.uis.edu/mba/

University of Illinois at Urbana–Champaign, Graduate College, Gies College of Business, Department of Business Administration, Champaign, IL 61820. Offers business administration (MS, PhD); technology management (MS). *Accreditation:* AACSB. *Expenses:* Contact institution.

University of Illinois at Urbana–Champaign, Graduate College, Gies College of Business, MBA Program, Champaign, IL 61820. Offers MBA, Ed M/MBA, JD/MBA, M Arch/MBA, MCS/MBA, MHRIR/MBA, MS/MBA. *Accreditation:* AACSB.

University of Indianapolis, Graduate Programs, School of Business, Indianapolis, IN 46227-3697. Offers EMBA, MBA, Graduate Certificate. *Program availability:* Part-time, evening/weekend. *Entrance requirements:* For master's, GMAT, interview, minimum GPA of 2.8, 2 letters of recommendation, resume. Additional exam requirements/recommendations for international students: Required—TOEFL (minimum score 550 paper-based).

The University of Iowa, Tippie College of Business, Department of Management and Organizations, Iowa City, IA 52242-1316. Offers PhD. *Accreditation:* AACSB. *Faculty:* 13 full-time (6 women), 2 part-time/adjunct (0 women). *Students:* 14 full-time (5 women); includes 1 minority (Asian, non-Hispanic/Latino), 5 international. Average age 30. 76 applicants, 8% accepted, 2 enrolled. In 2017, 2 doctorates awarded. *Degree requirements:* For doctorate, comprehensive exam, thesis/dissertation. *Entrance requirements:* For doctorate, GMAT or GRE. Additional exam requirements/recommendations for international students: Required—TOEFL (minimum score 100 iBT), IELTS (minimum score 7). *Application deadline:* For fall admission, 1/15 priority date for domestic and international students. Application fee: $60 ($100 for international students). Electronic applications accepted. *Financial support:* In 2017–18, 14 students received support, including 14 fellowships (averaging $3,000 per year), 3 research assistantships with full tuition reimbursements available (averaging $19,016 per year), 11 teaching assistantships with full tuition reimbursements available (averaging $19,016 per year); health care benefits and unspecified assistantships also available. Financial award application deadline: 1/15; financial award applicants required to submit FAFSA. *Faculty research:* Decision-making, human resources, personal selection, organizational behavior, training. *Unit head:* Prof. Amy E. Colbert, Department Executive Officer, 319-335-0932, Fax: 319-335-0860, E-mail: amy-colbert@uiowa.edu. *Application contact:* Renea L. Jay, Associate Director, Non-MBA Graduate Programs, 319-335-0830, Fax: 319-335-0860, E-mail: renea-jay@uiowa.edu.
Website: https://tippie.uiowa.edu/management-and-organizations

The University of Iowa, Tippie College of Business, Department of Management Sciences, Iowa City, IA 52242-1316. Offers PhD. *Accreditation:* AACSB. *Faculty:* 15 full-time (3 women). *Students:* 14 full-time (4 women), 13 international. Average age 29. 56 applicants, 18% accepted, 4 enrolled. In 2017, 1 doctorate awarded. *Degree requirements:* For doctorate, comprehensive exam, thesis/dissertation. *Entrance requirements:* For doctorate, GRE General Test or GMAT. Additional exam requirements/recommendations for international students: Required—TOEFL (minimum score 100 iBT) or IELTS (minimum score 7.0). *Application deadline:* For fall admission, 1/15 priority date for domestic and international students. Application fee: $60 ($100 for international students). Electronic applications accepted. *Financial support:* In 2017–18, 14 students received support, including 14 fellowships (averaging $3,000 per year), 1 research assistantship with full tuition reimbursement available (averaging $19,016 per year), 13 teaching assistantships with full tuition reimbursements available (averaging $19,016 per year); health care benefits and unspecified assistantships also available. Financial award application deadline: 1/15. *Faculty research:* Optimization, supply chain management, data mining, logistics, database management. *Unit head:* Prof. Nick Street, Department Executive Officer, 319-335-0858, Fax: 319-335-1956, E-mail: nick-street@uiowa.edu. *Application contact:* Renea L. Jay, Associate Director, Non-MBA Graduate Programs, 319-335-0830, Fax: 319-335-0860, E-mail: renea-jay@uiowa.edu.
Website: https://tippie.uiowa.edu/management-sciences

The University of Iowa, Tippie College of Business, Executive MBA Program, Iowa City, IA 52242. Offers EMBA. *Program availability:* Part-time-only, evening/weekend. *Faculty:* 19 full-time (7 women), 5 part-time/adjunct (2 women). *Students:* 91 part-time (31 women); includes 18 minority (5 Black or African American, non-Hispanic/Latino; 10 Asian, non-Hispanic/Latino; 3 Hispanic/Latino). Average age 40. 45 applicants, 89% accepted, 37 enrolled. In 2017, 24 master's awarded. *Application deadline:* Applications are processed on a rolling basis. Electronic applications accepted. *Expenses:* Contact institution. *Financial support:* Institutionally sponsored loans available. Financial award applicants required to submit FAFSA. *Unit head:* Dawn Kluber, Assistant Dean, 319-335-1043, E-mail: dawn-kluber@uiowa.edu.
Website: https://tippie.uiowa.edu/future-graduate-students/mba-programs/executive-mba

The University of Iowa, Tippie College of Business, Professional MBA Program, Iowa City, IA 52242-1316. Offers business administration (MBA); business analytics (MBA); finance (MBA); leadership (MBA); marketing (MBA). *Program availability:* Part-time-only, evening/weekend. *Faculty:* 50 full-time (11 women), 22 part-time/adjunct (2 women). *Students:* 873 part-time (325 women); includes 102 minority (16 Black or African American, non-Hispanic/Latino; 1 American Indian or Alaska Native, non-Hispanic/Latino; 54 Asian, non-Hispanic/Latino; 22 Hispanic/Latino; 9 Two or more races, non-Hispanic/Latino), 44 international. Average age 33. 155 applicants, 94% accepted, 137 enrolled. In 2017, 176 master's awarded. *Degree requirements:* For master's, successful completion of nine required courses and six electives totaling 45 credits, minimum GPA of 2.75. *Entrance requirements:* For master's, GMAT or GRE. Additional exam requirements/recommendations for international students: Required—TOEFL (minimum score 600 paper-based; 100 iBT), IELTS (minimum score 7). *Application deadline:* For fall admission, 7/30 for domestic and international students; for spring admission, 12/15 for domestic and international students; for summer admission, 4/30 for domestic and international students. Applications are processed on a rolling basis. Application fee: $60 ($100 for international students). Electronic applications accepted. *Expenses:* Contact institution. *Faculty research:* Capital markets; analytics techniques and applications; organizational and market systems analysis; applied econometrics; talent effectiveness. *Unit head:* Prof. Sarah Fisher Gardial, Dean, 319-335-0862, Fax: 319-335-0860, E-mail: sarah-gardial@uiowa.edu.
Website: https://tippie.uiowa.edu/future-graduate-students/21-mba-programs/professional-mba

The University of Kansas, Graduate Studies, School of Business, Program in Business, Lawrence, KS 66045. Offers business and organizational leadership (MS); decision sciences and supply chain management (PhD); finance (PhD); human resources management (PhD); marketing (PhD); organizational behavior (PhD); strategic management (PhD); supply chain management and logistics (MS). *Accreditation:* AACSB. *Program availability:* Part-time. *Students:* 66 full-time (18 women), 227 part-time (76 women); includes 59 minority (21 Black or African American, non-Hispanic/Latino; 2 American Indian or Alaska Native, non-Hispanic/Latino; 13 Asian, non-Hispanic/Latino; 3 Hispanic/Latino; 20 Two or more races, non-Hispanic/Latino), 29 international. Average age 32. 329 applicants, 71% accepted, 185 enrolled. In 2017, 30 master's, 8 doctorates awarded. *Entrance requirements:* For master's, GMAT, official transcript, three letters of recommendation, resume, statement of purpose; for doctorate, GMAT or GRE, official transcript, three letters of recommendation, resume, statement of purpose. Additional exam requirements/recommendations for international students: Required—TOEFL (minimum score 600 paper-based; 100 iBT). *Application deadline:* For fall admission, 1/10 for domestic and international students. Application fee: $65 ($85 for international students). Electronic applications accepted. *Financial support:* Fellowships, research assistantships, teaching assistantships, scholarships/grants, health care benefits, tuition waivers (full), and unspecified assistantships available. Financial award application deadline: 1/10. *Faculty research:* Strategic human resource management, business ethics, organizational theory/behavior, corporate strategy, international business, supply chain management, Bayesian networks, game theory, decision analysis and time/series analysis, pricing, consumer effects, advertising and emotion. *Unit head:* Charly Edmonds, Director, 785-864-3841, E-mail: bschoolphd@ku.edu. *Application contact:* Graduate Admission Contact, 785-864-7500, E-mail: bschoolphd@ku.edu.
Website: http://www.business.ku.edu

The University of Kansas, Graduate Studies, School of Business, Program in Business Administration and Management, Lawrence, KS 66045. Offers MBA, JD/MBA, MBA/MA, MBA/MM, MBA/MS, MBA/Pharm D. *Accreditation:* AACSB. *Program availability:* Part-time, online learning. *Students:* 85 full-time (28 women), 282 part-time (85 women); includes 57 minority (17 Black or African American, non-Hispanic/Latino; 3 American Indian or Alaska Native, non-Hispanic/Latino; 6 Asian, non-Hispanic/Latino; 13 Hispanic/Latino; 18 Two or more races, non-Hispanic/Latino), 11 international. Average age 32. 222 applicants, 75% accepted, 141 enrolled. In 2017, 95 master's awarded. *Entrance requirements:* For master's, GMAT, official transcript; two recommendation forms; current resume; three essays; acknowledge the University Honor Code. *Application deadline:* For fall admission, 8/4 for domestic students, 5/1 for international students. Application fee: $65 ($85 for international students). Electronic applications accepted. *Financial support:* Research assistantships, career-related internships or fieldwork, Federal Work-Study, institutionally sponsored loans, scholarships/grants, and unspecified assistantships available. Financial award application deadline: 1/15; financial award applicants required to submit FAFSA. *Unit head:* Dr. Duane Myer, Director of MBA Programs, 785-864-4276, E-mail: dmyer@ku.edu. *Application contact:* Marysa Sacerdote, Master's Admissions Coordinator, 785-864-7556, E-mail: marysa@ku.edu.
Website: http://www.business.ku.edu/

University of Kentucky, Graduate School, Gatton College of Business and Economics, Program in Business Administration, Lexington, KY 40506-0032. Offers MBA, PhD. *Accreditation:* AACSB. *Degree requirements:* For master's, comprehensive exam; for doctorate, comprehensive exam, thesis/dissertation. *Entrance requirements:* For master's, GMAT, minimum undergraduate GPA of 2.75; for doctorate, GMAT, minimum undergraduate GPA of 3.0. Additional exam requirements/recommendations for international students: Required—TOEFL (minimum score 550 paper-based). Electronic applications accepted. *Faculty research:* Expert systems in manufacturing, knowledge acquisition and management, financial institutions, market in service organizations, strategic planning.

University of La Verne, College of Business and Public Management, Graduate Programs in Business Administration, La Verne, CA 91750-4443. Offers accounting (MBA, MBA-EP); finance (MBA, MBA-EP); health services management (MBA); information technology (MBA, MBA-EP); international business (MBA, MBA-EP); management and leadership (MBA, MBA-EP); marketing (MBA, MBA-EP); supply chain management (MBA, MBA-EP). *Program availability:* Part-time, evening/weekend. *Faculty:* 24 full-time (11 women), 25 part-time/adjunct (6 women). *Students:* 390 full-time (193 women), 93 part-time (48 women); includes 96 minority (7 Black or African American, non-Hispanic/Latino; 1 American Indian or Alaska Native, non-Hispanic/Latino; 17 Asian, non-Hispanic/Latino; 67 Hispanic/Latino; 1 Native Hawaiian or other Pacific Islander, non-Hispanic/Latino; 3 Two or more races, non-Hispanic/Latino), 336 international. Average age 28. *Entrance requirements:* For master's, GMAT, MAT, or GRE, minimum undergraduate GPA of 3.0, 2 letters of recommendation, resume, statement of purpose. Additional exam requirements/recommendations for international students: Required—TOEFL (minimum score 550 paper-based; 85 iBT). *Application deadline:* Applications are processed on a rolling basis. Application fee: $50. Tuition and fees vary according to program. *Financial support:* Institutionally sponsored loans and scholarships/grants available. Financial award application deadline: 3/2; financial award applicants required to submit FAFSA. *Unit head:* Dr. Abe Helou, Chairperson, 909-448-4455, Fax: 909-392-2704, E-mail: ihelou@laverne.edu. *Application contact:* Rina Lazarian-Chehab, Senior Associate Director of Graduate Admissions, 909-448-4317, Fax: 909-971-2295, E-mail: rlazarian@laverne.edu.
Website: https://business.laverne.edu/mba/

University of La Verne, College of Business and Public Management, Program in Health Administration, La Verne, CA 91750-4443. Offers financial management (MHA); management and leadership (MHA); marketing and business development (MHA). *Program availability:* Part-time. *Faculty:* 4 full-time (3 women), 3 part-time/adjunct (1 woman). *Students:* 35 full-time (28 women), 34 part-time (23 women); includes 34 minority (7 Black or African American, non-Hispanic/Latino; 8 Asian, non-Hispanic/Latino; 19 Hispanic/Latino), 11 international. Average age 30. *Entrance requirements:* For master's, bachelor's degree, experience in health services industry (preferred). Additional exam requirements/recommendations for international students: Required—TOEFL (minimum score 550 paper-based). *Application deadline:* Applications are processed on a rolling basis. Application fee: $50. *Expenses:* Contact institution. *Financial support:* Federal Work-Study, institutionally sponsored loans, and scholarships/grants available. Financial award application deadline: 3/2; financial award applicants required to submit FAFSA. *Unit head:* Dr. Kathy Duncan, Program Chairperson, 909-448-4415, E-mail: kduncan2@laverne.edu. *Application contact:* Barbara Cox, Associate Director of Graduate Admission, 909-448-4004, Fax: 909-971-2295, E-mail: bcox@laverne.edu.
Website: https://business.laverne.edu/mha/

University of La Verne, College of Business and Public Management, Program in Leadership and Management, La Verne, CA 91750-4443. Offers human resource management (Certificate); leadership and management (MS), including human resource management, nonprofit management, organizational development; nonprofit management (Certificate); organizational leadership (Certificate). *Program availability:* Part-time. *Faculty:* 4 full-time (3 women), 5 part-time/adjunct (1 woman). *Students:* 49 full-time (25 women), 35 part-time (22 women); includes 47 minority (6 Black or African American, non-Hispanic/Latino; 4 Asian, non-Hispanic/Latino; 35 Hispanic/Latino; 2 Two or more races, non-Hispanic/Latino), 13 international. Average age 32. *Entrance requirements:* For master's, bachelor's degree, minimum undergraduate GPA of 2.75, 2 letters of recommendation, interview, resume. Additional exam requirements/recommendations for international students: Required—TOEFL (minimum score 550 paper-based). *Application deadline:* Applications are processed on a rolling basis. Application fee: $50. Tuition and fees vary according to program. *Financial support:* Federal Work-Study, institutionally sponsored loans, and scholarships/grants available. Financial award application deadline: 3/2; financial award applicants required to submit FAFSA. *Unit head:* Dr. Kathy Duncan, Program Director, 909-448-4415, E-mail: kduncan2@laverne.edu. *Application contact:* Barbara Cox, Associate Director of Graduate Admissions, 909-448-4004, E-mail: bcox@laverne.edu.
Website: https://business.laverne.edu/mslm/

Business Administration and Management—General

University of La Verne, Regional and Online Campuses, Graduate Programs, Central Coast/Vandenberg Air Force Base Campuses, La Verne, CA 91750-4443. Offers business administration for experienced professionals (MBA), including health services management, information technology; leadership and management (MS). *Program availability:* Part-time. *Students:* 6 full-time (1 woman), 37 part-time (20 women); includes 9 minority (1 Asian, non-Hispanic/Latino; 8 Hispanic/Latino). Average age 40. In 2017, 20 master's awarded. *Application deadline:* Applications are processed on a rolling basis. Application fee: $50. *Expenses:* Contact institution. *Financial support:* Application deadline: 3/2; applicants required to submit FAFSA. *Unit head:* Kitt Vincent, Director, Vandenberg AFB, 805-788-6202, Fax: 805-788-6201, E-mail: kvincent@laverne.edu. *Application contact:* Admissions, 805-734-6220, Fax: 805-734-6221, E-mail: vafb@laverne.edu.
Website: http://www.laverne.edu/locations

University of La Verne, Regional and Online Campuses, Graduate Programs, High Desert Campus, Victorville, CA 92392. Offers business administration for experienced professionals (MBA); educational (special emphasis) (M Ed); educational counseling (MS); leadership and management (MS); multiple subject (elementary) (Credential); preliminary administrative services (Credential); pupil personnel services (Credential); single subject (secondary) (Credential). *Students:* 7 full-time (3 women), 16 part-time (12 women); includes 14 minority (3 Black or African American, non-Hispanic/Latino; 1 American Indian or Alaska Native, non-Hispanic/Latino; 1 Asian, non-Hispanic/Latino; 9 Hispanic/Latino). Average age 41. In 2017, 9 master's awarded. *Application deadline:* Applications are processed on a rolling basis. Application fee: $50. *Expenses:* Contact institution. *Financial support:* Application deadline: 3/2; applicants required to submit FAFSA. *Unit head:* Juli Roberts, Regional Campus Director, 760-955-6448, Fax: 760-843-9505, E-mail: jroberts@laverne.edu. *Application contact:* Admissions, 760-955-6440, Fax: 760-955-6443, E-mail: hdcv@laverne.edu.
Website: https://laverne.edu/locations/

University of La Verne, Regional and Online Campuses, Graduate Programs, Inland Empire Campus, Ontario, CA 91730. Offers business administration (MBA, MBA-EP), including accounting (MBA), finance (MBA), health services management (MBA-EP), information technology (MBA-EP), international business (MBA), managed care (MBA), management and leadership (MBA-EP), marketing (MBA-EP), supply chain management (MBA); leadership and management (MS), including human resource management, nonprofit management, organizational development. *Program availability:* Part-time, evening/weekend. *Faculty:* 5 part-time/adjunct (1 woman). *Students:* 24 full-time (13 women), 72 part-time (44 women); includes 64 minority (12 Black or African American, non-Hispanic/Latino; 13 Asian, non-Hispanic/Latino; 36 Hispanic/Latino; 3 Two or more races, non-Hispanic/Latino). Average age 38. In 2017, 42 master's awarded. *Application deadline:* Applications are processed on a rolling basis. Application fee: $50. *Expenses:* Contact institution. *Financial support:* Application deadline: 3/2; applicants required to submit FAFSA. *Unit head:* Juli Roberts, Campus Director, Inland Empire Regional Campus in Ontario, 760-955-6448, E-mail: jroberts@laverne.edu. *Application contact:* Admissions, 877-468-6858, E-mail: gradadmission@laverne.edu.
Website: https://laverne.edu/locations/

University of La Verne, Regional and Online Campuses, Graduate Programs, Kern County Campus, Bakersfield, CA 93301. Offers business administration for experienced professionals (MBA-EP); education (special emphasis) (M Ed); educational counseling (MS); educational leadership (M Ed); health administration (MHA); leadership and management (MS); mild/moderate education specialist (Credential); multiple subject (elementary) (Credential); organizational leadership (Ed D); preliminary administrative services (Credential); single subject (secondary) (Credential); special education studies (MS). *Program availability:* Part-time, evening/weekend. *Students:* Average age 36. In 2017, 3 master's awarded. *Application deadline:* Applications are processed on a rolling basis. Application fee: $50. *Expenses:* Contact institution. *Financial support:* Institutionally sponsored loans available. Financial award application deadline: 3/2; financial award applicants required to submit FAFSA. *Unit head:* Nora Dominguez, Regional Campus Director, 661-861-6802, E-mail: ndominguez@laverne.edu. *Application contact:* Rebecca Murillo, Associate Director of Admissions, 661-861-6807, E-mail: rmurillo@laverne.edu.
Website: https://laverne.edu/locations/

University of La Verne, Regional and Online Campuses, Graduate Programs, Orange County Campus, Irvine, CA 92840. Offers business administration for experienced professionals (MBA); educational counseling (MS); educational leadership (M Ed); health administration (MHA); leadership and management (MS); preliminary administrative services (Credential); pupil personnel services (Credential). *Program availability:* Part-time. *Students:* 19 full-time (11 women), 51 part-time (30 women); includes 47 minority (12 Black or African American, non-Hispanic/Latino; 2 American Indian or Alaska Native, non-Hispanic/Latino; 12 Asian, non-Hispanic/Latino; 21 Hispanic/Latino). Average age 39. In 2017, 43 master's awarded. *Application deadline:* Applications are processed on a rolling basis. Application fee: $50. *Expenses:* Contact institution. *Financial support:* Application deadline: 3/2; applicants required to submit FAFSA. *Unit head:* Alison Rodriguez-Balles, Interim Campus Director, 714-505-6943, Fax: 909-505-6937, E-mail: arodriguez2@laverne.edu. *Application contact:* 877-468-6858, E-mail: gradadmission@laverne.edu.
Website: https://laverne.edu/locations/

University of La Verne, Regional and Online Campuses, Graduate Programs, San Fernando Valley Campus, Burbank, CA 91505. Offers business administration for experienced professionals (MBA-EP); educational counseling (MS); educational leadership (M Ed); leadership and management (MS); preliminary administrative services (Credential); pupil personnel services (Credential). *Program availability:* Part-time, evening/weekend. *Students:* 43 full-time (26 women), 97 part-time (49 women); includes 88 minority (21 Black or African American, non-Hispanic/Latino; 1 American Indian or Alaska Native, non-Hispanic/Latino; 15 Asian, non-Hispanic/Latino; 49 Hispanic/Latino; 1 Native Hawaiian or other Pacific Islander, non-Hispanic/Latino; 1 Two or more races, non-Hispanic/Latino). Average age 38. In 2017, 65 master's awarded. *Application deadline:* Applications are processed on a rolling basis. Application fee: $50. *Expenses:* Contact institution. *Financial support:* Application deadline: 3/2; applicants required to submit FAFSA. *Unit head:* Dr. Nelly Kazman, Senior Executive Director, 818-295-6502, E-mail: nkazman@laverne.edu. *Application contact:* Debi Hrboka, Associate Director of Admissions, 818-295-6508, E-mail: dhrboka@laverne.edu.
Website: https://laverne.edu/locations/

University of La Verne, Regional and Online Campuses, Graduate Programs, Ventura County/Point Mugu Naval Air Station Campuses, Oxnard, CA 93036. Offers business administration for experienced professionals (MS); educational counseling (MS); educational leadership (M Ed); leadership and management (MS); multiple subject (elementary) (Credential); pupil personnel services (Credential); single subject (secondary) (Credential). *Program availability:* Part-time, evening/weekend. *Students:* Average age 38. In 2017, 19 master's awarded. Application fee: $50. *Expenses:* Contact institution. *Financial support:* Institutionally sponsored loans available. Financial award application deadline: 3/2; financial award applicants required to submit FAFSA. *Unit head:* Kitt Vincent, Senior Executive Director, 805-788-6202, E-mail: kvincent@

laverne.edu. *Application contact:* Mike Stadler, Assistant Director/Academic Advisor, 805-986-6909, E-mail: mstadler3@laverne.edu.
Website: https://laverne.edu/locations/

University of La Verne, Regional and Online Campuses, Graduate Program, ULV Online, La Verne, CA 91750-4443. Offers business administration for experienced professionals (MBA); child development (MS); leadership and management (MS). *Program availability:* Part-time, evening/weekend, online learning. *Students:* Average age 37. In 2017, 57 master's awarded. *Entrance requirements:* For master's, GMAT, MAT, or GRE, minimum undergraduate GPA of 3.0, 2 letters of recommendation, resume, statement of purpose. *Application deadline:* Applications are processed on a rolling basis. Application fee: $50. Tuition and fees vary according to program. *Financial support:* Application deadline: 3/2; applicants required to submit FAFSA. *Unit head:* Barbara Colley, Coordinator, ULV Online, 909-448-4944, E-mail: bcolley@ulv.edu. *Application contact:* Jesse S. Martinez, Associate Director of Admission, 909-448-4961, E-mail: jmartinez@laverne.edu.
Website: http://laverne.edu/admission/online/

University of Lethbridge, School of Graduate Studies, Lethbridge, AB T1K 3M4, Canada. Offers addictions counseling (M Sc); agricultural biotechnology (M Sc); agricultural studies (M Sc, MA); anthropology (MA); archaeology (M Sc, MA); art (MA, MFA); biochemistry (M Sc); biological sciences (M Sc); biomolecular science (PhD); biosystems and biodiversity (PhD); Canadian studies (MA); chemistry (M Sc); computer science (M Sc); computer science and geographical information science (M Sc); counseling (MC); counseling psychology (M Ed); dramatic arts (MA); earth, space, and physical science (PhD); economics (MA); education (MA, PhD); educational leadership (M Ed); English (MA); environmental science (M Sc); evolution and behavior (PhD); exercise science (M Sc); French (MA); French/German (MA); French/Spanish (MA); general education (M Ed); geography (M Sc, MA); German (MA); health sciences (M Sc); individualized multidisciplinary (M Sc, MA); kinesiology (M Sc, MA); management (M Sc), including accounting, finance, human resource management and labor relations, information systems, international management, marketing, policy and strategy; mathematics (M Sc); music (M Mus, MA); Native American studies (MA); neuroscience (M Sc, PhD); new media (MA, MFA); nursing (M Sc, MN); philosophy (MA); physics (M Sc); political science (MA); psychology (M Sc, MA); religious studies (MA); sociology (MA); theatre and dramatic arts (MFA); theoretical and computational science (PhD); urban and regional studies (MA); women and gender studies (MA). *Program availability:* Part-time, evening/weekend. *Degree requirements:* For master's, thesis (for some programs); for doctorate, comprehensive exam, thesis/dissertation. *Entrance requirements:* For master's, GMAT (for M Sc in management), bachelor's degree in related field, minimum GPA of 3.0 during previous 20 graded semester courses, 2 years' teaching or related experience (M Ed); for doctorate, master's degree, minimum graduate GPA of 3.5. Additional exam requirements/recommendations for international students: Required—TOEFL (minimum score 580 paper-based; 93 iBT). Electronic applications accepted. *Faculty research:* Movement and brain plasticity, gibberellin physiology, photosynthesis, carbon cycling, molecular properties of main-group ring components.

University of Louisiana at Lafayette, BI Moody III College of Business Administration MBA Program, Lafayette, LA 70504. Offers MBA. *Accreditation:* AACSB. *Program availability:* Part-time, evening/weekend. *Entrance requirements:* For master's, GRE General Test. Additional exam requirements/recommendations for international students: Required—TOEFL (minimum score 550 paper-based).

University of Louisiana at Monroe, Graduate School, College of Business and Social Sciences, MBA Program, Monroe, LA 71209-0001. Offers MBA. Program also offered at Shue Yan University in Hong Kong. *Program availability:* Evening/weekend. *Faculty:* 11 full-time (4 women). *Students:* 30 full-time (11 women), 46 part-time (22 women); includes 15 minority (6 Black or African American, non-Hispanic/Latino; 1 Asian, non-Hispanic/Latino; 6 Hispanic/Latino; 2 Two or more races, non-Hispanic/Latino), 14 international. Average age 28. 60 applicants, 52% accepted, 17 enrolled. In 2017, 24 master's awarded. *Expenses:* Contact institution. *Financial support:* In 2017–18, 23 students received support. Teaching assistantships and unspecified assistantships available. *Unit head:* Dr. Ronald Berry, Dean, 318-342-1103, E-mail: rberry@ulm.edu.
Website: http://www.ulm.edu/cbss/mba

University of Louisiana at Monroe, Graduate School, College of Health and Pharmaceutical Sciences, Department of Gerontology, Monroe, LA 71209-0001. Offers aging studies (MA); gerontology (CGS); grief care management (MA); long-term care administration (MA); mental health (MA); program administration (MA); small business management (MA). *Program availability:* Part-time. *Faculty:* 1 (woman) full-time, 5 part-time/adjunct (3 women). *Students:* 6 full-time (5 women), 8 part-time (all women); includes 5 minority (all Black or African American, non-Hispanic/Latino). Average age 36. 7 applicants, 43% accepted, 3 enrolled. In 2017, 3 master's awarded. *Degree requirements:* For master's, thesis (for some programs), internship. *Entrance requirements:* For master's, GRE General Test (waived for students with a 2.5 GPA or above); for CGS, GRE General Test. Additional exam requirements/recommendations for international students: Required—TOEFL (minimum score 500 paper-based; 61 iBT). *Application deadline:* For fall admission, 8/24 priority date for domestic students, 7/1 for international students; for winter admission, 12/14 priority date for domestic students; for spring admission, 1/19 for domestic students, 11/1 for international students. Applications are processed on a rolling basis. Application fee: $20 ($30 for international students). Electronic applications accepted. *Expenses:* Tuition, state resident: full-time $6489; part-time $479 per hour. Tuition, nonresident: full-time $12,100; part-time $479 per hour. *Required fees:* $8860; $802 per hour. $3273 per semester. *Financial support:* In 2017–18, 2 students received support. Career-related internships or fieldwork, Federal Work-Study, and unspecified assistantships available. Financial award application deadline: 4/1; financial award applicants required to submit FAFSA. *Unit head:* Dr. Anita Sharma, Director, 318-342-1467, E-mail: sharma@ulm.edu.
Website: http://www.ulm.edu/gerontology/

University of Louisville, Graduate School, College of Business, MBA Programs, Louisville, KY 40292-0001. Offers entrepreneurship (MBA); global business (MBA); health sector management (MBA). *Accreditation:* AACSB. *Program availability:* Part-time, evening/weekend. *Students:* 253 full-time (99 women), 21 part-time (6 women); includes 49 minority (25 Black or African American, non-Hispanic/Latino; 1 American Indian or Alaska Native, non-Hispanic/Latino; 10 Asian, non-Hispanic/Latino; 8 Hispanic/Latino; 5 Two or more races, non-Hispanic/Latino), 27 international. Average age 32. 295 applicants, 63% accepted, 155 enrolled. In 2017, 85 master's awarded. *Degree requirements:* For master's, international learning experience. *Entrance requirements:* For master's, GMAT, 2 letters of reference, personal interview, resume, personal statement, college transcript(s). Additional exam requirements/recommendations for international students: Required—TOEFL (minimum score 83 iBT). *Application deadline:* For fall admission, 7/1 for domestic students; for spring admission, 12/1 for domestic students. Applications are processed on a rolling basis. Application fee: $65. *Expenses:* Tuition, state resident: full-time $12,246; part-time $681 per credit hour. Tuition, nonresident: full-time $25,486; part-time $1417 per credit hour. *Required fees:* $196. Tuition and fees vary according to course load, program and reciprocity agreements. *Financial support:* Fellowships with full tuition reimbursements, research assistantships

with full tuition reimbursements, health care benefits, and unspecified assistantships available. Financial award application deadline: 3/31; financial award applicants required to submit FAFSA. *Faculty research:* Entrepreneurship, venture capital, retailing/ franchising, corporate governance and leadership, supply chain management. *Total annual research expenditures:* $859,000. *Unit head:* Dr. Todd Mooradian, Dean, 502-852-6443, Fax: 502-852-7557, E-mail: todd.mooradian@louisville.edu. *Application contact:* Susan E. Hildebrand, Program Director, 502-852-7257, Fax: 502-852-4901, E-mail: s.hildebrand@louisville.edu.
Website: http://business.louisville.edu/mba

University of Lynchburg, Graduate Studies, MBA Program, Lynchburg, VA 24501-3199. Offers MBA. *Accreditation:* ACBSP. *Program availability:* Part-time, evening/ weekend, 100% online, blended/hybrid learning. *Faculty:* 9 full-time (2 women). *Students:* 5 full-time (1 woman), 45 part-time (16 women); includes 4 minority (all Black or African American, non-Hispanic/Latino), 1 international. Average age 30. 23 applicants, 100% accepted, 18 enrolled. In 2017, 36 master's awarded. *Degree requirements:* For master's, capstone course. *Entrance requirements:* For master's, GMAT (minimum score of 400) or GRE, personal essay, 3 letters of recommendation, official transcripts (bachelor's, others as relevant), career goals statement. Additional exam requirements/recommendations for international students: Required—TOEFL (minimum score 550 paper-based; 80 iBT), IELTS (minimum score 6). *Application deadline:* For fall admission, 7/31 for domestic students, 6/1 for international students; for spring admission, 11/30 for domestic students, 10/15 for international students. Applications are processed on a rolling basis. Application fee: $30. Electronic applications accepted. Application fee is waived when completed online. *Expenses:* $645 per credit hour tuition, $100 fees. *Financial support:* Federal Work-Study, scholarships/grants, health care benefits, and unspecified assistantships available. Support available to part-time students. Financial award application deadline: 7/31; financial award applicants required to submit FAFSA. *Unit head:* Dr. Lee Schimmoeller, Associate Professor/Director of MBA Program, 434-522-8897, E-mail: schimmoeller@lynchburg.edu. *Application contact:* Ellen Thompson, Graduate Admissions Counselor, 434-544-8841, E-mail: thompson_e@lynchburg.edu.
Website: http://www.lynchburg.edu/graduate/master-of-business-administration/

University of Maine, Graduate School, The Maine Business School, Orono, ME 04469. Offers MBA, CGS. *Accreditation:* AACSB. *Program availability:* Part-time, evening/ weekend, online learning. *Faculty:* 14 full-time (4 women), 6 part-time/adjunct (1 woman). *Students:* 42 full-time (15 women), 43 part-time (19 women); includes 4 minority (3 Asian, non-Hispanic/Latino; 1 Two or more races, non-Hispanic/Latino), 4 international. Average age 30. 69 applicants, 90% accepted, 44 enrolled. In 2017, 25 master's, 7 other advanced degrees awarded. *Entrance requirements:* For master's, GMAT. Additional exam requirements/recommendations for international students: Required—TOEFL (minimum score 550 paper-based; 80 iBT), IELTS (minimum score 6.5). *Application deadline:* For fall admission, 7/1 priority date for domestic and international students; for spring admission, 12/1 priority date for domestic and international students; for summer admission, 4/1 priority date for domestic and international students. Applications are processed on a rolling basis. Application fee: $65. Electronic applications accepted. *Expenses:* Contact institution. *Financial support:* In 2017–18, 15 students received support, including 1 research assistantship with full tuition reimbursement available (averaging $8,100 per year), 4 teaching assistantships with full tuition reimbursements available (averaging $13,600 per year); career-related internships or fieldwork, Federal Work-Study, institutionally sponsored loans, scholarships/grants, tuition waivers (full and partial), and unspecified assistantships also available. Financial award application deadline: 3/1. *Faculty research:* Audit, socially responsible investing, capital acquisition, international management, corporate social responsibility. *Unit head:* Scott Spolan, MBA Director and Lecturer in Management, 207-581-1973, E-mail: scott.spolan@maine.edu. *Application contact:* Scott G. Delcourt, Assistant Vice President for Graduate Studies and Senior Associate Dean, 207-581-3291, Fax: 207-581-3232, E-mail: graduate@maine.edu.
Website: http://www.umaine.edu/business/

University of Management and Technology, Program in Business Administration, Arlington, VA 22209-1609. Offers general management (MBA, DBA); project management (MBA). *Program availability:* Part-time, evening/weekend, online learning. *Degree requirements:* For master's, comprehensive exam; for doctorate, thesis/ dissertation. *Entrance requirements:* For master's, 3 recommendations, resume. Additional exam requirements/recommendations for international students: Required— TOEFL (minimum score 530 paper-based; 71 iBT). Electronic applications accepted.

University of Management and Technology, Program in Management, Arlington, VA 22209-1609. Offers acquisition management (MS, AC); criminal justice administration (MS); general management (MS); project management (MS, AC). *Program availability:* Part-time, evening/weekend, online learning. *Entrance requirements:* For master's, 3 recommendations, resume. Additional exam requirements/recommendations for international students: Required—TOEFL (minimum score 530 paper-based; 71 iBT). Electronic applications accepted.

The University of Manchester, Alliance Manchester Business School, M15 6PB, United Kingdom. Offers accounting and finance (M Sc); business (M Ent); business analysis and strategic management (M Sc); business analytics: operational research and risk analysis (M Sc); business psychology (M Sc); corporate communications and reputation management (M Sc); finance (M Sc); finance and business economics (M Sc); human resource management and industrial relations (M Sc); innovation management and entrepreneurship (M Sc); international business and management (M Sc); international human resource management and comparative industrial relations (M Sc); management (M Sc); marketing (M Sc); operations, project and supply chain management (M Sc); organizational psychology (M Sc); quantitative finance (M Sc). *Entrance requirements:* For master's, UK 2:1 honours degree or overseas equivalent. Additional exam requirements/recommendations for international students: Required— TOEFL (minimum score 100 iBT), IELTS (minimum score 7), PTE. Electronic applications accepted. *Faculty research:* Accounting and finance, management sciences and marketing, people management and organization, innovation management and policy, decision sciences.

University of Manitoba, Faculty of Graduate Studies, Asper School of Business, Winnipeg, MB R3T 2N2, Canada. Offers M Sc, MBA, PhD. *Accreditation:* AACSB.

University of Mary, Gary Tharaldson School of Business, Bismarck, ND 58504-9652. Offers business administration (MBA); energy management (MBA, MS); executive (MBA, MS); health care (MBA, MS); human resource management (MBA); project management (MBA, MPM, MS); virtuous leadership (MBA, MPM, MS). *Program availability:* Part-time, evening/weekend. *Entrance requirements:* For master's, minimum GPA of 2.5. Additional exam requirements/recommendations for international students: Required—TOEFL (minimum score 550 paper-based; 80 iBT). Electronic applications accepted.

University of Mary Hardin-Baylor, Graduate Studies in Business Administration, Belton, TX 76513. Offers accounting (MBA); information systems management (MBA); international business (MBA); management (MBA). *Program availability:* Part-time, evening/weekend. *Faculty:* 12 full-time (5 women), 6 part-time/adjunct (4 women).

Students: 16 full-time (10 women), 39 part-time (16 women); includes 15 minority (3 Black or African American, non-Hispanic/Latino; 1 Asian, non-Hispanic/Latino; 10 Hispanic/Latino; 1 Two or more races, non-Hispanic/Latino), 10 international. Average age 30. 72 applicants, 81% accepted, 16 enrolled. In 2017, 34 master's awarded. *Degree requirements:* For master's, comprehensive exam. *Entrance requirements:* For master's, minimum GPA of 3.0, interview. Additional exam requirements/ recommendations for international students: Required—TOEFL (minimum score 60 iBT), IELTS (minimum score 4.5). *Application deadline:* For fall admission, 6/1 for domestic students, 4/30 priority date for international students; for spring admission, 11/1 for domestic students, 9/30 priority date for international students. Applications are processed on a rolling basis. Application fee: $35 ($135 for international students). Electronic applications accepted. *Expenses:* Tuition: Full-time $15,570; part-time $10,380 per credit hour. *Required fees:* $1350; $75 per credit hour. $50 per term. Tuition and fees vary according to course load and degree level. *Financial support:* In 2017–18, 32 students received support. Federal Work-Study, institutionally sponsored loans, unspecified assistantships, and scholarships for some active duty military personnel available. Support available to part-time students. Financial award applicants required to submit FAFSA. *Faculty research:* Financial management, financial markets, supply chain management. *Unit head:* Dr. Kirk Fischer, Assistant Dean, Graduate Programs in McLane College of Business, 254-295-4655, E-mail: kfischer@umhb.edu. *Application contact:* Sharon Aguilera, Assistant Director, Graduate Admissions, 254-295-4835, E-mail: saguilera@umhb.edu.
Website: http://www.graduate.umhb.edu/mba

University of Maryland, College Park, Academic Affairs, Joint Program in Business and Management/Public Policy, College Park, MD 20742. Offers MBA/MPM. *Accreditation:* AACSB. Electronic applications accepted.

University of Maryland, College Park, Academic Affairs, Robert H. Smith School of Business, Combined MSW/MBA Program, College Park, MD 20742. Offers MSW/MBA. *Accreditation:* AACSB. *Entrance requirements:* Additional exam requirements/ recommendations for international students: Required—TOEFL.

University of Maryland, College Park, Academic Affairs, Robert H. Smith School of Business, Executive MBA Program, College Park, MD 20742. Offers EMBA. *Accreditation:* AACSB. *Entrance requirements:* For master's, minimum GPA of 3.0, 7-12 years of professional experience. Additional exam requirements/recommendations for international students: Required—TOEFL.

University of Maryland, College Park, Academic Affairs, Robert H. Smith School of Business, Joint Program in Business and Management, College Park, MD 20742. Offers MBA/MS. *Accreditation:* AACSB. *Entrance requirements:* Additional exam requirements/recommendations for international students: Required—TOEFL. Electronic applications accepted.

University of Maryland, College Park, Academic Affairs, Robert H. Smith School of Business, Program in Business Administration, College Park, MD 20742. Offers MBA. *Accreditation:* AACSB. *Program availability:* Part-time, evening/weekend, online learning. *Entrance requirements:* For master's, GMAT, minimum GPA of 3.0, resume, 3 letters of recommendation. Additional exam requirements/recommendations for international students: Required—TOEFL. Electronic applications accepted. *Faculty research:* Accounting, entrepreneurship, finance management and organization, management server and statistical information systems.

University of Maryland, College Park, Academic Affairs, Robert H. Smith School of Business, Program in Business and Management, College Park, MD 20742. Offers MS, PhD. *Accreditation:* AACSB. *Program availability:* Part-time. *Degree requirements:* For master's, thesis optional; for doctorate, comprehensive exam, thesis/dissertation. *Entrance requirements:* For master's, GMAT, minimum GPA of 3.0, resume, 2 letters of recommendation; for doctorate, GMAT or GRE General Test, minimum GPA of 3.0, resume, 2 letters of recommendation. Additional exam requirements/recommendations for international students: Required—TOEFL. Electronic applications accepted.

University of Maryland, College Park, Academic Affairs, Robert H. Smith School of Business, Program in Business Management/Law, College Park, MD 20742. Offers JD/ MBA. *Accreditation:* AACSB. *Entrance requirements:* Additional exam requirements/ recommendations for international students: Required—TOEFL.

University of Maryland University College, The Graduate School, Doctoral Program in Management, Adelphi, MD 20783. Offers DM. *Accreditation:* AACSB. *Program availability:* Part-time. *Students:* 58 full-time (33 women), 112 part-time (64 women); includes 91 minority (60 Black or African American, non-Hispanic/Latino; 1 American Indian or Alaska Native, non-Hispanic/Latino; 11 Asian, non-Hispanic/Latino; 14 Hispanic/Latino; 5 Two or more races, non-Hispanic/Latino), 3 international. Average age 45. 80 applicants, 100% accepted, 8 enrolled. In 2017, 27 doctorates awarded. *Degree requirements:* For doctorate, comprehensive exam, thesis/dissertation. *Application deadline:* Applications are processed on a rolling basis. Application fee: $100. Electronic applications accepted. *Financial support:* Federal Work-Study and scholarships/grants available. Support available to part-time students. Financial award application deadline: 6/1; financial award applicants required to submit FAFSA. *Unit head:* Dr. Leslie Dinauer, Program Director, 240-684-2400, Fax: 240-684-2401, E-mail: leslie.dinauer@umuc.edu. *Application contact:* Admissions Coordinator, 800-888-8682, Fax: 240-684-2151, E-mail: newgrad@umuc.edu.
Website: http://www.umuc.edu/academic-programs/doctor-of-management.cfm

University of Maryland University College, The Graduate School, Program in Business Administration, Adelphi, MD 20783. Offers MBA. *Accreditation:* AACSB. *Program availability:* Part-time, evening/weekend, online learning. *Students:* 2,187 full-time (1,198 women), 533 part-time (262 women); includes 1,546 minority (1,029 Black or African American, non-Hispanic/Latino; 10 American Indian or Alaska Native, non-Hispanic/Latino; 170 Asian, non-Hispanic/Latino; 212 Hispanic/Latino; 15 Native Hawaiian or other Pacific Islander, non-Hispanic/Latino; 110 Two or more races, non-Hispanic/Latino), 55 international. Average age 36. 1,254 applicants, 100% accepted, 571 enrolled. In 2017, 982 master's awarded. *Degree requirements:* For master's, thesis or alternative, capstone course. *Application deadline:* Applications are processed on a rolling basis. Application fee: $50. Electronic applications accepted. *Financial support:* Federal Work-Study and scholarships/grants available. Support available to part-time students. Financial award application deadline: 6/1; financial award applicants required to submit FAFSA. *Unit head:* Ravi Mittal, Professor, 240-684-2143, Fax: 240-684-2960, E-mail: ravi.mittal@umuc.edu. *Application contact:* Coordinator, Graduate Admissions, 800-888-8682, Fax: 240-684-2151, E-mail: newgrad@umuc.edu.
Website: http://www.umuc.edu/academic-programs/masters-degrees/master-of-business-administration.cfm

University of Maryland University College, The Graduate School, Program in Management, Adelphi, MD 20783. Offers MS, Certificate. *Program availability:* Part-time, online learning. *Students:* 19 full-time (14 women), 3,240 part-time (2,143 women); includes 2,030 minority (1,554 Black or African American, non-Hispanic/Latino; 16 American Indian or Alaska Native, non-Hispanic/Latino; 111 Asian, non-Hispanic/Latino; 241 Hispanic/Latino; 8 Native Hawaiian or other Pacific Islander, non-Hispanic/Latino; 100 Two or more races, non-Hispanic/Latino), 46 international. Average age 36. 872 applicants, 100% accepted, 660 enrolled. In 2017, 848 master's, 230 other advanced

Business Administration and Management—General

degrees awarded. *Degree requirements:* For master's, thesis or alternative. *Application deadline:* Applications are processed on a rolling basis. Application fee: $50. Electronic applications accepted. *Financial support:* Federal Work-Study and scholarships/grants available. Support available to part-time students. Financial award application deadline: 6/1; financial award applicants required to submit FAFSA. *Unit head:* Harriet Smith, Program Director, 240-684-2423, Fax: 240-684-2401, E-mail: harriet.smith@umuc.edu. *Application contact:* Coordinator, Graduate Admissions, 888-888-8682, Fax: 240-684-2151, E-mail: newgrad@umuc.edu.
Website: http://www.umuc.edu/academic-programs/masters-degrees/management.cfm

University of Mary Washington, College of Business, Fredericksburg, VA 22401-5300. Offers MBA. *Program availability:* Part-time-only, evening/weekend. *Entrance requirements:* For master's, GMAT or GRE, minimum GPA of 3.0. Additional exam requirements/recommendations for international students: Required—TOEFL (minimum score 570 paper-based; 80 iBT), IELTS (minimum score 6.5). Electronic applications accepted. Application fee is waived when completed online. *Expenses:* Contact institution. *Faculty research:* Power laws/CEO compensation, sustainable competitive advantage, resistance to security implementation, profiling sustainable curriculums, perceived customer value.

University of Massachusetts Amherst, Graduate School, Interdisciplinary Programs, Dual Degree Program in Management and Public Policy and Administration, Amherst, MA 01003. Offers MPPA/MBA. *Accreditation:* AACSB. *Program availability:* Part-time. *Entrance requirements:* Additional exam requirements/recommendations for international students: Required—TOEFL (minimum score 600 paper-based; 100 iBT), IELTS (minimum score 7). Electronic applications accepted.

University of Massachusetts Amherst, Graduate School, Interdisciplinary Programs, Dual Degree Program in Management and Sport Management, Amherst, MA 01003. Offers MBA/MS. *Program availability:* Part-time. *Entrance requirements:* Additional exam requirements/recommendations for international students: Required—TOEFL (minimum score 600 paper-based; 100 iBT), IELTS (minimum score 7). Electronic applications accepted.

University of Massachusetts Amherst, Graduate School, Interdisciplinary Programs, Dual Degree Programs in Management and Engineering, Amherst, MA 01003. Offers MBA/MIE, MBA/MSEWRE, MSCE/MBA, MSME/MBA. *Program availability:* Part-time. *Entrance requirements:* Additional exam requirements/recommendations for international students: Required—TOEFL (minimum score 600 paper-based; 100 iBT), IELTS (minimum score 7). Electronic applications accepted.

University of Massachusetts Amherst, Graduate School, Isenberg School of Management, Program in Management, Amherst, MA 01003. Offers accounting (PhD); business administration (MBA); entrepreneurship (MBA); finance (MBA, PhD); healthcare administration (MBA); hospitality and tourism management (PhD); management science (PhD); marketing (MBA, PhD); organization studies (PhD); sport management (PhD); strategic management (PhD); MBA/MS. *Accreditation:* AACSB. *Program availability:* Part-time, evening/weekend, online learning. Terminal master's awarded for partial completion of doctoral program. *Degree requirements:* For doctorate, comprehensive exam, thesis/dissertation. *Entrance requirements:* For master's and doctorate, GMAT or GRE General Test. Additional exam requirements/recommendations for international students: Required—TOEFL (minimum score 550 paper-based; 80 iBT), IELTS (minimum score 6.5). Electronic applications accepted.

University of Massachusetts Boston, College of Management, Program in Business Administration, Boston, MA 02125-3393. Offers MBA. *Accreditation:* AACSB. *Program availability:* Part-time, evening/weekend. *Students:* 136 full-time (59 women), 175 part-time (96 women); includes 70 minority (17 Black or African American, non-Hispanic/Latino; 22 Asian, non-Hispanic/Latino; 25 Hispanic/Latino; 6 Two or more races, non-Hispanic/Latino), 76 international. Average age 31. 219 applicants, 33% accepted, 55 enrolled. In 2017, 84 master's awarded. *Entrance requirements:* For master's, GMAT, minimum GPA of 3.0. *Application deadline:* For fall admission, 3/1 for domestic students; for spring admission, 11/1 for domestic students. *Expenses:* Tuition, state resident: full-time $17,375. Tuition, nonresident: full-time $33,915. *Required fees:* $355. *Financial support:* Research assistantships, teaching assistantships, career-related internships or fieldwork, Federal Work-Study, and unspecified assistantships available. Support available to part-time students. Financial award application deadline: 3/1; financial award applicants required to submit FAFSA. *Faculty research:* International finance, human resource management, management information systems, investment and corporate finance, international marketing. *Application contact:* Graduate Admissions Coordinator, 617-287-6400, Fax: 617-287-6236, E-mail: bos.gadm@dpc.umassp.edu.

University of Massachusetts Dartmouth, Graduate School, Charlton College of Business, North Dartmouth, MA 02747-2300. Offers accounting and finance (MS, Postbaccalaureate Certificate), including accounting, finance (Postbaccalaureate Certificate); business administration (MBA), including business administration; decision and information sciences (MS), including healthcare management, technology management. *Program availability:* Part-time, 100% online, blended/hybrid learning. *Faculty:* 46 full-time (18 women), 19 part-time/adjunct (5 women). *Students:* 169 full-time (77 women), 188 part-time (103 women); includes 70 minority (19 Black or African American, non-Hispanic/Latino; 1 American Indian or Alaska Native, non-Hispanic/Latino; 22 Asian, non-Hispanic/Latino; 19 Hispanic/Latino; 9 Two or more races, non-Hispanic/Latino), 105 international. Average age 32. 233 applicants, 86% accepted, 145 enrolled. In 2017, 190 master's, 21 other advanced degrees awarded. *Degree requirements:* For master's, thesis (for some programs), thesis or project (for healthcare management); e-portfolio (for business administration). *Entrance requirements:* For master's, GMAT (or waiver), statement of purpose (minimum of 300 words), resume, official transcripts, 2 letters of recommendation; for Postbaccalaureate Certificate, statement of purpose (minimum of 300 words), resume, official transcripts. Additional exam requirements/recommendations for international students: Required—TOEFL (minimum score 533 paper-based; 72 iBT), IELTS (minimum score 6). *Application deadline:* For fall admission, 8/1 priority date for domestic students, 7/1 priority date for international students; for spring admission, 11/15 priority date for domestic students, 10/15 priority date for international students. Application fee: $60. Electronic applications accepted. *Expenses:* Tuition, state resident: full-time $15,449; part-time $643.71 per credit. Tuition, nonresident: full-time $27,880; part-time $1161.67 per credit. *Required fees:* $405; $25.88 per credit. Tuition and fees vary according to course load and reciprocity agreements. *Financial support:* In 2017–18, 2 research assistantships (averaging $8,000 per year) were awarded; teaching assistantships, tuition waivers (full and partial), and unspecified assistantships also available. Support available to part-time students. Financial award application deadline: 3/1; financial award applicants required to submit FAFSA. *Faculty research:* Effects of managerial behaviors and personality on strategic decision making, asset pricing, applications in multivariate diagnosis/pattern recognition and data mining, sustainable development, social media marketing. *Total annual research expenditures:* $233,000. *Unit head:* Melissa Pacheco, Assistant Dean of Graduate Programs, 508-999-8543, Fax: 508-999-8646, E-mail: mpacheco@umassd.edu. *Application contact:* Steven Briggs, Director of Recruitment and Marketing for Graduate Studies, 508-999-8604, Fax: 508-999-8183, E-mail: graduate@umassd.edu.
Website: http://www.umassd.edu/charlton

University of Massachusetts Lowell, Manning School of Business, Lowell, MA 01854. Offers business administration (MBA, PhD); healthcare innovation and entrepreneurship (MS). *Accreditation:* AACSB. *Program availability:* Part-time, evening/weekend. *Entrance requirements:* For master's, GMAT.

University of Memphis, Graduate School, Fogelman College of Business and Economics, Program in Business Administration, Memphis, TN 38152. Offers accounting (MBA, PhD); business administration (IMBA); economics (PhD); executive business administration (MBA); finance (PhD); management (PhD); marketing (MS); marketing and supply chain management (PhD); real estate development (MS); JD/MBA. *Accreditation:* AACSB. *Faculty:* 2 part-time/adjunct (0 women). *Students:* 166 full-time (76 women), 361 part-time (142 women); includes 161 minority (91 Black or African American, non-Hispanic/Latino; 51 Asian, non-Hispanic/Latino; 10 Hispanic/Latino; 9 Two or more races, non-Hispanic/Latino), 89 international. Average age 32. 263 applicants, 83% accepted, 157 enrolled. In 2017, 186 master's, 14 doctorates awarded. *Degree requirements:* For master's, comprehensive exam; for doctorate, comprehensive exam, thesis/dissertation. *Entrance requirements:* For master's, GMAT, resume; for doctorate, GMAT, interview, minimum GPA of 3.4, resume, letter of recommendation. Additional exam requirements/recommendations for international students: Required—TOEFL (minimum score 550 paper-based). *Application deadline:* For fall admission, 8/1 for domestic students; for spring admission, 12/1 for domestic students. Application fee: $35 ($60 for international students). *Financial support:* In 2017–18, 164 students received support, including 17 research assistantships with full tuition reimbursements available (averaging $53,750 per year), 13 teaching assistantships with full tuition reimbursements available (averaging $20,798 per year); career-related internships or fieldwork, Federal Work-Study, scholarships/grants, and unspecified assistantships also available. Financial award application deadline: 2/15; financial award applicants required to submit FAFSA. *Faculty research:* Competitive business strategy, finance microstructures, supply chain management innovations, health care economics, litigation risks and corporate audits. *Unit head:* Dr. Rajiv Grover, Dean, 901-678-3759, E-mail: rgrover@memphis.edu. *Application contact:* Dr. Carol V. Danehower, Associate Dean, 901-678-5402, Fax: 901-678-3579, E-mail: fcbegp@memphis.edu.
Website: https://web0.memphis.edu/gradcatalog/degreeprog/fcbe/fcbe.php

University of Miami, Miami Business School, Coral Gables, FL 33146. Offers M Acc, MBA, MHA, MIBS, MS Tax, MSBA, MSF, PhD, JD/MBA, MD/MBA. *Accreditation:* AACSB; CAHME (one or more programs are accredited). *Program availability:* Part-time, evening/weekend, 100% online, blended/hybrid learning. *Faculty:* 155 full-time (47 women), 14 part-time/adjunct (5 women). *Students:* 987 full-time (411 women); includes 549 minority (79 Black or African American, non-Hispanic/Latino; 2 American Indian or Alaska Native, non-Hispanic/Latino; 174 Asian, non-Hispanic/Latino; 280 Hispanic/Latino; 14 Two or more races, non-Hispanic/Latino). Average age 30. 2,564 applicants, 38% accepted, 450 enrolled. In 2017, 476 master's, 7 doctorates awarded. Terminal master's awarded for partial completion of doctoral program. *Degree requirements:* For master's, comprehensive exam; for doctorate, comprehensive exam, thesis/dissertation. *Entrance requirements:* For master's, GMAT or GRE; for doctorate, GRE General Test. Additional exam requirements/recommendations for international students: Required—TOEFL (minimum score 587 paper-based, 94 iBT) or IELTS (7). *Application deadline:* For fall admission, 6/30 priority date for domestic students, 5/30 priority date for international students; for spring admission, 10/31 priority date for domestic students, 9/30 priority date for international students. Applications are processed on a rolling basis. Electronic applications accepted. *Expenses:* $1,960 per credit hour, $1,052 annual mandatory fees. *Financial support:* In 2017–18, 184 students received support, including 2 fellowships with full tuition reimbursements available (averaging $20,000 per year), 10 research assistantships with full and partial tuition reimbursements available (averaging $20,000 per year), 5 teaching assistantships with full and partial tuition reimbursements available (averaging $20,000 per year); career-related internships or fieldwork, Federal Work-Study, institutionally sponsored loans, scholarships/grants, and unspecified assistantships also available. Support available to part-time students. Financial award application deadline: 3/26; financial award applicants required to submit FAFSA. *Faculty research:* Behavioral finance; computational economics; consumer research; risk perception; consumer behavior; consumer choice research; behavioral decision theory; business analytics; point processes; longitudinal data analyses; international business; global business strategy, joint ventures, and alliances; emerging economies; global economic growth and development, money and financial markets, and computed dynamic models; health policy; innovative payment mechanisms. *Total annual research expenditures:* $703,773. *Unit head:* Dr. John Quelch, Dean, 305-284-6515, Fax: 305-284-6526, E-mail: jquelch@miami.edu. *Application contact:* Loubna Bouamane, Director of Graduate Business Recruiting and Admissions, 305-284-2510, Fax: 305-284-5905, E-mail: loubna@miami.edu.
Website: http://www.bus.miami.edu/grad

University of Michigan, Ross School of Business, Ann Arbor, MI 48109-1234. Offers accounting (M Acc); business (MBA); business administration (PhD); supply chain management (MSCM); JD/MBA; MBA/M Arch; MBA/M Eng; MBA/MA; MBA/MEM; MBA/MHSA; MBA/MM; MBA/MPP; MBA/MS; MBA/MSE; MBA/MSI; MBA/MSW; MBA/MUP; MD/MBA; MHSA/MBA. *Accreditation:* AACSB. *Program availability:* Part-time, evening/weekend. *Degree requirements:* For doctorate, comprehensive exam, thesis/dissertation, oral defense of dissertation, preliminary exam. *Entrance requirements:* For master's, GMAT or GRE, completion of equivalent of four-year U.S. bachelor's degree, two letters of recommendation, essays, resume; for doctorate, GMAT or GRE. Additional exam requirements/recommendations for international students: Required—TOEFL (minimum score 600 paper-based; 100 iBT). Electronic applications accepted. *Expenses:* Tuition, state resident: full-time $22,368; part-time $1201 per credit hour. Tuition, nonresident: full-time $45,156; part-time $2467 per credit hour. *Required fees:* $376 per term. Tuition and fees vary according to course load, degree level and program. *Faculty research:* Finance and accounting, marketing, technology and operations management, corporate strategy, management and organizations.

University of Michigan–Dearborn, College of Business, MBA Program, Dearborn, MI 48126. Offers MBA. *Accreditation:* AACSB. *Program availability:* Part-time, evening/weekend, 100% online. *Faculty:* 45 full-time (19 women), 4 part-time/adjunct (2 women). *Students:* 21 full-time (13 women), 199 part-time (61 women); includes 44 minority (9 Black or African American, non-Hispanic/Latino; 21 Asian, non-Hispanic/Latino; 11 Hispanic/Latino; 3 Two or more races, non-Hispanic/Latino), 17 international. Average age 30. 185 applicants, 55% accepted, 69 enrolled. In 2017, 55 master's awarded. *Entrance requirements:* For master's, GMAT or GRE, equivalent of four-year U.S. bachelor's degree from regionally-accredited institution, undergraduate course in finite math, pre-calculus, or calculus. Additional exam requirements/recommendations for international students: Required—TOEFL (minimum score 560 paper-based; 84 iBT), IELTS (minimum score 6.5). *Application deadline:* For fall admission, 8/1 for domestic students, 5/1 for international students; for winter admission, 12/1 for domestic students, 9/1 for international students; for spring admission, 4/1 for domestic students, 1/1 for international students. Applications are processed on a rolling basis. Application fee: $60. Electronic applications accepted. *Expenses:* $883 per credit hour in-state; $1,376 per credit hour out-state. *Financial support:* In 2017–18, 41 students received support. Scholarships/grants and non-resident tuition scholarships available. Financial award application deadline: 3/1; financial award applicants required to submit FAFSA. *Faculty*

research: Business intelligence, behavioral finance, brand management and new media, management education, operations strategy. *Unit head:* Dr. Michael Kamen, Director, College of Business Graduate Programs, 313-593-5460, E-mail: mkamen@umich.edu. *Application contact:* Joan Doherty, Academic Advisor/Counselor, 313-593-5460, Fax: 313-271-9838, E-mail: umd-gradbusiness@umich.edu.
Website: http://umdearborn.edu/cob/mba-program/

University of Michigan–Flint, School of Management, Flint, MI 48502-1950. Offers MBA, MS, MSA, Graduate Certificate, Post-Master's Certificate. *Accreditation:* AACSB. *Program availability:* Part-time, evening/weekend, mixed mode format. *Faculty:* 32 full-time (5 women), 8 part-time/adjunct (2 women). *Students:* 19 full-time (8 women), 179 part-time (62 women); includes 39 minority (18 Black or African American, non-Hispanic/Latino; 1 American Indian or Alaska Native, non-Hispanic/Latino; 13 Asian, non-Hispanic/Latino; 5 Hispanic/Latino; 2 Two or more races, non-Hispanic/Latino), 29 international. Average age 34. 141 applicants, 59% accepted, 41 enrolled. In 2017, 81 master's, 6 other advanced degrees awarded. *Degree requirements:* For master's, thesis or alternative. *Entrance requirements:* For master's, GMAT, GRE or GMAT waiver, bachelor's degree in arts, sciences, and engineering, or business administration from regionally-accredited college or university with minimum GPA of 3.0; for other advanced degree, bachelor's degree from regionally-accredited college with minimum GPA of 3.0 and completion of college-level math, statistics, or quantitative course (for Graduate Certificate); MBA or equivalent from accredited college or university (for Post-Master's Certificate). Additional exam requirements/recommendations for international students: Required—TOEFL (minimum score 84 iBT), IELTS (minimum score 6.5). *Application deadline:* For fall admission, 8/1 for domestic students, 5/1 for international students; for winter admission, 11/15 for domestic students, 9/1 for international students; for spring admission, 3/15 for domestic students, 1/1 for international students; for summer admission, 5/15 for domestic students. Applications are processed on a rolling basis. Application fee: $55. Electronic applications accepted. *Expenses:* Contact institution. *Financial support:* Federal Work-Study, scholarships/grants, and unspecified assistantships available. Support available to part-time students. Financial award application deadline: 3/1; financial award applicants required to submit FAFSA. *Unit head:* Dr. Scott Johnson, Dean, School of Management, 810-762-6579, Fax: 810-237-6685, E-mail: scotjohn@umflint.edu. *Application contact:* Bradley T. Maki, Director of Graduate Admissions, 810-762-3171, Fax: 810-766-6789, E-mail: bmaki@umflint.edu.
Website: https://www.umflint.edu/som/graduate-business-programs

University of Minnesota, Duluth, Graduate School, Labovitz School of Business and Economics, Program in Business Administration, Duluth, MN 55812-2496. Offers MBA. *Accreditation:* AACSB. *Program availability:* Part-time, evening/weekend. *Entrance requirements:* For master's, GMAT, minimum GPA of 3.0; course work in accounting, business administration, and economics. Additional exam requirements/recommendations for international students: Required—TOEFL (minimum score 550 paper-based; 79 iBT). *Expenses:* Contact institution. *Faculty research:* Regional economic analysis, marketing, management, human resources, organizational behavior.

University of Minnesota Rochester, Graduate Programs, Rochester, MN 55904. Offers bioinformatics and computational biology (MS, PhD); business administration (MBA); occupational therapy (MOT).

University of Minnesota, Twin Cities Campus, Carlson School of Management, Minneapolis, MN 55455. Offers EMBA, M Acc, MA, MBA, MBT, MS, PhD, JD/MBA, MBA/MPP, MBA/MSBA, MD/MBA, MHA/MBA, Pharm D/MBA. *Accreditation:* AACSB. *Program availability:* Part-time, evening/weekend. *Faculty:* 140 full-time (42 women), 46 part-time/adjunct (9 women). *Students:* 589 full-time (254 women), 1,059 part-time (366 women); includes 213 minority (25 Black or African American, non-Hispanic/Latino; 5 American Indian or Alaska Native, non-Hispanic/Latino; 106 Asian, non-Hispanic/Latino; 51 Hispanic/Latino; 1 Native Hawaiian or other Pacific Islander, non-Hispanic/Latino; 25 Two or more races, non-Hispanic/Latino), 333 international. Average age 28. 2,219 applicants, 42% accepted, 535 enrolled. In 2017, 559 master's, 14 doctorates awarded. Terminal master's awarded for partial completion of doctoral program. *Degree requirements:* For doctorate, comprehensive exam, thesis/dissertation. *Entrance requirements:* For master's, GMAT or GRE. Additional exam requirements/recommendations for international students: Required—TOEFL, IELTS, PTE. Application fee: $75 ($95 for international students). Electronic applications accepted. *Expenses:* Contact institution. *Financial support:* Fellowships with full and partial tuition reimbursements, research assistantships with full tuition reimbursements, teaching assistantships with full and partial tuition reimbursements, career-related internships or fieldwork, Federal Work-Study, institutionally sponsored loans, scholarships/grants, health care benefits, tuition waivers (full and partial), and unspecified assistantships available. Support available to part-time students. Financial award application deadline: 4/1; financial award applicants required to submit FAFSA. *Faculty research:* Finance and accounting: financial reporting, asset pricing models and corporate finance; information and decision sciences: on-line auctions, information transparency and recommender systems; marketing: psychological influences on consumer behavior, brand equity, pricing and marketing channels; operations: lean manufacturing, quality management and global supply chains; strategic management and organization: global strategy, networks, entrepreneurship and innovation, sustainability. *Unit head:* Prof. Alok Gupta, Associate Dean of Faculty and Research, 612-626-0276, Fax: 612-624-6374, E-mail: gupta037@umn.edu. *Application contact:* Graduate School Admissions, 612-625-3014, Fax: 612-625-6002, E-mail: gsquest@umn.edu.
Website: http://www.carlsonschool.umn.edu

University of Mississippi, Graduate School, School of Business Administration, University, MS 38677. Offers business administration (MBA, PhD); finance (PhD); management (PhD); management information systems (PhD); marketing (PhD); JD/MBA. *Accreditation:* AACSB. *Faculty:* 58 full-time (15 women), 8 part-time/adjunct (3 women). *Students:* 71 full-time (26 women), 112 part-time (27 women); includes 11 minority (4 Black or African American, non-Hispanic/Latino; 3 Asian, non-Hispanic/Latino; 1 Hispanic/Latino; 3 Two or more races, non-Hispanic/Latino), 17 international. Average age 29. In 2017, 83 master's, 6 doctorates awarded. *Entrance requirements:* For master's, GMAT, minimum GPA of 3.0; for doctorate, GMAT. Additional exam requirements/recommendations for international students: Required—TOEFL. *Application deadline:* For fall admission, 2/1 priority date for domestic students; for spring admission, 11/1 for domestic students; for summer admission, 4/1 for domestic students. Applications are processed on a rolling basis. Application fee: $50. Electronic applications accepted. *Financial support:* Fellowships, career-related internships or fieldwork, scholarships/grants, tuition waivers (full), and unspecified assistantships available. Financial award application deadline: 3/1; financial award applicants required to submit FAFSA. *Unit head:* Dr. Ken Cyree, Dean, 662-915-5820, Fax: 662-915-5821, E-mail: info@bus.olemiss.edu. *Application contact:* Ashley Jones McGee, Director of MBA and MHA Administration, 662-915-5483, E-mail: ajones@olemiss.edu.
Website: http://www.olemissbusiness.com/

University of Missouri, Office of Research and Graduate Studies, Robert J. Trulaske, Sr. College of Business, Program in Business Administration, Columbia, MO 65211. Offers business administration (MBA); executive business administration (MBA); finance (PhD); management (PhD); marketing (PhD); MBA/JD; MBA/MHA; MBA/MSIE. *Accreditation:* AACSB. *Degree requirements:* For doctorate, thesis/dissertation.

Entrance requirements: For master's and doctorate, GMAT, minimum GPA of 3.0. Additional exam requirements/recommendations for international students: Required—TOEFL (minimum score 500 paper-based; 61 iBT). Electronic applications accepted.

University of Missouri–Kansas City, Henry W. Bloch School of Management, Kansas City, MO 64110-2499. Offers accounting (MS); finance (MS); public affairs (MPA, PhD); JD/MBA; LL M/MPA. PhD (interdisciplinary) offered through the School of Graduate Studies. *Accreditation:* AACSB; NASPAA. *Program availability:* Part-time, evening/weekend. Terminal master's awarded for partial completion of doctoral program. *Entrance requirements:* For master's, GMAT, GRE, 2 essays, 2 references, support of employer; for doctorate, GRE, minimum GPA of 3.0. Additional exam requirements/recommendations for international students: Required—TOEFL (minimum score 550 paper-based; 80 iBT). Electronic applications accepted. *Faculty research:* Entrepreneurship, finance, non-profit, risk management.

University of Missouri–St. Louis, College of Business Administration, St. Louis, MO 63121. Offers accounting (M Acc); business administration (MBA, DBA, PhD, Certificate), including logistics and supply chain management (PhD); business intelligence (Certificate); cybersecurity (Certificate); digital and social media marketing (Certificate); human resources management (Certificate); information systems (MS); logistics and supply chain management (Certificate); marketing management (Certificate). *Program availability:* Part-time, evening/weekend. *Faculty:* 51 full-time (21 women), 25 part-time/adjunct (5 women). *Students:* 146 full-time (77 women), 326 part-time (143 women); includes 82 minority (32 Black or African American, non-Hispanic/Latino; 1 American Indian or Alaska Native, non-Hispanic/Latino; 34 Asian, non-Hispanic/Latino; 11 Hispanic/Latino; 4 Two or more races, non-Hispanic/Latino), 89 international. 276 applicants, 83% accepted, 142 enrolled. *Degree requirements:* For doctorate, thesis/dissertation. *Entrance requirements:* For master's, GMAT, 2 letters of recommendation; for doctorate, GMAT or GRE, 3 letters of recommendation. Additional exam requirements/recommendations for international students: Recommended—TOEFL (minimum score 550 paper-based; 79 iBT), IELTS (minimum score 6.5). *Application deadline:* For fall admission, 7/1 priority date for domestic and international students; for spring admission, 12/1 priority date for domestic and international students. Applications are processed on a rolling basis. Application fee: $50 ($40 for international students). Electronic applications accepted. *Expenses:* Tuition, state resident: part-time $476.50 per credit hour. Tuition, nonresident: part-time $1169.70 per credit hour. *Financial support:* Research assistantships with tuition reimbursements, teaching assistantships with tuition reimbursements, career-related internships or fieldwork, Federal Work-Study, and institutionally sponsored loans available. Support available to part-time students. Financial award application deadline: 4/1; financial award applicants required to submit FAFSA. *Faculty research:* Statistical decision aids, commercial banking, corporate finance, operations management, information systems. *Unit head:* Charles E. Hoffman, Dean, 314-516-6109, Fax: 314-516-6420. *Application contact:* 314-516-5458, Fax: 314-516-6996, E-mail: gradadm@umsl.edu.
Website: http://www.umsl.edu/divisions/business/

University of Missouri–St. Louis, Graduate School, Program in Public Policy Administration, St. Louis, MO 63121. Offers local government management (MPPA, Certificate); nonprofit management and leadership (MPPA, Certificate); policy and program evaluation (MPPA, Certificate). *Accreditation:* NASPAA. *Program availability:* Part-time, evening/weekend. *Faculty:* 2 full-time (1 woman), 4 part-time/adjunct (3 women). *Students:* 9 full-time (5 women), 34 part-time (19 women); includes 10 minority (6 Black or African American, non-Hispanic/Latino; 2 Asian, non-Hispanic/Latino; 1 Hispanic/Latino; 1 Two or more races, non-Hispanic/Latino). 34 applicants, 79% accepted, 14 enrolled. *Degree requirements:* For master's, exit project. *Entrance requirements:* For master's, 3 letters of recommendation, personal statement. Additional exam requirements/recommendations for international students: Recommended—TOEFL (minimum score 550 paper-based), IELTS (minimum score 6.5). *Application deadline:* For fall admission, 7/1 priority date for domestic and international students; for spring admission, 12/1 priority date for domestic and international students. Applications are processed on a rolling basis. Application fee: $50 ($40 for international students). Electronic applications accepted. *Expenses:* Tuition, state resident: part-time $476.50 per credit hour. Tuition, nonresident: part-time $1169.70 per credit hour. *Financial support:* Research assistantships with tuition reimbursements and career-related internships or fieldwork available. Financial award application deadline: 4/1; financial award applicants required to submit FAFSA. *Faculty research:* Urban policy, public finance, evaluation. *Unit head:* Daniel Sise, Interim Director, 314-516-6378, Fax: 314-516-5210, E-mail: sised@umsl.edu. *Application contact:* 314-516-5458, Fax: 314-516-6996, E-mail: gradadm@umsl.edu.
Website: http://www.umsl.edu/gradschool/ppa/

University of Mobile, Graduate Studies, Program in Business Administration, Mobile, AL 36613. Offers MBA. *Accreditation:* ACBSP. *Program availability:* Part-time, evening/weekend. *Degree requirements:* For master's, comprehensive exam. *Entrance requirements:* For master's, GMAT. Additional exam requirements/recommendations for international students: Required—TOEFL (minimum score 550 paper-based; 80 iBT). *Application deadline:* For fall admission, 8/3 priority date for domestic and international students; for spring admission, 12/23 priority date for domestic and international students. Applications are processed on a rolling basis. Application fee: $40 ($50 for international students). Electronic applications accepted. *Expenses:* $485 per credit hour. *Financial support:* Application deadline: 8/1; applicants required to submit FAFSA. *Faculty research:* Management, personnel management, small business, diversity. *Unit head:* Dr. Todd Greer, Dean, School of Business, 251-442-2701, Fax: 251-442-2523, E-mail: tgreer@umobile.edu. *Application contact:* Brian Boyle, Director of Recruitment, 251-442-2727, Fax: 251-442-2523.
Website: https://umobile.edu/academics/school-of-business/mba/

University of Montana, Graduate School, School of Business Administration, MBA Program, Missoula, MT 59812. Offers MBA, JD/MBA, MBA/Pharm D. *Accreditation:* AACSB. *Program availability:* Part-time, evening/weekend, online learning. *Degree requirements:* For master's, thesis optional. *Entrance requirements:* For master's, GMAT. Additional exam requirements/recommendations for international students: Required—TOEFL. *Faculty research:* Information systems, research methods, international business, human resource management, marketing.

University of Montevallo, Stephens College of Business, Montevallo, AL 35115. Offers MBA. *Accreditation:* AACSB. *Program availability:* Part-time, evening/weekend. *Students:* 14 full-time (6 women), 25 part-time (17 women); includes 7 minority (3 Black or African American, non-Hispanic/Latino; 1 Asian, non-Hispanic/Latino; 2 Hispanic/Latino; 1 Two or more races, non-Hispanic/Latino), 3 international. *Degree requirements:* For master's, comprehensive exam. *Entrance requirements:* Additional exam requirements/recommendations for international students: Required—TOEFL (minimum score 550 paper-based). *Application deadline:* For fall admission, 7/15 for domestic students; for spring admission, 11/15 for domestic students. Application fee: $30. *Expenses:* Tuition, state resident: full-time $9888. Tuition, nonresident: full-time $21,144. *Required fees:* $1920. *Unit head:* Dr. Stephen H. Craft, Dean, 205-665-6540, E-mail: scob@montevallo.edu. *Application contact:* 205-665-6540, E-mail: scob@montevallo.edu.
Website: https://www.montevallo.edu/academics/colleges/college-of-business/mba/

Business Administration and Management—General

University of Mount Olive, Graduate Programs, Mount Olive, NC 28365. Offers business (MBA); education (M Ed); nursing (MSN). *Program availability:* Online learning.

University of Nebraska at Kearney, College of Business and Technology, Department of Business, Kearney, NE 68849-0001. Offers accounting (MBA); generalist (MBA); human resources (MBA); human services (MBA); marketing (MBA). *Accreditation:* AACSB. *Program availability:* Part-time, evening/weekend. *Degree requirements:* For master's, thesis optional, capstone course. *Entrance requirements:* For master's, GRE or GMAT (if no significant managerial experience), letters of recommendation, essay, resume. Additional exam requirements/recommendations for international students: Recommended—TOEFL (minimum score 550 paper-based; 79 iBT), IELTS (minimum score 6.5). Electronic applications accepted. *Faculty research:* Small business financial management, employment law, expert systems, international trade and marketing, environmental economics.

University of Nebraska at Omaha, Graduate Studies, College of Business Administration, Program in Business Administration, Omaha, NE 68182. Offers business administration (MBA); business for bioscientists (Certificate); executive business administration (EMBA); human resources and training (Certificate). *Accreditation:* AACSB. *Program availability:* Part-time, evening/weekend. *Degree requirements:* For master's, thesis (for some programs), capstone course. *Entrance requirements:* For master's, GMAT or GRE, minimum GPA of 3.0, official transcripts, resume; for Certificate, minimum GPA of 3.0, official transcripts, resume, letter of recommendation, statement of purpose. Additional exam requirements/recommendations for international students: Required—TOEFL, IELTS, PTE. Electronic applications accepted.

University of Nebraska–Lincoln, Graduate College, College of Business Administration, Interdepartmental Area of Business, Lincoln, NE 68588. Offers accountancy (PhD); business (MBA); finance (MA, PhD), including business; management (MA, PhD), including business; marketing (MA, PhD), including business; JD/MBA; M Arch/MBA. *Accreditation:* AACSB. *Program availability:* Part-time, online learning. *Degree requirements:* For doctorate, comprehensive exam, thesis/dissertation. *Entrance requirements:* For master's and doctorate, GMAT. Additional exam requirements/recommendations for international students: Required—TOEFL (minimum score 550 paper-based). Electronic applications accepted.

University of Nevada, Las Vegas, Graduate College, Lee Business School, Program in Business Administration, Las Vegas, NV 89154-6031. Offers business administration (Certificate); DMD/MBA; MBA/JD; MBA/MS. *Accreditation:* AACSB. *Program availability:* Part-time, evening/weekend. *Faculty:* 1 full-time (0 women), 3 part-time/adjunct (2 women). *Students:* 124 full-time (51 women), 70 part-time (27 women); includes 60 minority (8 Black or African American, non-Hispanic/Latino; 24 Asian, non-Hispanic/Latino; 18 Hispanic/Latino; 10 Two or more races, non-Hispanic/Latino), 18 international. Average age 33. 86 applicants, 69% accepted, 48 enrolled. In 2017, 81 master's awarded. *Degree requirements:* For master's, capstone course. *Entrance requirements:* For master's, GMAT, 2 letters of recommendation; statement of purpose. Additional exam requirements/recommendations for international students: Required—TOEFL (minimum score 550 paper-based; 80 iBT), IELTS (minimum score 7). *Application deadline:* For fall admission, 7/15 for domestic students, 2/15 for international students; for spring admission, 11/15 for domestic students, 10/1 for international students; for summer admission, 4/1 for domestic students. Application fee: $60 ($95 for international students). Electronic applications accepted. *Expenses:* $275 per credit, $850 per course, $7,969 per year resident, $22,157 per year non-resident, $7,094 non-resident fee (7 credits or more), $1,307 annual health insurance fee. *Financial support:* In 2017–18, 19 students received support, including 12 research assistantships with full and partial tuition reimbursements available (averaging $13,188 per year), 7 teaching assistantships with full and partial tuition reimbursements available (averaging $11,250 per year); institutionally sponsored loans, scholarships/grants, health care benefits, and unspecified assistantships also available. Financial award application deadline: 3/15; financial award applicants required to submit FAFSA. *Faculty research:* Economic effects on wages; benefits and economic effects of risk, uncertainty; asymmetric information: adverse selection, moral hazard; business processes. *Unit head:* Dr. Vincent Hsu, Director of Academic Programs/Professor, 702-895-3842, Fax: 702-895-3632, E-mail: vincent.hsu@unlv.edu.
Website: http://business.unlv.edu/mba/

University of Nevada, Reno, Graduate School, College of Business Administration, Department of Business Administration, Reno, NV 89557. Offers MBA. *Accreditation:* AACSB. *Program availability:* Part-time, evening/weekend, online learning. *Entrance requirements:* For master's, GMAT, minimum GPA of 2.75. Additional exam requirements/recommendations for international students: Required—TOEFL (minimum score 500 paper-based; 61 iBT), IELTS (minimum score 6). Electronic applications accepted.

University of New Brunswick Fredericton, School of Graduate Studies, Faculty of Business Administration, Fredericton, NB E3B 5A3, Canada. Offers business administration (MBA); engineering management (MBA); entrepreneurship (MBA); sports and recreation management (MBA); MBA/LL B. *Program availability:* Part-time. *Degree requirements:* For master's, thesis optional. *Entrance requirements:* For master's, GMAT (minimum score 550), minimum GPA of 3.0; 3-5 years of work experience; 3 letters of reference with at least one academic reference. Additional exam requirements/recommendations for international students: Required—TOEFL (minimum score 580 paper-based; 92 iBT) or IELTS (minimum score 7). Electronic applications accepted. *Faculty research:* Entrepreneurship, finance, law, sport and recreation management, engineering management.

University of New Brunswick Saint John, Faculty of Business, Saint John, NB E2L 4L5, Canada. Offers administration (MBA); electronic commerce (MBA); international business (MBA); natural resource management (MBA). *Program availability:* Part-time. *Entrance requirements:* For master's, GMAT (minimum score of 550) or GRE (minimum 54th percentile), minimum GPA of 3.0. Additional exam requirements/recommendations for international students: Required—TOEFL (minimum score 580 paper-based; 93 iBT), TWE (minimum score 4.5). Electronic applications accepted. *Expenses:* Contact institution. *Faculty research:* International business, project management, innovation and technology management; business use of Weblogs and podcasts to communicate; corporate governance; high-involvement work systems; international competitiveness; supply chain management and logistics.

University of New Hampshire, Graduate School Manchester Campus, Manchester, NH 03101. Offers business administration (MBA); cybersecurity policy and risk management (MS); educational administration and supervision (Ed S); educational studies (M Ed); elementary education (M Ed); information technology (MS); public administration (MPA); public health (MPH, Certificate); secondary education (M Ed, MAT); social work (MSW); substance use disorders (Certificate). *Program availability:* Part-time, evening/weekend. *Students:* 13 full-time (6 women), 17 part-time (9 women); includes 7 minority (1 Black or African American, non-Hispanic/Latino; 4 Asian, non-Hispanic/Latino; 1 Hispanic/Latino; 1 Two or more races, non-Hispanic/Latino), 10 international. Average age 33. 42 applicants, 71% accepted, 8 enrolled. In 2017, 4 master's awarded. *Entrance requirements:* Additional exam requirements/recommendations for international students: Required—TOEFL (minimum score 550 paper-based; 80 iBT). *Application deadline:* For fall admission, 6/1 for domestic students, 4/1 for international students; for spring admission, 12/1 for domestic students. Application fee: $65. Electronic applications accepted. *Financial support:* Fellowships, research assistantships, teaching assistantships, Federal Work-Study, scholarships/grants, health care benefits, and unspecified assistantships available. Support available to part-time students. Financial award application deadline: 2/15; financial award applicants required to submit FAFSA. *Unit head:* Candice Morey, Educational Programs Coordinator, 603-641-4313, E-mail: unhm.gradcenter@unh.edu.
Website: http://www.gradschool.unh.edu/manchester/

University of New Hampshire, Graduate School, Peter T. Paul College of Business and Economics, Program in Business Administration, Durham, NH 03824. Offers MBA, MBA/JD. *Accreditation:* AACSB. *Program availability:* Part-time, evening/weekend, online learning. *Students:* 82 full-time (24 women), 172 part-time (52 women); includes 20 minority (5 Black or African American, non-Hispanic/Latino; 12 Asian, non-Hispanic/Latino; 2 Hispanic/Latino; 1 Two or more races, non-Hispanic/Latino), 15 international. Average age 33. 185 applicants, 68% accepted, 93 enrolled. In 2017, 105 master's awarded. *Entrance requirements:* For master's, GMAT. Additional exam requirements/recommendations for international students: Required—TOEFL (minimum score 550 paper-based; 80 iBT). *Application deadline:* For fall admission, 6/1 for domestic students, 4/1 for international students; for spring admission, 12/1 for domestic students. Application fee: $65. Electronic applications accepted. *Expenses:* Contact institution. *Financial support:* In 2017–18, 39 students received support, including 1 research assistantship; fellowships, teaching assistantships, career-related internships or fieldwork, Federal Work-Study, scholarships/grants, and tuition waivers (full and partial) also available. Financial award application deadline: 2/15. *Unit head:* Andrew Mitchell, Coordinator, 603-862-0809. *Application contact:* Wendy Harris, Administrative Assistant III, 603-862-3326, E-mail: mba.info@unh.edu.
Website: http://paulcollege.unh.edu/academics/graduate-programs/mba

★ **University of New Haven,** Graduate School, College of Business, Executive Program in Business Administration, West Haven, CT 06516. Offers EMBA. *Accreditation:* AACSB. *Program availability:* Part-time, evening/weekend. *Students:* 22 full-time (11 women); includes 6 minority (1 Black or African American, non-Hispanic/Latino; 2 Asian, non-Hispanic/Latino; 2 Hispanic/Latino; 1 Two or more races, non-Hispanic/Latino). Average age 45. 18 applicants, 100% accepted, 12 enrolled. *Entrance requirements:* Additional exam requirements/recommendations for international students: Required—TOEFL (minimum score 80 iBT), IELTS, PTE. *Application deadline:* Applications are processed on a rolling basis. Application fee: $50. Electronic applications accepted. Application fee is waived when completed online. *Expenses:* Contact institution. *Financial support:* Application deadline: 5/1. *Unit head:* Darell Singleterry, Program Director, 203-932-1085, E-mail: dsingleterry@newhaven.edu. *Application contact:* Michelle Mason, Director of Graduate Enrollment, 203-932-7067, E-mail: mmason@newhaven.edu.
Website: http://www.newhaven.edu/6465/

See Display on the next page and Close-Up on page 185.

★ **University of New Haven,** Graduate School, College of Business, Program in Business Administration, West Haven, CT 06516. Offers accounting (MBA); business administration (MBA); business intelligence (MBA); business policy and strategic leadership (MBA); finance (MBA), including chartered financial analyst; global marketing (MBA); human resources management (MBA); sport management (MBA). *Accreditation:* AACSB. *Program availability:* Part-time, evening/weekend. *Students:* 123 full-time (56 women), 67 part-time (28 women); includes 53 minority (27 Black or African American, non-Hispanic/Latino; 11 Asian, non-Hispanic/Latino; 12 Hispanic/Latino; 3 Two or more races, non-Hispanic/Latino), 50 international. Average age 28. 148 applicants, 89% accepted, 67 enrolled. In 2017, 106 master's awarded. *Entrance requirements:* For master's, GMAT. Additional exam requirements/recommendations for international students: Required—TOEFL (minimum score 80 iBT), IELTS, PTE. *Application deadline:* Applications are processed on a rolling basis. Application fee: $50. Electronic applications accepted. Application fee is waived when completed online. *Expenses: Tuition:* Full-time $16,020; part-time $890 per credit hour. *Required fees:* $220; $90 per term. *Financial support:* Research assistantships with partial tuition reimbursements, teaching assistantships with partial tuition reimbursements, career-related internships or fieldwork, Federal Work-Study, scholarships/grants, and unspecified assistantships available. Support available to part-time students. Financial award applicants required to submit FAFSA. *Unit head:* Darell Singleterry, Director, 203-932-1085, E-mail: dsingleterry@newhaven.edu. *Application contact:* Michelle Mason, Director of Graduate Enrollment, 203-932-7067, E-mail: mmason@newhaven.edu.
Website: http://www.newhaven.edu/business/graduate-programs/mba/index.php

See Display on the next page and Close-Up on page 185.

University of New Mexico, Anderson School of Management, Albuquerque, NM 87131. Offers EMBA, M Acct, MBA, MS, JD/M Acct, JD/MBA, MBA/MA, MBA/MEME, MBA/Pharm D. *Accreditation:* AACSB. *Program availability:* Part-time, evening/weekend. *Faculty:* 62 full-time (25 women), 42 part-time/adjunct (16 women). *Students:* 288 full-time (136 women), 364 part-time (206 women); includes 314 minority (10 Black or African American, non-Hispanic/Latino; 27 American Indian or Alaska Native, non-Hispanic/Latino; 28 Asian, non-Hispanic/Latino; 229 Hispanic/Latino; 1 Native Hawaiian or other Pacific Islander, non-Hispanic/Latino; 19 Two or more races, non-Hispanic/Latino), 59 international. Average age 31. 325 applicants, 60% accepted, 166 enrolled. In 2017, 274 master's awarded. *Degree requirements:* For master's, minimum of 33 credit hours, capstone course, minimum GPA of 3.0. *Entrance requirements:* For master's, GMAT or GRE (minimum score of 500), minimum GPA of 3.0 on last 60 hours of college coursework including any post baccalaureate work. Additional exam requirements/recommendations for international students: Required—TOEFL (minimum score 550 paper-based; 79 iBT), IELTS (minimum score 6.5). *Application deadline:* For fall admission, 4/1 priority date for domestic and international students; for spring admission, 10/1 priority date for domestic and international students. Applications are processed on a rolling basis. Application fee: $50. Electronic applications accepted. *Expenses:* Contact institution. *Financial support:* In 2017–18, 89 students received support, including 50 fellowships (averaging $15,746 per year), 52 research assistantships with partial tuition reimbursements available (averaging $15,400 per year); career-related internships or fieldwork, Federal Work-Study, scholarships/grants, and unspecified assistantships also available. Support available to part-time students. Financial award application deadline: 6/1; financial award applicants required to submit FAFSA. *Faculty research:* Organizational and social aspects of accounting, international management of technology and entrepreneurship, business ethics and corporate social responsibility, marketing, information assurance and fraud. *Unit head:* Dr. Craig White, Dean, 505-277-1792, E-mail: cwhite@unm.edu. *Application contact:* Lisa Beauchene, Student Recruitment Specialist, 505-277-6471, E-mail: andersonadvising@unm.edu.
Website: http://www.mgt.unm.edu

University of New Orleans, Graduate School, College of Business Administration, Program in Business Administration, New Orleans, LA 70148. Offers MBA. *Accreditation:* AACSB. *Degree requirements:* For master's, thesis optional. *Entrance* *requirements:* For master's, GMAT. Additional exam requirements/recommendations for international students: Required—TOEFL (minimum score 550 paper-based; 79 iBT). Electronic applications accepted.

University of North Alabama, College of Business, Florence, AL 35632-0001. Offers business administration (MBA), including accounting, enterprise resource planning systems, executive, finance, health care management, information systems, international business, project management. *Accreditation:* AACSB; ACBSP. *Program availability:* Part-time, 100% online, blended/hybrid learning. *Faculty:* 26 full-time (1 woman), 4 part-time/adjunct (0 women). *Students:* 178 full-time (78 women), 498 part-time (237 women); includes 229 minority (92 Black or African American, non-Hispanic/ Latino; 8 American Indian or Alaska Native, non-Hispanic/Latino; 104 Asian, non-Hispanic/Latino; 14 Hispanic/Latino; 11 Two or more races, non-Hispanic/Latino), 53 international. Average age 34. 354 applicants, 71% accepted, 190 enrolled. In 2017, 156 master's awarded. *Entrance requirements:* For master's, GMAT, GRE, minimum GPA of 2.75 in last 60 hours, 2.5 overall (on a 3.0 scale); 27 hours of course work in business and economics. Additional exam requirements/recommendations for international students: Required—TOEFL (minimum score 79 iBT), IELTS (minimum score 6), PTE (minimum score 54). *Application deadline:* Applications are processed on a rolling basis. Application fee: $50 ($100 for international students). Electronic applications accepted. *Expenses:* Tuition, state resident: full-time $7824; part-time $5943 per year. Tuition, nonresident: full-time $15,648; part-time $11,736 per year. *Required fees:* $3064; $2298 per unit. Tuition and fees vary according to course load and reciprocity agreements. *Financial support:* In 2017–18, 114 students received support. Scholarships/grants available. Financial award application deadline: 2/1; financial award applicants required to submit FAFSA. *Total annual research expenditures:* $193,193. *Unit head:* Dr. Gregory A. Carnes, Dean, 256-765-4261, Fax: 256-765-4170, E-mail: gacarnes@una.edu. *Application contact:* Hillary N. Coats, Graduate Admissions Coordinator, 256-765-4447, E-mail: graduate@una.edu.
Website: https://www.una.edu/mba/index.html

The University of North Carolina at Chapel Hill, Kenan-Flagler Business School, Doctoral Program in Business Administration, Chapel Hill, NC 27599. Offers accounting (PhD); finance (PhD); marketing (PhD); operations management (PhD); organizational behavior (PhD); strategy (PhD). *Accreditation:* AACSB. *Degree requirements:* For doctorate, thesis/dissertation. *Entrance requirements:* For doctorate, GMAT or GRE General Test. Electronic applications accepted. *Expenses:* Contact institution.

The University of North Carolina at Chapel Hill, Kenan-Flagler Business School, Executive MBA Programs, Chapel Hill, NC 27599. Offers MBA. *Accreditation:* AACSB. *Program availability:* Evening/weekend, online learning. *Degree requirements:* For master's, exams, project. *Entrance requirements:* For master's, GMAT, 5 years of full-time work experience, interview. Electronic applications accepted. *Expenses:* Contact institution.

The University of North Carolina at Chapel Hill, Kenan-Flagler Business School, MBA Program, Chapel Hill, NC 27599. Offers MBA, MBA/JD, MBA/MHA, MBA/MRP, MBA/MSIS. *Accreditation:* AACSB. *Degree requirements:* For master's, exams, practicum. *Entrance requirements:* For master's, GMAT, interview, minimum 2 years of work experience. Additional exam requirements/recommendations for international students: Required—TOEFL. Electronic applications accepted.

The University of North Carolina at Charlotte, Belk College of Business, Department of Management, Charlotte, NC 28223-0001. Offers business administration (MBA, DBA, PhD); business analytics (Graduate Certificate); management (MS). *Program availability:* Part-time, evening/weekend. *Faculty:* 13 full-time (5 women). *Students:* 85 full-time (38 women), 286 part-time (91 women); includes 69 minority (24 Black or African American, non-Hispanic/Latino; 1 American Indian or Alaska Native, non-Hispanic/Latino; 18 Asian, non-Hispanic/Latino; 18 Hispanic/Latino; 8 Two or more races, non-Hispanic/Latino), 127 international. Average age 33. 237 applicants, 58% accepted, 90 enrolled. In 2017, 128 master's, 1 doctorate awarded. Terminal master's awarded for partial completion of doctoral program. *Degree requirements:* For doctorate, comprehensive exam (for some programs), thesis/dissertation. *Entrance requirements:* For master's, GMAT or GRE, bachelor's degree from regionally-accredited college or university; at least three evaluations from persons familiar with applicant's personal and professional qualifications; essay describing applicant's experience and objectives; resume; for doctorate, GMAT (minimum score of 650) or GRE (minimum 700 on quantitative section, 500 on verbal), baccalaureate or master's degree in business, economics, or related field such as mathematical finance, mathematics, or physics with minimum undergraduate GPA of 3.5 (3.25 graduate); three letters of recommendation; statement of purpose; for Graduate Certificate, transcripts, minimum undergraduate GPA of 2.75, essay describing experience and objectives. Additional exam requirements/recommendations for international students: Required—TOEFL (minimum score 523 paper-based, 70 iBT) or IELTS (6.5). *Application deadline:* For fall admission, 1/15 for domestic and international students; for spring admission, 10/1 priority date for domestic and international students; for summer admission, 4/1 priority date for domestic and international students. Applications are processed on a rolling basis. Application fee: $75. Electronic applications accepted. *Expenses:* Contact institution. *Financial support:* Research assistantships, teaching assistantships, career-related internships or fieldwork, institutionally sponsored loans, scholarships/grants, and unspecified assistantships available. Support available to part-time students. Financial award application deadline: 3/1; financial award applicants required to submit FAFSA. *Total annual research expenditures:* $122,929. *Unit head:* Dr. David J. Woehr, Department Chair, 704-687-7684, Fax: 704-687-1380, E-mail: dwoehr@uncc.edu. *Application contact:* Kathy B. Giddings, Director of Graduate Admissions, 704-687-5503, Fax: 704-687-1668, E-mail: gradadm@uncc.edu.
Website: https://belkcollege.uncc.edu/departments/management

The University of North Carolina at Greensboro, Graduate School, Bryan School of Business and Economics, Department of Business Administration, Greensboro, NC 27412-5001. Offers MBA, PMC, Postbaccalaureate Certificate, MS/MBA, MSN/MBA. *Accreditation:* AACSB. *Entrance requirements:* For master's, GMAT, GRE General Test, managerial experience. Additional exam requirements/recommendations for international students: Required—TOEFL. Electronic applications accepted.

The University of North Carolina at Pembroke, The Graduate School, School of Business, Pembroke, NC 28372-1510. Offers MBA. *Accreditation:* AACSB. *Program availability:* Part-time, evening/weekend. *Entrance requirements:* For master's, GMAT, minimum GPA of 3.0 in major or 2.5 overall. Additional exam requirements/ recommendations for international students: Required—TOEFL. *Application deadline:* For fall admission, 7/15 priority date for domestic and international students; for spring admission, 12/1 priority date for domestic and international students. Applications are processed on a rolling basis. Application fee: $45 ($60 for international students). *Financial support:* Application deadline: 4/15; applicants required to submit FAFSA. *Unit head:* Christine Bell, Program Director, 910-521-6836, E-mail: christine.bell@uncp.edu.
Website: http://www.uncp.edu/business/

The University of North Carolina Wilmington, Cameron School of Business, Business Administration Program, Wilmington, NC 28403-3297. Offers business administration (MBA); business administration - international (MBA); business administration - professional (MBA). *Accreditation:* AACSB. *Program availability:* Part-time-only. *Faculty:* 37 full-time (10 women). *Students:* 104 full-time (35 women), 68 part-time (40 women); includes 28 minority (14 Black or African American, non-Hispanic/ Latino; 3 Asian, non-Hispanic/Latino; 6 Hispanic/Latino; 5 Two or more races, non-Hispanic/Latino), 20 international. Average age 31. 109 applicants, 82% accepted, 78

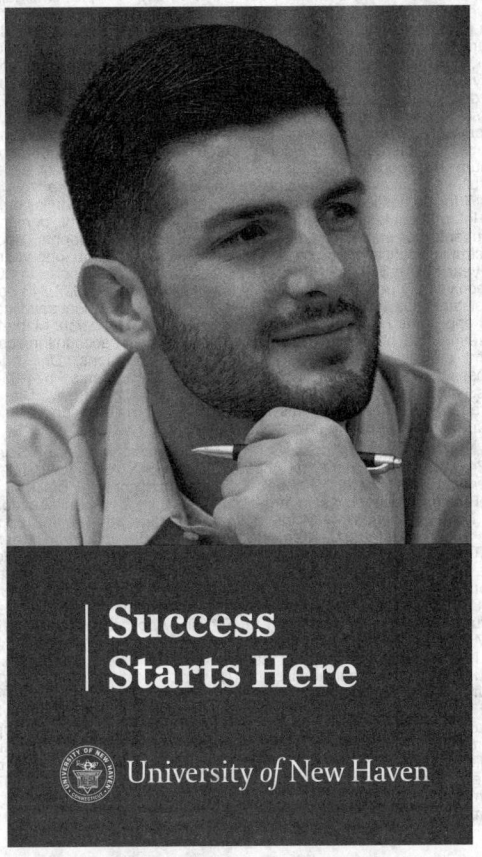

Business Administration and Management—General

enrolled. In 2017, 53 master's awarded. *Degree requirements:* For master's, thesis (for some programs), written case analysis and oral presentation (for professional), oral competency (for international). *Entrance requirements:* For master's, GMAT (for some programs), 2 years of appropriate work experience (for professional option), baccalaureate degree in the area of business and/or economics or six business prerequisite courses (for international option), resume, 3 letters of recommendation. Additional exam requirements/recommendations for international students: Required—TOEFL (minimum score 550 paper-based; 79 iBT), IELTS (minimum score 6.5). *Application deadline:* For fall admission, 6/1 for domestic students. Applications are processed on a rolling basis. Application fee: $75. Electronic applications accepted. *Expenses:* $4,042 in-state full-time, $10,512 out-of-state full-time; $292.15 per credit hour in-state students, $926.49 out-of-state(online); $435.86 per credit hour in-state, $1,083.32 per credit hour out-of-state (for Executive MBA). *Financial support:* Scholarships/grants and unspecified assistantships available. Financial award application deadline: 1/1; financial award applicants required to submit FAFSA. *Unit head:* Dr. Thom Porter, Interim MBA Director, 910-962-7466, E-mail: portert@uncw.edu. *Application contact:* Candace Wilhelm, Graduate Programs Coordinator, 910-962-3903, Fax: 910-962-2184, E-mail: wilhelmc@uncw.edu. Website: https://csb.uncw.edu/MBA/index.html

University of North Dakota, Graduate School, College of Business and Public Administration, Business Administration Program, Grand Forks, ND 58202. Offers MBA, MBA/JD. *Accreditation:* AACSB. *Program availability:* Part-time, evening/weekend, online learning. *Degree requirements:* For master's, comprehensive exam, thesis or alternative, project. *Entrance requirements:* For master's, GMAT, minimum GPA of 3.25. Additional exam requirements/recommendations for international students: Required—TOEFL (minimum score 550 paper-based; 79 iBT), IELTS (minimum score 6.5). Electronic applications accepted.

University of Northern Colorado, Graduate School, Monfort College of Business, Greeley, CO 80639. Offers accounting (MA); general business management (MBA); healthcare administration (MBA); human resources management (MBA). *Accreditation:* AACSB.

University of Northern Iowa, Graduate College, College of Business Administration, MBA Program, Cedar Falls, IA 50614. Offers MBA. *Accreditation:* AACSB. *Program availability:* Part-time, evening/weekend. *Entrance requirements:* For master's, GMAT (minimum score 500), minimum GPA of 3.0. Additional exam requirements/ recommendations for international students: Required—TOEFL (minimum score 500 paper-based; 61 iBT). Electronic applications accepted.

University of North Florida, Coggin College of Business, MBA Program, Jacksonville, FL 32224. Offers accounting (MBA); construction management (MBA); e-commerce (MBA); economics (MBA); finance (MBA); human resource management (MBA); international business (MBA); logistics (MBA); management applications (MBA). *Accreditation:* AACSB. *Program availability:* Part-time, evening/weekend. *Entrance requirements:* For master's, GMAT or GRE, U.S. bachelor's degree from regionally-accredited university or equivalent foreign degree. Additional exam requirements/ recommendations for international students: Required—TOEFL (minimum score 550 paper-based; 79 iBT). *Faculty research:* Performance measures, costing, and inventory issues in logistics and supply chain management; inter-organizational systems; international management and marketing practices; e-commerce; organizational learning and socialization processes.

University of North Georgia, Mike Cottrell College of Business, Dahlonega, GA 30597. Offers MBA. *Accreditation:* AACSB. *Program availability:* Part-time-only, evening/ weekend. *Faculty:* 5 full-time (3 women), 2 part-time/adjunct (1 woman). *Students:* 1 full-time (0 women), 79 part-time (40 women); includes 17 minority (5 Black or African American, non-Hispanic/Latino; 6 Asian, non-Hispanic/Latino; 5 Hispanic/Latino; 1 Two or more races, non-Hispanic/Latino). Average age 34. 60 applicants, 77% accepted, 37 enrolled. In 2017, 12 master's awarded. *Degree requirements:* For master's, capstone leadership experience. *Entrance requirements:* For master's, GRE or GMAT, 2 references, resume. Additional exam requirements/recommendations for international students: Required—TOEFL (minimum score 550 paper-based; 79 iBT), IELTS (minimum score 6.5). *Application deadline:* For fall admission, 4/1 priority date for domestic and international students. Application fee: $40. Electronic applications accepted. Application fee is waived when completed online. *Expenses:* Contact institution. *Financial support:* In 2017–18, 7 students received support. Unspecified assistantships available. Financial award application deadline: 3/17; financial award applicants required to submit CSS PROFILE or FAFSA. *Unit head:* Dr. Donna Mayo, Dean, 706-864-1620, E-mail: donna.mayo@ung.edu. *Application contact:* Melinda Maxwell, Director of Graduate Admissions, 706-864-1543, E-mail: melinda.maxwell@ung.edu. Website: http://www.ung.edu/graduate/MBA

University of North Texas, Robert B. Toulouse School of Graduate Studies, Denton, TX 76203-5459. Offers accounting (MS); applied anthropology (MA, MS); applied behavior analysis (Certificate); applied geography (MS); applied technology and performance improvement (M Ed, MS); art education (MA); art history (MA); art museum education (Certificate); arts leadership (Certificate); audiology (Au D); behavior analysis (MS); behavioral science (PhD); biochemistry and molecular biology (MS); biology (MA, MS); biomedical engineering (MS); business analysis (MS); chemistry (MS); clinical health psychology (PhD); communication studies (MA, MS); computer engineering (MS); computer science (MS); counseling (M Ed, MS), including clinical mental health counseling (MS), college and university counseling, elementary school counseling, secondary school counseling; creative writing (MA); criminal justice (MS); curriculum and instruction (M Ed); decision sciences (MBA); design (MA, MFA), including fashion design (MFA), innovation studies, interior design (MFA); early childhood studies (MS); economics (MS); educational leadership (M Ed, Ed D); educational psychology (MS, PhD), including family studies (MS), gifted and talented (MS), human development (MS), learning and cognition (MS), research, measurement and evaluation (MS); electrical engineering (MS); emergency management (MPA); engineering technology (MS); English (MA); English as a second language (MA); environmental science (MS); finance (MBA, MS); financial management (MPA); French (MA); health services management (MBA); higher education (M Ed, Ed D); history (MA, MS); hospitality management (MS); human resources management (MPA); information science (MS); information systems (PhD); information technologies (MBA); interdisciplinary studies (MA, MS); international studies (MA); international sustainable tourism (MS); jazz studies (MM); journalism (MA, MJ, Graduate Certificate), including interactive and virtual digital communication (Graduate Certificate), narrative journalism (Graduate Certificate), public relations (Graduate Certificate); kinesiology (MS); linguistics (MA); local government management (MPA); logistics (PhD); logistics and supply chain management (MBA); long-term care, senior housing, and aging services (MA); management (PhD); marketing (MBA); mathematics (MS); mechanical and energy engineering (MS, PhD); music (MA), including ethnomusicology, music theory, musicology, performance; music composition (PhD); music education (MM Ed, PhD); nonprofit management (MPA); operations and supply chain management (MBA); performance (MM, DMA); philosophy (MA); political science (MA); professional and technical communication (MA); radio, television and film (MA, MFA); rehabilitation counseling (Certificate); sociology (MA);

Spanish (MA); special education (M Ed); speech-language pathology (MA); strategic management (MBA); studio art (MFA); teaching (M Ed); MBA/MS. *Program availability:* Part-time, evening/weekend, online learning. Terminal master's awarded for partial completion of doctoral program. *Degree requirements:* For master's, variable foreign language requirement, comprehensive exam (for some programs), thesis (for some programs); for doctorate, variable foreign language requirement, comprehensive exam (for some programs), thesis/dissertation; for other advanced degree, variable foreign language requirement, comprehensive exam (for some programs). *Entrance requirements:* For master's and doctorate, GRE, GMAT. Additional exam requirements/ recommendations for international students: Required—TOEFL (minimum score 550 paper-based; 79 iBT). Electronic applications accepted.

University of North Texas at Dallas, Graduate School, Dallas, TX 75241. Offers accounting (MBA); counseling (M Ed, MS); criminal justice (MS); curriculum and instruction (M Ed); educational administration (M Ed); human resources and organizational behavior (MBA); public leadership (MS); strategic management (MBA).

University of Northwestern Ohio, Graduate College, Lima, OH 45805-1498. Offers business administration (MBA). *Program availability:* Evening/weekend, online learning.

University of Northwestern–St. Paul, Master of Business Administration Program, St. Paul, MN 55113-1598. Offers MBA. *Program availability:* Part-time, evening/weekend, online learning. *Application deadline:* Applications are processed on a rolling basis. Electronic applications accepted. *Application contact:* Graduate Studies Admissions, 651-631-5200, E-mail: gradstudies@unwsp.edu. Website: https://www.unwsp.edu/web/graduate-studies/master-of-business-administration

University of Notre Dame, Mendoza College of Business, Executive Master of Business Administration Program, Notre Dame, IN 46556. Offers MBA. Program offered at the Stayer Center for Executive Education in Notre Dame, Indiana and also at Notre Dame Chicago Commons in Chicago, Illinois on Michigan Avenue. *Accreditation:* AACSB. *Faculty:* 21 full-time (4 women), 8 part-time/adjunct (1 woman). *Students:* 139 full-time (30 women); includes 35 minority (15 Black or African American, non-Hispanic/ Latino; 1 American Indian or Alaska Native, non-Hispanic/Latino; 7 Asian, non-Hispanic/ Latino; 5 Hispanic/Latino; 7 Two or more races, non-Hispanic/Latino). Average age 38. In 2017, 119 master's awarded. *Entrance requirements:* For master's, five or more years of significant experience managing people, projects or business units. Additional exam requirements/recommendations for international students: Required—TOEFL, IELTS. *Application deadline:* For fall admission, 10/15 for domestic students, 6/1 for international students; for winter admission, 11/1 for international students; for summer admission, 6/1 for domestic students. Applications are processed on a rolling basis. Application fee: $100. Electronic applications accepted. Application fee is waived when completed online. *Expenses:* Contact institution. *Financial support:* In 2017–18, 57 fellowships (averaging $16,360 per year) were awarded. Financial award application deadline: 6/1; financial award applicants required to submit FAFSA. *Faculty research:* Economic determinants of multinational firm behavior and foreign direct investment; psychology of ethical decision making - examining why individuals behave unethically; role of corporate governance on voluntary financial statement disclosures; proactive personality and behavior at work; strategy design and implementation. *Unit head:* Michael Brach, Director of Degree Programs, 574-631-2717, Fax: 574-631-6783, E-mail: brach.8@nd.edu. *Application contact:* Terron J. Phillips, Admissions Coordinator, 574-631-3188, Fax: 574-631-6783, E-mail: terron.j.phillips.146@nd.edu. Website: https://mendoza.nd.edu

University of Notre Dame, Mendoza College of Business, Master of Business Administration Program, Notre Dame, IN 46556. Offers business analytics (MBA); business leadership (MBA); consulting (MBA); corporate finance (MBA); innovation and entrepreneurship (MBA); investments (MBA); marketing (MBA); MBA/MSBA. *Accreditation:* AACSB. *Faculty:* 60 full-time (10 women), 14 part-time/adjunct (1 woman). *Students:* 294 full-time (70 women); includes 46 minority (8 Black or African American, non-Hispanic/Latino; 3 American Indian or Alaska Native, non-Hispanic/ Latino; 12 Asian, non-Hispanic/Latino; 20 Hispanic/Latino; 1 Native Hawaiian or other Pacific Islander, non-Hispanic/Latino; 2 Two or more races, non-Hispanic/Latino), 74 international. Average age 29. 633 applicants, 42% accepted, 131 enrolled. In 2017, 182 master's awarded. *Entrance requirements:* For master's, GMAT or GRE, work experience, essay, four-slide presentation, two recommendations, transcripts from all colleges and/or universities attended, interview. Additional exam requirements/ recommendations for international students: Required—PTE (minimum score 68), TOEFL (minimum iBT score of 109), IELTS (7.5), or documentation of at least six semesters of full-time university education in English. *Application deadline:* For fall admission, 10/17 for domestic and international students; for winter admission, 1/9 for domestic and international students; for spring admission, 2/20 for domestic and international students; for summer admission, 3/17 for domestic students. Application fee: $175. Electronic applications accepted. *Expenses:* $74,133 (for one-year MBA); $106,526 (two-year MBA); $113,050 (for MBA/MSBA). *Financial support:* In 2017–18, 251 students received support, including 247 fellowships (averaging $27,748 per year); unspecified assistantships also available. Financial award application deadline: 2/28; financial award applicants required to submit FAFSA. *Faculty research:* Market micro-structure; marketing and public policy; corporate finance and accounting; corporate governance and ethical behavior; high performing organizations. *Unit head:* Dr. Katherine Spiess, Associate Dean, Graduate Business Programs, 574-631-7236, E-mail: spiess.1@nd.edu. *Application contact:* Kristin McAndrew, Director of Admissions, Graduate Business Programs, 574-631-8488, E-mail: kmcandre@nd.edu. Website: http://mendoza.nd.edu/programs/mba-programs/

University of Notre Dame, Mendoza College of Business, Master of Science in Management Program, Notre Dame, IN 46556. Offers MSM. *Faculty:* 13 full-time (3 women). *Students:* 45 full-time (21 women); includes 10 minority (4 Black or African American, non-Hispanic/Latino; 1 Asian, non-Hispanic/Latino; 2 Hispanic/Latino; 3 Two or more races, non-Hispanic/Latino), 4 international. Average age 23. 182 applicants, 49% accepted, 45 enrolled. In 2017, 46 master's awarded. *Entrance requirements:* For master's, GMAT or GRE, essay, two recommendations, transcript from all colleges or universities attended, resume, interview. Additional exam requirements/ recommendations for international students: Required—PTE (minimum score 68), TOEFL (minimum iBT score of 109), IELTS (7.5), or documentation of at least six semesters of full-time university education in English. *Application deadline:* For fall admission, 11/7 for domestic and international students; for winter admission, 1/16 for domestic and international students; for spring admission, 2/20 for domestic and international students; for summer admission, 4/17 for domestic students. Application fee: $50. Electronic applications accepted. *Expenses:* Contact institution. *Financial support:* In 2017–18, 38 students received support, including 38 fellowships (averaging $15,868 per year). Financial award application deadline: 2/28; financial award applicants required to submit FAFSA. *Unit head:* Dr. Katherine Spiess, Associate Dean, Graduate Business Programs, 574-631-7236, E-mail: spiess.1@nd.edu. *Application contact:* Kristin McAndrew, Director of Admissions, Graduate Business Programs, 574-631-8488, E-mail: kmcandre@nd.edu. Website: http://mendoza.nd.edu/msm

Business Administration and Management—General

University of Oklahoma, Price College of Business, Program in Business Administration, Oklahoma City, OK 73104. Offers business administration (MBA, PhD), including accounting (PhD), business administration, entrepreneurship and economic development (PhD), finance (PhD), management and international business (PhD), management of information systems (PhD), marketing/supply chain (PhD); JD/MBA; MBA/MS. *Accreditation:* AACSB. *Program availability:* Part-time, evening/weekend. *Students:* 100 full-time (27 women), 152 part-time (30 women); includes 36 minority (2 Black or African American, non-Hispanic/Latino; 4 American Indian or Alaska Native, non-Hispanic/Latino; 10 Asian, non-Hispanic/Latino; 13 Hispanic/Latino; 7 Two or more races, non-Hispanic/Latino), 32 international. Average age 31. 247 applicants, 29% accepted, 41 enrolled. In 2017, 118 master's, 9 doctorates awarded. *Degree requirements:* For doctorate, comprehensive exam, thesis/dissertation. *Entrance requirements:* For master's, GMAT or GRE, resume, 2 essays, interview; for doctorate, GMAT or GRE, resume, statement of goals, 3 letters of recommendation. Additional exam requirements/recommendations for international students: Required—TOEFL (minimum score 100 iBT) or IELTS (minimum score 7). *Application deadline:* For fall admission, 11/1 for domestic and international students; for summer admission, 11/1 for domestic and international students. Applications are processed on a rolling basis. Application fee: $50 ($100 for international students). Electronic applications accepted. *Expenses:* Contact institution. *Financial support:* In 2017–18, 107 students received support, including 6 fellowships with partial tuition reimbursements available (averaging $2,500 per year); research assistantships with full and partial tuition reimbursements available, teaching assistantships with full and partial tuition reimbursements available, career-related internships or fieldwork, scholarships/grants, health care benefits, and unspecified assistantships also available. Support available to part-time students. Financial award application deadline: 6/1; financial award applicants required to submit FAFSA. *Faculty research:* Energy finance; international accounting; organizational behavior and entrepreneurship; management information systems; supply chain. *Unit head:* Laku Chidambaram, Associate Dean for Academic Programs and Engagement, 405-325-8013. *Application contact:* Kate Hile, Associate Director of MBA Admissions, 405-325-4572, E-mail: khile@ou.edu.
Website: http://www.ou.edu/price/divisions/graduate-programs/graduate.html

University of Oregon, Graduate School, Charles H. Lundquist College of Business, Department of Management, Eugene, OR 97403. Offers PhD. *Accreditation:* AACSB. *Program availability:* Part-time. Terminal master's awarded for partial completion of doctoral program. *Degree requirements:* For doctorate, thesis/dissertation, 2 comprehensive exams. *Entrance requirements:* For doctorate, GMAT. Additional exam requirements/recommendations for international students: Required—TOEFL.

University of Oregon, Graduate School, Charles H. Lundquist College of Business, Department of Management: General Business, Eugene, OR 97403. Offers MBA. *Accreditation:* AACSB. *Entrance requirements:* For master's, GMAT. Additional exam requirements/recommendations for international students: Required—TOEFL.

University of Ottawa, Faculty of Graduate and Postdoctoral Studies, Telfer School of Management, Executive Business Administration Program, Ottawa, ON K1N 6N5, Canada. Offers EMBA. *Accreditation:* AACSB. *Program availability:* Evening/weekend. *Entrance requirements:* For master's, bachelor's degree or equivalent, minimum B average, business experience. Additional exam requirements/recommendations for international students: Recommended—TOEFL. Electronic applications accepted. *Expenses:* Contact institution.

University of Ottawa, Faculty of Graduate and Postdoctoral Studies, Telfer School of Management, MBA Program, Ottawa, ON K1N 6N5, Canada. Offers MBA. *Accreditation:* AACSB. *Program availability:* Part-time, evening/weekend. *Degree requirements:* For master's, thesis optional. *Entrance requirements:* For master's, GMAT, bachelor's degree or equivalent, minimum B average, minimum 2 years of work experience. Additional exam requirements/recommendations for international students: Recommended—TOEFL. Electronic applications accepted.

University of Pennsylvania, Wharton School, Management Department, Philadelphia, PA 19104. Offers MBA, PhD. *Accreditation:* AACSB. *Entrance requirements:* For master's, GMAT; for doctorate, GMAT or GRE. *Faculty research:* Cross-cultural leadership, international technology transfers, human resource management, financial services.

University of Pennsylvania, Wharton School, Wharton Doctoral Programs, Philadelphia, PA 19104. Offers accounting (PhD); applied economics (PhD); ethics and legal studies (PhD); finance (PhD); health care management and economics (PhD); management (PhD); marketing (PhD); operations and information management (PhD); statistics (PhD). *Accreditation:* AACSB. *Degree requirements:* For doctorate, thesis/dissertation. *Entrance requirements:* For doctorate, GMAT or GRE, letters of recommendation. Additional exam requirements/recommendations for international students: Required—TOEFL, TWE. Electronic applications accepted.

University of Pennsylvania, Wharton School, The Wharton MBA Program, Philadelphia, PA 19104. Offers MBA, DMD/MBA, JD/MBA, MBA/MA, MBA/MS, MBA/MSN, MBA/MSW, MBA/PhD, MD/MBA, VMD/MBA. *Accreditation:* AACSB. *Entrance requirements:* For master's, GMAT, interview, 2 letters of recommendation, resume/curriculum vitae. Additional exam requirements/recommendations for international students: Required—TOEFL. Electronic applications accepted. *Faculty research:* Entrepreneurial studies, finance, management of technology.

University of Pennsylvania, Wharton School, The Wharton MBA Program for Executives, Wharton Executive MBA East, Philadelphia, PA 19104. Offers MBA. *Accreditation:* AACSB. *Program availability:* Evening/weekend. *Entrance requirements:* For master's, GMAT. Additional exam requirements/recommendations for international students: Recommended—TOEFL.

University of Pennsylvania, Wharton School, The Wharton MBA Program for Executives, Wharton Executive MBA West, Philadelphia, PA 19104. Offers MBA. *Accreditation:* AACSB. *Program availability:* Evening/weekend. *Entrance requirements:* For master's, GMAT. Additional exam requirements/recommendations for international students: Recommended—TOEFL.

University of Phoenix–Bay Area Campus, School of Business, San Jose, CA 95134-1805. Offers accountancy (MS); accounting (MBA); business administration (MBA, DBA); energy management (MBA); global management (MBA); health care management (MBA); human resource management (MBA); human resources management (MM); management (MM); marketing (MBA); organizational leadership (DM); project management (MBA); public administration (MPA); technology management (MBA). *Accreditation:* ACBSP. *Program availability:* Evening/weekend, online learning. *Degree requirements:* For master's, thesis (for some programs). *Entrance requirements:* For master's, minimum undergraduate GPA of 3.0, 3 years of work experience. Additional exam requirements/recommendations for international students: Required—TOEFL (minimum score 550 paper-based; 79 iBT). Electronic applications accepted.

University of Phoenix–Central Valley Campus, School of Business, Fresno, CA 93720-1552. Offers accounting (MBA); business administration (MBA); global

management (MBA); human resources management (MBA, MM); management (MM); marketing (MBA); public administration (MBA, MM). *Accreditation:* ACBSP.

University of Phoenix–Dallas Campus, School of Business, Dallas, TX 75251. Offers accounting (MBA); business administration (MBA); global management (MBA); human resources management (MBA, MM); management (MM); marketing (MBA); public administration (MBA, MM). *Accreditation:* ACBSP. *Program availability:* Evening/weekend, online learning. *Degree requirements:* For master's, thesis (for some programs). *Entrance requirements:* For master's, 3 years of work experience, minimum undergraduate GPA of 3.0. Additional exam requirements/recommendations for international students: Required—TOEFL (minimum score 550 paper-based; 79 iBT). Electronic applications accepted.

University of Phoenix–Hawaii Campus, School of Business, Honolulu, HI 96813-3800. Offers accounting (MBA); business administration (MBA); global management (MBA); human resources management (MBA, MM); management (MM); marketing (MBA); public administration (MBA, MM). *Accreditation:* ACBSP. *Program availability:* Evening/weekend. *Degree requirements:* For master's, thesis (for some programs). *Entrance requirements:* For master's, minimum undergraduate GPA of 3.0, 3 years of work experience. Additional exam requirements/recommendations for international students: Required—TOEFL (minimum score 550 paper-based; 79 iBT). Electronic applications accepted.

University of Phoenix–Houston Campus, School of Business, Houston, TX 77079-2004. Offers accounting (MBA); business administration (MBA); global management (MBA); human resources management (MBA, MM); management (MM); marketing (MBA); public administration (MBA, MM). *Accreditation:* ACBSP. *Program availability:* Evening/weekend, online learning. *Degree requirements:* For master's, thesis (for some programs). *Entrance requirements:* For master's, 3 years of work experience, minimum undergraduate GPA of 3.0. Additional exam requirements/recommendations for international students: Required—TOEFL (minimum score 550 paper-based; 79 iBT). Electronic applications accepted.

University of Phoenix–Las Vegas Campus, School of Business, Las Vegas, NV 89135. Offers accounting (MBA); business administration (MBA); global management (MBA); human resources management (MBA, MM); management (MM); marketing (MBA); public administration (MM). *Accreditation:* ACBSP. *Program availability:* Evening/weekend, online learning. *Degree requirements:* For master's, thesis (for some programs). *Entrance requirements:* For master's, minimum undergraduate GPA of 3.0, 3 years of work experience. Additional exam requirements/recommendations for international students: Required—TOEFL (minimum score 550 paper-based; 79 iBT). Electronic applications accepted.

University of Phoenix–Online Campus, School of Advanced Studies, Phoenix, AZ 85034-7209. Offers business administration (DBA); education (Ed S); educational leadership (Ed D), including curriculum and instruction, education technology, educational leadership; health administration (DHA); higher education administration (PhD); industrial/organizational psychology (PhD); nursing (PhD); organizational leadership (DM), including information systems and technology, organizational leadership. *Program availability:* Evening/weekend, online learning. *Degree requirements:* For doctorate, thesis/dissertation. *Entrance requirements:* Additional exam requirements/recommendations for international students: Required—TOEFL, TOEIC (Test of English as an International Communication), Berlitz Online English Proficiency Exam, PTE, or IELTS. Electronic applications accepted. *Expenses:* Contact institution.

University of Phoenix–Online Campus, School of Business, Phoenix, AZ 85034-7209. Offers accountancy (MS); accounting (MBA, Certificate); business administration (MBA); energy management (MBA); global management (MBA); health care management (MBA); human resource management (MBA, Certificate); human resources management (MM); management (MM); marketing (MBA, Certificate); project management (MBA, Certificate); public administration (MBA, MM); technology management (MBA). *Program availability:* Evening/weekend, online learning. *Entrance requirements:* Additional exam requirements/recommendations for international students: Required—TOEFL, TOEIC (Test of English as an International Communication), Berlitz Online English Proficiency Exam, PTE, or IELTS. Electronic applications accepted. *Expenses:* Contact institution.

University of Phoenix–Phoenix Campus, School of Business, Tempe, AZ 85282-2371. Offers accounting (MBA, MS, Certificate); business administration (MBA); energy management (MBA); global management (MBA); health care management (MBA); human resource management (MBA, Certificate); management (MM); marketing (MBA); project management (MBA); technology management (MBA). *Program availability:* Evening/weekend, online learning. *Entrance requirements:* Additional exam requirements/recommendations for international students: Required—TOEFL, TOEIC (Test of English as an International Communication), Berlitz Online English Proficiency Exam, PTE, or IELTS. Electronic applications accepted. *Expenses:* Contact institution.

University of Phoenix–Sacramento Valley Campus, College of Information Systems and Technology, Sacramento, CA 95833-4334. Offers management (MIS); technology management (MBA). *Program availability:* Evening/weekend. *Degree requirements:* For master's, thesis (for some programs). *Entrance requirements:* For master's, minimum undergraduate GPA of 3.0, 3 years work experience. Additional exam requirements/recommendations for international students: Required—TOEFL (minimum score 550 paper-based; 79 iBT). Electronic applications accepted.

University of Phoenix–Sacramento Valley Campus, School of Business, Sacramento, CA 95833-4334. Offers accounting (MBA); business administration (MBA); global management (MBA); human resources management (MBA, MM); management (MM); marketing (MBA); public administration (MBA, MM). *Accreditation:* ACBSP. *Program availability:* Evening/weekend. *Degree requirements:* For master's, thesis (for some programs). *Entrance requirements:* For master's, minimum undergraduate GPA of 3.0, 3 years work experience. Additional exam requirements/recommendations for international students: Required—TOEFL (minimum score 550 paper-based; 79 iBT). Electronic applications accepted.

University of Phoenix–San Antonio Campus, School of Business, San Antonio, TX 78230. Offers accounting (MBA); business administration (MBA); e-business (MBA); global management (MBA); human resources management (MBA, MM); management (MM); marketing (MBA); public administration (MBA, MM). *Accreditation:* ACBSP.

University of Phoenix–San Diego Campus, College of Information Systems and Technology, San Diego, CA 92123. Offers management (MIS); technology management (MBA). *Program availability:* Evening/weekend. *Degree requirements:* For master's, thesis (for some programs). *Entrance requirements:* For master's, minimum undergraduate GPA of 3.0, 3 years work experience. Additional exam requirements/recommendations for international students: Required—TOEFL (minimum score 550 paper-based; 79 iBT). Electronic applications accepted.

University of Phoenix–San Diego Campus, School of Business, San Diego, CA 92123. Offers accounting (MBA); business administration (MBA); global management (MBA); human resources management (MBA, MM); management (MM); marketing (MBA); public administration (MBA). *Accreditation:* ACBSP. *Program availability:*

Business Administration and Management—General

Evening/weekend. *Degree requirements:* For master's, thesis (for some programs). *Entrance requirements:* For master's, 3 years of work experience, minimum undergraduate GPA of 3.0. Additional exam requirements/recommendations for international students: Required—TOEFL (minimum score 550 paper-based; 79 iBT). Electronic applications accepted.

University of Pikeville, Coleman College of Business, Pikeville, KY 41501. Offers business (MBA); entrepreneurship (MBA); healthcare (MBA). *Program availability:* Part-time, evening/weekend. *Faculty:* 5 part-time/adjunct (2 women). *Students:* 35 full-time (16 women), 2 part-time (both women); includes 3 minority (all Black or African American, non-Hispanic/Latino), 4 international. Average age 29. In 2017, 18 master's awarded. *Degree requirements:* For master's, comprehensive exam (for some programs). *Entrance requirements:* For master's, official transcripts, two professional letters of recommendation, three years of work experience. *Application deadline:* For fall admission, 8/15 for domestic students, 7/1 for international students. Applications are processed on a rolling basis. Application fee: $50. *Expenses:* Contact institution. *Financial support:* Tuition waivers (full) and university employee grants available. Financial award application deadline: 2/15; financial award applicants required to submit FAFSA. *Unit head:* Dr. Howard V. Roberts, Dean, 606-218-5019, Fax: 606-218-5031, E-mail: howardroberts@upike.edu. *Application contact:* Cathy Maynard, Secretary, Business and Economics, 606-218-5020, Fax: 606-218-5031, E-mail: cathymaynard@upike.edu.
Website: http://www.upike.edu/Colleges/CCOB/

University of Pittsburgh, Katz Graduate School of Business, Doctoral Program in Business Administration, Pittsburgh, PA 15260. Offers accounting (PhD); business analytics and operations (PhD); finance (PhD); information systems and technology management (PhD); marketing (PhD); organizational behavior and human resources (PhD); strategic management (PhD). *Accreditation:* AACSB. *Program availability:* Evening/weekend. *Faculty:* 91 full-time (30 women), 14 part-time/adjunct (4 women). *Students:* 51 full-time (26 women), 1 (woman) part-time; includes 5 minority (1 Black or African American, non-Hispanic/Latino; 3 Asian, non-Hispanic/Latino; 1 Two or more races, non-Hispanic/Latino), 30 international. Average age 31. 337 applicants, 3% accepted, 10 enrolled. In 2017, 7 doctorates awarded. *Degree requirements:* For doctorate, comprehensive exam, thesis/dissertation, student teaching. *Entrance requirements:* For doctorate, GMAT or GRE, 3 recommendations, statement of purpose, transcripts of all previous course work and degrees. Additional exam requirements/recommendations for international students: Required—TOEFL (minimum score 100 iBT) or IELTS (minimum score 7.0). *Application deadline:* For fall admission, 1/1 for domestic and international students. Applications are processed on a rolling basis. Application fee: $50. Electronic applications accepted. *Financial support:* In 2017–18, 43 students received support, including 33 research assistantships with full tuition reimbursements available (averaging $26,500 per year), 10 teaching assistantships with full tuition reimbursements available (averaging $28,220 per year); Federal Work-Study, scholarships/grants, health care benefits, and unspecified assistantships also available. Financial award application deadline: 1/1; financial award applicants required to submit FAFSA. *Faculty research:* Accounting systems/financial reporting, corporate finance, shopper marketing/consumer behavior, management information systems, organizational behavior and entrepreneurship. *Total annual research expenditures:* $475,077. *Unit head:* Dr. Arjang A. Assad, Dean, 412-648-1556, Fax: 412-648-1552, E-mail: aassad@katz.pitt.edu. *Application contact:* Dr. Dennis Galletta, Director, 412-648-1699, Fax: 412-648-3633, E-mail: galletta@katz.pitt.edu.
Website: http://www.katz.business.pitt.edu/degrees/phd/

See Display below and Close-Up on page 187.

University of Pittsburgh, Katz Graduate School of Business, Executive MBA Program, Pittsburgh, PA 15260. Offers EMBA. *Accreditation:* AACSB. *Faculty:* 91 full-time (30 women), 14 part-time/adjunct (4 women). *Students:* 113 full-time (26 women); includes 13 minority (2 Black or African American, non-Hispanic/Latino; 10 Asian, non-Hispanic/Latino; 1 Hispanic/Latino), 46 international. Average age 37. 80 applicants, 98% accepted, 66 enrolled. In 2017, 55 master's awarded. *Entrance requirements:* For master's, GMAT (for candidates with less than 10 years experience, GPA less than 3.0, or limited quantitative background), minimum 5 years of management experience, resume, 2 letters of recommendation, essay, interview. Additional exam requirements/recommendations for international students: Required—TOEFL (minimum score 100 iBT) or IELTS (minimum score 7.0). *Application deadline:* Applications are processed on a rolling basis. Application fee: $50. Electronic applications accepted. *Expenses:* Contact institution. *Financial support:* Scholarships/grants available. Financial award applicants required to submit FAFSA. *Faculty research:* Accounting systems/financial reporting, corporate finance, shopper marketing/consumer behavior, management information systems, organizational behavior and entrepreneurship. *Total annual research expenditures:* $475,077. *Unit head:* Dr. Arjang A. Assad, Dean, 412-648-1556, Fax: 412-648-1552, E-mail: aassad@katz.pitt.edu. *Application contact:* William T. Valenta, Jr., Assistant Dean, MBA and Executive Programs, 412-648-1610, Fax: 412-648-1787, E-mail: valenta@pitt.edu.
Website: http://www.katz.business.pitt.edu/degrees/emba/

See Display below and Close-Up on page 187.

University of Pittsburgh, Katz Graduate School of Business, Master of Business Administration Programs, Pittsburgh, PA 15260. Offers finance (MBA); information systems (MBA); marketing (MBA); operations (MBA); organizational behavior and human resources (MBA); strategy, environment and organizations (MBA); MBA/JD; MBA/MID; MBA/MIS; MBA/MSE. *Accreditation:* AACSB. *Program availability:* Part-time, evening/weekend, blended/hybrid learning. *Faculty:* 91 full-time (30 women), 14 part-time/adjunct (4 women). *Students:* 139 full-time (49 women), 294 part-time (94 women); includes 65 minority (27 Black or African American, non-Hispanic/Latino; 20 Asian, non-Hispanic/Latino; 11 Hispanic/Latino; 7 Two or more races, non-Hispanic/Latino), 54 international. Average age 29. 651 applicants, 44% accepted, 158 enrolled. In 2017, 217 master's awarded. *Degree requirements:* For master's, minimum GPA of 3.0. *Entrance requirements:* For master's, GMAT, GRE. Additional exam requirements/recommendations for international students: Required—TOEFL (minimum score 100 iBT) or IELTS (minimum score 7.0). *Application deadline:* For fall admission, 4/1 priority date for domestic students, 2/1 priority date for international students. Application fee: $50. Electronic applications accepted. *Financial support:* In 2017–18, 136 students received support. Scholarships/grants available. Financial award application deadline: 6/1; financial award applicants required to submit FAFSA. *Faculty research:* Accounting systems/financial reporting, corporate finance, shopper marketing/consumer behavior, management information systems, organizational behavior and entrepreneurship. *Total annual research expenditures:* $475,077. *Unit head:* Dr. Arjang A. Assad, Dean, 412-648-1556, Fax: 412-648-1552, E-mail: aassad@katz.pitt.edu. *Application contact:* Thomas Keller, Director of MBA Admissions, 412-648-1700, Fax: 412-648-1659, E-mail: mba@katz.pitt.edu.
Website: http://www.business.pitt.edu/katz/mba/

See Display below and Close-Up on page 187.

University of Pittsburgh, Katz Graduate School of Business, MBA/Juris Doctor Program, Pittsburgh, PA 15260. Offers MBA/JD. *Faculty:* 91 full-time (30 women), 14 part-time/adjunct (4 women). *Students:* 10 full-time (4 women); includes 2 minority (1 Black or African American, non-Hispanic/Latino; 1 Two or more races, non-Hispanic/Latino), 1 international. Average age 27. 7

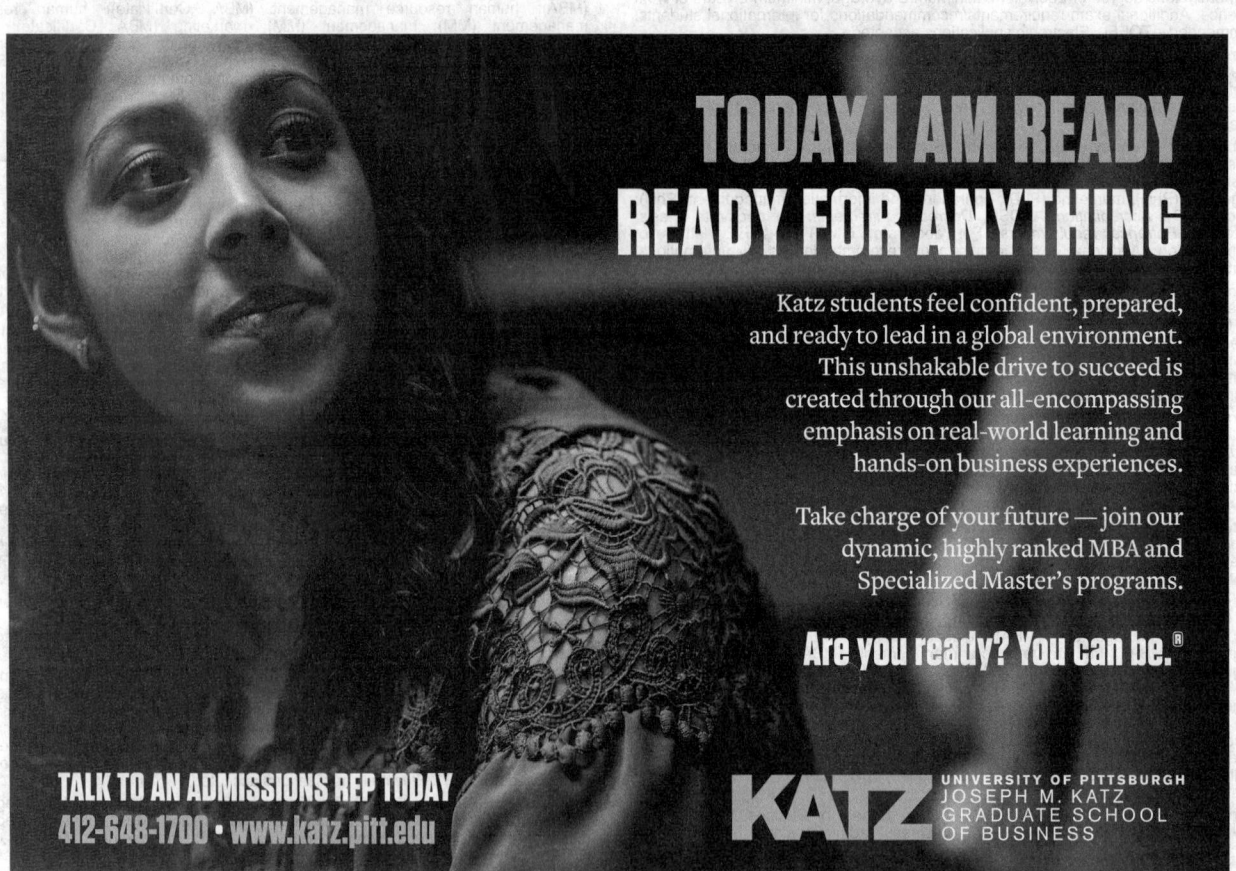

applicants, 71% accepted, 4 enrolled. *Entrance requirements:* Additional exam requirements/recommendations for international students: Required—TOEFL (minimum score 100 iBT) or IELTS (minimum score 7.0). *Application deadline:* For fall admission, 4/1 priority date for domestic students, 2/1 priority date for international students. Application fee: $50. Electronic applications accepted. *Financial support:* Scholarships/grants available. Financial award application deadline: 6/1; financial award applicants required to submit FAFSA. *Faculty research:* Accounting systems/financial reporting, corporate finance, shopper marketing/consumer behavior, management information systems, organizational behavior and entrepreneurship. *Total annual research expenditures:* $475,077. *Unit head:* Dr. Arjang A. Assad, Dean, 412-648-1556, Fax: 412-648-1552, E-mail: aassad@katz.pitt.edu. *Application contact:* Thomas Keller, Director of MBA Admissions, 412-648-1700, Fax: 412-648-1659, E-mail: mba@katz.pitt.edu.
Website: http://www.katz.business.pitt.edu/mba/joint-and-dual/juris-doc
See Display on the previous page and Close-Up on page 187.

University of Pittsburgh, Katz Graduate School of Business, MBA/Master of Health Administration in Health Policy and Management Program, Pittsburgh, PA 15260. Offers MBA/MHA. *Program availability:* Part-time, evening/weekend. *Faculty:* 91 full-time (30 women), 14 part-time/adjunct (4 women). *Students:* 8 full-time (6 women); includes 4 minority (2 Black or African American, non-Hispanic/Latino; 1 Asian, non-Hispanic/Latino; 1 Two or more races, non-Hispanic/Latino). Average age 25. 11 applicants, 73% accepted, 6 enrolled. *Entrance requirements:* Additional exam requirements/recommendations for international students: Required—TOEFL (minimum score 100 iBT), IELTS (minimum score 7). *Application deadline:* For fall admission, 4/1 priority date for domestic students, 2/1 priority date for international students. Application fee: $50. Electronic applications accepted. *Financial support:* Scholarships/grants available. Financial award application deadline: 6/1; financial award applicants required to submit FAFSA. *Faculty research:* Accounting systems/financial reporting, corporate finance, shopper marketing/consumer behavior, management information systems, organizational behavior and entrepreneurship. *Total annual research expenditures:* $475,077. *Unit head:* Dr. Arjang A. Assad, Dean, 412-648-1556, Fax: 412-648-1552, E-mail: aassad@katz.pitt.edu. *Application contact:* Thomas Keller, Director of MBA Admissions, 412-648-1700, Fax: 412-648-1659, E-mail: mba@katz.pitt.edu.
Website: http://www.katz.business.pitt.edu/mba/joint-and-dual/health-administration

University of Pittsburgh, Katz Graduate School of Business, MBA/Master of International Business Dual Degree Program, Pittsburgh, PA 15260. Offers MBA/MIB. *Program availability:* Part-time, evening/weekend. *Faculty:* 91 full-time (30 women), 14 part-time/adjunct (4 women). *Students:* 2 part-time (both women); includes 1 minority (Black or African American, non-Hispanic/Latino). Average age 32. 3 applicants. *Entrance requirements:* Additional exam requirements/recommendations for international students: Required—TOEFL (minimum score 100 iBT) or IELTS (minimum score 7.0). *Application deadline:* For fall admission, 4/1 priority date for domestic students, 2/1 priority date for international students. Application fee: $50. Electronic applications accepted. *Financial support:* Scholarships/grants available. Financial award application deadline: 6/1; financial award applicants required to submit FAFSA. *Faculty research:* Accounting systems/financial reporting, corporate finance, shopper marketing/consumer behavior, management information systems, organizational behavior and entrepreneurship. *Total annual research expenditures:* $475,077. *Unit head:* Dr. Arjang A. Assad, Dean, 412-648-1556, Fax: 412-648-1552, E-mail: aassad@katz.pitt.edu. *Application contact:* Thomas Keller, Director of MBA Admissions, 412-648-1700, Fax: 412-648-1659, E-mail: mba@katz.pitt.edu.
Website: https://www.katz.business.pitt.edu/mba/joint-and-dual/ib#section-1
See Display on the previous page and Close-Up on page 187.

University of Pittsburgh, Katz Graduate School of Business, MBA/Master of International Development Joint Degree Program, Pittsburgh, PA 15260. Offers MID/MBA. *Accreditation:* AACSB. *Program availability:* Part-time, evening/weekend. *Faculty:* 91 full-time (30 women), 14 part-time/adjunct (4 women). *Students:* 1 (woman) full-time. Average age 26. 8 applicants, 50% accepted. *Entrance requirements:* Additional exam requirements/recommendations for international students: Required—TOEFL (minimum score 100 iBT) or IELTS (minimum score 7.0). *Application deadline:* For fall admission, 4/1 priority date for domestic students, 2/1 priority date for international students. Application fee: $50. Electronic applications accepted. *Financial support:* Scholarships/grants available. Financial award application deadline: 6/1; financial award applicants required to submit FAFSA. *Faculty research:* Accounting systems/financial reporting, corporate finance, shopper marketing/consumer behavior, management information systems, organizational behavior and entrepreneurship. *Total annual research expenditures:* $475,077. *Unit head:* Dr. Arjang A. Assad, Dean, 412-648-1556, Fax: 412-648-1552, E-mail: aassad@katz.pitt.edu. *Application contact:* Thomas Keller, Director of MBA Admissions, 412-648-1700, Fax: 412-648-1659, E-mail: mba@katz.pitt.edu.
Website: https://www.katz.business.pitt.edu/mba/joint-and-dual/international-development#section-1
See Display on the previous page and Close-Up on page 187.

University of Pittsburgh, Katz Graduate School of Business, MBA/Master of Public and International Affairs Dual-Degree Program, Pittsburgh, PA 15260. Offers MBA/MPIA. *Accreditation:* AACSB. *Program availability:* Part-time, evening/weekend. *Faculty:* 91 full-time (30 women), 14 part-time/adjunct (4 women). *Students:* 1 (woman) full-time. Average age 24. 3 applicants, 33% accepted, 1 enrolled. *Entrance requirements:* Additional exam requirements/recommendations for international students: Required—TOEFL (minimum score 100 iBT) or IELTS (minimum score 7.0). *Application deadline:* For fall admission, 4/1 priority date for domestic students, 2/1 priority date for international students. Application fee: $50. Electronic applications accepted. *Financial support:* Scholarships/grants available. Financial award application deadline: 6/1; financial award applicants required to submit FAFSA. *Faculty research:* Accounting systems/financial reporting, corporate finance, shopper marketing/consumer behavior, management information systems, organizational behavior and entrepreneurship. *Total annual research expenditures:* $475,077. *Unit head:* Dr. Arjang A. Assad, Dean, 412-648-1556, Fax: 412-648-1552, E-mail: aassad@katz.pitt.edu. *Application contact:* Thomas Keller, Director of MBA Admissions, 412-648-1700, Fax: 412-648-1659, E-mail: mba@katz.pitt.edu.
Website: https://www.katz.business.pitt.edu/mba/joint-and-dual/international-affairs#section-1
See Display on the previous page and Close-Up on page 187.

University of Pittsburgh, Katz Graduate School of Business, MBA/Master of Science in Engineering Joint Degree Program, Pittsburgh, PA 15260. Offers MBA/MSE. *Accreditation:* AACSB. *Program availability:* Part-time, evening/weekend. *Faculty:* 91 full-time (30 women), 14 part-time/adjunct (4 women). *Students:* 14 full-time (2 women), 12 part-time (1 woman); includes 5 minority (1 Black or African American, non-Hispanic/Latino; 4 Hispanic/Latino), 3 international. Average age 27. 30 applicants, 57% accepted, 7 enrolled. *Entrance requirements:* Additional exam requirements/recommendations for international students: Required—TOEFL (minimum score 100 iBT) or IELTS (minimum score 7.0). *Application deadline:* For fall admission,

4/1 priority date for domestic students, 2/1 priority date for international students. Application fee: $50. Electronic applications accepted. *Financial support:* Scholarships/grants available. Financial award application deadline: 6/1; financial award applicants required to submit FAFSA. *Faculty research:* Accounting systems/financial reporting, corporate finance, shopper marketing/consumer behavior, management information systems, organizational behavior and entrepreneurship. *Total annual research expenditures:* $475,077. *Unit head:* Dr. Arjang A. Assad, Dean, 412-648-1556, Fax: 412-648-1552, E-mail: aassad@katz.pitt.edu. *Application contact:* Thomas Keller, Director of MBA Admissions, 412-648-1700, Fax: 412-648-1659, E-mail: mba@katz.pitt.edu.
Website: https://www.katz.business.pitt.edu/mba/joint-and-dual/engineering#section-1
See Display on the previous page and Close-Up on page 187.

University of Portland, Dr. Robert B. Pamplin, Jr. School of Business, Portland, OR 97203-5798. Offers entrepreneurship (MBA); finance (MBA, MS); health care management (MBA); marketing (MBA); nonprofit management (EMBA); operations and technology management (MBA, MS); sustainability (MBA). *Accreditation:* AACSB. *Program availability:* Part-time, evening/weekend. *Entrance requirements:* For master's, GMAT, minimum GPA of 3.0, resume, 2 letters of recommendation. Additional exam requirements/recommendations for international students: Required—TOEFL (minimum score 570 paper-based; 89 iBT), IELTS (minimum score 7). *Expenses:* Contact institution.

University of Puerto Rico–Mayagüez, Graduate Studies, College of Business Administration, Mayagüez, PR 00681-9000. Offers business administration (MBA); finance (MBA); human resources (MBA); industrial management (MBA). *Program availability:* Part-time, evening/weekend. *Degree requirements:* For master's, one foreign language, comprehensive exam, thesis (for some programs). *Entrance requirements:* For master's, GMAT or EXADEP, bachelor's degree with courses in calculus, microeconomics, accounting and statistics. Additional exam requirements/recommendations for international students: Required—TOEFL (minimum score 500 paper-based), GMAT or EXADEP. Electronic applications accepted. *Faculty research:* Organizational studies, management, accounting, entrepreneurship, leadership and motivation.

University of Puerto Rico–Río Piedras, College of Business Administration, San Juan, PR 00931-3300. Offers accounting (MBA); finance (MBA, PhD); general business (MBA); human resources management (MBA); international trade and business (MBA, PhD); marketing (MBA); operations management (MBA); quantitative methods (MBA). *Accreditation:* AACSB. *Program availability:* Part-time. *Degree requirements:* For master's, comprehensive exam, thesis or alternative, research project. *Entrance requirements:* For master's, GMAT or PAEG, minimum GPA of 3.0, letter of recommendation; for doctorate, GMAT, PAEG, minimum GPA of 3.0, master degree. *Faculty research:* Management.

University of Redlands, School of Business, Redlands, CA 92373-0999. Offers business (MBA); information technology (MS); management (MA). *Program availability:* Evening/weekend. *Entrance requirements:* For master's, minimum GPA of 3.0, 2 letters of recommendation. *Faculty research:* Human resources management, educational leadership, humanities, teacher education.

University of Regina, Faculty of Graduate Studies and Research, Kenneth Levene Graduate School of Business, Regina, SK S4S 0A2, Canada. Offers EMBA, M Admin, MBA, MHRM, Master's Certificate, PGD. *Program availability:* Part-time, evening/weekend. *Faculty:* 39 full-time (13 women), 12 part-time/adjunct (7 women). *Students:* 75 full-time (41 women), 109 part-time (78 women). 357 applicants, 41% accepted. In 2017, 57 master's, 15 other advanced degrees awarded. *Degree requirements:* For master's, project (for some programs). *Entrance requirements:* For master's, two years of relevant work experience (MHRM, M Admin); three years of relevant work experience (MBA); for other advanced degree, two years of relevant work experience (Master's Certificate); three years' relevant work experience (PGD). Additional exam requirements/recommendations for international students: Required—TOEFL (minimum score 580 paper-based; 80 iBT), IELTS (minimum score 6.5), PTE (minimum score 59). *Application deadline:* Applications are processed on a rolling basis. Application fee: $100. Electronic applications accepted. *Expenses:* CAD$20,150 per year. *Financial support:* In 2017–18, fellowships (averaging $6,000 per year), teaching assistantships (averaging $2,562 per year) were awarded; research assistantships, career-related internships or fieldwork, and scholarships/grants also available. Financial award application deadline: 6/15. *Faculty research:* Management of public and private sector organizations. *Unit head:* Dr. David Senkow, Dean, 306-585-4719, Fax: 306-585-4805, E-mail: david.senkow@uregina.ca. *Application contact:* Dr. Gina Grandy, Associate Dean, Research and Graduate Programs/Director of Kenneth Levene Graduate School, 306-585-5647, Fax: 306-585-5361, E-mail: gina.grandy@uregina.ca.
Website: http://www.uregina.ca/business/levene/

University of Rhode Island, Graduate School, College of Business, Program in Business Administration, Kingston, RI 02881. Offers finance (MBA); general business (MBA); management (MBA); marketing (MBA, PhD); operations and supply chain management (PhD); supply chain management (MBA); Pharm D/MBA. *Faculty:* 34 full-time (13 women). *Students:* 47 full-time (13 women), 146 part-time (72 women); includes 22 minority (3 Black or African American, non-Hispanic/Latino; 1 American Indian or Alaska Native, non-Hispanic/Latino; 11 Asian, non-Hispanic/Latino; 6 Hispanic/Latino; 1 Two or more races, non-Hispanic/Latino), 16 international. 131 applicants, 59% accepted, 58 enrolled. In 2017, 94 master's, 1 doctorate awarded. *Entrance requirements:* Additional exam requirements/recommendations for international students: Required—TOEFL. *Application deadline:* For fall admission, 6/30 for domestic students; for spring admission, 10/31 for domestic students; for summer admission, 3/31 for domestic students. Electronic applications accepted. *Expenses:* Tuition, state resident: full-time $12,706; part-time $786 per credit. Tuition, nonresident: full-time $25,216; part-time $1401 per credit. *Required fees:* $1598; $45 per credit. One-time fee: $30 part-time. *Financial support:* In 2017–18, 15 teaching assistantships (averaging $16,541 per year) were awarded. Financial award application deadline: 2/1. *Unit head:* Lisa Lancellotta, Coordinator, MBA Programs, 401-874-4241, E-mail: mba@uri.edu.
See Display on the next page and Close-Up on page 189.

University of Richmond, Robins School of Business, University of Richmond, VA 23173. Offers MBA, JD/MBA. *Accreditation:* AACSB. *Program availability:* Part-time, evening/weekend. *Degree requirements:* For master's, capstone project. *Entrance requirements:* For master's, GMAT or GRE, minimum of two years' professional work experience. Additional exam requirements/recommendations for international students: Required—TOEFL (minimum score 600 paper-based; 100 iBT). Electronic applications accepted. *Faculty research:* Entrepreneurship, investments, auditing, consumer behavior, strategic management.

University of Rochester, Simon Business School, Doctoral Program in Business Administration, Rochester, NY 14627. Offers accounting (PhD); computer information systems (PhD); finance (PhD); marketing (PhD); operations management (PhD). *Accreditation:* AACSB. *Faculty:* 70 full-time (12 women), 23 part-time/adjunct (6 women). *Students:* 50 full-time (17 women); includes 2 minority (both Asian, non-

Hispanic/Latino), 41 international. Average age 28. 199 applicants, 10% accepted, 9 enrolled. In 2017, 8 doctorates awarded. *Degree requirements:* For doctorate, comprehensive exam, thesis/dissertation, qualifying exam. *Entrance requirements:* For doctorate, GMAT or GRE. Additional exam requirements/recommendations for international students: Required—TOEFL. *Application deadline:* For fall admission, 1/5 for domestic and international students. Application fee: $100. Electronic applications accepted. *Expenses:* Contact institution. *Financial support:* In 2017–18, 50 students received support. Fellowships, research assistantships, teaching assistantships, health care benefits, and tuition waivers (full) available. Financial award application deadline: 1/5. *Faculty research:* Empirical industrial organization, risk management, financial disclosure and regulation, social media, health care management. *Unit head:* Dr. Ron Kaniel, Committee Chair, 585-275-2959. *Application contact:* Sue Harris, PhD Administrator, 585-275-2959, E-mail: phdoffice@simon.rochester.edu. Website: http://www.simon.rochester.edu/programs/phd/index.aspx

University of Rochester, Simon Business School, Executive MBA Program, Rochester, NY 14627. Offers MBA. *Program availability:* Part-time-only, evening/weekend. *Faculty:* 70 full-time (12 women), 23 part-time/adjunct (6 women). *Students:* 60 part-time (20 women); includes 7 minority (1 Black or African American, non-Hispanic/Latino; 5 Asian, non-Hispanic/Latino; 1 Hispanic/Latino). Average age 36. 39 applicants, 87% accepted, 32 enrolled. In 2017, 35 master's awarded. *Application deadline:* For fall admission, 6/15 for domestic students. Applications are processed on a rolling basis. Electronic applications accepted. *Expenses:* $91,800 tuition, $6,700 fees. *Financial support:* In 2017–18, 40 students received support. Tuition waivers (partial) available. Financial award application deadline: 6/15. *Faculty research:* Empirical industrial organization, risk management, financial disclosure and regulation, social media, health care management. *Unit head:* Andrew Ainslie, Dean, 585-275-3316, E-mail: andrew.ainslie@simon.rochester.edu. *Application contact:* Molly Mesko, Executive Director, EMBA and Part-Time Programs, 585-275-4277, E-mail: molly.mesko@simon.rochester.edu. Website: http://www.simon.rochester.edu/programs/executive-mba/index.aspx

University of Rochester, Simon Business School, Full-Time Master's Program in Business Administration, Rochester, NY 14627. Offers business systems consulting (MBA); competitive and organizational strategy (MBA); computers and information systems (MBA); corporate accounting (MBA); entrepreneurship (MBA); finance (MBA); health sciences management (MBA); marketing (MBA); operations management (MBA); public accounting (MBA); strategy and organizations (MBA). *Accreditation:* AACSB. *Faculty:* 70 full-time (12 women), 23 part-time/adjunct (6 women). *Students:* 208 full-time (70 women). Average age 28. *Entrance requirements:* For master's, GMAT or GRE. *Application deadline:* For fall admission, 10/15 for domestic and international students; for winter admission, 1/5 for domestic and international students; for spring admission, 3/15 for domestic and international students; for summer admission, 5/15 for domestic and international students. Application fee: $150. *Financial support:* Fellowships, institutionally sponsored loans, scholarships/grants, and tuition waivers (full and partial) available. Financial award application deadline: 1/5; financial award applicants required to submit FAFSA. *Faculty research:* Empirical industrial organization, risk management, financial disclosure and regulation, social media, health care management. *Unit head:* Andrew Ainslie, Dean, 585-275-3316, E-mail: andrew.ainslie@simon.rochester.edu. *Application contact:* Rebekah S. Lewin, Assistant Dean of Admissions and Financial Aid, 585-275-3533, E-mail: admissions@simon.rochester.edu. Website: http://www.simon.rochester.edu/programs/full-time-mba/index.aspx

University of Rochester, Simon Business School, Part-Time MBA Program, Rochester, NY 14627. Offers business systems consulting (MBA); competitive and organizational strategy (MBA); computers and information systems (MBA); corporate accounting (MBA); entrepreneurship (MBA); finance (MBA); health sciences management (MBA); marketing (MBA), including brand management, marketing strategy, pricing; operations management (MBA); public accounting (MBA). *Program availability:* Part-time-only, evening/weekend. *Faculty:* 70 full-time (12 women), 23 part-time/adjunct (6 women). *Students:* 159 part-time (62 women); includes 25 minority (5 Black or African American, non-Hispanic/Latino; 9 Asian, non-Hispanic/Latino; 9 Hispanic/Latino; 2 Two or more races, non-Hispanic/Latino), 4 international. Average age 32. 39 applicants, 92% accepted, 35 enrolled. In 2017, 59 master's awarded. *Entrance requirements:* For master's, GRE or GMAT. *Application deadline:* For fall admission, 8/1 for domestic students; for spring admission, 2/15 for domestic students. Applications are processed on a rolling basis. Application fee: $150. Electronic applications accepted. *Expenses:* $1,875 per credit, $1,385 fees. *Financial support:* In 2017–18, 69 students received support. Tuition waivers (partial) available. Financial award application deadline: 8/1. *Unit head:* Andrew Ainslie, Dean, 585-275-3316, E-mail: andrew.ainslie@simon.rochester.edu. *Application contact:* Molly Mesko, Executive Director, EMBA and Part-Time Programs, 585-275-4277, E-mail: molly.mesko@simon.rochester.edu. Website: http://www.simon.rochester.edu/programs/ptmba/index.aspx

University of Saint Francis, Graduate School, Keith Busse School of Business and Entrepreneurial Leadership, Fort Wayne, IN 46808-3994. Offers business administration (MBA), including sustainability; environmental health (MEH); healthcare administration (MHA); organizational leadership (MOL). *Accreditation:* ACBSP. *Program availability:* Part-time, evening/weekend, online only, 100% online. *Faculty:* 4 full-time (3 women), 11 part-time/adjunct (1 woman). *Students:* 75 full-time (43 women), 108 part-time (59 women); includes 37 minority (21 Black or African American, non-Hispanic/Latino; 1 Asian, non-Hispanic/Latino; 11 Hispanic/Latino; 1 Native Hawaiian or other Pacific Islander, non-Hispanic/Latino; 3 Two or more races, non-Hispanic/Latino). Average age 34. 101 applicants, 98% accepted, 75 enrolled. In 2017, 133 master's awarded. *Entrance requirements:* For master's, GMAT (if cumulative GPA is below 2.75 with less than five years' professional work experience), minimum undergraduate GPA of 2.75; statement of professional goals; resume. Additional exam requirements/recommendations for international students: Required—TOEFL (minimum score 550 paper-based) or IELTS (minimum score 6.5). *Application deadline:* For fall admission, 7/1 for international students; for spring admission, 11/1 for international students; for summer admission, 3/1 for international students. Applications are processed on a rolling basis. Application fee: $0. Electronic applications accepted. *Expenses:* $475 per hour. *Financial support:* Application deadline: 4/15; applicants required to submit FAFSA. *Unit head:* Dr. Robert Lee, Dean, 260-399-7700 Ext. 8304, Fax: 260-399-8174, E-mail: rlee@sf.edu. *Application contact:* Kyle Richardson, Associate Director of Enrollment Services for Adult Learning, 260-399-7700 Ext. 6310, Fax: 260-399-8152, E-mail: krichardson@sf.edu. Website: https://business.sf.edu/graduate/

University of Saint Joseph, Department of Business Administration, West Hartford, CT 06117-2700. Offers management (MS). *Program availability:* Part-time, evening/weekend. *Entrance requirements:* For master's, 2 letters of recommendation. *Application deadline:* Applications are processed on a rolling basis. Application fee: $50. Electronic applications accepted. Application fee is waived when completed online. *Financial support:* Career-related internships or fieldwork and unspecified assistantships available. Support available to part-time students. Financial award applicants required to submit FAFSA. *Unit head:* Steven B. Jarett, Chair, 860-231-5288, E-mail: sjarett@usj.edu. Website: https://www.usj.edu/academics/schools/sasbe/business-administration/

University of Saint Mary, Graduate Programs, Program in Business Administration, Leavenworth, KS 66048-5082. Offers enterprise risk management (MBA); finance (MBA); general management (MBA); health care management (MBA); human resource management (MBA); marketing and advertising management (MBA). *Program availability:* Part-time, evening/weekend, 100% online, blended/hybrid learning. *Degree requirements:* For master's, thesis. *Entrance requirements:* For master's, minimum undergraduate GPA of 2.75, official transcripts, two letters of recommendation. Electronic applications accepted. *Expenses:* Contact institution.

University of St. Thomas, Cameron School of Business, Houston, TX 77006-4696. Offers MBA, MCTM, MIB, MSA, MSF. *Program availability:* Part-time, evening/weekend. *Faculty:* 26 full-time (10 women), 7 part-time/adjunct (1 woman). *Students:* 136 full-time (73 women), 200 part-time (113 women); includes 155 minority (41 Black or African American, non-Hispanic/Latino; 1 American Indian or Alaska Native, non-Hispanic/Latino; 24 Asian, non-Hispanic/Latino; 81 Hispanic/Latino; 8 Two or more races, non-Hispanic/Latino), 99 international. Average age 31. 121 applicants, 97% accepted, 70 enrolled. In 2017, 186 master's awarded. *Degree requirements:* For master's, capstone (for some programs), additional course requirements for those sitting for state accountancy exam. *Entrance requirements:* For master's, minimum GPA of 2.5, 3 letters of recommendation. Additional exam requirements/recommendations for international students: Required—TOEFL (minimum score 550 paper-based; 79 iBT), IELTS (minimum score 6.5), PTE (minimum score 53). *Application deadline:* For fall admission, 7/15 for domestic and international students; for winter admission, 7/15 for domestic and international students; for spring admission, 11/15 for domestic students, 10/15 for international students. Applications are processed on a rolling basis. Application fee: $35. Electronic applications accepted. *Expenses:* Tuition: Full-time $20,934; part-time $1163 per credit hour. *Required fees:* $250; $210 per semester. *Financial support:* In 2017–18, 22 students received support, including research assistantships with partial tuition reimbursements available (averaging $3,000 per year); Federal Work-Study, scholarships/grants, unspecified assistantships, and state work-study, institutional employment also available. Support available to part-time students. Financial award application deadline: 4/15; financial award applicants required to submit FAFSA. *Unit head:* Dr. Beena George, Dean, 713-525-2100, Fax: 713-525-2110, E-mail: cameron@stthom.edu. *Application contact:* 713-525-2100, Fax: 713-525-2110, E-mail: cameron@stthom.edu.
Website: http://www.stthom.edu/Academics/Cameron_School_of_Business/Index.aqf

University of St. Thomas, Opus College of Business, Executive UST MBA Program, Minneapolis, MN 55403. Offers MBA. *Program availability:* Part-time. *Entrance requirements:* For master's, five years of significant management or leadership experience. *Application deadline:* For fall admission, 7/15 for domestic and international students. Applications are processed on a rolling basis. Application fee: $100. Electronic applications accepted. *Expenses:* Contact institution. *Financial support:* Applicants required to submit FAFSA. *Unit head:* Sandy Bauer, Coordinator, 651-962-8800, Fax: 651-962-4235, E-mail: execmba@stthomas.edu.
Website: http://www.stthomas.edu/execmba

University of St. Thomas, Opus College of Business, Full-time UST MBA Program, Minneapolis, MN 55403. Offers MBA. *Entrance requirements:* For master's, GMAT, GRE. Additional exam requirements/recommendations for international students: Required—TOEFL (minimum score 90 iBT), IELTS (minimum score 7), or Michigan English Language Assessment Battery. *Application deadline:* For fall admission, 12/15 priority date for domestic and international students. Applications are processed on a rolling basis. Application fee: $60. Electronic applications accepted. Tuition and fees vary according to course load, degree level, campus/location and program. *Financial support:* Scholarships/grants, tuition waivers (full and partial), and unspecified assistantships available. Financial award application deadline: 4/15. *Unit head:* Hannah Hedegard, Program Director, 651-962-8819. *Application contact:* Josie Visser, Associate Director of Recruiting and Admissions, 651-962-8825, Fax: 651-962-4129, E-mail: jtvisser@stthomas.edu.
Website: http://www.stthomas.edu/mba

University of St. Thomas, Opus College of Business, Part-time MBA Program, Minneapolis, MN 55403. Offers MBA, MSBA. *Program availability:* Part-time, evening/weekend, 100% online, blended/hybrid learning. *Entrance requirements:* For master's, GMAT. *Application deadline:* For fall admission, 5/1 priority date for domestic students; for spring admission, 11/1 priority date for domestic students; for summer admission, 4/1 priority date for domestic students. Applications are processed on a rolling basis. Application fee: $60. Electronic applications accepted. Tuition and fees vary according to course load, degree level, campus/location and program. *Financial support:* Scholarships/grants available. Financial award application deadline: 6/1. *Unit head:* Corey Eakins, Senior Program Director, 651-962-4228, Fax: 651-962-4129. *Application contact:* Susan Haun, Associate Director of Recruiting and Admissions, 651-962-4312, Fax: 651-962-4129.
Website: https://www.stthomas.edu/business/part-time-mba/

University of San Diego, School of Business, MBA Program, San Diego, CA 92110-2492. Offers MBA, JD/MBA. *Program availability:* Part-time, evening/weekend. *Students:* 112 full-time (37 women), 67 part-time (28 women); includes 39 minority (4 Black or African American, non-Hispanic/Latino; 12 Asian, non-Hispanic/Latino; 19 Hispanic/Latino; 2 Native Hawaiian or other Pacific Islander, non-Hispanic/Latino; 4 Two or more races, non-Hispanic/Latino), 48 international. Average age 30. In 2017, 65 master's awarded. *Degree requirements:* For master's, community service, capstone project. *Entrance requirements:* For master's, GMAT (minimum score 600 for full-time, 550 for part-time), minimum GPA of 3.0, minimum 2 years of full-time professional experience. Additional exam requirements/recommendations for international students: Required—TOEFL (minimum score 580 paper-based; 92 iBT), TWE. *Application deadline:* For fall admission, 11/1 priority date for domestic students; for spring admission, 10/1 priority date for domestic students. Applications are processed on a rolling basis. Application fee: $80. Electronic applications accepted. *Financial support:* In 2017–18, 118 students received support. Career-related internships or fieldwork, Federal Work-Study, institutionally sponsored loans, and unspecified assistantships available. Support available to part-time students. Financial award application deadline: 4/1; financial award applicants required to submit FAFSA. *Faculty research:* Exchange rate forecasting, corporate governance, performance of private equity funds, economic geography, food banking. *Unit head:* Dr. Manzur Rahman, Academic Director, MBA Programs, 619-260-2388, E-mail: mba@sandiego.edu. *Application contact:* Monica Mahon, Associate Director of Graduate Admissions, 619-260-4524, Fax: 619-260-4158, E-mail: grads@sandiego.edu.
Website: http://www.sandiego.edu/business/graduate/mba/

University of San Diego, School of Business, Program in Executive Leadership, San Diego, CA 92110-2492. Offers MS. *Program availability:* Evening/weekend. *Students:* 19 full-time (10 women), 18 part-time (6 women); includes 10 minority (2 Black or African American, non-Hispanic/Latino; 1 Asian, non-Hispanic/Latino; 7 Hispanic/Latino). Average age 44. In 2017, 16 master's awarded. *Entrance requirements:* For master's, GMAT (taken within the last 5 years) or professional product that demonstrates ability to analyze complex problems. Additional exam requirements/recommendations for international students: Required—TOEFL (minimum score 580 paper-based; 92 iBT),

TWE. *Application deadline:* For fall admission, 5/1 for domestic students. Applications are processed on a rolling basis. Application fee: $80. Electronic applications accepted. *Financial support:* In 2017–18, 11 students received support. Career-related internships or fieldwork and scholarships/grants available. Financial award application deadline: 4/1; financial award applicants required to submit FAFSA. *Unit head:* Director, MS in Executive Leadership, 619-260-4860, E-mail: msel@sandiego.edu. *Application contact:* Monica Mahon, Associate Director of Graduate Admissions, 619-260-4524, Fax: 619-260-4158, E-mail: grads@sandiego.edu.
Website: http://www.sandiego.edu/business/graduate/ms-executive-leadership/

University of San Francisco, School of Management, Executive Master of Business Administration Program, San Francisco, CA 94117. Offers MBA. *Accreditation:* AACSB. *Program availability:* Part-time, evening/weekend. *Entrance requirements:* For master's, GMAT (for applicants with less than eight years of post-undergraduate professional experience), resume demonstrating minimum of eight years of professional work experience, transcripts from each college or university attended, two letters of recommendation, essays, interview. Additional exam requirements/recommendations for international students: Required—TOEFL (minimum score 600 paper-based, 100 iBT), IELTS (minimum score 7) or PTE (minimum score 68). Electronic applications accepted. *Expenses:* Contact institution.

University of San Francisco, School of Management, Master of Business Administration Program, San Francisco, CA 94117. Offers entrepreneurship and innovation (MBA); finance (MBA); marketing (MBA); organization development (MBA); DDS/MBA; JD/MBA; MBA/MAPS. *Accreditation:* AACSB. *Program availability:* Part-time, evening/weekend. *Entrance requirements:* For master's, GMAT or GRE, resume (two years of professional work experience required for part-time students, preferred for full-time), transcripts from each college or university attended, two letters of recommendation, personal statement, interview. Additional exam requirements/recommendations for international students: Required—TOEFL (minimum score 600 paper-based, 100 iBT), IELTS (minimum score 7) or PTE (minimum score 68). Electronic applications accepted. *Expenses:* Contact institution. *Faculty research:* International financial markets, technology transfer licensing, international marketing, strategic planning.

University of Saskatchewan, College of Graduate Studies and Research, Edwards School of Business, Saskatoon, SK S7N 5A2, Canada. Offers M Sc, MBA, MP Acc. *Program availability:* Part-time. *Degree requirements:* For master's, thesis (for some programs). *Entrance requirements:* For master's, GMAT. Additional exam requirements/recommendations for international students: Required—TOEFL.

The University of Scranton, Kania School of Management, Program in Business Administration, Scranton, PA 18510. Offers accounting (MBA); finance (MBA); general business administration (MBA); health care management (MBA); international business (MBA); management information systems (MBA); marketing (MBA); operations management (MBA). *Accreditation:* AACSB. *Program availability:* Part-time, evening/weekend, 100% online. *Entrance requirements:* For master's, GMAT (for MBA). *Faculty research:* Financial markets, strategic impact of total quality management, internal accounting controls, consumer preference, information systems and the Internet.

University of Sioux Falls, Vucurevich School of Business, Sioux Falls, SD 57105-1699. Offers entrepreneurial leadership (MBA); general management (MBA); health care management (MBA); marketing (MBA). *Program availability:* Part-time, evening/weekend. *Degree requirements:* For master's, project. *Entrance requirements:* For master's, minimum GPA of 3.0. Additional exam requirements/recommendations for international students: Required—TOEFL. *Expenses:* Contact institution.

University of South Africa, College of Economic and Management Sciences, Pretoria, South Africa. Offers accounting (D Admin, D Com); accounting science (DA); auditing (D Admin, D Com); business administration (M Tech); business economics (D Admin); business leadership (DBL); business management (D Admin, D Com); economic management analysis (M Tech); economics (D Admin, D Com, PhD); human resource development (M Tech); industrial psychology (D Admin, D Com, PhD); logistics (D Com); marketing (M Tech); public administration (D Admin, D Com, DPA, PhD); public management (M Tech); quantitative management (D Admin, D Com); real estate (M Tech); statistics (D Admin, PhD); tourism management (D Admin, D Com); transport economics (D Admin, D Com).

University of South Africa, Graduate School of Business Leadership, Pretoria, South Africa. Offers MBA, MBL, DBL.

University of South Alabama, Mitchell College of Business, Program in Business Administration, Mobile, AL 36688. Offers business administration (MBA); management (DBA); marketing (DBA). *Accreditation:* AACSB. *Program availability:* Part-time, evening/weekend. *Faculty:* 9 full-time (2 women). *Students:* 67 full-time (35 women), 8 part-time (1 woman); includes 15 minority (7 Black or African American, non-Hispanic/Latino; 1 American Indian or Alaska Native, non-Hispanic/Latino; 5 Asian, non-Hispanic/Latino; 2 Hispanic/Latino), 8 international. Average age 34. 74 applicants, 43% accepted, 26 enrolled. In 2017, 18 master's, 2 doctorates awarded. *Degree requirements:* For master's, comprehensive exam; for doctorate, comprehensive exam, thesis/dissertation. *Entrance requirements:* For master's, GMAT (minimum score of 450, 3.0 in Analytical Writing section), minimum undergraduate GPA of 3.0; for doctorate, MBA/specialized master's degree, 5 years of professional experience, 3 letters of reference, curriculum vitae, interview. Additional exam requirements/recommendations for international students: Required—TOEFL (minimum score 525 paper-based; 71 iBT). *Application deadline:* For fall admission, 7/15 for domestic students, 6/15 for international students; for spring admission, 12/1 for domestic students; for summer admission, 1/31 for domestic students. Application fee: $35. Electronic applications accepted. *Expenses:* Contact institution. *Financial support:* Research assistantships and unspecified assistantships available. Support available to part-time students. Financial award application deadline: 3/31; financial award applicants required to submit FAFSA. *Unit head:* Dr. Bob Wood, Dean of Business, 251-460-7167, Fax: 251-460-6529, E-mail: bgwood@southalabama.edu. *Application contact:* Dr. Alex Sharland, Assistant Dean and Director of Graduate Studies, 251-460-6418, Fax: 251-460-6529, E-mail: mcobgraduate@southalabama.edu.

University of South Carolina, The Graduate School, Darla Moore School of Business, Columbia, SC 29208. Offers accountancy (M Acc), including business measurement and assurance; business administration (MBA, PhD), including business administration (PhD), economics (PhD); economics (MA); human resources (MHR); international business administration (IMBA); JD/M Acc; JD/MA; JD/MHR. *Accreditation:* AACSB. *Program availability:* Part-time, evening/weekend, online learning. *Degree requirements:* For doctorate, one foreign language, thesis/dissertation. *Entrance requirements:* For master's, GMAT, GRE, minimum GPA of 3.0; for doctorate, GMAT or GRE. Additional exam requirements/recommendations for international students: Required—TOEFL (minimum score 600 paper-based). Electronic applications accepted. *Expenses:* Contact institution. *Faculty research:* Finance, marketing, strategic management, international management, operations.

University of South Carolina Aiken, Program in Business Administration, Aiken, SC 29801. Offers MBA. *Program availability:* Part-time, evening/weekend, online only, 100% online. *Faculty:* 3 full-time (2 women). *Students:* 13 part-time (6 women), 1

Business Administration and Management—General

international. Average age 37. 1 applicant. *Degree requirements:* For master's, capstone course(s). *Entrance requirements:* For master's, GMAT or GRE. Additional exam requirements/recommendations for international students: Required—TOEFL (minimum score 551 paper-based, 80 iBT), IELTS (6), or PTE (53). *Application deadline:* For fall admission, 8/6 for domestic and international students; for spring admission, 12/14 for domestic and international students. Applications are processed on a rolling basis. Application fee: $45 ($100 for international students). Electronic applications accepted. *Expenses:* $466.67 per credit hour (online). *Financial support:* In 2017–18, 3 students received support. Scholarships/grants and tuition waivers (partial) available. Support available to part-time students. Financial award application deadline: 3/1; financial award applicants required to submit FAFSA. *Faculty research:* Accounting, economics, finance, management, marketing. *Unit head:* Dr. Michael J. Fekula, Dean for School of Business Administration, 803-641-3340, E-mail: mickf@usca.edu. *Application contact:* Dan Robb, Associate Vice Chancellor for Enrollment Management, 803-641-3487, Fax: 803-641-3727, E-mail: danr@usca.edu.
Website: https://online.usca.edu/programs/business-programs.aspx

University of South Dakota, Graduate School, Beacom School of Business, Department of Business Administration, Vermillion, SD 57069. Offers business administration (MBA); business analytics (MBA, Graduate Certificate); health services administration (MBA); long term care management (Graduate Certificate); marketing (MBA, Graduate Certificate); operations and supply chain management (MBA, Graduate Certificate); JD/MBA. *Accreditation:* AACSB. *Program availability:* Part-time, blended/hybrid learning. *Degree requirements:* For master's, thesis or alternative. *Entrance requirements:* For master's, GMAT, minimum GPA of 2.7, resume. Additional exam requirements/recommendations for international students: Required—TOEFL (minimum score 550 paper-based; 79 iBT), IELTS (minimum score 6). *Application deadline:* For fall admission, 6/1 priority date for domestic students, 5/1 priority date for international students; for spring admission, 10/1 priority date for domestic students, 9/1 priority date for international students; for summer admission, 3/1 priority date for domestic students. Applications are processed on a rolling basis. Application fee: $35. Electronic applications accepted. *Expenses:* Contact institution. *Financial support:* Research assistantships with partial tuition reimbursements, teaching assistantships with partial tuition reimbursements, career-related internships or fieldwork, Federal Work-Study, and unspecified assistantships available. Financial award applicants required to submit FAFSA. *Application contact:* Graduate School, 605-658-6140, Fax: 605-677-6118, E-mail: grad@usd.edu.
Website: http://www.usd.edu/business/business-administration/graduate

University of South Dakota, Graduate School, College of Arts and Sciences, Program in Administrative Studies, Vermillion, SD 57069. Offers addiction studies (MSA); criminal justice studies (MSA); health services administration (MSA); human resources (MSA); interdisciplinary studies (MSA); long term care administration (MSA); organizational leadership (MSA). *Program availability:* Part-time, evening/weekend, 100% online. *Degree requirements:* For master's, thesis or alternative. *Entrance requirements:* For master's, 3 years of work or experience, minimum GPA of 2.7, resume. Additional exam requirements/recommendations for international students: Required—TOEFL (minimum score 550 paper-based; 79 iBT). *Application deadline:* Applications are processed on a rolling basis. Application fee: $35. Electronic applications accepted. *Financial support:* Teaching assistantships with partial tuition reimbursements available. Financial award applicants required to submit FAFSA. *Application contact:* Graduate School, 605-658-6140, Fax: 605-677-6118, E-mail: grad@usd.edu.
Website: http://www.usd.edu/onlinemsa

University of Southern California, Graduate School, Marshall School of Business, Los Angeles, CA 90089. Offers M Acc, MBA, MBT, MBV, MMM, MS, PhD, DDS/MBA, JD/MBT, MBA/Ed D, MBA/M PI, MBA/MD, MBA/MRED, MBA/MS, MBA/MSW, MBA/Pharm D. *Accreditation:* AACSB. *Degree requirements:* For doctorate, thesis/dissertation. *Entrance requirements:* For master's, GMAT and/or CPA Exam; for doctorate, GMAT or GRE. Additional exam requirements/recommendations for international students: Required—TOEFL. Electronic applications accepted.

University of Southern Indiana, Graduate Studies, Romain College of Business, Program in Business Administration, Evansville, IN 47712-3590. Offers accounting (MBA); data analytics (MBA); engineering management (MBA); general business administration (MBA); healthcare administration (MBA); human resource management (MBA). *Accreditation:* AACSB. *Program availability:* Part-time, evening/weekend, 100% online, blended/hybrid learning. *Faculty:* 22 full-time (4 women), 2 part-time/adjunct (0 women). *Students:* 312 full-time (167 women), 148 part-time (56 women); includes 72 minority (43 Black or African American, non-Hispanic/Latino; 8 Asian, non-Hispanic/Latino; 13 Hispanic/Latino; 8 Two or more races, non-Hispanic/Latino), 10 international. Average age 33. In 2017, 34 master's awarded. *Entrance requirements:* For master's, GMAT or GRE, minimum GPA of 2.5, resume, 3 professional references. Additional exam requirements/recommendations for international students: Required—TOEFL (minimum score 550 paper-based; 79 iBT), IELTS (minimum score 6). *Application deadline:* For fall admission, 8/1 for domestic students, 3/1 priority date for international students. Applications are processed on a rolling basis. Application fee: $40. Electronic applications accepted. *Expenses:* Tuition, state resident: full-time $9394. Tuition, nonresident: full-time $17,917. *Required fees:* $510. *Financial support:* In 2017–18, 18 students received support. Federal Work-Study, scholarships/grants, tuition waivers (full and partial), and unspecified assistantships available. Financial award application deadline: 3/1; financial award applicants required to submit FAFSA. *Unit head:* Dr. Jack E. Smothers, Program Director, 812-461-5248, E-mail: jesmothers@usi.edu. *Application contact:* Michelle Simmons, MBA Program Assistant, 812-464-1926, Fax: 812-465-1044, E-mail: masimmons3@usi.edu.
Website: http://www.usi.edu/business/mba

University of Southern Maine, College of Management and Human Service, School of Business, Portland, ME 04104-9300. Offers accounting (MBA); business administration (MBA); finance (MBA); health management and policy (MBA); sustainability (MBA); JD/MBA; MBA/MSA; MBA/MSN; MS/MBA. *Accreditation:* AACSB. *Program availability:* Part-time, evening/weekend. *Entrance requirements:* For master's, GMAT or GRE, minimum AACSB index of 1100. Additional exam requirements/recommendations for international students: Required—TOEFL (minimum score 550 paper-based; 79 iBT). Electronic applications accepted. *Faculty research:* Economic development, management information systems, real options, system dynamics, simulation.

University of Southern Maine, Lewiston-Auburn College, Program in Leadership Studies, Portland, ME 04103. Offers creative leadership/global strategies (CGS); leadership studies (MA). *Program availability:* Part-time, online learning.

University of Southern Mississippi, College of Business, Program in Business Administration, Hattiesburg, MS 39406-0001. Offers business administration (MBA); sport security management (MBA). *Accreditation:* AACSB. *Program availability:* Part-time, evening/weekend. *Students:* 43 full-time (18 women), 4 part-time (3 women). 84 applicants, 75% accepted, 47 enrolled. In 2017, 10 master's awarded. *Degree requirements:* For master's, comprehensive exam. *Entrance requirements:* For master's, GMAT, minimum GPA of 2.75 on last 60 hours. Additional exam requirements/recommendations for international students: Required—TOEFL, IELTS. *Application deadline:* For fall admission, 7/15 priority date for domestic students, 7/15 for

international students; for spring admission, 11/15 priority date for domestic students, 11/15 for international students. Application fee: $60. Electronic applications accepted. *Expenses:* Tuition, state resident: full-time $3830. *Financial support:* Research assistantships with full and partial tuition reimbursements, teaching assistantships with full tuition reimbursements, Federal Work-Study, institutionally sponsored loans, scholarships/grants, health care benefits, and unspecified assistantships available. Support available to part-time students. Financial award application deadline: 3/15; financial award applicants required to submit FAFSA. *Faculty research:* Inflation accounting, self-esteem training, international trade policy, health care marketing, ethics in strategic planning. *Unit head:* Heather Adams Sison, Advisor, 601-266-3496, E-mail: h.l.adams@usm.edu. *Application contact:* Amy Yeend, Assistant Dean, Academic and Career Services, 601-266-4663, Fax: 601-266-5814.

University of South Florida, Muma College of Business, Department of Management, Tampa, FL 33620-9951. Offers management (MS), including human resources, management information systems. *Accreditation:* AACSB. *Program availability:* Part-time, online learning. *Faculty:* 3 full-time (2 women). *Students:* 15 full-time (2 women), 26 part-time (13 women); includes 5 minority (3 Black or African American, non-Hispanic/Latino; 2 Hispanic/Latino), 26 international. Average age 27. 62 applicants, 56% accepted, 18 enrolled. In 2017, 35 master's awarded. Terminal master's awarded for partial completion of doctoral program. *Degree requirements:* For master's, comprehensive exam, thesis (for some programs). *Entrance requirements:* For master's, GMAT, letters of recommendation, resume, statement of purpose, relevant work experience. Additional exam requirements/recommendations for international students: Required—TOEFL (minimum score 550 paper-based; 79 iBT) or IELTS (minimum score 6.5). *Application deadline:* For fall admission, 6/1 for domestic students, 2/1 for international students; for spring admission, 10/15 for domestic students, 7/1 for international students. Application fee: $30. Electronic applications accepted. *Financial support:* In 2017–18, 1 student received support, including 1 research assistantship with tuition reimbursement available (averaging $9,002 per year), 3 teaching assistantships with tuition reimbursements available (averaging $9,002 per year); tuition waivers also available. Financial award applicants required to submit FAFSA. *Faculty research:* Leadership and employment relations, time management, personal motivation, crew resource management in aviation, psychology of gambling, organizational culture, issues of fairness, employment law, marketing strategy/implementation, organizational diversity, ethics, environmentally-friendly business practices, green business, sustainable business plans, institutional theory, social movement theory, diffusion of innovations, stakeholder human resources management, social responsibility. *Unit head:* Dr. Sally Fuller, Interim Department Chair/Associate Professor, 813-974-1766, Fax: 813-905-9964, E-mail: sfuller@usf.edu. *Application contact:* Stacee Bender, 813-974-4516, Fax: 813-974-9964, E-mail: staceebender@usf.edu.
Website: http://www.usf.edu/business/masters/management/

University of South Florida, St. Petersburg, Kate Tiedemann College of Business, St. Petersburg, FL 33701. Offers MBA. *Accreditation:* AACSB. *Program availability:* Part-time. *Entrance requirements:* For master's, GMAT (minimum score of 500), bachelor's degree with minimum GPA of 3.0 overall or in upper two years from regionally-accredited institution; resume. Additional exam requirements/recommendations for international students: Required—TOEFL (minimum score 550 paper-based; 79 iBT); Recommended—IELTS. Electronic applications accepted.

University of South Florida Sarasota-Manatee, College of Business, Sarasota, FL 34243. Offers MBA. *Accreditation:* AACSB. *Program availability:* Part-time, evening/weekend. *Faculty:* 8 full-time (1 woman). *Students:* 42 full-time (15 women), 38 part-time (20 women); includes 30 minority (8 Black or African American, non-Hispanic/Latino; 8 Asian, non-Hispanic/Latino; 11 Hispanic/Latino; 3 Two or more races, non-Hispanic/Latino). Average age 32. 86 applicants, 23% accepted, 19 enrolled. In 2017, 30 master's awarded. *Degree requirements:* For master's, capstone project. *Entrance requirements:* For master's, GMAT (minimum score 500) or GRE (minimum score 1050 if taken before August 1, 2011 or 300 if taken after August 1, 2011), two years of full-time work experience (preferred); resume; two letters of recommendation; statement of purpose. Additional exam requirements/recommendations for international students: Required—TOEFL (minimum score 550 paper-based; 79 iBT), IELTS (minimum score 6.5). *Application deadline:* For fall admission, 3/1 priority date for domestic students, 3/1 for international students; for spring admission, 10/1 priority date for domestic students, 10/1 for international students. Applications are processed on a rolling basis. Application fee: $30. Electronic applications accepted. *Expenses:* $453.81 per credit hour. *Financial support:* In 2017–18, 2 students received support. Federal Work-Study, scholarships/grants, health care benefits, and unspecified assistantships available. Support available to part-time students. Financial award application deadline: 3/1; financial award applicants required to submit FAFSA. *Faculty research:* Mergers and acquisitions, customer loyalty, employment discrimination, measurement of quality, efficiency of markets. *Total annual research expenditures:* $35,000. *Unit head:* Dr. James M. Curran, Dean, 941-359-4605, Fax: 941-359-4367, E-mail: jmcurran@sar.usf.edu. *Application contact:* Andy Telatovich, Director, Admissions, 941-359-4330, E-mail: atelatovich@sar.usf.edu.
Website: http://usfsm.edu/college-of-business/

The University of Tampa, Sykes College of Business, Tampa, FL 33606-1490. Offers accounting (MS); business analytics (MBA); cybersecurity (MBA, MS); entrepreneurship (MBA, MS); finance (MBA, MS); information systems management (MBA); innovation management (MBA); international business (MBA); marketing (MBA, MS); nonprofit management (MBA, Certificate). *Accreditation:* AACSB. *Program availability:* Part-time, evening/weekend. *Faculty:* 38 full-time (14 women), 6 part-time/adjunct (1 woman). *Students:* 229 full-time (1 woman), 115 part-time (51 women); includes 51 minority (26 Black or African American, non-Hispanic/Latino; 11 Asian, non-Hispanic/Latino; 1 Native Hawaiian or other Pacific Islander, non-Hispanic/Latino; 13 Two or more races, non-Hispanic/Latino), 182 international. Average age 28. 1,305 applicants, 39% accepted, 192 enrolled. In 2017, 266 master's awarded. *Degree requirements:* For master's, capstone. *Entrance requirements:* For master's, GMAT or GRE, official transcripts from all colleges and/or universities previously attended, resume, personal statement, letters of recommendation. Additional exam requirements/recommendations for international students: Required—TOEFL (minimum score 577 paper-based; 90 iBT), IELTS (minimum score 7.5). *Application deadline:* Applications are processed on a rolling basis. Application fee: $40. Electronic applications accepted. *Expenses:* Contact institution. *Financial support:* In 2017–18, 116 students received support. Career-related internships or fieldwork, scholarships/grants, and unspecified assistantships available. Financial award applicants required to submit FAFSA. *Faculty research:* Job market signaling, on-line shopping behaviors and social media, the Tampa Bay economy, digital literacy, entrepreneurship in small businesses. *Unit head:* Dr. Natasha F. Veltri, Associate Dean, 813-253-6289, E-mail: nveltri@ut.edu. *Application contact:* Chanelle Cox, Staff Assistant, Admissions for Graduate and Continuing Studies, 813-253-6249, E-mail: ccox@ut.edu.
Website: http://www.ut.edu/business/

The University of Tennessee, Graduate School, College of Business Administration, Program in Business Administration, Knoxville, TN 37996. Offers accounting (PhD); finance (MBA, PhD); logistics and transportation (MBA, PhD); management (PhD);

marketing (MBA, PhD); operations management (MBA); professional business administration (MBA); statistics (PhD); JD/MBA; MS/MBA; Pharm D/MBA. Pharm D/MBA offered jointly with The University of Tennessee Health Science Center. *Accreditation:* AACSB. *Program availability:* Online learning. *Degree requirements:* For master's, thesis or alternative; for doctorate, thesis/dissertation. *Entrance requirements:* For master's and doctorate, GMAT, minimum GPA of 2.7. Additional exam requirements/recommendations for international students: Required—TOEFL. Electronic applications accepted.

The University of Tennessee, Graduate School, College of Business Administration, Program in Management Science, Knoxville, TN 37996. Offers MS, PhD. *Accreditation:* AACSB. *Degree requirements:* For master's, thesis or alternative; for doctorate, thesis/dissertation. *Entrance requirements:* For master's and doctorate, GMAT or GRE General Test, minimum GPA of 2.7. Additional exam requirements/recommendations for international students: Required—TOEFL. Electronic applications accepted.

The University of Tennessee at Chattanooga, Program in Business Administration, Chattanooga, TN 37403. Offers EMBA, MBA, PMBA. *Accreditation:* AACSB. *Program availability:* Part-time, evening/weekend. *Students:* 63 full-time (26 women), 238 part-time (110 women); includes 60 minority (21 Black or African American, non-Hispanic/Latino; 1 American Indian or Alaska Native, non-Hispanic/Latino; 9 Asian, non-Hispanic/Latino; 14 Hispanic/Latino; 15 Two or more races, non-Hispanic/Latino), 5 international. Average age 32. 150 applicants, 90% accepted, 98 enrolled. In 2017, 103 master's awarded. *Entrance requirements:* For master's, GMAT (minimum score 450) or GRE General Test (minimum score 146 on verbal and 144 on quantitative), minimum overall undergraduate GPA of 2.7 or 3.0 in final two years. Additional exam requirements/recommendations for international students: Required—TOEFL (minimum score 550 paper-based; 79 iBT), IELTS (minimum score 6). *Application deadline:* For fall admission, 6/15 priority date for domestic students, 7/1 for international students; for spring admission, 11/1 priority date for domestic students, 11/1 for international students. Applications are processed on a rolling basis. Application fee: $35 ($40 for international students). Electronic applications accepted. *Expenses:* Contact institution. *Financial support:* Research assistantships, teaching assistantships, career-related internships or fieldwork, scholarships/grants, health care benefits, tuition waivers (partial), and unspecified assistantships available. Support available to part-time students. Financial award application deadline: 7/1. *Faculty research:* Diversity, operations/production management, entrepreneurial processes, customer satisfaction and retention, branding. *Unit head:* Elizabeth Bell, Director of Graduate Programs, 423-425-2326, Fax: 423-425-5255, E-mail: elizabeth-bell@utc.edu. *Application contact:* Dr. Joanne Romagni, Dean of the Graduate School, 423-425-4478, Fax: 423-425-5223, E-mail: joanne-romagni@utc.edu.
Website: http://www.utc.edu/college-business/academic-programs/graduate-programs/index.php

The University of Tennessee at Martin, Graduate Programs, College of Business and Global Affairs, Program in Business, Martin, TN 38238. Offers agricultural business (MBA); financial services (MBA); general business (MBA). *Accreditation:* AACSB. *Program availability:* Part-time, online only, 100% online, blended/hybrid learning. *Faculty:* 31. *Students:* 12 full-time (5 women), 73 part-time (31 women); includes 12 minority (7 Black or African American, non-Hispanic/Latino; 2 Asian, non-Hispanic/Latino; 2 Hispanic/Latino; 1 Two or more races, non-Hispanic/Latino). Average age 34. 33 applicants, 24% accepted, 6 enrolled. In 2017, 38 master's awarded. *Degree requirements:* For master's, comprehensive exam. *Entrance requirements:* For master's, GMAT, GRE, minimum GPA of 2.5, resume. Additional exam requirements/recommendations for international students: Required—TOEFL (minimum score 525 paper-based; 71 iBT). *Application deadline:* For fall admission, 7/27 priority date for domestic students, 7/27 for international students; for spring admission, 12/17 priority date for domestic students, 12/17 for international students; for summer admission, 5/10 priority date for domestic and international students. Applications are processed on a rolling basis. Application fee: $30 ($130 for international students). Electronic applications accepted. *Expenses:* Tuition, state resident: full-time $8658; part-time $481 per credit hour. Tuition, nonresident: full-time $14,418; part-time $801 per credit hour. *International tuition:* $22,602 full-time. *Required fees:* $1404; $79 per credit hour. Part-time tuition and fees vary according to course load. *Financial support:* In 2017–18, 29 students received support, including 4 research assistantships with full tuition reimbursements available (averaging $7,226 per year), 2 teaching assistantships with full tuition reimbursements available (averaging $7,540 per year); scholarships/grants and tuition waivers (full and partial) also available. Financial award application deadline: 2/1; financial award applicants required to submit FAFSA. *Unit head:* Dr. Ashley Kilburn, Coordinator, 731-881-7245, Fax: 731-881-7231, E-mail: mba@utm.edu. *Application contact:* Jolene L. Cunningham, Student Services Specialist, 731-881-7012, Fax: 731-881-7499, E-mail: jcunningham@utm.edu.

The University of Texas at Austin, Graduate School, McCombs School of Business, Department of Management, Austin, TX 78712-1111. Offers PhD. *Accreditation:* AACSB. *Degree requirements:* For doctorate, thesis/dissertation. *Entrance requirements:* For doctorate, GMAT or GRE. Electronic applications accepted.

The University of Texas at Austin, Graduate School, McCombs School of Business, Executive MBA Program at Mexico City, Austin, TX 78712-1111. Offers MBA. Program offered jointly with Instituto Tecnológico y de Estudios Superiores de Monterrey, Campus Ciudad de México. *Accreditation:* AACSB. *Entrance requirements:* For master's, GMAT, 5 years of work experience. Additional exam requirements/recommendations for international students: Required—TOEFL.

The University of Texas at Austin, Graduate School, McCombs School of Business, MBA Programs, Austin, TX 78712-1111. Offers MBA, JD/MBA, MBA/MA, MBA/MP Aff, MBA/MSN. *Accreditation:* AACSB. *Program availability:* Part-time. *Entrance requirements:* For master's, GMAT, minimum 2 years of full-time work experience. Additional exam requirements/recommendations for international students: Required—TOEFL. Electronic applications accepted.

The University of Texas at Dallas, Naveen Jindal School of Management, Richardson, TX 75080. Offers EMBA, MBA, MS, PhD, MS/MBA, MSEE/MBA. *Program availability:* Part-time, evening/weekend, online learning. *Faculty:* 113 full-time (22 women), 71 part-time/adjunct (23 women). *Students:* 2,991 full-time (1,276 women), 1,677 part-time (746 women); includes 873 minority (142 Black or African American, non-Hispanic/Latino; 7 American Indian or Alaska Native, non-Hispanic/Latino; 459 Asian, non-Hispanic/Latino; 203 Hispanic/Latino; 1 Native Hawaiian or other Pacific Islander, non-Hispanic/Latino; 61 Two or more races, non-Hispanic/Latino), 2,884 international. Average age 28. 6,657 applicants, 43% accepted, 1485 enrolled. In 2017, 2,047 master's, 14 doctorates awarded. *Degree requirements:* For doctorate, thesis/dissertation. *Entrance requirements:* For master's and doctorate, GMAT. Additional exam requirements/recommendations for international students: Required—TOEFL (minimum score 550 paper-based). *Application deadline:* For fall admission, 7/15 for domestic students, 5/1 priority date for international students; for spring admission, 11/15 for domestic students, 9/1 priority date for international students. Applications are processed on a rolling basis. Application fee: $50 ($100 for international students). Electronic applications accepted. *Expenses:* Tuition, state resident: full-time $12,916; part-time $718 per credit hour. Tuition, nonresident: full-time $25,252; part-time $1403 per credit hour. *Financial*

support: In 2017–18, 1,288 students received support, including 26 research assistantships with partial tuition reimbursements available (averaging $33,146 per year), 175 teaching assistantships with partial tuition reimbursements available (averaging $17,697 per year); fellowships, career-related internships or fieldwork, Federal Work-Study, institutionally sponsored loans, scholarships/grants, and unspecified assistantships also available. Support available to part-time students. Financial award application deadline: 4/30; financial award applicants required to submit FAFSA. *Faculty research:* Finance, marketing and organization, strategy, management education for physicians. *Total annual research expenditures:* $3.9 million. *Unit head:* Dr. Hasan Pirkul, Dean, 972-883-2705, Fax: 972-883-2799, E-mail: hpirkul@utdallas.edu. *Application contact:* 972-883-2750, Fax: 972-883-6425, E-mail: jindal@utdallas.edu.
Website: http://jindal.utdallas.edu/

The University of Texas at El Paso, Graduate School, College of Business Administration, Programs in Business Administration, El Paso, TX 79968-0001. Offers business administration (MBA, Certificate); international business (PhD). *Accreditation:* AACSB. *Program availability:* Part-time, evening/weekend, online learning. *Degree requirements:* For master's, comprehensive exam. *Entrance requirements:* For master's and doctorate, GMAT. Additional exam requirements/recommendations for international students: Required—TOEFL. Electronic applications accepted. *Faculty research:* Cross-border modeling, human resources, and outsourcing and manufacturing; global information technology transfer; international investments and risk management.

The University of Texas at San Antonio, College of Business, Department of Information Systems and Cyber Security, San Antonio, TX 78249-0617. Offers cyber security (MSIT); information technology (MS, PhD); management of technology (MBA); technology entrepreneurship and management (Certificate). *Program availability:* Part-time, evening/weekend. *Faculty:* 12 full-time (2 women), 5 part-time/adjunct (0 women). *Students:* 73 full-time (23 women), 81 part-time (26 women); includes 53 minority (9 Black or African American, non-Hispanic/Latino; 8 Asian, non-Hispanic/Latino; 35 Hispanic/Latino; 1 Two or more races, non-Hispanic/Latino), 35 international. Average age 30. 106 applicants, 59% accepted, 42 enrolled. In 2017, 50 master's, 3 doctorates, 8 other advanced degrees awarded. *Degree requirements:* For master's, comprehensive exam (for some programs), thesis optional; for doctorate, comprehensive exam, thesis/dissertation. *Entrance requirements:* For master's and doctorate, GMAT/GRE, official transcripts, statement of purpose, letters of recommendation. Additional exam requirements/recommendations for international students: Required—TOEFL (minimum score 550 paper-based; 79 iBT), IELTS (minimum score 6.5). *Application deadline:* For fall admission, 7/31 for domestic students, 3/1 for international students; for spring admission, 10/15 for domestic students, 9/15 for international students. Applications are processed on a rolling basis. Application fee: $50 ($90 for international students). Electronic applications accepted. *Expenses:* Contact institution. *Financial support:* Fellowships, research assistantships, teaching assistantships, scholarships/grants, health care benefits, and unspecified assistantships available. Support available to part-time students. *Faculty research:* Cyber security, digital forensics, economics of information systems, information systems privacy, information technology adoption. *Total annual research expenditures:* $1.1 million. *Unit head:* Dr. David A. Dampier, Interim Chair, 210-458-6300, Fax: 210-458-6305, E-mail: david.dampier@utsa.edu.
Website: https://business.utsa.edu/information-systems-cyber-security/

The University of Texas at San Antonio, College of Business, Department of Management, San Antonio, TX 78249-0617. Offers management and organization studies (PhD). *Faculty:* 13 full-time (3 women). *Students:* 162 full-time (69 women), 79 part-time (31 women); includes 121 minority (17 Black or African American, non-Hispanic/Latino; 1 American Indian or Alaska Native, non-Hispanic/Latino; 18 Asian, non-Hispanic/Latino; 79 Hispanic/Latino; 1 Native Hawaiian or other Pacific Islander, non-Hispanic/Latino; 5 Two or more races, non-Hispanic/Latino), 9 international. Average age 32. 180 applicants, 64% accepted, 84 enrolled. In 2017, 1 doctorate awarded. Terminal master's awarded for partial completion of doctoral program. *Degree requirements:* For doctorate, comprehensive exam, thesis/dissertation. *Entrance requirements:* For doctorate, GMAT, GRE. Additional exam requirements/recommendations for international students: Required—TOEFL (minimum score 550 paper-based; 79 iBT), IELTS (minimum score 6.5). *Application deadline:* For fall admission, 7/31 for domestic students, 3/1 for international students; for spring admission, 10/15 for domestic students, 9/15 for international students. Application fee: $50 ($90 for international students). Electronic applications accepted. *Expenses:* Tuition, state resident: full-time $5495. Tuition, nonresident: full-time $21,938. *Required fees:* $1915. Tuition and fees vary according to program. *Unit head:* Dr. Robert L. Cardy, Chair, 210-458-4310, Fax: 210-458-5783, E-mail: robert.cardy@utsa.edu. *Application contact:* Caron Kiley, Assistant Director of Graduate Fiscal Services/PhD Program Manager, 210-458-7324, E-mail: caron.kiley@utsa.edu.
Website: https://business.utsa.edu/management/

The University of Texas at San Antonio, College of Business, Department of Management Science and Statistics, San Antonio, TX 78249-0617. Offers applied statistics (MS, PhD); management science (MBA). *Accreditation:* AACSB. *Program availability:* Part-time, evening/weekend. *Faculty:* 12 full-time (1 woman), 4 part-time/adjunct (0 women). *Students:* 30 full-time (18 women), 153 part-time (52 women); includes 81 minority (4 Black or African American, non-Hispanic/Latino; 24 Asian, non-Hispanic/Latino; 50 Hispanic/Latino; 3 Two or more races, non-Hispanic/Latino), 20 international. Average age 32. 196 applicants, 68% accepted, 103 enrolled. In 2017, 42 master's, 3 doctorates awarded. *Degree requirements:* For master's, comprehensive exam (for some programs), thesis or alternative; for doctorate, comprehensive exam, thesis/dissertation. *Entrance requirements:* For master's, GMAT, minimum of 36 semester credit hours of coursework beyond any hours acquired in the MBA-leveling courses; statement of purpose; for doctorate, GRE, minimum cumulative GPA of 3.3 in the last 60 hours of coursework; transcripts from all colleges and universities attended; curriculum vitae; statement of academic work experiences, interests, and goals; three letters of recommendation; BA, BS, or MS in mathematics, statistics, or closely-related field. Additional exam requirements/recommendations for international students: Required—TOEFL (minimum score 550 paper-based; 79 iBT), IELTS (minimum score 6.5). *Application deadline:* For fall admission, 7/31 for domestic students, 3/1 for international students; for spring admission, 10/15 for domestic students, 9/15 for international students. Applications are processed on a rolling basis. Application fee: $50 ($90 for international students). Electronic applications accepted. *Expenses:* Tuition, state resident: full-time $5495. Tuition, nonresident: full-time $21,938. *Required fees:* $1915. Tuition and fees vary according to program. *Faculty research:* Statistical signal processing, reliability and life-testing experiments, modeling decompression sickness using survival analysis. *Total annual research expenditures:* $209,168. *Unit head:* Dr. Mark Leung, Chair, 210-458-6345, Fax: 210-458-6350, E-mail: mark.leung@utsa.edu. *Application contact:* Katherine Pope, Director of Graduate Student Services, 210-458-7316, E-mail: katherine.pope@utsa.edu.
Website: https://business.utsa.edu/management-science-statistics/

The University of Texas at Tyler, College of Business and Technology, Program in Business Administration, Tyler, TX 75799-0001. Offers cyber security (MBA);

Business Administration and Management—General

engineering management (MBA); general management (MBA); healthcare management (MBA); internal assurance and consulting (MBA); marketing (MBA); oil, gas and energy (MBA); organizational development (MBA); quality management (MBA). *Accreditation:* AACSB. *Program availability:* Part-time, online learning. *Entrance requirements:* Additional exam requirements/recommendations for international students: Required—TOEFL (minimum score 550 paper-based). *Faculty research:* General business, inventory control, institutional markets, service marketing, product distribution, accounting fraud, financial reporting and recognition.

The University of Texas of the Permian Basin, Office of Graduate Studies, School of Business, Program in Management, Odessa, TX 79762-0001. Offers MBA. *Accreditation:* AACSB. *Entrance requirements:* For master's, GMAT. Additional exam requirements/recommendations for international students: Required—TOEFL (minimum score 550 paper-based).

The University of Texas Rio Grande Valley, Robert C. Vackar College of Business and Entrepreneurship, Edinburg, TX 78539. Offers M Acc, MBA, MS, PhD. *Accreditation:* AACSB. *Program availability:* Part-time, evening/weekend. *Degree requirements:* For master's, thesis optional; for doctorate, one foreign language, thesis/dissertation, internship. *Entrance requirements:* For master's, GMAT, minimum AACSB index of 1000 (based on last 60 semester hours); for doctorate, GMAT. Additional exam requirements/recommendations for international students: Required—TOEFL. *Expenses:* Tuition, state resident: full-time $5550; part-time $417 per credit hour. Tuition, nonresident: full-time $13,020; part-time $832 per credit hour. *Required fees:* $1169.

University of the Cumberlands, Hutton School of Business, Williamsburg, KY 40769-1372. Offers accounting (MBA); business (MBA). *Program availability:* Part-time, online learning. *Entrance requirements:* For master's, GMAT, GRE. Additional exam requirements/recommendations for international students: Required—TOEFL. Electronic applications accepted.

University of the District of Columbia, School of Business and Public Administration, Program in Business Administration, Washington, DC 20008-1175. Offers MBA. *Accreditation:* ACBSP. *Degree requirements:* For master's, comprehensive exam, thesis optional. *Entrance requirements:* For master's, GMAT, writing proficiency exam.

University of the Incarnate Word, H-E-B School of Business and Administration, San Antonio, TX 78209-6397. Offers MBA, MHA, MS. *Program availability:* Part-time, evening/weekend, online learning. *Faculty:* 22 full-time (11 women), 12 part-time/adjunct (4 women). *Students:* 240 full-time (118 women), 39 part-time (19 women); includes 151 minority (24 Black or African American, non-Hispanic/Latino; 5 Asian, non-Hispanic/Latino; 120 Hispanic/Latino; 2 Two or more races, non-Hispanic/Latino), 50 international. In 2017, 164 master's awarded. *Degree requirements:* For master's, capstone. *Entrance requirements:* For master's, GMAT, GRE, writing sample, interview. Additional exam requirements/recommendations for international students: Required—TOEFL (minimum score 560 paper-based; 83 iBT). *Application deadline:* Applications are processed on a rolling basis. Application fee: $20. Electronic applications accepted. *Expenses:* Tuition: Full-time $16,470; part-time $915 per credit hour. Tuition and fees vary according to degree level, program and student level. *Financial support:* In 2017–18, 4 research assistantships were awarded; Federal Work-Study, scholarships/grants, tuition waivers (partial), and unspecified assistantships also available. Financial award applicants required to submit FAFSA. *Faculty research:* Importance of business sustainability, comparison of tax/legal research services, fair trade branding as a tool for the marketing of developing society crafts, ethnocentrism and country of origin effects among immigrant consumers, international trade and investment. *Unit head:* Dr. Forrest Aven, Dean, 210-805-5884, Fax: 210-805-3564, E-mail: aven@uiwtx.edu. *Application contact:* Johnny Garcia, Assistant Director of Graduate Admissions, 210-805-3554, Fax: 210-829-3921, E-mail: jsgarcia@uiwtx.edu.

University of the Incarnate Word, School of Professional Studies, San Antonio, TX 78209-6397. Offers communication arts (MAA), including applied administration, communication arts, healthcare administration, industrial and organizational psychology, organizational development; organizational development and leadership (MS); professional studies (DBA). *Program availability:* Part-time, evening/weekend, 100% online, blended/hybrid learning. *Faculty:* 9 full-time (3 women), 25 part-time/adjunct (10 women). *Students:* 528 full-time (263 women), 348 part-time (141 women); includes 543 minority (122 Black or African American, non-Hispanic/Latino; 3 American Indian or Alaska Native, non-Hispanic/Latino; 26 Asian, non-Hispanic/Latino; 365 Hispanic/Latino; 6 Native Hawaiian or other Pacific Islander, non-Hispanic/Latino; 21 Two or more races, non-Hispanic/Latino). In 2017, 377 master's, 10 doctorates awarded. *Degree requirements:* For master's, comprehensive exam (for some programs), thesis or alternative. *Entrance requirements:* For master's, GMAT, GRE, official transcripts from all other colleges attended. Additional exam requirements/recommendations for international students: Required—TOEFL (minimum score 560 paper-based; 83 iBT). *Application deadline:* Applications are processed on a rolling basis. Electronic applications accepted. *Expenses:* $915 per credit hour (for master's programs); $940 per credit hour (for doctoral program). *Financial support:* Scholarships/grants and unspecified assistantships available. Financial award applicants required to submit FAFSA. *Unit head:* Dr. Cyndi Porter, Vice President, 877-603-1130, E-mail: porter@uiwtx.edu. *Application contact:* Julie Weber, Director of Marketing and Recruitment, 210-318-1876, Fax: 210-829-2756, E-mail: eapadmission@uiwtx.edu. Website: http://sps.uiw.edu/

University of the Pacific, Eberhardt School of Business, Stockton, CA 95211-0197. Offers M Acc, MBA, JD/MBA, Pharm D/MBA. *Accreditation:* AACSB. *Program availability:* Part-time. *Faculty:* 27 full-time (12 women). *Students:* 22 full-time (12 women), 1 (woman) part-time; includes 12 minority (6 Asian, non-Hispanic/Latino; 4 Hispanic/Latino; 2 Two or more races, non-Hispanic/Latino), 4 international. Average age 24. 69 applicants, 61% accepted, 16 enrolled. In 2017, 44 master's awarded. *Entrance requirements:* For master's, GMAT. Additional exam requirements/recommendations for international students: Required—TOEFL. *Application deadline:* For fall admission, 7/31 priority date for domestic students; for spring admission, 11/30 for domestic students. Applications are processed on a rolling basis. Application fee: $75. *Financial support:* Fellowships, research assistantships, Federal Work-Study, and institutionally sponsored loans available. Support available to part-time students. Financial award application deadline: 3/1; financial award applicants required to submit FAFSA. *Unit head:* Dr. David Dauwalder, Interim Dean, 209-946-7710, E-mail: ddauwalder@pacific.edu. *Application contact:* 209-946-2239, E-mail: business@pacific.edu. Website: http://www.pacific.edu/mba/

University of the People, Master of Business Administration Program, Pasadena, CA 91101. Offers MBA. *Program availability:* Online learning.

University of the Potomac, Program in Business Administration, Washington, DC 20005. Offers MBA. Program also offered at Vienna, VA campus. *Program availability:* Online learning.

University of the Sacred Heart, Graduate Programs, Department of Business Administration, San Juan, PR 00914-0383. Offers human resource management (MBA); information systems auditing (MS); information technology (Certificate); international marketing (MBA); management information systems (MBA); production and marketing of special events (Certificate); taxation (MBA). *Program availability:* Part-time, evening/weekend. *Degree requirements:* For master's, thesis. *Entrance requirements:* For master's, EXADEP, minimum undergraduate GPA of 2.75.

University of the Southwest, Graduate Programs, Hobbs, NM 88240-9129. Offers business administration (MBA); curriculum and instruction (MSE); curriculum and instruction: bilingual (MSE); curriculum and instruction: TESOL (MSE); early childhood education (MSE); educational administration (MSE); mental health counseling (MSE); school counseling (MSE); special education (MSE); sports management (MBA). *Program availability:* Part-time, evening/weekend, online learning. *Entrance requirements:* For master's, comprehensive exam, thesis (for some programs). *Entrance requirements:* Additional exam requirements/recommendations for international students: Recommended—TOEFL. Electronic applications accepted.

University of the Virgin Islands, School of Business, St. Thomas, VI 00802. Offers EMBA, MBA. *Program availability:* Part-time, evening/weekend. *Degree requirements:* For master's, comprehensive exam or thesis. *Entrance requirements:* For master's, GMAT, minimum GPA of 2.5. Additional exam requirements/recommendations for international students: Required—TOEFL (minimum score 550 paper-based). Electronic applications accepted. *Expenses:* Contact institution.

University of the West, Department of Business Administration, Rosemead, CA 91770. Offers business administration (EMBA); computer information systems (MBA); finance (MBA); international business (MBA); nonprofit organization management (MBA). *Program availability:* Part-time, evening/weekend. *Entrance requirements:* Additional exam requirements/recommendations for international students: Required—TOEFL.

The University of Toledo, College of Graduate Studies, College of Business and Innovation, Department of Management, Toledo, OH 43606-3390. Offers MBA. *Program availability:* Part-time, evening/weekend. *Entrance requirements:* For master's, GMAT, GRE, or LSAT, minimum GPA of 2.7 for all prior academic work, three letters of recommendation, statement of purpose, transcripts from all prior institutions attended. Additional exam requirements/recommendations for international students: Required—TOEFL (minimum score 550 paper-based; 80 iBT). Electronic applications accepted. *Faculty research:* Stress, deviation, workplace, globalization, recruitment.

University of Toronto, School of Graduate Studies, Rotman School of Management, Toronto, ON M5S 1A1, Canada. Offers MBA, MF, PhD, JD/MBA. *Accreditation:* AACSB. *Program availability:* Part-time, evening/weekend. *Degree requirements:* For doctorate, thesis/dissertation. *Entrance requirements:* For master's, GMAT (MBA), minimum mid-B average in final undergraduate year; minimum 2 years of full-time work experience; 2-3 letters of reference; for doctorate, GMAT or GRE, minimum B+ average, master's degree in business administration, 2-3 letters of reference. *Expenses:* Contact institution. *Faculty research:* Natural resources, organizational behavior, finance, marketing, strategic management.

The University of Tulsa, Graduate School, Collins College of Business, Business Administration/Computer Science Program, Tulsa, OK 74104-3189. Offers MBA/MS. *Program availability:* Part-time. *Entrance requirements:* Additional exam requirements/recommendations for international students: Required—TOEFL (minimum score 577 paper-based; 91 iBT), IELTS (minimum score 6.5). *Application deadline:* Applications are processed on a rolling basis. Application fee: $55. Electronic applications accepted. *Expenses:* Tuition: Full-time $22,230. *Required fees:* $2000. Tuition and fees vary according to course load and program. *Financial support:* Fellowships, research assistantships with full tuition reimbursements, teaching assistantships, career-related internships or fieldwork, Federal Work-Study, institutionally sponsored loans, scholarships/grants, health care benefits, tuition waivers (full and partial), and unspecified assistantships available. Support available to part-time students. Financial award application deadline: 2/1; financial award applicants required to submit FAFSA. *Unit head:* Dr. Ralph Jackson, Associate Dean, 918-631-2242, Fax: 918-631-2142, E-mail: ralph-jackson@utulsa.edu. *Application contact:* Information Contact, 918-631-2242, E-mail: graduate-business@utulsa.edu.

The University of Tulsa, Graduate School, Collins College of Business, Master of Business Administration Program, Tulsa, OK 74104-3189. Offers MBA, JD/MBA, MBA/MSCS, MBA/MSF. *Accreditation:* AACSB. *Program availability:* Part-time, evening/weekend. *Faculty:* 32 full-time (6 women). *Students:* 36 full-time (15 women), 56 part-time (18 women); includes 12 minority (1 Black or African American, non-Hispanic/Latino; 3 American Indian or Alaska Native, non-Hispanic/Latino; 1 Asian, non-Hispanic/Latino; 4 Hispanic/Latino; 3 Two or more races, non-Hispanic/Latino), 10 international. Average age 30. 93 applicants, 53% accepted, 30 enrolled. In 2017, 35 master's awarded. *Entrance requirements:* For master's, GMAT. Additional exam requirements/recommendations for international students: Required—TOEFL (minimum score 577 paper-based; 91 iBT), IELTS (minimum score 6.5). *Application deadline:* Applications are processed on a rolling basis. Application fee: $55. Electronic applications accepted. *Expenses:* Tuition: Full-time $22,230. *Required fees:* $2000. Tuition and fees vary according to course load and program. *Financial support:* In 2017–18, 25 students received support, including 25 teaching assistantships with full tuition reimbursements available (averaging $8,000 per year); fellowships, research assistantships with full tuition reimbursements available, career-related internships or fieldwork, institutionally sponsored loans, scholarships/grants, health care benefits, tuition waivers (full and partial), and unspecified assistantships also available. Support available to part-time students. Financial award application deadline: 2/1; financial award applicants required to submit FAFSA. *Faculty research:* Accounting, energy management, finance, international business, management information systems, taxation. *Unit head:* Dr. Ralph Jackson, Associate Dean of the Collins College of Business, 918-631-2242, Fax: 918-631-2142, E-mail: ralph-jackson@utulsa.edu. *Application contact:* Information Contact, 918-631-2242, E-mail: graduate-business@utulsa.edu.

University of Utah, Graduate School, David Eccles School of Business, Salt Lake City, UT 84112-8939. Offers EMBA, M Acc, MBA, MHA, MRED, MS, MSF, PMBA, PhD, Graduate Certificate, MBA/JD, MBA/MHA, MBA/MS, MHA/MPA, MPH/MHA, MRED/JD, MRED/M Arch, MRED/MCMP, MSF/MSBA, MSF/PMBA, PMBA/MHA. *Accreditation:* AACSB. *Program availability:* Part-time, evening/weekend. *Faculty:* 95 full-time (32 women), 89 part-time/adjunct (15 women). *Students:* 1,018 full-time (297 women), 383 part-time (98 women); includes 168 minority (5 Black or African American, non-Hispanic/Latino; 1 American Indian or Alaska Native, non-Hispanic/Latino; 44 Asian, non-Hispanic/Latino; 87 Hispanic/Latino; 2 Native Hawaiian or other Pacific Islander, non-Hispanic/Latino; 29 Two or more races, non-Hispanic/Latino), 242 international. Average age 25. 817 applicants, 77% accepted, 451 enrolled. In 2017, 750 master's, 7 doctorates awarded. *Degree requirements:* For master's, comprehensive exam (for some programs), thesis (for some programs); for doctorate, comprehensive exam (for some programs), thesis/dissertation. *Entrance requirements:* Additional exam requirements/recommendations for international students: Required—TOEFL. Application fee: $55 ($65 for international students). Electronic applications accepted. *Expenses:* Contact institution. *Financial support:* Fellowships with partial tuition reimbursements, research assistantships with partial tuition reimbursements, teaching assistantships with tuition reimbursements, scholarships/grants, tuition waivers (full and partial), and unspecified assistantships available. Financial award applicants required to

submit FAFSA. *Faculty research:* Information systems, investment, financial accounting, international strategy. *Unit head:* Dr. Taylor Randall, Dean, 801-587-3869, E-mail: dean@eccles.utah.edu. *Application contact:* Director of Graduate Admissions, 801-585-7366.
Website: http://www.business.utah.edu/

University of Vermont, Graduate College, Grossman School of Business, Burlington, VT 05405. Offers M Acc, MBA, MBA/JD. *Accreditation:* AACSB. *Program availability:* Part-time. *Students:* 65 full-time (28 women); includes 2 minority (both Asian, non-Hispanic/Latino), 7 international. 119 applicants, 79% accepted, 61 enrolled. In 2017, 39 master's awarded. *Entrance requirements:* For master's, GMAT or GRE, resume. Additional exam requirements/recommendations for international students: Required—TOEFL (minimum iBT score of 90) or IELTS (6.5). *Application deadline:* Applications are processed on a rolling basis. Application fee: $65. Electronic applications accepted. *Expenses:* Tuition, state resident: full-time $11,628; part-time $646 per credit. Tuition, nonresident: full-time $29,340; part-time $1630 per credit. *Required fees:* $1994; $10 per credit. Tuition and fees vary according to course load and program. *Financial support:* Federal Work-Study, scholarships/grants, and health care benefits available. Financial award application deadline: 3/1. *Unit head:* Dr. Sanjay Sharma, Dean, 802-656-3177, E-mail: sanjay.sharma@uvm.edu. *Application contact:* 802-656-4119, E-mail: studentservices@bsad.uvm.edu.
Website: https://www.uvm.edu/business

University of Victoria, Faculty of Graduate Studies, Peter B. Gustavson School of Business, Victoria, BC V8W 2Y2, Canada. Offers MBA, MBA/LL B. *Accreditation:* AACSB. *Program availability:* Part-time. *Entrance requirements:* For master's, GMAT, minimum B average. Additional exam requirements/recommendations for international students: Required—TOEFL (minimum score 575 paper-based), IELTS (minimum score 7). Electronic applications accepted. *Expenses:* Contact institution. *Faculty research:* Organizational design and analysis, negotiation and conflict management, human resources management, entrepreneurship, international marketing and tourism.

University of Virginia, Darden School of Business, Charlottesville, VA 22903. Offers MBA, PhD, MBA/JD, MBA/M Ed, MBA/MA, MBA/MD, MBA/ME, MBA/MPP, MBA/MS, MBA/MSDS, MBA/MSN. *Accreditation:* AACSB. *Faculty:* 62 full-time (17 women), 3 part-time/adjunct (1 woman). *Students:* 928 full-time (324 women), 7 part-time (3 women); includes 192 minority (57 Black or African American, non-Hispanic/Latino; 67 Asian, non-Hispanic/Latino; 48 Hispanic/Latino; 20 Two or more races, non-Hispanic/Latino), 203 international. Average age 30. 2,911 applicants, 28% accepted, 388 enrolled. In 2017, 424 master's, 1 doctorate awarded. *Degree requirements:* For doctorate, thesis/dissertation. *Entrance requirements:* For master's, GMAT, resume; 2 letters of recommendation; interview; for doctorate, GMAT, resume; essay; 2 letters of recommendation; interview. Additional exam requirements/recommendations for international students: Required—TOEFL. *Application deadline:* For fall admission, 3/1 for domestic students, 3/2 for international students. Applications are processed on a rolling basis. Application fee: $200. Electronic applications accepted. *Expenses:* Contact institution. *Financial support:* Career-related internships or fieldwork available. Financial award applicants required to submit FAFSA. *Unit head:* Scott C. Beardsley, Dean, 434-924-7481, E-mail: dean@virginia.edu. *Application contact:* Dawna Clarke, Executive Director of Admissions and Financial Aid, 434-924-3900, E-mail: darden@virginia.edu.
Website: http://www.darden.virginia.edu/

University of Virginia, McIntire School of Commerce, Charlottesville, VA 22904. Offers MS, MSC, Certificate, JD/MS. *Accreditation:* AACSB. *Entrance requirements:* For master's, GMAT, 2 letters of recommendation. Additional exam requirements/recommendations for international students: Required—TOEFL (minimum score 100 iBT) or IELTS (minimum score 7.5). Electronic applications accepted. *Expenses:* Contact institution.

University of Washington, Graduate School, Michael G. Foster School of Business, Seattle, WA 98195-3200. Offers auditing and assurance (MP Acc); business administration (MBA, PhD); entrepreneurship (MS); executive business administration (MBA); global executive business administration (MBA); information systems (MSIS); supply chain management (MSSCM); taxation (MP Acc); technology management (MBA); JD/MBA; MBA/MAIS; MBA/MHA. *Accreditation:* AACSB. *Program availability:* Part-time, evening/weekend, blended/hybrid learning. *Faculty:* 109 full-time (35 women), 54 part-time/adjunct (32 women). *Students:* 469 full-time (173 women), 638 part-time (216 women); includes 314 minority (15 Black or African American, non-Hispanic/Latino; 6 American Indian or Alaska Native, non-Hispanic/Latino; 246 Asian, non-Hispanic/Latino; 28 Hispanic/Latino; 5 Native Hawaiian or other Pacific Islander, non-Hispanic/Latino; 14 Two or more races, non-Hispanic/Latino), 125 international. Average age 32. 1,809 applicants, 84% accepted, 1107 enrolled. In 2017, 543 master's, 10 doctorates awarded. Terminal master's awarded for partial completion of doctoral program. *Degree requirements:* For doctorate, comprehensive exam, thesis/dissertation. *Entrance requirements:* For master's and doctorate, GMAT, GRE. Additional exam requirements/recommendations for international students: Required—TOEFL (minimum score 600 paper-based; 100 iBT). *Application deadline:* For fall admission, 3/15 for domestic students, 1/15 for international students. Application fee: $85. Electronic applications accepted. *Expenses:* Contact institution. *Financial support:* Fellowships with partial tuition reimbursements, research assistantships with partial tuition reimbursements, teaching assistantships with partial tuition reimbursements, Federal Work-Study, institutionally sponsored loans, and scholarships/grants available. Financial award application deadline: 2/28; financial award applicants required to submit FAFSA. *Faculty research:* Finance, consumer behavior, marketing analytics, technology management, supply chain. *Unit head:* Dr. James Jiambalvo, Dean, 206-543-4750, E-mail: jjiambal@uw.edu. *Application contact:* Erin Town, Director of Admissions, 206-543-4661, Fax: 206-616-7351, E-mail: mba@uw.edu.
Website: http://www.foster.washington.edu/

University of Washington, Bothell, School of Business, Bothell, WA 98011. Offers leadership (MBA); technology (MBA). *Accreditation:* AACSB. *Program availability:* Part-time, evening/weekend. *Degree requirements:* For master's, 72 credits, minimum cumulative GPA of 3.0. *Entrance requirements:* For master's, GMAT or GRE General Test. Additional exam requirements/recommendations for international students: Required—TOEFL (minimum score 580 paper-based; 92 iBT), IELTS (minimum score 7). Electronic applications accepted. *Expenses:* Contact institution. *Faculty research:* Leadership, supply chain management, entrepreneurship, game theory, corporate finance, marketing innovation.

University of Washington, Tacoma, Graduate Programs, MBA Programs, Tacoma, WA 98402-3100. Offers accounting (MBA); business administration (MBA); certified financial analyst (MBA). *Accreditation:* AACSB. *Program availability:* Part-time, evening/weekend. *Entrance requirements:* For master's, GMAT, minimum GPA of 3.0 in final graded 90 quarter credits or 60 graded semester credits; at least 2 years of professional/management work experience. Additional exam requirements/recommendations for international students: Required—TOEFL (minimum score 580 paper-based; 92 iBT). Electronic applications accepted. *Expenses:* Contact institution. *Faculty research:* International accounting, marketing, change management, investments, corporate social responsibility.

University of Waterloo, Graduate Studies, Faculty of Engineering, Conrad Business, Entrepreneurship and Technology Center, Waterloo, ON N2L 3G1, Canada. Offers MBET. *Entrance requirements:* For master's, honors degree. Additional exam requirements/recommendations for international students: Required—TOEFL (minimum score 90 iBT), IELTS (minimum score 7), PTE (minimum score 63). Electronic applications accepted.

The University of West Alabama, School of Graduate Studies, College of Business and Technology, Livingston, AL 35470. Offers finance (MBA); general business (MBA). *Program availability:* Part-time, evening/weekend, 100% online. *Faculty:* 2 full-time (1 woman), 9 part-time/adjunct (7 women). *Students:* 106 (73 women); includes 62 minority (57 Black or African American, non-Hispanic/Latino; 3 Hispanic/Latino; 2 Two or more races, non-Hispanic/Latino). Average age 30. 52 applicants, 98% accepted, 43 enrolled. In 2017, 9 master's awarded. *Degree requirements:* For master's, project or six additional hours in emphasis area and comprehensive examination. *Entrance requirements:* For master's, bachelor's degree with minimum GPA of 2.75. Additional exam requirements/recommendations for international students: Required—TOEFL (minimum score 500 paper-based; 61 iBT). *Application deadline:* Applications are processed on a rolling basis. Application fee: $40. Electronic applications accepted. *Expenses:* Tuition, state resident: part-time $371 per credit hour. Tuition, nonresident: part-time $742 per credit hour. *Required fees:* $130 per semester. *Financial support:* Federal Work-Study and scholarships/grants available. Support available to part-time students. Financial award application deadline: 3/1; financial award applicants required to submit FAFSA. *Unit head:* Dr. Aliquippa Allen, Interim Dean of College of Business and Technology, 205-652-3564, Fax: 205-652-3776, E-mail: aallen@uwa.edu. Website: http://www.uwa.edu/academics/collegeofbusinessandtechnology

The University of Western Ontario, Richard Ivey School of Business, London, ON N6A 3K7, Canada. Offers business (EMBA, PhD); corporate strategy and leadership elective (MBA); entrepreneurship elective (MBA); finance elective (MBA); health sector stream (MBA); international management elective (MBA); marketing elective (MBA); JD/MBA. *Degree requirements:* For master's, thesis (for some programs); for doctorate, thesis/dissertation. *Entrance requirements:* For master's, GMAT, 2 years of full-time work experience, interview. Additional exam requirements/recommendations for international students: Required—TOEFL (minimum score 100 iBT) or IELTS (minimum score 6). Electronic applications accepted. *Faculty research:* Strategy, organizational behavior, international business, finance, operations management.

University of West Florida, College of Business, Program in Business Administration, Pensacola, FL 32514-5750. Offers MBA. *Accreditation:* AACSB. *Program availability:* Part-time, evening/weekend. *Degree requirements:* For master's, industry portfolio project based on information from five of the core MBA courses. *Entrance requirements:* For master's, GMAT or GRE, official transcripts; minimum undergraduate GPA of 3.0; bachelor's degree; business course academic preparation; graduate-level motivation and writing abilities as noted in essay responses; two letters of recommendation; appropriate employment at increasing levels of responsibility via resume. Additional exam requirements/recommendations for international students: Required—TOEFL (minimum score 550 paper-based). *Faculty research:* Robotics, corporate behavior, international trade, franchising, counterfeiting.

University of West Georgia, Richards College of Business, Carrollton, GA 30118. Offers accounting (MP Acc); business administration (MBA). *Program availability:* Part-time, evening/weekend, 100% online, blended/hybrid learning. *Faculty:* 38 full-time (14 women). *Students:* 64 full-time (34 women), 123 part-time (61 women); includes 69 minority (48 Black or African American, non-Hispanic/Latino; 6 Asian, non-Hispanic/Latino; 13 Hispanic/Latino; 1 Native Hawaiian or other Pacific Islander, non-Hispanic/Latino; 1 Two or more races, non-Hispanic/Latino), 8 international. Average age 32. 129 applicants, 85% accepted, 74 enrolled. In 2017, 111 master's awarded. *Entrance requirements:* Additional exam requirements/recommendations for international students: Required—TOEFL (minimum score 550 paper-based; 79 iBT); Recommended—IELTS (minimum score 6.5). *Application deadline:* For fall admission, 7/15 for domestic students, 6/1 for international students; for spring admission, 11/15 for domestic students, 10/15 for international students; for summer admission, 5/15 for domestic students, 3/30 for international students. Applications are processed on a rolling basis. Application fee: $40. Electronic applications accepted. Tuition and fees vary according to degree level and program. *Financial support:* Fellowships, research assistantships, teaching assistantships, career-related internships or fieldwork, Federal Work-Study, institutionally sponsored loans, scholarships/grants, and unspecified assistantships available. Support available to part-time students. Financial award application deadline: 4/1; financial award applicants required to submit FAFSA. *Unit head:* Dr. Faye S. McIntyre, Dean of Richards College of Business, 678-839-6467, Fax: 678-839-5040, E-mail: fmcintyr@westga.edu. *Application contact:* Dr. Toby Ziglar, Assistant Dean of the Graduate School, 678-839-1394, Fax: 678-839-1395, E-mail: graduate@westga.edu.
Website: https://www.westga.edu/business

University of Windsor, Faculty of Graduate Studies, Odette School of Business, Windsor, ON N9B 3P4, Canada. Offers MBA, MM, MBA/LL B. *Program availability:* Evening/weekend. *Degree requirements:* For master's, thesis or alternative. *Entrance requirements:* For master's, GMAT, minimum B average. Additional exam requirements/recommendations for international students: Required—TOEFL (minimum score 600 paper-based). Electronic applications accepted. *Faculty research:* Accounting, administrative studies, finance, marketing, business policy and strategy.

University of Wisconsin–Eau Claire, College of Business, Program in Business Administration, Eau Claire, WI 54702-4004. Offers MBA. *Accreditation:* AACSB. *Program availability:* Part-time, evening/weekend, online learning. Terminal master's awarded for partial completion of doctoral program. *Degree requirements:* For master's, thesis optional, applied field project. *Entrance requirements:* For master's, GMAT or GRE, minimum GPA of 2.75 overall. Additional exam requirements/recommendations for international students: Required—TOEFL (minimum score 79 iBT). *Expenses:* Contact institution.

University of Wisconsin–Green Bay, Graduate Studies, Program in Management, Green Bay, WI 54311-7001. Offers MS. *Program availability:* Part-time, evening/weekend. *Degree requirements:* For master's, thesis or alternative. *Entrance requirements:* For master's, GMAT or GRE General Test, minimum GPA of 3.0. Electronic applications accepted. *Faculty research:* Planning methods, budgeting, decision-making, organizational behavior and theory, management.

University of Wisconsin–Madison, Graduate School, Wisconsin School of Business, Wisconsin Evening MBA Program, Madison, WI 53706. Offers general management (MBA). *Program availability:* Part-time-only, evening/weekend. *Faculty:* 15 full-time (4 women), 7 part-time/adjunct (0 women). *Students:* 158 part-time (48 women); includes 17 minority (2 Black or African American, non-Hispanic/Latino; 1 American Indian or Alaska Native, non-Hispanic/Latino; 11 Asian, non-Hispanic/Latino; 2 Hispanic/Latino; 1 Two or more races, non-Hispanic/Latino), 5 international. Average age 30. 76 applicants, 79% accepted, 46 enrolled. In 2017, 55 master's awarded. *Entrance requirements:* For master's, GMAT, essay, resume, 2 professional recommendations, official college transcripts, two years of professional experience. Additional exam

Business Administration and Management—General

requirements/recommendations for international students: Required—TOEFL (minimum score 600 paper-based; 106 iBT). *Application deadline:* For fall admission, 6/1 priority date for domestic and international students. Applications are processed on a rolling basis. Application fee: $75 ($81 for international students). Electronic applications accepted. *Expenses:* Contact institution. *Financial support:* In 2017–18, 25 students received support. Scholarships/grants available. Support available to part-time students. Financial award application deadline: 7/1. *Faculty research:* Creativity, leadership, healthcare operations, financial accounting, compensation. *Unit head:* Dr. Don Hausch, Associate Dean, 608-262-2535, Fax: 608-262-3607, E-mail: emba@wsb.wisc.edu. *Application contact:* Jean Sink, Director of Admissions, 608-262-9141, Fax: 608-262-3607, E-mail: emba@wsb.wisc.edu.
Website: https://wsb.wisc.edu/programs-degrees/mba/evening

University of Wisconsin–Madison, Graduate School, Wisconsin School of Business, Wisconsin Executive MBA Program, Madison, WI 53706. Offers general management (MBA). *Program availability:* Part-time-only, evening/weekend. *Faculty:* 14 full-time (1 woman), 5 part-time/adjunct (2 women). *Students:* 78 full-time (24 women); includes 16 minority (3 Black or African American, non-Hispanic/Latino; 7 Asian, non-Hispanic/Latino; 6 Hispanic/Latino), 6 international. Average age 41. 62 applicants, 82% accepted, 38 enrolled. In 2017, 37 master's awarded. *Entrance requirements:* For master's, essay, two professional recommendations, official college transcripts, resume, interview, eight years of professional work experience, five years of leadership experience, employer authorization form. Additional exam requirements/recommendations for international students: Required—TOEFL (minimum score 600 paper-based; 106 iBT). *Application deadline:* For fall admission, 6/1 priority date for domestic and international students. Applications are processed on a rolling basis. Application fee: $75 ($81 for international students). Electronic applications accepted. *Expenses:* Contact institution. *Financial support:* In 2017–18, 22 students received support. Scholarships/grants available. Support available to part-time students. Financial award application deadline: 7/1. *Faculty research:* Entrepreneurship, environmental issues in supply chain, leadership, marketing channels, strategic leadership. *Unit head:* Dr. Don Hausch, Associate Dean, 608-262-2535, Fax: 608-262-3607, E-mail: emba@wsb.wisc.edu. *Application contact:* Jean Sink, Director of Admissions, 608-262-9141, Fax: 608-262-3607, E-mail: emba@wsb.wisc.edu.
Website: https://wsb.wisc.edu/programs-degrees/mba/executive

University of Wisconsin–Madison, Graduate School, Wisconsin School of Business, Wisconsin Full-Time MBA Program, Madison, WI 53706. Offers applied security analysis (MBA); arts administration (MBA); brand and product management (MBA); corporate finance and investment banking (MBA); marketing research (MBA); operations and technology management (MBA); real estate (MBA); risk management and insurance (MBA); strategic human resource management (MBA); supply chain management (MBA). *Faculty:* 130 full-time (35 women), 42 part-time/adjunct (13 women). *Students:* 203 full-time (72 women); includes 34 minority (8 Black or African American, non-Hispanic/Latino; 10 Asian, non-Hispanic/Latino; 12 Hispanic/Latino; 4 Two or more races, non-Hispanic/Latino), 41 international. Average age 28. 556 applicants, 30% accepted, 104 enrolled. In 2017, 97 master's awarded. *Entrance requirements:* For master's, GMAT or GRE, bachelor's or equivalent degree, 2 years of work experience, essay, letter of recommendation, resume. Additional exam requirements/recommendations for international students: Required—TOEFL (minimum score 100 iBT), IELTS (minimum score 7.5). *Application deadline:* For fall admission, 11/2 for domestic and international students; for winter admission, 1/11 for domestic and international students; for spring admission, 3/1 for domestic and international students; for summer admission, 4/12 for domestic and international students. Applications are processed on a rolling basis. Application fee: $75 ($81 for international students). Electronic applications accepted. *Expenses:* $9,356 per semester resident, $18,288 non-resident. *Financial support:* In 2017–18, 183 students received support, including 14 fellowships with full tuition reimbursements available (averaging $25,420 per year), 7 research assistantships with full tuition reimbursements available (averaging $13,375 per year), 53 teaching assistantships with full tuition reimbursements available (averaging $13,375 per year); scholarships/grants, health care benefits, tuition waivers (full), and unspecified assistantships also available. Financial award application deadline: 4/11. *Faculty research:* Forms of competition and outcomes in dual distribution systems; explaining the accuracy of revised forecasts; supply chain planning for random demand surges; advanced demand information in a multi-product system; the effects of presentation salience and measurement subjectivity on nonprofessional investors' fair value judgments. *Unit head:* Dr. Don Hausch, Associate Dean, Full-time MBA Program, 608-262-9731, E-mail: don.hausch@wisc.edu. *Application contact:* Betsy Kacizak, Director of Admissions and Recruiting, Full-time MBA Program, 608-262-4000, E-mail: betsy.kacizak@wisc.edu.
Website: https://wsb.wisc.edu/

University of Wisconsin–Milwaukee, Graduate School, Lubar School of Business, Milwaukee, WI 53201. Offers business administration (MBA); executive business administration (EMBA); management science (MS, PhD, Graduate Certificate), including business analytics (Graduate Certificate), enterprise resource planning (Graduate Certificate), information technology management (MS), investment management (Graduate Certificate), nonprofit management (Graduate Certificate), nonprofit management and leadership (MS), state and local taxation (Graduate Certificate); technology entrepreneurship (Graduate Certificate). *Accreditation:* AACSB. *Program availability:* Part-time, evening/weekend. *Students:* 321 full-time (137 women), 252 part-time (93 women); includes 94 minority (25 Black or African American, non-Hispanic/Latino; 1 American Indian or Alaska Native, non-Hispanic/Latino; 28 Asian, non-Hispanic/Latino; 6 Hispanic/Latino; 34 Two or more races, non-Hispanic/Latino), 66 international. Average age 32. 426 applicants, 61% accepted, 191 enrolled. In 2017, 266 master's, 8 doctorates, 21 other advanced degrees awarded. *Degree requirements:* For master's, comprehensive exam (for some programs); for doctorate, comprehensive exam, thesis/dissertation. *Entrance requirements:* For master's and doctorate, GMAT or GRE General Test. Additional exam requirements/recommendations for international students: Required—TOEFL (minimum score 550 paper-based; 79 iBT), IELTS (minimum score 6.5). *Application deadline:* For fall admission, 1/1 priority date for domestic students; for spring admission, 9/1 for domestic students. Application fee: $56 ($96 for international students). Electronic applications accepted. *Expenses:* Contact institution. *Financial support:* Fellowships with full tuition reimbursements, research assistantships with full tuition reimbursements, teaching assistantships with full tuition reimbursements, career-related internships or fieldwork, Federal Work-Study, health care benefits, unspecified assistantships, and project assistantships available. Support available to part-time students. Financial award application deadline: 4/15; financial award applicants required to submit FAFSA. *Faculty research:* Applied management research in finance, management information systems, marketing, operations research, organizational sciences. *Unit head:* V. Kanti Prasad, Dean, 414-229-6256, E-mail: deanprasad@uwm.edu. *Application contact:* Business Graduate Student Services, 414-229-5403, E-mail: mba-ms@uwm.edu.
Website: https://uwm.edu/business/

University of Wisconsin–Oshkosh, Graduate Studies, College of Business, Program in Business Administration, Oshkosh, WI 54901. Offers MBA. *Accreditation:* AACSB. *Program availability:* Part-time. *Degree requirements:* For master's, integrative seminar.

Entrance requirements: For master's, GMAT, GRE, minimum undergraduate GPA of 2.75. Additional exam requirements/recommendations for international students: Required—TOEFL (minimum score 550 paper-based; 79 iBT). Electronic applications accepted.

University of Wisconsin–Parkside, College of Business, Economics, and Computing, Kenosha, WI 53141-2000. Offers MBA, MSCIS. *Accreditation:* AACSB. *Program availability:* Part-time, evening/weekend. *Entrance requirements:* For master's, GMAT. Additional exam requirements/recommendations for international students: Required—TOEFL (minimum score 550 paper-based; 79 iBT). Electronic applications accepted. *Expenses:* Contact institution. *Faculty research:* Business strategy, ethics in accounting and finance, mutual funds, decision analysis and neural networks, management skills.

University of Wisconsin–River Falls, Outreach and Graduate Studies, College of Business and Economics, River Falls, WI 54022. Offers MBA, MM. *Accreditation:* AACSB. *Degree requirements:* For master's, thesis or alternative. *Entrance requirements:* Additional exam requirements/recommendations for international students: Required—TOEFL (minimum score 550 paper-based; 79 iBT). Electronic applications accepted.

University of Wisconsin–Stevens Point, College of Letters and Science, Division of Business and Economics, Stevens Point, WI 54481-3897. Offers MBA. Program offered jointly with University of Wisconsin–Oshkosh.

University of Wisconsin–Whitewater, School of Graduate Studies, College of Business and Economics, Program in Business Administration, Whitewater, WI 53190-1790. Offers finance (MBA). *Accreditation:* AACSB. *Program availability:* Part-time, evening/weekend, online learning. *Entrance requirements:* For master's, GMAT or GRE, minimum AACSB index of 1000, minimum GPA of 2.75. Additional exam requirements/recommendations for international students: Required—TOEFL (minimum score 550 paper-based; 80 iBT), IELTS (minimum score 6). Electronic applications accepted. *Faculty research:* Interface between social institutions and individual behavior, technology and innovation management, occupational mental health, workplace deviance and workplace romance.

University of Wyoming, College of Business, Program in Business Administration, Laramie, WY 82071. Offers MBA. *Accreditation:* AACSB. *Program availability:* Part-time, evening/weekend, online learning. *Degree requirements:* For master's, comprehensive exam, thesis or alternative. *Entrance requirements:* For master's, GMAT, GRE General Test, minimum GPA of 3.0. Additional exam requirements/recommendations for international students: Required—TOEFL (minimum score 550 paper-based; 80 iBT). Electronic applications accepted. *Faculty research:* Natural resource marketing and product development, work place violence.

Upper Iowa University, Online Master's Programs, Fayette, IA 52142-1857. Offers accounting (MBA); corporate financial management (MBA); emergency management and homeland security (MPA); general management (MBA); general studies (MPA); government administration (MPA); health and human services (MPA); human resources management (MBA); nonprofit organizational management (MPA); organizational development (MBA); public management (MPA); sport administration (MSA). MBA also available at Madison, WI campus. *Program availability:* Part-time, online learning. *Degree requirements:* For master's, research project. *Entrance requirements:* For master's, GMAT, GRE, or minimum GPA of 2.7 during last 60 hours. Additional exam requirements/recommendations for international students: Required—TOEFL (minimum score 570 paper-based). Electronic applications accepted. *Faculty research:* Total quality management, teams, organization culture and climate, management.

Urbana University–A Branch Campus of Franklin University, Division of Business Administration, Urbana, OH 43078-2091. Offers MBA. *Program availability:* Part-time, evening/weekend. *Degree requirements:* For master's, comprehensive exam, thesis or alternative. *Entrance requirements:* For master's, GMAT, minimum GPA of 2.7, BS in business, 3 letters of recommendation, work experience. Additional exam requirements/recommendations for international students: Required—TOEFL (minimum score 550 paper-based). *Faculty research:* Organizational behavior, taxation, segmentation, information systems, retail gravitation.

Ursuline College, School of Graduate and Professional Studies, Program in Business Administration, Pepper Pike, OH 44124-4398. Offers ethical and entrepreneurial leadership (MBA); financial planning and accounting (MBA); health services management (MBA); management (MBA); management and leadership (MBA); marketing and communications management (MBA). *Program availability:* Part-time. *Faculty:* 3 full-time (2 women), 3 part-time/adjunct (2 women). *Students:* 3 full-time (all women), 26 part-time (23 women); includes 13 minority (12 Black or African American, non-Hispanic/Latino; 1 Two or more races, non-Hispanic/Latino). Average age 38. 13 applicants, 85% accepted, 6 enrolled. In 2017, 11 master's awarded. *Degree requirements:* For master's, comprehensive exam (for some programs). *Entrance requirements:* For master's, GRE. Additional exam requirements/recommendations for international students: Required—TOEFL (minimum score 500 paper-based) or GRE. *Application deadline:* Applications are processed on a rolling basis. Application fee: $25. Electronic applications accepted. *Expenses:* $842 per credit hour. *Financial support:* In 2017–18, 3 students received support. Scholarships/grants available. Financial award application deadline: 8/1; financial award applicants required to submit FAFSA. *Faculty research:* Gift economy; sharing economy; cooperative business models; collaborative leadership; corporate social responsibility and the triple bottom line, defined as the three P's: people, planet and profit. *Unit head:* Dr. Anthony Caffarelli, Associate Professor, 440-646-8134, Fax: 440-684-6088, E-mail: tcafarelli@ursuline.edu. *Application contact:* Melanie Steele, Director of Graduate Admission, 440-646-8146, Fax: 440-684-6138, E-mail: graduateadmissions@ursuline.edu.

Utah State University, School of Graduate Studies, Jon M. Huntsman School of Business, Program in Business Administration, Logan, UT 84322. Offers MBA. *Accreditation:* AACSB. *Program availability:* Part-time, evening/weekend, online learning. *Degree requirements:* For master's, comprehensive exam. *Entrance requirements:* For master's, GMAT or GRE, minimum GPA of 3.0. Additional exam requirements/recommendations for international students: Required—TOEFL. Electronic applications accepted. *Faculty research:* Marketing strategy, technology and innovation, public utility finance, international competitiveness.

Utah Valley University, MBA Program, Orem, UT 84058-5999. Offers accounting (MBA); management (MBA). *Accreditation:* AACSB. *Program availability:* Part-time, evening/weekend. *Entrance requirements:* For master's, GMAT, official transcripts, current resume, three letters of recommendation, essay. Additional exam requirements/recommendations for international students: Required—TOEFL (minimum score 79 iBT). Electronic applications accepted. *Expenses:* Contact institution.

Valdosta State University, Langdale College of Business, Valdosta, GA 31698. Offers accountancy (M Acc); business administration (MBA); healthcare administration (MBA). MBA program is a member of the Georgia WebMBA. *Accreditation:* AACSB. *Program availability:* Part-time, evening/weekend, 100% online, blended/hybrid learning. *Degree requirements:* For master's, comprehensive written and/or oral exams. *Entrance requirements:* For master's, GMAT or GRE, minimum GPA of 2.75. Additional exam requirements/recommendations for international students: Required—TOEFL (minimum

score 523 paper-based); Recommended—IELTS. *Application deadline:* For fall admission, 7/1 for domestic and international students; for spring admission, 11/1 for domestic and international students. Applications are processed on a rolling basis. Application fee: $45. Electronic applications accepted. *Expenses:* Contact institution. *Financial support:* Research assistantships with full tuition reimbursements, institutionally sponsored loans, and scholarships/grants available. Support available to part-time students. Financial award application deadline: 7/1; financial award applicants required to submit FAFSA. *Unit head:* Dr. Mel Schnake, Director, 229-245-2233, Fax: 229-245-2795, E-mail: mschnake@valdosta.edu. *Application contact:* Jessica Powers, Admission Specialist, 229-333-5694, Fax: 229-245-3853, E-mail: jldevane@valdosta.edu.
Website: http://www.valdosta.edu/academics/graduate-school/our-programs/business-administration.php

Valparaiso University, Graduate School and Continuing Education, College of Business, Valparaiso, IN 46383. Offers business administration (MBA); business decision-making (Certificate); business intelligence (Certificate); engineering management (Certificate); finance (Certificate); general business (Certificate); leading the global enterprise (Certificate); management (Certificate); JD/MBA; MSN/MBA. *Accreditation:* AACSB. *Program availability:* Part-time, evening/weekend, online learning. *Entrance requirements:* For master's, GMAT, GRE, minimum GPA of 3.0. Additional exam requirements/recommendations for international students: Required—TOEFL (minimum score 550 paper-based; 80 iBT), IELTS (minimum score 6). Electronic applications accepted. *Expenses:* Contact institution.

Vancouver Island University, Master of Business Administration Program, Nanaimo, BC V9R 5S5, Canada. Offers international business (MBA), including finance, marketing. Program offered jointly with University of Hertfordshire. *Accreditation:* ACBSP. *Program availability:* Part-time. *Degree requirements:* For master's, thesis. *Entrance requirements:* Additional exam requirements/recommendations for international students: Required—TOEFL (minimum score 88 iBT), IELTS (minimum score 6.5). Electronic applications accepted. *Expenses:* Contact institution. *Faculty research:* Tourism development, entrepreneurship, organizational development, strategic planning, international business strategy, intercultural team work.

Vanderbilt University, Vanderbilt University Owen Graduate School of Management, Vanderbilt Executive MBA Programs, Nashville, TN 37203. Offers EMBA, MBA. *Accreditation:* AACSB. *Program availability:* Evening/weekend. *Entrance requirements:* For master's, GMAT, minimum of 5 years of professional work experience. Electronic applications accepted. *Expenses:* Contact institution.

Vanderbilt University, Vanderbilt University Owen Graduate School of Management, Vanderbilt MBA Program, Nashville, TN 37203. Offers accounting (MBA); finance (MBA); general management (MBA); health care (MBA); human and organizational performance (MBA); marketing (MBA); operations (MBA); strategy (MBA); MBA/JD; MBA/M Div; MBA/MD; MBA/MSN; MBA/MTS; MBA/PhD. *Accreditation:* AACSB. *Degree requirements:* For master's, 62 credit hours of coursework; completion of ethics course; minimum GPA of 3.0. *Entrance requirements:* For master's, GMAT (preferred) or GRE, 2 years of work experience (recommended). Additional exam requirements/recommendations for international students: Required—TOEFL (minimum score 100 iBT). Electronic applications accepted. *Expenses:* Contact institution. *Faculty research:* Accounting and finance, business strategy and economics, marketing, operations management, organization studies.

Villanova University, Villanova School of Business, Executive MBA Program, Radnor, PA 19087. Offers EMBA. *Accreditation:* AACSB. *Program availability:* Evening/weekend. *Faculty:* 68 full-time (22 women), 65 part-time/adjunct (11 women). *Students:* 53 part-time (15 women); includes 9 minority (6 Black or African American, non-Hispanic/Latino; 1 Hispanic/Latino; 2 Two or more races, non-Hispanic/Latino), 2 international. Average age 39. 48 applicants, 98% accepted, 36 enrolled. In 2017, 28 master's awarded. *Degree requirements:* For master's, minimum cumulative GPA of 3.0. *Entrance requirements:* For master's, 2 letters of recommendation, essay, resume, official transcript, significant managerial or executive work experience, employer approval. Additional exam requirements/recommendations for international students: Required—TOEFL (minimum score 550 paper-based; 100 iBT). *Application deadline:* For fall admission, 6/30 for domestic and international students. Applications are processed on a rolling basis. Application fee: $65. Electronic applications accepted. *Expenses:* Contact institution. *Financial support:* Scholarships/grants available. Financial award application deadline: 6/30; financial award applicants required to submit FAFSA. *Faculty research:* Business analytics; creativity, innovation and entrepreneurship; global leadership; real estate; church management; business ethics. *Unit head:* Dr. Joyce Russell, Dean of Villanova School of Business, 610-519-5424, E-mail: joyce.russell@villanova.edu. *Application contact:* Jennifer Wiess, Director, Executive Programs, 610-523-1794, E-mail: jennifer.wiess@villanova.edu.
Website: http://www.emba.villanova.edu/

Villanova University, Villanova School of Business, MBA - The Fast Track Program, Villanova, PA 19085. Offers finance (MBA); healthcare (MBA); international business (MBA); strategic management (MBA). *Accreditation:* AACSB. *Program availability:* Part-time, evening/weekend. *Faculty:* 68 full-time (22 women), 65 part-time/adjunct (11 women). *Students:* 128 part-time (55 women); includes 11 minority (3 Black or African American, non-Hispanic/Latino; 4 Asian, non-Hispanic/Latino; 4 Hispanic/Latino), 4 international. Average age 30. 79 applicants, 96% accepted, 64 enrolled. In 2017, 58 master's awarded. *Degree requirements:* For master's, minimum GPA of 3.0. *Entrance requirements:* For master's, GMAT or GRE, work experience, 2 letters of recommendation, 2 essays, resume, official transcripts, interview. Additional exam requirements/recommendations for international students: Required—TOEFL (minimum score 550 paper-based; 100 iBT). *Application deadline:* For fall admission, 6/30 for domestic and international students. Applications are processed on a rolling basis. Application fee: $65. Electronic applications accepted. *Expenses:* $56,016 per year tuition, $1,167 per credit; $50 semester fee. *Financial support:* Scholarships/grants available. Financial award application deadline: 6/30; financial award applicants required to submit FAFSA. *Faculty research:* Business analytics; creativity, innovation and entrepreneurship; global leadership; real estate; church management; business ethics; marketing and consumer insights. *Unit head:* Dr. Joyce Russell, Dean of Villanova School of Business, 610-519-5424, Fax: 610-519-6273, E-mail: joyce.russell@villanova.edu. *Application contact:* Kimberly Kane, Manager of Admissions, 610-519-3701, Fax: 610-519-6273, E-mail: kimberly.kane@villanova.edu.
Website: http://www1.villanova.edu/villanova/business/graduate/mba.html

Villanova University, Villanova School of Business, MBA - The Flex Track Program, Villanova, PA 19085. Offers healthcare (MBA); international business (MBA); marketing (MBA); real estate (MBA); strategic management (MBA); JD/MBA. *Accreditation:* AACSB. *Program availability:* Part-time, evening/weekend, online learning. *Faculty:* 68 full-time (22 women), 65 part-time/adjunct (11 women). *Students:* 13 full-time (4 women), 410 part-time (137 women); includes 105 minority (28 Black or African American, non-Hispanic/Latino; 1 American Indian or Alaska Native, non-Hispanic/Latino; 41 Asian, non-Hispanic/Latino; 29 Hispanic/Latino; 6 Two or more races, non-Hispanic/Latino), 13 international. Average age 31. 94 applicants, 94% accepted, 79 enrolled. In 2017, 201 master's awarded. *Degree requirements:* For master's, minimum

GPA of 3.0. *Entrance requirements:* For master's, GMAT or GRE, work experience, 2 letters of recommendation, 2 essays, resume, official transcript. Additional exam requirements/recommendations for international students: Required—TOEFL (minimum score 550 paper-based; 100 iBT). *Application deadline:* For fall admission, 6/30 for domestic and international students; for spring admission, 11/15 for domestic and international students; for summer admission, 3/31 for domestic and international students. Applications are processed on a rolling basis. Application fee: $65. Electronic applications accepted. *Expenses:* $50,016 per year tuition, $1,167 per credit; $50 semester fee. *Financial support:* In 2017–18, 19 research assistantships with full tuition reimbursements (averaging $16,245 per year) were awarded; scholarships/grants also available. Financial award application deadline: 6/30; financial award applicants required to submit FAFSA. *Faculty research:* Business analytics; creativity, innovation and entrepreneurship; global leadership; real estate; church management; business ethics. *Unit head:* Dr. Joyce Russell, Dean of Villanova School of Business, 610-519-5424, Fax: 610-519-6273, E-mail: joyce.russell@villanova.edu. *Application contact:* Claire Bruno, Director of Recruitment and Enrollment Management, 610-519-4336, Fax: 610-519-6273, E-mail: claire.bruno@villanova.edu.
Website: http://www1.villanova.edu/villanova/business/graduate/mba.html

Villanova University, Villanova School of Business, Online MBA Program, Villanova, PA 19085-1699. Offers MBA. *Program availability:* Part-time-only, evening/weekend, 100% online, blended/hybrid learning. *Faculty:* 68 full-time (22 women), 65 part-time/adjunct (11 women). *Students:* 76 part-time (27 women); includes 28 minority (11 Black or African American, non-Hispanic/Latino; 1 American Indian or Alaska Native, non-Hispanic/Latino; 8 Asian, non-Hispanic/Latino; 4 Hispanic/Latino; 4 Two or more races, non-Hispanic/Latino), 2 international. Average age 33. 122 applicants, 84% accepted, 80 enrolled. In 2017, 76 master's awarded. *Degree requirements:* For master's, minimum cumulative GPA of 3.0. *Entrance requirements:* For master's, GMAT or GRE. Additional exam requirements/recommendations for international students: Required—TOEFL (minimum score 550 paper-based). *Application deadline:* For fall admission, 6/30 for domestic and international students; for spring admission, 11/15 for domestic and international students; for summer admission, 3/31 for domestic and international students. Applications are processed on a rolling basis. Application fee: $50. Electronic applications accepted. *Expenses:* $64,800 per year tuition, $1,350 per credit; $50 semester fee. *Financial support:* Institutionally sponsored loans and scholarships/grants available. Financial award application deadline: 6/30; financial award applicants required to submit FAFSA. *Faculty research:* Real estate; business analytics; global leadership; innovation, creativity and entrepreneurship; church management; business ethics; marketing and consumer insights. *Unit head:* Dr. Joyce Russell, Dean of Villanova School of Business, 610-519-5424, Fax: 610-519-6273, E-mail: joyce.russell@villanova.edu. *Application contact:* Claire Bruno, Director of Recruitment and Enrollment Management, 610-519-4336, Fax: 610-519-6273, E-mail: claire.bruno@villanova.edu.

Virginia Commonwealth University, Graduate School, School of Business, Program in Business Administration, Richmond, VA 23284-9005. Offers MBA, PhD. *Degree requirements:* For doctorate, thesis/dissertation. *Entrance requirements:* For master's and doctorate, GMAT. Additional exam requirements/recommendations for international students: Required—TOEFL (minimum score 600 paper-based; 100 iBT). Electronic applications accepted.

Virginia International University, School of Business, Fairfax, VA 22030. Offers accounting (MBA, MS); entrepreneurship (MBA); executive management (Graduate Certificate); global logistics (MBA); health care management (MBA); hospitality and tourism management (MBA); human resources management (MBA); international business management (MBA); international finance (MBA); marketing management (MBA); mass media and public relations (MBA); project management (MBA, MS). *Program availability:* Part-time, online learning. *Entrance requirements:* For master's and Graduate Certificate, bachelor's degree. Additional exam requirements/recommendations for international students: Required—TOEFL (minimum score 550 paper-based; 80 iBT), IELTS (minimum score 6). Electronic applications accepted.

Virginia Polytechnic Institute and State University, Graduate School, Pamplin College of Business, Blacksburg, VA 24061. Offers accounting and information systems (MACIS, PhD); business (PhD), including marketing (MS, PhD); business administration (MS), including business analytics, marketing (MS, PhD); business information technology (PhD); executive business research (PhD); finance (PhD); MS/MBA. *Faculty:* 131 full-time (42 women), 2 part-time/adjunct (1 woman). *Students:* 261 full-time (101 women), 189 part-time (76 women); includes 112 minority (32 Black or African American, non-Hispanic/Latino; 50 Asian, non-Hispanic/Latino; 15 Hispanic/Latino; 15 Two or more races, non-Hispanic/Latino), 80 international. Average age 32. 434 applicants, 57% accepted, 168 enrolled. In 2017, 142 master's, 11 doctorates awarded. *Degree requirements:* For master's, comprehensive exam (for some programs), thesis (for some programs); for doctorate, comprehensive exam (for some programs), thesis/dissertation (for some programs). *Entrance requirements:* For master's and doctorate, GRE/GMAT. Additional exam requirements/recommendations for international students: Required—TOEFL (minimum score 80 iBT). *Application deadline:* For fall admission, 8/1 for domestic students, 4/1 for international students; for spring admission, 1/1 for domestic students, 9/1 for international students. Applications are processed on a rolling basis. Application fee: $75. Electronic applications accepted. *Expenses:* Tuition, state resident: full-time $15,072; part-time $718.50 per credit hour. Tuition, nonresident: full-time $28,810; part-time $1448.25 per credit hour. *Required fees:* $2741; $502 per semester. Tuition and fees vary according to course load, campus/location and program. *Financial support:* In 2017–18, 9 research assistantships with full tuition reimbursements (averaging $18,588 per year), 48 teaching assistantships with full tuition reimbursements (averaging $22,706 per year) were awarded. Financial award application deadline: 3/1; financial award applicants required to submit FAFSA. *Total annual research expenditures:* $3.4 million. *Unit head:* Dr. Robert T. Sumichrast, Dean, 540-231-6601, Fax: 540-231-4487, E-mail: busdean@vt.edu. *Application contact:* Kimberly Ridpath, Executive Assistant, 540-231-9647, Fax: 540-231-4487, E-mail: ridpathk@vt.edu.
Website: http://www.pamplin.vt.edu/

Virginia Wesleyan University, Graduate Studies, Virginia Beach, VA 23455. Offers business administration (MBA); secondary and PreK-12 education (MA Ed). *Program availability:* Online learning.

Viterbo University, Master of Business Administration Program, La Crosse, WI 54601-4797. Offers general business administration (MBA); health care management (MBA); international business (MBA); leadership (MBA); project management (MBA). *Accreditation:* ACBSP. *Program availability:* Part-time, evening/weekend. *Degree requirements:* For master's, 34 semester credits. *Entrance requirements:* For master's, bachelor's degree, transcripts, minimum undergraduate cumulative GPA of 3.0, 2 letters of reference, 3-5 page essay. Additional exam requirements/recommendations for international students: Recommended—TOEFL (minimum score 550 paper-based). Electronic applications accepted. *Expenses:* Contact institution.

Wagner College, Division of Graduate Studies, Nicolais School of Business, Staten Island, NY 10301-4495. Offers accounting (MS); business administration (MBA); finance (MBA); management (Exec MBA); marketing (MBA); media management (MS). *Accreditation:* ACBSP. *Program availability:* Part-time, evening/weekend. *Faculty:* 8 full-

Business Administration and Management—General

time (3 women), 17 part-time/adjunct (5 women). *Students:* 90 full-time (41 women), 27 part-time (9 women); includes 18 minority (10 Black or African American, non-Hispanic/Latino; 2 Asian, non-Hispanic/Latino; 4 Hispanic/Latino; 2 Two or more races, non-Hispanic/Latino), 14 international. Average age 27. 85 applicants, 92% accepted, 58 enrolled. In 2017, 72 master's awarded. *Degree requirements:* For master's, thesis optional. *Entrance requirements:* For master's, minimum GPA of 2.75, proficiency in computers and math. Additional exam requirements/recommendations for international students: Required—TOEFL (minimum score 550 paper-based; 79 iBT), IELTS (minimum score 6.5). *Application deadline:* For fall admission, 5/1 priority date for domestic students, 3/1 priority date for international students; for spring admission, 12/1 for domestic students, 11/1 for international students. Applications are processed on a rolling basis. Application fee: $60. *Financial support:* In 2017–18, 93 students received support. Career-related internships or fieldwork, unspecified assistantships, and alumni fellowship grants available. Financial award application deadline: 4/1; financial award applicants required to submit FAFSA. *Unit head:* Dr. Donald Crooks, Director, 718-390-3429, Fax: 718-390-3429, E-mail: dcrooks@wagner.edu. *Application contact:* Patricia Clancy, Assistant Director for Enrollment, 718-420-4464, Fax: 718-390-3105, E-mail: patricia.clancy@wagner.edu.

Wake Forest University, School of Business, Master in Management Program, Winston-Salem, NC 27106. Offers MA. *Faculty:* 16 full-time (6 women), 7 part-time/adjunct (3 women). *Students:* 119 full-time (74 women); includes 30 minority (18 Black or African American, non-Hispanic/Latino; 4 Asian, non-Hispanic/Latino; 6 Hispanic/Latino; 2 Two or more races, non-Hispanic/Latino), 18 international. Average age 24. 279 applicants, 78% accepted, 119 enrolled. In 2017, 146 master's awarded. *Degree requirements:* For master's, 41.5 credit hours. *Entrance requirements:* For master's, GMAT or GRE, letters of recommendation, official transcripts, current resume or curriculum vitae, interview. Additional exam requirements/recommendations for international students: Required—TOEFL (minimum score 600 paper-based; 100 iBT). *Application deadline:* For fall admission, 6/15 for domestic and international students. Applications are processed on a rolling basis. Application fee: $100. Electronic applications accepted. *Expenses:* Contact institution. *Financial support:* Scholarships/grants available. Financial award application deadline: 4/1; financial award applicants required to submit FAFSA. *Faculty research:* Influence of personal relationships on business decision-making and management of change; drivers of perceived value and consumer behavior; impact of accounting on auditing, financial, managerial, systems and taxation stakeholders; corporate governance and executive compensation; impact of operations strategies on competitiveness. *Unit head:* Scott Shafer, Associate Dean, 336-758-5422, Fax: 336-758-5830, E-mail: busadmissions@wfu.edu. *Application contact:* John Montana, Director, Enrollment Management, 336-758-5422, Fax: 336-758-5830, E-mail: busadmissions@wfu.edu.
Website: http://www.business.wfu.edu/ma-management

Wake Forest University, School of Business, Working Professionals MBA Program, Winston-Salem, NC 27106. Offers MBA, PhD/MBA. *Accreditation:* AACSB. *Program availability:* Part-time-only, evening/weekend. *Faculty:* 14 full-time (1 woman), 1 part-time/adjunct (0 women). *Students:* 313 full-time (182 women); includes 81 minority (47 Black or African American, non-Hispanic/Latino; 19 Asian, non-Hispanic/Latino; 12 Hispanic/Latino; 3 Two or more races, non-Hispanic/Latino), 2 international. Average age 34. 242 applicants, 89% accepted, 167 enrolled. In 2017, 145 master's awarded. *Degree requirements:* For master's, 54 total credit hours. *Entrance requirements:* For master's, GMAT or GRE, letters of recommendation, official transcripts, current resume or curriculum vitae, two years of work experience, interview. Additional exam requirements/recommendations for international students: Required—TOEFL (minimum score 600 paper-based; 100 iBT). *Application deadline:* For fall admission, 8/1 for domestic and international students. Applications are processed on a rolling basis. Application fee: $100. Electronic applications accepted. *Expenses:* Contact institution. *Financial support:* Scholarships/grants available. Financial award application deadline: 4/15; financial award applicants required to submit FAFSA. *Faculty research:* Influence of personal relationships on business decision-making and management of change; drivers of perceived value and consumer behavior; impact of accounting on auditing, financial, managerial, systems and taxation stakeholders; corporate governance and executive compensation; impact of operations strategies on competitiveness. *Unit head:* Tim Janke, Associate Dean of Working Professional Programs, 336-758-5422, Fax: 336-758-5830, E-mail: busadmissions@wfu.edu. *Application contact:* Denise Kelly, Administrative Assistant, 336-758-5422, Fax: 336-758-5830, E-mail: busadmissions@wfu.edu.
Website: http://business.wfu.edu/evening-mba/

Walden University, Graduate Programs, School of Management, Minneapolis, MN 55401. Offers accounting (MBA, MS, DBA), including accounting for the professional (MS), accounting with CPA emphasis (MS), self-designed (MS); advanced project management (Graduate Certificate); applied project management (Graduate Certificate); auditing (Graduate Certificate); bridge to business administration (Post-Doctoral Certificate); bridge to management (Post-Doctoral Certificate); business management (Graduate Certificate); communication (MBA); corporate finance (MBA); digital marketing (Graduate Certificate); entrepreneurship (DBA); entrepreneurship and small business (MBA); finance (MS, DBA), including finance for the professional (MS), finance with CFA/investment (MS), finance with CPA emphasis (MS); global supply chain management (DBA); healthcare management (MBA, DBA); human resource management (MBA, MS, Graduate Certificate), including functional human resource management (MS), general program (MS), integrating functional and strategic human resource management (MS), organizational strategy (MS); human resources management (DBA); information systems management (DBA); international business (MBA, DBA); leadership (MBA, MS, DBA, Graduate Certificate), including general program (MS), human resource leadership (MS), leader development (MS), self-designed (MS); management (MS, PhD), including communications (MS), finance (PhD), general program (MS), healthcare management (MS), human resource management (MS), human resources management (PhD), information systems management (PhD), international business (MS), leadership (MS), leadership and organizational change (PhD), marketing (MS), project management (MS), strategy and operations (MS); managerial accounting (Graduate Certificate); marketing (MBA, MS, DBA); project management (MBA, MS, DBA); self-designed (MBA, DBA); social impact management (DBA); technology entrepreneurship (DBA). *Accreditation:* ACBSP. *Program availability:* Part-time, evening/weekend, online only, 100% online. *Degree requirements:* For master's, thesis (for some programs), residency (for EMBA); for doctorate, thesis/dissertation (for some programs), residency. *Entrance requirements:* For master's, bachelor's degree or higher; minimum GPA of 2.5; official transcripts; goal statement (for some programs); access to computer and Internet; for doctorate, master's degree or higher; three years of related professional or academic experience (preferred); minimum GPA of 3.0; goal statement and current resume (for select programs); official transcripts; access to computer and Internet; for other advanced degree, relevant work experience; access to computer and Internet. Additional exam requirements/recommendations for international students: Required—TOEFL (minimum score 550 paper-based, 79 iBT), IELTS (minimum score 6.5), Michigan English Language Assessment Battery (minimum score 82), or PTE (minimum score 53). Electronic applications accepted.

Walden University, Graduate Programs, School of Public Policy and Administration, Minneapolis, MN 55401. Offers criminal justice (MPA, MPP, MS, Graduate Certificate), including emergency management (MS), general program (MS), global leadership (MS, PhD), homeland security and policy coordination (MS, PhD), law and public policy (MS, PhD), policy analysis (MS, PhD), public management and leadership (MS, PhD), self-designed (MS), terrorism, mediation, and peace (MS, PhD); criminal justice and executive management (MS), including global leadership (MS, PhD); criminal justice leadership and executive management (MS), including emergency management (MS, PhD), general program, homeland security and policy coordination (MS, PhD), law and public policy (MS, PhD), policy analysis (MS, PhD), public management and leadership (MS, PhD), self-designed, terrorism, mediation, and peace (MS, PhD); emergency management (MPA, MPP, MS), including criminal justice (MS, PhD), general program (MS), homeland security (MS), public management and leadership (MS, PhD), terrorism and emergency management (MS); general program (MPA, MPP); global leadership (MPA, MPP); government management (Graduate Certificate); health policy (MPA, MPP); homeland security (Graduate Certificate); homeland security and policy coordination (MPA, MPP); international nongovernmental organizations (MPA, MPP); law and public policy (MPA, MPP); local government management for sustainable communities (MPA, MPP); nonprofit management (Graduate Certificate); nonprofit management and leadership (MPA, MPP, MS), including global leadership (MS, PhD), international nongovernmental organization (MS), local government for sustainable communities (MS), self designed (MS); online teaching in higher education (Post-Master's Certificate); policy analysis (MPA); public management and leadership (MPA, MPP, Graduate Certificate); public policy (Graduate Certificate); public policy and administration (PhD), including criminal justice (MS, PhD), emergency management (MS, PhD), global leadership (MS, PhD), health policy, homeland security and policy coordination (MS, PhD), international nongovernmental organizations, law and public policy (MS, PhD), local government management for sustainable communities, nonprofit management and leadership, policy analysis (MS, PhD), public management and leadership (MS, PhD), terrorism, mediation, and peace (MS, PhD); strategic planning and public policy (Graduate Certificate); terrorism, mediation, and peace (MPA, MPP). *Program availability:* Part-time, evening/weekend, online only, 100% online. *Degree requirements:* For doctorate, thesis/dissertation, residency. *Entrance requirements:* For master's, bachelor's degree or higher; minimum GPA of 2.5; official transcripts; goal statement (for some programs); access to computer and Internet; for doctorate, master's degree or higher; three years of related professional or academic experience (preferred); minimum GPA of 3.0; goal statement and current resume (for select programs); official transcripts; access to computer and Internet; for other advanced degree, relevant work experience; access to computer and Internet. Additional exam requirements/recommendations for international students: Required—TOEFL (minimum score 550 paper-based, 79 iBT), IELTS (minimum score 6.5), Michigan English Language Assessment Battery (minimum score 82), or PTE (minimum score 53). Electronic applications accepted.

Walsh College of Accountancy and Business Administration, Graduate Programs, Master of Arts in Business Program, Troy, MI 48083. Offers MAB. *Program availability:* Part-time, evening/weekend, 100% online, blended/hybrid learning. *Faculty:* 2 full-time (1 woman). *Students:* 25 part-time (16 women); includes 5 minority (4 Black or African American, non-Hispanic/Latino; 1 Two or more races, non-Hispanic/Latino). Average age 38. 26 applicants, 96% accepted, 17 enrolled. *Entrance requirements:* For master's, minimum overall cumulative GPA of 2.75 from all colleges previously attended. Additional exam requirements/recommendations for international students: Required—TOEFL (minimum score 550 paper-based, 79 iBT), IELTS (6.5), Michigan English Language Assessment Battery, or MTELP (80). *Application deadline:* Applications are processed on a rolling basis. Application fee: $35. Electronic applications accepted. *Expenses:* $770 per semester credit hour plus $125 registration fee per semester. *Financial support:* In 2017–18, 1 student received support. Career-related internships or fieldwork and scholarships/grants available. Financial award application deadline: 6/30; financial award applicants required to submit FAFSA. *Unit head:* Dr. Michael Rinkus, Chief Academic Officer/Executive Vice President, 248-823-1269, Fax: 248-689-0920, E-mail: mrinkus@walshcollege.edu. *Application contact:* Heather Rigby, Director, Admissions and Academic Advising, 248-823-1600, Fax: 248-823-1611, E-mail: hrigby@walshcollege.edu.
Website: https://mainbusiness.walshcollege.edu/

Walsh College of Accountancy and Business Administration, Graduate Programs, Program in Business Administration, Troy, MI 48083. Offers MBA, MBA/MSF, MBA/MSITL, MBA/MSM, MBA/MSMKT. *Accreditation:* ACBSP. *Program availability:* Part-time, evening/weekend, 100% online, blended/hybrid learning. *Faculty:* 12 full-time (7 women), 23 part-time/adjunct (9 women). *Students:* 513 (254 women); includes 119 minority (64 Black or African American, non-Hispanic/Latino; 1 American Indian or Alaska Native, non-Hispanic/Latino; 29 Asian, non-Hispanic/Latino; 18 Hispanic/Latino; 7 Two or more races, non-Hispanic/Latino), 11 international. Average age 33. 137 applicants, 85% accepted, 79 enrolled. In 2017, 152 master's awarded. *Entrance requirements:* For master's, minimum overall cumulative GPA of 2.75 from all colleges previously attended. Additional exam requirements/recommendations for international students: Required—TOEFL (minimum score 550 paper-based, 79 iBT), IELTS (6.5), Michigan English Language Assessment Battery, or MTELP (80). *Application deadline:* Applications are processed on a rolling basis. Application fee: $35. Electronic applications accepted. *Expenses:* $770 per semester credit hour plus $125 registration fee per semester. *Financial support:* In 2017–18, 13 students received support. Career-related internships or fieldwork and scholarships/grants available. Financial award application deadline: 6/30; financial award applicants required to submit FAFSA. *Faculty research:* Strategy practice and process, management learning and decision making, consumer behavior, data and decision making. *Unit head:* Dr. Michael Rinkus, Executive Vice President/Chief Academic Officer, 248-823-1269, Fax: 248-689-0920, E-mail: mrinkus@walshcollege.edu. *Application contact:* Heather Rigby, Director, Admissions and Academic Advising, 248-823-1600, Fax: 248-823-1611, E-mail: hrigby@walshcollege.edu.

Walsh College of Accountancy and Business Administration, Graduate Programs, Program in Management, Troy, MI 48083. Offers human resources management (MS); international business (MS); strategic management (MS). *Program availability:* Part-time, evening/weekend, 100% online, blended/hybrid learning. *Faculty:* 10 full-time (6 women), 13 part-time/adjunct (6 women). *Students:* 49 (37 women); includes 18 minority (14 Black or African American, non-Hispanic/Latino; 2 Asian, non-Hispanic/Latino; 2 Hispanic/Latino), 2 international. Average age 33. 17 applicants, 76% accepted, 6 enrolled. In 2017, 15 master's awarded. *Entrance requirements:* For master's, minimum overall cumulative GPA of 2.75 from all colleges previously attended. Additional exam requirements/recommendations for international students: Required—TOEFL (minimum score 550 paper-based, 79 iBT), IELTS (6.5), Michigan English Language Assessment Battery, or MTELP (80). *Application deadline:* Applications are processed on a rolling basis. Application fee: $35. Electronic applications accepted. *Expenses:* $770 per semester credit hour plus $125 registration fee per semester. *Financial support:* In 2017–18, 1 student received support. Career-related internships or fieldwork and scholarships/grants available. Financial award application deadline: 6/30; financial award applicants required to submit FAFSA. *Faculty research:* Strategy practice and process, management learning and decision-making, human capital development, global leadership and citizenship, use of systems and complexity theory and management practice. *Unit head:* Dr. Ann Saurbier, Chair, Management, 248-823-1635, Fax: 248-689-0920, E-mail: asaurbie@walshcollege.edu. *Application contact:* Heather Rigby, Director, Admissions and Academic Advising, 248-823-1610, Fax: 248-823-1611, E-mail: hrigby@walshcollege.edu.

Walsh University, Graduate Programs, MBA Program, North Canton, OH 44720-3396. Offers healthcare management (MBA); management (MBA); marketing (MBA). *Program availability:* Part-time, evening/weekend, online only, 100% online. *Degree requirements:* For master's, capstone course in strategic management. *Entrance requirements:* For master's, GMAT (minimum score of 490), minimum GPA of 3.0. Additional exam requirements/recommendations for international students: Required—TOEFL (minimum score 500 paper-based; 61 iBT). Electronic applications accepted. Application fee is waived when completed online. *Expenses:* Contact institution. *Faculty research:* Medical tourism, familial influence in financial fitness, pedagogy in finance courses, sociocultural aspects of women entrepreneurs, patient satisfaction.

Warner University, School of Business, Lake Wales, FL 33859. Offers accounting (MBA); business administration (MBA); human resource management (MBA); international business (MBA); management (MSMC). *Program availability:* Part-time, evening/weekend, online learning. *Degree requirements:* For master's, comprehensive exam, thesis. *Entrance requirements:* For master's, minimum GPA of 3.0, 2 letters of recommendation. Additional exam requirements/recommendations for international students: Required—TOEFL. Electronic applications accepted.

Washburn University, School of Business, Topeka, KS 66621. Offers accountancy (M Acc). *Accreditation:* AACSB. *Program availability:* Part-time, evening/weekend. *Entrance requirements:* For master's, GMAT, minimum GPA of 2.75. Additional exam requirements/recommendations for international students: Required—TOEFL (minimum score 550 paper-based; 80 iBT); Recommended—IELTS (minimum score 6.5). Electronic applications accepted. *Faculty research:* Ethics in information technology, forecasting for shareholder value creation, model for measuring expected losses from litigation contingencies, business vs. family commitment in family businesses, calculated intangible value and brand recognition.

Washington Adventist University, MBA Program, Takoma Park, MD 20912. Offers MBA. *Program availability:* Part-time, evening/weekend, online learning. *Students:* 13 full-time (6 women), 24 part-time (18 women); includes 20 minority (16 Black or African American, non-Hispanic/Latino; 1 Asian, non-Hispanic/Latino; 3 Hispanic/Latino). Average age 31. In 2017, 24 master's awarded. *Entrance requirements:* For master's, minimum undergraduate GPA of 2.75, curriculum vitae, interview, essay, personal statement. Additional exam requirements/recommendations for international students: Required—TOEFL (minimum score 550 paper-based), IELTS (minimum score 5). *Application deadline:* Applications are processed on a rolling basis. Application fee: $50. *Expenses: Tuition:* Part-time $625 per credit. *Financial support:* Institutionally sponsored loans available. Support available to part-time students. Financial award applicants required to submit FAFSA. *Unit head:* Dr. Patrick Williams, Associate Provost, 301-891-4116. *Application contact:* Jessica Ritchie, Program Coordinator, 301-891-4086, Fax: 301-891-4023, E-mail: jritchie@wau.edu.
Website: http://www.wau.edu/index.php?option-com_content&view-article&id-406temid-963

Washington State University, Carson College of Business, Pullman, WA 99164-4750. Offers M Acc, MBA, PhD. Programs also offered at the Tri-Cities, Vancouver, and Global (online) campuses. *Program availability:* Online learning. *Degree requirements:* For master's, comprehensive exam (for some programs), thesis (for some programs); for doctorate, comprehensive exam, thesis/dissertation. *Entrance requirements:* For master's and doctorate, GMAT (minimum score of 600), resume; statement of purpose identifying area of interest, experiences, and intended research focus; minimum GPA of 3.25. Additional exam requirements/recommendations for international students: Required—TOEFL (minimum score 580 paper-based), IELTS.

Washington University in St. Louis, Olin Business School, Executive MBA Program, St. Louis, MO 63130-4899. Offers EMBA. *Program availability:* Part-time, evening/weekend. *Faculty:* 98 full-time (25 women), 54 part-time/adjunct (12 women). *Students:* 170 part-time (54 women); includes 30 minority (11 Black or African American, non-Hispanic/Latino; 3 Asian, non-Hispanic/Latino; 5 Hispanic/Latino; 1 Native Hawaiian or other Pacific Islander, non-Hispanic/Latino; 10 Two or more races, non-Hispanic/Latino), 15 international. Average age 40. 57 applicants, 96% accepted, 44 enrolled. In 2017, 87 master's awarded. *Entrance requirements:* For master's, two letters of recommendation, letter of commitment/sponsorship, transcripts. Additional exam requirements/recommendations for international students: Required—TOEFL, IELTS. *Application deadline:* For fall admission, 8/19 for domestic and international students; for spring admission, 3/24 for domestic and international students. Applications are processed on a rolling basis. Application fee: $0. Electronic applications accepted. *Expenses:* Contact institution. *Financial support:* Applicants required to submit FAFSA. *Unit head:* Dr. Patrick Moreton, Senior Associate Dean of Graduate Programs, 314-935-6332, Fax: 314-935-7161, E-mail: moreton@wustl.edu. *Application contact:* Ruthie Pyles, Assistant Dean of Admissions, Recruiting and Financial Aid, 314-935-9009, Fax: 314-935-7161, E-mail: ruthie.pyles@wustl.edu.
Website: http://www.olin.wustl.edu/execed/emba.cfm

Washington University in St. Louis, Olin Business School, Full-time MBA Program, St. Louis, MO 63130-4899. Offers MBA, JD/MBA, M Arch/MBA, M Eng/MBA, MBA/MA, MBA/MPH, MBA/MSW. *Faculty:* 98 full-time (25 women), 54 part-time/adjunct (12 women). *Students:* 271 full-time (87 women); includes 55 minority (18 Black or African American, non-Hispanic/Latino; 17 Asian, non-Hispanic/Latino; 15 Hispanic/Latino; 1 Native Hawaiian or other Pacific Islander, non-Hispanic/Latino; 4 Two or more races, non-Hispanic/Latino), 106 international. Average age 28. 1,175 applicants, 40% accepted, 145 enrolled. In 2017, 138 master's awarded. *Entrance requirements:* For master's, GMAT or GRE, U.S. bachelor's degree or equivalent. Additional exam requirements/recommendations for international students: Required—TOEFL, IELTS. *Application deadline:* For fall admission, 10/3 for domestic and international students; for winter admission, 11/30 for domestic and international students; for spring admission, 2/1 for domestic students, 2/1 priority date for international students; for summer admission, 4/10 for domestic and international students. Applications are processed on a rolling basis. Application fee: $0. Electronic applications accepted. *Expenses:* $57,900. *Financial support:* Institutionally sponsored loans and scholarships/grants available. Financial award application deadline: 4/19; financial award applicants required to submit CSS PROFILE or FAFSA. *Unit head:* Dr. Patrick Moreton, Senior Associate Dean of Graduate Programs, 314-935-6322, Fax: 314-935-4464, E-mail: moreton@wustl.edu. *Application contact:* Ruthie Pyles, Assistant Dean and Director of Graduate Admissions, 314-935-7301, Fax: 314-935-4464, E-mail: ruthie.pyles@wustl.edu.
Website: http://www.olin.wustl.edu/mba/

Washington University in St. Louis, Olin Business School, IIT Bombay-Washington University Executive MBA Program, 400076, India. Offers EMBA. Program offered in partnership with Shailesh J. Mehta School of Management at the Indian Institute of Technology in Bombay. *Program availability:* Part-time-only. *Faculty:* 98 full-time (25

women), 54 part-time/adjunct (12 women). *Students:* 23 full-time (5 women). Average age 41. 29 applicants, 100% accepted, 23 enrolled. In 2017, 22 master's awarded. *Entrance requirements:* For master's, bachelor's degree with 7 years of work experience and 5 years of managerial experience. *Application deadline:* Applications are processed on a rolling basis. Application fee: $0. Electronic applications accepted. *Expenses:* Contact institution. *Unit head:* Dr. Mark Taylor, Dean, 314-935-6344, Fax: 314-935-4074. *Application contact:* Kiran Shesh, Academy Chief Executive Officer, 314-935-3383, E-mail: kiran.shesh@wustl.edu.

Washington University in St. Louis, Olin Business School, PhD Program in Business Administration, St. Louis, MO 63130-4899. Offers PhD. *Faculty:* 98 full-time (25 women), 54 part-time/adjunct (12 women). *Students:* 62 full-time (20 women); includes 8 minority (all Asian, non-Hispanic/Latino), 45 international. Average age 26. 412 applicants, 10% accepted, 16 enrolled. In 2017, 9 doctorates awarded. *Degree requirements:* For doctorate, comprehensive exam, thesis/dissertation, field exam, 2nd-year paper presentation, thesis proposal defense. *Entrance requirements:* For doctorate, GMAT or GRE. Additional exam requirements/recommendations for international students: Required—TOEFL or IELTS. *Application deadline:* For fall admission, 12/31 for domestic and international students. Application fee: $100. Electronic applications accepted. *Expenses:* Contact institution. *Financial support:* In 2017–18, fellowships with full tuition reimbursements (averaging $25,000 per year) were awarded; health care benefits and travel support for conferences also available. *Unit head:* Prof. Anjan Thakor, Professor/Director, 314-935-7197, Fax: 314-935-6359, E-mail: thakor@wust.edu. *Application contact:* Erin Murdock, Associate Director of Doctoral Admissions, 314-935-6340, Fax: 314-935-9484, E-mail: murdockel@wustl.edu.
Website: http://www.olin.wustl.edu/prospective/phd.cfm

Washington University in St. Louis, Olin Business School, Professional MBA Program, St. Louis, MO 63130-4899. Offers MBA. *Program availability:* Part-time, evening/weekend. *Faculty:* 98 full-time (25 women), 54 part-time/adjunct (12 women). *Students:* 258 part-time (80 women); includes 49 minority (9 Black or African American, non-Hispanic/Latino; 1 American Indian or Alaska Native, non-Hispanic/Latino; 24 Asian, non-Hispanic/Latino; 8 Hispanic/Latino; 7 Two or more races, non-Hispanic/Latino), 16 international. Average age 29. 106 applicants, 85% accepted, 65 enrolled. In 2017, 119 master's awarded. *Degree requirements:* For master's, 54 credits. *Entrance requirements:* For master's, GMAT or GRE, U.S. bachelor's degree or equivalent. Additional exam requirements/recommendations for international students: Required—TOEFL, IELTS. *Application deadline:* For fall admission, 10/3 for domestic and international students; for winter admission, 1/3 for domestic and international students; for spring admission, 4/10 for domestic and international students; for summer admission, 7/9 for domestic and international students. Applications are processed on a rolling basis. Application fee: $0. Electronic applications accepted. *Expenses:* Contact institution. *Financial support:* Applicants required to submit CSS PROFILE or FAFSA. *Unit head:* Dr. Patrick Moreton, Senior Associate Dean of Graduate Programs, 314-935-6322, Fax: 314-935-4464, E-mail: moreton@wustl.edu. *Application contact:* Ruthie Pyles, Assistant Dean and Director of Graduate Admissions, 314-935-7301, Fax: 314-935-4464, E-mail: olingradadmissions@wustl.edu.
Website: http://www.olin.wustl.edu/prospective/pmba.cfm

Washington University in St. Louis, Olin Business School, Washington University-Fudan University Executive MBA Program, 200040, China. Offers EMBA. *Program availability:* Part-time. *Faculty:* 98 full-time (25 women), 54 part-time/adjunct (12 women). *Students:* 66 part-time (30 women); includes 65 minority (all Asian, non-Hispanic/Latino). Average age 39. 248 applicants, 28% accepted, 66 enrolled. In 2017, 38 master's awarded. *Degree requirements:* For master's, thesis optional. *Entrance requirements:* Additional exam requirements/recommendations for international students: Required—TOEFL. *Application deadline:* For fall admission, 9/8 for domestic and international students; for winter admission, 1/26 for domestic and international students; for spring admission, 3/13 for domestic and international students; for summer admission, 6/20 for domestic and international students. Applications are processed on a rolling basis. Application fee: 1,200 Chinese yuans. Electronic applications accepted. *Expenses:* Contact institution. *Unit head:* Dr. Patrick Moreton, Senior Associate Dean of Graduate Programs, 314-935-3622, E-mail: moreton@wustl.edu. *Application contact:* Chen Zhang, Recruiting Director, 314-935-3622, E-mail: czhang30@wustl.edu.
Website: http://www.olin.wustl.edu/EN-US/executive-programs/executive-mba-shanghai/Pages/default.aspx

Wayland Baptist University, Graduate Programs, Programs in Business Administration/Management, Plainview, TX 79072-6998. Offers accounting (MBA); general business (MBA); health care administration (MAM, MBA); human resource management (MAM, MBA); international management (MBA); management (MBA, D Mgt); management information systems (MBA); organization management (MAM); project management (MBA). *Program availability:* Part-time, evening/weekend, online learning. *Faculty:* 30 full-time (5 women), 38 part-time/adjunct (9 women). *Students:* 42 full-time (20 women), 538 part-time (253 women); includes 311 minority (98 Black or African American, non-Hispanic/Latino; 4 American Indian or Alaska Native, non-Hispanic/Latino; 16 Asian, non-Hispanic/Latino; 153 Hispanic/Latino; 11 Native Hawaiian or other Pacific Islander, non-Hispanic/Latino; 29 Two or more races, non-Hispanic/Latino), 6 international. Average age 40. 100 applicants, 96% accepted, 60 enrolled. In 2017, 216 master's awarded. *Degree requirements:* For master's, capstone course. *Entrance requirements:* For master's, GMAT, GRE or MAT. Additional exam requirements/recommendations for international students: Required—TOEFL (minimum score 500 paper-based; 61 iBT). *Application deadline:* Applications are processed on a rolling basis. Application fee: $50. Electronic applications accepted. *Expenses: Tuition:* Full-time $11,250; part-time $625 per credit hour. *Required fees:* $1200. *Financial support:* Federal Work-Study, institutionally sponsored loans, and scholarships/grants available. Support available to part-time students. Financial award application deadline: 5/1; financial award applicants required to submit FAFSA. *Unit head:* Dr. Kelly Warren, Chairman, 806-291-1020, Fax: 806-291-1957, E-mail: warrenk@wbu.edu. *Application contact:* Amanda Stanton, Graduate Studies, 806-291-3423, Fax: 806-291-1950, E-mail: stanton@wbu.edu.

Waynesburg University, Graduate and Professional Studies, Canonsburg, PA 15370. Offers business (MBA), including energy management, finance, health systems, human resources, leadership, market development; counseling (MA), including addictions counseling, clinical mental health; counselor education and supervision (PhD); criminal investigation (MA); education (M Ed), including autism, curriculum and instruction, educational leadership, online teaching; nursing (MSN), including administration, education, informatics; nursing practice (DNP); special education (M Ed); technology (M Ed); MSN/MBA. *Accreditation:* AACN. *Program availability:* Part-time, evening/weekend. *Degree requirements:* For doctorate, thesis/dissertation. *Entrance requirements:* Additional exam requirements/recommendations for international students: Required—TOEFL. Electronic applications accepted.

Wayne State College, School of Business and Technology, Wayne, NE 68787. Offers MBA. *Program availability:* Part-time, evening/weekend, online learning. *Entrance requirements:* For master's, GMAT, minimum overall GPA of 3.0. Additional exam requirements/recommendations for international students: Required—TOEFL (minimum score 550 paper-based).

Business Administration and Management—General

Wayne State University, Mike Ilitch School of Business, Detroit, MI 48202. Offers accounting (MS, MSA, Postbaccalaureate Certificate); business (EMS, Graduate Certificate); business administration (MBA, PhD); data science (MS), including business analytics; entrepreneurship and innovation (Postbaccalaureate Certificate); finance (MS); information systems management (Postbaccalaureate Certificate); taxation (MST); JD/MBA. Application deadline for PhD is February 15. *Accreditation:* AACSB. *Program availability:* Part-time, evening/weekend. *Faculty:* 32. *Students:* 235 full-time (121 women), 1,082 part-time (480 women); includes 356 minority (202 Black or African American, non-Hispanic/Latino; 2 American Indian or Alaska Native, non-Hispanic/Latino; 79 Asian, non-Hispanic/Latino; 47 Hispanic/Latino; 26 Two or more races, non-Hispanic/Latino), 87 international. Average age 30. 1,285 applicants, 43% accepted, 308 enrolled. In 2017, 200 master's, 2 doctorates, 9 other advanced degrees awarded. *Degree requirements:* For doctorate, thesis/dissertation. *Entrance requirements:* For master's, GMAT, GRE, LSAT, MCAT, at least three years of relevant work experience that shows increased responsibility, or minimum GPA of 3.0 from AACSB-accredited program or 3.2 from regionally-accredited program, undergraduate degree from accredited institution; undergraduate degree in accounting, business administration, or area of business administration (for MS and MST); for doctorate, GMAT (minimum score of 600), minimum undergraduate GPA of 3.0, 3.5 upper-division or graduate; three letters of recommendation; brief essay; undergraduate degree from accredited institution; personal statement; for other advanced degree, bachelor's degree from accredited institution. Additional exam requirements/recommendations for international students: Required—TOEFL (minimum score 550 paper-based; 79 iBT), Michigan English Language Assessment Battery (minimum score 85); Recommended—IELTS (minimum score 6.5), TWE (minimum score 5.5). *Application deadline:* For fall admission, 7/1 for domestic students, 5/1 priority date for international students; for winter admission, 11/1 for domestic students, 9/1 priority date for international students; for spring admission, 3/1 for domestic students, 1/1 priority date for international students. Applications are processed on a rolling basis. Application fee: $50. Electronic applications accepted. *Expenses:* Contact institution. *Financial support:* In 2017–18, 165 students received support, including 1 fellowship with tuition reimbursement available (averaging $18,534 per year), 1 teaching assistantship with tuition reimbursement available (averaging $18,534 per year); research assistantships with tuition reimbursements available, scholarships/grants, health care benefits, and unspecified assistantships also available. Support available to part-time students. Financial award applicants required to submit FAFSA. *Faculty research:* Executive compensation and stock performance, consumer reactions to pricing strategies, communication across the automotive supply chain, performance of firms in sub-Saharan Africa, implementation issues with ERP software. *Unit head:* Dr. Robert Forsythe, Dean, School of Business Administration, 313-577-4501, E-mail: robert.forsythe@wayne.edu. *Application contact:* Kiantee N. Rupert-Jones, Director, 313-577-4511, Fax: 313-577-9442, E-mail: gradbusiness@wayne.edu. Website: http://ilitchbusiness.wayne.edu/

Webber International University, Graduate School of Business, Babson Park, FL 33827-0096. Offers accounting (MBA); business (MBA); criminal justice management (MBA); international business (MBA); sport business management (MBA). *Program availability:* Part-time, evening/weekend, 100% online. *Faculty:* 10 full-time (4 women), 1 part-time/adjunct (0 women). *Students:* 50 full-time (29 women), 6 part-time (2 women); includes 19 minority (12 Black or African American, non-Hispanic/Latino; 6 Hispanic/Latino; 1 Two or more races, non-Hispanic/Latino), 6 international. Average age 24. 64 applicants, 61% accepted, 32 enrolled. In 2017, 29 master's awarded. *Degree requirements:* For master's, class trip (for international business); practicum (for criminal justice management). *Entrance requirements:* For master's, three recommendation letters, résumé, essay, official transcripts from all colleges and universities attended. Additional exam requirements/recommendations for international students: Recommended—TOEFL (minimum score 500 paper-based; 61 iBT), IELTS (minimum score 6). *Application deadline:* For fall admission, 7/1 for international students. Applications are processed on a rolling basis. Application fee: $50 ($75 for international students). Electronic applications accepted. *Expenses:* Tuition: Part-time $688 per hour. *Financial support:* In 2017–18, 11 students received support. Scholarships/grants and unspecified assistantships available. Financial award application deadline: 8/1; financial award applicants required to submit FAFSA. *Unit head:* Dr. Nikos Orphanoudakis, Dean, 863-638-2910, Fax: 863-638-1591, E-mail: orphanoudakisn@webber.edu. *Application contact:* Lacy Edwards, Admissions Counselor and MBA Coordinator, 863-638-2910, Fax: 863-638-1591, E-mail: admissions@webber.edu.

Weber State University, Goddard School of Business and Economics, Program in Business Administration, Ogden, UT 84408-1001. Offers MBA, Graduate Certificate. *Accreditation:* AACSB. *Program availability:* Part-time, evening/weekend. *Faculty:* 13 full-time (3 women). *Students:* 60 full-time (16 women), 148 part-time (42 women); includes 12 minority (1 Black or African American, non-Hispanic/Latino; 2 American Indian or Alaska Native, non-Hispanic/Latino; 7 Hispanic/Latino; 2 Two or more races, non-Hispanic/Latino), 6 international. Average age 36. In 2017, 57 master's, 24 other advanced degrees awarded. *Entrance requirements:* For master's, GMAT or GRE, resume, letters of recommendation. Additional exam requirements/recommendations for international students: Required—TOEFL (minimum score 550 paper-based). *Application deadline:* For fall admission, 5/1 for domestic and international students; for spring admission, 11/1 for domestic and international students. Application fee: $60 ($90 for international students). Electronic applications accepted. *Expenses:* Tuition, state resident: full-time $7283. Tuition, nonresident: full-time $17,166. *Required fees:* $898. Tuition and fees vary according to program. *Financial support:* In 2017–18, 14 students received support. Scholarships/grants available. Financial award application deadline: 4/1; financial award applicants required to submit FAFSA. *Unit head:* Dr. Matt Mouritsen, MBA Program Director/Associate Professor of Accounting, 801-626-7811, Fax: 801-626-7423, E-mail: mmouritsen@weber.edu. *Application contact:* Dr. Mark A. Stevenson, MBA Enrollment Director, 801-395-3528, Fax: 801-395-3525, E-mail: mba@weber.edu. Website: http://www.weber.edu/mba/

Webster University, George Herbert Walker School of Business and Technology, Department of Business, St. Louis, MO 63119-3194. Offers business and organizational security management (MBA); decision support systems (MBA); environmental management (MBA); finance (MBA, MS); forensic accounting (MS); gerontology (MBA); human resources development (MBA); human resources management (MBA); information technology management (MBA); international business (MA, MBA); international relations (MBA); management and leadership (MBA); marketing (MBA); media communications (MBA); procurement and acquisitions management (MBA); Web services (MBA). *Accreditation:* ACBSP. *Program availability:* Part-time, evening/weekend, online learning. *Degree requirements:* For master's, comprehensive exam (for some programs), thesis (for some programs). *Entrance requirements:* Additional exam requirements/recommendations for international students: Required—TOEFL.

Webster University, George Herbert Walker School of Business and Technology, Department of Management, St. Louis, MO 63119-3194. Offers business and organizational security management (MA); digital marketing management (Graduate Certificate); government contracting (Graduate Certificate); health administration (MHA); health care management (MA); health services management (MA); human resources development (MA); human resources management (MA); information technology

management (MA, MS); management (D Mgt); management and leadership (MA); marketing (MA); nonprofit leadership (MA); nonprofit revenue development (Graduate Certificate); organizational development (Graduate Certificate); procurement and acquisitions management (MA); public administration (MPA); space systems operations management (MS). *Program availability:* Part-time, evening/weekend, online learning. *Degree requirements:* For master's, thesis (for some programs); for doctorate, thesis/dissertation, written exam. *Entrance requirements:* For doctorate, GMAT, 3 years of work experience, MBA. Additional exam requirements/recommendations for international students: Required—TOEFL.

Wesleyan College, Department of Business and Economics, EMBA Program, Macon, GA 31210-4462. Offers EMBA. *Program availability:* Evening/weekend. *Entrance requirements:* For master's, GMAT, LSAT, GRE or MAT, 5 years work experience, 5 years of management experience. Additional exam requirements/recommendations for international students: Required—TOEFL (minimum score 550 paper-based). Electronic applications accepted.

Wesley College, Business Program, Dover, DE 19901-3875. Offers environmental management (MBA); executive leadership (MBA); management (MBA). Executive leadership concentration also offered at New Castle, DE location. *Program availability:* Part-time, evening/weekend. *Entrance requirements:* For master's, GMAT or GRE, minimum undergraduate GPA of 2.75.

West Chester University of Pennsylvania, College of Business and Public Management, School of Business, West Chester, PA 19383. Offers business analytics (Certificate); business education (MBA). *Accreditation:* AACSB. *Program availability:* Part-time, evening/weekend, online only, 100% online. *Students:* 41 full-time (17 women), 388 part-time (150 women); includes 69 minority (33 Black or African American, non-Hispanic/Latino; 19 Asian, non-Hispanic/Latino; 14 Hispanic/Latino; 3 Two or more races, non-Hispanic/Latino). Average age 32. 268 applicants, 68% accepted, 153 enrolled. In 2017, 78 master's, 21 other advanced degrees awarded. *Degree requirements:* For master's, minimum GPA of 3.0. *Entrance requirements:* For master's, GMAT or GRE, statement of professional goals, resume, three letters of recommendation, transcripts. Additional exam requirements/recommendations for international students: Required—TOEFL or IELTS. *Application deadline:* For fall admission, 5/15 for international students; for spring admission, 10/15 for international students. Applications are processed on a rolling basis. Application fee: $50. Electronic applications accepted. *Expenses:* Tuition, state resident: full-time $9000; part-time $500 per credit. Tuition, nonresident: full-time $13,500; part-time $750 per credit. *Required fees:* $2959; $149.79 per credit. *Financial support:* Scholarships/grants and unspecified assistantships available. Financial award application deadline: 2/15; financial award applicants required to submit FAFSA. *Unit head:* Dr. Brian Halsey, MBA Director/Graduate Coordinator, 610-425-5000 Ext. 4444, E-mail: mba@wcupa.edu. *Application contact:* Office of Graduate Studies and Extended Education, 610-436-2943, Fax: 610-436-2763, E-mail: gradstudy@wcupa.edu. Website: http://www.wcupa.edu/mba

Western Carolina University, Graduate School, College of Business, Program in Business Administration, Cullowhee, NC 28723. Offers MBA. *Accreditation:* AACSB. *Program availability:* Part-time, evening/weekend. *Entrance requirements:* For master's, GMAT, appropriate undergraduate degree, 3 letters of recommendation. Additional exam requirements/recommendations for international students: Required—TOEFL (minimum score 550 paper-based; 79 iBT). *Expenses:* Tuition, state resident: full-time $4436. Tuition, nonresident: full-time $14,842. *Required fees:* $2926. *Faculty research:* Marketing strategy, biotechnology, executive education, business statistics, supply chain management, innovation.

Western Connecticut State University, Division of Graduate Studies, Ancell School of Business, Program in Business Administration, Danbury, CT 06810-6885. Offers accounting (MBA); business administration (MBA). *Program availability:* Part-time. *Degree requirements:* For master's, comprehensive exam, completion of program within 8 years. *Entrance requirements:* For master's, GMAT. Additional exam requirements/recommendations for international students: Recommended—TOEFL (minimum score 550 paper-based; 79 iBT), IELTS (minimum score 6). *Expenses:* Tuition, state resident: full-time $6757; part-time $374 per credit hour. Tuition, nonresident: full-time $18,102; part-time $374 per credit hour. *Required fees:* $4994; $190 per credit hour. $60 per term. Tuition and fees vary according to degree level and program. *Faculty research:* Global strategic marketing planning, project management and team coordination; email, discussion boards that act as blogs and videoconferencing.

Western Governors University, College of Business, Salt Lake City, UT 84107. Offers information technology management (MBA); integrated healthcare management (MS); management and strategy (MBA); strategic leadership (MBA). *Program availability:* Evening/weekend. *Degree requirements:* For master's, capstone project. *Entrance requirements:* For master's, Readiness Assessment, transcripts. Additional exam requirements/recommendations for international students: Required—TOEFL (minimum score 450 paper-based; 80 iBT). Electronic applications accepted.

Western Illinois University, School of Graduate Studies, College of Business and Technology, Program in Business Administration, Macomb, IL 61455-1390. Offers business administration (MBA, Certificate); supply chain management (Certificate). *Accreditation:* AACSB. *Program availability:* Part-time. *Students:* 44 full-time (20 women), 63 part-time (23 women); includes 14 minority (2 Black or African American, non-Hispanic/Latino; 2 Asian, non-Hispanic/Latino; 9 Hispanic/Latino; 1 Two or more races, non-Hispanic/Latino), 9 international. Average age 32. 94 applicants, 65% accepted, 24 enrolled. In 2017, 42 master's awarded. *Degree requirements:* For master's, thesis or alternative. *Entrance requirements:* For master's, GMAT. Additional exam requirements/recommendations for international students: Required—TOEFL (minimum score 550 paper-based; 80 iBT). *Application deadline:* Applications are processed on a rolling basis. Application fee: $30. Electronic applications accepted. *Financial support:* Research assistantships with full tuition reimbursements and unspecified assistantships available. Financial award applicants required to submit FAFSA. *Unit head:* Dr. Bill Polley, Associate Dean, 309-298-2442. *Application contact:* Dr. Nancy Parsons, Associate Provost and Director of Graduate Studies, 309-298-1806, Fax: 309-298-2345, E-mail: grad-office@wiu.edu. Website: http://wiu.edu/cbt

Western Kentucky University, Graduate Studies, Gordon Ford College of Business, MBA Program, Bowling Green, KY 42101. Offers MBA. *Accreditation:* AACSB. *Program availability:* Part-time, evening/weekend. *Degree requirements:* For master's, comprehensive exam, thesis optional. *Entrance requirements:* For master's, GMAT, minimum GPA of 2.5. Additional exam requirements/recommendations for international students: Required—TOEFL (minimum score 555 paper-based; 79 iBT). *Faculty research:* Business and international education, web page development, management training, international studies, globalization.

Western Michigan University, Graduate College, Haworth College of Business, Department of Interdisciplinary Business, Kalamazoo, MI 49008. Offers business administration (MBA). *Accreditation:* AACSB.

Western New England University, College of Business, Program in Business Administration, Springfield, MA 01119. Offers general business (MBA); sport

management (MBA); JD/MBA; MS/MBA; Pharm D/MBA. *Accreditation:* AACSB. *Program availability:* Part-time, evening/weekend, online learning. *Faculty:* 8 full-time (6 women). *Students:* 74 part-time (34 women); includes 7 minority (2 Black or African American, non-Hispanic/Latino; 2 Asian, non-Hispanic/Latino; 2 Hispanic/Latino; 1 Two or more races, non-Hispanic/Latino), 1 international. Average age 32. 79 applicants, 66% accepted, 47 enrolled. In 2017, 48 master's awarded. *Entrance requirements:* For master's, GMAT or GRE, official transcript, two letters of recommendation, essay, resume. Additional exam requirements/recommendations for international students: Required—TOEFL (minimum score 79 iBT). *Application deadline:* Applications are processed on a rolling basis. Application fee: $30. Electronic applications accepted. *Expenses:* Contact institution. *Financial support:* Application deadline: 4/15; applicants required to submit FAFSA. *Unit head:* Dr. Rob Kleine, Dean, 413-782-1395, E-mail: rob.kleine@wne.edu. *Application contact:* Matthew Fox, Director of Admissions for Graduate Students and Adult Learners, 413-782-1410, Fax: 413-782-1777, E-mail: study@wne.edu.
Website: http://www1.wne.edu/academics/graduate/mba.cfm

Western New Mexico University, Graduate Division, School of Business, Silver City, NM 88062-0680. Offers business administration (MBA). *Accreditation:* ACBSP. *Program availability:* Part-time, online learning. *Entrance requirements:* For master's, GMAT. Additional exam requirements/recommendations for international students: Required—TOEFL (minimum score 550 paper-based). Electronic applications accepted. *Faculty research:* Migration: an analysis of Puerto Rican interest to migrate to the United States using Internet search trends, entrepreneurship management in rural U.S. areas, exports and maritime ports: Puerto Rico and the port of Las Americas, female labor force participation in the border states.

Western Washington University, Graduate School, College of Business and Economics, Bellingham, WA 98225-5996. Offers MBA, MP Acc. *Accreditation:* AACSB. *Program availability:* Part-time, evening/weekend. *Degree requirements:* For master's, comprehensive exam. *Entrance requirements:* For master's, GMAT, minimum GPA of 3.0 in last 60 semester hours or last 90 quarter hours. Additional exam requirements/recommendations for international students: Required—TOEFL (minimum score 567 paper-based). Electronic applications accepted. *Faculty research:* Enterprise strategy/ corporate social performance, sustainability/environmental management/nonprofit marketing, managerial/environmental accounting, organizational applications of collaborative technology, environmental and resource economics.

Westminster College, The Bill and Vieve Gore School of Business, Salt Lake City, UT 84105-3697. Offers accountancy (M Acc); business administration (MBA, Certificate); technology commercialization (MBA). *Program availability:* Part-time, evening/weekend, blended/hybrid learning. *Faculty:* 20 full-time (6 women), 16 part-time/adjunct (6 women). *Students:* 89 full-time (36 women), 130 part-time (46 women); includes 52 minority (9 Black or African American, non-Hispanic/Latino; 1 American Indian or Alaska Native, non-Hispanic/Latino; 17 Asian, non-Hispanic/Latino; 21 Hispanic/Latino; 1 Native Hawaiian or other Pacific Islander, non-Hispanic/Latino; 3 Two or more races, non-Hispanic/Latino), 13 international. Average age 34. 67 applicants, 84% accepted, 47 enrolled. In 2017, 150 master's, 1 other advanced degree awarded. *Degree requirements:* For master's, International Context Tour (for MBA). *Entrance requirements:* For master's, GMAT (waived on a case-by-case basis), 2 professional recommendations, employer letter of support, personal resume, essay, official transcripts. Additional exam requirements/recommendations for international students: Required—TOEFL (minimum score 84 iBT), IELTS (minimum score 7). *Application deadline:* For fall admission, 5/1 priority date for domestic and international students; for spring admission, 10/1 priority date for domestic and international students; for summer admission, 2/1 priority date for domestic and international students. Applications are processed on a rolling basis. Application fee: $50. Electronic applications accepted. *Expenses:* Contact institution. *Financial support:* In 2017–18, 58 students received support. Career-related internships or fieldwork, scholarships/grants, unspecified assistantships, and tuition remission available. Financial award applicants required to submit FAFSA. *Faculty research:* Innovation and entrepreneurship, business strategy and change, financial analysis and capital budgeting, leadership development, knowledge management. *Unit head:* Melissa Koerner, Dean, Bill and Vieve Gore School of Business, 801-832-2600, Fax: 801-832-3106, E-mail: mkoerner@ westminstercollege.edu. *Application contact:* Ashley Williams, Director of Graduate and International Admissions, 801-832-2213, Fax: 801-832-3101, E-mail: awilliams@ westminstercollege.edu.
Website: https://www.westminstercollege.edu/graduate/programs

West Texas A&M University, College of Business, Department of Management, Marketing and General Business, Canyon, TX 79015. Offers business administration (MBA). *Accreditation:* AACSB. *Program availability:* Part-time, evening/weekend, 100% online. *Entrance requirements:* For master's, GMAT. Additional exam requirements/ recommendations for international students: Required—TOEFL (minimum score 550 paper-based). Electronic applications accepted. *Faculty research:* Human resources, international business, southern Asian markets, global strategies, international trade composition.

West Virginia University, College of Business and Economics, Morgantown, WV 26506. Offers accountancy (M Acc); accounting (PhD); business administration (MBA); business cyber security management (MS); business data analytics (MS); economics (MA, PhD); finance (MS, PhD); forensic and fraud examination (MS); industrial relations (MS); management (PhD); marketing (PhD). *Program availability:* Part-time, online learning. *Students:* 343 full-time (141 women), 43 part-time (12 women); includes 59 minority (22 Black or African American, non-Hispanic/Latino; 11 Asian, non-Hispanic/ Latino; 12 Hispanic/Latino; 14 Two or more races, non-Hispanic/Latino), 54 international. Terminal master's awarded for partial completion of doctoral program. *Degree requirements:* For master's, thesis optional; for doctorate, comprehensive exam, thesis/dissertation. *Entrance requirements:* For doctorate, GRE General Test, minimum GPA of 3.0. Additional exam requirements/recommendations for international students: Required—TOEFL (minimum score 550 paper-based; 92 iBT). *Application deadline:* For fall admission, 10/15 priority date for domestic and international students; for spring admission, 3/1 priority date for domestic and international students. Applications are processed on a rolling basis. Application fee: $60. Electronic applications accepted. *Expenses:* Contact institution. *Financial support:* Fellowships, research assistantships, teaching assistantships, career-related internships or fieldwork, Federal Work-Study, institutionally sponsored loans, scholarships/grants, health care benefits, tuition waivers (full and partial), unspecified assistantships, and administrative assistantships available. Financial award application deadline: 2/1; financial award applicants required to submit FAFSA. *Faculty research:* Regional labor market studies, economic development, market research, economic forecasting, energy analysis. *Unit head:* Dr. Javier Reyes, Dean, 304-293-7800, Fax: 304-293-4056, E-mail: javier.reyes@mail.wvu.edu. *Application contact:* Dr. Mark Gavin, Associate Dean for Graduate Programs, 304-293-7952, Fax: 304-293-7188, E-mail: mark.gavin@mail.wvu.edu.
Website: http://www.be.wvu.edu

West Virginia Wesleyan College, MBA Program, Buckhannon, WV 26201. Offers MBA. *Program availability:* Part-time, evening/weekend. *Degree requirements:* For

master's, exit evaluation. *Entrance requirements:* For master's, GMAT. Additional exam requirements/recommendations for international students: Required—TOEFL.

Wheeling Jesuit University, Department of Business, Wheeling, WV 26003-6295. Offers accounting (MSA); business administration (MBA). *Accreditation:* ACBSP. *Program availability:* Part-time, evening/weekend. *Entrance requirements:* For master's, minimum undergraduate GPA of 2.8. Additional exam requirements/recommendations for international students: Required—TOEFL (minimum score 600 paper-based; 100 iBT). Electronic applications accepted. *Faculty research:* Forensic economics, consumer behavior, economic development, capitalism, leadership.

Whitworth University, School of Business, Spokane, WA 99251-0001. Offers MBA. *Program availability:* Part-time, evening/weekend. *Degree requirements:* For master's, variable foreign language requirement. *Entrance requirements:* For master's, GMAT or GRE, minimum undergraduate GPA of 3.25, or alternate exam, two letters of recommendation; resume; completion of prerequisite courses in micro-economics, macro-economics, financial accounting, finance, and marketing; interview with director. Additional exam requirements/recommendations for international students: Required— TOEFL (minimum score 88 iBT), TWE. Electronic applications accepted. *Faculty research:* International business (European, Central America and Asian topics), entrepreneurship and business plan development.

WHU - Otto Beisheim School of Management, Graduate Programs, Vallendar, Germany. Offers EMBA, MBA, MS. EMBA offered jointly with Kellogg School of Management.

Wichita State University, Graduate School, W. Frank Barton School of Business, Department of Business, Wichita, KS 67260. Offers EMBA, MBA. *Accreditation:* AACSB. *Program availability:* Part-time, evening/weekend. *Unit head:* Liz McLain, Director, 316-978-3230, E-mail: liz.mclain@wichita.edu. *Application contact:* Jordan Oleson, Admissions Coordinator, 316-978-3095, Fax: 316-978-3253, E-mail: jordan.oleson@wichita.edu.
Website: http://www.wichita.edu/mba

Widener University, School of Business Administration, Chester, PA 19013-5792. Offers MBA, MHA, MS, JD/MBA, MD/MBA, MD/MHA, ME/MBA, Psy D/MBA, Psy D/ MHA. *Accreditation:* AACSB. *Program availability:* Part-time, evening/weekend, 100% online, blended/hybrid learning. *Faculty:* 14 full-time (6 women), 6 part-time/adjunct (2 women). *Students:* 47 full-time (18 women), 158 part-time (76 women); includes 58 minority (35 Black or African American, non-Hispanic/Latino; 11 Asian, non-Hispanic/ Latino; 9 Hispanic/Latino; 1 Native Hawaiian or other Pacific Islander, non-Hispanic/ Latino; 2 Two or more races, non-Hispanic/Latino), 33 international. Average age 32. 154 applicants, 49% accepted, 43 enrolled. In 2017, 45 master's awarded. *Entrance requirements:* For master's, minimum GPA of 2.5. *Application deadline:* For fall admission, 8/1 priority date for domestic students; for spring admission, 12/1 for domestic students. Applications are processed on a rolling basis. Application fee: $25 ($300 for international students). Electronic applications accepted. *Expenses:* Contact institution. *Financial support:* In 2017–18, 11 research assistantships with full tuition reimbursements were awarded; career-related internships or fieldwork, Federal Work-Study, and traineeships also available. Support available to part-time students. Financial award application deadline: 5/1. *Faculty research:* Cost containment in health care, human resource management, productivity, globalization. *Unit head:* Dr. Jayati Ghosh, Dean, 610-499-4300, Fax: 610-499-4615. *Application contact:* Ann Seltzer, Graduate Enrollment Administrator, 610-499-4305, E-mail: apseltzer@widener.edu.
Website: http://www.widener.edu

Wilfrid Laurier University, Faculty of Graduate and Postdoctoral Studies, School of Business and Economics, Business Administration Program, Waterloo, ON N2L 3C5, Canada. Offers co-op (MBA); full-time (MBA); part-time (MBA). *Accreditation:* AACSB. *Program availability:* Part-time, evening/weekend. *Degree requirements:* For master's, thesis. *Entrance requirements:* For master's, GMAT, minimum 2 years of business experience (for 12-month or part-time MBA formats), minimum B average in 4-year BA program. Additional exam requirements/recommendations for international students: Required—TOEFL (minimum score 89 iBT). Electronic applications accepted.

Wilfrid Laurier University, Faculty of Graduate and Postdoctoral Studies, School of Business and Economics, Department of Business, Waterloo, ON N2L 3C5, Canada. Offers accounting (PhD); finance (M Fin); financial economics (PhD); marketing (PhD); operations and supply chain management (PhD); organizational behavior and human resource management (M Sc); organizational behaviour and human resource management (PhD); supply chain management (M Sc); technology management (EMTM). *Accreditation:* AACSB. *Program availability:* Part-time, evening/weekend. *Degree requirements:* For master's, thesis optional; for doctorate, comprehensive exam, thesis/dissertation. *Entrance requirements:* For master's, GMAT, 4-year honors degree with minimum B+ average; for doctorate, GMAT, master's degree, minimum B+ average. Additional exam requirements/recommendations for international students: Required—TOEFL (minimum score 89 iBT). Electronic applications accepted. *Faculty research:* Financial economics, management and organizational behavior, operations and supply chain management.

Wilkes University, College of Graduate and Professional Studies, Jay S. Sidhu School of Business and Leadership, Wilkes-Barre, PA 18766-0002. Offers accounting (MBA); entrepreneurship (MBA); finance (MBA); health care administration (MBA); human resource management (MBA); international business (MBA); operations management (MBA); organizational leadership and development (MBA). *Accreditation:* ACBSP. *Program availability:* Part-time, evening/weekend. *Students:* 37 full-time (18 women), 87 part-time (45 women); includes 17 minority (4 Black or African American, non-Hispanic/ Latino; 5 Asian, non-Hispanic/Latino; 6 Hispanic/Latino; 2 Two or more races, non-Hispanic/Latino), 14 international. Average age 30. In 2017, 77 master's awarded. *Entrance requirements:* For master's, GMAT. Additional exam requirements/ recommendations for international students: Required—TOEFL (minimum score 550 paper-based; 79 iBT). *Application deadline:* Applications are processed on a rolling basis. Application fee: $45 ($65 for international students). Electronic applications accepted. *Expenses:* Contact institution. *Financial support:* Unspecified assistantships available. Financial award application deadline: 3/1; financial award applicants required to submit FAFSA. *Unit head:* Dr. Abel Adekola, Dean, 570-408-4701, Fax: 570-408-7846, E-mail: abel.adekola@wilkes.edu. *Application contact:* Kristin Donati, Associate Director of Graduate Admissions, 570-408-3338, Fax: 570-408-7846, E-mail: kristin.donati@wilkes.edu.
Website: http://www.wilkes.edu/academics/colleges/sidhu-school-of-business-leadership/index.aspx

Willamette University, Atkinson Graduate School of Management, Salem, OR 97301-3931. Offers MBA, JD/MBA. JD/MBA offered jointly with College of Law. *Accreditation:* AACSB; NASPAA. *Program availability:* Part-time, evening/weekend. *Faculty:* 18 full-time (5 women), 15 part-time/adjunct (5 women). *Students:* 131 full-time (59 women), 119 part-time (65 women); includes 51 minority (15 Black or African American, non-Hispanic/Latino; 2 American Indian or Alaska Native, non-Hispanic/Latino; 15 Asian, non-Hispanic/Latino; 15 Hispanic/Latino; 4 Native Hawaiian or other Pacific Islander, non-Hispanic/Latino), 33 international. Average age 28. 261 applicants, 67% accepted, 105 enrolled. In 2017, 138 master's awarded. *Degree requirements:* For master's, minimum cumulative GPA of 3.0, 60 semester credits. *Entrance requirements:* For master's, GMAT or GRE, essays, transcripts, references, resume, interview. Additional exam requirements/recommendations for international students: Required—TOEFL (minimum score 570 paper-based; 88 iBT), IELTS (minimum score 6.5). *Application deadline:* 5/1 priority date for domestic and international students. Applications are processed on a rolling basis. Application fee: $100. Electronic applications accepted. Application fee is waived when completed online. *Expenses:* Contact institution. *Financial support:* In 2017–18, 220 students received support. Federal Work-Study, scholarships/grants, and unspecified assistantships available. Financial award application deadline: 5/1; financial award applicants required to submit FAFSA. *Faculty research:* Entrepreneurship and angel investing, corporate finance and investment, political economy and public management, sustainability and corporate responsibility, marketing, operations, social networks for managers, managing interorganizational interactions, employer duty of care, values and leadership, statistical methods and computing, employee well being and conflict management. *Unit head:* Dr. Debra J. Ringold, Dean and Professor of Free Enterprise, 503-370-6790, Fax: 503-370-3011, E-mail: dringold@willamette.edu. *Application contact:* Juliet Valdez, Director of Recruitment, 503-370-6792, Fax: 503-370-3011, E-mail: jvaldez@willamette.edu. Website: http://www.willamette.edu/mba

William Carey University, School of Business, Hattiesburg, MS 39401. Offers MBA. *Program availability:* Part-time. *Entrance requirements:* For master's, GMAT. Additional exam requirements/recommendations for international students: Required—TOEFL (minimum score 500 paper-based).

William Paterson University of New Jersey, Cotsakos College of Business, Wayne, NJ 07470-8420. Offers applied business analytics (MS); business administration (MBA, Certificate); sales leadership (MS). *Accreditation:* AACSB. *Program availability:* Part-time, evening/weekend. *Faculty:* 16 full-time (3 women), 3 part-time/adjunct (1 woman). *Students:* 69 full-time (37 women), 194 part-time (96 women); includes 109 minority (27 Black or African American, non-Hispanic/Latino; 13 Asian, non-Hispanic/Latino; 57 Hispanic/Latino; 12 Two or more races, non-Hispanic/Latino), 26 international. Average age 31. 164 applicants, 87% accepted, 96 enrolled. In 2017, 73 master's awarded. *Entrance requirements:* For master's, GMAT (minimum score 500) or GRE (minimum 152 Verbal, 152 Quantitative), minimum GPA of 3.0, professional resume. Additional exam requirements/recommendations for international students: Required—TOEFL (minimum score 550 paper-based; 79 iBT), IELTS (minimum score 6). *Application deadline:* For fall admission, 6/1 for domestic students, 3/1 for international students; for spring admission, 11/1 for domestic students, 10/1 for international students. Applications are processed on a rolling basis. Application fee: $50. Electronic applications accepted. *Expenses:* Tuition, state resident: full-time $13,920; part-time $6264 per year. Tuition, nonresident: full-time $21,700; part-time $9765 per year. *Required fees:* $80; $36 per year. Tuition and fees vary according to course load, degree level and program. *Financial support:* In 2017–18, 5,300 students received support. Career-related internships or fieldwork, Federal Work-Study, scholarships/grants, and unspecified assistantships available. Support available to part-time students. Financial award application deadline: 3/15; financial award applicants required to submit FAFSA. *Faculty research:* Labor markets, job characteristics and ethical behavior, institutional trading of stocks and bonds, education funding, and pricing strategies in business to business markets. *Unit head:* Dr. Siamack Shojai, Dean, 973-720-2964, Fax: 973-720-2809, E-mail: shojais@wpunj.edu. *Application contact:* Tinu Adeniran, Assistant Director, Graduate Admissions, 973-720-2764, Fax: 973-720-2035, E-mail: adenirant@wpunj.edu.
Website: http://www.wpunj.edu/ccob

William Woods University, Graduate and Adult Studies, Fulton, MO 65251-1098. Offers administration (M Ed, Ed S); athletic/activities administration (M Ed); curriculum and instruction (M Ed, Ed S); educational leadership (Ed D); equestrian education (M Ed); health management (MBA); human resources (MBA); leadership (MBA); marketing, advertising, and public relations (MBA); teaching and technology (M Ed). *Program availability:* Part-time, evening/weekend. *Degree requirements:* For master's, capstone course (MBA), action research (M Ed); for Ed S, field experience. *Entrance requirements:* Additional exam requirements/recommendations for international students: Required—TOEFL (minimum score 550 paper-based). Electronic applications accepted. *Expenses:* Contact institution.

Wilmington University, College of Business, New Castle, DE 19720-6491. Offers accounting (MBA, MS); business administration (MBA, DBA); environmental stewardship (MBA); finance (MBA); health care administration (MBA, MSM); homeland security (MBA, MSM); human resource management (MSM); management information systems (MBA, MSN); marketing (MSM); marketing management (MBA); military leadership (MSM); organizational leadership (MBA, MSM); public administration (MSM). *Program availability:* Part-time, evening/weekend. *Faculty:* 16 full-time (8 women), 106 part-time/adjunct (49 women). *Students:* 525 full-time (294 women), 1,212 part-time (780 women); includes 557 minority (412 Black or African American, non-Hispanic/Latino; 14 American Indian or Alaska Native, non-Hispanic/Latino; 55 Asian, non-Hispanic/Latino; 25 Hispanic/Latino; 3 Native Hawaiian or other Pacific Islander, non-Hispanic/Latino; 48 Two or more races, non-Hispanic/Latino), 157 international. Average age 35. 1,484 applicants, 70% accepted, 685 enrolled. In 2017, 543 master's, 16 doctorates awarded. *Entrance requirements:* Additional exam requirements/recommendations for international students: Required—TOEFL (minimum score 500 paper-based). *Application deadline:* Applications are processed on a rolling basis. Application fee: $35. Electronic applications accepted. *Expenses:* Tuition: Part-time $466 per credit. *Required fees:* $25 per semester. Tuition and fees vary according to degree level and campus/location. *Financial support:* Applicants required to submit FAFSA. *Unit head:* Dr. Kathy S. Kennedy Ratajack, Dean, 302-356-2481. *Application contact:* Laura Morris, Director of Admissions, 877-967-5456, E-mail: infocenter@wilmu.edu.
Website: http://www.wilmu.edu/business/

Wilson College, Graduate Programs, Chambersburg, PA 17201-1285. Offers accounting (M Acc); choreography and visual art (MFA); education (M Ed); educational technology (MET); healthcare administration (MHA); humanities (MA), including art and culture, critical/cultural theory, English language and literature, women's studies; management (MSM); nursing (MSN), including nursing education, nursing leadership and management; special education (MSE). *Program availability:* Evening/weekend. *Degree requirements:* For master's, project. *Entrance requirements:* For master's, PRAXIS, minimum undergraduate cumulative GPA of 3.0, 2 letters of recommendation, current certification for eligibility to teach in grades K-12, resume, personal interview. Electronic applications accepted.

Wingate University, Porter B. Byrum School of Business, Wingate, NC 28174. Offers accounting (MAC); corporate innovation (MBA); finance (MBA); general management (MBA); healthcare management (MBA); marketing (MBA); project management (MBA). *Accreditation:* ACBSP. *Program availability:* Part-time, evening/weekend. *Entrance requirements:* For master's, GMAT, work experience, 2 letters of recommendation. Electronic applications accepted. *Expenses:* Contact institution. *Faculty research:* Stochastic processes, business ethics, regional economic development, municipal finance, consumer behavior.

Winston-Salem State University, Program in Business Administration, Winston-Salem, NC 27110-0003. Offers MBA. *Accreditation:* AACSB. *Program availability:* Part-time, evening/weekend, online learning. *Entrance requirements:* For master's, GMAT, resume, 3 letters of recommendation. Electronic applications accepted. *Faculty research:* Innovative entrepreneurship and customer service, econometrics and operations research.

Winthrop University, College of Business Administration, Program in Business Administration, Rock Hill, SC 29733. Offers MBA. *Accreditation:* AACSB. *Program availability:* Part-time. *Students:* 82 full-time (51 women), 48 part-time (23 women); includes 33 minority (29 Black or African American, non-Hispanic/Latino; 1 Asian, non-Hispanic/Latino; 2 Hispanic/Latino; 1 Two or more races, non-Hispanic/Latino), 44 international. Average age 34. In 2017, 85 master's awarded. *Entrance requirements:* For master's, GMAT. Additional exam requirements/recommendations for international students: Required—TOEFL (minimum score 550 paper-based; 79 iBT), IELTS (minimum score 6). Application fee: $50. *Unit head:* Keith Benson, Director of Graduate Studies, 803-323-2409, E-mail: bensonk@winthrop.edu. *Application contact:* 800-411-7041, Fax: 803-323-2292, E-mail: gradschool@winthrop.edu.
Website: http://www.winthrop.edu/cba/mba/

Woodbury University, School of Business, Burbank, CA 91504. Offers business administration (MBA); organizational leadership (MA). *Accreditation:* AACSB; ACBSP. *Program availability:* Part-time, evening/weekend. *Entrance requirements:* For master's, GMAT, transcripts, resume. Additional exam requirements/recommendations for international students: Required—TOEFL (minimum score 550 paper-based; 83 iBT), IELTS (minimum score 6.5). *Faculty research:* Total quality management, leadership.

Worcester Polytechnic Institute, Graduate Admissions, Foisie Business School, Worcester, MA 01609-2280. Offers business administration (PhD); information technology (MS), including information security management; management (Graduate Certificate); marketing and technological innovation (MS); operations design and leadership (MS); supply chain management (MS); technology (MS). *Accreditation:* AACSB. *Program availability:* Part-time, evening/weekend, 100% online, blended/hybrid learning. *Faculty:* 26 full-time (12 women), 9 part-time/adjunct (0 women). *Students:* 254 full-time (153 women), 150 part-time (52 women); includes 34 minority (3 Black or African American, non-Hispanic/Latino; 10 Asian, non-Hispanic/Latino; 14 Hispanic/Latino; 7 Two or more races, non-Hispanic/Latino), 230 international. Average age 29. 677 applicants, 71% accepted, 146 enrolled. In 2017, 188 master's, 14 doctorates awarded. *Degree requirements:* For master's, thesis optional. *Entrance requirements:* For master's and Graduate Certificate, GMAT or GRE General Test, 3 letters of recommendation, statement of purpose, resume. Additional exam requirements/recommendations for international students: Required—TOEFL (minimum score 563 paper-based; 84 iBT), IELTS (minimum score 7). *Application deadline:* For fall admission, 6/1 priority date for domestic and international students; for spring admission, 11/1 priority date for domestic students, 10/1 priority date for international students. Applications are processed on a rolling basis. Application fee: $70. Electronic applications accepted. *Expenses:* Tuition: Full-time $26,226; part-time $1457 per credit. *Required fees:* $60; $30 per credit. One-time fee: $15. Tuition and fees vary according to course load. *Financial support:* Career-related internships or fieldwork, institutionally sponsored loans, scholarships/grants, and unspecified assistantships available. Financial award application deadline: 6/1. *Unit head:* Melissa Terrio, Executive Director, 508-831-4665, Fax: 508-831-4665, E-mail: biz@wpi.edu. *Application contact:* Margaret Clancey, Recruiting Operations Coordinator, 508-831-4980, Fax: 508-831-5720, E-mail: maclancey@wpi.edu.
Website: https://www.wpi.edu/academics/business

Worcester State University, Graduate School, Program in Management, Worcester, MA 01602-2597. Offers accounting (MS); managerial leadership (MS); marketing (MS). *Program availability:* Part-time, evening/weekend. *Faculty:* 6 full-time, 1 part-time/adjunct. *Students:* 12 full-time (7 women), 44 part-time (26 women); includes 14 minority (7 Black or African American, non-Hispanic/Latino; 2 Asian, non-Hispanic/Latino; 5 Hispanic/Latino), 3 international. Average age 32. 50 applicants, 80% accepted, 21 enrolled. In 2017, 10 master's awarded. *Degree requirements:* For master's, comprehensive exam (for some programs), thesis optional. *Entrance requirements:* For master's, GMAT, 3 letters of recommendation from professors and/or supervisors. Additional exam requirements/recommendations for international students: Required—TOEFL (minimum score 550 paper-based; 79 iBT). *Application deadline:* For fall admission, 6/15 for domestic and international students; for spring admission, 11/1 for domestic and international students; for summer admission, 4/1 for domestic and international students. Applications are processed on a rolling basis. Application fee: $50. Electronic applications accepted. *Expenses:* Tuition, state resident: full-time $3042; part-time $169 per credit hour. Tuition, nonresident: full-time $3042; part-time $169 per credit hour. *Required fees:* $2754; $153 per credit hour. *Financial support:* Career-related internships or fieldwork, scholarships/grants, and unspecified assistantships available. Financial award application deadline: 3/1; financial award applicants required to submit FAFSA. *Unit head:* Dr. Elizabeth Wark, Program Coordinator, 508-929-8743, E-mail: ewark@worcester.edu. *Application contact:* Sara Grady, Associate Dean, Graduate Studies and Professional Development, 508-929-8130, E-mail: sara.grady@worcester.edu.

Wright State University, Graduate School, Raj Soin College of Business, Program in Business Administration, Dayton, OH 45435. Offers MBA.

Xavier University, Williams College of Business, Master of Business Administration Program, Cincinnati, OH 45207. Offers business administration (Exec MBA, MBA); business intelligence (MBA); finance (MBA); health industry (MBA); international business (MBA); marketing (MBA); values-based leadership (MBA); MBA/MHSA; MSN/MBA. *Accreditation:* AACSB. *Program availability:* Part-time, evening/weekend. *Degree requirements:* For master's, capstone course. *Entrance requirements:* For master's, GMAT or GRE, official transcript; resume. Additional exam requirements/recommendations for international students: Required—TOEFL (minimum score 550 paper-based; 79 iBT). Electronic applications accepted. Application fee is waived when completed online. *Expenses:* Contact institution.

Yale University, Yale School of Management and Graduate School of Arts and Sciences, Doctoral Program in Management, New Haven, CT 06520. Offers accounting (PhD); financial economics (PhD); marketing (PhD); organizations and management (PhD). *Accreditation:* AACSB. *Degree requirements:* For doctorate, comprehensive exam, thesis/dissertation. *Entrance requirements:* For doctorate, GMAT or GRE General Test. Additional exam requirements/recommendations for international students: Required—TOEFL or IELTS. Electronic applications accepted. *Expenses:* Contact institution. *Faculty research:* Pricing of options and futures, term structure of interest rates, use of accounting numbers in debt contracts, product differentiation, e-commerce and marketing, behavioral finance.

Yale University, Yale School of Management, Program in Business Administration, New Haven, CT 06520. Offers MBA, MBA/JD, MBA/M Arch, MBA/M Div, MBA/MA, MBA/MEM, MBA/MF, MBA/MFA, MBA/MPH, MBA/PhD, MD/MBA. *Accreditation:* AACSB. Terminal master's awarded for partial completion of doctoral program. *Degree requirements:* For master's, international experience. *Entrance requirements:* For master's, GMAT or GRE. Additional exam requirements/recommendations for international students: Required—TOEFL, PTE, or IELTS. Electronic applications accepted. *Expenses:* Contact institution. *Faculty research:* Finance, strategy, marketing, leadership, operations.

Yeshiva University, Sy Syms School of Business, New York, NY 10016. Offers accounting (MS); business (EMBA); marketing (MS); taxation (MS). *Program availability:* Part-time. *Entrance requirements:* For master's, minimum GPA of 3.5 or GMAT.

York College of Pennsylvania, Graham School of Business, York, PA 17403-3651. Offers accounting (M Acc); business (MBA); continuous improvement (MBA); financial management (MBA); health care management (MBA); management (MBA); marketing (MBA); self-designed (MBA). *Accreditation:* ACBSP. *Program availability:* Part-time, evening/weekend. *Faculty:* 9 full-time (2 women), 3 part-time/adjunct (0 women). *Students:* 3 full-time (2 women), 72 part-time (33 women); includes 14 minority (7 Black or African American, non-Hispanic/Latino; 3 Asian, non-Hispanic/Latino; 1 Hispanic/Latino; 3 Two or more races, non-Hispanic/Latino). Average age 35. 68 applicants, 76% accepted, 28 enrolled. In 2017, 17 master's awarded. *Degree requirements:* For master's, directed study. *Entrance requirements:* For master's, GMAT. Additional exam requirements/recommendations for international students: Required—TOEFL (minimum score 530 paper-based; 72 iBT), IELTS (minimum score 6). *Application deadline:* For fall admission, 7/15 priority date for domestic students, 5/1 for international students; for spring admission, 11/15 priority date for domestic students, 9/1 for international students; for summer admission, 4/15 priority date for domestic students. Applications are processed on a rolling basis. Application fee: $0. Electronic applications accepted. *Expenses:* $795 per credit. *Financial support:* In 2017–18, 3 students received support. Scholarships/grants available. Financial award applicants required to submit FAFSA.

Unit head: Nicole Cornell Sadowski, MBA Director, 717-815-1491, Fax: 717-600-3999, E-mail: ncornell@ycp.edu. *Application contact:* MBA Office, 717-815-1491, Fax: 717-600-3999, E-mail: mba@ycp.edu. Website: http://www.ycp.edu/mba

York University, Faculty of Graduate Studies, Schulich School of Business, Toronto, ON M3J 1P3, Canada. Offers accounting (M Acc); administration (PhD); business (MBA); business analytics (MBA); finance (MF); international business (IMBA); MBA/JD; MBA/MA; MBA/MFA. *Program availability:* Part-time, evening/weekend. *Degree requirements:* For master's, advanced proficiency in a second language, work term (IMBA); for doctorate, comprehensive exam, thesis/dissertation. *Entrance requirements:* For master's, GMAT or GRE, minimum GPA of 3.0 (3.3 for MF, MBA in business analytics, and IMBA); for doctorate, GMAT or GRE, minimum GPA of 3.3. Additional exam requirements/recommendations for international students: Required—TOEFL (minimum score 600 paper-based; 100 iBT), IELTS (minimum score 7), York English Language Test (minimum score 1); PearsonVUE (minimum score 64). Electronic applications accepted. *Faculty research:* Accounting, finance, marketing, operations management and information systems, organizational studies, strategic management.

Youngstown State University, Graduate School, Williamson College of Business Administration, Youngstown, OH 44555-0001. Offers MBA, Certificate. *Accreditation:* AACSB. *Program availability:* Part-time, evening/weekend. *Degree requirements:* For master's, thesis optional. *Entrance requirements:* For master's, GMAT, minimum GPA of 2.7. Additional exam requirements/recommendations for international students: Required—TOEFL. *Faculty research:* Taxation and compliance, business ethics, operations management, organizational behavior, gender issues.

JACKSONVILLE UNIVERSITY
Davis College of Business

Programs of Study

Jacksonville University's (JU) Davis College of Business offers daytime (Accelerated) and evening (Flex) Master of Business Administration (M.B.A.) programs designed for all types of working professionals. Graduates earn promotions into senior managerial roles in their professions by incorporating their accumulated theory and practice into their respective roles as managers and leaders. Management training serves as a foundation for both the Flex M.B.A. and Accelerated M.B.A. programs.

The M.B.A. Program: It combines accounting, decision sciences, economics, finance, information technology, international business, management, and marketing so that students are well-equipped for management and decision-making roles in both small companies and large organizations. Students can choose to follow a general M.B.A. path (36 credits) or concentrate in one of four concentration areas (39 credits): Accounting and Finance, Management, Management Accounting, or Consumer Goods and Services Marketing. More than half of the students choose to pursue one of the four concentration areas.

The Accelerated M.B.A. program is a full-time, structured cohort, enabling students to complete the program in just twelve months regardless of their undergraduate degree. The Flex program is highly adaptable for the student's career goals: students choose the pace of coursework based on how quickly they want to complete their program. Most students are able to complete the program in two years as part-time students.

Executive M.B.A. Program: With concentrations in Leadership Development, and Consumer Goods and Services, the JU Davis Executive Masters of Business Administration (E.M.B.A.) is an intensive 19-month program designed to develop a leader's strategic mindset, business expertise, and creative instincts. Grounded in a compelling holistic management framework, the program recognizes that sustainable high-performance in the business world today requires attention to mind, body, and spirit. The E.M.B.A. is designed for rising and midcareer executives, both in context and convenience. The curriculum is taught in a team-oriented environment where courses are integrated to emphasize broader strategic management and leadership skills.

Master of Science in Organizational Leadership: The Master of Science in Organizational Leadership (M.S.O.L.) degree program is a 30-credit program designed for experienced professionals who want the practical knowledge and skills to lead people engaged in innovation, change, and transformation initiatives. It is particularly appropriate for human resource, technical, or functional specialists who are preparing for greater leadership roles. It is tailored for nonbusiness undergraduate majors who seek to earn graduate degrees that focus more on management and leadership rather than the quantitative focus of the M.B.A. degree.

Doctor of Business Administration: The JU Davis D.B.A. program takes business intelligence and the art of informed intuition to a new level. The D.B.A. 63-credit program builds on the skills students have mastered professionally, while heightening their ability to be agile and fluid as managers. The JU D.B.A. program is based on three pillars of leadership, globalization, and business analytics. This three-year program prepares candidates to explore the best paths for data discovery, innovation, quantitative analysis, and global challenges.

Joint Program Graduate Business Degrees: There are three joint M.B.A. programs at Jacksonville University: the Master of Science in Nursing (M.S.N.)/M.B.A. degree program; the Master of Public Policy (M.P.P.)/M.B.A. degree program; and the Juris Doctor (J.D.)/M.B.A. degree program. The first two programs are offered entirely at JU, while the J.D./M.B.A. is conducted in conjunction with the Florida Coastal School of Law.

Four+1 Bachelor's/M.B.A.: Jacksonville University offers a unique 4-year+1 bachelor's/M.B.A. program that is designed for highly motivated high school students with interests in any major. If qualified, students are conditionally admitted to the Accelerated (full-time day) M.B.A. program when they apply to JU as high school seniors. Students who maintain at least 3.3 cumulative GPAs in their undergraduate studies are automatically accepted into the Accelerated M.B.A. program upon graduation from JU.

Accreditation

Jacksonville University is regionally accredited by the Southern Association of Colleges and Schools (SACS). In addition, the Davis College of Business has been accredited by the Association to Advance Collegiate Schools of Business (AACSB) since 2010. Only 5 percent of all the business schools in the world are accredited by AACSB, making it the most challenging, prestigious accreditation for a school to earn. Very strict standards apply in every area—faculty quality, teaching resources and technology, facilities, connections with the business community, and services for students.

Financial Aid

Most graduate students at Jacksonville University receive some type of financial aid through scholarships, loans, or assistantships. Many working students receive partial financial support for their education from their employers. JU is a voluntary participant in the Yellow Ribbon Program for Post-9/11 G.I. Bill recipients.

Cost of Study

The graduate programs at Jacksonville University are competitively priced. Costs shown are for the 2018–19 academic year and may vary depending on foundation needs, concentration(s) pursued, and the amount of time each student needs to complete the program.

The Flex and Accelerated M.B.A. programs cost $793 per credit hour, with a total program cost of $27,720 for a general M.B.A. with no foundation courses.

The Executive M.B.A.–Leadership Development program cost is $12,272 per semester for a total cost of $61,360 (five semesters).

The Master of Science in Organizational Leadership program costs $793 per credit hour and has a total cost of $23,000.

The Doctor of Business Administration program costs $31,000 per year, for a total cost of $93,000.

Student Group

More than 200 graduate students attend classes at the Davis College of Business (DCOB) and the majority of students enroll part-time.

Student Outcomes

The JU Career Resource Center supports all Jacksonville University students and alumni, including graduate students. Staff members provide a variety of services to help students and alumni succeed in graduate and professional school and in the world of work. These include individual career consulting and counseling, career assessments, career workshops, an annual career and internship expo, information sessions, special speakers and events, on-campus recruiting, job and internship postings, mock interviewing, resume/cover letter preparation and revision, and much more.

Jacksonville University

Location

Jacksonville is a rapidly growing metropolitan city, the largest in Florida, with approximately 850,000 residents. Miles of beaches and waterways, a major symphony orchestra, NFL football, a myriad of restaurants, and annual special events enhance the quality of life. Jacksonville is also a leading international business hub, with world-renowned port and air cargo facilities and rail and trucking routes. According to Forbes magazine, Jacksonville's growing population, strong economy, diverse cultural and recreational opportunities, abundant natural resources, and growing financial and tech environment make Jacksonville one of the nation's top-rated job markets.

The University and the Business School

Jacksonville University (JU) is located in a beautiful riverfront setting in suburban Jacksonville, across the St. Johns River from downtown and just minutes from the Atlantic Ocean. The 190-acre campus includes a riverfront, oak-lined paths, and a state-of-the-art business building. JU offers seven bachelor's degree programs and more than 70 majors, programs, and concentrations. There are graduate programs in nursing, business, education, marine science, fine arts, math, applied health sciences, and public policy. Doctoral programs include the Doctor of Nursing Practice (D.N.P.) program, a Doctor of Business Administration (D.B.A.) program, and a nationally known postgraduate certification in orthodontics.

A second location for graduate classes has opened in the heart of downtown Jacksonville. Students experience the benefits of proximity to leading companies and organizations for internships, job interviewing, and unique business events. Both the E.M.B.A. and D.B.A. programs are delivered in this urban setting. Convenient hotel lodging for non-resident students is located directly across the street.

The Davis College of Business (DCOB) offers both undergraduate and graduate business degrees. The college is the only private business college in North Florida that is accredited by the Association to Advance Collegiate Schools of Business (AACSB) International. The college has been recognized by *CEO Magazine* for having one of the Top 100 M.B.A. programs in North America.

The Faculty

Graduate students benefit from in-depth business instruction. Classes are taught by both Ph.D.-credentialed faculty members from the world's best universities and experienced professionals who have earned excellent records of accomplishment in the industry. The flexible graduate programs are tailored to each student's particular needs and goals.

Applying

Prospective students can apply to Jacksonville University's graduate business programs online at www.ju.edu/apply.

Correspondence and Information

For more information, students should contact:

Davis College of Business
Jacksonville University
2800 University Boulevard North
Jacksonville, Florida 32211
United States
Phone: 904-256-7426
E-mail: amurphy8@ju.edu
Website: www.ju.edu/dcob

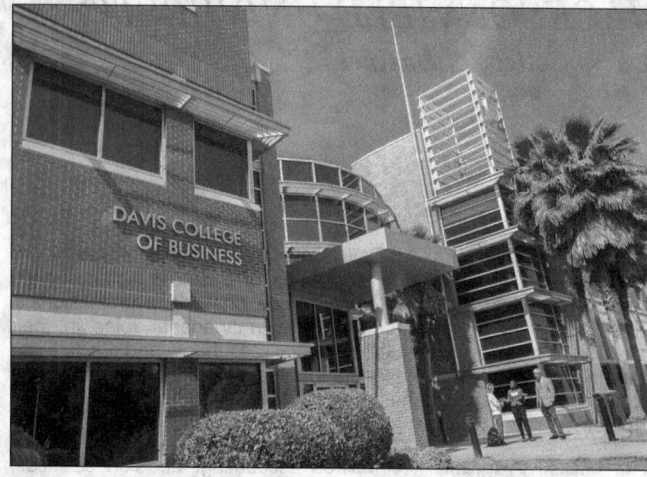

This Jacksonville University state-of-the-art campus building features executive training rooms, conference rooms, computer labs, media conference room, and study rooms.

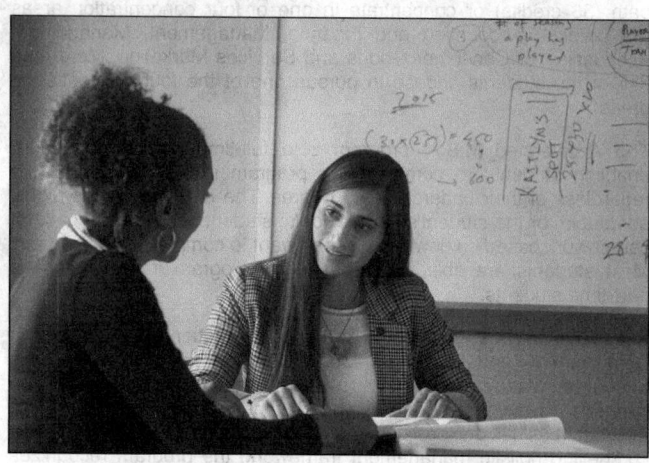

Jacksonville University's more than 25,000 alumni come from all 50 states and 92 countries.

MONMOUTH UNIVERSITY

Leon Hess Business School

MONMOUTH
UNIVERSITY

Programs of Study

Monmouth University is a leading private institution that helps students of all ages to increase their professional skills and enhance their intellectual development. Graduate programs are offered within six academic schools: the Leon Hess Business School (M.B.A.), the Wayne D. McMurray School of Humanities and Social Sciences (M.A., M.S.), the Marjorie K. Unterberg School of Nursing and Health Studies (M.S.N., P.A., D.N.P.), the School of Education (E.d.D, M.A.T., M.S.Ed., M.Ed., Ed.D.), the School of Science (M.S.), and the School of Social Work (M.S.W.).

Monmouth provides high-quality graduate and certificate programs in areas that are in demand in the work-place. The University also offers a Doctor of Nursing Practice (D.N.P.) and Doctor of Education in Educational Leadership (E.d.D.) program. M.B.A. students can customize their program by pursuing a concentration in accounting, finance, management, marketing, or real estate. Monmouth's programs offer hands-on, personalized attention to improve students' leadership qualities and prepare them for career advancement, career changes, or further study. Graduate students also have opportunities to engage in scholarly research with the University's innovative faculty. To view all of Monmouth's graduate studies offerings, visit monmouth.edu/graduate.

Many of Monmouth's graduate students work or intern on a full-time basis and attend classes in the evening. To provide flexibility, some programs offer courses in a hybrid format, consisting of face-to-face classes interspersed with online sessions on alternate weeks. The online component is asynchronous, allowing students to participate when it is most convenient for them. The University encourages students to accelerate their program by taking summer course work.

Research Facilities

The Monmouth University Library holds approximately 360,000 print and electronic monographs, 68,000 print and electronic periodicals, 157 databases, and 1,100 media assets (CDs and DVDs). All academic programs are amply supported by state-of-the-art computer hardware and software and classroom/laboratory facilities. The major components supporting Monmouth's academic programs include Windows, Mac OS, and Unix systems connected via an expansive wired and wireless network, which spans 23 buildings and encompasses more than 2,400 workstations in general and specialty labs and classrooms.

Financial Aid

To help students realize their goals, graduate scholarships are available to eligible matriculated students in most master's degree and doctoral programs and are renewable each semester. Qualified students may also be eligible for graduate assistantships in which on-campus work is performed in exchange for tuition. These positions include graduate teaching and research assistantship opportunities, and there is a competitive application process.

To obtain federal loans, applicants must file the FAFSA form at fafsa. ed.gov. Monmouth University participates in the Federal Direct Student Loan Program, which makes loans available to all students who file the FAFSA. Alternative loan funding sources are available to those students who might not otherwise qualify for federal funding or need additional funding above and beyond the amount that has already been provided.

Cost of Study

Tuition for study in 2018–19 is $1,187 per credit. A University fee is assessed each semester.

Living and Housing Costs

Due to Monmouth's proximity to the beach, there are ample off-campus housing opportunities that are conveniently located near the University. A rental listing website is maintained by the Office of Off-Campus and Commuter Services and can be found at monmouth.edu/commuter. Graduate students may also apply for University housing; these apartment-style accommodations are located in University-owned or -sponsored housing.

Student Group

Monmouth University enrolls approximately 6,400 students, roughly 1,600 of whom are enrolled in Graduate Studies. The diverse student body includes international students representing 30 different countries.

Location

Monmouth University is located less than a mile from the Atlantic Ocean on a 159-acre campus in the safe, suburban town of West Long Branch, New Jersey. The campus is approximately an hour from New York City and Philadelphia. The University's proximity to high-technology firms, financial institutions, and a thriving business-industrial sector provides Monmouth students and graduates with a wide variety of employment possibilities. The surrounding area also has numerous activities, theaters, restaurants, and cultural events.

The University

Monmouth University provides a learning environment that enables students to pursue their educational goals and realize their full potential as leaders. Small classes allow for individual attention and student-faculty dialogue, and the Center for Student Success offers a hub of academic and career counseling services.

At Monmouth, students enjoy one of the most beautiful campuses in New Jersey. The centerpiece of campus is Woodrow Wilson Hall, a National Historic Landmark, which was used as Daddy Warbucks' mansion in the film *Annie*. Other unique buildings include the Jules L. Plangere Jr. Center for Communication, which provides state-of-the-art studios and editing facilities, and Bey Hall, which houses the financial markets lab.

Throughout the year, students and employees cheer on Monmouth's Division I athletic teams. The school fields 23 teams for men and women. The University's basketball and track and field teams compete in the 153,200-square-foot OceanFirst Bank Center, which features a 4,100-seat arena with premium suites, as well as a fitness center and a 200-meter, six-lane indoor track.

Applying

An application for graduate admission includes a completed application form with fee, official transcripts of the undergraduate record, score reports from the appropriate entrance examination, and transcripts of any graduate work done elsewhere. Students should contact the Office of Graduate Admission for details, or visit monmouth.edu/graduate. International students must also provide evidence of English proficiency.

The application deadlines are July 15 for the fall term, December 1 for the spring term, and May 1 for the summer sessions. (Please note that some programs have different application deadlines and only accept students once per year.) An initial review of the complete application for admission is conducted by the Office of Graduate Admission; the file is then forwarded to the faculty program director for an admission decision. All correspondence should be directed to the Office of Graduate Admission.

Correspondence and Information

Office of Graduate Admission
Monmouth University
400 Cedar Avenue
West Long Branch, New Jersey 07764-1898
United States
Phone: 732-571-3452
Fax: 732-263-5123
E-mail: gradadm@monmouth.edu
Website: http://www.monmouth.edu/graduate

THE FACULTY AND THEIR RESEARCH AREAS

Faculty members at Monmouth University are committed teachers with extensive academic and professional experience who have established themselves as important scholars in their respective fields. Their work has been published in a variety of major journals, the proceedings of national and international conferences, books, and other outlets.

Students at Monmouth learn in small classes that promote close interaction with this knowledgeable faculty. Each faculty member strives to provide students with the foundation to succeed. Teaching and learning are not just confined to the classroom; professors and students often continue their discussions in the hallways, faculty offices, and dining facilities on campus.

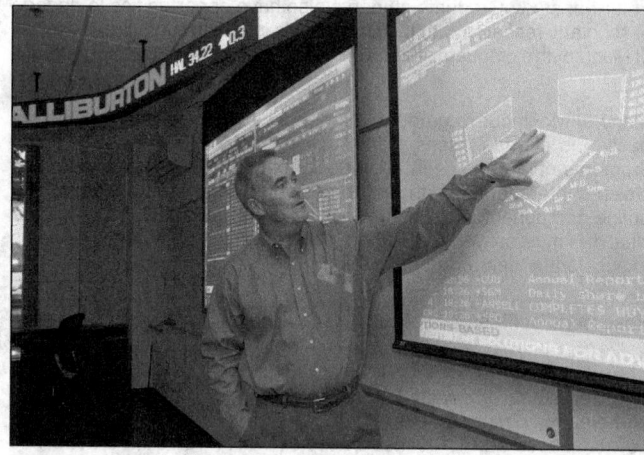

NORTH DAKOTA STATE UNIVERSITY
College of Business

 For more information, visit http://petersons.to/ndstatebusiness

NDSU GRADUATE SCHOOL

Programs of Study

The College of Business at North Dakota State University offers the following graduate programs:

- Master of Accountancy (M.Acc.)
- Master of Business Administration (M.B.A.)
- Master of Managerial Logistics (M.M.L.)
- Master of Transportation and Urban Systems (M.S., M.T.U.S.)
- Doctorate in Transportation and Logistics (Ph.D.)

These programs integrate case study and applied learning to prepare students for career advancement. Accreditation from AACSB International, which accredits less than five percent of the business schools worldwide, ensures that these programs meet the highest academic standards.

In addition to providing high-quality programs, the college offers a collaborative learning environment. Students learn from fellow students' experiences and network with leaders from top businesses.

Master of Accountancy program: The 30-credit M.Acc. program is ideal for students who want to advance their careers in corporate accounting, government accounting, or public accounting. The program's curriculum consists of four required courses, five additional accounting courses, and one management course. It emphasizes the analytical, decision-making, and research skills involved with identifying and solving accounting problems. It also prepares students for the Certified Public Accounting (CPA) exam.

Master of Business Administration program: The M.B.A. program provides analytical skills, an expansive view of how organizations operate, and in-depth understanding of business functional areas. Its curriculum consists of 16 credits of core courses in finance, information resources, management, marketing, and organizational behavior. The curriculum also includes 14 credits of elective courses from a variety of program areas. In addition, concentrations are offered in health care industry and in supply chain/logistics.

Required courses are generally offered during the evening to accommodate working professionals, while elective courses are offered during the day and in the evening, as well as in the summer. Options also may be available to students via teleconferencing technology.

Master of Managerial Logistics program: The online M.M.L. program targets aspiring logisticians, industry professionals, military officers, and DOD civilians who want to meet the logistical challenges of the 21st century. A wide range of career opportunities exists in the sectors of the logistics industry, including logistics and supply chain management, operations management, purchasing and demand management, emergency management, consulting, retail, and many more.

Master of Transportation and Urban Systems program: The online M.S./M.T.U.S. programs are valuable for students with backgrounds in transportation and logistics, as well as agribusiness, applied economics, civil engineering, construction management, emergency management, finance, geosciences, industrial/manufacturing engineering, and supply chain management.

Ph.D. in Transportation and Logistics: This program attracts the same profile students as the Master of Transportation and Urban Systems and takes them to the next level of research and application within this exciting field. The Ph.D. program is offered on-campus only.

All of the Transportation and Logistics graduate programs are offered through the Department of Transportation, Logistics and Finance and provide an interdisciplinary approach to transportation and logics that clearly appeal to students with a multitude of backgrounds. The degrees are awarded through the College of Business in collaboration with the Upper Great Plains Transportation Institute.

Research

Faculty members in the College of Business conduct innovative research to advance business education, theory, and practice. They investigate an extensive range of topics, including the following:

- auditing
- asset management
- big data analytics
- economic development
- entrepreneurship/small business strategy
- financial accounting
- fraud in nonprofits
- healthcare logistics
- intellectual capital
- international accounting
- logistics and supply chain management
- managerial accounting
- market structure and performance
- personal selling
- public-private partnerships
- sales management
- services marketing
- strategic leadership
- strategic management in nonprofit organizations
- transportation economics, planning, and policy

Students assist faculty members with their research and conduct their own research through course work. For example, the Marketing Research course emphasizes research design, data collection, and data analysis. The Applied Professional Research course focuses on the research methods used to address complex accounting issues.

Financial Aid

Graduate students in the College of Business may qualify for graduate assistantships and scholarships. Assistantships provide stipends and tuition waivers.

Students also may qualify for loans through federal programs or private lenders and receive tuition reimbursement from their employers.

Cost of Study

The most current information on tuition and fees can be found online at https://www.ndsu.edu/onestop/accounts/.

Living and Housing Costs

Information about on-campus housing for graduate students can be found at www.ndsu.edu/reslife/general_apartment_information/. While there is no specific residence hall for graduate students, they are able to live in the University apartments. There are also numerous housing options in the Fargo community.

Faculty

Graduate faculty members in the College of Business have considerable academic expertise and practical experience working at Fortune 500 companies.

For example, Professor of Accounting Peggy Andersen has more than 30 years of academic experience. A prolific researcher, she has investigated issues concerning corporate responsibility, business ethics, target costing, new product costing, real estate, and mutual funds. Her work has been published in numerous scholarly journals, and she has received several grants and awards for her research.

Associate Professor of Management Derek Lehmberg holds graduate degrees from schools in Asia, Europe, and North America. His research primarily examines issues relating to strategic management in the context of Japanese business. He has authored numerous academic journal articles and also written several widely used teaching case studies. Prior to entering academia, Lehmberg was a management consultant in areas of operations and strategic management, serving clients in the Consumer and Industrial Products industry based in Japan, the U.S., and Germany.

Student Life

The College of Business provides a supportive environment where students with diverse academic, cultural, and professional backgrounds thrive. Students build productive relationships with each other, faculty members, and business leaders. They have access to co-curricular activities that enhance academic and professional achievement, including student organizations, events, speakers, and study abroad opportunities.

Support services like the Career Center, Counseling Center, Disability Services, Military and Veterans Services, Office of Multicultural Programs, and Wallman Wellness Center also enhance students' academic, professional, and personal growth.

Students take classes in Richard H. Barry Hall in downtown Fargo. This 135,000-square-foot facility includes a state-of-the-art trading room, 250-seat auditorium, and a Business Learning Center, as well as wireless Internet. Its three-story atrium also has a coffee bar and study lounges.

Location

North Dakota State University is located on the eastern edge of North Dakota in Fargo, the state's largest community. With its sister city, Moorhead, Minnesota, directly across the Red River, Fargo is one of the largest metropolitan centers between Minneapolis and Seattle and offers a family-friendly environment with excellent schools, safe neighborhoods, and a low crime rate; an active arts and cultural scene, including a symphony, civic opera company, art museums, and community theater; and many places to shop and eat, including numerous restaurants, coffee shops, and a newly refurbished downtown district.

The University

North Dakota State University, a student-focused, land-grant, research institution provides student-centered education for more than 14,300 students (and more than 2,000 graduate students) who represent forty-eight states and eighty-two countries. Its rigorous academic programs integrate theory and practice to create a comprehensive learning experience. The National Science Foundation ranks several of its programs among the top 100 in the country. Challenging academic programs coupled with outstanding co-curricular activities allow students to achieve academic excellence and contribute to the world.

Applying

The North Dakota State University graduate school application procedure places responsibility on the applicant to gather all supporting credentials and verifying that the application file is complete. The deadline for submission is dependent upon the program. If no deadline is listed on the program's bulletin page, all application materials are due at least one month prior to the start of the semester.

Prospective students must file their application online. There is a $35 nonrefundable application fee. A statement of purpose—covering reasons for pursuing graduate study, special interests within the chosen discipline, and preparation, skills, and experience in the proposed field of study—is required for admission consideration and must be uploaded with the online application. Other requirements include three letters of recommendation; official transcripts from each college or university attended; and official GRE or GMAT scores if required. Some programs may have additional requirements, as stated on the individual program pages.

The online application and additional details regarding the application process are available at https://www.ndsu.edu/gradschool/prospective_students.

Correspondence and Information

College of Business
Graduate School
Department 2820, P.O. Box 6050
North Dakota State University
Fargo, North Dakota 58108-6050
Phone: 701-231-7033
        800-608-6378 (toll-free)
E-mail: ndsu.grad.school@ndsu.edu
Website: www.ndsu.edu/gradschool
   facebook.com/ndsugradschool (Facebook)
   @NDSUGradSchool (Twitter)

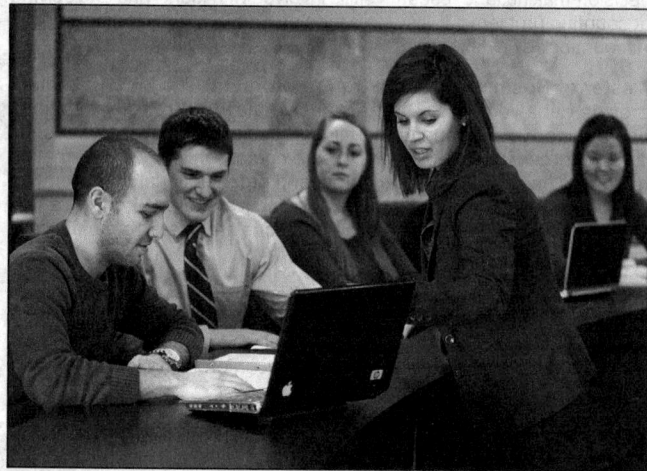

M.B.A. and M.Acc. students work with top NDSU graduate faculty members with extensive expertise from prominent research institutions and work experience—including management of billion-dollar portfolios and applied engineering management at Fortune 500 firms. NDSU's approach to learning combines case study and applied learning in a collaborative environment at an institution that has earned accreditation by AACSB International.

SAINT JOSEPH'S UNIVERSITY
Master of Business Administration

 For more information, visit http://petersons.to/sjumba

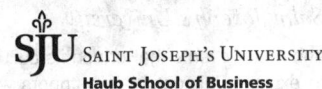 SAINT JOSEPH'S UNIVERSITY
Haub School of Business

Programs of Study

The Master of Business Administration (MBA) program at Saint Joseph's University's Haub School of Business (HSB) empowers students to succeed in an ever-changing world by deepening their business knowledge, developing their leadership potential, and strengthening their managerial acumen, enhancing their communications skills, and expanding their professional network.

The program provides immediately applicable skills for both working professionals who want to deepen their knowledge and advance their career and recent college graduates or early careerists who want to prepare for their next professional opportunity.

Offered in a variety of formats, students can attend full- or part-time and take courses online, on campus, or both. Classes are offered in the fall, spring, and summer terms, and students can begin any semester. Students can pace the program according to their needs, and can graduate in one year or take up to six years to complete the degree. Online courses include synchronous and asynchronous sessions along with other collaborative learning tools.

The MBA curriculum consists of 11 upper level courses (33 credits) which provide students with broad-based learning in core business disciplines and allow students to concentrate in a subject area, such as Business Intelligence and Analytics, Finance, Health and Medical Services, Marketing, International Business, and more. Optional, international study tours are available to complement the classroom experience.

Designed to strengthen leadership skills and managerial effectiveness, the curriculum also strives to foster a genuine sensitivity to the ethical, moral and cultural aspects of contemporary society. Focus is placed on key competencies including: leading, critical thinking, interpersonal and communication skills, value-based decision making, and global perspective.

MBA students come from all majors and backgrounds. For those whose undergraduate degree is in a non-business major, eight foundations courses (20 credits) are offered to prepare them for success in the program. Opportunities for foundation course waivers are determined for every applicant.

The Haub School of Business has more than 80 full-time faculty contribute scholarly research to the classroom along with part-time faculty who are senior executives in their field. Small classes allow for in-depth discussions, reflection, experiential exercises, writing assignments, and team projects, as well as facilitate interactions with fellow students, faculty, and guest lecturers.

Graduates of the program can connect with more than 67,000 SJU alumni around the globe. Numerous formal and informal events and activities allow students to network with their peers, alumni, lecturers, and business representatives. With lifetime access to the Career Development Center, students receive guidance on vital techniques including resume writing, interviewing, networking, and job search.

A recent survey of those who have earned a graduate business degree at Saint Joseph's University has shown that 73 percent report receiving a raise after completing their program; 76 percent say the program significantly helped them advance their career; 70 percent indicate that their degree from the Haub School provided them with more opportunities to increase their salary and gain professional recognition; and 86 percent say the program provided them with the strategic business acumen they needed to succeed in their chosen field.

Research Facilities

The Post Learning Commons and Drexel Library make up the Post Academic Center and support the academic programs of Saint Joseph's University with books and periodicals in both print and electronic formats, research databases, audio-visual materials, and microforms. Research resources and support are available on campus and fully online.

The Wall Street Trading Room at SJU's Haub School of Business supports the financial education programs and provides students with the knowledge and skills required for competing in a global job market. The room provides access to electronic sources of financial and investment data, analytical tools, and trading simulations. The room allows hands-on learning, curriculum enhancements, and more effective class projects. Trading simulations provide opportunities for real trading experiences. Continuous access to financial data and software provides an integrated learning environment to focus on analysis, synthesis, and evaluation.

Financial Aid

Financial aid is available and includes federal loans, university scholarships, graduate assistantships, employer tuition deferral programs, and loans from private lenders. SJU also offers tuition benefits to eligible military personnel and veterans through the Yellow Ribbon Program.

Cost of Study

Tuition for the 2018–19 academic year is $1,043 per credit for domestic and international students. Tuition is charged on a per credit basis, per semester, and is the same for online and on-campus courses. There are no additional fees for domestic students; international students may incur additional fees in regard to their visa, as well as a university health plan. Tuition is subject to change by the order of the Saint Joseph's University Board of Trustees.

Living and Housing Costs

The Office of Residence Life offers limited on-campus housing options for graduate students; availability is not guaranteed. The 2018–19 rates range from $5,120 to $6,120 per person per semester. Residence Life also assists students with off-campus housing recommendations. More information can be found at https://offcampushousing.sju.edu/.

Student Life

Students in the MBA program may choose to participate in SJU's Graduate Business Student Association (GBSA). The GBSA enhances the graduate experience by promoting professional development and a sense of community among graduate business students, faculty, and administration. All students are automatically members of the GBSA and no registration is required. This student-run organization aims to build strategic relationships by providing networking opportunities through social and service activities.

The Office of Adult Student Life assists graduate students by providing support in overcoming obstacles and resources to foster success. The ASL Office seeks to help adult students develop a personalized plan for success, coordinate adult student groups, organize programs to meet adult student needs, and provide adult student advocacy as needed.

Location

Located in Philadelphia, Pennsylvania, SJU's community enjoys the surroundings of one of America's first major cities. Widely known as "The City of Brotherly Love" Philadelphia's historical importance and vibrant communities create a charming and unique culture. The city is the fifth-largest metropolis in the U.S. and is home to historical landmarks and world-class museums, a number of professional sports teams and dining options,

Saint Joseph's University

and major events that enrich its cultural life. There are also opportunities to explore Philadelphia's outdoors with a wealth of year-round festivals and cultural events, parks, zoos, and aquariums. With eight Fortune 500 companies, Philadelphia offers numerous internship, networking, and post-graduation job opportunities.

The SJU campus is just a train ride away from Center City Philadelphia, allowing students to easily access the culture, art, nightlife, and opportunity that Philadelphia has to offer. The city is also conveniently located between New York City and Washington D.C., providing convenient access to additional cultural and employment opportunities.

The University and the School

For over 160 years, Saint Joseph's University has been engaging students in a rigorous Jesuit education that empowers them to become leaders in their industries and communities. Built upon the Ignatian credo of *cura personalis*, the Saint Joseph's education encompasses all aspects of personal growth and development: high achievement, deepening understanding, strengthening reasoning and communication skills, and developing moral character.

The university offers approximately 8,086 students 55 majors, 50 minors, 30-plus degree completion and certificate programs, and 52 graduate programs through two schools. The College of Arts and Sciences offers programs in the humanities, natural sciences, and social sciences.

The Erivan K. Haub School of Business provides a wide-range of programs including STEM master's degrees and graduate programs in analytics. It is an international AACSB-accredited institution in business and accounting, offering programs at the bachelor's, master's, and executive master's levels. *U.S. News & World Report* has ranked the school's part-time MBA, risk-management and insurance, marketing, management, and finance programs among the top in the nation. The Haub School was recently named one of the nation's top business schools in the Princeton Review's "The Best 294 Business Schools," and the undergraduate program was recently recognized by Bloomberg's Businessweek.

It is the largest Jesuit business school in the country with 3,600 students, 84 full-time faculty and more than 22,000 alumni.

Faculty

The professors in the SJU MBA program are full-time faculty engaged in cutting-edge research and part-time faculty who are senior executives in their fields. All instructors infuse their classes with relevant, real-world learning and scholarship, providing students with practical business knowledge that they can apply immediately in their careers.

Additional information regarding members of the MBA faculty can be found online at https://www.sju.edu/majors-programs/graduate-business/master-degrees/master-business-administration-mba/meet-faculty.

Applying

Applications are reviewed on a rolling basis. Students may apply to start the MBA program in the fall, spring, or summer terms. The priority application deadline is July 15 for fall semester, November 15 for spring semester, and March 15 for summer semester.

Applicants must have a baccalaureate degree from an accredited university and complete the official application. Required application materials include:

official transcripts for all credits earned (undergraduate and graduate), two letters of recommendation, a current resume, a $35 application fee, a personal statement (specifics available online), and official GMAT or GRE scores from within the past seven years (GMAT may be waived under certain circumstances; more details are available online).

Additional requirements and details for international students are available at https://www.sju.edu/majors-programs/graduate-business/master-degrees/master-business-administration-mba/admission.

Correspondence and Information

MBA Program
Saint Joseph's University
5600 City Avenue, MV 280
Philadelphia, PA 19131
Phone: 610-660-1690
Email: sjumba@sju.edu
Website: sju.edu/haubmba

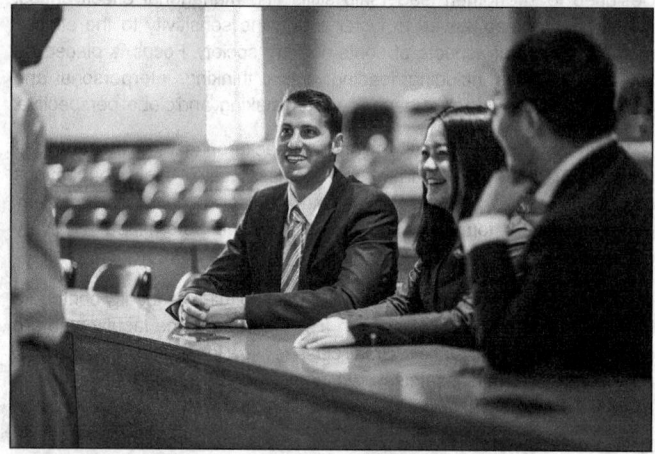

UNIVERSITY OF CONNECTICUT

Master of Business Administration

 For more information, visit http://petersons.to/uconnbus

UCONN
SCHOOL OF BUSINESS

Programs of Study

The Master of Business Administration (MBA) at the University of Connecticut (UConn) is a small, public, boutique degree program that provides students with the knowledge and skills to distinguish themselves in the competitive job market. UConn's MBA program offers a proven ROI—of all the *Forbes*-ranked MBA programs in the Northeast corridor with average starting salaries of $100k or more, UConn is the only one with public university tuition. The programs also provide intense experiential opportunities ranging from a multimillion-dollar student-managed fund to Innovation Quest (iQ) to international case competitions.

UConn's MBA offerings include flexible completion paths, as well as specialized MBA tracks and dual degrees in financial risk management, business analytics and project management, human resource management, and STEM-designations (select quantitative tracks in the Full-time MBA program option).

In 2016, the MBA program earned top rankings in the numerous college guides. *Financial Times, U.S. News & World Report*, and *BloombergBusinessweek* ranked it the #1 public MBA program in New England. *U.S. News & World Report* ranked it 23rd and *BloombergBusinessweek* ranked it 30th among the top MBA programs at public institutions. *Financial Times* ranked it 46th among global MBA programs (U.S.) and *Military Times* designated it the 48th best MBA program for veterans.

Full-time MBA: This 57-credit program is designed for those looking to become innovative leaders in the business world. Students complete 19 courses in four curriculum areas: business foundations, core functional knowledge, business leadership, and experiential learning. The program also has four elective tracks: business analytics, digital marketing strategy, financial analysis and investments, and general business.

Business foundations cover the fundamental theories and skills about managing quantitative business information and the key concepts and institutions that construct the business environment. Core functional knowledge covers core concepts about accounting, finance, marketing, operations, and information technology. Business leadership focuses on the concepts, perspectives, and skills critical to undertaking leadership positions. Experiential learning allows students to gain practical experience through projects, internships, and co-ops.

Part-time MBA: This program features the same curriculum and faculty scholars as the Full-time MBA program but employs a flexible schedule that allows working professionals to earn their degrees at their own pace. The 57-credit curriculum has 11 core and eight elective courses. Elective courses can be used to create one or more concentrations finance, health care management, international business, management, management of technology, marketing, or real estate.

Executive MBA Program (EMBA): This program was created for experienced managers and other professionals who seek leadership positions. The 48-credit curriculum represents a careful balance between management theory, practical applications, technical rigor, and realistic business situations. The curriculum is delivered in six terms over 20 months.

Dual-Degree Programs: These allow students to pursue two advanced degrees jointly, which reduces the time and credits required to earn both degrees individually. Students can choose from 11 dual degree programs such as:

- MBA/Master of Science (M.S.) in Financial Risk Management
- MBA/M.S. in Business Analytics and Project Management
- MBA/M.S. in Human Resources Management
- MBA/Jurist Doctor (J.D.)
- MBA/Doctor of Medicine (M.D.)
- MBA/Doctor of Pharmacy (Pharm.D.)

Graduates of UConn's MBA Program, particularly the full-time program, go "from knowing to being known." This makes it possible for them to obtain rewarding leadership positions in several industries or, in many cases, launch their own businesses. During the past three years, graduates have obtained positions at corporations such as Aetna, Bank of America, Cigna, Johnson & Johnson, Merrill Lynch, Kohler Co., Microsoft, PricewaterhouseCooper, Stanley Black & Decker, and T-Mobile USA.

In the class of 2016, 91 percent had obtained jobs within three months of graduating. The mean income for the class was $93,375, the median income was $97,500, and the high income was $145,000.

Financial Aid

MBA students may qualify for merit-based graduate assistantships and scholarships. Graduate assistantships include full tuition waivers, stipends, and subsidized healthcare benefits. Scholarships are offered on a one-time basis. Part-time employment is also available.

Other financial resources include federal student loans and work study employment.

Cost of Study

Graduate tuition for the 2018–19 academic year is $853 per credit for Connecticut residents, $1,442 per credit for regional students, and $20,054 per credit for out-of-state students. Including fees, costs per semester range from $1,360 to $8,830 for in-state students, $1,949 to $14,128 for regional students, and $2,561 to $19,636 for out-of-state students.

Part-time MBA courses are $900 per credit.

Student Life

UConn Graduate Business students are able to continue their growth and learning outside the classroom with several extra-curricular activities. Interacting with peers in the various MBA programs serves to supplement classroom training with an appreciation of diversity and collegiality. These interactions include social events and club activities. All the UConn graduate programs are active in Case Competitions and several teams place among the top in these competitions.

Location

Located in vibrant downtown Hartford, UConn's Full-time MBA program's central location allows easy access to both New York and Boston metro areas as well as New England beaches and ski resorts. The campus itself is integrated with the Hartford Public Library and surrounded by the Wadsworth Atheneum, Connecticut Science Center, Connecticut Convention Center, and state and city government offices. UConn graduate business students can also take classes in Waterbury and Stamford.

UConn's main campus is in Storrs, Connecticut in the northeastern region of the United States.

The University

Founded in 1881, the University of Connecticut is one of the nation's top public research universities. Its diverse and vibrant culture attracts the world's brightest students and most highly regarded faculty members.

University of Connecticut

The university has 30,000 students, 14 schools and colleges, 113 majors, 18 graduate programs, and six professional programs.

According to *U.S. News & World Report*'s 2018 rankings, the University of Connecticut is 56th among national universities, 18th among the nation's Top Public Schools, and 24th among the Best Colleges for Veterans.

Faculty

Over 96 percent of the School of Business's faculty members have doctoral or the highest degrees in their fields. They conduct research; author articles, books, college textbooks, and conference papers; and consult with businesses and government agencies.

David Souder, Ph.D., the associate dean for graduate programs and an associate professor of management, is an experienced teacher, researcher, and practitioner. His research focuses on the precursors and consequences of firms' long-term horizon investments. Prior to joining academia, he worked as a strategy consultant and finance director. He continues to advise businesses and community organizations.

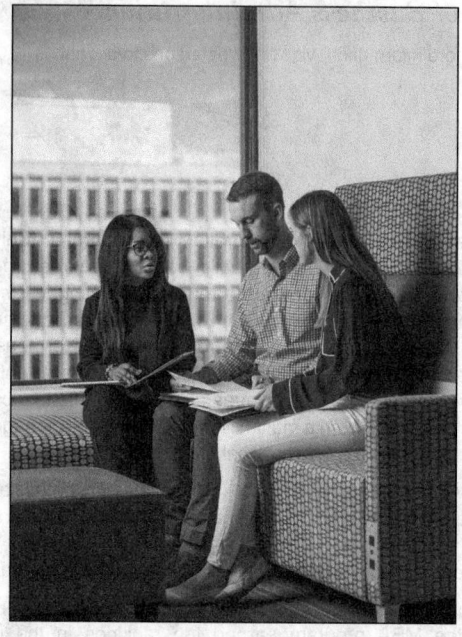

Applying

Applications to the UConn School of Business MBA programs are only taken via the the university's online application system. The application fee is $75 and must be paid online with a credit card or PayPal. A fee waiver will be automatically applied for all active duty, veterans, guardsmen and reservists, when their military service is indicated on their application.

Applicants must submit official academic credentials/transcripts of all previous undergraduate and graduate studies. A cumulative GPA or 3.0 or at least 3.0 for the last two undergraduate years or exceptional work—3.5 or better—in the final undergraduate year is required. A program-specific or supplemental essay is required for all but the Executive MBA program. GMAT or GRE scores are required for the Full-time MBA program and are preferred for the other programs. Interviews are required for applicants to the Full-time and Executive MBA programs and are conducted once the admissions committee has received a completed application. Two letters or recommendation are required for all programs. International applicants to the Full-time MBA must also support TOEFL, IELTS, or PTE scores.

After the online application and supporting materials have been submitted, applicants are able to track their status and access admissions decisions online.

Deadlines for fall entry are generally in June; deadlines for spring entry (Part-time MBA programs) are generally in late November.

Contact

UConn MBA Programs
Graduate Business Learning Center
100 Constitution Plaza
Hartford, Connecticut 06103
Phone: 860-728-2440
Fax: 860-728-2499
E-mail: mba@uconn.edu
Website: mba.uconn.edu

UNIVERSITY OF NEW HAVEN
College of Business Graduate Programs

University of
New Haven

Programs of Study

The College of Business at the University of New Haven belongs to an elite group of schools recognized worldwide for providing the highest quality academic business degree programs. Graduates have gone on to executive roles within a wide range of Fortune 500 companies, start-ups, and entrepreneurial ventures. The University of New Haven College of Business is accredited by AACSB International, the Association to Advance Collegiate Schools of Business.

The College of Business at University of New Haven offers the following graduate degree programs: Executive MBA (Master of Business Administration); Flexible MBA; Full-Time MBA; Master of Science (M.S.) in Accounting; M.S. in Finance; M.S. in Sport Management; M.S. in Taxation; and MBA/Master of Public Administration (M.P.A.) Dual Degree. Graduate certificates are available for students who seek a shortened graduate-level curriculum concentrated in a specific business area. Most programs are designed for working professionals, with real-time, hybrid, and online course delivery options.

Executive MBA (EMBA): This program is designed for experienced, full-time managers who want to enhance their ability to manage in a dynamic business environment and learn strategies that promote growth, creativity, and innovation. The Executive MBA curriculum contains six integrative modules that together reflect a representative and comprehensive spectrum of key elements of a business enterprise. It is designed to develop synergy across content, delivery, experiential and cognitive learning, and real-world application. Students receive guidance from faculty experts, entrepreneurial mentors, and class advisors. The program concludes with a series of capstone projects where participants utilize any one or a combination of the modules and apply it to ongoing and real-time organizational projects.

Flexible MBA: Designed for working professionals, the Flexible MBA program provides students the convenience of studying on a full- or part-time basis. The program transforms students into business leaders by building their knowledge base and honing the skills needed to become a strategic, collaborative, corporate thinker. Concentrations are offered in: MBA, Human Resource Management, Accounting, International Business, Business Intelligence, Marketing, Business Policy and Strategic Leadership, Sport Management, and Finance.

Full-Time MBA: The Full-Time MBA program is designed for recent college graduates with little or no professional experience. Coursework comprises core elements of business. Students develop the critical skills to analyze and solve modern business problems, think strategically, and manage all aspects of a modern business enterprise. Students may select from one of the eight aforementioned concentration areas.

M.S. in Accounting: Students in this program elect a specialty in a sub-discipline within the accounting field while obtaining the general knowledge base and skills to work in a variety of business environments. The Corporate Concentration prepares graduates to work in publicly- or privately-held companies. The Forensic concentration emphasizes skills to address financial crises and fraud, with a focus on investigative accounting. The Taxation concentration prepares students to advise clients on tax law as it relates to corporations, partnerships, and limited liability companies.

M.S. in Finance: This program prepares students to compete in the financial world in a variety of analytical roles. Students learn to apply the core areas of finance—investments, corporate finance, and derivatives—within a framework of making appropriate, ethically based decisions. Students gain real-world experience through a rigorous curriculum, internships, and real-world projects that allow them to become proficient with the same data sets and tools used by global financial firms.

M.S. in Sport Management: This program prepares students for careers in professional sports team management, collegiate athletic administration, sport marketing, sport finance, and sport facility management. Students select from concentrations in Collegiate Athletic Administration, Facility Management, and Sport Analytics. Graduates have gone on to work for Major League Soccer, WWE, ESPN, and Octagon.

M.S. in Taxation: This program was developed for accountants, attorneys, government employees, and executives seeking to gain advanced expertise in taxation law. The program satisfies the 150 credit hours of coursework needed to sit for the Certified Public Accountant (CPA) examination in Connecticut.

MBA/Master in Public Administration (M.P.A.) Dual Degree: Designed for both new and current working professionals the MBA/M.P.A. dual-degree program prepares students for managerial roles in the public and private sector. The curriculum emphasizes the use of management skills and analytic techniques applied to business, industrial, governmental, and not-for-profit organizations. Public administration courses cover a variety of topics in city management, personnel and labor relations, and community-clinical services, among others. All dual-degree students must choose to complete either a thesis or capstone project.

Graduate Certificates: Programs are available in Accounting; Business Administration (Management); Business Intelligence; Finance; Human Resources Management; International Business; Sport Management; Taxation; and Nonprofit Leadership, Innovation, and Organizational Leadership, Innovation, and Sustainability for Non-profits.

Career Support

Graduate students have access to the University's top-rated Career Development Center, which offers internship location help, interview practice, and other services. Program graduates have gone on to pursue work in public defense, risk-mitigation services, shelter and supportive housing programs, and mentorship programs.

Financial Aid

The University is committed to assisting graduate students by offering a comprehensive financial aid program. The financial aid that is offered generally consists of student loans and, when applicable, grants and student employment.

A number of merit-based assistantships are available for full-time graduate students to defray the cost of tuition and provide an earned wage. These include the Provost's Assistantship, which offsets 75 percent of tuition expenses and provides 15 to 20 hours per week of research or teaching experience, and the Dean's Scholarship, which covers up to half of the recipients' tuition.

Cost of Study

College of Business graduate tuition for the 2018–19 academic year is $915 per credit hour for most programs. The EMBA program is $1,120 per credit. The graduate student general fee is $220 per year for full-time students (9 credits or more) and $180 per year for part-time students.

Living and Housing

There are two graduate student housing options sponsored by the University. The Atwood Apartments are located just across the street from the northeast end of campus and the Savin Court apartments are

University of New Haven

located approximately 1.5 miles from campus. Other off-campus housing is also available.

The University's Office of Graduate Student Services offers many resources to assist participants in the program.

Location

The University's main campus is located on 82 acres in West Haven, Connecticut, a suburban hillside community minutes from the bustling city of New Haven and miles of Connecticut shoreline and beaches. The campus is 90 minutes from New York City and 2 1/2 hours from Boston and is also accessible by train from those cities.

Situated on 82 acres atop a hill overlooking the New Haven skyline with views of Long Island Sound, this residential campus is conveniently located a mile north of Interstate 95. The campus has experienced significant growth in the last decade with more than $220 million in construction projects completed or underway.

The University

The University of New Haven is a small private, secular school established in 1920 in West Haven, Connecticut. Today, the university has four campuses in Connecticut as well as one in Italy. It has been named one of U.S. News & World Report's "Best Regional Universities–North" and one of The Princeton Review's "Best 382 Colleges" and "Best Northeastern Colleges." The Princeton Review has also named the University of New Haven to its top-20 U.S. colleges for "Best Career Services." The institution has also been recognized by multiple organizations for its service to military veteran students.

The Graduate School offers over 60 graduate degree and certificate programs to help prepare students for success in their careers and lives. The various courses of study deliver skills and experiences that will help students make the most of real-world opportunities and maximize your career potential. Graduate programs follow a semester schedule. Courses are generally in the evenings, offering flexibility for those continuing to work while pursuing their studies.

Faculty

The University of New Haven College of Business graduate faculty members are seasoned practitioners who work in the cutting edge of research. The University is a recognized leader in experiential education, promoting a philosophy and methodology of education in which educators purposefully engage with learners in direct experience and focused reflection in order to increase knowledge, develop skills, and clarify values.

Applying

The Office of Graduate Admissions strives to provide a personalized admission process. Interested students are welcome to visit campus, meet with a graduate admissions counselor, go on a campus tour, meet a faculty advisor in the program, and meet with a financial aid officer.

Applicants to the College of Business programs must submit the following:

- Online application
- $50 nonrefundable fee
- Official university transcripts and proof of bachelor's degree completion. An explanation of the grading system that conferred the degree must be provided with the transcripts.
- Two letters of recommendation from professors or employers
- A statement of purpose is required. A resume is highly recommended.
- Students applying to the MBA, M.S. in Finance, and M.S. in Accounting programs are urged to submit GMAT scores as well.

Applications are considered on a rolling basis, but there are recommended deadlines: June 1 (domestic) and May 1 (international) for fall admission and November 15 for spring admission.

Conditional acceptance is offered in most majors to those who are academically admissible but who have not met the University's required English test scores. Students who do not submit proof of English proficiency will be recommended to enroll in the Academic English Preparatory Program (AEPP).

Contact

University of New Haven
Office of Graduate Admissions
Maxcy 129
300 Boston Post Road
West Haven, Connecticut 06516
Phone: 800-342-5864
   203-932-7148
Email: SOToole@newhaven.edu
Website: https://www.newhaven.edu/business/graduate-programs/index.php

The College of Business at the University of New Haven is accredited by AACSB, making it one of the best in the world.

The University of New Haven's College of Business offers 18 graduate programs and certificates.

UNIVERSITY OF PITTSBURGH
Graduate Programs in Education

 For more information, visit http://petersons.to//upittkatz

Programs of Study

The University of Pittsburgh's Joseph M. Katz Graduate School of Business believes two things to be universally true: business never stops reinventing itself, and neither should businesspersons. As a global, AACSB-accredited institution, Katz offers MBA, Executive MBA, and Ph.D., degrees, as well as specialized master's programs in accounting, business analytics, finance, marketing science, management information systems (MIS), and supply chain management that are continually ranked among the world's best by independent publications.

The **One-Year MBA** is a full-time, 51-credit program, with classes in person on campus. The program is designed to be completed in 12 months, beginning in May.

The **Two-Year MBA** is a full-time, 57-credit program, with classes in person on campus. The program requires 21 months of study and begins in August.

The **Professional MBA** is a part-time, 51-credit program, with classes in a blended online format. The program can be completed in 12 to 48 months, with sessions beginning in August, January, and May.

The **Specialized Master's** programs are full-time, 30–45-credit programs with classes on campus. The programs can be completed in 9–17 months and begin in August. Programs are available in accounting, business analytics, finance, marketing science, MIS, and supply chain management.

Research Facilities

Led by a world-renowned faculty, the curriculum incorporates groundbreaking research, the entrepreneurial spirit, and an emphasis on experience-based learning. As part of the University of Pittsburgh, Katz students and faculty enjoy an abundance of opportunities for cross-disciplinary collaboration.

Students have opportunities in several Katz research centers, including the Center for Branding, David Berg Center for Ethics and Leadership, Center for Executive Education, Center for Healthcare Management, International Business Center, Center for Supply Chain Management, and The Business of Humanity® Project.

Financial Aid

Tuition scholarships provide the primary source of financial assistance for incoming full-time Katz students. These merit-based scholarships are awarded in various dollar amounts and are directly applied to tuition charges.

Cost of Study

For full-time students who are Pennsylvania residents in the 2018–19 academic year, the One-Year MBA tuition is $45,564 and fees bring the total to $51,339; the Two-Year MBA tuition is $45,564 and fees bring the total to $53,264; and the Specialized Master's programs have tuition costs of $29,252 and fees bring the total to $31,802. Part-time Pennsylvania students in the Professional MBA program pay $66,708 in tuition and fees bring the total to $70,488; those in the Specialized Master's programs pay $33,300 in tuition and fees bring the total to $35,775.

For full-time students who are nonresidents in the 2018–19 academic year, the One-Year MBA tuition is $63,912 and fees bring the total to $69,687; the Two-Year MBA tuition is $63,912 and fees bring the total to $70,112; and the Specialized Master's programs have tuition costs of $40,500 and fees bring the total to $43,050. Part-time nonresident students in the Professional MBA program pay $103,224 in tuition and

fees bring the total to $107,004; those in the Specialized Master's programs pay $48,480 in tuition and fees bring the total to $50,955.

Living and Housing Costs

The University of Pittsburgh does not provide graduate student housing; however, there are numerous housing options available in the nearby area.

Living expenses are estimated at $15,920 for the One-Year MBA program, $31,840 for the Two-Year MBA, and $11,940 for the specialized master's programs. Health insurance costs are estimated at an additional $1,573 to $4,194 per program. Students should add $5,016 per year for each dependent family member.

Student Group

Katz students are part of a nurturing community of business professionals who use small class sizes, a collaborative environment, and student-led organizations to form friendships that last a lifetime.

For the Full-Time MBA programs, the most recent entering class had 70 students, with an average work experience of 48 months, average GMAT of 608, and average undergraduate GPA of 3.41. International students made up 31 percent of the group; 37 percent of the students were female; and 21 percent were diversity students.

For the Professional MBA program, the most recent entering class had 92 students, with an average work experience of 61 months, average GMAT of 544, and average undergraduate GPA of 3.16. International students made up 1 percent of the group; 32 percent of the students were female; and 4 percent were diversity students.

For the specialized master's programs, the most recent entering class had 144 students, with an average work experience of 7 months, average GMAT of 632, and average undergraduate GPA of 3.47. International students made up 60 percent of the group; 63 percent of the students were female; and 9 percent were diversity students.

Student Outcomes

The Katz leadership network spans the globe: over 30,000 Pitt Business alumni live in more than 90 countries. Through its Career Management Center, Katz builds partnerships with leading companies and assists students in all programs to realize their full career potential.

Students who have completed the various graduate-level programs in the Katz School of Business went on to further their careers in finance (investment management, banking and financial institutions, corporate finance, financial consulting, etc.), information systems and technology management (IS management, business analysis, IT consulting, product development management, etc.), marketing (brand and product management, marketing research and consumer insights, social media and digital marketing, business development and sales management, etc.), operations (supply chain/logistics management, project management, operations management), organizational behavior and HR management (human resources management, human resources consulting, etc.), and strategy (management consulting, business development analysis, entrepreneurship, etc.).

Firms that have hired Katz graduates include: Accenture, Alcoa, Amazon, American Eagle Outfitters, Anheuser-Busch, Aon, AT Kearney, Bank of America, Bank of New York Mellon, Barclays, Bayer, Booz Allen Hamilton, Bosch, Capgemini, Capital One, Citibank, Cognizant, Colgate Palmolive, Corning, Crane, Deloitte, Dick's Sporting Goods, Direct Energy, Eaton, eBay, EQT, Ericcson, Ernst & Young, FDIC, FedEx, Ford, General Electric, General Mills, Georgia Pacific, GNC, Goodyear, Highmark, Honeywell,

University of Pittsburgh

HSBC, IBM, Key Bank, KPMG, Kraft Heinz, McKinsey, Merck, Microsoft, Nationwide Insurance, Nielson, Olympus, Oracle, Philips, PNC, PPG, PricewaterhouseCoopers, Samsung, SDLC, Starkist, Sungard, Target, Texas Instruments, Hershey, The Vanguard Group, Thermo Fisher Scientific, TriState Capital Bank, Uber, United Technologies, UPMC, Volkswagen, Westinghouse Electric Company, Wipro Technologies, and others.

Location

Pittsburgh's unique and eclectic heritage, energy, and diversity are a source of inspiration and opportunity for Katz students. Nationally renowned for livability and natural beauty, Pittsburgh has a vibrant business community anchored by Fortune 500 companies in banking, manufacturing, consumer goods, and retail, and bolstered by new tech arrivals such as Google and Uber. University of Pittsburgh students can take advantage of all the amenities the city has to offer. Some students choose to stay in Pittsburgh after they graduate, while others pursue their careers in cities all over the world. Either way, Pittsburgh is a launch pad.

The University's urban campus is home to the Cathedral of Learning and the beautiful 300-acre Schenley Park. Students can also cheer on their Pitt Panthers as they compete for championships and renew rivalries in the Atlantic Coast Conference (ACC).

The University and the School

The University of Pittsburgh is a state-related research university, founded as the Pittsburgh Academy in 1787. Pitt is a member of the Association of American Universities (AAU), which comprises 62 pre-eminent doctorate-granting research institutions in North America.

The Katz School of Business was established in 1960, but has history dating to 1907, Katz is the first school to offer a one-year MBA and was among the first to offer an Executive MBA. Katz believes that success favors the agile, which is why students are immersed in real-world experiences so they graduate ready to build, lead, and contribute immediately.

Faculty

Katz faculty members anchor a strong research culture and collaborative atmosphere. Their teaching approach ties the latest in business theory to experience-based learning to prepare students to be catalysts for change. They pursue a wide variety of cutting-edge research streams and ask the bold questions needed to unearth and expand globally relevant insights for today's business leaders. Not only do faculty members frequently publish in top academic journals, many serve as journal editors and command leadership roles in academic organizations.

The University's urban location in Pittsburgh gives faculty members opportunities to collaborate with business leaders, which they leverage into opportunities for consulting-based projects, case studies, and guest speakers. Students find that faculty members genuinely care about their education and are committed to help them in their careers.

Applying

Prospective students are required to submit the following: application and fee (waived if entering FT18PE11 in the Fee Waiver Code field of the application), two letters of recommendation, an essay, resume, transcripts from all post-secondary schools attended, GMAT or GRE scores, and TOEFL or ITLTS scores (international applicants).

Application deadlines for the Full-Time MBA and M.S. in Accounting programs are: Round 1, October 1; Round 2, December 1; Round 3, February 1 (also deadline for scholarship consideration); and Round 4, April 1.

Application deadlines for the M.S. in Marketing Science, Finance, MIS, and Supply Chain Management programs are: Round 1, November 1; Round 2, January 1; Round 3, March 1 (also deadline for scholarship consideration); and Round 4, May 1.

Application deadlines for the part-time programs are: spring semester, November 1; summer semester, March 1; and fall semester, July 1.

Correspondence and Information

Admissions Office
Katz Graduate School of Business
University of Pittsburgh
301 Mervis Hall
3950 Roberto Clemente Drive
Pittsburgh, Pennsylvania 15260
Phone: 412-648-1700
E-mail: admissions@katz.pitt.edu
Website: business.pitt.edu

UNIVERSITY OF RHODE ISLAND

College of Business

 For more information, visit http://petersons.to/uri-business

THE
NIVE S TY
OF RHODE ISLAND

Programs of Study

The University of Rhode Island's (URI) College of Business, the first accredited business school in Rhode Island, is recognized for its leadership in business education, research, and outreach.

URI offers a variety of AACSB-accredited M.B.A. programs to a meet the needs of students with different goals and schedules. Other master degrees available at the College of Business include M.S. Accounting, M.S. Finance, M.S. Labor Relations and Human Resources, M.S. Textile, Fashion Merchandising and Design, and Ph.D.s in a variety of business areas. The University recognizes that students' time is valuable, so it has created programs to allow them to finish their degrees in a rapid timeframe and quickly move to the next phase of their careers. URI keeps its classes small, helping students feel more comfortable networking in a smaller environment and encouraging interaction and intellectual debate in a community atmosphere.

The URI M.B.A. programs offer personalized academic advising, faculty members with a broad range of experience and research, value, and technologically enhanced facilities.

One-Year Program in Strategic Innovation: To meet the needs of a global business environment that requires a workforce capable of critical and innovative thinking, URI redesigned its one-year M.B.A. that challenged the traditional look and feel of a full-time M.B.A. program. The program offers a unique, hands-on approach to learning that breaks down the functional barriers of business education, by offering cross-disciplined courses that directly map onto solving real business problems in a strategically innovative way. Students will meet Monday through Friday from 9 a.m. to 4:30 p.m. at the Providence campus during the fall and spring semesters, followed by a summer internship, electives, or research projects.

The URI One-Year M.B.A. program walks students through the strategic process of defining how to define their change goals, measure them, analyze the results, make improvements, and control that process to ensure that the goals have been met. This is accomplished by using a small dedicated group of faculty members that will work with the students for the entire year, combining forces within the classroom to integrate different disciplines; a live case study with a local global company; hands-on consulting projects with such companies as CVS Health, Fidelity Investments, Hasbro, IGT, Ocean State Job Lot, and Schneider Electric; and team and individual papers, homework, and exams. To complete the program, students will participate in a summer internship, electives, or research project.

Part-Time Evening M.B.A.: The URI evening M.B.A. program is aimed at individuals who want to pursue a degree while maintaining their professional commitments and who value flexibility, convenience, diversity, and a return on investment. The program is designed to emphasize conceptual, analytical, technical, and interpersonal skills. Material for this non-thesis program is presented through lectures, discussions, case studies, and both individual and group projects. Students learn from both the instructor and the network of fellow students who work in a broad range of industries. A goal of the program is to take the new ideas discussed and learned in class that evening straight to the workplace the next day.

This flexible program requires the completion of 45 credits, or 15 courses. Classes (with a maximum of 30 students) meet one night a week during the fall, spring, and summer sessions in Providence or Kingston. Students are allowed to enroll in as many classes as they wish per semester. Concentrations include finance, healthcare management, general management, marketing, and supply chain management. Web-based and Saturday courses are also available to enable students to finish in their desired timeframes. The M.B.A. program does not require previous instruction in business administration.

Blue M.B.A.—Dual Degree M.B.A. and Master of Oceanography: Climate change represents both a major challenge and opportunity to a broad range of businesses and the global economy. In turn, there is a growing demand for leaders with skills in both business and science, particularly climate-related sciences. To address this need, URI created a unique dual-degree program that merges the M.B.A. with a Master of Oceanography (M.B.A./M.O.) dubbed the Blue M.B.A.

The Blue M.B.A. program requires students to take both M.B.A. and M.O. classes at the Providence and Narragansett Bay campuses, choosing one of three schedule options. The program provides students with the knowledge and skills needed to develop business models to ensure an environmentally sustainable world for future generations. It allows for a summer internship anywhere in the world. At the end of the program, students graduate with two degrees: the M.B.A. and the M.O.

This program is designed for students with pure science, environmental science, or engineering undergraduate degrees who want to develop their management skills and broaden their marketability. Students are expected to be successful in both GSO science courses and M.B.A. courses. The program will be particularly beneficial to those seeking management careers in industries such as energy, ocean technology and engineering, hazard risk management, water resources, fisheries, marine navigation, and tourism, as well as ocean and human health.

Accreditation

The College of Business Administration has been accredited since 1972 by AACSB—The Association to Advance Collegiate Schools of Business. AACSB accreditation is highly sought-after by universities; its high level of academic merit and accreditation has been achieved by less than 15 percent of the institutions teaching management education.

Research

Research is central to the University of Rhode Island. Faculty research within the College of Business Administration covers a broad range of interests and specializations, and students have a variety of opportunities to benefit from it.

PACAP Research Center: The Sandra Ann Morsilli Pacific-Basin Capital Markets Research Center was established in 1989 at the University of Rhode Island to meet the growing demand for information on the capital markets in the Pacific-Basin region. The PACAP Research Center, which serves the securities industry, financial service industry, government, multilateral development institutions, and academia, has become recognized internationally as the leading research institute on Asian capital markets.

For current information on faculty research, prospective students should visit http://web.uri.edu/business/research/.

Financial Aid

Financial support is available in the form of assistantships, scholarships and fellowships.

Recommendations for the appointment of teaching, research, and administrative assistants are usually made by individual departments or programs. Assistantships are awarded with the expectation that service will be provided by the recipient.

Scholarships are available from a variety of professional societies and organizations, and often the best sources of advice for these awards will be the major professor, Graduate Director or Department Chair. The Graduate School provides a limited number of scholarships that are awarded on a competitive basis.

Fellowships are available from a number of organizations and agencies. Information on grants and loans is available from Enrollment Services/Financial Aid (www.uri.edu/es/menus/finaid.html).

Costs

Tuition and fees for full-time graduate students in the 2018–19 academic year are estimated at $22,925 for in-state students and $42,274 for out-of-state students. Part-time M.B.A. students are charged per credit: $735/credit for in-state students, $1,103/credit for regional students, and $1,436 for out-of-state students.

Student Outcomes

More than 220 students are currently enrolled in URI's M.B.A. programs. The average graduating salary in 2018 was approximately $85,000. Students work in a wide variety of companies including Amgen, Citizens Bank, CVS Health, Electric Boat, Fidelity Investments, FM Global, Lockheed Martin, Morgan Stanley, Pfizer RI Hospital, and Sensata Technologies.

Alumni of these programs are given exit surveys and here are just some of their comments about their experiences at URI:

"As I progressed through the program, I realized that I was not only getting a wonderful business education, but I was also getting a fantastic real-world education."

"The professors taught with passion and were always there for the students. It was evident that the professors wanted the students to excel."

"The education I received at URI's Providence campus provided some of the momentum I needed to launch my businesses. In fact, I visualized my marketing company during an entrepreneurship class project, and it is a dream that the business is now growing so fast. There's no doubt that I have URI to thank for laying a solid groundwork for the success I've achieved as a business owner."

"Having an engineering degree with no business background except on the job, the program was very effective at providing me with a broad yet in-depth knowledge that will be very useful in the future."

"Excellent exposure to public speaking and business interaction such as debating issues and negotiating. I have found this is the area where any person interacting with others in today's business world must excel at and feel comfortable with in order to succeed."

Location

The M.B.A courses are held at the Alan Shawn Feinstein Providence campus, conveniently located in downtown Providence, RI. The building houses a bookstore, breakout spaces, cafeteria, classrooms, computer center and library. Free validated parking is available to students at the RI Convention Center Parking Garage. URI also maintains 315 buildings on four campuses.

The University and the College

The University of Rhode Island is the State's public learner-centered research university. The University is committed to enriching the lives of its students through its land, sea, and urban grant traditions. URI is the only public institution in Rhode Island offering undergraduate, graduate, and professional students the distinctive educational opportunities of a major research university. Students, faculty, staff, and alumni are united in one common purpose: to learn and lead together.

The College of Business strives to be one of the leading business programs in New England, and highly responsive to the needs of the Rhode Island and regional business community. The College offers multi-disciplinary business programs that align with the financial, health, environmental, science, and technological sectors of the economy.

Applying

Applicants with a bachelor's degree in any major, from any accredited college or university may apply for admission to the Master of Business Administration Program. The application includes submission of the following: brief statement of purpose; a $65 non-refundable application fee; two letters of recommendation; current resume; official college transcript(s) from a baccalaureate degree at an accredited institution in the U.S. or the equivalent of a four-year degree at an international institution; official score report for the Graduate Management Admission Test (GMAT) or GRE taken within the last five years (waived for students who meet specific criteria listed on the M.B.A. website); Residency Application or Certificate of Residency for in-state or qualified regional students; and TOEFL or IELTS scores (taken within the last two years) for all international students who completed their bachelor's degree from a non-English speaking foreign University. Most of this material can be submitted online.

More specific information regarding the M.B.A. admission process is available at http://web.uri.edu/business/mba-admission/.

Correspondence and Information

Ms. Lisa Lancellotta, Coordinator
M.B.A. Programs
College of Business
University of Rhode Island
Kingston, Rhode Island 02881
United States
Phone: 401-874-4241
Fax: 401-874-4312
E-mail: mba@uri.edu
Website: http://web.uri.edu/business/mba/

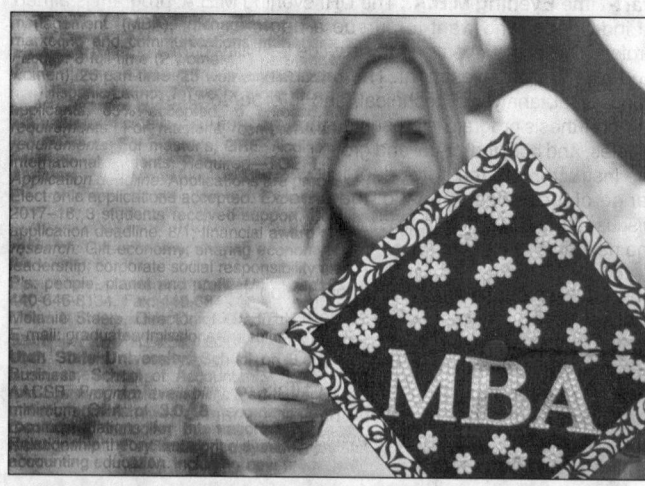

Section 2
Accounting and Finance

This section contains a directory of institutions offering graduate work in accounting and finance. Additional information about programs listed in the directory but not augmented by an in-depth entry may be obtained by writing directly to the dean of a graduate school or chair of a department at the address given in the directory.

For programs offering related work, see also in this book *Business Administration and Management, International Business,* and *Nonprofit Management.* In the other guides in this series:

Graduate Programs in the Humanities, Arts & Social Sciences
See *Economics* and *Family and Consumer Sciences (Consumer Economics)*

Graduate Programs in the Physical Sciences, Mathematics, Agricultural Sciences, the Environment & Natural Resources
See *Mathematical Sciences*

Graduate Programs in Engineering & Applied Sciences
See *Computer Science and Information Technology*

CONTENTS

Program Directories

Featured Schools: Displays and Close-Ups

See also:

Accounting

Abilene Christian University, Graduate Programs, College of Business Administration, Program in Accountancy, Abilene, TX 79699. Offers M Acc. *Program availability:* Part-time. *Faculty:* 7 part-time/adjunct (0 women). *Students:* 12 full-time (4 women), 1 (woman) part-time; includes 2 minority (1 American Indian or Alaska Native, non-Hispanic/Latino; 1 Hispanic/Latino). 26 applicants, 46% accepted, 9 enrolled. In 2017, 25 master's awarded. *Entrance requirements:* For master's, GMAT. Additional exam requirements/recommendations for international students: Required—TOEFL (minimum score 80 iBT), IELTS (minimum score 6). *Application deadline:* For fall admission, 8/11 for domestic students; for spring admission, 11/1 for domestic students. Applications are processed on a rolling basis. Application fee: $50. Electronic applications accepted. *Expenses:* $1,148 per hour. *Financial support:* In 2017–18, 7 students received support. Federal Work-Study and scholarships/grants available. Support available to part-time students. Financial award application deadline: 4/1; financial award applicants required to submit FAFSA. *Unit head:* John Neill, Graduate Director, 325-674-2053, Fax: 325-674-2507, E-mail: john.neill@acu.edu. *Application contact:* Graduate Admissions, 325-674-6911, Fax: 325-674-6717, E-mail: gradinfo@acu.edu.
Website: http://www.acu.edu/graduate/academics/accounting.html

Adelphi University, Robert B. Willumstad School of Business, MBA Program, Garden City, NY 11530-0701. Offers accounting (MBA); finance (MBA); health services administration (MBA); human resource management (MBA); management (MBA); management information systems (MBA); marketing (MBA); sport management (MBA). *Accreditation:* AACSB. *Program availability:* Part-time, evening/weekend. *Students:* 257 full-time (110 women), 78 part-time (38 women); includes 56 minority (18 Black or African American, non-Hispanic/Latino; 16 Asian, non-Hispanic/Latino; 19 Hispanic/Latino; 3 Two or more races, non-Hispanic/Latino), 181 international. Average age 28. 435 applicants, 61% accepted, 205 enrolled. In 2017, 130 master's awarded. *Degree requirements:* For master's, capstone course. *Entrance requirements:* For master's, GMAT, 2 letters of recommendation. Additional exam requirements/recommendations for international students: Required—TOEFL (minimum score 550 paper-based; 80 iBT), IELTS (minimum score 6.5). *Application deadline:* For fall admission, 4/1 for international students; for spring admission, 11/1 for international students. Applications are processed on a rolling basis. Application fee: $50. Electronic applications accepted. *Expenses:* Contact institution. *Financial support:* Research assistantships with partial tuition reimbursements, career-related internships or fieldwork, Federal Work-Study, institutionally sponsored loans, scholarships/grants, tuition waivers (partial), and unspecified assistantships available. Financial award application deadline: 3/1; financial award applicants required to submit FAFSA. *Faculty research:* Supply chain management, distribution channels, productivity benchmark analysis, data envelopment analysis, financial portfolio analysis. *Unit head:* Dr. Rakesh Gupta, Associate Dean, 516-877-4629. *Application contact:* E-mail: graduateadmissions@adelphi.edu.
Website: http://business.adelphi.edu/degree-programs/graduate-degree-programs/m-b-a/

Adrian College, Graduate Programs, Adrian, MI 49221-2575. Offers accounting (MS); athletic training (MS); criminal justice (MA). *Degree requirements:* For master's, comprehensive exam (for some programs), thesis (for some programs), thesis, internship or practicum with corresponding in-depth paper and/or presentation. *Entrance requirements:* For master's, appropriate undergraduate degree, minimum cumulative and major GPA of 3.0, personal statement.

Alabama State University, College of Business Administration, Department of Accounting and Finance, Montgomery, AL 36101-0271. Offers accountancy (M Acc). *Faculty:* 4 full-time (1 woman), 1 part-time/adjunct (0 women). *Students:* 18 full-time (12 women), 6 part-time (4 women); includes 17 minority (15 Black or African American, non-Hispanic/Latino; 2 Hispanic/Latino), 5 international. Average age 22. 16 applicants, 63% accepted, 8 enrolled. In 2017, 8 master's awarded. *Degree requirements:* For master's, comprehensive exam. *Entrance requirements:* For master's, minimum GPA of 2.75 (undergraduate), 3.0 (graduate). Additional exam requirements/recommendations for international students: Required—TOEFL (minimum score 500 paper-based). *Application deadline:* For fall admission, 4/15 for domestic and international students; for spring admission, 11/15 for domestic and international students; for summer admission, 3/15 for domestic and international students. Applications are processed on a rolling basis. Application fee: $25. Electronic applications accepted. *Expenses:* Tuition, state resident: part-time $412 per credit hour. Tuition, nonresident: part-time $824 per credit hour. *Required fees:* $685 per semester. *Financial support:* In 2017–18, 11 students received support. Fellowships and unspecified assistantships available. Financial award applicants required to submit FAFSA. *Unit head:* Dr. Dave Thompson, Chair, 334-229-4134, Fax: 334-229-4870, E-mail: dthompson@asunet.alasu.edu. *Application contact:* Dr. William Person, Dean of Graduate Studies, 334-229-4274, Fax: 334-229-4928, E-mail: wperson@alasu.edu.
Website: http://www.alasu.edu/academics/colleges—departments/college-of-business-administration/college-of-business-academics/accounting—finance/index.aspx

Albany State University, College of Business, Albany, GA 31705-2717. Offers accounting (MBA); general business administration (MBA); healthcare (MBA); public administration (MBA); supply chain and logistics (MBA). *Accreditation:* ACBSP. *Program availability:* Part-time, evening/weekend. *Degree requirements:* For master's, comprehensive exam, internship, 3 hours of physical education. *Entrance requirements:* For master's, GMAT (minimum score of 450)/GRE (minimum score of 800) for those without earned master's degree or higher, minimum undergraduate GPA of 2.5, 2 letters of reference, official transcript, pre-entrance medical record and certificate of immunization. Electronic applications accepted. *Faculty research:* Diversity issues, ancestry, understanding finance through use of technology.

Albertus Magnus College, Master of Business Administration Program, New Haven, CT 06511-1189. Offers accounting (MBA); general management (MBA); health care management (MBA); human resource management (MBA); leadership (MBA); project management (MBA). Program also offered in East Hartford, CT. *Program availability:* Part-time, evening/weekend, 100% online, blended/hybrid learning. *Degree requirements:* For master's, thesis, capstone project, business plan, minimum cumulative GPA of 3.0, completion of all requirements within seven years of matriculation. *Entrance requirements:* For master's, 3 years of management or related experience, minimum GPA of 2.5, 2 letters of recommendation, official transcripts. Additional exam requirements/recommendations for international students: Recommended—TOEFL (minimum score 550 paper-based; 80 iBT). *Application deadline:* Applications are processed on a rolling basis. Application fee: $50. Electronic applications accepted. *Expenses:* Contact institution. *Financial support:* Federal Work-Study and unspecified assistantships available. Support available to part-time students. Financial award applicants required to submit FAFSA. *Faculty research:* Finance, project management, accounting, business administration, generalist. *Unit head:* Dr. Wayne Gineo, Director, 203-672-6670, E-mail: wgineo@albertus.edu. *Application contact:* Anthony Reich, Director of Admission, Division of Professional and Graduate Studies, 203-773-5302, E-mail: arreich@albertus.edu.
Website: http://www.albertus.edu/business-administration/ms/

Albertus Magnus College, Master of Science in Accounting Program, New Haven, CT 06511-1189. Offers MSA. *Program availability:* Part-time, evening/weekend, 100% online, blended/hybrid learning. *Degree requirements:* For master's, project. *Entrance requirements:* For master's, bachelor's degree; minimum cumulative GPA of 3.0; 24 undergraduate credits in accounting, 22 in business (separate from accounting); 2 letters of recommendation; essay. Additional exam requirements/recommendations for international students: Recommended—TOEFL (minimum score 575 paper-based). *Application deadline:* Applications are processed on a rolling basis. Application fee: $50. Electronic applications accepted. *Expenses:* Contact institution. *Financial support:* Federal Work-Study and unspecified assistantships available. Support available to part-time students. Financial award applicants required to submit FAFSA. *Unit head:* Dr. Nancy Fallon, Director, 203-773-8567, E-mail: nfallon@albertus.edu. *Application contact:* Dr. Nancy Fallon, Director, 203-773-8567, E-mail: nfallon@albertus.edu.
Website: http://www.albertus.edu/graduate-degrees/graduate-degree-programs/accounting/

Alfred University, Graduate School, School of Business, Alfred, NY 14802-1205. Offers accounting (MBA); business administration (MBA). *Accreditation:* AACSB. *Program availability:* Part-time. *Entrance requirements:* For master's, GMAT. Additional exam requirements/recommendations for international students: Required—TOEFL (minimum score 590 paper-based; 90 iBT), IELTS (minimum score 6.5). Electronic applications accepted.

American Business & Technology University, Programs in Business Administration, Saint Joseph, MO 64506. Offers business administration (MBA); financial management (MBA); global business management (MBA); information systems management (MBA); marketing and social media (MBA); project and operations management (MBA); public accounting (MBA). *Program availability:* Online learning.

American InterContinental University Online, Program in Business Administration, Schaumburg, IL 60173. Offers accounting and finance (MBA); finance (MBA); healthcare management (MBA); human resource management (MBA); international business (MBA); management (MBA); marketing (MBA); operations management (MBA); organizational psychology and development (MBA); project management (MBA). *Accreditation:* ACBSP. *Program availability:* Evening/weekend, online learning. *Entrance requirements:* Additional exam requirements/recommendations for international students: Required—TOEFL (minimum score 550 paper-based). Electronic applications accepted.

American International College, School of Business, Arts and Sciences, Springfield, MA 01109-3189. Offers accounting and taxation (MS); business administration (MBA); clinical psychology (MA); educational psychology (Ed D); forensic psychology (MS); general psychology (MA, CAGS); management (CAGS); resort and casino management (MBA, CAGS). *Program availability:* Part-time, evening/weekend. *Faculty:* 4 full-time (2 women), 25 part-time/adjunct (13 women). *Students:* 178 full-time (120 women), 24 part-time (20 women); includes 94 minority (42 Black or African American, non-Hispanic/Latino; 1 American Indian or Alaska Native, non-Hispanic/Latino; 4 Asian, non-Hispanic/Latino; 39 Hispanic/Latino; 8 Two or more races, non-Hispanic/Latino), 13 international. Average age 28. 155 applicants, 83% accepted, 71 enrolled. In 2017, 87 master's, 3 doctorates awarded. *Degree requirements:* For master's, practicum; for doctorate, comprehensive exam, thesis/dissertation, practicum. *Entrance requirements:* For master's, BS or BA, minimum undergraduate GPA of 2.75, 2 letters of recommendation, official transcripts, personal goal statement or essay; for doctorate, 3 letters of recommendation; BS or BA; minimum undergraduate GPA of 3.0 (3.25 recommended); official transcripts; personal goal statement or essay. Additional exam requirements/recommendations for international students: Required—TOEFL (minimum score 550 paper-based; 80 iBT). *Application deadline:* For fall admission, 8/15 for domestic and international students; for spring admission, 12/15 for domestic and international students. Applications are processed on a rolling basis. Application fee: $50. *Expenses:* Contact institution. *Financial support:* In 2017–18, 6 students received support, including 6 research assistantships with full tuition reimbursements available (averaging $1,500 per year). Financial award application deadline: 4/1; financial award applicants required to submit FAFSA. *Faculty research:* Substance abuse, forensic psychology, special education. *Unit head:* Dr. Susanne Swanker, Dean, 413-205-3216, Fax: 413-205-3943, E-mail: susanne.swanker@aic.edu. *Application contact:* Kerry Barnes, Dean of Graduate Admissions, 413-205-3703, Fax: 413-205-3051, E-mail: kerry.barnes@aic.edu.
Website: http://www.aic.edu/school-of-business-arts-and-sciences/

American Public University System, AMU/APU Graduate Programs, Charles Town, WV 25414. Offers accounting (MS); applied business analytics (MS); business administration (MBA); criminal justice (MA); cybersecurity studies (MS); educational leadership (M Ed); environmental policy and management (MS); global security (DGS); health information management (MS); history (MA), including American military history, American Revolution, civil war, war since 1945, World War II; information technology (MS); international relations and conflict resolution (MA), including American politics and government, comparative government and development, general, international relations, public policy; national security studies (MA); nursing (MSN); political science (MA); public policy (MPP); reverse logistics management (MA), including comparative and security issues, conflict resolution, international and transnational security issues, peacekeeping; space studies (MS); sports management (MS); strategic intelligence (DSI); teaching (M Ed), including secondary social studies; transportation and logistics management (MA). *Program availability:* Part-time, evening/weekend, online only, 100% online. *Students:* 455 full-time (227 women), 7,939 part-time (3,353 women); includes 2,793 minority (1,429 Black or African American, non-Hispanic/Latino; 48 American Indian or Alaska Native, non-Hispanic/Latino; 205 Asian, non-Hispanic/Latino; 766 Hispanic/Latino; 62 Native Hawaiian or other Pacific Islander, non-Hispanic/Latino; 283 Two or more races, non-Hispanic/Latino), 101 international. Average age 37. In 2017, 2,977 master's awarded. *Degree requirements:* For master's, comprehensive exam or practicum. *Entrance requirements:* For master's, official transcript showing earned bachelor's degree from institution accredited by recognized accrediting body. Additional exam requirements/recommendations for international students: Required—TOEFL (minimum score 550 paper-based), IELTS (minimum score 6.5). *Application deadline:* Applications are processed on a rolling basis. Application fee: $0. Electronic applications accepted. *Expenses:* Tuition: Full-time $6300; part-time $350 per credit. *Required fees:* $300; $50 per course. *Financial support:* Scholarships/grants available. Financial award applicants required to submit FAFSA. *Unit head:* Dr. Wallace Boston, President, 877-468-6268, Fax: 304-728-2348, E-mail: president@apus.edu. *Application contact:* Yoci Deal, Associate Vice President, Graduate and International Admissions, 877-468-6268, Fax: 304-724-3764, E-mail: info@apus.edu.
Website: http://www.apus.edu

American University, Kogod School of Business, Department of Accounting, Washington, DC 20016-8044. Offers accounting (MS, Certificate), including accounting (MS), forensic accounting (Certificate); taxation (MS, Certificate), including tax (Certificate), taxation (MS). *Program availability:* Part-time, evening/weekend. *Students:* 53 full-time (31 women), 70 part-time (35 women); includes 45 minority (23 Black or African American, non-Hispanic/Latino; 7 Asian, non-Hispanic/Latino; 13 Hispanic/Latino; 2 Two or more races, non-Hispanic/Latino), 36 international. Average age 31. 139 applicants, 80% accepted, 62 enrolled. In 2017, 60 master's, 14 other advanced degrees awarded. *Entrance requirements:* For master's, GMAT/GRE, resume, interview, personal statement, 2 letters of recommendation, transcripts; for Certificate, bachelor's degree. Additional exam requirements/recommendations for international students: Required—TOEFL (minimum score 100 iBT). *Application deadline:* For fall admission, 1/15 priority date for domestic students, 1/15 for international students; for spring admission, 10/15 priority date for domestic students, 10/15 for international students. Applications are processed on a rolling basis. Application fee: $100. *Expenses:* Contact institution. *Financial support:* Application deadline: 2/1; applicants required to submit FAFSA. *Faculty research:* Harmonization of international accounting standards, federal accounting and financial reporting, taxation of U.S. corporations doing business abroad, tax planning for real estate transactions. *Unit head:* Dr. Donald T. Williamson, Chair, Department of Accounting, 202-885-1942, Fax: 202-885-1992, E-mail: dwillia@american.edu. *Application contact:* Jason Garner, Director of Admissions, 202-885-1926, E-mail: jgarner@american.edu. Website: http://www.american.edu/kogod/

American University of Sharjah, Graduate Programs, 26666, United Arab Emirates. Offers accounting (MS); biomedical engineering (MSBME); business administration (MBA); chemical engineering (MS Ch E); civil engineering (MSCE); computer engineering (MS); electrical engineering (MSEE); engineering systems management (MS, PhD); mathematics (MS); mechanical engineering (MSME); mechatronics engineering (MS); teaching English to speakers of other languages (MA); translation and interpreting (MA); urban planning (MUP). *Program availability:* Part-time, evening/weekend. *Students:* 108 full-time (73 women), 287 part-time (207 women). Average age 27. 203 applicants, 83% accepted, 121 enrolled. In 2017, 114 master's awarded. *Degree requirements:* For master's, thesis (for some programs). *Entrance requirements:* For master's, GMAT (for MBA). Additional exam requirements/recommendations for international students: Required—TOEFL (minimum score 550 paper-based; 80 iBT), TWE (minimum score 5); Recommended—IELTS (minimum score 6.5). *Application deadline:* For fall admission, 8/5 priority date for domestic students, 7/1 priority date for international students; for spring admission, 12/30 priority date for domestic students, 12/9 for international students; for summer admission, 5/21 for domestic and international students. Applications are processed on a rolling basis. Application fee: $110. Electronic applications accepted. *Expenses: Tuition:* Full-time $20,000; part-time $1350 per credit. Tuition and fees vary according to degree level and program. *Financial support:* In 2017–18, 82 students received support, including 54 research assistantships, 54 teaching assistantships; scholarships/grants also available. Financial award application deadline: 6/3. *Faculty research:* Water pollution, management and waste water treatment, energy and sustainability, air pollution, Islamic finance, family business and small and medium enterprises. *Unit head:* Salwa Mohammed, Office of Graduate Studies, 971-6515-2934, E-mail: ogs@aus.edu. *Application contact:* Salwa H. Mohammed, Office of Graduate Studies, 971-65152934, E-mail: ogs@aus.edu. Website: https://www.aus.edu/masters-degrees

Anderson University, Falls School of Business, Anderson, IN 46012-3495. Offers accountancy (MA); business administration (MBA, DBA). *Accreditation:* ACBSP.

Andrews University, School of Graduate Studies, School of Business, Graduate Programs in Business, Berrien Springs, MI 49104. Offers MBA, MSA. *Faculty:* 8 full-time (3 women). *Students:* 23 full-time (13 women), 32 part-time (15 women); includes 21 minority (7 Black or African American, non-Hispanic/Latino; 6 Asian, non-Hispanic/Latino; 6 Hispanic/Latino; 2 Two or more races, non-Hispanic/Latino), 21 international. Average age 31. 83 applicants, 43% accepted, 28 enrolled. In 2017, 23 master's awarded. *Entrance requirements:* For master's, GMAT. Additional exam requirements/recommendations for international students: Required—TOEFL (minimum score 550 paper-based). Application fee: $40. *Unit head:* Dr. Leonard K. Gashugi, Chair, 769-471-3429, E-mail: gashugi@andrews.edu. *Application contact:* Justina Clayburn, Supervisor of Graduate Admission, 800-253-2874, Fax: 269-471-6321, E-mail: graduate@andrews.edu.

Angelo State University, College of Graduate Studies and Research, College of Business, Department of Accounting, Economics and Finance, San Angelo, TX 76909. Offers professional accountancy (MPAC). *Program availability:* Part-time, evening/weekend. *Students:* 11 full-time (5 women), 3 part-time (2 women); includes 4 minority (1 American Indian or Alaska Native, non-Hispanic/Latino; 3 Hispanic/Latino), 2 international. Average age 26. *Degree requirements:* For master's, comprehensive exam. *Entrance requirements:* For master's, GMAT, essay. Additional exam requirements/recommendations for international students: Required—TOEFL or IELTS. *Application deadline:* For fall admission, 7/15 priority date for domestic students, 6/10 for international students; for spring admission, 12/1 priority date for domestic students, 11/1 for international students. Applications are processed on a rolling basis. Application fee: $40 ($50 for international students). Electronic applications accepted. *Expenses:* Tuition, state resident: full-time $3856. Tuition, nonresident: full-time $11,324. *Required fees:* $2650. *Financial support:* Career-related internships or fieldwork, Federal Work-Study, and scholarships/grants available. Support available to part-time students. Financial award application deadline: 3/1; financial award applicants required to submit FAFSA. *Unit head:* Dr. Charles Aaron Pier, Chair, 325-486-6479, Fax: 325-942-2285, E-mail: chuck.pier@angelo.edu. *Application contact:* Dr. Norman A. Sunderman, Graduate Advisor, 325-942-2046 Ext. 245, E-mail: norman.sunderman@angelo.edu. Website: http://www.angelo.edu/dept/aef/

Appalachian State University, Cratis D. Williams Graduate School, Department of Accounting, Boone, NC 28608. Offers taxation (MS). *Program availability:* Part-time. *Degree requirements:* For master's, comprehensive exam, thesis optional. *Entrance requirements:* For master's, GMAT, 3 letters of recommendation. Additional exam requirements/recommendations for international students: Required—TOEFL (minimum score 550 paper-based; 79 iBT), IELTS (minimum score 6.5). Electronic applications accepted. *Faculty research:* Audit assurance risk, state taxation, financial accounting inconsistencies, management information systems, charitable contribution taxation.

Argosy University, Atlanta, College of Business, Atlanta, GA 30328. Offers accounting (DBA); corporate compliance (MBA); customized professional concentration (MBA, DBA); finance (MBA); healthcare administration (MBA); information systems (DBA); information systems management (MBA); international business (MBA, DBA); management (MBA, MSM, DBA); marketing (MBA, DBA). *Accreditation:* ACBSP.

Argosy University, Chicago, College of Business, Chicago, IL 60601. Offers accounting (DBA); customized professional concentration (MBA, DBA); finance (MBA); fraud examination (MBA); global business sustainability (DBA); healthcare administration (MBA); information systems (DBA); information systems management (MBA); international business (MBA, DBA); management (MBA, MSM, DBA); marketing (MBA, DBA); organizational leadership (Ed D); public administration (MBA); sustainable management (MBA). *Accreditation:* ACBSP. *Program availability:* Online learning.

Argosy University, Hawai`i, College of Business, Honolulu, HI 96813. Offers accounting (DBA); corporate compliance (MBA); customized professional concentration (MBA, DBA); finance (MBA, Certificate); fraud examination (MBA); global business sustainability (DBA); healthcare administration (MBA, Certificate); information systems (DBA); information systems management (MBA, Certificate); international business (MBA, DBA, Certificate); management (MBA, MSM, DBA); marketing (MBA, DBA, Certificate); organizational leadership (Ed D); public administration (MBA); sustainable management (MBA).

Argosy University, Los Angeles, College of Business, Los Angeles, CA 90045. Offers accounting (DBA); corporate compliance (MBA); customized professional concentration (MBA, DBA); finance (MBA); fraud examination (MBA); global business sustainability (DBA); healthcare administration (MBA); information systems (DBA); information systems management (MBA); international business (MBA, DBA); management (MBA, MSM, DBA); marketing (MBA, DBA); organizational leadership (Ed D); public administration (MBA); sustainable management (MBA).

Argosy University, Northern Virginia, College of Business, Arlington, VA 22209. Offers accounting (DBA); customized professional concentration (MBA, DBA); finance (MBA); fraud examination (MBA); global business sustainability (DBA); healthcare administration (MBA); information systems (DBA); information systems management (MBA); international business (MBA, DBA, Certificate); management (MBA, MSM, DBA); marketing (MBA, DBA, Certificate); organizational leadership (Ed D); public administration (MBA); sustainable management (MBA).

Argosy University, Orange County, College of Business, Orange, CA 92868. Offers accounting (DBA, Adv C); corporate compliance (MBA); customized professional concentration (MBA, DBA); finance (MBA, Certificate); fraud examination (MBA); global business sustainability (DBA); healthcare administration (MBA, Certificate); information systems (DBA, Adv C, Certificate); information systems management (MBA); international business (MBA, DBA, Adv C, Certificate); management (MBA, MSM, DBA, Adv C); marketing (MBA, DBA, Adv C, Certificate); organizational leadership (Ed D); public administration (MBA, Certificate); sustainable management (MBA).

Argosy University, Phoenix, College of Business, Phoenix, AZ 85021. Offers accounting (DBA); corporate compliance (MBA); customized professional concentration (MBA, DBA); finance (MBA); fraud examination (MBA); global business sustainability (DBA); healthcare administration (MBA); information systems (DBA); information systems management (MBA); international business (MBA, DBA); management (MBA, DBA); marketing (MBA, DBA); public administration (MBA); sustainable management (MBA).

Argosy University, Seattle, College of Business, Seattle, WA 98121. Offers accounting (DBA); corporate compliance (MBA); customized professional concentration (MBA, DBA); finance (MBA); fraud examination (MBA); global business sustainability (DBA); healthcare administration (MBA); information systems (DBA); information systems management (MBA); international business (MBA, DBA); management (MBA, MSM, DBA); marketing (MBA, DBA); organizational leadership (Ed D); public administration (MBA); sustainable management (MBA).

Argosy University, Tampa, College of Business, Tampa, FL 33607. Offers accounting (DBA); corporate compliance (MBA); customized professional concentration (MBA, DBA); finance (MBA); fraud examination (MBA); global business sustainability (DBA); healthcare administration (MBA); information systems (DBA); information systems management (MBA); international business (MBA, DBA); management (MBA, MSM, DBA); marketing (MBA, DBA); organizational leadership (Ed D); public administration (MBA); sustainable management (MBA).

Argosy University, Twin Cities, College of Business, Eagan, MN 55121. Offers accounting (DBA); customized professional concentration (MBA, DBA); finance (MBA); fraud examination (MBA); global business sustainability (DBA); healthcare administration (MBA); information systems (DBA); information systems management (MBA); international business (MBA, DBA); management (MBA, MSM, DBA); marketing (MBA, DBA); organizational leadership (Ed D); public administration (MBA); sustainable management (MBA).

Arizona State University at the Tempe campus, W. P. Carey School of Business, School of Accountancy, Tempe, AZ 85287-3606. Offers accountancy (M Acc, M Tax); business administration (PhD), including accountancy. *Accreditation:* AACSB. *Program availability:* Part-time, evening/weekend. *Degree requirements:* For master's, thesis optional, interactive Program of Study (iPOS) submitted before completing 50 percent of required credit hours. *Entrance requirements:* For master's, GMAT (waivers may apply for ASU accountancy undergraduates), minimum GPA of 3.0 in last 2 years of work leading to bachelor's degree, 2 letters of recommendation, professional resume, official transcripts, responses to 3 essay questions. Additional exam requirements/recommendations for international students: Required—TOEFL (minimum score 550 paper-based; 80 iBT), IELTS (minimum score 6.5). Electronic applications accepted. *Expenses:* Contact institution.

Arkansas State University, Graduate School, College of Business, Department of Accounting, State University, AR 72467. Offers accountancy (M Acc). *Program availability:* Part-time. *Degree requirements:* For master's, comprehensive exam, thesis or alternative. *Entrance requirements:* For master's, GMAT, appropriate bachelor's degree, letters of reference, official transcript, immunization records. Additional exam requirements/recommendations for international students: Required—TOEFL (minimum score 550 paper-based; 79 iBT), IELTS (minimum score 6), PTE (minimum score 56). Electronic applications accepted. *Expenses:* Contact institution.

Ashland University, Dauch College of Business and Economics, Ashland, OH 44805-3702. Offers accounting (MBA); business analytics (MBA); entrepreneurship (MBA); financial management (MBA); global management (MBA); health care management and leadership (MBA); human resource management (MBA); human resources (MBA); management information systems (MBA); project management (MBA); sport management (MBA); supply chain management (MBA). *Accreditation:* ACBSP. *Program availability:* Part-time, evening/weekend, 100% online, blended/hybrid learning. *Faculty:* 20 full-time (8 women), 13 part-time/adjunct (2 women). *Students:* 458 full-time (210 women), 144 part-time (52 women); includes 88 minority (63 Black or African American, non-Hispanic/Latino; 1 American Indian or Alaska Native, non-Hispanic/Latino; 10 Asian, non-Hispanic/Latino; 14 Hispanic/Latino), 202 international. Average age 31. 216 applicants, 74% accepted, 115 enrolled. In 2017, 184 master's awarded. Terminal master's awarded for partial completion of doctoral program. *Degree requirements:* For master's, thesis optional, capstone course. *Entrance requirements:* For master's, 2 years of full-time work experience. Additional exam requirements/recommendations for international students: Required—TOEFL (minimum score 550 paper-based; 78 iBT). *Application deadline:* For fall admission, 8/1 priority date for domestic students; for spring admission, 12/1 priority date for domestic students. Applications are processed on a rolling basis. Application fee: $30. Electronic applications accepted. *Expenses:* $815 per credit hour, $15 technology fee for online sections. *Financial support:* Scholarships/grants, tuition waivers (partial), and unspecified assistantships available.

Accounting

Financial award application deadline: 4/15; financial award applicants required to submit FAFSA. *Faculty research:* Relationship marketing strategy, executive compensation and company performance, online marketplaces in electronic commerce, diversity training in campus recreation departments, entrepreneurship in developing and emerging economies. *Unit head:* Dr. Elad Granot, Dean, 419-289-5932, E-mail: egranot@ashland.edu. *Application contact:* Stephen W. Krispinsky, Executive Director of MBA Program, 419-289-5236, Fax: 419-289-5910, E-mail: skrispin@ashland.edu. Website: http://www.mba.ashland.edu

Assumption College, Business Studies Program, Worcester, MA 01609-1296. Offers accounting (MBA); business studies (CAGS); finance/economics (MBA); human resources (MBA); international business (MBA); management (MBA); marketing (MBA); nonprofit leadership (MBA). *Program availability:* Part-time, evening/weekend. *Faculty:* 5 full-time (1 woman), 21 part-time/adjunct (6 women). *Students:* 29 full-time (13 women), 87 part-time (50 women); includes 15 minority (1 Black or African American, non-Hispanic/Latino; 4 Asian, non-Hispanic/Latino; 8 Hispanic/Latino; 2 Two or more races, non-Hispanic/Latino), 4 international. Average age 29. 34 applicants, 100% accepted, 26 enrolled. In 2017, 81 master's, 2 other advanced degrees awarded. *Degree requirements:* For master's, capstone. *Entrance requirements:* For master's, bachelor's degree, three letters of recommendation, official transcripts, personal statement, current resume; for CAGS, MBA or equivalent degree in a closely related field, three letters of recommendation, official transcripts, personal statement, current resume. Additional exam requirements/recommendations for international students: Required—TOEFL (minimum score 540 paper-based; 76 iBT), IELTS (minimum score 6). *Application deadline:* For fall admission, 8/10 priority date for domestic and international students; for spring admission, 1/4 priority date for domestic and international students; for summer admission, 5/10 priority date for domestic and international students. Application fee: $30. Electronic applications accepted. *Expenses: Tuition:* Full-time $11,952; part-time $664 per credit. *Required fees:* $70 per term. *Financial support:* In 2017–18, 19 students received support. Tuition waivers (full and partial), unspecified assistantships, and institutional discounts available. Financial award applicants required to submit FAFSA. *Faculty research:* Workplace diversity, dynamics of team interaction, utilization of leased employees, experiential learning project on due diligence market for prostheses. *Unit head:* Dr. Robin Frkal, Director, 508-767-7622, E-mail: ra.frkal@assumption.edu. *Application contact:* Karen Stoyanoff, Director of Recruitment for Graduate Enrollment, 508-767-7442, Fax: 508-799-4412, E-mail: graduate@assumption.edu.
Website: http://graduate.assumption.edu/mba/assumption-mba

Auburn University, Graduate School, College of Business, School of Accountancy, Auburn University, AL 36849. Offers M Acc. *Accreditation:* AACSB. *Program availability:* Part-time. *Faculty:* 17 full-time (9 women). *Students:* 64 full-time (25 women), 66 part-time (34 women); includes 16 minority (3 Black or African American, non-Hispanic/Latino; 1 American Indian or Alaska Native, non-Hispanic/Latino; 3 Asian, non-Hispanic/Latino; 6 Hispanic/Latino; 3 Two or more races, non-Hispanic/Latino), 1 international. Average age 29. 160 applicants, 66% accepted, 89 enrolled. In 2017, 97 master's awarded. *Entrance requirements:* For master's, GMAT, GRE General Test. Additional exam requirements/recommendations for international students: Required—TOEFL. *Application deadline:* Applications are processed on a rolling basis. Application fee: $50 ($60 for international students). Electronic applications accepted. *Expenses:* Tuition, state resident: full-time $10,974; part-time $519 per credit hour. Tuition, nonresident: full-time $29,658; part-time $1557 per credit hour. *Required fees:* $816 per semester. Tuition and fees vary according to degree level and program. *Financial support:* Teaching assistantships and Federal Work-Study available. Support available to part-time students. Financial award application deadline: 3/15; financial award applicants required to submit FAFSA. *Unit head:* Jennifer Mueller-Phillips, Director, 334-844-5827. *Application contact:* Dr. George Flowers, Dean of the Graduate School, 334-844-2125. Website: http://business.auburn.edu/academics/departments/school-of-accountancy

Auburn University at Montgomery, College of Business, School of Accountancy, Montgomery, AL 36124-4023. Offers M Acc. *Program availability:* Part-time. *Faculty:* 4 full-time (3 women), 1 part-time/adjunct (0 women). *Students:* 13 full-time (7 women), 31 part-time (18 women); includes 8 minority (4 Black or African American, non-Hispanic/Latino; 1 American Indian or Alaska Native, non-Hispanic/Latino; 2 Asian, non-Hispanic/Latino; 1 Two or more races, non-Hispanic/Latino), 9 international. Average age 28. 34 applicants, 85% accepted, 23 enrolled. In 2017, 10 master's awarded. *Entrance requirements:* For master's, GMAT. Additional exam requirements/recommendations for international students: Required—TOEFL (minimum score 500 paper-based; 61 iBT), IELTS (minimum score 5.5), PTE (minimum score 44). *Application deadline:* Applications are processed on a rolling basis. Application fee: $25 ($0 for international students). Electronic applications accepted. *Expenses:* Tuition, state resident: full-time $6930; part-time $385 per credit hour. Tuition, nonresident: full-time $15,588; part-time $866 per credit hour. *Required fees:* $640. *Financial support:* Scholarships/grants available. Financial award applicants required to submit FAFSA. *Application contact:* Rhonda Seay, Graduate Advisor, 334-244-3115, E-mail: rseay@aum.edu.
Website: http://business.aum.edu/academic-departments/accounting

Augustana University, Master of Professional Accountancy Program, Sioux Falls, SD 57197. Offers MPA. *Program availability:* Part-time. *Faculty:* 5 full-time (3 women), 1 (woman) part-time/adjunct. *Students:* 6 full-time (2 women), 1 part-time (0 women); includes 1 minority (Hispanic/Latino). Average age 23. 11 applicants, 100% accepted, 10 enrolled. In 2017, 2 master's awarded. *Entrance requirements:* For master's, GRE or GMAT, essay. Additional exam requirements/recommendations for international students: Required—TOEFL. *Application deadline:* For fall admission, 4/1 for domestic students. Application fee: $60. Electronic applications accepted. *Expenses:* Contact institution. *Financial support:* In 2017–18, 6 students received support. Scholarships/grants available. Financial award applicants required to submit FAFSA. *Unit head:* Laura Hybertson, Associate Professor, 605-274-5495, E-mail: laura.hybertson@augie.edu. *Application contact:* Julia Paluch, Administrative Assistant, Graduate Education, 605-274-4043, Fax: 605-274-4450, E-mail: julia.paluch@augie.edu.
Website: http://www.augie.edu/academics/majors-and-programs/master-professional-accountancy

Aurora University, Dunham School of Business and Public Policy, Aurora, IL 60506-4892. Offers accountancy (MS); business (MBA). *Program availability:* Part-time, evening/weekend, 100% online. *Faculty:* 4 full-time (0 women), 22 part-time/adjunct (9 women). *Students:* 193 full-time (106 women), 34 part-time (20 women); includes 83 minority (31 Black or African American, non-Hispanic/Latino; 6 Asian, non-Hispanic/Latino; 36 Hispanic/Latino; 1 Native Hawaiian or other Pacific Islander, non-Hispanic/Latino; 9 Two or more races, non-Hispanic/Latino), 2 international. Average age 33. 135 applicants, 100% accepted, 52 enrolled. In 2017, 122 master's awarded. *Entrance requirements:* For master's, minimum GPA of 3.0, 2 years of work experience, resume. Additional exam requirements/recommendations for international students: Required—TOEFL (minimum score 550 paper-based; 79 iBT). *Application deadline:* For fall admission, 6/1 for international students; for spring admission, 10/1 for international students. Applications are processed on a rolling basis. Application fee: $0. Electronic applications accepted. *Expenses:* Contact institution. *Financial support:* In 2017–18, 58 students received support. Federal Work-Study, scholarships/grants, and unspecified

assistantships available. Support available to part-time students. Financial award applicants required to submit FAFSA. *Unit head:* Dr. Toby Arquette, Dean, School of Business and Policy, 630-844-5614, E-mail: tarquett@aurora.edu. *Application contact:* Tom Gergits, Recruiter for Graduate Programs, 630-947-8945, E-mail: tgergits@aurora.edu.

Averett University, Master of Accountancy Program, Danville, VA 24541-3692. Offers M Acc. *Program availability:* Part-time, online only, 100% online. *Faculty:* 2 full-time (1 woman). *Students:* 6 part-time (4 women); includes 1 minority (Black or African American, non-Hispanic/Latino). Average age 24. 1 applicant, 100% accepted, 1 enrolled. *Degree requirements:* For master's, 30 credit hours, minimum GPA of 3.0 throughout program, completion of degree requirements within six years from start of program. *Entrance requirements:* For master's, GMAT, minimum cumulative GPA of 3.0, undergraduate degree in accounting, work experience. Additional exam requirements/recommendations for international students: Required—TOEFL. *Application deadline:* Applications are processed on a rolling basis. Electronic applications accepted. *Expenses:* $10,170. *Financial support:* In 2017–18, 1 student received support. Application deadline: 3/1; applicants required to submit FAFSA. *Unit head:* Dr. Peggy C. Wright, Director of the Master in Accountancy Program, 434-791-7118, E-mail: pwright@averett.edu. *Application contact:* Melissa Anderson, Director of Admissions, Graduate and Professional Studies, 804-729-8285, E-mail: manderson@averett.edu.

Avila University, School of Business, Kansas City, MO 64145-1698. Offers accounting (MBA); finance (MBA); health care administration (MBA); international business (MBA); management (MBA); management information systems (MBA); marketing (MBA). *Program availability:* Part-time, evening/weekend. *Faculty:* 6 full-time (2 women), 6 part-time/adjunct (2 women). *Students:* 49 full-time (19 women), 29 part-time (14 women); includes 16 minority (12 Black or African American, non-Hispanic/Latino; 1 Asian, non-Hispanic/Latino; 3 Hispanic/Latino), 19 international. Average age 32. 51 applicants, 47% accepted, 20 enrolled. In 2017, 31 master's awarded. *Degree requirements:* For master's, comprehensive exam, capstone course. *Entrance requirements:* For master's, GMAT (minimum score 420), minimum GPA of 3.0, interview. Additional exam requirements/recommendations for international students: Required—TOEFL (minimum score 550 paper-based). *Application deadline:* For fall admission, 7/30 priority date for domestic and international students; for winter admission, 11/30 priority date for domestic and international students; for spring admission, 2/28 priority date for domestic and international students; for summer admission, 6/1 priority date for domestic and international students. Applications are processed on a rolling basis. Application fee: $0. Electronic applications accepted. *Expenses:* Contact institution. *Financial support:* In 2017–18, 18 students received support. Career-related internships or fieldwork and scholarships/grants available. Support available to part-time students. Financial award applicants required to submit FAFSA. *Faculty research:* Leadership characteristics, financial hedging, group dynamics. *Unit head:* Dr. Wendy L. Acker, Interim Dean, 816-501-3720, Fax: 816-501-2463, E-mail: wendy.acker@avila.edu. *Application contact:* Brandon Black, MBA Admission Advisor, 816-501-3601, Fax: 816-501-2463, E-mail: brandon.black@avila.edu.
Website: https://www.avila.edu/mrk/mba

Azusa Pacific University, School of Business and Management, Azusa, CA 91702-7000. Offers accounting (MBA); business administration (MBA); entrepreneurship (MBA); finance (MBA); international business (MBA); marketing (MBA); organizational science (MBA); professional accountancy (M Acc); sport management (MBA). *Program availability:* Part-time, evening/weekend. *Degree requirements:* For master's, thesis (for some programs), final project. *Entrance requirements:* For master's, GMAT, minimum GPA of 3.0. Additional exam requirements/recommendations for international students: Required—TOEFL (minimum score 600 paper-based). *Expenses:* Contact institution. *Faculty research:* Gender issues, financial risk, leadership and ethics, marketing strategy.

Babson College, F. W. Olin Graduate School of Business, Babson Park, MA 02457-0310. Offers accounting (MSA); advanced management (Certificate); business administration (MBA); business analytics (MS); finance (MS); global entrepreneurship (MS); technological entrepreneurship (MS). *Accreditation:* AACSB. *Program availability:* Part-time, evening/weekend, online learning. *Entrance requirements:* For master's, GMAT, 2 years of work experience, resume, letters of recommendation. Additional exam requirements/recommendations for international students: Required—TOEFL (minimum score 100 iBT), IELTS (minimum score 6.5). Electronic applications accepted. *Faculty research:* Entrepreneurship, sustainability, global markets, process of innovation, social media and advertising.

Baker College Center for Graduate Studies–Online, Graduate Programs, Flint, MI 48507. Offers accounting (MBA); business administration (DBA); finance (MBA); general business (MBA); health care management (MBA); human resources management (MBA); information management (MBA); leadership studies (MBA); management information systems (MSIS); marketing (MBA). *Program availability:* Part-time, evening/weekend, online learning. *Degree requirements:* For master's, portfolio. *Entrance requirements:* For master's, 3 years of work experience, minimum undergraduate GPA of 2.5, writing sample, 3 letters of recommendation; for doctorate, MBA or acceptable related master's degree from accredited association, 5 years work experience, minimum graduate GPA of 3.25, writing sample, 3 professional references. Additional exam requirements/recommendations for international students: Required—TOEFL (minimum score 550 paper-based). Electronic applications accepted.

Baldwin Wallace University, Graduate Programs, School of Business, Program in Accounting, Berea, OH 44017-2088. Offers MBA. *Program availability:* Part-time, evening/weekend. *Students:* 8 full-time (3 women), 6 part-time (5 women); includes 1 minority (Hispanic/Latino). Average age 34. 7 applicants, 57% accepted, 2 enrolled. In 2017, 35 master's awarded. *Degree requirements:* For master's, minimum overall GPA of 3.0. *Entrance requirements:* For master's, GMAT or minimum undergraduate GPA of 3.0, minimum GPA of 3.0, work experience, bachelor's degree in any field, undergraduate accounting coursework. Additional exam requirements/recommendations for international students: Required—TOEFL (minimum score 550 paper-based; 79 iBT). *Application deadline:* For fall admission, 7/25 priority date for domestic students, 4/30 priority date for international students; for spring admission, 12/15 priority date for domestic students, 9/30 priority date for international students. Applications are processed on a rolling basis. Application fee: $25. Electronic applications accepted. Application fee is waived when completed online. *Expenses:* $948 per credit hour. *Financial support:* Applicants required to submit FAFSA. *Unit head:* Linda Chase, Professor/Chair, Accounting and Finance, 440-826-3039, Fax: 440-826-3868, E-mail: lichase@bw.edu. *Application contact:* Laura Spencer, Graduate Application Specialist, 440-826-2191, Fax: 440-826-3868, E-mail: lspencer@bw.edu.
Website: http://www.bw.edu/graduate/business/mba-accounting

Ball State University, Graduate School, Miller College of Business, Department of Accounting, Muncie, IN 47306. Offers MS. *Accreditation:* AACSB. *Program availability:* Part-time. *Faculty:* 3 full-time (1 woman). *Students:* 29 full-time (11 women), 3 part-time (2 women); includes 3 minority (1 Black or African American, non-Hispanic/Latino; 1 Asian, non-Hispanic/Latino; 1 Two or more races, non-Hispanic/Latino), 3 international. Average age 23. 42 applicants, 81% accepted, 31 enrolled. In 2017, 24 master's awarded. *Entrance requirements:* For master's, GMAT, minimum baccalaureate GPA of

2.75 or 3.0 in latter half of baccalaureate. Additional exam requirements/recommendations for international students: Required—TOEFL (minimum score 550 paper-based; 79 iBT), IELTS (minimum score 6.5). *Application deadline:* For fall admission, 7/1 for domestic students; for spring admission, 12/1 for domestic students; for summer admission, 4/1 for domestic students. Applications are processed on a rolling basis. Application fee: $60. Electronic applications accepted. *Expenses:* Contact institution. *Financial support:* In 2017–18, 3 students received support, including 3 teaching assistantships with partial tuition reimbursements available (averaging $13,183 per year); research assistantships with partial tuition reimbursements available and unspecified assistantships also available. Financial award application deadline: 3/1; financial award applicants required to submit FAFSA. *Unit head:* Dr. Mark Myring, Chairperson, 765-285-5100, Fax: 765-285-4312, E-mail: mmyring@bsu.edu. Website: http://www.bsu.edu/accounting

Barry University, Andreas School of Business, Program in Accounting, Miami Shores, FL 33161-6695. Offers MSA.

Baruch College of the City University of New York, Zicklin School of Business, Department of Accounting, Program in Accounting, New York, NY 10010-5585. Offers MBA, MS, PhD. PhD offered jointly with Graduate School and University Center of the City University of New York. *Accreditation:* AACSB. *Program availability:* Part-time, evening/weekend. *Degree requirements:* For doctorate, comprehensive exam, thesis/dissertation. *Entrance requirements:* For master's, GMAT, 2 letters of recommendation, resume, 2 years of work experience; for doctorate, GMAT. Additional exam requirements/recommendations for international students: Required—TOEFL (minimum score 590 paper-based), TWE (minimum score 5).

Bayamón Central University, Graduate Programs, Program in Business Administration, Bayamón, PR 00960-1725. Offers accounting (MBA); finance (MBA); general business (MBA); management (MBA); marketing (MBA). *Program availability:* Part-time, evening/weekend. *Degree requirements:* For master's, comprehensive exam (for some programs). *Entrance requirements:* For master's, EXADEP, bachelor's degree in business or related field.

Baylor University, Graduate School, Hankamer School of Business, Department of Accounting and Business Law, Waco, TX 76798. Offers M Acc, MT, JD/MT. *Accreditation:* AACSB. *Program availability:* Part-time. *Students:* 94 full-time (44 women), 17 part-time (14 women); includes 22 minority (2 Black or African American, non-Hispanic/Latino; 1 American Indian or Alaska Native, non-Hispanic/Latino; 5 Asian, non-Hispanic/Latino; 7 Hispanic/Latino; 7 Two or more races, non-Hispanic/Latino), 3 international. In 2017, 94 master's awarded. *Entrance requirements:* For master's, GMAT. Additional exam requirements/recommendations for international students: Required—TOEFL (minimum score 100 iBT). Application fee: $50. Electronic applications accepted. *Financial support:* Research assistantships, career-related internships or fieldwork, Federal Work-Study, and institutionally sponsored loans available. *Faculty research:* Financial reporting, auditing, professional skepticism, tax policy, international financial reporting. *Unit head:* Dr. Gia Chevis, Adviser, 254-710-1328, Fax: 254-710-1067, E-mail: gia_chevis@baylor.edu. *Application contact:* Drew Snyder, Assistant Director of Admissions, 254-710-6281, E-mail: drew_snyder@baylor.edu.

Bay Path University, Program in Accounting, Longmeadow, MA 01106-2292. Offers forensic accounting (MS); private accounting (MS); public accounting (tax and audit) (MS). *Program availability:* Part-time, online only, 100% online. *Students:* 3 full-time (1 woman), 17 part-time (all women); includes 5 minority (2 Black or African American, non-Hispanic/Latino; 1 Asian, non-Hispanic/Latino; 2 Hispanic/Latino). Average age 29. In 2017, 3 master's awarded. *Entrance requirements:* For master's, minimum GPA of 3.0; completion of accounting principles I and II, intermediate accounting, cost accounting, accounting information systems, auditing, federal taxation, business law, and managerial finance. *Application deadline:* Applications are processed on a rolling basis. Application fee: $45. Electronic applications accepted. Application fee is waived when completed online. *Expenses:* $815 per credit. *Financial support:* In 2017–18, 2 students received support. Scholarships/grants and unspecified assistantships available. Financial award applicants required to submit FAFSA. *Unit head:* Kara Stevens, Director, 413-565-1344, E-mail: kastevens@baypath.edu. *Application contact:* Diane Ranaldi, Dean of Graduate Admissions, 413-565-1332, Fax: 413-565-1250, E-mail: dranaldi@baypath.edu. Website: http://graduate.baypath.edu/graduate-programs/programs-online/ms-programs/accounting

Belmont University, Jack C. Massey Graduate School of Business, Nashville, TN 37212. Offers accounting (M Acc); business (AMBA, PMBA); healthcare (MBA). *Accreditation:* AACSB. *Program availability:* Part-time, evening/weekend. *Faculty:* 29 full-time (9 women), 7 part-time/adjunct (3 women). *Students:* 163 full-time (72 women), 42 part-time (19 women); includes 36 minority (13 Black or African American, non-Hispanic/Latino; 9 Asian, non-Hispanic/Latino; 5 Hispanic/Latino; 9 Two or more races, non-Hispanic/Latino), 10 international. Average age 30. 135 applicants, 96% accepted, 102 enrolled. In 2017, 110 master's awarded. *Entrance requirements:* For master's, GMAT, 2 years of work experience (MBA). Additional exam requirements/recommendations for international students: Required—TOEFL (minimum score 550 paper-based). *Application deadline:* For fall admission, 7/1 for domestic and international students; for spring admission, 11/1 for domestic and international students. Applications are processed on a rolling basis. Application fee: $50. Electronic applications accepted. *Expenses:* Contact institution. *Financial support:* In 2017–18, 86 students received support. Scholarships/grants, tuition waivers (partial), and unspecified assistantships available. Financial award application deadline: 7/1; financial award applicants required to submit FAFSA. *Faculty research:* Music business, strategy, ethics, finance, accounting systems. *Unit head:* Dr. Patrick Raines, Dean, 615-460-6480, Fax: 615-460-6455, E-mail: pat.raines@belmont.edu. *Application contact:* 615-460-6480, E-mail: masseyadmissions@belmont.edu.

Benedictine University, Graduate Programs, Program in Accountancy, Lisle, IL 60532. Offers MS. *Program availability:* Evening/weekend. *Entrance requirements:* For master's, official transcripts, 2 letters of reference, resume. Additional exam requirements/recommendations for international students: Required—TOEFL. Electronic applications accepted.

Benedictine University, Graduate Programs, Program in Business Administration, Lisle, IL 60532. Offers accounting (MBA); entrepreneurship and managing innovation (MBA); financial management (MBA); health administration (MBA); human resource management (MBA); information systems security (MBA); international business (MBA); management consulting (MBA); management information systems (MBA); marketing management (MBA); operations management and logistics (MBA); organizational leadership (MBA). *Program availability:* Part-time, evening/weekend, online learning. *Entrance requirements:* For master's, GMAT. Additional exam requirements/recommendations for international students: Required—TOEFL (minimum score 550 paper-based). Electronic applications accepted. *Faculty research:* Strategic leadership in professional organizations, sociology of professions, organizational change, social identity theory, applications to change management.

Bentley University, McCallum Graduate School of Business, Master's Program in Accounting, Waltham, MA 02452-4705. Offers MSA. *Accreditation:* AACSB. *Program availability:* Part-time, evening/weekend. *Faculty:* 71 full-time (25 women), 33 part-time/adjunct (15 women). *Students:* 196 full-time (138 women), 51 part-time (31 women); includes 31 minority (3 Black or African American, non-Hispanic/Latino; 1 American Indian or Alaska Native, non-Hispanic/Latino; 20 Asian, non-Hispanic/Latino; 5 Hispanic/Latino; 2 Two or more races, non-Hispanic/Latino), 145 international. Average age 25. 317 applicants, 85% accepted, 108 enrolled. In 2017, 149 master's awarded. *Entrance requirements:* For master's, GMAT or GRE General Test, current resume; two letters of recommendation; official copies of all university-level transcripts; 2 essays; online interview (for international students). Additional exam requirements/recommendations for international students: Required—TOEFL (minimum score 100) or IELTS (minimum score 7). *Application deadline:* Applications are processed on a rolling basis. Application fee: $75. Electronic applications accepted. *Expenses: Tuition:* Part-time $4445 per course. *Required fees:* $170 per unit. *Financial support:* In 2017–18, 74 students received support. Scholarships/grants and unspecified assistantships available. Financial award application deadline: 6/1; financial award applicants required to submit FAFSA. *Faculty research:* Audit risk assessment; ethics in accounting; corporate governance; accounting information systems and management control; tax policy, forensic accounting. *Unit head:* Leonard Pepe, Lecturer, 781-891-2470, E-mail: lpepe@bentley.edu. *Application contact:* Graduate Admissions, 781-891-2108, Fax: 781-891-2464, E-mail: applygrad@bentley.edu. Website: https://admissions.bentley.edu/graduate/masters-in-accounting

Bentley University, McCallum Graduate School of Business, PhD Program in Accountancy, Waltham, MA 02452-4705. Offers PhD. *Faculty:* 11 full-time (4 women). *Students:* 6 full-time (all women), 2 international. Average age 28. 39 applicants, 10% accepted, 4 enrolled. In 2017, 5 doctorates awarded. *Degree requirements:* For doctorate, comprehensive exam, thesis/dissertation. *Entrance requirements:* For doctorate, GMAT or GRE General Test, master's degree; official copies of transcripts; research paper; personal statement; 3 letters of recommendation; curriculum vitae; interview. Additional exam requirements/recommendations for international students: Required—TOEFL. *Application deadline:* For fall admission, 1/15 for domestic and international students. Electronic applications accepted. *Expenses: Tuition:* Part-time $4445 per course. *Required fees:* $170 per unit. *Financial support:* In 2017–18, 12 students received support. Scholarships/grants available. Financial award application deadline: 6/1; financial award applicants required to submit FAFSA. *Faculty research:* Auditing; accounting information systems; capital markets; governance and control; judgment and decision-making. *Unit head:* Patricia A. Caffrey, Administrative Director of PhD Programs, 781-891-2541, E-mail: pacaffrey@bentley.edu. *Application contact:* PhD Program Office, 781-891-2404, E-mail: phd@bentley.edu. Website: https://www.bentley.edu/offices/phd/phd-accountancy

Binghamton University, State University of New York, Graduate School, School of Management, Program in Accounting, Binghamton, NY 13902-6000. Offers MS. *Program availability:* Part-time, evening/weekend. *Students:* 170 full-time (107 women), 20 part-time (16 women); includes 48 minority (2 Black or African American, non-Hispanic/Latino; 30 Asian, non-Hispanic/Latino; 8 Hispanic/Latino; 8 Two or more races, non-Hispanic/Latino), 88 international. Average age 24. 333 applicants, 67% accepted, 115 enrolled. In 2017, 215 master's awarded. *Entrance requirements:* For master's, GMAT. Additional exam requirements/recommendations for international students: Required—TOEFL (minimum score 90 iBT). *Application deadline:* For fall admission, 3/1 priority date for domestic and international students. Application fee: $75. Electronic applications accepted. *Financial support:* In 2017–18, 9 students received support, including 6 teaching assistantships (averaging $10,000 per year); career-related internships or fieldwork, Federal Work-Study, institutionally sponsored loans, scholarships/grants, health care benefits, and unspecified assistantships also available. Financial award applicants required to submit FAFSA. *Unit head:* Dr. Upinder Dhillon, Dean of School of Management, 607-777-2314, E-mail: dhillon@binghamton.edu. *Application contact:* Ben Balkaya, Assistant Dean and Director, 607-777-2151, Fax: 607-777-2501, E-mail: balkaya@binghamton.edu.

Bloomfield College, Program in Accounting, Bloomfield, NJ 07003-9981. Offers MS.

Bloomsburg University of Pennsylvania, School of Graduate Studies, Zeigler College of Business, Program in Accounting, Bloomsburg, PA 17815-1301. Offers M Acc. *Program availability:* Part-time, evening/weekend. *Faculty:* 3 full-time (2 women). *Students:* 14 full-time (7 women), 1 part-time (0 women); includes 1 minority (Hispanic/Latino). Average age 22. 23 applicants, 74% accepted, 15 enrolled. In 2017, 12 master's awarded. *Degree requirements:* For master's, minimum QPA of 3.0. *Entrance requirements:* For master's, GRE/GMAT (waived for BU accounting majors with minimum GPA of 3.0 in accounting classes and overall), 2 letters of recommendation, resume. Additional exam requirements/recommendations for international students: Required—TOEFL, IELTS. *Application deadline:* Applications are processed on a rolling basis. Application fee: $35 ($60 for international students). Electronic applications accepted. *Expenses: Tuition,* state resident: full-time $10,000; part-time $500 per credit hour. Tuition, nonresident: full-time $15,000; part-time $750 per credit hour. *Required fees:* $2484; $110.75 per credit hour. $75 per term. Tuition and fees vary according to program. *Financial support:* Federal Work-Study, scholarships/grants, and unspecified assistantships available. *Unit head:* Dr. Todd Shawver, Chair, 570-389-5322, Fax: 570-389-3892, E-mail: tshawver@bloomu.edu. *Application contact:* Jennifer Kessler, Administrative Assistant, 570-389-4015, Fax: 570-389-3054, E-mail: jkessler@bloomu.edu. Website: http://www.bloomu.edu/gradschool/accounting

Bluffton University, Programs in Business, Bluffton, OH 45817. Offers accounting and financial management (MBA); health care management (MBA); leadership (MAOM, MBA); production and operations management (MBA); sustainability management (MBA). *Program availability:* Evening/weekend, blended/hybrid learning, videoconference. *Faculty:* 5 full-time (2 women), 8 part-time/adjunct (2 women). *Students:* 48 full-time (31 women); includes 11 minority (5 Black or African American, non-Hispanic/Latino; 1 Asian, non-Hispanic/Latino; 3 Hispanic/Latino; 2 Two or more races, non-Hispanic/Latino), 1 international. Average age 33. 44 applicants, 70% accepted, 26 enrolled. In 2017, 41 master's awarded. *Degree requirements:* For master's, integrated research project (for some programs). *Entrance requirements:* For master's, current resume, official transcript, bachelor's degree, minimum GPA of 3.0, personal essay. Additional exam requirements/recommendations for international students: Recommended—TOEFL (minimum score 550 paper-based). *Application deadline:* For fall admission, 7/31 priority date for domestic and international students. Applications are processed on a rolling basis. Application fee: $0. Electronic applications accepted. *Expenses:* $550 per credit hour, $150 per semester technology fee, $25 per semester payment plan fee. *Financial support:* Unspecified assistantships and faculty/staff grants available. Financial award applicants required to submit FAFSA. *Unit head:* Dr. Melissa Green, Director of Graduate Programs in Business, 419-358-3447, E-mail: greenm@bluffton.edu. *Application contact:* Carrie Mast, Administrative Assistant, Graduate Programs in Business, 419-358-3065, E-mail: mastc@bluffton.edu. Website: http://www.bluffton.edu/grad/

Accounting

Bob Jones University, Graduate Programs, Greenville, SC 29614. Offers accountancy (MS); Bible (MA); Bible translation (MA); Biblical studies (Certificate); broadcast management (MS); business administration (MBA); church history (MA, PhD); church ministries (MA); church music (MM); cinema and video production (MA); counseling (MS); curriculum and instruction (Ed D); divinity (M Div); dramatic production (MA); educational leadership (MS, Ed D, Ed S); elementary education (M Ed, MAT); English (M Ed, MA, MAT); fine arts (MA); graphic design (MA); history (M Ed, MA); illustration (MA); interpretative speech (MA); mathematics (M Ed, MAT); medical missions (Certificate); ministry (MM, D Min); multi-categorical special education (M Ed, MAT); music (M Ed); New Testament interpretation (PhD); Old Testament interpretation (PhD); orchestral instrument performance (MM); organ performance (MM); pastoral studies (MA); personnel services (MS, Ed S); piano pedagogy (MM); piano performance (MM); platform arts (MA); radio and television broadcasting (MS); rhetoric and public address (MA); secondary education (M Ed); studio art (MA); teaching Bible (MA); theology (MA, PhD); voice performance (MM); youth ministries (MA); M Div/MM.

Boise State University, College of Business and Economics, Department of Accountancy, Boise, ID 83725-0399. Offers accountancy (MSA); accountancy taxation (MSAT). *Accreditation:* AACSB. *Program availability:* Part-time. *Faculty:* 7. *Students:* 18 full-time (8 women), 28 part-time (13 women); includes 5 minority (2 Asian, non-Hispanic/Latino; 3 Hispanic/Latino), 1 international. Average age 32. 27 applicants, 74% accepted, 12 enrolled. In 2017, 27 master's awarded. *Entrance requirements:* For master's, GMAT, minimum GPA of 3.0. Additional exam requirements/recommendations for international students: Required—TOEFL (minimum score 587 paper-based; 95 iBT), IELTS (minimum score 6.5). *Application deadline:* For fall admission, 6/1 for domestic and international students; for spring admission, 10/1 for domestic and international students; for summer admission, 3/1 for domestic and international students. Application fee: $65 ($95 for international students). Electronic applications accepted. *Expenses:* Tuition, state resident: full-time $6471; part-time $390 per credit. Tuition, nonresident: full-time $21,787; part-time $685 per credit. *Required fees:* $2283; $100 per term. Part-time tuition and fees vary according to course load and program. *Financial support:* Scholarships/grants and unspecified assistantships available. Financial award application deadline: 2/15; financial award applicants required to submit FAFSA. *Unit head:* Dr. Troy Hyatt, Director, 208-426-3412, E-mail: troyhyatt@boisestate.edu. *Application contact:* Trisha Stevens Lamb, Program Director, 208-426-1120, E-mail: trishastevenslamb@boisestate.edu.
Website: https://cobe.boisestate.edu/graduate-programs-overview/

Boston College, Carroll School of Management, Programs in Accounting, Chestnut Hill, MA 02467-3800. Offers MSA. *Entrance requirements:* For master's, GMAT, GRE, recommendations, resume, transcript. Additional exam requirements/recommendations for international students: Required—TOEFL (minimum score 600 paper-based; 100 iBT), IELTS (minimum score 7.5), or PTE (minimum score 68). Electronic applications accepted. *Faculty research:* Financial reporting, auditing, tax planning, financial statement analysis.

Bowling Green State University, Graduate College, College of Business, Program in Accountancy, Bowling Green, OH 43403. Offers M Acc. *Accreditation:* AACSB. *Program availability:* Part-time. *Degree requirements:* For master's, thesis or alternative. *Entrance requirements:* For master's, GMAT. Additional exam requirements/recommendations for international students: Required—TOEFL. Electronic applications accepted. *Faculty research:* Financial reporting and auditing, accounting information systems, taxation.

Bradley University, The Graduate School, Foster College of Business, Program in Accounting, Peoria, IL 61625-0002. Offers MSA. *Accreditation:* AACSB. *Program availability:* Part-time, evening/weekend. *Degree requirements:* For master's, comprehensive exam. *Entrance requirements:* For master's, GMAT, 2 letters of recommendation. Additional exam requirements/recommendations for international students: Required—TOEFL (minimum score 550 paper-based; 79 iBT), IELTS (minimum score 6.5). Electronic applications accepted.

Brandman University, School of Business and Professional Studies, Irvine, CA 92618. Offers accounting (MBA); business administration (MBA); business intelligence and data analytics (MBA); e-business strategic management (MBA); entrepreneurship (MBA); finance (MBA); health administration (MBA); human resources (MBA, MS); international business (MBA); marketing (MBA); organizational leadership (MA, MBA, MPA); public administration (MPA). *Expenses: Tuition:* Part-time $640 per credit hour. Tuition and fees vary according to degree level and program. *Unit head:* Dr. Glenn Worthington, Dean, 253-861-1024, E-mail: gworthin@brandman.edu. *Application contact:* Dr. Glenn Worthington, Dean, 253-861-1024, E-mail: gworthin@brandman.edu.
Website: https://www.brandman.edu/academic-programs/business-and-professional-studies

Brenau University, Sydney O. Smith Graduate School, College of Business and Mass Communication, Gainesville, GA 30501. Offers accounting (MBA); business administration (MBA); healthcare management (MBA); organizational leadership (MS); project management (MBA). *Accreditation:* ACBSP. *Program availability:* Part-time, evening/weekend, online learning. *Degree requirements:* For master's, comprehensive exam (for some programs). *Entrance requirements:* For master's, resume, minimum undergraduate GPA of 2.5. Additional exam requirements/recommendations for international students: Required—TOEFL (minimum score 500 paper-based; 61 iBT); Recommended—IELTS (minimum score 5). Electronic applications accepted. *Expenses:* Contact institution.

Bridgewater State University, College of Graduate Studies, Ricciardi College of Business, Department of Accounting and Finance, Bridgewater, MA 02325. Offers MSM. *Program availability:* Part-time, evening/weekend. *Entrance requirements:* For master's, GMAT.

Brock University, Faculty of Graduate Studies, Faculty of Business, Program in Accountancy, St. Catharines, ON L2S 3A1, Canada. Offers M Acc. *Degree requirements:* For master's, thesis or alternative. *Entrance requirements:* For master's, honours degree. Additional exam requirements/recommendations for international students: Required—TOEFL (minimum score 550 paper-based; 80 iBT), IELTS (minimum score 6.5), TWE (minimum score 4.5). Electronic applications accepted.

Brooklyn College of the City University of New York, School of Business, Brooklyn, NY 11210-2889. Offers accounting (MS); business administration (MS), including economic analysis, general business, global business and finance. *Program availability:* Part-time, evening/weekend. *Degree requirements:* For master's, comprehensive exam, thesis or alternative. *Entrance requirements:* For master's, GMAT, 2 letters of recommendation. Additional exam requirements/recommendations for international students: Required—TOEFL (minimum score 550 paper-based; 79 iBT). Electronic applications accepted. *Faculty research:* Econometrics, environmental economics, microeconomics, macroeconomics, taxation.

Bryant University, Graduate School of Business, Smithfield, RI 02917. Offers accounting (MPAC); business administration (MBA), including business analytics, general management, global finance, global supply chain management, international business; taxation (MST). *Program availability:* Part-time, 100% online. *Faculty:* 30 full-time (5 women), 7 part-time/adjunct (2 women). *Students:* 84 full-time (31 women), 91 part-time (35 women); includes 24 minority (4 Black or African American, non-Hispanic/

Latino; 1 American Indian or Alaska Native, non-Hispanic/Latino; 6 Asian, non-Hispanic/Latino; 8 Hispanic/Latino; 5 Two or more races, non-Hispanic/Latino), 6 international. Average age 26. 215 applicants, 66% accepted, 96 enrolled. In 2017, 118 master's awarded. *Degree requirements:* For master's, comprehensive exam (for some programs). *Entrance requirements:* For master's, GMAT, resume, recommendation, college transcripts. Additional exam requirements/recommendations for international students: Required—TOEFL (minimum score 580 paper-based; 95 iBT). *Application deadline:* For fall admission, 7/15 for domestic and international students; for spring admission, 11/15 for domestic and international students; for summer admission, 4/15 for domestic and international students. Applications are processed on a rolling basis. Application fee: $80. Electronic applications accepted. *Expenses:* $45,102 total, $1,118 per credit hour, $1,500 study abroad fee (for full-time MBA); $40,248 total, $1,118 per credit hour (for part-time MBA); $30,280 total, $1,176 per credit hour (for MP Ac and MST); $13,146, $1,118 per credit hour (for CGS). *Financial support:* In 2017–18, 95 fellowships with full and partial tuition reimbursements (averaging $9,825 per year), 9 research assistantships with full and partial tuition reimbursements (averaging $7,100 per year) were awarded; scholarships/grants and unspecified assistantships also available. Support available to part-time students. Financial award application deadline: 2/15; financial award applicants required to submit FAFSA. *Faculty research:* International business, public sector auditing, taxation of partnerships, information systems security, financial markets microstructure. *Unit head:* Bjorn Carlsson, Graduate Program Director, 401-232-6707, E-mail: bcarlsson@bryant.edu. *Application contact:* Terri Rogers, Admissions Assistant, 401-232-6230, Fax: 401-232-6494, E-mail: graduateprograms@bryant.edu.
Website: http://gradschool.bryant.edu/business/

Butler University, Lacy School of Business, Indianapolis, IN 46208-3485. Offers entrepreneurship and innovation (MBA); finance (MBA); international business (MBA); leadership (MBA); marketing (MBA); professional accounting (MP Ac). *Accreditation:* AACSB. *Program availability:* Part-time. *Faculty:* 14 full-time (4 women), 9 part-time/adjunct (2 women). *Students:* 35 full-time (16 women), 111 part-time (38 women); includes 15 minority (2 Black or African American, non-Hispanic/Latino; 5 Asian, non-Hispanic/Latino; 8 Hispanic/Latino), 6 international. Average age 30. 149 applicants, 64% accepted, 43 enrolled. In 2017, 90 master's awarded. *Degree requirements:* For master's, comprehensive exam, thesis optional. *Entrance requirements:* For master's, GMAT, minimum AACSB index of 950, personal statement, two letters of recommendation, official transcripts, current resume. Additional exam requirements/recommendations for international students: Required—TOEFL (minimum score 550 paper-based; 79 iBT), IELTS (minimum score 6), Michigan English Language Assessment Battery (minimum score of 80). *Application deadline:* For fall admission, 8/1 for domestic and international students; for spring admission, 12/1 for domestic and international students; for summer admission, 4/1 for domestic and international students. Applications are processed on a rolling basis. Application fee: $0. Electronic applications accepted. *Expenses:* $820 per credit. *Financial support:* In 2017–18, 22 students received support. Scholarships/grants, tuition waivers (full and partial), and unspecified assistantships available. Financial award application deadline: 7/15; financial award applicants required to submit FAFSA. *Faculty research:* Higher education and pedagogy; ecotourism; healthcare issues and marketing public policy; domestic public policy, international finance and banking, international and management entrepreneurship, organizational management. *Unit head:* Dr. Stephen Standifird, Dean, 317-940-6307. *Application contact:* Diane Dubord, Graduate Student Service Specialist, 317-940-8107, Fax: 317-940-8250, E-mail: ddubord@butler.edu.
Website: https://www.butler.edu/lacyschool

Cabrini University, Academic Affairs, Radnor, PA 19087. Offers accounting (M Acc); autism spectrum disorder (M Ed); biological sciences (MS), including civic leadership; criminology and criminal justice (MA); curriculum, instruction, and assessment (M Ed); educational leadership (M Ed, Ed D), including curriculum and instructional leadership (Ed D), preK-12 leadership (Ed D); English as a second language (M Ed); organizational leadership (DBA, PhD); preK to 4 (M Ed); reading specialist (M Ed); secondary education (M Ed), including biology, chemistry, English, English/communication, mathematics, social studies; special education grades 7-12 (M Ed); special education preK-8 (M Ed); teaching and learning (M Ed). *Program availability:* Part-time, evening/weekend. *Faculty:* 23 full-time (17 women), 46 part-time/adjunct (38 women). *Students:* 60 full-time (35 women), 559 part-time (435 women); includes 93 minority (66 Black or African American, non-Hispanic/Latino; 1 American Indian or Alaska Native, non-Hispanic/Latino; 8 Asian, non-Hispanic/Latino; 15 Hispanic/Latino; 3 Two or more races, non-Hispanic/Latino), 4 international. Average age 33. 290 applicants, 82% accepted, 154 enrolled. In 2017, 283 master's awarded. *Degree requirements:* For master's, comprehensive exam (for some programs), thesis (for some programs); for doctorate, comprehensive exam (for some programs), thesis/dissertation. *Entrance requirements:* For master's, professional resume, personal statement, two recommendations, official transcripts; for doctorate, official transcripts, minimum master's GPA of 3.0, two recommendations, interview with admissions committee. Additional exam requirements/recommendations for international students: Required—TOEFL (minimum score 80 iBT). *Application deadline:* For fall admission, 8/26 for domestic students, 8/1 for international students; for winter admission, 1/13 for domestic students, 12/20 for international students; for spring admission, 1/13 for domestic students, 12/20 for international students; for summer admission, 5/20 for domestic students, 4/30 for international students. Applications are processed on a rolling basis. Application fee: $50. Electronic applications accepted. Application fee is waived when completed online. *Expenses:* Contact institution. *Financial support:* In 2017–18, 1,459 students received support. Tuition waivers and unspecified assistantships available. Financial award application deadline: 5/1; financial award applicants required to submit FAFSA. *Unit head:* Dr. Maliha Zaman, 610-902-8502, Fax: 610-902-8797, E-mail: msz37@cabrini.edu. *Application contact:* Diane Greenwood, Director of Graduate Admissions, 610-902-8291, E-mail: diane.l.greenwood@cabrini.edu.
Website: http://cabrini.edu/graduate

Cairn University, School of Business, Langhorne, PA 19047-2990. Offers accounting (MBA); business administration (MBA); international entrepreneurship (MBA); nonprofit leadership (MBA); organizational leadership (MSOL, Postbaccalaureate Certificate). *Program availability:* Part-time, evening/weekend, 100% online, blended/hybrid learning. *Entrance requirements:* Additional exam requirements/recommendations for international students: Required—TOEFL (minimum score 550 paper-based). Electronic applications accepted. Application fee is waived when completed online. *Expenses:* Contact institution.

Caldwell University, School of Business and CIS, Caldwell, NJ 07006-6195. Offers accounting (MS); business administration (MBA). *Accreditation:* ACBSP. *Program availability:* Part-time. *Faculty:* 8 full-time (4 women), 12 part-time/adjunct (2 women). *Students:* 23 full-time (14 women), 54 part-time (37 women); includes 25 minority (11 Black or African American, non-Hispanic/Latino; 2 Asian, non-Hispanic/Latino; 11 Hispanic/Latino; 1 Two or more races, non-Hispanic/Latino), 4 international. Average age 31. 39 applicants, 100% accepted, 23 enrolled. In 2017, 20 master's awarded. *Entrance requirements:* For master's, undergraduate accounting, marketing, economics, and finance; minimum three years' relevant experience. Additional exam requirements/recommendations for international students: Required—TOEFL (minimum score 580 paper-based). *Application deadline:* Applications are processed on a rolling basis. Application fee: $50. Electronic applications accepted. *Expenses:* $975 per credit, $225 comprehensive fee per semester. *Financial support:* 1 general assistantship available. *Unit head:* Bernard O'Rourke, Associate Dean, 973-618-3409, Fax: 973-618-3355, E-mail: borourke@caldwell.edu. *Application contact:* Tom Disch, Senior Admissions Counselor, 973-618-3544, E-mail: graduate@caldwell.edu.

California Baptist University, Program in Accounting, Riverside, CA 92504-3206. Offers MS. *Program availability:* Part-time, evening/weekend, online only, 100% online. *Faculty:* 8 full-time (2 women). *Students:* 11 full-time (6 women), 15 part-time (11 women); includes 11 minority (1 Black or African American, non-Hispanic/Latino; 9 Hispanic/Latino; 1 Two or more races, non-Hispanic/Latino). Average age 31. 48 applicants, 56% accepted, 10 enrolled. In 2017, 12 master's awarded. *Degree requirements:* For master's, interdisciplinary capstone project. *Entrance requirements:* For master's, minimum cumulative GPA of 2.5, prerequisite courses completed with minimum C grade, two letters of recommendation, 500-word essay, current resume. Additional exam requirements/recommendations for international students: Required—TOEFL (minimum score 80 iBT). *Application deadline:* For fall admission, 8/1 priority date for domestic students, 7/1 priority date for international students; for spring admission, 12/1 priority date for domestic students, 11/1 priority date for international students. Applications are processed on a rolling basis. Application fee: $45. Electronic applications accepted. Application fee is waived when completed online. *Expenses:* Contact institution. *Financial support:* In 2017–18, 7 students received support. Federal Work-Study and scholarships/grants available. Financial award applicants required to submit CSS PROFILE or FAFSA. *Faculty research:* Financial stability, social entrepreneurship, cross-sector collaboration, business and government relations. *Unit head:* Dr. David Poole, Vice President, Online and Professional Studies, 951-343-3902, E-mail: dpoole@calbaptist.edu. *Application contact:* Karin Nelson, Program Director, Accounting, 951-552-8777, E-mail: knelson@calbaptist.edu.
Website: http://www.cbuonline.edu/programs/master-of-science-in-accounting

California Baptist University, Program in Business Administration, Riverside, CA 92504-3206. Offers accounting (MBA); construction management (MBA); healthcare management (MBA); management (MBA). *Accreditation:* ACBSP. *Program availability:* Part-time, evening/weekend, 100% online, blended/hybrid learning. *Faculty:* 19 full-time (7 women), 18 part-time/adjunct (6 women). *Students:* 123 full-time (64 women), 101 part-time (55 women); includes 108 minority (22 Black or African American, non-Hispanic/Latino; 15 Asian, non-Hispanic/Latino; 62 Hispanic/Latino; 1 Native Hawaiian or other Pacific Islander, non-Hispanic/Latino; 8 Two or more races, non-Hispanic/Latino), 29 international. Average age 30. 285 applicants, 62% accepted, 142 enrolled. In 2017, 147 master's awarded. *Degree requirements:* For master's, interdisciplinary capstone project. *Entrance requirements:* For master's, GMAT, minimum GPA of 2.5; two recommendations; comprehensive essay; resume; interview. Additional exam requirements/recommendations for international students: Required—TOEFL (minimum score 80 iBT). *Application deadline:* For fall admission, 8/1 priority date for domestic students, 7/1 for international students; for spring admission, 12/1 priority date for domestic students, 11/1 for international students. Applications are processed on a rolling basis. Application fee: $45. Electronic applications accepted. *Expenses:* Contact institution. *Financial support:* In 2017–18, 38 students received support. Federal Work-Study and scholarships/grants available. Financial award applicants required to submit CSS PROFILE or FAFSA. *Faculty research:* Behavioral economics, economic indicators, marketing ethics, international business, microfinance. *Unit head:* Dr. Andrea Scott, Dean, School of Business, 951-343-4701, Fax: 951-343-4361, E-mail: ascott@calbaptist.edu. *Application contact:* Deanna Meyer, Graduate Admissions Counselor, 951-343-4463, E-mail: dmeyer@calbaptist.edu.
Website: http://www.calbaptist.edu/mba/about/

California Polytechnic State University, San Luis Obispo, Orfalea College of Business, Program in Accounting, San Luis Obispo, CA 93407. Offers MS. *Students:* 25 full-time (14 women), 1 part-time (0 women); includes 8 minority (2 Asian, non-Hispanic/Latino; 5 Hispanic/Latino; 1 Two or more races, non-Hispanic/Latino). Average age 23. In 2017, 33 master's awarded. *Degree requirements:* For master's, comprehensive exam (for some programs), thesis (for some programs). *Entrance requirements:* For master's, GMAT. Additional exam requirements/recommendations for international students: Required—TOEFL (minimum score 80 iBT). *Application deadline:* For fall admission, 4/1 for domestic students, 3/1 for international students. Applications are processed on a rolling basis. *Expenses:* Tuition, state resident: full-time $7176; part-time $4164 per year. *Required fees:* $3690; $3219 per year. $1073 per trimester. *Financial support:* Fellowships, career-related internships or fieldwork, Federal Work-Study, institutionally sponsored loans, scholarships/grants, and unspecified assistantships available. Support available to part-time students. Financial award application deadline: 3/2; financial award applicants required to submit FAFSA. *Faculty research:* Management of high-tech firms, Pacific Rim, capital market structures, economics of environmental policy, marketing of services. *Unit head:* Dr. Scott Dawson, Dean, 805-756-2705, E-mail: scdawson@calpoly.edu. *Application contact:* Dr. Sanjiv Jaggia, Associate Dean, Graduate Programs, 805-756-7519, E-mail: sjaggia@calpoly.edu.
Website: http://www.cob.calpoly.edu/gradbusiness/degree-programs/ms-accounting/

California State Polytechnic University, Pomona, Master of Science in Business Administration Program, Pomona, CA 91768-2557. Offers information systems auditing (MS). *Accreditation:* AACSB. *Program availability:* Part-time, evening/weekend. *Students:* 5 part-time (2 women); includes 3 minority (1 Asian, non-Hispanic/Latino; 2 Hispanic/Latino), 1 international. Average age 28. 24 applicants, 38% accepted, 5 enrolled. In 2017, 4 master's awarded. *Entrance requirements:* Additional exam requirements/recommendations for international students: Required—TOEFL (minimum score 550 paper-based). *Application deadline:* Applications are processed on a rolling basis. Application fee: $55. Electronic applications accepted. *Expenses:* Contact institution. *Financial support:* Application deadline: 3/2; applicants required to submit FAFSA. *Unit head:* Dr. Tarique Hossain, Associate Professor/Director of Graduate Programs, 909-869-2362, Fax: 909-869-4559, E-mail: tmhossain@cpp.edu. *Application contact:* Deborah L. Brandon, Executive Director of Admissions and Enrollment Planning, 909-869-3427, Fax: 909-869-5315, E-mail: dlbrandon@cpp.edu.
Website: http://www.cpp.edu/~cba/graduate-business-programs/programs/MSBA.shtml

California State Polytechnic University, Pomona, Program in Accountancy, Pomona, CA 91768-2557. Offers MS. *Program availability:* Part-time, evening/weekend. *Students:* 14 full-time (5 women), 7 part-time (4 women); includes 10 minority (5 Asian, non-Hispanic/Latino; 5 Hispanic/Latino), 6 international. Average age 27. 51 applicants, 51% accepted, 14 enrolled. In 2017, 12 master's awarded. *Entrance requirements:* Additional exam requirements/recommendations for international students: Required—TOEFL (minimum score 550 paper-based). *Application deadline:* Applications are processed on a rolling basis. Application fee: $55. Electronic applications accepted. *Expenses:* Contact institution. *Financial support:* Application deadline: 3/2; applicants required to submit FAFSA. *Unit head:* Dr. Meihua Koo, Assistant Professor/MSA Coordinator, 909-869-4531, Fax: 909-869-4511, E-mail: mkoo@cpp.edu. *Application contact:* Deborah L. Brandon, Executive Director of Admissions and Enrollment Planning, 909-869-3427, Fax: 909-869-5315, E-mail: dlbrandon@cpp.edu.
Website: http://www.cpp.edu/~ceu/degree-programs/accountancy/index.shtml

California State University, East Bay, Office of Graduate Studies, College of Business and Economics, Department of Accounting and Finance, Hayward, CA 94542-3000. Offers accountancy (MS). *Program availability:* Part-time, evening/weekend. *Students:* 63 applicants, 19% accepted. In 2017, 33 master's awarded. *Degree requirements:* For master's, comprehensive exam or thesis. *Entrance requirements:* For master's, GMAT, minimum GPA of 2.75. Additional exam requirements/recommendations for international students: Required—TOEFL (minimum score 550 paper-based). *Application deadline:* For fall admission, 6/1 for domestic and international students. Applications are processed on a rolling basis. Application fee: $55. Electronic applications accepted. *Financial support:* Career-related internships or fieldwork, Federal Work-Study, and institutionally sponsored loans available. Support available to part-time students. Financial award application deadline: 3/2; financial award applicants required to submit FAFSA. *Unit head:* Nancy Mangold, Chair, 510-885-3315, Fax: 510-885-4796, E-mail: nancy.mangold@csueastbay.edu. *Application contact:* Philip Cole-Regis, Administrative Support Coordinator, 510-885-3286, E-mail: philip.coleregis@csueastbay.edu.
Website: http://www.csueastbay.edu/cbe/departments/accounting-and-finance/

California State University, Fullerton, Graduate Studies, College of Business and Economics, Department of Accounting, Fullerton, CA 92831-3599. Offers accounting (MBA, MS). *Accreditation:* AACSB. *Program availability:* Part-time. *Faculty:* 8 full-time (2 women), 6 part-time/adjunct (1 woman). *Students:* 102 full-time (68 women), 64 part-time (31 women); includes 63 minority (44 Asian, non-Hispanic/Latino; 15 Hispanic/Latino; 4 Two or more races, non-Hispanic/Latino), 81 international. Average age 28. 130 applicants, 55% accepted, 34 enrolled. *Degree requirements:* For master's, thesis or alternative, project. *Entrance requirements:* For master's, GMAT, minimum AACSB index of 950. *Application deadline:* Applications are processed on a rolling basis. Application fee: $55. Electronic applications accepted. *Financial support:* Career-related internships or fieldwork, Federal Work-Study, institutionally sponsored loans, and scholarships/grants available. Support available to part-time students. Financial award application deadline: 3/1; financial award applicants required to submit FAFSA. *Unit head:* Dr. Betty Chavis, Chair, 657-278-2225. *Application contact:* Admissions/Applications, 657-278-2371.

California State University, Los Angeles, Graduate Studies, College of Business and Economics, Department of Accounting, Los Angeles, CA 90032-8530. Offers MBA. *Program availability:* Part-time, evening/weekend. *Degree requirements:* For master's, comprehensive exam (MBA), thesis (MS). *Entrance requirements:* For master's, GMAT, minimum GPA of 2.5 during previous 2 years of course work. Additional exam requirements/recommendations for international students: Required—TOEFL (minimum score 550 paper-based). Electronic applications accepted.

California State University, Sacramento, College of Business Administration, Sacramento, CA 95819. Offers accountancy (MS); business administration (IMBA, MBA); human resources (MBA); urban land development (MBA). *Accreditation:* AACSB. *Program availability:* Part-time, evening/weekend, 100% online, blended/hybrid learning. *Students:* 122 full-time (62 women), 153 part-time (75 women); includes 114 minority (10 Black or African American, non-Hispanic/Latino; 2 American Indian or Alaska Native, non-Hispanic/Latino; 73 Asian, non-Hispanic/Latino; 25 Hispanic/Latino; 4 Native Hawaiian or other Pacific Islander, non-Hispanic/Latino), 6 international. Average age 34. 230 applicants, 75% accepted, 134 enrolled. In 2017, 123 master's awarded. *Degree requirements:* For master's, comprehensive exam, project, thesis, or writing proficiency exam. *Entrance requirements:* For master's, GMAT. Additional exam requirements/recommendations for international students: Required—TOEFL (minimum score 550 paper-based; 80 iBT). *Application deadline:* For fall admission, 2/1 for domestic students, 3/1 for international students; for spring admission, 9/15 for domestic students, 9/30 for international students. Applications are processed on a rolling basis. Application fee: $55. Electronic applications accepted. *Expenses:* Contact institution. *Financial support:* Teaching assistantships, career-related internships or fieldwork, Federal Work-Study, and scholarships/grants available. Support available to part-time students. Financial award application deadline: 3/1; financial award applicants required to submit FAFSA. *Unit head:* Dr. Pierre A. Balthazard, Dean, 916-278-6578, Fax: 916-278-5793, E-mail: cba@csus.edu. *Application contact:* Jose Martinez, Graduate Admissions Supervisor, 916-278-7871, E-mail: martinj@skymail.csus.edu.
Website: http://www.cba.csus.edu

California State University, San Bernardino, Graduate Studies, College of Business and Public Administration, Program in Accountancy, San Bernardino, CA 92407. Offers MSA. *Faculty:* 8 full-time (0 women). *Students:* 41 full-time (20 women), 54 part-time (26 women); includes 33 minority (2 Black or African American, non-Hispanic/Latino; 1 American Indian or Alaska Native, non-Hispanic/Latino; 9 Asian, non-Hispanic/Latino; 19 Hispanic/Latino; 2 Two or more races, non-Hispanic/Latino), 30 international. Average age 30. 50 applicants, 56% accepted, 23 enrolled. In 2017, 40 master's awarded. *Application deadline:* For fall admission, 7/16 for domestic students. Application fee: $55. *Unit head:* Dr. Lawrence C. Rose, Dean, 909-537-3703, E-mail: lrose@csusb.edu. *Application contact:* Dr. Dorota Huizinga, Dean of Graduate Studies, 909-537-3064, Fax: 909-537-5078, E-mail: dorota.huizinga@csusb.edu.

California State University, San Bernardino, Graduate Studies, College of Business and Public Administration, Program in Business Administration, San Bernardino, CA 92407. Offers accounting (MBA); entrepreneurship (MBA); finance (MBA); global business (MBA); information management (MBA); information security (MBA); management (MBA); supply chain management (MBA). *Accreditation:* AACSB. *Program availability:* Part-time, evening/weekend, online learning. *Faculty:* 4 full-time (3 women), 6 part-time/adjunct (4 women). *Students:* 21 full-time (5 women), 122 part-time (30 women); includes 82 minority (15 Black or African American, non-Hispanic/Latino; 1 American Indian or Alaska Native, non-Hispanic/Latino; 19 Asian, non-Hispanic/Latino; 44 Hispanic/Latino; 3 Two or more races, non-Hispanic/Latino), 37 international. Average age 33. 258 applicants, 44% accepted, 50 enrolled. In 2017, 134 master's awarded. *Degree requirements:* For master's, comprehensive exam, thesis. *Entrance requirements:* Additional exam requirements/recommendations for international students: Required—TOEFL. *Application deadline:* For fall admission, 7/16 for domestic students, 7/20 for international students; for winter admission, 10/23 for domestic students, 10/20 for international students; for spring admission, 1/22 for domestic students, 1/20 for international students. Application fee: $55. *Expenses:* Contact institution. *Financial support:* Application deadline: 3/1. *Unit head:* Dr. Lawrence C. Rose, Dean, 909-537-3703, Fax: 909-537-7026, E-mail: lrose@csusb.edu. *Application contact:* Dr. Vipin Gupta, Associate Dean/MBA Director, 909-537-7380, Fax: 909-537-7026, E-mail: vgupta@csusb.edu.
Website: http://mba.csusb.edu/

California Western School of Law, Graduate and Professional Programs, San Diego, CA 92101-3090. Offers law (JD); Spanish language in trial advocacy (LL M); JD/MBA; JD/MSW; MCL/LL M. JD/MSW and JD/MBA offered jointly with San Diego State University. *Accreditation:* ABA. *Program availability:* Part-time. *Entrance requirements:* For doctorate, LSAT. Additional exam requirements/recommendations for international students: Required—TOEFL. Electronic applications accepted. *Faculty research:* Biotechnology, health law, international law, labor and employment law, business law.

Accounting

Calvin College, Program in Accounting, Grand Rapids, MI 49546-4388. Offers M Acc. *Program availability:* Part-time.

Canisius College, Graduate Division, Richard J. Wehle School of Business, Department of Accounting, Buffalo, NY 14208-1098. Offers accounting (MBA); forensic accounting (MS); professional accounting (MBA). *Program availability:* Part-time, evening/weekend. *Faculty:* 6 full-time (0 women), 4 part-time/adjunct (0 women). *Students:* 27 full-time (10 women), 22 part-time (4 women); includes 2 minority (both Black or African American, non-Hispanic/Latino), 1 international. Average age 27. 47 applicants, 81% accepted, 24 enrolled. In 2017, 49 master's awarded. *Entrance requirements:* For master's, GMAT, GRE, official transcript from colleges attended, current resume. Additional exam requirements/recommendations for international students: Required—TOEFL (minimum score 550 paper-based, 80 iBT), IELTS (minimum score 6.5), or CAEL (minimum score 70). *Application deadline:* For fall admission, 7/1 priority date for domestic students; for spring admission, 11/1 priority date for domestic students. Applications are processed on a rolling basis. Application fee: $0. Electronic applications accepted. *Expenses: Tuition:* Full-time $22,860; part-time $820 per credit. *Required fees:* $720; $25 per credit. $65 per semester. One-time fee: $425. *Financial support:* Career-related internships or fieldwork, Federal Work-Study, scholarships/grants, and unspecified assistantships available. Financial award application deadline: 4/30; financial award applicants required to submit FAFSA. *Faculty research:* Auditing (process and operational factors), fraud from a global perspective, managing risk in software development, valuation of intellectual property. *Unit head:* Dr. Ian J. Redpath, Chair/Professor, 716-888-2880, E-mail: redpathi@canisius.edu. Website: http://www.canisius.edu/graduate/

Capella University, School of Business and Technology, Doctoral Programs in Business, Minneapolis, MN 55402. Offers accounting (DBA, PhD); business intelligence (DBA); finance (DBA, PhD); general business management (PhD); human resource management (DBA, PhD); leadership (DBA, PhD); management education (PhD); marketing (DBA, PhD); project management (DBA, PhD); strategy and innovation (DBA, PhD). *Accreditation:* ACBSP.

Capella University, School of Business and Technology, Master's Programs in Business, Minneapolis, MN 55402. Offers accounting (MBA); business analysis (MS); business intelligence (MBA); entrepreneurship (MBA); finance (MBA); general business administration (MBA); general human resource management (MS); general leadership (MS); health care management (MBA); human resource management (MBA); marketing (MBA); project management (MBA, MS). *Accreditation:* ACBSP.

Carnegie Mellon University, Tepper School of Business, Program in Accounting, Pittsburgh, PA 15213-3891. Offers PhD. *Accreditation:* AACSB. *Degree requirements:* For doctorate, thesis/dissertation. *Entrance requirements:* For doctorate, GRE.

Case Western Reserve University, Weatherhead School of Management, Department of Accountancy, Cleveland, OH 44106. Offers M Acc, PhD, MBA/M Acc. *Accreditation:* AACSB. *Program availability:* Evening/weekend. *Degree requirements:* For doctorate, thesis/dissertation. *Entrance requirements:* For master's and doctorate, GMAT. *Expenses: Tuition:* Full-time $43,854; part-time $1827 per credit hour. *Required fees:* $50; $50 per credit hour. Tuition and fees vary according to course load and program. *Faculty research:* Auditing, regulation, financial reporting, public interest, efficient markets.

The Catholic University of America, Busch School of Business and Economics, Washington, DC 20064. Offers accounting (MS); business analysis (MSBA); integral economic development management (MA); integral economic development policy (MA); management (MS), including Federal contract management, human resource management, leadership and management, project management, sales management. *Program availability:* Part-time. *Faculty:* 27 full-time (6 women), 45 part-time/adjunct (12 women). *Students:* 74 full-time (50 women), 9 part-time (3 women); includes 26 minority (5 Black or African American, non-Hispanic/Latino; 1 American Indian or Alaska Native, non-Hispanic/Latino; 3 Asian, non-Hispanic/Latino; 9 Hispanic/Latino; 8 Two or more races, non-Hispanic/Latino), 18 international. Average age 31. 99 applicants, 86% accepted, 61 enrolled. In 2017, 46 master's awarded. *Degree requirements:* For master's, comprehensive exam (for some programs). *Entrance requirements:* For master's, GRE General Test, statement of purpose, official copies of academic transcripts, three letters of recommendation. Additional exam requirements/recommendations for international students: Required—TOEFL (minimum score 550 paper-based; 80 iBT). *Application deadline:* For fall admission, 7/15 priority date for domestic students, 7/1 for international students; for spring admission, 11/15 priority date for domestic students, 11/1 for international students. Applications are processed on a rolling basis. Application fee: $55. Electronic applications accepted. *Expenses:* Contact institution. *Financial support:* Fellowships, research assistantships, teaching assistantships, Federal Work-Study, scholarships/grants, tuition waivers (full and partial), and unspecified assistantships available. Financial award application deadline: 2/1; financial award applicants required to submit FAFSA. *Faculty research:* Integrity of the marketing process, economics of energy and the environment, emerging markets, social change, international finance and economic development. *Total annual research expenditures:* $31,390. *Unit head:* Dr. William Bowman, Dean, 202-319-5290, Fax: 202-319-4426, E-mail: otey@cua.edu. *Application contact:* Dr. Steven Brown, Director of Graduate Admissions, 202-319-5057, Fax: 202-319-6533, E-mail: cua-admissions@cua.edu.
Website: https://business.catholic.edu/

Centenary University, Program in Professional Accounting, Hackettstown, NJ 07840-2100. Offers MS. *Program availability:* Part-time, evening/weekend, online learning.

Central Connecticut State University, School of Graduate Studies, School of Business, Department of Accounting, New Britain, CT 06050-4010. Offers MSA. *Program availability:* Part-time, evening/weekend. *Faculty:* 3 full-time (1 woman), 3 part-time/adjunct (0 women). *Students:* 25 full-time (13 women), 45 part-time (31 women); includes 28 minority (7 Black or African American, non-Hispanic/Latino; 12 Asian, non-Hispanic/Latino; 8 Hispanic/Latino; 1 Two or more races, non-Hispanic/Latino), 1 international. Average age 30. 55 applicants, 82% accepted, 27 enrolled. In 2017, 2 master's awarded. *Degree requirements:* For master's, thesis or alternative. *Entrance requirements:* For master's, GMAT or GRE, minimum undergraduate GPA of 2.7, resume. Additional exam requirements/recommendations for international students: Required—TOEFL (minimum score 550 paper-based; 79 iBT), Recommended—IELTS (minimum score 6.5). *Application deadline:* For fall admission, 8/1 for domestic students, 5/1 for international students; for spring admission, 11/1 for domestic and international students. Applications are processed on a rolling basis. Application fee: $50. Electronic applications accepted. *Expenses: Tuition, area resident:* Full-time $6757. Tuition, state resident: full-time $9750; part-time $374 per credit. Tuition, nonresident: full-time $18,102; part-time $374 per credit. *Required fees:* $4635; $255 per credit. *Financial support:* In 2017–18, 8 students received support. Career-related internships or fieldwork, Federal Work-Study, scholarships/grants, and unspecified assistantships available. Support available to part-time students. Financial award application deadline: 3/1; financial award applicants required to submit FAFSA. *Unit head:* Lawrence Grasso, Chair, 860-832-3220, E-mail: grassola@ccsu.edu. *Application contact:* Patricia Gardner, Associate Director of Graduate Admissions, 860-832-2350, Fax: 860-832-2362. Website: http://www.ccsu.edu/accounting/

Central Michigan University, College of Graduate Studies, College of Business Administration, Department of Business Information Systems, Mount Pleasant, MI 48859. Offers business computing (Graduate Certificate); information systems (MS), including accounting information systems, business informatics, enterprise systems using SAP software, information systems. *Program availability:* Part-time, evening/weekend. *Degree requirements:* For master's, thesis or alternative. Electronic applications accepted. *Faculty research:* Enterprise software, electronic commerce, decision support systems, ethical issues in information systems, information technology management and teaching issues.

Central Michigan University, College of Graduate Studies, College of Business Administration, MBA Program, Mount Pleasant, MI 48859. Offers accounting (MBA); business economics (MBA); consulting (MBA); finance (MBA); general business (MBA); human resource management (MBA); information systems (MBA); international business (MBA); logistics management (MBA); marketing (MBA); value-driven organization (MBA). *Program availability:* Part-time, evening/weekend, online learning. Electronic applications accepted. *Faculty research:* Accounting, consulting, international business, marketing, information systems.

Chaminade University of Honolulu, Office of Professional and Continuing Education, Program in Business Administration, Honolulu, HI 96816-1578. Offers accounting (MBA); business (MBA); island business (MBA); not-for-profit (MBA). *Program availability:* Part-time, evening/weekend, 100% online, blended/hybrid learning. *Faculty:* 5 full-time (2 women), 8 part-time/adjunct (2 women). *Students:* 80 full-time (44 women), 54 part-time (37 women); includes 95 minority (6 Black or African American, non-Hispanic/Latino; 2 American Indian or Alaska Native, non-Hispanic/Latino; 42 Asian, non-Hispanic/Latino; 8 Hispanic/Latino; 34 Native Hawaiian or other Pacific Islander, non-Hispanic/Latino; 3 Two or more races, non-Hispanic/Latino), 5 international. Average age 32. 36 applicants, 94% accepted, 24 enrolled. In 2017, 39 master's awarded. *Entrance requirements:* For master's, minimum GPA of 3.0, resume, two years or more of work experience. Additional exam requirements/recommendations for international students: Required—TOEFL (minimum score 550 paper-based; 79 iBT). *Application deadline:* Applications are processed on a rolling basis. Application fee: $40. Electronic applications accepted. *Expenses:* $900 per credit hour with $93 fee per online course. *Financial support:* Applicants required to submit FAFSA. *Unit head:* Dr. Scott J. Schroeder, Dean, 808-739-4612, Fax: 808-735-4734, E-mail: mba@chaminade.edu. *Application contact:* 808-735-4755, E-mail: gradserv@chaminade.edu.
Website: https://pace.chaminade.edu/graduate-programs/mba-program/

Chapman University, The George L. Argyros School of Business and Economics, Orange, CA 92866. Offers accounting (MS); behavioral and computational economics (MS); business administration (Exec MBA, MBA); JD/MBA. *Accreditation:* AACSB. *Program availability:* Part-time, evening/weekend. *Faculty:* 60 full-time (16 women), 46 part-time/adjunct (8 women). *Students:* 180 full-time (87 women), 100 part-time (45 women); includes 86 minority (4 Black or African American, non-Hispanic/Latino; 1 American Indian or Alaska Native, non-Hispanic/Latino; 39 Asian, non-Hispanic/Latino; 28 Hispanic/Latino; 1 Native Hawaiian or other Pacific Islander, non-Hispanic/Latino; 13 Two or more races, non-Hispanic/Latino), 89 international. Average age 28. 250 applicants, 75% accepted, 94 enrolled. In 2017, 119 master's awarded. Application fee: $60. Electronic applications accepted. *Expenses:* Contact institution. *Financial support:* Fellowships, Federal Work-Study, and scholarships/grants available. Financial award applicants required to submit FAFSA. *Unit head:* Thomas Turk, Interim Dean, 714-997-6819, E-mail: turk@chapman.edu. *Application contact:* Debra Gonda, Associate Dean, 714-997-6894, E-mail: gonda@chapman.edu.
Website: https://www.chapman.edu/business/index.aspx

Charleston Southern University, College of Business, Charleston, SC 29423-8087. Offers accounting (MBA); finance (MBA); general management (MBA); human resource management (MS); leadership (MBA); management information systems (MBA); organizational leadership (MA). *Program availability:* Part-time, evening/weekend. *Degree requirements:* For master's, thesis optional. *Entrance requirements:* For master's, GMAT. Additional exam requirements/recommendations for international students: Required—TOEFL (minimum score 550 paper-based; 79 iBT). *Application deadline:* Applications are processed on a rolling basis. Application fee: $40. Electronic applications accepted. *Expenses: Tuition:* Part-time $500 per credit hour. One-time fee: $30. Tuition and fees vary according to program. *Financial support:* Research assistantships with full tuition reimbursements available. Financial award application deadline: 4/15; financial award applicants required to submit FAFSA. *Unit head:* Dr. David Palmer, Dean, 843-863-7025, Fax: 843-863-7922, E-mail: dpalmer@csuniv.edu. *Application contact:* Dr. Darin L. Gerdes, Associate Professor of Management, 843-863-7814, Fax: 843-863-7922, E-mail: dgerdes@csuniv.edu.
Website: http://www.csuniv.edu/business/

Chatham University, Program in Accounting, Pittsburgh, PA 15232-2826. Offers M Acc, MAC. *Program availability:* Part-time, evening/weekend. *Faculty:* 1 full-time (0 women), 1 part-time/adjunct (0 women). *Students:* 4 full-time (3 women), 12 part-time (7 women); includes 4 minority (1 Black or African American, non-Hispanic/Latino; 2 Asian, non-Hispanic/Latino; 1 Hispanic/Latino), 2 international. Average age 31. 13 applicants, 54% accepted, 6 enrolled. In 2017, 10 master's awarded. *Entrance requirements:* Additional exam requirements/recommendations for international students: Required—TOEFL (minimum score 600 paper-based; 100 iBT), IELTS (minimum score 7), TWE. *Application deadline:* For fall admission, 4/1 for domestic and international students; for spring admission, 11/1 for domestic students, 10/1 for international students. Applications are processed on a rolling basis. Application fee: $45. Electronic applications accepted. Application fee is waived when completed online. *Expenses:* Contact institution. *Financial support:* Applicants required to submit FAFSA. *Unit head:* Dr. Rachel Chung, Director of Business and Entrepreneurship Program, 412-365-2433, E-mail: rchung@chatham.edu. *Application contact:* 412-365-1141, Fax: 412-365-1609, E-mail: gradadmissions@chatham.edu.
Website: http://www.chatham.edu/macc

Christian Brothers University, School of Business, Memphis, TN 38104-5581. Offers accountancy (M Acc); business (MBA); international business (MIB); project management (Certificate); MBA/MIB. *Program availability:* Part-time, evening/weekend. *Entrance requirements:* For master's, GMAT, GRE. Additional exam requirements/recommendations for international students: Required—TOEFL.

City University of Seattle, Graduate Division, School of Management, Seattle, WA 98121. Offers accounting (Certificate); change leadership (MBA, Certificate); computer systems (MS); finance (Certificate); financial management (MBA); general management (MBA); general management-Europe (MBA); global marketing (MBA); human resources management (Certificate); individualized study (MBA); information security (MS); information systems (MBA); leadership (MA); marketing (MBA, Certificate); project management (MBA, MS, Certificate); sustainable business (Certificate); technology management (MBA, Certificate). *Program availability:* Part-time, evening/weekend, online learning. *Degree requirements:* For master's, comprehensive exam (for some programs), thesis (for some programs). *Entrance requirements:* For master's, baccalaureate degree or equivalent from an accredited or otherwise recognized institution. Additional exam requirements/recommendations for international students: Required—TOEFL (minimum score 567 paper-based; 87 iBT); Recommended—IELTS. Electronic applications accepted.

Clarion University of Pennsylvania, College of Business Administration and Information Sciences, Master of Business Administration Program, Clarion, PA 16214. Offers accounting (MBA); finance (MBA); health care administration (MBA); innovation and entrepreneurship (MBA); non-profit business (MBA). *Accreditation:* AACSB. *Program availability:* Part-time, evening/weekend, 100% online. *Faculty:* 4 full-time (1 woman), 3 part-time/adjunct (0 women). *Students:* 19 full-time (7 women), 66 part-time (34 women); includes 10 minority (6 Black or African American, non-Hispanic/Latino; 1 Asian, non-Hispanic/Latino; 3 Hispanic/Latino), 2 international. Average age 31. 86 applicants, 63% accepted, 21 enrolled. In 2017, 33 master's awarded. *Degree requirements:* For master's, portfolio. *Entrance requirements:* For master's, GMAT, minimum QPA of 2.75. Additional exam requirements/recommendations for international students: Required—TOEFL (minimum score 550 paper-based, 80 iBT) or IELTS (7). *Application deadline:* For fall admission, 8/1 priority date for domestic students, 4/15 priority date for international students; for spring admission, 12/1 priority date for domestic students, 9/15 priority date for international students. Applications are processed on a rolling basis. Application fee: $40. Electronic applications accepted. *Expenses:* $655.05 per credit. *Financial support:* Unspecified assistantships available. Support available to part-time students. Financial award application deadline: 3/1; financial award applicants required to submit FAFSA. *Unit head:* Juanice Vega, Assistant to the Dean, 814-393-2600, Fax: 814-393-1910, E-mail: mba@clarion.edu. *Application contact:* Dana Bearer, Assistant Director, Graduate Programs, 814-393-2337, Fax: 814-393-2722, E-mail: gradstudies@clarion.edu.
Website: http://www.clarion.edu/admissions/graduate/index.html

Clarion University of Pennsylvania, College of Business Administration and Information Sciences, MS Program in Accounting, Clarion, PA 16214. Offers MS. *Program availability:* Part-time, evening/weekend, online only, 100% online. *Faculty:* 1 full-time (0 women), 1 part-time/adjunct (0 women). *Students:* 10 full-time (8 women), 16 part-time (10 women); includes 7 minority (2 Black or African American, non-Hispanic/Latino; 1 American Indian or Alaska Native, non-Hispanic/Latino; 3 Asian, non-Hispanic/Latino; 1 Two or more races, non-Hispanic/Latino). Average age 27. 45 applicants, 98% accepted, 14 enrolled. In 2017, 2 master's awarded. *Entrance requirements:* For master's, minimum undergraduate GPA of 3.0. Additional exam requirements/recommendations for international students: Required—TOEFL (minimum score 550 paper-based, 80 iBT) or IELTS (7). *Application deadline:* For fall admission, 8/15 priority date for domestic students, 7/15 priority date for international students; for winter admission, 11/1 priority date for domestic students; for spring admission, 1/7 priority date for domestic students, 11/15 priority date for international students; for summer admission, 4/1 priority date for domestic students. Applications are processed on a rolling basis. Application fee: $40. Electronic applications accepted. *Expenses:* $655.05 per credit. *Financial support:* Career-related internships or fieldwork and scholarships/grants available. Support available to part-time students. Financial award application deadline: 3/1; financial award applicants required to submit FAFSA. *Unit head:* Dr. Anthony Grenci, Department Chair, 814-393-2628, E-mail: agrenci@clarion.edu. *Application contact:* Dana Bearer, Associate Director for Transfer, Adult and Graduate Admissions, 814-393-2337, Fax: 814-393-2772, E-mail: gradstudies@clarion.edu.

Clark Atlanta University, School of Business Administration, Department of Accounting, Atlanta, GA 30314. Offers MA. *Program availability:* Part-time. *Faculty:* 8 full-time (6 women), 1 (woman) part-time/adjunct. *Students:* 5 full-time (3 women), 2 part-time (1 woman); includes 5 minority (4 Black or African American, non-Hispanic/Latino; 1 Asian, non-Hispanic/Latino), 2 international. Average age 31. 10 applicants, 50% accepted, 2 enrolled. In 2017, 17 master's awarded. *Entrance requirements:* For master's, GMAT, minimum undergraduate GPA of 2.5. Additional exam requirements/recommendations for international students: Required—TOEFL (minimum score 500 paper-based; 61 iBT). *Application deadline:* For fall admission, 4/1 for domestic and international students; for spring admission, 11/1 for domestic and international students. Applications are processed on a rolling basis. Application fee: $40 ($55 for international students). Electronic applications accepted. *Financial support:* Career-related internships or fieldwork, Federal Work-Study, scholarships/grants, and unspecified assistantships available. Support available to part-time students. Financial award application deadline: 4/30; financial award applicants required to submit FAFSA. *Unit head:* Dr. Kasim Alli, Chairperson, 404-880-8740, E-mail: kalli@cau.edu.

Clark University, Graduate School, Graduate School of Management, Business Administration Program, Worcester, MA 01610-1477. Offers accounting (MBA); finance (MBA); information management and business analytics (MBA); management (MBA); marketing (MBA); social change (MBA); sustainability (MBA). *Accreditation:* AACSB. *Program availability:* Part-time, evening/weekend. *Students:* 87 full-time (41 women), 41 part-time (26 women); includes 19 minority (10 Black or African American, non-Hispanic/Latino; 4 Asian, non-Hispanic/Latino; 4 Hispanic/Latino; 1 Two or more races, non-Hispanic/Latino), 40 international. Average age 30. 242 applicants, 50% accepted, 54 enrolled. In 2017, 102 master's awarded. *Degree requirements:* For master's, thesis optional. *Entrance requirements:* For master's, GMAT or GRE, 2 references, resume or curriculum vitae, personal statement. Additional exam requirements/recommendations for international students: Required—TOEFL (minimum score 575 paper-based; 90 iBT), IELTS (minimum score 6.5). *Application deadline:* For fall admission, 4/15 priority date for domestic and international students; for spring admission, 12/1 priority date for domestic and international students. Application fee: $75. Electronic applications accepted. *Expenses:* $4,490 tuition per 14-week course, $2,245 per half-unit (7-week course); $40 activity fee (full-time students only); $80 miscellaneous one-time fee; $1,750 student services fee. *Financial support:* Fellowships, research assistantships, teaching assistantships, career-related internships or fieldwork, Federal Work-Study, institutionally sponsored loans, and tuition waivers (partial) available. Support available to part-time students. Financial award application deadline: 5/31. *Faculty research:* Marketing, accounting, human resource management, management information systems, business finance. *Unit head:* Dr. Priscilla Elsass, Dean, 508-793-7543, Fax: 508-793-8822, E-mail: pelsass@clarku.edu. *Application contact:* Yingying Chen, Assistant Director of Graduate Admissions, 508-793-7373, Fax: 508-798-4386, E-mail: graduateadmissions@clarku.edu.
Website: http://www.clarku.edu/programs/masters-business-administration

Clark University, Graduate School, Graduate School of Management, Program in Accounting, Worcester, MA 01610-1477. Offers MSA. *Program availability:* Part-time, evening/weekend. *Students:* Average age 20. 238 applicants, 76% accepted, 15 enrolled. In 2017, 35 master's awarded. *Entrance requirements:* For master's, GMAT or GRE, statement of purpose, resume, two letters of recommendation. Additional exam requirements/recommendations for international students: Required—TOEFL (minimum score 575 paper-based; 90 iBT), IELTS (minimum score 6.5). *Application deadline:* For fall admission, 4/15 priority date for domestic and international students; for spring admission, 12/1 priority date for domestic and international students. Application fee: $100. Electronic applications accepted. *Expenses:* $4,920 tuition per 14-week course, $2,460 per half-unit (7-week course); $40 activity fee (full-time students only); $80 miscellaneous one-time fee; $1,800 student services fee. *Financial support:* Research assistantships and teaching assistantships available. *Unit head:* Dr. Priscilla Elsass, Dean, 508-793-7543, Fax: 508-793-8822, E-mail: pelsass@clarku.edu. *Application contact:* Yingying Chen, Assistant Director of Graduate Admissions, 508-793-7373, Fax: 508-798-4386, E-mail: graduateadmissions@clarku.edu.
Website: http://www.clarku.edu/programs/masters-accounting

Clayton State University, School of Graduate Studies, College of Business, Program in Business Administration, Morrow, GA 30260-0285. Offers accounting (MBA); human resource leadership (MBA); international business (MBA); sports and entertainment management (MBA); supply chain management (MBA). *Accreditation:* AACSB. *Program availability:* Part-time, evening/weekend. *Degree requirements:* For master's, thesis. *Entrance requirements:* For master's, GMAT, 3 letters of recommendation; statement of purpose; 2 official transcripts. Additional exam requirements/recommendations for international students: Required—TOEFL (minimum score 550 paper-based; 80 iBT). Electronic applications accepted. *Expenses:* Contact institution.

Clemson University, Graduate School, College of Business, School of Accountancy, Clemson, SC 29634. Offers accounting (MP Acc). *Accreditation:* AACSB. *Program availability:* Part-time. *Faculty:* 29 full-time (13 women), 10 part-time/adjunct (6 women). *Students:* 194 full-time (98 women), 22 part-time (12 women); includes 34 minority (10 Black or African American, non-Hispanic/Latino; 6 Asian, non-Hispanic/Latino; 16 Hispanic/Latino; 2 Two or more races, non-Hispanic/Latino), 16 international. Average age 23. 220 applicants, 70% accepted, 111 enrolled. In 2017, 206 master's awarded. *Entrance requirements:* For master's, GMAT, unofficial transcripts, letters of recommendation. Additional exam requirements/recommendations for international students: Required—TOEFL (minimum score 80 iBT), IELTS (minimum score 6.5), PTE (minimum score 54). *Application deadline:* For fall admission, 6/1 priority date for domestic students, 4/15 priority date for international students; for spring admission, 11/1 priority date for domestic students, 9/30 priority date for international students. Applications are processed on a rolling basis. Application fee: $80 ($90 for international students). Electronic applications accepted. *Expenses:* $5,767 per semester full-time resident, $10,918 per semester full-time non-resident, $656 per credit hour part-time resident, $1,310 per credit hour part-time non-resident, $915 per credit hour online; other fees may apply per session. *Financial support:* In 2017–18, 17 students received support, including 3 fellowships with partial tuition reimbursements available (averaging $2,000 per year); career-related internships or fieldwork and unspecified assistantships also available. Financial award application deadline: 12/31. *Faculty research:* Financial accounting, auditing, managerial accounting. *Unit head:* Dr. Sally Widener, Director, 864-656-1275, E-mail: kwidene@clemson.edu. *Application contact:* Suzanne Pearse, MP Acc Program Coordinator, 864-656-0131, E-mail: spearse@clemson.edu.
Website: https://www.clemson.edu/business/departments/accountancy/index.html

Cleveland State University, College of Graduate Studies, Monte Ahuja College of Business, Department of Accounting, Cleveland, OH 44115. Offers financial accounting/audit (M Acc). *Accreditation:* AACSB. *Program availability:* Part-time, evening/weekend. *Faculty:* 13 full-time (3 women), 11 part-time/adjunct (3 women). *Students:* 49 full-time (30 women), 71 part-time (40 women); includes 24 minority (10 Black or African American, non-Hispanic/Latino; 1 American Indian or Alaska Native, non-Hispanic/Latino; 9 Asian, non-Hispanic/Latino; 4 Hispanic/Latino), 19 international. Average age 31. 89 applicants, 85% accepted, 36 enrolled. In 2017, 56 master's awarded. *Entrance requirements:* For master's, GMAT, minimum GPA of 2.75. Additional exam requirements/recommendations for international students: Required—TOEFL (minimum score 550 paper-based; 78 iBT). *Application deadline:* For fall admission, 7/1 priority date for domestic students, 5/15 for international students; for spring admission, 11/15 priority date for domestic students, 11/1 for international students; for summer admission, 4/1 for domestic students, 3/15 for international students. Applications are processed on a rolling basis. Application fee: $40. Electronic applications accepted. *Financial support:* In 2017–18, 3 research assistantships with tuition reimbursements (averaging $6,960 per year) were awarded; career-related internships or fieldwork, Federal Work-Study, scholarships/grants, and unspecified assistantships also available. Financial award applicants required to submit FAFSA. *Faculty research:* Internal auditing, computer auditing, accounting education, managerial accounting. *Unit head:* Dr. Heidi Meier, Chair/Professor, 216-687-3671, Fax: 216-687-9212, E-mail: h.meier@csuohio.edu. *Application contact:* Marilyn Leadbetter, Administrative Secretary, 216-687-4721, Fax: 216-687-5311, E-mail: m.leadbetter@csuohio.edu.
Website: http://www.csuohio.edu/business/academics/master-accountancy

Coastal Carolina University, E. Craig Wall, Sr. College of Business Administration, Conway, SC 29528-6054. Offers accounting (M Acc); business administration (MBA); business foundations (Certificate); fraud examination (Certificate). *Accreditation:* AACSB. *Program availability:* Part-time, evening/weekend, 100% online, blended/hybrid learning. *Faculty:* 11 full-time (5 women), 2 part-time/adjunct (0 women). *Students:* 58 full-time (31 women), 34 part-time (16 women); includes 26 minority (19 Black or African American, non-Hispanic/Latino; 2 Asian, non-Hispanic/Latino; 1 Hispanic/Latino; 1 Native Hawaiian or other Pacific Islander, non-Hispanic/Latino; 3 Two or more races, non-Hispanic/Latino), 9 international. Average age 27. 103 applicants, 74% accepted, 54 enrolled. In 2017, 68 master's awarded. *Entrance requirements:* For master's, GMAT, official transcripts, 2 letters of recommendation, resume, baccalaureate degree, statement of purpose, minimum cumulative GPA of 3.0 overall from completed undergraduate and graduate coursework; for Certificate, GMAT, official transcripts; 2 letters of recommendation; baccalaureate degree or evidence of receiving a CPA certificate, law degree, or admittance to an accredited law school. Additional exam requirements/recommendations for international students: Required—TOEFL (minimum score 550 paper-based; 79 iBT), IELTS (minimum score 6.5). *Application deadline:* For fall admission, 6/15 priority date for domestic and international students; for spring admission, 11/15 priority date for domestic and international students; for summer admission, 4/15 priority date for domestic and international students. Applications are processed on a rolling basis. Application fee: $45. Electronic applications accepted. *Expenses:* Tuition, state resident: full-time $5184; part-time $576 per credit hour. Tuition, nonresident: full-time $9369; part-time $1041 per credit hour. *Required fees:* $90; $5 per credit hour. *Financial support:* Fellowships, research assistantships, teaching assistantships, and tuition waivers available. Financial award application deadline: 3/1; financial award applicants required to submit FAFSA. *Unit head:* Dr. Mark Mitchell, Associate Dean/Professor/Director of Graduate Programs and Executive Education, 843-349-2392, Fax: 843-349-2455, E-mail: mmitchel@coastal.edu. *Application contact:* Dr. James O. Luken, Associate Provost for Graduate Program/Interim Vice-Dean of the Coastal Environment, 843-349-2235, Fax: 843-349-6444, E-mail: joluken@coastal.edu.
Website: https://www.coastal.edu/business/

The College at Brockport, State University of New York, School of Business and Management, Brockport, NY 14420-2997. Offers accounting (MS); public administration (MPA, AGC), including arts administration (AGC), nonprofit management (AGC), public administration (MPA). *Program availability:* Part-time. *Faculty:* 6 full-time (2 women), 5 part-time/adjunct (3 women). *Students:* 76 full-time (49 women), 106 part-time (64 women); includes 45 minority (22 Black or African American, non-Hispanic/Latino; 6 Asian, non-Hispanic/Latino; 11 Hispanic/Latino; 6 Two or more races, non-Hispanic/

Accounting

Latino), 6 international. 29 applicants, 79% accepted, 19 enrolled. In 2017, 75 master's, 6 other advanced degrees awarded. *Entrance requirements:* For master's, GMAT or GRE General Test. Additional exam requirements/recommendations for international students: Required—TOEFL (minimum score 550 paper-based; 79 iBT), IELTS (minimum score 6.5). *Application deadline:* For fall admission, 7/1 priority date for domestic and international students; for spring admission, 12/1 priority date for domestic and international students. Application fee: $50. Electronic applications accepted. *Expenses:* Tuition, state resident: full-time $10,870; part-time $453 per credit hour. Tuition, nonresident: full-time $22,210. *Required fees:* $988; $246 per semester. *Financial support:* Career-related internships or fieldwork, Federal Work-Study, scholarships/grants, and unspecified assistantships available. Financial award application deadline: 3/15; financial award applicants required to submit FAFSA. *Unit head:* Dr. Joy Bhadury, School Dean, 585-395-2623, Fax: 585-395-2542. *Application contact:* Danielle A. Welch, Graduate Counselor, 585-395-5430, Fax: 585-395-2515, E-mail: dwelch@brockport.edu.
Website: http://www.brockport.edu/academics/school_business_management/

College of Charleston, Graduate School, School of Business, Program in Accountancy, Charleston, SC 29424-0001. Offers MS. *Accreditation:* AACSB. *Program availability:* Evening/weekend. *Entrance requirements:* For master's, GMAT, minimum GPA of 3.0 in last 60 hours of undergraduate course work, 24 hours of course work in accounting, 2 letters of reference. Additional exam requirements/recommendations for international students: Required—TOEFL (minimum score 81 iBT). Electronic applications accepted.

The College of Saint Rose, Graduate Studies, Huether School of Business, Program in Accounting, Albany, NY 12203-1419. Offers MS. *Program availability:* Part-time, evening/weekend. *Students:* 22 full-time (3 women), 7 part-time (6 women); includes 6 minority (3 Black or African American, non-Hispanic/Latino; 1 Hispanic/Latino; 2 Two or more races, non-Hispanic/Latino), 1 international. Average age 29. 8 applicants, 75% accepted, 6 enrolled. In 2017, 25 master's awarded. *Entrance requirements:* For master's, GMAT, graduate degree, or minimum undergraduate GPA of 3.0. Additional exam requirements/recommendations for international students: Required—TOEFL (minimum score 550 paper-based; 80 iBT), IELTS (minimum score 6), PTE (minimum score 56). *Application deadline:* For fall admission, 4/1 priority date for domestic and international students; for spring admission, 10/15 priority date for domestic and international students; for summer admission, 3/15 priority date for domestic and international students. Applications are processed on a rolling basis. Application fee: $40. Electronic applications accepted. *Expenses: Tuition:* Full-time $7191; part-time $799 per credit hour. *Required fees:* $924; $462 per credit hour. Tuition and fees vary according to course load. *Financial support:* Career-related internships or fieldwork, scholarships/grants, tuition waivers (partial), and unspecified assistantships available. Support available to part-time students. Financial award application deadline: 4/15; financial award applicants required to submit FAFSA. *Unit head:* Mike Mathews, Interim Dean, 518-454-5272, Fax: 518-458-5449, E-mail: mathewsm@strose.edu. *Application contact:* Cris Murray, Assistant Vice President for Graduate Recruitment and Enrollment, 518-485-3390, Fax: 518-458-5479, E-mail: grad@strose.edu.
Website: https://www.strose.edu/accounting-ms/

College of Staten Island of the City University of New York, Graduate Programs, School of Business, Program in Accounting, Staten Island, NY 10314-6600. Offers MS. *Program availability:* Part-time, evening/weekend. *Faculty:* 6 full-time, 2 part-time/adjunct. *Students:* 36. 15 applicants, 87% accepted, 11 enrolled. In 2017, 12 master's awarded. *Degree requirements:* For master's, 30 credits or 10 courses worth 3 credits each; significant written assignment in capstone course. *Entrance requirements:* For master's, GMAT or College of Staten Island degree with minimum GPA of 3.2 in accounting or business pre-major and major, baccalaureate degree in accounting or related field; letter of intent; minimum GPA of 3.0; two letters of recommendation from instructors or employers; proficiency in business fundamentals and in-depth knowledge of accounting through undergraduate coursework. Additional exam requirements/recommendations for international students: Required—TOEFL (minimum score 550 paper-based; 79 iBT), IELTS (minimum score 6.5). *Application deadline:* For fall admission, 6/30 priority date for domestic and international students; for spring admission, 11/25 priority date for domestic and international students. Applications are processed on a rolling basis. Application fee: $125. Electronic applications accepted. *Expenses:* Tuition, state resident: full-time $10,450; part-time $440 per credit. Tuition, nonresident: full-time $19,320; part-time $440 per credit. *Required fees:* $181.10 per semester. Tuition and fees vary according to program. *Faculty research:* Fair value reporting, forensic accounting, pension asset allocation, archival empirical analysis. *Unit head:* Prof. John Sandler, Graduate Program Coordinator, 718-982-2963, E-mail: john.sandler@csi.cuny.edu. *Application contact:* Sasha Spence, Associate Director for Graduate Admissions, 718-982-2019, Fax: 718-982-2500, E-mail: sasha.spence@csi.cuny.edu.
Website: http://www.csi.cuny.edu/schoolofbusiness/programs_graduate.php

The College of William and Mary, Raymond A. Mason School of Business, Master of Accounting Program, Williamsburg, VA 23185. Offers M Acc. *Accreditation:* AACSB. *Faculty:* 12 full-time (6 women), 3 part-time/adjunct (0 women). *Students:* 101 full-time (49 women); includes 27 minority (7 Black or African American, non-Hispanic/Latino; 9 Asian, non-Hispanic/Latino; 8 Hispanic/Latino; 3 Two or more races, non-Hispanic/Latino), 21 international. Average age 22. 384 applicants, 44% accepted, 91 enrolled. In 2017, 118 master's awarded. *Degree requirements:* For master's, 30 credit hours. *Entrance requirements:* For master's, GRE or GMAT (recommended), 2 written recommendations, interview, transcripts. Additional exam requirements/recommendations for international students: Required—TOEFL (minimum iBT score of 100), IELTS (7), or 4 years of studies in the U.S. *Application deadline:* For fall admission, 12/1 priority date for domestic and international students; for winter admission, 2/1 for domestic and international students; for spring admission, 4/1 for domestic and international students; for summer admission, 6/1 for domestic and international students. Application fee: $100. Electronic applications accepted. *Expenses:* $32,106 in-state tuition, $42,678 out-of-state (for two-semester degree program). *Financial support:* Fellowships, research assistantships, scholarships/grants, and unspecified assistantships available. Financial award application deadline: 8/1; financial award applicants required to submit FAFSA. *Faculty research:* Valuation, voluntary disclosure, auditing, taxation, executive compensation. *Unit head:* Denise Jones, Accounting Department Chair, 757-221-2876, Fax: 757-221-7862, E-mail: denise.jones@mason.wm.edu. *Application contact:* Midori Juarez, Associate Director, 757-221-2934, Fax: 757-221-7862, E-mail: midori.juarez@mason.wm.edu.
Website: http://mason.wm.edu/programs/macc/index.php

Colorado State University, College of Business, Department of Accounting, Fort Collins, CO 80523-1271. Offers accounting (M Acc). *Faculty:* 8 full-time (5 women), 1 part-time/adjunct (0 women). *Students:* 31 full-time (16 women), 10 part-time (6 women); includes 7 minority (2 Black or African American, non-Hispanic/Latino; 2 Asian, non-Hispanic/Latino; 2 Hispanic/Latino; 1 Two or more races, non-Hispanic/Latino), 3 international. Average age 30. 51 applicants, 65% accepted, 28 enrolled. In 2017, 25 master's awarded. *Entrance requirements:* For master's, GMAT (minimum score of 550), minimum GPA of 3.25, BA/BS, 3 letters of reference, official transcripts, statement

of purpose, resume. Additional exam requirements/recommendations for international students: Required—TOEFL (minimum score 95 iBT), IELTS (minimum score 7), PTE (minimum score 70). *Application deadline:* For fall admission, 5/1 for domestic and international students. Applications are processed on a rolling basis. Application fee: $60 ($70 for international students). Electronic applications accepted. *Expenses:* $303 per credit hour. *Financial support:* Scholarships/grants and unspecified assistantships available. *Faculty research:* Theoretical application of economics and psychology; internal and external auditing issues; taxation; accounting choices and social dynamics; managerial accounting; accounting practice and tax policy. *Unit head:* Dr. Audrey A. Gramling, Department Chair, 970-491-6268, E-mail: audrey.gramling@colostate.edu. *Application contact:* Megan Skeehan, Program Assistant, 970-491-5102, E-mail: megan.skeehan@colostate.edu.
Website: https://biz.colostate.edu/About/Departments/Department-of-Accounting

Colorado State University–Global Campus, Graduate Programs, Greenwood Village, CO 80111. Offers criminal justice and law enforcement administration (MS); education leadership (MS); finance (MS); healthcare administration and management (MS); human resource management (MHRM); information technology management (MITM); international management (MS); management (MS); organizational leadership (MS); professional accounting (MPA); project management (MS); teaching and learning (MS). *Accreditation:* ACBSP. *Program availability:* Online learning.

Colorado Technical University Aurora, Programs in Business Administration and Management, Aurora, CO 80014. Offers accounting (MBA); business administration (MBA); business administration and management (EMBA); finance (MBA); human resource management (MBA); marketing (MBA); mediation and dispute resolution (MBA); operations management (MBA); project management (MBA); technology management (MBA). *Program availability:* Part-time, evening/weekend. *Degree requirements:* For master's, thesis or alternative. *Entrance requirements:* For master's, minimum undergraduate GPA of 3.0, resume.

Colorado Technical University Colorado Springs, Graduate Studies, Program in Management, Colorado Springs, CO 80907. Offers accounting (MBA, MSA); business administration (MBA); finance (MBA); human resources management (MBA); logistics/supply chain management (MBA); management (DM); marketing (MBA); mediation and dispute resolution (MBA); operations management (MBA); project management (MBA); technology management (MBA). *Accreditation:* ACBSP. *Program availability:* Part-time, evening/weekend, online learning. *Degree requirements:* For master's, thesis or alternative; for doctorate, thesis/dissertation. *Entrance requirements:* For doctorate, minimum graduate GPA of 3.0, 5 years of related work experience. *Faculty research:* Sexual harassment, performance evaluation, critical thinking.

Columbia College, Master of Business Administration Program, Columbia, MO 65216-0002. Offers accounting (MBA); business administration (MBA); human resources (MBA). *Program availability:* Part-time, evening/weekend, 100% online, blended/hybrid learning. *Faculty:* 7 full-time (0 women), 76 part-time/adjunct (26 women). *Students:* 53 full-time (37 women), 389 part-time (241 women); includes 114 minority (60 Black or African American, non-Hispanic/Latino; 2 American Indian or Alaska Native, non-Hispanic/Latino; 7 Asian, non-Hispanic/Latino; 28 Hispanic/Latino; 1 Native Hawaiian or other Pacific Islander, non-Hispanic/Latino; 16 Two or more races, non-Hispanic/Latino), 22 international. Average age 37. 368 applicants, 99% accepted, 111 enrolled. In 2017, 209 master's awarded. *Entrance requirements:* For master's, 3 letters of recommendation, minimum cumulative undergraduate GPA of 3.0, resume, goal statement. Additional exam requirements/recommendations for international students: Required—TOEFL (minimum score 550 paper-based; 79 iBT). *Application deadline:* For fall admission, 8/9 priority date for domestic and international students; for spring admission, 12/27 priority date for domestic and international students. Applications are processed on a rolling basis. Application fee: $55. Electronic applications accepted. *Expenses:* Contact institution. *Financial support:* In 2017–18, 27 students received support. Federal Work-Study and scholarships/grants available. Financial award application deadline: 3/1; financial award applicants required to submit FAFSA. *Unit head:* Dr. Shanda Davis, Dean, School of Business Administration, 573-875-7561, Fax: 573-876-4493, E-mail: sdavis19@ccis.edu. *Application contact:* Stephanie Johnson, Director of Admissions, 573-875-7352, Fax: 573-875-7506, E-mail: sjohnson@ccis.edu.
Website: http://www.ccis.edu/graduate/academics/degrees.asp?MBA

Columbia University, Graduate School of Business, Doctoral Program in Business, New York, NY 10027. Offers business (PhD), including accounting, decision, risk, and operations, finance and economics, management, marketing. *Accreditation:* AACSB. *Degree requirements:* For doctorate, comprehensive exam, thesis/dissertation, major field exam, research paper, thesis proposal. *Entrance requirements:* For doctorate, GMAT or GRE (finance), 2 letters of reference, resume. Additional exam requirements/recommendations for international students: Required—TOEFL. Electronic applications accepted. *Expenses:* Contact institution. *Faculty research:* Human decision making and behavioral research; real estate market and mortgage defaults; financial crisis and corporate governance; international business; security analysis and accounting.

Columbia University, Graduate School of Business, MBA Program, New York, NY 10027. Offers accounting (MBA); decision, risk, and operations (MBA); entrepreneurship (MBA); finance and economics (MBA); healthcare and pharmaceutical management (MBA); human resource management (MBA); international business (MBA); leadership and ethics (MBA); management (MBA); marketing (MBA); media (MBA); private equity (MBA); real estate (MBA); social enterprise (MBA); value investing (MBA); DDS/MBA; JD/MBA; MBA/MIA; MBA/MPH; MBA/MS; MD/MBA. *Entrance requirements:* For master's, GMAT, 2 letters of recommendation. Additional exam requirements/recommendations for international students: Required—TOEFL. Electronic applications accepted. *Expenses:* Contact institution. *Faculty research:* Human decision making and behavioral research; real estate market and mortgage defaults; financial crisis and corporate governance; international business; security analysis and accounting.

Cornell University, Graduate School, Graduate Field of Management, Ithaca, NY 14853. Offers accounting (PhD); finance (PhD); marketing (PhD); organizational behavior (PhD); production and operations management (PhD). *Accreditation:* AACSB. *Degree requirements:* For doctorate, comprehensive exam, thesis/dissertation. *Entrance requirements:* For doctorate, GMAT or GRE General Test. Additional exam requirements/recommendations for international students: Required—TOEFL (minimum score 600 paper-based; 77 iBT). Electronic applications accepted. *Expenses:* Contact institution. *Faculty research:* Operations and manufacturing.

Cornell University, Samuel Curtis Johnson Graduate School of Management, Ithaca, NY 14853. Offers business administration (Exec MBA); management (MBA, PhD); management - accounting (MPS); JD/MBA; M Eng/MBA; MBA/MD; MBA/MHA; MBA/MILR; MBA/MPS. *Accreditation:* AACSB. *Faculty:* 65 full-time (17 women). *Students:* 573 full-time (165 women); includes 72 minority (11 Black or African American, non-Hispanic/Latino; 1 American Indian or Alaska Native, non-Hispanic/Latino; 36 Asian, non-Hispanic/Latino; 16 Hispanic/Latino; 8 Two or more races, non-Hispanic/Latino), 189 international. Average age 28. 1,653 applicants, 30% accepted, 277 enrolled. In 2017, 283 master's awarded. *Entrance requirements:* For master's, GMAT or GRE, resume, two essays, two recommendations. Additional exam requirements/recommendations for international students: Required—TOEFL. *Application deadline:*

For fall admission, 10/5 for domestic and international students; for winter admission, 11/15 for domestic and international students; for spring admission, 1/10 for domestic and international students; for summer admission, 4/5 for domestic and international students. Application fee: $200. Electronic applications accepted. *Expenses:* $66,894 per year. *Financial support:* Fellowships, institutionally sponsored loans, and scholarships/grants available. Financial award applicants required to submit FAFSA. *Faculty research:* Wholesale prices and revenue sharing contracts in markets with imperfect competition; differential access to information among traders in financial markets and how it impacts price efficiency; how corporate governance mechanisms matter for corporate financial policy choices and performance outcomes; conflict resolution in teams by conflict type, conflict management strategies, and team outcomes; information and incentive problems in operations and supply-chain management. *Unit head:* Dr. Mark Nelson, Dean, 607-255-6418, E-mail: dean@johnson.cornell.edu. *Application contact:* Admissions Office, 800-847-2082, Fax: 607-255-0065, E-mail: mba@johnson.cornell.edu.
Website: http://www.johnson.cornell.edu

Creighton University, Graduate School, Heider College of Business, Omaha, NE 68178-0001. Offers accounting (MAC); business administration (MBA, DBA); business intelligence and analytics (MS); finance (M Fin); investment management and financial analysis (MIMFA); JD/MBA; MBA/MIMFA; MD/MBA; Pharm D/MBA. *Accreditation:* AACSB. *Program availability:* Part-time, evening/weekend, 100% online, blended/hybrid learning. *Faculty:* 33 full-time (10 women), 22 part-time/adjunct (3 women). *Students:* 60 full-time (24 women), 308 part-time (95 women); includes 31 minority (14 Black or African American, non-Hispanic/Latino; 1 American Indian or Alaska Native, non-Hispanic/Latino; 9 Asian, non-Hispanic/Latino; 3 Hispanic/Latino; 2 Native Hawaiian or other Pacific Islander, non-Hispanic/Latino; 2 Two or more races, non-Hispanic/Latino), 28 international. Average age 32. 253 applicants, 74% accepted, 123 enrolled. In 2017, 139 master's awarded. *Degree requirements:* For master's, thesis optional; for doctorate, thesis/dissertation optional. *Entrance requirements:* For master's, GMAT, resume, 2 letters of recommendation. Additional exam requirements/recommendations for international students: Required—TOEFL (minimum score 90 iBT). *Application deadline:* For fall admission, 7/1 priority date for domestic students, 3/1 for international students; for winter admission, 10/1 priority date for domestic students, 7/1 for international students; for spring admission, 4/1 priority date for domestic students, 10/1 for international students; for summer admission, 5/1 for domestic and international students. Applications are processed on a rolling basis. Application fee: $50. Electronic applications accepted. *Expenses:* Contact institution. *Financial support:* In 2017–18, 10 fellowships with partial tuition reimbursements (averaging $8,448 per year) were awarded; career-related internships or fieldwork, tuition waivers (partial), and unspecified assistantships also available. Financial award application deadline: 3/1. *Faculty research:* Small business issues, economics, business analytics. *Unit head:* Dr. Deborah Wells, Associate Dean for Graduate Programs, 402-280-2841, E-mail: deborahwells@creighton.edu. *Application contact:* Chris Karasek, Assistant Dean, 402-280-2829, Fax: 402-280-2172, E-mail: chriskarasek@creighton.edu.
Website: http://business.creighton.edu

Culver-Stockton College, MBA Program, Canton, MO 63435-1299. Offers accounting and finance (MBA).

Daemen College, Department of Accounting/Information Systems, Amherst, NY 14226-3592. Offers global business (MS), including accounting, global business, management information systems, marketing. *Program availability:* Part-time, evening/weekend. *Degree requirements:* For master's, minimum GPA of 3.0. *Entrance requirements:* For master's, GMAT if undergraduate GPA is less than 3.0, 2 letters of recommendation; goal statement; transcripts; demonstration of satisfactory oral and written English. Additional exam requirements/recommendations for international students: Required—TOEFL (minimum score 500 paper-based; 63 iBT), IELTS (minimum score 5.5). Electronic applications accepted. *Faculty research:* Internationalization of small business, cultural influences on business practices, international human resource practices.

Dallas Baptist University, College of Business, Master of Business Administration Program, Dallas, TX 75211-9299. Offers accounting (MBA); business communication (MBA); conflict resolution management (MBA); entrepreneurship (MBA); finance (MBA); health care management (MBA); international business (MBA); leading the non-profit organization (MBA); management (MBA); management information systems (MBA); marketing (MBA); project management (MBA); technology and engineering management (MBA). *Accreditation:* ACBSP. *Program availability:* Part-time, evening/weekend, 100% online, blended/hybrid learning. *Application deadline:* Applications are processed on a rolling basis. Application fee: $25. Electronic applications accepted. Application fee is waived when completed online. *Expenses:* Tuition: Full-time $16,308; part-time $906 per credit hour. *Required fees:* $900; $450 per semester. Tuition and fees vary according to course load and degree level. *Unit head:* Dr. Sandra Reid, Chair of Graduate Business Programs, 214-333-5280, E-mail: sandra@dbu.edu. *Application contact:* Bobby Soto, Director of Admissions, 214-333-5242, E-mail: graduate@dbu.edu.
Website: http://www.dbu.edu/gsb/mba

Dallas Baptist University, Professional Development Program, Dallas, TX 75211-9299. Offers accounting (MA); church leadership (MA); communication (MA); counseling (MA); criminal justice (MA); English as a second language (MA); finance (MA); higher education (MA); leadership studies (MA); management (MA). *Program availability:* Part-time, evening/weekend. *Application deadline:* Applications are processed on a rolling basis. Application fee: $25. Electronic applications accepted. Application fee is waived when completed online. *Expenses:* Tuition: Full-time $16,308; part-time $906 per credit hour. *Required fees:* $900; $450 per semester. Tuition and fees vary according to course load and degree level. *Unit head:* Jared Ingram, Program Director, 214-333-5584, E-mail: jaredi@dbu.edu. *Application contact:* Bobby Soto, Director of Admissions, 214-333-5242, E-mail: bobby@dbu.edu.
Website: http://www3.dbu.edu/graduate/mapd.asp

Davenport University, Sneden Graduate School, Grand Rapids, MI 49512. Offers accounting (MBA); business administration (EMBA); finance (MBA); health care management (MBA); human resources (MBA); information assurance (MS); public health (MPH); strategic management (MBA). *Program availability:* Evening/weekend. *Entrance requirements:* For master's, GMAT, minimum undergraduate GPA of 2.75. Additional exam requirements/recommendations for international students: Required—TOEFL. Electronic applications accepted. *Faculty research:* Leadership, management, marketing, organizational culture.

Delaware Valley University, MBA Program, Doylestown, PA 18901-2697. Offers accounting (MBA); entrepreneurship (MBA); finance (MBA); food and agribusiness (MBA); general business (MBA); global executive leadership (MBA); human resource management (MBA); supply chain management (MBA). *Program availability:* Part-time, evening/weekend, online learning. *Entrance requirements:* For master's, minimum undergraduate GPA of 3.0. Electronic applications accepted. *Expenses:* Contact institution.

Delta State University, Graduate Programs, College of Business, Division of Accounting, Computer Information Systems, and Finance, Cleveland, MS 38733-0001. Offers accountancy (MPA).

DePaul University, Kellstadt Graduate School of Business, Chicago, IL 60604. Offers accountancy (MBA, MSA); applied economics (MBA); audit and advisory services (MS); business administration (DBA); business analytics (MS); business strategy and decision-making (MBA); computational finance (MS); economics and policy analysis (MS); enterprise risk management (MS); entrepreneurship (MBA, MS); finance (MBA, MS); general business (MBA); hospitality leadership (MBA); hospitality leadership and operational performance (MS); human resources (MS); international business (MBA); management (MBA, MS); management information systems (MBA); marketing (MBA, MS); marketing analysis (MS); marketing strategy and planning (MBA); real estate (MS); real estate finance and investment (MBA); strategy, execution and valuation (MBA); supply chain management (MS); sustainable management (MS); taxation (MS); JD/MBA. *Accreditation:* AACSB. *Program availability:* Part-time, evening/weekend, online learning. *Entrance requirements:* For master's, GMAT/GRE, 2 letters of recommendation, resume, essay, official transcripts. Additional exam requirements/recommendations for international students: Required—TOEFL (minimum score 550 paper-based; 80 iBT). *Application deadline:* For fall admission, 7/1 for domestic students, 6/1 for international students; for winter admission, 10/1 for domestic students, 9/1 for international students; for spring admission, 2/1 for domestic students, 1/1 for international students. Applications are processed on a rolling basis. Application fee: $60. Electronic applications accepted. *Expenses:* Contact institution. *Financial support:* Application deadline: 4/1; applicants required to submit FAFSA. *Unit head:* Christa Hinton, Assistant Dean and Director, 312-362-8810, Fax: 312-362-6677, E-mail: chinton@depaul.edu. *Application contact:* Garry Cooke, Director of Recruitment and Admissions, 312-362-8810, Fax: 312-362-6677, E-mail: kgsb@depaul.edu.
Website: http://kellstadt.depaul.edu

DeSales University, Division of Business, Center Valley, PA 18034-9568. Offers accounting (MBA); computer information systems (MBA); finance (MBA); health care systems management (MBA); human resources management (MBA); management (MBA); marketing (MBA); project management (MBA); self-design (MBA); supply chain management (MBA); DNP/MBA; MSN/MBA. *Accreditation:* ACBSP. *Program availability:* Part-time, evening/weekend, 100% online, blended/hybrid learning. *Faculty:* 9 full-time (3 women), 32 part-time/adjunct (8 women). *Students:* 78 full-time (44 women), 323 part-time (164 women); includes 71 minority (22 Black or African American, non-Hispanic/Latino; 17 Asian, non-Hispanic/Latino; 24 Hispanic/Latino; 8 Two or more races, non-Hispanic/Latino), 1 international. Average age 34. 213 applicants, 40% accepted, 64 enrolled. In 2017, 123 master's awarded. *Entrance requirements:* For master's, GMAT (waived if undergraduate GPA is 3.0 or better), minimum GPA of 3.0 in undergraduate work, literacy in basic software, background or interest in the field of study, personal statement, 2 years of work experience. Additional exam requirements/recommendations for international students: Required—TOEFL. *Application deadline:* Applications are processed on a rolling basis. Application fee: $50. Electronic applications accepted. *Expenses:* Contact institution. *Financial support:* Applicants required to submit FAFSA. *Faculty research:* Quality improvement, executive development, productivity, cross-cultural managerial differences, leadership. *Unit head:* Dr. David M. Gilfoil, Director, MBA Program, 610-282-1100 Ext. 1828, Fax: 610-282-2869, E-mail: david.gilfoil@desales.edu. *Application contact:* Julia Ferraro, Director of Graduate Admissions, 610-282-1100 Ext. 1768, E-mail: gradadmissions@desales.edu.

DeVry University–Folsom Campus, Graduate Programs, Folsom, CA 95630. Offers accounting (M Acc); accounting and financial management (MAFM); business administration (MBA); curriculum leadership (M Ed); educational leadership (M Ed); educational technology (M Ed); higher education leadership (M Ed); human resource management (MHRM); information systems management (MISM); network and communications management (MNCM); project management (MPM); public administration (MPA).

Dominican College, MBA Program, Orangeburg, NY 10962-1210. Offers accounting (MBA); healthcare management (MBA); management (MBA). *Program availability:* Part-time, evening/weekend. *Faculty:* 1 full-time (0 women). *Students:* 1 (woman) full-time, 21 part-time (15 women); includes 11 minority (6 Black or African American, non-Hispanic/Latino; 1 Asian, non-Hispanic/Latino; 3 Hispanic/Latino; 1 Two or more races, non-Hispanic/Latino), 1 international. In 2017, 14 master's awarded. *Entrance requirements:* For master's, GMAT, 2 letters of recommendation. Additional exam requirements/recommendations for international students: Required—TOEFL (minimum score 550 paper-based; 90 iBT). *Application deadline:* Applications are processed on a rolling basis. Application fee: $50. Electronic applications accepted. *Expenses:* Contact institution. *Financial support:* Application deadline: 2/1; applicants required to submit FAFSA. *Unit head:* Ken Mias, MBA Director, 845-848-4102, E-mail: ken.mias@dc.edu. *Application contact:* Christina Lifshey, Assistant Director of Graduate Admissions, 845-848-7908, Fax: 845-365-3150, E-mail: admissions@dc.edu.

Dominican University, Brennan School of Business, River Forest, IL 60305-1099. Offers MBA, MSA, JD/MBA, MBA/MLIS, MBA/MSW. JD/MBA offered jointly with John Marshall Law School. *Accreditation:* AACSB. *Program availability:* Part-time, evening/weekend, 100% online, blended/hybrid learning. *Faculty:* 20 full-time (8 women), 17 part-time/adjunct (6 women). *Students:* 68 full-time (52 women), 79 part-time (48 women); includes 34 minority (10 Black or African American, non-Hispanic/Latino; 7 Asian, non-Hispanic/Latino; 14 Hispanic/Latino; 1 Native Hawaiian or other Pacific Islander, non-Hispanic/Latino; 2 Two or more races, non-Hispanic/Latino), 25 international. Average age 29. 80 applicants, 78% accepted, 40 enrolled. In 2017, 77 master's awarded. *Entrance requirements:* For master's, GMAT. Additional exam requirements/recommendations for international students: Required—TOEFL (minimum score 550 paper-based; 79 iBT); Recommended—IELTS (minimum score 6). *Application deadline:* Applications are processed on a rolling basis. Application fee: $25. Electronic applications accepted. *Expenses:* $22,824. *Financial support:* Research assistantships, career-related internships or fieldwork, scholarships/grants, tuition waivers (partial), and unspecified assistantships available. Financial award application deadline: 3/1; financial award applicants required to submit FAFSA. *Faculty research:* Entrepreneurship, small business finance, business ethics, marketing strategy. *Unit head:* Dr. Roberto Curci, Dean, 708-524-6321, Fax: 708-524-6939, E-mail: rcurci@dom.edu. *Application contact:* Dr. Kathleen Odell, Associate Dean, Brennan School of Business, 708-488-5394, Fax: 708-524-6939, E-mail: kodell@dom.edu.
Website: http://business.dom.edu/

Drake University, College of Business and Public Administration, Des Moines, IA 50311-4516. Offers accounting (M Acc); business administration (MBA); public administration (MPA); JD/MBA; JD/MPA; Pharm D/MBA; Pharm D/MPA. *Program availability:* Part-time, evening/weekend. *Degree requirements:* For master's, comprehensive exam (for some programs), thesis (for some programs), internships. *Entrance requirements:* For master's, GMAT, letters of recommendation, resume. Additional exam requirements/recommendations for international students: Required—TOEFL (minimum score 550 paper-based). *Application deadline:* For fall admission, 8/15 priority date for domestic students; for winter admission, 12/20 priority date for domestic students; for spring admission, 12/1 priority date for domestic students.

Accounting

Applications are processed on a rolling basis. Application fee: $25. Electronic applications accepted. *Expenses:* Contact institution. *Financial support:* Fellowships with tuition reimbursements, teaching assistantships, career-related internships or fieldwork, and institutionally sponsored loans available. Support available to part-time students. Financial award application deadline: 3/1; financial award applicants required to submit FAFSA. *Faculty research:* Venture capital, online commerce, professional ethics, process improvement, project management. *Unit head:* Dr. Daniel J. Connolly, Dean, 515-271-2872, Fax: 515-271-4518, E-mail: daniel.connolly@drake.edu. *Application contact:* Danette Kenne, Assistant Dean, 515-271-2188, Fax: 515-271-4518, E-mail: cbpa.gradprograms@drake.edu. Website: http://www.drake.edu/cbpa/

Drexel University, LeBow College of Business, Department of Accounting, Program in Accounting, Philadelphia, PA 19104-2875. Offers MS. *Entrance requirements:* For master's, GMAT, minimum GPA of 2.75. Additional exam requirements/recommendations for international students: Required—TOEFL. Electronic applications accepted.

Drexel University, LeBow College of Business, Program in Business Administration, Philadelphia, PA 19104-2875. Offers business administration (MBA, PhD, APC), including accounting (MBA, PhD), decision sciences (PhD), economics (MBA, PhD), finance (MBA, PhD), legal studies (MBA), management (MBA), marketing (MBA, PhD), organizational sciences (PhD), quantitative methods (MBA), strategic management (PhD). *Accreditation:* AACSB. *Program availability:* Part-time, evening/weekend, online learning. Terminal master's awarded for partial completion of doctoral program. *Entrance requirements:* For master's, GMAT, minimum GPA of 2.75; for doctorate, GMAT. Additional exam requirements/recommendations for international students: Required—TOEFL. Electronic applications accepted. *Faculty research:* Decision support systems, individual and group behavior, operations research, techniques and strategy.

Duke University, The Fuqua School of Business, PhD Program, Durham, NC 27708-0586. Offers accounting (PhD); decision sciences (PhD); finance (PhD); management and organizations (PhD); marketing (PhD); operations management (PhD); strategy (PhD). *Faculty:* 96 full-time (19 women). *Students:* 64 full-time (25 women); includes 1 minority (Hispanic/Latino), 41 international. Average age 27. 617 applicants, 5% accepted, 14 enrolled. In 2017, 15 doctorates awarded. *Degree requirements:* For doctorate, thesis/dissertation, major field requirement (exam or major paper, depending upon the area). *Entrance requirements:* For doctorate, GMAT or GRE, transcripts, essays, recommendation letters, statement of purpose. Additional exam requirements/recommendations for international students: Required—TOEFL (minimum score 577 paper-based; 108 iBT), IELTS (minimum score 8). *Application deadline:* For fall admission, 12/31 priority date for domestic and international students. Application fee: $85. Electronic applications accepted. *Expenses:* $52,253. *Financial support:* In 2017–18, 66 students received support, including 66 fellowships with full tuition reimbursements available (averaging $29,200 per year), 63 research assistantships with full tuition reimbursements available (averaging $7,000 per year); institutionally sponsored loans, scholarships/grants, and tuition waivers (full) also available. Financial award applicants required to submit FAFSA. *Unit head:* William Boulding, Dean. *Application contact:* Qi Chen, Director of Graduate Studies, 919-660-7753, Fax: 919-660-7971, E-mail: qc2@duke.edu.

Duquesne University, Palumbo-Donahue School of Business, Pittsburgh, PA 15282-0001. Offers accounting (M Acc); finance (MBA); information systems management (MSISM); management (MBA, MS); marketing (MBA); sports business (MS); supply chain management (MS); sustainability (MBA); JD/MBA; MBA/M Acc; MBA/MA; MBA/MES; MBA/MHMS; MSISM/MBA; Pharm D/MBA. *Accreditation:* AACSB. *Program availability:* Part-time, evening/weekend, minimal on-campus study. *Faculty:* 59 full-time (23 women), 25 part-time/adjunct (6 women). *Students:* 232 full-time (83 women), 46 part-time (18 women); includes 28 minority (14 Black or African American, non-Hispanic/Latino; 8 Asian, non-Hispanic/Latino; 4 Hispanic/Latino; 2 Two or more races, non-Hispanic/Latino), 24 international. Average age 29. 220 applicants, 83% accepted, 121 enrolled. In 2017, 113 master's awarded. *Entrance requirements:* For master's, GMAT or GRE, undergraduate transcripts, 2 letters of recommendation, current resume, personal statement. Additional exam requirements/recommendations for international students: Required—TOEFL (minimum score 577 paper-based; 90 iBT), IELTS (minimum score 7). *Application deadline:* For fall admission, 7/1 priority date for domestic and international students; for spring admission, 12/1 for domestic and international students; for summer admission, 4/1 for domestic and international students. Applications are processed on a rolling basis. Application fee: $0. Electronic applications accepted. *Expenses:* $934 per credit (MS in management, sports business); $1,259 per credit (MBA, MS in accountancy, information systems management). *Financial support:* In 2017–18, 211 students received support, including 12 fellowships with partial tuition reimbursements available (averaging $14,200 per year), 20 research assistantships with partial tuition reimbursements available (averaging $22,662 per year); career-related internships or fieldwork, scholarships/grants, and unspecified assistantships also available. Support available to part-time students. Financial award application deadline: 7/1; financial award applicants required to submit FAFSA. *Faculty research:* Investment management, business ethics, technology management, supply chain management, entrepreneurship. *Unit head:* Dr. Karen Donovan, Associate Dean of Graduate Programs and Executive Education, 412-396-6276, Fax: 412-396-1726, E-mail: donovan6@duq.edu. *Application contact:* Jeff Jewett, Director of Admissions and Enrollment Management, 412-396-6244, Fax: 412-396-1726, E-mail: decrostam@duq.edu. Website: http://www.duq.edu/business/grad

East Carolina University, Graduate School, College of Business, Department of Accounting, Greenville, NC 27858-4353. Offers MSA. *Program availability:* Part-time. *Students:* 83 full-time (39 women), 8 part-time (5 women); includes 21 minority (11 Black or African American, non-Hispanic/Latino; 2 American Indian or Alaska Native, non-Hispanic/Latino; 4 Asian, non-Hispanic/Latino; 4 Hispanic/Latino), 1 international. Average age 26. 76 applicants, 79% accepted, 50 enrolled. In 2017, 56 master's awarded. *Entrance requirements:* For master's, GRE or GMAT. Additional exam requirements/recommendations for international students: Required—TOEFL (minimum score 78 iBT). Application fee: $75. Electronic applications accepted. *Expenses:* Tuition, state resident: full-time $4749; part-time $297 per credit hour. Tuition, nonresident: full-time $17,898; part-time $1119 per credit hour. *Required fees:* $2691; $224 per credit hour. Part-time tuition and fees vary according to course load and program. *Unit head:* Dr. Dan L. Schisler, Chair, 252-328-6055, E-mail: gradbus@ecu.edu. Website: https://business.ecu.edu/grad/msa/

Eastern Connecticut State University, School of Education and Professional Studies/Graduate Division, Program in Accounting, Willimantic, CT 06226-2295. Offers MS. *Accreditation:* NCATE. *Program availability:* Part-time, evening/weekend. *Faculty:* 3 full-time (1 woman), 3 part-time/adjunct (1 woman). *Students:* 11 full-time (5 women), 8 part-time (7 women); includes 9 minority (2 Black or African American, non-Hispanic/Latino; 6 Asian, non-Hispanic/Latino; 1 Hispanic/Latino). Average age 32. 6 applicants, 100% accepted, 5 enrolled. In 2017, 7 master's awarded. *Entrance requirements:* For

master's, minimum GPA of 2.7, bachelor's degree from accredited institution. Additional exam requirements/recommendations for international students: Required—TOEFL (minimum score 550 paper-based; 79 iBT); Recommended—IELTS (minimum score 6). *Application deadline:* For fall admission, 7/6 priority date for domestic and international students; for spring admission, 11/3 priority date for domestic and international students. Applications are processed on a rolling basis. Application fee: $50. Electronic applications accepted. *Expenses: Tuition, area resident:* Full-time $12,252. Tuition, state resident: Full-time $15,245; part-time $582 per credit hour. Tuition, nonresident: full-time $24,828; part-time $582 per credit hour. *Required fees:* $40 per semester. Full-time tuition and fees vary according to reciprocity agreements. *Financial support:* Research assistantships, career-related internships or fieldwork, institutionally sponsored loans, scholarships/grants, and unspecified assistantships available. Financial award application deadline: 3/1; financial award applicants required to submit FAFSA. *Unit head:* Dr. Moh'd RuJoub, Advisor, 860-465-5284, Fax: 860-465-5099, E-mail: rujoubm@easternct.edu. *Application contact:* Paula Goyette, Graduate Division, School of Education and Professional Studies, 860-465-5292, Fax: 860-465-4538, E-mail: graduateadmissions@easternct.edu.

Eastern Illinois University, Graduate School, Lumpkin College of Business and Technology, Program in Business Administration, Charleston, IL 61920. Offers accountancy (MBA); applied management (MBA); geographic information systems (MBA); research (MBA). *Accreditation:* AACSB. *Program availability:* Part-time, evening/weekend. *Entrance requirements:* For master's, GMAT or GRE. Additional exam requirements/recommendations for international students: Required—TOEFL (minimum score 500 paper-based; 61 iBT), IELTS (minimum score 6). *Application deadline:* For fall admission, 5/15 for domestic and international students; for spring admission, 10/15 for domestic and international students. Applications are processed on a rolling basis. Application fee: $30. Electronic applications accepted. *Financial support:* Research assistantships with full tuition reimbursements, teaching assistantships with full tuition reimbursements, career-related internships or fieldwork, Federal Work-Study, and unspecified assistantships available. Support available to part-time students. Financial award application deadline: 3/1; financial award applicants required to submit FAFSA. *Unit head:* Dr. Melody L. Wollan, Coordinator, 217-581-3028, Fax: 217-581-6642, E-mail: mlwollan@eiu.edu. *Application contact:* Dr. Melody L. Wollan, Coordinator, 217-581-3028, Fax: 217-581-6642, E-mail: mlwollan@eiu.edu. Website: http://www.eiu.edu/mba/index.php

Eastern Michigan University, Graduate School, College of Business, Department of Accounting and Finance, Ypsilanti, MI 48197. Offers accounting (MS); accounting information systems (MS). *Program availability:* Part-time, evening/weekend, online learning. *Faculty:* 26 full-time (11 women). *Students:* 44 full-time (23 women), 51 part-time (25 women); includes 13 minority (1 Black or African American, non-Hispanic/Latino; 1 American Indian or Alaska Native, non-Hispanic/Latino; 8 Asian, non-Hispanic/Latino; 3 Hispanic/Latino), 6 international. Average age 28. 50 applicants, 60% accepted, 24 enrolled. In 2017, 48 master's awarded. *Entrance requirements:* For master's, GMAT. Additional exam requirements/recommendations for international students: Required—TOEFL. *Application deadline:* Applications are processed on a rolling basis. Application fee: $45. *Financial support:* Fellowships, research assistantships with full tuition reimbursements, teaching assistantships with full tuition reimbursements, career-related internships or fieldwork, Federal Work-Study, institutionally sponsored loans, scholarships/grants, tuition waivers (partial), and unspecified assistantships available. Support available to part-time students. Financial award applicants required to submit FAFSA. *Unit head:* Dr. Phil Lewis, Interim Department Head, 734-487-3320, Fax: 734-487-0806, E-mail: plewis4@emich.edu. Website: http://www.accfin.emich.edu

Eastern Washington University, Graduate Studies, College of Business and Public Administration, Program in Professional Accounting, Cheney, WA 99004-2431. Offers MP Acc. Admissions temporarily suspended. *Accreditation:* NCATE. *Degree requirements:* For master's, comprehensive exam, thesis optional. *Expenses:* Tuition, state resident: full-time $11,191; part-time $373.06 per credit. Tuition, nonresident: full-time $25,995; part-time $866.52 per credit.

East Tennessee State University, School of Graduate Studies, College of Business and Technology, Department of Accountancy, Johnson City, TN 37614. Offers M Acc. *Accreditation:* AACSB. *Program availability:* Part-time, evening/weekend. *Degree requirements:* For master's, comprehensive exam, capstone, professional accounting experience. *Entrance requirements:* For master's, GMAT, minimum GPA of 2.5. Additional exam requirements/recommendations for international students: Required—TOEFL (minimum score 550 paper-based; 79 iBT). *Application deadline:* For fall admission, 6/1 for domestic students, 4/29 for international students; for spring admission, 11/1 for domestic students, 9/29 for international students. Application fee: $55 ($65 for international students). Electronic applications accepted. *Financial support:* Research assistantships with full tuition reimbursements, career-related internships or fieldwork, institutionally sponsored loans, scholarships/grants, and unspecified assistantships available. Financial award application deadline: 7/1; financial award applicants required to submit FAFSA. *Faculty research:* Smaller firm practice management, personal financial planning, accounting education, taxation issues. *Unit head:* Dr. Gary Burkette, Chair, 423-439-4432, Fax: 423-439-8659, E-mail: burkette@etsu.edu. *Application contact:* M Acc Program Director, 423-439-5314, Fax: 423-439-5274, E-mail: pointer@etsu.edu. Website: http://www.etsu.edu/cbat/acct/

Edgewood College, Program in Business, Madison, WI 53711-1997. Offers accountancy (MS); sustainability leadership (MBA). *Accreditation:* ACBSP. *Program availability:* Part-time, evening/weekend. *Students:* 19 full-time (12 women), 107 part-time (63 women); includes 16 minority (3 Black or African American, non-Hispanic/Latino; 5 Asian, non-Hispanic/Latino; 4 Hispanic/Latino; 4 Two or more races, non-Hispanic/Latino), 13 international. Average age 34. In 2017, 47 master's awarded. *Entrance requirements:* For master's, GMAT (minimum score 430), minimum GPA of 2.75, 2 letters of recommendation. Additional exam requirements/recommendations for international students: Required—TOEFL. *Application deadline:* For fall admission, 8/15 for domestic students, 5/1 for international students; for spring admission, 1/8 for domestic students, 11/1 for international students. Applications are processed on a rolling basis. Application fee: $30. Electronic applications accepted. *Expenses: Tuition:* Part-time $930 per credit. *Financial support:* Career-related internships or fieldwork and scholarships/grants available. *Unit head:* Dr. Stevie Watson, Dean, 608-663-2224, Fax: 608-663-3251, E-mail: swatson@edgewood.edu. *Application contact:* Joann Eastman, Admissions Counselor, 608-663-3250, Fax: 608-663-2214, E-mail: gps@edgewood.edu. Website: https://www.edgewood.edu/academics/schools/school-of-business

Elms College, Division of Business, Chicopee, MA 01013-2839. Offers accounting (MBA); accounting and finance (MS); financial planning (MBA, Certificate); healthcare leadership (MBA); lean entrepreneurship (MBA); management (MBA). *Program availability:* Part-time, evening/weekend. *Faculty:* 5 full-time (all women), 7 part-time/adjunct (4 women). *Students:* 51 part-time (30 women); includes 9 minority (4 Black or African American, non-Hispanic/Latino; 2 Asian, non-Hispanic/Latino; 3 Hispanic/Latino), 2 international. Average age 33. 14 applicants, 93% accepted, 10 enrolled. In

2017, 28 master's awarded. *Entrance requirements:* For master's, minimum GPA of 3.0. *Application deadline:* Applications are processed on a rolling basis. Application fee: $30. Electronic applications accepted. *Expenses: Tuition:* Full-time $13,860; part-time $770 per credit hour. *Required fees:* $200. Tuition and fees vary according to degree level and program. *Unit head:* Dr. David Kimball, Chair, Division of Business, 413-265-2300, E-mail: kimballd@elms.edu. *Application contact:* MBA Program Coordinator, 413-265-2592, E-mail: mba@elms.edu.

Emory University, Goizueta Business School, Doctoral Program in Business, Atlanta, GA 30322. Offers accounting (PhD); finance (PhD); information systems and operations management (PhD); marketing (PhD); organization and management (PhD). *Students:* 250 applicants, 5% accepted. *Degree requirements:* For doctorate, comprehensive exam, thesis/dissertation. *Entrance requirements:* For doctorate, GMAT, interview. Additional exam requirements/recommendations for international students: Required—TOEFL (minimum score 600 paper-based; 100 iBT). *Application deadline:* For fall admission, 1/3 priority date for domestic and international students. Applications are processed on a rolling basis. Application fee: $75. Electronic applications accepted. *Expenses:* Contact institution. *Financial support:* Fellowships, scholarships/grants, and health care benefits available. Financial award application deadline: 1/3. *Faculty research:* Financial and managerial accounting, asset pricing strategy and organizational behavior, information technology marketing analytics and consumer behavior. *Unit head:* Kathryn Kadous, Associate Dean, 404-727-2306, Fax: 404-727-5337, E-mail: kathryn.kadous@emory.edu. *Application contact:* Allison Gilmore, Director of Admissions and Student Services, 404-727-6353, Fax: 404-727-5337, E-mail: allison.gilmore@emory.edu.
Website: https://goizueta.emory.edu/degree/phd/index.html

Emory University, Goizueta Business School, Full Time MBA Program, Atlanta, GA 30322. Offers accounting (MBA); alternative investments (MBA); business process consulting (MBA); business technology management (MBA); capital markets (MBA); corporate finance (MBA); customer relationship management (MBA); decision analytics (MBA); entrepreneurship (MBA); finance (MBA); global management (MBA); investment banking (MBA); management consulting (MBA); marketing (MBA); marketing analytics (MBA); marketing consulting (MBA); operations management (MBA); organization and management (MBA); product and brand management (MBA); real estate (MBA); social enterprise (MBA); strategy consulting (MBA). *Accreditation:* AACSB. *Faculty:* 74 full-time (18 women), 18 part-time/adjunct (6 women). *Students:* 353 full-time (96 women); includes 80 minority (18 Black or African American, non-Hispanic/Latino; 2 American Indian or Alaska Native, non-Hispanic/Latino; 39 Asian, non-Hispanic/Latino; 16 Hispanic/Latino; 1 Native Hawaiian or other Pacific Islander, non-Hispanic/Latino; 4 Two or more races, non-Hispanic/Latino), 104 international. Average age 29. 1,380 applicants, 34% accepted, 172 enrolled. In 2017, 179 master's awarded. *Degree requirements:* For master's, 1 leadership course; 2 mid-semester module programs; 2 global components. *Entrance requirements:* For master's, GMAT/GRE, essays; recommendation letters; undergraduate degree; interview. Additional exam requirements/recommendations for international students: Required—TOEFL (minimum score 100 iBT), IELTS (minimum score 7), PTE (minimum score 68). *Application deadline:* For fall admission, 10/6 for domestic and international students; for winter admission, 11/17 for domestic and international students; for spring admission, 1/3 priority date for domestic and international students; for summer admission, 3/9 for domestic and international students. Application fee: $150. Electronic applications accepted. *Expenses:* $59,616. *Financial support:* In 2017–18, 273 students received support. Career-related internships or fieldwork, institutionally sponsored loans, and scholarships/grants available. Financial award application deadline: 4/1; financial award applicants required to submit FAFSA. *Faculty research:* Corporate finance, information systems, digital marketing, asset pricing, sports management. *Unit head:* Brian Mitchell, Associate Dean, 404-727-4824, Fax: 404-712-9648, E-mail: brian.mitchell@emory.edu. *Application contact:* Julie Barefoot, Associate Dean, 404-727-6311, Fax: 404-727-4612, E-mail: mbaadmissions@emory.edu.
Website: http://www.goizueta.emory.edu

Emporia State University, Program in Accountancy, Emporia, KS 66801-5415. Offers M Acc. *Program availability:* Part-time, 100% online, blended/hybrid learning. *Faculty:* 29 full-time (8 women). *Students:* 13 full-time (10 women), 33 part-time (15 women); includes 1 minority (Hispanic/Latino), 6 international. 26 applicants, 73% accepted, 18 enrolled. In 2017, 23 master's awarded. *Entrance requirements:* For master's, bachelor's degree in accounting. Additional exam requirements/recommendations for international students: Required—TOEFL (minimum score 550 paper-based). *Application deadline:* Applications are processed on a rolling basis. Application fee: $40. Electronic applications accepted. *Expenses:* Tuition, state resident: full-time $6084; part-time $253.50 per credit hour. Tuition, nonresident: full-time $18,924; part-time $788.50 per credit hour. *Required fees:* $1943; $80.95 per credit hour. Tuition and fees vary according to campus/location. *Financial support:* In 2017–18, 1 research assistantship with full tuition reimbursement (averaging $7,344 per year), 9 teaching assistantships with full tuition reimbursements (averaging $4,488 per year) were awarded; unspecified assistantships also available. Financial award applicants required to submit FAFSA. *Unit head:* Dr. Shawn Keough, Chair of the Faculty, 620-341-5408, E-mail: skeough@emporia.edu. *Application contact:* April Huddleston, Recruitment and Development Specialist, 800-950-GRAD, Fax: 620-341-5909, E-mail: ahuddles@emporia.edu.

Everglades University, Graduate Programs, Program in Business Administration, Boca Raton, FL 33431. Offers accounting for managers (MBA); aviation management (MBA); human resource management (MBA); project management (MBA). *Program availability:* Part-time, evening/weekend, 100% online. *Entrance requirements:* For master's, GMAT (minimum score of 400) or GRE (minimum score of 290), bachelor's or graduate degree from college accredited by an agency recognized by the U.S. Department of Education; minimum cumulative GPA of 2.0 at the baccalaureate level, 3.0 at the master's level. Additional exam requirements/recommendations for international students: Recommended—TOEFL (minimum score 500 paper-based). Electronic applications accepted. *Expenses:* Contact institution.

Fairfield University, Dolan School of Business, Fairfield, CT 06824. Offers accounting (MBA, MS, CAS); business analytics (MS); finance (MBA, MS, CAS); information systems and business analytics (MBA); management (MBA, CAS); marketing (MBA, CAS); taxation (CAS). *Accreditation:* AACSB. *Program availability:* Part-time, evening/weekend. *Faculty:* 18 full-time (6 women), 6 part-time/adjunct (2 women). *Students:* 120 full-time (57 women), 67 part-time (27 women); includes 20 minority (3 Black or African American, non-Hispanic/Latino; 1 American Indian or Alaska Native, non-Hispanic/Latino; 3 Asian, non-Hispanic/Latino; 11 Hispanic/Latino; 2 Two or more races, non-Hispanic/Latino), 33 international. Average age 26. 195 applicants, 87% accepted, 112 enrolled. In 2017, 93 master's awarded. *Degree requirements:* For master's, capstone course. *Entrance requirements:* For master's, GMAT (minimum score 500), 2 letters of reference, resume, minimum GPA of 3.0. Additional exam requirements/recommendations for international students: Required—TOEFL (minimum score 550 paper-based; 80 iBT) or IELTS (minimum score 6.5). *Application deadline:* For fall admission, 5/15 for international students; for spring admission, 10/15 for international students. Applications are processed on a rolling basis. Application fee: $60. Electronic applications accepted. *Expenses:* $925 per credit hour. *Financial support:* In 2017–18, 31 students received support. Scholarships/grants and unspecified assistantships available. Financial award applicants required to submit FAFSA. *Faculty research:* International finance, leadership and careers, ethics in accounting, emotions in consumer behavior and organizations, data analytics. *Unit head:* Dr. Mark Ligas, Interim Dean, 203-254-4070, Fax: 203-254-4105, E-mail: mligas@fairfield.edu. *Application contact:* Marianne Gumpper, Director of Graduate and Continuing Studies Admission, 203-254-4184, Fax: 203-254-4073, E-mail: gradadmis@fairfield.edu.
Website: http://fairfield.edu/mba

Fairleigh Dickinson University, Florham Campus, Silberman College of Business, Department of Accounting, Law, and Tax, Program in Accounting, Madison, NJ 07940-1099. Offers MS. *Entrance requirements:* For master's, GMAT.

Fairleigh Dickinson University, Metropolitan Campus, Silberman College of Business, Department of Accounting, Law, and Tax, Program in Accounting, Teaneck, NJ 07666-1914. Offers MBA, MS, Certificate. *Faculty research:* Corporate accounting, legal issues.

Fitchburg State University, Division of Graduate and Continuing Education, Program in Business Administration, Fitchburg, MA 01420-2697. Offers accounting (MBA); human resources management (MBA); management (MBA). *Program availability:* Part-time, evening/weekend, 100% online. *Faculty:* 7 full-time (2 women), 6 part-time/adjunct (2 women). *Students:* 356 full-time (179 women), 129 part-time (71 women); includes 132 minority (55 Black or African American, non-Hispanic/Latino; 1 American Indian or Alaska Native, non-Hispanic/Latino; 29 Asian, non-Hispanic/Latino; 42 Hispanic/Latino; 5 Two or more races, non-Hispanic/Latino). Average age 35. 332 applicants, 97% accepted, 259 enrolled. In 2017, 39 master's awarded. *Entrance requirements:* Additional exam requirements/recommendations for international students: Required—TOEFL (minimum score 550 paper-based; 79 iBT). *Application deadline:* For fall admission, 7/15 for international students; for spring admission, 12/1 for international students. Applications are processed on a rolling basis. Application fee: $50. Electronic applications accepted. *Expenses:* Contact institution. *Financial support:* In 2017–18, research assistantships with partial tuition reimbursements (averaging $5,500 per year) were awarded; Federal Work-Study, scholarships/grants, and unspecified assistantships also available. Support available to part-time students. Financial award application deadline: 3/1; financial award applicants required to submit FAFSA. *Unit head:* Joseph McAloon, Chair, 978-665-3745, Fax: 978-665-3658, E-mail: gce@fitchburgstate.edu. *Application contact:* Jinawa McNeil, Director of Admissions, 978-665-3140, Fax: 978-665-4540, E-mail: admissions@fitchburgstate.edu.
Website: http://www.fitchburgstate.edu

Florida Agricultural and Mechanical University, Division of Graduate Studies, Research, and Continuing Education, School of Business and Industry, Tallahassee, FL 32307-3200. Offers accounting (MBA); finance (MBA); management information systems (MBA); marketing (MBA). *Accreditation:* ACBSP. *Degree requirements:* For master's, residency. *Entrance requirements:* For master's, GMAT, minimum GPA of 3.0.

Florida Atlantic University, College of Business, School of Accounting, Boca Raton, FL 33431-0991. Offers MAC. *Accreditation:* AACSB. *Program availability:* Part-time, evening/weekend, online learning. *Faculty:* 15 full-time (5 women), 3 part-time/adjunct (2 women). *Students:* 145 full-time (62 women), 455 part-time (247 women); includes 288 minority (63 Black or African American, non-Hispanic/Latino; 1 American Indian or Alaska Native, non-Hispanic/Latino; 42 Asian, non-Hispanic/Latino; 158 Hispanic/Latino; 24 Two or more races, non-Hispanic/Latino), 23 international. Average age 31. 504 applicants, 63% accepted, 247 enrolled. In 2017, 242 master's awarded. *Degree requirements:* For master's, comprehensive exam, thesis optional. *Entrance requirements:* For master's, GMAT with minimum score 500 (preferred) or GRE (minimum score 1000 old test, 153 Verbal, 144 Quantitative, 4 Writing) taken within last 5 years, BS in accounting or equivalent, minimum GPA of 3.0 in last 60 hours of undergraduate study. Additional exam requirements/recommendations for international students: Required—TOEFL (minimum score 600 paper-based; 61 iBT), IELTS (minimum score 6). *Application deadline:* For fall admission, 7/1 priority date for domestic students, 2/15 priority date for international students; for spring admission, 11/1 priority date for domestic students, 7/15 priority date for international students. Applications are processed on a rolling basis. Application fee: $30. *Expenses:* Tuition, state resident: full-time $7400; part-time $369.82 per credit. Tuition, nonresident: full-time $20,496; part-time $1042.81 per credit. *Financial support:* Fellowships, research assistantships with partial tuition reimbursements, teaching assistantships, career-related internships or fieldwork, Federal Work-Study, institutionally sponsored loans, scholarships/grants, and tuition waivers (partial) available. Support available to part-time students. Financial award application deadline: 3/1. *Faculty research:* Systems and computer applications, accounting theory, information systems. *Unit head:* George Young, Director, 561-297-3636, E-mail: soa@fau.edu.
Website: http://business.fau.edu/departments/accounting/index.aspx

Florida Gulf Coast University, Lutgert College of Business, Program in Accounting and Taxation, Fort Myers, FL 33965-6565. Offers MS. *Program availability:* Part-time, evening/weekend. *Faculty:* 60 full-time (24 women), 31 part-time/adjunct (7 women). *Students:* 17 full-time (6 women), 27 part-time (16 women); includes 8 minority (1 Black or African American, non-Hispanic/Latino; 7 Hispanic/Latino), 1 international. Average age 29. 31 applicants, 77% accepted, 17 enrolled. In 2017, 18 master's awarded. *Degree requirements:* For master's, thesis or alternative. *Entrance requirements:* For master's, GMAT, minimum GPA of 3.0. Additional exam requirements/recommendations for international students: Required—TOEFL (minimum score 550 paper-based). *Application deadline:* For fall admission, 5/1 priority date for domestic students; for spring admission, 9/15 priority date for domestic students. Applications are processed on a rolling basis. Application fee: $30. Electronic applications accepted. *Expenses:* Tuition, state resident: part-time $290 per credit hour. Tuition, nonresident: part-time $1173 per credit hour. *Required fees:* $127 per credit hour. Tuition and fees vary according to course load. *Financial support:* In 2017–18, 2 students received support. Application deadline: 6/30; applicants required to submit FAFSA. *Faculty research:* Stock petitions, mergers and acquisitions, deferred taxes, fraud and accounting regulations, graphical reporting practices. *Unit head:* Dr. Tanya Benford, Chair, 239-590-7342, Fax: 239-590-7330, E-mail: tbenford@fgcu.edu. *Application contact:* Marisa Ouverson, Director of Enrollment Management, 239-590-7403, Fax: 239-590-7330, E-mail: mouverso@fgcu.edu.

Florida International University, Chapman Graduate School of Business, School of Accounting, Miami, FL 33199. Offers M Acc. *Program availability:* Part-time, evening/weekend. *Faculty:* 25 full-time (9 women), 18 part-time/adjunct (2 women). *Students:* 84 full-time (41 women), 19 part-time (8 women); includes 87 minority (5 Black or African American, non-Hispanic/Latino; 9 Asian, non-Hispanic/Latino; 72 Hispanic/Latino; 1 Two or more races, non-Hispanic/Latino), 4 international. Average age 26. 202 applicants, 48% accepted, 71 enrolled. In 2017, 139 master's awarded. *Entrance requirements:* For master's, GMAT or GRE, minimum GPA of 3.0 in upper-level coursework. Additional exam requirements/recommendations for international students: Required—TOEFL (minimum score 550 paper-based; 80 iBT) or IELTS (minimum score 6.5). *Application deadline:* For fall admission, 6/1 for domestic students, 4/1 for international students; for spring admission, 10/1 for domestic students, 9/1 for international students. Applications

Accounting

are processed on a rolling basis. Application fee: $30. Electronic applications accepted. *Expenses:* Contact institution. *Financial support:* Institutionally sponsored loans and scholarships/grants available. Financial award application deadline: 3/1; financial award applicants required to submit FAFSA. *Faculty research:* Financial and managerial accounting. *Unit head:* Ruth Ann McEewen, Director, 305-348-2581, E-mail: rmcewen@fiu.edu. *Application contact:* Cynthia Teijeiro, Program Manager, 305-348-7564, E-mail: cteijeir@fiu.edu.

Florida National University, Program in Business Administration, Hialeah, FL 33012. Offers accounting (MBA); finance (MBA); general management (MBA); health services administration (MBA); marketing (MBA); public management and leadership (MBA). *Program availability:* Part-time, blended/hybrid learning. *Degree requirements:* For master's, capstone. *Entrance requirements:* For master's, writing assessment, bachelor's degree from accredited institution; official undergraduate transcripts; minimum undergraduate GPA of 2.5, GMAT (minimum score of 400), or GRE (minimum score of 900); two letters of recommendation; resume. Additional exam requirements/recommendations for international students: Required—TOEFL (minimum score 500 paper-based; 62 iBT), IELTS (minimum score 5.5). *Application deadline:* Applications are processed on a rolling basis. Electronic applications accepted. *Expenses:* Contact institution. *Financial support:* Federal Work-Study, institutionally sponsored loans, scholarships/grants, and tuition waivers available. Financial award applicants required to submit FAFSA. *Unit head:* Dr. Ernesto Gonzalez, Business and Economics Department Head, 305-821-3333 Ext. 1070, Fax: 305-362-0595, E-mail: egonzalez@fnu.edu. Website: https://www.fnu.edu/prospective-students/our-programs/select-a-program/master-of-business-administration/business-administration-mba-masters/

Florida Southern College, Program in Accounting, Lakeland, FL 33801-5698. Offers M Acc. *Program availability:* Part-time, blended/hybrid learning. *Faculty:* 4 full-time (2 women). *Students:* 23 full-time (14 women), 3 part-time (1 woman); includes 6 minority (2 Black or African American, non-Hispanic/Latino; 4 Hispanic/Latino), 4 international. Average age 28. 25 applicants, 80% accepted, 18 enrolled. In 2017, 8 master's awarded. *Entrance requirements:* For master's, GMAT or GRE General Test, letter of reference, resume, personal statement. Additional exam requirements/recommendations for international students: Required—TOEFL (minimum score 550 paper-based, 79 iBT) or IELTS (6.5). *Application deadline:* For fall admission, 6/1 for domestic and international students; for spring admission, 10/1 for domestic and international students. Applications are processed on a rolling basis. Application fee: $30. Electronic applications accepted. *Expenses:* $775 per credit hour, $100 required fees. *Financial support:* Federal Work-Study and unspecified assistantships available. Financial award applicants required to submit FAFSA. *Unit head:* Dr. Lynn Clements, Director, 863-680-5022, E-mail: lclements@flsouthern.edu. *Application contact:* Jared Welling, Director, Office of Adult and Graduate Education, 863-680-4914, Fax: 863-680-3872, E-mail: jwelling@flsouthern.edu.
Website: http://www.flsouthern.edu/sage/graduate/programs/master-of-accountancy.aspx

Florida State University, The Graduate School, College of Business, Tallahassee, FL 32306-1110. Offers accounting (M Acc), including assurance and advisory services, generalist, taxation; business administration (MBA, PhD), including accounting (PhD), finance (PhD), management information systems (PhD), marketing (PhD), organizational behavior and human resources (PhD), risk management and insurance (PhD), strategy (PhD); finance (MS); management information systems (MS); risk management and insurance (MS); JD/MBA; MSW/MBA. *Accreditation:* AACSB. *Program availability:* Part-time, 100% online. *Faculty:* 93 full-time (23 women), 2 part-time/adjunct (1 woman). *Students:* 229 full-time (96 women), 423 part-time (154 women); includes 159 minority (44 Black or African American, non-Hispanic/Latino; 24 Asian, non-Hispanic/Latino; 75 Hispanic/Latino; 1 Native Hawaiian or other Pacific Islander, non-Hispanic/Latino; 15 Two or more races, non-Hispanic/Latino), 48 international. Average age 31. 300 applicants, 61% accepted, 133 enrolled. In 2017, 268 master's, 9 doctorates awarded. Terminal master's awarded for partial completion of doctoral program. *Degree requirements:* For doctorate, comprehensive exam, thesis/dissertation. *Entrance requirements:* For master's, GMAT, GRE (for all except MS in finance), work experience (MBA, MS); minimum GPA of 3.0, letters of recommendation; for doctorate, GMAT, GRE (for marketing, organizational behavior, risk management and insurance, management information systems, and human resources only), minimum graduate GPA of 3.5, letters of recommendation. Additional exam requirements/recommendations for international students: Required—TOEFL (minimum score 600 paper-based; 85 iBT); Recommended—IELTS (minimum score 6). *Application deadline:* For fall admission, 6/1 for domestic and international students; for spring admission, 10/1 for domestic and international students; for summer admission, 3/1 for domestic and international students. Applications are processed on a rolling basis. Application fee: $30. Electronic applications accepted. *Expenses:* Contact institution. *Financial support:* In 2017–18, 146 students received support, including 26 fellowships (averaging $1,500 per year), 77 research assistantships with full tuition reimbursements available (averaging $20,000 per year), 43 teaching assistantships with full tuition reimbursements available (averaging $20,000 per year); career-related internships or fieldwork, scholarships/grants, health care benefits, tuition waivers (full and partial), and unspecified assistantships also available. Support available to part-time students. Financial award application deadline: 1/1; financial award applicants required to submit FAFSA. *Faculty research:* Business strategy, marketing, finance, accounting, business analytics. *Total annual research expenditures:* $1.4 million. *Unit head:* Dr. Michael Hartline, Dean, 850-644-4405, Fax: 850-644-0915, E-mail: mhartline@business.fsu.edu. *Application contact:* Jennifer Clark, Director, 850-644-6458, E-mail: gradprograms@business.fsu.edu.
Website: http://business.fsu.edu/

Fontbonne University, Graduate Programs, St. Louis, MO 63105-3098. Offers accounting (MBA, MS); art (MA); art (K-12) (MAT); business (MBA); computer science (MS); deaf education (MA); early intervention in deaf education (MA); education (MA), including autism spectrum disorders, curriculum and instruction, diverse learners, early childhood education, reading, special education; elementary education (MAT); family and consumer sciences (MA), including multidisciplinary health communication studies; fine arts (MFA); instructional design and technology (MS); management and leadership (MM); middle school education (MAT); secondary education (MAT); special education (MAT); speech-language pathology (MS); supply chain management (MS); theatre (MA). *Program availability:* Part-time, evening/weekend, online learning. *Degree requirements:* For master's, comprehensive exam (for some programs), thesis (for some programs). *Entrance requirements:* Additional exam requirements/recommendations for international students: Required—TOEFL (minimum score 500 paper-based; 65 iBT). Electronic applications accepted.

Fordham University, Gabelli School of Business, New York, NY 10023. Offers accounting (MBA, MS); applied statistics and decision-making (MS); business economics (DPS); capital markets (DPS); communications and media management (MBA); electronic business (MBA); entrepreneurship (MBA); finance (MBA, PhD); global finance (MS); global sustainability (MBA); health administration (MS); healthcare management (MBA); information systems (MBA, MS); investor relations (MS); management (EMBA, MBA, MS, PhD); marketing (MBA); marketing intelligence (MS);

media management (MS); nonprofit leadership (MS); quantitative finance (MS); strategy and decision-making (DPS); taxation (MS); JD/MBA; MS/MBA. *Accreditation:* AACSB. *Program availability:* Part-time, evening/weekend. *Faculty:* 130 full-time (46 women), 42 part-time/adjunct (5 women). *Students:* 1,051 full-time (570 women), 563 part-time (313 women); includes 190 minority (48 Black or African American, non-Hispanic/Latino; 72 Asian, non-Hispanic/Latino; 69 Hispanic/Latino; 1 Native Hawaiian or other Pacific Islander, non-Hispanic/Latino), 1,106 international. Average age 27. 4,577 applicants, 58% accepted, 794 enrolled. In 2017, 937 master's awarded. Terminal master's awarded for partial completion of doctoral program. *Degree requirements:* For master's, internships (for some degrees); for doctorate, comprehensive exam (for some programs), thesis/dissertation. *Entrance requirements:* For master's, GMAT/GRE, 2 letters of recommendation, resume, 2 essays, transcripts, interview. Additional exam requirements/recommendations for international students: Required—TOEFL (minimum score 100 iBT), IELTS (minimum score 7). *Application deadline:* For fall admission, 11/15 priority date for domestic and international students; for winter admission, 1/19 priority date for domestic students, 1/1 priority date for international students; for spring admission, 4/15 for domestic students, 3/1 for international students; for summer admission, 6/1 for domestic students. Application fee: $130. Electronic applications accepted. *Expenses:* $1,495 per credit. *Financial support:* Career-related internships or fieldwork, institutionally sponsored loans, scholarships/grants, and unspecified assistantships available. Support available to part-time students. Financial award application deadline: 6/30; financial award applicants required to submit FAFSA. *Unit head:* Dr. Donna Rapaccioli, Dean, 212-636-6165, Fax: 212-307-1779, E-mail: rapaccioli@fordham.edu. *Application contact:* Lawrence Murray, Senior Assistant Dean of Graduate Admissions and Advising, 212-636-6200, Fax: 212-636-7076, E-mail: admissionsgb@fordham.edu.
Website: http://www.fordham.edu/gabelli

Franklin University, Accounting Program, Columbus, OH 43215-5399. Offers MSA. *Program availability:* Online learning.

Freed-Hardeman University, Program in Business Administration, Henderson, TN 38340-2399. Offers accounting (MBA); corporate responsibility (MBA); leadership (MBA). *Accreditation:* ACBSP. *Program availability:* Part-time, evening/weekend, online learning. *Entrance requirements:* For master's, GMAT. Additional exam requirements/recommendations for international students: Required—TOEFL (minimum score 500 paper-based).

Friends University, Graduate School, Wichita, KS 67213. Offers family therapy (MSFT); global business administration (MBA), including accounting, business law, change management, health care leadership, management information systems, supply chain management and logistics; health care leadership (MHCL); management information systems (MMIS); professional business administration (MBA), including accounting, business law, change management, health care leadership, management information systems, supply chain management and logistics. *Program availability:* Part-time, evening/weekend, online learning. *Degree requirements:* For master's, research project. *Entrance requirements:* For master's, bachelor's degree from accredited institution, official transcripts, interview with program director, letter(s) of recommendation. Additional exam requirements/recommendations for international students: Required—TOEFL (minimum score 560 paper-based). Electronic applications accepted.

George Fox University, College of Business, Newberg, OR 97132-2697. Offers accounting (DBA); finance (MBA); management (DBA); management and leadership (MBA); marketing (DBA); organizational strategy (MBA); strategic human resource management (MBA). MBA offered in Newberg, OR and in Portland, OR. *Accreditation:* ACBSP. *Program availability:* Part-time, evening/weekend, online learning. *Degree requirements:* For master's, capstone project; for doctorate, credit-applied research project. *Entrance requirements:* For master's, resume (5 years of professional experience); 3 professional references; interview; financial e-learning course; official transcripts; for doctorate, GRE or GMAT, resume; personal mission statement; academic research writing sample; official transcript from each college/university attended; three professional references. Additional exam requirements/recommendations for international students: Required—TOEFL (minimum score 577 paper-based; 90 iBT) or IELTS (minimum score 7). Electronic applications accepted. *Expenses:* Contact institution.

George Mason University, School of Business, Program in Accounting, Fairfax, VA 22030. Offers MS. *Accreditation:* AACSB. *Program availability:* Evening/weekend, 100% online. *Faculty:* 21 full-time (9 women), 14 part-time/adjunct (5 women). *Students:* 48 full-time (31 women), 46 part-time (33 women); includes 46 minority (15 Black or African American, non-Hispanic/Latino; 21 Asian, non-Hispanic/Latino; 9 Hispanic/Latino; 1 Two or more races, non-Hispanic/Latino), 19 international. Average age 30. 137 applicants, 74% accepted, 50 enrolled. In 2017, 34 master's awarded. *Entrance requirements:* For master's, GMAT/GRE, resume; official transcripts; 2 letters of recommendation; personal statement; professional essay; interview. Additional exam requirements/recommendations for international students: Required—TOEFL (minimum score 575 paper-based; 93 iBT), IELTS (minimum score 7), PTE (minimum score 59). *Application deadline:* For fall admission, 2/1 for domestic and international students. Application fee: $75 ($80 for international students). Electronic applications accepted. *Expenses:* $965 per credit in-state tuition, $1,778.25 out-of-state. *Financial support:* In 2017–18, 9 students received support, including 7 research assistantships with tuition reimbursements available (averaging $6,630 per year), 5 teaching assistantships with tuition reimbursements available (averaging $4,182 per year); career-related internships or fieldwork, Federal Work-Study, scholarships/grants, unspecified assistantships, and health care benefits (for full-time research or teaching assistantship recipients) also available. Support available to part-time students. Financial award application deadline: 3/1; financial award applicants required to submit FAFSA. *Faculty research:* Current leading global business issues, including offshore outsourcing, international financial risk, and comparative systems of innovation; business management/practices; emerging technology and generating new business. *Unit head:* JK Aier, Chair, 703-993-4546, Fax: 703-993-1809, E-mail: jaier@gmu.edu. *Application contact:* Mary Hayes Colllins, Program Manager, 703-993-9093, E-mail: mhayesco@gmu.edu.
Website: http://business.gmu.edu/masters-in-accounting/

The George Washington University, School of Business, Department of Accountancy, Washington, DC 20052. Offers M Accy. *Accreditation:* AACSB. *Program availability:* Part-time, evening/weekend. *Faculty:* 20 full-time (7 women), 7 part-time/adjunct (1 woman). *Students:* 137 full-time (93 women), 43 part-time (27 women); includes 36 minority (13 Black or African American, non-Hispanic/Latino; 12 Asian, non-Hispanic/Latino; 9 Hispanic/Latino; 2 Native Hawaiian or other Pacific Islander, non-Hispanic/Latino), 106 international. Average age 27. 715 applicants, 37% accepted, 81 enrolled. In 2017, 122 master's awarded. *Entrance requirements:* For master's, GMAT. Additional exam requirements/recommendations for international students: Required—TOEFL. *Application deadline:* For fall admission, 4/1 priority date for domestic students; for spring admission, 10/1 for domestic students. Applications are processed on a rolling basis. Application fee: $75. *Expenses: Tuition:* Full-time $28,800; part-time $1655 per credit hour. *Required fees:* $45; $2.75 per credit hour. *Financial support:* In 2017–18, 50 students received support. Fellowships, teaching assistantships, career-related internships or fieldwork, Federal Work-Study, and institutionally sponsored loans available. Financial award application deadline: 4/1. *Faculty research:* Management accounting and capital markets, financial accounting and the analytic hierarchy process, ethics and accounting, accounting information systems. *Unit head:* Dr. Angela Gore, Chair, 202-994-6195, E-mail: agore@gwu.edu. *Application contact:* Tatyana I. Kuzina, Administrative Manager, 202-994-4181, Fax: 202-994-5164, E-mail: tkuzina@gwu.edu. Website: http://business.gwu.edu/about-us/departments/department-of-accountancy/

Georgia College & State University, Graduate School, The J. Whitney Bunting School of Business, Program in Accounting, Milledgeville, GA 31061. Offers M Acc. *Program availability:* Part-time, evening/weekend. *Students:* 28 full-time (10 women), 6 part-time (3 women); includes 5 minority (3 Black or African American, non-Hispanic/Latino; 1 Hispanic/Latino; 1 Native Hawaiian or other Pacific Islander, non-Hispanic/Latino), 2 international. Average age 25. 16 applicants, 100% accepted, 13 enrolled. In 2017, 21 master's awarded. *Degree requirements:* For master's, minimum GPA of 3.0 on all business courses taken at Georgia College, complete program within 7 years of start date. *Entrance requirements:* For master's, GRE or GMAT (not required if graduated from AASCB-accredited business school with accounting degree, overall GPA of 3.25, and major GPA of 3.0), transcript, certification of immunization. *Application deadline:* For fall admission, 7/1 priority date for domestic students; for spring admission, 11/1 priority date for domestic students; for summer admission, 4/1 priority date for domestic students. Applications are processed on a rolling basis. Application fee: $40. Electronic applications accepted. *Expenses:* $288 per credit hour in-state tuition, $1,027 out-of-state; $1,011 per semester full-time fees. *Financial support:* In 2017–18, 17 students received support. Research assistantships, health care benefits, and unspecified assistantships available. Financial award application deadline: 3/1; financial award applicants required to submit FAFSA. *Unit head:* Dr. Dale Young, Dean, School of Business, 478-445-5497, E-mail: dale.younge@gcsu.edu. *Application contact:* Lynn Hanson, Director of Graduate Programs, 478-445-5115, E-mail: lynn.hanson@gcsu.edu.
Website: http://gcsu.edu/business/gradbusiness/macc

Georgia Southern University, Jack N. Averitt College of Graduate Studies, College of Business, Program in Accounting, Statesboro, GA 30460. Offers forensic accounting (M Acc). *Accreditation:* AACSB. *Program availability:* Part-time, 100% online. *Faculty:* 18 full-time (5 women). *Students:* 57 full-time (37 women), 68 part-time (48 women); includes 34 minority (18 Black or African American, non-Hispanic/Latino; 8 Asian, non-Hispanic/Latino; 4 Hispanic/Latino; 4 Two or more races, non-Hispanic/Latino), 3 international. Average age 28. 56 applicants, 89% accepted, 39 enrolled. In 2017, 59 master's awarded. *Entrance requirements:* For master's, GMAT. Additional exam requirements/recommendations for international students: Required—TOEFL (minimum score 550 paper-based; 80 iBT), IELTS (minimum score 6). *Application deadline:* For fall admission, 3/1 priority date for domestic and international students; for spring admission, 10/1 priority date for domestic students, 10/1 for international students. Applications are processed on a rolling basis. Application fee: $50. Electronic applications accepted. *Expenses:* $410 per credit in-state, $4,912 per semester; $1,286 per credit out-of-state, $14,856 per semester; $527 per credit online. *Financial support:* In 2017–18, 39 students received support, including 1 research assistantship with partial tuition reimbursement available (averaging $7,750 per year), 1 teaching assistantship with partial tuition reimbursement available (averaging $7,750 per year); career-related internships or fieldwork, Federal Work-Study, scholarships/grants, tuition waivers (partial), and unspecified assistantships also available. Support available to part-time students. Financial award application deadline: 4/15; financial award applicants required to submit FAFSA. *Faculty research:* Financial fraud in financial statements, determinants of firms switching auditors, whistle-blowing, impact of new tax code on firms, pedagogy issues in accounting and law courses. *Unit head:* Dr. Timothy Pearson, Graduate Program Director, 912-478-0103, Fax: 912-478-0292, E-mail: tpearson@georgiasouthern.edu. *Application contact:* 912-478-5767, Fax: 912-478-0740, E-mail: macccoordinator@georgiasouthern.edu.
Website: http://cob.georgiasouthern.edu/soa/graduate/

Georgia State University, J. Mack Robinson College of Business, School of Accountancy, Program in Professional Accountancy, Atlanta, GA 30303. Offers MPA. *Accreditation:* AACSB. *Program availability:* Part-time, evening/weekend. *Entrance requirements:* For master's, GRE or GMAT, transcripts from all institutions attended, resume, essays. Additional exam requirements/recommendations for international students: Required—TOEFL (minimum score 610 paper-based; 101 iBT), IELTS (minimum score 7). *Application deadline:* Applications are processed on a rolling basis. Application fee: $50. Electronic applications accepted. *Expenses:* Tuition, state resident: full-time $7020. Tuition, nonresident: full-time $22,518. *Required fees:* $2128. Tuition and fees vary according to degree level and program. *Financial support:* Research assistantships, scholarships/grants, tuition waivers, and unspecified assistantships available. *Unit head:* Dr. Galen R. Sevcik, Director of the School of Accountancy, 404-413-7200, Fax: 404-413-7203. *Application contact:* Toby McChesney, Assistant Dean for Graduate Recruiting and Student Services, 404-413-7167, Fax: 404-413-7162, E-mail: rcbgradadmissions@gsu.edu.
Website: http://robinson.gsu.edu/accountancy/mpa.html

Golden Gate University, Ageno School of Business, San Francisco, CA 94105-2968. Offers accounting (MBA); adaptive leadership (MBA); advanced financial planning (MS); business administration (EMBA, MBA, DBA); business analytics (MBA, MS); entrepreneurship (MBA); finance (MBA, MS, Certificate); financial life planning (Certificate); financial planning (MS, Certificate); global supply chain management (MBA, Certificate); human resource management (MBA, MS, Certificate); information technology management (MBA, MS, Certificate); international business (MBA); marketing (MBA, MS, Certificate); project management (MBA, MS, Certificate); psychology (MA, Certificate); public administration (EMPA, MPA); public administration leadership (Certificate); JD/MBA. *Program availability:* Part-time, evening/weekend. *Faculty:* 17 full-time (7 women), 280 part-time/adjunct (95 women). *Students:* 309 full-time (147 women), 527 part-time (266 women); includes 286 minority (56 Black or African American, non-Hispanic/Latino; 1 American Indian or Alaska Native, non-Hispanic/Latino; 131 Asian, non-Hispanic/Latino; 83 Hispanic/Latino; 4 Native Hawaiian or other Pacific Islander, non-Hispanic/Latino; 11 Two or more races, non-Hispanic/Latino), 209 international. Average age 35. 549 applicants, 66% accepted, 185 enrolled. *Degree requirements:* For doctorate, thesis/dissertation, qualifying examination. *Entrance requirements:* For master's, GMAT (for MBA), minimum GPA of 2.5 (MS). Additional exam requirements/recommendations for international students: Required—TOEFL (minimum score 550 paper-based; 79 iBT). *Application deadline:* For fall admission, 5/15 for domestic and international students; for winter admission, 1/15 for domestic and international students; for spring admission, 9/15 for domestic and international students. Applications are processed on a rolling basis. Application fee: $65 ($105 for international students). Electronic applications accepted. *Expenses:* $3,150 per 3-unit course. *Financial support:* Career-related internships or fieldwork, Federal Work-Study, institutionally sponsored loans, and scholarships/grants available. Support available to part-time students. Financial award applicants required to submit FAFSA. *Unit head:* Marianne Koch, Associate Dean, 415-442-6542, Fax: 415-442-6579, E-mail: mkoch@ggu.edu. *Application contact:* Angela Melero, Enrollment Services, 415-

442-7800, Fax: 415-442-7807, E-mail: info@ggu.edu.
Website: http://www.ggu.edu/programs/business-and-management

Golden Gate University, School of Accounting, San Francisco, CA 94105-2968. Offers financial accounting and reporting (M Ac, MSA, Graduate Certificate); forensic accounting (M Ac, MSA, Graduate Certificate); internal auditing (M Ac, MSA, Certificate); management accounting (M Ac, MSA); taxation (M Ac, MSA). *Program availability:* Part-time, evening/weekend. *Faculty:* 3 full-time (1 woman), 64 part-time/adjunct (21 women). *Students:* 76 full-time (51 women), 136 part-time (87 women); includes 63 minority (7 Black or African American, non-Hispanic/Latino; 35 Asian, non-Hispanic/Latino; 18 Hispanic/Latino; 1 Native Hawaiian or other Pacific Islander, non-Hispanic/Latino; 2 Two or more races, non-Hispanic/Latino), 76 international. Average age 32. 94 applicants, 69% accepted, 38 enrolled. *Entrance requirements:* For master's, minimum GPA of 3.0. Additional exam requirements/recommendations for international students: Required—TOEFL (minimum score 550 paper-based), IELTS (minimum score 6.5). *Application deadline:* For fall admission, 5/15 for international students; for winter admission, 1/15 for international students; for spring admission, 9/15 for international students. Applications are processed on a rolling basis. Application fee: $65 ($95 for international students). Electronic applications accepted. *Expenses:* $3,150 per 3-unit course. *Financial support:* Career-related internships or fieldwork, Federal Work-Study, institutionally sponsored loans, and scholarships/grants available. Support available to part-time students. Financial award applicants required to submit FAFSA. *Faculty research:* Forensic accounting, audit, tax, CPA exam. *Unit head:* Fred Sroka, Dean, 415-369-5285, Fax: 415-543-2607. *Application contact:* Angela Melero, Enrollment Services, 415-442-7800, Fax: 415-442-7807, E-mail: info@ggu.edu.

Gonzaga University, School of Business Administration, Spokane, WA 99258. Offers accountancy (M Acc); American Indian entrepreneurship (MBA); business administration (MBA); taxation (MS); JD/M Acc; JD/MBA. *Accreditation:* AACSB. *Program availability:* Part-time, evening/weekend. *Faculty:* 17 full-time (3 women), 11 part-time/adjunct (3 women). *Students:* 94 full-time (32 women), 118 part-time (64 women); includes 41 minority (2 Black or African American, non-Hispanic/Latino; 9 American Indian or Alaska Native, non-Hispanic/Latino; 8 Asian, non-Hispanic/Latino; 10 Hispanic/Latino; 1 Native Hawaiian or other Pacific Islander, non-Hispanic/Latino; 11 Two or more races, non-Hispanic/Latino), 11 international. Average age 29. 218 applicants, 75% accepted, 101 enrolled. In 2017, 96 master's awarded. *Degree requirements:* For master's, capstone course. *Entrance requirements:* For master's, GMAT or GRE, essay, two professional recommendations, resume/curriculum vitae, copy of official transcripts from all colleges attended, minimum GPA of 3.0. Additional exam requirements/recommendations for international students: Required—TOEFL (minimum score 570 paper-based, 89 iBT) or IELTS (minimum score 6.5). *Application deadline:* Applications are processed on a rolling basis. Application fee: $50. Electronic applications accepted. *Expenses:* Contact institution. *Financial support:* In 2017–18, 117 students received support. Scholarships/grants, tuition waivers, and unspecified assistantships available. Support available to part-time students. Financial award applicants required to submit FAFSA. *Unit head:* Dr. Ken Anderson, Dean, 509-313-5991, E-mail: anderson@gonzaga.edu. *Application contact:* Stacey Chatman, Assistant Director for Admissions, 509-313-4622, E-mail: chatman@gonzaga.edu.
Website: https://www.gonzaga.edu/school-of-business-administration

Governors State University, College of Business, Program in Accounting, University Park, IL 60484. Offers MS. *Program availability:* Part-time. *Faculty:* 13 full-time (4 women), 15 part-time/adjunct (7 women). *Students:* 13 full-time (10 women), 19 part-time (4 women); includes 10 minority (7 Black or African American, non-Hispanic/Latino; 3 Hispanic/Latino), 3 international. Average age 36. 18 applicants, 56% accepted, 9 enrolled. In 2017, 24 master's awarded. *Application deadline:* For fall admission, 4/1 for domestic students. Applications are processed on a rolling basis. Application fee: $50. Electronic applications accepted. *Expenses:* Contact institution. *Financial support:* Application deadline: 5/1; applicants required to submit FAFSA. *Unit head:* David Green, Chair, Division of Accounting, Finance, Management Information Systems, and Economics, 708-534-5000 Ext. 4967, E-mail: dgreen@govst.edu.

The Graduate Center, City University of New York, Graduate Studies, Program in Business, New York, NY 10016-4039. Offers accounting (PhD); behavioral science (PhD); finance (PhD); management planning systems (PhD). *Faculty:* 66 full-time (5 women). *Students:* 56 full-time (30 women); includes 6 minority (1 Black or African American, non-Hispanic/Latino; 1 American Indian or Alaska Native, non-Hispanic/Latino; 2 Asian, non-Hispanic/Latino; 2 Hispanic/Latino), 42 international. Average age 33. 177 applicants, 7% accepted, 10 enrolled. In 2017, 10 doctorates awarded. *Degree requirements:* For doctorate, thesis/dissertation. *Entrance requirements:* For doctorate, GMAT, writing sample (15 pages). Additional exam requirements/recommendations for international students: Required—TOEFL. *Application deadline:* For fall admission, 1/15 for domestic students. Application fee: $125. Electronic applications accepted. *Financial support:* In 2017–18, 50 students received support, including 54 fellowships, 5 teaching assistantships; research assistantships, career-related internships or fieldwork, Federal Work-Study, institutionally sponsored loans, and tuition waivers (full and partial) also available. Financial award application deadline: 2/1; financial award applicants required to submit FAFSA. *Unit head:* Dr. Joseph Weintrop, Executive Officer, 646-312-3092, Fax: 646-312-3031. *Application contact:* Les Gribben, Director of Admissions, 212-817-7470, Fax: 212-817-1624, E-mail: lgribben@gc.cuny.edu.

Grand Canyon University, Colangelo College of Business, Phoenix, AZ 85017-1097. Offers accounting (MBA, MS); business analytics (MS); disaster preparedness and executive fire service leadership (MS); finance (MBA); general management (MBA); health systems management (MS); information technology management (MS); leadership (MBA, MS); marketing (MBA); organizational leadership and entrepreneurship (MS); project management (MBA); sports business (MBA); strategic human resource management (MBA). *Accreditation:* ACBSP. *Program availability:* Part-time, evening/weekend, online learning. *Entrance requirements:* For master's, equivalent of two years' full-time professional work experience. Additional exam requirements/recommendations for international students: Required—TOEFL (minimum score 575 paper-based; 90 iBT), IELTS (minimum score 7). Electronic applications accepted.

Grand Valley State University, Seidman College of Business, Program in Accounting, Allendale, MI 49401-9403. Offers MSA. *Accreditation:* AACSB. *Program availability:* Part-time, evening/weekend. *Faculty:* 8 full-time (4 women), 4 part-time/adjunct (2 women). *Students:* 48 full-time (24 women), 30 part-time (9 women); includes 9 minority (5 Asian, non-Hispanic/Latino; 2 Hispanic/Latino; 2 Two or more races, non-Hispanic/Latino), 3 international. Average age 26. 30 applicants, 97% accepted, 19 enrolled. In 2017, 54 master's awarded. *Degree requirements:* For master's, comprehensive exam. *Entrance requirements:* For master's, GMAT, personal statement. Additional exam requirements/recommendations for international students: Required—TOEFL (minimum iBT score of 80), IELTS (6.5), or Michigan English Language Assessment Battery (77). *Application deadline:* For fall admission, 8/1 priority date for domestic students, 5/1 priority date for international students; for winter admission, 11/1 priority date for domestic and international students; for spring admission, 4/1 priority date for domestic students, 3/1 priority date for international students. Applications are processed on a rolling basis. Application fee: $30. *Expenses:* $686 per credit hour. *Financial support:* In

2017–18, 23 students received support, including 9 fellowships, 10 research assistantships with full and partial tuition reimbursements available (averaging $4,000 per year); Federal Work-Study, scholarships/grants, and unspecified assistantships also available. Support available to part-time students. Financial award application deadline: 2/15; financial award applicants required to submit FAFSA. *Faculty research:* Public trust, capacity measurement, theoretical capacity, economic order quantity. *Unit head:* Dr. Steve Goldberg, Director, 616-331-7410, Fax: 616-331-7412, E-mail: goldbers@gvsu.edu. *Application contact:* Koleta Moore, Assistant Dean of Student Engagement, Graduate Program Operations, 616-331-7386, Fax: 616-331-7389, E-mail: moorekol@gvsu.edu.
Website: http://www.gvsu.edu/business/

Harvard University, Harvard Business School, Doctoral Programs in Management, Boston, MA 02163. Offers accounting and management (DBA); business economics (PhD); health policy management (PhD); management (DBA); marketing (DBA); organizational behavior (PhD); science, technology and management (PhD); strategy (DBA); technology and operations management (DBA). *Degree requirements:* For doctorate, comprehensive exam (for some programs), thesis/dissertation. *Entrance requirements:* For doctorate, GRE General Test or GMAT. Additional exam requirements/recommendations for international students: Required—TOEFL.

HEC Montreal, School of Business Administration, Doctoral Program in Administration, Montréal, QC H3T 2A7, Canada. Offers accounting (PhD); applied economics (PhD); data science (PhD); finance (PhD); financial engineering (PhD); information technology (PhD); international business (PhD); logistics and operations management (PhD); management science (PhD); management, strategy and organizations (PhD); marketing (PhD); organizational behaviour and human resources (PhD). Program offered jointly with Concordia University, McGill University, and Universite du Quebec a Montreal. *Accreditation:* AACSB. *Students:* 114 full-time (47 women). 78 applicants, 42% accepted, 24 enrolled. In 2017, 23 doctorates awarded. *Entrance requirements:* For doctorate, TAGE MAGE, GMAT, or GRE, master's degree in administration or related field. *Application deadline:* For fall admission, 1/15 for domestic and international students. Application fee: $88 ($187 for international students). Electronic applications accepted. *Expenses:* Tuition, state resident: full-time $2869 Canadian dollars; part-time $79.70 Canadian dollars per credit. Tuition, nonresident: full-time $8883 Canadian dollars; part-time $246.76 Canadian dollars per credit. *International tuition:* $19,648 Canadian dollars full-time. *Required fees:* $41.20 Canadian dollars per credit. $67.94 Canadian dollars per term. Tuition and fees vary according to degree level and program. *Financial support:* Research assistantships, teaching assistantships, and scholarships/grants available. Financial award application deadline: 9/2. *Faculty research:* Art management, business policy, entrepreneurship, new technologies, transportation. *Unit head:* Jacques Robert, Director, 514-340-6853, E-mail: jacques.robert@hec.ca. *Application contact:* Julie Bilodeau, PhD Program Analyst, 514-340-6151, Fax: 514-340-6411, E-mail: analyste.phd@hec.ca.
Website: http://www.hec.ca/en/programs/phd/index.html

HEC Montreal, School of Business Administration, Graduate Diploma Programs in Administration, Program in Professional Accounting, Montréal, QC H3T 2A7, Canada. Offers Graduate Diploma. All courses are given in French. *Program availability:* Part-time. *Students:* 174 full-time (98 women), 81 part-time (39 women). 326 applicants, 76% accepted, 221 enrolled. In 2017, 229 Graduate Diplomas awarded. *Entrance requirements:* For degree, bachelor's degree in accounting. *Application deadline:* For winter admission, 9/15 for domestic and international students; for spring admission, 2/10 for domestic and international students. Application fee: $88 Canadian dollars ($184 Canadian dollars for international students). Electronic applications accepted. *Expenses:* Tuition, state resident: full-time $2869 Canadian dollars; part-time $79.70 Canadian dollars per credit. Tuition, nonresident: full-time $8883 Canadian dollars; part-time $246.76 Canadian dollars per credit. *International tuition:* $19,648 Canadian dollars full-time. *Required fees:* $41.20 Canadian dollars per credit. $67.94 Canadian dollars per term. Tuition and fees vary according to degree level and program. *Financial support:* Research assistantships, teaching assistantships, and scholarships/grants available. Financial award application deadline: 9/2. *Unit head:* Renaud Lachance, Director, 514-340-7165, E-mail: renaud.lachance@hec.ca. *Application contact:* Anny Caron, Administrative Director, 514-340-6151, Fax: 514-340-6411, E-mail: aide@hec.ca.
Website: http://www.hec.ca/programmes/dess/dess-comptabilite-professionnelle-cpa/index.html

HEC Montreal, School of Business Administration, Master of Science Programs in Administration, Program in Management Control, Montréal, QC H3T 2A7, Canada. Offers M Sc. Program offered in French. *Students:* 5 full-time (3 women), 5 part-time (4 women). 7 applicants, 14% accepted, 1 enrolled. In 2017, 3 master's awarded. *Entrance requirements:* For master's, BBA, undergraduate degree in another field, degree deemed equivalent by program director and minimum GPA of 3.0 on 4.3 scale. Additional exam requirements/recommendations for international students: Required—TAGE MAGE (minimum recommended score of 283), GMAT (minimum recommended score of 630), or GRE. *Application deadline:* For fall admission, 3/15 for domestic and international students; for winter admission, 9/15 for domestic and international students. Application fee: $88 Canadian dollars ($184 Canadian dollars for international students). Electronic applications accepted. *Expenses:* Tuition, state resident: full-time $2869 Canadian dollars; part-time $79.70 Canadian dollars per credit. Tuition, nonresident: full-time $8883 Canadian dollars; part-time $246.76 Canadian dollars per credit. *International tuition:* $19,648 Canadian dollars full-time. *Required fees:* $41.20 Canadian dollars per credit. $67.94 Canadian dollars per term. Tuition and fees vary according to degree level and program. *Financial support:* Research assistantships, teaching assistantships, and scholarships/grants available. Financial award application deadline: 9/2. *Unit head:* Dr. Marie-Helene Jobin, Director, 514-340-6283, E-mail: marie-helene.jobin@hec.ca. *Application contact:* Marianne de Moura, Administrative Director, 514-340-6151, Fax: 514-340-6411, E-mail: aide@hec.ca.
Website: http://www.hec.ca/programmes/maitrises/maitrise-comptabilite-controle-audit/index.html

HEC Montreal, School of Business Administration, Master of Science Programs in Administration, Program on Accounting, Management, Control and Audit, Montréal, QC H3T 2A7, Canada. Offers M Sc. *Students:* 3 full-time (2 women), 7 part-time (3 women). 10 applicants, 100% accepted, 6 enrolled. In 2017, 15 master's awarded. *Entrance requirements:* For master's, short graduate program in public accounting from HEC Montreal, minimum GPA of 3.0 on 4.3 scale. Additional exam requirements/recommendations for international students: Required—TAGE MAGE (minimum recommended score of 283), GMAT (minimum recommended score of 630), or GRE. *Application deadline:* For fall admission, 3/15 for domestic and international students; for winter admission, 9/15 for domestic and international students. Application fee: $88 ($184 for international students). Electronic applications accepted. *Expenses:* Tuition, state resident: full-time $2869 Canadian dollars; part-time $79.70 Canadian dollars per credit. Tuition, nonresident: full-time $8883 Canadian dollars; part-time $246.76 Canadian dollars per credit. *International tuition:* $19,648 Canadian dollars full-time. *Required fees:* $41.20 Canadian dollars per credit. $67.94 Canadian dollars per term. Tuition and fees vary according to degree level and program. *Financial support:*

Research assistantships, teaching assistantships, and scholarships/grants available. Financial award application deadline: 9/2. *Unit head:* Dr. Marie-Helene Jobin, Director, 514-340-6283, E-mail: marie-helene.jobin@hec.ca. *Application contact:* Marianne de Moura, Administrative Director, 514-340-6151, Fax: 514-340-6411, E-mail: aide@hec.ca.
Website: http://www.hec.ca/programmes/maitrises/maitrise-comptabilite-controle-audit/index.html

Hendrix College, Program in Accounting, Conway, AR 72032-3080. Offers MA. *Program availability:* Part-time. *Entrance requirements:* For master's, GMAT. Additional exam requirements/recommendations for international students: Required—TOEFL. *Faculty research:* Meta-analysis, utility regulatory entities.

Herzing University Online, Program in Business Administration, Menomonee Falls, WI 53051. Offers accounting (MBA); business administration (MBA); business management (MBA); healthcare management (MBA); human resources (MBA); marketing (MBA); project management (MBA); technology management (MBA). *Program availability:* Online learning.

Hodges University, Graduate Programs, Naples, FL 34119. Offers accounting (M Acc); business administration (MBA); clinical mental health counseling (MS); health services administration (MS); information systems management (MIS); legal studies (MS); management (MSM). *Program availability:* Part-time, evening/weekend, 100% online, blended/hybrid learning. *Degree requirements:* For master's, comprehensive exam (for some programs), thesis (for some programs). *Entrance requirements:* For master's, essay. Additional exam requirements/recommendations for international students: Recommended—TOEFL. Electronic applications accepted.

Hofstra University, Frank G. Zarb School of Business, Programs in Accounting and Taxation, Hempstead, NY 11549. Offers accounting (MS, Advanced Certificate); business administration (MBA), including accounting, professional accountancy, taxation; taxation (MS, Advanced Certificate). *Program availability:* Part-time, evening/weekend, blended/hybrid learning. *Students:* 161 full-time (89 women), 35 part-time (16 women); includes 28 minority (2 Black or African American, non-Hispanic/Latino; 1 American Indian or Alaska Native, non-Hispanic/Latino; 9 Asian, non-Hispanic/Latino; 12 Hispanic/Latino; 2 Native Hawaiian or other Pacific Islander, non-Hispanic/Latino; 2 Two or more races, non-Hispanic/Latino), 87 international. Average age 25. 328 applicants, 77% accepted, 82 enrolled. In 2017, 129 master's awarded. *Degree requirements:* For master's, capstone course (for MBA), thesis (for MS), minimum GPA of 3.0. *Entrance requirements:* For master's, GMAT/GRE, 2 letters of recommendation, resume, essay. Additional exam requirements/recommendations for international students: Required—TOEFL (minimum score 550 paper-based; 80 iBT); Recommended—IELTS (minimum score 6). *Application deadline:* Applications are processed on a rolling basis. Application fee: $75. Electronic applications accepted. *Expenses:* $1,322 per credit. *Financial support:* In 2017–18, 63 students received support, including 54 fellowships with full and partial tuition reimbursements available (averaging $4,794 per year); research assistantships with full and partial tuition reimbursements available, career-related internships or fieldwork, Federal Work-Study, institutionally sponsored loans, scholarships/grants, tuition waivers (full and partial), and unspecified assistantships also available. Support available to part-time students. Financial award applicants required to submit FAFSA. *Faculty research:* Corporate compliance, international accounting and auditing, financial accounting fraud, tax reform legislation, accounting analytics. *Unit head:* Dr. Jacqueline Burke, Chairperson, 516-463-6987, E-mail: jacqueline.a.burke@hofstra.edu. *Application contact:* Sunil Samuel, Assistant Vice President of Admissions, 516-463-4723, Fax: 516-463-4664, E-mail: graduateadmission@hofstra.edu.
Website: http://www.hofstra.edu/business/

Holy Family University, Graduate and Professional Programs, School of Business Administration, Philadelphia, PA 19114. Offers accountancy (MS); finance (MBA); health care administration (MBA); human resource management (MBA); information systems management (MBA). *Accreditation:* ACBSP. *Program availability:* Part-time, evening/weekend. *Degree requirements:* For master's, comprehensive exam, thesis. *Entrance requirements:* For master's, minimum GPA of 3.0, interview, essay/personal statement, current resume, official transcript of all college or university work. Additional exam requirements/recommendations for international students: Required—TOEFL (minimum score 550 paper-based; 79 iBT), IELTS (minimum score 6), PTE (minimum score 54). Electronic applications accepted. *Expenses: Tuition:* Full-time $13,518; part-time $9012 per credit hour. Tuition and fees vary according to degree level and program.

Hood College, Graduate School, Department of Economics and Business Administration, Frederick, MD 21701-8575. Offers accounting (MBA, Certificate); finance (MBA); financial management (Certificate); human resource management (MBA); information systems (MBA); marketing (MBA); organizational management (Certificate); public management (MBA). *Accreditation:* ACBSP. *Program availability:* Part-time, evening/weekend. *Faculty:* 4 full-time (2 women), 7 part-time/adjunct (1 woman). *Students:* 21 full-time (12 women), 91 part-time (47 women); includes 19 minority (8 Black or African American, non-Hispanic/Latino; 3 Asian, non-Hispanic/Latino; 8 Hispanic/Latino), 15 international. Average age 31. 34 applicants, 97% accepted, 23 enrolled. In 2017, 42 master's awarded. *Degree requirements:* For master's, capstone/final research project. *Entrance requirements:* For master's, minimum GPA of 3.0 (or resume and two letters of recommendation), copy of official transcripts, essay. Additional exam requirements/recommendations for international students: Required—TOEFL (minimum score 575 paper-based; 89 iBT), IELTS (minimum score 6.5). *Application deadline:* For fall admission, 8/15 for domestic students, 8/5 for international students; for spring admission, 12/1 for domestic and international students; for summer admission, 5/1 for domestic students, 4/15 for international students. Applications are processed on a rolling basis. Application fee: $35. Electronic applications accepted. *Expenses:* $550 per credit hour plus $110 per semester comprehensive fee. *Financial support:* Tuition waivers (partial) and unspecified assistantships available. Financial award applicants required to submit FAFSA. *Faculty research:* Corporate strategy and sustainable competitive advantages, business ethics, entrepreneurship, investments management, economic development. *Unit head:* Dr. April M. Boulton, Dean of the Graduate School, 301-696-3600, Fax: 301-696-3597, E-mail: gofurther@hood.edu. *Application contact:* Jan Marcus, Assistant Director of Graduate Admissions, 301-696-3603, E-mail: gofurther@hood.edu.

Howard University, School of Business, Graduate Programs in Business, Washington, DC 20059-0002. Offers accounting (MBA); entrepreneurship (MBA); finance (MBA); general management (MBA); human resources management (MBA); information systems (MBA); international business (MBA); marketing (MBA); supply chain management (MBA); JD/MBA. *Accreditation:* AACSB. *Program availability:* Part-time, evening/weekend, online learning. *Entrance requirements:* For master's, GMAT, minimum 1 year post undergraduate work experience, resume, 3 letters of recommendation, advanced college algebra. Additional exam requirements/recommendations for international students: Required—TOEFL. *Faculty research:* Marketing research in multi-ethnic populations, U.S. trade policies and international relations, risk management (finance).

Hunter College of the City University of New York, Graduate School, School of Arts and Sciences, Department of Economics, Program in Accounting, New York, NY 10065-5085. Offers MS. *Entrance requirements:* For master's, GMAT, statement of purpose, bachelor's degree, official transcripts, two letters of recommendation. Additional exam requirements/recommendations for international students: Required—TOEFL (minimum score 550 paper-based; 60 iBT). Electronic applications accepted.

IGlobal University, Graduate Programs, Vienna, VA 22182. Offers accounting (MBA); data management and analytics (MSIT); entrepreneurship (MBA); finance (MBA); global business management (MBA); health care management (MBA); hospitality and tourism management (MBA); human resources management (MBA); information technology (MBA); information technology systems and management (MSIT); leadership and management (MBA); project management (MBA); public service and administration (MBA); software design and management (MSIT).

Illinois State University, Graduate School, College of Business, Department of Accounting, Normal, IL 61790. Offers MPA, MS. *Accreditation:* AACSB. *Degree requirements:* For master's, comprehensive exam. *Entrance requirements:* For master's, GMAT, minimum GPA of 2.75 in last 60 hours of course work. Additional exam requirements/recommendations for international students: Required—TOEFL.

Indiana Tech, Program in Business Administration, Fort Wayne, IN 46803-1297. Offers accounting (MBA); health care management (MBA); human resources (MBA); management (MBA); marketing (MBA). *Program availability:* Part-time, evening/weekend, online learning. *Entrance requirements:* For master's, GMAT, bachelor's degree from regionally-accredited university; minimum undergraduate GPA of 2.5; 2 years of significant work experience; 3 letters of recommendation. Electronic applications accepted.

Indiana University Kokomo, School of Business, Kokomo, IN 46904. Offers accounting (Postbaccalaureate Certificate); business administration (MBA); business fundamentals (Postbaccalaureate Certificate). *Accreditation:* AACSB. *Program availability:* Part-time, evening/weekend. *Degree requirements:* For master's, thesis optional, research project. *Entrance requirements:* For master's, GMAT. Additional exam requirements/recommendations for international students: Required—TOEFL (minimum score 550 paper-based; 73 iBT). Electronic applications accepted. *Expenses:* Contact institution. *Faculty research:* Investments, outsourcing, technology, adoption.

Indiana University Northwest, School of Business and Economics, Gary, IN 46408. Offers accounting (Graduate Certificate); management (Certificate); management and administrative studies (MBA). *Accreditation:* AACSB. *Program availability:* Part-time, evening/weekend. *Entrance requirements:* For master's, GMAT (not for Weekend MBA for Professionals), letter of recommendation. Electronic applications accepted. *Expenses:* Contact institution. *Faculty research:* International finance, employment law and testing, business ethics, taxation, financial institutions.

Indiana University–Purdue University Indianapolis, Kelley School of Business, Evening MBA Program, Indianapolis, IN 46202-5151. Offers accounting (MBA); entrepreneurship (MBA); finance (MBA); general administration (MBA); marketing (MBA); supply chain management (MBA); MBA/JD; MBA/MD; MBA/MHA; MBA/MS; MBA/MSA; MBA/MSE. *Program availability:* Part-time-only, evening/weekend, online learning. *Entrance requirements:* For master's, GMAT or GRE, 2 years of professional work experience. Additional exam requirements/recommendations for international students: Required—TOEFL or IELTS. Electronic applications accepted. *Expenses:* Contact institution. *Faculty research:* Entrepreneurship; corporate finance; international business; consumer behavior; supply chain; business law.

Indiana University–Purdue University Indianapolis, Kelley School of Business, Graduate Accounting Program, Indianapolis, IN 46202-5151. Offers MBA, MSA. *Entrance requirements:* For master's, GMAT, previous coursework in accounting and statistics. *Faculty research:* Auditing analytics; international accounting; taxation; financial accounting; corporate finance.

Indiana University South Bend, Judd Leighton School of Business and Economics, South Bend, IN 46615. Offers accounting (MSA); business (Graduate Certificate); business administration (MBA), including finance, human resource management, marketing; MBA/MSA. *Program availability:* Part-time, evening/weekend. *Entrance requirements:* For master's, GMAT. Additional exam requirements/recommendations for international students: Required—TOEFL (minimum score 550 paper-based; 79 iBT). Electronic applications accepted. *Expenses:* Contact institution. *Faculty research:* Financial accounting, consumer research, capital budgeting research, business strategy research.

Indiana Wesleyan University, College of Adult and Professional Studies, Graduate Studies in Business, Marion, IN 46953. Offers accounting (MBA, Graduate Certificate); applied management (MBA); business administration (MBA); health care (MBA, Graduate Certificate); human resources (MBA, Graduate Certificate); management (MS); organizational leadership (MA). *Program availability:* Part-time, evening/weekend, online learning. *Degree requirements:* For master's, applied business or management project. *Entrance requirements:* For master's, minimum GPA of 2.5, 2 years of related work experience. Additional exam requirements/recommendations for international students: Required—TOEFL (minimum score 550 paper-based). Electronic applications accepted.

Instituto Tecnologico de Santo Domingo, Graduate School, Area of Humanities and Social Sciences, Santo Domingo, Dominican Republic. Offers accounting (Certificate); adult education (Certificate); applied linguistics (MA); economics (MA); education (M Ed); educational psychology (MA, Certificate); gender and development (MA, Certificate); humanistic studies (MA); international marketing management (Certificate); international relations in the Caribbean basin (Certificate); intervention systems in family therapy (MA); linguistic and literary communication (Certificate); pedagogical support (MA); social science education (M Ed); sustainable human development (MA); terminal illness and death psychology (Certificate); youth and adult education (M Ed).

Inter American University of Puerto Rico, Aguadilla Campus, Graduate School, Aguadilla, PR 00605. Offers accounting (MBA); counseling psychology specializing in family (MS); criminal justice (MA); educative management and leadership (MA); elementary education (M Ed); finance (MBA); human resources (MBA); industrial management (MBA); management information systems (MBA); marketing (MBA). *Program availability:* Part-time, evening/weekend. *Degree requirements:* For master's, comprehensive exam. *Entrance requirements:* For master's, EXADEP, 2 letters of recommendation, minimum GPA of 2.5. Electronic applications accepted.

Inter American University of Puerto Rico, Arecibo Campus, Program in Business Administration, Arecibo, PR 00614-4050. Offers accounting (MBA); finance (MBA); human resources (MBA).

Inter American University of Puerto Rico, Barranquitas Campus, Business Administration Program, Barranquitas, PR 00794. Offers accounting (MBA); human resources (MBA); managerial information systems (MBA). *Program availability:* Part-time, evening/weekend. *Faculty:* 2 full-time (1 woman), 2 part-time/adjunct (both women). *Students:* 11 full-time (9 women), 1 (woman) part-time; all minorities (all Hispanic/Latino). Average age 31. 6 applicants, 83% accepted, 5 enrolled. In 2017, 3 master's awarded. *Degree requirements:* For master's, 2 foreign languages,

comprehensive exam (for some programs), thesis or alternative, minimum GPA of 3.0. *Entrance requirements:* For master's, BBA or its equivalent from accredited institution, official academic transcript from institution that conferred bachelor's degree, minimum GPA of 2.5, interview (for some programs). *Application deadline:* Applications are processed on a rolling basis. Application fee: $31. Electronic applications accepted. *Expenses:* $3,392 full-time tuition plus $652 fees. *Financial support:* Applicants required to submit FAFSA. *Unit head:* Juan A. Negron-Berrios, PhD, Chancellor, 787-857-3600 Ext. 2002, Fax: 787-857-2125, E-mail: janegron@br.inter.edu. *Application contact:* Aramilda Cartagena-Santiago, Dean of Students, 787-857-3600 Ext. 2009, Fax: 787-857-2125, E-mail: aramildacartagena@br.inter.edu.

Inter American University of Puerto Rico, Metropolitan Campus, Graduate Programs, Program in Accounting, San Juan, PR 00919-1293. Offers MBA. *Degree requirements:* For master's, comprehensive exam. *Entrance requirements:* For master's, GRE or EXADEP, interview. Electronic applications accepted.

Inter American University of Puerto Rico, Ponce Campus, Graduate School, Mercedita, PR 00715-1602. Offers accounting (MBA); biology (M Ed); chemistry (M Ed); criminal justice (MA); elementary education (M Ed); English as a Second Language (M Ed); finance (MBA); history (M Ed); human resources (MBA); marketing (MBA); mathematics (M Ed); Spanish (M Ed). *Entrance requirements:* For master's, minimum GPA of 2.5.

Inter American University of Puerto Rico, San Germán Campus, Graduate Studies Center, Program in Business Administration, San Germán, PR 00683-5008. Offers accounting (MBA); finance (MBA); general business administration (MBA); human resources (MBA, PhD); industrial relations (MBA); information systems (MBA); international and interregional business (PhD); management (MBA); marketing (MBA). *Program availability:* Part-time, evening/weekend. *Degree requirements:* For master's, comprehensive exam. *Entrance requirements:* For master's, GRE General Test or EXADEP, minimum GPA of 3.0.

Iona College, School of Business, Department of Accounting, New Rochelle, NY 10801-1890. Offers accounting and information systems (MS); general accounting (MBA, AC); public accounting (MBA, MS, AC). *Program availability:* Part-time, evening/weekend. *Faculty:* 5 full-time (1 woman), 1 (woman) part-time/adjunct. *Students:* 25 full-time (13 women), 40 part-time (15 women); includes 26 minority (6 Black or African American, non-Hispanic/Latino; 1 American Indian or Alaska Native, non-Hispanic/Latino; 2 Asian, non-Hispanic/Latino; 16 Hispanic/Latino; 1 Two or more races, non-Hispanic/Latino), 4 international. Average age 28. 32 applicants, 100% accepted, 16 enrolled. In 2017, 59 master's, 6 other advanced degrees awarded. *Entrance requirements:* For master's and AC, minimum GPA of 3.0. Additional exam requirements/recommendations for international students: Required—TOEFL (minimum score 550 paper-based; 80 iBT), IELTS (minimum score 6.5). *Application deadline:* For fall admission, 8/15 priority date for domestic students, 8/1 priority date for international students; for winter admission, 11/15 priority date for domestic students, 11/1 priority date for international students; for spring admission, 2/15 priority date for domestic students, 2/1 priority date for international students; for summer admission, 5/15 priority date for domestic students, 5/1 priority date for international students. Applications are processed on a rolling basis. Application fee: $0. Electronic applications accepted. Tuition and fees vary according to program. *Financial support:* Scholarships/grants, tuition waivers (partial), and unspecified assistantships available. Support available to part-time students. Financial award application deadline: 4/15; financial award applicants required to submit FAFSA. *Faculty research:* Tax policy, investment returns, international accounting standards. *Unit head:* Dr. Jeffrey Haber, Chair, 914-633-2244, E-mail: jhaber@iona.edu. *Application contact:* Katelyn Brunck, Director of Graduate Admissions, 914-633-2451, Fax: 914-633-2277, E-mail: kbrunck@iona.edu. Website: https://www.iona.edu/academics/school-of-business/departments/accounting.aspx

Iona College, School of Business, Department of Information Systems, New Rochelle, NY 10801-1890. Offers accounting and information systems (MS); business continuity and risk management (AC); information systems (MBA, MS, PMC); project management (MS). *Program availability:* Part-time, evening/weekend. *Faculty:* 7 full-time (1 woman), 1 part-time/adjunct (0 women). *Students:* 15 full-time (7 women), 8 part-time (3 women); includes 5 minority (3 Asian, non-Hispanic/Latino; 2 Hispanic/Latino), 3 international. Average age 26. 13 applicants, 92% accepted, 8 enrolled. In 2017, 15 master's, 1 other advanced degree awarded. *Entrance requirements:* For master's, GMAT, 2 letters of recommendation, minimum GPA of 3.0; for other advanced degree, GMAT, minimum GPA of 3.0. Additional exam requirements/recommendations for international students: Required—TOEFL (minimum score 550 paper-based; 80 iBT), IELTS (minimum score 6.5). *Application deadline:* For fall admission, 8/15 priority date for domestic students, 8/1 priority date for international students; for winter admission, 11/15 priority date for domestic students, 11/1 priority date for international students; for spring admission, 2/15 priority date for domestic students, 2/1 priority date for international students; for summer admission, 5/15 priority date for domestic students, 5/1 priority date for international students. Applications are processed on a rolling basis. Application fee: $50. Electronic applications accepted. *Expenses:* Contact institution. *Financial support:* In 2017–18, 4 students received support. Scholarships/grants, tuition waivers (partial), and unspecified assistantships available. Support available to part-time students. Financial award application deadline: 4/15; financial award applicants required to submit FAFSA. *Faculty research:* Fuzzy sets, risk management, computer security, competence set analysis, investment strategies. *Unit head:* Dr. Shoshana Altschuller, Department Chair, 914-637-7726, E-mail: saltschuller@iona.edu. *Application contact:* Katelyn Brunck, Director of MBA Admissions, 914-633-2451, Fax: 914-633-2277, E-mail: kbrunck@iona.edu. Website: http://www.iona.edu/Academics/Hagan-School-of-Business/Departments/Information-Systems/Graduate-Programs.aspx

Iowa State University of Science and Technology, Department of Accounting, Ames, IA 50011. Offers M Acc. *Accreditation:* AACSB. *Degree requirements:* For master's, thesis or alternative. *Entrance requirements:* For master's, GMAT, resume. Additional exam requirements/recommendations for international students: Recommended—TOEFL (minimum score 600 paper-based; 100 iBT), IELTS (minimum score 7). Electronic applications accepted.

Ithaca College, School of Business, Program in Accounting, Ithaca, NY 14850. Offers MS. *Program availability:* Part-time. *Faculty:* 5 full-time (2 women), 1 (woman) part-time/adjunct. *Students:* 28 full-time (8 women); includes 3 minority (1 Asian, non-Hispanic/Latino; 2 Hispanic/Latino), 1 international. Average age 22. 32 applicants, 91% accepted, 28 enrolled. In 2017, 30 master's awarded. *Entrance requirements:* For master's, GMAT. Additional exam requirements/recommendations for international students: Required—TOEFL (minimum score 550 paper-based; 80 iBT). *Application deadline:* For fall admission, 5/15 for domestic and international students; for spring admission, 11/1 for domestic and international students. Applications are processed on a rolling basis. Application fee: $40. Electronic applications accepted. *Expenses:* Contact institution. *Financial support:* In 2017–18, 23 students received support, including 23 fellowships (averaging $7,782 per year); career-related internships or fieldwork, Federal Work-Study, and scholarships/grants also available. Support available to part-time students. Financial award application deadline: 3/1; financial

Accounting

award applicants required to submit FAFSA. *Unit head:* Dr. Rasoul Rezvanian, Associate Dean and Director, MBA Programs, 607-274-1762, Fax: 607-274-1263, E-mail: rrezvanian@ithaca.edu. *Application contact:* Nicole Eversley Bradwell, Director, Office of Admission, 607-274-3124, Fax: 607-274-1263, E-mail: admission@ithaca.edu. Website: https://www.ithaca.edu/business/programs/accounting

Jackson State University, Graduate School, College of Business, Department of Accounting, Jackson, MS 39217. Offers MPA. *Accreditation:* AACSB. *Program availability:* Part-time, evening/weekend. *Degree requirements:* For master's, comprehensive exam. *Entrance requirements:* For master's, GRE General Test, GMAT. Additional exam requirements/recommendations for international students: Required—TOEFL (minimum score 520 paper-based; 67 iBT).

Jacksonville University, Davis College of Business, Accelerated Day-time MBA Program, Jacksonville, FL 32211. Offers accounting and finance (MBA); business administration (MBA); consumer goods and services marketing (MBA); management (MBA); management accounting (MBA). *Faculty:* 5 full-time (2 women). *Students:* 43 full-time (17 women), 7 part-time (2 women); includes 9 minority (4 Black or African American, non-Hispanic/Latino; 4 Hispanic/Latino; 1 Two or more races, non-Hispanic/Latino), 18 international. Average age 26. 70 applicants, 90% accepted, 44 enrolled. In 2017, 42 master's awarded. *Entrance requirements:* For master's, GMAT or GRE, bachelor's degree from regionally-accredited institution, original transcripts of academic work, statement of intent, resume, 3 letters of recommendation; 3 years of work experience (recommended); interview with program advisor. Additional exam requirements/recommendations for international students: Required—TOEFL (minimum score 550 paper-based; 79 iBT), IELTS (minimum score 6), PTE (minimum score 53). *Application deadline:* For fall admission, 7/1 priority date for domestic students, 6/15 priority date for international students; for spring admission, 12/1 priority date for domestic students, 11/15 priority date for international students; for summer admission, 4/1 for domestic students, 3/15 for international students. Applications are processed on a rolling basis. Application fee: $50. Electronic applications accepted. *Expenses:* $793 per credit hour; $150-$250 books per course (estimated). *Financial support:* Scholarships/grants, health care benefits, and unspecified assistantships available. Financial award application deadline: 6/30; financial award applicants required to submit FAFSA. *Faculty research:* Behavioral finance, game theory, regional economic integration, information sabotage, public choice and public finance. *Unit head:* Dr. Douglas Johansen, Associate Dean and Graduate Programs Director, 904-256-7763, Fax: 904-256-7168, E-mail: djohans@ju.edu. *Application contact:* AnnaMaria Murphy, Assistant Director of Graduate Admissions, 904-256-7426, Fax: 904-256-7012, E-mail: mba@ju.edu.

See Display on page 104 and Close-Up on page 175.

Jacksonville University, Davis College of Business, FLEX Master of Business Administration Program, Jacksonville, FL 32211. Offers accounting and finance (MBA); business management (MBA); consumer goods and services marketing (MBA); management (MBA); management accounting (MBA); JD/MBA; MBA/MPP; MSN/MBA. MBA/JD offered jointly with Florida School of Law; MSN/MBA offered jointly with JU's Keigwin School of Nursing; MBA/MPP offered jointly with JU's Public Policy Institute. *Accreditation:* AACSB. *Program availability:* Part-time, evening/weekend, blended/hybrid learning. *Faculty:* 23 full-time (8 women), 4 part-time/adjunct (2 women). *Students:* 32 full-time (7 women), 80 part-time (30 women); includes 34 minority (15 Black or African American, non-Hispanic/Latino; 1 American Indian or Alaska Native, non-Hispanic/Latino; 6 Asian, non-Hispanic/Latino; 10 Hispanic/Latino; 2 Two or more races, non-Hispanic/Latino), 2 international. Average age 33. 43 applicants, 91% accepted, 32 enrolled. In 2017, 56 master's awarded. *Entrance requirements:* For master's, GMAT or GRE, bachelor's degree from regionally-accredited institution, 3 years of full-time work experience (recommended), resume, statement of intent, 3 letters of recommendation, interview with program advisor. Additional exam requirements/recommendations for international students: Required—TOEFL (minimum score 550 paper-based; 79 iBT), IELTS (minimum score 6), PTE (minimum score 53). *Application deadline:* For fall admission, 7/1 priority date for domestic students, 6/15 priority date for international students; for spring admission, 12/1 priority date for domestic students, 11/15 priority date for international students; for summer admission, 4/1 priority date for domestic students, 3/15 priority date for international students. Applications are processed on a rolling basis. Application fee: $50. Electronic applications accepted. *Expenses:* $793 per credit hour; $150-$250 books per course (estimated). *Financial support:* Scholarships/grants and health care benefits available. Financial award application deadline: 6/30; financial award applicants required to submit FAFSA. *Faculty research:* Downsizing with integrity; impact of YouTube videos; game theory; analysis of effective tax rates; creativity innovation and change. *Unit head:* Dr. Douglas Johansen, Associate Dean and Director of Graduate Studies, 904-256-7763, Fax: 904-256-7168, E-mail: djohans@ju.edu. *Application contact:* AnnaMaria Murphy, Assistant Director of Graduate Admissions, 904-256-7426, Fax: 904-256-7012, E-mail: mba@ju.edu.

See Display on page 104 and Close-Up on page 175.

James Madison University, The Graduate School, College of Business, Program in Accounting, Harrisonburg, VA 22801. Offers accounting information systems (MS); taxation (MS). *Accreditation:* AACSB. *Program availability:* Part-time, evening/weekend. *Students:* 71 full-time (28 women), 1 (woman) part-time; includes 10 minority (2 Black or African American, non-Hispanic/Latino; 5 Asian, non-Hispanic/Latino; 3 Hispanic/Latino), 1 international. Average age 30. In 2017, 24 master's awarded. Application fee: $55. Electronic applications accepted. *Expenses:* Tuition, state resident: full-time $10,512; part-time $438 per credit hour. Tuition, nonresident: full-time $28,358; part-time $1162 per credit hour. *Required fees:* $1128. *Financial support:* In 2017–18, 24 students received support, including 23 fellowships; Federal Work-Study and 23 assistantships (averaging $6911); 1 service assistantship also available. Financial award application deadline: 3/1; financial award applicants required to submit FAFSA. *Unit head:* Dr. Tim J. Louwers, Director of the School of Accounting, 540-568-3027, E-mail: louwertj@jmu.edu. *Application contact:* Lynette D. Michael, Director of Graduate Admissions, 540-568-6131 Ext. 6395, Fax: 540-568-7860, E-mail: michaeld@jmu.edu. Website: https://www.jmu.edu/cob/accounting/masters/index.shtml

John Carroll University, Graduate Studies, John M. and Mary Jo Boler School of Business, University Heights, OH 44118. Offers accountancy (MS); business (MBA); laboratory administration (MS). *Accreditation:* AACSB. *Program availability:* Part-time, evening/weekend. *Faculty:* 11 full-time (1 woman), 9 part-time/adjunct (3 women). *Students:* 63 full-time (21 women), 67 part-time (22 women); includes 18 minority (10 Black or African American, non-Hispanic/Latino; 4 Asian, non-Hispanic/Latino; 3 Hispanic/Latino; 1 Two or more races, non-Hispanic/Latino), 10 international. Average age 26. In 2017, 50 master's awarded. *Entrance requirements:* For master's, GMAT, minimum GPA of 2.5. Additional exam requirements/recommendations for international students: Required—TOEFL (minimum score 550 paper-based). *Application deadline:* Applications are processed on a rolling basis. Application fee: $25 ($35 for international students). Electronic applications accepted. *Expenses:* Contact institution. *Financial support:* Research assistantships with full tuition reimbursements, scholarships/grants, and unspecified assistantships available. Financial award application deadline: 3/15; financial award applicants required to submit FAFSA. *Faculty research:* Accounting,

economics and finance, management, marketing and logistics. *Unit head:* Dr. Alan R. Miciak, Dean, 216-397-4391, Fax: 216-397-1833. *Application contact:* Gayle T. Bruno-Gannon, Assistant to the Dean, 216-397-1970, Fax: 216-397-1728, E-mail: ggannon@jcu.edu.
Website: http://www.jcu.edu/boler/grads

Johnson & Wales University, Graduate Studies, MBA Program, Providence, RI 02903-3703. Offers accounting (MBA); business administration (MBA); finance (MBA); global fashion merchandising and management (MBA); hospitality (MBA); human resource management (MBA); information security/assurance (MBA); information technology (MBA); nonprofit management (MBA); operations and supply chain management (MBA); organizational leadership (MBA); organizational psychology (MBA); sport leadership (MBA). Program also offered on Denver campus. *Program availability:* Part-time, online learning. *Entrance requirements:* For master's, minimum GPA of 2.75. Additional exam requirements/recommendations for international students: Required—TOEFL (minimum score 550 paper-based); Recommended—IELTS, TWE. *Application deadline:* For fall admission, 8/15 priority date for domestic students, 6/28 priority date for international students; for winter admission, 11/10 priority date for domestic students, 9/20 priority date for international students; for spring admission, 2/5 priority date for domestic students, 12/20 priority date for international students. Applications are processed on a rolling basis. *Expenses:* Tuition: Full-time $12,636; part-time $702 per credit hour. *Financial support:* Tuition waivers (partial) and unspecified assistantships available. Support available to part-time students. Financial award application deadline: 5/1. *Faculty research:* International banking, global economy, international trade, cultural differences. *Unit head:* Dr. Karen Silva, Director, 401-598-2849, Fax: 401-598-1125. *Application contact:* Graduate School Admissions, 401-598-1015, Fax: 401-598-1286, E-mail: gradadm@jwu.edu.

Juniata College, Department of Accounting, Business, and Economics, Huntingdon, PA 16652-2119. Offers accounting (M Acc). *Students:* 8 full-time (2 women), 1 part-time (0 women). Average age 22. 9 applicants, 100% accepted, 7 enrolled. In 2017, 5 master's awarded. *Entrance requirements:* For master's, GMAT. *Application deadline:* Applications are processed on a rolling basis. *Unit head:* Dr. Dominick Peruso, Chair, 814-641-3661, E-mail: peruso@juniata.edu.
Website: https://www.juniata.edu/academics/departments/accounting-business-economics/master-of-accounting/

Kansas State University, Graduate School, College of Business, Department of Accounting, Manhattan, KS 66506. Offers M Acc. *Accreditation:* AACSB. *Program availability:* Part-time. *Entrance requirements:* For master's, GMAT (minimum score of 500), minimum undergraduate GPA of 3.0. Additional exam requirements/recommendations for international students: Required—TOEFL (minimum score 550 paper-based; 79 iBT); Recommended—IELTS (minimum score 7). Electronic applications accepted. *Faculty research:* Accounting education, accounting ethics, capital markets (empirical/archival), research in tax and financial reporting, behavioral research in accounting.

Kean University, College of Business and Public Management, Program in Accounting, Union, NJ 07083. Offers MS. *Program availability:* Part-time, evening/weekend. *Faculty:* 11 full-time (2 women). *Students:* 24 full-time (18 women), 20 part-time (9 women); includes 22 minority (9 Black or African American, non-Hispanic/Latino; 6 Asian, non-Hispanic/Latino; 7 Hispanic/Latino), 7 international. Average age 30. 19 applicants, 100% accepted, 12 enrolled. In 2017, 18 master's awarded. *Entrance requirements:* For master's, GMAT/GRE, two letters of recommendation; professional resume/curriculum vitae; personal statement; minimum cumulative GPA of 3.0; official transcripts from all institutions attended. Additional exam requirements/recommendations for international students: Required—TOEFL (minimum score 550 paper-based; 79 iBT), IELTS (minimum score 6.5). *Application deadline:* For fall admission, 6/1 for domestic and international students; for spring admission, 12/1 for domestic and international students. Applications are processed on a rolling basis. Application fee: $75. Electronic applications accepted. *Expenses:* Tuition, state resident: full-time $13,419; part-time $653 per credit. Tuition, nonresident: full-time $18,188; part-time $801 per credit. *Required fees:* $3382; $154 per credit. Tuition and fees vary according to course level, course load, degree level and program. *Financial support:* Scholarships/grants and unspecified assistantships available. Financial award applicants required to submit FAFSA. *Unit head:* Dr. Veysel Yucetepe, Program Coordinator, 908-737-4762, E-mail: vyucetep@kean.edu. *Application contact:* Pedro Lopes, Office of Graduate Admissions, 908-737-7100, E-mail: gradadmissions@kean.edu.
Website: http://grad.kean.edu/masters-programs/accounting

Keiser University, Master of Accountancy Program, Fort Lauderdale, FL 33309. Offers forensic accounting (M Acc). *Entrance requirements:* For master's, baccalaureate degree from accredited institution in accounting, business or a related discipline.
Website: http://www.keiseruniversity.edu/graduateschool/master-of-accountancy-macc.php

Keiser University, Master of Business Administration Program, Fort Lauderdale, FL 33309. Offers accounting (MBA); health services administration (MBA); international business (MBA); management (MBA); marketing (MBA); technology management (MBA). All concentrations except technology management also offered in Mandarin. *Program availability:* Part-time, online learning. *Unit head:* Yan Luo-Beitler, Department Chair.
Website: http://www.keiseruniversity.edu/graduateschool/mba.php#accounting

Kennesaw State University, Michael J. Coles College of Business, Program in Accounting, Kennesaw, GA 30144. Offers M Acc. *Accreditation:* AACSB. *Program availability:* Part-time, evening/weekend. *Entrance requirements:* For master's, GMAT, minimum GPA of 2.8. Additional exam requirements/recommendations for international students: Required—TOEFL (minimum score 550 paper-based; 80 iBT), IELTS (minimum score 6.5). Electronic applications accepted.

Kent State University, College of Business Administration, Doctoral Program in Accounting, Kent, OH 44242. Offers PhD. *Faculty:* 12 full-time (6 women). *Students:* 12 full-time (5 women); includes 1 minority (Asian, non-Hispanic/Latino), 9 international. Average age 33. 16 applicants, 25% accepted, 2 enrolled. In 2017, 2 doctorates awarded. *Degree requirements:* For doctorate, comprehensive exam, thesis/dissertation, oral defense. *Entrance requirements:* For doctorate, GMAT. Additional exam requirements/recommendations for international students: Required—TOEFL (minimum score 600 paper-based; 100 iBT), IELTS (minimum score 7). *Application deadline:* For fall admission, 1/1 for domestic students, 2/1 for international students. Application fee: $45 ($70 for international students). Electronic applications accepted. *Expenses:* $11,300 per academic year. *Financial support:* In 2017–18, 10 students received support, including 10 teaching assistantships with full tuition reimbursements available (averaging $23,000 per year). Financial award application deadline: 2/1; financial award applicants required to submit FAFSA. *Faculty research:* Information economics, capital management, use of accounting information, curriculum design. *Unit head:* Steven Dennis, Interim Chair, Department of Accounting, 330-672-2545, Fax: 330-672-2548, E-mail: gradbus@kent.edu. *Application contact:* Felecia A. Urbanek, Assistant Director, 330-672-2282, Fax: 330-672-7303, E-mail: gradbus@kent.edu.
Website: http://www.kent.edu/business/phd

Kent State University, College of Business Administration, Master of Science Program in Accounting, Kent, OH 44242. Offers MS. *Program availability:* Part-time, evening/weekend. *Faculty:* 12 full-time (6 women). *Students:* 24 full-time (9 women), 3 part-time (2 women); includes 1 minority (Black or African American, non-Hispanic/Latino), 6 international. Average age 27. 18 applicants, 83% accepted, 11 enrolled. In 2017, 23 master's awarded. *Degree requirements:* For master's, internship. *Entrance requirements:* For master's, GMAT, minimum GPA of 3.0. Additional exam requirements/recommendations for international students: Required—TOEFL (minimum score 550 paper-based; 79 iBT), IELTS (minimum score 6.5). *Application deadline:* For fall admission, 3/15 priority date for domestic students, 3/15 for international students; for spring admission, 10/15 for domestic and international students; for summer admission, 5/1 for domestic and international students. Applications are processed on a rolling basis. Application fee: $45 ($70 for international students). Electronic applications accepted. *Expenses:* $515 per credit resident; $928 per credit non-resident. *Financial support:* In 2017–18, 5 students received support, including 5 research assistantships with full tuition reimbursements available (averaging $4,000 per year); Federal Work-Study also available. Financial award application deadline: 3/15; financial award applicants required to submit FAFSA. *Faculty research:* Financial accounting, managerial accounting, auditing, accounting systems. *Unit head:* Steven Dennis, Interim Chair, Department of Accounting, 330-672-2545, Fax: 330-672-2548, E-mail: gradbus@kent.edu. *Application contact:* Louise M. Ditchey, Administrative Director, 330-672-2282, Fax: 330-672-7303, E-mail: gradbus@kent.edu.
Website: http://www.kent.edu/business/ms-accounting

Keystone College, Program in Accountancy, La Plume, PA 18440. Offers M Acc. *Program availability:* Part-time, online only, 100% online. *Faculty:* 1 (woman) full-time, 2 part-time/adjunct (both women). *Students:* 10 part-time (5 women); includes 1 minority (Hispanic/Latino). 5 applicants, 80% accepted, 3 enrolled. In 2017, 5 master's awarded. *Degree requirements:* For master's, thesis. *Entrance requirements:* For master's, GMAT, college transcripts, resume or curriculum vitae. Additional exam requirements/recommendations for international students: Required—TOEFL (minimum score 80 iBT) or IELTS (minimum score 6.5). *Application deadline:* For fall admission, 8/1 for domestic students; for spring admission, 12/1 for domestic students; for summer admission, 5/1 for domestic students. Applications are processed on a rolling basis. Application fee: $0. Electronic applications accepted. *Expenses:* $650 per credit. *Financial support:* Unspecified assistantships available. Financial award application deadline: 5/1; financial award applicants required to submit FAFSA. *Unit head:* Patricia Davis, PhD, Professor, 570-945-8424, E-mail: patricia.davis@keystone.edu. *Application contact:* Jennifer Sekol, Director of Admissions, 570-945-8117, Fax: 570-945-7916, E-mail: jennifer.sekol@keystone.edu.

King University, School of Business and Economics, Bristol, TN 37620-2699. Offers accounting (MBA); finance (MBA); healthcare management (MBA); human resources management (MBA); leadership (MBA); management (MBA); marketing (MBA); project management (MBA). *Program availability:* Part-time, evening/weekend, online learning. *Degree requirements:* For master's, comprehensive exam, thesis optional. *Entrance requirements:* For master's, GMAT, 2 years of work experience. Additional exam requirements/recommendations for international students: Required—TOEFL (minimum score 550 paper-based). Electronic applications accepted. *Faculty research:* International monetary policy.

Lakeland University, Graduate Studies Division, Program in Business Administration, Plymouth, WI 53073. Offers accounting (MBA); finance (MBA); healthcare management (MBA); project management (MBA). *Entrance requirements:* For master's, GMAT. *Expenses:* Contact institution.

Lamar University, College of Graduate Studies, College of Business, Beaumont, TX 77701. Offers accounting (MBA); experiential business and entrepreneurship (MBA); healthcare administration (MBA); MSA/MBA. *Accreditation:* AACSB. *Program availability:* Part-time, evening/weekend. *Faculty:* 50 full-time (14 women), 6 part-time/adjunct (2 women). *Students:* 20 full-time (11 women), 228 part-time (118 women); includes 98 minority (58 Black or African American, non-Hispanic/Latino; 10 Asian, non-Hispanic/Latino; 26 Hispanic/Latino; 4 Two or more races, non-Hispanic/Latino), 32 international. Average age 32. 205 applicants, 92% accepted, 78 enrolled. In 2017, 69 master's awarded. *Degree requirements:* For master's, comprehensive exam (for some programs), thesis optional. *Entrance requirements:* For master's, GMAT. Additional exam requirements/recommendations for international students: Required—TOEFL (minimum score 550 paper-based; 79 iBT), IELTS (minimum score 6.5). *Application deadline:* For fall admission, 8/10 for domestic students, 7/1 for international students; for spring admission, 1/5 for domestic students, 12/1 for international students. Applications are processed on a rolling basis. Application fee: $25 ($50 for international students). Electronic applications accepted. *Expenses:* Contact institution. *Financial support:* Fellowships with tuition reimbursements, research assistantships with partial tuition reimbursements, career-related internships or fieldwork, Federal Work-Study, institutionally sponsored loans, scholarships/grants, and tuition waivers (partial) available. Support available to part-time students. Financial award application deadline: 4/1; financial award applicants required to submit FAFSA. *Faculty research:* Marketing, finance, quantitative methods, management information systems, legal, environmental. *Unit head:* Dr. Enrique R. Venta, Dean, 409-880-8603, Fax: 409-880-8088, E-mail: henry.venta@lamar.edu. *Application contact:* Deidre Mayer, Interim Director, Admissions and Academic Services, 409-880-8888, Fax: 409-880-7419, E-mail: gradmissions@lamar.edu.
Website: http://business.lamar.edu

La Roche College, School of Graduate Studies and Adult Education, Program in Accounting, Pittsburgh, PA 15237-5898. Offers MS. *Program availability:* Part-time, evening/weekend. *Faculty:* 2 full-time (1 woman), 3 part-time/adjunct (0 women). *Students:* 7 full-time (6 women), 9 part-time (8 women); includes 1 minority (Hispanic/Latino), 4 international. Average age 34. 34 applicants, 65% accepted, 8 enrolled. In 2017, 7 master's awarded. *Entrance requirements:* For master's, baccalaureate degree in business, accounting or finance from accredited college or university; two letters of recommendation; resume; personal essay. *Application deadline:* For fall admission, 8/15 for domestic and international students; for spring admission, 12/15 for domestic and international students. Applications are processed on a rolling basis. Application fee: $50. Electronic applications accepted. *Expenses: Tuition:* Part-time $715 per credit hour. *Required fees:* $80 per credit hour. *Unit head:* Mark Dawson, Professor/Department Chair of Accounting and Finance, 412-536-1190, Fax: 412-536-1179, E-mail: mark.dawson@laroche.edu. *Application contact:* Hope Schiffgens, Director of Graduate Studies and Adult Education, 412-536-1266, Fax: 412-536-1283, E-mail: schombh1@laroche.edu.

La Salle University, School of Business, Master of Business Administration Program, Philadelphia, PA 19141-1199. Offers accounting (MBA, Post-MBA Certificate); business systems and analytics (MBA, Post-MBA Certificate); finance (MBA, Post-MBA Certificate); general business administration (MBA, Post-MBA Certificate); human resource management (MBA, Post-MBA Certificate); management (MBA, Post-MBA Certificate); marketing (Post-MBA Certificate); MBA/MSN. Program also offered in Switzerland. *Accreditation:* AACSB. *Program availability:* Part-time, evening/weekend, online learning. *Faculty:* 22 full-time (10 women), 10 part-time/adjunct (3 women). *Students:* 59 full-time (25 women), 200 part-time (109 women); includes 66 minority (36 Black or African American, non-Hispanic/Latino; 21 Asian, non-Hispanic/Latino; 7 Hispanic/Latino; 2 Two or more races, non-Hispanic/Latino), 22 international. Average age 31. 216 applicants, 57% accepted, 74 enrolled. In 2017, 146 master's awarded. *Entrance requirements:* For master's, GMAT or GRE, two letters of reference; resume; for Post-MBA Certificate, MBA with minimum GPA of 3.0. Additional exam requirements/recommendations for international students: Required—TOEFL. *Application deadline:* For fall admission, 8/15 priority date for domestic students, 7/15 for international students; for spring admission, 12/15 priority date for domestic students, 11/15 for international students; for summer admission, 4/15 priority date for domestic students, 3/15 for international students. Applications are processed on a rolling basis. Application fee: $35. Electronic applications accepted. Application fee is waived when completed online. *Expenses:* Contact institution. *Financial support:* In 2017–18, 51 students received support. Scholarships/grants available. Support available to part-time students. Financial award application deadline: 8/31; financial award applicants required to submit FAFSA. *Unit head:* Dr. MarySheila McDonald, Interim Dean, 215-951-1040, Fax: 215-951-1886, E-mail: mcdonaldms@lasalle.edu. *Application contact:* Elizabeth Heenan, Director, Graduate and Adult Enrollment, 215-951-1100, Fax: 215-951-1462, E-mail: heenan@lasalle.edu.

La Sierra University, School of Business and Management, Riverside, CA 92505. Offers accounting (MBA); finance (MBA); general management (MBA); human resources management (MBA); leadership, values, and ethics for business and management (Certificate); marketing (MBA). *Degree requirements:* For master's, research project. *Entrance requirements:* For master's, GMAT, minimum GPA of 3.0. Additional exam requirements/recommendations for international students: Required—TOEFL. *Faculty research:* Financial econometrics, institutional assessment and strategic planning, legal issues in management, behavioral finance, content of financial reports.

Lehigh University, College of Business and Economics, Department of Accounting, Bethlehem, PA 18015. Offers accounting and information analysis (MS). *Accreditation:* AACSB. *Faculty:* 10 full-time (1 woman). *Students:* 36 full-time (25 women), 5 part-time (3 women); includes 6 minority (3 Asian, non-Hispanic/Latino; 3 Hispanic/Latino), 27 international. Average age 23. 103 applicants, 51% accepted, 25 enrolled. In 2017, 21 master's awarded. *Entrance requirements:* For master's, GMAT. Additional exam requirements/recommendations for international students: Required—TOEFL (minimum score 105 iBT). *Application deadline:* For fall admission, 4/15 for domestic and international students. Application fee: $75. Electronic applications accepted. *Expenses:* $1,235 per credit hour. *Financial support:* In 2017–18, 19 students received support. Scholarships/grants and tuition waivers (partial) available. Financial award application deadline: 1/15. *Faculty research:* Behavioral accounting, internal control, information systems, supply chain management, financial accounting. *Unit head:* Dr. C. Bryan Cloyd, Chairman, 610-758-2816, Fax: 610-758-6429, E-mail: cbc215@lehigh.edu. *Application contact:* Michael Tarantino, Director of Recruitment and Admissions, 610-758-3418, Fax: 610-758-5283, E-mail: mgt215@lehigh.edu.
Website: http://www4.lehigh.edu/business/academics/depts/accounting

Lehman College of the City University of New York, School of Natural and Social Sciences, Department of Economics and Accounting, Bronx, NY 10468-1589. Offers accounting (MS). *Entrance requirements:* For master's, GMAT.

Lenoir-Rhyne University, Graduate Programs, Charles M. Snipes School of Business, Hickory, NC 28601. Offers accounting (MBA); business analytics and information technology (MBA); entrepreneurship (MBA); global business (MBA); healthcare administration (MBA); innovation and change management (MBA); leadership development (MBA). *Accreditation:* ACBSP. *Program availability:* Part-time, evening/weekend, online learning. *Degree requirements:* For master's, capstone course. *Entrance requirements:* For master's, GMAT, GRE, MAT, minimum undergraduate GPA of 2.7, graduate 3.0. Additional exam requirements/recommendations for international students: Required—TOEFL (minimum score 600 paper-based). Electronic applications accepted. *Expenses:* Contact institution.

Lewis University, College of Business, Program in Business Administration, Romeoville, IL 60446. Offers accounting (MBA); custom elective option (MBA); e-business (MBA); finance (MBA); healthcare management (MBA); human resources management (MBA); international business (MBA); management information systems (MBA); marketing (MBA); project management (MBA); technology and operations management (MBA). *Program availability:* Part-time, evening/weekend. *Students:* 130 full-time (77 women), 187 part-time (107 women); includes 83 minority (27 Black or African American, non-Hispanic/Latino; 3 American Indian or Alaska Native, non-Hispanic/Latino; 7 Asian, non-Hispanic/Latino; 40 Hispanic/Latino; 6 Two or more races, non-Hispanic/Latino), 31 international. Average age 31. In 2017, 99 master's awarded. *Degree requirements:* For master's, comprehensive exam. *Entrance requirements:* For master's, interview, bachelor's degree, resume, two recommendations. Additional exam requirements/recommendations for international students: Required—TOEFL (minimum score 550 paper-based), IELTS. *Application deadline:* For fall admission, 8/15 priority date for domestic students, 5/1 priority date for international students; for spring admission, 11/15 priority date for international students. Applications are processed on a rolling basis. Application fee: $40. Electronic applications accepted. Tuition and fees vary according to program. *Financial support:* Career-related internships or fieldwork, Federal Work-Study, scholarships/grants, and unspecified assistantships available. Financial award application deadline: 5/1; financial award applicants required to submit FAFSA. *Unit head:* Dr. Maureen Culleeney, Academic Program Director, 815-838-0500 Ext. 5631, E-mail: culleema@lewisu.edu. *Application contact:* Michele Ryan, Director of Admission, 815-838-0500 Ext. 5384, E-mail: ryanml@lewisu.edu.

Liberty University, School of Business, Lynchburg, VA 24515. Offers accounting (MBA, MS), including audit and financial reporting (MS), business (MS), financial services (MS), forensic accounting (MS), leadership (MS), taxation (MS); criminal justice (MBA); cyber security (MS); executive leadership (MA); information systems (MS), including information assurance, technology management; international business (MBA, DBA); leadership (DBA); marketing (MBA, MS, DBA), including digital marketing and advertising (MS), project management (MS), public relations (MS), sports marketing and media (MS); project management (MBA, DBA); public administration (MBA); public relations (MBA). *Program availability:* Part-time, online learning. *Students:* 1,887 full-time (1,003 women), 4,223 part-time (1,950 women); includes 1,570 minority (1,133 Black or African American, non-Hispanic/Latino; 30 American Indian or Alaska Native, non-Hispanic/Latino; 118 Asian, non-Hispanic/Latino; 149 Hispanic/Latino; 13 Native Hawaiian or other Pacific Islander, non-Hispanic/Latino; 127 Two or more races, non-Hispanic/Latino), 109 international. Average age 35. 5,680 applicants, 51% accepted, 1510 enrolled. In 2017, 1,290 master's, 17 doctorates awarded. *Entrance requirements:* For master's, minimum undergraduate GPA of 3.0, 15 hours of upper-level business courses. Additional exam requirements/recommendations for international students: Required—TOEFL (minimum score 600 paper-based; 100 iBT). *Application deadline:* Applications are processed on a rolling basis. Application fee: $50. Electronic applications accepted. *Expenses:* Contact institution. *Financial support:* Applicants required to submit FAFSA. *Unit head:* Dr. Scott Hicks, Dean, 434-592-4808, Fax: 434-582-2366, E-mail: smhicks@liberty.edu. *Application contact:* Jay Bridge, Director of Graduate Admissions, 800-424-9595, Fax: 800-628-7977, E-mail: gradadmissions@liberty.edu.
Website: http://www.liberty.edu/academics/business/index.cfm?PID=149

Accounting

Lincoln University, Graduate Studies, Jefferson City, MO 65101. Offers business administration (MBA), including accounting, management, management information systems, public administration/policy; elementary teaching (M Ed); environmental science (MS); guidance and counseling (M Ed), including community/agency counseling, elementary school, secondary school; higher education (MA); history (MA); integrated agricultural systems (MS); middle school (M Ed); natural sciences (MS); secondary teaching (M Ed); sociology (MA); sociology/criminal justice (MA). *Program availability:* Part-time, evening/weekend, 100% online, blended/hybrid learning. *Students:* 40 full-time (23 women), 64 part-time (32 women); includes 33 minority (30 Black or African American, non-Hispanic/Latino; 2 Hispanic/Latino; 1 Two or more races, non-Hispanic/Latino), 12 international. Average age 33. 48 applicants, 81% accepted, 22 enrolled. In 2017, 46 master's awarded. *Degree requirements:* For master's, comprehensive exam, thesis optional. *Entrance requirements:* For master's, GRE, MAT, or GMAT, minimum GPA of 2.75 overall, 3.0 in courses related to specialization; 3 letters of recommendation; minimum C average in English composition; personal statement of purpose. Additional exam requirements/recommendations for international students: Required—TOEFL (minimum score 500 paper-based; 61 iBT), IELTS (minimum score 5.5), Michigan English Language Assessment Battery (minimum score 80). *Application deadline:* For fall admission, 7/1 priority date for domestic students, 5/1 priority date for international students; for spring admission, 11/1 priority date for domestic students, 10/1 priority date for international students; for summer admission, 6/1 priority date for domestic students. Applications are processed on a rolling basis. Application fee: $30. Electronic applications accepted. *Expenses:* Tuition, state resident: part-time $291 per credit hour. Tuition, nonresident: part-time $541.50 per credit hour. *Financial support:* In 2017–18, 2 fellowships with tuition reimbursements, 3 research assistantships with tuition reimbursements were awarded; Federal Work-Study, scholarships/grants, and unspecified assistantships also available. Support available to part-time students. Financial award application deadline: 3/1; financial award applicants required to submit FAFSA. *Unit head:* Dr. Debra F. Greene, Interim Provost, 573-681-5247, Fax: 573-681-5106, E-mail: gradschool@lincolnu.edu. *Application contact:* Irasema Steck, Administrative Assistant, 573-681-5247, Fax: 573-681-5106, E-mail: gradschool@lincolnu.edu.
Website: http://www.lincolnu.edu/web/graduate-studies/graduate-studies

Lindenwood University, Graduate Programs, Plaster School of Business and Entrepreneurship, St. Charles, MO 63301-1695. Offers accountancy (M Acc); accounting (MBA); business administration (MBA); entrepreneurial studies (MBA); finance (MBA, MS); human resource management (MBA); international business (MBA); leadership (MA); management (MBA); marketing (MBA, MS); nonprofit administration (MA); public administration (MBA); sport management (MA); supply chain management (MBA). *Accreditation:* ACBSP. *Program availability:* Part-time, evening/weekend, 100% online. *Faculty:* 15 full-time (8 women), 26 part-time/adjunct (9 women). *Students:* 201 full-time (116 women), 253 part-time (153 women); includes 102 minority (80 Black or African American, non-Hispanic/Latino; 2 American Indian or Alaska Native, non-Hispanic/Latino; 6 Asian, non-Hispanic/Latino; 7 Hispanic/Latino; 7 Two or more races, non-Hispanic/Latino), 61 international. Average age 32. 370 applicants, 42% accepted, 134 enrolled. In 2017, 178 master's awarded. *Degree requirements:* For master's, comprehensive exam (for some programs), thesis (for some programs), minimum GPA of 3.0. *Entrance requirements:* For master's, interview, minimum undergraduate cumulative GPA of 3.0, letter of recommendation. Additional exam requirements/recommendations for international students: Required—TOEFL (minimum score 550 paper-based; 80 iBT); Recommended—IELTS (minimum score 6.5). *Application deadline:* For fall admission, 8/27 priority date for domestic and international students; for winter admission, 1/14 priority date for domestic and international students; for spring admission, 3/18 for domestic students, 3/18 priority date for international students; for summer admission, 6/3 priority date for domestic and international students. Applications are processed on a rolling basis. Application fee: $30 ($100 for international students). Electronic applications accepted. *Expenses:* Contact institution. *Financial support:* In 2017–18, 439 students received support. Career-related internships or fieldwork, Federal Work-Study, institutionally sponsored loans, scholarships/grants, tuition waivers (partial), and unspecified assistantships available. Financial award application deadline: 6/30; financial award applicants required to submit FAFSA. *Unit head:* Roger Ellis, Dean, School of Business and Entrepreneurship, 636-949-4839, E-mail: rellis@lindenwood.edu. *Application contact:* Kara Schilli, Director, Evening and Graduate Admissions, 636-949-4349, Fax: 636-949-4109, E-mail: adultadmissions@lindenwood.edu.
Website: http://www.lindenwood.edu/academics/academic-schools/robert-w-plaster-school-of-business-entrepreneurship/

Lipscomb University, College of Business, Nashville, TN 37204-3951. Offers accounting and finance (MBA); audit/accounting (M Acc); business (Certificate); business administration (MM); healthcare management (MBA); leadership (MBA); tax (M Acc); MBA/MS; Pharm D/MM. *Accreditation:* ACBSP. *Program availability:* Part-time, evening/weekend. *Faculty:* 14 full-time (2 women), 8 part-time/adjunct (1 woman). *Students:* 157 full-time (68 women), 9 part-time (6 women); includes 26 minority (9 Black or African American, non-Hispanic/Latino; 7 Asian, non-Hispanic/Latino; 8 Hispanic/Latino; 2 Two or more races, non-Hispanic/Latino), 9 international. Average age 30. 249 applicants, 49% accepted, 52 enrolled. In 2017, 130 master's awarded. *Entrance requirements:* For master's, GMAT, transcripts, interview, 2 references, resume. Additional exam requirements/recommendations for international students: Required—TOEFL (minimum score 570 paper-based). *Application deadline:* For fall admission, 6/15 for domestic students, 2/1 for international students; for winter admission, 6/1 for international students; for spring admission, 11/15 for domestic students. Applications are processed on a rolling basis. Application fee: $50 ($75 for international students). Electronic applications accepted. *Expenses:* Contact institution. *Financial support:* Career-related internships or fieldwork, scholarships/grants, tuition waivers (partial), and unspecified assistantships available. Support available to part-time students. Financial award application deadline: 7/1; financial award applicants required to submit FAFSA. *Faculty research:* Impact of spirituality on organization commitment, women in corporate leadership, psychological empowerment, training. *Unit head:* Allison Duke, Associate Dean of Graduate Business Programs, 615-966-5732, Fax: 615-966-1818, E-mail: allison.duke@lipscomb.edu. *Application contact:* Karen Risley, Manager, Graduate Business Recruiting, 615-966-5145, E-mail: karen.risley@lipscomb.edu.
Website: http://www.lipscomb.edu/business/Graduate-Programs

Long Island University–LIU Brooklyn, School of Business, Public Administration and Information Sciences, Brooklyn, NY 11201-8423. Offers accounting (MBA); accounting (MS); business administration (MBA); computer science (MS); gerontology (Advanced Certificate); health administration (MPA); human resources management (MS); not-for-profit management (Advanced Certificate); public administration (MPA); taxation (MS). *Program availability:* Part-time, evening/weekend. *Faculty:* 18 full-time (7 women), 28 part-time/adjunct (8 women). *Students:* 226 full-time (140 women), 232 part-time (150 women); includes 272 minority (192 Black or African American, non-Hispanic/Latino; 2 American Indian or Alaska Native, non-Hispanic/Latino; 35 Asian, non-Hispanic/Latino; 40 Hispanic/Latino; 3 Two or more races, non-Hispanic/Latino), 88 international. Average age 32. 495 applicants, 64% accepted, 149 enrolled. In 2017, 189 master's, 13 other advanced degrees awarded. *Entrance requirements:* Additional exam requirements/recommendations for international students: Required—TOEFL (minimum score 550 paper-based; 75 iBT). *Application deadline:* Applications are processed on a rolling basis. Application fee: $50. Electronic applications accepted. *Expenses:* Tuition: Full-time $21,618; part-time $1201 per credit. *Required fees:* $1840; $920 per term. Tuition and fees vary according to course load. *Financial support:* In 2017–18, 78 students received support. Career-related internships or fieldwork, Federal Work-Study, scholarships/grants, and unspecified assistantships available. Support available to part-time students. Financial award application deadline: 2/15; financial award applicants required to submit FAFSA. *Faculty research:* Tax policy; public sector budgeting and gender inequities; technology and innovation; game theory; knowledge management. *Unit head:* Dr. Edward Rogoff, Dean, 718-488-1159, E-mail: edward.rogoff@liu.edu. *Application contact:* Luis Santiago, Dean of Enrollment, 718-488-1011, Fax: 718-780-6110, E-mail: bkln-admissions@liu.edu.
Website: http://liu.edu/Brooklyn/Academics/School-of-Business-Public-Administration-and-Information-Sciences

Long Island University–LIU Post, College of Management, Brookville, NY 11548-1300. Offers accountancy (MS); finance (MBA); information systems (MS); international business (MBA); management (MBA); management engineering (MS); marketing (MBA); taxation (MS); technical project management (MS); JD/MBA. *Accreditation:* AACSB. *Program availability:* Part-time, evening/weekend, blended/hybrid learning. *Faculty:* 23 full-time (7 women), 7 part-time/adjunct (1 woman). *Students:* 119 full-time (47 women), 62 part-time (23 women); includes 33 minority (11 Black or African American, non-Hispanic/Latino; 8 Asian, non-Hispanic/Latino; 13 Hispanic/Latino; 1 Two or more races, non-Hispanic/Latino), 56 international. Average age 28. 162 applicants, 62% accepted, 41 enrolled. In 2017, 91 master's awarded. *Entrance requirements:* For master's, GMAT, GRE, or LSAT. Additional exam requirements/recommendations for international students: Required—TOEFL (minimum score 550 paper-based, 75 iBT) or IELTS. *Application deadline:* Applications are processed on a rolling basis. Application fee: $50. Electronic applications accepted. *Expenses:* Tuition: Full-time $21,618; part-time $1201 per credit. *Required fees:* $1840; $920 per term. Tuition and fees vary according to course load. *Financial support:* In 2017–18, 47 students received support. Career-related internships or fieldwork, Federal Work-Study, and scholarships/grants available. Support available to part-time students. Financial award application deadline: 2/15; financial award applicants required to submit FAFSA. *Faculty research:* Innovation and property rights, knowledge sourcing, sustainability and firm performance, China and growth markets, corporate social responsibility, workforce compensation and issues. *Unit head:* Dr. Robert M. Valli, Dean, 516-299-3004, E-mail: rob.valli@liu.edu. *Application contact:* Rita Langdon, Graduate Admissions, 516-299-2900, Fax: 516-299-2137, E-mail: post-enroll@liu.edu.
Website: http://liu.edu/CWPost/Academics/Schools/COM

Louisiana State University and Agricultural & Mechanical College, Graduate School, E. J. Ourso College of Business, Department of Accounting, Baton Rouge, LA 70803. Offers MS. *Faculty:* 12 full-time (5 women), 1 part-time/adjunct (0 women). *Students:* 54 full-time (35 women), 5 part-time (4 women); includes 10 minority (4 Black or African American, non-Hispanic/Latino; 1 American Indian or Alaska Native, non-Hispanic/Latino; 3 Asian, non-Hispanic/Latino; 1 Hispanic/Latino; 1 Two or more races, non-Hispanic/Latino), 6 international. Average age 26. 67 applicants, 54% accepted, 27 enrolled. In 2017, 60 master's, 1 doctorate awarded. *Financial support:* In 2017–18, 6 research assistantships (averaging $9,583 per year), 16 teaching assistantships (averaging $25,021 per year) were awarded. *Total annual research expenditures:* $12,352.

Louisiana Tech University, Graduate School, College of Business, Ruston, LA 71272. Offers accounting (M Acc, DBA); computer information systems (DBA); finance (MBA, DBA); information assurance (MBA); innovation (MBA); management (DBA); marketing (MBA, DBA). *Accreditation:* AACSB. *Program availability:* Part-time, evening/weekend, 100% online, blended/hybrid learning. *Faculty:* 36 full-time (7 women), 8 part-time/adjunct (3 women). *Students:* 104 full-time (43 women), 40 part-time (16 women); includes 22 minority (13 Black or African American, non-Hispanic/Latino; 2 Asian, non-Hispanic/Latino; 7 Two or more races, non-Hispanic/Latino), 32 international. Average age 29. 104 applicants, 58% accepted, 25 enrolled. In 2017, 71 master's, 4 doctorates awarded. *Degree requirements:* For doctorate, thesis/dissertation. *Entrance requirements:* For master's and doctorate, GMAT, transcript with bachelor's degree awarded. Additional exam requirements/recommendations for international students: Required—TOEFL (minimum score 550 paper-based; 80 iBT), IELTS (minimum score 6.5). *Application deadline:* For fall admission, 8/1 priority date for domestic students, 6/1 for international students; for winter admission, 11/1 priority date for domestic students, 9/1 for international students; for spring admission, 2/1 priority date for domestic students, 12/1 for international students; for summer admission, 5/1 priority date for domestic students, 3/1 for international students. Application fee: $40. Electronic applications accepted. *Expenses:* Tuition, state resident: full-time $5146. Tuition, nonresident: full-time $10,147. *International tuition:* $10,267 full-time. *Required fees:* $2273. *Financial support:* In 2017–18, 24 students received support, including 17 research assistantships with partial tuition reimbursements available (averaging $12,500 per year), 7 teaching assistantships with partial tuition reimbursements available (averaging $12,500 per year); scholarships/grants and unspecified assistantships also available. Financial award application deadline: 2/1. *Faculty research:* Consumer environmental behavior; identifying and analyzing current issues and future concerns in real estate; information assurance and related areas in business for Northwest Louisiana and the United States (business continuity, disaster recovery, accounting controls, auditing, computer forensics, and security attribution); value creation driven by the consumer and employee interface within exchange environments. *Unit head:* Dr. Christopher D. Martin, Dean, 318-257-4526, Fax: 318-257-4253. *Application contact:* Samantha J. Bailey, Graduate Management Admissions Specialist, 318-257-2924, Fax: 318-257-4487, E-mail: samantha@latech.edu.
Website: http://www.business.latech.edu/

Loyola Marymount University, College of Business Administration, Master of Science in Accounting Program, Los Angeles, CA 90045-2659. Offers MS. *Unit head:* Dr. Michael Moore, Director, Master of Science in Accounting Program, 310-568-6266, E-mail: michael.moore@lmu.edu. *Application contact:* Chake H. Kouyoumjian, Associate Dean of Graduate Studies, 310-338-2721, Fax: 310-338-6086, E-mail: graduateinfo@lmu.edu.
Website: http://cba.lmu.edu/academics/msinaccounting

Loyola University Chicago, Quinlan School of Business, Master of Science in Accountancy Program, Chicago, IL 60611. Offers MSA. *Accreditation:* AACSB. *Program availability:* Part-time, evening/weekend. *Faculty:* 11 full-time (3 women), 8 part-time/adjunct (1 woman). *Students:* 102 full-time (75 women), 11 part-time (4 women); includes 16 minority (5 Black or African American, non-Hispanic/Latino; 6 Asian, non-Hispanic/Latino; 5 Hispanic/Latino), 75 international. Average age 24. 182 applicants, 64% accepted, 26 enrolled. In 2017, 51 master's awarded. *Entrance requirements:* For master's, GMAT or GRE, official transcripts, two letters of recommendation, statement of purpose, resume. Additional exam requirements/recommendations for international students: Required—TOEFL (minimum score 90 iBT) or IELTS (minimum score 6.5). *Application deadline:* For fall admission, 7/15 for domestic and international students; for

winter admission, 10/1 for domestic and international students; for spring admission, 1/15 for domestic and international students; for summer admission, 4/1 for domestic and international students. Applications are processed on a rolling basis. Application fee: $50. Electronic applications accepted. Application fee is waived when completed online. *Expenses:* $4,488 per course. *Financial support:* In 2017–18, 27 students received support. Research assistantships, career-related internships or fieldwork, Federal Work-Study, scholarships/grants, and health care benefits available. *Faculty research:* Investigate taxonomy of financial ratios across industries and financial reporting standards, federal transfer taxation, federal fiduciary taxation, estate planning, fraud in local governments, multi-disciplinary instructional cases for class use, impact of changes in accounting standards and business practices on the use of financial ratios, employment attributes for college graduates, credit relevance of litigation materiality disclosures. *Unit head:* Dr. Brian Stanko, Chair, 312-915-7106, Fax: 312-915-7224, E-mail: bstanko@luc.edu.
Website: http://www.luc.edu/quinlan/mba/masters-in-accounting/

Loyola University Chicago, Quinlan School of Business, MBA Programs, Chicago, IL 60611. Offers accounting (MBA); business ethics (MBA); derivative markets (MBA); economics (MBA); entrepreneurship (MBA); finance (MBA); healthcare management (MBA); human resources management (MBA); information systems management (MBA); international business (MBA); management (MBA); marketing (MBA); risk management (MBA); supply chain management (MBA). *Program availability:* Part-time, evening/weekend. *Faculty:* 84 full-time (28 women), 12 part-time/adjunct (3 women). *Students:* 253 full-time (118 women), 76 part-time (35 women); includes 83 minority (21 Black or African American, non-Hispanic/Latino; 1 American Indian or Alaska Native, non-Hispanic/Latino; 33 Asian, non-Hispanic/Latino; 24 Hispanic/Latino; 4 Two or more races, non-Hispanic/Latino), 37 international. Average age 30. 334 applicants, 52% accepted, 80 enrolled. In 2017, 220 master's awarded. *Entrance requirements:* For master's, GMAT or GRE, official transcripts, two letters of recommendation, statement of purpose, resume. Additional exam requirements/recommendations for international students: Required—TOEFL (minimum score 90 iBT) or IELTS (minimum score 6.5). *Application deadline:* For fall admission, 7/15 for domestic and international students; for winter admission, 10/1 for domestic and international students; for spring admission, 1/15 for domestic and international students; for summer admission, 4/1 for domestic and international students. Applications are processed on a rolling basis. Application fee: $50. Electronic applications accepted. Application fee is waived when completed online. *Expenses:* $4,488 per course. *Financial support:* In 2017–18, 11 students received support. Research assistantships, career-related internships or fieldwork, Federal Work-Study, scholarships/grants, and health care benefits available. *Faculty research:* Social enterprise and responsibility, emerging markets, supply chain management, risk management. *Unit head:* Katherine Acles, Assistant Dean for Graduate Programs, 312-915-6124, Fax: 312-915-7207, E-mail: kacles@luc.edu.

Maharishi University of Management, Graduate Studies, Program in Business Administration, Fairfield, IA 52557. Offers accounting (MBA); management (PhD); sustainability (MBA). *Program availability:* Evening/weekend, online learning. *Degree requirements:* For doctorate, thesis/dissertation. *Entrance requirements:* For master's, GMAT, minimum GPA of 3.0; for doctorate, minimum GPA of 3.0. Additional exam requirements/recommendations for international students: Required—TOEFL. *Faculty research:* Leadership, effects of the group dynamics of consciousness on the economy, innovation, employee development, cooperative strategy.

Manhattanville College, School of Business, Master of Science in Finance Program, Purchase, NY 10577-2132. Offers finance (MS, Advanced Certificate), including accounting (MS); corporate finance (MS); investment management (MS). *Program availability:* Part-time, evening/weekend. *Faculty:* 4 part-time/adjunct (2 women). *Students:* 23 full-time (7 women), 6 part-time (3 women); includes 9 minority (3 Black or African American, non-Hispanic/Latino; 6 Hispanic/Latino), 2 international. Average age 29. 35 applicants, 37% accepted, 11 enrolled. In 2017, 12 master's awarded. *Degree requirements:* For master's, thesis (for some programs), final project. *Entrance requirements:* For master's, personal essay, transcripts, 2 letters of recommendation (academic or professional), resume, health form with proof of immunization (for those born after 1957). Additional exam requirements/recommendations for international students: Required—TOEFL (minimum score 563 paper-based, 85 iBT), IELTS (7), or iTEP (B2). *Application deadline:* Applications are processed on a rolling basis. Application fee: $75. Electronic applications accepted. *Expenses:* $915 per credit. *Financial support:* Federal Work-Study, institutionally sponsored loans, scholarships/grants, and unspecified assistantships available. Financial award application deadline: 3/15; financial award applicants required to submit FAFSA. *Unit head:* Laura Persky, Graduate Program Director, 914-323-5188, E-mail: laura.persky@mville.edu. *Application contact:* Monika Pottgen, Assistant Director, Recruitment and Admissions, 914-323-5150, E-mail: business@mville.edu.
Website: https://www.mville.edu/programs/ms-finance

Marquette University, Graduate School of Management, Program in Accounting, Milwaukee, WI 53201-1881. Offers MSA. *Accreditation:* AACSB. *Program availability:* Part-time, evening/weekend. *Entrance requirements:* For master's, GMAT or GRE, letters of recommendation (if applying for financial aid). Additional exam requirements/recommendations for international students: Required—TOEFL (minimum score 550 paper-based; 88 iBT), IELTS (minimum score 6.5), PTE. Electronic applications accepted. *Faculty research:* Financial (accounting) literacy, international perception of corruption, effect of carbon credits on accounting and tax transactions, targeted tax breaks.

Marshall University, Academic Affairs Division, College of Business, Program in Accountancy, Huntington, WV 25755. Offers MS. *Students:* 13 full-time (10 women), 2 part-time (both women); includes 2 minority (both Asian, non-Hispanic/Latino). Average age 25. In 2017, 11 master's awarded. *Entrance requirements:* For master's, undergraduate degree in accounting with minimum GPA of 3.0 or GMAT. *Unit head:* Dr. Jeffrey Archambault, Director, 304-696-2655. *Application contact:* Wesley Spradlin, Information Contact, 304-746-8964, Fax: 304-746-1902, E-mail: spradlin2@marshall.edu.
Website: http://www.marshall.edu/cob/graduate/accountancy/

Maryville University of Saint Louis, The John E. Simon School of Business, St. Louis, MO 63141-7299. Offers accounting (MBA, MS, Certificate); business studies (Certificate); cybersecurity (MBA, MS, Certificate); financial services (MBA, Certificate); healthcare practice management (MBA, Certificate); human resource management (MBA, Certificate); information technology (MBA, Certificate); management (MBA, Certificate); management and leadership (MA); marketing (MBA, Certificate); project management (MBA, Certificate); sport business management (MBA); supply chain management (Certificate); supply chain management/logistics (MBA). *Accreditation:* ACBSP. *Program availability:* Part-time, 100% online, blended/hybrid learning. *Faculty:* 5 full-time (3 women), 51 part-time/adjunct (16 women). *Students:* 222 full-time (96 women), 498 part-time (222 women); includes 185 minority (104 Black or African American, non-Hispanic/Latino; 5 American Indian or Alaska Native, non-Hispanic/Latino; 30 Asian, non-Hispanic/Latino; 37 Hispanic/Latino; 9 Two or more races, non-Hispanic/Latino), 26 international. Average age 33. In 2017, 106 master's awarded. *Degree requirements:* For master's, capstone course (for MBA). *Entrance requirements:*

Additional exam requirements/recommendations for international students: Required—TOEFL (minimum score 563 paper-based; 85 iBT). *Application deadline:* Applications are processed on a rolling basis. Electronic applications accepted. *Expenses:* Contact institution. *Financial support:* Career-related internships or fieldwork, Federal Work-Study, tuition waivers (partial), and campus employment available. Financial award application deadline: 4/1; financial award applicants required to submit FAFSA. *Unit head:* Pam Horwitz, Interim Dean, 314-529-9680, Fax: 314-529-9975. *Application contact:* Dustin Loeffler, Director for Graduate Studies in Business, 314-529-9571, Fax: 314-529-9975, E-mail: dloeffler@maryville.edu.
Website: http://www.maryville.edu/bu/business-administration-masters/

McGill University, Faculty of Graduate and Postdoctoral Studies, Desautels Faculty of Management, Montréal, QC H3A 2T5, Canada. Offers administration (PhD); entrepreneurial studies (MBA); finance (MBA); general management (Post Master's Certificate); information systems (MBA); international business (MBA); international practicing management (MM); management (MBA); management for development (MBA); manufacturing management (MMM); marketing (MBA); operations management (MBA); public accountancy (Diploma); strategic management (MBA); MBA/LL B; MD/MBA. MMM offered jointly with Faculty of Engineering; PhD with Concordia University, HEC Montreal, Université de Montréal, Université du Québec à Montréal.

Mercer University, Graduate Studies, Cecil B. Day Campus, Eugene W. Stetson School of Business and Economics (Atlanta), Atlanta, GA 30341. Offers accounting (M Acc); innovation (PMBA), including entrepreneurship; international business (MBA); DPT/MBA; M Div/MBA; MBA/M Acc; Pharm D/MBA. *Accreditation:* AACSB. *Program availability:* Part-time, evening/weekend, 100% online, blended/hybrid learning. *Faculty:* 22 full-time (8 women), 7 part-time/adjunct (3 women). *Students:* 222 full-time (130 women), 138 part-time (72 women); includes 154 minority (114 Black or African American, non-Hispanic/Latino; 1 American Indian or Alaska Native, non-Hispanic/Latino; 27 Asian, non-Hispanic/Latino; 8 Hispanic/Latino; 4 Two or more races, non-Hispanic/Latino), 76 international. Average age 31. 207 applicants, 77% accepted, 110 enrolled. In 2017, 124 master's awarded. *Entrance requirements:* For master's, GMAT or GRE. Additional exam requirements/recommendations for international students: Required—TOEFL (minimum score 550 paper-based, 80 iBT) or IELTS. *Application deadline:* For fall admission, 6/15 priority date for domestic and international students; for spring admission, 11/1 priority date for domestic and international students; for summer admission, 3/15 priority date for domestic and international students. Applications are processed on a rolling basis. Application fee: $50 ($100 for international students). Electronic applications accepted. *Expenses:* $740 per credit (for evening, online and 2-year MBA); $818 per credit (for full-time MBA); $42,500 per degree (for PMBA); $727 per credit (for MSBA and M Acc). *Financial support:* In 2017–18, 25 students received support. Federal Work-Study and tuition discounts available. Financial award application deadline: 5/1; financial award applicants required to submit FAFSA. *Faculty research:* Entrepreneurship, market studies, international business strategy, financial analysis. *Unit head:* Dr. Susan P. Gilbert, Dean, 678-547-6438, Fax: 678-547-6337, E-mail: gilbert_sp@mercer.edu. *Application contact:* Lael Whiteside, Director of Admissions, 678-547-6300, Fax: 678-547-6160, E-mail: whiteside_l@mercer.edu.
Website: http://business.mercer.edu

Mercy College, School of Business, Program in Public Accounting, Dobbs Ferry, NY 10522-1189. Offers accounting (MS). *Program availability:* Part-time, evening/weekend. *Students:* 22 full-time (11 women), 2 part-time (1 woman); includes 14 minority (2 Black or African American, non-Hispanic/Latino; 3 Asian, non-Hispanic/Latino; 7 Hispanic/Latino; 2 Two or more races, non-Hispanic/Latino). Average age 32. 30 applicants, 20% accepted, 5 enrolled. In 2017, 22 master's awarded. *Degree requirements:* For master's, thesis or alternative. *Entrance requirements:* For master's, interview, essay, two letters of reference, undergraduate transcripts. Additional exam requirements/recommendations for international students: Required—TOEFL (minimum score 600 paper-based; 100 iBT), IELTS (minimum score 8). *Application deadline:* For fall admission, 8/1 for international students. Applications are processed on a rolling basis. Application fee: $40. Electronic applications accepted. *Expenses:* Contact institution. *Financial support:* Career-related internships or fieldwork, Federal Work-Study, scholarships/grants, and unspecified assistantships available. Support available to part-time students. Financial award applicants required to submit FAFSA. *Unit head:* Ed Weis, Dean, School of Business, 914-674-7490, E-mail: eweis@mercy.edu. *Application contact:* Allison Gurdineer, Senior Director of Admissions, 877-637-2946, Fax: 914-674-7382, E-mail: admissions@mercy.edu.
Website: https://www.mercy.edu/degrees-programs/ms-public-accounting

Mercyhurst University, Graduate Studies, Program in Organizational Leadership, Erie, PA 16546. Offers accounting (MS); higher education administration (MS); human resources (MS); organizational leadership (MS, Certificate); sports leadership (MS); strategy and innovation (MS). *Program availability:* Part-time, evening/weekend. *Degree requirements:* For master's, thesis. *Entrance requirements:* For master's, GRE General Test or MAT, interview, resume, essay, three professional references, transcripts. Additional exam requirements/recommendations for international students: Required—TOEFL (minimum score 80 iBT), IELTS (minimum score 6.5). Electronic applications accepted. *Faculty research:* Leadership training, organizational communication, leadership pedagogy.

Merrimack College, Girard School of Business, North Andover, MA 01845-5800. Offers accounting (MS); business analytics (MS); management (MS). *Program availability:* Part-time, evening/weekend, 100% online. *Faculty:* 13 full-time, 19 part-time/adjunct. *Students:* 86 full-time (33 women), 31 part-time (11 women); includes 10 minority (2 Black or African American, non-Hispanic/Latino; 2 Asian, non-Hispanic/Latino; 6 Hispanic/Latino), 34 international. Average age 31. 139 applicants, 78% accepted, 61 enrolled. In 2017, 74 master's awarded. *Degree requirements:* For master's, comprehensive exam (for some programs), thesis optional, capstone. *Entrance requirements:* For master's, official college transcripts, resume, personal statement, 2 recommendations. Additional exam requirements/recommendations for international students: Required—TOEFL (minimum score 84 iBT), IELTS (minimum score 6.5), PTE (minimum score 56). *Application deadline:* For fall admission, 8/24 for domestic students, 7/30 for international students; for spring admission, 1/10 for domestic and international students; for summer admission, 5/10 for domestic students, 4/10 for international students. Applications are processed on a rolling basis. Application fee: $0. Electronic applications accepted. *Expenses:* Contact institution. *Financial support:* Career-related internships or fieldwork, scholarships/grants, health care benefits, and unspecified assistantships available. Support available to part-time students. Financial award application deadline: 5/1; financial award applicants required to submit FAFSA. *Application contact:* Jennifer Greenwood, Graduate Admission Counselor, 978-837-3563, E-mail: graduate@merrimack.edu.
Website: http://www.merrimack.edu/academics/graduate/

Metropolitan State University of Denver, School of Business, Denver, CO 80204. Offers accounting (MP Acc); fraud and forensic auditing (MP Acc); internal audit (MP Acc); public accounting (MP Acc); taxation (MP Acc). *Accreditation:* AACSB. *Entrance requirements:* For master's, GMAT. *Expenses:* Contact institution.

Miami University, Farmer School of Business, Department of Accountancy, Oxford, OH 45056. Offers M Acc. *Accreditation:* AACSB. *Students:* 24 full-time (10 women);

Accounting

includes 1 minority (Two or more races, non-Hispanic/Latino), 3 international. Average age 22. In 2017, 35 master's awarded. *Expenses:* Tuition, state resident: full-time $13,812; part-time $575 per credit hour. Tuition, nonresident: full-time $30,860; part-time $1286 per credit hour. *Unit head:* Andrew Reffett, Chair and Professor, 513-529-6212, E-mail: reffeta@miamioh.edu. *Application contact:* Amanda Pyzoha, Academic Program Coordinator, 513-529-3372, E-mail: shickar@miamioh.edu.
Website: http://www.MiamiOH.edu/accountancy

Michigan State University, The Graduate School, Eli Broad College of Business, Department of Accounting and Information Systems, East Lansing, MI 48224. Offers accounting (MS, PhD), including information systems (MS), public and corporate accounting (MS), taxation (MS); business information systems (PhD). *Accreditation:* AACSB. *Degree requirements:* For doctorate, comprehensive exam, thesis/dissertation. *Entrance requirements:* For master's, GMAT (minimum score 550), bachelor's degree in accounting; minimum cumulative GPA of 3.0 at any institution attended and in any junior-/senior-level accounting courses taken; 3 letters of recommendation (at least 1 from faculty); working knowledge of computers including word processing, spreadsheets, networking, and database management system; for doctorate, GMAT (minimum score 600), bachelor's degree; transcripts; 3 letters of recommendation; statement of purpose; resume; on-campus interview; personal qualifications of sound character, perseverance, intellectual curiosity, and interest in scholarly research. Additional exam requirements/recommendations for international students: Required—TOEFL (minimum score 600 paper-based; 100 iBT), IELTS (minimum score 7) accepted for MS only. Electronic applications accepted.

Michigan Technological University, Graduate School, School of Business and Economics, Houghton, MI 49931. Offers accounting (MS); applied natural resource economics (MS); business administration (MBA). *Accreditation:* AACSB. *Program availability:* Part-time, evening/weekend. *Faculty:* 24 full-time (6 women), 1 part-time/adjunct. *Students:* 25 full-time (12 women), 21 part-time (13 women); includes 1 minority (Two or more races, non-Hispanic/Latino), 14 international. Average age 27. 165 applicants, 23% accepted, 22 enrolled. In 2017, 24 master's awarded. *Degree requirements:* For master's, thesis (for some programs). *Entrance requirements:* For master's, GMAT/GRE (recommended minimum score in the 55th percentile), statement of purpose, personal statement, official transcripts, 2 letters of recommendation, resume/curriculum vitae. Additional exam requirements/recommendations for international students: Required—TOEFL (recommended minimum score 95 iBT) or IELTS (minimum score 7). *Application deadline:* For fall admission, 7/1 for domestic and international students; for spring admission, 12/1 for domestic and international students. Applications are processed on a rolling basis. Electronic applications accepted. *Expenses:* Tuition, state resident: full-time $17,100; part-time $950 per credit. Tuition, nonresident: full-time $17,100; part-time $950 per credit. *Required fees:* $248; $124 per term. Tuition and fees vary according to course load and program. *Financial support:* In 2017–18, 22 students received support. Health care benefits and unspecified assistantships available. Financial award application deadline: 2/1; financial award applicants required to submit FAFSA. *Faculty research:* Natural resource and mineral economics, entrepreneurship, management of technology and innovation, engineering management, management information systems. *Total annual research expenditures:* $5,749. *Unit head:* Dr. Dean Johnson, Dean, 906-487-2668, Fax: 906-487-1863, E-mail: dean@mtu.edu. *Application contact:* Carol T. Wingerson, Administrative Aide, 906-487-2328, Fax: 906-487-2284, E-mail: gradadms@mtu.edu.
Website: http://www.mtu.edu/business/

Middle Tennessee State University, College of Graduate Studies, Jennings A. Jones College of Business, Department of Accounting, Murfreesboro, TN 37132. Offers M Acc. *Accreditation:* AACSB. *Program availability:* Part-time, evening/weekend, online learning. *Entrance requirements:* For master's, GMAT (minimum score of 400). Additional exam requirements/recommendations for international students: Required—TOEFL (minimum score 525 paper-based; 71 iBT) or IELTS (minimum score 6). Electronic applications accepted.

Millennia Atlantic University, Graduate Programs, Doral, FL 33178. Offers accounting (MBA); business administration (MBA); health information management (MS); human resource management (MA). *Program availability:* Online learning.

Millsaps College, Else School of Management, Jackson, MS 39210-0001. Offers accounting (M Acc); business administration (MBA). *Accreditation:* AACSB. *Program availability:* Part-time. *Entrance requirements:* For master's, GMAT. Additional exam requirements/recommendations for international students: Required—TOEFL. Electronic applications accepted. *Faculty research:* Ethics, audit independence, satisfaction with assurance services, political business cycles, economic development, commercialization of new products.

Minnesota State University Mankato, College of Graduate Studies and Research, College of Business, Mankato, MN 56001. Offers accounting (MSA); business (MBA). *Accreditation:* AACSB. *Entrance requirements:* For master's, GMAT, 2 letters of reference, resume. Additional exam requirements/recommendations for international students: Required—TOEFL. Electronic applications accepted.

Minnesota State University Moorhead, Graduate Studies, College of Business and Innovation, Moorhead, MN 56563. Offers accounting and finance (MBA); business administration (MBA); health care management (MBA). *Accreditation:* AACSB. *Program availability:* Part-time. *Faculty:* 13. *Students:* 17 full-time (5 women), 26 part-time (17 women). Average age 29. 21 applicants, 81% accepted. In 2017, 13 master's awarded. *Degree requirements:* For master's, comprehensive exam (for some programs), thesis, final oral defense. *Entrance requirements:* For master's, GMAT, minimum GPA of 3.0. Additional exam requirements/recommendations for international students: Required—TOEFL (minimum score 550 paper-based); Recommended—IELTS (minimum score 6.5). *Application deadline:* For fall admission, 3/15 for domestic students; for spring admission, 10/15 for domestic students. Applications are processed on a rolling basis. Application fee: $20. Electronic applications accepted. *Expenses:* Tuition, state resident: full-time $9000; part-time $374 per credit. Tuition, nonresident: full-time $18,000; part-time $748 per credit. *Required fees:* $1055; $43.96 per credit. Tuition and fees vary according to degree level, program and reciprocity agreements. *Financial support:* Federal Work-Study and unspecified assistantships available. Financial award application deadline: 10/1; financial award applicants required to submit FAFSA. *Faculty research:* Union decertification, small business development, business innovation, pedagogy, curriculum design. *Unit head:* Denise Gorsline, Interim Dean, 218-477-4623, E-mail: gorsline@mnstate.edu. *Application contact:* Karla Wenger, Coordinator, 218-477-2344, E-mail: wengerk@mnstate.edu.
Website: http://www.mnstate.edu/cbi/

Misericordia University, College of Business, Master of Business Administration Program, Dallas, PA 18612-1098. Offers accounting (MBA); healthcare management (MBA); human resource management (MBA); management (MBA); sport management (MBA). *Program availability:* Part-time, evening/weekend, online learning. *Entrance requirements:* For master's, GMAT, MAT, GRE (50th percentile or higher), or minimum undergraduate GPA of 3.0, interview. Additional exam requirements/recommendations for international students: Required—TOEFL. Electronic applications accepted. Application fee is waived when completed online. *Expenses:* Contact institution.

Mississippi College, Graduate School, School of Business, Clinton, MS 39058. Offers accounting (Certificate); business administration (MBA), including accounting; business education (M Ed); finance (MBA, Certificate); JD/MBA. *Accreditation:* ACBSP. *Program availability:* Part-time, evening/weekend. *Degree requirements:* For master's, comprehensive exam, thesis optional. *Entrance requirements:* For master's, GMAT, minimum GPA of 2.5, 24 hours of undergraduate course work in business. Additional exam requirements/recommendations for international students: Recommended—TOEFL, IELTS. Electronic applications accepted.

Mississippi State University, College of Business, Adkerson School of Accountancy, Mississippi State, MS 39762. Offers accountancy (MPA); systems (MPA). *Accreditation:* AACSB. *Faculty:* 10 full-time (0 women). *Students:* 61 full-time (38 women), 3 part-time (0 women); includes 8 minority (5 Black or African American, non-Hispanic/Latino; 1 Asian, non-Hispanic/Latino; 2 Hispanic/Latino), 3 international. Average age 23. 40 applicants, 70% accepted, 26 enrolled. In 2017, 51 master's awarded. *Degree requirements:* For master's, comprehensive exam. *Entrance requirements:* For master's, GMAT (minimum score of 510), minimum GPA of 3.0 over last 60 hours of undergraduate course work. Additional exam requirements/recommendations for international students: Required—TOEFL (minimum score 575 paper-based; 84 iBT); Recommended—IELTS (minimum score 7). *Application deadline:* For fall admission, 7/1 for domestic students, 5/1 for international students; for spring admission, 11/1 for domestic students, 9/1 for international students. Applications are processed on a rolling basis. Application fee: $60 ($80 for international students). Electronic applications accepted. *Expenses:* Tuition, state resident: full-time $8318; part-time $462.12 per credit hour. Tuition, nonresident: full-time $22,358; part-time $1242.12 per credit hour. *Required fees:* $110; $12.24 per credit hour. $6.12 per semester. *Financial support:* Career-related internships or fieldwork, Federal Work-Study, institutionally sponsored loans, scholarships/grants, and unspecified assistantships available. Support available to part-time students. Financial award application deadline: 4/1; financial award applicants required to submit FAFSA. *Faculty research:* Income tax, financial accounting system, managerial accounting, auditing. *Unit head:* Dr. Shawn Mauldin, Professor and Director, 662-325-3710, Fax: 662-325-1646, E-mail: smauldin@business.msstate.edu. *Application contact:* Lakan Drinker, Admissions and Enrollment Assistant, 662-325-8951, E-mail: ldrinker@grad.msstate.edu.
Website: http://www.business.msstate.edu/programs/adkerson

Missouri State University, Graduate College, College of Business, School of Accountancy, Springfield, MO 65897. Offers M Acc. *Accreditation:* AACSB. *Program availability:* Part-time, evening/weekend. *Faculty:* 13 full-time (3 women). *Students:* 40 full-time (25 women), 13 part-time (10 women); includes 6 minority (1 Black or African American, non-Hispanic/Latino; 3 Asian, non-Hispanic/Latino; 1 Hispanic/Latino; 1 Two or more races, non-Hispanic/Latino), 11 international. Average age 22. 39 applicants, 38% accepted, 14 enrolled. In 2017, 48 master's awarded. *Entrance requirements:* For master's, GMAT (minimum composite score of 500), minimum GPA of 3.2 in last 60 hours of coursework. Additional exam requirements/recommendations for international students: Required—TOEFL (minimum score 90 iBT). *Application deadline:* For fall admission, 7/20 priority date for domestic students, 5/1 for international students; for spring admission, 12/20 priority date for domestic students, 9/1 for international students; for summer admission, 5/20 priority date for domestic students. Applications are processed on a rolling basis. Application fee: $35 ($50 for international students). Electronic applications accepted. *Expenses:* Tuition, state resident: full-time $2915; part-time $2021 per credit hour. Tuition, nonresident: full-time $5354; part-time $3647 per credit hour. *International tuition:* $11,992 full-time. *Required fees:* $173; $173 per credit hour. Tuition and fees vary according to class time, course level, course load, degree level, campus/location and program. *Financial support:* Career-related internships or fieldwork, Federal Work-Study, institutionally sponsored loans, scholarships/grants, tuition waivers (partial), and unspecified assistantships available. Support available to part-time students. Financial award application deadline: 3/31; financial award applicants required to submit FAFSA. *Faculty research:* Forensic accounting, accounting information systems, accounting education, tax compliance. *Unit head:* Dr. John R. Williams, Director, 417-836-5414, Fax: 417-836-6337, E-mail: accountancy@missouristate.edu. *Application contact:* Stephanie Praschan, Director, Graduate Enrollment Management, 417-836-5330, Fax: 417-836-6200, E-mail: stephaniepraschan@missouristate.edu.
Website: http://www.missouristate.edu/soa/

Missouri Western State University, Program in Business Administration, St. Joseph, MO 64507-2294. Offers animal and life sciences (MBA); enterprise resource planning (MBA); forensic accounting (MBA); general business (MBA). *Program availability:* Part-time. *Students:* 4 full-time (3 women), 24 part-time (8 women); includes 5 minority (3 Black or African American, non-Hispanic/Latino; 1 Asian, non-Hispanic/Latino; 1 Two or more races, non-Hispanic/Latino). Average age 35. 30 applicants, 93% accepted, 18 enrolled. *Entrance requirements:* Additional exam requirements/recommendations for international students: Recommended—TOEFL (minimum score 79 iBT), IELTS (minimum score 6). *Application deadline:* For fall admission, 7/15 for domestic and international students; for spring admission, 10/1 for domestic and international students; for summer admission, 3/15 for domestic students. Applications are processed on a rolling basis. Application fee: $45 ($50 for international students). Electronic applications accepted. *Expenses:* Tuition, state resident: full-time $6391; part-time $336 per credit hour. Tuition, nonresident: full-time $11,483; part-time $604 per credit hour. *Required fees:* $542; $99 per credit hour. $176 per semester. One-time fee: $45. Tuition and fees vary according to course load and program. *Financial support:* Scholarships/grants and unspecified assistantships available. Support available to part-time students. *Unit head:* Dr. Logan Jones, Director, 816-271-4351, E-mail: jjones81@missouriwestern.edu. *Application contact:* Dr. Benjamin D. Caldwell, Dean of the Graduate School, 816-271-4394, Fax: 816-271-4525, E-mail: graduate@missouriwestern.edu.
Website: http://www.missouriwestern.edu/mba/

Molloy College, Graduate Business Program, Rockville Centre, NY 11571-5002. Offers accounting (MBA); finance (MBA, Post-Master's Certificate, Postbaccalaureate Certificate); healthcare (MBA, Post-Master's Certificate, Postbaccalaureate Certificate); management (MBA); marketing (MBA, Post-Master's Certificate, Postbaccalaureate Certificate); personal financial planning (MBA). *Program availability:* Part-time, evening/weekend. *Faculty:* 8 full-time (3 women), 7 part-time/adjunct (2 women). *Students:* 53 full-time (29 women), 175 part-time (89 women); includes 88 minority (38 Black or African American, non-Hispanic/Latino; 18 Asian, non-Hispanic/Latino; 30 Hispanic/Latino; 2 Two or more races, non-Hispanic/Latino), 3 international. Average age 39. 128 applicants, 68% accepted, 81 enrolled. In 2017, 125 master's awarded. *Entrance requirements:* Additional exam requirements/recommendations for international students: Required—TOEFL (minimum score 550 paper-based; 79 iBT). *Application deadline:* Applications are processed on a rolling basis. Application fee: $60. Electronic applications accepted. *Expenses:* Tuition: Full-time $19,980; part-time $1110 per credit. *Required fees:* $1040. Tuition and fees vary according to course load and degree level. *Financial support:* Application deadline: 3/1; applicants required to submit FAFSA. *Faculty research:* Graduate education - pedagogy and the capstone experience; Freedom of Speech in the workplace; employer liability for sexual harassment in the workplace; educational economics and industrial organization; corporate governance

and distressed debt analysis; social network analysis; market segmentation. *Unit head:* Dr. Maureen Mackenzie, Dean, Division of Business/Director of Graduate Programs, 516-323-3080, E-mail: mmackenzie@molloy.edu. *Application contact:* Jaclyn Machowicz, Assistant Director for Admissions, 516-323-4010, E-mail: jmachowicz@molloy.edu.
Website: http://www.molloy.edu/academics/graduate-programs/graduate-business

Monmouth University, Graduate Studies, Leon Hess Business School, West Long Branch, NJ 07764-1898. Offers accounting (MBA, Certificate); business administration (MBA); finance (MBA); management (MBA); marketing (MBA); real estate (MBA). *Accreditation:* AACSB. *Program availability:* Part-time, evening/weekend. *Faculty:* 20 full-time (4 women), 8 part-time/adjunct (0 women). *Students:* 101 full-time (55 women), 107 part-time (44 women); includes 19 minority (3 Black or African American, non-Hispanic/Latino; 6 Asian, non-Hispanic/Latino; 6 Hispanic/Latino; 1 Native Hawaiian or other Pacific Islander, non-Hispanic/Latino; 3 Two or more races, non-Hispanic/Latino), 13 international. Average age 30. In 2017, 61 master's, 1 other advanced degree awarded. *Degree requirements:* For master's, capstone course. *Entrance requirements:* For master's, GMAT or GRE, current resume; essay (500 words or less). Additional exam requirements/recommendations for international students: Required—TOEFL (minimum score 550 paper-based; 79 iBT), IELTS (minimum score 6), Michigan English Language Assessment Battery (minimum score 77) or Certificate of Advanced English (minimum score 160). *Application deadline:* For fall admission, 7/15 priority date for domestic students, 6/1 for international students; for spring admission, 12/1 priority date for domestic students, 11/1 for international students; for summer admission, 5/1 for domestic students. Applications are processed on a rolling basis. Application fee: $50. Electronic applications accepted. *Expenses: Tuition:* Full-time $21,366; part-time $7122 per credit. *Required fees:* $700; $175 per term. *Financial support:* In 2017–18, 42 students received support. Institutionally sponsored loans, scholarships/grants, and unspecified assistantships available. Support available to part-time students. Financial award applicants required to submit FAFSA. *Faculty research:* Information technology and marketing, behavioral research in accounting, human resources, management of technology. *Unit head:* Dr. Susan Gupta, MBA Program Director, 732-571-3639, Fax: 732-263-5517, E-mail: sgupta@monmouth.edu. *Application contact:* Laurie Kuhn, Associate Director of Graduate Admission, 732-571-3452, Fax: 732-263-5123, E-mail: gradadm@monmouth.edu.
Website: https://www.monmouth.edu/business-school/leon-hess-business-school.aspx
See Display on page 115 and Close-Up on page 177.

Monroe College, King Graduate School, Bronx, NY 10468. Offers accounting (MS); business administration (MBA), including entrepreneurship, finance, general business administration, healthcare management, human resources, information technology, marketing; computer science (MS); criminal justice (MS); hospitality management (MS); public health (MPH), including biostatistics and epidemiology, community health, health administration and leadership. *Program availability:* Online learning. Application fee: $50.
Website: https://www.monroecollege.edu/Degrees/King-Graduate-School/

Montana State University, The Graduate School, College of Business, Bozeman, MT 59717. Offers professional accountancy (MP Ac). *Accreditation:* AACSB. *Program availability:* Part-time. *Degree requirements:* For master's, comprehensive exam. *Entrance requirements:* For master's, GRE General Test, GMAT, minimum undergraduate GPA of 3.1 (preferred). Additional exam requirements/recommendations for international students: Required—TOEFL (minimum score 550 paper-based). Electronic applications accepted. *Faculty research:* Tax research, accounting education, fraud issues, CPA exams.

Montclair State University, The Graduate School, Feliciano School of Business, Post Master's Certificate Program in Accounting, Montclair, NJ 07043-1624. Offers Post Master's Certificate. *Program availability:* Part-time, evening/weekend. *Entrance requirements:* For degree, 2 letters of recommendation, essay. Additional exam requirements/recommendations for international students: Required—TOEFL (minimum score 83 iBT), IELTS (minimum score 6.5). Electronic applications accepted. *Faculty research:* Economic costs and benefits of tax incentive programs, sustainability and financial accounting, auditors' expanded role post-Great Recession, revising rules for restructuring charges, aggressive accounting and ethical behavior.

Montclair State University, The Graduate School, Feliciano School of Business, Program in Accounting, Montclair, NJ 07043-1624. Offers MS. *Program availability:* Part-time, evening/weekend. *Degree requirements:* For master's, culminating experience. *Entrance requirements:* For master's, GMAT, 2 letters of recommendation, resume, essay. Additional exam requirements/recommendations for international students: Required—TOEFL (minimum score 83 iBT), IELTS (minimum score 6.5). Electronic applications accepted. *Faculty research:* Economic costs and benefits of tax incentive programs, sustainability and financial accounting, auditors' expanded role post-Great Recession, revising rules for restructuring charges, aggressive accounting and ethical behavior.

Montclair State University, The Graduate School, Feliciano School of Business, Program in Forensic Accounting, Montclair, NJ 07043-1624. Offers Graduate Certificate.

Moravian College, Graduate and Continuing Studies, Business and Management Programs, Bethlehem, PA 18018-6650. Offers accounting (MBA); business analytics (MBA); business management (MBA); health administration (MHA); healthcare management (MBA); HR leadership (MSHRM); human resource management (MBA); learning and performance management (MSHRM); supply chain management (MBA). *Program availability:* Part-time, evening/weekend. *Faculty:* 5 full-time (2 women), 9 part-time/adjunct (3 women). *Students:* 13 full-time (10 women), 80 part-time (45 women); includes 13 minority (6 Black or African American, non-Hispanic/Latino; 6 Hispanic/Latino; 1 Two or more races, non-Hispanic/Latino). Average age 31. 55 applicants, 91% accepted, 31 enrolled. In 2017, 29 master's awarded. *Entrance requirements:* For master's, current resume, official transcripts, 2 letters of recommendation. Additional exam requirements/recommendations for international students: Required—TOEFL (minimum score 550 paper-based), IELTS (minimum score 6.5). *Application deadline:* For fall admission, 8/1 priority date for domestic and international students; for spring admission, 1/1 priority date for domestic and international students; for summer admission, 5/1 priority date for domestic and international students. Applications are processed on a rolling basis. Electronic applications accepted. *Expenses: Tuition:* Full-time $15,714; part-time $2619 per course. *Required fees:* $45 per semester. Tuition and fees vary according to program. *Financial support:* In 2017–18, 3 students received support, including 2 research assistantships with full tuition reimbursements available. Financial award applicants required to submit FAFSA. *Faculty research:* Leadership, change management, human resources. *Unit head:* Dr. Liz Kleintop, Associate Chair of Graduate Business, 610-861-1400, Fax: 610-861-1466, E-mail: graduate@moravian.edu. *Application contact:* Sean Rossi, Student Experience Mentor, 610-861-1400, Fax: 610-861-1466, E-mail: graduate@moravian.edu.
Website: http://www.moravian.edu/graduate

Morgan State University, School of Graduate Studies, Earl G. Graves School of Business and Management, PhD Program in Business Administration, Baltimore, MD 21251. Offers business administration (PhD), including accounting, information systems,

management and marketing. *Accreditation:* AACSB. *Entrance requirements:* For doctorate, GMAT. Additional exam requirements/recommendations for international students: Required—TOEFL (minimum score 550 paper-based). *Application deadline:* For fall admission, 2/1 priority date for domestic students; for spring admission, 10/1 priority date for domestic students. Applications are processed on a rolling basis. Application fee: $0. *Expenses:* Tuition, state resident: part-time $433 per credit. Tuition, nonresident: part-time $851 per credit. *Required fees:* $81.50 per credit. *Financial support:* Application deadline: 2/1. *Unit head:* Dr. Augustus Abbey, Department Chair, 443-885-3285, E-mail: augustus.abbey@morgan.edu. *Application contact:* Dr. Dean Campbell, Graduate Recruitment Specialist, 443-885-3185, Fax: 443-885-8226, E-mail: dean.campbell@morgan.edu.

Morgan State University, School of Graduate Studies, Earl G. Graves School of Business and Management, Program in Accounting, Baltimore, MD 21251. Offers MS. *Expenses:* Tuition, state resident: part-time $433 per credit. Tuition, nonresident: part-time $851 per credit. *Required fees:* $81.50 per credit.

Mount Aloysius College, Program in Business Administration, Cresson, PA 16630. Offers accounting (MBA); health and human services administration (MBA); non-profit management (MBA); project management (MBA). *Program availability:* Part-time, evening/weekend. *Entrance requirements:* Additional exam requirements/recommendations for international students: Required—IELTS (minimum score 5.5); Recommended—TOEFL. *Application deadline:* For fall admission, 8/1 for domestic students; for spring admission, 12/1 for domestic students. Applications are processed on a rolling basis. Application fee: $30. Electronic applications accepted. Application fee is waived when completed online. *Expenses: Tuition:* Full-time $14,000; part-time $790 per credit hour. *Financial support:* Unspecified assistantships available. Financial award applicants required to submit FAFSA. *Application contact:* Matthew P. Bodenschatz, Director of Graduate and Continuing Education Admissions, 814-886-6556, Fax: 814-886-6441, E-mail: mbodenschatz@mtaloy.edu.
Website: http://www.mtaloy.edu

Murray State University, Arthur J. Bauernfeind College of Business, MBA Program, Murray, KY 42071. Offers accounting (MBA); finance (MBA); global communications (MBA); human resource management (MBA); marketing (MBA). *Accreditation:* AACSB. *Program availability:* Part-time, evening/weekend, 100% online, blended/hybrid learning. *Faculty:* 49 full-time (18 women), 3 part-time/adjunct (0 women). *Students:* 54 full-time (22 women), 79 part-time (37 women); includes 13 minority (6 Black or African American, non-Hispanic/Latino; 1 American Indian or Alaska Native, non-Hispanic/Latino; 2 Asian, non-Hispanic/Latino; 2 Hispanic/Latino; 2 Two or more races, non-Hispanic/Latino), 30 international. Average age 29. 70 applicants, 81% accepted, 34 enrolled. In 2017, 61 master's awarded. *Entrance requirements:* For master's, GRE or GMAT, minimum university GPA of 2.75. Additional exam requirements/recommendations for international students: Required—TOEFL (minimum score 527 paper-based; 71 iBT). *Application deadline:* Applications are processed on a rolling basis. Application fee: $40 ($50 for international students). *Expenses:* Tuition, state resident: full-time $9504. Tuition, nonresident: full-time $26,811. *International tuition:* $14,400 full-time. Tuition and fees vary according to course load, degree level and reciprocity agreements. *Financial support:* In 2017–18, 5 research assistantships, 5 teaching assistantships were awarded; Federal Work-Study also available. Financial award applicants required to submit FAFSA. *Faculty research:* Human resource management, e-commerce, supply-chain management, investment management, accounting. *Unit head:* Dr. Joy Humphreys, Assistant Dean and MBA Director, 270-809-4259, Fax: 270-809-3482, E-mail: jumphreys4@murraystate.edu. *Application contact:* Kaitlyn Burzynski, Interim Assistant Director for Graduate Admission and Records, 270-809-5732, Fax: 270-809-3780, E-mail: msu.graduateadmissions@murraystate.edu.
Website: http://www.murraystate.edu/academics/CollegesDepartments/CollegeOfBusiness/Programs/mba/index.aspx

National American University, Roueche Graduate Center, Austin, TX 78731. Offers accounting (MBA); aviation management (MBA, MM); care coordination (MSN); community college leadership (Ed D); criminal justice (MM); e-marketing (MBA, MM); health care administration (MBA, MM); higher education (MM); human resources management (MBA, MM); information technology management (MBA, MM); international business (MBA); leadership (EMBA); management (MBA); nursing administration (MSN); nursing education (MSN); nursing informatics (MSN); operations and configuration management (MBA, MM); project and process management (MBA, MM). Master's programs offered online through the Harold D. Buckingham Graduate School. *Program availability:* Part-time, evening/weekend, online learning. *Entrance requirements:* For master's, minimum undergraduate GPA of 2.75. Additional exam requirements/recommendations for international students: Required—TOEFL, TWE. Electronic applications accepted. *Faculty research:* Tourism, finance, marketing.

National University, Academic Affairs, School of Business and Management, La Jolla, CA 92037-1011. Offers accountancy (M Acc, Certificate); business administration (GMBA, MBA); business analytics (MS); cause leadership (MA); global management (MGM); human resource management (MA); management information systems (MS); marketing (MS); organizational leadership (MS). GMBA offered in Spanish. *Program availability:* Part-time, evening/weekend, 100% online, blended/hybrid learning. *Degree requirements:* For master's, thesis (for some programs). *Entrance requirements:* For master's, interview, minimum GPA of 2.5. Additional exam requirements/recommendations for international students: Required—TOEFL (minimum score 550 paper-based; 79 iBT), IELTS (minimum score 6). *Application deadline:* Applications are processed on a rolling basis. Application fee: $60 ($65 for international students). Electronic applications accepted. *Expenses: Tuition:* Part-time $430 per quarter hour. *Financial support:* Career-related internships or fieldwork, scholarships/grants, and tuition waivers (partial) available. Support available to part-time students. Financial award application deadline: 6/30; financial award applicants required to submit FAFSA. *Unit head:* Dr. Alfred Ntoko, Dean, 858-642-8400, Fax: 858-642-8719, E-mail: sobm@nu.edu. *Application contact:* Brandon Jouganatos, Vice President for Enrollment Services, 800-628-8648, E-mail: advisor@nu.edu.
Website: http://www.nu.edu/OurPrograms/SchoolOfBusinessAndManagement.html

Neumann University, Graduate Programs in Business and Information Management, Aston, PA 19014-1298. Offers accounting (MS), including forensic and fraud detection; sport business (MS). *Program availability:* Part-time, evening/weekend. *Faculty:* 2 full-time (both women), 4 part-time/adjunct (1 woman). *Students:* 7 full-time (1 woman), 29 part-time (14 women); includes 12 minority (10 Black or African American, non-Hispanic/Latino; 1 Asian, non-Hispanic/Latino; 1 Hispanic/Latino). Average age 30. 35 applicants, 37% accepted, 7 enrolled. In 2017, 16 master's awarded. *Degree requirements:* For master's, thesis (for some programs). *Entrance requirements:* For master's, official transcripts from all institutions attended, resume, letter of intent, 2-3 letters of recommendation. Additional exam requirements/recommendations for international students: Required—TOEFL (minimum score 70 iBT). *Application deadline:* Applications are processed on a rolling basis. Application fee: $0. Electronic applications accepted. *Expenses:* $600 per credit hour (for accounting program); $495 per credit hour (for sport business program). *Financial support:* Scholarships/grants and health care benefits available. Support available to part-time students. Financial award application deadline: 3/15; financial award applicants required to submit FAFSA. *Unit head:* Dr. Eric R.

Accounting

Wellington, Dean of Business and Information Management, 610-558-5596, Fax: 610-558-5574, E-mail: wellinge@neumann.edu. *Application contact:* Dr. Erika K. Davis, Director of Adult and Graduate Admissions, 800-9-NEUMANN Ext. 5208, Fax: 610-361-2548, E-mail: gradadultadmiss@neumann.edu.

New England College, Program in Management, Henniker, NH 03242-3293. Offers accounting (MSA); healthcare administration (MS); international relations (MA); marketing management (MS); nonprofit leadership (MS); project management (MS); strategic leadership (MS). *Program availability:* Part-time, evening/weekend. *Degree requirements:* For master's, independent research project. Electronic applications accepted.

New Jersey City University, School of Business, Program in Accounting, Jersey City, NJ 07305-1597. Offers MS, Graduate Certificate. *Program availability:* Part-time, evening/weekend. *Entrance requirements:* Additional exam requirements/recommendations for international students: Required—TOEFL (minimum score 79 iBT).

New Mexico State University, College of Business, Department of Accounting and Information Systems, Las Cruces, NM 88003. Offers accountancy (MACCT). *Accreditation:* AACSB. *Program availability:* Part-time. *Faculty:* 12 full-time (4 women). *Students:* 29 full-time (14 women), 10 part-time (6 women); includes 20 minority (1 Black or African American, non-Hispanic/Latino; 2 Asian, non-Hispanic/Latino; 16 Hispanic/Latino; 1 Two or more races, non-Hispanic/Latino), 4 international. Average age 27. 20 applicants, 75% accepted, 11 enrolled. In 2017, 22 master's awarded. *Entrance requirements:* For master's, GMAT, minimum undergraduate accounting GPA of 3.0 (upper-division). Additional exam requirements/recommendations for international students: Required—TOEFL (minimum score 550 paper-based; 79 iBT), IELTS (minimum score 6.5). *Application deadline:* For fall admission, 7/1 priority date for domestic students, 3/1 priority date for international students; for spring admission, 11/1 priority date for domestic students. Applications are processed on a rolling basis. Application fee: $40 ($50 for international students). Electronic applications accepted. *Expenses:* Tuition, state resident: full-time $4390. Tuition, nonresident: full-time $15,309. *Required fees:* $853. *Financial support:* In 2017–18, 29 students received support, including 1 fellowship (averaging $4,390 per year), 14 teaching assistantships (averaging $9,391 per year); career-related internships or fieldwork, Federal Work-Study, scholarships/grants, traineeships, health care benefits, and unspecified assistantships also available. Support available to part-time students. Financial award application deadline: 3/1. *Faculty research:* Taxation, financial accounting, managerial accounting, accounting systems, accounting education. *Unit head:* Dr. Larry Tunnell, Head, 575-646-4901, Fax: 575-646-1552, E-mail: ltunnell@nmsu.edu. *Application contact:* Cindy Seipel, Director, Master of Accountancy Program, 575-646-5206, Fax: 575-646-1552, E-mail: cseipel@nmsu.edu.
Website: http://business.nmsu.edu/departments/accounting

New York University, Leonard N. Stern School of Business, Department of Accounting, New York, NY 10012-1019. Offers MBA, PhD. *Accreditation:* AACSB. *Expenses: Tuition:* Full-time $41,352; part-time $19,968 per year. *Required fees:* $2496; $1628 per unit. $814 per term. Tuition and fees vary according to course load and program. *Faculty research:* Earnings management and financial analysis effectiveness and accounting policy, value-relevance of financial reporting, intangibles-related reporting and analysis, equity.

Niagara University, Graduate Division of Business Administration, Niagara University, NY 14109. Offers accounting (MBA); business administration (MBA); finance (MBA, MS); financial planning (MBA); healthcare administration (MBA, MHA); human resources (MBA); international business (MBA); marketing (MBA); professional accountancy (MBA); strategic management (MBA); supply chain management (MBA). *Accreditation:* AACSB. *Program availability:* Part-time, evening/weekend. *Faculty:* 17 full-time, 11 part-time/adjunct. *Students:* 173 full-time (92 women), 77 part-time (43 women); includes 38 minority (8 Black or African American, non-Hispanic/Latino; 3 American Indian or Alaska Native, non-Hispanic/Latino; 8 Asian, non-Hispanic/Latino; 8 Hispanic/Latino; 11 Two or more races, non-Hispanic/Latino), 46 international. Average age 27. In 2017, 139 master's awarded. *Entrance requirements:* For master's, GMAT. Additional exam requirements/recommendations for international students: Required—TOEFL (minimum score 550 paper-based; 79 iBT), IELTS (minimum score 6). *Application deadline:* For fall admission, 8/1 for domestic students; for spring admission, 11/1 for domestic students. Applications are processed on a rolling basis. Electronic applications accepted. *Expenses:* Contact institution. *Financial support:* Fellowships, research assistantships, career-related internships or fieldwork, and Federal Work-Study available. Support available to part-time students. Financial award application deadline: 4/15; financial award applicants required to submit FAFSA. *Faculty research:* Capital flows, Federal Reserve policy, human resource management, public policy, issues in marketing, auctions, economics of information, risk and capital markets, management strategy, consumer behavior, Internet and social media marketing. *Unit head:* Dr. Paul Richardson, MBA Director/Chair of the Marketing Department, 716-286-8169, Fax: 716-286-8206, E-mail: psr@niagara.edu. *Application contact:* Evan Pierce, Associate Director for Graduate Recruitment, 716-286-8769, Fax: 716-286-8170, E-mail: epierce@niagara.edu.
Website: http://mba.niagara.edu

North Carolina Agricultural and Technical State University, School of Graduate Studies, School of Business and Economics, Greensboro, NC 27411. Offers accounting (MBA); business education (MAT); human resources management (MBA); supply chain systems (MBA).

North Carolina State University, Graduate School, Poole College of Management, Program in Accounting, Raleigh, NC 27695. Offers MAC. *Program availability:* Part-time. *Degree requirements:* For master's, thesis optional. *Entrance requirements:* For master's, GMAT, interview. Additional exam requirements/recommendations for international students: Required—TOEFL. Electronic applications accepted. *Faculty research:* Financial reporting issues using positive economic models and empirical studies of human behavior related to accounting decisions.

North Dakota State University, College of Graduate and Interdisciplinary Studies, College of Business, Fargo, ND 58102. Offers accountancy (M Acc); business administration (MBA). *Accreditation:* AACSB. *Program availability:* Part-time, evening/weekend. *Entrance requirements:* For master's, GMAT. Additional exam requirements/recommendations for international students: Required—TOEFL (minimum score 550 paper-based; 79 iBT). Electronic applications accepted. *Faculty research:* Labor management, operations, international finance, agency, Internet marketing.

See Display on page 119 and Close-Up on page 179.

Northeastern Illinois University, College of Graduate Studies and Research, College of Business and Management, Master of Science in Accounting Program, Chicago, IL 60625. Offers MSA. *Expenses:* Tuition, state resident: full-time $7274; part-time $404.11 per credit hour. Tuition, nonresident: full-time $14,548; part-time $808.23 per credit hour. *Required fees:* $1284. *Unit head:* Dr. Essam Elshafie, Coordinator/Advisor, 773-442-6118, E-mail: e-elshafie@neiu.edu. *Application contact:* Martha Narvaez, Graduate Admission Representative, 773-442-6006, E-mail: m-narvaez@neiu.edu.

Northeastern State University, College of Business and Technology, Program in Accounting and Financial Analysis, Tahlequah, OK 74464-2399. Offers MS. *Program availability:* Part-time, evening/weekend. *Faculty:* 4 full-time (1 woman). *Students:* 12 full-time (7 women), 46 part-time (26 women); includes 19 minority (4 Black or African American, non-Hispanic/Latino; 3 American Indian or Alaska Native, non-Hispanic/Latino; 2 Hispanic/Latino; 10 Two or more races, non-Hispanic/Latino), 2 international. Average age 32. In 2017, 19 master's awarded. *Entrance requirements:* For master's, GMAT. Additional exam requirements/recommendations for international students: Required—TOEFL. *Application deadline:* For fall admission, 6/1 priority date for domestic students. Applications are processed on a rolling basis. Application fee: $25. Electronic applications accepted. *Expenses:* Tuition, state resident: part-time $222 per credit hour. Tuition, nonresident: part-time $501.75 per credit hour. *Required fees:* $37.40 per credit hour. Tuition and fees vary according to degree level. *Faculty research:* Information systems and organizational performance, capital markets, sustainability. *Unit head:* Dr. Gary Freeman, Director, Master of Accounting and Financial Analysis, 918-449-6524, E-mail: freemadg@nsuok.edu. *Application contact:* Josh McCollum, Graduate Coordinator, 918-444-2093, E-mail: mccollu@nsuok.edu. Website: http://academics.nsuok.edu/businesstechnology/Graduate/MAFA.aspx

Northeastern University, D'Amore-McKim School of Business, Boston, MA 02115-5096. Offers accounting (MS); business administration (EMBA, MBA); finance (MS); innovation (MS); international business (MS); international management (MS); taxation (MS); technological entrepreneurship (MS); JD/MBA; LL M/MBA; MBA/MSN; MS/MBA. *Accreditation:* AACSB. *Program availability:* Part-time, evening/weekend, online learning. *Faculty:* 184. *Students:* 1,489. In 2017, 800 master's awarded. *Entrance requirements:* For master's, GMAT or GRE. Application fee: $75. Electronic applications accepted. *Expenses:* Contact institution. *Financial support:* Scholarships/grants available. Financial award applicants required to submit FAFSA. *Unit head:* Dr. Raj Echambadi, Dean, D'Amore-McKim School of Business, 617-373-3232, Fax: 617-373-2056. *Application contact:* Evelyn Tate, Director, Graduate Recruitment and Admissions, 617-373-3258, E-mail: e.tate@northeastern.edu.
Website: http://damore-mckim.northeastern.edu/

Northern Illinois University, Graduate School, College of Business, Department of Accountancy, De Kalb, IL 60115-2854. Offers MAC, MAS, MST. *Accreditation:* AACSB. *Program availability:* Part-time, evening/weekend. *Faculty:* 14 full-time (4 women). *Students:* 138 full-time (58 women), 84 part-time (44 women); includes 63 minority (6 Black or African American, non-Hispanic/Latino; 23 Asian, non-Hispanic/Latino; 27 Hispanic/Latino; 7 Two or more races, non-Hispanic/Latino), 27 international. Average age 27. 109 applicants, 89% accepted, 58 enrolled. In 2017, 140 master's awarded. *Degree requirements:* For master's, thesis optional. *Entrance requirements:* For master's, GMAT, minimum GPA of 2.75. Additional exam requirements/recommendations for international students: Required—TOEFL (minimum score 550 paper-based). *Application deadline:* For fall admission, 4/1 priority date for domestic students, 5/1 for international students; for spring admission, 9/15 priority date for domestic students, 10/1 for international students. Applications are processed on a rolling basis. Application fee: $40. Electronic applications accepted. *Financial support:* In 2017–18, 5 research assistantships with full tuition reimbursements, 31 teaching assistantships with full tuition reimbursements were awarded; fellowships with full tuition reimbursements, career-related internships or fieldwork, Federal Work-Study, scholarships/grants, tuition waivers (full), and unspecified assistantships also available. Support available to part-time students. Financial award applicants required to submit FAFSA. *Faculty research:* Accounting fraud, governmental accounting, corporate income tax planning, auditing, ethics. *Unit head:* Rebecca Shortridge, Chair, 815-753-1250, Fax: 815-753-8515. *Application contact:* Graduate Advising, 815-753-1325, E-mail: cobadvising@niu.edu.
Website: http://www.cob.niu.edu/accy/

Northern Kentucky University, Office of Graduate Programs, College of Business, Program in Accountancy, Highland Heights, KY 41099. Offers accountancy (M Acc); advanced taxation (Certificate). *Program availability:* Part-time, evening/weekend. *Degree requirements:* For master's, capstone course. *Entrance requirements:* For master's, GMAT, master's degree, MD, or PhD, official transcripts, current resume, 3 years of work experience (strongly suggested), statement of purpose. Additional exam requirements/recommendations for international students: Required—TOEFL (minimum score 79 iBT); Recommended—IELTS (minimum score 6.5). Electronic applications accepted. *Faculty research:* Ethics, accounting history, financial reporting.

Northwest Christian University, School of Business and Management, Eugene, OR 97401-3745. Offers accounting (MBA); management (MBA). *Program availability:* Part-time, evening/weekend, online only, 100% online. *Faculty:* 6 full-time (1 woman), 8 part-time/adjunct (3 women). *Students:* 61 full-time (30 women), 10 part-time (4 women); includes 21 minority (2 Black or African American, non-Hispanic/Latino; 1 American Indian or Alaska Native, non-Hispanic/Latino; 4 Asian, non-Hispanic/Latino; 8 Hispanic/Latino; 1 Native Hawaiian or other Pacific Islander, non-Hispanic/Latino; 5 Two or more races, non-Hispanic/Latino). Average age 33. In 2017, 36 master's awarded. *Entrance requirements:* For master's, GMAT, GRE, MAT, minimum undergraduate GPA of 3.0, 500-word essay, resume. Additional exam requirements/recommendations for international students: Required—TOEFL (minimum score 550 paper-based; 80 iBT). *Application deadline:* Applications are processed on a rolling basis. Electronic applications accepted. *Expenses:* $630 per credit. *Unit head:* Dr. Peter Diffenderfer, Assistant Dean, 541-684-7441, Fax: 541-684-7336, E-mail: pdiffenderfer@nwcu.edu. *Application contact:* Billy Dorsch, Admission Counselor for Graduate Studies, 541-684-7279, Fax: 541-349-5281, E-mail: wdorsch@nwcu.edu.

Northwestern University, The Graduate School, Kellogg School of Management, Department of Accounting Information and Management, Evanston, IL 60208. Offers PhD. Admissions and degree offered through The Graduate School. *Accreditation:* AACSB. *Degree requirements:* For doctorate, comprehensive exam, thesis/dissertation. *Entrance requirements:* For doctorate, GMAT or GRE General Test. Additional exam requirements/recommendations for international students: Required—TOEFL. Electronic applications accepted. *Faculty research:* Managerial and financial accounting theory, financial accounting/theory, managerial accounting and performance measurement, international accounting, joint cost allocation.

Northwestern University, The Graduate School, Kellogg School of Management, Management Programs, Evanston, IL 60208. Offers accounting information and management (MBA, PhD); analytical finance (MBA); business administration (MBA); decision sciences (MBA); entrepreneurship and innovation (MBA); finance (MBA, PhD); health enterprise management (MBA); human resources management (MBA); international business (MBA); management and organizations (MBA, PhD); management and organizations and sociology (PhD); management and strategy (MBA); management studies (MS); managerial analytics (MBA); managerial economics (MBA); managerial economics and strategy (PhD); marketing (MBA, PhD); marketing management (MBA); media management (MBA); operations management (MBA, PhD); real estate (MBA); social enterprise at Kellogg (MBA); JD/MBA. *Program availability:* Part-time, evening/weekend. Terminal master's awarded for partial completion of doctoral program. *Degree requirements:* For doctorate, thesis/dissertation, 2 years of coursework, qualifying (field) exam and candidacy, summer research papers and presentations to faculty, proposal defense, final exam/defense. *Entrance requirements:* For master's, GMAT, GRE, interview, 2 letters of recommendation, college transcripts, resume, essays, Kellogg honor code; for doctorate, GMAT, GRE, statement of purpose, transcripts, 2 letters of recommendation, resume, interview. Additional exam requirements/recommendations for international students: Required—TOEFL, IELTS. Electronic applications accepted. *Expenses:* Contact institution. *Faculty research:* Business cycles and international finance, health policy, networks, non-market strategy, consumer psychology.

Nova Southeastern University, H. Wayne Huizenga College of Business and Entrepreneurship, Fort Lauderdale, FL 33314-7796. Offers accounting (M Acc); business (MBA); business intelligence/analytics (MBA); complex health systems (MBA); enterprise informatics (MBA); entrepreneurship (MBA); finance (MBA); human resource management (MBA); international business (MBA); management (MBA); marketing (MBA); process improvement (MBA); public administration (MPA); real estate development (MS); sport revenue generation (MBA); supply chain management (MBA). *Accreditation:* NASPAA. *Program availability:* Part-time, evening/weekend, 100% online, blended/hybrid learning. *Faculty:* 85 full-time (37 women), 59 part-time/adjunct (19 women). *Students:* 1,999 full-time (1,225 women), 335 part-time (210 women); includes 1,516 minority (597 Black or African American, non-Hispanic/Latino; 4 American Indian or Alaska Native, non-Hispanic/Latino; 92 Asian, non-Hispanic/Latino; 789 Hispanic/Latino; 3 Native Hawaiian or other Pacific Islander, non-Hispanic/Latino; 31 Two or more races, non-Hispanic/Latino), 291 international. Average age 34. 1,269 applicants, 59% accepted, 551 enrolled. In 2017, 1,055 master's awarded. *Entrance requirements:* For master's, GMAT, GMAT or GRE (depending on undergraduate GPA), official transcripts from all schools attended while in pursuit of bachelor's degree; minimum GPA of 2.5 from regionally-accredited institution. Additional exam requirements/recommendations for international students: Required—TOEFL (minimum score 550 paper-based; 79 iBT), IELTS (minimum score 6), PTE (minimum score 54). *Application deadline:* For fall admission, 8/5 priority date for domestic students, 7/29 priority date for international students; for winter admission, 12/16 priority date for domestic students, 12/9 priority date for international students; for summer admission, 4/21 priority date for domestic and international students. Applications are processed on a rolling basis. Application fee: $50. Electronic applications accepted. *Expenses:* $37,785 (online), $35,640 (in-classroom). *Financial support:* In 2017–18, 325 students received support. Federal Work-Study and scholarships/grants available. Support available to part-time students. Financial award application deadline: 4/15; financial award applicants required to submit FAFSA. *Faculty research:* Entrepreneurship and venture capital, ethics and social responsibility, global commerce and cultures, business process management. *Unit head:* Dr. J. Preston Jones, Dean, 954-262-5127, E-mail: prestonj@nova.edu. *Application contact:* Zeida Rodriguez, Associate Director of Enrollment Services, 954-262-5163, Fax: 954-262-3822, E-mail: zeida@nova.edu.
Website: http://www.huizenga.nova.edu

Oakland University, Graduate Study and Lifelong Learning, School of Business Administration, Department of Accounting and Finance, Rochester, MI 48309-4401. Offers accounting (M Acc, Certificate); finance (Certificate). *Expenses:* Tuition, state resident: full-time $16,950; part-time $706.25 per credit. Tuition, nonresident: full-time $24,648; part-time $1027 per credit.

Ohio Christian University, Graduate Programs, Circleville, OH 43113. Offers accounting (MBA); business administration (MBA); digital marketing (MBA); finance (MBA); healthcare management (MBA); human resources (MBA); management (MM); organizational leadership (MBA); pastoral care and counseling (MAM); practical theology (MAM).

Ohio Dominican University, Division of Business, Program in Business Administration, Columbus, OH 43219-2099. Offers accounting (MBA); data analytics (MBA); finance (MBA); leadership (MBA); risk management (MBA); sport management (MBA). *Program availability:* Part-time, evening/weekend, 100% online, blended/hybrid learning. *Faculty:* 7 full-time (4 women), 9 part-time/adjunct (2 women). *Students:* 53 full-time (21 women), 112 part-time (49 women); includes 37 minority (20 Black or African American, non-Hispanic/Latino; 1 American Indian or Alaska Native, non-Hispanic/Latino; 6 Asian, non-Hispanic/Latino; 5 Two or more races, non-Hispanic/Latino), 5 international. Average age 31. 110 applicants, 45% accepted, 40 enrolled. In 2017, 93 master's awarded. *Entrance requirements:* For master's, minimum overall GPA of 3.0 in undergraduate degree from regionally-accredited institution or 2.75 in last 60 semester hours of bachelor's degree. Additional exam requirements/recommendations for international students: Required—TOEFL (minimum score 550 paper-based), IELTS (minimum score 6.5). *Application deadline:* For fall admission, 8/15 for domestic students, 6/10 for international students; for spring admission, 1/4 for domestic students, 11/2 for international students; for summer admission, 5/30 for domestic students. Applications are processed on a rolling basis. Application fee: $25. Electronic applications accepted. *Expenses:* $600 per credit hour, $175 per semester technology fee, $50 per semester activity fee. *Financial support:* Applicants required to submit FAFSA. *Unit head:* Dr. Steve Vickner, Director of Master of Business Administration Program, 614-251-4569, E-mail: vickners@ohiodominican.edu. *Application contact:* John W. Naughton, Associate Vice President for Enrollment Management, 614-251-4721, Fax: 614-251-6654, E-mail: grad@ohiodominican.edu.
Website: http://www.ohiodominican.edu/academics/graduate/mba

Ohio Northern University, College of Business, Ada, OH 45810-1599. Offers MSA. *Students:* 21 part-time (15 women); includes 4 minority (3 Black or African American, non-Hispanic/Latino; 1 Two or more races, non-Hispanic/Latino), 2 international. Average age 25. In 2017, 23 master's awarded. *Unit head:* Dr. John C. Navin, Dean, 419-772-2070, E-mail: j-navin@onu.edu. *Application contact:* Deborah Miller, Director of Admissions, 419-772-2464, E-mail: d-miller@onu.edu.

The Ohio State University, Graduate School, Max M. Fisher College of Business, Department of Accounting and Management Information Systems, Program in Accounting, Columbus, OH 43210. Offers M Acc. *Faculty:* 23. *Students:* 91 full-time (50 women). Average age 23. In 2017, 79 master's awarded. *Entrance requirements:* For master's, GMAT. Additional exam requirements/recommendations for international students: Required—TOEFL (minimum score 600 paper-based; 100 iBT), Michigan English Language Assessment Battery (minimum score 86); Recommended—IELTS (minimum score 7). *Application deadline:* For fall admission, 11/18 priority date for domestic and international students. Applications are processed on a rolling basis. Application fee: $60 ($70 for international students). Electronic applications accepted. *Financial support:* Fellowships with tuition reimbursements available. *Unit head:* Dr. Brian Mittendorf, Professor and Chair, 614-292-1720, E-mail: mittendorf.3@osu.edu. *Application contact:* 614-292-8511, Fax: 614-292-9006, E-mail: fisher_macc@fisher.osu.edu.
Website: http://fisher.osu.edu/macc

Oklahoma Christian University, Graduate School of Business, Oklahoma City, OK 73136-1100. Offers accounting (M Acc, MBA); financial services (MBA); general business (MBA); health services management (MBA); human resources (MBA); international business (MBA); leadership and organizational development (MBA); marketing (MBA); nonprofit management (MBA); project management (MBA). *Accreditation:* ACBSP. *Program availability:* Part-time, 100% online. *Entrance requirements:* For master's, bachelor's degree. Additional exam requirements/

recommendations for international students: Required—TOEFL (minimum score 550 paper-based). Electronic applications accepted. *Expenses:* Contact institution.

Oklahoma State University, Spears School of Business, School of Accounting, Stillwater, OK 74078. Offers MS, PhD. *Accreditation:* AACSB. *Program availability:* Part-time. *Faculty:* 16 full-time (8 women), 4 part-time/adjunct (3 women). *Students:* 32 full-time (20 women), 7 part-time (4 women); includes 8 minority (2 American Indian or Alaska Native, non-Hispanic/Latino; 1 Asian, non-Hispanic/Latino; 1 Hispanic/Latino; 4 Two or more races, non-Hispanic/Latino), 3 international. Average age 23. 34 applicants, 50% accepted, 12 enrolled. In 2017, 39 master's awarded. *Entrance requirements:* For master's and doctorate, GRE or GMAT. Additional exam requirements/recommendations for international students: Required—TOEFL (minimum score 550 paper-based; 79 iBT). *Application deadline:* For fall admission, 3/1 priority date for international students; for spring admission, 8/1 priority date for international students. Applications are processed on a rolling basis. Application fee: $40 ($75 for international students). Electronic applications accepted. *Expenses:* Tuition, state resident: full-time $4019; part-time $2679.60 per year. Tuition, nonresident: full-time $15,286; part-time $10,190.40 per year. *Required fees:* $2129; $1419 per unit. Tuition and fees vary according to program. *Financial support:* Research assistantships, teaching assistantships, career-related internships or fieldwork, Federal Work-Study, scholarships/grants, health care benefits, tuition waivers (partial), and unspecified assistantships available. Support available to part-time students. Financial award application deadline: 3/1; financial award applicants required to submit FAFSA. *Faculty research:* International accounting, accounting education, cost-management, taxation, oil and gas. *Unit head:* Dr. Rick Wilson, Department Head, 405-744-3551, Fax: 405-744-1680, E-mail: rick.wilson@okstate.edu. *Application contact:* Dr. Alyssa Vowell, Graduate Coordinator, 405-744-6635, Fax: 405-744-1680, E-mail: alyssa.vowell@okstate.edu.
Website: https://business.okstate.edu/accounting

Old Dominion University, Strome College of Business, Program in Accounting, Norfolk, VA 23529. Offers MS. *Accreditation:* AACSB. *Program availability:* Part-time, evening/weekend. *Faculty:* 7 full-time (3 women), 4 part-time/adjunct (2 women). *Students:* 16 full-time (9 women), 31 part-time (21 women); includes 25 minority (9 Black or African American, non-Hispanic/Latino; 10 Asian, non-Hispanic/Latino; 1 Hispanic/Latino; 1 Native Hawaiian or other Pacific Islander, non-Hispanic/Latino; 4 Two or more races, non-Hispanic/Latino), 5 international. Average age 34. 21 applicants, 81% accepted, 16 enrolled. In 2017, 21 master's awarded. *Degree requirements:* For master's, comprehensive exam. *Entrance requirements:* For master's, GMAT, minimum GPA of 3.0. Additional exam requirements/recommendations for international students: Required—TOEFL (minimum score 550 paper-based). *Application deadline:* For fall admission, 7/1 priority date for domestic students, 4/15 priority date for international students; for spring admission, 11/1 priority date for domestic students, 10/1 priority date for international students. Applications are processed on a rolling basis. Application fee: $50. Electronic applications accepted. *Expenses:* Contact institution. *Financial support:* In 2017–18, 4 students received support, including 8 research assistantships with partial tuition reimbursements available (averaging $6,400 per year); career-related internships or fieldwork and unspecified assistantships also available. Financial award application deadline: 2/15; financial award applicants required to submit FAFSA. *Faculty research:* Assurance services, auditing, managerial accounting, financial accounting, accounting history. *Unit head:* Dr. Yin Xu, Graduate Program Director, 757-683-3554, Fax: 757-683-5639, E-mail: yxu@odu.edu.
Website: http://www.odu.edu/business/departments/accounting

Oral Roberts University, School of Business, Tulsa, OK 74171. Offers accounting (MBA); entrepreneurship (MBA); finance (MBA); international business (MBA); management (MBA); marketing (MBA); not for profit management (MNM). *Accreditation:* ACBSP. *Program availability:* Part-time, online learning. *Faculty:* 7 full-time (0 women), 5 part-time/adjunct (4 women). *Students:* 71 applicants, 94% accepted, 56 enrolled. *Degree requirements:* For master's, thesis optional. *Entrance requirements:* For master's, minimum cumulative GPA of 3.0 from regionally-accredited institution. *Application deadline:* Applications are processed on a rolling basis. Application fee: $35. Electronic applications accepted. Application fee is waived when completed online. *Financial support:* In 2017–18, 39 students received support. Scholarships/grants and unspecified assistantships available. Financial award application deadline: 6/1. *Faculty research:* Social media, international business and marketing. *Unit head:* Dr. Marshal Wright, Chair of the Graduate School of Business, 918-495-6988, E-mail: mwright@oru.edu. *Application contact:* Sam Park, Enrollment Counselor, 918-495-7179, E-mail: sampark@oru.edu.
Website: http://www.oru.edu/university/departments/schools/bus

Oregon State University, College of Business, Program in Business Administration, Corvallis, OR 97331. Offers business administration (PhD), including accounting; corporate finance (MBA). *Program availability:* Part-time, blended/hybrid learning. *Entrance requirements:* For master's, GMAT. Additional exam requirements/recommendations for international students: Required—TOEFL (minimum score 91 iBT), IELTS (minimum score 7). *Application deadline:* For fall admission, 2/1 priority date for domestic and international students; for winter admission, 9/15 priority date for domestic and international students; for spring admission, 1/1 priority date for domestic and international students. Applications are processed on a rolling basis. Application fee: $75 ($85 for international students). *Expenses:* Contact institution. *Financial support:* Application deadline: 1/15. *Unit head:* Matt Alex, Associate Director, 541-737-5340, E-mail: matt.alex@oregonstate.edu. *Application contact:* Matt Alex, Associate Director, 541-737-5340, E-mail: matt.alex@oregonstate.edu.
Website: http://business.oregonstate.edu/graduate-programs

Our Lady of the Lake University, School of Business and Leadership, Program in Accounting, San Antonio, TX 78207-4689. Offers MS. *Program availability:* Part-time, evening/weekend. *Faculty:* 4 full-time (2 women), 4 part-time/adjunct (0 women). *Students:* 10 full-time (5 women); includes 7 minority (all Hispanic/Latino). Average age 26. 4 applicants, 100% accepted, 2 enrolled. In 2017, 14 master's awarded. *Entrance requirements:* For master's, GMAT, GRE General Test, or MAT, official transcripts showing undergraduate degree in accounting or 30 hours of accounting courses previously taken with minimum cumulative GPA of 2.5; 2 letters of recommendation; resume highlighting managerial or professional work experience. Additional exam requirements/recommendations for international students: Required—TOEFL. *Application deadline:* For fall admission, 6/15 for domestic and international students; for spring admission, 11/15 for domestic and international students; for summer admission, 4/15 for domestic and international students. Applications are processed on a rolling basis. Application fee: $40 ($50 for international students). Electronic applications accepted. Application fee is waived when completed online. *Expenses:* Tuition: Full-time $10,668; part-time $5334 per year. *Required fees:* $816; $816 per year. $408 per semester. *Financial support:* In 2017–18, 8 students received support. Federal Work-Study, scholarships/grants, unspecified assistantships, and tuition discounts available. Support available to part-time students. Financial award application deadline: 5/1; financial award applicants required to submit FAFSA. *Unit head:* Kathryn Winney, Associate Dean, 210-434-6711 Ext. 2297, E-mail: kmwinney@ollusa.edu. *Application contact:* Graduate Admission, 210-431-3995, Fax: 210-431-3945, E-mail: gradadm@ollusa.edu.
Website: http://www.ollusa.edu/s/1190/hybrid/default-hybrid-ollu.aspx?sid=1190&gid-1&pgid-7870

Accounting

Pace University, Lubin School of Business, Accounting Program, New York, NY 10038. Offers public accounting (MBA, MS). *Accreditation:* AACSB. *Program availability:* Part-time, evening/weekend. *Students:* 123 full-time (86 women), 60 part-time (32 women); includes 34 minority (7 Black or African American, non-Hispanic/Latino; 16 Asian, non-Hispanic/Latino; 10 Hispanic/Latino; 1 Two or more races, non-Hispanic/Latino), 115 international. Average age 27. 197 applicants, 66% accepted, 32 enrolled. In 2017, 87 master's awarded. *Entrance requirements:* For master's, GMAT, GRE, undergraduate degree, transcripts from all accredited colleges/universities attended, two letters of recommendation, resume, personal statement. Additional exam requirements/recommendations for international students: Required—TOEFL (minimum score 90 iBT), IELTS (minimum score 7) or PTE (minimum score 61). *Application deadline:* For fall admission, 8/1 priority date for domestic students, 6/1 for international students; for spring admission, 12/1 priority date for domestic students, 10/1 for international students. Applications are processed on a rolling basis. Application fee: $70. Electronic applications accepted. *Expenses:* Contact institution. *Financial support:* Research assistantships, career-related internships or fieldwork, Federal Work-Study, and unspecified assistantships available. Support available to part-time students. Financial award application deadline: 2/15; financial award applicants required to submit FAFSA. *Unit head:* Dr. Rudolph Jacob, Chairperson, 212-618-6425, E-mail: rjacob@pace.edu. *Application contact:* Susan Ford-Goldschein, Director of Graduate Admissions, 212-346-1531, Fax: 212-346-1585, E-mail: graduateadmission@pace.edu. Website: http://www.pace.edu/lubin/departments-and-research-centers/accounting-department/graduate-accounting-programs

Pace University, Lubin School of Business, Advanced Professional Certificate Program, New York, NY 10038. Offers business economics (APC); e-business (APC); financial management (APC); international business (APC); international economics (APC); investment management (APC); marketing (APC); public accounting (APC). *Program availability:* Part-time, evening/weekend. *Students:* 1 applicant, 100% accepted. *Entrance requirements:* For degree, MBA or MS in business discipline, relevant professional experience. Additional exam requirements/recommendations for international students: Required—TOEFL (minimum score 90 iBT), IELTS (minimum score 7) or PTE (minimum score 61). *Application deadline:* For fall admission, 8/1 priority date for domestic students, 6/1 for international students; for spring admission, 12/1 for domestic students, 10/1 for international students. Applications are processed on a rolling basis. Application fee: $70. Electronic applications accepted. *Unit head:* Dr. Jack Yurkiewicz, Director, 212-618-6567, E-mail: jyurkiewicz@pace.edu. *Application contact:* Susan Ford-Goldschein, Director of Graduate Admissions, 212-346-1531, Fax: 212-346-1585, E-mail: graduateadmission@pace.edu. Website: http://www.pace.edu/lubin/agc

Pacific Lutheran University, School of Business, Master of Science in Accounting Program, Tacoma, WA 98447. Offers MSA. *Program availability:* Part-time. *Entrance requirements:* For master's, GMAT or GRE. Additional exam requirements/recommendations for international students: Required—TOEFL (minimum score 550 paper-based; 88 iBT). *Expenses:* Contact institution.

Pacific States University, College of Business, Los Angeles, CA 90010. Offers accounting (MBA, Certificate); beauty management (MBA); finance (MBA); international business (MBA); management of information technology (MBA); project management (Certificate); real estate management (MBA). *Program availability:* Part-time, evening/weekend, online learning. *Entrance requirements:* For master's, minimum undergraduate GPA of 2.5 during last 90 quarter units of course work, bachelor's degree in business administration or economics. Additional exam requirements/recommendations for international students: Required—TOEFL (minimum score 500 paper-based; 61 iBT), IELTS (minimum score 5.5). *Application deadline:* For fall admission, 9/1 priority date for domestic students, 8/1 priority date for international students; for winter admission, 12/1 priority date for domestic students, 11/1 priority date for international students; for spring admission, 3/1 priority date for domestic students, 2/1 priority date for international students; for summer admission, 6/1 priority date for domestic students, 5/1 priority date for international students. Applications are processed on a rolling basis. Application fee: $100. *Expenses:* Tuition: Part-time $380 per unit. *Financial support:* Scholarships/grants available. Financial award applicants required to submit FAFSA. *Unit head:* Chase C. Rhee, MBA Program Administrator, 323-731-2383 Ext. 208, Fax: 323-731-7276, E-mail: ccrhee@psuca.edu. *Application contact:* Maawiya Ayeva, Director of Admissions, 323-731-2383 Ext. 204, Fax: 323-731-7276, E-mail: admissions@psuca.edu.

Penn State Erie, The Behrend College, Graduate School, Erie, PA 16563. Offers accounting (MPAC); applied clinical psychology (MA); business administration (MBA); quality and manufacturing management (MMM). *Accreditation:* AACSB. *Program availability:* Part-time. *Students:* 31 full-time (15 women), 126 part-time (39 women); includes 10 minority (4 Black or African American, non-Hispanic/Latino; 1 Hispanic/Latino; 5 Two or more races, non-Hispanic/Latino). Average age 31. 104 applicants, 75% accepted, 75 enrolled. In 2017, 72 master's awarded. *Entrance requirements:* Additional exam requirements/recommendations for international students: Required—TOEFL (minimum score 550 paper-based; 80 iBT), IELTS. *Application deadline:* Applications are processed on a rolling basis. Application fee: $65. Electronic applications accepted. *Financial support:* Federal Work-Study available. Financial award application deadline: 2/15; financial award applicants required to submit FAFSA. *Unit head:* Dr. Ralph M. Ford, Chancellor, 814-898-6160, Fax: 814-898-6461. *Application contact:* Ann M. Burbules, Assistant Director, Graduate Admissions, 866-374-3378, Fax: 814-898-6044, E-mail: behrend.admissions@psu.edu. Website: http://behrend.psu.edu/

Penn State Harrisburg, Graduate School, School of Business Administration, Middletown, PA 17057. Offers accounting (MPAC, Certificate); business administration (MBA); information systems (MS); operations and supply chain management (Certificate). *Program availability:* Part-time, evening/weekend. *Unit head:* Dr. Mukund S. Kulkarni, Chancellor, 717-948-6105, Fax: 717-948-6452. *Application contact:* Robert W. Coffman, Jr., Director of Enrollment Management, Recruitment and Admissions, 717-948-6250, Fax: 717-948-6325, E-mail: hbgadmit@psu.edu. Website: https://harrisburg.psu.edu/business-administration/

Penn State University Park, Graduate School, Smeal College of Business, University Park, PA 16802. Offers accounting (M Acc); business administration (MBA, MS, PhD); management and organizational leadership (MPS). *Accreditation:* AACSB. *Program availability:* Part-time, evening/weekend. *Students:* 290 full-time (97 women), 7 part-time (2 women). Average age 29. 1,125 applicants, 27% accepted, 236 enrolled. In 2017, 235 master's, 10 doctorates awarded. *Entrance requirements:* Additional exam requirements/recommendations for international students: Required—TOEFL (minimum score 550 paper-based; 80 iBT), IELTS. *Application deadline:* Applications are processed on a rolling basis. Application fee: $65. Electronic applications accepted. *Expenses:* Contact institution. *Financial support:* Fellowships, research assistantships, teaching assistantships, career-related internships or fieldwork, Federal Work-Study, scholarships/grants, traineeships, health care benefits, and unspecified assistantships available. Support available to part-time students. Financial award application deadline: 2/15; financial award applicants required to submit FAFSA. *Unit head:* Dr. Charles H. Whiteman, Dean, 814-863-0448, Fax: 814-865-7064. *Application contact:* Lori Hawn,

Director, Graduate Student Services, 814-865-1795, Fax: 814-863-4627, E-mail: l-gswww@lists.psu.edu. Website: http://smeal.psu.edu/

Pepperdine University, Graziadio Business School, Master of Science Programs, Malibu, CA 90263. Offers accounting (MS); applied analytics (MS); applied finance (MS); global business (MS); human resources (MS); management and leadership (MS); organization development (MS); real estate investment and finance (MS). *Accreditation:* AACSB. *Students:* 462 full-time (277 women), 104 part-time (68 women); includes 67 minority (23 Black or African American, non-Hispanic/Latino; 1 American Indian or Alaska Native, non-Hispanic/Latino; 41 Asian, non-Hispanic/Latino; 2 Hispanic/Latino), 380 international. Average age 27. 2,180 applicants, 63% accepted, 336 enrolled. In 2017, 291 master's awarded. *Entrance requirements:* For master's, GMAT or GRE, two letters of recommendation. Additional exam requirements/recommendations for international students: Required—TOEFL. *Application deadline:* For fall admission, 5/1 for domestic students, 4/1 for international students. Application fee: $75. Electronic applications accepted. *Financial support:* Applicants required to submit FAFSA. *Unit head:* Dr. Michael L. Williams, Associate Dean, 310-506-4112, Fax: 310-506-4126, E-mail: michael.williams@pepperdine.edu. Website: http://bschool.pepperdine.edu/masters-degree/

Pepperdine University, Seaver College, Division of Business, Malibu, CA 90263. Offers accounting (MS). *Entrance requirements:* For master's, GRE General Test, statement of purpose and intent for writing as a vocation, script writing sample, letters of recommendation. Additional exam requirements/recommendations for international students: Required—TOEFL. *Application deadline:* For fall admission, 2/1 priority date for domestic students. Application fee: $55. Electronic applications accepted. *Unit head:* Dr. Dean Baim, Divisional Dean/Professor of Economics and Finance, 310-506-4237, E-mail: dean.baim@pepperdine.edu. *Application contact:* Hayley Wolf, Director of Admission, 310-506-4392, E-mail: hayley.wolf@pepperdine.edu. Website: http://seaver.pepperdine.edu/humanities/graduate/screenwriting/

Pittsburg State University, Graduate School, Kelce College of Business, Department of Accounting, Pittsburg, KS 66762. Offers MBA. *Program availability:* Part-time. *Students:* 11. In 2017, 12 master's awarded. *Degree requirements:* For master's, thesis or alternative. *Entrance requirements:* For master's, GMAT or GRE. Additional exam requirements/recommendations for international students: Required—TOEFL (minimum score 550 paper-based; 79 iBT), IELTS (minimum score 6.5), PTE (minimum score 53). *Application deadline:* For fall admission, 7/15 for domestic students, 7/1 for international students; for spring admission, 12/15 for domestic students, 10/15 for international students; for summer admission, 5/15 for domestic students, 4/1 for international students. Applications are processed on a rolling basis. Application fee: $35 ($60 for international students). Electronic applications accepted. *Expenses:* Contact institution. *Financial support:* In 2017–18, 5 teaching assistantships with full tuition reimbursements (averaging $5,500 per year) were awarded; research assistantships, career-related internships or fieldwork, Federal Work-Study, and unspecified assistantships also available. Financial award application deadline: 2/1; financial award applicants required to submit FAFSA. *Faculty research:* Accountant's legal liability, computer audit. *Unit head:* Dr. Bienvenido Cortes, MBA Coordinator, 620-235-4594, E-mail: bcortes@pittstate.edu. *Application contact:* Lisa Allen, Assistant Director of Graduate and Continuing Studies, 620-235-4218, Fax: 620-235-4219, E-mail: lallen@pittstate.edu.

Polytechnic University of Puerto Rico, Miami Campus, Graduate School, Miami, FL 33166. Offers accounting (MBA); business administration (MBA); construction management (MEM); environmental management (MEM); finance (MBA); human resources management (MBA); logistics and supply chain management (MBA); management of international enterprises (MBA); manufacturing management (MEM); marketing management (MBA); project management (MBA). *Program availability:* Part-time, evening/weekend, online learning. *Entrance requirements:* For master's, minimum GPA of 3.0. Electronic applications accepted.

Polytechnic University of Puerto Rico, Orlando Campus, Graduate School, Orlando, FL 32825. Offers accounting (MBA); business administration (MBA); construction management (MEM); engineering management (MEM); environmental management (MEM); finance (MBA); human resources management (MBA); management of international enterprises (MBA); management of technology (MBA); manufacturing management (MEM). *Program availability:* Part-time, evening/weekend, online learning. *Entrance requirements:* For master's, minimum GPA of 3.0. Additional exam requirements/recommendations for international students: Recommended—TOEFL. Electronic applications accepted.

Pontifical Catholic University of Puerto Rico, College of Business Administration, Program in Accounting, Ponce, PR 00717-0777. Offers MBA. *Program availability:* Part-time, evening/weekend. *Degree requirements:* For master's, thesis. *Entrance requirements:* For master's, GRE, interview, minimum GPA of 2.75.

Pontifical Catholic University of Puerto Rico, College of Business Administration, Program in Management and Accounting, Ponce, PR 00717-0777. Offers Professional Certificate.

Post University, Program in Business Administration, Waterbury, CT 06723-2540. Offers accounting (MSA); business administration (MBA); corporate finance (MBA); corporate innovation (MBA); healthcare systems leadership (MBA); leadership (MBA); marketing (MBA); project management (MBA, MS). *Accreditation:* ACBSP. *Program availability:* Online learning. *Entrance requirements:* For master's, resume. *Expenses:* Tuition: Part-time $730 per credit hour. Part-time tuition and fees vary according to degree level and program. *Application contact:* Veronica Montalvo, Vice President, Online Education Enrollment Management and Admissions, 203-596-6164, E-mail: vmontalvo@post.edu.

Prairie View A&M University, College of Business, Prairie View, TX 77446. Offers accounting (MS); business administration (MBA). *Accreditation:* AACSB. *Program availability:* Part-time, evening/weekend. *Faculty:* 18 full-time (3 women). *Students:* 82 full-time (48 women), 143 part-time (81 women); includes 192 minority (174 Black or African American, non-Hispanic/Latino; 10 Asian, non-Hispanic/Latino; 8 Hispanic/Latino), 17 international. Average age 29. 180 applicants, 84% accepted, 106 enrolled. In 2017, 98 master's awarded. *Degree requirements:* For master's, comprehensive exam, thesis optional. *Entrance requirements:* For master's, GMAT, GRE, minimum GPA of 2.45, essay. Additional exam requirements/recommendations for international students: Required—TOEFL (minimum score 550 paper-based; 79 iBT). *Application deadline:* For fall admission, 5/1 for domestic students, 5/1 priority date for international students; for spring admission, 10/1 for domestic students, 9/1 priority date for international students; for summer admission, 3/1 for domestic students, 2/1 for international students. Applications are processed on a rolling basis. Application fee: $50. Electronic applications accepted. *Expenses:* $1,167 per semester credit hour (for EMBA). *Financial support:* Research assistantships, teaching assistantships, scholarships/grants, and unspecified assistantships available. Financial award application deadline: 4/1; financial award applicants required to submit FAFSA. *Faculty research:* Accounting (energy, oil and gas); finance (international finance, personal finance, real estate markets and institutions); marketing management (supply chain, human resources, entrepreneurship, small business ownership, ethics); management information systems (cyber-security, managing social media during crises). *Unit head:* Dr. Munir Quddus, Dean, 936-261-9200, Fax: 936-261-9241, E-mail: cob@pvamu.edu. *Application contact:* Gabriel Crosby, Director, Graduate Programs in Business, 936-261-9217, Fax: 936-261-9232, E-mail: mba@pvamu.edu. Website: http://www.pvamu.edu/business/

Providence College, School of Business, Providence, RI 02918. Offers accounting (MBA); finance (MBA); international business (MBA); management (MBA); marketing (MBA). *Accreditation:* AACSB. *Program availability:* Part-time, evening/weekend. *Entrance requirements:* For master's, GMAT. Additional exam requirements/recommendations for international students: Required—TOEFL (minimum score 577 paper-based; 90 iBT). *Expenses:* Contact institution.

Purdue University Northwest, Graduate Studies Office, School of Management, Hammond, IN 46323-2094. Offers accountancy (M Acc); business administration (MBA); business administration for executives (EMBA). *Accreditation:* AACSB. *Program availability:* Part-time, evening/weekend. *Entrance requirements:* For master's, GMAT. Additional exam requirements/recommendations for international students: Required—TOEFL. Electronic applications accepted.

Queens College of the City University of New York, Division of Social Sciences, Department of Accounting and Information Systems, Queens, NY 11367-1597. Offers accounting (MS). *Program availability:* Part-time. *Students:* 24 full-time (9 women), 171 part-time (102 women); includes 135 minority (12 Black or African American, non-Hispanic/Latino; 1 American Indian or Alaska Native, non-Hispanic/Latino; 79 Asian, non-Hispanic/Latino; 39 Hispanic/Latino; 1 Native Hawaiian or other Pacific Islander, non-Hispanic/Latino; 3 Two or more races, non-Hispanic/Latino), 18 international. Average age 30. *Degree requirements:* For master's, comprehensive exam. *Entrance requirements:* For master's, minimum GPA of 3.0. Additional exam requirements/recommendations for international students: Required—TOEFL (minimum score 100 iBT), IELTS (minimum score 7). *Application deadline:* For fall admission, 4/1 for domestic students; for spring admission, 11/1 for domestic students. Application fee: $125. Electronic applications accepted. *Financial support:* Career-related internships or fieldwork and unspecified assistantships available. *Unit head:* Dr. Israel Blumenfrucht, Chair, 718-997-5070, E-mail: israel.blumenfrucht@qc.cuny.edu. *Application contact:* Elizabeth D'Amico-Ramirez, Assistant Director of Graduate Admissions, 718-997-5203, E-mail: elizabeth.damicoramirez@qc.cuny.edu.

Queens College of the City University of New York, Division of Social Sciences, Department of Economics, Queens, NY 11367-1597. Offers risk management: accounting (MS); risk management: dynamic financial analysis (MS); risk management: finance (MS). *Students:* 11 full-time (4 women), 38 part-time (21 women); includes 29 minority (6 Black or African American, non-Hispanic/Latino; 15 Asian, non-Hispanic/Latino; 5 Hispanic/Latino; 3 Two or more races, non-Hispanic/Latino), 12 international. Average age 31. *Degree requirements:* For master's, thesis. *Entrance requirements:* For master's, minimum GPA of 3.0. Additional exam requirements/recommendations for international students: Required—TOEFL (minimum score 100 iBT), IELTS (minimum score 7). *Financial support:* Federal Work-Study, institutionally sponsored loans, and tuition waivers (partial) available. Support available to part-time students. Financial award application deadline: 4/1; financial award applicants required to submit FAFSA. *Faculty research:* Business economics, urban economic problems, international economics, economics of nonprofit sector. *Unit head:* Dr. John Devereux, Chair, 718-997-5440, E-mail: john.devereux@qc.cuny.edu. *Application contact:* Elvira Casper, Program Coordinator, 718-997-5507, E-mail: elvira.casper@qc.cuny.edu.

Quinnipiac University, School of Business, Program in Accounting, Hamden, CT 06518-1940. Offers MS. *Entrance requirements:* For master's, GMAT/GRE, BS in accounting or prerequisite course work in accounting. Additional exam requirements/recommendations for international students: Required—TOEFL (minimum score 575 paper-based; 90 iBT), IELTS (minimum score 6.5). *Application deadline:* For fall admission, 7/30 priority date for domestic students, 4/30 priority date for international students; for spring admission, 12/15 priority date for domestic students, 9/15 priority date for international students. Applications are processed on a rolling basis. Application fee: $45. Electronic applications accepted. *Financial support:* Tuition waivers (partial) and unspecified assistantships available. Support available to part-time students. Financial award application deadline: 4/15; financial award applicants required to submit FAFSA. *Unit head:* Dr. Jennifer Boutin, 203-582-3443, E-mail: jennifer.boutin@quinnipiac.edu. Website: https://www.qu.edu/schools/business/programs/ms-accounting.html

Ramapo College of New Jersey, Master of Science in Accounting Program, Mahwah, NJ 07430-1680. Offers MS. *Program availability:* Part-time. *Faculty:* 3 full-time (3 women). *Students:* 12 full-time (4 women), 11 part-time (8 women); includes 7 minority (1 Asian, non-Hispanic/Latino; 6 Hispanic/Latino). Average age 31. 41 applicants, 85% accepted, 23 enrolled. *Degree requirements:* For master's, capstone course, including research project. *Entrance requirements:* For master's, undergraduate degree in business with accounting or finance major or accounting minor from accredited institution with minimum GPA of 3.0; personal statement; letter of recommendation. Additional exam requirements/recommendations for international students: Required—TOEFL (minimum score 550 paper-based; 79 iBT); Recommended—IELTS (minimum score 6). *Application deadline:* For fall admission, 5/1 for domestic and international students; for spring admission, 12/1 for domestic and international students; for summer admission, 5/1 for domestic and international students. Applications are processed on a rolling basis. Application fee: $65. Electronic applications accepted. *Expenses:* $785.95 per credit tuition, $56.95 per credit fees. *Financial support:* Career-related internships or fieldwork available. Financial award application deadline: 3/1; financial award applicants required to submit FAFSA. *Faculty research:* Leadership, accountability and ethics; tax strategy and regulatory compliance; accounting pedagogy and curriculum development; earnings, forecasting and financial statement analysis; fraud detection and audit implications; cyber security threats and audit planning. *Unit head:* Dr. Edward Petkus, Dean of the Anisfield School of Business, 201-684-7377, E-mail: epetkus@ramapo.edu. *Application contact:* Constance Crawford, Director of the Master of Science in Accounting Program, 201-684-7396, E-mail: ccrawfor@ramapo.edu. Website: http://www.ramapo.edu/ms-accounting

Regent University, Graduate School, School of Business and Leadership, Virginia Beach, VA 23464-9800. Offers business administration (MBA), including accounting, economics, entrepreneurship, finance and investing, general management, healthcare management (MA, MBA), human resource management (MA, MBA), innovation management, leadership, marketing, not-for-profit management (MA, MBA); business analytics (MS); business and design management (MA); church leadership (MA); leadership (Certificate); organizational leadership (MA, PhD), including ecclesial leadership (DSL, PhD), entrepreneurial leadership (PhD), healthcare management (MA, MBA), human resource development (PhD), human resource management (MA, MBA), individualized studies (DSL, PhD), interdisciplinary studies (MA), leadership coaching and mentoring (MA), not-for-profit management (MA, MBA), organizational development consulting (MA), servant leadership (MA, DSL); strategic leadership (DSL), including ecclesial leadership (DSL, PhD), global consulting, healthcare leadership, individualized studies (DSL, PhD), leadership coaching, servant leadership (MA, DSL), strategic foresight. *Program availability:* Part-time, evening/weekend, 100% online, blended/

hybrid learning. *Faculty:* 9 full-time (2 women), 38 part-time/adjunct (11 women). *Students:* 129 full-time (80 women), 1,152 part-time (598 women); includes 685 minority (546 Black or African American, non-Hispanic/Latino; 10 American Indian or Alaska Native, non-Hispanic/Latino; 29 Asian, non-Hispanic/Latino; 65 Hispanic/Latino; 6 Native Hawaiian or other Pacific Islander, non-Hispanic/Latino; 29 Two or more races, non-Hispanic/Latino), 62 international. Average age 41. 1,721 applicants, 48% accepted, 624 enrolled. In 2017, 125 master's, 69 doctorates awarded. *Degree requirements:* For master's, thesis or alternative, 3-credit hour culminating experience; for doctorate, thesis/dissertation. *Entrance requirements:* For master's, college transcripts, resume, essay; for doctorate, college transcripts, resume, essay, writing sample; for Certificate, writing sample, resume, transcripts. Additional exam requirements/recommendations for international students: Required—TOEFL (minimum score 577 paper-based). *Application deadline:* For fall admission, 5/1 priority date for domestic students; for spring admission, 10/1 priority date for domestic students. Applications are processed on a rolling basis. Application fee: $50. Electronic applications accepted. *Expenses:* $650 per credit (MA, MS, MBA); $995 per credit (PhD); $300 per semester technology fee. *Financial support:* In 2017–18, 829 students received support. Career-related internships or fieldwork, scholarships/grants, and unspecified assistantships available. Support available to part-time students. *Faculty research:* Servant leadership, global business, team effectiveness, technology utilization, leadership development. *Unit head:* Dr. Doris Gomez, Dean, 757-352-4686, Fax: 757-352-4634, E-mail: dorigom@regent.edu. *Application contact:* Heidi Cece, Assistant Vice President of Enrollment Management, 800-373-5504, Fax: 757-352-4381, E-mail: admissions@regent.edu. Website: https://www.regent.edu/school-of-business-and-leadership/

Regis University, College of Business and Economics, Denver, CO 80221-1099. Offers accounting (MS); executive leadership (Certificate); finance (MS); finance and accounting (MBA); health industry leadership (MBA); human resource management and leadership (MSOL); management (MBA); marketing (MBA); nonprofit leadership (Post-Graduate Certificate); nonprofit management (MNM); nonprofit organizational capacity building (Certificate); operations management (MBA); organizational leadership and management (MSOL); project leadership and management (MS, MSOL); strategic business management (Certificate); strategic human resource integration (Certificate); strategic management (MBA). Programs offered at Colorado Springs Campus, Northwest Denver Campus, Southeast Denver Campus, Fort Collins Campus, Broomfield Campus, Henderson (Nevada) Campus, and Summerlin (Nevada) Campus. *Program availability:* Part-time, evening/weekend, 100% online, blended/hybrid learning. *Degree requirements:* For master's, thesis (for some programs), capstone or final research project. *Entrance requirements:* For master's, official transcript reflecting baccalaureate degree awarded from regionally-accredited college or university, interview, 2 years of full-time related work experience, resume, letters of recommendation. Additional exam requirements/recommendations for international students: Required—TOEFL (minimum score 550 paper-based; 82 iBT). Electronic applications accepted. *Expenses:* Contact institution. *Faculty research:* Impact of information technology on small business regulation of accounting, international project financing, mineral development, delivery of healthcare to rural indigenous communities.

Rhode Island College, School of Graduate Studies, School of Business, Department of Accounting and Computer Information Systems, Providence, RI 02908-1991. Offers accounting (MP Ac); financial planning (CGS). *Program availability:* Part-time, evening/weekend. *Faculty:* 1 (woman) full-time. *Students:* 1 full-time (0 women), 15 part-time (8 women); includes 5 minority (3 Black or African American, non-Hispanic/Latino; 2 Hispanic/Latino). Average age 32. In 2017, 17 master's, 2 CGSs awarded. *Entrance requirements:* For master's, GMAT (unless applicant is a CPA or has passed a state bar exam); for CGS, GMAT, bachelor's degree from an accredited college or university, official transcripts of all undergraduate and graduate records. Additional exam requirements/recommendations for international students: Recommended—TOEFL (minimum score 550 paper-based; 79 iBT). *Application deadline:* For fall admission, 3/1 for domestic students. Applications are processed on a rolling basis. Application fee: $50. Electronic applications accepted. *Expenses:* Tuition, state resident: full-time $9768; part-time $407 per credit. Tuition, nonresident: full-time $19,008; part-time $792 per credit. *Required fees:* $696; $29 per credit. One-time fee: $200 full-time; $100 part-time. Tuition and fees vary according to course load. *Financial support:* In 2017–18, 1 teaching assistantship with full tuition reimbursement (averaging $1,500 per year) was awarded; Federal Work-Study, scholarships/grants, and health care benefits also available. Support available to part-time students. Financial award application deadline: 5/15; financial award applicants required to submit FAFSA. *Unit head:* Dr. Lisa Bain, Chair, 401-456-9829. *Application contact:* Graduate Studies, 401-456-8700. Website: http://www.ric.edu/accountingComputerInformationSystems/

Rhodes College, Department of Commerce and Business, Memphis, TN 38112-1690. Offers accounting (MS). *Program availability:* Part-time. *Entrance requirements:* For master's, GMAT. Additional exam requirements/recommendations for international students: Required—TOEFL (minimum score 550 paper-based).

Rider University, College of Business Administration, Program in Accountancy, Lawrenceville, NJ 08648-3001. Offers M Acc. *Accreditation:* AACSB. *Program availability:* Online learning. *Entrance requirements:* For master's, GMAT, resume. Additional exam requirements/recommendations for international students: Required—TOEFL (minimum score 550 paper-based). Electronic applications accepted. *Faculty research:* Financial reporting, corporate governance, information technology, ethics, pedagogy.

Robert Morris University Illinois, Morris Graduate School of Management, Chicago, IL 60605. Offers accounting (MBA); accounting/finance (MBA); business analytics (MIS); health care administration (MM); higher education administration (MM); human performance (MS); human resource management (MBA); information security (MIS); information systems management (MIS); law enforcement administration (MM); management (MBA); management/finance (MBA); management/human resource management (MBA); sports administration (MM). *Program availability:* Part-time, evening/weekend. *Faculty:* 2 full-time (0 women), 26 part-time/adjunct (8 women). *Students:* 186 full-time (108 women), 114 part-time (57 women); includes 167 minority (88 Black or African American, non-Hispanic/Latino; 15 Asian, non-Hispanic/Latino; 62 Hispanic/Latino; 1 Native Hawaiian or other Pacific Islander, non-Hispanic/Latino; 1 Two or more races, non-Hispanic/Latino), 18 international. Average age 32. 157 applicants, 78% accepted, 72 enrolled. In 2017, 191 master's awarded. *Entrance requirements:* For master's, official transcripts and letters of recommendation (for some programs); written personal statement. Additional exam requirements/recommendations for international students: Required—TOEFL (minimum score 550 paper-based). *Application deadline:* Applications are processed on a rolling basis. Application fee: $20 ($100 for international students). Electronic applications accepted. *Expenses:* Tuition: Full-time $17,100; part-time $2850 per course. *Financial support:* In 2017–18, 381 students received support. Federal Work-Study, scholarships/grants, and unspecified assistantships available. Support available to part-time students. Financial award applicants required to submit FAFSA. *Unit head:* Kayed Akkawi, Dean, 312-935-6050, Fax: 312-935-6020, E-mail: kakkawi@robertmorris.edu. *Application contact:* Mark Daugherty, Director of Admissions, 312-935-4814, Fax: 312-935-6020, E-mail: mdaugherty@robertmorris.edu.

Accounting

Rochester Institute of Technology, Graduate Enrollment Services, Saunders College of Business, Accounting and Finance Department, MBA Program in Accounting, Rochester, NY 14623-5603. Offers MBA. *Program availability:* Part-time, evening/weekend. *Students:* 9 full-time (3 women), 3 part-time (2 women); includes 1 minority (Two or more races, non-Hispanic/Latino), 4 international. Average age 26. 24 applicants, 50% accepted, 6 enrolled. In 2017, 12 master's awarded. *Entrance requirements:* For master's, GRE or GMAT, minimum GPA of 3.0 (recommended). Additional exam requirements/recommendations for international students: Required—TOEFL (minimum score 580 paper-based; 92 iBT), IELTS (minimum score 7), PTE (minimum score 63). *Application deadline:* Applications are processed on a rolling basis. Application fee: $65. Electronic applications accepted. *Expenses:* $1,815 per credit hour. *Financial support:* In 2017–18, 8 students received support. Research assistantships with partial tuition reimbursements available, teaching assistantships with partial tuition reimbursements available, career-related internships or fieldwork, scholarships/grants, and unspecified assistantships available. Support available to part-time students. Financial award applicants required to submit FAFSA. *Faculty research:* Corporate financial reporting disclosure and quality, fraud and litigation risk, audit quality, opinion, and pricing decision, financial regulations, information technology performance. *Unit head:* Matt Cornwell, Assistant Director of Student Services and Outreach, 585-475-6916, E-mail: gradbus@saunders.rit.edu. *Application contact:* Diane Ellison, Senior Associate Vice President, Graduate Enrollment Services, 585-475-2229, Fax: 585-475-7164, E-mail: gradinfo@rit.edu.
Website: http://saunders.rit.edu/programs/graduate/mba_accounting.php

Rochester Institute of Technology, Graduate Enrollment Services, Saunders College of Business, Accounting and Finance Department, MS Program in Accounting, Rochester, NY 14623. Offers MS. *Program availability:* Part-time, evening/weekend. *Students:* 9 full-time (6 women), 1 part-time (0 women); includes 2 minority (1 Hispanic/Latino; 1 Two or more races, non-Hispanic/Latino), 6 international. Average age 26. 23 applicants, 52% accepted, 7 enrolled. In 2017, 2 master's awarded. *Entrance requirements:* For master's, GMAT or GRE, minimum GPA of 3.0 (recommended). Additional exam requirements/recommendations for international students: Required—TOEFL (minimum score 92 iBT), IELTS (minimum score 7), PTE (minimum score 63). *Application deadline:* Applications are processed on a rolling basis. Application fee: $65. Electronic applications accepted. *Expenses:* $1,815 per credit hour. *Financial support:* In 2017–18, 6 students received support. Research assistantships with partial tuition reimbursements available, teaching assistantships with partial tuition reimbursements available, career-related internships or fieldwork, and unspecified assistantships available. Support available to part-time students. Financial award applicants required to submit FAFSA. *Faculty research:* Corporate financial reporting disclosure and quality, fraud and litigation risk, audit quality, opinion, and pricing decision, financial regulations, information technology performance. *Unit head:* Matt Cornwell, Assistant Director of Student Services and Outreach, 585-475-6916, E-mail: mcornwell@saunders.rit.edu. *Application contact:* Diane Ellison, Senior Associate Vice President, Graduate Enrollment Services, 585-475-2229, Fax: 585-475-7164, E-mail: gradinfo@rit.edu.
Website: http://saunders.rit.edu/programs/graduate/ms_accounting.php

Rockhurst University, Helzberg School of Management, Kansas City, MO 64110-2561. Offers accounting (MBA); business intelligence (MBA, Certificate); business intelligence and analytics (MS); data science (MBA, Certificate); entrepreneurship (MBA); finance (MBA); fundraising leadership (MBA, Certificate); healthcare management (MBA, Certificate); human capital (Certificate); international business (Certificate); management (MA, MBA, Certificate); nonprofit administration (Certificate); organizational development (Certificate); science leadership (Certificate). *Accreditation:* AACSB. *Program availability:* Part-time, evening/weekend. *Faculty:* 18 full-time (4 women), 20 part-time/adjunct (9 women). *Students:* 99 full-time (30 women), 355 part-time (132 women); includes 95 minority (30 Black or African American, non-Hispanic/Latino; 29 Asian, non-Hispanic/Latino; 25 Hispanic/Latino; 11 Two or more races, non-Hispanic/Latino), 8 international. Average age 32. 249 applicants, 81% accepted, 175 enrolled. In 2017, 145 master's, 17 other advanced degrees awarded. *Entrance requirements:* For master's, GMAT or GRE. Additional exam requirements/recommendations for international students: Required—TOEFL (minimum score 550 paper-based; 79 iBT). *Application deadline:* Applications are processed on a rolling basis. Application fee: $0. Electronic applications accepted. *Financial support:* Applicants required to submit FAFSA. *Faculty research:* Offshoring/outsourcing, systems analysis/synthesis, work teams, multilateral trade, path dependencies/creation. *Unit head:* Cheryl McConnell, Dean, 816-501-4201, Fax: 816-501-4650, E-mail: cheryl.mcconnell@rockhurst.edu. *Application contact:* Jonnae Hill, Director of Graduate Business Advising, 816-501-4823, E-mail: jonnae.hill@rockhurst.edu.
Website: https://www.rockhurst.edu/helzberg

Rocky Mountain College, Program in Accountancy, Billings, MT 59102-1796. Offers M Acc. *Program availability:* Part-time-only. *Faculty:* 2 full-time (0 women). *Students:* 1 (woman) part-time. Average age 32. In 2017, 4 master's awarded. *Entrance requirements:* Additional exam requirements/recommendations for international students: Required—TOEFL (minimum score 570 paper-based; 88 iBT), IELTS (minimum score 6.5). *Application deadline:* Applications are processed on a rolling basis. Application fee: $35 ($40 for international students). Electronic applications accepted. Application fee is waived when completed online. *Expenses:* Contact institution. *Financial support:* Applicants required to submit FAFSA. *Unit head:* Anthony Piltz, Professor of Business Administration and Economics, 406-657-1069, E-mail: piltza@rocky.edu. *Application contact:* Austin Mapston, Dean of Enrollment Services, 406-657-1026, Fax: 406-657-1189, E-mail: admissions@rocky.edu.
Website: http://www.rocky.edu/academics/academic-programs/undergraduate-majors/accountancy/index.php

Roosevelt University, Graduate Division, Walter E. Heller College of Business, Program in Accounting, Chicago, IL 60605. Offers accounting (MSA); accounting forensics (MSAF). *Program availability:* Part-time, evening/weekend. *Students:* 28 full-time (18 women), 58 part-time (28 women); includes 36 minority (19 Black or African American, non-Hispanic/Latino; 8 Asian, non-Hispanic/Latino; 7 Hispanic/Latino; 2 Two or more races, non-Hispanic/Latino), 19 international. Average age 32. 48 applicants, 92% accepted, 24 enrolled. In 2017, 34 master's awarded. *Application deadline:* Applications are processed on a rolling basis. Application fee: $40. Electronic applications accepted. *Financial support:* Scholarships/grants and unspecified assistantships available. *Application contact:* Michael Conwell, Graduate Admission Counselor, 312-281-3250, E-mail: mconwell@roosevelt.edu.
Website: https://www.roosevelt.edu/

Rutgers University–Newark, Graduate School, Program in Management, Newark, NJ 07102. Offers accounting (PhD); accounting information systems (PhD); computer information systems (PhD); finance (PhD); information technology (PhD); international business (PhD); management science (PhD); marketing (PhD); organization management (PhD). Program offered jointly with New Jersey Institute of Technology. *Accreditation:* AACSB. *Degree requirements:* For doctorate, thesis/dissertation, cumulative exams. *Entrance requirements:* For doctorate, GMAT or GRE General Test, minimum undergraduate B average. Additional exam requirements/recommendations for international students: Required—TOEFL. Electronic applications accepted. *Faculty*

research: Technology management, leadership and teams, consumer behavior, financial and markets, logistics.

Rutgers University–Newark, Rutgers Business School–Newark and New Brunswick, Doctoral Programs in Management, Newark, NJ 07102. Offers accounting (PhD); accounting information systems (PhD); economics (PhD); finance (PhD); individualized study (PhD); information technology (PhD); international business (PhD); management science (PhD); marketing science (PhD); organizational management (PhD); science, technology and management (PhD); supply chain management (PhD). *Degree requirements:* For doctorate, comprehensive exam, thesis/dissertation. *Entrance requirements:* For doctorate, GRE or GMAT. Additional exam requirements/recommendations for international students: Required—TOEFL (minimum score 550 paper-based; 79 iBT). Electronic applications accepted.

Rutgers University–Newark, Rutgers Business School–Newark and New Brunswick, Program in Accountancy, Newark, NJ 07102. Offers M Accy. *Accreditation:* AACSB. *Program availability:* Online learning.

Rutgers University–Newark, Rutgers Business School–Newark and New Brunswick, Program in Professional Accounting, Newark, NJ 07102. Offers MBA. *Accreditation:* AACSB. *Entrance requirements:* For master's, GMAT. Additional exam requirements/recommendations for international students: Required—TOEFL. Electronic applications accepted.

Sacred Heart University, Graduate Programs, Jack Welch College of Business, Department of Accounting, Fairfield, CT 06825. Offers MBA, MS, Graduate Certificate. *Program availability:* Part-time, evening/weekend. *Faculty:* 5 full-time (2 women), 1 part-time/adjunct (0 women). *Students:* 39 full-time (20 women), 1 part-time (0 women); includes 7 minority (2 Black or African American, non-Hispanic/Latino; 5 Hispanic/Latino). Average age 23. 50 applicants, 92% accepted, 40 enrolled. In 2017, 33 master's awarded. *Entrance requirements:* For master's, bachelor's degree with minimum GPA of 3.0. Additional exam requirements/recommendations for international students: Required—TOEFL (minimum score 570 paper-based, 80 iBT), TWE, or IELTS (6.5). *Application deadline:* Applications are processed on a rolling basis. Application fee: $75. Electronic applications accepted. *Expenses:* Contact institution. *Financial support:* Unspecified assistantships available. Financial award applicants required to submit FAFSA. *Unit head:* Barbara Tarasovich, Director of MS in Accounting Program, 203-416-3513, E-mail: tarasovichb@sacredheart.edu. *Application contact:* Pam Pillo, Executive Director of Graduate Admissions, 203-365-7619, Fax: 203-365-4732, E-mail: graduatestudies@sacredheart.edu.
Website: http://www.sacredheart.edu/academics/johnfwelchcollegeofbusiness/graduateprogramscertificates/msinaccounting/

St. Ambrose University, College of Business, Program in Accounting, Davenport, IA 52803-2898. Offers MAC. *Program availability:* Part-time, evening/weekend. *Degree requirements:* For master's, comprehensive exam (for some programs), thesis or alternative, capstone seminar. *Entrance requirements:* For master's, GMAT. Electronic applications accepted.

St. Bonaventure University, School of Graduate Studies, School of Business, St. Bonaventure, NY 14778-2284. Offers general business (MBA); professional accountancy (MBA). *Accreditation:* AACSB. *Program availability:* Part-time, evening/weekend, 100% online. *Faculty:* 14 full-time (4 women), 4 part-time/adjunct (1 woman). *Students:* 81 full-time (33 women), 92 part-time (47 women); includes 16 minority (3 Black or African American, non-Hispanic/Latino; 1 American Indian or Alaska Native, non-Hispanic/Latino; 4 Asian, non-Hispanic/Latino; 5 Hispanic/Latino; 1 Native Hawaiian or other Pacific Islander, non-Hispanic/Latino; 2 Two or more races, non-Hispanic/Latino), 7 international. Average age 28. 104 applicants, 98% accepted, 79 enrolled. In 2017, 78 master's awarded. *Entrance requirements:* For master's, GMAT or GRE, undergraduate degree, transcripts, current resume. Additional exam requirements/recommendations for international students: Required—TOEFL (minimum score 550 paper-based; 79 iBT). *Application deadline:* For fall admission, 6/15 priority date for domestic students, 2/1 priority date for international students; for spring admission, 11/1 priority date for domestic students, 7/1 priority date for international students. Applications are processed on a rolling basis. Application fee: $0. Electronic applications accepted. *Expenses:* $733 per credit hour, $100 graduation fee. *Financial support:* Career-related internships or fieldwork, Federal Work-Study, scholarships/grants, health care benefits, and unspecified assistantships available. Support available to part-time students. Financial award application deadline: 4/15; financial award applicants required to submit FAFSA. *Faculty research:* High performance computing, sports economics, influence of crowd-sourcing from virtual brand communities on brand perception. *Unit head:* Dr. Matrecia James, Dean, 716-375-2200, Fax: 716-372-2191, E-mail: mjames@sbu.edu. *Application contact:* Bruce Campbell, Director of Graduate Admissions, 716-375-2429, Fax: 716-375-4015, E-mail: gradsch@sbu.edu.
Website: http://www.sbu.edu/academics/schools/business/graduate-degrees/master-of-business-administration-(mba)

St. Edward's University, Bill Munday School of Business, Master of Accounting Program, Austin, TX 78704. Offers M Ac. *Program availability:* Part-time, evening/weekend. *Students:* 9 full-time (6 women), 19 part-time (9 women); includes 14 minority (1 Black or African American, non-Hispanic/Latino; 1 Asian, non-Hispanic/Latino; 11 Hispanic/Latino; 1 Two or more races, non-Hispanic/Latino), 2 international. Average age 30. 27 applicants, 48% accepted, 6 enrolled. In 2017, 11 master's awarded. *Entrance requirements:* Additional exam requirements/recommendations for international students: Required—TOEFL, IELTS. *Application deadline:* For fall admission, 6/1 priority date for domestic and international students; for spring admission, 10/1 priority date for domestic and international students. Applications are processed on a rolling basis. Application fee: $50. Electronic applications accepted. *Expenses: Tuition:* Full-time $26,406; part-time $1467 per hour. *Required fees:* $75 per trimester. Full-time tuition and fees vary according to course load and program. *Unit head:* Dr. Louise Single, Program Director/Chair of Accounting Department, 512-492-3114, E-mail: louises@stedwards.edu. *Application contact:* Mike Leveriza, Graduate Admissions Advisor, 512-448-8745, E-mail: mleveriz@stedwards.edu.
Website: http://www.stedwards.edu

St. Edward's University, Bill Munday School of Business, Master of Business Administration Program, Austin, TX 78704. Offers accounting (MBA); digital management (MBA). *Program availability:* Part-time, evening/weekend. *Students:* 34 full-time (19 women), 108 part-time (50 women); includes 61 minority (3 Black or African American, non-Hispanic/Latino; 5 Asian, non-Hispanic/Latino; 48 Hispanic/Latino; 5 Two or more races, non-Hispanic/Latino), 11 international. Average age 32. 115 applicants, 58% accepted, 41 enrolled. In 2017, 94 master's awarded. *Entrance requirements:* Additional exam requirements/recommendations for international students: Required—TOEFL, IELTS. *Application deadline:* For fall admission, 6/1 priority date for domestic and international students; for spring admission, 10/1 priority date for domestic and international students. Applications are processed on a rolling basis. Application fee: $50. Electronic applications accepted. *Expenses: Tuition:* Full-time $26,406; part-time $1467 per hour. *Required fees:* $75 per trimester. Full-time tuition and fees vary according to course load and program. *Unit head:* Dr. David Altounian, Associate Dean and MBA Director, 512-448-8678, E-mail: davida@stedwards.edu. *Application contact:* Mike Leveriza, Graduate Admissions Advisor, 512-448-8745, E-mail: mleveriz@stedwards.edu.

St. Francis College, Program in Professional Accountancy, Brooklyn Heights, NY 11201-4398. Offers MS.

St. John's University, The Peter J. Tobin College of Business, Department of Accountancy, Program in Accounting, Queens, NY 11439. Offers MS. *Accreditation:* AACSB. *Program availability:* Part-time, evening/weekend, 100% online, blended/hybrid learning. *Students:* 142 full-time (83 women), 48 part-time (27 women); includes 52 minority (12 Black or African American, non-Hispanic/Latino; 28 Asian, non-Hispanic/Latino; 7 Hispanic/Latino; 5 Two or more races, non-Hispanic/Latino), 74 international. Average age 27. In 2017, 145 master's awarded. *Degree requirements:* For master's, thesis (for some programs). *Entrance requirements:* For master's, GMAT or GRE, 2 letters of recommendation, essay, resume, unofficial transcripts. Additional exam requirements/recommendations for international students: Required—TOEFL (minimum score 80 iBT), IELTS (minimum score 6.5). *Application deadline:* For fall admission, 11/1 for domestic and international students; for winter admission, 3/1 for domestic and international students; for spring admission, 6/1 for domestic and international students. Applications are processed on a rolling basis. Application fee: $70. Electronic applications accepted. *Expenses:* $22,410 per year. *Financial support:* Research assistantships, teaching assistantships, scholarships/grants, and unspecified assistantships available. Support available to part-time students. Financial award application deadline: 2/1; financial award applicants required to submit FAFSA. *Faculty research:* Accounting theory, auditing, managerial accounting, accounting information systems, accounting education. *Unit head:* Nina T. Dorata, PhD, Chair, 718-990-6460, E-mail: doratan@stjohns.edu. *Application contact:* Amber Steiger, Associate Director of Enrollment Management, 718-990-1345, E-mail: steigera@stjohns.edu.
Website: http://www.stjohns.edu/academics/schools-and-colleges/peter-j-tobin-college-business/programs-and-majors/accounting-master-science

St. Joseph's College, Long Island Campus, Programs in Business Management and Administration, Program in Accounting, Patchogue, NY 11772-2399. Offers MBA. *Program availability:* Part-time, evening/weekend. *Faculty:* 15 full-time (7 women), 22 part-time/adjunct (7 women). *Students:* 37 full-time (20 women), 48 part-time (19 women); includes 16 minority (1 Black or African American, non-Hispanic/Latino; 1 American Indian or Alaska Native, non-Hispanic/Latino; 3 Asian, non-Hispanic/Latino; 10 Hispanic/Latino; 1 Native Hawaiian or other Pacific Islander, non-Hispanic/Latino). Average age 29. 51 applicants, 80% accepted, 27 enrolled. In 2017, 35 master's awarded. *Entrance requirements:* For master's, official college transcripts, two letters of recommendation, resume, verification of employment letter and form, 200-250 word essay or personal statement. Additional exam requirements/recommendations for international students: Recommended—TOEFL (minimum score 550 paper-based; 80 iBT), IELTS (minimum score 7). *Application deadline:* Applications are processed on a rolling basis. Application fee: $25. Electronic applications accepted. *Expenses:* Tuition: Full-time $17,550; part-time $975 per credit. *Required fees:* $362. *Financial support:* In 2017–18, 17 students received support. Federal Work-Study available. *Unit head:* Mary A. Chance, Assistant Professor/Interim Director of Graduate Management Studies, 631-687-1297, E-mail: mchance@sjcny.edu.
Website: http://www.sjcny.edu

St. Joseph's College, New York, Programs in Business Management and Administration, Program in Accounting, Brooklyn, NY 11205-3688. Offers MBA. *Program availability:* Part-time, evening/weekend. *Faculty:* 1 full-time (0 women), 6 part-time/adjunct (4 women). *Students:* 2 full-time (1 woman), 8 part-time (4 women); includes 7 minority (6 Black or African American, non-Hispanic/Latino; 1 Hispanic/Latino). Average age 28. 17 applicants, 59% accepted, 7 enrolled. In 2017, 2 master's awarded. *Entrance requirements:* For master's, two letters of recommendation, 250-word essay, official college transcripts. Additional exam requirements/recommendations for international students: Required—TOEFL (minimum score 80 iBT). *Application deadline:* Applications are processed on a rolling basis. Application fee: $25. Electronic applications accepted. *Expenses:* Tuition: Full-time $17,550; part-time $975 per credit. *Required fees:* $362. *Financial support:* In 2017–18, 3 students received support. *Unit head:* Christopher Smith, Assistant Professor/Associate Chair, 718-940-5786, E-mail: csmith2@sjcny.edu.
Website: http://www.sjcny.edu

Saint Joseph's College of Maine, Master of Accountancy Program, Standish, ME 04084. Offers M Acc. *Program availability:* Part-time, online learning. *Entrance requirements:* For master's, baccalaureate degree with minimum cumulative GPA of 2.5; successful completion of each of the following prior to program enrollment: financial accounting, managerial accounting, introduction of finance/business finance and macroeconomics. Electronic applications accepted.

Saint Joseph's University, Erivan K. Haub School of Business, MBA Program, Philadelphia, PA 19131-1395. Offers accounting (MBA); business intelligence analytics (MBA); finance (MBA); financial analysis reporting (Postbaccalaureate Certificate); general business (MBA); health and medical services administration (MBA); international business (MBA); international marketing (MBA); leading (MBA); marketing (MBA); DO/MBA. DO/MBA offered jointly with Philadelphia College of Osteopathic Medicine. *Program availability:* Part-time-only, evening/weekend, 100% online. *Students:* 85 full-time (36 women), 371 part-time (153 women); includes 74 minority (32 Black or African American, non-Hispanic/Latino; 15 Asian, non-Hispanic/Latino; 19 Hispanic/Latino; 1 Native Hawaiian or other Pacific Islander, non-Hispanic/Latino; 7 Two or more races, non-Hispanic/Latino), 36 international. Average age 30. 247 applicants, 76% accepted, 112 enrolled. In 2017, 163 master's awarded. *Degree requirements:* For master's, minimum GPA of 3.0. *Entrance requirements:* For master's, GMAT or GRE, 2 letters of recommendation, resume, personal statement, official undergraduate and graduate transcripts. Additional exam requirements/recommendations for international students: Required—PTE, TOEFL, IELTS, or PTE. *Application deadline:* For fall admission, 7/15 priority date for domestic students, 5/15 priority date for international students; for spring admission, 11/15 priority date for domestic students, 10/15 priority date for international students; for summer admission, 4/15 priority date for domestic students, 2/15 priority date for international students. Applications are processed on a rolling basis. Application fee: $35. Electronic applications accepted. *Expenses:* Contact institution. *Financial support:* Scholarships/grants and unspecified assistantships available. Financial award application deadline: 5/1; financial award applicants required to submit FAFSA. *Unit head:* Jeannine Lajeunesse, Director, 610-660-1626, Fax: 610-660-1599, E-mail: jlajeune@sju.edu. *Application contact:* Christine Anderson, Assistant Director, 610-660-2252, Fax: 610-660-1599, E-mail: chris.anderson@sju.edu.
Website: http://www.sju.edu/haubmba

Saint Leo University, Graduate Studies in Business, Saint Leo, FL 33574-6665. Offers accounting (M Acc, MBA); cybersecurity (MS); cybersecurity management (MBA); data analytics (MBA); health care management (MBA); human resource management (MBA); international and experiential business administration (MBA); management (MBA, DBA); marketing (MBA); marketing research and social media analytics (MBA); project management (MBA); social media marketing (MBA); sport business (MBA); supply chain global integration management (MBA). *Accreditation:* ACBSP. *Program availability:* Part-time, evening/weekend, 100% online, blended/hybrid learning. *Faculty:* 54 full-time (18 women), 52 part-time/adjunct (18 women). *Students:* 9 full-time (3 women), 1,867 part-time (1,079 women); includes 861 minority (598 Black or African American, non-

Hispanic/Latino; 3 American Indian or Alaska Native, non-Hispanic/Latino; 38 Asian, non-Hispanic/Latino; 186 Hispanic/Latino; 3 Native Hawaiian or other Pacific Islander, non-Hispanic/Latino; 33 Two or more races, non-Hispanic/Latino), 68 international. Average age 37. 868 applicants, 63% accepted, 537 enrolled. In 2017, 859 master's, 3 doctorates awarded. *Degree requirements:* For doctorate, comprehensive exam, thesis/dissertation. *Entrance requirements:* For master's, GMAT with minimum score 500 (for M Acc), official transcripts, current resume, 2 professional recommendations, personal statement, bachelor's degree from regionally-accredited university; undergraduate degree in accounting and minimum undergraduate GPA of 3.0 (for M Acc); minimum undergraduate GPA of 3.0 in final 2 years of undergraduate study and 2 years' work experience (for MBA); for doctorate, GMAT (minimum score of 550) if master's GPA is under 3.25, official transcripts, current resume, 2 professional recommendations, personal statement, master's degree from regionally-accredited university with minimum GPA of 3.25, 3 years' work experience, interview. Additional exam requirements/recommendations for international students: Required—TOEFL (minimum score 550 paper-based; 78 iBT). *Application deadline:* For fall admission, 7/1 priority date for domestic and international students; for spring admission, 11/12 priority date for domestic students, 11/1 for international students. Applications are processed on a rolling basis. Application fee: $80. Electronic applications accepted. *Expenses:* Contact institution. *Financial support:* In 2017–18, 106 students received support. Career-related internships or fieldwork, health care benefits, and tuition remission for Saint Leo employees and their dependents available. Financial award application deadline: 3/1; financial award applicants required to submit FAFSA. *Faculty research:* Servant leadership, work/life balance, emotional intelligence, pricing, marketing. *Unit head:* Dr. Charles Hale, Dean, School of Business, 352-588-8599, Fax: 352-588-8912, E-mail: mbaslu@saintleo.edu. *Application contact:* Mark Russum, Assistant Vice President, Enrollment, 800-707-8846, Fax: 352-588-7873, E-mail: grad.admissions@saintleo.edu.
Website: https://www.saintleo.edu/school-of-business

Saint Louis University, Graduate Programs, John Cook School of Business, Department of Accounting, St. Louis, MO 63103. Offers M Acct, MBA. *Program availability:* Part-time, evening/weekend. *Entrance requirements:* For master's, GMAT. Additional exam requirements/recommendations for international students: Required—TOEFL (minimum score 570 paper-based; 88 iBT). Electronic applications accepted. *Expenses:* Contact institution. *Faculty research:* Tax policy, market valuation/corporate governance, foreign currency translation, accounting for income taxes, earnings quality.

Saint Mary's College of California, School of Economics and Business Administration, MS in Accounting Program, Moraga, CA 94575. Offers MS.

Saint Mary's University of Minnesota, Schools of Graduate and Professional Programs, Graduate School of Business and Technology, Accountancy Program, Winona, MN 55987-1399. Offers MS. *Program availability:* Online learning. *Unit head:* Melanie Torborg, Program Director, 612-238-4525, E-mail: mtorborg@smumn.edu. *Application contact:* James Callinan, Director of Admissions for Graduate and Professional Programs, 612-728-5158, Fax: 612-728-5121, E-mail: jcallina@smumn.edu.
Website: http://www.smumn.edu/graduate-home/areas-of-study/graduate-school-of-business-technology/ms-in-accountancy

Saint Peter's University, Graduate Business Programs, Program in Accountancy, Jersey City, NJ 07306-5997. Offers MS, MBA/MS. *Program availability:* Part-time, evening/weekend. *Entrance requirements:* Additional exam requirements/recommendations for international students: Required—TOEFL. Electronic applications accepted.

St. Thomas University, School of Business, Department of Management, Miami Gardens, FL 33054-6459. Offers accounting (MBA); general management (MSM, Certificate); health management (MBA, MSM, Certificate); human resource management (MBA, MSM, Certificate); international business (MBA, MIB, MSM, Certificate); justice administration (MSM, Certificate); management accounting (MSM, Certificate); public management (MSM, Certificate); sports administration (MS). *Program availability:* Part-time, evening/weekend. *Degree requirements:* For master's, comprehensive exam. *Entrance requirements:* For master's, interview, minimum GPA of 3.0 or GMAT. Additional exam requirements/recommendations for international students: Required—TOEFL (minimum score 550 paper-based; 79 iBT). Electronic applications accepted.

Samford University, Brock School of Business, Birmingham, AL 35229. Offers accountancy (M Acc); entrepreneurship (MBA); finance (MBA); marketing (MBA); JD/M Acc; JD/MBA; MBA/M Acc; MBA/M Div; MBA/MSEM; MBA/Pharm D. Programs offered jointly with Cumberland School of Law, Beeson School of Divinity, Howard College of Arts and Sciences, and McWhorter School of Pharmacy. *Accreditation:* AACSB. *Program availability:* Part-time, 100% online, blended/hybrid learning. *Faculty:* 8 full-time (1 woman), 5 part-time/adjunct (0 women). *Students:* 79 full-time (31 women), 18 part-time (8 women); includes 7 minority (2 Black or African American, non-Hispanic/Latino; 1 Asian, non-Hispanic/Latino; 3 Hispanic/Latino; 1 Two or more races, non-Hispanic/Latino), 8 international. Average age 28. 46 applicants, 78% accepted, 16 enrolled. In 2017, 78 master's awarded. *Degree requirements:* For master's, capstone course. *Entrance requirements:* For master's, GMAT or GRE, resume, transcripts; essay (international applicants only). Additional exam requirements/recommendations for international students: Required—TOEFL (minimum score 90 iBT), IELTS (minimum score 6.5). *Application deadline:* For fall admission, 8/1 for domestic and international students; for spring admission, 12/1 for domestic and international students; for summer admission, 5/1 for domestic and international students. Applications are processed on a rolling basis. Application fee: $35. Electronic applications accepted. Application fee is waived when completed online. *Expenses:* $813 per credit hour tuition; $425 per semester fees. *Financial support:* In 2017–18, 59 students received support. Scholarships/grants available. Financial award application deadline: 2/15; financial award applicants required to submit FAFSA. *Unit head:* Dr. Barbara Cartledge, Assistant Dean, 205-726-2935, Fax: 205-726-2540, E-mail: bhcartle@samford.edu. *Application contact:* Elizabeth Anne Gambrell, Associate Director, 205-726-2040, Fax: 205-726-2540, E-mail: eagambre@samford.edu.
Website: http://www.samford.edu/business

Sam Houston State University, College of Business Administration, Department of Accounting, Huntsville, TX 77341. Offers MS. *Program availability:* Part-time. *Degree requirements:* For master's, comprehensive exam. *Entrance requirements:* For master's, GMAT. Additional exam requirements/recommendations for international students: Required—TOEFL (minimum score 550 paper-based; 79 iBT), IELTS (minimum score 6.5). Electronic applications accepted.

San Diego State University, Graduate and Research Affairs, College of Business Administration, Charles W. Lamden School of Accountancy, San Diego, CA 92182. Offers MS. *Accreditation:* AACSB. *Degree requirements:* For master's, thesis or alternative. *Entrance requirements:* For master's, GMAT, resume, letters of reference. Additional exam requirements/recommendations for international students: Required—TOEFL. Electronic applications accepted.

San Francisco State University, Division of Graduate Studies, College of Business, Department of Accounting, San Francisco, CA 94132-1722. Offers MSA. *Program*

Accounting

availability: Part-time. *Entrance requirements:* For master's, GMAT, copy of transcripts, written statement of purpose, resume, two letters of reference. Additional exam requirements/recommendations for international students: Required—TOEFL or IELTS. Electronic applications accepted. *Unit head:* Dr. Sanjit Sengupta, Faculty Director, 415-817-4366, Fax: 415-817-4340, E-mail: sengupta@sfsu.edu. *Application contact:* Dr. Theresa Hammond, Graduate Coordinator, 415-338-6283, Fax: 415-817-4340, E-mail: thammond@sfsu.edu.
Website: http://cob.sfsu.edu/graduate-programs/MSA

San Jose State University, Graduate Studies and Research, Lucas Graduate School of Business, San Jose, CA 95192-0065. Offers accountancy (MS); business administration (MBA); taxation (MS); transportation management (MS). *Program availability:* Part-time, evening/weekend, online learning. *Faculty:* 15 full-time (7 women), 6 part-time/adjunct (3 women). *Students:* 85 full-time (49 women), 51 part-time (28 women); includes 77 minority (2 Black or African American, non-Hispanic/Latino; 44 Asian, non-Hispanic/Latino; 16 Hispanic/Latino; 1 Native Hawaiian or other Pacific Islander, non-Hispanic/Latino; 14 Two or more races, non-Hispanic/Latino), 42 international. Average age 28. 328 applicants, 43% accepted, 88 enrolled. In 2017, 155 master's awarded. *Degree requirements:* For master's, graduate writing assessment, culminating project. *Entrance requirements:* Additional exam requirements/recommendations for international students: Required—TOEFL (minimum score 80 iBT), IELTS (minimum score 6.5), PTE (minimum score 53). *Application deadline:* For fall admission, 2/1 for domestic and international students. Applications are processed on a rolling basis. Application fee: $55. Electronic applications accepted. *Expenses:* Contact institution. *Financial support:* Fellowships, research assistantships, career-related internships or fieldwork, Federal Work-Study, institutionally sponsored loans, scholarships/grants, and unspecified assistantships available. Support available to part-time students. Financial award application deadline: 4/28; financial award applicants required to submit FAFSA. *Faculty research:* Financial effects of cyber-security breaches, health care analytics, innovation and teamwork, corporate bankruptcy prediction, multi-domain executive coaching. *Unit head:* Dr. Dan Moshavi, Dean, 408-924-3400, Fax: 408-924-3426, E-mail: dan.moshavi@sjsu.edu.
Website: http://www.sjsu.edu/lucasschool/

Seattle University, Albers School of Business and Economics, Master of Professional Accounting Program, Seattle, WA 98122-1090. Offers MPAC, JD/MPAC, MBA/MPAC, MPAC/MSF. *Program availability:* Part-time, evening/weekend. *Faculty:* 9 full-time (4 women), 3 part-time/adjunct (1 woman). *Students:* 56 full-time (39 women), 29 part-time (19 women); includes 11 minority (2 Black or African American, non-Hispanic/Latino; 8 Asian, non-Hispanic/Latino; 1 Hispanic/Latino), 62 international. Average age 26. 80 applicants, 64% accepted, 21 enrolled. In 2017, 43 master's awarded. *Entrance requirements:* For master's, GMAT, minimum GPA of 3.0. Additional exam requirements/recommendations for international students: Required—TOEFL (minimum score 580 paper-based; 92 iBT). *Application deadline:* For fall admission, 5/1 priority date for domestic students, 4/1 priority date for international students; for winter admission, 11/20 priority date for domestic students, 9/1 priority date for international students; for spring admission, 2/20 priority date for domestic students, 12/1 priority date for international students. Applications are processed on a rolling basis. Application fee: $55. Electronic applications accepted. *Expenses:* Contact institution. *Financial support:* In 2017–18, 30 students received support. Career-related internships or fieldwork and Federal Work-Study available. Support available to part-time students. Financial award applicants required to submit FAFSA. *Unit head:* Dr. Bruce Koch, Program Director, 206-296-5700, Fax: 206-296-5795, E-mail: kochb@seattleu.edu. *Application contact:* Janet Shandley, Director of Graduate Admissions, 206-296-5900, Fax: 206-298-5656, E-mail: grad_admissions@seattleu.edu.
Website: http://www.seattleu.edu/albers/mpac/

Seton Hall University, Stillman School of Business, Programs in Accounting, South Orange, NJ 07079-2697. Offers accounting (MS, Certificate); professional accounting (MS). *Program availability:* Part-time, evening/weekend. *Faculty:* 7 full-time (0 women), 2 part-time/adjunct (0 women). *Students:* 29 full-time (10 women), 46 part-time (15 women); includes 11 minority (1 Black or African American, non-Hispanic/Latino; 7 Asian, non-Hispanic/Latino; 2 Hispanic/Latino; 1 Two or more races, non-Hispanic/Latino), 20 international. Average age 28. 66 applicants, 61% accepted, 27 enrolled. In 2017, 57 master's awarded. *Entrance requirements:* For master's, GMAT or GRE (waived based on work experience), MS in business discipline, professional degree or designation (MD, JD, PhD, DVM, DDS, CPA, etc.), minimum undergraduate GPA of 3.0. Additional exam requirements/recommendations for international students: Required—TOEFL (minimum score 607 paper-based; 80 iBT), IELTS (minimum score 6), PTE. *Application deadline:* For fall admission, 5/31 priority date for domestic students, 3/31 for international students; for spring admission, 10/31 for domestic students, 9/30 for international students; for summer admission, 4/30 priority date for domestic students, 3/31 priority date for international students. Applications are processed on a rolling basis. Application fee: $75. Electronic applications accepted. *Expenses:* $1,305 per credit; $126 fees (fall and spring semester); $51 (summer semester). *Financial support:* In 2017–18, 12 students received support, including 12 research assistantships with full tuition reimbursements available (averaging $3,988 per year); career-related internships or fieldwork, scholarships/grants, and unspecified assistantships also available. Financial award application deadline: 6/30; financial award applicants required to submit FAFSA. *Faculty research:* Nonfinancial metrics, pension accounting, integrated reporting, multinational enterprises. *Unit head:* Dr. Mark Holtzman, Chair, 973-761-9133, Fax: 973-761-9217, E-mail: mark.holtzman@shu.edu. *Application contact:* Alfred Ayoub, Director of Graduate Admissions, 973-761-9262, Fax: 973-761-9208, E-mail: alfred.ayoub@shu.edu.
Website: http://www.shu.edu/business/ms-programs.cfm

Seton Hall University, Stillman School of Business, Programs in Business Administration, South Orange, NJ 07079-2697. Offers accounting (MBA); entrepreneurial studies (Certificate); finance (MBA); financial decision making (Certificate); information technology management (MBA); international business (MBA); management (MBA); marketing (MBA); sport management (MBA); supply chain management (MBA, Certificate). *Program availability:* Part-time, evening/weekend. *Faculty:* 29 full-time (4 women), 18 part-time/adjunct (0 women). *Students:* 140 full-time (58 women), 154 part-time (49 women); includes 66 minority (25 Black or African American, non-Hispanic/Latino; 14 Asian, non-Hispanic/Latino; 23 Hispanic/Latino; 4 Two or more races, non-Hispanic/Latino), 88 international. Average age 32. 406 applicants, 75% accepted, 100 enrolled. In 2017, 132 master's awarded. *Degree requirements:* For master's, 20 hours of community service (Social Responsibility Project). *Entrance requirements:* For master's, GMAT or CPA, GRE (waived based on work experience or advanced degree from AACSB institution), MS in business discipline, professional degree or designation (MD, JD, PhD, DVM, DDS, CPA, etc.), minimum undergraduate GPA of 3.0. Additional exam requirements/recommendations for international students: Required—TOEFL (minimum score 607 paper-based; 80 iBT), IELTS (minimum score 6), PTE. *Application deadline:* For fall admission, 5/31 priority date for domestic students, 4/30 priority date for international students; for spring admission, 10/31 priority date for domestic students, 9/30 priority date for international students; for summer admission, 3/31 priority date for domestic students. Applications are processed on a rolling basis. Application fee: $75. Electronic applications accepted. *Expenses:* $1,305 per credit; $126 fees (fall and spring semester), $51 (summer semester). *Financial support:* In 2017–18, 41 students received support, including 25 research assistantships with full tuition reimbursements available (averaging $3,644 per year); career-related internships or fieldwork, scholarships/grants, and unspecified assistantships also available. Financial award application deadline: 6/30; financial award applicants required to submit FAFSA. *Faculty research:* Sport, hedge funds, executive compensation, social media, legal studies. *Unit head:* Dr. Joyce Strawser, Dean, 973-761-9013, Fax: 973-761-9217, E-mail: joyce.strawser@shu.edu. *Application contact:* Alfred Ayoub, Director of Graduate Admissions, 973-761-9262, Fax: 973-761-9208, E-mail: alfred.ayoub@shu.edu.
Website: http://www.shu.edu/business/mba-programs.cfm

Seton Hill University, MBA Program, Greensburg, PA 15601. Offers entrepreneurship (MBA); forensic accounting and fraud examination (MBA); healthcare administration (MBA); management (MBA). *Program availability:* Part-time, evening/weekend. *Entrance requirements:* For master's, resume, 3 letters of recommendation, personal statement, transcripts. Additional exam requirements/recommendations for international students: Required—TOEFL (minimum score 600 paper-based; 100 iBT), IELTS (minimum score 6.5). *Application deadline:* Applications are processed on a rolling basis. Application fee: $0. Electronic applications accepted. *Expenses:* Tuition: Part-time $734 per credit. Tuition and fees vary according to class time, course level, course load and program. *Financial support:* Federal Work-Study, scholarships/grants, and tuition discounts available. Financial award application deadline: 8/15; financial award applicants required to submit FAFSA. *Unit head:* Dr. Douglas Nelson, Associate Professor, Business/MBA Program Director, E-mail: dnelson@setonhill.edu.
Website: http://www.setonhill.edu/academics/graduate_programs/mba

Shorter University, Professional Studies, Rome, GA 30165. Offers accountancy (MAC); business administration (MBA); management (MM). *Program availability:* Evening/weekend. *Degree requirements:* For master's, project. *Entrance requirements:* For master's, minimum undergraduate GPA of 2.75 in last 60 hours, 3 years of work experience. Additional exam requirements/recommendations for international students: Required—TOEFL (minimum score 550 paper-based; 79 iBT). Electronic applications accepted.

Siena College, School of Business, Loudonville, NY 12211-1462. Offers accounting (MS). *Program availability:* Evening/weekend. *Degree requirements:* For master's, internship.

Slippery Rock University of Pennsylvania, Graduate Studies (Recruitment), College of Business, School of Business, Slippery Rock, PA 16057-1383. Offers accounting/finance (MBA); general (MBA); marketing/management (MBA). *Program availability:* Part-time, evening/weekend. *Degree requirements:* For master's, comprehensive exam (for some programs), thesis (for some programs). *Entrance requirements:* For master's, minimum cumulative GPA of 3.0, official transcripts, three references. Additional exam requirements/recommendations for international students: Required—TOEFL (minimum score 550 paper-based; 80 iBT). Electronic applications accepted. *Expenses:* Contact institution.

Southeast Missouri State University, School of Graduate Studies, Harrison College of Business, Cape Girardeau, MO 63701-4799. Offers accounting (MBA); entrepreneurship (MBA); financial management (MBA); sport management (MBA). *Accreditation:* AACSB. *Program availability:* Part-time, evening/weekend, 100% online. *Faculty:* 27 full-time (7 women), 1 (woman) part-time/adjunct. *Students:* 71 full-time (38 women), 68 part-time (31 women); includes 13 minority (7 Black or African American, non-Hispanic/Latino; 4 Asian, non-Hispanic/Latino; 2 Two or more races, non-Hispanic/Latino), 47 international. Average age 30. 51 applicants, 100% accepted, 51 enrolled. In 2017, 95 master's awarded. *Degree requirements:* For master's, variable foreign language requirement, comprehensive exam (for some programs), thesis or alternative. *Entrance requirements:* For master's, GMAT or GRE, minimum undergraduate GPA of 2.5, minimum grade of C in prerequisite courses. Additional exam requirements/recommendations for international students: Required—TOEFL (minimum score 550 paper-based; 79 iBT), IELTS (minimum score 6), PTE (minimum score 53). *Application deadline:* For fall admission, 8/1 for domestic students, 6/1 for international students; for spring admission, 11/21 for domestic students, 10/1 for international students; for summer admission, 5/15 for domestic students. Applications are processed on a rolling basis. Application fee: $30 ($40 for international students). Electronic applications accepted. *Expenses:* $270.35 per credit hour in-state tuition, $33.40 per credit hour fees. *Financial support:* In 2017–18, 26 students received support. Career-related internships or fieldwork, Federal Work-Study, scholarships/grants, traineeships, tuition waivers (full), and unspecified assistantships available. Financial award application deadline: 6/30; financial award applicants required to submit FAFSA. *Faculty research:* Organizational justice, ethics, leadership, corporate finance, generational differences. *Unit head:* Dr. Judy A. Wiles, Interim Dean, Harrison College of Business, 573-651-2913, Fax: 573-651-5032, E-mail: jwiles@semo.edu.
Website: http://www.semo.edu/mba

Southern Adventist University, School of Business, Collegedale, TN 37315-0370. Offers accounting (MBA); finance (MBA); healthcare administration (MBA); management (MBA); marketing management (MBA). *Program availability:* Part-time, evening/weekend, 100% online. *Entrance requirements:* For master's, GMAT, minimum cumulative undergraduate GPA of 3.0. Additional exam requirements/recommendations for international students: Required—TOEFL (minimum score 600 paper-based; 100 iBT). *Application deadline:* For fall admission, 7/1 for domestic students, 5/1 for international students; for winter admission, 11/1 for domestic students, 9/1 for international students; for summer admission, 4/1 for domestic students, 2/1 for international students. Applications are processed on a rolling basis. Application fee: $40. Electronic applications accepted. *Expenses:* Tuition: Full-time $11,430; part-time $635 per credit hour. Tuition and fees vary according to degree level and program. *Financial support:* Scholarships/grants and unspecified assistantships available. Financial award application deadline: 9/1; financial award applicants required to submit FAFSA. *Unit head:* Dr. Stephanie Sheehan, Dean, 423-236-2659, Fax: 423-236-1527, E-mail: ssheehan@southern.edu. *Application contact:* Teshia Price, Graduate Studies Coordinator, 423-236-2751, Fax: 423-236-1527, E-mail: tprice@southern.edu.
Website: https://www.southern.edu/academics/business.html

Southern Illinois University Carbondale, Graduate School, College of Business and Administration, School of Accountancy, Carbondale, IL 62901-4701. Offers M Acc, PhD, JD/M Acc. *Accreditation:* AACSB. *Program availability:* Part-time. *Degree requirements:* For doctorate, thesis/dissertation. *Entrance requirements:* For master's, GMAT, minimum GPA of 2.7; for doctorate, GMAT, minimum graduate GPA of 3.25. Additional exam requirements/recommendations for international students: Required—TOEFL (minimum score 550 paper-based; 80 iBT). Electronic applications accepted. *Faculty research:* Not-for-profit accounting, SEC regulations, computers and accounting education, taxation.

Southern Illinois University Edwardsville, Graduate School, School of Business, Department of Accounting, Edwardsville, IL 62026. Offers accountancy (MSA); taxation (MSA). *Accreditation:* AACSB. *Program availability:* Part-time, evening/weekend. *Degree requirements:* For master's, thesis or alternative, final exam. *Entrance requirements:* For master's, GMAT. Additional exam requirements/recommendations for international students: Required—TOEFL (minimum score 550 paper-based; 79 iBT), IELTS (minimum score 6.5). Electronic applications accepted.

Southern Methodist University, Cox School of Business, MBA Program, Dallas, TX 75275. Offers accounting (MBA, PMBA); business administration (EMBA); finance (MBA); financial statement analysis (PMBA); general business (MBA); information technology and operations management (MBA); management (MBA); marketing (MBA); real estate (MBA); strategy (MBA); strategy and entrepreneurship (MBA); JD/MBA; MA/MBA. *Program availability:* Part-time, evening/weekend. *Entrance requirements:* For master's, GMAT. Additional exam requirements/recommendations for international students: Required—TOEFL. Electronic applications accepted. *Expenses:* Contact institution. *Faculty research:* Corporate finance, financial reporting, modeling consumer decision-making, competition between national brands and store brands, institutional determinants of firms' strategy.

Southern Methodist University, Cox School of Business, Program in Accounting, Dallas, TX 75275. Offers MSA. *Program availability:* Part-time, evening/weekend. *Entrance requirements:* For master's, GMAT. Additional exam requirements/recommendations for international students: Required—TOEFL. *Expenses:* Contact institution. *Faculty research:* Capital markets, taxation, business combinations, intangibles accounting, accounting history.

Southern New Hampshire University, School of Business, Manchester, NH 03106-1045. Offers accounting (MBA, Graduate Certificate); accounting finance (MS); accounting/auditing (MS); accounting/forensic accounting (MS); accounting/management accounting (MS); accounting/taxation (MS); applied economics (MS); athletic administration (MBA, Graduate Certificate); business administration (IMBA, Certificate), including business information systems (Certificate), human resource management (Certificate); business analytics (MBA); business intelligence (MBA); communication (MA), including new media and marketing, public relations; community economic development (MBA); criminal justice (MBA); data analytics (MS); economics (MBA); engineering management (MBA); entrepreneurship (MBA); finance (MBA, MS, Graduate Certificate); finance/corporate finance (MS); finance/investments (MS); forensic accounting (MBA); forensic accounting and fraud examination (Graduate Certificate); healthcare informatics (MBA); healthcare management (MBA); human resource management (MS); human resources (MBA); information technology (MS); information technology management (MBA); international business (PhD); Internet marketing (MBA); leadership (MBA); leadership of nonprofit organizations (Graduate Certificate); management (MS); marketing (MBA, MS, Graduate Certificate); music business (MBA); operations and project management (MS); operations and supply chain management (MBA, Graduate Certificate); organizational leadership (MBA); project management (MBA, Graduate Certificate); public administration (MBA, Graduate Certificate); quantitative analysis (MBA); Six Sigma (Graduate Certificate); Six Sigma quality (MBA); social media marketing (MBA, Graduate Certificate); sport management (MBA, MS, Graduate Certificate); sustainability and environmental compliance (MBA); MBA/Certificate. *Accreditation:* ACBSP. *Program availability:* Part-time, evening/weekend, online learning. Terminal master's awarded for partial completion of doctoral program. *Degree requirements:* For master's, one foreign language, comprehensive exam (for some programs), thesis or alternative; for doctorate, one foreign language, comprehensive exam, thesis/dissertation. *Entrance requirements:* For master's, minimum GPA of 2.5; for doctorate, GMAT. Additional exam requirements/recommendations for international students: Required—TOEFL (minimum score 500 paper-based). *Application deadline:* Applications are processed on a rolling basis. Application fee: $40. Electronic applications accepted. *Expenses: Tuition:* Part-time $627 per credit hour. Part-time tuition and fees vary according to campus/location and program. *Financial support:* Career-related internships or fieldwork, Federal Work-Study, institutionally sponsored loans, scholarships/grants, tuition waivers (partial), and unspecified assistantships available. Support available to part-time students. Financial award applicants required to submit FAFSA. *Unit head:* Dr. Bill Lightfoot, Dean, 603-644-3102, Fax: 603-644-3144. *Application contact:* Office of Graduate Admission, 888-327-SNHU, Fax: 603-644-3144, E-mail: enroll@snhu.edu.

Southern Oregon University, Graduate Studies, School of Business, Ashland, OR 97520. Offers accounting (Postbaccalaureate Certificate); business administration (MBA); international management (MIM). *Accreditation:* ACBSP. *Program availability:* Part-time, evening/weekend, online learning. *Degree requirements:* For master's, comprehensive exam. *Entrance requirements:* For master's, GMAT, minimum cumulative GPA of 3.0 in the last 90 quarter credits (60 semester credits) of undergraduate coursework. Additional exam requirements/recommendations for international students: Required—TOEFL (minimum score 540 paper-based; 76 iBT), IELTS (minimum score 6), ELPT (minimum score 964) or ELS (minimum score 112). Electronic applications accepted.

Southern Utah University, Master of Accountancy/MBA Dual Degree Program, Cedar City, UT 84720-2498. Offers MBA/M Acc. *Program availability:* Part-time, 100% online. *Students:* 3 full-time (1 woman), 1 (woman) part-time. Average age 26. 8 applicants, 75% accepted. *Entrance requirements:* Additional exam requirements/recommendations for international students: Required—TOEFL (minimum score 550 paper-based, 79 iBT) or IELTS (minimum score 6). *Application deadline:* For fall admission, 3/1 for domestic and international students; for spring admission, 10/1 for domestic and international students; for summer admission, 3/1 for domestic and international students. Applications are processed on a rolling basis. Application fee: $60 ($65 for international students). Electronic applications accepted. *Expenses:* Contact institution. *Financial support:* Unspecified assistantships available. *Application contact:* Patricia Palmer, Academic Advisor and Graduate Program Coordinator, 435-865-8167, Fax: 435-586-5493, E-mail: patriciapalmer@suu.edu. Website: https://www.suu.edu/business/graduate/

Southern Utah University, Program in Accounting, Cedar City, UT 84720-2498. Offers M Acc. *Program availability:* Part-time, 100% online. *Faculty:* 5 full-time (0 women), 2 part-time/adjunct (0 women). *Students:* 63 full-time (22 women), 48 part-time (14 women); includes 17 minority (2 Black or African American, non-Hispanic/Latino; 3 Asian, non-Hispanic/Latino; 12 Hispanic/Latino). Average age 29. 64 applicants, 83% accepted, 46 enrolled. In 2017, 62 master's awarded. *Entrance requirements:* For master's, GMAT or GRE, official transcripts of all academic work prior to admission with transcripts verifying minimum GPA of 3.0 for all work completed; three letters of recommendation from former/current college professors, assigned mentors, supervisors or associates (for non-SUU business majors). Additional exam requirements/recommendations for international students: Required—TOEFL (minimum scores: 550 paper-based, 79 iBT) or IELTS (minimum score 6). *Application deadline:* For fall admission, 3/1 for domestic and international students; for spring admission, 10/1 for domestic and international students; for summer admission, 3/1 for domestic and international students. Applications are processed on a rolling basis. Application fee: $60 ($65 for international students). Electronic applications accepted. *Expenses:* Contact institution. *Financial support:* Unspecified assistantships available. *Faculty research:* Cost accounting, intermediate accounting text, GAAP policy, Statements on Standards for Accounting and Review Services (SSARS). *Unit head:* Dr. Robin Boneck, Chair, Accounting Department, 435-586-7773, Fax: 435-586-5493, E-mail: boneck@suu.edu. *Application contact:* Patricia Palmer, Academic Advisor and Graduate Program Coordinator, 435-865-8167, Fax: 435-586-5493, E-mail: patriciapalmer@suu.edu. Website: https://www.suu.edu/business/acct/macc.html

Southwestern Adventist University, Business Administration Department, Keene, TX 76059. Offers accounting (MBA); finance (MBA); management/leadership (MBA). *Program availability:* Part-time, evening/weekend. *Degree requirements:* For master's, capstone course. *Entrance requirements:* For master's, GMAT, GRE General Test.

State University of New York at New Paltz, Graduate and Extended Learning School, School of Business, New Paltz, NY 12561. Offers business administration (MBA); public accountancy (MBA). *Accreditation:* AACSB. *Program availability:* Part-time, evening/weekend. *Faculty:* 15 full-time (3 women), 2 part-time/adjunct (0 women). *Students:* 62 full-time (27 women), 36 part-time (24 women); includes 28 minority (8 Black or African American, non-Hispanic/Latino; 6 Asian, non-Hispanic/Latino; 11 Hispanic/Latino; 3 Two or more races, non-Hispanic/Latino), 12 international. 59 applicants, 68% accepted, 28 enrolled. In 2017, 43 master's awarded. *Entrance requirements:* For master's, GMAT or GRE, minimum GPA of 3.0. Additional exam requirements/recommendations for international students: Required—TOEFL (minimum score 550 paper-based; 80 iBT), IELTS (minimum score 6.5). *Application deadline:* Applications are processed on a rolling basis. Application fee: $50. Electronic applications accepted. *Expenses:* Contact institution. *Financial support:* In 2017–18, 6 research assistantships with partial tuition reimbursements (averaging $5,000 per year), 1 teaching assistantship with partial tuition reimbursement (averaging $5,000 per year) were awarded; scholarships/grants, traineeships, and unspecified assistantships also available. Financial award application deadline: 8/1. *Faculty research:* Cognitive styles in management education, supporting SME e-commerce migration through e-learning, earnings management and board activity, trading future spread portfolio, global equity market correlation and volatility. *Unit head:* Dr. Kristin Backhaus, Dean, 845-257-2930, E-mail: mba@newpaltz.edu. *Application contact:* Aaron Hines, Director of MBA Program, 845-257-2968, E-mail: mba@newpaltz.edu.
Website: http://mba.newpaltz.edu

State University of New York College at Geneseo, Graduate Studies, School of Business, Geneseo, NY 14454. Offers accounting (MS). *Accreditation:* AACSB. *Faculty:* 3 full-time (1 woman), 2 part-time/adjunct (0 women). *Students:* 19 full-time (7 women); includes 2 minority (both Asian, non-Hispanic/Latino). Average age 22. 39 applicants, 59% accepted, 19 enrolled. In 2017, 17 master's awarded. *Degree requirements:* For master's, thesis. *Entrance requirements:* For master's, GMAT, bachelor's degree in accounting. Additional exam requirements/recommendations for international students: Required—TOEFL (minimum score 525 paper-based; 71 iBT), IELTS (minimum score 6.5), PTE, iTEP. *Application deadline:* For fall admission, 6/1 priority date for domestic students. Applications are processed on a rolling basis. Application fee: $50. Electronic applications accepted. *Expenses:* Contact institution. *Financial support:* In 2017–18, 9 students received support. Research assistantships with partial tuition reimbursements available and scholarships/grants available. Financial award application deadline: 4/1; financial award applicants required to submit FAFSA. *Unit head:* Dr. Michael Schinski, Dean of the School of Business, 585-245-5367, Fax: 585-245-5467, E-mail: schinski@geneseo.edu. *Application contact:* Michael R. George, Director of Graduate Admissions, 585-245-5148, Fax: 585-245-5550, E-mail: georgem@geneseo.edu.
Website: http://www.geneseo.edu/business/accounting_ms

State University of New York College at Old Westbury, School of Business, Old Westbury, NY 11568-0210. Offers accounting (MS); taxation (MS). *Program availability:* Part-time, evening/weekend. *Faculty:* 10 full-time (2 women), 1 part-time/adjunct (0 women). *Students:* 30 full-time (13 women), 47 part-time (15 women); includes 19 minority (3 Black or African American, non-Hispanic/Latino; 11 Asian, non-Hispanic/Latino; 5 Hispanic/Latino). Average age 31. 35 applicants, 91% accepted, 25 enrolled. In 2017, 25 master's awarded. *Entrance requirements:* For master's, GMAT, 2 letters of recommendation. Additional exam requirements/recommendations for international students: Required—TOEFL (minimum score 550 paper-based). *Application deadline:* For fall admission, 6/15 priority date for domestic students; for spring admission, 11/15 priority date for domestic students. Applications are processed on a rolling basis. Application fee: $50. Electronic applications accepted. *Financial support:* Applicants required to submit FAFSA. *Faculty research:* Corporate governance, asset pricing, corporate finance, hedge funds, taxation. *Unit head:* Rita Buttermilch, Director of Graduate Business Programs, 516-876-3900, E-mail: langec@oldwestbury.edu. *Application contact:* Philip D'Angelo, Graduate Admissions Office, 516-876-3073, E-mail: enroll@oldwestbury.edu.
Website: http://www.oldwestbury.edu/schools/business

State University of New York Polytechnic Institute, MBA Program in Technology Management, Utica, NY 13502. Offers accounting and finance (MBA); business management (MBA); health informatics (MBA); human resource management (MBA); marketing management (MBA). *Program availability:* Part-time, online only, 100% online. *Faculty:* 8 full-time (2 women), 2 part-time/adjunct (1 woman). *Students:* 29 full-time (13 women), 85 part-time (41 women); includes 18 minority (4 Black or African American, non-Hispanic/Latino; 8 Asian, non-Hispanic/Latino; 6 Hispanic/Latino). Average age 32. 83 applicants, 55% accepted, 37 enrolled. In 2017, 41 master's awarded. *Degree requirements:* For master's, comprehensive exam, capstone project. *Entrance requirements:* For master's, GMAT, resume, letter of reference. Additional exam requirements/recommendations for international students: Required—TOEFL (minimum score 550 paper-based; 79 iBT), IELTS (minimum score 6.5). *Application deadline:* For fall admission, 7/1 priority date for domestic students; 7/1 for international students; for spring admission, 12/1 for domestic students, 11/1 for international students. Applications are processed on a rolling basis. Application fee: $60. Electronic applications accepted. *Expenses:* Contact institution. *Financial support:* Fellowships, research assistantships, and unspecified assistantships available. Financial award application deadline: 6/1; financial award applicants required to submit FAFSA. *Faculty research:* Economic development and design thinking, transfer of training, trade intensity and liquidity, enforcement and punishment, acculturation attitudes and consumption behavior. Total annual research expenditures: $20,000. *Unit head:* Dr. Rafael Romero, Program Coordinator, 315-792-7207, E-mail: rafael.romero@sunyit.edu. *Application contact:* Alicia Foster, Director of Graduate Admissions, E-mail: alicia.foster@sunyit.edu.
Website: https://sunypoly.edu/academics/majors-and-programs/technology-management.html

State University of New York Polytechnic Institute, Program in Accountancy, Utica, NY 13502. Offers MS. *Accreditation:* AACSB. *Program availability:* Part-time, online only, 100% online. *Faculty:* 3 full-time (1 woman). *Students:* 27 full-time (14 women), 48 part-time (28 women); includes 24 minority (4 Black or African American, non-Hispanic/Latino; 1 American Indian or Alaska Native, non-Hispanic/Latino; 10 Asian, non-Hispanic/Latino; 8 Hispanic/Latino; 1 Two or more races, non-Hispanic/Latino). Average age 33. 86 applicants, 51% accepted, 27 enrolled. In 2017, 14 master's awarded. *Degree requirements:* For master's, capstone courses. *Entrance requirements:* For master's, GMAT, letter of reference, resume. Additional exam requirements/recommendations for international students: Required—TOEFL. *Application deadline:* For fall admission, 7/1 priority date for domestic students, 7/1 for international students; for spring admission, 12/1 for domestic students, 11/1 for international students. Applications are processed on a rolling basis. Application fee: $60. Electronic applications accepted. *Expenses:* Tuition, state resident: full-time $8154; part-time

Accounting

$2718 per year. Tuition, nonresident: full-time $16,650; part-time $5550 per year. *Required fees:* $993; $331 per unit. Tuition and fees vary according to course load, degree level, campus/location and program. *Financial support:* Fellowships, research assistantships, and unspecified assistantships available. Financial award application deadline: 6/1; financial award applicants required to submit FAFSA. *Faculty research:* Business interruption insurance claims, social security and income planning, income equality and pay ratio disclosure, Medicaid and the nursing home dilemma, fake news. *Unit head:* Peter Karl, Program Coordinator, 315-792-7120, E-mail: pak3rd@sunyit.edu. *Application contact:* Alicia Foster, Director of Graduate Admissions, E-mail: alicia.foster@sunyit.edu.
Website: https://sunypoly.edu/academics/majors-and-programs/ms-accountancy.html

Stephen F. Austin State University, Graduate School, College of Business, Program in Professional Accountancy, Nacogdoches, TX 75962. Offers MPAC. Students admitted at the undergraduate level. *Degree requirements:* For master's, comprehensive exam. *Entrance requirements:* For master's, GMAT. Additional exam requirements/recommendations for international students: Required—TOEFL.

Stetson University, School of Business Administration, Program in Accounting, DeLand, FL 32723. Offers M Acc. *Accreditation:* AACSB. *Program availability:* Part-time, online learning. *Faculty:* 16 full-time (4 women), 3 part-time/adjunct (1 woman). *Students:* 20 full-time (8 women), 2 part-time (1 woman); includes 7 minority (2 Black or African American, non-Hispanic/Latino; 1 Asian, non-Hispanic/Latino; 1 Hispanic/Latino; 3 Two or more races, non-Hispanic/Latino), 2 international. Average age 29. 38 applicants, 53% accepted, 13 enrolled. In 2017, 20 master's awarded. *Entrance requirements:* For master's, GMAT, GRE, transcripts, resume, two letters of recommendation, personal statement. Additional exam requirements/recommendations for international students: Required—TOEFL (minimum score 90 iBT), IELTS (minimum score 7.5). *Application deadline:* For fall admission, 8/1 for domestic students; for spring admission, 1/1 for domestic students; for summer admission, 5/1 for domestic students. Applications are processed on a rolling basis. Application fee: $50. Electronic applications accepted. *Expenses:* $1,009 per credit hour (DeLand Campus); $784 per credit hour (online). *Financial support:* In 2017–18, 13 students received support. Career-related internships or fieldwork, Federal Work-Study, institutionally sponsored loans, unspecified assistantships, and tuition waivers (for staff and dependents) available. Support available to part-time students. Financial award application deadline: 3/15; financial award applicants required to submit FAFSA. *Faculty research:* Oil and gas reserve accounting, the impact of dependent tuition policies on behavior, tax scams and frauds, auditor conservatism in going concern decisions, tax implications of NCAA travel benefits. *Unit head:* Dr. Michael E. Bitter, Director, 386-822-7410. *Application contact:* Jamie Vanderlip, Director of Admissions for Graduate, Transfer and Adult Programs, 386-822-7100, Fax: 386-822-7112, E-mail: jlvander@stetson.edu.

Stony Brook University, State University of New York, Graduate School, College of Business, Program in Accounting, Stony Brook, NY 11794. Offers MS. *Program availability:* Part-time. *Students:* 26 full-time (14 women), 8 part-time (5 women); includes 11 minority (6 Asian, non-Hispanic/Latino; 4 Hispanic/Latino; 1 Two or more races, non-Hispanic/Latino), 4 international. 111 applicants, 49% accepted, 34 enrolled. In 2017, 23 master's awarded. *Degree requirements:* For master's, capstone. *Entrance requirements:* For master's, GMAT or GRE. Additional exam requirements/recommendations for international students: Required—TOEFL (minimum score 85 iBT). *Application deadline:* For fall admission, 5/15 for domestic students, 3/15 for international students; for spring admission, 11/15 for domestic students, 10/15 for international students. *Expenses:* Contact institution. *Unit head:* Dr. Manuel London, Dean, 631-632-7159, E-mail: manuel.london@stonybrook.edu. *Application contact:* Erica Robey, Graduate Coordinator, 631-632-7171, Fax: 631-632-8181, E-mail: oss@stonybrook.edu.
Website: https://www.stonybrook.edu/commcms/business/academics/_graduate-program/ms-accounting.php

Stony Brook University, State University of New York, Graduate School, College of Business, Program in Business Administration, Stony Brook, NY 11794. Offers accounting (MBA); business administration (MBA); finance (MBA, Certificate); health care management (MBA); human resources (MBA); innovation (MBA); management (MBA); marketing (MBA); operations management (MBA). *Faculty:* 39 full-time (13 women), 14 part-time/adjunct (5 women). *Students:* 181 full-time (98 women), 145 part-time (73 women); includes 68 minority (16 Black or African American, non-Hispanic/Latino; 1 American Indian or Alaska Native, non-Hispanic/Latino; 35 Asian, non-Hispanic/Latino; 11 Hispanic/Latino; 1 Native Hawaiian or other Pacific Islander, non-Hispanic/Latino; 4 Two or more races, non-Hispanic/Latino), 69 international. Average age 29. 154 applicants, 66% accepted, 58 enrolled. In 2017, 105 master's awarded. *Entrance requirements:* For master's, GMAT, 3 letters of recommendation from current or former employers or professors, transcripts, personal statement, resume. Additional exam requirements/recommendations for international students: Required—TOEFL (minimum score 550 paper-based; 90 iBT), IELTS (minimum score 6.5). *Application deadline:* For fall admission, 5/15 for domestic students, 3/15 for international students; for spring admission, 11/15 for domestic students, 10/15 for international students. Application fee: $100. *Expenses:* Contact institution. *Financial support:* Teaching assistantships available. *Total annual research expenditures:* $2,070. *Unit head:* Dr. Manuel London, Dean, 631-632-7159, E-mail: manuel.london@stonybrook.edu. *Application contact:* Dr. Dmytro Holod, Associate Dean for Academic Programs/Graduate Director, 631-632-7183, Fax: 631-632-8181, E-mail: dmytro.holod@stonybrook.edu.
Website: https://www.stonybrook.edu/commcms/business/

Stratford University, School of Graduate Studies, Falls Church, VA 22043. Offers accounting (MS); business administration (MBA, DBA); cyber security (MS); cyber security leadership and policy (MS); digital forensics (MS); healthcare administration (MS); information systems (MS); information technology (DIT); networking and telecommunications (MS); software engineering (MS). *Program availability:* Part-time, evening/weekend, 100% online, blended/hybrid learning. *Students:* 272 full-time (110 women), 204 part-time (89 women). *Degree requirements:* For master's, comprehensive exam, capstone project. *Entrance requirements:* For master's, GRE or GMAT, baccalaureate degree. Additional exam requirements/recommendations for international students: Required—TOEFL (minimum score 79 iBT), IELTS (minimum score 6.5), PTE (minimum score 5). *Application deadline:* Applications are processed on a rolling basis. Application fee: $50. Electronic applications accepted. *Expenses: Tuition:* Full-time $33,405; part-time $11,135 per credit hour. One-time fee: $385 full-time. Tuition and fees vary according to degree level and program. *Financial support:* Federal Work-Study and scholarships/grants available. Financial award applicants required to submit FAFSA. *Unit head:* Dr. Valarie Trimarchi, Campus President, 703-539-6890, Fax: 703-539-6960. *Application contact:* Lori Smith, Admissions, 214-649-7113, E-mail: lasmith@stratford.edu.

Strayer University, Graduate Studies, Washington, DC 20005-2603. Offers accounting (MS); acquisition (MBA); business administration (MBA); communications technology (MS); educational management (M Ed); finance (MBA); health services administration (MHSA); hospitality and tourism management (MBA); human resource management (MBA); information systems (MS), including computer security management, decision support system management, enterprise resource management, network management, software engineering management, systems development management; management (MBA); management information systems (MS); marketing (MBA); professional accounting (MS), including accounting information systems, controllership, taxation; public administration (MPA); supply chain management (MBA); technology in education (M Ed). Programs also offered at campus locations in Birmingham, AL; Chamblee, GA; Cobb County, GA; Morrow, GA; White Marsh, MD; Charleston, SC; Columbia, SC; Greensboro, NC; Greenville, SC; Lexington, KY; Louisville, KY; Nashville, TN; North Raleigh, NC; Washington, DC. *Accreditation:* ACBSP. *Program availability:* Part-time, evening/weekend, online learning. *Degree requirements:* For master's, thesis. *Entrance requirements:* For master's, GMAT, GRE General Test, bachelor's degree from an accredited college or university, minimum undergraduate GPA of 2.75. Electronic applications accepted.

Suffolk University, Sawyer Business School, Department of Accounting, Boston, MA 02108-2770. Offers accounting (MSA, Graduate Certificate); taxation (MST); MBA/MSA; MBA/MST. *Accreditation:* AACSB. *Program availability:* Part-time, evening/weekend, 100% online. *Faculty:* 12 full-time (6 women), 4 part-time/adjunct (1 woman). *Students:* 60 full-time (43 women), 125 part-time (80 women); includes 57 minority (17 Black or African American, non-Hispanic/Latino; 27 Asian, non-Hispanic/Latino; 12 Hispanic/Latino; 1 Two or more races, non-Hispanic/Latino), 38 international. Average age 29. 113 applicants, 71% accepted, 35 enrolled. In 2017, 88 master's awarded. *Entrance requirements:* For master's, GMAT. Additional exam requirements/recommendations for international students: Required—TOEFL (minimum score 550 paper-based; 80 iBT). *Application deadline:* For fall admission, 3/15 priority date for domestic and international students; for spring admission, 10/15 priority date for domestic and international students. Applications are processed on a rolling basis. Application fee: $50. Electronic applications accepted. *Expenses:* $43,980 per year full-time tuition; $1,466 per credit part-time. *Financial support:* In 2017–18, 98 students received support, including 1 fellowship (averaging $6,200 per year); career-related internships or fieldwork, Federal Work-Study, institutionally sponsored loans, and scholarships/grants also available. Support available to part-time students. Financial award application deadline: 4/1; financial award applicants required to submit FAFSA. *Faculty research:* Tax policy, tax research, decision-making in accounting, accounting information systems, capital markets and strategic planning. *Unit head:* Tracy Riley, Chair, 617-994-4276, E-mail: triley@suffolk.edu. *Application contact:* Mara Marzocchi, Associate Director of Graduate Admissions, 617-573-8302, Fax: 617-305-1733, E-mail: grad.admission@suffolk.edu.
Website: http://www.suffolk.edu/msa

Suffolk University, Sawyer Business School, Master of Business Administration Program, Boston, MA 02108-2770. Offers accounting (MBA); entrepreneurship (MBA); executive business administration (EMBA); finance (MBA); global business administration (GMBA); health administration (MBA); international business (MBA); marketing (MBA); nonprofit management (MBA); organizational behavior (MBA); strategic management (MBA); supply chain management (MBA); taxation (MBA); JD/MBA; MBA/MHA; MBA/MSA; MBA/MSF; MBA/MST. *Accreditation:* AACSB. *Program availability:* Part-time, evening/weekend, 100% online. *Faculty:* 16 full-time (6 women), 9 part-time/adjunct (1 woman). *Students:* 106 full-time (57 women), 236 part-time (135 women); includes 80 minority (23 Black or African American, non-Hispanic/Latino; 23 Asian, non-Hispanic/Latino; 28 Hispanic/Latino; 6 Two or more races, non-Hispanic/Latino), 41 international. Average age 30. 354 applicants, 69% accepted, 115 enrolled. In 2017, 170 master's awarded. *Entrance requirements:* For master's, GMAT, minimum undergraduate GPA of 2.75 (MBA), 5 years of managerial experience (EMBA). Additional exam requirements/recommendations for international students: Required—TOEFL (minimum score 550 paper-based; 80 iBT). *Application deadline:* For fall admission, 3/15 priority date for domestic students, 10/15 priority date for international students; for spring admission, 10/15 priority date for domestic and international students. Applications are processed on a rolling basis. Application fee: $50. Electronic applications accepted. *Expenses:* $43,980 per year full-time, $1,466 per credit part-time (for MBA); $1,794 per credit part-time (for Executive MBA). *Financial support:* In 2017–18, 198 students received support, including 1 fellowship (averaging $2,325 per year); career-related internships or fieldwork, Federal Work-Study, institutionally sponsored loans, and scholarships/grants also available. Support available to part-time students. Financial award application deadline: 4/1; financial award applicants required to submit FAFSA. *Faculty research:* Foreign investments; career strategies and boundaryless careers; corporate ethics codes; interest rates, inflation, and growth options; innovation and product development performance. *Unit head:* Jodi Detjen, Director of MBA Programs, 617-573-8306, E-mail: jdetjen@suffolk.edu. *Application contact:* Mara Marzocchi, Associate Director of Graduate Admissions, 617-573-8302, Fax: 617-305-1733, E-mail: grad.admission@suffolk.edu.
Website: http://www.suffolk.edu/mba

Syracuse University, Martin J. Whitman School of Management, Master of Business Administration Program, Syracuse, NY 13244. Offers accounting (MBA); business analytics (MBA); entrepreneurship (MBA); marketing management (MBA); real estate (MBA); supply chain management (MBA); JD/MBA. *Program availability:* Part-time, 100% online. *Students:* 22 full-time (9 women), 495 part-time (147 women); includes 182 minority (81 Black or African American, non-Hispanic/Latino; 3 American Indian or Alaska Native, non-Hispanic/Latino; 42 Asian, non-Hispanic/Latino; 52 Hispanic/Latino; 4 Native Hawaiian or other Pacific Islander, non-Hispanic/Latino). Average age 32. 1,086 applicants, 73% accepted, 516 enrolled. In 2017, 84 master's awarded. *Entrance requirements:* For master's, GMAT or GRE, resume, essay, 5-minute video interview, two letters of recommendation, transcripts (unofficial). Additional exam requirements/recommendations for international students: Required—TOEFL (minimum score 100 iBT), IELTS (minimum score 7), PTE (minimum score 68). *Application deadline:* For fall admission, 11/30 for domestic students, 11/30 priority date for international students; for winter admission, 1/1 for domestic students, 1/1 priority date for international students; for spring admission, 2/15 for domestic and international students; for summer admission, 4/19 for domestic students. Application fee: $75. Electronic applications accepted. *Expenses:* Contact institution. *Financial support:* In 2017–18, 22 students received support. Merit scholarships available. Financial award application deadline: 2/15. *Faculty research:* Data analysis, economics of international business, financial markets and institutions, operations management, supply chain management. *Unit head:* Dr. Alexander McKelvie, Associate Dean for Undergraduate and Full-time Master's Education, 315-443-7252, E-mail: mckelvie@syr.edu. *Application contact:* Shri Ramakrishnan, Assistant Director, Graduate Recruitment, 315-443-3497, Fax: 315-443-9517, E-mail: busgrad@syr.edu.
Website: http://whitman.syr.edu/ftmba/

Syracuse University, Martin J. Whitman School of Management, MS Program in Professional Accounting, Syracuse, NY 13244. Offers MS. *Program availability:* Part-time, evening/weekend, 100% online. *Students:* Average age 23. 429 applicants, 55% accepted, 103 enrolled. In 2017, 76 master's awarded. *Entrance requirements:* For master's, GMAT or GRE, resume, essay, 5-minute video interview, two letters of recommendation, transcripts (unofficial). Additional exam requirements/recommendations for international students: Required—TOEFL (minimum score 100 iBT), IELTS (minimum score 7), PTE (minimum score 68). *Application deadline:* For fall admission, 11/30 for domestic students, 11/30 priority date for international students; for winter admission, 1/1 for domestic students, 1/1 priority date for international students; for spring admission, 2/15 for domestic and international students; for summer admission, 4/19 for domestic students. Application fee: $75. Electronic applications accepted. *Expenses:* Contact institution. *Financial support:* In 2017–18, 41 students received support. Merit-based scholarships available. Financial award application deadline: 2/15. *Faculty research:* Financial statement analysis, international reporting and analysis, advanced auditing, taxes and business strategy, principles of fraud examination. *Unit head:* Dr. Joseph Comprix, Chair/Associate Professor, 315-443-3674, E-mail: jjcompri@syr.edu. *Application contact:* Shri Ramakrishnan, Assistant Director, Graduate Recruitment, 315-443-3497, Fax: 315-443-9517, E-mail: busgrad@syr.edu. Website: http://whitman.syr.edu/msacc/

Tabor College, Graduate Program, Hillsboro, KS 67063. Offers accounting (MBA). Program offered at the Wichita campus only.

Tarleton State University, College of Graduate Studies, College of Business Administration, Department of Accounting, Finance and Economics, Stephenville, TX 76402. Offers accounting (M Acc). *Program availability:* Part-time, evening/weekend. *Faculty:* 11 full-time (3 women), 1 part-time/adjunct (0 women). *Students:* 16 full-time (12 women), 20 part-time (12 women); includes 8 minority (3 Black or African American, non-Hispanic/Latino; 1 Asian, non-Hispanic/Latino; 4 Hispanic/Latino), 1 international. Average age 30. 21 applicants, 95% accepted, 13 enrolled. In 2017, 5 master's awarded. *Degree requirements:* For master's, comprehensive exam, thesis (for some programs). *Entrance requirements:* For master's, GRE or GMAT, minimum GPA of 3.0. Additional exam requirements/recommendations for international students: Required— TOEFL (minimum score 550 paper-based; 80 iBT), IELTS (minimum score 6). *Application deadline:* For fall admission, 8/5 priority date for domestic students; for spring admission, 12/1 for domestic students. Applications are processed on a rolling basis. Application fee: $45 ($145 for international students). Electronic applications accepted. *Expenses:* Contact institution. *Financial support:* Research assistantships and teaching assistantships available. Financial award application deadline: 5/1; financial award applicants required to submit FAFSA. *Unit head:* Dr. Keldon Bauer, Department Head, 254-968-9909, Fax: 254-968-9665, E-mail: kbauer@tarleton.edu. *Application contact:* Information Contact, 254-968-9104, Fax: 254-968-9670, E-mail: gradoffice@tarleton.edu.
Website: http://www.tarleton.edu/afe/

Temple University, Fox School of Business, Doctoral Programs in Business, Philadelphia, PA 19122-6096. Offers accounting (PhD); entrepreneurship (PhD); finance (PhD); international business (PhD); management information systems (PhD); marketing (PhD); risk management and insurance (PhD); statistics (PhD); strategic management (PhD); tourism and sport (PhD). *Accreditation:* AACSB. *Degree requirements:* For doctorate, thesis/dissertation. *Entrance requirements:* For doctorate, GRE General Test, GMAT, minimum GPA of 3.0, master's degree. Additional exam requirements/recommendations for international students: Required—TOEFL (minimum score 600 paper-based; 100 iBT), IELTS (minimum score 7.5). Electronic applications accepted. *Expenses:* Tuition, state resident: full-time $16,164; part-time $898 per credit hour. Tuition, nonresident: full-time $22,158; part-time $1231 per credit hour. *Required fees:* $890; $445 per semester. Full-time tuition and fees vary according to course load, degree level, campus/location and program.

Temple University, Fox School of Business, MBA Programs, Philadelphia, PA 19122-6096. Offers accounting (MBA); business management (MBA); financial management (MBA); healthcare and life sciences innovation (MBA); human resource management (MBA); international business (IMBA); IT management (MBA); marketing management (MBA); pharmaceutical management (MBA); strategic management (EMBA, MBA). EMBA offered in Philadelphia, PA and Tokyo, Japan. *Accreditation:* AACSB. *Program availability:* Part-time, evening/weekend, online learning. *Entrance requirements:* For master's, GMAT, minimum undergraduate GPA of 3.0. Additional exam requirements/recommendations for international students: Required—TOEFL (minimum score 600 paper-based; 100 iBT), IELTS (minimum score 7.5). *Expenses:* Tuition, state resident: full-time $16,164; part-time $898 per credit hour. Tuition, nonresident: full-time $22,158; part-time $1231 per credit hour. *Required fees:* $890; $445 per semester. Full-time tuition and fees vary according to course load, degree level, campus/location and program.

Temple University, Fox School of Business, Specialized Master's Programs, Philadelphia, PA 19122-6096. Offers accountancy (MS); actuarial science (MS); finance (MS); financial engineering (MS); human resource management (MS); innovation management and entrepreneurship (MS); marketing (MS); statistics (MS). MS in innovation management and entrepreneurship delivered jointly with College of Engineering. *Accreditation:* AACSB. *Program availability:* Part-time. *Entrance requirements:* For master's, GRE General Test or GMAT, minimum undergraduate GPA of 3.0. Additional exam requirements/recommendations for international students: Required—TOEFL (minimum score 600 paper-based; 100 iBT), IELTS (minimum score 7.5). *Expenses:* Tuition, state resident: full-time $16,164; part-time $898 per credit hour. Tuition, nonresident: full-time $22,158; part-time $1231 per credit hour. *Required fees:* $890; $445 per semester. Full-time tuition and fees vary according to course load, degree level, campus/location and program.

Tennessee Technological University, College of Graduate Studies, College of Business, Master of Accountancy Program, Cookeville, TN 38505. Offers M Acc. *Program availability:* Part-time, evening/weekend. *Students:* 5 full-time (2 women), 8 part-time (3 women); includes 1 minority (Asian, non-Hispanic/Latino). 17 applicants, 71% accepted, 12 enrolled. *Entrance requirements:* For master's, GMAT or GRE. *Application deadline:* For fall admission, 7/1 for domestic students, 5/1 for international students; for spring admission, 12/1 for domestic students, 10/1 for international students; for summer admission, 5/1 for domestic students, 2/1 for international students. Applications are processed on a rolling basis. Application fee: $35 ($40 for international students). Electronic applications accepted. *Expenses:* Tuition, state resident: full-time $9925; part-time $565 per credit hour. Tuition, nonresident: full-time $22,993; part-time $1291 per credit hour. *Financial support:* In 2017–18, 1 teaching assistantship (averaging $7,500 per year) was awarded; fellowships, research assistantships, and unspecified assistantships also available. Financial award application deadline: 4/1; financial award applicants required to submit FAFSA. *Unit head:* Kate Nicewicz, Director, 931-372-3600, E-mail: knicewicz@tntech.edu. *Application contact:* Shelia K. Kendrick, Coordinator of Graduate Studies, 931-372-3808, Fax: 931-372-3497, E-mail: skendrick@tntech.edu.
Website: https://www.tntech.edu/cob/macc/

Tennessee Wesleyan University, Graduate Programs, Athens, TN 37303. Offers accounting (MBA); management (MBA). *Program availability:* Evening/weekend. *Faculty:* 4 full-time (1 woman), 1 (woman) part-time/adjunct. *Students:* 2 full-time (1 woman), 14 part-time (10 women). *Entrance requirements:* For master's, GMAT, official transcripts, three letters of recommendation, current curriculum vitae or resume. *Expenses:* Tuition: Part-time $500 per semester hour. *Application contact:* Mark Bucco, Adult and Graduate Admissions Counselor, 423-252-1114, Fax: 423-745-9335, E-mail: mbucco@tnwesleyan.edu.
Website: http://www.tnwesleyan.edu/academics/graduate-programs/

Texas A&M International University, Office of Graduate Studies and Research, A.R. Sanchez, Jr. School of Business, Division of International Banking and Finance Studies, Laredo, TX 78041. Offers accounting (MP Acc); international banking and finance (MBA). *Entrance requirements:* For master's, GMAT or GRE General Test. Additional exam requirements/recommendations for international students: Required—TOEFL (minimum score 550 paper-based; 79 iBT).

Texas A&M University, Mays Business School, Department of Accounting, College Station, TX 77843. Offers MS. *Accreditation:* AACSB. *Faculty:* 28. *Students:* 161 full-time (90 women), 2 part-time (1 woman); includes 35 minority (3 Black or African American, non-Hispanic/Latino; 1 American Indian or Alaska Native, non-Hispanic/Latino; 7 Asian, non-Hispanic/Latino; 19 Hispanic/Latino; 5 Two or more races, non-Hispanic/Latino), 7 international. Average age 24. 199 applicants, 16% accepted, 16 enrolled. In 2017, 150 master's awarded. Terminal master's awarded for partial completion of doctoral program. *Degree requirements:* For master's, comprehensive exam. *Entrance requirements:* For master's, GMAT or GRE. Additional exam requirements/recommendations for international students: Required—TOEFL (minimum score 550 paper-based; 80 iBT), IELTS (minimum score 6), PTE (minimum score 53). *Application deadline:* For fall admission, 3/15 for domestic students, 2/15 for international students; for spring admission, 10/15 for domestic and international students. Applications are processed on a rolling basis. Application fee: $50 ($90 for international students). *Expenses:* Contact institution. *Financial support:* In 2017–18, 88 students received support, including 1 fellowship with tuition reimbursement available (averaging $13,600 per year), 13 research assistantships with tuition reimbursements available (averaging $14,670 per year); career-related internships or fieldwork, institutionally sponsored loans, scholarships/grants, traineeships, health care benefits, tuition waivers (full and partial), and unspecified assistantships also available. Support available to part-time students. Financial award application deadline: 3/15; financial award applicants required to submit FAFSA. *Faculty research:* Financial reporting, taxation management, decision-making, accounting information systems, government accounting. *Unit head:* Dr. James J. Benjamin, Head, 979-845-0356, Fax: 979-845-0028, E-mail: jbenjamin@mays.tamu.edu. *Application contact:* Dr. Bala Shetty, Interim Associate Dean for Graduate Programs, 979-845-7024, Fax: 979-845-0028, E-mail: bshetty@mays.tamu.edu.
Website: http://mays.tamu.edu/acct/

Texas A&M University–Central Texas, Graduate Studies and Research, Killeen, TX 76549. Offers accounting (MS); business administration (MBA); clinical mental health counseling (MS); criminal justice (MCJ); curriculum and instruction (M Ed); educational administration (M Ed); educational psychology - experimental psychology (MS); history (MA); human resource management (MS); information systems (MS); liberal studies (MS); management and leadership (MS); marriage and family therapy (MS); mathematics (MS); political science (MA); school counseling (M Ed); school psychology (Ed S).

Texas A&M University–Commerce, College of Business, Commerce, TX 75429. Offers accounting (MSA); business administration (MBA); business analytics (MS); finance (MSF); management (MS); marketing (MS). *Accreditation:* AACSB. *Program availability:* Part-time, evening/weekend, 100% online, blended/hybrid learning. *Faculty:* 50 full-time (19 women), 7 part-time/adjunct (0 women). *Students:* 479 full-time (248 women), 1,056 part-time (556 women); includes 660 minority (281 Black or African American, non-Hispanic/Latino; 4 American Indian or Alaska Native, non-Hispanic/Latino; 120 Asian, non-Hispanic/Latino; 222 Hispanic/Latino; 33 Two or more races, non-Hispanic/Latino), 224 international. Average age 33. 930 applicants, 61% accepted, 363 enrolled. In 2017, 686 master's awarded. *Degree requirements:* For master's, comprehensive exam. *Entrance requirements:* For master's, GRE General Test, GMAT, letter of recommendation. Additional exam requirements/recommendations for international students: Required—TOEFL (minimum score 550 paper-based; 79 iBT), IELTS (minimum score 6). *Application deadline:* For fall admission, 6/1 priority date for international students; for spring admission, 10/15 priority date for international students; for summer admission, 3/15 priority date for international students. Applications are processed on a rolling basis. Application fee: $50 ($75 for international students). Electronic applications accepted. *Expenses:* Contact institution. *Financial support:* In 2017–18, 46 students received support, including 20 research assistantships with partial tuition reimbursements available (averaging $8,000 per year); Federal Work-Study, institutionally sponsored loans, scholarships/grants, health care benefits, and unspecified assistantships also available. Financial award application deadline: 5/1; financial award applicants required to submit FAFSA. *Faculty research:* Applied economics with emphasis on industries that are important to the region including health, energy and agriculture; finance research on banking, investments, financial institutions and risk management; marketing and big data decisions of product choice behavior and channel behavior of consumers; strategic management and organizational behavior phenomena; international accounting in governmental sectors. *Total annual research expenditures:* $1,920. *Unit head:* Dr. Shanan Gwaltney Gibson, Dean of College of Business, 903-886-5191, Fax: 903-886-5650, E-mail: shanan.gibson@tamuc.edu. *Application contact:* Vicky Turner, Doctoral Degree and Special Programs Coordinator, 903-886-5167, E-mail: vicky.turner@tamuc.edu.
Website: http://www.tamuc.edu/academics/graduateSchool/programs/businessEntrepreneurship/default.aspx

Texas A&M University–Corpus Christi, College of Graduate Studies, College of Business, Corpus Christi, TX 78412. Offers accounting (M Acc); business (MBA); finance (MBA); health care administration (MBA); international business (MBA). *Accreditation:* AACSB. *Program availability:* Part-time, evening/weekend, 100% online, blended/hybrid learning. *Faculty:* 31 full-time (11 women), 2 part-time/adjunct (0 women). *Students:* 107 full-time (50 women), 583 part-time (283 women); includes 259 minority (80 Black or African American, non-Hispanic/Latino; 85 Asian, non-Hispanic/Latino; 83 Hispanic/Latino; 11 Two or more races, non-Hispanic/Latino), 77 international. Average age 34. 485 applicants, 57% accepted, 236 enrolled. In 2017, 310 master's awarded. *Degree requirements:* For master's, 30 to 42 hours (for MBA; varies by concentration area, delivery format, and necessity for foundational courses for students with nonbusiness degrees). *Entrance requirements:* For master's, GMAT, GRE. Additional exam requirements/recommendations for international students: Required—TOEFL (minimum score 550 paper-based; 79 iBT), IELTS (minimum score 6.5). *Application deadline:* For fall admission, 7/15 priority date for domestic students, 5/1 priority date for international students; for spring admission, 11/15 priority date for domestic students, 9/1 priority date for international students; for summer admission, 4/15 priority date for domestic and international students. Applications are processed on a rolling basis. Application fee: $50 ($70 for international students). Electronic applications accepted. *Expenses:* Tuition, state resident: full-time $3568; part-time $198.24 per credit hour. Tuition, nonresident: full-time $11,038; part-time $613.24 per credit hour. *Required fees:* $2129; $1422.58 per semester. Tuition and fees vary according to program. *Financial support:* Research assistantships, teaching assistantships, career-related internships or fieldwork, Federal Work-Study, institutionally sponsored loans, scholarships/grants, health care benefits, and unspecified assistantships available. Support available to part-time students. Financial award application deadline: 3/15; financial award applicants required to submit FAFSA. *Unit head:* Dr. John Gamble, Dean, 361-825-6045, Fax: 361-825-2725, E-mail: john.gamble@tamucc.edu. *Application contact:* Sharon Polansky, Director of Master's Programs, 361-825-3448, Fax: 361-825-2755, E-mail: gradweb@tamucc.edu.
Website: http://cob.tamucc.edu

Accounting

Texas A&M University–San Antonio, School of Business, San Antonio, TX 78224. Offers business administration (MBA); professional accounting (MPA). *Program availability:* Part-time, evening/weekend, online learning. *Faculty:* 19 full-time (7 women), 2 part-time/adjunct (1 woman). *Students:* 104 full-time (54 women), 391 part-time (200 women); includes 355 minority (43 Black or African American, non-Hispanic/Latino; 21 Asian, non-Hispanic/Latino; 280 Hispanic/Latino; 2 Native Hawaiian or other Pacific Islander, non-Hispanic/Latino; 9 Two or more races, non-Hispanic/Latino), 11 international. Average age 32. 365 applicants, 71% accepted, 160 enrolled. In 2017, 128 master's awarded. *Degree requirements:* For master's, comprehensive exam. *Entrance requirements:* For master's, GMAT. Additional exam requirements/recommendations for international students: Required—TOEFL (minimum score 550 paper-based; 79 iBT), IELTS (minimum score 6). *Application deadline:* For fall admission, 3/15 priority date for domestic and international students; for spring admission, 11/1 priority date for domestic and international students; for summer admission, 4/1 priority date for domestic and international students. Applications are processed on a rolling basis. Application fee: $35 ($50 for international students). Electronic applications accepted. *Expenses:* Tuition, state resident: full-time $3475; part-time $1930 per semester. Tuition, nonresident: full-time $10,945; part-time $6080 per semester. *Required fees:* $2148; $1412 per year. $706 per semester. Tuition and fees vary according to course load. *Financial support:* In 2017–18, 29 students received support. Federal Work-Study, scholarships/grants, and tuition waivers available. Financial award application deadline: 3/15; financial award applicants required to submit FAFSA. *Faculty research:* Culture and its effect on organizational processes; diversity and teams. *Unit head:* Dr. Tracy Hurley, Dean of the College of Business. *Application contact:* Caitie Garza, Graduate Admissions Coordinator, 210-784-1300, E-mail: beajaguar@tamusa.edu.
Website: http://www.tamusa.edu/collegeofbusiness/index.html

Texas A&M University–Texarkana, Graduate Studies and Research, College of Business, Texarkana, TX 75503. Offers accounting (MSA); business administration (MBA, MS). *Program availability:* Part-time, evening/weekend. *Degree requirements:* For master's, thesis or alternative. *Entrance requirements:* For master's, minimum GPA of 2.5 in last 60 hours of bachelor's degree. Additional exam requirements/recommendations for international students: Required—TOEFL. Electronic applications accepted.

Texas Christian University, Neeley School of Business, Master of Accounting Program, Fort Worth, TX 76129. Offers audit (M Ac); taxation (M Ac); valuation and reporting (M Ac). *Accreditation:* AACSB. *Faculty:* 17 full-time (8 women). *Students:* 65 full-time (25 women); includes 6 minority (all Hispanic/Latino), 6 international. Average age 22. 81 applicants, 99% accepted, 65 enrolled. In 2017, 63 master's awarded. *Entrance requirements:* Additional exam requirements/recommendations for international students: Recommended—TOEFL. *Application deadline:* For fall admission, 2/15 for domestic and international students; for spring admission, 9/15 for domestic and international students. Application fee: $0. Electronic applications accepted. *Expenses:* $1,555 per hour tuition, $1,450 per semester fees. *Financial support:* In 2017–18, 33 students received support. Unspecified assistantships available. Financial award application deadline: 1/31. *Faculty research:* Financial accounting, market valuation of accounting information, corporate governance, managerial compensation and incentives, taxation. *Unit head:* Dr. Mary A. Stanford, Department Chair, 817-257-7483, Fax: 817-257-7227, E-mail: m.stanford@tcu.edu. *Application contact:* Renee Olvera, Director, 817-257-7578, Fax: 817-257-7227, E-mail: renee.olvera@tcu.edu.
Website: http://www.neeley.tcu.edu/Academics/Master_of_Accounting/MAc.aspx

Texas Lutheran University, Program in Accounting, Seguin, TX 78155-5999. Offers M Acy.

Texas State University, The Graduate College, Emmett and Miriam McCoy College of Business Administration, Program in Accounting, San Marcos, TX 78666. Offers M Acy. *Program availability:* Part-time. *Faculty:* 14 full-time (7 women), 2 part-time/adjunct (0 women). *Students:* 62 full-time (36 women), 18 part-time (8 women); includes 29 minority (3 Black or African American, non-Hispanic/Latino; 7 Asian, non-Hispanic/Latino; 17 Hispanic/Latino; 2 Two or more races, non-Hispanic/Latino), 3 international. Average age 24. 78 applicants, 40% accepted, 9 enrolled. In 2017, 65 master's awarded. *Degree requirements:* For master's, comprehensive exam. *Entrance requirements:* For master's, GMAT or GRE, baccalaureate degree from regionally-accredited university; two forms of recommendation from persons best able to assess the applicant's ability to succeed in graduate school; essays; resume showing work experience, extracurricular and community activities, and honors and achievements. Additional exam requirements/recommendations for international students: Required—TOEFL (minimum score 550 paper-based; 78 iBT); Recommended—IELTS (minimum score 6.5). *Application deadline:* For fall admission, 2/1 priority date for domestic and international students; for spring admission, 10/1 for domestic and international students; for summer admission, 4/1 for domestic students, 3/15 for international students. Application fee: $40 ($90 for international students). Electronic applications accepted. *Expenses:* Tuition, state resident: full-time $7868; part-time $3934 per semester. Tuition, nonresident: full-time $17,828; part-time $8914 per semester. *Required fees:* $2092; $1435 per semester. Tuition and fees vary according to course load. *Financial support:* In 2017–18, 55 students received support, including 1 research assistantship (averaging $12,152 per year), 12 teaching assistantships (averaging $12,465 per year); Federal Work-Study, institutionally sponsored loans, scholarships/grants, health care benefits, and unspecified assistantships also available. Support available to part-time students. Financial award application deadline: 3/1; financial award applicants required to submit FAFSA. *Unit head:* Dr. William Chittenden, Graduate Advisor, 512-245-3591, Fax: 512-245-8365, E-mail: wc10@txstate.edu. *Application contact:* Dr. Andrea Golato, Dean of Graduate School, 512-245-2581, Fax: 512-245-8365, E-mail: gradcollege@txstate.edu.
Website: http://accounting.mccoy.txstate.edu/

Texas State University, The Graduate College, Emmett and Miriam McCoy College of Business Administration, Program in Accounting and Information Technology, San Marcos, TX 78666. Offers MS. *Program availability:* Part-time. *Faculty:* 13 full-time (2 women), 2 part-time/adjunct (0 women). *Students:* 9 full-time (5 women), 6 part-time (4 women); includes 6 minority (1 Asian, non-Hispanic/Latino; 5 Hispanic/Latino), 4 international. Average age 36. 21 applicants, 43% accepted, 3 enrolled. In 2017, 6 master's awarded. *Degree requirements:* For master's, comprehensive exam. *Entrance requirements:* For master's, GMAT or GRE, baccalaureate degree from regionally-accredited university; two letters or forms of recommendation from persons best able to assess applicant's ability to succeed in graduate school; essay; resume showing work experience, extracurricular and community activities, and honors and achievements. Additional exam requirements/recommendations for international students: Required—TOEFL (minimum score 550 paper-based; 78 iBT), IELTS (minimum score 6.5). *Application deadline:* For fall admission, 2/1 priority date for domestic and international students; for spring admission, 10/1 for domestic and international students. Application fee: $40 ($90 for international students). Electronic applications accepted. *Expenses:* Tuition, state resident: full-time $7868; part-time $3934 per semester. Tuition, nonresident: full-time $17,828; part-time $8914 per semester. *Required fees:* $2092; $1435 per semester. Tuition and fees vary according to course load. *Financial support:* In 2017–18, 7 students received support, including 4 teaching assistantships (averaging

$12,407 per year); research assistantships, Federal Work-Study, institutionally sponsored loans, scholarships/grants, health care benefits, and unspecified assistantships also available. Support available to part-time students. Financial award application deadline: 3/1; financial award applicants required to submit FAFSA. *Unit head:* Dr. William Chittenden, Graduate Advisor, 512-245-3591, Fax: 512-245-8365, E-mail: wc10@txstate.edu. *Application contact:* Dr. Andrea Golato, Dean of Graduate School, 512-245-2581, Fax: 512-245-8365, E-mail: gradcollege@txstate.edu.
Website: http://www.gradcollege.txstate.edu/programs/msait.html

Texas Tech University, Rawls College of Business Administration, Lubbock, TX 79409-2101. Offers accounting (MSA, PhD), including audit/financial reporting (MSA), taxation (MSA); data science (MS); finance (PhD); general business (MBA); healthcare management (MS); information systems and operations management (PhD); management (PhD); marketing (PhD); STEM (MBA); JD/MBA; JD/MSA; MBA/M Arch; MBA/MD; MBA/MS; MBA/Pharm D. *Accreditation:* AACSB. *Program availability:* Evening/weekend, 100% online, blended/hybrid learning. *Faculty:* 89 full-time (22 women). *Students:* 660 full-time (252 women); includes 174 minority (30 Black or African American, non-Hispanic/Latino; 3 American Indian or Alaska Native, non-Hispanic/Latino; 20 Asian, non-Hispanic/Latino; 104 Hispanic/Latino; 17 Two or more races, non-Hispanic/Latino), 99 international. Average age 29. 492 applicants, 51% accepted, 148 enrolled. In 2017, 439 master's, 6 doctorates awarded. *Degree requirements:* For master's, thesis (for MS); capstone course; for doctorate, comprehensive exam, thesis/dissertation, qualifying exams. *Entrance requirements:* For master's, GMAT, GRE, MCAT, PCAT, LSAT, or DAT, holistic review of academic credentials, resume, essay, letters of recommendation; for doctorate, GMAT, GRE, holistic review of academic credentials, resume, statement of purpose, letters of recommendation. Additional exam requirements/recommendations for international students: Required—TOEFL (minimum score 550 paper-based; 79 iBT), IELTS (minimum score 6.5), PTE (minimum score 60). *Application deadline:* For fall admission, 7/1 priority date for domestic students, 1/15 for international students; for spring admission, 12/1 priority date for domestic students, 6/15 for international students; for summer admission, 5/1 for domestic students. Applications are processed on a rolling basis. Application fee: $60. Electronic applications accepted. *Expenses:* $5,167.50 full-time; $9,000 per semester (for hybrid MBA). *Financial support:* In 2017–18, 81 students received support, including 1 research assistantship with full tuition reimbursement available (averaging $22,725 per year), 63 teaching assistantships with full tuition reimbursements available (averaging $22,725 per year); career-related internships or fieldwork, Federal Work-Study, scholarships/grants, health care benefits, and unspecified assistantships also available. Financial award application deadline: 3/1; financial award applicants required to submit FAFSA. *Faculty research:* Governmental and nonprofit accounting, securities and options futures, statistical analysis and design, leadership, consumer behavior. *Total annual research expenditures:* $230,000. *Unit head:* Dr. Margaret Williams, Dean, 806-834-2839, Fax: 806-742-1092, E-mail: margaret.l.williams@ttu.edu. *Application contact:* Jennifer Yack, Applications Manager, Graduate and Professional Programs, 806-742-3184, E-mail: rawlsgrad@ttu.edu.
Website: http://www.depts.ttu.edu/rawlsbusiness/graduate/

Texas Woman's University, Graduate School, College of Business, Denton, TX 76204. Offers business administration (MBA), including accounting, business analytics, healthcare administration (MBA, MHA), human resources management, management; health systems management (MHSM); healthcare administration (MHA), including healthcare administration (MBA, MHA). *Accreditation:* ACBSP. *Program availability:* Part-time. *Faculty:* 32 full-time (12 women), 13 part-time/adjunct (9 women). *Students:* 373 full-time (312 women), 432 part-time (368 women); includes 569 minority (312 Black or African American, non-Hispanic/Latino; 1 American Indian or Alaska Native, non-Hispanic/Latino; 116 Asian, non-Hispanic/Latino; 118 Hispanic/Latino; 3 Native Hawaiian or other Pacific Islander, non-Hispanic/Latino; 19 Two or more races, non-Hispanic/Latino), 35 international. Average age 35. 314 applicants, 82% accepted, 184 enrolled. In 2017, 443 master's awarded. *Degree requirements:* For master's, thesis or alternative, capstone. *Entrance requirements:* For master's, minimum GPA of 3.0 in last 60 hours of undergraduate coursework and prior graduate coursework, 2 letters of reference, resume, 5 years of relevant experience (EMBA only). Additional exam requirements/recommendations for international students: Required—TOEFL (minimum score 550 paper-based; 79 iBT); Recommended—IELTS (minimum score 6.5), TSE (minimum score 53). *Application deadline:* For fall admission, 3/1 priority date for domestic students, 3/1 for international students; for spring admission, 11/1 priority date for domestic students, 7/1 for international students. Applications are processed on a rolling basis. Application fee: $50 ($75 for international students). Electronic applications accepted. *Expenses:* $7,520 per year full-time in-state; $16,820 per year full-time out-of-state. *Financial support:* In 2017–18, 198 students received support. Career-related internships or fieldwork, Federal Work-Study, institutionally sponsored loans, scholarships/grants, traineeships, health care benefits, and unspecified assistantships available. Support available to part-time students. Financial award application deadline: 3/1; financial award applicants required to submit FAFSA. *Faculty research:* Marketing and market research, economics, accounting, logistics and supply chain management, health systems. *Unit head:* Dr. Margaret A. Young, Director, 940-898-2458, Fax: 940-898-2120, E-mail: mba@twu.edu. *Application contact:* Korie Hawkins, Associate Director of Admissions, Graduate Recruitment, 940-898-3188, Fax: 940-898-3081, E-mail: admissions@twu.edu.
Website: http://www.twu.edu/business/

Thomas Edison State University, School of Business and Management, Program in Management, Trenton, NJ 08608. Offers accounting (MSM); organizational leadership (MSM); project management (MSM). *Program availability:* Part-time, 100% online. *Degree requirements:* For master's, final capstone project. *Entrance requirements:* For master's, bachelor's degree from a regionally-accredited college or university; minimum 2 letters of recommendation; 3-5 years of related working experience; current resume. Additional exam requirements/recommendations for international students: Required—TOEFL (minimum score 550 paper-based; 79 iBT). Electronic applications accepted.

Towson University, College of Business and Economics, Program in Accounting, Towson, MD 21252-0001. Offers MS. *Accreditation:* AACSB. *Program availability:* Part-time, evening/weekend. *Students:* 25 full-time (13 women), 8 part-time (4 women); includes 12 minority (4 Black or African American, non-Hispanic/Latino; 3 Asian, non-Hispanic/Latino; 3 Hispanic/Latino; 2 Two or more races, non-Hispanic/Latino), 5 international. *Entrance requirements:* For master's, GMAT, GRE General Test, minimum GPA of 3.0; prerequisite courses in accounting, economics, communications, math, marketing, finance, business law, and business ethics. *Application deadline:* For fall admission, 1/17 for domestic students, 5/15 for international students; for spring admission, 10/15 for domestic students, 12/1 for international students. Applications are processed on a rolling basis. Application fee: $45. Electronic applications accepted. *Expenses:* Tuition, state resident: full-time $7960; part-time $398 per unit. Tuition, nonresident: full-time $16,480; part-time $824 per unit. *Required fees:* $2600; $130 per year. $390 per term. *Unit head:* Dr. Martin Freedman, Program Director, 410-704-4143, E-mail: mfreedman@towson.edu. *Application contact:* Coverley Beidleman, Assistant Director of Graduate Admissions, 410-704-5630, Fax: 410-704-3030, E-mail: cbeidleman@towson.edu.
Website: https://www.towson.edu/cbe/departments/accounting/gradaccounting/

Trinity University, School of Business, San Antonio, TX 78212-7200. Offers accounting (MS). *Accreditation:* AACSB. *Entrance requirements:* For master's, GMAT, minimum GPA of 3.0, course work in accounting and business law, letters of recommendation. *Application deadline:* For fall admission, 2/1 for domestic and international students. Electronic applications accepted. *Financial support:* Institutionally sponsored loans and scholarships/grants available. Financial award application deadline: 5/1; financial award applicants required to submit FAFSA. *Unit head:* Dr. Julie Persellin, Chair, Department of Accounting, 210-999-7230, E-mail: jpersell@trinity.edu. *Application contact:* Dr. Julie Persellin, Chair, Department of Accounting, 210-999-7230, E-mail: jpersell@trinity.edu. Website: https://new.trinity.edu/academics/departments/school-business/graduate-accounting-program

Troy University, Graduate School, College of Business, Program in Accountancy, Troy, AL 36082. Offers M Acc. *Program availability:* Part-time, evening/weekend. *Faculty:* 5 full-time (3 women). *Students:* 19 full-time (8 women), 8 part-time (7 women); includes 2 minority (1 Black or African American, non-Hispanic/Latino; 1 Asian, non-Hispanic/Latino). Average age 24. 20 applicants, 95% accepted, 8 enrolled. In 2017, 16 master's awarded. *Degree requirements:* For master's, minimum GPA of 3.0, research course. *Entrance requirements:* For master's, GMAT (minimum score of 500), bachelor's degree; minimum undergraduate GPA of 2.5 or 3.0 on last 30 semester hours, letter of recommendation. Additional exam requirements/recommendations for international students: Required—TOEFL (minimum score 523 paper-based; 70 iBT), IELTS (minimum score 6). *Application deadline:* Applications are processed on a rolling basis. Application fee: $50. Electronic applications accepted. *Expenses:* Tuition, state resident: part-time $417 per credit hour. Tuition, nonresident: part-time $834 per credit hour. *Required fees:* $42 per credit hour. $50 per semester. Tuition and fees vary according to campus/location. *Financial support:* Fellowships, career-related internships or fieldwork, and scholarships/grants available. Support available to part-time students. Financial award applicants required to submit FAFSA. *Unit head:* Dr. Steve Grice, Chairman, Master of Accountancy, 334-670-3154, Fax: 334-670-3592, E-mail: sgrice@troy.edu. *Application contact:* Jessica A. Kimbro, Director of Graduate Admissions, 334-670-3178, E-mail: jacord@troy.edu.

Troy University, Graduate School, College of Business, Program in Business Administration, Troy, AL 36082. Offers accounting (EMBA, MBA); criminal justice (EMBA); finance (MBA); general management (EMBA, MBA); healthcare management (EMBA); information systems (EMBA, MBA); international economic development (MBA). *Accreditation:* ACBSP. *Program availability:* Part-time, evening/weekend. *Faculty:* 6 full-time (2 women), 1 part-time/adjunct (0 women). *Students:* 43 full-time (22 women), 115 part-time (55 women); includes 50 minority (31 Black or African American, non-Hispanic/Latino; 12 Asian, non-Hispanic/Latino; 6 Hispanic/Latino; 1 Two or more races, non-Hispanic/Latino). Average age 30. 156 applicants, 76% accepted, 36 enrolled. In 2017, 95 master's awarded. *Degree requirements:* For master's, minimum GPA of 3.0, capstone course, research course. *Entrance requirements:* For master's, GMAT (minimum score 500) or GRE (minimum score 900 on old exam or 294 on new exam), bachelor's degree; minimum undergraduate GPA of 2.5 or 3.0 on last 30 semester hours, letter of recommendation. Additional exam requirements/recommendations for international students: Required—TOEFL (minimum score 523 paper-based; 70 iBT), IELTS (minimum score 6). *Application deadline:* Applications are processed on a rolling basis. Application fee: $50. Electronic applications accepted. *Expenses:* Tuition, state resident: part-time $417 per credit hour. Tuition, nonresident: part-time $834 per credit hour. *Required fees:* $42 per credit hour. $50 per semester. Tuition and fees vary according to campus/location. *Financial support:* Fellowships, career-related internships or fieldwork, and scholarships/grants available. Support available to part-time students. Financial award applicants required to submit FAFSA. *Unit head:* Dr. Phillip Mixon, MBA Director, 334-670-3140, Fax: 334-670-3708, E-mail: pamixon@troy.edu. *Application contact:* Jessica A. Kimbro, Director of Graduate Admissions, 334-670-3178, E-mail: jacord@troy.edu.

Truman State University, Graduate School, School of Business, Program in Accounting, Kirksville, MO 63501-4221. Offers M Ac. *Accreditation:* AACSB. *Degree requirements:* For master's, comprehensive exam. *Entrance requirements:* For master's, GMAT, minimum GPA of 3.0. Additional exam requirements/recommendations for international students: Required—TOEFL (minimum score 550 paper-based). Electronic applications accepted.

Tulane University, A. B. Freeman School of Business, New Orleans, LA 70118-5669. Offers accounting (M Acct); analytics (MBA); banking and financial services (M Fin); energy (M Fin, MBA); entrepreneurship (MBA); finance (MBA, PhD); financial accounting (PhD); international business (MBA); international management (MBA); strategic management and leadership (MBA); JD/M Acct; JD/MBA; MBA/M Acc; MBA/MA; MBA/MD; MBA/ME; MBA/MPH. *Accreditation:* AACSB. *Program availability:* Part-time, evening/weekend. *Faculty:* 51 full-time (15 women), 38 part-time/adjunct (3 women). *Students:* 561 full-time (287 women), 297 part-time (151 women); includes 112 minority (43 Black or African American, non-Hispanic/Latino; 2 American Indian or Alaska Native, non-Hispanic/Latino; 24 Asian, non-Hispanic/Latino; 38 Hispanic/Latino; 5 Two or more races, non-Hispanic/Latino), 515 international. Average age 27. 2,021 applicants, 74% accepted, 476 enrolled. In 2017, 632 master's, 9 doctorates awarded. Terminal master's awarded for partial completion of doctoral program. *Degree requirements:* For master's, one foreign language, comprehensive exam (for some programs); for doctorate, one foreign language, comprehensive exam, thesis/dissertation. *Entrance requirements:* For master's and doctorate, GMAT or GRE, interview. Additional exam requirements/recommendations for international students: Required—TOEFL or IELTS. *Application deadline:* For fall admission, 11/1 priority date for domestic and international students; for winter admission, 1/6 for domestic and international students; for spring admission, 3/1 priority date for domestic and international students; for summer admission, 5/5 for domestic students. Applications are processed on a rolling basis. Application fee: $125. Electronic applications accepted. *Expenses:* Contact institution. *Financial support:* In 2017–18, 176 students received support. Fellowships with tuition reimbursements available, research assistantships, teaching assistantships, career-related internships or fieldwork, Federal Work-Study, tuition waivers (full and partial), and unspecified assistantships available. Support available to part-time students. Financial award application deadline: 4/15; financial award applicants required to submit FAFSA. *Faculty research:* Corporate finance, managerial accounting and financial reporting, strategic management and leadership, consumer behavior and decision making, organizational behavior and human resource management. *Unit head:* Ira Solomon, PhD, Dean, 504-865-5407, Fax: 504-865-5491, E-mail: businessdean@tulane.edu. *Application contact:* Melissa Booth, Assistant Dean for Graduate Admissions, 800-223-5402, E-mail: freeman.admissions@tulane.edu. Website: http://www.freeman.tulane.edu

Union University, McAfee School of Business Administration, Jackson, TN 38305-3697. Offers accountancy (M Acc). Program also available at Germantown campus. *Program availability:* Evening/weekend, online learning. *Entrance requirements:* For master's, GMAT, minimum GPA of 2.5. Electronic applications accepted. *Expenses:* Contact institution. *Faculty research:* Personal financial management, strategy, accounting, marketing, economics.

Universidad del Este, Graduate School, Carolina, PR 00984. Offers accounting (MBA); adult education (M Ed); agribusiness (MBA); criminal justice and criminology (MA); curriculum and instruction - early education (M Ed); curriculum and instruction - elementary (M Ed); curriculum and instruction - English (M Ed); curriculum and instruction - Spanish (M Ed); human resources (MBA); information security management (MBA); information technology and Web business development (MBA); management (MBA); public policy (MPA); social work (MA), including clinical social work; special education (M Ed); strategic leadership (MBA).

Universidad del Turabo, Graduate Programs, School of Business and Entrepreneurship, Program in Accounting, Gurabo, PR 00778-3030. Offers MBA. *Program availability:* Part-time, evening/weekend. *Entrance requirements:* For master's, GRE, EXADEP, GMAT, interview, essay, official transcript, recommendation letters. Electronic applications accepted.

Universidad Metropolitana, School of Business Administration, Program in Accounting, San Juan, PR 00928-1150. Offers MBA. *Program availability:* Part-time. *Degree requirements:* For master's, thesis or alternative. *Entrance requirements:* For master's, GMAT, PAEG, interview. Electronic applications accepted.

Université de Sherbrooke, Faculty of Administration, Program in Accounting, Sherbrooke, QC J1K 2R1, Canada. Offers M Sc. *Degree requirements:* For master's, one foreign language, thesis. *Entrance requirements:* For master's, bachelor's degree in related field, minimum GPA of 3.0 (on 4.3 scale). Electronic applications accepted. *Faculty research:* Financial analysis, management accounting, certification, system and control.

Université du Québec à Montréal, Graduate Programs, Program in Accounting, Montréal, QC H3C 3P8, Canada. Offers M Sc, MPA, Diploma. *Program availability:* Part-time. *Degree requirements:* For master's, thesis (for some programs). *Entrance requirements:* For master's, appropriate bachelor's degree or equivalent and proficiency in French.

Université du Québec à Trois-Rivières, Graduate Programs, Program in Accounting Science, Trois-Rivières, QC G9A 5H7, Canada. Offers MBA.

Université du Québec en Outaouais, Graduate Programs, Program in Accounting, Gatineau, QC J8X 3X7, Canada. Offers MA, DESS, Diploma. *Program availability:* Part-time, evening/weekend.

Université du Québec en Outaouais, Graduate Programs, Program in Executive Certified Management Accounting, Gatineau, QC J8X 3X7, Canada. Offers MA, MBA, DESS. *Program availability:* Part-time, evening/weekend. *Degree requirements:* For master's, thesis (for some programs).

Université Laval, Faculty of Administrative Sciences, Programs in Business Administration, Québec, QC G1K 7P4, Canada. Offers accounting (MBA); agri-food management (MBA); electronic business (MBA, Diploma); factory management and logistics (MBA); finance (MBA); firm management (MBA); geomatic management (MBA); information technology management (MBA); international management (MBA); management (MBA); management accounting (MBA, Diploma); marketing (MBA); modeling and organizational decision (MBA); occupational health and safety management (MBA); pharmacy management (MBA); social and environmental responsibility (MBA); technological entrepreneurship (Diploma). *Accreditation:* AACSB. *Program availability:* Part-time, evening/weekend, online learning. *Entrance requirements:* For master's and Diploma, knowledge of French and English. Electronic applications accepted.

Université Laval, Faculty of Administrative Sciences, Programs in Public Accountancy, Québec, QC G1K 7P4, Canada. Offers MBA, Diploma. *Program availability:* Part-time. *Entrance requirements:* For master's and Diploma, knowledge of French and English. Electronic applications accepted.

University at Buffalo, the State University of New York, Graduate School, School of Management, Buffalo, NY 14260. Offers accounting (MS); analytics (MBA); business administration (PMBA); consulting (MBA); finance (MBA, MS), including financial risk management (MS); quantitative finance (MS); healthcare (MBA); information assurance (MBA); information systems (MBA); international management (MBA); management (EMBA, PhD); management information systems (MS); marketing (MBA); supply chain and operations (MBA); supply chains and operations management (MS); Au D/MBA; DDS/MBA; JD/MBA; M Arch/MBA; MD/MBA; MPH/MBA; MSW/MBA; Pharm D/MBA. *Accreditation:* AACSB. *Program availability:* Part-time, evening/weekend. *Faculty:* 80 full-time (26 women), 45 part-time/adjunct (12 women). *Students:* 597 full-time (251 women); includes 83 minority (19 Black or African American, non-Hispanic/Latino; 59 Asian, non-Hispanic/Latino; 5 Hispanic/Latino), 306 international. Average age 25. 2,109 applicants, 46% accepted, 376 enrolled. In 2017, 371 master's, 13 doctorates awarded. *Degree requirements:* For master's, capstone courses or projects; for doctorate, comprehensive exam, thesis/dissertation. *Entrance requirements:* For master's, GMAT (for MS in accounting, finance); GRE or GMAT (for MBA, MS in management information systems, supply chains and operations management), essays, letters of recommendation; for doctorate, GMAT or GRE, essays, writing sample, letters of recommendation. Additional exam requirements/recommendations for international students: Required—TOEFL (minimum score 95 iBT) or IELTS (minimum score 6.5); Recommended—TSE (minimum score 73). *Application deadline:* For fall admission, 10/15 priority date for domestic and international students; for winter admission, 2/1 priority date for domestic and international students; for spring admission, 4/15 for domestic students; for summer admission, 5/15 for domestic students. Application fee: $100. Electronic applications accepted. *Expenses:* Varies by program. *Financial support:* Fellowships with full and partial tuition reimbursements, research assistantships with full and partial tuition reimbursements, teaching assistantships with full and partial tuition reimbursements, career-related internships or fieldwork, Federal Work-Study, institutionally sponsored loans, scholarships/grants, health care benefits, and unspecified assistantships available. Financial award application deadline: 2/15. *Faculty research:* Data analytics, accounting and law, rate finance, consumer behavior, supply chain logistics, leadership and team effectiveness. *Total annual research expenditures:* $968,376. *Unit head:* Erin K. O'Brien, Assistant Dean and Director of Graduate Programs, 716-645-3204, Fax: 716-645-2341, E-mail: ekobrien@buffalo.edu. *Application contact:* Meghan Felser, Director of Admissions and Recruiting, 716-645-3204, Fax: 716-645-2341, E-mail: mpwood@buffalo.edu. Website: http://mgt.buffalo.edu/

The University of Akron, Graduate School, College of Business Administration, The George W. Daverio School of Accountancy, Program in Accounting, Akron, OH 44325. Offers MSA. *Students:* 25 full-time (9 women), 11 part-time (5 women); includes 4 minority (1 Black or African American, non-Hispanic/Latino; 2 Hispanic/Latino; 1 Two or more races, non-Hispanic/Latino), 6 international. Average age 28. 24 applicants, 92% accepted, 20 enrolled. In 2017, 14 master's awarded. *Entrance requirements:* For master's, GMAT, GRE, MCAT, LSAT, PCAT, or CAT, minimum GPA of 3.0 (preferred), two letters of recommendation, resume, statement of purpose. Additional exam requirements/recommendations for international students: Required—TOEFL (minimum score 79 iBT), IELTS (minimum score 6.5). *Unit head:* Dr. Thomas Calderon, Chair, 330-972-6099, E-mail: tcalderon@uakron.edu. *Application contact:* Dr. William Hauser, Director of Graduate Business Programs, 330-972-7043, Fax: 330-972-6588, E-mail: whauser@uakron.edu.

Accounting

The University of Alabama, Graduate School, Manderson Graduate School of Business, Culverhouse School of Accountancy, Tuscaloosa, AL 35487. Offers accounting (M Acc, PhD); tax accounting (MTA). *Accreditation:* AACSB. *Faculty:* 20 full-time (5 women). *Students:* 104 full-time (46 women), 2 part-time (both women); includes 11 minority (5 Black or African American, non-Hispanic/Latino; 1 American Indian or Alaska Native, non-Hispanic/Latino; 2 Asian, non-Hispanic/Latino; 2 Hispanic/Latino; 1 Two or more races, non-Hispanic/Latino), 2 international. Average age 24. 185 applicants, 58% accepted, 89 enrolled. In 2017, 103 master's, 1 doctorate awarded. *Degree requirements:* For doctorate, thesis/dissertation. *Entrance requirements:* For master's, GMAT, minimum GPA of 3.0 overall or on last 60 hours; for doctorate, GMAT, minimum GPA of 3.0. Additional exam requirements/recommendations for international students: Required—TOEFL. *Application deadline:* For fall admission, 7/1 priority date for domestic students, 6/1 priority date for international students; for spring admission, 11/1 priority date for domestic students, 9/1 priority date for international students. Applications are processed on a rolling basis. Application fee: $50 ($60 for international students). Electronic applications accepted. *Financial support:* In 2017–18, 42 students received support, including fellowships with full tuition reimbursements available (averaging $15,000 per year), research assistantships with tuition reimbursements available (averaging $9,765 per year), teaching assistantships with tuition reimbursements available (averaging $13,352 per year); career-related internships or fieldwork, Federal Work-Study, institutionally sponsored loans, scholarships/grants, health care benefits, and unspecified assistantships also available. Financial award application deadline: 3/31. *Faculty research:* Corporate governance, audit decision-making, earning management, valuation, executive compensation. *Unit head:* Dr. Richard Houston, Director, 205-348-8392, E-mail: rhouston@culverhouse.ua.edu. *Application contact:* Candace Peters, Advisor, 205-348-6131, Fax: 205-348-8453, E-mail: cpeters@cba.ua.edu.
Website: http://www.cba.ua.edu/accounting/

The University of Alabama at Birmingham, Collat School of Business, Program in Accounting, Birmingham, AL 35294. Offers accounting (M Acct), including internal auditing. *Accreditation:* AACSB. *Program availability:* Part-time, evening/weekend, 100% online, blended/hybrid learning. *Faculty:* 12 full-time (1 woman), 1 (woman) part-time/adjunct. *Students:* 29 full-time (8 women), 114 part-time (71 women); includes 41 minority (21 Black or African American, non-Hispanic/Latino; 1 American Indian or Alaska Native, non-Hispanic/Latino; 9 Asian, non-Hispanic/Latino; 8 Hispanic/Latino; 2 Two or more races, non-Hispanic/Latino), 2 international. Average age 33. 83 applicants, 62 enrolled. In 2017, 83 master's awarded. *Entrance requirements:* For master's, GMAT (minimum score of 500). Additional exam requirements/recommendations for international students: Required—TOEFL (minimum score 80 iBT). *Application deadline:* For fall admission, 7/1 for domestic and international students; for spring admission, 11/1 for domestic students, 10/1 for international students; for summer admission, 4/1 for domestic and international students. Application fee: $60 ($75 for international students). Electronic applications accepted. *Financial support:* Applicants required to submit FAFSA. *Faculty research:* Capital markets, accounting information systems, international accounting, regulatory oversight, earnings forecasts. *Unit head:* Dr. Arline Savage, Director, Master of Accounting Program, 205-934-8825, Fax: 205-975-4429, E-mail: arlsav@uab.edu. *Application contact:* Christy Manning, Admissions Counselor, 205-934-8815, Fax: 205-975-5933, E-mail: cmanning@uab.edu.
Website: http://www.uab.edu/business/degrees-certificates/master-of-accounting

The University of Alabama in Huntsville, School of Graduate Studies, College of Business Administration, Program in Accounting, Huntsville, AL 35899. Offers accounting (M Acc), including CPA preparatory with an emphasis in taxation, CPA preparatory with emphasis in assurance and financial reporting, general accounting, information systems audit and control (ISAC). *Accreditation:* AACSB. *Program availability:* Part-time, evening/weekend. *Degree requirements:* For master's, comprehensive exam, thesis or alternative. *Entrance requirements:* For master's, GMAT (minimum score 500), minimum AACSB index of 1080. Additional exam requirements/recommendations for international students: Required—TOEFL (minimum score 550 paper-based; 80 iBT), IELTS (minimum score 6.5). Electronic applications accepted. *Faculty research:* Accounting information systems, managerial accounting, behavioral accounting, state and local taxation, financial accounting.

The University of Alabama in Huntsville, School of Graduate Studies, College of Business Administration, Programs in Business and Management, Huntsville, AL 35899. Offers business analytics (MSMS); federal contracting and procurement management (Certificate); human resource management (MSM); management (MBA), including acquisition management, entrepreneurship, federal contract accounting, finance, human resource management, logistics and supply chain management, marketing, project management; supply chain management (Certificate); technology and innovation management (Certificate). *Accreditation:* AACSB. *Program availability:* Part-time, evening/weekend. *Degree requirements:* For master's, comprehensive exam, thesis or alternative. *Entrance requirements:* For master's, GMAT (minimum score 500), minimum AACSB index of 1080. Additional exam requirements/recommendations for international students: Required—TOEFL (minimum score 550 paper-based; 80 iBT), IELTS (minimum score 6.5). Electronic applications accepted. *Faculty research:* Supply chain management, management of research and development, international marketing and branding, organizational behavior and human resource management, social networks and computational economics.

University of Alberta, Faculty of Graduate Studies and Research, Doctoral Program in Business, Edmonton, AB T6G 2E1, Canada. Offers accounting (PhD); finance (PhD); human resources/industrial relations (PhD); management science (PhD); marketing (PhD); organizational analysis (PhD); MBA/PhD. *Accreditation:* AACSB. *Program availability:* Part-time. *Degree requirements:* For doctorate, comprehensive exam, thesis/dissertation. *Entrance requirements:* For doctorate, GMAT. Additional exam requirements/recommendations for international students: Required—TOEFL (minimum score 550 paper-based). Electronic applications accepted. *Faculty research:* Accounting, capital markets and corporate finance, organizational change and human resource management, marketing, strategic management.

The University of Arizona, Eller College of Management, Department of Accounting, Tucson, AZ 85721. Offers M Ac, MS. *Accreditation:* AACSB. *Program availability:* Part-time. *Degree requirements:* For master's, comprehensive exam, 1-year residency. *Entrance requirements:* For master's, GMAT (minimum score 550), 2 letters of recommendation, 3 writing samples, resume. Additional exam requirements/recommendations for international students: Required—TOEFL (minimum score 600 paper-based; 100 iBT). Electronic applications accepted. *Expenses:* Contact institution. *Faculty research:* Auditing, financial reporting and financial markets, taxation policy and markets, behavioral research in accounting.

University of Arkansas, Graduate School, Sam M. Walton College of Business Administration, Department of Accounting, Fayetteville, AR 72701. Offers M Acc. *Accreditation:* AACSB. In 2017, 51 master's awarded. *Entrance requirements:* For master's, GMAT. *Application deadline:* For fall admission, 8/1 for domestic students, 4/1 for international students; for spring admission, 12/1 for domestic students, 10/1 for international students; for summer admission, 4/15 for domestic students, 3/1 for

international students. Application fee: $60. Electronic applications accepted. *Expenses:* Tuition, state resident: full-time $3782. Tuition, nonresident: full-time $10,238. *Financial support:* In 2017–18, 18 research assistantships, 2 teaching assistantships were awarded; fellowships with tuition reimbursements, career-related internships or fieldwork, and Federal Work-Study also available. Support available to part-time students. Financial award application deadline: 4/1; financial award applicants required to submit FAFSA. *Unit head:* Dr. Gary Peters, Department Chair, 479-575-4117, Fax: 479-575-2863, E-mail: gfpeters@walton.uark.edu.
Website: https://accounting.uark.edu/

University of Baltimore, Graduate School, Merrick School of Business, Department of Accounting, Baltimore, MD 21201-5779. Offers accounting and business advisory services (MS); accounting fundamentals (Graduate Certificate); forensic accounting (Graduate Certificate); taxation (MS). *Program availability:* Part-time, evening/weekend. *Entrance requirements:* For master's, GMAT. Additional exam requirements/recommendations for international students: Required—TOEFL (minimum score 550 paper-based). Electronic applications accepted. *Faculty research:* Health care, accounting and administration, managerial accounting, financial accounting theory, accounting information.

University of Baltimore, Graduate School, Merrick School of Business, Department of Information Systems and Decision Science, Baltimore, MD 21201-5779. Offers accounting and business advisory services (MS).

University of Bridgeport, School of Business, Bridgeport, CT 06604. Offers accounting (MBA); finance (MBA); general business (MBA); global financial services (MBA); human resource management (MBA); information systems and knowledge management (MBA); international business (MBA); management (MBA); marketing (MBA); operations management (MBA); small business and entrepreneurship (MBA); specialized business (MBA). *Accreditation:* ACBSP. *Program availability:* Part-time, evening/weekend. *Degree requirements:* For master's, thesis optional. *Entrance requirements:* For master's, GMAT. Additional exam requirements/recommendations for international students: Recommended—TOEFL (minimum score 550 paper-based; 80 iBT), IELTS (minimum score 6.5). Electronic applications accepted. *Expenses:* Contact institution.

The University of British Columbia, Sauder School of Business, Doctoral Program in Business Administration, Vancouver, BC V6T 1Z2, Canada. Offers accounting (PhD); finance (PhD); management information systems (PhD); management science (PhD); marketing (PhD); organizational behavior (PhD); strategy and business economics (PhD); transportation and logistics (PhD); urban land economics (PhD). *Degree requirements:* For doctorate, comprehensive exam, thesis/dissertation. *Entrance requirements:* For doctorate, GMAT or GRE. Additional exam requirements/recommendations for international students: Required—TOEFL (minimum score 600 paper-based; 100 iBT). Electronic applications accepted. *Expenses:* Contact institution.

University of California, Berkeley, Graduate Division, Haas School of Business, PhD in Business Administration Program, Berkeley, CA 94720-1500. Offers accounting (PhD); business and public policy (PhD); finance (PhD); management of organizations (PhD); marketing (PhD); real estate (PhD). *Accreditation:* AACSB. *Students:* 72 full-time (20 women); includes 30 minority (26 Asian, non-Hispanic/Latino; 4 Hispanic/Latino). Average age 27. *Degree requirements:* For doctorate, comprehensive exam, thesis/dissertation, written preliminary exams, oral qualifying exam. *Entrance requirements:* For doctorate, GMAT or GRE, minimum GPA of 3.0 in undergraduate and graduate coursework. Additional exam requirements/recommendations for international students: Required—TOEFL (minimum score 570 paper-based; 70 iBT), IELTS (minimum score 7). *Application deadline:* For fall admission, 12/1 for domestic and international students. Application fee: $105 ($125 for international students). Electronic applications accepted. *Expenses:* Contact institution. *Financial support:* Fellowships with tuition reimbursements, research assistantships with tuition reimbursements, teaching assistantships with tuition reimbursements, scholarships/grants, health care benefits, tuition waivers (full), unspecified assistantships, and transit passes, travel grants available. Financial award application deadline: 12/1. *Faculty research:* Accounting, business and public policy, entrepreneurship, finance, management of organizations, marketing, operations and information technology management, real estate. *Unit head:* Dr. Nicolae Garleanu, Director, 510-643-6349, Fax: 510-643-4255. *Application contact:* Melissa Hacker, Director, Student Affairs, 510-642-3944, Fax: 510-643-4255, E-mail: melhacker@haas.berkeley.edu.
Website: http://www.haas.berkeley.edu/Phd/

University of California, Berkeley, UC Berkeley Extension, Certificate Programs in Business, Berkeley, CA 94720-1500. Offers accounting (Certificate); business administration (Certificate); finance (Certificate); human resource management (Certificate); management (Certificate); marketing (Certificate); project management (Certificate). *Accreditation:* AACSB. *Program availability:* Online learning.

University of California, Davis, Graduate School of Management, Full-Time MBA Program, Davis, CA 95616. Offers business analytics and technologies (MBA); entrepreneurship and innovation (MBA); finance and accounting (MBA); general management (MBA); marketing (MBA); organizational behavior (MBA); public health management (MBA); strategy (MBA); technology management (MBA); DVM/MBA; JD/MBA; M Engr/MBA; MBA/MPH; MBA/MS; MD/MBA; MSN/MBA; PhD/MBA. *Faculty:* 52 full-time (15 women). *Students:* 96 full-time (42 women); includes 31 minority (1 Black or African American, non-Hispanic/Latino; 17 Asian, non-Hispanic/Latino; 5 Hispanic/Latino; 8 Two or more races, non-Hispanic/Latino), 36 international. Average age 29. 290 applicants, 37% accepted, 45 enrolled. In 2017, 44 master's awarded. *Degree requirements:* For master's, integrated management project. *Entrance requirements:* For master's, GMAT or GRE, letters of recommendation, resume, essays, equivalent of a 4-year U.S. undergraduate degree, transcript. Additional exam requirements/recommendations for international students: Required—TOEFL (minimum score 600 paper-based; 100 iBT), IELTS (minimum score 7). *Application deadline:* For fall admission, 5/18 priority date for domestic and international students. Application fee: $125. Electronic applications accepted. *Expenses:* Contact institution. *Financial support:* In 2017–18, 90 students received support. Fellowships, research assistantships, teaching assistantships with partial tuition reimbursements available, institutionally sponsored loans, scholarships/grants, health care benefits, tuition waivers (partial), and unspecified assistantships available. Financial award application deadline: 3/1; financial award applicants required to submit FAFSA. *Faculty research:* Finance, marketing, management, business analytics, accounting. *Unit head:* James Stevens, Senior Assistant Dean of Student Affairs, 530-752-7658, Fax: 530-754-9355, E-mail: admissions@gsm.ucdavis.edu. *Application contact:* Kristy Bird MaKieve, Interim Director of Admissions, 530-754-5476, Fax: 530-754-9355, E-mail: admissions@gsm.ucdavis.edu.
Website: http://gsm.ucdavis.edu/daytime-mba-program

University of California, Davis, Graduate School of Management, Master of Professional Accountancy Program, Davis, CA 95616. Offers audit analytics (MP Ac); financial accounting (MP Ac). *Faculty:* 11 full-time (4 women). *Students:* 50 full-time (37 women); includes 12 minority (1 Black or African American, non-Hispanic/Latino; 7 Asian, non-Hispanic/Latino; 4 Hispanic/Latino), 19 international. Average age 24. 449 applicants, 21% accepted, 50 enrolled. In 2017, 55 master's awarded. *Entrance*

requirements: For master's, GMAT or GRE, letters of recommendation, resume, essays, equivalent of a 4-year U.S. undergraduate degree. Additional exam requirements/recommendations for international students: Required—TOEFL (minimum score 600 paper-based; 100 iBT), IELTS (minimum score 7). *Application deadline:* For fall admission, 5/18 priority date for domestic and international students. Application fee: $125. Electronic applications accepted. *Expenses:* Contact institution. *Financial support:* In 2017–18, 34 students received support. Fellowships, research assistantships, teaching assistantships with partial tuition reimbursements available, scholarships/grants, and tuition waivers (partial) available. Financial award application deadline: 3/1; financial award applicants required to submit FAFSA. *Faculty research:* Financial accounting, audit, audit analytics, business ethics, taxation. *Unit head:* James Stevens, Senior Assistant Dean of Student Affairs, 530-752-7658, Fax: 530-754-9355, E-mail: admissions@gsm.ucdavis.edu. *Application contact:* Kristy Bird MaKieve, Interim Director of Admissions, 530-754-5476, Fax: 530-754-9355, E-mail: admissions@gsm.ucdavis.edu.
Website: http://gsm.ucdavis.edu/master-professional-accountancy

University of California, Davis, Graduate School of Management, MBA Programs in Sacramento and San Francisco Bay Area, Davis, CA 95616. Offers business analytics and technologies (MBA); entrepreneurship and innovation (MBA); finance and accounting (MBA); general management (MBA); marketing (MBA); organizational behavior (MBA); public health management (MBA); strategy (MBA); technology management (MBA). *Program availability:* Part-time-only, evening/weekend. *Faculty:* 99 part-time/adjunct (30 women). *Students:* 323 part-time (133 women); includes 148 minority (7 Black or African American, non-Hispanic/Latino; 96 Asian, non-Hispanic/Latino; 26 Hispanic/Latino; 1 Native Hawaiian or other Pacific Islander, non-Hispanic/Latino; 18 Two or more races, non-Hispanic/Latino), 37 international. Average age 30. 202 applicants, 75% accepted, 111 enrolled. In 2017, 112 master's awarded. *Degree requirements:* For master's, integrated management project. *Entrance requirements:* For master's, GMAT or GRE, letters of recommendation, resume, equivalent of a 4-year undergraduate degree. Additional exam requirements/recommendations for international students: Required—TOEFL (minimum score 600 paper-based; 100 iBT), IELTS (minimum score 7). *Application deadline:* For fall admission, 5/18 priority date for domestic and international students. Application fee: $125. Electronic applications accepted. *Expenses:* Contact institution. *Financial support:* In 2017–18, 67 students received support. Fellowships, teaching assistantships with partial tuition reimbursements available, scholarships/grants, and unspecified assistantships available. Support available to part-time students. Financial award application deadline: 3/1; financial award applicants required to submit FAFSA. *Faculty research:* Accounting, finance, marketing, management, business analytics. *Unit head:* James Stevens, Senior Assistant Dean of Student Affairs, 530-752-7658, Fax: 530-754-9355, E-mail: admissions@gsm.ucdavis.edu. *Application contact:* Kristy Bird MaKieve, Interim Director of Admissions, 530-754-5476, Fax: 530-754-9355, E-mail: admissions@gsm.ucdavis.edu.
Website: http://gsm.ucdavis.edu/mba-programs

University of California, Irvine, The Paul Merage School of Business, Program in Professional Accountancy, Irvine, CA 92697. Offers MPA. *Students:* 137 full-time (93 women), 2 part-time (both women); includes 38 minority (2 Black or African American, non-Hispanic/Latino; 2 American Indian or Alaska Native, non-Hispanic/Latino; 33 Asian, non-Hispanic/Latino; 1 Hispanic/Latino), 39 international. Average age 25. 771 applicants, 35% accepted, 139 enrolled. In 2017, 107 master's awarded. Application fee: $105 ($125 for international students). *Unit head:* Morton Pincus, Director, 949-824-4062, E-mail: mpincus@uci.edu. *Application contact:* Burt Slusher, Senior Associate Director, Recruitment and Admissions, 949-824-1609, E-mail: bslusher@uci.edu.
Website: http://merage.uci.edu/MPAc/

University of California, Los Angeles, Graduate Division, UCLA Anderson School of Management, Los Angeles, CA 90095-1481. Offers accounting (PhD); behavioral decision making (PhD); business administration (EMBA, MBA); business analytics (MSBA); decisions, operations, and technology management (PhD); finance (PhD); financial engineering (MFE); global economics and management (PhD); management and organizations (PhD); marketing (PhD); strategy and policy (PhD); DDS/MBA; MBA/JD; MBA/MD; MBA/MLAS; MBA/MLIS; MBA/MN; MBA/MPH; MBA/MPP; MBA/MSCS; MBA/MURP. *Accreditation:* AACSB. *Program availability:* Part-time, evening/weekend. *Faculty:* 88 full-time (20 women), 107 part-time/adjunct (21 women). *Students:* 918 full-time (314 women), 1,269 part-time (399 women); includes 743 minority (38 Black or African American, non-Hispanic/Latino; 3 American Indian or Alaska Native, non-Hispanic/Latino; 531 Asian, non-Hispanic/Latino; 115 Hispanic/Latino; 4 Native Hawaiian or other Pacific Islander, non-Hispanic/Latino; 52 Two or more races, non-Hispanic/Latino), 544 international. Average age 31. 5,842 applicants, 29% accepted, 1015 enrolled. In 2017, 855 master's, 14 doctorates awarded. Terminal master's awarded for partial completion of doctoral program. *Degree requirements:* For master's, comprehensive exam, field consulting project (for MBA, FEMBA, EMBA and GEMBA); internship (for MBA only); thesis/dissertation (for MFE); 10 capstone (for MSBA); for doctorate, comprehensive exam, thesis/dissertation, oral and written qualifying exams. *Entrance requirements:* For master's, GMAT or GRE, 4-year bachelor's degree or equivalent; 2 letters of recommendation; interview (by invitation only); 2 essays; 4-8 years of full-time work experience (for FEMBA only); minimum eight years of work experience with at least three years at management level (for EMBA only); for doctorate, GMAT or GRE, bachelor's degree from college or university of fully-recognized standing, minimum B average during junior and senior undergraduate years, 3 letters of recommendation, statement of purpose. Additional exam requirements/recommendations for international students: Required—TOEFL (minimum score 560 paper-based; 87 iBT), IELTS (minimum score 7), TOEFL with minimum iBT score of 100 (for MSBA). *Application deadline:* For fall admission, 10/2 for domestic and international students; for winter admission, 1/8 for domestic and international students; for spring admission, 4/16 for domestic and international students. Applications are processed on a rolling basis. Application fee: $200. Electronic applications accepted. *Expenses:* Contact institution. *Financial support:* In 2017–18, 649 students received support, including 440 fellowships (averaging $29,273 per year); research assistantships with partial tuition reimbursements available, teaching assistantships with partial tuition reimbursements available, career-related internships or fieldwork, institutionally sponsored loans, and scholarships/grants also available. Support available to part-time students. *Faculty research:* Finance/global economics, entrepreneurship, accounting, human resources/organizational behavior, marketing and behavioral decision-making. *Total annual research expenditures:* $1.3 million. *Unit head:* Dean, 310-825-7982, Fax: 310-206-2073. *Application contact:* Alex Lawrence, Assistant Dean and Director of MBA Admissions, 310-825-6944, Fax: 310-825-8582, E-mail: mba.admissions@anderson.ucla.edu.
Website: http://www.anderson.ucla.edu/

University of California, Riverside, Graduate Division, The A. Gary Anderson Graduate School of Management, Riverside, CA 92521-0102. Offers accounting (MPAC); business administration (MBA, PhD); finance (M Fin). *Accreditation:* AACSB. *Program availability:* Part-time, evening/weekend. *Faculty:* 32 full-time (8 women), 18 part-time/adjunct (7 women). *Students:* 180 full-time (92 women), 114 part-time (48 women); includes 75 minority (13 Black or African American, non-Hispanic/Latino; 1

American Indian or Alaska Native, non-Hispanic/Latino; 33 Asian, non-Hispanic/Latino; 28 Hispanic/Latino), 187 international. Average age 27. 722 applicants, 63% accepted, 169 enrolled. In 2017, 133 master's, 1 doctorate awarded. Terminal master's awarded for partial completion of doctoral program. *Degree requirements:* For master's, thesis optional; for doctorate, comprehensive exam, thesis/dissertation. *Entrance requirements:* For master's and doctorate, GMAT or GRE. Additional exam requirements/recommendations for international students: Required—TOEFL (minimum score 550 paper-based; 80 iBT), IELTS (minimum score 7). *Application deadline:* For fall admission, 9/1 for domestic students, 5/1 for international students; for winter admission, 12/1 for domestic students, 9/1 for international students; for spring admission, 3/1 for domestic students, 10/1 for international students. Applications are processed on a rolling basis. Application fee: $100 ($125 for international students). Electronic applications accepted. *Expenses:* Contact institution. *Financial support:* Fellowships with partial tuition reimbursements, research assistantships with full tuition reimbursements, teaching assistantships with partial tuition reimbursements, career-related internships or fieldwork, institutionally sponsored loans, scholarships/grants, and tuition waivers (full) available. Financial award application deadline: 5/1; financial award applicants required to submit FAFSA. *Faculty research:* Finance, management, marketing, operations and supply chain management, accounting and information systems. *Unit head:* Yunzeng Wang, Dean, School of Business, 951-827-3704, E-mail: yunzeng.wang@ucr.edu. *Application contact:* Mark Estrada, Director of Graduate Admissions, 951-827-2915, E-mail: mark.estrada@ucr.edu.
Website: http://agsm.ucr.edu/

University of Central Arkansas, Graduate School, College of Business Administration, Program in Accounting, Conway, AR 72035-0001. Offers M Acc. *Program availability:* Part-time. *Degree requirements:* For master's, capstone course. *Entrance requirements:* For master's, GMAT or GRE, minimum GPA of 2.7. Additional exam requirements/recommendations for international students: Required—TOEFL (minimum score 550 paper-based; 80 iBT).

University of Central Florida, College of Business Administration, Kenneth G. Dixon School of Accounting, Orlando, FL 32816. Offers MSA. *Accreditation:* AACSB. *Program availability:* Part-time, evening/weekend. *Students:* 91 full-time (43 women), 60 part-time (32 women); includes 47 minority (4 Black or African American, non-Hispanic/Latino; 20 Asian, non-Hispanic/Latino; 17 Hispanic/Latino; 6 Two or more races, non-Hispanic/Latino), 3 international. Average age 28. 119 applicants, 56% accepted, 49 enrolled. In 2017, 79 master's awarded. *Degree requirements:* For master's, comprehensive exam. *Entrance requirements:* For master's, GMAT, minimum GPA of 3.0 in last 60 hours, resume. Additional exam requirements/recommendations for international students: Required—TOEFL. *Application deadline:* For fall admission, 7/15 for domestic students; for spring admission, 12/1 for domestic students; for summer admission, 4/15 for domestic students. Application fee: $30. Electronic applications accepted. *Expenses:* Tuition, state resident: part-time $288.16 per credit hour. Tuition, nonresident: part-time $1073.31 per credit hour. Tuition and fees vary according to program. *Financial support:* In 2017–18, 20 students received support, including 1 research assistantship with partial tuition reimbursement available (averaging $180 per year), 20 teaching assistantships with partial tuition reimbursements available (averaging $9,445 per year); fellowships, career-related internships or fieldwork, Federal Work-Study, institutionally sponsored loans, health care benefits, tuition waivers (partial), and unspecified assistantships also available. Financial award application deadline: 3/1; financial award applicants required to submit FAFSA. *Unit head:* Dr. Gregory Trompeter, Director, 407-823-2876, Fax: 407-823-3881, E-mail: trompete@ucf.edu. *Application contact:* Associate Director, Graduate Admissions, 407-823-2766, Fax: 407-823-6442, E-mail: gradadmissions@ucf.edu.
Website: https://business.ucf.edu/departments-schools/kenneth-g-dixon-school-of-accounting/

University of Central Missouri, The Graduate School, Warrensburg, MO 64093. Offers accountancy (MA); accounting (MBA); applied mathematics (MS); aviation safety (MA); biology (MS); business administration (MBA); career and technical education leadership (MS); college student personnel administration (MS); communication (MA); computer science (MS); counseling (MS); criminal justice (MS); educational leadership (Ed D); educational technology (MS); elementary and early childhood education (MSE); English (MA); environmental studies (MA); finance (MBA); history (MA); human services/educational technology (Ed S); human services/learning resources (Ed S); human services/professional counseling (Ed S); industrial hygiene (MS); industrial management (MS); information systems (MBA); information technology (MS); kinesiology (MS); library science and information services (MS); literacy education (MSE); marketing (MBA); mathematics (MS); music (MA); occupational safety management (MS); psychology (MS); rural family nursing (MS); school administration (MSE); social gerontology (MS); sociology (MA); special education (MSE); speech language pathology (MS); superintendency (Ed S); teaching (MAT); teaching English as a second language (MA); technology (MS); technology management (PhD); theatre (MA). *Program availability:* Part-time, 100% online, blended/hybrid learning. *Faculty:* 337 full-time (145 women), 41 part-time/adjunct (28 women). *Students:* 785 full-time (398 women), 1,633 part-time (1,063 women); includes 231 minority (102 Black or African American, non-Hispanic/Latino; 4 American Indian or Alaska Native, non-Hispanic/Latino; 16 Asian, non-Hispanic/Latino; 52 Hispanic/Latino; 57 Two or more races, non-Hispanic/Latino), 692 international. Average age 30. In 2017, 2,605 master's, 122 other advanced degrees awarded. *Degree requirements:* For master's and Ed S, comprehensive exam (for some programs), thesis (for some programs). *Entrance requirements:* Additional exam requirements/recommendations for international students: Required—TOEFL (minimum score 550 paper-based; 79 iBT). *Application deadline:* For fall admission, 6/1 priority date for domestic and international students; for spring admission, 10/1 priority date for domestic and international students; for summer admission, 4/1 priority date for domestic and international students. Applications are processed on a rolling basis. Application fee: $30 ($75 for international students). Electronic applications accepted. *Expenses:* Tuition, state resident: full-time $8771; part-time $292.35 per credit hour. Tuition, nonresident: full-time $17,541; part-time $584.70 per credit hour. *Required fees:* $372; $24.78 per credit hour. *Financial support:* In 2017–18, 99 students received support. Research assistantships, teaching assistantships, career-related internships or fieldwork, Federal Work-Study, scholarships/grants, and administrative and laboratory assistantships available. Support available to part-time students. Financial award application deadline: 3/1; financial award applicants required to submit FAFSA. *Unit head:* Shellie Hewitt, Director of Graduate and International Student Services, 660-543-4621, Fax: 660-543-4778, E-mail: hewitt@ucmo.edu. *Application contact:* 660-543-4621, E-mail: admit_intl@ucmo.edu.
Website: http://www.ucmo.edu/graduate/

University of Charleston, Master of Forensic Accounting Program, Charleston, WV 25304-1099. Offers EMFA. *Program availability:* Part-time, blended/hybrid learning. *Entrance requirements:* Additional exam requirements/recommendations for international students: Required—TOEFL. Electronic applications accepted.

University of Chicago, Booth School of Business, Full-Time MBA Program, Chicago, IL 60637. Offers accounting (MBA); analytic finance (MBA); analytic management (MBA); econometrics and statistics (MBA); economics (MBA); entrepreneurship (MBA); finance (MBA); general management (MBA); health administration and policy (Certificate);

international business (MBA); managerial and organizational behavior (MBA); marketing analytics (MBA); marketing management (MBA); operations management (MBA); strategic management (MBA); MBA/AM; MBA/JD; MBA/MA; MBA/MD; MBA/MPP. *Accreditation:* AACSB. *Faculty:* 154 full-time (26 women), 61 part-time/adjunct (12 women). *Students:* 1,176 full-time (481 women). In 2017, 586 master's awarded. *Entrance requirements:* For master's, GMAT or GRE, transcripts, resume, 2 letters of recommendation, essays, interview. Additional exam requirements/recommendations for international students: Required—TOEFL, IELTS, or PTE. *Application deadline:* for fall admission, 9/1 for domestic and international students; for winter admission, 1/1 for domestic and international students; for spring admission, 4/1 for domestic and international students. Application fee: $250. Electronic applications accepted. *Expenses:* Contact institution. *Unit head:* Stacey Kole, Deputy Dean for Alumni, Corporate Relations, and the Full-time MBA Program, 773-702-7121. *Application contact:* Kurt Ahlm, Associate Dean for Student Recruitment and Admissions, 773-702-7369, Fax: 773-702-9085, E-mail: admissions@chicagobooth.edu. Website: https://www.chicagobooth.edu/programs/full-time

University of Cincinnati, Carl H. Lindner College of Business, MS Program, Cincinnati, OH 45221. Offers accounting (MS); applied economics (MS); business analytics (MS); finance (MS); information systems (MS); marketing (MS); taxation (MS). *Program availability:* Part-time, evening/weekend. *Faculty:* 65 full-time (20 women), 27 part-time/adjunct (6 women). *Students:* 324 full-time (132 women), 204 part-time (77 women); includes 50 minority (18 Black or African American, non-Hispanic/Latino; 21 Asian, non-Hispanic/Latino; 5 Hispanic/Latino; 1 Native Hawaiian or other Pacific Islander, non-Hispanic/Latino; 5 Two or more races, non-Hispanic/Latino), 299 international. Average age 28. 1,756 applicants, 24% accepted, 351 enrolled. In 2017, 369 master's awarded. *Degree requirements:* For master's, thesis (for some programs), capstone. *Entrance requirements:* For master's, GMAT, GRE, resume, transcripts, essays, letters of recommendation. Additional exam requirements/recommendations for international students: Required—TOEFL (minimum score 577 paper-based; 90 iBT), IELTS (minimum score 6.5). *Application deadline:* For fall admission, 6/30 priority date for domestic students, 3/15 for international students; for spring admission, 12/15 for domestic students, 9/15 for international students; for summer admission, 4/15 for domestic and international students. Applications are processed on a rolling basis. Application fee: $65 ($70 for international students). Electronic applications accepted. *Expenses:* $10,479 per term full-time resident, $14,398 per term full-time nonresident, $890 per credit hour part-time. *Financial support:* In 2017–18, 251 students received support, including 12 teaching assistantships with full and partial tuition reimbursements available (averaging $3,500 per year); scholarships/grants, tuition waivers (full and partial), and unspecified assistantships also available. Financial award application deadline: 2/1; financial award applicants required to submit FAFSA. *Faculty research:* Business analytics, financial management, organizational behavior, financial accounting, consumer insights. *Total annual research expenditures:* $24,842. *Unit head:* Dr. David Szymanski, Dean, 513-556-7001, Fax: 513-556-4891, E-mail: david.szymanski@uc.edu. *Application contact:* Dona Clary, Executive Director, Graduate Programs, 513-556-3546, Fax: 513-558-7006, E-mail: dona.clary@uc.edu. Website: http://business.uc.edu/graduate/masters.html

University of Cincinnati, Carl H. Lindner College of Business, PhD Programs, Cincinnati, OH 45221. Offers accounting (PhD); business analytics (PhD); economics (PhD); finance (PhD); information systems (PhD); management (PhD); marketing (PhD); operations and business analytics (PhD); operations research (PhD). *Faculty:* 37 full-time (13 women). *Students:* 29 full-time (12 women), 12 part-time (6 women); includes 5 minority (1 Black or African American, non-Hispanic/Latino; 4 Asian, non-Hispanic/Latino), 20 international. Average age 30. 123 applicants, 16% accepted, 11 enrolled. In 2017, 3 doctorates awarded. *Degree requirements:* For doctorate, comprehensive exam, thesis/dissertation. *Entrance requirements:* For doctorate, GMAT, GRE, transcripts, essays, resume, letters of recommendation. Additional exam requirements/recommendations for international students: Required—TOEFL (minimum score 600 paper-based; 100 iBT), IELTS (minimum score 7). *Application deadline:* For fall admission, 1/15 for domestic and international students. Application fee: $65 ($70 for international students). Electronic applications accepted. *Expenses:* $7,234 resident per term, $13,105 nonresident per term. *Financial support:* In 2017–18, 41 students received support, including 29 research assistantships with full tuition reimbursements available (averaging $23,250 per year); scholarships/grants, health care benefits, tuition waivers (full), and unspecified assistantships also available. Financial award application deadline: 1/15; financial award applicants required to submit FAFSA. *Faculty research:* Bayesian Prediction Theory, organizational fairness, consumer insight and market research, consumer insight and market research, density estimation from correlated data. *Unit head:* Dr. Suzanne Masterson, Director, 513-556-7125, Fax: 513-556-5499, E-mail: suzanne.masterson@uc.edu. *Application contact:* Angel Elvin, Assistant Director, 513-556-7190, Fax: 513-558-7006, E-mail: angel.elvin@uc.edu. Website: http://business.uc.edu/graduate/phd.html

University of Colorado Denver, Business School, Program in Accounting, Denver, CO 80217. Offers accounting and information systems audit control (MS); auditing and forensic accounting (MS); controllership and financial leadership (MS). *Accreditation:* AACSB. *Program availability:* Part-time, evening/weekend. *Degree requirements:* For master's, 30 semester hours. *Entrance requirements:* For master's, GMAT (waived for students who already hold a graduate degree, or an undergraduate degree from CU Denver), essay, resume, two letters of recommendation; financial statements for international students). Additional exam requirements/recommendations for international students: Required—TOEFL (minimum score 537 paper-based; 75 iBT); Recommended—IELTS (minimum score 6.5). Electronic applications accepted. *Expenses:* Contact institution. *Faculty research:* Transportation, energy, communications, healthcare, nano-science and engineering, unmanned aircraft systems, biomedical applications, aerosol mechanics, interface mechanics during rapid evaporation, low SWAP-C inertial navigation systems.

University of Colorado Denver, Business School, Program in Information Systems, Denver, CO 80217. Offers accounting and information systems audit and control (MS); business intelligence systems (MS); digital health entrepreneurship (MS); enterprise risk management (MS); enterprise technology management (MS); geographic information systems (MS); health information technology (MS); technology innovation and entrepreneurship (MS); Web and mobile computing (MS). *Program availability:* Part-time, evening/weekend, online learning. *Degree requirements:* For master's, 30 credit hours. *Entrance requirements:* For master's, GMAT, resume, essay, two letters of recommendation, financial statements (for international applicants). Additional exam requirements/recommendations for international students: Required—TOEFL (minimum score 525 paper-based; 71 iBT); Recommended—IELTS (minimum score 6.5). Electronic applications accepted. *Expenses:* Contact institution. *Faculty research:* Human-computer interaction, expert systems, database management, electronic commerce, object-oriented software development.

University of Connecticut, Graduate School, School of Business, Field of Accounting, Storrs, CT 06269. Offers MS. *Accreditation:* AACSB. *Entrance requirements:* Additional exam requirements/recommendations for international students: Required—TOEFL (minimum score 550 paper-based). Electronic applications accepted.

University of Dallas, Satish and Yasmin Gupta College of Business, Irving, TX 75062-4736. Offers accounting (MBA, MS); business administration (DBA); business analytics (MS); business management (MBA); corporate finance (MBA); cybersecurity (MS); finance (MS); financial services (MBA); global business (MBA, MS); health services management (MBA); human resource management (MBA); information and technology management (MS); information assurance (MBA); information technology (MBA); information technology service management (MBA); marketing management (MBA); organization development (MBA); project management (MBA); sports and entertainment management (MBA); strategic leadership (MBA); supply chain management (MBA). *Accreditation:* AACSB. *Program availability:* Part-time, evening/weekend, online learning. *Entrance requirements:* Additional exam requirements/recommendations for international students: Required—TOEFL. *Application deadline:* Applications are processed on a rolling basis. Application fee: $50. Electronic applications accepted. *Expenses:* Contact institution. *Financial support:* Application deadline: 2/15; applicants required to submit FAFSA. *Unit head:* Brett J.L. Landry, Dean, 972-721-5356, E-mail: blandry@udallas.edu. *Application contact:* Dr. David Sweet, Dean, Braniff Graduate School, 972-721-5288, Fax: 972-721-5280, E-mail: dsweet@udallas.edu. Website: http://www.udallas.edu/cob/

University of Dayton, School of Business Administration, Dayton, OH 45469. Offers accounting (MBA); cyber security (MBA); finance (MBA); marketing (MBA); JD/MBA. *Accreditation:* AACSB. *Program availability:* Part-time, evening/weekend, blended/hybrid learning. *Faculty:* 23 full-time (8 women), 12 part-time/adjunct (2 women). *Students:* 57 full-time (24 women), 82 part-time (32 women); includes 10 minority (5 Black or African American, non-Hispanic/Latino; 2 Asian, non-Hispanic/Latino; 3 Hispanic/Latino), 18 international. Average age 31. 269 applicants, 31% accepted. In 2017, 88 master's awarded. *Entrance requirements:* For master's, GMAT (minimum score of 500 total, 19 verbal); GRE (minimum score of 149 verbal, 146 quantitative), minimum GPA of 3.0, current resume. Additional exam requirements/recommendations for international students: Required—TOEFL (minimum score 550 paper-based; 80 iBT); Recommended—IELTS (minimum score 6.5). *Application deadline:* For fall admission, 5/1 for international students; for spring admission, 11/1 for international students. Applications are processed on a rolling basis. Application fee: $0 ($50 for international students). Electronic applications accepted. *Expenses:* Contact institution. *Financial support:* In 2017–18, 10 research assistantships with partial tuition reimbursements (averaging $9,295 per year) were awarded; teaching assistantships, career-related internships or fieldwork, institutionally sponsored loans, scholarships/grants, traineeships, tuition waivers, and unspecified assistantships also available. Financial award application deadline: 3/1; financial award applicants required to submit FAFSA. *Faculty research:* Management information systems, economics, finance, marketing, entrepreneurship, accounting, cyber security, analytics. *Unit head:* Scott MacDonald, Director, MBA Program, 937-229-3733, Fax: 937-229-3882, E-mail: smacdonald1@udayton.edu. *Application contact:* Mandy Bingaman, MBA Program Manager, 937-229-3733, Fax: 937-229-3882, E-mail: mbingaman1@udayton.edu. Website: https://www.udayton.edu/business/academics/master_of_business_administration/index.php

University of Delaware, Alfred Lerner College of Business and Economics, Department of Accounting and Management Information Systems, Newark, DE 19716. Offers accounting (MS); information systems and technology management (MS). *Accreditation:* AACSB. *Program availability:* Part-time, evening/weekend. *Degree requirements:* For master's, thesis optional. *Entrance requirements:* For master's, GMAT. Additional exam requirements/recommendations for international students: Required—TOEFL (minimum score 550 paper-based). Electronic applications accepted. *Faculty research:* External reporting, managerial accounting, auditing information systems, taxation.

University of Denver, Daniels College of Business, School of Accountancy, Denver, CO 80208. Offers accounting (M Acc, MBA). *Accreditation:* AACSB. *Program availability:* Part-time, evening/weekend. *Faculty:* 19 full-time (8 women), 7 part-time/adjunct (1 woman). *Students:* 31 full-time (19 women), 42 part-time (31 women); includes 17 minority (1 Black or African American, non-Hispanic/Latino; 1 American Indian or Alaska Native, non-Hispanic/Latino; 6 Asian, non-Hispanic/Latino; 8 Hispanic/Latino; 1 Two or more races, non-Hispanic/Latino), 31 international. Average age 26. 189 applicants, 46% accepted, 28 enrolled. In 2017, 110 master's awarded. *Entrance requirements:* For master's, GRE General Test or GMAT, bachelor's degree, transcripts, resume, two letters of recommendation, essays, interview. Additional exam requirements/recommendations for international students: Required—TOEFL (minimum score 570 paper-based; 88 iBT). *Application deadline:* For fall admission, 11/15 priority date for domestic and international students; for spring admission, 10/1 priority date for domestic and international students. Applications are processed on a rolling basis. Application fee: $100. Electronic applications accepted. *Expenses:* $47,823 per year full-time; $1,320 per credit. *Financial support:* In 2017–18, 70 students received support, including 3 teaching assistantships with tuition reimbursements available (averaging $1,242 per year); career-related internships or fieldwork, Federal Work-Study, institutionally sponsored loans, scholarships/grants, and unspecified assistantships also available. Support available to part-time students. Financial award application deadline: 2/15; financial award applicants required to submit FAFSA. *Faculty research:* Financial accounting and reporting, performance measurement, corporate governance, auditing, data security. *Unit head:* Dr. Sharon Lassar, Professor/Director, School of Accountancy, 303-871-2032, Fax: 303-871-2016, E-mail: slassar@du.edu. *Application contact:* Jacquelyn Villa, Assistant to the Director, 303-871-2032, E-mail: jacquelyn.villa@du.edu. Website: https://daniels.du.edu/accountancy

University of Detroit Mercy, College of Business Administration, Detroit, MI 48221. Offers business administration (MBA); business fundamentals (Certificate); business turnaround management (Certificate); ethical leadership and change management (Certificate); finance (Certificate); forensic accounting (Certificate); JD/MBA; MBA/MHSA. *Program availability:* Part-time, evening/weekend, 100% online, blended/hybrid learning. *Entrance requirements:* For master's, GMAT, resume, letter of recommendation, transcripts; for Certificate, resume, letter of recommendation, transcripts. Electronic applications accepted. Application fee is waived when completed online. *Expenses:* Contact institution. *Faculty research:* Ethics, international finance, trade policy, leadership, information technology.

The University of Findlay, Office of Graduate Admissions, Findlay, OH 45840. Offers applied security and analytics (MSAS); athletic training (MAT); business (MBA), including certified management accountant, certified public accountant, health care management, hospitality management; education (MA Ed, Ed D), including children's literature (MA Ed), curriculum and teaching (MA Ed), education (MA Ed), educational administration (MA Ed), human resource development (MA Ed), mathematics (MA Ed), reading (MA Ed), science education (MA Ed), superintendent (Ed D), teaching (Ed D), technology (MA Ed); environmental, safety, and health management (MSEM); health informatics (MS); occupational therapy (MOT); pharmacy (Pharm D); physical therapy (DPT); physician assistant (MPA); rhetoric and writing (MA); teaching English to speakers of other languages (TESOL) and applied linguistics (MA). *Program availability:* Part-time, evening/weekend, 100% online, blended/hybrid learning. *Students:* 688 full-time (430 women), 553 part-time (308 women), 170 international. Average age 28. In

2017, 366 master's, 137 doctorates awarded. *Degree requirements:* For master's, comprehensive exam (for some programs), thesis (for some programs), cumulative project, capstone project; for doctorate, thesis/dissertation (for some programs). *Entrance requirements:* For master's, GRE/GMAT, bachelor's degree from accredited institution, minimum undergraduate GPA of 2.5 in last 64 hours of course work; for doctorate, GRE, MAT, minimum cumulative GPA of 3.0. Additional exam requirements/recommendations for international students: Required—TOEFL (minimum score 79 iBT), IELTS (minimum score 7), PTE (minimum score 61). *Application deadline:* Applications are processed on a rolling basis. Electronic applications accepted. *Financial support:* In 2017–18, 10 research assistantships with partial tuition reimbursements (averaging $7,200 per year), 35 teaching assistantships with partial tuition reimbursements (averaging $7,200 per year) were awarded; Federal Work-Study, institutionally sponsored loans, and unspecified assistantships also available. Financial award applicants required to submit FAFSA. *Unit head:* Christopher M. Harris, Director of Admissions, 419-434-4347, E-mail: harrisc1@findlay.edu. *Application contact:* Madeline Fauser Brennan, Graduate Admissions Counselor, 419-434-4636, Fax: 419-434-4898, E-mail: fauserbrennan@findlay.edu.
Website: http://www.findlay.edu/admissions/graduate/Pages/default.aspx

University of Florida, Graduate School, Warrington College of Business Administration, Fisher School of Accounting, Gainesville, FL 32611. Offers M Acc, PhD, JD/M Acc. *Accreditation:* AACSB. *Program availability:* Part-time. *Degree requirements:* For master's, comprehensive exam, thesis optional; for doctorate, comprehensive exam, thesis/dissertation. *Entrance requirements:* For master's, GMAT (minimum score of 465) or GRE General Test, minimum GPA of 3.0. Additional exam requirements/recommendations for international students: Required—TOEFL (minimum score 550 paper-based; 80 iBT), IELTS (minimum score 6). Electronic applications accepted. *Faculty research:* Financial reporting, managerial accounting, auditing, taxation.

University of Georgia, Terry College of Business, J.M. Tull School of Accounting, Athens, GA 30602. Offers M Acc. *Accreditation:* AACSB. *Entrance requirements:* For master's, GMAT. Electronic applications accepted.

University of Hartford, Barney School of Business, Department of Accounting and Taxation, West Hartford, CT 06117-1599. Offers professional accounting (Certificate); taxation (MSAT). *Program availability:* Part-time, evening/weekend. *Entrance requirements:* For master's, GMAT, 2 letters of recommendation, resume. Additional exam requirements/recommendations for international students: Required—TOEFL (minimum score 550 paper-based). Electronic applications accepted.

University of Hawaii at Manoa, Office of Graduate Education, Shidler College of Business, Program in Accounting, Honolulu, HI 96822. Offers accounting (M Acc); accounting law (M Acc); information systems (M Acc); taxation (M Acc). *Program availability:* Part-time. *Entrance requirements:* For master's, GMAT, bachelor's degree in accounting, minimum GPA of 3.0. Additional exam requirements/recommendations for international students: Required—TOEFL (minimum score 550 paper-based; 79 iBT), IELTS (minimum score 5). *Faculty research:* International accounting, current tax topics, insurance industry financial reporting, behavioral accounting, auditing.

University of Hawaii at Manoa, Office of Graduate Education, Shidler College of Business, Program in International Management, Honolulu, HI 96822. Offers Asian finance (PhD); global information technology management (PhD); international accounting (PhD); international marketing (PhD); international organization and strategy (PhD). *Program availability:* Part-time. *Degree requirements:* For doctorate, comprehensive exam, thesis/dissertation. *Entrance requirements:* For doctorate, GMAT or GRE General Test, minimum GPA of 3.0. Additional exam requirements/recommendations for international students: Required—TOEFL (minimum score 600 paper-based; 100 iBT), IELTS (minimum score 7). *Expenses:* Contact institution.

University of Houston, Bauer College of Business, Accountancy and Taxation Program, Houston, TX 77204. Offers accountancy (MS Accy); accountancy and taxation (PhD). *Accreditation:* AACSB. *Program availability:* Part-time, evening/weekend. *Degree requirements:* For master's, 30 hours completed in residence, minimum cumulative GPA of 3.0 at UH, no more than 11 semester hours of 'C' grades or below in graduate courses taken at UH; for doctorate, continuous full time enrollment, dissertation defense within 6 years of entering the program. *Entrance requirements:* For master's, GMAT, official transcripts from all higher education institutions attended, letters of recommendation, resume, goals statement; for doctorate, GMAT or GRE, letter of financial backing, statement of understanding, reference letters, statement of academic and research interests. Additional exam requirements/recommendations for international students: Required—TOEFL (minimum score 550 paper-based; 79 iBT), IELTS (minimum score 6.5), PTE (minimum score 70). Electronic applications accepted. *Faculty research:* Accountancy and taxation, finance, international business, management.

University of Houston–Clear Lake, School of Business, Program in Accounting, Houston, TX 77058-1002. Offers accounting (MS); professional accounting (MS). *Accreditation:* AACSB. *Program availability:* Part-time, evening/weekend. *Degree requirements:* For master's, thesis optional. *Entrance requirements:* For master's, GMAT. Additional exam requirements/recommendations for international students: Required—TOEFL (minimum score 550 paper-based). Electronic applications accepted.

University of Houston–Downtown, Marilyn Davies College of Business, MBA Program, Houston, TX 77002. Offers accounting (MBA); finance (MBA); human resource management (MBA); international business (MBA); investment management (MBA); leadership (MBA); project management and process improvement (MBA); sales management and business development (MBA); supply chain management (MBA). *Accreditation:* AACSB. *Program availability:* Part-time, evening/weekend. *Faculty:* 36 full-time (13 women), 11 part-time/adjunct (6 women). *Students:* 4 full-time (2 women), 1,065 part-time (605 women); includes 821 minority (383 Black or African American, non-Hispanic/Latino; 3 American Indian or Alaska Native, non-Hispanic/Latino; 136 Asian, non-Hispanic/Latino; 299 Hispanic/Latino), 33 international. Average age 33. 418 applicants, 89% accepted, 308 enrolled. In 2017, 310 master's awarded. *Entrance requirements:* For master's, GMAT, two letters of recommendation from professional references, personal statement, resume. Additional exam requirements/recommendations for international students: Required—TOEFL (minimum score 81 iBT). *Application deadline:* For fall admission, 8/1 for domestic and international students. Application fee: $35 ($60 for international students). Electronic applications accepted. *Expenses:* $360 per credit resident; $725 per credit non-resident. *Financial support:* Federal Work-Study and scholarships/grants available. Financial award application deadline: 4/1; financial award applicants required to submit FAFSA. *Unit head:* Dr. Charles E. Gengler, Dean, 713-221-8179, Fax: 713-221-8675. *Application contact:* Ceshia Love, Director of Admissions, 713-221-8093, Fax: 713-223-7408, E-mail: gradadmissions@uhd.edu.
Website: http://mba.uhd.edu/

University of Houston–Victoria, School of Business Administration, Victoria, TX 77901-4450. Offers accounting (MBA); economic development and entrepreneurship (MS); finance (GMBA, MBA); general business (MBA); international business (MBA); management (GMBA, MBA); marketing (MBA). *Accreditation:* AACSB. *Program availability:* Part-time, evening/weekend, online learning. *Entrance requirements:* For

master's, GMAT. Additional exam requirements/recommendations for international students: Required—TOEFL (minimum score 550 paper-based). Electronic applications accepted. *Faculty research:* Economic development, marketing, finance.

University of Idaho, College of Graduate Studies, College of Business and Economics, Department of Accounting, Moscow, ID 83844. Offers accountancy (M Acct). *Accreditation:* AACSB. *Faculty:* 5 full-time. *Students:* 22 full-time, 5 part-time. Average age 29. In 2017, 19 master's awarded. *Entrance requirements:* For master's, minimum GPA of 3.0. Additional exam requirements/recommendations for international students: Required—TOEFL (minimum score 88 iBT). *Application deadline:* For fall admission, 7/1 for domestic students; for spring admission, 11/1 for domestic students. Applications are processed on a rolling basis. Application fee: $60. Electronic applications accepted. *Expenses:* Tuition, state resident: full-time $6722; part-time $430 per credit hour. Tuition, nonresident: full-time $23,046; part-time $1337 per credit hour. *Required fees:* $2142; $63 per credit hour. *Financial support:* Research assistantships and teaching assistantships available. Financial award applicants required to submit FAFSA. *Unit head:* Dr. Marla Kraut, Head, 208-885-6453, Fax: 208-885-6296, E-mail: amberg@uidaho.edu. *Application contact:* Sean Scoggin, Graduate Recruitment Coordinator, 208-885-4001, Fax: 208-885-4406, E-mail: graduateadmissions@uidaho.edu.
Website: http://www.uidaho.edu/cbe

University of Illinois at Chicago, Liautaud Graduate School of Business, Department of Accounting, Chicago, IL 60607-7128. Offers MS, MBA/MS. *Accreditation:* AACSB. *Program availability:* Part-time. *Entrance requirements:* For master's, GMAT, minimum GPA of 2.75. Additional exam requirements/recommendations for international students: Required—TOEFL. Electronic applications accepted. *Expenses:* Contact institution. *Faculty research:* Governmental accounting, managerial accounting, auditing.

University of Illinois at Springfield, Graduate Programs, College of Business and Management, Program in Accountancy, Springfield, IL 62703-5407. Offers MA. *Program availability:* Part-time, evening/weekend. *Faculty:* 10 full-time (1 woman), 1 part-time/adjunct (0 women). *Students:* 50 full-time (27 women), 41 part-time (25 women); includes 5 minority (2 Black or African American, non-Hispanic/Latino; 3 Asian, non-Hispanic/Latino), 28 international. Average age 28. 61 applicants, 62% accepted, 23 enrolled. In 2017, 37 master's awarded. *Degree requirements:* For master's, closure exercise including capstone courses, thesis or projects. *Entrance requirements:* For master's, minimum undergraduate GPA of 2.7 in prerequisite coursework; introductory course in financial and managerial accounting, college math through business calculus, principles of economics (micro and macro), and statistics. Additional exam requirements/recommendations for international students: Required—TOEFL (minimum score 550 paper-based). *Application deadline:* Applications are processed on a rolling basis. Application fee: $60 ($75 for international students). Electronic applications accepted. *Expenses:* Tuition, state resident: full-time $7896; part-time $329 per credit hour. Tuition, nonresident: full-time $16,200; part-time $675 per credit hour. Tuition and fees vary according to program. *Financial support:* In 2017–18, research assistantships with full tuition reimbursements (averaging $10,249 per year), teaching assistantships with full tuition reimbursements (averaging $10,303 per year) were awarded; fellowships, career-related internships or fieldwork, Federal Work-Study, scholarships/grants, health care benefits, and unspecified assistantships also available. Support available to part-time students. Financial award application deadline: 11/15; financial award applicants required to submit FAFSA. *Unit head:* Dr. Mark Buxton, Program Administrator, 217-206-6299, Fax: 217-206-7914, E-mail: mbuxt2@uis.edu.
Website: http://www.uis.edu/accountancy

University of Illinois at Urbana–Champaign, Graduate College, Gies College of Business, Department of Accountancy, Champaign, IL 61820. Offers accountancy (MS, PhD); accounting science (MAS). *Accreditation:* AACSB.

The University of Iowa, Tippie College of Business, M Ac Program in Accounting, Iowa City, IA 52242-1316. Offers M Ac, JD/M Ac. *Faculty:* 2 full-time (1 woman). *Students:* 33 full-time (13 women); includes 3 minority (1 Hispanic/Latino; 2 Two or more races, non-Hispanic/Latino), 5 international. Average age 25. 121 applicants, 26% accepted, 27 enrolled. In 2017, 32 master's awarded. *Entrance requirements:* Additional exam requirements/recommendations for international students: Required—TOEFL (minimum score 100 iBT). *Application deadline:* For fall admission, 7/15 for domestic students, 4/15 priority date for international students; for spring admission, 12/1 for domestic students, 10/1 priority date for international students; for summer admission, 4/1 for domestic students, 3/1 priority date for international students. Application fee: $60 ($100 for international students). Electronic applications accepted. *Expenses:* Contact institution. *Financial support:* In 2017–18, 39 students received support, including 18 fellowships (averaging $4,400 per year), 15 teaching assistantships with partial tuition reimbursements available (averaging $19,016 per year); scholarships/grants and health care benefits also available. Financial award application deadline: 3/1; financial award applicants required to submit FAFSA. *Unit head:* Prof. Daniel W. Collins, Dean, 319-335-0910, Fax: 319-335-1956, E-mail: daniel-collins@uiowa.edu. *Application contact:* Renea L. Jay, Associate Director, Non-MBA Graduate Programs, 319-335-0930, Fax: 319-335-0860, E-mail: renea-jay@uiowa.edu.
Website: https://tippie.uiowa.edu/accounting

The University of Iowa, Tippie College of Business, PhD Program in Accounting, Iowa City, IA 52242-1316. Offers PhD. *Accreditation:* AACSB. *Faculty:* 11 full-time (3 women). *Students:* 11 full-time (4 women); includes 3 minority (1 American Indian or Alaska Native, non-Hispanic/Latino; 2 Asian, non-Hispanic/Latino), 5 international. Average age 32. 54 applicants, 6% accepted, 2 enrolled. In 2017, 3 doctorates awarded. *Degree requirements:* For doctorate, comprehensive exam, thesis/dissertation. *Entrance requirements:* For doctorate, GMAT. Additional exam requirements/recommendations for international students: Required—TOEFL (minimum score 100 iBT), IELTS (minimum score 7). *Application deadline:* For fall admission, 1/15 priority date for domestic students, 1/15 for international students. Application fee: $60 ($100 for international students). Electronic applications accepted. *Financial support:* In 2017–18, 11 students received support, including 11 fellowships with full tuition reimbursements available (averaging $11,500 per year), 11 teaching assistantships with full tuition reimbursements available (averaging $19,016 per year); scholarships/grants, health care benefits, and unspecified assistantships also available. Financial award application deadline: 1/15. *Faculty research:* Corporate financial reporting issues; financial statement information and capital markets; cost structure: analysis, estimation, and management; experimental and prediction economics; income taxes and interaction of financial and tax reporting systems. *Unit head:* Prof. Daniel W. Collins, Department Executive Officer, 319-335-0910, Fax: 319-335-1956, E-mail: daniel-collins@uiowa.edu. *Application contact:* Renea L. Jay, Associate Director, Non-MBA Graduate Programs, 319-335-0830, Fax: 319-335-0860, E-mail: renea-jay@uiowa.edu.
Website: https://tippie.uiowa.edu/accounting/

The University of Kansas, Graduate Studies, School of Business, Master of Accounting Program, Lawrence, KS 66045. Offers M Acc. *Accreditation:* AACSB. *Program availability:* Part-time. *Students:* 127 full-time (63 women), 42 part-time (24 women); includes 25 minority (10 Asian, non-Hispanic/Latino; 8 Hispanic/Latino; 7 Two or more races, non-Hispanic/Latino), 11 international. Average age 26. 107 applicants, 74% accepted, 71 enrolled. In 2017, 142 master's awarded. *Entrance requirements:* For master's, GMAT, official transcript, two letters of recommendation, pledge to support

Accounting

Honor System of School of Business, current resume, three essays. *Application deadline:* For fall admission, 9/15 for domestic students, 12/15 for international students; for spring admission, 8/1 for domestic and international students; for summer admission, 12/15 for domestic and international students. Application fee: $65 ($85 for international students). Electronic applications accepted. *Financial support:* Fellowships, research assistantships, teaching assistantships, career-related internships or fieldwork, Federal Work-Study, institutionally sponsored loans, and scholarships/grants available. Financial award application deadline: 2/15; financial award applicants required to submit FAFSA. *Faculty research:* Earnings quality, financial reporting conservatism, internal control systems, auditing and corporate governance, financial reporting restatements. *Unit head:* Dr. John T. Sweeney, Director, 785-864-7507, E-mail: jtsweeney@ku.edu. *Application contact:* Karen Heintzen, Assistant Director, M Acc Program, 785-864-7558, E-mail: heintzen@ku.edu.
Website: https://business.ku.edu/degrees/accounting/macc/

University of Kentucky, Graduate School, Gatton College of Business and Economics, Program in Accounting, Lexington, KY 40506-0032. Offers MSACC. *Accreditation:* AACSB. *Degree requirements:* For master's, comprehensive exam. *Entrance requirements:* For master's, GRE General Test, minimum undergraduate GPA of 2.75. Additional exam requirements/recommendations for international students: Required—TOEFL (minimum score 550 paper-based). Electronic applications accepted. *Faculty research:* Taxation, financial accounting and auditing, managerial accounting, not-for-profit accounting.

University of La Verne, College of Business and Public Management, Graduate Programs in Business Administration, La Verne, CA 91750-4443. Offers accounting (MBA, MBA-EP); finance (MBA, MBA-EP); health services management (MBA); information technology (MBA, MBA-EP); international business (MBA, MBA-EP); management and leadership (MBA, MBA-EP); marketing (MBA, MBA-EP); supply chain management (MBA, MBA-EP). *Program availability:* Part-time, evening/weekend. *Faculty:* 24 full-time (11 women), 25 part-time/adjunct (6 women). *Students:* 390 full-time (193 women), 93 part-time (48 women); includes 96 minority (7 Black or African American, non-Hispanic/Latino; 1 American Indian or Alaska Native, non-Hispanic/Latino; 17 Asian, non-Hispanic/Latino; 67 Hispanic/Latino; 1 Native Hawaiian or other Pacific Islander, non-Hispanic/Latino; 3 Two or more races, non-Hispanic/Latino), 336 international. Average age 28. *Entrance requirements:* For master's, GMAT, MAT, or GRE, minimum undergraduate GPA of 3.0, 2 letters of recommendation, resume, statement of purpose. Additional exam requirements/recommendations for international students: Required—TOEFL (minimum score 550 paper-based; 85 iBT). *Application deadline:* Applications are processed on a rolling basis. Application fee: $50. Tuition and fees vary according to program. *Financial support:* Institutionally sponsored loans and scholarships/grants available. Financial award application deadline: 3/2; financial award applicants required to submit FAFSA. *Unit head:* Dr. Abe Helou, Chairperson, 909-448-4455, Fax: 909-392-2704, E-mail: ihelou@laverne.edu. *Application contact:* Rina Lazarian-Chehab, Senior Associate Director of Graduate Admissions, 909-448-4317, Fax: 909-971-2295, E-mail: rlazarian@laverne.edu.
Website: https://business.laverne.edu/mba/

University of La Verne, College of Business and Public Management, Program in Accounting, La Verne, CA 91750-4443. Offers MS. *Program availability:* Part-time. *Faculty:* 3 full-time (1 woman), 2 part-time/adjunct (0 women). *Students:* 73 full-time (50 women), 13 part-time (7 women); includes 12 minority (1 Black or African American, non-Hispanic/Latino; 1 Asian, non-Hispanic/Latino; 9 Hispanic/Latino; 1 Two or more races, non-Hispanic/Latino), 67 international. Average age 28. *Entrance requirements:* For master's, GMAT, MAT, or GRE, minimum undergraduate GPA of 3.0, 2 letters of recommendation, resume, statement of purpose. Additional exam requirements/recommendations for international students: Required—TOEFL (minimum score 550 paper-based; 85 iBT). *Application deadline:* Applications are processed on a rolling basis. Application fee: $50. *Expenses:* Contact institution. *Financial support:* Institutionally sponsored loans and scholarships/grants available. Financial award application deadline: 3/2; financial award applicants required to submit FAFSA. *Unit head:* Renee Miller, Program Chair, 909-448-4766, E-mail: rmiller@laverne.edu. *Application contact:* Rina Lazarian-Chehab, Senior Associate Director of Graduate Admissions, 909-448-4317, Fax: 909-971-2295, E-mail: rlazarian@laverne.edu.
Website: https://business.laverne.edu/accounting/

University of La Verne, Regional and Online Campuses, Graduate Programs, Inland Empire Campus, Ontario, CA 91730. Offers business administration (MBA, MBA-EP), including accounting (MBA), finance (MBA), health services management (MBA-EP), information technology (MBA-EP), international business (MBA), managed care (MBA), management and leadership (MBA-EP), marketing (MBA-EP), supply chain management (MBA); leadership and management (MS), including human resource management, nonprofit management, organizational development. *Program availability:* Part-time, evening/weekend. *Faculty:* 5 part-time/adjunct (1 woman). *Students:* 24 full-time (13 women), 72 part-time (44 women); includes 64 minority (12 Black or African American, non-Hispanic/Latino; 13 Asian, non-Hispanic/Latino; 36 Hispanic/Latino; 3 Two or more races, non-Hispanic/Latino). Average age 38. In 2017, 42 master's awarded. *Application deadline:* Applications are processed on a rolling basis. Application fee: $50. *Expenses:* Contact institution. *Financial support:* Application deadline: 3/2; applicants required to submit FAFSA. *Unit head:* Juli Roberts, Campus Director, Inland Empire Regional Campus in Ontario, 760-955-6448, E-mail: jroberts@laverne.edu. *Application contact:* Admissions, 877-468-6858, E-mail: gradadmission@laverne.edu.
Website: https://laverne.edu/locations/

University of Lethbridge, School of Graduate Studies, Lethbridge, AB T1K 3M4, Canada. Offers addictions counseling (M Sc); agricultural biotechnology (M Sc); agricultural studies (M Sc, MA); anthropology (MA); archaeology (M Sc, MA); art (MA, MFA); biochemistry (M Sc); biological sciences (M Sc); biomolecular science (PhD); biosystems and biodiversity (PhD); Canadian studies (MA); chemistry (M Sc); computer science (M Sc); computer science and geographical information science (M Sc); counseling (MC); counseling psychology (M Ed); dramatic arts (MA); earth, space, and physical science (PhD); economics (MA); education (MA, PhD); educational leadership (M Ed); English (MA); environmental science (M Sc); evolution and behavior (PhD); exercise science (M Sc); French (MA); French/German (MA); French/Spanish (MA); general education (M Ed); geography (M Sc, MA); German (MA); health sciences (M Sc); individualized multidisciplinary (M Sc, MA); kinesiology (M Sc, MA); management (M Sc), including accounting, finance, human resource management and labor relations, information systems, international management, marketing, policy and strategy; mathematics (M Sc); music (M Mus, MA); Native American studies (MA); neuroscience (M Sc, PhD); new media (MA, MFA); nursing (M Sc, MN); philosophy (MA); physics (M Sc); political science (MA); psychology (M Sc, MA); religious studies (MA); sociology (MA); theatre and dramatic arts (MFA); theoretical and computational science (PhD); urban and regional studies (MA); women and gender studies (MA). *Program availability:* Part-time, evening/weekend. *Degree requirements:* For master's, thesis (for some programs); for doctorate, comprehensive exam, thesis/dissertation. *Entrance requirements:* For master's, GMAT (for M Sc in management), bachelor's degree in related field, minimum GPA of 3.0 during previous 20 graded semester

courses, 2 years' teaching or related experience (M Ed); for doctorate, master's degree, minimum graduate GPA of 3.5. Additional exam requirements/recommendations for international students: Required—TOEFL (minimum score 580 paper-based; 93 iBT). Electronic applications accepted. *Faculty research:* Movement and brain plasticity, gibberellin physiology, photosynthesis, carbon cycling, molecular properties of main-group ring components.

University of Louisville, Graduate School, College of Business, School of Accountancy, Louisville, KY 40292-0001. Offers MAC, MBA/MAC. *Accreditation:* AACSB. *Program availability:* Part-time, evening/weekend. *Faculty:* 11 full-time (5 women), 3 part-time/adjunct (2 women). *Students:* 22 full-time (13 women), 29 part-time (17 women); includes 7 minority (2 Black or African American, non-Hispanic/Latino; 2 Asian, non-Hispanic/Latino; 3 Hispanic/Latino). Average age 29. 34 applicants, 85% accepted, 20 enrolled. In 2017, 1 master's awarded. *Entrance requirements:* For master's, GMAT, 2 letters of reference, resume, personal statement, personal interview, transcript. Additional exam requirements/recommendations for international students: Required—TOEFL (minimum score 83 iBT). *Application deadline:* For fall admission, 5/15 priority date for domestic students. Applications are processed on a rolling basis. Application fee: $65. *Expenses:* Tuition, state resident: full-time $12,246; part-time $681 per credit hour. Tuition, nonresident: full-time $25,486; part-time $1417 per credit hour. *Required fees:* $196. Tuition and fees vary according to course load, program and reciprocity agreements. *Financial support:* In 2017–18, research assistantships with full tuition reimbursements (averaging $1,200 per year) were awarded; health care benefits and unspecified assistantships also available. Financial award application deadline: 3/15; financial award applicants required to submit FAFSA. *Faculty research:* Audit judgment and decision-making, information systems, taxation, cost and managerial accounting. *Total annual research expenditures:* $19,347. *Unit head:* Dr. Todd Mooradian, Dean, 502-852-6443, Fax: 502-852-7557, E-mail: todd.mooradian@louisville.edu. *Application contact:* Susan E. Hildebrand, Director of IT and Master's Programs Admissions/Recruiting Manager, 502-852-7257, Fax: 502-852-4901, E-mail: s.hildebrand@louisville.edu.
Website: http://business.louisville.edu/graduate-programs/

The University of Manchester, Alliance Manchester Business School, M15 6PB, United Kingdom. Offers accounting and finance (M Sc); business (M Ent); business analysis and strategic management (M Sc); business analytics: operational research and risk analysis (M Sc); business psychology (M Sc); corporate communications and reputation management (M Sc); finance (M Sc); finance and business economics (M Sc); human resource management and industrial relations (M Sc); innovation management and entrepreneurship (M Sc); international business and management (M Sc); international human resource management and comparative industrial relations (M Sc); management (M Sc); marketing (M Sc); operations, project and supply chain management (M Sc); organizational psychology (M Sc); quantitative finance (M Sc). *Entrance requirements:* For master's, UK 2:1 honours degree or overseas equivalent. Additional exam requirements/recommendations for international students: Required—TOEFL (minimum score 100 iBT), IELTS (minimum score 7), PTE. Electronic applications accepted. *Faculty research:* Accounting and finance, management sciences and marketing, people management and organization, innovation management and policy, decision sciences.

University of Mary Hardin-Baylor, Graduate Studies in Business Administration, Belton, TX 76513. Offers accounting (MBA); information systems management (MBA); international business (MBA); management (MBA). *Program availability:* Part-time, evening/weekend. *Faculty:* 12 full-time (5 women), 6 part-time/adjunct (4 women). *Students:* 16 full-time (10 women), 39 part-time (16 women); includes 15 minority (3 Black or African American, non-Hispanic/Latino; 1 Asian, non-Hispanic/Latino; 10 Hispanic/Latino; 1 Two or more races, non-Hispanic/Latino), 10 international. Average age 30. 72 applicants, 81% accepted, 16 enrolled. In 2017, 34 master's awarded. *Degree requirements:* For master's, comprehensive exam. *Entrance requirements:* For master's, minimum GPA of 3.0, interview. Additional exam requirements/recommendations for international students: Required—TOEFL (minimum score 60 iBT), IELTS (minimum score 4.5). *Application deadline:* For fall admission, 6/1 for domestic students, 4/30 priority date for international students; for spring admission, 11/1 for domestic students, 9/30 priority date for international students. Applications are processed on a rolling basis. Application fee: $35 ($135 for international students). Electronic applications accepted. *Expenses:* Tuition: Full-time $15,570; part-time $10,380 per credit hour. *Required fees:* $1350; $75 per credit hour. $50 per term. Tuition and fees vary according to course load and degree level. *Financial support:* In 2017–18, 32 students received support. Federal Work-Study, institutionally sponsored loans, unspecified assistantships, and scholarships for some active duty military personnel available. Support available to part-time students. Financial award applicants required to submit FAFSA. *Faculty research:* Financial management, financial markets, supply chain management. *Unit head:* Dr. Kirk Fischer, Assistant Dean, Graduate Programs in McLane College of Business, 254-295-4655, E-mail: kfischer@umhb.edu. *Application contact:* Sharon Aguilera, Assistant Director, Graduate Admissions, 254-295-4835, E-mail: saguilera@umhb.edu.
Website: http://www.graduate.umhb.edu/mba

University of Maryland University College, The Graduate School, Program in Accounting and Financial Management, Adelphi, MD 20783. Offers MS. *Accreditation:* AACSB. *Program availability:* Part-time, evening/weekend, online learning. *Students:* 13 full-time (8 women), 442 part-time (287 women); includes 281 minority (189 Black or African American, non-Hispanic/Latino; 5 American Indian or Alaska Native, non-Hispanic/Latino; 35 Asian, non-Hispanic/Latino; 36 Hispanic/Latino; 1 Native Hawaiian or other Pacific Islander, non-Hispanic/Latino; 15 Two or more races, non-Hispanic/Latino), 15 international. Average age 36. 131 applicants, 100% accepted, 105 enrolled. In 2017, 88 master's awarded. *Degree requirements:* For master's, thesis or alternative, capstone course. *Application deadline:* Applications are processed on a rolling basis. Application fee: $50. Electronic applications accepted. *Financial support:* Federal Work-Study and scholarships/grants available. Support available to part-time students. Financial award application deadline: 6/1; financial award applicants required to submit FAFSA. *Unit head:* Dr. Kirby Cundiff, Program Chair, 240-684-2400, E-mail: kirby.cundiff@umuc.edu. *Application contact:* Coordinator, Graduate Admissions, 800-888-8682, Fax: 240-684-2151, E-mail: newgrad@umuc.edu.
Website: http://www.umuc.edu/academic-programs/masters-degrees/accounting-and-financial-management.cfm

University of Massachusetts Amherst, Graduate School, Isenberg School of Management, Department of Accounting, Amherst, MA 01003. Offers MSA. *Accreditation:* AACSB. *Program availability:* Part-time. *Entrance requirements:* For master's, GMAT. Additional exam requirements/recommendations for international students: Required—TOEFL (minimum score 550 paper-based; 80 iBT), IELTS (minimum score 6.5). Electronic applications accepted.

University of Massachusetts Amherst, Graduate School, Isenberg School of Management, Program in Management, Amherst, MA 01003. Offers accounting (PhD); business administration (MBA); entrepreneurship (MBA); finance (MBA, PhD); healthcare administration (MBA); hospitality and tourism management (PhD); management science (PhD); marketing (MBA, PhD); organization studies (PhD); sport management (PhD); strategic management (PhD); MBA/MS. *Accreditation:* AACSB. *Program availability:* Part-time, evening/weekend, online learning. Terminal master's awarded for partial completion of doctoral program. *Degree requirements:* For doctorate, comprehensive exam, thesis/dissertation. *Entrance requirements:* For master's and doctorate, GMAT or GRE General Test. Additional exam requirements/recommendations for international students: Required—TOEFL (minimum score 550 paper-based; 80 iBT), IELTS (minimum score 6.5). Electronic applications accepted.

University of Massachusetts Boston, College of Management, Program in Accounting, Boston, MA 02125-3393. Offers MS. *Faculty:* 25 full-time (9 women), 8 part-time/adjunct (1 woman). *Students:* 35 full-time (14 women), 33 part-time (12 women); includes 18 minority (3 Black or African American, non-Hispanic/Latino; 13 Asian, non-Hispanic/Latino; 2 Hispanic/Latino), 23 international. Average age 30. 67 applicants, 48% accepted, 14 enrolled. In 2017, 38 master's awarded. *Expenses:* Tuition, state resident: full-time $17,375. Tuition, nonresident: full-time $33,915. *Required fees:* $355. *Application contact:* Graduate Admissions Coordinator, 617-287-6400, Fax: 617-287-6236, E-mail: bos.gadm@dpc.umassp.edu.

University of Massachusetts Dartmouth, Graduate School, Charlton College of Business, Department of Accounting and Finance, North Dartmouth, MA 02747-2300. Offers accounting (MS, Postbaccalaureate Certificate); finance (Postbaccalaureate Certificate). *Program availability:* Part-time. *Faculty:* 15 full-time (5 women), 4 part-time/adjunct (1 woman). *Students:* 36 full-time (21 women), 17 part-time (12 women); includes 17 minority (3 Black or African American, non-Hispanic/Latino; 7 Asian, non-Hispanic/Latino; 5 Hispanic/Latino; 2 Two or more races, non-Hispanic/Latino), 8 international. Average age 31. 33 applicants, 91% accepted, 25 enrolled. In 2017, 23 master's, 1 other advanced degree awarded. *Entrance requirements:* For master's, GMAT or waiver, statement of purpose (minimum 300 words), resume, official transcript, 2 letters of recommendation; for Postbaccalaureate Certificate, statement of purpose (minimum 300 words), resume, official transcript. Additional exam requirements/recommendations for international students: Required—TOEFL (minimum score 550 paper-based; 79 iBT), IELTS (minimum score 6.5). *Application deadline:* For fall admission, 8/1 priority date for domestic students, 6/1 priority date for international students; for spring admission, 11/15 priority date for domestic students, 10/15 priority date for international students. Application fee: $60. Electronic applications accepted. *Expenses:* Tuition, state resident: full-time $15,449; part-time $643.71 per credit. Tuition, nonresident: full-time $27,880; part-time $1161.67 per credit. *Required fees:* $405; $25.88 per credit. Tuition and fees vary according to course load and reciprocity agreements. *Financial support:* Research assistantships, teaching assistantships, tuition waivers, and unspecified assistantships available. Support available to part-time students. Financial award application deadline: 3/1; financial award applicants required to submit FAFSA. *Faculty research:* Accounting information systems, analytical controls in continuous auditing, accounting education, managerial accounting, e-commerce. *Unit head:* Dr. Jia Wu, Program Coordinator, Accounting, 508-999-8428, E-mail: jwu@umassd.edu. *Application contact:* Steven Briggs, Director of Marketing and Recruitment for Graduate Studies, 508-999-8604, Fax: 508-999-8183, E-mail: graduate@umassd.edu.
Website: http://www.umassd.edu/charlton/programs/graduate/msaccounting/

University of Memphis, Graduate School, Fogelman College of Business and Economics, Program in Business Administration, Memphis, TN 38152. Offers accounting (MBA, PhD); business administration (IMBA); economics (PhD); executive business administration (MBA); finance (PhD); management (PhD); marketing (MS); marketing and supply chain management (PhD); real estate development (MS); JD/MBA. *Accreditation:* AACSB. *Faculty:* 2 part-time/adjunct (0 women). *Students:* 166 full-time (76 women), 361 part-time (142 women); includes 161 minority (91 Black or African American, non-Hispanic/Latino; 51 Asian, non-Hispanic/Latino; 10 Hispanic/Latino; 9 Two or more races, non-Hispanic/Latino), 89 international. Average age 32. 263 applicants, 83% accepted, 157 enrolled. In 2017, 186 master's, 14 doctorates awarded. *Degree requirements:* For master's, comprehensive exam; for doctorate, comprehensive exam, thesis/dissertation. *Entrance requirements:* For master's, GMAT, resume; for doctorate, GMAT, interview, minimum GPA of 3.4, resume, letter of recommendation. Additional exam requirements/recommendations for international students: Required—TOEFL (minimum score 550 paper-based). *Application deadline:* For fall admission, 8/1 for domestic students; for spring admission, 12/1 for domestic students. Application fee: $35 ($60 for international students). *Financial support:* In 2017–18, 164 students received support, including 17 research assistantships with full tuition reimbursements available (averaging $53,750 per year), 13 teaching assistantships with full tuition reimbursements available (averaging $20,798 per year); career-related internships or fieldwork, Federal Work-Study, scholarships/grants, and unspecified assistantships also available. Financial award application deadline: 2/15; financial award applicants required to submit FAFSA. *Faculty research:* Competitive business strategy, finance microstructures, supply chain management innovations, health care economics, litigation risks and corporate audits. *Unit head:* Dr. Rajiv Grover, Dean, 901-678-3759, E-mail: rgrover@memphis.edu. *Application contact:* Dr. Carol V. Danehower, Associate Dean, 901-678-5402, Fax: 901-678-3579, E-mail: fcbegp@memphis.edu.
Website: https://web0.memphis.edu/gradcatalog/degreeprog/fcbe/fcbe.php

University of Memphis, Graduate School, Fogelman College of Business and Economics, School of Accountancy, Memphis, TN 38152. Offers accounting (MS). *Accreditation:* AACSB. *Faculty:* 7 full-time (0 women). *Students:* 43 full-time (20 women), 31 part-time (16 women); includes 28 minority (15 Black or African American, non-Hispanic/Latino; 6 Asian, non-Hispanic/Latino; 4 Hispanic/Latino; 3 Two or more races, non-Hispanic/Latino), 5 international. Average age 28. 43 applicants, 98% accepted, 34 enrolled. In 2017, 32 master's awarded. *Degree requirements:* For master's, comprehensive exam. *Entrance requirements:* For master's, GMAT. Additional exam requirements/recommendations for international students: Required—TOEFL (minimum score 550 paper-based; 79 iBT). *Application deadline:* For fall admission, 8/1 for domestic students; for spring admission, 12/1 for domestic students. Application fee: $35 ($60 for international students). Electronic applications accepted. *Expenses:* Contact institution. *Financial support:* In 2017–18, 32 students received support, including 12 research assistantships with full tuition reimbursements available (averaging $11,500 per year); teaching assistantships with full tuition reimbursements available, Federal Work-Study, scholarships/grants, and unspecified assistantships also available. Financial award application deadline: 2/1; financial award applicants required to submit FAFSA. *Faculty research:* Financial accounting, corporate governance, EDP auditing, evolution of system analysis, investor behavior and investment decisions. *Unit head:* Dr. Kenton Walker, Director, 901-678-4569, E-mail: kbwalker@memphis.edu. *Application contact:* Dr. Zabihollah Rezaee, PhD Program Coordinator, 901-678-4652, E-mail: zrezaee@memphis.edu.
Website: http://www.memphis.edu/accountancy/

University of Michigan, Ross School of Business, Ann Arbor, MI 48109-1234. Offers accounting (M Acc); business (MBA); business administration (PhD); supply chain management (MSCM); JD/MBA; MBA/M Arch; MBA/M Eng; MBA/MA; MBA/MEM; MBA/MHSA; MBA/MM; MBA/MPP; MBA/MS; MBA/MSE; MBA/MSI; MBA/MSW; MBA/MUP; MD/MBA; MHSA/MBA. *Accreditation:* AACSB. *Program availability:* Part-time, evening/

weekend. *Degree requirements:* For doctorate, comprehensive exam, thesis/dissertation, oral defense of dissertation, preliminary exam. *Entrance requirements:* For master's, GMAT or GRE, completion of equivalent of four-year U.S. bachelor's degree, two letters of recommendation, essays, resume; for doctorate, GMAT or GRE. Additional exam requirements/recommendations for international students: Required—TOEFL (minimum score 600 paper-based; 100 iBT). Electronic applications accepted. *Expenses:* Tuition, state resident: full-time $22,368; part-time $1201 per credit hour. Tuition, nonresident: full-time $45,156; part-time $2467 per credit hour. *Required fees:* $376 per term. Tuition and fees vary according to course load, degree level and program. *Faculty research:* Finance and accounting, marketing, technology and operations management, corporate strategy, management and organizations.

University of Michigan–Dearborn, College of Business, MS Program in Accounting, Dearborn, MI 48126. Offers MS. *Program availability:* Part-time, evening/weekend. *Faculty:* 45 full-time (19 women), 4 part-time/adjunct (2 women). *Students:* 9 full-time (6 women), 25 part-time (15 women); includes 10 minority (2 Black or African American, non-Hispanic/Latino; 6 Asian, non-Hispanic/Latino; 1 Hispanic/Latino; 1 Two or more races, non-Hispanic/Latino), 6 international. Average age 31. 40 applicants, 55% accepted, 12 enrolled. In 2017, 8 master's awarded. *Entrance requirements:* For master's, GMAT or GRE, equivalent of four-year U.S. bachelor's degree from regionally-accredited institution, undergraduate course in finite math, pre-calculus, or calculus. Additional exam requirements/recommendations for international students: Required—TOEFL (minimum score 560 paper-based; 84 iBT), IELTS (minimum score 6.5). *Application deadline:* For fall admission, 8/1 for domestic students, 5/1 for international students; for winter admission, 12/1 for domestic students, 9/1 for international students; for spring admission, 4/1 for domestic students, 1/1 for international students. Applications are processed on a rolling basis. Application fee: $60. Electronic applications accepted. *Expenses:* $883 per credit hour in-state; $1,376 per credit hour out-state. *Financial support:* In 2017–18, 14 students received support. Scholarships/grants and non-resident tuition scholarships available. Financial award application deadline: 3/1; financial award applicants required to submit FAFSA. *Faculty research:* Business intelligence, behavioral finance, brand management and new media, management education, operations strategy. *Unit head:* Dr. Michael Kamen, Director, College of Business Graduate Programs, 313-593-5460, E-mail: mkamen@umich.edu. *Application contact:* Joan Doherty, Academic Advisor/Counselor, 313-593-5460, Fax: 313-271-9838, E-mail: umd-gradbusiness@umich.edu.
Website: http://umdearborn.edu/cob/ms-accounting

University of Michigan–Flint, School of Management, Program in Accounting, Flint, MI 48502-1950. Offers MSA, Post-Master's Certificate. *Program availability:* Part-time, evening/weekend, mixed mode format. *Faculty:* 32 full-time (5 women), 8 part-time/adjunct (2 women). *Students:* 2 full-time (1 woman), 26 part-time (10 women); includes 7 minority (3 Black or African American, non-Hispanic/Latino; 3 Asian, non-Hispanic/Latino; 1 Two or more races, non-Hispanic/Latino), 6 international. Average age 32. 18 applicants, 83% accepted, 8 enrolled. In 2017, 22 master's awarded. *Entrance requirements:* For master's, GMAT or GRE, bachelor's degree in arts, sciences, engineering, or business administration from regionally-accredited college or university with minimum GPA of 3.0; for Post-Master's Certificate, MBA or equivalent degree from accredited college or university (for Post-Master's Certificate). Additional exam requirements/recommendations for international students: Required—TOEFL (minimum score 84 iBT), IELTS (minimum score 3.5). *Application deadline:* For fall admission, 8/1 for domestic students, 5/1 for international students; for winter admission, 11/15 for domestic students, 9/1 for international students; for spring admission, 3/15 for domestic students, 1/1 for international students; for summer admission, 5/15 for domestic students. Applications are processed on a rolling basis. Application fee: $55. Electronic applications accepted. *Expenses:* Contact institution. *Financial support:* Federal Work-Study, scholarships/grants, and unspecified assistantships available. Support available to part-time students. Financial award application deadline: 3/1; financial award applicants required to submit FAFSA. *Unit head:* Dr. Scott Johnson, Dean, School of Management, 810-762-3164, Fax: 810-237-6685, E-mail: scotjohn@umflint.edu. *Application contact:* Bradley T. Maki, Director of Graduate Admissions, 810-762-3171, Fax: 810-766-6789, E-mail: bmaki@umflint.edu.
Website: http://www.umflint.edu/graduateprograms/accounting-msa

University of Michigan–Flint, School of Management, Program in Business Administration, Flint, MI 48502-1950. Offers accounting (MBA); computer information systems (MBA); finance (MBA, Post-Master's Certificate); general business (Graduate Certificate); general business administration (MBA); health care management (MBA); international business (MBA, Post-Master's Certificate); lean manufacturing (MBA); marketing (Post-Master's Certificate); marketing and innovation management (MBA); organizational leadership (MBA). *Program availability:* Part-time, evening/weekend, mixed mode format. *Faculty:* 32 full-time (5 women), 8 part-time/adjunct (2 women). *Students:* 12 full-time (7 women), 147 part-time (51 women); includes 31 minority (15 Black or African American, non-Hispanic/Latino; 1 American Indian or Alaska Native, non-Hispanic/Latino; 9 Asian, non-Hispanic/Latino; 5 Hispanic/Latino; 1 Two or more races, non-Hispanic/Latino), 18 international. Average age 34. 110 applicants, 52% accepted, 29 enrolled. In 2017, 59 master's, 6 other advanced degrees awarded. *Entrance requirements:* For master's, GMAT or GRE, bachelor's degree in arts, sciences, engineering, or business administration from regionally-accredited college or university with minimum GPA of 3.0; for other advanced degree, bachelor's degree in arts, sciences, engineering, or business administration from regionally-accredited college or university with minimum GPA of 3.0, college-level math, statistics, or quantitative course (for Graduate Certificate); MBA or equivalent degree from regionally-accredited college or university (for Post Master's Certificate). Additional exam requirements/recommendations for international students: Required—TOEFL (minimum score 84 iBT), IELTS (minimum score 6.5). *Application deadline:* For fall admission, 8/1 for domestic students, 5/1 for international students; for winter admission, 11/15 for domestic students, 9/1 for international students; for spring admission, 3/15 for domestic students, 1/1 for international students; for summer admission, 5/15 for domestic students. Applications are processed on a rolling basis. Application fee: $55. Electronic applications accepted. *Expenses:* Contact institution. *Financial support:* Federal Work-Study, scholarships/grants, and unspecified assistantships available. Support available to part-time students. Financial award application deadline: 3/1; financial award applicants required to submit FAFSA. *Unit head:* Dr. Scott Johnson, Dean, School of Management, 810-762-3164, Fax: 810-237-6685, E-mail: scotjohn@umflint.edu. *Application contact:* Bradley T. Maki, Director of Graduate Admissions, 810-762-3171, E-mail: bmaki@umflint.edu.
Website: http://www.umflint.edu/graduateprograms/business-administration-mba

University of Minnesota, Twin Cities Campus, Carlson School of Management, Doctoral Program in Business Administration, Minneapolis, MN 55455. Offers accounting (PhD); finance (PhD); information and decision sciences (PhD); marketing (PhD); strategic management and entrepreneurship (PhD); supply chain and operations (PhD); work and organizations (PhD). *Faculty:* 102 full-time (32 women). *Students:* 95 full-time (32 women); includes 10 minority (2 Black or African American, non-Hispanic/Latino; 7 Asian, non-Hispanic/Latino; 1 Hispanic/Latino), 68 international. Average age 30. 357 applicants, 6% accepted, 17 enrolled. In 2017, 14 doctorates awarded. *Degree requirements:* For doctorate, comprehensive exam, thesis/dissertation, written and oral

Accounting

preliminary exams, proposal defense, final defense. *Entrance requirements:* For doctorate, GMAT, GRE General Test, minimum undergraduate GPA of 3.0, graduate 3.5 (recommended). Additional exam requirements/recommendations for international students: Required—TOEFL (minimum score 600 paper-based, 100 iBT) or IELTS (minimum score 7.0). *Application deadline:* For fall admission, 12/15 for domestic students, 12/15 priority date for international students. Applications are processed on a rolling basis. Application fee: $75 ($95 for international students). Electronic applications accepted. *Expenses:* Contact institution. *Financial support:* In 2017–18, 80 students received support, including 80 fellowships with full tuition reimbursements available (averaging $13,000 per year), 73 research assistantships with full tuition reimbursements available (averaging $7,520 per year), 73 teaching assistantships with full tuition reimbursements available (averaging $7,520 per year); institutionally sponsored loans, scholarships/grants, health care benefits, unspecified assistantships, and full student service fee waivers also available. Financial award application deadline: 12/15. *Faculty research:* Finance, strategy and entrepreneurship, marketing, information and decision science, operations, accounting, supply chain, human resources and industrial relations, organizational behavior. *Unit head:* Dr. Shawn P. Curley, Director, 612-624-6546, Fax: 612-624-8221, E-mail: curley@umn.edu. *Application contact:* Sandy Herzan, Associate Director, 612-624-0875, Fax: 612-624-8221, E-mail: herza002@umn.edu.
Website: http://carlsonschool.umn.edu/degrees/phd

University of Minnesota, Twin Cities Campus, Carlson School of Management, Master's Program in Accountancy, Minneapolis, MN 55455-0213. Offers M Acc. *Accreditation:* AACSB. *Program availability:* Part-time, evening/weekend. *Faculty:* 23 full-time (5 women), 1 part-time/adjunct (0 women). *Students:* 59 full-time (31 women), 10 part-time (3 women); includes 9 minority (1 American Indian or Alaska Native, non-Hispanic/Latino; 7 Asian, non-Hispanic/Latino; 1 Hispanic/Latino), 25 international. Average age 26. 190 applicants, 31% accepted, 48 enrolled. In 2017, 39 master's awarded. *Entrance requirements:* For master's, GMAT, letters of recommendation. Additional exam requirements/recommendations for international students: Required—TOEFL (minimum score 550 paper-based; 79 iBT), IELTS (minimum score 6.5). *Application deadline:* For fall admission, 2/1 priority date for domestic and international students; for spring admission, 10/1 priority date for domestic and international students. Applications are processed on a rolling basis. Application fee: $75 ($95 for international students). Electronic applications accepted. *Expenses:* Contact institution. *Financial support:* In 2017–18, 35 students received support, including 3 fellowships (averaging $3,000 per year), 6 teaching assistantships with partial tuition reimbursements available (averaging $9,000 per year); institutionally sponsored loans and scholarships/grants also available. Financial award application deadline: 7/15. *Faculty research:* Capital market-based accounting, cognitive skill acquisition in auditing, incentives and control in organizations, economic consequences of securities regulation, earnings management. *Unit head:* Clayton Forester, Director of Graduate Studies, 612-626-7532, E-mail: claytonf@umn.edu. *Application contact:* Rhonda Bjurlin, Information Contact, 612-625-6516, E-mail: macct@umn.edu.
Website: http://carlsonschool.umn.edu/degrees/master-accountancy

University of Mississippi, Graduate School, School of Accountancy, University, MS 38677. Offers accountancy (M Acc, PhD); accounting and data analytics (MA); taxation accounting (M Tax). *Accreditation:* AACSB. *Faculty:* 17 full-time (4 women), 5 part-time/adjunct (3 women). *Students:* 116 full-time (48 women), 7 part-time (3 women); includes 10 minority (7 Black or African American, non-Hispanic/Latino; 1 Asian, non-Hispanic/Latino; 1 Native Hawaiian or other Pacific Islander, non-Hispanic/Latino; 1 Two or more races, non-Hispanic/Latino), 3 international. Average age 24. *Entrance requirements:* For master's, GMAT, minimum GPA of 3.0; for doctorate, GMAT. Additional exam requirements/recommendations for international students: Required—TOEFL. *Application deadline:* For fall admission, 8/1 for domestic students; for spring admission, 12/1 for domestic students; for summer admission, 5/1 for domestic students. Applications are processed on a rolling basis. Application fee: $50. *Financial support:* Scholarships/grants available. Financial award application deadline: 3/1; financial award applicants required to submit FAFSA. *Unit head:* Dr. W. Mark Wilder, Dean, School of Accountancy, 662-915-7468, Fax: 662-915-7483, E-mail: umaccy@olemiss.edu. *Application contact:* Dr. Dale Flesher, Associate Dean/Professor/Chair, 662-915-7623, E-mail: acdlf@olemiss.edu.
Website: https://www.olemiss.edu

University of Missouri, Office of Research and Graduate Studies, Robert J. Trulaske, Sr. College of Business, School of Accountancy, Columbia, MO 65211. Offers accountancy (M Acc, PhD); taxation (Certificate). *Accreditation:* AACSB. *Program availability:* Part-time. *Degree requirements:* For master's, thesis or alternative; for doctorate, thesis/dissertation. *Entrance requirements:* For master's and doctorate, GMAT, minimum GPA of 3.0. Additional exam requirements/recommendations for international students: Required—TOEFL (minimum score 600 paper-based; 100 iBT). Electronic applications accepted.

University of Missouri–Kansas City, Henry W. Bloch School of Management, Kansas City, MO 64110-2499. Offers accounting (MS); finance (MS); public affairs (MPA, PhD); JD/MBA; LL M/MPA. PhD (interdisciplinary) offered through the School of Graduate Studies. *Accreditation:* AACSB; NASPAA. *Program availability:* Part-time, evening/weekend. Terminal master's awarded for partial completion of doctoral program. *Entrance requirements:* For master's, GMAT, GRE, 2 essays, 2 references, support of employer; for doctorate, GRE, minimum GPA of 3.0. Additional exam requirements/recommendations for international students: Required—TOEFL (minimum score 550 paper-based; 80 iBT). Electronic applications accepted. *Faculty research:* Entrepreneurship, finance, non-profit, risk management.

University of Missouri–St. Louis, College of Business Administration, St. Louis, MO 63121. Offers accounting (M Acc); business administration (MBA, DBA, PhD, Certificate), including logistics and supply chain management (PhD); business intelligence (Certificate); cybersecurity (Certificate); digital and social media marketing (Certificate); human resources management (Certificate); information systems (MS); logistics and supply chain management (Certificate); marketing management (Certificate). *Program availability:* Part-time, evening/weekend. *Faculty:* 51 full-time (21 women), 25 part-time/adjunct (5 women). *Students:* 146 full-time (77 women), 326 part-time (143 women); includes 82 minority (32 Black or African American, non-Hispanic/Latino; 1 American Indian or Alaska Native, non-Hispanic/Latino; 34 Asian, non-Hispanic/Latino; 11 Hispanic/Latino; 4 Two or more races, non-Hispanic/Latino), 89 international. 276 applicants, 83% accepted, 142 enrolled. *Degree requirements:* For doctorate, thesis/dissertation. *Entrance requirements:* For master's, GMAT, 2 letters of recommendation; for doctorate, GMAT or GRE, 3 letters of recommendation. Additional exam requirements/recommendations for international students: Recommended—TOEFL (minimum score 550 paper-based; 79 iBT), IELTS (minimum score 6.5). *Application deadline:* For fall admission, 7/1 priority date for domestic and international students; for spring admission, 12/1 priority date for domestic and international students. Applications are processed on a rolling basis. Application fee: $50 ($40 for international students). Electronic applications accepted. *Expenses:* Tuition, state resident: part-time $476.50 per credit hour. Tuition, nonresident: part-time $1169.70 per credit hour. *Financial support:* Research assistantships with tuition reimbursements, teaching assistantships with tuition reimbursements, career-related internships or fieldwork, Federal Work-Study, and institutionally sponsored loans available. Support available to part-time students. Financial award application deadline: 4/1; financial award applicants required to submit FAFSA. *Faculty research:* Statistical decision aids, commercial banking, corporate finance, operations management, information systems. *Unit head:* Charles E. Hoffman, Dean, 314-516-6109, Fax: 314-516-6420. *Application contact:* 314-516-5458, Fax: 314-516-6996, E-mail: gradadm@umsl.edu.
Website: http://www.umsl.edu/divisions/business/

University of Montana, Graduate School, School of Business Administration, Department of Accounting and Finance, Missoula, MT 59812. Offers accounting (M Acct). *Accreditation:* AACSB. *Degree requirements:* For master's, thesis optional. *Entrance requirements:* For master's, GMAT. Additional exam requirements/recommendations for international students: Required—TOEFL (minimum score 580 paper-based). *Faculty research:* Income tax, financial markets, nonprofit accounting, accounting information systems, auditing.

University of Nebraska at Kearney, College of Business and Technology, Department of Business, Kearney, NE 68849-0001. Offers accounting (MBA); generalist (MBA); human resources (MBA); human services (MBA); marketing (MBA). *Accreditation:* AACSB. *Program availability:* Part-time, evening/weekend. *Degree requirements:* For master's, thesis optional, capstone course. *Entrance requirements:* For master's, GRE or GMAT (if no significant managerial experience), letters of recommendation, essay, resume. Additional exam requirements/recommendations for international students: Recommended—TOEFL (minimum score 550 paper-based; 79 iBT), IELTS (minimum score 6.5). Electronic applications accepted. *Faculty research:* Small business financial management, employment law, expert systems, international trade and marketing, environmental economics.

University of Nebraska at Omaha, Graduate Studies, College of Business Administration, Department of Accounting, Omaha, NE 68182. Offers M Acc. *Program availability:* Part-time, evening/weekend. *Degree requirements:* For master's, comprehensive exam (for some programs), thesis (for some programs). *Entrance requirements:* For master's, GMAT, minimum GPA of 3.0 in undergraduate courses related to accounting, official transcript. Additional exam requirements/recommendations for international students: Required—TOEFL, IELTS, PTE. Electronic applications accepted.

University of Nebraska–Lincoln, Graduate College, College of Business Administration, Interdepartmental Area of Business, Lincoln, NE 68588. Offers accountancy (PhD); business (MBA); finance (MA, PhD), including business; management (MA, PhD), including business; marketing (MA, PhD), including business; JD/MBA; M Arch/MBA. *Accreditation:* AACSB. *Program availability:* Part-time, online learning. *Degree requirements:* For doctorate, comprehensive exam, thesis/dissertation. *Entrance requirements:* For master's and doctorate, GMAT. Additional exam requirements/recommendations for international students: Required—TOEFL (minimum score 550 paper-based). Electronic applications accepted.

University of Nebraska–Lincoln, Graduate College, College of Business Administration, School of Accountancy, Lincoln, NE 68588. Offers MPA, PhD, JD/MPA. *Accreditation:* AACSB. *Entrance requirements:* For master's, GMAT. Additional exam requirements/recommendations for international students: Required—TOEFL (minimum score 550 paper-based). Electronic applications accepted. *Faculty research:* Auditing, financial accounting, managerial accounting, capital markets, tax accounting.

University of Nevada, Las Vegas, Graduate College, Lee Business School, Department of Accounting, Las Vegas, NV 89154-6003. Offers accountancy (MS); accounting (Advanced Certificate, Certificate). *Accreditation:* AACSB. *Program availability:* Part-time. *Faculty:* 10 full-time (5 women), 7 part-time/adjunct (2 women). *Students:* 71 full-time (33 women), 26 part-time (16 women); includes 38 minority (1 Black or African American, non-Hispanic/Latino; 20 Asian, non-Hispanic/Latino; 12 Hispanic/Latino; 5 Two or more races, non-Hispanic/Latino), 14 international. Average age 28. 46 applicants, 74% accepted, 25 enrolled. In 2017, 63 master's awarded. *Entrance requirements:* For master's, GMAT, bachelor's degree with minimum GPA 3.0. Additional exam requirements/recommendations for international students: Required—TOEFL (minimum score 550 paper-based; 80 iBT), IELTS (minimum score 7). *Application deadline:* For fall admission, 8/1 for domestic students, 5/1 for international students; for spring admission, 12/1 for domestic students, 10/1 for international students; for summer admission, 5/15 for domestic students, 4/15 for international students. Application fee: $60 ($95 for international students). Electronic applications accepted. *Expenses:* $275 per credit, $850 per course, $7,969 per year resident, $22,157 per year non-resident fee (7 credits or more), $1,307 annual health insurance fee. *Financial support:* In 2017–18, 19 students received support, including 4 research assistantships with full and partial tuition reimbursements available (averaging $11,363 per year), 15 teaching assistantships with full and partial tuition reimbursements available (averaging $11,167 per year); institutionally sponsored loans, scholarships/grants, health care benefits, and unspecified assistantships also available. Financial award application deadline: 3/15; financial award applicants required to submit FAFSA. *Faculty research:* Audit judgments and decision-making, fraud, corporate governance, information systems technology and decision-making, internal audit. *Total annual research expenditures:* $681. *Unit head:* Dr. Bob Cornell, Chair/Associate Professor, 702-895-4323, E-mail: robert.cornell@unlv.edu. *Application contact:* Dr. Kim Charron, Graduate Coordinator, 702-895-3975, E-mail: kim.charron@unlv.edu.
Website: http://business.unlv.edu/accounting/

University of Nevada, Reno, Graduate School, College of Business Administration, Department of Accounting and Information Systems, Reno, NV 89557. Offers M Acc. *Accreditation:* AACSB. *Entrance requirements:* For master's, GMAT or GRE (if undergraduate degree is not from an AACSB-accredited business school with minimum GPA of 3.5), minimum GPA of 2.75. Additional exam requirements/recommendations for international students: Required—TOEFL (minimum score 500 paper-based; 61 iBT), IELTS (minimum score 6). Electronic applications accepted. *Faculty research:* Financial reporting/auditing, taxation.

University of New Hampshire, Graduate School, Peter T. Paul College of Business and Economics, Department of Accounting and Finance, Durham, NH 03824. Offers accounting (MS). *Program availability:* Part-time. *Students:* 28 full-time (12 women), 1 part-time (0 women); includes 1 minority (Asian, non-Hispanic/Latino), 4 international. Average age 23. 56 applicants, 68% accepted, 27 enrolled. In 2017, 26 master's awarded. *Entrance requirements:* For master's, GMAT. Additional exam requirements/recommendations for international students: Required—TOEFL (minimum score 550 paper-based; 80 iBT). *Application deadline:* For fall admission, 4/1 for domestic and international students; for spring admission, 10/15 for domestic students. Application fee: $65. Electronic applications accepted. *Financial support:* In 2017–18, 20 students received support. Fellowships, research assistantships, and teaching assistantships available. Financial award application deadline: 2/15. *Unit head:* Stephen Ciccone, Chair, 603-862-3343, E-mail: stephen.ciccone@unh.edu. *Application contact:* Sinthy Kounlasa, Administrative Assistant III, 603-862-3380, E-mail: sinthy.kounlasa@unh.edu.
Website: http://paulcollege.unh.edu/academics/graduate-programs/ms-accounting

University of New Haven, Graduate School, College of Business, Program in Accounting, West Haven, CT 06516. Offers MS, Graduate Certificate. *Accreditation:* AACSB. *Students:* 6 full-time (1 woman), 2 part-time (1 woman), 1 international. Average age 30. 13 applicants, 85% accepted, 6 enrolled. *Application deadline:* Applications are processed on a rolling basis. Application fee: $50. *Expenses: Tuition:* Full-time $16,020; part-time $890 per credit hour. *Required fees:* $220; $90 per term. *Financial support:* Research assistantships with partial tuition reimbursements, teaching assistantships with partial tuition reimbursements, and Federal Work-Study available. Support available to part-time students. Financial award application deadline: 5/1; financial award applicants required to submit FAFSA. *Unit head:* Michael Rolleri, Chair of Accounting, 203-932-7092, E-mail: mrolleri@newhaven.edu. *Application contact:* Michelle Mason, Director of Graduate Enrollment, 203-932-7067, E-mail: mmason@newhaven.edu.

See Display on page 154 and Close-Up on page 185.

University of New Haven, Graduate School, College of Business, Program in Business Administration, West Haven, CT 06516. Offers accounting (MBA); business administration (MBA); business intelligence (MBA); business policy and strategic leadership (MBA); finance (MBA), including chartered financial analyst; global marketing (MBA); human resources management (MBA); sport management (MBA). *Accreditation:* AACSB. *Program availability:* Part-time, evening/weekend. *Students:* 123 full-time (56 women), 67 part-time (28 women); includes 53 minority (27 Black or African American, non-Hispanic/Latino; 11 Asian, non-Hispanic/Latino; 12 Hispanic/Latino; 3 Two or more races, non-Hispanic/Latino), 50 international. Average age 28. 148 applicants, 89% accepted, 67 enrolled. In 2017, 106 master's awarded. *Entrance requirements:* For master's, GMAT. Additional exam requirements/recommendations for international students: Required—TOEFL (minimum score 80 iBT), IELTS, PTE. *Application deadline:* Applications are processed on a rolling basis. Application fee: $50. Electronic applications accepted. Application fee is waived when completed online. *Expenses: Tuition:* Full-time $16,020; part-time $890 per credit hour. *Required fees:* $220; $90 per term. *Financial support:* Research assistantships with partial tuition reimbursements, teaching assistantships with partial tuition reimbursements, career-related internships or fieldwork, Federal Work-Study, scholarships/grants, and unspecified assistantships available. Support available to part-time students. Financial award applicants required to submit FAFSA. *Unit head:* Darell Singleterry, Director, 203-932-1085, E-mail: dsingleterry@newhaven.edu. *Application contact:* Michelle Mason, Director of Graduate Enrollment, 203-932-7067, E-mail: mmason@newhaven.edu. Website: http://www.newhaven.edu/business/graduate-programs/mba/index.php

See Display on page 154 and Close-Up on page 185.

University of New Mexico, Anderson School of Management, Department of Accounting, Albuquerque, NM 87131. Offers accounting (MBA); advanced accounting (M Acct); information assurance (M Acct); professional accounting (M Acct); tax accounting (M Acct); JD/M Acct. *Accreditation:* AACSB. *Program availability:* Part-time, evening/weekend. *Faculty:* 16 full-time (8 women), 5 part-time/adjunct (2 women). *Students:* 67 applicants, 66% accepted, 35 enrolled. In 2017, 68 master's awarded. *Entrance requirements:* For master's, GMAT/GRE (minimum score of 500), minimum GPA of 3.25, 3.0 on last 60 hours of coursework (for M Acct in professional accounting). Additional exam requirements/recommendations for international students: Required— TOEFL (minimum score 550 paper-based; 79 iBT), IELTS (minimum score 6.5). *Application deadline:* For fall admission, 4/1 priority date for domestic and international students; for spring admission, 10/1 priority date for domestic and international students. Applications are processed on a rolling basis. Application fee: $50. Electronic applications accepted. *Expenses:* Contact institution. *Financial support:* In 2017–18, 16 students received support, including 5 fellowships (averaging $16,744 per year), 14 research assistantships with partial tuition reimbursements available (averaging $15,345 per year); career-related internships or fieldwork, Federal Work-Study, scholarships/ grants, and unspecified assistantships also available. Support available to part-time students. Financial award application deadline: 6/1; financial award applicants required to submit FAFSA. *Faculty research:* Critical accounting, accounting pedagogy, theory, taxation, information fraud. *Unit head:* Dr. Richard Brody, Interim Chair, 505-277-6471, E-mail: tmarmijo@unm.edu. *Application contact:* Dr. Rich Brody, Professor, 505-277-6471, E-mail: tmarmijo@unm.edu. Website: https://www.mgt.unm.edu/acct/default.asp?mm-faculty

University of New Orleans, Graduate School, College of Business Administration, Department of Accounting, Program in Accounting, New Orleans, LA 70148. Offers MS. *Accreditation:* AACSB. *Program availability:* Part-time, evening/weekend. *Degree requirements:* For master's, thesis optional. *Entrance requirements:* For master's, GMAT. Additional exam requirements/recommendations for international students: Required—TOEFL (minimum score 550 paper-based; 79 iBT). Electronic applications accepted.

University of North Alabama, College of Business, Florence, AL 35632-0001. Offers business administration (MBA), including accounting, enterprise resource planning systems, executive, finance, health care management, information systems, international business, project management. *Accreditation:* AACSB; ACBSP. *Program availability:* Part-time, 100% online, blended/hybrid learning. *Faculty:* 26 full-time (1 woman), 4 part-time/adjunct (0 women). *Students:* 178 full-time (78 women), 498 part-time (237 women); includes 229 minority (92 Black or African American, non-Hispanic/ Latino; 8 American Indian or Alaska Native, non-Hispanic/Latino; 104 Asian, non-Hispanic/Latino; 14 Hispanic/Latino; 11 Two or more races, non-Hispanic/Latino), 53 international. Average age 34. 354 applicants, 71% accepted, 190 enrolled. In 2017, 156 master's awarded. *Entrance requirements:* For master's, GMAT, GRE, minimum GPA of 2.75 in last 60 hours, 2.5 overall (on a 3.0 scale); 27 hours of course work in business and economics. Additional exam requirements/recommendations for international students: Required—TOEFL (minimum score 79 iBT), IELTS (minimum score 6), PTE (minimum score 54). *Application deadline:* Applications are processed on a rolling basis. Application fee: $50 ($100 for international students). Electronic applications accepted. *Expenses:* Tuition, state resident: full-time $7824; part-time $5943 per year. Tuition, nonresident: full-time $15,648; part-time $11,736 per year. *Required fees:* $3064; $2298 per unit. Tuition and fees vary according to course load and reciprocity agreements. *Financial support:* In 2017–18, 114 students received support. Scholarships/grants available. Financial award application deadline: 2/1; financial award applicants required to submit FAFSA. *Total annual research expenditures:* $193,193. *Unit head:* Dr. Gregory A. Carnes, Dean, 256-765-4261, Fax: 256-765-4170, E-mail: gacarnes@una.edu. *Application contact:* Hillary N. Coats, Graduate Admissions Coordinator, 256-765-4447, E-mail: graduate@una.edu. Website: https://www.una.edu/mba/index.html

The University of North Carolina at Chapel Hill, Kenan-Flagler Business School, Accounting Program, Chapel Hill, NC 27599. Offers MAC. *Entrance requirements:* For master's, GMAT. Additional exam requirements/recommendations for international students: Required—TOEFL. *Expenses:* Contact institution. *Faculty research:* Corporate taxation, international taxation, financial accounting, corporate governance, strategy.

The University of North Carolina at Chapel Hill, Kenan-Flagler Business School, Doctoral Program in Business Administration, Chapel Hill, NC 27599. Offers accounting

(PhD); finance (PhD); marketing (PhD); operations management (PhD); organizational behavior (PhD); strategy (PhD). *Accreditation:* AACSB. *Degree requirements:* For doctorate, thesis/dissertation. *Entrance requirements:* For doctorate, GMAT or GRE General Test. Electronic applications accepted. *Expenses:* Contact institution.

The University of North Carolina at Charlotte, Belk College of Business, Turner School of Accountancy, Charlotte, NC 28223-0001. Offers M Acct. *Accreditation:* AACSB. *Program availability:* Part-time, evening/weekend. *Faculty:* 10 full-time (3 women), 1 part-time/adjunct (0 women). *Students:* 63 full-time (35 women), 48 part-time (22 women); includes 22 minority (5 Black or African American, non-Hispanic/Latino; 11 Asian, non-Hispanic/Latino; 5 Hispanic/Latino; 1 Two or more races, non-Hispanic/ Latino), 13 international. Average age 27. 149 applicants, 69% accepted, 76 enrolled. In 2017, 63 master's awarded. *Degree requirements:* For master's, thesis or alternative. *Entrance requirements:* For master's, GMAT or GRE, bachelor's degree from accredited college or university; official transcript of all previous academic work; minimum overall GPA of 3.0 on previous work beyond high school; completion of a principles of financial accounting course with minimum B grade; at least three evaluations; essay. Additional exam requirements/recommendations for international students: Required—TOEFL (minimum score 523 paper-based, 70 iBT) or IELTS (6.5). *Application deadline:* For fall admission, 3/1 priority date for domestic and international students; for spring admission, 10/1 priority date for domestic and international students; for summer admission, 4/1 priority date for domestic and international students. Applications are processed on a rolling basis. Application fee: $75. Electronic applications accepted. *Expenses:* Contact institution. *Financial support:* Research assistantships, teaching assistantships, career-related internships or fieldwork, institutionally sponsored loans, scholarships/grants, and unspecified assistantships available. Support available to part-time students. Financial award application deadline: 3/1; financial award applicants required to submit FAFSA. *Faculty research:* Corporate financial reporting trends, use of latest software for accounting and business applications, latest developments in federal and international taxation. *Unit head:* Dr. Hughlene Burton, Chair, 704-687-7701, Fax: 704-687-1382, E-mail: haburton@uncc.edu. *Application contact:* Kathy B. Giddings, Director of Graduate Admissions, 704-687-5503, Fax: 704-687-1668, E-mail: gradadm@uncc.edu. Website: http://belkcollege.uncc.edu/departments/accounting

The University of North Carolina at Greensboro, Graduate School, Bryan School of Business and Economics, Department of Accounting and Finance, Greensboro, NC 27412-5001. Offers accounting (MS); financial analysis (PMC). *Accreditation:* AACSB. *Entrance requirements:* For master's, GMAT, GRE General Test, previous course work in accounting and business. Additional exam requirements/recommendations for international students: Required—TOEFL. Electronic applications accepted.

The University of North Carolina Wilmington, Cameron School of Business, Accountancy Program, Wilmington, NC 28403-3297. Offers MSA. *Faculty:* 11 full-time (5 women). *Students:* 57 full-time (27 women), 1 part-time (0 women); includes 6 minority (2 Black or African American, non-Hispanic/Latino; 2 Hispanic/Latino; 2 Two or more races, non-Hispanic/Latino). Average age 23. 85 applicants, 68% accepted, 56 enrolled. In 2017, 64 master's awarded. *Degree requirements:* For master's, written and oral comprehensive case analysis. *Entrance requirements:* For master's, GMAT, 3 letters of recommendation, resume. Additional exam requirements/recommendations for international students: Required—TOEFL (minimum score 550 paper-based; 79 iBT), IELTS (minimum score 6.5). *Application deadline:* For fall admission, 4/1 for domestic students; for summer admission, 4/1 for domestic students. Applications are processed on a rolling basis. Application fee: $75. Electronic applications accepted. *Expenses:* Contact institution. *Financial support:* Scholarships/grants and unspecified assistantships available. Financial award application deadline: 1/1; financial award applicants required to submit FAFSA. *Unit head:* Dr. David Mautz, Department Chair, 910-962-2280, Fax: 910-962-3663, E-mail: mautzr@uncw.edu. *Application contact:* Dr. William Kerler, Program Director, 910-962-7632, Fax: 910-962-3663, E-mail: kerlerw@uncw.edu. Website: https://csb.uncw.edu/MSA/index.html

University of Northern Colorado, Graduate School, Monfort College of Business, Greeley, CO 80639. Offers accounting (MA); general business management (MBA); healthcare administration (MBA); human resources management (MBA). *Accreditation:* AACSB.

University of Northern Iowa, Graduate College, College of Business Administration, M Acc Program in Accounting, Cedar Falls, IA 50614. Offers M Acc. *Degree requirements:* For master's, thesis or alternative. *Entrance requirements:* For master's, GMAT. Additional exam requirements/recommendations for international students: Required— TOEFL (minimum score 575 paper-based; 89 iBT).

University of North Florida, Coggin College of Business, M Acc Program, Jacksonville, FL 32224. Offers M Acc. *Accreditation:* AACSB. *Program availability:* Part-time, evening/ weekend. *Entrance requirements:* For master's, GMAT or GRE, U.S. bachelor's degree from regionally-accredited university or equivalent foreign degree. Additional exam requirements/recommendations for international students: Required—TOEFL (minimum score 550 paper-based; 79 iBT). Electronic applications accepted. *Faculty research:* Enterprise-wide risk management, accounting input in the strategic planning process, accounting information systems, taxation issues in lawsuits and damage awards, database design.

University of North Florida, Coggin College of Business, MBA Program, Jacksonville, FL 32224. Offers accounting (MBA); construction management (MBA); e-commerce (MBA); economics (MBA); finance (MBA); human resource management (MBA); international business (MBA); logistics (MBA); management applications (MBA). *Accreditation:* AACSB. *Program availability:* Part-time, evening/weekend. *Entrance requirements:* For master's, GMAT or GRE, U.S. bachelor's degree from regionally-accredited university or equivalent foreign degree. Additional exam requirements/ recommendations for international students: Required—TOEFL (minimum score 550 paper-based; 79 iBT). *Faculty research:* Performance measures, costing, and inventory issues in logistics and supply chain management; inter-organizational systems; international management and marketing practices; e-commerce; organizational learning and socialization processes.

University of North Texas, Robert B. Toulouse School of Graduate Studies, Denton, TX 76203-5459. Offers accounting (MS); applied anthropology (MA, MS); applied behavior analysis (Certificate); applied geography (MA); applied technology and performance improvement (M Ed, MS); art education (MA); art history (MA); art museum education (Certificate); arts leadership (Certificate); audiology (Au D); behavior analysis (MS); behavioral science (PhD); biochemistry and molecular biology (MS); biology (MA, MS); biomedical engineering (MS); business analysis (MS); chemistry (MS); clinical health psychology (PhD); communication studies (MA, MS); computer engineering (MS); computer science (MS); counseling (M Ed, MS), including clinical mental health counseling (MS), college and university counseling, elementary school counseling, secondary school counseling; creative writing (MA); criminal justice (MS); curriculum and instruction (M Ed); decision sciences (MBA); design (MA, MFA), including fashion design (MFA), innovation studies, interior design (MFA); early childhood studies (MS); economics (MS); educational leadership (M Ed, Ed D); educational psychology (MS,

Accounting

PhD), including family studies (MS), gifted and talented (MS), human development (MS), learning and cognition (MS), research, measurement and evaluation (MS); electrical engineering (MS); emergency management (MPA); engineering technology (MS); English (MA); English as a second language (MA); environmental science (MS); finance (MBA, MS); financial management (MPA); French (MA); health services management (MBA); higher education (M Ed, Ed D); history (MA, MS); hospitality management (MS); human resources management (MPA); information science (MS); information systems (PhD); information technologies (MBA); interdisciplinary studies (MA, MS); international studies (MA); international sustainable tourism (MS); jazz studies (MM); journalism (MA, MJ, Graduate Certificate), including interactive and virtual digital communication (Graduate Certificate), narrative journalism (Graduate Certificate), public relations (Graduate Certificate); kinesiology (MS); linguistics (MA); local government management (MPA); logistics (PhD); logistics and supply chain management (MBA); long-term care, senior housing, and aging services (MA); management (PhD); marketing (MBA); mathematics (MA, MS); mechanical and energy engineering (MS, PhD); music (MA), including ethnomusicology, music theory, musicology, performance; music composition (PhD); music education (MM Ed, PhD); nonprofit management (MPA); operations and supply chain management (MBA); performance (MM, DMA); philosophy (MA); political science (MA); professional and technical communication (MA); radio, television and film (MA, MFA); rehabilitation counseling (Certificate); sociology (MA); Spanish (MA); special education (M Ed); speech-language pathology (MA); strategic management (MBA); studio art (MFA); teaching (M Ed); MBA/MS. *Program availability:* Part-time, evening/weekend, online learning. Terminal master's awarded for partial completion of doctoral program. *Degree requirements:* For master's, variable foreign language requirement, comprehensive exam (for some programs), thesis (for some programs); for doctorate, variable foreign language requirement, comprehensive exam (for some programs), thesis/dissertation; for other advanced degree, variable foreign language requirement, comprehensive exam (for some programs). *Entrance requirements:* For master's and doctorate, GRE, GMAT. Additional exam requirements/recommendations for international students: Required—TOEFL (minimum score 550 paper-based; 79 iBT). Electronic applications accepted.

University of North Texas at Dallas, Graduate School, Dallas, TX 75241. Offers accounting (MBA); counseling (M Ed, MS); criminal justice (MS); curriculum and instruction (M Ed); educational administration (M Ed); human resources and organizational behavior (MBA); public leadership (MS); strategic management (MBA).

University of Notre Dame, Mendoza College of Business, Master of Science in Accountancy Program, Notre Dame, IN 46556. Offers assurance and advisory services (MSA); tax services (MSA). *Accreditation:* AACSB. *Faculty:* 40 full-time (8 women), 7 part-time/adjunct (0 women). *Students:* 92 full-time (41 women); includes 14 minority (1 Black or African American, non-Hispanic/Latino; 2 American Indian or Alaska Native, non-Hispanic/Latino; 4 Asian, non-Hispanic/Latino; 7 Hispanic/Latino), 17 international. Average age 23. 316 applicants, 41% accepted, 92 enrolled. In 2017, 95 master's awarded. *Entrance requirements:* For master's, GMAT, essay, two recommendations, transcripts from all colleges or universities attended, resume, interview, course descriptions for accounting prerequisites. Additional exam requirements/ recommendations for international students: Required—PTE (minimum score 68), TOEFL (minimum iBT score of 109), IELTS (7.5), or documentation of at least six semesters of full-time university education in English. *Application deadline:* For fall admission, 10/1 for domestic and international students; for spring admission, 5/1 for domestic and international students. Applications are processed on a rolling basis. Application fee: $50 ($100 for international students). Electronic applications accepted. *Expenses:* Contact institution. *Financial support:* In 2017–18, 88 students received support, including 88 fellowships (averaging $15,748 per year); scholarships/grants and unspecified assistantships also available. Financial award application deadline: 2/28; financial award applicants required to submit FAFSA. *Faculty research:* Stock valuation, accounting information in decision-making, choice of accounting method, taxes cost on capital. *Unit head:* Dr. Katherine Spiess, Associate Dean, Graduate Business Programs, 574-631-7236, E-mail: spiess.1@nd.edu. *Application contact:* Kristin McAndrew, Director of Admissions, Graduate Business Programs, 574-631-8488, E-mail: kmcandre@nd.edu. Website: http://msa.nd.edu

University of Oklahoma, Price College of Business, John T. Steed School of Accounting, Norman, OK 73019. Offers M Acc. *Accreditation:* AACSB. *Program availability:* Part-time, 100% online. *Faculty:* 13 full-time (5 women). *Students:* 19 full-time (11 women), 29 part-time (12 women); includes 17 minority (5 Black or African American, non-Hispanic/Latino; 1 American Indian or Alaska Native, non-Hispanic/Latino; 4 Asian, non-Hispanic/Latino; 3 Hispanic/Latino; 4 Two or more races, non-Hispanic/Latino), 5 international. Average age 31. 49 applicants, 80% accepted, 32 enrolled. In 2017, 10 master's awarded. *Entrance requirements:* For master's, GMAT or GRE, resume, statement of goals, 3 letters of recommendation. Additional exam requirements/recommendations for international students: Required—TOEFL (minimum score 100 iBT) or IELTS (minimum score 7). *Application deadline:* For fall admission, 6/15 for domestic students, 3/1 for international students; for spring admission, 11/15 for domestic students, 8/1 for international students; for summer admission, 3/15 for domestic students, 1/1 for international students. Applications are processed on a rolling basis. Application fee: $50 ($100 for international students). Electronic applications accepted. *Expenses:* Contact institution. *Financial support:* In 2017–18, 15 students received support, including 1 fellowship (averaging $5,000 per year), 5 research assistantships (averaging $14,940 per year), 9 teaching assistantships (averaging $13,701 per year); career-related internships or fieldwork, scholarships/grants, and unspecified assistantships also available. Support available to part-time students. Financial award application deadline: 6/1; financial award applicants required to submit FAFSA. *Faculty research:* Tax professional judgment and taxpayer compliance; financial disclosure and reporting decisions; regulation and auditing profession; behavioral issues of auditor-client dyad; market based accounting research. *Unit head:* Wayne Thomas, Director/Chair, 405-325-5799, Fax: 405-325-7348, E-mail: wthomas@ou.edu. *Application contact:* Jennifer Aragon, Academic Advisor, 405-325-2074, Fax: 405-325-7118, E-mail: jhardman@ou.edu. Website: http://www.ou.edu/content/price/accounting.html

University of Oklahoma, Price College of Business, Program in Business Administration, Oklahoma City, OK 73104. Offers business administration (MBA, PhD), including accounting (PhD), business administration, entrepreneurship and economic development (PhD), finance (PhD), management and international business (PhD), management of information systems (PhD), marketing/supply chain (PhD); JD/MBA; MBA/MS. *Accreditation:* AACSB. *Program availability:* Part-time, evening/weekend. *Students:* 100 full-time (27 women), 152 part-time (30 women); includes 36 minority (2 Black or African American, non-Hispanic/Latino; 4 American Indian or Alaska Native, non-Hispanic/Latino; 10 Asian, non-Hispanic/Latino; 13 Hispanic/Latino; 7 Two or more races, non-Hispanic/Latino), 32 international. Average age 31. 247 applicants, 29% accepted, 41 enrolled. In 2017, 118 master's, 9 doctorates awarded. *Degree requirements:* For doctorate, comprehensive exam, thesis/dissertation. *Entrance requirements:* For master's, GMAT or GRE, resume, 2 essays, interview; for doctorate, GMAT or GRE, resume, statement of goals, 3 letters of recommendation. Additional exam requirements/recommendations for international students: Required—TOEFL (minimum score 100 iBT) or IELTS (minimum score 7). *Application deadline:* For fall

admission, 11/1 for domestic and international students; for summer admission, 11/1 for domestic and international students. Applications are processed on a rolling basis. Application fee: $50 ($100 for international students). Electronic applications accepted. *Expenses:* Contact institution. *Financial support:* In 2017–18, 107 students received support, including 6 fellowships with partial tuition reimbursements available (averaging $2,500 per year); research assistantships with full and partial tuition reimbursements available, teaching assistantships with full and partial tuition reimbursements available, career-related internships or fieldwork, scholarships/grants, health care benefits, and unspecified assistantships also available. Support available to part-time students. Financial award application deadline: 6/1; financial award applicants required to submit FAFSA. *Faculty research:* Energy finance; international accounting; organizational behavior and entrepreneurship; management information systems; supply chain. *Unit head:* Laku Chidambaram, Associate Dean for Academic Programs and Engagement, 405-325-8013. *Application contact:* Kate Hile, Associate Director of MBA Admissions, 405-325-4572, E-mail: khile@ou.edu. Website: http://www.ou.edu/price/divisions/graduate-programs/graduate.html

University of Oregon, Graduate School, Charles H. Lundquist College of Business, Department of Accounting, Eugene, OR 97403. Offers M Actg, PhD. *Accreditation:* AACSB. *Program availability:* Part-time. *Degree requirements:* For doctorate, thesis/ dissertation, 2 comprehensive exams. *Entrance requirements:* For master's, GMAT, minimum GPA of 3.0, bachelor's degree in accounting or equivalent; for doctorate, GMAT. Additional exam requirements/recommendations for international students: Required— TOEFL. *Faculty research:* Empirical financial accounting, effects of regulation on accounting standards, use of protocol analysis as a research methodology in accounting.

University of Pennsylvania, Wharton School, Accounting Department, Philadelphia, PA 19104. Offers MBA, PhD. *Accreditation:* AACSB. Terminal master's awarded for partial completion of doctoral program. *Degree requirements:* For doctorate, thesis/ dissertation. *Entrance requirements:* For master's, GMAT; for doctorate, GMAT or GRE. *Faculty research:* Financial reporting, information disclosure, performance measurement, executive compensation, corporate governance.

University of Phoenix–Bay Area Campus, School of Business, San Jose, CA 95134-1805. Offers accountancy (MS); accounting (MBA); business administration (MBA, DBA); energy management (MBA); global management (MBA); health care management (MBA); human resource management (MBA); human resources management (MM); management (MM); marketing (MBA); organizational leadership (DM); project management (MBA); public administration (MPA); technology management (MBA). *Accreditation:* ACBSP. *Program availability:* Evening/weekend, online learning. *Degree requirements:* For master's, thesis (for some programs). *Entrance requirements:* For master's, minimum undergraduate GPA of 3.0, 3 years of work experience. Additional exam requirements/recommendations for international students: Required—TOEFL (minimum score 550 paper-based; 79 iBT). Electronic applications accepted.

University of Phoenix–Central Valley Campus, School of Business, Fresno, CA 93720-1552. Offers accounting (MBA); business administration (MBA); global management (MBA); human resources management (MBA, MM); management (MM); marketing (MBA); public administration (MBA, MM). *Accreditation:* ACBSP.

University of Phoenix–Dallas Campus, School of Business, Dallas, TX 75251. Offers accounting (MBA); business administration (MBA); global management (MBA); human resources management (MBA, MM); management (MM); marketing (MBA); public administration (MBA, MM). *Accreditation:* ACBSP. *Program availability:* Evening/ weekend, online learning. *Degree requirements:* For master's, thesis (for some programs). *Entrance requirements:* For master's, 3 years of work experience, minimum undergraduate GPA of 3.0. Additional exam requirements/recommendations for international students: Required—TOEFL (minimum score 550 paper-based; 79 iBT). Electronic applications accepted.

University of Phoenix–Hawaii Campus, School of Business, Honolulu, HI 96813-3800. Offers accounting (MBA); business administration (MBA); global management (MBA); human resources management (MBA, MM); management (MM); marketing (MBA); public administration (MBA, MM). *Accreditation:* ACBSP. *Program availability:* Evening/weekend. *Degree requirements:* For master's, thesis (for some programs). *Entrance requirements:* For master's, minimum undergraduate GPA of 3.0, 3 years of work experience. Additional exam requirements/recommendations for international students: Required—TOEFL (minimum score 550 paper-based; 79 iBT). Electronic applications accepted.

University of Phoenix–Houston Campus, School of Business, Houston, TX 77079-2004. Offers accounting (MBA); business administration (MBA); global management (MBA); human resources management (MBA, MM); management (MM); marketing (MBA); public administration (MBA, MM). *Accreditation:* ACBSP. *Program availability:* Evening/weekend, online learning. *Degree requirements:* For master's, thesis (for some programs). *Entrance requirements:* For master's, 3 years of work experience, minimum undergraduate GPA of 3.0. Additional exam requirements/recommendations for international students: Required—TOEFL (minimum score 550 paper-based; 79 iBT). Electronic applications accepted.

University of Phoenix–Las Vegas Campus, School of Business, Las Vegas, NV 89135. Offers accounting (MBA); business administration (MBA); global management (MBA); human resources management (MBA, MM); management (MM); marketing (MBA); public administration (MM). *Accreditation:* ACBSP. *Program availability:* Evening/weekend, online learning. *Degree requirements:* For master's, thesis (for some programs). *Entrance requirements:* For master's, minimum undergraduate GPA of 3.0, 3 years of work experience. Additional exam requirements/recommendations for international students: Required—TOEFL (minimum score 550 paper-based; 79 iBT). Electronic applications accepted.

University of Phoenix–Online Campus, School of Business, Phoenix, AZ 85034-7209. Offers accountancy (MS); accounting (MBA, Certificate); business administration (MBA); energy management (MBA); global management (MBA); health care management (MBA); human resource management (MBA, Certificate); human resources management (MM); management (MM); marketing (MBA, Certificate); project management (MBA, Certificate); public administration (MBA, MM); technology management (MBA). *Program availability:* Evening/weekend, online learning. *Entrance requirements:* Additional exam requirements/recommendations for international students: Required—TOEFL, TOEIC (Test of English as an International Communication), Berlitz Online English Proficiency Exam, PTE, or IELTS. Electronic applications accepted. *Expenses:* Contact institution.

University of Phoenix–Phoenix Campus, School of Business, Tempe, AZ 85282-2371. Offers accounting (MBA, MS, Certificate); business administration (MBA); energy management (MBA); global management (MBA); health care management (MBA); human resource management (MBA, Certificate); management (MM); marketing (MBA); project management (MBA); technology management (MBA). *Program availability:* Evening/weekend, online learning. *Entrance requirements:* Additional exam requirements/recommendations for international students: Required—TOEFL, TOEIC (Test of English as an International Communication), Berlitz Online English Proficiency Exam, PTE, or IELTS. Electronic applications accepted. *Expenses:* Contact institution.

University of Phoenix–Sacramento Valley Campus, School of Business, Sacramento, CA 95833-4334. Offers accounting (MBA); business administration (MBA); global management (MBA); human resources management (MBA, MM); management (MM); marketing (MBA); public administration (MBA, MM). *Accreditation:* ACBSP. *Program availability:* Evening/weekend. *Degree requirements:* For master's, thesis (for some programs). *Entrance requirements:* For master's, minimum undergraduate GPA of 3.0, 3 years work experience. Additional exam requirements/recommendations for international students: Required—TOEFL (minimum score 550 paper-based; 79 iBT). Electronic applications accepted.

University of Phoenix–San Antonio Campus, School of Business, San Antonio, TX 78230. Offers accounting (MBA); business administration (MBA); e-business (MBA); global management (MBA); human resources management (MBA, MM); management (MM); marketing (MBA); public administration (MBA, MM). *Accreditation:* ACBSP.

University of Phoenix–San Diego Campus, School of Business, San Diego, CA 92123. Offers accounting (MBA); business administration (MBA); global management (MBA); human resources management (MBA, MM); management (MM); marketing (MBA); public administration (MBA). *Accreditation:* ACBSP. *Program availability:* Evening/weekend. *Degree requirements:* For master's, thesis (for some programs). *Entrance requirements:* For master's, 3 years of work experience, minimum undergraduate GPA of 3.0. Additional exam requirements/recommendations for international students: Required—TOEFL (minimum score 550 paper-based; 79 iBT). Electronic applications accepted.

University of Pittsburgh, Katz Graduate School of Business, Doctoral Program in Business Administration, Pittsburgh, PA 15260. Offers accounting (PhD); business analytics and operations (PhD); finance (PhD); information systems and technology management (PhD); marketing (PhD); organizational behavior and human resources (PhD); strategic management (PhD). *Accreditation:* AACSB. *Program availability:* Evening/weekend. *Faculty:* 91 full-time (30 women), 14 part-time/adjunct (4 women). *Students:* 51 full-time (26 women), 1 (woman) part-time; includes 5 minority (1 Black or African American, non-Hispanic/Latino; 3 Asian, non-Hispanic/Latino; 1 Two or more races, non-Hispanic/Latino), 30 international. Average age 31. 337 applicants, 3% accepted, 10 enrolled. In 2017, 7 doctorates awarded. *Degree requirements:* For doctorate, comprehensive exam, thesis/dissertation, student teaching. *Entrance requirements:* For doctorate, GMAT or GRE, 3 recommendations, statement of purpose, transcripts of all previous course work and degrees. Additional exam requirements/recommendations for international students: Required—TOEFL (minimum score 100 iBT) or IELTS (minimum score 7.0). *Application deadline:* For fall admission, 1/1 for domestic and international students. Applications are processed on a rolling basis. Application fee: $50. Electronic applications accepted. *Financial support:* In 2017–18, 43 students received support, including 33 research assistantships with full tuition reimbursements available (averaging $26,500 per year), 10 teaching assistantships with full tuition reimbursements available (averaging $28,220 per year); Federal Work-Study, scholarships/grants, health care benefits, and unspecified assistantships also available. Financial award application deadline: 1/1; financial award applicants required to submit FAFSA. *Faculty research:* Accounting systems/financial reporting, corporate finance, shopper marketing/consumer behavior, management information systems, organizational behavior and entrepreneurship. *Total annual research expenditures:* $475,077. *Unit head:* Dr. Arjang A. Assad, Dean, 412-648-1556, Fax: 412-648-1552, E-mail: aassad@katz.pitt.edu. *Application contact:* Dr. Dennis Galletta, Director, 412-648-1699, Fax: 412-648-3633, E-mail: galletta@katz.pitt.edu. Website: http://www.katz.business.pitt.edu/degrees/phd/

See Display on page 158 and Close-Up on page 187.

University of Pittsburgh, Katz Graduate School of Business, Master of Science in Accounting Program, Pittsburgh, PA 15260. Offers MS. *Program availability:* Part-time, blended/hybrid learning. *Faculty:* 91 full-time (30 women), 14 part-time/adjunct (4 women). *Students:* 129 full-time (85 women), 6 part-time (4 women); includes 7 minority (2 Black or African American, non-Hispanic/Latino; 1 Asian, non-Hispanic/Latino; 3 Hispanic/Latino; 1 Two or more races, non-Hispanic/Latino), 85 international. Average age 23. 357 applicants, 56% accepted, 94 enrolled. In 2017, 83 master's awarded. *Degree requirements:* For master's, 30 credits; minimum cumulative GPA of 3.0. *Entrance requirements:* For master's, GMAT, GRE. Additional exam requirements/recommendations for international students: Required—TOEFL (minimum score 100 iBT) or IELTS (minimum score 7.0). *Application deadline:* For fall admission, 4/1 priority date for domestic students, 2/1 priority date for international students. Application fee: $50. Electronic applications accepted. *Financial support:* Scholarships/grants available. Financial award application deadline: 6/1; financial award applicants required to submit FAFSA. *Faculty research:* Accounting systems/financial reporting, corporate finance, shopper marketing/consumer behavior, management information systems, organizational behavior and entrepreneurship. *Total annual research expenditures:* $475,077. *Unit head:* Sandra Douglas, Director, 412-648-1556, Fax: 412-624-5198, E-mail: srdouglas@katz.pitt.edu. *Application contact:* Jessica Quarterman, Assistant Director, 412-624-0147, E-mail: macc@katz.pitt.edu. Website: http://www.katz.business.pitt.edu/degrees/ms/accounting

University of Puerto Rico–Río Piedras, College of Business Administration, San Juan, PR 00931-3300. Offers accounting (MBA); finance (MBA, PhD); general business (MBA); human resources management (MBA); international trade and business (MBA, PhD); marketing (MBA); operations management (MBA); quantitative methods (MBA). *Accreditation:* AACSB. *Program availability:* Part-time. *Degree requirements:* For master's, comprehensive exam, thesis or alternative, research project. *Entrance requirements:* For master's, GMAT or PAEG, minimum GPA of 3.0, letter of recommendation; for doctorate, GMAT, PAEG, minimum GPA of 3.0, master degree. *Faculty research:* Management.

University of Rhode Island, Graduate School, College of Business, Program in Accounting, Kingston, RI 02881. Offers MS. *Accreditation:* AACSB. *Faculty:* 11 full-time (6 women). *Students:* 27 full-time (13 women), 8 part-time (5 women); includes 5 minority (2 Black or African American, non-Hispanic/Latino; 1 Asian, non-Hispanic/Latino; 1 Hispanic/Latino; 1 Two or more races, non-Hispanic/Latino). 38 applicants, 87% accepted, 27 enrolled. In 2017, 27 master's awarded. *Entrance requirements:* Additional exam requirements/recommendations for international students: Required—TOEFL. *Application deadline:* For fall admission, 7/15 for domestic students, 2/15 for international students. Application fee: $35. Electronic applications accepted. *Expenses:* Tuition, state resident: full-time $12,706; part-time $786 per credit. Tuition, nonresident: full-time $25,216; part-time $1401 per credit. *Required fees:* $1598; $45 per credit. One-time fee: $30 part-time. *Financial support:* Application deadline: 2/1. *Unit head:* Prof. Judy Beckman, Area Coordinator, 401-874-4327, E-mail: beckman@uri.edu. Website: https://web.uri.edu/business/m-s-in-accounting/

University of Rochester, Simon Business School, Doctoral Program in Business Administration, Rochester, NY 14627. Offers accounting (PhD); computer information systems (PhD); finance (PhD); marketing (PhD); operations management (PhD). *Accreditation:* AACSB. *Faculty:* 70 full-time (12 women), 23 part-time/adjunct (6 women). *Students:* 50 full-time (17 women); includes 2 minority (both Asian, non-Hispanic/Latino), 41 international. Average age 28. 199 applicants, 10% accepted, 9

enrolled. In 2017, 8 doctorates awarded. *Degree requirements:* For doctorate, comprehensive exam, thesis/dissertation, qualifying exam. *Entrance requirements:* For doctorate, GMAT or GRE. Additional exam requirements/recommendations for international students: Required—TOEFL. *Application deadline:* For fall admission, 1/5 for domestic and international students. Application fee: $100. Electronic applications accepted. *Expenses:* Contact institution. *Financial support:* In 2017–18, 50 students received support. Fellowships, research assistantships, teaching assistantships, health care benefits, and tuition waivers (full) available. Financial award application deadline: 1/5. *Faculty research:* Empirical industrial organization, risk management, financial disclosure and regulation, social media, health care management. *Unit head:* Dr. Ron Kaniel, Committee Chair, 585-275-2959. *Application contact:* Sue Harris, PhD Administrator, 585-275-2959, E-mail: phdoffice@simon.rochester.edu. Website: http://www.simon.rochester.edu/programs/phd/index.aspx

University of Rochester, Simon Business School, Full-Time Master's Program in Business Administration, Rochester, NY 14627. Offers business systems consulting (MBA); competitive and organizational strategy (MBA); computers and information systems (MBA); corporate accounting (MBA); entrepreneurship (MBA); finance (MBA); health sciences management (MBA); marketing (MBA); operations management (MBA); public accounting (MBA); strategy and organizations (MBA). *Accreditation:* AACSB. *Faculty:* 70 full-time (12 women), 23 part-time/adjunct (6 women). *Students:* 208 full-time (70 women). Average age 28. *Entrance requirements:* For master's, GMAT or GRE. *Application deadline:* For fall admission, 10/15 for domestic and international students; for winter admission, 1/5 for domestic and international students; for spring admission, 3/15 for domestic and international students; for summer admission, 5/15 for domestic and international students. Application fee: $150. *Financial support:* Fellowships, institutionally sponsored loans, scholarships/grants, and tuition waivers (full and partial) available. Financial award application deadline: 1/5; financial award applicants required to submit FAFSA. *Faculty research:* Empirical industrial organization, risk management, financial disclosure and regulation, social media, health care management. *Unit head:* Andrew Ainslie, Dean, 585-275-3316, E-mail: andrew.ainslie@simon.rochester.edu. *Application contact:* Rebekah S. Lewin, Assistant Dean of Admissions and Financial Aid, 585-275-3533, E-mail: admissions@simon.rochester.edu. Website: http://www.simon.rochester.edu/programs/full-time-mba/index.aspx

University of Rochester, Simon Business School, Master of Science Program in Accountancy, Rochester, NY 14627. Offers MS. *Faculty:* 70 full-time (12 women), 23 part-time/adjunct (6 women). *Students:* 49 full-time (38 women). Average age 22. *Entrance requirements:* For master's, GMAT or GRE. *Application deadline:* For fall admission, 10/15 for domestic and international students; for winter admission, 1/5 for domestic and international students; for spring admission, 3/15 for domestic and international students; for summer admission, 5/15 for domestic and international students. Application fee: $150. *Financial support:* Scholarships/grants available. Financial award application deadline: 1/1. *Faculty research:* Empirical industrial organization, risk management, financial disclosure and regulation, social media, health care management. *Unit head:* Andrew Ainslie, Dean, 585-275-3316, E-mail: andrew.ainslie@simon.rochester.edu. *Application contact:* Rebekah S. Lewin, Assistant Dean of Admissions and Financial Aid, 585-275-3533, E-mail: admissions@simon.rochester.edu. Website: http://www.simon.rochester.edu/programs/full-time-ms-in-accountancy/index.aspx

University of Rochester, Simon Business School, Part-Time MBA Program, Rochester, NY 14627. Offers business systems consulting (MBA); competitive and organizational strategy (MBA); computers and information systems (MBA); corporate accounting (MBA); entrepreneurship (MBA); finance (MBA); health sciences management (MBA); marketing (MBA), including brand management, marketing strategy, pricing; operations management (MBA); public accounting (MBA). *Program availability:* Part-time-only, evening/weekend. *Faculty:* 70 full-time (12 women), 23 part-time/adjunct (6 women). *Students:* 159 part-time (62 women); includes 25 minority (5 Black or African American, non-Hispanic/Latino; 9 Asian, non-Hispanic/Latino; 9 Hispanic/Latino; 2 Two or more races, non-Hispanic/Latino), 4 international. Average age 32. 39 applicants, 92% accepted, 35 enrolled. In 2017, 59 master's awarded. *Entrance requirements:* For master's, GRE or GMAT. *Application deadline:* For fall admission, 8/1 for domestic students; for spring admission, 2/15 for domestic students. Applications are processed on a rolling basis. Application fee: $150. Electronic applications accepted. *Expenses:* $1,875 per credit, $1,385 fees. *Financial support:* In 2017–18, 69 students received support. Tuition waivers (partial) available. Financial award application deadline: 8/1. *Unit head:* Andrew Ainslie, Dean, 585-275-3316, E-mail: andrew.ainslie@simon.rochester.edu. *Application contact:* Molly Mesko, Executive Director, EMBA and Part-Time Programs, 585-275-4277, E-mail: molly.mesko@simon.rochester.edu. Website: http://www.simon.rochester.edu/programs/ptmba/index.aspx

University of St. Thomas, Cameron School of Business, Houston, TX 77006-4696. Offers MBA, MCTM, MIB, MSA, MSF. *Program availability:* Part-time, evening/weekend. *Faculty:* 26 full-time (10 women), 7 part-time/adjunct (1 woman). *Students:* 136 full-time (73 women), 200 part-time (113 women); includes 155 minority (41 Black or African American, non-Hispanic/Latino; 1 American Indian or Alaska Native, non-Hispanic/Latino; 24 Asian, non-Hispanic/Latino; 81 Hispanic/Latino; 8 Two or more races, non-Hispanic/Latino), 99 international. Average age 31. 121 applicants, 97% accepted, 70 enrolled. In 2017, 186 master's awarded. *Degree requirements:* For master's, capstone (for some programs), additional course requirements for those sitting for state accountancy exam. *Entrance requirements:* For master's, minimum GPA of 2.5, 3 letters of recommendation. Additional exam requirements/recommendations for international students: Required—TOEFL (minimum score 550 paper-based; 79 iBT), IELTS (minimum score 6.5), PTE (minimum score 53). *Application deadline:* For fall admission, 7/15 for domestic and international students; for winter admission, 7/15 for domestic and international students; for spring admission, 11/15 for domestic students, 10/15 for international students. Applications are processed on a rolling basis. Application fee: $35. Electronic applications accepted. *Expenses:* Tuition: Full-time $20,934; part-time $1163 per credit hour. *Required fees:* $250; $210 per semester. *Financial support:* In 2017–18, 22 students received support, including research assistantships with partial tuition reimbursements available (averaging $3,000 per year); Federal Work-Study, scholarships/grants, unspecified assistantships, and state work-study, institutional employment also available. Support available to part-time students. Financial award application deadline: 4/15; financial award applicants required to submit FAFSA. *Unit head:* Dr. Beena George, Dean, 713-525-2100, Fax: 713-525-2110, E-mail: cameron@stthom.edu. *Application contact:* 713-525-2100, Fax: 713-525-2110, E-mail: cameron@stthom.edu. Website: http://www.stthom.edu/Academics/Cameron_School_of_Business/Index.aqf

University of St. Thomas, Opus College of Business, Master of Science in Accountancy Program, Minneapolis, MN 55403. Offers MS. *Entrance requirements:* For master's, GMAT. Additional exam requirements/recommendations for international students: Required—TOEFL (minimum score 94 iBT), IELTS (minimum score 7). *Application deadline:* For spring admission, 5/4 for domestic students, 1/13 for international students. Applications are processed on a rolling basis. Application fee:

$60. Electronic applications accepted. Tuition and fees vary according to course load, degree level, campus/location and program. *Financial support:* Career-related internships or fieldwork and scholarships/grants available. *Unit head:* Kristine Sharockman DeVinck, Director, 651-962-4124, Fax: 651-962-4141, E-mail: msacct@stthomas.edu. *Application contact:* Josie Visser, Associate Director of Admissions, 651-962-8825, Fax: 651-962-4141, E-mail: jtvisser@stthomas.edu. Website: http://www.stthomas.edu/accountancy

University of San Diego, School of Business, Programs in Accountancy and Taxation, San Diego, CA 92110-2492. Offers accountancy (MS); taxation (MS). *Program availability:* Part-time, evening/weekend. *Students:* 14 full-time (13 women), 15 part-time (12 women); includes 3 minority (2 Hispanic/Latino; 1 Two or more races, non-Hispanic/Latino), 21 international. Average age 25. In 2017, 27 master's awarded. *Entrance requirements:* For master's, GMAT (minimum score of 550), minimum GPA of 3.0. Additional exam requirements/recommendations for international students: Required—TOEFL (minimum score 580 paper-based; 92 iBT), TWE. *Application deadline:* For fall admission, 4/1 for domestic students, 6/1 for international students; for spring admission, 10/1 for domestic students, 12/1 for international students. Application fee: $80. *Financial support:* In 2017–18, 8 students received support. Career-related internships or fieldwork, Federal Work-Study, institutionally sponsored loans, scholarships/grants, and unspecified assistantships available. Support available to part-time students. Financial award application deadline: 4/1; financial award applicants required to submit FAFSA. *Faculty research:* Accounting, financial report, taxation, Sarbanes-Oxley. *Unit head:* Dr. Diane Pattison, Academic Director, Accountancy Programs, 619-260-4850, E-mail: pattison@sandiego.edu. *Application contact:* Monica Mahon, Associate Director of Graduate Admissions, 619-260-4524, Fax: 619-260-4158, E-mail: grads@sandiego.edu. Website: http://www.sandiego.edu/business/graduate/accounting-tax/

University of Saskatchewan, College of Graduate Studies and Research, Edwards School of Business, Department of Accounting, Saskatoon, SK S7N 5A2, Canada. Offers M Sc, MP Acc. *Program availability:* Part-time. *Degree requirements:* For master's, thesis (for some programs). *Entrance requirements:* For master's, GMAT. Additional exam requirements/recommendations for international students: Required—TOEFL.

The University of Scranton, Kania School of Management, Program in Accountancy, Scranton, PA 18510. Offers M Acc.

The University of Scranton, Kania School of Management, Program in Business Administration, Scranton, PA 18510. Offers accounting (MBA); finance (MBA); general business administration (MBA); health care management (MBA); international business (MBA); management information systems (MBA); marketing (MBA); operations management (MBA). *Accreditation:* AACSB. *Program availability:* Part-time, evening/weekend, 100% online. *Entrance requirements:* For master's, GMAT (for MBA). *Faculty research:* Financial markets, strategic impact of total quality management, internal accounting controls, consumer preference, information systems and the Internet.

University of South Africa, College of Economic and Management Sciences, Pretoria, South Africa. Offers accounting (D Admin, D Com); accounting science (DA); auditing (D Admin, D Com); business administration (M Tech); business economics (D Admin); business leadership (DBL); business management (D Admin, D Com); economic management analysis (M Tech); economics (D Admin, D Com, PhD); human resource development (M Tech); industrial psychology (D Admin, D Com, PhD); logistics (D Com); marketing (M Tech); public administration (D Admin, D Com, DPA, PhD); public management (M Tech); quantitative management (D Admin, D Com); real estate (M Tech); statistics (D Admin, PhD); tourism management (D Admin, D Com); transport economics (D Admin, D Com).

University of South Alabama, Mitchell College of Business, Department of Accounting, Mobile, AL 36688. Offers M Acc. *Program availability:* Part-time, evening/weekend. *Faculty:* 3 full-time (1 woman). *Students:* 12 full-time (8 women), 1 part-time (0 women); includes 1 minority (Black or African American, non-Hispanic/Latino), 2 international. Average age 26. 28 applicants, 18% accepted, 3 enrolled. In 2017, 10 master's awarded. *Degree requirements:* For master's, comprehensive exam. *Entrance requirements:* For master's, GMAT (minimum score of 450, 3.0 in Analytical Writing section), minimum undergraduate GPA of 3.0. Additional exam requirements/recommendations for international students: Required—TOEFL (minimum score 525 paper-based; 71 iBT), IELTS (minimum score 6). *Application deadline:* For fall admission, 7/15 for domestic students, 6/15 for international students; for spring admission, 12/1 for domestic students, 11/1 for international students. Application fee: $35. Electronic applications accepted. *Expenses:* Contact institution. *Financial support:* Fellowships, research assistantships, teaching assistantships, career-related internships or fieldwork, Federal Work-Study, institutionally sponsored loans, scholarships/grants, and unspecified assistantships available. Support available to part-time students. Financial award application deadline: 3/31; financial award applicants required to submit FAFSA. *Unit head:* Dr. Russell Hardin, Chair, 251-460-7410, E-mail: mcobgraduate@southalabama.edu. *Application contact:* Dr. Alex Sharland, Assistant Dean and Director of Graduate Studies, 251-460-6418, Fax: 251-460-6529, E-mail: mcobgraduate@southalabama.edu. Website: http://www.southalabama.edu/colleges/mcob/macc/index.html

University of South Carolina, The Graduate School, Darla Moore School of Business, Master of Accountancy Program, Columbia, SC 29208. Offers business measurement and assurance (M Acc); JD/M Acc. *Accreditation:* AACSB. *Program availability:* Part-time. *Degree requirements:* For master's, comprehensive exam. *Entrance requirements:* For master's, GMAT. Additional exam requirements/recommendations for international students: Required—TOEFL (minimum score 100 iBT); Recommended—IELTS. Electronic applications accepted. *Faculty research:* Judgment modeling, international accounting, accounting information systems, behavioral accounting, cost/management accounting.

University of South Dakota, Graduate School, Beacom School of Business, Department of Accounting, Vermillion, SD 57069. Offers professional accountancy (MP Acc); JD/MP Acc. *Program availability:* Part-time, evening/weekend, online learning. *Degree requirements:* For master's, comprehensive exam. *Entrance requirements:* For master's, GMAT, minimum GPA of 2.7, resume. Additional exam requirements/recommendations for international students: Required—TOEFL (minimum score 550 paper-based; 79 iBT), IELTS (minimum score 6). *Application deadline:* For fall admission, 6/1 priority date for domestic students; for spring admission, 10/1 priority date for domestic students; for summer admission, 3/1 priority date for domestic students. Applications are processed on a rolling basis. Application fee: $35. Electronic applications accepted. *Financial support:* Research assistantships with partial tuition reimbursements, teaching assistantships with partial tuition reimbursements, Federal Work-Study, and unspecified assistantships available. Financial award applicants required to submit FAFSA. *Application contact:* Graduate School, 605-658-6140, Fax: 605-677-6118, E-mail: grad@usd.edu. Website: http://www.usd.edu/business/accounting/graduate

University of Southern California, Graduate School, Marshall School of Business, Leventhal School of Accounting, Los Angeles, CA 90089. Offers accounting (M Acc);

business taxation (MBT); JD/MBT. *Program availability:* Part-time. *Degree requirements:* For master's, 30-48 units of study. *Entrance requirements:* For master's, GMAT, undergraduate degree, communication skills. Additional exam requirements/recommendations for international students: Required—TOEFL. Electronic applications accepted. *Faculty research:* State and local taxation, Securities and Exchange Commission, governance, auditing fees, financial accounting, enterprise zones, women in business.

University of Southern Indiana, Graduate Studies, Romain College of Business, Program in Business Administration, Evansville, IN 47712-3590. Offers accounting (MBA); data analytics (MBA); engineering management (MBA); general business administration (MBA); healthcare administration (MBA); human resource management (MBA). *Accreditation:* AACSB. *Program availability:* Part-time, evening/weekend, 100% online, blended/hybrid learning. *Faculty:* 22 full-time (4 women), 2 part-time/adjunct (0 women). *Students:* 312 full-time (167 women), 148 part-time (56 women); includes 72 minority (43 Black or African American, non-Hispanic/Latino; 8 Asian, non-Hispanic/Latino; 13 Hispanic/Latino; 8 Two or more races, non-Hispanic/Latino), 10 international. Average age 33. In 2017, 34 master's awarded. *Entrance requirements:* For master's, GMAT or GRE, minimum GPA of 2.5, resume, 3 professional references. Additional exam requirements/recommendations for international students: Required—TOEFL (minimum score 550 paper-based; 79 iBT), IELTS (minimum score 6). *Application deadline:* For fall admission, 8/1 for domestic students, 3/1 priority date for international students. Applications are processed on a rolling basis. Application fee: $40. Electronic applications accepted. *Expenses:* Tuition, state resident: full-time $9394. Tuition, nonresident: full-time $17,917. *Required fees:* $510. *Financial support:* In 2017–18, 18 students received support. Federal Work-Study, scholarships/grants, tuition waivers (full and partial), and unspecified assistantships available. Financial award application deadline: 3/1; financial award applicants required to submit FAFSA. *Unit head:* Dr. Jack E. Smothers, Program Director, 812-461-5248, E-mail: jesmothers@usi.edu. *Application contact:* Michelle Simmons, MBA Program Assistant, 812-464-1926, Fax: 812-465-1044, E-mail: masimmons3@usi.edu. Website: http://www.usi.edu/business/mba

University of Southern Maine, College of Management and Human Service, School of Business, Portland, ME 04104-9300. Offers accounting (MBA); business administration (MBA); finance (MBA); health management and policy (MBA); sustainability (MBA); JD/MBA; MBA/MSA; MBA/MSN; MS/MBA. *Accreditation:* AACSB. *Program availability:* Part-time, evening/weekend. *Entrance requirements:* For master's, GMAT or GRE, minimum AACSB index of 1100. Additional exam requirements/recommendations for international students: Required—TOEFL (minimum score 550 paper-based; 79 iBT). Electronic applications accepted. *Faculty research:* Economic development, management information systems, real options, system dynamics, simulation.

University of Southern Mississippi, College of Business, School of Accountancy, Hattiesburg, MS 39406-0001. Offers accountancy (MPA). *Accreditation:* AACSB. *Program availability:* Part-time, evening/weekend. *Students:* 11 full-time (7 women). 18 applicants, 67% accepted, 11 enrolled. In 2017, 6 master's awarded. *Degree requirements:* For master's, comprehensive exam. *Entrance requirements:* For master's, GMAT, minimum GPA of 2.75 on last 60 hours. Additional exam requirements/recommendations for international students: Required—TOEFL, IELTS. *Application deadline:* For fall admission, 7/15 priority date for domestic students, 7/15 for international students; for spring admission, 11/15 priority date for domestic students, 11/15 for international students. Applications are processed on a rolling basis. Application fee: $60. Electronic applications accepted. *Expenses:* Tuition, state resident: full-time $3830. *Financial support:* Research assistantships with full tuition reimbursements, Federal Work-Study, institutionally sponsored loans, scholarships/grants, health care benefits, and unspecified assistantships available. Support available to part-time students. Financial award application deadline: 3/15; financial award applicants required to submit FAFSA. *Faculty research:* Bank liquidity, subchapter S corporations, internal auditing, governmental accounting, inflation accounting. *Unit head:* Gwen Pate, Director, 601-266-4641, Fax: 601-266-4642. *Application contact:* Amy Yeend, Assistant Dean, Academic and Career Services, 601-266-4663, Fax: 601-266-5814. Website: https://www.usm.edu/business/accounting

University of South Florida, Muma College of Business, Lynn Pippenger School of Accountancy, Tampa, FL 33620-9951. Offers accountancy (M Acc, PhD), including assurance (M Acc), corporate accounting (M Acc), tax (M Acc). *Accreditation:* AACSB. *Program availability:* Part-time, evening/weekend. *Faculty:* 13 full-time (4 women). *Students:* 74 full-time (35 women), 26 part-time (15 women); includes 32 minority (4 Black or African American, non-Hispanic/Latino; 6 Asian, non-Hispanic/Latino; 19 Hispanic/Latino; 3 Two or more races, non-Hispanic/Latino), 10 international. Average age 25. 102 applicants, 53% accepted, 43 enrolled. In 2017, 58 master's, 1 doctorate awarded. Terminal master's awarded for partial completion of doctoral program. *Degree requirements:* For master's, comprehensive exam, thesis or alternative; for doctorate, comprehensive exam, thesis/dissertation. *Entrance requirements:* For master's, GMAT, minimum overall GPA of 3.0 in general upper-level coursework and in upper-level accounting coursework (minimum of 21 hours at a U.S. accredited program within past 5 years); for doctorate, GMAT or GRE, personal statement, recommendations, interview. Additional exam requirements/recommendations for international students: Required—TOEFL (minimum score 550 paper-based; 79 iBT) or IELTS (minimum score 6.5). *Application deadline:* For fall admission, 3/1 priority date for domestic students, 3/1 for international students; for spring admission, 10/1 for domestic students, 9/15 for international students; for summer admission, 2/15 for domestic and international students. Application fee: $30. Electronic applications accepted. *Financial support:* In 2017–18, 43 students received support, including 18 teaching assistantships with tuition reimbursements available (averaging $12,273 per year); scholarships/grants, health care benefits, and unspecified assistantships also available. Financial award applicants required to submit FAFSA. *Faculty research:* Auditing, auditor independence, audit committee decisions, fraud detection and reporting, disclosure effects, effects of information technology on accounting, governmental accounting/auditing, accounting information systems, data modeling and design methodologies for accounting systems, auditing computer-based systems, expert systems, group support systems in accounting, fair value accounting issues, corporate governance, financial accounting, financial reporting quality. *Unit head:* Dr. Uday Murthy, Interim Director, School of Accountancy, 813-974-6516, Fax: 813-974-6528, E-mail: umurthy@usf.edu. *Application contact:* Stacee Bender, 813-974-4516, E-mail: staceebender@usf.edu. Website: http://business.usf.edu/departments/accountancy/

The University of Tampa, Sykes College of Business, Tampa, FL 33606-1490. Offers accounting (MS); business analytics (MBA); cybersecurity (MBA, MS); entrepreneurship (MBA, MS); finance (MBA, MS); information systems management (MBA); innovation management (MBA); international business (MBA); marketing (MBA, MS); nonprofit management (MBA, Certificate). *Accreditation:* AACSB. *Program availability:* Part-time, evening/weekend. *Faculty:* 38 full-time (14 women), 6 part-time/adjunct (1 woman). *Students:* 229 full-time (1 woman), 115 part-time (51 women); includes 51 minority (26 Black or African American, non-Hispanic/Latino; 11 Asian, non-Hispanic/Latino; 1 Native Hawaiian or other Pacific Islander, non-Hispanic/Latino; 13 Two or more races, non-

Hispanic/Latino), 182 international. Average age 28. 1,305 applicants, 39% accepted, 192 enrolled. In 2017, 266 master's awarded. *Degree requirements:* For master's, capstone. *Entrance requirements:* For master's, GMAT, or GRE, official transcripts from all colleges and/or universities previously attended, resume, personal statement, letters of recommendation. Additional exam requirements/recommendations for international students: Required—TOEFL (minimum score 577 paper-based; 90 iBT), IELTS (minimum score 7.5). *Application deadline:* Applications are processed on a rolling basis. Application fee: $40. Electronic applications accepted. *Expenses:* Contact institution. *Financial support:* In 2017–18, 116 students received support. Career-related internships or fieldwork, scholarships/grants, and unspecified assistantships available. Financial award applicants required to submit FAFSA. *Faculty research:* Job market signaling, on-line shopping behaviors and social media, the Tampa Bay economy, digital literacy, entrepreneurship in small businesses. *Unit head:* Dr. Natasha F. Veltri, Associate Dean, 813-253-6289, E-mail: nveltri@ut.edu. *Application contact:* Chanelle Cox, Staff Assistant, Admissions for Graduate and Continuing Studies, 813-253-6249, E-mail: ccox@ut.edu.
Website: http://www.ut.edu/business/

The University of Tennessee, Graduate School, College of Business Administration, Department of Accounting, Knoxville, TN 37996. Offers accounting (M Acc), including assurance; systems (M Acc); taxation (M Acc). *Accreditation:* AACSB. *Degree requirements:* For master's, thesis or alternative. *Entrance requirements:* For master's, GMAT, minimum GPA of 2.7. Additional exam requirements/recommendations for international students: Required—TOEFL. Electronic applications accepted.

The University of Tennessee, Graduate School, College of Business Administration, Program in Business Administration, Knoxville, TN 37996. Offers accounting (PhD); finance (MBA, PhD); logistics and transportation (MBA, PhD); management (PhD); marketing (MBA, PhD); operations management (MBA); professional business administration (MBA); statistics (PhD); JD/MBA; MS/MBA; Pharm D/MBA. Pharm D/MBA offered jointly with The University of Tennessee Health Science Center. *Accreditation:* AACSB. *Program availability:* Online learning. *Degree requirements:* For master's, thesis or alternative; for doctorate, thesis/dissertation. *Entrance requirements:* For master's and doctorate, GMAT, minimum GPA of 2.7. Additional exam requirements/recommendations for international students: Required—TOEFL. Electronic applications accepted.

The University of Tennessee at Chattanooga, Program in Accountancy, Chattanooga, TN 37403. Offers M Acc. *Accreditation:* AACSB. *Program availability:* Part-time, evening/weekend. *Students:* 8 full-time (6 women), 20 part-time (12 women); includes 5 minority (1 Black or African American, non-Hispanic/Latino; 3 Asian, non-Hispanic/Latino; 1 Two or more races, non-Hispanic/Latino). Average age 26. 19 applicants, 63% accepted, 11 enrolled. In 2017, 10 master's awarded. *Entrance requirements:* For master's, GMAT (minimum score 450). Additional exam requirements/recommendations for international students: Required—TOEFL (minimum score 550 paper-based; 79 iBT), IELTS (minimum score 6). *Application deadline:* For fall admission, 6/15 priority date for domestic students, 7/1 for international students; for spring admission, 11/1 priority date for domestic students, 11/1 for international students. Applications are processed on a rolling basis. Application fee: $35 ($40 for international students). Electronic applications accepted. *Expenses:* Contact institution. *Financial support:* Research assistantships, teaching assistantships, career-related internships or fieldwork, scholarships/grants, and unspecified assistantships available. Support available to part-time students. Financial award application deadline: 7/1; financial award applicants required to submit FAFSA. *Faculty research:* Performance measurement, auditing, income taxation, corporate efficiency, portfolio management and performance. *Unit head:* Dr. Dan Hollingsworth, Department Head, 423-425-4664, Fax: 423-425-5255, E-mail: dan-hollingsworth@utc.edu. *Application contact:* Dr. Joanne Romagni, Dean of the Graduate School, 413-425-4478, Fax: 423-425-5223, E-mail: randy-walker@utc.edu.
Website: http://www.utc.edu/college-business/academic-programs/graduate-programs/macc/index.php

The University of Texas at Arlington, Graduate School, College of Business, Accounting Department, Arlington, TX 76019. Offers accounting (MP Acc, MS, PhD); taxation (MS). *Accreditation:* AACSB. *Program availability:* Part-time, evening/weekend. *Degree requirements:* For master's, thesis optional; for doctorate, comprehensive exam, thesis/dissertation. *Entrance requirements:* For master's and doctorate, GMAT. Additional exam requirements/recommendations for international students: Required—TOEFL (minimum score 550 paper-based; 79 iBT).

The University of Texas at Austin, Graduate School, McCombs School of Business, Department of Accounting, Austin, TX 78712-1111. Offers MPA, PhD. *Accreditation:* AACSB. *Degree requirements:* For doctorate, comprehensive exam, thesis/dissertation. *Entrance requirements:* For master's and doctorate, GMAT. Additional exam requirements/recommendations for international students: Required—TOEFL. Electronic applications accepted.

The University of Texas at Dallas, Naveen Jindal School of Management, Program in Accounting, Richardson, TX 75080. Offers MS. *Accreditation:* AACSB. *Faculty:* 21 full-time (8 women), 14 part-time/adjunct (8 women). *Students:* 440 full-time (277 women), 239 part-time (136 women); includes 163 minority (18 Black or African American, non-Hispanic/Latino; 3 American Indian or Alaska Native, non-Hispanic/Latino; 85 Asian, non-Hispanic/Latino; 48 Hispanic/Latino; 9 Two or more races, non-Hispanic/Latino), 376 international. Average age 27. 569 applicants, 61% accepted, 165 enrolled. In 2017, 380 master's awarded. *Entrance requirements:* For master's, GMAT, minimum GPA of 3.0 in upper-level course work in field. Additional exam requirements/recommendations for international students: Required—TOEFL (minimum score 550 paper-based). *Application deadline:* For fall admission, 7/15 for domestic students, 5/1 priority date for international students; for spring admission, 11/15 for domestic students, 9/1 priority date for international students. Applications are processed on a rolling basis. Application fee: $50 ($100 for international students). Electronic applications accepted. *Expenses:* Tuition, state resident: full-time $12,916; part-time $718 per credit hour. Tuition, nonresident: full-time $25,252; part-time $1403 per credit hour. *Financial support:* In 2017–18, 160 students received support, including 15 teaching assistantships with partial tuition reimbursements available (averaging $10,050 per year); research assistantships with partial tuition reimbursements available, career-related internships or fieldwork, Federal Work-Study, institutionally sponsored loans, scholarships/grants, and unspecified assistantships also available. Support available to part-time students. Financial award application deadline: 4/30; financial award applicants required to submit FAFSA. *Faculty research:* Privatization and accounting/auditing, corporate performance and executive compensation, risk management, information technology in accounting. *Unit head:* Dr. Daniel Cohen, Area Coordinator, 972-883-4772, Fax: 972-883-6823, E-mail: dcohen@utdallas.edu. *Application contact:* Mary Guan, Program Director, 972-883-5031, Fax: 972-883-6823, E-mail: mary.guan@utdallas.edu.
Website: http://jindal.utdallas.edu/accounting

The University of Texas at El Paso, Graduate School, College of Business Administration, Department of Accounting, El Paso, TX 79968-0001. Offers M Acc. *Accreditation:* AACSB. *Program availability:* Part-time, evening/weekend. *Entrance requirements:* For master's, GMAT, minimum GPA of 3.0. Additional exam

requirements/recommendations for international students: Required—TOEFL; Recommended—IELTS. Electronic applications accepted. *Faculty research:* Financial and managerial accounting, auditing and accounting information systems.

The University of Texas at San Antonio, College of Business, Department of Accounting, San Antonio, TX 78249-0617. Offers M Acy, PhD. *Accreditation:* AACSB. *Program availability:* Part-time, evening/weekend. *Faculty:* 10 full-time (3 women), 5 part-time/adjunct (3 women). *Students:* 93 full-time (58 women), 53 part-time (28 women); includes 67 minority (6 Black or African American, non-Hispanic/Latino; 9 Asian, non-Hispanic/Latino; 49 Hispanic/Latino; 3 Two or more races, non-Hispanic/Latino), 11 international. Average age 28. 114 applicants, 51% accepted, 18 enrolled. In 2017, 54 master's, 3 doctorates awarded. *Degree requirements:* For master's, thesis or alternative. *Entrance requirements:* For master's, GMAT, bachelor's degree, transcripts, statement of purpose. Additional exam requirements/recommendations for international students: Required—TOEFL (minimum score 550 paper-based; 79 iBT), IELTS (minimum score 6.5). *Application deadline:* For fall admission, 7/31 for domestic students, 3/1 for international students; for spring admission, 10/15 for domestic students, 9/15 for international students. Application fee: $50 ($90 for international students). Electronic applications accepted. *Expenses:* Contact institution. *Financial support:* Teaching assistantships, Federal Work-Study, and scholarships/grants available. *Faculty research:* Capital markets, corporate governance, auditing, health care accounting, fraud. *Total annual research expenditures:* $29,207. *Unit head:* Dr. Sharad Asthana, Chair, 210-458-4320, E-mail: sharad.asthana@utsa.edu. *Application contact:* Dr. Jeff Boone, Advisor of Record for Accounting Doctoral Programs, 210-458-7091, E-mail: jeff.boone@utsa.edu.
Website: http://business.utsa.edu/accounting/

The University of Texas at Tyler, College of Business and Technology, Program in Accountancy, Tyler, TX 75799-0001. Offers M Acc. *Entrance requirements:* For master's, GMAT, official transcripts, current resume.

The University of Texas of the Permian Basin, Office of Graduate Studies, School of Business, Program in Accountancy, Odessa, TX 79762-0001. Offers MPA. *Entrance requirements:* For master's, GMAT. Additional exam requirements/recommendations for international students: Required—TOEFL (minimum score 550 paper-based).

The University of Texas Rio Grande Valley, Robert C. Vackar College of Business and Entrepreneurship, Program in Accounting, Edinburg, TX 78539. Offers M Acc, MS. *Program availability:* Part-time, evening/weekend. *Entrance requirements:* For master's, GMAT. Additional exam requirements/recommendations for international students: Required—TOEFL (minimum score 500 paper-based). Electronic applications accepted. *Expenses:* Tuition, state resident: full-time $5550; part-time $417 per credit hour. Tuition, nonresident: full-time $13,020; part-time $832 per credit hour. *Required fees:* $1169. *Faculty research:* Financial and managerial accounting, international accounting, taxation, ethics.

University of the Cumberlands, Hutton School of Business, Williamsburg, KY 40769-1372. Offers accounting (MBA); business (MBA). *Program availability:* Part-time, online learning. *Entrance requirements:* For master's, GMAT, GRE. Additional exam requirements/recommendations for international students: Required—TOEFL. Electronic applications accepted.

University of the Sacred Heart, Graduate Programs, Department of Business Administration, San Juan, PR 00914-0383. Offers human resource management (MBA); information systems auditing (MS); information technology (Certificate); international marketing (MBA); management information systems (MBA); production and marketing of special events (Certificate); taxation (MBA). *Program availability:* Part-time, evening/weekend. *Degree requirements:* For master's, thesis. *Entrance requirements:* For master's, EXADEP, minimum undergraduate GPA of 2.75, interview.

The University of Toledo, College of Graduate Studies, College of Business and Innovation, Department of Accounting, Toledo, OH 43606-3390. Offers MBA, MSA. *Accreditation:* AACSB. *Program availability:* Part-time, evening/weekend. *Entrance requirements:* For master's, GMAT, GRE, or LSAT, minimum GPA of 2.7 for all prior academic work, three letters of recommendation, statement of purpose, transcripts from all prior institutions attended. Additional exam requirements/recommendations for international students: Required—TOEFL (minimum score 550 paper-based; 80 iBT). Electronic applications accepted. *Faculty research:* Estate gift tax, audit and legal liability, corporate tax, accounting information systems.

The University of Tulsa, Graduate School, Collins College of Business, Program in Accounting, Tulsa, OK 74104-3189. Offers M Acc. *Program availability:* Part-time. *Faculty:* 10 full-time (4 women). *Students:* 19 full-time (6 women), 4 part-time (1 woman); includes 3 minority (1 American Indian or Alaska Native, non-Hispanic/Latino; 1 Hispanic/Latino; 1 Two or more races, non-Hispanic/Latino), 6 international. Average age 25. 29 applicants, 41% accepted, 7 enrolled. In 2017, 10 master's awarded. *Entrance requirements:* For master's, GMAT. Additional exam requirements/recommendations for international students: Required—TOEFL (minimum score 577 paper-based; 91 iBT). *Application deadline:* Applications are processed on a rolling basis. Application fee: $55. Electronic applications accepted. *Expenses:* Tuition: Full-time $22,230. *Required fees:* $2000. Tuition and fees vary according to course load and program. *Financial support:* In 2017–18, 13 students received support, including 13 teaching assistantships with full tuition reimbursements available (averaging $10,951 per year); fellowships, research assistantships, career-related internships or fieldwork, Federal Work-Study, scholarships/grants, health care benefits, tuition waivers (full and partial), and unspecified assistantships also available. Support available to part-time students. Financial award application deadline: 2/1; financial award applicants required to submit FAFSA. *Faculty research:* Capital markets, financial reporting, innovation in accounting. *Unit head:* Dr. Ralph Jackson, Associate Dean, 918-631-2242, Fax: 918-631-2142, E-mail: ralph-jackson@utulsa.edu. *Application contact:* Information Contact, 918-631-2242, E-mail: graduate-business@utulsa.edu.

University of Utah, Graduate School, David Eccles School of Business, Business Administration Program, Salt Lake City, UT 84112. Offers accounting (PhD); business administration (EMBA, MBA, PMBA); finance (PhD); information systems (PhD); marketing (PhD); operations management (PhD); organizational behavior (PhD); strategic management (PhD); MBA/JD; MBA/MHA; MBA/MS. *Program availability:* Part-time, evening/weekend, online learning. *Faculty:* 58 full-time (21 women), 37 part-time/adjunct (7 women). *Students:* 558 full-time (149 women), 103 part-time (21 women); includes 66 minority (1 Black or African American, non-Hispanic/Latino; 16 Asian, non-Hispanic/Latino; 41 Hispanic/Latino; 8 Two or more races, non-Hispanic/Latino), 50 international. Average age 27. 442 applicants, 70% accepted, 226 enrolled. In 2017, 298 master's, 7 doctorates awarded. *Entrance requirements:* For master's, GMAT or GRE; for doctorate, GMAT. Additional exam requirements/recommendations for international students: Required—TOEFL (minimum score 600 paper-based; 100 iBT), IELTS (minimum score 7). *Application deadline:* Applications are processed on a rolling basis. Application fee: $55 ($65 for international students). Electronic applications accepted. *Expenses:* Contact institution. *Financial support:* In 2017–18, 53 students received support. Fellowships, scholarships/grants, and unspecified assistantships available. Financial award application deadline: 2/1; financial award applicants required to submit FAFSA. *Faculty research:* Corporate finance, strategy services, consumer behavior,

Accounting

financial disclosures, operations. *Unit head:* Kristina Diekmann, Department Chair, 801-581-8524, Fax: 801-581-3380, E-mail: mastersinfo@business.utah.edu. *Application contact:* Christine Harris, Coordinator, 801-581-7785, Fax: 801-585-3962, E-mail: execch@business.utah.edu.
Website: http://www.business.utah.edu/

University of Utah, Graduate School, David Eccles School of Business, School of Accounting, Salt Lake City, UT 84112. Offers accounting (PhD); accounting information systems (M Acc); financial/audit (M Acc); tax (M Acc). *Accreditation:* AACSB. *Program availability:* Part-time, evening/weekend. *Faculty:* 15 full-time (6 women), 13 part-time/adjunct (5 women). *Students:* 135 full-time (51 women), 36 part-time (17 women); includes 35 minority (1 Black or African American, non-Hispanic/Latino; 12 Asian, non-Hispanic/Latino; 16 Hispanic/Latino; 1 Native Hawaiian or other Pacific Islander, non-Hispanic/Latino; 5 Two or more races, non-Hispanic/Latino), 21 international. Average age 26. 153 applicants, 87% accepted, 103 enrolled. In 2017, 162 master's awarded. *Degree requirements:* For doctorate, comprehensive exam, thesis/dissertation, oral qualifying exams, written qualifying exams. *Entrance requirements:* For master's, minimum undergraduate GPA of 3.0. Additional exam requirements/recommendations for international students: Required—TOEFL (minimum score 600 paper-based; 100 iBT), IELTS (minimum score 7). *Application deadline:* For fall admission, 3/1 priority date for domestic and international students; for spring admission, 10/15 priority date for domestic students, 8/1 priority date for international students. Applications are processed on a rolling basis. Application fee: $55 ($65 for international students). Electronic applications accepted. *Expenses:* Contact institution. *Financial support:* In 2017–18, 78 students received support. Scholarships/grants and tuition waivers (partial) available. Financial award application deadline: 3/1; financial award applicants required to submit FAFSA. *Faculty research:* Auditing, taxation, information systems, financial accounting, accounting theory, international accounting. *Total annual research expenditures:* $125,000. *Unit head:* Dr. Rachel M. Hayes, Chair, 801-581-4409, Fax: 801-581-3581, E-mail: rachel.hayes@Eccles.utah.edu. *Application contact:* Brittany Wonsor, M Acc Admissions Coordinator, 801-581-7324, E-mail: brittany.wonsor@eccles.utah.edu.
Website: https://eccles.utah.edu/faculty/school-of-accounting/

University of Vermont, Graduate College, Grossman School of Business, Program in Accountancy, Burlington, VT 05405. Offers M Acc. *Students:* 34 (14 women). 58 applicants, 74% accepted, 29 enrolled. In 2017, 23 master's awarded. *Entrance requirements:* For master's, GMAT (500 minimum) or GRE, resume. Additional exam requirements/recommendations for international students: Required—TOEFL (minimum score 550 paper-based, 90 iBT) or IELTS (6.5). *Application deadline:* Applications are processed on a rolling basis. Application fee: $65. Electronic applications accepted. *Expenses:* Tuition, state resident: full-time $11,628; part-time $646 per credit. Tuition, nonresident: full-time $29,340; part-time $1630 per credit. *Required fees:* $1994; $10 per credit. Tuition and fees vary according to course load and program. *Financial support:* In 2017–18, 19 students received support. Scholarships/grants available. *Application contact:* Dr. Susan Hughes, Coordinator, 802-656-4119, E-mail: macc@uvm.edu.
Website: https://www.uvm.edu/business/macc_master_accountancy

University of Virginia, McIntire School of Commerce, Program in Accounting, Charlottesville, VA 22903. Offers MS, JD/MS. *Accreditation:* AACSB. *Entrance requirements:* For master's, GMAT, 2 letters of recommendation, 12 hours of accounting courses. Additional exam requirements/recommendations for international students: Required—TOEFL (minimum score 600 paper-based; 100 iBT), IELTS (minimum score 7). Electronic applications accepted. *Expenses:* Contact institution.

University of Washington, Graduate School, Michael G. Foster School of Business, Seattle, WA 98195-3200. Offers auditing and assurance (MP Acc); business administration (MBA, PhD); entrepreneurship (MS); executive business administration (MBA); global executive business administration (MBA); information systems (MSIS); supply chain management (MSSCM); taxation (MP Acc); technology management (MBA); JD/MBA; MBA/MAIS; MBA/MHA. *Accreditation:* AACSB. *Program availability:* Part-time, evening/weekend, blended/hybrid learning. *Faculty:* 109 full-time (35 women), 54 part-time/adjunct (32 women). *Students:* 469 full-time (173 women), 638 part-time (216 women); includes 314 minority (15 Black or African American, non-Hispanic/Latino; 6 American Indian or Alaska Native, non-Hispanic/Latino; 246 Asian, non-Hispanic/Latino; 28 Hispanic/Latino; 5 Native Hawaiian or other Pacific Islander, non-Hispanic/Latino; 14 Two or more races, non-Hispanic/Latino), 125 international. Average age 32. 1,809 applicants, 84% accepted, 1107 enrolled. In 2017, 543 master's, 10 doctorates awarded. Terminal master's awarded for partial completion of doctoral program. *Degree requirements:* For doctorate, comprehensive exam, thesis/dissertation. *Entrance requirements:* For master's and doctorate, GMAT, GRE. Additional exam requirements/recommendations for international students: Required—TOEFL (minimum score 600 paper-based; 100 iBT). *Application deadline:* For fall admission, 3/15 for domestic students, 1/15 for international students. Application fee: $85. Electronic applications accepted. *Expenses:* Contact institution. *Financial support:* Fellowships with partial tuition reimbursements, research assistantships with partial tuition reimbursements, teaching assistantships with partial tuition reimbursements, Federal Work-Study, institutionally sponsored loans, and scholarships/grants available. Financial award application deadline: 2/28; financial award applicants required to submit FAFSA. *Faculty research:* Finance, consumer behavior, marketing analytics, technology management, supply chain. *Unit head:* Dr. James Jiambalvo, Dean, 206-543-4750, E-mail: jjiambal@uw.edu. *Application contact:* Erin Town, Director of Admissions, 206-543-4661, Fax: 206-616-7351, E-mail: mba@uw.edu.
Website: http://www.foster.washington.edu/

University of Washington, Tacoma, Graduate Programs, MBA Programs, Tacoma, WA 98402-3100. Offers accounting (MBA); business administration (MBA); certified financial analyst (MBA). *Accreditation:* AACSB. *Program availability:* Part-time, evening/weekend. *Entrance requirements:* For master's, GMAT, minimum GPA of 3.0 in final graded 90 quarter credits or 60 graded semester credits; at least 2 years of professional/management work experience. Additional exam requirements/recommendations for international students: Required—TOEFL (minimum score 580 paper-based; 92 iBT). Electronic applications accepted. *Expenses:* Contact institution. *Faculty research:* International accounting, marketing, change management, investments, corporate social responsibility.

University of Waterloo, Graduate Studies, Faculty of Arts, School of Accounting and Finance, Waterloo, ON N2L 3G1, Canada. Offers accounting (M Acc, PhD); finance (M Acc); taxation (M Tax). *Degree requirements:* For master's, thesis or alternative; for doctorate, thesis/dissertation. *Entrance requirements:* For master's, honors degree, minimum B average, resume; for doctorate, GMAT, master's degree, minimum A-average, resume. Additional exam requirements/recommendations for international students: Required—TOEFL, IELTS, PTE. Electronic applications accepted. *Expenses:* Contact institution. *Faculty research:* Auditing, management accounting.

University of West Florida, College of Business, Program in Accounting, Pensacola, FL 32514-5750. Offers M Acc. *Program availability:* Part-time, evening/weekend. *Entrance requirements:* For master's, GMAT (minimum score 450) or equivalent GRE score, official transcripts; bachelor's degree; two letters of recommendation; letter of intent. Additional exam requirements/recommendations for international students:

Required—TOEFL (minimum score 550 paper-based). *Faculty research:* Audit risk, tax legislation, product costing, bank core deposit intangibles, financial reporting.

University of West Georgia, Richards College of Business, Carrollton, GA 30118. Offers accounting (MP Acc); business administration (MBA). *Program availability:* Part-time, evening/weekend, 100% online, blended/hybrid learning. *Faculty:* 38 full-time (14 women). *Students:* 64 full-time (34 women), 123 part-time (61 women); includes 69 minority (48 Black or African American, non-Hispanic/Latino; 6 Asian, non-Hispanic/Latino; 13 Hispanic/Latino; 1 Native Hawaiian or other Pacific Islander, non-Hispanic/Latino; 1 Two or more races, non-Hispanic/Latino), 8 international. Average age 32. 129 applicants, 85% accepted, 74 enrolled. In 2017, 111 master's awarded. *Entrance requirements:* Additional exam requirements/recommendations for international students: Required—TOEFL (minimum score 550 paper-based; 79 iBT). Recommended—IELTS (minimum score 6.5). *Application deadline:* For fall admission, 7/15 for domestic students, 6/1 for international students; for spring admission, 11/15 for domestic students, 10/15 for international students; for summer admission, 5/15 for domestic students, 3/30 for international students. Applications are processed on a rolling basis. Application fee: $40. Electronic applications accepted. Tuition and fees vary according to degree level and program. *Financial support:* Fellowships, research assistantships, teaching assistantships, career-related internships or fieldwork, Federal Work-Study, institutionally sponsored loans, scholarships/grants, and unspecified assistantships available. Support available to part-time students. Financial award application deadline: 4/1; financial award applicants required to submit FAFSA. *Unit head:* Dr. Faye S. McIntyre, Dean of Richards College of Business, 678-839-6467, Fax: 678-839-5040, E-mail: fmcintyr@westga.edu. *Application contact:* Dr. Toby Ziglar, Assistant Dean of the Graduate School, 678-839-1394, Fax: 678-839-1395, E-mail: graduate@westga.edu.
Website: https://www.westga.edu/business

University of Wisconsin–Madison, Graduate School, Wisconsin School of Business, Doctoral Program in Accounting and Information Systems, Madison, WI 53706-1380. Offers PhD. *Accreditation:* AACSB. *Degree requirements:* For doctorate, comprehensive exam, thesis/dissertation. *Entrance requirements:* For doctorate, GMAT or GRE. Additional exam requirements/recommendations for international students: Recommended—TOEFL (minimum score 623 paper-based; 106 iBT), IELTS (minimum score 7.5). Electronic applications accepted. *Expenses:* Contact institution. *Faculty research:* Auditing, financial reporting, economic theory, strategy, computer models, internal audit and fraud, health care fiscal management, tax reporting, incentives used in nonprofit hospitals, CFO compensation, state and local taxation, audit quality, FASB pronouncements, financial statement analysis.

University of Wisconsin–Madison, Graduate School, Wisconsin School of Business, Master of Accountancy Program, Madison, WI 53706-1380. Offers accountancy (M Acc); taxation (M Acc). *Degree requirements:* For master's, minimum GPA of 3.0. *Entrance requirements:* For master's, GMAT, essays. Additional exam requirements/recommendations for international students: Required—TOEFL (minimum score 104 iBT), IELTS (minimum score 8), GMAT. Electronic applications accepted. *Faculty research:* Tax reserves, audit committee incentives, internal audit, accounting report's impact on management decisions.

University of Wisconsin–Whitewater, School of Graduate Studies, College of Business and Economics, Department of Accounting, Whitewater, WI 53190-1790. Offers MPA. *Program availability:* Part-time, evening/weekend, online learning. *Degree requirements:* For master's, thesis or alternative. *Entrance requirements:* For master's, GMAT or GRE, minimum AACSB index of 1000, minimum GPA of 2.75. Additional exam requirements/recommendations for international students: Required—TOEFL (minimum score 550 paper-based; 80 iBT), IELTS (minimum score 6). Electronic applications accepted. *Faculty research:* Laws/economy/quality of life; tax, accounting and public policy.

University of Wyoming, College of Business, Program in Accounting, Laramie, WY 82071. Offers MS. *Degree requirements:* For master's, thesis optional. *Entrance requirements:* For master's, GMAT or GRE, minimum GPA of 3.0. Additional exam requirements/recommendations for international students: Required—TOEFL (minimum score 540 paper-based; 76 iBT). Electronic applications accepted. *Faculty research:* Taxation, accounting education, assessment, not-for-profit accounting, fraud examination, ethics, management accounting.

Upper Iowa University, Online Master's Programs, Fayette, IA 52142-1857. Offers accounting (MBA); corporate financial management (MBA); emergency management and homeland security (MPA); general management (MBA); general studies (MPA); government administration (MPA); health and human services (MPA); human resources management (MBA); nonprofit organizational management (MPA); organizational development (MBA); public management (MPA); sport administration (MSA). MBA also available at Madison, WI campus. *Program availability:* Part-time, online learning. *Degree requirements:* For master's, research project. *Entrance requirements:* For master's, GMAT, GRE, or minimum GPA of 2.7 during last 60 hours. Additional exam requirements/recommendations for international students: Required—TOEFL (minimum score 570 paper-based). Electronic applications accepted. *Faculty research:* Total quality management, teams, organization culture and climate, management.

Ursuline College, School of Graduate and Professional Studies, Program in Business Administration, Pepper Pike, OH 44124-4398. Offers ethical and entrepreneurial leadership (MBA); financial planning and accounting (MBA); health services management (MBA); management (MBA); management and leadership (MBA); marketing and communications management (MBA). *Program availability:* Part-time. *Faculty:* 3 full-time (2 women), 3 part-time/adjunct (2 women). *Students:* 3 full-time (all women), 26 part-time (23 women); includes 13 minority (12 Black or African American, non-Hispanic/Latino; 1 Two or more races, non-Hispanic/Latino). Average age 38. 13 applicants, 85% accepted, 6 enrolled. In 2017, 11 master's awarded. *Degree requirements:* For master's, comprehensive exam (for some programs). *Entrance requirements:* For master's, GRE. Additional exam requirements/recommendations for international students: Required—TOEFL (minimum score 500 paper-based) or GRE. *Application deadline:* Applications are processed on a rolling basis. Application fee: $25. Electronic applications accepted. *Expenses:* $842 per credit hour. *Financial support:* In 2017–18, 3 students received support. Scholarships/grants available. Financial award application deadline: 8/1; financial award applicants required to submit FAFSA. *Faculty research:* Gift economy; sharing economy; cooperative business models; collaborative leadership; corporate social responsibility and the triple bottom line, defined as the three P's: people, planet and profit. *Unit head:* Dr. Anthony Caffarelli, Associate Professor, 440-646-8134, Fax: 440-684-6088, E-mail: tcafarelli@ursuline.edu. *Application contact:* Melanie Steele, Director of Graduate Admission, 440-646-8146, Fax: 440-684-6138, E-mail: graduateadmissions@ursuline.edu.

Utah State University, School of Graduate Studies, Jon M. Huntsman School of Business, School of Accountancy, Logan, UT 84322. Offers M Acc. *Accreditation:* AACSB. *Program availability:* Part-time. *Entrance requirements:* For master's, GMAT, minimum GPA of 3.0, 3 recommendation letters. Additional exam requirements/recommendations for international students: Required—TOEFL. *Faculty research:* Relationship theory, enterprise systems, just in time/loan, reported earnings measures, accounting education.

Utah Valley University, MBA Program, Orem, UT 84058-5999. Offers accounting (MBA); management (MBA). *Accreditation:* AACSB. *Program availability:* Part-time, evening/weekend. *Entrance requirements:* For master's, GMAT, official transcripts, current resume, three letters of recommendation, essay. Additional exam requirements/recommendations for international students: Required—TOEFL (minimum score 79 iBT). Electronic applications accepted. *Expenses:* Contact institution.

Utica College, Program in Accountancy, Utica, NY 13502-4892. Offers MBA. *Program availability:* Part-time, evening/weekend. *Faculty:* 3 full-time (1 woman). *Students:* 8 full-time (4 women), 7 part-time (all women); includes 7 minority (1 Black or African American, non-Hispanic/Latino; 4 Asian, non-Hispanic/Latino; 2 Hispanic/Latino). Average age 25. 16 applicants, 88% accepted, 11 enrolled. In 2017, 11 master's awarded. *Entrance requirements:* For master's, BS, minimum GPA of 3.0. Additional exam requirements/recommendations for international students: Required—TOEFL (minimum score 525 paper-based). *Application deadline:* Applications are processed on a rolling basis. Application fee: $50. Electronic applications accepted. *Expenses:* Contact institution. *Financial support:* Career-related internships or fieldwork, scholarships/grants, tuition waivers (partial), and unspecified assistantships available. Support available to part-time students. Financial award application deadline: 3/15; financial award applicants required to submit FAFSA. *Unit head:* Dr. Zhaodan Huang, MBA Director, 315-792-3247, E-mail: zhuang@utica.edu. *Application contact:* John D. Rowe, Director of Graduate Admissions, 315-792-3824, Fax: 315-792-3003, E-mail: jrowe@utica.edu.
Website: http://www.utica.edu/academic/ssm/accounting/mba/

Valdosta State University, Langdale College of Business, Valdosta, GA 31698. Offers accountancy (M Acc); business administration (MBA); healthcare administration (MBA). MBA program is a member of the Georgia WebMBA. *Accreditation:* AACSB. *Program availability:* Part-time, evening/weekend, 100% online, blended/hybrid learning. *Degree requirements:* For master's, comprehensive written and/or oral exams. *Entrance requirements:* For master's, GMAT or GRE, minimum GPA of 2.75. Additional exam requirements/recommendations for international students: Required—TOEFL (minimum score 523 paper-based); Recommended—IELTS. *Application deadline:* For fall admission, 7/1 for domestic and international students; for spring admission, 11/1 for domestic and international students. Applications are processed on a rolling basis. Application fee: $45. Electronic applications accepted. *Expenses:* Contact institution. *Financial support:* Research assistantships with full tuition reimbursements, institutionally sponsored loans, and scholarships/grants available. Support available to part-time students. Financial award application deadline: 7/1; financial award applicants required to submit FAFSA. *Unit head:* Dr. Mel Schnake, Director, 229-245-2233, Fax: 229-245-2795, E-mail: mschnake@valdosta.edu. *Application contact:* Jessica Powers, Admission Specialist, 229-333-5694, Fax: 229-245-3853, E-mail: jldevane@valdosta.edu.
Website: http://www.valdosta.edu/academics/graduate-school/our-programs/business-administration.php

Vanderbilt University, Vanderbilt University Owen Graduate School of Management, Master of Accountancy in Valuation Program, Nashville, TN 37203. Offers M Acc. *Entrance requirements:* For master's, GMAT or GRE. Additional exam requirements/recommendations for international students: Required—TOEFL, IELTS. Electronic applications accepted.

Vanderbilt University, Vanderbilt University Owen Graduate School of Management, Master of Accountancy Program, Nashville, TN 37240-1001. Offers M Acc. *Accreditation:* AACSB. *Entrance requirements:* For master's, GMAT or GRE. Additional exam requirements/recommendations for international students: Required—TOEFL, IELTS. Electronic applications accepted. *Expenses:* Contact institution.

Vanderbilt University, Vanderbilt University Owen Graduate School of Management, Vanderbilt MBA Program, Nashville, TN 37203. Offers accounting (MBA); finance (MBA); general management (MBA); health care (MBA); human and organizational performance (MBA); marketing (MBA); operations (MBA); strategy (MBA); MBA/JD; MBA/M Div; MBA/MD; MBA/MSN; MBA/MTS; MBA/PhD. *Accreditation:* AACSB. *Degree requirements:* For master's, 62 credit hours of coursework; completion of ethics course; minimum GPA of 3.0. *Entrance requirements:* For master's, GMAT (preferred) or GRE, 2 years of work experience (recommended). Additional exam requirements/recommendations for international students: Required—TOEFL (minimum score 100 iBT). Electronic applications accepted. *Expenses:* Contact institution. *Faculty research:* Accounting and finance, business strategy and economics, marketing, operations management, organization studies.

Villanova University, Villanova School of Business, Master of Accountancy Program, Villanova, PA 19085. Offers MAC. *Accreditation:* AACSB. *Faculty:* 68 full-time (22 women), 65 part-time/adjunct (11 women). *Students:* 52 part-time (27 women); includes 8 minority (1 Black or African American, non-Hispanic/Latino; 4 Asian, non-Hispanic/Latino; 3 Hispanic/Latino). Average age 23. 21 applicants, 76% accepted, 12 enrolled. In 2017, 28 master's awarded. *Degree requirements:* For master's, minimum cumulative GPA of 3.0. *Entrance requirements:* For master's, undergraduate accounting major or the following prerequisite courses: intermediate accounting I and II, federal income tax and auditing; 2 letters of recommendation; 2 essays; resume; official transcripts. Additional exam requirements/recommendations for international students: Required—TOEFL (minimum score 550 paper-based; 100 iBT). *Application deadline:* For fall admission, 6/30 for domestic and international students; for spring admission, 11/15 for domestic and international students; for summer admission, 3/31 for domestic and international students. Applications are processed on a rolling basis. Application fee: $65. Electronic applications accepted. *Expenses:* $1,400 per credit tuition, $50 per semester fees. *Financial support:* Scholarships/grants available. Financial award application deadline: 6/30; financial award applicants required to submit FAFSA. *Faculty research:* Business analytics; creativity, innovation and entrepreneurship; global leadership; real estate; church management; business ethics; marketing and consumer insights. *Unit head:* Dr. Joyce Russell, Dean of Villanova School of Business, 610-519-5424, Fax: 610-519-6273, E-mail: joyce.russell@villanova.edu. *Application contact:* Claire Bruno, Manager of Recruiting, 610-519-4336, Fax: 610-519-6273, E-mail: claire.bruno@villanova.edu.
Website: http://www1.villanova.edu/villanova/business/graduate/specializedprograms/mac.html

Virginia Commonwealth University, Graduate School, School of Business, Program in Accounting, Richmond, VA 23284-9005. Offers M Acc. *Accreditation:* AACSB. *Entrance requirements:* For master's, GMAT. Additional exam requirements/recommendations for international students: Required—TOEFL (minimum score 600 paper-based; 100 iBT). Electronic applications accepted.

Virginia International University, School of Business, Fairfax, VA 22030. Offers accounting (MBA, MS); entrepreneurship (MBA); executive management (Graduate Certificate); global logistics (MBA); health care management (MBA); hospitality and tourism management (MBA); human resources management (MBA); international business management (MBA); international finance (MBA); marketing management (MBA); mass media and public relations (MBA); project management (MBA, MS). *Program availability:* Part-time, online learning. *Entrance requirements:* For master's

and Graduate Certificate, bachelor's degree. Additional exam requirements/recommendations for international students: Required—TOEFL (minimum score 550 paper-based; 80 iBT), IELTS (minimum score 6). Electronic applications accepted.

Virginia Polytechnic Institute and State University, Graduate School, Pamplin College of Business, Blacksburg, VA 24061. Offers accounting and information systems (MACIS, PhD); business (PhD), including marketing (MS, PhD); business administration (MS), including business analytics, marketing (MS, PhD); business information technology (PhD); executive business research (PhD); finance (PhD); MS/MBA. *Faculty:* 131 full-time (42 women), 2 part-time/adjunct (1 woman). *Students:* 261 full-time (101 women), 189 part-time (76 women); includes 112 minority (32 Black or African American, non-Hispanic/Latino; 50 Asian, non-Hispanic/Latino; 15 Hispanic/Latino; 15 Two or more races, non-Hispanic/Latino), 80 international. Average age 32. 434 applicants, 57% accepted, 168 enrolled. In 2017, 142 master's, 11 doctorates awarded. *Degree requirements:* For master's, comprehensive exam (for some programs), thesis (for some programs); for doctorate, comprehensive exam (for some programs), thesis/dissertation (for some programs). *Entrance requirements:* For master's and doctorate, GRE/GMAT. Additional exam requirements/recommendations for international students: Required—TOEFL (minimum score 80 iBT). *Application deadline:* For fall admission, 8/1 for domestic students, 4/1 for international students; for spring admission, 1/1 for domestic students, 9/1 for international students. Applications are processed on a rolling basis. Application fee: $75. Electronic applications accepted. *Expenses:* Tuition, state resident: full-time $15,072; part-time $718.50 per credit hour. Tuition, nonresident: full-time $28,810; part-time $1448.25 per credit hour. *Required fees:* $2741; $502 per semester. Tuition and fees vary according to course load, campus/location and program. *Financial support:* In 2017–18, 9 research assistantships with full tuition reimbursements (averaging $18,588 per year), 48 teaching assistantships with full tuition reimbursements (averaging $22,706 per year) were awarded. Financial award application deadline: 3/1; financial award applicants required to submit FAFSA. *Total annual research expenditures:* $3.4 million. *Unit head:* Dr. Robert T. Sumichrast, Dean, 540-231-6601, Fax: 540-231-4487, E-mail: busdean@vt.edu. *Application contact:* Kimberly Ridpath, Executive Assistant, 540-231-9647, Fax: 540-231-4487, E-mail: ridpathk@vt.edu.
Website: http://www.pamplin.vt.edu/

Wagner College, Division of Graduate Studies, Nicolais School of Business, Staten Island, NY 10301-4495. Offers accounting (MS); business administration (MBA); finance (MBA); management (Exec MBA); marketing (MBA); media management (MS). *Accreditation:* ACBSP. *Program availability:* Part-time, evening/weekend. *Faculty:* 8 full-time (3 women), 17 part-time/adjunct (5 women). *Students:* 90 full-time (41 women), 27 part-time (9 women); includes 18 minority (10 Black or African American, non-Hispanic/Latino; 2 Asian, non-Hispanic/Latino; 4 Hispanic/Latino; 2 Two or more races, non-Hispanic/Latino), 14 international. Average age 27. 85 applicants, 92% accepted, 58 enrolled. In 2017, 72 master's awarded. *Degree requirements:* For master's, thesis optional. *Entrance requirements:* For master's, minimum GPA of 2.75, proficiency in computers and math. Additional exam requirements/recommendations for international students: Required—TOEFL (minimum score 550 paper-based; 79 iBT), IELTS (minimum score 6.5). *Application deadline:* For fall admission, 5/1 priority date for domestic students, 3/1 priority date for international students; for spring admission, 12/1 for domestic students, 11/1 for international students. Applications are processed on a rolling basis. Application fee: $60. *Financial support:* In 2017–18, 93 students received support. Career-related internships or fieldwork, unspecified assistantships, and alumni fellowship grants available. Financial award application deadline: 4/1; financial award applicants required to submit FAFSA. *Unit head:* Dr. Donald Crooks, Director, 718-390-3429, Fax: 718-390-3429, E-mail: dcrooks@wagner.edu. *Application contact:* Patricia Clancy, Assistant Director for Enrollment, 718-420-4464, Fax: 718-390-3105, E-mail: patricia.clancy@wagner.edu.

Wake Forest University, Graduate School of Arts and Sciences, Department of Accountancy, Winston-Salem, NC 27109. Offers MSA. *Accreditation:* AACSB. *Entrance requirements:* For master's, GMAT. Additional exam requirements/recommendations for international students: Required—TOEFL. Electronic applications accepted.

Wake Forest University, School of Business, MS in Accountancy Program, Winston-Salem, NC 27106. Offers assurance services (MSA); tax consulting (MSA); transaction services (MSA). *Faculty:* 19 full-time (3 women), 2 part-time/adjunct (0 women). *Students:* 178 full-time (95 women); includes 34 minority (14 Black or African American, non-Hispanic/Latino; 8 Asian, non-Hispanic/Latino; 7 Hispanic/Latino; 5 Two or more races, non-Hispanic/Latino), 45 international. Average age 24. 453 applicants, 47% accepted, 108 enrolled. In 2017, 132 master's awarded. *Degree requirements:* For master's, 30 credit hours. *Entrance requirements:* For master's, GMAT/GRE, letters of recommendation, official transcripts, current resume or curriculum vitae, interview. Additional exam requirements/recommendations for international students: Required—TOEFL (minimum score 600 paper-based; 100 iBT). *Application deadline:* For fall admission, 6/1 for domestic students, 1/1 for international students. Applications are processed on a rolling basis. Application fee: $100. Electronic applications accepted. *Expenses:* Contact institution. *Financial support:* Career-related internships or fieldwork and scholarships/grants available. Financial award application deadline: 4/15; financial award applicants required to submit FAFSA. *Faculty research:* Influence of personal relationships on business decision-making and management of change; drivers of perceived value and consumer behavior; impact of accounting on auditing, financial, managerial, systems and taxation stakeholders; corporate governance and executive compensation; impact of operations strategies on competitiveness. *Unit head:* James Willis, Associate Dean for Accountancy, 336-758-5422, Fax: 336-758-5830, E-mail: busadmissions@wfu.edu. *Application contact:* Denise Kelly, Administrative Assistant, 336-758-5422, Fax: 336-758-5830, E-mail: busadmissions@wfu.edu.
Website: http://business.wfu.edu/ms-accountancy

Walden University, Graduate Programs, School of Management, Minneapolis, MN 55401. Offers accounting (MBA, MS, DBA), including accounting for the professional (MS), accounting with CPA emphasis (MS), self-designed (MS); advanced project management (Graduate Certificate); applied project management (Graduate Certificate); auditing (Graduate Certificate); bridge to business administration (Post-Doctoral Certificate); bridge to management (Post-Doctoral Certificate); business management (Graduate Certificate); communication (MBA); corporate finance (MBA); digital marketing (Graduate Certificate); entrepreneurship (DBA); entrepreneurship and small business (MBA); finance (MS, DBA), including finance for the professional (MS), finance with CFA/investment (MS), finance with CPA emphasis (MS); global supply chain management (DBA); healthcare management (MBA, DBA); human resource management (MBA, MS, Graduate Certificate), including functional human resource management (MS), general program (MS), integrating functional and strategic human resource management (MS), organizational strategy (MS); human resources management (DBA); information systems management (DBA); international business (MBA, DBA); leadership (MBA, MS, DBA, Graduate Certificate), including general program (MS), human resource leadership (MS), leader development (MS), self-designed (MS); management (MS, PhD), including communications (MS), finance (PhD), general program (MS), healthcare management (MS), human resource management (MS), human resources management (PhD), information systems

Accounting

management (PhD), international business (MS), leadership (MS), leadership and organizational change (PhD), marketing (MS), project management (MS), strategy and operations (MS); managerial accounting (Graduate Certificate); marketing (MBA, MS, DBA); project management (MBA, MS, DBA); self-designed (MBA, DBA); social impact management (DBA); technology entrepreneurship (DBA). *Accreditation:* ACBSP. *Program availability:* Part-time, evening/weekend, online only, 100% online. *Degree requirements:* For master's, thesis (for some programs), residency (for EMBA); for doctorate, thesis/dissertation (for some programs), residency. *Entrance requirements:* For master's, bachelor's degree or higher; minimum GPA of 2.5; official transcripts; goal statement (for some programs); access to computer and Internet; for doctorate, master's degree or higher; three years of related professional or academic experience (preferred); minimum GPA of 3.0; goal statement and current resume (for select programs); official transcripts; access to computer and Internet; for other advanced degree, relevant work experience; access to computer and Internet. Additional exam requirements/recommendations for international students: Required—TOEFL (minimum score 550 paper-based, 79 iBT), IELTS (minimum score 6.5), Michigan English Language Assessment Battery (minimum score 82), or PTE (minimum score 53). Electronic applications accepted.

Walsh College of Accountancy and Business Administration, Graduate Programs, Program in Accountancy, Troy, MI 48083. Offers data analytics (MAC); finance (MAC); taxation (MAC). *Program availability:* Part-time, evening/weekend. *Students:* 252 (139 women); includes 64 minority (22 Black or African American, non-Hispanic/Latino; 30 Asian, non-Hispanic/Latino; 11 Hispanic/Latino; 1 Two or more races, non-Hispanic/Latino), 21 international. Average age 32. 94 applicants, 76% accepted, 71 enrolled. In 2017, 93 master's awarded. *Degree requirements:* For master's, thesis optional. *Entrance requirements:* For master's, minimum overall cumulative GPA of 2.75 from all colleges previously attended. Additional exam requirements/recommendations for international students: Required—TOEFL (minimum score 550 paper-based, 79 iBT), IELTS (6.5), Michigan English Language Assessment Battery, or MTELP (80). *Application deadline:* Applications are processed on a rolling basis. Application fee: $35. Electronic applications accepted. *Expenses:* $770 per semester credit hour plus $125 registration fee per semester. *Financial support:* In 2017–18, 19 students received support. Career-related internships or fieldwork and scholarships/grants available. Financial award application deadline: 6/30; financial award applicants required to submit FAFSA. *Unit head:* John Black, Chair, Accounting, Tax and Business Law, 248-823-1635, Fax: 248-689-0920, E-mail: jblack@walshcollege.edu. *Application contact:* Heather Rigby, Director, Admissions and Academic Advising, 248-823-1600, Fax: 248-823-1611, E-mail: hrigby@walshcollege.edu.

Warner University, School of Business, Lake Wales, FL 33859. Offers accounting (MBA); business administration (MBA); human resource management (MBA); international business (MBA); management (MSMC). *Program availability:* Part-time, evening/weekend, online learning. *Degree requirements:* For master's, comprehensive exam, thesis. *Entrance requirements:* For master's, minimum GPA of 3.0, 2 letters of recommendation. Additional exam requirements/recommendations for international students: Required—TOEFL. Electronic applications accepted.

Washburn University, School of Business, Topeka, KS 66621. Offers accountancy (M Acc). *Accreditation:* AACSB. *Program availability:* Part-time, evening/weekend. *Entrance requirements:* For master's, GMAT, minimum GPA of 2.75. Additional exam requirements/recommendations for international students: Required—TOEFL (minimum score 550 paper-based; 80 iBT); Recommended—IELTS (minimum score 6.5). Electronic applications accepted. *Faculty research:* Ethics in information technology, forecasting for shareholder value creation, model for measuring expected losses from litigation contingencies, business vs. family commitment in family businesses, calculated intangible value and brand recognition.

Washington & Jefferson College, Graduate and Continuing Studies, Washington, PA 15301. Offers applied health care economics and outcomes management (MS); professional accounting (MAC); professional writing (Graduate Certificate); thanatology (Graduate Certificate).

Washington State University, Carson College of Business, Department of Accounting, Pullman, WA 99164-4729. Offers M Acc. Program also offered at the Vancouver campus. *Accreditation:* AACSB. *Program availability:* Part-time. *Degree requirements:* For master's, comprehensive exam, thesis or alternative. *Entrance requirements:* For master's, GMAT (minimum score of 500), minimum GPA of 3.0, statement of purpose. Additional exam requirements/recommendations for international students: Required—TOEFL (minimum score 580 paper-based; 93 iBT), IELTS (minimum score 7.5). Electronic applications accepted. *Faculty research:* Ethics, taxation, auditing, finance.

Washington University in St. Louis, Olin Business School, Program in Accounting, St. Louis, MO 63130-4899. Offers MS. *Program availability:* Part-time. *Faculty:* 98 full-time (25 women), 54 part-time/adjunct (12 women). *Students:* 101 full-time (79 women); includes 3 minority (all Asian, non-Hispanic/Latino), 91 international. 395 applicants, 41% accepted, 75 enrolled. In 2017, 50 master's awarded. *Entrance requirements:* For master's, GMAT or GRE. Additional exam requirements/recommendations for international students: Required—TOEFL, IELTS. *Application deadline:* For fall admission, 10/3 for domestic students, 2/1 priority date for international students; for winter admission, 12/1 for domestic students; for spring admission, 4/3 for domestic students. Applications are processed on a rolling basis. Application fee: $100. Electronic applications accepted. *Financial support:* Institutionally sponsored loans and scholarships/grants available. Financial award applicants required to submit FAFSA. *Unit head:* Dr. Patrick Moreton, Senior Associate Dean of Graduate Programs, 314-935-6322, Fax: 314-935-4464, E-mail: moreton@wustl.edu. *Application contact:* 314-935-7301, E-mail: olingradadmissions@wustl.edu.
Website: http://www.olin.wustl.edu

Wayland Baptist University, Graduate Programs, Programs in Business Administration/Management, Plainview, TX 79072-6998. Offers accounting (MBA); general business (MBA); health care administration (MAM, MBA); human resource management (MAM, MBA); international management (MBA); management (MBA, D Mgt); management information systems (MBA); organization management (MAM); project management (MBA). *Program availability:* Part-time, evening/weekend, online learning. *Faculty:* 30 full-time (5 women), 38 part-time/adjunct (9 women). *Students:* 42 full-time (20 women), 538 part-time (253 women); includes 311 minority (98 Black or African American, non-Hispanic/Latino; 4 American Indian or Alaska Native, non-Hispanic/Latino; 16 Asian, non-Hispanic/Latino; 153 Hispanic/Latino; 11 Native Hawaiian or other Pacific Islander, non-Hispanic/Latino; 29 Two or more races, non-Hispanic/Latino), 6 international. Average age 40. 100 applicants, 96% accepted, 60 enrolled. In 2017, 216 master's awarded. *Degree requirements:* For master's, capstone course. *Entrance requirements:* For master's, GMAT, GRE or MAT. Additional exam requirements/recommendations for international students: Required—TOEFL (minimum score 500 paper-based; 61 iBT). *Application deadline:* Applications are processed on a rolling basis. Application fee: $50. Electronic applications accepted. *Expenses:* Tuition: Full-time $11,250; part-time $625 per credit hour. *Required fees:* $1200. *Financial support:* Federal Work-Study, institutionally sponsored loans, and scholarships/grants available. Support available to part-time students. Financial award application deadline: 5/1; financial award applicants required to submit FAFSA. *Unit head:* Dr. Kelly Warren,

Chairman, 806-291-1020, Fax: 806-291-1957, E-mail: warrenk@wbu.edu. *Application contact:* Amanda Stanton, Graduate Studies, 806-291-3423, Fax: 806-291-1950, E-mail: stanton@wbu.edu.

Wayne State University, Mike Ilitch School of Business, Detroit, MI 48202. Offers accounting (MS, MSA, Postbaccalaureate Certificate); business (EMS, Graduate Certificate); business administration (MBA, PhD); data science (MS), including business analytics; entrepreneurship and innovation (Postbaccalaureate Certificate); finance (MS); information systems management (Postbaccalaureate Certificate); taxation (MST); JD/MBA. Application deadline for PhD is February 15. *Accreditation:* AACSB. *Program availability:* Part-time, evening/weekend. *Faculty:* 32. *Students:* 235 full-time (121 women), 1,082 part-time (480 women); includes 356 minority (202 Black or African American, non-Hispanic/Latino; 2 American Indian or Alaska Native, non-Hispanic/Latino; 79 Asian, non-Hispanic/Latino; 47 Hispanic/Latino; 26 Two or more races, non-Hispanic/Latino), 87 international. Average age 30. 1,285 applicants, 43% accepted, 308 enrolled. In 2017, 200 master's, 2 doctorates, 9 other advanced degrees awarded. *Degree requirements:* For doctorate, thesis/dissertation. *Entrance requirements:* For master's, GMAT, GRE, LSAT, MCAT, at least three years of relevant work experience that shows increased responsibility, or minimum GPA of 3.0 from AACSB-accredited program or 3.2 from regionally-accredited program, undergraduate degree from accredited institution; undergraduate degree in accounting, business administration, or area of business administration (for MS and MST); for doctorate, GMAT (minimum score of 600), minimum undergraduate GPA of 3.0, 3.5 upper-division or graduate; three letters of recommendation; brief essay; undergraduate degree from accredited institution; personal statement; for other advanced degree, bachelor's degree from accredited institution. Additional exam requirements/recommendations for international students: Required—TOEFL (minimum score 550 paper-based; 79 iBT), Michigan English Language Assessment Battery (minimum score 85); Recommended—IELTS (minimum score 6.5), TWE (minimum score 5.5). *Application deadline:* For fall admission, 7/1 for domestic students, 5/1 priority date for international students; for winter admission, 11/1 for domestic students, 9/1 priority date for international students; for spring admission, 3/1 for domestic students, 1/1 priority date for international students. Applications are processed on a rolling basis. Application fee: $50. Electronic applications accepted. *Expenses:* Contact institution. *Financial support:* In 2017–18, 165 students received support, including 1 fellowship with tuition reimbursement available (averaging $18,534 per year), 1 teaching assistantship with tuition reimbursement available (averaging $18,534 per year); research assistantships with tuition reimbursements available, scholarships/grants, health care benefits, and unspecified assistantships also available. Support available to part-time students. Financial award applicants required to submit FAFSA. *Faculty research:* Executive compensation and stock performance, consumer reactions to pricing strategies, communication across the automotive supply chain, performance of firms in sub-Saharan Africa, implementation issues with ERP software. *Unit head:* Dr. Robert Forsythe, Dean, School of Business Administration, 313-577-4501, E-mail: robert.forsythe@wayne.edu. *Application contact:* Kiantee N. Rupert-Jones, Director, 313-577-4511, Fax: 313-577-9442, E-mail: gradbusiness@wayne.edu.
Website: http://ilitchbusiness.wayne.edu/

Webber International University, Graduate School of Business, Babson Park, FL 33827-0096. Offers accounting (MBA); business (MBA); criminal justice management (MBA); international business (MBA); sport business management (MBA). *Program availability:* Part-time, evening/weekend, 100% online. *Faculty:* 10 full-time (4 women), 1 part-time/adjunct (0 women). *Students:* 50 full-time (29 women), 6 part-time (2 women); includes 19 minority (12 Black or African American, non-Hispanic/Latino; 6 Hispanic/Latino; 1 Two or more races, non-Hispanic/Latino), 6 international. Average age 24. 64 applicants, 61% accepted, 32 enrolled. In 2017, 29 master's awarded. *Degree requirements:* For master's, class trip (for international business); practicum (for criminal justice management). *Entrance requirements:* For master's, three recommendation letters, résumé, essay, official transcripts from all colleges and universities attended. Additional exam requirements/recommendations for international students: Recommended—TOEFL (minimum score 500 paper-based; 61 iBT), IELTS (minimum score 6). *Application deadline:* For fall admission, 7/1 for international students. Applications are processed on a rolling basis. Application fee: $50 ($75 for international students). Electronic applications accepted. *Expenses: Tuition:* Part-time $688 per hour. *Financial support:* In 2017–18, 11 students received support. Scholarships/grants and unspecified assistantships available. Financial award application deadline: 8/1; financial award applicants required to submit FAFSA. *Unit head:* Dr. Nikos Orphanoudakis, Dean, 863-638-2910, Fax: 863-638-1591, E-mail: orphanoudakisn@webber.edu. *Application contact:* Lacy Edwards, Admissions Counselor and MBA Coordinator, 863-638-2910, Fax: 863-638-1591, E-mail: admissions@webber.edu.

Weber State University, Goddard School of Business and Economics, School of Accounting and Taxation, Ogden, UT 84408-1001. Offers accounting (M Acc); taxation (M Tax). *Accreditation:* AACSB. *Program availability:* Part-time, evening/weekend. *Faculty:* 7 full-time (2 women). *Students:* 37 full-time (10 women), 28 part-time (15 women); includes 4 minority (2 Asian, non-Hispanic/Latino; 2 Hispanic/Latino), 1 international. Average age 32. In 2017, 28 master's awarded. *Entrance requirements:* For master's, GMAT. Additional exam requirements/recommendations for international students: Required—TOEFL (minimum score 80 iBT). *Application deadline:* For fall admission, 8/1 for domestic students; for spring admission, 12/1 for domestic students; for summer admission, 4/1 for domestic students. Application fee: $60 ($90 for international students). Electronic applications accepted. *Expenses:* Tuition, state resident: full-time $7283. Tuition, nonresident: full-time $17,166. *Required fees:* $898. Tuition and fees vary according to program. *Financial support:* In 2017–18, 32 students received support. Scholarships/grants available. Financial award application deadline: 4/1; financial award applicants required to submit FAFSA. *Unit head:* Dr. Ryan Pace, Program Director, 801-626-7562, Fax: 801-626-7423, E-mail: rpace@weber.edu. *Application contact:* Dr. Larry A. Deppe, Graduate Coordinator, 801-626-7838, Fax: 801-626-7423, E-mail: ldeppe1@weber.edu.
Website: http://www.weber.edu/goddard/accounting-taxation.html

Webster University, George Herbert Walker School of Business and Technology, Department of Business, St. Louis, MO 63119-3194. Offers business and organizational security management (MBA); decision support systems (MBA); environmental management (MBA); finance (MBA, MS); forensic accounting (MS); gerontology (MBA); human resources development (MBA); human resources management (MBA); information technology management (MBA); international business (MA, MBA); international relations (MBA); management and leadership (MBA); marketing (MBA); media communications (MBA); procurement and acquisitions management (MBA); Web services (MBA). *Accreditation:* ACBSP. *Program availability:* Part-time, evening/weekend, online learning. *Degree requirements:* For master's, comprehensive exam (for some programs), thesis (for some programs). *Entrance requirements:* Additional exam requirements/recommendations for international students: Required—TOEFL.

Western Carolina University, Graduate School, College of Business, Program in Accountancy, Cullowhee, NC 28723. Offers M Ac. *Program availability:* Part-time, evening/weekend. *Entrance requirements:* For master's, GMAT, appropriate undergraduate degree, 3 letters of recommendation. Additional exam requirements/

recommendations for international students: Required—TOEFL (minimum score 550 paper-based; 79 iBT). *Expenses:* Tuition, state resident: full-time $4436. Tuition, nonresident: full-time $14,842. *Required fees:* $2926.

Western Connecticut State University, Division of Graduate Studies, Ancell School of Business, Program in Business Administration, Danbury, CT 06810-6885. Offers accounting (MBA); business administration (MBA). *Program availability:* Part-time. *Degree requirements:* For master's, comprehensive exam, completion of program within 8 years. *Entrance requirements:* For master's, GMAT. Additional exam requirements/recommendations for international students: Recommended—TOEFL (minimum score 550 paper-based; 79 iBT), IELTS (minimum score 6). *Expenses:* Tuition, state resident: full-time $6757; part-time $374 per credit hour. Tuition, nonresident: full-time $18,102; part-time $374 per credit hour. *Required fees:* $4994; $190 per credit hour. $60 per term. Tuition and fees vary according to degree level and program. *Faculty research:* Global strategic marketing planning, project management and team coordination; email, discussion boards that act as blogs and videoconferencing.

Western Illinois University, School of Graduate Studies, College of Business and Technology, Department of Accountancy, Macomb, IL 61455-1390. Offers M Acct. *Accreditation:* AACSB. *Program availability:* Part-time. *Students:* 18 full-time (13 women), 8 part-time (6 women); includes 7 minority (4 Black or African American, non-Hispanic/Latino; 1 Asian, non-Hispanic/Latino; 2 Hispanic/Latino), 3 international. Average age 29. 13 applicants, 77% accepted, 5 enrolled. In 2017, 10 master's awarded. *Degree requirements:* For master's, thesis or alternative. *Entrance requirements:* For master's, GMAT. Additional exam requirements/recommendations for international students: Required—TOEFL (minimum score 550 paper-based; 80 iBT). *Application deadline:* Applications are processed on a rolling basis. Application fee: $30. Electronic applications accepted. *Financial support:* Unspecified assistantships available. Financial award applicants required to submit FAFSA. *Unit head:* Dr. Gregg Woodruff, Chairperson, 309-298-1152. *Application contact:* Dr. Nancy Parsons, Assistant Director of Graduate Studies, 309-298-1806, Fax: 309-298-2345, E-mail: grad-office@wiu.edu.
Website: http://wiu.edu/accountancy

Western Michigan University, Graduate College, Haworth College of Business, Department of Accountancy, Kalamazoo, MI 49008. Offers MSA. *Accreditation:* AACSB.

Western New England University, College of Business, Program in Accounting, Springfield, MA 01119. Offers MSA, JD/MSA. *Program availability:* Part-time, evening/weekend. *Faculty:* 10 full-time (3 women). *Students:* 31 part-time (15 women); includes 2 minority (1 Black or African American, non-Hispanic/Latino; 1 Asian, non-Hispanic/Latino). Average age 25. 47 applicants, 64% accepted, 26 enrolled. In 2017, 21 master's awarded. *Entrance requirements:* For master's, GMAT, official transcript, two letters of recommendation, essay, resume. Additional exam requirements/recommendations for international students: Required—TOEFL (minimum score 79 iBT). *Application deadline:* Applications are processed on a rolling basis. Application fee: $30. Electronic applications accepted. *Expenses:* Contact institution. *Financial support:* Application deadline: 4/15; applicants required to submit FAFSA. *Unit head:* Dr. William Bosworth, Chair, Accounting and Finance, 413-782-1738, E-mail: william.bosworth@wne.edu. *Application contact:* Matthew Fox, Director of Admissions for Graduate Students and Adult Learners, 413-782-1410, Fax: 413-782-1779, E-mail: study@wne.edu.
Website: http://www1.wne.edu/academics/graduate/msa.cfm

Westfield State University, College of Graduate and Continuing Education, Department of Economics and Business Management, Westfield, MA 01086. Offers accounting (MS). *Program availability:* Part-time, evening/weekend. *Faculty:* 4 full-time (3 women), 4 part-time/adjunct (1 woman). *Students:* 6 full-time (4 women), 17 part-time (8 women); includes 6 minority (1 Black or African American, non-Hispanic/Latino; 1 American Indian or Alaska Native, non-Hispanic/Latino; 2 Asian, non-Hispanic/Latino; 2 Hispanic/Latino; 1 Two or more races, non-Hispanic/Latino), 2 international. Average age 29. 14 applicants, 93% accepted, 12 enrolled. In 2017, 9 master's awarded. *Degree requirements:* For master's, comprehensive exam, thesis (for some programs). *Entrance requirements:* For master's, GRE General Test or MAT, minimum undergraduate GPA of 2.8. Additional exam requirements/recommendations for international students: Recommended—TOEFL (minimum score 550 paper-based; 79 iBT). *Application deadline:* For fall admission, 7/1 for domestic students; for spring admission, 11/1 for domestic students; for summer admission, 4/1 for domestic students. Applications are processed on a rolling basis. Application fee: $50. *Expenses:* Tuition, state resident: part-time $332 per credit. Tuition, nonresident: part-time $332 per credit. *Required fees:* $75 per semester. Tuition and fees vary according to program. *Financial support:* Unspecified assistantships available. Financial award application deadline: 3/1; financial award applicants required to submit FAFSA. *Unit head:* Dr. Cornelia Daniel, Chair, 413-572-5696, Fax: 413-572-8787, E-mail: cdaniel@westfield.ma.edu. *Application contact:* Shelly Henrichon, Admissions Coordinator, 413-572-8022, Fax: 413-572-5227, E-mail: mhenrichon@westfield.ma.edu.

Westminster College, The Bill and Vieve Gore School of Business, Salt Lake City, UT 84105-3697. Offers accountancy (M Acc); business administration (MBA, Certificate); technology commercialization (MBA). *Program availability:* Part-time, evening/weekend, blended/hybrid learning. *Faculty:* 20 full-time (6 women), 16 part-time/adjunct (4 women). *Students:* 89 full-time (36 women), 130 part-time (46 women); includes 52 minority (9 Black or African American, non-Hispanic/Latino; 1 American Indian or Alaska Native, non-Hispanic/Latino; 17 Asian, non-Hispanic/Latino; 21 Hispanic/Latino; 1 Native Hawaiian or other Pacific Islander, non-Hispanic/Latino; 3 Two or more races, non-Hispanic/Latino), 13 international. Average age 34. 67 applicants, 84% accepted, 47 enrolled. In 2017, 150 master's, 1 other advanced degree awarded. *Degree requirements:* For master's, International Context Tour (for MBA). *Entrance requirements:* For master's, GMAT (waived on a case-by-case basis), 2 professional recommendations, employer letter of support, personal resume, essay, official transcripts. Additional exam requirements/recommendations for international students: Required—TOEFL (minimum score 84 iBT), IELTS (minimum score 7). *Application deadline:* For fall admission, 5/1 priority date for domestic and international students; for spring admission, 10/1 priority date for domestic and international students; for summer admission, 2/1 priority date for domestic and international students. Applications are processed on a rolling basis. Application fee: $50. Electronic applications accepted. *Expenses:* Contact institution. *Financial support:* In 2017–18, 58 students received support. Career-related internships or fieldwork, scholarships/grants, unspecified assistantships, and tuition remission available. Financial award applicants required to submit FAFSA. *Faculty research:* Innovation and entrepreneurship, business strategy and change, financial analysis and capital budgeting, leadership development, knowledge management. *Unit head:* Melissa Koerner, Dean, Bill and Vieve Gore School of Business, 801-832-2600, E-mail: mkoerner@westminstercollege.edu. *Application contact:* Ashley Williams, Director of Graduate and International Admissions, 801-832-2213, Fax: 801-832-3101, E-mail: awilliams@westminstercollege.edu.
Website: https://www.westminstercollege.edu/graduate/programs

West Texas A&M University, College of Business, Department of Accounting, Economics and Finance, Canyon, TX 79015. Offers accounting (MPA); finance and economics (MS). *Program availability:* Part-time, evening/weekend, online learning. *Degree requirements:* For master's, comprehensive exam, thesis optional. *Entrance*

requirements: For master's, GMAT. Additional exam requirements/recommendations for international students: Required—TOEFL (minimum score 550 paper-based). Electronic applications accepted. *Faculty research:* Texas economy, decision report service learning and entrepreneurship, small business, trade effects of financial flow.

West Virginia University, College of Business and Economics, Morgantown, WV 26506. Offers accountancy (M Acc); accounting (PhD); business administration (MBA); business cyber security management (MS); business data analytics (MS); economics (MA, PhD); finance (MS, PhD); forensic and fraud examination (MS); industrial relations (MS); management (PhD); marketing (PhD). *Program availability:* Part-time, online learning. *Students:* 343 full-time (141 women), 43 part-time (12 women); includes 59 minority (22 Black or African American, non-Hispanic/Latino; 11 Asian, non-Hispanic/Latino; 12 Hispanic/Latino; 14 Two or more races, non-Hispanic/Latino), 54 international. Terminal master's awarded for partial completion of doctoral program. *Degree requirements:* For master's, thesis optional; for doctorate, comprehensive exam, thesis/dissertation. *Entrance requirements:* For doctorate, GRE General Test, minimum GPA of 3.0. Additional exam requirements/recommendations for international students: Required—TOEFL (minimum score 550 paper-based; 92 iBT). *Application deadline:* For fall admission, 10/15 priority date for domestic and international students; for spring admission, 3/1 priority date for domestic and international students. Applications are processed on a rolling basis. Application fee: $60. Electronic applications accepted. *Expenses:* Contact institution. *Financial support:* Fellowships, research assistantships, teaching assistantships, career-related internships or fieldwork, Federal Work-Study, institutionally sponsored loans, scholarships/grants, health care benefits, tuition waivers (full and partial), unspecified assistantships, and administrative assistantships available. Financial award application deadline: 2/1; financial award applicants required to submit FAFSA. *Faculty research:* Regional labor market studies, economic development, market research, economic forecasting, energy analysis. *Unit head:* Dr. Javier Reyes, Dean, 304-293-7800, Fax: 304-293-4056, E-mail: javier.reyes@mail.wvu.edu. *Application contact:* Dr. Mark Gavin, Associate Dean for Graduate Programs, 304-293-7952, Fax: 304-293-7188, E-mail: mark.gavin@mail.wvu.edu.
Website: http://www.be.wvu.edu

Wheeling Jesuit University, Department of Business, Wheeling, WV 26003-6295. Offers accounting (MSA); business administration (MBA). *Accreditation:* ACBSP. *Program availability:* Part-time, evening/weekend. *Entrance requirements:* For master's, minimum undergraduate GPA of 2.8. Additional exam requirements/recommendations for international students: Required—TOEFL (minimum score 600 paper-based; 100 iBT). Electronic applications accepted. *Faculty research:* Forensic economics, consumer behavior, economic development, capitalism, leadership.

Wichita State University, Graduate School, W. Frank Barton School of Business, School of Accountancy, Wichita, KS 67260. Offers accounting information systems (M Acc); taxation (M Acc). *Accreditation:* AACSB. *Program availability:* Part-time, evening/weekend. *Unit head:* Dr. Paul D. Harrison, Director, 316-978-3215, Fax: 316-978-3660, E-mail: paul.harrison@wichita.edu. *Application contact:* Jordan Oleson, Admissions Coordinator, 316-978-3095, Fax: 316-978-3253, E-mail: jordan.oleson@wichita.edu.
Website: http://www.wichita.edu/acct

Wilfrid Laurier University, Faculty of Graduate and Postdoctoral Studies, School of Business and Economics, Department of Business, Waterloo, ON N2L 3C5, Canada. Offers accounting (PhD); finance (M Fin); financial economics (PhD); marketing (PhD); operations and supply chain management (PhD); organizational behavior and human resource management (M Sc); organizational behaviour and human resource management (PhD); supply chain management (M Sc); technology management (EMTM). *Accreditation:* AACSB. *Program availability:* Part-time, evening/weekend. *Degree requirements:* For master's, thesis optional; for doctorate, comprehensive exam, thesis/dissertation. *Entrance requirements:* For master's, GMAT, 4-year honors degree with minimum B+ average; for doctorate, GMAT, master's degree, minimum B+ average. Additional exam requirements/recommendations for international students: Required—TOEFL (minimum score 89 iBT). Electronic applications accepted. *Faculty research:* Financial economics, management and organizational behavior, operations and supply chain management.

Wilkes University, College of Graduate and Professional Studies, Jay S. Sidhu School of Business and Leadership, Wilkes-Barre, PA 18766-0002. Offers accounting (MBA); entrepreneurship (MBA); finance (MBA); health care administration (MBA); human resource management (MBA); international business (MBA); operations management (MBA); organizational leadership and development (MBA). *Accreditation:* ACBSP. *Program availability:* Part-time, evening/weekend. *Students:* 37 full-time (18 women), 87 part-time (45 women); includes 17 minority (4 Black or African American, non-Hispanic/Latino; 5 Asian, non-Hispanic/Latino; 6 Hispanic/Latino; 2 Two or more races, non-Hispanic/Latino), 14 international. Average age 30. In 2017, 77 master's awarded. *Entrance requirements:* For master's, GMAT. Additional exam requirements/recommendations for international students: Required—TOEFL (minimum score 550 paper-based; 79 iBT). *Application deadline:* Applications are processed on a rolling basis. Application fee: $45 ($65 for international students). Electronic applications accepted. *Expenses:* Contact institution. *Financial support:* Unspecified assistantships available. Financial award application deadline: 3/1; financial award applicants required to submit FAFSA. *Unit head:* Dr. Abel Adekola, Dean, 570-408-4701, Fax: 570-408-7846, E-mail: abel.adekola@wilkes.edu. *Application contact:* Kristin Donati, Associate Director of Graduate Admissions, 570-408-3338, Fax: 570-408-7846, E-mail: kristin.donati@wilkes.edu.
Website: http://www.wilkes.edu/academics/colleges/sidhu-school-of-business-leadership/index.aspx

Wilmington University, College of Business, New Castle, DE 19720-6491. Offers accounting (MBA, MS); business administration (MBA, DBA); environmental stewardship (MBA); finance (MBA); health care administration (MBA, MSM); homeland security (MBA, MSM); human resource management (MSM); management information systems (MBA, MSN); marketing (MSM); marketing management (MBA); military leadership (MSM); organizational leadership (MBA, MSM); public administration (MSM). *Program availability:* Part-time, evening/weekend. *Faculty:* 16 full-time (8 women), 106 part-time/adjunct (49 women). *Students:* 525 full-time (294 women), 1,212 part-time (780 women); includes 557 minority (412 Black or African American, non-Hispanic/Latino; 14 American Indian or Alaska Native, non-Hispanic/Latino; 55 Asian, non-Hispanic/Latino; 25 Hispanic/Latino; 3 Native Hawaiian or other Pacific Islander, non-Hispanic/Latino; 48 Two or more races, non-Hispanic/Latino), 157 international. Average age 35. 1,484 applicants, 70% accepted, 685 enrolled. In 2017, 543 master's, 16 doctorates awarded. *Entrance requirements:* Additional exam requirements/recommendations for international students: Required—TOEFL (minimum score 500 paper-based). *Application deadline:* Applications are processed on a rolling basis. Application fee: $35. Electronic applications accepted. *Expenses: Tuition:* Part-time $466 per credit. *Required fees:* $25 per semester. Tuition and fees vary according to degree level and campus/location. *Financial support:* Applicants required to submit FAFSA. *Unit head:* Dr. Kathy S. Kennedy Ratajack, Dean, 302-356-2481. *Application contact:* Laura Morris, Director of Admissions, 877-967-5456, E-mail: infocenter@wilmu.edu.
Website: http://www.wilmu.edu/business/

Accounting

Wilson College, Graduate Programs, Chambersburg, PA 17201-1285. Offers accounting (M Acc); choreography and visual art (MFA); education (M Ed); educational technology (MET); healthcare administration (MHA); humanities (MA), including art and culture, critical/cultural theory, English language and literature, women's studies; management (MSM); nursing (MSN), including nursing education, nursing leadership and management; special education (MSE). *Program availability:* Evening/weekend. *Degree requirements:* For master's, project. *Entrance requirements:* For master's, PRAXIS, minimum undergraduate cumulative GPA of 3.0, 2 letters of recommendation, current certification for eligibility to teach in grades K-12, resume, personal interview. Electronic applications accepted.

Wingate University, Porter B. Byrum School of Business, Wingate, NC 28174. Offers accounting (MAC); corporate innovation (MBA); finance (MBA); general management (MBA); healthcare management (MBA); marketing (MBA); project management (MBA). *Accreditation:* ACBSP. *Program availability:* Part-time, evening/weekend. *Entrance requirements:* For master's, GMAT, work experience, 2 letters of recommendation. Electronic applications accepted. *Expenses:* Contact institution. *Faculty research:* Stochastic processes, business ethics, regional economic development, municipal finance, consumer behavior.

Worcester State University, Graduate School, Program in Management, Worcester, MA 01602-2597. Offers accounting (MS); managerial leadership (MS); marketing (MS). *Program availability:* Part-time, evening/weekend. *Faculty:* 6 full-time, 1 part-time/adjunct. *Students:* 12 full-time (7 women), 44 part-time (26 women); includes 14 minority (7 Black or African American, non-Hispanic/Latino; 2 Asian, non-Hispanic/Latino; 5 Hispanic/Latino), 3 international. Average age 32. 50 applicants, 80% accepted, 21 enrolled. In 2017, 10 master's awarded. *Degree requirements:* For master's, comprehensive exam (for some programs), thesis optional. *Entrance requirements:* For master's, GMAT, 3 letters of recommendation from professors and/or supervisors. Additional exam requirements/recommendations for international students: Required—TOEFL (minimum score 550 paper-based; 79 iBT). *Application deadline:* For fall admission, 6/15 for domestic and international students; for spring admission, 11/1 for domestic and international students; for summer admission, 4/1 for domestic and international students. Applications are processed on a rolling basis. Application fee: $50. Electronic applications accepted. *Expenses:* Tuition, state resident: full-time $3042; part-time $169 per credit hour. Tuition, nonresident: full-time $3042; part-time $169 per credit hour. *Required fees:* $2754; $153 per credit hour. *Financial support:* Career-related internships or fieldwork, scholarships/grants, and unspecified assistantships available. Financial award application deadline: 3/1; financial award applicants required to submit FAFSA. *Unit head:* Dr. Elizabeth Wark, Program Coordinator, 508-929-8743, E-mail: ewark@worcester.edu. *Application contact:* Sara Grady, Associate Dean, Graduate Studies and Professional Development, 508-929-8130, E-mail: sara.grady@worcester.edu.

Wright State University, Graduate School, Raj Soin College of Business, Department of Accountancy, Accountancy Program, Dayton, OH 45435. Offers M Acc.

Xavier University, Williams College of Business, Master of Science in Accountancy Program, Cincinnati, OH 45207. Offers MS. *Entrance requirements:* For master's, GMAT, official transcript; resume; 3 letters of recommendation. Additional exam requirements/recommendations for international students: Required—TOEFL (minimum score 550 paper-based; 70 iBT) or IELTS. Electronic applications accepted. Application fee is waived when completed online. *Expenses:* Contact institution.

Yale University, Yale School of Management and Graduate School of Arts and Sciences, Doctoral Program in Management, New Haven, CT 06520. Offers accounting (PhD); financial economics (PhD); marketing (PhD); organizations and management (PhD). *Accreditation:* AACSB. *Degree requirements:* For doctorate, comprehensive exam, thesis/dissertation. *Entrance requirements:* For doctorate, GMAT or GRE General Test. Additional exam requirements/recommendations for international students: Required—TOEFL or IELTS. Electronic applications accepted. *Expenses:* Contact institution. *Faculty research:* Pricing of options and futures, term structure of interest rates, use of accounting numbers in debt contracts, product differentiation, e-commerce and marketing, behavioral finance.

Yeshiva University, Sy Syms School of Business, New York, NY 10016. Offers accounting (MS); business (EMBA); marketing (MS); taxation (MS). *Program availability:* Part-time. *Entrance requirements:* For master's, minimum GPA of 3.5 or GMAT.

York College of Pennsylvania, Graham School of Business, York, PA 17403-3651. Offers accounting (M Acc); business (MBA); continuous improvement (MBA); financial management (MBA); health care management (MBA); management (MBA); marketing (MBA); self-designed (MBA). *Accreditation:* ACBSP. *Program availability:* Part-time, evening/weekend. *Faculty:* 9 full-time (2 women), 3 part-time/adjunct (0 women). *Students:* 3 full-time (2 women), 72 part-time (33 women); includes 14 minority (7 Black or African American, non-Hispanic/Latino; 3 Asian, non-Hispanic/Latino; 1 Hispanic/Latino; 3 Two or more races, non-Hispanic/Latino). Average age 35. 68 applicants, 76% accepted, 28 enrolled. In 2017, 17 master's awarded. *Degree requirements:* For master's, directed study. *Entrance requirements:* For master's, GMAT. Additional exam requirements/recommendations for international students: Required—TOEFL (minimum score 530 paper-based; 72 iBT), IELTS (minimum score 6). *Application deadline:* For fall admission, 7/15 priority date for domestic students, 5/1 for international students; for spring admission, 11/15 priority date for domestic students, 9/1 for international students; for summer admission, 4/15 priority date for domestic students. Applications are processed on a rolling basis. Application fee: $0. Electronic applications accepted. *Expenses:* $795 per credit. *Financial support:* In 2017–18, 3 students received support. Scholarships/grants available. Financial award applicants required to submit FAFSA. *Unit head:* Nicole Cornell Sadowski, MBA Director, 717-815-1491, Fax: 717-600-3999, E-mail: ncornell@ycp.edu. *Application contact:* MBA Office, 717-815-1491, Fax: 717-600-3999, E-mail: mba@ycp.edu.
Website: http://www.ycp.edu/mba

York University, Faculty of Graduate Studies, Schulich School of Business, Toronto, ON M3J 1P3, Canada. Offers accounting (M Acc); administration (PhD); business (MBA); business analytics (MBA); finance (MF); international business (IMBA); MBA/JD; MBA/MA; MBA/MFA. *Program availability:* Part-time, evening/weekend. *Degree requirements:* For master's, advanced proficiency in a second language, work term (IMBA); for doctorate, comprehensive exam, thesis/dissertation. *Entrance requirements:* For master's, GMAT or GRE, minimum GPA of 3.0 (3.3 for MF, MBA in business analytics, and IMBA); for doctorate, GMAT or GRE, minimum GPA of 3.3. Additional exam requirements/recommendations for international students: Required—TOEFL (minimum score 600 paper-based; 100 iBT), IELTS (minimum score 7), York English Language Test (minimum score 1); PearsonVUE (minimum score 64). Electronic applications accepted. *Faculty research:* Accounting, finance, marketing, operations management and information systems, organizational studies, strategic management.

Youngstown State University, Graduate School, Williamson College of Business Administration, Department of Accounting and Finance, Youngstown, OH 44555-0001. Offers accounting (MBA). *Accreditation:* AACSB. *Program availability:* Part-time, evening/weekend. *Degree requirements:* For master's, thesis optional. *Entrance requirements:* For master's, GMAT, minimum GPA of 2.7. Additional exam requirements/recommendations for international students: Required—TOEFL. *Faculty research:* Taxation and compliance, capital markets, accounting information systems, accounting theory, tax and government accounting.

Finance and Banking

Abilene Christian University, College of Graduate and Professional Studies, Program in Business Administration, Addison, TX 75001. Offers business analytics (MBA); corporate finance (MBA); general management (MBA); healthcare administration (MBA); human resource management (MBA); international business (MBA); management: business analytics (MS); management: healthcare administration (MS); management: international business (MS); management: marketing (MS); management: operations and supply chain management (MS); marketing (MBA); nonprofit leadership (MBA); operations and supply chain management (MBA). *Program availability:* Part-time, online only, 100% online. *Faculty:* 2 full-time (0 women), 6 part-time/adjunct (2 women). *Students:* 109 full-time (47 women), 51 part-time (22 women); includes 42 minority (33 Black or African American, non-Hispanic/Latino; 1 American Indian or Alaska Native, non-Hispanic/Latino; 2 Asian, non-Hispanic/Latino; 6 Hispanic/Latino). 125 applicants, 65% accepted, 58 enrolled. *Entrance requirements:* Additional exam requirements/recommendations for international students: Required—TOEFL (minimum score 80 iBT), IELTS (minimum score 6). *Application deadline:* For fall admission, 8/14 priority date for domestic students; for winter admission, 10/1 priority date for domestic students; for spring admission, 12/15 priority date for domestic students; for summer admission, 4/15 priority date for domestic students. Applications are processed on a rolling basis. Application fee: $50. Electronic applications accepted. *Expenses:* $700 per hour. *Financial support:* In 2017–18, 2 students received support. Application deadline: 4/1; applicants required to submit FAFSA. *Faculty research:* Organizational structure, financial management, cost accounting, unit analysis management. *Unit head:* Phil Vardiman, Program Director, 325-674-2153, E-mail: pxv02b@acu.edu. *Application contact:* Graduate Advisor, 817-219-7300, E-mail: gradonline@acu.edu.
Website: http://www.acu.edu/online/academics/mba-business-administration.html

Adelphi University, Robert B. Willumstad School of Business, MBA Program, Garden City, NY 11530-0701. Offers accounting (MBA); finance (MBA); health services administration (MBA); human resource management (MBA); management (MBA); management information systems (MBA); marketing (MBA); sport management (MBA). *Accreditation:* AACSB. *Program availability:* Part-time, evening/weekend. *Students:* 257 full-time (110 women), 78 part-time (38 women); includes 56 minority (18 Black or African American, non-Hispanic/Latino; 16 Asian, non-Hispanic/Latino; 19 Hispanic/Latino; 3 Two or more races, non-Hispanic/Latino), 181 international. Average age 28. 435 applicants, 61% accepted, 205 enrolled. In 2017, 130 master's awarded. *Degree requirements:* For master's, capstone course. *Entrance requirements:* For master's, GMAT, 2 letters of recommendation. Additional exam requirements/recommendations for international students: Required—TOEFL (minimum score 550 paper-based; 80 iBT), IELTS (minimum score 6.5). *Application deadline:* For fall admission, 4/1 for international students; for spring admission, 11/1 for international students. Applications are processed on a rolling basis. Application fee: $50. Electronic applications accepted.

Expenses: Contact institution. *Financial support:* Research assistantships with partial tuition reimbursements, career-related internships or fieldwork, Federal Work-Study, institutionally sponsored loans, scholarships/grants, tuition waivers (partial), and unspecified assistantships available. Financial award application deadline: 3/1; financial award applicants required to submit FAFSA. *Faculty research:* Supply chain management, distribution channels, productivity benchmark analysis, data envelopment analysis, financial portfolio analysis. *Unit head:* Dr. Rakesh Gupta, Associate Dean, 516-877-4629. *Application contact:* E-mail: graduateadmissions@adelphi.edu.
Website: http://business.adelphi.edu/degree-programs/graduate-degree-programs/m-b-a/

American Business & Technology University, Programs in Business Administration, Saint Joseph, MO 64506. Offers business administration (MBA); financial management (MBA); global business management (MBA); information systems management (MBA); marketing and social media (MBA); project and operations management (MBA); public accounting (MBA). *Program availability:* Online learning.

The American College of Financial Services, Graduate Programs, Bryn Mawr, PA 19010-2105. Offers financial services (MSFS); leadership (MSM). *Program availability:* Part-time, evening/weekend, online learning. Electronic applications accepted. *Faculty research:* Retirement counseling, social security, aging, family composition, inflation.

American College of Thessaloniki, Department of Business Administration, Pylea, Greece. Offers banking and finance (MBA); entrepreneurship (MBA, Certificate); finance (Certificate); management (MBA, Certificate); marketing (MBA, Certificate). *Program availability:* Part-time, evening/weekend. *Degree requirements:* For master's, thesis. *Entrance requirements:* For master's, bachelor's degree. Additional exam requirements/recommendations for international students: Recommended—TOEFL. Electronic applications accepted.

American InterContinental University Online, Program in Business Administration, Schaumburg, IL 60173. Offers accounting and finance (MBA); finance (MBA); healthcare management (MBA); human resource management (MBA); international business (MBA); management (MBA); marketing (MBA); operations management (MBA); organizational psychology and development (MBA); project management (MBA). *Accreditation:* ACBSP. *Program availability:* Evening/weekend, online learning. *Entrance requirements:* Additional exam requirements/recommendations for international students: Required—TOEFL (minimum score 550 paper-based). Electronic applications accepted.

American University, Kogod School of Business, Department of Finance, Washington, DC 20016-8044. Offers finance (MS, Certificate); real estate (MS, Certificate). *Program availability:* Part-time, evening/weekend. *Students:* 40 full-time (16 women), 24 part-time

(10 women); includes 13 minority (8 Black or African American, non-Hispanic/Latino; 4 Asian, non-Hispanic/Latino; 1 Two or more races, non-Hispanic/Latino), 32 international. Average age 28. 130 applicants, 72% accepted, 36 enrolled. In 2017, 49 master's, 2 other advanced degrees awarded. *Degree requirements:* For master's, comprehensive exam (for some programs). *Entrance requirements:* For master's, GMAT/GRE, resume, personal statement, interview, 2 letters of recommendation, transcripts. Additional exam requirements/recommendations for international students: Required—TOEFL (minimum score 100 iBT). *Application deadline:* For fall admission, 1/15 priority date for domestic students, 1/15 for international students; for spring admission, 10/15 priority date for domestic students, 10/15 for international students. Applications are processed on a rolling basis. Application fee: $100. *Expenses:* Contact institution, *Financial support:* Application deadline: 2/1; applicants required to submit FAFSA. *Unit head:* Dr. Jeffrey Harris, Department Chair, Finance and Real Estate, 202-885-6669, Fax: 202-885-1946, E-mail: jharris@american.edu. *Application contact:* Jason Garner, Director of Admissions, 202-885-1926, E-mail: jgarner@american.edu.
Website: http://www.american.edu/kogod

The American University in Cairo, School of Business, Cairo, Egypt. Offers business administration (MBA); economics (MA); economics in international development (MA, Diploma); finance (MS). *Program availability:* Part-time, evening/weekend. *Faculty:* 30 full-time (10 women), 8 part-time/adjunct (3 women). *Students:* 49 full-time (25 women), 67 part-time (38 women), 5 international. Average age 29. 112 applicants, 35% accepted, 26 enrolled. In 2017, 51 master's awarded. *Degree requirements:* For master's, comprehensive exam (for some programs), thesis (for some programs). *Entrance requirements:* For master's, GMAT, GRE. Additional exam requirements/recommendations for international students: Required—TOEFL (minimum score 450 paper-based; 45 iBT), IELTS (minimum score 5). *Application deadline:* For fall admission, 2/1 priority date for domestic and international students; for spring admission, 10/15 priority date for domestic and international students. Applications are processed on a rolling basis. Application fee: $85. Electronic applications accepted. *Expenses:* Contact institution. *Financial support:* Fellowships with partial tuition reimbursements, scholarships/grants, tuition waivers (partial), and unspecified assistantships available. Financial award application deadline: 3/10. *Faculty research:* Marketing and quality management, banking operations management, economics, finance. *Unit head:* Dr. Sherif Kamel, Dean, 20-2-2615-2118, E-mail: skamel@aucegypt.edu. *Application contact:* Maha Hegazi, Director of Graduate Admissions, 20-2-2615-1462, E-mail: mahahegazi@aucegypt.edu.
Website: http://www.aucegypt.edu/Business/Pages/default.aspx

The American University in Dubai, Graduate Programs, Dubai, United Arab Emirates. Offers construction management (MS); education (M Ed); finance (MBA); generalist (MBA); marketing (MBA). *Program availability:* Part-time, evening/weekend. *Degree requirements:* For master's, thesis optional. *Entrance requirements:* For master's, GMAT (for MBA); GRE (for M Ed and MS), minimum undergraduate GPA of 3.0, official transcripts, two reference forms, curriculum vitae/resume, statement of career objectives, work experience. Additional exam requirements/recommendations for international students: Required—TOEFL (minimum score 550 paper-based; 79 iBT). Electronic applications accepted.

American University of Beirut, Graduate Programs, Faculty of Arts and Sciences, 1107 2020, Lebanon. Offers anthropology (MA); Arab and Middle Eastern history (PhD); Arabic language and literature (MA, PhD); archaeology (MA); art history and curating (MA); biology (MS); cell and molecular biology (PhD); chemistry (MS); clinical psychology (MA); computational sciences (MS); computer science (MS); economics (MA); education (MA), including administration and policy studies, elementary education, mathematics education, psychology school guidance, psychology test and measurements, science education, teaching English as a foreign language; English language (MA); English literature (MA); environmental policy planning (MS); financial economics (MAFE); general psychology (MA); geology (MS); history (MA); Islamic studies (MA); mathematics (MS); media studies (MA); Middle East studies (MA); philosophy (MA); physics (MS); political studies (MA); public administration (MA); public policy and international affairs (MA); sociology (MA); theoretical physics (PhD). *Program availability:* Part-time. *Faculty:* 108 full-time (36 women), 5 part-time/adjunct (4 women). *Students:* 251 full-time (180 women), 233 part-time (172 women). Average age 26. 425 applicants, 65% accepted, 121 enrolled. In 2017, 47 master's, 2 doctorates awarded. *Degree requirements:* For master's, one foreign language, comprehensive exam, thesis (for some programs), project; for doctorate, one foreign language, comprehensive exam, thesis/dissertation. *Entrance requirements:* For master's, GRE General Test (for some programs); for doctorate, GRE General Test (GRE Subject Test for theoretical physics). Additional exam requirements/recommendations for international students: Required—TOEFL (minimum score 583 paper-based; 97 iBT), IELTS (minimum score 7). *Application deadline:* For fall admission, 2/8 for domestic students; for spring admission, 11/3 for domestic students. Application fee: $50. Electronic applications accepted. *Expenses:* Contact institution. *Financial support:* In 2017–18, 29 fellowships, 40 research assistantships were awarded; teaching assistantships, scholarships/grants, tuition waivers (full and partial), and unspecified assistantships also available. Financial award application deadline: 4/4. *Unit head:* Dr. Nadia Maria El Cheikh, Dean, Faculty of Arts and Sciences, 961-1-374374 Ext. 3800, Fax: 961-1-744461, E-mail: nmcheikh@aub.edu.lb. *Application contact:* Rima Rassi, Graduate Studies Officer, 961-1-350000 Ext. 3833, Fax: 961-1-744461, E-mail: rr46@aub.edu.lb.
Website: http://www.aub.edu.lb/fas/pages/default.aspx

American University of Beirut, Graduate Programs, Suliman S. Olayan School of Business, Master's in Finance Program, 1107 2020, Lebanon. Offers M Fin. *Program availability:* Part-time. *Faculty:* 8 full-time (1 woman), 1 part-time/adjunct (0 women). *Students:* 27 full-time (14 women), 24 part-time (16 women). Average age 24. 144 applicants, 70% accepted, 51 enrolled. In 2017, 26 master's awarded. *Entrance requirements:* Additional exam requirements/recommendations for international students: Required—TOEFL (minimum score 583 paper-based; 97 iBT), IELTS (minimum score 7). *Application deadline:* For fall admission, 2/8 for domestic students; for spring admission, 4/4 for domestic students. Applications are processed on a rolling basis. Application fee: $50. Electronic applications accepted. *Expenses: Tuition:* Full-time $17,244; part-time $958 per credit. *Required fees:* $740. Tuition and fees vary according to course load and program. *Financial support:* In 2017–18, 17 research assistantships with full tuition reimbursements (averaging $21,000 per year) were awarded; fellowships, teaching assistantships, scholarships/grants, health care benefits, tuition waivers (full and partial), and unspecified assistantships also available. Financial award application deadline: 4/4; financial award applicants required to submit CSS PROFILE. *Unit head:* Maya Naim El-Helou, Director of Graduate Programs, 961-1-352700 Ext. 3955, Fax: 961-1-750214, E-mail: helou@aub.edu.lb. *Application contact:* Maya Naim El-Helou, Director of Graduate Programs, 961-1-352700 Ext. 3955, Fax: 961-1-750214, E-mail: helou@aub.edu.lb.
Website: https://www.aub.edu.lb/osb/osb_home/program/MFIN/Pages/programOverview.aspx

Andrews University, School of Graduate Studies, School of Business, Graduate Programs in Business, Berrien Springs, MI 49104. Offers MBA, MSA. *Faculty:* 8 full-time (3 women). *Students:* 23 full-time (13 women), 32 part-time (15 women); includes 21

minority (7 Black or African American, non-Hispanic/Latino; 6 Asian, non-Hispanic/Latino; 6 Hispanic/Latino; 2 Two or more races, non-Hispanic/Latino), 21 international. Average age 31. 83 applicants, 43% accepted, 28 enrolled. In 2017, 23 master's awarded. *Entrance requirements:* For master's, GMAT. Additional exam requirements/recommendations for international students: Required—TOEFL (minimum score 550 paper-based). Application fee: $40. *Unit head:* Dr. Leonard K. Gashugi, Chair, 769-471-3429, E-mail: gashugi@andrews.edu. *Application contact:* Justina Clayburn, Supervisor of Graduate Admission, 800-253-2874, Fax: 269-471-6321, E-mail: graduate@andrews.edu.

Argosy University, Atlanta, College of Business, Atlanta, GA 30328. Offers accounting (DBA); corporate compliance (MBA); customized professional concentration (MBA, DBA); finance (MBA); healthcare administration (MBA); information systems (DBA); information systems management (MBA); international business (MBA, DBA); management (MBA, MSM, DBA); marketing (MBA, DBA). *Accreditation:* ACBSP.

Argosy University, Chicago, College of Business, Chicago, IL 60601. Offers accounting (DBA); customized professional concentration (MBA, DBA); finance (MBA); fraud examination (MBA); global business sustainability (DBA); healthcare administration (MBA); information systems (DBA); information systems management (MBA); international business (MBA, DBA); management (MBA, MSM, DBA); marketing (MBA, DBA); organizational leadership (Ed D); public administration (MBA); sustainable management (MBA). *Accreditation:* ACBSP. *Program availability:* Online learning.

Argosy University, Hawai`i, College of Business, Honolulu, HI 96813. Offers accounting (DBA); corporate compliance (MBA); customized professional concentration (MBA, DBA); finance (MBA, Certificate); fraud examination (MBA); global business sustainability (DBA); healthcare administration (MBA, Certificate); information systems management (MBA, Certificate); international business (MBA, DBA, Certificate); management (MBA, MSM, DBA); marketing (MBA, DBA, Certificate); organizational leadership (Ed D); public administration (MBA); sustainable management (MBA).

Argosy University, Los Angeles, College of Business, Los Angeles, CA 90045. Offers accounting (DBA); corporate compliance (MBA); customized professional concentration (MBA, DBA); finance (MBA); fraud examination (MBA); global business sustainability (DBA); healthcare administration (MBA); information systems (DBA); information systems management (MBA); international business (MBA, DBA); management (MBA, MSM, DBA); marketing (MBA, DBA); organizational leadership (Ed D); public administration (MBA); sustainable management (MBA).

Argosy University, Northern Virginia, College of Business, Arlington, VA 22209. Offers accounting (DBA); customized professional concentration (MBA, DBA); finance (MBA); fraud examination (MBA); global business sustainability (DBA); healthcare administration (MBA); information systems (DBA); information systems management (MBA); international business (MBA, DBA, Certificate); management (MBA, MSM, DBA); marketing (MBA, DBA, Certificate); organizational leadership (Ed D); public administration (MBA); sustainable management (MBA).

Argosy University, Orange County, College of Business, Orange, CA 92868. Offers accounting (DBA, Adv C); corporate compliance (MBA); customized professional concentration (MBA, DBA); finance (MBA, Certificate); fraud examination (MBA); global business sustainability (DBA); healthcare administration (MBA, Certificate); information systems (DBA, Adv C, Certificate); information systems management (MBA); international business (MBA, DBA, Adv C, Certificate); management (MBA, MSM, DBA, Adv C); marketing (MBA, DBA, Adv C, Certificate); organizational leadership (Ed D); public administration (MBA, Certificate); sustainable management (MBA).

Argosy University, Phoenix, College of Business, Phoenix, AZ 85021. Offers accounting (DBA); corporate compliance (MBA); customized professional concentration (MBA, DBA); finance (MBA); fraud examination (MBA); global business sustainability (DBA); healthcare administration (MBA); information systems (DBA); information systems management (MBA); international business (MBA, DBA); management (MBA, DBA); marketing (MBA, DBA); public administration (MBA); sustainable management (MBA).

Argosy University, Seattle, College of Business, Seattle, WA 98121. Offers accounting (DBA); corporate compliance (MBA); customized professional concentration (MBA, DBA); finance (MBA); fraud examination (MBA); global business sustainability (DBA); healthcare administration (MBA); information systems (DBA); information systems management (MBA); international business (MBA, DBA); management (MBA, MSM, DBA); marketing (MBA, DBA); organizational leadership (Ed D); public administration (MBA); sustainable management (MBA).

Argosy University, Tampa, College of Business, Tampa, FL 33607. Offers accounting (DBA); corporate compliance (MBA); customized professional concentration (MBA, DBA); finance (MBA); fraud examination (MBA); global business sustainability (DBA); healthcare administration (MBA); information systems (DBA); information systems management (MBA); international business (MBA, DBA); management (MBA, MSM, DBA); marketing (MBA, DBA); organizational leadership (Ed D); public administration (MBA); sustainable management (MBA).

Argosy University, Twin Cities, College of Business, Eagan, MN 55121. Offers accounting (DBA); customized professional concentration (MBA, DBA); finance (MBA); fraud examination (MBA); global business sustainability (DBA); healthcare administration (MBA); information systems (DBA); information systems management (MBA); international business (MBA, DBA); management (MBA, MSM, DBA); marketing (MBA, DBA); organizational leadership (Ed D); public administration (MBA); sustainable management (MBA).

Arizona State University at the Tempe campus, W. P. Carey School of Business, Program in Business Administration, Tempe, AZ 85287-4906. Offers entrepreneurship (MBA); finance (MBA); health sector management (MBA); international business (MBA); leadership (MBA); marketing (MBA); organizational behavior (PhD); strategic management (PhD); supply chain management (MBA, PhD); JD/MBA; MBA/M Acc; MBA/M Arch. *Accreditation:* AACSB. *Program availability:* Part-time, evening/weekend, online learning. Terminal master's awarded for partial completion of doctoral program. *Degree requirements:* For master's, thesis or alternative, internship, interactive Program of Study (iPOS) submitted before completing 50 percent of required credit hours; for doctorate, comprehensive exam, thesis/dissertation, interactive Program of Study (iPOS) submitted before completing 50 percent of required credit hours. *Entrance requirements:* For master's, GMAT, minimum GPA of 3.0 in last 2 years of work leading to bachelor's degree, 2 letters of recommendation, professional resume, official transcripts, 3 essays; for doctorate, GMAT or GRE, minimum GPA of 3.0 in last 2 years of work leading to bachelor's degree, 3 letters of recommendation, resume, personal statement/essay. Additional exam requirements/recommendations for international students: Required—TOEFL (minimum score 550 paper-based; 80 iBT), IELTS (minimum score 6.5). Electronic applications accepted. *Expenses:* Contact institution.

Ashland University, Dauch College of Business and Economics, Ashland, OH 44805-3702. Offers accounting (MBA); business analytics (MBA); entrepreneurship (MBA); financial management (MBA); global management (MBA); health care management and leadership (MBA); human resource management (MBA); human resources (MBA);

management information systems (MBA); project management (MBA); sport management (MBA); supply chain management (MBA). *Accreditation:* ACBSP. *Program availability:* Part-time, evening/weekend, 100% online, blended/hybrid learning. *Faculty:* 20 full-time (8 women), 13 part-time/adjunct (2 women). *Students:* 458 full-time (210 women), 144 part-time (52 women); includes 88 minority (63 Black or African American, non-Hispanic/Latino; 1 American Indian or Alaska Native, non-Hispanic/Latino; 10 Asian, non-Hispanic/Latino; 14 Hispanic/Latino), 202 international. Average age 31. 216 applicants, 74% accepted, 115 enrolled. In 2017, 184 master's awarded. Terminal master's awarded for partial completion of doctoral program. *Degree requirements:* For master's, thesis optional, capstone course. *Entrance requirements:* For master's, 2 years of full-time work experience. Additional exam requirements/recommendations for international students: Required—TOEFL (minimum score 550 paper-based; 78 iBT). *Application deadline:* For fall admission, 8/1 priority date for domestic students; for spring admission, 12/1 priority date for domestic students. Applications are processed on a rolling basis. Application fee: $30. Electronic applications accepted. *Expenses:* $815 per credit hour, $15 technology fee for online sections. *Financial support:* Scholarships/grants, tuition waivers (partial), and unspecified assistantships available. Financial award application deadline: 4/15; financial award applicants required to submit FAFSA. *Faculty research:* Relationship marketing strategy, executive compensation and company performance, online marketplaces in electronic commerce, diversity training in campus recreation departments, entrepreneurship in developing and emerging economies. *Unit head:* Dr. Elad Granot, Dean, 419-289-5932, E-mail: egranot@ashland.edu. *Application contact:* Stephen W. Krispinsky, Executive Director of MBA Program, 419-289-5236, Fax: 419-289-5910, E-mail: skrispin@ashland.edu. Website: http://www.mba.ashland.edu

Aspen University, Program in Business Administration, Denver, CO 80246-1930. Offers business administration (MBA); finance (MBA); information management (MBA); project management (MBA, Certificate). *Program availability:* Part-time, evening/weekend, online learning. *Entrance requirements:* Additional exam requirements/recommendations for international students: Required—TOEFL (minimum score 530 paper-based). Electronic applications accepted.

Assumption College, Business Studies Program, Worcester, MA 01609-1296. Offers accounting (MBA); business studies (CAGS); finance/economics (MBA); human resources (MBA); international business (MBA); management (MBA); marketing (MBA); nonprofit leadership (MBA). *Program availability:* Part-time, evening/weekend. *Faculty:* 5 full-time (1 woman), 21 part-time/adjunct (6 women). *Students:* 29 full-time (13 women), 87 part-time (50 women); includes 15 minority (1 Black or African American, non-Hispanic/Latino; 4 Asian, non-Hispanic/Latino; 8 Hispanic/Latino; 2 Two or more races, non-Hispanic/Latino), 4 international. Average age 29. 34 applicants, 100% accepted, 26 enrolled. In 2017, 81 master's, 2 other advanced degrees awarded. *Degree requirements:* For master's, capstone. *Entrance requirements:* For master's, bachelor's degree, three letters of recommendation, official transcripts, personal statement, current resume; for CAGS, MBA or equivalent degree in a closely related field, three letters of recommendation, official transcripts, personal statement, current resume. Additional exam requirements/recommendations for international students: Required—TOEFL (minimum score 540 paper-based; 76 iBT), IELTS (minimum score 6). *Application deadline:* For fall admission, 8/10 priority date for domestic and international students; for spring admission, 1/4 priority date for domestic and international students; for summer admission, 5/10 priority date for domestic and international students. Application fee: $30. Electronic applications accepted. *Expenses: Tuition:* Full-time $11,952; part-time $664 per credit. *Required fees:* $70 per term. *Financial support:* In 2017–18, 19 students received support. Tuition waivers (full and partial), unspecified assistantships, and institutional discounts available. Financial award applicants required to submit FAFSA. *Faculty research:* Workplace diversity, dynamics of team interaction, utilization of leased employees, experiential learning project on due diligence market for prostheses. *Unit head:* Dr. Robin Frkal, Director, 508-767-7622, E-mail: ra.frkal@assumption.edu. *Application contact:* Karen Stoyanoff, Director of Recruitment for Graduate Enrollment, 508-767-7442, Fax: 508-799-4412, E-mail: graduate@assumption.edu.
Website: http://graduate.assumption.edu/mba/assumption-mba

Auburn University, Graduate School, College of Business, Department of Finance, Auburn University, AL 36849. Offers MS. *Faculty:* 13 full-time (3 women), 3 part-time/adjunct (1 woman). *Students:* 8 full-time (1 woman), 24 part-time (9 women); includes 1 minority (Asian, non-Hispanic/Latino), 11 international. Average age 30. 80 applicants, 33% accepted, 5 enrolled. In 2017, 21 master's awarded. Application fee: $50 ($60 for international students). *Expenses:* Tuition, state resident: full-time $10,974; part-time $519 per credit hour. Tuition, nonresident: full-time $29,658; part-time $1557 per credit hour. *Required fees:* $816 per semester. Tuition and fees vary according to degree level and program. *Financial support:* Applicants required to submit FAFSA. *Unit head:* Dr. Larry L. Colquitt, Jr., Chair, 334-844-3000. *Application contact:* Dr. George Flowers, Dean of the Graduate School, 334-844-2125.

Avila University, School of Business, Kansas City, MO 64145-1698. Offers accounting (MBA); finance (MBA); health care administration (MBA); international business (MBA); management (MBA); management information systems (MBA); marketing (MBA). *Program availability:* Part-time, evening/weekend. *Faculty:* 6 full-time (2 women), 6 part-time/adjunct (2 women). *Students:* 49 full-time (19 women), 29 part-time (14 women); includes 16 minority (12 Black or African American, non-Hispanic/Latino; 1 Asian, non-Hispanic/Latino; 3 Hispanic/Latino), 19 international. Average age 32. 51 applicants, 47% accepted, 20 enrolled. In 2017, 31 master's awarded. *Degree requirements:* For master's, comprehensive exam, capstone course. *Entrance requirements:* For master's, GMAT (minimum score 420), minimum GPA of 3.0, interview. Additional exam requirements/recommendations for international students: Required—TOEFL (minimum score 550 paper-based). *Application deadline:* For fall admission, 7/30 priority date for domestic and international students; for winter admission, 11/30 priority date for domestic and international students; for spring admission, 2/28 priority date for domestic and international students; for summer admission, 6/1 priority date for domestic and international students. Applications are processed on a rolling basis. Application fee: $0. Electronic applications accepted. *Expenses:* Contact institution. *Financial support:* In 2017–18, 18 students received support. Career-related internships or fieldwork and scholarships/grants available. Support available to part-time students. Financial award applicants required to submit FAFSA. *Faculty research:* Leadership characteristics, financial hedging, group dynamics. *Unit head:* Dr. Wendy L. Acker, Interim Dean, 816-501-3720, Fax: 816-501-2463, E-mail: wendy.acker@avila.edu. *Application contact:* Brandon Black, MBA Admission Advisor, 816-501-3601, Fax: 816-501-2463, E-mail: brandon.black@avila.edu.
Website: https://www.avila.edu/mrk/mba

Azusa Pacific University, School of Business and Management, Azusa, CA 91702-7000. Offers accounting (MBA); business administration (MBA); entrepreneurship (MBA); finance (MBA); international business (MBA); marketing (MBA); organizational science (MBA); professional accountancy (M Acc); sport management (MBA). *Program availability:* Part-time, evening/weekend. *Degree requirements:* For master's, thesis (for some programs), final project. *Entrance requirements:* For master's, GMAT, minimum GPA of 3.0. Additional exam requirements/recommendations for international students:

Required—TOEFL (minimum score 600 paper-based). *Expenses:* Contact institution. *Faculty research:* Gender issues, financial risk, leadership and ethics, marketing strategy.

Babson College, F. W. Olin Graduate School of Business, Babson Park, MA 02457-0310. Offers accounting (MSA); advanced management (Certificate); business administration (MBA); business analytics (MS); finance (MS); global entrepreneurship (MS); technological entrepreneurship (MS). *Accreditation:* AACSB. *Program availability:* Part-time, evening/weekend, online learning. *Entrance requirements:* For master's, GMAT, 2 years of work experience, resume, letters of recommendation. Additional exam requirements/recommendations for international students: Required—TOEFL (minimum score 100 iBT), IELTS (minimum score 6.5). Electronic applications accepted. *Faculty research:* Entrepreneurship, sustainability, global markets, process of innovation, social media and advertising.

Baker College Center for Graduate Studies–Online, Graduate Programs, Flint, MI 48507. Offers accounting (MBA); business administration (DBA); finance (MBA); general business (MBA); health care management (MBA); human resources management (MBA); information management (MBA); leadership studies (MBA); management information systems (MSIS); marketing (MBA). *Program availability:* Part-time, evening/weekend, online learning. *Degree requirements:* For master's, portfolio. *Entrance requirements:* For master's, 3 years of work experience, minimum undergraduate GPA of 2.5, writing sample, 3 letters of recommendation; for doctorate, MBA or acceptable related master's degree from accredited association, 5 years work experience, minimum graduate GPA of 3.25, writing sample, 3 professional references. Additional exam requirements/recommendations for international students: Required—TOEFL (minimum score 550 paper-based). Electronic applications accepted.

Barry University, Andreas School of Business, Graduate Certificate Programs, Miami Shores, FL 33161-6695. Offers finance (Certificate); health services administration (Certificate); international business (Certificate); management (Certificate); management information systems (Certificate); marketing (Certificate).

Baruch College of the City University of New York, Zicklin School of Business, Department of Economics and Finance, Program in Finance, New York, NY 10010-5585. Offers MBA, MS, PhD. PhD offered jointly with Graduate School and University Center of the City University of New York. *Program availability:* Part-time, evening/weekend. *Degree requirements:* For doctorate, comprehensive exam, thesis/dissertation. *Entrance requirements:* For master's, GMAT, 2 letters of recommendation, resume, 2 years of work experience; for doctorate, GMAT. Additional exam requirements/recommendations for international students: Required—TOEFL (minimum score 590 paper-based), TWE (minimum score 5).

Baruch College of the City University of New York, Zicklin School of Business, Zicklin Executive Programs, Executive Program in Finance, New York, NY 10010-5585. Offers MS. *Program availability:* Evening/weekend. *Entrance requirements:* For master's, personal interview, work experience. *Expenses:* Contact institution. *Faculty research:* Corporate finance, investments, options, securities, system risk.

Bayamón Central University, Graduate Programs, Program in Business Administration, Bayamón, PR 00960-1725. Offers accounting (MBA); finance (MBA); general business (MBA); management (MBA); marketing (MBA). *Program availability:* Part-time, evening/weekend. *Degree requirements:* For master's, comprehensive exam (for some programs). *Entrance requirements:* For master's, EXADEP, bachelor's degree in business or related field.

Bellevue University, Graduate School, College of Business, Bellevue, NE 68005-3098. Offers acquisition and contract management (MS); business administration (MBA); finance (MS); human capital management (PhD); management (MSM).

Benedictine University, Graduate Programs, Program in Business Administration, Lisle, IL 60532. Offers accounting (MBA); entrepreneurship and managing innovation (MBA); financial management (MBA); health administration (MBA); human resource management (MBA); information systems security (MBA); international business (MBA); management consulting (MBA); management information systems (MBA); marketing management (MBA); operations management and logistics (MBA); organizational leadership (MBA). *Program availability:* Part-time, evening/weekend, online learning. *Entrance requirements:* For master's, GMAT. Additional exam requirements/recommendations for international students: Required—TOEFL (minimum score 550 paper-based). Electronic applications accepted. *Faculty research:* Strategic leadership in professional organizations, sociology of professions, organizational change, social identity theory, applications to change management.

Bentley University, McCallum Graduate School of Business, Master's Program in Finance, Waltham, MA 02452-4705. Offers MSF. *Program availability:* Part-time, evening/weekend. *Faculty:* 71 full-time (25 women), 33 part-time/adjunct (15 women). *Students:* 83 full-time (42 women), 25 part-time (7 women); includes 5 minority (all Asian, non-Hispanic/Latino), 84 international. Average age 25. 176 applicants, 79% accepted, 45 enrolled. In 2017, 38 master's awarded. *Entrance requirements:* For master's, GMAT or GRE General Test, current resume; two letters of recommendation; official copies of all university-level transcripts. Additional exam requirements/recommendations for international students: Required—TOEFL (minimum score 100) or IELTS (minimum score 7). *Application deadline:* Applications are processed on a rolling basis. Application fee: $75. Electronic applications accepted. *Expenses: Tuition:* Part-time $4445 per course. *Required fees:* $170 per unit. *Financial support:* In 2017–18, 28 students received support. Scholarships/grants and unspecified assistantships available. Financial award application deadline: 6/1; financial award applicants required to submit FAFSA. *Faculty research:* Management of financial institutions; corporate governance and executive compensation; asset valuation; international mergers and acquisitions; hedging, risk management and derivatives. *Unit head:* Claude Cicchetti, Lecturer/MS Director, 781-891-2511, E-mail: ccicchetti@bentley.edu. *Application contact:* Graduate Admissions, 781-891-2108, Fax: 781-891-2464, E-mail: applygrad@bentley.edu.
Website: https://admissions.bentley.edu/graduate/masters-in-finance

Bentley University, McCallum Graduate School of Business, Master's Program in Financial Planning, Waltham, MA 02452-4705. Offers MSFP. *Program availability:* Part-time, evening/weekend, 100% online, blended/hybrid learning. *Faculty:* 71 full-time (25 women), 33 part-time/adjunct (15 women). *Students:* 7 full-time (3 women), 18 part-time (10 women); includes 4 minority (2 Black or African American, non-Hispanic/Latino; 2 Asian, non-Hispanic/Latino), 4 international. Average age 31. 20 applicants, 80% accepted, 8 enrolled. In 2017, 19 master's awarded. *Entrance requirements:* For master's, GMAT or GRE General Test, current resume; two letters of recommendation; official copies of all university-level transcripts; 2 essays. Additional exam requirements/recommendations for international students: Required—TOEFL (minimum score 100) or IELTS (minimum score 7). *Application deadline:* Applications are processed on a rolling basis. Application fee: $75. Electronic applications accepted. *Expenses: Tuition:* Part-time $4445 per course. *Required fees:* $170 per unit. *Financial support:* In 2017–18, 4 students received support. Scholarships/grants available. Financial award application deadline: 6/1; financial award applicants required to submit FAFSA. *Faculty research:* International financial planning, compensation and benefits, retirement planning. *Unit head:* John Lynch, Senior Lecturer/Director, 781-891-2624, E-mail: jlynch@bentley.edu. *Application contact:* Graduate Admissions, 781-891-2108, Fax: 781-891-2464, E-mail: applygrad@bentley.edu.
Website: https://admissions.bentley.edu/graduate/masters-in-financial-planning

Binghamton University, State University of New York, Graduate School, School of Management, Program in Management, Binghamton, NY 13902-6000. Offers finance (PhD); management information systems (PhD); marketing (PhD); organizational studies (PhD); supply chain management (PhD). *Students:* 8 full-time (5 women), 12 part-time (5 women), 19 international. Average age 30. 57 applicants, 21% accepted, 7 enrolled. In 2017, 3 doctorates awarded. *Degree requirements:* For doctorate, thesis/ dissertation. *Entrance requirements:* For doctorate, GMAT. *Application deadline:* For fall admission, 2/1 for domestic students. *Financial support:* In 2017–18, 18 students received support. *Unit head:* Dr. Upinder Dhillon, Dean, 607-777-2314, E-mail: dhillon@binghamton.edu. *Application contact:* Marianne Ferry, Administrative Assistant, Executive Education and PhD Programs, 607-777-2342, E-mail: mferry@binghamton.edu.

Bluffton University, Programs in Business, Bluffton, OH 45817. Offers accounting and financial management (MBA); health care management (MBA); leadership (MAOM, MBA); production and operations management (MBA); sustainability management (MBA). *Program availability:* Evening/weekend, blended/hybrid learning, videoconference. *Faculty:* 5 full-time (2 women), 8 part-time/adjunct (2 women). *Students:* 48 full-time (31 women); includes 11 minority (5 Black or African American, non-Hispanic/Latino; 1 Asian, non-Hispanic/Latino; 3 Hispanic/Latino; 2 Two or more races, non-Hispanic/Latino), 1 international. Average age 33. 44 applicants, 70% accepted, 26 enrolled. In 2017, 41 master's awarded. *Degree requirements:* For master's, integrated research project (for some programs). *Entrance requirements:* For master's, current resume, official transcript, bachelor's degree, minimum GPA of 3.0, personal essay. Additional exam requirements/recommendations for international students: Recommended—TOEFL (minimum score 550 paper-based). *Application deadline:* For fall admission, 7/31 priority date for domestic and international students. Applications are processed on a rolling basis. Application fee: $0. Electronic applications accepted. *Expenses:* $550 per credit hour, $150 per semester technology fee, $25 per semester payment plan fee. *Financial support:* Unspecified assistantships and faculty/staff grants available. Financial award applicants required to submit FAFSA. *Unit head:* Dr. Melissa Green, Director of Graduate Programs in Business, 419-358-3447, E-mail: greenm@bluffton.edu. *Application contact:* Carrie Mast, Administrative Assistant, Graduate Programs in Business, 419-358-3065, E-mail: mastc@bluffton.edu. Website: http://www.bluffton.edu/grad/

Boston College, Carroll School of Management, Graduate Finance Programs, Chestnut Hill, MA 02467-3800. Offers MSF, PhD, MBA/MSF. *Program availability:* Part-time. *Degree requirements:* For doctorate, thesis/dissertation. *Entrance requirements:* For master's, GMAT or GRE, resume, recommendations; for doctorate, GMAT or GRE, curriculum vitae, recommendations. Additional exam requirements/recommendations for international students: Required—TOEFL (minimum score 600 paper-based, 100 iBT), IELTS (minimum score 7.5), or PTE (minimum score 68). Electronic applications accepted. *Faculty research:* Security and derivative markets, financial institutions, corporate finance and capital markets, market macrostructure, investments, portfolio analysis.

Boston University, Metropolitan College, Department of Administrative Sciences, Boston, MA 02215. Offers applied business analytics (MS); economic development and tourism management (MSAS); enterprise risk management (MS); financial management (MS); global marketing management (MS); innovation and technology (MSAS); insurance management (MS); project management (MS); supply chain management (MS). *Accreditation:* AACSB. *Program availability:* Part-time, evening/weekend, 100% online, blended/hybrid learning. *Faculty:* 21 full-time (5 women), 34 part-time/adjunct (5 women). *Students:* 297 full-time (156 women), 597 part-time (298 women); includes 183 minority (58 Black or African American, non-Hispanic/Latino; 2 American Indian or Alaska Native, non-Hispanic/Latino; 56 Asian, non-Hispanic/Latino; 51 Hispanic/Latino; 2 Native Hawaiian or other Pacific Islander, non-Hispanic/Latino; 14 Two or more races, non-Hispanic/Latino), 391 international. Average age 30. 963 applicants, 64% accepted, 209 enrolled. In 2017, 372 master's awarded. *Degree requirements:* For master's, thesis optional. *Entrance requirements:* For master's, 1 year of work experience, minimum GPA of 3.0. Additional exam requirements/recommendations for international students: Required—TOEFL (minimum score 84 iBT). *Application deadline:* Applications are processed on a rolling basis. Application fee: $85. Electronic applications accepted. *Expenses:* Contact institution. *Financial support:* In 2017–18, 15 students received support, including 18 research assistantships (averaging $8,400 per year), 12 teaching assistantships (averaging $2,700 per year); career-related internships or fieldwork, Federal Work-Study, and unspecified assistantships also available. Financial award applicants required to submit FAFSA. *Faculty research:* International business, innovative process. *Unit head:* Dr. John Sullivan, Chair, 617-353-3016, E-mail: adminsc@bu.edu. *Application contact:* Fiona Niven, Administrative Sciences Department, 617-353-3016, E-mail: adminsc@bu.edu. Website: http://www.bu.edu/met/academic-community/departments/administrative-sciences/

Brandeis University, International Business School (IBS), Master of Arts in International Economics and Finance Program, Waltham, MA 02454-9110. Offers applied economic analysis (MA). *Faculty:* 40 full-time (16 women), 31 part-time/adjunct (7 women). *Students:* 158 full-time (96 women); includes 8 minority (1 American Indian or Alaska Native, non-Hispanic/Latino; 6 Asian, non-Hispanic/Latino; 1 Hispanic/Latino), 140 international. Average age 23. 649 applicants, 45% accepted, 92 enrolled. In 2017, 103 master's awarded. *Entrance requirements:* For master's, GMAT or GRE. Additional exam requirements/recommendations for international students: Required—TOEFL (minimum score 600 paper-based; 100 iBT), IELTS (minimum score 7), PTE (minimum score 68). *Application deadline:* For fall admission, 11/1 priority date for domestic and international students; for winter admission, 1/15 priority date for domestic and international students; for spring admission, 3/15 priority date for domestic and international students; for summer admission, 4/15 for domestic and international students. Application fee: $100. Electronic applications accepted. *Expenses:* Contact institution. *Financial support:* In 2017–18, 81 students received support. Institutionally sponsored loans and scholarships (averaging $18,384 annually) available. Financial award application deadline: 4/15; financial award applicants required to submit FAFSA. *Faculty research:* International economic policy analysis, macroeconomics, econometrics, business economics, economic development. *Unit head:* Peter Petri, Dean, 781-736-2256. *Application contact:* Kelly Sugrue, Assistant Dean of Admissions, 781-736-2252, Fax: 781-736-2263, E-mail: globaladmissions@brandeis.edu. Website: http://www.brandeis.edu/global/ma

Brandeis University, International Business School (IBS), Master of Business Administration Program, Waltham, MA 02454-9110. Offers data analytics (MBA); finance (MBA); marketing (MBA); real estate (MBA). *Faculty:* 40 full-time (16 women), 31 part-time/adjunct (7 women). *Students:* 35 full-time (18 women), 1 (woman) part-time; includes 3 minority (1 Black or African American, non-Hispanic/Latino; 2 Asian, non-Hispanic/Latino), 30 international. Average age 27. 75 applicants, 49% accepted, 17 enrolled. In 2017, 21 master's awarded. *Entrance requirements:* For master's, GMAT or GRE, minimum two years of full-time work experience. Additional exam requirements/recommendations for international students: Required—TOEFL (minimum score 600 paper-based; 100 iBT), IELTS (minimum score 7), PTE (minimum score 68). *Application deadline:* For fall admission, 11/1 priority date for domestic and international students; for winter admission, 1/15 priority date for domestic and international students; for spring admission, 3/15 priority date for domestic and international students; for summer admission, 4/15 for domestic and international students. Application fee: $100. Electronic applications accepted. *Expenses:* Contact institution. *Financial support:* In 2017–18, 32 students received support. Institutionally sponsored loans and scholarships (averaging $29,641 annually) available. Financial award application deadline: 4/15; financial award applicants required to submit FAFSA. *Faculty research:* Strategic alliances, IPO and venture capital financing, real estate, risk management, data analytics. *Unit head:* Peter Petri, Interim Dean, 781-736-2256. *Application contact:* Kelly Sugrue, Assistant Dean of Admissions, 781-736-2252, Fax: 781-736-2263, E-mail: globaladmissions@brandeis.edu.

Brandeis University, International Business School (IBS), Master of Science in Finance Program, Waltham, MA 02454-9110. Offers asset management (MSF); corporate finance (MSF); risk management (MSF). *Faculty:* 40 full-time (16 women), 31 part-time (7 women). *Students:* 115 full-time (66 women), 71 part-time (51 women); includes 1 minority (Asian, non-Hispanic/Latino), 180 international. Average age 22. 876 applicants, 36% accepted, 109 enrolled. In 2017, 33 master's awarded. *Entrance requirements:* For master's, GMAT or GRE. Additional exam requirements/ recommendations for international students: Required—TOEFL (minimum score 600 paper-based; 100 iBT), IELTS (minimum score 7), PTE (minimum score 68). *Application deadline:* For fall admission, 11/1 priority date for domestic and international students; for winter admission, 1/15 priority date for domestic and international students; for spring admission, 3/15 priority date for domestic and international students; for summer admission, 4/15 for domestic and international students. Application fee: $100. Electronic applications accepted. *Expenses:* Contact institution. *Financial support:* In 2017–18, 75 students received support. Institutionally sponsored loans and scholarships (averaging $11,479 annually) available. Financial award application deadline: 4/15; financial award applicants required to submit FAFSA. *Faculty research:* Asset management, municipal finance, corporate finance, venture capital, international trade. *Unit head:* Peter Petri, Interim Dean, 781-736-2256. *Application contact:* Kelly Sugrue, Assistant Dean of Admissions, 781-736-2252, Fax: 781-736-2263, E-mail: admission@lemberg.edu. Website: https://www.brandeis.edu/global/msf

Brandeis University, International Business School (IBS), PhD in International Economics and Finance Program, Waltham, MA 02454-9110. Offers advanced macroeconomics (PhD); applied microeconomics (PhD). *Faculty:* 40 full-time (16 women), 31 part-time/adjunct (7 women). *Students:* 20 full-time (7 women); includes 2 minority (1 American Indian or Alaska Native, non-Hispanic/Latino; 1 Hispanic/Latino), 10 international. Average age 32. 107 applicants, 19% accepted, 7 enrolled. In 2017, 5 doctorates awarded. *Degree requirements:* For doctorate, thesis/dissertation. *Entrance requirements:* Additional exam requirements/recommendations for international students: Required—TOEFL (minimum score 600 paper-based; 100 iBT), IELTS (minimum score 7), PTE (minimum score 68). *Application deadline:* For winter admission, 1/15 priority date for domestic and international students. Application fee: $55. *Expenses:* Contact institution. *Financial support:* In 2017–18, 16 students received support, including research assistantships (averaging $6,000 per year), teaching assistantships (averaging $6,000 per year); scholarships/grants and health care benefits also available. Financial award application deadline: 1/15; financial award applicants required to submit FAFSA. *Faculty research:* Global business, global trade, global finance, macroeconomics, development and institutions. *Unit head:* Peter Petri, Interim Dean, 781-736-2256. *Application contact:* Kelly Sugrue, Assistant Dean of Admissions, 781-736-2252, Fax: 781-736-2263, E-mail: globaladmissions@brandeis.edu. Website: https://www.brandeis.edu/global/academics/phd/

Brandman University, School of Business and Professional Studies, Irvine, CA 92618. Offers accounting (MBA); business administration (MBA); business intelligence and data analytics (MBA); e-business strategic management (MBA); entrepreneurship (MBA); finance (MBA); health administration (MBA); human resources (MBA, MS); international business (MBA); marketing (MBA); organizational leadership (MA, MBA, MPA); public administration (MPA). *Expenses: Tuition:* Part-time $640 per credit hour. Tuition and fees vary according to degree level and program. *Unit head:* Dr. Glenn Worthington, Dean, 253-861-1024, E-mail: gworthin@brandman.edu. *Application contact:* Dr. Glenn Worthington, Dean, 253-861-1024, E-mail: gworthin@brandman.edu. Website: https://www.brandman.edu/academic-programs/business-and-professional-studies

Bridgewater State University, College of Graduate Studies, Ricciardi College of Business, Department of Accounting and Finance, Bridgewater, MA 02325. Offers MSM. *Program availability:* Part-time, evening/weekend. *Entrance requirements:* For master's, GMAT.

Brigham Young University, Graduate Studies, BYU Marriott School of Business, MBA Program, Provo, UT 84602. Offers entrepreneurship (MBA); finance (MBA); global supply chain management (MBA); marketing (MBA); strategic human resources (MBA); JD/MBA; MBA/MS. *Accreditation:* AACSB. *Faculty:* 134 full-time (15 women), 65 part-time/adjunct (16 women). *Students:* 303 full-time (65 women); includes 26 minority (3 American Indian or Alaska Native, non-Hispanic/Latino; 8 Asian, non-Hispanic/Latino; 11 Hispanic/Latino; 4 Native Hawaiian or other Pacific Islander, non-Hispanic/Latino), 58 international. Average age 30. 339 applicants, 52% accepted, 136 enrolled. In 2017, 163 master's awarded. *Entrance requirements:* For master's, GMAT or GRE, commitment to BYU Honor Code, undergraduate degree. Additional exam requirements/recommendations for international students: Required—TOEFL (minimum score 590 paper-based; 100 iBT), IELTS (minimum score 7). *Application deadline:* For fall admission, 5/1 for domestic students, 3/1 for international students. Applications are processed on a rolling basis. Application fee: $50. Electronic applications accepted. *Expenses:* Contact institution. *Financial support:* Research assistantships, teaching assistantships, career-related internships or fieldwork, institutionally sponsored loans, and scholarships/grants available. Financial award application deadline: 3/1; financial award applicants required to submit FAFSA. *Faculty research:* Finance, marketing, supply chain management, entrepreneurship, strategic human resources. *Unit head:* Dr. Grant McQueen, Director, 801-422-3500, E-mail: mba@byu.edu. *Application contact:* Yvette Anderson, MBA Program Admissions Director, 801-422-3500, Fax: 801-422-0513, E-mail: mba@byu.edu. Website: http://mba.byu.edu

Brooklyn College of the City University of New York, School of Business, Brooklyn, NY 11210-2889. Offers accounting (MS); business administration (MS), including economic analysis, general business, global business and finance. *Program availability:* Part-time, evening/weekend. *Degree requirements:* For master's, comprehensive exam, thesis or alternative. *Entrance requirements:* For master's, GMAT, 2 letters of recommendation. Additional exam requirements/recommendations for international students: Required—TOEFL (minimum score 550 paper-based; 79 iBT). Electronic applications accepted. *Faculty research:* Econometrics, environmental economics, microeconomics, macroeconomics, taxation.

Bryant University, Graduate School of Business, Smithfield, RI 02917. Offers accounting (MPAC); business administration (MBA), including business analytics,

Finance and Banking

general management, global finance, global supply chain management, international business; taxation (MST). *Program availability:* Part-time, 100% online. *Faculty:* 30 full-time (5 women), 7 part-time/adjunct (2 women). *Students:* 84 full-time (31 women), 91 part-time (35 women); includes 24 minority (4 Black or African American, non-Hispanic/Latino; 1 American Indian or Alaska Native, non-Hispanic/Latino; 6 Asian, non-Hispanic/Latino; 8 Hispanic/Latino; 5 Two or more races, non-Hispanic/Latino), 6 international. Average age 26. 215 applicants, 66% accepted, 96 enrolled. In 2017, 118 master's awarded. *Degree requirements:* For master's, comprehensive exam (for some programs). *Entrance requirements:* For master's, GMAT, resume, recommendation, college transcripts. Additional exam requirements/recommendations for international students: Required—TOEFL (minimum score 580 paper-based; 95 iBT). *Application deadline:* For fall admission, 7/15 for domestic and international students; for spring admission, 11/15 for domestic and international students; for summer admission, 4/15 for domestic and international students. Applications are processed on a rolling basis. Application fee: $80. Electronic applications accepted. *Expenses:* $45,102 total, $1,118 per credit hour, $1,500 study abroad fee (for full-time MBA); $40,248 total, $1,118 per credit hour (for part-time MBA); $30,280 total, $1,176 per credit hour (for MP Ac and MST); $13,146, $1,118 per credit hour (for CGS). *Financial support:* In 2017–18, 95 fellowships with full and partial tuition reimbursements (averaging $9,825 per year), 9 research assistantships with full and partial tuition reimbursements (averaging $7,100 per year) were awarded; scholarships/grants and unspecified assistantships also available. Support available to part-time students. Financial award application deadline: 2/15; financial award applicants required to submit FAFSA. *Faculty research:* International business, public sector auditing, taxation of partnerships, information systems security, financial markets microstructure. *Unit head:* Bjorn Carlsson, Graduate Program Director, 401-232-6707, E-mail: bcarlsson@bryant.edu. *Application contact:* Terri Rogers, Admissions Assistant, 401-232-6230, Fax: 401-232-6494, E-mail: graduateprograms@bryant.edu.
Website: http://gradschool.bryant.edu/business/

Butler University, Lacy School of Business, Indianapolis, IN 46208-3485. Offers entrepreneurship and innovation (MBA); finance (MBA); international business (MBA); leadership (MBA); marketing (MBA); professional accounting (MP Acc). *Accreditation:* AACSB. *Program availability:* Part-time. *Faculty:* 14 full-time (4 women), 9 part-time/adjunct (2 women). *Students:* 35 full-time (16 women), 111 part-time (38 women); includes 15 minority (2 Black or African American, non-Hispanic/Latino; 5 Asian, non-Hispanic/Latino; 8 Hispanic/Latino), 6 international. Average age 30. 149 applicants, 64% accepted, 43 enrolled. In 2017, 90 master's awarded. *Degree requirements:* For master's, comprehensive exam, thesis optional. *Entrance requirements:* For master's, GMAT, minimum AACSB index of 950, personal statement, two letters of recommendation, official transcripts, current resume. Additional exam requirements/recommendations for international students: Required—TOEFL (minimum score 550 paper-based; 79 iBT), IELTS (minimum score 6), Michigan English Language Assessment Battery (minimum score of 80). *Application deadline:* For fall admission, 8/1 for domestic and international students; for spring admission, 12/1 for domestic and international students; for summer admission, 4/1 for domestic and international students. Applications are processed on a rolling basis. Application fee: $0. Electronic applications accepted. *Expenses:* $820 per credit. *Financial support:* In 2017–18, 22 students received support. Scholarships/grants, tuition waivers (full and partial), and unspecified assistantships available. Financial award application deadline: 7/15; financial award applicants required to submit FAFSA. *Faculty research:* Higher education and pedagogy; ecotourism; healthcare issues and marketing public policy; domestic public policy, international finance and banking, international and management entrepreneurship, organizational management. *Unit head:* Dr. Stephen Standifird, Dean, 317-940-6307. *Application contact:* Diane Dubord, Graduate Student Service Specialist, 317-940-8107, Fax: 317-940-8250, E-mail: ddubord@butler.edu.
Website: https://www.butler.edu/lacyschool

California College of the Arts, Graduate Programs, MBA in Design Strategy Program, San Francisco, CA 94107. Offers MBA. *Accreditation:* NASAD. *Faculty:* 1 (woman) full-time, 16 part-time/adjunct (5 women). *Students:* 88 full-time (62 women); includes 24 minority (3 Black or African American, non-Hispanic/Latino; 14 Asian, non-Hispanic/Latino; 6 Hispanic/Latino; 1 Native Hawaiian or other Pacific Islander, non-Hispanic/Latino), 26 international. Average age 30. 187 applicants, 68% accepted, 49 enrolled. In 2017, 53 master's awarded. *Degree requirements:* For master's, thesis. *Entrance requirements:* Additional exam requirements/recommendations for international students: Required—TOEFL, IELTS, or PTE. *Application deadline:* For fall admission, 1/31 priority date for domestic and international students. Applications are processed on a rolling basis. Application fee: $70. Electronic applications accepted. *Expenses:* $49,230 per year full-time tuition, $490 per year fees; $1,641 per unit part-time tuition. *Financial support:* Federal Work-Study and scholarships/grants available. Financial award application deadline: 7/31; financial award applicants required to submit FAFSA. *Unit head:* Andy Dong, Program Chair, 800-447-1ART, E-mail: andy@cca.edu. *Application contact:* Wes Fanelli, Assistant Director of Graduate Admissions, 415-703-9533, Fax: 415-703-9539, E-mail: wfanelli@cca.edu.

California Intercontinental University, School of Business, Irvine, CA 92614. Offers banking and finance (MBA); entrepreneurship and business management (DBA); global business leadership (DBA); international management and marketing (MBA); organizational management and human resource management (MBA).

California Lutheran University, Graduate Studies, School of Management, Thousand Oaks, CA 91360-2787. Offers business (IMBA); entrepreneurship (MBA, Certificate); finance (MBA, Certificate); financial planning (MBA, MS, Certificate); human capital management (MBA, Certificate); information technology (MS); information technology management (MBA, Certificate); international business (MBA, Certificate); marketing (MBA, Certificate); public policy and administration (MPPA); quantitative economics (MS). *Program availability:* Part-time, evening/weekend, 100% online, blended/hybrid learning. *Faculty:* 17 full-time (4 women), 40 part-time/adjunct (9 women). *Students:* 423 full-time (168 women), 153 part-time (72 women); includes 124 minority (11 Black or African American, non-Hispanic/Latino; 1 American Indian or Alaska Native, non-Hispanic/Latino; 21 Asian, non-Hispanic/Latino; 75 Hispanic/Latino; 16 Two or more races, non-Hispanic/Latino), 294 international. Average age 31. 467 applicants, 72% accepted, 108 enrolled. In 2017, 306 master's awarded. *Degree requirements:* For master's, comprehensive exam (for some programs). *Entrance requirements:* For master's, GMAT, interview, minimum GPA of 3.0. *Application deadline:* Applications are processed on a rolling basis. Application fee: $50. Electronic applications accepted. *Expenses:* Contact institution. *Unit head:* Dr. Gerhard Apfelthaler, Dean, 805-493-3360. *Application contact:* 805-493-3325, Fax: 805-493-3861, E-mail: clugrad@callutheran.edu.
Website: http://www.callutheran.edu/management/

California State University, East Bay, Office of Graduate Studies, College of Business and Economics, MBA Program, Option in Finance, Hayward, CA 94542-3000. Offers MBA. *Students:* 23 full-time (8 women), 34 part-time (14 women); includes 29 minority (4 Black or African American, non-Hispanic/Latino; 17 Asian, non-Hispanic/Latino; 2 Hispanic/Latino; 3 Native Hawaiian or other Pacific Islander, non-Hispanic/Latino; 3 Two or more races, non-Hispanic/Latino), 17 international. Average age 33. 42 applicants,

48% accepted, 13 enrolled. In 2017, 26 master's awarded. *Degree requirements:* For master's, comprehensive exam or thesis. *Entrance requirements:* For master's, GMAT, minimum GPA of 2.75. Additional exam requirements/recommendations for international students: Required—TOEFL (minimum score 550 paper-based). *Application deadline:* For fall admission, 6/1 for domestic and international students. Applications are processed on a rolling basis. Application fee: $55. Electronic applications accepted. *Financial support:* Career-related internships or fieldwork, Federal Work-Study, and institutionally sponsored loans available. Support available to part-time students. Financial award application deadline: 3/2; financial award applicants required to submit FAFSA. *Application contact:* Philip Cole-Regis, Administrative Support Coordinator, 510-885-3286, Fax: 510-885-4777, E-mail: philip.coleregis@csueastbay.edu.

California State University, Fullerton, Graduate Studies, College of Business and Economics, Department of Finance, Fullerton, CA 92831-3599. Offers MBA. *Program availability:* Part-time. *Faculty:* 5 full-time (3 women), 2 part-time/adjunct (1 woman). *Students:* 13 full-time (5 women), 28 part-time (9 women); includes 22 minority (12 Asian, non-Hispanic/Latino; 8 Hispanic/Latino; 2 Two or more races, non-Hispanic/Latino), 3 international. Average age 29. 24 applicants, 33% accepted. *Entrance requirements:* For master's, GMAT, minimum AACSB index of 950. Application fee: $55. *Financial support:* Career-related internships or fieldwork, Federal Work-Study, institutionally sponsored loans, and scholarships/grants available. Support available to part-time students. Financial award application deadline: 3/1; financial award applicants required to submit FAFSA. *Unit head:* Mark Hoven Stohs, Chair, 657-278-2217. *Application contact:* Admissions/Applications, 657-278-2371.

California State University, Los Angeles, Graduate Studies, College of Business and Economics, Department of Finance and Law, Los Angeles, CA 90032-8530. Offers finance and banking (MBA, MS). *Program availability:* Part-time, evening/weekend. *Degree requirements:* For master's, comprehensive exam (MBA), thesis (MS). *Entrance requirements:* For master's, GMAT, minimum GPA of 2.5 during previous 2 years of course work. Additional exam requirements/recommendations for international students: Required—TOEFL (minimum score 550 paper-based). Electronic applications accepted.

California State University, San Bernardino, Graduate Studies, College of Business and Public Administration, Program in Business Administration, San Bernardino, CA 92407. Offers accounting (MBA); entrepreneurship (MBA); finance (MBA); global business (MBA); information management (MBA); information security (MBA); management (MBA); supply chain management (MBA). *Accreditation:* AACSB. *Program availability:* Part-time, evening/weekend, online learning. *Faculty:* 4 full-time (3 women), 6 part-time/adjunct (4 women). *Students:* 21 full-time (15 women), 122 part-time (30 women); includes 82 minority (15 Black or African American, non-Hispanic/Latino; 1 American Indian or Alaska Native, non-Hispanic/Latino; 19 Asian, non-Hispanic/Latino; 44 Hispanic/Latino; 3 Two or more races, non-Hispanic/Latino), 37 international. Average age 33. 258 applicants, 44% accepted, 50 enrolled. In 2017, 134 master's awarded. *Degree requirements:* For master's, comprehensive exam, thesis. *Entrance requirements:* Additional exam requirements/recommendations for international students: Required—TOEFL. *Application deadline:* For fall admission, 7/16 for domestic students, 7/20 for international students; for winter admission, 10/23 for domestic students, 10/20 for international students; for spring admission, 1/22 for domestic students, 1/20 for international students. Application fee: $55. *Expenses:* Contact institution. *Financial support:* Application deadline: 3/1. *Unit head:* Dr. Lawrence C. Rose, Dean, 909-537-3703, Fax: 909-537-7026, E-mail: lrose@csusb.edu. *Application contact:* Dr. Vipin Gupta, Associate Dean/MBA Director, 909-537-7380, Fax: 909-537-7026, E-mail: vgupta@csusb.edu.
Website: http://mba.csusb.edu/

Capella University, School of Business and Technology, Doctoral Programs in Business, Minneapolis, MN 55402. Offers accounting (DBA, PhD); business intelligence (DBA); finance (DBA, PhD); general business management (PhD); human resource management (DBA, PhD); leadership (DBA, PhD); management education (PhD); marketing (DBA, PhD); project management (DBA, PhD); strategy and innovation (DBA, PhD). *Accreditation:* ACBSP.

Capella University, School of Business and Technology, Master's Programs in Business, Minneapolis, MN 55402. Offers accounting (MBA); business analysis (MS); business intelligence (MBA); entrepreneurship (MBA); finance (MBA); general business administration (MBA); general human resource management (MS); general leadership (MS); health care management (MBA); human resource management (MBA); marketing (MBA); project management (MBA, MS). *Accreditation:* ACBSP.

Carnegie Mellon University, Tepper School of Business, Program in Financial Economics, Pittsburgh, PA 15213-3891. Offers PhD. *Degree requirements:* For doctorate, thesis/dissertation. *Entrance requirements:* For doctorate, GRE General Test.

Case Western Reserve University, Weatherhead School of Management, Department of Banking and Finance, Cleveland, OH 44106. Offers finance (MSM). *Entrance requirements:* For master's, GMAT. *Expenses:* Tuition: Full-time $43,854; part-time $1827 per credit hour. *Required fees:* $50; $50 per credit hour. Tuition and fees vary according to course load and program. *Faculty research:* Monetary and fiscal policy, corporate finance, future markets, derivative pricing, capital market efficiency.

Central European University, Department of Economics, 1051, Hungary. Offers business administration (PhD); business analytics (M Sc); economic policy in global markets (MA); economics (MA, PhD); finance (MS); global economic relations (MA); technology management and innovation (MS). *Program availability:* Part-time. *Faculty:* 23 full-time (2 women), 25 part-time/adjunct (4 women). *Students:* 177 full-time (77 women), 125 part-time (39 women). Average age 31. 530 applicants, 49% accepted, 144 enrolled. In 2017, 150 master's, 6 doctorates awarded. *Degree requirements:* For master's, one foreign language, thesis; for doctorate, one foreign language, comprehensive exam, thesis/dissertation. *Entrance requirements:* For master's and doctorate, interview. Additional exam requirements/recommendations for international students: Required—TOEFL (minimum score 570 paper-based); Recommended—IELTS (minimum score 6.5). *Application deadline:* For fall admission, 2/4 for domestic and international students. Application fee: $30. Electronic applications accepted. *Expenses: Tuition:* Full-time 12,000 euros. *Required fees:* 230 euros. One-time fee: 30 euros full-time. Tuition and fees vary according to course level, course load, degree level and program. *Financial support:* Fellowships, teaching assistantships, career-related internships or fieldwork, institutionally sponsored loans, scholarships/grants, health care benefits, and tuition waivers (full and partial) available. *Faculty research:* Economic theory (microeconomics and macroeconomics) and econometrics, as well as study of many applied fields, including labor economics, health economics and economics of education, industrial organization, monetary economics, international economics, law and economics, comparative institutional economics, corporate governance, and economics of transition. *Unit head:* Miklos Koren, Head of Department, 36 1 327-3000 Ext. 2212, E-mail: econbusi@ceu.edu. *Application contact:* Zsuzsanna Jaszberenyi, Admissions Officer, 361-324-3009, Fax: 367-327-3211, E-mail: admissions@ceu.edu.
Website: http://economics.ceu.edu/

Central Michigan University, College of Graduate Studies, College of Business Administration, MBA Program, Mount Pleasant, MI 48859. Offers accounting (MBA); business economics (MBA); consulting (MBA); finance (MBA); general business (MBA);

human resource management (MBA); information systems (MBA); international business (MBA); logistics management (MBA); marketing (MBA); value-driven organization (MBA). *Program availability:* Part-time, evening/weekend, online learning. Electronic applications accepted. *Faculty research:* Accounting, consulting, international business, marketing, information systems.

Charleston Southern University, College of Business, Charleston, SC 29423-8087. Offers accounting (MBA); finance (MBA); general management (MBA); human resource management (MS); leadership (MBA); management information systems (MBA); organizational leadership (MA). *Program availability:* Part-time, evening/weekend. *Degree requirements:* For master's, thesis optional. *Entrance requirements:* For master's, GMAT. Additional exam requirements/recommendations for international students: Required—TOEFL (minimum score 550 paper-based; 79 iBT). *Application deadline:* Applications are processed on a rolling basis. Application fee: $40. Electronic applications accepted. *Expenses: Tuition:* Part-time $500 per credit hour. One-time fee: $30. Tuition and fees vary according to program. *Financial support:* Research assistantships with full tuition reimbursements available. Financial award application deadline: 4/15; financial award applicants required to submit FAFSA. *Unit head:* Dr. David Palmer, Dean, 843-863-7025, Fax: 843-863-7922, E-mail: dpalmer@csuniv.edu. *Application contact:* Dr. Darin L. Gerdes, Associate Professor of Management, 843-863-7814, Fax: 843-863-7922, E-mail: dgerdes@csuniv.edu.
Website: http://www.csuniv.edu/business/

City University of Seattle, Graduate Division, School of Management, Seattle, WA 98121. Offers accounting (Certificate); change leadership (MBA, Certificate); computer systems (MS); finance (Certificate); financial management (MBA); general management (MBA); general management-Europe (MBA); global marketing (MBA); human resources management (Certificate); individualized study (MBA); information security (MS); information systems (MBA); leadership (MA); marketing (MBA, Certificate); project management (MBA, MS, Certificate); sustainable business (Certificate); technology management (MBA, Certificate). *Program availability:* Part-time, evening/weekend, online learning. *Degree requirements:* For master's, comprehensive exam (for some programs), thesis (for some programs). *Entrance requirements:* For master's, baccalaureate degree or equivalent from an accredited or otherwise recognized institution. Additional exam requirements/recommendations for international students: Required—TOEFL (minimum score 567 paper-based; 87 iBT); Recommended—IELTS. Electronic applications accepted.

Clarion University of Pennsylvania, College of Business Administration and Information Sciences, Master of Business Administration Program, Clarion, PA 16214. Offers accounting (MBA); finance (MBA); health care administration (MBA); innovation and entrepreneurship (MBA); non-profit business (MBA). *Accreditation:* AACSB. *Program availability:* Part-time, evening/weekend, 100% online. *Faculty:* 4 full-time (1 woman), 3 part-time/adjunct (0 women). *Students:* 19 full-time (7 women), 66 part-time (34 women); includes 10 minority (6 Black or African American, non-Hispanic/Latino; 1 Asian, non-Hispanic/Latino; 3 Hispanic/Latino), 2 international. Average age 31. 86 applicants, 63% accepted, 21 enrolled. In 2017, 33 master's awarded. *Degree requirements:* For master's, portfolio. *Entrance requirements:* For master's, GMAT, minimum QPA of 2.75. Additional exam requirements/recommendations for international students: Required—TOEFL (minimum score 550 paper-based, 80 iBT) or IELTS (7). *Application deadline:* For fall admission, 8/1 priority date for domestic students, 4/15 priority date for international students; for spring admission, 12/1 priority date for domestic students, 9/15 priority date for international students. Applications are processed on a rolling basis. Application fee: $40. Electronic applications accepted. *Expenses:* $655.05 per credit. *Financial support:* Unspecified assistantships available. Support available to part-time students. Financial award application deadline: 3/1; financial award applicants required to submit FAFSA. *Unit head:* Juanice Vega, Assistant to the Dean, 814-393-2600, Fax: 814-393-1910, E-mail: mba@clarion.edu. *Application contact:* Dana Bearer, Assistant Director, Graduate Programs, 814-393-2337, Fax: 814-393-2722, E-mail: gradstudies@clarion.edu.
Website: http://www.clarion.edu/admissions/graduate/index.html

Clark University, Graduate School, Graduate School of Management, Business Administration Program, Worcester, MA 01610-1477. Offers accounting (MBA); finance (MBA); information management and business analytics (MBA); management (MBA); marketing (MBA); social change (MBA); sustainability (MBA). *Accreditation:* AACSB. *Program availability:* Part-time, evening/weekend. *Students:* 87 full-time (41 women), 41 part-time (26 women); includes 19 minority (10 Black or African American, non-Hispanic/Latino; 4 Asian, non-Hispanic/Latino; 4 Hispanic/Latino; 1 Two or more races, non-Hispanic/Latino), 40 international. Average age 30. 242 applicants, 50% accepted, 54 enrolled. In 2017, 102 master's awarded. *Degree requirements:* For master's, thesis optional. *Entrance requirements:* For master's, GMAT or GRE, 2 references, resume or curriculum vitae, personal statement. Additional exam requirements/recommendations for international students: Required—TOEFL (minimum score 575 paper-based; 90 iBT), IELTS (minimum score 6.5). *Application deadline:* For fall admission, 4/15 priority date for domestic and international students; for spring admission, 12/1 priority date for domestic and international students. Application fee: $75. Electronic applications accepted. *Expenses:* $4,490 tuition per 14-week course, $2,245 per half-unit (7-week course); $40 activity fee (full-time students only); $80 miscellaneous one-time fee; $1,750 student services fee. *Financial support:* Fellowships, research assistantships, teaching assistantships, career-related internships or fieldwork, Federal Work-Study, institutionally sponsored loans, and tuition waivers (partial) available. Support available to part-time students. Financial award application deadline: 5/31. *Faculty research:* Marketing, accounting, human resource management, management information systems, business finance. *Unit head:* Dr. Priscilla Elsass, Dean, 508-793-7543, Fax: 508-793-8822, E-mail: pelsass@clarku.edu. *Application contact:* Yingying Chen, Assistant Director of Graduate Admissions, 508-793-7373, Fax: 508-798-4386, E-mail: graduateadmissions@clarku.edu.
Website: http://www.clarku.edu/programs/masters-business-administration

Clark University, Graduate School, Graduate School of Management, Program in Finance, Worcester, MA 01610-1477. Offers MSF. *Students:* 97 full-time (45 women), 95 international. Average age 24. 562 applicants, 63% accepted, 42 enrolled. In 2017, 65 master's awarded. *Degree requirements:* For master's, thesis optional. *Entrance requirements:* For master's, GMAT or GRE, 2 references, resume or curriculum vitae, personal statement. Additional exam requirements/recommendations for international students: Required—TOEFL (minimum score 575 paper-based; 90 iBT), IELTS (minimum score 6.5). *Application deadline:* For fall admission, 4/15 priority date for domestic and international students; for spring admission, 12/1 priority date for domestic and international students. Application fee: $100. Electronic applications accepted. *Expenses:* $4,920 tuition per 14-week course, $2,460 per half-unit (7-week course); $40 activity fee (full-time students only); $80 miscellaneous one-time fee; $1,800 student services fee. *Financial support:* Fellowships, research assistantships, teaching assistantships, and tuition waivers (partial) available. *Faculty research:* Marketing, accounting, human resource management, management information systems, business finance. *Unit head:* Dr. Priscilla Elsass, Dean, 508-793-8822, Fax: 508-793-8822, E-mail: pelsass@clarku.edu. *Application contact:* Yingying Chen, Assistant Director of Graduate Admissions, 508-793-7373, Fax: 508-798-4386, E-mail: graduateadmissions@clarku.edu.
Website: http://www.clarku.edu/programs/masters-finance

Cleary University, Online Program in Business Administration, Howell, MI 48843. Offers analytics, technology, and innovation (MBA, Graduate Certificate); financial planning (Graduate Certificate); global leadership (MBA, Graduate Certificate); health care leadership (MBA, Graduate Certificate). *Program availability:* Part-time, evening/weekend, online learning. *Degree requirements:* For master's, thesis. *Entrance requirements:* For master's, bachelor's degree; minimum GPA of 2.5; professional resume indicating minimum of 2 years of management or related experience; undergraduate degree from accredited college or university with at least 18 quarter hours (or 12 semester hours) of accounting study (for MBA in accounting). Additional exam requirements/recommendations for international students: Required—TOEFL (minimum score 550 paper-based; 79 iBT), Michigan English Language Assessment Battery (minimum score 75). Electronic applications accepted.

College for Financial Planning, Graduate Programs, Centennial, CO 80112. Offers finance (MSF); personal financial planning (MS). *Program availability:* Part-time, evening/weekend, online only, 100% online. *Faculty:* 9 full-time (2 women), 24 part-time/adjunct (4 women). *Students:* 5,000 full-time. *Degree requirements:* For master's, capstone course or thesis. *Entrance requirements:* Additional exam requirements/recommendations for international students: Required—TOEFL (minimum score 550 paper-based). *Application deadline:* Applications are processed on a rolling basis. Electronic applications accepted. *Expenses: Tuition:* Full-time $7000; part-time $1400 per course. *Unit head:* John Sears, President, 303-220-4918, E-mail: john.sears@cffp.edu. *Application contact:* Alicia Christensen, Director of Enrollment, 303-220-4835, Fax: 303-220-1810, E-mail: alicia.mead@cffp.edu.
Website: http://www.cffpinfo.com/graduate-education-programs.html

The College of Saint Rose, Graduate Studies, Huether School of Business, Program in Financial Planning, Albany, NY 12203-1419. Offers Advanced Certificate. *Program availability:* Part-time, evening/weekend. *Students:* 2 part-time (0 women). Average age 41. 3 applicants, 100% accepted. In 2017, 3 Advanced Certificates awarded. *Degree requirements:* For Advanced Certificate, comprehensive exam. *Entrance requirements:* Additional exam requirements/recommendations for international students: Required—TOEFL (minimum score 550 paper-based; 80 iBT), IELTS (minimum score 6), PTE (minimum score 56). *Application deadline:* For fall admission, 4/1 priority date for domestic and international students; for spring admission, 10/15 priority date for domestic students, 10/15 for international students; for summer admission, 3/15 priority date for domestic and international students. Applications are processed on a rolling basis. Application fee: $40. Electronic applications accepted. *Expenses: Tuition:* Full-time $7191; part-time $799 per credit hour. *Required fees:* $924; $462 per credit hour. Tuition and fees vary according to course load. *Financial support:* Career-related internships or fieldwork and scholarships/grants available. Support available to part-time students. Financial award application deadline: 4/15. *Unit head:* John F. Dion, Program Coordinator, 518-458-5488, E-mail: dionj@strose.edu. *Application contact:* Cris Murray, Assistant Vice President for Graduate Recruitment and Enrollment, 518-485-3390, Fax: 518-458-5479, E-mail: grad@strose.edu.
Website: https://www.strose.edu/academics/graduate-programs/graduate-studies/financial-planning/

Colorado State University, College of Business, Program in Finance, Fort Collins, CO 80523-1201. Offers M Fin. *Program availability:* Part-time. *Faculty:* 11 full-time (3 women), 2 part-time/adjunct (1 woman). *Students:* 22 full-time (10 women), 14 part-time (3 women); includes 4 minority (1 Black or African American, non-Hispanic/Latino; 2 Asian, non-Hispanic/Latino; 1 Hispanic/Latino), 16 international. Average age 29. 39 applicants, 44% accepted, 10 enrolled. In 2017, 19 master's awarded. *Entrance requirements:* For master's, GMAT (minimum score 620) or GRE (minimum score 315), undergraduate degree with minimum GPA of 3.0; current resume; 3 letters of recommendation; official transcripts; statement of purpose. Additional exam requirements/recommendations for international students: Required—TOEFL (minimum score 86 iBT), IELTS (minimum score 6.5), PTE (minimum score 58). *Application deadline:* For fall admission, 6/1 for domestic students, 5/1 for international students. Applications are processed on a rolling basis. Application fee: $60 ($70 for international students). Electronic applications accepted. *Expenses:* $313 per credit hour. *Financial support:* Scholarships/grants and unspecified assistantships available. *Faculty research:* Individual risk management and insurance decision-making; corporate finance; quantitative and empirical finance; equity offerings; equity creation and preservation including taxation. *Unit head:* Dr. Sanjay Ramchander, Department Chair, 970-491-5027, E-mail: gradadmissions@business.colostate.edu. *Application contact:* Hilary Klein, Program Assistant, 970-491-5062, E-mail: hilary.klein@colostate.edu.
Website: https://biz.colostate.edu/Academics/Graduate-Programs/Master-of-Finance#Overview

Colorado State University–Global Campus, Graduate Programs, Greenwood Village, CO 80111. Offers criminal justice and law enforcement administration (MS); education leadership (MS); finance (MS); healthcare administration and management (MS); human resource management (MHRM); information technology management (MITM); international management (MS); management (MS); organizational leadership (MS); professional accounting (MPA); project management (MS); teaching and learning (MS). *Accreditation:* ACBSP. *Program availability:* Online learning.

Colorado Technical University Aurora, Programs in Business Administration and Management, Aurora, CO 80014. Offers accounting (MBA); business administration (MBA); business administration and management (EMBA); finance (MBA); human resource management (MBA); marketing (MBA); mediation and dispute resolution (MBA); operations management (MBA); project management (MBA); technology management (MBA). *Program availability:* Part-time, evening/weekend. *Degree requirements:* For master's, thesis or alternative. *Entrance requirements:* For master's, minimum undergraduate GPA of 3.0.

Colorado Technical University Colorado Springs, Graduate Studies, Program in Management, Colorado Springs, CO 80907. Offers accounting (MBA, MSA); business administration (MBA); finance (MBA); human resources management (MBA); logistics/supply chain management (MBA); management (DM); marketing (MBA); mediation and dispute resolution (MBA); operations management (MBA); project management (MBA); technology management (MBA). *Accreditation:* ACBSP. *Program availability:* Part-time, evening/weekend, online learning. *Degree requirements:* For master's, thesis or alternative; for doctorate, thesis/dissertation. *Entrance requirements:* For doctorate, minimum graduate GPA of 3.0, 5 years of related work experience. *Faculty research:* Sexual harassment, performance evaluation, critical thinking.

Columbia Southern University, MBA Program, Orange Beach, AL 36561. Offers finance (MBA); health care management (MBA); human resource management (MBA); marketing (MBA); project management (MBA); public administration (MBA). *Program availability:* Part-time, evening/weekend, online learning. *Entrance requirements:* For master's, bachelor's degree from accredited/approved institution. Additional exam requirements/recommendations for international students: Required—TOEFL. Electronic applications accepted.

Finance and Banking

Columbia University, Graduate School of Arts and Sciences, New York, NY 10027. Offers African-American studies (MA); American studies (MA); anthropology (MA, PhD); art history and archaeology (MA, PhD); astronomy (PhD); biological sciences (PhD); biotechnology (MA); chemical physics (PhD); chemistry (PhD); classical studies (MA, PhD); classics (MA, PhD); climate and society (MA); conservation biology (MA); earth and environmental sciences (PhD); East Asia: regional studies (MA); East Asian languages and cultures (MA, PhD); ecology, evolution and environmental biology (MA), including conservation biology; ecology, evolution, and environmental biology (PhD), including ecology and evolutionary biology, evolutionary primatology; economics (MA, PhD); English and comparative literature (MA, PhD); French and Romance philology (MA, PhD); Germanic languages (MA, PhD); global French studies (MA); global thought (MA); Hispanic cultural studies (MA); history (PhD); history and literature (MA); human rights studies (MA); Islamic studies (MA); Italian (MA, PhD); Japanese pedagogy (MA); Jewish studies (MA); Latin America and the Caribbean: regional studies (MA); Latin American and Iberian cultures (PhD); mathematics (MA, PhD), including finance (MA); medieval and Renaissance studies (MA); Middle Eastern, South Asian, and African studies (MA, PhD); modern art: critical and curatorial studies (MA); modern European studies (MA); museum anthropology (MA); music (DMA, PhD); oral history (MA); philosophical foundations of physics (MA); philosophy (MA, PhD); physics (PhD); political science (MA, PhD); psychology (PhD); quantitative methods in the social sciences (MA); religion (MA); Russia, Eurasia and East Europe: regional studies (MA); Russian translation (MA); Slavic cultures (MA); Slavic languages (MA, PhD); sociology (MA, PhD); South Asian studies (MA); statistics (MA, PhD); theatre (PhD). Dual-degree programs require admission to both Graduate School of Arts and Sciences and another Columbia school. *Program availability:* Part-time. Terminal master's awarded for partial completion of doctoral program. *Degree requirements:* For master's, variable foreign language requirement, comprehensive exam (for some programs), thesis (for some programs); for doctorate, variable foreign language requirement, comprehensive exam (for some programs), thesis/dissertation. *Entrance requirements:* For master's and doctorate, GRE General Test, GRE Subject Test (for some programs). Additional exam requirements/recommendations for international students: Required—TOEFL, IELTS. Electronic applications accepted. *Expenses: Tuition:* Full-time $44,864; part-time $1704 per credit. *Required fees:* $2370 per semester. One-time fee: $105.

Columbia University, Graduate School of Business, Doctoral Program in Business, New York, NY 10027. Offers business (PhD), including accounting, decision, risk, and operations, finance and economics, management, marketing. *Accreditation:* AACSB. *Degree requirements:* For doctorate, comprehensive exam, thesis/dissertation, major field exam, research paper, thesis proposal. *Entrance requirements:* For doctorate, GMAT or GRE (finance), 2 letters of reference, resume. Additional exam requirements/recommendations for international students: Required—TOEFL. Electronic applications accepted. *Expenses:* Contact institution. *Faculty research:* Human decision making and behavioral research; real estate market and mortgage defaults; financial crisis and corporate governance; international business; security analysis and accounting.

Columbia University, Graduate School of Business, MBA Program, New York, NY 10027. Offers accounting (MBA); decision, risk, and operations (MBA); entrepreneurship (MBA); finance and economics (MBA); healthcare and pharmaceutical management (MBA); human resource management (MBA); international business (MBA); leadership and ethics (MBA); management (MBA); marketing (MBA); media (MBA); private equity (MBA); real estate (MBA); social enterprise (MBA); value investing (MBA); DDS/MBA; JD/MBA; MBA/MIA; MBA/MPH; MBA/MS; MD/MBA. *Entrance requirements:* For master's, GMAT, 2 letters of recommendation. Additional exam requirements/recommendations for international students: Required—TOEFL. Electronic applications accepted. *Expenses:* Contact institution. *Faculty research:* Human decision making and behavioral research; real estate market and mortgage defaults; financial crisis and corporate governance; international business; security analysis and accounting.

Concordia University, School of Graduate Studies, John Molson School of Business, Montreal, QC H3H 0A1, Canada. Offers administration (M Sc), including finance, management, marketing; business administration (MBA, PhD, Certificate, Diploma); executive business administration (EMBA); supply chain management (MSCM). PhD program offered jointly with HEC Montreal, McGill University, and Université du Québec à Montréal. *Program availability:* Part-time, evening/weekend. *Degree requirements:* For master's, one foreign language, thesis (for some programs), research project; for doctorate, one foreign language, thesis/dissertation; for other advanced degree, one foreign language. *Entrance requirements:* For master's, GMAT, minimum 2 years of work experience (for MBA); letters of recommendation, bachelor's degree from recognized university with minimum GPA of 3.0, curriculum vitae; for doctorate, GMAT (minimum score of 600), official transcripts, curriculum vitae, 3 letters of reference, statement of purpose; for other advanced degree, minimum GPA of 2.7, 2 letters of reference, statement of purpose, resume. Additional exam requirements/recommendations for international students: Required—TOEFL (minimum score 90 iBT), IELTS (minimum score 7). Electronic applications accepted. *Expenses:* Contact institution. *Faculty research:* General business, capital markets, international business.

Concordia University Wisconsin, Graduate Programs, School of Business Administration, MBA Program, Mequon, WI 53097-2402. Offers finance (MBA); health care administration (MBA); human resource management (MBA); international business (MBA); international business-bilingual English/Chinese (MBA); management (MBA); management information systems (MBA); managerial communications (MBA); marketing (MBA); public administration (MBA); risk management (MBA). *Program availability:* Online learning. *Degree requirements:* For master's, comprehensive exam, thesis or alternative. *Entrance requirements:* Additional exam requirements/recommendations for international students: Required—TOEFL. *Expenses:* Contact institution.

Cornell University, Graduate School, Graduate Field of Management, Ithaca, NY 14853. Offers accounting (PhD); finance (PhD); marketing (PhD); organizational behavior (PhD); production and operations management (PhD). *Accreditation:* AACSB. *Degree requirements:* For doctorate, comprehensive exam, thesis/dissertation. *Entrance requirements:* For doctorate, GMAT or GRE General Test. Additional exam requirements/recommendations for international students: Required—TOEFL (minimum score 600 paper-based; 77 iBT). Electronic applications accepted. *Expenses:* Contact institution. *Faculty research:* Operations and manufacturing.

Cornell University, Graduate School, Graduate Fields of Arts and Sciences, Field of Economics, Ithaca, NY 14853. Offers applied economics (PhD); basic analytical economics (PhD); econometrics and economic statistics (PhD); economic development and planning (PhD); economic theory (PhD); industrial organization and control (PhD); international economics (PhD); labor economics (PhD); monetary and macro economics (PhD); public finance (PhD). *Degree requirements:* For doctorate, comprehensive exam, thesis/dissertation. *Entrance requirements:* For doctorate, GRE General Test, 3 letters of recommendation. Additional exam requirements/recommendations for international students: Required—TOEFL (minimum score 550 paper-based; 77 iBT). Electronic applications accepted. *Faculty research:* Learning and games, economics of education, political economy, transfer payments, time series and nonparametrics.

Creighton University, Graduate School, Heider College of Business, Omaha, NE 68178-0001. Offers accounting (MAC); business administration (MBA, DBA); business intelligence and analytics (MS); finance (M Fin); investment management and financial analysis (MIMFA); JD/MBA; MBA/MIMFA; MD/MBA; Pharm D/MBA. *Accreditation:* AACSB. *Program availability:* Part-time, evening/weekend, 100% online, blended/hybrid learning. *Faculty:* 33 full-time (10 women), 22 part-time/adjunct (3 women). *Students:* 60 full-time (24 women), 308 part-time (95 women); includes 31 minority (14 Black or African American, non-Hispanic/Latino; 1 American Indian or Alaska Native, non-Hispanic/Latino; 9 Asian, non-Hispanic/Latino; 3 Hispanic/Latino; 2 Native Hawaiian or other Pacific Islander, non-Hispanic/Latino; 2 Two or more races, non-Hispanic/Latino), 28 international. Average age 32. 253 applicants, 74% accepted, 123 enrolled. In 2017, 139 master's awarded. *Degree requirements:* For master's, thesis optional; for doctorate, thesis/dissertation optional. *Entrance requirements:* For master's, GMAT, resume, 2 letters of recommendation. Additional exam requirements/recommendations for international students: Required—TOEFL (minimum score 90 iBT). *Application deadline:* For fall admission, 7/1 priority date for domestic students, 3/1 for international students; for winter admission, 10/1 priority date for domestic students, 7/1 for international students; for spring admission, 4/1 priority date for domestic students, 10/1 for international students; for summer admission, 5/1 for domestic and international students. Applications are processed on a rolling basis. Application fee: $50. Electronic applications accepted. *Expenses:* Contact institution. *Financial support:* In 2017–18, 10 fellowships with partial tuition reimbursements (averaging $8,448 per year) were awarded; career-related internships or fieldwork, tuition waivers (partial), and unspecified assistantships also available. Financial award application deadline: 3/1. *Faculty research:* Small business issues, economics, business analytics. *Unit head:* Dr. Deborah Wells, Associate Dean for Graduate Programs, 402-280-2841, E-mail: deborahwells@creighton.edu. *Application contact:* Chris Karasek, Assistant Dean, 402-280-2829, Fax: 402-280-2172, E-mail: chriskarasek@creighton.edu. Website: http://business.creighton.edu

Culver-Stockton College, MBA Program, Canton, MO 63435-1299. Offers accounting and finance (MBA).

Curry College, Graduate Studies, Program in Business Administration, Milton, MA 02186-9984. Offers business administration (MBA); finance (Certificate). *Program availability:* Part-time, evening/weekend. *Degree requirements:* For master's, capstone applied project. *Entrance requirements:* For master's, resume, recommendations, interview, written statement. Additional exam requirements/recommendations for international students: Required—TOEFL (minimum score 550 paper-based; 80 iBT). *Expenses:* Contact institution.

Dalhousie University, Faculty of Management, Centre for Advanced Management Education, Halifax, NS B3H 3J5, Canada. Offers financial services (MBA); information management (MIM); management (MPA); natural resources (MBA). *Program availability:* Part-time, online learning. *Entrance requirements:* For master's, GMAT, minimum GPA of 3.0, resume. Additional exam requirements/recommendations for international students: Required—TOEFL, IELTS, CANTEST, CAEL, or Michigan English Language Assessment Battery. Electronic applications accepted.

Dalhousie University, Faculty of Management, Rowe School of Business, Halifax, NS B3H 3J5, Canada. Offers business administration (MBA); financial services (MBA); LL B/MBA; MBA/MLIS. *Program availability:* Part-time. *Entrance requirements:* For master's, GMAT, letter of non-financial guarantee for non-Canadian students, resume, Corporate Residency Preference Form. Additional exam requirements/recommendations for international students: Required—TOEFL, IELTS, CANTEST, CAEL, or Michigan English Language Assessment Battery. Electronic applications accepted. *Faculty research:* International business, quantitative methods, operations research, MIS, marketing, finance.

Dallas Baptist University, College of Business, Master of Business Administration Program, Dallas, TX 75211-9299. Offers accounting (MBA); business communication (MBA); conflict resolution management (MBA); entrepreneurship (MBA); finance (MBA); health care management (MBA); international business (MBA); leading the non-profit organization (MBA); management (MBA); management information systems (MBA); marketing (MBA); project management (MBA); technology and engineering management (MBA). *Accreditation:* ACBSP. *Program availability:* Part-time, evening/weekend, 100% online, blended/hybrid learning. *Application deadline:* Applications are processed on a rolling basis. Application fee: $25. Electronic applications accepted. Application fee is waived when completed online. *Expenses: Tuition:* Full-time $16,308; part-time $906 per credit hour. *Required fees:* $900; $450 per semester. Tuition and fees vary according to course load and degree level. *Unit head:* Dr. Sandra Reid, Chair of Graduate Business Programs, 214-333-5280, E-mail: sandra@dbu.edu. *Application contact:* Bobby Soto, Director of Admissions, 214-333-5242, E-mail: graduate@dbu.edu. Website: http://www.dbu.edu/gsb/mba

Dallas Baptist University, Professional Development Program, Dallas, TX 75211-9299. Offers accounting (MA); church leadership (MA); communication (MA); counseling (MA); criminal justice (MA); English as a second language (MA); finance (MA); higher education (MA); leadership studies (MA); management (MA). *Program availability:* Part-time, evening/weekend. *Application deadline:* Applications are processed on a rolling basis. Application fee: $25. Electronic applications accepted. Application fee is waived when completed online. *Expenses: Tuition:* Full-time $16,308; part-time $906 per credit hour. *Required fees:* $900; $450 per semester. Tuition and fees vary according to course load and degree level. *Unit head:* Jared Ingram, Program Director, 214-333-5584, E-mail: jaredi@dbu.edu. *Application contact:* Bobby Soto, Director of Admissions, 214-333-5242, E-mail: bobby@dbu.edu. Website: http://www3.dbu.edu/graduate/mapd.asp

Davenport University, Sneden Graduate School, Grand Rapids, MI 49512. Offers accounting (MBA); business administration (EMBA); finance (MBA); health care management (MBA); human resources (MBA); information assurance (MS); public health (MPH); strategic management (MBA). *Program availability:* Evening/weekend. *Entrance requirements:* For master's, GMAT, minimum undergraduate GPA of 2.75. Additional exam requirements/recommendations for international students: Required—TOEFL. Electronic applications accepted. *Faculty research:* Leadership, management, marketing, organizational culture.

Delaware Valley University, MBA Program, Doylestown, PA 18901-2697. Offers accounting (MBA); entrepreneurship (MBA); finance (MBA); food and agribusiness (MBA); general business (MBA); global executive leadership (MBA); human resource management (MBA); supply chain management (MBA). *Program availability:* Part-time, evening/weekend, online learning. *Entrance requirements:* For master's, minimum undergraduate GPA of 3.0. Electronic applications accepted. *Expenses:* Contact institution.

DePaul University, Kellstadt Graduate School of Business, Chicago, IL 60604. Offers accountancy (MBA, MSA); applied economics (MBA); audit and advisory services (MS); business administration (DBA); business analytics (MS); business strategy and decision-making (MBA); computational finance (MS); economics and policy analysis (MS); enterprise risk management (MS); entrepreneurship (MBA, MS); finance (MBA, MS); general business (MBA); hospitality leadership (MBA); hospitality leadership and operational performance (MS); human resources (MS); international business (MBA);

management (MBA, MS); management information systems (MBA); marketing (MBA, MS); marketing analysis (MS); marketing strategy and planning (MBA); real estate (MS); real estate finance and investment (MBA); strategy, execution and valuation (MBA); supply chain management (MS); sustainable management (MS); taxation (MS); JD/MBA. *Accreditation:* AACSB. *Program availability:* Part-time, evening/weekend, online learning. *Entrance requirements:* For master's, GMAT/GRE, 2 letters of recommendation, resume, essay, official transcripts. Additional exam requirements/recommendations for international students: Required—TOEFL (minimum score 550 paper-based; 80 iBT). *Application deadline:* For fall admission, 7/1 for domestic students, 6/1 for international students; for winter admission, 10/1 for domestic students, 9/1 for international students; for spring admission, 2/1 for domestic students, 1/1 for international students. Applications are processed on a rolling basis. Application fee: $60. Electronic applications accepted. *Expenses:* Contact institution. *Financial support:* Application deadline: 4/1; applicants required to submit FAFSA. *Unit head:* Christa Hinton, Assistant Dean and Director, 312-362-8810, Fax: 312-362-6677, E-mail: chinton@depaul.edu. *Application contact:* Garry Cooke, Director of Recruitment and Admissions, 312-362-8810, Fax: 312-362-6677, E-mail: kgsb@depaul.edu. Website: http://kellstadt.depaul.edu

DeSales University, Division of Business, Center Valley, PA 18034-9568. Offers accounting (MBA); computer information systems (MBA); finance (MBA); health care systems management (MBA); human resources management (MBA); management (MBA); marketing (MBA); project management (MBA); self-design (MBA); supply chain management (MBA); DNP/MBA; MSN/MBA. *Accreditation:* ACBSP. *Program availability:* Part-time, evening/weekend, 100% online, blended/hybrid learning. *Faculty:* 9 full-time (3 women), 32 part-time/adjunct (8 women). *Students:* 78 full-time (44 women), 323 part-time (164 women); includes 71 minority (22 Black or African American, non-Hispanic/Latino; 17 Asian, non-Hispanic/Latino; 24 Hispanic/Latino; 8 Two or more races, non-Hispanic/Latino), 1 international. Average age 34. 213 applicants, 40% accepted, 64 enrolled. In 2017, 123 master's awarded. *Entrance requirements:* For master's, GMAT (waived if undergraduate GPA is 3.0 or better), minimum GPA of 3.0 in undergraduate work, literacy in basic software, background or interest in the field of study, personal statement, 2 years of work experience. Additional exam requirements/recommendations for international students: Required—TOEFL. *Application deadline:* Applications are processed on a rolling basis. Application fee: $50. Electronic applications accepted. *Expenses:* Contact institution. *Financial support:* Applicants required to submit FAFSA. *Faculty research:* Quality improvement, executive development, productivity, cross-cultural managerial differences, leadership. *Unit head:* Dr. David M. Gilfoil, Director, MBA Program, 610-282-1100 Ext. 1828, Fax: 610-282-2869, E-mail: david.gilfoil@desales.edu. *Application contact:* Julia Ferraro, Director of Graduate Admissions, 610-282-1100 Ext. 1768, E-mail: gradadmissions@desales.edu.

DeVry University–Folsom Campus, Graduate Programs, Folsom, CA 95630. Offers accounting (M Acc); accounting and financial management (MAFM); business administration (MBA); curriculum leadership (M Ed); educational leadership (M Ed); educational technology (M Ed); higher education leadership (M Ed); human resource management (MHRM); information systems management (MISM); network and communications management (MNCM); project management (MPM); public administration (MPA).

Drew University, Caspersen School of Graduate Studies, Madison, NJ 07940-1493. Offers conflict resolution and leadership (Certificate), including community leadership, moderation, peace building; education (M Ed); finance (MA); history and culture (MA, PhD), including American history, book history, British history, European history, Holocaust and genocide (M Litt, MA, D Litt, PhD), intellectual history, Irish history, print culture, public history; K-12 education (MAT), including art, biology, chemistry, elementary education, English, French, Italian, math, secondary education, special education, teacher of students with disabilities; liberal studies (M Litt, D Litt), including history, Holocaust and genocide (M Litt, MA, D Litt, PhD), Irish/Irish-American studies, literature (M Litt, MMH, D Litt, DMH, CMH), religion, spirituality, teaching in the two-year college, writing; medical humanities (MMH, DMH, CMH), including arts, health, healthcare, literature (M Litt, MMH, D Litt, DMH, CMH), scientific research; poetry (MFA). *Program availability:* Part-time, evening/weekend. *Faculty:* 4 full-time (2 women), 29 part-time/adjunct (15 women). *Students:* 77 full-time (42 women), 175 part-time (114 women); includes 39 minority (12 Black or African American, non-Hispanic/Latino; 6 Asian, non-Hispanic/Latino; 16 Hispanic/Latino; 5 Two or more races, non-Hispanic/Latino), 11 international. Average age 41. 126 applicants, 75% accepted, 52 enrolled. In 2017, 38 master's, 23 doctorates, 35 other advanced degrees awarded. Terminal master's awarded for partial completion of doctoral program. *Degree requirements:* For master's and other advanced degree, thesis (for some programs); for doctorate, one foreign language, comprehensive exam (for some programs), thesis/dissertation. *Entrance requirements:* For master's, PRAXIS Core and Subject Area tests (for MAT), GRE/GMAT (for M Fin), resume, transcripts, writing sample, personal statement, letters of recommendation; for doctorate, GRE (PhD in history and culture), resume, transcripts, writing sample, personal statement, letters of recommendation; for other advanced degree, resume, transcripts, personal statement. Additional exam requirements/recommendations for international students: Required—TOEFL (minimum score 587 paper-based; 80 iBT), IELTS (minimum score 6), TWE (minimum score 4). *Application deadline:* For fall admission, 8/1 for domestic students, 6/1 for international students; for spring admission, 12/1 for domestic students, 10/1 for international students. Applications are processed on a rolling basis. Application fee: $35. Electronic applications accepted. *Financial support:* Fellowships, research assistantships, teaching assistantships, career-related internships or fieldwork, Federal Work-Study, scholarships/grants, and unspecified assistantships available. Support available to part-time students. Financial award applicants required to submit FAFSA. *Faculty research:* Irish history and culture, conflict resolution and leadership. *Application contact:* Leanne Horinko, Director of Caspersen Admissions, 973-408-3280, E-mail: gradm@drew.edu. Website: http://www.drew.edu/caspersen

Drexel University, LeBow College of Business, Department of Finance, Philadelphia, PA 19104-2875. Offers MS. *Degree requirements:* For master's, seminar paper. *Entrance requirements:* For master's, GMAT, minimum GPA of 2.75. Additional exam requirements/recommendations for international students: Required—TOEFL. Electronic applications accepted. *Faculty research:* Investment analysis, portfolio mix, capital budgeting, banking and financial institutions, international finance.

Drexel University, LeBow College of Business, Program in Business Administration, Philadelphia, PA 19104-2875. Offers business administration (MBA, PhD, APC), including accounting (MBA, PhD), decision sciences (PhD), economics (MBA, PhD), finance (MBA, PhD), legal studies (MBA), management (MBA), marketing (MBA, PhD), organizational sciences (PhD), quantitative methods (MBA), strategic management (PhD). *Accreditation:* AACSB. *Program availability:* Part-time, evening/weekend, online learning. Terminal master's awarded for partial completion of doctoral program. *Entrance requirements:* For master's, GMAT, minimum GPA of 2.75; for doctorate, GMAT. Additional exam requirements/recommendations for international students: Required—TOEFL. Electronic applications accepted. *Faculty research:* Decision support systems, individual and group behavior, operations research, techniques and strategy.

Duke University, The Fuqua School of Business, The Duke MBA-Daytime Program, Durham, NC 27708-0586. Offers academic excellence in finance (Certificate); business administration (MBA); decision sciences (MBA); energy and environment (MBA); energy finance (MBA); entrepreneurship and innovation (MBA); finance (MBA); financial analysis (MBA); health sector management (Certificate); leadership and ethics (MBA); management (MBA); management science and technology management (Certificate); marketing (MBA); operations management (MBA); social entrepreneurship (MBA); strategy (MBA). *Faculty:* 96 full-time (19 women), 48 part-time/adjunct (15 women). *Students:* 876 full-time (297 women); includes 180 minority (39 Black or African American, non-Hispanic/Latino; 2 American Indian or Alaska Native, non-Hispanic/Latino; 83 Asian, non-Hispanic/Latino; 50 Hispanic/Latino; 6 Two or more races, non-Hispanic/Latino), 321 international. Average age 29. In 2017, 445 master's awarded. *Entrance requirements:* For master's, GMAT or GRE, transcripts, essays, resume, recommendation letters, interview. *Application deadline:* For fall admission, 9/12 for domestic and international students; for winter admission, 10/10 for domestic and international students; for spring admission, 1/3 for domestic and international students; for summer admission, 3/20 for domestic and international students. Application fee: $225. Electronic applications accepted. *Expenses:* $69,342 first-year tuition and fees. *Financial support:* In 2017–18, 423 students received support. Scholarships/grants available. Financial award applicants required to submit FAFSA. *Unit head:* Steve Misuraca, Assistant Dean, Daytime MBA Program. *Application contact:* Shari Hubert, Associate Dean, Office of Admissions, 919-660-7705, Fax: 919-681-8026, E-mail: admissions-info@fuqua.duke.edu. Website: https://www.fuqua.duke.edu/programs/daytime-mba

Duke University, The Fuqua School of Business, The Duke MBA-Global Executive Program, Durham, NC 27708-0586. Offers business administration (MBA); energy and environment (MBA); entrepreneurship and innovation (MBA); finance (MBA); health sector management (Certificate); marketing (MBA); strategy (MBA). *Faculty:* 96 full-time (19 women), 48 part-time/adjunct (15 women). *Students:* 94 full-time (26 women); includes 34 minority (8 Black or African American, non-Hispanic/Latino; 21 Asian, non-Hispanic/Latino; 4 Hispanic/Latino; 1 Two or more races, non-Hispanic/Latino), 25 international. Average age 39. In 2017, 27 master's awarded. *Entrance requirements:* For master's, Executive Assessment, GMAT, or GRE, transcripts, essays, resume, recommendation letters, letter of company support, interview. *Application deadline:* For fall admission, 10/12 priority date for domestic and international students; for winter admission, 12/7 priority date for domestic and international students; for spring admission, 3/20 priority date for domestic and international students; for summer admission, 5/31 for domestic and international students. Applications are processed on a rolling basis. Application fee: $225. Electronic applications accepted. *Expenses:* Contact institution. *Financial support:* In 2017–18, 31 students received support. Scholarships/grants available. Financial award applicants required to submit FAFSA. *Unit head:* Karen Courtney, Associate Dean, Executive Programs. *Application contact:* Shari Hubert, Associate Dean, Office of Admissions, 919-660-7705, Fax: 919-681-8026, E-mail: admissions-info@fuqua.duke.edu. Website: https://www.fuqua.duke.edu/programs/global-executive-mba

Duke University, The Fuqua School of Business, The Duke MBA-Weekend Executive Program, Durham, NC 27708-0586. Offers business administration (MBA); energy and environment (MBA); entrepreneurship and innovation (MBA); finance (MBA); health sector management (Certificate); marketing (MBA); strategy (MBA). *Faculty:* 96 full-time (19 women), 48 part-time/adjunct (15 women). *Students:* 219 full-time (59 women); includes 80 minority (13 Black or African American, non-Hispanic/Latino; 3 American Indian or Alaska Native, non-Hispanic/Latino; 45 Asian, non-Hispanic/Latino; 13 Hispanic/Latino; 6 Two or more races, non-Hispanic/Latino), 32 international. Average age 35. In 2017, 92 master's awarded. *Entrance requirements:* For master's, Executive Assessment, GMAT or GRE, transcripts, essays, resume, recommendation letters, letter of company support, interview. *Application deadline:* For fall admission, 10/12 priority date for domestic and international students; for winter admission, 12/7 priority date for domestic and international students; for spring admission, 2/7 priority date for domestic and international students; for summer admission, 3/20 for domestic and international students. Applications are processed on a rolling basis. Application fee: $225. Electronic applications accepted. *Expenses:* Contact institution. *Financial support:* In 2017–18, 44 students received support. Scholarships/grants available. Financial award applicants required to submit FAFSA. *Unit head:* Karen Courtney, Associate Dean, Executive Programs. *Application contact:* Shari Hubert, Associate Dean, Office of Admissions, 919-660-7705, Fax: 919-681-8026, E-mail: admissions-info@fuqua.duke.edu. Website: https://www.fuqua.duke.edu/programs/weekend-executive-mba

Duke University, The Fuqua School of Business, Master of Quantitative Management Program: Business Analytics, Durham, NC 27708-0586. Offers finance (MQM); forensics (MQM); marketing (MQM); strategy (MQM). *Faculty:* 96 full-time (19 women), 48 part-time/adjunct (15 women). *Students:* 140 full-time (81 women); includes 11 minority (9 Asian, non-Hispanic/Latino; 2 Hispanic/Latino), 118 international. Average age 24. *Entrance requirements:* For master's, GMAT/GRE, transcripts, essays, resume, recommendation letters. *Application deadline:* For fall admission, 9/13 for domestic and international students; for winter admission, 1/17 for domestic and international students; for spring admission, 2/28 for domestic and international students; for summer admission, 4/4 for domestic and international students. Application fee: $125. Electronic applications accepted. *Expenses:* $66,907 tuition and fees. *Financial support:* In 2017–18, 46 students received support. Scholarships/grants available. Financial award applicants required to submit FAFSA. *Unit head:* Jeremy Petranka, Associate Dean. *Application contact:* Shari Hubert, Associate Dean, Office of Admissions, 919-660-7705, Fax: 919-681-8026, E-mail: admissions-info@fuqua.duke.edu. Website: https://www.fuqua.duke.edu/programs/mqm-business-analytics

Duke University, The Fuqua School of Business, PhD Program, Durham, NC 27708-0586. Offers accounting (PhD); decision sciences (PhD); finance (PhD); management and organizations (PhD); marketing (PhD); operations management (PhD); strategy (PhD). *Faculty:* 96 full-time (19 women). *Students:* 64 full-time (25 women); includes 1 minority (Hispanic/Latino), 41 international. Average age 27. 617 applicants, 5% accepted, 14 enrolled. In 2017, 15 doctorates awarded. *Degree requirements:* For doctorate, thesis/dissertation, major field requirement (exam or major paper, depending upon the area). *Entrance requirements:* For doctorate, GMAT or GRE, transcripts, essays, recommendation letters, statement of purpose. Additional exam requirements/recommendations for international students: Required—TOEFL (minimum score 577 paper-based; 108 iBT), IELTS (minimum score 8). *Application deadline:* For fall admission, 12/31 priority date for domestic and international students. Application fee: $85. Electronic applications accepted. *Expenses:* $52,253. *Financial support:* In 2017–18, 66 students received support, including 66 fellowships with full tuition reimbursements available (averaging $29,200 per year), 63 research assistantships with full tuition reimbursements available (averaging $7,000 per year); institutionally sponsored loans, scholarships/grants, and tuition waivers (full) also available. Financial award applicants required to submit FAFSA. *Unit head:* William Boulding, Dean. *Application contact:* Qi Chen, Director of Graduate Studies, 919-660-7753, Fax: 919-660-7971, E-mail: qc2@duke.edu.

SECTION 2: ACCOUNTING AND FINANCE

Finance and Banking

Duquesne University, Palumbo-Donahue School of Business, Pittsburgh, PA 15282-0001. Offers accounting (M Acc); finance (MBA); information systems management (MSISM); management (MBA, MS); marketing (MBA); sports business (MS); supply chain management (MS); sustainability (MBA); JD/MBA; MBA/M Acc; MBA/MA; MBA/MES; MBA/MHMS; MSISM/MBA; Pharm D/MBA. *Accreditation:* AACSB. *Program availability:* Part-time, evening/weekend, minimal on-campus study. *Faculty:* 59 full-time (23 women), 25 part-time/adjunct (6 women). *Students:* 232 full-time (83 women), 46 part-time (18 women); includes 28 minority (14 Black or African American, non-Hispanic/Latino; 8 Asian, non-Hispanic/Latino; 4 Hispanic/Latino; 2 Two or more races, non-Hispanic/Latino), 24 international. Average age 29. 220 applicants, 83% accepted, 121 enrolled. In 2017, 113 master's awarded. *Entrance requirements:* For master's, GMAT or GRE, undergraduate transcripts, 2 letters of recommendation, current resume, personal statement. Additional exam requirements/recommendations for international students: Required—TOEFL (minimum score 577 paper-based; 90 iBT), IELTS (minimum score 7). *Application deadline:* For fall admission, 7/1 priority date for domestic and international students; for spring admission, 12/1 for domestic and international students; for summer admission, 4/1 for domestic and international students. Applications are processed on a rolling basis. Application fee: $0. Electronic applications accepted. *Expenses:* $934 per credit (MS in management, sports business); $1,259 per credit (MBA, MS in accountancy, information systems management). *Financial support:* In 2017–18, 211 students received support, including 12 fellowships with partial tuition reimbursements available (averaging $14,200 per year), 20 research assistantships with partial tuition reimbursements available (averaging $22,662 per year); career-related internships or fieldwork, scholarships/grants, and unspecified assistantships also available. Support available to part-time students. Financial award application deadline: 7/1; financial award applicants required to submit FAFSA. *Faculty research:* Investment management, business ethics, technology management, supply chain management, entrepreneurship. *Unit head:* Dr. Karen Donovan, Associate Dean of Graduate Programs and Executive Education, 412-396-6276, Fax: 412-396-1726, E-mail: donovan6@duq.edu. *Application contact:* Jeff Jewett, Director of Admissions and Enrollment Management, 412-396-6244, Fax: 412-396-1726, E-mail: decrostam@duq.edu.
Website: http://www.duq.edu/business/grad

Eastern Michigan University, Graduate School, College of Business, Programs in Business Administration, Ypsilanti, MI 48197. Offers business administration (MBA, Graduate Certificate); computer information systems (Graduate Certificate); e-business (MBA, Graduate Certificate); enterprise business intelligence (MBA); entrepreneurship (MBA, Graduate Certificate); finance (MBA, Graduate Certificate); human resources (MBA); human resources management (Graduate Certificate); information systems (MBA); internal auditing (MBA); international business (MBA, Graduate Certificate); marketing management (Graduate Certificate); nonprofit management (MBA); organizational development (Graduate Certificate); supply chain management (MBA, Graduate Certificate). *Accreditation:* AACSB. *Program availability:* Part-time, online learning. *Students:* 53 full-time (30 women), 297 part-time (170 women); includes 121 minority (72 Black or African American, non-Hispanic/Latino; 4 American Indian or Alaska Native, non-Hispanic/Latino; 15 Asian, non-Hispanic/Latino; 20 Hispanic/Latino; 10 Two or more races, non-Hispanic/Latino), 20 international. Average age 31. 247 applicants, 74% accepted, 94 enrolled. In 2017, 71 master's, 34 other advanced degrees awarded. *Entrance requirements:* For master's, GMAT (minimum score 450), minimum cumulative undergraduate GPA of 2.75. Additional exam requirements/recommendations for international students: Required—TOEFL. *Application deadline:* For fall admission, 5/15 priority date for domestic students, 2/15 priority date for international students; for winter admission, 10/15 priority date for domestic students, 9/1 priority date for international students; for summer admission, 3/15 priority date for domestic students, 3/1 priority date for international students. Applications are processed on a rolling basis. Application fee: $45. *Financial support:* Fellowships, research assistantships with full tuition reimbursements, teaching assistantships with full tuition reimbursements, career-related internships or fieldwork, Federal Work-Study, institutionally sponsored loans, scholarships/grants, tuition waivers (partial), and unspecified assistantships available. Support available to part-time students. Financial award applicants required to submit FAFSA. *Unit head:* K. Michelle Henry, Director, Graduate Business Programs, 734-487-4444, Fax: 734-483-1316, E-mail: cob.graduate@emich.edu.
Website: http://www.emich.edu/cob/mba/

Elms College, Division of Business, Chicopee, MA 01013-2839. Offers accounting (MBA); accounting and finance (MS); financial planning (MBA, Certificate); healthcare leadership (MBA); lean entrepreneurship (MBA); management (MBA). *Program availability:* Part-time, evening/weekend. *Faculty:* 5 full-time (all women), 7 part-time/adjunct (4 women). *Students:* 51 part-time (30 women); includes 9 minority (4 Black or African American, non-Hispanic/Latino; 2 Asian, non-Hispanic/Latino; 3 Hispanic/Latino), 2 international. Average age 33. 14 applicants, 93% accepted, 10 enrolled. In 2017, 28 master's awarded. *Entrance requirements:* For master's, minimum GPA of 3.0. *Application deadline:* Applications are processed on a rolling basis. Application fee: $30. Electronic applications accepted. *Expenses:* Tuition: Full-time $13,860; part-time $770 per credit hour. *Required fees:* $200. Tuition and fees vary according to degree level and program. *Unit head:* Dr. David Kimball, Chair, Division of Business, 413-265-2300, E-mail: kimballd@elms.edu. *Application contact:* MBA Program Coordinator, 413-265-2592, E-mail: mba@elms.edu.

Embry-Riddle Aeronautical University–Daytona, College of Business, Daytona Beach, FL 32114-3900. Offers airline management (MBA); airport management (MBA); aviation finance (MSAF); aviation human resources (MBA); aviation management (MBA-AM); aviation system management (MBA); finance (MBA). *Accreditation:* ACBSP. *Faculty:* 14 full-time (2 women). *Students:* 95 full-time (31 women), 19 part-time (8 women); includes 15 minority (5 Black or African American, non-Hispanic/Latino; 1 Asian, non-Hispanic/Latino; 1 Hispanic/Latino; 8 Two or more races, non-Hispanic/Latino), 65 international. Average age 27. 141 applicants, 38% accepted, 41 enrolled. In 2017, 49 master's awarded. *Degree requirements:* For master's, thesis (for some programs). *Entrance requirements:* For master's, GRE (for some programs). Additional exam requirements/recommendations for international students: Required—TOEFL (minimum score 550 paper-based, 79 iBT) or IELTS (6). *Application deadline:* For fall admission, 1/15 priority date for domestic students; for spring admission, 11/1 priority date for domestic students; for summer admission, 4/1 priority date for domestic students. Applications are processed on a rolling basis. Application fee: $50. Electronic applications accepted. *Expenses:* Tuition: Full-time $16,704; part-time $1392 per credit hour. *Required fees:* $1314; $657 per semester. Tuition and fees vary according to degree level. *Financial support:* Research assistantships, teaching assistantships, career-related internships or fieldwork, scholarships/grants, unspecified assistantships, and on-campus employment available. Financial award application deadline: 3/15; financial award applicants required to submit FAFSA. *Unit head:* Michael J. Williams, PhD, Dean of the College of Business and Professor of Information Systems, 386-226-6293, E-mail: michael.williams@erau.edu. *Application contact:* Graduate Admissions, 386-226-6176, E-mail: graduate.admissions@erau.edu.
Website: https://daytonabeach.erau.edu/college-business/index.html

Embry-Riddle Aeronautical University–Worldwide, Department of Decision Sciences, Daytona Beach, FL 32114-3900. Offers aviation and aerospace (MSPM); aviation/aerospace management (MSEM); financial management (MSEM, MSPM); general management (MSPM); global management (MSPM); human resources management (MSPM); information systems (MSPM); leadership (MSEM, MSPM); logistics and supply chain management (MSEM, MSLSCM, MSPM); management (MSEM, MSPM); project management (MSEM); systems engineering (MSEM, MSPM); technical management (MSPM). *Program availability:* Part-time, evening/weekend, EagleVision Classroom (between classrooms), EagleVision Home (faculty and students at home), and a blend of Classroom or Home. *Faculty:* 12 full-time (3 women), 53 part-time/adjunct (10 women). *Students:* 514 full-time (141 women), 476 part-time (111 women); includes 337 minority (136 Black or African American, non-Hispanic/Latino; 6 American Indian or Alaska Native, non-Hispanic/Latino; 39 Asian, non-Hispanic/Latino; 81 Hispanic/Latino; 4 Native Hawaiian or other Pacific Islander, non-Hispanic/Latino; 71 Two or more races, non-Hispanic/Latino), 21 international. Average age 36. 297 applicants, 72% accepted, 209 enrolled. In 2017, 292 master's awarded. *Degree requirements:* For master's, comprehensive exam (for some programs), thesis (for some programs). *Entrance requirements:* Additional exam requirements/recommendations for international students: Required—TOEFL (minimum score 550 paper-based; 79 iBT), IELTS (minimum score 6). *Application deadline:* Applications are processed on a rolling basis. Application fee: $50. Electronic applications accepted. *Expenses:* Contact institution. *Financial support:* Career-related internships or fieldwork and scholarships/grants available. Financial award applicants required to submit FAFSA. *Unit head:* Aman Gupta, PhD, Department Chair, E-mail: aman.gupta@erau.edu. *Application contact:* Worldwide Campus, 800-522-6787, E-mail: worldwide@erau.edu.

Emory University, Goizueta Business School, Doctoral Program in Business, Atlanta, GA 30322. Offers accounting (PhD); finance (PhD); information systems and operations management (PhD); marketing (PhD); organization and management (PhD). *Students:* 250 applicants, 5% accepted. *Degree requirements:* For doctorate, comprehensive exam, thesis/dissertation. *Entrance requirements:* For doctorate, GMAT, interview. Additional exam requirements/recommendations for international students: Required—TOEFL (minimum score 600 paper-based; 100 iBT). *Application deadline:* For fall admission, 1/3 priority date for domestic and international students. Applications are processed on a rolling basis. Application fee: $75. Electronic applications accepted. *Expenses:* Contact institution. *Financial support:* Fellowships, scholarships/grants, and health care benefits available. Financial award application deadline: 1/3. *Faculty research:* Financial and managerial accounting, asset pricing strategy and organizational behavior, information technology marketing analytics and consumer behavior. *Unit head:* Kathryn Kadous, Associate Dean, 404-727-2306, Fax: 404-727-5337, E-mail: kathryn.kadous@emory.edu. *Application contact:* Allison Gilmore, Director of Admissions and Student Services, 404-727-6353, Fax: 404-727-5337, E-mail: allison.gilmore@emory.edu.
Website: https://goizueta.emory.edu/degree/phd/index.html

Emory University, Goizueta Business School, Full Time MBA Program, Atlanta, GA 30322. Offers accounting (MBA); alternative investments (MBA); business process consulting (MBA); business technology management (MBA); capital markets (MBA); corporate finance (MBA); customer relationship management (MBA); decision analytics (MBA); entrepreneurship (MBA); finance (MBA); global management (MBA); investment banking (MBA); management consulting (MBA); marketing (MBA); marketing analytics (MBA); marketing consulting (MBA); operations management (MBA); organization and management (MBA); product and brand management (MBA); real estate (MBA); social enterprise (MBA); strategy consulting (MBA). *Accreditation:* AACSB. *Faculty:* 74 full-time (18 women), 18 part-time/adjunct (6 women). *Students:* 353 full-time (96 women); includes 80 minority (18 Black or African American, non-Hispanic/Latino; 2 American Indian or Alaska Native, non-Hispanic/Latino; 39 Asian, non-Hispanic/Latino; 16 Hispanic/Latino; 1 Native Hawaiian or other Pacific Islander, non-Hispanic/Latino; 4 Two or more races, non-Hispanic/Latino), 104 international. Average age 29. 1,380 applicants, 34% accepted, 172 enrolled. In 2017, 179 master's awarded. *Degree requirements:* For master's, 1 leadership course; 2 mid-semester module programs; 2 global components. *Entrance requirements:* For master's, GMAT/GRE, essays; recommendation letters; undergraduate degree; interview. Additional exam requirements/recommendations for international students: Required—TOEFL (minimum score 100 iBT), IELTS (minimum score 7), PTE (minimum score 68). *Application deadline:* For fall admission, 10/6 for domestic and international students; for winter admission, 11/17 for domestic and international students; for spring admission, 1/3 priority date for domestic and international students; for summer admission, 3/9 for domestic and international students. Application fee: $150. Electronic applications accepted. *Expenses:* $59,616. *Financial support:* In 2017–18, 273 students received support. Career-related internships or fieldwork, institutionally sponsored loans, and scholarships/grants available. Financial award application deadline: 4/1; financial award applicants required to submit FAFSA. *Faculty research:* Corporate finance, information systems, digital marketing, asset pricing, sports management. *Unit head:* Brian Mitchell, Associate Dean, 404-727-4824, Fax: 404-712-9648, E-mail: brian.mitchell@emory.edu. *Application contact:* Julie Barefoot, Associate Dean, 404-727-6311, Fax: 404-727-4612, E-mail: mbaadmissions@emory.edu.
Website: http://www.goizueta.emory.edu

Fairfield University, Dolan School of Business, Fairfield, CT 06824. Offers accounting (MBA, MS, CAS); business analytics (MS); finance (MBA, MS, CAS); information systems and business analytics (MBA); management (MBA, CAS); marketing (MBA, CAS); taxation (CAS). *Accreditation:* AACSB. *Program availability:* Part-time, evening/weekend. *Faculty:* 18 full-time (6 women), 6 part-time/adjunct (2 women). *Students:* 120 full-time (57 women), 67 part-time (27 women); includes 20 minority (3 Black or African American, non-Hispanic/Latino; 1 American Indian or Alaska Native, non-Hispanic/Latino; 3 Asian, non-Hispanic/Latino; 11 Hispanic/Latino; 2 Two or more races, non-Hispanic/Latino), 33 international. Average age 26. 195 applicants, 87% accepted, 112 enrolled. In 2017, 93 master's awarded. *Degree requirements:* For master's, capstone course. *Entrance requirements:* For master's, GMAT (minimum score 500), 2 letters of reference, resume, minimum GPA of 3.0. Additional exam requirements/recommendations for international students: Required—TOEFL (minimum score 550 paper-based; 80 iBT) or IELTS (minimum score 6.5). *Application deadline:* For fall admission, 5/15 for international students; for spring admission, 10/15 for international students. Applications are processed on a rolling basis. Application fee: $60. Electronic applications accepted. *Expenses:* $925 per credit hour. *Financial support:* In 2017–18, 31 students received support. Scholarships/grants and unspecified assistantships available. Financial award applicants required to submit FAFSA. *Faculty research:* International finance, leadership and careers, ethics in accounting, emotions in consumer behavior and organizations, data analytics. *Unit head:* Dr. Mark Ligas, Interim Dean, 203-254-4070, Fax: 203-254-4105, E-mail: mligas@fairfield.edu. *Application contact:* Marianne Gumpper, Director of Graduate and Continuing Studies Admission, 203-254-4184, Fax: 203-254-4073, E-mail: gradadmis@fairfield.edu.
Website: http://fairfield.edu/mba

Fairleigh Dickinson University, Florham Campus, Silberman College of Business, Department of Economics, Finance, and International Business, Program in Finance, Madison, NJ 07940-1099. Offers MBA, Certificate.

Fairleigh Dickinson University, Metropolitan Campus, Silberman College of Business, Department of Economics, Finance and International Business, Program in Finance, Teaneck, NJ 07666-1914. Offers MBA, Certificate.

Florida Agricultural and Mechanical University, Division of Graduate Studies, Research, and Continuing Education, School of Business and Industry, Tallahassee, FL 32307-3200. Offers accounting (MBA); finance (MBA); management information systems (MBA); marketing (MBA). *Accreditation:* ACBSP. *Degree requirements:* For master's, residency. *Entrance requirements:* For master's, GMAT, minimum GPA of 3.0.

Florida International University, Chapman Graduate School of Business, Department of Finance, Miami, FL 33199. Offers MSF. *Program availability:* Part-time, evening/weekend. *Faculty:* 25 full-time (5 women), 9 part-time/adjunct (1 woman). *Students:* 84 full-time (36 women), 8 part-time (3 women); includes 55 minority (5 Black or African American, non-Hispanic/Latino; 5 Asian, non-Hispanic/Latino; 43 Hispanic/Latino; 2 Two or more races, non-Hispanic/Latino), 28 international. Average age 29. 205 applicants, 46% accepted, 60 enrolled. In 2017, 111 master's awarded. *Entrance requirements:* For master's, GMAT or GRE, minimum GPA of 3.0 in upper-level coursework; letter of intent; resume. Additional exam requirements/recommendations for international students: Required—TOEFL (minimum score 550 paper-based; 80 iBT) or IELTS (minimum score 6.5). *Application deadline:* For fall admission, 6/1 for domestic students, 4/1 for international students; for spring admission, 10/1 for domestic students, 9/1 for international students. Applications are processed on a rolling basis. Application fee: $30. Electronic applications accepted. *Expenses:* Contact institution. *Financial support:* Institutionally sponsored loans and scholarships/grants available. Financial award application deadline: 3/1; financial award applicants required to submit FAFSA. *Faculty research:* Investment, corporate and international finance. *Unit head:* Shahid Hamid, Chair, 305-348-2681, E-mail: hamids@fiu.edu. *Application contact:* Paula Alger, Program Manager, 305-348-7466, E-mail: palger@fiu.edu.

Florida National University, Program in Business Administration, Hialeah, FL 33012. Offers accounting (MBA); finance (MBA); general management (MBA); health services administration (MBA); marketing (MBA); public management and leadership (MBA). *Program availability:* Part-time, blended/hybrid learning. *Degree requirements:* For master's, capstone. *Entrance requirements:* For master's, writing assessment, bachelor's degree from accredited institution; official undergraduate transcripts; minimum undergraduate GPA of 2.5, GMAT (minimum score of 400), or GRE (minimum score of 900); two letters of recommendation; resume. Additional exam requirements/recommendations for international students: Required—TOEFL (minimum score 500 paper-based; 62 iBT), IELTS (minimum score 5.5). *Application deadline:* Applications are processed on a rolling basis. Electronic applications accepted. *Expenses:* Contact institution. *Financial support:* Federal Work-Study, institutionally sponsored loans, scholarships/grants, and tuition waivers available. Financial award applicants required to submit FAFSA. *Unit head:* Dr. Ernesto Gonzalez, Business and Economics Department Head, 305-821-3333 Ext. 1070, Fax: 305-362-0595, E-mail: egonzalez@fnu.edu. Website: https://www.fnu.edu/prospective-students/our-programs/select-a-program/master-of-business-administration/business-administration-mba-masters/

Florida State University, The Graduate School, College of Business, Tallahassee, FL 32306-1110. Offers accounting (M Acc), including assurance and advisory services, generalist, taxation; business administration (MBA, PhD), including accounting (PhD), finance (PhD), management information systems (PhD), marketing (PhD), organizational behavior and human resources (PhD), risk management and insurance (PhD), strategy (PhD); finance (MS); management information systems (MS); risk management and insurance (MS); JD/MBA; MSW/MBA. *Accreditation:* AACSB. *Program availability:* Part-time, 100% online. *Faculty:* 93 full-time (23 women), 2 part-time/adjunct (1 woman). *Students:* 229 full-time (96 women), 423 part-time (154 women); includes 159 minority (44 Black or African American, non-Hispanic/Latino; 24 Asian, non-Hispanic/Latino; 75 Hispanic/Latino; 1 Native Hawaiian or other Pacific Islander, non-Hispanic/Latino; 15 Two or more races, non-Hispanic/Latino), 48 international. Average age 31. 300 applicants, 61% accepted, 133 enrolled. In 2017, 268 master's, 9 doctorates awarded. Terminal master's awarded for partial completion of doctoral program. *Degree requirements:* For doctorate, comprehensive exam, thesis/dissertation. *Entrance requirements:* For master's, GMAT, GRE (for all except MS in finance), work experience (MBA, MS); minimum GPA of 3.0, letters of recommendation; for doctorate, GMAT, GRE (for marketing, organizational behavior, risk management and insurance, management information systems, and human resources only), minimum graduate GPA of 3.5, letters of recommendation. Additional exam requirements/recommendations for international students: Required—TOEFL (minimum score 600 paper-based; 85 iBT); Recommended—IELTS (minimum score 6). *Application deadline:* For fall admission, 6/1 for domestic and international students; for spring admission, 10/1 for domestic and international students; for summer admission, 3/1 for domestic and international students. Applications are processed on a rolling basis. Application fee: $30. Electronic applications accepted. *Expenses:* Contact institution. *Financial support:* In 2017–18, 146 students received support, including 26 fellowships (averaging $1,500 per year), 77 research assistantships with full tuition reimbursements available (averaging $20,000 per year), 43 teaching assistantships with full tuition reimbursements available (averaging $20,000 per year); career-related internships or fieldwork, scholarships/grants, health care benefits, tuition waivers (full and partial), and unspecified assistantships also available. Support available to part-time students. Financial award application deadline: 1/1; financial award applicants required to submit FAFSA. *Faculty research:* Business strategy, marketing, finance, accounting, business analytics. *Total annual research expenditures:* $1.4 million. *Unit head:* Dr. Michael Hartline, Dean, 850-644-4405, Fax: 850-644-0915, E-mail: mhartline@business.fsu.edu. *Application contact:* Jennifer Clark, Director, 850-644-6458, E-mail: gradprograms@business.fsu.edu.
Website: http://business.fsu.edu/

Fordham University, Gabelli School of Business, New York, NY 10023. Offers accounting (MBA, MS); applied statistics and decision-making (MS); business economics (DPS); capital markets (DPS); communications and media management (MBA); electronic business (MBA); entrepreneurship (MBA); finance (MBA, PhD); global finance (MS); global sustainability (MBA); health administration (MS); healthcare management (MBA); information systems (MBA, MS); investor relations (MS); management (EMBA, MBA, MS, PhD); marketing (MBA); marketing intelligence (MS); media management (MS); nonprofit leadership (MS); quantitative finance (MS); strategy and decision-making (DPS); taxation (MS); JD/MBA; MS/MBA. *Accreditation:* AACSB. *Program availability:* Part-time, evening/weekend. *Faculty:* 130 full-time (46 women), 42 part-time/adjunct (9 women). *Students:* 1,051 full-time (570 women), 563 part-time (313 women); includes 190 minority (48 Black or African American, non-Hispanic/Latino; 72 Asian, non-Hispanic/Latino; 69 Hispanic/Latino; 1 Native Hawaiian or other Pacific Islander, non-Hispanic/Latino), 1,106 international. Average age 27. 4,577 applicants, 58% accepted, 794 enrolled. In 2017, 937 master's awarded. Terminal master's awarded for partial completion of doctoral program. *Degree requirements:* For master's, internships (for some degrees); for doctorate, comprehensive exam (for some programs), thesis/dissertation. *Entrance requirements:* For master's, GMAT/GRE, 2 letters of recommendation, resume, 2 essays, transcripts, interview. Additional exam requirements/recommendations for international students: Required—TOEFL (minimum score 100 iBT), IELTS (minimum score 7). *Application deadline:* For fall admission, 11/15 priority date for domestic and international students; for

winter admission, 1/19 priority date for domestic students, 1/1 priority date for international students; for spring admission, 4/15 for domestic students, 3/1 for international students; for summer admission, 6/1 for domestic students. Application fee: $130. Electronic applications accepted. *Expenses:* $1,495 per credit. *Financial support:* Career-related internships or fieldwork, institutionally sponsored loans, scholarships/grants, and unspecified assistantships available. Support available to part-time students. Financial award application deadline: 6/30; financial award applicants required to submit FAFSA. *Unit head:* Dr. Donna Rapaccioli, Dean, 212-636-6165, Fax: 212-307-1779, E-mail: rapaccioli@fordham.edu. *Application contact:* Lawrence Murray, Senior Assistant Dean of Graduate Admissions and Advising, 212-636-6200, Fax: 212-636-7076, E-mail: admissionsgb@fordham.edu.
Website: http://www.fordham.edu/gabelli

Gannon University, School of Graduate Studies, College of Engineering and Business, Dahlkemper School of Business, Program in Business Administration, Erie, PA 16541-0001. Offers business administration (MBA); finance (MBA); human resources management (MBA); marketing (MBA). *Accreditation:* ACBSP. *Program availability:* Part-time, evening/weekend, 100% online, blended/hybrid learning. *Entrance requirements:* For master's, GMAT, bachelor's degree in any discipline from any accredited college or university, resume, transcripts, 3 letters of recommendation. Additional exam requirements/recommendations for international students: Required—TOEFL (minimum score 79 iBT). Electronic applications accepted. Application fee is waived when completed online.

Geneva College, Program in Business Administration, Beaver Falls, PA 15010-3599. Offers business administration (MBA); finance (MBA); marketing (MBA); operations (MBA). *Accreditation:* ACBSP. *Program availability:* Part-time, evening/weekend. *Faculty:* 5 full-time (1 woman), 3 part-time/adjunct (0 women). *Students:* 33 full-time (13 women), 8 part-time (2 women); includes 6 minority (4 Black or African American, non-Hispanic/Latino; 1 American Indian or Alaska Native, non-Hispanic/Latino; 1 Asian, non-Hispanic/Latino). Average age 37. 25 applicants, 52% accepted, 10 enrolled. In 2017, 14 master's awarded. *Degree requirements:* For master's, 36 credit hours of course work (30 of which are required of all students). *Entrance requirements:* For master's, GMAT (if college GPA less than 2.5), undergraduate transcript, 2 letters of recommendation, resume, goals statement. Additional exam requirements/recommendations for international students: Required—TOEFL. *Application deadline:* For fall admission, 3/1 priority date for domestic students; for spring admission, 11/1 priority date for domestic students. Applications are processed on a rolling basis. Electronic applications accepted. *Expenses:* $710 per credit. *Financial support:* In 2017–18, 1 student received support. Scholarships/grants available. Financial award application deadline: 8/1; financial award applicants required to submit FAFSA. *Unit head:* Dr. Dan Vander Plaats, Director of the MBA Program, 724-847-6619, E-mail: gpvander@geneva.edu. *Application contact:* Marina Frazier, Director of Graduate Enrollment, 724-847-6697, E-mail: mba@geneva.edu.
Website: http://www.geneva.edu/page/masters_business

George Fox University, College of Business, Newberg, OR 97132-2697. Offers accounting (DBA); finance (MBA); management (DBA); management and leadership (MBA); marketing (DBA); organizational strategy (MBA); strategic human resource management (MBA). MBA offered in Newberg, OR and in Portland, OR. *Accreditation:* ACBSP. *Program availability:* Part-time, evening/weekend, online learning. *Degree requirements:* For master's, capstone project; for doctorate, credit-applied research project. *Entrance requirements:* For master's, resume (5 years of professional experience); 3 professional references; interview; financial e-learning course; official transcripts; for doctorate, GRE or GMAT, resume; personal mission statement; academic research writing sample; official transcript from each college/university attended; three professional references. Additional exam requirements/recommendations for international students: Required—TOEFL (minimum score 577 paper-based; 90 iBT) or IELTS (minimum score 7). Electronic applications accepted. *Expenses:* Contact institution.

Georgetown University, Graduate School of Arts and Sciences, Department of Economics, Washington, DC 20057. Offers econometrics (PhD); economic development (PhD); economic theory (PhD); industrial organization (PhD); international macro and finance (PhD); international trade (PhD); labor economics (PhD); macroeconomics (PhD); public economics and political economy (PhD); MA/PhD; MS/MA. *Degree requirements:* For doctorate, comprehensive exam, thesis/dissertation. *Entrance requirements:* For doctorate, GRE General Test. Additional exam requirements/recommendations for international students: Required—TOEFL. *Faculty research:* International economics, economic development.

Georgetown University, Graduate School of Arts and Sciences, McDonough School of Business, Washington, DC 20057. Offers business administration (EMBA, GEMBA, MBA); finance (MS); leadership (EML). *Accreditation:* AACSB. *Entrance requirements:* For master's, GMAT. Additional exam requirements/recommendations for international students: Required—TOEFL. *Expenses:* Contact institution.

The George Washington University, School of Business, Department of Finance, Washington, DC 20052. Offers finance (MSF, PhD); finance and investments (MBA). *Program availability:* Part-time, evening/weekend. *Faculty:* 19 full-time (3 women), 14 part-time/adjunct (1 woman). *Students:* 200 full-time (101 women), 7 part-time (2 women); includes 10 minority (2 Black or African American, non-Hispanic/Latino; 1 American Indian or Alaska Native, non-Hispanic/Latino; 6 Asian, non-Hispanic/Latino; 1 Hispanic/Latino), 191 international. Average age 26. 901 applicants, 38% accepted, 74 enrolled. In 2017, 138 master's awarded. *Entrance requirements:* For master's, GMAT; for doctorate, GMAT or GRE. Additional exam requirements/recommendations for international students: Required—TOEFL. *Application deadline:* For fall admission, 4/1 priority date for domestic students; for spring admission, 10/1 for domestic students. Applications are processed on a rolling basis. Application fee: $75. *Expenses: Tuition:* Full-time $28,800; part-time $1655 per credit hour. *Required fees:* $45; $2.75 per credit hour. *Financial support:* In 2017–18, 38 students received support. Fellowships, teaching assistantships, career-related internships or fieldwork, Federal Work-Study, and institutionally sponsored loans available. Financial award application deadline: 4/1. *Unit head:* Robert Van Order, Chair, 202-994-3427, E-mail: rvo@gwu.edu. *Application contact:* Christopher Storer, Executive Director, Graduate Admissions, 202-994-1212, E-mail: gwmba@gwu.edu.

The George Washington University, School of Business, Program in Government Contracts, Washington, DC 20052. Offers MS. *Program availability:* Part-time, evening/weekend. *Students:* 4 full-time (1 woman), 54 part-time (34 women); includes 26 minority (19 Black or African American, non-Hispanic/Latino; 1 Asian, non-Hispanic/Latino; 5 Hispanic/Latino; 1 Two or more races, non-Hispanic/Latino), 2 international. Average age 40. 44 applicants, 82% accepted, 16 enrolled. In 2017, 18 master's awarded. *Entrance requirements:* For master's, GMAT/GRE or seven years of full-time, relevant professional work experience. *Application deadline:* For fall admission, 7/31 for domestic students. *Expenses: Tuition:* Full-time $28,800; part-time $1655 per credit hour. *Required fees:* $45; $2.75 per credit hour. *Unit head:* Dr. George Jabbour, Associate Dean, 202-994-3879, E-mail: wemba@gwu.edu. *Application contact:* Neal Couture, Director, 202-994-2693, E-mail: ncouture@gwu.edu.
Website: http://gwsbwebsite.com/programs/specialized-masters/m-s-in-government-contracts/

Georgia State University, Andrew Young School of Policy Studies, Department of Economics, Atlanta, GA 30302. Offers economics (MA); environmental economics (PhD); experimental economics (PhD); labor economics (PhD); policy (MA); public finance (PhD); urban and regional economics (PhD). MA offered through the College of Arts and Sciences. *Program availability:* Part-time. *Faculty:* 26 full-time (4 women). *Students:* 110 full-time (39 women), 14 part-time (5 women); includes 26 minority (14 Black or African American, non-Hispanic/Latino; 4 Asian, non-Hispanic/Latino; 4 Hispanic/Latino; 4 Two or more races, non-Hispanic/Latino), 61 international. Average age 28. 204 applicants, 50% accepted, 37 enrolled. In 2017, 26 master's, 13 doctorates awarded. Terminal master's awarded for partial completion of doctoral program. *Degree requirements:* For master's, thesis optional; for doctorate, comprehensive exam, thesis/dissertation. *Entrance requirements:* For master's and doctorate, GRE. Additional exam requirements/recommendations for international students: Required—TOEFL (minimum score 603 paper-based; 100 iBT) or IELTS (minimum score 7). *Application deadline:* For fall admission, 1/15 for domestic and international students. Application fee: $50. Electronic applications accepted. *Expenses:* Tuition, state resident: full-time $7020. Tuition, nonresident: full-time $22,518. *Required fees:* $2128. Tuition and fees vary according to degree level and program. *Financial support:* In 2017–18, fellowships with full tuition reimbursements (averaging $11,333 per year), research assistantships with full tuition reimbursements (averaging $9,788 per year), teaching assistantships with full tuition reimbursements (averaging $3,000 per year) were awarded; career-related internships or fieldwork also available. Financial award application deadline: 2/15; financial award applicants required to submit FAFSA. *Faculty research:* Public, experimental, urban/environmental, labor, and health economics. *Unit head:* Dr. Rusty Tchernis, Director of the Doctoral Program, 404-413-0154, Fax: 404-413-0145, E-mail: rtchernis@gsu.edu.
Website: http://economics.gsu.edu/

Georgia State University, Andrew Young School of Policy Studies, Department of Public Management and Policy, Atlanta, GA 30303. Offers criminal justice (MPA); disaster management (Certificate); disaster policy (MPA); environmental policy (PhD); health policy (PhD); management and finance (MPA); nonprofit management (MPA, Certificate); nonprofit policy (MPA); planning and economic development (MPP, Certificate); policy analysis and evaluation (MPA), including planning and economic development; public and nonprofit management (PhD); public finance and budgeting (PhD), including science and technology policy, urban and regional economic development; public finance policy (MPA), including social policy; public health (MPA). *Accreditation:* NASPAA (one or more programs are accredited). *Program availability:* Part-time. *Faculty:* 17 full-time (9 women). *Students:* 125 full-time (75 women), 78 part-time (51 women); includes 90 minority (67 Black or African American, non-Hispanic/Latino; 5 Asian, non-Hispanic/Latino; 9 Two or more races, non-Hispanic/Latino), 34 international. Average age 30. 275 applicants, 62% accepted, 88 enrolled. In 2017, 71 master's, 5 doctorates, 12 other advanced degrees awarded. Terminal master's awarded for partial completion of doctoral program. *Degree requirements:* For master's, thesis optional; for doctorate, comprehensive exam, thesis/dissertation. *Entrance requirements:* For master's and doctorate, GRE. Additional exam requirements/recommendations for international students: Required—TOEFL (minimum score 603 paper-based; 100 iBT) or IELTS (minimum score 7). *Application deadline:* For fall admission, 1/15 for domestic and international students. Application fee: $50. Electronic applications accepted. *Expenses:* Tuition, state resident: full-time $7020. Tuition, nonresident: full-time $22,518. *Required fees:* $2128. Tuition and fees vary according to degree level and program. *Financial support:* In 2017–18, fellowships (averaging $8,194 per year), research assistantships (averaging $8,068 per year), teaching assistantships (averaging $3,600 per year) were awarded; institutionally sponsored loans, scholarships/grants, health care benefits, and unspecified assistantships also available. Financial award application deadline: 2/1. *Faculty research:* Public budgeting and finance, public management, nonprofit management, performance measurement and management, urban development. *Unit head:* Dr. Carolyn Bourdeaux, Chair and Professor, 404-413-0013, Fax: 404-413-0104, E-mail: cbourdeaux@gsu.edu.
Website: http://aysps.gsu.edu/pmap/

Georgia State University, J. Mack Robinson College of Business, Department of Finance, Atlanta, GA 30302-3083. Offers MBA, MS, PhD. *Program availability:* Part-time, evening/weekend. *Faculty:* 20 full-time (4 women). *Students:* 41 full-time (14 women), 13 part-time (5 women); includes 7 minority (2 Black or African American, non-Hispanic/Latino; 2 Asian, non-Hispanic/Latino; 2 Hispanic/Latino; 1 Two or more races, non-Hispanic/Latino), 38 international. Average age 26. 144 applicants, 45% accepted, 24 enrolled. In 2017, 20 master's, 2 doctorates awarded. *Entrance requirements:* For master's, GRE or GMAT, transcripts from all institutions attended, resume, essays; for doctorate, GRE or GMAT, three letters of recommendation, personal statement, transcripts from all institutions attended, resume. Additional exam requirements/recommendations for international students: Required—TOEFL (minimum score 610 paper-based; 101 iBT), IELTS (minimum score 7). *Application deadline:* For fall admission, 5/1 priority date for domestic students, 2/1 priority date for international students; for spring admission, 9/15 priority date for domestic students, 4/1 priority date for international students. Applications are processed on a rolling basis. Application fee: $50. Electronic applications accepted. *Expenses:* Tuition, state resident: full-time $7020. Tuition, nonresident: full-time $22,518. *Required fees:* $2128. Tuition and fees vary according to degree level and program. *Financial support:* Research assistantships, teaching assistantships, scholarships/grants, tuition waivers, and unspecified assistantships available. *Faculty research:* Mergers and acquisitions, asset pricing, mutual and hedge funds, derivatives, corporate governance. *Unit head:* Dr. Gerald D. Gay, Professor/Chair, 404-413-7310, Fax: 404-413-7312. *Application contact:* Toby McChesney, Assistant Dean for Graduate Recruiting and Student Services, 404-413-7167, Fax: 404-413-7162, E-mail: rcbgradadmissions@gsu.edu.
Website: http://www.robinson.gsu.edu/finance/

Georgia State University, J. Mack Robinson College of Business, Department of Risk Management and Insurance, Program in Risk Management and Insurance, Atlanta, GA 30302-3083. Offers enterprise risk management (MBA, Certificate); financial risk management (MBA); mathematical risk management (MS); risk and insurance (MS); risk management and insurance (MBA, PhD); MAS/MRM. *Program availability:* Part-time, evening/weekend. *Entrance requirements:* For master's, GRE or GMAT, transcripts from all institutions attended, resume, essays. Additional exam requirements/recommendations for international students: Required—TOEFL (minimum score 610 paper-based; 101 iBT), IELTS (minimum score 7). *Application deadline:* Applications are processed on a rolling basis. Application fee: $50. Electronic applications accepted. *Expenses:* Tuition, state resident: full-time $7020. Tuition, nonresident: full-time $22,518. *Required fees:* $2128. Tuition and fees vary according to degree level and program. *Financial support:* Research assistantships, scholarships/grants, tuition waivers, and unspecified assistantships available. *Faculty research:* Insurance economics, structure and performance of insurance markets, regulation and policy in insurance markets, asset pricing theory, financial econometrics. *Unit head:* Dr. Martin Grace, Professor of Risk Management and Legal Studies/Chair of the Department of Risk Management and Insurance, 404-413-7500, Fax: 404-413-7499. *Application contact:* Toby McChesney, Graduate Recruiting Contact, 404-413-7167, Fax: 404-413-

7162, E-mail: rcbgradadmissions@gsu.edu.
Website: http://rmi.robinson.gsu.edu/academic-programs/ms-rmi/

Golden Gate University, Ageno School of Business, San Francisco, CA 94105-2968. Offers accounting (MBA); adaptive leadership (MBA); advanced financial planning (MS); business administration (EMBA, MBA, DBA); business analytics (MBA, MS); entrepreneurship (MBA); finance (MBA, MS, Certificate); financial life planning (Certificate); financial planning (MS, Certificate); global supply chain management (MBA, Certificate); human resource management (MBA, MS, Certificate); information technology management (MBA, MS, Certificate); international business (MBA); marketing (MBA, MS, Certificate); project management (MBA, MS, Certificate); psychology (MA, Certificate); public administration (EMPA, MBA); public administration leadership (Certificate); JD/MBA. *Program availability:* Part-time, evening/weekend. *Faculty:* 17 full-time (7 women), 280 part-time/adjunct (95 women). *Students:* 309 full-time (147 women), 527 part-time (266 women); includes 286 minority (56 Black or African American, non-Hispanic/Latino; 1 American Indian or Alaska Native, non-Hispanic/Latino; 131 Asian, non-Hispanic/Latino; 83 Hispanic/Latino; 4 Native Hawaiian or other Pacific Islander, non-Hispanic/Latino; 11 Two or more races, non-Hispanic/Latino), 209 international. Average age 35. 549 applicants, 66% accepted, 185 enrolled. *Degree requirements:* For doctorate, thesis/dissertation, qualifying examination. *Entrance requirements:* For master's, GMAT (for MBA), minimum GPA of 2.5 (MS). Additional exam requirements/recommendations for international students: Required—TOEFL (minimum score 550 paper-based; 79 iBT). *Application deadline:* For fall admission, 5/15 for domestic and international students; for winter admission, 1/15 for domestic and international students; for spring admission, 9/15 for domestic and international students. Applications are processed on a rolling basis. Application fee: $65 ($105 for international students). Electronic applications accepted. *Expenses:* $3,150 per 3-unit course. *Financial support:* Career-related internships or fieldwork, Federal Work-Study, institutionally sponsored loans, and scholarships/grants available. Support available to part-time students. Financial award applicants required to submit FAFSA. *Unit head:* Marianne Koch, Associate Dean, 415-442-6542, Fax: 415-442-6579, E-mail: mkoch@ggu.edu. *Application contact:* Angela Melero, Enrollment Services, 415-442-7800, Fax: 415-442-7807, E-mail: info@ggu.edu.
Website: http://www.ggu.edu/programs/business-and-management

Golden Gate University, School of Taxation, San Francisco, CA 94105-2968. Offers advanced studies in taxation (Certificate); estate planning (Certificate); financial planning and taxation (MS); international taxation (Certificate); state and local taxation (Certificate); taxation (MS, Certificate). *Program availability:* Part-time, evening/weekend. *Faculty:* 7 full-time (1 woman), 65 part-time/adjunct (19 women). *Students:* 72 full-time (44 women), 539 part-time (281 women); includes 156 minority (17 Black or African American, non-Hispanic/Latino; 3 American Indian or Alaska Native, non-Hispanic/Latino; 100 Asian, non-Hispanic/Latino; 23 Hispanic/Latino; 7 Native Hawaiian or other Pacific Islander, non-Hispanic/Latino; 6 Two or more races, non-Hispanic/Latino), 82 international. Average age 36. 252 applicants, 84% accepted, 105 enrolled. In 2017, 193 master's awarded. *Entrance requirements:* For master's, minimum GPA of 3.0. Additional exam requirements/recommendations for international students: Required—TOEFL (minimum score 550 paper-based), IELTS (minimum score 6.5). *Application deadline:* For fall admission, 5/15 for international students; for winter admission, 1/15 for international students; for spring admission, 9/15 for international students. Applications are processed on a rolling basis. Application fee: $70 ($100 for international students). Electronic applications accepted. *Expenses:* Contact institution. *Financial support:* In 2017–18, 66 students received support. Career-related internships or fieldwork, Federal Work-Study, institutionally sponsored loans, and scholarships/grants available. Support available to part-time students. Financial award applicants required to submit FAFSA. *Unit head:* Fred Sroka, Dean, 415-369-5285, Fax: 415-442-7807. *Application contact:* Angela Melero, Enrollment Services, 415-442-7800, Fax: 415-442-7807, E-mail: info@ggu.edu.
Website: http://www.ggu.edu/programs/taxation/master-of-science-in-taxation

Goldey-Beacom College, Graduate Program, Wilmington, DE 19808-1999. Offers business administration (MBA); finance (MS); financial management (MBA); health care management (MBA); human resource management (MBA); information technology (MBA); international business management (MBA); major finance (MBA); major taxation (MBA); management (MM); marketing management (MBA); taxation (MBA, MS). *Accreditation:* ACBSP. *Program availability:* Part-time, evening/weekend. *Entrance requirements:* For master's, GMAT, MAT, GRE, minimum GPA of 3.0. Additional exam requirements/recommendations for international students: Required—TOEFL (minimum score 65 iBT); Recommended—IELTS (minimum score 6). Electronic applications accepted.

Gordon College, Graduate Financial Analysis Program, Wenham, MA 01984-1899. Offers MS. *Program availability:* Part-time, evening/weekend. *Faculty:* 1 full-time (0 women), 9 part-time/adjunct (1 woman). *Students:* 9 part-time (3 women); includes 2 minority (both Black or African American, non-Hispanic/Latino), 2 international. Average age 23. *Entrance requirements:* For master's, two academic references; one personal reference; resume; academic transcript(s). Additional exam requirements/recommendations for international students: Required—TOEFL, IELTS, or PTE. *Application deadline:* For fall admission, 4/30 for domestic and international students; for spring admission, 12/10 for domestic and international students. Applications are processed on a rolling basis. Application fee: $75. Electronic applications accepted. *Expenses:* $800 per credit tuition; $250 per semester administrative fee. *Financial support:* Applicants required to submit FAFSA. *Faculty research:* International trade, international monetary, security analysis, accounting, financial analysis. *Unit head:* Alexander Lowry, Executive Director, E-mail: alexander.lowry@gordon.edu. *Application contact:* Alexander Lowry, Executive Director, E-mail: alexander.lowry@gordon.edu.
Website: http://www.gordon.edu/graduate/finance

The Graduate Center, City University of New York, Graduate Studies, Program in Business, New York, New York, NY 10016-4039. Offers accounting (PhD); behavioral science (PhD); finance (PhD); management planning systems (PhD). *Faculty:* 66 full-time (5 women). *Students:* 56 full-time (30 women); includes 6 minority (1 Black or African American, non-Hispanic/Latino; 1 American Indian or Alaska Native, non-Hispanic/Latino; 2 Asian, non-Hispanic/Latino; 2 Hispanic/Latino), 42 international. Average age 33. 177 applicants, 7% accepted, 10 enrolled. In 2017, 10 doctorates awarded. *Degree requirements:* For doctorate, thesis/dissertation. *Entrance requirements:* For doctorate, GMAT, writing sample (15 pages). Additional exam requirements/recommendations for international students: Required—TOEFL. *Application deadline:* For fall admission, 1/15 for domestic students. Application fee: $125. Electronic applications accepted. *Financial support:* In 2017–18, 50 students received support, including 54 fellowships, 5 teaching assistantships; research assistantships, career-related internships or fieldwork, Federal Work-Study, institutionally sponsored loans, and tuition waivers (full and partial) also available. Financial award application deadline: 2/1; financial award applicants required to submit FAFSA. *Unit head:* Dr. Joseph Weintrop, Executive Officer, 646-312-3092, Fax: 646-312-3031. *Application contact:* Les Gribben, Director of Admissions, 212-817-7470, Fax: 212-817-1624, E-mail: lgribben@gc.cuny.edu.

Grand Canyon University, Colangelo College of Business, Phoenix, AZ 85017-1097. Offers accounting (MBA, MS); business analytics (MS); disaster preparedness and executive fire service leadership (MS); finance (MBA); general management (MBA); health systems management (MBA); information technology management (MS); leadership (MBA, MS); marketing (MBA); organizational leadership and entrepreneurship (MS); project management (MBA); sports business (MBA); strategic human resource management (MBA). *Accreditation:* ACBSP. *Program availability:* Part-time, evening/weekend, online learning. *Entrance requirements:* For master's, equivalent of two years' full-time professional work experience. Additional exam requirements/recommendations for international students: Required—TOEFL (minimum score 575 paper-based; 90 iBT), IELTS (minimum score 7). Electronic applications accepted.

Hawai`i Pacific University, College of Business, Program in Business Administration, Honolulu, HI 96813. Offers finance (MBA); human resource management (MBA); information systems (MBA); international business (MBA); management (MBA); marketing (MBA); organizational change and development (MBA). *Program availability:* Part-time, evening/weekend, 100% online, blended/hybrid learning. *Faculty:* 7 full-time (3 women), 3 part-time/adjunct (0 women). *Students:* 88 full-time (34 women), 28 part-time (18 women); includes 63 minority (9 Black or African American, non-Hispanic/Latino; 17 Asian, non-Hispanic/Latino; 14 Hispanic/Latino; 1 Native Hawaiian or other Pacific Islander, non-Hispanic/Latino; 22 Two or more races, non-Hispanic/Latino), 29 international. Average age 32. 82 applicants, 78% accepted, 40 enrolled. In 2017, 87 master's awarded. *Entrance requirements:* For master's, GMAT or GRE. Additional exam requirements/recommendations for international students: Recommended—TOEFL (minimum score 550 paper-based; 80 iBT), IELTS (minimum score 6), TWE (minimum score 5). *Application deadline:* For fall admission, 1/15 priority date for domestic students; for spring admission, 10/15 priority date for domestic students. Applications are processed on a rolling basis. Application fee: $50. Electronic applications accepted. *Expenses: Tuition:* Full-time $18,000; part-time $1000 per credit. *Required fees:* $200; $26 per credit. Tuition and fees vary according to course load and program. *Financial support:* In 2017–18, 24 students received support. Research assistantships, career-related internships or fieldwork, Federal Work-Study, scholarships/grants, tuition waivers (partial), and unspecified assistantships available. Financial award application deadline: 3/1; financial award applicants required to submit FAFSA. *Unit head:* Dr. Daewoo Park, Department Chair, 808-544-1463, E-mail: dwpark@hpu.edu. *Application contact:* Danny Lam, Assistant Director of Graduate Admissions, 808-544-1135, E-mail: graduate@hpu.edu.
Website: https://www.hpu.edu/cob/grad-programs/mba.html

HEC Montreal, School of Business Administration, Doctoral Program in Administration, Montréal, QC H3T 2A7, Canada. Offers accounting (PhD); applied economics (PhD); data science (PhD); finance (PhD); financial engineering (PhD); information technology (PhD); international business (PhD); logistics and operations management (PhD); management science (PhD); management, strategy and organizations (PhD); marketing (PhD); organizational behaviour and human resources (PhD). Program offered jointly with Concordia University, McGill University, and Universite du Quebec a Montreal. *Accreditation:* AACSB. *Students:* 114 full-time (47 women). 78 applicants, 42% accepted, 24 enrolled. In 2017, 23 doctorates awarded. *Entrance requirements:* For doctorate, TAGE MAGE, GMAT, or GRE, master's degree in administration or related field. *Application deadline:* For fall admission, 1/15 for domestic and international students. Application fee: $88 ($187 for international students). Electronic applications accepted. *Expenses:* Tuition, state resident: full-time $2869 Canadian dollars; part-time $79.70 Canadian dollars per credit. Tuition, nonresident: full-time $8883 Canadian dollars; part-time $246.76 Canadian dollars per credit. *International tuition:* $19,648 Canadian dollars full-time. *Required fees:* $41.20 Canadian dollars per credit. $67.94 Canadian dollars per term. Tuition and fees vary according to degree level and program. *Financial support:* Research assistantships, teaching assistantships, and scholarships/grants available. Financial award application deadline: 9/2. *Faculty research:* Art management, business policy, entrepreneurship, new technologies, transportation. *Unit head:* Jacques Robert, Director, 514-340-6853, E-mail: jacques.robert@hec.ca. *Application contact:* Julie Bilodeau, PhD Program Analyst, 514-340-6151, Fax: 514-340-6411, E-mail: analyste.phd@hec.ca.
Website: http://www.hec.ca/en/programs/phd/index.html

HEC Montreal, School of Business Administration, Graduate Diploma Programs in Administration, Program in Financial Professions, Montréal, QC H3T 2A7, Canada. Offers Graduate Diploma. All courses are given in French. *Students:* 23 full-time (8 women), 3 part-time (2 women). 74 applicants, 66% accepted, 26 enrolled. In 2017, 16 Graduate Diplomas awarded. *Entrance requirements:* For master's, bachelor's degree in administration (finance option). *Application deadline:* For fall admission, 4/15 for domestic and international students. Application fee: $88 ($184 for international students). Electronic applications accepted. *Expenses:* Tuition, state resident: full-time $2869 Canadian dollars; part-time $79.70 Canadian dollars per credit. Tuition, nonresident: full-time $8883 Canadian dollars; part-time $246.76 Canadian dollars per credit. *International tuition:* $19,648 Canadian dollars full-time. *Required fees:* $41.20 Canadian dollars per credit. $67.94 Canadian dollars per term. Tuition and fees vary according to degree level and program. *Financial support:* Research assistantships, teaching assistantships, and scholarships/grants available. Financial award application deadline: 9/2. *Unit head:* Renaud Lachance, Academic Supervisor, 514-340-7165, E-mail: renaud.lachance@hec.ca. *Application contact:* Anny Caron, Administrative Director, 514-340-6151, Fax: 514-340-6411, E-mail: aide@hec.ca.
Website: http://www.hec.ca/programmes/dess/dess-professions-financieres/index.html

HEC Montreal, School of Business Administration, Master of Science Programs in Administration, Program in Applied Financial Economics, Montréal, QC H3T 2A7, Canada. Offers M Sc. Program offered in French and also in English. *Students:* 37 full-time (12 women), 12 part-time (4 women). 39 applicants, 79% accepted, 17 enrolled. In 2017, 4 master's awarded. *Entrance requirements:* For master's, BBA, undergraduate degree in another field, degree deemed equivalent by program director and minimum GPA of 3.0 on 4.3 scale. Additional exam requirements/recommendations for international students: Required—TAGE MAGE (minimum recommended score of 283), GMAT (minimum recommended score of 630), or GRE. *Application deadline:* For fall admission, 3/15 for domestic and international students; for winter admission, 9/15 for domestic and international students. Application fee: $88 Canadian dollars ($184 Canadian dollars for international students). Electronic applications accepted. *Expenses:* Tuition, state resident: full-time $2869 Canadian dollars; part-time $79.70 Canadian dollars per credit. Tuition, nonresident: full-time $8883 Canadian dollars; part-time $246.76 Canadian dollars per credit. *International tuition:* $19,648 Canadian dollars full-time. *Required fees:* $41.20 Canadian dollars per credit. $67.94 Canadian dollars per term. Tuition and fees vary according to degree level and program. *Financial support:* Research assistantships, teaching assistantships, and scholarships/grants available. Financial award application deadline: 9/2. *Unit head:* Dr. Marie-Helene Jobin, Director, 514-340-6283, E-mail: marie-helene.jobin@hec.ca. *Application contact:* Marianne de Moura, Administrative Director, 514-340-6151, Fax: 514-340-6411, E-mail: aide@hec.ca.
Website: http://www.hec.ca/en/programs/masters/master-applied-financial-economics/index.html

HEC Montreal, School of Business Administration, Master of Science Programs in Administration, Program in Finance, Montréal, QC H3T 2A7, Canada. Offers M Sc. Program offered in French and also in English. *Students:* 77 full-time (20 women), 17 part-time (6 women). 76 applicants, 70% accepted, 34 enrolled. In 2017, 32 master's awarded. *Entrance requirements:* For master's, BBA, undergraduate degree in another field, degree deemed equivalent by program director and minimum GPA of 3.0 on 4.3 scale. Additional exam requirements/recommendations for international students: Required—TAGE MAGE (minimum recommended score of 283), GMAT (minimum recommended score of 630), or GRE. *Application deadline:* For fall admission, 3/15 for domestic and international students; for winter admission, 9/15 for domestic and international students. Application fee: $88 Canadian dollars ($184 Canadian dollars for international students). Electronic applications accepted. *Expenses:* Tuition, state resident: full-time $2869 Canadian dollars; part-time $79.70 Canadian dollars per credit. Tuition, nonresident: full-time $8883 Canadian dollars; part-time $246.76 Canadian dollars per credit. *International tuition:* $19,648 Canadian dollars full-time. *Required fees:* $41.20 Canadian dollars per credit. $67.94 Canadian dollars per term. Tuition and fees vary according to degree level and program. *Financial support:* Research assistantships, teaching assistantships, and scholarships/grants available. Financial award application deadline: 9/2. *Unit head:* Dr. Marie-Helene Jobin, Director, 514-340-6283, E-mail: marie-helene.jobin@hec.ca. *Application contact:* Marianne de Moura, Administrative Director, 514-340-6151, Fax: 514-340-6411, E-mail: aide@hec.ca.
Website: http://www.hec.ca/en/programs/masters/master-finance/index.html

Hofstra University, Frank G. Zarb School of Business, Programs in Finance, Hempstead, NY 11549. Offers business administration (MBA), including finance; corporate finance (Advanced Certificate); finance (MS), including financial and risk management, investment analysis; investment management (Advanced Certificate); quantitative finance (MS). *Program availability:* Part-time, evening/weekend, blended/hybrid learning. *Students:* 157 full-time (55 women), 44 part-time (11 women); includes 23 minority (6 Black or African American, non-Hispanic/Latino; 1 American Indian or Alaska Native, non-Hispanic/Latino; 7 Asian, non-Hispanic/Latino; 8 Hispanic/Latino; 1 Two or more races, non-Hispanic/Latino), 134 international. Average age 25. 530 applicants, 75% accepted, 71 enrolled. In 2017, 103 master's awarded. *Degree requirements:* For master's, capstone course (for MBA), thesis (for MS), minimum GPA of 3.0. *Entrance requirements:* For master's, GMAT/GRE, 2 letters of recommendation, resume, essay. Additional exam requirements/recommendations for international students: Required—TOEFL (minimum score 550 paper-based; 80 iBT); Recommended—IELTS (minimum score 6). *Application deadline:* Applications are processed on a rolling basis. Application fee: $75. Electronic applications accepted. *Expenses:* $1,322 per credit. *Financial support:* In 2017–18, 57 students received support, including 51 fellowships with full and partial tuition reimbursements available (averaging $5,604 per year); research assistantships with full and partial tuition reimbursements available, career-related internships or fieldwork, Federal Work-Study, institutionally sponsored loans, scholarships/grants, tuition waivers (full and partial), and unspecified assistantships also available. Support available to part-time students. Financial award applicants required to submit FAFSA. *Faculty research:* Individual investors and financial crisis; short-sale constraints and futures trading; social media and sentiment in financial markets; external monitoring of firms; CEO inside debt and insider trading. *Unit head:* Dr. K. G. Viswanathan, Chairperson, 516-463-5699, Fax: 516-463-4834, E-mail: k.g.viswanathan@hofstra.edu. *Application contact:* Sunil Samuel, Assistant Vice President of Admissions, 516-463-4723, Fax: 516-463-4664, E-mail: graduateadmission@hofstra.edu.
Website: http://www.hofstra.edu/business/

Holy Family University, Graduate and Professional Programs, School of Business Administration, Philadelphia, PA 19114. Offers accountancy (MS); finance (MBA); health care administration (MBA); human resource management (MBA); information systems management (MBA). *Accreditation:* ACBSP. *Program availability:* Part-time, evening/weekend. *Degree requirements:* For master's, comprehensive exam, thesis optional. *Entrance requirements:* For master's, minimum GPA of 3.0, interview, essay/personal statement, current resume, official transcript of all college or university work. Additional exam requirements/recommendations for international students: Required—TOEFL (minimum score 550 paper-based; 79 iBT), IELTS (minimum score 6), PTE (minimum score 54). Electronic applications accepted. *Expenses: Tuition:* Full-time $13,518; part-time $9012 per credit hour. Tuition and fees vary according to degree level and program.

Holy Names University, Graduate Division, Department of Business, Oakland, CA 94619-1699. Offers finance (MBA); management and leadership (MBA); marketing (MBA). *Program availability:* Part-time, evening/weekend. *Entrance requirements:* For master's, minimum undergraduate GPA of 2.6 overall, 3.0 in major; two recommendations (letter or form) from previous professors or current or previous work supervisors; 1-3 page personal statement; resume. Additional exam requirements/recommendations for international students: Required—TOEFL (minimum score 550 paper-based; 79 iBT). Electronic applications accepted. Application fee is waived when completed online. *Expenses:* Contact institution. *Faculty research:* Business ethics, sustainable economics, accounting models, cross-cultural management, diversity in organizations.

Hood College, Graduate School, Department of Economics and Business Administration, Frederick, MD 21701-8575. Offers accounting (MBA, Certificate); finance (MBA); financial management (Certificate); human resource management (MBA); information systems (MBA); marketing (MBA); organizational management (Certificate); public management (MBA). *Accreditation:* ACBSP. *Program availability:* Part-time, evening/weekend. *Faculty:* 4 full-time (2 women), 7 part-time/adjunct (1 woman). *Students:* 21 full-time (12 women), 91 part-time (47 women); includes 19 minority (8 Black or African American, non-Hispanic/Latino; 3 Asian, non-Hispanic/Latino; 8 Hispanic/Latino), 15 international. Average age 31. 34 applicants, 97% accepted, 23 enrolled. In 2017, 42 master's awarded. *Degree requirements:* For master's, capstone/final research project. *Entrance requirements:* For master's, minimum GPA of 3.0 (or resume and two letters of recommendation), copy of official transcripts, essay. Additional exam requirements/recommendations for international students: Required—TOEFL (minimum score 550 paper-based; 89 iBT), IELTS (minimum score 6.5). *Application deadline:* For fall admission, 8/15 for domestic students, 8/5 for international students; for spring admission, 12/1 for domestic and international students; for summer admission, 5/1 for domestic students, 4/15 for international students. Applications are processed on a rolling basis. Application fee: $35. Electronic applications accepted. *Expenses:* $550 per credit hour plus $110 per semester comprehensive fee. *Financial support:* Tuition waivers (partial) and unspecified assistantships available. Financial award applicants required to submit FAFSA. *Faculty research:* Corporate strategy and sustainable competitive advantages, business ethics, entrepreneurship, investments management, economic development. *Unit head:* Dr. April M. Boulton, Dean of the Graduate School, 301-696-3600, Fax: 301-696-3597, E-mail: gofurther@hood.edu. *Application contact:* Jan Marcus, Assistant Director of Graduate Admissions, 301-696-3603, E-mail: gofurther@hood.edu.

Howard University, School of Business, Graduate Programs in Business, Washington, DC 20059-0002. Offers accounting (MBA); entrepreneurship (MBA); finance (MBA); general management (MBA); human resources management (MBA); information

Finance and Banking

systems (MBA); international business (MBA); marketing (MBA); supply chain management (MBA); JD/MBA. *Accreditation:* AACSB. *Program availability:* Part-time, evening/weekend, online learning. *Entrance requirements:* For master's, GMAT, minimum 1 year post undergraduate work experience, resume, 3 letters of recommendation, advanced college algebra. Additional exam requirements/recommendations for international students: Required—TOEFL. *Faculty research:* Marketing research in multi-ethnic populations, U.S. trade policies and international relations, risk management (finance).

Hult International Business School, Graduate Programs, Cambridge, MA 02141. Offers business administration (EMBA); business analytics (MBA, MIB); business statistics (MBS); disruptive innovation (MDI); entrepreneurship (MBA, MIB); family business (MBA, MIB); finance (MBA, MF, MIB); international marketing (MIM); marketing (MBA, MIB); project management (MBA, MIB). MDI and MBS offered in San Francisco; MBA also offered in Boston, San Francisco, Dubai, Shanghai, and New York. *Entrance requirements:* For master's, GMAT, 3 years of work experience. Additional exam requirements/recommendations for international students: Required—TOEFL. Electronic applications accepted. *Expenses:* Contact institution.

IGlobal University, Graduate Programs, Vienna, VA 22182. Offers accounting (MBA); data management and analytics (MSIT); entrepreneurship (MBA); finance (MBA); global business management (MBA); health care management (MBA); hospitality and tourism management (MBA); human resources management (MBA); information technology (MBA); information technology systems and management (MSIT); leadership and management (MBA); project management (MBA); public service and administration (MBA); software design and management (MSIT).

Illinois Institute of Technology, Chicago-Kent College of Law, Chicago, IL 60661-3691. Offers family law (LL M); financial services law (LL M); international intellectual property law (LL M); law (JD); legal studies (JSD); taxation (LL M); U.S., international, and transnational law (LL M); JD/LL M; JD/MBA; JD/MPA; JD/MPH; JD/MS. *Accreditation:* ABA. *Program availability:* Part-time, evening/weekend. Terminal master's awarded for partial completion of doctoral program. *Entrance requirements:* For master's, 1st degree in law or certified license to practice law; for doctorate, LSAT. Additional exam requirements/recommendations for international students: Required—TOEFL (minimum score 600 paper-based; 100 iBT); Recommended—IELTS (minimum score 7). Electronic applications accepted. *Expenses:* Contact institution. *Faculty research:* Constitutional law, bioethics, environmental law, intellectual property.

Illinois Institute of Technology, Graduate College, College of Science, Department of Computer Science, Chicago, IL 60616. Offers business (MCS); computational intelligence (MCS); computer science (MCS, MS, PhD); cyber-physical systems (MCS); data analytics (MCS); data science (MAS); database systems (MCS); distributed and cloud computing (MCS); education (MCS); finance (MCS); information security and assurance (MCS); networking and communications (MCS); software engineering (MCS); telecommunications and software engineering (MAS); MS/MAS. *Program availability:* Part-time, evening/weekend, online learning. Terminal master's awarded for partial completion of doctoral program. *Degree requirements:* For master's, thesis optional; for doctorate, comprehensive exam, thesis/dissertation. *Entrance requirements:* For master's, GRE General Test with minimum scores of 298 Quantitative and Verbal, 3.0 Analytical Writing (for MS; GRE General Test with minimum scores of 292 Quantitative and Verbal, 2.5 Analytical Writing (for MAS), minimum undergraduate GPA of 3.0; for doctorate, GRE General Test (minimum scores: 304 Quantitative and Verbal, 3.5 Analytical Writing), minimum undergraduate GPA of 3.0. Additional exam requirements/recommendations for international students: Required—TOEFL (minimum score 523 paper-based; 70 iBT). Electronic applications accepted. *Faculty research:* Parallel and distributed processing, high-performance computing, computational linguistics, information retrieval, data mining, grid computing.

Illinois Institute of Technology, Stuart School of Business, Program in Finance, Chicago, IL 60661. Offers MS, JD/MS, MBA/MS. *Program availability:* Part-time, evening/weekend. *Entrance requirements:* For master's, GRE (minimum score 1200) or GMAT (600). Additional exam requirements/recommendations for international students: Required—TOEFL (minimum score 600 paper-based; 85 iBT); Recommended—IELTS (minimum score 7). Electronic applications accepted. *Expenses:* Contact institution. *Faculty research:* Factor models for investment management, credit rating and credit risk management, hedge fund performance analysis, option trading and risk management, global asset allocation strategies.

Indiana University Bloomington, School of Public and Environmental Affairs, Public Affairs Programs, Bloomington, IN 47405. Offers economic development (MPA); energy (MPA); environmental policy (PhD); environmental policy and natural resource management (MPA); information systems (MPA); international development (MPA); local government management (MPA); nonprofit management (MPA, Certificate); policy analysis (MPA); public budgeting and financial management (Certificate); public finance (PhD); public financial administration (MPA); public management (MPA, PhD, Certificate); public policy analysis (PhD); social entrepreneurship (Certificate); specialized public affairs (MPA); sustainability and sustainable development (MPA); JD/MPA; MPA/MA; MPA/MIS; MPA/MLS; MSES/MPA. *Accreditation:* NASPAA (one or more programs are accredited). *Program availability:* Part-time. *Degree requirements:* For master's, capstone, internship; for doctorate, comprehensive exam, thesis/dissertation. *Entrance requirements:* For master's, GRE General Test or GMAT, official transcripts, 3 letters of recommendation, resume, personal statement; for doctorate, GRE General Test, official transcripts, 3 letters of recommendation, statement of purpose. Additional exam requirements/recommendations for international students: Required—TOEFL (minimum score 600 paper-based; 96 iBT); Recommended—IELTS (minimum score 7). Electronic applications accepted. *Faculty research:* International development, environmental policy and resource management, policy analysis, public finance, public management, urban management, nonprofit management, energy policy, social policy, public finance.

Indiana University–Purdue University Indianapolis, Kelley School of Business, Evening MBA Program, Indianapolis, IN 46202-5151. Offers accounting (MBA); entrepreneurship (MBA); finance (MBA); general administration (MBA); marketing (MBA); supply chain management (MBA); MBA/JD; MBA/MD; MBA/MHA; MBA/MS; MBA/MSA; MBA/MSE. *Program availability:* Part-time-only, evening/weekend, online learning. *Entrance requirements:* For master's, GMAT or GRE, 2 years of professional work experience. Additional exam requirements/recommendations for international students: Required—TOEFL or IELTS. Electronic applications accepted. *Expenses:* Contact institution. *Faculty research:* Entrepreneurship; corporate finance; international business; consumer behavior; supply chain; business law.

Indiana University South Bend, Judd Leighton School of Business and Economics, South Bend, IN 46615. Offers accounting (MSA); business (Graduate Certificate); business administration (MBA), including finance, human resource management, marketing; MBA/MSA. *Program availability:* Part-time, evening/weekend. *Entrance requirements:* For master's, GMAT. Additional exam requirements/recommendations for international students: Required—TOEFL (minimum score 550 paper-based; 79 iBT). Electronic applications accepted. *Expenses:* Contact institution. *Faculty research:* Financial accounting, consumer research, capital budgeting research, business strategy research.

Indiana University Southeast, School of Business, New Albany, IN 47150-6405. Offers business administration (MBA); strategic finance (MS). *Accreditation:* AACSB. *Program availability:* Part-time. *Degree requirements:* For master's, community service. *Entrance requirements:* For master's, GMAT, work experience. Additional exam requirements/recommendations for international students: Required—TOEFL.

Instituto Centroamericano de Administración de Empresas, Graduate Programs, La Garita, Costa Rica. Offers agribusiness management (MIAM); business administration (EMBA); finance (MBA); real estate management (MGREM); sustainable development (MBA); technology (MBA). *Degree requirements:* For master's, comprehensive exam, essay. *Entrance requirements:* For master's, GMAT or GRE General Test, fluency in Spanish, interview, letters of recommendation, minimum 1 year of work experience. Additional exam requirements/recommendations for international students: Recommended—TOEFL. Electronic applications accepted. *Faculty research:* Competitiveness, production.

Instituto Tecnologico de Santo Domingo, Graduate School, Area of Business, Santo Domingo, Dominican Republic. Offers banking and securities markets (M Mgmt); corporate finance (M Mgmt); human resources management (M Mgmt, Certificate); international trade management (M Mgmt); marketing (M Mgmt); organizational development (M Mgmt); quality and productivity management (Certificate); tax management and planning (M Mgmt); upper management (M Mgmt).

Instituto Tecnológico y de Estudios Superiores de Monterrey, Campus Central de Veracruz, Graduate Programs, Córdoba, Mexico. Offers administration (MA); administration of information technologies (MTI); computer sciences (MCC); education (MEE); educational institution administration (MAD); educational technology (MTE); electronic commerce (MCE); finance (MAF); humanistic studies (MEH); international business for Latin America (MNL); marketing (MMT); science (MCP). *Program availability:* Part-time, evening/weekend, online learning. *Degree requirements:* For master's, thesis (for some programs). *Entrance requirements:* For master's, PAEP College Board. Electronic applications accepted.

Instituto Tecnológico y de Estudios Superiores de Monterrey, Campus Ciudad de México, School of Business Administration, Ciudad de Mexico, Mexico. Offers business administration (EMBA, MBA, PhD); economy (MBA); finance (MBA). EMBA program offered jointly with The University of Texas at Austin. *Program availability:* Part-time, evening/weekend, online learning. *Entrance requirements:* For master's and doctorate, Instituto entrance exam. Additional exam requirements/recommendations for international students: Required—TOEFL.

Instituto Tecnológico y de Estudios Superiores de Monterrey, Campus Ciudad Obregón, Program in Finance, Ciudad Obregón, Mexico. Offers MF.

Instituto Tecnológico y de Estudios Superiores de Monterrey, Campus Cuernavaca, Programs in Business Administration, Temixco, Mexico. Offers finance (MA); human resources management (MA); international business (MA); marketing (MA).

Instituto Tecnológico y de Estudios Superiores de Monterrey, Campus Estado de México, Professional and Graduate Division, Estado de Mexico, Mexico. Offers administration of information technologies (MITA); architecture (M Arch); business administration (GMBA, MBA); computer sciences (MCS, PhD); education (M Ed); educational institution administration (MAD); educational technology and innovation (PhD); electronic commerce (MEC); environmental systems (MS); finance (MAF); humanistic studies (MHS); information sciences and knowledge management (MISKM); information systems (MS); manufacturing systems (MS); marketing (MEM); quality systems and productivity (MS); science and materials engineering (PhD); telecommunications management (MTM). *Program availability:* Part-time, online learning. *Degree requirements:* For master's, one foreign language, thesis (for some programs); for doctorate, one foreign language, thesis/dissertation. *Entrance requirements:* For master's, E-PAEP 500, interview; for doctorate, E-PAEP 500, research proposal. Additional exam requirements/recommendations for international students: Required—TOEFL (minimum score 550 paper-based). *Faculty research:* Surface treatments by plasmas, mechanical properties, robotics, graphical computing, mechatronics security protocols.

Instituto Tecnológico y de Estudios Superiores de Monterrey, Campus Guadalajara, Program in Finance, Zapopan, Mexico. Offers MF. *Degree requirements:* For master's, one foreign language, thesis. *Entrance requirements:* For master's, ITESM admission test.

Instituto Tecnológico y de Estudios Superiores de Monterrey, Campus Irapuato, Graduate Programs, Irapuato, Mexico. Offers administration (MBA); administration of information technology (MAIT); administration of telecommunications (MAT); architecture (M Arch); computer science (MCS); education (M Ed); educational administration (MEA); educational innovation and technology (DEIT); educational technology (MET); electronic commerce (MBA); environmental administration and planning (MEAP); environmental systems (MES); finances (MBA); humanistic studies (MHS); international management for Latin American executives (MIMLAE); library and information science (MLIS); manufacturing quality management (MMQM); marketing research (MBA).

Instituto Tecnológico y de Estudios Superiores de Monterrey, Campus Monterrey, Graduate School of Business Administration and Leadership, Program in Business Administration, Monterrey, Mexico. Offers business administration (MA, MBA); finance (M Sc); international business (M Sc); marketing (M Sc). *Program availability:* Part-time. *Degree requirements:* For master's, one foreign language, thesis. *Entrance requirements:* For master's, GMAT. Additional exam requirements/recommendations for international students: Required—TOEFL. *Faculty research:* Technology management, quality management, organizational theory and behavior.

Inter American University of Puerto Rico, Aguadilla Campus, Graduate School, Aguadilla, PR 00605. Offers accounting (MBA); counseling psychology specializing in family (MS); criminal justice (MA); educative management and leadership (MA); elementary education (M Ed); finance (MBA); human resources (MBA); industrial management (MBA); management information systems (MBA); marketing (MBA). *Program availability:* Part-time, evening/weekend. *Degree requirements:* For master's, comprehensive exam. *Entrance requirements:* For master's, EXADEP, 2 letters of recommendation, minimum GPA of 2.5. Electronic applications accepted.

Inter American University of Puerto Rico, Arecibo Campus, Program in Business Administration, Arecibo, PR 00614-4050. Offers accounting (MBA); finance (MBA); human resources (MBA).

Inter American University of Puerto Rico, Metropolitan Campus, Graduate Programs, Program in Finance, San Juan, PR 00919-1293. Offers MBA. *Degree requirements:* For master's, comprehensive exam. *Entrance requirements:* For master's, GRE or EXADEP, interview. Electronic applications accepted.

Inter American University of Puerto Rico, Ponce Campus, Graduate School, Mercedita, PR 00715-1602. Offers accounting (MBA); biology (M Ed); chemistry (M Ed); criminal justice (MA); elementary education (M Ed); English as a Second Language (M Ed); finance (MBA); history (M Ed); human resources (MBA); marketing (MBA); mathematics (M Ed); Spanish (M Ed). *Entrance requirements:* For master's, minimum GPA of 2.5.

Inter American University of Puerto Rico, San Germán Campus, Graduate Studies Center, Program in Business Administration, San Germán, PR 00683-5008. Offers accounting (MBA); finance (MBA); general business administration (MBA); human resources (MBA, PhD); industrial relations (MBA); information systems (MBA); international and interregional business (PhD); management (MBA); marketing (MBA). *Program availability:* Part-time, evening/weekend. *Degree requirements:* For master's, comprehensive exam. *Entrance requirements:* For master's, GRE General Test or EXADEP, minimum GPA of 3.0.

The International University of Monaco, Graduate Programs, Monte Carlo, Monaco. Offers entrepreneurship (EMBA, MBA); financial engineering (M Sc); hedge fund and private equity (M Sc); international marketing (EMBA, MBA); international wealth management (M Sc); luxury goods and services (EMBA, M Sc, MBA); wealth and asset management (EMBA, MBA). *Program availability:* Part-time. *Degree requirements:* For master's, comprehensive exam (for some programs), applied research project. *Entrance requirements:* Additional exam requirements/recommendations for international students: Required—TOEFL (minimum score 550 paper-based), IELTS. Electronic applications accepted. *Faculty research:* Gaming, leadership, disintermediation.

Iona College, School of Business, Department of Finance, Business Economics and Legal Studies, New Rochelle, NY 10801-1890. Offers finance (MS); financial management (MBA, PMC); financial services (MS); international finance (MS). *Program availability:* Part-time, evening/weekend. *Faculty:* 7 full-time (3 women), 4 part-time/adjunct (1 woman). *Students:* 33 full-time (10 women), 31 part-time (15 women); includes 21 minority (8 Black or African American, non-Hispanic/Latino; 1 American Indian or Alaska Native, non-Hispanic/Latino; 3 Asian, non-Hispanic/Latino; 9 Hispanic/Latino), 6 international. Average age 27. 23 applicants, 91% accepted, 15 enrolled. In 2017, 88 master's awarded. *Entrance requirements:* For master's, GMAT, 2 letters of recommendation, minimum GPA of 3.0; for PMC, minimum GPA of 3.0. Additional exam requirements/recommendations for international students: Required—TOEFL (minimum score 550 paper-based; 80 iBT), IELTS (minimum score 6.5). *Application deadline:* For fall admission, 8/15 priority date for domestic students, 8/1 priority date for international students; for winter admission, 11/15 priority date for domestic students, 11/1 priority date for international students; for spring admission, 2/15 priority date for domestic students, 2/1 priority date for international students; for summer admission, 5/15 priority date for domestic students, 5/1 priority date for international students. Applications are processed on a rolling basis. Application fee: $50. Electronic applications accepted. *Expenses:* Contact institution. *Financial support:* In 2017–18, 15 students received support. Scholarships/grants, tuition waivers (partial), and unspecified assistantships available. Support available to part-time students. Financial award application deadline: 4/15; financial award applicants required to submit FAFSA. *Faculty research:* Options, insurance financing, asset depreciation ranges, international finance, emerging markets. *Unit head:* Dr. John F. Manley, Department Chair, 914-633-2284, E-mail: jmanley@iona.edu. *Application contact:* Katelyn Brunck, Director of MBA Admissions, 914-633-2451, Fax: 914-633-2277, E-mail: kbrunck@iona.edu.
Website: http://www.iona.edu/Academics/Hagan-School-of-Business/Departments/Finance-Business-Economics-Legal-Studies/Graduate-Programs.aspx

Iowa State University of Science and Technology, Program in Finance, Ames, IA 50011. Offers M Fin. *Entrance requirements:* For master's, GMAT, GRE Writing Test, minimum undergraduate GPA of 3.25, resume, three letters of recommendation, personal essay. Additional exam requirements/recommendations for international students: Required—TOEFL (minimum score 600 paper-based; 100 iBT), IELTS (minimum score 7). *Expenses:* Contact institution.

Jacksonville University, Davis College of Business, Accelerated Day-time MBA Program, Jacksonville, FL 32211. Offers accounting and finance (MBA); business administration (MBA); consumer goods and services marketing (MBA); management (MBA); management accounting (MBA). *Faculty:* 5 full-time (2 women). *Students:* 43 full-time (17 women), 7 part-time (2 women); includes 9 minority (4 Black or African American, non-Hispanic/Latino; 4 Hispanic/Latino; 1 Two or more races, non-Hispanic/Latino), 18 international. Average age 26. 70 applicants, 90% accepted, 44 enrolled. In 2017, 42 master's awarded. *Entrance requirements:* For master's, GMAT or GRE, bachelor's degree from regionally-accredited institution, original transcripts of academic work, statement of intent, resume, 3 letters of recommendation; 3 years of work experience (recommended); interview with program advisor. Additional exam requirements/recommendations for international students: Required—TOEFL (minimum score 550 paper-based; 79 iBT), IELTS (minimum score 6), PTE (minimum score 53). *Application deadline:* For fall admission, 7/1 priority date for domestic students, 6/15 priority date for international students; for spring admission, 12/1 priority date for domestic students, 11/15 priority date for international students; for summer admission, 4/1 for domestic students, 3/15 for international students. Applications are processed on a rolling basis. Application fee: $50. Electronic applications accepted. *Expenses:* $793 per credit hour; $150-$250 books per course (estimated). *Financial support:* Scholarships/grants, health care benefits, and unspecified assistantships available. Financial award application deadline: 6/30; financial award applicants required to submit FAFSA. *Faculty research:* Behavioral finance, game theory, regional economic integration, information sabotage, public choice and public finance. *Unit head:* Dr. Douglas Johansen, Associate Dean and Graduate Programs Director, 904-256-7763, Fax: 904-256-7168, E-mail: djohans@ju.edu. *Application contact:* AnnaMaria Murphy, Assistant Director of Graduate Admissions, 904-256-7426, Fax: 904-256-7012, E-mail: mba@ju.edu.

See Display on page 104 and Close-Up on page 175.

Jacksonville University, Davis College of Business, FLEX Master of Business Administration Program, Jacksonville, FL 32211. Offers accounting and finance (MBA); business management (MBA); consumer goods and services marketing (MBA); management (MBA); management accounting (MBA); JD/MBA; MBA/MPP; MSN/MBA. MBA/JD offered jointly with Florida School of Law; MSN/MBA offered jointly with JU's Keigwin School of Nursing; MBA/MPP offered jointly with JU's Public Policy Institute. *Accreditation:* AACSB. *Program availability:* Part-time, evening/weekend, blended/hybrid learning. *Faculty:* 23 full-time (8 women), 4 part-time/adjunct (2 women). *Students:* 32 full-time (7 women), 80 part-time (30 women); includes 34 minority (15 Black or African American, non-Hispanic/Latino; 1 American Indian or Alaska Native, non-Hispanic/Latino; 6 Asian, non-Hispanic/Latino; 10 Hispanic/Latino; 2 Two or more races, non-Hispanic/Latino), 2 international. Average age 33. 43 applicants, 91% accepted, 32 enrolled. In 2017, 56 master's awarded. *Entrance requirements:* For master's, GMAT or GRE, bachelor's degree from regionally-accredited institution, 3 years of full-time work experience (recommended), resume, statement of intent, 3 letters of recommendation, interview with program advisor. Additional exam requirements/recommendations for international students: Required—TOEFL (minimum score 550 paper-based; 79 iBT), IELTS (minimum score 6), PTE (minimum score 53). *Application deadline:* For fall admission, 7/1 priority date for domestic students, 6/15 priority date for international students; for spring admission, 12/1 priority date for domestic students, 11/15 priority date for international students; for summer admission, 4/1 priority date for domestic students, 3/15 priority date for international students. Applications are processed on a rolling basis. Application fee: $50. Electronic applications accepted. *Expenses:* $793 per credit hour; $150-$250 books per course (estimated). *Financial support:* Scholarships/grants and health care benefits available. Financial award application deadline: 6/30; financial award applicants required to submit FAFSA. *Faculty research:* Downsizing with integrity; impact of YouTube videos; game theory; analysis of effective tax rates; creativity innovation and change. *Unit head:* Dr. Douglas Johansen, Associate Dean and Director of Graduate Studies, 904-256-7763, Fax: 904-256-7168, E-mail: djohans@ju.edu. *Application contact:* AnnaMaria Murphy, Assistant Director of Graduate Admissions, 904-256-7426, Fax: 904-256-7012, E-mail: mba@ju.edu.

See Display on page 104 and Close-Up on page 175.

Johns Hopkins University, Carey Business School, Certificate Programs, Baltimore, MD 21218. Offers financial management (Certificate); investments (Certificate). *Program availability:* Part-time, evening/weekend. *Faculty:* 93 full-time (33 women), 45 part-time/adjunct (11 women). *Students:* 19 part-time (10 women); includes 7 minority (2 Black or African American, non-Hispanic/Latino; 2 Asian, non-Hispanic/Latino; 2 Hispanic/Latino; 1 Two or more races, non-Hispanic/Latino), 3 international. Average age 34. 12 applicants, 83% accepted, 3 enrolled. In 2017, 31 Certificates awarded. *Degree requirements:* For Certificate, 16 credits. *Entrance requirements:* Additional exam requirements/recommendations for international students: Required—TOEFL, IELTS. *Application deadline:* Applications are processed on a rolling basis. Application fee: $100. Electronic applications accepted. *Expenses:* Contact institution. *Unit head:* Dr. Kevin Frick, Vice Dean of Education, 410-234-9272, E-mail: kfrick@jhu.edu. *Application contact:* Office of Admissions, 410-234-9220, Fax: 443-529-1554, E-mail: carey.admissions@jhu.edu.
Website: http://carey.jhu.edu/academics/certificate-programs/

Johns Hopkins University, Carey Business School, MS in Finance Program, Baltimore, MD 21218. Offers finance (MS). *Program availability:* Part-time, evening/weekend, blended/hybrid learning, on-site residency requirement. *Faculty:* 93 full-time (33 women), 45 part-time/adjunct (11 women). *Students:* 489 full-time (262 women), 122 part-time (33 women); includes 58 minority (22 Black or African American, non-Hispanic/Latino; 22 Asian, non-Hispanic/Latino; 10 Hispanic/Latino; 4 Two or more races, non-Hispanic/Latino), 485 international. Average age 23. 2,340 applicants, 69% accepted, 521 enrolled. In 2017, 526 master's awarded. *Degree requirements:* For master's, 36 credits. *Entrance requirements:* For master's, GMAT or GRE. Additional exam requirements/recommendations for international students: Required—TOEFL, IELTS. *Application deadline:* For fall admission, 4/3 for domestic and international students. Applications are processed on a rolling basis. Application fee: $100. Electronic applications accepted. *Expenses:* $66,500 (full-time); $1,330 per credit (part-time). *Financial support:* In 2017–18, 26 students received support. Scholarships/grants available. Support available to part-time students. Financial award application deadline: 4/15; financial award applicants required to submit FAFSA. *Faculty research:* Derivatives, financial institutions, fixed income securities, international finance, investments. *Unit head:* Dr. Kevin Frick, Vice Dean of Education, 410-234-9272, E-mail: kfrick@jhu.edu. *Application contact:* Office of Admissions, 410-234-9220, Fax: 443-529-1554, E-mail: carey.admissions@jhu.edu.
Website: http://carey.jhu.edu/academics/master-of-science/ms-in-finance

Johns Hopkins University, School of Advanced International Studies, Washington, DC 20036. Offers global risk (MA); international development (MA, Certificate), including international economics (MA); international economics (Certificate); international economics and finance (MA); international public policy (MIPP); international relations (PhD); international studies (Certificate); Japan studies (MA), including international economics; Korea studies (MA), including international economics; South Asia studies (MA), including international economics; Southeast Asia studies (MA), including international economics; JD/MA; MBA/MA; MHS/MA. Terminal master's awarded for partial completion of doctoral program. *Degree requirements:* For master's, 4-6 international economics courses, 5-6 functional or regional concentration courses, 2 core examinations, proficiency in language other than native language, capstone project; for doctorate, 2 foreign languages, thesis/dissertation, 3 comprehensive exams, economics, quantitative and qualitative course, dissertation prospectus and defense. *Entrance requirements:* For master's, GMAT or GRE General Test, previous course work in economics, foreign language, undergraduate degree; for doctorate, GRE General Test, master's degree. Additional exam requirements/recommendations for international students: Required—TOEFL (minimum score 600 paper-based; 100 iBT) or IELTS (minimum score 7). Electronic applications accepted. *Expenses:* Contact institution. *Faculty research:* International economics; international relations/regional studies; international development; energy, resources, and environment; international security/strategic studies.

Johnson & Wales University, Graduate Studies, MBA Program, Providence, RI 02903-3703. Offers accounting (MBA); business administration (MBA); finance (MBA); global fashion merchandising and management (MBA); hospitality (MBA); human resource management (MBA); information security/assurance (MBA); information technology (MBA); nonprofit management (MBA); operations and supply chain management (MBA); organizational leadership (MBA); organizational psychology (MBA); sport leadership (MBA). Program also offered on Denver campus. *Program availability:* Part-time, online learning. *Entrance requirements:* For master's, minimum GPA of 2.75. Additional exam requirements/recommendations for international students: Required—TOEFL (minimum score 550 paper-based); Recommended—IELTS, TWE. *Application deadline:* For fall admission, 8/15 priority date for domestic students, 6/28 priority date for international students; for winter admission, 11/10 priority date for domestic students, 9/20 priority date for international students; for spring admission, 2/5 priority date for domestic students, 12/20 priority date for international students. Applications are processed on a rolling basis. *Expenses: Tuition:* Full-time $12,636; part-time $702 per credit hour. *Financial support:* Tuition waivers (partial) and unspecified assistantships available. Support available to part-time students. Financial award application deadline: 5/1. *Faculty research:* International banking, global economy, international trade, cultural differences. *Unit head:* Dr. Karen Silva, Director, 401-598-2849, Fax: 401-598-1125. *Application contact:* Graduate School Admissions, 401-598-1015, Fax: 401-598-1286, E-mail: gradadm@jwu.edu.

Johnson & Wales University, Graduate Studies, MS Program in Finance, Providence, RI 02903-3703. Offers MS. *Program availability:* Online learning. *Expenses: Tuition:* Full-time $12,636; part-time $702 per credit hour. *Unit head:* Dr. Karen Silva, Director, 401-598-2849, Fax: 401-598-1125. *Application contact:* Graduate School Admissions, 401-598-1015, Fax: 401-598-1286, E-mail: pvdgrad@admissions.jwu.edu.
Website: https://www.jwu.edu/academics/programs-by-campus/providence-programs/finance-ms.html

Kansas State University, Graduate School, College of Business, Program in Business Administration, Manhattan, KS 66506. Offers data analytics (MBA); finance (MBA); management (MBA); marketing (MBA); technology entrepreneurship (MBA). *Accreditation:* AACSB. *Program availability:* Part-time, 100% online. *Entrance requirements:* For master's, GMAT (minimum score of 500), minimum undergraduate GPA of 3.0. Additional exam requirements/recommendations for international students: Required—TOEFL (minimum score 550 paper-based; 79 iBT); Recommended—IELTS (minimum score 7). Electronic applications accepted. *Expenses:* Contact institution. *Faculty research:* Organizational citizenship behavior, service marketing, impression management, human resources management, lean manufacturing and supply chain management, financial market behavior and investment management, data analytics, corporate responsibility, technology entrepreneurship.

Finance and Banking

Kansas State University, Graduate School, College of Human Ecology, School of Family Studies and Human Services, Manhattan, KS 66506-1403. Offers applied family sciences (MS); communication sciences and disorders (MS); conflict resolution (Graduate Certificate); couple and family therapy (MS); early childhood education (MS); family and community service (MS); life-span human development (MS); personal financial planning (MS, PhD, Graduate Certificate); youth development (MS, Graduate Certificate). *Accreditation:* AAMFT/COAMFTE; ASHA. *Program availability:* Part-time, online learning. *Degree requirements:* For master's, comprehensive exam (for some programs), thesis optional. *Entrance requirements:* For master's, GRE, minimum GPA of 3.0 in last 2 years (60 semester hours) of undergraduate study; for doctorate, GRE. Additional exam requirements/recommendations for international students: Required—TOEFL (minimum score 600 paper-based). Electronic applications accepted. *Faculty research:* Health and security of military families, training in and evaluation of professional human services (marriage and couple therapy, family life education, treatment of speech and swallowing disorders, financial therapy), disorders of communication and swallowing, family and relationship development and health, financial decision-making.

Kent State University, College of Business Administration, Doctoral Program in Finance, Kent, OH 44242-0001. Offers PhD. *Faculty:* 8 full-time (3 women). *Students:* 15 full-time (6 women), 13 international. Average age 33. 18 applicants, 22% accepted, 2 enrolled. *Degree requirements:* For doctorate, comprehensive exam, thesis/dissertation, oral defense. *Entrance requirements:* For doctorate, GMAT or GRE. Additional exam requirements/recommendations for international students: Required—TOEFL (minimum score 600 paper-based; 100 iBT), IELTS (minimum score 7). *Application deadline:* For fall admission, 1/1 for domestic students, 2/1 for international students. Application fee: $45 ($70 for international students). Electronic applications accepted. *Expenses:* $11,330 per academic year. *Financial support:* In 2017–18, 11 students received support, including 11 teaching assistantships with full tuition reimbursements available (averaging $23,000 per year). Financial award application deadline: 2/1; financial award applicants required to submit FAFSA. *Faculty research:* Corporate finance, investments, international finance, futures and options, risk and insurance. *Unit head:* Steven Dennis, Chair and Associate Professor, 330-672-2426, Fax: 330-672-9806, E-mail: sdenni14@kent.edu. *Application contact:* Felecia A. Urbanek, Assistant Director, 330-672-2282, Fax: 330-672-7303, E-mail: gradbus@kent.edu.
Website: http://www.kent.edu/business/phd

King University, School of Business and Economics, Bristol, TN 37620-2699. Offers accounting (MBA); finance (MBA); healthcare management (MBA); human resources management (MBA); leadership (MBA); management (MBA); marketing (MBA); project management (MBA). *Program availability:* Part-time, evening/weekend, online learning. *Degree requirements:* For master's, comprehensive exam, thesis optional. *Entrance requirements:* For master's, GMAT, 2 years of work experience. Additional exam requirements/recommendations for international students: Required—TOEFL (minimum score 550 paper-based). Electronic applications accepted. *Faculty research:* International monetary policy.

Lake Forest Graduate School of Management, The Leadership MBA Program, Lake Forest, IL 60045. Offers finance (MBA); global business (MBA); healthcare management (MBA); management (MBA); marketing (MBA); organizational behavior (MBA). *Program availability:* Part-time, evening/weekend. *Entrance requirements:* For master's, 4 years of work experience in field, interview, 2 letters of recommendation. Electronic applications accepted.

Lakeland University, Graduate Studies Division, Program in Business Administration, Plymouth, WI 53073. Offers accounting (MBA); finance (MBA); healthcare management (MBA); project management (MBA). *Entrance requirements:* For master's, GMAT. *Expenses:* Contact institution.

La Salle University, School of Business, Master of Business Administration Program, Philadelphia, PA 19141-1199. Offers accounting (MBA, Post-MBA Certificate); business systems and analytics (MBA, Post-MBA Certificate); finance (MBA, Post-MBA Certificate); general business administration (MBA, Post-MBA Certificate); human resource management (MBA, Post-MBA Certificate); management (MBA, Post-MBA Certificate); marketing (Post-MBA Certificate); MBA/MSN. Program also offered in Switzerland. *Accreditation:* AACSB. *Program availability:* Part-time, evening/weekend, online learning. *Faculty:* 22 full-time (10 women), 10 part-time/adjunct (3 women). *Students:* 59 full-time (25 women), 200 part-time (109 women); includes 66 minority (36 Black or African American, non-Hispanic/Latino; 21 Asian, non-Hispanic/Latino; 7 Hispanic/Latino; 2 Two or more races, non-Hispanic/Latino), 22 international. Average age 31. 216 applicants, 57% accepted, 74 enrolled. In 2017, 146 master's awarded. *Entrance requirements:* For master's, GMAT or GRE, two letters of reference; resume; for Post-MBA Certificate, MBA with minimum GPA of 3.0. Additional exam requirements/recommendations for international students: Required—TOEFL. *Application deadline:* For fall admission, 8/15 priority date for domestic students, 7/15 for international students; for spring admission, 12/15 priority date for domestic students, 11/15 for international students; for summer admission, 4/15 priority date for domestic students, 3/15 for international students. Applications are processed on a rolling basis. Application fee: $35. Electronic applications accepted. Application fee is waived when completed online. *Expenses:* Contact institution. *Financial support:* In 2017–18, 51 students received support. Scholarships/grants available. Support available to part-time students. Financial award application deadline: 8/31; financial award applicants required to submit FAFSA. *Unit head:* Dr. MarySheila McDonald, Interim Dean, 215-951-1040, Fax: 215-951-1886, E-mail: mcdonaldms@lasalle.edu. *Application contact:* Elizabeth Heenan, Director, Graduate and Adult Enrollment, 215-951-1100, Fax: 215-951-1462, E-mail: heenan@lasalle.edu.

La Sierra University, School of Business and Management, Riverside, CA 92505. Offers accounting (MBA); finance (MBA); general management (MBA); human resources management (MBA); leadership, values, and ethics for business and management (Certificate); marketing (MBA). *Degree requirements:* For master's, research project. *Entrance requirements:* For master's, GMAT, minimum GPA of 3.0. Additional exam requirements/recommendations for international students: Required—TOEFL. *Faculty research:* Financial econometrics, institutional assessment and strategic planning, legal issues in management, behavioral finance, content of financial reports.

Lawrence Technological University, College of Management, Southfield, MI 48075-1058. Offers business administration (MBA, DBA), including business analytics (MBA, MS), cybersecurity (MBA, MS), finance (MBA), information systems (MBA), information technology (MBA), marketing (MBA), project management (MBA, MS); cybersecurity (Graduate Certificate); health IT management (Graduate Certificate); information assurance mangement (Graduate Certificate); information systems (MS), including enterprise resource planning, enterprise security management, project management (MBA, MS); information technology (MS, DM), including business analytics (MBA, MS), cybersecurity (MBA, MS), information assurance (MS), project management (MBA, MS); management (PhD); nonprofit management and leadership (Graduate Certificate); operations management (MS), including manufacturing operations, service operations; project management (Graduate Certificate). *Accreditation:* ACBSP. *Program availability:*

Part-time, evening/weekend, 100% online. *Faculty:* 13 full-time (6 women), 7 part-time/adjunct (1 woman). *Students:* 8 full-time (3 women), 280 part-time (102 women); includes 70 minority (34 Black or African American, non-Hispanic/Latino; 2 American Indian or Alaska Native, non-Hispanic/Latino; 18 Asian, non-Hispanic/Latino; 11 Hispanic/Latino; 5 Two or more races, non-Hispanic/Latino), 73 international. Average age 34. 143 applicants, 50% accepted, 68 enrolled. In 2017, 114 master's, 7 doctorates, 10 other advanced degrees awarded. Terminal master's awarded for partial completion of doctoral program. *Degree requirements:* For master's, thesis (for some programs); for doctorate, comprehensive exam, thesis/dissertation. *Entrance requirements:* Additional exam requirements/recommendations for international students: Required—TOEFL (minimum score 550 paper-based; 79 iBT), IELTS (minimum score 6.5). *Application deadline:* For fall admission, 5/27 for international students; for spring admission, 10/8 for international students; for summer admission, 2/14 for international students. Applications are processed on a rolling basis. Application fee: $50. Electronic applications accepted. *Expenses: Tuition:* Full-time $15,274; part-time $1091 per credit. One-time fee: $150. *Financial support:* In 2017–18, 35 students received support, including 8 research assistantships with partial tuition reimbursements available (averaging $3,360 per year); career-related internships or fieldwork, unspecified assistantships, and corporate tuition incentives also available. Financial award application deadline: 4/1; financial award applicants required to submit FAFSA. *Faculty research:* Cybersecurity; risk management; IT governance; security controls and countermeasures; threat modeling cyber resilience; autonomous cars; natural language processing; text mining; machine learning; reflective leadership; emerging leadership theories and practice; motivational studies; teaching effectiveness strategies; teamwork; organization development; strategic planning; strengths-based and positive organizational scholarship; global leadership; globalization; corporate governance. *Unit head:* Dr. Bahman Mirshab, Dean, 248-204-3050, E-mail: mgtdean@ltu.edu. *Application contact:* Jane Rohrback, Director of Admissions, 248-204-3160, Fax: 248-204-2228, E-mail: admissions@ltu.edu.
Website: http://www.ltu.edu/management/index.asp

Lehigh University, College of Business and Economics, Department of Finance, Bethlehem, PA 18015. Offers analytical finance (MS). *Faculty:* 6 full-time (1 woman). *Students:* 60 full-time (30 women), 1 (woman) part-time, 59 international. Average age 23. 278 applicants, 42% accepted, 24 enrolled. In 2017, 41 master's awarded. *Degree requirements:* For master's, capstone project. *Entrance requirements:* For master's, GMAT or GRE, bachelor's degree from a mathematically rigorous program, minimum GPA of 3.0. Additional exam requirements/recommendations for international students: Required—TOEFL (minimum score 600 paper-based; 94 iBT), IELTS (minimum score 7). *Application deadline:* For fall admission, 7/15 for domestic students, 4/15 for international students. Application fee: $75. Electronic applications accepted. *Financial support:* Fellowships, research assistantships, teaching assistantships, and health care benefits available. *Total annual research expenditures:* $334,916. *Unit head:* Nandu Nayar, Department Chair, 610-758-4161, E-mail: nan2@lehigh.edu. *Application contact:* Michael Tarantino, Director of Recruitment and Admissions, 610-758-3418, Fax: 610-758-5283, E-mail: mgt215@lehigh.edu.
Website: http://www4.lehigh.edu/business/academics/depts/finance

Lewis University, College of Business, Program in Business Administration, Romeoville, IL 60446. Offers accounting (MBA); custom elective option (MBA); e-business (MBA); finance (MBA); healthcare management (MBA); human resources management (MBA); international business (MBA); management information systems (MBA); marketing (MBA); project management (MBA); technology and operations management (MBA). *Program availability:* Part-time, evening/weekend. *Students:* 130 full-time (77 women), 187 part-time (107 women); includes 83 minority (27 Black or African American, non-Hispanic/Latino; 3 American Indian or Alaska Native, non-Hispanic/Latino; 7 Asian, non-Hispanic/Latino; 40 Hispanic/Latino; 6 Two or more races, non-Hispanic/Latino), 31 international. Average age 31. In 2017, 99 master's awarded. *Degree requirements:* For master's, comprehensive exam. *Entrance requirements:* For master's, interview, bachelor's degree, resume, two recommendations. Additional exam requirements/recommendations for international students: Required—TOEFL (minimum score 550 paper-based), IELTS. *Application deadline:* For fall admission, 8/15 priority date for domestic students, 5/1 priority date for international students; for spring admission, 11/15 priority date for international students. Applications are processed on a rolling basis. Application fee: $40. Electronic applications accepted. Tuition and fees vary according to program. *Financial support:* Career-related internships or fieldwork, Federal Work-Study, scholarships/grants, and unspecified assistantships available. Financial award application deadline: 5/1; financial award applicants required to submit FAFSA. *Unit head:* Dr. Maureen Culleeney, Academic Program Director, 815-838-0500 Ext. 5631, E-mail: culleema@lewisu.edu. *Application contact:* Michele Ryan, Director of Admission, 815-838-0500 Ext. 5384, E-mail: ryanml@lewisu.edu.

Lewis University, College of Business, Program in Finance, Romeoville, IL 60446. Offers MS. *Program availability:* Part-time, evening/weekend. *Students:* 7 full-time (3 women), 12 part-time (6 women); includes 6 minority (2 Black or African American, non-Hispanic/Latino; 1 Asian, non-Hispanic/Latino; 3 Hispanic/Latino), 4 international. Average age 30. *Entrance requirements:* For master's, bachelor's degree, interview, resume, two letters of recommendation, minimum GPA of 2.75. Additional exam requirements/recommendations for international students: Required—TOEFL (minimum score 550 paper-based; 80 iBT), IELTS. *Application deadline:* For fall admission, 5/1 priority date for international students; for spring admission, 11/15 priority date for international students. Applications are processed on a rolling basis. Application fee: $40. Electronic applications accepted. Tuition and fees vary according to program. *Financial support:* Career-related internships or fieldwork, Federal Work-Study, scholarships/grants, and unspecified assistantships available. Financial award application deadline: 5/1; financial award applicants required to submit FAFSA. *Unit head:* Dr. Robert Atra, Academic Program Director, 815-838-0500 Ext. 5804, E-mail: atraro@lewisu.edu. *Application contact:* Michele Ryan, Director of Admission, 815-838-5384, E-mail: ryanml@lewisu.edu.

Liberty University, School of Business, Lynchburg, VA 24515. Offers accounting (MBA, MS), including audit and financial reporting (MS), business (MS), financial services (MS), forensic accounting (MS), leadership (MS), taxation (MS); criminal justice (MBA); cyber security (MS); executive leadership (MA); information systems (MS), including information assurance, technology management; international business (MBA, DBA); leadership (DBA); marketing (MBA, MS, DBA), including digital marketing and advertising (MS), project management (MS), public relations (MS), sports marketing and media (MS); project management (MBA, DBA); public administration (MBA); public relations (MBA). *Program availability:* Part-time, online learning. *Students:* 1,887 full-time (1,003 women), 4,223 part-time (1,950 women); includes 1,570 minority (1,133 Black or African American, non-Hispanic/Latino; 30 American Indian or Alaska Native, non-Hispanic/Latino; 118 Asian, non-Hispanic/Latino; 149 Hispanic/Latino; 13 Native Hawaiian or other Pacific Islander, non-Hispanic/Latino; 127 Two or more races, non-Hispanic/Latino), 109 international. Average age 35. 5,680 applicants, 51% accepted, 1510 enrolled. In 2017, 1,290 master's, 17 doctorates awarded. *Entrance requirements:* For master's, minimum undergraduate GPA of 3.0, 15 hours of upper-level business courses. Additional exam requirements/recommendations for international students: Required—TOEFL (minimum score 600 paper-based; 100 iBT). *Application deadline:*

Applications are processed on a rolling basis. Application fee: $50. Electronic applications accepted. *Expenses:* Contact institution. *Financial support:* Applicants required to submit FAFSA. *Unit head:* Dr. Scott Hicks, Dean, 434-592-4808, Fax: 434-582-2366, E-mail: smhicks@liberty.edu. *Application contact:* Jay Bridge, Director of Graduate Admissions, 800-424-9595, Fax: 800-628-7977, E-mail: gradadmissions@liberty.edu.
Website: http://www.liberty.edu/academics/business/index.cfm?PID-149

Lincoln University, Graduate Programs, Philadelphia, PA 19104. Offers counseling (MSC); early childhood education (M Ed), including PreK-4; early childhood education and special education (M Ed); educational leadership (M Ed), including principal certification; finance (MBA); human resources management (MBA); human services delivery (MAHS). *Program availability:* Part-time, evening/weekend. *Faculty:* 9 full-time (3 women), 25 part-time/adjunct (15 women). *Students:* 196 full-time (138 women), 68 part-time (46 women); includes 236 minority (227 Black or African American, non-Hispanic/Latino; 1 American Indian or Alaska Native, non-Hispanic/Latino; 7 Hispanic/Latino; 1 Two or more races, non-Hispanic/Latino), 3 international. Average age 34. 120 applicants, 100% accepted, 95 enrolled. In 2017, 126 master's awarded. *Degree requirements:* For master's, comprehensive exam, thesis or alternative, capstone, grant proposal. *Entrance requirements:* For master's, official academic transcript(s), letters of recommendation, personal statement, resume, supervisor's evaluation form. Additional exam requirements/recommendations for international students: Recommended—TOEFL (minimum score 500 paper-based; 71 iBT), IELTS. *Application deadline:* For fall admission, 8/1 priority date for domestic students, 7/1 priority date for international students; for spring admission, 12/1 priority date for domestic students, 10/1 for international students. Applications are processed on a rolling basis. Application fee: $50. Electronic applications accepted. *Expenses:* Contact institution. *Financial support:* Scholarships/grants available. Financial award application deadline: 6/30; financial award applicants required to submit FAFSA. *Unit head:* Dr. Patricia Pierce Ramsey, Provost, 484-365-7437, Fax: 484-365-8108, E-mail: provost@lincoln.edu. *Application contact:* Jernice Lea, Director, University City Student Services and Admissions, 215-590-8231, Fax: 215-387-3859, E-mail: jlea@lincoln.edu.
Website: http://www.lincoln.edu/admissions/graduate-admissions

Lincoln University, Graduate Studies, Oakland, CA 94612. Offers finance and investments (DBA); finance management (MS); finance management and investments (MBA); general business (MBA); human resource management (MBA, DBA); international business (MBA, MS); management information systems (MBA). *Program availability:* Part-time. *Faculty:* 14 full-time (2 women), 20 part-time/adjunct (6 women). *Students:* 606 full-time (222 women), 31 part-time (14 women); includes 10 minority (8 Asian, non-Hispanic/Latino; 1 Hispanic/Latino; 1 Two or more races, non-Hispanic/Latino), 623 international. Average age 26. *Degree requirements:* For master's, research project (thesis), internship report, or comprehensive exam; for doctorate, comprehensive exam, thesis/dissertation. *Entrance requirements:* For master's, minimum GPA of 2.7; for doctorate, GMAT (minimum score: 550), GRE (minimum score: 1000), or equivalent test results (waived for master's degree with minimum cumulative GPA of 3.3). Additional exam requirements/recommendations for international students: Required—TOEFL minimum score 525 paper-based; 71 iBT or IELTS minimum score 5.5 (for MBA); TOEFL minimum score 550 paper-based; 79 iBT or IELTS minimum score 6 (for MS and DBA). *Application deadline:* For fall admission, 8/7 for domestic students, 7/14 for international students; for spring admission, 11/30 for domestic students, 10/31 for international students; for summer admission, 5/29 for domestic students, 5/5 for international students. Applications are processed on a rolling basis. Application fee: $75. Electronic applications accepted. *Expenses:* Tuition: Full-time $8100; part-time $450 per unit. *Required fees:* $360; $180 per semester. Tuition and fees vary according to course level, course load, degree level and program. *Financial support:* Teaching assistantships, career-related internships or fieldwork, and scholarships/grants available. Financial award applicants required to submit FAFSA. *Unit head:* Dr. Marshall Burak, Provost, 510-628-8016, Fax: 510-628-8012, E-mail: mburak@lincolnuca.edu. *Application contact:* Reenu Shrestha, Assistant to the President, 510-628-8017, Fax: 510-208-2826, E-mail: sreenu@lincolnuca.edu.

Lindenwood University, Graduate Programs, Plaster School of Business and Entrepreneurship, St. Charles, MO 63301-1695. Offers accountancy (M Acc); accounting (MBA); business administration (MBA); entrepreneurial studies (MBA); finance (MBA, MS); human resource management (MBA); international business (MBA); leadership (MA); management (MBA); marketing (MBA, MS); nonprofit administration (MA); public administration (MBA); sport management (MBA); supply chain management (MBA). *Accreditation:* ACBSP. *Program availability:* Part-time, evening/weekend, 100% online. *Faculty:* 15 full-time (8 women), 26 part-time/adjunct (9 women). *Students:* 201 full-time (116 women), 253 part-time (153 women); includes 102 minority (80 Black or African American, non-Hispanic/Latino; 2 American Indian or Alaska Native, non-Hispanic/Latino; 6 Asian, non-Hispanic/Latino; 7 Hispanic/Latino; 7 Two or more races, non-Hispanic/Latino), 61 international. Average age 32. 370 applicants, 42% accepted, 134 enrolled. In 2017, 178 master's awarded. *Degree requirements:* For master's, comprehensive exam (for some programs), thesis (for some programs), minimum GPA of 3.0. *Entrance requirements:* For master's, interview, minimum undergraduate cumulative GPA of 3.0, letter of recommendation. Additional exam requirements/recommendations for international students: Required—TOEFL (minimum score 550 paper-based; 80 iBT); Recommended—IELTS (minimum score 6.5). *Application deadline:* For fall admission, 8/27 priority date for domestic and international students; for winter admission, 1/14 priority date for domestic and international students; for spring admission, 3/18 for domestic students, 3/18 priority date for international students; for summer admission, 6/3 priority date for domestic and international students. Applications are processed on a rolling basis. Application fee: $30 ($100 for international students). Electronic applications accepted. *Expenses:* Contact institution. *Financial support:* In 2017–18, 439 students received support. Career-related internships or fieldwork, Federal Work-Study, institutionally sponsored loans, scholarships/grants, tuition waivers (partial), and unspecified assistantships available. Financial award application deadline: 6/30; financial award applicants required to submit FAFSA. *Unit head:* Roger Ellis, Dean, School of Business and Entrepreneurship, 636-949-4839, E-mail: rellis@lindenwood.edu. *Application contact:* Kara Schilli, Director, Evening and Graduate Admissions, 636-949-4349, Fax: 636-949-4109, E-mail: adultadmissions@lindenwood.edu.
Website: http://www.lindenwood.edu/academics/academic-schools/robert-w-plaster-school-of-business-entrepreneurship/

Lipscomb University, College of Business, Nashville, TN 37204-3951. Offers accounting and finance (MBA); audit/accounting (M Acc); business (Certificate); business administration (MM); healthcare management (MBA); leadership (MBA); tax (M Acc); MBA/MS; Pharm D/MM. *Accreditation:* ACBSP. *Program availability:* Part-time, evening/weekend. *Faculty:* 14 full-time (2 women), 8 part-time/adjunct (1 woman). *Students:* 157 full-time (68 women), 9 part-time (6 women); includes 26 minority (9 Black or African American, non-Hispanic/Latino; 7 Asian, non-Hispanic/Latino; 8 Hispanic/Latino; 2 Two or more races, non-Hispanic/Latino), 9 international. Average age 30. 249 applicants, 49% accepted, 52 enrolled. In 2017, 130 master's awarded. *Entrance requirements:* For master's, GMAT, transcripts, interview, 2 references, resume. Additional exam requirements/recommendations for international students: Required—

TOEFL (minimum score 570 paper-based). *Application deadline:* For fall admission, 6/15 for domestic students, 2/1 for international students; for winter admission, 6/1 for international students; for spring admission, 11/15 for domestic students. Applications are processed on a rolling basis. Application fee: $50 ($75 for international students). Electronic applications accepted. *Expenses:* Contact institution. *Financial support:* Career-related internships or fieldwork, scholarships/grants, tuition waivers (partial), and unspecified assistantships available. Support available to part-time students. Financial award application deadline: 7/1; financial award applicants required to submit FAFSA. *Faculty research:* Impact of spirituality on organization commitment, women in corporate leadership, psychological empowerment, training. *Unit head:* Allison Duke, Associate Dean of Graduate Business Programs, 615-966-5732, Fax: 615-966-1818, E-mail: allison.duke@lipscomb.edu. *Application contact:* Karen Risley, Manager, Graduate Business Recruiting, 615-966-5145, E-mail: karen.risley@lipscomb.edu.
Website: http://www.lipscomb.edu/business/Graduate-Programs

Long Island University–LIU Post, College of Management, Brookville, NY 11548-1300. Offers accountancy (MS); finance (MBA); information systems (MS); international business (MBA); management (MBA); management engineering (MS); marketing (MBA); taxation (MS); technical project management (MS); JD/MBA. *Accreditation:* AACSB. *Program availability:* Part-time, evening/weekend, blended/hybrid learning. *Faculty:* 23 full-time (7 women), 7 part-time/adjunct (1 woman). *Students:* 119 full-time (47 women), 62 part-time (23 women); includes 33 minority (11 Black or African American, non-Hispanic/Latino; 8 Asian, non-Hispanic/Latino; 13 Hispanic/Latino; 1 Two or more races, non-Hispanic/Latino), 56 international. Average age 28. 162 applicants, 62% accepted, 41 enrolled. In 2017, 91 master's awarded. *Entrance requirements:* For master's, GMAT, GRE, or LSAT. Additional exam requirements/recommendations for international students: Required—TOEFL (minimum score 550 paper-based, 75 iBT) or IELTS. *Application deadline:* Applications are processed on a rolling basis. Application fee: $50. Electronic applications accepted. *Expenses:* Tuition: Full-time $21,618; part-time $1201 per credit. *Required fees:* $1840; $920 per term. Tuition and fees vary according to course load. *Financial support:* In 2017–18, 47 students received support. Career-related internships or fieldwork, Federal Work-Study, and scholarships/grants available. Support available to part-time students. Financial award application deadline: 2/15; financial award applicants required to submit FAFSA. *Faculty research:* Innovation and property rights, knowledge sourcing, sustainability and firm performance, China and growth markets, corporate social responsibility, workforce compensation and issues. *Unit head:* Dr. Robert M. Valli, Dean, 516-299-3004, E-mail: rob.valli@liu.edu. *Application contact:* Rita Langdon, Graduate Admissions, 516-299-2900, Fax: 516-299-2137, E-mail: post-enroll@liu.edu.
Website: http://liu.edu/CWPost/Academics/Schools/COM

Louisiana State University and Agricultural & Mechanical College, Graduate School, E. J. Ourso College of Business, Department of Finance, Baton Rouge, LA 70803. Offers business administration (PhD), including finance; finance (MS). *Faculty:* 12 full-time (2 women). *Students:* 20 full-time (5 women), 6 part-time (1 woman); includes 4 minority (1 Black or African American, non-Hispanic/Latino; 2 Hispanic/Latino; 1 Two or more races, non-Hispanic/Latino). Average age 26. 32 applicants, 72% accepted, 12 enrolled. In 2017, 18 master's awarded. *Financial support:* In 2017–18, 2 teaching assistantships (averaging $17,700 per year) were awarded. *Total annual research expenditures:* $18,685.

Louisiana Tech University, Graduate School, College of Business, Ruston, LA 71272. Offers accounting (M Acc, DBA); computer information systems (DBA); finance (MBA, DBA); information assurance (MBA); innovation (MBA); management (DBA); marketing (MBA, DBA). *Accreditation:* AACSB. *Program availability:* Part-time, evening/weekend, 100% online, blended/hybrid learning. *Faculty:* 36 full-time (7 women), 8 part-time/adjunct (3 women). *Students:* 104 full-time (43 women), 40 part-time (16 women); includes 22 minority (13 Black or African American, non-Hispanic/Latino; 2 Asian, non-Hispanic/Latino; 7 Two or more races, non-Hispanic/Latino), 32 international. Average age 29. 104 applicants, 58% accepted, 25 enrolled. In 2017, 71 master's, 4 doctorates awarded. *Degree requirements:* For doctorate, thesis/dissertation. *Entrance requirements:* For master's and doctorate, GMAT, transcript with bachelor's degree awarded. Additional exam requirements/recommendations for international students: Required—TOEFL (minimum score 550 paper-based; 80 iBT), IELTS (minimum score 6.5). *Application deadline:* For fall admission, 8/1 priority date for domestic students, 6/1 for international students; for winter admission, 11/1 priority date for domestic students, 9/1 for international students; for spring admission, 2/1 priority date for domestic students, 12/1 for international students; for summer admission, 5/1 priority date for domestic students, 3/1 for international students. Application fee: $40. Electronic applications accepted. *Expenses:* Tuition, state resident: full-time $5146. Tuition, nonresident: full-time $10,147. *International tuition:* $10,267 full-time. *Required fees:* $2273. *Financial support:* In 2017–18, 24 students received support, including 17 research assistantships with partial tuition reimbursements available (averaging $12,500 per year), 7 teaching assistantships with partial tuition reimbursements available (averaging $12,500 per year); scholarships/grants and unspecified assistantships also available. Financial award application deadline: 2/1. *Faculty research:* Consumer environmental behavior; identifying and analyzing current issues and future concerns in real estate; information assurance and related areas in business for Northwest Louisiana and the United States (business continuity, disaster recovery, accounting controls, auditing, computer forensics, and security attribution); value creation driven by the consumer and employee interface within exchange environments. *Unit head:* Dr. Christopher D. Martin, Dean, 318-257-4526, Fax: 318-257-4253. *Application contact:* Samantha J. Bailey, Graduate Management Admissions Specialist, 318-257-2924, Fax: 318-257-4487, E-mail: samantha@latech.edu.
Website: http://www.business.latech.edu/

Loyola University Chicago, Quinlan School of Business, Master of Science in Finance Program, Chicago, IL 60611. Offers asset management (MSF). *Program availability:* Part-time, evening/weekend. *Faculty:* 11 full-time (3 women), 6 part-time/adjunct (0 women). *Students:* 36 full-time (16 women), 3 part-time (0 women); includes 3 minority (1 Asian, non-Hispanic/Latino; 2 Two or more races, non-Hispanic/Latino), 26 international. Average age 24. 168 applicants, 49% accepted, 22 enrolled. In 2017, 23 master's awarded. *Entrance requirements:* For master's, GMAT or GRE, official transcripts, letters of recommendation, statement of purpose, resume. Additional exam requirements/recommendations for international students: Required—TOEFL (minimum score 90 iBT) or IELTS (minimum score 6.5). *Application deadline:* For fall admission, 7/15 for domestic and international students; for winter admission, 10/1 for domestic and international students; for spring admission, 1/15 for domestic and international students; for summer admission, 4/1 for domestic and international students. Applications are processed on a rolling basis. Application fee: $50. Electronic applications accepted. Application fee is waived when completed online. *Expenses:* $4,488 per course. *Financial support:* In 2017–18, 13 students received support. Research assistantships, career-related internships or fieldwork, Federal Work-Study, scholarships/grants, and health care benefits available. *Faculty research:* Corporate finance, banking, risk management and derivatives, investment, theoretical finance. *Unit head:* Dr. Suk Hun Lee, Chair, Department of Finance, 312-915-7101, Fax: 312-915-8508, E-mail: slee2@luc.edu.
Website: http://www.luc.edu/quinlan/mba/masters/masters-in-finance/

Finance and Banking

Loyola University Chicago, Quinlan School of Business, MBA Programs, Chicago, IL 60611. Offers accounting (MBA); business ethics (MBA); derivative markets (MBA); economics (MBA); entrepreneurship (MBA); finance (MBA); healthcare management (MBA); human resources management (MBA); information systems management (MBA); international business (MBA); management (MBA); marketing (MBA); risk management (MBA); supply chain management (MBA). *Program availability:* Part-time, evening/weekend. *Faculty:* 84 full-time (28 women), 12 part-time/adjunct (3 women). *Students:* 253 full-time (118 women), 76 part-time (35 women); includes 83 minority (21 Black or African American, non-Hispanic/Latino; 1 American Indian or Alaska Native, non-Hispanic/Latino; 33 Asian, non-Hispanic/Latino; 24 Hispanic/Latino; 4 Two or more races, non-Hispanic/Latino), 37 international. Average age 30. 334 applicants, 52% accepted, 80 enrolled. In 2017, 220 master's awarded. *Entrance requirements:* For master's, GMAT or GRE, official transcripts, two letters of recommendation, statement of purpose, resume. Additional exam requirements/recommendations for international students: Required—TOEFL (minimum score 90 iBT) or IELTS (minimum score 6.5). *Application deadline:* For fall admission, 7/15 for domestic and international students; for winter admission, 10/1 for domestic and international students; for spring admission, 1/15 for domestic and international students; for summer admission, 4/1 for domestic and international students. Applications are processed on a rolling basis. Application fee: $50. Electronic applications accepted. Application fee is waived when completed online. *Expenses:* $4,488 per course. *Financial support:* In 2017–18, 11 students received support. Research assistantships, career-related internships or fieldwork, Federal Work-Study, scholarships/grants, and health care benefits available. *Faculty research:* Social enterprise and responsibility, emerging markets, supply chain management, risk management. *Unit head:* Katherine Acles, Assistant Dean for Graduate Programs, 312-915-6124, Fax: 312-915-7207, E-mail: kacles@luc.edu.

Loyola University Maryland, Graduate Programs, Sellinger School of Business, Professional MBA Program, Baltimore, MD 21210-2699. Offers finance (MBA); information systems (MBA); investments and applied portfolio management (MBA); management (MBA); marketing (MBA). *Accreditation:* AACSB. *Program availability:* Part-time, evening/weekend. *Entrance requirements:* For master's, GMAT, resume, essay, official transcripts, professional letter of recommendation. Additional exam requirements/recommendations for international students: Required—TOEFL (minimum score 550 paper-based, 80 iBT) or IELTS (minimum score 7). *Application deadline:* For fall admission, 8/1 priority date for domestic students, 4/1 for international students; for spring admission, 12/1 priority date for domestic students, 9/1 for international students; for summer admission, 5/1 priority date for domestic students. Applications are processed on a rolling basis. Application fee: $60. Electronic applications accepted. *Expenses:* Contact institution. *Financial support:* In 2017–18, 26 students received support. Scholarships/grants available. Financial award application deadline: 4/15; financial award applicants required to submit FAFSA. *Unit head:* Kelly Fader, Director of Graduate Cohort Program, 410-617-1617, E-mail: kgfader@loyola.edu. *Application contact:* Office of Graduate Business Programs, 410-617-5067, E-mail: mba@loyola.edu.

Manhattanville College, School of Business, Master of Science in Finance Program, Purchase, NY 10577-2132. Offers finance (MS, Advanced Certificate), including accounting (MS), corporate finance (MS), investment management (MS). *Program availability:* Part-time, evening/weekend. *Faculty:* 4 part-time/adjunct (2 women). *Students:* 23 full-time (7 women), 6 part-time (3 women); includes 9 minority (3 Black or African American, non-Hispanic/Latino; 6 Hispanic/Latino), 2 international. Average age 29. 35 applicants, 37% accepted, 11 enrolled. In 2017, 12 master's awarded. *Degree requirements:* For master's, thesis (for some programs), final project. *Entrance requirements:* For master's, personal essay, transcripts, 2 letters of recommendation (academic or professional), resume, health form with proof of immunization (for those born after 1957). Additional exam requirements/recommendations for international students: Required—TOEFL (minimum score 563 paper-based, 85 iBT), IELTS (7), or iTEP (B2). *Application deadline:* Applications are processed on a rolling basis. Application fee: $75. Electronic applications accepted. *Expenses:* $915 per credit. *Financial support:* Federal Work-Study, institutionally sponsored loans, scholarships/grants, and unspecified assistantships available. Financial award application deadline: 3/15; financial award applicants required to submit FAFSA. *Unit head:* Laura Persky, Graduate Program Director, 914-323-5188, E-mail: laura.persky@mville.edu. *Application contact:* Monika Pottgen, Assistant Director, Recruitment and Admissions, 914-323-5150, E-mail: business@mville.edu. Website: https://www.mville.edu/programs/ms-finance

Manhattanville College, School of Business, Master of Science in International Management Program, Purchase, NY 10577-2132. Offers international management (MS, Advanced Certificate), including business leadership (MS), finance (MS), human resource management (MS), marketing communication management (MS). *Program availability:* Part-time, evening/weekend. *Faculty:* 2 part-time/adjunct (0 women). *Students:* 6 full-time (3 women), 2 part-time (1 woman); includes 2 minority (1 Black or African American, non-Hispanic/Latino; 1 Two or more races, non-Hispanic/Latino), 2 international. Average age 34. 6 applicants, 67% accepted, 1 enrolled. In 2017, 2 master's awarded. *Degree requirements:* For master's, thesis (for some programs), final project. *Entrance requirements:* For master's, personal essay, transcripts, 2 letters of recommendation (academic or professional), resume, health form with proof of immunization (for those born after 1957). Additional exam requirements/recommendations for international students: Required—TOEFL (minimum score 563 paper-based, 85 iBT), IELTS (7), or iTEP (B2). *Application deadline:* Applications are processed on a rolling basis. Application fee: $75. Electronic applications accepted. *Expenses:* $915 per credit. *Financial support:* Federal Work-Study, institutionally sponsored loans, scholarships/grants, and unspecified assistantships available. Financial award application deadline: 3/15; financial award applicants required to submit FAFSA. *Unit head:* Laura Persky, Graduate Program Director, 914-323-5188, E-mail: laura.persky@mville.edu. *Application contact:* Monika Pottgen, Assistant Director, Recruitment and Admissions, 914-323-5150, E-mail: business@mville.edu. Website: https://www.mville.edu/programs/ms-international-management

Marquette University, Graduate School of Management, Executive MBA Program, Milwaukee, WI 53201-1881. Offers economics (MBA); finance (MBA); human resources (MBA); international business (MBA); management information systems (MBA); marketing (MBA); operations and supply chain management (MBA); sports business (MBA). *Accreditation:* AACSB. *Degree requirements:* For master's, international trip. *Entrance requirements:* For master's, GMAT or GRE, two letters of recommendation, official transcripts from current and previous colleges/universities. Additional exam requirements/recommendations for international students: Required—TOEFL (minimum score 550 paper-based; 88 iBT), IELTS (minimum score 6.5), PTE. Electronic applications accepted. *Expenses:* Contact institution. *Faculty research:* International trade and finance, customer relationship management, consumer satisfaction, customer service.

Marquette University, Graduate School of Management, Program in Business Administration, Milwaukee, WI 53201-1881. Offers business administration (MBA); economics (MBA); entrepreneurship (Certificate); finance (MBA); human resources (MBA); international business (MBA); management information systems (MBA); operations and supply chain management (MBA); sports business (MBA); JD/MBA; MBA/MA; MBA/MSN. *Accreditation:* AACSB. *Program availability:* Part-time, evening/weekend. *Degree requirements:* For Certificate, business plan. *Entrance requirements:* For master's, GMAT or GRE, letters of recommendation. Additional exam requirements/recommendations for international students: Required—TOEFL (minimum score 550 paper-based; 88 iBT), IELTS (minimum score 6.5), PTE. Electronic applications accepted. *Faculty research:* Ethics in the professions, services marketing, technology impact on decision-making, mentoring.

Maryville University of Saint Louis, The John E. Simon School of Business, St. Louis, MO 63141-7299. Offers accounting (MBA, MS, Certificate); business studies (Certificate); cybersecurity (MBA, MS, Certificate); financial services (MBA, Certificate); healthcare practice management (MBA, Certificate); human resource management (MBA, Certificate); information technology (MBA, Certificate); management (MBA, Certificate); management and leadership (MA); marketing (MBA, Certificate); project management (MBA, Certificate); sport business management (MBA); supply chain management (Certificate); supply chain management/logistics (MBA). *Accreditation:* ACBSP. *Program availability:* Part-time, 100% online, blended/hybrid learning. *Faculty:* 5 full-time (3 women), 51 part-time/adjunct (16 women). *Students:* 222 full-time (96 women), 498 part-time (222 women); includes 185 minority (104 Black or African American, non-Hispanic/Latino; 5 American Indian or Alaska Native, non-Hispanic/Latino; 30 Asian, non-Hispanic/Latino; 37 Hispanic/Latino; 9 Two or more races, non-Hispanic/Latino), 26 international. Average age 33. In 2017, 106 master's awarded. *Degree requirements:* For master's, capstone course (for MBA). *Entrance requirements:* Additional exam requirements/recommendations for international students: Required—TOEFL (minimum score 563 paper-based; 85 iBT). *Application deadline:* Applications are processed on a rolling basis. Electronic applications accepted. *Expenses:* Contact institution. *Financial support:* Career-related internships or fieldwork, Federal Work-Study, tuition waivers (partial), and campus employment available. Financial award application deadline: 4/1; financial award applicants required to submit FAFSA. *Unit head:* Pam Horwitz, Interim Dean, 314-529-9680, Fax: 314-529-9975. *Application contact:* Dustin Loeffler, Director for Graduate Studies in Business, 314-529-9571, Fax: 314-529-9975, E-mail: dloeffler@maryville.edu. Website: http://www.maryville.edu/bu/business-administration-masters/

Marywood University, Academic Affairs, Munley College of Liberal Arts and Sciences, School of Business and Global Innovation, Emphasis in Finance/Investment, Scranton, PA 18509-1598. Offers MBA. *Entrance requirements:* For master's, GMAT. Electronic applications accepted.

McGill University, Faculty of Graduate and Postdoctoral Studies, Desautels Faculty of Management, Montréal, QC H3A 2T5, Canada. Offers administration (PhD); entrepreneurial studies (MBA); finance (MBA); general management (Post Master's Certificate); information systems (MBA); international business (MBA); international practicing management (MM); management (MBA); management for development (MBA); manufacturing management (MMM); marketing (MBA); operations management (MBA); public accountancy (Diploma); strategic management (MBA); MBA/LL B; MD/MBA. MMM offered jointly with Faculty of Engineering; PhD with Concordia University, HEC Montreal, Université de Montréal, Université du Québec à Montréal.

Metropolitan College of New York, Program in Business Administration, New York, NY 10006. Offers financial services (MBA); general management (MBA); healthcare systems and risk management (MBA); media management (MBA). *Accreditation:* ACBSP. *Program availability:* Evening/weekend. *Students:* 164 full-time (106 women), 37 part-time (31 women); includes 153 minority (112 Black or African American, non-Hispanic/Latino; 3 American Indian or Alaska Native, non-Hispanic/Latino; 10 Asian, non-Hispanic/Latino; 24 Hispanic/Latino; 1 Native Hawaiian or other Pacific Islander, non-Hispanic/Latino; 3 Two or more races, non-Hispanic/Latino), 31 international. Average age 37. 133 applicants, 62% accepted, 66 enrolled. In 2017, 100 master's awarded. *Degree requirements:* For master's, thesis, 10-day study abroad. *Entrance requirements:* For master's, GMAT. Additional exam requirements/recommendations for international students: Required—TOEFL (minimum score 600 paper-based). *Application deadline:* For fall admission, 7/15 priority date for domestic students; for winter admission, 11/15 priority date for domestic students; for spring admission, 3/30 priority date for domestic students. Applications are processed on a rolling basis. Application fee: $45. Electronic applications accepted. *Expenses:* $926 per credit, $395 fee per semester. *Financial support:* Scholarships/grants available. Financial award application deadline: 8/15; financial award applicants required to submit FAFSA. *Unit head:* Dr. Tilokie Depoo, Dean and Professor, School for Business, 212-343-1234 Ext. 2204. *Application contact:* Steebo Varghese, Assistant Director of Admissions, 212-343-1234 Ext. 2708, Fax: 212-343-8470.

Michigan State University, The Graduate School, Eli Broad College of Business, Department of Finance, East Lansing, MI 48224. Offers MS, PhD. PhD program admits students only in odd-numbered years. *Degree requirements:* For doctorate, comprehensive exam, thesis/dissertation. *Entrance requirements:* For master's, GMAT (minimum score 550) or GRE (minimum score 1050 verbal and quantitative taken within 5 years), 4-year bachelor's degree or equivalent with minimum cumulative GPA of 3.0, transcripts, at least 2 years' work experience, 2 letters of recommendation, working knowledge of computers, laptop computer; for doctorate, GMAT or GRE, transcripts from all colleges/universities attended, 3 letters of recommendation, statement of purpose. Additional exam requirements/recommendations for international students: Required—TOEFL (minimum score 600 paper-based; 100 iBT), IELTS (minimum score 7) accepted for MS only. Electronic applications accepted.

Michigan State University, The Graduate School, Eli Broad College of Business, Program in Business Administration, East Lansing, MI 48224. Offers finance (MBA); human resource management (MBA); integrative management (MBA); marketing (MBA); supply chain management (MBA). MBA in integrative management is through Weekend MBA Program; other 4 concentrations are through Full-Time MBA Program. *Program availability:* Evening/weekend. *Degree requirements:* For master's, enrichment experience. *Entrance requirements:* For master's, GMAT or GRE, 4-year bachelor's degree; resume; work experience (minimum of 5 years for Weekend MBA); 2-3 personal essays; 2 letters of recommendation; personal interview. Additional exam requirements/recommendations for international students: Required—PTE (minimum score 70), TOEFL (minimum score 100 iBT) or IELTS (minimum score 7) for full-time MBA applicants. Electronic applications accepted. *Expenses:* Contact institution.

Minnesota State University Moorhead, Graduate Studies, College of Business and Innovation, Moorhead, MN 56563. Offers accounting and finance (MS); business administration (MBA); health care management (MBA). *Accreditation:* AACSB. *Program availability:* Part-time. *Faculty:* 13. *Students:* 17 full-time (5 women), 26 part-time (17 women). Average age 29. 21 applicants, 81% accepted. In 2017, 13 master's awarded. *Degree requirements:* For master's, comprehensive exam (for some programs), thesis, final oral defense. *Entrance requirements:* For master's, GMAT, minimum GPA of 3.0. Additional exam requirements/recommendations for international students: Required—TOEFL (minimum score 550 paper-based); Recommended—IELTS (minimum score 6.5). *Application deadline:* For fall admission, 3/15 for domestic students; for spring admission, 10/15 for domestic students. Applications are processed on a rolling basis. Application fee: $20. Electronic applications accepted. *Expenses:* Tuition, state

resident: full-time $9000; part-time $374 per credit. Tuition, nonresident: full-time $18,000; part-time $748 per credit. *Required fees:* $1055; $43.96 per credit. Tuition and fees vary according to degree level, program and reciprocity agreements. Financial support: Federal Work-Study and unspecified assistantships available. Financial award application deadline: 10/1; financial award applicants required to submit FAFSA. *Faculty research:* Union decertification, small business development, business innovation, pedagogy, curriculum design. *Unit head:* Denise Gorsline, Interim Dean, 218-477-4623, E-mail: gorsline@mnstate.edu. *Application contact:* Karla Wenger, Coordinator, 218-477-2344, E-mail: wengerk@mnstate.edu.
Website: http://www.mnstate.edu/cbi/

Mississippi College, Graduate School, School of Business, Clinton, MS 39058. Offers accounting (Certificate); business administration (MBA), including accounting; business education (M Ed); finance (MBA, Certificate); JD/MBA. *Accreditation:* ACBSP. *Program availability:* Part-time, evening/weekend. *Degree requirements:* For master's, comprehensive exam, thesis optional. *Entrance requirements:* For master's, GMAT, minimum GPA of 2.5, 24 hours of undergraduate course work in business. Additional exam requirements/recommendations for international students: Recommended—TOEFL, IELTS. Electronic applications accepted.

Mississippi State University, College of Business, Department of Finance and Economics, Mississippi State, MS 39762. Offers applied economics (PhD); economics (MA). PhD in applied economics offered jointly with Department of Agricultural Economics. *Program availability:* Part-time. *Faculty:* 18 full-time (5 women), 1 part-time/adjunct (0 women). *Students:* 11 full-time (3 women), 1 part-time (0 women), 10 international. Average age 30. 36 applicants, 25% accepted, 5 enrolled. In 2017, 1 master's, 1 doctorate awarded. Terminal master's awarded for partial completion of doctoral program. *Degree requirements:* For master's, comprehensive exam, thesis optional; for doctorate, comprehensive exam, thesis/dissertation, written and oral exams. *Entrance requirements:* For master's, GRE, previously-completed intermediate microeconomics and macroeconomics; for doctorate, GRE, BS with minimum GPA of 3.0 cumulative and over last 60 hours of undergraduate work, 3.25 on all graduate work. Additional exam requirements/recommendations for international students: Required—TOEFL (minimum score 575 paper-based; 84 iBT); Recommended—IELTS (minimum score 6.5). *Application deadline:* For fall admission, 7/1 for domestic students, 5/1 for international students; for spring admission, 11/1 for domestic students, 10/1 for international students. Applications are processed on a rolling basis. Application fee: $60 ($80 for international students). Electronic applications accepted. *Expenses:* Tuition, state resident: full-time $8318; part-time $462.12 per credit hour. Tuition, nonresident: full-time $22,358; part-time $1242.12 per credit hour. *Required fees:* $110; $12.24 per credit hour. $6.12 per semester. *Financial support:* Federal Work-Study, scholarships/grants, health care benefits, and unspecified assistantships available. Financial award application deadline: 4/1; financial award applicants required to submit FAFSA. *Faculty research:* Economics development, mergers, event studies, economic education, bank performance. *Total annual research expenditures:* $1 million. *Unit head:* Dr. Mike Highfield, Professor/Head, 662-325-1984, Fax: 662-325-1977, E-mail: m.highfield@msstate.edu. *Application contact:* Lakan Drinker, Admissions and Enrollment Assistant, 662-325-8951, E-mail: ldrinker@grad.msstate.edu.
Website: http://www.business.msstate.edu/programs/fe/index.php

Molloy College, Graduate Business Program, Rockville Centre, NY 11571-5002. Offers accounting (MBA); finance (MBA, Post-Master's Certificate, Postbaccalaureate Certificate); healthcare (MBA, Post-Master's Certificate, Postbaccalaureate Certificate); management (MBA); marketing (MBA, Post-Master's Certificate, Postbaccalaureate Certificate); personal financial planning (MBA). *Program availability:* Part-time, evening/weekend. *Faculty:* 8 full-time (3 women), 7 part-time/adjunct (2 women). *Students:* 53 full-time (29 women), 175 part-time (89 women); includes 88 minority (38 Black or African American, non-Hispanic/Latino; 18 Asian, non-Hispanic/Latino; 30 Hispanic/Latino; 2 Two or more races, non-Hispanic/Latino), 3 international. Average age 39. 128 applicants, 68% accepted, 81 enrolled. In 2017, 125 master's awarded. *Entrance requirements:* Additional exam requirements/recommendations for international students: Required—TOEFL (minimum score 550 paper-based; 79 iBT). *Application deadline:* Applications are processed on a rolling basis. Application fee: $60. Electronic applications accepted. *Expenses: Tuition:* Full-time $19,980; part-time $1110 per credit. *Required fees:* $1040. Tuition and fees vary according to course load and degree level. *Financial support:* Application deadline: 3/1; applicants required to submit FAFSA. *Faculty research:* Graduate education - pedagogy and the capstone experience; Freedom of Speech in the workplace; employer liability for sexual harassment in the workplace; educational economics and industrial organization; corporate governance and distressed debt analysis; social network analysis; market segmentation. *Unit head:* Dr. Maureen Mackenzie, Dean, Division of Business/Director of Graduate Programs, 516-323-3080, E-mail: mmackenzie@molloy.edu. *Application contact:* Jaclyn Machowicz, Assistant Director for Admissions, 516-323-4010, E-mail: jmachowicz@molloy.edu.
Website: http://www.molloy.edu/academics/graduate-programs/graduate-business

Monmouth University, Graduate Studies, Leon Hess Business School, West Long Branch, NJ 07764-1898. Offers accounting (MBA, Certificate); business administration (MBA); finance (MBA); management (MBA); marketing (MBA); real estate (MBA). *Accreditation:* AACSB. *Program availability:* Part-time, evening/weekend. *Faculty:* 20 full-time (4 women), 8 part-time/adjunct (0 women). *Students:* 101 full-time (55 women), 107 part-time (44 women); includes 19 minority (3 Black or African American, non-Hispanic/Latino; 6 Asian, non-Hispanic/Latino; 6 Hispanic/Latino; 1 Native Hawaiian or other Pacific Islander, non-Hispanic/Latino; 3 Two or more races, non-Hispanic/Latino), 13 international. Average age 30. In 2017, 61 master's, 1 other advanced degree awarded. *Degree requirements:* For master's, capstone course. *Entrance requirements:* For master's, GMAT or GRE, current resume; essay (500 words or less). Additional exam requirements/recommendations for international students: Required—TOEFL (minimum score 550 paper-based; 79 iBT), IELTS (minimum score 6), Michigan English Language Assessment Battery (minimum score 77) or Certificate of Advanced English (minimum score 160). *Application deadline:* For fall admission, 7/15 priority date for domestic students, 6/1 for international students; for spring admission, 12/1 priority date for domestic students, 11/1 for international students; for summer admission, 5/1 for domestic students. Applications are processed on a rolling basis. Application fee: $50. Electronic applications accepted. *Expenses: Tuition:* Full-time $21,366; part-time $7122 per credit. *Required fees:* $700; $175 per term. *Financial support:* In 2017–18, 42 students received support. Institutionally sponsored loans, scholarships/grants, and unspecified assistantships available. Support available to part-time students. Financial award applicants required to submit FAFSA. *Faculty research:* Information technology and marketing, behavioral research in accounting, human resources, management of technology. *Unit head:* Dr. Susan Gupta, MBA Program Director, 732-571-3639, Fax: 732-263-5517, E-mail: sgupta@monmouth.edu. *Application contact:* Laurie Kuhn, Associate Director of Graduate Admission, 732-571-3452, Fax: 732-263-5123, E-mail: gradadm@monmouth.edu.
Website: https://www.monmouth.edu/business-school/leon-hess-business-school.aspx
See Display on page 115 and Close-Up on page 177.

Monroe College, King Graduate School, Bronx, NY 10468. Offers accounting (MS); business administration (MBA), including entrepreneurship, finance, general business administration, healthcare management, human resources, information technology, marketing; computer science (MS); criminal justice (MS); hospitality management (MS); public health (MPH), including biostatistics and epidemiology, community health, health administration and leadership. *Program availability:* Online learning. Application fee: $50.
Website: https://www.monroecollege.edu/Degrees/King-Graduate-School/

Mount Saint Mary College, School of Business, Newburgh, NY 12550-3494. Offers business (MBA); financial planning (MBA); health care management (MBA). *Program availability:* Part-time, evening/weekend. *Faculty:* 4 full-time (1 woman), 8 part-time/adjunct (4 women). *Students:* 48 full-time (21 women), 30 part-time (21 women); includes 20 minority (6 Black or African American, non-Hispanic/Latino; 1 Asian, non-Hispanic/Latino; 12 Hispanic/Latino; 1 Two or more races, non-Hispanic/Latino). Average age 32. 17 applicants, 65% accepted, 6 enrolled. In 2017, 41 master's awarded. *Degree requirements:* For master's, thesis or alternative. *Entrance requirements:* For master's, GMAT or minimum undergraduate GPA of 2.7. Additional exam requirements/recommendations for international students: Required—TOEFL (minimum score 80 iBT). *Application deadline:* Applications are processed on a rolling basis. Application fee: $45. Electronic applications accepted. Application fee is waived when completed online. *Expenses: Tuition:* Full-time $14,454; part-time $803 per credit. *Required fees:* $172; $86 per semester. *Financial support:* In 2017–18, 18 students received support. Unspecified assistantships available. Financial award application deadline: 4/15; financial award applicants required to submit FAFSA. *Faculty research:* Financial reform, entrepreneurship and small business development, global business relations, technology's impact on business decision-making, college-assisted business education. *Unit head:* Dr. Moira Tolan, Graduate Coordinator, 845-569-3121, Fax: 845-562-6762, E-mail: moira.tolan@msmc.edu. *Application contact:* Lisa Alvarez, Director of Admissions for Graduate Programs and Adult Degree Completion, 845-569-3166, Fax: 845-569-3450, E-mail: lisa.gallina@msmc.edu.
Website: http://www.msmc.edu/Academics/Graduate_Programs/master_of_business_administration.be

Murray State University, Arthur J. Bauernfeind College of Business, Department of Economics and Finance, Murray, KY 42071. Offers economic development (MS); economics (MS), including finance. *Program availability:* Part-time. *Faculty:* 13 full-time (4 women), 1 part-time/adjunct (0 women). *Students:* 10 full-time (6 women), 2 part-time (0 women); includes 2 minority (1 Black or African American, non-Hispanic/Latino; 1 Two or more races, non-Hispanic/Latino), 5 international. Average age 26. 7 applicants, 86% accepted, 1 enrolled. In 2017, 5 master's awarded. *Entrance requirements:* For master's, GRE General Test or GMAT, minimum university GPA of 2.75. Additional exam requirements/recommendations for international students: Required—TOEFL (minimum score 527 paper-based; 71 iBT). *Application deadline:* Applications are processed on a rolling basis. Application fee: $40 ($50 for international students). Electronic applications accepted. *Expenses:* Tuition, state resident: full-time $9504. Tuition, nonresident: full-time $26,811. *International tuition:* $14,400 full-time. Tuition and fees vary according to course load, degree level and reciprocity agreements. *Financial support:* In 2017–18, 1 research assistantship, 1 teaching assistantship were awarded; Federal Work-Study and unspecified assistantships also available. Financial award applicants required to submit FAFSA. *Unit head:* Dr. David Eaton, Chair, Department of Economics and Finance, 270-809-4290, Fax: 270-809-5478, E-mail: deaton@murraystate.edu. *Application contact:* Kaitlyn Burzynski, Interim Assistant Director for Graduate Admission and Records, 270-809-5732, Fax: 270-809-3780, E-mail: msu.graduateadmissions@murraystate.edu.
Website: https://www.murraystate.edu/academics/CollegesDepartments/CollegeOfBusiness/Programs/EconomicsAndFinance/

Murray State University, Arthur J. Bauernfeind College of Business, MBA Program, Murray, KY 42071. Offers accounting (MBA); finance (MBA); global communications (MBA); human resource management (MBA); marketing (MBA). *Accreditation:* AACSB. *Program availability:* Part-time, evening/weekend, 100% online, blended/hybrid learning. *Faculty:* 49 full-time (18 women), 3 part-time/adjunct (0 women). *Students:* 54 full-time (22 women), 79 part-time (37 women); includes 13 minority (6 Black or African American, non-Hispanic/Latino; 1 American Indian or Alaska Native, non-Hispanic/Latino; 2 Asian, non-Hispanic/Latino; 2 Hispanic/Latino; 2 Two or more races, non-Hispanic/Latino), 30 international. Average age 29. 70 applicants, 81% accepted, 34 enrolled. In 2017, 61 master's awarded. *Entrance requirements:* For master's, GRE or GMAT, minimum university GPA of 2.75. Additional exam requirements/recommendations for international students: Required—TOEFL (minimum score 527 paper-based; 71 iBT). *Application deadline:* Applications are processed on a rolling basis. Application fee: $40 ($50 for international students). *Expenses:* Tuition, state resident: full-time $9504. Tuition, nonresident: full-time $26,811. *International tuition:* $14,400 full-time. Tuition and fees vary according to course load, degree level and reciprocity agreements. *Financial support:* In 2017–18, 5 research assistantships, 5 teaching assistantships were awarded; Federal Work-Study also available. Financial award applicants required to submit FAFSA. *Faculty research:* Human resource management, e-commerce, supply-chain management, investment management, accounting. *Unit head:* Dr. Joy Humphreys, Assistant Dean and MBA Director, 270-809-4259, Fax: 270-809-3482, E-mail: jumphreys4@murraystate.edu. *Application contact:* Kaitlyn Burzynski, Interim Assistant Director for Graduate Admission and Records, 270-809-5732, Fax: 270-809-3780, E-mail: msu.graduateadmissions@murraystate.edu.
Website: http://www.murraystate.edu/academics/CollegesDepartments/CollegeOfBusiness/Programs/mba/index.aspx

Naval Postgraduate School, Departments and Academic Groups, Department of Defense Analysis, Monterey, CA 93943. Offers command and control (MS); communications (MS); defense analysis (MS), including astronautics; financial management (MS); information operations (MS); irregular warfare (MS); national security affairs (MS); operations analysis (MS); special operations (MA, MS), including command and control (MS), communications (MS), financial management (MS), information operations (MS), irregular warfare (MS), national security affairs, operations analysis (MS), tactile missiles (MS), terrorist operations and financing (MS); tactile missiles (MS); terrorist operations and financing (MS). Program only open to commissioned officers of the United States and friendly nations and selected United States federal civilian employees. *Program availability:* Part-time. *Degree requirements:* For master's, thesis. *Faculty research:* CTF Global Ecco Project, Afghanistan endgames, core lab Philippines project, Defense Manpower Data Center (DMDC) data vulnerability.

Naval Postgraduate School, Departments and Academic Groups, Graduate School of Business and Public Policy, Monterey, CA 93943. Offers acquisition and contract management (MBA); business administration (EMBA, MBA); contract management (MS); defense business management (MBA); defense systems analysis (MS), including management; defense systems management (international) (MBA); financial management (MBA); information management (MBA); manpower systems analysis (MS); material logistics support management (MBA); program management (MS); resource planning and management for international defense (MBA); supply chain

Finance and Banking

management (MBA); systems acquisition management (MBA); transportation management (MBA). Program only open to commissioned officers of the United States and friendly nations and selected United States federal civilian employees. *Accreditation:* AACSB; NASPAA. *Program availability:* Part-time, online learning. *Degree requirements:* For master's, thesis (for some programs), terminal project/capstone (for some programs). *Faculty research:* U.S. and European public procurement policies for small and medium-sized enterprises, examining external validity criticisms in the choice of students as subjects in accounting experiment studies, assurance of learning in contract management education, contracting for cloud computing: opportunities and risks, NPS, Apple App Store as a business model supporting U.S. Navy requirements.

New Charter University, College of Business, Salt Lake City, UT 84101. Offers finance (MBA); health care management (MBA); management (MBA). *Program availability:* Part-time, evening/weekend, online learning. *Entrance requirements:* For master's, course work in calculus, statistics, macroeconomics. Additional exam requirements/recommendations for international students: Required—TOEFL (minimum score 550 paper-based). Electronic applications accepted.

New England College of Business and Finance, Program in Finance, Boston, MA 02111-2645. Offers MSF. *Program availability:* Online learning.

New Jersey City University, School of Business, Program in Finance, Jersey City, NJ 07305-1597. Offers MBA, MS, Graduate Certificate. *Program availability:* Part-time, evening/weekend. *Degree requirements:* For master's, thesis. *Entrance requirements:* Additional exam requirements/recommendations for international students: Required—TOEFL (minimum score 79 iBT).

Newman University, MBA Program, Wichita, KS 67213-2097. Offers finance (MBA); international business (MBA); leadership (MBA); management (MBA); management information technology (MBA). *Program availability:* Part-time. *Degree requirements:* For master's, thesis optional. *Entrance requirements:* For master's, minimum GPA of 3.0; 2 letters of recommendation; course work in algebra, statistics, macroeconomics, and financial accounting. Additional exam requirements/recommendations for international students: Required—TOEFL (minimum score 600 paper-based; 100 iBT). Electronic applications accepted. *Expenses:* Contact institution.

New Mexico State University, College of Business, Department of Finance, Las Cruces, NM 88003. Offers finance (MBA, Graduate Certificate). *Program availability:* Part-time. *Faculty:* 9 full-time (2 women). *Students:* 2 full-time (both women), 1 part-time (0 women), 2 international. Average age 34. 2 applicants, 50% accepted, 1 enrolled. *Entrance requirements:* Additional exam requirements/recommendations for international students: Required—TOEFL (minimum score 550 paper-based; 79 iBT), IELTS (minimum score 6.5). *Application deadline:* Applications are processed on a rolling basis. Application fee: $40 ($50 for international students). Electronic applications accepted. *Expenses:* Tuition, state resident: full-time $4390. Tuition, nonresident: full-time $15,309. *Required fees:* $853. *Financial support:* In 2017–18, 1 student received support. Career-related internships or fieldwork, Federal Work-Study, scholarships/grants, traineeships, health care benefits, and unspecified assistantships available. Support available to part-time students. Financial award application deadline: 3/1. *Faculty research:* Tribal finance, international business finance and trade, market microstructure issues, business law, executive compensation. *Unit head:* Dr. Harikumar Sankaran, Department Head, 575-646-3201, Fax: 575-646-2820, E-mail: sankaran@nmsu.edu.
Website: http://business.nmsu.edu/departments/finance/

New Mexico State University, College of Business, MBA Program, Las Cruces, NM 88003. Offers agribusiness (MBA); finance (MBA); information systems (MBA). *Accreditation:* AACSB. *Program availability:* Part-time-only, evening/weekend, online with required 2-3 day orientation and 2-3 day concluding session in Las Cruces. *Students:* 47 full-time (24 women), 123 part-time (74 women); includes 69 minority (2 Black or African American, non-Hispanic/Latino; 3 American Indian or Alaska Native, non-Hispanic/Latino; 4 Asian, non-Hispanic/Latino; 85 Hispanic/Latino; 1 Native Hawaiian or other Pacific Islander, non-Hispanic/Latino; 3 Two or more races, non-Hispanic/Latino), 6 international. Average age 33. 166 applicants, 82% accepted, 19 enrolled. In 2017, 79 master's awarded. *Entrance requirements:* For master's, GMAT or GRE (depending upon undergraduate or graduate degree institution and GPA), minimum GPA of 3.5 from AACSB international or ACBSP-accredited institution or graduate degree from regionally-accredited U.S. university (without GMAT or GRE). Additional exam requirements/recommendations for international students: Required—TOEFL (minimum score 550 paper-based; 79 iBT), IELTS (minimum score 6.5). *Application deadline:* For fall admission, 7/15 priority date for domestic students, 4/15 priority date for international students; for spring admission, 4/15 priority date for domestic students, 9/15 priority date for international students; for summer admission, 4/15 for domestic students, 1/15 for international students. Applications are processed on a rolling basis. Application fee: $40 ($50 for international students). Electronic applications accepted. *Expenses:* Tuition, state resident: full-time $4390. Tuition, nonresident: full-time $15,309. *Required fees:* $853. *Financial support:* In 2017–18, 29 students received support. Fellowships, Federal Work-Study, institutionally sponsored loans, scholarships/grants, health care benefits, and unspecified assistantships available. Financial award application deadline: 3/1. *Unit head:* Dr. Kathy Brook, Associate Dean, 575-646-8003, Fax: 575-646-7977, E-mail: kbrook@nmsu.edu. *Application contact:* John Shonk, MBA Advisor, 575-646-8003, Fax: 575-646-7977, E-mail: mbaprog@nmsu.edu.
Website: http://business.nmsu.edu/mba

The New School, The New School for Social Research, Department of Economics, New York, NY 10003. Offers economics (MA, MS, PhD); global political economy and finance (MA). *Program availability:* Part-time. *Faculty:* 9 full-time (3 women), 2 part-time/adjunct (both women). *Students:* 80 full-time (22 women), 20 part-time (8 women); includes 17 minority (4 Black or African American, non-Hispanic/Latino; 6 Asian, non-Hispanic/Latino; 7 Hispanic/Latino), 53 international. Average age 32. 146 applicants, 66% accepted, 21 enrolled. In 2017, 23 master's, 8 doctorates awarded. Terminal master's awarded for partial completion of doctoral program. *Degree requirements:* For master's, comprehensive exam (for some programs), mentored research/internship; for doctorate, one foreign language, comprehensive exam, thesis/dissertation. *Entrance requirements:* For master's, GRE, letters of recommendation, writing sample, essays, transcript; for doctorate, letters of recommendation, writing sample, essays, transcript. Additional exam requirements/recommendations for international students: Required—TOEFL (minimum score 100 iBT), IELTS (minimum score 7), PTE (minimum score 68). *Application deadline:* For fall admission, 1/5 priority date for domestic and international students; for spring admission, 10/15 priority date for domestic and international students. Applications are processed on a rolling basis. Application fee: $50. Electronic applications accepted. *Expenses:* $2,180 per credit. *Financial support:* In 2017–18, 72 students received support, including 14 fellowships (averaging $16,694 per year), 7 research assistantships (averaging $13,681 per year), 23 teaching assistantships with full and partial tuition reimbursements available (averaging $7,340 per year); career-related internships or fieldwork, Federal Work-Study, scholarships/grants, tuition waivers (full and partial), and unspecified assistantships also available. Support available to part-time students. Financial award application deadline: 2/1; financial

award applicants required to submit FAFSA. *Unit head:* Dr. William Milberg, Dean, The New School for Social Research, 212-229-5777, E-mail: milbergw@newschool.edu. *Application contact:* Dana Messinger, Director of Graduate Admission, 212-229-5150 Ext. 2300, E-mail: socialresearchadmit@newschool.edu.
Website: https://www.newschool.edu/nssr/economics/

New York Institute of Technology, School of Management, Department of Business Administration, Old Westbury, NY 11568-8000. Offers executive management (MBA), including finance, marketing, operations and supply chain management. *Accreditation:* AACSB. *Program availability:* Part-time. *Faculty:* 25 full-time (4 women), 20 part-time/adjunct (6 women). *Students:* 398 full-time (187 women), 138 part-time (63 women); includes 43 minority (9 Black or African American, non-Hispanic/Latino; 1 American Indian or Alaska Native, non-Hispanic/Latino; 22 Asian, non-Hispanic/Latino; 9 Hispanic/Latino; 2 Two or more races, non-Hispanic/Latino), 432 international. Average age 26. 635 applicants, 75% accepted, 196 enrolled. In 2017, 230 master's awarded. *Entrance requirements:* For master's, bachelor's degree; minimum undergraduate GPA of 3.0. Additional exam requirements/recommendations for international students: Required—TOEFL (minimum score 79 iBT), IELTS (minimum score 6). *Application deadline:* Applications are processed on a rolling basis. Application fee: $50. Electronic applications accepted. *Expenses:* $1,285 per credit plus fees. *Financial support:* Career-related internships or fieldwork, Federal Work-Study, scholarships/grants, tuition waivers (full and partial), and unspecified assistantships available. Support available to part-time students. Financial award application deadline: 2/15; financial award applicants required to submit FAFSA. *Faculty research:* Accounting, economics, finance, management, marketing. *Unit head:* Dr. Jess Boronico, Dean, 516-686-7838, E-mail: som@nyit.edu. *Application contact:* Alice Dolitsky, Director, Graduate Admissions, 516-686-7520, Fax: 516-686-1116, E-mail: nyitgrad@nyit.edu.
Website: http://www.nyit.edu/degrees/management_mba

New York University, Leonard N. Stern School of Business, Department of Finance, New York, NY 10012-1019. Offers MBA, PhD. *Expenses: Tuition:* Full-time $41,352; part-time $19,968 per year. *Required fees:* $2496; $1628 per unit. $814 per term. Tuition and fees vary according to course load and program. *Faculty research:* Derivative securities, pricing of assets, credit risk, portfolio management, international finance.

New York University, School of Professional Studies, Jonathan M. Tisch Center of Hospitality, Program in Hospitality Industry Studies, New York, NY 10012-1019. Offers hospitality industry studies (MS), including brand strategy, hotel finance, lodging operations, revenue management. *Program availability:* Part-time, evening/weekend. *Students:* 42 full-time (28 women), 21 part-time (15 women); includes 11 minority (2 Black or African American, non-Hispanic/Latino; 7 Asian, non-Hispanic/Latino; 2 Hispanic/Latino), 35 international. Average age 26. 78 applicants, 54% accepted, 23 enrolled. In 2017, 62 master's awarded. *Degree requirements:* For master's, thesis. *Entrance requirements:* For master's, GRE or GMAT (only upon request), bachelor's degree, resume with relevant professional work, internship or volunteer experience, two letters of recommendation, statement of purpose. Additional exam requirements/recommendations for international students: Required—TOEFL (minimum score 600 paper-based; 100 iBT), IELTS (minimum score 7). *Application deadline:* For fall admission, 2/1 priority date for domestic and international students; for spring admission, 10/15 priority date for domestic students, 8/15 priority date for international students. Applications are processed on a rolling basis. Application fee: $150. Electronic applications accepted. *Expenses:* $20,244 per term. *Financial support:* Fellowships, career-related internships or fieldwork, Federal Work-Study, scholarships/grants, and health care benefits available. Support available to part-time students. Financial award application deadline: 6/30; financial award applicants required to submit FAFSA. *Unit head:* Nicolas Graf, Associate Dean/Clinical Associate Professor, 212-998-9100. *Application contact:* Admissions Office, 212-998-7100, E-mail: sps.gradadmissions@nyu.edu.
Website: http://www.sps.nyu.edu/areas-of-study/tisch/graduate-programs/ms-hospitality-industry-studies/

New York University, School of Professional Studies, Schack Institute of Real Estate, Program in Real Estate, New York, NY 10012-1019. Offers real estate (MS), including finance and investment, real estate asset management. *Program availability:* Part-time, evening/weekend. *Students:* 182 full-time (72 women), 297 part-time (60 women); includes 67 minority (5 Black or African American, non-Hispanic/Latino; 37 Asian, non-Hispanic/Latino; 21 Hispanic/Latino; 1 Native Hawaiian or other Pacific Islander, non-Hispanic/Latino; 3 Two or more races, non-Hispanic/Latino), 158 international. Average age 28. 267 applicants, 67% accepted, 96 enrolled. In 2017, 330 master's awarded. *Degree requirements:* For master's, thesis, capstone project. *Entrance requirements:* For master's, GRE or GMAT (only upon request), bachelor's degree, resume with relevant professional work, internship or volunteer experience, two letters of recommendation, statement of purpose. Additional exam requirements/recommendations for international students: Required—TOEFL (minimum score 600 paper-based; 100 iBT), IELTS (minimum score 7). *Application deadline:* For fall admission, 2/1 priority date for domestic and international students; for spring admission, 10/15 priority date for domestic students, 8/15 priority date for international students; for summer admission, 5/1 priority date for domestic students, 1/15 priority date for international students. Applications are processed on a rolling basis. Application fee: $150. Electronic applications accepted. *Expenses:* $20,244 per term. *Financial support:* Fellowships, career-related internships or fieldwork, Federal Work-Study, scholarships/grants, and health care benefits available. Support available to part-time students. Financial award application deadline: 6/30; financial award applicants required to submit FAFSA. *Unit head:* Sam Chandan, Associate Dean/Chair/Clinical Professor, 212-992-3335. *Application contact:* Office of Admissions, 212-998-7100, E-mail: sps.gradadmissions@nyu.edu.
Website: http://www.sps.nyu.edu/content/scps/academics/departments/schack/academic-offerings/graduate.html

New York University, Tandon School of Engineering, Department of Finance and Risk Engineering, New York, NY 10012-1019. Offers financial engineering (MS), including capital markets, computational finance, financial technology. *Program availability:* Part-time, evening/weekend. *Faculty:* 9 full-time (3 women), 16 part-time/adjunct (4 women). *Students:* 304 full-time (137 women), 7 part-time (1 woman); includes 8 minority (all Asian, non-Hispanic/Latino), 297 international. Average age 23. 1,604 applicants, 28% accepted, 163 enrolled. In 2017, 101 master's awarded. *Degree requirements:* For master's, comprehensive exam (for some programs), thesis (for some programs). *Entrance requirements:* For master's, GMAT, minimum B average in undergraduate course work. Additional exam requirements/recommendations for international students: Required—TOEFL (minimum score 550 paper-based; 90 iBT); Recommended—IELTS (minimum score 7). *Application deadline:* For fall admission, 2/15 priority date for domestic and international students; for spring admission, 11/1 priority date for domestic and international students. Applications are processed on a rolling basis. Application fee: $75. Electronic applications accepted. *Expenses:* $1,720 per credit tuition plus $89 per credit fees. *Financial support:* Institutionally sponsored loans, scholarships/grants, and unspecified assistantships available. Support available to part-time students. Financial award applicants required to submit FAFSA. *Faculty research:* Optimal control theory, general modeling and analysis, risk parity optimality, a new algorithmic approach to entangled political economy. *Total annual research expenditures:* $730,638. *Unit head:* Dr. Peter Paul Carr, Department Chair, 646-997-3539, E-mail: petercarr@nyu.edu. *Application contact:* Elizabeth Ensweiler, Senior Director of Graduate Enrollment and Graduate Admissions, 646-997-3182, E-mail: elizabeth.ensweiler@nyu.edu.

Niagara University, Graduate Division of Business Administration, Niagara University, NY 14109. Offers accounting (MBA); business administration (MBA); finance (MBA, MS); financial planning (MBA); healthcare administration (MBA, MHA); human resources (MBA); international business (MBA); marketing (MBA); professional accountancy (MBA); strategic management (MBA); supply chain management (MBA). *Accreditation:* AACSB. *Program availability:* Part-time, evening/weekend. *Faculty:* 17 full-time, 11 part-time/adjunct. *Students:* 173 full-time (92 women), 77 part-time (39 women); includes 38 minority (8 Black or African American, non-Hispanic/Latino; 3 American Indian or Alaska Native, non-Hispanic/Latino; 8 Asian, non-Hispanic/Latino; 8 Hispanic/Latino; 11 Two or more races, non-Hispanic/Latino), 46 international. Average age 27. In 2017, 139 master's awarded. *Entrance requirements:* For master's, GMAT. Additional exam requirements/recommendations for international students: Required—TOEFL (minimum score 550 paper-based; 79 iBT), IELTS (minimum score 6). *Application deadline:* For fall admission, 8/1 for domestic students; for spring admission, 11/1 for domestic students. Applications are processed on a rolling basis. Electronic applications accepted. *Expenses:* Contact institution. *Financial support:* Fellowships, research assistantships, career-related internships or fieldwork, and Federal Work-Study available. Support available to part-time students. Financial award application deadline: 4/15; financial award applicants required to submit FAFSA. *Faculty research:* Capital flows, Federal Reserve policy, human resource management, public policy, issues in marketing, auctions, economics of information, risk and capital markets, management strategy, consumer behavior, Internet and social media marketing. *Unit head:* Dr. Paul Richardson, MBA Director/Chair of the Marketing Department, 716-286-8169, Fax: 716-286-8206, E-mail: psr@niagara.edu. *Application contact:* Evan Pierce, Associate Director for Graduate Recruitment, 716-286-8769, Fax: 716-286-8170, E-mail: epierce@niagara.edu.
Website: http://mba.niagara.edu

North Central College, School of Graduate and Professional Studies, Program in Business Administration, Naperville, IL 60566-7063. Offers change management (MBA); finance (MBA); human resource management (MBA); management (MBA). *Program availability:* Part-time, evening/weekend. *Degree requirements:* For master's, thesis optional, project. *Entrance requirements:* For master's, interview. Additional exam requirements/recommendations for international students: Required—TOEFL (minimum score 550 paper-based; 80 iBT), IELTS (minimum score 6.5). Electronic applications accepted. Application fee is waived when completed online. *Expenses:* Contact institution.

Northeastern State University, College of Business and Technology, Program in Accounting and Financial Analysis, Tahlequah, OK 74464-2399. Offers MS. *Program availability:* Part-time, evening/weekend. *Faculty:* 4 full-time (1 woman). *Students:* 12 full-time (7 women), 46 part-time (26 women); includes 19 minority (4 Black or African American, non-Hispanic/Latino; 3 American Indian or Alaska Native, non-Hispanic/Latino; 2 Hispanic/Latino; 10 Two or more races, non-Hispanic/Latino), 2 international. Average age 32. In 2017, 19 master's awarded. *Entrance requirements:* For master's, GMAT. Additional exam requirements/recommendations for international students: Required—TOEFL. *Application deadline:* For fall admission, 6/1 priority date for domestic students. Applications are processed on a rolling basis. Application fee: $25. Electronic applications accepted. *Expenses:* Tuition, state resident: part-time $222 per credit hour. Tuition, nonresident: part-time $501.75 per credit hour. *Required fees:* $37.40 per credit hour. Tuition and fees vary according to degree level. *Faculty research:* Information systems and organizational performance, capital markets, sustainability. *Unit head:* Dr. Gary Freeman, Director, Master of Accounting and Financial Analysis, 918-449-6524, E-mail: freemadg@nsuok.edu. *Application contact:* Josh McCollum, Graduate Coordinator, 918-444-2093, E-mail: mccolluj@nsuok.edu.
Website: http://academics.nsuok.edu/businesstechnology/Graduate/MAFA.aspx

Northeastern University, D'Amore-McKim School of Business, Boston, MA 02115-5096. Offers accounting (MS); business administration (EMBA, MBA); finance (MS); innovation (MS); international business (MS); international management (MS); taxation (MS); technological entrepreneurship (MS); JD/MBA; LL M/MBA; MBA/MSN; MS/MBA. *Accreditation:* AACSB. *Program availability:* Part-time, evening/weekend, online learning. *Faculty:* 184. *Students:* 1,489. In 2017, 800 master's awarded. *Entrance requirements:* For master's, GMAT or GRE. Application fee: $75. Electronic applications accepted. *Expenses:* Contact institution. *Financial support:* Scholarships/grants available. Financial award applicants required to submit FAFSA. *Unit head:* Dr. Raj Echambadi, Dean, D'Amore-McKim School of Business, 617-373-3232, Fax: 617-373-2056. *Application contact:* Evelyn Tate, Director, Graduate Recruitment and Admissions, 617-373-3258, E-mail: e.tate@northeastern.edu.
Website: http://damore-mckim.northeastern.edu/

Northern State University, MS Program in Banking and Financial Services, Aberdeen, SD 57401-7198. Offers MS. *Program availability:* Part-time, online learning. *Degree requirements:* For master's, capstone course. *Entrance requirements:* For master's, GMAT or GRE, minimum GPA of 2.75. Additional exam requirements/recommendations for international students: Required—TOEFL (minimum score 550 paper-based; 78 iBT), IELTS (minimum score 6). Electronic applications accepted.

North Greenville University, T. Walter Brashier Graduate School, Greer, SC 29651. Offers Christian ministry (MCM, D Min); education (M Ed, MAT); financial planning (MBA); human resources (MBA). *Program availability:* Part-time, evening/weekend, online learning. *Degree requirements:* For master's, comprehensive exam (for some programs), thesis or alternative, capstone course. *Entrance requirements:* For master's, minimum GPA of 2.25 overall, 2.5 in major; for doctorate, MAT. Additional exam requirements/recommendations for international students: Required—TOEFL (minimum score 550 paper-based). Electronic applications accepted. *Faculty research:* Organizational behavior, church growth, homiletics, human resources, business strategy.

Northwestern University, The Graduate School, Kellogg School of Management, Department of Finance, Evanston, IL 60208. Offers PhD. Admissions and degree offered through The Graduate School. *Degree requirements:* For doctorate, comprehensive exam, thesis/dissertation. *Entrance requirements:* For doctorate, GMAT or GRE General Test, 2 years of undergraduate course work in mathematics. Additional exam requirements/recommendations for international students: Required—TOEFL. Electronic applications accepted. *Faculty research:* Corporate finance, asset pricing, international finance, micro-structure, empirical finance.

Northwestern University, The Graduate School, Kellogg School of Management, Management Programs, Evanston, IL 60208. Offers accounting information and management (MBA, PhD); analytical finance (MBA); business administration (MBA); decision sciences (MBA); entrepreneurship and innovation (MBA); finance (MBA, PhD); health enterprise management (MBA); human resources management (MBA); international business (MBA); management and organizations (MBA, PhD); management and organizations and sociology (PhD); management and strategy (MBA); management studies (MS); managerial analytics (MBA); managerial economics (MBA); managerial economics and strategy (PhD); marketing (MBA, PhD); marketing management (MBA); media management (MBA); operations management (MBA, PhD); real estate (MBA); social enterprise at Kellogg (MBA); JD/MBA. *Program availability:* Part-time, evening/weekend. Terminal master's awarded for partial completion of doctoral program. *Degree requirements:* For doctorate, thesis/dissertation, 2 years of coursework, qualifying (field) exam and candidacy, summer research papers and presentations to faculty, proposal defense, final exam/defense. *Entrance requirements:* For master's, GMAT, GRE, interview, 2 letters of recommendation, college transcripts, resume, essays, Kellogg honor code; for doctorate, GMAT, GRE, statement of purpose, transcripts, 2 letters of recommendation, resume, interview. Additional exam requirements/recommendations for international students: Required—TOEFL, IELTS. Electronic applications accepted. *Expenses:* Contact institution. *Faculty research:* Business cycles and international finance, health policy, networks, non-market strategy, consumer psychology.

Norwich University, College of Graduate and Continuing Studies, Master of Business Administration Program, Northfield, VT 05663. Offers construction management (MBA); energy management (MBA); finance (MBA); logistics (MBA); organizational leadership (MBA); project management (MBA); supply chain management (MBA). *Accreditation:* ACBSP. *Program availability:* Evening/weekend, online only, mostly all online with a week-long residency requirement. *Degree requirements:* For master's, comprehensive exam. *Entrance requirements:* For master's, minimum undergraduate GPA of 2.75. Additional exam requirements/recommendations for international students: Required—TOEFL (minimum score 550 paper-based; 80 iBT), IELTS (minimum score 6.5). Electronic applications accepted. *Expenses:* Contact institution.

Notre Dame de Namur University, Division of Academic Affairs, School of Business and Management, Program in Business Administration, Belmont, CA 94002-1908. Offers finance (MBA); human resource management (MBA); marketing (MBA); media and promotion (MBA). *Accreditation:* ACBSP. *Program availability:* Part-time, evening/weekend. *Students:* 28 full-time (24 women), 93 part-time (56 women). Average age 35. *Entrance requirements:* For master's, minimum GPA of 2.5. Additional exam requirements/recommendations for international students: Required—TOEFL (minimum score 550 paper-based; 79 iBT). *Application deadline:* For fall admission, 8/1 priority date for domestic students; for spring admission, 12/1 priority date for domestic students. Applications are processed on a rolling basis. Application fee: $60. Electronic applications accepted. *Expenses:* Tuition: Full-time $16,128; part-time $8064 per credit hour. *Required fees:* $80; $80 per credit hour. $40 per semester. *Financial support:* Available to part-time students. Applicants required to submit FAFSA. *Unit head:* Jordan Holtzman, Program Director, Graduate Business Programs, 510-375-1348, E-mail: jholtzman@ndnu.edu.
Website: http://www.ndnu.edu/academics/schools-programs/school-business/

Nova Southeastern University, H. Wayne Huizenga College of Business and Entrepreneurship, Fort Lauderdale, FL 33314-7796. Offers accounting (M Acc); business (MBA); business intelligence/analytics (MBA); complex health systems (MBA); enterprise informatics (MBA); entrepreneurship (MBA); finance (MBA); human resource management (MBA); international business (MBA); management (MBA); marketing (MBA); process improvement (MBA); public administration (MPA); real estate development (MS); sport revenue generation (MBA); supply chain management (MBA). *Accreditation:* NASPAA. *Program availability:* Part-time, evening/weekend, 100% online, blended/hybrid learning. *Faculty:* 85 full-time (37 women), 59 part-time/adjunct (19 women). *Students:* 1,999 full-time (1,225 women), 335 part-time (210 women); includes 1,516 minority (597 Black or African American, non-Hispanic/Latino; 4 American Indian or Alaska Native, non-Hispanic/Latino; 92 Asian, non-Hispanic/Latino; 789 Hispanic/Latino; 3 Native Hawaiian or other Pacific Islander, non-Hispanic/Latino; 31 Two or more races, non-Hispanic/Latino), 291 international. Average age 34. 1,269 applicants, 59% accepted, 551 enrolled. In 2017, 1,055 master's awarded. *Entrance requirements:* For master's, GMAT or GRE (depending on undergraduate GPA), official transcripts from all schools attended while in pursuit of bachelor's degree; minimum GPA of 2.5 from regionally-accredited institution. Additional exam requirements/recommendations for international students: Required—TOEFL (minimum score 550 paper-based; 79 iBT), IELTS (minimum score 6), PTE (minimum score 54). *Application deadline:* For fall admission, 8/5 priority date for domestic students, 7/29 priority date for international students; for winter admission, 12/16 priority date for domestic students, 12/9 priority date for international students; for summer admission, 4/21 priority date for domestic and international students. Applications are processed on a rolling basis. Application fee: $50. Electronic applications accepted. *Expenses:* $37,785 (online), $35,640 (in-classroom). *Financial support:* In 2017–18, 325 students received support. Federal Work-Study and scholarships/grants available. Support available to part-time students. Financial award application deadline: 4/15; financial award applicants required to submit FAFSA. *Faculty research:* Entrepreneurship and venture capital, ethics and social responsibility, global commerce and cultures, business process management. *Unit head:* Dr. J. Preston Jones, Dean, 954-262-5127, E-mail: prestonj@nova.edu. *Application contact:* Zeida Rodriguez, Associate Director of Enrollment Services, 954-262-5163, Fax: 954-262-3822, E-mail: zeida@nova.edu.
Website: http://www.huizenga.nova.edu

Oakland University, Graduate Study and Lifelong Learning, School of Business Administration, Department of Accounting and Finance, Rochester, MI 48309-4401. Offers accounting (M Acc, Certificate); finance (Certificate). *Expenses:* Tuition, state resident: full-time $16,950; part-time $706.25 per credit. Tuition, nonresident: full-time $24,648; part-time $1027 per credit.

Ohio Christian University, Graduate Programs, Circleville, OH 43113. Offers accounting (MBA); business administration (MBA); digital marketing (MBA); finance (MBA); healthcare management (MBA); human resources (MBA); management (MM); organizational leadership (MBA); pastoral care and counseling (MAM); practical theology (MAM).

Ohio Dominican University, Division of Business, Program in Business Administration, Columbus, OH 43219-2099. Offers accounting (MBA); data analytics (MBA); finance (MBA); leadership (MBA); risk management (MBA); sport management (MBA). *Program availability:* Part-time, evening/weekend, 100% online, blended/hybrid learning. *Faculty:* 7 full-time (4 women), 9 part-time/adjunct (2 women). *Students:* 53 full-time (21 women), 112 part-time (49 women); includes 37 minority (20 Black or African American, non-Hispanic/Latino; 1 American Indian or Alaska Native, non-Hispanic/Latino; 6 Asian, non-Hispanic/Latino; 5 Hispanic/Latino; 5 Two or more races, non-Hispanic/Latino), 5 international. Average age 31. 110 applicants, 45% accepted, 40 enrolled. In 2017, 93 master's awarded. *Entrance requirements:* For master's, minimum overall GPA of 3.0 in undergraduate degree from regionally-accredited institution or 2.75 in last 60 semester hours of bachelor's degree. Additional exam requirements/recommendations for international students: Required—TOEFL (minimum score 550 paper-based), IELTS (minimum score 6.5). *Application deadline:* For fall admission, 8/15 for domestic students, 6/10 for international students; for spring admission, 1/4 for domestic students, 11/2 for international students; for summer admission, 5/30 for domestic students. Applications are processed on a rolling basis. Application fee: $25. Electronic

applications accepted. *Expenses:* $600 per credit hour, $175 per semester technology fee, $50 per semester activity fee. *Financial support:* Applicants required to submit FAFSA. *Unit head:* Dr. Steve Vickner, Director of Master of Business Administration Program, 614-251-4569, E-mail: vickners@ohiodominican.edu. *Application contact:* John W. Naughton, Associate Vice President for Enrollment Management, 614-251-4721, Fax: 614-251-6654, E-mail: grad@ohiodominican.edu.
Website: http://www.ohiodominican.edu/academics/graduate/mba

The Ohio State University, Graduate School, Max M. Fisher College of Business, Program in Finance, Columbus, OH 43210. Offers MF. *Students:* 52 full-time (21 women). Average age 23. In 2017, 50 master's awarded. *Entrance requirements:* For master's, GMAT (preferred with minimum score of 550 recommended, 600 preferred) or GRE. Additional exam requirements/recommendations for international students: Required—TOEFL (minimum score 600 paper-based; 100 iBT). *Application deadline:* For fall admission, 11/15 priority date for domestic and international students; for spring admission, 10/1 for domestic students. Applications are processed on a rolling basis. Application fee: $60 ($70 for international students). Electronic applications accepted. *Financial support:* Fellowships with tuition reimbursements available. *Unit head:* George Pinteris, Graduate Studies Chair, 614-292-4334, E-mail: pinteris.1@osu.edu. *Application contact:* Graduate and Professional Admissions, 614-292-9444, Fax: 614-292-3895, E-mail: gpadmissions@osu.edu.
Website: http://fisher.osu.edu/smf

Ohio University, Graduate College, College of Arts and Sciences, Department of Economics, Athens, OH 45701-2979. Offers applied economics (MA); financial economics (MFE). *Program availability:* Part-time, evening/weekend. *Degree requirements:* For master's, thesis or alternative. *Entrance requirements:* For master's, GRE or GMAT (recommended), minimum GPA of 3.0. Additional exam requirements/recommendations for international students: Required—TOEFL (minimum score 550 paper-based; 80 iBT) or IELTS (minimum score 6.5). Electronic applications accepted. *Faculty research:* Macroeconomics, public finance, international economics and finance, monetary theory, healthcare economics.

Oklahoma Christian University, Graduate School of Business, Oklahoma City, OK 73136-1100. Offers accounting (M Acc, MBA); financial services (MBA); general business (MBA); health services management (MBA); human resources (MBA); international business (MBA); leadership and organizational development (MBA); marketing (MBA); nonprofit management (MBA); project management (MBA). *Accreditation:* ACBSP. *Program availability:* Part-time, 100% online. *Entrance requirements:* For master's, bachelor's degree. Additional exam requirements/recommendations for international students: Required—TOEFL (minimum score 550 paper-based). Electronic applications accepted. *Expenses:* Contact institution.

Oklahoma State University, Spears School of Business, Department of Finance, Stillwater, OK 74078. Offers MS, PhD. *Program availability:* Part-time. *Faculty:* 13 full-time (3 women), 2 part-time/adjunct (0 women). *Students:* 18 full-time (6 women), 1 part-time (0 women); includes 1 minority (Hispanic/Latino), 14 international. Average age 26. 31 applicants, 35% accepted, 10 enrolled. In 2017, 9 master's, 4 doctorates awarded. *Entrance requirements:* For master's and doctorate, GRE or GMAT. Additional exam requirements/recommendations for international students: Required—TOEFL (minimum score 550 paper-based; 79 iBT). *Application deadline:* For fall admission, 3/1 priority date for international students; for spring admission, 8/1 priority date for international students. Applications are processed on a rolling basis. Application fee: $40 ($75 for international students). Electronic applications accepted. *Expenses:* Tuition, state resident: full-time $4019; part-time $2679.60 per year. Tuition, nonresident: full-time $15,286; part-time $10,190.40 per year. *Required fees:* $2129; $1419 per unit. Tuition and fees vary according to program. *Financial support:* Research assistantships, teaching assistantships, career-related internships or fieldwork, Federal Work-Study, scholarships/grants, health care benefits, tuition waivers (partial), and unspecified assistantships available. Support available to part-time students. Financial award application deadline: 3/1; financial award applicants required to submit FAFSA. *Faculty research:* Corporate risk management, derivatives banking, investments and securities issuance, corporate governance, banking. *Unit head:* Dr. Betty Simkins, Interim Department Head, 405-744-8625, Fax: 405-744-5180, E-mail: betty.simkins@okstate.edu.
Website: https://business.okstate.edu/finance/

Old Dominion University, Strome College of Business, Doctoral Program in Business Administration, Norfolk, VA 23529. Offers business administration (PhD), including finance, IT and supply chain management, marketing, strategic innovation. *Accreditation:* AACSB. *Faculty:* 35 full-time (6 women). *Students:* 27 full-time (8 women), 25 part-time (6 women); includes 1 minority (Asian, non-Hispanic/Latino), 41 international. Average age 35. 63 applicants, 30% accepted, 8 enrolled. In 2017, 9 doctorates awarded. *Degree requirements:* For doctorate, comprehensive exam, thesis/dissertation. *Entrance requirements:* For doctorate, GMAT or GRE. Additional exam requirements/recommendations for international students: Required—TOEFL (minimum score 550 paper-based; 79 iBT). *Application deadline:* For fall admission, 3/1 priority date for domestic and international students. Application fee: $50. Electronic applications accepted. *Expenses:* Tuition, state resident: full-time $8928; part-time $496 per credit. Tuition, nonresident: full-time $22,482; part-time $1249 per credit. *Required fees:* $66 per semester. *Financial support:* In 2017–18, 36 students received support, including 15 research assistantships with full tuition reimbursements available (averaging $18,500 per year), 13 teaching assistantships with full tuition reimbursements available (averaging $18,500 per year); unspecified assistantships and tuition grants (for fourth-year students) also available. Financial award application deadline: 3/1; financial award applicants required to submit FAFSA. *Faculty research:* International business, buyer behavior, financial markets, strategy, operations research. *Unit head:* Dr. John B. Ford, Graduate Program Director, 757-683-3587, Fax: 757-683-4076, E-mail: jbford@odu.edu. *Application contact:* Katrina Davenport, Program Coordinator, 757-683-5138, Fax: 757-683-4076, E-mail: kdavenpo@odu.edu.
Website: http://www.odu.edu/business/academics/graduate/scb-phd

Oral Roberts University, School of Business, Tulsa, OK 74171. Offers accounting (MBA); entrepreneurship (MBA); finance (MBA); international business (MBA); management (MBA); marketing (MBA); not for profit management (MNM). *Accreditation:* ACBSP. *Program availability:* Part-time, online learning. *Faculty:* 7 full-time (0 women), 5 part-time/adjunct (4 women). *Students:* 71 applicants, 94% accepted, 56 enrolled. *Degree requirements:* For master's, thesis optional. *Entrance requirements:* For master's, minimum cumulative GPA of 3.0 from regionally-accredited institution. *Application deadline:* Applications are processed on a rolling basis. Application fee: $35. Electronic applications accepted. Application fee is waived when completed online. *Financial support:* In 2017–18, 39 students received support. Scholarships/grants and unspecified assistantships available. Financial award application deadline: 6/1. *Faculty research:* Social media, international business and marketing. *Unit head:* Dr. Marshal Wright, Chair of the Graduate School of Business, 918-495-6988, E-mail: mwright@oru.edu. *Application contact:* Sam Park, Enrollment Counselor, 918-495-7179, E-mail: sampark@oru.edu.
Website: http://www.oru.edu/university/departments/schools/bus

Oregon State University, College of Business, Program in Business Administration, Corvallis, OR 97331. Offers business administration (PhD), including accounting; corporate finance (MBA). *Program availability:* Part-time, blended/hybrid learning. *Entrance requirements:* For master's, GMAT. Additional exam requirements/recommendations for international students: Required—TOEFL (minimum score 91 iBT), IELTS (minimum score 7). *Application deadline:* For fall admission, 2/1 priority date for domestic and international students; for winter admission, 9/15 priority date for domestic and international students; for spring admission, 1/1 priority date for domestic and international students. Applications are processed on a rolling basis. Application fee: $75 ($85 for international students). *Expenses:* Contact institution. *Financial support:* Application deadline: 1/15. *Unit head:* Matt Alex, Associate Director, 541-737-5340, E-mail: matt.alex@oregonstate.edu. *Application contact:* Matt Alex, Associate Director, 541-737-5340, E-mail: matt.alex@oregonstate.edu.
Website: http://business.oregonstate.edu/graduate-programs

Ottawa University, Graduate Studies-Arizona, Programs in Business, Ottawa, KS 66067-3399. Offers business administration (MBA); finance (MBA); human resources (MA, MBA); leadership (MBA); marketing (MBA). Programs offered in Mesa, Phoenix, Tempe and West Valley, AZ. *Program availability:* Part-time, evening/weekend, online learning. *Degree requirements:* For master's, thesis or alternative. *Entrance requirements:* For master's, minimum undergraduate GPA of 3.0. Additional exam requirements/recommendations for international students: Required—TOEFL (minimum score 550 paper-based). Electronic applications accepted.

Our Lady of the Lake University, School of Business and Leadership, Program in Finance, San Antonio, TX 78207-4689. Offers MBA. *Program availability:* Part-time, evening/weekend. *Faculty:* 2 full-time (both women), 1 part-time/adjunct (0 women). *Students:* 13 full-time (6 women), 4 part-time (2 women); includes 11 minority (all Hispanic/Latino). Average age 35. 4 applicants, 75% accepted, 2 enrolled. In 2017, 1 master's awarded. *Entrance requirements:* For master's, official transcripts showing 6 hours of coursework in economics and 3 hours of coursework in each of the following areas: statistics, management, business law, and finance; résumé including detailed work history describing managerial or professional work experience. Additional exam requirements/recommendations for international students: Required—TOEFL. *Application deadline:* For fall admission, 6/15 for domestic students, 7/15 for international students; for spring admission, 11/15 for domestic and international students; for summer admission, 4/15 for domestic and international students. Applications are processed on a rolling basis. Application fee: $40 ($50 for international students). Electronic applications accepted. Application fee is waived when completed online. *Expenses:* Tuition: Full-time $10,668; part-time $5334 per year. *Required fees:* $816; $816 per year. $408 per semester. *Financial support:* In 2017–18, 3 students received support. Federal Work-Study, unspecified assistantships, and tuition discounts available. Support available to part-time students. Financial award application deadline: 5/1; financial award applicants required to submit FAFSA. *Unit head:* Dr. Ronald Crowe, Business Programs Chair, E-mail: rcrowe@ollusa.edu. *Application contact:* Office of Graduate Admissions, 210-431-3995, Fax: 210-431-3945, E-mail: gradadm@ollusa.edu.

Pace University, Lubin School of Business, Advanced Professional Certificate Program, New York, NY 10038. Offers business economics (APC); e-business (APC); financial management (APC); international business (APC); international economics (APC); investment management (APC); marketing (APC); public accounting (APC). *Program availability:* Part-time, evening/weekend. *Students:* 1 applicant, 100% accepted. *Entrance requirements:* For degree, MBA or MS in business discipline, relevant professional experience. Additional exam requirements/recommendations for international students: Required—TOEFL (minimum score 90 iBT), IELTS (minimum score 7) or PTE (minimum score 61). *Application deadline:* For fall admission, 8/1 priority date for domestic students, 6/1 for international students; for spring admission, 12/1 for domestic students, 10/1 for international students. Applications are processed on a rolling basis. Application fee: $70. Electronic applications accepted. *Unit head:* Dr. Jack Yurkiewicz, Director, 212-618-6567, E-mail: jyurkiewicz@pace.edu. *Application contact:* Susan Ford-Goldschein, Director of Graduate Admissions, 212-346-1531, Fax: 212-346-1585, E-mail: graduateadmission@pace.edu.
Website: http://www.pace.edu/lubin/agc

Pace University, Lubin School of Business, Doctor of Professional Studies Program, New York, NY 10038. Offers finance (DPS); management (DPS); marketing (DPS). *Program availability:* Part-time. *Students:* 12 full-time (5 women), 67 part-time (29 women); includes 22 minority (12 Black or African American, non-Hispanic/Latino; 5 Asian, non-Hispanic/Latino; 4 Hispanic/Latino; 1 Two or more races, non-Hispanic/Latino), 3 international. Average age 50. 31 applicants, 81% accepted, 13 enrolled. In 2017, 4 doctorates awarded. *Degree requirements:* For doctorate, thesis/dissertation, oral and written exam. *Entrance requirements:* For doctorate, MBA or similar master's degree, 10 years of experience in business, transcripts from all accredited colleges/universities attended, 4 letters of recommendation, interview. Additional exam requirements/recommendations for international students: Required—TOEFL (minimum score 90 iBT), IELTS (minimum score 7) or PTE (minimum score 61). *Application deadline:* For fall admission, 6/1 priority date for domestic students, 6/1 for international students. Applications are processed on a rolling basis. Application fee: $70. Electronic applications accepted. *Unit head:* Dr. John P. Dory, Director, Doctoral Program in Business, 212-618-6660, E-mail: jdory@pace.edu. *Application contact:* Margaret Hanson, Program Coordinator for Doctoral Programs, 212-618-6660, E-mail: dps.bus@pace.edu.
Website: http://www.pace.edu/lubin/dps/

Pace University, Lubin School of Business, Financial Management Program, New York, NY 10038. Offers financial management (MBA, MS); financial risk management (MS); international finance (MBA); investment management (MBA, MS). *Program availability:* Part-time, evening/weekend. *Students:* 103 full-time (41 women), 53 part-time (26 women); includes 24 minority (5 Black or African American, non-Hispanic/Latino; 11 Asian, non-Hispanic/Latino; 6 Hispanic/Latino; 1 Native Hawaiian or other Pacific Islander, non-Hispanic/Latino; 1 Two or more races, non-Hispanic/Latino), 103 international. Average age 26. 251 applicants, 61% accepted, 43 enrolled. In 2017, 108 master's awarded. *Entrance requirements:* For master's, GMAT, GRE (GMAT not required for MS with passing of Level 1 of Chartered Financial Analyst exam or Level 1 of Financial Risk Manager Exam), undergraduate degree, transcripts from all accredited colleges/universities attended, two letters of recommendation, resume, personal statement. Additional exam requirements/recommendations for international students: Required—TOEFL (minimum score 90 iBT), IELTS (minimum score 7) or PTE (minimum score 61). *Application deadline:* For fall admission, 8/1 priority date for domestic students, 6/1 for international students; for spring admission, 12/1 for domestic students, 10/1 for international students. Applications are processed on a rolling basis. Application fee: $70. Electronic applications accepted. *Financial support:* Research assistantships, career-related internships or fieldwork, Federal Work-Study, and tuition waivers (full and partial) available. Support available to part-time students. Financial award application deadline: 2/15; financial award applicants required to submit FAFSA. *Unit head:* Dr. P. V. Viswanath, Chairperson, 212-618-6518, E-mail: pviswanath@pace.edu. *Application contact:* Susan Ford-Goldschein, Director of Graduate Admissions, 212-346-1531, Fax: 212-346-1585, E-mail: graduateadmissions@pace.edu.
Website: http://www.pace.edu/lubin/financial-management-mba

Pacific Lutheran University, School of Business, Master of Science in Finance Program, Tacoma, WA 98447. Offers MSF. *Entrance requirements:* For master's, GRE or GMAT. Additional exam requirements/recommendations for international students: Required—TOEFL (minimum score 550 paper-based; 88 iBT). Electronic applications accepted. *Expenses:* Contact institution.

Pacific States University, College of Business, Los Angeles, CA 90010. Offers accounting (MBA, Certificate); beauty management (MBA); finance (MBA); international business (MBA); management of information technology (MBA); project management (Certificate); real estate management (MBA). *Program availability:* Part-time, evening/weekend, online learning. *Entrance requirements:* For master's, minimum undergraduate GPA of 2.5 during last 90 quarter units of course work, bachelor's degree in business administration or economics. Additional exam requirements/recommendations for international students: Required—TOEFL (minimum score 500 paper-based; 61 iBT), IELTS (minimum score 5.5). *Application deadline:* For fall admission, 9/1 priority date for domestic students, 8/1 priority date for international students; for winter admission, 12/1 priority date for domestic students, 11/1 priority date for international students; for spring admission, 3/1 priority date for domestic students, 2/1 priority date for international students; for summer admission, 6/1 priority date for domestic students, 5/1 priority date for international students. Applications are processed on a rolling basis. Application fee: $100. *Expenses: Tuition:* Part-time $380 per unit. *Financial support:* Scholarships/grants available. Financial award applicants required to submit FAFSA. *Unit head:* Chase C. Rhee, MBA Program Administrator, 323-731-2383 Ext. 208, Fax: 323-731-7276, E-mail: ccrhee@psuca.edu. *Application contact:* Maawiya Ayeva, Director of Admissions, 323-731-2383 Ext. 204, Fax: 323-731-7276, E-mail: admissions@psuca.edu.

Pacific University, College of Business, Forest Grove, OR 97116-1797. Offers business administration (MBA); finance (MSF).

Park University, School of Graduate and Professional Studies, Kansas City, MO 54105. Offers adult education (M Ed); business and government leadership (Graduate Certificate); business, government, and global society (MPA); communication and leadership (MA); creative and life writing (Graduate Certificate); disaster and emergency management (MPA, Graduate Certificate); educational leadership (M Ed); finance (MBA, Graduate Certificate); general business (MBA); global business (Graduate Certificate); healthcare administration (MHA); healthcare services management and leadership (Graduate Certificate); international business (MBA); language and literacy (M Ed), including English for speakers of other languages, special reading teacher/literacy coach; leadership of international healthcare organizations (Graduate Certificate); management information systems (MBA, Graduate Certificate); music performance (ADP, Graduate Certificate), including cello (MM, ADP), piano (MM, ADP), viola (MM, ADP), violin (MM, ADP); nonprofit and community services management (MPA); nonprofit leadership (Graduate Certificate); performance (MM), including cello (MM, ADP), piano (MM, ADP), viola (MM, ADP), violin (MM, ADP); public management (MPA); social work (MSW); teacher leadership (M Ed), including curriculum and assessment, instructional leader. *Program availability:* Part-time, evening/weekend, online learning. *Degree requirements:* For master's, comprehensive exam (for some programs), thesis (for some programs), internship (for some programs); exam (for some programs). *Entrance requirements:* For master's, GRE or GMAT (for some programs), teacher certification (for some M Ed programs), letters of recommendation, essay, resume (for some programs). Additional exam requirements/recommendations for international students: Required—TOEFL (minimum score 550 paper-based; 79 iBT), IELTS (minimum score 6). Electronic applications accepted.

Penn State Great Valley, Graduate Studies, Management Division, Malvern, PA 19355-1488. Offers business administration (MBA); cyber security (Certificate); data analytics (MPS, MS, Certificate); distributed energy and grid modernization (Certificate); finance (M Fin); health sector management (Certificate); human resource management (Certificate); information science (MSIS); leadership development (MLD); new ventures and entrepreneurship (Certificate); sustainable management practices (Certificate). *Accreditation:* AACSB. *Unit head:* Dr. James A. Nemes, Chancellor, 610-648-3202, Fax: 610-725-5296. *Application contact:* JoAnn Kelly, Director of Admissions, 610-648-3315, Fax: 610-725-5296, E-mail: jek2@psu.edu.
Website: http://greatvalley.psu.edu/academics/masters-degrees/engineering-management

Penn State Harrisburg, Graduate School, School of Public Affairs, Middletown, PA 17057. Offers criminal justice (MA); health administration (MHA); health administration: long term care (Certificate); homeland security (MPS, Certificate); public administration (MPA, PhD); public administration: non-profit administration (Certificate); public budgeting and financial management (Certificate); public sector human resource management (Certificate). *Accreditation:* NASPAA. *Unit head:* Dr. Mukund S. Kulkarni, Chancellor, 717-948-6105, Fax: 717-948-6452. *Application contact:* Robert W. Coffman, Jr., Director of Enrollment Management, Recruitment and Admissions, 717-948-6250, Fax: 717-948-6325, E-mail: hbgadmit@psu.edu.
Website: https://harrisburg.psu.edu/public-affairs

Pepperdine University, Graziadio Business School, Master of Science Programs, Malibu, CA 90263. Offers accounting (MS); applied analytics (MS); applied finance (MS); global business (MS); human resources (MS); management and leadership (MS); organization development (MS); real estate investment and finance (MS). *Accreditation:* AACSB. *Students:* 462 full-time (277 women), 104 part-time (68 women); includes 67 minority (23 Black or African American, non-Hispanic/Latino; 1 American Indian or Alaska Native, non-Hispanic/Latino; 41 Asian, non-Hispanic/Latino; 2 Hispanic/Latino), 380 international. Average age 27. 2,180 applicants, 63% accepted, 336 enrolled. In 2017, 291 master's awarded. *Entrance requirements:* For master's, GMAT or GRE, two letters of recommendation. Additional exam requirements/recommendations for international students: Required—TOEFL. *Application deadline:* For fall admission, 5/1 for domestic students, 4/1 for international students. Application fee: $75. Electronic applications accepted. *Financial support:* Applicants required to submit FAFSA. *Unit head:* Dr. Michael L. Williams, Associate Dean, 310-506-4112, Fax: 310-506-4126, E-mail: michael.williams@pepperdine.edu.
Website: http://bschool.pepperdine.edu/masters-degree/

Polytechnic University of Puerto Rico, Miami Campus, Graduate School, Miami, FL 33166. Offers accounting (MBA); business administration (MBA); construction management (MEM); environmental management (MEM); finance (MBA); human resources management (MBA); logistics and supply chain management (MBA); management of international enterprises (MBA); manufacturing management (MEM); marketing management (MBA); project management (MBA). *Program availability:* Part-time, evening/weekend, online learning. *Entrance requirements:* For master's, minimum GPA of 3.0. Electronic applications accepted.

Polytechnic University of Puerto Rico, Orlando Campus, Graduate School, Orlando, FL 32825. Offers accounting (MBA); business administration (MBA); construction management (MEM); engineering management (MEM); environmental management (MEM); finance (MBA); human resources management (MBA); management of international enterprises (MBA); management of technology (MBA); manufacturing management (MEM). *Program availability:* Part-time, evening/weekend, online learning.

Entrance requirements: For master's, minimum GPA of 3.0. Additional exam requirements/recommendations for international students: Recommended—TOEFL. Electronic applications accepted.

Pontifical Catholic University of Puerto Rico, College of Business Administration, Program in Finance, Ponce, PR 00717-0777. Offers MBA. *Program availability:* Part-time, evening/weekend. *Degree requirements:* For master's, thesis. *Entrance requirements:* For master's, GRE, interview, minimum GPA of 2.75.

Pontificia Universidad Catolica Madre y Maestra, Graduate School, Faculty of Social and Administrative Sciences, Santiago, Dominican Republic. Offers business administration (MBA), including business development, finance, international business, management skills (M Mgmt, MBA), marketing, operations, strategic cost management, strategy, tourist destination planning and management; law (LL M), including civil law, corporate business law, criminal law, international relations, real estate law; management (M Mgmt), including higher financial management, insurance program administration, management skills (M Mgmt, MBA); psychology (MA), including clinical child and adolescent psychology, forensic psychology; strategic human resources (EMBA).

Portland State University, Graduate Studies, The School of Business, Master of Science in Financial Analysis Program, Portland, OR 97207-0751. Offers MSF. *Program availability:* Part-time, evening/weekend. *Students:* 20 full-time (9 women), 22 part-time (14 women); includes 9 minority (5 Asian, non-Hispanic/Latino; 2 Hispanic/Latino; 2 Two or more races, non-Hispanic/Latino), 10 international. Average age 33. 1 applicant, 100% accepted, 1 enrolled. In 2017, 38 master's awarded. *Entrance requirements:* For master's, GMAT or GRE, minimum GPA of 2.75, 2 recommendations, statement of purpose, resume, interview. Additional exam requirements/recommendations for international students: Required—TOEFL (minimum score 550 paper-based; 80 iBT). *Application deadline:* For fall admission, 2/1 priority date for domestic and international students. Applications are processed on a rolling basis. Application fee: $65. Electronic applications accepted. *Expenses:* Contact institution. *Financial support:* In 2017–18, 9 students received support. Career-related internships or fieldwork, Federal Work-Study, and scholarships/grants available. Financial award application deadline: 3/1; financial award applicants required to submit FAFSA. *Unit head:* David Nickel, Academic Director, 503-725-5931, Fax: 503-725-5850, E-mail: nickel@pdx.edu. *Application contact:* Pamela Dusschee, Director, Graduate Business Programs, 503-725-3714, E-mail: pamela.dusschee@pdx.edu.
Website: https://www.pdx.edu/sba/master-of-science-in-finance

Post University, Program in Business Administration, Waterbury, CT 06723-2540. Offers accounting (MSA); business administration (MBA); corporate finance (MBA); corporate innovation (MBA); healthcare systems leadership (MBA); leadership (MBA); marketing (MBA); project management (MBA, MS). *Accreditation:* ACBSP. *Program availability:* Online learning. *Entrance requirements:* For master's, resume. *Expenses: Tuition:* Part-time $730 per credit hour. Part-time tuition and fees vary according to degree level and program. *Application contact:* Veronica Montalvo, Vice President, Online Education Enrollment Management and Admissions, 203-596-6164, E-mail: vmontalvo@post.edu.

Princeton University, Graduate School, Bendheim Center for Finance, Princeton, NJ 08544-1019. Offers M Fin. *Entrance requirements:* For master's, GRE General Test. Additional exam requirements/recommendations for international students: Required—TOEFL (minimum score 600 paper-based). Electronic applications accepted.

Providence College, School of Business, Providence, RI 02918. Offers accounting (MBA); finance (MBA); international business (MBA); management (MBA); marketing (MBA). *Accreditation:* AACSB. *Program availability:* Part-time, evening/weekend. *Entrance requirements:* For master's, GMAT. Additional exam requirements/recommendations for international students: Required—TOEFL (minimum score 577 paper-based; 90 iBT). *Expenses:* Contact institution.

Purdue University, Graduate School, Krannert School of Management, Master of Science in Finance Program, West Lafayette, IN 47907. Offers MSF. *Faculty:* 143 full-time (32 women), 6 part-time/adjunct (1 woman). *Students:* 40 full-time (23 women); includes 3 minority (2 Asian, non-Hispanic/Latino; 1 Two or more races, non-Hispanic/Latino), 35 international. Average age 24. 199 applicants, 67% accepted, 40 enrolled. In 2017, 51 master's awarded. *Entrance requirements:* For master's, GMAT or GRE, minimum GPA of 3.0, four-year baccalaureate degree, essays, letters of recommendation. Additional exam requirements/recommendations for international students: Required—TOEFL (minimum score 600 paper-based; 93 iBT), IELTS (minimum score 7.5). *Application deadline:* For fall admission, 11/15 priority date for domestic students, 11/15 for international students; for winter admission, 1/15 for domestic and international students; for spring admission, 3/1 for domestic and international students. Applications are processed on a rolling basis. Application fee: $60 ($75 for international students). Electronic applications accepted. *Expenses:* Contact institution. *Financial support:* In 2017–18, 5 students received support. Scholarships/grants available. Financial award application deadline: 3/1; financial award applicants required to submit FAFSA. *Faculty research:* Capital market imperfections and sensitivity of investment to stock prices, identifying beneficial collaboration in decentralized logistics systems, performance periods and the dynamics of the performance-risk relationship, applications of global optimization to process and molecular design. *Unit head:* Dr. David Hummels, Dean/Professor of Economics, 765-494-4366, E-mail: krannertdean@purdue.edu. *Application contact:* Thomas Bates, Associate Director of Admissions, 765-494-0773, Fax: 765-494-9841, E-mail: krannertmasters@purdue.edu.
Website: http://www.krannert.purdue.edu/masters/programs/ms-f/

Purdue University Global, School of Business, Davenport, IA 52807. Offers business administration (MBA); change leadership (MS); entrepreneurship (MBA); finance (MBA); health care management (MBA, MS); human resource (MBA); international business (MBA); management (MS); marketing (MBA); project management (MBA, MS); supply chain management and logistics (MBA, MS). *Accreditation:* ACBSP. *Program availability:* Part-time, evening/weekend, online learning. *Entrance requirements:* Additional exam requirements/recommendations for international students: Required—TOEFL (minimum score 500 paper-based; 80 iBT). Electronic applications accepted.

Queens College of the City University of New York, Division of Social Sciences, Department of Economics, Queens, NY 11367-1597. Offers risk management: accounting (MS); risk management: dynamic financial analysis (MS); risk management: finance (MS). *Students:* 11 full-time (4 women), 38 part-time (21 women); includes 29 minority (6 Black or African American, non-Hispanic/Latino; 15 Asian, non-Hispanic/Latino; 5 Hispanic/Latino; 3 Two or more races, non-Hispanic/Latino), 12 international. Average age 31. *Degree requirements:* For master's, thesis. *Entrance requirements:* For master's, minimum GPA of 3.0. Additional exam requirements/recommendations for international students: Required—TOEFL (minimum score 100 iBT), IELTS (minimum score 7). *Financial support:* Federal Work-Study, institutionally sponsored loans, and tuition waivers (partial) available. Support available to part-time students. Financial award application deadline: 4/1; financial award applicants required to submit FAFSA. *Faculty research:* Business economics, urban economic problems, international economics, economics of nonprofit sector. *Unit head:* Dr. John Devereux, Chair, 718-997-5440, E-mail: john.devereux@qc.cuny.edu. *Application contact:* Elvira Casper, Program Coordinator, 718-997-5507, E-mail: elvira.casper@qc.cuny.edu.

SECTION 2: ACCOUNTING AND FINANCE

Finance and Banking

Queen's University at Kingston, Queens School of Business, Program in Business Administration, Kingston, ON K7L 3N6, Canada. Offers consulting and project management (MBA); finance (MBA); innovation and entrepreneurship (MBA); marketing (MBA). *Degree requirements:* For master's, thesis optional, research project. *Entrance requirements:* For master's, GMAT, minimum B+ average. Additional exam requirements/recommendations for international students: Required—TOEFL. Electronic applications accepted. *Faculty research:* Management fundamentals, strategic thinking, global business, innovation and change, leadership.

Quinnipiac University, School of Business, Program in Business Administration, Hamden, CT 06518-1940. Offers finance (MBA); health care management (MBA); supply chain management (MBA); JD/MBA. *Accreditation:* AACSB. *Program availability:* Part-time, evening/weekend, 100% online, blended/hybrid learning. *Faculty:* 32 full-time (11 women), 8 part-time/adjunct (3 women). *Students:* 201 full-time (95 women), 215 part-time (95 women); includes 48 minority (9 Black or African American, non-Hispanic/Latino; 12 Asian, non-Hispanic/Latino; 20 Hispanic/Latino; 7 Two or more races, non-Hispanic/Latino), 19 international. 307 applicants, 79% accepted, 223 enrolled. In 2017, 264 master's awarded. *Entrance requirements:* For master's, GMAT or GRE, minimum GPA of 3.0. Additional exam requirements/recommendations for international students: Required—TOEFL (minimum score 575 paper-based; 90 iBT), IELTS (minimum score 6.5). *Application deadline:* For fall admission, 7/30 priority date for domestic students, 4/30 priority date for international students; for spring admission, 12/15 priority date for domestic students, 9/30 priority date for international students. Applications are processed on a rolling basis. Application fee: $45. Electronic applications accepted. *Expenses:* Contact institution. *Financial support:* Career-related internships or fieldwork, Federal Work-Study, scholarships/grants, and unspecified assistantships available. Financial award application deadline: 6/1; financial award applicants required to submit FAFSA. *Faculty research:* Financial markets and investments, international business, supply chain management, health care management, corporate governance. *Unit head:* Lisa Braiewa, Director of the MBA Program, 800-462-1944, Fax: 203-582-3443, E-mail: graduate@qu.edu. *Application contact:* Office of Graduate Admissions, 800-462-1944, Fax: 203-582-3443, E-mail: graduate@qu.edu. Website: http://www.qu.edu/mba

Regent's University London, Webster Graduate School, London, United Kingdom. Offers business (MBA); finance (MS); human resources (MA); information technology management (MA); international business (MA); international non-governmental organizations (MA); international relations (MA); management and leadership (MA); marketing (MA). *Program availability:* Part-time.

Regent University, Graduate School, School of Business and Leadership, Virginia Beach, VA 23464-9800. Offers business administration (MBA), including accounting, economics, entrepreneurship, finance and investing, general management, healthcare management (MA, MBA), human resource management (MA, MBA), innovation management, leadership, marketing, not-for-profit management (MA, MBA); business analytics (MS); business and design management (MA); church leadership (MA); leadership (Certificate); organizational leadership (MA, PhD), including ecclesia leadership (DSL, PhD), entrepreneurial leadership (PhD), healthcare management (MA, MBA), human resource development (PhD), human resource management (MA, MBA), individualized studies (DSL, PhD), interdisciplinary studies (MA), leadership coaching and mentoring (MA), not-for-profit management (MA, MBA), organizational development consulting (MA), servant leadership (MA, DSL); strategic leadership (DSL), including ecclesial leadership (DSL, PhD), global consulting, healthcare leadership, individualized studies (DSL, PhD), leadership coaching, servant leadership (MA, DSL), strategic foresight. *Program availability:* Part-time, evening/weekend, 100% online, blended/hybrid learning. *Faculty:* 9 full-time (2 women), 38 part-time/adjunct (11 women). *Students:* 129 full-time (80 women), 1,152 part-time (598 women); includes 685 minority (546 Black or African American, non-Hispanic/Latino; 10 American Indian or Alaska Native, non-Hispanic/Latino; 29 Asian, non-Hispanic/Latino; 65 Hispanic/Latino; 6 Native Hawaiian or other Pacific Islander, non-Hispanic/Latino; 29 Two or more races, non-Hispanic/Latino), 62 international. Average age 41. 1,721 applicants, 48% accepted, 624 enrolled. In 2017, 125 master's, 69 doctorates awarded. *Degree requirements:* For master's, thesis or alternative, 3-credit hour culminating experience; for doctorate, thesis/dissertation. *Entrance requirements:* For master's, college transcripts, resume, essay; for doctorate, college transcripts, resume, essay, writing sample; for Certificate, writing sample, resume, transcripts. Additional exam requirements/recommendations for international students: Required—TOEFL (minimum score 577 paper-based). *Application deadline:* For fall admission, 5/1 priority date for domestic students; for spring admission, 10/1 priority date for domestic students. Applications are processed on a rolling basis. Application fee: $50. Electronic applications accepted. *Expenses:* $650 per credit (MA, MS, MBA); $995 per credit (PhD); $300 per semester technology fee. *Financial support:* In 2017–18, 829 students received support. Career-related internships or fieldwork, scholarships/grants, and unspecified assistantships available. Support available to part-time students. *Faculty research:* Servant leadership, global business, team effectiveness, technology utilization, leadership development. *Unit head:* Dr. Doris Gomez, Dean, 757-352-4686, Fax: 757-352-4634, E-mail: dorigom@regent.edu. *Application contact:* Heidi Cece, Assistant Vice President of Enrollment Management, 800-373-5504, Fax: 757-352-4381, E-mail: admissions@regent.edu. Website: https://www.regent.edu/school-of-business-and-leadership/

Regis University, College of Business and Economics, Denver, CO 80221-1099. Offers accounting (MS); executive leadership (Certificate); finance (MS); finance and accounting (MBA); health industry leadership (MBA); human resource management and leadership (MSOL); management (MBA); marketing (MBA); nonprofit leadership (Post-Graduate Certificate); nonprofit management (MNM); nonprofit organizational capacity building (Certificate); operations management (MBA); organizational leadership and management (MSOL); project leadership and management (MS, MSOL); strategic business management (Certificate); strategic human resource integration (Certificate); strategic management (MBA). Programs offered at Colorado Springs Campus, Northwest Denver Campus, Southeast Denver Campus, Fort Collins Campus, Broomfield Campus, Henderson (Nevada) Campus, and Summerlin (Nevada) Campus. *Program availability:* Part-time, evening/weekend, 100% online, blended/hybrid learning. *Degree requirements:* For master's, thesis (for some programs), capstone or final research project. *Entrance requirements:* For master's, official transcript reflecting baccalaureate degree awarded from regionally-accredited college or university, interview, 2 years of full-time related work experience, resume, letters of recommendation. Additional exam requirements/recommendations for international students: Required—TOEFL (minimum score 550 paper-based; 82 iBT). Electronic applications accepted. *Expenses:* Contact institution. *Faculty research:* Impact of information technology on small business regulation of accounting, international project financing, mineral development, delivery of healthcare to rural indigenous communities.

Rhode Island College, School of Graduate Studies, School of Business, Department of Accounting and Computer Information Systems, Providence, RI 02908-1991. Offers accounting (MP Ac); financial planning (CGS). *Program availability:* Part-time, evening/weekend. *Faculty:* 1 (woman) full-time. *Students:* 1 full-time (0 women), 15 part-time (8 women); includes 5 minority (3 Black or African American, non-Hispanic/Latino; 2

Hispanic/Latino). Average age 32. In 2017, 17 master's, 2 CGSs awarded. *Entrance requirements:* For master's, GMAT (unless applicant is a CPA or has passed a state bar exam); for CGS, GMAT, bachelor's degree from an accredited college or university, official transcripts of all undergraduate and graduate records. Additional exam requirements/recommendations for international students: Recommended—TOEFL (minimum score 550 paper-based; 79 iBT). *Application deadline:* For fall admission, 3/1 for domestic students. Applications are processed on a rolling basis. Application fee: $50. Electronic applications accepted. *Expenses:* Tuition, state resident: full-time $9768; part-time $407 per credit. Tuition, nonresident: full-time $19,008; part-time $792 per credit. *Required fees:* $696; $29 per credit. One-time fee: $200 full-time; $100 part-time. Tuition and fees vary according to course load. *Financial support:* In 2017–18, 1 teaching assistantship with full tuition reimbursement (averaging $1,500 per year) was awarded; Federal Work-Study, scholarships/grants, and health care benefits also available. Support available to part-time students. Financial award application deadline: 5/15; financial award applicants required to submit FAFSA. *Unit head:* Dr. Lisa Bain, Chair, 401-456-9829. *Application contact:* Graduate Studies, 401-456-8700. Website: http://www.ric.edu/accountingComputerInformationSystems/

Rider University, College of Business Administration, Program in Corporate Finance, Lawrenceville, NJ 08648-3001. Offers MS. *Program availability:* Evening/weekend, online learning.

Robert Morris University Illinois, Morris Graduate School of Management, Chicago, IL 60605. Offers accounting (MBA); accounting/finance (MBA); business analytics (MIS); health care administration (MM); higher education administration (MM); human performance (MS); human resource management (MBA); information security (MIS); information systems management (MIS); law enforcement administration (MM); management (MBA); management/finance (MBA); management/human resource management (MBA); sports administration (MM). *Program availability:* Part-time, evening/weekend. *Faculty:* 2 full-time (0 women), 26 part-time/adjunct (8 women). *Students:* 186 full-time (108 women), 114 part-time (57 women); includes 167 minority (88 Black or African American, non-Hispanic/Latino; 15 Asian, non-Hispanic/Latino; 62 Hispanic/Latino; 1 Native Hawaiian or other Pacific Islander, non-Hispanic/Latino; 1 Two or more races, non-Hispanic/Latino), 18 international. Average age 32. 157 applicants, 78% accepted, 72 enrolled. In 2017, 191 master's awarded. *Entrance requirements:* For master's, official transcripts and letters of recommendation (for some programs); written personal statement. Additional exam requirements/recommendations for international students: Required—TOEFL (minimum score 550 paper-based). *Application deadline:* Applications are processed on a rolling basis. Application fee: $20 ($100 for international students). Electronic applications accepted. *Expenses:* Tuition: Full-time $17,100; part-time $2850 per course. *Financial support:* In 2017–18, 381 students received support. Federal Work-Study, scholarships/grants, and unspecified assistantships available. Support available to part-time students. Financial award applicants required to submit FAFSA. *Unit head:* Kayed Akkawi, Dean, 312-935-6050, Fax: 312-935-6020, E-mail: kakkawi@robertmorris.edu. *Application contact:* Mark Daugherty, Director of Admissions, 312-935-4814, Fax: 312-935-6020, E-mail: mdaugherty@robertmorris.edu.

Rochester Institute of Technology, Graduate Enrollment Services, Saunders College of Business, Accounting and Finance Department, MS Program in Finance, Rochester, NY 14623. Offers MS. *Program availability:* Part-time, evening/weekend. *Students:* 12 full-time (6 women), 5 part-time (2 women); includes 1 minority (Asian, non-Hispanic/Latino), 8 international. Average age 28. 94 applicants, 43% accepted, 10 enrolled. In 2017, 5 master's awarded. *Entrance requirements:* For master's, GMAT or GRE, minimum GPA of 3.0 (recommended). Additional exam requirements/recommendations for international students: Required—TOEFL (minimum score 580 paper-based; 92 iBT), IELTS (minimum score 7), PTE (minimum score 63). *Application deadline:* Applications are processed on a rolling basis. Application fee: $65. Electronic applications accepted. *Expenses:* $1,815 per credit hour. *Financial support:* In 2017–18, 10 students received support. Research assistantships with partial tuition reimbursements available, teaching assistantships with partial tuition reimbursements available, career-related internships or fieldwork, scholarships/grants, and unspecified assistantships available. Support available to part-time students. Financial award applicants required to submit FAFSA. *Faculty research:* Trading algorithms, short selling effects, corporate governance effects, optimal incentive compensation contracts, debt contract parameters, tax policy. *Unit head:* Matt Cornwell, Assistant Director of Student Services and Outreach, 585-475-6916, E-mail: mcornwell@saunders.rit.edu. *Application contact:* Diane Ellison, Senior Associate Vice President, Graduate Enrollment Services, 585-475-2229, Fax: 585-475-7164, E-mail: gradinfo@rit.edu. Website: http://saunders.rit.edu/programs/graduate/ms_finance.php

Rockhurst University, Helzberg School of Management, Kansas City, MO 64110-2561. Offers accounting (MBA); business intelligence (MBA, Certificate); business intelligence and analytics (MS); data science (MBA, Certificate); entrepreneurship (MBA); finance (MBA); fundraising leadership (MBA, Certificate); healthcare management (MBA, Certificate); human capital (Certificate); international business (Certificate); management (MA, MBA, Certificate); nonprofit administration (Certificate); organizational development (Certificate); science leadership (Certificate). *Accreditation:* AACSB. *Program availability:* Part-time, evening/weekend. *Faculty:* 18 full-time (4 women), 20 part-time/adjunct (9 women). *Students:* 99 full-time (30 women), 355 part-time (132 women); includes 95 minority (30 Black or African American, non-Hispanic/Latino; 29 Asian, non-Hispanic/Latino; 25 Hispanic/Latino; 11 Two or more races, non-Hispanic/Latino), 8 international. Average age 32. 249 applicants, 81% accepted, 175 enrolled. In 2017, 145 master's, 17 other advanced degrees awarded. *Entrance requirements:* For master's, GMAT or GRE. Additional exam requirements/recommendations for international students: Required—TOEFL (minimum score 550 paper-based; 79 iBT). *Application deadline:* Applications are processed on a rolling basis. Application fee: $0. Electronic applications accepted. *Financial support:* Applicants required to submit FAFSA. *Faculty research:* Offshoring/outsourcing, systems analysis/synthesis, work teams, multilateral trade, path dependencies/creation. *Unit head:* Cheryl McConnell, Dean, 816-501-4201, Fax: 816-501-4650, E-mail: cheryl.mcconnell@rockhurst.edu. *Application contact:* Jonnae Hill, Director of Graduate Business Advising, 816-501-4823, E-mail: jonnae.hill@rockhurst.edu. Website: https://www.rockhurst.edu/helzberg

Rollins College, Crummer Graduate School of Business, Winter Park, FL 32789-4499. Offers entrepreneurship (MBA); finance (MBA); international business (MBA); management (MBA). *Accreditation:* AACSB. *Program availability:* Part-time, evening/weekend, online learning. *Faculty:* 20 full-time (4 women). *Students:* 261 full-time (119 women), 114 part-time (45 women); includes 86 minority (24 Black or African American, non-Hispanic/Latino; 13 Asian, non-Hispanic/Latino; 44 Hispanic/Latino; 5 Two or more races, non-Hispanic/Latino), 31 international. Average age 32. In 2017, 134 master's awarded. *Degree requirements:* For master's, minimum GPA of 2.85. *Entrance requirements:* For master's, GMAT or GRE, official transcripts, two letters of recommendation, essay, current resume/curriculum vitae, interview. Additional exam requirements/recommendations for international students: Required—TOEFL (minimum score 100 iBT) or IELTS (minimum score 7). *Application deadline:* Applications are processed on a rolling basis. Application fee: $50. Electronic applications accepted. *Expenses:* Contact institution. *Financial support:* Scholarships/grants available. Support

available to part-time students. Financial award applicants required to submit FAFSA. *Faculty research:* Sustainability, world financial markets, international business, market research, strategic marketing. *Unit head:* Deborah Crown, Dean, 407-646-2249, Fax: 407-646-1550, E-mail: dcrown@rollins.edu. *Application contact:* Maralyn E. Graham, Admissions Coordinator, 407-646-2405, Fax: 407-646-1550, E-mail: mbaadmissions@rollins.edu.
Website: http://www.rollins.edu/mba/

Rutgers University–Newark, Graduate School, Program in Management, Newark, NJ 07102. Offers accounting (PhD); accounting information systems (PhD); computer information systems (PhD); finance (PhD); information technology (PhD); international business (PhD); management science (PhD); marketing (PhD); organization management (PhD). Program offered jointly with New Jersey Institute of Technology. *Accreditation:* AACSB. *Degree requirements:* For doctorate, thesis/dissertation, cumulative exams. *Entrance requirements:* For doctorate, GMAT or GRE General Test, minimum undergraduate B average. Additional exam requirements/recommendations for international students: Required—TOEFL. Electronic applications accepted. *Faculty research:* Technology management, leadership and teams, consumer behavior, financial and markets, logistics.

Rutgers University–Newark, Rutgers Business School–Newark and New Brunswick, Doctoral Programs in Management, Newark, NJ 07102. Offers accounting (PhD); accounting information systems (PhD); economics (PhD); finance (PhD); individualized study (PhD); information technology (PhD); international business (PhD); management science (PhD); marketing science (PhD); organizational management (PhD); science, technology and management (PhD); supply chain management (PhD). *Degree requirements:* For doctorate, comprehensive exam, thesis/dissertation. *Entrance requirements:* For doctorate, GRE or GMAT. Additional exam requirements/recommendations for international students: Required—TOEFL (minimum score 550 paper-based; 79 iBT). Electronic applications accepted.

Rutgers University–Newark, Rutgers Business School–Newark and New Brunswick, Program in Financial Analysis, Newark, NJ 07102. Offers MFA. *Entrance requirements:* For master's, GMAT. Additional exam requirements/recommendations for international students: Required—TOEFL.

Rutgers University–Newark, Rutgers Business School–Newark and New Brunswick, Program in Quantitative Finance, Newark, NJ 07102. Offers MQF. *Entrance requirements:* For master's, GMAT (MBA), GRE General Test (MQF). Additional exam requirements/recommendations for international students: Required—TOEFL.

Sacred Heart University, Graduate Programs, Jack Welch College of Business, Department of Finance, Fairfield, CT 06825. Offers administration (DBA); finance (MBA, Graduate Certificate); finance and investment management (MS). *Program availability:* Part-time, evening/weekend. *Faculty:* 8 full-time (2 women), 5 part-time/adjunct (1 woman). *Students:* 19 full-time (7 women), 55 part-time (16 women); includes 13 minority (8 Black or African American, non-Hispanic/Latino; 3 Asian, non-Hispanic/Latino; 2 Two or more races, non-Hispanic/Latino), 31 international. Average age 36. 54 applicants, 94% accepted, 24 enrolled. In 2017, 14 master's awarded. *Degree requirements:* For doctorate, comprehensive exam. *Entrance requirements:* For master's, GMAT or GRE, official transcripts from all institutions attended; for doctorate, GMAT or GRE with master's degree and 5 years' experience. Additional exam requirements/recommendations for international students: Required—TOEFL (minimum score 570 paper-based, 80 iBT), TWE, or IELTS (6.5). *Application deadline:* Applications are processed on a rolling basis. Application fee: $75. Electronic applications accepted. *Expenses:* Contact institution. *Financial support:* Unspecified assistantships available. Financial award applicants required to submit FAFSA. *Unit head:* Dr. Kwamie Dunbar, Assistant Professor of Finance/Director of MS in Finance and Investment Management, 203-396-8068, E-mail: dunbark@sacredheart.edu. *Application contact:* Pam Pillo, Executive Director of Graduate Admissions, 203-365-7619, E-mail: gradstudies@sacredheart.edu.
Website: http://www.sacredheart.edu/academics/johnfwelchcollegeofbusiness/aboutthecollege/

St. John's University, The Peter J. Tobin College of Business, Department of Economics and Finance, Queens, NY 11439. Offers finance (MBA, MS). *Program availability:* Part-time, evening/weekend, 100% online, blended/hybrid learning. *Faculty:* 25 full-time (4 women), 11 part-time/adjunct (1 woman). *Students:* 62 full-time (21 women), 38 part-time (11 women); includes 19 minority (6 Black or African American, non-Hispanic/Latino; 8 Asian, non-Hispanic/Latino; 5 Hispanic/Latino), 37 international. Average age 27. 88 applicants, 66% accepted, 39 enrolled. In 2017, 59 master's awarded. *Degree requirements:* For master's, 36 credit hours. *Entrance requirements:* For master's, GMAT or GRE, 2 letters of recommendation, essay, resume, unofficial transcripts. Additional exam requirements/recommendations for international students: Required—TOEFL (minimum score 80 iBT), IELTS (minimum score 6.5). *Application deadline:* For fall admission, 11/1 for domestic and international students; for winter admission, 3/1 for domestic and international students; for spring admission, 6/1 for domestic and international students. Applications are processed on a rolling basis. Application fee: $70. Electronic applications accepted. *Expenses:* $22,410 per year. *Financial support:* Research assistantships, teaching assistantships, scholarships/grants, and unspecified assistantships available. Support available to part-time students. Financial award application deadline: 2/1; financial award applicants required to submit FAFSA. *Faculty research:* Exchange rate exposure, corporate default likelihood, credit derivatives, emerging markets, stock returns predictability. *Total annual research expenditures:* $26,883. *Unit head:* Dr. Charles Clark, Chair, 718-990-7343, E-mail: clarkc@stjohns.edu. *Application contact:* Amber Steiger, Associate Director of Enrollment Management, 718-990-1345, E-mail: steigera@stjohns.edu.
Website: http://www.stjohns.edu/academics/schools-and-colleges/peter-j-tobin-college-business/economics-and-finance

Saint Joseph's University, Erivan K. Haub School of Business, MBA Program, Philadelphia, PA 19131-1395. Offers accounting (MBA); business intelligence analytics (MBA); finance (MBA); financial analysis reporting (Postbaccalaureate Certificate); general business (MBA); health and medical services administration (MBA); international business (MBA); international marketing (MBA); leading (MBA); marketing (MBA); DO/MBA. DO/MBA offered jointly with Philadelphia College of Osteopathic Medicine. *Program availability:* Part-time-only, evening/weekend, 100% online. *Students:* 85 full-time (36 women), 371 part-time (153 women); includes 74 minority (32 Black or African American, non-Hispanic/Latino; 15 Asian, non-Hispanic/Latino; 19 Hispanic/Latino; 1 Native Hawaiian or other Pacific Islander, non-Hispanic/Latino; 7 Two or more races, non-Hispanic/Latino), 36 international. Average age 30. 247 applicants, 76% accepted, 112 enrolled. In 2017, 163 master's awarded. *Degree requirements:* For master's, minimum GPA of 3.0. *Entrance requirements:* For master's, GMAT or GRE, 2 letters of recommendation, resume, personal statement, official undergraduate and graduate transcripts. Additional exam requirements/recommendations for international students: Required—PTE, TOEFL, IELTS, or PTE. *Application deadline:* For fall admission, 7/15 priority date for domestic students, 5/15 priority date for international students; for spring admission, 11/15 priority date for domestic students, 10/15 priority date for international students; for summer admission, 4/15 priority date for domestic students, 2/15 priority date for international students. Applications are processed on a

rolling basis. Application fee: $35. Electronic applications accepted. *Expenses:* Contact institution. *Financial support:* Scholarships/grants and unspecified assistantships available. Financial award application deadline: 5/1; financial award applicants required to submit FAFSA. *Unit head:* Jeannine Lajeunesse, Director, 610-660-1626, Fax: 610-660-1599, E-mail: jlajeune@sju.edu. *Application contact:* Christine Anderson, Assistant Director, 610-660-2252, Fax: 610-660-1599, E-mail: chris.anderson@sju.edu.
Website: http://www.sju.edu/haubmba

★ **Saint Joseph's University,** Erivan K. Haub School of Business, MS in Financial Services Program, Philadelphia, PA 19131-1395. Offers MS. *Program availability:* Part-time, evening/weekend, online learning. *Faculty:* 9 full-time (2 women), 6 part-time/adjunct (1 woman). *Students:* 32 full-time (11 women), 31 part-time (4 women); includes 4 minority (1 Black or African American, non-Hispanic/Latino; 3 Hispanic/Latino), 27 international. Average age 30. 81 applicants, 56% accepted, 18 enrolled. In 2017, 30 master's awarded. *Degree requirements:* For master's, minimum GPA of 3.0. *Entrance requirements:* For master's, GMAT or GRE, 2 letters of recommendation, resume, personal statement, official undergraduate and graduate transcripts. Additional exam requirements/recommendations for international students: Required—PTE, TOEFL, IELTS, or PTE. *Application deadline:* For fall admission, 7/15 priority date for domestic students, 5/15 priority date for international students; for spring admission, 11/15 priority date for domestic students, 10/15 priority date for international students; for summer admission, 4/15 priority date for domestic students. Applications are processed on a rolling basis. Application fee: $35. Electronic applications accepted. *Expenses:* Contact institution. *Financial support:* Scholarships/grants and unspecified assistantships available. Financial award application deadline: 5/1; financial award applicants required to submit FAFSA. *Unit head:* Jeannine Lajeunesse, Director, 610-660-1626, Fax: 610-660-1599, E-mail: jlajeune@sju.edu. *Application contact:* Christine Anderson, Assistant Director, 610-660-2252, Fax: 610-660-1599, E-mail: chris.anderson@sju.edu.
Website: http://www.sju.edu/msfs

See Display on the next page and Close-Up on page 299.

Saint Louis University, Graduate Programs, John Cook School of Business, Department of Finance, St. Louis, MO 63103. Offers MBA, MSF. *Program availability:* Part-time, evening/weekend. *Degree requirements:* For master's, thesis. *Entrance requirements:* For master's, GMAT or GRE General Test, letters of recommendation, resume. Additional exam requirements/recommendations for international students: Required—TOEFL (minimum score 570 paper-based; 88 iBT). Electronic applications accepted. *Expenses:* Contact institution. *Faculty research:* Market microstructure, corporate governance, banking, portfolio performance and asset allocation.

Saint Mary's College of California, School of Economics and Business Administration, MS in Financial Analysis and Investment Management Program, Moraga, CA 94556. Offers MS. *Expenses:* Contact institution.

Saint Peter's University, Graduate Business Programs, MBA Program, Jersey City, NJ 07306-5997. Offers finance (MBA); health care administration (MBA); human resource management (MBA); international business (MBA); management (MBA); management information systems (MBA); marketing (MBA); risk management (MBA); MBA/MS. *Program availability:* Part-time, evening/weekend. *Entrance requirements:* Additional exam requirements/recommendations for international students: Required—TOEFL. Electronic applications accepted. *Faculty research:* Finance, health care management, human resource management, international business, management, management information systems, marketing, risk management.

St. Thomas Aquinas College, Division of Business Administration, Sparkill, NY 10976. Offers business administration (MBA); finance (MBA); management (MBA); marketing (MBA). *Program availability:* Part-time, evening/weekend. *Entrance requirements:* For master's, GMAT. Additional exam requirements/recommendations for international students: Required—TOEFL. Electronic applications accepted.

Saint Xavier University, Graduate Studies, Graham School of Management, Chicago, IL 60655-3105. Offers employee health benefits (Certificate); finance (MBA); financial fraud examination and management (MBA, Certificate); financial planning (MBA, Certificate); generalist/individualized (MBA); health administration (MBA); managed care (Certificate); management (MBA); marketing (MBA); project management (MBA, Certificate); MBA/MS. *Accreditation:* AACSB. *Program availability:* Part-time, evening/weekend. *Entrance requirements:* For master's, GMAT, minimum GPA of 3.0, 2 years of work experience. Electronic applications accepted. *Expenses:* Contact institution.

Samford University, Brock School of Business, Birmingham, AL 35229. Offers accountancy (M Acc); entrepreneurship (MBA); finance (MBA); marketing (MBA); JD/M Acc; JD/MBA; MBA/M Acc; MBA/M Div; MBA/MSEM; MBA/Pharm D. Programs offered jointly with Cumberland School of Law, Beeson School of Divinity, Howard College of Arts and Sciences, and McWhorter School of Pharmacy. *Accreditation:* AACSB. *Program availability:* Part-time, 100% online, blended/hybrid learning. *Faculty:* 8 full-time (1 woman), 5 part-time/adjunct (0 women). *Students:* 79 full-time (31 women), 18 part-time (8 women); includes 7 minority (2 Black or African American, non-Hispanic/Latino; 1 Asian, non-Hispanic/Latino; 3 Hispanic/Latino; 1 Two or more races, non-Hispanic/Latino), 8 international. Average age 28. 46 applicants, 78% accepted, 16 enrolled. In 2017, 78 master's awarded. *Degree requirements:* For master's, capstone course. *Entrance requirements:* For master's, GMAT or GRE, resume, transcripts; essay (international applicants only). Additional exam requirements/recommendations for international students: Required—TOEFL (minimum score 90 iBT), IELTS (minimum score 6.5). *Application deadline:* For fall admission, 8/1 for domestic and international students; for spring admission, 12/1 for domestic and international students; for summer admission, 5/1 for domestic and international students. Applications are processed on a rolling basis. Application fee: $35. Electronic applications accepted. Application fee is waived when completed online. *Expenses:* $813 per credit hour tuition; $425 per semester fees. *Financial support:* In 2017–18, 59 students received support. Scholarships/grants available. Financial award application deadline: 2/15; financial award applicants required to submit FAFSA. *Unit head:* Dr. Barbara Cartledge, Assistant Dean, 205-726-2935, Fax: 205-726-2540, E-mail: bhcartle@samford.edu. *Application contact:* Elizabeth Anne Gambrell, Associate Director, 205-726-2040, Fax: 205-726-2540, E-mail: eagambre@samford.edu.
Website: http://www.samford.edu/business

Sam Houston State University, College of Business Administration, Department of General Business and Finance, Huntsville, TX 77341. Offers banking and financial institutions (EMBA); business administration (MBA). *Accreditation:* AACSB. *Program availability:* Part-time, evening/weekend, online learning. *Degree requirements:* For master's, comprehensive exam (for some programs). *Entrance requirements:* For master's, GMAT, interview (for EMBA); resume, transcript(s). Additional exam requirements/recommendations for international students: Required—TOEFL (minimum score 550 paper-based; 79 iBT), IELTS (minimum score 6.5). Electronic applications accepted.

San Diego State University, Graduate and Research Affairs, College of Business Administration, Department of Finance, San Diego, CA 92182. Offers MS. *Program availability:* Part-time, evening/weekend. *Degree requirements:* For master's, thesis or

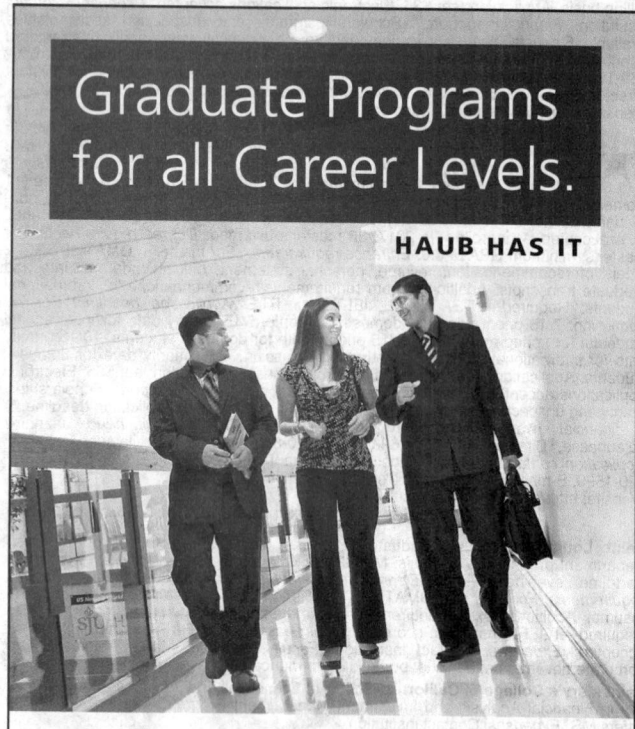

alternative. *Entrance requirements:* For master's, GMAT, resume, letters of reference. Additional exam requirements/recommendations for international students: Required—TOEFL. Electronic applications accepted.

San Francisco State University, Division of Graduate Studies, College of Business, Program in Business Administration, San Francisco, CA 94132-1722. Offers decision sciences/operations research (MBA); ethics and compliance (MBA); finance (MBA); global business and innovation (MBA); healthcare administration (MBA); hospitality and tourism management (MBA); information systems (MBA); leadership (MBA); marketing (MBA); nonprofit and social enterprise leadership (MBA); sustainable business (MBA). *Accreditation:* AACSB. *Program availability:* Part-time, evening/weekend. *Degree requirements:* For master's, thesis, essay test. *Entrance requirements:* For master's, GMAT, minimum GPA of 2.7 in last 60 units. Additional exam requirements/recommendations for international students: Required—TOEFL (minimum score 550 paper-based). *Application deadline:* For fall admission, 5/1 priority date for domestic students, 4/1 for international students; for spring admission, 11/1 for domestic students, 10/15 for international students. Applications are processed on a rolling basis. Application fee: $55. *Financial support:* Application deadline: 3/1. *Unit head:* Dr. Sanjit Sengupta, Faculty Director, 415-817-4366, Fax: 415-817-4340, E-mail: sengupta@sfsu.edu. *Application contact:* Christopher Kingston, Director of Student Advising, 415-817-4322, Fax: 415-817-4340, E-mail: cak@sfsu.edu.
Website: http://cob.sfsu.edu/graduate-programs/mba

Santa Clara University, Leavey School of Business, Santa Clara, CA 95053. Offers business administration (MBA); business analytics (MS); finance (MS); information systems (MS); supply chain management and analytics (MS); JD/MBA. *Accreditation:* AACSB. *Program availability:* Part-time, evening/weekend, online curriculum with 2 on-campus intensives. *Faculty:* 100 full-time (30 women), 42 part-time/adjunct (16 women). *Students:* 413 full-time (226 women), 308 part-time (131 women); includes 246 minority (10 Black or African American, non-Hispanic/Latino; 175 Asian, non-Hispanic/Latino; 40 Hispanic/Latino; 2 Native Hawaiian or other Pacific Islander, non-Hispanic/Latino; 19 Two or more races, non-Hispanic/Latino), 256 international. Average age 31. 761 applicants, 63% accepted, 271 enrolled. In 2017, 267 master's awarded. *Entrance requirements:* For master's, GMAT, resume, essays, 2 letters of recommendation, 2 official transcripts. Additional exam requirements/recommendations for international students: Required—TOEFL (minimum score 100 iBT) or IELTS (7.0). Application fee: $100 ($150 for international students). Electronic applications accepted. *Expenses:* Contact institution. *Financial support:* In 2017–18, 192 students received support. Career-related internships or fieldwork, scholarships/grants, and unspecified assistantships available. Financial award applicants required to submit FAFSA. *Faculty research:* Digital marketing, database mining and retail, product innovation, industry disruption, entrepreneurship and cluster dynamics, innovation and temporary advantage, platform strategy, ethics and leadership, bank regulation, monetary policy, poverty alleviation, costs of financial crises, information technology and business intelligence, supply chain management, corporate social responsibility and institutional ownership, audits and financial reporting. *Unit head:* Caryn Beck-Dudley, Dean, 408-554-4523, E-mail: cbeckdudley@scu.edu. *Application contact:* Lenore Grant, Director, Graduate Business Recruitment and Admissions, 408-551-1633, E-mail: lgrant@scu.edu.
Website: http://www.scu.edu/business/

Schiller International University, MBA Programs, Florida, Largo, FL 33771. Offers financial planning (MBA); information technology (MBA); international business (MBA); international hotel and tourism management (MBA). *Program availability:* Part-time, evening/weekend, online learning. *Degree requirements:* For master's, thesis optional. *Entrance requirements:* Additional exam requirements/recommendations for international students: Required—TOEFL (minimum score 550 paper-based).

Seattle University, Albers School of Business and Economics, Master of Science in Finance Program, Seattle, WA 98122-1090. Offers MSF, Certificate, JD/MSF, MPAC/MSF, MSF/MSBA. *Program availability:* Part-time, evening/weekend. *Faculty:* 9 full-time (3 women), 2 part-time/adjunct (0 women). *Students:* 35 full-time (9 women), 38 part-time (13 women); includes 13 minority (1 Black or African American, non-Hispanic/Latino; 10 Asian, non-Hispanic/Latino; 2 Hispanic/Latino), 32 international. Average age 27. 69 applicants, 51% accepted, 15 enrolled. In 2017, 21 master's, 20 Certificates awarded. *Entrance requirements:* For master's, GMAT, minimum GPA of 3.0, 2 years of related work experience. Additional exam requirements/recommendations for international students: Required—TOEFL (minimum score 580 paper-based; 92 iBT). *Application deadline:* For fall admission, 8/20 priority date for domestic students, 4/1 priority date for international students; for winter admission, 11/20 priority date for domestic students, 9/1 priority date for international students; for spring admission, 2/20 priority date for domestic students, 12/1 priority date for international students. Applications are processed on a rolling basis. Application fee: $55. Electronic applications accepted. *Expenses:* Contact institution. *Financial support:* In 2017–18, 16 students received support. Career-related internships or fieldwork and Federal Work-Study available. Support available to part-time students. Financial award applicants required to submit FAFSA. *Unit head:* Dr. Fiona Robertson, Chair, 206-296-5791, Fax: 206-296-5795, E-mail: robertsf@seattleu.edu. *Application contact:* Janet Shandley, Director of Graduate Admissions, 206-296-5900, Fax: 206-298-5656, E-mail: grad_admissions@seattleu.edu.
Website: http://www.seattleu.edu/albers/msf/

Seton Hall University, Stillman School of Business, Programs in Business Administration, South Orange, NJ 07079-2697. Offers accounting (MBA); entrepreneurial studies (Certificate); finance (MBA); financial decision making (Certificate); information technology management (MBA); international business (MBA); management (MBA); marketing (MBA); sport management (MBA); supply chain management (MBA, Certificate). *Program availability:* Part-time, evening/weekend. *Faculty:* 29 full-time (4 women), 18 part-time/adjunct (0 women). *Students:* 140 full-time (58 women), 154 part-time (49 women); includes 66 minority (25 Black or African American, non-Hispanic/Latino; 14 Asian, non-Hispanic/Latino; 23 Hispanic/Latino; 4 Two or more races, non-Hispanic/Latino), 88 international. Average age 32. 406 applicants, 75% accepted, 100 enrolled. In 2017, 132 master's awarded. *Degree requirements:* For master's, 20 hours of community service (Social Responsibility Project). *Entrance requirements:* For master's, GMAT or CPA, GRE (waived based on work experience or advanced degree from AACSB institution), MS in business discipline, professional degree or designation (MD, JD, PhD, DVM, DDS, CPA, etc.), minimum undergraduate GPA of 3.0. Additional exam requirements/recommendations for international students: Required—TOEFL (minimum score 607 paper-based; 80 iBT), IELTS (minimum score 6), PTE. *Application deadline:* For fall admission, 5/31 priority date for domestic students, 4/30 priority date for international students; for spring admission, 10/31 priority date for domestic students, 9/30 priority date for international students; for summer admission, 3/31 priority date for domestic students. Applications are processed on a rolling basis. Application fee: $75. Electronic applications accepted. *Expenses:* $1,305 per credit; $126 fees (fall and spring semester), $51 (summer semester). *Financial support:* In 2017–18, 41 students received support, including 25 research assistantships with full tuition reimbursements available (averaging $3,644 per year); career-related internships or fieldwork, scholarships/grants, and unspecified

assistantships also available. Financial award application deadline: 6/30; financial award applicants required to submit FAFSA. *Faculty research:* Sport, hedge funds, executive compensation, social media, legal studies. *Unit head:* Dr. Joyce Strawser, Dean, 973-761-9013, Fax: 973-761-9217, E-mail: joyce.strawser@shu.edu. *Application contact:* Alfred Ayoub, Director of Graduate Admissions, 973-761-9262, Fax: 973-761-9208, E-mail: alfred.ayoub@shu.edu.
Website: http://www.shu.edu/business/mba-programs.cfm

Shippensburg University of Pennsylvania, School of Graduate Studies, John L. Grove College of Business, Shippensburg, PA 17257-2299. Offers advanced studies in business (Certificate); advanced supply chain and logistics management (Certificate); business administration (MBA, DBA), including business administration (MBA), business analytics (MBA), finance (MBA), healthcare management (MBA), management information systems (MBA), supply chain management (MBA); finance (Certificate); health care management (Certificate); management information systems (Certificate). *Accreditation:* AACSB. *Program availability:* Part-time, evening/weekend, 100% online, blended/hybrid learning. *Faculty:* 23 full-time (5 women), 1 part-time/adjunct (0 women). *Students:* 46 full-time (14 women), 201 part-time (71 women); includes 35 minority (12 Black or African American, non-Hispanic/Latino; 10 Asian, non-Hispanic/Latino; 11 Hispanic/Latino; 2 Two or more races, non-Hispanic/Latino), 22 international. Average age 32. 169 applicants, 65% accepted, 77 enrolled. In 2017, 105 master's, 82 other advanced degrees awarded. *Degree requirements:* For master's, thesis optional, practicum; for doctorate, comprehensive exam, thesis/dissertation. *Entrance requirements:* For master's, GMAT (minimum score 450 if less than 5 years of mid-level experience, including management experience), current resume; relevant work/classroom experience; 500-word statement of purpose; prerequisites of quantitative analysis, computer usage, and oral and written communications; laptop computer; for doctorate, GMAT (minimum score of 600 if less than 5 years of substantive professional or teaching experience), 2 letters of recommendation from professionals in academia or industry; 2-3 page personal and professional statement; interview; resume. Additional exam requirements/recommendations for international students: Required—TOEFL (minimum score 550 paper-based, 68 iBT) or IELTS (minimum score 6). *Application deadline:* For fall admission, 4/30 for international students; for spring admission, 9/30 for international students. Applications are processed on a rolling basis. Application fee: $45. Electronic applications accepted. *Expenses:* Tuition, state resident: part-time $500 per credit. Tuition, nonresident: part-time $750 per credit. *Required fees:* $145 per credit. *Financial support:* In 2017–18, 14 students received support. Career-related internships or fieldwork, scholarships/grants, unspecified assistantships, and resident hall director and student payroll positions available. Support available to part-time students. Financial award application deadline: 3/1; financial award applicants required to submit FAFSA. *Unit head:* Dr. John G. Kooti, Dean of the College of Business, 717-477-1435, Fax: 717-477-4003, E-mail: jgkooti@ship.edu. *Application contact:* Maya T. Mapp, Director of Admissions, 717-477-1231, Fax: 717-477-4016, E-mail: mtmapp@ship.edu.
Website: http://www.ship.edu/business

Simon Fraser University, Office of Graduate Studies and Postdoctoral Fellows, Faculty of Business Administration, Vancouver, BC V6B 5K3, Canada. Offers business administration (EMBA, PhD, Graduate Diploma); finance (M Sc); management of technology (MBA); management of technology/biotechnology (MBA). *Program availability:* Online learning. *Degree requirements:* For master's, thesis (for some programs); for doctorate, comprehensive exam, thesis/dissertation. *Entrance requirements:* For master's, GMAT, minimum GPA of 3.0 (on scale of 4.33) or 3.33 based on last 60 credits of undergraduate courses; for doctorate, minimum GPA of 3.5 (on scale of 4.33); for Graduate Diploma, minimum GPA of 2.5 (on scale of 4.33) or 2.67 based on last 60 credits of undergraduate courses. Additional exam requirements/recommendations for international students: Recommended—TOEFL (minimum score 580 paper-based; 93 iBT), IELTS (minimum score 7), TWE (minimum score 5). *Expenses:* Contact institution. *Faculty research:* Accounting, management and organizational studies, technology and operations management, finance, international business.

Slippery Rock University of Pennsylvania, Graduate Studies (Recruitment), College of Business, School of Business, Slippery Rock, PA 16057-1383. Offers accounting/finance (MBA); general (MBA); marketing/management (MBA). *Program availability:* Part-time, evening/weekend. *Degree requirements:* For master's, comprehensive exam (for some programs), thesis (for some programs). *Entrance requirements:* For master's, minimum cumulative GPA of 3.0, official transcripts, three references. Additional exam requirements/recommendations for international students: Required—TOEFL (minimum score 550 paper-based; 80 iBT). Electronic applications accepted. *Expenses:* Contact institution.

Southeast Missouri State University, School of Graduate Studies, Harrison College of Business, Cape Girardeau, MO 63701-4799. Offers accounting (MBA); entrepreneurship (MBA); financial management (MBA); sport management (MBA). *Accreditation:* AACSB. *Program availability:* Part-time, evening/weekend, 100% online. *Faculty:* 27 full-time (7 women), 1 (woman) part-time/adjunct. *Students:* 71 full-time (38 women), 68 part-time (31 women); includes 13 minority (7 Black or African American, non-Hispanic/Latino; 4 Asian, non-Hispanic/Latino; 2 Two or more races, non-Hispanic/Latino), 47 international. Average age 30. 51 applicants, 100% accepted, 51 enrolled. In 2017, 95 master's awarded. *Degree requirements:* For master's, variable foreign language requirement, comprehensive exam (for some programs), thesis or alternative. *Entrance requirements:* For master's, GMAT or GRE, minimum undergraduate GPA of 2.5, minimum grade of C in prerequisite courses. Additional exam requirements/recommendations for international students: Required—TOEFL (minimum score 550 paper-based; 79 iBT), IELTS (minimum score 6), PTE (minimum score 53). *Application deadline:* For fall admission, 8/1 for domestic students, 6/1 for international students; for spring admission, 11/21 for domestic students, 10/1 for international students; for summer admission, 5/15 for domestic students. Applications are processed on a rolling basis. Application fee: $30 ($40 for international students). Electronic applications accepted. *Expenses:* $270.35 per credit hour in-state tuition, $33.40 per credit hour fees. *Financial support:* In 2017–18, 26 students received support. Career-related internships or fieldwork, Federal Work-Study, scholarships/grants, traineeships, tuition waivers (full), and unspecified assistantships available. Financial award application deadline: 6/30; financial award applicants required to submit FAFSA. *Faculty research:* Organizational justice, ethics, leadership, corporate finance, generational differences. *Unit head:* Dr. Judy A. Wiles, Interim Dean, Harrison College of Business, 573-651-2913, Fax: 573-651-5032, E-mail: jwiles@semo.edu.
Website: http://www.semo.edu/mba

Southern Adventist University, School of Business, Collegedale, TN 37315-0370. Offers accounting (MBA); finance (MBA); healthcare administration (MBA); management (MBA); marketing management (MBA). *Program availability:* Part-time, evening/weekend, 100% online. *Entrance requirements:* For master's, GMAT, minimum cumulative undergraduate GPA of 3.0. Additional exam requirements/recommendations for international students: Required—TOEFL (minimum score 600 paper-based; 100 iBT). *Application deadline:* For fall admission, 7/1 for domestic students, 5/1 for international students; for winter admission, 11/1 for domestic students, 9/1 for

international students; for summer admission, 4/1 for domestic students, 2/1 for international students. Applications are processed on a rolling basis. Application fee: $40. Electronic applications accepted. *Expenses: Tuition:* Full-time $11,430; part-time $635 per credit hour. Tuition and fees vary according to degree level and program. *Financial support:* Scholarships/grants and unspecified assistantships available. Financial award application deadline: 9/1; financial award applicants required to submit FAFSA. *Unit head:* Dr. Stephanie Sheehan, Dean, 423-236-2659, Fax: 423-236-1527, E-mail: ssheehan@southern.edu. *Application contact:* Teshia Price, Graduate Studies Coordinator, 423-236-2751, Fax: 423-236-1527, E-mail: tprice@southern.edu.
Website: https://www.southern.edu/academics/business.html

Southern Illinois University Edwardsville, Graduate School, School of Business, Department of Economics and Finance, Edwardsville, IL 62026. Offers MA, MS. *Program availability:* Part-time, evening/weekend. *Degree requirements:* For master's, thesis or alternative, final exam, portfolio. *Entrance requirements:* For master's, GMAT or GRE. Additional exam requirements/recommendations for international students: Required—TOEFL (minimum score 550 paper-based; 79 iBT), IELTS (minimum score 6.5). Electronic applications accepted.

Southern Methodist University, Cox School of Business, MBA Program, Dallas, TX 75275. Offers accounting (MBA, PMBA); business administration (EMBA); finance (MBA); financial statement analysis (PMBA); general business (MBA); information technology and operations management (MBA); management (MBA); marketing (MBA); real estate (MBA); strategy (MBA); strategy and entrepreneurship (MBA); JD/MBA; MA/MBA. *Program availability:* Part-time, evening/weekend. *Entrance requirements:* For master's, GMAT. Additional exam requirements/recommendations for international students: Required—TOEFL. Electronic applications accepted. *Expenses:* Contact institution. *Faculty research:* Corporate finance, financial reporting, modeling consumer decision-making, competition between national brands and store brands, institutional determinants of firms' strategy.

Southern New Hampshire University, School of Business, Manchester, NH 03106-1045. Offers accounting (MBA, Graduate Certificate); accounting finance (MS); accounting/auditing (MS); accounting/forensic accounting (MS); accounting/management accounting (MS); accounting/taxation (MS); applied economics (MS); athletic administration (MBA, Graduate Certificate); business administration (IMBA, Certificate), including business information systems (Certificate), human resource management (Certificate); business analytics (MBA); business intelligence (MBA); communication (MA), including new media and marketing, public relations; community economic development (MBA); criminal justice (MBA); data analytics (MS); economics (MBA); engineering management (MBA); entrepreneurship (MBA); finance (MBA, MS, Graduate Certificate); finance/corporate finance (MS); finance/investments (MS); forensic accounting (MBA); forensic accounting and fraud examination (Graduate Certificate); healthcare informatics (MBA); healthcare management (MBA); human resource management (MS); human resources (MBA); information technology (MS); information technology management (MBA); international business (PhD); Internet marketing (MBA); leadership (MBA); leadership of nonprofit organizations (Graduate Certificate); management (MS); marketing (MBA, MS, Graduate Certificate); music business (MBA); operations and project management (MS); operations and supply chain management (MBA, Graduate Certificate); organizational leadership (MS); project management (MBA, Graduate Certificate); public administration (MBA, Graduate Certificate); quantitative analysis (MBA); Six Sigma (Graduate Certificate); Six Sigma quality (MBA); social media marketing (MBA, Graduate Certificate); sport management (MBA, MS, Graduate Certificate); sustainability and environmental compliance (MBA); MBA/Certificate. *Accreditation:* ACBSP. *Program availability:* Part-time, evening/weekend, online learning. Terminal master's awarded for partial completion of doctoral program. *Degree requirements:* For master's, one foreign language, comprehensive exam (for some programs), thesis or alternative; for doctorate, one foreign language, comprehensive exam, thesis/dissertation. *Entrance requirements:* For master's, minimum GPA of 2.5; for doctorate, GMAT. Additional exam requirements/recommendations for international students: Required—TOEFL (minimum score 500 paper-based). *Application deadline:* Applications are processed on a rolling basis. Application fee: $40. Electronic applications accepted. *Expenses: Tuition:* Part-time $627 per credit hour. Part-time tuition and fees vary according to campus/location and program. *Financial support:* Career-related internships or fieldwork, Federal Work-Study, institutionally sponsored loans, scholarships/grants, tuition waivers (partial), and unspecified assistantships available. Support available to part-time students. Financial award applicants required to submit FAFSA. *Unit head:* Dr. Bill Lightfoot, Dean, 603-644-3102, Fax: 603-644-3144. *Application contact:* Office of Graduate Admission, 888-327-SNHU, Fax: 603-644-3144, E-mail: enroll@snhu.edu.

Southwestern Adventist University, Business Administration Department, Keene, TX 76059. Offers accounting (MBA); finance (MBA); management/leadership (MBA). *Program availability:* Part-time, evening/weekend. *Degree requirements:* For master's, capstone course. *Entrance requirements:* For master's, GMAT, GRE General Test.

State University of New York Polytechnic Institute, MBA Program in Technology Management, Utica, NY 13502. Offers accounting and finance (MBA); business management (MBA); health informatics (MBA); human resource management (MBA); marketing management (MBA). *Program availability:* Part-time, online only, 100% online. *Faculty:* 8 full-time (2 women), 2 part-time/adjunct (1 woman). *Students:* 29 full-time (13 women), 85 part-time (41 women); includes 18 minority (4 Black or African American, non-Hispanic/Latino; 8 Asian, non-Hispanic/Latino; 6 Hispanic/Latino). Average age 32. 83 applicants, 55% accepted, 37 enrolled. In 2017, 41 master's awarded. *Degree requirements:* For master's, comprehensive exam, capstone project. *Entrance requirements:* For master's, GMAT, resume, letter of reference. Additional exam requirements/recommendations for international students: Required—TOEFL (minimum score 550 paper-based; 79 iBT), IELTS (minimum score 6.5). *Application deadline:* For fall admission, 7/1 priority date for domestic students, 7/1 for international students; for spring admission, 12/1 for domestic students, 11/1 for international students. Applications are processed on a rolling basis. Application fee: $60. Electronic applications accepted. *Expenses:* Contact institution. *Financial support:* Fellowships, research assistantships, and unspecified assistantships available. Financial award application deadline: 6/1; financial award applicants required to submit FAFSA. *Faculty research:* Economic development and design thinking, transfer of training, trade intensity and liquidity, enforcement and punishment, acculturation attitudes and consumption behavior. *Total annual research expenditures:* $20,000. *Unit head:* Dr. Rafael Romero, Program Coordinator, 315-792-7207, E-mail: rafael.romero@sunyit.edu. *Application contact:* Alicia Foster, Director of Graduate Admissions, E-mail: alicia.foster@sunyit.edu.
Website: https://sunypoly.edu/academics/majors-and-programs/technology-management.html

Stevens Institute of Technology, Graduate School, School of Business, Program in Business Administration, Hoboken, NJ 07030. Offers business intelligence and analytics (MBA); engineering management (MBA); finance (MBA); information systems (MBA); innovation and entrepreneurship (MBA); marketing (MBA); pharmaceutical management (MBA); project management (MBA, Certificate); technology management (MBA); telecommunications management (MBA). *Accreditation:* AACSB. *Program availability:*

Finance and Banking

Part-time, evening/weekend. *Students:* 46 full-time (19 women), 179 part-time (88 women); includes 46 minority (10 Black or African American, non-Hispanic/Latino; 2 American Indian or Alaska Native, non-Hispanic/Latino; 30 Asian, non-Hispanic/Latino; 4 Hispanic/Latino), 45 international. Average age 36. 218 applicants, 49% accepted, 53 enrolled. In 2017, 33 master's awarded. *Degree requirements:* For master's, thesis optional, minimum B average in major field and overall; for Certificate, minimum B average. *Entrance requirements:* Additional exam requirements/recommendations for international students: Required—TOEFL (minimum score 74 iBT), IELTS (minimum score 6). *Application deadline:* For fall admission, 7/1 for domestic students, 4/15 for international students; for spring admission, 12/1 for domestic and international students. Applications are processed on a rolling basis. Application fee: $60. Electronic applications accepted. *Expenses: Tuition:* Full-time $34,494; part-time $1554 per credit. *Required fees:* $291 per semester. *Financial support:* Fellowships, research assistantships, teaching assistantships, career-related internships or fieldwork, Federal Work-Study, scholarships/grants, and unspecified assistantships available. Financial award application deadline: 2/15; financial award applicants required to submit FAFSA. *Unit head:* Dr. Gregory Prastacos, Dean, 201-216-8366, E-mail: gprastac@stevens.edu. *Application contact:* Graduate Admissions, 888-783-8367, Fax: 888-511-1306, E-mail: graduate@stevens.edu.
Website: https://www.stevens.edu/school-business/masters-programs/mbaemba

Stevens Institute of Technology, Graduate School, School of Business, Program in Finance, Hoboken, NJ 07030. Offers MS. *Program availability:* Part-time, evening/weekend. *Students:* 50 full-time (18 women), 8 part-time (3 women); includes 1 minority (Asian, non-Hispanic/Latino), 46 international. Average age 24. 427 applicants, 53% accepted, 32 enrolled. In 2017, 12 master's awarded. *Degree requirements:* For master's, thesis optional, minimum B average in major field and overall. *Entrance requirements:* Additional exam requirements/recommendations for international students: Required—TOEFL (minimum score 74 iBT), IELTS (minimum score 6). *Application deadline:* For fall admission, 7/1 for domestic students, 4/15 for international students; for spring admission, 12/1 for domestic and international students. Application fee: $60. *Expenses: Tuition:* Full-time $34,494; part-time $1554 per credit. *Required fees:* $291 per semester. *Financial support:* Fellowships, research assistantships, teaching assistantships, career-related internships or fieldwork, Federal Work-Study, scholarships/grants, and unspecified assistantships available. Financial award application deadline: 2/15; financial award applicants required to submit FAFSA. *Unit head:* Dr. Michael Muehlen, Dean, 201-216-8293, E-mail: michael.zurmuehlen@stevens.edu. *Application contact:* Graduate Admissions, 888-793-8367, Fax: 888-511-1306, E-mail: graduate@stevens.edu.
Website: http://www.stevens.edu/school-business/masters-programs/finance

Stony Brook University, State University of New York, Graduate School, College of Business, Program in Business Administration, Stony Brook, NY 11794. Offers accounting (MBA); business administration (MBA); finance (MBA, Certificate); health care management (MBA); human resources (MBA); innovation (MBA); management (MBA); marketing (MBA); operations management (MBA). *Faculty:* 39 full-time (13 women), 14 part-time/adjunct (5 women). *Students:* 181 full-time (98 women), 145 part-time (73 women); includes 68 minority (16 Black or African American, non-Hispanic/Latino; 1 American Indian or Alaska Native, non-Hispanic/Latino; 35 Asian, non-Hispanic/Latino; 11 Hispanic/Latino; 1 Native Hawaiian or other Pacific Islander, non-Hispanic/Latino; 4 Two or more races, non-Hispanic/Latino), 69 international. Average age 29. 154 applicants, 66% accepted, 58 enrolled. In 2017, 105 master's awarded. *Entrance requirements:* For master's, GMAT, 3 letters of recommendation from current or former employers or professors, transcripts, personal statement, resume. Additional exam requirements/recommendations for international students: Required—TOEFL (minimum score 550 paper-based; 90 iBT), IELTS (minimum score 6.5). *Application deadline:* For fall admission, 5/15 for domestic students, 3/15 for international students; for spring admission, 11/15 for domestic students, 10/15 for international students. Application fee: $100. *Expenses:* Contact institution. *Financial support:* Teaching assistantships available. *Total annual research expenditures:* $2,070. *Unit head:* Dr. Manuel London, Dean, 631-632-7159, E-mail: manuel.london@stonybrook.edu. *Application contact:* Dr. Dmytro Holod, Associate Dean for Academic Programs/Graduate Director, 631-632-7183, Fax: 631-632-8181, E-mail: dmytro.holod@stonybrook.edu.
Website: https://www.stonybrook.edu/commcms/business/

Stony Brook University, State University of New York, Graduate School, College of Business, Program in Finance, Stony Brook, NY 11794. Offers MS, AGC. *Program availability:* Part-time. *Students:* 11 full-time (4 women), 5 part-time (0 women); includes 3 minority (1 Black or African American, non-Hispanic/Latino; 2 Asian, non-Hispanic/Latino), 10 international. 205 applicants, 54% accepted, 32 enrolled. In 2017, 45 master's, 5 other advanced degrees awarded. *Degree requirements:* For master's, capstone course. *Entrance requirements:* For master's, GMAT or GRE, letters of recommendation, minimum GPA of 3.0 in prior academic work. Additional exam requirements/recommendations for international students: Required—TOEFL (minimum score 85 iBT). *Application deadline:* For fall admission, 5/15 for domestic students, 3/15 for international students; for spring admission, 11/15 for domestic students, 10/15 for international students; for summer admission, 3/15 for domestic students. *Expenses:* Contact institution. *Unit head:* Dr. Manuel London, Dean, 631-632-7159, E-mail: manuel.london@stonybrook.edu. *Application contact:* Erica Robey, Graduate Coordinator, 631-632-7171, Fax: 631-632-8181, E-mail: oss@stonybrook.edu.
Website: https://www.stonybrook.edu/commcms/business/academics/graduate-programs.php

Strayer University, Graduate Studies, Washington, DC 20005-2603. Offers accounting (MS); acquisition (MBA); business administration (MBA); communications technology (MS); educational management (M Ed); finance (MBA); health services administration (MHSA); hospitality and tourism management (MBA); human resource management (MBA); information systems (MS), including computer security management, decision support system management, enterprise resource management, network management, software engineering management, systems development management; management (MBA); management information systems (MS); marketing (MBA); professional accounting (MS), including accounting information systems, controllership, taxation; public administration (MPA); supply chain management (MBA); technology in education (M Ed). Programs also offered at campus locations in Birmingham, AL; Chamblee, GA; Cobb County, GA; Morrow, GA; White Marsh, MD; Charleston, SC; Columbia, SC; Greensboro, NC; Greenville, SC; Lexington, KY; Louisville, KY; Nashville, TN; North Raleigh, NC; Washington, DC. *Accreditation:* ACBSP. *Program availability:* Part-time, evening/weekend, online learning. *Degree requirements:* For master's, thesis. *Entrance requirements:* For master's, GMAT, GRE General Test, bachelor's degree from an accredited college or university, minimum undergraduate GPA of 2.75. Electronic applications accepted.

Suffolk University, Sawyer Business School, Master of Business Administration Program, Boston, MA 02108-2770. Offers accounting (MBA); entrepreneurship (MBA); executive business administration (EMBA); finance (MBA); global business administration (GMBA); health administration (MBA); international business (MBA); marketing (MBA); nonprofit management (MBA); organizational behavior (MBA);

strategic management (MBA); supply chain management (MBA); taxation (MBA); JD/MBA; MBA/MHA; MBA/MSA; MBA/MSF; MBA/MST. *Accreditation:* AACSB. *Program availability:* Part-time, evening/weekend, 100% online. *Faculty:* 16 full-time (6 women), 9 part-time/adjunct (1 woman). *Students:* 106 full-time (57 women), 236 part-time (135 women); includes 80 minority (23 Black or African American, non-Hispanic/Latino; 23 Asian, non-Hispanic/Latino; 28 Hispanic/Latino; 6 Two or more races, non-Hispanic/Latino), 41 international. Average age 30. 354 applicants, 69% accepted, 115 enrolled. In 2017, 170 master's awarded. *Entrance requirements:* For master's, GMAT, minimum undergraduate GPA of 2.75 (MBA), 5 years of managerial experience (EMBA). Additional exam requirements/recommendations for international students: Required—TOEFL (minimum score 550 paper-based; 80 iBT). *Application deadline:* For fall admission, 3/15 priority date for domestic students, 10/15 priority date for international students; for spring admission, 10/15 priority date for domestic and international students. Applications are processed on a rolling basis. Application fee: $50. Electronic applications accepted. *Expenses:* $43,980 per year full-time, $1,466 per credit part-time (for MBA); $1,794 per credit part-time (for Executive MBA). *Financial support:* In 2017–18, 198 students received support, including 1 fellowship (averaging $2,325 per year); career-related internships or fieldwork, Federal Work-Study, institutionally sponsored loans, and scholarships/grants also available. Support available to part-time students. Financial award application deadline: 4/1; financial award applicants required to submit FAFSA. *Faculty research:* Foreign investments; career strategies and boundaryless careers; corporate ethics codes; interest rates, inflation, and growth options; innovation and product development performance. *Unit head:* Jodi Detjen, Director of MBA Programs, 617-573-8306, E-mail: jdetjen@suffolk.edu. *Application contact:* Mara Marzocchi, Associate Director of Graduate Admissions, 617-573-8302, Fax: 617-305-1733, E-mail: grad.admission@suffolk.edu.
Website: http://www.suffolk.edu/mba

Suffolk University, Sawyer Business School, Programs in Finance, Boston, MA 02108-2770. Offers MSF, MSFSB, JD/MSF, MBA/MSF, MSF/MSA. *Accreditation:* AACSB. *Program availability:* Part-time, evening/weekend. *Faculty:* 7 full-time (4 women), 1 part-time/adjunct (0 women). *Students:* 29 full-time (14 women), 26 part-time (10 women); includes 10 minority (2 Black or African American, non-Hispanic/Latino; 6 Asian, non-Hispanic/Latino; 2 Hispanic/Latino), 26 international. Average age 27. 138 applicants, 68% accepted, 37 enrolled. In 2017, 43 master's awarded. *Entrance requirements:* For master's, GMAT, interview. Additional exam requirements/recommendations for international students: Required—TOEFL (minimum score 550 paper-based; 80 iBT). *Application deadline:* For fall admission, 3/15 priority date for domestic and international students; for spring admission, 10/15 priority date for domestic and international students. Applications are processed on a rolling basis. Application fee: $50. Electronic applications accepted. *Expenses:* Contact institution. *Financial support:* In 2017–18, 33 students received support. Fellowships, career-related internships or fieldwork, Federal Work-Study, institutionally sponsored loans, and scholarships/grants available. Support available to part-time students. Financial award application deadline: 4/1; financial award applicants required to submit FAFSA. *Faculty research:* Financial institutions, corporate finance, ownership structure, dividend policy, corporate restructuring. *Unit head:* Dr. Shahriar Khaksari, Chairperson/Professor of Finance, 617-573-8366, E-mail: skhaksari@suffolk.edu. *Application contact:* Mara Marzocchi, Associate Director of Graduate Admissions, 617-573-8302, Fax: 617-305-1733, E-mail: grad.admission@suffolk.edu.
Website: http://www.suffolk.edu/msf

Syracuse University, Martin J. Whitman School of Management, MS in Finance Program, Syracuse, NY 13244. Offers MS. *Students:* Average age 23. 454 applicants, 42% accepted, 26 enrolled. In 2017, 43 master's awarded. *Entrance requirements:* For master's, GMAT or GRE, resume, essay, 5-minute video interview, two letters of recommendation, transcripts (unofficial). Additional exam requirements/recommendations for international students: Required—TOEFL (minimum score 100 iBT), IELTS (minimum score 7), PTE (minimum score 68). *Application deadline:* For fall admission, 11/30 for domestic students, 11/30 priority date for international students; for winter admission, 1/1 for domestic students, 1/1 priority date for international students; for spring admission, 2/15 for domestic and international students; for summer admission, 4/19 for domestic students. Application fee: $75. Electronic applications accepted. *Expenses:* Contact institution. *Financial support:* Merit scholarships available. Financial award application deadline: 2/15. *Faculty research:* Financial accounting, investment analysis, corporate financial policy and strategy, data analysis/business statistics, managerial finance. *Unit head:* Tom Barkley, Director, MS in Finance Program/Professor of Finance Practice, 315-443-8107, E-mail: tbarkley@syr.edu. *Application contact:* Shri Ramakrishnan, Assistant Director, Graduate Recruitment, 315-443-3497, Fax: 315-443-9517, E-mail: sramak01@syr.edu.
Website: http://whitman.syr.edu/msfin/

Syracuse University, Martin J. Whitman School of Management, PhD Programs, Syracuse, NY 13244. Offers finance (PhD); management information systems (PhD). In 2017, 2 doctorates awarded. *Degree requirements:* For doctorate, comprehensive exam, thesis/dissertation, summer research paper. *Entrance requirements:* For doctorate, GMAT (preferred) or GRE, master's degree (preferred), transcripts, three recommendation letters, personal statement. Additional exam requirements/recommendations for international students: Required—TOEFL (minimum score 600 paper-based; 100 iBT). *Application deadline:* For fall admission, 1/15 for domestic and international students. Application fee: $75. Electronic applications accepted. *Financial support:* Fellowships with full tuition reimbursements, research assistantships with full tuition reimbursements, teaching assistantships with full tuition reimbursements, and scholarships/grants available. *Faculty research:* Marketing models, market microstructure, supply chain, auditing, corporate governance. *Unit head:* Dr. Michel Benaroch, Associate Dean for Research and PhD Programs, 315-443-3492, E-mail: mbenaroc@syr.edu. *Application contact:* Lisa Svegl, Executive Assistant for Development and PhD Programs, 315-443-9141, E-mail: lmsvegl@syr.edu.

Télé-université, Graduate Programs, Québec, QC G1K 9H5, Canada. Offers computer science (PhD); corporate finance (MS); distance learning (MS). *Program availability:* Part-time.

Temple University, Fox School of Business, Doctoral Programs in Business, Philadelphia, PA 19122-6096. Offers accounting (PhD); entrepreneurship (PhD); finance (PhD); international business (PhD); management information systems (PhD); marketing (PhD); risk management and insurance (PhD); statistics (PhD); strategic management (PhD); tourism and sport (PhD). *Accreditation:* AACSB. *Degree requirements:* For doctorate, thesis/dissertation. *Entrance requirements:* For doctorate, GRE General Test, GMAT, minimum GPA of 3.0, master's degree. Additional exam requirements/recommendations for international students: Required—TOEFL (minimum score 600 paper-based; 100 iBT), IELTS (minimum score 7.5). Electronic applications accepted. *Expenses:* Tuition, state resident: full-time $16,164; part-time $898 per credit hour. Tuition, nonresident: full-time $22,158; part-time $1231 per credit hour. *Required fees:* $890; $445 per semester. Full-time tuition and fees vary according to course load, degree level, campus/location and program.

Temple University, Fox School of Business, Specialized Master's Programs, Philadelphia, PA 19122-6096. Offers accountancy (MS); actuarial science (MS); finance

(MS); financial engineering (MS); human resource management (MS); innovation management and entrepreneurship (MS); marketing (MS); statistics (MS). MS in innovation management and entrepreneurship delivered jointly with College of Engineering. *Accreditation:* AACSB. *Program availability:* Part-time. *Entrance requirements:* For master's, GRE General Test or GMAT, minimum undergraduate GPA of 3.0. Additional exam requirements/recommendations for international students: Required—TOEFL (minimum score 600 paper-based; 100 iBT), IELTS (minimum score 7.5). *Expenses:* Tuition, state resident: full-time $16,164; part-time $898 per credit hour. Tuition, nonresident: full-time $22,158; part-time $1231 per credit hour. *Required fees:* $890; $445 per semester. Full-time tuition and fees vary according to course load, degree level, campus/location and program.

Tennessee Technological University, College of Graduate Studies, College of Business, MBA Program, Cookeville, TN 38505. Offers finance (MBA); human resource management (MBA); international business (MBA); management information systems (MBA). *Program availability:* Part-time, evening/weekend. In 2017, 77 master's awarded. *Entrance requirements:* For master's, GMAT or GRE. *Expenses:* Tuition, state resident: full-time $9925; part-time $565 per credit hour. Tuition, nonresident: full-time $32,993; part-time $1291 per credit hour. *Financial support:* In 2017–18, 2 research assistantships, 3 teaching assistantships were awarded; fellowships and unspecified assistantships also available. Financial award application deadline: 4/1; financial award applicants required to submit FAFSA. *Unit head:* Kate Nicewicz, Director, E-mail: knicewicz@tntech.edu. *Application contact:* Shelia K. Kendrick, Coordinator of Graduate Studies, 931-372-3808, Fax: 931-372-3497, E-mail: skendrick@tntech.edu. Website: https://www.tntech.edu/cob/mba/

Texas A&M International University, Office of Graduate Studies and Research, A.R. Sanchez, Jr. School of Business, Division of International Banking and Finance Studies, Laredo, TX 78041. Offers accounting (MP Acc); international banking and finance (MBA). *Entrance requirements:* For master's, GMAT or GRE General Test. Additional exam requirements/recommendations for international students: Required—TOEFL (minimum score 550 paper-based; 79 iBT).

Texas A&M University, Mays Business School, Department of Finance, College Station, TX 77843. Offers finance (MS); financial management (MFM); land economics and real estate (MRE); management information systems (MS). *Faculty:* 21. *Students:* 235 full-time (72 women), 10 part-time (4 women); includes 43 minority (2 Black or African American, non-Hispanic/Latino; 2 American Indian or Alaska Native, non-Hispanic/Latino; 11 Asian, non-Hispanic/Latino; 24 Hispanic/Latino; 4 Two or more races, non-Hispanic/Latino), 19 international. Average age 24. 179 applicants, 33% accepted, 50 enrolled. In 2017, 163 master's awarded. Terminal master's awarded for partial completion of doctoral program. *Degree requirements:* For master's, comprehensive exam. *Entrance requirements:* For master's, GMAT or GRE. Additional exam requirements/recommendations for international students: Required—TOEFL (minimum score 550 paper-based; 80 iBT), IELTS (minimum score 6), PTE (minimum score 53). *Application deadline:* For fall admission, 4/7 for domestic students. Applications are processed on a rolling basis. Application fee: $50 ($90 for international students). Electronic applications accepted. *Expenses:* Contact institution. *Financial support:* In 2017–18, 165 students received support, including 14 fellowships with tuition reimbursements available (averaging $2,232 per year), 23 research assistantships with tuition reimbursements available (averaging $10,754 per year), 12 teaching assistantships with tuition reimbursements available (averaging $3,926 per year); career-related internships or fieldwork, institutionally sponsored loans, scholarships/grants, traineeships, health care benefits, tuition waivers (full and partial), and unspecified assistantships also available. Support available to part-time students. Financial award application deadline: 3/15; financial award applicants required to submit FAFSA. *Unit head:* Dr. Sorin Sorescu, Head, 979-458-0380, Fax: 979-845-3884, E-mail: smsorescu@mays.tamu.edu. *Application contact:* Angela G. Degelman, Program Coordinator/Graduate Academic Advisor, 979-845-4858, Fax: 979-845-3884, E-mail: adegelman@mays.tamu.edu.
Website: http://mays.tamu.edu/finc/

Texas A&M University–Commerce, College of Business, Commerce, TX 75429. Offers accounting (MSA); business administration (MBA); business analytics (MS); finance (MSF); management (MS); marketing (MS). *Accreditation:* AACSB. *Program availability:* Part-time, evening/weekend, 100% online, blended/hybrid learning. *Faculty:* 50 full-time (19 women), 7 part-time/adjunct (0 women). *Students:* 479 full-time (248 women), 1,056 part-time (556 women); includes 660 minority (281 Black or African American, non-Hispanic/Latino; 4 American Indian or Alaska Native, non-Hispanic/Latino; 120 Asian, non-Hispanic/Latino; 222 Hispanic/Latino; 33 Two or more races, non-Hispanic/Latino), 224 international. Average age 33. 930 applicants, 61% accepted, 363 enrolled. In 2017, 686 master's awarded. *Degree requirements:* For master's, comprehensive exam. *Entrance requirements:* For master's, GRE General Test, GMAT, letter of recommendation. Additional exam requirements/recommendations for international students: Required—TOEFL (minimum score 550 paper-based; 79 iBT), IELTS (minimum score 6). *Application deadline:* For fall admission, 6/1 priority date for international students; for spring admission, 10/15 priority date for international students; for summer admission, 3/15 priority date for international students. Applications are processed on a rolling basis. Application fee: $50 ($75 for international students). Electronic applications accepted. *Expenses:* Contact institution. *Financial support:* In 2017–18, 46 students received support, including 20 research assistantships with partial tuition reimbursements available (averaging $8,000 per year); Federal Work-Study, institutionally sponsored loans, scholarships/grants, health care benefits, and unspecified assistantships also available. Financial award application deadline: 5/1; financial award applicants required to submit FAFSA. *Faculty research:* Applied economics with emphasis on industries that are important to the region including health, energy and agriculture; finance research on banking, investments, financial institutions and risk management; marketing and big data decisions of product choice behavior and channel behavior of consumers; strategic management and organizational behavior phenomena; international accounting in governmental sectors. *Total annual research expenditures:* $1,920. *Unit head:* Dr. Shanan Gwaltney Gibson, Dean of College of Business, 903-886-5191, Fax: 903-886-5650, E-mail: shanan.gibson@tamuc.edu. *Application contact:* Vicky Turner, Doctoral Degree and Special Programs Coordinator, 903-886-5167, E-mail: vicky.turner@tamuc.edu.
Website: http://www.tamuc.edu/academics/graduateSchool/programs/businessEntrepreneurship/default.aspx

Texas A&M University–Corpus Christi, College of Graduate Studies, College of Business, Corpus Christi, TX 78412. Offers accounting (M Acc); business (MBA); finance (MBA); health care administration (MBA); international business (MBA). *Accreditation:* AACSB. *Program availability:* Part-time, evening/weekend, 100% online, blended/hybrid learning. *Faculty:* 31 full-time (11 women), 2 part-time/adjunct (4 women). *Students:* 107 full-time (50 women), 583 part-time (283 women); includes 259 minority (80 Black or African American, non-Hispanic/Latino; 85 Asian, non-Hispanic/Latino; 83 Hispanic/Latino; 11 Two or more races, non-Hispanic/Latino), 77 international. Average age 34. 485 applicants, 57% accepted, 236 enrolled. In 2017, 310 master's awarded. *Degree requirements:* For master's, 30 to 42 hours (for MBA; varies by concentration area, delivery format, and necessity for foundational courses for

students with nonbusiness degrees). *Entrance requirements:* For master's, GMAT, GRE. Additional exam requirements/recommendations for international students: Required—TOEFL (minimum score 550 paper-based; 79 iBT), IELTS (minimum score 6.5). *Application deadline:* For fall admission, 7/15 priority date for domestic students, 5/1 priority date for international students; for spring admission, 11/15 priority date for domestic students, 9/1 priority date for international students; for summer admission, 4/15 priority date for domestic and international students. Applications are processed on a rolling basis. Application fee: $50 ($70 for international students). Electronic applications accepted. *Expenses:* Tuition, state resident: full-time $3568; part-time $198.24 per credit hour. Tuition, nonresident: full-time $11,038; part-time $613.24 per credit hour. *Required fees:* $2129; $1422.58 per semester. Tuition and fees vary according to program. *Financial support:* Research assistantships, teaching assistantships, career-related internships or fieldwork, Federal Work-Study, institutionally sponsored loans, scholarships/grants, health care benefits, and unspecified assistantships available. Support available to part-time students. Financial award application deadline: 3/15; financial award applicants required to submit FAFSA. *Unit head:* Dr. John Gamble, Dean, 361-825-6045, Fax: 361-825-2725, E-mail: john.gamble@tamucc.edu. *Application contact:* Sharon Polansky, Director of Master's Programs, 361-825-3448, Fax: 361-825-2755, E-mail: gradweb@tamucc.edu.
Website: http://cob.tamucc.edu

Texas Tech University, Rawls College of Business Administration, Lubbock, TX 79409-2101. Offers accounting (MSA, PhD), including audit/financial reporting (MSA), taxation (MSA); data science (MS); finance (PhD); general business (MBA); healthcare management (MS); information systems and operations management (PhD); management (PhD); marketing (PhD); STEM (MBA); JD/MBA; JD/MSA; MBA/M Arch; MBA/MD; MBA/MS; MBA/Pharm D. *Accreditation:* AACSB. *Program availability:* Evening/weekend, 100% online, blended/hybrid learning. *Faculty:* 89 full-time (22 women). *Students:* 660 full-time (252 women); includes 174 minority (30 Black or African American, non-Hispanic/Latino; 3 American Indian or Alaska Native, non-Hispanic/Latino; 20 Asian, non-Hispanic/Latino; 104 Hispanic/Latino; 17 Two or more races, non-Hispanic/Latino), 99 international. Average age 29. 492 applicants, 51% accepted, 148 enrolled. In 2017, 439 master's, 6 doctorates awarded. *Degree requirements:* For master's, thesis (for MS); capstone course; for doctorate, comprehensive exam, thesis/dissertation, qualifying exams. *Entrance requirements:* For master's, GMAT, GRE, MCAT, PCAT, LSAT, or DAT, holistic review of academic credentials, resume, essay, letters of recommendation; for doctorate, GMAT, GRE, holistic review of academic credentials, resume, statement of purpose, letters of recommendation. Additional exam requirements/recommendations for international students: Required—TOEFL (minimum score 550 paper-based; 79 iBT), IELTS (minimum score 6.5), PTE (minimum score 60). *Application deadline:* For fall admission, 7/1 priority date for domestic students, 1/15 for international students; for spring admission, 12/1 priority date for domestic students, 6/15 for international students; for summer admission, 5/1 for domestic students. Applications are processed on a rolling basis. Application fee: $60. Electronic applications accepted. *Expenses:* $5,167.50 full-time; $9,000 per semester (for hybrid MBA). *Financial support:* In 2017–18, 81 students received support, including 1 research assistantship with full tuition reimbursement available (averaging $22,725 per year), 63 teaching assistantships with full tuition reimbursements available (averaging $22,725 per year); career-related internships or fieldwork, Federal Work-Study, scholarships/grants, health care benefits, and unspecified assistantships also available. Financial award application deadline: 3/1; financial award applicants required to submit FAFSA. *Faculty research:* Governmental and nonprofit accounting, securities and options futures, statistical analysis and design, leadership, consumer behavior. *Total annual research expenditures:* $230,000. *Unit head:* Dr. Margaret Williams, Dean, 806-834-2839, Fax: 806-742-1092, E-mail: margaret.l.williams@ttu.edu. *Application contact:* Jennifer Yack, Applications Manager, Graduate and Professional Programs, 806-742-3184, E-mail: rawlsgrad@ttu.edu.
Website: http://www.depts.ttu.edu/rawlsbusiness/graduate/

Thomas Edison State University, School of Business and Management, Program in International Business Finance, Trenton, NJ 08608. Offers MS. *Program availability:* Online learning. *Entrance requirements:* For master's, undergraduate coursework in financial accounting, microeconomics, finance and statistics.

Tiffin University, Program in Business Administration, Tiffin, OH 44883-2161. Offers finance (MBA); general management (MBA); healthcare administration (MBA); human resource management (MBA); international business (MBA); leadership (MBA); marketing (MBA); non-profit management (MBA); sports management (MBA). *Accreditation:* ACBSP. *Program availability:* Part-time, evening/weekend, online learning. *Entrance requirements:* For master's, minimum undergraduate GPA of 2.5, work experience. Additional exam requirements/recommendations for international students: Required—TOEFL (minimum score 550 paper-based; 79 iBT), IELTS. Electronic applications accepted. Application fee is waived when completed online. *Faculty research:* Small business, executive development operations, research and statistical analysis, market research, management information systems.

Trident University International, College of Business Administration, Program in Business Administration, Cypress, CA 90630. Offers business administration (PhD); conflict and negotiation management (MBA); criminal justice administration (MBA); entrepreneurship (MBA); finance (MBA); general management (MBA); government accounting (MBA); human resource management (MBA); information security and digital assurance management (MBA); information technology management (MBA); international business (MBA); logistics management (MBA); marketing (MBA); project management (MBA); public management (MBA); quality management (MBA); strategic leadership (MBA). *Program availability:* Part-time, evening/weekend, online learning. *Degree requirements:* For doctorate, comprehensive exam, thesis/dissertation, defense of dissertation. *Entrance requirements:* For master's, minimum GPA of 2.5 (students with GPA 3.0 or greater may transfer up to 30% of graduate level credits); for doctorate, minimum GPA of 3.4, curriculum vitae, course work in research methods or statistics. Additional exam requirements/recommendations for international students: Required—TOEFL. Electronic applications accepted.

Troy University, Graduate School, College of Business, Program in Business Administration, Troy, AL 36082. Offers accounting (EMBA, MBA); criminal justice (EMBA); finance (MBA); general management (EMBA, MBA); healthcare management (EMBA); information systems (EMBA, MBA); international economic development (MBA). *Accreditation:* ACBSP. *Program availability:* Part-time, evening/weekend. *Faculty:* 6 full-time (2 women), 1 part-time/adjunct (0 women). *Students:* 43 full-time (22 women), 115 part-time (55 women); includes 50 minority (31 Black or African American, non-Hispanic/Latino; 12 Asian, non-Hispanic/Latino; 6 Hispanic/Latino; 1 Two or more races, non-Hispanic/Latino). Average age 30. 156 applicants, 76% accepted, 36 enrolled. In 2017, 95 master's awarded. *Degree requirements:* For master's, minimum GPA of 3.0, capstone course, research course. *Entrance requirements:* For master's, GMAT (minimum score 500) or GRE (minimum score 900 on old exam or 294 on new exam), bachelor's degree; minimum undergraduate GPA of 2.5 or 3.0 on last 30 semester hours, letter of recommendation. Additional exam requirements/recommendations for international students: Required—TOEFL (minimum score 523 paper-based; 70 iBT), IELTS (minimum score 6). *Application deadline:* Applications are

Finance and Banking

processed on a rolling basis. Application fee: $50. Electronic applications accepted. *Expenses:* Tuition, state resident: part-time $417 per credit hour. Tuition, nonresident: part-time $834 per credit hour. *Required fees:* $42 per credit hour. $50 per semester. Tuition and fees vary according to campus/location. *Financial support:* Fellowships, career-related internships or fieldwork, and scholarships/grants available. Support available to part-time students. Financial award applicants required to submit FAFSA. *Unit head:* Dr. Phillip Mixon, MBA Director, 334-670-3140, Fax: 334-670-3708, E-mail: pamixon@troy.edu. *Application contact:* Jessica A. Kimbro, Director of Graduate Admissions, 334-670-3178, E-mail: jacord@troy.edu.

Tulane University, A. B. Freeman School of Business, New Orleans, LA 70118-5669. Offers accounting (M Acct); analytics (MBA); banking and financial services (M Fin); energy (M Fin, MBA); entrepreneurship (MBA); finance (MBA, PhD); financial accounting (PhD); international business (MBA); international management (MBA); strategic management and leadership (MBA); JD/M Acct; JD/MBA; MBA/M Acc; MBA/MA; MBA/MD; MBA/ME; MBA/MPH. *Accreditation:* AACSB. *Program availability:* Part-time, evening/weekend. *Faculty:* 51 full-time (15 women), 38 part-time/adjunct (3 women). *Students:* 561 full-time (287 women), 297 part-time (151 women); includes 112 minority (43 Black or African American, non-Hispanic/Latino; 2 American Indian or Alaska Native, non-Hispanic/Latino; 24 Asian, non-Hispanic/Latino; 38 Hispanic/Latino; 5 Two or more races, non-Hispanic/Latino), 515 international. Average age 27. 2,021 applicants, 74% accepted, 476 enrolled. In 2017, 632 master's, 9 doctorates awarded. Terminal master's awarded for partial completion of doctoral program. *Degree requirements:* For master's, one foreign language, comprehensive exam (for some programs); for doctorate, one foreign language, comprehensive exam, thesis/ dissertation. *Entrance requirements:* For master's and doctorate, GMAT or GRE, interview. Additional exam requirements/recommendations for international students: Required—TOEFL or IELTS. *Application deadline:* For fall admission, 11/1 priority date for domestic and international students; for winter admission, 1/6 for domestic and international students; for spring admission, 3/1 priority date for domestic and international students; for summer admission, 5/5 for domestic students. Applications are processed on a rolling basis. Application fee: $125. Electronic applications accepted. *Expenses:* Contact institution. *Financial support:* In 2017–18, 176 students received support. Fellowships with tuition reimbursements available, research assistantships, teaching assistantships, career-related internships or fieldwork, Federal Work-Study, tuition waivers (full and partial), and unspecified assistantships available. Support available to part-time students. Financial award application deadline: 4/15; financial award applicants required to submit FAFSA. *Faculty research:* Corporate finance, managerial accounting and financial reporting, strategic management and leadership, consumer behavior and decision making, organizational behavior and human resource management. *Unit head:* Ira Solomon, PhD, Dean, 504-865-5407, Fax: 504-865-5491, E-mail: businessdean@tulane.edu. *Application contact:* Melissa Booth, Assistant Dean for Graduate Admissions, 800-223-5402, E-mail: freeman.admissions@tulane.edu. Website: http://www.freeman.tulane.edu

United States International University–Africa, School of Business Administration, Nairobi, Kenya. Offers business administration (GEMBA); entrepreneurship (MBA); finance (MBA); human resource management (MBA); information technology management (MBA); integrated studies (MBA); international business administration (MBA); management and organizational development (MS); marketing (MBA); organizational development (EMS); strategic management (MBA). *Program availability:* Part-time, evening/weekend. *Degree requirements:* For master's, thesis. *Entrance requirements:* For master's, GMAT, 2 letters of reference, resume. Additional exam requirements/recommendations for international students: Required—TOEFL (minimum score 550 paper-based). *Faculty research:* Marketing in small business enterprises, total quality management in Kenya.

Universidad Central del Este, Graduate School, San Pedro de Macoris, Dominican Republic. Offers environmental engineering (ME); financial management (M Ad); higher education (M Ed), including higher education management, higher education pedagogy; human resources (M Ad). *Entrance requirements:* For master's, letters of recommendation.

Universidad de las Americas, A.C., Program in Business Administration, Mexico City, Mexico. Offers finance (MBA); marketing research (MBA); production and quality (MBA).

Universidad de las Américas Puebla, Division of Graduate Studies, School of Business and Economics, Puebla, Mexico. Offers business administration (MBA); finance (M Adm). *Program availability:* Part-time, evening/weekend. *Degree requirements:* For master's, one foreign language, thesis. *Entrance requirements:* Additional exam requirements/recommendations for international students: Required— TOEFL. *Faculty research:* System dynamics, information technology, marketing, international business, strategic planning, quality.

Universidad de las Américas Puebla, Division of Graduate Studies, School of Social Sciences, Program in Economics, Puebla, Mexico. Offers economics (MA); finance (M Adm). *Program availability:* Part-time, evening/weekend. *Degree requirements:* For master's, one foreign language, thesis. *Faculty research:* Economic models (mathematics), industrial organization, assets and values market.

Universidad Metropolitana, School of Business Administration, Program in Finance, San Juan, PR 00928-1150. Offers MBA.

Université de Sherbrooke, Faculty of Administration, Program in Finance, Sherbrooke, QC J1K 2R1, Canada. Offers M Sc. *Degree requirements:* For master's, one foreign language, thesis. *Entrance requirements:* For master's, bachelor's degree in related field, minimum GPA of 3.0 (on 4.3 scale). Electronic applications accepted. *Faculty research:* Public projects analysis, financial econometrics, risk management, portfolio management.

Université du Québec à Montréal, Graduate Programs, Program in Finance, Montréal, QC H3C 3P8, Canada. Offers Diploma. *Program availability:* Part-time. *Entrance requirements:* For degree, appropriate bachelor's degree or equivalent, proficiency in French.

Université du Québec à Trois-Rivières, Graduate Programs, Program in Finance, Trois-Rivières, QC G9A 5H7, Canada. Offers DESS.

Université du Québec en Outaouais, Graduate Programs, Program in Financial Services, Gatineau, QC J8X 3X7, Canada. Offers MBA, DESS, Diploma. *Program availability:* Part-time, evening/weekend. *Degree requirements:* For master's, thesis (for some programs).

Université Laval, Faculty of Administrative Sciences, Programs in Business Administration, Québec, QC G1K 7P4, Canada. Offers accounting (MBA); agri-food management (MBA); electronic business (MBA, Diploma); factory management and logistics (MBA); finance (MBA); firm management (MBA); geomatic management (MBA); information technology management (MBA); international management (MBA); management (MBA); management accounting (MBA, Diploma); marketing (MBA); modeling and organizational decision (MBA); occupational health and safety management (MBA); pharmacy management (MBA); social and environmental responsibility (MBA); technological entrepreneurship (Diploma). *Accreditation:* AACSB. *Program availability:* Part-time, evening/weekend, online learning. *Entrance*

requirements: For master's and Diploma, knowledge of French and English. Electronic applications accepted.

University at Albany, State University of New York, Nelson A. Rockefeller College of Public Affairs and Policy, Department of Public Administration and Policy, Albany, NY 12222-0001. Offers financial management and public economics (MPA); financial market regulation (MPA); health policy (MPA); healthcare management (MPA); homeland security (MPA); human resources management (MPA); information strategy and management (MPA); local government management (MPA); nonprofit management (MPA); nonprofit management and leadership (Certificate); organizational behavior and theory (MPA, PhD); planning and policy analysis (CAS); policy analysis (MPA); politics and administration (PhD); public finance (PhD); public management (PhD); public policy (PhD); public sector management (Certificate); women and public policy (Certificate); JD/MPA. JD/MPA offered jointly with Albany Law School. *Accreditation:* NASPAA (one or more programs are accredited). *Faculty:* 21 full-time (7 women), 14 part-time/adjunct (7 women). *Students:* 115 full-time (59 women), 93 part-time (56 women); includes 41 minority (11 Black or African American, non-Hispanic/Latino; 9 Asian, non-Hispanic/ Latino; 18 Hispanic/Latino; 3 Two or more races, non-Hispanic/Latino), 32 international. 236 applicants, 69% accepted, 86 enrolled. In 2017, 57 master's, 1 doctorate, 14 other advanced degrees awarded. *Degree requirements:* For doctorate, one foreign language, thesis/dissertation. *Entrance requirements:* For doctorate, GRE General Test. Additional exam requirements/recommendations for international students: Required—TOEFL (minimum score 550 paper-based). *Application deadline:* For fall admission, 2/1 priority date for domestic students, 5/1 for international students; for spring admission, 12/1 for domestic students. Applications are processed on a rolling basis. Application fee: $75. Electronic applications accepted. *Expenses:* Tuition, state resident: full-time $10,870; part-time $453 per credit hour. Tuition, nonresident: full-time $22,210; part-time $925 per credit hour. *Required fees:* $84.68 per credit hour. $508.06 per semester. Part-time tuition and fees vary according to course load and program. *Financial support:* Application deadline: 2/1. *Unit head:* Victor Asal, Chair, 518-591-8729, E-mail: vasal@ albany.edu.
Website: http://www.albany.edu/rockefeller/pad.shtml

University at Albany, State University of New York, School of Business, MBA Programs, Albany, NY 12222. Offers business administration (MBA); cyber security (MBA); entrepreneurship (MBA); finance (MBA); human resource information systems (MBA); information systems and business analytics (MBA); marketing (MBA); JD/MBA. JD/MBA offered jointly with Albany Law School. *Program availability:* Part-time, evening/weekend. *Faculty:* 29 full-time (13 women), 9 part-time/adjunct (2 women). *Students:* 103 full-time (36 women), 188 part-time (69 women); includes 76 minority (27 Black or African American, non-Hispanic/Latino; 33 Asian, non-Hispanic/Latino; 16 Hispanic/ Latino), 16 international. Average age 25. 181 applicants, 80% accepted, 114 enrolled. In 2017, 103 master's awarded. *Degree requirements:* For master's, thesis (for some programs), field or research project. *Entrance requirements:* For master's, GMAT, minimum undergraduate GPA of 3.0; 3 letters of recommendation; resume; statement of goals. Additional exam requirements/recommendations for international students: Required—TOEFL (minimum score 100 iBT); Recommended—IELTS (minimum score 7). *Application deadline:* For fall admission, 4/1 priority date for domestic students, 2/15 for international students; for spring admission, 12/1 for domestic students; for summer admission, 5/1 for domestic students. Applications are processed on a rolling basis. Application fee: $75. Electronic applications accepted. *Expenses:* $16,622.00 per year (for Full-Time MBA); $645 per credit hour (for Evening MBA). *Financial support:* In 2017–18, 25 students received support, including 7 fellowships with partial tuition reimbursements available (averaging $6,000 per year), 4 research assistantships with partial tuition reimbursements available, 21 teaching assistantships with partial tuition reimbursements available; unspecified assistantships also available. Financial award application deadline: 4/1; financial award applicants required to submit FAFSA. *Faculty research:* Social goods, information assurance, social computing, corporate entrepreneurship, asset pricing. *Total annual research expenditures:* $136,000. *Unit head:* Dr. Hany A. Shawky, Interim Dean, 518-956-8337, Fax: 518-442-3273, E-mail: hshawky@albany.edu. *Application contact:* Zina Mega Lawrence, Assistant Dean of Graduate Student Services, 518-956-8320, Fax: 518-442-4042, E-mail: zlawrence@ albany.edu.
Website: https://graduatebusiness.albany.edu/

University at Buffalo, the State University of New York, Graduate School, School of Management, Buffalo, NY 14260. Offers accounting (MS); analytics (MBA); business administration (PMBA); consulting (MBA); finance (MBA, MS), including financial risk management (MS), quantitative finance (MS); healthcare (MBA); information assurance (MBA); information systems (MBA); international management (MBA); management (EMBA, PhD); management information systems (MS); marketing (MBA); supply chain and operations (MBA); supply chains and operations management (MS); Au D/MBA; DDS/MBA; JD/MBA; M Arch/MBA; MD/MBA; MPH/MBA; MSW/MBA; Pharm D/MBA. *Accreditation:* AACSB. *Program availability:* Part-time, evening/weekend. *Faculty:* 80 full-time (26 women), 45 part-time/adjunct (12 women). *Students:* 597 full-time (251 women); includes 83 minority (19 Black or African American, non-Hispanic/Latino; 59 Asian, non-Hispanic/Latino; 5 Hispanic/Latino), 306 international. Average age 25. 2,109 applicants, 46% accepted, 376 enrolled. In 2017, 371 master's, 13 doctorates awarded. *Degree requirements:* For master's, capstone courses or projects; for doctorate, comprehensive exam, thesis/dissertation. *Entrance requirements:* For master's, GMAT (for MS in accounting, finance); GRE or GMAT (for MBA, MS in management information systems, supply chains and operations management), essays, letters of recommendation; for doctorate, GMAT or GRE, essays, writing sample, letters of recommendation. Additional exam requirements/recommendations for international students: Required—TOEFL (minimum score 95 iBT) or IELTS (minimum score 6.5); Recommended—TSE (minimum score 73). *Application deadline:* For fall admission, 10/ 15 priority date for domestic and international students; for winter admission, 2/1 priority date for domestic and international students; for spring admission, 4/15 for domestic students; for summer admission, 5/15 for domestic students. Application fee: $100. Electronic applications accepted. *Expenses:* Varies by program. *Financial support:* Fellowships with full and partial tuition reimbursements, research assistantships with full and partial tuition reimbursements, teaching assistantships with full and partial tuition reimbursements, career-related internships or fieldwork, Federal Work-Study, institutionally sponsored loans, scholarships/grants, health care benefits, and unspecified assistantships available. Financial award application deadline: 2/15. *Faculty research:* Data analytics, accounting and law, rate finance, consumer behavior, supply chain logistics, leadership and team effectiveness. *Total annual research expenditures:* $968,376. *Unit head:* Erin K. O'Brien, Assistant Dean and Director of Graduate Programs, 716-645-3204, Fax: 716-645-2341, E-mail: ekobrien@buffalo.edu. *Application contact:* Meghan Felser, Director of Admissions and Recruiting, 716-645-3204, Fax: 716-645-2341, E-mail: mpwood@buffalo.edu.
Website: http://mgt.buffalo.edu/

The University of Akron, Graduate School, College of Business Administration, Department of Finance, Akron, OH 44325. Offers MBA. *Program availability:* Part-time, evening/weekend. *Faculty:* 9 full-time (4 women), 2 part-time/adjunct (0 women). *Students:* 11 full-time (1 woman), 12 part-time (5 women); includes 4 minority (3 Black or African American, non-Hispanic/Latino; 1 Asian, non-Hispanic/Latino), 3 international.

Average age 26. 8 applicants, 88% accepted, 3 enrolled. In 2017, 15 master's awarded. *Entrance requirements:* For master's, GMAT, GRE, MCAT, LSAT, PCAT, or CAT, minimum GPA of 3.0 (preferred), two letters of recommendation, statement of purpose, resume. Additional exam requirements/recommendations for international students: Required—TOEFL (minimum score 79 iBT), IELTS (minimum score 6.5). *Application deadline:* For fall admission, 7/15 for domestic and international students; for spring admission, 11/15 for domestic and international students; for summer admission, 4/15 for domestic and international students. Application fee: $45 ($75 for international students). Electronic applications accepted. *Financial support:* In 2017–18, 1 teaching assistantship with full and partial tuition reimbursement was awarded. *Faculty research:* Corporate finance, financial markets and institutions, investment and equity market analysis, personal financial planning, real estate. *Total annual research expenditures:* $15,809. *Unit head:* Dr. James Thomson, Chair, 330-972-6329, E-mail: thomson1@uakron.edu. *Application contact:* Dr. William Hauser, Director of Graduate Business Programs, 330-972-7043, Fax: 330-972-6588, E-mail: whauser@uakron.edu. Website: http://www.uakron.edu/cba/departments/finance/

The University of Alabama, Graduate School, Manderson Graduate School of Business, Economics, Finance and Legal Studies Department, Tuscaloosa, AL 35487. Offers economics (MA, PhD); finance (MS, PhD). *Faculty:* 37 full-time (6 women), 1 part-time/adjunct (0 women). *Students:* 49 full-time (14 women), 6 part-time (1 woman); includes 2 minority (1 Asian, non-Hispanic/Latino; 1 Two or more races, non-Hispanic/Latino), 35 international. Average age 29. 117 applicants, 33% accepted, 14 enrolled. In 2017, 26 master's, 6 doctorates awarded. Terminal master's awarded for partial completion of doctoral program. *Degree requirements:* For master's, comprehensive exam (MA), thesis (MS); for doctorate, comprehensive exam, thesis/dissertation. *Entrance requirements:* For master's, GMAT, GRE; for doctorate, GRE or GMAT. Additional exam requirements/recommendations for international students: Required—TOEFL (minimum score 550 paper-based; 79 iBT). *Application deadline:* For fall admission, 7/1 priority date for domestic students, 1/15 for international students; for spring admission, 11/1 priority date for domestic students, 6/1 for international students. Applications are processed on a rolling basis. Application fee: $50 ($60 for international students). Electronic applications accepted. *Financial support:* In 2017–18, 41 students received support, including research assistantships with tuition reimbursements available (averaging $15,000 per year), teaching assistantships with tuition reimbursements available (averaging $15,000 per year); fellowships, Federal Work-Study, institutionally sponsored loans, and unspecified assistantships also available. Financial award application deadline: 1/15. *Faculty research:* Taxation, futures market, monetary theory and policy, income distribution. *Unit head:* Dr. Laura Razzolini, Department Head, 205-348-6683, E-mail: kcwise@cba.ua.edu. *Application contact:* Debra F. Wheatley, Graduate Programs Secretary, 205-348-6683, Fax: 205-348-0590, E-mail: dwheatle@cba.ua.edu. Website: http://www.cba.ua.edu/

The University of Alabama at Birmingham, Collat School of Business, Program in Business Administration, Birmingham, AL 35294. Offers business administration (MBA), including finance, health care management, information technology management, marketing; MD/MBA. *Program availability:* Part-time, evening/weekend, 100% online, blended/hybrid learning. *Faculty:* 44 full-time (8 women), 11 part-time/adjunct (4 women). *Students:* 111 full-time (46 women), 308 part-time (136 women); includes 107 minority (73 Black or African American, non-Hispanic/Latino; 21 Asian, non-Hispanic/Latino; 8 Hispanic/Latino; 5 Two or more races, non-Hispanic/Latino), 56 international. Average age 33. 222 applicants, 89% accepted, 143 enrolled. In 2017, 114 master's awarded. *Entrance requirements:* For master's, GMAT. Additional exam requirements/recommendations for international students: Required—TOEFL (minimum score 80 iBT), IELTS (minimum score 6.5). *Application deadline:* For fall admission, 7/1 for domestic and international students; for spring admission, 11/1 for domestic and international students; for summer admission, 4/1 for domestic and international students. Applications are processed on a rolling basis. Application fee: $60 ($75 for international students). Electronic applications accepted. *Faculty research:* Open innovation, workplace issues, leadership, supply chain management, capital markets. *Total annual research expenditures:* $240,000. *Unit head:* Dr. Ken Miller, Executive Director, MBA Programs, 205-934-8855, E-mail: klmiller@uab.edu. *Application contact:* Christy Manning, Coordinator of Graduate Programs in Business, 205-934-8817, E-mail: cmanning@uab.edu. Website: http://www.uab.edu/business/home/mba

The University of Alabama in Huntsville, School of Graduate Studies, College of Business Administration, Program in Accounting, Huntsville, AL 35899. Offers accounting (M Acc), including CPA preparatory with an emphasis in taxation, CPA preparatory with emphasis in assurance and financial reporting, general accounting, information systems audit and control (ISAC). *Accreditation:* AACSB. *Program availability:* Part-time, evening/weekend. *Degree requirements:* For master's, comprehensive exam, thesis or alternative. *Entrance requirements:* For master's, GMAT (minimum score 500), minimum AACSB index of 1080. Additional exam requirements/recommendations for international students: Required—TOEFL (minimum score 550 paper-based; 80 iBT), IELTS (minimum score 6.5). Electronic applications accepted. *Faculty research:* Accounting information systems, managerial accounting, behavioral accounting, state and local taxation, financial accounting.

The University of Alabama in Huntsville, School of Graduate Studies, College of Business Administration, Programs in Business and Management, Huntsville, AL 35899. Offers business analytics (MSMS); federal contracting and procurement management (Certificate); human resource management (MSM); management (MBA), including acquisition management, entrepreneurship, federal contract accounting, finance, human resource management, logistics and supply chain management, marketing, project management; supply chain management (Certificate); technology and innovation management (Certificate). *Accreditation:* AACSB. *Program availability:* Part-time, evening/weekend. *Degree requirements:* For master's, comprehensive exam, thesis or alternative. *Entrance requirements:* For master's, GMAT (minimum score 500), minimum AACSB index of 1080. Additional exam requirements/recommendations for international students: Required—TOEFL (minimum score 550 paper-based; 80 iBT), IELTS (minimum score 6.5). Electronic applications accepted. *Faculty research:* Supply chain management, management of research and development, international marketing and branding, organizational behavior and human resource management, social networks and computational economics.

University of Alaska Fairbanks, School of Management, Department of Business Administration, Fairbanks, AK 99775-6080. Offers capital markets (MBA); general management (MBA). *Accreditation:* AACSB. *Program availability:* Part-time, online only, 100% online. *Degree requirements:* For master's, comprehensive exam, thesis or alternative. *Entrance requirements:* For master's, GRE General Test, GMAT, bachelor's degree from accredited institution with minimum cumulative undergraduate and major GPA of 3.0. Additional exam requirements/recommendations for international students: Required—TOEFL (minimum score 550 paper-based; 79 iBT), IELTS (minimum score 6.5). Electronic applications accepted. *Expenses:* Contact institution. *Faculty research:* Consumer behavior, marketing, international finance and business, strategic risk, organization theory.

University of Alberta, Faculty of Graduate Studies and Research, Department of Economics, Edmonton, AB T6G 2E1, Canada. Offers economics (MA, PhD); economics and finance (MA); environmental and natural resource economics (PhD). *Program availability:* Part-time. *Degree requirements:* For doctorate, thesis/dissertation. *Entrance requirements:* For master's and doctorate, GRE. Additional exam requirements/recommendations for international students: Required—TOEFL. *Faculty research:* Public finance, international trade, industrial organization, Pacific Rim economics, monetary economics.

University of Alberta, Faculty of Graduate Studies and Research, Doctoral Program in Business, Edmonton, AB T6G 2E1, Canada. Offers accounting (PhD); finance (PhD); human resources/industrial relations (PhD); management science (PhD); marketing (PhD); organizational analysis (PhD); MBA/PhD. *Accreditation:* AACSB. *Program availability:* Part-time. *Degree requirements:* For doctorate, comprehensive exam, thesis/dissertation. *Entrance requirements:* For doctorate, GMAT. Additional exam requirements/recommendations for international students: Required—TOEFL (minimum score 550 paper-based). Electronic applications accepted. *Faculty research:* Accounting, capital markets and corporate finance, organizational change and human resource management, marketing, strategic management.

The University of Arizona, Eller College of Management, Department of Finance, Tucson, AZ 85721. Offers MS. *Program availability:* Part-time. Terminal master's awarded for partial completion of doctoral program. *Degree requirements:* For master's, project. *Entrance requirements:* Additional exam requirements/recommendations for international students: Required—TOEFL (minimum score 550 paper-based; 79 iBT). Electronic applications accepted. *Expenses:* Contact institution. *Faculty research:* Corporate finance, banking, investments, stock market.

University of Baltimore, Graduate School, Merrick School of Business, Department of Finance and Economics, Baltimore, MD 21201-5779. Offers business/finance (MS). *Program availability:* Part-time, evening/weekend. *Entrance requirements:* For master's, GMAT. Additional exam requirements/recommendations for international students: Required—TOEFL (minimum score 550 paper-based). Electronic applications accepted. *Faculty research:* International finance, corporate finance, health care, regional economics, small business.

University of Bridgeport, School of Business, Bridgeport, CT 06604. Offers accounting (MBA); finance (MBA); general business (MBA); global financial services (MBA); human resource management (MBA); information systems and knowledge management (MBA); international business (MBA); management (MBA); marketing (MBA); operations management (MBA); small business and entrepreneurship (MBA); specialized business (MBA). *Accreditation:* ACBSP. *Program availability:* Part-time, evening/weekend. *Degree requirements:* For master's, thesis optional. *Entrance requirements:* For master's, GMAT. Additional exam requirements/recommendations for international students: Recommended—TOEFL (minimum score 550 paper-based; 80 iBT), IELTS (minimum score 6.5). Electronic applications accepted. *Expenses:* Contact institution.

The University of British Columbia, Sauder School of Business, Doctoral Program in Business Administration, Vancouver, BC V6T 1Z2, Canada. Offers accounting (PhD); finance (PhD); management information systems (PhD); management science (PhD); marketing (PhD); organizational behavior (PhD); strategy and business economics (PhD); transportation and logistics (PhD); urban land economics (PhD). *Degree requirements:* For doctorate, comprehensive exam, thesis/dissertation. *Entrance requirements:* For doctorate, GMAT or GRE. Additional exam requirements/recommendations for international students: Required—TOEFL (minimum score 600 paper-based; 100 iBT). Electronic applications accepted. *Expenses:* Contact institution.

University of California, Berkeley, Graduate Division, Haas School of Business, PhD in Business Administration Program, Berkeley, CA 94720-1500. Offers accounting (PhD); business and public policy (PhD); finance (PhD); management of organizations (PhD); marketing (PhD); real estate (PhD). *Accreditation:* AACSB. *Students:* 72 full-time (20 women); includes 30 minority (26 Asian, non-Hispanic/Latino; 4 Hispanic/Latino). Average age 27. *Degree requirements:* For doctorate, comprehensive exam, thesis/dissertation, written preliminary exams, oral qualifying exam. *Entrance requirements:* For doctorate, GMAT or GRE, minimum GPA of 3.0 in undergraduate and graduate coursework. Additional exam requirements/recommendations for international students: Required—TOEFL (minimum score 570 paper-based; 70 iBT), IELTS (minimum score 7). *Application deadline:* For fall admission, 12/1 for domestic and international students. Application fee: $105 ($125 for international students). Electronic applications accepted. *Expenses:* Contact institution. *Financial support:* Fellowships with tuition reimbursements, research assistantships with tuition reimbursements, teaching assistantships with tuition reimbursements, scholarships/grants, health care benefits, tuition waivers (full), unspecified assistantships, and transit passes, travel grants available. Financial award application deadline: 12/1. *Faculty research:* Accounting, business and public policy, entrepreneurship, finance, management of organizations, marketing, operations and information technology management, real estate. *Unit head:* Dr. Nicolae Garleanu, Director, 510-643-6349, Fax: 510-643-4255. *Application contact:* Melissa Hacker, Director, Student Affairs, 510-642-3944, Fax: 510-643-4255, E-mail: melhacker@haas.berkeley.edu. Website: http://www.haas.berkeley.edu/Phd/

University of California, Berkeley, UC Berkeley Extension, Certificate Programs in Business, Berkeley, CA 94720-1500. Offers accounting (Certificate); business administration (Certificate); finance (Certificate); human resource management (Certificate); management (Certificate); marketing (Certificate); project management (Certificate). *Accreditation:* AACSB. *Program availability:* Online learning.

University of California, Berkeley, UC Berkeley Extension, International Diploma Programs, Berkeley, CA 94720-1500. Offers business administration (Certificate); finance (Certificate); global business management (Certificate); marketing (Certificate); project management (Certificate). *Accreditation:* AACSB.

University of California, Davis, Graduate School of Management, Full-Time MBA Program, Davis, CA 95616. Offers business analytics and technologies (MBA); entrepreneurship and innovation (MBA); finance and accounting (MBA); general management (MBA); marketing (MBA); organizational behavior (MBA); public health management (MBA); strategy (MBA); technology management (MBA); DVM/MBA; JD/MBA; M Engr/MBA; MBA/MPH; MBA/MS; MD/MBA; MSN/MBA; PhD/MBA. *Faculty:* 52 full-time (15 women). *Students:* 96 full-time (42 women); includes 31 minority (1 Black or African American, non-Hispanic/Latino; 17 Asian, non-Hispanic/Latino; 5 Hispanic/Latino; 8 Two or more races, non-Hispanic/Latino), 36 international. Average age 29. 290 applicants, 37% accepted, 45 enrolled. In 2017, 44 master's awarded. *Degree requirements:* For master's, integrated management project. *Entrance requirements:* For master's, GMAT or GRE, letters of recommendation, resume, essays, equivalent of a 4-year U.S. undergraduate degree, transcript. Additional exam requirements/recommendations for international students: Required—TOEFL (minimum score 600 paper-based; 100 iBT), IELTS (minimum score 7). *Application deadline:* For fall admission, 5/18 priority date for domestic and international students. Application fee: $125. Electronic applications accepted. *Expenses:* Contact institution. *Financial support:* In 2017–18, 90 students received support. Fellowships, research assistantships, teaching assistantships with partial tuition reimbursements available, institutionally

Finance and Banking

sponsored loans, scholarships/grants, health care benefits, tuition waivers (partial), and unspecified assistantships available. Financial award application deadline: 3/1; financial award applicants required to submit FAFSA. *Faculty research:* Finance, marketing, management, business analytics, accounting. *Unit head:* James Stevens, Senior Assistant Dean of Student Affairs, 530-752-7658, Fax: 530-754-9355, E-mail: admissions@gsm.ucdavis.edu. *Application contact:* Kristy Bird MaKieve, Interim Director of Admissions, 530-754-5476, Fax: 530-754-9355, E-mail: admissions@gsm.ucdavis.edu.
Website: http://gsm.ucdavis.edu/daytime-mba-program

University of California, Davis, Graduate School of Management, MBA Programs in Sacramento and San Francisco Bay Area, Davis, CA 95616. Offers business analytics and technologies (MBA); entrepreneurship and innovation (MBA); finance and accounting (MBA); general management (MBA); marketing (MBA); organizational behavior (MBA); public health management (MBA); strategy (MBA); technology management (MBA). *Program availability:* Part-time-only, evening/weekend. *Faculty:* 99 part-time/adjunct (30 women). *Students:* 323 part-time (133 women); includes 148 minority (7 Black or African American, non-Hispanic/Latino; 96 Asian, non-Hispanic/Latino; 26 Hispanic/Latino; 1 Native Hawaiian or other Pacific Islander, non-Hispanic/Latino; 18 Two or more races, non-Hispanic/Latino), 37 international. Average age 30. 202 applicants, 75% accepted, 111 enrolled. In 2017, 112 master's awarded. *Degree requirements:* For master's, integrated management project. *Entrance requirements:* For master's, GMAT or GRE, letters of recommendation, resume, equivalent of a 4-year undergraduate degree. Additional exam requirements/recommendations for international students: Required—TOEFL (minimum score 600 paper-based; 100 iBT), IELTS (minimum score 7). *Application deadline:* For fall admission, 5/18 priority date for domestic and international students. Application fee: $125. Electronic applications accepted. *Expenses:* Contact institution. *Financial support:* In 2017–18, 67 students received support. Fellowships, teaching assistantships with partial tuition reimbursements available, scholarships/grants, and unspecified assistantships available. Support available to part-time students. Financial award application deadline: 3/1; financial award applicants required to submit FAFSA. *Faculty research:* Accounting, finance, marketing, management, business analytics. *Unit head:* James Stevens, Senior Assistant Dean of Student Affairs, 530-752-7658, Fax: 530-754-9355, E-mail: admissions@gsm.ucdavis.edu. *Application contact:* Kristy Bird MaKieve, Interim Director of Admissions, 530-754-5476, Fax: 530-754-9355, E-mail: admissions@gsm.ucdavis.edu.
Website: http://gsm.ucdavis.edu/mba-programs

University of California, Los Angeles, Graduate Division, UCLA Anderson School of Management, Los Angeles, CA 90095-1481. Offers accounting (PhD); behavioral decision making (PhD); business administration (EMBA, MBA); business analytics (MSBA); decisions, operations, and technology management (PhD); finance (PhD); financial engineering (MFE); global economics and management (PhD); management and organizations (PhD); marketing (PhD); strategy and policy (PhD); DDS/MBA; MBA/JD; MBA/MD; MBA/MLAS; MBA/MLIS; MBA/MN; MBA/MPH; MBA/MPP; MBA/MSCS; MBA/MURP. *Accreditation:* AACSB. *Program availability:* Part-time, evening/weekend. *Faculty:* 88 full-time (21 women), 107 part-time/adjunct (21 women). *Students:* 918 full-time (314 women), 1,269 part-time (399 women); includes 743 minority (38 Black or African American, non-Hispanic/Latino; 3 American Indian or Alaska Native, non-Hispanic/Latino; 531 Asian, non-Hispanic/Latino; 115 Hispanic/Latino; 4 Native Hawaiian or other Pacific Islander, non-Hispanic/Latino; 52 Two or more races, non-Hispanic/Latino), 544 international. Average age 31. 5,842 applicants, 29% accepted, 1015 enrolled. In 2017, 855 master's, 14 doctorates awarded. Terminal master's awarded for partial completion of doctoral program. *Degree requirements:* For master's, comprehensive exam, field consulting project (for MBA, FEMBA, EMBA and GEMBA); internship (for MBA only); thesis/dissertation (for MFE); 10 capstone (for MSBA); for doctorate, comprehensive exam, thesis/dissertation, oral and written qualifying exams. *Entrance requirements:* For master's, GMAT or GRE, 4-year bachelor's degree or equivalent; 2 letters of recommendation; interview (by invitation only); 2 essays; 4-8 years of full-time work experience (for FEMBA only); minimum eight years of work experience with at least three years at management level (for EMBA only); for doctorate, GMAT or GRE, bachelor's degree from college or university of fully-recognized standing, minimum B average during junior and senior undergraduate years, 3 letters of recommendation, statement of purpose. Additional exam requirements/recommendations for international students: Required—TOEFL (minimum score 560 paper-based; 87 iBT), IELTS (minimum score 7), TOEFL with minimum iBT score of 100 (for MSBA). *Application deadline:* For fall admission, 10/2 for domestic and international students; for winter admission, 1/8 for domestic and international students; for spring admission, 4/16 for domestic and international students. Applications are processed on a rolling basis. Application fee: $200. Electronic applications accepted. *Expenses:* Contact institution. *Financial support:* In 2017–18, 649 students received support, including 440 fellowships (averaging $29,273 per year); research assistantships with partial tuition reimbursements available, teaching assistantships with partial tuition reimbursements available, career-related internships or fieldwork, institutionally sponsored loans, and scholarships/grants also available. Support available to part-time students. *Faculty research:* Finance/global economics, entrepreneurship, accounting, human resources/organizational behavior, marketing and behavioral decision-making. *Total annual research expenditures:* $1.3 million. *Unit head:* Dean, 310-825-7982, Fax: 310-206-2073. *Application contact:* Alex Lawrence, Assistant Dean and Director of MBA Admissions, 310-825-6944, Fax: 310-825-8582, E-mail: mba.admissions@anderson.ucla.edu.
Website: http://www.anderson.ucla.edu/

University of California, Riverside, Graduate Division, The A. Gary Anderson Graduate School of Management, Riverside, CA 92521-0102. Offers accounting (MPAC); business administration (MBA, PhD); finance (M Fin). *Accreditation:* AACSB. *Program availability:* Part-time, evening/weekend. *Faculty:* 32 full-time (8 women), 38 part-time/adjunct (7 women). *Students:* 180 full-time (92 women), 114 part-time (48 women); includes 75 minority (13 Black or African American, non-Hispanic/Latino; 1 American Indian or Alaska Native, non-Hispanic/Latino; 33 Asian, non-Hispanic/Latino; 28 Hispanic/Latino), 187 international. Average age 27. 722 applicants, 63% accepted, 169 enrolled. In 2017, 133 master's, 1 doctorate awarded. Terminal master's awarded for partial completion of doctoral program. *Degree requirements:* For master's, thesis optional; for doctorate, comprehensive exam, thesis/dissertation. *Entrance requirements:* For master's and doctorate, GMAT or GRE. Additional exam requirements/recommendations for international students: Required—TOEFL (minimum score 550 paper-based; 80 iBT), IELTS (minimum score 7). *Application deadline:* For fall admission, 9/1 for domestic students, 5/1 for international students; for winter admission, 12/1 for domestic students, 9/1 for international students; for spring admission, 3/1 for domestic students, 10/1 for international students. Applications are processed on a rolling basis. Application fee: $100 ($125 for international students). Electronic applications accepted. *Expenses:* Contact institution. *Financial support:* Fellowships with partial tuition reimbursements, research assistantships with full tuition reimbursements, teaching assistantships with partial tuition reimbursements, career-related internships or fieldwork, institutionally sponsored loans, scholarships/grants, and tuition waivers (full) available. Financial award application deadline: 5/1; financial award

applicants required to submit FAFSA. *Faculty research:* Finance, management, marketing, operations and supply chain management, accounting and information systems. *Unit head:* Yunzeng Wang, Dean, School of Business, 951-827-3704, E-mail: yunzeng.wang@ucr.edu. *Application contact:* Mark Estrada, Director of Graduate Admissions, 951-827-2915, E-mail: mark.estrada@ucr.edu.
Website: http://agsm.ucr.edu/

University of California, San Diego, Graduate Division, Rady School of Management, La Jolla, CA 92093. Offers business administration (MBA); business analytics (MS); finance (MF); management (PhD). *Accreditation:* AACSB. *Program availability:* Part-time, evening/weekend. *Faculty:* 28 full-time (5 women), 5 part-time/adjunct (1 woman). *Students:* 436 full-time (201 women), 119 part-time (60 women). 2,265 applicants, 33% accepted, 307 enrolled. In 2017, 193 master's, 2 doctorates awarded. *Degree requirements:* For master's, capstone project; for doctorate, comprehensive exam, thesis/dissertation. *Entrance requirements:* For master's, GMAT (for MBA); GMAT or GRE General Test (for MF); for doctorate, GMAT or GRE General Test. Additional exam requirements/recommendations for international students: Required—TOEFL (minimum score 550 paper-based; 80 iBT), IELTS (minimum score 7). *Application deadline:* Applications are processed on a rolling basis. Application fee: $200. Electronic applications accepted. *Expenses:* Contact institution. *Financial support:* Fellowships, teaching assistantships, and scholarships/grants available. Financial award applicants required to submit FAFSA. *Faculty research:* Innovation technology, operations management, finance, behavioral economics, organizational strategy, marketing, business analytics. *Unit head:* Robert Sullivan, Dean, 858-822-0830, E-mail: rssullivan@ucsd.edu. *Application contact:* Jay Bryant, Director of Graduate Recruitment and Admissions, 858-534-0864, E-mail: radygradadmissions@ucsd.edu.
Website: http://rady.ucsd.edu/

University of California, Santa Barbara, Graduate Division, College of Letters and Sciences, Division of Social Sciences, Department of Economics, Santa Barbara, CA 93106-9210. Offers economics (MA); mathematical economics (PhD); public finance (PhD); MA/PhD. Terminal master's awarded for partial completion of doctoral program. *Degree requirements:* For master's, comprehensive exam; for doctorate, comprehensive exam, thesis/dissertation. *Entrance requirements:* For master's and doctorate, GRE General Test, 3 letters of recommendation, statement of purpose, personal achievements/contributions statement, resume/curriculum vitae, transcripts for post-secondary institutions attended. Additional exam requirements/recommendations for international students: Required—TOEFL (minimum score 550 paper-based; 80 iBT), IELTS (minimum score 7), TOEFL (minimum score 600 paper-based or 100 iBT) for PhD. Electronic applications accepted. *Faculty research:* Labor economics, econometrics, macroeconomic theory and policy, environmental and natural resources economics, experimental and behavioral economics.

University of California, Santa Cruz, Division of Graduate Studies, Division of Social Sciences, Program in Applied Economics and Finance, Santa Cruz, CA 95064. Offers MS. *Degree requirements:* For master's, thesis or alternative, project. *Entrance requirements:* For master's, GRE General Test, GRE Subject Test. Additional exam requirements/recommendations for international students: Required—TOEFL (minimum score 550 paper-based; 83 iBT); Recommended—IELTS (minimum score 8). Electronic applications accepted. *Faculty research:* Economic decision-making skills for the design and operation of complex institutional systems.

University of Central Missouri, The Graduate School, Warrensburg, MO 64093. Offers accountancy (MA); accounting (MBA); applied mathematics (MS); aviation safety (MA); biology (MS); business administration (MBA); career and technical education leadership (MS); college student personnel administration (MS); communication (MA); computer science (MS); counseling (MS); criminal justice (MS); educational leadership (Ed D); educational technology (MS); elementary and early childhood education (MSE); English (MA); environmental studies (MA); finance (MBA); history (MA); human services/educational technology (Ed S); human services/learning resources (Ed S); human services/professional counseling (Ed S); industrial hygiene (MS); industrial management (MS); information systems (MBA); information technology (MS); kinesiology (MS); library science and information services (MS); literacy education (MSE); marketing (MBA); mathematics (MS); music (MA); occupational safety management (MS); psychology (MS); rural family nursing (MS); school administration (MSE); social gerontology (MS); sociology (MA); special education (MSE); speech language pathology (MS); superintendency (Ed S); teaching (MAT); teaching English as a second language (MA); technology (MS); technology management (PhD); theatre (MA). *Program availability:* Part-time, 100% online, blended/hybrid learning. *Faculty:* 337 full-time (145 women), 41 part-time/adjunct (28 women). *Students:* 785 full-time (398 women), 1,633 part-time (1,063 women); includes 231 minority (102 Black or African American, non-Hispanic/Latino; 4 American Indian or Alaska Native, non-Hispanic/Latino; 16 Asian, non-Hispanic/Latino; 52 Hispanic/Latino; 57 Two or more races, non-Hispanic/Latino), 692 international. Average age 30. In 2017, 2,605 master's, 122 other advanced degrees awarded. *Degree requirements:* For master's and Ed S, comprehensive exam (for some programs), thesis (for some programs). *Entrance requirements:* Additional exam requirements/recommendations for international students: Required—TOEFL (minimum score 550 paper-based; 79 iBT). *Application deadline:* For fall admission, 6/1 priority date for domestic and international students; for spring admission, 10/1 priority date for domestic and international students; for summer admission, 4/1 priority date for domestic and international students. Applications are processed on a rolling basis. Application fee: $30 ($75 for international students). Electronic applications accepted. *Expenses:* Tuition, state resident: full-time $8771; part-time $292.35 per credit hour. Tuition, nonresident: full-time $17,541; part-time $584.70 per credit hour. *Required fees:* $372; $24.78 per credit hour. *Financial support:* In 2017–18, 99 students received support. Research assistantships, teaching assistantships, career-related internships or fieldwork, Federal Work-Study, scholarships/grants, and administrative and laboratory assistantships available. Support available to part-time students. Financial award application deadline: 3/1; financial award applicants required to submit FAFSA. *Unit head:* Shellie Hewitt, Director of Graduate and International Student Services, 660-543-4621, Fax: 660-543-4778, E-mail: hewitt@ucmo.edu. *Application contact:* 660-543-4621, E-mail: admit_intl@ucmo.edu.
Website: http://www.ucmo.edu/graduate/

University of Chicago, Booth School of Business, Full-Time MBA Program, Chicago, IL 60637. Offers accounting (MBA); analytic finance (MBA); analytic management (MBA); econometrics and statistics (MBA); economics (MBA); entrepreneurship (MBA); finance (MBA); general management (MBA); health administration and policy (Certificate); international business (MBA); managerial and organizational behavior (MBA); marketing analytics (MBA); marketing management (MBA); operations management (MBA); strategic management (MBA); MBA/AM; MBA/JD; MBA/MA; MBA/MD; MBA/MPP. *Accreditation:* AACSB. *Faculty:* 154 full-time (26 women), 61 part-time/adjunct (12 women). *Students:* 1,176 full-time (481 women). In 2017, 586 master's awarded. *Entrance requirements:* For master's, GMAT or GRE, transcripts, resume, 2 letters of recommendation, essays, interview. Additional exam requirements/recommendations for international students: Required—TOEFL, IELTS, or PTE. *Application deadline:* For fall admission, 9/1 for domestic and international students; for winter admission, 1/1 for domestic and international students; for spring admission, 4/1 for domestic and international students. Application fee: $250. Electronic applications accepted. *Expenses:* Contact institution. *Unit head:* Stacey Kole, Deputy Dean for Alumni, Corporate Relations, and the Full-time MBA Program, 773-702-7121. *Application contact:* Kurt Ahlm, Associate Dean for Student Recruitment and Admissions, 773-702-7369, Fax: 773-702-9085, E-mail: admissions@chicagobooth.edu. Website: https://www.chicagobooth.edu/programs/full-time

University of Cincinnati, Carl H. Lindner College of Business, MS Program, Cincinnati, OH 45221. Offers accounting (MS); applied economics (MS); business analytics (MS); finance (MS); information systems (MS); marketing (MS); taxation (MS). *Program availability:* Part-time, evening/weekend. *Faculty:* 65 full-time (20 women), 27 part-time/adjunct (6 women). *Students:* 324 full-time (132 women), 204 part-time (77 women); includes 50 minority (18 Black or African American, non-Hispanic/Latino; 21 Asian, non-Hispanic/Latino; 5 Hispanic/Latino; 1 Native Hawaiian or other Pacific Islander, non-Hispanic/Latino; 5 Two or more races, non-Hispanic/Latino), 299 international. Average age 28. 1,756 applicants, 24% accepted, 351 enrolled. In 2017, 369 master's awarded. *Degree requirements:* For master's, thesis (for some programs), capstone. *Entrance requirements:* For master's, GMAT, GRE, resume, transcripts, essays, letters of recommendation. Additional exam requirements/recommendations for international students: Required—TOEFL (minimum score 577 paper-based; 90 iBT), IELTS (minimum score 6.5). *Application deadline:* For fall admission, 6/30 priority date for domestic students, 3/15 for international students; for spring admission, 12/15 for domestic students, 9/15 for international students; for summer admission, 4/15 for domestic and international students. Applications are processed on a rolling basis. Application fee: $65 ($70 for international students). Electronic applications accepted. *Expenses:* $10,479 per term full-time resident, $14,398 per term full-time nonresident, $890 per credit hour part-time. *Financial support:* In 2017–18, 251 students received support, including 12 teaching assistantships with full and partial tuition reimbursements available (averaging $3,500 per year); scholarships/grants, tuition waivers (full and partial), and unspecified assistantships also available. Financial award application deadline: 2/1; financial award applicants required to submit FAFSA. *Faculty research:* Business analytics, financial management, organizational behavior, financial accounting, consumer insights. *Total annual research expenditures:* $24,842. *Unit head:* Dr. David Szymanski, Dean, 513-556-7001, Fax: 513-556-4891, E-mail: david.szymanski@uc.edu. *Application contact:* Dona Clary, Executive Director, Graduate Programs, 513-556-3546, Fax: 513-558-7006, E-mail: dona.clary@uc.edu. Website: http://business.uc.edu/graduate/masters.html

University of Cincinnati, Carl H. Lindner College of Business, PhD Programs, Cincinnati, OH 45221. Offers accounting (PhD); business analytics (PhD); economics (PhD); finance (PhD); information systems (PhD); management (PhD); marketing (PhD); operations and business analytics (PhD); operations research (PhD). *Faculty:* 37 full-time (13 women). *Students:* 29 full-time (12 women), 12 part-time (6 women); includes 5 minority (1 Black or African American, non-Hispanic/Latino; 4 Asian, non-Hispanic/Latino), 20 international. Average age 30. 123 applicants, 16% accepted, 11 enrolled. In 2017, 5 doctorates awarded. *Degree requirements:* For doctorate, comprehensive exam, thesis/dissertation. *Entrance requirements:* For doctorate, GMAT, GRE, transcripts, essays, resume, letters of recommendation. Additional exam requirements/recommendations for international students: Required—TOEFL (minimum score 600 paper-based; 100 iBT), IELTS (minimum score 7). *Application deadline:* For fall admission, 1/15 for domestic and international students. Application fee: $65 ($70 for international students). Electronic applications accepted. *Expenses:* $7,234 resident per term, $13,105 nonresident per term. *Financial support:* In 2017–18, 41 students received support, including 29 research assistantships with full tuition reimbursements available (averaging $23,250 per year); scholarships/grants, health care benefits, tuition waivers (full), and unspecified assistantships also available. Financial award application deadline: 1/15; financial award applicants required to submit FAFSA. *Faculty research:* Bayesian Prediction Theory, organizational fairness, consumer insight and market research, consumer insight and market research, density estimation from correlated data. *Unit head:* Dr. Suzanne Masterson, Director, 513-556-7125, Fax: 513-556-5499, E-mail: suzanne.masterson@uc.edu. *Application contact:* Angel Elvin, Assistant Director, 513-556-7190, Fax: 513-558-7006, E-mail: angel.elvin@uc.edu. Website: http://business.uc.edu/graduate/phd.html

University of Colorado Denver, Business School, Master of Business Administration Program, Denver, CO 80217. Offers bioinnovation and entrepreneurship (MBA); business intelligence (MBA); business strategy (MBA); business to business marketing (MBA); business to consumer marketing (MBA); change management (MBA); corporate financial management (MBA); enterprise technology management (MBA); entrepreneurship (MBA); health administration (MBA), including financial management, health administration, health information technologies, international health management and policy; human resources management (MBA); international business (MBA); investment management (MBA); managing for sustainability (MBA); sports and entertainment management (MBA). *Accreditation:* AACSB. *Program availability:* Part-time, evening/weekend, 100% online, blended/hybrid learning. *Degree requirements:* For master's, 48 semester hours, including 30 of core courses, 3 in international business, and 15 in electives from over 50 other business courses. *Entrance requirements:* For master's, GMAT, resume, official transcripts, essay, two letters of recommendation, financial statements (for international applicants). Additional exam requirements/recommendations for international students: Required—TOEFL (minimum score 560 paper-based; 83 iBT); Recommended—IELTS (minimum score 6.5). Electronic applications accepted. *Expenses:* Contact institution. *Faculty research:* Marketing, management, entrepreneurship, finance, health administration.

University of Colorado Denver, Business School, Program in Finance, Denver, CO 80217. Offers economics (MS); finance (MS); financial analysis and management (MS); financial and commodities risk management (MS); risk management and insurance (MS); MS/MA; MS/MBA. *Program availability:* Part-time, evening/weekend. *Degree requirements:* For master's, 30 semester hours (18 of required core courses, 9 of finance electives, and 3 of free elective). *Entrance requirements:* For master's, GMAT, essay, resume, two letters of recommendation; financial statements (for international students). Additional exam requirements/recommendations for international students: Required—TOEFL (minimum score 537 paper-based; 75 iBT); Recommended—IELTS (minimum score 6.5). Electronic applications accepted. *Expenses:* Contact institution. *Faculty research:* Corporate governance, debt maturity policies, regulation and financial markets, option management strategies.

University of Connecticut, Graduate School, College of Liberal Arts and Sciences, Department of Public Policy, Storrs, CT 06269. Offers public administration (MPA, Graduate Certificate), including nonprofit management (Graduate Certificate), public financial management (Graduate Certificate); survey research (MA, Graduate Certificate), including quantitative research methods (Graduate Certificate), survey research (MA); JD/MPA; MPA/MSW. *Degree requirements:* For master's, comprehensive exam. *Entrance requirements:* For master's, GRE General Test. Additional exam requirements/recommendations for international students: Required—TOEFL (minimum score 550 paper-based). Electronic applications accepted.

University of Connecticut, Graduate School, School of Business, Storrs, CT 06269. Offers accounting (MS, PhD); business administration (MBA, PhD); finance (PhD);

health care management and insurance studies (MBA); management (PhD); management consulting (MBA); marketing (PhD); marketing intelligence (MBA). *Accreditation:* AACSB. *Degree requirements:* For master's, comprehensive exam; for doctorate, thesis/dissertation. *Entrance requirements:* For master's and doctorate, GMAT. Additional exam requirements/recommendations for international students: Required—TOEFL (minimum score 550 paper-based). Electronic applications accepted.
See Display on page 146 and Close-Up on page 183.

University of Dallas, Satish and Yasmin Gupta College of Business, Irving, TX 75062-4736. Offers accounting (MBA, MS); business administration (DBA); business analytics (MS); business management (MBA); corporate finance (MBA); cybersecurity (MS); finance (MS); financial services (MBA); global business (MBA, MS); health services management (MBA); human resource management (MBA); information and technology management (MS); information assurance (MBA); information technology (MBA); information technology service management (MBA); marketing management (MBA); organization development (MBA); project management (MBA); sports and entertainment management (MBA); strategic leadership (MBA); supply chain management (MBA). *Accreditation:* AACSB. *Program availability:* Part-time, evening/weekend, online learning. *Entrance requirements:* Additional exam requirements/recommendations for international students: Required—TOEFL. *Application deadline:* Applications are processed on a rolling basis. Application fee: $50. Electronic applications accepted. *Expenses:* Contact institution. *Financial support:* Application deadline: 2/15; applicants required to submit FAFSA. *Unit head:* Brett J.L. Landry, Dean, 972-721-5356, E-mail: blandry@udallas.edu. *Application contact:* Dr. David Sweet, Dean, Braniff Graduate School, 972-721-5288, Fax: 972-721-5280, E-mail: dsweet@udallas.edu. Website: http://www.udallas.edu/cob/

University of Dayton, School of Business Administration, Dayton, OH 45469. Offers accounting (MBA); cyber security (MBA); finance (MBA); marketing (MBA); JD/MBA. *Accreditation:* AACSB. *Program availability:* Part-time, evening/weekend, blended/hybrid learning. *Faculty:* 23 full-time (8 women), 12 part-time/adjunct (2 women). *Students:* 57 full-time (24 women), 82 part-time (32 women); includes 10 minority (5 Black or African American, non-Hispanic/Latino; 2 Asian, non-Hispanic/Latino; 3 Hispanic/Latino), 18 international. Average age 31. 269 applicants, 31% accepted. In 2017, 88 master's awarded. *Entrance requirements:* For master's, GMAT (minimum score of 500 total, 19 verbal); GRE (minimum score of 149 verbal, 146 quantitative), minimum GPA of 3.0, current resume. Additional exam requirements/recommendations for international students: Required—TOEFL (minimum score 550 paper-based; 80 iBT); Recommended—IELTS (minimum score 6.5). *Application deadline:* For fall admission, 5/1 for international students; for spring admission, 11/1 for international students. Applications are processed on a rolling basis. Application fee: $0 ($50 for international students). Electronic applications accepted. *Expenses:* Contact institution. *Financial support:* In 2017–18, 10 research assistantships with partial tuition reimbursements (averaging $9,295 per year) were awarded; teaching assistantships, career-related internships or fieldwork, institutionally sponsored loans, scholarships/grants, traineeships, tuition waivers, and unspecified assistantships also available. Financial award application deadline: 3/1; financial award applicants required to submit FAFSA. *Faculty research:* Management information systems, economics, finance, marketing, entrepreneurship, accounting, cyber security, analytics. *Unit head:* Scott MacDonald, Director, MBA Program, 937-229-3733, Fax: 937-229-3882, E-mail: smacdonald1@udayton.edu. *Application contact:* Mandy Bingaman, MBA Program Manager, 937-229-3733, Fax: 937-229-3882, E-mail: mbingaman1@udayton.edu. Website: https://www.udayton.edu/business/academics/master_of_business_administration/index.php

University of Delaware, Alfred Lerner College of Business and Economics, Department of Finance, Newark, DE 19716. Offers MS.

University of Denver, Daniels College of Business, Reiman School of Finance, Denver, CO 80208. Offers applied quantitative finance (MS); finance (MBA). *Program availability:* Part-time, evening/weekend. *Faculty:* 18 full-time (4 women), 3 part-time/adjunct (0 women). *Students:* 32 full-time (13 women), 25 part-time (10 women); includes 1 minority (Hispanic/Latino), 35 international. Average age 26. 232 applicants, 43% accepted, 25 enrolled. In 2017, 53 master's awarded. *Entrance requirements:* For master's, GRE General Test or GMAT, bachelor's degree, transcripts, resume, two letters of recommendation, essays, interview. Additional exam requirements/recommendations for international students: Required—TOEFL (minimum score 570 paper-based; 88 iBT). *Application deadline:* For fall admission, 11/15 priority date for domestic and international students; for spring admission, 10/1 priority date for domestic and international students. Applications are processed on a rolling basis. Application fee: $100. Electronic applications accepted. *Expenses:* $47,823 per year full-time; $1,320 per credit. *Financial support:* In 2017–18, 53 students received support. Teaching assistantships with tuition reimbursements available, career-related internships or fieldwork, Federal Work-Study, institutionally sponsored loans, scholarships/grants, tuition waivers, and unspecified assistantships available. Support available to part-time students. Financial award application deadline: 2/15; financial award applicants required to submit FAFSA. *Faculty research:* Sector forecasting, analysts estimates and guidance, derivatives, SEC comment letters, corporate governance. *Unit head:* Dr. Conrad Ciccotello, Director, 303-871-2282, E-mail: conrad.ciccotello@du.edu. *Application contact:* Kay Brisch, Assistant to Director, 303-871-3222, E-mail: ebrisch@du.edu. Website: https://daniels.du.edu/finance

University of Detroit Mercy, College of Business Administration, Detroit, MI 48221. Offers business administration (MBA); business fundamentals (Certificate); business turnaround management (Certificate); ethical leadership and change management (Certificate); finance (Certificate); forensic accounting (Certificate); JD/MBA; MBA/MHSA. *Program availability:* Part-time, evening/weekend, 100% online, blended/hybrid learning. *Entrance requirements:* For master's, GMAT, resume, letter of recommendation, transcripts; for Certificate, resume, letter of recommendation, transcripts. Electronic applications accepted. Application fee is waived when completed online. *Expenses:* Contact institution. *Faculty research:* Ethics, international finance, trade policy, leadership, information technology.

University of Detroit Mercy, College of Liberal Arts and Education, Detroit, MI 48221. Offers addiction counseling (MA); addiction studies (Certificate); clinical mental health counseling (MA); clinical psychology (MA, PhD); computer and information systems (MS); criminal justice (MA); curriculum and instruction (MA); economics (MA); educational administration (MA); financial economics (MA); industrial/organizational psychology (MA); information assurance (MS); intelligence analysis (MA); liberal studies (MALS); religious studies (MA); school counseling (MA, Certificate); school psychology (Spec); security administration (MS); special education: emotionally impaired/behaviorally disordered (MA); special education: learning disabilities (MA). *Program availability:* Part-time, evening/weekend. *Degree requirements:* For doctorate, departmental qualifying exam. *Faculty research:* Psychology of aging, history of technology, Renaissance humanism, U.S. and Japanese economic relations.

University of Florida, Graduate School, Warrington College of Business Administration, Hough Graduate School of Business, Department of Finance, Insurance

Finance and Banking

and Real Estate, Gainesville, FL 32611. Offers entrepreneurship (MS); finance (MS, PhD); financial services (Certificate); insurance (PhD); quantitative finance (PhD); real estate (MS); real estate and urban analysis (PhD); JD/MBA; JD/MS. Terminal master's awarded for partial completion of doctoral program. *Degree requirements:* For master's, comprehensive exam, thesis; for doctorate, comprehensive exam, thesis/dissertation. *Entrance requirements:* For master's, GMAT (minimum score of 465) or GRE General Test, minimum GPA of 3.0 for last 60 hours of undergraduate degree, work experience (preferred); for doctorate, GMAT (minimum score of 465) or GRE General Test, minimum GPA of 3.0. Additional exam requirements/recommendations for international students: Required—TOEFL (minimum score 550 paper-based; 80 iBT), IELTS (minimum score 6). Electronic applications accepted. *Faculty research:* Banking, empirical corporate finance, hedge funds.

University of Florida, Graduate School, Warrington College of Business Administration, Hough Graduate School of Business, Programs in Business Administration, Gainesville, FL 32611. Offers business administration (MA, MS, PhD); competitive strategy (MBA); finance (MBA); global management (MBA); Graham-Buffett security analysis (MBA); human resource management (MBA); information systems and operations management (MBA); international studies (MBA); management (MBA); real estate (MBA); JD/MBA; MBA/MS; MBA/PhD; MBA/Pharm D; MD/MBA. *Accreditation:* AACSB. *Program availability:* Part-time, evening/weekend, online learning. *Degree requirements:* For master's, capstone course. *Entrance requirements:* For master's and doctorate, GMAT (minimum score 465), minimum GPA of 3.0, interview. Additional exam requirements/recommendations for international students: Required—TOEFL (minimum score 550 paper-based; 80 iBT), IELTS (minimum score 6). Electronic applications accepted. *Faculty research:* Accounting, finance, insurance, management, real estate, urban analysis marketing.

University of Hawaii at Manoa, Office of Graduate Education, Shidler College of Business, Program in Business Administration, Honolulu, HI 96822. Offers Asian business studies (MBA); Chinese business studies (MBA); decision sciences (MBA); entrepreneurship (MBA); finance (MBA); finance and banking (MBA); human resources management (MBA); information management (MBA); information technology (MBA); international business (MBA); Japanese business studies (MBA); marketing (MBA); organizational behavior (MBA); organizational management (MBA); real estate (MBA); student-designed track (MBA). *Accreditation:* AACSB. *Program availability:* Part-time, evening/weekend. *Degree requirements:* For master's, thesis optional. *Entrance requirements:* For master's, GMAT, minimum GPA of 3.0. Additional exam requirements/recommendations for international students: Required—TOEFL (minimum score 600 paper-based; 100 iBT), IELTS (minimum score 7). *Expenses:* Contact institution.

University of Hawaii at Manoa, Office of Graduate Education, Shidler College of Business, Program in International Management, Honolulu, HI 96822. Offers Asian finance (PhD); global information technology management (PhD); international accounting (PhD); international marketing (PhD); international organization and strategy (PhD). *Program availability:* Part-time. *Degree requirements:* For doctorate, comprehensive exam, thesis/dissertation. *Entrance requirements:* For doctorate, GMAT or GRE General Test, minimum GPA of 3.0. Additional exam requirements/recommendations for international students: Required—TOEFL (minimum score 600 paper-based; 100 iBT), IELTS (minimum score 7). *Expenses:* Contact institution.

University of Houston, Bauer College of Business, Finance Program, Houston, TX 77204. Offers MS. *Program availability:* Part-time, evening/weekend. *Degree requirements:* For master's, 30 hours completed in residence, minimum cumulative GPA of 3.0 at UH, no more than 11 semester hours of 'C' grades or below in graduate courses taken at UH. *Entrance requirements:* For master's, GMAT or GRE, official transcripts from all higher education institutions attended, resume, goal statement, letters of recommendation. Additional exam requirements/recommendations for international students: Required—TOEFL (minimum score 620 paper-based; 105 iBT), IELTS (minimum score 7.5). Electronic applications accepted. *Faculty research:* Accountancy and taxation, finance, international business, management.

University of Houston–Clear Lake, School of Business, Program in Finance, Houston, TX 77058-1002. Offers MS. *Program availability:* Part-time, evening/weekend. *Degree requirements:* For master's, thesis optional. *Entrance requirements:* For master's, GMAT. Additional exam requirements/recommendations for international students: Required—TOEFL (minimum score 550 paper-based). Electronic applications accepted.

University of Houston–Downtown, Marilyn Davies College of Business, MBA Program, Houston, TX 77002. Offers accounting (MBA); finance (MBA); human resource management (MBA); international business (MBA); investment management (MBA); leadership (MBA); project management and process improvement (MBA); sales management and business development (MBA); supply chain management (MBA). *Accreditation:* AACSB. *Program availability:* Part-time, evening/weekend. *Faculty:* 36 full-time (13 women), 11 part-time/adjunct (6 women). *Students:* 4 full-time (2 women), 1,065 part-time (605 women); includes 821 minority (383 Black or African American, non-Hispanic/Latino; 3 American Indian or Alaska Native, non-Hispanic/Latino; 136 Asian, non-Hispanic/Latino; 299 Hispanic/Latino), 33 international. Average age 33. 418 applicants, 89% accepted, 308 enrolled. In 2017, 310 master's awarded. *Entrance requirements:* For master's, GMAT, two letters of recommendation from professional references, personal statement, resume. Additional exam requirements/recommendations for international students: Required—TOEFL (minimum score 81 iBT). *Application deadline:* For fall admission, 8/1 for domestic and international students. Application fee: $35 ($60 for international students). Electronic applications accepted. *Expenses:* $360 per credit resident; $725 per credit non-resident. *Financial support:* Federal Work-Study and scholarships/grants available. Financial award application deadline: 4/1; financial award applicants required to submit FAFSA. *Unit head:* Dr. Charles E. Gengler, Dean, 713-221-8179, Fax: 713-221-8675. *Application contact:* Ceshia Love, Director of Admissions, 713-221-8093, Fax: 713-223-7408, E-mail: gradadmissions@uhd.edu.
Website: http://mba.uhd.edu/

University of Houston–Victoria, School of Business Administration, Victoria, TX 77901-4450. Offers accounting (MBA); economic development and entrepreneurship (MS); finance (GMBA, MBA); general business (MBA); international business (MBA); management (GMBA, MBA); marketing (MBA). *Accreditation:* AACSB. *Program availability:* Part-time, evening/weekend, online learning. *Entrance requirements:* For master's, GMAT. Additional exam requirements/recommendations for international students: Required—TOEFL (minimum score 550 paper-based). Electronic applications accepted. *Faculty research:* Economic development, marketing, finance.

University of Illinois at Chicago, Liautaud Graduate School of Business, Department of Finance, Chicago, IL 60607-7128. Offers MS. *Entrance requirements:* Additional exam requirements/recommendations for international students: Required—TOEFL. Electronic applications accepted. *Expenses:* Contact institution. *Faculty research:* Global financial markets.

University of Illinois at Urbana–Champaign, Graduate College, Gies College of Business, Department of Finance, Champaign, IL 61820. Offers MS, PhD.

The University of Iowa, Tippie College of Business, Department of Finance, Iowa City, IA 52242-1316. Offers PhD. *Faculty:* 20 full-time (3 women), 2 part-time/adjunct (0 women). *Students:* 10 full-time (2 women), 7 international. Average age 30. 82 applicants, 5% accepted, 1 enrolled. In 2017, 1 doctorate awarded. *Degree requirements:* For doctorate, comprehensive exam, thesis/dissertation. *Entrance requirements:* For doctorate, GMAT or GRE. Additional exam requirements/recommendations for international students: Required—TOEFL (minimum score 100 iBT) or IELTS (minimum score 7.0). *Application deadline:* For fall admission, 1/15 priority date for domestic and international students. Application fee: $60 ($100 for international students). Electronic applications accepted. *Financial support:* In 2017–18, 15 students received support, including 10 fellowships (averaging $6,000 per year), 10 teaching assistantships with full tuition reimbursements available (averaging $19,016 per year); health care benefits and unspecified assistantships also available. Financial award application deadline: 1/15. *Faculty research:* International finance, real estate finance, theoretical and empirical corporate finance, theoretical and empirical asset pricing, bond pricing and derivatives. *Unit head:* Prof. Thomas Rietz, Department Executive Officer, 319-335-0929, Fax: 319-335-3690, E-mail: thomas-rietz@uiowa.edu. *Application contact:* Renea L. Jay, Associate Director, Non-MBA Graduate Programs, 319-335-0830, Fax: 319-335-0860, E-mail: renea-jay@uiowa.edu.
Website: https://tippie.uiowa.edu/finance

The University of Iowa, Tippie College of Business, MS Program in Finance, Iowa City, IA 52242-1316. Offers MS. *Expenses:* Contact institution. *Unit head:* Prof. Thomas Rietz, Finance Department Executive Officer, 319-335-0856, E-mail: tippie-mfin@uiowa.edu.
Website: https://tippie.uiowa.edu/future-graduate-students/masters-programs/finance

The University of Iowa, Tippie College of Business, Professional MBA Program, Iowa City, IA 52242-1316. Offers business administration (MBA); business analytics (MBA); finance (MBA); leadership (MBA); marketing (MBA). *Program availability:* Part-time-only, evening/weekend. *Faculty:* 50 full-time (11 women), 22 part-time/adjunct (2 women). *Students:* 873 part-time (325 women); includes 102 minority (16 Black or African American, non-Hispanic/Latino; 1 American Indian or Alaska Native, non-Hispanic/Latino; 54 Asian, non-Hispanic/Latino; 22 Hispanic/Latino; 9 Two or more races, non-Hispanic/Latino), 44 international. Average age 33. 155 applicants, 94% accepted, 137 enrolled. In 2017, 176 master's awarded. *Degree requirements:* For master's, successful completion of nine required courses and six electives totaling 45 credits, minimum GPA of 2.75. *Entrance requirements:* For master's, GMAT or GRE. Additional exam requirements/recommendations for international students: Required—TOEFL (minimum score 600 paper-based; 100 iBT), IELTS (minimum score 7). *Application deadline:* For fall admission, 7/30 for domestic and international students; for spring admission, 12/15 for domestic and international students; for summer admission, 4/30 for domestic and international students. Applications are processed on a rolling basis. Application fee: $60 ($100 for international students). Electronic applications accepted. *Expenses:* Contact institution. *Faculty research:* Capital markets; analytics techniques and applications; organizational and market systems analysis; applied econometrics; talent effectiveness. *Unit head:* Prof. Sarah Fisher Gardial, Dean, 319-335-0862, Fax: 319-335-0860, E-mail: sarah-gardial@uiowa.edu.
Website: https://tippie.uiowa.edu/future-graduate-students/mba-programs/professional-mba

The University of Kansas, Graduate Studies, School of Business, Program in Business, Lawrence, KS 66045. Offers business and organizational leadership (MS); decision sciences and supply chain management (PhD); finance (PhD); human resources management (PhD); marketing (PhD); organizational behavior (PhD); strategic management (PhD); supply chain management and logistics (MS). *Accreditation:* AACSB. *Program availability:* Part-time. *Students:* 66 full-time (18 women), 227 part-time (76 women); includes 59 minority (21 Black or African American, non-Hispanic/Latino; 2 American Indian or Alaska Native, non-Hispanic/Latino; 13 Asian, non-Hispanic/Latino; 3 Hispanic/Latino; 20 Two or more races, non-Hispanic/Latino), 29 international. Average age 32. 329 applicants, 71% accepted, 185 enrolled. In 2017, 30 master's, 8 doctorates awarded. *Entrance requirements:* For master's, GMAT, official transcript, three letters of recommendation, resume, statement of purpose; for doctorate, GMAT or GRE, official transcript, three letters of recommendation, resume, statement of purpose. Additional exam requirements/recommendations for international students: Required—TOEFL (minimum score 600 paper-based; 100 iBT). *Application deadline:* For fall admission, 1/10 for domestic and international students. Application fee: $65 ($85 for international students). Electronic applications accepted. *Financial support:* Fellowships, research assistantships, teaching assistantships, scholarships/grants, health care benefits, tuition waivers (full), and unspecified assistantships available. Financial award application deadline: 1/10. *Faculty research:* Strategic human resource management, business ethics, organizational theory/behavior, corporate strategy, international business, supply chain management, Bayesian networks, game theory, decision analysis and time/series analysis, pricing, consumer effects, advertising and emotion. *Unit head:* Charly Edmonds, Director, 785-864-3841, E-mail: bschoolphd@ku.edu. *Application contact:* Graduate Admission Contact, 785-864-7500, E-mail: bschoolphd@ku.edu.
Website: http://www.business.ku.edu/

University of La Verne, College of Business and Public Management, Graduate Programs in Business Administration, La Verne, CA 91750-4443. Offers accounting (MBA, MBA-EP); finance (MBA, MBA-EP); health services management (MBA); information technology (MBA, MBA-EP); international business (MBA, MBA-EP); management and leadership (MBA, MBA-EP); marketing (MBA, MBA-EP); supply chain management (MBA, MBA-EP). *Program availability:* Part-time, evening/weekend. *Faculty:* 24 full-time (11 women), 25 part-time/adjunct (6 women). *Students:* 390 full-time (193 women), 93 part-time (48 women); includes 96 minority (7 Black or African American, non-Hispanic/Latino; 1 American Indian or Alaska Native, non-Hispanic/Latino; 17 Asian, non-Hispanic/Latino; 67 Hispanic/Latino; 1 Native Hawaiian or other Pacific Islander, non-Hispanic/Latino; 3 Two or more races, non-Hispanic/Latino), 336 international. Average age 28. *Entrance requirements:* For master's, GMAT, MAT, or GRE, minimum undergraduate GPA of 3.0, 2 letters of recommendation, resume, statement of purpose. Additional exam requirements/recommendations for international students: Required—TOEFL (minimum score 550 paper-based; 85 iBT). *Application deadline:* Applications are processed on a rolling basis. Application fee: $50. Tuition and fees vary according to program. *Financial support:* Institutionally sponsored loans and scholarships/grants available. Financial award application deadline: 3/2; financial award applicants required to submit FAFSA. *Unit head:* Dr. Abe Helou, Chairperson, 909-448-4455, Fax: 909-392-2704, E-mail: ihelou@laverne.edu. *Application contact:* Rina Lazarian-Chehab, Senior Associate Director of Graduate Admissions, 909-448-4317, Fax: 909-971-2295, E-mail: rlazarian@laverne.edu.
Website: https://business.laverne.edu/mba/

University of La Verne, College of Business and Public Management, Program in Finance, La Verne, CA 91750-4443. Offers MS. *Program availability:* Part-time. *Faculty:* 3 full-time (1 woman). *Students:* 53 full-time (17 women), 8 part-time (1 woman); includes 9 minority (1 Black or African American, non-Hispanic/Latino; 2 Asian, non-Hispanic/Latino; 5 Hispanic/Latino; 1 Two or more races, non-Hispanic/Latino), 49

international. Average age 26. *Entrance requirements:* For master's, bachelor's degree, minimum preferred GPA of 3.0, 2 recommendations, resume, personal statement. Additional exam requirements/recommendations for international students: Required—TOEFL (minimum score 550 paper-based; 79 iBT). *Application deadline:* Applications are processed on a rolling basis. Application fee: $50. *Expenses:* Contact institution. *Financial support:* Federal Work-Study, institutionally sponsored loans, and scholarships/grants available. *Unit head:* Paul Abbondante, Director, 909-448-4452, E-mail: pabbondante@laverne.edu. *Application contact:* Rina Lazarian-Chehab, Senior Associate Director of Graduate Admissions, 909-448-4317, Fax: 909-971-2295, E-mail: rlazarian@laverne.edu.
Website: https://business.laverne.edu/finance/

University of La Verne, Regional and Online Campuses, Graduate Programs, Inland Empire Campus, Ontario, CA 91730. Offers business administration (MBA, MBA-EP), including accounting (MBA), finance (MBA), health services management (MBA-EP), information technology (MBA-EP), international business (MBA), managed care (MBA), management and leadership (MBA-EP), marketing (MBA-EP), supply chain management (MBA); leadership and management (MS), including human resource management, nonprofit management, organizational development. *Program availability:* Part-time, evening/weekend. *Faculty:* 5 part-time/adjunct (1 woman). *Students:* 24 full-time (13 women), 72 part-time (44 women); includes 64 minority (12 Black or African American, non-Hispanic/Latino; 13 Asian, non-Hispanic/Latino; 36 Hispanic/Latino; 3 Two or more races, non-Hispanic/Latino). Average age 38. In 2017, 42 master's awarded. *Application deadline:* Applications are processed on a rolling basis. Application fee: $50. *Expenses:* Contact institution. *Financial support:* Application deadline: 3/2; applicants required to submit FAFSA. *Unit head:* Juli Roberts, Campus Director, Inland Empire Regional Campus in Ontario, 760-955-6448, E-mail: jroberts@laverne.edu. *Application contact:* Admissions, 877-468-6858, E-mail: gradadmission@laverne.edu.
Website: https://laverne.edu/locations/

University of Lethbridge, School of Graduate Studies, Lethbridge, AB T1K 3M4, Canada. Offers addictions counseling (M Sc); agricultural biotechnology (M Sc); agricultural studies (M Sc, MA); anthropology (MA); archaeology (M Sc, MA); art (MA, MFA); biochemistry (M Sc); biological sciences (M Sc); biomolecular science (PhD); biosystems and biodiversity (PhD); Canadian studies (MA); chemistry (M Sc); computer science (M Sc); computer science and geographical information science (M Sc); counseling (MC); counseling psychology (M Ed); dramatic arts (MA); earth, space, and physical science (PhD); economics (MA); education (MA, PhD); educational leadership (M Ed); English (MA); environmental science (M Sc); evolution and behavior (PhD); exercise science (M Sc); French (MA); French/German (MA); French/Spanish (MA); general education (M Ed); geography (M Sc, MA); German (MA); health sciences (M Sc); individualized multidisciplinary (M Sc, MA); kinesiology (M Sc, MA); management (M Sc), including accounting, finance, human resource management and labor relations, information systems, international management, marketing, policy and strategy; mathematics (M Sc); music (M Mus, MA); Native American studies (MA); neuroscience (M Sc, PhD); new media (MA, MFA); nursing (M Sc, MN); philosophy (MA); physics (M Sc); political science (MA); psychology (M Sc, MA); religious studies (MA); sociology (MA); theatre and dramatic arts (MFA); theoretical and computational science (PhD); urban and regional studies (MA); women and gender studies (MA). *Program availability:* Part-time, evening/weekend. *Degree requirements:* For master's, thesis (for some programs); for doctorate, comprehensive exam, thesis/dissertation. *Entrance requirements:* For master's, GMAT (for M Sc in management), bachelor's degree in related field, minimum GPA of 3.0 during previous 20 graded semester courses, 2 years' teaching or related experience (M Ed); for doctorate, master's degree, minimum graduate GPA of 3.5. Additional exam requirements/recommendations for international students: Required—TOEFL (minimum score 580 paper-based; 93 iBT). Electronic applications accepted. *Faculty research:* Movement and brain plasticity, gibberellin physiology, photosynthesis, carbon cycling, molecular properties of main-group ring components.

University of Maine, Graduate School, College of Natural Sciences, Forestry, and Agriculture, School of Economics, Orono, ME 04469. Offers economics (MA); financial economics (MA); resource economics and policy (MS). *Program availability:* Part-time. *Faculty:* 11 full-time (3 women). *Students:* 22 full-time (9 women), 1 (woman) part-time, 9 international. Average age 24. 25 applicants, 84% accepted, 11 enrolled. In 2017, 12 master's awarded. *Degree requirements:* For master's, thesis (for some programs). *Entrance requirements:* For master's, GRE General Test. Additional exam requirements/recommendations for international students: Required—TOEFL (minimum score 580 paper-based; 93 iBT), IELTS (minimum score 6.9), TWE (minimum score 4.9), PTE (minimum score 67). *Application deadline:* For fall admission, 2/15 for domestic students, 2/1 for international students; for spring admission, 9/15 for domestic students, 8/15 for international students. Applications are processed on a rolling basis. Application fee: $65. Electronic applications accepted. *Expenses:* Tuition, state resident: full-time $7722; part-time $429 per credit hour. Tuition, nonresident: full-time $25,146; part-time $1397 per credit hour. *Required fees:* $1162; $581 per credit hour. *Financial support:* In 2017–18, 27 students received support, including 12 research assistantships with full tuition reimbursements available (averaging $20,500 per year), 13 teaching assistantships with full tuition reimbursements available (averaging $15,200 per year); career-related internships or fieldwork, Federal Work-Study, institutionally sponsored loans, scholarships/grants, and tuition waivers (full and partial) also available. Support available to part-time students. Financial award application deadline: 3/1. *Faculty research:* Economics of: health, energy, transportation, marine resource, consumer behavior. *Total annual research expenditures:* $848,400. *Unit head:* Dr. Mario Teisl, Director, 207-581-3151, Fax: 207-581-4278. *Application contact:* Scott G. Delcourt, Assistant Vice President for Graduate Studies and Senior Associate Dean, 207-581-3291, Fax: 207-581-3232, E-mail: graduate@maine.edu.
Website: http://umaine.edu/soe/

The University of Manchester, Alliance Manchester Business School, M15 6PB, United Kingdom. Offers accounting and finance (M Sc); business (M Ent); business analysis and strategic management (M Sc); business analytics: operational research and risk analysis (M Sc); business psychology (M Sc); corporate communications and reputation management (M Sc); finance (M Sc); finance and business economics (M Sc); human resource management and industrial relations (M Sc); innovation management and entrepreneurship (M Sc); international business and management (M Sc); international human resource management and comparative industrial relations (M Sc); management (M Sc); marketing (M Sc); operations, project and supply chain management (M Sc); organizational psychology (M Sc); quantitative finance (M Sc). *Entrance requirements:* For master's, UK 2:1 honours degree or overseas equivalent. Additional exam requirements/recommendations for international students: Required—TOEFL (minimum score 100 iBT), IELTS (minimum score 7), PTE. Electronic applications accepted. *Faculty research:* Accounting and finance, management sciences and marketing, people management and organization, innovation management and policy, decision sciences.

University of Maryland University College, The Graduate School, Program in Accounting and Financial Management, Adelphi, MD 20783. Offers MS. *Accreditation:* AACSB. *Program availability:* Part-time, evening/weekend, online learning. *Students:* 13 full-time (8 women), 442 part-time (287 women); includes 281 minority (189 Black or African American, non-Hispanic/Latino; 5 American Indian or Alaska Native, non-Hispanic/Latino; 35 Asian, non-Hispanic/Latino; 36 Hispanic/Latino; 1 Native Hawaiian or other Pacific Islander, non-Hispanic/Latino; 15 Two or more races, non-Hispanic/Latino), 15 international. Average age 36. 131 applicants, 100% accepted, 105 enrolled. In 2017, 88 master's awarded. *Degree requirements:* For master's, thesis or alternative, capstone course. *Application deadline:* Applications are processed on a rolling basis. Application fee: $50. Electronic applications accepted. *Financial support:* Federal Work-Study and scholarships/grants available. Support available to part-time students. Financial award application deadline: 6/1; financial award applicants required to submit FAFSA. *Unit head:* Dr. Kirby Cundiff, Program Chair, 240-684-2400, E-mail: kirby.cundiff@umuc.edu. *Application contact:* Coordinator, Graduate Admissions, 800-888-8682, Fax: 240-684-2151, E-mail: newgrad@umuc.edu.
Website: http://www.umuc.edu/academic-programs/masters-degrees/accounting-and-financial-management.cfm

University of Massachusetts Amherst, Graduate School, Isenberg School of Management, Program in Management, Amherst, MA 01003. Offers accounting (PhD); business administration (MBA); entrepreneurship (MBA); finance (MBA, PhD); healthcare administration (MBA); hospitality and tourism management (PhD); management science (PhD); marketing (MBA, PhD); organization studies (PhD); sport management (PhD); strategic management (PhD); MBA/MS. *Accreditation:* AACSB. *Program availability:* Part-time, evening/weekend, online learning. Terminal master's awarded for partial completion of doctoral program. *Degree requirements:* For doctorate, comprehensive exam, thesis/dissertation. *Entrance requirements:* For master's and doctorate, GMAT or GRE General Test. Additional exam requirements/recommendations for international students: Required—TOEFL (minimum score 550 paper-based; 80 iBT), IELTS (minimum score 6.5). Electronic applications accepted.

University of Massachusetts Boston, College of Management, Program in Finance, Boston, MA 02125-3393. Offers MS. *Faculty:* 27 full-time (9 women), 13 part-time/adjunct (1 woman). *Students:* 36 full-time (17 women), 17 part-time (8 women); includes 7 minority (2 Black or African American, non-Hispanic/Latino; 3 Asian, non-Hispanic/Latino; 2 Hispanic/Latino), 35 international. Average age 28. 91 applicants, 36% accepted, 15 enrolled. In 2017, 20 master's awarded. *Expenses:* Tuition, state resident: full-time $17,375. Tuition, nonresident: full-time $33,915. *Required fees:* $355. *Application contact:* Graduate Admissions Coordinator, 617-287-6400, Fax: 617-287-6236, E-mail: bos.gadm@dpc.umassp.edu.

University of Massachusetts Dartmouth, Graduate School, Charlton College of Business, Department of Accounting and Finance, North Dartmouth, MA 02747-2300. Offers accounting (MS, Postbaccalaureate Certificate); finance (Postbaccalaureate Certificate). *Program availability:* Part-time. *Faculty:* 15 full-time (5 women), 4 part-time/adjunct (1 woman). *Students:* 36 full-time (21 women), 17 part-time (12 women); includes 17 minority (3 Black or African American, non-Hispanic/Latino; 7 Asian, non-Hispanic/Latino; 5 Hispanic/Latino; 2 Two or more races, non-Hispanic/Latino), 8 international. Average age 31. 33 applicants, 91% accepted, 25 enrolled. In 2017, 23 master's, 1 other advanced degree awarded. *Entrance requirements:* For master's, GMAT or waiver, statement of purpose (minimum 300 words), resume, official transcript, 2 letters of recommendation; for Postbaccalaureate Certificate, statement of purpose (minimum 300 words), resume, official transcript. Additional exam requirements/recommendations for international students: Required—TOEFL (minimum score 550 paper-based; 79 iBT), IELTS (minimum score 6.5). *Application deadline:* For fall admission, 8/1 priority date for domestic students, 6/1 priority date for international students; for spring admission, 11/15 priority date for domestic students, 10/15 priority date for international students. Application fee: $60. Electronic applications accepted. *Expenses:* Tuition, state resident: full-time $15,449; part-time $643.71 per credit. Tuition, nonresident: full-time $27,880; part-time $1161.67 per credit. *Required fees:* $405; $25.88 per credit. Tuition and fees vary according to course load and reciprocity agreements. *Financial support:* Research assistantships, teaching assistantships, tuition waivers, and unspecified assistantships available. Support available to part-time students. Financial award application deadline: 3/1; financial award applicants required to submit FAFSA. *Faculty research:* Accounting information systems, analytical controls in continuous auditing, accounting education, managerial accounting, e-commerce. *Unit head:* Dr. Jia Wu, Program Coordinator, Accounting, 508-999-8428, E-mail: jwu@umassd.edu. *Application contact:* Steven Briggs, Director of Marketing and Recruitment for Graduate Studies, 508-999-8604, Fax: 508-999-8183, E-mail: graduate@umassd.edu.
Website: http://www.umassd.edu/charlton/programs/graduate/msaccounting

University of Memphis, Graduate School, Fogelman College of Business and Economics, Program in Business Administration, Memphis, TN 38152. Offers accounting (MBA, PhD); business administration (IMBA); economics (PhD); executive business administration (MBA); finance (PhD); management (PhD); marketing (MS); marketing and supply chain management (PhD); real estate development (MS); JD/MBA. *Accreditation:* AACSB. *Faculty:* 2 part-time/adjunct (0 women). *Students:* 166 full-time (76 women), 361 part-time (142 women); includes 161 minority (91 Black or African American, non-Hispanic/Latino; 51 Asian, non-Hispanic/Latino; 10 Hispanic/Latino; 9 Two or more races, non-Hispanic/Latino), 89 international. Average age 32. 263 applicants, 83% accepted, 157 enrolled. In 2017, 186 master's, 14 doctorates awarded. *Degree requirements:* For master's, comprehensive exam; for doctorate, comprehensive exam, thesis/dissertation. *Entrance requirements:* For master's, GMAT, resume; for doctorate, GMAT, interview, minimum GPA of 3.4, resume, letter of recommendation. Additional exam requirements/recommendations for international students: Required—TOEFL (minimum score 550 paper-based). *Application deadline:* For fall admission, 8/1 for domestic students; for spring admission, 12/1 for domestic students. Application fee: $35 ($60 for international students). *Financial support:* In 2017–18, 164 students received support, including 17 research assistantships with full tuition reimbursements available (averaging $53,750 per year), 13 teaching assistantships with full tuition reimbursements available (averaging $20,798 per year); career-related internships or fieldwork, Federal Work-Study, scholarships/grants, and unspecified assistantships also available. Financial award application deadline: 2/15; financial award applicants required to submit FAFSA. *Faculty research:* Competitive business strategy, finance microstructures, supply chain management innovations, health care economics, litigation risks and corporate audits. *Unit head:* Dr. Rajiv Grover, Dean, 901-678-3759, E-mail: rgrover@memphis.edu. *Application contact:* Dr. Carol V. Danehower, Associate Dean, 901-678-5402, Fax: 901-678-3579, E-mail: fcbegp@memphis.edu.
Website: https://web0.memphis.edu/gradcatalog/degreeprog/fcbe/fcbe.php

University of Michigan–Dearborn, College of Business, MS Program in Finance, Dearborn, MI 48126. Offers MS. *Program availability:* Part-time, evening/weekend, 100% online. *Faculty:* 45 full-time (19 women), 4 part-time/adjunct (2 women). *Students:* 8 full-time (4 women), 30 part-time (10 women); includes 9 minority (3 Black or African American, non-Hispanic/Latino; 5 Asian, non-Hispanic/Latino; 1 Hispanic/Latino), 6 international. Average age 31. 50 applicants, 56% accepted, 13 enrolled. In 2017, 21 master's awarded. *Entrance requirements:* For master's, GRE or GMAT, equivalent of

four-year U.S. bachelor's degree from regionally-accredited institution, undergraduate course in finite math, pre-calculus, or calculus. Additional exam requirements/recommendations for international students: Required—TOEFL (minimum score 560 paper-based; 84 iBT), IELTS (minimum score 6.5). *Application deadline:* For fall admission, 8/1 for domestic students, 5/1 for international students; for winter admission, 12/1 for domestic students, 9/1 for international students; for spring admission, 4/1 for domestic students, 1/1 for international students. Applications are processed on a rolling basis. Application fee: $60. Electronic applications accepted. *Expenses:* $883 per credit hour in-state; $1,376 per credit hour out-state. *Financial support:* In 2017–18, 5 students received support. Scholarships/grants and non-resident tuition scholarships available. Financial award application deadline: 3/1; financial award applicants required to submit FAFSA. *Faculty research:* Business intelligence, behavioral finance, brand management and new media, management education, operations strategy. *Unit head:* Dr. Michael Kamen, Director, Graduate Programs, 313-593-5460, E-mail: mkamen@ umich.edu. *Application contact:* Joan Doherty, Academic Advisor/Counselor, 313-593-5460, Fax: 313-271-9838, E-mail: umd-gradbusiness@umich.edu.
Website: http://umdearborn.edu/cob/ms-finance/

University of Michigan–Flint, School of Management, Program in Business Administration, Flint, MI 48502-1950. Offers accounting (MBA); computer information systems (MBA); finance (MBA, Post-Master's Certificate); general business (Graduate Certificate); general business administration (MBA); health care management (MBA); international business (MBA, Post-Master's Certificate); lean manufacturing (MBA); marketing (Post-Master's Certificate); marketing and innovation management (MBA); organizational leadership (MBA). *Program availability:* Part-time, evening/weekend, mixed mode format. *Faculty:* 32 full-time (5 women), 8 part-time/adjunct (2 women). *Students:* 12 full-time (7 women), 147 part-time (51 women); includes 31 minority (15 Black or African American, non-Hispanic/Latino; 1 American Indian or Alaska Native, non-Hispanic/Latino; 9 Asian, non-Hispanic/Latino; 5 Hispanic/Latino; 1 Two or more races, non-Hispanic/Latino), 18 international. Average age 34. 110 applicants, 52% accepted, 29 enrolled. In 2017, 59 master's, 6 other advanced degrees awarded. *Entrance requirements:* For master's, GMAT or GRE, bachelor's degree in arts, sciences, engineering, or business administration from regionally-accredited college or university with minimum GPA of 3.0; for other advanced degree, bachelor's degree in arts, sciences, engineering, or business administration from regionally-accredited college or university with minimum GPA of 3.0, college-level math, statistics, or quantitative course (for Graduate Certificate); MBA or equivalent degree from regionally-accredited college or university (for Post Master's Certificate). Additional exam requirements/recommendations for international students: Required—TOEFL (minimum score 84 iBT), IELTS (minimum score 6.5). *Application deadline:* For fall admission, 8/1 for domestic students, 5/1 for international students; for winter admission, 11/15 for domestic students, 9/1 for international students; for spring admission, 3/15 for domestic students, 1/1 for international students; for summer admission, 5/15 for domestic students. Applications are processed on a rolling basis. Application fee: $55. Electronic applications accepted. *Expenses:* Contact institution. *Financial support:* Federal Work-Study, scholarships/grants, and unspecified assistantships available. Support available to part-time students. Financial award application deadline: 3/1; financial award applicants required to submit FAFSA. *Unit head:* Dr. Scott Johnson, Dean, School of Management, 810-762-3164, Fax: 810-237-6685, E-mail: scotjohn@umflint.edu. *Application contact:* Bradley T. Maki, Director of Graduate Admissions, 810-762-3171, E-mail: bmaki@umflint.edu.
Website: http://www.umflint.edu/graduateprograms/business-administration-mba

University of Minnesota, Twin Cities Campus, Carlson School of Management, Carlson Full-Time MBA Program, Minneapolis, MN 55455. Offers finance (MBA); information technology (MBA); management (MBA); marketing (MBA); medical industry orientation (MBA); supply chain and operations (MBA); JD/MBA; MBA/MPP; MBA/MSBA; MD/MBA; MHA/MBA; Pharm D/MBA. *Accreditation:* AACSB. *Faculty:* 143 full-time (42 women), 24 part-time/adjunct (6 women). *Students:* 200 full-time (63 women); includes 25 minority (4 Black or African American, non-Hispanic/Latino; 13 Asian, non-Hispanic/Latino; 5 Hispanic/Latino; 3 Two or more races, non-Hispanic/Latino), 41 international. Average age 29. 606 applicants, 45% accepted, 104 enrolled. In 2017, 85 master's awarded. *Entrance requirements:* For master's, GMAT or GRE. Additional exam requirements/recommendations for international students: Required—TOEFL (minimum score 580 paper-based; 84 iBT), IELTS (minimum score 7), PTE. *Application deadline:* For fall admission, 4/1 for domestic students, 2/1 for international students. Application fee: $75. Electronic applications accepted. *Expenses:* $19,104 per semester resident tuition, $24,468 per semester non-resident tuition; $1,138 per semester fees; $1,050 per semester student health plan; $179 per semester (for international students). *Financial support:* In 2017–18, 147 students received support, including 147 fellowships with tuition reimbursements available (averaging $23,479 per year); research assistantships with partial tuition reimbursements available, teaching assistantships with partial tuition reimbursements available, career-related internships or fieldwork, Federal Work-Study, institutionally sponsored loans, scholarships/grants, health care benefits, and unspecified assistantships also available. Financial award application deadline: 4/1; financial award applicants required to submit FAFSA. *Faculty research:* Market regulation and asset pricing, social networks and data analytics, consumer behavior, innovation and entrepreneurship, workplace wellbeing and labor relationships. *Total annual research expenditures:* $577,440. *Unit head:* Philip J. Miller, Assistant Dean, MBA and MS Programs, 612-625-5555, Fax: 612-625-1012, E-mail: mba@umn.edu. *Application contact:* Linh Gilles, Director of Admissions and Recruiting, 612-625-5555, Fax: 612-625-1012, E-mail: ftmba@umn.edu.
Website: http://www.csom.umn.edu/MBA/full-time/

University of Minnesota, Twin Cities Campus, Carlson School of Management, Carlson Part-Time MBA Program, Minneapolis, MN 55455. Offers finance (MBA); information technology (MBA); management (MBA); marketing (MBA); medical industry orientation (MBA); supply chain and operations (MBA). *Program availability:* Part-time-only, evening/weekend, 100% online, blended/hybrid learning. *Faculty:* 143 full-time (42 women), 26 part-time/adjunct (6 women). *Students:* 919 part-time (291 women); includes 120 minority (14 Black or African American, non-Hispanic/Latino; 2 American Indian or Alaska Native, non-Hispanic/Latino; 55 Asian, non-Hispanic/Latino; 26 Hispanic/Latino; 1 Native Hawaiian or other Pacific Islander, non-Hispanic/Latino; 22 Two or more races, non-Hispanic/Latino), 57 international. Average age 28. 226 applicants, 85% accepted, 167 enrolled. In 2017, 289 master's awarded. *Entrance requirements:* For master's, GMAT or GRE. Additional exam requirements/recommendations for international students: Required—TOEFL (minimum score 580 paper-based; 84 iBT), IELTS (minimum score 7), PTE. *Application deadline:* For fall admission, 5/15 priority date for domestic and international students; for spring admission, 10/15 priority date for domestic and international students. Applications are processed on a rolling basis. Application fee: $75. Electronic applications accepted. *Expenses:* $1,375 per credit tuition, $314 per semester fees. *Financial support:* Applicants required to submit FAFSA. *Faculty research:* Market regulation and asset pricing, social networks and data analytics, consumer behavior, innovation and entrepreneurship, workplace wellbeing and labor relationships. *Total annual research expenditures:* $577,440. *Unit head:* Philip J. Miller, Assistant Dean, MBA and MS Programs, 612-624-2039, Fax: 612-625-1012, E-mail: mba@umn.edu. *Application*

contact: Linh Gilles, Director of Admissions and Recruiting, 612-625-5555, Fax: 612-625-1012, E-mail: ptmba@umn.edu.
Website: http://www.carlsonschool.umn.edu/ptmba

University of Minnesota, Twin Cities Campus, Carlson School of Management, Doctoral Program in Business Administration, Minneapolis, MN 55455. Offers accounting (PhD); finance (PhD); information and decision sciences (PhD); marketing (PhD); strategic management and entrepreneurship (PhD); supply chain and operations (PhD); work and organizations (PhD). *Faculty:* 102 full-time (32 women). *Students:* 95 full-time (32 women); includes 10 minority (2 Black or African American, non-Hispanic/Latino; 7 Asian, non-Hispanic/Latino; 1 Hispanic/Latino), 68 international. Average age 30. 357 applicants, 6% accepted, 17 enrolled. In 2017, 14 doctorates awarded. *Degree requirements:* For doctorate, comprehensive exam, thesis/dissertation, written and oral preliminary exams, proposal defense, final defense. *Entrance requirements:* For doctorate, GMAT, GRE General Test, minimum undergraduate GPA of 3.0, graduate 3.5 (recommended). Additional exam requirements/recommendations for international students: Required—TOEFL (minimum score 600 paper-based, 100 iBT) or IELTS (minimum score 7.0). *Application deadline:* For fall admission, 12/15 for domestic students, 12/15 priority date for international students. Applications are processed on a rolling basis. Application fee: $75 ($95 for international students). Electronic applications accepted. *Expenses:* Contact institution. *Financial support:* In 2017–18, 80 students received support, including 80 fellowships with full tuition reimbursements available (averaging $13,000 per year), 73 research assistantships with full tuition reimbursements available (averaging $7,520 per year), 73 teaching assistantships with full tuition reimbursements available (averaging $7,520 per year); institutionally sponsored loans, scholarships/grants, health care benefits, unspecified assistantships, and full student service fee waivers also available. Financial award application deadline: 12/15. *Faculty research:* Finance, strategy and entrepreneurship, marketing, information and decision science, operations, accounting, supply chain, human resources and industrial relations, organizational behavior. *Unit head:* Dr. Shawn P. Curley, Director, 612-624-6546, Fax: 612-624-8221, E-mail: curley@umn.edu. *Application contact:* Sandy Herzan, Associate Director, 612-624-0875, Fax: 612-624-8221, E-mail: herza002@umn.edu.
Website: http://carlsonschool.umn.edu/degrees/phd

University of Mississippi, Graduate School, School of Business Administration, University, MS 38677. Offers business administration (MBA, PhD); finance (PhD); management (PhD); management information systems (PhD); marketing (PhD); JD/MBA. *Accreditation:* AACSB. *Faculty:* 58 full-time (15 women), 8 part-time/adjunct (3 women). *Students:* 71 full-time (26 women), 112 part-time (27 women); includes 11 minority (4 Black or African American, non-Hispanic/Latino; 3 Asian, non-Hispanic/Latino; 1 Hispanic/Latino; 3 Two or more races, non-Hispanic/Latino), 17 international. Average age 29. In 2017, 83 master's, 6 doctorates awarded. *Entrance requirements:* For master's, GMAT, minimum GPA of 3.0; for doctorate, GMAT. Additional exam requirements/recommendations for international students: Required—TOEFL. *Application deadline:* For fall admission, 2/1 priority date for domestic students; for spring admission, 11/1 for domestic students; for summer admission, 4/1 for domestic students. Applications are processed on a rolling basis. Application fee: $50. Electronic applications accepted. *Financial support:* Fellowships, career-related internships or fieldwork, scholarships/grants, tuition waivers (full), and unspecified assistantships available. Financial award application deadline: 3/1; financial award applicants required to submit FAFSA. *Unit head:* Dr. Ken Cyree, Dean, 662-915-5820, Fax: 662-915-5821, E-mail: info@bus.olemiss.edu. *Application contact:* Ashley Jones McGee, Director of MBA and MHA Administration, 662-915-5483, E-mail: ajones@olemiss.edu.
Website: http://www.olemissbusiness.com/

University of Missouri, Office of Research and Graduate Studies, Robert J. Trulaske, Sr. College of Business, Program in Business Administration, Columbia, MO 65211. Offers business administration (MBA); executive business administration (MBA); finance (PhD); management (PhD); marketing (PhD); MBA/JD; MBA/MHA; MBA/MSIE. *Accreditation:* AACSB. *Degree requirements:* For doctorate, thesis/dissertation. *Entrance requirements:* For master's and doctorate, GMAT, minimum GPA of 3.0. Additional exam requirements/recommendations for international students: Required—TOEFL (minimum score 500 paper-based; 61 iBT). Electronic applications accepted.

University of Missouri–Kansas City, Henry W. Bloch School of Management, Kansas City, MO 64110-2499. Offers accounting (MS); finance (MS); public affairs (MPA, PhD); JD/MBA; LL M/MPA. PhD (interdisciplinary) offered through the School of Graduate Studies. *Accreditation:* AACSB; NASPAA. *Program availability:* Part-time, evening/weekend. Terminal master's awarded for partial completion of doctoral program. *Entrance requirements:* For master's, GMAT, GRE, 2 essays, 2 references, support of employer; for doctorate, GRE, minimum GPA of 3.0. Additional exam requirements/recommendations for international students: Required—TOEFL (minimum score 550 paper-based; 80 iBT). Electronic applications accepted. *Faculty research:* Entrepreneurship, finance, non-profit, risk management.

University of Nebraska–Lincoln, Graduate College, College of Business Administration, Interdepartmental Area of Business, Department of Finance, Lincoln, NE 68588. Offers business (MA, PhD). *Degree requirements:* For doctorate, comprehensive exam, thesis/dissertation. *Entrance requirements:* For master's and doctorate, GMAT. Additional exam requirements/recommendations for international students: Required—TOEFL (minimum score 100 iBT). Electronic applications accepted. *Faculty research:* Banking, investments, international finance, insurance, corporate finance.

University of Nevada, Reno, Graduate School, College of Business Administration, Department of Finance, Reno, NV 89557. Offers MS. *Program availability:* Part-time. *Degree requirements:* For master's, thesis optional. *Entrance requirements:* For master's, GMAT or GRE, minimum GPA of 2.75. Additional exam requirements/recommendations for international students: Required—TOEFL (minimum score 500 paper-based; 61 iBT), IELTS (minimum score 6). Electronic applications accepted. *Faculty research:* Financial business problems, economic theory, financial concepts theory.

University of New Haven, Graduate School, College of Business, Program in Business Administration, West Haven, CT 06516. Offers accounting (MBA); business administration (MBA); business intelligence (MBA); business policy and strategic leadership (MBA); finance (MBA), including chartered financial analyst; global marketing (MBA); human resources management (MBA); sport management (MBA). *Accreditation:* AACSB. *Program availability:* Part-time, evening/weekend. *Students:* 123 full-time (56 women), 67 part-time (28 women); includes 53 minority (27 Black or African American, non-Hispanic/Latino; 11 Asian, non-Hispanic/Latino; 12 Hispanic/Latino; 3 Two or more races, non-Hispanic/Latino), 50 international. Average age 28. 148 applicants, 89% accepted, 67 enrolled. In 2017, 106 master's awarded. *Entrance requirements:* For master's, GMAT. Additional exam requirements/recommendations for international students: Required—TOEFL (minimum score 80 iBT), IELTS, PTE. *Application deadline:* Applications are processed on a rolling basis. Application fee: $50. Electronic applications accepted. Application fee is waived when completed online. *Expenses:* Tuition: Full-time $16,020; part-time $890 per credit hour. *Required fees:* $220; $90 per term. *Financial support:* Research assistantships with partial tuition reimbursements, teaching assistantships with partial tuition reimbursements, career-related internships or

fieldwork, Federal Work-Study, scholarships/grants, and unspecified assistantships available. Support available to part-time students. Financial award applicants required to submit FAFSA. *Unit head:* Darell Singleterry, Director, 203-932-1085, E-mail: dsingleterry@newhaven.edu. *Application contact:* Michelle Mason, Director of Graduate Enrollment, 203-932-7067, E-mail: mmason@newhaven.edu.
Website: http://www.newhaven.edu/business/graduate-programs/mba/index.php

See Display on page 154 and Close-Up on page 185.

University of New Haven, Graduate School, College of Business, Program in Finance, West Haven, CT 06516. Offers MS. *Students:* 13 full-time (5 women), 2 part-time (0 women); includes 1 minority (Two or more races, non-Hispanic/Latino), 9 international. Average age 27. 25 applicants, 88% accepted, 4 enrolled. *Application deadline:* Applications are processed on a rolling basis. Application fee: $50. *Expenses: Tuition:* Full-time $16,020; part-time $890 per credit hour. *Required fees:* $220; $90 per term. *Financial support:* Research assistantships with partial tuition reimbursements, teaching assistantships with partial tuition reimbursements, and Federal Work-Study available. Financial award application deadline: 5/1; financial award applicants required to submit FAFSA. *Unit head:* Dr. Charlie Boynton, Chair, 203-932-7356, E-mail: cboynton@newhaven.edu. *Application contact:* Michelle Mason, Director of Graduate Enrollment, 203-932-7067, E-mail: mmason@newhaven.edu.
Website: http://www.newhaven.edu/business/programs/graduate/finance/

See Display on page 154 and Close-Up on page 185.

University of New Haven, Graduate School, Henry C. Lee College of Criminal Justice and Forensic Sciences, Program in Public Administration, West Haven, CT 06516. Offers fire and emergency medical services (MPA); municipal management (MPA); nonprofit organization management (MPA); public administration (MPA, Graduate Certificate); public finance (MPA); public safety (MPA). *Program availability:* Part-time, evening/weekend. *Students:* 36 full-time (20 women), 25 part-time (10 women); includes 21 minority (15 Black or African American, non-Hispanic/Latino; 1 American Indian or Alaska Native, non-Hispanic/Latino; 1 Asian, non-Hispanic/Latino; 3 Hispanic/Latino; 1 Two or more races, non-Hispanic/Latino), 3 international. Average age 37. 46 applicants, 91% accepted, 21 enrolled. In 2017, 15 master's, 1 other advanced degree awarded. *Entrance requirements:* Additional exam requirements/recommendations for international students: Required—TOEFL (minimum score 80 iBT), IELTS, PTE. *Application deadline:* Applications are processed on a rolling basis. Application fee: $50. Electronic applications accepted. Application fee is waived when completed online. *Expenses: Tuition:* Full-time $16,020; part-time $890 per credit hour. *Required fees:* $220; $90 per term. *Financial support:* Research assistantships with partial tuition reimbursements, teaching assistantships with partial tuition reimbursements, career-related internships or fieldwork, Federal Work-Study, scholarships/grants, and unspecified assistantships available. Support available to part-time students. Financial award application deadline: 5/1; financial award applicants required to submit FAFSA. *Unit head:* Dr. Cynthia Conrad, Associate Professor, 203-932-7486, E-mail: cconrad@newhaven.edu. *Application contact:* Michelle Mason, Director of Graduate Enrollment, 203-932-7067, E-mail: mmason@newhaven.edu.
Website: http://www.newhaven.edu/lee-college/graduate-programs/public-administration/

University of New Mexico, Anderson School of Management, Department of Finance, International, Technology and Entrepreneurship, Albuquerque, NM 87131-1221. Offers entrepreneurship (MBA); finance (MBA); international management (MBA); international management in Latin America (MBA); management of technology (MBA). *Program availability:* Part-time. *Faculty:* 13 full-time (1 woman), 6 part-time/adjunct (1 woman). In 2017, 47 master's awarded. *Entrance requirements:* For master's, GMAT or GRE, minimum GPA of 3.0 on last 60 hours of coursework; bachelor's degree from regionally-accredited college or university in U.S. or its equivalent in another country. Additional exam requirements/recommendations for international students: Required—TOEFL (minimum score 550 paper-based; 79 iBT), IELTS (minimum score 6.5). *Application deadline:* For fall admission, 4/1 priority date for domestic and international students; for spring admission, 10/1 priority date for domestic and international students. Applications are processed on a rolling basis. Application fee: $50. Electronic applications accepted. *Expenses:* Contact institution. *Financial support:* In 2017–18, 17 students received support, including 9 fellowships (averaging $18,720 per year), 12 research assistantships with partial tuition reimbursements available (averaging $15,291 per year); career-related internships or fieldwork, Federal Work-Study, scholarships/grants, and unspecified assistantships also available. Support available to part-time students. Financial award application deadline: 6/1; financial award applicants required to submit FAFSA. *Faculty research:* Corporate finance, investments, management in Latin America, management of technology, entrepreneurship. *Unit head:* Dr. Raul Gouvea, Chair, 505-277-6471, E-mail: rauldg@unm.edu. *Application contact:* Lisa Beauchene, Student Recruitment Specialist, 505-277-6471, E-mail: andersonadvising@unm.edu.
Website: https://www.mgt.unm.edu/fite/default.asp?mm-faculty

University of New Orleans, Graduate School, College of Business Administration, Department of Economics and Finance, New Orleans, LA 70148. Offers economics and finance (MS); financial economics (PhD). *Accreditation:* AACSB. Terminal master's awarded for partial completion of doctoral program. *Degree requirements:* For master's, thesis optional; for doctorate, one foreign language, comprehensive exam, thesis/dissertation, general exams. *Entrance requirements:* For doctorate, GRE General Test, minimum GPA of 3.0. Additional exam requirements/recommendations for international students: Required—TOEFL (minimum score 550 paper-based; 79 iBT). *Faculty research:* Monetary economics, international economics, urban economics, real estate.

University of North Alabama, College of Business, Florence, AL 35632-0001. Offers business administration (MBA), including accounting, enterprise resource planning systems, executive, finance, health care management, information systems, international business, project management. *Accreditation:* AACSB; ACBSP. *Program availability:* Part-time, 100% online, blended/hybrid learning. *Faculty:* 26 full-time (1 woman), 4 part-time/adjunct (0 women). *Students:* 178 full-time (78 women), 498 part-time (237 women); includes 229 minority (92 Black or African American, non-Hispanic/Latino; 8 American Indian or Alaska Native, non-Hispanic/Latino; 104 Asian, non-Hispanic/Latino; 14 Hispanic/Latino; 11 Two or more races, non-Hispanic/Latino), 53 international. Average age 34. 354 applicants, 71% accepted, 190 enrolled. In 2017, 156 master's awarded. *Entrance requirements:* For master's, GMAT, GRE, minimum GPA of 2.75 in last 60 hours, 2.5 overall (on a 3.0 scale); 27 hours of course work in business and economics. Additional exam requirements/recommendations for international students: Required—TOEFL (minimum score 79 iBT), IELTS (minimum score 6), PTE (minimum score 54). *Application deadline:* Applications are processed on a rolling basis. Application fee: $50 ($100 for international students). Electronic applications accepted. *Expenses:* Tuition, state resident: full-time $7824; part-time $5943 per year. Tuition, nonresident: full-time $15,648; part-time $11,736 per year. *Required fees:* $3064; $2298 per unit. Tuition and fees vary according to course load and reciprocity agreements. *Financial support:* In 2017–18, 114 students received support. Scholarships/grants available. Financial award application deadline: 2/1; financial award applicants required to submit FAFSA. *Total annual research expenditures:* $193,193. *Unit head:* Dr. Gregory A. Carnes, Dean, 256-765-4261, Fax: 256-765-4170, E-mail: gacarnes@una.edu.

Application contact: Hillary N. Coats, Graduate Admissions Coordinator, 256-765-4447, E-mail: graduate@una.edu.
Website: https://www.una.edu/mba/index.html

The University of North Carolina at Chapel Hill, Kenan-Flagler Business School, Doctoral Program in Business Administration, Chapel Hill, NC 27599. Offers accounting (PhD); finance (PhD); marketing (PhD); operations management (PhD); organizational behavior (PhD); strategy (PhD). *Accreditation:* AACSB. *Degree requirements:* For doctorate, thesis/dissertation. *Entrance requirements:* For doctorate, GMAT or GRE General Test. Electronic applications accepted. *Expenses:* Contact institution.

The University of North Carolina at Charlotte, College of Liberal Arts and Sciences, Department of Political Science and Public Administration, Charlotte, NC 28223-0001. Offers emergency management (Graduate Certificate); non-profit management (Graduate Certificate); public administration (MPA), including arts administration, emergency management, non-profit management, public budgeting and finance, urban management and policy; public budgeting and finance (Graduate Certificate); urban management and policy (Graduate Certificate). *Accreditation:* NASPAA. *Program availability:* Part-time, evening/weekend. *Faculty:* 19 full-time (9 women), 4 part-time/adjunct (1 woman). *Students:* 20 full-time (11 women), 61 part-time (41 women); includes 21 minority (12 Black or African American, non-Hispanic/Latino; 2 American Indian or Alaska Native, non-Hispanic/Latino; 1 Asian, non-Hispanic/Latino; 4 Hispanic/Latino; 2 Two or more races, non-Hispanic/Latino), 1 international. Average age 28. 48 applicants, 67% accepted, 22 enrolled. In 2017, 25 master's, 15 other advanced degrees awarded. *Degree requirements:* For master's, research project or thesis. *Entrance requirements:* For master's, GRE General Test, bachelor's degree, or its equivalent, from accredited college or university; minimum undergraduate GPA of 3.0; 3 letters of recommendation; statement of purpose; for Graduate Certificate, statement of purpose (1-2 pages in length) explaining applicant's career goals, how the Graduate Certificate fits into achieving those goals, and any relevant work experience; official transcripts; letters of recommendation. Additional exam requirements/recommendations for international students: Required—TOEFL (minimum score 523 paper-based, 70 iBT) or IELTS (6.5). *Application deadline:* For fall admission, 8/1 for domestic and international students; for spring admission, 12/1 for domestic and international students. Applications are processed on a rolling basis. Application fee: $75. Electronic applications accepted. *Expenses:* Tuition, state resident: full-time $4337. Tuition, nonresident: full-time $17,771. *Required fees:* $3211. Tuition and fees vary according to course load and program. *Financial support:* In 2017–18, 14 students received support, including 13 research assistantships (averaging $9,015 per year), 1 teaching assistantship (averaging $19,500 per year); career-related internships or fieldwork, Federal Work-Study, institutionally sponsored loans, scholarships/grants, and unspecified assistantships also available. Support available to part-time students. Financial award application deadline: 3/1; financial award applicants required to submit FAFSA. *Total annual research expenditures:* $419,411. *Unit head:* Dr. Greg Weeks, Chair, 704-687-7574, E-mail: gbweeks@uncc.edu. *Application contact:* Kathy B. Giddings, Director of Graduate Admissions, 704-687-5503, Fax: 704-687-1668, E-mail: gradadm@uncc.edu.
Website: http://politicalscience.uncc.edu/

The University of North Carolina at Greensboro, Graduate School, Bryan School of Business and Economics, Department of Accounting and Finance, Greensboro, NC 27412-5001. Offers accounting (PMC); financial analysis (PMC). *Accreditation:* AACSB. *Entrance requirements:* For master's, GMAT, GRE General Test, previous course work in accounting and business. Additional exam requirements/recommendations for international students: Required—TOEFL. Electronic applications accepted.

University of North Florida, Coggin College of Business, MBA Program, Jacksonville, FL 32224. Offers accounting (MBA); construction management (MBA); e-commerce (MBA); economics (MBA); finance (MBA); human resource management (MBA); international business (MBA); logistics (MBA); management applications (MBA). *Accreditation:* AACSB. *Program availability:* Part-time, evening/weekend. *Entrance requirements:* For master's, GMAT or GRE, U.S. bachelor's degree from regionally-accredited university or equivalent foreign degree. Additional exam requirements/recommendations for international students: Required—TOEFL (minimum score 550 paper-based; 79 iBT). *Faculty research:* Performance measures, costing, and inventory issues in logistics and supply chain management; inter-organizational systems; international management and marketing practices; e-commerce; organizational learning and socialization processes.

University of North Texas, Robert B. Toulouse School of Graduate Studies, Denton, TX 76203-5459. Offers accounting (MS); applied anthropology (MA, MS); applied behavior analysis (Certificate); applied geography (MA); applied technology and performance improvement (M Ed, MS); art education (MA); art history (MA); art museum education (Certificate); arts leadership (Certificate); audiology (Au D); behavior analysis (MS); behavioral science (PhD); biochemistry and molecular biology (MS); biology (MA, MS); biomedical engineering (MS); business analysis (MS); chemistry (MS); clinical health psychology (PhD); communication studies (MA, MS); computer engineering (MS); computer science (MS); counseling (M Ed, MS), including clinical mental health counseling (MS), college and university counseling, elementary school counseling, secondary school counseling; creative writing (MA); criminal justice (MS); curriculum and instruction (M Ed); decision sciences (MBA); design (MA, MFA), including fashion design (MFA), innovation studies, interior design (MFA); early childhood studies (MS); economics (MS); educational leadership (M Ed, Ed D); educational psychology (MS, PhD), including family studies (MS), gifted and talented (MS), human development (MS), learning and cognition (MS), research, measurement and evaluation (MS); electrical engineering (MS); emergency management (MPA); engineering technology (MS); English (MA); English as a second language (MA); environmental science (MS); finance (MBA, MS); financial management (MPA); French (MA); health services management (MBA); higher education (M Ed, Ed D); history (MA, MS); hospitality management (MS); human resources management (MPA); information science (MS); information systems (PhD); information technologies (MBA); interdisciplinary studies (MA, MS); international studies (MA); international sustainable tourism (MS); jazz studies (MM); journalism (MA, MJ, Graduate Certificate), including interactive and virtual digital communication (Graduate Certificate), narrative journalism (Graduate Certificate), public relations (Graduate Certificate); kinesiology (MS); linguistics (MA); local government management (MPA); logistics (PhD); logistics and supply chain management (MBA); long-term care, senior housing, and aging services (MA); management (PhD); marketing (MBA); mathematics (MA, MS); mechanical and energy engineering (MS, PhD); music (MA), including ethnomusicology, music theory, musicology, performance; music composition (PhD); music education (MM Ed, PhD); nonprofit management (MPA); operations and supply chain management (MBA); performance (MM, DMA); philosophy (MA); political science (MA); professional and technical communication (MA); radio, television and film (MA, MFA); rehabilitation counseling (Certificate); sociology (MA); Spanish (MA); special education (M Ed); speech-language pathology (MA); strategic management (MBA); studio art (MFA); teaching (M Ed); MBA/MS. *Program availability:* Part-time, evening/weekend, online learning. Terminal master's awarded for partial completion of doctoral program. *Degree requirements:* For master's, variable foreign language requirement, comprehensive exam (for some programs), thesis (for some programs); for doctorate, variable foreign language requirement, comprehensive exam (for some programs), thesis/dissertation; for other advanced degree, variable foreign language requirement, comprehensive exam (for some programs). *Entrance requirements:* For master's and doctorate, GRE, GMAT. Additional exam requirements/recommendations for international students: Required—TOEFL (minimum score 550 paper-based; 79 iBT). Electronic applications accepted.

University of Notre Dame, Mendoza College of Business, Master of Business Administration Program, Notre Dame, IN 46556. Offers business analytics (MBA); business leadership (MBA); consulting (MBA); corporate finance (MBA); innovation and entrepreneurship (MBA); investments (MBA); marketing (MBA); MBA/MSBA. *Accreditation:* AACSB. *Faculty:* 60 full-time (10 women), 14 part-time/adjunct (1 woman). *Students:* 294 full-time (70 women); includes 46 minority (8 Black or African American, non-Hispanic/Latino; 3 American Indian or Alaska Native, non-Hispanic/Latino; 12 Asian, non-Hispanic/Latino; 20 Hispanic/Latino; 1 Native Hawaiian or other Pacific Islander, non-Hispanic/Latino; 2 Two or more races, non-Hispanic/Latino), 74 international. Average age 29. 633 applicants, 42% accepted, 131 enrolled. In 2017, 182 master's awarded. *Entrance requirements:* For master's, GMAT or GRE, work experience, essay, four-slide presentation, two recommendations, transcripts from all colleges and/or universities attended, interview. Additional exam requirements/recommendations for international students: Required—PTE (minimum score 68), TOEFL (minimum iBT score of 109), IELTS (7.5), or documentation of at least six semesters of full-time university education in English. *Application deadline:* For fall admission, 10/17 for domestic and international students; for winter admission, 1/9 for domestic and international students; for spring admission, 2/20 for domestic and international students; for summer admission, 3/17 for domestic students. Application fee: $175. Electronic applications accepted. *Expenses:* $74,133 (for one-year MBA); $106,526 (two-year MBA); $113,050 (for MBA/MSBA). *Financial support:* In 2017–18, 251 students received support, including 247 fellowships (averaging $27,748 per year); unspecified assistantships also available. Financial award application deadline: 2/28; financial award applicants required to submit FAFSA. *Faculty research:* Market microstructure; marketing and public policy; corporate finance and accounting; corporate governance and ethical behavior; high performing organizations. *Unit head:* Dr. Katherine Spiess, Associate Dean, Graduate Business Programs, 574-631-7236, E-mail: spiess.1@nd.edu. *Application contact:* Kristin McAndrew, Director of Admissions, Graduate Business Programs, 574-631-8488, E-mail: kmcandre@nd.edu. Website: http://mendoza.nd.edu/programs/mba-programs/

University of Notre Dame, Mendoza College of Business, Master of Science in Finance Program, Notre Dame, IN 46556. Offers MSF. *Faculty:* 4 full-time (2 women), 3 part-time/adjunct (0 women). *Students:* 26 full-time (6 women); includes 9 minority (2 Black or African American, non-Hispanic/Latino; 4 Asian, non-Hispanic/Latino; 3 Hispanic/Latino). Average age 30. In 2017, 40 master's awarded. *Entrance requirements:* For master's, minimum of two years' work experience and active employment. Additional exam requirements/recommendations for international students: Required—TOEFL, IELTS. *Application deadline:* For fall admission, 10/15 for domestic students; for summer admission, 7/15 for domestic students. Applications are processed on a rolling basis. Application fee: $50. Electronic applications accepted. *Expenses:* Contact institution. *Financial support:* In 2017–18, 24 students received support, including 24 fellowships (averaging $7,222 per year). Financial award application deadline: 10/15; financial award applicants required to submit FAFSA. *Unit head:* Gianna Bern, Academic Director, Master of Science in Finance, 574-631-0434, E-mail: gbern@nd.edu. *Application contact:* Kaitlyn Reeves, Admissions Coordinator, 574-631-1593, Fax: 574-631-6783, E-mail: kreeves@nd.edu.
Website: http://mendoza.nd.edu/programs/specialized-masters/ms-in-finance/

University of Oklahoma, Price College of Business, Program in Business Administration, Oklahoma City, OK 73104. Offers business administration (MBA, PhD), including accounting (PhD), business administration, entrepreneurship and economic development (PhD), finance (PhD), management and international business (PhD), management of information systems (PhD), marketing/supply chain (PhD); JD/MBA; MBA/MS. *Accreditation:* AACSB. *Program availability:* Part-time, evening/weekend. *Students:* 100 full-time (27 women), 152 part-time (30 women); includes 36 minority (2 Black or African American, non-Hispanic/Latino; 4 American Indian or Alaska Native, non-Hispanic/Latino; 10 Asian, non-Hispanic/Latino; 13 Hispanic/Latino; 7 Two or more races, non-Hispanic/Latino), 32 international. Average age 31. 247 applicants, 29% accepted, 41 enrolled. In 2017, 118 master's, 9 doctorates awarded. *Degree requirements:* For doctorate, comprehensive exam, thesis/dissertation. *Entrance requirements:* For master's, GMAT or GRE, resume, 2 essays, interview; for doctorate, GMAT or GRE, resume, statement of goals, 3 letters of recommendation. Additional exam requirements/recommendations for international students: Required—TOEFL (minimum score 100 iBT) or IELTS (minimum score 7). *Application deadline:* For fall admission, 11/1 for domestic and international students; for summer admission, 11/1 for domestic and international students. Applications are processed on a rolling basis. Application fee: $50 ($100 for international students). Electronic applications accepted. *Expenses:* Contact institution. *Financial support:* In 2017–18, 107 students received support, including 6 fellowships with partial tuition reimbursements available (averaging $2,500 per year); research assistantships with full and partial tuition reimbursements available, teaching assistantships with full and partial tuition reimbursements available, career-related internships or fieldwork, scholarships/grants, health care benefits, and unspecified assistantships also available. Support available to part-time students. Financial award application deadline: 6/1; financial award applicants required to submit FAFSA. *Faculty research:* Energy finance; international accounting; organizational behavior and entrepreneurship; management information systems; supply chain. *Unit head:* Laku Chidambaram, Associate Dean for Academic Programs and Engagement, 405-325-8013. *Application contact:* Kate Hile, Associate Director of MBA Admissions, 405-325-4572, E-mail: khile@ou.edu.
Website: http://www.ou.edu/price/divisions/graduate-programs/graduate.html

University of Oregon, Graduate School, Charles H. Lundquist College of Business, Department of Finance, Eugene, OR 97403. Offers PhD. *Program availability:* Part-time. Terminal master's awarded for partial completion of doctoral program. *Degree requirements:* For doctorate, thesis/dissertation, 2 comprehensive exams. *Entrance requirements:* For doctorate, GMAT. Additional exam requirements/recommendations for international students: Required—TOEFL. *Faculty research:* Changes in firm value in response to corporate takeovers and defenses, capital structure, regulatory changes, financial intermediaries.

University of Ottawa, Faculty of Graduate and Postdoctoral Studies, Interdisciplinary Programs, Ottawa, ON K1N 6N5, Canada. Offers e-business (Certificate); e-commerce (Certificate); finance (Certificate); health services and policies research (Diploma); population health (PhD); population health risk assessment and management (Certificate); public management and governance (Certificate); systems science (Certificate).

University of Pennsylvania, Wharton School, Finance Department, Philadelphia, PA 19104. Offers MBA, PhD. *Degree requirements:* For doctorate, thesis/dissertation. *Entrance requirements:* For doctorate, GMAT or GRE. *Faculty research:* Corporate finance, investments, macroeconomics, international finance.

University of Pittsburgh, Katz Graduate School of Business, Doctoral Program in Business Administration, Pittsburgh, PA 15260. Offers accounting (PhD); business analytics and operations (PhD); finance (PhD); information systems and technology management (PhD); marketing (PhD); organizational behavior and human resources (PhD); strategic management (PhD). *Accreditation:* AACSB. *Program availability:* Evening/weekend. *Faculty:* 91 full-time (30 women), 14 part-time/adjunct (4 women). *Students:* 51 full-time (26 women), 1 (woman) part-time; includes 5 minority (1 Black or African American, non-Hispanic/Latino; 3 Asian, non-Hispanic/Latino; 1 Two or more races, non-Hispanic/Latino), 30 international. Average age 31. 337 applicants, 3% accepted, 10 enrolled. In 2017, 7 doctorates awarded. *Degree requirements:* For doctorate, comprehensive exam, thesis/dissertation, student teaching. *Entrance requirements:* For doctorate, GMAT or GRE, 3 recommendations, statement of purpose, transcripts of all previous course work and degrees. Additional exam requirements/recommendations for international students: Required—TOEFL (minimum score 100 iBT) or IELTS (minimum score 7.0). *Application deadline:* For fall admission, 1/1 for domestic and international students. Applications are processed on a rolling basis. Application fee: $50. Electronic applications accepted. *Financial support:* In 2017–18, 43 students received support, including 33 research assistantships with full tuition reimbursements available (averaging $26,500 per year), 10 teaching assistantships with full tuition reimbursements available (averaging $28,220 per year); Federal Work-Study, scholarships/grants, health care benefits, and unspecified assistantships also available. Financial award application deadline: 1/1; financial award applicants required to submit FAFSA. *Faculty research:* Accounting systems/financial reporting, corporate finance, shopper marketing/consumer behavior, management information systems, organizational behavior and entrepreneurship. *Total annual research expenditures:* $475,077. *Unit head:* Dr. Arjang A. Assad, Dean, 412-648-1556, Fax: 412-648-1552, E-mail: aassad@katz.pitt.edu. *Application contact:* Dr. Dennis Galletta, Director, 412-648-1699, Fax: 412-648-3633, E-mail: galletta@katz.pitt.edu.
Website: http://www.katz.business.pitt.edu/degrees/phd/

See Display on page 158 and Close-Up on page 187.

University of Pittsburgh, Katz Graduate School of Business, Master of Business Administration Programs, Pittsburgh, PA 15260. Offers finance (MBA); information systems (MBA); marketing (MBA); operations (MBA); organizational behavior and human resources (MBA); strategy, environment and organizations (MBA); MBA/JD; MBA/MID; MBA/MIS; MBA/MSE. *Accreditation:* AACSB. *Program availability:* Part-time, evening/weekend, blended/hybrid learning. *Faculty:* 91 full-time (30 women), 14 part-time/adjunct (4 women). *Students:* 139 full-time (49 women), 294 part-time (94 women); includes 65 minority (27 Black or African American, non-Hispanic/Latino; 20 Asian, non-Hispanic/Latino; 11 Hispanic/Latino; 7 Two or more races, non-Hispanic/Latino), 54 international. Average age 29. 651 applicants, 44% accepted, 158 enrolled. In 2017, 217 master's awarded. *Degree requirements:* For master's, minimum GPA of 3.0. *Entrance requirements:* For master's, GMAT, GRE. Additional exam requirements/recommendations for international students: Required—TOEFL (minimum score 100 iBT) or IELTS (minimum score 7.0). *Application deadline:* For fall admission, 4/1 priority date for domestic students, 2/1 priority date for international students. Application fee: $50. Electronic applications accepted. *Financial support:* In 2017–18, 136 students received support. Scholarships/grants available. Financial award application deadline: 6/1; financial award applicants required to submit FAFSA. *Faculty research:* Accounting systems/financial reporting, corporate finance, shopper marketing/consumer behavior, management information systems, organizational behavior and entrepreneurship. *Total annual research expenditures:* $475,077. *Unit head:* Dr. Arjang A. Assad, Dean, 412-648-1556, Fax: 412-648-1552, E-mail: aassad@katz.pitt.edu. *Application contact:* Thomas Keller, Director of MBA Admissions, 412-648-1700, Fax: 412-648-1659, E-mail: mba@katz.pitt.edu.
Website: http://www.business.pitt.edu/katz/mba/

See Display on page 158 and Close-Up on page 187.

University of Pittsburgh, Katz Graduate School of Business, Master of Science in Finance Program, Pittsburgh, PA 15260. Offers MS. *Faculty:* 91 full-time (30 women), 14 part-time/adjunct (4 women). *Students:* 19 full-time (17 women), 1 (woman) part-time, 18 international. Average age 23. 293 applicants, 40% accepted, 19 enrolled. In 2017, 24 master's awarded. *Degree requirements:* For master's, minimum GPA of 3.0. *Entrance requirements:* For master's, GMAT, GRE. Additional exam requirements/recommendations for international students: Required—TOEFL (minimum score 100 iBT), IELTS (minimum score 7). *Application deadline:* For fall admission, 7/1 priority date for domestic students, 5/1 priority date for international students. Applications are processed on a rolling basis. Application fee: $50. Electronic applications accepted. *Expenses:* Contact institution. *Financial support:* Scholarships/grants available. Financial award application deadline: 6/1; financial award applicants required to submit FAFSA. *Faculty research:* Accounting systems/financial reporting, corporate finance, shopper marketing/consumer behavior, management information systems, organizational behavior and entrepreneurship. *Total annual research expenditures:* $475,077. *Unit head:* Dr. Arjang A. Assad, Dean, 412-648-1556, Fax: 412-648-1552, E-mail: aassad@katz.pitt.edu. *Application contact:* Thomas Keller, Director of MBA Admissions, 412-648-1700, Fax: 412-648-1659, E-mail: mba@katz.pitt.edu.
Website: http://www.business.pitt.edu/katz/ms-programs/finance

University of Portland, Dr. Robert B. Pamplin, Jr. School of Business, Portland, OR 97203-5798. Offers entrepreneurship (MBA); finance (MBA, MS); health care management (MBA); marketing (MBA); nonprofit management (EMBA); operations and technology management (MBA, MS); sustainability (MBA). *Accreditation:* AACSB. *Program availability:* Part-time, evening/weekend. *Entrance requirements:* For master's, GMAT, minimum GPA of 3.0, resume, 2 letters of recommendation. Additional exam requirements/recommendations for international students: Required—TOEFL (minimum score 570 paper-based; 89 iBT), IELTS (minimum score 7). *Expenses:* Contact institution.

University of Puerto Rico–Mayagüez, Graduate Studies, College of Business Administration, Mayagüez, PR 00681-9000. Offers business administration (MBA); finance (MBA); human resources (MBA); industrial management (MBA). *Program availability:* Part-time, evening/weekend. *Degree requirements:* For master's, one foreign language, comprehensive exam, thesis (for some programs). *Entrance requirements:* For master's, GMAT or EXADEP, bachelor's degree with courses in calculus, microeconomics, accounting and statistics. Additional exam requirements/recommendations for international students: Required—TOEFL (minimum score 500 paper-based), GMAT or EXADEP. Electronic applications accepted. *Faculty research:* Organizational studies, management, accounting, entrepreneurship, leadership and motivation.

University of Puerto Rico–Río Piedras, College of Business Administration, San Juan, PR 00931-3300. Offers accounting (MBA); finance (MBA, PhD); general business (MBA); human resources management (MBA); international trade and business (MBA, PhD); marketing (MBA); operations management (MBA); quantitative methods (MBA). *Accreditation:* AACSB. *Program availability:* Part-time. *Degree requirements:* For master's, comprehensive exam, thesis or alternative, research project. *Entrance requirements:* For master's, GMAT or PAEG, minimum GPA of 3.0, letter of recommendation; for doctorate, GMAT, PAEG, minimum GPA of 3.0, master degree. *Faculty research:* Management.

University of Rhode Island, Graduate School, College of Business, Program in Business Administration, Kingston, RI 02881. Offers finance (MBA); general business (MBA); management (MBA); marketing (MBA, PhD); operations and supply chain management (PhD); supply chain management (MBA); Pharm D/MBA. *Faculty:* 34 full-time (13 women). *Students:* 47 full-time (13 women), 146 part-time (72 women); includes 22 minority (3 Black or African American, non-Hispanic/Latino; 1 American Indian or Alaska Native, non-Hispanic/Latino; 11 Asian, non-Hispanic/Latino; 6 Hispanic/Latino; 1 Two or more races, non-Hispanic/Latino), 16 international. 131 applicants, 59% accepted, 58 enrolled. In 2017, 94 master's, 1 doctorate awarded. *Entrance requirements:* Additional exam requirements/recommendations for international students: Required—TOEFL. *Application deadline:* For fall admission, 6/30 for domestic students; for spring admission, 10/31 for domestic students; for summer admission, 3/31 for domestic students. Electronic applications accepted. *Expenses:* Tuition, state resident: full-time $12,706; part-time $786 per credit. Tuition, nonresident: full-time $25,216; part-time $1401 per credit. *Required fees:* $1598; $45 per credit. One-time fee: $30 part-time. *Financial support:* In 2017–18, 15 teaching assistantships (averaging $16,541 per year) were awarded. Financial award application deadline: 2/1. *Unit head:* Lisa Lancellotta, Coordinator, MBA Programs, 401-874-4241, E-mail: mba@uri.edu.

University of Rhode Island, Graduate School, College of Business, Program in Finance, Kingston, RI 02881. Offers MS, PhD. *Program availability:* Part-time, evening/weekend, blended/hybrid learning. *Faculty:* 7 full-time (2 women). *Students:* 4 part-time (0 women); includes 2 minority (1 American Indian or Alaska Native, non-Hispanic/Latino; 1 Asian, non-Hispanic/Latino). 3 applicants, 33% accepted. *Entrance requirements:* Additional exam requirements/recommendations for international students: Required—TOEFL. *Application deadline:* For fall admission, 2/1 for domestic and international students. Electronic applications accepted. *Expenses:* Tuition, state resident: full-time $12,706; part-time $786 per credit. Tuition, nonresident: full-time $25,216; part-time $1401 per credit. *Required fees:* $1598; $45 per credit. One-time fee: $30 part-time. *Financial support:* Application deadline: 2/1. *Unit head:* Dr. Bingxuan Lin, Professor/Area Coordinator for Finance, E-mail: bingxuan@uri.edu. *Application contact:* Dr. Shingo Goto, Graduate Program Director, E-mail: shingo_goto@uri.edu. Website: https://web.uri.edu/business/msf/

University of Rochester, Simon Business School, Doctoral Program in Business Administration, Rochester, NY 14627. Offers accounting (PhD); computer information systems (PhD); finance (PhD); marketing (PhD); operations management (PhD). *Accreditation:* AACSB. *Faculty:* 70 full-time (12 women), 23 part-time/adjunct (6 women). *Students:* 50 full-time (17 women); includes 2 minority (both Asian, non-Hispanic/Latino), 41 international. Average age 28. 199 applicants, 10% accepted, 9 enrolled. In 2017, 8 doctorates awarded. *Degree requirements:* For doctorate, comprehensive exam, thesis/dissertation, qualifying exam. *Entrance requirements:* For doctorate, GMAT or GRE. Additional exam requirements/recommendations for international students: Required—TOEFL. *Application deadline:* For fall admission, 1/5 for domestic and international students. Application fee: $100. Electronic applications accepted. *Expenses:* Contact institution. *Financial support:* In 2017–18, 50 students received support. Fellowships, research assistantships, teaching assistantships, health care benefits, and tuition waivers (full) available. Financial award application deadline: 1/5. *Faculty research:* Empirical industrial organization, risk management, financial disclosure and regulation, social media, health care management. *Unit head:* Dr. Ron Kaniel, Committee Chair, 585-275-2959. *Application contact:* Sue Harris, PhD Administrator, 585-275-2959, E-mail: phdoffice@simon.rochester.edu. Website: http://www.simon.rochester.edu/programs/phd/index.aspx

University of Rochester, Simon Business School, Full-Time Master's Program in Business Administration, Rochester, NY 14627. Offers business systems consulting (MBA); competitive and organizational strategy (MBA); computers and information systems (MBA); corporate accounting (MBA); entrepreneurship (MBA); finance (MBA); health sciences management (MBA); marketing (MBA); operations management (MBA); public accounting (MBA); strategy and organizations (MBA). *Accreditation:* AACSB. *Faculty:* 70 full-time (12 women), 23 part-time/adjunct (6 women). *Students:* 208 full-time (70 women). Average age 28. *Entrance requirements:* For master's, GMAT or GRE. *Application deadline:* For fall admission, 10/15 for domestic and international students; for winter admission, 1/5 for domestic and international students; for spring admission, 3/15 for domestic and international students; for summer admission, 5/15 for domestic and international students. Application fee: $150. *Financial support:* Fellowships, institutionally sponsored loans, scholarships/grants, and tuition waivers (full and partial) available. Financial award application deadline: 1/5; financial award applicants required to submit FAFSA. *Faculty research:* Empirical industrial organization, risk management, financial disclosure and regulation, social media, health care management. *Unit head:* Andrew Ainslie, Dean, 585-275-3316, E-mail: andrew.ainslie@simon.rochester.edu. *Application contact:* Rebekah S. Lewin, Assistant Dean of Admissions and Financial Aid, 585-275-3533, E-mail: admissions@simon.rochester.edu. Website: http://www.simon.rochester.edu/programs/full-time-mba/index.aspx

University of Rochester, Simon Business School, Master of Science Program in Finance, Rochester, NY 14627. Offers MS. *Faculty:* 70 full-time (12 women), 23 part-time/adjunct (6 women). *Students:* 177 full-time (87 women). Average age 22. *Entrance requirements:* For master's, GMAT or GRE. *Application deadline:* For fall admission, 10/15 for domestic and international students; for winter admission, 1/5 for domestic and international students; for spring admission, 3/15 for domestic and international students; for summer admission, 5/15 for domestic and international students. Application fee: $150. *Financial support:* Scholarships/grants available. Financial award application deadline: 1/1. *Unit head:* Andrew Ainslie, Dean, 585-275-3316, E-mail: andrew.ainslie@simon.rochester.edu. *Application contact:* Rebekah S. Lewin, Assistant Dean of Admissions and Financial Aid, 585-275-3533, E-mail: admissions@simon.rochester.edu. Website: http://www.simon.rochester.edu/programs/full-time-ms-in-finance/index.aspx

University of Rochester, Simon Business School, Part-Time MBA Program, Rochester, NY 14627. Offers business systems consulting (MBA); competitive and organizational strategy (MBA); computers and information systems (MBA); corporate accounting (MBA); entrepreneurship (MBA); finance (MBA); health sciences management (MBA); marketing (MBA), including brand management, marketing strategy, pricing; operations management (MBA); public accounting (MBA). *Program availability:* Part-time-only, evening/weekend. *Faculty:* 70 full-time (12 women), 23 part-time/adjunct (6 women). *Students:* 159 part-time (62 women); includes 25 minority (5 Black or African American, non-Hispanic/Latino; 9 Asian, non-Hispanic/Latino; 9 Hispanic/Latino; 2 Two or more races, non-Hispanic/Latino), 4 international. Average age 32. 39 applicants, 92% accepted, 35 enrolled. In 2017, 59 master's awarded. *Entrance requirements:* For master's, GRE or GMAT. *Application deadline:* For fall admission, 8/1 for domestic students; for spring admission, 2/15 for domestic students. Applications are processed on a rolling basis. Application fee: $150. Electronic applications accepted. *Expenses:* $1,875 per credit, $1,385 fees. *Financial support:* In 2017–18, 69 students received support. Tuition waivers (partial) available. Financial award application deadline: 8/1. *Unit head:* Andrew Ainslie, Dean, 585-275-3316, E-mail: andrew.ainslie@simon.rochester.edu. *Application contact:* Molly Mesko, Executive Director, EMBA and Part-Time Programs, 585-275-4277, E-mail: molly.mesko@simon.rochester.edu. Website: http://www.simon.rochester.edu/programs/ptmba/index.aspx

University of Saint Mary, Graduate Programs, Program in Business Administration, Leavenworth, KS 66048-5082. Offers enterprise risk management (MBA); finance (MBA); general management (MBA); health care management (MBA); human resource management (MBA); marketing and advertising management (MBA). *Program availability:* Part-time, evening/weekend, 100% online, blended/hybrid learning. *Degree requirements:* For master's, thesis. *Entrance requirements:* For master's, minimum undergraduate GPA of 2.75, official transcripts, two letters of recommendation. Electronic applications accepted. *Expenses:* Contact institution.

University of St. Thomas, Cameron School of Business, Houston, TX 77006-4696. Offers MBA, MCTM, MIB, MSA, MSF. *Program availability:* Part-time, evening/weekend. *Faculty:* 26 full-time (10 women), 7 part-time/adjunct (1 woman). *Students:* 136 full-time (73 women), 200 part-time (113 women); includes 155 minority (41 Black or African American, non-Hispanic/Latino; 1 American Indian or Alaska Native, non-Hispanic/Latino; 24 Asian, non-Hispanic/Latino; 81 Hispanic/Latino; 8 Two or more races, non-Hispanic/Latino), 99 international. Average age 31. 121 applicants, 97% accepted, 70 enrolled. In 2017, 186 master's awarded. *Degree requirements:* For master's, capstone (for some programs), additional course requirements for those sitting for state accountancy exam. *Entrance requirements:* For master's, minimum GPA of 2.5, 3 letters of recommendation. Additional exam requirements/recommendations for international students: Required—TOEFL (minimum score 550 paper-based; 79 iBT), IELTS (minimum score 6.5), PTE (minimum score 53). *Application deadline:* For fall admission, 7/15 for domestic and international students; for winter admission, 7/15 for domestic and international students; for spring admission, 11/15 for domestic students, 10/15 for international students. Applications are processed on a rolling basis. Application fee: $35. Electronic applications accepted. *Expenses:* Tuition: Full-time $20,934; part-time $1163 per credit hour. *Required fees:* $250; $210 per semester. *Financial support:* In 2017–18, 22 students received support, including research assistantships with partial tuition reimbursements available (averaging $3,000 per year); Federal Work-Study, scholarships/grants, unspecified assistantships, and state work-study, institutional employment also available. Support available to part-time students. Financial award application deadline: 4/15; financial award applicants required to submit FAFSA. *Unit head:* Dr. Beena George, Dean, 713-525-2100, Fax: 713-525-2110, E-mail: cameron@stthom.edu. *Application contact:* 713-525-2100, Fax: 713-525-2110, E-mail: cameron@stthom.edu. Website: http://www.stthom.edu/Academics/Cameron_School_of_Business/Index.aqf

University of San Diego, School of Business, Program in Finance, San Diego, CA 92110-2492. Offers MSF. *Program availability:* Part-time, evening/weekend. *Students:* 49 full-time (20 women); includes 11 minority (3 Asian, non-Hispanic/Latino; 7 Hispanic/Latino; 1 Two or more races, non-Hispanic/Latino), 35 international. Average age 25. In 2017, 29 master's awarded. *Entrance requirements:* For master's, GMAT (minimum score of 560), minimum GPA of 3.0. Additional exam requirements/recommendations for international students: Required—TOEFL (minimum score 92 iBT), IELTS (minimum score 7). *Application deadline:* For fall admission, 7/1 for domestic students, 5/1 for international students. Applications are processed on a rolling basis. Application fee: $80. Electronic applications accepted. *Financial support:* In 2017–18, 1 student received support. Career-related internships or fieldwork, Federal Work-Study, institutionally sponsored loans, scholarships/grants, and unspecified assistantships available. Support available to part-time students. Financial award application deadline: 4/1; financial award applicants required to submit FAFSA. *Faculty research:* Asset pricing, mergers and acquisitions, option implied volatility, corporate governance, payout policy. *Unit head:* Dr. Marko Svetina, Academic Director, Finance Program, 619-260-7586, E-mail: msf@sandiego.edu. *Application contact:* Monica Mahon, Associate Director of Graduate Admissions, 619-260-4524, Fax: 619-260-4158, E-mail: grads@sandiego.edu. Website: http://www.sandiego.edu/business/graduate/ms-finance/

University of San Francisco, School of Management, Master of Business Administration Program, San Francisco, CA 94117. Offers entrepreneurship and innovation (MBA); finance (MBA); marketing (MBA); organization development (MBA); DDS/MBA; JD/MBA; MBA/MAPS. *Accreditation:* AACSB. *Program availability:* Part-time, evening/weekend. *Entrance requirements:* For master's, GMAT or GRE, resume (two years of professional work experience required for part-time students, preferred for full-time), transcripts from each college or university attended, two letters of recommendation, personal statement, interview. Additional exam requirements/recommendations for international students: Required—TOEFL (minimum score 600 paper-based, 100 iBT), IELTS (minimum score 7) or PTE (minimum score 68). Electronic applications accepted. *Expenses:* Contact institution. *Faculty research:* International financial markets, technology transfer licensing, international marketing, strategic planning.

University of San Francisco, School of Management, Master of Science in Financial Analysis Program, San Francisco, CA 94117. Offers MSFA, MS/MBA. *Program availability:* Part-time, evening/weekend. *Entrance requirements:* For master's, GMAT or GRE, resume (minimum of two years of professional work experience for working professionals format), transcripts from each college or university attended showing completion of required foundation courses, two letters of recommendation, personal statement. Additional exam requirements/recommendations for international students: Required—TOEFL (minimum score 600 paper-based, 100 iBT), IELTS (minimum score 7) or PTE (minimum score 68). Electronic applications accepted. *Expenses:* Contact institution.

University of Saskatchewan, College of Graduate Studies and Research, Edwards School of Business, Department of Finance and Management Science, Saskatoon, SK S7N 5A2, Canada. Offers finance (M Sc). *Program availability:* Part-time. *Degree requirements:* For master's, thesis. *Entrance requirements:* For master's, GMAT. Additional exam requirements/recommendations for international students: Required—TOEFL.

The University of Scranton, Kania School of Management, Program in Business Administration, Scranton, PA 18510. Offers accounting (MBA); finance (MBA); general business administration (MBA); health care management (MBA); international business (MBA); management information systems (MBA); marketing (MBA); operations management (MBA). *Accreditation:* AACSB. *Program availability:* Part-time, evening/weekend, 100% online. *Entrance requirements:* For master's, GMAT (for MBA). *Faculty research:* Financial markets, strategic impact of total quality management, internal accounting controls, consumer preference, information systems and the Internet.

University of Southern Maine, College of Management and Human Service, School of Business, Portland, ME 04104-9300. Offers accounting (MBA); business administration (MBA); finance (MBA); health management and policy (MBA); sustainability (MBA); JD/MBA; MBA/MSA; MBA/MSN; MS/MBA. *Accreditation:* AACSB. *Program availability:* Part-time, evening/weekend. *Entrance requirements:* For master's, GMAT or GRE, minimum AACSB index of 1100. Additional exam requirements/recommendations for international students: Required—TOEFL (minimum score 550 paper-based; 79 iBT). Electronic applications accepted. *Faculty research:* Economic development, management information systems, real options, system dynamics, simulation.

Finance and Banking

University of South Florida, Muma College of Business, Department of Finance, Tampa, FL 33620-9951. Offers business administration (PhD), including finance; finance (MS); real estate (MSRE). *Program availability:* Part-time, evening/weekend. *Faculty:* 14 full-time (3 women). *Students:* 99 full-time (30 women), 26 part-time (13 women); includes 8 minority (4 Asian, non-Hispanic/Latino; 4 Hispanic/Latino), 94 international. Average age 25. 142 applicants, 58% accepted, 57 enrolled. In 2017, 57 master's, 1 doctorate awarded. Terminal master's awarded for partial completion of doctoral program. *Degree requirements:* For master's, comprehensive exam, thesis or alternative; for doctorate, comprehensive exam, thesis/dissertation. *Entrance requirements:* For master's, GMAT, minimum undergraduate GPA of 3.0 in upper-division coursework; for doctorate, GMAT or GRE, minimum undergraduate GPA of 3.0 in upper-division coursework, personal statement, recommendations, interview. Additional exam requirements/recommendations for international students: Required—TOEFL (minimum score 550 paper-based; 79 iBT) or IELTS (minimum score 6.5). *Application deadline:* For fall admission, 6/1 for domestic students, 1/2 for international students; for spring admission, 10/15 for domestic students, 7/1 for international students; for summer admission, 2/15 for domestic students, 1/1 for international students. Application fee: $30. Electronic applications accepted. *Financial support:* In 2017–18, 16 students received support, including 8 research assistantships (averaging $14,357 per year), 9 teaching assistantships with tuition reimbursements available (averaging $11,972 per year); scholarships/grants, health care benefits, and unspecified assistantships also available. Financial award application deadline: 6/30. *Faculty research:* International corporate finance, corporate finance, market efficiency, mergers and acquisitions, agency theory, corporate governance, investments, mutual fund industry, mergers and acquisitions, corporate creditworthiness, credit risk issues, empirical asset pricing, financial intermediation, corporate finance theory, public offerings, business strategy. *Unit head:* Dr. Scott Besley, Chairperson and Associate Professor, 813-974-6341, Fax: 813-974-3084, E-mail: sbesley@usf.edu. *Application contact:* Yuting DiGiovanni, 813-974-6358, Fax: 813-974-3084, E-mail: yuting2@usf.edu.
Website: http://business.usf.edu/departments/finance/

The University of Tampa, Sykes College of Business, Tampa, FL 33606-1490. Offers accounting (MS); business analytics (MBA); cybersecurity (MBA, MS); entrepreneurship (MBA, MS); finance (MBA, MS); information systems management (MBA); innovation management (MBA); international business (MBA); marketing (MBA, MS); nonprofit management (MBA, Certificate). *Accreditation:* AACSB. *Program availability:* Part-time, evening/weekend. *Faculty:* 38 full-time (14 women), 6 part-time/adjunct (1 woman). *Students:* 229 full-time (1 woman), 115 part-time (51 women); includes 51 minority (26 Black or African American, non-Hispanic/Latino; 11 Asian, non-Hispanic/Latino; 1 Native Hawaiian or other Pacific Islander, non-Hispanic/Latino; 13 Two or more races, non-Hispanic/Latino), 182 international. Average age 28. 1,305 applicants, 39% accepted, 192 enrolled. In 2017, 266 master's awarded. *Degree requirements:* For master's, capstone. *Entrance requirements:* For master's, GMAT or GRE, official transcripts from all colleges and/or universities previously attended, resume, personal statement, letters of recommendation. Additional exam requirements/recommendations for international students: Required—TOEFL (minimum score 577 paper-based; 90 iBT), IELTS (minimum score 7.5). *Application deadline:* Applications are processed on a rolling basis. Application fee: $40. Electronic applications accepted. *Expenses:* Contact institution. *Financial support:* In 2017–18, 116 students received support. Career-related internships or fieldwork, scholarships/grants, and unspecified assistantships available. Financial award applicants required to submit FAFSA. *Faculty research:* Job market signaling, on-line shopping behaviors and social media, the Tampa Bay economy, digital literacy, entrepreneurship in small businesses. *Unit head:* Dr. Natasha F. Veltri, Associate Dean, 813-253-6289, E-mail: nveltri@ut.edu. *Application contact:* Chanelle Cox, Staff Assistant, Admissions for Graduate and Continuing Studies, 813-253-6249, E-mail: ccox@ut.edu.
Website: http://www.ut.edu/business/

The University of Tennessee, Graduate School, College of Business Administration, Program in Business Administration, Knoxville, TN 37996. Offers accounting (PhD); finance (MBA, PhD); logistics and transportation (MBA, PhD); management (PhD); marketing (MBA, PhD); operations management (MBA); professional business administration (MBA); statistics (PhD); JD/MBA; MS/MBA; Pharm D/MBA. Pharm D/MBA offered jointly with The University of Tennessee Health Science Center. *Accreditation:* AACSB. *Program availability:* Online learning. *Degree requirements:* For master's, thesis or alternative; for doctorate, thesis/dissertation. *Entrance requirements:* For master's and doctorate, GMAT, minimum GPA of 2.7. Additional exam requirements/recommendations for international students: Required—TOEFL. Electronic applications accepted.

The University of Tennessee at Martin, Graduate Programs, College of Business and Global Affairs, Program in Business, Martin, TN 38238. Offers agricultural business (MBA); financial services (MBA); general business (MBA). *Accreditation:* AACSB. *Program availability:* Part-time, online only, 100% online, blended/hybrid learning. *Faculty:* 31. *Students:* 12 full-time (5 women), 73 part-time (31 women); includes 12 minority (7 Black or African American, non-Hispanic/Latino; 2 Asian, non-Hispanic/Latino; 2 Hispanic/Latino; 1 Two or more races, non-Hispanic/Latino). Average age 34. 33 applicants, 24% accepted, 6 enrolled. In 2017, 38 master's awarded. *Degree requirements:* For master's, comprehensive exam. *Entrance requirements:* For master's, GMAT, GRE, minimum GPA of 2.5, resume. Additional exam requirements/recommendations for international students: Required—TOEFL (minimum score 525 paper-based; 71 iBT). *Application deadline:* For fall admission, 7/27 priority date for domestic students, 7/27 for international students; for spring admission, 12/17 priority date for domestic students, 12/17 for international students; for summer admission, 5/10 priority date for domestic and international students. Applications are processed on a rolling basis. Application fee: $30 ($130 for international students). Electronic applications accepted. *Expenses:* Tuition, state resident: full-time $8658; part-time $481 per credit hour. Tuition, nonresident: full-time $14,418; part-time $801 per credit hour. *International tuition:* $22,602 full-time. *Required fees:* $1404; $79 per credit hour. Part-time tuition and fees vary according to course load. *Financial support:* In 2017–18, 29 students received support, including 4 research assistantships with full tuition reimbursements available (averaging $7,226 per year), 2 teaching assistantships with full tuition reimbursements available (averaging $7,540 per year); scholarships/grants and tuition waivers (full and partial) also available. Financial award application deadline: 2/1; financial award applicants required to submit FAFSA. *Unit head:* Dr. Ashley Kilburn, Coordinator, 731-881-7245, Fax: 731-881-7231, E-mail: mba@utm.edu. *Application contact:* Jolene L. Cunningham, Student Services Specialist, 731-881-7012, Fax: 731-881-7499, E-mail: jcunningham@utm.edu.

The University of Texas at Arlington, Graduate School, College of Business, Department of Finance and Real Estate, Arlington, TX 76019. Offers finance (PhD); quantitative finance (MS); real estate (MS). *Program availability:* Part-time, evening/weekend. *Degree requirements:* For master's, thesis optional; for doctorate, comprehensive exam, thesis/dissertation. *Entrance requirements:* For master's, GMAT/GRE, minimum GPA of 3.0; for doctorate, GMAT/GRE. Additional exam requirements/recommendations for international students: Required—TOEFL (minimum score 550 paper-based; 79 iBT).

The University of Texas at Austin, Graduate School, McCombs School of Business, Department of Finance, Austin, TX 78712-1111. Offers MSF, PhD. *Entrance requirements:* For doctorate, GMAT or GRE. Electronic applications accepted.

The University of Texas at Dallas, Naveen Jindal School of Management, Program in Finance and Managerial Economics, Richardson, TX 75080. Offers finance (MS), including energy risk management, enterprise risk management, real estate, risk management insurance. *Program availability:* Part-time, evening/weekend. *Faculty:* 27 full-time (2 women), 10 part-time/adjunct (4 women). *Students:* 291 full-time (103 women), 80 part-time (33 women); includes 64 minority (7 Black or African American, non-Hispanic/Latino; 32 Asian, non-Hispanic/Latino; 17 Hispanic/Latino; 8 Two or more races, non-Hispanic/Latino), 227 international. Average age 26. 717 applicants, 48% accepted, 140 enrolled. In 2017, 190 master's awarded. *Entrance requirements:* For master's, GMAT or GRE. Additional exam requirements/recommendations for international students: Required—TOEFL (minimum score 550 paper-based). *Application deadline:* For fall admission, 7/15 for domestic students, 5/1 priority date for international students; for spring admission, 11/15 for domestic students, 9/1 priority date for international students. Applications are processed on a rolling basis. Application fee: $50 ($100 for international students). Electronic applications accepted. *Expenses:* Tuition, state resident: full-time $12,916; part-time $718 per credit hour. Tuition, nonresident: full-time $25,252; part-time $1403 per credit hour. *Financial support:* In 2017–18, 96 students received support, including 8 teaching assistantships with partial tuition reimbursements available (averaging $10,050 per year); research assistantships with partial tuition reimbursements available, career-related internships or fieldwork, Federal Work-Study, institutionally sponsored loans, scholarships/grants, and unspecified assistantships also available. Support available to part-time students. Financial award application deadline: 4/30; financial award applicants required to submit FAFSA. *Faculty research:* Econometrics, industrial organization, auction theory, file-sharing copyrights and bundling, international financial management, entrepreneurial finance. *Unit head:* Dr. Vikram Nanda, Area Coordinator, 972-883-5004, E-mail: vikram.nanda@utdallas.edu.
Website: http://jindal.utdallas.edu/finance

The University of Texas at San Antonio, College of Business, Department of Finance, San Antonio, TX 78249-0617. Offers MBA, MS, PhD. *Program availability:* Part-time, evening/weekend. *Faculty:* 9 full-time (0 women), 2 part-time/adjunct (0 women). *Students:* 36 full-time (9 women), 68 part-time (17 women); includes 45 minority (4 Black or African American, non-Hispanic/Latino; 2 Asian, non-Hispanic/Latino; 38 Hispanic/Latino; 1 Two or more races, non-Hispanic/Latino), 12 international. Average age 29. 96 applicants, 60% accepted, 38 enrolled. In 2017, 32 master's awarded. *Degree requirements:* For master's, comprehensive exam, thesis or alternative, 33 semester credit hours to be taken from a specified list of courses; for doctorate, comprehensive exam, thesis/dissertation. *Entrance requirements:* For master's and doctorate, GMAT or GRE, statement of purpose; 3 letters of recommendation. Additional exam requirements/recommendations for international students: Required—TOEFL (minimum score 550 paper-based; 79 iBT), IELTS (minimum score 6.5). *Application deadline:* For fall admission, 7/31 for domestic students, 3/1 for international students; for spring admission, 10/15 for domestic students, 9/15 for international students. Applications are processed on a rolling basis. Application fee: $50 ($90 for international students). Electronic applications accepted. *Expenses:* Tuition, state resident: full-time $5495. Tuition, nonresident: full-time $21,938. *Required fees:* $1915. Tuition and fees vary according to program. *Financial support:* Research assistantships and teaching assistantships available. *Faculty research:* Corporate finance, international finance, options and futures, market microstructure, financial institutions. *Total annual research expenditures:* $70,629. *Unit head:* Dr. Karan Bhanot, Chair, 210-458-6315, E-mail: karan.bhanot@utsa.edu. *Application contact:* Monica Rodriguez, Director of Graduate Admissions, 210-458-4331, Fax: 210-458-4332, E-mail: graduate.admissions@utsa.edu.
Website: https://business.utsa.edu/finance/

The University of Texas Rio Grande Valley, Robert C. Vackar College of Business and Entrepreneurship, Program in Business Administration, Edinburg, TX 78539. Offers business administration (MBA); finance (PhD); management (PhD); marketing (PhD). *Program availability:* Part-time, evening/weekend, online learning. *Degree requirements:* For master's, thesis optional. *Entrance requirements:* For master's, GMAT, minimum GPA of 3.0. Additional exam requirements/recommendations for international students: Required—TOEFL (minimum score 500 paper-based). Electronic applications accepted. *Expenses:* Tuition, state resident: full-time $5550; part-time $417 per credit hour. Tuition, nonresident: full-time $13,020; part-time $832 per credit hour. *Required fees:* $1169. *Faculty research:* Human resources, border region, entrepreneurship, marketing.

University of the West, Department of Business Administration, Rosemead, CA 91770. Offers business administration (EMBA); computer information systems (MBA); finance (MBA); international business (MBA); nonprofit organization management (MBA). *Program availability:* Part-time, evening/weekend. *Entrance requirements:* Additional exam requirements/recommendations for international students: Required—TOEFL.

The University of Toledo, College of Graduate Studies, College of Business and Innovation, Department of Finance, Toledo, OH 43606-3390. Offers MBA. *Program availability:* Part-time, evening/weekend. *Entrance requirements:* For master's, GMAT, GRE, or LSAT, minimum GPA of 2.7 for all prior academic work, three letters of recommendation, statement of purpose, transcripts from all prior institutions attended. Additional exam requirements/recommendations for international students: Required—TOEFL (minimum score 550 paper-based; 80 iBT). Electronic applications accepted. *Faculty research:* Financial management, banking, international finance, investments.

University of Toronto, School of Graduate Studies, Faculty of Arts and Science, Department of Economics, Program in Financial Economics, Toronto, ON M5S 1A1, Canada. Offers MFE. *Entrance requirements:* Additional exam requirements/recommendations for international students: Required—TOEFL (minimum score 102 iBT), TWE. Electronic applications accepted.

The University of Tulsa, Graduate School, Collins College of Business, Finance/Applied Mathematics Program, Tulsa, OK 74104-3189. Offers MS/MS. *Program availability:* Part-time. *Students:* 1 full-time (0 women); minority (Asian, non-Hispanic/Latino). Average age 29. 5 applicants. *Entrance requirements:* Additional exam requirements/recommendations for international students: Required—TOEFL (minimum score 577 paper-based; 91 iBT), IELTS (minimum score 6.5). *Application deadline:* Applications are processed on a rolling basis. Application fee: $55. Electronic applications accepted. *Expenses:* Tuition: Full-time $22,230. *Required fees:* $2000. Tuition and fees vary according to course load and program. *Financial support:* In 2017–18, 1 student received support, including 1 teaching assistantship with full tuition reimbursement available (averaging $6,705 per year); fellowships, career-related internships or fieldwork, Federal Work-Study, institutionally sponsored loans, scholarships/grants, health care benefits, tuition waivers (full and partial), and unspecified assistantships also available. Support available to part-time students. Financial award application deadline: 2/1; financial award applicants required to submit FAFSA. *Unit head:* Dr. Ralph Jackson, Associate Dean, 918-631-2242, Fax: 918-631-2142, E-mail: ralph-jackson@utulsa.edu. *Application contact:* Information Contact, 918-631-2242, E-mail: graduate-business@utulsa.edu.

The University of Tulsa, Graduate School, Collins College of Business, MBA/MS Program in Finance, Tulsa, OK 74104-3189. Offers MBA/MS. *Program availability:* Part-time, evening/weekend. *Students:* 2 full-time (1 woman); includes 1 minority (Two or more races, non-Hispanic/Latino), 1 international. Average age 24. 11 applicants, 18% accepted. *Entrance requirements:* Additional exam requirements/recommendations for international students: Required—TOEFL (minimum score 577 paper-based; 91 iBT), IELTS (minimum score 6.5). *Application deadline:* Applications are processed on a rolling basis. Application fee: $55. Electronic applications accepted. *Expenses:* Tuition: Full-time $22,230. *Required fees:* $2000. Tuition and fees vary according to course load and program. *Financial support:* In 2017–18, teaching assistantships with full tuition reimbursements (averaging $13,410 per year) were awarded; fellowships, career-related internships or fieldwork, Federal Work-Study, institutionally sponsored loans, scholarships/grants, health care benefits, tuition waivers (full and partial), and unspecified assistantships also available. Support available to part-time students. Financial award application deadline: 2/1. *Unit head:* Dr. Ralph Jackson, Associate Dean, 918-631-2242, Fax: 918-631-2142, E-mail: ralph-jackson@utulsa.edu. *Application contact:* Information Contact, 918-631-2242, E-mail: graduate-business@utulsa.edu.
Website: http://business.utulsa.edu/academics/graduate-business/

The University of Tulsa, Graduate School, Collins College of Business, Program in Finance, Tulsa, OK 74104-3189. Offers corporate finance (MS); risk management (MS); JD/MSF; MBA/MSF; MSF/MSAM. *Program availability:* Part-time, evening/weekend. *Faculty:* 9 full-time (1 woman). *Students:* 4 full-time (1 woman), 2 part-time (0 women); includes 2 minority (both Asian, non-Hispanic/Latino). Average age 26. 61 applicants, 44% accepted, 3 enrolled. In 2017, 7 master's awarded. *Degree requirements:* For master's, thesis optional. *Entrance requirements:* For master's, GMAT. Additional exam requirements/recommendations for international students: Required—TOEFL (minimum score 577 paper-based; 91 iBT), IELTS (minimum score 6.5). *Application deadline:* Applications are processed on a rolling basis. Application fee: $55. Electronic applications accepted. *Expenses:* Tuition: Full-time $22,230. *Required fees:* $2000. Tuition and fees vary according to course load and program. *Financial support:* In 2017–18, 3 students received support, including 3 teaching assistantships with full tuition reimbursements available (averaging $10,347 per year); fellowships with full tuition reimbursements available, research assistantships with tuition reimbursements available, career-related internships or fieldwork, Federal Work-Study, institutionally sponsored loans, scholarships/grants, health care benefits, tuition waivers (full and partial), and unspecified assistantships also available. Support available to part-time students. Financial award application deadline: 2/1; financial award applicants required to submit FAFSA. *Unit head:* Dr. Ralph Jackson, Associate Dean, 918-631-2242, Fax: 918-631-2142, E-mail: ralph-jackson@utulsa.edu. *Application contact:* Information Contact, 918-631-2242, E-mail: graduate-business@utulsa.edu.

University of Utah, Graduate School, David Eccles School of Business, Business Administration Program, Salt Lake City, UT 84112. Offers accounting (PhD); business administration (EMBA, MBA, PMBA); finance (PhD); information systems (PhD); marketing (PhD); operations management (PhD); organizational behavior (PhD); strategic management (PhD); MBA/JD; MBA/MHA; MBA/MS. *Program availability:* Part-time, evening/weekend, online learning. *Faculty:* 58 full-time (21 women), 37 part-time/adjunct (7 women). *Students:* 558 full-time (149 women), 103 part-time (21 women); includes 66 minority (1 Black or African American, non-Hispanic/Latino; 16 Asian, non-Hispanic/Latino; 41 Hispanic/Latino; 8 Two or more races, non-Hispanic/Latino), 50 international. Average age 27. 442 applicants, 70% accepted, 226 enrolled. In 2017, 298 master's, 7 doctorates awarded. *Entrance requirements:* For master's, GMAT or GRE; for doctorate, GMAT. Additional exam requirements/recommendations for international students: Required—TOEFL (minimum score 600 paper-based; 100 iBT), IELTS (minimum score 7). *Application deadline:* Applications are processed on a rolling basis. Application fee: $55 ($65 for international students). Electronic applications accepted. *Expenses:* Contact institution. *Financial support:* In 2017–18, 53 students received support. Fellowships, scholarships/grants, and unspecified assistantships available. Financial award application deadline: 2/1; financial award applicants required to submit FAFSA. *Faculty research:* Corporate finance, strategy services, consumer behavior, financial disclosures, operations. *Unit head:* Kristina Diekmann, Department Chair, 801-581-8524, Fax: 801-531-3380, E-mail: mastersinfo@business.utah.edu. *Application contact:* Christine Harris, Coordinator, 801-581-7785, Fax: 801-585-3962, E-mail: execch@business.utah.edu.
Website: http://www.business.utah.edu/

University of Utah, Graduate School, David Eccles School of Business, Master of Science in Finance Program, Salt Lake City, UT 84112. Offers MSF, MSF/MSBA, MSF/PMBA. *Program availability:* Part-time. *Faculty:* 20 full-time (4 women), 24 part-time/adjunct (2 women). *Students:* 84 full-time (23 women), 82 part-time (14 women); includes 53 minority (1 Black or African American, non-Hispanic/Latino; 1 American Indian or Alaska Native, non-Hispanic/Latino; 40 Asian, non-Hispanic/Latino; 9 Hispanic/Latino; 2 Native Hawaiian or other Pacific Islander, non-Hispanic/Latino), 43 international. Average age 26. 135 applicants, 94% accepted, 85 enrolled. In 2017, 95 master's awarded. *Degree requirements:* For master's, comprehensive exam. *Entrance requirements:* For master's, GMAT or GRE, minimum undergraduate GPA of 3.0. Additional exam requirements/recommendations for international students: Required—TOEFL (minimum score 90 iBT), IELTS (minimum score 6.5). *Application deadline:* For fall admission, 7/28 for domestic students, 4/1 for international students; for winter admission, 12/7 for domestic students, 10/1 for international students. Applications are processed on a rolling basis. Application fee: $53 ($24 for international students). Electronic applications accepted. *Expenses:* Contact institution. *Financial support:* In 2017–18, 77 students received support, including 77 fellowships with partial tuition reimbursements available (averaging $7,771 per year); tuition waivers (partial) and unspecified assistantships also available. Financial award application deadline: 4/15; financial award applicants required to submit FAFSA. *Faculty research:* Investment, corporate finance, risk management, financial analysis, venture capital. *Total annual research expenditures:* $43,423. *Unit head:* Danny Wall, Director, 801-581-8903, E-mail: danny.wall@eccles.utah.edu. *Application contact:* Regina Mavis, Admissions Coordinator, 801-585-0005, E-mail: regina.mavis@eccles.utah.edu.
Website: http://msf.eccles.utah.edu/

University of Virginia, McIntire School of Commerce, Master's Program in Commerce, Charlottesville, VA 22903. Offers business analytics (MSC); finance (MSC); marketing and management (MSC). *Entrance requirements:* For master's, GMAT, 2 letters of recommendation; prerequisite course work in financial accounting, microeconomics, and introduction to statistics. Additional exam requirements/recommendations for international students: Required—TOEFL (minimum score 600 paper-based; 100 iBT), IELTS (minimum score 7.5). Electronic applications accepted. *Expenses:* Contact institution.

University of Washington, Tacoma, Graduate Programs, MBA Programs, Tacoma, WA 98402-3100. Offers accounting (MBA); business administration (MBA); certified financial analyst (MBA). *Accreditation:* AACSB. *Program availability:* Part-time, evening/weekend. *Entrance requirements:* For master's, GMAT, minimum GPA of 3.0 in final graded 90 quarter credits or 60 graded semester credits; at least 2 years of professional/

management work experience. Additional exam requirements/recommendations for international students: Required—TOEFL (minimum score 580 paper-based; 92 iBT). Electronic applications accepted. *Expenses:* Contact institution. *Faculty research:* International accounting, marketing, change management, investments, corporate social responsibility.

University of Waterloo, Graduate Studies, Faculty of Arts, School of Accounting and Finance, Waterloo, ON N2L 3G1, Canada. Offers accounting (M Acc, PhD); finance (M Acc); taxation (M Tax). *Degree requirements:* For master's, thesis or alternative; for doctorate, thesis/dissertation. *Entrance requirements:* For master's, honors degree, minimum B average, resume; for doctorate, GMAT, master's degree, minimum A-average, resume. Additional exam requirements/recommendations for international students: Required—TOEFL, IELTS, PTE. Electronic applications accepted. *Expenses:* Contact institution. *Faculty research:* Auditing, management accounting.

The University of West Alabama, School of Graduate Studies, College of Business and Technology, Livingston, AL 35470. Offers finance (MBA); general business (MBA). *Program availability:* Part-time, evening/weekend, 100% online. *Faculty:* 2 full-time (1 woman), 9 part-time/adjunct (7 women). *Students:* 106 (73 women); includes 62 minority (57 Black or African American, non-Hispanic/Latino; 3 Hispanic/Latino; 2 Two or more races, non-Hispanic/Latino). Average age 30. 52 applicants, 98% accepted, 43 enrolled. In 2017, 9 master's awarded. *Degree requirements:* For master's, project or six additional hours in emphasis area and comprehensive examination. *Entrance requirements:* For master's, bachelor's degree with minimum GPA of 2.75. Additional exam requirements/recommendations for international students: Required—TOEFL (minimum score 500 paper-based; 61 iBT). *Application deadline:* Applications are processed on a rolling basis. Application fee: $40. Electronic applications accepted. *Expenses:* Tuition, state resident: part-time $371 per credit hour. Tuition, nonresident: part-time $742 per credit hour. *Required fees:* $130 per semester. *Financial support:* Federal Work-Study and scholarships/grants available. Support available to part-time students. Financial award application deadline: 3/1; financial award applicants required to submit FAFSA. *Unit head:* Dr. Aliquippa Allen, Interim Dean of College of Business and Technology, 205-652-3564, Fax: 205-652-3776, E-mail: aallen@uwa.edu.
Website: http://www.uwa.edu/academics/collegeofbusinessandtechnology

The University of Western Ontario, Richard Ivey School of Business, London, ON N6A 3K7, Canada. Offers business (EMBA, PhD); corporate strategy and leadership elective (MBA); entrepreneurship elective (MBA); finance elective (MBA); health sector stream (MBA); international management elective (MBA); marketing elective (MBA); JD/MBA. *Degree requirements:* For master's, thesis (for some programs); for doctorate, thesis/dissertation. *Entrance requirements:* For master's, GMAT, 2 years of full-time work experience, interview. Additional exam requirements/recommendations for international students: Required—TOEFL (minimum score 100 iBT) or IELTS (minimum score 6). Electronic applications accepted. *Faculty research:* Strategy, organizational behavior, international business, finance, operations management.

University of Wisconsin–Madison, Graduate School, Wisconsin School of Business, Doctoral Program in Finance, Investment and Banking, Madison, WI 53706-1380. Offers PhD. *Degree requirements:* For doctorate, comprehensive exam, thesis/dissertation. *Entrance requirements:* For doctorate, GMAT or GRE. Additional exam requirements/recommendations for international students: Recommended—TOEFL (minimum score 623 paper-based; 106 iBT), IELTS (minimum score 7.5), TSE (minimum score 73). Electronic applications accepted. *Expenses:* Contact institution. *Faculty research:* Banking and financial institutions, business cycles, investments, derivatives, corporate finance, economics, bankruptcy, foreclosures, mergers and acquisitions, portfolio theory.

University of Wisconsin–Madison, Graduate School, Wisconsin School of Business, Wisconsin Full-Time MBA Program, Madison, WI 53706. Offers applied security analysis (MBA); arts administration (MBA); brand and product management (MBA); corporate finance and investment banking (MBA); marketing research (MBA); operations and technology management (MBA); real estate (MBA); risk management and insurance (MBA); strategic human resource management (MBA); supply chain management (MBA). *Faculty:* 130 full-time (35 women), 42 part-time/adjunct (13 women). *Students:* 203 full-time (72 women); includes 34 minority (8 Black or African American, non-Hispanic/Latino; 10 Asian, non-Hispanic/Latino; 12 Hispanic/Latino; 4 Two or more races, non-Hispanic/Latino), 41 international. Average age 28. 556 applicants, 30% accepted, 104 enrolled. In 2017, 97 master's awarded. *Entrance requirements:* For master's, GMAT or GRE, bachelor's or equivalent degree, 2 years of work experience, essay, letter of recommendation, resume. Additional exam requirements/recommendations for international students: Required—TOEFL (minimum score 100 iBT), IELTS (minimum score 7.5). *Application deadline:* For fall admission, 11/2 for domestic and international students; for winter admission, 1/11 for domestic and international students; for spring admission, 3/1 for domestic and international students; for summer admission, 4/12 for domestic and international students. Applications are processed on a rolling basis. Application fee: $75 ($81 for international students). Electronic applications accepted. *Expenses:* $9,356 per semester resident, $18,288 non-resident. *Financial support:* In 2017–18, 183 students received support, including 14 fellowships with full tuition reimbursements available (averaging $25,420 per year), 7 research assistantships with full tuition reimbursements available (averaging $13,375 per year), 53 teaching assistantships with full tuition reimbursements available (averaging $13,375 per year); scholarships/grants, health care benefits, tuition waivers (full), and unspecified assistantships also available. Financial award application deadline: 4/11. *Faculty research:* Forms of competition and outcomes in dual distribution systems; explaining the accuracy of revised forecasts; supply chain planning for random demand surges; advanced demand information in a multi-product system; the effects of presentation salience and measurement subjectivity on nonprofessional investors' fair value judgments. *Unit head:* Dr. Don Hausch, Associate Dean, Full-time MBA Program, 608-262-9731, E-mail: don.hausch@wisc.edu. *Application contact:* Betsy Kacizak, Director of Admissions and Recruiting, Full-time MBA Program, 608-262-4000, E-mail: betsy.kacizak@wisc.edu.
Website: https://wsb.wisc.edu/

University of Wisconsin–Whitewater, School of Graduate Studies, College of Business and Economics, Program in Business Administration, Whitewater, WI 53190-1790. Offers finance (MBA). *Accreditation:* AACSB. *Program availability:* Part-time, evening/weekend, online learning. *Entrance requirements:* For master's, GMAT or GRE, minimum AACSB index of 1000, minimum GPA of 2.75. Additional exam requirements/recommendations for international students: Required—TOEFL (minimum score 550 paper-based; 80 iBT), IELTS (minimum score 6). Electronic applications accepted. *Faculty research:* Interface between social institutions and individual behavior, technology and innovation management, occupational mental health, workplace deviance and corporate romance.

University of Wyoming, College of Business, Department of Economics and Finance, Program in Economics and Finance, Laramie, WY 82071. Offers MS. *Degree requirements:* For master's, thesis. *Entrance requirements:* For master's, GRE, minimum GPA of 3.0. Additional exam requirements/recommendations for international students: Required—TOEFL (minimum score 540 paper-based; 76 iBT). *Faculty research:* Financial economics.

Finance and Banking

University of Wyoming, College of Business, Department of Economics and Finance, Program in Finance, Laramie, WY 82071. Offers MS. *Program availability:* Part-time. *Degree requirements:* For master's, thesis. *Entrance requirements:* For master's, GMAT, GRE, minimum GPA of 3.0. Additional exam requirements/recommendations for international students: Required—TOEFL (minimum score 540 paper-based; 76 iBT). *Faculty research:* Banking.

Upper Iowa University, Online Master's Programs, Fayette, IA 52142-1857. Offers accounting (MBA); corporate financial management (MBA); emergency management and homeland security (MPA); general management (MBA); general studies (MPA); government administration (MPA); health and human services (MPA); human resources management (MBA); nonprofit organizational management (MPA); organizational development (MBA); public management (MPA); sport administration (MSA). MBA also available at Madison, WI campus. *Program availability:* Part-time, online learning. *Degree requirements:* For master's, research project. *Entrance requirements:* For master's, GMAT, GRE, or minimum GPA of 2.7 during last 60 hours. Additional exam requirements/recommendations for international students: Required—TOEFL (minimum score 570 paper-based). Electronic applications accepted. *Faculty research:* Total quality management, teams, organization culture and climate, management.

Ursuline College, School of Graduate and Professional Studies, Program in Business Administration, Pepper Pike, OH 44124-4398. Offers ethical and entrepreneurial leadership (MBA); financial planning and accounting (MBA); health services management (MBA); management (MBA); management and leadership (MBA); marketing and communications management (MBA). *Program availability:* Part-time. *Faculty:* 3 full-time (2 women), 3 part-time/adjunct (2 women). *Students:* 3 full-time (all women), 26 part-time (23 women); includes 13 minority (12 Black or African American, non-Hispanic/Latino; 1 Two or more races, non-Hispanic/Latino). Average age 38. 13 applicants, 85% accepted, 6 enrolled. In 2017, 11 master's awarded. *Degree requirements:* For master's, comprehensive exam (for some programs). *Entrance requirements:* For master's, GRE. Additional exam requirements/recommendations for international students: Required—TOEFL (minimum score 500 paper-based) or GRE. *Application deadline:* Applications are processed on a rolling basis. Application fee: $25. Electronic applications accepted. *Expenses:* $842 per credit hour. *Financial support:* In 2017–18, 3 students received support. Scholarships/grants available. Financial award application deadline: 8/1; financial award applicants required to submit FAFSA. *Faculty research:* Gift economy; sharing economy; cooperative business models; collaborative leadership; corporate social responsibility and the triple bottom line, defined as the three P's: people, planet and profit. *Unit head:* Dr. Anthony Caffarelli, Associate Professor, 440-646-8134, Fax: 440-684-6088, E-mail: tcafarelli@ursuline.edu. *Application contact:* Melanie Steele, Director of Graduate Admission, 440-646-8146, Fax: 440-684-6138, E-mail: graduateadmissions@ursuline.edu.

Utah State University, School of Graduate Studies, Jon M. Huntsman School of Business, Department of Economics and Finance, Logan, UT 84322. Offers economics (MS); financial economics (MS). *Degree requirements:* For master's, thesis (for some programs). *Entrance requirements:* For master's, GRE General Test, GMAT, minimum GPA of 3.0. Additional exam requirements/recommendations for international students: Required—TOEFL. Electronic applications accepted. *Faculty research:* Resource economics, economic theory, international trade, industrial organization, development.

Valparaiso University, Graduate School and Continuing Education, College of Business, Valparaiso, IN 46383. Offers business administration (MBA); business decision-making (Certificate); business intelligence (Certificate); engineering management (Certificate); finance (Certificate); general business (Certificate); leading the global enterprise (Certificate); management (Certificate); JD/MBA; MSN/MBA. *Accreditation:* AACSB. *Program availability:* Part-time, evening/weekend, online learning. *Entrance requirements:* For master's, GMAT, GRE, minimum GPA of 3.0. Additional exam requirements/recommendations for international students: Required—TOEFL (minimum score 550 paper-based; 80 iBT), IELTS (minimum score 6). Electronic applications accepted. *Expenses:* Contact institution.

Valparaiso University, Graduate School and Continuing Education, Program in International Economics and Finance, Valparaiso, IN 46383. Offers MS. *Program availability:* Part-time, evening/weekend. *Entrance requirements:* For master's, 1 semester of college-level calculus; 1 statistics or quantitative methods class; 2 semesters of introductory economics (course content in introductory economics must include both introductory microeconomics and macroeconomics); 1 introductory accounting course; minimum undergraduate GPA of 3.0; 2 letters of recommendation. Additional exam requirements/recommendations for international students: Required—TOEFL (minimum score 550 paper-based; 80 iBT), IELTS (minimum score 6). *Expenses: Tuition:* Full-time $11,340; part-time $630 per credit hour. *Required fees:* $520; $250 per year. $125 per semester. Tuition and fees vary according to program and reciprocity agreements.

Vancouver Island University, Master of Business Administration Program, Nanaimo, BC V9R 5S5, Canada. Offers international business (MBA), including finance, marketing. Program offered jointly with University of Hertfordshire. *Accreditation:* ACBSP. *Program availability:* Part-time. *Degree requirements:* For master's, thesis. *Entrance requirements:* Additional exam requirements/recommendations for international students: Required—TOEFL (minimum score 88 iBT), IELTS (minimum score 6.5). Electronic applications accepted. *Expenses:* Contact institution. *Faculty research:* Tourism development, entrepreneurship, organizational development, strategic planning, international business strategy, intercultural team work.

Vanderbilt University, Vanderbilt University Owen Graduate School of Management, MS in Finance Program, Nashville, TN 37203. Offers MS. *Entrance requirements:* For master's, GMAT and/or GRE. Additional exam requirements/recommendations for international students: Required—TOEFL (minimum score 105 iBT). Electronic applications accepted. *Expenses:* Contact institution.

Vanderbilt University, Vanderbilt University Owen Graduate School of Management, Vanderbilt MBA Program, Nashville, TN 37203. Offers accounting (MBA); finance (MBA); general management (MBA); health care (MBA); human and organizational performance (MBA); marketing (MBA); operations (MBA); strategy (MBA); MBA/JD; MBA/M Div; MBA/MD; MBA/MSN; MBA/MTS; MBA/PhD. *Accreditation:* AACSB. *Degree requirements:* For master's, 62 credit hours of coursework; completion of ethics course; minimum GPA of 3.0. *Entrance requirements:* For master's, GMAT (preferred) or GRE, 2 years of work experience (recommended). Additional exam requirements/recommendations for international students: Required—TOEFL (minimum score 100 iBT). Electronic applications accepted. *Expenses:* Contact institution. *Faculty research:* Accounting and finance, business strategy and economics, marketing, operations management, organization studies.

Villanova University, Villanova School of Business, Master of Science in Finance Program, Villanova, PA 19085. Offers MSF. *Faculty:* 68 full-time (22 women), 65 part-time/adjunct (11 women). *Students:* 25 full-time (5 women); includes 6 minority (4 Asian, non-Hispanic/Latino; 1 Hispanic/Latino; 1 Native Hawaiian or other Pacific Islander, non-Hispanic/Latino), 4 international. Average age 23. 94 applicants, 47% accepted, 25 enrolled. In 2017, 22 master's awarded. *Degree requirements:* For master's, minimum cumulative GPA of 3.0. *Entrance requirements:* For master's, GMAT, prerequisite course in principles of finance, 2 letters of recommendation, 2 essays, resume, official transcripts, interview. Additional exam requirements/recommendations for international students: Required—TOEFL (minimum score 550 paper-based; 100 iBT). *Application deadline:* For spring admission, 3/15 for domestic and international students. Applications are processed on a rolling basis. Application fee: $65. Electronic applications accepted. *Expenses:* $1,400 per credit tuition. *Financial support:* In 2017–18, 4 research assistantships (averaging $6,550 per year) were awarded; scholarships/grants also available. Financial award applicants required to submit FAFSA. *Faculty research:* Business analytics; creativity, innovation and entrepreneurship; global leadership; real estate; church management; business ethics; marketing and consumer insights. *Unit head:* Dr. Joyce Russell, Dean of Villanova School of Business, 610-519-5424, Fax: 610-519-6273, E-mail: joyce.russell@villanova.edu. *Application contact:* Claire Bruno, Director of Recruitment and Enrollment Management, 610-519-4336, Fax: 610-519-6273, E-mail: claire.bruno@villanova.edu.
Website: http://www1.villanova.edu/villanova/business/graduate/specializedprograms/msf.html

Villanova University, Villanova School of Business, MBA - The Fast Track Program, Villanova, PA 19085. Offers finance (MBA); healthcare (MBA); international business (MBA); strategic management (MBA). *Accreditation:* AACSB. *Program availability:* Part-time, evening/weekend. *Faculty:* 68 full-time (22 women), 65 part-time/adjunct (11 women). *Students:* 128 part-time (55 women); includes 11 minority (3 Black or African American, non-Hispanic/Latino; 4 Asian, non-Hispanic/Latino; 4 Hispanic/Latino), 4 international. Average age 30. 79 applicants, 96% accepted, 64 enrolled. In 2017, 58 master's awarded. *Degree requirements:* For master's, minimum GPA of 3.0. *Entrance requirements:* For master's, GMAT or GRE, work experience, 2 letters of recommendation, 2 essays, resume, official transcripts, interview. Additional exam requirements/recommendations for international students: Required—TOEFL (minimum score 550 paper-based; 100 iBT). *Application deadline:* For fall admission, 6/30 for domestic and international students. Applications are processed on a rolling basis. Application fee: $65. Electronic applications accepted. *Expenses:* $56,016 per year tuition, $1,167 per credit; $50 semester fee. *Financial support:* Scholarships/grants available. Financial award application deadline: 6/30; financial award applicants required to submit FAFSA. *Faculty research:* Business analytics; creativity, innovation and entrepreneurship; global leadership; real estate; church management; business ethics; marketing and consumer insights. *Unit head:* Dr. Joyce Russell, Dean of Villanova School of Business, 610-519-5424, Fax: 610-519-6273, E-mail: joyce.russell@villanova.edu. *Application contact:* Kimberly Kane, Manager of Admissions, 610-519-3701, Fax: 610-519-6273, E-mail: kimberly.kane@villanova.edu.
Website: http://www1.villanova.edu/villanova/business/graduate/mba.html

Virginia Commonwealth University, Graduate School, L. Douglas Wilder School of Government and Public Affairs, Program in Public Administration, Richmond, VA 23284-9005. Offers financial management (MPA); human resource management (MPA); state and local government management (MPA). *Accreditation:* NASPAA. *Program availability:* Part-time. *Entrance requirements:* For master's, GRE, GMAT or LSAT. Additional exam requirements/recommendations for international students: Required—TOEFL (minimum score 600 paper-based; 100 iBT); Recommended—IELTS (minimum score 6.5). Electronic applications accepted. *Faculty research:* Environmental policy, executive leadership, human resource management, local government management, nonprofit management, public financial management, public policy analysis and evaluation.

Virginia International University, School of Business, Fairfax, VA 22030. Offers accounting (MBA, MS); entrepreneurship (MBA); executive management (Graduate Certificate); global logistics (MBA); health care management (MBA); hospitality and tourism management (MBA); human resources management (MBA); international business management (MBA); international finance (MBA); marketing management (MBA); mass media and public relations (MBA); project management (MBA, MS). *Program availability:* Part-time, online learning. *Entrance requirements:* For master's and Graduate Certificate, bachelor's degree. Additional exam requirements/recommendations for international students: Required—TOEFL (minimum score 550 paper-based; 80 iBT), IELTS (minimum score 6). Electronic applications accepted.

Virginia Polytechnic Institute and State University, Graduate School, Pamplin College of Business, Blacksburg, VA 24061. Offers accounting and information systems (MACIS, PhD); business (PhD), including marketing (MS, PhD); business administration (MS), including business analytics, marketing (MS, PhD); business information technology (PhD); executive business research (PhD); finance (PhD); MS/MBA. *Faculty:* 131 full-time (42 women), 2 part-time/adjunct (1 woman). *Students:* 261 full-time (101 women), 189 part-time (76 women); includes 112 minority (32 Black or African American, non-Hispanic/Latino; 50 Asian, non-Hispanic/Latino; 15 Hispanic/Latino; 15 Two or more races, non-Hispanic/Latino), 80 international. Average age 32. 434 applicants, 57% accepted, 168 enrolled. In 2017, 142 master's, 11 doctorates awarded. *Degree requirements:* For master's, comprehensive exam (for some programs), thesis (for some programs); for doctorate, comprehensive exam (for some programs), thesis/dissertation (for some programs). *Entrance requirements:* For master's and doctorate, GRE/GMAT. Additional exam requirements/recommendations for international students: Required—TOEFL (minimum score 80 iBT). *Application deadline:* For fall admission, 8/1 for domestic students, 4/1 for international students; for spring admission, 1/1 for domestic students, 9/1 for international students. Applications are processed on a rolling basis. Application fee: $75. Electronic applications accepted. *Expenses:* Tuition, state resident: full-time $15,072; part-time $718.50 per credit hour. Tuition, nonresident: full-time $28,810; part-time $1448.25 per credit hour. *Required fees:* $2741; $502 per semester. Tuition and fees vary according to course load, campus/location and program. *Financial support:* In 2017–18, 9 research assistantships with full tuition reimbursements (averaging $18,588 per year), 48 teaching assistantships with full tuition reimbursements (averaging $22,706 per year) were awarded. Financial award application deadline: 3/1; financial award applicants required to submit FAFSA. *Total annual research expenditures:* $3.4 million. *Unit head:* Dr. Robert T. Sumichrast, Dean, 540-231-6601, Fax: 540-231-4487, E-mail: busdean@vt.edu. *Application contact:* Kimberly Ridpath, Executive Assistant, 540-231-9647, Fax: 540-231-4487, E-mail: ridpathk@vt.edu.
Website: http://www.pamplin.vt.edu/

Wagner College, Division of Graduate Studies, Nicolais School of Business, Staten Island, NY 10301-4495. Offers accounting (MS); business administration (MBA); finance (MBA); management (Exec MBA); marketing (MBA); media management (MS). *Accreditation:* ACBSP. *Program availability:* Part-time, evening/weekend. *Faculty:* 8 full-time (3 women), 17 part-time/adjunct (5 women). *Students:* 90 full-time (41 women), 27 part-time (9 women); includes 18 minority (10 Black or African American, non-Hispanic/Latino; 2 Asian, non-Hispanic/Latino; 4 Hispanic/Latino; 2 Two or more races, non-Hispanic/Latino), 14 international. Average age 27. 85 applicants, 92% accepted, 58 enrolled. In 2017, 72 master's awarded. *Degree requirements:* For master's, thesis optional. *Entrance requirements:* For master's, minimum GPA of 2.75, proficiency in computers and math. Additional exam requirements/recommendations for international students: Required—TOEFL (minimum score 550 paper-based; 79 iBT), IELTS (minimum score 6.5). *Application deadline:* For fall admission, 5/1 priority date for domestic students, 3/1 priority date for international students; for spring admission, 12/1 for domestic students, 11/1 for international students. Applications are processed on a rolling basis. Application fee: $60. *Financial support:* In 2017–18, 93 students received support. Career-related internships or fieldwork, unspecified assistantships, and alumni fellowship grants available. Financial award application deadline: 4/1; financial award applicants required to submit FAFSA. *Unit head:* Dr. Donald Crooks, Director, 718-390-3429, Fax: 718-390-3429, E-mail: dcrooks@wagner.edu. *Application contact:* Patricia Clancy, Assistant Director for Enrollment, 718-420-4464, Fax: 718-390-3105, E-mail: patricia.clancy@wagner.edu.

Walden University, Graduate Programs, School of Management, Minneapolis, MN 55401. Offers accounting (MBA, MS, DBA), including accounting for the professional (MS), accounting with CPA emphasis (MS), self-designed (MS); advanced project management (Graduate Certificate); applied project management (Graduate Certificate); auditing (Graduate Certificate); bridge to business administration (Post-Doctoral Certificate); bridge to management (Post-Doctoral Certificate); business management (Graduate Certificate); communication (MBA); corporate finance (MBA); digital marketing (Graduate Certificate); entrepreneurship (DBA); entrepreneurship and small business (MBA); finance (MS, DBA), including finance for the professional (MS), finance with CFA/investment (MS), finance with CPA emphasis (MS); global supply chain management (DBA); healthcare management (MBA, DBA); human resource management (MBA, MS, Graduate Certificate), including functional human resource management (MS), general program (MS), integrating functional and strategic human resource management (MS), organizational strategy (MS); human resources management (DBA); information systems management (DBA); international business (MBA, DBA); leadership (MBA, MS, DBA, Graduate Certificate), including general program (MS), human resource leadership (MS), leader development (MS), self-designed (MS); management (MS, PhD), including communications (MS), finance (PhD), general program (MS), healthcare management (MS), human resource management (MS), human resources management (PhD), information systems management (PhD), international business (MS), leadership (MS), leadership and organizational change (PhD), marketing (MS), project management (MS), strategy and operations (MS); managerial accounting (Graduate Certificate); marketing (MBA, MS, DBA); project management (MBA, MS, DBA); self-designed (MBA, MS, DBA); social impact management (DBA); technology entrepreneurship (DBA). *Accreditation:* ACBSP. *Program availability:* Part-time, evening/weekend, online only, 100% online. *Degree requirements:* For master's, thesis (for some programs), residency (for EMBA); for doctorate, thesis/dissertation, (for some programs), residency. *Entrance requirements:* For master's, bachelor's degree or higher; minimum GPA of 2.5; official transcripts; goal statement (for some programs); access to computer and Internet; for doctorate, master's degree or higher; three years of related professional or academic experience (preferred); minimum GPA of 3.0; goal statement and current resume (for select programs); official transcripts; access to computer and Internet; for other advanced degree, relevant work experience; access to computer and Internet. Additional exam requirements/recommendations for international students: Required—TOEFL (minimum score 550 paper-based, 79 iBT), IELTS (minimum score 6.5), Michigan English Language Assessment Battery (minimum score 82), or PTE (minimum score 53). Electronic applications accepted.

Walsh College of Accountancy and Business Administration, Graduate Programs, Program in Accountancy, Troy, MI 48083. Offers data analytics (MAC); finance (MAC); taxation (MAC). *Program availability:* Part-time, evening/weekend. *Students:* 252 (139 women); includes 64 minority (22 Black or African American, non-Hispanic/Latino; 30 Asian, non-Hispanic/Latino; 11 Hispanic/Latino; 1 Two or more races, non-Hispanic/Latino), 21 international. Average age 32. 94 applicants, 76% accepted, 71 enrolled. In 2017, 93 master's awarded. *Degree requirements:* For master's, thesis optional. *Entrance requirements:* For master's, minimum overall cumulative GPA of 2.75 from all colleges previously attended. Additional exam requirements/recommendations for international students: Required—TOEFL (minimum score 550 paper-based, 79 iBT), IELTS (6.5), Michigan English Language Assessment Battery, or MTELP (80). *Application deadline:* Applications are processed on a rolling basis. Application fee: $35. Electronic applications accepted. *Expenses:* $770 per semester credit hour plus $125 registration fee per semester. *Financial support:* In 2017–18, 19 students received support. Career-related internships or fieldwork and scholarships/grants available. Financial award application deadline: 6/30; financial award applicants required to submit FAFSA. *Unit head:* John Black, Chair, Accounting, Tax and Business Law, 248-823-1635, Fax: 248-689-0920, E-mail: jblack@walshcollege.edu. *Application contact:* Heather Rigby, Director, Admissions and Academic Advising, 248-823-1600, Fax: 248-823-1611, E-mail: hrigby@walshcollege.edu.

Walsh College of Accountancy and Business Administration, Graduate Programs, Program in Finance, Troy, MI 48083. Offers financial investments (MSF); financial management (MSF); financial services (MSF). *Program availability:* Part-time, evening/weekend, 100% online, blended/hybrid learning. *Faculty:* 8 full-time (5 women), 16 part-time/adjunct (4 women). *Students:* 92 (40 women); includes 16 minority (12 Black or African American, non-Hispanic/Latino; 1 American Indian or Alaska Native, non-Hispanic/Latino; 2 Asian, non-Hispanic/Latino; 1 Two or more races, non-Hispanic/Latino), 6 international. Average age 33. 31 applicants, 81% accepted, 23 enrolled. In 2017, 32 master's awarded. *Entrance requirements:* For master's, minimum overall cumulative GPA of 2.75 from all colleges previously attended. Additional exam requirements/recommendations for international students: Required—TOEFL (minimum score 550 paper-based, 79 iBT), IELTS (6.5), Michigan English Language Assessment Battery, or MTELP (80). *Application deadline:* Applications are processed on a rolling basis. Application fee: $35. Electronic applications accepted. *Expenses:* $770 per semester credit hour plus $125 registration fee per semester. *Financial support:* In 2017–18, 9 students received support. Career-related internships or fieldwork and scholarships/grants available. Financial award application deadline: 6/30; financial award applicants required to submit FAFSA. *Unit head:* Dr. John Moore, Interim Chair, Finance and Economics, 248-823-1635, Fax: 248-689-0920, E-mail: john.moore@walshcollege.edu. *Application contact:* Heather Rigby, Director, Admissions and Academic Advising, 248-823-1600, Fax: 248-823-1611, E-mail: hrigby@walshcollege.edu.

Washington University in St. Louis, Olin Business School, DBA Program in Finance, St. Louis, MO 63130-4899. Offers DBA. *Program availability:* Part-time. *Faculty:* 98 full-time (25 women), 54 part-time/adjunct (12 women). *Students:* 9 full-time (3 women), 6 part-time (2 women); includes 3 minority (1 Black or African American, non-Hispanic/Latino; 1 Asian, non-Hispanic/Latino; 1 Hispanic/Latino), 11 international. Average age 34. 27 applicants, 48% accepted, 4 enrolled. In 2017, 1 doctorate awarded. *Degree requirements:* For doctorate, comprehensive exam, thesis/dissertation. *Entrance requirements:* For doctorate, GRE or GMAT. Additional exam requirements/recommendations for international students: Required—TOEFL or IELTS. *Application deadline:* For fall admission, 6/1 for domestic and international students. Applications are processed on a rolling basis. Application fee: $99. Electronic applications accepted. *Unit head:* Prof. Anjan Thakor, Director, 314-935-7197, E-mail: thakor@wustl.edu. *Application contact:* Erin Murdock, Associate Director of Doctoral Admissions and Student Affairs, 314-935-6340, Fax: 314-935-9484, E-mail: murdockel@wustl.edu. Website: http://www.olin.wustl.edu/EN-US/academic-programs/dba-in-finance/

Washington University in St. Louis, Olin Business School, Program in Finance, St. Louis, MO 63130-4899. Offers corporate finance and investments (MS); quantitative finance (MS). *Program availability:* Part-time. *Faculty:* 98 full-time (25 women), 54 part-time/adjunct (12 women). *Students:* 161 full-time (68 women), 1 part-time (0 women); includes 26 minority (16 Asian, non-Hispanic/Latino; 9 Hispanic/Latino; 1 Two or more races, non-Hispanic/Latino), 125 international. Average age 25. 1,468 applicants, 20% accepted, 124 enrolled. In 2017, 61 master's awarded. *Entrance requirements:* For master's, GMAT or GRE. Additional exam requirements/recommendations for international students: Required—TOEFL, IELTS. *Application deadline:* For fall admission, 10/3 for domestic students, 2/1 priority date for international students; for winter admission, 12/1 for domestic students; for spring admission, 4/3 for domestic students. Applications are processed on a rolling basis. Application fee: $100. Electronic applications accepted. *Financial support:* Institutionally sponsored loans and scholarships/grants available. Financial award applicants required to submit FAFSA. *Unit head:* Dr. Patrick Moreton, Senior Associate Dean of Graduate Programs, 314-935-6322, Fax: 314-935-4464, E-mail: moreton@wustl.edu. *Application contact:* 314-935-7301, Fax: 314-935-4464, E-mail: olingradadmissions@wustl.edu. Website: http://www.olin.wustl.edu/prospective/

Waynesburg University, Graduate and Professional Studies, Canonsburg, PA 15370. Offers business (MBA), including energy management, finance, health systems, human resources, leadership, market development; counseling (MA), including addictions counseling, clinical mental health; counselor education and supervision (PhD); criminal investigation (MA); education (M Ed), including autism, curriculum and instruction, educational leadership, online teaching; nursing (MSN), including administration, education, informatics; nursing practice (DNP); special education (M Ed); technology (M Ed); MSN/MBA. *Accreditation:* AACN. *Program availability:* Part-time, evening/weekend. *Degree requirements:* For doctorate, thesis/dissertation. *Entrance requirements:* Additional exam requirements/recommendations for international students: Required—TOEFL. Electronic applications accepted.

Wayne State University, Law School, Detroit, MI 48202. Offers corporate and finance law (LL M); labor and employment law (LL M); law (JD); taxation (LL M); United States law (LL M); JD/MA; JD/MADR; JD/MBA; JD/MS. *Accreditation:* ABA. *Program availability:* Part-time, evening/weekend. *Faculty:* 43 full-time (18 women), 17 part-time/adjunct (9 women). *Students:* 409 full-time (184 women), 46 part-time (22 women); includes 61 minority (33 Black or African American, non-Hispanic/Latino; 1 American Indian or Alaska Native, non-Hispanic/Latino; 14 Asian, non-Hispanic/Latino; 3 Hispanic/Latino; 10 Two or more races, non-Hispanic/Latino), 11 international. Average age 26. 811 applicants, 54% accepted, 146 enrolled. In 2017, 4 master's, 113 doctorates awarded. *Degree requirements:* For master's, thesis (for some programs). *Entrance requirements:* For master's, JD or LL B from ABA-accredited and member institution of the AALS; for doctorate, LSAT, LDAS report, bachelor's degree from accredited institution, personal statement, transcripts from all U.S. undergraduate schools attended and an analysis and summary of the transcripts; letter of recommendation (up to two are accepted). Additional exam requirements/recommendations for international students: Required—TOEFL, Michigan English Language Assessment Battery (minimum score 85); Recommended—IELTS. *Application deadline:* For fall admission, 7/1 for domestic students, 5/1 priority date for international students. Applications are processed on a rolling basis. Application fee: $0. Electronic applications accepted. *Expenses:* Contact institution. *Financial support:* In 2017–18, 386 students received support. Fellowships, Federal Work-Study, and scholarships/grants available. Support available to part-time students. Financial award application deadline: 6/30; financial award applicants required to submit FAFSA. *Unit head:* Richard A. Bierschbach, Dean and Professor of Law, 313-577-3933, E-mail: rbierschbach@wayne.edu. *Application contact:* Kathy Fox, Assistant Dean of Admissions, 313-577-3937, Fax: 313-993-8129, E-mail: lawinquire@wayne.edu. Website: http://law.wayne.edu/

Wayne State University, Mike Ilitch School of Business, Detroit, MI 48202. Offers accounting (MS, MSA, Postbaccalaureate Certificate); business (EMS, Graduate Certificate); business administration (MBA, PhD); data science (MS), including business analytics; entrepreneurship and innovation (Postbaccalaureate Certificate); finance (MS); information systems management (Postbaccalaureate Certificate); taxation (MST); JD/MBA. Application deadline for PhD is February 15. *Accreditation:* AACSB. *Program availability:* Part-time, evening/weekend. *Faculty:* 32. *Students:* 235 full-time (121 women), 1,082 part-time (480 women); includes 356 minority (202 Black or African American, non-Hispanic/Latino; 2 American Indian or Alaska Native, non-Hispanic/Latino; 79 Asian, non-Hispanic/Latino; 47 Hispanic/Latino; 26 Two or more races, non-Hispanic/Latino), 87 international. Average age 30. 1,285 applicants, 43% accepted, 308 enrolled. In 2017, 200 master's, 2 doctorates, 9 other advanced degrees awarded. *Degree requirements:* For doctorate, thesis/dissertation. *Entrance requirements:* For master's, GMAT, GRE, LSAT, MCAT, at least three years of relevant work experience that shows increased responsibility, or minimum GPA of 3.0 from AACSB-accredited program or 3.2 from regionally-accredited program, undergraduate degree from accredited institution; undergraduate degree in accounting, business administration, or area of business administration (for MS and MST); for doctorate, GMAT (minimum score of 600), minimum undergraduate GPA of 3.0, 3.5 upper-division or graduate; three letters of recommendation; brief essay; undergraduate degree from accredited institution; personal statement; for other advanced degree, bachelor's degree from accredited institution. Additional exam requirements/recommendations for international students: Required—TOEFL (minimum score 550 paper-based; 79 iBT), Michigan English Language Assessment Battery (minimum score 85); Recommended—IELTS (minimum score 6.5), TWE (minimum score 5.5). *Application deadline:* For fall admission, 7/1 for domestic students, 5/1 priority date for international students; for winter admission, 11/1 for domestic students, 9/1 priority date for international students; for spring admission, 3/1 for domestic students, 1/1 priority date for international students. Applications are processed on a rolling basis. Application fee: $50. Electronic applications accepted. *Expenses:* Contact institution. *Financial support:* In 2017–18, 165 students received support, including 1 fellowship with tuition reimbursement available (averaging $18,534 per year), 1 teaching assistantship with tuition reimbursement available (averaging $18,534 per year); research assistantships with tuition reimbursements available, scholarships/grants, health care benefits, and unspecified assistantships also available. Support available to part-time students. Financial award applicants required to submit FAFSA. *Faculty research:* Executive compensation and stock performance, consumer reactions to pricing strategies, communication across the automotive supply chain, performance of firms in sub-Saharan Africa, implementation issues with ERP software. *Unit head:* Dr. Robert Forsythe, Dean, School of Business Administration, 313-577-4501, E-mail: robert.forsythe@wayne.edu. *Application contact:* Kiantee N. Rupert-Jones, Director, 313-577-4511, Fax: 313-577-9442, E-mail: gradbusiness@wayne.edu. Website: http://ilitchbusiness.wayne.edu/

Webster University, George Herbert Walker School of Business and Technology, Department of Business, St. Louis, MO 63119-3194. Offers business and organizational security management (MBA); decision support systems (MBA); environmental management (MBA); finance (MBA, MS); forensic accounting (MS); gerontology (MBA); human resources development (MBA); human resources management (MBA);

information technology management (MBA); international business (MA, MBA); international relations (MBA); management and leadership (MBA); marketing (MBA); media communications (MBA); procurement and acquisitions management (MBA); Web services (MBA). *Accreditation:* ACBSP. *Program availability:* Part-time, evening/weekend, online learning. *Degree requirements:* For master's, comprehensive exam (for some programs), thesis (for some programs). *Entrance requirements:* Additional exam requirements/recommendations for international students: Required—TOEFL.

Western Michigan University Thomas M. Cooley Law School, Graduate Programs, Lansing, MI 48901-3038. Offers administrative law (public law) (JD); business transactions (JD); Canadian law practice (JD); corporate law and finance (LL M); environmental law (public law) (JD); general practice (JD), including solo and small firm; general studies (LL M); homeland and national security law (LL M); insurance law (LL M); intellectual property (JD); intellectual property law (LL M); international law (JD); litigation (JD); taxation (LL M); U.S. legal studies for foreign attorneys (LL M); JD/LL M; JD/MBA; JD/MHA; JD/MPA; JD/MSW. *Program availability:* Part-time, evening/weekend, 100% online, blended/hybrid learning. *Degree requirements:* For master's, thesis (for some programs); for doctorate, minimum of 3 credits of clinical experience. *Entrance requirements:* For master's, JD or LL B; for doctorate, LSAT. Additional exam requirements/recommendations for international students: Required—TOEFL (for U.S. legal studies for foreign attorneys LL M program); Recommended—TOEFL. Electronic applications accepted. *Expenses:* Contact institution. *Faculty research:* Wrongful convictions, civil rights, environmental law, litigation techniques, data mining, intellectual property, practical and skills-based legal education.

West Texas A&M University, College of Business, Department of Accounting, Economics and Finance, Canyon, TX 79015. Offers accounting (MPA); finance and economics (MS). *Program availability:* Part-time, evening/weekend, online learning. *Degree requirements:* For master's, comprehensive exam, thesis optional. *Entrance requirements:* For master's, GMAT. Additional exam requirements/recommendations for international students: Required—TOEFL (minimum score 550 paper-based). Electronic applications accepted. *Faculty research:* Texas economy, decision report service learning and entrepreneurship, small business, trade effects of financial flow.

West Virginia University, College of Business and Economics, Morgantown, WV 26506. Offers accountancy (M Acc); accounting (PhD); business administration (MBA); business cyber security management (MS); business data analytics (MS); economics (MA, PhD); finance (MS, PhD); forensic and fraud examination (MS); industrial relations (MS); management (PhD); marketing (PhD). *Program availability:* Part-time, online learning. *Students:* 343 full-time (141 women), 43 part-time (12 women); includes 59 minority (22 Black or African American, non-Hispanic/Latino; 11 Asian, non-Hispanic/Latino; 12 Hispanic/Latino; 14 Two or more races, non-Hispanic/Latino), 54 international. Terminal master's awarded for partial completion of doctoral program. *Degree requirements:* For master's, thesis optional; for doctorate, comprehensive exam, thesis/dissertation. *Entrance requirements:* For doctorate, GRE General Test, minimum GPA of 3.0. Additional exam requirements/recommendations for international students: Required—TOEFL (minimum score 550 paper-based; 92 iBT). *Application deadline:* For fall admission, 10/15 priority date for domestic and international students; for spring admission, 3/1 priority date for domestic and international students. Applications are processed on a rolling basis. Application fee: $60. Electronic applications accepted. *Expenses:* Contact institution. *Financial support:* Fellowships, research assistantships, teaching assistantships, career-related internships or fieldwork, Federal Work-Study, institutionally sponsored loans, scholarships/grants, health care benefits, tuition waivers (full and partial), unspecified assistantships, and administrative assistantships available. Financial award application deadline: 2/1; financial award applicants required to submit FAFSA. *Faculty research:* Regional labor market studies, economic development, market research, economic forecasting, energy analysis. *Unit head:* Dr. Javier Reyes, Dean, 304-293-7800, Fax: 304-293-4056, E-mail: javier.reyes@mail.wvu.edu. *Application contact:* Dr. Mark Gavin, Associate Dean for Graduate Programs, 304-293-7952, Fax: 304-293-7188, E-mail: mark.gavin@mail.wvu.edu.
Website: http://www.be.wvu.edu

Wilfrid Laurier University, Faculty of Graduate and Postdoctoral Studies, School of Business and Economics, Department of Business, Waterloo, ON N2L 3C5, Canada. Offers accounting (PhD); finance (M Fin); financial economics (PhD); marketing (PhD); operations and supply chain management (PhD); organizational behavior and human resource management (M Sc); organizational behaviour and human resource management (PhD); supply chain management (M Sc); technology management (EMTM). *Accreditation:* AACSB. *Program availability:* Part-time, evening/weekend. *Degree requirements:* For master's, thesis optional; for doctorate, comprehensive exam, thesis/dissertation. *Entrance requirements:* For master's, GMAT, 4-year honors degree with minimum B+ average; for doctorate, GMAT, master's degree, minimum B+ average. Additional exam requirements/recommendations for international students: Required—TOEFL (minimum score 89 iBT). Electronic applications accepted. *Faculty research:* Financial economics, management and organizational behavior, operations and supply chain management.

Wilkes University, College of Graduate and Professional Studies, Jay S. Sidhu School of Business and Leadership, Wilkes-Barre, PA 18766-0002. Offers accounting (MBA); entrepreneurship (MBA); finance (MBA); health care administration (MBA); human resource management (MBA); international business (MBA); operations management (MBA); organizational leadership and development (MBA). *Accreditation:* ACBSP. *Program availability:* Part-time, evening/weekend. *Students:* 37 full-time (18 women), 87 part-time (45 women); includes 17 minority (4 Black or African American, non-Hispanic/Latino; 5 Asian, non-Hispanic/Latino; 6 Hispanic/Latino; 2 Two or more races, non-Hispanic/Latino), 14 international. Average age 30. In 2017, 77 master's awarded. *Entrance requirements:* For master's, GMAT. Additional exam requirements/recommendations for international students: Required—TOEFL (minimum score 550 paper-based; 79 iBT). *Application deadline:* Applications are processed on a rolling basis. Application fee: $45 ($65 for international students). Electronic applications accepted. *Expenses:* Contact institution. *Financial support:* Unspecified assistantships available. Financial award application deadline: 3/1; financial award applicants required to submit FAFSA. *Unit head:* Dr. Abel Adekola, Dean, 570-408-4701, Fax: 570-408-7846, E-mail: abel.adekola@wilkes.edu. *Application contact:* Kristin Donati, Associate Director of Graduate Admissions, 570-408-3338, Fax: 570-408-7846, E-mail: kristin.donati@wilkes.edu.
Website: http://www.wilkes.edu/academics/colleges/sidhu-school-of-business-leadership/index.aspx

Wilmington University, College of Business, New Castle, DE 19720-6491. Offers accounting (MBA, MS); business administration (MBA, DBA); environmental stewardship (MBA); finance (MBA); health care administration (MBA, MSM); homeland security (MBA, MSM); human resource management (MSM); management information systems (MBA, MSN); marketing (MSM); marketing management (MBA); military

leadership (MSM); organizational leadership (MBA, MSM); public administration (MSM). *Program availability:* Part-time, evening/weekend. *Faculty:* 16 full-time (8 women), 106 part-time/adjunct (49 women). *Students:* 525 full-time (294 women), 1,212 part-time (780 women); includes 557 minority (412 Black or African American, non-Hispanic/Latino; 14 American Indian or Alaska Native, non-Hispanic/Latino; 55 Asian, non-Hispanic/Latino; 25 Hispanic/Latino; 3 Native Hawaiian or other Pacific Islander, non-Hispanic/Latino; 48 Two or more races, non-Hispanic/Latino), 157 international. Average age 35. 1,484 applicants, 70% accepted, 685 enrolled. In 2017, 543 master's, 16 doctorates awarded. *Entrance requirements:* Additional exam requirements/recommendations for international students: Required—TOEFL (minimum score 500 paper-based). *Application deadline:* Applications are processed on a rolling basis. Application fee: $35. Electronic applications accepted. *Expenses: Tuition:* Part-time $466 per credit. *Required fees:* $25 per semester. Tuition and fees vary according to degree level and campus/location. *Financial support:* Applicants required to submit FAFSA. *Unit head:* Dr. Kathy S. Kennedy Ratajack, Dean, 302-356-2481. *Application contact:* Laura Morris, Director of Admissions, 877-967-5456, E-mail: infocenter@wilmu.edu.
Website: http://www.wilmu.edu/

Wingate University, Porter B. Byrum School of Business, Wingate, NC 28174. Offers accounting (MAC); corporate innovation (MBA); finance (MBA); general management (MBA); healthcare management (MBA); marketing (MBA); project management (MBA). *Accreditation:* ACBSP. *Program availability:* Part-time, evening/weekend. *Entrance requirements:* For master's, GMAT, work experience, 2 letters of recommendation. Electronic applications accepted. *Expenses:* Contact institution. *Faculty research:* Stochastic processes, business ethics, regional economic development, municipal finance, consumer behavior.

Xavier University, Williams College of Business, Master of Business Administration Program, Cincinnati, OH 45207. Offers business administration (Exec MBA, MBA); business intelligence (MBA); finance (MBA); health industry (MBA); international business (MBA); marketing (MBA); values-based leadership (MBA); MBA/MHSA; MSN/MBA. *Accreditation:* AACSB. *Program availability:* Part-time, evening/weekend. *Degree requirements:* For master's, capstone course. *Entrance requirements:* For master's, GMAT or GRE, official transcript; resume. Additional exam requirements/recommendations for international students: Required—TOEFL (minimum score 550 paper-based; 79 iBT). Electronic applications accepted. Application fee is waived when completed online. *Expenses:* Contact institution.

Yale University, Yale School of Management and Graduate School of Arts and Sciences, Doctoral Program in Management, New Haven, CT 06520. Offers accounting (PhD); financial economics (PhD); marketing (PhD); organizations and management (PhD). *Accreditation:* AACSB. *Degree requirements:* For doctorate, comprehensive exam, thesis/dissertation. *Entrance requirements:* For doctorate, GMAT or GRE General Test. Additional exam requirements/recommendations for international students: Required—TOEFL or IELTS. Electronic applications accepted. *Expenses:* Contact institution. *Faculty research:* Pricing of options and futures, term structure of interest rates, use of accounting numbers in debt contracts, product differentiation, e-commerce and marketing, behavioral finance.

York College of Pennsylvania, Graham School of Business, York, PA 17403-3651. Offers accounting (M Acc); business (MBA); continuous improvement (MBA); financial management (MBA); health care management (MBA); management (MBA); marketing (MBA); self-designed (MBA). *Accreditation:* ACBSP. *Program availability:* Part-time, evening/weekend. *Faculty:* 9 full-time (2 women), 3 part-time/adjunct (0 women). *Students:* 3 full-time (2 women), 72 part-time (33 women); includes 14 minority (7 Black or African American, non-Hispanic/Latino; 3 Asian, non-Hispanic/Latino; 1 Hispanic/Latino; 3 Two or more races, non-Hispanic/Latino). Average age 35. 68 applicants, 76% accepted, 28 enrolled. In 2017, 17 master's awarded. *Degree requirements:* For master's, directed study. *Entrance requirements:* For master's, GMAT. Additional exam requirements/recommendations for international students: Required—TOEFL (minimum score 530 paper-based; 72 iBT), IELTS (minimum score 6). *Application deadline:* For fall admission, 7/15 priority date for domestic students, 5/1 for international students; for spring admission, 11/15 priority date for domestic students, 9/1 for international students; for summer admission, 4/15 priority date for domestic students. Applications are processed on a rolling basis. Application fee: $0. Electronic applications accepted. *Expenses:* $795 per credit. *Financial support:* In 2017–18, 3 students received support. Scholarships/grants available. Financial award applicants required to submit FAFSA. *Unit head:* Nicole Cornell Sadowski, MBA Director, 717-815-1491, Fax: 717-600-3999, E-mail: ncornell@ycp.edu. *Application contact:* MBA Office, 717-815-1491, Fax: 717-600-3999, E-mail: mba@ycp.edu.
Website: http://www.ycp.edu/mba

York University, Faculty of Graduate Studies, Schulich School of Business, Toronto, ON M3J 1P3, Canada. Offers accounting (M Acc); administration (PhD); business (MBA); business analytics (MBA); finance (MF); international business (IMBA); MBA/JD; MBA/MA; MBA/MFA. *Program availability:* Part-time, evening/weekend. *Degree requirements:* For master's, advanced proficiency in a second language, work term (IMBA); for doctorate, comprehensive exam, thesis/dissertation. *Entrance requirements:* For master's, GMAT or GRE, minimum GPA of 3.0 (3.3 for MF, MBA in business analytics, and IMBA); for doctorate, GMAT or GRE, minimum GPA of 3.3. Additional exam requirements/recommendations for international students: Required—TOEFL (minimum score 600 paper-based; 100 iBT), IELTS (minimum score 7), York English Language Test (minimum score 1); PearsonVUE (minimum score 64). Electronic applications accepted. *Faculty research:* Accounting, finance, marketing, operations management and information systems, organizational strategy, strategic management.

Youngstown State University, Graduate School, College of Liberal Arts and Social Sciences, Department of Economics, Youngstown, OH 44555-0001. Offers economics (MA); financial economics (MA). *Program availability:* Part-time. *Degree requirements:* For master's, comprehensive exam, thesis optional. *Entrance requirements:* For master's, minimum GPA of 2.7, 21 hours in economics. Additional exam requirements/recommendations for international students: Required—TOEFL. *Faculty research:* Forecasting, applied econometrics, labor economics, applied macroeconomics, industrial organization.

Youngstown State University, Graduate School, Williamson College of Business Administration, Department of Accounting and Finance, Youngstown, OH 44555-0001. Offers accounting (MBA). *Accreditation:* AACSB. *Program availability:* Part-time, evening/weekend. *Degree requirements:* For master's, thesis optional. *Entrance requirements:* For master's, GMAT, minimum GPA of 2.7. Additional exam requirements/recommendations for international students: Required—TOEFL. *Faculty research:* Taxation and compliance, capital markets, accounting information systems, accounting theory, tax and government accounting.

Investment Management

Alaska Pacific University, Graduate Programs, Business Administration Department, Anchorage, AK 99508-4672. Offers business administration (MBA), including business administration, health services administration; information and communication technology (MBAICT); investment (CGS). *Program availability:* Part-time, evening/weekend. *Degree requirements:* For master's, capstone course. *Entrance requirements:* For master's, GMAT or GRE General Test, minimum GPA of 3.0. Additional exam requirements/recommendations for international students: Required—TOEFL (minimum score 550 paper-based).

Creighton University, Graduate School, Heider College of Business, Omaha, NE 68178-0001. Offers accounting (MAC); business administration (MBA, DBA); business intelligence and analytics (MS); finance (M Fin); investment management and financial analysis (MIMFA); JD/MBA; MBA/MIMFA; MD/MBA; Pharm D/MBA. *Accreditation:* AACSB. *Program availability:* Part-time, evening/weekend, 100% online, blended/hybrid learning. *Faculty:* 33 full-time (10 women), 22 part-time/adjunct (3 women). *Students:* 60 full-time (24 women), 308 part-time (95 women); includes 31 minority (14 Black or African American, non-Hispanic/Latino; 1 American Indian or Alaska Native, non-Hispanic/Latino; 9 Asian, non-Hispanic/Latino; 3 Hispanic/Latino; 2 Native Hawaiian or other Pacific Islander, non-Hispanic/Latino; 2 Two or more races, non-Hispanic/Latino), 28 international. Average age 32. 253 applicants, 74% accepted, 123 enrolled. In 2017, 139 master's awarded. *Degree requirements:* For master's, thesis optional; for doctorate, thesis/dissertation optional. *Entrance requirements:* For master's, GMAT, resume, 2 letters of recommendation. Additional exam requirements/recommendations for international students: Required—TOEFL (minimum score 90 iBT). *Application deadline:* For fall admission, 7/1 priority date for domestic students, 3/1 for international students; for winter admission, 10/1 priority date for domestic students, 7/1 for international students; for spring admission, 4/1 priority date for domestic students, 10/1 for international students; for summer admission, 5/1 for domestic and international students. Applications are processed on a rolling basis. Application fee: $50. Electronic applications accepted. *Expenses:* Contact institution. *Financial support:* In 2017–18, 10 fellowships with partial tuition reimbursements (averaging $8,448 per year) were awarded; career-related internships or fieldwork, tuition waivers (partial), and unspecified assistantships also available. Financial award application deadline: 3/1. *Faculty research:* Small business issues, economics, business analytics. *Unit head:* Dr. Deborah Wells, Associate Dean for Graduate Programs, 402-280-2841, E-mail: deborahwells@creighton.edu. *Application contact:* Chris Karasek, Assistant Dean, 402-280-2829, Fax: 402-280-2172, E-mail: chriskarasek@creighton.edu.
Website: http://business.creighton.edu

Fordham University, Gabelli School of Business, New York, NY 10023. Offers accounting (MBA, MS); applied statistics and decision-making (MS); business economics (DPS); capital markets (DPS); communications and media management (MBA); electronic business (MBA); entrepreneurship (MBA); finance (MBA, PhD); global finance (MS); global sustainability (MBA); health administration (MS); healthcare management (MBA); information systems (MBA, MS); investor relations (MS); management (EMBA, MBA, MS, PhD); marketing (MBA); marketing intelligence (MS); media management (MS); nonprofit leadership (MS); quantitative finance (MS); strategy and decision-making (DPS); taxation (MS); JD/MBA; MS/MBA. *Accreditation:* AACSB. *Program availability:* Part-time, evening/weekend. *Faculty:* 130 full-time (46 women), 42 part-time/adjunct (5 women). *Students:* 1,051 full-time (570 women), 563 part-time (313 women); includes 190 minority (48 Black or African American, non-Hispanic/Latino; 72 Asian, non-Hispanic/Latino; 69 Hispanic/Latino; 1 Native Hawaiian or other Pacific Islander, non-Hispanic/Latino), 1,106 international. Average age 27. 4,577 applicants, 58% accepted, 794 enrolled. In 2017, 937 master's awarded. Terminal master's awarded for partial completion of doctoral program. *Degree requirements:* For master's, internships (for some degrees); for doctorate, comprehensive exam (for some programs), thesis/dissertation. *Entrance requirements:* For master's, GMAT/GRE, 2 letters of recommendation, resume, 2 essays, transcripts, interview. Additional exam requirements/recommendations for international students: Required—TOEFL (minimum score 100 iBT), IELTS (minimum score 7). *Application deadline:* For fall admission, 11/15 priority date for domestic and international students; for winter admission, 1/19 priority date for domestic students, 1/1 priority date for international students; for spring admission, 4/15 for domestic students, 3/1 for international students; for summer admission, 6/1 for domestic students. Application fee: $130. Electronic applications accepted. *Expenses:* $1,495 per credit. *Financial support:* Career-related internships or fieldwork, institutionally sponsored loans, scholarships/grants, and unspecified assistantships available. Support available to part-time students. Financial award application deadline: 6/30; financial award applicants required to submit FAFSA. *Unit head:* Dr. Donna Rapaccioli, Dean, 212-636-6165, Fax: 212-307-1779, E-mail: rapaccioli@fordham.edu. *Application contact:* Lawrence Murray, Senior Assistant Dean of Graduate Admissions and Advising, 212-636-6200, Fax: 212-636-7076, E-mail: admissionsgb@fordham.edu.
Website: http://www.fordham.edu/gabelli

The George Washington University, School of Business, Department of Finance, Washington, DC 20052. Offers finance (MSF, PhD); finance and investments (MBA). *Program availability:* Part-time, evening/weekend. *Faculty:* 19 full-time (3 women), 14 part-time/adjunct (1 woman). *Students:* 200 full-time (101 women), 7 part-time (2 women); includes 10 minority (2 Black or African American, non-Hispanic/Latino; 1 American Indian or Alaska Native, non-Hispanic/Latino; 6 Asian, non-Hispanic/Latino; 1 Hispanic/Latino), 191 international. Average age 26. 901 applicants, 38% accepted, 74 enrolled. In 2017, 138 master's awarded. *Entrance requirements:* For master's, GMAT; for doctorate, GMAT or GRE. Additional exam requirements/recommendations for international students: Required—TOEFL. *Application deadline:* For fall admission, 4/1 priority date for domestic students; for spring admission, 10/1 for domestic students. Applications are processed on a rolling basis. Application fee: $75. *Expenses: Tuition:* Full-time $28,800; part-time $1655 per credit hour. *Required fees:* $45; $2.75 per credit hour. *Financial support:* In 2017–18, 38 students received support. Fellowships, teaching assistantships, career-related internships or fieldwork, Federal Work-Study, and institutionally sponsored loans available. Financial award application deadline: 4/1. *Unit head:* Robert Van Order, Chair, 202-994-3427, E-mail: rvo@gwu.edu. *Application contact:* Christopher Storer, Executive Director, Graduate Admissions, 202-994-1212, E-mail: gwmba@gwu.edu.

Hofstra University, Frank G. Zarb School of Business, Programs in Finance, Hempstead, NY 11549. Offers business administration (MBA), including finance; corporate finance (Advanced Certificate); finance (MS), including financial and risk management, investment analysis; investment management (Advanced Certificate); quantitative finance (MS). *Program availability:* Part-time, evening/weekend, blended/hybrid learning. *Students:* 157 full-time (55 women), 44 part-time (11 women); includes 23 minority (6 Black or African American, non-Hispanic/Latino; 1 American Indian or

Alaska Native, non-Hispanic/Latino; 7 Asian, non-Hispanic/Latino; 8 Hispanic/Latino; 1 Two or more races, non-Hispanic/Latino), 134 international. Average age 25. 530 applicants, 75% accepted, 71 enrolled. In 2017, 103 master's awarded. *Degree requirements:* For master's, capstone course (for MBA), thesis (for MS), minimum GPA of 3.0. *Entrance requirements:* For master's, GMAT/GRE, 2 letters of recommendation, resume, essay. Additional exam requirements/recommendations for international students: Required—TOEFL (minimum score 550 paper-based; 80 iBT); Recommended—IELTS (minimum score 6). *Application deadline:* Applications are processed on a rolling basis. Application fee: $75. Electronic applications accepted. *Expenses:* $1,322 per credit. *Financial support:* In 2017–18, 57 students received support, including 51 fellowships with full and partial tuition reimbursements available (averaging $5,604 per year); research assistantships with full and partial tuition reimbursements available, career-related internships or fieldwork, Federal Work-Study, institutionally sponsored loans, scholarships/grants, tuition waivers (full and partial), and unspecified assistantships also available. Support available to part-time students. Financial award applicants required to submit FAFSA. *Faculty research:* Individual investors and financial crisis; short-sale constraints and futures trading; social media and sentiment in financial markets; external monitoring of firms; CEO inside debt and insider trading. *Unit head:* Dr. K. G. Viswanathan, Chairperson, 516-463-5699, Fax: 516-463-4834, E-mail: k.g.viswanathan@hofstra.edu. *Application contact:* Sunil Samuel, Assistant Vice President of Admissions, 516-463-4723, Fax: 516-463-4664, E-mail: graduateadmission@hofstra.edu.
Website: http://www.hofstra.edu/business/

Johns Hopkins University, Carey Business School, Certificate Programs, Baltimore, MD 21218. Offers financial management (Certificate); investments (Certificate). *Program availability:* Part-time, evening/weekend. *Faculty:* 93 full-time (33 women), 45 part-time/adjunct (11 women). *Students:* 19 part-time (10 women); includes 7 minority (2 Black or African American, non-Hispanic/Latino; 2 Asian, non-Hispanic/Latino; 2 Hispanic/Latino; 1 Two or more races, non-Hispanic/Latino), 3 international. Average age 34. 12 applicants, 83% accepted, 3 enrolled. In 2017, 31 Certificates awarded. *Degree requirements:* For Certificate, 16 credits. *Entrance requirements:* Additional exam requirements/recommendations for international students: Required—TOEFL, IELTS. *Application deadline:* Applications are processed on a rolling basis. Application fee: $100. Electronic applications accepted. *Expenses:* Contact institution. *Unit head:* Dr. Kevin Frick, Vice Dean of Education, 410-234-9272, E-mail: kfrick@jhu.edu. *Application contact:* Office of Admissions, 410-234-9220, Fax: 443-529-1554, E-mail: carey.admissions@jhu.edu.
Website: http://carey.jhu.edu/academics/certificate-programs/

Johns Hopkins University, Carey Business School, MS in Business Analytics and Risk Management Program, Baltimore, MD 21218. Offers MS. *Program availability:* Part-time, evening/weekend. *Faculty:* 93 full-time (33 women), 45 part-time/adjunct (11 women). *Students:* 39 full-time (25 women), 11 part-time (4 women); includes 7 minority (4 Black or African American, non-Hispanic/Latino; 1 Asian, non-Hispanic/Latino; 2 Hispanic/Latino), 38 international. Average age 24. 158 applicants, 70% accepted, 42 enrolled. In 2017, 26 master's awarded. *Degree requirements:* For master's, 36 credits. *Entrance requirements:* For master's, GMAT or GRE. Additional exam requirements/recommendations for international students: Required—TOEFL, IELTS. *Application deadline:* For fall admission, 5/1 for domestic and international students. Applications are processed on a rolling basis. Application fee: $100. Electronic applications accepted. *Expenses:* $66,500 (full-time); $1,330 per credit (part-time). *Financial support:* In 2017–18, 7 students received support. Scholarships/grants available. Support available to part-time students. Financial award application deadline: 4/15; financial award applicants required to submit FAFSA. *Faculty research:* Emerging issues in risk management, health care/medical services, strategic options and simulation. *Unit head:* Dr. Kevin Frick, Vice Dean of Education, 410-234-9272, E-mail: kfrick@jhu.edu. *Application contact:* Office of Admissions, 410-234-9220, Fax: 443-529-1554, E-mail: carey.admissions@jhu.edu.

Lincoln University, Graduate Studies, Oakland, CA 94612. Offers finance and investments (DBA); finance management (MS); finance management and investments (MBA); general business (MBA); human resource management (MBA, DBA); international business (MBA, MS); management information systems (MBA). *Program availability:* Part-time. *Faculty:* 14 full-time (2 women), 20 part-time/adjunct (6 women). *Students:* 606 full-time (222 women), 31 part-time (14 women); includes 10 minority (8 Asian, non-Hispanic/Latino; 1 Hispanic/Latino; 1 Two or more races, non-Hispanic/Latino), 623 international. Average age 26. *Degree requirements:* For master's, research project (thesis), internship report, or comprehensive exam; for doctorate, comprehensive exam, thesis/dissertation. *Entrance requirements:* For master's, minimum GPA of 2.7; for doctorate, GMAT (minimum score: 550), GRE (minimum score: 1000), or equivalent test results (waived for master's degree with minimum cumulative GPA of 3.3). Additional exam requirements/recommendations for international students: Required—TOEFL minimum score 525 paper-based; 71 iBT or IELTS minimum score 5.5 (for MBA); TOEFL minimum score 550 paper-based; 79 iBT or IELTS minimum score 6 (for MS and DBA). *Application deadline:* For fall admission, 8/7 for domestic students, 7/14 for international students; for spring admission, 11/30 for domestic students, 10/31 for international students; for summer admission, 5/29 for domestic students, 5/5 for international students. Applications are processed on a rolling basis. Application fee: $75. Electronic applications accepted. *Expenses: Tuition:* Full-time $8100; part-time $450 per unit. *Required fees:* $360; $180 per semester. Tuition and fees vary according to course level, course load, degree level and program. *Financial support:* Teaching assistantships, career-related internships or fieldwork, and scholarships/grants available. Financial award applicants required to submit FAFSA. *Unit head:* Dr. Marshall Burak, Provost, 510-628-8016, Fax: 510-628-8012, E-mail: mburak@lincolnuca.edu. *Application contact:* Reenu Shrestha, Assistant to the President, 510-628-8017, Fax: 510-208-2826, E-mail: sreenu@lincolnuca.edu.

Loyola University Maryland, Graduate Programs, Sellinger School of Business, Professional MBA Program, Baltimore, MD 21210-2699. Offers finance (MBA); information systems (MBA); investments and applied portfolio management (MBA); management (MBA); marketing (MBA). *Accreditation:* AACSB. *Program availability:* Part-time, evening/weekend. *Entrance requirements:* For master's, GMAT, resume, essay, official transcripts, professional letter of recommendation. Additional exam requirements/recommendations for international students: Required—TOEFL (minimum score 550 paper-based, 80 iBT) or IELTS (minimum score 7). *Application deadline:* For fall admission, 8/1 priority date for domestic students, 4/1 for international students; for spring admission, 12/1 priority date for domestic students, 9/1 for international students; for summer admission, 5/1 priority date for domestic students. Applications are processed on a rolling basis. Application fee: $60. Electronic applications accepted. *Expenses:* Contact institution. *Financial support:* In 2017–18, 26 students received support. Scholarships/grants available. Financial award application deadline: 4/15; financial award applicants required to submit FAFSA. *Unit head:* Kelly Fader, Director of Graduate Cohort Program, 410-617-1617, E-mail: kgfader@loyola.edu. *Application contact:* Office of Graduate Business Programs, 410-617-5067, E-mail: mba@loyola.edu.

Lynn University, College of Business and Management, Boca Raton, FL 33431-5598. Offers business administration (MBA), including aviation management, entrepreneurial management, financial valuation and investment management, hospitality management, human resource management, international business management, marketing, media management, social innovation management, sports management, Web development. *Program availability:* Part-time, evening/weekend, 100% online, blended/hybrid learning. *Faculty:* 29 full-time (11 women), 19 part-time/adjunct (7 women). *Students:* 287 full-time (124 women), 195 part-time (105 women); includes 110 minority (44 Black or African American, non-Hispanic/Latino; 2 American Indian or Alaska Native, non-Hispanic/Latino; 11 Asian, non-Hispanic/Latino; 47 Hispanic/Latino; 6 Two or more races, non-Hispanic/Latino), 135 international. Average age 28. 293 applicants, 94% accepted, 192 enrolled. In 2017, 236 master's awarded. *Degree requirements:* For master's, thesis, minimum GPA of 3.0, strategic management seminar, written presentation reflecting the integration and application of theory to practice. *Entrance requirements:* For master's, bachelor's degree from accredited institution, minimum undergraduate GPA of 2.5, official undergraduate transcripts, resume, personal statement, letter of recommendation from academic or professional sources, writing sample demonstrating capacity to perform at graduate level. Additional exam requirements/recommendations for international students: Required—TOEFL (minimum score 550 paper-based; 80 iBT), IELTS (minimum score 6.5). *Application deadline:* For fall admission, 8/18 for domestic students, 8/4 for international students; for spring admission, 12/15 for domestic students, 12/1 for international students; for summer admission, 4/17 for domestic students, 4/3 for international students. Applications are processed on a rolling basis. Application fee: $45. Electronic applications accepted. *Expenses:* $740 per credit. *Financial support:* Career-related internships or fieldwork, Federal Work-Study, scholarships/grants, tuition waivers (full and partial), and unspecified assistantships available. Support available to part-time students. Financial award application deadline: 3/1; financial award applicants required to submit FAFSA. *Faculty research:* Knowledge economy, urban economy, U.S. manufacturing industries, leadership personality, stock market reactions to terrorism, personality psychology, industrial/organizational psychology. *Unit head:* Dr. RT Good, Dean of the College of Business and Management, 561-237-7458, E-mail: rgood@lynn.edu. *Application contact:* Steven Pruitt, Director of Graduate and Undergraduate Evening Admission, 561-237-7834, Fax: 561-237-7100, E-mail: spruitt@lynn.edu.
Website: http://www.lynn.edu/academics/colleges/business-and-management

Manhattanville College, School of Business, Master of Science in Finance Program, Purchase, NY 10577-2132. Offers finance (MS, Advanced Certificate), including accounting (MS), corporate finance (MS), investment management (MS). *Program availability:* Part-time, evening/weekend. *Faculty:* 4 part-time/adjunct (2 women). *Students:* 23 full-time (7 women), 6 part-time (3 women); includes 9 minority (3 Black or African American, non-Hispanic/Latino; 6 Hispanic/Latino), 2 international. Average age 29. 35 applicants, 37% accepted, 11 enrolled. In 2017, 12 master's awarded. *Degree requirements:* For master's, thesis (for some programs), final project. *Entrance requirements:* For master's, personal essay, transcripts, 2 letters of recommendation (academic or professional), resume, health form with proof of immunization (for those born after 1957). Additional exam requirements/recommendations for international students: Required—TOEFL (minimum score 563 paper-based, 85 iBT), IELTS (7), or iTEP (B2). *Application deadline:* Applications are processed on a rolling basis. Application fee: $75. Electronic applications accepted. *Expenses:* $915 per credit. *Financial support:* Federal Work-Study, institutionally sponsored loans, scholarships/grants, and unspecified assistantships available. Financial award application deadline: 3/15; financial award applicants required to submit FAFSA. *Unit head:* Laura Persky, Graduate Program Director, 914-323-5188, E-mail: laura.persky@mville.edu. *Application contact:* Monika Pottgen, Assistant Director, Recruitment and Admissions, 914-323-5150, E-mail: business@mville.edu.
Website: https://www.mville.edu/programs/ms-finance

Marywood University, Academic Affairs, Munley College of Liberal Arts and Sciences, School of Business and Global Innovation, Emphasis in Finance/Investment, Scranton, PA 18509-1598. Offers MBA. *Entrance requirements:* For master's, GMAT. Electronic applications accepted.

New York University, School of Professional Studies, Schack Institute of Real Estate, Program in Real Estate, New York, NY 10012-1019. Offers real estate (MS), including finance and investment, real estate asset management. *Program availability:* Part-time, evening/weekend. *Students:* 182 full-time (72 women), 297 part-time (60 women); includes 67 minority (5 Black or African American, non-Hispanic/Latino; 37 Asian, non-Hispanic/Latino; 21 Hispanic/Latino; 1 Native Hawaiian or other Pacific Islander, non-Hispanic/Latino; 3 Two or more races, non-Hispanic/Latino), 158 international. Average age 28. 267 applicants, 67% accepted, 96 enrolled. In 2017, 330 master's awarded. *Degree requirements:* For master's, thesis, capstone project. *Entrance requirements:* For master's, GRE or GMAT (only upon request), bachelor's degree, resume with relevant professional work, internship or volunteer experience, two letters of recommendation, statement of purpose. Additional exam requirements/recommendations for international students: Required—TOEFL (minimum score 600 paper-based; 100 iBT), IELTS (minimum score 7). *Application deadline:* For fall admission, 2/1 priority date for domestic and international students; for spring admission, 10/15 priority date for domestic students, 8/15 priority date for international students; for summer admission, 5/1 priority date for domestic students, 1/15 priority date for international students. Applications are processed on a rolling basis. Application fee: $150. Electronic applications accepted. *Expenses:* $20,244 per term. *Financial support:* Fellowships, career-related internships or fieldwork, Federal Work-Study, scholarships/grants, and health care benefits available. Support available to part-time students. Financial award application deadline: 6/30; financial award applicants required to submit FAFSA. *Unit head:* Sam Chandan, Associate Dean/Chair/Clinical Professor, 212-992-3335. *Application contact:* Office of Admissions, 212-998-7100, E-mail: sps.gradadmissions@nyu.edu.
Website: http://www.sps.nyu.edu/content/scps/academics/departments/schack/academic-offerings/graduate.html

Pace University, Lubin School of Business, Advanced Professional Certificate Program, New York, NY 10038. Offers business economics (APC); e-business (APC); financial management (APC); international business (APC); international economics (APC); investment management (APC); marketing (APC); public accounting (APC). *Program availability:* Part-time, evening/weekend. *Students:* 1 applicant, 100% accepted. *Entrance requirements:* For degree, MBA or MS in business discipline, relevant professional experience. Additional exam requirements/recommendations for international students: Required—TOEFL (minimum score 90 iBT), IELTS (minimum score 7) or PTE (minimum score 61). *Application deadline:* For fall admission, 8/1 priority date for domestic students, 6/1 for international students; for spring admission, 12/1 for domestic students, 10/1 for international students. Applications are processed

on a rolling basis. Application fee: $70. Electronic applications accepted. *Unit head:* Dr. Jack Yurkiewicz, Director, 212-618-6567, E-mail: jyurkiewicz@pace.edu. *Application contact:* Susan Ford-Goldschein, Director of Graduate Admissions, 212-346-1531, Fax: 212-346-1585, E-mail: graduateadmission@pace.edu.
Website: http://www.pace.edu/lubin/agc

Pace University, Lubin School of Business, Financial Management Program, New York, NY 10038. Offers financial management (MBA, MS); financial risk management (MS); international finance (MBA); investment management (MBA, MS). *Program availability:* Part-time, evening/weekend. *Students:* 103 full-time (41 women), 53 part-time (26 women); includes 24 minority (5 Black or African American, non-Hispanic/Latino; 11 Asian, non-Hispanic/Latino; 6 Hispanic/Latino; 1 Native Hawaiian or other Pacific Islander, non-Hispanic/Latino; 1 Two or more races, non-Hispanic/Latino), 103 international. Average age 26. 251 applicants, 61% accepted, 43 enrolled. In 2017, 108 master's awarded. *Entrance requirements:* For master's, GMAT, GRE (GMAT not required for MS with passing of Level 1 of Chartered Financial Analyst exam or Level 1 of Financial Risk Manager Exam), undergraduate degree, transcripts from all accredited colleges/universities attended, two letters of recommendation, resume, personal statement. Additional exam requirements/recommendations for international students: Required—TOEFL (minimum score 90 iBT), IELTS (minimum score 7) or PTE (minimum score 61). *Application deadline:* For fall admission, 8/1 priority date for domestic students, 6/1 for international students; for spring admission, 12/1 for domestic students, 10/1 for international students. Applications are processed on a rolling basis. Application fee: $70. Electronic applications accepted. *Financial support:* Research assistantships, career-related internships or fieldwork, Federal Work-Study, and tuition waivers (full and partial) available. Support available to part-time students. Financial award application deadline: 2/15; financial award applicants required to submit FAFSA. *Unit head:* Dr. P. V. Viswanath, Chairperson, 212-618-6518, E-mail: pviswanath@pace.edu. *Application contact:* Susan Ford-Goldschein, Director of Graduate Admissions, 212-346-1531, Fax: 212-346-1585, E-mail: graduateadmissions@pace.edu.
Website: http://www.pace.edu/lubin/financial-management-mba

Regent University, Graduate School, School of Business and Leadership, Virginia Beach, VA 23464-9800. Offers business administration (MBA), including accounting, economics, entrepreneurship, finance and investing, general management, healthcare management (MA, MBA), human resource management (MA, MBA), innovation management, leadership, marketing, not-for-profit management (MA, MBA); business analytics (MS); business and design management (MA); church leadership (MA); leadership (Certificate); organizational leadership (MA, PhD), including ecclesial leadership (DSL, PhD), entrepreneurial leadership (PhD), healthcare management (MA, MBA), human resource development (PhD), human resource management (MA, MBA), individualized studies (DSL, PhD), interdisciplinary studies (MA), leadership coaching and mentoring (MA), not-for-profit management (MA, MBA), organizational development consulting (MA), servant leadership (MA, DSL); strategic leadership (DSL), including ecclesial leadership (DSL, PhD), global consulting, healthcare leadership, individualized studies (DSL, PhD), leadership coaching, servant leadership (MA, DSL), strategic foresight. *Program availability:* Part-time, evening/weekend, 100% online, blended/hybrid learning. *Faculty:* 9 full-time (2 women), 38 part-time/adjunct (11 women). *Students:* 129 full-time (80 women), 1,152 part-time (598 women); includes 685 minority (546 Black or African American, non-Hispanic/Latino; 10 American Indian or Alaska Native, non-Hispanic/Latino; 29 Asian, non-Hispanic/Latino; 65 Hispanic/Latino; 6 Native Hawaiian or other Pacific Islander, non-Hispanic/Latino; 29 Two or more races, non-Hispanic/Latino), 62 international. Average age 41. 1,721 applicants, 48% accepted, 624 enrolled. In 2017, 125 master's, 69 doctorates awarded. *Degree requirements:* For master's, thesis or alternative, 3-credit hour culminating experience; for doctorate, thesis/dissertation. *Entrance requirements:* For master's, college transcripts, resume, essay; for doctorate, college transcripts, resume, essay, writing sample; for Certificate, writing sample, resume, transcripts. Additional exam requirements/recommendations for international students: Required—TOEFL (minimum score 577 paper-based). *Application deadline:* For fall admission, 5/1 priority date for domestic students; for spring admission, 10/1 priority date for domestic students. Applications are processed on a rolling basis. Application fee: $50. Electronic applications accepted. *Expenses:* $650 per credit (MA, MS, MBA); $995 per credit (PhD); $300 per semester technology fee. *Financial support:* In 2017–18, 829 students received support. Career-related internships or fieldwork, scholarships/grants, and unspecified assistantships available. Support available to part-time students. *Faculty research:* Servant leadership, global business, team effectiveness, technology utilization, leadership development. *Unit head:* Dr. Doris Gomez, Dean, 757-352-4686, Fax: 757-352-4634, E-mail: dorigom@regent.edu. *Application contact:* Heidi Cece, Assistant Vice President of Enrollment Management, 800-373-5504, Fax: 757-352-4381, E-mail: admissions@regent.edu.
Website: https://www.regent.edu/school-of-business-and-leadership/

Sacred Heart University, Graduate Programs, Jack Welch College of Business, Department of Finance, Fairfield, CT 06825. Offers administration (DBA); finance (MBA, Graduate Certificate); finance and investment management (MS). *Program availability:* Part-time, evening/weekend. *Faculty:* 8 full-time (2 women), 5 part-time/adjunct (1 woman). *Students:* 19 full-time (7 women), 55 part-time (16 women); includes 13 minority (8 Black or African American, non-Hispanic/Latino; 3 Asian, non-Hispanic/Latino; 2 Two or more races, non-Hispanic/Latino), 31 international. Average age 36. 54 applicants, 94% accepted, 24 enrolled. In 2017, 14 master's awarded. *Degree requirements:* For doctorate, comprehensive exam. *Entrance requirements:* For master's, GMAT or GRE, official transcripts from all institutions attended; for doctorate, GMAT or GRE with master's degree and 5 years' experience. Additional exam requirements/recommendations for international students: Required—TOEFL (minimum score 570 paper-based, 80 iBT), TWE, or IELTS (6.5). *Application deadline:* Applications are processed on a rolling basis. Application fee: $75. Electronic applications accepted. *Expenses:* Contact institution. *Financial support:* Unspecified assistantships available. Financial award applicants required to submit FAFSA. *Unit head:* Dr. Kwamie Dunbar, Assistant Professor of Finance/Director of MS in Finance and Investment Management, 203-396-8068, E-mail: dunbark@sacredheart.edu. *Application contact:* Pam Pillo, Executive Director of Graduate Admissions, 203-365-7619, E-mail: gradstudies@sacredheart.edu.
Website: http://www.sacredheart.edu/academics/johnfwelchcollegeofbusiness/aboutthecollege/

Saint Mary's College of California, School of Economics and Business Administration, MS in Financial Analysis and Investment Management Program, Moraga, CA 94556. Offers MS. *Expenses:* Contact institution.

Southern New Hampshire University, School of Business, Manchester, NH 03106-1045. Offers accounting (MBA, Graduate Certificate); accounting finance (MS); accounting/auditing (MS); accounting/forensic accounting (MS); accounting/management accounting (MS); accounting/taxation (MS); applied economics (MS); athletic administration (IMBA, Graduate Certificate); business administration (IMBA, Certificate), including business information systems (Certificate), human resource management (Certificate); business analytics (MBA); business intelligence (MBA); communication (MA), including new media and marketing, public relations; community economic development (MBA); criminal justice (MBA); data analytics (MS); economics (MBA); engineering management (MBA); entrepreneurship (MBA); finance (MBA, MS, Graduate Certificate); finance/corporate finance (MS); finance/investments (MS); forensic accounting (MBA); forensic accounting and fraud examination (Graduate Certificate); healthcare informatics (MBA); healthcare management (MBA); human resource management (MS); human resources (MBA); information technology (MS); information technology management (MBA); international business (PhD); Internet marketing (MBA); leadership (MBA); leadership of nonprofit organizations (Graduate Certificate); management (MS); marketing (MBA, MS, Graduate Certificate); music business (MBA); operations and project management (MS); operations and supply chain management (MBA, Graduate Certificate); organizational leadership (MS); project management (MBA, Graduate Certificate); public administration (MBA, Graduate Certificate); quantitative analysis (MBA); Six Sigma (Graduate Certificate); Six Sigma quality (MBA); social media marketing (MBA, Graduate Certificate); sport management (MBA, MS, Graduate Certificate); sustainability and environmental compliance (MBA); MBA/Certificate. *Accreditation:* ACBSP. *Program availability:* Part-time, evening/weekend, online learning. Terminal master's awarded for partial completion of doctoral program. *Degree requirements:* For master's, one foreign language, comprehensive exam (for some programs), thesis or alternative; for doctorate, one foreign language, comprehensive exam, thesis/dissertation. *Entrance requirements:* For master's, minimum GPA of 2.5; for doctorate, GMAT. Additional exam requirements/recommendations for international students: Required—TOEFL (minimum score 500 paper-based). *Application deadline:* Applications are processed on a rolling basis. Application fee: $40. Electronic applications accepted. *Expenses: Tuition:* Part-time $627 per credit hour. Part-time tuition and fees vary according to campus/location and program. *Financial support:* Career-related internships or fieldwork, Federal Work-Study, institutionally sponsored loans, scholarships/grants, tuition waivers (partial), and unspecified assistantships available. Support available to part-time students. Financial award applicants required to submit FAFSA. *Unit head:* Dr. Bill Lightfoot, Dean, 603-644-3102, Fax: 603-644-3144. *Application contact:* Office of Graduate Admission, 888-327-SNHU, Fax: 603-644-3144, E-mail: enroll@snhu.edu.

Temple University, Beasley School of Law, Master's and Certificate Programs, Philadelphia, PA 19122-6096. Offers Asian law (LL M); business law (Certificate); employee benefits (Certificate); estate planning (Certificate); trial advocacy (LL M); trial advocacy and litigation (Certificate). *Expenses:* Tuition, state resident: full-time $16,164; part-time $898 per credit hour. Tuition, nonresident: full-time $22,158; part-time $1231 per credit hour. *Required fees:* $890; $445 per semester. Full-time tuition and fees vary according to course load, degree level, campus/location and program.

University of Colorado Denver, Business School, Master of Business Administration Program, Denver, CO 80217. Offers bioinnovation and entrepreneurship (MBA); business intelligence (MBA); business strategy (MBA); business to business marketing (MBA); business to consumer marketing (MBA); change management (MBA); corporate financial management (MBA); enterprise technology management (MBA); entrepreneurship (MBA); health administration (MBA), including financial management, health administration, health information technologies, international health management and policy; human resources management (MBA); international business (MBA); investment management (MBA); managing for sustainability (MBA); sports and entertainment management (MBA). *Accreditation:* AACSB. *Program availability:* Part-time, evening/weekend, 100% online, blended/hybrid learning. *Degree requirements:* For master's, 48 semester hours, including 30 of core courses, 3 in international business, and 15 in electives from over 50 other business courses. *Entrance requirements:* For master's, GMAT, resume, official transcripts, essay, two letters of recommendation, financial statements (for international applicants). Additional exam requirements/recommendations for international students: Required—TOEFL (minimum score 560 paper-based; 83 iBT); Recommended—IELTS (minimum score 6.5). Electronic applications accepted. *Expenses:* Contact institution. *Faculty research:* Marketing, management, entrepreneurship, finance, health administration.

University of Houston–Downtown, Marilyn Davies College of Business, MBA Program, Houston, TX 77002. Offers accounting (MBA); finance (MBA); human resource management (MBA); international business (MBA); investment management (MBA); leadership (MBA); project management and process improvement (MBA); sales management and business development (MBA); supply chain management (MBA). *Accreditation:* AACSB. *Program availability:* Part-time, evening/weekend. *Faculty:* 36 full-time (13 women), 11 part-time/adjunct (6 women). *Students:* 4 full-time (2 women), 1,065 part-time (605 women); includes 821 minority (383 Black or African American, non-Hispanic/Latino; 3 American Indian or Alaska Native, non-Hispanic/Latino; 136 Asian, non-Hispanic/Latino; 299 Hispanic/Latino), 33 international. Average age 33. 418 applicants, 89% accepted, 308 enrolled. In 2017, 310 master's awarded. *Entrance requirements:* For master's, GMAT, two letters of recommendation from professional references, personal statement, resume. Additional exam requirements/recommendations for international students: Required—TOEFL (minimum score 81 iBT). *Application deadline:* For fall admission, 8/1 for domestic and international students. Application fee: $35 ($60 for international students). Electronic applications accepted. *Expenses:* $360 per credit resident; $725 per credit non-resident. *Financial support:* Federal Work-Study and scholarships/grants available. Financial award application deadline: 4/1; financial award applicants required to submit FAFSA. *Unit head:* Dr. Charles E. Gengler, Dean, 713-221-8179, Fax: 713-221-8675. *Application contact:* Ceshia Love, Director of Admissions, 713-221-8093, Fax: 713-223-7408, E-mail: gradadmissions@uhd.edu.
Website: http://mba.uhd.edu/

University of Notre Dame, Mendoza College of Business, Master of Business Administration Program, Notre Dame, IN 46556. Offers business analytics (MBA); business leadership (MBA); consulting (MBA); corporate finance (MBA); innovation and entrepreneurship (MBA); investments (MBA); marketing (MBA); MBA/MSBA. *Accreditation:* AACSB. *Faculty:* 60 full-time (10 women), 14 part-time/adjunct (1 woman). *Students:* 294 full-time (70 women); includes 46 minority (8 Black or African American, non-Hispanic/Latino; 3 American Indian or Alaska Native, non-Hispanic/Latino; 12 Asian, non-Hispanic/Latino; 20 Hispanic/Latino; 1 Native Hawaiian or other Pacific Islander, non-Hispanic/Latino; 2 Two or more races, non-Hispanic/Latino), 74 international. Average age 29. 633 applicants, 42% accepted, 131 enrolled. In 2017, 182 master's awarded. *Entrance requirements:* For master's, GMAT or GRE, work experience, essay, four-slide presentation, two recommendations, transcripts from all colleges and/or universities attended, interview. Additional exam requirements/recommendations for international students: Required—PTE (minimum score 68), TOEFL (minimum iBT score of 109), IELTS (7.5), or documentation of at least six semesters of full-time university education in English. *Application deadline:* For fall admission, 10/17 for domestic and international students; for winter admission, 1/9 for domestic and international students; for spring admission, 2/20 for domestic and international students; for summer admission, 3/17 for domestic students. Application fee: $175. Electronic applications accepted. *Expenses:* $74,133 (for one-year MBA); $106,526 (two-year MBA); $113,050 (for MBA/MSBA). *Financial support:* In 2017–18, 251 students received support, including 247 fellowships (averaging $27,748 per year); unspecified assistantships also available. Financial award application deadline: 2/28; financial award applicants required to submit FAFSA. *Faculty research:* Market microstructure; marketing and public policy; corporate finance and accounting; corporate governance and ethical behavior; high performing organizations. *Unit head:* Dr. Katherine Spiess, Associate Dean, Graduate Business Programs, 574-631-7236, E-mail: spiess.1@nd.edu. *Application contact:* Kristin McAndrew, Director of Admissions, Graduate Business Programs, 574-631-8488, E-mail: kmcandre@nd.edu. Website: http://mendoza.nd.edu/programs/mba-programs/

University of Wisconsin–Madison, Graduate School, Wisconsin School of Business, Doctoral Program in Finance, Investment and Banking, Madison, WI 53706-1380. Offers PhD. *Degree requirements:* For doctorate, comprehensive exam, thesis/dissertation. *Entrance requirements:* For doctorate, GMAT or GRE. Additional exam requirements/recommendations for international students: Recommended—TOEFL (minimum score 623 paper-based; 106 iBT), IELTS (minimum score 7.5), TSE (minimum score 73). Electronic applications accepted. *Expenses:* Contact institution. *Faculty research:* Banking and financial institutions, business cycles, investments, derivatives, corporate finance, economics, bankruptcy, foreclosures, mergers and acquisitions, portfolio theory.

University of Wisconsin–Milwaukee, Graduate School, Lubar School of Business, MS and Certificate Business Programs, Milwaukee, WI 53201-0413. Offers business analytics (Graduate Certificate); enterprise resource planning (Graduate Certificate); information technology management (MS); investment management (Graduate Certificate); nonprofit management (Graduate Certificate); nonprofit management and leadership (MS); state and local taxation (Graduate Certificate). *Students:* 164 full-time (87 women), 120 part-time (51 women); includes 51 minority (15 Black or African American, non-Hispanic/Latino; 18 Asian, non-Hispanic/Latino; 3 Hispanic/Latino; 15 Two or more races, non-Hispanic/Latino), 55 international. Average age 31. 227 applicants, 54% accepted, 74 enrolled. In 2017, 157 master's, 21 other advanced degrees awarded. *Entrance requirements:* Additional exam requirements/recommendations for international students: Required—TOEFL (minimum score 550 paper-based; 79 iBT), IELTS (minimum score 6.5). Application fee: $56 ($96 for international students). Electronic applications accepted. *Financial support:* Fellowships, research assistantships, teaching assistantships, health care benefits, unspecified assistantships, and project assistantships available. Financial award applicants required to submit FAFSA. *Application contact:* General Information Contact, 414-229-4982, Fax: 414-229-6967, E-mail: gradschool@uwm.edu.

Walsh College of Accountancy and Business Administration, Graduate Programs, Program in Finance, Troy, MI 48083. Offers financial investments (MSF); financial management (MSF); financial services (MSF). *Program availability:* Part-time, evening/weekend, 100% online, blended/hybrid learning. *Faculty:* 8 full-time (5 women), 16 part-time/adjunct (4 women). *Students:* 92 (40 women); includes 16 minority (12 Black or African American, non-Hispanic/Latino; 1 American Indian or Alaska Native, non-Hispanic/Latino; 2 Asian, non-Hispanic/Latino; 1 Two or more races, non-Hispanic/Latino), 6 international. Average age 33. 31 applicants, 81% accepted, 23 enrolled. In 2017, 32 master's awarded. *Entrance requirements:* For master's, minimum overall cumulative GPA of 2.75 from all colleges previously attended. Additional exam requirements/recommendations for international students: Required—TOEFL (minimum score 550 paper-based, 79 iBT), IELTS (6.5), Michigan English Language Assessment Battery, or MTELP (80). *Application deadline:* Applications are processed on a rolling basis. Application fee: $35. Electronic applications accepted. *Expenses:* $770 per semester credit hour plus $125 registration fee per semester. *Financial support:* In 2017–18, 9 students received support. Career-related internships or fieldwork and scholarships/grants available. Financial award application deadline: 6/30; financial award applicants required to submit FAFSA. *Unit head:* Dr. John Moore, Interim Chair, Finance and Economics, 248-823-1635, Fax: 248-689-0920, E-mail: john.moore@walshcollege.edu. *Application contact:* Heather Rigby, Director, Admissions and Academic Advising, 248-823-1600, Fax: 248-823-1611, E-mail: hrigby@walshcollege.edu.

Taxation

American International College, School of Business, Arts and Sciences, Springfield, MA 01109-3189. Offers accounting and taxation (MS); business administration (MBA); clinical psychology (MA); educational psychology (Ed D); forensic psychology (MS); general psychology (MA, CAGS); management (CAGS); resort and casino management (MBA, CAGS). *Program availability:* Part-time, evening/weekend. *Faculty:* 4 full-time (2 women), 25 part-time/adjunct (13 women). *Students:* 178 full-time (120 women), 24 part-time (20 women); includes 94 minority (42 Black or African American, non-Hispanic/Latino; 1 American Indian or Alaska Native, non-Hispanic/Latino; 4 Asian, non-Hispanic/Latino; 39 Hispanic/Latino; 8 Two or more races, non-Hispanic/Latino), 13 international. Average age 28. 155 applicants, 83% accepted, 71 enrolled. In 2017, 87 master's, 3 doctorates awarded. *Degree requirements:* For master's, practicum; for doctorate, comprehensive exam, thesis/dissertation, practicum. *Entrance requirements:* For master's, BS or BA, minimum undergraduate GPA of 2.75, 2 letters of recommendation, official transcripts, personal goal statement or essay; for doctorate, 3 letters of recommendation; BS or BA; minimum undergraduate GPA of 3.0 (3.25 recommended); official transcripts; personal goal statement or essay. Additional exam requirements/recommendations for international students: Required—TOEFL (minimum score 550 paper-based; 80 iBT). *Application deadline:* For fall admission, 8/15 for domestic and international students; for spring admission, 12/15 for domestic and international students. Applications are processed on a rolling basis. Application fee: $50. *Expenses:* Contact institution. *Financial support:* In 2017–18, 6 students received support, including 6 research assistantships with full tuition reimbursements available (averaging $1,500 per year). Financial award application deadline: 4/1; financial award applicants required to submit FAFSA. *Faculty research:* Substance abuse, forensic psychology, special education. *Unit head:* Dr. Susanne Swanker, Dean, 413-205-3216, Fax: 413-205-3943, E-mail: susanne.swanker@aic.edu. *Application contact:* Kerry Barnes, Dean of Graduate Admissions, 413-205-3703, Fax: 413-205-3051, E-mail: kerry.barnes@aic.edu.
Website: http://www.aic.edu/school-of-business-arts-and-sciences/

Taxation

American University, Kogod School of Business, Department of Accounting, Washington, DC 20016-8044. Offers accounting (MS, Certificate), including accounting (MS), forensic accounting (Certificate); taxation (MS, Certificate), including tax (Certificate), taxation (MS). *Program availability:* Part-time, evening/weekend. *Students:* 53 full-time (31 women), 70 part-time (35 women); includes 45 minority (23 Black or African American, non-Hispanic/Latino; 7 Asian, non-Hispanic/Latino; 13 Hispanic/Latino; 2 Two or more races, non-Hispanic/Latino), 36 international. Average age 31. 139 applicants, 80% accepted, 62 enrolled. In 2017, 60 master's, 14 other advanced degrees awarded. *Entrance requirements:* For master's, GMAT/GRE, resume, interview, personal statement, 2 letters of recommendation, transcripts; for Certificate, bachelor's degree. Additional exam requirements/recommendations for international students: Required—TOEFL (minimum score 100 iBT). *Application deadline:* For fall admission, 1/15 priority date for domestic students, 1/15 for international students; for spring admission, 10/15 priority date for domestic students, 10/15 for international students. Applications are processed on a rolling basis. Application fee: $100. *Expenses:* Contact institution. *Financial support:* Application deadline: 2/1; applicants required to submit FAFSA. *Faculty research:* Harmonization of international accounting standards, federal accounting and financial reporting, taxation of U.S. corporations doing business abroad, tax planning for real estate transactions. *Unit head:* Dr. Donald T. Williamson, Chair, Department of Accounting, 202-885-1942, Fax: 202-885-1992, E-mail: dwillia@american.edu. *Application contact:* Jason Garner, Director of Admissions, 202-885-1926, E-mail: jgarner@american.edu.
Website: http://www.american.edu/kogod/

Appalachian State University, Cratis D. Williams Graduate School, Department of Accounting, Boone, NC 28608. Offers taxation (MS). *Program availability:* Part-time. *Degree requirements:* For master's, comprehensive exam, thesis optional. *Entrance requirements:* For master's, GMAT, 3 letters of recommendation. Additional exam requirements/recommendations for international students: Required—TOEFL (minimum score 550 paper-based; 79 iBT), IELTS (minimum score 6.5). Electronic applications accepted. *Faculty research:* Audit assurance risk, state taxation, financial accounting inconsistencies, management information systems, charitable contribution taxation.

Baruch College of the City University of New York, Zicklin School of Business, Department of Accounting, Program in Taxation, New York, NY 10010-5585. Offers MBA, MS. *Program availability:* Part-time, evening/weekend. *Entrance requirements:* For master's, GMAT, 2 letters of recommendation, resume, 2 years of work experience. Additional exam requirements/recommendations for international students: Required—TOEFL (minimum score 590 paper-based), TWE.

Bentley University, McCallum Graduate School of Business, Master's Program in Audit Analytics, Waltham, MA 02452-4705. Offers MS. *Program availability:* Part-time, evening/weekend. *Faculty:* 71 full-time (25 women), 33 part-time/adjunct (15 women). *Entrance requirements:* For master's, GMAT or GRE General Test, current resume; two letters of recommendation; official copies of all university-level transcripts; 2 essays. Additional exam requirements/recommendations for international students: Required—TOEFL (minimum score 100) or IELTS (minimum score 7). *Application deadline:* Applications are processed on a rolling basis. Application fee: $75. Electronic applications accepted. *Expenses: Tuition:* Full-time $4445 per course. *Required fees:* $170 per unit. *Financial support:* In 2017–18, 1 student received support. Scholarships/grants available. Financial award application deadline: 6/1; financial award applicants required to submit FAFSA. *Application contact:* Graduate Admissions, 781-891-2108, Fax: 781-891-2464, E-mail: applygrad@bentley.edu.
Website: https://admissions.bentley.edu/graduate/masters-in-analytics

Bentley University, McCallum Graduate School of Business, Master's Program in Taxation, Waltham, MA 02452-4705. Offers MST. *Program availability:* Part-time, evening/weekend, 100% online, blended/hybrid learning. *Faculty:* 71 full-time (25 women), 33 part-time/adjunct (15 women). *Students:* 41 full-time (28 women), 57 part-time (24 women); includes 15 minority (3 Black or African American, non-Hispanic/Latino; 7 Asian, non-Hispanic/Latino; 3 Hispanic/Latino; 2 Two or more races, non-Hispanic/Latino), 17 international. Average age 31. 53 applicants, 87% accepted, 32 enrolled. In 2017, 59 master's awarded. *Entrance requirements:* For master's, GMAT or GRE General Test, current resume, two letters of recommendation, official copies of all university-level transcripts, 2 essays. Additional exam requirements/recommendations for international students: Required—TOEFL (minimum score 100) or IELTS (minimum score 7). *Application deadline:* Applications are processed on a rolling basis. Application fee: $75. Electronic applications accepted. *Expenses: Tuition:* Part-time $4445 per course. *Required fees:* $170 per unit. *Financial support:* In 2017–18, 29 students received support. Scholarships/grants and unspecified assistantships available. Financial award application deadline: 6/1; financial award applicants required to submit FAFSA. *Faculty research:* Taxation of intellectual property, tax dispute resolution, corporate tax planning and advocacy, estate and financial planning. *Unit head:* John Lynch, Senior Lecturer/Director, 781-891-2624, E-mail: jlynch@bentley.edu. *Application contact:* Graduate Admissions, 781-891-2108, Fax: 781-891-2464, E-mail: applygrad@bentley.edu.
Website: https://admissions.bentley.edu/graduate/masters-in-taxation

Boise State University, College of Business and Economics, Department of Accountancy, Boise, ID 83725-0399. Offers accountancy (MSA); accountancy taxation (MSAT). *Accreditation:* AACSB. *Program availability:* Part-time. *Faculty:* 7. *Students:* 18 full-time (8 women), 28 part-time (13 women); includes 5 minority (2 Asian, non-Hispanic/Latino; 3 Hispanic/Latino), 1 international. Average age 32. 27 applicants, 74% accepted, 12 enrolled. In 2017, 27 master's awarded. *Entrance requirements:* For master's, GMAT, minimum GPA of 3.0. Additional exam requirements/recommendations for international students: Required—TOEFL (minimum score 587 paper-based; 95 iBT), IELTS (minimum score 6.5). *Application deadline:* For fall admission, 6/1 for domestic and international students; for spring admission, 10/1 for domestic and international students; for summer admission, 4/1 for domestic and international students. Application fee: $65 ($95 for international students). Electronic applications accepted. *Expenses: Tuition,* state resident: Full-time $6471; part-time $390 per credit. *Tuition,* nonresident: full-time $21,787; part-time $685 per credit. *Required fees:* $2283; $100 per term. Part-time tuition and fees vary according to course load and program. *Financial support:* Scholarships/grants and unspecified assistantships available. Financial award application deadline: 2/15; financial award applicants required to submit FAFSA. *Unit head:* Dr. Troy Hyatt, Director, 208-426-3412, E-mail: troyhyatt@boisestate.edu. *Application contact:* Trisha Stevens Lamb, Program Director, 208-426-1120, E-mail: trishastevenslamb@boisestate.edu.
Website: https://cobe.boisestate.edu/graduate-programs-overview/

Bryant University, Graduate School of Business, Smithfield, RI 02917. Offers accounting (MPAC); business administration (MBA), including business analytics, general management, global finance, global supply chain management, international business; taxation (MST). *Program availability:* Part-time, 100% online. *Faculty:* 30 full-time (5 women), 7 part-time/adjunct (2 women). *Students:* 84 full-time (31 women), 91 part-time (35 women); includes 24 minority (4 Black or African American, non-Hispanic/Latino; 1 American Indian or Alaska Native, non-Hispanic/Latino; 6 Asian, non-Hispanic/Latino; 8 Hispanic/Latino; 5 Two or more races, non-Hispanic/Latino), 6 international. Average age 26. 215 applicants, 66% accepted, 96 enrolled. In 2017, 118 master's

awarded. *Degree requirements:* For master's, comprehensive exam (for some programs). *Entrance requirements:* For master's, GMAT, resume, recommendation, college transcripts. Additional exam requirements/recommendations for international students: Required—TOEFL (minimum score 580 paper-based; 95 iBT). *Application deadline:* For fall admission, 7/15 for domestic and international students; for spring admission, 11/15 for domestic and international students; for summer admission, 4/15 for domestic and international students. Applications are processed on a rolling basis. Application fee: $80. Electronic applications accepted. *Expenses:* $45,102 total, $1,118 per credit hour, $1,500 study abroad fee (for full-time MBA); $40,248 total, $1,118 per credit hour (for part-time MBA); $30,280 total, $1,176 per credit hour (for MP Ac and MST); $13,146, $1,118 per credit hour (for CGS). *Financial support:* In 2017–18, 95 fellowships with full and partial tuition reimbursements (averaging $9,825 per year), 9 research assistantships with full and partial tuition reimbursements (averaging $7,100 per year) were awarded; scholarships/grants and unspecified assistantships also available. Support available to part-time students. Financial award application deadline: 2/15; financial award applicants required to submit FAFSA. *Faculty research:* International business, public sector auditing, taxation of partnerships, information systems security, financial markets microstructure. *Unit head:* Bjorn Carlsson, Graduate Program Director, 401-232-6707, E-mail: bcarlsson@bryant.edu. *Application contact:* Terri Rogers, Admissions Assistant, 401-232-6230, Fax: 401-232-6494, E-mail: graduateprograms@bryant.edu.
Website: http://gradschool.bryant.edu/business/

California Miramar University, Program in Taxation and Trade for Executives, San Diego, CA 92108. Offers MT.

California Polytechnic State University, San Luis Obispo, Orfalea College of Business, Program in Taxation, San Luis Obispo, CA 93407. Offers MS. *Students:* 16 full-time (7 women); includes 6 minority (4 Asian, non-Hispanic/Latino; 1 Hispanic/Latino; 1 Two or more races, non-Hispanic/Latino). Average age 23. In 2017, 17 master's awarded. *Degree requirements:* For master's, comprehensive exam (for some programs), thesis (for some programs). *Entrance requirements:* For master's, GMAT. Additional exam requirements/recommendations for international students: Required—TOEFL. *Application deadline:* Applications are processed on a rolling basis. Application fee: $55. Electronic applications accepted. *Expenses:* Tuition, state resident $7176; part-time $4164 per year. *Required fees:* $3690; $3219 per year. $1073 per trimester. *Financial support:* Fellowships, career-related internships or fieldwork, Federal Work-Study, institutionally sponsored loans, scholarships/grants, and unspecified assistantships available. Support available to part-time students. Financial award application deadline: 3/2; financial award applicants required to submit FAFSA. *Unit head:* Dr. Scott Dawson, Dean, 805-756-2705, E-mail: scdawson@calpoly.edu. *Application contact:* Dr. Sanjiv Jaggia, Associate Dean, Graduate Programs, 805-756-7519, E-mail: sjaggia@calpoly.edu.
Website: http://www.cob.calpoly.edu/gradbusiness/degree-programs/ms-tax/

California State University, Fullerton, Graduate Studies, College of Business and Economics, Department of Accounting, Fullerton, CA 92831-3599. Offers accounting (MBA, MS). *Accreditation:* AACSB. *Program availability:* Part-time. *Faculty:* 8 full-time (2 women), 6 part-time/adjunct (1 woman). *Students:* 102 full-time (68 women), 64 part-time (31 women); includes 63 minority (44 Asian, non-Hispanic/Latino; 15 Hispanic/Latino; 4 Two or more races, non-Hispanic/Latino), 81 international. Average age 28. 130 applicants, 55% accepted, 34 enrolled. *Degree requirements:* For master's, thesis or alternative, project. *Entrance requirements:* For master's, GMAT, minimum AACSB index of 950. *Application deadline:* Applications are processed on a rolling basis. Application fee: $55. Electronic applications accepted. *Financial support:* Career-related internships or fieldwork, Federal Work-Study, institutionally sponsored loans, and scholarships/grants available. Support available to part-time students. Financial award application deadline: 3/1; financial award applicants required to submit FAFSA. *Unit head:* Dr. Betty Chavis, Chair, 657-278-2225. *Application contact:* Admissions/Applications, 657-278-2371.

California State University, Northridge, Graduate Studies, Tseng College, Northridge, CA 91330. Offers business administration (Graduate Certificate); health administration (MPA); health education (MPH); knowledge management (MKM); music industry administration (MA); nonprofit-sector management (Graduate Certificate); public administration (MPA); public sector management and leadership (MPA); social work (MSW); taxation (MS); tourism, hospitality and recreation management (MS). *Students:* 4 part-time (all women); includes 1 minority (Black or African American, non-Hispanic/Latino). Average age 37. In 2017, 2 master's awarded. *Entrance requirements:* For master's, GRE (if cumulative undergraduate GPA less than 3.0). *Unit head:* Joyce Feucht-Haviar, Dean, 866-873-6439.

Capital University, Law School, Program in Business Law and Taxation, Columbus, OH 43209-2394. Offers business (LL M); business and taxation (LL M); taxation (LL M); JD/LL M. *Program availability:* Part-time, evening/weekend. *Degree requirements:* For master's, thesis or alternative. *Entrance requirements:* For master's, previous course work in accounting, business law, and taxation. Additional exam requirements/recommendations for international students: Required—TOEFL (minimum score 600 paper-based). Electronic applications accepted.

Capital University, Law School, Program in Taxation, Columbus, OH 43209-2394. Offers taxation (MT). *Program availability:* Part-time, evening/weekend. *Degree requirements:* For master's, thesis or alternative. *Entrance requirements:* For master's, previous course work in accounting, business law, and taxation. Additional exam requirements/recommendations for international students: Required—TOEFL (minimum score 600 paper-based). Electronic applications accepted. *Expenses:* Contact institution.

Chapman University, Dale E. Fowler School of Law, Orange, CA 92866. Offers advocacy and dispute resolution (JD); business law (LL M, JD); criminal law (JD); entertainment and media law (LL M); entertainment law (JD); environmental, land use, and real estate law (JD); international and comparative law (LL M); international law (JD); law (JD); prosecutorial science (LL M); tax law (JD); taxation (LL M); trial advocacy (LL M); JD/MBA; JD/MFA. *Accreditation:* ABA. *Program availability:* Part-time. *Faculty:* 44 full-time (18 women), 34 part-time/adjunct (9 women). *Students:* 478 full-time (262 women), 37 part-time (24 women); includes 217 minority (9 Black or African American, non-Hispanic/Latino; 1 American Indian or Alaska Native, non-Hispanic/Latino; 69 Asian, non-Hispanic/Latino; 104 Hispanic/Latino; 34 Two or more races, non-Hispanic/Latino), 11 international. Average age 26. 1,499 applicants, 50% accepted, 190 enrolled. In 2017, 17 master's, 149 doctorates awarded. *Entrance requirements:* For doctorate, LSAT. Additional exam requirements/recommendations for international students: Required—TOEFL (minimum score 600 paper-based; 100 iBT). *Application deadline:* For fall admission, 4/17 priority date for domestic students. Applications are processed on a rolling basis. Electronic applications accepted. *Expenses:* Contact institution. *Financial support:* Fellowships, Federal Work-Study, and scholarships/grants available. Financial award applicants required to submit FAFSA. *Unit head:* Matthew J. Parlow, Dean, 714-628-2678, E-mail: parlow@chapman.edu. *Application contact:* Justin Cruz, Assistant Dean of Admissions and Diversity Initiatives, 714-628-2594, E-mail: lawadmission@chapman.edu.
Website: https://www.chapman.edu/law/index.aspx

DePaul University, College of Law, Chicago, IL 60604. Offers business law and taxation (MJ); criminal law (MJ); health and intellectual property law (MJ); health care compliance (MJ); health law (LL M, MJ); intellectual property law (LL M); international and comparative law (MJ); international law (LL M); law (JD); public interest law (MJ); taxation (LL M); U.S. legal studies (LL M); JD/LL M; JD/MA; JD/MBA; JD/MS. *Accreditation:* ABA. *Program availability:* Part-time, evening/weekend. *Entrance requirements:* For doctorate, LSAT, LSAC applicant evaluation/letter of recommendation, personal statement, resume. Additional exam requirements/recommendations for international students: Required—TOEFL (minimum score 577 paper-based; 90 iBT), IELTS (minimum score 6.5). *Application deadline:* For fall admission, 3/1 for domestic and international students. Applications are processed on a rolling basis. Electronic applications accepted. *Expenses:* Contact institution. *Financial support:* Application deadline: 3/1; applicants required to submit FAFSA. *Unit head:* Jennifer Rosato Perea, Dean, 312-362-8701, E-mail: jrosato@depaul.edu. *Application contact:* Amanda Noascono, Director of Law Admissions/Assistant Dean, 312-362-8807, Fax: 312-362-5280, E-mail: lawinfo@depaul.edu.
Website: http://law.depaul.edu

DePaul University, Kellstadt Graduate School of Business, Chicago, IL 60604. Offers accountancy (MBA, MSA); applied economics (MBA); audit and advisory services (MS); business administration (DBA); business analytics (MS); business strategy and decision-making (MBA); computational finance (MS); economics and policy analysis (MS); enterprise risk management (MS); entrepreneurship (MBA, MS); finance (MBA, MS); general business (MBA); hospitality leadership (MBA); hospitality leadership and operational performance (MBA); human resources (MS); international business (MBA); management (MBA, MS); management information systems (MBA); marketing (MBA, MS); marketing analysis (MS); marketing strategy and planning (MBA); real estate (MS); real estate finance and investment (MBA); strategy, execution and valuation (MBA); supply chain management (MS); sustainable management (MS); taxation (MS); JD/MBA. *Accreditation:* AACSB. *Program availability:* Part-time, evening/weekend, online learning. *Entrance requirements:* For master's, GMAT/GRE, 2 letters of recommendation, resume, essay, official transcripts. Additional exam requirements/recommendations for international students: Required—TOEFL (minimum score 550 paper-based; 80 iBT). *Application deadline:* For fall admission, 7/1 for domestic students, 6/1 for international students; for winter admission, 10/1 for domestic students, 9/1 for international students; for spring admission, 2/1 for domestic students, 1/1 for international students. Applications are processed on a rolling basis. Application fee: $60. Electronic applications accepted. *Expenses:* Contact institution. *Financial support:* Application deadline: 4/1; applicants required to submit FAFSA. *Unit head:* Christa Hinton, Assistant Dean and Director, 312-362-8810, Fax: 312-362-6677, E-mail: chinton@depaul.edu. *Application contact:* Garry Cooke, Director of Recruitment and Admissions, 312-362-8810, Fax: 312-362-6677, E-mail: kgsb@depaul.edu.
Website: http://kellstadt.depaul.edu

Fairfield University, Dolan School of Business, Fairfield, CT 06824. Offers accounting (MBA, MS, CAS); business analytics (MS); finance (MBA, MS, CAS); information systems and business analytics (MBA); management (MBA, CAS); marketing (MBA, CAS); taxation (CAS). *Accreditation:* AACSB. *Program availability:* Part-time, evening/weekend. *Faculty:* 18 full-time (6 women), 6 part-time/adjunct (2 women). *Students:* 120 full-time (57 women), 67 part-time (27 women); includes 20 minority (3 Black or African American, non-Hispanic/Latino; 1 American Indian or Alaska Native, non-Hispanic/Latino; 3 Asian, non-Hispanic/Latino; 11 Hispanic/Latino; 2 Two or more races, non-Hispanic/Latino), 33 international. Average age 26. 195 applicants, 87% accepted, 112 enrolled. In 2017, 93 master's awarded. *Degree requirements:* For master's, capstone course. *Entrance requirements:* For master's, GMAT (minimum score 500), 2 letters of reference, resume, minimum GPA of 3.0. Additional exam requirements/recommendations for international students: Required—TOEFL (minimum score 550 paper-based; 80 iBT) or IELTS (minimum score 6.5). *Application deadline:* For fall admission, 5/15 for international students; for spring admission, 10/15 for international students. Applications are processed on a rolling basis. Application fee: $60. Electronic applications accepted. *Expenses:* $925 per credit hour. *Financial support:* In 2017–18, 31 students received support. Scholarships/grants and unspecified assistantships available. Financial award applicants required to submit FAFSA. *Faculty research:* International finance, leadership and careers, ethics in accounting, emotions in consumer behavior and organizations, data analytics. *Unit head:* Dr. Mark Ligas, Interim Dean, 203-254-4070, Fax: 203-254-4105, E-mail: mligas@fairfield.edu. *Application contact:* Marianne Gumpper, Director of Graduate and Continuing Studies Admission, 203-254-4184, Fax: 203-254-4073, E-mail: gradadmis@fairfield.edu.
Website: http://fairfield.edu/mba

Fairleigh Dickinson University, Florham Campus, Silberman College of Business, Department of Accounting, Law, and Tax, Program in Taxation, Madison, NJ 07940-1099. Offers MS, Certificate.

Fairleigh Dickinson University, Metropolitan Campus, Silberman College of Business, Department of Accounting, Law, and Tax, Program in Taxation, Teaneck, NJ 07666-1914. Offers MS.

Florida Gulf Coast University, Lutgert College of Business, Program in Accounting and Taxation, Fort Myers, FL 33965-6565. Offers MS. *Program availability:* Part-time, evening/weekend. *Faculty:* 60 full-time (24 women), 31 part-time/adjunct (7 women). *Students:* 17 full-time (6 women), 27 part-time (16 women); includes 8 minority (1 Black or African American, non-Hispanic/Latino; 7 Hispanic/Latino), 1 international. Average age 29. 31 applicants, 77% accepted, 17 enrolled. In 2017, 18 master's awarded. *Degree requirements:* For master's, thesis or alternative. *Entrance requirements:* For master's, GMAT, minimum GPA of 3.0. Additional exam requirements/recommendations for international students: Required—TOEFL (minimum score 550 paper-based). *Application deadline:* For fall admission, 5/1 priority date for domestic students; for spring admission, 9/15 priority date for domestic students. Applications are processed on a rolling basis. Application fee: $30. Electronic applications accepted. *Expenses:* Tuition, state resident: part-time $290 per credit hour. Tuition, nonresident: part-time $1173 per credit hour. *Required fees:* $127 per credit hour. Tuition and fees vary according to course load. *Financial support:* In 2017–18, 2 students received support. Application deadline: 6/30; applicants required to submit FAFSA. *Faculty research:* Stock petitions, mergers and acquisitions, deferred taxes, fraud and accounting regulations, graphical reporting practices. *Unit head:* Dr. Tanya Benford, Chair, 239-590-7342, Fax: 239-590-7330, E-mail: tbenford@fgcu.edu. *Application contact:* Marisa Ouverson, Director of Enrollment Management, 239-590-7403, Fax: 239-590-7330, E-mail: mouverso@fgcu.edu.

Florida State University, The Graduate School, College of Business, Tallahassee, FL 32306-1110. Offers accounting (M Acc), including assurance and advisory services, generalist, taxation; business administration (MBA, PhD), including accounting (PhD), finance (PhD), management (PhD), management information systems (PhD), marketing (PhD), organizational behavior and human resources (PhD), risk management and insurance (PhD), strategy (PhD); finance (MS); management information systems (MS); risk management and insurance (MS); JD/MBA; MSW/MBA. *Accreditation:* AACSB. *Program availability:* Part-time, 100% online. *Faculty:* 93 full-time (23 women), 2 part-time/adjunct (1 woman). *Students:* 229 full-time (96 women), 423 part-time (154 women); includes 159 minority (44 Black or African American, non-Hispanic/Latino; 24 Asian, non-Hispanic/Latino; 75 Hispanic/Latino; 1 Native Hawaiian or other Pacific Islander, non-Hispanic/Latino; 15 Two or more races, non-Hispanic/Latino), 48 international. Average age 31. 300 applicants, 61% accepted, 133 enrolled. In 2017, 268 master's, 9 doctorates awarded. Terminal master's awarded for partial completion of doctoral program. *Degree requirements:* For doctorate, comprehensive exam, thesis/dissertation. *Entrance requirements:* For master's, GMAT, GRE (for all except MS in finance), work experience (MBA, MS); minimum GPA of 3.0, letters of recommendation; for doctorate, GMAT, GRE (for marketing, organizational behavior, risk management and insurance, management information systems, and human resources only), minimum graduate GPA of 3.5, letters of recommendation. Additional exam requirements/recommendations for international students: Required—TOEFL (minimum score 600 paper-based; 85 iBT); Recommended—IELTS (minimum score 6). *Application deadline:* For fall admission, 6/1 for domestic and international students; for spring admission, 10/1 for domestic and international students; for summer admission, 3/1 for domestic and international students. Applications are processed on a rolling basis. Application fee: $30. Electronic applications accepted. *Expenses:* Contact institution. *Financial support:* In 2017–18, 146 students received support, including 26 fellowships (averaging $1,500 per year), 77 research assistantships with full tuition reimbursements available (averaging $20,000 per year), 43 teaching assistantships with full tuition reimbursements available (averaging $20,000 per year); career-related internships or fieldwork, scholarships/grants, health care benefits, tuition waivers (full and partial), and unspecified assistantships also available. Support available to part-time students. Financial award application deadline: 1/1; financial award applicants required to submit FAFSA. *Faculty research:* Business strategy, marketing, finance, accounting, business analytics. *Total annual research expenditures:* $1.4 million. *Unit head:* Dr. Michael Hartline, Dean, 850-644-4405, Fax: 850-644-0915, E-mail: mhartline@business.fsu.edu. *Application contact:* Jennifer Clark, Director, 850-644-6458, E-mail: gradprograms@business.fsu.edu.
Website: http://business.fsu.edu/

Fordham University, Gabelli School of Business, New York, NY 10023. Offers accounting (MBA, MS); applied statistics and decision-making (MS); business economics (DPS); capital markets (DPS); communications and media management (MBA); electronic business (MBA); entrepreneurship (MBA); finance (MBA, PhD); global finance (MS); global sustainability (MBA); health administration (MBA); healthcare management (MBA); information systems (MBA, MS); investor relations (MS); management (EMBA, MBA, MS, PhD); marketing (MBA); marketing intelligence (MS); media management (MS); nonprofit leadership (MS); quantitative finance (MS); strategy and decision-making (DPS); taxation (MS); JD/MBA; MS/MBA. *Accreditation:* AACSB. *Program availability:* Part-time, evening/weekend. *Faculty:* 130 full-time (46 women), 42 part-time/adjunct (5 women). *Students:* 1,051 full-time (570 women), 563 part-time (313 women); includes 190 minority (48 Black or African American, non-Hispanic/Latino; 72 Asian, non-Hispanic/Latino; 69 Hispanic/Latino; 1 Native Hawaiian or other Pacific Islander, non-Hispanic/Latino), 1,106 international. Average age 27. 4,577 applicants, 58% accepted, 794 enrolled. In 2017, 937 master's awarded. Terminal master's awarded for partial completion of doctoral program. *Degree requirements:* For master's, internships (for some degrees); for doctorate, comprehensive exam (for some programs), thesis/dissertation. *Entrance requirements:* For master's, GMAT/GRE, 2 letters of recommendation, resume, 2 essays, transcripts, interview. Additional exam requirements/recommendations for international students: Required—TOEFL (minimum score 100 iBT), IELTS (minimum score 7). *Application deadline:* For fall admission, 11/15 priority date for domestic and international students; for winter admission, 1/19 priority date for domestic students, 1/1 priority date for international students; for spring admission, 4/15 for domestic students, 3/1 for international students; for summer admission, 6/1 for domestic students. Application fee: $130. Electronic applications accepted. *Expenses:* $1,495 per credit. *Financial support:* Career-related internships or fieldwork, institutionally sponsored loans, scholarships/grants, and unspecified assistantships available. Support available to part-time students. Financial award application deadline: 6/30; financial award applicants required to submit FAFSA. *Unit head:* Dr. Donna Rapaccioli, Dean, 212-636-6165, Fax: 212-307-1779, E-mail: rapaccioli@fordham.edu. *Application contact:* Lawrence Murray, Senior Assistant Dean of Graduate Admissions and Advising, 212-636-6200, Fax: 212-636-7076, E-mail: admissionsgb@fordham.edu.
Website: http://www.fordham.edu/gabelli

Georgetown University, Law Center, Washington, DC 20001. Offers environmental law (LL M); global health law (LL M); global health law and international institutions (LL M); individualized study (LL M); international business and economic law (LL M); law (JD, SJD); national security law (LL M); securities and financial regulation (LL M); taxation (LL M); JD/LL M; JD/MA; JD/MBA; JD/MPH; JD/PhD. *Accreditation:* ABA. *Program availability:* Part-time, evening/weekend. *Degree requirements:* For master's, thesis; for doctorate, thesis/dissertation (for some programs). *Entrance requirements:* For master's, JD, LL B, or first law degree earned in country of origin; for doctorate, LSAT (for JD). Additional exam requirements/recommendations for international students: Required—TOEFL. *Expenses:* Contact institution. *Faculty research:* Constitutional law, legal history, jurisprudence.

Georgia State University, J. Mack Robinson College of Business, School of Accountancy, Program in Taxation, Atlanta, GA 30303. Offers M Tax, JD/M Tax. *Program availability:* Part-time, evening/weekend. *Entrance requirements:* For master's, GRE or GMAT, transcripts from all institutions attended, resume, essays. Additional exam requirements/recommendations for international students: Required—TOEFL (minimum score 610 paper-based; 101 iBT), IELTS (minimum score 7). *Application deadline:* Applications are processed on a rolling basis. Application fee: $50. Electronic applications accepted. *Expenses:* Tuition, state resident: full-time $7020. Tuition, nonresident: full-time $22,518. *Required fees:* $2128. Tuition and fees vary according to degree level and program. *Financial support:* Research assistantships, career-related internships or fieldwork, scholarships/grants, tuition waivers, and unspecified assistantships available. Financial award application deadline: 5/1. *Unit head:* Dr. Tad Ransoper, Director, 404-413-7229, Fax: 404-651-1033. *Application contact:* Toby McChesney, Assistant Dean for Graduate Recruiting and Student Services, 404-413-7167, Fax: 404-413-7162, E-mail: rcbgradadmissions@gsu.edu.
Website: http://robinson.gsu.edu/accountancy/mtx.html

Golden Gate University, School of Accounting, San Francisco, CA 94105-2968. Offers financial accounting and reporting (M Ac, MSA, Graduate Certificate); forensic accounting (M Ac, MSA, Graduate Certificate); internal auditing (M Ac, MSA, Certificate); management accounting (M Ac, MSA); taxation (M Ac, MSA). *Program availability:* Part-time, evening/weekend. *Faculty:* 3 full-time (1 woman), 64 part-time/adjunct (21 women). *Students:* 76 full-time (51 women), 136 part-time (87 women); includes 63 minority (7 Black or African American, non-Hispanic/Latino; 35 Asian, non-Hispanic/Latino; 18 Hispanic/Latino; 1 Native Hawaiian or other Pacific Islander, non-Hispanic/Latino; 2 Two or more races, non-Hispanic/Latino), 76 international. Average age 32. 94 applicants, 69% accepted, 38 enrolled. *Entrance requirements:* For master's, minimum GPA of 3.0. Additional exam requirements/recommendations for international students: Required—TOEFL (minimum score 550 paper-based), IELTS (minimum score 6.5). *Application deadline:* For fall admission, 5/15 for international students; for winter admission, 1/15 for international students; for spring admission, 9/15 for international students. Applications are processed on a rolling basis. Application fee: $65 ($95 for international students). Electronic applications accepted. *Expenses:* $3,150 per 3-unit course. *Financial support:* Career-related internships or fieldwork, Federal Work-Study, institutionally sponsored loans, and scholarships/grants available. Support available to part-time students. Financial award applicants required to submit FAFSA. *Faculty research:* Forensic accounting, audit, tax, CPA exam. *Unit head:* Fred Sroka, Dean, 415-369-5285, Fax: 415-543-2607. *Application contact:* Angela Melero, Enrollment Services, 415-442-7800, Fax: 415-442-7807, E-mail: info@ggu.edu.

Golden Gate University, School of Law, San Francisco, CA 94105. Offers environmental law (LL M); estate planning (LL M); intellectual property law (LL M); international legal studies (LL M, SJD); law (JD); taxation law (LL M); U.S. legal studies (LL M); JD/MBA. *Accreditation:* ABA. *Program availability:* Part-time, evening/weekend. *Faculty:* 31 full-time (19 women), 160 part-time/adjunct (77 women). *Students:* 286 full-time (184 women), 245 part-time (134 women); includes 242 minority (48 Black or African American, non-Hispanic/Latino; 4 American Indian or Alaska Native, non-Hispanic/Latino; 69 Asian, non-Hispanic/Latino; 95 Hispanic/Latino; 7 Native Hawaiian or other Pacific Islander, non-Hispanic/Latino; 19 Two or more races, non-Hispanic/Latino), 71 international. Average age 31. 1,354 applicants, 66% accepted, 227 enrolled. *Degree requirements:* For doctorate, thesis/dissertation (for some programs). *Entrance requirements:* For doctorate, LSAT (for JD). Additional exam requirements/recommendations for international students: Required—TOEFL (minimum score 600 paper-based). *Application deadline:* For fall admission, 6/30 for domestic students. Applications are processed on a rolling basis. Electronic applications accepted. *Expenses:* Contact institution. *Financial support:* Fellowships, research assistantships, teaching assistantships, career-related internships or fieldwork, Federal Work-Study, institutionally sponsored loans, scholarships/grants, tuition waivers (full and partial), and unspecified assistantships available. Support available to part-time students. Financial award applicants required to submit FAFSA. *Faculty research:* International law, intellectual property law, environmental law, real estate, civil rights. *Unit head:* Anthony Niedwiecki, Dean, 415-442-6601, Fax: 415-442-6609. *Application contact:* Greg Egertson, Associate Dean and Director of Admissions, 415-442-6636, Fax: 415-442-6609, E-mail: lawadmit@ggu.edu.
Website: http://law.ggu.edu/

Golden Gate University, School of Taxation, San Francisco, CA 94105-2968. Offers advanced studies in taxation (Certificate); estate planning (Certificate); financial planning and taxation (MS); international taxation (Certificate); state and local taxation (Certificate); taxation (MS, Certificate). *Program availability:* Part-time, evening/weekend. *Faculty:* 7 full-time (1 woman), 65 part-time/adjunct (19 women). *Students:* 72 full-time (44 women), 539 part-time (281 women); includes 156 minority (17 Black or African American, non-Hispanic/Latino; 3 American Indian or Alaska Native, non-Hispanic/Latino; 100 Asian, non-Hispanic/Latino; 23 Hispanic/Latino; 7 Native Hawaiian or other Pacific Islander, non-Hispanic/Latino; 6 Two or more races, non-Hispanic/Latino), 82 international. Average age 36. 252 applicants, 84% accepted, 105 enrolled. In 2017, 193 master's awarded. *Entrance requirements:* For master's, minimum GPA of 3.0. Additional exam requirements/recommendations for international students: Required—TOEFL (minimum score 550 paper-based), IELTS (minimum score 6.5). *Application deadline:* For fall admission, 5/15 for international students; for winter admission, 1/15 for international students; for spring admission, 9/15 for international students. Applications are processed on a rolling basis. Application fee: $70 ($100 for international students). Electronic applications accepted. *Expenses:* Contact institution. *Financial support:* In 2017–18, 66 students received support. Career-related internships or fieldwork, Federal Work-Study, institutionally sponsored loans, and scholarships/grants available. Support available to part-time students. Financial award applicants required to submit FAFSA. *Unit head:* Fred Sroka, Dean, 415-369-5285, Fax: 415-442-7807. *Application contact:* Angela Melero, Enrollment Services, 415-442-7800, Fax: 415-442-7807, E-mail: info@ggu.edu.
Website: http://www.ggu.edu/programs/taxation/master-of-science-in-taxation

Goldey-Beacom College, Graduate Program, Wilmington, DE 19808-1999. Offers business administration (MBA); finance (MS); financial management (MBA); health care management (MBA); human resource management (MBA); information technology (MBA); international business management (MBA); major finance (MBA); major taxation (MBA); management (MM); marketing management (MBA); taxation (MBA, MS). *Accreditation:* ACBSP. *Program availability:* Part-time, evening/weekend. *Entrance requirements:* For master's, GMAT, MAT, GRE, minimum GPA of 3.0. Additional exam requirements/recommendations for international students: Required—TOEFL (minimum score 65 iBT); Recommended—IELTS (minimum score 6). Electronic applications accepted.

Gonzaga University, School of Business Administration, Spokane, WA 99258. Offers accountancy (M Acc); American Indian entrepreneurship (MBA); business administration (MBA); taxation (MS); JD/M Acc; JD/MBA. *Accreditation:* AACSB. *Program availability:* Part-time, evening/weekend. *Faculty:* 17 full-time (3 women), 11 part-time/adjunct (3 women). *Students:* 94 full-time (32 women), 118 part-time (64 women); includes 41 minority (2 Black or African American, non-Hispanic/Latino; 9 American Indian or Alaska Native, non-Hispanic/Latino; 8 Asian, non-Hispanic/Latino; 10 Hispanic/Latino; 1 Native Hawaiian or other Pacific Islander, non-Hispanic/Latino; 11 Two or more races, non-Hispanic/Latino), 11 international. Average age 29. 218 applicants, 75% accepted, 101 enrolled. In 2017, 96 master's awarded. *Degree requirements:* For master's, capstone course. *Entrance requirements:* For master's, GMAT or GRE, essay, two professional recommendations, resume/curriculum vitae, copy of official transcripts from all colleges attended, minimum GPA of 3.0. Additional exam requirements/recommendations for international students: Required—TOEFL (minimum score 570 paper-based, 89 iBT) or IELTS (minimum score 6.5). *Application deadline:* Applications are processed on a rolling basis. Application fee: $50. Electronic applications accepted. *Expenses:* Contact institution. *Financial support:* In 2017–18, 117 students received support. Scholarships/grants, tuition waivers, and unspecified assistantships available. Support available to part-time students. Financial award applicants required to submit FAFSA. *Unit head:* Dr. Ken Anderson, Dean, 509-313-5991, E-mail: anderson@gonzaga.edu. *Application contact:* Stacey Chatman, Assistant Director for Admissions, 509-313-4622, E-mail: chatman@gonzaga.edu.
Website: https://www.gonzaga.edu/school-of-business-administration

Grand Valley State University, Seidman College of Business, Program in Taxation, Allendale, MI 49401-9403. Offers MST. *Program availability:* Part-time, evening/weekend. *Students:* 3 full-time (1 woman), 13 part-time (6 women); includes 2 minority (1 Black or African American, non-Hispanic/Latino; 1 Two or more races, non-Hispanic/Latino), 2 international. Average age 29. 5 applicants, 100% accepted, 4 enrolled. In 2017, 5 master's awarded. *Degree requirements:* For master's, capstone course. *Entrance requirements:* For master's, GMAT, personal statement. Additional exam requirements/recommendations for international students: Required—TOEFL (minimum iBT score of 80), IELTS (6.5), or Michigan English Language Assessment Battery (77). *Application deadline:* For fall admission, 8/1 priority date for domestic students, 5/1 priority date for international students; for winter admission, 12/1 priority date for domestic students, 11/1 priority date for international students; for spring admission, 4/1

priority date for domestic students, 3/1 priority date for international students. Applications are processed on a rolling basis. Application fee: $30. Electronic applications accepted. *Expenses:* Contact institution. *Financial support:* In 2017–18, 1 student received support, including 1 fellowship; Federal Work-Study, institutionally sponsored loans, and unspecified assistantships also available. Financial award application deadline: 2/15. *Faculty research:* Individual income taxation, state taxation, pass-through entities, estate and gift taxation, sale-leasebacks. *Unit head:* Dr. Steve Goldberg, Director, 616-331-7410, Fax: 616-331-7412, E-mail: goldbers@gvsu.edu. *Application contact:* Koleta Moore, Assistant Dean of Student Engagement, Graduate Program Operations, 616-331-7386, Fax: 616-331-7389, E-mail: moorekol@gvsu.edu.
Website: http://www.gvsu.edu/business/

HEC Montreal, School of Business Administration, Graduate Diploma Programs in Administration, Program in Taxation, Montréal, QC H3T 2A7, Canada. Offers Graduate Diploma. All courses are given in French. *Program availability:* Part-time. *Students:* 36 full-time (18 women), 72 part-time (32 women). 97 applicants, 66% accepted, 48 enrolled. In 2017, 43 Graduate Diplomas awarded. *Entrance requirements:* For degree, bachelor's diploma in law, accounting, or economics. *Application deadline:* For fall admission, 3/15 for domestic and international students; for winter admission, 9/15 for domestic and international students. Application fee: $88 Canadian dollars ($184 Canadian dollars for international students). Electronic applications accepted. *Expenses:* Tuition, state resident: full-time $2869 Canadian dollars; part-time $79.70 Canadian dollars per credit. Tuition, nonresident: full-time $8883 Canadian dollars; part-time $246.76 Canadian dollars per credit. *International tuition:* $19,648 Canadian dollars full-time. *Required fees:* $41.20 Canadian dollars per credit. $67.94 Canadian dollars per term. Tuition and fees vary according to degree level and program. *Financial support:* Research assistantships, teaching assistantships, and scholarships/grants available. Financial award application deadline: 9/2. *Unit head:* Renaud Lachance, Director, 514-340-7165, E-mail: renaud.lachance@hec.ca. *Application contact:* Anny Caron, Administrative Director, 514-340-6151, Fax: 514-340-6411, E-mail: aide@hec.ca.
Website: http://www.hec.ca/programmes/dess/dess-fiscalite/index.html

HEC Montreal, School of Business Administration, Master of Laws in Taxation Program, Montréal, QC H3T 2A7, Canada. Offers LL M. All courses are given in French. *Program availability:* Part-time. *Students:* 6 full-time (2 women), 23 part-time (16 women). 6 applicants, 100% accepted, 3 enrolled. In 2017, 23 master's awarded. *Entrance requirements:* For master's, bachelor's degree in taxation from HEC Montreal. *Application deadline:* For fall admission, 8/1 for domestic and international students; for winter admission, 11/15 for domestic and international students; for summer admission, 3/15 for domestic and international students. Application fee: $88 ($184 for international students). Electronic applications accepted. *Expenses:* Tuition, state resident: full-time $2869 Canadian dollars; part-time $79.70 Canadian dollars per credit. Tuition, nonresident: full-time $8883 Canadian dollars; part-time $246.76 Canadian dollars per credit. *International tuition:* $19,648 Canadian dollars full-time. *Required fees:* $41.20 Canadian dollars per credit. $67.94 Canadian dollars per term. Tuition and fees vary according to degree level and program. *Financial support:* Research assistantships, teaching assistantships, and scholarships/grants available. Financial award application deadline: 9/2. *Unit head:* Renaud Lachance, Director, 514-340-7165, E-mail: renaud.lachance@hec.ca. *Application contact:* Anny Caron, Administrative Director, 514-340-6151, Fax: 514-340-6411, E-mail: aide@hec.ca.
Website: http://www.hec.ca/programmes/maitrises/maitrise-droit-llm-fiscalite/index.html

Hofstra University, Frank G. Zarb School of Business, Programs in Accounting and Taxation, Hempstead, NY 11549. Offers accounting (MS, Advanced Certificate); business administration (MBA), including accounting, professional accountancy, taxation; taxation (MS, Advanced Certificate). *Program availability:* Part-time, evening/weekend, blended/hybrid learning. *Students:* 161 full-time (89 women), 35 part-time (16 women); includes 28 minority (2 Black or African American, non-Hispanic/Latino; 1 American Indian or Alaska Native, non-Hispanic/Latino; 9 Asian, non-Hispanic/Latino; 12 Hispanic/Latino; 2 Native Hawaiian or other Pacific Islander, non-Hispanic/Latino; 2 Two or more races, non-Hispanic/Latino), 87 international. Average age 25. 328 applicants, 77% accepted, 82 enrolled. In 2017, 129 master's awarded. *Degree requirements:* For master's, capstone course (for MBA), thesis (for MS), minimum GPA of 3.0. *Entrance requirements:* For master's, GMAT/GRE, 2 letters of recommendation, resume, essay. Additional exam requirements/recommendations for international students: Required—TOEFL (minimum score 550 paper-based; 80 iBT); Recommended—IELTS (minimum score 6). *Application deadline:* Applications are processed on a rolling basis. Application fee: $75. Electronic applications accepted. *Expenses:* $1,322 per credit. *Financial support:* In 2017–18, 63 students received support, including 54 fellowships with full and partial tuition reimbursements available (averaging $4,794 per year); research assistantships with full and partial tuition reimbursements available, career-related internships or fieldwork, Federal Work-Study, institutionally sponsored loans, scholarships/grants, tuition waivers (full and partial), and unspecified assistantships also available. Support available to part-time students. Financial award applicants required to submit FAFSA. *Faculty research:* Corporate compliance, international accounting and auditing, financial accounting fraud, tax reform legislation, accounting analytics. *Unit head:* Dr. Jacqueline Burke, Chairperson, 516-463-6987, E-mail: jacqueline.a.burke@hofstra.edu. *Application contact:* Sunil Samuel, Assistant Vice President of Admissions, 516-463-4723, Fax: 516-463-4664, E-mail: graduateadmission@hofstra.edu.
Website: http://www.hofstra.edu/business/

Illinois Institute of Technology, Chicago-Kent College of Law, Chicago, IL 60661-3691. Offers family law (LL M); financial services law (LL M); international intellectual property law (LL M); law (JD); legal studies (JSD); taxation (LL M); U.S., international, and transnational law (LL M); JD/LL M; JD/MBA; JD/MPA; JD/MPH; JD/MS. *Accreditation:* ABA. *Program availability:* Part-time, evening/weekend. Terminal master's awarded for partial completion of doctoral program. *Entrance requirements:* For master's, 1st degree in law or certified license to practice law; for doctorate, LSAT. Additional exam requirements/recommendations for international students: Required—TOEFL (minimum score 600 paper-based; 100 iBT); Recommended—IELTS (minimum score 7). Electronic applications accepted. *Expenses:* Contact institution. *Faculty research:* Constitutional law, bioethics, environmental law, intellectual property.

Instituto Tecnologico de Santo Domingo, Graduate School, Area of Business, Santo Domingo, Dominican Republic. Offers banking and securities markets (M Mgmt); corporate finance (M Mgmt); human resources management (M Mgmt, Certificate); international trade management (M Mgmt); marketing (M Mgmt); organizational development (M Mgmt); quality and productivity management (Certificate); tax management and planning (M Mgmt); upper management (M Mgmt).

James Madison University, The Graduate School, College of Business, Program in Accounting, Harrisonburg, VA 22801. Offers accounting information systems (MS); taxation (MS). *Accreditation:* AACSB. *Program availability:* Part-time, evening/weekend. *Students:* 71 full-time (28 women), 1 (woman) part-time; includes 10 minority (2 Black or African American, non-Hispanic/Latino; 5 Asian, non-Hispanic/Latino; 3 Hispanic/Latino), 1 international. Average age 30. In 2017, 24 master's awarded. Application fee: $55. Electronic applications accepted. *Expenses:* Tuition, state resident: full-time

$10,512; part-time $438 per credit hour. Tuition, nonresident: full-time $28,358; part-time $1162 per credit hour. *Required fees:* $1128. *Financial support:* In 2017–18, 24 students received support, including 23 fellowships; Federal Work-Study and 23 assistantships (averaging $6911), 1 service assistantship also available. Financial award application deadline: 3/1; financial award applicants required to submit FAFSA. *Unit head:* Dr. Tim J. Louwers, Director of the School of Accounting, 540-568-3027, E-mail: louwertj@jmu.edu. *Application contact:* Lynette D. Michael, Director of Graduate Admissions, 540-568-6131 Ext. 6395, Fax: 540-568-7860, E-mail: michaeld@jmu.edu. Website: https://www.jmu.edu/cob/accounting/masters/index.shtml

Liberty University, School of Business, Lynchburg, VA 24515. Offers accounting (MBA, MS), including audit and financial reporting (MS), business (MS), financial services (MS), forensic accounting (MS), leadership (MS), taxation (MS); criminal justice (MBA); cyber security (MS); executive leadership (MA); information systems (MS), including information assurance, technology management; international business (MBA, DBA); leadership (DBA); marketing (MBA, MS, DBA), including digital marketing and advertising (MS), project management (MS), public relations (MS), sports marketing and media (MS); project management (MBA, DBA); public administration (MBA); public relations (MBA). *Program availability:* Part-time, online learning. *Students:* 1,887 full-time (1,003 women), 4,223 part-time (1,950 women); includes 1,570 minority (1,133 Black or African American, non-Hispanic/Latino; 30 American Indian or Alaska Native, non-Hispanic/Latino; 118 Asian, non-Hispanic/Latino; 149 Hispanic/Latino; 13 Native Hawaiian or other Pacific Islander, non-Hispanic/Latino; 127 Two or more races, non-Hispanic/Latino), 109 international. Average age 35. 5,680 applicants, 51% accepted, 1510 enrolled. In 2017, 1,290 master's, 17 doctorates awarded. *Entrance requirements:* For master's, minimum undergraduate GPA of 3.0, 15 hours of upper-level business courses. Additional exam requirements/recommendations for international students: Required—TOEFL (minimum score 600 paper-based; 100 iBT). *Application deadline:* Applications are processed on a rolling basis. Application fee: $50. Electronic applications accepted. *Expenses:* Contact institution. *Financial support:* Applicants required to submit FAFSA. *Unit head:* Dr. Scott Hicks, Dean, 434-592-4808, Fax: 434-582-2366, E-mail: smhicks@liberty.edu. *Application contact:* Jay Bridge, Director of Graduate Admissions, 800-424-9595, Fax: 800-628-7977, E-mail: gradadmissions@liberty.edu.
Website: http://www.liberty.edu/academics/business/index.cfm?PID-149

Lipscomb University, College of Business, Nashville, TN 37204-3951. Offers accounting and finance (MBA); audit/accounting (M Acc); business (Certificate); business administration (MM); healthcare management (MBA); leadership (MBA); tax (M Acc); MBA/MS; Pharm D/MM. *Accreditation:* ACBSP. *Program availability:* Part-time, evening/weekend. *Faculty:* 14 full-time (2 women), 8 part-time/adjunct (1 woman). *Students:* 157 full-time (68 women), 9 part-time (6 women); includes 26 minority (9 Black or African American, non-Hispanic/Latino; 7 Asian, non-Hispanic/Latino; 8 Hispanic/Latino; 2 Two or more races, non-Hispanic/Latino), 9 international. Average age 30. 249 applicants, 49% accepted, 52 enrolled. In 2017, 130 master's awarded. *Entrance requirements:* For master's, GMAT, transcripts, interview, 2 references, resume. Additional exam requirements/recommendations for international students: Required—TOEFL (minimum score 570 paper-based). *Application deadline:* For fall admission, 6/15 for domestic students, 2/1 for international students; for winter admission, 6/1 for international students; for spring admission, 11/15 for domestic students. Applications are processed on a rolling basis. Application fee: $50 ($75 for international students). Electronic applications accepted. *Expenses:* Contact institution. *Financial support:* Career-related internships or fieldwork, scholarships/grants, tuition waivers (partial), and unspecified assistantships available. Support available to part-time students. Financial award application deadline: 7/1; financial award applicants required to submit FAFSA. *Faculty research:* Impact of spirituality on organization commitment, women in corporate leadership, psychological empowerment, training. *Unit head:* Allison Duke, Associate Dean of Graduate Business Programs, 615-966-5732, Fax: 615-966-1818, E-mail: allison.duke@lipscomb.edu. *Application contact:* Karen Risley, Manager, Graduate Business Recruiting, 615-966-5145, E-mail: karen.risley@lipscomb.edu.
Website: http://www.lipscomb.edu/business/Graduate-Programs

Long Island University–LIU Brooklyn, School of Business, Public Administration and Information Sciences, Brooklyn, NY 11201-8423. Offers accounting (MBA); accounting (MS); business administration (MBA); computer science (MS); gerontology (Advanced Certificate); health administration (MPA); human resources management (MS); not-for-profit management (Advanced Certificate); public administration (MPA); taxation (MS). *Program availability:* Part-time, evening/weekend. *Faculty:* 18 full-time (7 women), 28 part-time/adjunct (8 women). *Students:* 226 full-time (140 women), 232 part-time (150 women); includes 272 minority (192 Black or African American, non-Hispanic/Latino; 2 American Indian or Alaska Native, non-Hispanic/Latino; 35 Asian, non-Hispanic/Latino; 40 Hispanic/Latino; 3 Two or more races, non-Hispanic/Latino), 88 international. Average age 32. 495 applicants, 64% accepted, 149 enrolled. In 2017, 189 master's, 13 other advanced degrees awarded. *Entrance requirements:* Additional exam requirements/recommendations for international students: Required—TOEFL (minimum score 550 paper-based; 75 iBT). *Application deadline:* Applications are processed on a rolling basis. Application fee: $50. Electronic applications accepted. *Expenses:* Tuition: Full-time $21,618; part-time $1201 per credit. *Required fees:* $1840; $920 per term. Tuition and fees vary according to course load. *Financial support:* In 2017–18, 78 students received support. Career-related internships or fieldwork, Federal Work-Study, scholarships/grants, and unspecified assistantships available. Support available to part-time students. Financial award application deadline: 2/15; financial award applicants required to submit FAFSA. *Faculty research:* Tax policy; public sector budgeting and gender inequities; technology and innovation; game theory; knowledge management. *Unit head:* Dr. Edward Rogoff, Dean, 718-488-1159, E-mail: edward.rogoff@liu.edu. *Application contact:* Luis Santiago, Dean of Enrollment, 718-488-1011, Fax: 718-780-6110, E-mail: bkln-admissions@liu.edu.
Website: http://liu.edu/Brooklyn/Academics/School-of-Business-Public-Administration-and-Information-Sciences

Long Island University–LIU Post, College of Management, Brookville, NY 11548-1300. Offers accountancy (MS); finance (MBA); information systems (MS); international business (MBA); management (MBA); management engineering (MS); marketing (MBA); taxation (MS); technical project management (MS); JD/MBA. *Accreditation:* AACSB. *Program availability:* Part-time, evening/weekend, blended/hybrid learning. *Faculty:* 23 full-time (9 women), 7 part-time/adjunct (1 woman). *Students:* 119 full-time (47 women), 62 part-time (23 women); includes 33 minority (11 Black or African American, non-Hispanic/Latino; 8 Asian, non-Hispanic/Latino; 13 Hispanic/Latino; 1 Two or more races, non-Hispanic/Latino), 56 international. Average age 28. 162 applicants, 62% accepted, 41 enrolled. In 2017, 91 master's awarded. *Entrance requirements:* For master's, GMAT, GRE, or LSAT. Additional exam requirements/recommendations for international students: Required—TOEFL (minimum score 550 paper-based, 75 iBT) or IELTS. *Application deadline:* Applications are processed on a rolling basis. Application fee: $50. Electronic applications accepted. *Expenses:* Tuition: Full-time $21,618; part-time $1201 per credit. *Required fees:* $1840; $920 per term. Tuition and fees vary according to course load. *Financial support:* In 2017–18, 47 students received support. Career-related internships or fieldwork, Federal Work-Study, and scholarships/grants available. Support available to part-time students. Financial award application deadline:

2/15; financial award applicants required to submit FAFSA. *Faculty research:* Innovation and property rights, knowledge sourcing, sustainability and firm performance, China and growth markets, corporate social responsibility, workforce compensation and issues. *Unit head:* Dr. Robert M. Valli, Dean, 516-299-3004, E-mail: rob.valli@liu.edu. *Application contact:* Rita Langdon, Graduate Admissions, 516-299-2900, Fax: 516-299-2137, E-mail: post-enroll@liu.edu.
Website: http://liu.edu/CWPost/Academics/Schools/COM

Loyola University Chicago, School of Law, Chicago, IL 60611. Offers advocacy (LL M); business and compliance (MJ); business law (LL M); child and family (LL M); child and family law (MJ, Certificate); global competition (LL M, MJ); health law (LL M, MJ, Certificate); international law (LL M); law (JD); public interest law (Certificate); rule of law for development (LL M, MJ); tax (LL M); tax law (Certificate); transactional law (Certificate); trial advocacy (Certificate); JD/MA; JD/MBA; JD/MPP; JD/MSW; MJ/MSW; MS/MJ. *Accreditation:* ABA. *Program availability:* Part-time, evening/weekend, 100% online, blended/hybrid learning. *Faculty:* 69 full-time (36 women), 306 part-time/adjunct (148 women). *Students:* 823 full-time (483 women), 262 part-time (201 women); includes 334 minority (124 Black or African American, non-Hispanic/Latino; 1 American Indian or Alaska Native, non-Hispanic/Latino; 54 Asian, non-Hispanic/Latino; 114 Hispanic/Latino; 1 Native Hawaiian or other Pacific Islander, non-Hispanic/Latino; 40 Two or more races, non-Hispanic/Latino), 42 international. Average age 31. 2,670 applicants, 48% accepted, 372 enrolled. In 2017, 187 master's, 222 doctorates, 104 Certificates awarded. *Degree requirements:* For master's and Certificate, thesis (for some programs); for doctorate, thesis/dissertation (for some programs). *Entrance requirements:* For doctorate, LSAT. Additional exam requirements/recommendations for international students: Required—TOEFL (minimum score 100 iBT); Recommended—IELTS (minimum score 7). *Application deadline:* For fall admission, 4/1 for domestic and international students. Applications are processed on a rolling basis. Application fee: $0. Electronic applications accepted. *Expenses:* $46,460 full-time, $34,860 weekend (for JD). *Financial support:* In 2017–18, 598 students received support, including 67 fellowships; research assistantships, Federal Work-Study, scholarships/grants, and health care benefits also available. Financial award application deadline: 3/1; financial award applicants required to submit FAFSA. *Faculty research:* Constitutional law including hate speech and supreme court advocacy; early childhood education including law policy and pedagogy; hedonic psychology - legal and social determinants of happiness; racial inequality; intersection of law, science, and technology. *Unit head:* James Faught, JD, Associate Dean for Administration, Law School, 312-915-7131, Fax: 312-915-6911, E-mail: law-admissions@luc.edu. *Application contact:* Jill Schur, Director, Graduate Enrollment Management, 312-915-8902, E-mail: gradinfo@luc.edu.
Website: http://www.luc.edu/law/

Metropolitan State University of Denver, School of Business, Denver, CO 80204. Offers accounting (MP Acc); fraud examination and forensic auditing (MP Acc); internal audit (MP Acc); public accounting (MP Acc); taxation (MP Acc). *Accreditation:* AACSB. *Entrance requirements:* For master's, GMAT. *Expenses:* Contact institution.

Michigan State University, The Graduate School, Eli Broad College of Business, Department of Accounting and Information Systems, East Lansing, MI 48224. Offers accounting (MS, PhD), including information systems (MS), public and corporate accounting (MS), taxation (MS); business information systems (PhD). *Accreditation:* AACSB. *Degree requirements:* For doctorate, comprehensive exam, thesis/dissertation. *Entrance requirements:* For master's, GMAT (minimum score 550), bachelor's degree in accounting; minimum cumulative GPA of 3.0 at any institution attended and in any junior-/senior-level accounting courses taken; 3 letters of recommendation (at least 1 from faculty); working knowledge of computers including word processing, spreadsheets, networking, and database management system; for doctorate, GMAT (minimum score 600), bachelor's degree; transcripts; 3 letters of recommendation; statement of purpose; resume; on-campus interview; personal qualifications of sound character, perseverance, intellectual curiosity, and interest in scholarly research. Additional exam requirements/recommendations for international students: Required—TOEFL (minimum score 600 paper-based; 100 iBT), IELTS (minimum score 7) accepted for MS only. Electronic applications accepted.

Mississippi State University, College of Business, Adkerson School of Accountancy, Mississippi State, MS 39762. Offers accountancy (MPA); systems (MPA). *Accreditation:* AACSB. *Faculty:* 10 full-time (0 women). *Students:* 61 full-time (38 women), 3 part-time (0 women); includes 8 minority (5 Black or African American, non-Hispanic/Latino; 1 Asian, non-Hispanic/Latino; 2 Hispanic/Latino), 3 international. Average age 23. 40 applicants, 70% accepted, 26 enrolled. In 2017, 51 master's awarded. *Degree requirements:* For master's, comprehensive exam. *Entrance requirements:* For master's, GMAT (minimum score of 510), minimum GPA of 3.0 over last 60 hours of undergraduate course work. Additional exam requirements/recommendations for international students: Required—TOEFL (minimum score 575 paper-based; 84 iBT); Recommended—IELTS (minimum score 7). *Application deadline:* For fall admission, 7/1 for domestic students, 5/1 for international students; for spring admission, 11/1 for domestic students, 9/1 for international students. Applications are processed on a rolling basis. Application fee: $60 ($80 for international students). Electronic applications accepted. *Expenses:* Tuition, state resident: full-time $8318; part-time $462.12 per credit hour. Tuition, nonresident: full-time $22,358; part-time $1242.12 per credit hour. *Required fees:* $110; $12.24 per credit hour. $6.12 per semester. *Financial support:* Career-related internships or fieldwork, Federal Work-Study, institutionally sponsored loans, scholarships/grants, and unspecified assistantships available. Support available to part-time students. Financial award application deadline: 4/1; financial award applicants required to submit FAFSA. *Faculty research:* Income tax, financial accounting system, managerial accounting, auditing. *Unit head:* Dr. Shawn Mauldin, Professor and Director, 662-325-3710, Fax: 662-325-1646, E-mail: smauldin@business.msstate.edu. *Application contact:* Lakan Drinker, Admissions and Enrollment Assistant, 662-325-8951, E-mail: ldrinker@grad.msstate.edu.
Website: http://www.business.msstate.edu/programs/adkerson

National Paralegal College, Graduate Programs, Phoenix, AZ 85014. Offers compliance law (MS); legal studies (MS); taxation (MS). *Program availability:* Part-time. Electronic applications accepted.

New York University, School of Law, New York, NY 10012-1019. Offers law (LL M, JD, JSD); law and business (Advanced Certificate); taxation (MSL, Advanced Certificate); JD/LL M; JD/MA; JD/MBA; JD/MPA; JD/MPP; JD/MSW; JD/MUP; JD/PhD. *Accreditation:* ABA. *Program availability:* Part-time, blended/hybrid learning. *Faculty:* 158 full-time (51 women), 204 part-time/adjunct (55 women). *Students:* 1,364 full-time (728 women); includes 394 minority (72 Black or African American, non-Hispanic/Latino; 147 Asian, non-Hispanic/Latino; 124 Hispanic/Latino; 51 Two or more races, non-Hispanic/Latino), 127 international. 6,534 applicants, 427 enrolled. In 2017, 516 master's, 484 doctorates awarded. *Entrance requirements:* For doctorate, LSAT (for JD). *Application deadline:* For fall admission, 2/15 for domestic students. Applications are processed on a rolling basis. Application fee: $85. Electronic applications accepted. *Expenses:* Contact institution. *Financial support:* Fellowships, research assistantships, teaching assistantships, career-related internships or fieldwork, Federal Work-Study, scholarships/grants, and loan repayment assistance available. Financial award application deadline: 4/15; financial award applicants required to submit FAFSA. *Faculty*

research: International law, environmental law, corporate law, globalization of law, philosophy of law. *Unit head:* Trevor Morrison, Dean, 212-998-6000, Fax: 212-995-3150. *Application contact:* Cassandra Williams, Assistant Dean for Admissions, 212-998-6060, Fax: 212-995-4527.
Website: http://www.law.nyu.edu/

Northeastern University, D'Amore-McKim School of Business, Boston, MA 02115-5096. Offers accounting (MS); business administration (EMBA, MBA); finance (MS); innovation (MS); international business (MS); international management (MS); taxation (MS); technological entrepreneurship (MS); JD/MBA; LL M/MBA; MBA/MSN; MS/MBA. *Accreditation:* AACSB. *Program availability:* Part-time, evening/weekend, online learning. *Faculty:* 184. *Students:* 1,489. In 2017, 800 master's awarded. *Entrance requirements:* For master's, GMAT or GRE. Application fee: $75. Electronic applications accepted. *Expenses:* Contact institution. *Financial support:* Scholarships/grants available. Financial award applicants required to submit FAFSA. *Unit head:* Dr. Raj Echambadi, Dean, D'Amore-McKim School of Business, 617-373-3232, Fax: 617-373-2056. *Application contact:* Evelyn Tate, Director, Graduate Recruitment and Admissions, 617-373-3258, E-mail: e.tate@northeastern.edu.
Website: http://damore-mckim.northeastern.edu/

Northern Illinois University, Graduate School, College of Business, Department of Accountancy, De Kalb, IL 60115-2854. Offers MAC, MAS, MST. *Accreditation:* AACSB. *Program availability:* Part-time, evening/weekend. *Faculty:* 14 full-time (4 women). *Students:* 138 full-time (58 women), 84 part-time (44 women); includes 63 minority (6 Black or African American, non-Hispanic/Latino; 23 Asian, non-Hispanic/Latino; 27 Hispanic/Latino; 7 Two or more races, non-Hispanic/Latino), 27 international. Average age 27. 109 applicants, 89% accepted, 58 enrolled. In 2017, 140 master's awarded. *Degree requirements:* For master's, thesis optional. *Entrance requirements:* For master's, GMAT, minimum GPA of 2.75. Additional exam requirements/recommendations for international students: Required—TOEFL (minimum score 550 paper-based). *Application deadline:* For fall admission, 4/1 priority date for domestic students, 5/1 for international students; for spring admission, 9/15 priority date for domestic students, 10/1 for international students. Applications are processed on a rolling basis. Application fee: $40. Electronic applications accepted. *Financial support:* In 2017–18, 5 research assistantships with full tuition reimbursements, 31 teaching assistantships with full tuition reimbursements were awarded; fellowships with full tuition reimbursements, career-related internships or fieldwork, Federal Work-Study, scholarships/grants, tuition waivers (full), and unspecified assistantships also available. Support available to part-time students. Financial award applicants required to submit FAFSA. *Faculty research:* Accounting fraud, governmental accounting, corporate income tax planning, auditing, ethics. *Unit head:* Rebecca Shortridge, Chair, 815-753-1250, Fax: 815-753-8515. *Application contact:* Graduate Advising, 815-753-1325, E-mail: cobadvising@niu.edu.
Website: http://www.cob.niu.edu/accy/

Northern Kentucky University, Office of Graduate Programs, College of Business, Program in Accountancy, Highland Heights, KY 41099. Offers accountancy (M Acc); advanced taxation (Certificate). *Program availability:* Part-time, evening/weekend. *Degree requirements:* For master's, capstone course. *Entrance requirements:* For master's, GMAT, master's degree, MD, or PhD, official transcripts, current resume, 3 years of work experience (strongly suggested), statement of purpose. Additional exam requirements/recommendations for international students: Required—TOEFL (minimum score 79 iBT); Recommended—IELTS (minimum score 6.5). Electronic applications accepted. *Faculty research:* Ethics, accounting history, financial reporting.

Northwestern University, Pritzker School of Law, Chicago, IL 60611-3069. Offers international human rights (LL M); law (JD); law and business (LL M); science law (MSL); tax (LL M in Tax); JD/LL M; JD/MBA; JD/PhD; LL M/Certificate. Executive LL M programs offered in Madrid (Spain), Seoul (South Korea), and Tel Aviv (Israel). *Accreditation:* ABA. *Entrance requirements:* For master's, law degree or equivalent, letter of recommendation, resume; for doctorate, LSAT, 1 letter of recommendation, resume. Additional exam requirements/recommendations for international students: Required—TOEFL. Electronic applications accepted. *Expenses:* Contact institution. *Faculty research:* Constitutional law, corporate law, international law, law and social policy, ethical studies.

Pace University, Lubin School of Business, Taxation Program, New York, NY 10038. Offers taxation (MBA, MS). *Program availability:* Part-time, evening/weekend. *Students:* 11 full-time (5 women), 28 part-time (11 women); includes 24 minority (2 Black or African American, non-Hispanic/Latino; 1 American Indian or Alaska Native, non-Hispanic/Latino; 17 Asian, non-Hispanic/Latino; 4 Hispanic/Latino), 5 international. Average age 31. 19 applicants, 84% accepted, 9 enrolled. In 2017, 18 master's awarded. *Entrance requirements:* For master's, GMAT or GRE (waived for anyone who has passed the CPA), undergraduate degree, transcripts from all accredited colleges/universities attended, two letters of recommendation, resume, personal statement. Additional exam requirements/recommendations for international students: Required—TOEFL (minimum score 90 iBT), IELTS (minimum score 7) or PTE (minimum score 61). *Application deadline:* For fall admission, 8/1 priority date for domestic students, 6/1 for international students; for spring admission, 12/1 for domestic students, 10/1 for international students. Applications are processed on a rolling basis. Application fee: $70. Electronic applications accepted. *Financial support:* Research assistantships, career-related internships or fieldwork, Federal Work-Study, and unspecified assistantships available. Support available to part-time students. Financial award application deadline: 2/15; financial award applicants required to submit FAFSA. *Unit head:* Dr. Walter G. Antognini, Chairperson, Legal Studies and Taxation Department, 212-618-6480, E-mail: wantognini@pace.edu. *Application contact:* Susan Ford-Goldschein, Director of Graduate Admissions, 212-346-1531, Fax: 212-346-1585, E-mail: graduateadmission@pace.edu.
Website: http://www.pace.edu/lubin/lubin-academic-programs/graduate-programs

Robert Morris University, School of Business, Moon Township, PA 15108-1189. Offers business administration (MBA); human resource management (MS); taxation (MS); MBA/MS. *Accreditation:* AACSB. *Program availability:* Part-time-only, evening/weekend, 100% online. *Faculty:* 12 full-time (4 women), 3 part-time/adjunct (2 women). *Students:* 163 part-time (61 women); includes 13 minority (6 Black or African American, non-Hispanic/Latino; 6 Asian, non-Hispanic/Latino; 1 Two or more races, non-Hispanic/Latino), 8 international. Average age 30. 167 applicants, 40% accepted, 32 enrolled. In 2017, 87 master's awarded. *Entrance requirements:* For master's, GMAT, letters of recommendation. Additional exam requirements/recommendations for international students: Required—TOEFL (minimum score 550 paper-based; 79 iBT). *Application deadline:* For fall admission, 7/1 priority date for domestic and international students; for spring admission, 11/1 priority date for domestic and international students. Applications are processed on a rolling basis. Application fee: $35. Electronic applications accepted. Application fee is waived when completed online. *Expenses:* $955 tuition per credit plus fees of $80 per credit. *Financial support:* Institutionally sponsored loans available. Support available to part-time students. Financial award application deadline: 5/1; financial award applicants required to submit FAFSA. *Unit head:* Dr. Michelle L. Patrick, Dean, 412-397-5445, Fax: 412-397-2585, E-mail: patrick@rmu.edu. *Application contact:*

E-mail: graduateadmissions@rmu.edu.
Website: http://sbus.rmu.edu

St. John's University, The Peter J. Tobin College of Business, Department of Accountancy, Program in Taxation, Queens, NY 11439. Offers MBA, MS. *Program availability:* Part-time, evening/weekend, 100% online, blended/hybrid learning. *Students:* 32 full-time (13 women), 26 part-time (10 women); includes 25 minority (6 Black or African American, non-Hispanic/Latino; 9 Asian, non-Hispanic/Latino; 9 Hispanic/Latino; 1 Two or more races, non-Hispanic/Latino), 4 international. Average age 29. In 2017, 35 master's awarded. *Degree requirements:* For master's, thesis. *Entrance requirements:* For master's, GMAT or GRE, 2 letters of recommendation, essay, resume, unofficial transcripts. Additional exam requirements/recommendations for international students: Required—TOEFL (minimum score 80 iBT), IELTS (minimum score 6.5). *Application deadline:* For fall admission, 11/1 for domestic and international students; for winter admission, 3/1 for domestic and international students; for spring admission, 6/1 for domestic and international students. Applications are processed on a rolling basis. Application fee: $70. Electronic applications accepted. *Expenses:* $22,410 per year. *Financial support:* Research assistantships, teaching assistantships, scholarships/grants, and unspecified assistantships available. Support available to part-time students. Financial award application deadline: 2/1; financial award applicants required to submit FAFSA. *Faculty research:* Tax policy, taxation systems. *Unit head:* Nina T. Dorata, PhD, Chair, 718-990-6460, E-mail: doratan@stjohns.edu. *Application contact:* Amber Steiger, Associate Director of Enrollment Management, 718-990-1345, E-mail: steigera@stjohns.edu.
Website: http://www.stjohns.edu/academics/schools-and-colleges/peter-j-tobin-college-business/programs-and-majors/taxation-master-science

St. Thomas University, School of Law, Miami Gardens, FL 33054-6459. Offers international human rights (LL M); international taxation (LL M); law (JD); JD/MBA; JD/MS. *Accreditation:* ABA. *Program availability:* Online learning. *Degree requirements:* For master's, thesis (international taxation). *Entrance requirements:* For doctorate, LSAT. Electronic applications accepted. *Expenses:* Contact institution.

San Jose State University, Graduate Studies and Research, Lucas Graduate School of Business, San Jose, CA 95192-0065. Offers accountancy (MS); business administration (MBA); taxation (MS); transportation management (MS). *Program availability:* Part-time, evening/weekend, online learning. *Faculty:* 15 full-time (7 women), 6 part-time/adjunct (3 women). *Students:* 85 full-time (49 women), 51 part-time (28 women); includes 77 minority (2 Black or African American, non-Hispanic/Latino; 44 Asian, non-Hispanic/Latino; 16 Hispanic/Latino; 1 Native Hawaiian or other Pacific Islander, non-Hispanic/Latino; 14 Two or more races, non-Hispanic/Latino), 42 international. Average age 28. 328 applicants, 43% accepted, 88 enrolled. In 2017, 155 master's awarded. *Degree requirements:* For master's, graduate writing assessment, culminating project. *Entrance requirements:* Additional exam requirements/recommendations for international students: Required—TOEFL (minimum score 80 iBT), IELTS (minimum score 6.5), PTE (minimum score 53). *Application deadline:* For fall admission, 2/1 for domestic and international students. Applications are processed on a rolling basis. Application fee: $55. Electronic applications accepted. *Expenses:* Contact institution. *Financial support:* Fellowships, research assistantships, career-related internships or fieldwork, Federal Work-Study, institutionally sponsored loans, scholarships/grants, and unspecified assistantships available. Support available to part-time students. Financial award application deadline: 4/28; financial award applicants required to submit FAFSA. *Faculty research:* Financial effects of cyber-security breaches, health care analytics, innovation and teamwork, corporate bankruptcy prediction, multi-domain executive coaching. *Unit head:* Dr. Dan Moshavi, Dean, 408-924-3400, Fax: 408-924-3426, E-mail: dan.moshavi@sjsu.edu.
Website: http://www.sjsu.edu/lucasschool/

Seton Hall University, Stillman School of Business, Program in Taxation, South Orange, NJ 07079-2697. Offers Certificate. *Program availability:* Part-time-only, evening/weekend, blended/hybrid learning. *Faculty:* 1 full-time (0 women), 2 part-time/adjunct (0 women). *Entrance requirements:* For degree, GMAT or GRE (waived based on work experience or advanced degree from AACSB institution), MS in business discipline, professional degree or designation (MD, JD, PhD, DVM, DDS, CPA, etc.), minimum undergraduate GPA of 3.0. Additional exam requirements/recommendations for international students: Required—TOEFL (minimum score 607 paper-based; 80 iBT), IELTS (minimum score 6), PTE. *Application deadline:* For fall admission, 6/1 priority date for domestic students, 4/11 priority date for international students; for spring admission, 10/31 priority date for domestic students, 9/30 priority date for international students; for summer admission, 4/30 priority date for domestic students, 3/31 priority date for international students. Applications are processed on a rolling basis. Application fee: $75. Electronic applications accepted. *Expenses:* $1,305 per credit; $126 fees (fall and spring semester), $51 (summer semester). *Financial support:* Research assistantships available. Financial award application deadline: 6/1; financial award applicants required to submit FAFSA. *Faculty research:* Third-party settled trusts, family partnership, estate valuation discounts, remainder purchase, marital trusts, offshore asset protection trusts. *Unit head:* Dr. Mark Holtzman, Department Chair, 973-761-9133, Fax: 973-761-9217, E-mail: mark.holtzman@shu.edu. *Application contact:* Alfred Ayoub, Director of Graduate Admissions, 973-761-9220, Fax: 973-761-9208, E-mail: alfred.ayoub@shu.edu.
Website: http://www.shu.edu/academics/business/certificate-graduate-taxation.cfm

Southern Illinois University Edwardsville, Graduate School, School of Business, Department of Accounting, Edwardsville, IL 62026. Offers accountancy (MSA); taxation (MSA). *Accreditation:* AACSB. *Program availability:* Part-time, evening/weekend. *Degree requirements:* For master's, thesis or alternative, final exam. *Entrance requirements:* For master's, GMAT. Additional exam requirements/recommendations for international students: Required—TOEFL (minimum score 550 paper-based; 79 iBT), IELTS (minimum score 6.5). Electronic applications accepted.

Southern Methodist University, Dedman School of Law, Dallas, TX 75275-0110. Offers law (JD, SJD); law (for foreign law school graduates) (LL M); law (general) (LL M); taxation (LL M); JD/MA; JD/MBA. *Accreditation:* ABA. *Program availability:* Part-time, evening/weekend. *Degree requirements:* For master's, thesis optional; for doctorate, thesis/dissertation (for some programs), 30 hours of public service (for JD). *Entrance requirements:* For master's, JD; for doctorate, LSAT (for JD). Additional exam requirements/recommendations for international students: Required—TOEFL (minimum score 575 paper-based; 91 iBT). Electronic applications accepted. *Expenses:* Contact institution. *Faculty research:* Corporate law, intellectual property, international law, commercial law, dispute resolution.

Southern New Hampshire University, School of Business, Manchester, NH 03106-1045. Offers accounting (MBA, Graduate Certificate); accounting finance (MS); accounting/auditing (MS); accounting/forensic accounting (MS); accounting/management accounting (MS); accounting/taxation (MS); applied economics (MS); athletic administration (MBA, Graduate Certificate); business administration (IMBA, Certificate), including business information systems (Certificate), human resource management (Certificate); business analytics (MBA); business intelligence (MBA); communication (MA), including new media and marketing, public relations; community economic development (MBA); criminal justice (MBA); data analytics (MS); economics

(MBA); engineering management (MBA); entrepreneurship (MBA); finance (MBA, MS, Graduate Certificate); finance/corporate finance (MS); finance/investments (MS); forensic accounting (MBA); forensic accounting and fraud examination (Graduate Certificate); healthcare informatics (MBA); healthcare management (MBA); human resource management (MS); human resources (MBA); information technology (MS); information technology management (MBA); international business (PhD); Internet marketing (MBA); leadership (MBA); leadership of nonprofit organizations (Graduate Certificate); management (MS); marketing (MBA, MS, Graduate Certificate); music business (MBA); operations and project management (MS); operations and supply chain management (MBA, Graduate Certificate); organizational leadership (MS); project management (MBA, Graduate Certificate); public administration (MBA, Graduate Certificate); quantitative analysis (MBA); Six Sigma (Graduate Certificate); Six Sigma quality (MBA); social media marketing (MBA, Graduate Certificate); sport management (MBA, MS, Graduate Certificate); sustainability and environmental compliance (MBA); MBA/Certificate. *Accreditation:* ACBSP. *Program availability:* Part-time, evening/weekend, online learning. Terminal master's awarded for partial completion of doctoral program. *Degree requirements:* For master's, one foreign language, comprehensive exam (for some programs), thesis or alternative; for doctorate, one foreign language, comprehensive exam, thesis/dissertation. *Entrance requirements:* For master's, minimum GPA of 2.5; for doctorate, GMAT. Additional exam requirements/recommendations for international students: Required—TOEFL (minimum score 500 paper-based). *Application deadline:* Applications are processed on a rolling basis. Application fee: $40. Electronic applications accepted. *Expenses:* Tuition: Part-time $627 per credit hour. Part-time tuition and fees vary according to campus/location and program. *Financial support:* Career-related internships or fieldwork, Federal Work-Study, institutionally sponsored loans, scholarships/grants, tuition waivers (partial), and unspecified assistantships available. Support available to part-time students. Financial award applicants required to submit FAFSA. *Unit head:* Dr. Bill Lightfoot, Dean, 603-644-3102, Fax: 603-644-3144. *Application contact:* Office of Graduate Admission, 888-327-SNHU, Fax: 603-644-3144, E-mail: enroll@snhu.edu.

State University of New York College at Old Westbury, School of Business, Old Westbury, NY 11568-0210. Offers accounting (MS); taxation (MS). *Program availability:* Part-time, evening/weekend. *Faculty:* 10 full-time (2 women), 1 part-time/adjunct (0 women). *Students:* 30 full-time (13 women), 47 part-time (15 women); includes 19 minority (3 Black or African American, non-Hispanic/Latino; 11 Asian, non-Hispanic/Latino; 5 Hispanic/Latino). Average age 31. 35 applicants, 91% accepted, 25 enrolled. In 2017, 25 master's awarded. *Entrance requirements:* For master's, GMAT, 2 letters of recommendation. Additional exam requirements/recommendations for international students: Required—TOEFL (minimum score 550 paper-based). *Application deadline:* For fall admission, 6/15 priority date for domestic students; for spring admission, 11/15 priority date for domestic students. Applications are processed on a rolling basis. Application fee: $50. Electronic applications accepted. *Financial support:* Applicants required to submit FAFSA. *Faculty research:* Corporate governance, asset pricing, corporate finance, hedge funds, taxation. *Unit head:* Rita Buttermilch, Director of Graduate Business Programs, 516-876-3900, E-mail: langec@oldwestbury.edu. *Application contact:* Philip D'Angelo, Graduate Admissions Office, 516-876-3073, E-mail: enroll@oldwestbury.edu.
Website: http://www.oldwestbury.edu/schools/business

Strayer University, Graduate Studies, Washington, DC 20005-2603. Offers accounting (MS); acquisition (MBA); business administration (MBA); communications technology (MS); educational management (M Ed); finance (MBA); health services administration (MHSA); hospitality and tourism management (MBA); human resource management (MBA); information systems (MS), including computer security management, decision support system management, enterprise resource management, network management, software engineering management, systems development management; management (MBA); management information systems (MS); marketing (MBA); professional accounting (MS), including accounting information systems, controllership, taxation; public administration (MPA); supply chain management (MBA); technology in education (M Ed). Programs also offered at campus locations in Birmingham, AL; Chamblee, GA; Cobb County, GA; Morrow, GA; White Marsh, MD; Charleston, SC; Columbia, SC; Greensboro, NC; Greenville, SC; Lexington, KY; Louisville, KY; Nashville, TN; North Raleigh, NC; Washington, DC. *Accreditation:* ACBSP. *Program availability:* Part-time, evening/weekend, online learning. *Degree requirements:* For master's, thesis. *Entrance requirements:* For master's, GMAT, GRE General Test, bachelor's degree from an accredited college or university, minimum undergraduate GPA of 2.75. Electronic applications accepted.

Suffolk University, Sawyer Business School, Department of Accounting, Boston, MA 02108-2770. Offers accounting (MSA, Graduate Certificate); taxation (MST); MBA/MSA; MBA/MST. *Accreditation:* AACSB. *Program availability:* Part-time, evening/weekend, 100% online. *Faculty:* 12 full-time (6 women), 4 part-time/adjunct (1 woman). *Students:* 60 full-time (43 women), 125 part-time (80 women); includes 57 minority (17 Black or African American, non-Hispanic/Latino; 27 Asian, non-Hispanic/Latino; 12 Hispanic/Latino; 1 Two or more races, non-Hispanic/Latino), 38 international. Average age 29. 113 applicants, 71% accepted, 35 enrolled. In 2017, 88 master's awarded. *Entrance requirements:* For master's, GMAT. Additional exam requirements/recommendations for international students: Required—TOEFL (minimum score 550 paper-based; 80 iBT). *Application deadline:* For fall admission, 3/15 priority date for domestic and international students; for spring admission, 10/15 priority date for domestic and international students. Applications are processed on a rolling basis. Application fee: $50. Electronic applications accepted. *Expenses:* $43,980 per year full-time tuition; $1,466 per credit part-time. *Financial support:* In 2017–18, 98 students received support, including 1 fellowship (averaging $6,200 per year); career-related internships or fieldwork, Federal Work-Study, institutionally sponsored loans, and scholarships/grants also available. Support available to part-time students. Financial award application deadline: 4/1; financial award applicants required to submit FAFSA. *Faculty research:* Tax policy, tax research, decision-making in accounting, accounting information systems, capital markets and strategic planning. *Unit head:* Tracy Riley, Chair, 617-994-4276, E-mail: triley@suffolk.edu. *Application contact:* Mara Marzocchi, Associate Director of Graduate Admissions, 617-573-8302, Fax: 617-305-1733, E-mail: grad.admission@suffolk.edu.
Website: http://www.suffolk.edu/msa

Suffolk University, Sawyer Business School, Master of Business Administration Program, Boston, MA 02108-2770. Offers accounting (MBA); entrepreneurship (MBA); executive business administration (EMBA); finance (MBA); global business administration (GMBA); health administration (MBA); international business (MBA); marketing (MBA); nonprofit management (MBA); organizational behavior (MBA); strategic management (MBA); supply chain management (MBA); taxation (MBA); JD/MBA; MBA/MHA; MBA/MSA; MBA/MSF; MBA/MST. *Accreditation:* AACSB. *Program availability:* Part-time, evening/weekend, 100% online. *Faculty:* 16 full-time (6 women), 9 part-time/adjunct (1 woman). *Students:* 106 full-time (57 women), 236 part-time (135 women); includes 80 minority (23 Black or African American, non-Hispanic/Latino; 23 Asian, non-Hispanic/Latino; 28 Hispanic/Latino; 6 Two or more races, non-Hispanic/Latino), 41 international. Average age 30. 354 applicants, 69% accepted, 115 enrolled. In 2017, 170 master's awarded. *Entrance requirements:* For master's, GMAT, minimum undergraduate GPA of 2.75 (MBA), 5 years of managerial experience (EMBA).

Additional exam requirements/recommendations for international students: Required—TOEFL (minimum score 550 paper-based; 80 iBT). *Application deadline:* For fall admission, 3/15 priority date for domestic students, 10/15 priority date for international students; for spring admission, 10/15 priority date for domestic and international students. Applications are processed on a rolling basis. Application fee: $50. Electronic applications accepted. *Expenses:* $43,980 per year full-time, $1,466 per credit part-time (for MBA); $1,794 per credit part-time (for Executive MBA). *Financial support:* In 2017–18, 198 students received support, including 1 fellowship (averaging $2,325 per year); career-related internships or fieldwork, Federal Work-Study, institutionally sponsored loans, and scholarships/grants also available. Support available to part-time students. Financial award application deadline: 4/1; financial award applicants required to submit FAFSA. *Faculty research:* Foreign investments; career strategies and boundaryless careers; corporate ethics codes; interest rates, inflation, and growth options; innovation and product development performance. *Unit head:* Jodi Detjen, Director of MBA Programs, 617-573-8306, E-mail: jdetjen@suffolk.edu. *Application contact:* Mara Marzocchi, Associate Director of Graduate Admissions, 617-573-8302, Fax: 617-305-1733, E-mail: grad.admission@suffolk.edu.
Website: http://www.suffolk.edu/mba

Taft University System, Taft Law School, Denver, CO 80246. Offers American jurisprudence (LL M); law (JD); taxation (LL M).

Taft University System, W. Edwards Deming School of Business, Denver, CO 80246. Offers taxation (MS).

Temple University, Beasley School of Law, Philadelphia, PA 19122. Offers Asian law (LL M); law (JD); legal education (SJD); taxation (LL M); transnational law (LL M); trial advocacy (LL M); JD/LL M; JD/MBA; JD/MPH. *Accreditation:* ABA. *Program availability:* Part-time, evening/weekend. *Faculty:* 66 full-time (33 women), 136 part-time/adjunct (51 women). *Students:* 541 full-time (288 women), 147 part-time (62 women); includes 197 minority (65 Black or African American, non-Hispanic/Latino; 2 American Indian or Alaska Native, non-Hispanic/Latino; 52 Asian, non-Hispanic/Latino; 73 Hispanic/Latino; 5 Two or more races, non-Hispanic/Latino), 11 international. Average age 27. 2,096 applicants, 41% accepted, 223 enrolled. In 2017, 218 doctorates awarded. *Entrance requirements:* For doctorate, LSAT (for JD). Additional exam requirements/recommendations for international students: Recommended—TOEFL. *Application deadline:* For fall admission, 3/1 for domestic and international students. Applications are processed on a rolling basis. Application fee: $65. Electronic applications accepted. *Expenses:* $26,103 resident full-time, $21,107 resident part-time; $39,793 nonresident full-time, $32,065 nonresident part-time. *Financial support:* In 2017–18, 506 students received support, including research assistantships (averaging $5,500 per year), teaching assistantships (averaging $5,500 per year); Federal Work-Study, scholarships/grants, tuition waivers (full and partial), and unspecified assistantships also available. Support available to part-time students. Financial award application deadline: 3/1; financial award applicants required to submit FAFSA. *Faculty research:* Cybersecurity, gender issues, health care law, immigration law, intellectual property law. *Unit head:* Gregory N. Mandel, Dean, 215-204-7863, Fax: 215-204-1185, E-mail: law@temple.edu. *Application contact:* Johanne L. Johnston, Assistant Dean for Admissions and Financial Aid, 800-560-1428, Fax: 215-204-9319, E-mail: lawadmis@temple.edu.
Website: http://www.law.temple.edu

Texas Christian University, Neeley School of Business, Master of Accounting Program, Fort Worth, TX 76129. Offers audit (M Ac); taxation (M Ac); valuation and reporting (M Ac). *Accreditation:* AACSB. *Faculty:* 17 full-time (8 women). *Students:* 65 full-time (25 women); includes 6 minority (all Hispanic/Latino), 6 international. Average age 22. 81 applicants, 99% accepted, 65 enrolled. In 2017, 63 master's awarded. *Entrance requirements:* Additional exam requirements/recommendations for international students: Recommended—TOEFL. *Application deadline:* For fall admission, 2/15 for domestic and international students; for spring admission, 9/15 for domestic and international students. Application fee: $0. Electronic applications accepted. *Expenses:* $1,555 per hour tuition, $1,450 per semester fees. *Financial support:* In 2017–18, 33 students received support. Unspecified assistantships available. Financial award application deadline: 1/31. *Faculty research:* Financial accounting, market valuation of accounting information, corporate governance, managerial compensation and incentives, taxation. *Unit head:* Dr. Mary A. Stanford, Department Chair, 817-257-7483, Fax: 817-257-7227, E-mail: m.stanford@tcu.edu. *Application contact:* Renee Olvera, Director, 817-257-7578, Fax: 817-257-7227, E-mail: renee.olvera@tcu.edu.
Website: http://www.neeley.tcu.edu/Academics/Master_of_Accounting/MAc.aspx

Texas Tech University, Rawls College of Business Administration, Lubbock, TX 79409-2101. Offers accounting (MSA, PhD), including audit/financial reporting (MSA), taxation (MSA); data science (MS); finance (PhD); general business (MBA); healthcare management (MS); information systems and operations management (PhD); management (PhD); marketing (PhD); STEM (MBA); JD/MBA; JD/MSA; MBA/M Arch; MBA/MD; MBA/MS; MBA/Pharm D. *Accreditation:* AACSB. *Program availability:* Evening/weekend, 100% online, blended/hybrid learning. *Faculty:* 89 full-time (22 women). *Students:* 660 full-time (252 women); includes 174 minority (30 Black or African American, non-Hispanic/Latino; 3 American Indian or Alaska Native, non-Hispanic/Latino; 20 Asian, non-Hispanic/Latino; 104 Hispanic/Latino; 17 Two or more races, non-Hispanic/Latino), 99 international. Average age 29. 492 applicants, 51% accepted, 148 enrolled. In 2017, 439 master's, 6 doctorates awarded. *Degree requirements:* For master's, thesis (for MS); capstone course; for doctorate, comprehensive exam, thesis/dissertation, qualifying exams. *Entrance requirements:* For master's, GMAT, GRE, MCAT, PCAT, LSAT, or DAT, holistic review of academic credentials, resume, essay, letters of recommendation; for doctorate, GMAT, GRE, holistic review of academic credentials, resume, statement of purpose, letters of recommendation. Additional exam requirements/recommendations for international students: Required—TOEFL (minimum score 550 paper-based; 79 iBT), IELTS (minimum score 6.5), PTE (minimum score 60). *Application deadline:* For fall admission, 7/1 priority date for domestic students, 1/15 for international students; for spring admission, 12/1 priority date for domestic students, 6/15 for international students; for summer admission, 5/1 for domestic students. Applications are processed on a rolling basis. Application fee: $60. Electronic applications accepted. *Expenses:* $5,167.50 full-time; $9,000 per semester (for hybrid MBA). *Financial support:* In 2017–18, 81 students received support, including 1 research assistantship with full tuition reimbursement available (averaging $22,725 per year), 63 teaching assistantships with full tuition reimbursements available (averaging $22,725 per year); career-related internships or fieldwork, Federal Work-Study, scholarships/grants, health care benefits, and unspecified assistantships also available. Financial award application deadline: 3/1; financial award applicants required to submit FAFSA. *Faculty research:* Governmental and nonprofit accounting, securities and options futures, statistical analysis and design, leadership, consumer behavior. *Total annual research expenditures:* $230,000. *Unit head:* Dr. Margaret Williams, Dean, 806-834-2839, Fax: 806-742-1092, E-mail: margaret.l.williams@ttu.edu. *Application contact:* Jennifer Yack, Applications Manager, Graduate and Professional Programs, 806-742-3184, E-mail: rawlsgrad@ttu.edu.
Website: http://www.depts.ttu.edu/rawlsbusiness/graduate/

Taxation

Thomas Jefferson University, Kanbar College of Design, Engineering and Commerce, Program in Taxation, Philadelphia, PA 19107. Offers MS. *Program availability:* Part-time, evening/weekend. *Entrance requirements:* For master's, GMAT. Additional exam requirements/recommendations for international students: Required—TOEFL (minimum score 550 paper-based; 79 iBT). Electronic applications accepted.

Université de Montréal, Faculty of Law, Montréal, QC H3C 3J7, Canada. Offers business law (DESS); common law (North America) (JD); international law (DESS); law (LL M, LL D, DDN, DESS, LL B); tax law (LL M). *Program availability:* Part-time. *Degree requirements:* For master's, thesis; for doctorate, thesis/dissertation, project; for other advanced degree, thesis (for some programs). Electronic applications accepted. *Faculty research:* Legal theory; constitutional, private, and public law.

Université de Sherbrooke, Faculty of Administration, Program in Taxation, Sherbrooke, QC J1K 2R1, Canada. Offers M Tax, Diploma. *Program availability:* Part-time, evening/weekend. *Degree requirements:* For master's, one foreign language, thesis. *Entrance requirements:* For master's, bachelor's degree in business, law or economics; basic knowledge of Canadian taxation (2 courses). Electronic applications accepted. *Faculty research:* Taxation research, public finances.

The University of Akron, Graduate School, College of Business Administration, The George W. Daverio School of Accountancy, Program in Taxation, Akron, OH 44325. Offers MT, JD/MT. *Students:* 18 full-time (6 women), 15 part-time (6 women); includes 3 minority (2 Black or African American, non-Hispanic/Latino; 1 Hispanic/Latino), 4 international. Average age 32. 24 applicants, 100% accepted, 24 enrolled. In 2017, 34 master's awarded. *Entrance requirements:* For master's, GMAT, GRE, MCAT, LSAT, PCAT, or CAT, minimum GPA of 3.0 (preferred), two letters of recommendation, resume, statement of purpose. Additional exam requirements/recommendations for international students: Required—TOEFL (minimum score 79 iBT), IELTS (minimum score 6.5). *Application deadline:* For fall admission, 8/3 for domestic and international students; for spring admission, 11/15 for domestic and international students; for summer admission, 4/15 for domestic and international students. Application fee: $45 ($75 for international students). Electronic applications accepted. *Unit head:* Dr. Thomas Calderon, Department Chair, 330-972-6228, E-mail: tcalderon@uakron.edu. *Application contact:* Dr. William Hauser, Director of Graduate Business Programs, 330-972-7043, Fax: 330-972-6588, E-mail: whauser@uakron.edu.
Website: http://www.uakron.edu/cba/graduate/programs/mtax/index.dot

The University of Alabama, Graduate School, Manderson Graduate School of Business, Culverhouse School of Accountancy, Tuscaloosa, AL 35487. Offers accounting (M Acc, PhD); tax accounting (MTA). *Accreditation:* AACSB. *Faculty:* 20 full-time (5 women). *Students:* 104 full-time (46 women), 2 part-time (both women); includes 11 minority (5 Black or African American, non-Hispanic/Latino; 1 American Indian or Alaska Native, non-Hispanic/Latino; 2 Asian, non-Hispanic/Latino; 2 Hispanic/Latino; 1 Two or more races, non-Hispanic/Latino), 2 international. Average age 24. 185 applicants, 58% accepted, 89 enrolled. In 2017, 103 master's, 1 doctorate awarded. *Degree requirements:* For doctorate, thesis/dissertation. *Entrance requirements:* For master's, GMAT, minimum GPA of 3.0 overall or on last 60 hours; for doctorate, GMAT, minimum GPA of 3.0. Additional exam requirements/recommendations for international students: Required—TOEFL. *Application deadline:* For fall admission, 7/1 priority date for domestic students, 6/1 priority date for international students; for spring admission, 11/1 priority date for domestic students, 9/1 priority date for international students. Applications are processed on a rolling basis. Application fee: $50 ($60 for international students). Electronic applications accepted. *Financial support:* In 2017–18, 42 students received support, including fellowships with full tuition reimbursements available (averaging $15,000 per year), research assistantships with tuition reimbursements available (averaging $9,765 per year), teaching assistantships with tuition reimbursements available (averaging $13,352 per year); career-related internships or fieldwork, Federal Work-Study, institutionally sponsored loans, scholarships/grants, health care benefits, and unspecified assistantships also available. Financial award application deadline: 3/31. *Faculty research:* Corporate governance, audit decision-making, earning management, valuation, executive compensation. *Unit head:* Dr. Richard Houston, Director, 205-348-8392, E-mail: rhouston@culverhouse.ua.edu. *Application contact:* Candace Peters, Advisor, 205-348-6131, Fax: 205-348-8453, E-mail: cpeters@cba.ua.edu.
Website: http://www.cba.ua.edu/accounting/

The University of Alabama, School of Law, Tuscaloosa, AL 35487. Offers business transactions (LL M); comparative law (LL M, JSD); law (JD, JSD); taxation (LL M); JD/MBA. *Accreditation:* ABA. *Faculty:* 40 full-time (17 women), 33 part-time/adjunct (7 women). *Students:* 412 full-time (175 women), 56 part-time (17 women); includes 94 minority (53 Black or African American, non-Hispanic/Latino; 4 American Indian or Alaska Native, non-Hispanic/Latino; 9 Asian, non-Hispanic/Latino; 22 Hispanic/Latino; 6 Two or more races, non-Hispanic/Latino), 6 international. Average age 27. 1,532 applicants, 25% accepted, 165 enrolled. In 2017, 45 master's, 132 doctorates awarded. *Degree requirements:* For master's, 24 hours, exams; for doctorate, 90 hours, including 6 hours of experiential learning, 1 seminar, and 34 required hours. *Entrance requirements:* For master's, LSAT, JD (for business transactions and taxation); undergraduate degree in law, letters of recommendation, personal statement, resume, and official transcripts (for comparative law); for doctorate, LSAT (for JD), undergraduate degree, letter of recommendation, resume, personal statement, and CAS report (for JD). Additional exam requirements/recommendations for international students: Required—TOEFL, IELTS. *Application deadline:* Applications are processed on a rolling basis. Application fee: $40. Electronic applications accepted. *Expenses:* Contact institution. *Financial support:* Applicants required to submit FAFSA. *Faculty research:* Public interest law, Constitutional law, civil rights, international law, tax law. *Unit head:* Claude R. Arrington, Associate Dean for Admissions, 205-348-6557, Fax: 205-348-3077, E-mail: carrington@law.ua.edu. *Application contact:* Martha Griffith, Assistant Director for Admissions, 205-348-7945, Fax: 205-348-3917, E-mail: mgriffith@law.ua.edu.
Website: http://www.law.ua.edu/

The University of Alabama in Huntsville, School of Graduate Studies, College of Business Administration, Program in Accounting, Huntsville, AL 35899. Offers accounting (M Acc), including CPA preparatory with an emphasis in taxation, CPA preparatory with emphasis in assurance and financial reporting, general accounting, information systems audit and control (ISAC). *Accreditation:* AACSB. *Program availability:* Part-time, evening/weekend. *Degree requirements:* For master's, comprehensive exam, thesis or alternative. *Entrance requirements:* For master's, GMAT (minimum score 500), minimum AACSB index of 1080. Additional exam requirements/recommendations for international students: Required—TOEFL (minimum score 550 paper-based; 80 iBT), IELTS (minimum score 6.5). Electronic applications accepted. *Faculty research:* Accounting information systems, managerial accounting, behavioral accounting, state and local taxation, financial accounting.

University of Baltimore, Graduate School, Merrick School of Business, Department of Accounting, Program in Taxation, Baltimore, MD 21201-5779. Offers MS. *Program availability:* Part-time, evening/weekend. *Entrance requirements:* For master's, GMAT, minimum GPA of 3.0. Additional exam requirements/recommendations for international students: Required—TOEFL (minimum score 550 paper-based). *Expenses:* Contact institution. *Faculty research:* Taxation of not-for-profit entities.

University of Baltimore, School of Law, Baltimore, MD 21201. Offers business law (JD); criminal practice (JD); estate planning (JD); family law (JD); intellectual property (JD); international law (JD); law (JD); law of the United States (LL M); litigation and advocacy (JD); public service (JD); real estate practice (JD); taxation (LL M); JD/LL M; JD/MBA; JD/MPA; JD/MS; JD/PhD. JD/PhD with University of Maryland, Baltimore. *Accreditation:* ABA. *Program availability:* Part-time, evening/weekend. *Entrance requirements:* For doctorate, LSAT. Additional exam requirements/recommendations for international students: Required—TOEFL (for LL M in law of the United States). Electronic applications accepted. *Expenses:* Contact institution. *Faculty research:* Plain view doctrine, statute of limitations, bankruptcy, family law, international and comparative law, Constitutional law.

The University of British Columbia, Peter A. Allard School of Law, Vancouver, BC V6T 1Z1, Canada. Offers common law (LL M CL); law (LL M, PhD); taxation (LL M). *Program availability:* Part-time. *Degree requirements:* For master's, variable foreign language requirement, thesis, seminar; for doctorate, variable foreign language requirement, comprehensive exam, thesis/dissertation, seminar. *Entrance requirements:* For master's, LL B or JD, thesis proposal, 3 letters of reference; for doctorate, LL B or JD, LL M, thesis proposal, 3 letters of reference. Additional exam requirements/recommendations for international students: Required—TOEFL, IELTS. Electronic applications accepted. *Expenses:* Contact institution. *Faculty research:* Aboriginal rights/native law, Asian legal studies, criminal law, environmental law, international law, corporate, human rights, intellectual property, dispute resolution, entertainment.

University of Cincinnati, Carl H. Lindner College of Business, MS Program, Cincinnati, OH 45221. Offers accounting (MS); applied economics (MS); business analytics (MS); finance (MS); information systems (MS); marketing (MS); taxation (MS). *Program availability:* Part-time, evening/weekend. *Faculty:* 65 full-time (20 women), 27 part-time/adjunct (6 women). *Students:* 324 full-time (132 women), 204 part-time (77 women); includes 50 minority (18 Black or African American, non-Hispanic/Latino; 21 Asian, non-Hispanic/Latino; 5 Hispanic/Latino; 1 Native Hawaiian or other Pacific Islander, non-Hispanic/Latino; 5 Two or more races, non-Hispanic/Latino), 299 international. Average age 28. 1,756 applicants, 24% accepted, 351 enrolled. In 2017, 369 master's awarded. *Degree requirements:* For master's, thesis (for some programs), capstone. *Entrance requirements:* For master's, GMAT, GRE, resume, transcripts, essays, letters of recommendation. Additional exam requirements/recommendations for international students: Required—TOEFL (minimum score 577 paper-based; 90 iBT), IELTS (minimum score 6.5). *Application deadline:* For fall admission, 6/30 priority date for domestic students, 3/15 for international students; for spring admission, 12/15 for domestic students, 9/15 for international students; for summer admission, 4/15 for domestic and international students. Applications are processed on a rolling basis. Application fee: $65 ($70 for international students). Electronic applications accepted. *Expenses:* $10,479 per term full-time resident, $14,398 per term full-time nonresident, $890 per credit hour part-time. *Financial support:* In 2017–18, 251 students received support, including 12 teaching assistantships with full and partial tuition reimbursements available (averaging $3,500 per year); scholarships/grants, tuition waivers (full and partial), and unspecified assistantships also available. Financial award application deadline: 2/1; financial award applicants required to submit FAFSA. *Faculty research:* Business analytics, financial management, organizational behavior, financial accounting, consumer insights. *Total annual research expenditures:* $24,842. *Unit head:* Dr. David Szymanski, Dean, 513-556-7001, Fax: 513-556-4891, E-mail: david.szymanski@uc.edu. *Application contact:* Dona Clary, Executive Director, Graduate Programs, 513-556-3546, Fax: 513-558-7006, E-mail: dona.clary@uc.edu.
Website: http://business.uc.edu/graduate/masters.html

University of Colorado Denver, Business School, Program in Taxation, Denver, CO 80217. Offers MS. *Degree requirements:* For master's, 30 semester hours of course work. *Entrance requirements:* For master's, GMAT, resume, essay, transcripts from all universities or colleges attended, letters of recommendation (strongly encouraged). Additional exam requirements/recommendations for international students: Required—TOEFL (minimum score 525 paper-based; 71 iBT); Recommended—IELTS (minimum score 6.5). Electronic applications accepted.

University of Denver, Sturm College of Law, Graduate Tax Program, Denver, CO 80208. Offers LL M, MT. *Program availability:* Part-time, evening/weekend. *Faculty:* 4 full-time (2 women), 4 part-time/adjunct (0 women). *Students:* 23 full-time (11 women), 77 part-time (47 women); includes 21 minority (3 Black or African American, non-Hispanic/Latino; 8 Asian, non-Hispanic/Latino; 8 Hispanic/Latino; 2 Two or more races, non-Hispanic/Latino), 11 international. Average age 33. 75 applicants, 77% accepted, 37 enrolled. In 2017, 53 master's awarded. *Entrance requirements:* For master's, LSAT (for LL M), GMAT (for MT), transcripts; JD from ABA-approved institution (for LL M). Additional exam requirements/recommendations for international students: Required—TOEFL (minimum score 550 paper-based; 80 iBT). *Application deadline:* Applications are processed on a rolling basis. Application fee: $65. Electronic applications accepted. *Expenses:* $47,874 per year full-time; $16,071 per year part-time. *Financial support:* In 2017–18, 87 students received support. Federal Work-Study, institutionally sponsored loans, and scholarships/grants available. Support available to part-time students. Financial award application deadline: 6/30; financial award applicants required to submit FAFSA. *Faculty research:* Individual, estate and gift, and state and local tax; qualified plans; partnerships; c corporations and s corporations; procedural and ethical aspects of the practice of tax. *Unit head:* John Wilson, Professor of the Practice of Taxation/Director, 303-871-6000, E-mail: john.r.wilson@du.edu. *Application contact:* Information Contact, 303-871-6239, Fax: 303-871-6358, E-mail: gtp@du.edu.
Website: http://www.du.edu/tax

University of Florida, Levin College of Law, Gainesville, FL 32611. Offers comparative law (LL M), including tropical conservation and development; environmental and land use law (LL M); international taxation (LL M); law (JD); taxation (LL M, SJD). *Accreditation:* ABA. *Entrance requirements:* For doctorate, LSAT (for JD). Electronic applications accepted. *Faculty research:* Environmental and land use law, taxation, dispute resolution, family law, Constitutional law.

University of Hartford, Barney School of Business, Department of Accounting and Taxation, West Hartford, CT 06117-1599. Offers professional accounting (Certificate); taxation (MSAT). *Program availability:* Part-time, evening/weekend. *Entrance requirements:* For master's, GMAT, 2 letters of recommendation, resume. Additional exam requirements/recommendations for international students: Required—TOEFL (minimum score 550 paper-based). Electronic applications accepted.

University of Hawaii at Manoa, Office of Graduate Education, Shidler College of Business, Program in Accounting, Honolulu, HI 96822. Offers accounting (M Acc); accounting law (M Acc); information systems (M Acc); taxation (M Acc). *Program availability:* Part-time. *Entrance requirements:* For master's, GMAT, bachelor's degree in accounting, minimum GPA of 3.0. Additional exam requirements/recommendations for international students: Required—TOEFL (minimum score 550 paper-based; 79 iBT), IELTS (minimum score 5). *Faculty research:* International accounting, current tax topics, insurance industry financial reporting, behavioral accounting, auditing.

University of Houston, University of Houston Law Center, Houston, TX 77204-6060. Offers energy, environment, and natural resources (LL M); health law (LL M); intellectual property and information law (LL M); international law (LL M); law (JD); tax law (LL M); U.S. law (LL M). *Accreditation:* ABA. *Program availability:* Part-time, evening/weekend. *Faculty:* 58 full-time (23 women), 130 part-time/adjunct (36 women). *Students:* 695 full-time (331 women), 120 part-time (55 women); includes 319 minority (62 Black or African American, non-Hispanic/Latino; 10 American Indian or Alaska Native, non-Hispanic/Latino; 73 Asian, non-Hispanic/Latino; 172 Hispanic/Latino; 2 Native Hawaiian or other Pacific Islander, non-Hispanic/Latino), 33 international. Average age 26. 2,751 applicants, 33% accepted, 227 enrolled. In 2017, 75 master's, 231 doctorates awarded. *Degree requirements:* For master's, thesis optional; for doctorate, senior writing requirement. *Entrance requirements:* For doctorate, LSAT. Additional exam requirements/recommendations for international students: Required—TOEFL (minimum score 600 paper-based; 100 iBT). *Application deadline:* For fall admission, 2/15 for domestic and international students. Applications are processed on a rolling basis. Application fee: $0. Electronic applications accepted. *Expenses:* Contact institution. *Financial support:* In 2017–18, 442 students received support, including 20 fellowships (averaging $2,980 per year); research assistantships, career-related internships or fieldwork, Federal Work-Study, scholarships/grants, and tuition waivers also available. Support available to part-time students. Financial award application deadline: 3/15; financial award applicants required to submit FAFSA. *Faculty research:* Health law, international law, tax, environmental law/energy, information law/intellectual property. *Total annual research expenditures:* $472,551. *Unit head:* Leonard M. Baynes, Dean and Professor of Law, 713-743-2100, Fax: 713-743-2122, E-mail: lbaynes@central.uh.edu. *Application contact:* Pilar Mensah, Assistant Dean for Admissions, 713-743-2280, Fax: 713-743-2194, E-mail: lpmensah@central.uh.edu.
Website: http://www.law.uh.edu/

University of Miami, Graduate School, University of Miami School of Law, Coral Gables, FL 33146. Offers entertainment, arts, and sports law (LL M); estate planning (LL M); intensive English (LL M); international arbitration (LL M); international law (LL M), including general international law, inter-American law; law (JD); maritime law (LL M); real estate/property development (LL M); taxation (LL M); taxation of cross-border investment (LL M); the business of innovation, law and technology (BILT) (JD); U.S. and transnational law for foreign-trained lawyers (LL M); JD/LL M; JD/MA; JD/MBA; JD/MBA/LL M; JD/MD; JD/MM; JD/MPA; JD/MPH; JD/MPS; JD/MS Ed; JD/PhD. *Accreditation:* ABA. *Program availability:* Part-time. *Faculty:* 89 full-time (45 women), 115 part-time/adjunct (27 women). *Students:* 1,099 full-time (534 women), 93 part-time (48 women); includes 455 minority (63 Black or African American, non-Hispanic/Latino; 3 American Indian or Alaska Native, non-Hispanic/Latino; 25 Asian, non-Hispanic/Latino; 330 Hispanic/Latino; 1 Native Hawaiian or other Pacific Islander, non-Hispanic/Latino; 33 Two or more races, non-Hispanic/Latino), 53 international. 2,356 applicants, 59% accepted, 316 enrolled. *Entrance requirements:* For doctorate, LSAT, 2 letters of recommendation. Additional exam requirements/recommendations for international students: Required—TOEFL (minimum score 580 paper-based; 92 iBT), IELTS (minimum score 7). *Application deadline:* For fall admission, 7/31 for domestic and international students. Applications are processed on a rolling basis. Application fee: $60. Electronic applications accepted. *Expenses:* Contact institution. *Financial support:* Fellowships, research assistantships, career-related internships or fieldwork, Federal Work-Study, institutionally sponsored loans, scholarships/grants, and unspecified assistantships available. Financial award application deadline: 3/1; financial award applicants required to submit FAFSA. *Faculty research:* Energy/climate change, international finance, Internet law/law of electronic commerce, race/social justice, art law/cultural heritage law. *Unit head:* Michael Goodnight, Associate Dean of Admissions and Enrollment Management, 305-284-2527, Fax: 305-284-3084, E-mail: mgoodnig@law.miami.edu. *Application contact:* Therese Lambert, Director of Student Recruitment, 305-284-6746, Fax: 305-284-3084, E-mail: tlambert@law.miami.edu.
Website: http://www.law.miami.edu/

See Display on page 1510 and Close-Up on page 1527.

University of Michigan, Law School, Ann Arbor, MI 48109-1215. Offers comparative law (MCL); international tax (LL M); law (LL M, JD, SJD); JD/MA; JD/MBA; JD/MHSA; JD/MPH; JD/MPP; JD/MS; JD/MSI; JD/MSW; JD/MUP; JD/PhD. *Accreditation:* ABA. *Faculty:* 113 full-time (40 women), 33 part-time/adjunct (7 women). *Students:* 931 full-time (435 women); includes 194 minority (36 Black or African American, non-Hispanic/Latino; 7 American Indian or Alaska Native, non-Hispanic/Latino; 65 Asian, non-Hispanic/Latino; 44 Hispanic/Latino; 42 Two or more races, non-Hispanic/Latino), 52 international. 5,284 applicants, 22% accepted, 320 enrolled. In 2017, 41 master's, 331 doctorates awarded. *Entrance requirements:* For doctorate, LSAT. *Application deadline:* For fall admission, 2/15 for domestic students. Applications are processed on a rolling basis. Application fee: $75. Electronic applications accepted. *Expenses:* Contact institution. *Financial support:* In 2017–18, 777 students received support. Career-related internships or fieldwork, Federal Work-Study, institutionally sponsored loans, and scholarships/grants available. Financial award applicants required to submit FAFSA. *Unit head:* Mark D. West, Dean, 734-764-1358. *Application contact:* Sarah C. Zearfoss, Assistant Dean and Director of Admissions, 734-764-0537, Fax: 734-647-3218, E-mail: law.jd.admissions@umich.edu.
Website: http://www.law.umich.edu/

University of Minnesota, Twin Cities Campus, Carlson School of Management, Master of Business Taxation Program, Minneapolis, MN 55455-0213. Offers MBT. *Program availability:* Part-time, evening/weekend. *Faculty:* 3 full-time (1 woman), 17 part-time/adjunct (4 women). *Students:* 17 full-time (5 women), 60 part-time (28 women); includes 6 minority (all Asian, non-Hispanic/Latino), 11 international. Average age 30. 46 applicants, 89% accepted, 33 enrolled. In 2017, 36 master's awarded. *Entrance requirements:* For master's, GMAT or LSAT. Additional exam requirements/recommendations for international students: Required—TOEFL (minimum score 550 paper-based; 79 iBT), IELTS (minimum score 6.5). *Application deadline:* For fall admission, 6/15 priority date for domestic and international students; for spring admission, 10/15 priority date for domestic and international students; for summer admission, 3/15 priority date for domestic and international students. Applications are processed on a rolling basis. Application fee: $75 ($95 for international students). Electronic applications accepted. *Expenses:* $1,295 per credit; Carlson School fee: 1-8 credits $290, 9+ credits $580; some additional fees. *Financial support:* In 2017–18, 19 students received support, including 17 fellowships (averaging $2,000 per year), 2 teaching assistantships with partial tuition reimbursements available (averaging $7,500 per year). Support available to part-time students. Financial award application deadline: 8/1. *Unit head:* Paul Gutterman, Director of Graduate Studies, 612-624-8515, Fax: 612-626-7795, E-mail: pgutterm@umn.edu. *Application contact:* Rhonda Bjurlin, Information Contact, 612-625-6516, E-mail: mbt@umn.edu.
Website: http://carlsonschool.umn.edu/degrees/master-business-taxation

University of Mississippi, Graduate School, School of Accountancy, University, MS 38677. Offers accountancy (M Acc, PhD); accounting and data analytics (MA); taxation accounting (M Tax). *Accreditation:* AACSB. *Faculty:* 17 full-time (4 women), 5 part-time/adjunct (3 women). *Students:* 116 full-time (48 women), 7 part-time (3 women); includes 10 minority (7 Black or African American, non-Hispanic/Latino; 1 Asian, non-Hispanic/

Latino; 1 Native Hawaiian or other Pacific Islander, non-Hispanic/Latino; 1 Two or more races, non-Hispanic/Latino), 3 international. Average age 24. *Entrance requirements:* For master's, GMAT, minimum GPA of 3.0; for doctorate, GMAT. Additional exam requirements/recommendations for international students: Required—TOEFL. *Application deadline:* For fall admission, 8/1 for domestic students; for spring admission, 12/1 for domestic students; for summer admission, 5/1 for domestic students. Applications are processed on a rolling basis. Application fee: $50. *Financial support:* Scholarships/grants available. Financial award application deadline: 3/1; financial award applicants required to submit FAFSA. *Unit head:* Dr. W. Mark Wilder, Dean, School of Accountancy, 662-915-7468, Fax: 662-915-7483, E-mail: umaccy@olemiss.edu. *Application contact:* Dr. Dale Flesher, Associate Dean/Professor/Chair, 662-915-7623, E-mail: acdlf@olemiss.edu.
Website: https://www.olemiss.edu

University of Missouri, Office of Research and Graduate Studies, Robert J. Trulaske, Sr. College of Business, School of Accountancy, Columbia, MO 65211. Offers accountancy (M Acc, PhD); taxation (Certificate). *Accreditation:* AACSB. *Program availability:* Part-time. *Degree requirements:* For master's, thesis or alternative; for doctorate, thesis/dissertation. *Entrance requirements:* For master's and doctorate, GMAT, minimum GPA of 3.0. Additional exam requirements/recommendations for international students: Required—TOEFL (minimum score 600 paper-based; 100 iBT). Electronic applications accepted.

University of New Haven, Graduate School, College of Business, Program in Taxation, West Haven, CT 06516. Offers MS, Graduate Certificate. *Program availability:* Part-time, evening/weekend. *Students:* 15 full-time (7 women), 14 part-time (7 women); includes 9 minority (5 Black or African American, non-Hispanic/Latino; 2 Asian, non-Hispanic/Latino; 1 Hispanic/Latino; 1 Two or more races, non-Hispanic/Latino), 1 international. Average age 32. 24 applicants, 100% accepted, 18 enrolled. In 2017, 12 master's awarded. *Degree requirements:* For master's, thesis or alternative. *Entrance requirements:* For master's, GMAT. Additional exam requirements/recommendations for international students: Required—TOEFL (minimum score 80 iBT), IELTS, PTE. *Application deadline:* Applications are processed on a rolling basis. Application fee: $50. Electronic applications accepted. Application fee is waived when completed online. *Expenses:* Contact institution. *Financial support:* Research assistantships with partial tuition reimbursements, teaching assistantships with partial tuition reimbursements, career-related internships or fieldwork, Federal Work-Study, scholarships/grants, and unspecified assistantships available. Support available to part-time students. Financial award application deadline: 5/1; financial award applicants required to submit FAFSA. *Unit head:* Robert E. Wnek, Chair, 203-932-7111, E-mail: rwnek@newhaven.edu. *Application contact:* Michelle Mason, Director of Graduate Enrollment, 203-932-7067, E-mail: mmason@newhaven.edu.
Website: http://www.newhaven.edu/6856/

See Display on page 154 and Close-Up on page 185.

University of New Mexico, Anderson School of Management, Department of Accounting, Albuquerque, NM 87131. Offers accounting (MBA); advanced accounting (M Acct); information assurance (M Acct); professional accounting (M Acct); tax accounting (M Acct); JD/M Acct. *Accreditation:* AACSB. *Program availability:* Part-time, evening/weekend. *Faculty:* 16 full-time (8 women), 5 part-time/adjunct (2 women). *Students:* 67 applicants, 66% accepted, 35 enrolled. In 2017, 68 master's awarded. *Entrance requirements:* For master's, GMAT/GRE (minimum score of 500), minimum GPA of 3.25, 3.0 on last 60 hours of coursework (for M Acct in professional accounting). Additional exam requirements/recommendations for international students: Required—TOEFL (minimum score 550 paper-based; 79 iBT), IELTS (minimum score 6.5). *Application deadline:* For fall admission, 4/1 priority date for domestic and international students; for spring admission, 10/1 priority date for domestic and international students. Applications are processed on a rolling basis. Application fee: $50. Electronic applications accepted. *Expenses:* Contact institution. *Financial support:* In 2017–18, 16 students received support, including 5 fellowships (averaging $16,744 per year), 14 research assistantships with partial tuition reimbursements available (averaging $15,345 per year); career-related internships or fieldwork, Federal Work-Study, scholarships/grants, and unspecified assistantships also available. Support available to part-time students. Financial award application deadline: 6/1; financial award applicants required to submit FAFSA. *Faculty research:* Critical accounting, accounting pedagogy, theory, taxation, information fraud. *Unit head:* Dr. Richard Brody, Interim Chair, 505-277-6471, E-mail: tmarmijo@unm.edu. *Application contact:* Dr. Rich Brody, Professor, 505-277-6471, E-mail: tmarmijo@unm.edu.
Website: https://www.mgt.unm.edu/acct/default.asp?mm-faculty

University of New Orleans, Graduate School, College of Business Administration, Department of Accounting, Program in Taxation, New Orleans, LA 70148. Offers MS. *Program availability:* Part-time, evening/weekend. *Degree requirements:* For master's, thesis optional. *Entrance requirements:* For master's, GMAT. Additional exam requirements/recommendations for international students: Required—TOEFL (minimum score 550 paper-based; 79 iBT). Electronic applications accepted.

University of Notre Dame, Mendoza College of Business, Master of Science in Accountancy Program, Notre Dame, IN 46556. Offers assurance and advisory services (MSA); tax services (MSA). *Accreditation:* AACSB. *Faculty:* 40 full-time (8 women), 7 part-time/adjunct (0 women). *Students:* 92 full-time (41 women); includes 14 minority (1 Black or African American, non-Hispanic/Latino; 2 American Indian or Alaska Native, non-Hispanic/Latino; 4 Asian, non-Hispanic/Latino; 7 Hispanic/Latino), 17 international. Average age 23. 316 applicants, 41% accepted, 92 enrolled. In 2017, 95 master's awarded. *Entrance requirements:* For master's, GMAT, essay, two recommendations, transcripts from all colleges or universities attended, resume, interview, course descriptions for accounting prerequisites. Additional exam requirements/recommendations for international students: Required—PTE (minimum score 68), TOEFL (minimum iBT score of 109), IELTS (7.5), or documentation of at least six semesters of full-time university education in English. *Application deadline:* For fall admission, 10/1 for domestic and international students; for spring admission, 5/1 for domestic and international students. Applications are processed on a rolling basis. Application fee: $50 ($100 for international students). Electronic applications accepted. *Expenses:* Contact institution. *Financial support:* In 2017–18, 88 students received support, including 88 fellowships (averaging $15,748 per year); scholarships/grants and unspecified assistantships also available. Financial award application deadline: 2/28; financial award applicants required to submit FAFSA. *Faculty research:* Stock valuation, accounting information in decision-making, choice of accounting method, taxes cost on capital. *Unit head:* Dr. Katherine Spiess, Associate Dean, Graduate Business Programs, 574-631-7236, E-mail: spiess.1@nd.edu. *Application contact:* Kristin McAndrew, Director of Admissions, Graduate Business Programs, 574-631-8488, E-mail: kmcandre@nd.edu.
Website: http://msa.nd.edu

University of San Diego, School of Business, Programs in Accountancy and Taxation, San Diego, CA 92110-2492. Offers accountancy (MS); taxation (MS). *Program availability:* Part-time, evening/weekend. *Students:* 14 full-time (13 women), 15 part-time (12 women); includes 3 minority (2 Hispanic/Latino; 1 Two or more races, non-Hispanic/

Latino), 21 international. Average age 25. In 2017, 27 master's awarded. *Entrance requirements:* For master's, GMAT (minimum score of 550), minimum GPA of 3.0. Additional exam requirements/recommendations for international students: Required—TOEFL (minimum score 580 paper-based; 92 iBT), TWE. *Application deadline:* For fall admission, 4/1 for domestic students, 6/1 for international students; for spring admission, 10/1 for domestic students, 12/1 for international students. Application fee: $80. *Financial support:* In 2017–18, 8 students received support. Career-related internships or fieldwork, Federal Work-Study, institutionally sponsored loans, scholarships/grants, and unspecified assistantships available. Support available to part-time students. Financial award application deadline: 4/1; financial award applicants required to submit FAFSA. *Faculty research:* Accounting, financial report, taxation, Sarbanes-Oxley. *Unit head:* Dr. Diane Pattison, Academic Director, Accountancy Programs, 619-260-4850, E-mail: pattison@sandiego.edu. *Application contact:* Monica Mahon, Associate Director of Graduate Admissions, 619-260-4524, Fax: 619-260-4158, E-mail: grads@sandiego.edu.
Website: http://www.sandiego.edu/business/graduate/accounting-tax/

University of San Diego, School of Law, San Diego, CA 92110. Offers business and corporate law (LL M); comparative law (LL M); general studies (LL M); international law (LL M); law (JD); taxation (LL M, Diploma); JD/IMBA; JD/MA; JD/MBA. *Accreditation:* ABA. *Program availability:* Part-time, evening/weekend. *Faculty:* 45 full-time (13 women), 46 part-time/adjunct (13 women). *Students:* 693 full-time (371 women), 96 part-time (40 women); includes 265 minority (31 Black or African American, non-Hispanic/Latino; 15 American Indian or Alaska Native, non-Hispanic/Latino; 97 Asian, non-Hispanic/Latino; 107 Hispanic/Latino; 4 Native Hawaiian or other Pacific Islander, non-Hispanic/Latino; 11 Two or more races, non-Hispanic/Latino), 28 international. Average age 27. 3,260 applicants, 238 enrolled. In 2017, 57 master's, 206 doctorates awarded. *Entrance requirements:* For master's, JD, LL B or equivalent from an ABA-accredited law school; for doctorate, LSAT (less than 5 years old), bachelor's degree, registration with the Credential Assemble Service (CAS). Additional exam requirements/recommendations for international students: Required—TOEFL (minimum score 600 paper-based; 100 iBT). *Application deadline:* For fall admission, 2/1 priority date for domestic students. Applications are processed on a rolling basis. Electronic applications accepted. *Expenses:* Contact institution. *Financial support:* In 2017–18, 617 students received support. Career-related internships or fieldwork, Federal Work-Study, institutionally sponsored loans, and scholarships/grants available. Support available to part-time students. Financial award application deadline: 3/1; financial award applicants required to submit FAFSA. *Faculty research:* Corporate law, children's advocacy, Constitutional and criminal law, international and comparative law, public interest law, intellectual property and tax law. *Unit head:* Dr. Stephen C. Ferruolo, Dean, 619-260-4527, E-mail: lawdean@sandiego.edu. *Application contact:* Jorge Garcia, Assistant Dean, JD Admissions, 619-260-4528, Fax: 619-260-2218, E-mail: jdinfo@sandiego.edu.
Website: http://www.sandiego.edu/law/

University of Southern California, Graduate School, Marshall School of Business, Leventhal School of Accounting, Los Angeles, CA 90089. Offers accounting (M Acc); business taxation (MBT); JD/MBT. *Program availability:* Part-time. *Degree requirements:* For master's, 30-48 units of study. *Entrance requirements:* For master's, GMAT, undergraduate degree, communication skills. Additional exam requirements/recommendations for international students: Required—TOEFL. Electronic applications accepted. *Faculty research:* State and local taxation, Securities and Exchange Commission, governance, auditing fees, financial accounting, enterprise zones, women in business.

University of South Florida, Muma College of Business, Lynn Pippenger School of Accountancy, Tampa, FL 33620-9951. Offers accountancy (M Acc, PhD), including assurance (M Acc), corporate accounting (M Acc), tax (M Acc). *Accreditation:* AACSB. *Program availability:* Part-time, evening/weekend. *Faculty:* 13 full-time (4 women). *Students:* 74 full-time (35 women), 26 part-time (15 women); includes 32 minority (4 Black or African American, non-Hispanic/Latino; 6 Asian, non-Hispanic/Latino; 19 Hispanic/Latino; 3 Two or more races, non-Hispanic/Latino), 10 international. Average age 25. 102 applicants, 53% accepted, 43 enrolled. In 2017, 58 master's, 1 doctorate awarded. Terminal master's awarded for partial completion of doctoral program. *Degree requirements:* For master's, comprehensive exam, thesis or alternative; for doctorate, comprehensive exam, thesis/dissertation. *Entrance requirements:* For master's, GMAT, minimum overall GPA of 3.0 in general upper-level coursework and in upper-level accounting coursework (minimum of 21 hours at a U.S. accredited program within past 5 years); for doctorate, GMAT or GRE, personal statement, recommendations, interview. Additional exam requirements/recommendations for international students: Required—TOEFL (minimum score 550 paper-based; 79 iBT) or IELTS (minimum score 6.5). *Application deadline:* For fall admission, 3/1 priority date for domestic students, 3/1 for international students; for spring admission, 10/1 for domestic students, 9/15 for international students; for summer admission, 2/15 for domestic and international students. Application fee: $30. Electronic applications accepted. *Financial support:* In 2017–18, 43 students received support, including 18 teaching assistantships with tuition reimbursements available (averaging $12,273 per year); scholarships/grants, health care benefits, and unspecified assistantships also available. Financial award applicants required to submit FAFSA. *Faculty research:* Auditing, auditor independence, audit committee decisions, fraud detection and reporting, disclosure effects, effects of information technology on accounting, governmental accounting/auditing, accounting information systems, data modeling and design methodologies for accounting systems, auditing computer-based systems, expert systems, group support systems in accounting, fair value accounting issues, corporate governance, financial accounting, financial reporting quality. *Unit head:* Dr. Uday Murthy, Interim Director, School of Accountancy, 813-974-6516, Fax: 813-974-6528, E-mail: umurthy@usf.edu. *Application contact:* Stacee Bender, 813-974-4516, E-mail: staceebender@usf.edu.
Website: http://business.usf.edu/departments/accountancy/

The University of Texas at Arlington, Graduate School, College of Business, Accounting Department, Arlington, TX 76019. Offers accounting (MP Acc, MS, PhD); taxation (MS). *Accreditation:* AACSB. *Program availability:* Part-time, evening/weekend. *Degree requirements:* For master's, thesis optional; for doctorate, comprehensive exam, thesis/dissertation. *Entrance requirements:* For master's and doctorate, GMAT. Additional exam requirements/recommendations for international students: Required—TOEFL (minimum score 550 paper-based; 79 iBT).

University of the Sacred Heart, Graduate Programs, Department of Business Administration, Program in Taxation, San Juan, PR 00914-0383. Offers MBA. *Program availability:* Part-time, evening/weekend. *Degree requirements:* For master's, thesis. *Entrance requirements:* For master's, EXADEP, minimum undergraduate GPA of 2.75, interview.

University of Washington, Graduate School, Michael G. Foster School of Business, Seattle, WA 98195-3200. Offers auditing and assurance (MP Acc); business administration (MBA, PhD); entrepreneurship (MS); executive business administration (MBA); global executive business administration (MBA); information systems (MSIS); supply chain management (MSSCM); taxation (MP Acc); technology management (MBA); JD/MBA; MBA/MAIS; MBA/MHA. *Accreditation:* AACSB. *Program availability:* Part-time, evening/weekend, blended/hybrid learning. *Faculty:* 109 full-time (35 women),

54 part-time/adjunct (32 women). *Students:* 469 full-time (173 women), 638 part-time (216 women); includes 314 minority (15 Black or African American, non-Hispanic/Latino; 6 American Indian or Alaska Native, non-Hispanic/Latino; 246 Asian, non-Hispanic/Latino; 28 Hispanic/Latino; 5 Native Hawaiian or other Pacific Islander, non-Hispanic/Latino; 14 Two or more races, non-Hispanic/Latino), 125 international. Average age 32. 1,809 applicants, 84% accepted, 1107 enrolled. In 2017, 543 master's, 10 doctorates awarded. Terminal master's awarded for partial completion of doctoral program. *Degree requirements:* For doctorate, comprehensive exam, thesis/dissertation. *Entrance requirements:* For master's and doctorate, GMAT, GRE. Additional exam requirements/recommendations for international students: Required—TOEFL (minimum score 600 paper-based; 100 iBT). *Application deadline:* For fall admission, 3/15 for domestic students, 1/15 for international students. Application fee: $85. Electronic applications accepted. *Expenses:* Contact institution. *Financial support:* Fellowships with partial tuition reimbursements, research assistantships with partial tuition reimbursements, teaching assistantships with partial tuition reimbursements, Federal Work-Study, institutionally sponsored loans, and scholarships/grants available. Financial award application deadline: 2/28; financial award applicants required to submit FAFSA. *Faculty research:* Finance, consumer behavior, marketing analytics, technology management, supply chain. *Unit head:* Dr. James Jiambalvo, Dean, 206-543-4750, E-mail: jjiambal@uw.edu. *Application contact:* Erin Town, Director of Admissions, 206-543-4661, Fax: 206-616-7351, E-mail: mba@uw.edu.
Website: http://www.foster.washington.edu/

University of Washington, Graduate School, School of Law, Seattle, WA 98195-3020. Offers Asian law (LL M, PhD); intellectual property law and policy (LL M); law (JD); law of sustainable international development (LL M); taxation (LL M); JD/LL M; JD/MA; JD/MAIS; JD/MBA; JD/MPA; JD/MS; JD/PhD. *Accreditation:* ABA. *Degree requirements:* For master's, thesis; for doctorate, thesis/dissertation (for some programs). *Entrance requirements:* For master's, language proficiency (LL M in Asian law); for doctorate, LSAT (for JD). Additional exam requirements/recommendations for international students: Required—TOEFL. *Expenses:* Contact institution. *Faculty research:* Asian, international and comparative law, intellectual property law, health law, environmental law, taxation.

University of Waterloo, Graduate Studies, Faculty of Arts, School of Accounting and Finance, Waterloo, ON N2L 3G1, Canada. Offers accounting (M Acc, PhD); finance (M Acc); taxation (M Tax). *Degree requirements:* For master's, thesis or alternative; for doctorate, thesis/dissertation. *Entrance requirements:* For master's, honors degree, minimum B average, resume; for doctorate, GMAT, master's degree, minimum A-average, resume. Additional exam requirements/recommendations for international students: Required—TOEFL, IELTS, PTE. Electronic applications accepted. *Expenses:* Contact institution. *Faculty research:* Auditing, management accounting.

University of Wisconsin–Madison, Graduate School, Wisconsin School of Business, Master of Accountancy Program, Madison, WI 53706-1380. Offers accountancy (M Acc); taxation (M Acc). *Degree requirements:* For master's, minimum GPA of 3.0. *Entrance requirements:* For master's, GMAT, essays. Additional exam requirements/recommendations for international students: Required—TOEFL (minimum score 104 iBT), IELTS (minimum score 8), GMAT. Electronic applications accepted. *Faculty research:* Tax reserves, audit committee incentives, internal audit, accounting report's impact on management decisions.

University of Wisconsin–Milwaukee, Graduate School, Lubar School of Business, MS and Certificate Business Programs, Milwaukee, WI 53201-0413. Offers business analytics (Graduate Certificate); enterprise resource planning (Graduate Certificate); information technology management (MS); investment management (Graduate Certificate); nonprofit management (Graduate Certificate); nonprofit management and leadership (MS); state and local taxation (Graduate Certificate). *Students:* 164 full-time (87 women), 120 part-time (51 women); includes 51 minority (15 Black or African American, non-Hispanic/Latino; 18 Asian, non-Hispanic/Latino; 3 Hispanic/Latino; 15 Two or more races, non-Hispanic/Latino), 55 international. Average age 31. 227 applicants, 54% accepted, 74 enrolled. In 2017, 157 master's, 21 other advanced degrees awarded. *Entrance requirements:* Additional exam requirements/recommendations for international students: Required—TOEFL (minimum score 550 paper-based; 79 iBT), IELTS (minimum score 6.5). Application fee: $56 ($96 for international students). Electronic applications accepted. *Financial support:* Fellowships, research assistantships, teaching assistantships, health care benefits, unspecified assistantships, and project assistantships available. Financial award applicants required to submit FAFSA. *Application contact:* General Information Contact, 414-229-4982, Fax: 414-229-6967, E-mail: gradschool@uwm.edu.

Villanova University, Charles Widger School of Law and Villanova School of Business, Tax Program, Villanova, PA 19085-1699. Offers LL M, JD/LL M. *Program availability:* Part-time, evening/weekend. *Entrance requirements:* For master's, LSAT, JD (for LL M). Additional exam requirements/recommendations for international students: Required—TOEFL (minimum score 600 paper-based). Electronic applications accepted. *Expenses:* Contact institution. *Faculty research:* Taxation and estate planning, corporate tax planning, international taxation, state taxation.

Wake Forest University, School of Business, MS in Accountancy Program, Winston-Salem, NC 27106. Offers assurance services (MSA); tax consulting (MSA); transaction services (MSA). *Faculty:* 19 full-time (3 women), 2 part-time/adjunct (0 women). *Students:* 178 full-time (95 women); includes 34 minority (14 Black or African American, non-Hispanic/Latino; 8 Asian, non-Hispanic/Latino; 7 Hispanic/Latino; 5 Two or more races, non-Hispanic/Latino), 45 international. Average age 24. 453 applicants, 47% accepted, 108 enrolled. In 2017, 132 master's awarded. *Degree requirements:* For master's, 30 credit hours. *Entrance requirements:* For master's, GMAT/GRE, letters of recommendation, official transcripts, current resume or curriculum vitae, interview. Additional exam requirements/recommendations for international students: Required—TOEFL (minimum score 600 paper-based; 100 iBT). *Application deadline:* For fall admission, 6/1 for domestic students, 1/1 for international students. Applications are processed on a rolling basis. Application fee: $100. Electronic applications accepted. *Expenses:* Contact institution. *Financial support:* Career-related internships or fieldwork and scholarships/grants available. Financial award application deadline: 4/15; financial award applicants required to submit FAFSA. *Faculty research:* Influence of personal relationships on business decision-making and management of change; drivers of perceived value and consumer behavior; impact of accounting on auditing, financial, managerial, systems and taxation stakeholders; corporate governance and executive compensation; impact of operations strategies on competitiveness. *Unit head:* James Willis, Associate Dean for Accountancy, 336-758-5422, Fax: 336-758-5830, E-mail: busadmissions@wfu.edu. *Application contact:* Denise Kelly, Administrative Assistant, 336-758-5422, Fax: 336-758-5830, E-mail: busadmissions@wfu.edu.
Website: http://business.wfu.edu/ms-accountancy

Walsh College of Accountancy and Business Administration, Graduate Programs, Program in Accountancy, Troy, MI 48083. Offers data analytics (MAC); finance (MAC); taxation (MAC). *Program availability:* Part-time, evening/weekend. *Students:* 252 (139 women); includes 64 minority (22 Black or African American, non-Hispanic/Latino; 30 Asian, non-Hispanic/Latino; 11 Hispanic/Latino; 1 Two or more races, non-Hispanic/Latino), 21 international. Average age 32. 94 applicants, 76% accepted, 71 enrolled. In

2017, 93 master's awarded. *Degree requirements:* For master's, thesis optional. *Entrance requirements:* For master's, minimum overall cumulative GPA of 2.75 from all colleges previously attended. Additional exam requirements/recommendations for international students: Required—TOEFL (minimum score 550 paper-based, 79 iBT), IELTS (6.5), Michigan English Language Assessment Battery, or MTELP (80). *Application deadline:* Applications are processed on a rolling basis. Application fee: $35. Electronic applications accepted. *Expenses:* $770 per semester credit hour plus $125 registration fee per semester. *Financial support:* In 2017–18, 19 students received support. Career-related internships or fieldwork and scholarships/grants available. Financial award application deadline: 6/30; financial award applicants required to submit FAFSA. *Unit head:* John Black, Chair, Accounting, Tax and Business Law, 248-823-1635, Fax: 248-689-0920, E-mail: jblack@walshcollege.edu. *Application contact:* Heather Rigby, Director, Admissions and Academic Advising, 248-823-1600, Fax: 248-823-1611, E-mail: hrigby@walshcollege.edu.

Walsh College of Accountancy and Business Administration, Graduate Programs, Program in Taxation, Troy, MI 48083. Offers MST. *Program availability:* Part-time, evening/weekend. *Faculty:* 1 full-time (0 women), 6 part-time/adjunct (0 women). *Students:* 53 (23 women); includes 15 minority (7 Black or African American, non-Hispanic/Latino; 6 Asian, non-Hispanic/Latino; 2 Hispanic/Latino), 2 international. Average age 35. 20 applicants, 85% accepted, 8 enrolled. In 2017, 25 master's awarded. *Entrance requirements:* For master's, minimum overall cumulative GPA of 2.75 from all colleges previously attended. Additional exam requirements/recommendations for international students: Required—TOEFL (minimum score 550 paper-based, 79 iBT), IELTS (6.5), Michigan English Language Assessment Battery, or MTELP (80). *Application deadline:* Applications are processed on a rolling basis. Application fee: $35. Electronic applications accepted. *Expenses:* $770 per semester credit hour plus $125 registration fee per semester. *Financial support:* Career-related internships or fieldwork and scholarships/grants available. Financial award application deadline: 6/30; financial award applicants required to submit FAFSA. *Unit head:* Richard Davidson, Chair, Taxation and Business Law, 248-823-1635, Fax: 248-689-0920, E-mail: rdavidson@walshcollege.edu. *Application contact:* Heather Rigby, Director, Admissions and Academic Advising, 248-823-1610, Fax: 248-823-1611, E-mail: hrigby@walshcollege.edu.

Wayne State University, Law School, Detroit, MI 48202. Offers corporate and finance law (LL M); labor and employment law (LL M); law (JD); taxation (LL M); United States law (LL M); JD/MA; JD/MADR; JD/MBA; JD/MS. *Accreditation:* ABA. *Program availability:* Part-time, evening/weekend. *Faculty:* 43 full-time (18 women), 17 part-time/adjunct (9 women). *Students:* 409 full-time (184 women), 46 part-time (22 women); includes 61 minority (33 Black or African American, non-Hispanic/Latino; 1 American Indian or Alaska Native, non-Hispanic/Latino; 14 Asian, non-Hispanic/Latino; 3 Hispanic/Latino; 10 Two or more races, non-Hispanic/Latino), 11 international. Average age 26. 811 applicants, 54% accepted, 146 enrolled. In 2017, 4 master's, 113 doctorates awarded. *Degree requirements:* For master's, thesis (for some programs). *Entrance requirements:* For master's, JD or LL B from ABA-accredited institution and member institution of the AALS; for doctorate, LSAT, LDAS report, bachelor's degree from accredited institution, personal statement, transcripts from all U.S. undergraduate schools attended and an analysis and summary of the transcripts; letter of recommendation (up to two are accepted). Additional exam requirements/recommendations for international students: Required—TOEFL, Michigan English Language Assessment Battery (minimum score 85); Recommended—IELTS. *Application deadline:* For fall admission, 7/1 for domestic students, 5/1 priority date for international students. Applications are processed on a rolling basis. Application fee: $0. Electronic applications accepted. *Expenses:* Contact institution. *Financial support:* In 2017–18, 386 students received support. Fellowships, Federal Work-Study, and scholarships/grants available. Support available to part-time students. Financial award application deadline: 6/30; financial award applicants required to submit FAFSA. *Unit head:* Richard A. Bierschbach, Dean and Professor of Law, 313-577-3933, E-mail: rbierschbach@wayne.edu. *Application contact:* Kathy Fox, Assistant Dean of Admissions, 313-577-3937, Fax: 313-993-8129, E-mail: lawinquire@wayne.edu. Website: http://law.wayne.edu/

Wayne State University, Mike Ilitch School of Business, Detroit, MI 48202. Offers accounting (MS, MSA, Postbaccalaureate Certificate); business (EMS, Graduate Certificate); business administration (MBA, PhD); data science (MS, including business analytics; entrepreneurship and innovation (Postbaccalaureate Certificate); finance (MS); information systems management (Postbaccalaureate Certificate); taxation (MST); JD/MBA. Application deadline for PhD is February 15. *Accreditation:* AACSB. *Program availability:* Part-time, evening/weekend. *Faculty:* 32. *Students:* 235 full-time (121 women), 1,082 part-time (480 women); includes 356 minority (202 Black or African American, non-Hispanic/Latino; 2 American Indian or Alaska Native, non-Hispanic/Latino; 79 Asian, non-Hispanic/Latino; 47 Hispanic/Latino; 26 Two or more races, non-Hispanic/Latino), 87 international. Average age 30. 1,285 applicants, 43% accepted, 308 enrolled. In 2017, 200 master's, 2 doctorates, 9 other advanced degrees awarded. *Degree requirements:* For doctorate, thesis/dissertation. *Entrance requirements:* For master's, GMAT, GRE, LSAT, MCAT, at least three years of relevant work experience that shows increased responsibility, or minimum GPA of 3.0 from AACSB-accredited program or 3.2 from regionally-accredited program, undergraduate degree from accredited institution; undergraduate degree in accounting, business administration, or area of business administration (for MS and MST); for doctorate, GMAT (minimum score of 600), minimum undergraduate GPA of 3.0, 3.5 upper-division or graduate; three letters of recommendation; brief essay; undergraduate degree from accredited institution; personal statement; for other advanced degree, bachelor's degree from accredited institution. Additional exam requirements/recommendations for international

students: Required—TOEFL (minimum score 550 paper-based; 79 iBT), Michigan English Language Assessment Battery (minimum score 85); Recommended—IELTS (minimum score 6.5), TWE (minimum score 5.5). *Application deadline:* For fall admission, 7/1 for domestic students, 5/1 priority date for international students; for winter admission, 11/1 for domestic students, 9/1 priority date for international students; for spring admission, 3/1 for domestic students, 1/1 priority date for international students. Applications are processed on a rolling basis. Application fee: $50. Electronic applications accepted. *Expenses:* Contact institution. *Financial support:* In 2017–18, 165 students received support, including 1 fellowship with tuition reimbursement available (averaging $18,534 per year), 1 teaching assistantship with tuition reimbursement available (averaging $18,534 per year); research assistantships with tuition reimbursements available, scholarships/grants, health care benefits, and unspecified assistantships also available. Support available to part-time students. Financial award applicants required to submit FAFSA. *Faculty research:* Executive compensation and stock performance, consumer reactions to pricing strategies, communication across the automotive supply chain, performance of firms in sub-Saharan Africa, implementation issues with ERP software. *Unit head:* Dr. Robert Forsythe, Dean, School of Business Administration, 313-577-4501, E-mail: robert.forsythe@wayne.edu. *Application contact:* Kiantee N. Rupert-Jones, Director, 313-577-4511, Fax: 313-577-9442, E-mail: gradbusiness@wayne.edu. Website: http://ilitchbusiness.wayne.edu

Weber State University, Goddard School of Business and Economics, School of Accounting and Taxation, Ogden, UT 84408-1001. Offers accounting (M Acc); taxation (M Tax). *Accreditation:* AACSB. *Program availability:* Part-time, evening/weekend. *Faculty:* 7 full-time (2 women). *Students:* 37 full-time (10 women), 28 part-time (15 women); includes 4 minority (2 Asian, non-Hispanic/Latino; 2 Hispanic/Latino), 1 international. Average age 32. In 2017, 28 master's awarded. *Entrance requirements:* For master's, GMAT. Additional exam requirements/recommendations for international students: Required—TOEFL (minimum score 80 iBT). *Application deadline:* For fall admission, 8/1 for domestic students; for spring admission, 12/1 for domestic students; for summer admission, 4/1 for domestic students. Application fee: $60 ($90 for international students). Electronic applications accepted. *Expenses:* Tuition, state resident: full-time $7283. Tuition, nonresident: full-time $17,166. *Required fees:* $898. Tuition and fees vary according to program. *Financial support:* In 2017–18, 32 students received support. Scholarships/grants available. Financial award application deadline: 4/1; financial award applicants required to submit FAFSA. *Unit head:* Dr. Ryan Pace, Program Director, 801-626-7562, Fax: 801-626-7423, E-mail: rpace@weber.edu. *Application contact:* Dr. Larry A. Deppe, Graduate Coordinator, 801-626-7838, Fax: 801-626-7423, E-mail: ldeppe1@weber.edu. Website: http://www.weber.edu/goddard/accounting-taxation.html

Western Michigan University Thomas M. Cooley Law School, Graduate Programs, Lansing, MI 48901-3038. Offers administrative law (public law) (JD); business transactions (JD); Canadian law practice (JD); corporate law and finance (LL M); environmental law (public law) (JD); general practice (JD), including solo and small firm; general studies (LL M); homeland and national security law (LL M); insurance law (LL M); intellectual property (JD); intellectual property law (LL M); international law (JD); litigation (JD); taxation (LL M); U.S. legal studies for foreign attorneys (LL M); JD/LL M; JD/MBA; JD/MHA; JD/MPA; JD/MSW. *Program availability:* Part-time, evening/weekend, 100% online, blended/hybrid learning. *Degree requirements:* For master's, thesis (for some programs); for doctorate, minimum of 3 credits of clinical experience. *Entrance requirements:* For master's, JD or LL B; for doctorate, LSAT. Additional exam requirements/recommendations for international students: Required—TOEFL (for U.S. legal studies for foreign attorneys LL M program); Recommended—TOEFL. Electronic applications accepted. *Expenses:* Contact institution. *Faculty research:* Wrongful convictions, civil rights, environmental law, litigation techniques, data mining, intellectual property, practical and skills-based legal education.

Wichita State University, Graduate School, W. Frank Barton School of Business, School of Accountancy, Wichita, KS 67260. Offers accounting information systems (M Acc); taxation (M Acc). *Accreditation:* AACSB. *Program availability:* Part-time, evening/weekend. *Unit head:* Dr. Paul D. Harrison, Director, 316-978-3215, Fax: 316-978-3660, E-mail: paul.harrison@wichita.edu. *Application contact:* Jordan Oleson, Admissions Coordinator, 316-978-3095, Fax: 316-978-3253, E-mail: jordan.oleson@wichita.edu. Website: http://www.wichita.edu/acct

Widener University, School of Business Administration, Program in Taxation, Chester, PA 19013-5792. Offers MS. *Program availability:* Part-time, evening/weekend. *Faculty:* 2 full-time (1 woman), 2 part-time/adjunct (1 woman). *Students:* 8 full-time (3 women), 19 part-time (7 women); includes 7 minority (all Black or African American, non-Hispanic/Latino), 1 international. Average age 32. 10 applicants, 60% accepted, 4 enrolled. In 2017, 11 master's awarded. *Entrance requirements:* For master's, Certified Public Accountant Exam or GMAT. *Application deadline:* For fall admission, 8/1 priority date for domestic students; for spring admission, 12/1 for domestic students. Applications are processed on a rolling basis. Application fee: $25 ($300 for international students). Electronic applications accepted. *Financial support:* Available to part-time students. Application deadline: 5/1. *Faculty research:* Financial planning, taxation fraud. *Application contact:* Ann Seltzer, Graduate Enrollment Administrator, 610-499-4305, E-mail: apseltzer@widener.edu.

Yeshiva University, Sy Syms School of Business, New York, NY 10016. Offers accounting (MS); business (EMBA); marketing (MS); taxation (MS). *Program availability:* Part-time. *Entrance requirements:* For master's, minimum GPA of 3.5 or GMAT.

SAINT JOSEPH'S UNIVERSITY
Financial Services

 For more information, visit http://petersons.to/sjufinservices

SJU SAINT JOSEPH'S UNIVERSITY
Haub School of Business

Programs of Study

The Master of Science in Financial Services (M.S.F.S.) program at Saint Joseph's University's Haub School of Business (HSB) is designed to prepare students for success in the fast-paced, dynamic financial industry. The curriculum is rich enough to prepare professionals to engage in financial planning services or to pursue careers in financial analysis and corporate finance. As one of the few programs in the nation that is both AACSB accredited and CFP® certified, this top-ranked program offers students advanced credentials by building on professional planning, analytical, and financial experience, along with the strong ethical foundation that is crucial in today's financial environment. In addition, seven courses in the M.S.F.S. program fulfill the educational requirements so students can sit for the CFP® exam.

The program provides immediately applicable skills for professionals in the finance or financial planning field who want to deepen their knowledge and advance their career; professionals pursuing the Certified Financial Planner® (CFP) certification; and recent college graduates or early careerists who want to prepare for their next professional opportunity.

The M.S.F.S. program is offered in a variety of formats. Students can attend part- or full-time and take courses online, on campus, or both. Classes are offered in the fall, spring, and summer terms, and students can begin any semester. Students can pace the program according to their needs, and can graduate in one year or take up to six years to complete the degree. Online courses include synchronous and asynchronous sessions along with other collaborative learning tools.

The curriculum consists of 10 upper-level courses (30 credits) which provide students with in-depth learning in core finance principles, including: portfolio management, financial institutions and capital markets, mergers and acquisitions, risk management, security analysis, derivative markets, and international finance.

Students in the M.S.F.S. program come from all majors and backgrounds. For students whose undergraduate degree is in a non-business major, there are four foundations courses (10 credits) available to prepare them for success in the program. Opportunities for foundation course waivers are determined for every applicant.

The Haub School of Business has over 80 full-time faculty members who contribute scholarly research to the classroom, as well as part-time faculty who are senior executives in their field. Small classes allow for in-depth discussions, reflection, experiential exercises, writing assignments, and team projects, as well as facilitate interactions with fellow students, faculty, and guest lecturers. Optional, international study tours are available to complement the classroom experience.

Students of the M.S.F.S. program graduate prepared to create solutions, introduce new capabilities, improve client relationships, and ultimately, contribute to their organization's bottom line.

Graduates of the program can connect with more than 67,000 SJU alumni around the globe. Numerous formal and informal events and activities allow students to network with their peers, alumni, lecturers, and business representatives. With lifetime access to the Career Development Center, students receive guidance on vital techniques including resume writing, interviewing, networking, and job search.

A recent survey of those who have earned a graduate business degree at Saint Joseph's University has shown that 73 percent report receiving a raise after completing their program; 76 percent say the program significantly helped them advance their career; 70 percent indicate that their degree from the Haub School provided them with more opportunities to increase their salary and gain professional recognition; and 86 percent say the program provided them with the strategic business acumen they needed to succeed in their chosen field.

Research Facilities

The Post Learning Commons and Drexel Library make up the Post Academic Center and support the academic programs of Saint Joseph's University with books and periodicals in both print and electronic formats, research databases, audio-visual materials, and microforms. Research resources and support are available on campus and fully online.

The Wall Street Trading Room at SJU's Haub School of Business supports the financial education programs and provides students with the knowledge and skills required for competing in a global job market. The room provides access to electronic sources of financial and investment data, analytical tools, and trading simulations. The room allows hands-on learning, curriculum enhancements, and more effective class projects. Trading simulations provide opportunities for real trading experiences. Continuous access to financial data and software provides an integrated learning environment to focus on analysis, synthesis, and evaluation.

Financial Aid

Financial aid is available and includes federal loans, university scholarships, graduate assistantships, employer tuition deferral programs, and loans from private lenders. SJU also offers tuition benefits to eligible military personnel and veterans through the Yellow Ribbon Program.

Cost of Study

Tuition for the 2018–19 academic year is $1,043 per credit for domestic and international students. Tuition is charged on a per credit basis, per semester, and is the same for online and on-campus courses. There are no additional fees for domestic students; international students may incur additional fees in regard to their visa, as well as a university health plan. Tuition is subject to change by the order of the Saint Joseph's University Board of Trustees.

Living and Housing Costs

The Office of Residence Life offers limited on-campus housing options for graduate students; availability is not guaranteed. The 2018–19 rates range from $5,120 to $6,120 per person per semester. Residence Life also assists students with off-campus housing recommendations. More information can be found at https://offcampushousing.sju.edu/.

Student Life

Students in the M.S.F.S. program may choose to participate in SJU's Graduate Business Student Association (GBSA). The GBSA enhances the graduate experience by promoting professional development and a sense of community among graduate business students, faculty, and administration. All students are automatically members of the GBSA and no registration is required. This student-run organization aims to build strategic relationships by providing networking opportunities through social and service activities.

The Office of Adult Student Life assists graduate students by providing support in overcoming obstacles and resources to foster success. The ASL Office seeks to help adult students develop a personalized plan for success, coordinate adult student groups, organize programs to meet adult student needs, and provide adult student advocacy as needed.

Location

Located in Philadelphia, Pennsylvania, SJU's community enjoys the surroundings of one of America's first major cities. Widely known as "The City of Brotherly Love" Philadelphia's historical importance and vibrant

Saint Joseph's University

communities create a charming and unique culture. The city is the fifth-largest metropolis in the U.S. and is home to historical landmarks and world-class museums, a number of professional sports teams and dining options, and major events that enrich its cultural life. There are also opportunities to explore Philadelphia's outdoors with a wealth of year-round festivals and cultural events, parks, zoos, and aquariums. With eight Fortune 500 companies, Philadelphia offers numerous internship, networking, and post-graduation job opportunities.

The SJU campus is just a train ride away from Center City Philadelphia, allowing students to easily access the culture, art, nightlife, and opportunity that Philadelphia has to offer. The city is also conveniently located between New York City and Washington D.C., providing convenient access to additional cultural and employment opportunities.

The University and the School

For over 160 years, Saint Joseph's University has been engaging students in a rigorous Jesuit education that empowers them to become leaders in their industries and communities. Built upon the Ignatian credo of *cura personalis*, the Saint Joseph's education encompasses all aspects of personal growth and development: high achievement, deepening understanding, strengthening reasoning and communication skills, and developing moral character.

The university offers approximately 8,086 students 55 majors, 50 minors, 30-plus degree completion and certificate programs, and 52 graduate programs through two schools. The College of Arts and Sciences offers programs in the humanities, natural sciences, and social sciences.

The Erivan K. Haub School of Business provides a wide-range of programs including STEM master's degrees and graduate programs in analytics. It is an international AACSB-accredited institution in business and accounting, offering programs at the bachelor's, master's, and executive master's levels. *U.S. News & World Report* has ranked the school's part-time MBA, risk-management and insurance, marketing, management, and finance programs among the top in the nation. The Haub School was recently named one of the nation's top business schools in the Princeton Review's "The Best 294 Business Schools," and the undergraduate program was recently recognized by Bloomberg's Businessweek.

It is the largest Jesuit business school in the country with 3,600 students, 84 full-time faculty and more than 22,000 alumni.

Faculty

The professors in the M.S.F.S. program are full-time faculty engaged in cutting-edge research and part-time faculty who are senior executives in their fields. All instructors infuse their classes with relevant, real-world learning and scholarship, providing students with practical business knowledge that they can apply immediately in their careers.

Additional information regarding members of the M.S.F.S. faculty can be found online at sju.edu/msfs.

Applying

Applications are reviewed on a rolling basis. Students may apply to start the M.S.F.S. program in the fall, spring, or summer terms. The priority application deadline is July 15 for fall semester, November 15 for spring semester, and March 15 for summer semester.

Applicants must have a baccalaureate degree from an accredited university and complete the official application. Required application materials include: official transcripts for all credits earned (undergraduate and graduate), two letters of recommendation, a current resume, a $35 application fee, a personal statement (specifics available online), and official GMAT or GRE scores from within the past seven years (GMAT may be waived under certain circumstances; more details are available online).

Additional requirements and details for international students are available at https://www.sju.edu/majors-programs/graduate-business/master-degrees/financial-services-ms/admission-requirements.

Correspondence and Information

Graduate Business Office
Master of Science in Financial Services
Saint Joseph's University
5600 City Avenue, MV 280
Philadelphia, Pennsylvania 19131
Phone: 610-660-1690
E-mail: sjumba@sju.edu
Website: sju.edu/msfs

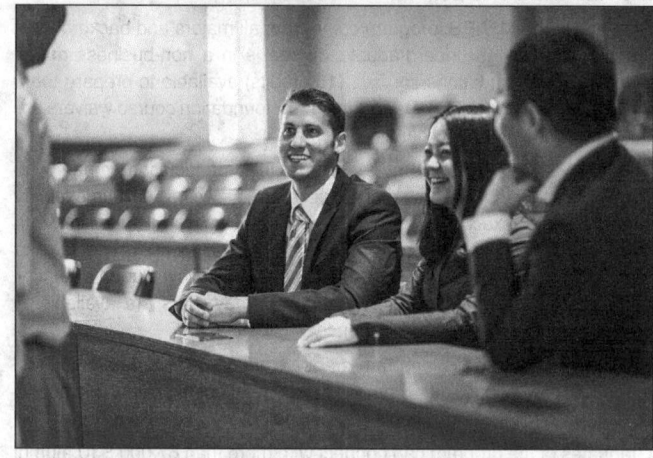

Section 3
Advertising and Public Relations

This section contains a directory of institutions offering graduate work in electronic commerce. Additional information about programs listed in the directory but not augmented by an in-depth entry may be obtained by writing directly to the dean of a graduate school or chair of a department at the address given in the directory.

For programs offering related work, see also in this book *Business Administration* and *Management and Marketing*. In another guide in this series:

Graduate Programs in the Humanities, Arts & Social Sciences
See *Communication and Media*

CONTENTS

Advertising and Public Relations

Academy of Art University, Graduate Programs, School of Advertising, San Francisco, CA 94105-3410. Offers advertising (MFA); advertising and branded media technology (MA). *Program availability:* Part-time, 100% online. *Faculty:* 5 full-time (2 women), 13 part-time/adjunct (6 women). *Students:* 59 full-time (41 women), 34 part-time (24 women); includes 16 minority (5 Black or African American, non-Hispanic/Latino; 6 Asian, non-Hispanic/Latino; 5 Hispanic/Latino), 57 international. Average age 28. 29 applicants, 100% accepted, 23 enrolled. In 2017, 61 master's awarded. *Degree requirements:* For master's, final review. *Entrance requirements:* For master's, statement of intent; resume; portfolio/reel; official college transcripts. *Application deadline:* Applications are processed on a rolling basis. Application fee: $50. Electronic applications accepted. *Expenses: Tuition:* Part-time $982 per unit. *Financial support:* Career-related internships or fieldwork, Federal Work-Study, and scholarships/grants available. Financial award application deadline: 8/10; financial award applicants required to submit FAFSA. *Unit head:* 800-544-ARTS, E-mail: info@academyart.edu. *Application contact:* 800-544-ARTS, E-mail: info@academyart.edu.
Website: https://www.academyart.edu/academics/advertising

Arcadia University, College of Arts and Sciences, Program in International Public Relations, Glenside, PA 19038-3295. Offers MA. *Degree requirements:* For master's, thesis, internship. *Expenses:* Contact institution.

Ball State University, Graduate School, College of Communication, Information, and Media, Department of Journalism, Program in Public Relations, Muncie, IN 47306. Offers MA. *Program availability:* Part-time, 100% online, blended/hybrid learning. *Students:* 11 full-time (7 women), 17 part-time (14 women); includes 4 minority (3 Black or African American, non-Hispanic/Latino; 1 Hispanic/Latino), 3 international. Average age 31. 30 applicants, 37% accepted, 9 enrolled. In 2017, 13 master's awarded. *Entrance requirements:* For master's, GRE General Test (minimum score 150 verbal), minimum baccalaureate GPA of 2.75 or 3.0 in latter half of baccalaureate, transcripts of all prior course work, current resume or curriculum vitae, statement of purpose, writing sample. Additional exam requirements/recommendations for international students: Required—TOEFL (minimum score 550 paper-based; 79 iBT), IELTS (minimum score 6.5). *Application deadline:* Applications are processed on a rolling basis. Application fee: $60. Electronic applications accepted. *Financial support:* Research assistantships with partial tuition reimbursements and unspecified assistantships available. Financial award application deadline: 3/1; financial award applicants required to submit FAFSA. *Unit head:* Dr. Johnny Sparks, Chairperson, 765-285-8278, Fax: 765-285-7997, E-mail: jvsparks@bsu.edu. *Application contact:* Dr. Deborah Davis, Graduate Advisor, 765-285-9104, Fax: 765-285-7997, E-mail: dadavis@bsu.edu.
Website: http://cms.bsu.edu/academics/collegesanddepartments/journalism/graduateprograms/mapublicrelations

Boston University, College of Communication, Department of Mass Communication, Advertising, and Public Relations, Boston, MA 02215. Offers advertising (MS); mass communication (MS), including communication studies, marketing communication research; public relations (MS); JD/MS. *Program availability:* Part-time. *Faculty:* 26 full-time, 33 part-time/adjunct. *Students:* 231 full-time (195 women), 8 part-time (6 women); includes 22 minority (8 Black or African American, non-Hispanic/Latino; 2 Asian, non-Hispanic/Latino; 8 Hispanic/Latino; 4 Two or more races, non-Hispanic/Latino), 173 international. Average age 23. 529 applicants, 67% accepted, 126 enrolled. In 2017, 106 master's awarded. *Degree requirements:* For master's, comprehensive exam (for some programs), thesis (for some programs). *Entrance requirements:* For master's, GRE General Test, resume, letters of recommendation, personal statement. Additional exam requirements/recommendations for international students: Required—TOEFL (minimum score 600 paper-based; 100 iBT), IELTS (minimum score 7). *Application deadline:* For fall admission, 5/1 for domestic and international students. Applications are processed on a rolling basis. Application fee: $95. Electronic applications accepted. *Financial support:* Research assistantships, teaching assistantships with partial tuition reimbursements, career-related internships or fieldwork, Federal Work-Study, scholarships/grants, and unspecified assistantships available. Support available to part-time students. Financial award application deadline: 5/1; financial award applicants required to submit FAFSA. *Unit head:* Christopher Beaudoin, Chairperson, 617-353-3482, E-mail: mcadvpr@bu.edu. *Application contact:* Jackie Cummings, Admission and Financial Aid Counselor, 617-353-3481, E-mail: comgrad@bu.edu.
Website: http://www.bu.edu/com/academics/masscomm-ad-pr/

Boston University, Metropolitan College, Program in Advertising, Boston, MA 02215. Offers MS. *Program availability:* Part-time, evening/weekend. *Faculty:* 1 full-time (0 women), 15 part-time/adjunct (6 women). *Students:* 15 part-time (11 women); includes 4 minority (1 Black or African American, non-Hispanic/Latino; 1 Hispanic/Latino; 2 Two or more races, non-Hispanic/Latino). Average age 28. 9 applicants, 11% accepted, 1 enrolled. In 2017, 24 master's awarded. *Entrance requirements:* For master's, undergraduate degree in appropriate field of study. *Application deadline:* Applications are processed on a rolling basis. Application fee: $85. Electronic applications accepted. *Expenses:* Contact institution. *Financial support:* Unspecified assistantships available. Support available to part-time students. Financial award applicants required to submit FAFSA. *Faculty research:* Communication and advertising. *Unit head:* Dr. Christopher Cakebread, Associate Professor, 617-353-3476, E-mail: ccakebr@bu.edu.
Website: http://www.bu.edu/met/advertising

California Baptist University, Program in Public Relations, Riverside, CA 92503. Offers MA. *Program availability:* Part-time, evening/weekend. *Faculty:* 2 full-time (both women). *Students:* 16 full-time (14 women), 8 part-time (all women); includes 17 minority (5 Black or African American, non-Hispanic/Latino; 1 Asian, non-Hispanic/Latino; 9 Hispanic/Latino; 2 Two or more races, non-Hispanic/Latino). Average age 33. 19 applicants, 68% accepted, 11 enrolled. In 2017, 10 master's awarded. *Degree requirements:* For master's, comprehensive capstone. *Entrance requirements:* For master's, minimum undergraduate GPA of 2.5, 2 recommendations, current resume, 500-word essay. Additional exam requirements/recommendations for international students: Required—TOEFL (minimum score 80 iBT). *Application deadline:* For fall admission, 8/1 priority date for domestic students, 7/1 for international students; for spring admission, 12/1 priority date for domestic students, 11/1 priority date for international students. Applications are processed on a rolling basis. Application fee: $45. Electronic applications accepted. *Expenses:* Contact institution. *Financial support:* Applicants required to submit CSS PROFILE or FAFSA. *Faculty research:* New media technologies, media relations, journalism, media effects. *Unit head:* Dr. Mary Ann Pearson, Program Director, MA in Public Relations, 951-343-3967, E-mail: mpearson@calbaptist.edu. *Application contact:* Ted Meyer, Dean of Enrollment Services, Online and Professional Studies, 951-343-3909, E-mail: tmeyer@calbaptist.edu.
Website: http://www.cbuonline.edu/programs/program/master-of-arts-in-public-relations

Central Connecticut State University, School of Graduate Studies, College of Liberal Arts and Social Sciences, Department of Communication, New Britain, CT 06050-4010. Offers communication (MS); public relations/promotions (Certificate). *Program availability:* Part-time, evening/weekend. *Faculty:* 6 full-time (1 woman). *Students:* 8 full-time (3 women), 24 part-time (19 women); includes 11 minority (5 Black or African American, non-Hispanic/Latino; 6 Hispanic/Latino), 2 international. Average age 28. 22 applicants, 77% accepted, 10 enrolled. In 2017, 9 master's awarded. *Degree requirements:* For master's, comprehensive exam, thesis or alternative, special project; for Certificate, qualifying exam. *Entrance requirements:* For master's, minimum undergraduate GPA of 3.0, resume, references, essay. Additional exam requirements/recommendations for international students: Required—TOEFL (minimum score 550 paper-based; 79 iBT); Recommended—IELTS (minimum score 6.5). *Application deadline:* For fall admission, 8/1 for domestic students, 5/1 for international students; for spring admission, 11/1 for domestic and international students. Applications are processed on a rolling basis. Application fee: $50. Electronic applications accepted. *Expenses: Tuition, area resident:* Full-time $6757. Tuition, state resident: full-time $9750; part-time $374 per credit. Tuition, nonresident: full-time $18,102; part-time $374 per credit. *Required fees:* $4635; $255 per credit. *Financial support:* In 2017–18, 5 students received support. Career-related internships or fieldwork, Federal Work-Study, scholarships/grants, and unspecified assistantships available. Support available to part-time students. Financial award application deadline: 3/1; financial award applicants required to submit FAFSA. *Faculty research:* Organizational communication, mass communication, intercultural communication, political communication, information management. *Unit head:* Dr. Christopher Pudlinski, Chair, 860-832-2690, E-mail: pudlinskic@ccsu.edu. *Application contact:* Patricia Gardner, Associate Director of Graduate Studies, 860-832-2350, Fax: 860-832-2362.
Website: http://comm.ccsu.edu/

Clarion University of Pennsylvania, College of Arts, Education and Sciences, Certificate Program in Public Relations, Clarion, PA 16214. Offers Certificate. *Accreditation:* ALA. *Program availability:* Part-time-only, evening/weekend, online only, 100% online. *Faculty:* 2 full-time (both women). *Students:* 3 part-time (all women); includes 1 minority (Asian, non-Hispanic/Latino). Average age 46. 3 applicants, 67% accepted, 1 enrolled. In 2017, 2 Certificates awarded. *Entrance requirements:* Additional exam requirements/recommendations for international students: Required—TOEFL (minimum score 550 paper-based, 80 iBT) or IELTS (7). *Application deadline:* For fall admission, 8/15 priority date for domestic students, 7/15 priority date for international students; for winter admission, 11/1 priority date for domestic students; for spring admission, 1/7 priority date for domestic students, 11/15 priority date for international students; for summer admission, 4/1 priority date for domestic students. Applications are processed on a rolling basis. Application fee: $40. Electronic applications accepted. *Expenses:* $655.05 per credit. *Financial support:* Available to part-time students. Application deadline: 3/1; applicants required to submit FAFSA. *Unit head:* Dr. Steven Harris, Interim Dean of Arts, Education, and Sciences, 814-393-2197, E-mail: harris@clarion.edu. *Application contact:* Dana Bearer, Associate Director, Transfer, Adult, and Graduate Programs, 814-393-2337, Fax: 814-393-2722, E-mail: gradstudies@clarion.edu.

Colorado State University, College of Liberal Arts, Department of Journalism and Media Communication, Fort Collins, CO 80523-1785. Offers communications and media management (MCMM); public communication and technology (MS, PhD). *Program availability:* Part-time, blended/hybrid learning. *Faculty:* 12 full-time (7 women), 2 part-time/adjunct (both women). *Students:* 27 full-time (22 women), 38 part-time (25 women); includes 11 minority (1 Black or African American, non-Hispanic/Latino; 2 American Indian or Alaska Native, non-Hispanic/Latino; 1 Asian, non-Hispanic/Latino; 5 Hispanic/Latino; 2 Two or more races, non-Hispanic/Latino), 12 international. Average age 32. 40 applicants, 73% accepted, 20 enrolled. In 2017, 11 master's, 4 doctorates awarded. Terminal master's awarded for partial completion of doctoral program. *Degree requirements:* For master's, thesis (for some programs), research project; for doctorate, comprehensive exam, thesis/dissertation. *Entrance requirements:* For master's, GRE General Test (for MS program only), minimum GPA of 3.0; transcripts; letters of recommendation; writing sample, curriculum vitae/resume; statement of purpose; for doctorate, GRE General Test, minimum GPA of 3.0; transcripts; letters of recommendation; writing sample, curriculum vitae/resume; statement of purpose. Additional exam requirements/recommendations for international students: Required—TOEFL (minimum score 550 paper-based; 80 iBT), IELTS (minimum score 6.5); Recommended—TWE. Application fee: $60 ($70 for international students). Electronic applications accepted. *Expenses:* Contact institution. *Financial support:* In 2017–18, 2 research assistantships with full and partial tuition reimbursements (averaging $14,102 per year), 33 teaching assistantships with full and partial tuition reimbursements (averaging $14,861 per year) were awarded; scholarships/grants, health care benefits, and unspecified assistantships also available. *Faculty research:* Food marketing communication models of influence; sports media and journalism; health and science communication; social interaction in online contexts; public discourse and media sociology. *Total annual research expenditures:* $668,408. *Unit head:* Greg Luft, Professor and Department Chair, 970-491-1979, Fax: 970-491-2908, E-mail: greg.luft@colostate.edu. *Application contact:* Linda Kidder, Graduate Program Administrator, 970-491-5132, Fax: 970-491-2908, E-mail: linda.kidder@colostate.edu.
Website: http://journalism.colostate.edu/

DePaul University, College of Communication, Chicago, IL 60604. Offers digital communication and media arts (MA); health communication (MA); journalism (MA); media and cinema studies (MA); multicultural communication (MA); organizational communication (MA); public relations and advertising (MA); relational communication (MA). *Program availability:* Part-time, evening/weekend. *Entrance requirements:* Additional exam requirements/recommendations for international students: Required—TOEFL (minimum score 590 paper-based; 96 iBT), IELTS (minimum score 7.5) or PTE. *Application deadline:* For fall admission, 6/1 priority date for domestic students; for winter admission, 10/1 priority date for domestic students; for spring admission, 2/15 priority date for domestic students. Applications are processed on a rolling basis. Application fee: $40. Electronic applications accepted. *Financial support:* Applicants required to submit FAFSA. *Unit head:* Salma Ghanem, Dean, 312-362-8600, Fax: 312-362-8620. *Application contact:* Ann Spittle, Director of Graduate Admission, 773-325-7315, Fax: 312-362-8620, E-mail: graddepaul@depaul.edu.
Website: http://communication.depaul.edu/

Georgetown University, Graduate School of Arts and Sciences, School of Continuing Studies, Program in Public Relations and Corporate Communications, Washington, DC 20057. Offers MPS. *Degree requirements:* For master's, capstone course.

Hofstra University, Lawrence Herbert School of Communication, Programs in Journalism and Public Relations, Hempstead, NY 11549. Offers journalism (MA); public relations (MA). *Program availability:* Part-time, evening/weekend. *Students:* 46 full-time (29

women), 19 part-time (14 women); includes 38 minority (20 Black or African American, non-Hispanic/Latino; 2 Asian, non-Hispanic/Latino; 14 Hispanic/Latino; 1 Native Hawaiian or other Pacific Islander, non-Hispanic/Latino; 1 Two or more races, non-Hispanic/Latino), 3 international. Average age 27. 61 applicants, 85% accepted, 25 enrolled. In 2017, 42 master's awarded. *Degree requirements:* For master's, thesis. *Entrance requirements:* For master's, minimum GPA of 2.75; bachelor's degree. Additional exam requirements/recommendations for international students: Required—TOEFL (minimum score 550 paper-based; 95 iBT). *Application deadline:* Applications are processed on a rolling basis. Application fee: $75. Electronic applications accepted. *Expenses: Tuition:* Full-time $1292. *Required fees:* $970. Tuition and fees vary according to program. *Financial support:* In 2017–18, 42 students received support, including 32 fellowships with full and partial tuition reimbursements available (averaging $3,199 per year), 2 research assistantships with full and partial tuition reimbursements available (averaging $7,045 per year); career-related internships or fieldwork, Federal Work-Study, institutionally sponsored loans, scholarships/grants, tuition waivers (full and partial), and unspecified assistantships also available. Support available to part-time students. Financial award applicants required to submit FAFSA. *Faculty research:* Hybrid media theory, particularly as it relates to journalism and politics; political communication, public relations and international communication; impact of convergence and interactive-based technologies and the impact of immigration and globalization on health information campaigns; mediated message design; rational and emotional appeals in strategic messaging; crisis communications; public relations; persuasion; the crossroads of popular culture, politics, new media, and civic engagement. *Unit head:* Dr. Cliff Jernigan, Chairperson, 516-463-4873, E-mail: cliff.jernigan@hofstra.edu. *Application contact:* Sunil Samuel, Assistant Vice President of Admissions, 516-463-4723, Fax: 516-463-4664, E-mail: graduateadmission@hofstra.edu.
Website: http://www.hofstra.edu/academics/colleges/soc/

Iona College, School of Arts and Science, Department of Mass Communication, New Rochelle, NY 10801-1890. Offers non-profit public relations (Certificate); public relations (MA); sports communication and media (MA). *Accreditation:* ACEJMC (one or more programs are accredited). *Program availability:* Part-time, evening/weekend. *Faculty:* 4 full-time (1 woman), 5 part-time/adjunct (0 women). *Students:* 21 full-time (12 women), 13 part-time (8 women); includes 16 minority (11 Black or African American, non-Hispanic/Latino; 1 Asian, non-Hispanic/Latino; 4 Hispanic/Latino), 1 international. Average age 27. 18 applicants, 100% accepted, 11 enrolled. In 2017, 18 master's, 3 other advanced degrees awarded. *Degree requirements:* For master's, comprehensive exam (for some programs), thesis or alternative. *Entrance requirements:* For master's, GRE General Test if undergraduate GPA is below 3.0. Additional exam requirements/recommendations for international students: Required—TOEFL (minimum score 550 paper-based; 80 iBT), IELTS (minimum score 6). *Application deadline:* For fall admission, 8/1 for domestic students, 5/1 for international students; for spring admission, 1/1 for domestic students, 9/1 for international students. Applications are processed on a rolling basis. Electronic applications accepted. *Expenses:* Contact institution. *Financial support:* In 2017–18, 8 students received support. Scholarships/grants, tuition waivers (partial), and unspecified assistantships available. Support available to part-time students. Financial award application deadline: 4/15; financial award applicants required to submit FAFSA. *Faculty research:* Media ecology, new media, corporate communication, media images, organizational learning in public relations, media law, medicine ethics. *Unit head:* Anthony Kelso, PhD, Chair, 914-633-7795, E-mail: akelso@iona.edu. *Application contact:* Katelyn Brunck, Assistant Director of Graduate Admissions, 914-633-2492, Fax: 914-633-2277, E-mail: kbrunck@iona.edu.
Website: http://www.iona.edu/Academics/School-of-Arts-Science/Departments/Mass-Communication/Graduate-Programs.aspx

Kansas State University, Graduate School, College of Arts and Sciences, A.Q. Miller School of Journalism and Mass Communications, Manhattan, KS 66506. Offers advertising (MS); community journalism (MS); global communication (MS); health communication (MS); media management (MS); public relations (MS). *Program availability:* Part-time, evening/weekend. *Degree requirements:* For master's, comprehensive exam, thesis. *Entrance requirements:* For master's, GRE General Test, minimum GPA of 3.0. Additional exam requirements/recommendations for international students: Required—TOEFL (minimum score 79 iBT). Electronic applications accepted. *Faculty research:* Health communication, risk communication, strategic communications, community journalism, global communication.

Kent State University, College of Communication and Information, School of Journalism and Mass Communication, Kent, OH 44242-0001. Offers journalism and mass communication (MA), including media management, public relations, reporting and editing-broadcast, reporting and editing-convergence, reporting and editing-journalism educators, reporting and editing-magazine, reporting and editing-newspaper. *Program availability:* Part-time, online learning. *Faculty:* 15 full-time (8 women), 14 part-time/adjunct (7 women). *Students:* 13 full-time (8 women), 74 part-time (51 women); includes 14 minority (11 Black or African American, non-Hispanic/Latino; 2 Hispanic/Latino; 1 Two or more races, non-Hispanic/Latino), 4 international. Average age 35. 24 applicants, 71% accepted, 13 enrolled. In 2017, 58 master's awarded. *Degree requirements:* For master's, thesis or project. *Entrance requirements:* For master's, GRE, minimum GPA of 3.0, statement of purpose, 3 online recommendations, resume. Additional exam requirements/recommendations for international students: Required—TOEFL (minimum score 587 paper-based; 94 iBT), Michigan English Language Assessment Battery (minimum score 82), IELTS (minimum score 7.0) or PTE (minimum score 65). *Application deadline:* For fall admission, 7/1 for domestic and international students. Applications are processed on a rolling basis. Application fee: $45 ($70 for international students). Electronic applications accepted. *Expenses:* Tuition, state resident: full-time $11,310; part-time $515 per credit hour. Tuition, nonresident: full-time $20,396; part-time $928 per credit hour. *International tuition:* $18,544 full-time. *Financial support:* Research assistantships with full tuition reimbursements, teaching assistantships with full tuition reimbursements, scholarships/grants, and unspecified assistantships available. Financial award application deadline: 2/16. *Unit head:* Jeff Fruit, Interim Director and Professor, 330-672-2572, E-mail: jmc@kent.edu. *Application contact:* Mark Goodman, Graduate Coordinator/Professor, 330-672-6239, E-mail: mgoodm10@kent.edu.
Website: http://www.kent.edu/jmc

La Salle University, School of Arts and Sciences, Program in Strategic Communication, Philadelphia, PA 19141-1199. Offers communication consulting and development (MA); communication management (MA); general professional communication (MA); professional and business communication (Certificate); public relations (MA); social and new media (Certificate). *Program availability:* Part-time, evening/weekend, online learning. *Faculty:* 4 full-time (3 women), 1 (woman) part-time/adjunct. *Students:* 11 full-time (4 women), 22 part-time (16 women); includes 10 minority (9 Black or African American, non-Hispanic/Latino; 1 Two or more races, non-Hispanic/Latino). Average age 27. 40 applicants, 93% accepted, 23 enrolled. In 2017, 34 master's, 1 other advanced degree awarded. *Degree requirements:* For master's, practicum. *Entrance requirements:* For master's, writing assessment, professional resume; minimum overall B average; two letters of recommendation (if GPA below 3.25); brief personal statement (about 500 words); interview; for Certificate, writing assessment, minimum GPA of 2.75 in undergraduate studies; brief personal statement (about 500 words); interview. Additional exam requirements/recommendations for international students: Required—

TOEFL. *Application deadline:* For fall admission, 8/15 priority date for domestic students, 7/15 for international students; for spring admission, 12/15 priority date for domestic students, 11/15 for international students; for summer admission, 4/15 priority date for domestic students, 3/15 for international students. Applications are processed on a rolling basis. Application fee: $35. Electronic applications accepted. Application fee is waived when completed online. *Expenses:* Contact institution. *Financial support:* In 2017–18, 12 students received support. Scholarships/grants available. Support available to part-time students. Financial award application deadline: 8/31; financial award applicants required to submit FAFSA. *Unit head:* Dr. Pamela Lannutti, Director, 215-951-1935, Fax: 215-951-5043, E-mail: annutti95@lasalle.edu. *Application contact:* Elizabeth Heenan, Director, Graduate and Adult Enrollment, 215-951-1100, Fax: 214-951-1462, E-mail: heenan@lasalle.edu.
Website: http://www.lasalle.edu/strategic-communication/

Lasell College, Graduate and Professional Studies in Communication, Newton, MA 02466-2709. Offers health communication (MSC, Graduate Certificate); integrated marketing communication (MSC, Graduate Certificate); public relations (MSC, Graduate Certificate). *Program availability:* Part-time, evening/weekend, 100% online, blended/hybrid learning. *Faculty:* 3 full-time (2 women), 7 part-time/adjunct (5 women). *Students:* 25 full-time (16 women), 35 part-time (28 women); includes 12 minority (6 Black or African American, non-Hispanic/Latino; 1 Asian, non-Hispanic/Latino; 4 Hispanic/Latino; 1 Two or more races, non-Hispanic/Latino), 16 international. Average age 30. 53 applicants, 45% accepted, 22 enrolled. In 2017, 28 master's awarded. *Degree requirements:* For master's, comprehensive exam, thesis or alternative, minimum GPA of 3.0; special project or internship. *Entrance requirements:* For master's, one-page personal statement, 2 letters of recommendation, resume, bachelor's degree transcript; for Graduate Certificate, bachelor's degree transcript, 2 letters of recommendation, 1-page personal statement, resume. Additional exam requirements/recommendations for international students: Required—TOEFL (minimum score 550 paper-based, 79 iBT) or IELTS (minimum score 6). *Application deadline:* For fall admission, 8/31 priority date for domestic students, 6/30 priority date for international students; for spring admission, 12/31 priority date for domestic students, 10/31 priority date for international students. Applications are processed on a rolling basis. Electronic applications accepted. *Expenses:* $600 per credit. *Financial support:* Federal Work-Study, scholarships/grants, and tuition discounts available. Support available to part-time students. Financial award application deadline: 8/31; financial award applicants required to submit FAFSA. *Faculty research:* Terrorists' use of the Internet; refugees' use of cell phones as means of communication in Jordan and Germany; political communication; analysis of the media coverage of the conflict and peace process in northern Ireland; interpersonal communication; strategies to address bullying in online communities, in schools and in the workplace. *Unit head:* Eric Turner, Vice President of Graduate and Professional Studies, 617-243-2071, Fax: 617-243-2450, E-mail: gradinfo@lasell.edu. *Application contact:* Adrienne Franciosi, Director of Graduate Enrollment, 617-243-2214, Fax: 617-243-2450, E-mail: gradinfo@lasell.edu.
Website: http://www.lasell.edu/academics/graduate-and-professional-studies/programs-of-study/master-of-science-in-communication.html

La Sierra University, College of Arts and Sciences, Department of English and Communication, Riverside, CA 92505. Offers communication (MA), including public relations/advertising, theory emphasis; English (MA), including literary emphasis, writing emphasis. *Program availability:* Part-time. *Degree requirements:* For master's, one foreign language. *Entrance requirements:* For master's, GRE General Test.

Liberty University, School of Business, Lynchburg, VA 24515. Offers accounting (MBA, MS), including audit and financial reporting (MS), business (MS), financial services (MS), forensic accounting (MS), leadership (MS), taxation (MS); criminal justice (MBA); cyber security (MS); executive leadership (MA); information systems (MS), including information assurance, technology management; international business (MBA, DBA); leadership (DBA); marketing (MBA, MS, DBA), including digital marketing and advertising (MS), project management (MS), public relations (MS), sports marketing and media (MS); project management (MBA, DBA); public administration (MBA); public relations (MBA). *Program availability:* Part-time, online learning. *Students:* 1,887 full-time (1,003 women), 4,223 part-time (1,950 women); includes 1,570 minority (1,133 Black or African American, non-Hispanic/Latino; 30 American Indian or Alaska Native, non-Hispanic/Latino; 118 Asian, non-Hispanic/Latino; 149 Hispanic/Latino; 13 Native Hawaiian or other Pacific Islander, non-Hispanic/Latino; 127 Two or more races, non-Hispanic/Latino), 109 international. Average age 35. 5,680 applicants, 51% accepted, 1510 enrolled. In 2017, 1,290 master's, 17 doctorates awarded. *Entrance requirements:* For master's, minimum undergraduate GPA of 3.0, 15 hours of upper-level business courses. Additional exam requirements/recommendations for international students: Required—TOEFL (minimum score 600 paper-based; 100 iBT). *Application deadline:* Applications are processed on a rolling basis. Application fee: $50. Electronic applications accepted. *Expenses:* Contact institution. *Financial support:* Applicants required to submit FAFSA. *Unit head:* Dr. Scott Hicks, Dean, 434-592-4808, Fax: 434-582-2366, E-mail: smhicks@liberty.edu. *Application contact:* Jay Bridge, Director of Graduate Admissions, 800-424-9595, Fax: 800-628-7977, E-mail: gradadmissions@liberty.edu.
Website: http://www.liberty.edu/academics/business/index.cfm?PID-149

Lindenwood University, Graduate Programs, School of Arts, Media, and Communications, St. Charles, MO 63301-1695. Offers advertising (MA); art history (MA); cinema and media arts (MFA); communications (MA); digital and Web design (MA); fashion and business design (MS); journalism (MA); mass communications (MA); social media and digital content (MS). *Program availability:* Part-time. *Faculty:* 23 full-time (6 women), 8 part-time/adjunct (4 women). *Students:* 26 full-time (13 women), 11 part-time (8 women); includes 3 minority (1 American Indian or Alaska Native, non-Hispanic/Latino; 2 Hispanic/Latino), 7 international. Average age 33. 60 applicants, 45% accepted, 16 enrolled. In 2017, 11 master's awarded. *Degree requirements:* For master's, thesis (for some programs), minimum cumulative GPA of 3.0. *Entrance requirements:* For master's, audition or interview, minimum GPA of 3.0, portfolio, letter of recommendation. Additional exam requirements/recommendations for international students: Required—TOEFL (minimum score 550 paper-based; 80 iBT); Recommended—IELTS (minimum score 6.5). *Application deadline:* For fall admission, 8/27 priority date for domestic and international students; for spring admission, 1/14 for domestic students, 1/14 priority date for international students; for summer admission, 6/4 priority date for domestic and international students. Applications are processed on a rolling basis. Application fee: $30 ($100 for international students). Electronic applications accepted. *Expenses: Tuition:* Full-time $16,300; part-time $460 per credit. *Required fees:* $660; $330 per credit. Tuition and fees vary according to degree level and program. *Financial support:* In 2017–18, 34 students received support. Career-related internships or fieldwork, institutionally sponsored loans, scholarships/grants, tuition waivers (partial), and unspecified assistantships available. Financial award application deadline: 6/30; financial award applicants required to submit FAFSA. *Unit head:* Dr. Joseph Alsobrook, Dean, School of Arts, Media, and Communications, 636-949-4164, Fax: 636-949-4910, E-mail: jalsobrook@lindenwood.edu. *Application contact:* Kara Schilli, Director, Evening and Graduate Admissions, 636-949-4349, Fax: 636-949-4109, E-mail: adultadmissions@lindenwood.edu.
Website: http://www.lindenwood.edu/academics/academic-schools/school-of-arts-media-and-communications/

Advertising and Public Relations

Marquette University, Graduate School, College of Communication, Milwaukee, WI 53201-1881. Offers advertising and public relations (MA); communication studies (MA); digital storytelling (Certificate); journalism (MA); mass communication (MA); science, health and environmental communication (MA). *Accreditation:* ACEJMC (one or more programs are accredited). *Program availability:* Part-time, evening/weekend. *Degree requirements:* For master's, comprehensive exam, thesis or alternative. *Entrance requirements:* For master's, GRE, official transcripts from all current and previous colleges/universities except Marquette, three letters of recommendation, statement of academic and professional goals. Additional exam requirements/recommendations for international students: Required—TOEFL (minimum score 530 paper-based). Electronic applications accepted. *Faculty research:* Urban journalism, gender and communication, intercultural communication, religious communication.

Marshall University, Academic Affairs Division, College of Arts and Media, Program in Journalism, Huntington, WV 25755. Offers journalism (MAJ, Certificate), including health care public relations (MAJ). *Faculty:* 6 full-time (2 women). *Students:* 8 full-time (3 women), 4 part-time (0 women); includes 1 minority (Two or more races, non-Hispanic/Latino). Average age 33. In 2017, 5 master's awarded. *Degree requirements:* For master's, thesis optional. *Entrance requirements:* For master's, GRE General Test. Application fee: $40. *Unit head:* Dr. Janet Dooley, Chair, 304-696-2734, E-mail: dooley@marshall.edu. *Application contact:* Dr. Robert Rabe, Graduate Coordinator, 304-696-4636, E-mail: rabe@marshall.edu.

Michigan State University, The Graduate School, College of Communication Arts and Sciences, Department of Advertising, Public Relations and Retailing, East Lansing, MI 48824. Offers advertising (MA); public relations (MA); retailing (MS, PhD). *Entrance requirements:* Additional exam requirements/recommendations for international students: Required—TOEFL. Electronic applications accepted.

Mississippi College, Graduate School, College of Arts and Sciences, School of Christian Studies and the Arts, Department of Communication, Clinton, MS 39058. Offers applied communication (MSC); public relations and corporate communication (MSC). *Program availability:* Part-time. *Degree requirements:* For master's, comprehensive exam, thesis optional. *Entrance requirements:* For master's, GRE or NTE, minimum GPA of 2.5. Additional exam requirements/recommendations for international students: Recommended—TOEFL, IELTS. Electronic applications accepted.

Monmouth University, Graduate Studies, Department of Communication, West Long Branch, NJ 07764-1898. Offers corporate and public communication (MA); human resources management and communication (Certificate); public service communication specialist (Certificate); strategic public relations and new media (Certificate). *Program availability:* Part-time, evening/weekend, online learning. *Faculty:* 4 full-time (3 women), 2 part-time/adjunct (both women). *Students:* 10 full-time (7 women), 18 part-time (14 women); includes 9 minority (5 Black or African American, non-Hispanic/Latino; 1 Asian, non-Hispanic/Latino; 3 Hispanic/Latino). Average age 28. In 2017, 18 master's, 1 other advanced degree awarded. Terminal master's awarded for partial completion of doctoral program. *Degree requirements:* For master's, comprehensive exam (for some programs), thesis (for some programs), project. *Entrance requirements:* For master's, GRE, baccalaureate degree with minimum GPA of 3.0 in major, 2.75 overall; two letters of recommendation; personal essay (750 words or less describing preparation for study and personal objectives); digital or hard copy portfolio of select samples of work including writing sample; resume. Additional exam requirements/recommendations for international students: Required—TOEFL (minimum score 550 paper-based; 79 iBT), IELTS (minimum score 6), Michigan English Language Assessment Battery (minimum score 77). *Application deadline:* For fall admission, 7/15 priority date for domestic students, 6/1 for international students; for spring admission, 12/1 priority date for domestic students, 11/1 for international students; for summer admission, 5/1 for domestic students. Applications are processed on a rolling basis. Application fee: $50. Electronic applications accepted. *Expenses: Tuition:* Full-time $21,366; part-time $7122 per credit. *Required fees:* $700; $175 per term. *Financial support:* In 2017–18, 2 students received support. Institutionally sponsored loans, scholarships/grants, and unspecified assistantships available. Support available to part-time students. Financial award applicants required to submit FAFSA. *Faculty research:* Service-learning, history of television, feminism and the media, executive communication, public relations pedagogy. *Unit head:* Dr. Marina Vujnovic, Program Director, 732-263-5667, Fax: 732-571-5667, E-mail: mvujnovi@monmouth.edu. *Application contact:* Andrea Thompson, Graduate Admission Counselor, 732-571-3452, Fax: 732-263-5123, E-mail: gradadm@monmouth.edu.
Website: http://www.monmouth.edu/cpc

Montana State University Billings, College of Arts and Sciences, Department of Communication and Theatre, Billings, MT 59101. Offers public relations (MS). *Program availability:* Part-time, 100% online, blended/hybrid learning. *Degree requirements:* For master's, comprehensive exam, thesis optional. *Entrance requirements:* For master's, GRE General Test, minimum undergraduate GPA of 3.0, letters of recommendation, letter of intent, resume. Additional exam requirements/recommendations for international students: Required—TOEFL (minimum score 79 iBT), IELTS (minimum score 6.5). *Application deadline:* For fall admission, 3/15 for domestic students, 7/15 for international students; for spring admission, 10/15 for domestic students, 12/1 for international students. Applications are processed on a rolling basis. Application fee: $40. Electronic applications accepted. *Expenses:* Tuition, state resident: full-time $11,740; part-time $7880 per year. Tuition, nonresident: full-time $32,200; part-time $24,140 per year. *Financial support:* Research assistantships with partial tuition reimbursements, teaching assistantships with partial tuition reimbursements, career-related internships or fieldwork, Federal Work-Study, institutionally sponsored loans, scholarships/grants, and unspecified assistantships available. Support available to part-time students. Financial award application deadline: 5/1; financial award applicants required to submit FAFSA. *Unit head:* Dr. Stephen L. Coffman, Chair, 406-657-1726, E-mail: scoffman@msubillings.edu. *Application contact:* Dr. Stephen L. Coffman, Chair, 406-657-1726, E-mail: scoffman@msubillings.edu.
Website: http://www.msubillings.edu/cas/comt/

Montclair State University, The Graduate School, College of the Arts, MA Program in Public and Organizational Relations, Montclair, NJ 07043-1624. Offers MA. *Program availability:* Part-time, evening/weekend. *Degree requirements:* For master's, comprehensive exam. *Entrance requirements:* For master's, GRE General Test, 2 letters of recommendation. Additional exam requirements/recommendations for international students: Required—TOEFL (minimum score 83 iBT) or IELTS (minimum score 6.5). Electronic applications accepted. *Faculty research:* Organizational problem solving and innovation, social media, health communication, globalization, organizational change management.

Murray State University, Arthur J. Bauernfeind College of Business, Department of Journalism and Mass Communications, Murray, KY 42071. Offers mass communications (MA, MS), including public relations. *Program availability:* Part-time. *Faculty:* 7 full-time (4 women), 2 part-time/adjunct (0 women). *Students:* 18 full-time (6 women), 11 part-time (9 women); includes 1 minority (Two or more races, non-Hispanic/Latino), 15 international. Average age 28. 41 applicants, 90% accepted, 10 enrolled. In 2017, 6 master's awarded. *Entrance requirements:* For master's, GRE or GMAT,

minimum university GPA of 2.75. Additional exam requirements/recommendations for international students: Required—TOEFL (minimum score 527 paper-based; 51 iBT). *Application deadline:* Applications are processed on a rolling basis. Application fee: $40 ($50 for international students). Electronic applications accepted. *Expenses:* Tuition, state resident: full-time $9504. Tuition, nonresident: full-time $26,811. *International tuition:* $14,400 full-time. Tuition and fees vary according to course load, degree level and reciprocity agreements. *Financial support:* Research assistantships, Federal Work-Study, and unspecified assistantships available. Financial award applicants required to submit FAFSA. *Faculty research:* Mass media, audience analysis, press and politics, government open records laws, public relations. *Unit head:* Dr. Debbie Owens, Associate Professor/Interim Chair, 270-809-6318, Fax: 270-809-2390, E-mail: dowens@murraystate.edu. *Application contact:* Kaitlyn Burzysnki, Interim Assistant Director for Graduate Admission and Records, 270-809-5732, Fax: 270-809-3780, E-mail: msu.graduateadmissions@murraystate.edu.
Website: http://www.murraystate.edu/academics/CollegesDepartments/CollegeOfBusiness/Programs/JournalismAndMassCommunications/graduate/masscomm.aspx

New York University, School of Professional Studies, Division of Programs in Business, Programs in Marketing and Public Relations, New York, NY 10012-1019. Offers public relations and corporate communication (MS), including corporate and organizational communication, public relations management. *Program availability:* Part-time, evening/weekend. *Students:* 224 full-time (197 women), 62 part-time (56 women); includes 40 minority (18 Black or African American, non-Hispanic/Latino; 1 American Indian or Alaska Native, non-Hispanic/Latino; 7 Asian, non-Hispanic/Latino; 11 Hispanic/Latino; 3 Two or more races, non-Hispanic/Latino), 219 international. Average age 25. 355 applicants, 69% accepted, 110 enrolled. In 2017, 316 master's awarded. *Degree requirements:* For master's, thesis. *Entrance requirements:* For master's, GRE or GMAT (only upon request), bachelor's degree, resume with relevant professional work, internship or volunteer experience, two letters of recommendation, statement of purpose. Additional exam requirements/recommendations for international students: Required—TOEFL (minimum score 600 paper-based; 100 iBT), IELTS (minimum score 7). *Application deadline:* For fall admission, 2/1 priority date for domestic and international students; for spring admission, 10/15 priority date for domestic students, 8/15 priority date for international students. Applications are processed on a rolling basis. Application fee: $150. Electronic applications accepted. *Expenses:* $20,244 per term. *Financial support:* Fellowships, career-related internships or fieldwork, Federal Work-Study, scholarships/grants, and health care benefits available. Support available to part-time students. Financial award application deadline: 6/30; financial award applicants required to submit FAFSA. *Unit head:* Martin Ihrig, Associate Dean/Clinical Professor, 212-992-3288. *Application contact:* Admissions Office, 212-998-7100, E-mail: sps.gradadmissions@nyu.edu.
Website: http://www.sps.nyu.edu/academics/departments/marketing-and-pr.html

Northern Kentucky University, Office of Graduate Programs, College of Informatics, Program in Communication, Highland Heights, KY 41099. Offers communication (MA); communication teaching (Certificate); documentary studies (Certificate); public relations (Certificate); relationships (Certificate). *Program availability:* Part-time, evening/weekend. Terminal master's awarded for partial completion of doctoral program. *Degree requirements:* For master's, comprehensive exams, thesis or applied capstone project. *Entrance requirements:* For master's, GRE, minimum GPA of 3.0, 3 letters of recommendation, letter of intent. Additional exam requirements/recommendations for international students: Required—TOEFL (minimum score 79 iBT). Recommended—IELTS (minimum score 6.5). Electronic applications accepted. *Faculty research:* Mediating effect of health communication, organizational communication, quantitative and qualitative research methods, family and interpersonal communication.

Quinnipiac University, School of Communications, Program in Public Relations, Hamden, CT 06518-1940. Offers public relations (MS), including social media. *Program availability:* Part-time, evening/weekend. *Faculty:* 5 full-time (3 women), 1 (woman) part-time/adjunct. *Students:* 16 full-time (13 women), 6 part-time (5 women); includes 4 minority (1 Black or African American, non-Hispanic/Latino; 1 Hispanic/Latino; 2 Two or more races, non-Hispanic/Latino), 2 international. 22 applicants, 86% accepted, 9 enrolled. In 2017, 9 master's awarded. *Entrance requirements:* Additional exam requirements/recommendations for international students: Required—TOEFL (minimum score 575 paper-based; 90 iBT), IELTS (minimum score 6.5). *Application deadline:* For fall admission, 7/31 priority date for domestic students, 4/30 for international students. Applications are processed on a rolling basis. Application fee: $45. Electronic applications accepted. *Financial support:* Federal Work-Study, scholarships/grants, and unspecified assistantships available. Financial award application deadline: 6/1; financial award applicants required to submit FAFSA. *Faculty research:* Social media, corporate social responsibility, ethics, international communications and international public relations, public diplomacy, non-profit management, crisis management, investor relations. *Unit head:* Phillip Simon, Program Director, 203-582-8672, E-mail: graduate@qu.edu. *Application contact:* Office of Graduate Admissions, 203-582-8672, Fax: 203-582-3443, E-mail: graduate@qu.edu.
Website: http://www.qu.edu/gradpr

Rowan University, Graduate School, College of Communication and Creative Arts, Program in Public Relations/Advertising, Glassboro, NJ 08028-1701. Offers MA. *Program availability:* Part-time, evening/weekend. *Degree requirements:* For master's, thesis. *Entrance requirements:* For master's, GRE General Test. Additional exam requirements/recommendations for international students: Required—TOEFL. Electronic applications accepted. *Expenses:* Tuition, state resident: full-time $15,020; part-time $751 per semester hour. Tuition, nonresident: full-time $15,020; part-time $751 per semester hour. *Required fees:* $3158; $157.90 per semester hour. Tuition and fees vary according to course load, campus/location and program.

San Diego State University, Graduate and Research Affairs, College of Professional Studies and Fine Arts, School of Communication, San Diego, CA 92182. Offers advertising and public relations (MA); critical-cultural studies (MA); interaction studies (MA); intercultural and international studies (MA); new media studies (MA); news and information studies (MA); telecommunications and media management (MA). *Degree requirements:* For master's, thesis. *Entrance requirements:* For master's, GRE General Test, 3 letters of recommendation. Additional exam requirements/recommendations for international students: Required—TOEFL. Electronic applications accepted.

Savannah College of Art and Design, Program in Advertising, Savannah, GA 31402-3146. Offers MA, MFA. *Program availability:* Part-time. *Faculty:* 10 full-time (3 women), 5 part-time/adjunct (2 women). *Students:* 21 full-time (11 women), 9 part-time (4 women); includes 14 minority (9 Black or African American, non-Hispanic/Latino; 2 Asian, non-Hispanic/Latino; 3 Hispanic/Latino), 11 international. Average age 27. 59 applicants, 22% accepted, 9 enrolled. In 2017, 23 master's awarded. *Degree requirements:* For master's, final project (for MA); thesis (for MFA). *Entrance requirements:* For master's, GRE (recommended), portfolio (submitted in digital format), audition or writing submission, resume, statement of purpose, two letters of recommendation. Additional exam requirements/recommendations for international students: Recommended—TOEFL (minimum score 550 paper-based; 85 iBT), IELTS (minimum score 6.5). *Application deadline:* For fall admission, 4/1 for domestic and

international students. Applications are processed on a rolling basis. Application fee: $40. Electronic applications accepted. *Expenses: Tuition:* Full-time $36,765; part-time $817 per credit hour. One-time fee: $500. *Financial support:* Career-related internships or fieldwork, Federal Work-Study, and scholarships/grants available. Financial award application deadline: 4/1; financial award applicants required to submit FAFSA. *Unit head:* Emily Sander, Chair of Advertising Design. *Application contact:* Jenny Jaquillard, Executive Director of Admissions, Recruitment and Events, 912-525-5100, Fax: 912-525-5985, E-mail: admission@scad.edu.
Website: http://www.scad.edu/academics/programs/advertising

Seton Hall University, College of Communication and the Arts, Program in Public Relations, South Orange, NJ 07079-2697. Offers MA. *Program availability:* Part-time, evening/weekend, online learning. *Degree requirements:* For master's, thesis (for some programs). *Entrance requirements:* For master's, GRE or MAT, official transcripts, resume, personal statement, 3 letters of recommendation. Additional exam requirements/recommendations for international students: Required—TOEFL (minimum iBT score 80) or IELTS (6.5). Electronic applications accepted. *Faculty research:* Leadership, art history, reputation management, image management, public relations.

Southeastern Louisiana University, College of Arts, Humanities and Social Sciences, Department of Languages and Communication, Hammond, LA 70402. Offers health communications (MA); journalism (MA); marketing (MA); public relations (MA); sociology (MA). *Program availability:* Part-time, evening/weekend. *Faculty:* 5 full-time (3 women). *Students:* 7 full-time (6 women), 11 part-time (7 women); includes 10 minority (5 Black or African American, non-Hispanic/Latino; 3 Hispanic/Latino; 2 Two or more races, non-Hispanic/Latino). Average age 28. 133 applicants, 51% accepted, 10 enrolled. In 2017, 36 master's awarded. *Degree requirements:* For master's, comprehensive exam. *Entrance requirements:* For master's, GRE (minimum score 148 on Verbal section, 3.5 Written). Additional exam requirements/recommendations for international students: Required—TOEFL (minimum score 525 paper-based; 75 iBT). *Application deadline:* For fall admission, 7/15 priority date for domestic students, 6/1 priority date for international students; for spring admission, 12/1 priority date for domestic students, 10/1 priority date for international students. Applications are processed on a rolling basis. Application fee: $20 ($30 for international students). Electronic applications accepted. *Expenses:* Tuition, state resident: full-time $6684. Tuition, nonresident: full-time $19,162. *Required fees:* $2088. *Financial support:* In 2017–18, 12 students received support, including 7 research assistantships (averaging $6,082 per year); career-related internships or fieldwork, Federal Work-Study, institutionally sponsored loans, scholarships/grants, traineeships, health care benefits, tuition waivers, and unspecified assistantships also available. Financial award application deadline: 5/1; financial award applicants required to submit FAFSA. *Faculty research:* Communicate with the millennial generation to enhance organizational effectiveness, conflict resolution and mediation among nations, journalism history, media law, media writing, media convergence, external compliances accreditation and strategic planning. *Unit head:* Dr. Lucia Harrison, Department Head, 985-549-2105, Fax: 985-549-5014, E-mail: lharrison@southeastern.edu. *Application contact:* Amanda Harper, Graduate Admissions Analyst, 985-549-5620, Fax: 985-549-5632, E-mail: admissions@southeastern.edu.
Website: http://www.southeastern.edu/acad_research/depts/lang_comm/index.html

Southern Illinois University Edwardsville, Graduate School, College of Arts and Sciences, Department of Applied Communication Studies, Program in Public Relations, Edwardsville, IL 62026. Offers MA. *Program availability:* Part-time, evening/weekend. *Degree requirements:* For master's, comprehensive exam (for some programs), thesis (for some programs). *Entrance requirements:* Additional exam requirements/recommendations for international students: Required—TOEFL (minimum score 550 paper-based, 79 iBT), IELTS (minimum score 6.5), Michigan Test of English Language Proficiency or PTE. Electronic applications accepted.

Southern Methodist University, Meadows School of the Arts, Temerlin Advertising Institute, Dallas, TX 75275. Offers MA. *Entrance requirements:* For master's, GRE, GMAT. Additional exam requirements/recommendations for international students: Required—TOEFL (minimum score 550 paper-based; 80 iBT). Electronic applications accepted.

Southern New Hampshire University, School of Business, Manchester, NH 03106-1045. Offers accounting (MBA, Graduate Certificate); accounting finance (MS); accounting/auditing (MS); accounting/forensic accounting (MS); accounting/management accounting (MS); accounting/taxation (MS); applied economics (MS); athletic administration (MBA, Graduate Certificate); business administration (IMBA, Certificate, including business information systems (Certificate), human resource management (Certificate); business analytics (MBA); business intelligence (MBA); communication (MA), including new media and marketing, public relations; community economic development (MBA); criminal justice (MBA); data analytics (MS); economics (MBA); engineering management (MBA); entrepreneurship (MBA); finance (MBA, MS, Graduate Certificate); finance/corporate finance (MS); finance/investments (MS); forensic accounting (MBA); forensic accounting and fraud examination (Graduate Certificate); healthcare informatics (MBA); healthcare management (MBA); human resource management (MS); human resources (MBA); information technology (MS); information technology management (MBA); international business (PhD); Internet marketing (MBA); leadership (MBA); leadership of nonprofit organizations (Graduate Certificate); management (MS); marketing (MBA, MS, Graduate Certificate); music business (MBA); operations and project management (MS); operations and supply chain management (MBA, Graduate Certificate); organizational leadership (MS); project management (MBA, Graduate Certificate); public administration (MBA, Graduate Certificate); quantitative analysis (MBA); Six Sigma (Graduate Certificate); Six Sigma quality (MBA); social media marketing (MBA, Graduate Certificate); sport management (MBA, MS, Graduate Certificate); sustainability and environmental compliance (MBA); MBA/Certificate. *Accreditation:* ACBSP. *Program availability:* Part-time, evening/weekend, online learning. Terminal master's awarded for partial completion of doctoral program. *Degree requirements:* For master's, one foreign language, comprehensive exam (for some programs), thesis or alternative; for doctorate, one foreign language, comprehensive exam, thesis/dissertation. *Entrance requirements:* For master's, minimum GPA of 2.5; for doctorate, GMAT. Additional exam requirements/recommendations for international students: Required—TOEFL (minimum score 500 paper-based). *Application deadline:* Applications are processed on a rolling basis. Application fee: $40. Electronic applications accepted. *Expenses: Tuition:* Part-time $627 per credit hour. Part-time tuition and fees vary according to campus/location and program. *Financial support:* Career-related internships or fieldwork, Federal Work-Study, institutionally sponsored loans, scholarships/grants, tuition waivers (partial), and unspecified assistantships available. Support available to part-time students. Financial award applicants required to submit FAFSA. *Unit head:* Dr. Bill Lightfoot, Dean, 603-644-3102, Fax: 603-644-3144. *Application contact:* Office of Graduate Admission, 888-327-SNHU, Fax: 603-644-3144, E-mail: enroll@snhu.edu.

Suffolk University, College of Arts and Sciences, Advertising and Public Relations Department, Boston, MA 02108-2770. Offers communication studies (MAC); integrated marketing communication (MAC); public relations and advertising (MAC). *Program availability:* Part-time, evening/weekend. *Faculty:* 4 full-time (3 women). *Students:* 25 full-time (18 women), 14 part-time (13 women); includes 10 minority (4 Black or African

American, non-Hispanic/Latino; 5 Hispanic/Latino; 1 Two or more races, non-Hispanic/Latino), 9 international. Average age 26. 41 applicants, 71% accepted, 2 enrolled. In 2017, 10 master's awarded. *Degree requirements:* For master's, thesis optional. *Entrance requirements:* For master's, GRE General Test, MAT, or GMAT, 2 letters of recommendation, resume. Additional exam requirements/recommendations for international students: Required—TOEFL (minimum score 550 paper-based; 80 iBT). *Application deadline:* For fall admission, 3/15 priority date for domestic and international students; for spring admission, 10/15 priority date for domestic and international students. Applications are processed on a rolling basis. Application fee: $50. Electronic applications accepted. *Expenses:* $29,520 per year full-time tuition; $1,230 per credit part-time. *Financial support:* In 2017–18, 31 students received support, including 4 fellowships (averaging $6,200 per year); career-related internships or fieldwork, Federal Work-Study, institutionally sponsored loans, and scholarships/grants also available. Support available to part-time students. Financial award application deadline: 4/1; financial award applicants required to submit FAFSA. *Faculty research:* Branding law and management, health care communication, gender roles and violence in video games, new media, political communication. *Unit head:* Robert Rosenthal, Chair, 617-573-8502, E-mail: rrosenthal@suffolk.edu. *Application contact:* Mara Marzocchi, Associate Director of Graduate Admissions, 617-573-8302, Fax: 617-305-1733, E-mail: grad.admission@suffolk.edu.
Website: http://www.suffolk.edu/college/graduate/69298.php

Syracuse University, S. I. Newhouse School of Public Communications, MA Program in Advertising, Syracuse, NY 13244. Offers MA. *Students:* Average age 24. *Entrance requirements:* For master's, GRE General Test, resume, official transcripts, personal statement, three letters of recommendation. Additional exam requirements/recommendations for international students: Required—TOEFL (minimum score 600 paper-based; 100 iBT). *Application deadline:* For summer admission, 1/15 for domestic and international students. Application fee: $45. Electronic applications accepted. *Financial support:* Fellowships with full tuition reimbursements, research assistantships with partial tuition reimbursements, and teaching assistantships with full tuition reimbursements available. Financial award application deadline: 1/1. *Faculty research:* Advertising management, digital advertising and branding, marketing communication, strategic media planning, advertising campaigns. *Unit head:* Prof. James Tsao, Chair, 315-443-7362, E-mail: jctsao@syr.edu. *Application contact:* Martha Coria, Graduate Records Office, 315-443-4039, Fax: 315-443-1834, E-mail: pcgrad@syr.edu.
Website: http://newhouse.syr.edu/academics/degrees/masters/advertising

Syracuse University, S. I. Newhouse School of Public Communications, MS in Public Relations Program, Syracuse, NY 13244. Offers MS. *Students:* Average age 24. *Entrance requirements:* For master's, GRE General Test, resume, official transcripts, personal statement, three letters of recommendation. Additional exam requirements/recommendations for international students: Required—TOEFL (minimum score 600 paper-based; 100 iBT). *Application deadline:* For summer admission, 1/15 priority date for domestic and international students. Application fee: $45. Electronic applications accepted. *Financial support:* Fellowships with full tuition reimbursements, research assistantships with partial tuition reimbursements, and teaching assistantships with partial tuition reimbursements available. Financial award application deadline: 2/1. *Faculty research:* Media law, visual communication, public relations, financial markets and institutions. *Unit head:* Prof. Rochelle Ford, Chair, 315-443-9347, E-mail: pcgrad@syr.edu. *Application contact:* Martha Coria, Graduate Records Office, 315-443-4039, Fax: 315-443-1834, E-mail: pcgrad@syr.edu.
Website: http://newhouse.syr.edu/academics/degrees/masters/public-relations

Universidad Autonoma de Guadalajara, Graduate Programs, Guadalajara, Mexico. Offers administrative law and justice (LL M); advertising and corporate communications (MA); architecture (M Arch); business (MBA); computational science (MCC); education (Ed M, Ed D); English-Spanish translation (MA); entrepreneurship and management (MBA); integrated management of digital animation (MA); international business (MIB); international corporate law (LL M); internet technologies (MS); manufacturing systems (MMS); occupational health (MS); philosophy (MA, PhD); power electronics (MS); quality systems (MQS); renewable energy (MS); social evaluation of projects (MBA); strategic market research (MBA); tax law (MA); teaching mathematics (MA).

Université Laval, Faculty of Letters, Program in Public Relations, Québec, QC G1K 7P4, Canada. Offers Diploma. *Program availability:* Part-time, evening/weekend. *Entrance requirements:* For degree, knowledge of French, comprehension of written English. Electronic applications accepted.

University of Colorado Boulder, Graduate School, College of Media, Communication and Information, Department of Advertising, Public Relations and Media Design, Boulder, CO 80309. Offers media research and practice (PhD); strategic communication design (MA). *Faculty:* 10 full-time (5 women). *Students:* 20 full-time (11 women), 1 (woman) part-time; includes 4 minority (2 Asian, non-Hispanic/Latino; 2 Hispanic/Latino), 2 international. Average age 30. 39 applicants, 79% accepted, 20 enrolled. In 2017, 14 master's awarded. *Application deadline:* For fall admission, 1/10 for domestic students; for spring admission, 12/1 for domestic students. Application fee: $60 ($80 for international students). Electronic applications accepted. *Financial support:* In 2017–18, 10 students received support, including 3 fellowships (averaging $1,333 per year), 1 research assistantship with full and partial tuition reimbursement available (averaging $25,432 per year), 2 teaching assistantships with full and partial tuition reimbursements available (averaging $32,310 per year); institutionally sponsored loans, scholarships/grants, health care benefits, and unspecified assistantships also available. Financial award application deadline: 2/15; financial award applicants required to submit FAFSA. *Faculty research:* Advertising; mass communication/media; electronic media; communications; consumer behavior. *Application contact:* E-mail: gharsha@colorado.edu.
Website: http://www.colorado.edu/cmci/academics/advertising-pr-and-media-design

University of Florida, Graduate School, College of Journalism and Communications, Program in Advertising, Gainesville, FL 32611. Offers M Adv. *Degree requirements:* For master's, thesis or terminal project. *Entrance requirements:* For master's, GRE General Test, minimum GPA of 3.0. Additional exam requirements/recommendations for international students: Required—TOEFL (minimum score 550 paper-based; 80 iBT), IELTS (minimum score 6). Electronic applications accepted. *Faculty research:* Branding, information flow between clients and suppliers, message and media strategies, emotional response.

University of Florida, Graduate School, College of Journalism and Communications, Program in Mass Communication, Gainesville, FL 32611. Offers international/intercultural communication (MAMC); journalism (MAMC); mass communication (MAMC, PhD), including clinical translational science (MAMC); public relations (MAMC); science/health communication (MAMC); telecommunication (MAMC). *Accreditation:* ACEJMC. *Entrance requirements:* For master's and doctorate, GRE General Test, minimum GPA of 3.0.

University of Houston, College of Liberal Arts and Social Sciences, Jack J. Valenti School of Communication, Houston, TX 77204. Offers health communication (MA); mass communication studies (MA); public relations studies (MA); speech communication (MA). *Program availability:* Part-time. *Degree requirements:* For

Advertising and Public Relations

master's, comprehensive exam (for some programs), thesis (for some programs), 30-33 hours. *Entrance requirements:* For master's, GRE. Additional exam requirements/recommendations for international students: Required—TOEFL. Electronic applications accepted.

University of Illinois at Urbana–Champaign, Graduate College, College of Media, Charles H. Sandage Department of Advertising, Champaign, IL 61820. Offers MS.

University of Maryland, College Park, Academic Affairs, College of Arts and Humanities, Department of Communication, College Park, MD 20742. Offers MA, PhD. *Degree requirements:* For master's, thesis optional; for doctorate, comprehensive exam, thesis/dissertation. *Entrance requirements:* For master's, GRE General Test, minimum GPA of 3.0, sample of scholarly writing, 3 letters of recommendation, statement of goals and experiences; for doctorate, GRE General Test. Additional exam requirements/recommendations for international students: Required—TOEFL. Electronic applications accepted. *Faculty research:* Health communication, interpersonal communication, persuasion, intercultural communication, contemporary rhetoric theory.

University of Miami, Graduate School, School of Communication, Coral Gables, FL 33124. Offers communication (PhD); communication studies (MA); film studies (MA, PhD); motion pictures (MFA), including production, producing, and screenwriting; print journalism (MA); public relations (MA); Spanish language journalism (MA); television broadcast journalism (MA). *Program availability:* Part-time. *Degree requirements:* For master's, comprehensive exam (for some programs), thesis (for some programs); for doctorate, comprehensive exam, thesis/dissertation. *Entrance requirements:* For master's, GRE General Test; for doctorate, GRE General Test, master's thesis or scholarly research. Additional exam requirements/recommendations for international students: Required—TOEFL (minimum score 600 paper-based; 100 iBT). Electronic applications accepted. *Faculty research:* Communication studies, mass communication, international/interpersonal communication, film studies, journalism.

University of Nebraska–Lincoln, Graduate College, College of Arts and Sciences, Department of Communication Studies, Lincoln, NE 68588. Offers instructional communication (MA, PhD); interpersonal communication (MA, PhD); marketing, communication studies, and advertising (MA, PhD); organizational communication (MA, PhD); rhetoric and culture (MA, PhD). *Degree requirements:* For master's, thesis optional; for doctorate, comprehensive exam, thesis/dissertation. *Entrance requirements:* For master's and doctorate, GRE General Test, writing sample. Additional exam requirements/recommendations for international students: Required—TOEFL (minimum score 600 paper-based). Electronic applications accepted. *Faculty research:* Message strategies, gender communication, political communication, organizational communication, instructional communication.

University of Nebraska–Lincoln, Graduate College, College of Journalism and Mass Communications, Lincoln, NE 68588. Offers marketing, communication and advertising (MA); professional journalism (MA). *Program availability:* Online learning. *Degree requirements:* For master's, thesis. *Entrance requirements:* For master's, samples of work. Additional exam requirements/recommendations for international students: Required—TOEFL (minimum score 600 paper-based). Electronic applications accepted. *Faculty research:* Interactive media and the Internet, community newspapers, children's radio, advertising involvement, telecommunications policy.

University of North Texas, Robert B. Toulouse School of Graduate Studies, Denton, TX 76203-5459. Offers accounting (MS); applied anthropology (MA, MS); applied behavior analysis (Certificate); applied geography (MA); applied technology and performance improvement (M Ed, MS); art education (MA); art history (MA); art museum education (Certificate); arts leadership (Certificate); audiology (Au D); behavior analysis (MS); behavioral science (PhD); biochemistry and molecular biology (MS); biology (MA, MS); biomedical engineering (MS); business analysis (MS); chemistry (MS); clinical health psychology (PhD); communication studies (MA, MS); computer engineering (MS); computer science (MS); counseling (M Ed, MS), including clinical mental health counseling (MS), college and university counseling, elementary school counseling, secondary school counseling; creative writing (MA); criminal justice (MS); curriculum and instruction (M Ed); decision sciences (MBA); design (MA, MFA), including fashion design (MFA), innovation studies, interior design (MFA); early childhood studies (MS); economics (MS); educational leadership (M Ed, Ed D); educational psychology (MS, PhD), including family studies (MS), gifted and talented (MS), human development (MS), learning and cognition (MS), research, measurement and evaluation (MS); electrical engineering (MS); emergency management (MPA); engineering technology (MS); English (MA); English as a second language (MA); environmental science (MS); finance (MBA, MS); financial management (MPA); French (MA); health services management (MBA); higher education (M Ed, Ed D); history (MA, MS); hospitality management (MS); human resources management (MPA); information science (MS); information systems (PhD); information technologies (MBA); interdisciplinary studies (MA, MS); international studies (MA); international sustainable tourism (MS); jazz studies (MM); journalism (MA, MJ, Graduate Certificate), including interactive and virtual digital communication (Graduate Certificate), narrative journalism (Graduate Certificate), public relations (Graduate Certificate); kinesiology (MS); linguistics (MA); local government management (MPA); logistics (PhD); logistics and supply chain management (MBA); long-term care, senior housing, and aging services (MA); management (PhD); marketing (MBA); mathematics (MA, MS); mechanical and energy engineering (MS, PhD); music (MA), including ethnomusicology, music theory, musicology, performance; music composition (PhD); music education (MM Ed, PhD); nonprofit management (MPA); operations and supply chain management (MBA); performance (MM, DMA); philosophy (MA); political science (MA); professional and technical communication (MA); radio, television and film (MA, MFA); rehabilitation counseling (Certificate); sociology (MA); Spanish (MA); special education (M Ed); speech-language pathology (MA); strategic management (MBA); studio art (MFA); teaching (M Ed); MBA/MS. *Program availability:* Part-time, evening/weekend, online learning. Terminal master's awarded for partial completion of doctoral program. *Degree requirements:* For master's, variable foreign language requirement, comprehensive exam (for some programs), thesis (for some programs); for doctorate, variable foreign language requirement, comprehensive exam (for some programs), thesis/dissertation; for other advanced degree, variable foreign language requirement, comprehensive exam (for some programs). *Entrance requirements:* For master's and doctorate, GRE, GMAT. Additional exam requirements/recommendations for international students: Required—TOEFL (minimum score 550 paper-based; 79 iBT). Electronic applications accepted.

University of Saint Mary, Graduate Programs, Program in Business Administration, Leavenworth, KS 66048-5082. Offers enterprise risk management (MBA); finance (MBA); general management (MBA); health care management (MBA); human resource management (MBA); marketing and advertising management (MBA). *Program availability:* Part-time, evening/weekend, 100% online, blended/hybrid learning. *Degree requirements:* For master's, thesis. *Entrance requirements:* For master's, minimum undergraduate GPA of 2.75, official transcripts, two letters of recommendation. Electronic applications accepted. *Expenses:* Contact institution.

University of Southern California, Graduate School, Annenberg School for Communication and Journalism, School of Journalism, Program in Strategic Public Relations, Los Angeles, CA 90089. Offers MA. *Program availability:* Part-time, evening/

weekend. *Degree requirements:* For master's, comprehensive exam (for some programs), thesis optional. *Entrance requirements:* For master's, GRE General Test, resume, writing samples, letters of recommendation, statement of purpose. Additional exam requirements/recommendations for international students: Required—TOEFL (minimum score 114 iBT), IELTS (minimum score 8). Electronic applications accepted.

The University of Tennessee, Graduate School, College of Communication and Information, Knoxville, TN 37996. Offers advertising (MS, PhD); broadcasting (MS, PhD); communications (MS, PhD); information sciences (MS, PhD); journalism (MS, PhD); public relations (MS, PhD); speech communication (MS, PhD). *Program availability:* Part-time, evening/weekend, online learning. *Degree requirements:* For master's, thesis or alternative; for doctorate, thesis/dissertation. *Entrance requirements:* For master's and doctorate, GRE General Test, minimum GPA of 2.7. Additional exam requirements/recommendations for international students: Required—TOEFL. Electronic applications accepted.

The University of Texas at Austin, Graduate School, College of Communication, Department of Advertising, Austin, TX 78712-1111. Offers MA, PhD. *Entrance requirements:* For master's and doctorate, GRE General Test. Electronic applications accepted. *Faculty research:* Interactive advertising, advertising laws and ethics, advertising creativity, media planning and modeling, international advertising.

University of the Sacred Heart, Graduate Programs, Department of Communication, Program in Public Relations, San Juan, PR 00914-0383. Offers MA. *Program availability:* Part-time, evening/weekend. *Degree requirements:* For master's, thesis. *Entrance requirements:* For master's, EXADEP, minimum undergraduate GPA of 2.75, interview.

University of Wisconsin–Stevens Point, College of Fine Arts and Communication, Division of Communication, Stevens Point, WI 54481-3897. Offers interpersonal communication (MA); media studies (MA); organizational communication (MA); public relations (MA). *Program availability:* Part-time. *Degree requirements:* For master's, thesis or alternative. *Entrance requirements:* For master's, GRE. Additional exam requirements/recommendations for international students: Required—TOEFL (minimum score 575 paper-based). *Faculty research:* Communication theory and research, film history.

Virginia Commonwealth University, Graduate School, College of Humanities and Sciences, Richard T. Robertson School of Media and Culture, Program in Mass Communications, Richmond, VA 23284-9005. Offers multimedia journalism (MS); strategic public relations (MS). *Degree requirements:* For master's, comprehensive exam, thesis optional. *Entrance requirements:* For master's, GRE General Test. Additional exam requirements/recommendations for international students: Required—TOEFL (minimum score 600 paper-based; 100 iBT); Recommended—IELTS (minimum score 6.5). Electronic applications accepted. *Faculty research:* Multimedia journalism, strategic public relations.

Virginia International University, School of Business, Fairfax, VA 22030. Offers accounting (MBA, MS); entrepreneurship (MBA); executive management (Graduate Certificate); global logistics (MBA); health care management (MBA); hospitality and tourism management (MBA); human resources management (MBA); international business management (MBA); international finance (MBA); marketing management (MBA); mass media and public relations (MBA); project management (MBA, MS). *Program availability:* Part-time, online learning. *Entrance requirements:* For master's and Graduate Certificate, bachelor's degree. Additional exam requirements/recommendations for international students: Required—TOEFL (minimum score 550 paper-based; 80 iBT), IELTS (minimum score 6). Electronic applications accepted.

Wayne State University, College of Fine, Performing and Communication Arts, Department of Communication, Detroit, MI 48202. Offers communication (PhD), including democratic participation and culture, identity and representation, media, society and culture, risk, crisis and conflict, wellness, work life and relationships; communication and new media (Graduate Certificate); communication studies (MA); dispute resolution (MADR, Graduate Certificate), including community and urban studies (MADR), conflict area studies (MADR), health and family (MADR), international conflict and cooperation (MADR), professional practice (MADR), theory of conflict (MADR), workplace (MADR); health communication (Graduate Certificate); journalism (MA); media arts (MA); media studies (MA); public relations and organizational communication (MA); JD/MADR. Doctoral program admits for fall only. *Program availability:* Online learning. *Faculty:* 21. *Students:* 63 full-time (35 women), 87 part-time (55 women); includes 54 minority (39 Black or African American, non-Hispanic/Latino; 2 Asian, non-Hispanic/Latino; 7 Hispanic/Latino; 6 Two or more races, non-Hispanic/Latino), 10 international. Average age 34. 153 applicants, 39% accepted, 27 enrolled. In 2017, 26 master's, 7 doctorates, 8 other advanced degrees awarded. *Degree requirements:* For master's, thesis (for some programs), thesis or essay; for doctorate, thesis/dissertation. *Entrance requirements:* For master's, GRE (for MA if undergraduate GPA less than 3.2), personal statement; BA or BS in communication or related field with minimum upper-division GPA of 3.2 and minimum upper-division undergraduate GPA of 3.0, and sample of academic writing (for MA); undergraduate degree with minimum upper-division GPA of 3.0 and three letters of recommendation (for MADR); for doctorate, GRE, undergraduate degree in communication or related field; master's degree in communication or related field with minimum GPA of 3.5; letters of recommendation; personal statement; sample of written scholarship. Additional exam requirements/recommendations for international students: Required—TOEFL (minimum score 100 iBT), IELTS, TWE. Application fee: $50. Electronic applications accepted. *Expenses:* Contact institution. *Financial support:* In 2017–18, 57 students received support, including 5 fellowships with tuition reimbursements available (averaging $17,400 per year), 2 research assistantships with tuition reimbursements available (averaging $20,388 per year), 20 teaching assistantships with tuition reimbursements available (averaging $18,534 per year); scholarships/grants and unspecified assistantships also available. Financial award applicants required to submit FAFSA. *Faculty research:* Democratic participation and culture; identity and representation; media, society and culture; risk, crisis and conflict; wellness, work life, and relationships. *Unit head:* Dr. Lee Wilkins, Professor and Chair, 313-577-2943, E-mail: eh8899@wayne.edu. *Application contact:* E-mail: communication@wayne.edu.
Website: http://comm.wayne.edu/

Webster University, School of Communications, Program in Advertising and Marketing Communications, St. Louis, MO 63119-3194. Offers MA. *Program availability:* Online learning.

Webster University, School of Communications, Program in Public Relations, St. Louis, MO 63119-3194. Offers MA.

Western New England University, College of Arts and Sciences, Program in Communication, Springfield, MA 01119. Offers public relations (MA). *Program availability:* Part-time, evening/weekend. *Faculty:* 6 full-time (5 women). *Students:* 11 part-time (6 women); includes 3 minority (1 Black or African American, non-Hispanic/Latino; 1 Asian, non-Hispanic/Latino; 1 Hispanic/Latino). Average age 31. 7 applicants, 100% accepted, 5 enrolled. In 2017, 7 master's awarded. *Degree requirements:* For master's, independent study or thesis. *Entrance requirements:* For master's, official transcript, personal statement, resume, three letters of recommendation. Additional

exam requirements/recommendations for international students: Required—TOEFL (minimum score 79 iBT). *Application deadline:* Applications are processed on a rolling basis. Application fee: $30. Electronic applications accepted. *Expenses:* Contact institution. *Financial support:* Application deadline: 4/15; applicants required to submit FAFSA. *Unit head:* Dr. Saeed Ghahramani, Dean, 413-782-1218, Fax: 413-796-2118, E-mail: sghahram@wne.edu. *Application contact:* Matthew Fox, Director of Graduate Admissions, Enrollment Management Group, 413-782-1410, Fax: 413-782-1777, E-mail: study@wne.edu.
Website: http://www1.wne.edu/academics/graduate/ma-communication.cfm

William Woods University, Graduate and Adult Studies, Fulton, MO 65251-1098. Offers administration (M Ed, Ed S); athletic/activities administration (M Ed); curriculum and instruction (M Ed, Ed S); educational leadership (Ed D); equestrian education (M Ed); health management (MBA); human resources (MBA); leadership (MBA); marketing, advertising, and public relations (MBA); teaching and technology (M Ed). *Program availability:* Part-time, evening/weekend. *Degree requirements:* For master's, capstone course (MBA), action research (M Ed); for Ed S, field experience. *Entrance requirements:* Additional exam requirements/recommendations for international students: Required—TOEFL (minimum score 550 paper-based). Electronic applications accepted. *Expenses:* Contact institution.

Section 4
Electronic Commerce

This section contains a directory of institutions offering graduate work in electronic commerce. Additional information about programs listed in the directory but not augmented by an in-depth entry may be obtained by writing directly to the dean of a graduate school or chair of a department at the address given in the directory.

CONTENTS

Program Directory

Electronic Commerce

California State University, Fullerton, Graduate Studies, College of Business and Economics, Department of Information Systems and Decision Sciences, Fullerton, CA 92831-3599. Offers decision science (MBA); information systems (MBA, MS); information systems and decision sciences (MS); information systems and e-commerce (MS); information technology (MS). *Program availability:* Part-time. *Faculty:* 14 full-time (4 women), 1 (woman) part-time/adjunct. *Students:* 164 full-time (81 women), 95 part-time (27 women); includes 63 minority (5 Black or African American, non-Hispanic/Latino; 33 Asian, non-Hispanic/Latino; 19 Hispanic/Latino; 6 Two or more races, non-Hispanic/Latino), 165 international. Average age 28. 589 applicants, 52% accepted, 93 enrolled. *Entrance requirements:* For master's, GMAT, minimum AACSB index of 950. Application fee: $55. *Financial support:* Career-related internships or fieldwork, Federal Work-Study, institutionally sponsored loans, and scholarships/grants available. Support available to part-time students. Financial award application deadline: 3/1; financial award applicants required to submit FAFSA. *Unit head:* Dr. Bhushan Kapoor, Chair, 657-278-2221. *Application contact:* Admissions/Applications, 657-278-2371. Website: http://business.fullerton.edu/isds/

Claremont Graduate University, Graduate Programs, Center for Information Systems and Technology, Claremont, CA 91711-6160. Offers cybersecurity and networking (MS); data science and analytics (MS); electronic commerce (PhD); geographic information systems (MS); health informatics (MS); information systems (Certificate); IT strategy and innovation (MS); knowledge management (PhD); systems development (PhD); telecommunications and networking (PhD); MBA/MS. *Program availability:* Part-time. *Degree requirements:* For doctorate, comprehensive exam, thesis/dissertation, portfolio. *Entrance requirements:* For master's and doctorate, GMAT, GRE General Test. Additional exam requirements/recommendations for international students: Required—TOEFL (minimum score 75 iBT). Electronic applications accepted. *Faculty research:* Man-machine interaction, organizational aspects of computing, implementation of information systems, information systems practice.

Dalhousie University, Faculty of Computer Science, Halifax, NS B3H 1W5, Canada. Offers computational biology and bioinformatics (M Sc); computer science (MA Sc, MC Sc, PhD); electronic commerce (MEC); health informatics (MHI). *Degree requirements:* For master's, thesis (for some programs); for doctorate, thesis/dissertation. *Entrance requirements:* Additional exam requirements/recommendations for international students: Required—1 of 5 approved tests: TOEFL, IELTS, CANTEST, CAEL, Michigan English Language Assessment Battery. Electronic applications accepted.

DePaul University, College of Computing and Digital Media, Chicago, IL 60604. Offers animation (MA, MFA); applied technology (MS); business information technology (MS); computational finance (MS); computer and information sciences (PhD); computer science (MS); creative producing (MFA); cybersecurity (MS); data science (MS); digital communication and media arts (MA); documentary (MFA); e-commerce technology (MS); experience design (MA); film and television (MS); film and television directing (MFA); game design (MFA); game programming (MS); health informatics (MS); human centered design (PhD); human-computer interaction (MS); information systems (MS); network engineering and security (MS); product innovation and computing (MS); screenwriting (MFA); software engineering (MS); JD/MS. *Program availability:* Part-time, evening/weekend, online learning. *Degree requirements:* For master's, thesis (for some programs); for doctorate, comprehensive exam, thesis/dissertation. *Entrance requirements:* For master's, GRE or GMAT (for MS in computational finance only), bachelor's degree, resume (MS in predictive analytics only), IT experience (MS in information technology project management only), portfolio review (all MFA programs and MA in animation); for doctorate, GRE, master's degree in computer science. Additional exam requirements/recommendations for international students: Required—TOEFL (minimum score 590 paper-based; 80 iBT), IELTS (minimum score 6.5), PTE (minimum score 53). *Application deadline:* For fall admission, 8/1 priority date for domestic students, 6/15 priority date for international students; for winter admission, 12/1 priority date for domestic students, 10/15 priority date for international students; for spring admission, 3/1 priority date for domestic students, 1/15 priority date for international students; for summer admission, 5/1 for domestic students, 4/15 for international students. Applications are processed on a rolling basis. Application fee: $25. Electronic applications accepted. *Expenses:* Contact institution. *Financial support:* Fellowships with full tuition reimbursements, research assistantships with full and partial tuition reimbursements, teaching assistantships with full and partial tuition reimbursements, Federal Work-Study, scholarships/grants, tuition waivers (full and partial), and unspecified assistantships available. Support available to part-time students. Financial award application deadline: 4/20; financial award applicants required to submit FAFSA. *Faculty research:* Data mining, computer science, human-computer interaction, security, animation and film. *Unit head:* Elly Kafritsas-Wessels, Communications Manager, 312-362-5816, Fax: 312-362-5185, E-mail: ekafrits@cdm.depaul.edu. *Application contact:* Office of Admission, 312-362-8714, E-mail: admission@cdm.depaul.edu.
Website: http://cdm.depaul.edu

Eastern Michigan University, Graduate School, College of Business, Department of Marketing, Ypsilanti, MI 48197. Offers e-business (MBA); integrated marketing communications (MS, Postbaccalaureate Certificate); international business (MBA); marketing management (MBA); supply chain management (MBA). *Program availability:* Part-time, evening/weekend, online learning. *Faculty:* 21 full-time (8 women). *Students:* 24 full-time (20 women), 33 part-time (26 women); includes 15 minority (11 Black or African American, non-Hispanic/Latino; 3 Hispanic/Latino; 1 Two or more races, non-Hispanic/Latino). Average age 31. 41 applicants, 66% accepted, 23 enrolled. In 2017, 22 master's, 1 other advanced degree awarded. *Entrance requirements:* For master's, GMAT. Additional exam requirements/recommendations for international students: Required—TOEFL. *Application deadline:* For fall admission, 5/15 priority date for domestic students, 2/15 priority date for international students; for winter admission, 10/15 priority date for domestic students, 9/1 priority date for international students; for summer admission, 3/15 priority date for domestic students, 3/1 priority date for international students. Applications are processed on a rolling basis. Application fee: $45. *Financial support:* Fellowships, research assistantships with full tuition reimbursements, teaching assistantships with full tuition reimbursements, career-related internships or fieldwork, Federal Work-Study, institutionally sponsored loans, scholarships/grants, tuition waivers (partial), and unspecified assistantships available. Support available to part-time students. Financial award applicants required to submit FAFSA. *Unit head:* Dr. Lewis Hershey, Department Head, 734-487-3323, Fax: 734-487-7099, E-mail: lhershe1@emich.edu. *Application contact:* K. Michelle Henry, Director, Graduate Business Programs, 734-487-4444, Fax: 734-483-1316, E-mail: cob.graduate@emich.edu.
Website: http://www.mkt.emich.edu/index.html

Eastern Michigan University, Graduate School, College of Business, Programs in Business Administration, Ypsilanti, MI 48197. Offers business administration (MBA, Graduate Certificate); computer information systems (Graduate Certificate); e-business (MBA, Graduate Certificate); enterprise business intelligence (MBA); entrepreneurship (MBA, Graduate Certificate); finance (MBA, Graduate Certificate); human resources (MBA); human resources management (Graduate Certificate); information systems (MBA); internal auditing (MBA); international business (MBA, Graduate Certificate); marketing management (Graduate Certificate); nonprofit management (MBA); organizational development (Graduate Certificate); supply chain management (MBA, Graduate Certificate). *Accreditation:* AACSB. *Program availability:* Part-time, online learning. *Students:* 53 full-time (30 women), 297 part-time (170 women); includes 121 minority (72 Black or African American, non-Hispanic/Latino; 4 American Indian or Alaska Native, non-Hispanic/Latino; 15 Asian, non-Hispanic/Latino; 20 Hispanic/Latino; 10 Two or more races, non-Hispanic/Latino), 20 international. Average age 31. 247 applicants, 74% accepted, 94 enrolled. In 2017, 71 master's, 34 other advanced degrees awarded. *Entrance requirements:* For master's, GMAT (minimum score 450), minimum cumulative undergraduate GPA of 2.75. Additional exam requirements/recommendations for international students: Required—TOEFL. *Application deadline:* For fall admission, 5/15 priority date for domestic students, 2/15 priority date for international students; for winter admission, 10/15 priority date for domestic students, 9/1 priority date for international students; for summer admission, 3/15 priority date for domestic students, 3/1 priority date for international students. Applications are processed on a rolling basis. Application fee: $45. *Financial support:* Fellowships, research assistantships with full tuition reimbursements, teaching assistantships with full tuition reimbursements, career-related internships or fieldwork, Federal Work-Study, institutionally sponsored loans, scholarships/grants, tuition waivers (partial), and unspecified assistantships available. Support available to part-time students. Financial award applicants required to submit FAFSA. *Unit head:* K. Michelle Henry, Director, Graduate Business Programs, 734-487-4444, Fax: 734-483-1316, E-mail: cob.graduate@emich.edu.
Website: http://www.emich.edu/cob/mba/

Fairleigh Dickinson University, Metropolitan Campus, University College: Arts, Sciences, and Professional Studies, School of Computer Sciences and Engineering, Program in E-Commerce, Teaneck, NJ 07666-1914. Offers MS.

Florida Institute of Technology, Extended Studies Division, Melbourne, FL 32901-6975. Offers acquisition and contract management (MS); aerospace engineering (MS); business administration (MBA, DBA); computer information systems (MS); computer science (MS); electrical engineering (MS); engineering management (MS); human resources management (MS); logistics management (MS), including humanitarian and disaster relief logistics; management (MS), including acquisition and contract management, e-business, human resources management, information systems, logistics management, management, transportation management; material acquisition management (MS); mechanical engineering (MS); operations research (MS); project management (MS), including information systems, operations research; public administration (MPA); quality management (MS); software engineering (MS); space systems (MS); space systems management (MS); supply chain management (MS); systems management (MS), including information systems, operations research; technology management (MS). *Program availability:* Part-time, evening/weekend, online learning. *Students:* Average age 36. 962 applicants, 48% accepted, 323 enrolled. In 2017, 403 master's awarded. *Entrance requirements:* For master's, GMAT or resume showing 8 years of supervised experience, minimum GPA of 3.0, 2 letters of recommendation, resume. Additional exam requirements/recommendations for international students: Required—TOEFL (minimum score 550 paper-based; 79 iBT). *Application deadline:* For fall admission, 4/1 for international students; for spring admission, 9/30 for international students. Applications are processed on a rolling basis. Electronic applications accepted. *Expenses:* Contact institution. *Financial support:* Application deadline: 3/1; applicants required to submit FAFSA. *Unit head:* Dr. Theodore R. Richardson, III, Dean, 321-674-8123, Fax: 321-674-7597, E-mail: trichardson@fit.edu. *Application contact:* Carolyn Farrior, Director of Graduate Admissions, Online Learning and Off-Campus Programs, 321-674-7118, Fax: 321-674-8216, E-mail: cfarrior@fit.edu.
Website: http://es.fit.edu

Fordham University, Gabelli School of Business, New York, NY 10023. Offers accounting (MBA, MS); applied statistics and decision-making (MS); business economics (DPS); capital markets (DPS); communications and media management (MBA); electronic business (MBA); entrepreneurship (MBA); finance (MBA, PhD); global finance (MS); global sustainability (MBA); health administration (MS); healthcare management (MBA); information systems (MBA, MS); investor relations (MS); management (EMBA, MBA, MS, PhD); marketing (MBA); marketing intelligence (MS); media management (MS); nonprofit leadership (MS); quantitative finance (MS); strategy and decision-making (DPS); taxation (MS); JD/MBA; MS/MBA. *Accreditation:* AACSB. *Program availability:* Part-time, evening/weekend. *Faculty:* 130 full-time (46 women), 42 part-time/adjunct (5 women). *Students:* 1,051 full-time (570 women), 563 part-time (313 women); includes 190 minority (48 Black or African American, non-Hispanic/Latino; 72 Asian, non-Hispanic/Latino; 69 Hispanic/Latino; 1 Native Hawaiian or other Pacific Islander, non-Hispanic/Latino), 1,106 international. Average age 27. 4,577 applicants, 58% accepted, 794 enrolled. In 2017, 937 master's awarded. Terminal master's awarded for partial completion of doctoral program. *Degree requirements:* For master's, internships (for some degrees); for doctorate, comprehensive exam (for some programs), thesis/dissertation. *Entrance requirements:* For master's, GMAT/GRE, 2 letters of recommendation, resume, 2 essays, transcripts, interview. Additional exam requirements/recommendations for international students: Required—TOEFL (minimum score 100 iBT), IELTS (minimum score 7). *Application deadline:* For fall admission, 11/15 priority date for domestic and international students; for winter admission, 1/19 priority date for domestic students, 1/1 priority date for international students; for spring admission, 4/15 for domestic students, 3/1 for international students; for summer admission, 6/1 for domestic students. Application fee: $130. Electronic applications accepted. *Expenses:* $1,495 per credit. *Financial support:* Career-related internships or fieldwork, institutionally sponsored loans, scholarships/grants, and unspecified assistantships available. Support available to part-time students. Financial award application deadline: 6/30; financial award applicants required to submit FAFSA. *Unit head:* Dr. Donna Rapaccioli, Dean, 212-636-6165, Fax: 212-307-1779, E-mail: rapaccioli@fordham.edu. *Application contact:* Lawrence Murray, Senior Assistant Dean of Graduate Admissions and Advising, 212-636-6200, Fax: 212-636-7076, E-mail: admissionsgb@fordham.edu.
Website: http://www.fordham.edu/gabelli

HEC Montreal, School of Business Administration, Graduate Diploma Programs in Administration, Program in E-Business, Montréal, QC H3T 2A7, Canada. Offers Graduate Diploma. All courses are given in French. *Program availability:* Part-time. *Students:* 17 full-time (8 women), 35 part-time (20 women). 90 applicants, 70% accepted, 48 enrolled. In 2017, 18 Graduate Diplomas awarded. *Entrance requirements:* For degree, bachelor's degree in administration or equivalent. *Application deadline:* For fall admission, 4/15 for domestic and international students; for winter admission, 9/15 for domestic and international students. Application fee: $88 Canadian dollars ($184 Canadian dollars for international students). Electronic applications accepted. *Expenses:* Tuition, state resident: full-time $2869 Canadian dollars; part-time $79.70 Canadian dollars per credit. Tuition, nonresident: full-time $8883 Canadian dollars; part-time $246.76 Canadian dollars per credit. *International tuition:* $19,648 Canadian dollars full-time. *Required fees:* $41.20 Canadian dollars per credit. $67.94 Canadian dollars per term. Tuition and fees vary according to degree level and program. *Financial support:* Research assistantships, teaching assistantships, and scholarships/grants available. Financial award application deadline: 9/2. *Unit head:* Renaud Lachance, Director, 514-340-7165, E-mail: renaud.lachance@hec.ca. *Application contact:* Anny Caron, Administrative Director, 514-340-6151, Fax: 514-340-6411, E-mail: aide@hec.ca.
Website: http://www.hec.ca/programmes/dess/dess-gestion-commerce-electronique/index.html

HEC Montreal, School of Business Administration, Master of Science Programs in Administration, Program in Electronic Commerce, Montréal, QC H3T 2A7, Canada. Offers M Sc. Program offered in French. *Students:* 23 full-time (10 women), 22 part-time (11 women). 55 applicants, 53% accepted, 26 enrolled. In 2017, 28 master's awarded. *Entrance requirements:* For master's, bachelor's degree in law, management, information systems or related field with minimum GPA of 3.0 out of 4.3. Additional requirements/recommendations for international students: Required—TAGE MAGE (minimum recommended score of 283), GMAT (minimum recommended score of 630), or GRE. *Application deadline:* For fall admission, 3/1 for domestic and international students; for winter admission, 9/15 for domestic and international students. Application fee: $88 Canadian dollars ($184 Canadian dollars for international students). Electronic applications accepted. *Expenses:* Tuition, state resident: full-time $2869 Canadian dollars; part-time $79.70 Canadian dollars per credit. Tuition, nonresident: full-time $8883 Canadian dollars; part-time $246.76 Canadian dollars per credit. *International tuition:* $19,648 Canadian dollars full-time. *Required fees:* $41.20 Canadian dollars per credit. $67.94 Canadian dollars per term. Tuition and fees vary according to degree level and program. *Financial support:* Research assistantships, teaching assistantships, and scholarships/grants available. Financial award application deadline: 9/2. *Unit head:* Dr. Marie-Helene Jobin, Director, 514-340-6283, E-mail: marie-helene.jobin@hec.ca. *Application contact:* Marianne de Moura, Administrative Director, 514-340-6151, Fax: 514-340-6411, E-mail: aide@hec.ca.
Website: http://www.hec.ca/programmes/maitrises/maitrise-commerce-electronique/index.html

Instituto Tecnológico y de Estudios Superiores de Monterrey, Campus Central de Veracruz, Graduate Programs, Córdoba, Mexico. Offers administration (MA); administration of information technologies (MTI); computer sciences (MCC); education (MEE); educational institution administration (MAD); educational technology (MTE); electronic commerce (MCE); finance (MAF); humanistic studies (MEH); international business for Latin America (MNL); marketing (MMT); science (MCP). *Program availability:* Part-time, evening/weekend, online learning. *Degree requirements:* For master's, thesis (for some programs). *Entrance requirements:* For master's, PAEP College Board. Electronic applications accepted.

Instituto Tecnológico y de Estudios Superiores de Monterrey, Campus Ciudad Juárez, Program in Electronic Commerce, Ciudad Juárez, Mexico. Offers MEC.

Instituto Tecnológico y de Estudios Superiores de Monterrey, Campus Estado de México, Professional and Graduate Division, Estado de Mexico, Mexico. Offers administration of information technologies (MITA); architecture (M Arch); business administration (GMBA, MBA); computer sciences (MCS, PhD); education (M Ed); educational institution administration (MAD); educational technology and innovation (PhD); electronic commerce (MEC); environmental systems (MS); finance (MAF); humanistic studies (MHS); information sciences and knowledge management (MISKM); information systems (MS); manufacturing systems (MS); marketing (MEM); quality systems and productivity (MS); science and materials engineering (PhD); telecommunications management (MTM). *Program availability:* Part-time, online learning. *Degree requirements:* For master's, one foreign language, thesis (for some programs); for doctorate, one foreign language, thesis/dissertation. *Entrance requirements:* For master's, E-PAEP 500, interview; for doctorate, E-PAEP 500, research proposal. Additional exam requirements/recommendations for international students: Required—TOEFL (minimum score 550 paper-based). *Faculty research:* Surface treatments by plasmas, mechanical properties, robotics, graphical computing, mechatronics security protocols.

Instituto Tecnológico y de Estudios Superiores de Monterrey, Campus Irapuato, Graduate Programs, Irapuato, Mexico. Offers administration (MBA); administration of information technology (MAIT); administration of telecommunications (MAT); architecture (M Arch); computer science (MCS); education (M Ed); educational administration (MEA); educational innovation and technology (DEIT); educational technology (MET); electronic commerce (MBA); environmental administration and planning (MEAP); environmental systems (MES); finances (MBA); humanistic studies (MHS); international management for Latin American executives (MIMLAE); library and information science (MLIS); manufacturing quality management (MMQM); marketing research (MBA).

Lewis University, College of Business, Program in Business Administration, Romeoville, IL 60446. Offers accounting (MBA); custom elective option (MBA); e-business (MBA); finance (MBA); healthcare management (MBA); human resources management (MBA); international business (MBA); management information systems (MBA); marketing (MBA); project management (MBA); technology and operations management (MBA). *Program availability:* Part-time, evening/weekend. *Students:* 130 full-time (77 women), 187 part-time (107 women); includes 83 minority (27 Black or African American, non-Hispanic/Latino; 3 American Indian or Alaska Native, non-Hispanic/Latino; 7 Asian, non-Hispanic/Latino; 40 Hispanic/Latino; 6 Two or more races, non-Hispanic/Latino), 31 international. Average age 31. In 2017, 99 master's awarded. *Degree requirements:* For master's, comprehensive exam. *Entrance requirements:* For master's, interview, bachelor's degree, resume, two recommendations. Additional exam requirements/recommendations for international students: Required—TOEFL (minimum score 550 paper-based), IELTS. *Application deadline:* For fall admission, 8/15 priority date for domestic students, 5/1 priority date for international students; for spring admission, 11/15 priority date for international students. Applications are processed on a rolling basis. Application fee: $40. Electronic applications accepted. Tuition and fees vary according to program. *Financial support:* Career-related internships or fieldwork, Federal Work-Study, scholarships/grants, and unspecified assistantships available. Financial award application deadline: 5/1; financial award applicants required to submit FAFSA. *Unit head:* Dr. Maureen Culleeney, Academic Program Director, 815-838-0500 Ext. 5631, E-mail: culleema@lewisu.edu. *Application contact:* Michele Ryan, Director of Admission, 815-838-0500 Ext. 5384, E-mail: ryanml@lewisu.edu.

Northwestern University, Medill School of Journalism, Media, and Integrated Marketing Communications, Integrated Marketing Communications Program, Evanston, IL 60208. Offers brand strategy (MSIMC); content marketing (MSIMC); direct and interactive marketing (MSIMC); marketing analytics (MSIMC); strategic communications (MSIMC). *Program availability:* Part-time. *Entrance requirements:* For master's, GRE General Test or GMAT, full-time work experience (preferred). Additional exam requirements/recommendations for international students: Required—TOEFL. Electronic applications accepted. *Faculty research:* Data mining, business to business marketing, values in advertising, political advertising.

Northwestern University, School of Professional Studies, Program in Data Science, Evanston, IL 60208. Offers computer-based data mining (MS); marketing analytics (MS); predictive modeling (MS); risk analytics (MS); Web analytics (MS). *Program availability:* Online learning. *Entrance requirements:* For master's, official transcripts, two letters of recommendation, statement of purpose, current resume or curriculum vitae. Additional exam requirements/recommendations for international students: Required—TOEFL (minimum score 600 paper-based; 100 iBT) or IELTS (minimum score 7).

Pace University, Lubin School of Business, Advanced Professional Certificate Program, New York, NY 10038. Offers business economics (APC); e-business (APC); financial management (APC); international business (APC); international economics (APC); investment management (APC); marketing (APC); public accounting (APC). *Program availability:* Part-time, evening/weekend. *Students:* 1 applicant, 100% accepted. *Entrance requirements:* For degree, MBA or MS in business discipline, relevant professional experience. Additional exam requirements/recommendations for international students: Required—TOEFL (minimum score 90 iBT), IELTS (minimum score 7) or PTE (minimum score 61). *Application deadline:* For fall admission, 8/1 priority date for domestic students, 6/1 for international students; for spring admission, 12/1 for domestic students, 10/1 for international students. Applications are processed on a rolling basis. Application fee: $70. Electronic applications accepted. *Unit head:* Dr. Jack Yurkiewicz, Director, 212-618-6567, E-mail: jyurkiewicz@pace.edu. *Application contact:* Susan Ford-Goldschein, Director of Graduate Admissions, 212-346-1531, Fax: 212-346-1585, E-mail: graduateadmission@pace.edu.
Website: http://www.pace.edu/lubin/agc

Stevens Institute of Technology, Graduate School, School of Business, Program in Information Systems, Hoboken, NJ 07030. Offers computer science (MS); e-commerce (MS); enterprise systems (MS); entrepreneurial information technology (MS); information architecture (MS); information management (MS, Certificate); information security (MS); information technology in financial services industry (MS); information technology in the pharmaceutical industry (MS); information technology outsourcing management (MS); project management (MS, Certificate); software engineering (MS); telecommunications (MS). *Program availability:* Part-time, evening/weekend. *Students:* 321 full-time (110 women), 58 part-time (18 women); includes 22 minority (7 Black or African American, non-Hispanic/Latino; 15 Asian, non-Hispanic/Latino), 321 international. Average age 26. 877 applicants, 67% accepted, 117 enrolled. In 2017, 168 master's, 2 other advanced degrees awarded. *Degree requirements:* For master's, thesis optional, minimum B average in major field and overall; for Certificate, minimum B average. *Entrance requirements:* Additional exam requirements/recommendations for international students: Required—TOEFL (minimum score 74 iBT), IELTS (minimum score 6). *Application deadline:* For fall admission, 7/1 for domestic students, 4/15 for international students; for spring admission, 12/1 for domestic and international students. Applications are processed on a rolling basis. Application fee: $60. Electronic applications accepted. *Expenses: Tuition:* Full-time $34,494; part-time $1554 per credit. *Required fees:* $291 per semester. *Financial support:* Fellowships, research assistantships, teaching assistantships, career-related internships or fieldwork, Federal Work-Study, scholarships/grants, and unspecified assistantships available. Financial award application deadline: 2/15; financial award applicants required to submit FAFSA. *Unit head:* Dr. Gregory Prastacos, Dean, 201-216-8366, E-mail: gprastac@stevens.edu. *Application contact:* Graduate Admissions, 888-783-8367, Fax: 888-511-1306, E-mail: graduate@stevens.edu.
Website: https://www.stevens.edu/school-business/masters-programs/information-systems

Towson University, College of Business and Economics, Program in e-Business and Technology Management, Towson, MD 21252-0001. Offers project, program and portfolio management (Postbaccalaureate Certificate); supply chain management (MS). *Students:* 3 full-time (1 woman), 23 part-time (12 women); includes 5 minority (2 Black or African American, non-Hispanic/Latino; 1 Asian, non-Hispanic/Latino; 2 Two or more races, non-Hispanic/Latino), 3 international. *Entrance requirements:* For master's and Postbaccalaureate Certificate, GRE or GMAT, bachelor's degree in relevant field and/or three years of post-bachelor's experience working in supply chain related areas; minimum cumulative GPA of 3.0; resume; 2 reference letters. Additional exam requirements/recommendations for international students: Required—TOEFL (minimum score 550 paper-based). *Application deadline:* For fall admission, 1/17 for domestic students, 5/15 for international students; for spring admission, 10/15 for domestic students, 12/1 for international students. Applications are processed on a rolling basis. Application fee: $45. Electronic applications accepted. *Expenses:* Tuition, state resident: full-time $7960; part-time $398 per unit. Tuition, nonresident: full-time $16,480; part-time $824 per unit. *Required fees:* $2600; $130 per year. $390 per term. *Unit head:* Dr. Tobin Porterfield, Program Director, 410-704-3265, E-mail: tporterfield@towson.edu. *Application contact:* Coverley Beidleman, Assistant Director of Graduate Admissions, 410-704-5630, Fax: 410-704-3030, E-mail: cbeidleman@towson.edu.
Website: http://www.towson.edu/cbe/departments/ebusiness/grad/

Universidad del Este, Graduate School, Carolina, PR 00984. Offers accounting (MBA); adult education (M Ed); agribusiness (MBA); criminal justice and criminology (MA); curriculum and instruction - early education (M Ed); curriculum and instruction - elementary (M Ed); curriculum and instruction - English (M Ed); curriculum and instruction - Spanish (M Ed); human resources (MBA); information security management (MBA); information technology and Web business development (MBA); management (MBA); public policy (MPA); social work (MA), including clinical social work; special education (M Ed); strategic leadership (MBA).

Université de Montréal, Faculty of Arts and Sciences, Department of Computer Science and Operational Research, Montréal, QC H3C 3J7, Canada. Offers computer systems (M Sc, PhD); electronic commerce (M Sc). *Program availability:* Part-time. Terminal master's awarded for partial completion of doctoral program. *Degree requirements:* For master's, one foreign language, thesis; for doctorate, one foreign language, thesis/dissertation, general exam. *Entrance requirements:* For master's, B Sc in related field; for doctorate, MA or M Sc in related field. Electronic applications accepted. *Faculty research:* Optimization statistics, programming languages, telecommunications, theoretical computer science, artificial intelligence.

Université de Sherbrooke, Faculty of Administration, Program in E-Commerce, Sherbrooke, QC J1K 2R1, Canada. Offers M Sc. *Degree requirements:* For master's, one foreign language, thesis. *Entrance requirements:* For master's, bachelor's degree in

Electronic Commerce

related field, minimum GPA of 3.0 (on 4.3 scale), letters of reference, fluency in French. Electronic applications accepted. *Faculty research:* Radio frequency identification (RFID), Web value concept.

Université Laval, Faculty of Administrative Sciences, Programs in Business Administration, Québec, QC G1K 7P4, Canada. Offers accounting (MBA); agri-food management (MBA); electronic business (MBA, Diploma); factory management and logistics (MBA); finance (MBA); firm management (MBA); geomatic management (MBA); information technology management (MBA); international management (MBA); management (MBA); management accounting (MBA, Diploma); marketing (MBA); modeling and organizational decision (MBA); occupational health and safety management (MBA); pharmacy management (MBA); social and environmental responsibility (MBA); technological entrepreneurship (Diploma). *Accreditation:* AACSB. *Program availability:* Part-time, evening/weekend, online learning. *Entrance requirements:* For master's and Diploma, knowledge of French and English. Electronic applications accepted.

University at Buffalo, the State University of New York, Graduate School, College of Arts and Sciences, Department of Economics, Buffalo, NY 14260. Offers econometrics and quantitative economics (MS); economics (MA, PhD); financial economics (Certificate); health services (Certificate); information and Internet economics (Certificate); international economics (Certificate); law and regulation (Certificate); urban and regional economics (Certificate). *Program availability:* Part-time. *Faculty:* 17 full-time (3 women), 5 part-time/adjunct (2 women). *Students:* 119 full-time (42 women); includes 14 minority (8 Black or African American, non-Hispanic/Latino; 6 Asian, non-Hispanic/Latino), 75 international. Average age 27. 229 applicants, 28% accepted, 30 enrolled. In 2017, 28 master's, 5 doctorates, 2 other advanced degrees awarded. Terminal master's awarded for partial completion of doctoral program. *Degree requirements:* For master's, comprehensive exam; for doctorate, comprehensive exam, thesis/dissertation, field and theory exams. *Entrance requirements:* For master's, GRE General Test or GMAT; for doctorate, GRE General Test. Additional exam requirements/recommendations for international students: Required—TOEFL (minimum score 550 paper-based; 79 iBT), TWE. *Application deadline:* For fall admission, 1/15 priority date for domestic and international students. Applications are processed on a rolling basis. Application fee: $75. Electronic applications accepted. *Financial support:* In 2017–18, 8 students received support, including 3 fellowships with full tuition reimbursements available (averaging $13,594 per year), 1 research assistantship with full tuition reimbursement available (averaging $13,594 per year), 20 teaching assistantships with full tuition reimbursements available (averaging $13,594 per year); Federal Work-Study, health care benefits, and unspecified assistantships also available. Financial award application deadline: 2/1; financial award applicants required to submit FAFSA. *Faculty research:* Human capital, international economics, econometrics, applied economics, urban economics, economic growth and development. *Unit head:* Dr. Alex Anas, Chair, 716-645-8663, Fax: 716-645-2127, E-mail: alexanas@buffalo.edu. *Application contact:* Dr. Nagesh Revankar, Director of Graduate Studies, 716-645-2121 Ext. 428, Fax: 716-645-2127, E-mail: ecorevan@buffalo.edu.
Website: http://www.economics.buffalo.edu/

University of New Brunswick Saint John, Faculty of Business, Saint John, NB E2L 4L5, Canada. Offers administration (MBA); electronic commerce (MBA); international business (MBA); natural resource management (MBA). *Program availability:* Part-time. *Entrance requirements:* For master's, GMAT (minimum score of 550) or GRE (minimum

54th percentile), minimum GPA of 3.0. Additional exam requirements/recommendations for international students: Required—TOEFL (minimum score 580 paper-based; 93 iBT), TWE (minimum score 4.5). Electronic applications accepted. *Expenses:* Contact institution. *Faculty research:* International business, project management, innovation and technology management; business use of Weblogs and podcasts to communicate; corporate governance; high-involvement work systems; international competitiveness; supply chain management and logistics.

University of North Florida, Coggin College of Business, MBA Program, Jacksonville, FL 32224. Offers accounting (MBA); construction management (MBA); e-commerce (MBA); economics (MBA); finance (MBA); human resource management (MBA); international business (MBA); logistics (MBA); management applications (MBA). *Accreditation:* AACSB. *Program availability:* Part-time, evening/weekend. *Entrance requirements:* For master's, GMAT or GRE, U.S. bachelor's degree from regionally-accredited university or equivalent foreign degree. Additional exam requirements/recommendations for international students: Required—TOEFL (minimum score 550 paper-based; 79 iBT). *Faculty research:* Performance measures, costing, and inventory issues in logistics and supply chain management; inter-organizational systems; international management and marketing practices; e-commerce; organizational learning and socialization processes.

University of Ottawa, Faculty of Graduate and Postdoctoral Studies, Interdisciplinary Programs, Ottawa, ON K1N 6N5, Canada. Offers e-business (Certificate); e-commerce (Certificate); finance (Certificate); health services and policies research (Diploma); population health (PhD); population health risk assessment and management (Certificate); public management and governance (Certificate); systems science (Certificate).

University of Ottawa, Faculty of Graduate and Postdoctoral Studies, Program in E-Business Technologies, Ottawa, ON K1N 6N5, Canada. Offers M Sc, MEBT. *Degree requirements:* For master's, thesis or alternative, project. *Entrance requirements:* For master's, honours degree or equivalent, minimum B average.

University of Phoenix–Dallas Campus, College of Information Systems and Technology, Dallas, TX 75251. Offers e-business (MBA); information systems (MIS); technology management (MBA). *Program availability:* Evening/weekend. *Degree requirements:* For master's, thesis (for some programs). *Entrance requirements:* For master's, minimum undergraduate GPA of 3.0, 3 years of work experience. Additional exam requirements/recommendations for international students: Required—TOEFL (minimum score 550 paper-based; 79 iBT). Electronic applications accepted.

University of Phoenix–Houston Campus, College of Information Systems and Technology, Houston, TX 77079-2004. Offers e-business (MBA); information systems (MIS); technology management (MBA). *Program availability:* Evening/weekend, online learning. *Degree requirements:* For master's, comprehensive exam (for some programs), thesis. *Entrance requirements:* For master's, minimum undergraduate GPA of 3.0, 3 years of work experience. Additional exam requirements/recommendations for international students: Required—TOEFL (minimum score 550 paper-based; 79 iBT). Electronic applications accepted.

University of Phoenix–San Antonio Campus, School of Business, San Antonio, TX 78230. Offers accounting (MBA); business administration (MBA); e-business (MBA); global management (MBA); human resources management (MBA, MM); management (MM); marketing (MBA); public administration (MBA, MM). *Accreditation:* ACBSP.

Section 5
Entrepreneurship

This section contains a directory of institutions offering graduate work in entrepreneurship. Additional information about programs listed in the directory but not augmented by an in-depth entry may be obtained by writing directly to the dean of a graduate school or chair of a department at the address given in the directory.

For programs offering related work, see also in this book *Business Administration and Management, International Business,* and *Education (Business Education)*

CONTENTS

Program Directory

Entrepreneurship

American College of Thessaloniki, Department of Business Administration, Pylea, Greece. Offers banking and finance (MBA); entrepreneurship (MBA, Certificate); finance (Certificate); management (MBA, Certificate); marketing (MBA, Certificate). *Program availability:* Part-time, evening/weekend. *Degree requirements:* For master's, thesis. *Entrance requirements:* For master's, bachelor's degree. Additional exam requirements/ recommendations for international students: Recommended—TOEFL. Electronic applications accepted.

American University, School of International Service, Washington, DC 20016-8071. Offers comparative and regional studies (Certificate); cross-cultural communication (Certificate); development management (MS); ethics, peace, and global affairs (MA); European studies (Certificate); global environmental policy (MA, Certificate); global information technology (Certificate); global media (MA); international affairs (MA), including comparative and regional studies, global governance, politics, and security, international economic relations, natural resources and sustainable development, U.S. foreign policy and national security; international arts management (Certificate); international communication (MA, Certificate); international development (MA); international economic policy (Certificate); international economic relations (Certificate); international economics (MA); international peace and conflict resolution (MA, Certificate); international politics (Certificate); international relations (MA, PhD); international service (MIS); peacebuilding (Certificate); social enterprise (MA); the Americas (Certificate); United States foreign policy (Certificate); JD/MA. *Program availability:* Part-time, evening/weekend, 100% online. *Faculty:* 112 full-time (50 women), 46 part-time/adjunct (19 women). *Students:* 495 full-time (333 women), 518 part-time (276 women); includes 360 minority (95 Black or African American, non-Hispanic/Latino; 2 American Indian or Alaska Native, non-Hispanic/Latino; 60 Asian, non-Hispanic/Latino; 164 Hispanic/Latino; 39 Two or more races, non-Hispanic/Latino), 98 international. Average age 30. 1,559 applicants, 81% accepted, 356 enrolled. In 2017, 427 master's, 9 doctorates, 5 other advanced degrees awarded. Terminal master's awarded for partial completion of doctoral program. *Degree requirements:* For master's, one foreign language, comprehensive exam, thesis or alternative; for doctorate, one foreign language, comprehensive exam, thesis/dissertation. *Entrance requirements:* For master's, GRE; GMAT or GRE (for MA in social enterprise), transcripts, resume, 2 letters of recommendation, statement of purpose; for doctorate, GRE, transcripts, resume, 3 letters of recommendation, statement of purpose. Additional exam requirements/recommendations for international students: Required—TOEFL (minimum score 600 paper-based; 100 iBT). *Application deadline:* For fall admission, 1/15 for domestic students, 1/1 for international students; for spring admission, 10/1 for domestic students, 9/15 for international students. Application fee: $55. Electronic applications accepted. *Expenses:* Contact institution. *Financial support:* Research assistantships, teaching assistantships, institutionally sponsored loans, scholarships/ grants, and unspecified assistantships available. Financial award application deadline: 1/15; financial award applicants required to submit FAFSA. *Application contact:* 202-885-1646, Fax: 202-885-1109, E-mail: sisgrad@american.edu.
Website: http://www.american.edu/sis/

Anaheim University, Programs in Business Administration, Anaheim, CA 92806-5150. Offers entrepreneurship (ME, DBA); global sustainable management (MBA); international business (MBA, DBA, Certificate, Diploma); management (DBA); sustainable management (DBA, Certificate, Diploma). *Program availability:* Part-time, evening/weekend, online only, 100% online. Electronic applications accepted.

Arizona State University at the Tempe campus, W. P. Carey School of Business, Program in Business Administration, Tempe, AZ 85287-4906. Offers entrepreneurship (MBA); finance (MBA); health sector management (MBA); international business (MBA); leadership (MBA); marketing (MBA); organizational behavior (PhD); strategic management (PhD); supply chain management (MBA, PhD); JD/MBA; MBA/M Acc; MBA/M Arch. *Accreditation:* AACSB. *Program availability:* Part-time, evening/weekend, online learning. Terminal master's awarded for partial completion of doctoral program. *Degree requirements:* For master's, thesis or alternative, internship, interactive Program of Study (iPOS) submitted before completing 50 percent of required credit hours; for doctorate, comprehensive exam, thesis/dissertation, interactive Program of Study (iPOS) submitted before completing 50 percent of required credit hours. *Entrance requirements:* For master's, GMAT, minimum GPA of 3.0 in last 2 years of work leading to bachelor's degree, 2 letters of recommendation, professional resume, official transcripts, 3 essays; for doctorate, GMAT or GRE, minimum GPA of 3.0 in last 2 years of work leading to bachelor's degree, 3 letters of recommendation, resume, personal statement/essay. Additional exam requirements/recommendations for international students: Required—TOEFL (minimum score 550 paper-based; 80 iBT), IELTS (minimum score 6.5). Electronic applications accepted. *Expenses:* Contact institution.

Ashland University, Dauch College of Business and Economics, Ashland, OH 44805-3702. Offers accounting (MBA); business analytics (MBA); entrepreneurship (MBA); financial management (MBA); global management (MBA); health care management and leadership (MBA); human resource management (MBA); human resources (MBA); management information systems (MBA); project management (MBA); sport management (MBA); supply chain management (MBA). *Accreditation:* ACBSP. *Program availability:* Part-time, evening/weekend, 100% online, blended/hybrid learning. *Faculty:* 20 full-time (8 women), 13 part-time/adjunct (2 women). *Students:* 458 full-time (210 women), 144 part-time (52 women); includes 88 minority (63 Black or African American, non-Hispanic/Latino; 1 American Indian or Alaska Native, non-Hispanic/Latino; 10 Asian, non-Hispanic/Latino; 14 Hispanic/Latino), 202 international. Average age 31. 216 applicants, 74% accepted, 115 enrolled. In 2017, 184 master's awarded. Terminal master's awarded for partial completion of doctoral program. *Degree requirements:* For master's, thesis optional, capstone course. *Entrance requirements:* For master's, 2 years of full-time work experience. Additional exam requirements/recommendations for international students: Required—TOEFL (minimum score 550 paper-based; 78 iBT). *Application deadline:* For fall admission, 8/1 priority date for domestic students; for spring admission, 12/1 priority date for domestic students. Applications are processed on a rolling basis. Application fee: $30. Electronic applications accepted. *Expenses:* $815 per credit hour, $15 technology fee for online sections. *Financial support:* Scholarships/grants, tuition waivers (partial), and unspecified assistantships available. Financial award application deadline: 4/15; financial award applicants required to submit FAFSA. *Faculty research:* Relationship marketing strategy, executive compensation and company performance, online marketplaces in electronic commerce, diversity training in campus recreation departments, entrepreneurship in developing and emerging economies. *Unit head:* Dr. Elad Granot, Dean, 419-289-5932, E-mail: egranot@ ashland.edu. *Application contact:* Stephen W. Krispinsky, Executive Director of MBA Program, 419-289-5236, Fax: 419-289-5910, E-mail: skrispin@ashland.edu.
Website: http://www.mba.ashland.edu

Azusa Pacific University, School of Business and Management, Azusa, CA 91702-7000. Offers accounting (MBA); business administration (MBA); entrepreneurship (MBA); finance (MBA); international business (MBA); marketing (MBA); organizational science (MBA); professional accountancy (M Acc); sport management (MBA). *Program availability:* Part-time, evening/weekend. *Degree requirements:* For master's, thesis (for some programs), final project. *Entrance requirements:* For master's, GMAT, minimum GPA of 3.0. Additional exam requirements/recommendations for international students: Required—TOEFL (minimum score 600 paper-based). *Expenses:* Contact institution. *Faculty research:* Gender issues, financial risk, leadership and ethics, marketing strategy.

Babson College, F. W. Olin Graduate School of Business, Babson Park, MA 02457-0310. Offers accounting (MSA); advanced management (Certificate); business administration (MBA); business analytics (MS); finance (MS); global entrepreneurship (MS); technological entrepreneurship (MS). *Accreditation:* AACSB. *Program availability:* Part-time, evening/weekend, online learning. *Entrance requirements:* For master's, GMAT, 2 years of work experience, resume, letters of recommendation. Additional exam requirements/recommendations for international students: Required—TOEFL (minimum score 100 iBT), IELTS (minimum score 6.5). Electronic applications accepted. *Faculty research:* Entrepreneurship, sustainability, global markets, process of innovation, social media and advertising.

Bakke Graduate University, Programs in Pastoral Ministry and Business, Dallas, TX 75243-7039. Offers business administration (MBA); church and ministry multiplication (D Min); global urban leadership (MA); leadership (D Min); ministry in complex contexts (D Min); social and civic entrepreneurship (MA); theology of work (D Min); theology reflection (D Min); transformational leadership (DTL); urban youth ministry (D Min). *Program availability:* Part-time, online learning. *Faculty:* 5 full-time (3 women), 27 part-time/adjunct (12 women). *Students:* 120 full-time (48 women), 54 part-time (24 women). *Degree requirements:* For master's, thesis; for doctorate, thesis/dissertation. *Entrance requirements:* For master's, 2 years of ministry experience, BA in Biblical studies or theology; for doctorate, 3 years of ministry experience, M Div. Additional exam requirements/recommendations for international students: Required—TOEFL. *Application deadline:* For fall admission, 7/1 priority date for domestic students; for winter admission, 12/1 for domestic students; for spring admission, 3/15 for domestic students. Applications are processed on a rolling basis. Application fee: $50. Electronic applications accepted. *Expenses:* Tuition: Full-time $6120; part-time $3000 per credit. *Required fees:* $50 per course. $50 per quarter. *Financial support:* Scholarships/grants and tuition waivers (partial) available. Financial award applicants required to submit FAFSA. *Faculty research:* Theological systems, church management, worship. *Unit head:* Dr. Gwen Dewey, Senior Vice President of International Partnerships, 214-329-4447 Ext. 119, E-mail: gwen.dewey@bgu.edu. *Application contact:* Traci Tucker, Director of Admissions, 214-329-4447 Ext. 122, Fax: 214-347-9367, E-mail: traci.tucker@bgu.edu.
Website: http://www.bgu.edu/

Baruch College of the City University of New York, Zicklin School of Business, Department of Management, New York, NY 10010-5585. Offers entrepreneurship (MBA); management (PhD); operations management (MBA); organizational behavior/ human resources management (MBA); sustainable business (MBA). PhD offered jointly with Graduate School and University Center of the City University of New York. *Program availability:* Part-time, evening/weekend. *Degree requirements:* For doctorate, comprehensive exam, thesis/dissertation. *Entrance requirements:* For master's, GMAT, 2 letters of recommendation, resume, 2 years of work experience; for doctorate, GMAT. Additional exam requirements/recommendations for international students: Required— TOEFL (minimum score 590 paper-based), TWE.

Baruch College of the City University of New York, Zicklin School of Business, International Executive MS Programs, New York, NY 10010-5585. Offers entrepreneurship (MS). *Program availability:* Part-time, evening/weekend. *Entrance requirements:* For master's, GMAT, 2 letters of recommendation, resume, 2 years of work experience. Additional exam requirements/recommendations for international students: Required—TOEFL (minimum score 590 paper-based), TWE (minimum score 5).

Baylor University, Graduate School, Hankamer School of Business, Department of Entrepreneurship, Waco, TX 76798. Offers PhD. *Students:* 3 full-time (1 woman), 2 international. *Entrance requirements:* For doctorate, GMAT or GRE. *Unit head:* Kendall Artz, Chairman, E-mail: kendall_artz@baylor.edu. *Application contact:* Laurie Wilson, Director, Graduate Business Programs, 254-710-4163, Fax: 254-710-1066, E-mail: laurie_wilson@baylor.edu.
Website: http://www.baylor.edu/business/entrepreneurship/

Bay Path University, Program in Entrepreneurial Thinking and Innovative Practices, Longmeadow, MA 01106-2292. Offers MBA. *Program availability:* Part-time, 100% online. *Students:* 19 full-time (16 women), 57 part-time (53 women); includes 20 minority (11 Black or African American, non-Hispanic/Latino; 1 Asian, non-Hispanic/Latino; 5 Hispanic/Latino; 3 Two or more races, non-Hispanic/Latino). Average age 34. In 2017, 34 master's awarded. *Degree requirements:* For master's, 12 courses - eight core courses and four electives (each course is eight weeks long). *Application deadline:* Applications are processed on a rolling basis. Application fee: $45. Electronic applications accepted. Application fee is waived when completed online. *Expenses:* $815 per credit. *Financial support:* Unspecified assistantships available. Financial award applicants required to submit FAFSA. *Unit head:* Mo Sattar, Program Director, 413-565-1228, E-mail: msattar@baypath.edu. *Application contact:* Diane Ranaldi, Dean of Graduate Admissions, 413-565-1332, Fax: 413-565-1250, E-mail: dranaldi@ baypath.edu.
Website: http://graduate.baypath.edu/Graduate-Programs/Programs-On-Campus/MBA-Program/Entrepreneurial-Thinking-and-Innovative-Practices

Benedictine University, Graduate Programs, Program in Business Administration, Lisle, IL 60532. Offers accounting (MBA); entrepreneurship and managing innovation (MBA); financial management (MBA); health administration (MBA); human resource management (MBA); information systems security (MBA); international business (MBA); management consulting (MBA); management information systems (MBA); marketing management (MBA); operations management and logistics (MBA); organizational leadership (MBA). *Program availability:* Part-time, evening/weekend, online learning. *Entrance requirements:* For master's, GMAT. Additional exam requirements/ recommendations for international students: Required—TOEFL (minimum score 550 paper-based). Electronic applications accepted. *Faculty research:* Strategic leadership in professional organizations, sociology of professions, organizational change, social identity theory, applications to change management.

Brandeis University, Rabb School of Continuing Studies, Division of Graduate Professional Studies, Master of Science in Digital Innovation for Finance Technology Program, Waltham, MA 02454-9110. Offers MS. *Program availability:* Part-time-only. *Faculty:* 55 part-time/adjunct (18 women). *Students:* 2 part-time (1 woman); includes 1 minority (Hispanic/Latino). Average age 40. 2 applicants, 50% accepted, 1 enrolled. *Entrance requirements:* For master's, undergraduate coursework in general finance or economics and at least some basic experience with a programming language; four-year bachelor's degree from regionally-accredited U.S. institution or equivalent; official transcript(s) from every college or university attended; resume or curriculum vitae; statement of goals; letter of recommendation. Additional exam requirements/recommendations for international students: Required—TWE (minimum score 4.5), TOEFL (minimum scores: 600 paper-based, 100 iBT), IELTS (7), or PTE (68). *Application deadline:* For fall admission, 6/20 priority date for domestic and international students; for winter admission, 9/12 priority date for domestic and international students; for spring admission, 12/19 priority date for domestic and international students; for summer admission, 3/13 priority date for domestic and international students. Applications are processed on a rolling basis. Application fee: $75. Electronic applications accepted. *Expenses:* $1,178 per credit. *Financial support:* Applicants required to submit FAFSA. *Unit head:* Ashley Nagle Eknaian, Program Chair, E-mail: aeknaian@brandeis.edu. *Application contact:* Frances Stearns, Director of Student and Faculty Operations, 781-736-8785, E-mail: fstearns@brandeis.edu. Website: http://www.brandeis.edu/gps/future-students/learn-about-our-programs/fintech-digital-innovation.html

Brandman University, School of Business and Professional Studies, Irvine, CA 92618. Offers accounting (MBA); business administration (MBA); business intelligence and data analytics (MBA); e-business strategic management (MBA); entrepreneurship (MBA); finance (MBA); health administration (MBA); human resources (MBA, MS); international business (MBA); marketing (MBA); organizational leadership (MA, MBA, MPA); public administration (MPA). *Expenses:* Tuition: Part-time $640 per credit hour. Tuition and fees vary according to degree level and program. *Unit head:* Dr. Glenn Worthington, Dean, 253-861-1024, E-mail: gworthin@brandman.edu. *Application contact:* Dr. Glenn Worthington, Dean, 253-861-1024, E-mail: gworthin@brandman.edu. Website: https://www.brandman.edu/academic-programs/business-and-professional-studies

Brigham Young University, Graduate Studies, BYU Marriott School of Business, MBA Program, Provo, UT 84602. Offers entrepreneurship (MBA); finance (MBA); global supply chain management (MBA); marketing (MBA); strategic human resources (MBA); JD/MBA; MBA/MS. *Accreditation:* AACSB. *Faculty:* 134 full-time (15 women), 65 part-time/adjunct (16 women). *Students:* 303 full-time (65 women); includes 26 minority (3 American Indian or Alaska Native, non-Hispanic/Latino; 8 Asian, non-Hispanic/Latino; 11 Hispanic/Latino; 4 Native Hawaiian or other Pacific Islander, non-Hispanic/Latino), 58 international. Average age 30. 339 applicants, 52% accepted, 136 enrolled. In 2017, 163 master's awarded. *Entrance requirements:* For master's, GMAT or GRE, commitment to BYU Honor Code, undergraduate degree. Additional exam requirements/recommendations for international students: Required—TOEFL (minimum score 590 paper-based; 100 iBT), IELTS (minimum score 7). *Application deadline:* For fall admission, 5/1 for domestic students, 3/1 for international students. Applications are processed on a rolling basis. Application fee: $50. Electronic applications accepted. *Expenses:* Contact institution. *Financial support:* Research assistantships, teaching assistantships, career-related internships or fieldwork, institutionally sponsored loans, and scholarships/grants available. Financial award application deadline: 3/1; financial award applicants required to submit FAFSA. *Faculty research:* Finance, marketing, supply chain management, entrepreneurship, strategic human resources. *Unit head:* Dr. Grant McQueen, Director, 801-422-3500, E-mail: mba@byu.edu. *Application contact:* Yvette Anderson, MBA Program Admissions Director, 801-422-3500, Fax: 801-422-0513, E-mail: mba@byu.edu. Website: http://mba.byu.edu

Butler University, Lacy School of Business, Indianapolis, IN 46208-3485. Offers entrepreneurship and innovation (MBA); finance (MBA); international business (MBA); leadership (MBA); marketing (MBA); professional accounting (MP Acc). *Accreditation:* AACSB. *Program availability:* Part-time. *Faculty:* 14 full-time (4 women), 9 part-time/adjunct (2 women). *Students:* 35 full-time (16 women), 111 part-time (38 women); includes 15 minority (2 Black or African American, non-Hispanic/Latino; 5 Asian, non-Hispanic/Latino; 8 Hispanic/Latino), 6 international. Average age 30. 149 applicants, 64% accepted, 43 enrolled. In 2017, 90 master's awarded. *Degree requirements:* For master's, comprehensive exam, thesis optional. *Entrance requirements:* For master's, GMAT, minimum AACSB index of 950, personal statement, two letters of recommendation, official transcripts, current resume. Additional exam requirements/recommendations for international students: Required—TOEFL (minimum score 550 paper-based; 79 iBT), IELTS (minimum score 6), Michigan English Language Assessment Battery (minimum score of 80). *Application deadline:* For fall admission, 8/1 for domestic and international students; for spring admission, 12/1 for domestic and international students; for summer admission, 4/1 for domestic and international students. Applications are processed on a rolling basis. Application fee: $0. Electronic applications accepted. *Expenses:* $820 per credit. *Financial support:* In 2017–18, 22 students received support. Scholarships/grants, tuition waivers (full and partial), and unspecified assistantships available. Financial award application deadline: 7/15; financial award applicants required to submit FAFSA. *Faculty research:* Higher education and pedagogy; ecotourism; healthcare issues and marketing public policy; domestic public policy, international finance and banking, international and management entrepreneurship, organizational management. *Unit head:* Dr. Stephen Standifird, Dean, 317-940-6307. *Application contact:* Diane Dubord, Graduate Student Service Specialist, 317-940-8107, Fax: 317-940-8250, E-mail: ddubord@butler.edu. Website: https://www.butler.edu/lacyschool

Cairn University, School of Business, Langhorne, PA 19047-2990. Offers accounting (MBA); business administration (MBA); international entrepreneurship (MBA); nonprofit leadership (MBA); organizational leadership (MSOL, Postbaccalaureate Certificate). *Program availability:* Part-time, evening/weekend, 100% online, blended/hybrid learning. *Entrance requirements:* Additional exam requirements/recommendations for international students: Required—TOEFL (minimum score 550 paper-based). Electronic applications accepted. Application fee is waived when completed online. *Expenses:* Contact institution.

California Institute of Advanced Management, The MBA Program, El Monte, CA 91731. Offers executive management and entrepreneurship (MBA).

California Intercontinental University, School of Business, Irvine, CA 92614. Offers banking and finance (MBA); entrepreneurship and business management (DBA); global business leadership (DBA); international management and marketing (MBA); organizational management and human resource management (MBA).

California Lutheran University, Graduate Studies, School of Management, Thousand Oaks, CA 91360-2787. Offers business (IMBA); entrepreneurship (MBA, Certificate); finance (MBA, Certificate); financial planning (MBA, MS, Certificate); human capital management (MBA, Certificate); information technology (MS); information technology management (MBA, Certificate); international business (MBA, Certificate); marketing (MBA, Certificate); public policy and administration (MPPA); quantitative economics (MS). *Program availability:* Part-time, evening/weekend, 100% online, blended/hybrid learning. *Faculty:* 17 full-time (4 women), 40 part-time/adjunct (9 women). *Students:* 423 full-time (168 women), 153 part-time (72 women); includes 124 minority (11 Black or African American, non-Hispanic/Latino; 1 American Indian or Alaska Native, non-Hispanic/Latino; 21 Asian, non-Hispanic/Latino; 75 Hispanic/Latino; 16 Two or more races, non-Hispanic/Latino), 294 international. Average age 31. 467 applicants, 72% accepted, 108 enrolled. In 2017, 306 master's awarded. *Degree requirements:* For master's, comprehensive exam (for some programs). *Entrance requirements:* For master's, GMAT, interview, minimum GPA of 3.0. *Application deadline:* Applications are processed on a rolling basis. Application fee: $50. Electronic applications accepted. *Expenses:* Contact institution. *Unit head:* Dr. Gerhard Apfelthaler, Dean, 805-493-3360. *Application contact:* 805-493-3325, Fax: 805-493-3861, E-mail: clugrad@callutheran.edu. Website: http://www.callutheran.edu/management/

California State University, San Bernardino, Graduate Studies, College of Business and Public Administration, Program in Business Administration, San Bernardino, CA 92407. Offers accounting (MBA); entrepreneurship (MBA); finance (MBA); global business (MBA); information management (MBA); information security (MBA); management (MBA); supply chain management (MBA). *Accreditation:* AACSB. *Program availability:* Part-time, evening/weekend, online learning. *Faculty:* 4 full-time (3 women), 6 part-time/adjunct (4 women). *Students:* 21 full-time (15 women), 122 part-time (30 women); includes 82 minority (15 Black or African American, non-Hispanic/Latino; 1 American Indian or Alaska Native, non-Hispanic/Latino; 19 Asian, non-Hispanic/Latino; 44 Hispanic/Latino; 3 Two or more races, non-Hispanic/Latino), 37 international. Average age 33. 258 applicants, 44% accepted, 50 enrolled. In 2017, 134 master's awarded. *Degree requirements:* For master's, comprehensive exam, thesis. *Entrance requirements:* Additional exam requirements/recommendations for international students: Required—TOEFL. *Application deadline:* For fall admission, 7/16 for domestic students, 7/20 for international students; for winter admission, 10/23 for domestic students, 10/20 for international students; for spring admission, 1/22 for domestic students, 1/20 for international students. Application fee: $55. *Expenses:* Contact institution. *Financial support:* Application deadline: 3/1. *Unit head:* Dr. Lawrence C. Rose, Dean, 909-537-3703, Fax: 909-537-7026, E-mail: lrose@csusb.edu. *Application contact:* Dr. Vipin Gupta, Associate Dean/MBA Director, 909-537-7380, Fax: 909-537-7026, E-mail: vgupta@csusb.edu. Website: http://mba.csusb.edu/

California University of Pennsylvania, School of Graduate Studies and Research, Eberly College of Science and Technology, Program in Business Administration, California, PA 15419-1394. Offers business analytics (MBA); entrepreneurship (MBA); healthcare management (MBA). *Program availability:* Part-time, evening/weekend. *Degree requirements:* For master's, comprehensive exam. *Entrance requirements:* For master's, minimum GPA of 3.0, official transcripts. Additional exam requirements/recommendations for international students: Required—TOEFL (minimum score 550 paper-based). *Application deadline:* For fall admission, 8/1 priority date for domestic and international students; for winter admission, 12/1 priority date for domestic and international students; for spring admission, 5/1 priority date for domestic and international students. Applications are processed on a rolling basis. Application fee: $25. Electronic applications accepted. *Financial support:* Applicants required to submit FAFSA. *Faculty research:* Economics, applied economics, consumer behavior, technology and business, impact of technology. *Unit head:* Dr. Arshad Chawdhry, Graduate Coordinator, 724-938-5990, Fax: 724-938-5908, E-mail: chawdhry@cup.edu. *Application contact:* Suzanne C. Powers, Director of Graduate Admissions and Recruitment, 724-938-4029, Fax: 724-938-5712, E-mail: powers_s@cup.edu.

Cambridge College, School of Management, Boston, MA 02129. Offers business negotiation and conflict resolution (M Mgt); general business (M Mgt); health care informatics (M Mgt); health care management (M Mgt); leadership in human and organizational dynamics (M Mgt); non-profit and public organization management (M Mgt); small business development (M Mgt); technology management (M Mgt). *Program availability:* Part-time, evening/weekend. *Degree requirements:* For master's, thesis, seminars. *Entrance requirements:* For master's, resume, 2 professional references. Additional exam requirements/recommendations for international students: Required—TOEFL (minimum score 550 paper-based; 79 iBT), Michigan English Language Assessment Battery (minimum score 85); Recommended—IELTS (minimum score 6). Electronic applications accepted. *Expenses:* Contact institution. *Faculty research:* Negotiation, mediation and conflict resolution; leadership; management of diverse organizations; case studies and simulation methodologies for management education, digital as a second language: social networking for digital immigrants, non-profit and public management.

Cameron University, Office of Graduate Studies, Program in Entrepreneurial Studies, Lawton, OK 73505-6377. Offers MS. *Program availability:* Part-time, evening/weekend, online learning. *Degree requirements:* For master's, comprehensive exam. *Entrance requirements:* Additional exam requirements/recommendations for international students: Required—TOEFL (minimum score 550 paper-based). Electronic applications accepted. *Faculty research:* Entrepreneurial competition, new venture creation, legal issues, electronic commerce.

Capella University, School of Business and Technology, Doctoral Programs in Business, Minneapolis, MN 55402. Offers accounting (DBA, PhD); business intelligence (DBA); finance (DBA, PhD); general business management (PhD); human resource management (DBA, PhD); leadership (DBA, PhD); management education (PhD); marketing (DBA, PhD); project management (DBA, PhD); strategy and innovation (DBA, PhD). *Accreditation:* ACBSP.

Capella University, School of Business and Technology, Master's Programs in Business, Minneapolis, MN 55402. Offers accounting (MBA); business analysis (MS); business intelligence (MBA); entrepreneurship (MBA); finance (MBA); general business administration (MBA); general human resource management (MS); general leadership (MS); health care management (MBA); human resource management (MBA); marketing (MBA); project management (MBA, MS). *Accreditation:* ACBSP.

Carlos Albizu University, Miami Campus, Graduate Programs, Miami, FL 33172-2209. Offers clinical psychology (PhD, Psy D); entrepreneurship (MBA); exceptional student education (MS); human services (PhD); industrial/organizational psychology (MS); marriage and family therapy (MS); mental health counseling (MS); nonprofit management (MBA); organizational management (MBA); psychology (MS); speech and language pathology (MS); teaching English for speakers of other languages (MS). *Accreditation:* APA. *Program availability:* Part-time, evening/weekend, 100% online, blended/hybrid learning. *Faculty:* 32 full-time (24 women), 27 part-time/adjunct (15 women). *Students:* 411 full-time (345 women), 248 part-time (215 women); includes 562 minority (53 Black or African American, non-Hispanic/Latino; 4 Asian, non-Hispanic/Latino; 498 Hispanic/Latino; 7 Two or more races, non-Hispanic/Latino), 23 international. Average age 34. 391 applicants, 42% accepted, 154 enrolled. In 2017, 96 master's, 54 doctorates awarded. Terminal master's awarded for partial completion of doctoral program. *Degree requirements:* For master's, comprehensive exam (for some programs), integrative project (for MBA); research project (for exceptional student

Entrepreneurship

education, teaching English as a second language); for doctorate, comprehensive examinations, internship, project/dissertation. *Entrance requirements:* For master's, GRE/EXADEP, bachelor's degree from accredited institution, minimum GPA of 3.0, 3 letters of recommendation, interview, resume, statement of purpose, official transcripts; for doctorate, GRE (for Psy D), 3 letters of recommendation, resume, interview, statement of purpose, official transcripts; bachelor's degree and minimum GPA of 3.25 (for Psy D); master's degree and minimum GPA of 3.0 (for PhD). Additional exam requirements/recommendations for international students: Required—Michigan Test of English Language Proficiency. *Application deadline:* For fall admission, 4/1 priority date for domestic students, 5/1 priority date for international students; for spring admission, 11/1 priority date for domestic students, 9/1 priority date for international students. Applications are processed on a rolling basis. Application fee: $50. Electronic applications accepted. Application fee is waived when completed online. *Expenses:* Contact institution. *Financial support:* In 2017–18, 145 students received support. Federal Work-Study, scholarships/grants, unspecified assistantships, and tuition discounts available. Financial award application deadline: 6/1; financial award applicants required to submit FAFSA. *Faculty research:* Psychotherapy, forensic psychology, neuropsychology, special education, speech-language pathology, criminal justice. *Unit head:* Dr. Etiony Aldarondo, Provost, 305-593-1223 Ext. 3138, Fax: 305-592-7930, E-mail: ealdarondo@albizu.edu. *Application contact:* Sonia Feliciano, Institutional Director of Student Recruitment, 305-593-1223 Ext. 3108, Fax: 305-477-8983, E-mail: sfeliciano@albizu.edu.

Carnegie Mellon University, Dietrich College of Humanities and Social Sciences, Department of Social and Decision Sciences, Pittsburgh, PA 15213-3891. Offers behavioral decision research (PhD); social and decision science (PhD); strategy, entrepreneurship, and technological change (PhD). Terminal master's awarded for partial completion of doctoral program. *Degree requirements:* For doctorate, comprehensive exam, thesis/dissertation, research paper. *Entrance requirements:* For doctorate, GRE General Test. Additional exam requirements/recommendations for international students: Required—TOEFL. Electronic applications accepted. *Faculty research:* Organization theory, political science, sociology, technology studies.

City Vision University, Program in Technology and Ministry, Kansas City, MO 64109-1845. Offers MS. *Program availability:* Online learning. *Degree requirements:* For master's, capstone project.

Clarion University of Pennsylvania, College of Business Administration and Information Sciences, Master of Business Administration Program, Clarion, PA 16214. Offers accounting (MBA); finance (MBA); health care administration (MBA); innovation and entrepreneurship (MBA); non-profit business (MBA). *Accreditation:* AACSB. *Program availability:* Part-time, evening/weekend, 100% online. *Faculty:* 4 full-time (1 woman), 3 part-time/adjunct (0 women). *Students:* 19 full-time (7 women), 66 part-time (34 women); includes 10 minority (6 Black or African American, non-Hispanic/Latino; 1 Asian, non-Hispanic/Latino; 3 Hispanic/Latino), 2 international. Average age 31. 86 applicants, 63% accepted, 21 enrolled. In 2017, 33 master's awarded. *Degree requirements:* For master's, portfolio. *Entrance requirements:* For master's, GMAT, minimum QPA of 2.75. Additional exam requirements/recommendations for international students: Required—TOEFL (minimum score 550 paper-based, 80 iBT) or IELTS (7). *Application deadline:* For fall admission, 8/1 priority date for domestic students, 4/15 priority date for international students; for spring admission, 12/1 priority date for domestic students, 9/15 priority date for international students. Applications are processed on a rolling basis. Application fee: $40. Electronic applications accepted. *Expenses:* $655.05 per credit. *Financial support:* Unspecified assistantships available. Support available to part-time students. Financial award application deadline: 3/1; financial award applicants required to submit FAFSA. *Unit head:* Juanice Vega, Assistant to the Dean, 814-393-2600, Fax: 814-393-1910, E-mail: mba@clarion.edu. *Application contact:* Dana Bearer, Assistant Director, Graduate Programs, 814-393-2337, Fax: 814-393-2722, E-mail: gradstudies@clarion.edu.
Website: http://www.clarion.edu/admissions/graduate/index.html

Clemson University, Graduate School, College of Business, Department of Management, Clemson, SC 29634. Offers business administration (PhD), including management information systems, strategy, entrepreneurship and organizational behavior, supply chain and operations management; management (MS). *Accreditation:* AACSB. *Faculty:* 34 full-time (12 women), 1 part-time/adjunct (0 women). *Students:* 14 full-time (3 women), 1 part-time (0 women), 9 international. Average age 33. 30 applicants, 13% accepted. In 2017, 4 master's, 4 doctorates awarded. Terminal master's awarded for partial completion of doctoral program. *Degree requirements:* For master's, comprehensive exam, thesis optional; for doctorate, comprehensive exam, thesis/dissertation. *Entrance requirements:* For master's and doctorate, GMAT or GRE General Test, unofficial transcripts, two letters of reference, curriculum vitae. Additional exam requirements/recommendations for international students: Required—TOEFL (minimum score 94 iBT), IELTS (minimum score 7), PTE (minimum score 64). *Application deadline:* For fall admission, 1/15 priority date for domestic and international students. Application fee: $80 ($90 for international students). Electronic applications accepted. *Expenses:* $6,564 per semester full-time resident, $12,538 per semester full-time non-resident, $743 per credit hour part-time resident, $1,486 per credit hour part-time non-resident, $1,203 per credit hour online, other fees may apply per session. *Financial support:* In 2017–18, 10 students received support, including 1 fellowship with partial tuition reimbursement available (averaging $1,000 per year), 1 research assistantship with partial tuition reimbursement available (averaging $12,000 per year), 2 teaching assistantships with partial tuition reimbursements available (averaging $18,770 per year); unspecified assistantships also available. Financial award application deadline: 1/15. *Faculty research:* Effective use of information technology in business, manufacturing and service operations strategy, lean operations and quality management, healthcare operations, behavioral market design. *Total annual research expenditures:* $89,179. *Unit head:* Dr. V. Sridharan, Department Chair, 864-656-2624, E-mail: suhas@clemson.edu. *Application contact:* Dr. Janis Miller, Graduate Program Coordinator, 864-656-3757, E-mail: janism@clemson.edu.
Website: https://www.clemson.edu/business/departments/management/

Clemson University, Graduate School, College of Business, Master of Business Administration Program, Greenville, SC 29634. Offers business administration (MBA); business analytics (MBA); entrepreneurship and innovation (MBA). *Accreditation:* AACSB. *Program availability:* Part-time, evening/weekend. *Faculty:* 2 full-time (1 woman), 8 part-time/adjunct (1 woman). *Students:* 242 full-time (96 women), 736 part-time (222 women); includes 81 minority (46 Black or African American, non-Hispanic/Latino; 13 Asian, non-Hispanic/Latino; 17 Hispanic/Latino; 1 Native Hawaiian or other Pacific Islander, non-Hispanic/Latino; 4 Two or more races, non-Hispanic/Latino), 35 international. Average age 31. 413 applicants, 82% accepted, 233 enrolled. In 2017, 364 master's awarded. *Entrance requirements:* For master's, GMAT, resume, unofficial transcripts, personal statement, letters of recommendation. Additional exam requirements/recommendations for international students: Required—TOEFL (minimum score 80 iBT), IELTS (minimum score 6.5), PTE (minimum score 54). *Application deadline:* For fall admission, 7/15 for domestic students, 4/15 for international students; for spring admission, 12/1 for domestic students. Applications are processed on a rolling basis. Application fee: $80 ($90 for international students). Electronic applications

accepted. *Expenses:* Contact institution. *Unit head:* Dr. Gregory Pickett, Senior Associate Dean, 864-656-3975, E-mail: pgregor@clemson.edu. *Application contact:* Laura Fischman, Assistant Director of Admissions, 864-365-0604, E-mail: ann6@clemson.edu.
Website: https://www.clemson.edu/business/departments/mba/

Cogswell Polytechnic College, Program in Entrepreneurship and Innovation, San Jose, CA 95134. Offers MA.

Columbia University, Graduate School of Business, MBA Program, New York, NY 10027. Offers accounting (MBA); decision, risk, and operations (MBA); entrepreneurship (MBA); finance and economics (MBA); healthcare and pharmaceutical management (MBA); human resource management (MBA); international business (MBA); leadership and ethics (MBA); management (MBA); marketing (MBA); media (MBA); private equity (MBA); real estate (MBA); social enterprise (MBA); value investing (MBA); DDS/MBA; JD/MBA; MBA/MIA; MBA/MPH; MBA/MS; MD/MBA. *Entrance requirements:* For master's, GMAT, 2 letters of recommendation. Additional exam requirements/recommendations for international students: Required—TOEFL. Electronic applications accepted. *Expenses:* Contact institution. *Faculty research:* Human decision making and behavioral research; real estate market and mortgage defaults; financial crisis and corporate governance; international business; security analysis and accounting.

Dallas Baptist University, College of Business, Management Program, Dallas, TX 75211-9299. Offers conflict resolution management (MA); general management (MA, MS); health care management (MA); human resource management (MA); organizational communication (MA); performance management (MA); professional sales and management optimization (MA). *Program availability:* Part-time, evening/weekend, online learning. *Application deadline:* Applications are processed on a rolling basis. Application fee: $25. Electronic applications accepted. Application fee is waived when completed online. *Expenses: Tuition:* Full-time $16,308; part-time $906 per credit hour. *Required fees:* $900; $450 per semester. Tuition and fees vary according to course load and degree level. *Unit head:* Dr. Sandra Reid, Chair, Graduate School of Business, 214-333-6860, E-mail: sandra@dbu.edu. *Application contact:* Richard Nassar, Director, 214-333-6801, E-mail: richardn@dbu.edu.
Website: http://www.dbu.edu/gsb/ma-in-management

Dallas Baptist University, College of Business, Master of Business Administration Program, Dallas, TX 75211-9299. Offers accounting (MBA); business communication (MBA); conflict resolution management (MBA); entrepreneurship (MBA); finance (MBA); health care management (MBA); international business (MBA); leading the non-profit organization (MBA); management (MBA); management information systems (MBA); marketing (MBA); project management (MBA); technology and engineering management (MBA). *Accreditation:* ACBSP. *Program availability:* Part-time, evening/weekend, 100% online, blended/hybrid learning. *Application deadline:* Applications are processed on a rolling basis. Application fee: $25. Electronic applications accepted. Application fee is waived when completed online. *Expenses: Tuition:* Full-time $16,308; part-time $906 per credit hour. *Required fees:* $900; $450 per semester. Tuition and fees vary according to course load and degree level. *Unit head:* Dr. Sandra Reid, Chair of Graduate Business Programs, 214-333-5280, E-mail: sandra@dbu.edu. *Application contact:* Bobby Soto, Director of Admissions, 214-333-5242, E-mail: graduate@dbu.edu.
Website: http://www.dbu.edu/gsb/mba

Dartmouth College, Thayer School of Engineering, PhD in Innovation Program, Hanover, NH 03755. Offers PhD. *Degree requirements:* For doctorate, internship. *Entrance requirements:* For doctorate, curriculum vitae. *Application deadline:* For fall admission, 1/1 for domestic students. *Financial support:* Fellowships and research assistantships available. *Total annual research expenditures:* $523,948. *Unit head:* Prof. Eric Fossum, Director, 603-646-2238, Fax: 603-646-2580, E-mail: eric.r.fossum@dartmouth.edu. *Application contact:* Candace S. Potter, Graduate Admissions and Financial Aid Administrator, 603-646-3844, Fax: 603-646-1620, E-mail: candace.s.potter@dartmouth.edu.
Website: http://engineering.dartmouth.edu/academics/graduate/innovation

Delaware Valley University, MBA Program, Doylestown, PA 18901-2697. Offers accounting (MBA); entrepreneurship (MBA); finance (MBA); food and agribusiness (MBA); general business (MBA); global executive leadership (MBA); human resource management (MBA); supply chain management (MBA). *Program availability:* Part-time, evening/weekend, online learning. *Entrance requirements:* For master's, minimum undergraduate GPA of 3.0. Electronic applications accepted. *Expenses:* Contact institution.

DePaul University, Kellstadt Graduate School of Business, Chicago, IL 60604. Offers accountancy (MBA, MSA); applied economics (MBA); audit and advisory services (MS); business administration (DBA); business analytics (MS); business strategy and decision-making (MBA); computational finance (MS); economics and policy analysis (MS); enterprise risk management (MS); entrepreneurship (MBA, MS); finance (MBA, MS); general business (MBA); hospitality leadership (MBA); hospitality leadership and operational performance (MS); human resources (MS); international business (MBA); management (MBA, MS); management information systems (MBA); marketing (MBA, MS); marketing analysis (MS); marketing strategy and planning (MBA); real estate (MS); real estate finance and investment (MBA); strategy, execution and valuation (MBA); supply chain management (MS); sustainable management (MS); taxation (MS); JD/MBA. *Accreditation:* AACSB. *Program availability:* Part-time, evening/weekend, online learning. *Entrance requirements:* For master's, GMAT/GRE, 2 letters of recommendation, resume, essay, official transcripts. Additional exam requirements/recommendations for international students: Required—TOEFL (minimum score 550 paper-based; 80 iBT). *Application deadline:* For fall admission, 7/1 for domestic students, 6/1 for international students; for winter admission, 10/1 for domestic students, 9/1 for international students; for spring admission, 2/1 for domestic students, 1/1 for international students. Applications are processed on a rolling basis. Application fee: $60. Electronic applications accepted. *Expenses:* Contact institution. *Financial support:* Application deadline: 4/1; applicants required to submit FAFSA. *Unit head:* Christa Hinton, Assistant Dean and Director, 312-362-8810, Fax: 312-362-6677, E-mail: chinton@depaul.edu. *Application contact:* Garry Cooke, Director of Recruitment and Admissions, 312-362-8810, Fax: 312-362-6677, E-mail: kgsb@depaul.edu.
Website: http://kellstadt.depaul.edu

Drexel University, Goodwin College of Professional Studies, School of Technology and Professional Studies, Philadelphia, PA 19104-2875. Offers construction management (MS); creativity and innovation (MS); engineering technology (MS); food science (MS); hospitality management (MS); professional studies: creativity studies (MS); professional studies: e-learning leadership (MS); professional studies: homeland security management (MS); project management (MS); property management (MS); sport management (MS). *Program availability:* Part-time, evening/weekend. *Entrance requirements:* Additional exam requirements/recommendations for international students: Required—TOEFL, IELTS. Electronic applications accepted. Application fee is waived when completed online.

Duke University, The Fuqua School of Business, The Duke MBA-Daytime Program, Durham, NC 27708-0586. Offers academic excellence in finance (Certificate); business

administration (MBA); decision sciences (MBA); energy and environment (MBA); energy finance (MBA); entrepreneurship and innovation (MBA); finance (MBA); financial analysis (MBA); health sector management (Certificate); leadership and ethics (MBA); management (MBA); management science and technology management (Certificate); marketing (MBA); operations management (MBA); social entrepreneurship (MBA); strategy (MBA). *Faculty:* 96 full-time (19 women), 48 part-time/adjunct (15 women). *Students:* 876 full-time (297 women); includes 180 minority (39 Black or African American, non-Hispanic/Latino; 2 American Indian or Alaska Native, non-Hispanic/Latino; 83 Asian, non-Hispanic/Latino; 50 Hispanic/Latino; 6 Two or more races, non-Hispanic/Latino), 321 international. Average age 29. In 2017, 445 master's awarded. *Entrance requirements:* For master's, GMAT or GRE, transcripts, essays, resume, recommendation letters, interview. *Application deadline:* For fall admission, 9/12 for domestic and international students; for winter admission, 10/10 for domestic and international students; for spring admission, 1/3 for domestic and international students; for summer admission, 3/20 for domestic and international students. Application fee: $225. Electronic applications accepted. *Expenses:* $69,342 first-year tuition and fees. *Financial support:* In 2017–18, 423 students received support. Scholarships/grants available. Financial award applicants required to submit FAFSA. *Unit head:* Steve Misuraca, Assistant Dean, Daytime MBA Program. *Application contact:* Shari Hubert, Associate Dean, Office of Admissions, 919-660-7705, Fax: 919-681-8026, E-mail: admissions-info@fuqua.duke.edu.
Website: https://www.fuqua.duke.edu/programs/daytime-mba

Duke University, The Fuqua School of Business, The Duke MBA-Global Executive Program, Durham, NC 27708-0586. Offers business administration (MBA); energy and environment (MBA); entrepreneurship and innovation (MBA); finance (MBA); health sector management (Certificate); marketing (MBA); strategy (MBA). *Faculty:* 96 full-time (19 women), 48 part-time/adjunct (15 women). *Students:* 94 full-time (26 women); includes 34 minority (8 Black or African American, non-Hispanic/Latino; 21 Asian, non-Hispanic/Latino; 4 Hispanic/Latino; 1 Two or more races, non-Hispanic/Latino), 25 international. Average age 39. In 2017, 27 master's awarded. *Entrance requirements:* For master's, Executive Assessment, GMAT, or GRE, transcripts, essays, resume, recommendation letters, letter of company support, interview. *Application deadline:* For fall admission, 10/12 priority date for domestic and international students; for winter admission, 12/7 priority date for domestic and international students; for spring admission, 3/20 priority date for domestic and international students; for summer admission, 5/31 for domestic and international students. Applications are processed on a rolling basis. Application fee: $225. Electronic applications accepted. *Expenses:* Contact institution. *Financial support:* In 2017–18, 31 students received support. Scholarships/grants available. Financial award applicants required to submit FAFSA. *Unit head:* Karen Courtney, Associate Dean, Executive Programs. *Application contact:* Shari Hubert, Associate Dean, Office of Admissions, 919-660-7705, Fax: 919-681-8026, E-mail: admissions-info@fuqua.duke.edu.
Website: https://www.fuqua.duke.edu/programs/global-executive-mba

Duke University, The Fuqua School of Business, The Duke MBA-Weekend Executive Program, Durham, NC 27708-0586. Offers business administration (MBA); energy and environment (MBA); entrepreneurship and innovation (MBA); finance (MBA); health sector management (Certificate); marketing (MBA); strategy (MBA). *Faculty:* 96 full-time (19 women), 48 part-time/adjunct (15 women). *Students:* 219 full-time (59 women); includes 80 minority (13 Black or African American, non-Hispanic/Latino; 3 American Indian or Alaska Native, non-Hispanic/Latino; 45 Asian, non-Hispanic/Latino; 13 Hispanic/Latino; 6 Two or more races, non-Hispanic/Latino), 32 international. Average age 35. In 2017, 92 master's awarded. *Entrance requirements:* For master's, Executive Assessment, GMAT or GRE, transcripts, essays, resume, recommendation letters, letter of company support, interview. *Application deadline:* For fall admission, 10/12 priority date for domestic and international students; for winter admission, 12/7 priority date for domestic and international students; for spring admission, 2/7 priority date for domestic and international students; for summer admission, 3/20 for domestic and international students. Applications are processed on a rolling basis. Application fee: $225. Electronic applications accepted. *Expenses:* Contact institution. *Financial support:* In 2017–18, 44 students received support. Scholarships/grants available. Financial award applicants required to submit FAFSA. *Unit head:* Karen Courtney, Associate Dean, Executive Programs. *Application contact:* Shari Hubert, Associate Dean, Office of Admissions, 919-660-7705, Fax: 919-681-8026, E-mail: admissions-info@fuqua.duke.edu.
Website: https://www.fuqua.duke.edu/programs/weekend-executive-mba

Eastern Michigan University, Graduate School, College of Business, Department of Management, Ypsilanti, MI 48197. Offers entrepreneurship (Postbaccalaureate Certificate); human resources management and organizational development (MSHROD). *Program availability:* Part-time, evening/weekend, online learning. *Faculty:* 21 full-time (11 women). *Students:* 10 full-time (4 women), 58 part-time (40 women); includes 19 minority (11 Black or African American, non-Hispanic/Latino; 2 Asian, non-Hispanic/Latino; 3 Hispanic/Latino; 3 Two or more races, non-Hispanic/Latino), 4 international. Average age 31. 41 applicants, 76% accepted, 18 enrolled. In 2017, 92 master's awarded. *Degree requirements:* For master's, thesis optional. *Entrance requirements:* For master's, GMAT. Additional exam requirements/recommendations for international students: Required—TOEFL. *Application deadline:* For fall admission, 5/15 priority date for domestic students, 2/15 priority date for international students; for winter admission, 10/15 priority date for domestic students, 9/1 priority date for international students; for summer admission, 3/15 priority date for domestic students, 3/1 priority date for international students. Applications are processed on a rolling basis. Application fee: $45. *Financial support:* Fellowships, research assistantships with full tuition reimbursements, teaching assistantships with full tuition reimbursements, career-related internships or fieldwork, Federal Work-Study, institutionally sponsored loans, scholarships/grants, tuition waivers (partial), and unspecified assistantships available. Support available to part-time students. Financial award applicants required to submit FAFSA. *Unit head:* Dr. Fraya Wagner-Marsh, Department Head, 734-487-3240, Fax: 734-487-4100, E-mail: fraya.wagner@emich.edu.

Eastern Michigan University, Graduate School, College of Business, Programs in Business Administration, Ypsilanti, MI 48197. Offers business administration (MBA, Graduate Certificate); computer information systems (Graduate Certificate); e-business (MBA, Graduate Certificate); enterprise business intelligence (MBA); entrepreneurship (MBA, Graduate Certificate); finance (MBA, Graduate Certificate); human resources (MBA); human resources management (Graduate Certificate); information systems (MBA); internal auditing (MBA); international business (MBA, Graduate Certificate); marketing management (Graduate Certificate); nonprofit management (MBA); organizational development (Graduate Certificate); supply chain management (MBA, Graduate Certificate). *Accreditation:* AACSB. *Program availability:* Part-time, online learning. *Students:* 53 full-time (30 women), 297 part-time (170 women); includes 121 minority (72 Black or African American, non-Hispanic/Latino; 4 American Indian or Alaska Native, non-Hispanic/Latino; 15 Asian, non-Hispanic/Latino; 20 Hispanic/Latino; 10 Two or more races, non-Hispanic/Latino), 20 international. Average age 31. 247 applicants, 74% accepted, 94 enrolled. In 2017, 71 master's, 34 other advanced degrees awarded. *Entrance requirements:* For master's, GMAT (minimum score 450), minimum cumulative undergraduate GPA of 2.75. Additional exam requirements/recommendations for international students: Required—TOEFL. *Application deadline:* For fall admission, 5/15

priority date for domestic students, 2/15 priority date for international students; for winter admission, 10/15 priority date for domestic students, 9/1 priority date for international students; for summer admission, 3/15 priority date for domestic students, 3/1 priority date for international students. Applications are processed on a rolling basis. Application fee: $45. *Financial support:* Fellowships, research assistantships with full tuition reimbursements, teaching assistantships with full tuition reimbursements, career-related internships or fieldwork, Federal Work-Study, institutionally sponsored loans, scholarships/grants, tuition waivers (partial), and unspecified assistantships available. Support available to part-time students. Financial award applicants required to submit FAFSA. *Unit head:* K. Michelle Henry, Director, Graduate Business Programs, 734-487-4444, Fax: 734-483-1316, E-mail: cob.graduate@emich.edu.
Website: http://www.emich.edu/cob/mba/

East Tennessee State University, School of Graduate Studies, College of Business and Technology, Department of Management and Marketing, Johnson City, TN 37614. Offers business administration (MBA, Postbaccalaureate Certificate); digital marketing (MS); entrepreneurial leadership (Postbaccalaureate Certificate); health care management (Postbaccalaureate Certificate). *Program availability:* Part-time, evening/weekend. *Degree requirements:* For master's, comprehensive exam, capstone. *Entrance requirements:* For master's, GMAT, minimum GPA of 2.5 (for MBA, 3.0 (for MS); current resume; three letters of recommendation; for Postbaccalaureate Certificate, minimum GPA of 2.5, undergraduate degree. Additional exam requirements/recommendations for international students: Required—TOEFL (minimum score 550 paper-based; 79 iBT). *Application deadline:* For fall admission, 6/1 for domestic students, 4/29 for international students; for spring admission, 11/1 for domestic students, 9/29 for international students. Application fee: $55 ($65 for international students). Electronic applications accepted. *Financial support:* Research assistantships with full tuition reimbursements, teaching assistantships with full tuition reimbursements, career-related internships or fieldwork, institutionally sponsored loans, scholarships/grants, and unspecified assistantships available. Financial award application deadline: 7/1; financial award applicants required to submit FAFSA. *Faculty research:* Sustainability, healthcare effectiveness, consumer behavior, merchandising trends, organizational management issues. *Unit head:* Charles Gorman, Chair, 423-439-4433, Fax: 423-439-5661, E-mail: gormanc@etsu.edu. *Application contact:* Charles Gorman, Chair, 423-439-4433, Fax: 423-439-5661, E-mail: gormanc@etsu.edu.
Website: http://www.etsu.edu/cbat/mgmtmktr/

Elms College, Division of Business, Chicopee, MA 01013-2839. Offers accounting (MBA); accounting and finance (MS); financial planning (MBA, Certificate); healthcare leadership (MBA); lean entrepreneurship (MBA); management (MBA). *Program availability:* Part-time, evening/weekend. *Faculty:* 5 full-time (all women), 7 part-time/adjunct (4 women). *Students:* 51 part-time (30 women); includes 9 minority (4 Black or African American, non-Hispanic/Latino; 2 Asian, non-Hispanic/Latino; 3 Hispanic/Latino), 2 international. Average age 33. 14 applicants, 93% accepted, 10 enrolled. In 2017, 28 master's awarded. *Entrance requirements:* For master's, minimum GPA of 3.0. *Application deadline:* Applications are processed on a rolling basis. Application fee: $30. Electronic applications accepted. *Expenses: Tuition:* Full-time $13,860; part-time $770 per credit hour. *Required fees:* $200. Tuition and fees vary according to degree level and program. *Unit head:* Dr. David Kimball, Chair, Division of Business, 413-265-2300, E-mail: kimballd@elms.edu. *Application contact:* MBA Program Coordinator, 413-265-2592, E-mail: mba@elms.edu.

Embry-Riddle Aeronautical University–Worldwide, Department of Engineering and Technology, Daytona Beach, FL 32114-3900. Offers aerospace engineering (MS); entrepreneurship in technology (MS); systems engineering (M Sys E), including engineering management, technical. *Program availability:* Part-time, evening/weekend, 100% online, blended/hybrid learning. *Faculty:* 6 full-time (1 woman), 5 part-time/adjunct (0 women). *Students:* 29 full-time (5 women), 39 part-time (6 women); includes 16 minority (3 Black or African American, non-Hispanic/Latino; 4 Asian, non-Hispanic/Latino; 5 Hispanic/Latino; 4 Two or more races, non-Hispanic/Latino). Average age 32. 76 applicants, 28% accepted, 15 enrolled. In 2017, 34 master's awarded. *Entrance requirements:* For master's, GRE (for MS in aerospace engineering). Additional exam requirements/recommendations for international students: Required—TOEFL (minimum score 550 paper-based; 79 iBT), IELTS (minimum score 6). *Application deadline:* Applications are processed on a rolling basis. Application fee: $50. Electronic applications accepted. *Expenses:* Contact institution. *Financial support:* Career-related internships or fieldwork and scholarships/grants available. Financial award applicants required to submit FAFSA. *Unit head:* Brian Sanders, PhD, Department Chair, E-mail: brian.sanders1@erau.edu. *Application contact:* Worldwide Campus, 800-522-6787, E-mail: worldwide@erau.edu.

Emory University, Goizueta Business School, Full Time MBA Program, Atlanta, GA 30322. Offers accounting (MBA); alternative investments (MBA); business process consulting (MBA); business technology management (MBA); capital markets (MBA); corporate finance (MBA); customer relationship management (MBA); decision analytics (MBA); entrepreneurship (MBA); finance (MBA); global management (MBA); investment banking (MBA); management consulting (MBA); marketing (MBA); marketing analytics (MBA); marketing consulting (MBA); operations management (MBA); organization and management (MBA); product and brand management (MBA); real estate (MBA); social enterprise (MBA); strategy consulting (MBA). *Accreditation:* AACSB. *Faculty:* 74 full-time (18 women), 18 part-time/adjunct (6 women). *Students:* 353 full-time (96 women); includes 80 minority (18 Black or African American, non-Hispanic/Latino; 2 American Indian or Alaska Native, non-Hispanic/Latino; 39 Asian, non-Hispanic/Latino; 16 Hispanic/Latino; 1 Native Hawaiian or other Pacific Islander, non-Hispanic/Latino; 4 Two or more races, non-Hispanic/Latino), 104 international. Average age 29. 1,380 applicants, 34% accepted, 172 enrolled. In 2017, 179 master's awarded. *Degree requirements:* For master's, 1 leadership course; 2 mid-semester module programs; 2 global components. *Entrance requirements:* For master's, GMAT/GRE, essays; recommendation letters; undergraduate degree; interview. Additional exam requirements/recommendations for international students: Required—TOEFL (minimum score 100 iBT), IELTS (minimum score 7), PTE (minimum score 68). *Application deadline:* For fall admission, 10/6 for domestic and international students; for winter admission, 11/17 for domestic and international students; for spring admission, 1/3 priority date for domestic and international students; for summer admission, 3/9 for domestic and international students. Application fee: $150. Electronic applications accepted. *Expenses:* $59,616. *Financial support:* In 2017–18, 273 students received support. Career-related internships or fieldwork, institutionally sponsored loans, and scholarships/grants available. Financial award application deadline: 4/1; financial award applicants required to submit FAFSA. *Faculty research:* Corporate finance, information systems, digital marketing, asset pricing, sports management. *Unit head:* Brian Mitchell, Associate Dean, 404-727-4824, Fax: 404-712-9648, E-mail: brian.mitchell@emory.edu. *Application contact:* Julie Barefoot, Associate Dean, 404-727-6311, Fax: 404-727-4612, E-mail: mbaadmissions@emory.edu.
Website: http://www.goizueta.emory.edu

Everglades University, Graduate Programs, Program in Entrepreneurship, Boca Raton, FL 33431. Offers MS. *Program availability:* Part-time, evening/weekend, 100% online. *Degree requirements:* For master's, capstone course. *Entrance requirements:*

Entrepreneurship

For master's, GMAT (minimum score of 400) or GRE (minimum score of 290), bachelor's or graduate degree from college accredited by an agency recognized by the U.S. Department of Education; minimum cumulative GPA of 2.0 at the baccalaureate level, 3.0 at the master's level. Additional exam requirements/recommendations for international students: Recommended—TOEFL (minimum score 500 paper-based). Electronic applications accepted. *Expenses:* Contact institution.

Fairleigh Dickinson University, Florham Campus, Silberman College of Business, Departments of Management, Marketing, and Entrepreneurial Studies, Program in Entrepreneurial Studies, Madison, NJ 07940-1099. Offers MBA, Certificate.

Fairleigh Dickinson University, Metropolitan Campus, Silberman College of Business, Departments of Management, Marketing, and Entrepreneurial Studies, Program in Entrepreneurial Studies, Teaneck, NJ 07666-1914. Offers MBA, Certificate.

Felician University, Program in Business, Lodi, NJ 07644-2117. Offers business administration (DBA); innovation and entrepreneurial leadership (MBA). *Program availability:* Part-time-only, evening/weekend, online learning. *Faculty:* 5 full-time (0 women), 17 part-time/adjunct (3 women). *Students:* 17 full-time (11 women), 94 part-time (59 women); includes 59 minority (25 Black or African American, non-Hispanic/Latino; 10 Asian, non-Hispanic/Latino; 24 Hispanic/Latino), 5 international. Average age 34. 68 applicants, 81% accepted, 34 enrolled. In 2017, 20 master's awarded. Terminal master's awarded for partial completion of doctoral program. *Degree requirements:* For master's, comprehensive exam, thesis, presentation; for doctorate, thesis/dissertation, scholarly project. *Entrance requirements:* For master's and doctorate, GMAT, resume, personal statement, graduation from accredited baccalaureate program. Additional exam requirements/recommendations for international students: Required—TOEFL (minimum score 550 paper-based; 79 iBT), IELTS (minimum score 6.5), PTE (minimum score 56). *Application deadline:* Applications are processed on a rolling basis. Application fee: $40. Electronic applications accepted. Application fee is waived when completed online. *Expenses:* Contact institution. *Financial support:* Federal Work-Study and scholarships/grants available. Financial award applicants required to submit FAFSA. *Faculty research:* Social media, assessment, small business management, mission integration. *Unit head:* Dr. David M. Turi, Associate Dean/Associate Professor, School of Business, 201-559-3327, E-mail: turid@felician.edu. *Application contact:* Michael Szarek, Assistant Vice-President of Graduate Admissions, 201-355-1450, E-mail: szarekm@felician.edu.

Florida Atlantic University, College of Business, Department of Management, Boca Raton, FL 33431-0991. Offers business administration (MBA); entrepreneurship (MBA); health administration (MBA); international business (MBA); sport management (MBA). *Faculty:* 4 full-time (1 woman). *Students:* 122 full-time (86 women), 81 part-time (67 women); includes 117 minority (61 Black or African American, non-Hispanic/Latino; 12 Asian, non-Hispanic/Latino; 44 Hispanic/Latino), 3 international. Average age 35. 124 applicants, 73% accepted, 75 enrolled. In 2017, 70 master's awarded. *Entrance requirements:* For master's, GMAT or GRE General Test, minimum GPA of 3.0 in last 60 hours of course work. Additional exam requirements/recommendations for international students: Required—TOEFL (minimum score 600 paper-based; 64 iBT), IELTS (minimum score 6). *Application deadline:* For fall admission, 7/25 for domestic students, 2/15 for international students; for spring admission, 12/10 for domestic students, 7/15 for international students. Applications are processed on a rolling basis. Application fee: $30. Electronic applications accepted. *Expenses:* Tuition, state resident: full-time $7400; part-time $369.82 per credit. Tuition, nonresident: full-time $20,496; part-time $1042.81 per credit. *Financial support:* Research assistantships with full tuition reimbursements, career-related internships or fieldwork, tuition waivers (partial), and unspecified assistantships available. *Faculty research:* Sports administration, healthcare, policy, finance, real estate, senior living. *Unit head:* Dr. Roland Kidwell, Chair, 561-297-5634, E-mail: kidwellr@fau.edu.
Website: http://business.fau.edu/departments/management/index.aspx

Florida Institute of Technology, Nathan M. Bisk College of Business, Program in Innovation and Entrepreneurship, Melbourne, FL 32901-6975. Offers MS. *Program availability:* Part-time, evening/weekend. *Students:* 18 applicants, 11% accepted, 1 enrolled. In 2017, 5 master's awarded. *Degree requirements:* For master's, comprehensive exam (for some programs), thesis optional, 30 credit hours. *Entrance requirements:* For master's, GMAT (minimum score of 500), GRE, or equivalent, bachelor's degree from regionally-accredited institution with minimum GPA of 3.0, 2 letters of recommendation, statement of objectives. Additional exam requirements/recommendations for international students: Required—TOEFL (minimum score 550 paper-based; 79 iBT). *Application deadline:* For fall admission, 4/1 for international students; for spring admission, 9/1 for international students. *Expenses: Tuition:* Part-time $1241 per credit hour. Part-time tuition and fees vary according to campus/location. *Financial support:* Application deadline: 3/1. *Unit head:* Dr. Abram Walton, Associate Professor, 321-674-7327, Fax: 321-674-7494, E-mail: awalton@fit.edu. *Application contact:* Cheryl A. Brown, Associate Director of Graduate Admissions, 321-674-7581, Fax: 321-723-9468, E-mail: cbrown@fit.edu.
Website: http://www.fit.edu/programs/grad/ms_innovation_entrepreneurship

Fordham University, Gabelli School of Business, New York, NY 10023. Offers accounting (MBA, MS); applied statistics and decision-making (MS); business economics (DPS); capital markets (DPS); communications and media management (MBA); electronic business (MBA); entrepreneurship (MBA); finance (MBA, PhD); global finance (MS); global sustainability (MBA); health administration (MS); healthcare management (MBA); information systems (MBA, MS); investor relations (MS); management (EMBA, MBA, MS, PhD); marketing (MBA); marketing intelligence (MS); media management (MS); nonprofit leadership (MS); quantitative finance (MS); strategy and decision-making (DPS); taxation (MS); JD/MBA; MS/MBA. *Accreditation:* AACSB. *Program availability:* Part-time, evening/weekend. *Faculty:* 130 full-time (46 women), 42 part-time/adjunct (5 women). *Students:* 1,051 full-time (570 women), 563 part-time (313 women); includes 190 minority (48 Black or African American, non-Hispanic/Latino; 72 Asian, non-Hispanic/Latino; 69 Hispanic/Latino; 1 Native Hawaiian or other Pacific Islander, non-Hispanic/Latino), 1,106 international. Average age 27. 4,577 applicants, 58% accepted, 794 enrolled. In 2017, 937 master's awarded. Terminal master's awarded for partial completion of doctoral program. *Degree requirements:* For master's, internships (for some degrees); for doctorate, comprehensive exam (for some programs), thesis/dissertation. *Entrance requirements:* For master's, GMAT/GRE, 2 letters of recommendation, resume, 2 essays, transcripts, interview. Additional exam requirements/recommendations for international students: Required—TOEFL (minimum score 100 iBT), IELTS (minimum score 7). *Application deadline:* For fall admission, 11/15 priority date for domestic and international students; for winter admission, 1/19 priority date for domestic students, 1/1 priority date for international students; for spring admission, 4/15 for domestic students, 3/1 for international students; for summer admission, 6/1 for domestic students. Application fee: $130. Electronic applications accepted. *Expenses:* $1,495 per credit. *Financial support:* Career-related internships or fieldwork, institutionally sponsored loans, scholarships/grants, and unspecified assistantships available. Support available to part-time students. Financial award application deadline: 6/30; financial award applicants required to submit FAFSA. *Unit head:* Dr. Donna Rapaccioli, Dean, 212-636-6165, Fax: 212-307-1779, E-mail: rapaccioli@fordham.edu. *Application contact:* Lawrence Murray, Senior Assistant Dean

of Graduate Admissions and Advising, 212-636-6200, Fax: 212-636-7076, E-mail: admissionsgb@fordham.edu.
Website: http://www.fordham.edu/gabelli

Georgia State University, J. Mack Robinson College of Business, Department of Managerial Sciences, Atlanta, GA 30302-3083. Offers business analysis (MBA, MS); entrepreneurship (MBA); human resources management (MBA, MS); operations management (MBA, MS); organization behavior/human resource management (PhD); organization management (MBA); organizational change (MS); strategic management (PhD). *Accreditation:* AACSB. *Program availability:* Part-time, evening/weekend. *Faculty:* 25 full-time (11 women). *Students:* 20 full-time (12 women); includes 7 minority (4 Black or African American, non-Hispanic/Latino; 2 Hispanic/Latino; 1 Two or more races, non-Hispanic/Latino), 6 international. Average age 33. 77 applicants, 18% accepted, 10 enrolled. In 2017, 25 master's, 1 doctorate awarded. *Entrance requirements:* For master's, GRE or GMAT, transcripts from all institutions attended, resume, essays; for doctorate, GMAT, three letters of recommendation, personal statement, transcripts from all institutions attended, resume. Additional exam requirements/recommendations for international students: Required—TOEFL (minimum score 610 paper-based; 101 iBT), IELTS (minimum score 7). *Application deadline:* For fall admission, 5/1 priority date for domestic students, 2/1 priority date for international students; for spring admission, 9/15 priority date for domestic students, 4/1 priority date for international students. Applications are processed on a rolling basis. Application fee: $50. Electronic applications accepted. *Expenses:* Tuition, state resident: full-time $7020. Tuition, nonresident: full-time $22,518. *Required fees:* $2128. Tuition and fees vary according to degree level and program. *Financial support:* Research assistantships, teaching assistantships, scholarships/grants, tuition waivers, and unspecified assistantships available. Financial award applicants required to submit FAFSA. *Faculty research:* Entrepreneurship and innovation; strategy process; workplace interactions, relationships, and processes; leadership and culture; supply chain management. *Unit head:* Dr. Pamela S. Barr, Interim Chair, 404-413-7525, Fax: 404-413-7571. *Application contact:* Toby McChesney, Assistant Dean for Graduate Recruiting and Student Services, 404-413-7167, Fax: 404-413-7162, E-mail: rcbgradadmissions@gsu.edu.
Website: http://mgmt.robinson.gsu.edu/

Georgia State University, J. Mack Robinson College of Business, Institute of International Business, Atlanta, GA 30303. Offers international business (GMBA, MBA, MIB); international business and information technology (MBA); international entrepreneurship (MBA); MIB/MIA. *Program availability:* Part-time, evening/weekend. *Faculty:* 11 full-time (4 women). *Students:* 37 full-time (21 women); includes 19 minority (16 Black or African American, non-Hispanic/Latino; 1 Asian, non-Hispanic/Latino; 1 Hispanic/Latino; 1 Two or more races, non-Hispanic/Latino), 10 international. Average age 27. 44 applicants, 86% accepted, 18 enrolled. In 2017, 33 master's awarded. *Entrance requirements:* For master's, GRE or GMAT, transcripts from all institutions attended, resume, essays. Additional exam requirements/recommendations for international students: Required—TOEFL (minimum score 610 paper-based; 101 iBT), IELTS (minimum score 7). *Application deadline:* For fall admission, 5/1 priority date for domestic students, 2/1 priority date for international students; for spring admission, 9/15 priority date for domestic students, 5/1 priority date for international students. Applications are processed on a rolling basis. Application fee: $50. Electronic applications accepted. *Expenses:* Tuition, state resident: full-time $7020. Tuition, nonresident: full-time $22,518. *Required fees:* $2128. Tuition and fees vary according to degree level and program. *Financial support:* Research assistantships, teaching assistantships, scholarships/grants, tuition waivers (partial), and unspecified assistantships available. Financial award application deadline: 5/1. *Faculty research:* Business challenges in emerging markets (especially in India and China); interorganizational relationships in an international context, such as strategic alliances and global supply chain relations; globalization and entry mode strategy or new (or emerging) multinationals; emerging market development and business environments; cross-cultural effects on business processes and performance. *Unit head:* Dr. Daniel Bello, Professor/Director of the Institute of International Business, 404-413-7275, Fax: 404-413-7276. *Application contact:* Toby McChesney, Assistant Dean for Graduate Recruiting and Student Services, 404-413-7167, Fax: 404-413-7162, E-mail: rcbgradadmissions@gsu.edu.
Website: http://iib.gsu.edu/

Golden Gate University, Ageno School of Business, San Francisco, CA 94105-2968. Offers accounting (MBA); adaptive leadership (MBA); advanced financial planning (MS); business administration (EMBA, MBA, DBA); business analytics (MBA, MS); entrepreneurship (MBA); finance (MBA, MS, Certificate); financial life planning (Certificate); financial planning (MS, Certificate); global supply chain management (MBA, Certificate); human resource management (MBA, MS, Certificate); information technology management (MBA, MS, Certificate); international business (MBA); marketing (MBA, MS, Certificate); project management (MBA, MS, Certificate); psychology (MA, Certificate); public administration (EMPA, MBA); public administration leadership (Certificate); JD/MBA. *Program availability:* Part-time, evening/weekend. *Faculty:* 17 full-time (7 women), 280 part-time/adjunct (95 women). *Students:* 309 full-time (147 women), 527 part-time (266 women); includes 286 minority (56 Black or African American, non-Hispanic/Latino; 1 American Indian or Alaska Native, non-Hispanic/Latino; 131 Asian, non-Hispanic/Latino; 83 Hispanic/Latino; 4 Native Hawaiian or other Pacific Islander, non-Hispanic/Latino; 11 Two or more races, non-Hispanic/Latino), 209 international. Average age 35. 549 applicants, 66% accepted, 185 enrolled. *Degree requirements:* For doctorate, thesis/dissertation, qualifying examination. *Entrance requirements:* For master's, GMAT (for MBA), minimum GPA of 2.5 (MS). Additional exam requirements/recommendations for international students: Required—TOEFL (minimum score 550 paper-based; 79 iBT). *Application deadline:* For fall admission, 5/15 for domestic and international students; for winter admission, 1/15 for domestic and international students; for spring admission, 9/15 for domestic and international students. Applications are processed on a rolling basis. Application fee: $65 ($105 for international students). Electronic applications accepted. *Expenses:* $3,150 per 3-unit course. *Financial support:* Career-related internships or fieldwork, Federal Work-Study, institutionally sponsored loans, and scholarships/grants available. Support available to part-time students. Financial award applicants required to submit FAFSA. *Unit head:* Marianne Koch, Associate Dean, 415-442-6542, Fax: 415-442-6579, E-mail: mkoch@ggu.edu. *Application contact:* Angela Melero, Enrollment Services, 415-442-7800, Fax: 415-442-7807, E-mail: info@ggu.edu.
Website: http://www.ggu.edu/programs/business-and-management

Grand Canyon University, Colangelo College of Business, Phoenix, AZ 85017-1097. Offers accounting (MBA, MS); business analytics (MS); disaster preparedness and executive fire service leadership (MS); finance (MBA); general management (MBA); health systems management (MBA); information technology management (MS); leadership (MBA, MS); marketing (MBA); organizational leadership and entrepreneurship (MS); project management (MBA); sports business (MBA); strategic human resource management (MBA). *Accreditation:* ACBSP. *Program availability:* Part-time, evening/weekend, online learning. *Entrance requirements:* For master's, equivalent of two years' full-time professional work experience. Additional exam requirements/recommendations for international students: Required—TOEFL (minimum score 575 paper-based; 90 iBT), IELTS (minimum score 7). Electronic applications accepted.

Harrisburg University of Science and Technology, Program in Information Systems Engineering and Management, Harrisburg, PA 17101. Offers analytics (MS); digital government (MS); digital health (MS); entrepreneurship (MS); information security (MS); software engineering and systems development (MS). *Program availability:* Part-time, evening/weekend. *Degree requirements:* For master's, thesis optional. *Entrance requirements:* For master's, baccalaureate degree. Additional exam requirements/recommendations for international students: Required—TOEFL (minimum score 520 paper-based; 80 iBT). Recommended—IELTS (minimum score 6). Electronic applications accepted. *Faculty research:* Healthcare Informatics, material analysis, enterprise systems, circuit design, enterprise architectures.

Harrisburg University of Science and Technology, Program in Techpreneurship, Philadelphia, PA 19130. Offers MS.

HEC Montreal, School of Business Administration, Graduate Diploma Programs in Administration, Montréal, QC H3T 2A7, Canada. Offers business administration (Graduate Diploma); business analysis - information technology (Graduate Diploma); e-business (Graduate Diploma); entrepreneurship (Graduate Diploma); financial professions (Graduate Diploma); human resources (Graduate Diploma); management (Graduate Diploma); management and sustainable development (Graduate Diploma); management of cultural organizations (Graduate Diploma); marketing communication (Graduate Diploma); organizational development (Graduate Diploma); professional accounting (Graduate Diploma); supply chain management (Graduate Diploma); taxation (Graduate Diploma). All courses are given in French. *Students:* 380 full-time (210 women), 819 part-time (501 women). 1,195 applicants, 72% accepted, 673 enrolled. In 2017, 629 Graduate Diplomas awarded. *Entrance requirements:* For degree, bachelor's degree. Application fee: $88 Canadian dollars ($184 Canadian dollars for international students). Electronic applications accepted. *Expenses:* Tuition, state resident: full-time $2869 Canadian dollars; part-time $79.70 Canadian dollars per credit. Tuition, nonresident: full-time $8883 Canadian dollars; part-time $246.76 Canadian dollars per credit. *International tuition:* $19,648 Canadian dollars full-time. *Required fees:* $41.20 Canadian dollars per credit. $67.94 Canadian dollars per term. Tuition and fees vary according to degree level and program. *Financial support:* Research assistantships, teaching assistantships, and scholarships/grants available. Financial award application deadline: 9/2. *Faculty research:* Art management, business policy, entrepreneurship, new technologies, transportation. *Unit head:* Renaud Lachance, Director, 514-340-7165, E-mail: renaud.lachance@hec.ca. *Application contact:* Anny Caron, Administrative Director, 514-340-6151, Fax: 514-340-6411, E-mail: aide@hec.ca.
Website: http://www.hec.ca/programmes/dess/index.html

HEC Montreal, School of Business Administration, Master of Science Programs in Administration, Montréal, QC H3T 2A7, Canada. Offers accounting, management, control, and audit (M Sc); applied economics (M Sc); applied financial economics (M Sc); business analysis and information technologies (M Sc); business analysis (M Sc); business intelligence (M Sc); electronic commerce (M Sc); entrepreneurship-intrapreneurship-innovation (M Sc); finance (M Sc); financial engineering (M Sc); global supply chain management (M Sc); human resources management (M Sc); international business (M Sc); international logistics (M Sc); management (M Sc); management and social innovations (M Sc); management control (M Sc); marketing (M Sc); operations management (M Sc); organizational development (M Sc); strategy (M Sc); user exprerience in business context (M Sc). Most courses are given in French. *Accreditation:* AACSB. *Students:* 906 full-time (436 women), 259 part-time (136 women). 950 applicants, 63% accepted, 418 enrolled. In 2017, 440 master's awarded. *Entrance requirements:* For master's, bachelor's degree in business administration or equivalent. Additional exam requirements/recommendations for international students: Required—TAGE MAGE (minimum recommended score of 283), GMAT (minimum recommended score of 630), or GRE. *Application deadline:* For fall admission, 3/15 for domestic and international students; for winter admission, 9/15 for domestic and international students. Application fee: $88 Canadian dollars ($184 Canadian dollars for domestic and international students). Electronic applications accepted. *Expenses:* Tuition, state resident: full-time $2869 Canadian dollars; part-time $79.70 Canadian dollars per credit. Tuition, nonresident: full-time $8883 Canadian dollars; part-time $246.76 Canadian dollars per credit. *International tuition:* $19,648 Canadian dollars full-time. *Required fees:* $41.20 Canadian dollars per credit. $67.94 Canadian dollars per term. Tuition and fees vary according to degree level and program. *Financial support:* Research assistantships, teaching assistantships, and scholarships/grants available. Financial award application deadline: 9/2. *Unit head:* Dr. Marie-Helene Jobin, Director, 514-340-6283, E-mail: marie-helene.jobin@hec.ca. *Application contact:* Marianne de Moura, Administrative Director, 514-340-6151, Fax: 514-340-6411, E-mail: aide@hec.ca.
Website: http://www.hec.ca/programmes/maitrises/index.html

Hult International Business School, Graduate Programs, Cambridge, MA 02141. Offers business administration (EMBA); business analytics (MBA, MIB); business statistics (MBS); disruptive innovation (MDI); entrepreneurship (MBA, MIB); family business (MBA, MIB); finance (MBA, MF, MIB); international marketing (MIM); marketing (MBA, MIB); project management (MBA, MIB). MDI and MBS offered in San Francisco; MBA also offered in Boston, San Francisco, Dubai, Shanghai, and New York. *Entrance requirements:* For master's, GMAT, 3 years of work experience. Additional exam requirements/recommendations for international students: Required—TOEFL. Electronic applications accepted. *Expenses:* Contact institution.

IGlobal University, Graduate Programs, Vienna, VA 22182. Offers accounting (MBA); data management and analytics (MSIT); entrepreneurship (MBA); finance (MBA); global business management (MBA); health care management (MBA); hospitality and tourism management (MBA); human resources management (MBA); information technology (MBA); information technology systems and management (MSIT); leadership and management (MBA); project management (MBA); public service and administration (MBA); software design and management (MSIT).

Illinois Institute of Technology, Stuart School of Business, Program in Technological Entrepreneurship, Chicago, IL 60616. Offers MTE.

Indiana University–Purdue University Indianapolis, Kelley School of Business, Evening MBA Program, Indianapolis, IN 46202-5151. Offers accounting (MBA); entrepreneurship (MBA); finance (MBA); general administration (MBA); marketing (MBA); supply chain management (MBA); MBA/JD; MBA/MD; MBA/MHA; MBA/MS; MBA/MSA; MBA/MSE. *Program availability:* Part-time-only, evening/weekend, online learning. *Entrance requirements:* For master's, GMAT or GRE, 2 years of professional work experience. Additional exam requirements/recommendations for international students: Required—TOEFL or IELTS. Electronic applications accepted. *Expenses:* Contact institution. *Faculty research:* Entrepreneurship; corporate finance; international business; consumer behavior; supply chain; business law.

International University in Geneva, Business Programs, Geneva, Switzerland. Offers business administration (MBA, DBA); entrepreneurship (MBA); international business (MIB); international trade (MIT); sales and marketing (MBA). *Accreditation:* ACBSP. *Program availability:* Part-time, evening/weekend. *Degree requirements:* For master's, comprehensive exam. *Entrance requirements:* For master's, GMAT. Additional exam requirements/recommendations for international students: Required—TOEFL. Electronic applications accepted.

The International University of Monaco, Graduate Programs, Monte Carlo, Monaco. Offers entrepreneurship (EMBA, MBA); financial engineering (M Sc); hedge fund and private equity (M Sc); international marketing (EMBA, MBA); international wealth management (M Sc); luxury goods and services (EMBA, M Sc, MBA); wealth and asset management (EMBA, MBA). *Program availability:* Part-time. *Degree requirements:* For master's, comprehensive exam (for some programs), applied research project. *Entrance requirements:* Additional exam requirements/recommendations for international students: Required—TOEFL (minimum score 550 paper-based), IELTS. Electronic applications accepted. *Faculty research:* Gaming, leadership, disintermediation.

James Madison University, The Graduate School, College of Business, Program in Business Administration, Harrisonburg, VA 22801. Offers business (MBA), including executive leadership, information security, innovation. *Accreditation:* AACSB. *Program availability:* Part-time, evening/weekend, blended/hybrid learning. *Students:* 34 full-time (12 women), 96 part-time (33 women); includes 29 minority (10 Black or African American, non-Hispanic/Latino; 9 Asian, non-Hispanic/Latino; 8 Hispanic/Latino; 2 Two or more races, non-Hispanic/Latino), 3 international. Average age 30. In 2017, 39 master's awarded. Application fee: $55. Electronic applications accepted. *Expenses:* Tuition, state resident: full-time $10,512; part-time $438 per credit hour. Tuition, nonresident: full-time $28,358; part-time $1162 per credit hour. *Required fees:* $1128. *Financial support:* In 2017–18, 1 student received support. Federal Work-Study and 1 assistantship (averaging $7911) available. Financial award application deadline: 3/1; financial award applicants required to submit FAFSA. *Unit head:* Dr. Matthew A. Rutherford, Department Head, 540-568-8777, E-mail: rutherma@jmu.edu. *Application contact:* Lynette D. Michael, Director of Graduate Admissions, 540-568-6131 Ext. 6395, Fax: 540-568-7860, E-mail: michaeld@jmu.edu.
Website: http://www.jmu.edu/cob/graduate/mba/index.shtml

Kansas State University, Graduate School, College of Business, Program in Business Administration, Manhattan, KS 66506. Offers data analytics (MBA); finance (MBA); management (MBA); marketing (MBA); technology entrepreneurship (MBA). *Accreditation:* AACSB. *Program availability:* Part-time, 100% online. *Entrance requirements:* For master's, GMAT (minimum score of 500), minimum undergraduate GPA of 3.0. Additional exam requirements/recommendations for international students: Required—TOEFL (minimum score 550 paper-based; 79 iBT); Recommended—IELTS (minimum score 7). Electronic applications accepted. *Expenses:* Contact institution. *Faculty research:* Organizational citizenship behavior, service marketing, impression management, human resources management, lean manufacturing and supply chain management, financial market behavior and investment management, data analytics, corporate responsibility, technology entrepreneurship.

Lamar University, College of Graduate Studies, College of Business, Beaumont, TX 77701. Offers accounting (MBA); experiential business and entrepreneurship (MBA); healthcare administration (MBA); MSA/MBA. *Accreditation:* AACSB. *Program availability:* Part-time, evening/weekend. *Faculty:* 50 full-time (14 women), 6 part-time/adjunct (2 women). *Students:* 20 full-time (11 women), 228 part-time (118 women); includes 98 minority (58 Black or African American, non-Hispanic/Latino; 10 Asian, non-Hispanic/Latino; 26 Hispanic/Latino; 4 Two or more races, non-Hispanic/Latino), 32 international. Average age 32. 205 applicants, 92% accepted, 78 enrolled. In 2017, 69 master's awarded. *Degree requirements:* For master's, comprehensive exam (for some programs), thesis optional. *Entrance requirements:* For master's, GMAT. Additional exam requirements/recommendations for international students: Required—TOEFL (minimum score 550 paper-based; 79 iBT), IELTS (minimum score 6.5). *Application deadline:* For fall admission, 8/10 for domestic students, 7/1 for international students; for spring admission, 1/5 for domestic students, 12/1 for international students. Applications are processed on a rolling basis. Application fee: $25 ($50 for international students). Electronic applications accepted. *Expenses:* Contact institution. *Financial support:* Fellowships with tuition reimbursements, research assistantships with partial tuition reimbursements, career-related internships or fieldwork, Federal Work-Study, institutionally sponsored loans, scholarships/grants, and tuition waivers (partial) available. Support available to part-time students. Financial award application deadline: 4/1; financial award applicants required to submit FAFSA. *Faculty research:* Marketing, finance, quantitative methods, management information systems, legal, environmental. *Unit head:* Dr. Enrique R. Venta, Dean, 409-880-8603, Fax: 409-880-8088, E-mail: henry.venta@lamar.edu. *Application contact:* Deidre Mayer, Interim Director, Admissions and Academic Services, 409-880-8888, Fax: 409-880-7419, E-mail: gradmissions@lamar.edu.
Website: http://business.lamar.edu

Lehigh University, P.C. Rossin College of Engineering and Applied Science, Technical Entrepreneurship Program, Bethlehem, PA 18015. Offers M Eng. *Faculty:* 3 full-time (1 woman). *Students:* 19 full-time (7 women); includes 5 minority (2 Black or African American, non-Hispanic/Latino; 3 Hispanic/Latino), 3 international. Average age 23. 30 applicants, 100% accepted, 18 enrolled. In 2017, 23 master's awarded. *Entrance requirements:* For master's, bachelor's degree. Additional exam requirements/recommendations for international students: Required—TOEFL (minimum score 79 iBT). *Application deadline:* For fall admission, 4/15 for domestic and international students. Application fee: $75. Electronic applications accepted. *Financial support:* In 2017–18, 6 fellowships were awarded. Financial award application deadline: 2/15. *Unit head:* Dr. John B. Ochs, Director, 610-758-4593, Fax: 610-758-6131, E-mail: jbo0@lehigh.edu. *Application contact:* Jodie L. Johnson, Assistant Director, 610-758-4789, Fax: 610-758-6131, E-mail: jlk4@lehigh.edu.
Website: http://www.lehigh.edu/innovate

Lenoir-Rhyne University, Graduate Programs, Charles M. Snipes School of Business, Hickory, NC 28601. Offers accounting (MBA); business analytics and information technology (MBA); entrepreneurship (MBA); global business (MBA); healthcare administration (MBA); innovation and change management (MBA); leadership development (MBA). *Accreditation:* ACBSP. *Program availability:* Part-time, evening/weekend, online learning. *Degree requirements:* For master's, capstone course. *Entrance requirements:* For master's, GMAT, GRE, MAT, minimum undergraduate GPA of 2.7, graduate 3.0. Additional exam requirements/recommendations for international students: Required—TOEFL (minimum score 600 paper-based). Electronic applications accepted. *Expenses:* Contact institution.

Lindenwood University, Graduate Programs, Plaster School of Business and Entrepreneurship, St. Charles, MO 63301-1695. Offers accountancy (M Acc); accounting (MBA); business administration (MBA); entrepreneurial studies (MBA); finance (MBA, MS); human resource management (MBA); international business (MBA); leadership (MA); management (MBA); marketing (MBA, MS); nonprofit administration (MA); public administration (MBA); sport management (MA); supply chain management (MBA). *Accreditation:* ACBSP. *Program availability:* Part-time, evening/weekend, 100% online. *Faculty:* 15 full-time (8 women), 26 part-time/adjunct (9 women). *Students:* 201 full-time (116 women), 253 part-time (153 women); includes 102 minority (80 Black or African American, non-Hispanic/Latino; 2 American Indian or Alaska Native, non-Hispanic/Latino; 6 Asian, non-Hispanic/Latino; 7 Two or more races, non-Hispanic/Latino), 61 international. Average age 32. 370 applicants, 42% accepted, 134 enrolled. In 2017, 178 master's awarded. *Degree requirements:* For master's, comprehensive exam (for some programs), thesis (for some programs), minimum GPA

Entrepreneurship

of 3.0. *Entrance requirements:* For master's, interview, minimum undergraduate cumulative GPA of 3.0, letter of recommendation. Additional exam requirements/recommendations for international students: Required—TOEFL (minimum score 550 paper-based; 80 iBT); Recommended—IELTS (minimum score 6.5). *Application deadline:* For fall admission, 8/27 priority date for domestic and international students; for winter admission, 1/14 priority date for domestic and international students; for spring admission, 3/18 for domestic students, 3/18 priority date for international students; for summer admission, 6/3 priority date for domestic and international students. Applications are processed on a rolling basis. Application fee: $30 ($100 for international students). Electronic applications accepted. *Expenses:* Contact institution. *Financial support:* In 2017–18, 439 students received support. Career-related internships or fieldwork, Federal Work-Study, institutionally sponsored loans, scholarships/grants, tuition waivers (partial), and unspecified assistantships available. Financial award application deadline: 6/30; financial award applicants required to submit FAFSA. *Unit head:* Roger Ellis, Dean, School of Business and Entrepreneurship, 636-949-4839, E-mail: rellis@lindenwood.edu. *Application contact:* Kara Schilli, Director, Evening and Graduate Admissions, 636-949-4349, Fax: 636-949-4109, E-mail: adultadmissions@lindenwood.edu.
Website: http://www.lindenwood.edu/academics/academic-schools/robert-w-plaster-school-of-business-entrepreneurship/

Loyola University Chicago, Quinlan School of Business, MBA Programs, Chicago, IL 60611. Offers accounting (MBA); business ethics (MBA); derivative markets (MBA); economics (MBA); entrepreneurship (MBA); finance (MBA); healthcare management (MBA); human resources management (MBA); information systems management (MBA); international business (MBA); management (MBA); marketing (MBA); risk management (MBA); supply chain management (MBA). *Program availability:* Part-time, evening/weekend. *Faculty:* 84 full-time (28 women), 12 part-time/adjunct (3 women). *Students:* 253 full-time (118 women), 76 part-time (35 women); includes 83 minority (21 Black or African American, non-Hispanic/Latino; 1 American Indian or Alaska Native, non-Hispanic/Latino; 33 Asian, non-Hispanic/Latino; 24 Hispanic/Latino; 4 Two or more races, non-Hispanic/Latino), 37 international. Average age 30. 334 applicants, 52% accepted, 80 enrolled. In 2017, 220 master's awarded. *Entrance requirements:* For master's, GMAT or GRE, official transcripts, two letters of recommendation, statement of purpose, resume. Additional exam requirements/recommendations for international students: Required—TOEFL (minimum score 90 iBT) or IELTS (minimum score 6.5). *Application deadline:* For fall admission, 7/15 for domestic and international students; for winter admission, 10/1 for domestic and international students; for spring admission, 1/15 for domestic and international students; for summer admission, 4/1 for domestic and international students. Applications are processed on a rolling basis. Application fee: $50. Electronic applications accepted. Application fee is waived when completed online. *Expenses:* $4,488 per course. *Financial support:* In 2017–18, 11 students received support. Research assistantships, career-related internships or fieldwork, Federal Work-Study, scholarships/grants, and health care benefits available. *Faculty research:* Social enterprise and responsibility, emerging markets, supply chain management, risk management. *Unit head:* Katherine Acles, Assistant Dean for Graduate Programs, 312-915-6124, Fax: 312-915-7207, E-mail: kacles@luc.edu.

Lynn University, College of Business and Management, Boca Raton, FL 33431-5598. Offers business administration (MBA), including aviation management, entrepreneurial management, financial valuation and investment management, hospitality management, human resource management, international business management, marketing, media management, social innovation management, sports management, Web development. *Program availability:* Part-time, evening/weekend, 100% online, blended/hybrid learning. *Faculty:* 29 full-time (11 women), 19 part-time/adjunct (7 women). *Students:* 287 full-time (124 women), 195 part-time (105 women); includes 110 minority (44 Black or African American, non-Hispanic/Latino; 2 American Indian or Alaska Native, non-Hispanic/Latino; 11 Asian, non-Hispanic/Latino; 47 Hispanic/Latino; 6 Two or more races, non-Hispanic/Latino), 135 international. Average age 28. 293 applicants, 94% accepted, 192 enrolled. In 2017, 236 master's awarded. *Degree requirements:* For master's, thesis, minimum GPA of 3.0, strategic management seminar, written presentation reflecting the integration and application of theory to practice. *Entrance requirements:* For master's, bachelor's degree from accredited institution, minimum undergraduate GPA of 2.5, official undergraduate transcripts, resume, personal statement, letter of recommendation from academic or professional sources, writing sample demonstrating capacity to perform at graduate level. Additional exam requirements/recommendations for international students: Required—TOEFL (minimum score 550 paper-based; 80 iBT), IELTS (minimum score 6.5). *Application deadline:* For fall admission, 8/18 for domestic students, 8/4 for international students; for spring admission, 12/15 for domestic students, 12/1 for international students; for summer admission, 4/17 for domestic students, 4/3 for international students. Applications are processed on a rolling basis. Application fee: $45. Electronic applications accepted. *Expenses:* $740 per credit. *Financial support:* Career-related internships or fieldwork, Federal Work-Study, scholarships/grants, tuition waivers (full and partial), and unspecified assistantships available. Support available to part-time students. Financial award application deadline: 3/1; financial award applicants required to submit FAFSA. *Faculty research:* Knowledge economy, urban economy, U.S. manufacturing industries, leadership personality, stock market reactions to terrorism, personality psychology, industrial/organizational psychology. *Unit head:* Dr. RT Good, Dean of the College of Business and Management, 561-237-7458, E-mail: rgood@lynn.edu. *Application contact:* Steven Pruitt, Director of Graduate and Undergraduate Evening Admission, 561-237-7834, Fax: 561-237-7100, E-mail: spruitt@lynn.edu.
Website: http://www.lynn.edu/academics/colleges/business-and-management

Manhattanville College, School of Education, Program in Education Entrepreneurship, Purchase, NY 10577-2132. Offers M Ed. Program offered jointly with the School of Business. *Program availability:* Part-time, evening/weekend. *Faculty:* 1 full-time (0 women), 3 part-time/adjunct (1 woman). *Students:* 1 applicant, 100% accepted. *Degree requirements:* For master's, comprehensive exam (for some programs), thesis (for some programs), student teaching, research seminars, portfolios, internships, writing assessment. *Entrance requirements:* For master's, GRE or MAT (for programs leading to certification), minimum GPA of 3.0, 2 letters of recommendation, interview, essay (2-3 page personal statement that describes reasons for choosing teaching or educational leadership as profession and philosophy of education), proof of immunization (for those born after 1957). Additional exam requirements/recommendations for international students: Required—TOEFL (minimum score 600 paper-based; 110 iBT); Recommended—IELTS (minimum score 8). *Application deadline:* Applications are processed on a rolling basis. Application fee: $75. Electronic applications accepted. *Expenses:* $915 per credit. *Financial support:* Teaching assistantships, career-related internships or fieldwork, Federal Work-Study, institutionally sponsored loans, scholarships/grants, and unspecified assistantships available. Financial award application deadline: 3/15; financial award applicants required to submit FAFSA. *Unit head:* Dr. Shelly Wepner, Dean, 914-323-3153, Fax: 914-323-5493. *Application contact:* Alissa Wilson, Director, Graduate Admissions, 914-323-3150, Fax: 914-694-1732, E-mail: edschool@mville.edu.
Website: http://www.mville.edu/programs/educational-studies-education-entrepreneurship

Marlboro College, Graduate and Professional Studies, Program in Business Administration, Marlboro, VT 05344. Offers mission-driven organizations (MBA); project management (MBA); social innovation (MBA). *Program availability:* Part-time, evening/weekend, blended/hybrid learning. *Degree requirements:* For master's, 45 credits including a Master Workshop. *Entrance requirements:* For master's, letter of intent, essay, transcripts, 2 letters of recommendation. *Application deadline:* For fall admission, 7/1 priority date for domestic students; for winter admission, 11/1 priority date for domestic students. Applications are processed on a rolling basis. Application fee: $0. Electronic applications accepted. *Expenses:* $794 per credit. *Financial support:* Scholarships/grants available. Financial award applicants required to submit FAFSA. *Unit head:* Tristan Toleno, Co-Chair, 802-258-9200, Fax: 802-258-9201, E-mail: tristant@gradschool.marlboro.edu. *Application contact:* Amanda Mehegan, Assistant Director of Graduate Admissions, 802-258-9209, Fax: 802-258-9201, E-mail: graduateadmissions@marlboro.edu.
Website: https://www.marlboro.edu/academics/graduate/management

Marlboro College, Graduate and Professional Studies, Program in Management, Marlboro, VT 05344. Offers mission-driven organizations (MS); project management (MS); social innovation (MS). *Program availability:* Part-time, evening/weekend, blended/hybrid learning. *Degree requirements:* For master's, capstone project. *Entrance requirements:* For master's, statement of intent, 2 letters of recommendation. Additional exam requirements/recommendations for international students: Recommended—TOEFL (minimum score 577 paper-based; 90 iBT), IELTS (minimum score 7). *Application deadline:* For fall admission, 8/5 for domestic students; for winter admission, 12/5 for domestic students; for spring admission, 4/5 for domestic students. Applications are processed on a rolling basis. Application fee: $0. Electronic applications accepted. *Expenses:* $794 per credit. *Financial support:* Scholarships/grants available. Financial award applicants required to submit FAFSA. *Unit head:* Tristan Toleno, Co-Chair, 802-258-9200, Fax: 802-258-9201, E-mail: tristant@gradschool.marlboro.edu. *Application contact:* Amanda Mehegan, Assistant Director of Graduate Admissions, 802-258-9209, Fax: 802-258-9201, E-mail: graduateadmissions@marlboro.edu.
Website: https://www.marlboro.edu/academics/graduate/management

Marquette University, Graduate School of Management, Program in Business Administration, Milwaukee, WI 53201-1881. Offers business administration (MBA); economics (MBA); entrepreneurship (Certificate); finance (MBA); human resources (MBA); international business (MBA); management information systems (MBA); marketing (MBA); operations and supply chain management (MBA); sports business (MBA); JD/MBA; MBA/MA; MBA/MSN. *Accreditation:* AACSB. *Program availability:* Part-time, evening/weekend. *Degree requirements:* For Certificate, business plan. *Entrance requirements:* For master's, GMAT or GRE, letters of recommendation. Additional exam requirements/recommendations for international students: Required—TOEFL (minimum score 550 paper-based; 88 iBT), IELTS (minimum score 6.5), PTE. Electronic applications accepted. *Faculty research:* Ethics in the professions, services marketing, technology impact on decision-making, mentoring.

McGill University, Faculty of Graduate and Postdoctoral Studies, Desautels Faculty of Management, Montréal, QC H3A 2T5, Canada. Offers administration (PhD); entrepreneurial studies (MBA); finance (MBA); general management (Post Master's Certificate); information systems (MBA); international business (MBA); international practicing management (MM); management (MBA); management for development (MBA); manufacturing management (MMM); marketing (MBA); operations management (MBA); public accountancy (Diploma); strategic management (MBA); MBA/LL B; MD/MBA. MMM offered jointly with Faculty of Engineering; PhD with Concordia University, HEC Montreal, Université de Montréal, Université du Québec à Montréal.

Mercer University, Graduate Studies, Cecil B. Day Campus, Eugene W. Stetson School of Business and Economics (Atlanta), Atlanta, GA 30341. Offers accounting (M Acc); innovation (PMBA), including entrepreneurship; international business (MBA); DPT/MBA; M Div/MBA; MBA/M Acc; Pharm D/MBA. *Accreditation:* AACSB. *Program availability:* Part-time, evening/weekend, 100% online, blended/hybrid learning. *Faculty:* 22 full-time (8 women), 7 part-time/adjunct (3 women). *Students:* 222 full-time (130 women), 138 part-time (72 women); includes 154 minority (114 Black or African American, non-Hispanic/Latino; 1 American Indian or Alaska Native, non-Hispanic/Latino; 27 Asian, non-Hispanic/Latino; 8 Hispanic/Latino; 4 Two or more races, non-Hispanic/Latino), 76 international. Average age 31. 207 applicants, 77% accepted, 110 enrolled. In 2017, 124 master's awarded. *Entrance requirements:* For master's, GMAT or GRE. Additional exam requirements/recommendations for international students: Required—TOEFL (minimum score 550 paper-based, 80 iBT) or IELTS. *Application deadline:* For fall admission, 6/15 priority date for domestic and international students; for spring admission, 11/1 priority date for domestic and international students; for summer admission, 3/15 priority date for domestic and international students. Applications are processed on a rolling basis. Application fee: $50 ($100 for international students). Electronic applications accepted. *Expenses:* $740 per credit (for evening, online and 2-year MBA); $818 per credit (for full-time MBA); $42,500 per degree (for PMBA); $727 per credit (for MSBA and M Acc). *Financial support:* In 2017–18, 25 students received support. Federal Work-Study and tuition discounts available. Financial award application deadline: 5/1; financial award applicants required to submit FAFSA. *Faculty research:* Entrepreneurship, market studies, international business strategy, financial analysis. *Unit head:* Dr. Susan P. Gilbert, Dean, 678-547-6438, Fax: 678-547-6337, E-mail: gilbert_sp@mercer.edu. *Application contact:* Lael Whiteside, Director of Admissions, 678-547-6300, Fax: 678-547-6160, E-mail: whiteside_l@mercer.edu.
Website: http://business.mercer.edu

Mercyhurst University, Graduate Studies, Program in Organizational Leadership, Erie, PA 16546. Offers accounting (MS); higher education administration (MS); human resources (MS); organizational leadership (MS, Certificate); sports leadership (MS); strategy and innovation (MS). *Program availability:* Part-time, evening/weekend. *Degree requirements:* For master's, thesis. *Entrance requirements:* For master's, GRE General Test or MAT, interview, resume, essay, three professional references, transcripts. Additional exam requirements/recommendations for international students: Required—TOEFL (minimum score 80 iBT), IELTS (minimum score 6.5). Electronic applications accepted. *Faculty research:* Leadership training, organizational communication, leadership pedagogy.

Meredith College, School of Business, Raleigh, NC 27607-5298. Offers entrepreneurship and family business (MBA); human resource management (MBA); project management (MBA). *Accreditation:* AACSB. *Program availability:* Part-time, evening/weekend. *Students:* 5 full-time (all women), 88 part-time (73 women); includes 33 minority (24 Black or African American, non-Hispanic/Latino; 1 Asian, non-Hispanic/Latino; 6 Hispanic/Latino; 2 Two or more races, non-Hispanic/Latino), 4 international. Average age 34. 62 applicants, 63% accepted, 29 enrolled. In 2017, 18 master's awarded. *Degree requirements:* For master's, thesis optional. *Entrance requirements:* For master's, GMAT, interview, minimum GPA of 2.5, letters of recommendation. Additional exam requirements/recommendations for international students: Required—TOEFL. *Application deadline:* For fall admission, 7/1 priority date for domestic and international students; for spring admission, 11/1 priority date for domestic and international students. Applications are processed on a rolling basis. Application fee: $50. Electronic applications accepted. *Expenses:* Contact institution. *Financial support:*

Career-related internships or fieldwork, institutionally sponsored loans, scholarships/grants, and tuition waivers (partial) available. Support available to part-time students. Financial award application deadline: 2/15; financial award applicants required to submit FAFSA. *Unit head:* Kristie Ogilvie, Dean, 919-760-8432, Fax: 919-760-8470. Website: https://www.meredith.edu/school-of-business

Monroe College, King Graduate School, Bronx, NY 10468. Offers accounting (MS); business administration (MBA), including entrepreneurship, finance, general business administration, healthcare management, human resources, information technology, marketing; computer science (MS); criminal justice (MS); hospitality management (MS); public health (MPH), including biostatistics and epidemiology, community health, health administration and leadership. *Program availability:* Online learning. Application fee: $50. Website: https://www.monroecollege.edu/Degrees/King-Graduate-School/

New York University, Tandon School of Engineering, Major in Biotechnology and Entrepreneurship, New York, NY 10012-1019. Offers MS. *Faculty:* 20 full-time (4 women), 23 part-time/adjunct (4 women). *Students:* 12 full-time (5 women), 2 part-time (1 woman); includes 3 minority (all Asian, non-Hispanic/Latino), 10 international. Average age 25. 48 applicants, 56% accepted, 7 enrolled. In 2017, 8 master's awarded. *Entrance requirements:* Additional exam requirements/recommendations for international students: Required—TOEFL (minimum score 550 paper-based; 90 iBT); Recommended—IELTS (minimum score 7). *Application deadline:* For fall admission, 2/15 priority date for domestic and international students; for spring admission, 11/1 priority date for domestic and international students. Applications are processed on a rolling basis. Application fee: $75. Electronic applications accepted. *Expenses:* Tuition: Full-time $41,352; part-time $19,968 per year. *Required fees:* $2496; $1628 per unit. $814 per term. Tuition and fees vary according to course load and program. *Financial support:* Institutionally sponsored loans, scholarships/grants, and unspecified assistantships available. Support available to part-time students. Financial award applicants required to submit FAFSA. *Total annual research expenditures:* $1.6 million. *Unit head:* Dr. Evgeny Vulfson, Program Director, 646-997-3096, E-mail: ev494@nyu.edu. *Application contact:* Elizabeth Ensweiler, Senior Director of Graduate Enrollment and Graduate Admissions, 646-997-3182, E-mail: elizabeth.ensweiler@nyu.edu.

North Carolina State University, Graduate School, Poole College of Management, Program in Business Administration, Raleigh, NC 27695. Offers biosciences management (MBA); entrepreneurship and technology commercialization (MBA); financial management (MBA); innovation management (MBA); marketing management (MBA); services management (MBA); supply chain management (MBA). *Accreditation:* AACSB. *Program availability:* Part-time. *Degree requirements:* For master's, thesis optional. *Entrance requirements:* For master's, GMAT, interview, 3 letters of recommendation. Additional exam requirements/recommendations for international students: Required—TOEFL (minimum score 600 paper-based; 100 iBT). Electronic applications accepted. *Faculty research:* Manufacturing strategy, information systems, technology commercialization, managing research and development, historical stock returns.

Northeastern University, D'Amore-McKim School of Business, Boston, MA 02115-5096. Offers accounting (MS); business administration (EMBA, MBA); finance (MS); innovation (MS); international business (MS); international management (MS); taxation (MS); technological entrepreneurship (MS); JD/MBA; LL M/MBA; MBA/MSN; MS/MBA. *Accreditation:* AACSB. *Program availability:* Part-time, evening/weekend, online learning. *Faculty:* 184. *Students:* 1,489. In 2017, 800 master's awarded. *Entrance requirements:* For master's, GMAT or GRE. Application fee: $75. Electronic applications accepted. *Expenses:* Contact institution. *Financial support:* Scholarships/grants available. Financial award applicants required to submit FAFSA. *Unit head:* Dr. Raj Echambadi, Dean, D'Amore-McKim School of Business, 617-373-3232, Fax: 617-373-2056. *Application contact:* Evelyn Tate, Director, Graduate Recruitment and Admissions, 617-373-3258, E-mail: e.tate@northeastern.edu. Website: http://damore-mckim.northeastern.edu/

Northwestern University, The Graduate School, Kellogg School of Management, Management Programs, Evanston, IL 60208. Offers accounting information and management (MBA, PhD); analytical finance (MBA); business administration (MBA); decision sciences (MBA); entrepreneurship and innovation (MBA); finance (MBA, PhD); health enterprise management (MBA); human resources management (MBA); international business (MBA); management and organizations (MBA, PhD); management and organizations and sociology (PhD); management and strategy (MBA); management studies (MS); managerial analytics (MBA); managerial economics (MBA); managerial economics and strategy (PhD); marketing (MBA, PhD); marketing management (MBA); media management (MBA); operations management (MBA, PhD); real estate (MBA); social enterprise at Kellogg (MBA); JD/MBA. *Program availability:* Part-time, evening/weekend. Terminal master's awarded for partial completion of doctoral program. *Degree requirements:* For doctorate, thesis/dissertation, 2 years of coursework, qualifying (field) exam and candidacy, summer research papers and presentations to faculty, proposal defense, final exam/defense. *Entrance requirements:* For master's, GMAT, GRE, interview, 2 letters of recommendation, college transcripts, resume, essays, Kellogg honor code; for doctorate, GMAT, GRE, statement of purpose, transcripts, 2 letters of recommendation, resume, interview. Additional exam requirements/recommendations for international students: Required—TOEFL, IELTS. Electronic applications accepted. *Expenses:* Contact institution. *Faculty research:* Business cycles and international finance, health policy, networks, non-market strategy, consumer psychology.

Nova Southeastern University, H. Wayne Huizenga College of Business and Entrepreneurship, Fort Lauderdale, FL 33314-7796. Offers accounting (M Acc); business (MBA); business intelligence/analytics (MBA); complex health systems (MBA); enterprise informatics (MBA); entrepreneurship (MBA); finance (MBA); human resource management (MBA); international business (MBA); management (MBA); marketing (MBA); process improvement (MBA); public administration (MPA); real estate development (MS); sport revenue generation (MBA); supply chain management (MBA). *Accreditation:* NASPAA. *Program availability:* Part-time, evening/weekend, 100% online, blended/hybrid learning. *Faculty:* 85 full-time (37 women), 59 part-time/adjunct (19 women). *Students:* 1,999 full-time (1,225 women), 335 part-time (210 women); includes 1,516 minority (597 Black or African American, non-Hispanic/Latino; 4 American Indian or Alaska Native, non-Hispanic/Latino; 92 Asian, non-Hispanic/Latino; 789 Hispanic/Latino; 3 Native Hawaiian or other Pacific Islander, non-Hispanic/Latino; 31 Two or more races, non-Hispanic/Latino), 291 international. Average age 34. 1,269 applicants, 59% accepted, 551 enrolled. In 2017, 1,055 master's awarded. *Entrance requirements:* For master's, GMAT or GRE (depending on undergraduate GPA), official transcripts from all schools attended while in pursuit of bachelor's degree; minimum GPA of 2.5 from regionally-accredited institution. Additional exam requirements/recommendations for international students: Required—TOEFL (minimum score 550 paper-based; 79 iBT), IELTS (minimum score 6), PTE (minimum score 54). *Application deadline:* For fall admission, 8/5 priority date for domestic students, 7/29 priority date for international students; for winter admission, 12/16 priority date for domestic students, 12/9 priority date for international students; for summer admission, 4/21 priority date for domestic and international students. Applications are processed on a rolling basis. Application fee: $50. Electronic applications accepted. *Expenses:* $37,785 (online), $35,640 (in-classroom). *Financial support:* In 2017–18, 325 students received support. Federal

Work-Study and scholarships/grants available. Support available to part-time students. Financial award application deadline: 4/15; financial award applicants required to submit FAFSA. *Faculty research:* Entrepreneurship and venture capital, ethics and social responsibility, global commerce and cultures, business process management. *Unit head:* Dr. J. Preston Jones, Dean, 954-262-5127, E-mail: prestonj@nova.edu. *Application contact:* Zeida Rodriguez, Associate Director of Enrollment Services, 954-262-5163, Fax: 954-262-3822, E-mail: zeida@nova.edu. Website: http://www.huizenga.nova.edu/

Oakland University, Graduate Study and Lifelong Learning, School of Business Administration, Department of Management and Marketing, Rochester, MI 48309-4401. Offers business administration (MBA); entrepreneurship (Certificate); general management (Certificate); human resource management (Certificate); international business (Certificate); management and marketing (EMBA); marketing (Certificate). *Expenses:* Tuition, state resident: full-time $16,950; part-time $706.25 per credit. Tuition, nonresident: full-time $24,648; part-time $1027 per credit.

Oklahoma State University, Spears School of Business, School of Entrepreneurship, Stillwater, OK 74078. Offers MBA, MS, PhD. *Program availability:* Part-time. *Faculty:* 8 full-time (0 women). *Students:* 12 full-time (6 women), 18 part-time (3 women); includes 7 minority (3 Black or African American, non-Hispanic/Latino; 3 Hispanic/Latino; 1 Two or more races, non-Hispanic/Latino), 4 international. Average age 31. 9 applicants, 78% accepted, 7 enrolled. In 2017, 20 master's, 1 doctorate awarded. *Entrance requirements:* For master's and doctorate, GMAT. Additional exam requirements/recommendations for international students: Required—TOEFL (minimum score 550 paper-based; 89 iBT). *Application deadline:* For fall admission, 3/1 priority date for international students; for spring admission, 8/1 priority date for international students. Applications are processed on a rolling basis. Application fee: $40 ($75 for international students). Electronic applications accepted. *Expenses:* Tuition, state resident: full-time $4019; part-time $2679.60 per year. Tuition, nonresident: full-time $15,286; part-time $10,190.40 per year. *Required fees:* $2129; $1419 per unit. Tuition and fees vary according to program. *Financial support:* Research assistantships, teaching assistantships, career-related internships or fieldwork, Federal Work-Study, scholarships/grants, health care benefits, tuition waivers (partial), and unspecified assistantships available. Support available to part-time students. Financial award application deadline: 3/1; financial award applicants required to submit FAFSA. *Unit head:* Dr. Bruce Barringer, Department Head, 405-744-9702, E-mail: bruce.barringer@okstate.edu. Website: https://business.okstate.edu/entrepreneurship/

Old Dominion University, College of Arts and Letters, Institute for the Humanities, Norfolk, VA 23529. Offers arts and entrepreneurship (Certificate); cultural and human geography (MA); cultural studies (MA); gender and sexuality studies (MA); health, communication and culture (Certificate); media and popular culture studies (MA); philosophy and religious studies (MA); social justice and entrepreneurship (Certificate); visual studies (MA); world cultures (MA). *Program availability:* Part-time, evening/weekend. *Faculty:* 1 full-time (0 women), 1 part-time/adjunct (0 women). *Students:* 20 full-time (16 women), 13 part-time (8 women); includes 15 minority (8 Black or African American, non-Hispanic/Latino; 2 Asian, non-Hispanic/Latino; 2 Hispanic/Latino; 3 Two or more races, non-Hispanic/Latino). Average age 35. 27 applicants, 96% accepted, 22 enrolled. In 2017, 3 master's awarded. *Degree requirements:* For master's, thesis optional, project. *Entrance requirements:* For master's, GRE General Test, minimum GPA of 3.25. *Application deadline:* For fall admission, 6/15 for domestic students; for spring admission, 11/15 for domestic students; for summer admission, 4/15 for domestic students. Applications are processed on a rolling basis. Application fee: $50. Electronic applications accepted. *Expenses:* Tuition, state resident: full-time $8928; part-time $496 per credit. Tuition, nonresident: full-time $22,482; part-time $1249 per credit. *Required fees:* $66 per semester. *Financial support:* In 2017–18, 3 students received support, including 5 research assistantships (averaging $10,000 per year); career-related internships or fieldwork, scholarships/grants, and unspecified assistantships also available. Financial award application deadline: 3/15; financial award applicants required to submit FAFSA. *Faculty research:* Media studies, cultural studies, gender studies, American literature, philosophy, art history, cultural geography. *Unit head:* Dr. Avi D. Santo, Graduate Program Director, 757-683-3719, Fax: 757-683-6191, E-mail: humgpd@odu.edu. *Application contact:* Dr. David C. Earnest, Associate Dean, 757-683-6077, Fax: 757-683-5746, E-mail: dearnest@odu.edu. Website: http://al.odu.edu/hum/

Oral Roberts University, School of Business, Tulsa, OK 74171. Offers accounting (MBA); entrepreneurship (MBA); finance (MBA); international business (MBA); management (MBA); marketing (MBA); not for profit management (MNM). *Accreditation:* ACBSP. *Program availability:* Part-time, online learning. *Faculty:* 7 full-time (0 women), 5 part-time/adjunct (4 women). *Students:* 71 applicants, 94% accepted, 56 enrolled. *Degree requirements:* For master's, thesis optional. *Entrance requirements:* For master's, minimum cumulative GPA of 3.0 from regionally-accredited institution. *Application deadline:* Applications are processed on a rolling basis. Application fee: $35. Electronic applications accepted. Application fee is waived when completed online. *Financial support:* In 2017–18, 39 students received support. Scholarships/grants and unspecified assistantships available. Financial award application deadline: 6/1. *Faculty research:* Social media, international business and marketing. *Unit head:* Dr. Marshal Wright, Chair of the Graduate School of Business, 918-495-6988, E-mail: mwright@oru.edu. *Application contact:* Sam Park, Enrollment Counselor, 918-495-7179, E-mail: sampark@oru.edu. Website: http://www.oru.edu/university/departments/schools/bus

Pace University, Lubin School of Business, Program in Management, New York, NY 10038. Offers entrepreneurial studies (MBA); entrepreneurship (MBA); human resource management (MBA, MS); strategic management (MBA, MS). *Program availability:* Part-time, evening/weekend. *Students:* 58 full-time (37 women), 72 part-time (40 women); includes 38 minority (15 Black or African American, non-Hispanic/Latino; 7 Asian, non-Hispanic/Latino; 12 Hispanic/Latino; 4 Two or more races, non-Hispanic/Latino), 40 international. Average age 30. 160 applicants, 56% accepted, 38 enrolled. In 2017, 47 master's awarded. *Entrance requirements:* For master's, GMAT, GRE (GMAT not required for MS with 3 years of HR experience in a management position), undergraduate degree, transcripts from all accredited colleges/universities attended, two letters of recommendation, resume, personal statement. Additional exam requirements/recommendations for international students: Required—TOEFL (minimum score 90 iBT), IELTS (minimum score 7) or PTE (minimum score 61). *Application deadline:* For fall admission, 8/1 priority date for domestic students, 6/1 for international students; for spring admission, 12/1 for domestic students, 10/1 for international students. Applications are processed on a rolling basis. Application fee: $70. Electronic applications accepted. *Financial support:* Research assistantships, career-related internships or fieldwork, Federal Work-Study, and unspecified assistantships available. Support available to part-time students. Financial award application deadline: 2/15; financial award applicants required to submit FAFSA. *Unit head:* Dr. John C. Byrne, Chairperson, 212-618-6581, E-mail: jbyrne@pace.edu. *Application contact:* Susan Ford-Goldschein, Director of Graduate Admissions, 212-346-1531, Fax: 212-346-1585, E-mail: graduateadmission@pace.edu. Website: http://www.pace.edu/lubin/management-concentration-mba

Entrepreneurship

Penn State Great Valley, Graduate Studies, Management Division, Malvern, PA 19355-1488. Offers business administration (MBA); cyber security (Certificate); data analytics (MPS, MS, Certificate); distributed energy and grid modernization (Certificate); finance (M Fin); health sector management (Certificate); human resource management (Certificate); information science (MSIS); leadership development (MLD); new ventures and entrepreneurship (Certificate); sustainable management practices (Certificate). *Accreditation:* AACSB. *Unit head:* Dr. James A. Nemes, Chancellor, 610-648-3202, Fax: 610-725-5296. *Application contact:* JoAnn Kelly, Director of Admissions, 610-648-3315, Fax: 610-725-5296, E-mail: jek2@psu.edu.
Website: http://greatvalley.psu.edu/academics/masters-degrees/engineering-management

Penn State University Park, Graduate School, College of Engineering, Program in Engineering Leadership and Innovation Management, University Park, PA 16802. Offers M Eng. *Unit head:* Dr. Dena Lang, Associate Director of Engineering Leadership Research, E-mail: engrleadership@engr.psu.edu. *Application contact:* Lori Hawn, Director, Graduate Student Services, 814-865-1795, Fax: 814-863-4627, E-mail: l-gswww@lists.psu.edu.
Website: http://www.engr.psu.edu/students/grad-prospective/academic-areas/elim.aspx

Peru State College, Graduate Programs, Program in Organizational Management, Peru, NE 68421. Offers MS. Program offered online only. *Program availability:* Part-time, online learning. *Degree requirements:* For master's, thesis (for some programs). *Expenses:* Contact institution. *Faculty research:* Emotional intelligence.

Point Loma Nazarene University, Fermanian School of Business, San Diego, CA 92106-2899. Offers general business (MBA); healthcare management (MBA); innovation and entrepreneurship (MBA); organizational leadership (MBA); project management (MBA). *Accreditation:* ACBSP. *Program availability:* Part-time, evening/weekend. *Faculty:* 7 full-time (0 women), 5 part-time/adjunct (3 women). *Students:* 27 full-time (8 women), 94 part-time (45 women); includes 52 minority (6 Black or African American, non-Hispanic/Latino; 1 American Indian or Alaska Native, non-Hispanic/Latino; 7 Asian, non-Hispanic/Latino; 33 Hispanic/Latino; 5 Two or more races, non-Hispanic/Latino), 11 international. Average age 31. 74 applicants, 99% accepted, 56 enrolled. In 2017, 45 master's awarded. *Entrance requirements:* For master's, GMAT, letters of recommendation, essay, interview. Additional exam requirements/recommendations for international students: Required—TOEFL. *Application deadline:* For fall admission, 7/26 priority date for domestic students; for spring admission, 11/29 priority date for domestic students; for summer admission, 4/2 priority date for domestic students. Applications are processed on a rolling basis. Application fee: $50. Electronic applications accepted. *Expenses:* Contact institution. *Financial support:* Applicants required to submit FAFSA. *Unit head:* Jamie McIlwaine, Associate Dean, Graduate Business, 619-849-2721, E-mail: jmcilwai@pointloma.edu. *Application contact:* Joanie Joy, Senior Director of Enrollment Management, 619-329-6785, E-mail: gradinfo@pointloma.edu.
Website: https://www.pointloma.edu/schools-departments-colleges/fermanian-school-business

Pontificia Universidad Catolica Madre y Maestra, Graduate School, Faculty of Social and Administrative Sciences, Santiago, Dominican Republic. Offers business administration (MBA), including business development, finance, international business, management skills (M Mgmt, MBA), marketing, operations, strategic cost management, strategy, tourist destination planning and management; law (LL M), including civil law, corporate business law, criminal law, international relations, real estate law; management (M Mgmt), including higher financial management, insurance program administration, management skills (M Mgmt, MBA); psychology (MA), including clinical child and adolescent psychology, forensic psychology; strategic human resources (EMBA).

Purchase College, State University of New York, School of the Arts, Purchase, NY 10577-1400. Offers entrepreneurship in the arts (MA). *Program availability:* Part-time. *Degree requirements:* For master's, thesis. *Unit head:* Dr. Peggy De Cooke, Acting Dean, 914-251-4455, Fax: 914-251-4457, E-mail: peggy.decooke@purchase.edu.
Website: https://www.purchase.edu/academics/arts/

Purdue University Global, School of Business, Davenport, IA 52807. Offers business administration (MBA); change leadership (MS); entrepreneurship (MBA); finance (MBA); health care management (MBA, MS); human resource (MBA); international business (MBA); management (MS); marketing (MBA); project management (MBA, MS); supply chain management and logistics (MBA, MS). *Accreditation:* ACBSP. *Program availability:* Part-time, evening/weekend, online learning. *Entrance requirements:* Additional exam requirements/recommendations for international students: Required—TOEFL (minimum score 550 paper-based; 80 iBT). Electronic applications accepted.

Queen's University at Kingston, Queens School of Business, Program in Business Administration, Kingston, ON K7L 3N6, Canada. Offers consulting and project management (MBA); finance (MBA); innovation and entrepreneurship (MBA); marketing (MBA). *Degree requirements:* For master's, thesis optional, research project. *Entrance requirements:* For master's, GMAT, minimum B+ average. Additional exam requirements/recommendations for international students: Required—TOEFL. Electronic applications accepted. *Faculty research:* Management fundamentals, strategic thinking, global business, innovation and change, leadership.

Regent University, Graduate School, School of Business and Leadership, Virginia Beach, VA 23464-9800. Offers business administration (MBA), including accounting, economics, entrepreneurship, finance and investing, general management, healthcare management (MA, MBA), human resource management (MA, MBA), innovation management, leadership, marketing, not-for-profit management (MA, MBA); business analytics (MS); business and design management (MA); church leadership (MA); leadership (Certificate); organizational leadership (MA, PhD), including ecclesial leadership (DSL, PhD), entrepreneurial leadership (PhD), healthcare management (MA, MBA), human resource development (PhD), human resource management (MA, MBA), individualized studies (DSL, PhD), interdisciplinary studies (MA), leadership coaching and mentoring (MA), not-for-profit management (MA, MBA), organizational development consulting (MA), servant leadership (MA, DSL); strategic leadership (DSL), including ecclesial leadership (DSL, PhD), global consulting, healthcare leadership, individualized studies (DSL, PhD), leadership coaching, servant leadership (MA, DSL), strategic foresight. *Program availability:* Part-time, evening/weekend, 100% online, blended/hybrid learning. *Faculty:* 9 full-time (2 women), 38 part-time/adjunct (11 women). *Students:* 129 full-time (80 women), 1,152 part-time (598 women); includes 685 minority (546 Black or African American, non-Hispanic/Latino; 10 American Indian or Alaska Native, non-Hispanic/Latino; 29 Asian, non-Hispanic/Latino; 65 Hispanic/Latino; 6 Native Hawaiian or other Pacific Islander, non-Hispanic/Latino; 29 Two or more races, non-Hispanic/Latino), 62 international. Average age 41. 1,721 applicants, 48% accepted, 624 enrolled. In 2017, 125 master's, 69 doctorates awarded. *Degree requirements:* For master's, thesis or alternative, 3-credit hour culminating experience; for doctorate, thesis/dissertation. *Entrance requirements:* For master's, college transcripts, resume, essay; for doctorate, college transcripts, resume, essay, writing sample; for Certificate, writing sample, resume, transcripts. Additional exam requirements/recommendations for international students: Required—TOEFL (minimum score 577 paper-based). *Application deadline:* For fall admission, 5/1 priority date for domestic students; for spring admission, 10/1 priority date for domestic students. Applications are processed on a rolling basis. Application fee: $50. Electronic applications accepted. *Expenses:* $650 per credit (MA, MS, MBA); $995 per credit (PhD); $300 per semester technology fee. *Financial support:* In 2017–18, 829 students received support. Career-related internships or fieldwork, scholarships/grants, and unspecified assistantships available. Support available to part-time students. *Faculty research:* Servant leadership, global business, team effectiveness, technology utilization, leadership development. *Unit head:* Dr. Doris Gomez, Dean, 757-352-4886, Fax: 757-352-4634, E-mail: dorigom@regent.edu. *Application contact:* Heidi Cece, Assistant Vice President of Enrollment Management, 800-373-5504, Fax: 757-352-4381, E-mail: admissions@regent.edu.
Website: https://www.regent.edu/school-of-business-and-leadership/

Rensselaer Polytechnic Institute, Graduate School, Lally School of Management, Program in Technology Commercialization and Entrepreneurship, Troy, NY 12180-3590. Offers MS, MS/MBA. *Program availability:* Part-time. *Faculty:* 36 full-time (9 women), 5 part-time/adjunct (0 women). *Students:* 15 full-time (7 women), 3 part-time (1 woman); includes 7 minority (1 Black or African American, non-Hispanic/Latino; 3 Asian, non-Hispanic/Latino; 2 Hispanic/Latino; 1 Two or more races, non-Hispanic/Latino), 3 international. Average age 25. 17 applicants, 59% accepted, 6 enrolled. *Entrance requirements:* For master's, GMAT or GRE, personal statement. Additional exam requirements/recommendations for international students: Required—TOEFL (minimum score 570 paper-based; 88 iBT), IELTS (minimum score 6.5), PTE (minimum score 60). *Application deadline:* For fall admission, 1/1 for domestic and international students. Applications are processed on a rolling basis. Application fee: $75. Electronic applications accepted. *Expenses:* Tuition: Full-time $52,550; part-time $2125 per credit hour. *Required fees:* $2890. *Financial support:* Scholarships/grants available. Financial award application deadline: 1/1. *Unit head:* Dr. Hao Zhao, Graduate Program Director, 518-276-6818, E-mail: zhaoh@rpi.edu.
Website: https://lallyschool.rpi.edu/graduate-programs/ms-tce

Rochester Institute of Technology, Graduate Enrollment Services, Saunders College of Business, Marketing and Management Department, MS Program in Entrepreneurship and Innovative Ventures, Rochester, NY 14623. Offers MS. *Program availability:* Part-time, evening/weekend. *Students:* 15 full-time (6 women), 9 part-time (5 women), 4 international. Average age 28. 58 applicants, 47% accepted, 17 enrolled. In 2017, 12 master's awarded. *Entrance requirements:* For master's, GMAT or GRE, minimum GPA of 3.0 (recommended). Additional exam requirements/recommendations for international students: Required—TOEFL (minimum score 580 paper-based; 92 iBT), IELTS (minimum score 7), PTE (minimum score 63). *Application deadline:* Applications are processed on a rolling basis. Application fee: $65. Electronic applications accepted. *Expenses:* $1,815 per credit hour. *Financial support:* In 2017–18, 1 student received support. Research assistantships with partial tuition reimbursements available, teaching assistantships with partial tuition reimbursements available, career-related internships or fieldwork, scholarships/grants, and unspecified assistantships available. Support available to part-time students. Financial award applicants required to submit FAFSA. *Faculty research:* Technology management, creativity, and innovation; corporate social responsibility and business ethics; entrepreneurship; leadership; social capital/work relationships; social media and entrepreneurship. *Unit head:* Matt Cornwell, Assistant Director of Student Services and Outreach, 585-475-6916, E-mail: mcornwell@saunders.rit.edu. *Application contact:* Diane Ellison, Senior Associate Vice President, Graduate Enrollment Services, 585-475-2229, Fax: 585-475-7164, E-mail: gradinfo@rit.edu.
Website: http://saunders.rit.edu/programs/graduate/ms_eiv.php

Rockhurst University, Helzberg School of Management, Kansas City, MO 64110-2561. Offers accounting (MBA); business intelligence (MBA, Certificate); business intelligence and analytics (MS); data science (MBA, Certificate); entrepreneurship (MBA); finance (MBA); fundraising leadership (MBA, Certificate); healthcare management (MBA, Certificate); human capital (Certificate); international business (Certificate); management (MA, MBA, Certificate); nonprofit administration (Certificate); organizational development (Certificate); science leadership (Certificate). *Accreditation:* AACSB. *Program availability:* Part-time, evening/weekend. *Faculty:* 18 full-time (4 women), 20 part-time/adjunct (9 women). *Students:* 99 full-time (30 women), 355 part-time (132 women); includes 95 minority (30 Black or African American, non-Hispanic/Latino; 29 Asian, non-Hispanic/Latino; 25 Hispanic/Latino; 11 Two or more races, non-Hispanic/Latino), 8 international. Average age 32. 249 applicants, 81% accepted, 175 enrolled. In 2017, 145 master's, 17 other advanced degrees awarded. *Entrance requirements:* For master's, GMAT or GRE. Additional exam requirements/recommendations for international students: Required—TOEFL (minimum score 550 paper-based; 79 iBT). *Application deadline:* Applications are processed on a rolling basis. Application fee: $0. Electronic applications accepted. *Financial support:* Applicants required to submit FAFSA. *Faculty research:* Offshoring/outsourcing, systems analysis/synthesis, work teams, multilateral trade, path dependencies/creation. *Unit head:* Cheryl McConnell, Dean, 816-501-4201, Fax: 816-501-4650, E-mail: cheryl.mcconnell@rockhurst.edu. *Application contact:* Jonnae Hill, Director of Graduate Business Advising, 816-501-4823, E-mail: jonnae.hill@rockhurst.edu.
Website: https://www.rockhurst.edu/helzberg

Rollins College, Crummer Graduate School of Business, Winter Park, FL 32789-4499. Offers entrepreneurship (MBA); finance (MBA); international business (MBA); management (MBA). *Accreditation:* AACSB. *Program availability:* Part-time, evening/weekend, online learning. *Faculty:* 20 full-time (4 women). *Students:* 261 full-time (119 women), 114 part-time (45 women); includes 86 minority (24 Black or African American, non-Hispanic/Latino; 13 Asian, non-Hispanic/Latino; 44 Hispanic/Latino; 5 Two or more races, non-Hispanic/Latino), 31 international. Average age 32. In 2017, 134 master's awarded. *Degree requirements:* For master's, minimum GPA of 2.85. *Entrance requirements:* For master's, GMAT or GRE, official transcripts, two letters of recommendation, essay, current resume/curriculum vitae, interview. Additional exam requirements/recommendations for international students: Required—TOEFL (minimum score 100 iBT) or IELTS (minimum score 7). *Application deadline:* Applications are processed on a rolling basis. Application fee: $50. Electronic applications accepted. *Expenses:* Contact institution. *Financial support:* Scholarships/grants available. Support available to part-time students. Financial award applicants required to submit FAFSA. *Faculty research:* Sustainability, world financial markets, international business, market research, strategic marketing. *Unit head:* Deborah Crown, Dean, 407-646-2249, Fax: 407-646-1550, E-mail: dcrown@rollins.edu. *Application contact:* Maralyn E. Graham, Admissions Coordinator, 407-646-2405, Fax: 407-646-1550, E-mail: mbaadmissions@rollins.edu.
Website: http://www.rollins.edu/mba/

Salve Regina University, Program in Business Administration, Newport, RI 02840-4192. Offers cybersecurity issues in business (MBA); entrepreneurial enterprise (MBA); health care administration and management (MBA); nonprofit management (MBA); social ventures (MBA). *Program availability:* Part-time, evening/weekend, online learning. *Entrance requirements:* For master's, GMAT, GRE General Test, or MAT, 6 undergraduate credits each in accounting, economics, quantitative analysis and calculus or statistics. Additional exam requirements/recommendations for international students: Required—TOEFL (minimum score 600 paper-based; 100 iBT) or IELTS. Electronic applications accepted.

Samford University, Brock School of Business, Birmingham, AL 35229. Offers accountancy (M Acc); entrepreneurship (MBA); finance (MBA); marketing (MBA); JD/M Acc; JD/MBA; MBA/M Acc; MBA/M Div; MBA/MSEM; MBA/Pharm D. Programs offered jointly with Cumberland School of Law, Beeson School of Divinity, Howard College of Arts and Sciences, and McWhorter School of Pharmacy. *Accreditation:* AACSB. *Program availability:* Part-time, 100% online, blended/hybrid learning. *Faculty:* 8 full-time (1 woman), 5 part-time/adjunct (0 women). *Students:* 79 full-time (31 women), 18 part-time (8 women); includes 7 minority (2 Black or African American, non-Hispanic/Latino; 1 Asian, non-Hispanic/Latino; 3 Hispanic/Latino; 1 Two or more races, non-Hispanic/Latino), 8 international. Average age 28. 46 applicants, 78% accepted, 16 enrolled. In 2017, 78 master's awarded. *Degree requirements:* For master's, capstone course. *Entrance requirements:* For master's, GMAT or GRE, resume, transcripts; essay (international applicants only). Additional exam requirements/recommendations for international students: Required—TOEFL (minimum score 90 iBT), IELTS (minimum score 6.5). *Application deadline:* For fall admission, 8/1 for domestic and international students; for spring admission, 12/1 for domestic and international students; for summer admission, 5/1 for domestic and international students. Applications are processed on a rolling basis. Application fee: $35. Electronic applications accepted. Application fee is waived when completed online. *Expenses:* $813 per credit hour tuition; $425 per semester fees. *Financial support:* In 2017–18, 59 students received support. Scholarships/grants available. Financial award application deadline: 2/15; financial award applicants required to submit FAFSA. *Unit head:* Dr. Barbara Cartledge, Assistant Dean, 205-726-2935, Fax: 205-726-2540, E-mail: bhcartle@samford.edu. *Application contact:* Elizabeth Anne Gambrell, Associate Director, 205-726-2040, Fax: 205-726-2540, E-mail: eagambre@samford.edu.
Website: http://www.samford.edu/business

San Diego State University, Graduate and Research Affairs, College of Business Administration, Department of Management, San Diego, CA 92182. Offers entrepreneurship (MS); human resources management (MS); management science (MS). *Program availability:* Part-time, evening/weekend. *Degree requirements:* For master's, thesis or alternative. *Entrance requirements:* For master's, GMAT, resume, letters of reference. Additional exam requirements/recommendations for international students: Required—TOEFL. Electronic applications accepted.

San Francisco State University, Division of Graduate Studies, College of Business, Program in Business Administration, San Francisco, CA 94132-1722. Offers decision sciences/operations research (MBA); ethics and compliance (MBA); finance (MBA); global business and innovation (MBA); healthcare administration (MBA); hospitality and tourism management (MBA); information systems (MBA); leadership (MBA); marketing (MBA); nonprofit and social enterprise leadership (MBA); sustainable business (MBA). *Accreditation:* AACSB. *Program availability:* Part-time, evening/weekend. *Degree requirements:* For master's, thesis, essay test. *Entrance requirements:* For master's, GMAT, minimum GPA of 2.7 in last 60 units. Additional exam requirements/recommendations for international students: Required—TOEFL (minimum score 550 paper-based). *Application deadline:* For fall admission, 5/1 priority date for domestic students, 4/1 for international students; for spring admission, 11/1 for domestic students, 10/15 for international students. Applications are processed on a rolling basis. Application fee: $55. *Financial support:* Application deadline: 3/1. *Unit head:* Dr. Sanjit Sengupta, Faculty Director, 415-817-4366, Fax: 415-817-4340, E-mail: sengupta@sfsu.edu. *Application contact:* Christopher Kingston, Director of Student Advising, 415-817-4322, Fax: 415-817-4340, E-mail: cak@sfsu.edu.
Website: http://cob.sfsu.edu/graduate-programs/mba

Seton Hall University, Stillman School of Business, Programs in Business Administration, South Orange, NJ 07079-2697. Offers accounting (MBA); entrepreneurial studies (Certificate); finance (MBA); financial decision making (Certificate); information technology management (MBA); international business (MBA); management (MBA); marketing (MBA); sport management (MBA); supply chain management (MBA, Certificate). *Program availability:* Part-time, evening/weekend. *Faculty:* 29 full-time (4 women), 18 part-time/adjunct (0 women). *Students:* 140 full-time (58 women), 154 part-time (49 women); includes 66 minority (25 Black or African American, non-Hispanic/Latino; 14 Asian, non-Hispanic/Latino; 23 Hispanic/Latino; 4 Two or more races, non-Hispanic/Latino), 88 international. Average age 32. 406 applicants, 75% accepted, 100 enrolled. In 2017, 132 master's awarded. *Degree requirements:* For master's, 20 hours of community service (Social Responsibility Project). *Entrance requirements:* For master's, GMAT or CPA, GRE (waived based on work experience or advanced degree from AACSB institution), MS in business discipline, professional degree or designation (MD, JD, PhD, DVM, DDS, CPA, etc.), minimum undergraduate GPA of 3.0. Additional exam requirements/recommendations for international students: Required—TOEFL (minimum score 607 paper-based; 80 iBT), IELTS (minimum score 6), PTE. *Application deadline:* For fall admission, 5/31 priority date for domestic students, 4/30 priority date for international students; for spring admission, 10/31 priority date for domestic students, 9/30 priority date for international students; for summer admission, 3/31 priority date for domestic students. Applications are processed on a rolling basis. Application fee: $75. Electronic applications accepted. *Expenses:* $1,305 per credit; $126 fees (fall and spring semester), $51 (summer semester). *Financial support:* In 2017–18, 41 students received support, including 25 research assistantships with full tuition reimbursements available (averaging $3,644 per year); career-related internships or fieldwork, scholarships/grants, and unspecified assistantships also available. Financial award application deadline: 6/30; financial award applicants required to submit FAFSA. *Faculty research:* Sport, hedge funds, executive compensation, social media, legal studies. *Unit head:* Dr. Joyce Strawser, Dean, 973-761-9013, Fax: 973-761-9217, E-mail: joyce.strawser@shu.edu. *Application contact:* Alfred Ayoub, Director of Graduate Admissions, 973-761-9262, Fax: 973-761-9208, E-mail: alfred.ayoub@shu.edu.
Website: http://www.shu.edu/business/mba-programs.cfm

Seton Hill University, MBA Program, Greensburg, PA 15601. Offers entrepreneurship (MBA); forensic accounting and fraud examination (MBA); healthcare administration (MBA); management (MBA). *Program availability:* Part-time, evening/weekend. *Entrance requirements:* For master's, resume, 3 letters of recommendation, personal statement, transcripts. Additional exam requirements/recommendations for international students: Required—TOEFL (minimum score 600 paper-based; 100 iBT), IELTS (minimum score 6.5). *Application deadline:* Applications are processed on a rolling basis. Application fee: $0. Electronic applications accepted. *Expenses:* Tuition: Part-time $734 per credit. Tuition and fees vary according to class time, course level, course load and program. *Financial support:* Federal Work-Study, scholarships/grants, and tuition discounts available. Financial award application deadline: 8/15; financial award applicants required to submit FAFSA. *Unit head:* Dr. Douglas Nelson, Associate Professor, Business/MBA Program Director, E-mail: dnelson@setonhill.edu.
Website: http://www.setonhill.edu/academics/graduate_programs/mba

SIT Graduate Institute, Graduate Programs, Master's Program in Global Leadership and Social Innovation, Brattleboro, VT 05302-0676. Offers MA. *Program availability:* Online learning.

South Carolina State University, College of Graduate and Professional Studies, School of Business, Orangeburg, SC 29117-0001. Offers agribusiness (MBA);

entrepreneurship (MBA); general business administration (MBA); healthcare management (MBA). *Program availability:* Part-time, evening/weekend. *Faculty:* 7 full-time (3 women), 2 part-time/adjunct (0 women). *Students:* 20 full-time (10 women), 11 part-time (7 women); all minorities (all Black or African American, non-Hispanic/Latino). Average age 27. 12 applicants, 92% accepted, 11 enrolled. In 2017, 10 master's awarded. *Degree requirements:* For master's, comprehensive exam, business plan. *Entrance requirements:* For master's, GMAT, minimum GPA of 2.8. Additional exam requirements/recommendations for international students: Required—TOEFL. *Application deadline:* For fall admission, 6/15 for domestic and international students; for spring admission, 11/1 for domestic and international students. Application fee: $25. Electronic applications accepted. *Expenses:* Tuition, state resident: full-time $9388; part-time $607 per credit hour. Tuition, nonresident: full-time $19,968; part-time $1194 per credit hour. *Required fees:* $766; $766 per credit hour. *Financial support:* Fellowships, research assistantships, career-related internships or fieldwork, Federal Work-Study, scholarships/grants, and unspecified assistantships available. Financial award application deadline: 6/1. *Unit head:* Dr. David Jamison, Interim Chair, 803-536-8443, Fax: 803-536-8078, E-mail: djamison@scsu.edu. *Application contact:* Ellen R. Ricoma, MBA Program Director, 803-533-3777, Fax: 803-516-4651, E-mail: ericoma1@scsu.edu.

Southeastern University, Jannetides College of Business and Entrepreneurial Leadership, Lakeland, FL 33801-6099. Offers executive leadership (MBA); global business administration (MBA); healthcare administration (MBA); missional leadership (MBA); organizational leadership (PhD); sport management (MBA); strategic leadership (DSL). *Accreditation:* ACBSP. *Program availability:* Evening/weekend, online learning. *Faculty:* 10 full-time (2 women), 8 part-time/adjunct (1 woman). *Students:* 80 full-time (38 women), 110 part-time (54 women); includes 51 minority (18 Black or African American, non-Hispanic/Latino; 5 Asian, non-Hispanic/Latino; 28 Hispanic/Latino), 7 international. Average age 31. *Entrance requirements:* For master's, GMAT, minimum cumulative GPA of 3.0, writing sample. *Application fee:* $50. Electronic applications accepted. *Unit head:* Lyle L. Bowlin, Dean, 863-667-5118, E-mail: llbowlin@seu.edu.
Website: http://www.seu.edu/business/

Southeast Missouri State University, School of Graduate Studies, Harrison College of Business, Cape Girardeau, MO 63701-4799. Offers accounting (MBA); entrepreneurship (MBA); financial management (MBA); sport management (MBA). *Accreditation:* AACSB. *Program availability:* Part-time, evening/weekend, 100% online. *Faculty:* 27 full-time (7 women), 1 (woman) part-time/adjunct. *Students:* 71 full-time (38 women), 68 part-time (31 women); includes 13 minority (7 Black or African American, non-Hispanic/Latino; 4 Asian, non-Hispanic/Latino; 2 Two or more races, non-Hispanic/Latino), 47 international. Average age 30. 51 applicants, 100% accepted, 51 enrolled. In 2017, 95 master's awarded. *Degree requirements:* For master's, variable foreign language requirement, comprehensive exam (for some programs), thesis or alternative. *Entrance requirements:* For master's, GMAT or GRE, minimum undergraduate GPA of 2.5, minimum grade of C in prerequisite courses. Additional exam requirements/recommendations for international students: Required—TOEFL (minimum score 550 paper-based; 79 iBT), IELTS (minimum score 6), PTE (minimum score 53). *Application deadline:* For fall admission, 8/1 for domestic students, 6/1 for international students; for spring admission, 11/21 for domestic students, 10/1 for international students; for summer admission, 5/15 for domestic students. Applications are processed on a rolling basis. Application fee: $30 ($40 for international students). Electronic applications accepted. *Expenses:* $270.35 per credit hour in-state tuition, $33.40 per credit hour fees. *Financial support:* In 2017–18, 26 students received support. Career-related internships or fieldwork, Federal Work-Study, scholarships/grants, traineeships, tuition waivers (full), and unspecified assistantships available. Financial award application deadline: 6/30; financial award applicants required to submit FAFSA. *Faculty research:* Organizational justice, ethics, leadership, corporate finance, generational differences. *Unit head:* Dr. Judy A. Wiles, Interim Dean, Harrison College of Business, 573-651-2913, Fax: 573-651-5032, E-mail: jwiles@semo.edu.
Website: http://www.semo.edu/mba

Southern Methodist University, Cox School of Business, MBA Program, Dallas, TX 75275. Offers accounting (MBA, PMBA); business administration (EMBA); finance (MBA); financial statement analysis (PMBA); general business (MBA); information technology and operations management (MBA); management (MBA); marketing (MBA); real estate (MBA); strategy (MBA); strategy and entrepreneurship (MBA); JD/MBA; MA/MBA. *Program availability:* Part-time, evening/weekend. *Entrance requirements:* For master's, GMAT. Additional exam requirements/recommendations for international students: Required—TOEFL. Electronic applications accepted. *Expenses:* Contact institution. *Faculty research:* Corporate finance, financial reporting, modeling consumer decision-making, competition between national brands and store brands, institutional determinants of firms' strategy.

Southern Methodist University, Cox School of Business, Program in Entrepreneurship, Dallas, TX 75275. Offers MS.

Southern New Hampshire University, School of Business, Manchester, NH 03106-1045. Offers accounting (MBA, Graduate Certificate); accounting finance (MS); accounting/auditing (MS); accounting/forensic accounting (MS); accounting/management accounting (MS); accounting/taxation (MS); applied economics (MS); athletic administration (MBA, Graduate Certificate); business administration (IMBA, Certificate), including business information systems (Certificate), human resource management (Certificate); business analytics (MBA); business intelligence (MBA); communication (MA), including new media and marketing, public relations; community economic development (MBA); criminal justice (MA); data analytics (MS); economics (MBA); engineering management (MBA); entrepreneurship (MBA); finance (MBA, MS, Graduate Certificate); finance/corporate finance (MS); finance/investments (MS); forensic accounting (MBA); forensic accounting and fraud examination (Graduate Certificate); healthcare informatics (MBA); healthcare management (MBA); human resource management (MS); human resources (MBA); information technology (MS); information technology management (MBA); international business (PhD); Internet marketing (MBA); leadership (MBA); leadership of nonprofit organizations (Graduate Certificate); management (MS); marketing (MBA, MS, Graduate Certificate); music business (MBA); operations and project management (MS); operations and supply chain management (MBA, Graduate Certificate); organizational leadership (MS); project management (MBA, Graduate Certificate); public administration (MBA, Graduate Certificate); quantitative analysis (MBA); Six Sigma (Graduate Certificate); Six Sigma quality (MBA); social media marketing (MBA, Graduate Certificate); sport management (MBA, MS, Graduate Certificate); sustainability and environmental compliance (MBA); MBA/Certificate. *Accreditation:* ACBSP. *Program availability:* Part-time, evening/weekend, online learning. Terminal master's awarded for partial completion of doctoral program. *Degree requirements:* For master's, one foreign language, comprehensive exam (for some programs), thesis or alternative; for doctorate, one foreign language, comprehensive exam, thesis/dissertation. *Entrance requirements:* For master's, minimum GPA of 2.5; for doctorate, GMAT. Additional exam requirements/recommendations for international students: Required—TOEFL (minimum score 500 paper-based). *Application deadline:* Applications are processed on a rolling basis. Application fee: $40. Electronic applications accepted. *Expenses:* Tuition: Part-time

Entrepreneurship

$627 per credit hour. Part-time tuition and fees vary according to campus/location and program. *Financial support:* Career-related internships or fieldwork, Federal Work-Study, institutionally sponsored loans, scholarships/grants, tuition waivers (partial), and unspecified assistantships available. Support available to part-time students. Financial award applicants required to submit FAFSA. *Unit head:* Dr. Bill Lightfoot, Dean, 603-644-3102, Fax: 603-644-3144. *Application contact:* Office of Graduate Admission, 888-327-SNHU, Fax: 603-644-3144, E-mail: enroll@snhu.edu.

South University, Graduate Programs, College of Business, Savannah, GA 31406. Offers corrections (MBA); entrepreneurship and small business (MBA); healthcare administration (MBA); hospitality management (MBA); leadership (MS); public administration (MPA); sustainability (MBA).

Stevens Institute of Technology, Graduate School, School of Business, Program in Business Administration, Hoboken, NJ 07030. Offers business intelligence and analytics (MBA); engineering management (MBA); finance (MBA); information systems (MBA); innovation and entrepreneurship (MBA); marketing (MBA); pharmaceutical management (MBA); project management (MBA, Certificate); technology management (MBA); telecommunications management (MBA). *Accreditation:* AACSB. *Program availability:* Part-time, evening/weekend. *Students:* 46 full-time (19 women), 179 part-time (88 women); includes 46 minority (10 Black or African American, non-Hispanic/Latino; 2 American Indian or Alaska Native, non-Hispanic/Latino; 30 Asian, non-Hispanic/Latino; 4 Hispanic/Latino), 45 international. Average age 36. 218 applicants, 49% accepted, 53 enrolled. In 2017, 33 master's awarded. *Degree requirements:* For master's, thesis optional, minimum B average in major field and overall; for Certificate, minimum B average. *Entrance requirements:* Additional exam requirements/recommendations for international students: Required—TOEFL (minimum score 74 iBT), IELTS (minimum score 6). *Application deadline:* For fall admission, 7/1 for domestic students, 4/15 for international students; for spring admission, 12/1 for domestic and international students. Applications are processed on a rolling basis. Application fee: $60. Electronic applications accepted. *Expenses: Tuition:* Full-time $34,494; part-time $1554 per credit. *Required fees:* $291 per semester. *Financial support:* Fellowships, research assistantships, teaching assistantships, career-related internships or fieldwork, Federal Work-Study, scholarships/grants, and unspecified assistantships available. Financial award application deadline: 2/15; financial award applicants required to submit FAFSA. *Unit head:* Dr. Gregory Prastacos, Dean, 201-216-8366, E-mail: gprastac@stevens.edu. *Application contact:* Graduate Admissions, 888-783-8367, Fax: 888-511-1306, E-mail: graduate@stevens.edu.
Website: https://www.stevens.edu/school-business/masters-programs/mbaemba

Stevens Institute of Technology, Graduate School, School of Business, Program in Information Systems, Hoboken, NJ 07030. Offers computer science (MS); e-commerce (MS); enterprise systems (MS); entrepreneurial information technology (MS); information architecture (MS); information management (MS, Certificate); information security (MS); information technology in financial services industry (MS); information technology in the pharmaceutical industry (MS); information technology outsourcing management (MS); project management (MS); software engineering (MS); telecommunications management (MS, Certificate). *Program availability:* Part-time, evening/weekend. *Students:* 321 full-time (110 women), 58 part-time (18 women); includes 22 minority (7 Black or African American, non-Hispanic/Latino; 15 Asian, non-Hispanic/Latino), 321 international. Average age 26. 877 applicants, 67% accepted, 117 enrolled. In 2017, 168 master's, 2 other advanced degrees awarded. *Degree requirements:* For master's, thesis optional, minimum B average in major field and overall; for Certificate, minimum B average. *Entrance requirements:* Additional exam requirements/recommendations for international students: Required—TOEFL (minimum score 74 iBT), IELTS (minimum score 6). *Application deadline:* For fall admission, 7/1 for domestic students, 4/15 for international students; for spring admission, 12/1 for domestic and international students. Applications are processed on a rolling basis. Application fee: $60. Electronic applications accepted. *Expenses: Tuition:* Full-time $34,494; part-time $1554 per credit. *Required fees:* $291 per semester. *Financial support:* Fellowships, research assistantships, teaching assistantships, career-related internships or fieldwork, Federal Work-Study, scholarships/grants, and unspecified assistantships available. Financial award application deadline: 2/15; financial award applicants required to submit FAFSA. *Unit head:* Dr. Gregory Prastacos, Dean, 201-216-8366, E-mail: gprastac@stevens.edu. *Application contact:* Graduate Admissions, 888-783-8367, Fax: 888-511-1306, E-mail: graduate@stevens.edu.
Website: https://www.stevens.edu/school-business/masters-programs/information-systems

Stony Brook University, State University of New York, Graduate School, College of Business, Program in Business Administration, Stony Brook, NY 11794. Offers accounting (MBA); business administration (MBA); finance (MBA, Certificate); health care management (MBA); human resources (MBA); innovation (MBA); management (MBA); marketing (MBA); operations management (MBA). *Faculty:* 39 full-time (13 women), 14 part-time/adjunct (5 women). *Students:* 181 full-time (98 women), 145 part-time (73 women); includes 68 minority (16 Black or African American, non-Hispanic/Latino; 1 American Indian or Alaska Native, non-Hispanic/Latino; 35 Asian, non-Hispanic/Latino; 11 Hispanic/Latino; 1 Native Hawaiian or other Pacific Islander, non-Hispanic/Latino; 4 Two or more races, non-Hispanic/Latino), 69 international. Average age 29. 154 applicants, 66% accepted, 58 enrolled. In 2017, 105 master's awarded. *Entrance requirements:* For master's, GMAT, 3 letters of recommendation from current or former employers or professors, transcripts, personal statement, resume. Additional exam requirements/recommendations for international students: Required—TOEFL (minimum score 550 paper-based; 90 iBT), IELTS (minimum score 6.5). *Application deadline:* For fall admission, 5/15 for domestic students, 3/15 for international students; for spring admission, 11/15 for domestic students, 10/15 for international students. Application fee: $100. *Expenses:* Contact institution. *Financial support:* Teaching assistantships available. *Total annual research expenditures:* $2,070. *Unit head:* Dr. Manuel London, Dean, 631-632-7159, E-mail: manuel.london@stonybrook.edu. *Application contact:* Dr. Dmytro Holod, Associate Dean for Academic Programs/Graduate Director, 631-632-7183, Fax: 631-632-8181, E-mail: dmytro.holod@stonybrook.edu.
Website: https://www.stonybrook.edu/commcms/business/

Suffolk University, Sawyer Business School, Master of Business Administration Program, Boston, MA 02108-2770. Offers accounting (MBA); entrepreneurship (MBA); executive business administration (EMBA); finance (MBA); global business administration (GMBA); health administration (MBA); international business (MBA); marketing (MBA); nonprofit management (MBA); organizational behavior (MBA); strategic management (MBA); supply chain management (MBA); taxation (MBA); JD/MBA; MBA/MHA; MBA/MSA; MBA/MSF; MBA/MST. *Accreditation:* AACSB. *Program availability:* Part-time, evening/weekend, 100% online. *Faculty:* 16 full-time (6 women), 9 part-time/adjunct (1 woman). *Students:* 106 full-time (57 women), 236 part-time (135 women); includes 80 minority (23 Black or African American, non-Hispanic/Latino; 23 Asian, non-Hispanic/Latino; 28 Hispanic/Latino; 6 Two or more races, non-Hispanic/Latino), 41 international. Average age 30. 354 applicants, 69% accepted, 115 enrolled. In 2017, 170 master's awarded. *Entrance requirements:* For master's, GMAT, minimum undergraduate GPA of 2.75 (MBA), 5 years of managerial experience (EMBA).

Additional exam requirements/recommendations for international students: Required—TOEFL (minimum score 550 paper-based; 80 iBT). *Application deadline:* For fall admission, 3/15 priority date for domestic students, 10/15 priority date for international students; for spring admission, 10/15 priority date for domestic and international students. Applications are processed on a rolling basis. Application fee: $50. Electronic applications accepted. *Expenses:* $43,980 per year full-time, $1,466 per credit part-time (for MBA); $1,794 per credit part-time (for Executive MBA). *Financial support:* In 2017–18, 198 students received support, including 1 fellowship (averaging $2,325 per year); career-related internships or fieldwork, Federal Work-Study, institutionally sponsored loans, and scholarships/grants also available. Support available to part-time students. Financial award application deadline: 4/1; financial award applicants required to submit FAFSA. *Faculty research:* Foreign investments; career strategies and boundaryless careers; corporate ethics codes; interest rates, inflation, and growth options; innovation and product development performance. *Unit head:* Jodi Detjen, Director of MBA Programs, 617-573-8306, E-mail: jdetjen@suffolk.edu. *Application contact:* Mara Marzocchi, Associate Director of Graduate Admissions, 617-573-8302, Fax: 617-305-1733, E-mail: grad.admission@suffolk.edu.
Website: http://www.suffolk.edu/mba

Syracuse University, Martin J. Whitman School of Management, Master of Business Administration Program, Syracuse, NY 13244. Offers accounting (MBA); business analytics (MBA); entrepreneurship (MBA); marketing management (MBA); real estate (MBA); supply chain management (MBA); JD/MBA. *Program availability:* Part-time, 100% online. *Students:* 22 full-time (9 women), 495 part-time (147 women); includes 182 minority (81 Black or African American, non-Hispanic/Latino; 3 American Indian or Alaska Native, non-Hispanic/Latino; 42 Asian, non-Hispanic/Latino; 52 Hispanic/Latino; 4 Native Hawaiian or other Pacific Islander, non-Hispanic/Latino). Average age 32. 1,086 applicants, 73% accepted, 516 enrolled. In 2017, 84 master's awarded. *Entrance requirements:* For master's, GMAT or GRE, resume, essay, 5-minute video interview, two letters of recommendation, transcripts (unofficial). Additional exam requirements/recommendations for international students: Required—TOEFL (minimum score 100 iBT), IELTS (minimum score 7), PTE (minimum score 68). *Application deadline:* For fall admission, 11/30 for domestic students, 11/30 priority date for international students; for winter admission, 1/1 for domestic students, 1/1 priority date for international students; for spring admission, 2/15 for domestic and international students; for summer admission, 4/19 for domestic students. Application fee: $75. Electronic applications accepted. *Expenses:* Contact institution. *Financial support:* In 2017–18, 22 students received support. Merit scholarships available. Financial award application deadline: 2/15. *Faculty research:* Data analysis, economics of international business, financial markets and institutions, operations management, supply chain management. *Unit head:* Dr. Alexander McKelvie, Associate Dean for Undergraduate and Full-time Master's Education, 315-443-7252, E-mail: mckelvie@syr.edu. *Application contact:* Shri Ramakrishnan, Assistant Director, Graduate Recruitment, 315-443-3497, Fax: 315-443-9517, E-mail: busgrad@syr.edu.
Website: http://whitman.syr.edu/ftmba/

Syracuse University, Martin J. Whitman School of Management, MS in Entrepreneurship Program, Syracuse, NY 13244. Offers MS. *Program availability:* Part-time, 100% online. *Students:* Average age 22. 24 applicants, 38% accepted, 4 enrolled. In 2017, 7 master's awarded. *Entrance requirements:* For master's, GMAT or GRE, resume, essay, one-page business plan, 5-minute video interview, two letters of recommendation, transcripts (unofficial). Additional exam requirements/recommendations for international students: Required—TOEFL (minimum score 100 iBT), IELTS (minimum score 7), PTE (minimum score 68), GMAT or GRE. *Application deadline:* For fall admission, 11/30 for domestic students, 11/30 priority date for international students; for winter admission, 1/1 for domestic students, 1/1 priority date for international students; for spring admission, 2/15 for domestic and international students; for summer admission, 4/19 for domestic students. Application fee: $75. Electronic applications accepted. *Expenses:* Contact institution. *Financial support:* In 2017–18, 4 students received support. Merit scholarships available. Financial award application deadline: 2/15. *Faculty research:* Entrepreneurship, emerging enterprises, financial markets and institutions, competitive strategy, opportunity recognition and ideation. *Unit head:* Dr. Alexander McKelvie, Chair, Department of Entrepreneurship and Emerging Enterprises, 315-443-7252, E-mail: mckelvie@syr.edu. *Application contact:* Shri Ramakrishnan, Assistant Director, Graduate Recruitment, 315-443-3497, Fax: 315-443-9517, E-mail: sramak01@syr.edu.
Website: http://whitman.syr.edu/programs-and-academics/programs/ms/eee/index.aspx

Temple University, Fox School of Business, Doctoral Programs in Business, Philadelphia, PA 19122-6096. Offers accounting (PhD); entrepreneurship (PhD); finance (PhD); international business (PhD); management information systems (PhD); marketing (PhD); risk management and insurance (PhD); statistics (PhD); strategic management (PhD); tourism and sport (PhD). *Accreditation:* AACSB. *Degree requirements:* For doctorate, thesis/dissertation. *Entrance requirements:* For doctorate, GRE General Test, GMAT, minimum GPA of 3.0, master's degree. Additional exam requirements/recommendations for international students: Required—TOEFL (minimum score 600 paper-based; 100 iBT), IELTS (minimum score 7.5). Electronic applications accepted. *Expenses:* Tuition, state resident: full-time $16,164; part-time $898 per credit hour. Tuition, nonresident: full-time $22,158; part-time $1231 per credit hour. *Required fees:* $890; $445 per semester. Full-time tuition and fees vary according to course load, degree level, campus/location and program.

Temple University, Fox School of Business, Specialized Master's Programs, Philadelphia, PA 19122-6096. Offers accountancy (MS); actuarial science (MS); finance (MS); financial engineering (MS); human resource management (MS); innovation management and entrepreneurship (MS); marketing (MS); statistics (MS). MS in innovation management and entrepreneurship delivered jointly with College of Engineering. *Accreditation:* AACSB. *Program availability:* Part-time. *Entrance requirements:* For master's, GRE General Test or GMAT, minimum undergraduate GPA of 3.0. Additional exam requirements/recommendations for international students: Required—TOEFL (minimum score 600 paper-based; 100 iBT), IELTS (minimum score 7.5). *Expenses:* Tuition, state resident: full-time $16,164; part-time $898 per credit hour. Tuition, nonresident: full-time $22,158; part-time $1231 per credit hour. *Required fees:* $890; $445 per semester. Full-time tuition and fees vary according to course load, degree level, campus/location and program.

Texas A&M University, Mays Business School, Department of Management, College Station, TX 77843. Offers entrepreneurial leadership (MS); human resource management (MS). *Faculty:* 32. *Students:* 90 full-time (63 women); includes 20 minority (3 Black or African American, non-Hispanic/Latino; 2 American Indian or Alaska Native, non-Hispanic/Latino; 2 Asian, non-Hispanic/Latino; 10 Hispanic/Latino; 3 Two or more races, non-Hispanic/Latino), 5 international. Average age 26. 163 applicants, 31% accepted, 40 enrolled. In 2017, 45 master's awarded. Terminal master's awarded for partial completion of doctoral program. *Degree requirements:* For master's, comprehensive exam. *Entrance requirements:* For master's, GMAT or GRE. Additional exam requirements/recommendations for international students: Required—TOEFL (minimum score 550 paper-based; 80 iBT), IELTS (minimum score 6), PTE (minimum score 53). *Application deadline:* For fall admission, 5/26 for domestic and international

students. Applications are processed on a rolling basis. Application fee: $50 ($90 for international students). Electronic applications accepted. *Expenses:* Contact institution. *Financial support:* In 2017–18, 76 students received support, including 28 research assistantships with tuition reimbursements available (averaging $8,154 per year), 24 teaching assistantships with tuition reimbursements available (averaging $4,822 per year); career-related internships or fieldwork, institutionally sponsored loans, scholarships/grants, traineeships, health care benefits, tuition waivers (full and partial), and unspecified assistantships also available. Support available to part-time students. Financial award application deadline: 3/15; financial award applicants required to submit FAFSA. *Faculty research:* Strategic and human resource management, business and public policy, organizational behavior, organizational theory. *Unit head:* Dr. Wendy R. Boswell, Head, 979-845-4045, Fax: 979-845-9641, E-mail: wboswell@mays.tamu.edu. *Application contact:* Kristi R. Mora, Senior Academic Advisor II, 979-845-6127, Fax: 979-845-9641, E-mail: kmora@mays.tamu.edu.
Website: http://mays.tamu.edu/mgmt/

Tufts University, School of Engineering, The Gordon Institute, Medford, MA 02155. Offers engineering management (MS); innovation and management (MS). *Program availability:* Part-time. *Faculty:* 7 full-time, 25 part-time/adjunct. *Students:* 204 full-time (68 women), 20 part-time (2 women); includes 54 minority (9 Black or African American, non-Hispanic/Latino; 28 Asian, non-Hispanic/Latino; 14 Hispanic/Latino; 3 Two or more races, non-Hispanic/Latino), 35 international. Average age 31. 118 applicants, 62% accepted, 62 enrolled. In 2017, 65 master's awarded. *Entrance requirements:* Additional exam requirements/recommendations for international students: Required—TOEFL (minimum score 550 paper-based; 80 iBT), IELTS (minimum score 6.5). *Application deadline:* For fall admission, 3/15 for domestic students, 1/15 for international students. Applications are processed on a rolling basis. Application fee: $85. Electronic applications accepted. *Expenses:* Contact institution. *Faculty research:* Engineering management, engineering leadership. *Unit head:* Nancy Buczko, Graduate Program Director. *Application contact:* Carla Eberle, Admissions Manager, 617-627-3395, E-mail: tgi@tufts.edu.
Website: http://gordon.tufts.edu/

Tulane University, A. B. Freeman School of Business, New Orleans, LA 70118-5669. Offers accounting (M Acct); analytics (MBA); banking and financial services (M Fin); energy (M Fin, MBA); entrepreneurship (MBA); finance (MBA, PhD); financial accounting (PhD); international business (MBA); international management (MBA); strategic management and leadership (MBA); JD/M Acct; JD/MBA; MBA/M Acc; MBA/MA; MBA/MD; MBA/ME; MBA/MPH. *Accreditation:* AACSB. *Program availability:* Part-time, evening/weekend. *Faculty:* 51 full-time (15 women), 38 part-time/adjunct (3 women). *Students:* 561 full-time (287 women), 297 part-time (151 women); includes 112 minority (43 Black or African American, non-Hispanic/Latino; 2 American Indian or Alaska Native, non-Hispanic/Latino; 24 Asian, non-Hispanic/Latino; 38 Hispanic/Latino; 5 Two or more races, non-Hispanic/Latino), 515 international. Average age 27. 2,021 applicants, 74% accepted, 476 enrolled. In 2017, 632 master's, 9 doctorates awarded. Terminal master's awarded for partial completion of doctoral program. *Degree requirements:* For master's, one foreign language, comprehensive exam (for some programs); for doctorate, one foreign language, comprehensive exam, thesis/dissertation. *Entrance requirements:* For master's and doctorate, GMAT or GRE, interview. Additional exam requirements/recommendations for international students: Required—TOEFL or IELTS. *Application deadline:* For fall admission, 11/1 priority date for domestic and international students; for winter admission, 1/6 for domestic and international students; for spring admission, 3/1 priority date for domestic and international students; for summer admission, 5/5 for domestic students. Applications are processed on a rolling basis. Application fee: $125. Electronic applications accepted. *Expenses:* Contact institution. *Financial support:* In 2017–18, 176 students received support. Fellowships with tuition reimbursements available, research assistantships, teaching assistantships, career-related internships or fieldwork, Federal Work-Study, tuition waivers (full and partial), and unspecified assistantships available. Support available to part-time students. Financial award application deadline: 4/15; financial award applicants required to submit FAFSA. *Faculty research:* Corporate finance, managerial accounting and financial reporting, strategic management and leadership, consumer behavior and decision making, organizational behavior and human resource management. *Unit head:* Ira Solomon, PhD, Dean, 504-865-5407, Fax: 504-865-5491, E-mail: businessdean@tulane.edu. *Application contact:* Melissa Booth, Assistant Dean for Graduate Admissions, 800-223-5402, E-mail: freeman.admissions@tulane.edu.
Website: http://www.freeman.tulane.edu

United States International University–Africa, School of Business Administration, Nairobi, Kenya. Offers business administration (GEMBA); entrepreneurship (MBA); finance (MBA); human resource management (MBA); information technology management (MBA); integrated studies (MBA); international business administration (MBA); management and organizational development (MBA); marketing (MBA); organizational development (EMS); strategic management (MBA). *Program availability:* Part-time, evening/weekend. *Degree requirements:* For master's, thesis. *Entrance requirements:* For master's, GMAT, 2 letters of reference, resume. Additional exam requirements/recommendations for international students: Required—TOEFL (minimum score 550 paper-based). *Faculty research:* Marketing in small business enterprises, total quality management in Kenya.

Université Laval, Faculty of Administrative Sciences, Programs in Business Administration, Québec, QC G1K 7P4, Canada. Offers accounting (MBA); agri-food management (MBA); electronic business (MBA, Diploma); factory management and logistics (MBA); finance (MBA); firm management (MBA); geomatic management (MBA); information technology management (MBA); international management (MBA); management (MBA); management accounting (MBA, Diploma); marketing (MBA); modeling and organizational decision (MBA); occupational health and safety management (MBA); pharmacy management (MBA); social and environmental responsibility (MBA); technological entrepreneurship (Diploma). *Accreditation:* AACSB. *Program availability:* Part-time, evening/weekend, online learning. *Entrance requirements:* For master's and Diploma, knowledge of French and English. Electronic applications accepted.

University at Albany, State University of New York, School of Business, MBA Programs, Albany, NY 12222. Offers business administration (MBA); cyber security (MBA); entrepreneurship (MBA); finance (MBA); human resource information systems (MBA); information systems and business analytics (MBA); marketing (MBA); JD/MBA. JD/MBA offered jointly with Albany Law School. *Program availability:* Part-time, evening/weekend. *Faculty:* 29 full-time (13 women), 9 part-time/adjunct (2 women). *Students:* 103 full-time (36 women), 188 part-time (69 women); includes 76 minority (27 Black or African American, non-Hispanic/Latino; 33 Asian, non-Hispanic/Latino; 16 Hispanic/Latino), 16 international. Average age 25. 181 applicants, 80% accepted, 114 enrolled. In 2017, 103 master's awarded. *Degree requirements:* For master's, thesis (for some programs), field or research project. *Entrance requirements:* For master's, GMAT, minimum undergraduate GPA of 3.0; 3 letters of recommendation; resume; statement of goals. Additional exam requirements/recommendations for international students: Required—TOEFL (minimum score 100 iBT); Recommended—IELTS (minimum score 7). *Application deadline:* For fall admission, 4/1 priority date for domestic students, 2/15 for international students; for spring admission, 12/1 for domestic students; for summer admission, 5/1 for domestic students. Applications are processed on a rolling basis. Application fee: $75. Electronic applications accepted. *Expenses:* $16,622.00 per year (for Full-Time MBA); $645 per credit hour (for Evening MBA). *Financial support:* In 2017–18, 25 students received support, including 7 fellowships with partial tuition reimbursements available (averaging $6,000 per year), 4 research assistantships with partial tuition reimbursements available, 21 teaching assistantships with partial tuition reimbursements available; unspecified assistantships also available. Financial award application deadline: 4/1; financial award applicants required to submit FAFSA. *Faculty research:* Social goods, information assurance, social computing, corporate entrepreneurship, asset pricing. *Total annual research expenditures:* $136,000. *Unit head:* Dr. Hany A. Shawky, Interim Dean, 518-956-8337, Fax: 518-442-3273, E-mail: hshawky@albany.edu. *Application contact:* Zina Mega Lawrence, Assistant Dean of Graduate Student Services, 518-956-8320, Fax: 518-442-4042, E-mail: zlawrence@albany.edu.
Website: https://graduatebusiness.albany.edu/

The University of Alabama in Huntsville, School of Graduate Studies, College of Business Administration, Programs in Business and Management, Huntsville, AL 35899. Offers business analytics (MSMS); federal contracting and procurement management (Certificate); human resource management (MSM); management (MBA), including acquisition management, entrepreneurship, federal contract accounting, finance, human resource management, logistics and supply chain management, marketing, project management; supply chain management (Certificate); technology and innovation management (Certificate). *Accreditation:* AACSB. *Program availability:* Part-time, evening/weekend. *Degree requirements:* For master's, comprehensive exam, thesis or alternative. *Entrance requirements:* For master's, GMAT (minimum score 500), minimum AACSB index of 1080. Additional exam requirements/recommendations for international students: Required—TOEFL (minimum score 550 paper-based; 80 iBT), IELTS (minimum score 6.5). Electronic applications accepted. *Faculty research:* Supply chain management, management of research and development, international marketing and branding, organizational behavior and human resource management, social networks and computational economics.

University of Arkansas at Little Rock, Graduate School, George W. Donaghey College of Engineering and Information Technology, Graduate Certificate in Technology Innovation Program, Little Rock, AR 72204-1099. Offers Graduate Certificate. *Program availability:* Part-time, evening/weekend. *Degree requirements:* For Graduate Certificate, 1 year of full-time study. *Entrance requirements:* For degree, minimum GPA of 2.75 on undergraduate work or 3.0 in the last 60 hours of undergraduate credit. Additional exam requirements/recommendations for international students: Required—TOEFL (minimum score 525 paper-based). Electronic applications accepted. *Faculty research:* Web computing, robotics, text mining, technology foresight, biotechnology.

University of Baltimore, Graduate School, Merrick School of Business, Department of Marketing and Entrepreneurship, Baltimore, MD 21201-5779. Offers innovation management and technology commercialization (MS). *Program availability:* Part-time, evening/weekend. *Entrance requirements:* For master's, GMAT. Additional exam requirements/recommendations for international students: Required—TOEFL (minimum score 550 paper-based). Electronic applications accepted.

University of Bridgeport, School of Business, Bridgeport, CT 06604. Offers accounting (MBA); finance (MBA); general business (MBA); global financial services (MBA); human resource management (MBA); information systems and knowledge management (MBA); international business (MBA); management (MBA); marketing (MBA); operations management (MBA); small business and entrepreneurship (MBA); specialized business (MBA). *Accreditation:* ACBSP. *Program availability:* Part-time, evening/weekend. *Degree requirements:* For master's, thesis optional. *Entrance requirements:* For master's, GMAT. Additional exam requirements/recommendations for international students: Recommended—TOEFL (minimum score 550 paper-based; 80 iBT), IELTS (minimum score 6.5). Electronic applications accepted. *Expenses:* Contact institution.

University of California, Davis, Graduate School of Management, Full-Time MBA Program, Davis, CA 95616. Offers business analytics and technologies (MBA); entrepreneurship and innovation (MBA); finance and accounting (MBA); general management (MBA); marketing (MBA); organizational behavior (MBA); public health management (MBA); strategy (MBA); technology management (MBA); DVM/MBA; JD/MBA; M Engr/MBA; MBA/MPH; MBA/MS; MD/MBA; MSN/MBA; PhD/MBA. *Faculty:* 52 full-time (15 women). *Students:* 96 full-time (42 women); includes 31 minority (1 Black or African American, non-Hispanic/Latino; 17 Asian, non-Hispanic/Latino; 5 Hispanic/Latino; 8 Two or more races, non-Hispanic/Latino), 36 international. Average age 29. 290 applicants, 37% accepted, 45 enrolled. In 2017, 44 master's awarded. *Degree requirements:* For master's, integrated management project. *Entrance requirements:* For master's, GMAT or GRE, letters of recommendation, resume, essays, equivalent of a 4-year U.S. undergraduate degree, transcript. Additional exam requirements/recommendations for international students: Required—TOEFL (minimum score 600 paper-based; 100 iBT), IELTS (minimum score 7). *Application deadline:* For fall admission, 5/18 priority date for domestic and international students. Application fee: $125. Electronic applications accepted. *Expenses:* Contact institution. *Financial support:* In 2017–18, 90 students received support. Fellowships, research assistantships, teaching assistantships with partial tuition reimbursements available, institutionally sponsored loans, scholarships/grants, health care benefits, tuition waivers (partial), and unspecified assistantships available. Financial award application deadline: 3/1; financial award applicants required to submit FAFSA. *Faculty research:* Finance, marketing, management, business analytics, accounting. *Unit head:* James Stevens, Senior Assistant Dean of Student Affairs, 530-752-7658, Fax: 530-754-9355, E-mail: admissions@gsm.ucdavis.edu. *Application contact:* Kristy Bird MaKieve, Interim Director of Admissions, 530-754-5476, Fax: 530-754-9355, E-mail: admissions@gsm.ucdavis.edu.
Website: http://gsm.ucdavis.edu/daytime-mba-program

University of California, Davis, Graduate School of Management, MBA Programs in Sacramento and San Francisco Bay Area, Davis, CA 95616. Offers business analytics and technologies (MBA); entrepreneurship and innovation (MBA); finance and accounting (MBA); general management (MBA); marketing (MBA); organizational behavior (MBA); public health management (MBA); strategy (MBA); technology management (MBA). *Program availability:* Part-time-only, evening/weekend. *Faculty:* 99 part-time/adjunct (30 women). *Students:* 323 part-time (133 women); includes 148 minority (7 Black or African American, non-Hispanic/Latino; 96 Asian, non-Hispanic/Latino; 26 Hispanic/Latino; 1 Native Hawaiian or other Pacific Islander, non-Hispanic/Latino; 18 Two or more races, non-Hispanic/Latino), 37 international. Average age 30. 202 applicants, 75% accepted, 111 enrolled. In 2017, 112 master's awarded. *Degree requirements:* For master's, integrated management project. *Entrance requirements:* For master's, GMAT or GRE, letters of recommendation, resume, equivalent of a 4-year undergraduate degree. Additional exam requirements/recommendations for international students: Required—TOEFL (minimum score 600 paper-based; 100 iBT), IELTS (minimum score 7). *Application deadline:* For fall admission, 5/18 priority date for domestic and international students. Application fee: $125. Electronic applications accepted. *Expenses:* Contact institution. *Financial support:* In 2017–18, 67 students

Entrepreneurship

received support. Fellowships, teaching assistantships with partial tuition reimbursements available, scholarships/grants, and unspecified assistantships available. Support available to part-time students. Financial award application deadline: 3/1; financial award applicants required to submit FAFSA. *Faculty research:* Accounting, finance, marketing, management, business analytics. *Unit head:* James Stevens, Senior Assistant Dean of Student Affairs, 530-752-7658, Fax: 530-754-9355, E-mail: admissions@gsm.ucdavis.edu. *Application contact:* Kristy Bird MaKieve, Interim Director of Admissions, 530-754-5476, Fax: 530-754-9355, E-mail: admissions@gsm.ucdavis.edu.
Website: http://gsm.ucdavis.edu/mba-programs

University of California, Merced, Graduate Division, School of Engineering, Merced, CA 95343. Offers biological engineering and small scale technologies (MS, PhD); electrical engineering and computer science (MS, PhD); environmental systems (MS, PhD); management of innovation, sustainability, and technology (MM); mechanical engineering (MS); mechanical engineering and applied mechanics (PhD). *Faculty:* 55 full-time (13 women), 2 part-time/adjunct (1 woman). *Students:* 184 full-time (60 women), 1 part-time (0 women); includes 41 minority (2 Black or African American, non-Hispanic/Latino; 16 Asian, non-Hispanic/Latino; 18 Hispanic/Latino; 1 Native Hawaiian or other Pacific Islander, non-Hispanic/Latino; 4 Two or more races, non-Hispanic/Latino; 112 international. Average age 28. 348 applicants, 35% accepted, 55 enrolled. In 2017, 13 master's, 15 doctorates awarded. Terminal master's awarded for partial completion of doctoral program. *Degree requirements:* For master's, variable foreign language requirement, comprehensive exam, thesis or alternative; for doctorate, variable foreign language requirement, comprehensive exam, thesis/dissertation. *Entrance requirements:* For master's and doctorate, GRE. Additional exam requirements/recommendations for international students: Required—TOEFL (minimum score 550 paper-based; 80 iBT); Recommended—IELTS (minimum score 7). *Application deadline:* For fall admission, 1/15 priority date for domestic and international students. Applications are processed on a rolling basis. Application fee: $90 ($110 for international students). Electronic applications accepted. *Expenses:* Contact institution. *Financial support:* In 2017–18, 150 students received support, including 16 fellowships with full tuition reimbursements available (averaging $19,088 per year), 45 research assistantships with full tuition reimbursements available (averaging $18,389 per year), 89 teaching assistantships with full tuition reimbursements available (averaging $19,249 per year); scholarships/grants, traineeships, and health care benefits also available. Financial award application deadline: 1/15. *Faculty research:* Water resources, biotechnology, renewable energy, big data, cyber-physical systems. *Total annual research expenditures:* $3.3 million. *Unit head:* Dr. Mark Matsumoto, Dean, 209-228-4047, Fax: 209-228-4047, E-mail: mmatsumoto@ucmerced.edu. *Application contact:* Tsu Ya, Director of Admissions and Academic Services, 209-228-4521, Fax: 209-228-6906, E-mail: tya@ucmerced.edu.

University of Central Florida, College of Arts and Humanities, School of Visual Arts and Design, Orlando, FL 32816. Offers digital media (MA); emerging media (MFA), including animation and visual effects, digital media, entrepreneurial digital cinema, studio art and the computer. *Program availability:* Part-time. *Students:* 38 full-time (13 women), 9 part-time (3 women); includes 16 minority (6 Black or African American, non-Hispanic/Latino; 2 Asian, non-Hispanic/Latino; 8 Hispanic/Latino), 3 international. Average age 30. 61 applicants, 54% accepted, 20 enrolled. In 2017, 8 master's awarded. *Degree requirements:* For master's, comprehensive exam, thesis or alternative. *Entrance requirements:* For master's, GRE, letter of recommendation. Additional exam requirements/recommendations for international students: Required—TOEFL. *Application deadline:* For fall admission, 7/1 for domestic students. Application fee: $30. Electronic applications accepted. *Expenses:* Tuition, state resident: part-time $288.16 per credit hour. Tuition, nonresident: part-time $1073.31 per credit hour. Tuition and fees vary according to program. *Financial support:* In 2017–18, 17 students received support, including 7 fellowships with partial tuition reimbursements available (averaging $10,000 per year), 3 research assistantships with partial tuition reimbursements available (averaging $6,355 per year), 15 teaching assistantships with partial tuition reimbursements available (averaging $8,208 per year); scholarships/grants, health care benefits, and unspecified assistantships also available. Financial award application deadline: 3/1; financial award applicants required to submit FAFSA. *Unit head:* Dr. Rudy McDaniel, Director, 407-823-3145, E-mail: rudy@ucf.edu. *Application contact:* Associate Director, Graduate Admissions, 407-823-2766, Fax: 407-823-6442, E-mail: gradadmissions@ucf.edu.
Website: http://svad.cah.ucf.edu/

University of Central Florida, College of Business Administration, Department of Management, Orlando, FL 32816. Offers entrepreneurship (Graduate Certificate); management (MSM); technology ventures (Graduate Certificate). *Accreditation:* AACSB. *Program availability:* Part-time. *Students:* 73 part-time (38 women); includes 33 minority (10 Black or African American, non-Hispanic/Latino; 5 Asian, non-Hispanic/Latino; 15 Hispanic/Latino; 3 Two or more races, non-Hispanic/Latino). Average age 30. 68 applicants, 72% accepted, 39 enrolled. In 2017, 35 master's, 29 other advanced degrees awarded. *Degree requirements:* For master's, capstone course. *Entrance requirements:* For master's, GMAT, minimum GPA of 3.0 in last 60 hours, letters of recommendation, resume, goal statement. Additional exam requirements/recommendations for international students: Required—TOEFL. *Application deadline:* For fall admission, 6/15 for domestic students; for spring admission, 11/15 for domestic students. Application fee: $30. Electronic applications accepted. *Expenses:* Tuition, state resident: part-time $288.16 per credit hour. Tuition, nonresident: part-time $1073.31 per credit hour. Tuition and fees vary according to program. *Financial support:* Fellowships available. Financial award application deadline: 3/1; financial award applicants required to submit FAFSA. *Unit head:* Dr. Stephen Goodman, Chair, 407-823-2675, Fax: 407-823-3725, E-mail: sgoodman@ucf.edu. *Application contact:* Associate Director, Graduate Admissions, 407-823-2766, Fax: 407-823-6442, E-mail: gradadmissions@ucf.edu.
Website: http://business.ucf.edu/departments-schools/management/

University of Chicago, Booth School of Business, Full-Time MBA Program, Chicago, IL 60637. Offers accounting (MBA); analytic finance (MBA); analytic management (MBA); econometrics and statistics (MBA); economics (MBA); entrepreneurship (MBA); finance (MBA); general management (MBA); health administration and policy (Certificate); international business (MBA); managerial and organizational behavior (MBA); marketing analytics (MBA); marketing management (MBA); operations management (MBA); strategic management (MBA); MBA/AM; MBA/JD; MBA/MA; MBA/MD; MBA/MPP. *Accreditation:* AACSB. *Faculty:* 154 full-time (26 women), 61 part-time/adjunct (12 women). *Students:* 1,176 full-time (481 women). In 2017, 586 master's awarded. *Entrance requirements:* For master's, GMAT or GRE, transcripts, resume, 2 letters of recommendation, essays, interview. Additional exam requirements/recommendations for international students: Required—TOEFL, IELTS, or PTE. *Application deadline:* For fall admission, 9/1 for domestic and international students; for winter admission, 1/1 for domestic and international students; for spring admission, 4/1 for domestic and international students. Application fee: $250. Electronic applications accepted. *Expenses:* Contact institution. *Unit head:* Stacey Kole, Deputy Dean for Alumni, Corporate Relations, and the Full-time MBA Program, 773-702-7121. *Application contact:* Kurt Ahlm, Associate Dean for Student Recruitment and Admissions, 773-702-7369, Fax: 773-702-9085, E-mail: admissions@chicagobooth.edu.
Website: https://www.chicagobooth.edu/programs/full-time

University of Colorado Denver, Business School, Master of Business Administration Program, Denver, CO 80217. Offers bioinnovation and entrepreneurship (MBA); business intelligence (MBA); business strategy (MBA); business to business marketing (MBA); business to consumer marketing (MBA); change management (MBA); corporate financial management (MBA); enterprise technology management (MBA); entrepreneurship (MBA); health administration (MBA), including financial management, health administration, health information technologies, international health management and policy; human resources management (MBA); international business (MBA); investment management (MBA); managing for sustainability (MBA); sports and entertainment management (MBA). *Accreditation:* AACSB. *Program availability:* Part-time, evening/weekend, 100% online, blended/hybrid learning. *Degree requirements:* For master's, 48 semester hours, including 30 of core courses, 3 in international business, and 15 in electives from over 50 other business courses. *Entrance requirements:* For master's, GMAT, resume, official transcripts, essay, two letters of recommendation, financial statements (for international applicants). Additional exam requirements/recommendations for international students: Required—TOEFL (minimum score 560 paper-based; 83 iBT); Recommended—IELTS (minimum score 6.5). Electronic applications accepted. *Expenses:* Contact institution. *Faculty research:* Marketing, management, entrepreneurship, finance, health administration.

University of Colorado Denver, Business School, Program in Information Systems, Denver, CO 80217. Offers accounting and information systems audit and control (MS); business intelligence systems (MS); digital health entrepreneurship (MS); enterprise risk management (MS); enterprise technology management (MS); geographic information systems (MS); health information technology (MS); technology innovation and entrepreneurship (MS); Web and mobile computing (MS). *Program availability:* Part-time, evening/weekend, online learning. *Degree requirements:* For master's, 30 credit hours. *Entrance requirements:* For master's, GMAT, resume, essay, two letters of recommendation, financial statements (for international applicants). Additional exam requirements/recommendations for international students: Required—TOEFL (minimum score 525 paper-based; 71 iBT); Recommended—IELTS (minimum score 6.5). Electronic applications accepted. *Expenses:* Contact institution. *Faculty research:* Human-computer interaction, expert systems, database management, electronic commerce, object-oriented software development.

University of Colorado Denver, Business School, Program in Management and Organization, Denver, CO 80217. Offers business strategy (MS); change and innovation (MS); enterprise technology management (MS); entrepreneurship and innovation (MS); global management (MS); leadership (MS); managing for sustainability (MS); managing human resources (MS); sports and entertainment management (MS). *Accreditation:* AACSB. *Program availability:* Part-time, evening/weekend, online learning. *Degree requirements:* For master's, 30 semester hours (12 of required courses, 12 of management electives, and 6 of free electives). *Entrance requirements:* For master's, GMAT, resume, two letters of recommendation, essay, financial statements (for international applicants). Additional exam requirements/recommendations for international students: Required—TOEFL (minimum score 525 paper-based; 71 iBT); Recommended—IELTS (minimum score 6.5). Electronic applications accepted. *Expenses:* Contact institution. *Faculty research:* Human resource management, management of catastrophe, turnaround strategies.

University of Delaware, Alfred Lerner College of Business and Economics, Department of Economics, Newark, DE 19716. Offers economic education (PhD); economics (MA, MS, PhD); economics for entrepreneurship and educators (MA); MA/MBA. *Program availability:* Part-time. *Degree requirements:* For master's, comprehensive exam, thesis (for some programs), mathematics review exam, research project; for doctorate, comprehensive exam, thesis/dissertation, field exam. *Entrance requirements:* For master's, GMAT or GRE General Test, minimum GPA of 2.5; for doctorate, GRE General Test, minimum GPA of 3.5 in graduate economics course work. Additional exam requirements/recommendations for international students: Required—TOEFL (minimum score 550 paper-based). Electronic applications accepted. *Faculty research:* Applied quantitative economics, industrial organization, resource economics, monetary economics, labor economics.

University of Florida, Graduate School, Warrington College of Business Administration, Hough Graduate School of Business, Department of Finance, Insurance and Real Estate, Gainesville, FL 32611. Offers entrepreneurship (MS); finance (MS, PhD); financial services (Certificate); insurance (PhD); quantitative finance (PhD); real estate (MS); real estate and urban analysis (PhD); JD/MBA; JD/MS. Terminal master's awarded for partial completion of doctoral program. *Degree requirements:* For master's, comprehensive exam, thesis; for doctorate, comprehensive exam, thesis/dissertation. *Entrance requirements:* For master's, GMAT (minimum score of 465) or GRE General Test, minimum GPA of 3.0 for last 60 hours of undergraduate degree, work experience (preferred); for doctorate, GMAT (minimum score of 465) or GRE General Test, minimum GPA of 3.0. Additional exam requirements/recommendations for international students: Required—TOEFL (minimum score 550 paper-based; 80 iBT), IELTS (minimum score 6). Electronic applications accepted. *Faculty research:* Banking, empirical corporate finance, hedge funds.

University of Hawaii at Manoa, Office of Graduate Education, Shidler College of Business, The Pacific Asian Center for Entrepreneurship and E-Business (PACE), Honolulu, HI 96822. Offers entrepreneurship (Graduate Certificate). *Program availability:* Part-time. *Entrance requirements:* Additional exam requirements/recommendations for international students: Required—TOEFL (minimum score 500 paper-based; 61 iBT).

University of Hawaii at Manoa, Office of Graduate Education, Shidler College of Business, Program in Business Administration, Honolulu, HI 96822. Offers Asian business studies (MBA); Chinese business studies (MBA); decision sciences (MBA); entrepreneurship (MBA); finance (MBA); finance and banking (MBA); human resources management (MBA); information management (MBA); information technology (MBA); international business (MBA); Japanese business studies (MBA); marketing (MBA); organizational behavior (MBA); organizational management (MBA); real estate (MBA); student-designed track (MBA). *Accreditation:* AACSB. *Program availability:* Part-time, evening/weekend. *Degree requirements:* For master's, thesis optional. *Entrance requirements:* For master's, GMAT, minimum GPA of 3.0. Additional exam requirements/recommendations for international students: Required—TOEFL (minimum score 600 paper-based; 100 iBT), IELTS (minimum score 7). *Expenses:* Contact institution.

University of Houston–Victoria, School of Business Administration, Victoria, TX 77901-4450. Offers accounting (MBA); economic development and entrepreneurship (MS); (GMBA, MBA); general business (MBA); international business (MBA); management (GMBA, MBA); marketing (MBA). *Accreditation:* AACSB. *Program availability:* Part-time, evening/weekend, online learning. *Entrance requirements:* For master's, GMAT. Additional exam requirements/recommendations for international students: Required—TOEFL (minimum score 550 paper-based). Electronic applications accepted. *Faculty research:* Economic development, marketing, finance.

University of Louisville, Graduate School, College of Business, MBA Programs, Louisville, KY 40292-0001. Offers entrepreneurship (MBA); global business (MBA); health sector management (MBA). *Accreditation:* AACSB. *Program availability:* Part-time, evening/weekend. *Students:* 253 full-time (99 women), 21 part-time (6 women); includes 49 minority (25 Black or African American, non-Hispanic/Latino; 1 American Indian or Alaska Native, non-Hispanic/Latino; 10 Asian, non-Hispanic/Latino; 8 Hispanic/Latino; 5 Two or more races, non-Hispanic/Latino), 27 international. Average age 32. 295 applicants, 63% accepted, 155 enrolled. In 2017, 85 master's awarded. *Degree requirements:* For master's, international learning experience. *Entrance requirements:* For master's, GMAT, 2 letters of reference, personal interview, resume, personal statement, college transcript(s). Additional exam requirements/recommendations for international students: Required—TOEFL (minimum score 83 iBT). *Application deadline:* For fall admission, 7/1 for domestic students; for spring admission, 12/1 for domestic students. Applications are processed on a rolling basis. Application fee: $65. *Expenses:* Tuition, state resident: full-time $12,246; part-time $681 per credit hour. Tuition, nonresident: full-time $25,486; part-time $1417 per credit hour. *Required fees:* $196. Tuition and fees vary according to course load, program and reciprocity agreements. *Financial support:* Fellowships with full tuition reimbursements, research assistantships with full tuition reimbursements, health care benefits, and unspecified assistantships available. Financial award application deadline: 3/31; financial award applicants required to submit FAFSA. *Faculty research:* Entrepreneurship, venture capital, retailing/franchising, corporate governance and leadership, supply chain management. *Total annual research expenditures:* $859,000. *Unit head:* Dr. Todd Mooradian, Dean, 502-852-6443, Fax: 502-852-7557, E-mail: todd.mooradian@louisville.edu. *Application contact:* Susan E. Hildebrand, Program Director, 502-852-7257, Fax: 502-852-4901, E-mail: s.hildebrand@louisville.edu.
Website: http://business.louisville.edu/mba

University of Louisville, Graduate School, College of Business, PhD Program in Entrepreneurship, Louisville, KY 40292-0001. Offers PhD. *Faculty:* 4 full-time (1 woman). *Students:* 13 full-time (5 women), 1 part-time (0 women); includes 1 minority (Black or African American, non-Hispanic/Latino), 6 international. Average age 35. 17 applicants, 35% accepted, 5 enrolled. *Degree requirements:* For doctorate, comprehensive exam, thesis/dissertation, paper of sufficient quality for journal publication. *Entrance requirements:* For doctorate, GMAT, 3 letters of recommendation, curriculum vitae, personal interview. Additional exam requirements/recommendations for international students: Required—TOEFL (minimum score 83 iBT). *Application deadline:* For fall admission, 12/31 priority date for domestic students, 3/31 for international students. Applications are processed on a rolling basis. Application fee: $65. Electronic applications accepted. *Expenses:* Tuition, state resident: full-time $12,246; part-time $681 per credit hour. Tuition, nonresident: full-time $25,486; part-time $1417 per credit hour. *Required fees:* $196. Tuition and fees vary according to course load, program and reciprocity agreements. *Financial support:* Fellowships with full tuition reimbursements, research assistantships with full tuition reimbursements, teaching assistantships with full tuition reimbursements, scholarships/grants, health care benefits, and unspecified assistantships available. Financial award application deadline: 3/15; financial award applicants required to submit FAFSA. *Faculty research:* Entrepreneurship, supply chain management, venture capital, retailing/franchising, corporate governance. *Total annual research expenditures:* $133,436. *Unit head:* Dr. Todd Mooradian, Dean, 502-852-6443, Fax: 502-852-7557, E-mail: todd.mooradian@louisville.edu. *Application contact:* Susan E. Hildebrand, Program Director, 502-852-7257, Fax: 502-852-4901, E-mail: s.hildebrand@louisville.edu.
Website: http://business.louisville.edu/entrepreneurshipphd

University of Louisville, J. B. Speed School of Engineering, Department of Bioengineering, Louisville, KY 40292-0001. Offers advancing bioengineering technologies through entrepreneurship (PhD); bioengineering (M Eng, PhD). *Accreditation:* ABET. *Students:* 26 full-time (11 women), 13 part-time (4 women); includes 7 minority (1 Black or African American, non-Hispanic/Latino; 4 Asian, non-Hispanic/Latino; 1 Hispanic/Latino; 1 Two or more races, non-Hispanic/Latino). Average age 24. In 2017, 5 master's awarded. *Degree requirements:* For master's, thesis; for doctorate, comprehensive exam, thesis/dissertation. *Entrance requirements:* For master's, GRE, letters of recommendation, final official transcripts; for doctorate, GRE, three letters of recommendation, written statement describing previous experience related to bioengineering, written statement as to how the PhD in bioengineering will allow the applicant to fulfill their career goals. Additional exam requirements/recommendations for international students: Required—TOEFL (minimum score 550 paper-based; 80 iBT), IELTS (minimum score 6.5), GRE. *Application deadline:* For fall admission, 5/1 priority date for domestic and international students; for spring admission, 11/1 priority date for domestic and international students; for summer admission, 3/1 priority date for domestic and international students. Applications are processed on a rolling basis. Application fee: $65. Electronic applications accepted. *Expenses:* Tuition, state resident: full-time $12,246; part-time $681 per credit hour. Tuition, nonresident: full-time $25,486; part-time $1417 per credit hour. *Required fees:* $196. Tuition and fees vary according to course load, program and reciprocity agreements. *Financial support:* Fellowships with full tuition reimbursements, research assistantships with full tuition reimbursements, teaching assistantships with full tuition reimbursements, scholarships/grants, and health care benefits available. Financial award application deadline: 2/3. *Faculty research:* Injury risk assessment and prevention, bioimaging, interdisciplinary oncology, biomedical devices, biomes and cardiovascular mechanics, advanced heart failure research, nanotherapeutics, biomimetics and tissue engineering, vascular mechanics, drug, gene and protein delivery, bioinstrumentation and controls research and development, orthopedic bioengineering. *Total annual research expenditures:* $5.2 million. *Unit head:* Dr. Ayman El-Baz, Chair, 502-852-5092, E-mail: aselba01@louisville.edu. *Application contact:* Gina Bertocci, Director of Graduate Studies, 502-852-0296, E-mail: gina.bertocci@louisville.edu.
Website: https://louisville.edu/speed/bioengineering/

The University of Manchester, Alliance Manchester Business School, M15 6PB, United Kingdom. Offers accounting and finance (M Sc); business (M Ent); business analysis and strategic management (M Sc); business analytics: operational research and risk analysis (M Sc); business psychology (M Sc); corporate communications and reputation management (M Sc); finance (M Sc); finance and business economics (M Sc); human resource management and industrial relations (M Sc); innovation management and entrepreneurship (M Sc); international business and management (M Sc); international human resource management and comparative industrial relations (M Sc); management (M Sc); marketing (M Sc); operations, project and supply chain management (M Sc); organizational psychology (M Sc); quantitative finance (M Sc). *Entrance requirements:* For master's, UK 2:1 honours degree or overseas equivalent. Additional exam requirements/recommendations for international students: Required—TOEFL (minimum score 100 iBT), IELTS (minimum score 7), PTE. Electronic applications accepted. *Faculty research:* Accounting and finance, management sciences and marketing, people management and organization, innovation management and policy, decision sciences.

University of Massachusetts Amherst, Graduate School, Isenberg School of Management, Program in Management, Amherst, MA 01003. Offers accounting (PhD); business administration (MBA); entrepreneurship (MBA); finance (MBA, PhD); healthcare administration (MBA); hospitality and tourism management (PhD); management science (PhD); marketing (MBA, PhD); organization studies (PhD); sport management (PhD); strategic management (PhD); MBA/MS. *Accreditation:* AACSB. *Program availability:* Part-time, evening/weekend, online learning. Terminal master's awarded for partial completion of doctoral program. *Degree requirements:* For doctorate, comprehensive exam, thesis/dissertation. *Entrance requirements:* For master's and doctorate, GMAT or GRE General Test. Additional exam requirements/recommendations for international students: Required—TOEFL (minimum score 550 paper-based; 80 iBT), IELTS (minimum score 6.5). Electronic applications accepted.

University of Massachusetts Lowell, Manning School of Business, Lowell, MA 01854. Offers business administration (MBA, PhD); healthcare innovation and entrepreneurship (MS). *Accreditation:* AACSB. *Program availability:* Part-time, evening/weekend. *Entrance requirements:* For master's, GMAT.

University of Minnesota, Twin Cities Campus, Carlson School of Management, Doctoral Program in Business Administration, Minneapolis, MN 55455. Offers accounting (PhD); finance (PhD); information and decision sciences (PhD); marketing (PhD); strategic management and entrepreneurship (PhD); supply chain and operations (PhD); work and organizations (PhD). *Faculty:* 102 full-time (32 women). *Students:* 95 full-time (32 women); includes 10 minority (2 Black or African American, non-Hispanic/Latino; 7 Asian, non-Hispanic/Latino; 1 Hispanic/Latino), 68 international. Average age 30. 357 applicants, 6% accepted, 17 enrolled. In 2017, 14 doctorates awarded. *Degree requirements:* For doctorate, comprehensive exam, thesis/dissertation, written and oral preliminary exams, proposal defense, final defense. *Entrance requirements:* For doctorate, GMAT, GRE General Test, minimum undergraduate GPA of 3.0, graduate 3.5 (recommended). Additional exam requirements/recommendations for international students: Required—TOEFL (minimum score 600 paper-based, 100 iBT) or IELTS (minimum score 7.0). *Application deadline:* For fall admission, 12/15 for domestic students, 12/15 priority date for international students. Applications are processed on a rolling basis. Application fee: $75 ($95 for international students). Electronic applications accepted. *Expenses:* Contact institution. *Financial support:* In 2017–18, 80 students received support, including 80 fellowships with full tuition reimbursements available (averaging $13,000 per year), 73 research assistantships with full tuition reimbursements available (averaging $7,520 per year), 73 teaching assistantships with full tuition reimbursements available (averaging $7,520 per year); institutionally sponsored loans, scholarships/grants, health care benefits, unspecified assistantships, and full student service fee waivers also available. Financial award application deadline: 12/15. *Faculty research:* Finance, strategy and entrepreneurship, marketing, information and decision science, operations, accounting, supply chain, human resources and industrial relations, organizational behavior. *Unit head:* Dr. Shawn P. Curley, Director, 612-624-6546, Fax: 612-624-8221, E-mail: curley@umn.edu. *Application contact:* Sandy Herzan, Associate Director, 612-624-0875, Fax: 612-624-8221, E-mail: herza002@umn.edu.
Website: http://carlsonschool.umn.edu/degrees/phd

University of New Brunswick Fredericton, School of Graduate Studies, Faculty of Business Administration, Fredericton, NB E3B 5A3, Canada. Offers business administration (MBA); engineering management (MBA); entrepreneurship (MBA); sports and recreation management (MBA); MBA/LL B. *Program availability:* Part-time. *Degree requirements:* For master's, thesis optional. *Entrance requirements:* For master's, GMAT (minimum score 550), minimum GPA of 3.0; 3-5 years of work experience; 3 letters of reference with at least one academic reference. Additional exam requirements/recommendations for international students: Required—TOEFL (minimum score 580 paper-based; 92 iBT) or IELTS (minimum score 7). Electronic applications accepted. *Faculty research:* Entrepreneurship, finance, law, sport and recreation management, engineering management.

University of New Mexico, Anderson School of Management, Department of Finance, International, Technology and Entrepreneurship, Albuquerque, NM 87131-1221. Offers entrepreneurship (MBA); finance (MBA); international management (MBA); international management in Latin America (MBA); management of technology (MBA). *Program availability:* Part-time. *Faculty:* 13 full-time (1 woman), 6 part-time/adjunct (1 woman). In 2017, 47 master's awarded. *Entrance requirements:* For master's, GMAT or GRE, minimum GPA of 3.0 on last 60 hours of coursework; bachelor's degree from regionally-accredited college or university in U.S. or its equivalent in another country. Additional exam requirements/recommendations for international students: Required—TOEFL (minimum score 550 paper-based; 79 iBT), IELTS (minimum score 6.5). *Application deadline:* For fall admission, 4/1 priority date for domestic and international students; for spring admission, 10/1 priority date for domestic and international students. Applications are processed on a rolling basis. Application fee: $50. Electronic applications accepted. *Expenses:* Contact institution. *Financial support:* In 2017–18, 17 students received support, including 9 fellowships (averaging $18,720 per year), 12 research assistantships with partial tuition reimbursements available (averaging $15,291 per year); career-related internships or fieldwork, Federal Work-Study, scholarships/grants, and unspecified assistantships also available. Support available to part-time students. Financial award application deadline: 6/1; financial award applicants required to submit FAFSA. *Faculty research:* Corporate finance, investments, management in Latin America, management of technology, entrepreneurship. *Unit head:* Dr. Raul Gouvea, Chair, 505-277-6471, E-mail: rauldg@unm.edu. *Application contact:* Lisa Beauchene, Student Recruitment Specialist, 505-277-6471, E-mail: andersonadvising@unm.edu.
Website: https://www.mgt.unm.edu/fite/default.asp?mm-faculty

University of Notre Dame, Mendoza College of Business, Master of Business Administration Program, Notre Dame, IN 46556. Offers business analytics (MBA); business leadership (MBA); consulting (MBA); corporate finance (MBA); innovation and entrepreneurship (MBA); investments (MBA); marketing (MBA); MBA/MSBA. *Accreditation:* AACSB. *Faculty:* 60 full-time (10 women), 14 part-time/adjunct (1 woman). *Students:* 294 full-time (70 women); includes 46 minority (8 Black or African American, non-Hispanic/Latino; 3 American Indian or Alaska Native, non-Hispanic/Latino; 12 Asian, non-Hispanic/Latino; 20 Hispanic/Latino; 1 Native Hawaiian or other Pacific Islander, non-Hispanic/Latino; 2 Two or more races, non-Hispanic/Latino), 74 international. Average age 29. 633 applicants, 42% accepted, 131 enrolled. In 2017, 182 master's awarded. *Entrance requirements:* For master's, GMAT or GRE, work experience, essay, four-slide presentation, two recommendations, transcripts from all colleges and/or universities attended, interview. Additional exam requirements/recommendations for international students: Required—PTE (minimum score 68), TOEFL (minimum iBT score of 109), IELTS (7.5), or documentation of at least six semesters of full-time university education in English. *Application deadline:* For fall admission, 10/17 for domestic and international students; for winter admission, 1/9 for domestic and international students; for spring admission, 2/20 for domestic and international students; for summer admission, 3/17 for domestic students. Application fee: $175. Electronic applications accepted. *Expenses:* $74,133 (for one-year MBA); $106,526 (two-year MBA); $113,050 (for MBA/MSBA). *Financial support:* In 2017–18, 251 students received support, including 247 fellowships (averaging $27,748 per year); unspecified assistantships also available. Financial award application deadline: 2/28; financial award applicants required to submit FAFSA. *Faculty research:* Market micro-

Entrepreneurship

structure; marketing and public policy; corporate finance and accounting; corporate governance and ethical behavior; high performing organizations. *Unit head:* Dr. Katherine Spiess, Associate Dean, Graduate Business Programs, 574-631-7236, E-mail: spiess.1@nd.edu. *Application contact:* Kristin McAndrew, Director of Admissions, Graduate Business Programs, 574-631-8488, E-mail: kmcandre@nd.edu. Website: http://mendoza.nd.edu/programs/mba-programs/

University of Oklahoma, Price College of Business, Program in Business Administration, Oklahoma City, OK 73104. Offers business administration (MBA, PhD), including accounting (PhD), business administration, entrepreneurship and economic development (PhD), finance (PhD), management and international business (PhD), management of information systems (PhD), marketing/supply chain (PhD); JD/MBA; MBA/MS. *Accreditation:* AACSB. *Program availability:* Part-time, evening/weekend. *Students:* 100 full-time (27 women), 152 part-time (30 women); includes 36 minority (2 Black or African American, non-Hispanic/Latino; 4 American Indian or Alaska Native, non-Hispanic/Latino; 10 Asian, non-Hispanic/Latino; 13 Hispanic/Latino; 7 Two or more races, non-Hispanic/Latino), 32 international. Average age 31. 247 applicants, 29% accepted, 41 enrolled. In 2017, 118 master's, 9 doctorates awarded. *Degree requirements:* For doctorate, comprehensive exam, thesis/dissertation. *Entrance requirements:* For master's, GMAT or GRE, resume, 2 essays, interview; for doctorate, GMAT or GRE, resume, statement of goals, 3 letters of recommendation. Additional exam requirements/recommendations for international students: Required—TOEFL (minimum score 100 iBT) or IELTS (minimum score 7). *Application deadline:* For fall admission, 11/1 for domestic and international students; for summer admission, 11/1 for domestic and international students. Applications are processed on a rolling basis. Application fee: $50 ($100 for international students). Electronic applications accepted. *Expenses:* Contact institution. *Financial support:* In 2017–18, 107 students received support, including 6 fellowships with partial tuition reimbursements available (averaging $2,500 per year); research assistantships with full and partial tuition reimbursements available, teaching assistantships with full and partial tuition reimbursements available, career-related internships or fieldwork, scholarships/grants, health care benefits, and unspecified assistantships also available. Support available to part-time students. Financial award application deadline: 6/1; financial award applicants required to submit FAFSA. *Faculty research:* Energy finance; international accounting; organizational behavior and entrepreneurship; management information systems; supply chain. *Unit head:* Laku Chidambaram, Associate Dean for Academic Programs and Engagement, 405-325-8013. *Application contact:* Kate Hile, Associate Director of MBA Admissions, 405-325-4572, E-mail: khile@ou.edu. Website: http://www.ou.edu/price/divisions/graduate-programs/graduate.html

University of Pennsylvania, Graduate School of Education, Division of Teaching, Learning, and Leadership, Program in Education Entrepreneurship, Philadelphia, PA 19104. Offers MS Ed. *Program availability:* Evening/weekend. *Degree requirements:* For master's, thesis or alternative, capstone project. *Entrance requirements:* For master's, bachelor's degree; at least 3 years of work experience. Additional exam requirements/recommendations for international students: Required—TOEFL, IELTS. *Application deadline:* For summer admission, 2/1 priority date for domestic and international students. Application fee: $75. Electronic applications accepted. *Financial support:* Scholarships/grants available. *Unit head:* Dr. Jenny Zapf, Director, 215-898-3265, E-mail: jzapf@upenn.edu. *Application contact:* Ayoung Lee, Administrative Coordinator, 215-573-8149, E-mail: ayoungl@upenn.edu. Website: http://www.gse.upenn.edu/tll/ee

University of Pennsylvania, School of Engineering and Applied Science, Program in Integrated Product Design, Philadelphia, PA 19104. Offers MIPD, MSE. *Program availability:* Part-time. *Students:* 17 full-time (6 women), 12 part-time (4 women); includes 7 minority (2 Black or African American, non-Hispanic/Latino; 1 Asian, non-Hispanic/Latino; 3 Hispanic/Latino; 1 Two or more races, non-Hispanic/Latino), 10 international. Average age 27. 105 applicants, 35% accepted, 22 enrolled. In 2017, 14 master's awarded. *Degree requirements:* For master's, comprehensive exam, thesis optional. *Entrance requirements:* For master's, GRE, bachelor's degree, letters of recommendation, resume, personal statement, portfolio. Additional exam requirements/recommendations for international students: Required—TOEFL (minimum score 100 iBT), IELTS (minimum score 7). *Application deadline:* For fall admission, 2/1 priority date for domestic and international students. Applications are processed on a rolling basis. Application fee: $80. Electronic applications accepted. *Expenses:* $7,022 per course. *Faculty research:* Technology and manufacturing processes, mechatronics, product design and design thinking. *Application contact:* William Fenton, Assistant Director of Graduate Admissions, 215-898-4542, Fax: 215-573-5577, E-mail: gradstudies@seas.upenn.edu. Website: http://ipd.me.upenn.edu/

University of Pikeville, Coleman College of Business, Pikeville, KY 41501. Offers business (MBA); entrepreneurship (MBA); healthcare (MBA). *Program availability:* Part-time, evening/weekend. *Faculty:* 5 part-time/adjunct (2 women). *Students:* 35 full-time (16 women), 2 part-time (both women); includes 3 minority (all Black or African American, non-Hispanic/Latino), 4 international. Average age 29. In 2017, 18 master's awarded. *Degree requirements:* For master's, comprehensive exam (for some programs). *Entrance requirements:* For master's, official transcripts, two professional letters of recommendation, three years of work experience. *Application deadline:* For fall admission, 8/15 for domestic students, 7/1 for international students. Applications are processed on a rolling basis. Application fee: $50. *Expenses:* Contact institution. *Financial support:* Tuition waivers (full) and university employee grants available. Financial award application deadline: 2/15; financial award applicants required to submit FAFSA. *Unit head:* Dr. Howard V. Roberts, Dean, 606-218-5019, Fax: 606-218-5031, E-mail: howardroberts@upike.edu. *Application contact:* Cathy Maynard, Secretary, Business and Economics, 606-218-5020, Fax: 606-218-5031, E-mail: cathymaynard@upike.edu. Website: http://www.upike.edu/Colleges/CCOB/

University of Portland, Dr. Robert B. Pamplin, Jr. School of Business, Portland, OR 97203-5798. Offers entrepreneurship (MBA); finance (MBA, MS); health care management (MBA); marketing (MBA); nonprofit management (EMBA); operations and technology management (MBA, MS); sustainability (MBA). *Accreditation:* AACSB. *Program availability:* Part-time, evening/weekend. *Entrance requirements:* For master's, GMAT, minimum GPA of 3.0, resume, 2 letters of recommendation. Additional exam requirements/recommendations for international students: Required—TOEFL (minimum score 570 paper-based; 89 iBT), IELTS (minimum score 7). *Expenses:* Contact institution.

University of Rhode Island, Graduate School, College of Business, Kingston, RI 02881. Offers accounting (MS); business administration (MBA, PhD), including finance (MBA), general business (MBA), management (MBA), marketing, operations and supply chain management (PhD), supply chain management (MBA); finance (MBA, MS, PhD); general business (MBA); health care management (MBA); labor research (MS, Graduate Certificate), including labor relations and human resources; management (MBA); marketing (MBA); strategic innovation (MBA); supply chain management (MBA); textiles, fashion merchandising and design (MS, Certificate), including fashion merchandising (Certificate), master seamstress (Certificate), textiles, fashion

merchandising and design (MS); MS/JD; Pharm D/MBA. *Accreditation:* AACSB. *Program availability:* Part-time, evening/weekend. *Faculty:* 61 full-time (28 women), 2 part-time/adjunct (1 woman). *Students:* 88 full-time (37 women), 180 part-time (94 women); includes 36 minority (9 Black or African American, non-Hispanic/Latino; 2 American Indian or Alaska Native, non-Hispanic/Latino; 13 Asian, non-Hispanic/Latino; 10 Hispanic/Latino; 2 Two or more races, non-Hispanic/Latino), 20 international. 205 applicants, 68% accepted, 97 enrolled. In 2017, 128 master's, 1 doctorate, 20 other advanced degrees awarded. *Entrance requirements:* Additional exam requirements/recommendations for international students: Required—TOEFL. Application fee: $65. Electronic applications accepted. *Expenses:* Tuition, state resident: full-time $12,706; part-time $786 per credit. Tuition, nonresident: full-time $25,216; part-time $1401 per credit. *Required fees:* $1598; $45 per credit. One-time fee: $30 part-time. *Financial support:* In 2017–18, 19 teaching assistantships with tuition reimbursements (averaging $14,589 per year) were awarded; research assistantships also available. Financial award applicants required to submit FAFSA. *Unit head:* Dr. Maling Ebrahimpour, Dean, 401-874-4348, Fax: 401-874-4312, E-mail: mebrahimpour@uri.edu. *Application contact:* Lisa Lancellotta, Coordinator, MBA Programs, 401-874-4241, Fax: 401-874-4312, E-mail: mba@uri.edu. Website: https://web.uri.edu/business/

See Display on page 159 and Close-Up on page 189.

University of Rochester, Hajim School of Engineering and Applied Sciences, Master of Science in Technical Entrepreneurship and Management Program, Rochester, NY 14627-0360. Offers biomedical engineering (MS). Program offered in collaboration with the Simon School of Business and administered by the University of Rochester Ain Center for Entrepreneurship. *Program availability:* Part-time. *Students:* 33 full-time (12 women), 8 part-time (4 women); includes 3 minority (2 Black or African American, non-Hispanic/Latino; 1 Asian, non-Hispanic/Latino), 29 international. Average age 25. 235 applicants, 67% accepted, 28 enrolled. In 2017, 36 master's awarded. *Degree requirements:* For master's, comprehensive exam. *Entrance requirements:* For master's, GRE or GMAT (strongly recommended), 3 letters of recommendation, personal statement, official transcript. Additional exam requirements/recommendations for international students: Required—TOEFL. *Application deadline:* For fall admission, 2/1 for domestic and international students. Application fee: $60. Electronic applications accepted. *Expenses:* $1,875 per credit hour. *Financial support:* In 2017–18, 38 students received support, including 1 fellowship (averaging $20,000 per year); career-related internships or fieldwork, scholarships/grants, and health care benefits also available. Support available to part-time students. Financial award application deadline: 2/1. *Unit head:* Duncan T. Moore, Vice Provost for Entrepreneurship, 585-275-5248, E-mail: duncan.moore@rochester.edu. *Application contact:* Andrea Barrett, Executive Director, 585-276-3407, E-mail: andrea.barrett@rochester.edu. Website: http://www.rochester.edu/team/

University of Rochester, Simon Business School, Full-Time Master's Program in Business Administration, Rochester, NY 14627. Offers business systems consulting (MBA); competitive and organizational strategy (MBA); computers and information systems (MBA); corporate accounting (MBA); entrepreneurship (MBA); finance (MBA); health sciences management (MBA); marketing (MBA); operations management (MBA); public accounting (MBA); strategy and organizations (MBA). *Accreditation:* AACSB. *Faculty:* 70 full-time (12 women), 23 part-time/adjunct (6 women). *Students:* 208 full-time (70 women). Average age 28. *Entrance requirements:* For master's, GMAT or GRE. *Application deadline:* For fall admission, 10/15 for domestic and international students; for winter admission, 1/5 for domestic and international students; for spring admission, 3/15 for domestic and international students; for summer admission, 5/15 for domestic and international students. Application fee: $150. *Financial support:* Fellowships, institutionally sponsored loans, scholarships/grants, and tuition waivers (full and partial) available. Financial award application deadline: 1/5; financial award applicants required to submit FAFSA. *Faculty research:* Empirical industrial organization, risk management, financial disclosure and regulation, social media, health care management. *Unit head:* Andrew Ainslie, Dean, 585-275-3316, E-mail: andrew.ainslie@simon.rochester.edu. *Application contact:* Rebekah S. Lewin, Assistant Dean of Admissions and Financial Aid, 585-275-3533, E-mail: admissions@simon.rochester.edu. Website: http://www.simon.rochester.edu/programs/full-time-mba/index.aspx

University of Rochester, Simon Business School, Part-Time MBA Program, Rochester, NY 14627. Offers business systems consulting (MBA); competitive and organizational strategy (MBA); computers and information systems (MBA); corporate accounting (MBA); entrepreneurship (MBA); finance (MBA); health sciences management (MBA); marketing (MBA), including brand management, marketing strategy, pricing; operations management (MBA); public accounting (MBA). *Program availability:* Part-time-only, evening/weekend. *Faculty:* 70 full-time (12 women), 23 part-time/adjunct (6 women). *Students:* 159 part-time (62 women); includes 25 minority (5 Black or African American, non-Hispanic/Latino; 9 Asian, non-Hispanic/Latino; 9 Hispanic/Latino; 2 Two or more races, non-Hispanic/Latino), 4 international. Average age 32. 39 applicants, 92% accepted, 35 enrolled. In 2017, 59 master's awarded. *Entrance requirements:* For master's, GRE or GMAT. *Application deadline:* For fall admission, 8/1 for domestic students; for spring admission, 2/15 for domestic students. Applications are processed on a rolling basis. Application fee: $150. Electronic applications accepted. *Expenses:* $1,875 per credit, $1,385 fees. *Financial support:* In 2017–18, 69 students received support. Tuition waivers (partial) available. Financial award application deadline: 8/1. *Unit head:* Andrew Ainslie, Dean, 585-275-3316, E-mail: andrew.ainslie@simon.rochester.edu. *Application contact:* Molly Mesko, Executive Director, EMBA and Part-Time Programs, 585-275-4277, E-mail: molly.mesko@simon.rochester.edu. Website: http://www.simon.rochester.edu/programs/ptmba/index.aspx

University of San Francisco, School of Management, Master in Global Entrepreneurial Management Program, San Francisco, CA 94117. Offers MGEM. Program offered jointly with IQS in Barcelona, Spain and Fu Jen Catholic University in Taipei, Taiwan. *Entrance requirements:* For master's, resume, transcripts from each college or university attended, two letters of recommendation, personal statement. Additional exam requirements/recommendations for international students: Required—TOEFL (minimum score 550 paper-based, 79 iBT), IELTS (minimum score 6), or PTE (minimum score 53). Electronic applications accepted. *Expenses:* Contact institution.

University of San Francisco, School of Management, Master of Business Administration Program, San Francisco, CA 94117. Offers entrepreneurship and innovation (MBA); finance (MBA); marketing (MBA); organization development (MBA); DDS/MBA; JD/MBA; MBA/MAPS. *Accreditation:* AACSB. *Program availability:* Part-time, evening/weekend. *Entrance requirements:* For master's, GMAT or GRE, resume (two years of professional work experience required for part-time students, preferred for full-time), transcripts from each college or university attended, two letters of recommendation, personal statement, interview. Additional exam requirements/recommendations for international students: Required—TOEFL (minimum score 600 paper-based, 100 iBT), IELTS (minimum score 7) or PTE (minimum score 68). Electronic applications accepted. *Expenses:* Contact institution. *Faculty research:* International financial markets, technology transfer licensing, international marketing, strategic planning.

University of San Francisco, School of Management, Master of Science in Entrepreneurship and Innovation Program, San Francisco, CA 94117-1080. Offers MS. *Expenses:* Contact institution.

University of Sioux Falls, Vucurevich School of Business, Sioux Falls, SD 57105-1699. Offers entrepreneurial leadership (MBA); general management (MBA); health care management (MBA); marketing (MBA). *Program availability:* Part-time, evening/weekend. *Degree requirements:* For master's, project. *Entrance requirements:* For master's, minimum GPA of 3.0. Additional exam requirements/recommendations for international students: Required—TOEFL. *Expenses:* Contact institution.

University of Southern California, Graduate School, Marshall School of Business, Program in Entrepreneurship and Innovation, Los Angeles, CA 90089. Offers MS.

University of South Florida, College of Global Sustainability, Tampa, FL 33620-9951. Offers energy, global, water and sustainable tourism (Graduate Certificate); global sustainability (MA), including building sustainable enterprise, climate change and sustainability, coastal sustainability, entrepreneurship, food sustainability and security, sustainability policy, sustainable energy, sustainable tourism, water. *Faculty:* 2 full-time (0 women). *Students:* 124 full-time (64 women), 77 part-time (45 women); includes 33 minority (12 Black or African American, non-Hispanic/Latino; 1 American Indian or Alaska Native, non-Hispanic/Latino; 1 Asian, non-Hispanic/Latino; 14 Hispanic/Latino; 5 Two or more races, non-Hispanic/Latino), 87 international. Average age 28. 220 applicants, 65% accepted, 101 enrolled. In 2017, 50 master's awarded. *Degree requirements:* For master's, comprehensive exam (for some programs), thesis or alternative, internship. *Entrance requirements:* For master's, minimum GPA of 3.0 in undergraduate coursework; at least two letters of recommendation (one must be academic); 200-250 word essay on student's background, professional goals, and reasons for seeking degree. Additional exam requirements/recommendations for international students: Required—TOEFL (minimum score 550 paper-based; 79 iBT). *Application deadline:* For fall admission, 6/1 for domestic students, 5/1 for international students; for spring admission, 10/15 for domestic students, 9/15 for international students. Electronic applications accepted. *Financial support:* In 2017–18, 22 students received support. *Faculty research:* Global sustainability, integrated resource management, systems thinking, green communities, entrepreneurship, ecotourism. *Total annual research expenditures:* $107,829. *Unit head:* Dr. Govindan Parayil, Dean, 813-974-9694, E-mail: gparayil@usf.edu.
Website: http://psgs.usf.edu/

University of South Florida, Innovative Education, Tampa, FL 33620-9951. Offers adult, career and higher education (Graduate Certificate), including college teaching, leadership in developing human resources, leadership in higher education; Africana studies (Graduate Certificate), including diasporas and health disparities, genocide and human rights; aging studies (Graduate Certificate), including gerontology; art research (Graduate Certificate), including museum studies; business foundations (Graduate Certificate); chemical and biomedical engineering (Graduate Certificate), including materials science and engineering, water, health and sustainability; child and family studies (Graduate Certificate), including positive behavior support; civil and industrial engineering (Graduate Certificate), including transportation systems analysis; community and family health (Graduate Certificate), including maternal and child health, social marketing and public health, violence and injury: prevention and intervention, women's health; criminology (Graduate Certificate), including criminal justice administration; data science for public administration (Graduate Certificate); digital humanities (Graduate Certificate); educational measurement and research (Graduate Certificate), including evaluation; English (Graduate Certificate), including comparative literary studies, creative writing, professional and technical communication; entrepreneurship (Graduate Certificate); environmental health (Graduate Certificate), including safety management; epidemiology and biostatistics (Graduate Certificate), including applied biostatistics, biostatistics, concepts and tools of epidemiology, epidemiology, epidemiology of infectious diseases; geography, environment and planning (Graduate Certificate), including community development, environmental policy and management, geographical information systems; geology (Graduate Certificate), including hydrogeology; global health (Graduate Certificate), including disaster management, global health and Latin American and Caribbean studies, global health practice, humanitarian assistance, infection control; government and international affairs (Graduate Certificate), including Cuban studies, globalization studies; health policy and management (Graduate Certificate), including health management and leadership, public health policy and programs; hearing specialist: early intervention (Graduate Certificate); industrial and management systems engineering (Graduate Certificate), including systems engineering, technology management; information studies (Graduate Certificate), including school library media specialist; information systems/decision sciences (Graduate Certificate), including analytics and business intelligence; instructional technology (Graduate Certificate), including distance education, Florida digital/virtual educator, instructional design, multimedia design, Web design; internal medicine, bioethics and medical humanities (Graduate Certificate), including biomedical ethics; Latin American and Caribbean studies (Graduate Certificate); leadership for coastal resiliency planning (Graduate Certificate); mass communications (Graduate Certificate), including multimedia journalism; mathematics and statistics (Graduate Certificate), including mathematics; medicine (Graduate Certificate), including aging and neuroscience, bioinformatics, biotechnology, brain fitness and memory management, clinical investigation, hand and upper limb rehabilitation, health informatics, health sciences, integrative weight management, intellectual property, medicine and gender, metabolic and nutritional medicine, metabolic cardiology, pharmacy sciences; national and competitive intelligence (Graduate Certificate); nursing (Graduate Certificate), including simulation based academic fellowship in advanced pain management; psychological and social foundations (Graduate Certificate), including career counseling, college teaching, diversity in education, mental health counseling, school counseling; public affairs (Graduate Certificate), including nonprofit management, public management, research administration; public health (Graduate Certificate), including assessing chemical toxicity and public health risks, health equity, pharmacoepidemiology, public health generalist, toxicology, translational research in adolescent behavioral health; public health practices (Graduate Certificate), including planning for healthy communities; rehabilitation and mental health counseling (Graduate Certificate), including integrative mental health care, marriage and family therapy, rehabilitation technology; secondary education (Graduate Certificate), including ESOL, foreign language education: culture and content, foreign language education: professional; social work (Graduate Certificate), including geriatric social work/clinical gerontology; special education (Graduate Certificate), including autism spectrum disorder, disabilities education: severe/profound; world languages (Graduate Certificate), including teaching English as a second language (TESL) or foreign language. *Unit head:* Dr. Cynthia DeLuca, Associate Vice President and Assistant Vice Provost, 813-974-3077, Fax: 813-974-7061, E-mail: deluca@usf.edu. *Application contact:* Owen Hooper, Director, Summer and Alternative Calendar Programs, 813-974-6917, E-mail: hooper@usf.edu.
Website: http://www.usf.edu/innovative-education/

University of South Florida, Muma College of Business, Center for Entrepreneurship, Tampa, FL 33620-9951. Offers entrepreneurship and applied technologies (MS).

Program availability: Part-time, evening/weekend. *Faculty:* 4 full-time (2 women). *Students:* 51 full-time (17 women), 7 part-time (3 women); includes 19 minority (9 Black or African American, non-Hispanic/Latino; 2 Asian, non-Hispanic/Latino; 7 Hispanic/Latino; 1 Two or more races, non-Hispanic/Latino), 40 international. Average age 29. In 2017, 55 master's awarded. *Degree requirements:* For master's, thesis optional. *Entrance requirements:* For master's, GMAT or GRE (preferred), MCAT or LSAT, minimum undergraduate GPA of 3.0 in upper-division course work, two letters of recommendation, letter of interest, statement of purpose, personal interview. Additional exam requirements/recommendations for international students: Required—TOEFL (minimum score 550 paper-based; 79 iBT) or IELTS (minimum score 6.5). *Application deadline:* For fall admission, 6/1 for domestic students, 2/1 for international students; for spring admission, 10/15 for domestic students, 7/1 for international students. Applications are processed on a rolling basis. Application fee: $30. Electronic applications accepted. *Faculty research:* Underlying success factors which drive the creation, growth and failures of businesses and technologies in the life sciences industry; influences of individual company geographic location, financial parameters, intellectual property, FDA and regulatory compliance, and press coverage on stock performance of over 1,000 publicly-traded life sciences companies. *Unit head:* Dr. Michael W. Fountain, Director, Center for Entrepreneurship, 813-974-7825, Fax: 813-974-6175, E-mail: fountain@usf.edu. *Application contact:* Dr. Tapas Das, Assistant Director/Professor, 813-974-5585, Fax: 813-974-5953, E-mail: das@usf.edu.
Website: http://www.ce.usf.edu/

The University of Tampa, Sykes College of Business, Tampa, FL 33606-1490. Offers accounting (MS); business analytics (MBA); cybersecurity (MBA, MS); entrepreneurship (MBA, MS); finance (MBA, MS); information systems management (MBA); innovation management (MBA); international business (MBA); marketing (MBA, MS); nonprofit management (MBA, Certificate). *Accreditation:* AACSB. *Program availability:* Part-time, evening/weekend. *Faculty:* 38 full-time (14 women), 6 part-time/adjunct (1 woman). *Students:* 229 full-time (1 woman), 115 part-time (51 women); includes 51 minority (26 Black or African American, non-Hispanic/Latino; 11 Asian, non-Hispanic/Latino; 1 Native Hawaiian or other Pacific Islander, non-Hispanic/Latino; 13 Two or more races, non-Hispanic/Latino), 182 international. Average age 28. 1,305 applicants, 39% accepted, 192 enrolled. In 2017, 266 master's awarded. *Degree requirements:* For master's, capstone. *Entrance requirements:* For master's, GMAT or GRE, official transcripts from all colleges and/or universities previously attended, resume, personal statement, letters of recommendation. Additional exam requirements/recommendations for international students: Required—TOEFL (minimum score 577 paper-based; 90 iBT), IELTS (minimum score 7.5). *Application deadline:* Applications are processed on a rolling basis. Application fee: $40. Electronic applications accepted. *Expenses:* Contact institution. *Financial support:* In 2017–18, 116 students received support. Career-related internships or fieldwork, scholarships/grants, and unspecified assistantships available. Financial award applicants required to submit FAFSA. *Faculty research:* Job market signaling, on-line shopping behaviors and social media, the Tampa Bay economy, digital literacy, entrepreneurship in small businesses. *Unit head:* Dr. Natasha F. Veltri, Associate Dean, 813-253-6289, E-mail: nveltri@ut.edu. *Application contact:* Chanelle Cox, Staff Assistant, Admissions for Graduate and Continuing Studies, 813-253-6249, E-mail: ccox@ut.edu.
Website: http://www.ut.edu/business/

The University of Texas at Austin, Graduate School, McCombs School of Business, Program in Technology Commercialization, Austin, TX 78712-1111. Offers MS. Twelve-month program, beginning in May, with classes held every other Friday and Saturday. *Program availability:* Evening/weekend, online learning. *Degree requirements:* For master's, year-long global teaming project. *Entrance requirements:* For master's, GRE General Test or GMAT. Additional exam requirements/recommendations for international students: Required—TOEFL (minimum score 550 paper-based; 79 iBT). Electronic applications accepted. *Expenses:* Contact institution. *Faculty research:* Technology transfer; entrepreneurship; commercialization; research, development and innovation.

The University of Texas at Dallas, Naveen Jindal School of Management, Program in Organizations, Strategy and International Management, Richardson, TX 75080. Offers business administration (MBA); executive business administration (EMBA); global leadership (EMBA); healthcare leadership and management (MS); healthcare management (EMBA); innovation and entrepreneurship (MS); international management studies (MS, PhD); management science (MS, PhD); project management (EMBA); systems engineering and management (MS); MS/MBA. *Program availability:* Part-time, evening/weekend. *Faculty:* 18 full-time (6 women), 17 part-time/adjunct (2 women). *Students:* 608 full-time (232 women), 711 part-time (326 women); includes 446 minority (93 Black or African American, non-Hispanic/Latino; 3 American Indian or Alaska Native, non-Hispanic/Latino; 212 Asian, non-Hispanic/Latino; 107 Hispanic/Latino; 31 Two or more races, non-Hispanic/Latino), 339 international. Average age 32. 1,665 applicants, 36% accepted, 398 enrolled. In 2017, 473 master's, 14 doctorates awarded. *Degree requirements:* For doctorate, thesis/dissertation. *Entrance requirements:* For master's and doctorate, GMAT. Additional exam requirements/recommendations for international students: Required—TOEFL (minimum score 550 paper-based). *Application deadline:* For fall admission, 7/15 for domestic students, 5/1 priority date for international students; for spring admission, 11/15 for domestic students, 9/1 priority date for international students. Applications are processed on a rolling basis. Application fee: $50 ($100 for international students). Electronic applications accepted. *Expenses:* Tuition, state resident: full-time $12,916; part-time $718 per credit hour. Tuition, nonresident: full-time $25,252; part-time $1403 per credit hour. *Financial support:* In 2017–18, 369 students received support, including 22 research assistantships with partial tuition reimbursements available (averaging $36,554 per year), 88 teaching assistantships with partial tuition reimbursements available (averaging $25,176 per year); Federal Work-Study, institutionally sponsored loans, scholarships/grants, and unspecified assistantships also available. Support available to part-time students. Financial award application deadline: 4/30; financial award applicants required to submit FAFSA. *Faculty research:* International accounting, international trade and finance, economic development, international economics. *Unit head:* Dr. Erik W.K. Tsang, Area Coordinator, 972-883-4386, Fax: 972-883-5977, E-mail: ewktsang@utdallas.edu.
Website: http://jindal.utdallas.edu/osim/

University of Washington, Graduate School, Michael G. Foster School of Business, Seattle, WA 98195-3200. Offers auditing and assurance (MP Acc); business administration (MBA, PhD); entrepreneurship (MS); executive business administration (MBA); global executive business administration (MBA); information systems (MSIS); supply chain management (MSSCM); taxation (MP Acc); technology management (MBA); JD/MBA; MBA/MAIS; MBA/MHA. *Accreditation:* AACSB. *Program availability:* Part-time, evening/weekend, blended/hybrid learning. *Faculty:* 109 full-time (35 women), 54 part-time/adjunct (32 women). *Students:* 469 full-time (173 women), 638 part-time (216 women); includes 314 minority (15 Black or African American, non-Hispanic/Latino; 6 American Indian or Alaska Native, non-Hispanic/Latino; 246 Asian, non-Hispanic/Latino; 28 Hispanic/Latino; 5 Native Hawaiian or other Pacific Islander, non-Hispanic/Latino; 14 Two or more races, non-Hispanic/Latino), 125 international. Average age 32. 1,809 applicants, 84% accepted, 1107 enrolled. In 2017, 543 master's, 10 doctorates

Entrepreneurship

awarded. Terminal master's awarded for partial completion of doctoral program. *Degree requirements:* For doctorate, comprehensive exam, thesis/dissertation. *Entrance requirements:* For master's and doctorate, GMAT, GRE. Additional exam requirements/recommendations for international students: Required—TOEFL (minimum score 600 paper-based; 100 iBT). *Application deadline:* For fall admission, 3/15 for domestic students, 1/15 for international students. Application fee: $85. Electronic applications accepted. *Expenses:* Contact institution. *Financial support:* Fellowships with partial tuition reimbursements, research assistantships with partial tuition reimbursements, teaching assistantships with partial tuition reimbursements, Federal Work-Study, institutionally sponsored loans, and scholarships/grants available. Financial award application deadline: 2/28; financial award applicants required to submit FAFSA. *Faculty research:* Finance, consumer behavior, marketing analytics, technology management, supply chain. *Unit head:* Dr. James Jiambalvo, Dean, 206-543-4750, E-mail: jjiambal@uw.edu. *Application contact:* Erin Town, Director of Admissions, 206-543-4661, Fax: 206-616-7351, E-mail: mba@uw.edu.
Website: http://www.foster.washington.edu/

University of Waterloo, Graduate Studies, Faculty of Engineering, Conrad Business, Entrepreneurship and Technology Center, Waterloo, ON N2L 3G1, Canada. Offers MBET. *Entrance requirements:* For master's, honors degree. Additional exam requirements/recommendations for international students: Required—TOEFL (minimum score 90 iBT), IELTS (minimum score 7), PTE (minimum score 63). Electronic applications accepted.

The University of Western Ontario, Richard Ivey School of Business, London, ON N6A 3K7, Canada. Offers business (EMBA, PhD); corporate strategy and leadership elective (MBA); entrepreneurship elective (MBA); finance elective (MBA); health sector stream (MBA); international management elective (MBA); marketing elective (MBA); JD/MBA. *Degree requirements:* For master's, thesis (for some programs); for doctorate, thesis/dissertation. *Entrance requirements:* For master's, GMAT, 2 years of full-time work experience, interview. Additional exam requirements/recommendations for international students: Required—TOEFL (minimum score 100 iBT) or IELTS (minimum score 6). Electronic applications accepted. *Faculty research:* Strategy, organizational behavior, international business, finance, operations management.

University of Wisconsin–Milwaukee, Graduate School, Lubar School of Business, Milwaukee, WI 53201. Offers business administration (MBA); executive business administration (EMBA); management science (MS, PhD, Graduate Certificate), including business analytics (Graduate Certificate), enterprise resource planning (Graduate Certificate), information technology management (MS), investment management (Graduate Certificate), nonprofit management (Graduate Certificate), nonprofit management and leadership (MS), state and local taxation (Graduate Certificate); technology entrepreneurship (Graduate Certificate). *Accreditation:* AACSB. *Program availability:* Part-time, evening/weekend. *Students:* 321 full-time (137 women), 252 part-time (93 women); includes 94 minority (25 Black or African American, non-Hispanic/Latino; 1 American Indian or Alaska Native, non-Hispanic/Latino; 28 Asian, non-Hispanic/Latino; 6 Hispanic/Latino; 34 Two or more races, non-Hispanic/Latino), 66 international. Average age 32. 426 applicants, 61% accepted, 191 enrolled. In 2017, 266 master's, 8 doctorates, 21 other advanced degrees awarded. *Degree requirements:* For master's, comprehensive exam (for some programs); for doctorate, comprehensive exam, thesis/dissertation. *Entrance requirements:* For master's and doctorate, GMAT or GRE General Test. Additional exam requirements/recommendations for international students: Required—TOEFL (minimum score 550 paper-based; 79 iBT), IELTS (minimum score 6.5). *Application deadline:* For fall admission, 1/1 priority date for domestic students; for spring admission, 9/1 for domestic students. Application fee: $56 ($96 for international students). Electronic applications accepted. *Expenses:* Contact institution. *Financial support:* Fellowships with full tuition reimbursements, research assistantships with full tuition reimbursements, teaching assistantships with full tuition reimbursements, career-related internships or fieldwork, Federal Work-Study, health care benefits, unspecified assistantships, and project assistantships available. Support available to part-time students. Financial award application deadline: 4/15; financial award applicants required to submit FAFSA. *Faculty research:* Applied management research in finance, management information systems, marketing, operations research, organizational sciences. *Unit head:* V. Kanti Prasad, Dean, 414-229-6256, E-mail: deanprasad@uwm.edu. *Application contact:* Business Graduate Student Services, 414-229-5403, E-mail: mba-ms@uwm.edu.
Website: https://uwm.edu/business/

Ursuline College, School of Graduate and Professional Studies, Program in Business Administration, Pepper Pike, OH 44124-4398. Offers ethical and entrepreneurial leadership (MBA); financial planning and accounting (MBA); health services management (MBA); management (MBA); management and leadership (MBA); marketing and communications management (MBA). *Program availability:* Part-time. *Faculty:* 3 full-time (2 women), 3 part-time/adjunct (2 women). *Students:* 3 full-time (all women), 26 part-time (23 women); includes 13 minority (12 Black or African American, non-Hispanic/Latino; 1 Two or more races, non-Hispanic/Latino). Average age 38. 13 applicants, 85% accepted, 6 enrolled. In 2017, 11 master's awarded. *Degree requirements:* For master's, comprehensive exam (for some programs). *Entrance requirements:* For master's, GRE. Additional exam requirements/recommendations for international students: Required—TOEFL (minimum score 500 paper-based) or GRE. *Application deadline:* Applications are processed on a rolling basis. Application fee: $25. Electronic applications accepted. *Expenses:* $842 per credit hour. *Financial support:* In 2017–18, 3 students received support. Scholarships/grants available. Financial award application deadline: 8/1; financial award applicants required to submit FAFSA. *Faculty research:* Gift economy; sharing economy; cooperative business models; collaborative leadership; corporate social responsibility and the triple bottom line, defined as the three P's: people, planet and profit. *Unit head:* Dr. Anthony Caffarelli, Associate Professor, 440-646-8134, Fax: 440-684-6088, E-mail: tcafarelli@ursuline.edu. *Application contact:* Melanie Steele, Director of Graduate Admission, 440-646-8146, Fax: 440-684-6138, E-mail: graduateadmissions@ursuline.edu.

Virginia International University, School of Business, Fairfax, VA 22030. Offers accounting (MBA, MS); entrepreneurship (MBA); executive management (Graduate Certificate); global logistics (MBA); health care management (MBA); hospitality and tourism management (MBA); human resources management (MBA); international business management (MBA); international finance (MBA); marketing management (MBA); mass media and public relations (MBA); project management (MBA, MS). *Program availability:* Part-time, online learning. *Entrance requirements:* For master's and Graduate Certificate, bachelor's degree. Additional exam requirements/recommendations for international students: Required—TOEFL (minimum score 550 paper-based; 80 iBT), IELTS (minimum score 6). Electronic applications accepted.

Walden University, Graduate Programs, School of Management, Minneapolis, MN 55401. Offers accounting (MBA, MS, DBA), including accounting for the professional (MS), accounting with CPA emphasis (MS), self-designed (MS); advanced project management (Graduate Certificate); applied project management (Graduate Certificate); auditing (Graduate Certificate); bridge to business administration (Post-Doctoral Certificate); bridge to management (Post-Doctoral Certificate); business management (Graduate Certificate); communication (MBA); corporate finance (MBA);

digital marketing (Graduate Certificate); entrepreneurship (DBA); entrepreneurship and small business (MBA); finance (MS, DBA), including finance for the professional (MS), finance with CFA/investment (MS), finance with CPA emphasis (MS); global supply chain management (DBA); healthcare management (MBA, DBA); human resource management (MBA, MS, Graduate Certificate), including functional human resource management (MS), general program (MS), integrating functional and strategic human resource management (MS), organizational strategy (MS); human resources management (DBA); information systems management (DBA); international business (MBA, DBA); leadership (MBA, MS, DBA, Graduate Certificate), including general program (MS), human resource leadership (MS), leader development (MS), self-designed (MS); management (MS, PhD), including communications (MS), finance (PhD), general program (MS), healthcare management (MS), human resource management (MS), human resources management (PhD), information systems management (PhD), international business (MS), leadership (MS), leadership and organizational change (PhD), marketing (MS), project management (MS), strategy and operations (MS); managerial accounting (Graduate Certificate); marketing (MBA, MS, DBA); project management (MBA, MS, DBA); self-designed (MBA, DBA); social impact management (DBA); technology entrepreneurship (DBA). *Accreditation:* ACBSP. *Program availability:* Part-time, evening/weekend, online only, 100% online. *Degree requirements:* For master's, thesis (for some programs), residency (for EMBA); for doctorate, thesis/dissertation (for some programs), residency. *Entrance requirements:* For master's, bachelor's degree or higher; minimum GPA of 2.5; official transcripts; goal statement (for some programs); access to computer and Internet; for doctorate, master's degree or higher; three years of related professional or academic experience (preferred); minimum GPA of 3.0; goal statement and current resume (for select programs); official transcripts; access to computer and Internet; for other advanced degree, relevant work experience; access to computer and Internet. Additional exam requirements/recommendations for international students: Required—TOEFL (minimum score 550 paper-based, 79 iBT), IELTS (minimum score 6.5), Michigan English Language Assessment Battery (minimum score 82), or PTE (minimum score 53). Electronic applications accepted.

Washington University in St. Louis, School of Medicine, Program in Clinical Investigation, St. Louis, MO 63130-4899. Offers clinical investigation (MS), including bioethics, entrepreneurship, genetics/genomics, translational medicine. *Program availability:* Part-time, evening/weekend. *Degree requirements:* For master's, thesis. *Entrance requirements:* For master's, doctoral-level degree or in process of obtaining doctoral-level degree. Electronic applications accepted. *Faculty research:* Anesthesiology, infectious diseases, neurology, obstetrics and gynecology, orthopedic surgery.

Wayne State University, Mike Ilitch School of Business, Detroit, MI 48202. Offers accounting (MS, MSA, Postbaccalaureate Certificate); business (EMS, Graduate Certificate); business administration (MBA, PhD); data science (MS), including business analytics; entrepreneurship and innovation (Postbaccalaureate Certificate); finance (MS); information systems management (Postbaccalaureate Certificate); taxation (MST); JD/MBA. Application deadline for PhD is February 15. *Accreditation:* AACSB. *Program availability:* Part-time, evening/weekend. *Faculty:* 32. *Students:* 235 full-time (121 women), 1,082 part-time (480 women); includes 356 minority (202 Black or African American, non-Hispanic/Latino; 2 American Indian or Alaska Native, non-Hispanic/Latino; 79 Asian, non-Hispanic/Latino; 47 Hispanic/Latino; 26 Two or more races, non-Hispanic/Latino), 87 international. Average age 30. 1,285 applicants, 43% accepted, 308 enrolled. In 2017, 200 master's, 2 doctorates, 9 other advanced degrees awarded. *Degree requirements:* For doctorate, thesis/dissertation. *Entrance requirements:* For master's, GMAT, GRE, LSAT, MCAT, at least three years of relevant work experience that shows increased responsibility, or minimum GPA of 3.0 from AACSB-accredited program or 3.2 from regionally-accredited program, undergraduate degree from accredited institution; undergraduate degree in accounting, business administration, or area of business administration (for MS and MST); for doctorate, GMAT (minimum score of 600), minimum undergraduate GPA of 3.0, 3.5 upper-division or graduate; three letters of recommendation; brief essay; undergraduate degree from accredited institution; personal statement; for other advanced degree, bachelor's degree from accredited institution. Additional exam requirements/recommendations for international students: Required—TOEFL (minimum score 550 paper-based; 79 iBT), Michigan English Language Assessment Battery (minimum score 85); Recommended—IELTS (minimum score 6.5), TWE (minimum score 5.5). *Application deadline:* For fall admission, 7/1 for domestic students, 5/1 priority date for international students; for winter admission, 11/1 for domestic students, 9/1 priority date for international students; for spring admission, 3/1 for domestic students, 1/1 priority date for international students. Applications are processed on a rolling basis. Application fee: $50. Electronic applications accepted. *Expenses:* Contact institution. *Financial support:* In 2017–18, 165 students received support, including 1 fellowship with tuition reimbursement available (averaging $18,534 per year), 1 teaching assistantship with tuition reimbursement available (averaging $18,534 per year); research assistantships with tuition reimbursements available, scholarships/grants, health care benefits, and unspecified assistantships also available. Support available to part-time students. Financial award applicants required to submit FAFSA. *Faculty research:* Executive compensation and stock performance, consumer reactions to pricing strategies, communication across the automotive supply chain, performance of firms in sub-Saharan Africa, implementation issues with ERP software. *Unit head:* Dr. Robert Forsythe, Dean, School of Business Administration, 313-577-4501, E-mail: robert.forsythe@wayne.edu. *Application contact:* Kiantee N. Rupert-Jones, Director, 313-577-4511, Fax: 313-577-9442, E-mail: gradbusiness@wayne.edu.
Website: http://ilitchbusiness.wayne.edu/

Western Carolina University, Graduate School, College of Business, Program in Entrepreneurship, Cullowhee, NC 28723. Offers ME. *Program availability:* Part-time, evening/weekend, online learning. *Entrance requirements:* For master's, GMAT or GRE General Test. Additional exam requirements/recommendations for international students: Required—TOEFL (minimum score 550 paper-based; 79 iBT). *Expenses:* Tuition, state resident: full-time $4436. Tuition, nonresident: full-time $14,842. *Required fees:* $2926.

Wichita State University, Graduate School, Institute for Interdisciplinary Creativity, Wichita, KS 67260. Offers innovation design (MID). *Unit head:* Dr. Jeremy Patterson, Graduate Coordinator, 316-978-3010, E-mail: jeremy.patterson@wichita.edu. *Application contact:* Jordan Oleson, Admissions Coordinator, 316-978-3095, Fax: 316-978-3253, E-mail: jordan.oleson@wichita.edu.
Website: http://www.wichita.edu/iic

Wilkes University, College of Graduate and Professional Studies, Jay S. Sidhu School of Business and Leadership, Wilkes-Barre, PA 18766-0002. Offers accounting (MBA); entrepreneurship (MBA); finance (MBA); health care administration (MBA); human resource management (MBA); international business (MBA); operations management (MBA); organizational leadership and development (MBA). *Accreditation:* ACBSP. *Program availability:* Part-time, evening/weekend. *Students:* 37 full-time (18 women), 87 part-time (45 women); includes 17 minority (4 Black or African American, non-Hispanic/Latino; 5 Asian, non-Hispanic/Latino; 6 Hispanic/Latino; 2 Two or more races, non-

Hispanic/Latino), 14 international. Average age 30. In 2017, 77 master's awarded. *Entrance requirements:* For master's, GMAT. Additional exam requirements/recommendations for international students: Required—TOEFL (minimum score 550 paper-based; 79 iBT). *Application deadline:* Applications are processed on a rolling basis. Application fee: $45 ($65 for international students). Electronic applications accepted. *Expenses:* Contact institution. *Financial support:* Unspecified assistantships available. Financial award application deadline: 3/1; financial award applicants required to submit FAFSA. *Unit head:* Dr. Abel Adekola, Dean, 570-408-4701, Fax: 570-408-7846, E-mail: abel.adekola@wilkes.edu. *Application contact:* Kristin Donati, Associate Director of Graduate Admissions, 570-408-3338, Fax: 570-408-7846, E-mail: kristin.donati@wilkes.edu.

Website: http://www.wilkes.edu/academics/colleges/sidhu-school-of-business-leadership/index.aspx

Wingate University, Porter B. Byrum School of Business, Wingate, NC 28174. Offers accounting (MAC); corporate innovation (MBA); finance (MBA); general management (MBA); healthcare management (MBA); marketing (MBA); project management (MBA). *Accreditation:* ACBSP. *Program availability:* Part-time, evening/weekend. *Entrance requirements:* For master's, GMAT, work experience, 2 letters of recommendation. Electronic applications accepted. *Expenses:* Contact institution. *Faculty research:* Stochastic processes, business ethics, regional economic development, municipal finance, consumer behavior.

Section 6
Facilities and Entertainment Management

This section contains a directory of institutions offering graduate work in facilities management. Additional information about programs listed in the directory but not augmented by an in-depth entry may be obtained by writing directly to the dean of a graduate school or chair of a department at the address given in the directory.

For programs offering related work, see also in this book *Business Administration and Management.*

CONTENTS

Entertainment Management

Berklee College of Music, Berklee Graduate Programs, Boston, MA 46013, Spain. Offers contemporary performance (MM), including global jazz; production; global entertainment and music business (MA); music production, technology, and innovation (MM); scoring for film, television, and video games (MM). Production; global entertainment and music business; music production, technology, and innovation; and scoring for film, television, and video games programs offered at Valencia, Spain campus. *Program availability:* Part-time, blended/hybrid learning. *Faculty:* 45 full-time (12 women), 41 part-time/adjunct (6 women). *Students:* 196 full-time (75 women), 24 part-time (22 women); includes 36 minority (5 Black or African American, non-Hispanic/Latino; 9 Asian, non-Hispanic/Latino; 17 Hispanic/Latino; 5 Two or more races, non-Hispanic/Latino), 109 international. Average age 27. 735 applicants, 38% accepted, 162 enrolled. In 2017, 170 master's awarded. *Degree requirements:* For master's, thesis, culminating experience project. *Entrance requirements:* Additional exam requirements/recommendations for international students: Required—TOEFL (minimum score 600 paper-based; 100 iBT), IELTS (minimum score 7.5), PTE (minimum score 73). *Application deadline:* For fall admission, 1/15 for domestic and international students. Application fee: $150. Electronic applications accepted. *Expenses:* Contact institution. *Financial support:* In 2017–18, 153 students received support, including 123 fellowships with full and partial tuition reimbursements available (averaging $15,943 per year), 30 research assistantships (averaging $5,429 per year); career-related internships or fieldwork, scholarships/grants, and tuition waivers (full and partial) also available. Support available to part-time students. Financial award application deadline: 1/15; financial award applicants required to submit CSS PROFILE or FAFSA. *Faculty research:* Neuroscience, integrative medicine, music therapy practice, music cognition, ethnomusicology. *Unit head:* Camille Colatosti, PhD, Dean, Institutional Research and Assessment/Graduate Studies, 617-536-6340, E-mail: ccolatosti@berklee.edu. *Application contact:* Office of Admissions, 617-747-2221, E-mail: admissions@berklee.edu.
Website: https://www.berklee.edu/graduate

California Intercontinental University, Hollywood College of the Entertainment Industry, Irvine, CA 92614. Offers Hollywood and entertainment management (MBA).

California State University, Northridge, Graduate Studies, Tseng College, Northridge, CA 91330. Offers business administration (Graduate Certificate); health administration (MPA); health education (MPH); knowledge management (MKM); music industry administration (MA); nonprofit-sector management (Graduate Certificate); public administration (MPA); public sector management and leadership (MPA); social work (MSW); taxation (MS); tourism, hospitality and recreation management (MS). *Students:* 4 part-time (all women); includes 1 minority (Black or African American, non-Hispanic/Latino). Average age 37. In 2017, 2 master's awarded. *Entrance requirements:* For master's, GRE (if cumulative undergraduate GPA less than 3.0). *Unit head:* Joyce Feucht-Haviar, Dean, 866-873-6439.

Carnegie Mellon University, Heinz College, School of Public Policy and Management, Master of Entertainment Industry Management Program, Pittsburgh, PA 15213-3891. Offers MEIM. *Accreditation:* AACSB. *Entrance requirements:* For master's, GRE or GMAT, college-level course in advanced algebra/pre-calculus; college-level courses in economics and statistics (recommended). Additional exam requirements/recommendations for international students: Required—TOEFL or IELTS.

Columbia College Chicago, School of Graduate Studies, Business and Entrepreneurship Department, Chicago, IL 60605-1996. Offers arts, entertainment and media management (MAM). *Students:* 40 full-time (30 women); includes 7 minority (4 Black or African American, non-Hispanic/Latino; 1 Asian, non-Hispanic/Latino; 2 Hispanic/Latino), 17 international. 82 applicants, 54% accepted, 20 enrolled. *Entrance requirements:* For master's, self-assessment essay, resume, letters of recommendation, transcripts. Additional exam requirements/recommendations for international students: Required—TOEFL, IELTS. *Application deadline:* For fall admission, 1/15 priority date for domestic and international students. Applications are processed on a rolling basis. Application fee: $55 ($100 for international students). Electronic applications accepted. *Expenses:* Contact institution. *Financial support:* In 2017–18, 16 students received support. Federal Work-Study, scholarships/grants, and unspecified assistantships available. Financial award application deadline: 1/15. *Unit head:* Mary Filice, Chair, 312-369-7882, E-mail: mfilice@colum.edu. *Application contact:* Emily Schmidt, Graduate Admissions, 312-369-7298, E-mail: eschmidt@colum.edu.
Website: https://www.colum.edu/academics/fine-and-performing-arts/business-and-entrepreneurship/index.html

Full Sail University, Entertainment Business Master of Science Program - Campus, Winter Park, FL 32792-7437. Offers MS.

Full Sail University, Entertainment Business Master of Science Program - Online, Winter Park, FL 32792-7437. Offers MS. *Program availability:* Online learning. *Entrance requirements:* Additional exam requirements/recommendations for international students: Required—TOEFL (minimum score 550 paper-based; 79 iBT).

Hofstra University, Frank G. Zarb School of Business, Programs in Management and General Business, Hempstead, NY 11549. Offers business administration (MBA), including health services management, management, sports and entertainment management, strategic business management, strategic healthcare management; general management (Advanced Certificate); human resource management (MS, Advanced Certificate). *Program availability:* Part-time, evening/weekend, blended/hybrid learning. *Students:* 131 full-time (58 women), 145 part-time (65 women); includes 102 minority (23 Black or African American, non-Hispanic/Latino; 39 Asian, non-Hispanic/Latino; 37 Hispanic/Latino; 3 Two or more races, non-Hispanic/Latino), 25 international. Average age 33. 327 applicants, 72% accepted, 104 enrolled. In 2017, 116 master's awarded. *Degree requirements:* For master's, thesis optional, capstone course (for MBA), thesis (for MS), minimum GPA of 3.0. *Entrance requirements:* For master's, GMAT/GRE, 2 letters of recommendation, resume, essay. Additional exam requirements/recommendations for international students: Required—TOEFL (minimum score 550 paper-based; 80 iBT); Recommended—IELTS (minimum score 6). *Application deadline:* Applications are processed on a rolling basis. Application fee: $75. Electronic applications accepted. *Expenses:* $1,322 per credit. *Financial support:* In 2017–18, 78 students received support, including 75 fellowships with full and partial tuition reimbursements available (averaging $4,785 per year); research assistantships with full and partial tuition reimbursements available, career-related internships or fieldwork, Federal Work-Study, institutionally sponsored loans, scholarships/grants, tuition waivers (full and partial), and unspecified assistantships also available. Support available to part-time students. Financial award applicants required to submit FAFSA. *Faculty research:* Organizational change; sustainability; entrepreneurial spawning; family business; global supply chain strategies. *Unit head:* Dr. Kaushik Sengupta, Chairperson, 516-463-7825, Fax: 516-463-4834, E-mail: kaushik.sengupta@hofstra.edu. *Application contact:* Sunil Samuel, Assistant Vice President of Admissions, 516-463-4723, Fax: 516-463-4664, E-mail: graduateadmission@hofstra.edu.
Website: http://www.hofstra.edu/business/

Manhattanville College, School of Business, Master of Science in Sport Business and Entertainment Management Program, Purchase, NY 10577-2132. Offers sport business and entertainment management (MS, Advanced Certificate), including entertainment management (MS), sport business (MS). *Program availability:* Part-time, evening/weekend. *Faculty:* 9 part-time/adjunct (0 women). *Students:* 36 full-time (11 women), 4 part-time (1 woman); includes 12 minority (2 Black or African American, non-Hispanic/Latino; 1 American Indian or Alaska Native, non-Hispanic/Latino; 9 Hispanic/Latino), 7 international. Average age 27. 35 applicants, 51% accepted, 12 enrolled. In 2017, 25 master's awarded. *Degree requirements:* For master's, thesis (for some programs), internship, portfolio. *Entrance requirements:* For master's, personal essay, transcripts, 2 letters of recommendation (academic or professional), resume, health form with proof of immunization (for those born after 1957). Additional exam requirements/recommendations for international students: Required—TOEFL (minimum score 563 paper-based, 85 iBT), IELTS (7), or iTEP (B2). *Application deadline:* Applications are processed on a rolling basis. Application fee: $75. Electronic applications accepted. *Expenses:* $915 per credit. *Financial support:* Federal Work-Study, institutionally sponsored loans, scholarships/grants, and unspecified assistantships available. Financial award application deadline: 3/15; financial award applicants required to submit FAFSA. *Unit head:* David Torromeo, Program Director, 914-323-5301, Fax: 914-694-3488, E-mail: david.torromeo@mville.edu. *Application contact:* Monika Pottgen, Assistant Director, Recruitment and Admissions, 914-323-5150, E-mail: business@mville.edu.
Website: https://www.mville.edu/programs/ms-sport-business-and-entertainment-management

Point Park University, Rowland School of Business, Program in Business Administration, Pittsburgh, PA 15222-1984. Offers business analytics (MBA); global management and administration (MBA); health systems management (MBA); international business (MBA); management (MBA); management information systems (MBA); sports, arts and entertainment management (MBA). *Program availability:* Evening/weekend, 100% online.

Southern New Hampshire University, School of Business, Manchester, NH 03106-1045. Offers accounting (MBA, Graduate Certificate); accounting finance (MS); accounting/auditing (MS); accounting/forensic accounting (MS); accounting/management accounting (MS); accounting/taxation (MS); applied economics (MS); athletic administration (MBA, Graduate Certificate); business administration (IMBA, Certificate), including business information systems (Certificate), human resource management (Certificate); business analytics (MBA); business intelligence (MBA); communication (MA), including new media and marketing, public relations; community economic development (MBA); criminal justice (MBA); data analytics (MS); economics (MBA); engineering management (MBA); entrepreneurship (MBA); finance (MBA, MS, Graduate Certificate); finance/corporate finance (MS); finance/investments (MS); forensic accounting (MBA); forensic accounting and fraud examination (Graduate Certificate); healthcare informatics (MBA); healthcare management (MBA); human resource management (MS); human resources (MBA); information technology (MS); information technology management (MBA); international business (PhD); Internet marketing (MBA); leadership (MBA); leadership of nonprofit organizations (Graduate Certificate); management (MS); marketing (MBA, MS, Graduate Certificate); music business (MBA); operations and project management (MS); operations and supply chain management (MBA, Graduate Certificate); organizational leadership (MS); project management (MBA, Graduate Certificate); public administration (MBA, Graduate Certificate); quantitative analysis (MBA); Six Sigma (Graduate Certificate); Six Sigma quality (MBA); social media marketing (MBA, Graduate Certificate); sport management (MBA, MS, Graduate Certificate); sustainability and environmental compliance (MBA); MBA/Certificate. *Accreditation:* ACBSP. *Program availability:* Part-time, evening/weekend, online learning. Terminal master's awarded for partial completion of doctoral program. *Degree requirements:* For master's, one foreign language, comprehensive exam (for some programs), thesis or alternative; for doctorate, one foreign language, comprehensive exam, thesis/dissertation. *Entrance requirements:* For master's, minimum GPA of 2.5; for doctorate, GMAT. Additional exam requirements/recommendations for international students: Required—TOEFL (minimum score 500 paper-based). *Application deadline:* Applications are processed on a rolling basis. Application fee: $40. Electronic applications accepted. *Expenses: Tuition:* Part-time $627 per credit hour. Part-time tuition and fees vary according to campus/location and program. *Financial support:* Career-related internships or fieldwork, Federal Work-Study, institutionally sponsored loans, scholarships/grants, tuition waivers (partial), and unspecified assistantships available. Support available to part-time students. Financial award applicants required to submit FAFSA. *Unit head:* Dr. Bill Lightfoot, Dean, 603-644-3102, Fax: 603-644-3144. *Application contact:* Office of Graduate Admission, 888-327-SNHU, Fax: 603-644-3144, E-mail: enroll@snhu.edu.

Syracuse University, College of Visual and Performing Arts, MA Program in Audio Arts, Syracuse, NY 13244. Offers audio arts (MA), including audio recording, music industry, music video, radio horizons. Program taught in conjunction with the S.I. Newhouse School of Public Communications. *Entrance requirements:* For master's, resume, sample of work, personal statement, three letters of recommendation. Additional exam requirements/recommendations for international students: Required—TOEFL (minimum score 100 iBT). *Application deadline:* For summer admission, 2/1 priority date for domestic and international students. Application fee: $75. Electronic applications accepted. *Financial support:* Fellowships, teaching assistantships, and scholarships/grants available. Financial award application deadline: 1/1. *Faculty research:* Audio practice, music industry, audio recording, radio horizons, music video. *Unit head:* Prof. James Abbott, Professor of Practice, Music Industry and Technologies/Program Coordinator, Sound Recording Technology, 315-443-4107, E-mail: jsabbott@syr.edu. *Application contact:* Caitlin Jarvis, Graduate Recruitment Specialist, 315-443-2769, E-mail: admissg@syr.edu.
Website: http://vpa.syr.edu/academics/setnor/graduate/audio-arts/

Universidad Autonoma de Guadalajara, Graduate Programs, Guadalajara, Mexico. Offers administrative law and justice (LL M); advertising and corporate communications (MA); architecture (M Arch); business (MBA); computational science (MCC); education (Ed M, Ed D); English-Spanish translation (MA); entrepreneurship and management (MBA); integrated management of digital animation (MA); international business (MIB); international corporate law (LL M); internet technologies (MS); manufacturing systems (MMS); occupational health (MS); philosophy (MA, PhD); power electronics (MS); quality systems (MQS); renewable energy (MS); social evaluation of projects (MBA); strategic market research (MBA); tax law (MA); teaching mathematics (MA).

University of Colorado Denver, Business School, Master of Business Administration Program, Denver, CO 80217. Offers bioinnovation and entrepreneurship (MBA); business intelligence (MBA); business strategy (MBA); business to business marketing (MBA); business to consumer marketing (MBA); change management (MBA); corporate financial management (MBA); enterprise technology management (MBA); entrepreneurship (MBA); health administration (MBA), including financial management, health administration, health information technologies, international health management and policy; human resources management (MBA); international business (MBA); investment management (MBA); managing for sustainability (MBA); sports and entertainment management (MBA). *Accreditation:* AACSB. *Program availability:* Part-time, evening/weekend, 100% online, blended/hybrid learning. *Degree requirements:* For master's, 48 semester hours, including 30 of core courses, 3 in international business, and 15 in electives from over 50 other business courses. *Entrance requirements:* For master's, GMAT, resume, official transcripts, essay, two letters of recommendation, financial statements (for international applicants). Additional exam requirements/recommendations for international students: Required—TOEFL (minimum score 560 paper-based; 83 iBT); Recommended—IELTS (minimum score 6.5). Electronic applications accepted. *Expenses:* Contact institution. *Faculty research:* Marketing, management, entrepreneurship, finance, health administration.

University of Colorado Denver, Business School, Program in Management and Organization, Denver, CO 80217. Offers business strategy (MS); change and innovation (MS); enterprise technology management (MS); entrepreneurship and innovation (MS); global management (MS); leadership (MS); managing for sustainability (MS); managing human resources (MS); sports and entertainment management (MS). *Accreditation:* AACSB. *Program availability:* Part-time, evening/weekend, online learning. *Degree requirements:* For master's, 30 semester hours (12 of required courses, 12 of management electives, and 6 of free electives). *Entrance requirements:* For master's, GMAT, resume, two letters of recommendation, essay, financial statements (for international applicants). Additional exam requirements/recommendations for international students: Required—TOEFL (minimum score 525 paper-based; 71 iBT); Recommended—IELTS (minimum score 6.5). Electronic applications accepted. *Expenses:* Contact institution. *Faculty research:* Human resource management, management of catastrophe, turnaround strategies.

University of Colorado Denver, Business School, Program in Marketing, Denver, CO 80217. Offers brand management and marketing communication (MS); global marketing (MS); high-tech and entrepreneurial marketing (MS); marketing for sustainability (MS); marketing research (MS); sports and entertainment marketing (MS). *Program availability:* Part-time, evening/weekend. *Degree requirements:* For master's, 30 semester hours (21 of marketing core courses, 9 of marketing electives). *Entrance requirements:* For master's, GMAT, resume, essay, two letters of recommendation, financial statements (for international applicants). Additional exam requirements/recommendations for international students: Required—TOEFL (minimum score 525 paper-based; 71 iBT); Recommended—IELTS (minimum score 6.5). Electronic applications accepted. *Expenses:* Contact institution. *Faculty research:* Marketing issues in the Chinese environment, impact of individual difference and contextual factors on the risk-taking behaviors of managers making new-business creation decisions, attribution theory perspective of conflict between marketers and engineers, organizational identity and identification, international market entry strategies.

University of Dallas, Satish and Yasmin Gupta College of Business, Irving, TX 75062-4736. Offers accounting (MBA, MS); business administration (DBA); business analytics (MS); business management (MBA); corporate finance (MBA); cybersecurity (MS); finance (MS); financial services (MBA); global business (MBA, MS); health services management (MBA); human resource management (MBA); information and technology management (MS); information assurance (MBA); information technology (MBA); information technology service management (MBA); marketing management (MBA); organization development (MBA); project management (MBA); sports and entertainment management (MBA); strategic leadership (MBA); supply chain management (MBA). *Accreditation:* AACSB. *Program availability:* Part-time, evening/weekend, online learning. *Entrance requirements:* Additional exam requirements/recommendations for international students: Required—TOEFL. *Application deadline:* Applications are processed on a rolling basis. Application fee: $50. Electronic applications accepted. *Expenses:* Contact institution. *Financial support:* Application deadline: 2/15; applicants required to submit FAFSA. *Unit head:* Brett J.L. Landry, Dean, 972-721-5356, E-mail: blandry@udallas.edu. *Application contact:* Dr. David Sweet, Dean, Braniff Graduate School, 972-721-5288, Fax: 972-721-5280, E-mail: dsweet@udallas.edu. Website: http://www.udallas.edu/cob/

University of Massachusetts Amherst, Graduate School, Interdisciplinary Programs, Dual Degree Programs in Management and Engineering, Amherst, MA 01003. Offers MBA/MIE, MBA/MSEWRE, MSCE/MBA, MSME/MBA. *Program availability:* Part-time. *Entrance requirements:* Additional exam requirements/recommendations for international students: Required—TOEFL (minimum score 600 paper-based; 100 iBT), IELTS (minimum score 7). Electronic applications accepted.

University of South Carolina, The Graduate School, College of Hospitality, Retail, and Sport Management, Department of Sport and Entertainment Management, Columbia, SC 29208. Offers live sport and entertainment events (MS); public assembly facilities management (MS). *Program availability:* Part-time. *Degree requirements:* For master's, comprehensive exam, thesis optional. *Entrance requirements:* For master's, GRE General Test or GMAT (preferred), minimum GPA of 3.0. Additional exam requirements/recommendations for international students: Required—TOEFL (minimum score 570 paper-based; 70 iBT). Electronic applications accepted. *Expenses:* Contact institution. *Faculty research:* Public assembly marketing, operations, box office, booking and scheduling, law/economic impacts.

Valparaiso University, Graduate School and Continuing Education, Program in Arts and Entertainment Administration, Valparaiso, IN 46383. Offers MA. *Program availability:* Part-time, evening/weekend. *Degree requirements:* For master's, internship or research project. *Entrance requirements:* Additional exam requirements/recommendations for international students: Required—TOEFL (minimum score 550 paper-based; 80 iBT), IELTS (minimum score 6). Electronic applications accepted. *Expenses:* Tuition: Full-time $11,340; part-time $630 per credit hour. *Required fees:* $520; $250 per year. $125 per semester. Tuition and fees vary according to program and reciprocity agreements.

Facilities Management

Cornell University, Graduate School, Graduate Fields of Human Ecology, Field of Design and Environmental Analysis, Ithaca, NY 14853. Offers applied research in human-environment relations (MS); facilities planning and management (MS); housing and design (MS); human factors and ergonomics (MS); human-environment relations (MS); interior design (MA, MPS). *Degree requirements:* For master's, thesis. *Entrance requirements:* For master's, GRE General Test, portfolio or slides of recent work; bachelor's degree in interior design, architecture or related design discipline; 2 letters of recommendation. Additional exam requirements/recommendations for international students: Required—TOEFL (minimum score 600 paper-based; 105 iBT). Electronic applications accepted. *Faculty research:* Facility planning and management, environmental psychology, housing, interior design, ergonomics and human factors.

Indiana University–Purdue University Fort Wayne, College of Engineering, Technology, and Computer Science, Program in Technology, Fort Wayne, IN 46805-1499. Offers facilities/construction management (MS); industrial technology/manufacturing (MS); information technology/advanced computer applications (MS). *Program availability:* Part-time. *Entrance requirements:* For master's, minimum GPA of 3.0. Additional exam requirements/recommendations for international students: Required—TOEFL (minimum score 550 paper-based; 79 iBT), TWE. Electronic applications accepted.

Liberty University, School of Business, Lynchburg, VA 24515. Offers accounting (MBA, MS), including audit and financial reporting (MS); business (MS); financial services (MS); forensic accounting (MS); leadership (MS); taxation (MS); criminal justice (MBA); cyber security (MS); executive leadership (MA); information systems (MS), including information assurance, technology management; international business (MBA, DBA); leadership (DBA); marketing (MBA, MS, DBA), including digital marketing and advertising (MS); project management (MS), public relations (MS); sports marketing and media (MS); project management (MBA, DBA); public administration (MBA); public relations (MBA). *Program availability:* Part-time, online learning. *Students:* 1,887 full-time (1,003 women), 4,223 part-time (1,950 women); includes 1,570 minority (1,133 Black or African American, non-Hispanic/Latino; 30 American Indian or Alaska Native, non-Hispanic/Latino; 118 Asian, non-Hispanic/Latino; 149 Hispanic/Latino; 13 Native Hawaiian or other Pacific Islander, non-Hispanic/Latino; 127 Two or more races, non-Hispanic/Latino), 109 international. Average age 35. 5,680 applicants, 51% accepted, 1510 enrolled. In 2017, 1,290 master's, 17 doctorates awarded. *Entrance requirements:* For master's, minimum undergraduate GPA of 3.0, 15 hours of upper-level business courses. Additional exam requirements/recommendations for international students: Required—TOEFL (minimum score 600 paper-based; 100 iBT). *Application deadline:* Applications are processed on a rolling basis. Application fee: $50. Electronic applications accepted. *Expenses:* Contact institution. *Financial support:* Applicants required to submit FAFSA. *Unit head:* Dr. Scott Hicks, Dean, 434-592-4808, Fax: 434-582-2366, E-mail: smhicks@liberty.edu. *Application contact:* Jay Bridge, Director of Graduate Admissions, 800-424-9595, Fax: 800-628-7977, E-mail: gradadmissions@liberty.edu.
Website: http://www.liberty.edu/academics/business/index.cfm?PID-149

Maastricht School of Management, Graduate Programs, Maastricht, Netherlands. Offers business administration (MBA, DBA, PhD); facility management (Exec MBA); management (M Sc); sustainability (Exec MBA).

Massachusetts Maritime Academy, Program in Facilities Management, Buzzards Bay, MA 02532-1803. Offers MS. *Program availability:* Part-time-only, evening/weekend. *Entrance requirements:* For master's, GRE or GMAT, interview. Electronic applications accepted.

Pratt Institute, School of Architecture, Program in Facilities Management, New York, NY 10011. Offers MS. *Program availability:* Part-time. *Students:* 12 full-time (7 women), 4 part-time (0 women); includes 8 minority (2 Black or African American, non-Hispanic/Latino; 2 Asian, non-Hispanic/Latino; 3 Hispanic/Latino; 1 Two or more races, non-Hispanic/Latino), 6 international. Average age 31. 15 applicants, 87% accepted, 4 enrolled. In 2017, 7 master's awarded. *Degree requirements:* For master's, thesis. *Entrance requirements:* For master's, writing sample, bachelor's degree, transcripts, letters of recommendation, portfolio. Additional exam requirements/recommendations for international students: Required—TOEFL (minimum score 550 paper-based; 79 iBT). *Application deadline:* For fall admission, 1/5 for domestic and international students; for spring admission, 10/1 for domestic and international students. Application fee: $50 ($90 for international students). Electronic applications accepted. *Expenses:* Tuition: Full-time $30,834. *Required fees:* $1974. *Financial support:* Career-related internships or fieldwork, Federal Work-Study, institutionally sponsored loans, scholarships/grants, health care benefits, and unspecified assistantships available. Support available to part-time students. Financial award application deadline: 2/1; financial award applicants required to submit FAFSA. *Faculty research:* Benchmarking, organizational studies, resource planning and management, computer-aided facilities management, value analysis. *Unit head:* Regina Ford Cahill, Chairperson, 212-647-7524, E-mail: rcahill8@pratt.edu. *Application contact:* Natalie Capannelli, Director of Graduate Admissions, 718-636-3551, Fax: 718-399-4242, E-mail: ncapanne@pratt.edu.
Website: https://www.pratt.edu/academics/architecture/facilities-management/

Université Laval, Faculty of Administrative Sciences, Programs in Business Administration, Québec, QC G1K 7P4, Canada. Offers accounting (MBA); agri-food management (MBA); electronic business (MBA, Diploma); factory management and logistics (MBA); finance (MBA); firm management (MBA); geomatic management (MBA); information technology management (MBA); international management (MBA); management (MBA); management accounting (MBA, Diploma); marketing (MBA); modeling and organizational decision (MBA); occupational health and safety management (MBA); pharmacy management (MBA); social and environmental responsibility (MBA); technological entrepreneurship (Diploma). *Accreditation:* AACSB. *Program availability:* Part-time, evening/weekend, online learning. *Entrance requirements:* For master's and Diploma, knowledge of French and English. Electronic applications accepted.

University of California, Berkeley, UC Berkeley Extension, Certificate Programs in Engineering, Construction and Facilities Management, Berkeley, CA 94720-1500. Offers construction management (Certificate); HVAC (Certificate); integrated circuit design and techniques (online) (Certificate). *Program availability:* Online learning.

University of New Haven, Graduate School, College of Business, Program in Sport Management, West Haven, CT 06516. Offers collegiate athletic administration (MS); facility management (MS); sport analytics (MS); sport management (Graduate Certificate). *Program availability:* Part-time, evening/weekend. *Students:* 16 full-time (4 women), 7 part-time (5 women); includes 5 minority (4 Black or African American, non-

Facilities Management

Hispanic/Latino; 1 Native Hawaiian or other Pacific Islander, non-Hispanic/Latino), 3 international. Average age 26. 34 applicants, 88% accepted, 12 enrolled. In 2017, 15 master's awarded. *Entrance requirements:* For master's, GMAT. Additional exam requirements/recommendations for international students: Required—TOEFL (minimum score 80 iBT), IELTS, PTE. *Application deadline:* Applications are processed on a rolling basis. Application fee: $50. Electronic applications accepted. Application fee is waived when completed online. *Expenses: Tuition:* Full-time $16,020; part-time $890 per credit hour. *Required fees:* $220; $90 per term. *Financial support:* Research assistantships with partial tuition reimbursements, teaching assistantships with partial tuition reimbursements, Federal Work-Study, scholarships/grants, and unspecified assistantships available. Support available to part-time students. Financial award applicants required to submit FAFSA. *Unit head:* Gil B. Fried, Professor, 203-932-7081, E-mail: gfried@newhaven.edu.
Website: http://www.newhaven.edu/6851/

See Display on page 154 and Close-Up on page 185.

The University of North Carolina at Charlotte, William States Lee College of Engineering, Department of Engineering Technology and Construction Management, Charlotte, NC 28223-0001. Offers applied energy (Graduate Certificate); applied energy and electromechanical systems (MS); construction and facilities management (MS); fire protection and administration (MS). *Program availability:* Part-time. *Faculty:* 29 full-time (7 women). *Students:* 46 full-time (13 women), 32 part-time (3 women); includes 7 minority (3 Black or African American, non-Hispanic/Latino; 2 Asian, non-Hispanic/Latino; 2 Hispanic/Latino), 44 international. Average age 25. 126 applicants, 80% accepted, 33 enrolled. In 2017, 34 master's awarded. *Degree requirements:* For master's, thesis, capstone, or comprehensive exam. *Entrance requirements:* For master's, GRE, minimum undergraduate GPA of 3.0, recommendations, statistics; integral and differential calculus (for students pursuing fire protection concentration or applied energy and electromechanical systems program); for Graduate Certificate, bachelor's degree in engineering, engineering technology, construction management or a closely-related technical or scientific field; undergraduate coursework of at least 3 semesters in engineering analysis or calculus; minimum GPA of 3.0. Additional exam requirements/recommendations for international students: Required—TOEFL (minimum score 523 paper-based, 70 iBT) or IELTS (6.5). *Application deadline:* For fall admission, 3/1 priority date for domestic and international students; for spring admission, 10/1 priority date for domestic and international students. Applications are processed on a rolling basis. Application fee: $75. Electronic applications accepted. *Expenses:* Contact institution. *Financial support:* In 2017–18, 29 students received support, including 29 research assistantships (averaging $4,723 per year); career-related internships or fieldwork, institutionally sponsored loans, scholarships/grants, and unspecified assistantships also available. Support available to part-time students. Financial award application deadline: 3/1; financial award applicants required to submit FAFSA. *Total annual research expenditures:* $1.8 million. *Unit head:* Dr. Anthony Brizendine, Chair, 704-687-5050, E-mail: albrizen@uncc.edu. *Application contact:* Kathy B. Giddings, Director of Graduate Admissions, 704-687-5503, Fax: 704-687-1668, E-mail: gradadm@uncc.edu.
Website: http://et.uncc.edu/

Wentworth Institute of Technology, Master of Science in Facility Management Program, Boston, MA 02115-5998. Offers MS. *Program availability:* Part-time, evening/weekend, online only, 100% online, blended/hybrid learning. *Faculty:* 10 part-time/adjunct (4 women). *Students:* 15 part-time (3 women); includes 12 minority (all Hispanic/Latino). Average age 37. 17 applicants, 71% accepted, 9 enrolled. In 2017, 9 master's awarded. *Degree requirements:* For master's, thesis optional, capstone. *Entrance requirements:* For master's, current resume; two professional recommendation forms from current or former employer; statement of purpose; undergraduate degree in one of the following: architecture, facility management, engineering, construction management, business or interior design; one year of professional experience in technical role and/or technical organization. Additional exam requirements/recommendations for international students: Recommended—TOEFL (minimum score 550 paper-based). *Application deadline:* For fall admission, 8/1 for domestic and international students. Applications are processed on a rolling basis. Application fee: $50. Electronic applications accepted. *Expenses:* $1,135 per credit hour. *Financial support:* In 2017–18, 4 students received support. Scholarships/grants available. Support available to part-time students. Financial award application deadline: 8/1; financial award applicants required to submit FAFSA. *Unit head:* Philip Hammond, Director of Graduate Programs, 617-989-4594, Fax: 617-989-4399, E-mail: hammondp1@wit.edu. *Application contact:* Martha Sheehan, Director of Admissions and Marketing, 617-989-4661, Fax: 617-989-4399, E-mail: sheehanm@wit.edu.
Website: https://wit.edu/continuing-ed/programs/masters/master-science-facility-management

Section 7
Hospitality Management

This section contains a directory of institutions offering graduate work in hospitality management. Additional information about programs listed in the directory may be obtained by writing directly to the dean of a graduate school or chair of a department at the address given in the directory.

For programs offering related work, see also in this book *Business Administration and Management* and *Advertising and Public Relations*.

In the other guides in this series:

Graduate Programs in the Biological/Biomedical Sciences & Health-Related Medical Professions
See *Health Services*

Graduate Programs in the Physical Sciences, Mathematics, Agricultural Sciences, the Environment & Natural Resources
See *Agricultural and Food Sciences (Food Science and Technology)*

CONTENTS

Program Directories

Hospitality Management

Alabama Agricultural and Mechanical University, School of Graduate Studies, College of Agricultural, Life and Natural Sciences, Department of Family and Consumer Sciences, Huntsville, AL 35811. Offers apparel, merchandising and design (MS); family and consumer sciences (MS); human development and family studies (MS); nutrition and hospitality management (MS). *Program availability:* Part-time, evening/weekend. *Degree requirements:* For master's, comprehensive exam, thesis optional. *Entrance requirements:* For master's, GRE General Test. Additional exam requirements/recommendations for international students: Required—TOEFL (minimum score 500 paper-based; 61 iBT). Electronic applications accepted. *Faculty research:* Food biotechnology, nutrition, food microbiology, food engineering, food chemistry.

American International College, School of Business, Arts and Sciences, Springfield, MA 01109-3189. Offers accounting and taxation (MS); business administration (MBA); clinical psychology (MA); educational psychology (Ed D); forensic psychology (MS); general psychology (MA, CAGS); management (CAGS); resort and casino management (MBA, CAGS). *Program availability:* Part-time, evening/weekend. *Faculty:* 4 full-time (2 women), 25 part-time/adjunct (13 women). *Students:* 178 full-time (120 women), 24 part-time (20 women); includes 94 minority (42 Black or African American, non-Hispanic/Latino; 1 American Indian or Alaska Native, non-Hispanic/Latino; 4 Asian, non-Hispanic/Latino; 39 Hispanic/Latino; 8 Two or more races, non-Hispanic/Latino), 13 international. Average age 28. 155 applicants, 83% accepted, 71 enrolled. In 2017, 87 master's, 3 doctorates awarded. *Degree requirements:* For master's, practicum; for doctorate, comprehensive exam, thesis/dissertation, practicum. *Entrance requirements:* For master's, BS or BA, minimum undergraduate GPA of 2.75, 2 letters of recommendation, official transcripts, personal goal statement or essay; for doctorate, 3 letters of recommendation; BS or BA; minimum undergraduate GPA of 3.0 (3.25 recommended); official transcripts; personal goal statement or essay. Additional exam requirements/recommendations for international students: Required—TOEFL (minimum score 550 paper-based; 80 iBT). *Application deadline:* For fall admission, 8/15 for domestic and international students; for spring admission, 12/15 for domestic and international students. Applications are processed on a rolling basis. Application fee: $50. *Expenses:* Contact institution. *Financial support:* In 2017–18, 6 students received support, including 6 research assistantships with full tuition reimbursements available (averaging $1,500 per year). Financial award application deadline: 4/1; financial award applicants required to submit FAFSA. *Faculty research:* Substance abuse, forensic psychology, special education. *Unit head:* Dr. Susanne Swanker, Dean, 413-205-3216, Fax: 413-205-3943, E-mail: susanne.swanker@aic.edu. *Application contact:* Kerry Barnes, Dean of Graduate Admissions, 413-205-3703, Fax: 413-205-3051, E-mail: kerry.barnes@aic.edu.
Website: http://www.aic.edu/school-of-business-arts-and-sciences/

Boston University, School of Hospitality Administration, Boston, MA 02215. Offers MMH. *Program availability:* Part-time. *Faculty:* 9 full-time, 17 part-time/adjunct. *Students:* 30 full-time (21 women), 3 part-time (2 women); includes 6 minority (4 Black or African American, non-Hispanic/Latino; 1 Asian, non-Hispanic/Latino; 1 Hispanic/Latino), 20 international. Average age 26. *Entrance requirements:* For master's, GRE or GMAT. Additional exam requirements/recommendations for international students: Required—TOEFL (minimum score 84 iBT), IELTS (minimum score 6.5). *Application deadline:* For summer admission, 3/1 priority date for domestic and international students. Applications are processed on a rolling basis. Application fee: $95. Electronic applications accepted. *Financial support:* In 2017–18, 32 students received support. Scholarships/grants and unspecified assistantships available. Financial award application deadline: 3/1; financial award applicants required to submit FAFSA. *Unit head:* Dr. Arun Upneja, Dean, 617-353-3261, E-mail: aupneja@bu.edu. *Application contact:* Micah Sieber, Director of Graduate Affairs, 617-353-1011, E-mail: shagrad@bu.edu.
Website: http://www.bu.edu/hospitality/

California State Polytechnic University, Pomona, Program in Hospitality Management, Pomona, CA 91768-2557. Offers MS. *Program availability:* Part-time, evening/weekend. *Students:* 14 full-time (12 women), 24 part-time (16 women); includes 10 minority (2 Black or African American, non-Hispanic/Latino; 6 Asian, non-Hispanic/Latino; 2 Two or more races, non-Hispanic/Latino), 21 international. Average age 30. 22 applicants, 45% accepted, 6 enrolled. In 2017, 16 master's awarded. *Degree requirements:* For master's, thesis or professional paper. *Entrance requirements:* Additional exam requirements/recommendations for international students: Required—TOEFL (minimum score 550 paper-based). *Application deadline:* Applications are processed on a rolling basis. Application fee: $55. Electronic applications accepted. *Expenses:* Contact institution. *Financial support:* Application deadline: 3/2; applicants required to submit FAFSA. *Unit head:* Dr. Neha Singh, Associate Professor/MSHM Program Director, 909-869-4565, Fax: 909-869-4805, E-mail: nsingh@cpp.edu. *Application contact:* Deborah L. Brandon, Executive Director of Admissions and Enrollment Planning, 909-869-3427, Fax: 909-869-5315, E-mail: dlbrandon@cpp.edu.
Website: http://www.cpp.edu/~ceu/degree-programs/hospitality-management/index.shtml

California State University, Northridge, Graduate Studies, College of Health and Human Development, Department of Recreation and Tourism Management, Northridge, CA 91330. Offers hospitality and tourism (MS); recreational sport management/campus recreation (MS). *Students:* 19 full-time (6 women), 12 part-time (10 women); includes 12 minority (9 Hispanic/Latino; 1 Native Hawaiian or other Pacific Islander, non-Hispanic/Latino; 2 Two or more races, non-Hispanic/Latino), 7 international. Average age 29. 36 applicants, 67% accepted, 12 enrolled. In 2017, 17 master's awarded. *Degree requirements:* For master's, thesis (for some programs). *Entrance requirements:* For master's, GRE (if cumulative undergraduate GPA less than 3.0). Additional exam requirements/recommendations for international students: Required—TOEFL. *Application deadline:* For fall admission, 11/30 for domestic students. Application fee: $55. *Financial support:* Application deadline: 3/1. *Unit head:* Dr. Mechelle Best, Chair, 818-677-3202.
Website: http://www.csun.edu/hhd/rtm/

California State University, Northridge, Graduate Studies, Tseng College, Northridge, CA 91330. Offers business administration (Graduate Certificate); health administration (MPA); health education (MPH); knowledge management (MKM); music industry administration (MA); nonprofit-sector management (Graduate Certificate); public administration (MPA); public sector management and leadership (MPA); social work (MSW); taxation (MS); tourism, hospitality and recreation management (MS). *Students:* 4 part-time (all women); includes 1 minority (Black or African American, non-Hispanic/Latino). Average age 37. In 2017, 2 master's awarded. *Entrance requirements:* For master's, GRE (if cumulative undergraduate GPA less than 3.0). *Unit head:* Joyce Feucht-Haviar, Dean, 866-873-6439.

Cornell University, Graduate School, Field of Hotel Administration, Ithaca, NY 14853. Offers hospitality management (MMH); hotel administration (MS, PhD). Terminal master's awarded for partial completion of doctoral program. *Degree requirements:* For master's, thesis (MS); for doctorate, comprehensive exam, thesis/dissertation. *Entrance requirements:* For master's and doctorate, GMAT, 1 academic and 1 employer letter of recommendation, 2 interviews. Additional exam requirements/recommendations for international students: Required—TOEFL (minimum score 600 paper-based). Electronic applications accepted. *Faculty research:* Hospitality finance; property-asset management; real estate; management, strategy, and human resources; organizational communication.

Cornell University, Graduate School, Graduate Fields of Agriculture and Life Sciences, Field of Applied Economics and Management, Ithaca, NY 14853. Offers agricultural finance (MS, PhD); applied econometrics and qualitative analysis (MS, PhD); economics of development (MS, PhD); environmental economics (MS, PhD); environmental management (MPS); farm management and production economics (MS, PhD); marketing and food distribution (MS, PhD); public policy analysis (MS, PhD); resource economics (PhD). *Entrance requirements:* For master's and doctorate, GRE. Additional exam requirements/recommendations for international students: Required—TOEFL.

DePaul University, Kellstadt Graduate School of Business, Chicago, IL 60604. Offers accountancy (MBA, MSA); applied economics (MBA); audit and advisory services (MS); business administration (DBA); business analytics (MS); business strategy and decision-making (MBA); computational finance (MS); economics and policy analysis (MS); enterprise risk management (MS); entrepreneurship (MBA, MS); finance (MBA, MS); general business (MBA); hospitality leadership (MBA); hospitality leadership and operational performance (MS); human resources (MS); international business (MBA); management (MBA, MS); management information systems (MBA); marketing (MBA, MS); marketing analysis (MS); marketing strategy and planning (MBA); real estate (MS); real estate finance and investment (MBA); strategy, execution and valuation (MBA); supply chain management (MS); sustainable management (MS); taxation (MS); JD/MBA. *Accreditation:* AACSB. *Program availability:* Part-time, evening/weekend, online learning. *Entrance requirements:* For master's, GMAT/GRE, 2 letters of recommendation, resume, essay, official transcripts. Additional exam requirements/recommendations for international students: Required—TOEFL (minimum score 550 paper-based; 80 iBT). *Application deadline:* For fall admission, 7/1 for domestic students, 6/1 for international students; for winter admission, 10/1 for domestic students, 9/1 for international students; for spring admission, 2/1 for domestic students, 1/1 for international students. Applications are processed on a rolling basis. Application fee: $60. Electronic applications accepted. *Expenses:* Contact institution. *Financial support:* Application deadline: 4/1; applicants required to submit FAFSA. *Unit head:* Christa Hinton, Assistant Dean and Director, 312-362-8810, Fax: 312-362-6677, E-mail: chinton@depaul.edu. *Application contact:* Garry Cooke, Director of Recruitment and Admissions, 312-362-8810, Fax: 312-362-6677, E-mail: kgsb@depaul.edu.
Website: http://kellstadt.depaul.edu

Drexel University, Goodwin College of Professional Studies, School of Technology and Professional Studies, Philadelphia, PA 19104-2875. Offers construction management (MS); creativity and innovation (MS); engineering technology (MS); food science (MS); hospitality management (MS); professional studies: creativity studies (MS); professional studies: e-learning leadership (MS); professional studies: homeland security management (MS); project management (MS); property management (MS); sport management (MS). *Program availability:* Part-time, evening/weekend. *Entrance requirements:* Additional exam requirements/recommendations for international students: Required—TOEFL, IELTS. Electronic applications accepted. Application fee is waived when completed online.

East Carolina University, Graduate School, College of Business, School of Hospitality Leadership, Greenville, NC 27858-4353. Offers hospitality management (Postbaccalaureate Certificate); sustainable tourism and hospitality (MS). *Students:* 4 part-time (all women); includes 1 minority (Black or African American, non-Hispanic/Latino). Average age 37. 2 applicants, 100% accepted, 1 enrolled. In 2017, 4 master's awarded. *Entrance requirements:* For master's, GRE or GMAT. Additional exam requirements/recommendations for international students: Recommended—TOEFL (minimum score 78 iBT), IELTS (minimum score 6.5). Application fee: $75. Electronic applications accepted. *Expenses:* Tuition, state resident: full-time $4749; part-time $297 per credit hour. Tuition, nonresident: full-time $17,898; part-time $1119 per credit hour. *Required fees:* $2691; $224 per credit hour. Part-time tuition and fees vary according to course load and program. *Unit head:* Dr. Robert O'Halloran, Director, 252-737-1604, E-mail: ohalloranr@ecu.edu.
Website: http://www.ecu.edu/business/shl/

Eastern Michigan University, Graduate School, College of Technology, School of Technology and Professional Services Management, Program in Hotel and Restaurant Management, Ypsilanti, MI 48197. Offers Graduate Certificate. *Program availability:* Part-time, evening/weekend, online learning. *Students:* 1 full-time (0 women), 3 part-time (2 women); includes 1 minority (Two or more races, non-Hispanic/Latino). Average age 33. *Entrance requirements:* Additional exam requirements/recommendations for international students: Required—TOEFL. *Application deadline:* Applications are processed on a rolling basis. Application fee: $45. *Financial support:* Fellowships, research assistantships with full tuition reimbursements, teaching assistantships with full tuition reimbursements, career-related internships or fieldwork, Federal Work-Study, institutionally sponsored loans, scholarships/grants, tuition waivers (partial), and unspecified assistantships available. Support available to part-time students. Financial award applicants required to submit FAFSA. *Application contact:* Dr. Tierney Orfgen McCleary, Program Advisor, 734-487-2326, Fax: 734-487-7690, E-mail: cot_hrm@emich.edu.

Ecole Hôtelière de Lausanne, Program in Hospitality Administration, Lausanne, Switzerland. Offers MHA. *Degree requirements:* For master's, project.

ESSEC Business School, Graduate Programs, Paris, France. Offers business administration (PhD); executive business administration (MBA); global business administration (MBA); hospitality management (MBA); international luxury brand management (MBA); management (MSM).

Fairleigh Dickinson University, Florham Campus, Anthony J. Petrocelli College of Continuing Studies, International School of Hospitality and Tourism Management, Madison, NJ 07940-1099. Offers hospitality management studies (MS).

Fairleigh Dickinson University, Metropolitan Campus, Anthony J. Petrocelli College of Continuing Studies, International School of Hospitality and Tourism Management, Teaneck, NJ 07666-1914. Offers hospitality management (MS).

Florida International University, Chaplin School of Hospitality and Tourism Management, North Miami, FL 33181-3000. Offers MS. *Program availability:* Part-time, evening/weekend, online learning. *Faculty:* 22 full-time (6 women), 36 part-time/adjunct (11 women). *Students:* 193 full-time (124 women), 89 part-time (67 women); includes 94 minority (20 Black or African American, non-Hispanic/Latino; 3 Asian, non-Hispanic/Latino; 67 Hispanic/Latino; 4 Two or more races, non-Hispanic/Latino), 150 international. Average age 27. 216 applicants, 82% accepted, 115 enrolled. In 2017, 143 master's awarded. *Degree requirements:* For master's, thesis (for some programs). *Entrance requirements:* For master's, minimum GPA of 3.0, 5 years of management experience (for executive track). Additional exam requirements/recommendations for international students: Required—TOEFL (minimum score 550 paper-based; 80 iBT). *Application deadline:* For fall admission, 6/1 for domestic students, 4/1 for international students; for spring admission, 10/1 for domestic students, 9/1 for international students. Applications are processed on a rolling basis. Application fee: $30. Electronic applications accepted. *Expenses:* Tuition, state resident: full-time $8912; part-time $446 per credit hour. Tuition, nonresident: full-time $21,393; part-time $992 per credit hour. *Required fees:* $390; $195 per semester. *Financial support:* Institutionally sponsored loans and scholarships/grants available. Financial award application deadline: 3/1; financial award applicants required to submit FAFSA. *Faculty research:* Environmental sustainability in hospitality/lodging, casino marketing and management, management philosophy, strategic management and competitive advantage, legal liabilities of hotels and resorts for waterfront amenities. *Unit head:* Dr. Michael Cheng, Interim Dean, 305-919-4506, E-mail: michael.cheng@fiu.edu. *Application contact:* Nanett Rojas, Manager, Admissions Operations, 305-348-7464, Fax: 305-348-7441, E-mail: gradadm@fiu.edu. Website: http://hospitality.fiu.edu/

Georgetown University, Graduate School of Arts and Sciences, School of Continuing Studies, Washington, DC 20057. Offers American studies (MALS); applied intelligence (MPS); Catholic studies (MALS); classical civilizations (MALS); emergency and disaster management (MPS); ethics and the professions (MALS); global strategic communications (MPS); hospitality management (MPS); human resources management (MPS); humanities (MALS); individualized study (MALS); integrated marketing communications (MPS); international affairs (MALS); Islam and Muslim-Christian relations (MALS); journalism (MPS); liberal studies (DLS); literature and society (MALS); medieval and early modern European studies (MALS); public relations and corporate communications (MPS); real estate (MPS); religious studies (MALS); social and public policy (MALS); sports industry management (MPS); systems engineering management (MPS); technology management (MPS); the theory and practice of American democracy (MALS); urban and regional planning (MPS); visual culture (MALS). MPS in systems engineering management offered jointly with Stevens Institute of Technology. *Entrance requirements:* Additional exam requirements/recommendations for international students: Required—TOEFL.

The George Washington University, School of Business, Department of Tourism and Hospitality Management, Washington, DC 20052. Offers destination management (Professional Certificate); event and meeting management (MTA); event management (Professional Certificate); hospitality management (MTA); individualized studies (MTA); sport management (MTA); sustainable tourism destination management (MTA); tourism and hospitality management (MBA). *Program availability:* Part-time, online learning. *Students:* 69 full-time (46 women), 51 part-time (36 women); includes 35 minority (23 Black or African American, non-Hispanic/Latino; 3 Asian, non-Hispanic/Latino; 6 Hispanic/Latino; 3 Two or more races, non-Hispanic/Latino), 46 international. Average age 28. 185 applicants, 74% accepted, 53 enrolled. In 2017, 51 master's awarded. *Degree requirements:* For master's, comprehensive exam, thesis. *Entrance requirements:* For master's, GRE General Test. Additional exam requirements/recommendations for international students: Required—TOEFL. *Application deadline:* For fall admission, 4/1 priority date for domestic students; for spring admission, 10/1 for domestic students. Applications are processed on a rolling basis. Application fee: $75. *Expenses:* Tuition: Full-time $28,800; part-time $1655 per credit hour. *Required fees:* $45; $2.75 per credit hour. *Financial support:* In 2017–18, 32 students received support. Fellowships, teaching assistantships, career-related internships or fieldwork, Federal Work-Study, institutionally sponsored loans, and tuition waivers (partial) available. Financial award application deadline: 4/1. *Faculty research:* Tourism policy, tourism impact forecasting, geotourism. *Unit head:* Prof. Lisa Delpy Neirotti, Faculty Director, 202-994-6623, E-mail: delpy@gwu.edu. *Application contact:* Christopher Storer, Executive Director, Graduate Admissions, 202-994-1212, E-mail: gwmba@gwu.edu. Website: http://business.gwu.edu/tourism/

Glion Institute of Higher Education, Graduate Programs, Glion-sur-Montreux, Switzerland. Offers hospitality organizational training (M Ed); hotel management with leadership (MBA); hotel management with marketing (MBA); international hospitality management (MBA). *Program availability:* Evening/weekend.

Husson University, Master of Business Administration Program, Bangor, ME 04401-2999. Offers athletic administration (MBA); biotechnology and innovation (MBA); general business administration (MBA); healthcare management (MBA); hospitality and tourism management (MBA); organizational management (MBA); risk management (MBA). *Program availability:* Part-time, evening/weekend, 100% online, blended/hybrid learning. *Faculty:* 11 full-time (5 women), 19 part-time/adjunct (4 women). *Students:* 83 full-time (44 women), 287 part-time (176 women); includes 25 minority (7 Black or African American, non-Hispanic/Latino; 11 Asian, non-Hispanic/Latino; 4 Hispanic/Latino; 3 Two or more races, non-Hispanic/Latino), 16 international. Average age 35. 158 applicants, 77% accepted, 49 enrolled. In 2017, 120 master's awarded. *Degree requirements:* For master's, comprehensive exam (for some programs), thesis optional. *Entrance requirements:* For master's, minimum GPA of 3.0, letter of recommendation. Additional exam requirements/recommendations for international students: Required—TOEFL (minimum score 550 paper-based; 80 iBT), IELTS (minimum score 6.5). *Application deadline:* Applications are processed on a rolling basis. Application fee: $50. Electronic applications accepted. *Expenses:* $464 per credit. *Financial support:* In 2017–18, 13 students received support. Career-related internships or fieldwork, Federal Work-Study, scholarships/grants, and unspecified assistantships available. Financial award application deadline: 4/15; financial award applicants required to submit FAFSA. *Unit head:* Prof. Stephanie Shayne, Director, Graduate and Online Programs, 207-404-5632, Fax: 207-992-4987, E-mail: shaynes@husson.edu. *Application contact:* Kristen Card, Director of Graduate Admissions, 207-404-5660, Fax: 207-941-7935, E-mail: cardk@husson.edu. Website: http://www.husson.edu/college-of-business/school-of-business-and-management/master-of-business-administration-mba/

IGlobal University, Graduate Programs, Vienna, VA 22182. Offers accounting (MBA); data management and analytics (MSIT); entrepreneurship (MBA); finance (MBA); global business management (MBA); health care management (MBA); hospitality and tourism management (MBA); human resources management (MBA); information technology (MBA); information technology systems and management (MSIT); leadership and management (MBA); project management (MBA); public service and administration (MBA); software design and management (MSIT).

Johnson & Wales University, Graduate Studies, MBA Program, Providence, RI 02903-3703. Offers accounting (MBA); business administration (MBA); finance (MBA);

global fashion merchandising and management (MBA); hospitality (MBA); human resource management (MBA); information security/assurance (MBA); information technology (MBA); nonprofit management (MBA); operations and supply chain management (MBA); organizational leadership (MBA); organizational psychology (MBA); sport leadership (MBA). Program also offered on Denver campus. *Program availability:* Part-time, online learning. *Entrance requirements:* For master's, minimum GPA of 2.75. Additional exam requirements/recommendations for international students: Required—TOEFL (minimum score 550 paper-based); Recommended—IELTS, TWE. *Application deadline:* For fall admission, 8/15 priority date for domestic students, 6/28 priority date for international students; for winter admission, 11/10 priority date for domestic students, 9/20 priority date for international students; for spring admission, 2/5 priority date for domestic students, 12/20 priority date for international students. Applications are processed on a rolling basis. *Expenses: Tuition:* Full-time $12,636; part-time $702 per credit hour. *Financial support:* Tuition waivers (partial) and unspecified assistantships available. Support available to part-time students. Financial award application deadline: 5/1. *Faculty research:* International banking, global economy, international trade, cultural differences. *Unit head:* Dr. Karen Silva, Director, 401-598-2849, Fax: 401-598-1125. *Application contact:* Graduate School Admissions, 401-598-1015, Fax: 401-598-1286, E-mail: gradadm@jwu.edu.

Kansas State University, Graduate School, College of Human Ecology, Department of Hospitality Management, Manhattan, KS 66506. Offers hospitality and dietetics administration (MS). *Program availability:* Part-time. *Degree requirements:* For master's, comprehensive exam (for some programs), thesis or alternative, residency. *Entrance requirements:* For master's, GRE or GMAT. Additional exam requirements/recommendations for international students: Required—TOEFL (minimum score 550 paper-based; 79 iBT). Electronic applications accepted. *Expenses:* Contact institution. *Faculty research:* Food and beverage management; lodging management; event management; sustainability; customer behaviors; human resource management; food safety in food service operations; gerontology and the hospitality industry; education, training, and career development in hospitality administration.

Kansas State University, Graduate School, College of Human Ecology, Doctorate in Human Ecology Program, Manhattan, KS 66506-1407. Offers apparel and textiles (PhD); applied family sciences (PhD); couple and family therapy (PhD); hospitality administration (PhD); kinesiology (PhD); life-span human development (PhD). *Program availability:* Part-time. *Degree requirements:* For doctorate, thesis/dissertation. *Entrance requirements:* Additional exam requirements/recommendations for international students: Required—TOEFL. Electronic applications accepted.

Kent State University, College of Education, Health and Human Services, School of Foundations, Leadership and Administration, Program in Hospitality and Tourism Management, Kent, OH 44242-0001. Offers MS. *Program availability:* Part-time. *Degree requirements:* For master's, thesis optional. *Entrance requirements:* For master's, minimum GPA of 3.0, 3 letters of recommendation, resume, goals statement. Additional exam requirements/recommendations for international students: Required—TOEFL (minimum score 550 paper-based; 80 iBT). Electronic applications accepted. *Expenses:* Tuition, state resident: full-time $11,310; part-time $515 per credit hour. Tuition, nonresident: full-time $20,396; part-time $928 per credit hour. *International tuition:* $18,544 full-time. *Faculty research:* Training human service workers, health care services for older adults, early adolescent development, care-giving arrangements with aging families, peace and war.

Lasell College, Graduate and Professional Studies in Management, Newton, MA 02466-2709. Offers business administration (MBA); elder care management (MSM); hospitality and event management (MSM); human resources management (MSM, Graduate Certificate); management (MSM, Graduate Certificate); marketing (MS, Graduate Certificate); project management (MSM, Graduate Certificate). *Accreditation:* ACBSP. *Program availability:* Part-time, evening/weekend, 100% online, blended/hybrid learning. *Faculty:* 1 full-time (0 women), 15 part-time/adjunct (11 women). *Students:* 41 full-time (25 women), 102 part-time (70 women); includes 34 minority (19 Black or African American, non-Hispanic/Latino; 5 Asian, non-Hispanic/Latino; 8 Hispanic/Latino; 2 Two or more races, non-Hispanic/Latino), 29 international. Average age 32. 128 applicants, 46% accepted, 38 enrolled. In 2017, 66 master's, 3 other advanced degrees awarded. *Degree requirements:* For master's, minimum GPA of 3.0; internship or research paper (for MSM). *Entrance requirements:* For master's, one-page personal statement, 2 letters of recommendation, resume, bachelor's degree transcript; proof of microeconomics and statistics (for MBA); for Graduate Certificate, bachelor's degree transcript, 2 letters of recommendation, 1-page personal statement, resume. Additional exam requirements/recommendations for international students: Required—TOEFL (minimum score 550 paper-based, 79 iBT) or IELTS (minimum score 6). *Application deadline:* For fall admission, 8/31 priority date for domestic students, 6/30 priority date for international students; for spring admission, 12/31 priority date for domestic students, 10/31 priority date for international students. Applications are processed on a rolling basis. Electronic applications accepted. *Expenses:* $600 per credit. *Financial support:* Federal Work-Study, scholarships/grants, and tuition discounts available. Support available to part-time students. Financial award application deadline: 8/31; financial award applicants required to submit FAFSA. *Unit head:* Eric Turner, Vice President of Graduate and Professional Studies, 617-243-2071, Fax: 617-243-2450, E-mail: gradinfo@lasell.edu. *Application contact:* Adrienne Franciosi, Director of Graduate Enrollment, 617-243-2214, Fax: 617-243-2450, E-mail: gradinfo@lasell.edu. Website: http://www.lasell.edu/academics/graduate-and-professional-studies/programs-of-study/master-of-science-in-management.html

Lasell College, Graduate and Professional Studies in Sport Management, Newton, MA 02466-2709. Offers athletic administration (MS); parks and recreation (MS); sport leadership (MS, Graduate Certificate); sport tourism and hospitality (MS). *Program availability:* Part-time, evening/weekend, online only, 100% online. *Faculty:* 5 full-time (1 woman), 2 part-time/adjunct (1 woman). *Students:* 10 full-time (6 women), 25 part-time (8 women); includes 12 minority (9 Black or African American, non-Hispanic/Latino; 3 Hispanic/Latino). Average age 29. 35 applicants, 46% accepted, 11 enrolled. In 2017, 26 master's awarded. *Degree requirements:* For master's, minimum GPA of 3.0; internship or thesis. *Entrance requirements:* For master's, one-page personal statement, 2 letters of recommendation, resume, bachelor's degree transcript; for Graduate Certificate, bachelor's degree transcript, 2 letters of recommendation, 1-page personal statement, resume. Additional exam requirements/recommendations for international students: Required—TOEFL (minimum score 550 paper-based, 79 iBT) or IELTS (minimum score 6). *Application deadline:* For fall admission, 8/31 priority date for domestic students, 6/30 priority date for international students; for spring admission, 12/31 priority date for domestic students, 10/31 priority date for international students. Applications are processed on a rolling basis. Electronic applications accepted. *Expenses:* $600 per credit. *Financial support:* Federal Work-Study, scholarships/grants, and tuition discounts available. Support available to part-time students. Financial award application deadline: 8/31; financial award applicants required to submit FAFSA. *Faculty research:* How do fans attribute team failure; investigating cross-cultural difference in attribution; sense of ownership as a key predictor of fan loyalty; fans' normative beliefs about sponsorship and sponsors; investigation of new attitudinal variables in sponsorship. *Unit head:* Eric Turner, Vice President of Graduate and Professional

Hospitality Management

Studies, 617-243-2071, Fax: 617-243-2450, E-mail: gradinfo@lasell.edu. *Application contact:* Adrienne Franciosi, Director of Graduate Enrollment, 617-243-2214, Fax: 617-243-2450, E-mail: gradinfo@lasell.edu.
Website: http://www.lasell.edu/academics/graduate-and-professional-studies/programs-of-study/master-of-science-in-sport-management.html

Les Roches International School of Hotel Management, Program in Hospitality Management, Bluche, Switzerland. Offers MBA. Available only at Switzerland campus.

Lynn University, College of Business and Management, Boca Raton, FL 33431-5598. Offers business administration (MBA), including aviation management, entrepreneurial management, financial valuation and investment management, hospitality management, human resource management, international business management, marketing, media management, social innovation management, sports management, Web development. *Program availability:* Part-time, evening/weekend, 100% online, blended/hybrid learning. *Faculty:* 29 full-time (11 women), 19 part-time/adjunct (7 women). *Students:* 287 full-time (124 women), 195 part-time (105 women); includes 110 minority (44 Black or African American, non-Hispanic/Latino; 2 American Indian or Alaska Native, non-Hispanic/Latino; 11 Asian, non-Hispanic/Latino; 47 Hispanic/Latino; 6 Two or more races, non-Hispanic/Latino), 135 international. Average age 28. 293 applicants, 94% accepted, 192 enrolled. In 2017, 236 master's awarded. *Degree requirements:* For master's, thesis, minimum GPA of 3.0, strategic management seminar, written presentation reflecting the integration and application of theory to practice. *Entrance requirements:* For master's, bachelor's degree from accredited institution, minimum undergraduate GPA of 2.5, official undergraduate transcripts, resume, personal statement, letter of recommendation from academic or professional sources, writing sample demonstrating capacity to perform at graduate level. Additional exam requirements/recommendations for international students: Required—TOEFL (minimum score 550 paper-based; 80 iBT), IELTS (minimum score 6.5). *Application deadline:* For fall admission, 8/18 for domestic students, 8/4 for international students; for spring admission, 12/15 for domestic students, 12/1 for international students; for summer admission, 4/17 for domestic students, 4/3 for international students. Applications are processed on a rolling basis. Application fee: $45. Electronic applications accepted. *Expenses:* $740 per credit. *Financial support:* Career-related internships or fieldwork, Federal Work-Study, scholarships/grants, tuition waivers (full and partial), and unspecified assistantships available. Support available to part-time students. Financial award application deadline: 3/1; financial award applicants required to submit FAFSA. *Faculty research:* Knowledge economy, urban economy, U.S. manufacturing industries, leadership personality, stock market reactions to terrorism, personality psychology, industrial/organizational psychology. *Unit head:* Dr. RT Good, Dean of the College of Business and Management, 561-237-7458, E-mail: rgood@lynn.edu. *Application contact:* Steven Pruitt, Director of Graduate and Undergraduate Evening Admission, 561-237-7834, Fax: 561-237-7100, E-mail: spruitt@lynn.edu.
Website: http://www.lynn.edu/academics/colleges/business-and-management

Michigan State University, The Graduate School, Eli Broad College of Business, The School of Hospitality Business, East Lansing, MI 48224. Offers foodservice business management (MS); hospitality business management (MS). *Degree requirements:* For master's, comprehensive exam, research project. *Entrance requirements:* For master's, GMAT or GRE, minimum GPA of 3.0 in last 2 years of undergraduate course work, resume, 3 letters of recommendation, 2 official transcripts, at least 1 year of professional work experience. Additional exam requirements/recommendations for international students: Required—TOEFL (minimum score 580 paper-based; 87 iBT). Electronic applications accepted. *Faculty research:* Corporate food service management, entrepreneurial and food service management, hospitality business.

Monroe College, King Graduate School, Bronx, NY 10468. Offers accounting (MS); business administration (MBA), including entrepreneurship, finance, general business administration, healthcare management, human resources, information technology, marketing; computer science (MS); criminal justice (MS); hospitality management (MS); public health (MPH), including biostatistics and epidemiology, community health, health administration and leadership. *Program availability:* Online learning. Application fee: $50.
Website: https://www.monroecollege.edu/Degrees/King-Graduate-School/

Morgan State University, School of Graduate Studies, Earl G. Graves School of Business and Management, Program in Hospitality Management, Baltimore, MD 21251. Offers MS. *Expenses:* Tuition, state resident: part-time $433 per credit. Tuition, nonresident: part-time $851 per credit. *Required fees:* $81.50 per credit.

New York University, School of Professional Studies, Jonathan M. Tisch Center of Hospitality, Program in Hospitality Industry Studies, New York, NY 10012-1019. Offers hospitality industry studies (MS), including brand strategy, hotel finance, lodging operations, revenue management. *Program availability:* Part-time, evening/weekend. *Students:* 42 full-time (28 women), 21 part-time (15 women); includes 11 minority (2 Black or African American, non-Hispanic/Latino; 7 Asian, non-Hispanic/Latino; 2 Hispanic/Latino), 35 international. Average age 26. 78 applicants, 54% accepted, 23 enrolled. In 2017, 62 master's awarded. *Degree requirements:* For master's, thesis. *Entrance requirements:* For master's, GRE or GMAT (only upon request), bachelor's degree, resume with relevant professional work, internship or volunteer experience, two letters of recommendation, statement of purpose. Additional exam requirements/recommendations for international students: Required—TOEFL (minimum score 600 paper-based; 100 iBT), IELTS (minimum score 7). *Application deadline:* For fall admission, 2/1 priority date for domestic and international students; for spring admission, 10/15 priority date for domestic students, 8/15 priority date for international students. Applications are processed on a rolling basis. Application fee: $150. Electronic applications accepted. *Expenses:* $20,244 per term. *Financial support:* Fellowships, career-related internships or fieldwork, Federal Work-Study, scholarships/grants, and health care benefits available. Support available to part-time students. Financial award application deadline: 6/30; financial award applicants required to submit FAFSA. *Unit head:* Nicolas Graf, Associate Dean/Clinical Associate Professor, 212-998-9100. *Application contact:* Admissions Office, 212-998-7100, E-mail: sps.gradadmissions@nyu.edu.
Website: http://www.sps.nyu.edu/areas-of-study/tisch/graduate-programs/ms-hospitality-industry-studies/

New York University, Steinhardt School of Culture, Education, and Human Development, Department of Nutrition, Food Studies, and Public Health, Program in Food Studies, New York, NY 10012. Offers food studies (MA, PhD), including food culture (MA), food systems (MA). *Program availability:* Part-time. *Faculty:* 6 full-time (5 women). *Students:* 48 full-time (44 women), 119 part-time (110 women); includes 41 minority (2 Black or African American, non-Hispanic/Latino; 1 American Indian or Alaska Native, non-Hispanic/Latino; 11 Asian, non-Hispanic/Latino; 19 Hispanic/Latino; 1 Native Hawaiian or other Pacific Islander, non-Hispanic/Latino; 7 Two or more races, non-Hispanic/Latino), 18 international. Average age 29. 158 applicants, 64% accepted, 55 enrolled. In 2017, 38 master's, 2 doctorates awarded. *Degree requirements:* For master's, thesis (for some programs); for doctorate, thesis/dissertation. *Entrance requirements:* For doctorate, GRE General Test, interview. Additional exam requirements/recommendations for international students: Required—TOEFL (minimum score 100 iBT). *Application deadline:* For fall admission, 12/1 priority date for domestic students, 12/1 for international students; for spring admission, 10/1 for domestic and

international students. Applications are processed on a rolling basis. Application fee: $75. Electronic applications accepted. *Expenses: Tuition:* Full-time $41,352; part-time $19,968 per year. *Required fees:* $2496; $1628 per unit. Tuition and fees vary according to course load and program. *Financial support:* Fellowships with full and partial tuition reimbursements, career-related internships or fieldwork, Federal Work-Study, institutionally sponsored loans, scholarships/grants, tuition waivers (partial), and unspecified assistantships available. Financial award application deadline: 2/1; financial award applicants required to submit FAFSA. *Faculty research:* Cultural and social history of food, food systems and agriculture, food and aesthetics, political economy of food. *Unit head:* Prof. Jennifer Berg, Director, 212-998-5597, Fax: 212-995-4194, E-mail: jennifer.berg@nyu.edu. *Application contact:* 212-998-5030, Fax: 212-995-4328, E-mail: steinhardt.gradadmissions@nyu.edu.
Website: http://steinhardt.nyu.edu/nutrition/food

Oklahoma State University, College of Human Sciences, School of Hospitality and Tourism Management, Stillwater, OK 74078. Offers MS, PhD. *Faculty:* 16 full-time (9 women), 7 part-time/adjunct (1 woman). *Students:* 16 full-time (11 women), 12 part-time (8 women); includes 4 minority (2 Black or African American, non-Hispanic/Latino; 2 Asian, non-Hispanic/Latino), 20 international. Average age 28. 17 applicants, 65% accepted, 8 enrolled. In 2017, 3 master's, 2 doctorates awarded. *Entrance requirements:* For master's and doctorate, GRE or GMAT. Additional exam requirements/recommendations for international students: Required—TOEFL (minimum score 550 paper-based; 79 iBT). *Application deadline:* For fall admission, 3/1 priority date for international students; for spring admission, 8/1 priority date for international students. Applications are processed on a rolling basis. Application fee: $40 ($75 for international students). Electronic applications accepted. *Expenses:* Tuition, state resident: full-time $4019; part-time $2679.60 per year. Tuition, nonresident: full-time $15,286; part-time $10,190.40 per year. *Required fees:* $2129; $1419 per unit. Tuition and fees vary according to program. *Financial support:* Research assistantships, teaching assistantships, career-related internships or fieldwork, Federal Work-Study, scholarships/grants, health care benefits, tuition waivers (partial), and unspecified assistantships available. Support available to part-time students. Financial award application deadline: 3/1; financial award applicants required to submit FAFSA. *Faculty research:* Hotel operations and management, restaurant/food service management, hospitality education, hospitality human resources management, tourism. *Unit head:* Dr. Ben Goh, Director, 405-744-7651, Fax: 405-744-6299, E-mail: ben.goh@okstate.edu. *Application contact:* Dr. Li Miao, Graduate Coordinator, 405-744-1277, Fax: 405-744-6299, E-mail: lm@okstate.edu.
Website: https://humansciences.okstate.edu/htm/index.html

Penn State University Park, Graduate School, College of Health and Human Development, School of Hospitality Management, University Park, PA 16802. Offers MS, PhD. *Unit head:* Dr. Ann C. Crouter, Dean, 814-865-1420, Fax: 814-865-3282. *Application contact:* Lori Hawn, Director, Graduate Student Services, 814-865-1795, Fax: 814-863-4627, E-mail: l-gswww@lists.psu.edu.
Website: http://hhd.psu.edu/shm

Pontificia Universidad Catolica Madre y Maestra, Graduate School, Faculty of Social and Administrative Sciences, Santiago, Dominican Republic. Offers business administration (MBA), including business development, finance, international business, management skills (M Mgmt, MBA), marketing, operations, strategic cost management, strategy, tourist destination planning and management; law (LL M), including civil law, corporate business law, criminal law, international relations, real estate law; management (M Mgmt), including higher financial management, insurance program administration, management skills (M Mgmt, MBA); psychology (MA), including clinical child and adolescent psychology, forensic psychology; strategic human resources (EMBA).

Purdue University, Graduate School, College of Health and Human Sciences, School of Hospitality and Tourism Management, West Lafayette, IN 47907. Offers MS, PhD. *Program availability:* Online learning. *Faculty:* 17 full-time (6 women), 1 part-time/adjunct (0 women). *Students:* 38 full-time (26 women), 15 part-time (9 women); includes 3 minority (1 Asian, non-Hispanic/Latino; 2 Hispanic/Latino), 43 international. Average age 29. 79 applicants, 61% accepted, 12 enrolled. In 2017, 18 master's, 7 doctorates awarded. *Degree requirements:* For master's, thesis; for doctorate, thesis/dissertation. *Entrance requirements:* For master's, GMAT (minimum score of 550) or GRE General Test (minimum combined verbal and quantitative score of 290 new scoring, minimum of 145 each section, or 1000 with 500 each section, old scoring), minimum GPA of 3.0; for doctorate, GMAT (minimum score of 550) or GRE General Test (minimum combined verbal and quantitative score of 290 new scoring, minimum of 145 each section, or 1000 with 500 each section, old scoring), minimum undergraduate GPA of 3.0; master's degree with minimum GPA of 3.0 or equivalent. Additional exam requirements/recommendations for international students: Required—TOEFL (minimum score 77 iBT), TWE. *Application deadline:* For fall admission, 3/5 priority date for domestic and international students; for spring admission, 9/20 for domestic and international students. Applications are processed on a rolling basis. Application fee: $60 ($75 for international students). Electronic applications accepted. *Financial support:* Research assistantships, teaching assistantships, and career-related internships or fieldwork available. Support available to part-time students. Financial award applicants required to submit FAFSA. *Faculty research:* Human resources, marketing, hotel and restaurant operations, food product and equipment development, tourism development. *Unit head:* Dr. Richard F. Ghiselli, Head, 765-494-2636, E-mail: ghiselli@purdue.edu. *Application contact:* Ayrielle K. Espinosa, Graduate Contact, 765-494-9811, E-mail: camposm@purdue.edu.
Website: http://www.purdue.edu/hhs/htm/

Rochester Institute of Technology, Graduate Enrollment Services, College of Applied Science and Technology, School of International Hospitality and Service Innovation, MS Program in Hospitality and Tourism Management, Rochester, NY 14623. Offers MS. *Program availability:* Part-time, evening/weekend. *Students:* 10 full-time (5 women), 5 part-time (1 woman); includes 1 minority (Hispanic/Latino), 11 international. Average age 28. 22 applicants, 64% accepted, 4 enrolled. In 2017, 4 master's awarded. *Degree requirements:* For master's, thesis or alternative. *Entrance requirements:* For master's, minimum GPA of 3.0 (recommended). Additional exam requirements/recommendations for international students: Required—TOEFL (minimum score 570 paper-based; 88 iBT), IELTS (minimum score 6.5), PTE (minimum score 61). *Application deadline:* Applications are processed on a rolling basis. Application fee: $65. Electronic applications accepted. *Expenses:* $1,815 per credit hour. *Financial support:* In 2017–18, 9 students received support. Teaching assistantships with partial tuition reimbursements available, career-related internships or fieldwork, scholarships/grants, and unspecified assistantships available. Support available to part-time students. Financial award applicants required to submit FAFSA. *Faculty research:* Service innovation and technology integration, innovative food product development, hospitality employees' occupational health and wellness, tourist behaviors, destination management. *Unit head:* Yu-Chin Hsieh, Department Chair, 585-475-2355, E-mail: yhsieh@rit.edu. *Application contact:* Diane Ellison, Senior Associate Vice President, Graduate Enrollment Services, 585-475-2229, Fax: 585-475-7164, E-mail: gradinfo@rit.edu.
Website: http://www.rit.edu/cast/htm/graduate-program

Rochester Institute of Technology, Graduate Enrollment Services, College of Applied Science and Technology, School of International Hospitality and Service Innovation, MS Program in Service Leadership and Innovation, Rochester, NY 14623. Offers MS. *Program availability:* Part-time, evening/weekend, 100% online. *Students:* 13 full-time (10 women), 17 part-time (10 women); includes 3 minority (1 Black or African American, non-Hispanic/Latino; 1 Asian, non-Hispanic/Latino; 1 Hispanic/Latino), 2 international. Average age 31. 38 applicants, 42% accepted, 2 enrolled. In 2017, 2 master's awarded. *Degree requirements:* For master's, thesis or alternative. *Entrance requirements:* For master's, minimum GPA of 3.0 (recommended). Additional exam requirements/recommendations for international students: Required—TOEFL (minimum score 570 paper-based; 88 iBT), IELTS (minimum score 6.5), PTE (minimum score 62). *Application deadline:* Applications are processed on a rolling basis. Application fee: $65. Electronic applications accepted. *Expenses:* $1,815 per credit hour (classroom), $1,035 per credit hour (online study). *Financial support:* In 2017–18, 3 students received support. Teaching assistantships with partial tuition reimbursements available, career-related internships or fieldwork, scholarships/grants, and unspecified assistantships available. Support available to part-time students. Financial award applicants required to submit FAFSA. *Faculty research:* Leadership development, customer service/patient satisfaction, program evaluation, knowledge construction, diversity, individual creativity, healthcare applications. *Unit head:* Dr. Linda Underhill, Department Chair, 585-475-7359, E-mail: lmuism@rit.edu. *Application contact:* Diane Ellison, Senior Associate Vice President, Graduate Enrollment Services, 585-475-2229, Fax: 585-475-7164, E-mail: gradinfo@rit.edu.
Website: http://www.rit.edu/cast/servicesystems/service-leadership-innovation

Roosevelt University, Graduate Division, Walter E. Heller College of Business, Program in Hospitality and Tourism Management, Chicago, IL 60605. Offers MS. *Program availability:* Part-time, evening/weekend. *Students:* 12 full-time (10 women), 6 part-time (5 women); includes 11 minority (7 Black or African American, non-Hispanic/Latino; 2 Asian, non-Hispanic/Latino; 2 Two or more races, non-Hispanic/Latino), 3 international. Average age 30. 46 applicants, 96% accepted, 24 enrolled. In 2017, 7 master's awarded. *Degree requirements:* For master's, thesis. *Application deadline:* Applications are processed on a rolling basis. Application fee: $40. Electronic applications accepted. *Expenses:* $19,509 annual full-time. *Financial support:* Scholarships/grants and unspecified assistantships available. *Unit head:* Carol Brown, Director, 312-281-3181. *Application contact:* Michael Conwell, Graduate Admission Counselor, 312-281-3250, E-mail: mconwell@roosevelt.edu.
Website: https://www.roosevelt.edu/

San Francisco State University, Division of Graduate Studies, College of Business, Program in Business Administration, San Francisco, CA 94132-1722. Offers decision sciences/operations research (MBA); ethics and compliance (MBA); finance (MBA); global business and innovation (MBA); healthcare administration (MBA); hospitality and tourism management (MBA); information systems (MBA); leadership (MBA); marketing (MBA); nonprofit and social enterprise leadership (MBA); sustainable business (MBA). *Accreditation:* AACSB. *Program availability:* Part-time, evening/weekend. *Degree requirements:* For master's, thesis, essay test. *Entrance requirements:* For master's, GMAT, minimum GPA of 2.7 in last 60 units. Additional exam requirements/recommendations for international students: Required—TOEFL (minimum score 550 paper-based). *Application deadline:* For fall admission, 5/1 priority date for domestic students, 4/1 for international students; for spring admission, 11/1 for domestic students, 10/15 for international students. Applications are processed on a rolling basis. Application fee: $55. *Financial support:* Application deadline: 3/1. *Unit head:* Dr. Sanjit Sengupta, Faculty Director, 415-817-4366, Fax: 415-817-4340, E-mail: sengupta@sfsu.edu. *Application contact:* Christopher Kingston, Director of Student Advising, 415-817-4322, Fax: 415-817-4340, E-mail: cak@sfsu.edu.
Website: http://cob.sfsu.edu/graduate-programs/mba

San Ignacio University, Graduate Programs, Doral, FL 33178. Offers business administration (MBA), including human resources management, international business, marketing management; education (M Ed), including early childhood education, educational leadership, special education; hospitality management (MA), including gastronomy and restaurant management, tourism management.

Schiller International University, MBA Programs, Florida, Program in International Hotel and Tourism Management, Largo, FL 33771. Offers MBA. *Degree requirements:* For master's, thesis optional. *Entrance requirements:* Additional exam requirements/recommendations for international students: Required—TOEFL (minimum score 550 paper-based).

South University, Graduate Programs, College of Business, Savannah, GA 31406. Offers corrections (MBA); entrepreneurship and small business (MBA); healthcare administration (MBA); hospitality management (MBA); leadership (MS); public administration (MPA); sustainability (MBA).

Stratford University, Program in International Hospitality Management, Baltimore, MD 21202. Offers MS. *Program availability:* Part-time, evening/weekend, online learning.

Strayer University, Graduate Studies, Washington, DC 20005-2603. Offers accounting (MS); acquisition (MBA); business administration (MBA); communications technology (MS); educational management (M Ed); finance (MBA); health services administration (MHSA); hospitality and tourism management (MBA); human resource management (MBA); information systems (MS), including computer security management, decision support system management, enterprise resource management, network management, software engineering management, systems development management; management (MBA); management information systems (MS); marketing (MBA); professional accounting (MS), including accounting information systems, controllership, taxation; public administration (MPA); supply chain management (MBA); technology in education (M Ed). Programs also offered at campus locations in Birmingham, AL; Chamblee, GA; Cobb County, GA; Morrow, GA; White Marsh, MD; Charleston, SC; Columbia, SC; Greensboro, NC; Greenville, SC; Lexington, KY; Louisville, KY; Nashville, TN; North Raleigh, NC; Washington, DC. *Accreditation:* ACBSP. *Program availability:* Part-time, evening/weekend, online learning. *Degree requirements:* For master's, thesis. *Entrance requirements:* For master's, GMAT, GRE General Test, bachelor's degree from an accredited college or university, minimum undergraduate GPA of 2.75. Electronic applications accepted.

Syracuse University, David B. Falk College of Sport and Human Dynamics, Program in Food Studies, Syracuse, NY 13244. Offers MS, CAS. *Program availability:* Part-time. *Degree requirements:* For master's, thesis or final practicum project. *Entrance requirements:* For master's, GRE, three letters of recommendation, resume, personal statement, official transcripts. *Application deadline:* For fall admission, 2/15 priority date for domestic and international students; for spring admission, 11/15 priority date for domestic and international students. Application fee: $75. Electronic applications accepted. *Financial support:* Fellowships, research assistantships, teaching assistantships, career-related internships or fieldwork, and scholarships/grants available. Financial award application deadline: 1/1. *Faculty research:* Food and nutrition systems and economies, linkages between sustainable agriculture and development, human rights and the right to adequate food and nutrition, food sovereignty, urban-rural food linkages in terms of production for trade and household

consumption. *Unit head:* Anne C. Bellows, Director, 315-443-4228, E-mail: acbellow@syr.edu. *Application contact:* Felicia Otero, Director of College Admissions, 315-443-5555, Fax: 315-443-2562, E-mail: falk@syr.edu.
Website: https://falk.syr.edu/food-studies/academic-programs/#msfs

Temple University, Fox School of Business, Doctoral Programs in Business, Philadelphia, PA 19122-6096. Offers accounting (PhD); entrepreneurship (PhD); finance (PhD); international business (PhD); management information systems (PhD); marketing (PhD); risk management and insurance (PhD); statistics (PhD); strategic management (PhD); tourism and sport (PhD). *Accreditation:* AACSB. *Degree requirements:* For doctorate, thesis/dissertation. *Entrance requirements:* For doctorate, GRE General Test, GMAT, minimum GPA of 3.0, master's degree. Additional exam requirements/recommendations for international students: Required—TOEFL (minimum score 600 paper-based; 100 iBT), IELTS (minimum score 7.5). Electronic applications accepted. *Expenses:* Tuition, state resident: full-time $16,164; part-time $898 per credit hour. Tuition, nonresident: full-time $22,158; part-time $1231 per credit hour. *Required fees:* $890; $445 per semester. Full-time tuition and fees vary according to course load, degree level, campus/location and program.

Temple University, School of Sport, Tourism and Hospitality Management, Philadelphia, PA 19122-6096. Offers sport business (MS); tourism and hospitality management (MTHM); tourism and sport (PhD); travel and tourism (MS). *Program availability:* Part-time, evening/weekend. *Faculty:* 28 full-time (9 women), 9 part-time/adjunct (2 women). *Students:* 158 full-time (72 women), 32 part-time (19 women); includes 46 minority (29 Black or African American, non-Hispanic/Latino; 4 Asian, non-Hispanic/Latino; 11 Hispanic/Latino; 2 Two or more races, non-Hispanic/Latino), 31 international. 235 applicants, 74% accepted, 96 enrolled. In 2017, 37 master's awarded. *Entrance requirements:* For master's, GRE General Test, GMAT, or MAT, bachelor's degree or equivalent with minimum GPA of 3.0, 500-word essay, 2 letters of recommendation, resume; for doctorate, GMAT or GRE. Additional exam requirements/recommendations for international students: Required—TOEFL (minimum score 550 paper-based; 79 iBT), IELTS (minimum score 6.5). *Application deadline:* For fall admission, 3/1 priority date for domestic students, 1/15 priority date for international students; for spring admission, 8/15 priority date for domestic students, 6/30 priority date for international students. Applications are processed on a rolling basis. Application fee: $60. Electronic applications accepted. *Expenses:* Contact institution. *Financial support:* Fellowships, research assistantships, and teaching assistantships available. Financial award application deadline: 3/1; financial award applicants required to submit FAFSA. *Unit head:* Dr. M. Moshe Porat, Dean, 215-204-1836, Fax: 215-204-8705, E-mail: porat@temple.edu. *Application contact:* James Alton, Manager of Graduate Student Services, 215-204-7140, Fax: 215-204-8705, E-mail: jim.alton@temple.edu.
Website: http://sthm.temple.edu/

Texas Tech University, Graduate School, College of Human Sciences, Department of Hospitality and Retail Management, Lubbock, TX 79409-1240. Offers hospitality administration (PhD); hospitality and retail management (MS). *Program availability:* Part-time, evening/weekend. *Faculty:* 22 full-time (11 women), 1 (woman) part-time/adjunct. *Students:* 27 full-time (13 women), 6 part-time (2 women); includes 6 minority (2 Black or African American, non-Hispanic/Latino; 3 Hispanic/Latino; 1 Two or more races, non-Hispanic/Latino), 7 international. Average age 30. 31 applicants, 58% accepted, 13 enrolled. In 2017, 12 master's, 7 doctorates awarded. Terminal master's awarded for partial completion of doctoral program. *Degree requirements:* For master's, thesis or alternative; for doctorate, thesis/dissertation. *Entrance requirements:* For master's, GRE, professional experience (restaurant, hotel, and institutional management); for doctorate, GRE General Test, professional experience. Additional exam requirements/recommendations for international students: Required—TOEFL (minimum score 550 paper-based; 79 iBT), IELTS (minimum score 6.5). *Application deadline:* For fall admission, 6/1 priority date for domestic students, 1/15 priority date for international students; for spring admission, 9/1 priority date for domestic students, 6/15 priority date for international students. Applications are processed on a rolling basis. Application fee: $60. Electronic applications accepted. *Expenses:* Contact institution. *Financial support:* In 2017–18, 33 students received support, including 29 fellowships (averaging $5,707 per year), 8 research assistantships (averaging $8,711 per year), 23 teaching assistantships (averaging $9,354 per year); Federal Work-Study and scholarships/grants also available. Financial award application deadline: 4/15; financial award applicants required to submit FAFSA. *Faculty research:* Cultural intelligence, lodging, emotional intelligence, consumer behavior, beverage. *Total annual research expenditures:* $40,780. *Unit head:* Dr. Audrey C. McCool, Interim Chairperson, 806-834-6256, Fax: 806-742-3042, E-mail: audreyc.mccool@ttu.edu. *Application contact:* Dr. David Rivera, Jr., Graduate Coordinator, Hospitality and Retail Management, 806-834-8187, Fax: 806-742-3042, E-mail: david.rivera@ttu.edu.
Website: http://www.depts.ttu.edu/hs/hrm/

Thomas Edison State University, School of Business and Management, Program in Hospitality Management, Trenton, NJ 08608. Offers MS. *Program availability:* Online learning.

The University of Alabama, Graduate School, College of Human Environmental Sciences, Department of Human Nutrition and Hospitality Management, Tuscaloosa, AL 35487. Offers MSHES. *Program availability:* Part-time, online only, 100% online. *Faculty:* 16 full-time (13 women), 2 part-time/adjunct (1 woman). *Students:* 21 full-time (all women), 112 part-time (110 women); includes 10 minority (2 Asian, non-Hispanic/Latino; 4 Hispanic/Latino; 1 Native Hawaiian or other Pacific Islander, non-Hispanic/Latino; 3 Two or more races, non-Hispanic/Latino). Average age 29. 84 applicants, 68% accepted, 46 enrolled. In 2017, 52 master's awarded. *Degree requirements:* For master's, comprehensive exam, thesis optional. *Entrance requirements:* For master's, minimum GPA of 3.0. Additional exam requirements/recommendations for international students: Required—TOEFL, IELTS. *Application deadline:* For fall admission, 6/1 for domestic students; for spring admission, 11/1 for domestic students; for summer admission, 4/1 for domestic students. Applications are processed on a rolling basis. Application fee: $50 ($60 for international students). Electronic applications accepted. *Financial support:* In 2017–18, 11 students received support, including research assistantships (averaging $8,100 per year), teaching assistantships (averaging $8,100 per year); career-related internships or fieldwork also available. Financial award application deadline: 3/15. *Faculty research:* Maternal and child nutrition, childhood obesity, community nutrition interventions, geriatric nutrition, family eating patterns, food chemistry, phytochemicals, dietary antioxidants. *Total annual research expenditures:* $52,184. *Unit head:* Dr. Jeannine C. Lawrence, Chair/Associate Professor, 205-348-6252, Fax: 205-348-2982, E-mail: jlawrence@ches.ua.edu. *Application contact:* Patrick D. Fuller, Admissions Officer, 205-348-5923, Fax: 205-348-0400, E-mail: patrick.d.fuller@ua.edu.
Website: http://www.nhm.ches.ua.edu/

The University of Alabama, Graduate School, College of Human Environmental Sciences, Program in Human Environmental Science, Tuscaloosa, AL 35487. Offers interactive technology (MS); quality management (MS); restaurant and meeting management (MS); rural community health (MS); sport management (MS). *Program availability:* Part-time, evening/weekend, online learning. *Students:* 90 full-time (44 women), 158 part-time (86 women); includes 60 minority (42 Black or African American,

Hospitality Management

non-Hispanic/Latino; 1 American Indian or Alaska Native, non-Hispanic/Latino; 2 Asian, non-Hispanic/Latino; 7 Hispanic/Latino; 3 Native Hawaiian or other Pacific Islander, non-Hispanic/Latino; 5 Two or more races, non-Hispanic/Latino). Average age 34. 147 applicants, 84% accepted, 110 enrolled. In 2017, 108 master's awarded. *Degree requirements:* For master's, comprehensive exam. *Entrance requirements:* For master's, GRE (for some specializations), minimum GPA of 3.0. Additional exam requirements/recommendations for international students: Required—TOEFL. *Application deadline:* For fall admission, 7/1 for domestic students; for spring admission, 11/1 for domestic students; for summer admission, 4/15 for domestic students. Applications are processed on a rolling basis. Application fee: $50 ($60 for international students). Electronic applications accepted. *Financial support:* Teaching assistantships with full tuition reimbursements available. Financial award application deadline: 7/1. *Faculty research:* Rural health, hospitality management, sport management, interactive technology, consumer quality management, environmental health and safety. *Unit head:* Dr. Milla D. Boschung, Dean, 205-348-6250, Fax: 205-348-1786, E-mail: mboschun@ches.ua.edu. *Application contact:* Dr. Stuart Usdan, Associate Dean, 205-348-6150, Fax: 205-348-3789, E-mail: susdan@ches.ua.edu.
Website: http://www.ches.ua.edu/programs-of-study.html

University of Central Florida, Rosen College of Hospitality Management, Orlando, FL 32816. Offers destination marketing and management (Certificate); event management (Certificate); hospitality and tourism management (MS); hospitality management (PhD). *Program availability:* Part-time. *Faculty:* 71 full-time (29 women), 30 part-time/adjunct (8 women). *Students:* 76 full-time (50 women), 161 part-time (111 women); includes 72 minority (28 Black or African American, non-Hispanic/Latino; 1 American Indian or Alaska Native, non-Hispanic/Latino; 7 Asian, non-Hispanic/Latino; 31 Hispanic/Latino; 5 Two or more races, non-Hispanic/Latino), 24 international. Average age 30. 195 applicants, 65% accepted, 82 enrolled. In 2017, 31 master's, 5 doctorates, 32 other advanced degrees awarded. *Degree requirements:* For master's, thesis or alternative; for doctorate, thesis/dissertation, candidacy exam. *Entrance requirements:* For master's and doctorate, GMAT or GRE, letters of recommendation, goal statement, resume. Additional exam requirements/recommendations for international students: Required—TOEFL. *Application deadline:* For fall admission, 7/15 for domestic students; for spring admission, 12/1 for domestic students. Application fee: $30. Electronic applications accepted. *Expenses:* Tuition, state resident: part-time $288.16 per credit hour. Tuition, nonresident: part-time $1073.31 per credit hour. Tuition and fees vary according to program. *Financial support:* In 2017–18, 24 students received support, including 7 fellowships with partial tuition reimbursements available (averaging $1,971 per year), 2 research assistantships with partial tuition reimbursements available (averaging $9,323 per year), 22 teaching assistantships with partial tuition reimbursements available (averaging $12,876 per year); health care benefits also available. Financial award application deadline: 3/1; financial award applicants required to submit FAFSA. *Unit head:* Dr. Abraham C. Pizam, Dean, 407-903-8010, E-mail: abraham.pizam@ucf.edu. *Application contact:* Associate Director, Graduate Admissions, 407-823-2766, Fax: 407-823-6442, E-mail: gradadmissions@ucf.edu.
Website: http://www.hospitality.ucf.edu

University of Delaware, Alfred Lerner College of Business and Economics, Program in Hospitality Information Management, Newark, DE 19716. Offers MS. *Entrance requirements:* Additional exam requirements/recommendations for international students: Required—TOEFL (minimum score 550 paper-based). Electronic applications accepted. *Faculty research:* Foodservice, lodging and tourism management.

The University of Findlay, Office of Graduate Admissions, Findlay, OH 45840. Offers applied security and analytics (MSAS); athletic training (MAT); business (MBA), including certified management accountant, certified public accountant, health care management, hospitality management; education (MA Ed, Ed D), including children's literature (MA Ed); curriculum and teaching (MA Ed), education (MA Ed), educational administration (MA Ed), human resource development (MA Ed), mathematics (MA Ed), reading (MA Ed), science education (MA Ed), superintendent (Ed D), teaching (Ed D), technology (MA Ed); environmental, safety, and health management (MSEM); health informatics (MS); occupational therapy (MOT); pharmacy (Pharm D); physical therapy (DPT); physician assistant (MPA); rhetoric and writing (MA); teaching English to speakers of other languages (TESOL) and applied linguistics (MA). *Program availability:* Part-time, evening/weekend, 100% online, blended/hybrid learning. *Students:* 688 full-time (430 women), 553 part-time (308 women), 170 international. Average age 28. In 2017, 366 master's, 137 doctorates awarded. *Degree requirements:* For master's, comprehensive exam (for some programs), thesis (for some programs), cumulative project, capstone project; for doctorate, thesis/dissertation (for some programs). *Entrance requirements:* For master's, GRE/GMAT, bachelor's degree from accredited institution, minimum undergraduate GPA of 2.5 in last 64 hours of course work; for doctorate, GRE, MAT, minimum cumulative GPA of 3.0. Additional exam requirements/recommendations for international students: Required—TOEFL (minimum score 79 iBT), IELTS (minimum score 7), PTE (minimum score 61). *Application deadline:* Applications are processed on a rolling basis. Electronic applications accepted. *Financial support:* In 2017–18, 10 research assistantships with partial tuition reimbursements (averaging $7,200 per year), 35 teaching assistantships with partial tuition reimbursements (averaging $7,200 per year) were awarded; Federal Work-Study, institutionally sponsored loans, and unspecified assistantships also available. Financial award applicants required to submit FAFSA. *Unit head:* Christopher M. Harris, Director of Admissions, 419-434-4347, E-mail: harrisc1@findlay.edu. *Application contact:* Madeline Fauser Brennan, Graduate Admissions Counselor, 419-434-4636, Fax: 419-434-4898, E-mail: fauserbrennan@findlay.edu.
Website: http://www.findlay.edu/admissions/graduate/Pages/default.aspx

University of Guelph, Graduate Studies, College of Management and Economics, MBA Program, Guelph, ON N1G 2W1, Canada. Offers food and agribusiness management (MBA); hospitality and tourism management (MBA). *Program availability:* Part-time, evening/weekend, online learning. *Entrance requirements:* For master's, minimum B-average, minimum of 3 years of relevant work experience. Additional exam requirements/recommendations for international students: Required—TOEFL (minimum score 550 paper-based). Electronic applications accepted. *Faculty research:* Marketing, operations management, business policy, financial management, organizational behavior.

University of Houston, Conrad N. Hilton College of Hotel and Restaurant Management, Houston, TX 77204. Offers hospitality management (MS). *Program availability:* Part-time. *Degree requirements:* For master's, practicum or thesis. *Entrance requirements:* For master's, GMAT or GRE General Test. Additional exam requirements/recommendations for international students: Required—TOEFL (minimum score 100 iBT) or IELTS (minimum score 7). Electronic applications accepted. *Faculty research:* Catering, tourism, hospitality marketing, security and risk management, purchasing and financial information usage.

University of Kentucky, Graduate School, College of Agriculture, Food and Environment, Program in Hospitality and Dietetics Administration, Lexington, KY 40506-0032. Offers MS. *Degree requirements:* For master's, comprehensive exam, thesis optional. *Entrance requirements:* For master's, GRE General Test, minimum undergraduate GPA of 2.75. Additional exam requirements/recommendations for

international students: Required—TOEFL (minimum score 550 paper-based). Electronic applications accepted.

University of Massachusetts Amherst, Graduate School, Isenberg School of Management, Program in Management, Amherst, MA 01003. Offers accounting (PhD); business administration (MBA); entrepreneurship (MBA); finance (MBA, PhD); healthcare administration (MBA); hospitality and tourism management (PhD); management science (PhD); marketing (MBA, PhD); organization studies (PhD); sport management (PhD); strategic management (PhD); MBA/MS. *Accreditation:* AACSB. *Program availability:* Part-time, evening/weekend, online learning. Terminal master's awarded for partial completion of doctoral program. *Degree requirements:* For doctorate, comprehensive exam, thesis/dissertation. *Entrance requirements:* For master's and doctorate, GMAT or GRE General Test. Additional exam requirements/recommendations for international students: Required—TOEFL (minimum score 550 paper-based; 80 iBT), IELTS (minimum score 6.5). Electronic applications accepted.

University of Memphis, Graduate School, Kemmons Wilson School of Hospitality and Resort Management, Memphis, TN 38152. Offers hospitality management specialist (Graduate Certificate); sports commerce (MS). *Program availability:* Part-time. *Faculty:* 6 full-time (1 woman), 2 part-time/adjunct (0 women). *Students:* 11 full-time (3 women), 27 part-time (12 women); includes 18 minority (16 Black or African American, non-Hispanic/Latino; 1 Hispanic/Latino; 1 Two or more races, non-Hispanic/Latino), 1 international. Average age 28. 24 applicants, 100% accepted, 19 enrolled. In 2017, 19 master's awarded. *Degree requirements:* For master's, comprehensive exam, thesis and alternative. *Entrance requirements:* For master's, letters of recommendation, curriculum vitae or resume, statement of goals, minimum undergraduate GPA of 2.5. Additional exam requirements/recommendations for international students: Required—TOEFL (minimum score 550 paper-based; 79 iBT). *Application deadline:* For fall admission, 7/1 for domestic students, 5/1 for international students; for spring admission, 12/1 for domestic students, 9/1 for international students; for summer admission, 5/1 for domestic students, 2/1 for international students. Application fee: $35 ($60 for international students). Electronic applications accepted. *Expenses:* Contact institution. *Financial support:* In 2017–18, 5 research assistantships (averaging $8,400 per year), 6 teaching assistantships (averaging $9,000 per year) were awarded; career-related internships or fieldwork, Federal Work-Study, scholarships/grants, and unspecified assistantships also available. Support available to part-time students. Financial award application deadline: 2/1. *Unit head:* Dr. Radesh Palakurthi, Director, 901-678-3430, E-mail: rplkrthi@memphis.edu. *Application contact:* Dr. Timothy Ryan, Coordinator of Graduate Studies, 901-678-5003, E-mail: tdryan@memphis.edu.
Website: http://www.memphis.edu/wilson/programs

University of Mississippi, Graduate School, School of Applied Sciences, University, MS 38677. Offers communicative disorders (MS); criminal justice (MCJ); exercise science (MS); food and nutrition services (MS); health and kinesiology (PhD); health promotion (MS); nutrition and hospitality management (PhD); park and recreation management (MA); social welfare (PhD); social work (MSW). *Faculty:* 66 full-time (38 women), 33 part-time/adjunct (14 women). *Students:* 182 full-time (139 women), 41 part-time (27 women); includes 49 minority (41 Black or African American, non-Hispanic/Latino; 1 American Indian or Alaska Native, non-Hispanic/Latino; 3 Asian, non-Hispanic/Latino; 3 Hispanic/Latino; 1 Two or more races, non-Hispanic/Latino), 13 international. Average age 26. *Entrance requirements:* For master's, GRE General Test, minimum GPA of 3.0. Additional exam requirements/recommendations for international students: Required—TOEFL. *Application deadline:* For fall admission, 4/1 for domestic students; for spring admission, 10/1 for domestic students. Applications are processed on a rolling basis. Application fee: $50. Electronic applications accepted. *Financial support:* Scholarships/grants available. Financial award application deadline: 3/1; financial award applicants required to submit FAFSA. *Unit head:* Dr. Teresa C. Carithers, Dean, 662-915-1081, Fax: 662-915-5717, E-mail: applsci@olemiss.edu.

University of Missouri, Office of Research and Graduate Studies, College of Agriculture, Food and Natural Resources, Department of Food Science, Columbia, MO 65211. Offers MS, PhD. Terminal master's awarded for partial completion of doctoral program. *Degree requirements:* For doctorate, comprehensive exam, thesis/dissertation. *Entrance requirements:* For master's, GRE General Test (minimum score: Verbal and Quantitative 1000 with neither section below 400, 297 combined under new scoring; Analytical 3.5), minimum GPA of 3.0; BS in food science from accredited university; for doctorate, GRE General Test (minimum score: Verbal and Quantitative 1000 with neither section below 400, Analytical 3.5), minimum GPA of 3.0; BS and MS in food science from accredited university. Additional exam requirements/recommendations for international students: Required—TOEFL (minimum score 550 paper-based; 80 iBT). Electronic applications accepted. *Faculty research:* Food chemistry, food analysis, food microbiology, food engineering and process control, functional foods, meat science and processing technology.

University of Nevada, Las Vegas, Graduate College, William F. Harrah College of Hospitality, Las Vegas, NV 89154-6013. Offers hospitality administration (MHA, PhD); hotel administration (MS). *Program availability:* Part-time, evening/weekend, 100% online, blended/hybrid learning. *Faculty:* 15 full-time (6 women), 2 part-time/adjunct (1 woman). *Students:* 42 full-time (21 women), 54 part-time (25 women); includes 25 minority (4 Black or African American, non-Hispanic/Latino; 10 Asian, non-Hispanic/Latino; 5 Hispanic/Latino; 1 Native Hawaiian or other Pacific Islander, non-Hispanic/Latino; 5 Two or more races, non-Hispanic/Latino), 23 international. Average age 35. 131 applicants, 50% accepted, 32 enrolled. In 2017, 44 master's, 8 doctorates awarded. *Degree requirements:* For master's, thesis (for some programs), professional paper, oral examination; for doctorate, comprehensive exam, thesis/dissertation, dissertation defense. *Entrance requirements:* For master's, GRE or GMAT, bachelor's degree with minimum GPA 2.75; minimum of one year of full-time work experience; brief essay; 2 letters of recommendation; for doctorate, GRE or GMAT, master's degree with minimum GPA of 3.0; statement of purpose; 3 letters of recommendation. Additional exam requirements/recommendations for international students: Required—TOEFL (minimum score 550 paper-based; 80 iBT), IELTS (minimum score 7). *Application deadline:* For fall admission, 8/1 for domestic students, 5/1 for international students; for spring admission, 11/15 for domestic students, 10/1 for international students. Application fee: $60 ($95 for international students). Electronic applications accepted. *Expenses:* $275 per credit, $850 per course, $7,969 per year resident, $22,157 per year non-resident, $7,094 non-resident fee (7 credits or more), $1,307 annual health insurance fee. *Financial support:* In 2017–18, 34 students received support, including 4 research assistantships with full and partial tuition reimbursements available (averaging $13,438 per year), 30 teaching assistantships with full and partial tuition reimbursements available (averaging $12,768 per year); institutionally sponsored loans, scholarships/grants, health care benefits, and unspecified assistantships also available. Financial award application deadline: 3/15; financial award applicants required to submit FAFSA. *Faculty research:* Marketing, human resources, financial analysis, tourism, gaming. *Total annual research expenditures:* $127,492. *Unit head:* Dr. Stowe Shoemaker, Dean, 702-895-3308, Fax: 702-895-4109, E-mail: stowe.shoemaker@unlv.edu.
Website: http://hotel.unlv.edu/

University of New Orleans, Graduate School, College of Business Administration, Lester E. Kabacoff School of Hotel, Restaurant, and Tourism Administration, Program in

Hospitality and Tourism Management, New Orleans, LA 70148. Offers MS. *Program availability:* Online learning. *Entrance requirements:* Additional exam requirements/recommendations for international students: Required—TOEFL (minimum score 550 paper-based; 79 iBT).

University of North Texas, Robert B. Toulouse School of Graduate Studies, Denton, TX 76203-5459. Offers accounting (MS); applied anthropology (MA, MS); applied behavior analysis (Certificate); applied geography (MA); applied technology and performance improvement (M Ed, MS); art education (MA); art history (MA); art museum education (Certificate); arts leadership (Certificate); audiology (Au D); behavior analysis (MS); behavioral science (PhD); biochemistry and molecular biology (MS); biology (MA, MS); biomedical engineering (MS); business analysis (MS); chemistry (MS); clinical health psychology (PhD); communication studies (MA, MS); computer engineering (MS); computer science (MS); counseling (M Ed, MS), including clinical mental health counseling (MS), college and university counseling, elementary school counseling, secondary school counseling; creative writing (MA); criminal justice (MS); curriculum and instruction (M Ed); decision sciences (MBA); design (MA, MFA), including fashion design (MFA), innovation studies, interior design (MFA), early childhood studies (MS); economics (MS); educational leadership (M Ed, Ed D); educational psychology (MS, PhD), including family studies (MS), gifted and talented (MS), human development (MS), learning and cognition (MS), research, measurement and evaluation (MS); electrical engineering (MS); emergency management (MPA); engineering technology (MS); English (MA); English as a second language (MA); environmental science (MS); finance (MBA, MS); financial management (MPA); French (MA); health services management (MBA); higher education (M Ed, Ed D); history (MA, MS); hospitality management (MS); human resources management (MPA); information science (MS); information systems (PhD); information technologies (MBA); interdisciplinary studies (MA, MS); international studies (MA); international sustainable tourism (MS); jazz studies (MM); journalism (MA, MJ, Graduate Certificate), including interactive and virtual digital communication (Graduate Certificate), narrative journalism (Graduate Certificate), public relations (Graduate Certificate); kinesiology (MS); linguistics (MA); local government management (MPA); logistics (PhD); logistics and supply chain management (MBA); long-term care, senior housing, and aging services (MA); management (PhD); marketing (MBA); mathematics (MA, MS); mechanical and energy engineering (MS, PhD); music (MA), including ethnomusicology, music theory, musicology, performance; music composition (PhD); music education (MM Ed, PhD); nonprofit management (MPA); operations and supply chain management (MBA); performance (MM, DMA); philosophy (MA); political science (MA); professional and technical communication (MA); radio, television and film (MA, MFA); rehabilitation counseling (Certificate); sociology (MA); Spanish (MA); special education (M Ed); speech-language pathology (MA); strategic management (MBA); studio art (MFA); teaching (M Ed); MBA/MS. *Program availability:* Part-time, evening/weekend, online learning. Terminal master's awarded for partial completion of doctoral program. *Degree requirements:* For master's, variable foreign language requirement, comprehensive exam (for some programs), thesis (for some programs); for doctorate, variable foreign language requirement, comprehensive exam (for some programs), thesis/dissertation; for other advanced degree, variable foreign language requirement, comprehensive exam (for some programs). *Entrance requirements:* For master's and doctorate, GRE, GMAT. Additional exam requirements/recommendations for international students: Required—TOEFL (minimum score 550 paper-based; 79 iBT). Electronic applications accepted.

University of South Carolina, The Graduate School, College of Hospitality, Retail, and Sport Management, School of Hotel, Restaurant and Tourism Management, Columbia, SC 29208. Offers MIHTM. *Entrance requirements:* For master's, GMAT or GRE General Test, minimum GPA of 3.0, 2 letters of recommendation. Electronic applications accepted. *Faculty research:* Corporate strategy and management practices, sustainable tourism, club management, tourism technology, revenue management.

University of South Florida Sarasota-Manatee, College of Hospitality and Technology Leadership, Sarasota, FL 34243. Offers hospitality management (MS). *Program availability:* Part-time. *Faculty:* 3 full-time (1 woman). *Students:* 13 full-time (6 women), 2 part-time (both women); includes 2 minority (1 Black or African American, non-Hispanic/Latino; 1 Hispanic/Latino), 5 international. Average age 32. 17 applicants, 29% accepted, 3 enrolled. In 2017, 15 master's awarded. *Degree requirements:* For master's, thesis or professional project. *Entrance requirements:* For master's, GRE or GMAT (taken within last five years) if overall or upper-division GPA is less than 3.0, current resume, essay. Additional exam requirements/recommendations for international students: Required—TOEFL (minimum score 550 paper-based; 79 iBT), IELTS (minimum score 6.5). *Application deadline:* For fall admission, 3/1 priority date for domestic students, 3/1 for international students; for spring admission, 10/1 priority date for domestic students, 10/1 for international students. Applications are processed on a rolling basis. Application fee: $30. Electronic applications accepted. *Expenses:* Tuition, state resident: full-time $8350; part-time $418 per credit hour. Tuition, nonresident: full-time $19,047; part-time $863 per credit hour. *Required fees:* $1689. Tuition and fees vary according to degree level and program. *Financial support:* In 2017–18, 5 research assistantships with tuition reimbursements (averaging $7,831 per year) were awarded; teaching assistantships with tuition reimbursements, career-related internships or fieldwork, institutionally sponsored loans, health care benefits, and unspecified assistantships also available. Support available to part-time students. Financial award application deadline: 3/1; financial award applicants required to submit FAFSA. *Faculty research:* Technology's impact on hospitality industry, hospitality accounting and cost control, international tourism development, service quality. *Unit head:* Dr. Pat Moreo, Dean, 941-359-4327, E-mail: pmoreo@sar.usf.edu. *Application contact:* Andy Telatovich, Director, Admissions, 941-359-4330, E-mail: atelatovich@sar.usf.edu. Website: http://www.usfsm.edu/chtl/

The University of Tennessee, Graduate School, College of Education, Health and Human Sciences, Department of Consumer and Industry Services Management, Program in Hotel, Restaurant, and Tourism Management, Knoxville, TN 37996. Offers hospitality management (MS); tourism (MS). *Program availability:* Part-time. *Degree requirements:* For master's, thesis or alternative. *Entrance requirements:* For master's, GRE General Test, minimum GPA of 2.7. Additional exam requirements/recommendations for international students: Required—TOEFL. Electronic applications accepted.

University of the Pacific, College of the Pacific, Program in Food Studies, Stockton, CA 95211-0197. Offers MA. *Students:* 22 part-time (all women); includes 8 minority (1 Black or African American, non-Hispanic/Latino; 2 Asian, non-Hispanic/Latino; 4 Hispanic/Latino; 1 Two or more races, non-Hispanic/Latino). Average age 35. 27 applicants, 89% accepted, 7 enrolled. *Unit head:* Dr. Polly Adema, Director, 209-946-2434, E-mail: foodstudies@pacific.edu. *Application contact:* Information Contact, 209-946-2261.
Website: http://www.pacific.edu/Documents/school-graduate/acrobat/Pacific-MA-Food-Studies-Fact-Sheet-17-18.pdf

Virginia International University, School of Business, Fairfax, VA 22030. Offers accounting (MBA, MS); entrepreneurship (MBA); executive management (Graduate Certificate); global logistics (MBA); health care management (MBA); hospitality and tourism management (MBA); human resources management (MBA); international business management (MBA); international finance (MBA); marketing management (MBA); mass media and public relations (MBA); project management (MBA, MS). *Program availability:* Part-time, online learning. *Entrance requirements:* For master's and Graduate Certificate, bachelor's degree. Additional exam requirements/recommendations for international students: Required—TOEFL (minimum score 550 paper-based; 80 iBT), IELTS (minimum score 6). Electronic applications accepted.

Travel and Tourism

Arizona State University at the Tempe campus, College of Public Programs, School of Community Resources and Development, Phoenix, AZ 85004-0685. Offers community resources and development (MS, PhD); nonprofit leadership and management (Graduate Certificate); nonprofit studies (MNpS); sustainable tourism (MAS). *Program availability:* Part-time, evening/weekend. Terminal master's awarded for partial completion of doctoral program. *Degree requirements:* For master's, thesis or alternative, interactive Program of Study (iPOS) submitted before completing 50 percent of required credit hours; for doctorate, comprehensive exam, thesis/dissertation, interactive Program of Study (iPOS) submitted before completing 50 percent of required credit hours. *Entrance requirements:* For master's and doctorate, GRE, minimum GPA of 3.0 or equivalent in last 2 years of work leading to bachelor's degree. Additional exam requirements/recommendations for international students: Required—TOEFL, IELTS, or PTE. Electronic applications accepted. *Expenses:* Contact institution.

Boston University, Metropolitan College, Department of Administrative Sciences, Boston, MA 02215. Offers applied business analytics (MS); economic development and tourism management (MSAS); enterprise risk management (MS); financial management (MS); global marketing management (MS); innovation and technology (MSAS); insurance management (MS); project management (MS); supply chain management (MS). *Accreditation:* AACSB. *Program availability:* Part-time, evening/weekend, 100% online, blended/hybrid learning. *Faculty:* 21 full-time (5 women), 34 part-time/adjunct (5 women). *Students:* 297 full-time (156 women), 597 part-time (298 women); includes 183 minority (58 Black or African American, non-Hispanic/Latino; 2 American Indian or Alaska Native, non-Hispanic/Latino; 56 Asian, non-Hispanic/Latino; 51 Hispanic/Latino; 2 Native Hawaiian or other Pacific Islander, non-Hispanic/Latino; 14 Two or more races, non-Hispanic/Latino), 391 international. Average age 30. 963 applicants, 64% accepted, 209 enrolled. In 2017, 372 master's awarded. *Degree requirements:* For master's, thesis optional. *Entrance requirements:* For master's, 1 year of work experience, minimum GPA of 3.0. Additional exam requirements/recommendations for international students: Required—TOEFL (minimum score 84 iBT). *Application deadline:* Applications are processed on a rolling basis. Application fee: $85. Electronic applications accepted. *Expenses:* Contact institution. *Financial support:* In 2017–18, 15 students received support, including 18 research assistantships (averaging $8,400 per year), 12 teaching assistantships (averaging $2,700 per year); career-related internships or fieldwork, Federal Work-Study, and unspecified assistantships also available. Financial award applicants required to submit FAFSA. *Faculty research:* International business, innovative process. *Unit head:* Dr. John Sullivan, Chair, 617-353-3016, E-mail: adminsc@bu.edu. *Application contact:* Fiona Niven, Administrative Sciences Department, 617-353-3016, E-mail: adminsc@bu.edu.

Website: http://www.bu.edu/met/academic-community/departments/administrative-sciences/

California State University, Chico, Office of Graduate Studies, College of Communication and Education, Recreation, Hospitality and Parks Management Department, Chico, CA 95929-0722. Offers recreation, parks, and tourism (MS). *Program availability:* Part-time. *Degree requirements:* For master's, thesis or project. *Entrance requirements:* For master's, GRE General Test, 3 letters of recommendation, statement of purpose, resume. Additional exam requirements/recommendations for international students: Required—TOEFL (minimum score 550 paper-based; 80 iBT), IELTS (minimum score 6.5), PTE. Electronic applications accepted.

California State University, East Bay, Office of Graduate Studies, College of Education and Allied Studies, Department of Hospitality, Recreation and Tourism, Hayward, CA 94542-3000. Offers recreation and tourism (MS). *Program availability:* Part-time, evening/weekend, online learning. *Faculty:* 11 full-time (6 women), 16 part-time/adjunct (9 women). *Students:* 20 full-time (13 women), 9 part-time (7 women); includes 20 minority (8 Black or African American, non-Hispanic/Latino; 6 Asian, non-Hispanic/Latino; 4 Hispanic/Latino; 2 Two or more races, non-Hispanic/Latino). Average age 35. 23 applicants, 48% accepted, 7 enrolled. In 2017, 17 master's awarded. *Degree requirements:* For master's, thesis optional. *Entrance requirements:* For master's, minimum GPA of 2.75; 2 years' related work experience; 3 letters of recommendation; resume; baccalaureate degree. Additional exam requirements/recommendations for international students: Required—TOEFL (minimum score 550 paper-based). *Application deadline:* For fall admission, 6/1 for domestic and international students. Applications are processed on a rolling basis. Application fee: $55. Electronic applications accepted. *Financial support:* Federal Work-Study, institutionally sponsored loans, and scholarships/grants available. Support available to part-time students. Financial award application deadline: 3/2; financial award applicants required to submit FAFSA. *Faculty research:* Leisure, online vs. face-to-face (F2F) learning, risk management, leadership, tourism consumer behavior. *Unit head:* Dr. Chris Chamberlain, Chair, 510-885-2101, E-mail: chris.chamberlain@csueastbay.edu. *Application contact:* Philip Cole-Regis, Administrative Support Coordinator, 510-885-3716, Fax: 510-885-4777, E-mail: philip.coleregis@csueastbay.edu.

California State University, Fullerton, Graduate Studies, College of Communications, Department of Communications, Fullerton, CA 92831-3599. Offers communications in tourism and entertainment (MA); mass communications research and theory (MA); professional communications (MA). *Program availability:* Part-time. *Faculty:* 4 full-time (3 women), 1 part-time/adjunct (0 women). *Students:* 23 full-time (18 women), 17 part-time (8 women); includes 21 minority (4 Black or African American, non-Hispanic/Latino; 1

Asian, non-Hispanic/Latino; 15 Hispanic/Latino; 1 Two or more races, non-Hispanic/Latino), 2 international. Average age 27. 41 applicants, 56% accepted, 13 enrolled. *Entrance requirements:* For master's, GRE General Test. Application fee: $55. *Financial support:* Teaching assistantships, career-related internships or fieldwork, Federal Work-Study, institutionally sponsored loans, and scholarships/grants available. Support available to part-time students. Financial award application deadline: 3/1; financial award applicants required to submit FAFSA. *Unit head:* Jason Shepard, Chair, 657-278-5301, E-mail: jshepard@fullerton.edu. *Application contact:* Coordinator, 657-278-3832.

California State University, Northridge, Graduate Studies, College of Health and Human Development, Department of Recreation and Tourism Management, Northridge, CA 91330. Offers hospitality and tourism (MS); recreational sport management/campus recreation (MS). *Students:* 19 full-time (6 women), 12 part-time (10 women); includes 12 minority (9 Hispanic/Latino; 1 Native Hawaiian or other Pacific Islander, non-Hispanic/Latino; 2 Two or more races, non-Hispanic/Latino), 7 international. Average age 29. 36 applicants, 67% accepted, 12 enrolled. In 2017, 17 master's awarded. *Degree requirements:* For master's, thesis (for some programs). *Entrance requirements:* For master's, GRE (if cumulative undergraduate GPA less than 3.0). Additional exam requirements/recommendations for international students: Required—TOEFL. *Application deadline:* For fall admission, 11/30 for domestic students. Application fee: $55. *Financial support:* Application deadline: 3/1. *Unit head:* Dr. Mechelle Best, Chair, 818-677-3202.
Website: http://www.csun.edu/hhd/rtm/

Clemson University, Graduate School, College of Behavioral, Social and Health Sciences, Department of Parks, Recreation, and Tourism Management, Clemson, SC 29634. Offers international parks and tourism (Certificate); parks, recreation and tourism management (MS, PhD), including recreational therapy (PhD); public administration (MPA, Certificate); recreational therapy (MS); youth development leadership (MS, Certificate). *Program availability:* Part-time, evening/weekend, 100% online. *Faculty:* 31 full-time (10 women), 3 part-time/adjunct (0 women). *Students:* 90 full-time (62 women), 193 part-time (114 women); includes 57 minority (44 Black or African American, non-Hispanic/Latino; 1 American Indian or Alaska Native, non-Hispanic/Latino; 1 Asian, non-Hispanic/Latino; 8 Hispanic/Latino; 3 Two or more races, non-Hispanic/Latino), 14 international. Average age 32. 245 applicants, 80% accepted, 129 enrolled. In 2017, 37 master's, 5 doctorates, 38 other advanced degrees awarded. *Degree requirements:* For master's, comprehensive exam (for some programs), thesis (for some programs); for doctorate, comprehensive exam, thesis/dissertation; for Certificate, portfolio. *Entrance requirements:* For master's and doctorate, GRE General Test, unofficial transcripts, letter of intent, letters of reference; for Certificate, letter of recommendation, unofficial transcripts, personal statement, resume. Additional exam requirements/recommendations for international students: Required—TOEFL (minimum score 610 paper-based; 80 iBT), IELTS (minimum score 6.5), PTE (minimum score 54). *Application deadline:* For fall admission, 1/15 priority date for domestic and international students; for spring admission, 11/15 priority date for domestic and international students. Applications are processed on a rolling basis. Application fee: $80 ($90 for international students). Electronic applications accepted. *Expenses:* $5,767 per semester full-time resident, $10,918 per semester full-time non-resident, $656 per credit hour part-time resident, $1,310 per credit hour part-time non-resident, $915 per credit hour online; $5,174 per semester full-time resident, $9,714 per semester full-time non-resident, $511 per credit hour part-time resident, $1,017 per credit hour part-time non-resident, $741 per credit hour online (for online non-thesis ms and doctoral programs); $613 per credit hour (for online youth development leadership); other fees may apply per session. *Financial support:* In 2017–18, 68 students received support, including 4 fellowships with partial tuition reimbursements available (averaging $5,250 per year), 7 research assistantships with partial tuition reimbursements available (averaging $11,653 per year), 52 teaching assistantships with partial tuition reimbursements available (averaging $8,517 per year); career-related internships or fieldwork and unspecified assistantships also available. Financial award application deadline: 1/15. *Faculty research:* Human behavior, land use, recreational therapy, sustainability, tourism. *Total annual research expenditures:* $400,772. *Unit head:* Dr. Fran McGuire, Interim Chair, 864-656-3036, E-mail: lefty@clemson.edu. *Application contact:* Dr. Jeff Hallo, Graduate Coordinator, 864-656-3237, E-mail: jhallo@clemson.edu.
Website: http://www.clemson.edu/hehd/departments/prtm/

Colorado State University, Warner College of Natural Resources, Department of Human Dimensions of Natural Resources, Fort Collins, CO 80523-1480. Offers human dimensions of natural resources (MS, PhD); tourism management (MTM). *Program availability:* Part-time, evening/weekend, 100% online. *Faculty:* 15 full-time (6 women). *Students:* 49 full-time (32 women), 132 part-time (67 women); includes 23 minority (6 Black or African American, non-Hispanic/Latino; 1 American Indian or Alaska Native, non-Hispanic/Latino; 1 Asian, non-Hispanic/Latino; 9 Hispanic/Latino; 6 Two or more races, non-Hispanic/Latino), 14 international. Average age 29. 159 applicants, 77% accepted, 84 enrolled. In 2017, 58 master's awarded. Terminal master's awarded for partial completion of doctoral program. *Degree requirements:* For master's, thesis (for some programs); for doctorate, comprehensive exam, thesis/dissertation. *Entrance requirements:* For master's, GRE General Test, minimum GPA of 3.0, 3 letters of recommendation, statement of interest, official transcripts; for doctorate, GRE General Test, minimum GPA of 3.0, 3 letters of recommendation, copy of master's thesis or professional paper, statement of interest, official transcripts. *Application deadline:* For fall admission, 2/15 for domestic and international students. Applications are processed on a rolling basis. Application fee: $60 ($70 for international students). Electronic applications accepted. *Expenses:* $749 per credit hour (for online MTM); $1,200 per semester (for MS in conservation leadership and on-campus MTM). *Financial support:* In 2017–18, 8 research assistantships with full and partial tuition reimbursements (averaging $21,923 per year), 9 teaching assistantships with full and partial tuition reimbursements (averaging $14,256 per year) were awarded; scholarships/grants and unspecified assistantships also available. Financial award application deadline: 2/15. *Faculty research:* Biocultural approaches to conservation; conservation governance; dimensions of wildlife management; marine conservation; park recreation and management. *Total annual research expenditures:* $1.4 million. *Unit head:* Dr. Michael J. Manfredo, Professor and Department Head, 970-491-6591, Fax: 970-491-2255, E-mail: michael.manfredo@colostate.edu. *Application contact:* Jesse Striegel, Administrative Assistant, 970-491-6591, Fax: 970-491-2255, E-mail: jessie.striegel@colostate.edu.
Website: http://warnercnr.colostate.edu/hdnr-home

The George Washington University, School of Business, Department of Tourism and Hospitality Management, Washington, DC 20052. Offers destination management (Professional Certificate); event and meeting management (MTA); event management (Professional Certificate); hospitality management (MTA); individualized studies (MTA); sport management (MTA); sustainable tourism destination management (MTA); tourism and hospitality management (MBA). *Program availability:* Part-time, online learning. *Students:* 69 full-time (46 women), 51 part-time (36 women); includes 35 minority (23 Black or African American, non-Hispanic/Latino; 3 Asian, non-Hispanic/Latino; 6 Hispanic/Latino; 3 Two or more races, non-Hispanic/Latino), 46 international. Average age 28. 185 applicants, 74% accepted, 53 enrolled. In 2017, 51 master's awarded. *Degree requirements:* For master's, comprehensive exam, thesis. *Entrance*

requirements: For master's, GRE General Test. Additional exam requirements/recommendations for international students: Required—TOEFL. *Application deadline:* For fall admission, 4/1 priority date for domestic students; for spring admission, 10/1 for domestic students. Applications are processed on a rolling basis. Application fee: $75. *Expenses: Tuition:* Full-time $28,800; part-time $1655 per credit hour. *Required fees:* $45; $2.75 per credit hour. *Financial support:* In 2017–18, 32 students received support. Fellowships, teaching assistantships, career-related internships or fieldwork, Federal Work-Study, institutionally sponsored loans, and tuition waivers (partial) available. Financial award application deadline: 4/1. *Faculty research:* Tourism policy, tourism impact forecasting, geotourism. *Unit head:* Prof. Lisa Delpy Neirotti, Faculty Director, 202-994-6623, E-mail: delpy@gwu.edu. *Application contact:* Christopher Storer, Executive Director, Graduate Admissions, 202-994-1212, E-mail: gwmba@gwu.edu.
Website: http://business.gwu.edu/tourism/

IGlobal University, Graduate Programs, Vienna, VA 22182. Offers accounting (MBA); data management and analytics (MSIT); entrepreneurship (MBA); finance (MBA); global business management (MBA); health care management (MBA); hospitality and tourism management (MBA); human resources management (MBA); information technology (MBA); information technology systems and management (MSIT); leadership and management (MBA); project management (MBA); public service and administration (MBA); software design and management (MSIT).

Indiana University Bloomington, School of Public Health, Department of Recreation, Park, and Tourism Studies, Bloomington, IN 47405-7000. Offers leisure behavior (PhD); outdoor recreation (MS); park and public lands management (MS); recreation administration (MS); recreational sports administration (MS); recreational therapy (MS); tourism management (MS). Terminal master's awarded for partial completion of doctoral program. *Degree requirements:* For master's, thesis optional; for doctorate, comprehensive exam, thesis/dissertation. *Entrance requirements:* For master's, GRE General Test, minimum GPA of 2.8; for doctorate, GRE General Test, minimum GPA of 3.0 (undergraduate), 3.5 (graduate). Additional exam requirements/recommendations for international students: Required—TOEFL (minimum score 550 paper-based; 80 iBT). Electronic applications accepted. *Faculty research:* Leisure counseling, gerontology, special populations, planning and development.

Johnson & Wales University, Graduate Studies, MS Program in Global Tourism and Sustainable Economic Development, Providence, RI 02903-3703. Offers MS. *Program availability:* Online learning. *Expenses: Tuition:* Full-time $12,636; part-time $702 per credit hour. *Unit head:* Dr. Eldad Boker, Director, 401-598-4638, E-mail: eldad.boker@jwu.edu. *Application contact:* Graduate School Admissions, 401-598-1015, Fax: 401-598-1286, E-mail: pvdgrad@admissions.jwu.edu.
Website: https://www.jwu.edu/academics/programs-by-campus/providence-programs/global-tourism-and-sustainable-economic-development-ms.html

Kent State University, College of Education, Health and Human Services, School of Foundations, Leadership and Administration, Program in Hospitality and Tourism Management, Kent, OH 44242-0001. Offers MS. *Program availability:* Part-time. *Degree requirements:* For master's, thesis optional. *Entrance requirements:* For master's, minimum GPA of 3.0, 3 letters of recommendation, resume, goals statement. Additional exam requirements/recommendations for international students: Required—TOEFL (minimum score 550 paper-based; 80 iBT). Electronic applications accepted. *Expenses:* Tuition, state resident: full-time $11,310; part-time $515 per credit hour. Tuition, nonresident: full-time $20,396; part-time $928 per credit hour. *International tuition:* $18,544 full-time. *Faculty research:* Training human service workers, health care services for older adults, early adolescent development, care-giving arrangements with aging families, peace and war.

Lasell College, Graduate and Professional Studies in Management, Newton, MA 02466-2709. Offers business administration (MBA); elder care management (MSM); hospitality and event management (MSM); human resources management (MSM, Graduate Certificate); management (MSM, Graduate Certificate); marketing (MS, Graduate Certificate); project management (MSM, Graduate Certificate). *Accreditation:* ACBSP. *Program availability:* Part-time, evening/weekend, 100% online, blended/hybrid learning. *Faculty:* 1 full-time (0 women), 15 part-time/adjunct (11 women). *Students:* 41 full-time (25 women), 102 part-time (70 women); includes 34 minority (19 Black or African American, non-Hispanic/Latino; 5 Asian, non-Hispanic/Latino; 8 Hispanic/Latino; 2 Two or more races, non-Hispanic/Latino), 29 international. Average age 32. 128 applicants, 46% accepted, 38 enrolled. In 2017, 66 master's, 3 other advanced degrees awarded. *Degree requirements:* For master's, minimum GPA of 3.0; internship or research paper (for MSM). *Entrance requirements:* For master's, one-page personal statement, 2 letters of recommendation, resume, bachelor's degree transcript; proof of microeconomics and statistics (for MBA); for Graduate Certificate, bachelor's degree transcript, 2 letters of recommendation, 1-page personal statement, resume. Additional exam requirements/recommendations for international students: Required—TOEFL (minimum score 550 paper-based, 79 iBT) or IELTS (minimum score 6). *Application deadline:* For fall admission, 8/1 priority date for domestic students, 6/30 priority date for international students; for spring admission, 12/31 priority date for domestic students, 10/31 priority date for international students. Applications are processed on a rolling basis. Electronic applications accepted. *Expenses:* $600 per credit. *Financial support:* Federal Work-Study, scholarships/grants, and tuition discounts available. Support available to part-time students. Financial award application deadline: 8/31; financial award applicants required to submit FAFSA. *Unit head:* Eric Turner, Vice President of Graduate and Professional Studies, 617-243-2071, Fax: 617-243-2450, E-mail: gradinfo@lasell.edu. *Application contact:* Adrienne Franciosi, Director of Graduate Enrollment, 617-243-2214, Fax: 617-243-2450, E-mail: gradinfo@lasell.edu.
Website: http://www.lasell.edu/academics/graduate-and-professional-studies/programs-of-study/master-of-science-in-management.html

Lasell College, Graduate and Professional Studies in Sport Management, Newton, MA 02466-2709. Offers athletic administration (MS); parks and recreation (MS); sport leadership (MS, Graduate Certificate); sport tourism and hospitality (MS). *Program availability:* Part-time, evening/weekend, online only, 100% online. *Faculty:* 5 full-time (1 woman), 2 part-time/adjunct (1 woman). *Students:* 10 full-time (6 women), 25 part-time (8 women); includes 12 minority (9 Black or African American, non-Hispanic/Latino; 3 Hispanic/Latino). Average age 29. 35 applicants, 46% accepted, 11 enrolled. In 2017, 26 master's awarded. *Degree requirements:* For master's, minimum GPA of 3.0; internship or thesis. *Entrance requirements:* For master's, one-page personal statement, 2 letters of recommendation, resume, bachelor's degree transcript; for Graduate Certificate, bachelor's degree transcript, 2 letters of recommendation, 1-page personal statement, resume. Additional exam requirements/recommendations for international students: Required—TOEFL (minimum score 550 paper-based, 79 iBT) or IELTS (minimum score 6). *Application deadline:* For fall admission, 8/31 priority date for domestic students, 6/30 priority date for international students; for spring admission, 12/31 priority date for domestic students, 10/31 priority date for international students. Applications are processed on a rolling basis. Electronic applications accepted. *Expenses:* $600 per credit. *Financial support:* Federal Work-Study, scholarships/grants, and tuition discounts available. Support available to part-time students. Financial award application deadline: 8/31; financial award applicants required to submit FAFSA. *Faculty research:* How do fans attribute team failure; investigating cross-cultural difference in

attribution; sense of ownership as a key predictor of fan loyalty; fans' normative beliefs about sponsorship and sponsors; investigation of new attitudinal variables in sponsorship. *Unit head:* Eric Turner, Vice President of Graduate and Professional Studies, 617-243-2071, Fax: 617-243-2450, E-mail: gradinfo@lasell.edu. *Application contact:* Adrienne Franciosi, Director of Graduate Enrollment, 617-243-2214, Fax: 617-243-2450, E-mail: gradinfo@lasell.edu.
Website: http://www.lasell.edu/academics/graduate-and-professional-studies/programs-of-study/master-of-science-in-sport-management.html

Liberty University, School of Education, Lynchburg, VA 24515. Offers curriculum and instruction (Ed D, Ed S), including elementary education, middle grades education, secondary education, special education; educational leadership (Ed D); gifted education (Certificate); math specialist (M Ed); middle grades (MAT, Certificate); reading specialist (M Ed); school leadership (Certificate); secondary education (MAT); sport management (MS), including coaching and athletic administration, outdoor adventure sport, sport administration, tourism. *Accreditation:* NCATE. *Program availability:* Part-time, online learning. *Students:* 1,966 full-time (1,428 women), 3,484 part-time (2,528 women); includes 1,323 minority (1,026 Black or African American, non-Hispanic/Latino; 29 American Indian or Alaska Native, non-Hispanic/Latino; 49 Asian, non-Hispanic/Latino; 100 Hispanic/Latino; 9 Native Hawaiian or other Pacific Islander, non-Hispanic/Latino; 110 Two or more races, non-Hispanic/Latino), 58 international. Average age 37. 3,748 applicants, 58% accepted, 1167 enrolled. In 2017, 656 master's, 110 doctorates, 316 other advanced degrees awarded. *Degree requirements:* For doctorate, comprehensive exam, thesis/dissertation. *Entrance requirements:* For master's, GRE General Test or MAT (if taken in or before 1999), 2 letters of recommendation, minimum undergraduate GPA of 3.0, curriculum vitae; for doctorate and other advanced degree, GRE General Test or MAT (if taken before 1999), minimum master's GPA of 3.0, 3 years of teaching experience. Additional exam requirements/recommendations for international students: Required—TOEFL (minimum score 600 paper-based; 100 iBT). *Application deadline:* For fall admission, 6/1 for domestic students; for spring admission, 11/1 for domestic students. Applications are processed on a rolling basis. Application fee: $50. Electronic applications accepted. *Expenses:* Contact institution. *Financial support:* Federal Work-Study and tuition waivers (partial) available. *Faculty research:* Self-determination, character education, bibliotherapy, learning styles, distance education. *Unit head:* Dr. Heather Schoffstall, Dean, 434-582-2445, Fax: 434-582-2468, E-mail: awgunter@liberty.edu. *Application contact:* Jay Bridge, Director of Graduate Admissions, 800-424-9595, Fax: 800-628-7977, E-mail: gradadmissions@liberty.edu.
Website: http://www.liberty.edu/academics/education/graduate/

New Mexico State University, College of Agricultural, Consumer and Environmental Sciences, Department of Family and Consumer Sciences, Las Cruces, NM 88003. Offers clothing, textiles, and merchandising (MS); family and child science (MS); family and consumer science education (MS); family and consumer sciences (MS); food science and technology (MS); hotel, restaurant, and tourism management (MS); human nutrition and dietetic sciences (MS). *Program availability:* Part-time. *Faculty:* 9 full-time (6 women), 1 (woman) part-time/adjunct. *Students:* 38 full-time (30 women), 3 part-time (all women); includes 28 minority (3 Black or African American, non-Hispanic/Latino; 1 American Indian or Alaska Native, non-Hispanic/Latino; 1 Asian, non-Hispanic/Latino; 23 Hispanic/Latino). Average age 29. 26 applicants, 69% accepted, 17 enrolled. In 2017, 15 master's awarded. *Degree requirements:* For master's, comprehensive exam (for some programs), thesis (for some programs), oral exam. *Entrance requirements:* For master's, GRE, 3 letters of reference from faculty members or employers, resume, letter of interest. Additional exam requirements/recommendations for international students: Required—TOEFL (minimum score 550 paper-based; 79 iBT), IELTS (minimum score 6.5). *Application deadline:* For fall admission, 2/1 priority date for domestic and international students; for spring admission, 10/1 for domestic and international students. Applications are processed on a rolling basis. Application fee: $40 ($50 for international students). Electronic applications accepted. *Expenses:* Tuition, state resident: full-time $4390. Tuition, nonresident: full-time $15,309. *Required fees:* $853. *Financial support:* In 2017–18, 30 students received support, including 8 research assistantships (averaging $13,150 per year), 8 teaching assistantships (averaging $14,082 per year); career-related internships or fieldwork, Federal Work-Study, scholarships/grants, traineeships, health care benefits, and unspecified assistantships also available. Support available to part-time students. Financial award application deadline: 3/1. *Faculty research:* Food product analysis, childhood obesity, dietary decision-making, military families, equine assisted psychotherapy. *Total annual research expenditures:* $356,004. *Unit head:* Dr. Priscilla Bloomquist, Interim Department Head, 575-646-3936, Fax: 575-646-8100, E-mail: pbloomqu@nmsu.edu. *Application contact:* Dr. Kourtney Vaillancourt, Graduate Program Contact, 575-646-3383, Fax: 575-646-1889, E-mail: kvaillan@nmsu.edu.
Website: http://aces.nmsu.edu/academics/fcs

New York University, School of Professional Studies, Jonathan M. Tisch Center of Hospitality, Program in Tourism Management, New York, NY 10012-1019. Offers MS. *Program availability:* Part-time, evening/weekend. *Students:* 14 full-time (11 women), 5 part-time (4 women); includes 1 minority (Native Hawaiian or other Pacific Islander, non-Hispanic/Latino), 13 international. Average age 25. 31 applicants, 55% accepted, 8 enrolled. In 2017, 24 master's awarded. *Degree requirements:* For master's, thesis. *Entrance requirements:* For master's, GRE or GMAT (only upon request), bachelor's degree, resume with relevant professional work, internship or volunteer experience, two letters of recommendation, statement of purpose. Additional exam requirements/recommendations for international students: Required—TOEFL (minimum score 600 paper-based; 100 iBT), IELTS (minimum score 7). *Application deadline:* For fall admission, 2/1 priority date for domestic and international students; for spring admission, 10/15 priority date for domestic students, 8/15 priority date for international students. Applications are processed on a rolling basis. Application fee: $150. Electronic applications accepted. *Expenses:* $20,244 per term. *Financial support:* Fellowships, career-related internships or fieldwork, Federal Work-Study, scholarships/grants, and health care benefits available. Support available to part-time students. Financial award application deadline: 6/30; financial award applicants required to submit FAFSA. *Unit head:* Nicolas Graf, Associate Dean/Clinical Associate Professor, 212-998-9100. *Application contact:* Office of Admissions, 212-998-7100, E-mail: sps.gradadmissions@nyu.edu.
Website: http://www.sps.nyu.edu/content/scps/academics/departments/tisch/academic-offerings/graduate.html

North Carolina State University, Graduate School, College of Natural Resources, Department of Parks, Recreation and Tourism Management, Raleigh, NC 27695. Offers natural resource management (MPRTM, MS); park and recreation management (MPRTM, MS); parks, recreation and tourism management (PhD); recreational sport management (MPRTM, MS); spatial information science (MPRTM, MS); tourism policy and development (MPRTM, MS). *Degree requirements:* For master's, thesis (for some programs); for doctorate, thesis/dissertation. *Entrance requirements:* For master's and doctorate, GRE General Test. Additional exam requirements/recommendations for international students: Required—TOEFL. Electronic applications accepted. *Faculty research:* Tourism policy and development, spatial information systems, natural resource management, recreational sports management, park and recreation management.

Penn State University Park, Graduate School, College of Health and Human Development, Department of Recreation, Park and Tourism Management, University Park, PA 16802. Offers MS, PhD. *Unit head:* Dr. Ann C. Crouter, Dean, 814-865-1420, Fax: 814-865-3282. *Application contact:* Lori Hawn, Director, Graduate Student Services, 814-865-1795, Fax: 814-863-4627, E-mail: l-gswww@lists.psu.edu.
Website: http://hhd.psu.edu/rptm

Pontificia Universidad Catolica Madre y Maestra, Graduate School, Faculty of Social and Administrative Sciences, Santiago, Dominican Republic. Offers business administration (MBA), including business development, finance, international business, management skills (M Mgmt, MBA), marketing, operations, strategic cost management, strategy, tourist destination planning and management; law (LL M), including civil law, corporate business law, criminal law, international relations, real estate law; management (M Mgmt), including higher financial management, insurance program administration, management skills (M Mgmt, MBA); psychology (MA), including clinical child and adolescent psychology, forensic psychology; strategic human resources (EMBA).

Purdue University, Graduate School, College of Health and Human Sciences, School of Hospitality and Tourism Management, West Lafayette, IN 47907. Offers MS, PhD. *Program availability:* Online learning. *Faculty:* 17 full-time (6 women), 1 part-time/adjunct (0 women). *Students:* 38 full-time (26 women), 15 part-time (9 women); includes 3 minority (1 Asian, non-Hispanic/Latino; 2 Hispanic/Latino), 43 international. Average age 29. 79 applicants, 61% accepted, 12 enrolled. In 2017, 18 master's, 7 doctorates awarded. *Degree requirements:* For master's, thesis; for doctorate, thesis/dissertation. *Entrance requirements:* For master's, GMAT (minimum score of 550) or GRE General Test (minimum combined verbal and quantitative score of 290 new scoring, minimum of 145 each section, or 1000 with 500 each section, old scoring), minimum GPA of 3.0; for doctorate, GMAT (minimum score of 550) or GRE General Test (minimum combined verbal and quantitative score of 290 new scoring, minimum of 145 each section, or 1000 with 500 each section, old scoring), minimum undergraduate GPA of 3.0; master's degree with minimum GPA of 3.0 or equivalent. Additional exam requirements/recommendations for international students: Required—TOEFL (minimum score 77 iBT), TWE. *Application deadline:* For fall admission, 3/5 priority date for domestic and international students; for spring admission, 9/20 for domestic and international students. Applications are processed on a rolling basis. Application fee: $60 ($75 for international students). Electronic applications accepted. *Financial support:* Research assistantships, teaching assistantships, and career-related internships or fieldwork available. Support available to part-time students. Financial award applicants required to submit FAFSA. *Faculty research:* Human resources, marketing, hotel and restaurant operations, food product and equipment development, tourism development. *Unit head:* Dr. Richard F. Ghiselli, Head, 765-494-2636, E-mail: ghiselli@purdue.edu. *Application contact:* Ayrielle K. Espinosa, Graduate Contact, 765-494-9811, E-mail: camposm@purdue.edu.
Website: http://www.purdue.edu/hhs/htm/

Rochester Institute of Technology, Graduate Enrollment Services, College of Applied Science and Technology, School of International Hospitality and Service Innovation, MS Program in Hospitality and Tourism Management, Rochester, NY 14623. Offers MS. *Program availability:* Part-time, evening/weekend. *Students:* 10 full-time (5 women), 5 part-time (1 woman); includes 1 minority (Hispanic/Latino), 11 international. Average age 28. 22 applicants, 64% accepted, 4 enrolled. In 2017, 4 master's awarded. *Degree requirements:* For master's, thesis or alternative. *Entrance requirements:* For master's, minimum GPA of 3.0 (recommended). Additional exam requirements/recommendations for international students: Required—TOEFL (minimum score 570 paper-based; 88 iBT), IELTS (minimum score 6.5), PTE (minimum score 61). *Application deadline:* Applications are processed on a rolling basis. Application fee: $65. Electronic applications accepted. *Expenses:* $1,815 per credit hour. *Financial support:* In 2017–18, 9 students received support. Teaching assistantships with partial tuition reimbursements available, career-related internships or fieldwork, scholarships/grants, and unspecified assistantships available. Support available to part-time students. Financial award applicants required to submit FAFSA. *Faculty research:* Service innovation and technology integration, innovative food product development, hospitality employees' occupational health and wellness, tourist behaviors, destination management. *Unit head:* Yu-Chin Hsieh, Department Chair, 585-475-2355, E-mail: yhsieh@rit.edu. *Application contact:* Diane Ellison, Senior Associate Vice President, Graduate Enrollment Services, 585-475-2229, Fax: 585-475-7164, E-mail: gradinfo@rit.edu.
Website: http://www.rit.edu/cast/htm/graduate-program

Rochester Institute of Technology, Graduate Enrollment Services, College of Applied Science and Technology, School of International Hospitality and Service Innovation, MS Program in Service Leadership and Innovation, Rochester, NY 14623. Offers MS. *Program availability:* Part-time, evening/weekend, 100% online. *Students:* 13 full-time (10 women), 17 part-time (10 women); includes 3 minority (1 Black or African American, non-Hispanic/Latino; 1 Asian, non-Hispanic/Latino; 1 Hispanic/Latino), 2 international. Average age 31. 38 applicants, 42% accepted, 2 enrolled. In 2017, 2 master's awarded. *Degree requirements:* For master's, thesis or alternative. *Entrance requirements:* For master's, minimum GPA of 3.0 (recommended). Additional exam requirements/recommendations for international students: Required—TOEFL (minimum score 570 paper-based; 88 iBT), IELTS (minimum score 6.5), PTE (minimum score 62). *Application deadline:* Applications are processed on a rolling basis. Application fee: $65. Electronic applications accepted. *Expenses:* $1,815 per credit hour (classroom), $1,035 per credit hour (online study). *Financial support:* In 2017–18, 3 students received support. Teaching assistantships with partial tuition reimbursements available, career-related internships or fieldwork, scholarships/grants, and unspecified assistantships available. Support available to part-time students. Financial award applicants required to submit FAFSA. *Faculty research:* Leadership development, customer service/patient satisfaction, program evaluation, knowledge construction, diversity, individual creativity, healthcare applications. *Unit head:* Dr. Linda Underhill, Department Chair, 585-475-7359, E-mail: lmuism@rit.edu. *Application contact:* Diane Ellison, Senior Associate Vice President, Graduate Enrollment Services, 585-475-2229, Fax: 585-475-7164, E-mail: gradinfo@rit.edu.
Website: http://www.rit.edu/cast/servicesystems/service-leadership-innovation

Royal Roads University, Graduate Studies, Tourism and Hospitality Management Program, Victoria, BC V9B 5Y2, Canada. Offers tourism management (MA, Graduate Certificate). Application fee: $120 ($240 for international students). *Financial support:* Career-related internships or fieldwork, institutionally sponsored loans, scholarships/grants, and bursaries available. *Unit head:* William Holmes, Dean, 250-391-2511, E-mail: admissions@royalroads.ca. *Application contact:* E-mail: admissions@royalroads.ca.

San Francisco State University, Division of Graduate Studies, College of Business, Program in Business Administration, San Francisco, CA 94132-1722. Offers decision sciences/operations research (MBA); ethics and compliance (MBA); finance (MBA); global business and innovation (MBA); healthcare administration (MBA); hospitality and tourism management (MBA); information systems (MBA); leadership (MBA); marketing (MBA); nonprofit and social enterprise leadership (MBA); sustainable business (MBA).

Accreditation: AACSB. *Program availability:* Part-time, evening/weekend. *Degree requirements:* For master's, thesis, essay test. *Entrance requirements:* For master's, GMAT, minimum GPA of 2.7 in last 60 units. Additional exam requirements/recommendations for international students: Required—TOEFL (minimum score 550 paper-based). *Application deadline:* For fall admission, 5/1 priority date for domestic students, 4/1 for international students; for spring admission, 11/1 for domestic students, 10/15 for international students. Applications are processed on a rolling basis. Application fee: $55. *Financial support:* Application availability: 3/1. *Unit head:* Dr. Sanjit Sengupta, Faculty Director, 415-817-4366, Fax: 415-817-4340, E-mail: sengupta@sfsu.edu. *Application contact:* Christopher Kingston, Director of Student Advising, 415-817-4322, Fax: 415-817-4340, E-mail: cak@sfsu.edu.
Website: http://cob.sfsu.edu/graduate-programs/mba

San Francisco State University, Division of Graduate Studies, College of Health and Social Sciences, Department of Recreation, Parks, and Tourism, San Francisco, CA 94132-1722. Offers MS. *Program availability:* Part-time. *Application deadline:* Applications are processed on a rolling basis. *Financial support:* Career-related internships or fieldwork available. *Unit head:* Dr. Erik Rosegard, Chair, 415-338-7529, Fax: 415-338-0543, E-mail: rosegard@sfsu.edu. *Application contact:* Dr. Jackson Wilson, Graduate Coordinator, 415-338-1487, Fax: 415-338-0543, E-mail: wilsonj@sfsu.edu.
Website: http://recdept.sfsu.edu/graduate

San Ignacio University, Graduate Programs, Doral, FL 33178. Offers business administration (MBA), including human resources management, international business, marketing management; education (M Ed), including early childhood education, educational leadership, special education; hospitality management (MA), including gastronomy and restaurant management, tourism management.

Savannah College of Art and Design, Program in Themed Entertainment Design, Savannah, GA 31402-3146. Offers MFA. *Program availability:* Part-time. *Faculty:* 1 full-time (0 women). *Students:* 28 full-time (18 women), 1 (woman) part-time; includes 2 minority (1 Asian, non-Hispanic/Latino; 1 Hispanic/Latino), 8 international. Average age 26. 44 applicants, 57% accepted, 14 enrolled. In 2017, 13 master's awarded. *Degree requirements:* For master's, thesis. *Entrance requirements:* For master's, GRE (recommended), portfolio (submitted in digital format), audition or writing submission, resume, statement of purpose, two letters of recommendation. Additional exam requirements/recommendations for international students: Recommended—TOEFL (minimum score 550 paper-based; 85 iBT), IELTS (minimum score 6.5). *Application deadline:* For fall admission, 4/1 for domestic and international students. Applications are processed on a rolling basis. Application fee: $40. Electronic applications accepted. *Expenses: Tuition:* Full-time $36,765; part-time $817 per credit hour. One-time fee: $500. *Financial support:* Career-related internships or fieldwork, Federal Work-Study, and scholarships/grants available. Financial award application deadline: 4/1; financial award applicants required to submit FAFSA. *Unit head:* Gregory Beck, Chair, Production Design and Themed Entertainment. *Application contact:* Jenny Jaquillard, Executive Director of Admissions, Recruitment and Events, 912-525-5100, Fax: 912-525-5985, E-mail: admission@scad.edu.
Website: http://www.scad.edu/academics/programs/themed-entertainment-design

Schiller International University, MBA Programs, Florida, Program in International Hotel and Tourism Management, Largo, FL 33771. Offers MBA. *Degree requirements:* For master's, thesis optional. *Entrance requirements:* Additional exam requirements/recommendations for international students: Required—TOEFL (minimum score 550 paper-based).

Strayer University, Graduate Studies, Washington, DC 20005-2603. Offers accounting (MS); acquisition (MBA); business administration (MBA); communications technology (MS); educational management (M Ed); finance (MBA); health services administration (MHSA); hospitality and tourism management (MBA); human resource management (MBA); information systems (MS), including computer security management, decision support system management, enterprise resource management, network management, software engineering management, systems development management; management (MBA); management information systems (MS); marketing (MBA); professional accounting (MS), including accounting information systems, controllership, taxation; public administration (MPA); supply chain management (MBA); technology in education (M Ed). Programs also offered at campus locations in Birmingham, AL; Chamblee, GA; Cobb County, GA; Morrow, GA; White Marsh, MD; Charleston, SC; Columbia, SC; Greensboro, NC; Greenville, SC; Lexington, KY; Louisville, KY; Nashville, TN; North Raleigh, NC; Washington, DC. *Accreditation:* ACBSP. *Program availability:* Part-time, evening/weekend, online learning. *Degree requirements:* For master's, thesis. *Entrance requirements:* For master's, GMAT, GRE General Test, bachelor's degree from an accredited college or university, minimum undergraduate GPA of 2.75. Electronic applications accepted.

Syracuse University, David B. Falk College of Sport and Human Dynamics, MS Program in Sport Venue and Event Management, Syracuse, NY 13244. Offers MS. *Entrance requirements:* For master's, GRE, undergraduate transcripts, three recommendations, resume, personal statement. Additional exam requirements/recommendations for international students: Required—TOEFL (minimum score 100 iBT). *Application deadline:* For fall admission, 2/15 for domestic students; for spring admission, 11/1 priority date for domestic and international students. Application fee: $75. Electronic applications accepted. *Financial support:* Fellowships, research assistantships, teaching assistantships, and career-related internships or fieldwork available. Financial award application deadline: 1/1; financial award applicants required to submit FAFSA. *Faculty research:* Managing and operating sport and entertainment facilities and events, sociology of sport, psychological and social issues in sport. *Unit head:* Jeff Pauline, Graduate Program Director, 315-443-0364, Fax: 315-443-9811, E-mail: jspaulin@syr.edu. *Application contact:* Felicia Otero, Director of Admissions, 315-443-5555, E-mail: falk@syr.edu.
Website: https://falk.syr.edu/sport-management/academic-programs/#mssvem

Temple University, School of Sport, Tourism and Hospitality Management, Philadelphia, PA 19122-6096. Offers sport business (MS); tourism and hospitality management (MTHM); tourism and sport (PhD); travel and tourism (MS). *Program availability:* Part-time, evening/weekend. *Faculty:* 28 full-time (9 women), 9 part-time/adjunct (2 women). *Students:* 158 full-time (72 women), 32 part-time (19 women); includes 46 minority (29 Black or African American, non-Hispanic/Latino; 4 Asian, non-Hispanic/Latino; 11 Hispanic/Latino; 2 Two or more races, non-Hispanic/Latino), 31 international. 235 applicants, 74% accepted, 96 enrolled. In 2017, 37 master's awarded. *Entrance requirements:* For master's, GRE General Test, GMAT, or MAT, bachelor's degree or equivalent with minimum GPA of 3.0, 500-word essay, 2 letters of recommendation, resume; for doctorate, GMAT or GRE. Additional exam requirements/recommendations for international students: Required—TOEFL (minimum score 550 paper-based; 79 iBT), IELTS (minimum score 6.5). *Application deadline:* For fall admission, 3/1 priority date for domestic students, 1/15 priority date for international students; for spring admission, 8/15 priority date for domestic students, 6/30 priority date for international students. Applications are processed on a rolling basis. Application fee: $60. Electronic applications accepted. *Expenses:* Contact institution. *Financial support:* Fellowships, research assistantships, and teaching assistantships available. Financial

award application deadline: 3/1; financial award applicants required to submit FAFSA. *Unit head:* Dr. M. Moshe Porat, Dean, 215-204-1836, Fax: 215-204-8705, E-mail: porat@temple.edu. *Application contact:* James Alton, Manager of Graduate Student Services, 215-204-7140, Fax: 215-204-8705, E-mail: jim.alton@temple.edu.
Website: http://sthm.temple.edu/

Tropical Agriculture Research and Higher Education Center, Graduate School, Turrialba, Costa Rica. Offers agribusiness management (MS); agroforestry systems (PhD); development practices (MS); ecological agriculture (MS); environmental socioeconomics (MS); forestry in tropical and subtropical zones (PhD); integrated watershed management (MS); international sustainable tourism (MS); management and conservation of tropical rainforests and biodiversity (MS); tropical agriculture (PhD); tropical agroforestry (MS). *Entrance requirements:* For master's, GRE, 2 years of related professional experience, letters of recommendation; for doctorate, GRE, 4 letters of recommendation, letter of support from employing organization, master's degree in agronomy, biological sciences, forestry, natural resources or related field. Additional exam requirements/recommendations for international students: Required—TOEFL (minimum score 550 paper-based). Electronic applications accepted. *Faculty research:* Biodiversity in fragmented landscapes, ecosystem management, integrated pest management, environmental livestock production, biotechnology carbon balances in diverse land uses.

Université du Québec à Trois-Rivières, Graduate Programs, Program in Leisure, Culture and Tourism Sciences, Trois-Rivières, QC G9A 5H7, Canada. Offers MA, DESS. *Program availability:* Part-time. *Degree requirements:* For master's, thesis optional. *Entrance requirements:* For master's, appropriate bachelor's degree, proficiency in French.

University of Central Florida, Rosen College of Hospitality Management, Orlando, FL 32816. Offers destination marketing and management (Certificate); event management (Certificate); hospitality and tourism management (MS); hospitality management (PhD). *Program availability:* Part-time. *Faculty:* 71 full-time (29 women), 30 part-time/adjunct (8 women). *Students:* 76 full-time (50 women), 161 part-time (111 women); includes 72 minority (28 Black or African American, non-Hispanic/Latino; 1 American Indian or Alaska Native, non-Hispanic/Latino; 7 Asian, non-Hispanic/Latino; 31 Hispanic/Latino; 5 Two or more races, non-Hispanic/Latino), 24 international. Average age 30. 195 applicants, 65% accepted, 82 enrolled. In 2017, 31 master's, 5 doctorates, 32 other advanced degrees awarded. *Degree requirements:* For master's, thesis or alternative; for doctorate, thesis/dissertation, candidacy exam. *Entrance requirements:* For master's and doctorate, GMAT or GRE, letters of recommendation, goal statement, resume. Additional exam requirements/recommendations for international students: Required—TOEFL. *Application deadline:* For fall admission, 7/15 for domestic students; for spring admission, 12/1 for domestic students. Application fee: $30. Electronic applications accepted. *Expenses:* Tuition, state resident: part-time $288.16 per credit hour. Tuition, nonresident: part-time $1073.31 per credit hour. Tuition and fees vary according to program. *Financial support:* In 2017–18, 24 students received support, including 7 fellowships with partial tuition reimbursements available (averaging $1,971 per year), 2 research assistantships with partial tuition reimbursements available (averaging $9,323 per year), 22 teaching assistantships with partial tuition reimbursements available (averaging $12,876 per year); health care benefits also available. Financial award application deadline: 3/1; financial award applicants required to submit FAFSA. *Unit head:* Dr. Abraham C. Pizam, Dean, 407-903-8010, E-mail: abraham.pizam@ucf.edu. *Application contact:* Associate Director, Graduate Admissions, 407-823-2766, Fax: 407-823-6442, E-mail: gradadmissions@ucf.edu.
Website: http://www.hospitality.ucf.edu/

University of Florida, Graduate School, College of Health and Human Performance, Department of Tourism, Recreation and Sport Management, Gainesville, FL 32611. Offers health and human performance (PhD), including historic preservation (MS, PhD), recreation, parks and tourism (MS, PhD), sport management; recreation, parks and tourism (MS), including historic preservation (MS, PhD), natural resource recreation, recreation, parks and tourism (MS, PhD), therapeutic recreation, tourism, tropical conservation and development; sport management (MS), including historic preservation (MS, PhD), tropical conservation and development; JD/MS, MSM/MS. *Degree requirements:* For master's, comprehensive exam (for some programs), thesis (for some programs); for doctorate, comprehensive exam, thesis/dissertation. *Entrance requirements:* For master's and doctorate, GRE General Test, minimum GPA of 3.0. Additional exam requirements/recommendations for international students: Required—TOEFL (minimum score 550 paper-based; 80 iBT), IELTS (minimum score 6). Electronic applications accepted. *Faculty research:* Hospitality, natural resource management, sport management, tourism.

University of Hawaii at Manoa, Office of Graduate Education, School of Travel Industry Management, Honolulu, HI 96822. Offers MS. *Program availability:* Part-time. *Degree requirements:* For master's, thesis optional. *Entrance requirements:* For master's, GRE General Test, minimum GPA of 3.0. Additional exam requirements/recommendations for international students: Required—TOEFL (minimum score 560 paper-based; 83 iBT), IELTS (minimum score 5). Electronic applications accepted. *Faculty research:* Travel information technology, tourism development and policy, transportation management and policy, hospitality management, sustainable tourism development.

University of Idaho, College of Graduate Studies, College of Education, Health and Human Sciences, Department of Movement Sciences, Moscow, ID 83844. Offers athletic training (MSAT, DAT); exercise science and health (MS); physical education teacher education (M Ed, MS); recreation, sport, and tourism management (MS). *Faculty:* 22. *Students:* 89 full-time (41 women), 18 part-time (7 women). Average age 28. In 2017, 24 master's awarded. *Degree requirements:* For doctorate, thesis/dissertation. *Entrance requirements:* For master's and doctorate, minimum GPA of 3.0. Additional exam requirements/recommendations for international students: Required—TOEFL. *Application deadline:* For fall admission, 8/1 for domestic students; for spring admission, 12/15 for domestic students. Applications are processed on a rolling basis. Application fee: $60. Electronic applications accepted. *Expenses:* Tuition, state resident: full-time $6722; part-time $430 per credit hour. Tuition, nonresident: full-time $23,046; part-time $1337 per credit hour. *Required fees:* $2142; $63 per credit hour. *Financial support:* Research assistantships and teaching assistantships available. Financial award applicants required to submit FAFSA. *Unit head:* Dr. Philip W. Scruggs, Chair, 208-885-7921, E-mail: movementsciences@uidaho.edu. *Application contact:* Sean Scoggin, Graduate Recruitment Coordinator, 208-885-4001, Fax: 208-885-4406, E-mail: graduateadmissions@uidaho.edu.
Website: https://www.uidaho.edu/ed/mvsc

University of Massachusetts Amherst, Graduate School, Isenberg School of Management, Program in Management, Amherst, MA 01003. Offers accounting (PhD); business administration (MBA); entrepreneurship (MBA); finance (MBA, PhD); healthcare administration (MBA); hospitality and tourism management (PhD); management science (PhD); marketing (MBA, PhD); organization studies (PhD); sport management (PhD); strategic management (PhD); MBA/MS. *Accreditation:* AACSB. *Program availability:* Part-time, evening/weekend, online learning. Terminal master's awarded for partial completion of doctoral program. *Degree requirements:* For doctorate, comprehensive exam, thesis/dissertation. *Entrance requirements:* For master's and doctorate, GMAT or GRE General Test. Additional exam requirements/recommendations for international students: Required—TOEFL (minimum score 550 paper-based; 80 iBT), IELTS (minimum score 6.5). Electronic applications accepted.

University of Minnesota, Twin Cities Campus, Graduate School, College of Food, Agricultural and Natural Resource Sciences, Program in Natural Resources Science and Management, St. Paul, MN 55108. Offers assessment, monitoring, and geospatial analysis (MS, PhD); economics, policy, management, and society (MS, PhD); forest hydrology and watershed management (MS, PhD); forest products (MS, PhD); forests: biology, ecology, conservation, and management (MS, PhD); natural resources science and management (MS, PhD); paper science and engineering (MS, PhD); recreation resources, tourism, and environmental education (MS, PhD). *Program availability:* Part-time. *Faculty:* 72 full-time (29 women), 52 part-time/adjunct (8 women). *Students:* 88 full-time (49 women), 21 part-time (12 women); includes 11 minority (2 Black or African American, non-Hispanic/Latino; 2 American Indian or Alaska Native, non-Hispanic/Latino; 3 Asian, non-Hispanic/Latino; 4 Hispanic/Latino), 12 international. Average age 30. 69 applicants, 54% accepted, 30 enrolled. In 2017, 18 master's, 4 doctorates awarded. Terminal master's awarded for partial completion of doctoral program. *Degree requirements:* For master's, comprehensive exam, thesis (for some programs); for doctorate, comprehensive exam, thesis/dissertation. *Entrance requirements:* For master's and doctorate, GRE General Test. Additional exam requirements/recommendations for international students: Required—TOEFL (minimum score 550 paper-based; 79 iBT); Recommended—IELTS (minimum score 6.5). *Application deadline:* For fall admission, 12/15 priority date for domestic and international students; for spring admission, 10/15 for domestic and international students. Applications are processed on a rolling basis. Application fee: $75 ($95 for international students). Electronic applications accepted. *Financial support:* In 2017–18, 6 students received support, including fellowships with full tuition reimbursements available (averaging $41,000 per year), research assistantships with full tuition reimbursements available (averaging $41,000 per year), teaching assistantships with full tuition reimbursements available (averaging $36,000 per year); scholarships/grants, health care benefits, and unspecified assistantships also available. *Faculty research:* Forest hydrology, biology, ecology, conservation, and management; recreation resources and environmental education; wildlife ecology; economics, policy, and society; geographic information systems (GIS); forest products and paper science. *Unit head:* Dr. Mae Davenport, Director of Graduate Studies, 612-624-2721, E-mail: mdaven@umn.edu. *Application contact:* Toni Abts, Graduate Program Coordinator, 612-624-7683, Fax: 612-625-5212, E-mail: twheeler@umn.edu.
Website: http://www.nrsm.umn.edu

University of New Orleans, Graduate School, College of Business Administration, Lester E. Kabacoff School of Hotel, Restaurant, and Tourism Administration, Program in Hospitality and Tourism Management, New Orleans, LA 70148. Offers MS. *Program availability:* Online learning. *Entrance requirements:* Additional exam requirements/recommendations for international students: Required—TOEFL (minimum score 550 paper-based; 79 iBT).

University of North Texas, Robert B. Toulouse School of Graduate Studies, Denton, TX 76203-5459. Offers accounting (MS); applied anthropology (MA, MS); applied behavior analysis (Certificate); applied geography (MA); applied technology and performance improvement (M Ed, MS); art education (MA); art history (MA); art museum education (Certificate); arts leadership (Certificate); audiology (Au D); behavior analysis (MS); behavioral science (PhD); biochemistry and molecular biology (MS); biology (MA, MS); biomedical engineering (MS); business analysis (MS); chemistry (MS); clinical health psychology (PhD); communication studies (MA, MS); computer engineering (MS); computer science (MS); counseling (M Ed, MS), including clinical mental health counseling (MS), college and university counseling, elementary school counseling, secondary school counseling; creative writing (MA); criminal justice (MS); curriculum and instruction (M Ed); decision sciences (MBA); design (MA, MFA), including fashion design (MFA), innovation studies, interior design (MFA); early childhood studies (MS); economics (MS); educational leadership (M Ed, Ed D); educational psychology (MS, PhD), including family studies (MS), gifted and talented (MS), human development (MS), learning and cognition (MS), research, measurement and evaluation (MS); electrical engineering (MS); emergency management (MPA); engineering technology (MS); English (MA); English as a second language (MA); environmental science (MS); finance (MBA, MS); financial management (MPA); French (MA); health services management (MBA); higher education (M Ed, Ed D); history (MA, MS); hospitality management (MS); human resources management (MPA); information science (MS); information systems (PhD); information technologies (MBA); interdisciplinary studies (MA, MS); international studies (MA); international sustainable tourism (MS); jazz studies (MM); journalism (MA, MJ, Graduate Certificate), including interactive and virtual digital communication (Graduate Certificate), narrative journalism (Graduate Certificate), public relations (Graduate Certificate); kinesiology (MS); linguistics (MA); local government management (MPA); logistics (PhD); logistics and supply chain management (MBA); long-term care, senior housing, and aging services (MA); management (PhD); marketing (MBA); mathematics (MA, MS); mechanical and energy engineering (MS, PhD); music (MA), including ethnomusicology, music theory, musicology, performance; music composition (PhD); music education (MM Ed, PhD); nonprofit management (MPA); operations and supply chain management (MBA); performance (MM, DMA); philosophy (MA); political science (MA); professional and technical communication (MA); radio, television and film (MA, MFA); rehabilitation counseling (Certificate); sociology (MA); Spanish (MA); special education (M Ed); speech-language pathology (MS); strategic management (MBA); studio art (MFA); teaching (M Ed); MBA/MS. *Program availability:* Part-time, evening/weekend, online learning. Terminal master's awarded for partial completion of doctoral program. *Degree requirements:* For master's, variable foreign language requirement, comprehensive exam, thesis (for some programs); for doctorate, variable foreign language requirement, comprehensive exam (for some programs), thesis/dissertation; for other advanced degree, variable foreign language requirement, comprehensive exam (for some programs). *Entrance requirements:* For master's and doctorate, GRE, GMAT. Additional exam requirements/recommendations for international students: Required—TOEFL (minimum score 550 paper-based; 79 iBT). Electronic applications accepted.

University of South Africa, College of Economic and Management Sciences, Pretoria, South Africa. Offers accounting (D Admin, D Com); accounting science (DA); auditing (D Admin, D Com); business administration (M Tech); business economics (D Admin); business leadership (DBL); business management (D Admin, D Com); economic management analysis (M Tech); economics (D Admin, D Com, PhD); human resource development (M Tech); industrial psychology (D Admin, D Com, PhD); logistics (D Com); marketing (M Tech); public administration (D Admin, D Com, DPA, PhD); public management (D Admin, D Com); quantitative management (D Admin, D Com); real estate (M Tech); statistics (D Admin, PhD); tourism management (D Admin, D Com); transport economics (D Admin, D Com).

University of South Carolina, The Graduate School, College of Hospitality, Retail, and Sport Management, School of Hotel, Restaurant and Tourism Management, Columbia, SC 29208. Offers MIHTM. *Entrance requirements:* For master's, GMAT or GRE General Test, minimum GPA of 3.0, 2 letters of recommendation. Electronic applications accepted. *Faculty research:* Corporate strategy and management practices, sustainable tourism, club management, tourism technology, revenue management.

University of South Florida, College of Global Sustainability, Tampa, FL 33620-9951. Offers energy, global, water and sustainable tourism (Graduate Certificate); global sustainability (MA), including building sustainable enterprise, climate change and sustainability, coastal sustainability, entrepreneurship, food sustainability and security, sustainability policy, sustainable energy, sustainable tourism, water. *Faculty:* 2 full-time (0 women). *Students:* 124 full-time (64 women), 77 part-time (45 women); includes 33 minority (12 Black or African American, non-Hispanic/Latino; 1 American Indian or Alaska Native, non-Hispanic/Latino; 1 Asian, non-Hispanic/Latino; 14 Hispanic/Latino; 5 Two or more races, non-Hispanic/Latino), 87 international. Average age 28. 220 applicants, 65% accepted, 101 enrolled. In 2017, 50 master's awarded. *Degree requirements:* For master's, comprehensive exam (for some programs), thesis or alternative, internship. *Entrance requirements:* For master's, minimum GPA of 3.0 in undergraduate coursework; at least two letters of recommendation (one must be academic); 200-250 word essay on student's background, professional goals, and reasons for seeking degree. Additional exam requirements/recommendations for international students: Required—TOEFL (minimum score 550 paper-based; 79 iBT). *Application deadline:* For fall admission, 6/1 for domestic students, 5/1 for international students; for spring admission, 10/15 for domestic students, 9/15 for international students. Electronic applications accepted. *Financial support:* In 2017–18, 22 students received support. *Faculty research:* Global sustainability, integrated resource management, systems thinking, green communities, entrepreneurship, ecotourism. *Total annual research expenditures:* $107,829. *Unit head:* Dr. Govindan Parayil, Dean, 813-974-9694, E-mail: gparayil@usf.edu.
Website: http://psgs.usf.edu/

The University of Tennessee, Graduate School, College of Education, Health and Human Sciences, Department of Consumer and Industry Services Management, Program in Hotel, Restaurant, and Tourism Management, Knoxville, TN 37996. Offers hospitality management (MS); tourism (MS). *Program availability:* Part-time. *Degree requirements:* For master's, thesis or alternative. *Entrance requirements:* For master's, GRE General Test, minimum GPA of 2.7. Additional exam requirements/recommendations for international students: Required—TOEFL. Electronic applications accepted.

Western Illinois University, School of Graduate Studies, College of Education and Human Services, Department of Recreation, Park, and Tourism Administration, Macomb, IL 61455-1390. Offers MS. *Program availability:* Part-time. *Degree requirements:* For master's, thesis or alternative. *Entrance requirements:* Additional exam requirements/recommendations for international students: Required—TOEFL (minimum score 550 paper-based; 80 iBT). *Application deadline:* Applications are processed on a rolling basis. Application fee: $30. Electronic applications accepted. *Financial support:* Unspecified assistantships available. Financial award applicants required to submit FAFSA. *Unit head:* Dr. Dan Yoder, Chairperson, 309-298-1584. *Application contact:* Dr. Nancy Parsons, Assistant Director of Graduate Studies, 309-298-1806, Fax: 309-298-2345, E-mail: grad-office@wiu.edu.
Website: http://www.wiu.edu/rpta

West Virginia University, Davis College of Agriculture, Forestry and Consumer Sciences, Morgantown, WV 26506. Offers agricultural and extension education (MS, PhD); agriculture and resource management (MS); agriculture, natural resources and design (M Agr); agronomy (MS); animal and food science (PhD); animal physiology (MS); applied and environmental microbiology (MS); design and merchandising (MS); entomology (MS); forest resource science (PhD); forestry (MSF); genetics and developmental biology (MS, PhD); horticulture (MS); human and community development (PhD); landscape architecture (MLA); natural resource economics (PhD); nutritional and food science (MS); plant and soil science (PhD); plant pathology (MS); recreation, parks and tourism resources (MS); reproductive physiology (MS, PhD); wildlife and fisheries resources (PhD). *Program availability:* Part-time. *Students:* 200 full-time (97 women), 53 part-time (32 women); includes 27 minority (6 Black or African American, non-Hispanic/Latino; 1 American Indian or Alaska Native, non-Hispanic/Latino; 4 Asian, non-Hispanic/Latino; 11 Hispanic/Latino; 5 Two or more races, non-Hispanic/Latino), 67 international. *Degree requirements:* For master's, thesis; for doctorate, thesis/dissertation. *Entrance requirements:* Additional exam requirements/recommendations for international students: Required—TOEFL (minimum score 550 paper-based). *Application deadline:* For fall admission, 6/1 priority date for domestic students, 6/1 for international students; for spring admission, 1/5 for domestic and international students. Applications are processed on a rolling basis. Application fee: $60. Electronic applications accepted. *Expenses:* Tuition, state resident: full-time $9450. Tuition, nonresident: full-time $24,390. *Financial support:* Fellowships, research assistantships, teaching assistantships, career-related internships or fieldwork, Federal Work-Study, institutionally sponsored loans, tuition waivers (full and partial), and unspecified assistantships available. Financial award application deadline: 2/1; financial award applicants required to submit FAFSA. *Faculty research:* Reproductive physiology, soil and water quality, human nutrition, aquaculture, wildlife management. *Unit head:* Dr. Dan J. Robison, Dean, 304-293-2395, Fax: 304-293-3740, E-mail: dan.robison@mail.wvu.edu. *Application contact:* Dr. Dennis K. Smith, Associate Dean, 304-293-2275, Fax: 304-293-3740, E-mail: denny.smith@mail.wvu.edu.
Website: https://www.davis.wvu.edu

Section 8
Human Resources

This section contains a directory of institutions offering graduate work in human resources, followed by in-depth entries submitted by institutions that chose to prepare detailed program descriptions. Additional information about programs listed in the directory but not augmented by an in-depth entry may be obtained by writing directly to the dean of a graduate school or chair of a department at the address given in the directory.

For programs offering related work, see also in this book *Business Administration and Management, Advertising and Public Relations, Hospitality Management, Industrial and Manufacturing Management,* and *Organizational Behavior.* In another guide in this series:

Graduate Programs in the Humanities, Arts & Social Sciences

See *Public, Regional, and Industrial Affairs (Industrial and Labor Relations)*

CONTENTS

Program Directories

Featured Schools: Displays and Close-Ups

See:

Human Resources Development

Abilene Christian University, College of Graduate and Professional Studies, Program in Organizational Development, Addison, TX 75001. Offers MS. *Program availability:* Part-time, evening/weekend, online only, 100% online. *Students:* 40 full-time (36 women), 31 part-time (21 women); includes 29 minority (19 Black or African American, non-Hispanic/Latino; 2 Asian, non-Hispanic/Latino; 8 Hispanic/Latino). 23 applicants, 70% accepted, 11 enrolled. In 2017, 41 master's awarded. *Degree requirements:* For master's, thesis. *Entrance requirements:* Additional exam requirements/recommendations for international students: Required—TOEFL (minimum score 80 iBT), IELTS (minimum score 6), PTE. *Application deadline:* For fall admission, 8/11 priority date for domestic students; for winter admission, 10/1 priority date for domestic students; for spring admission, 12/15 priority date for domestic students; for summer admission, 4/5 priority date for domestic students. Applications are processed on a rolling basis. Application fee: $50. Electronic applications accepted. *Expenses:* $775 per hour. *Financial support:* Scholarships/grants available. Support available to part-time students. Financial award application deadline: 4/1; financial award applicants required to submit FAFSA. *Unit head:* Dr. Kipi Fleming, Program Director, 214-305-9451, E-mail: klw07b@acu.edu. *Application contact:* Graduate Advisor, 855-219-7300, E-mail: gradonline@acu.edu.
Website: http://www.acu.edu/online/academics/organizational-development.html

Amberton University, Graduate School, Program in Human Relations and Business, Garland, TX 75041-5595. Offers MS. *Program availability:* Part-time, evening/weekend. *Entrance requirements:* For master's, minimum GPA of 3.0. *Application deadline:* Applications are processed on a rolling basis. Application fee: $0. *Expenses: Tuition:* Part-time $795 per course. *Unit head:* Dr. Don Hebbard, Academic Dean, 972-635-8641 Ext. 157, Fax: 972-279-9773, E-mail: dhebbard@amberton.edu. *Application contact:* Adviser, 972-279-6511 Ext. 180, Fax: 972-279-9773, E-mail: advisor@amberton.edu.
Website: http://www.amberton.edu/programs-and-courses/masters-degree-programs/human-relations-and-business/index.html

Amberton University, Graduate School, Program in Human Resources Training and Development, Garland, TX 75041-5595. Offers MS. Application fee: $0. *Expenses: Tuition:* Part-time $795 per course. *Unit head:* Academic Dean, 972-279-6511 Ext. 153, Fax: 972-279-9773. *Application contact:* Adviser, 972-279-6511 Ext. 180, Fax: 972-279-9773, E-mail: advisor@amberton.edu.
Website: http://www.amberton.edu/programs-and-courses/masters-degree-programs/human-resources-training—development/index.html

Antioch University Los Angeles, Program in Leadership, Management and Business, Culver City, CA 90230. Offers human resource development (MA); leadership (MA); organizational development (MA). *Program availability:* Part-time, evening/weekend. *Faculty:* 7. *Students:* 25 full-time (20 women); includes 16 minority (5 Black or African American, non-Hispanic/Latino; 2 Asian, non-Hispanic/Latino; 7 Hispanic/Latino; 2 Two or more races, non-Hispanic/Latino), 1 international. Average age 33. In 2017, 8 master's awarded. *Entrance requirements:* For master's, interview. Additional exam requirements/recommendations for international students: Required—TOEFL. *Application deadline:* For fall admission, 8/4 for domestic students; for winter admission, 11/3 for domestic students; for spring admission, 2/2 for domestic students. *Financial support:* In 2017–18, 23 students received support. Career-related internships or fieldwork, Federal Work-Study, and scholarships/grants available. Support available to part-time students. Financial award application deadline: 3/24; financial award applicants required to submit CSS PROFILE or FAFSA. *Faculty research:* Systems thinking and chaos theory, technology and organizational structure, nonprofit management, power and empowerment. *Unit head:* Dr. Susan Nero, Chair, 310-578-1080 Ext. 226, Fax: 310-882-4824, E-mail: susan_nero@antiochla.edu. *Application contact:* Information Contact, 310-578-1090, Fax: 310-822-4824, E-mail: admissions@antiochla.edu.
Website: http://www.antiochla.edu

Barry University, School of Education, Program in Human Resource Development and Administration, Miami Shores, FL 33161-6695. Offers MS. *Program availability:* Part-time, evening/weekend. *Degree requirements:* For master's, comprehensive exam, practicum. *Entrance requirements:* For master's, GRE General Test or MAT, minimum GPA of 3.0. Electronic applications accepted.

Barry University, School of Education, Program in Leadership and Education, Miami Shores, FL 33161-6695. Offers educational technology (PhD); exceptional student education (PhD); higher education administration (PhD); human resource development (PhD); leadership (PhD). *Program availability:* Part-time, evening/weekend. *Degree requirements:* For doctorate, thesis/dissertation. *Entrance requirements:* For doctorate, GRE General Test, minimum GPA of 3.25. Electronic applications accepted.

Bowie State University, Graduate Programs, Program in Human Resource Development, Bowie, MD 20715-9465. Offers MA. *Program availability:* Part-time, evening/weekend. *Degree requirements:* For master's, comprehensive exam, thesis optional, research paper. *Entrance requirements:* For master's, minimum GPA of 2.5. Electronic applications accepted.

California State University, Sacramento, College of Business Administration, Sacramento, CA 95819. Offers accountancy (MS); business administration (IMBA, MBA); human resources (MBA); urban land development (MBA). *Accreditation:* AACSB. *Program availability:* Part-time, evening/weekend, 100% online, blended/hybrid learning. *Students:* 122 full-time (62 women), 153 part-time (75 women); includes 114 minority (10 Black or African American, non-Hispanic/Latino; 2 American Indian or Alaska Native, non-Hispanic/Latino; 73 Asian, non-Hispanic/Latino; 25 Hispanic/Latino; 4 Native Hawaiian or other Pacific Islander, non-Hispanic/Latino), 6 international. Average age 34. 230 applicants, 75% accepted, 134 enrolled. In 2017, 123 master's awarded. *Degree requirements:* For master's, comprehensive exam, project, thesis, or writing proficiency exam. *Entrance requirements:* For master's, GMAT. Additional exam requirements/recommendations for international students: Required—TOEFL (minimum score 550 paper-based; 80 iBT). *Application deadline:* For fall admission, 2/1 for domestic students, 3/1 for international students; for spring admission, 9/15 for domestic students, 9/30 for international students. Applications are processed on a rolling basis. Application fee: $55. Electronic applications accepted. *Expenses:* Contact institution. *Financial support:* Teaching assistantships, career-related internships or fieldwork, Federal Work-Study, and scholarships/grants available. Support available to part-time students. Financial award application deadline: 3/1; financial award applicants required to submit FAFSA. *Unit head:* Dr. Pierre A. Balthazard, Dean, 916-278-6578, Fax: 916-278-5793, E-mail: cba@csus.edu. *Application contact:* Jose Martinez, Graduate Admissions Supervisor, 916-278-7871, E-mail: martinj@skymail.csus.edu.
Website: http://www.cba.csus.edu

Claremont Graduate University, Graduate Programs, School of Social Science, Policy and Evaluation, Department of Psychology, Claremont, CA 91711-6160. Offers advanced study in evaluation (Certificate); cognitive psychology (MA, PhD); developmental psychology (MA, PhD); evaluation and applied research methods (MA, PhD); health behavior research and evaluation (MA, PhD); human resource development and evaluation (MA); industrial/organizational psychology (MA, PhD); organizational behavior (MA, PhD); organizational psychology (MA, PhD); social psychology (MA, PhD); MBA/PhD. *Program availability:* Part-time. Terminal master's awarded for partial completion of doctoral program. *Entrance requirements:* For master's and doctorate, GRE General Test. Additional exam requirements/recommendations for international students: Required—TOEFL (minimum score 75 iBT). Electronic applications accepted. *Faculty research:* Social intervention, diversity in organizations, eyewitness memory, aging and cognition, drug policy.

Clemson University, Graduate School, College of Education, Department of Educational and Organizational Leadership Development, Clemson, SC 29634. Offers administration and supervision (M Ed, Ed S); athletic leadership (MS, Certificate); education systems improvement science (Ed D); educational leadership (PhD), including higher education, P-12; human resource development (MHRD), including human resource development; leadership (Certificate); student affairs (M Ed). *Program availability:* Part-time, evening/weekend, 100% online. *Faculty:* 21 full-time (14 women), 1 part-time/adjunct (0 women). *Students:* 55 full-time (32 women), 285 part-time (169 women); includes 89 minority (71 Black or African American, non-Hispanic/Latino; 1 American Indian or Alaska Native, non-Hispanic/Latino; 1 Asian, non-Hispanic/Latino; 13 Hispanic/Latino; 3 Two or more races, non-Hispanic/Latino), 2 international. Average age 35. 216 applicants, 69% accepted, 100 enrolled. In 2017, 58 master's, 16 doctorates, 20 other advanced degrees awarded. *Degree requirements:* For master's, thesis (for some programs); for doctorate, comprehensive exam, thesis/dissertation. *Entrance requirements:* For master's, doctorate, and other advanced degree, GRE General Test, unofficial transcripts, letters of recommendation. Additional exam requirements/recommendations for international students: Required—TOEFL (minimum score 80 iBT), IELTS (minimum score 7), PTE (minimum score 54). *Application deadline:* For fall admission, 3/1 priority date for domestic and international students; for spring admission, 10/1 priority date for domestic and international students. Applications are processed on a rolling basis. Application fee: $80 ($90 for international students). Electronic applications accepted. *Expenses:* $5,174 per semester full-time resident, $9,714 per semester full-time non-resident, $511 per credit hour part-time resident, $1,017 per credit hour part-time non-resident; $741 per credit hour online; other fees may apply per session. *Financial support:* In 2017–18, 20 students received support, including 4 fellowships with partial tuition reimbursements available (averaging $8,750 per year), 1 research assistantship with partial tuition reimbursement available (averaging $9,378 per year); career-related internships or fieldwork and unspecified assistantships also available. Financial award application deadline: 3/1. *Total annual research expenditures:* $31,201. *Unit head:* Dr. Roy Jones, Interim Department Chair, 864-656-7915, E-mail: royj@clemson.edu. *Application contact:* Alison Search, Student Services Program Coordinator, 864-250-8880, E-mail: alisonp@clemson.edu.
Website: http://www.clemson.edu/education/departments/educational-organizational-leadership-development/index.html

The College of New Rochelle, Graduate School, Division of Human Services, Program in Career Development, New Rochelle, NY 10805-2308. Offers MS, Advanced Certificate. *Program availability:* Part-time. *Degree requirements:* For master's and Advanced Certificate, internship. *Entrance requirements:* For master's, interview, minimum GPA of 3.0, writing sample. *Expenses: Tuition:* Full-time $17,406. *Required fees:* $1120.

Drexel University, Goodwin College of Professional Studies, School of Education, Philadelphia, PA 19104-2875. Offers applied behavior analysis (MS); creativity and innovation (MS); education improvement and transformation (MS); educational administration (MS); educational leadership and management (Ed D); educational leadership development and learning technologies (PhD); global and international education (MS); higher education (MS); human resources development (MS); learning technologies (MS); mathematics, learning and teaching (MS); special education (MS); teaching, learning and curriculum (MS). *Program availability:* Part-time, evening/weekend, online learning. *Degree requirements:* For doctorate, thesis/dissertation. *Entrance requirements:* For doctorate, GRE or GMAT. Additional exam requirements/recommendations for international students: Required—TOEFL, IELTS. Electronic applications accepted. Application fee is waived when completed online. *Expenses:* Contact institution. *Faculty research:* Leadership development, mathematics education, literacy, autism, educational technology.

See Display on page 654 and Close-Up on page 719.

Florida International University, College of Arts, Sciences, and Education, Department of Leadership and Professional Studies, Miami, FL 33199. Offers adult education and human resource development (MS, Ed D); counseling (MS), including rehabilitation counseling, school counseling; counselor education (MS), including clinical mental health counseling; educational administration and supervision (Ed D); educational leadership (MS, Certificate, Ed S); higher education (Ed D); higher education administration (MS); international and comparative education (MS); recreation and sport management (MS), including recreation and sport management, recreational therapy; school psychology (Ed S); urban education (MS), including instruction in urban settings, learning technologies, multicultural/bilingual, multicultural/TESOL, urban education. *Program availability:* Part-time, evening/weekend. *Faculty:* 60 full-time (41 women), 112 part-time/adjunct (77 women). *Students:* 221 full-time (162 women), 301 part-time (239 women); includes 418 minority (127 Black or African American, non-Hispanic/Latino; 9 Asian, non-Hispanic/Latino; 271 Hispanic/Latino; 11 Two or more races, non-Hispanic/Latino), 10 international. Average age 31. 330 applicants, 55% accepted, 100 enrolled. In 2017, 181 master's, 6 doctorates awarded. *Degree requirements:* For doctorate, thesis/dissertation. *Entrance requirements:* For master's, minimum GPA of 3.0; for doctorate and other advanced degree, GRE General Test. Additional exam requirements/recommendations for international students: Required—TOEFL (minimum score 550 paper-based; 80 iBT), IELTS (minimum score 6.3). *Application deadline:* For fall admission, 6/1 priority date for domestic students, 4/1 for international students; for winter admission, 10/1 priority date for domestic students, 9/1 for international students; for spring admission, 3/1 priority date for domestic students, 2/1 for international students. Applications are processed on a rolling basis. Application fee: $30. Electronic applications accepted. *Expenses:* Tuition, state resident: full-time $8912; part-time $446 per credit hour. Tuition, nonresident: full-time $21,393; part-time $992 per credit hour. *Required fees:* $390; $195 per semester. *Financial support:* Fellowships, research assistantships with tuition reimbursements, teaching assistantships with tuition reimbursements, Federal Work-Study, and tuition waivers (full and partial) available. Support available to part-time students. Financial award

applicants required to submit FAFSA. *Unit head:* Dr. Benjamin Baez, Chair, 305-348-3214, Fax: 305-348-1515, E-mail: benjamin.baez@fiu.edu. *Application contact:* Nanett Rojas, Assistant Director, Graduate Admissions, 305-348-7464, Fax: 305-348-7441, E-mail: gradadm@fiu.edu.
Website: http://education.fiu.edu

The George Washington University, Graduate School of Education and Human Development, Department of Human and Organizational Learning, Program in Human Resource Development, Washington, DC 20052. Offers MA. *Program availability:* Part-time, evening/weekend. *Students:* 1 (woman) part-time. Average age 49. 1 applicant. *Entrance requirements:* For master's, GRE, MAT, or GMAT, two letters of recommendation, statement of purpose, official transcripts, resume. Additional exam requirements/recommendations for international students: Required—TOEFL or IELTS. Electronic applications accepted. *Expenses: Tuition:* Full-time $28,800; part-time $1655 per credit hour. *Required fees:* $45; $2.75 per credit hour. *Financial support:* Fellowships available. *Unit head:* Kristin Furio, Program Manager, 202-994-1040, E-mail: kfurio@gwu.edu. *Application contact:* Sarah Lang, Director of Graduate Admissions, 202-994-1447, Fax: 202-994-7207, E-mail: slang@gwu.edu.
Website: http://gsehd.gwu.edu/

The George Washington University, Graduate School of Education and Human Development, Department of Human and Organizational Learning, Program in Leadership Development, Washington, DC 20052. Offers Graduate Certificate. *Students:* 16 part-time (11 women); includes 6 minority (3 Black or African American, non-Hispanic/Latino; 3 Asian, non-Hispanic/Latino), 3 international. Average age 39. 21 applicants, 86% accepted, 16 enrolled. In 2017, 12 Graduate Certificates awarded. *Entrance requirements:* For degree, two letters of recommendation, resume, statement of purpose. Electronic applications accepted. *Expenses: Tuition:* Full-time $28,800; part-time $1655 per credit hour. *Required fees:* $45; $2.75 per credit hour. *Unit head:* Michael Feuer, Dean, 202-994-6161, E-mail: mjfeuer@gwu.edu. *Application contact:* Sarah Lang, Director of Graduate Admissions, 202-994-1447, Fax: 202-994-7207, E-mail: slang@gwu.edu.
Website: http://gsehd.gwu.edu/academics/programs/certificates/leadership-development/overview

The George Washington University, Graduate School of Education and Human Development, Department of Human and Organizational Learning, Programs in Human and Organizational Learning, Washington, DC 20052. Offers Ed D, Ed S. *Students:* 39 full-time (24 women), 120 part-time (66 women); includes 64 minority (41 Black or African American, non-Hispanic/Latino; 4 Asian, non-Hispanic/Latino; 12 Hispanic/Latino; 7 Two or more races, non-Hispanic/Latino), 7 international. Average age 46. 56 applicants, 75% accepted, 22 enrolled. In 2017, 19 doctorates, 3 other advanced degrees awarded. *Degree requirements:* For doctorate, comprehensive exam, thesis/dissertation; for Ed S, comprehensive exam. *Entrance requirements:* For doctorate, GRE General Test or MAT, interview, minimum GPA of 3.3; for Ed S, GRE General Test or MAT, minimum GPA of 3.3. *Application deadline:* For fall admission, 1/15 priority date for domestic students; for spring admission, 10/1 for domestic students. Applications are processed on a rolling basis. Application fee: $75. *Expenses: Tuition:* Full-time $28,800; part-time $1655 per credit hour. *Required fees:* $45; $2.75 per credit hour. *Financial support:* Fellowships, research assistantships, teaching assistantships, career-related internships or fieldwork, Federal Work-Study, and tuition waivers (partial) available. Financial award application deadline: 1/15; financial award applicants required to submit FAFSA. *Faculty research:* Organizational learning, program evaluation. *Unit head:* David Schwandt, Program Manager, 571-553-3770, E-mail: schwandt@gwu.edu. *Application contact:* Sarah Lang, Director of Graduate Admissions, 202-994-1447, E-mail: slang@gwu.edu.
Website: http://gsehd.gwu.edu/

Grantham University, Mark Skousen School of Business, Lenexa, KS 66219. Offers business administration (MBA); business intelligence (MS); human resources (Certificate); information management (MBA); performance improvement (MS); project management (MBA, Certificate). *Program availability:* Part-time, evening/weekend, online only, 100% online. *Faculty:* 1 full-time, 34 part-time/adjunct. *Students:* 610 full-time (231 women), 333 part-time (128 women); includes 466 minority (321 Black or African American, non-Hispanic/Latino; 12 American Indian or Alaska Native, non-Hispanic/Latino; 29 Asian, non-Hispanic/Latino; 71 Hispanic/Latino; 4 Native Hawaiian or other Pacific Islander, non-Hispanic/Latino; 29 Two or more races, non-Hispanic/Latino). Average age 40. 273 applicants, 87% accepted, 202 enrolled. In 2017, 362 master's awarded. *Degree requirements:* For master's, comprehensive exam (for some programs), PMP Prep Exams throughout the term (for MBA in project management); for Certificate, comprehensive exam (for some programs), PMP Prep Exam (for project management). *Entrance requirements:* For master's, baccalaureate or master's degree with minimum cumulative GPA of 2.5 from institution accredited by agency recognized by U.S. DOE or foreign equivalent; official transcripts showing proof of degree. Additional exam requirements/recommendations for international students: Required—TOEFL (minimum score 530 paper-based; 71 iBT), IELTS (minimum score 6.5), PTE (minimum score 50). *Application deadline:* Applications are processed on a rolling basis. Application fee: $0. Electronic applications accepted. *Expenses: Tuition:* $325 per credit hour. *Financial support:* Scholarships/grants available. Financial award applicants required to submit FAFSA. *Faculty research:* How chronic diseases contribute to the rising costs of healthcare, marketing for entrepreneurs, managers' hiring practices of workers with disability, organizational structures, organizational change, online pedagogy, impact of instructor video tips in the online classroom, decision-making techniques. *Unit head:* Dr. David Marker, Dean of the Mark Skousen School of Business, 913-309-4747, Fax: 844-260-6287, E-mail: dmarker@grantham.edu. *Application contact:* Jared Parlette, Vice President of Student Enrollment, 800-955-2527 Ext. 803, Fax: 866-914-4557, E-mail: admissions@grantham.edu.
Website: https://www.grantham.edu/school-of-business/

HEC Montreal, School of Business Administration, Graduate Diploma Programs in Administration, Montréal, QC H3T 2A7, Canada. Offers business administration (Graduate Diploma); business analysis - information technology (Graduate Diploma); e-business (Graduate Diploma); entrepreneurship (Graduate Diploma); financial professions (Graduate Diploma); human resources (Graduate Diploma); management (Graduate Diploma); management and sustainable development (Graduate Diploma); management of cultural organizations (Graduate Diploma); marketing communication (Graduate Diploma); organizational development (Graduate Diploma); professional accounting (Graduate Diploma); supply chain management (Graduate Diploma); taxation (Graduate Diploma). All courses are given in French. *Students:* 380 full-time (210 women), 819 part-time (501 women). 1,195 applicants, 72% accepted, 673 enrolled. In 2017, 629 Graduate Diplomas awarded. *Entrance requirements:* For degree, bachelor's degree. Application fee: $88 Canadian dollars ($184 Canadian dollars for international students). Electronic applications accepted. *Expenses: Tuition,* state resident: full-time $2869 Canadian dollars; part-time $79.70 Canadian dollars per credit. Tuition, nonresident: full-time $8883 Canadian dollars; part-time $246.76 Canadian dollars per credit. *International tuition:* $19,648 Canadian dollars full-time. *Required fees:* $41.20 Canadian dollars per credit. $67.94 Canadian dollars per term. Tuition and fees vary according to degree level and program. *Financial support:* Research

assistantships, teaching assistantships, and scholarships/grants available. Financial award application deadline: 9/2. *Faculty research:* Art management, business policy, entrepreneurship, new technologies, transportation. *Unit head:* Renaud Lachance, Director, 514-340-7165, E-mail: renaud.lachance@hec.ca. *Application contact:* Anny Caron, Administrative Director, 514-340-6151, Fax: 514-340-6411, E-mail: aide@hec.ca.
Website: http://www.hec.ca/programmes/dess/index.html

Illinois Institute of Technology, Graduate College, Lewis College of Human Sciences, Department of Psychology, Chicago, IL 60616. Offers clinical psychology (PhD); industrial and organizational psychology (PhD); personnel and human resource development (MS); rehabilitation and mental health counseling (MS); rehabilitation counseling education (PhD). *Accreditation:* APA (one or more programs are accredited); CORE. *Program availability:* Part-time, evening/weekend. Terminal master's awarded for partial completion of doctoral program. *Degree requirements:* For master's, thesis (for some programs); for doctorate, comprehensive exam, thesis/dissertation, minimum of 107 credit hours, 1-year full-time internship. *Entrance requirements:* For master's, GRE General Test (minimum score 298 Quantitative and Verbal, 3.0 Analytical Writing), minimum GPA of 3.0; 3 letters of recommendation; bachelor's degree from accredited institution (for personnel and human resource development); for doctorate, GRE General Test (minimum score 298 Quantitative and Verbal, 3.0 Analytical Writing), bachelor's or master's degree from accredited institution, recommendations. Additional exam requirements/recommendations for international students: Required—TOEFL (minimum score 550 paper-based; 80 iBT). Electronic applications accepted. *Faculty research:* Clinical psychology, rehabilitation and mental health counseling, industrial organizational psychology.

Indiana State University, College of Graduate and Professional Studies, College of Technology, Department of Human Resource Development and Performance Technologies, Terre Haute, IN 47809. Offers career and technical education (MS); human resource development (MS).

Indiana Tech, Program in Business Administration, Fort Wayne, IN 46803-1297. Offers accounting (MBA); health care management (MBA); human resources (MBA); management (MBA); marketing (MBA). *Program availability:* Part-time, evening/weekend, online learning. *Entrance requirements:* For master's, GMAT, bachelor's degree from regionally-accredited university; minimum undergraduate GPA of 2.5; 2 years of significant work experience; 3 letters of recommendation. Electronic applications accepted.

Indiana University of Pennsylvania, School of Graduate Studies and Research, College of Education and Communications, Department of Adult and Community Education, Program in Business/Workforce Development, Indiana, PA 15705. Offers M Ed. *Program availability:* Part-time. *Faculty:* 2 full-time (both women). *Students:* 3 full-time (2 women), 8 part-time (3 women). Average age 35. 2 applicants, 50% accepted. *Degree requirements:* For master's, thesis optional. *Entrance requirements:* For master's, GMAT or GRE. Additional exam requirements/recommendations for international students: Required—TOEFL (minimum score 540 paper-based). *Application deadline:* Applications are processed on a rolling basis. Application fee: $50. Electronic applications accepted. *Expenses:* Tuition, state resident: full-time $12,000; part-time $500 per credit. Tuition, nonresident: full-time $18,000; part-time $750 per credit. *Required fees:* $4073; $165.55 per credit. $64 per term. *Financial support:* In 2017–18, 1 research assistantship with tuition reimbursement (averaging $5,440 per year) was awarded; career-related internships or fieldwork and Federal Work-Study also available. Support available to part-time students. Financial award application deadline: 4/15; financial award applicants required to submit FAFSA. *Unit head:* Prof. Jacqueline McGinty, Coordinator, 724-357-2470, E-mail: jacqueline.mcginty@iup.edu.
Website: http://www.iup.edu/ace/grad/default.aspx

Inter American University of Puerto Rico, Metropolitan Campus, Graduate Programs, Program in Human Resources, San Juan, PR 00919-1293. Offers MBA. *Degree requirements:* For master's, comprehensive exam. *Entrance requirements:* For master's, GRE or EXADEP, interview. Electronic applications accepted.

Inter American University of Puerto Rico, San Germán Campus, Graduate Studies Center, Program in Business Administration, San Germán, PR 00683-5008. Offers accounting (MBA); finance (MBA); general business administration (MBA); human resources (MBA, PhD); industrial relations (MBA); information systems (MBA); international and interregional business (PhD); management (MBA); marketing (MBA). *Program availability:* Part-time, evening/weekend. *Degree requirements:* For master's, comprehensive exam. *Entrance requirements:* For master's, GRE General Test or EXADEP, minimum GPA of 3.0.

Iowa State University of Science and Technology, Department of Educational Leadership and Policy Studies, Ames, IA 50011. Offers counselor education (M Ed, MS); educational administration (M Ed, MS); educational leadership (PhD); higher education (M Ed, MS); organizational learning and human resource development (M Ed, MS); research and evaluation (MS); student affairs (MS). *Degree requirements:* For master's, thesis or alternative; for doctorate, thesis/dissertation. *Entrance requirements:* For master's and doctorate, GRE General Test. Additional exam requirements/recommendations for international students: Required—TOEFL (minimum score 560 paper-based; 83 iBT), IELTS (minimum score 6.5). Electronic applications accepted.

John F. Kennedy University, School of Management, Program in Career Development, Pleasant Hill, CA 94523-4817. Offers career coaching (Certificate); career development (MA, Certificate). *Program availability:* Part-time, evening/weekend. *Degree requirements:* For master's, thesis or alternative. *Entrance requirements:* For master's, interview. Additional exam requirements/recommendations for international students: Required—TOEFL.

Kentucky State University, College of Professional Studies, Frankfort, KY 40601. Offers nursing (DNP); public administration (MPA), including human resource management; special education (MA). *Program availability:* Part-time, evening/weekend, 100% online, blended/hybrid learning. *Faculty:* 9 full-time (7 women), 3 part-time/adjunct (all women). *Students:* 29 full-time (18 women), 29 part-time (24 women); includes 42 minority (40 Black or African American, non-Hispanic/Latino; 1 Asian, non-Hispanic/Latino; 1 Two or more races, non-Hispanic/Latino). Average age 35. 17 applicants, 53% accepted, 7 enrolled. In 2017, 11 master's, 4 doctorates awarded. *Degree requirements:* For master's, comprehensive exam, thesis optional; for doctorate, comprehensive exam, thesis/dissertation optional, 180 clinical hours. *Entrance requirements:* For master's, GMAT, GRE, transcript, essay, letters of recommendation; for doctorate, RN license; resume; graduate research and statistics courses (strongly recommended). Additional exam requirements/recommendations for international students: Required—TOEFL (minimum score 525 paper-based, 41 iBT) or IELTS (minimum score 4). *Application deadline:* For fall admission, 7/1 for domestic students, 4/1 for international students; for spring admission, 11/15 for domestic students, 8/15 for international students; for summer admission, 5/1 for domestic students, 2/1 for international students. Applications are processed on a rolling basis. Application fee: $30 ($100 for international students). Electronic applications accepted. *Expenses:* Contact institution. *Financial support:* In 2017–18, 54 students received support, including 1 research assistantship (averaging $1,350 per year); scholarships/grants,

Human Resources Development

tuition waivers (partial), and unspecified assistantships also available. Financial award application deadline: 4/15; financial award applicants required to submit FAFSA. *Faculty research:* Risk assessment and failure modeling for the public sector implication of property rights on economic development, the social stability of communities, civil peace of nations. *Total annual research expenditures:* $414,831. *Unit head:* Dr. Kristen Broady, Assistant Vice President and Dean of Graduate Programs, 502-597-6386, E-mail: kristen.broady@kysu.edu. *Application contact:* Dr. James Obielodan, Director of Graduate Studies, 502-597-4723, E-mail: james.obielodan@kysu.edu.
Website: http://kysu.edu/academics/college-of-professional-studies/

La Salle University, School of Business, Program in Human Capital Development, Philadelphia, PA 19141-1199. Offers MS, Certificate. *Program availability:* Part-time, evening/weekend, online only, 100% online. *Faculty:* 3 part-time/adjunct (2 women). *Students:* 1 (woman) full-time, 21 part-time (17 women); includes 12 minority (11 Black or African American, non-Hispanic/Latino; 1 Two or more races, non-Hispanic/Latino). Average age 38. 6 applicants, 100% accepted, 6 enrolled. In 2017, 11 master's awarded. *Degree requirements:* For master's, capstone project. *Entrance requirements:* For master's and Certificate, professional resume; 2 letters of recommendation; 500-word essay stating interest in program and goals; baccalaureate degree. Additional exam requirements/recommendations for international students: Required—TOEFL. *Application deadline:* For fall admission, 8/15 priority date for domestic students; for spring admission, 12/15 for domestic students; for summer admission, 4/14 for domestic students. Applications are processed on a rolling basis. Application fee: $35. Electronic applications accepted. Application fee is waived when completed online. *Expenses:* Contact institution. *Financial support:* In 2017–18, 2 students received support. Scholarships/grants and unspecified assistantships available. Support available to part-time students. Financial award application deadline: 8/31; financial award applicants required to submit FAFSA. *Unit head:* Lynnette Clement, Program Director, 215-991-3682, E-mail: clement@lasalle.edu. *Application contact:* Elizabeth Heenan, Director, Graduate and Adult Enrollment, 215-951-1100, Fax: 215-951-1462, E-mail: heenan@lasalle.edu.
Website: http://www.lasalle.edu/human-capital-development/

Lawrence Technological University, College of Arts and Sciences, Southfield, MI 48075-1058. Offers bioinformatics (Graduate Certificate); computer science (MS), including data science, big data, and data mining, intelligent systems; educational technology (MA), including robotics; instructional design, communication, and presentation (Graduate Certificate); integrated science (MA); science education (MA); technical and professional communication (MS, Graduate Certificate); writing for the digital age (Graduate Certificate). *Program availability:* Part-time, evening/weekend. *Faculty:* 6 full-time (2 women), 7 part-time/adjunct (3 women). *Students:* 34 part-time (15 women); includes 4 minority (1 Black or African American, non-Hispanic/Latino; 2 Asian, non-Hispanic/Latino; 1 Hispanic/Latino; 7 international. Average age 31. 84 applicants, 15% accepted, 10 enrolled. In 2017, 14 master's awarded. *Degree requirements:* For master's, thesis (for some programs). *Entrance requirements:* Additional exam requirements/recommendations for international students: Required—TOEFL (minimum score 550 paper-based; 79 iBT), IELTS (minimum score 6.5). *Application deadline:* For fall admission, 5/27 for international students; for spring admission, 10/8 for international students; for summer admission, 2/14 for international students. Applications are processed on a rolling basis. Application fee: $50. Electronic applications accepted. *Expenses: Tuition:* Full-time $15,274; part-time $1091 per credit. One-time fee: $150. *Financial support:* In 2017–18, 8 students received support. Scholarships/grants and tuition reduction available. Financial award application deadline: 4/1; financial award applicants required to submit FAFSA. *Faculty research:* Computer analysis of music, machine learning of literature and lyrics, customer sentiments and response analysis through social media, peta-scale computing in astronomical databases, early detection of diseases with pattern recognition. *Total annual research expenditures:* $242,460. *Unit head:* Glen Bauer, Interim Dean, 248-204-3532, Fax: 248-204-3518, E-mail: scidean@ltu.edu. *Application contact:* Jane Rohrback, Director of Admissions, 248-204-3160, Fax: 248-204-2228, E-mail: admissions@ltu.edu.

Lincoln Memorial University, Carter and Moyers School of Education, Harrogate, TN 37752-1901. Offers administration and supervision (M Ed, Ed S); counseling and guidance (M Ed); curriculum and instruction (M Ed, Ed D, Ed S); English (M Ed); executive leadership (Ed D); higher education administration (Ed D); human resource development (Ed D); leadership and administration (Ed D). *Program availability:* Part-time, evening/weekend, online learning. *Degree requirements:* For master's, comprehensive exam, thesis optional; for Ed S, comprehensive exam. *Entrance requirements:* For master's, PRAXIS, NTE, GRE, MAT, letters of recommendation; for Ed S, graduate transcripts. Additional exam requirements/recommendations for international students: Recommended—TOEFL. *Faculty research:* Brain compatible teaching and learning; poverty in Appalachia; leadership for change; ethics, moral responsibility and social justice; human and organizational learning.

Louisiana State University and Agricultural & Mechanical College, Graduate School, College of Human Sciences and Education, School of Human Resource Education and Workforce Development, Baton Rouge, LA 70803. Offers agriculture and extension education and youth development (MS, PhD); career and technical education (MS, PhD); comprehensive vocational education (MS, PhD); extension and international education (MS, PhD); human resource and leadership development (MS, PhD); industrial education (MS); vocational agriculture education (MS, PhD); vocational business education (MS); vocational home economics education (MS). *Accreditation:* NCATE. *Faculty:* 11 full-time (6 women). *Students:* 102 full-time (71 women), 130 part-time (92 women); includes 89 minority (63 Black or African American, non-Hispanic/Latino; 3 American Indian or Alaska Native, non-Hispanic/Latino; 8 Asian, non-Hispanic/Latino; 14 Hispanic/Latino; 1 Two or more races, non-Hispanic/Latino), 6 international. Average age 35. 98 applicants, 69% accepted, 52 enrolled. In 2017, 94 master's, 15 doctorates awarded. *Financial support:* In 2017–18, 1 fellowship (averaging $18,238 per year), 16 teaching assistantships (averaging $15,341 per year) were awarded. *Total annual research expenditures:* $1,998.

Marquette University, Graduate School of Management, Program in Human Resources, Milwaukee, WI 53201-1881. Offers MSHR. *Program availability:* Part-time, evening/weekend. *Entrance requirements:* For master's, GMAT or GRE General Test, letters of recommendation. Additional exam requirements/recommendations for international students: Required—TOEFL (minimum score 550 paper-based; 88 iBT), IELTS (minimum score 6.5), PTE. Electronic applications accepted. *Faculty research:* Diversity, mentoring, executive compensation.

McDaniel College, Graduate and Professional Studies, Program in Human Resources Development, Westminster, MD 21157-4390. Offers MS. *Program availability:* Part-time, evening/weekend. *Faculty:* 1 (woman) full-time, 4 part-time/adjunct (2 women). *Students:* 2 full-time (both women), 13 part-time (7 women); includes 4 minority (2 Black or African American, non-Hispanic/Latino; 1 Asian, non-Hispanic/Latino; 1 Hispanic/Latino), 2 international. Average age 29. 7 applicants, 100% accepted, 6 enrolled. In 2017, 6 master's awarded. *Degree requirements:* For master's, portfolio, internship. *Entrance requirements:* For master's, 3 recommendations; essay. Additional exam requirements/recommendations for international students: Required—TOEFL (minimum score 79 iBT), IELTS (minimum score 6). *Application deadline:* For fall admission, 6/1

priority date for domestic students. Applications are processed on a rolling basis. Application fee: $75. Electronic applications accepted. *Expenses: Tuition:* Full-time $11,760; part-time $490 per credit hour. Tuition and fees vary according to course load and program. *Financial support:* Application deadline: 3/1; applicants required to submit FAFSA. *Unit head:* E-mail: gradadms@mcdaniel.edu. *Application contact:* Crystal L. Perry, Assistant Director, Graduate Enrollment Management, 410-857-2516, Fax: 410-857-2515, E-mail: cperry@mcdaniel.edu.

Midwestern State University, Billie Doris McAda Graduate School, West College of Education, Program in Counseling, Wichita Falls, TX 76308. Offers counseling (MA); human resource development (MA); school counseling (M Ed); training and development (MA). *Program availability:* Part-time, evening/weekend. *Degree requirements:* For master's, comprehensive exam, thesis (for some programs). *Entrance requirements:* For master's, GRE General Test, MAT, or GMAT, valid teaching certificate (M Ed). Additional exam requirements/recommendations for international students: Required—TOEFL (minimum score 550 paper-based). Electronic applications accepted. *Faculty research:* Social development of students with disabilities, autism, criminal justice counseling, conflict resolution issues, leadership.

Mississippi State University, College of Education, Department of Instructional Systems and Workforce Development, Mississippi State, MS 39762. Offers instructional systems and workforce development (MSIT, PhD); technology (MST, Ed S). *Faculty:* 10 full-time (6 women). *Students:* 13 full-time (5 women), 45 part-time (34 women); includes 35 minority (34 Black or African American, non-Hispanic/Latino; 1 Two or more races, non-Hispanic/Latino), 1 international. Average age 37. 28 applicants, 68% accepted, 14 enrolled. In 2017, 4 master's, 6 doctorates, 4 other advanced degrees awarded. *Degree requirements:* For master's, thesis optional, comprehensive oral or written exam; for doctorate, thesis/dissertation, comprehensive oral and written exam; for Ed S, thesis, comprehensive written exam. *Entrance requirements:* For master's, GRE, minimum GPA of 2.75 on undergraduate work, 3.0 graduate; for doctorate, GRE, minimum GPA of 3.4 on graduate work; for Ed S, GRE, minimum GPA of 3.2, master's degree. Additional exam requirements/recommendations for international students: Required—TOEFL (minimum score 550 paper-based; 79 iBT); Recommended—IELTS (minimum score 6.5). *Application deadline:* For fall admission, 7/1 for domestic students, 5/1 for international students; for spring admission, 11/1 for domestic students, 9/1 for international students. Applications are processed on a rolling basis. Application fee: $60 ($80 for international students). Electronic applications accepted. *Expenses:* Tuition, state resident: full-time $8318; part-time $462.12 per credit hour. Tuition, nonresident: full-time $22,358; part-time $1242.12 per credit hour. *Required fees:* $110; $12.24 per credit hour. $6.12 per semester. *Financial support:* In 2017–18, 2 teaching assistantships with full tuition reimbursements (averaging $10,575 per year) were awarded; Federal Work-Study, institutionally sponsored loans, scholarships/grants, and unspecified assistantships also available. Financial award application deadline: 4/1; financial award applicants required to submit FAFSA. *Faculty research:* Computer technology, nontraditional students, interactive video, instructional technology, educational leadership. *Unit head:* Dr. Trey Martindale, Associate Professor and Head, 662-325-7258, Fax: 662-325-7599, E-mail: tmartindale@colled.msstate.edu. *Application contact:* Angie Campbell, Admissions and Enrollment Assistant, 662-325-9514, E-mail: acampbell@grad.msstate.edu.
Website: http://www.iswd.msstate.edu

Moravian College, Graduate and Continuing Studies, Business and Management Programs, Bethlehem, PA 18018-6650. Offers accounting (MBA); business analytics (MBA); business management (MBA); health administration (MHA); healthcare management (MBA); HR leadership (MSHRM); human resource management (MBA); learning and performance management (MSHRM); supply chain management (MBA). *Program availability:* Part-time, evening/weekend. *Faculty:* 5 full-time (2 women), 9 part-time/adjunct (3 women). *Students:* 13 full-time (10 women), 80 part-time (45 women); includes 13 minority (6 Black or African American, non-Hispanic/Latino; 6 Hispanic/Latino; 1 Two or more races, non-Hispanic/Latino). Average age 31. 55 applicants, 91% accepted, 31 enrolled. In 2017, 29 master's awarded. *Entrance requirements:* For master's, current resume, official transcripts, 2 letters of recommendation. Additional exam requirements/recommendations for international students: Required—TOEFL (minimum score 550 paper-based), IELTS (minimum score 6.5). *Application deadline:* For fall admission, 8/1 priority date for domestic and international students; for spring admission, 1/1 priority date for domestic and international students; for summer admission, 5/1 priority date for domestic and international students. Applications are processed on a rolling basis. Electronic applications accepted. *Expenses: Tuition:* Full-time $15,714; part-time $2619 per course. *Required fees:* $45 per semester. Tuition and fees vary according to program. *Financial support:* In 2017–18, 3 students received support, including 2 research assistantships with full tuition reimbursements available. Financial award applicants required to submit FAFSA. *Faculty research:* Leadership, change management, human resources. *Unit head:* Dr. Liz Kleintop, Associate Chair of Graduate Business, 610-861-1400, Fax: 610-861-1466, E-mail: graduate@moravian.edu. *Application contact:* Sean Rossi, Student Experience Mentor, 610-861-1400, Fax: 610-861-1466, E-mail: graduate@moravian.edu.
Website: https://www.moravian.edu/graduate

National Louis University, College of Management and Business, Chicago, IL 60603. Offers business administration (MBA); human resource management and development (MS); management (MS). *Program availability:* Part-time, evening/weekend. *Entrance requirements:* For master's, college-administered critical thinking and writing skills test, minimum GPA of 3.0, resume, 3 references. Additional exam requirements/recommendations for international students: Required—TOEFL (minimum score 550 paper-based; 79 iBT).

New York University, School of Professional Studies, Division of Programs in Business, Program in Leadership and Human Capital Management, New York, NY 10012-1019. Offers human resource management and development (MS), including global talent management, human resource management, learning, development, and executive coaching, organizational effectiveness. *Program availability:* Part-time, evening/weekend, 100% online, blended/hybrid learning. *Students:* 101 full-time (88 women), 107 part-time (93 women); includes 68 minority (19 Black or African American, non-Hispanic/Latino; 25 Asian, non-Hispanic/Latino; 21 Hispanic/Latino; 3 Two or more races, non-Hispanic/Latino), 93 international. Average age 29. 251 applicants, 52% accepted, 60 enrolled. In 2017, 180 master's awarded. *Degree requirements:* For master's, thesis. *Entrance requirements:* For master's, GRE or GMAT (only upon request), bachelor's degree, resume with relevant professional work, internship or volunteer experience, two letters of recommendation, statement of purpose. Additional exam requirements/recommendations for international students: Required—TOEFL (minimum score 600 paper-based; 100 iBT), IELTS (minimum score 7). *Application deadline:* For fall admission, 2/1 priority date for domestic and international students; for spring admission, 10/15 priority date for domestic students, 8/15 priority date for international students; for summer admission, 5/1 priority date for domestic students, 1/15 priority date for international students. Applications are processed on a rolling basis. Application fee: $150. Electronic applications accepted. *Expenses:* $20,244 per term. *Financial support:* Fellowships, career-related internships or fieldwork, Federal Work-Study, scholarships/grants, and health care benefits available. Support available to part-

time students. Financial award application deadline: 6/30; financial award applicants required to submit FAFSA. *Unit head:* Martin Ihrig, Associate Dean/Clinical Professor, 212-992-3288. *Application contact:* Admissions Office, 212-998-7100, E-mail: sps.gradadmissions@nyu.edu.
Website: http://www.sps.nyu.edu/academics/departments/leadership.html

North Carolina State University, Graduate School, College of Education, Department of Adult and Higher Education, Program in Human Resource Development, Raleigh, NC 27695. Offers MS. *Degree requirements:* For master's, thesis. *Entrance requirements:* For master's, GRE, 3 letters of recommendation, resume.

Northeastern Illinois University, College of Graduate Studies and Research, Daniel L. Goodwin College of Education, Program in Human Resource Development, Chicago, IL 60625. Offers human resource development (MA). *Program availability:* Part-time, evening/weekend. *Entrance requirements:* For master's, minimum GPA of 2.75, BA in human resource development. Additional exam requirements/recommendations for international students: Required—TOEFL (minimum score 550 paper-based; 79 iBT). *Application deadline:* For fall admission, 4/1 priority date for domestic students; for spring admission, 8/15 for domestic students. Applications are processed on a rolling basis. Application fee: $30. Electronic applications accepted. *Expenses:* Tuition, state resident: full-time $7274; part-time $404.11 per credit hour. Tuition, nonresident: full-time $14,548; part-time $808.23 per credit hour. *Required fees:* $1284. *Faculty research:* Analogics, development of expertise, case-based instruction, action science organizational development, theoretical model building. *Unit head:* Dr. Howard Bultinck, Department Chair, 773-442-5809, E-mail: h-bultinck@neiu.edu. *Application contact:* Martha Narvaez, Graduate Admission Representative, 773-442-6008, E-mail: m-narvaez@neiu.edu.

Ottawa University, Graduate Studies-Kansas City, Overland Park, KS 66211. Offers business administration (MBA); human resources (MA). *Program availability:* Part-time, evening/weekend, online learning. *Degree requirements:* For master's, thesis or alternative. *Entrance requirements:* For master's, resume, 3 letters of recommendation. Additional exam requirements/recommendations for international students: Required—TOEFL (minimum score 550 paper-based). Electronic applications accepted. *Expenses:* Contact institution.

Penn State Great Valley, Graduate Studies, Management Division, Malvern, PA 19355-1488. Offers business administration (MBA); cyber security (Certificate); data analytics (MPS, MS, Certificate); distributed energy and grid modernization (Certificate); finance (M Fin); health sector management (Certificate); human resource management (Certificate); information science (MSIS); leadership development (MLD); new ventures and entrepreneurship (Certificate); sustainable management practices (Certificate). *Accreditation:* AACSB. *Unit head:* Dr. James A. Nemes, Chancellor, 610-648-3202, Fax: 610-725-5296. *Application contact:* JoAnn Kelly, Director of Admissions, 610-648-3315, Fax: 610-725-5296, E-mail: jek2@psu.edu.
Website: http://greatvalley.psu.edu/academics/masters-degrees/engineering-management

Penn State University Park, Graduate School, College of the Liberal Arts, School of Labor and Employment Relations, University Park, PA 16802. Offers human resources and employment relations (MS); labor and global workers' rights (MPS). *Unit head:* Dr. Susan Welch, Dean, 814-865-7691, Fax: 814-863-2085. *Application contact:* Lori Hawn, Director, Graduate Student Services, 814-865-1795, Fax: 814-863-4627, E-mail: l-gswww@lists.psu.edu.
Website: http://lser.la.psu.edu/

Pittsburg State University, Graduate School, College of Technology, Department of Technology and Workforce Learning, Program in Human Resource Development, Pittsburg, KS 66762. Offers MS. *Program availability:* Part-time, online only, 100% online. *Students:* 45. In 2017, 32 master's awarded. *Degree requirements:* For master's, thesis or alternative. *Entrance requirements:* Additional exam requirements/recommendations for international students: Required—TOEFL (minimum score 520 paper-based; 68 iBT), IELTS (minimum score 6), PTE (minimum score 47). *Application deadline:* For fall admission, 7/15 for domestic students, 6/1 for international students; for spring admission, 12/15 for domestic students, 10/15 for international students; for summer admission, 5/15 for domestic students, 4/1 for international students. Applications are processed on a rolling basis. Application fee: $35 ($60 for international students). Electronic applications accepted. *Expenses:* Contact institution. *Financial support:* In 2017–18, 1 teaching assistantship with full tuition reimbursement (averaging $5,500 per year) was awarded; career-related internships or fieldwork and Federal Work-Study also available. Financial award application deadline: 2/1; financial award applicants required to submit FAFSA. *Unit head:* Dr. MeLisa Rogers, Program Coordinator, 620-235-4371, E-mail: mrogers@pittstate.edu. *Application contact:* Lisa Allen, Assistant Director of Graduate and Continuing Studies, 620-235-4218, Fax: 620-235-4219, E-mail: lallen@pittstate.edu.
Website: http://www.pittstate.edu/tm/hrd/masters.html

Regent University, Graduate School, School of Business and Leadership, Virginia Beach, VA 23464-9800. Offers business administration (MBA), including accounting, economics, entrepreneurship, finance and investing, general management, healthcare management (MA, MBA), human resource management (MA, MBA), innovation management, leadership, marketing, not-for-profit management (MA, MBA); business analytics (MS); business and design management (MA); church leadership (MA); leadership (Certificate); organizational leadership (MA, PhD), including ecclesial leadership (DSL, PhD), entrepreneurial leadership (PhD), healthcare management (MA, MBA), human resource development (PhD), human resource management (MA, MBA), individualized studies (DSL, PhD), interdisciplinary studies (MA), leadership coaching and mentoring (MA), not-for-profit management (MA, MBA), organizational development consulting (MA), servant leadership (MA, DSL); strategic leadership (DSL), including ecclesial leadership (DSL, PhD), global consulting, healthcare leadership, individualized studies (DSL, PhD), leadership coaching, servant leadership (MA, DSL), strategic foresight. *Program availability:* Part-time, evening/weekend, 100% online, blended/hybrid learning. *Faculty:* 9 full-time (2 women), 38 part-time/adjunct (11 women). *Students:* 129 full-time (80 women), 1,152 part-time (598 women); includes 685 minority (546 Black or African American, non-Hispanic/Latino; 10 American Indian or Alaska Native, non-Hispanic/Latino; 29 Asian, non-Hispanic/Latino; 65 Hispanic/Latino; 6 Native Hawaiian or other Pacific Islander, non-Hispanic/Latino; 29 Two or more races, non-Hispanic/Latino), 62 international. Average age 41. 1,721 applicants, 48% accepted, 624 enrolled. In 2017, 125 master's, 69 doctorates awarded. *Degree requirements:* For master's, thesis or alternative, 3-credit hour culminating experience; for doctorate, thesis/dissertation. *Entrance requirements:* For master's, college transcripts, resume, essay; for doctorate, college transcripts, resume, essay, writing sample; for Certificate, writing sample, resume, transcripts. Additional exam requirements/recommendations for international students: Required—TOEFL (minimum score 577 paper-based). *Application deadline:* For fall admission, 5/1 priority date for domestic students; for spring admission, 10/1 priority date for domestic students. Applications are processed on a rolling basis. Application fee: $50. Electronic applications accepted. *Expenses:* $650 per credit (MA, MS, MBA); $995 per credit (PhD); $300 per semester technology fee. *Financial support:* In 2017–18, 829 students received support. Career-related internships or fieldwork, scholarships/grants, and

unspecified assistantships available. Support available to part-time students. *Faculty research:* Servant leadership, global business, team effectiveness, technology utilization, leadership development. *Unit head:* Dr. Doris Gomez, Dean, 757-352-4686, Fax: 757-352-4634, E-mail: dorigom@regent.edu. *Application contact:* Heidi Cece, Assistant Vice President of Enrollment Management, 800-373-5504, Fax: 757-352-4381, E-mail: admissions@regent.edu.
Website: https://www.regent.edu/school-of-business-and-leadership/

Rochester Institute of Technology, Graduate Enrollment Services, College of Applied Science and Technology, School of International Hospitality and Service Innovation, MS Program in Human Resources Development, Rochester, NY 14623. Offers MS. *Program availability:* Part-time, evening/weekend, 100% online. *Students:* 13 full-time (6 women), 14 part-time (10 women); includes 1 minority (Asian, non-Hispanic/Latino), 9 international. Average age 30. 43 applicants, 30% accepted, 5 enrolled. In 2017, 8 master's awarded. *Degree requirements:* For master's, thesis or alternative. *Entrance requirements:* For master's, minimum GPA of 3.0 (recommended). Additional exam requirements/recommendations for international students: Required—TOEFL (minimum score 570 paper-based; 88 iBT), IELTS (minimum score 6.5), PTE (minimum score 62). *Application deadline:* Applications are processed on a rolling basis. Application fee: $65. Electronic applications accepted. *Expenses:* $1,815 per credit hour (classroom), $1,035 per credit hour (online study). *Financial support:* In 2017–18, 10 students received support. Teaching assistantships with partial tuition reimbursements available, career-related internships or fieldwork, scholarships/grants, and unspecified assistantships available. Support available to part-time students. Financial award applicants required to submit FAFSA. *Faculty research:* Diversity recruitment: higher education and corporate America; equity and social justice issues in graduate employability; leadership development. *Unit head:* Dr. Linda Underhill, Director, 585-475-7359, Fax: 585-475-5099, E-mail: lmuish@rit.edu. *Application contact:* Diane Ellison, Senior Associate Vice President, Graduate Enrollment Services, 585-475-2229, Fax: 585-475-7164, E-mail: gradinfo@rit.edu.
Website: http://www.rit.edu/cast/servicesystems/human-resources-development

Rockhurst University, Helzberg School of Management, Kansas City, MO 64110-2561. Offers accounting (MBA); business intelligence (MBA, Certificate); business intelligence and analytics (MS); data science (MBA, Certificate); entrepreneurship (MBA); finance (MBA); fundraising leadership (MBA, Certificate); healthcare management (MBA, Certificate); human capital (Certificate); international business (Certificate); management (MA, MBA, Certificate); nonprofit administration (Certificate); organizational development (Certificate); science leadership (Certificate). *Accreditation:* AACSB. *Program availability:* Part-time, evening/weekend. *Faculty:* 18 full-time (4 women), 20 part-time/adjunct (9 women). *Students:* 99 full-time (30 women), 355 part-time (132 women); includes 95 minority (30 Black or African American, non-Hispanic/Latino; 29 Asian, non-Hispanic/Latino; 25 Hispanic/Latino; 11 Two or more races, non-Hispanic/Latino), 8 international. Average age 32. 249 applicants, 81% accepted, 175 enrolled. In 2017, 145 master's, 17 other advanced degrees awarded. *Entrance requirements:* For master's, GMAT or GRE. Additional exam requirements/recommendations for international students: Required—TOEFL (minimum score 550 paper-based; 79 iBT). *Application deadline:* Applications are processed on a rolling basis. Application fee: $0. Electronic applications accepted. *Financial support:* Applicants required to submit FAFSA. *Faculty research:* Offshoring/outsourcing, systems analysis/synthesis, work teams, multilateral trade, path dependencies/creation. *Unit head:* Cheryl McConnell, Dean, 816-501-4201, Fax: 816-501-4650, E-mail: cheryl.mcconnell@rockhurst.edu. *Application contact:* Jonnae Hill, Director of Graduate Business Advising, 816-501-4823, E-mail: jonnae.hill@rockhurst.edu.
Website: https://www.rockhurst.edu/helzberg

Rollins College, Hamilton Holt School, Master of Human Resources Program, Winter Park, FL 32789. Offers MHR. *Program availability:* Part-time, evening/weekend. *Faculty:* 4 full-time (0 women), 1 (woman) part-time/adjunct. *Students:* 9 full-time (6 women), 40 part-time (31 women); includes 15 minority (3 Black or African American, non-Hispanic/Latino; 2 American Indian or Alaska Native, non-Hispanic/Latino; 3 Asian, non-Hispanic/Latino; 6 Hispanic/Latino; 1 Two or more races, non-Hispanic/Latino), 8 international. Average age 31. In 2017, 21 master's awarded. *Degree requirements:* For master's, thesis optional. *Entrance requirements:* For master's, GMAT or GRE, official transcripts, two letters of recommendation, essay, current resume. Additional exam requirements/recommendations for international students: Required—TOEFL (minimum score 550 paper-based; 80 iBT). *Application deadline:* For fall admission, 4/1 for domestic students; for spring admission, 12/1 for domestic students. Application fee: $50. *Expenses:* $2,556 per course. *Financial support:* Scholarships/grants and unspecified assistantships available. Support available to part-time students. Financial award applicants required to submit FAFSA. *Unit head:* Dr. Donald Rogers, Faculty Director, 407-646-2348, E-mail: drogers@rollins.edu. *Application contact:* Graduate Coordinator, 407-646-2653, Fax: 407-646-1551, E-mail: eveningadmission@rollins.edu.
Website: http://www.rollins.edu/holt/graduate/mhr.html

Roosevelt University, Graduate Division, College of Education, Program in Training and Development, Chicago, IL 60605. Offers MA. *Program availability:* Part-time, evening/weekend. *Students:* 10 full-time (5 women), 36 part-time (28 women); includes 20 minority (14 Black or African American, non-Hispanic/Latino; 1 Asian, non-Hispanic/Latino; 3 Hispanic/Latino; 2 Two or more races, non-Hispanic/Latino), 1 international. Average age 40. 9 applicants, 89% accepted, 6 enrolled. In 2017, 24 master's awarded. *Application deadline:* Applications are processed on a rolling basis. Application fee: $40. Electronic applications accepted. *Expenses:* $19,509 annual full-time. *Financial support:* Scholarships/grants available. *Application contact:* Laura Lag, Assistant Dean for Graduate Admission, 312-853-4753, E-mail: llag@roosevelt.edu.
Website: https://www.roosevelt.edu/

South Dakota State University, Graduate School, College of Education and Human Sciences, Department of Counseling and Human Resource Development, Brookings, SD 57007. Offers counseling and human resource development (M Ed, MS); human sciences (MS). *Accreditation:* ACA (one or more programs are accredited); NCATE. *Program availability:* Part-time, evening/weekend. *Degree requirements:* For master's, comprehensive exam, thesis (for some programs), oral exams. *Entrance requirements:* For master's, minimum GPA of 2.75. Additional exam requirements/recommendations for international students: Required—TOEFL (minimum score 525 paper-based; 71 iBT). *Faculty research:* Rural mental health, family issues, character education, student affairs, solution focused therapy.

Texas A&M University, College of Education and Human Development, Department of Educational Administration and Human Resource Development, College Station, TX 77843. Offers educational administration (M Ed, MS, Ed D); educational human resource development (MS, PhD). *Program availability:* Part-time. *Faculty:* 29. *Students:* 100 full-time (70 women), 275 part-time (169 women); includes 141 minority (45 Black or African American, non-Hispanic/Latino; 10 Asian, non-Hispanic/Latino; 78 Hispanic/Latino; 2 Native Hawaiian or other Pacific Islander, non-Hispanic/Latino; 6 Two or more races, non-Hispanic/Latino), 27 international. Average age 36. 144 applicants, 69% accepted, 81 enrolled. In 2017, 98 master's, 14 doctorates awarded. *Degree requirements:* For master's, thesis optional; for doctorate, thesis/dissertation. *Entrance requirements:* For master's, GRE General Test, writing exam, interview, professional

Human Resources Development

experience; for doctorate, GRE General Test, writing exam, interview/presentation, professional experience. Additional exam requirements/recommendations for international students: Required—TOEFL (minimum score 550 paper-based; 80 iBT), IELTS (minimum score 6), PTE (minimum score 53). *Application deadline:* For fall admission, 12/1 for domestic and international students; for spring admission, 8/15 for domestic and international students. Application fee: $50 ($90 for international students). Electronic applications accepted. *Expenses:* Contact institution. *Financial support:* In 2017–18, 182 students received support, including 4 fellowships with tuition reimbursements available (averaging $1,170 per year), 38 research assistantships with tuition reimbursements available (averaging $9,628 per year), 21 teaching assistantships with tuition reimbursements available (averaging $11,667 per year); career-related internships or fieldwork, institutionally sponsored loans, scholarships/grants, traineeships, health care benefits, tuition waivers (full and partial), and unspecified assistantships also available. Support available to part-time students. Financial award application deadline: 3/15; financial award applicants required to submit FAFSA. *Faculty research:* Higher education administration, public school administration, student affairs. *Unit head:* Dr. Fred M. Nafukho, Head, 979-862-3395, Fax: 979-862-4347, E-mail: fnafukho@tamu.edu. *Application contact:* Joyce Nelson, Director of Academic Advising, 979-845-3017, Fax: 979-862-4347, E-mail: eahradvisor@tamu.edu. Website: http://eahr.tamu.edu

Towson University, College of Liberal Arts, Program in Human Resource Development, Towson, MD 21252-0001. Offers education leadership (MS); general human resource management (MS). *Program availability:* Part-time, evening/weekend. *Students:* 23 full-time (19 women), 252 part-time (195 women); includes 63 minority (39 Black or African American, non-Hispanic/Latino; 11 Asian, non-Hispanic/Latino; 7 Hispanic/Latino; 6 Two or more races, non-Hispanic/Latino), 2 international. *Degree requirements:* For master's, comprehensive exam. *Entrance requirements:* For master's, bachelor's degree, 2 letters of recommendation, minimum GPA of 3.0, essay, resume. Additional exam requirements/recommendations for international students: Required—TOEFL. *Application deadline:* For fall admission, 1/17 for domestic students, 5/15 for international students; for spring admission, 10/15 for domestic students, 12/1 for international students. Applications are processed on a rolling basis. Application fee: $45. Electronic applications accepted. *Expenses:* Tuition, state resident: full-time $7960; part-time $398 per unit. Tuition, nonresident: full-time $16,480; part-time $824 per unit. *Required fees:* $2600; $130 per year. $390 per term. *Financial support:* Application deadline: 4/1. *Unit head:* Dr. Abby Mello, Graduate Program Director, 410-704-3364, E-mail: amello@towson.edu. *Application contact:* Coverley Beidleman, Assistant Director of Graduate Admissions, 410-704-5630, Fax: 410-704-3030, E-mail: cbeidleman@towson.edu.
Website: http://www.towson.edu/cla/departments/interdisciplinary/grad/hr/

Tusculum College, Program in Talent Development, Greeneville, TN 37743-9997. Offers MA. *Program availability:* Online learning. *Application contact:* Lindsey Seal, Director of Enrollment, 423-636-7300 Ext. 5006, E-mail: lseal@tusculum.edu.

Universidad Central del Este, Graduate School, San Pedro de Macoris, Dominican Republic. Offers environmental engineering (ME); financial management (M Ad); higher education (M Ed), including higher education management, higher education pedagogy; human resources (M Ad). *Entrance requirements:* For master's, letters of recommendation.

Universidad Iberoamericana, Graduate School, Santo Domingo D.N., Dominican Republic. Offers business administration (MBA, PMBA); constitutional law (LL M); dentistry (DMD); educational management (MA); integrated marketing communication (MA); psychopedagogical intervention (M Ed); real estate law (LL M); strategic management of human talent (MM).

University of Arkansas, Graduate School, College of Education and Health Professions, Department of Rehabilitation, Human Resources and Communication Disorders, Fayetteville, AR 72701. Offers adult and lifelong learning (M Ed, Ed D); communication disorders (MS); counselor education (MS, PhD); educational statistics and research methods (MS, PhD); higher education (M Ed, Ed D, Ed S); human resource and workforce development education (M Ed, Ed D); rehabilitation (MS, PhD). *Program availability:* Part-time. In 2017, 92 master's, 17 doctorates awarded. *Degree requirements:* For doctorate, thesis/dissertation. *Application deadline:* For fall admission, 8/1 for domestic students, 4/1 for international students; for spring admission, 12/1 for domestic students, 10/1 for international students; for summer admission, 4/15 for domestic students, 3/1 for international students. Applications are processed on a rolling basis. Application fee: $60. Electronic applications accepted. *Expenses:* Tuition, state resident: full-time $3782. Tuition, nonresident: full-time $10,238. *Financial support:* In 2017–18, 55 research assistantships, 3 teaching assistantships were awarded; fellowships with tuition reimbursements, career-related internships or fieldwork, and Federal Work-Study also available. Support available to part-time students. Financial award application deadline: 4/1; financial award applicants required to submit FAFSA. *Unit head:* Dr. Michael Hevel, Interim Department Head, 479-575-4924, Fax: 479-575-3319, E-mail: hevel@uark.edu. *Application contact:* Dr. Brent Williams, Graduate Coordinator, 479-575-4758, E-mail: btwilli@uark.edu.
Website: http://rhrc.uark.edu/

University of Bridgeport, School of Arts and Sciences, Department of Counseling, Bridgeport, CT 06604. Offers clinical mental health counseling (MS); college student personnel (MS); community counseling (MS); human resource development (MS); human service (MS). *Program availability:* Part-time, evening/weekend. *Degree requirements:* For master's, thesis, project. *Entrance requirements:* Additional exam requirements/recommendations for international students: Recommended—TOEFL (minimum score 550 paper-based; 80 iBT), IELTS (minimum score 6.5). Electronic applications accepted. *Expenses:* Contact institution.

University of Houston, College of Technology, Department of Human Development and Consumer Science, Houston, TX 77204. Offers future studies in commerce (MS); human resources development (MS). *Program availability:* Part-time. *Degree requirements:* For master's, project or thesis. *Entrance requirements:* For master's, GMAT, MAT. Additional exam requirements/recommendations for international students: Required—TOEFL (minimum score 550 paper-based; 79 iBT). Electronic applications accepted.

University of Louisville, Graduate School, College of Education and Human Development, Department of Educational Leadership, Evaluation and Organizational Development, Louisville, KY 40292-0001. Offers educational leadership and organizational development (Ed D, PhD), including evaluation (PhD), human resource development (PhD), P-12 administration (PhD), post-secondary administration (PhD), sport administration (PhD); health professions education (Certificate); higher education administration (MA); human resources and organization development (MS), including health professions education, human resource leadership, workplace learning and performance; P-12 educational administration (Ed S), including principalship, supervisor of instruction. *Accreditation:* NCATE. *Program availability:* Part-time, evening/weekend, online learning. *Students:* 190 full-time (64 women), 516 part-time (298 women); includes 218 minority (131 Black or African American, non-Hispanic/Latino; 1 American Indian or Alaska Native, non-Hispanic/Latino; 16 Asian, non-Hispanic/Latino; 47

Hispanic/Latino; 2 Native Hawaiian or other Pacific Islander, non-Hispanic/Latino; 21 Two or more races, non-Hispanic/Latino), 3 international. Average age 36. 232 applicants, 84% accepted, 141 enrolled. In 2017, 68 master's, 2 doctorates, 17 other advanced degrees awarded. Application fee: $65. *Expenses:* Tuition, state resident: full-time $12,246; part-time $681 per credit hour. Tuition, nonresident: full-time $25,486; part-time $1417 per credit hour. *Required fees:* $196. Tuition and fees vary according to course load, program and reciprocity agreements. *Financial support:* Application deadline: 6/1; applicants required to submit FAFSA. *Faculty research:* Urban educational leadership and policy, human resource and organizational development, program evaluation, community and military partnerships, higher education, and economic education. *Total annual research expenditures:* $256,111. *Unit head:* Dr. Jeffrey Sun, Chair and Professor, 502-852-0618, E-mail: jeffrey.sun@louisville.edu. *Application contact:* Betty Hampton, Director of Graduate Student Services, 502-852-5597, Fax: 502-852-1465, E-mail: edadvise@louisville.edu.
Website: http://louisville.edu/education/departments/eleod

University of Louisville, Graduate School, College of Education and Human Development, Departments of Early Childhood and Elementary Education, Middle and Secondary Education, and Special Education, Louisville, KY 40292-0001. Offers art education (MAT); autism and applied behavior analysis (Certificate); curriculum and instruction (PhD); early elementary education (MAT); exercise physiology (MS); health and physical education (MAT); health professions education (Certificate); higher education (MA); human resources and organization development (MS); instructional technology (M Ed); interdisciplinary early childhood education (MAT); middle school education (MAT); music education (MAT); secondary education (MAT); special education (MAT); sport administration (MS); teacher leadership (M Ed). *Program availability:* Part-time, evening/weekend. *Students:* 114 full-time (73 women), 173 part-time (114 women); includes 49 minority (19 Black or African American, non-Hispanic/Latino; 5 Asian, non-Hispanic/Latino; 13 Hispanic/Latino; 12 Two or more races, non-Hispanic/Latino), 7 international. Average age 29. 132 applicants, 73% accepted, 57 enrolled. In 2017, 70 master's, 2 doctorates, 2 other advanced degrees awarded. *Application deadline:* For spring admission, 1/1 priority date for international students. Application fee: $65. *Expenses:* Tuition, state resident: full-time $12,246; part-time $681 per credit hour. Tuition, nonresident: full-time $25,486; part-time $1417 per credit hour. *Required fees:* $196. Tuition and fees vary according to course load, program and reciprocity agreements. *Financial support:* Application deadline: 6/1; applicants required to submit FAFSA. *Faculty research:* STEM teaching and learning; content literacy for English language learners; social justice in teacher education; adolescent literacy; mathematics teacher development. *Total annual research expenditures:* $1.7 million. *Unit head:* Dr. Ann E. Larson, Dean, College of Education and Human Development, 502-852-6411, Fax: 502-852-1464, E-mail: ann@louisville.edu. *Application contact:* Betty Hampton, Director of Graduate Student Services, 502-852-5597, Fax: 502-852-1465, E-mail: edadvise@louisville.edu.
Website: http://louisville.edu/delphi

University of Minnesota, Twin Cities Campus, Graduate School, College of Education and Human Development, Department of Organizational Leadership, Policy and Development, Program in Human Resource Development, Minneapolis, MN 55455-0213. Offers M Ed, MA, Ed D, PhD, Certificate. *Students:* 89 full-time (62 women), 47 part-time (31 women); includes 23 minority (6 Black or African American, non-Hispanic/Latino; 2 American Indian or Alaska Native, non-Hispanic/Latino; 7 Asian, non-Hispanic/Latino; 2 Hispanic/Latino; 1 Native Hawaiian or other Pacific Islander, non-Hispanic/Latino; 5 Two or more races, non-Hispanic/Latino), 47 international. Average age 33. 113 applicants, 67% accepted, 62 enrolled. In 2017, 32 master's, 5 doctorates, 7 other advanced degrees awarded. Application fee: $75 ($95 for international students). *Unit head:* Dr. Heidi Barajas, Chair, 612-625-4823, E-mail: hbarajas@umn.edu. *Application contact:* Dr. Jeremy J. Hernandez, Director of Graduate Studies, 612-626-9377, E-mail: herna220@umn.edu.
Website: http://www.cehd.umn.edu/OLPD/grad-programs/HRD/

University of Nebraska at Omaha, Graduate Studies, College of Arts and Sciences, Department of Psychology, Omaha, NE 68182. Offers applied behavior analysis (Certificate); human resources and training (Certificate); industrial/organizational psychology (MS); psychology (MA, PhD); school psychology (MS, Ed S). *Program availability:* Part-time. *Degree requirements:* For master's, comprehensive exam, thesis (for some programs); for doctorate, comprehensive exam, thesis/dissertation. *Entrance requirements:* For master's and doctorate, GRE, minimum GPA of 3.0, official transcripts, 3 letters of recommendation, statement of purpose, writing sample, resume. Additional exam requirements/recommendations for international students: Required—TOEFL, IELTS, PTE. Electronic applications accepted.

University of Nebraska at Omaha, Graduate Studies, College of Business Administration, Program in Business Administration, Omaha, NE 68182. Offers business administration (MBA); business for bioscientists (Certificate); executive business administration (EMBA); human resources and training (Certificate). *Accreditation:* AACSB. *Program availability:* Part-time, evening/weekend. *Degree requirements:* For master's, thesis (for some programs), capstone course. *Entrance requirements:* For master's, GMAT or GRE, minimum GPA of 3.0, official transcripts, resume; for Certificate, minimum GPA of 3.0, official transcripts, resume, letter of recommendation, statement of purpose. Additional exam requirements/recommendations for international students: Required—TOEFL, IELTS, PTE. Electronic applications accepted.

University of Nebraska at Omaha, Graduate Studies, College of Communication, Fine Arts and Media, School of Communication, Omaha, NE 68182. Offers communication (MA); human resources and training (Certificate); technical communication (Certificate). *Program availability:* Part-time, evening/weekend. *Degree requirements:* For master's, comprehensive exam, thesis (for some programs). *Entrance requirements:* For master's, minimum GPA of 3.0, 15 undergraduate communication courses, resume, statement of purpose, 3 letters of recommendation. Additional exam requirements/recommendations for international students: Required—TOEFL, IELTS, PTE. Electronic applications accepted.

University of Regina, Faculty of Graduate Studies and Research, Faculty of Education, Department of Human Resource Development, Regina, SK S4S 0A2, Canada. Offers MHRD. *Program availability:* Part-time. *Faculty:* 5 full-time (2 women), 20 part-time/adjunct (11 women). *Students:* 10 full-time (7 women), 7 part-time (4 women). 22 applicants, 36% accepted. In 2017, 6 master's awarded. *Degree requirements:* For master's, thesis (for some programs), course, project or thesis. *Entrance requirements:* For master's, 4-year undergraduate degree in related field (e.g. adult education or administration). Additional exam requirements/recommendations for international students: Required—TOEFL (minimum score 580 paper-based; 80 iBT), IELTS (minimum score 6.5), PTE (minimum score 59). *Application deadline:* For fall admission, 2/15 for domestic and international students; for winter admission, 10/15 for domestic and international students; for spring admission, 2/15 for domestic and international students. Application fee: $100. Electronic applications accepted. *Expenses:* $10,681. *Financial support:* In 2017–18, fellowships (averaging $6,000 per year), teaching assistantships (averaging $2,562 per year) were awarded; research assistantships and scholarships/grants also available. Financial award application deadline: 6/15. *Faculty research:* Foundations of adult development, theory and practice of adult education and

human resource development, design and assessment of curriculum and instruction, planning and curriculum development, learning and the workplace. *Unit head:* Dr. Paul Clarke, Dean, Research and Graduate Programs in Education, 306-585-5353, Fax: 306-585-5330, E-mail: paul.clarke@uregina.ca. *Application contact:* Linda Jiang, Graduate Program Coordinator, 306-585-4506, Fax: 306-585-5387, E-mail: ed.grad.programs@uregina.ca.
Website: http://www.uregina.ca/education/

The University of Scranton, Panuska College of Professional Studies, Department of Health Administration and Human Resources, Program in Human Resources, Scranton, PA 18510. Offers MS. *Program availability:* Part-time, evening/weekend, 100% online.

University of South Africa, College of Economic and Management Sciences, Pretoria, South Africa. Offers accounting (D Admin, D Com); accounting science (DA); auditing (D Admin, D Com); business administration (M Tech); business economics (D Admin); business leadership (DBL); business management (D Admin, D Com); economic management analysis (M Tech); economics (D Admin, D Com, PhD); human resource development (M Tech); industrial psychology (D Admin, D Com, PhD); logistics (D Com); marketing (M Tech); public administration (D Admin, D Com, DPA, PhD); public management (M Tech); quantitative management (D Admin, D Com); real estate (M Tech); statistics (D Admin, PhD); tourism management (D Admin, D Com); transport economics (D Admin, D Com).

University of South Florida, Innovative Education, Tampa, FL 33620-9951. Offers adult, career and higher education (Graduate Certificate), including college teaching, leadership in developing human resources, leadership in higher education; Africana studies (Graduate Certificate), including diasporas and health disparities, genocide and human rights; aging studies (Graduate Certificate), including gerontology; art research (Graduate Certificate), including museum studies; business foundations (Graduate Certificate); chemical and biomedical engineering (Graduate Certificate), including materials science and engineering, water, health and sustainability; child and family studies (Graduate Certificate), including positive behavior support; civil and industrial engineering (Graduate Certificate), including transportation systems analysis; community and family health (Graduate Certificate), including maternal and child health, social marketing and public health, violence and injury: prevention and intervention, women's health; criminology (Graduate Certificate), including criminal justice administration; data science for public administration (Graduate Certificate); digital humanities (Graduate Certificate); educational measurement and research (Graduate Certificate), including evaluation; English (Graduate Certificate), including comparative literary studies, creative writing, professional and technical communication; entrepreneurship (Graduate Certificate); environmental health (Graduate Certificate), including safety management; epidemiology and biostatistics (Graduate Certificate), including applied biostatistics, biostatistics, concepts and tools of epidemiology, epidemiology, epidemiology of infectious diseases; geography, environment and planning (Graduate Certificate), including community development, environmental policy and management, geographical information systems; geology (Graduate Certificate), including hydrogeology; global health (Graduate Certificate), including disaster management, global health and Latin American and Caribbean studies, global health practice, humanitarian assistance, infection control; government and international affairs (Graduate Certificate), including Cuban studies, globalization studies; health policy and management (Graduate Certificate), including health management and leadership, public health policy and programs; hearing specialist: early intervention (Graduate Certificate); industrial and management systems engineering (Graduate Certificate), including systems engineering, technology management; information studies (Graduate Certificate), including school library media specialist; information systems/decision sciences (Graduate Certificate), including analytics and business intelligence; instructional technology (Graduate Certificate), including distance education, Florida digital/virtual educator, instructional design, multimedia design, Web design; internal medicine, bioethics and medical humanities (Graduate Certificate), including biomedical ethics; Latin American and Caribbean studies (Graduate Certificate); leadership for coastal resiliency planning (Graduate Certificate); mass communications (Graduate Certificate), including multimedia journalism; mathematics and statistics (Graduate Certificate), including mathematics; medicine (Graduate Certificate), including aging and neuroscience, bioinformatics, biotechnology, brain fitness and memory management, clinical investigation, hand and upper limb rehabilitation, health informatics, health sciences, integrative weight management, intellectual property, medicine and gender, metabolic and nutritional medicine, metabolic cardiology, pharmacy sciences; national and competitive intelligence (Graduate Certificate); nursing (Graduate Certificate), including simulation based academic fellowship in advanced pain management; psychological and social foundations (Graduate Certificate), including career counseling, college teaching, diversity in education, mental health counseling, school counseling; public affairs (Graduate Certificate), including nonprofit management, public management, research administration; public health (Graduate Certificate), including assessing chemical toxicity and public health risks, health equity, pharmacoepidemiology, public health generalist, toxicology, translational research in adolescent behavioral health; public health practices (Graduate Certificate), including planning for healthy communities; rehabilitation and mental health counseling (Graduate Certificate), including integrative mental health care, marriage and family therapy, rehabilitation technology; secondary education (Graduate Certificate), including ESOL, foreign language education: culture and content, foreign language education: professional; social work (Graduate Certificate), including geriatric social work/clinical gerontology; special education (Graduate Certificate), including autism spectrum disorder, disabilities education: severe/profound; world languages (Graduate Certificate), including teaching English as a second language (TESL) or foreign language. *Unit head:* Dr. Cynthia DeLuca, Associate Vice President and Assistant Vice Provost, 813-974-3077, Fax: 813-974-7061, E-mail: deluca@usf.edu. *Application contact:* Owen Hooper, Director, Summer and Alternative Calendar Programs, 813-974-6917, E-mail: hooper@usf.edu.
Website: http://www.usf.edu/innovative-education/

The University of Tennessee, Graduate School, College of Business Administration, Program in Human Resource Development, Knoxville, TN 37996. Offers teacher licensure (MS); training and development (MS). *Program availability:* Part-time. *Degree requirements:* For master's, thesis. *Entrance requirements:* For master's, GRE General Test, minimum GPA of 2.7. Electronic applications accepted.

The University of Texas at Tyler, College of Business and Technology, Program in Human Resource Development, Tyler, TX 75799-0001. Offers MS, PhD. *Program availability:* Part-time, evening/weekend, online learning. *Degree requirements:* For master's, comprehensive exam. *Entrance requirements:* For master's, GRE General Test or MAT. Additional exam requirements/recommendations for international students:

Required—TOEFL. Electronic applications accepted. *Faculty research:* Human resource development.

University of Wisconsin–Stout, Graduate School, College of Management, Program in Training and Human Resource Development, Menomonie, WI 54751. Offers MS. *Program availability:* Part-time, online learning. *Degree requirements:* For master's, thesis. *Entrance requirements:* For master's, minimum GPA 2.75. Additional exam requirements/recommendations for international students: Required—TOEFL (minimum score 500 paper-based; 61 iBT). Electronic applications accepted. *Faculty research:* Organizational behavior, performance, learning and performance, strategic planning.

Villanova University, Graduate School of Liberal Arts and Sciences, Department of Human Resource Development, Villanova, PA 19085-1699. Offers MS. *Program availability:* Part-time, evening/weekend, 100% online. *Faculty:* 31. *Students:* 204 full-time (156 women), 148 part-time (113 women); includes 109 minority (43 Black or African American, non-Hispanic/Latino; 1 American Indian or Alaska Native, non-Hispanic/Latino; 16 Asian, non-Hispanic/Latino; 39 Hispanic/Latino; 2 Native Hawaiian or other Pacific Islander, non-Hispanic/Latino; 8 Two or more races, non-Hispanic/Latino), 5 international. Average age 36. 116 applicants, 83% accepted, 77 enrolled. In 2017, 185 master's awarded. *Degree requirements:* For master's, comprehensive exam. *Entrance requirements:* For master's, GRE General Test, minimum GPA of 3.0, statement of goals, resume, 3 letters of recommendation. Additional exam requirements/recommendations for international students: Required—TOEFL. *Application deadline:* For fall admission, 5/1 priority date for international students; for spring admission, 10/15 priority date for international students. Applications are processed on a rolling basis. Application fee: $50. Electronic applications accepted. *Financial support:* Research assistantships, scholarships/grants, and unspecified assistantships available. Financial award applicants required to submit FAFSA. *Unit head:* Dr. Gerarad Brandon, Director, 610-519-8861, E-mail: gerard.brandon@villanova.edu.
Website: http://www.villanova.edu/artsci/hrd/

Virginia Commonwealth University, Graduate School, School of Education, Program in Adult Learning, Richmond, VA 23284-9005. Offers adult literacy (M Ed); human resource development (M Ed); teaching and learning with technology (M Ed). *Accreditation:* NCATE. *Program availability:* Part-time. *Entrance requirements:* For master's, GRE General Test or MAT. Additional exam requirements/recommendations for international students: Required—TOEFL (minimum score 600 paper-based; 100 iBT). Electronic applications accepted. *Faculty research:* Adult development and learning, program planning and evaluation.

Waldorf University, Program in Organizational Leadership, Forest City, IA 50436. Offers criminal justice leadership (MA); emergency management leadership (MA); fire/rescue executive leadership (MA); human resource development (MA); public administration (MA); sport management (MA); teacher leader (MA).

Webster University, George Herbert Walker School of Business and Technology, Department of Business, St. Louis, MO 63119-3194. Offers business and organizational security management (MBA); decision support systems (MBA); environmental management (MBA); finance (MBA, MS); forensic accounting (MS); gerontology (MBA); human resources development (MBA); human resources management (MBA); information technology management (MBA); international business (MA, MBA); international relations (MBA); management and leadership (MBA); marketing (MBA); media communications (MBA); procurement and acquisitions management (MBA); Web services (MBA). *Accreditation:* ACBSP. *Program availability:* Part-time, evening/weekend, online learning. *Degree requirements:* For master's, comprehensive exam (for some programs), thesis (for some programs). *Entrance requirements:* Additional exam requirements/recommendations for international students: Required—TOEFL.

Webster University, George Herbert Walker School of Business and Technology, Department of Management, St. Louis, MO 63119-3194. Offers business and organizational security management (MA); digital marketing management (Graduate Certificate); government contracting (Graduate Certificate); health administration (MHA); health care management (MA); health services management (MA); human resources development (MA); human resources management (MA); information technology management (MA, MS); management (D Mgt); management and leadership (MA); marketing (MA); nonprofit leadership (MA); nonprofit revenue development (Graduate Certificate); organizational development (Graduate Certificate); procurement and acquisitions management (MA); public administration (MPA); space systems operations management (MS). *Program availability:* Part-time, evening/weekend, online learning. *Degree requirements:* For master's, thesis (for some programs); for doctorate, thesis/dissertation, written exam. *Entrance requirements:* For doctorate, GMAT, 3 years of work experience, MBA. Additional exam requirements/recommendations for international students: Required—TOEFL.

Western Seminary, Graduate Programs, Program in Ministry and Leadership, Portland, OR 97215-3367. Offers chaplaincy (MA); coaching (MA); Jewish ministry (MA); pastoral care to women (MA); youth ministry (MA). *Degree requirements:* For master's, practicum. *Entrance requirements:* Additional exam requirements/recommendations for international students: Required—TOEFL.

William Woods University, Graduate and Adult Studies, Fulton, MO 65251-1098. Offers administration (M Ed, Ed S); athletic/activities administration (M Ed); curriculum and instruction (M Ed, Ed S); educational leadership (Ed D); equestrian education (M Ed); health management (MBA); human resources (MBA); leadership (MBA); marketing, advertising, and public relations (MBA); teaching and technology (M Ed). *Program availability:* Part-time, evening/weekend. *Degree requirements:* For master's, capstone course (MBA), action research (M Ed); for Ed S, field experience. *Entrance requirements:* Additional exam requirements/recommendations for international students: Required—TOEFL (minimum score 550 paper-based). Electronic applications accepted. *Expenses:* Contact institution.

Xavier University, College of Social Sciences, Health and Education, School of Education, Department of Educational Leadership and Human Resource Development, Cincinnati, OH 45207. Offers educational administration (M Ed); human resource development (MS). *Program availability:* Part-time, evening/weekend. *Degree requirements:* For master's, internship; for doctorate, comprehensive exam, thesis/dissertation. *Entrance requirements:* For master's, GRE or MAT, resume; 2 letters of recommendation; goal statement; official transcript; for doctorate, GRE, GMAT, LSAT or MAT, official transcript; 1,000-word goal statement; resume; 3 letters of recommendation. Additional exam requirements/recommendations for international students: Required—TOEFL (minimum score 550 paper-based; 79 iBT). Electronic applications accepted. Application fee is waived when completed online. *Expenses:* Contact institution.

Human Resources Management

Abilene Christian University, College of Graduate and Professional Studies, Program in Business Administration, Addison, TX 75001. Offers business analytics (MBA); corporate finance (MBA); general management (MBA); healthcare administration (MBA); human resource management (MBA); international business (MBA); management: business analytics (MS); management: healthcare administration (MS); management: international business (MS); management: marketing (MS); management: operations and supply chain management (MS); marketing (MBA); nonprofit leadership (MBA); operations and supply chain management (MBA). *Program availability:* Part-time, online only, 100% online. *Faculty:* 2 full-time (0 women), 6 part-time/adjunct (2 women). *Students:* 109 full-time (47 women), 51 part-time (22 women); includes 42 minority (33 Black or African American, non-Hispanic/Latino; 1 American Indian or Alaska Native, non-Hispanic/Latino; 2 Asian, non-Hispanic/Latino; 6 Hispanic/Latino). 125 applicants, 65% accepted, 58 enrolled. *Entrance requirements:* Additional exam requirements/recommendations for international students: Required—TOEFL (minimum score 80 iBT), IELTS (minimum score 6). *Application deadline:* For fall admission, 8/14 priority date for domestic students; for winter admission, 10/1 priority date for domestic students; for spring admission, 12/15 priority date for domestic students; for summer admission, 4/15 priority date for domestic students. Applications are processed on a rolling basis. Application fee: $50. Electronic applications accepted. *Expenses:* $700 per hour. *Financial support:* In 2017–18, 2 students received support. Application deadline: 4/1; applicants required to submit FAFSA. *Faculty research:* Organizational structure, financial management, cost accounting, unit analysis management. *Unit head:* Phil Vardiman, Program Director, 325-674-2153, E-mail: pxv02b@acu.edu. *Application contact:* Graduate Advisor, 817-219-7300, E-mail: gradonline@acu.edu.
Website: http://www.acu.edu/online/academics/mba-business-administration.html

Adelphi University, Robert B. Willumstad School of Business, Certificate Program in Human Resource Management, Garden City, NY 11530-0701. Offers Certificate. *Program availability:* Part-time, evening/weekend. *Students:* 3 part-time (2 women). Average age 35. 8 applicants, 50% accepted, 3 enrolled. In 2017, 11 Certificates awarded. *Entrance requirements:* For degree, GMAT or master's degree. Additional exam requirements/recommendations for international students: Required—TOEFL (minimum score 550 paper-based; 80 iBT), IELTS (minimum score 6.5). *Application deadline:* For fall admission, 4/1 for international students; for spring admission, 11/1 for international students. Applications are processed on a rolling basis. Application fee: $50. Electronic applications accepted. *Expenses:* Contact institution. *Financial support:* Career-related internships or fieldwork, Federal Work-Study, tuition waivers, and unspecified assistantships available. Financial award application deadline: 3/1; financial award applicants required to submit FAFSA. *Unit head:* Brian Rothschild, Assistant Dean, 516-877-4670, Fax: 516-877-4607, E-mail: gradbusinquiries@adelphi.edu. *Application contact:* E-mail: graduateadmissions@adelphi.edu.
Website: http://business.adelphi.edu/academics/certificate-programs/advanced-certificate-in-human-resource-management/

Adelphi University, Robert B. Willumstad School of Business, MBA Program, Garden City, NY 11530-0701. Offers accounting (MBA); finance (MBA); health services administration (MBA); human resource management (MBA); management (MBA); management information systems (MBA); marketing (MBA); sport management (MBA). *Accreditation:* AACSB. *Program availability:* Part-time, evening/weekend. *Students:* 257 full-time (110 women), 78 part-time (38 women); includes 56 minority (18 Black or African American, non-Hispanic/Latino; 16 Asian, non-Hispanic/Latino; 19 Hispanic/Latino; 3 Two or more races, non-Hispanic/Latino), 181 international. Average age 28. 435 applicants, 61% accepted, 205 enrolled. In 2017, 130 master's awarded. *Degree requirements:* For master's, capstone course. *Entrance requirements:* For master's, GMAT, 2 letters of recommendation. Additional exam requirements/recommendations for international students: Required—TOEFL (minimum score 550 paper-based; 80 iBT), IELTS (minimum score 6.5). *Application deadline:* For fall admission, 4/1 for international students; for spring admission, 11/1 for international students. Applications are processed on a rolling basis. Application fee: $50. Electronic applications accepted. *Expenses:* Contact institution. *Financial support:* Research assistantships with partial tuition reimbursements, career-related internships or fieldwork, Federal Work-Study, institutionally sponsored loans, scholarships/grants, tuition waivers (partial), and unspecified assistantships available. Financial award application deadline: 3/1; financial award applicants required to submit FAFSA. *Faculty research:* Supply chain management, distribution channels, productivity benchmark analysis, data envelopment analysis, financial portfolio analysis. *Unit head:* Dr. Rakesh Gupta, Associate Dean, 516-877-4629. *Application contact:* E-mail: graduateadmissions@adelphi.edu.
Website: http://business.adelphi.edu/degree-programs/graduate-degree-programs/m-b-a/

Albany State University, College of Arts and Humanities, Albany, GA 31705-2717. Offers criminal justice (MS); English education (M Ed); public administration (MPA), including community and economic development, criminal justice administration, health administration and policy, human resources management, public management, public policy, water resources management and policy; social work (MSW). *Accreditation:* NASPAA. *Program availability:* Part-time. *Degree requirements:* For master's, comprehensive exam, professional portfolio (for MPA), internship, capstone report. *Entrance requirements:* For master's, GRE, MAT, minimum GPA of 3.0, official transcript, pre-medical record/certificate of immunization, letters of reference. Electronic applications accepted. *Faculty research:* HIV prevention for minority students.

Albertus Magnus College, Master of Business Administration Program, New Haven, CT 06511-1189. Offers accounting (MBA); general management (MBA); health care management (MBA); human resource management (MBA); leadership (MBA); project management (MBA). Program also offered in East Hartford, CT. *Program availability:* Part-time, evening/weekend, 100% online, blended/hybrid learning. *Degree requirements:* For master's, thesis, capstone project, business plan, minimum cumulative GPA of 3.0, completion of all requirements within seven years of matriculation. *Entrance requirements:* For master's, 3 years of management or related experience, minimum GPA of 2.5, 2 letters of recommendation, official transcripts. Additional exam requirements/recommendations for international students: Recommended—TOEFL (minimum score 550 paper-based; 80 iBT). *Application deadline:* Applications are processed on a rolling basis. Application fee: $50. Electronic applications accepted. *Expenses:* Contact institution. *Financial support:* Federal Work-Study and unspecified assistantships available. Support available to part-time students. Financial award applicants required to submit FAFSA. *Faculty research:* Finance, project management, accounting, business administration, generalist. *Unit head:* Dr. Wayne Gineo, Director, 203-672-6670, E-mail: wgineo@albertus.edu. *Application contact:* Anthony Reich, Director of Admission, Division of Professional and Graduate Studies, 203-773-5302, E-mail: arreich@albertus.edu.
Website: http://www.albertus.edu/business-administration/ms/

Amberton University, Graduate School, Program in Human Relations and Business, Garland, TX 75041-5595. Offers MS. *Program availability:* Part-time, evening/weekend. *Entrance requirements:* For master's, minimum GPA of 3.0. *Application deadline:* Applications are processed on a rolling basis. Application fee: $0. *Expenses: Tuition:* Part-time $795 per course. *Unit head:* Dr. Don Hebbard, Academic Dean, 972-635-8641 Ext. 157, Fax: 972-279-9773, E-mail: dhebbard@amberton.edu. *Application contact:* Adviser, 972-279-6511 Ext. 180, Fax: 972-279-9773, E-mail: advisor@amberton.edu. Website: http://www.amberton.edu/programs-and-courses/masters-degree-programs/human-relations-and-business/index.html

American InterContinental University Online, Program in Business Administration, Schaumburg, IL 60173. Offers accounting and finance (MBA); finance (MBA); healthcare management (MBA); human resource management (MBA); international business (MBA); management (MBA); marketing (MBA); operations management (MBA); organizational psychology and development (MBA); project management (MBA). *Accreditation:* ACBSP. *Program availability:* Evening/weekend, online learning. *Entrance requirements:* Additional exam requirements/recommendations for international students: Required—TOEFL (minimum score 550 paper-based). Electronic applications accepted.

American University, School of Professional and Extended Studies, Washington, DC 20016-8030. Offers agile project management (MS); healthcare management (MS, Graduate Certificate); human resource analytics and management (MS, Graduate Certificate); instructional design and learning analytics (MS); measurement and evaluation (MS); project monitoring and evaluation (Graduate Certificate); sports analytics and management (MS, Graduate Certificate). *Program availability:* Part-time, evening/weekend, 100% online. *Faculty:* 27 full-time (13 women), 21 part-time/adjunct (10 women). *Students:* 17 full-time (8 women), 59 part-time (34 women); includes 9 minority (5 Black or African American, non-Hispanic/Latino; 2 Asian, non-Hispanic/Latino; 1 Hispanic/Latino; 1 Two or more races, non-Hispanic/Latino), 5 international. Average age 31. 55 applicants, 89% accepted, 38 enrolled. In 2017, 8 other advanced degrees awarded. *Entrance requirements:* For master's, official transcript(s), resume. Additional exam requirements/recommendations for international students: Required—TOEFL (minimum score 600 paper-based; 100 iBT). *Application deadline:* Applications are processed on a rolling basis. Application fee: $55. Electronic applications accepted. *Expenses:* Contact institution. *Financial support:* Applicants required to submit FAFSA. *Unit head:* Carola Weil, Dean, 202-885-5990, Fax: 202-895-4960, E-mail: weil@american.edu. *Application contact:* Emily Aronoff, Assistant Director for Recruitment and Admission, 202-895-4953, E-mail: aronoff@american.edu.
Website: http://www.american.edu/spexs/

American University of Beirut, Graduate Programs, Suliman S. Olayan School of Business, Master in Human Resource Management Program, 1107 2020, Lebanon. Offers MHRM. *Program availability:* Part-time. *Faculty:* 5 full-time (3 women), 3 part-time/adjunct (1 woman). *Students:* 20 full-time (11 women). Average age 26. 68 applicants, 60% accepted, 20 enrolled. In 2017, 15 master's awarded. *Degree requirements:* For master's, thesis. *Entrance requirements:* Additional exam requirements/recommendations for international students: Required—TOEFL (minimum score 583 paper-based; 97 iBT), IELTS (minimum score 7). *Application deadline:* For fall admission, 2/8 for domestic students; for spring admission, 4/4 for domestic students. Applications are processed on a rolling basis. Application fee: $50. Electronic applications accepted. *Expenses: Tuition:* Full-time $17,244; part-time $958 per credit. *Required fees:* $740. Tuition and fees vary according to course load and program. *Financial support:* In 2017–18, 6 research assistantships with full tuition reimbursements (averaging $21,000 per year) were awarded; fellowships, teaching assistantships, scholarships/grants, health care benefits, tuition waivers, and unspecified assistantships also available. Financial award application deadline: 4/4; financial award applicants required to submit CSS PROFILE. *Unit head:* Maya Naim El-Helou, Director of Graduate Programs, 961-1-352700 Ext. 3955, Fax: 961-1-750214, E-mail: helou@aub.edu.lb. *Application contact:* Maya Naim El-Helou, Director of Graduate Programs, 961-1-352700 Ext. 3955, Fax: 961-1-750214, E-mail: helou@aub.edu.lb.
Website: http://www.aub.edu.lb/osb/osb_home/program/MHRM/Pages/index.aspx

Anderson University, College of Business, Anderson, SC 29621-4035. Offers business administration (MBA); healthcare leadership (MBA); human resources (MBA); marketing (MBA); organizational leadership (MOL); supply chain management (MBA). *Accreditation:* ACBSP. *Expenses:* Contact institution. *Financial support:* Tuition waivers available. Financial award application deadline: 3/1; financial award applicants required to submit FAFSA. *Unit head:* Steve Nail, Dean, 864-MBA-6000. *Application contact:* Mallory Knight, Graduate Admission Counselor, 864-231-2182, Fax: 864-231-2115, E-mail: malloryknight@andersonuniversity.edu.
Website: http://www.andersonuniversity.edu/business

Ashland University, Dauch College of Business and Economics, Ashland, OH 44805-3702. Offers accounting (MBA); business analytics (MBA); entrepreneurship (MBA); financial management (MBA); global management (MBA); health care management and leadership (MBA); human resource management (MBA); human resources (MBA); management information systems (MBA); project management (MBA); sport management (MBA); supply chain management (MBA). *Accreditation:* ACBSP. *Program availability:* Part-time, evening/weekend, 100% online, blended/hybrid learning. *Faculty:* 20 full-time (8 women), 13 part-time/adjunct (2 women). *Students:* 458 full-time (210 women), 144 part-time (52 women); includes 88 minority (63 Black or African American, non-Hispanic/Latino; 1 American Indian or Alaska Native, non-Hispanic/Latino; 10 Asian, non-Hispanic/Latino; 14 Hispanic/Latino), 202 international. Average age 31. 216 applicants, 74% accepted, 115 enrolled. In 2017, 184 master's awarded. Terminal master's awarded for partial completion of doctoral program. *Degree requirements:* For master's, thesis optional, capstone course. *Entrance requirements:* For master's, 2 years of full-time work experience. Additional exam requirements/recommendations for international students: Required—TOEFL (minimum score 550 paper-based; 78 iBT). *Application deadline:* For fall admission, 8/1 priority date for domestic students; for spring admission, 12/1 priority date for domestic students. Applications are processed on a rolling basis. Application fee: $30. Electronic applications accepted. *Expenses:* $815 per credit hour, $15 technology fee for online sections. *Financial support:* Scholarships/grants, tuition waivers (partial), and unspecified assistantships available. Financial award application deadline: 4/15; financial award applicants required to submit FAFSA. *Faculty research:* Relationship marketing strategy, executive compensation and company performance, online marketplaces in electronic commerce, diversity training in campus recreation departments, entrepreneurship in developing and emerging economies. *Unit head:* Dr. Elad Granot, Dean, 419-289-5932, E-mail: egranot@ashland.edu. *Application contact:* Stephen W. Krispinsky, Executive Director of MBA Program, 419-289-5236, Fax: 419-289-5910, E-mail: skrispin@ashland.edu.
Website: http://www.mba.ashland.edu

Ashworth College, Graduate Programs, Norcross, GA 30092. Offers business administration (MBA); criminal justice (MS); health care administration (MBA, MS); human resource management (MBA, MS); international business (MBA); management (MS); marketing (MBA, MS).

Assumption College, Business Studies Program, Worcester, MA 01609-1296. Offers accounting (MBA); business studies (CAGS); finance/economics (MBA); human resources (MBA); international business (MBA); management (MBA); marketing (MBA); nonprofit leadership (MBA). *Program availability:* Part-time, evening/weekend. *Faculty:* 5 full-time (1 woman), 21 part-time/adjunct (6 women). *Students:* 29 full-time (13 women), 87 part-time (50 women); includes 15 minority (1 Black or African American, non-Hispanic/Latino; 4 Asian, non-Hispanic/Latino; 8 Hispanic/Latino; 2 Two or more races, non-Hispanic/Latino), 4 international. Average age 29. 34 applicants, 100% accepted, 26 enrolled. In 2017, 81 master's, 2 other advanced degrees awarded. *Degree requirements:* For master's, capstone. *Entrance requirements:* For master's, bachelor's degree, three letters of recommendation, official transcripts, personal statement, current resume; for CAGS, MBA or equivalent degree in a closely related field, three letters of recommendation, official transcripts, personal statement, current resume. Additional exam requirements/recommendations for international students: Required—TOEFL (minimum score 540 paper-based; 76 iBT), IELTS (minimum score 6). *Application deadline:* For fall admission, 8/10 priority date for domestic and international students; for spring admission, 1/4 priority date for domestic and international students; for summer admission, 5/10 priority date for domestic and international students. Application fee: $30. Electronic applications accepted. *Expenses: Tuition:* Full-time $11,952; part-time $664 per credit. *Required fees:* $70 per term. *Financial support:* In 2017–18, 19 students received support. Tuition waivers (full and partial), unspecified assistantships, and institutional discounts available. Financial award applicants required to submit FAFSA. *Faculty research:* Workplace diversity, dynamics of team interaction, utilization of leased employees, experiential learning project on due diligence market for prostheses. *Unit head:* Dr. Robin Frkal, Director, 508-767-7622, E-mail: ra.frkal@assumption.edu. *Application contact:* Karen Stoyanoff, Director of Recruitment for Graduate Enrollment, 508-767-7442, Fax: 508-799-4412, E-mail: graduate@assumption.edu.
Website: http://graduate.assumption.edu/mba/assumption-mba

Averett University, Master of Business Administration Program, Danville, VA 24541. Offers business administration (MBA); human resources management (MBA); leadership (MBA); marketing (MBA). *Program availability:* Part-time, evening/weekend, 100% online, blended/hybrid learning. *Faculty:* 7 full-time (0 women), 12 part-time/adjunct (4 women). *Students:* 53 full-time (28 women), 129 part-time (83 women); includes 82 minority (65 Black or African American, non-Hispanic/Latino; 1 American Indian or Alaska Native, non-Hispanic/Latino; 5 Asian, non-Hispanic/Latino; 4 Hispanic/Latino; 7 Two or more races, non-Hispanic/Latino). Average age 38. 88 applicants, 81% accepted, 65 enrolled. In 2017, 129 master's awarded. *Degree requirements:* For master's, 41-credit core curriculum, minimum GPA of 3.0 throughout program, no more than 2 grades of C, completion of degree requirements within six years from start of program. *Entrance requirements:* For master's, minimum cumulative GPA of 3.0 over the last 60 semester hours of undergraduate study toward a baccalaureate degree, official transcripts, three years of full-time work experience, three letters of recommendation, current resume. Additional exam requirements/recommendations for international students: Required—TOEFL (minimum score 600 paper-based; 100 iBT). *Application deadline:* Applications are processed on a rolling basis. Electronic applications accepted. *Expenses:* $11,790. *Financial support:* Application deadline: 3/1; applicants required to submit FAFSA. *Unit head:* Dr. Peggy C. Wright, Chair, Business Department, 434-791-7118, E-mail: pwright@averett.edu. *Application contact:* Melissa Anderson, Director of Admissions, Graduate and Professional Studies, 804-729-8285, E-mail: manderson@averett.edu.
Website: http://gps.averett.edu/programs/master-degrees/

Avila University, School of Professional Studies, Kansas City, MO 64145-1698. Offers executive leadership (MS); fundraising (MA); instructional design and technology (MA, MS); leadership coaching (MS); project management (MA); strategic human resources (MS). *Program availability:* Part-time-only, evening/weekend, 100% online, blended/hybrid learning. *Faculty:* 14 part-time/adjunct (8 women). *Students:* 85 full-time (61 women), 45 part-time (33 women); includes 42 minority (35 Black or African American, non-Hispanic/Latino; 2 Asian, non-Hispanic/Latino; 4 Hispanic/Latino; 1 Two or more races, non-Hispanic/Latino), 3 international. Average age 37. 63 applicants, 60% accepted, 29 enrolled. In 2017, 39 master's awarded. *Degree requirements:* For master's, thesis optional. *Entrance requirements:* For master's, 2 letters of recommendation, minimum GPA of 3.0 during last 60 hours, resume, statement of intent. Additional exam requirements/recommendations for international students: Required—TOEFL (minimum score 550 paper-based; 79 iBT). *Application deadline:* Applications are processed on a rolling basis. Application fee: $0. Electronic applications accepted. *Expenses:* Contact institution. *Financial support:* In 2017–18, 14 students received support. Unspecified assistantships available. Support available to part-time students. Financial award applicants required to submit FAFSA. *Unit head:* Kari Clevenger, Associate Dean/Director, 816-501-3675, Fax: 816-941-4650, E-mail: advantage@avila.edu. *Application contact:* Jessica Burson, Graduate Admission Advisor, 816-501-2482, Fax: 816-941-4650, E-mail: advantage@avila.edu.
Website: https://www.avila.edu/mrk/advantage-3

Baker College Center for Graduate Studies–Online, Graduate Programs, Flint, MI 48507. Offers accounting (MBA); business administration (DBA); finance (MBA); general business (MBA); health care management (MBA); human resources management (MBA); information management (MBA); leadership studies (MBA); management information systems (MSIS); marketing (MBA). *Program availability:* Part-time, evening/weekend, online learning. *Degree requirements:* For master's, portfolio. *Entrance requirements:* For master's, 3 years of work experience, minimum undergraduate GPA of 2.5, writing sample, 3 letters of recommendation; for doctorate, MBA or acceptable related master's degree from accredited association, 5 years work experience, minimum graduate GPA of 3.25, writing sample, 3 professional references. Additional exam requirements/recommendations for international students: Required—TOEFL (minimum score 550 paper-based). Electronic applications accepted.

Baldwin Wallace University, Graduate Programs, School of Business, Program in Human Resources, Berea, OH 44017-2088. Offers MBA. *Program availability:* Part-time, evening/weekend. *Students:* 17 full-time (14 women), 20 part-time (14 women); includes 12 minority (7 Black or African American, non-Hispanic/Latino; 2 Asian, non-Hispanic/Latino; 3 Hispanic/Latino). Average age 37. 9 applicants, 67% accepted, 3 enrolled. In 2017, 4 master's awarded. *Degree requirements:* For master's, minimum overall GPA of 3.0. *Entrance requirements:* For master's, GMAT or minimum GPA of 3.0, bachelor's degree in any field, work experience. Additional exam requirements/recommendations for international students: Required—TOEFL (minimum score 550 paper-based; 79 iBT). *Application deadline:* For fall admission, 7/25 priority date for domestic students, 4/30 priority date for international students; for spring admission, 12/15 priority date for domestic students, 9/30 priority date for international students; for summer admission, 4/15 priority date for domestic students. Applications are processed on a rolling basis. Application fee: $25. Electronic applications accepted. Application fee is waived when completed online. *Expenses:* $948 per credit hour. *Financial support:* Applicants required to submit FAFSA. *Unit head:* Dale Kramer, Director, 440-826-3331, Fax: 440-826-3868, E-mail: dkramer@bw.edu. *Application contact:* Laura Spencer, Graduate Application Specialist, 440-826-2191, Fax: 440-826-3868, E-mail: lspencer@bw.edu.
Website: http://www.bw.edu/graduate/business/mba/

Barry University, School of Education, Graduate Certificate Programs, Miami Shores, FL 33161-6695. Offers advanced teaching and learning with technology (Certificate); distance education (Certificate); higher education technology integration (Certificate); human resources: not for profit and religious organizations (Certificate); K-12 technology integration (Certificate).

Baruch College of the City University of New York, Zicklin School of Business, Department of Management, New York, NY 10010-5585. Offers entrepreneurship (MBA); management (PhD); operations management (MBA); organizational behavior/human resources management (MBA); sustainable business (MBA). PhD offered jointly with Graduate School and University Center of the City University of New York. *Program availability:* Part-time, evening/weekend. *Degree requirements:* For doctorate, comprehensive exam, thesis/dissertation. *Entrance requirements:* For master's, GMAT, 2 letters of recommendation, resume, 2 years of work experience; for doctorate, GMAT. Additional exam requirements/recommendations for international students: Required—TOEFL (minimum score 590 paper-based), TWE.

Belhaven University, School of Business, Jackson, MS 39202-1789. Offers business administration (MBA); health administration (MBA, MHA); human resources (MBA, MSL); leadership (MBA); public administration (MPA); sports administration (MBA, MSA). *Program availability:* Part-time, evening/weekend, 100% online. *Faculty:* 11 full-time (4 women), 93 part-time/adjunct (39 women). *Students:* 20 full-time (12 women), 1,441 part-time (1,061 women); includes 1,168 minority (1,100 Black or African American, non-Hispanic/Latino; 22 American Indian or Alaska Native, non-Hispanic/Latino; 2 Asian, non-Hispanic/Latino; 23 Hispanic/Latino; 1 Native Hawaiian or other Pacific Islander, non-Hispanic/Latino; 20 Two or more races, non-Hispanic/Latino), 21 international. Average age 35. 501 applicants, 74% accepted, 261 enrolled. In 2017, 326 master's awarded. *Degree requirements:* For master's, comprehensive exam (for some programs), thesis or alternative. *Entrance requirements:* For master's, minimum GPA of 2.8 (for MBA and MHA), 2.5 (for MSL, MPA and MSA). *Application deadline:* Applications are processed on a rolling basis. Application fee: $25. Electronic applications accepted. *Expenses:* Contact institution. *Financial support:* Applicants required to submit FAFSA. *Unit head:* Dr. Ralph Mason, Dean, 601-968-8949, Fax: 601-968-8951, E-mail: cmason@belhaven.edu. *Application contact:* Dr. Audrey Kelleher, Vice President of Adult and Graduate Marketing and Development, 407-804-1424, Fax: 407-620-5210, E-mail: akelleher@belhaven.edu.
Website: http://www.belhaven.edu/campuses/index.htm

Bellevue University, Graduate School, College of Business, Bellevue, NE 68005-3098. Offers acquisition and contract management (MS); business administration (MBA); finance (MS); human capital management (PhD); management (MSM).

Benedictine University, Graduate Programs, Program in Business Administration, Lisle, IL 60532. Offers accounting (MBA); entrepreneurship and managing innovation (MBA); financial management (MBA); health administration (MBA); human resource management (MBA); information systems security (MBA); international business (MBA); management consulting (MBA); management information systems (MBA); marketing management (MBA); operations management and logistics (MBA); organizational leadership (MBA). *Program availability:* Part-time, evening/weekend, online learning. *Entrance requirements:* For master's, GMAT. Additional exam requirements/recommendations for international students: Required—TOEFL (minimum score 550 paper-based). Electronic applications accepted. *Faculty research:* Strategic leadership in professional organizations, sociology of professions, organizational change, social identity theory, applications to change management.

Brandman University, School of Business and Professional Studies, Irvine, CA 92618. Offers accounting (MBA); business administration (MBA); business intelligence and data analytics (MBA); e-business strategic management (MBA); entrepreneurship (MBA); finance (MBA); health administration (MBA); human resources (MBA, MS); international business (MBA); marketing (MBA); organizational leadership (MA, MBA, MPA); public administration (MPA). *Expenses: Tuition:* Part-time $640 per credit hour. Tuition and fees vary according to degree level and program. *Unit head:* Dr. Glenn Worthington, Dean, 253-861-1024, E-mail: gworthin@brandman.edu. *Application contact:* Dr. Glenn Worthington, Dean, 253-861-1024, E-mail: gworthin@brandman.edu.
Website: https://www.brandman.edu/academic-programs/business-and-professional-studies

Brigham Young University, Graduate Studies, BYU Marriott School of Business, MBA Program, Provo, UT 84602. Offers entrepreneurship (MBA); finance (MBA); global supply chain management (MBA); marketing (MBA); strategic human resources (MBA); JD/MBA; MBA/MS. *Accreditation:* AACSB. *Faculty:* 134 full-time (15 women), 65 part-time/adjunct (16 women). *Students:* 303 full-time (65 women); includes 26 minority (3 American Indian or Alaska Native, non-Hispanic/Latino; 8 Asian, non-Hispanic/Latino; 11 Hispanic/Latino; 4 Native Hawaiian or other Pacific Islander, non-Hispanic/Latino), 58 international. Average age 30. 339 applicants, 52% accepted, 136 enrolled. In 2017, 163 master's awarded. *Entrance requirements:* For master's, GMAT or GRE, commitment to BYU Honor Code, undergraduate degree. Additional exam requirements/recommendations for international students: Required—TOEFL (minimum score 590 paper-based; 100 iBT), IELTS (minimum score 7). *Application deadline:* For fall admission, 5/1 for domestic students, 3/1 for international students. Applications are processed on a rolling basis. Application fee: $50. Electronic applications accepted. *Expenses:* Contact institution. *Financial support:* Research assistantships, teaching assistantships, career-related internships or fieldwork, institutionally sponsored loans, and scholarships/grants available. Financial award application deadline: 3/1; financial award applicants required to submit FAFSA. *Faculty research:* Finance, marketing, supply chain management, entrepreneurship, strategic human resources. *Unit head:* Dr. Grant McQueen, Director, 801-422-3500, E-mail: mba@byu.edu. *Application contact:* Yvette Anderson, MBA Program Admissions Director, 801-422-3500, Fax: 801-422-0513, E-mail: mba@byu.edu.
Website: http://mba.byu.edu

Bryan College, MBA Program, Dayton, TN 37321. Offers business administration (MBA); healthcare administration (MBA); human resources (MBA); marketing (MBA); ministry (MBA); sports management (MBA). *Program availability:* Online only, 100% online. *Entrance requirements:* For master's, resume, 2 letters of recommendation. Additional exam requirements/recommendations for international students: Required—TOEFL. *Application deadline:* For fall admission, 7/1 for domestic and international students; for winter admission, 11/15 for domestic and international students; for spring admission, 12/1 for domestic and international students; for summer admission, 5/1 for domestic and international students. Applications are processed on a rolling basis. Application fee: $50. Electronic applications accepted. *Expenses:* Contact institution. *Financial support:* Scholarships/grants available. Financial award applicants required to submit FAFSA. *Unit head:* Dr. Adina Scruggs, Dean of Adult and Graduate Studies, 423-634-2057, E-mail: adina.scruggs@bryan.edu. *Application contact:* Mandi K Sullivan, Director of Academic Programs, 423-634-9880, E-mail: mandi.sullivan@bryan.edu.
Website: http://www.bryan.edu/academics/adult-education/graduate/online-mba/

Human Resources Management

Buffalo State College, State University of New York, The Graduate School, Faculty of Applied Science and Education, Department of Educational Foundations, Program in Adult Education, Buffalo, NY 14222-1095. Offers adult education (MS, Certificate); human resources development (Certificate). *Program availability:* Part-time, evening/weekend, online learning. *Degree requirements:* For master's, comprehensive exam. *Entrance requirements:* Additional exam requirements/recommendations for international students: Required—TOEFL (minimum score 550 paper-based).

California Coast University, School of Administration and Management, Santa Ana, CA 92701. Offers business marketing (MBA); health care management (MBA); human resource management (MBA); management (MBA, MS). *Program availability:* Online learning. Electronic applications accepted.

California Intercontinental University, School of Business, Irvine, CA 92614. Offers banking and finance (MBA); entrepreneurship and business management (DBA); global business leadership (DBA); international management and marketing (MBA); organizational management and human resource management (MBA).

California State University, East Bay, Office of Graduate Studies, College of Business and Economics, MBA Program, Option in Human Resources and Organizational Behavior, Hayward, CA 94542-3000. Offers MBA. *Program availability:* Part-time, evening/weekend. *Students:* 5 full-time (4 women), 17 part-time (15 women); includes 18 minority (4 Black or African American, non-Hispanic/Latino; 6 Asian, non-Hispanic/Latino; 5 Hispanic/Latino; 3 Two or more races, non-Hispanic/Latino), 2 international. Average age 33. 20 applicants, 35% accepted, 6 enrolled. In 2017, 10 master's awarded. *Degree requirements:* For master's, comprehensive exam or thesis. *Entrance requirements:* For master's, GMAT, minimum GPA of 2.75. Additional exam requirements/recommendations for international students: Required—TOEFL (minimum score 550 paper-based). *Application deadline:* For fall admission, 6/1 for domestic and international students. Application fee: $55. Electronic applications accepted. *Financial support:* Fellowships, career-related internships or fieldwork, Federal Work-Study, institutionally sponsored loans, and scholarships/grants available. Support available to part-time students. Financial award application deadline: 3/2; financial award applicants required to submit FAFSA. *Unit head:* Dr. Asha Rao, Program Advisor, 510-885-3290, E-mail: asha.rao@csueastbay.edu. *Application contact:* Philip Wiley, Administrative Support Coordinator, 510-885-3286, E-mail: philip.coleregis@csueastbay.edu. Website: http://www20.csueastbay.edu/cbe/mba-options/Human-Resources-Management-Option.html

California State University, Sacramento, College of Business Administration, Sacramento, CA 95819. Offers accountancy (MS); business administration (IMBA, MBA); human resources (MBA); urban land development (MBA). *Accreditation:* AACSB. *Program availability:* Part-time, evening/weekend, online, blended/hybrid learning. *Students:* 122 full-time (62 women), 153 part-time (75 women); includes 114 minority (10 Black or African American, non-Hispanic/Latino; 2 American Indian or Alaska Native, non-Hispanic/Latino; 73 Asian, non-Hispanic/Latino; 25 Hispanic/Latino; 4 Native Hawaiian or other Pacific Islander, non-Hispanic/Latino), 6 international. Average age 34. 230 applicants, 75% accepted, 134 enrolled. In 2017, 123 master's awarded. *Degree requirements:* For master's, comprehensive exam, project, thesis, or writing proficiency exam. *Entrance requirements:* For master's, GMAT. Additional exam requirements/recommendations for international students: Required—TOEFL (minimum score 550 paper-based; 80 iBT). *Application deadline:* For fall admission, 2/1 for domestic students, 3/1 for international students; for spring admission, 9/15 for domestic students, 9/30 for international students. Applications are processed on a rolling basis. Application fee: $55. Electronic applications accepted. *Expenses:* Contact institution. *Financial support:* Teaching assistantships, career-related internships or fieldwork, Federal Work-Study, and scholarships/grants available. Support available to part-time students. Financial award application deadline: 3/1; financial award applicants required to submit FAFSA. *Unit head:* Dr. Pierre A. Balthazard, Dean, 916-278-6578, Fax: 916-278-5793, E-mail: cba@csus.edu. *Application contact:* Jose Martinez, Graduate Admissions Supervisor, 916-278-7871, E-mail: martinj@skymail.csus.edu. Website: http://www.cba.csus.edu

Capella University, School of Business and Technology, Doctoral Programs in Business, Minneapolis, MN 55402. Offers accounting (DBA, PhD); business intelligence (DBA); finance (DBA, PhD); general business management (PhD); human resource management (DBA, PhD); leadership (DBA, PhD); management education (PhD); marketing (DBA, PhD); project management (DBA, PhD); strategy and innovation (DBA, PhD). *Accreditation:* ACBSP.

Capella University, School of Business and Technology, Master's Programs in Business, Minneapolis, MN 55402. Offers accounting (MBA); business analysis (MS); business intelligence (MBA); entrepreneurship (MBA); finance (MBA); general business administration (MBA); general human resource management (MS); general leadership (MS); health care management (MBA); human resource management (MBA); marketing (MBA); project management (MBA, MS). *Accreditation:* ACBSP.

Caribbean University, Graduate School, Bayamón, PR 00960-0493. Offers administration and supervision (MA Ed); criminal justice (MA); curriculum and instruction (MA Ed, PhD), including elementary education (MA Ed), English education (MA Ed), history education (MA Ed), mathematics education (MA Ed), primary education (MA Ed), science education (MA Ed), Spanish education (MA Ed); educational technology in instructional systems (MA Ed); gerontology (MSN); human resources (MBA); museology, archiving and art history (MA Ed); neonatal pediatrics (MSN); physical education (MA Ed); special education (MA Ed). *Entrance requirements:* For master's, interview, minimum GPA of 2.5.

Carlow University, College of Leadership and Social Change, MBA Program, Pittsburgh, PA 15213-3165. Offers fraud and forensics (MBA); healthcare management (MBA); human resource management (MBA); leadership and management (MBA); project management (MBA). *Program availability:* Part-time, evening/weekend, 100% online, blended/hybrid learning. *Students:* 81 full-time (62 women), 28 part-time (18 women); includes 32 minority (26 Black or African American, non-Hispanic/Latino; 2 Asian, non-Hispanic/Latino; 1 Hispanic/Latino; 3 Two or more races, non-Hispanic/Latino). Average age 32. 46 applicants, 98% accepted, 32 enrolled. In 2017, 57 master's awarded. *Entrance requirements:* For master's, minimum undergraduate GPA of 3.0 (preferred); personal essay; resume; official transcripts; two professional recommendations. Additional exam requirements/recommendations for international students: Required—TOEFL (minimum score 550 paper-based). *Application deadline:* Applications are processed on a rolling basis. Electronic applications accepted. *Expenses: Tuition:* Full-time $12,103; part-time $825 per credit hour. Tuition and fees vary according to program. *Financial support:* Application deadline: 4/1; applicants required to submit FAFSA. *Unit head:* Dr. Howard Stern, Chair, MBA Program, 412-578-8828, E-mail: hastern@carlow.edu. *Application contact:* 412-578-6059, Fax: 412-578-6321, E-mail: gradstudies@carlow.edu. Website: http://www.carlow.edu/Business_Administration.aspx

The Catholic University of America, Busch School of Business and Economics, Washington, DC 20064. Offers accounting (MS); business analysis (MSBA); integral economic development management (MA); integral economic development policy (MA); management (MS), including Federal contract management, human resource

management, leadership and management, project management, sales management. *Program availability:* Part-time. *Faculty:* 27 full-time (6 women), 45 part-time/adjunct (12 women). *Students:* 74 full-time (50 women), 9 part-time (3 women); includes 26 minority (5 Black or African American, non-Hispanic/Latino; 1 American Indian or Alaska Native, non-Hispanic/Latino; 3 Asian, non-Hispanic/Latino; 9 Hispanic/Latino; 8 Two or more races, non-Hispanic/Latino), 18 international. Average age 31. 99 applicants, 86% accepted, 61 enrolled. In 2017, 46 master's awarded. *Degree requirements:* For master's, comprehensive exam (for some programs). *Entrance requirements:* For master's, GRE General Test, statement of purpose, official copies of academic transcripts, three letters of recommendation. Additional exam requirements/recommendations for international students: Required—TOEFL (minimum score 550 paper-based; 80 iBT). *Application deadline:* For fall admission, 7/15 priority date for domestic students, 7/1 for international students; for spring admission, 11/15 priority date for domestic students, 11/1 for international students. Applications are processed on a rolling basis. Application fee: $55. Electronic applications accepted. *Expenses:* Contact institution. *Financial support:* Fellowships, research assistantships, teaching assistantships, Federal Work-Study, scholarships/grants, tuition waivers (full and partial), and unspecified assistantships available. Financial award application deadline: 2/1; financial award applicants required to submit FAFSA. *Faculty research:* Integrity of the marketing process, economics of energy and the environment, emerging markets, social change, international finance and economic development. *Total annual research expenditures:* $31,390. *Unit head:* Dr. William Bowman, Dean, 202-319-5290, Fax: 202-319-4426, E-mail: otey@cua.edu. *Application contact:* Dr. Steven Brown, Director of Graduate Admissions, 202-319-5057, Fax: 202-319-6533, E-mail: cua-admissions@cua.edu.
Website: https://business.catholic.edu/

Central Michigan University, Central Michigan University Global Campus, Program in Administration, Mount Pleasant, MI 48859. Offers acquisitions administration (MSA, Certificate); engineering management administration (MSA, Certificate); general administration (MSA, Certificate); health services administration (MSA, Certificate); human resources administration (MSA, Certificate); information resource management (MSA); information resource management administration (Certificate); international administration (MSA, Certificate); leadership (MSA, Certificate); philanthropy and fundraising administration (MSA, Certificate); public administration (MSA, Certificate); recreation and park administration (MSA); research administration (MSA, Certificate). *Program availability:* Part-time, evening/weekend, online learning. *Entrance requirements:* For master's, minimum GPA of 2.7 in major. Electronic applications accepted.

Central Michigan University, Central Michigan University Global Campus, Program in Business Administration, Mount Pleasant, MI 48859. Offers enterprise resource planning (MBA, Certificate); human resource management (MBA); logistics management (MBA, Certificate); marketing (MBA); value-driven organization (MBA). *Program availability:* Part-time, evening/weekend. *Entrance requirements:* For master's, GMAT.

Central Michigan University, College of Graduate Studies, College of Business Administration, MBA Program, Mount Pleasant, MI 48859. Offers accounting (MBA); business economics (MBA); consulting (MBA); finance (MBA); general business (MBA); human resource management (MBA); information systems (MBA); international business (MBA); logistics management (MBA); marketing (MBA); value-driven organization (MBA). *Program availability:* Part-time, evening/weekend, online learning. Electronic applications accepted. *Faculty research:* Accounting, consulting, international business, marketing, information systems.

Central Michigan University, College of Graduate Studies, Interdisciplinary Administration Programs, Mount Pleasant, MI 48859. Offers acquisitions administration (MSA, Graduate Certificate); general administration (MSA, Graduate Certificate); health services administration (MSA, Graduate Certificate); human resource administration (Graduate Certificate); human resources administration (MSA); information resource management (MSA, Graduate Certificate); international administration (MSA, Graduate Certificate); leadership (MSA, Graduate Certificate); public administration (MSA, Graduate Certificate); research administration (Graduate Certificate); sport administration (MSA). *Accreditation:* AACSB. *Program availability:* Part-time, evening/weekend, online learning. *Degree requirements:* For master's, thesis or alternative. *Entrance requirements:* For master's, bachelor's degree with minimum GPA of 2.7. Electronic applications accepted. *Faculty research:* Interdisciplinary studies in acquisitions administration, health services administration, sport administration, recreation and park administration, and international administration.

Charleston Southern University, College of Business, Charleston, SC 29423-8087. Offers accounting (MBA); finance (MBA); general management (MBA); human resource management (MS); leadership (MBA); management information systems (MBA); organizational leadership (MA). *Program availability:* Part-time, evening/weekend. *Degree requirements:* For master's, thesis optional. *Entrance requirements:* For master's, GMAT. Additional exam requirements/recommendations for international students: Required—TOEFL (minimum score 550 paper-based; 79 iBT). *Application deadline:* Applications are processed on a rolling basis. Application fee: $40. Electronic applications accepted. *Expenses: Tuition:* Part-time $500 per credit hour. One-time fee: $30. Tuition and fees vary according to program. *Financial support:* Research assistantships with full tuition reimbursements available. Financial award application deadline: 4/15; financial award applicants required to submit FAFSA. *Unit head:* Dr. David Palmer, Dean, 843-863-7025, Fax: 843-863-7922, E-mail: dpalmer@csuniv.edu. *Application contact:* Dr. Darin L. Gerdes, Associate Professor of Management, 843-863-7814, Fax: 843-863-7922, E-mail: dgerdes@csuniv.edu.
Website: http://www.csuniv.edu/business/

City University of Seattle, Graduate Division, School of Management, Seattle, WA 98121. Offers accounting (Certificate); change leadership (MBA, Certificate); computer systems (MS); finance (Certificate); financial management (MBA); general management (MBA); general management-Europe (MBA); global marketing (MBA); human resources management (Certificate); individualized study (MBA); information security (MS); information systems (MBA); leadership (MA); marketing (MBA, Certificate); project management (MBA, MS, Certificate); sustainable business (Certificate); technology management (MBA, Certificate). *Program availability:* Part-time, evening/weekend, online learning. *Degree requirements:* For master's, comprehensive exam (for some programs), thesis (for some programs). *Entrance requirements:* For master's, baccalaureate degree or equivalent from an accredited or otherwise recognized institution. Additional exam requirements/recommendations for international students: Required—TOEFL (minimum score 567 paper-based; 87 iBT); Recommended—IELTS. Electronic applications accepted.

Claremont Graduate University, Graduate Programs, School of Social Science, Policy and Evaluation, Human Resource Management Program, Claremont, CA 91711-6160. Offers MS. *Program availability:* Part-time, evening/weekend. *Entrance requirements:* For master's, GMAT or GRE General Test. Additional exam requirements/recommendations for international students: Required—TOEFL (minimum score 75 iBT). Electronic applications accepted.

Clarkson University, David D. Reh School of Business, Master's Program in Business Administration, Potsdam, NY 13699. Offers business fundamentals (Advanced Certificate); global supply chain management (Advanced Certificate); human resource management (Advanced Certificate); management and leadership (Advanced Certificate). *Accreditation:* AACSB. *Program availability:* Part-time, evening/weekend, 100% online, blended/hybrid learning. *Faculty:* 55 full-time (14 women), 38 part-time/adjunct (10 women). *Students:* 92 full-time (31 women), 50 part-time (24 women); includes 20 minority (5 Black or African American, non-Hispanic/Latino; 1 American Indian or Alaska Native, non-Hispanic/Latino; 8 Asian, non-Hispanic/Latino; 5 Hispanic/Latino; 1 Two or more races, non-Hispanic/Latino), 11 international. 174 applicants, 55% accepted, 67 enrolled. In 2017, 1 Advanced Certificate awarded. *Entrance requirements:* Additional exam requirements/recommendations for international students: Required—TOEFL (minimum score 550 paper-based, 80 iBT) or IELTS (6.5). *Application deadline:* Applications are processed on a rolling basis. Application fee: $50. Electronic applications accepted. *Expenses:* Tuition: Full-time $24,210; part-time $1345 per credit hour. Tuition and fees vary according to campus/location and program. *Financial support:* Scholarships/grants available. *Unit head:* Dr. Alan Bowman, Senior Associate Dean of Graduate Business Programs, 518-631-9887, E-mail: abowman@clarkson.edu. *Application contact:* Dan Capogna, Director of Graduate Admissions, 518-631-9910, E-mail: graduate@clarkson.edu.
Website: https://www.clarkson.edu/academics/graduate

Clayton State University, School of Graduate Studies, College of Business, Program in Business Administration, Morrow, GA 30260-0285. Offers accounting (MBA); human resource leadership (MBA); international business (MBA); sports and entertainment management (MBA); supply chain management (MBA). *Accreditation:* AACSB. *Program availability:* Part-time, evening/weekend. *Degree requirements:* For master's, thesis. *Entrance requirements:* For master's, GMAT, 3 letters of recommendation; statement of purpose; 2 official transcripts. Additional exam requirements/recommendations for international students: Required—TOEFL (minimum score 550 paper-based; 80 iBT). Electronic applications accepted. *Expenses:* Contact institution.

Cleveland State University, College of Graduate Studies, Monte Ahuja College of Business, Department of Management, Cleveland, OH 44115. Offers health care administration (MBA); labor relations and human resources (MLRHR). *Program availability:* Part-time, evening/weekend. *Faculty:* 6 full-time (3 women), 8 part-time/adjunct (1 woman). *Students:* 101 full-time (45 women), 41 part-time (22 women); includes 19 minority (9 Black or African American, non-Hispanic/Latino; 6 Asian, non-Hispanic/Latino; 3 Hispanic/Latino; 1 Two or more races, non-Hispanic/Latino), 81 international. Average age 27. In 2017, 12 master's awarded. *Entrance requirements:* For master's, GMAT or GRE, minimum GPA of 3.0. Additional exam requirements/recommendations for international students: Required—TOEFL (minimum score 550 paper-based; 78 iBT). *Application deadline:* For fall admission, 7/15 for domestic students; for spring admission, 12/15 for domestic students. Applications are processed on a rolling basis. Application fee: $40. Electronic applications accepted. *Financial support:* In 2017–18, 3 students received support. Career-related internships or fieldwork, scholarships/grants, and unspecified assistantships available. Financial award application deadline: 5/1; financial award applicants required to submit FAFSA. *Faculty research:* Employee selection, individual differences, leadership, emotions, interviews. *Unit head:* Dr. Kenneth J. Dunegan, Chairperson, 216-687-4747, Fax: 216-687-4708, E-mail: t.degroot@csuohio.edu. *Application contact:* Lisa Marie Sample, Administrative Assistant, 216-687-4726, Fax: 216-687-6888, E-mail: l.m.sample@csuohio.edu.
Website: https://www.csuohio.edu/business/management/management

College of Saint Elizabeth, Department of Business Administration and Management, Morristown, NJ 07960-6989. Offers human resource management (MS); organizational change (MS). *Program availability:* Part-time. *Faculty:* 1 (woman) full-time, 5 part-time/adjunct (3 women). *Students:* 5 full-time (all women), 19 part-time (14 women); includes 8 minority (4 Black or African American, non-Hispanic/Latino; 1 Asian, non-Hispanic/Latino; 2 Hispanic/Latino; 1 Two or more races, non-Hispanic/Latino), 3 international. Average age 37. 11 applicants, 100% accepted, 5 enrolled. In 2017, 5 master's awarded. *Degree requirements:* For master's, thesis. *Entrance requirements:* Additional exam requirements/recommendations for international students: Required—TOEFL (minimum score 550 paper-based; 79 iBT), IELTS (minimum score 6.5). *Application deadline:* For fall admission, 5/1 for international students. Applications are processed on a rolling basis. Application fee: $35. Electronic applications accepted. Application fee is waived when completed online. *Financial support:* Career-related internships or fieldwork, scholarships/grants, tuition waivers (partial), and unspecified assistantships available. Financial award applicants required to submit FAFSA. *Unit head:* Dr. Regina Riccioni, Program Chair and Director, 973-290-4271, E-mail: rriccioni@cse.edu. *Application contact:* Lori J. Fragoso, Director of Graduate and Continuing Studies Admissions, 973-290-4413, Fax: 973-290-4710, E-mail: apply@cse.edu.
Website: http://www.cse.edu/academics/prof-studies/

Colorado State University–Global Campus, Graduate Programs, Greenwood Village, CO 80111. Offers criminal justice and law enforcement administration (MS); education leadership (MS); finance (MS); healthcare administration and management (MS); human resource management (MHRM); information technology management (MITM); international management (MS); management (MS); organizational leadership (MS); professional accounting (MPA); project management (MS); teaching and learning (MS). *Accreditation:* ACBSP. *Program availability:* Online learning.

Colorado Technical University Aurora, Programs in Business Administration and Management, Aurora, CO 80014. Offers accounting (MBA); business administration (MBA); business administration and management (EMBA); finance (MBA); human resource management (MBA); marketing (MBA); mediation and dispute resolution (MBA); operations management (MBA); project management (MBA); technology management (MBA). *Program availability:* Part-time, evening/weekend. *Degree requirements:* For master's, thesis or alternative. *Entrance requirements:* For master's, minimum undergraduate GPA of 3.0, resume.

Colorado Technical University Colorado Springs, Graduate Studies, Program in Management, Colorado Springs, CO 80907. Offers accounting (MBA, MSA); business administration (MBA); finance (MBA); human resources management (MBA); logistics/supply chain management (MBA); management (DM); marketing (MBA); mediation and dispute resolution (MBA); operations management (MBA); project management (MBA); technology management (MBA). *Accreditation:* ACBSP. *Program availability:* Part-time, evening/weekend, online learning. *Degree requirements:* For master's, thesis or alternative; for doctorate, thesis/dissertation. *Entrance requirements:* For doctorate, minimum graduate GPA of 3.0, 5 years of related work experience. *Faculty research:* Sexual harassment, performance evaluation, critical thinking.

Columbia College, Master of Business Administration Program, Columbia, MO 65216-0002. Offers accounting (MBA); business administration (MBA); human resources (MBA). *Program availability:* Part-time, evening/weekend, 100% online, blended/hybrid learning. *Faculty:* 7 full-time (0 women), 76 part-time/adjunct (26 women). *Students:* 53 full-time (37 women), 389 part-time (241 women); includes 114 minority (60 Black or African American, non-Hispanic/Latino; 2 American Indian or Alaska Native, non-Hispanic/Latino; 7 Asian, non-Hispanic/Latino; 28 Hispanic/Latino; 1 Native Hawaiian or other Pacific Islander, non-Hispanic/Latino; 16 Two or more races, non-Hispanic/Latino),

22 international. Average age 37. 368 applicants, 99% accepted, 111 enrolled. In 2017, 209 master's awarded. *Entrance requirements:* For master's, 3 letters of recommendation, minimum cumulative undergraduate GPA of 3.0, resume, goal statement. Additional exam requirements/recommendations for international students: Required—TOEFL (minimum score 550 paper-based; 79 iBT). *Application deadline:* For fall admission, 8/9 priority date for domestic and international students; for spring admission, 12/27 priority date for domestic and international students. Applications are processed on a rolling basis. Application fee: $55. Electronic applications accepted. *Expenses:* Contact institution. *Financial support:* In 2017–18, 27 students received support. Federal Work-Study and scholarships/grants available. Financial award application deadline: 3/1; financial award applicants required to submit FAFSA. *Unit head:* Dr. Shanda Davis, Dean, School of Business Administration, 573-875-7561, Fax: 573-876-4493, E-mail: sdavis19@ccis.edu. *Application contact:* Stephanie Johnson, Director of Admissions, 573-875-7352, Fax: 573-875-7506, E-mail: sjohnson@ccis.edu. Website: http://www.ccis.edu/graduate/academics/degrees.asp?MBA

Columbia Southern University, MBA Program, Orange Beach, AL 36561. Offers finance (MBA); health care management (MBA); human resource management (MBA); marketing (MBA); project management (MBA); public administration (MBA). *Program availability:* Part-time, evening/weekend, online learning. *Entrance requirements:* For master's, bachelor's degree from accredited/approved institution. Additional exam requirements/recommendations for international students: Required—TOEFL. Electronic applications accepted.

Columbia University, Graduate School of Business, MBA Program, New York, NY 10027. Offers accounting (MBA); decision, risk, and operations (MBA); entrepreneurship (MBA); finance and economics (MBA); healthcare and pharmaceutical management (MBA); human resource management (MBA); international business (MBA); leadership and ethics (MBA); management (MBA); marketing (MBA); media (MBA); private equity (MBA); real estate (MBA); social enterprise (MBA); value investing (MBA); DDS/MBA; JD/MBA; MBA/MIA; MBA/MPH; MBA/MS; MD/MBA. *Entrance requirements:* For master's, GMAT, 2 letters of recommendation. Additional exam requirements/recommendations for international students: Required—TOEFL. Electronic applications accepted. *Expenses:* Contact institution. *Faculty research:* Human decision making and behavioral research; real estate market and mortgage defaults; financial crisis and corporate governance; international business; security analysis and accounting.

Columbus State University, Graduate Studies, Turner College of Business, Columbus, GA 31907-5645. Offers applied computer science (MS), including informational assurance, modeling and simulation, software development; business administration (MBA); cyber security (MS); human resource management (Certificate); information systems security (Certificate); modeling and simulation (Certificate); organizational leadership (MS), including human resource management, leader development, servant leadership; servant leadership (Certificate). *Accreditation:* AACSB. *Program availability:* Part-time, evening/weekend, 100% online, blended/hybrid learning. *Faculty:* 20 full-time (5 women), 1 (woman) part-time/adjunct. *Students:* 70 full-time (20 women), 134 part-time (44 women); includes 76 minority (34 Black or African American, non-Hispanic/Latino; 2 American Indian or Alaska Native, non-Hispanic/Latino; 11 Asian, non-Hispanic/Latino; 20 Hispanic/Latino; 9 Two or more races, non-Hispanic/Latino), 30 international. Average age 30. 218 applicants, 56% accepted, 73 enrolled. In 2017, 110 master's, 1 other advanced degree awarded. *Entrance requirements:* For master's, GMAT, GRE, minimum undergraduate GPA of 2.75, letters of recommendation. Additional exam requirements/recommendations for international students: Required—TOEFL (minimum score 550 paper-based; 79 iBT). *Application deadline:* For fall admission, 6/30 for domestic students, 5/1 for international students; for spring admission, 11/1 for domestic and international students; for summer admission, 3/1 for domestic and international students. Applications are processed on a rolling basis. Application fee: $50. Electronic applications accepted. *Expenses:* Contact institution. *Financial support:* In 2017–18, 20 students received support, including 18 research assistantships (averaging $3,000 per year); Federal Work-Study also available. Financial award application deadline: 5/1; financial award applicants required to submit FAFSA. *Unit head:* Dr. Linda U. Hadley, Dean, 706-507-8153, Fax: 706-568-2184, E-mail: hadley_linda@columbusstate.edu. *Application contact:* Catrina Smith-Edmond, Assistant Director for Graduate and Global Admission, 706-507-8824, Fax: 706-568-5091, E-mail: smithedmond_catrina@columbusstate.edu.
Website: http://turner.columbusstate.edu/

Concordia University, St. Paul, College of Business and Technology, St. Paul, MN 55104-5494. Offers business administration (MBA), including cyber-security leadership; health care management (MBA); human resource management (MA); information technology (MBA); leadership and management (MA); strategic communication management (MA). *Accreditation:* ACBSP. *Program availability:* Part-time, evening/weekend, 100% online, blended/hybrid learning. *Faculty:* 12 full-time (5 women), 33 part-time/adjunct (16 women). *Students:* 475 full-time (293 women), 35 part-time (17 women); includes 122 minority (57 Black or African American, non-Hispanic/Latino; 1 American Indian or Alaska Native, non-Hispanic/Latino; 34 Asian, non-Hispanic/Latino; 12 Hispanic/Latino; 1 Native Hawaiian or other Pacific Islander, non-Hispanic/Latino; 17 Two or more races, non-Hispanic/Latino), 47 international. Average age 33. 203 applicants, 70% accepted, 136 enrolled. In 2017, 172 master's awarded. *Degree requirements:* For master's, thesis (for some programs). *Entrance requirements:* For master's, official transcripts from regionally-accredited institution stating the conferral of a bachelor's degree with minimum cumulative GPA of 3.0; personal statement; professional resume. Additional exam requirements/recommendations for international students: Recommended—TOEFL (minimum score 547 paper-based; 78 iBT), IELTS (minimum score 6). *Application deadline:* For fall admission, 8/1 for domestic and international students; for spring admission, 12/1 for domestic and international students; for summer admission, 5/1 for domestic and international students. Applications are processed on a rolling basis. Application fee: $0. Electronic applications accepted. *Expenses:* $625 per credit (for MBA); $475 per credit (for MA). *Financial support:* In 2017–18, 292 students received support. Scholarships/grants and unspecified assistantships available. Financial award applicants required to submit FAFSA. *Faculty research:* Alternative dispute resolution, franchising, entrepreneurship, applied business ethics, strategic leadership development. *Unit head:* Dr. Kevin Hall, Dean, 651-603-6165, Fax: 651-641-8807, E-mail: khall@csp.edu. *Application contact:* Amber Faletti, Director of Enrollment Management, 651-641-8838, Fax: 651-603-6320, E-mail: faletti@csp.edu.

Concordia University Wisconsin, Graduate Programs, School of Business Administration, MBA Program, Mequon, WI 53097-2402. Offers finance (MBA); health care administration (MBA); human resource management (MBA); international business (MBA); international business-bilingual English/Chinese (MBA); management (MBA); management information systems (MBA); managerial communications (MBA); marketing (MBA); public administration (MBA); risk management (MBA). *Program availability:* Online learning. *Degree requirements:* For master's, comprehensive exam, thesis or alternative. *Entrance requirements:* Additional exam requirements/recommendations for international students: Required—TOEFL. *Expenses:* Contact institution.

Human Resources Management

Cornell University, Graduate School, Graduate Fields of Industrial and Labor Relations, Ithaca, NY 14853. Offers collective bargaining, labor law and labor history (MILR, MPS, MS, PhD); economic and social statistics (MILR); human resource studies (MILR, MPS, MS, PhD); industrial and labor relations problems (MILR, MPS, MS, PhD); international and comparative labor (MILR, MPS, MS, PhD); labor economics (MILR, MPS, MS, PhD); organizational behavior (MILR, MPS, MS, PhD). *Degree requirements:* For master's, thesis (MS); for doctorate, comprehensive exam, thesis/dissertation, teaching experience. *Entrance requirements:* For master's and doctorate, GMAT or GRE General Test, 2 academic recommendations. Additional exam requirements/recommendations for international students: Required—TOEFL (minimum score 550 paper-based; 77 iBT). Electronic applications accepted. *Expenses:* Contact institution.

Dallas Baptist University, College of Business, Management Program, Dallas, TX 75211-9299. Offers conflict resolution management (MA); general management (MA, MS); health care management (MA); human resource management (MA); organizational communication (MA); performance management (MA); professional sales and management optimization (MA). *Program availability:* Part-time, evening/weekend, online learning. *Application deadline:* Applications are processed on a rolling basis. Application fee: $25. Electronic applications accepted. Application fee is waived when completed online. *Expenses: Tuition:* Full-time $16,308; part-time $906 per credit hour. *Required fees:* $900; $450 per semester. Tuition and fees vary according to course load and degree level. *Unit head:* Dr. Sandra Reid, Chair, Graduate School of Business, 214-333-6860, E-mail: sandra@dbu.edu. *Application contact:* Richard Nassar, Director, 214-333-6801, E-mail: richardn@dbu.edu.
Website: http://www.dbu.edu/gsb/ma-in-management

Davenport University, Sneden Graduate School, Grand Rapids, MI 49512. Offers accounting (MBA); business administration (EMBA); finance (MBA); health care management (MBA); human resources (MBA); information assurance (MS); public health (MPH); strategic management (MBA). *Program availability:* Evening/weekend. *Entrance requirements:* For master's, GMAT, minimum undergraduate GPA of 2.75. Additional exam requirements/recommendations for international students: Required—TOEFL. Electronic applications accepted. *Faculty research:* Leadership, management, marketing, organizational culture.

Delaware Valley University, MBA Program, Doylestown, PA 18901-2697. Offers accounting (MBA); entrepreneurship (MBA); finance (MBA); food and agribusiness (MBA); general business (MBA); global executive leadership (MBA); human resource management (MBA); supply chain management (MBA). *Program availability:* Part-time, evening/weekend, online learning. *Entrance requirements:* For master's, minimum undergraduate GPA of 3.0. Electronic applications accepted. *Expenses:* Contact institution.

DePaul University, Kellstadt Graduate School of Business, Chicago, IL 60604. Offers accountancy (MBA, MSA); applied economics (MBA); audit and advisory services (MS); business administration (DBA); business analytics (MS); business strategy and decision-making (MBA); computational finance (MS); economics and policy analysis (MS); enterprise risk management (MS); entrepreneurship (MBA, MS); finance (MBA, MS); general business (MBA); hospitality leadership (MBA); hospitality leadership and operational performance (MS); human resources (MS); international business (MBA); management (MBA, MS); management information systems (MBA); marketing (MBA, MS); marketing analysis (MS); marketing strategy and planning (MBA); real estate (MS); real estate finance and investment (MBA); strategy, execution and valuation (MBA); supply chain management (MS); sustainable management (MS); taxation (MS); JD/MBA. *Accreditation:* AACSB. *Program availability:* Part-time, evening/weekend, online learning. *Entrance requirements:* For master's, GMAT/GRE, 2 letters of recommendation, resume, essay, official transcripts. Additional exam requirements/recommendations for international students: Required—TOEFL (minimum score 550 paper-based; 80 iBT). *Application deadline:* For fall admission, 7/1 for domestic students, 6/1 for international students; for winter admission, 10/1 for domestic students, 9/1 for international students; for spring admission, 2/1 for domestic students, 1/1 for international students. Applications are processed on a rolling basis. Application fee: $60. Electronic applications accepted. *Expenses:* Contact institution. *Financial support:* Application deadline: 4/1; applicants required to submit FAFSA. *Unit head:* Christa Hinton, Assistant Dean and Director, 312-362-8810, Fax: 312-362-6677, E-mail: chinton@depaul.edu. *Application contact:* Garry Cooke, Director of Recruitment and Admissions, 312-362-8810, Fax: 312-362-6677, E-mail: kgsb@depaul.edu.
Website: http://kellstadt.depaul.edu

DeSales University, Division of Business, Center Valley, PA 18034-9568. Offers accounting (MBA); computer information systems (MBA); finance (MBA); health care systems management (MBA); human resources management (MBA); management (MBA); marketing (MBA); project management (MBA); self-design (MBA); supply chain management (MBA); DNP/MBA; MSN/MBA. *Accreditation:* ACBSP. *Program availability:* Part-time, evening/weekend, 100% online, blended/hybrid learning. *Faculty:* 9 full-time (3 women), 32 part-time/adjunct (8 women). *Students:* 78 full-time (44 women), 323 part-time (164 women); includes 71 minority (22 Black or African American, non-Hispanic/Latino; 17 Asian, non-Hispanic/Latino; 24 Hispanic/Latino; 8 Two or more races, non-Hispanic/Latino), 1 international. Average age 34. 213 applicants, 40% accepted, 64 enrolled. In 2017, 123 master's awarded. *Entrance requirements:* For master's, GMAT (waived if undergraduate GPA is 3.0 or better), minimum GPA of 3.0 in undergraduate work, literacy in basic software, background or interest in the field of study, personal statement, 2 years of work experience. Additional exam requirements/recommendations for international students: Required—TOEFL. *Application deadline:* Applications are processed on a rolling basis. Application fee: $50. Electronic applications accepted. *Expenses:* Contact institution. *Financial support:* Applicants required to submit FAFSA. *Faculty research:* Quality improvement, executive development, productivity, cross-cultural managerial differences, leadership. *Unit head:* Dr. David M. Gilfoil, Director, MBA Program, 610-282-1100 Ext. 1828, Fax: 610-282-2869, E-mail: david.gilfoil@desales.edu. *Application contact:* Julia Ferraro, Director of Graduate Admissions, 610-282-1100 Ext. 1768, E-mail: gradadmissions@desales.edu.

DeVry University–Folsom Campus, Graduate Programs, Folsom, CA 95630. Offers accounting (M Acc); accounting and financial management (MAFM); business administration (MBA); curriculum leadership (M Ed); educational leadership (M Ed); educational technology (M Ed); higher education leadership (M Ed); human resource management (MHRM); information systems management (MISM); network and communications management (MNCM); project management (MPM); public administration (MPA).

East Central University, School of Graduate Studies, Department of Professional Programs in Human Services, Ada, OK 74820. Offers clinical rehabilitation and clinical mental health counseling (MSHR); criminal justice (MSHR); human resources (MSHR). *Accreditation:* CORE. *Program availability:* Part-time, evening/weekend. *Degree requirements:* For master's, thesis optional. *Entrance requirements:* For master's, GRE General Test, MAT, minimum GPA of 2.5. *Application deadline:* Applications are processed on a rolling basis. Application fee: $0 ($50 for international students). Electronic applications accepted. *Unit head:* Regina Robertson, Chair, 580-559-5647, E-mail: rrobrtsn@ecok.edu. *Application contact:* Regina Robertson, Chair, 580-559-5647, E-mail: rrobrtsn@ecok.edu.

Website: http://www.ecok.edu/academics/colleges-and-schools/college-liberal-arts-and-social-sciences/department-human-resources

Eastern Michigan University, Graduate School, College of Business, Department of Management, Program in Human Resources Management and Organizational Development, Ypsilanti, MI 48197. Offers MSHROD. *Program availability:* Part-time, evening/weekend, online learning. *Students:* 10 full-time (4 women), 58 part-time (40 women); includes 19 minority (11 Black or African American, non-Hispanic/Latino; 2 Asian, non-Hispanic/Latino; 3 Hispanic/Latino; 3 Two or more races, non-Hispanic/Latino), 4 international. Average age 31. 41 applicants, 76% accepted, 18 enrolled. In 2017, 92 master's awarded. *Degree requirements:* For master's, thesis optional. *Entrance requirements:* For master's, GMAT. Additional exam requirements/recommendations for international students: Required—TOEFL. *Application deadline:* Applications are processed on a rolling basis. Application fee: $45. *Financial support:* Fellowships, research assistantships with full tuition reimbursements, teaching assistantships with full tuition reimbursements, career-related internships or fieldwork, Federal Work-Study, institutionally sponsored loans, scholarships/grants, tuition waivers (partial), and unspecified assistantships available. Support available to part-time students. Financial award applicants required to submit FAFSA. *Unit head:* Dr. Fraya Wagner-Marsh, Department Head, 734-487-3240, Fax: 734-487-4100, E-mail: fraya.wagner@emich.edu.
Website: http://www.emich.edu/cob/departments_centers/management/mshrod.php

Eastern Michigan University, Graduate School, College of Business, Programs in Business Administration, Ypsilanti, MI 48197. Offers business administration (MBA, Graduate Certificate); computer information systems (Graduate Certificate); e-business (MBA, Graduate Certificate); enterprise business intelligence (MBA); entrepreneurship (MBA, Graduate Certificate); finance (MBA, Graduate Certificate); human resources (MBA); human resources management (Graduate Certificate); information systems (MBA); internal auditing (MBA); international business (MBA, Graduate Certificate); marketing management (Graduate Certificate); nonprofit management (MBA); organizational development (Graduate Certificate); supply chain management (MBA, Graduate Certificate). *Accreditation:* AACSB. *Program availability:* Part-time, online learning. *Students:* 53 full-time (30 women), 297 part-time (170 women); includes 121 minority (72 Black or African American, non-Hispanic/Latino; 4 American Indian or Alaska Native, non-Hispanic/Latino; 15 Asian, non-Hispanic/Latino; 20 Hispanic/Latino; 10 Two or more races, non-Hispanic/Latino), 20 international. Average age 31. 247 applicants, 74% accepted, 94 enrolled. In 2017, 71 master's, 34 other advanced degrees awarded. *Entrance requirements:* For master's, GMAT (minimum score 450), minimum cumulative undergraduate GPA of 2.75. Additional exam requirements/recommendations for international students: Required—TOEFL. *Application deadline:* For fall admission, 5/15 priority date for domestic students, 2/15 priority date for international students; for winter admission, 10/15 priority date for domestic students, 9/1 priority date for international students; for summer admission, 3/15 priority date for domestic students, 3/1 priority date for international students. Applications are processed on a rolling basis. Application fee: $45. *Financial support:* Fellowships, research assistantships with full tuition reimbursements, teaching assistantships with full tuition reimbursements, career-related internships or fieldwork, Federal Work-Study, institutionally sponsored loans, scholarships/grants, tuition waivers (partial), and unspecified assistantships available. Support available to part-time students. Financial award applicants required to submit FAFSA. *Unit head:* K. Michelle Henry, Director, Graduate Business Programs, 734-487-4444, Fax: 734-483-1316, E-mail: cob.graduate@emich.edu.
Website: http://www.emich.edu/cob/mba/

Embry-Riddle Aeronautical University–Daytona, College of Business, Daytona Beach, FL 32114-3900. Offers airline management (MBA); airport management (MBA); aviation finance (MSAF); aviation human resources (MBA); aviation management (MBA-AM); aviation system management (MBA); finance (MBA). *Accreditation:* ACBSP. *Faculty:* 14 full-time (2 women). *Students:* 95 full-time (31 women), 19 part-time (8 women); includes 15 minority (5 Black or African American, non-Hispanic/Latino; 1 Asian, non-Hispanic/Latino; 1 Hispanic/Latino; 8 Two or more races, non-Hispanic/Latino), 65 international. Average age 27. 141 applicants, 38% accepted, 41 enrolled. In 2017, 49 master's awarded. *Degree requirements:* For master's, thesis (for some programs). *Entrance requirements:* For master's, GRE (for some programs). Additional exam requirements/recommendations for international students: Required—TOEFL (minimum score 550 paper-based, 79 iBT) or IELTS (6). *Application deadline:* For fall admission, 1/15 priority date for domestic students; for spring admission, 11/1 priority date for domestic students; for summer admission, 4/1 priority date for domestic students. Applications are processed on a rolling basis. Application fee: $50. Electronic applications accepted. *Expenses: Tuition:* Full-time $16,704; part-time $1392 per credit hour. *Required fees:* $1314; $657 per semester. Tuition and fees vary according to degree level. *Financial support:* Research assistantships, teaching assistantships, career-related internships or fieldwork, scholarships/grants, unspecified assistantships, and on-campus employment available. Financial award application deadline: 3/15; financial award applicants required to submit FAFSA. *Unit head:* Michael J. Williams, PhD, Dean of the College of Business and Professor of Information Systems, 386-226-6293, E-mail: michael.williams@erau.edu. *Application contact:* Graduate Admissions, 386-226-6176, E-mail: graduate.admissions@erau.edu.
Website: https://daytonabeach.erau.edu/college-business/index.html

Embry-Riddle Aeronautical University–Worldwide, Department of Decision Sciences, Daytona Beach, FL 32114-3900. Offers aviation and aerospace (MSPM); aviation/aerospace management (MSEM); financial management (MSEM, MSPM); general management (MSPM); global management (MSPM); human resources management (MSPM); information systems (MSEM, MSPM); leadership (MSEM, MSPM); logistics and supply chain management (MSEM, MSLSCM, MSPM); management (MSEM, MSPM); project management (MSEM); systems engineering (MSEM, MSPM); technical management (MSPM). *Program availability:* Part-time, evening/weekend, EagleVision Classroom (between classrooms), EagleVision Home (faculty and students at home), and a blend of Classroom or Home. *Faculty:* 12 full-time (3 women), 53 part-time/adjunct (10 women). *Students:* 514 full-time (141 women), 476 part-time (111 women); includes 337 minority (136 Black or African American, non-Hispanic/Latino; 6 American Indian or Alaska Native, non-Hispanic/Latino; 39 Asian, non-Hispanic/Latino; 81 Hispanic/Latino; 4 Native Hawaiian or other Pacific Islander, non-Hispanic/Latino; 71 Two or more races, non-Hispanic/Latino), 21 international. Average age 36. 297 applicants, 72% accepted, 209 enrolled. In 2017, 292 master's awarded. *Degree requirements:* For master's, comprehensive exam (for some programs), thesis (for some programs). *Entrance requirements:* Additional exam requirements/recommendations for international students: Required—TOEFL (minimum score 550 paper-based; 79 iBT), IELTS (minimum score 6). *Application deadline:* Applications are processed on a rolling basis. Application fee: $50. Electronic applications accepted. *Expenses:* Contact institution. *Financial support:* Career-related internships or fieldwork and scholarships/grants available. Financial award applicants required to submit FAFSA. *Unit head:* Aman Gupta, PhD, Department Chair, E-mail: aman.gupta@erau.edu. *Application contact:* Worldwide Campus, 800-522-6787, E-mail: worldwide@erau.edu.

Embry-Riddle Aeronautical University–Worldwide, Department of Management, Daytona Beach, FL 32114-3900. Offers global management (MS); human resources management (MS); leadership (MS); operations management (MS); project management (MS). *Program availability:* Part-time, evening/weekend, EagleVision Classroom (between classrooms), EagleVision Home (faculty and students at home), and a blend of Classroom or Home. *Students:* 148 full-time (48 women), 192 part-time (52 women); includes 91 minority (46 Black or African American, non-Hispanic/Latino; 1 American Indian or Alaska Native, non-Hispanic/Latino; 11 Asian, non-Hispanic/Latino; 16 Hispanic/Latino; 17 Two or more races, non-Hispanic/Latino), 7 international. Average age 39. In 2017, 104 master's awarded. *Entrance requirements:* Additional exam requirements/recommendations for international students: Required—TOEFL (minimum score 550 paper-based, 79 iBT) or IELTS (6). *Application deadline:* Applications are processed on a rolling basis. Application fee: $50. Electronic applications accepted. *Expenses:* Contact institution. *Financial support:* Career-related internships or fieldwork and scholarships/grants available. Financial award applicants required to submit FAFSA. *Unit head:* Thomas Henkel, PhD, Department Chair, E-mail: thomas.henkel@erau.edu. *Application contact:* Worldwide Campus, 800-522-6787, E-mail: worldwide@erau.edu.

Emmanuel College, Graduate and Professional Programs, Graduate Programs in Human Resource Management, Boston, MA 02115. Offers MS, Graduate Certificate. *Program availability:* Part-time, evening/weekend, blended/hybrid learning. *Faculty:* 9 part-time/adjunct (2 women). *Students:* 3 full-time (2 women), 34 part-time (29 women); includes 9 minority (4 Black or African American, non-Hispanic/Latino; 5 Hispanic/Latino). Average age 33. 16 applicants, 44% accepted, 6 enrolled. In 2017, 18 master's, 3 other advanced degrees awarded. *Degree requirements:* For master's, 36 credits. *Entrance requirements:* For master's and Graduate Certificate, transcripts from all regionally-accredited institutions attended (showing proof of bachelor's degree completion), 2 letters of recommendation, essay, resume. Additional exam requirements/recommendations for international students: Required—TOEFL. *Application deadline:* Applications are processed on a rolling basis. Electronic applications accepted. *Expenses:* $24,112 (for MS); $13,152 (for Graduate Certificate). *Financial support:* Application deadline: 2/15; applicants required to submit FAFSA. *Unit head:* Cindy O'Callaghan, Dean of Academic Administration and Graduate and Professional Programs, 617-735-9700, E-mail: gpp@emmanuel.edu. *Application contact:* Helen Muterperl, Director of Graduate and Professional Programs, 617-735-9700, Fax: 617-507-0434, E-mail: gpp@emmanuel.edu.
Website: http://www.emmanuel.edu/graduate-professional-programs/academics/management/human-resource-management.html

Everglades University, Graduate Programs, Program in Business Administration, Boca Raton, FL 33431. Offers accounting for managers (MBA); aviation management (MBA); human resource management (MBA); project management (MBA). *Program availability:* Part-time, evening/weekend, 100% online. *Entrance requirements:* For master's, GMAT (minimum score of 400) or GRE (minimum score of 290), bachelor's or graduate degree from college accredited by an agency recognized by the U.S. Department of Education; minimum cumulative GPA of 2.0 at the baccalaureate level, 3.0 at the master's level. Additional exam requirements/recommendations for international students: Recommended—TOEFL (minimum score 500 paper-based). Electronic applications accepted. *Expenses:* Contact institution.

Excelsior College, School of Business and Technology, Albany, NY 12203-5159. Offers business administration (MBA); cybersecurity - information assurance (MS); cybersecurity - medical data security (MS); cybersecurity - policy administration (MS); cybersecurity management (MBA, Graduate Certificate); general business management (MS); health care management (MBA); human performance technology (MBA); human resource management (MS); human resources management (MBA); leadership (MBA, MS); mediation and arbitration (MBA, MS); social media management (MBA); technology management (MBA). *Program availability:* Part-time, evening/weekend, online learning. *Faculty:* 30 part-time/adjunct (12 women). *Students:* 1,204 part-time (333 women); includes 560 minority (310 Black or African American, non-Hispanic/Latino; 7 American Indian or Alaska Native, non-Hispanic/Latino; 42 Asian, non-Hispanic/Latino; 140 Hispanic/Latino; 10 Native Hawaiian or other Pacific Islander, non-Hispanic/Latino; 51 Two or more races, non-Hispanic/Latino). Average age 40. In 2017, 294 master's awarded. *Application deadline:* Applications are processed on a rolling basis. Application fee: $50. Electronic applications accepted. *Expenses: Tuition:* Part-time $645 per credit. *Required fees:* $265 per credit. *Financial support:* Scholarships/grants available. *Unit head:* Dr. Lifang Shih, Dean, 888-647-2388. *Application contact:* Admissions, 888-647-2388 Ext. 133, Fax: 518-464-8777, E-mail: admissions@excelsior.edu.

Fairleigh Dickinson University, Florham Campus, Silberman College of Business, Center for Human Resource Management Studies, Program in Human Resource Management, Madison, NJ 07940-1099. Offers MBA, MA/MBA.

Fairleigh Dickinson University, Metropolitan Campus, Silberman College of Business, Center for Human Resources Management Studies, Program in Human Resource Management, Teaneck, NJ 07666-1914. Offers MBA, Certificate.

Fitchburg State University, Division of Graduate and Continuing Education, Program in Business Administration, Fitchburg, MA 01420-2697. Offers accounting (MBA); human resources management (MBA); management (MBA). *Program availability:* Part-time, evening/weekend, 100% online. *Faculty:* 7 full-time (2 women), 6 part-time/adjunct (2 women). *Students:* 356 full-time (179 women), 129 part-time (71 women); includes 132 minority (55 Black or African American, non-Hispanic/Latino; 1 American Indian or Alaska Native, non-Hispanic/Latino; 29 Asian, non-Hispanic/Latino; 42 Hispanic/Latino; 5 Two or more races, non-Hispanic/Latino). Average age 35. 332 applicants, 97% accepted, 259 enrolled. In 2017, 39 master's awarded. *Entrance requirements:* Additional exam requirements/recommendations for international students: Required—TOEFL (minimum score 550 paper-based; 79 iBT). *Application deadline:* For fall admission, 7/15 for international students; for spring admission, 12/1 for international students. Applications are processed on a rolling basis. Application fee: $50. Electronic applications accepted. *Expenses:* Contact institution. *Financial support:* In 2017–18, research assistantships with partial tuition reimbursements (averaging $5,500 per year) were awarded; Federal Work-Study, scholarships/grants, and unspecified assistantships also available. Support available to part-time students. Financial award application deadline: 3/1; financial award applicants required to submit FAFSA. *Unit head:* Joseph McAloon, Chair, 978-665-3745, Fax: 978-665-3658, E-mail: gce@fitchburgstate.edu. *Application contact:* Jinawa McNeil, Director of Admissions, 978-665-3140, Fax: 978-665-4540, E-mail: admissions@fitchburgstate.edu.
Website: http://www.fitchburgstate.edu

Florida Institute of Technology, Extended Studies Division, Melbourne, FL 32901-6975. Offers acquisition and contract management (MS); aerospace engineering (MS); business administration (MBA, DBA); computer information systems (MS); computer science (MS); electrical engineering (MS); engineering management (MS); human resources management (MS); logistics management (MS), including humanitarian and disaster relief logistics; management (MS), including acquisition and contract management, e-business, human resources management, information systems, logistics management, management, transportation management; material acquisition management (MS); mechanical engineering (MS); operations research (MS); project management (MS), including information systems, operations research; public administration (MPA); quality management (MS); software engineering (MS); space systems (MS); space systems management (MS); supply chain management (MS); systems management (MS), including information systems, operations research; technology management (MS). *Program availability:* Part-time, evening/weekend, online learning. *Students:* Average age 36. 962 applicants, 48% accepted, 323 enrolled. In 2017, 403 master's awarded. *Entrance requirements:* For master's, GMAT or resume showing 8 years of supervised experience, minimum GPA of 3.0, 2 letters of recommendation, resume. Additional exam requirements/recommendations for international students: Required—TOEFL (minimum score 550 paper-based; 79 iBT). *Application deadline:* For fall admission, 4/1 for international students; for spring admission, 9/30 for international students. Applications are processed on a rolling basis. Electronic applications accepted. *Expenses:* Contact institution. *Financial support:* Application deadline: 3/1; applicants required to submit FAFSA. *Unit head:* Dr. Theodore R. Richardson, III, Dean, 321-674-8123, Fax: 321-674-7597, E-mail: trichardson@fit.edu. *Application contact:* Carolyn Farrior, Director of Graduate Admissions, Online Learning and Off-Campus Programs, 321-674-7118, Fax: 321-674-8216, E-mail: cfarrior@fit.edu.
Website: http://es.fit.edu

Florida International University, Chapman Graduate School of Business, Department of Management and International Business, Miami, FL 33199. Offers human resources management (MSHRM); international business (MIB); management and international business (EMBA, IMBA, MBA, PhD). *Program availability:* Part-time, evening/weekend. *Faculty:* 28 full-time (10 women), 30 part-time/adjunct (10 women). *Students:* 970 full-time (565 women), 596 part-time (301 women); includes 1,119 minority (220 Black or African American, non-Hispanic/Latino; 45 Asian, non-Hispanic/Latino; 823 Hispanic/Latino; 5 Native Hawaiian or other Pacific Islander, non-Hispanic/Latino; 26 Two or more races, non-Hispanic/Latino), 180 international. Average age 32. 1,326 applicants, 45% accepted, 429 enrolled. In 2017, 795 master's, 13 doctorates awarded. *Degree requirements:* For doctorate, comprehensive exam, thesis/dissertation. *Entrance requirements:* For master's, GMAT or GRE (depending on program), minimum GPA of 3.0 in upper-level coursework; for doctorate, GMAT or GRE, letter of intent; 3 letters of recommendation; resume. Additional exam requirements/recommendations for international students: Required—TOEFL (minimum score 550 paper-based; 80 iBT) or IELTS (minimum score 6.5). *Application deadline:* For fall admission, 6/1 for domestic students, 4/1 for international students; for spring admission, 10/1 for domestic students, 9/1 for international students. Applications are processed on a rolling basis. Application fee: $30. Electronic applications accepted. *Expenses:* Contact institution. *Financial support:* Institutionally sponsored loans and scholarships/grants available. Financial award application deadline: 3/1; financial award applicants required to submit FAFSA. *Faculty research:* International business, strategy, entrepreneurship, human resource management. *Unit head:* Dr. Willam Newburry, Chair, 305-348-2791, E-mail: newburry@fiu.edu. *Application contact:* Jessica Aristizabal, Associate Director, Academic Support Services, 305-348-6880, E-mail: palger@fiu.edu.

Florida State University, The Graduate School, College of Business, Tallahassee, FL 32306-1110. Offers accounting (M Acc), including assurance and advisory services, generalist, taxation; business administration (MBA, PhD), including accounting (PhD), finance (PhD), management information systems (PhD), marketing (PhD), organizational behavior and human resources (PhD), risk management and insurance (PhD), strategy (PhD); finance (MS); management information systems (MS); risk management and insurance (MS); JD/MBA; MSW/MBA. *Accreditation:* AACSB. *Program availability:* Part-time, 100% online. *Faculty:* 93 full-time (23 women), 2 part-time/adjunct (1 woman). *Students:* 229 full-time (96 women), 423 part-time (154 women); includes 159 minority (44 Black or African American, non-Hispanic/Latino; 24 Asian, non-Hispanic/Latino; 75 Hispanic/Latino; 1 Native Hawaiian or other Pacific Islander, non-Hispanic/Latino; 15 Two or more races, non-Hispanic/Latino), 48 international. Average age 31. 300 applicants, 61% accepted, 133 enrolled. In 2017, 268 master's, 9 doctorates awarded. Terminal master's awarded for partial completion of doctoral program. *Degree requirements:* For doctorate, comprehensive exam, thesis/dissertation. *Entrance requirements:* For master's, GMAT, GRE (for all except MS in finance), work experience (MBA, MS); minimum GPA of 3.0, letters of recommendation; for doctorate, GMAT, GRE (for marketing, organizational behavior, risk management and insurance, management information systems, and human resources only), minimum graduate GPA of 3.5, letters of recommendation. Additional exam requirements/recommendations for international students: Required—TOEFL (minimum score 600 paper-based; 85 iBT); Recommended—IELTS (minimum score 6). *Application deadline:* For fall admission, 6/1 for domestic and international students; for spring admission, 10/1 for domestic and international students; for summer admission, 3/1 for domestic and international students. Applications are processed on a rolling basis. Application fee: $30. Electronic applications accepted. *Expenses:* Contact institution. *Financial support:* In 2017–18, 146 students received support, including 26 fellowships (averaging $1,500 per year), 77 research assistantships with full tuition reimbursements available (averaging $20,000 per year), 43 teaching assistantships with full tuition reimbursements available (averaging $20,000 per year); career-related internships or fieldwork, scholarships/grants, health care benefits, tuition waivers (full and partial), and unspecified assistantships also available. Support available to part-time students. Financial award application deadline: 1/1; financial award applicants required to submit FAFSA. *Faculty research:* Business strategy, marketing, finance, accounting, business analytics. *Total annual research expenditures:* $1.4 million. *Unit head:* Dr. Michael Hartline, Dean, 850-644-4405, Fax: 850-644-0915, E-mail: mhartline@business.fsu.edu. *Application contact:* Jennifer Clark, Director, 850-644-6458, E-mail: gradprograms@business.fsu.edu.
Website: http://business.fsu.edu/

Framingham State University, Graduate Studies, Program in Human Resource Management, Framingham, MA 01701-9101. Offers MHR. *Program availability:* Part-time, evening/weekend. *Unit head:* Dr. Robert J. Awkward, Program Coordinator, E-mail: rawkward@framingham.edu. *Application contact:* 508-626-4550, Fax: 508-626-4030, E-mail: dgce@frc.mass.edu.

Franklin Pierce University, Graduate and Professional Studies, Rindge, NH 03461-0060. Offers curriculum and instruction (M Ed); elementary education (MS Ed); emerging network technologies (Graduate Certificate); energy and sustainability studies (MBA, Graduate Certificate); health administration (MBA, Graduate Certificate); human resource management (MBA, Graduate Certificate); information technology (MBA); leadership (MBA); nursing education (MS); nursing leadership (MS); physical therapy (DPT); physician assistant studies (MPAS); special education (M Ed); sports management (MBA). *Accreditation:* APTA. *Program availability:* Part-time, 100% online, blended/hybrid learning. *Degree requirements:* For master's, concentrated original research projects; student teaching; fieldwork and/or internship; leadership project; PRAXIS I and II (for M Ed); for doctorate, concentrated original research projects, clinical fieldwork and/or internship, leadership project. *Entrance requirements:* For master's, minimum GPA of 2.5, 3 letters of recommendation; competencies in accounting, economics, statistics, and computer skills through life experience or undergraduate coursework (for MBA); certification/e-portfolio, minimum C grade in all education courses (for M Ed); license to practice as RN (for MS); for doctorate, GRE, 80 hours of observation/work in PT settings; completion of anatomy, chemistry, physics, and statistics; minimum GPA of 3.0. Additional exam requirements/recommendations for international students: Required—TOEFL (minimum score 550 paper-based; 61 iBT). Electronic applications accepted. *Faculty research:* Evidence-based practice in sports physical therapy, human resource management in economic crisis, leadership in nursing, innovation in sports facility management, differentiated learning and understanding by design.

Gannon University, School of Graduate Studies, College of Engineering and Business, Dahlkemper School of Business, Program in Business Administration, Erie, PA 16541-0001. Offers business administration (MBA); finance (MBA); human resources management (MBA); marketing (MBA). *Accreditation:* ACBSP. *Program availability:* Part-time, evening/weekend, 100% online, blended/hybrid learning. *Entrance requirements:* For master's, GMAT, bachelor's degree in any discipline from any accredited college or university, resume, transcripts, 3 letters of recommendation. Additional exam requirements/recommendations for international students: Required—TOEFL (minimum score 79 iBT). Electronic applications accepted. Application fee is waived when completed online.

George Fox University, College of Business, Newberg, OR 97132-2697. Offers accounting (DBA); finance (MBA); management (DBA); management and leadership (MBA); marketing (DBA); organizational strategy (MBA); strategic human resource management (MBA). MBA offered in Newberg, OR and in Portland, OR. *Accreditation:* ACBSP. *Program availability:* Part-time, evening/weekend, online learning. *Degree requirements:* For master's, capstone project; for doctorate, credit-applied research project. *Entrance requirements:* For master's, resume (5 years of professional experience); 3 professional references; interview; financial e-learning course; official transcripts; for doctorate, GRE or GMAT, resume; personal mission statement; academic research writing sample; official transcript from each college/university attended; three professional references. Additional exam requirements/recommendations for international students: Required—TOEFL (minimum score 577 paper-based; 90 iBT) or IELTS (minimum score 7). Electronic applications accepted. *Expenses:* Contact institution.

George Mason University, Schar School of Policy and Government, Program in Organization Development and Knowledge Management, Arlington, VA 22201. Offers MS. *Faculty:* 3 full-time (1 woman), 3 part-time/adjunct (1 woman). *Students:* 1 (woman) full-time, 47 part-time (38 women); includes 20 minority (10 Black or African American, non-Hispanic/Latino; 3 Asian, non-Hispanic/Latino; 4 Hispanic/Latino; 1 Native Hawaiian or other Pacific Islander, non-Hispanic/Latino; 2 Two or more races, non-Hispanic/Latino). Average age 35. 37 applicants, 95% accepted, 24 enrolled. In 2017, 23 master's awarded. *Degree requirements:* For master's, thesis or alternative, internship. *Entrance requirements:* For master's, GRE (for students seeking merit-based scholarships), bachelor's degree with minimum GPA of 3.0, current resume, 2 letters of recommendation, expanded goals statement, 2 copies of official transcripts. Additional exam requirements/recommendations for international students: Required—TOEFL (minimum score 575 paper-based; 88 iBT), IELTS (minimum score 6.5), PTE (minimum score 59). *Application deadline:* For fall admission, 2/1 priority date for domestic and international students. Applications are processed on a rolling basis. Application fee: $75 ($80 for international students). Electronic applications accepted. *Expenses:* $795 per credit in-state tuition, $1,516 out-of-state. *Financial support:* Career-related internships or fieldwork, Federal Work-Study, scholarships/grants, unspecified assistantships, and health care benefits (for full-time research or teaching assistantship recipients) available. Financial award application deadline: 3/1; financial award applicants required to submit FAFSA. *Faculty research:* Organization development; appreciative intelligence; leadership; collaborative learning; knowledge management. *Unit head:* Tojo Joseph Thatchenkery, Director, 703-993-3808, Fax: 703-993-8215, E-mail: thatchen@gmu.edu. *Application contact:* Stephanie Ellis, Graduate Admissions Coordinator, 703-993-4478, E-mail: sellis11@gmu.edu.
Website: http://spgia.gmu.edu/programs/graduate-degrees/organization-development-knowledge-management-odkm/

Georgetown University, Graduate School of Arts and Sciences, School of Continuing Studies, Washington, DC 20057. Offers American studies (MALS); applied intelligence (MPS); Catholic studies (MALS); classical civilizations (MALS); emergency and disaster management (MPS); ethics and the professions (MALS); global strategic communications (MPS); hospitality management (MPS); human resources management (MPS); humanities (MALS); individualized study (MALS); integrated marketing communications (MPS); international affairs (MALS); Islam and Muslim-Christian relations (MALS); journalism (MPS); liberal studies (DLS); literature and society (MALS); medieval and early modern European studies (MALS); public relations and corporate communications (MPS); real estate (MPS); religious studies (MALS); social and public policy (MALS); sports industry management (MPS); systems engineering management (MPS); technology management (MPS); the theory and practice of American democracy (MALS); urban and regional planning (MPS); visual culture (MALS). MPS in systems engineering management offered jointly with Stevens Institute of Technology. *Entrance requirements:* Additional exam requirements/recommendations for international students: Required—TOEFL.

The George Washington University, Columbian College of Arts and Sciences, Department of Organizational Sciences and Communication, Washington, DC 20052. Offers human resources management (MA); non-profit management (Graduate Certificate); organizational management (Graduate Certificate). *Program availability:* Part-time, evening/weekend. *Faculty:* 10 full-time (6 women), 6 part-time/adjunct (4 women). *Students:* 50 full-time (26 women), 26 part-time (20 women); includes 25 minority (8 Black or African American, non-Hispanic/Latino; 6 Asian, non-Hispanic/Latino; 6 Hispanic/Latino; 1 Native Hawaiian or other Pacific Islander, non-Hispanic/Latino; 4 Two or more races, non-Hispanic/Latino), 8 international. Average age 27. 138 applicants, 67% accepted, 39 enrolled. In 2017, 31 master's, 19 other advanced degrees awarded. *Degree requirements:* For master's, comprehensive exam. *Entrance requirements:* For master's, GRE General Test, minimum GPA of 3.0; for Graduate Certificate, minimum GPA of 3.0. Additional exam requirements/recommendations for international students: Required—TOEFL (minimum score 500 paper-based; 80 iBT). *Application deadline:* For fall admission, 1/15 priority date for domestic and international students; for spring admission, 10/1 priority date for domestic students, 9/1 priority date for international students. Applications are processed on a rolling basis. Application fee: $75. Electronic applications accepted. *Expenses: Tuition:* Full-time $28,800; part-time $1655 per credit hour. *Required fees:* $45; $2.75 per credit hour. *Financial support:* Federal Work-Study and institutionally sponsored loans available. *Unit head:* Dr. Lynn Offermann, Chair, 202-994-8507, E-mail: lro@gwu.edu. *Application contact:* Information Contact, 202-994-1878, Fax: 202-994-1881.
Website: http://www.gwu.edu/~orgsci/

Georgia State University, J. Mack Robinson College of Business, Department of Managerial Sciences, Atlanta, GA 30302-3083. Offers business analysis (MBA, MS); entrepreneurship (MBA); human resources management (MBA, MS); operations management (MBA, MS); organization behavior/human resource management (PhD); organization management (MBA); organizational change (MS); strategic management

(PhD). *Accreditation:* AACSB. *Program availability:* Part-time, evening/weekend. *Faculty:* 25 full-time (11 women). *Students:* 20 full-time (12 women); includes 7 minority (4 Black or African American, non-Hispanic/Latino; 2 Hispanic/Latino; 1 Two or more races, non-Hispanic/Latino), 6 international. Average age 33. 77 applicants, 18% accepted, 10 enrolled. In 2017, 25 master's, 1 doctorate awarded. *Entrance requirements:* For master's, GRE or GMAT, transcripts from all institutions attended, resume, essays; for doctorate, GMAT, three letters of recommendation, personal statement, transcripts from all institutions attended, resume. Additional exam requirements/recommendations for international students: Required—TOEFL (minimum score 610 paper-based; 101 iBT), IELTS (minimum score 7). *Application deadline:* For fall admission, 5/1 priority date for domestic students, 2/1 priority date for international students; for spring admission, 9/15 priority date for domestic students, 4/1 priority date for international students. Applications are processed on a rolling basis. Application fee: $50. Electronic applications accepted. *Expenses:* Tuition, state resident: full-time $7020. Tuition, nonresident: full-time $22,518. *Required fees:* $2128. Tuition and fees vary according to degree level and program. *Financial support:* Research assistantships, teaching assistantships, scholarships/grants, tuition waivers, and unspecified assistantships available. Financial award applicants required to submit FAFSA. *Faculty research:* Entrepreneurship and innovation; strategy process; workplace interactions, relationships, and processes; leadership and culture; supply chain management. *Unit head:* Dr. Pamela S. Barr, Interim Chair, 404-413-7525, Fax: 404-413-7571. *Application contact:* Toby McChesney, Assistant Dean for Graduate Recruiting and Student Services, 404-413-7167, Fax: 404-413-7162, E-mail: rcbgradadmissions@gsu.edu.
Website: http://mgmt.robinson.gsu.edu/

Golden Gate University, Ageno School of Business, San Francisco, CA 94105-2968. Offers accounting (MBA); adaptive leadership (MBA); advanced financial planning (MS); business administration (EMBA, MBA, DBA); business analytics (MBA, MS); entrepreneurship (MBA); finance (MBA, MS, Certificate); financial life planning (Certificate); financial planning (MS, Certificate); global supply chain management (MBA, Certificate); human resource management (MBA, MS, Certificate); information technology management (MBA, MS, Certificate); international business (MBA); marketing (MBA, MS, Certificate); project management (MBA, MS, Certificate); psychology (MA, Certificate); public administration (EMPA, MBA); public administration leadership (Certificate); JD/MBA. *Program availability:* Part-time, evening/weekend. *Faculty:* 17 full-time (7 women), 280 part-time/adjunct (95 women). *Students:* 309 full-time (147 women), 527 part-time (266 women); includes 286 minority (56 Black or African American, non-Hispanic/Latino; 1 American Indian or Alaska Native, non-Hispanic/Latino; 131 Asian, non-Hispanic/Latino; 83 Hispanic/Latino; 4 Native Hawaiian or other Pacific Islander, non-Hispanic/Latino; 11 Two or more races, non-Hispanic/Latino), 209 international. Average age 35. 549 applicants, 66% accepted, 185 enrolled. *Degree requirements:* For doctorate, thesis/dissertation, qualifying examination. *Entrance requirements:* For master's, GMAT (for MBA), minimum GPA of 2.5 (MS). Additional exam requirements/recommendations for international students: Required—TOEFL (minimum score 550 paper-based; 79 iBT). *Application deadline:* For fall admission, 5/15 for domestic and international students; for winter admission, 1/15 for domestic and international students; for spring admission, 9/15 for domestic and international students. Applications are processed on a rolling basis. Application fee: $65 ($105 for international students). Electronic applications accepted. *Expenses:* $3,150 per 3-unit course. *Financial support:* Career-related internships or fieldwork, Federal Work-Study, institutionally sponsored loans, and scholarships/grants available. Support available to part-time students. Financial award applicants required to submit FAFSA. *Unit head:* Marianne Koch, Associate Dean, 415-442-6542, Fax: 415-442-6579, E-mail: mkoch@ggu.edu. *Application contact:* Angela Melero, Enrollment Services, 415-442-7800, Fax: 415-442-7807, E-mail: info@ggu.edu.
Website: http://www.ggu.edu/programs/business-and-management

Goldey-Beacom College, Graduate Program, Wilmington, DE 19808-1999. Offers business administration (MBA); finance (MS); financial management (MBA); health care management (MBA); human resource management (MBA); information technology (MBA); international business management (MBA); major finance (MBA); major taxation (MBA); management (MM); marketing management (MBA); taxation (MBA, MS). *Accreditation:* ACBSP. *Program availability:* Part-time, evening/weekend. *Entrance requirements:* For master's, GMAT, MAT, GRE, minimum GPA of 3.0. Additional exam requirements/recommendations for international students: Required—TOEFL (minimum score 65 iBT); Recommended—IELTS (minimum score 6). Electronic applications accepted.

Grambling State University, School of Graduate Studies and Research, College of Arts and Sciences, Department of Political Science and Public Administration, Grambling, LA 71270. Offers health services administration (MPA); human resource management (MPA); public management (MPA); state and local government (MPA). *Accreditation:* NASPAA. *Program availability:* Part-time. *Degree requirements:* For master's, comprehensive exam (for some programs), thesis optional. *Entrance requirements:* For master's, GRE, minimum GPA of 2.75 on last degree. Additional exam requirements/recommendations for international students: Required—TOEFL (minimum score 500 paper-based; 62 iBT). Electronic applications accepted.

Grand Canyon University, Colangelo College of Business, Phoenix, AZ 85017-1097. Offers accounting (MBA, MS); business analytics (MS); disaster preparedness and executive fire service leadership (MS); finance (MBA); general management (MBA); health systems management (MBA); information technology management (MS); leadership (MBA, MS); marketing (MBA); organizational leadership and entrepreneurship (MS); project management (MBA); sports business (MBA); strategic human resource management (MBA). *Accreditation:* ACBSP. *Program availability:* Part-time, evening/weekend, online learning. *Entrance requirements:* For master's, equivalent of two years' full-time professional work experience. Additional exam requirements/recommendations for international students: Required—TOEFL (minimum score 575 paper-based; 90 iBT), IELTS (minimum score 7). Electronic applications accepted.

Grantham University, Mark Skousen School of Business, Lenexa, KS 66219. Offers business administration (MBA); business intelligence (MS); human resources (Certificate); information management (MBA); performance improvement (MS); project management (MBA, Certificate). *Program availability:* Part-time, evening/weekend, online only, 100% online. *Faculty:* 1 full-time, 34 part-time/adjunct. *Students:* 610 full-time (231 women), 333 part-time (128 women); includes 466 minority (321 Black or African American, non-Hispanic/Latino; 12 American Indian or Alaska Native, non-Hispanic/Latino; 29 Asian, non-Hispanic/Latino; 71 Hispanic/Latino; 4 Native Hawaiian or other Pacific Islander, non-Hispanic/Latino; 29 Two or more races, non-Hispanic/Latino). Average age 40. 273 applicants, 87% accepted, 202 enrolled. In 2017, 362 master's awarded. *Degree requirements:* For master's, comprehensive exam (for some programs), PMP Prep Exams throughout the term (for MBA in project management); for Certificate, comprehensive exam (for some programs), PMP Prep Exam (for project management). *Entrance requirements:* For master's, baccalaureate or master's degree with minimum cumulative GPA of 2.5 from institution accredited by agency recognized by U.S. DOE or foreign equivalent; official transcripts showing proof of degree.

Additional exam requirements/recommendations for international students: Required—TOEFL (minimum score 530 paper-based; 71 iBT), IELTS (minimum score 6.5), PTE (minimum score 50). *Application deadline:* Applications are processed on a rolling basis. Application fee: $0. Electronic applications accepted. *Expenses:* $325 per credit hour. *Financial support:* Scholarships/grants available. Financial award applicants required to submit FAFSA. *Faculty research:* How chronic diseases contribute to the rising costs of healthcare, marketing for entrepreneurs, managers' hiring practices of workers with disability, organizational structures, organizational change, online pedagogy, impact of instructor video tips in the online classroom, decision-making techniques. *Unit head:* Dr. David Marker, Dean of the Mark Skousen School of Business, 913-309-4747, Fax: 844-260-6287, E-mail: dmarker@grantham.edu. *Application contact:* Jared Parlette, Vice President of Student Enrollment, 800-955-2527 Ext. 803, Fax: 866-914-4557, E-mail: admissions@grantham.edu.
Website: https://www.grantham.edu/school-of-business/

Hawai`i Pacific University, College of Business, Program in Business Administration, Honolulu, HI 96813. Offers finance (MBA); human resource management (MBA); information systems (MBA); international business (MBA); management (MBA); marketing (MBA); organizational change and development (MBA). *Program availability:* Part-time, evening/weekend, 100% online, blended/hybrid learning. *Faculty:* 7 full-time (3 women), 3 part-time/adjunct (0 women). *Students:* 88 full-time (34 women), 28 part-time (18 women); includes 63 minority (9 Black or African American, non-Hispanic/Latino; 17 Asian, non-Hispanic/Latino; 14 Hispanic/Latino; 1 Native Hawaiian or other Pacific Islander, non-Hispanic/Latino; 22 Two or more races, non-Hispanic/Latino), 29 international. Average age 32. 82 applicants, 78% accepted, 40 enrolled. In 2017, 87 master's awarded. *Entrance requirements:* For master's, GMAT or GRE. Additional exam requirements/recommendations for international students: Recommended—TOEFL (minimum score 550 paper-based; 80 iBT), IELTS (minimum score 6), TWE (minimum score 5). *Application deadline:* For fall admission, 1/15 priority date for domestic students; for spring admission, 10/15 priority date for domestic students. Applications are processed on a rolling basis. Application fee: $50. Electronic applications accepted. *Expenses: Tuition:* Full-time $18,000; part-time $1000 per credit. *Required fees:* $200; $26 per credit. Tuition and fees vary according to course load and program. *Financial support:* In 2017–18, 24 students received support. Research assistantships, career-related internships or fieldwork, Federal Work-Study, scholarships/grants, tuition waivers (partial), and unspecified assistantships available. Financial award application deadline: 3/1; financial award applicants required to submit FAFSA. *Unit head:* Dr. Daewoo Park, Department Chair, 808-544-1463, E-mail: dwpark@hpu.edu. *Application contact:* Danny Lam, Assistant Director of Graduate Admissions, 808-544-1135, E-mail: graduate@hpu.edu.
Website: https://www.hpu.edu/cob/grad-programs/mba.html

HEC Montreal, School of Business Administration, Doctoral Program in Administration, Montréal, QC H3T 2A7, Canada. Offers accounting (PhD); applied economics (PhD); data science (PhD); finance (PhD); financial engineering (PhD); information technology (PhD); international business (PhD); logistics and operations management (PhD); management science (PhD); management, strategy and organizations (PhD); marketing (PhD); organizational behaviour and human resources (PhD). Program offered jointly with Concordia University, McGill University, and Universite du Quebec a Montreal. *Accreditation:* AACSB. *Students:* 114 full-time (47 women). 78 applicants, 42% accepted, 24 enrolled. In 2017, 23 doctorates awarded. *Entrance requirements:* For doctorate, TAGE MAGE, GMAT, or GRE, master's degree in administration or related field. *Application deadline:* For fall admission, 1/15 for domestic and international students. Application fee: $88 ($187 for international students). Electronic applications accepted. *Expenses:* Tuition, state resident: full-time $2869 Canadian dollars; part-time $79.70 Canadian dollars per credit. Tuition, nonresident: full-time $8883 Canadian dollars; part-time $246.76 Canadian dollars per credit. *International tuition:* $19,648 Canadian dollars full-time. *Required fees:* $41.20 Canadian dollars per credit. $67.94 Canadian dollars per term. Tuition and fees vary according to degree level and program. *Financial support:* Research assistantships, teaching assistantships, and scholarships/grants available. Financial award application deadline: 9/2. *Faculty research:* Art management, business policy, entrepreneurship, new technologies, transportation. *Unit head:* Jacques Robert, Director, 514-340-6853, E-mail: jacques.robert@hec.ca. *Application contact:* Julie Bilodeau, PhD Program Analyst, 514-340-6151, Fax: 514-340-6411, E-mail: analyste.phd@hec.ca.
Website: http://www.hec.ca/en/programs/phd/index.html

HEC Montreal, School of Business Administration, Graduate Diploma Programs in Administration, Montréal, QC H3T 2A7, Canada. Offers business administration (Graduate Diploma); business analysis - information technology (Graduate Diploma); e-business (Graduate Diploma); entrepreneurship (Graduate Diploma); financial professions (Graduate Diploma); human resources (Graduate Diploma); management (Graduate Diploma); management and sustainable development (Graduate Diploma); management of cultural organizations (Graduate Diploma); marketing communication (Graduate Diploma); organizational development (Graduate Diploma); professional accounting (Graduate Diploma); supply chain management (Graduate Diploma); taxation (Graduate Diploma). All courses are given in French. *Students:* 380 full-time (210 women), 819 part-time (501 women). 1,195 applicants, 72% accepted, 673 enrolled. In 2017, 629 Graduate Diplomas awarded. *Entrance requirements:* For degree, bachelor's degree. Application fee: $88 Canadian dollars ($184 Canadian dollars for international students). Electronic applications accepted. *Expenses:* Tuition, state resident: full-time $2869 Canadian dollars; part-time $79.70 Canadian dollars per credit. Tuition, nonresident: full-time $8883 Canadian dollars; part-time $246.76 Canadian dollars per credit. *International tuition:* $19,648 Canadian dollars full-time. *Required fees:* $41.20 Canadian dollars per credit. $67.94 Canadian dollars per term. Tuition and fees vary according to degree level and program. *Financial support:* Research assistantships, teaching assistantships, and scholarships/grants available. Financial award application deadline: 9/2. *Faculty research:* Art management, business policy, entrepreneurship, new technologies, transportation. *Unit head:* Renaud Lachance, Director, 514-340-7165, E-mail: renaud.lachance@hec.ca. *Application contact:* Anny Caron, Administrative Director, 514-340-6151, Fax: 514-340-6411, E-mail: aide@hec.ca.
Website: http://www.hec.ca/programmes/dess/index.html

HEC Montreal, School of Business Administration, Master of Science Programs in Administration, Program in Human Resources Management, Montréal, QC H3T 2A7, Canada. Offers M Sc. All courses are given in French. *Students:* 42 full-time (39 women), 23 part-time (18 women). 38 applicants, 71% accepted, 19 enrolled. In 2017, 20 master's awarded. *Entrance requirements:* For master's, BBA, undergraduate degree in another field, degree deemed equivalent by program director and minimum GPA of 3.0 on 4.3 scale. Additional exam requirements/recommendations for international students: Required—TAGE MAGE (minimum recommended score of 283), GMAT (minimum recommended score of 630), or GRE. *Application deadline:* For fall admission, 3/15 for domestic and international students; for winter admission, 9/15 for domestic and international students. Application fee: $88 Canadian dollars ($184 Canadian dollars for international students). Electronic applications accepted. *Expenses:* Tuition, state resident: full-time $2869 Canadian dollars; part-time $79.70 Canadian dollars per credit. Tuition, nonresident: full-time $8883 Canadian dollars; part-time $246.76 Canadian dollars

per credit. *International tuition:* $19,648 Canadian dollars full-time. *Required fees:* $41.20 Canadian dollars per credit. $67.94 Canadian dollars per term. Tuition and fees vary according to degree level and program. *Financial support:* Research assistantships, teaching assistantships, and scholarships/grants available. Financial award application deadline: 9/2. *Unit head:* Dr. Marie-Helene Jobin, Director, 514-340-6283, E-mail: marie-helene.jobin@hec.ca. *Application contact:* Marianne de Moura, Administrative Director, 514-340-6151, Fax: 514-340-6411, E-mail: aide@hec.ca.
Website: http://www.hec.ca/programmes/maitrises/maitrise-gestion-ressources-humaines/index.html

Herzing University Online, Program in Business Administration, Menomonee Falls, WI 53051. Offers accounting (MBA); business administration (MBA); business management (MBA); healthcare management (MBA); human resources (MBA); marketing (MBA); project management (MBA); technology management (MBA). *Program availability:* Online learning.

Hofstra University, Frank G. Zarb School of Business, Programs in Management and General Business, Hempstead, NY 11549. Offers business administration (MBA), including health services management, management, sports and entertainment management, strategic business management, strategic healthcare management; general management (Advanced Certificate); human resource management (MS, Advanced Certificate). *Program availability:* Part-time, evening/weekend, blended/hybrid learning. *Students:* 131 full-time (58 women), 145 part-time (65 women); includes 102 minority (23 Black or African American, non-Hispanic/Latino; 39 Asian, non-Hispanic/Latino; 37 Hispanic/Latino; 3 Two or more races, non-Hispanic/Latino), 25 international. Average age 33. 327 applicants, 72% accepted, 104 enrolled. In 2017, 116 master's awarded. *Degree requirements:* For master's, thesis optional, capstone course (for MBA), thesis (for MS), minimum GPA of 3.0. *Entrance requirements:* For master's, GMAT/GRE, 2 letters of recommendation, resume, essay. Additional exam requirements/recommendations for international students: Required—TOEFL (minimum score 550 paper-based; 80 iBT); Recommended—IELTS (minimum score 6). *Application deadline:* Applications are processed on a rolling basis. Application fee: $75. Electronic applications accepted. *Expenses:* $1,322 per credit. *Financial support:* In 2017–18, 78 students received support, including 75 fellowships with full and partial tuition reimbursements available (averaging $4,785 per year); research assistantships with full and partial tuition reimbursements available, career-related internships or fieldwork, Federal Work-Study, institutionally sponsored loans, scholarships/grants, tuition waivers (full and partial), and unspecified assistantships also available. Support available to part-time students. Financial award applicants required to submit FAFSA. *Faculty research:* Organizational change; sustainability; entrepreneurial spawning; family business; global supply chain strategies. *Unit head:* Dr. Kaushik Sengupta, Chairperson, 516-463-7825, Fax: 516-463-4834, E-mail: kaushik.sengupta@hofstra.edu. *Application contact:* Sunil Samuel, Assistant Vice President of Admissions, 516-463-4723, Fax: 516-463-4664, E-mail: graduateadmission@hofstra.edu.
Website: http://www.hofstra.edu/business/

Holy Family University, Graduate and Professional Programs, School of Business Administration, Philadelphia, PA 19114. Offers accountancy (MS); finance (MBA); health care administration (MBA); human resource management (MBA); information systems management (MBA). *Accreditation:* ACBSP. *Program availability:* Part-time, evening/weekend. *Degree requirements:* For master's, comprehensive exam, thesis optional. *Entrance requirements:* For master's, minimum GPA of 3.0, interview, essay/personal statement, current resume, official transcript of all college or university work. Additional exam requirements/recommendations for international students: Required—TOEFL (minimum score 550 paper-based; 79 iBT), IELTS (minimum score 6), PTE (minimum score 54). Electronic applications accepted. *Expenses: Tuition:* Full-time $13,518; part-time $9012 per credit hour. Tuition and fees vary according to degree level and program.

Hood College, Graduate School, Department of Economics and Business Administration, Frederick, MD 21701-8575. Offers accounting (MBA, Certificate); finance (MBA); financial management (Certificate); human resource management (MBA); information systems (MBA); marketing (MBA); organizational management (Certificate); public management (MBA). *Accreditation:* ACBSP. *Program availability:* Part-time, evening/weekend. *Faculty:* 4 full-time (2 women), 7 part-time/adjunct (1 woman). *Students:* 21 full-time (12 women), 91 part-time (47 women); includes 19 minority (8 Black or African American, non-Hispanic/Latino; 3 Asian, non-Hispanic/Latino; 8 Hispanic/Latino), 15 international. Average age 31. 34 applicants, 97% accepted, 23 enrolled. In 2017, 42 master's awarded. *Degree requirements:* For master's, capstone/final research project. *Entrance requirements:* For master's, minimum GPA of 3.0 (or resume and two letters of recommendation), copy of official transcripts, essay. Additional exam requirements/recommendations for international students: Required—TOEFL (minimum score 575 paper-based; 89 iBT), IELTS (minimum score 6.5). *Application deadline:* For fall admission, 8/15 for domestic students, 8/5 for international students; for spring admission, 12/1 for domestic and international students; for summer admission, 5/1 for domestic students, 4/15 for international students. Applications are processed on a rolling basis. Application fee: $35. Electronic applications accepted. *Expenses:* $550 per credit hour plus $110 per semester comprehensive fee. *Financial support:* Tuition waivers (partial) and unspecified assistantships available. Financial award applicants required to submit FAFSA. *Faculty research:* Corporate strategy and sustainable competitive advantages, business ethics, entrepreneurship, investments management, economic development. *Unit head:* Dr. April M. Boulton, Dean of the Graduate School, 301-696-3600, Fax: 301-696-3597, E-mail: gofurther@hood.edu. *Application contact:* Jan Marcus, Assistant Director of Graduate Admissions, 301-696-3603, E-mail: gofurther@hood.edu.

Houston Baptist University, Archie W. Dunham College of Business, Program in Human Resources Management, Houston, TX 77074-3298. Offers MSHRM. *Program availability:* Part-time, evening/weekend, 100% online. *Students:* 48 full-time (37 women), 39 part-time (34 women); includes 63 minority (38 Black or African American, non-Hispanic/Latino; 7 Asian, non-Hispanic/Latino; 14 Hispanic/Latino; 4 Two or more races, non-Hispanic/Latino), 9 international. Average age 30. 148 applicants, 46% accepted, 33 enrolled. In 2017, 52 master's awarded. *Entrance requirements:* For master's, minimum GPA of 2.5, essay/personal statement, resume, bachelor's degree conferred transcript. Additional exam requirements/recommendations for international students: Required—TOEFL (minimum score 80 iBT), IELTS (minimum score 6.5). *Application deadline:* For fall admission, 8/1 for domestic students, 6/1 for international students; for spring admission, 1/1 for domestic students, 11/1 for international students; for summer admission, 5/1 for domestic students, 3/1 for international students. Applications are processed on a rolling basis. Application fee: $0 ($100 for international students). Electronic applications accepted. Application fee is waived when completed online. *Expenses:* Contact institution. *Financial support:* In 2017–18, 20 students received support. Federal Work-Study and scholarships/grants available. Support available to part-time students. Financial award application deadline: 4/1; financial award applicants required to submit FAFSA. *Unit head:* Dr. Michael Weeks, Dean, Archie W. Dunham College of Business, 281-649-3014, E-mail: mweeks@hbu.edu. *Application contact:* Laurel Motal, Graduate Student Services Coordinator, 281-649-3306, Fax: 281-649-3436, E-mail: lmotal@hbu.edu.
Website: http://www.hbu.edu/mshrm

Human Resources Management

Howard University, School of Business, Graduate Programs in Business, Washington, DC 20059-0002. Offers accounting (MBA); entrepreneurship (MBA); finance (MBA); general management (MBA); human resources management (MBA); information systems (MBA); international business (MBA); marketing (MBA); supply chain management (MBA); JD/MBA. *Accreditation:* AACSB. *Program availability:* Part-time, evening/weekend, online learning. *Entrance requirements:* For master's, GMAT, minimum 1 year post undergraduate work experience, resume, 3 letters of recommendation, advanced college algebra. Additional exam requirements/recommendations for international students: Required—TOEFL. *Faculty research:* Marketing research in multi-ethnic populations, U.S. trade policies and international relations, risk management (finance).

Idaho State University, Office of Graduate Studies, College of Education, Department of Organizational Learning and Performance, Pocatello, ID 83209. Offers human resource development (MS); instructional design (PhD); instructional technology (M Ed). *Program availability:* Part-time. *Degree requirements:* For master's, comprehensive exam, thesis optional, minimum 36 credits; for doctorate, comprehensive exam, thesis/dissertation (for some programs). *Entrance requirements:* For master's, GRE or MAT, bachelor's degree; for doctorate, GRE or MAT, master's degree. Additional exam requirements/recommendations for international students: Required—TOEFL (minimum score 550 paper-based; 80 iBT). Electronic applications accepted.

IGlobal University, Graduate Programs, Vienna, VA 22182. Offers accounting (MBA); data management and analytics (MSIT); entrepreneurship (MBA); finance (MBA); global business management (MBA); health care management (MBA); hospitality and tourism management (MBA); human resources management (MBA); information technology (MBA); information technology systems and management (MSIT); leadership and management (MBA); project management (MBA); public service and administration (MBA); software design and management (MSIT).

Indiana Tech, Program in Business Administration, Fort Wayne, IN 46803-1297. Offers accounting (MBA); health care management (MBA); human resources (MBA); management (MBA); marketing (MBA). *Program availability:* Part-time, evening/weekend, online learning. *Entrance requirements:* For master's, GMAT, bachelor's degree from regionally-accredited university; minimum undergraduate GPA of 2.5; 2 years of significant work experience; 3 letters of recommendation. Electronic applications accepted.

Indiana University South Bend, Judd Leighton School of Business and Economics, South Bend, IN 46615. Offers accounting (MSA); business (Graduate Certificate); business administration (MBA), including finance, human resource management, marketing; MBA/MSA. *Program availability:* Part-time, evening/weekend. *Entrance requirements:* For master's, GMAT. Additional exam requirements/recommendations for international students: Required—TOEFL (minimum score 550 paper-based; 79 iBT). Electronic applications accepted. *Expenses:* Contact institution. *Faculty research:* Financial accounting, consumer research, capital budgeting research, business strategy research.

Indiana Wesleyan University, College of Adult and Professional Studies, Graduate Studies in Business, Marion, IN 46953. Offers accounting (MBA, Graduate Certificate); applied management (MBA); business administration (MBA); health care (MBA, Graduate Certificate); human resources (MBA, Graduate Certificate); management (MS); organizational leadership (MA). *Program availability:* Part-time, evening/weekend, online learning. *Degree requirements:* For master's, applied business or management project. *Entrance requirements:* For master's, minimum GPA of 2.5, 2 years of related work experience. Additional exam requirements/recommendations for international students: Required—TOEFL (minimum score 550 paper-based). Electronic applications accepted.

Instituto Tecnologico de Santo Domingo, Graduate School, Area of Business, Santo Domingo, Dominican Republic. Offers banking and securities markets (M Mgmt); corporate finance (M Mgmt); human resources management (M Mgmt, Certificate); international trade management (M Mgmt); marketing (M Mgmt); organizational development (M Mgmt); quality and productivity management (Certificate); tax management and planning (M Mgmt); upper management (M Mgmt).

Instituto Tecnologico de Santo Domingo, Graduate School, Area of Engineering, Santo Domingo, Dominican Republic. Offers construction administration (MS, Certificate); data telecommunications (M Eng, MS, Certificate); industrial engineering (M Eng, Certificate); industrial management (M Mgmt); information technology (Certificate); maintenance engineering (M Eng); occupational hazard prevention (M Mgmt); production management (Certificate); quantitative methods (Certificate); sanitary and environmental engineering (M Eng); structural engineering (M Eng); systems engineering and electronic data processing (Certificate); transportation (Certificate).

Instituto Tecnológico y de Estudios Superiores de Monterrey, Campus Cuernavaca, Programs in Business Administration, Temixco, Mexico. Offers finance (MA); human resources management (MA); international business (MA); marketing (MA).

Inter American University of Puerto Rico, Aguadilla Campus, Graduate School, Aguadilla, PR 00605. Offers accounting (MBA); counseling psychology specializing in family (MS); criminal justice (MA); educative management and leadership (MA); elementary education (M Ed); finance (MBA); human resources (MBA); industrial management (MBA); management information systems (MBA); marketing (MBA). *Program availability:* Part-time, evening/weekend. *Degree requirements:* For master's, comprehensive exam. *Entrance requirements:* For master's, EXADEP, 2 letters of recommendation, minimum GPA of 2.5. Electronic applications accepted.

Inter American University of Puerto Rico, Arecibo Campus, Program in Business Administration, Arecibo, PR 00614-4050. Offers accounting (MBA); finance (MBA); human resources (MBA).

Inter American University of Puerto Rico, Barranquitas Campus, Business Administration Program, Barranquitas, PR 00794. Offers accounting (MBA); human resources (MBA); managerial information systems (MBA). *Program availability:* Part-time, evening/weekend. *Faculty:* 2 full-time (1 woman), 2 part-time/adjunct (both women). *Students:* 11 full-time (9 women), 1 (woman) part-time; all minorities (all Hispanic/Latino). Average age 31. 6 applicants, 83% accepted, 5 enrolled. In 2017, 3 master's awarded. *Degree requirements:* For master's, 2 foreign languages, comprehensive exam (for some programs), thesis or alternative, minimum GPA of 3.0. *Entrance requirements:* For master's, BBA or its equivalent from accredited institution, official academic transcript from institution that conferred bachelor's degree, minimum GPA of 2.5, interview (for some programs). *Application deadline:* Applications are processed on a rolling basis. Application fee: $31. Electronic applications accepted. *Expenses:* $3,392 full-time tuition plus $652 fees. *Financial support:* Applicants required to submit FAFSA. *Unit head:* Juan A. Negron-Berrios, PhD, Chancellor, 787-857-3600 Ext. 2002, Fax: 787-857-2125, E-mail: janegron@br.inter.edu. *Application contact:* Aramilda Cartagena-Santiago, Dean of Students, 787-857-3600 Ext. 2009, Fax: 787-857-2125, E-mail: aramildacartagena@br.inter.edu.

Inter American University of Puerto Rico, Bayamón Campus, Graduate School, Bayamón, PR 00957. Offers biology (MS), including environmental sciences and ecology, molecular biotechnology; electrical engineering (ME), including control system, potence system; human resources (MBA); mechanical engineering (ME, MS), including aerospace, energy. *Program availability:* Part-time, evening/weekend. *Faculty:* 12 full-time (2 women), 3 part-time/adjunct (2 women). *Students:* 6 full-time (5 women), 99 part-time (62 women); includes 104 minority (1 Black or African American, non-Hispanic/Latino; 103 Hispanic/Latino). Average age 29. 46 applicants, 98% accepted, 34 enrolled. In 2017, 29 master's awarded. *Degree requirements:* For master's, comprehensive exam, research project. *Entrance requirements:* For master's, EXADEP, GRE General Test, letters of recommendation. *Application deadline:* For fall admission, 7/1 for domestic students, 5/1 priority date for international students; for winter admission, 11/15 priority date for domestic and international students; for spring admission, 2/15 priority date for domestic and international students. Application fee: $31. *Unit head:* Dr. Carlos J. Olivares, Acting Chancellor, 787-279-1200 Ext. 2295, Fax: 787-279-2205, E-mail: colivares@bayamon.inter.edu. *Application contact:* Aurelis Báez, Director of Student Services, 787-279-1912 Ext. 2017, Fax: 787-279-2205, E-mail: abaez@bayamon.inter.edu.

Inter American University of Puerto Rico, Fajardo Campus, Graduate Programs, Fajardo, PR 00738-7003. Offers computer science (MS); educational management and leadership (MA Ed); general business (MBA); human resources (MBA); management information systems (MBA); marketing (MBA); special education (MA Ed). *Program availability:* Online learning. *Faculty:* 1 full-time (0 women), 25 part-time/adjunct (13 women). *Students:* 1 (woman) full-time, 126 part-time (81 women).

Inter American University of Puerto Rico, Metropolitan Campus, Graduate Programs, Program in Human Resources, San Juan, PR 00919-1293. Offers MBA. *Degree requirements:* For master's, comprehensive exam. *Entrance requirements:* For master's, GRE or EXADEP, interview. Electronic applications accepted.

Inter American University of Puerto Rico, Ponce Campus, Graduate School, Mercedita, PR 00715-1602. Offers accounting (MBA); biology (M Ed); chemistry (M Ed); criminal justice (MA); elementary education (M Ed); English as a Second Language (M Ed); finance (MBA); history (M Ed); human resources (MBA); marketing (MBA); mathematics (M Ed); Spanish (M Ed). *Entrance requirements:* For master's, minimum GPA of 2.5.

Inter American University of Puerto Rico, San Germán Campus, Graduate Studies Center, Program in Business Administration, San Germán, PR 00683-5008. Offers accounting (MBA); finance (MBA); general business administration (MBA); human resources (MBA, PhD); industrial relations (MBA); information systems (MBA); international and interregional business (PhD); management (MBA); marketing (MBA). *Program availability:* Part-time, evening/weekend. *Degree requirements:* For master's, comprehensive exam. *Entrance requirements:* For master's, GRE General Test or EXADEP, minimum GPA of 3.0.

Iona College, School of Arts and Science, Department of Psychology, New Rochelle, NY 10801-1890. Offers general-experimental psychology (MA); human resources (Certificate); industrial-organizational psychology (MA); mental health counseling (MA); organizational behavior (Certificate); psychology (MA); school psychology (MA). *Program availability:* 9 full-time (5 women), 7 part-time/adjunct (5 women). *Students:* 75 full-time (55 women), 37 part-time (24 women); includes 46 minority (9 Black or African American, non-Hispanic/Latino; 2 Asian, non-Hispanic/Latino; 34 Hispanic/Latino; 1 Two or more races, non-Hispanic/Latino), 1 international. Average age 25. 88 applicants, 88% accepted, 40 enrolled. In 2017, 23 master's awarded. *Degree requirements:* For master's, thesis (for some programs), literature review (for some programs). *Entrance requirements:* For master's, BA in psychology including 3 credits each in psychology statistics and experimental research methods, or 9 credits in psychology including 3 credits each in psychology statistics, psychology research methods and upper-level coursework. Additional exam requirements/recommendations for international students: Required—TOEFL (minimum score 550 paper-based), IELTS (minimum score 6.5). *Application deadline:* For fall admission, 8/15 for domestic students, 5/1 for international students; for spring admission, 1/15 for domestic students, 9/1 for international students. Applications are processed on a rolling basis. Electronic applications accepted. Tuition and fees vary according to program. *Financial support:* In 2017–18, 27 students received support. Research assistantships with partial tuition reimbursements available, tuition waivers (partial), and unspecified assistantships available. Support available to part-time students. Financial award application deadline: 4/15; financial award applicants required to submit FAFSA. *Faculty research:* Non-suicidal self-injury, trauma response, performance appraisal and evaluation, diversity infusion, assessment and treatment of sexual offenders. *Unit head:* Patricia Oswald, PhD, Chair, 914-633-2374, E-mail: poswald@iona.edu. *Application contact:* Katelyn Brunck, Assistant Director, Graduate Admissions, 914-633-2451, Fax: 914-633-2277, E-mail: kbrunck@iona.edu.
Website: http://www.iona.edu/Academics/School-of-Arts-Science/Departments/Psychology/Graduate-Programs.aspx

Iona College, School of Business, Department of Management, Business Administration and Health Care Management, New Rochelle, NY 10801-1890. Offers business administration (MBA); health care analytics (AC); health care management (MBA, AC); human resource management (MBA, PMC); long term care services management (AC); management (MBA, PMC). *Program availability:* Part-time, evening/weekend. *Faculty:* 11 full-time (0 women), 6 part-time/adjunct (3 women). *Students:* 27 full-time (17 women), 62 part-time (41 women); includes 29 minority (14 Black or African American, non-Hispanic/Latino; 1 Asian, non-Hispanic/Latino; 13 Hispanic/Latino; 1 Native Hawaiian or other Pacific Islander, non-Hispanic/Latino), 4 international. Average age 29. 31 applicants, 94% accepted, 17 enrolled. In 2017, 40 master's, 30 other advanced degrees awarded. *Entrance requirements:* For master's, GMAT, 2 letters of recommendation, minimum GPA of 3.0; for other advanced degree, GMAT, minimum GPA of 3.0. Additional exam requirements/recommendations for international students: Required—TOEFL (minimum score 550 paper-based; 80 iBT), IELTS (minimum score 6.5). *Application deadline:* For fall admission, 8/15 priority date for domestic students, 8/1 priority date for international students; for winter admission, 11/15 priority date for domestic students, 11/1 priority date for international students; for spring admission, 2/15 priority date for domestic students, 2/1 priority date for international students; for summer admission, 5/15 priority date for domestic students, 5/1 priority date for international students. Applications are processed on a rolling basis. Application fee: $50. Electronic applications accepted. *Expenses:* Contact institution. *Financial support:* In 2017–18, 20 students received support. Scholarships/grants, tuition waivers (partial), and unspecified assistantships available. Support available to part-time students. Financial award application deadline: 4/15; financial award applicants required to submit FAFSA. *Faculty research:* Information systems, strategic management, corporate values and ethics. *Unit head:* George DeFeis, Chair, 914-633-2631, E-mail: gdefeis@iona.edu. *Application contact:* Katelyn Brunck, Director of MBA Admissions, 914-633-2451, Fax: 914-633-2277, E-mail: kbrunck@iona.edu.
Website: http://www.iona.edu/Academics/Hagan-School-of-Business/Departments/Management-Business-Administration-Health-Car/Graduate-Programs.aspx

James Madison University, The Graduate School, College of Education, Program in Adult Education and Human Resource Development, Harrisonburg, VA 22801. Offers higher education (MS Ed); human resource management (MS Ed); individualized (MS Ed); instructional design (MS Ed); leadership and facilitation (MS Ed); program evaluation and measurement (MS Ed). *Accreditation:* NCATE. *Program availability:* Part-time, evening/weekend. *Students:* 11 full-time (7 women), 12 part-time (10 women); includes 7 minority (4 Black or African American, non-Hispanic/Latino; 1 Hispanic/Latino; 2 Two or more races, non-Hispanic/Latino), 1 international. Average age 30. In 2017, 3 master's awarded. *Application fee:* $55. Electronic applications accepted. *Expenses:* Tuition, state resident: full-time $10,512; part-time $438 per credit hour. Tuition, nonresident: full-time $28,358; part-time $1162 per credit hour. *Required fees:* $1128. *Financial support:* In 2017–18, 10 students received support. Teaching assistantships, Federal Work-Study, and 10 assistantships (averaging $7911) available. Financial award application deadline: 3/1; financial award applicants required to submit FAFSA. *Unit head:* Dr. Jane B. Thall, Department Head, 540-568-5531, E-mail: thalljb@jmu.edu. *Application contact:* Lynette D. Michael, Director of Graduate Admissions, 540-568-6131 Ext. 6395, Fax: 540-568-7860, E-mail: michaeld@jmu.edu.

Johnson & Wales University, Graduate Studies, MBA Program, Providence, RI 02903-3703. Offers accounting (MBA); business administration (MBA); finance (MBA); global fashion merchandising and management (MBA); hospitality (MBA); human resource management (MBA); information security/assurance (MBA); information technology (MBA); nonprofit management (MBA); operations and supply chain management (MBA); organizational leadership (MBA); organizational psychology (MBA); sport leadership (MBA). Program also offered on Denver campus. *Program availability:* Part-time, online learning. *Entrance requirements:* For master's, minimum GPA of 2.75. Additional exam requirements/recommendations for international students: Required—TOEFL (minimum score 550 paper-based); Recommended—IELTS, TWE. *Application deadline:* For fall admission, 8/15 priority date for domestic students, 6/28 priority date for international students; for winter admission, 11/10 priority date for domestic students, 9/20 priority date for international students; for spring admission, 2/5 priority date for domestic students, 12/20 priority date for international students. Applications are processed on a rolling basis. *Expenses: Tuition:* Full-time $12,636; part-time $702 per credit hour. *Financial support:* Tuition waivers (partial) and unspecified assistantships available. Support available to part-time students. Financial award application deadline: 5/1. *Faculty research:* International banking, global economy, international trade, cultural differences. *Unit head:* Dr. Karen Silva, Director, 401-598-2849, Fax: 401-598-1125. *Application contact:* Graduate School Admissions, 401-598-1015, Fax: 401-598-1286, E-mail: gradadm@jwu.edu.

Johnson & Wales University, Graduate Studies, MS Program in Human Resource Management, Providence, RI 02903-3703. Offers MS. *Program availability:* Online learning. *Expenses: Tuition:* Full-time $12,636; part-time $702 per credit hour. *Unit head:* Dr. Karen Silva, Director, 401-598-2849, E-mail: karen.silva@jwu.edu. *Application contact:* Graduate School Admissions, 401-598-1015, Fax: 401-598-1286, E-mail: pvdgrad@admissions.jwu.edu.
Website: https://www.jwu.edu/academics/programs-by-campus/providence-programs/human-resource-management-ms.html

King University, School of Business and Economics, Bristol, TN 37620-2699. Offers accounting (MBA); finance (MBA); healthcare management (MBA); human resources management (MBA); leadership (MBA); management (MBA); marketing (MBA); project management (MBA). *Program availability:* Part-time, evening/weekend, online learning. *Degree requirements:* For master's, comprehensive exam, thesis optional. *Entrance requirements:* For master's, GMAT, 2 years of work experience. Additional exam requirements/recommendations for international students: Required—TOEFL (minimum score 550 paper-based). Electronic applications accepted. *Faculty research:* International monetary policy.

La Roche College, School of Graduate Studies and Adult Education, Program in Human Resources Management, Pittsburgh, PA 15237-5898. Offers MS, Certificate. *Program availability:* Part-time, evening/weekend. *Faculty:* 1 (woman) full-time, 6 part-time/adjunct (2 women). *Students:* 7 full-time (all women), 28 part-time (19 women); includes 3 minority (1 Hispanic/Latino; 2 Two or more races, non-Hispanic/Latino), 8 international. Average age 36. 44 applicants, 57% accepted, 14 enrolled. In 2017, 15 master's awarded. *Entrance requirements:* For master's, GMAT, GRE or MAT, minimum GPA of 3.0 during previous 2 years, resume, 2 letters of recommendation, interview. Additional exam requirements/recommendations for international students: Recommended—TOEFL (minimum score 550 paper-based). *Application deadline:* For fall admission, 8/15 priority date for domestic students, 8/15 for international students; for spring admission, 12/15 priority date for domestic students, 12/15 for international students. Applications are processed on a rolling basis. Application fee: $50. Electronic applications accepted. *Expenses: Tuition:* Part-time $715 per credit hour. *Required fees:* $80 per credit hour. *Financial support:* Unspecified assistantships available. Financial award application deadline: 3/31; financial award applicants required to submit FAFSA. *Faculty research:* Human resources development. *Unit head:* Dr. Jean Forti, Coordinator, 412-536-1193, Fax: 412-536-1179, E-mail: fortij1@laroche.edu. *Application contact:* Hope Schiffgens, Director of Graduate Studies and Adult Education, 412-536-1266, Fax: 412-536-1283, E-mail: schombh1@laroche.edu.

La Salle University, School of Business, Master of Business Administration Program, Philadelphia, PA 19141-1199. Offers accounting (MBA, Post-MBA Certificate); business systems and analytics (MBA, Post-MBA Certificate); finance (MBA, Post-MBA Certificate); general business administration (MBA, Post-MBA Certificate); human resource management (MBA, Post-MBA Certificate); management (MBA, Post-MBA Certificate); marketing (Post-MBA Certificate); MBA/MSN. Program also offered in Switzerland. *Accreditation:* AACSB. *Program availability:* Part-time, evening/weekend, online learning. *Faculty:* 22 full-time (10 women), 10 part-time/adjunct (3 women). *Students:* 59 full-time (25 women), 200 part-time (109 women); includes 66 minority (36 Black or African American, non-Hispanic/Latino; 21 Asian, non-Hispanic/Latino; 7 Hispanic/Latino; 2 Two or more races, non-Hispanic/Latino), 22 international. Average age 31. 216 applicants, 57% accepted, 74 enrolled. In 2017, 146 master's awarded. *Entrance requirements:* For master's, GMAT or GRE, two letters of reference; resume; for Post-MBA Certificate, MBA with minimum GPA of 3.0. Additional exam requirements/recommendations for international students: Required—TOEFL. *Application deadline:* For fall admission, 8/15 priority date for domestic students, 7/15 for international students; for spring admission, 12/15 priority date for domestic students, 11/15 for international students; for summer admission, 4/15 priority date for domestic students, 3/15 for international students. Applications are processed on a rolling basis. Application fee: $35. Electronic applications accepted. Application fee is waived when completed online. *Expenses:* Contact institution. *Financial support:* In 2017–18, 51 students received support. Scholarships/grants available. Support available to part-time students. Financial award application deadline: 8/31; financial award applicants required to submit FAFSA. *Unit head:* Dr. MarySheila McDonald, Interim Dean, 215-951-1040, Fax: 215-951-1886, E-mail: mcdonaldms@lasalle.edu. *Application contact:* Elizabeth Heenan, Director, Graduate and Adult Enrollment, 215-951-1100, Fax: 215-951-1462, E-mail: heenan@lasalle.edu.

Lasell College, Graduate and Professional Studies in Management, Newton, MA 02466-2709. Offers business administration (MBA); elder care management (MSM); hospitality and event management (MSM); human resources management (MSM, Graduate Certificate); management (MSM, Graduate Certificate); marketing (MS, Graduate Certificate); project management (MSM, Graduate Certificate). *Accreditation:* ACBSP. *Program availability:* Part-time, evening/weekend, 100% online, blended/hybrid learning. *Faculty:* 1 full-time (0 women), 15 part-time/adjunct (11 women). *Students:* 41 full-time (25 women), 102 part-time (70 women); includes 34 minority (19 Black or African American, non-Hispanic/Latino; 5 Asian, non-Hispanic/Latino; 8 Hispanic/Latino; 2 Two or more races, non-Hispanic/Latino), 29 international. Average age 32. 128 applicants, 46% accepted, 38 enrolled. In 2017, 66 master's, 3 other advanced degrees awarded. *Degree requirements:* For master's, minimum GPA 3.0; internship or research paper (for MSM). *Entrance requirements:* For master's, one-page personal statement, 2 letters of recommendation, resume, bachelor's degree transcript; proof of microeconomics and statistics (for MBA); for Graduate Certificate, bachelor's degree transcript, 2 letters of recommendation, 1-page personal statement, resume. Additional exam requirements/recommendations for international students: Required—TOEFL (minimum score 550 paper-based, 79 iBT) or IELTS (minimum score 6). *Application deadline:* For fall admission, 8/1 priority date for domestic students, 6/30 priority date for international students; for spring admission, 12/31 priority date for domestic students, 10/31 priority date for international students. Applications are processed on a rolling basis. Electronic applications accepted. *Expenses:* $600 per credit. *Financial support:* Federal Work-Study, scholarships/grants, and tuition discounts available. Support available to part-time students. Financial award application deadline: 8/31; financial award applicants required to submit FAFSA. *Unit head:* Eric Turner, Vice President of Graduate and Professional Studies, 617-243-2071, Fax: 617-243-2450, E-mail: gradinfo@lasell.edu. *Application contact:* Adrienne Franciosi, Director of Graduate Enrollment, 617-243-2214, Fax: 617-243-2450, E-mail: gradinfo@lasell.edu.
Website: http://www.lasell.edu/academics/graduate-and-professional-studies/programs-of-study/master-of-science-in-management.html

La Sierra University, School of Business and Management, Riverside, CA 92505. Offers accounting (MBA); finance (MBA); general management (MBA); human resources management (MBA); leadership, values, and ethics for business and management (Certificate); marketing (MBA). *Degree requirements:* For master's, research project. *Entrance requirements:* For master's, GMAT, minimum GPA of 3.0. Additional exam requirements/recommendations for international students: Required—TOEFL. *Faculty research:* Financial econometrics, institutional assessment and strategic planning, legal issues in management, behavioral finance, content of financial reports.

Lebanon Valley College, Program in Business Administration, Annville, PA 17003-1400. Offers business administration (MBA); healthcare management (MBA); human resources (MBA); leadership and ethics (MBA); project management (MBA). *Program availability:* Part-time, evening/weekend. *Faculty:* 7 full-time (1 woman), 8 part-time/adjunct (1 woman). *Students:* 11 full-time (5 women), 66 part-time (28 women); includes 11 minority (3 Black or African American, non-Hispanic/Latino; 4 Asian, non-Hispanic/Latino; 4 Hispanic/Latino), 3 international. Average age 34. 21 applicants, 81% accepted, 16 enrolled. In 2017, 32 master's awarded. *Degree requirements:* For master's, capstone course. *Entrance requirements:* For master's, GMAT, 3 years of work experience, resume, professional statement (application form, resume, personal statement, transcripts). Additional exam requirements/recommendations for international students: Required—TOEFL (minimum score 80 iBT), IELTS (minimum score 6.5) or STEP Eiken (grade 1). *Application deadline:* Applications are processed on a rolling basis. Application fee: $0. Electronic applications accepted. *Expenses:* $660 per credit hour. *Financial support:* Career-related internships or fieldwork and scholarships/grants available. Financial award application deadline: 3/1; financial award applicants required to submit FAFSA. *Faculty research:* Leadership, motivation, BI, information systems strategies, emerging market development, the role of informational business education, economic growth. *Unit head:* Dr. David Setley, Associate Professor/Chair of Business Administration/Director of the MBA Program, 717-867-6104, Fax: 717-867-6018, E-mail: setley@lvc.edu. *Application contact:* Christine M. Martin, Enrollment and Operations Specialist, 717-867-6486, Fax: 717-867-6013, E-mail: cmartin@lvc.edu.
Website: http://www.lvc.edu/mba

Lewis University, College of Business, Program in Business Administration, Romeoville, IL 60446. Offers accounting (MBA); custom elective option (MBA); e-business (MBA); finance (MBA); healthcare management (MBA); human resources management (MBA); international business (MBA); management information systems (MBA); marketing (MBA); project management (MBA); technology and operations management (MBA). *Program availability:* Part-time, evening/weekend. *Students:* 130 full-time (77 women), 187 part-time (107 women); includes 83 minority (27 Black or African American, non-Hispanic/Latino; 3 American Indian or Alaska Native, non-Hispanic/Latino; 7 Asian, non-Hispanic/Latino; 40 Hispanic/Latino; 6 Two or more races, non-Hispanic/Latino), 31 international. Average age 31. In 2017, 99 master's awarded. *Degree requirements:* For master's, comprehensive exam. *Entrance requirements:* For master's, interview, bachelor's degree, resume, two recommendations. Additional exam requirements/recommendations for international students: Required—TOEFL (minimum score 550 paper-based), IELTS. *Application deadline:* For fall admission, 8/15 priority date for domestic students, 5/1 priority date for international students; for spring admission, 11/15 priority date for international students. Applications are processed on a rolling basis. Application fee: $40. Electronic applications accepted. Tuition and fees vary according to program. *Financial support:* Career-related internships or fieldwork, Federal Work-Study, scholarships/grants, and unspecified assistantships available. Financial award application deadline: 5/1; financial award applicants required to submit FAFSA. *Unit head:* Dr. Maureen Culleeney, Academic Program Director, 815-838-0500 Ext. 5631, E-mail: culleema@lewisu.edu. *Application contact:* Michele Ryan, Director of Admission, 815-838-0500 Ext. 5384, E-mail: ryanml@lewisu.edu.

Lincoln University, Graduate Programs, Philadelphia, PA 19104. Offers counseling (MSC); early childhood education (M Ed), including PreK-4; early childhood education and special education (M Ed), including principal certification; finance (MBA); human resources management (MBA); human services delivery (MAHS). *Program availability:* Part-time, evening/weekend. *Faculty:* 9 full-time (3 women), 25 part-time/adjunct (15 women). *Students:* 196 full-time (138 women), 68 part-time (46 women); includes 236 minority (227 Black or African American, non-Hispanic/Latino; 1 American Indian or Alaska Native, non-Hispanic/Latino; 7 Hispanic/Latino; 1 Two or more races, non-Hispanic/Latino), 3 international. Average age 34. 120 applicants, 100% accepted, 95 enrolled. In 2017, 126 master's awarded. *Degree requirements:* For master's, comprehensive exam, thesis or alternative, capstone, grant proposal. *Entrance requirements:* For master's, official academic transcript(s), letters of recommendation, personal statement, resume, supervisor's evaluation form. Additional exam requirements/recommendations for international students: Recommended—TOEFL (minimum score 500 paper-based; 71 iBT), IELTS. *Application deadline:* For fall admission, 8/1 priority date for domestic students, 7/1 priority date for international students; for spring admission, 12/1 priority date for domestic students, 10/1 for international students. Applications are processed on a rolling basis. Application fee:

$50. Electronic applications accepted. *Expenses:* Contact institution. *Financial support:* Scholarships/grants available. Financial award application deadline: 6/30; financial award applicants required to submit FAFSA. *Unit head:* Dr. Patricia Pierce Ramsey, Provost, 484-365-7437, Fax: 484-365-8108, E-mail: provost@lincoln.edu. *Application contact:* Jernice Lea, Director, University City Student Services and Admissions, 215-590-8231, Fax: 215-387-3859, E-mail: jlea@lincoln.edu.
Website: http://www.lincoln.edu/admissions/graduate-admissions

Lincoln University, Graduate Studies, Oakland, CA 94612. Offers finance and investments (DBA); finance management (MS); finance management and investments (MBA); general business (MBA); human resource management (MBA, DBA); international business (MBA, MS); management information systems (MBA). *Program availability:* Part-time. *Faculty:* 14 full-time (2 women), 20 part-time/adjunct (6 women). *Students:* 606 full-time (222 women), 31 part-time (14 women); includes 10 minority (8 Asian, non-Hispanic/Latino; 1 Hispanic/Latino; 1 Two or more races, non-Hispanic/Latino), 623 international. Average age 26. *Degree requirements:* For master's, research project (thesis), internship report, or comprehensive exam; for doctorate, comprehensive exam, thesis/dissertation. *Entrance requirements:* For master's, minimum GPA of 2.7; for doctorate, GMAT (minimum score: 550), GRE (minimum score: 1000), or equivalent test results (waived for master's degree with minimum cumulative GPA of 3.3). Additional exam requirements/recommendations for international students: Required—TOEFL minimum score 525 paper-based; 71 iBT or IELTS minimum score 5.5 (for MBA); TOEFL minimum score 550 paper-based; 79 iBT or IELTS minimum score 6 (for MS and DBA). *Application deadline:* For fall admission, 8/7 for domestic students, 7/14 for international students; for spring admission, 11/30 for domestic students, 10/31 for international students; for summer admission, 5/29 for domestic students, 5/5 for international students. Applications are processed on a rolling basis. Application fee: $75. Electronic applications accepted. *Expenses: Tuition:* Full-time $8100; part-time $450 per unit. *Required fees:* $360; $180 per semester. Tuition and fees vary according to course level, course load, degree level and program. *Financial support:* Teaching assistantships, career-related internships or fieldwork, and scholarships/grants available. Financial award applicants required to submit FAFSA. *Unit head:* Dr. Marshall Burak, Provost, 510-628-8016, Fax: 510-628-8012, E-mail: mburak@lincolnuca.edu. *Application contact:* Reenu Shrestha, Assistant to the President, 510-628-8017, Fax: 510-208-2826, E-mail: sreenu@lincolnuca.edu.

Lindenwood University, Graduate Programs, Plaster School of Business and Entrepreneurship, St. Charles, MO 63301-1695. Offers accountancy (M Acc); accounting (MBA); business administration (MBA); entrepreneurial studies (MBA); finance (MBA, MS); human resource management (MBA); international business (MBA); leadership (MA); management (MBA); marketing (MBA, MS); nonprofit administration (MA); public administration (MBA); sport management (MA); supply chain management (MBA). *Accreditation:* ACBSP. *Program availability:* Part-time, evening/weekend, 100% online. *Faculty:* 15 full-time (8 women), 26 part-time/adjunct (9 women). *Students:* 201 full-time (116 women), 253 part-time (153 women); includes 102 minority (80 Black or African American, non-Hispanic/Latino; 2 American Indian or Alaska Native, non-Hispanic/Latino; 6 Asian, non-Hispanic/Latino; 7 Hispanic/Latino; 7 Two or more races, non-Hispanic/Latino), 61 international. Average age 32. 370 applicants, 42% accepted, 134 enrolled. In 2017, 178 master's awarded. *Degree requirements:* For master's, comprehensive exam (for some programs), thesis (for some programs), minimum GPA of 3.0. *Entrance requirements:* For master's, interview, minimum undergraduate cumulative GPA of 3.0, letter of recommendation. Additional exam requirements/recommendations for international students: Required—TOEFL (minimum score 550 paper-based; 80 iBT); Recommended—IELTS (minimum score 6.5). *Application deadline:* For fall admission, 8/27 priority date for domestic and international students; for winter admission, 1/14 priority date for domestic and international students; for spring admission, 3/18 for domestic students, 3/18 priority date for international students; for summer admission, 6/3 priority date for domestic and international students. Applications are processed on a rolling basis. Application fee: $30 ($100 for international students). Electronic applications accepted. *Expenses:* Contact institution. *Financial support:* In 2017–18, 439 students received support. Career-related internships or fieldwork, Federal Work-Study, institutionally sponsored loans, scholarships/grants, tuition waivers (partial), and unspecified assistantships available. Financial award application deadline: 6/30; financial award applicants required to submit FAFSA. *Unit head:* Roger Ellis, Dean, School of Business and Entrepreneurship, 636-949-4839, E-mail: rellis@lindenwood.edu. *Application contact:* Kara Schilli, Director, Evening and Graduate Admissions, 636-949-4349, Fax: 636-949-4109, E-mail: adultadmissions@lindenwood.edu.
Website: http://www.lindenwood.edu/academics/academic-schools/robert-w-plaster-school-of-business-entrepreneurship/

Lindenwood University, Graduate Programs, School of Accelerated Degree Programs, St. Charles, MO 63301-1695. Offers administration (MSA), including management, marketing, project management; business administration (MBA); communications (MA), including digital and multimedia, media management, promotions, training and development; criminal justice and administration (MS); healthcare administration (MS); human resource management (MS); information technology (Certificate); managing information security (MS); managing information technology (MS); managing virtualization and cloud computing (MS); writing (MFA). *Program availability:* Part-time, evening/weekend, 100% online. *Faculty:* 12 full-time (5 women), 90 part-time/adjunct (37 women). *Students:* 597 full-time (383 women), 202 part-time (138 women); includes 248 minority (206 Black or African American, non-Hispanic/Latino; 3 American Indian or Alaska Native, non-Hispanic/Latino; 6 Asian, non-Hispanic/Latino; 21 Hispanic/Latino; 1 Native Hawaiian or other Pacific Islander, non-Hispanic/Latino; 11 Two or more races, non-Hispanic/Latino), 69 international. Average age 36. 526 applicants, 46% accepted, 204 enrolled. In 2017, 537 master's awarded. *Degree requirements:* For master's, thesis (for some programs), minimum cumulative GPA of 3.0; for Certificate, minimum cumulative GPA of 3.0. *Entrance requirements:* For master's, resume, personal statement, official undergraduate transcript, minimum undergraduate cumulative GPA of 3.0. Additional exam requirements/recommendations for international students: Required—TOEFL (minimum score 550 paper-based; 80 iBT); Recommended—IELTS (minimum score 6.5). *Application deadline:* For fall admission, 9/24 priority date for domestic and international students; for winter admission, 1/7 priority date for domestic and international students; for spring admission, 4/8 priority date for domestic and international students; for summer admission, 7/8 priority date for domestic and international students. Applications are processed on a rolling basis. Application fee: $30 ($100 for international students). Electronic applications accepted. *Expenses: Tuition:* Full-time $16,300; part-time $460 per credit. *Required fees:* $660; $330 per credit. Tuition and fees vary according to degree level and program. *Financial support:* In 2017–18, 738 students received support. Career-related internships or fieldwork, institutionally sponsored loans, scholarships/grants, tuition waivers (partial), and unspecified assistantships available. Financial award application deadline: 6/30; financial award applicants required to submit FAFSA. *Unit head:* Dr. Gina Ganahl, Dean, Accelerated Degree Programs, 636-949-4501, Fax: 636-949-4505, E-mail: gganahl@lindenwood.edu. *Application contact:* Kara Schilli, Director, Evening and Graduate Admissions, 636-949-4349, Fax: 636-949-4109, E-mail: adultadmissions@lindenwood.edu.

Website: http://www.lindenwood.edu/academics/academic-schools/school-of-accelerated-degree-programs/

Lindenwood University–Belleville, Graduate Programs, Belleville, IL 62226. Offers business administration (MBA); communications (MA), including digital and multimedia, media management, promotions, training and development; counseling (MA); criminal justice administration (MS); education (MA); healthcare administration (MS); human resource management (MS); school administration (MA); teaching (MAT).

London Metropolitan University, Graduate Programs, London, United Kingdom. Offers applied psychology (M Sc); architecture (MA); biomedical science (M Sc); blood science (M Sc); cancer pharmacology (M Sc); computer networking and cyber security (M Sc); computing and information systems (M Sc); conference interpreting (MA); counter-terrorism studies (M Sc); creative, digital and professional writing (MA); crime, violence and prevention (M Sc); criminology (M Sc); curating contemporary art (MA); data analytics (M Sc); digital media (MA); early childhood studies (MA); education (MA, Ed D); financial services law, regulation and compliance (LL M); food science (M Sc); forensic psychology (M Sc); health and social care management and policy (M Sc); human nutrition (M Sc); human resource management (MA); human rights and international conflict (MA); information technology (M Sc); intelligence and security studies (M Sc); international oil, gas and energy law (LL M); international relations (MA); interpreting (MA); learning and teaching in higher education (MA); legal practice (LL M); media and entertainment law (LL M); organizational and consumer psychology (M Sc); psychological therapy (M Sc); psychology of mental health (M Sc); public health (M Sc); public policy and management (MPA); security studies (M Sc); social work (M Sc); spatial planning and urban design (MA); sports therapy (M Sc); supporting older children and young people with dyslexia (MA); teaching languages (MA), including Arabic, English; translation (MA); woman and child abuse (MA).

Long Island University–LIU Brooklyn, School of Business, Public Administration and Information Sciences, Brooklyn, NY 11201-8423. Offers accounting (MBA); accounting (MS); business administration (MBA); computer science (MS); gerontology (Advanced Certificate); health administration (MPA); human resources management (MS); not-for-profit management (Advanced Certificate); public administration (MPA); taxation (MS). *Program availability:* Part-time, evening/weekend. *Faculty:* 18 full-time (7 women), 28 part-time/adjunct (8 women). *Students:* 226 full-time (140 women), 232 part-time (150 women); includes 272 minority (192 Black or African American, non-Hispanic/Latino; 2 American Indian or Alaska Native, non-Hispanic/Latino; 35 Asian, non-Hispanic/Latino; 40 Hispanic/Latino; 3 Two or more races, non-Hispanic/Latino), 88 international. Average age 32. 495 applicants, 64% accepted, 149 enrolled. In 2017, 189 master's, 13 other advanced degrees awarded. *Entrance requirements:* Additional exam requirements/recommendations for international students: Required—TOEFL (minimum score 550 paper-based; 75 iBT). *Application deadline:* Applications are processed on a rolling basis. Application fee: $50. Electronic applications accepted. *Expenses: Tuition:* Full-time $21,618; part-time $1201 per credit. *Required fees:* $1840; $920 per term. Tuition and fees vary according to course load. *Financial support:* In 2017–18, 78 students received support. Career-related internships or fieldwork, Federal Work-Study, scholarships/grants, and unspecified assistantships available. Support available to part-time students. Financial award application deadline: 2/15; financial award applicants required to submit FAFSA. *Faculty research:* Tax policy; public sector budgeting and gender inequities; technology and innovation; game theory; knowledge management. *Unit head:* Dr. Edward Rogoff, Dean, 718-488-1159, E-mail: edward.rogoff@liu.edu. *Application contact:* Luis Santiago, Dean of Enrollment, 718-488-1011, Fax: 718-780-6110, E-mail: bkln-admissions@liu.edu.
Website: http://liu.edu/Brooklyn/Academics/School-of-Business-Public-Administration-and-Information-Sciences

Loyola University Chicago, Quinlan School of Business, Master of Science in Human Resources Program, Chicago, IL 60611. Offers MSHR. *Program availability:* Part-time, evening/weekend. *Faculty:* 4 full-time (0 women), 6 part-time/adjunct (3 women). *Students:* 27 full-time (23 women), 12 part-time (8 women); includes 19 minority (10 Black or African American, non-Hispanic/Latino; 3 Asian, non-Hispanic/Latino; 6 Hispanic/Latino), 6 international. Average age 29. 87 applicants, 61% accepted, 16 enrolled. In 2017, 18 master's awarded. *Entrance requirements:* For master's, GMAT or GRE, official transcripts, two letters of recommendation, statement of purpose, resume. Additional exam requirements/recommendations for international students: Required—TOEFL (minimum score 90 iBT) or IELTS (minimum score 6.5). *Application deadline:* For fall admission, 7/15 for domestic and international students; for winter admission, 10/1 for domestic and international students; for spring admission, 1/15 for domestic and international students; for summer admission, 4/1 for domestic and international students. Applications are processed on a rolling basis. Application fee: $50. Electronic applications accepted. Application fee is waived when completed online. *Expenses:* $4,488 per course. *Financial support:* In 2017–18, 5 students received support. Research assistantships, career-related internships or fieldwork, Federal Work-Study, scholarships/grants, and health care benefits available. *Faculty research:* Encouraging innovation with reward programs, alternative dispute resolution, performance appraisal, global human resources, work of Independent contractors. *Unit head:* Dr. Sung Min Kim, Chair, 312-915-7052, E-mail: skim@luc.edu.
Website: http://www.luc.edu/quinlan/mba/masters-degree-in-human-resources/index.shtml

Loyola University Chicago, Quinlan School of Business, MBA Programs, Chicago, IL 60611. Offers accounting (MBA); business ethics (MBA); derivative markets (MBA); economics (MBA); entrepreneurship (MBA); finance (MBA); healthcare management (MBA); human resources management (MBA); information systems management (MBA); international business (MBA); management (MBA); marketing (MBA); risk management (MBA); supply chain management (MBA). *Program availability:* Part-time, evening/weekend. *Faculty:* 84 full-time (28 women), 12 part-time/adjunct (3 women). *Students:* 253 full-time (118 women), 76 part-time (35 women); includes 83 minority (21 Black or African American, non-Hispanic/Latino; 1 American Indian or Alaska Native, non-Hispanic/Latino; 33 Asian, non-Hispanic/Latino; 24 Hispanic/Latino; 4 Two or more races, non-Hispanic/Latino), 37 international. Average age 30. 334 applicants, 52% accepted, 80 enrolled. In 2017, 220 master's awarded. *Entrance requirements:* For master's, GMAT or GRE, official transcripts, two letters of recommendation, statement of purpose, resume. Additional exam requirements/recommendations for international students: Required—TOEFL (minimum score 90 iBT) or IELTS (minimum score 6.5). *Application deadline:* For fall admission, 7/15 for domestic and international students; for winter admission, 10/1 for domestic and international students; for spring admission, 1/15 for domestic and international students; for summer admission, 4/1 for domestic and international students. Applications are processed on a rolling basis. Application fee: $50. Electronic applications accepted. Application fee is waived when completed online. *Expenses:* $4,488 per course. *Financial support:* In 2017–18, 11 students received support. Research assistantships, career-related internships or fieldwork, Federal Work-Study, scholarships/grants, and health care benefits available. *Faculty research:* Social enterprise and responsibility, emerging markets, supply chain management, risk management. *Unit head:* Katherine Acles, Assistant Dean for Graduate Programs, 312-915-6124, Fax: 312-915-7207, E-mail: kacles@luc.edu.

Lynn University, College of Business and Management, Boca Raton, FL 33431-5598. Offers business administration (MBA), including aviation management, entrepreneurial management, financial valuation and investment management, hospitality management, human resource management, international business management, marketing, media management, social innovation management, sports management, Web development. *Program availability:* Part-time, evening/weekend, 100% online, blended/hybrid learning. *Faculty:* 29 full-time (11 women), 19 part-time/adjunct (7 women). *Students:* 287 full-time (124 women), 195 part-time (105 women); includes 110 minority (44 Black or African American, non-Hispanic/Latino; 2 American Indian or Alaska Native, non-Hispanic/Latino; 11 Asian, non-Hispanic/Latino; 47 Hispanic/Latino; 6 Two or more races, non-Hispanic/Latino), 135 international. Average age 28. 293 applicants, 94% accepted, 192 enrolled. In 2017, 236 master's awarded. *Degree requirements:* For master's, thesis, minimum GPA of 3.0, strategic management seminar, written presentation reflecting the integration and application of theory to practice. *Entrance requirements:* For master's, bachelor's degree from accredited institution, minimum undergraduate GPA of 2.5, official undergraduate transcripts, resume, personal statement, letter of recommendation from academic or professional sources, writing sample demonstrating capacity to perform at graduate level. Additional exam requirements/recommendations for international students: Required—TOEFL (minimum score 550 paper-based; 80 iBT), IELTS (minimum score 6.5). *Application deadline:* For fall admission, 8/18 for domestic students, 8/4 for international students; for spring admission, 12/15 for domestic students, 12/1 for international students; for summer admission, 4/17 for domestic students, 4/3 for international students. Applications are processed on a rolling basis. Application fee: $45. Electronic applications accepted. *Expenses:* $740 per credit. *Financial support:* Career-related internships or fieldwork, Federal Work-Study, scholarships/grants, tuition waivers (full and partial), and unspecified assistantships available. Support available to part-time students. Financial award application deadline: 3/1; financial award applicants required to submit FAFSA. *Faculty research:* Knowledge economy, urban economy, U.S. manufacturing industries, leadership personality, stock market reactions to terrorism, personality psychology, industrial/organizational psychology. *Unit head:* Dr. RT Good, Dean of the College of Business and Management, 561-237-7834, E-mail: rgood@lynn.edu. *Application contact:* Steven Pruitt, Director of Graduate and Undergraduate Evening Admission, 561-237-7834, Fax: 561-237-7100, E-mail: spruitt@lynn.edu.
Website: http://www.lynn.edu/academics/colleges/business-and-management

Manhattanville College, School of Business, Master of Science in Human Resource Management and Organizational Effectiveness Program, Purchase, NY 10577-2132. Offers human resource management (Advanced Certificate); human resource management and organizational effectiveness (MS), including human resource management, organizational effectiveness. *Program availability:* Part-time, evening/weekend. *Faculty:* 8 part-time/adjunct (2 women). *Students:* 14 full-time (11 women), 7 part-time (all women); includes 7 minority (2 Asian, non-Hispanic/Latino; 5 Hispanic/Latino), 1 international. Average age 33. 23 applicants, 39% accepted, 7 enrolled. In 2017, 15 master's awarded. *Degree requirements:* For master's, thesis (for some programs), final project. *Entrance requirements:* For master's, personal essay, transcripts, 2 letters of recommendation (academic or professional), resume, health form with proof of immunization (for those born after 1957). Additional exam requirements/recommendations for international students: Required—TOEFL (minimum score 563 paper-based, 85 iBT), IELTS (7), or iTEP (B2). *Application deadline:* Applications are processed on a rolling basis. Application fee: $75. Electronic applications accepted. *Expenses:* $915 per credit. *Financial support:* Federal Work-Study, institutionally sponsored loans, scholarships/grants, and unspecified assistantships available. Financial award application deadline: 3/15; financial award applicants required to submit FAFSA. *Unit head:* Laura Persky, Graduate Program Director, 914-323-5188, E-mail: laura.persky@mville.edu. *Application contact:* Monika Pottgen, Assistant Director, Recruitment and Admissions, 914-323-5150, E-mail: business@mville.edu.
Website: https://www.mville.edu/programs/ms-human-resource-management

Manhattanville College, School of Business, Master of Science in International Management Program, Purchase, NY 10577-2132. Offers international management (MS, Advanced Certificate), including business leadership (MS), finance (MS), human resource management (MS), marketing communication management (MS). *Program availability:* Part-time, evening/weekend. *Faculty:* 2 part-time/adjunct (0 women). *Students:* 6 full-time (3 women), 2 part-time (1 woman); includes 2 minority (1 Black or African American, non-Hispanic/Latino; 1 Two or more races, non-Hispanic/Latino), 2 international. Average age 34. 6 applicants, 67% accepted, 1 enrolled. In 2017, 2 master's awarded. *Degree requirements:* For master's, thesis (for some programs), final project. *Entrance requirements:* For master's, personal essay, transcripts, 2 letters of recommendation (academic or professional), resume, health form with proof of immunization (for those born after 1957). Additional exam requirements/recommendations for international students: Required—TOEFL (minimum score 563 paper-based, 85 iBT), IELTS (7), or iTEP (B2). *Application deadline:* Applications are processed on a rolling basis. Application fee: $75. Electronic applications accepted. *Expenses:* $915 per credit. *Financial support:* Federal Work-Study, institutionally sponsored loans, scholarships/grants, and unspecified assistantships available. Financial award application deadline: 3/15; financial award applicants required to submit FAFSA. *Unit head:* Laura Persky, Graduate Program Director, 914-323-5188, E-mail: laura.persky@mville.edu. *Application contact:* Monika Pottgen, Assistant Director, Recruitment and Admissions, 914-323-5150, E-mail: business@mville.edu.
Website: https://www.mville.edu/programs/ms-international-management

Marquette University, Graduate School of Management, Executive MBA Program, Milwaukee, WI 53201-1881. Offers economics (MBA); finance (MBA); human resources (MBA); international business (MBA); management information systems (MBA); marketing (MBA); operations and supply chain management (MBA); sports business (MBA). *Accreditation:* AACSB. *Degree requirements:* For master's, international trip. *Entrance requirements:* For master's, GMAT or GRE, two letters of recommendation, official transcripts from current and previous colleges/universities. Additional exam requirements/recommendations for international students: Required—TOEFL (minimum score 550 paper-based; 88 iBT), IELTS (minimum score 6.5), PTE. Electronic applications accepted. *Expenses:* Contact institution. *Faculty research:* International trade and finance, customer relationship management, consumer satisfaction, customer service.

Marquette University, Graduate School of Management, Program in Business Administration, Milwaukee, WI 53201-1881. Offers business administration (MBA); economics (MBA); entrepreneurship (Certificate); finance (MBA); human resources (MBA); international business (MBA); management information systems (MBA); marketing (MBA); operations and supply chain management (MBA); sports business (MBA); JD/MBA; MBA/MA; MBA/MSN. *Accreditation:* AACSB. *Program availability:* Part-time, evening/weekend. *Degree requirements:* For Certificate, business plan. *Entrance requirements:* For master's, GMAT or GRE, letters of recommendation. Additional exam requirements/recommendations for international students: Required—TOEFL (minimum score 550 paper-based; 88 iBT), IELTS (minimum score 6.5), PTE. Electronic applications accepted. *Faculty research:* Ethics in the professions, services marketing, technology impact on decision-making, mentoring.

Marquette University, Graduate School of Management, Program in Human Resources, Milwaukee, WI 53201-1881. Offers MSHR. *Program availability:* Part-time, evening/weekend. *Entrance requirements:* For master's, GMAT or GRE General Test, letters of recommendation. Additional exam requirements/recommendations for international students: Required—TOEFL (minimum score 550 paper-based; 88 iBT), IELTS (minimum score 6.5), PTE. Electronic applications accepted. *Faculty research:* Diversity, mentoring, executive compensation.

Marshall University, Academic Affairs Division, College of Business, Program in Human Resource Management, Huntington, WV 25755. Offers MS. *Program availability:* Part-time, evening/weekend. *Students:* 40 full-time (25 women), 19 part-time (11 women); includes 4 minority (3 Black or African American, non-Hispanic/Latino; 1 Asian, non-Hispanic/Latino). Average age 31. In 2017, 31 master's awarded. *Entrance requirements:* For master's, GMAT or GRE General Test. *Application deadline:* Applications are processed on a rolling basis. Application fee: $40. *Financial support:* Tuition waivers (full) available. Support available to part-time students. Financial award applicants required to submit FAFSA. *Unit head:* Dr. Margie McInerney, Associate Dean, 304-696-2675, E-mail: mcinerney@marshall.edu. *Application contact:* Wesley Spradlin, Information Contact, 304-746-8964, Fax: 304-746-1902, E-mail: spradlin2@marshall.edu.

Marygrove College, Graduate Studies, Detroit, MI 48221-2599. Offers autism spectrum disorders (M Ed, Certificate); curriculum instruction and assessment (MAT); educational leadership (MA); educational technology (M Ed); effective teaching in the 21st century-classroom focus (MAT); effective teaching in the 21st century-technology focus (MAT); human resource management (MA, Certificate); mathematics 6-8 (MAT); mathematics K-5 (MAT); reading and literacy K-6 (MAT); reading specialist (M Ed); school administrator (Certificate); social justice (MA); special education (MAT); special education - learning disabilities (M Ed); teaching - pre-elementary education (M Ed); teaching - pre-secondary education (M Ed). *Program availability:* Part-time, evening/weekend, 100% online, blended/hybrid learning. *Students:* 163 full-time (123 women), 264 part-time (186 women). Average age 34. *Entrance requirements:* For master's, all official bachelor's transcripts. Additional exam requirements/recommendations for international students: Required—TOEFL (minimum score 550 paper-based; 80 iBT). *Application deadline:* Applications are processed on a rolling basis. Electronic applications accepted. *Expenses:* Tuition: Part-time $590 per credit hour. *Required fees:* $120 per semester. One-time fee: $25 part-time. *Financial support:* Applicants required to submit FAFSA. *Unit head:* Marygrove College Admissions, 313-927-1240, E-mail: info@marygrove.edu. *Application contact:* Marygrove College Admissions, 313-927-1240, E-mail: info@marygrove.edu.

Marymount University, School of Business Administration, Program in Human Resource Management, Arlington, VA 22207-4299. Offers human resource management (Certificate); organization development (Certificate); MBA/MA. *Program availability:* Part-time, evening/weekend. *Faculty:* 3 full-time (1 woman), 1 (woman) part-time/adjunct. *Students:* 9 full-time (7 women), 29 part-time (24 women); includes 22 minority (8 Black or African American, non-Hispanic/Latino; 2 Asian, non-Hispanic/Latino; 11 Hispanic/Latino; 1 Native Hawaiian or other Pacific Islander, non-Hispanic/Latino), 4 international. Average age 33. 21 applicants, 100% accepted, 10 enrolled. In 2017, 8 Certificates awarded. *Entrance requirements:* For degree, resume. Additional exam requirements/recommendations for international students: Required—TOEFL (minimum score 600 paper-based; 96 iBT), IELTS (minimum score 6.5). *Application deadline:* For fall admission, 7/16 priority date for domestic and international students; for spring admission, 11/16 priority date for domestic and international students; for summer admission, 4/16 for domestic and international students. Applications are processed on a rolling basis. Application fee: $40. Electronic applications accepted. *Expenses:* $990 per credit. *Financial support:* In 2017–18, 1 student received support. Career-related internships or fieldwork, Federal Work-Study, scholarships/grants, and unspecified assistantships available. Support available to part-time students. Financial award application deadline: 3/1; financial award applicants required to submit FAFSA. *Unit head:* Dr. Virginia Bianco-Mathis, Chair/Director, 703-284-5957, Fax: 703-527-3830, E-mail: virginia.bianco-mathis@marymount.edu. *Application contact:* Francesca Reed, Director, Graduate Admissions, 703-284-5901, Fax: 703-527-3815, E-mail: grad.admissions@marymount.edu.
Website: http://www.marymount.edu/Academics/School-of-Business-Administration/Graduate-Programs/Human-Resource-Management-(M-A-)

Maryville University of Saint Louis, The John E. Simon School of Business, St. Louis, MO 63141-7299. Offers accounting (MBA, MS, Certificate); business studies (Certificate); cybersecurity (MBA, MS, Certificate); financial services (MBA, Certificate); healthcare practice management (MBA, Certificate); human resource management (MBA, Certificate); information technology (MBA, Certificate); management (MBA, Certificate); management and leadership (MA); marketing (MBA, Certificate); project management (MBA, Certificate); sport business management (MBA); supply chain management (Certificate); supply chain management/logistics (MBA). *Accreditation:* ACBSP. *Program availability:* Part-time, 100% online, blended/hybrid learning. *Faculty:* 5 full-time (3 women), 51 part-time/adjunct (16 women). *Students:* 222 full-time (96 women), 498 part-time (222 women); includes 185 minority (104 Black or African American, non-Hispanic/Latino; 5 American Indian or Alaska Native, non-Hispanic/Latino; 30 Asian, non-Hispanic/Latino; 37 Hispanic/Latino; 9 Two or more races, non-Hispanic/Latino), 26 international. Average age 33. In 2017, 106 master's awarded. *Degree requirements:* For master's, capstone course (for MBA). *Entrance requirements:* Additional exam requirements/recommendations for international students: Required—TOEFL (minimum score 563 paper-based; 85 iBT). *Application deadline:* Applications are processed on a rolling basis. Electronic applications accepted. *Expenses:* Contact institution. *Financial support:* Career-related internships or fieldwork, Federal Work-Study, tuition waivers (partial), and campus employment available. Financial award application deadline: 4/1; financial award applicants required to submit FAFSA. *Unit head:* Pam Horwitz, Interim Dean, 314-529-9680, Fax: 314-529-9975. *Application contact:* Dustin Loeffler, Director for Graduate Studies in Business, 314-529-9571, Fax: 314-529-9975, E-mail: dloeffler@maryville.edu.
Website: http://www.maryville.edu/bu/business-administration-masters/

McKendree University, Graduate Programs, Master of Business Administration Program, Lebanon, IL 62254-1299. Offers business administration (MBA); human resource management (MBA); international business (MBA). *Program availability:* Part-time, evening/weekend, online learning. *Entrance requirements:* For master's, official transcripts from all institutions attended, essay, minimum GPA of 3.0, three references, resume. Additional exam requirements/recommendations for international students: Required—TOEFL. Electronic applications accepted.

McMaster University, School of Graduate Studies, DeGroote School of Business, Program in Human Resources and Management, Hamilton, ON L8S 4M2, Canada. Offers MBA, PhD. *Program availability:* Part-time. *Degree requirements:* For doctorate, comprehensive exam, thesis/dissertation. *Entrance requirements:* For master's, GMAT; for doctorate, GMAT or GRE, master's degree, minimum B+ average. Additional exam requirements/recommendations for international students: Required—TOEFL (minimum score 580 paper-based). *Faculty research:* Leadership, occupational mental health, work attitudes, human resources recruitment, change and stress management strategies.

Human Resources Management

Mercy College, School of Business, Program in Human Resource Management, Dobbs Ferry, NY 10522-1189. Offers MS. *Program availability:* Part-time, evening/weekend, 100% online, blended/hybrid learning. *Students:* 43 full-time (35 women), 22 part-time (19 women); includes 44 minority (15 Black or African American, non-Hispanic/Latino; 1 American Indian or Alaska Native, non-Hispanic/Latino; 6 Asian, non-Hispanic/Latino; 21 Hispanic/Latino; 1 Two or more races, non-Hispanic/Latino), 6 international. Average age 32. 58 applicants, 79% accepted, 22 enrolled. In 2017, 18 master's awarded. *Entrance requirements:* For master's, interview, two letters of reference, undergraduate transcripts. Additional exam requirements/recommendations for international students: Required—TOEFL (minimum score 600 paper-based; 100 iBT), IELTS (minimum score 8). *Application deadline:* For fall admission, 8/1 for international students. Applications are processed on a rolling basis. Application fee: $40. Electronic applications accepted. *Expenses:* Contact institution. *Financial support:* Career-related internships or fieldwork, Federal Work-Study, scholarships/grants, and unspecified assistantships available. Support available to part-time students. Financial award applicants required to submit FAFSA. *Unit head:* Ed Weis, Dean, School of Business, 914-674-7490, E-mail: eweis@mercy.edu. *Application contact:* Allison Gurdineer, Senior Director of Admissions, 877-637-2946, Fax: 914-674-7382, E-mail: admissions@mercy.edu. Website: https://www.mercy.edu/degrees-programs/ms-human-resource-management

Mercyhurst University, Graduate Studies, Program in Organizational Leadership, Erie, PA 16546. Offers accounting (MS); higher education administration (MS); human resources (MS); organizational leadership (MS, Certificate); sports leadership (MS); strategy and innovation (MS). *Program availability:* Part-time, evening/weekend. *Degree requirements:* For master's, thesis. *Entrance requirements:* For master's, GRE General Test or MAT, interview, resume, essay, three professional references, transcripts. Additional exam requirements/recommendations for international students: Required—TOEFL (minimum score 80 iBT), IELTS (minimum score 6.5). Electronic applications accepted. *Faculty research:* Leadership training, organizational communication, leadership pedagogy.

Meredith College, School of Business, Raleigh, NC 27607-5298. Offers entrepreneurship and family business (MBA); human resource management (MBA); project management (MBA). *Accreditation:* AACSB. *Program availability:* Part-time, evening/weekend. *Students:* 5 full-time (all women), 88 part-time (73 women); includes 33 minority (24 Black or African American, non-Hispanic/Latino; 1 Asian, non-Hispanic/Latino; 6 Hispanic/Latino; 2 Two or more races, non-Hispanic/Latino), 4 international. Average age 34. 62 applicants, 63% accepted, 29 enrolled. In 2017, 18 master's awarded. *Degree requirements:* For master's, thesis optional. *Entrance requirements:* For master's, GMAT, interview, minimum GPA of 2.5, letters of recommendation. Additional exam requirements/recommendations for international students: Required—TOEFL. *Application deadline:* For fall admission, 7/1 priority date for domestic and international students; for spring admission, 11/1 priority date for domestic and international students. Applications are processed on a rolling basis. Application fee: $50. Electronic applications accepted. *Expenses:* Contact institution. *Financial support:* Career-related internships or fieldwork, institutionally sponsored loans, scholarships/grants, and tuition waivers (partial) available. Support available to part-time students. Financial award application deadline: 2/15; financial award applicants required to submit FAFSA. *Unit head:* Kristie Ogilvie, Dean, 919-760-8432, Fax: 919-760-8470. Website: https://www.meredith.edu/school-of-business

Michigan State University, The Graduate School, College of Social Science, School of Labor and Industrial Relations, East Lansing, MI 48824. Offers human resources and labor relations (MLRHR); industrial relations and human resources (PhD). *Entrance requirements:* Additional exam requirements/recommendations for international students: Required—TOEFL.

Michigan State University, The Graduate School, Eli Broad College of Business, Program in Business Administration, East Lansing, MI 48224. Offers finance (MBA); human resource management (MBA); integrative management (MBA); marketing (MBA); supply chain management (MBA). MBA in integrative management is through Weekend MBA Program; other 4 concentrations are through Full-Time MBA Program. *Program availability:* Evening/weekend. *Degree requirements:* For master's, enrichment experience. *Entrance requirements:* For master's, GMAT or GRE, 4-year bachelor's degree; resume; work experience (minimum of 5 years for Weekend MBA); 2-3 personal essays; 2 letters of recommendation; personal interview. Additional exam requirements/recommendations for international students: Required—PTE (minimum score 70), TOEFL (minimum score 100 iBT) or IELTS (minimum score 7) for full-time MBA applicants. Electronic applications accepted. *Expenses:* Contact institution.

Middle Tennessee State University, College of Graduate Studies, University College, Murfreesboro, TN 37132. Offers advanced studies in teaching and learning (M Ed); human resources leadership (MPS); nursing administration (MSN); nursing education (MSN); strategic leadership (MPS); training and development (MPS). *Program availability:* Part-time, evening/weekend, online learning. *Entrance requirements:* Additional exam requirements/recommendations for international students: Required—TOEFL (minimum score 525 paper-based; 71 iBT) or IELTS (minimum score 6).

Millennia Atlantic University, Graduate Programs, Doral, FL 33178. Offers accounting (MBA); business administration (MBA); health information management (MS); human resource management (MA). *Program availability:* Online learning.

Misericordia University, College of Business, Master of Business Administration Program, Dallas, PA 18612-1098. Offers accounting (MBA); healthcare management (MBA); human resource management (MBA); management (MBA); sport management (MBA). *Program availability:* Part-time, evening/weekend, online learning. *Entrance requirements:* For master's, GMAT, MAT, GRE (50th percentile or higher), or minimum undergraduate GPA of 3.0, interview. Additional exam requirements/recommendations for international students: Required—TOEFL. Electronic applications accepted. Application fee is waived when completed online. *Expenses:* Contact institution.

Misericordia University, College of Business, Program in Organizational Management, Dallas, PA 18612-1098. Offers healthcare management (MS); human resource management (MS); management (MS). *Program availability:* Part-time, evening/weekend, online learning. *Entrance requirements:* For master's, GRE General Test, MAT (35th percentile or higher), or minimum undergraduate GPA of 3.0. Additional exam requirements/recommendations for international students: Required—TOEFL. Electronic applications accepted. Application fee is waived when completed online. *Expenses:* Contact institution.

Monmouth University, Graduate Studies, Department of Communication, West Long Branch, NJ 07764-1898. Offers corporate and public communication (MA); human resources management and communication (Certificate); public service communication specialist (Certificate); strategic public relations and new media (Certificate). *Program availability:* Part-time, evening/weekend, online learning. *Faculty:* 4 full-time (3 women), 2 part-time/adjunct (both women). *Students:* 10 full-time (7 women), 18 part-time (14 women); includes 9 minority (5 Black or African American, non-Hispanic/Latino; 1 Asian, non-Hispanic/Latino; 3 Hispanic/Latino). Average age 28. In 2017, 18 master's, 1 other advanced degree awarded. Terminal master's awarded for partial completion of doctoral program. *Degree requirements:* For master's, comprehensive exam (for some programs), thesis (for some programs), project. *Entrance requirements:* For master's,

GRE, baccalaureate degree with minimum GPA of 3.0 in major, 2.75 overall; two letters of recommendation; personal essay (750 words or less describing preparation for study and personal objectives); digital or hard copy portfolio of select samples of work including writing sample; resume. Additional exam requirements/recommendations for international students: Required—TOEFL (minimum score 550 paper-based; 79 iBT), IELTS (minimum score 6), Michigan English Language Assessment Battery (minimum score 77). *Application deadline:* For fall admission, 7/15 priority date for domestic students, 6/1 for international students; for spring admission, 12/1 priority date for domestic students, 11/1 for international students; for summer admission, 5/1 for domestic students. Applications are processed on a rolling basis. Application fee: $50. Electronic applications accepted. *Expenses:* Tuition: Full-time $21,366; part-time $7122 per credit. *Required fees:* $700; $175 per term. *Financial support:* In 2017–18, 2 students received support. Institutionally sponsored loans, scholarships/grants, and unspecified assistantships available. Support available to part-time students. Financial award applicants required to submit FAFSA. *Faculty research:* Service-learning, history of television, feminism and the media, executive communication, public relations pedagogy. *Unit head:* Dr. Marina Vujnovic, Program Director, 732-263-5667, Fax: 732-571-5667, E-mail: mvujnovi@monmouth.edu. *Application contact:* Andrea Thompson, Graduate Admission Counselor, 732-571-3452, Fax: 732-263-5123, E-mail: gradadm@monmouth.edu.
Website: http://www.monmouth.edu/cpc

Monroe College, King Graduate School, Bronx, NY 10468. Offers accounting (MS); business administration (MBA), including entrepreneurship, finance, general business administration, healthcare management, human resources, information technology, marketing; computer science (MS); criminal justice (MS); hospitality management (MS); public health (MPH), including biostatistics and epidemiology, community health, health administration and leadership. *Program availability:* Online learning. Application fee: $50.
Website: https://www.monroecollege.edu/Degrees/King-Graduate-School/

Moravian College, Graduate and Continuing Studies, Business and Management Programs, Bethlehem, PA 18018-6650. Offers accounting (MBA); business analytics (MBA); business management (MBA); health administration (MHA); healthcare management (MBA); HR leadership (MSHRM); human resource management (MBA); learning and performance management (MSHRM); supply chain management (MBA). *Program availability:* Part-time, evening/weekend. *Faculty:* 5 full-time (2 women), 9 part-time/adjunct (3 women). *Students:* 13 full-time (10 women), 80 part-time (45 women); includes 13 minority (6 Black or African American, non-Hispanic/Latino; 6 Hispanic/Latino; 1 Two or more races, non-Hispanic/Latino). Average age 31. 55 applicants, 91% accepted, 31 enrolled. In 2017, 29 master's awarded. *Entrance requirements:* For master's, current resume, official transcripts, 2 letters of recommendation. Additional exam requirements/recommendations for international students: Required—TOEFL (minimum score 550 paper-based), IELTS (minimum score 6.5). *Application deadline:* For fall admission, 8/1 priority date for domestic and international students; for spring admission, 1/1 priority date for domestic and international students; for summer admission, 5/1 priority date for domestic and international students. Applications are processed on a rolling basis. Electronic applications accepted. *Expenses:* Tuition: Full-time $15,714; part-time $2619 per course. *Required fees:* $45 per semester. Tuition and fees vary according to program. *Financial support:* In 2017–18, 3 students received support, including 2 research assistantships with full tuition reimbursements available. Financial award applicants required to submit FAFSA. *Faculty research:* Leadership, change management, human resources. *Unit head:* Dr. Liz Kleintop, Associate Chair of Graduate Business, 610-861-1400, Fax: 610-861-1466, E-mail: graduate@moravian.edu. *Application contact:* Sean Rossi, Student Experience Mentor, 610-861-1400, Fax: 610-861-1466, E-mail: graduate@moravian.edu.
Website: https://www.moravian.edu/graduate

Mount Mercy University, Program in Business Administration, Cedar Rapids, IA 52402-4797. Offers human resource (MBA); quality management (MBA). *Program availability:* Evening/weekend. *Entrance requirements:* For master's, minimum cumulative GPA of 3.0, 2 letters of recommendation, resume. Additional exam requirements/recommendations for international students: Required—TOEFL (minimum score 570 paper-based; 88 iBT). Electronic applications accepted.

Murray State University, Arthur J. Bauernfeind College of Business, MBA Program, Murray, KY 42071. Offers accounting (MBA); finance (MBA); global communications (MBA); human resource management (MBA); marketing (MBA). *Accreditation:* AACSB. *Program availability:* Part-time, evening/weekend, 100% online, blended/hybrid learning. *Faculty:* 49 full-time (15 women), 3 part-time/adjunct (0 women). *Students:* 54 full-time (22 women), 79 part-time (37 women); includes 13 minority (6 Black or African American, non-Hispanic/Latino; 1 American Indian or Alaska Native, non-Hispanic/Latino; 2 Asian, non-Hispanic/Latino; 2 Hispanic/Latino; 2 Two or more races, non-Hispanic/Latino), 30 international. Average age 29. 70 applicants, 81% accepted, 34 enrolled. In 2017, 61 master's awarded. *Entrance requirements:* For master's, GRE or GMAT, minimum university GPA of 2.75. Additional exam requirements/recommendations for international students: Required—TOEFL (minimum score 527 paper-based; 71 iBT). *Application deadline:* Applications are processed on a rolling basis. Application fee: $40 ($50 for international students). *Expenses:* Tuition, state resident: full-time $9504. Tuition, nonresident: full-time $26,811. *International tuition:* $14,400 full-time. Tuition and fees vary according to course load, degree level and reciprocity agreements. *Financial support:* In 2017–18, 5 research assistantships, 5 teaching assistantships were awarded; Federal Work-Study also available. Financial award applicants required to submit FAFSA. *Faculty research:* Human resource management, e-commerce, supply-chain management, investment management, accounting. *Unit head:* Dr. Joy Humphreys, Assistant Dean and MBA Director, 270-809-4259, Fax: 270-809-3482, E-mail: jumphreys4@murraystate.edu. *Application contact:* Kaitlyn Burzynski, Interim Assistant Director for Graduate Admission and Records, 270-809-5732, Fax: 270-809-3780, E-mail: msu.graduateadmissions@murraystate.edu.
Website: http://www.murraystate.edu/academics/CollegesDepartments/CollegeOfBusiness/Programs/mba/index.aspx

National American University, Roueche Graduate Center, Austin, TX 78731. Offers accounting (MBA); aviation management (MBA, MM); care coordination (MSN); community college leadership (Ed D); criminal justice (MM); e-marketing (MBA, MM); health care administration (MBA, MM); higher education (MM); human resources management (MBA, MM); information technology management (MBA, MM); international business (MBA); leadership (EMBA); management (MBA); nursing administration (MSN); nursing education (MSN); nursing informatics (MSN); operations and configuration management (MBA, MM); project and process management (MBA, MM). Master's programs offered online through the Harold D. Buckingham Graduate School. *Program availability:* Part-time, evening/weekend, online learning. *Entrance requirements:* For master's, minimum undergraduate GPA of 2.75. Additional exam requirements/recommendations for international students: Required—TOEFL, TWE. Electronic applications accepted. *Faculty research:* Tourism, finance, marketing.

National Louis University, College of Management and Business, Chicago, IL 60603. Offers business administration (MBA); human resource management and development (MS); management (MS). *Program availability:* Part-time, evening/weekend. *Entrance *requirements:* For master's, college-administered critical thinking and writing skills test, minimum GPA of 3.0, resume, 3 references. Additional exam requirements/recommendations for international students: Required—TOEFL (minimum score 550 paper-based; 79 iBT).

National University, Academic Affairs, School of Business and Management, La Jolla, CA 92037-1011. Offers accountancy (M Acc, Certificate); business administration (GMBA, MBA); business analytics (MS); cause leadership (MA); global management (MGM); human resource management (MA); management information systems (MS); marketing (MS); organizational leadership (MS). GMBA offered in Spanish. *Program availability:* Part-time, evening/weekend, 100% online, blended/hybrid learning. *Degree requirements:* For master's, thesis (for some programs). *Entrance requirements:* For master's, interview, minimum GPA of 2.5. Additional exam requirements/recommendations for international students: Required—TOEFL (minimum score 550 paper-based; 79 iBT), IELTS (minimum score 6). *Application deadline:* Applications are processed on a rolling basis. Application fee: $60 ($65 for international students). Electronic applications accepted. *Expenses: Tuition:* Part-time $430 per quarter hour. *Financial support:* Career-related internships or fieldwork, scholarships/grants, and tuition waivers (partial) available. Support available to part-time students. Financial award application deadline: 6/30; financial award applicants required to submit FAFSA. *Unit head:* Dr. Alfred Ntoko, Dean, 858-642-8400, Fax: 858-642-8719, E-mail: sobm@nu.edu. *Application contact:* Brandon Jouganatos, Vice President for Enrollment Services, 800-628-8648, E-mail: advisor@nu.edu.
Website: http://www.nu.edu/OurPrograms/SchoolOfBusinessAndManagement.html

National University, Academic Affairs, School of Professional Studies, La Jolla, CA 92037-1011. Offers criminal justice (MCJ); digital cinema production (MFA); digital journalism (MA); homeland security and emergency management (MS); juvenile justice (MS); professional screenwriting (MFA); public administration (MPA), including human resource management, organizational leadership. *Program availability:* Part-time, evening/weekend, 100% online, blended/hybrid learning. *Degree requirements:* For master's, thesis (for some programs). *Entrance requirements:* For master's, interview, minimum GPA of 2.5. Additional exam requirements/recommendations for international students: Required—TOEFL (minimum score 550 paper-based; 79 iBT), IELTS (minimum score 6). *Application deadline:* Applications are processed on a rolling basis. Application fee: $60 ($65 for international students). Electronic applications accepted. *Expenses: Tuition:* Part-time $430 per quarter hour. *Financial support:* Career-related internships or fieldwork, institutionally sponsored loans, scholarships/grants, and tuition waivers (partial) available. Support available to part-time students. Financial award application deadline: 6/30; financial award applicants required to submit FAFSA. *Unit head:* Dr. Daniel Donaldson, Dean, 858-642-8480, E-mail: sops@nu.edu. *Application contact:* Brandon Jouganatos, Vice President for Enrollment Services, 800-628-8648, E-mail: advisor@nu.edu.
Website: http://www.nu.edu/OurPrograms/School-of-Professional-Studies.html

Nazareth College of Rochester, Graduate Studies, Department of Business, Program in Human Resource Management, Rochester, NY 14618. Offers MS. *Program availability:* Part-time, evening/weekend. *Entrance requirements:* For master's, minimum GPA of 3.0. Additional exam requirements/recommendations for international students: Required—TOEFL (minimum score 550 paper-based, 79 iBT) or IELTS (6.5). Electronic applications accepted.

New Mexico Highlands University, Graduate Studies, School of Business, Media and Technology, Las Vegas, NM 87701. Offers business administration (MBA), including human resource management, international business, management; media arts and technology (MA), including media arts and computer science. *Accreditation:* ACBSP. *Degree requirements:* For master's, comprehensive exam, thesis or alternative. *Entrance requirements:* For master's, minimum undergraduate GPA of 3.0. Additional exam requirements/recommendations for international students: Required—TOEFL (minimum score 540 paper-based). *Faculty research:* Real estate valuation, studying expert judgments in complex accounting, decision environments, green marketing, environmentalism, marketing research methodology.

New York Institute of Technology, School of Management, Department of Human Resource Management Studies, Old Westbury, NY 11568-8000. Offers human resource management (Advanced Certificate); human resource management and labor relations (MS). *Program availability:* Part-time. *Faculty:* 5 full-time (1 woman), 4 part-time/adjunct (1 woman). *Students:* 16 full-time (15 women), 29 part-time (25 women); includes 23 minority (7 Black or African American, non-Hispanic/Latino; 6 Asian, non-Hispanic/Latino; 10 Hispanic/Latino), 10 international. Average age 30. 57 applicants, 61% accepted, 10 enrolled. In 2017, 18 master's, 1 other advanced degree awarded. *Degree requirements:* For master's, seminar and comprehensive exam, or thesis. *Entrance requirements:* For master's, bachelor's degree; minimum undergraduate GPA of 3.0; interview; for Advanced Certificate, bachelor's degree; minimum undergraduate GPA of 3.0. Additional exam requirements/recommendations for international students: Required—TOEFL (minimum score 79 iBT), IELTS (minimum score 6). *Application deadline:* Applications are processed on a rolling basis. Application fee: $50. Electronic applications accepted. *Expenses:* $1,285 per credit plus fees. *Financial support:* Career-related internships or fieldwork, Federal Work-Study, scholarships/grants, tuition waivers (full and partial), and unspecified assistantships available. Support available to part-time students. Financial award application deadline: 2/15; financial award applicants required to submit FAFSA. *Faculty research:* Conflict resolution; adapting human resource practices to the needs of a global workforce; effect of leadership styles and human resource practices on employee productivity; human resource management practices as a source of competitive advantage; influence of personality on work-life balance and work-home domain boundaries. *Unit head:* Dr. Maya Kroumova, Chairperson, 212-261-1667, Fax: 516-686-7425, E-mail: mkroumov@nyit.edu. *Application contact:* Alice Dolitsky, Director, Graduate Admissions, 516-686-7520, Fax: 516-686-1116, E-mail: nyitgrad@nyit.edu.
Website: http://www.nyit.edu/degrees/human_resources_management_labor_relations_ms

New York University, School of Professional Studies, Division of Programs in Business, Program in Leadership and Human Capital Management, New York, NY 10012-1019. Offers human resource management and development (MS), including global talent management, human resource management, learning, development, and executive coaching, organizational effectiveness. *Program availability:* Part-time, evening/weekend, 100% online, blended/hybrid learning. *Students:* 101 full-time (88 women), 107 part-time (93 women); includes 68 minority (19 Black or African American, non-Hispanic/Latino; 25 Asian, non-Hispanic/Latino; 21 Hispanic/Latino; 3 Two or more races, non-Hispanic/Latino), 93 international. Average age 29. 251 applicants, 52% accepted, 60 enrolled. In 2017, 180 master's awarded. *Degree requirements:* For master's, thesis. *Entrance requirements:* For master's, GRE or GMAT (only upon request), bachelor's degree, resume with relevant professional work, internship or volunteer experience, two letters of recommendation, statement of purpose. Additional exam requirements/recommendations for international students: Required—TOEFL (minimum score 600 paper-based; 100 iBT), IELTS (minimum score 7). *Application deadline:* For fall admission, 2/1 priority date for domestic and international students; for spring admission, 10/15 priority date for domestic students, 8/15 priority date for international students; for summer admission, 5/1 priority date for domestic students, 1/15 priority date for international students. Applications are processed on a rolling basis. Application fee: $150. Electronic applications accepted. *Expenses:* $20,244 per term. *Financial support:* Fellowships, career-related internships or fieldwork, Federal Work-Study, scholarships/grants, and health care benefits available. Support available to part-time students. Financial award application deadline: 6/30; financial award applicants required to submit FAFSA. *Unit head:* Martin Ihrig, Associate Dean/Clinical Professor, 212-992-3288. *Application contact:* Admissions Office, 212-998-7100, E-mail: sps.gradadmissions@nyu.edu.
Website: http://www.sps.nyu.edu/academics/departments/leadership.html

Niagara University, Graduate Division of Business Administration, Niagara University, NY 14109. Offers accounting (MBA); business administration (MBA); finance (MBA, MS); financial planning (MBA); healthcare administration (MBA, MHA); human resources (MBA); international business (MBA); marketing (MBA); professional accountancy (MBA); strategic management (MBA); supply chain management (MBA). *Accreditation:* AACSB. *Program availability:* Part-time, evening/weekend. *Faculty:* 17 full-time, 11 part-time/adjunct. *Students:* 173 full-time (92 women), 77 part-time (39 women); includes 38 minority (8 Black or African American, non-Hispanic/Latino; 3 American Indian or Alaska Native, non-Hispanic/Latino; 8 Asian, non-Hispanic/Latino; 8 Hispanic/Latino; 11 Two or more races, non-Hispanic/Latino), 46 international. Average age 27. In 2017, 139 master's awarded. *Entrance requirements:* For master's, GMAT. Additional exam requirements/recommendations for international students: Required—TOEFL (minimum score 550 paper-based; 79 iBT), IELTS (minimum score 6). *Application deadline:* For fall admission, 8/1 for domestic students; for spring admission, 11/1 for domestic students. Applications are processed on a rolling basis. Electronic applications accepted. *Expenses:* Contact institution. *Financial support:* Fellowships, research assistantships, career-related internships or fieldwork, and Federal Work-Study available. Support available to part-time students. Financial award application deadline: 4/15; financial award applicants required to submit FAFSA. *Faculty research:* Capital flows, Federal Reserve policy, human resource management, public policy, issues in marketing, auctions, economics of information, risk and capital markets, management strategy, consumer behavior, Internet and social media marketing. *Unit head:* Dr. Paul Richardson, MBA Director/Chair of the Marketing Department, 716-286-8169, Fax: 716-286-8206, E-mail: psr@niagara.edu. *Application contact:* Evan Pierce, Associate Director for Graduate Recruitment, 716-286-8769, Fax: 716-286-8170, E-mail: epierce@niagara.edu.
Website: http://mba.niagara.edu

North Carolina Agricultural and Technical State University, School of Graduate Studies, School of Business and Economics, Greensboro, NC 27411. Offers accounting (MBA); business education (MAT); human resources management (MBA); supply chain systems (MBA).

North Central College, School of Graduate and Professional Studies, Program in Business Administration, Naperville, IL 60566-7063. Offers change management (MBA); finance (MBA); human resource management (MBA); management (MBA). *Program availability:* Part-time, evening/weekend. *Degree requirements:* For master's, thesis optional, project. *Entrance requirements:* For master's, interview. Additional exam requirements/recommendations for international students: Required—TOEFL (minimum score 550 paper-based; 80 iBT), IELTS (minimum score 6.5). Electronic applications accepted. Application fee is waived when completed online. *Expenses:* Contact institution.

North Greenville University, T. Walter Brashier Graduate School, Greer, SC 29651. Offers Christian ministry (MCM, D Min); education (M Ed, MAT); financial planning (MBA); human resources (MBA). *Program availability:* Part-time, evening/weekend, online learning. *Degree requirements:* For master's, comprehensive exam (for some programs), thesis or alternative, capstone course. *Entrance requirements:* For master's, minimum GPA of 2.25 overall, 2.5 in major; for doctorate, MAT. Additional exam requirements/recommendations for international students: Required—TOEFL (minimum score 550 paper-based). Electronic applications accepted. *Faculty research:* Organizational behavior, church growth, homiletics, human resources, business strategy.

Northwestern University, The Graduate School, Kellogg School of Management, Management Programs, Evanston, IL 60208. Offers accounting information and management (MBA, PhD); analytical finance (MBA); business administration (MBA); decision sciences (MBA); entrepreneurship and innovation (MBA); finance (MBA, PhD); health enterprise management (MBA); human resources management (MBA); international business (MBA); management and organizations (MBA, PhD); management and organizations and sociology (PhD); management and strategy (MBA); management studies (MS); managerial analytics (MBA); managerial economics (MBA); managerial economics and strategy (PhD); marketing (MBA, PhD); marketing management (MBA); media management (MBA); operations management (MBA, PhD); real estate (MBA); social enterprise at Kellogg (MBA); JD/MBA. *Program availability:* Part-time, evening/weekend. Terminal master's awarded for partial completion of doctoral program. *Degree requirements:* For doctorate, thesis/dissertation, 2 years of coursework, qualifying (field) exam and candidacy, summer research papers and presentations to faculty, proposal defense, final exam/defense. *Entrance requirements:* For master's, GMAT, GRE, interview, 2 letters of recommendation, college transcripts, resume, essays, Kellogg honor code; for doctorate, GMAT, GRE, statement of purpose, transcripts, 2 letters of recommendation, resume, interview. Additional exam requirements/recommendations for international students: Required—TOEFL, IELTS. Electronic applications accepted. *Expenses:* Contact institution. *Faculty research:* Business cycles and international finance, health policy, networks, non-market strategy, consumer psychology.

Northwest Missouri State University, Graduate School, Melvin and Valorie Booth College of Business and Professional Studies, Maryville, MO 64468-6001. Offers agricultural economics (MBA); business decision and analytics (MBA); general management (MBA); human resource management (MBA); marketing (MBA). *Program availability:* Part-time. *Faculty:* 17 full-time (6 women). *Students:* 40 full-time (13 women), 95 part-time (48 women); includes 16 minority (8 Black or African American, non-Hispanic/Latino; 1 American Indian or Alaska Native, non-Hispanic/Latino; 2 Asian, non-Hispanic/Latino; 3 Hispanic/Latino; 2 Two or more races, non-Hispanic/Latino), 15 international. Average age 31. 142 applicants, 66% accepted, 70 enrolled. In 2017, 53 master's awarded. *Degree requirements:* For master's, comprehensive exam. *Entrance requirements:* For master's, GMAT, GRE, minimum GPA of 2.5. Additional exam requirements/recommendations for international students: Required—TOEFL (minimum score 550 paper-based). *Application deadline:* For fall admission, 7/1 for domestic and international students; for spring admission, 11/15 for domestic and international students; for summer admission, 4/1 for domestic and international students. Applications are processed on a rolling basis. Application fee: $0 ($50 for international students). Electronic applications accepted. *Expenses:* $389.11 per credit in-state tuition; $641.97 per credit out-of-state tuition. *Financial support:* Research assistantships with full tuition reimbursements, teaching assistantships with full tuition reimbursements, career-related internships or fieldwork, and administrative assistantships, tutorial assistantships available. Financial award application deadline: 4/

Human Resources Management

1; financial award applicants required to submit FAFSA. *Unit head:* Dr. Steve Ludwig, Director of the Melvin And Valorie Booth School of Business, 660-562-1749, Fax: 660-562-1096, E-mail: sludwig@nwmissouri.edu.
Website: https://www.nwmissouri.edu/business/index.htm

Norwich University, College of Graduate and Continuing Studies, Master of Science in Leadership Program, Northfield, VT 05663. Offers leadership (MS), including human resources leadership, leading change management consulting, organizational leadership, public sector/government/military leadership. *Program availability:* Evening/weekend, online only, mostly all online with a week-long residency requirement. *Degree requirements:* For master's, capstone. *Entrance requirements:* For master's, minimum undergraduate GPA of 2.75. Additional exam requirements/recommendations for international students: Required—TOEFL (minimum score 550 paper-based; 80 iBT), IELTS (minimum score 6.5). Electronic applications accepted. *Expenses:* Contact institution.

Notre Dame de Namur University, Division of Academic Affairs, School of Business and Management, Program in Business Administration, Belmont, CA 94002-1908. Offers finance (MBA); human resource management (MBA); marketing (MBA); media and promotion (MBA). *Accreditation:* ACBSP. *Program availability:* Part-time, evening/weekend. *Students:* 28 full-time (24 women), 93 part-time (56 women). Average age 35. *Entrance requirements:* For master's, minimum GPA of 2.5. Additional exam requirements/recommendations for international students: Required—TOEFL (minimum score 550 paper-based; 79 iBT). *Application deadline:* For fall admission, 8/1 priority date for domestic students; for spring admission, 12/1 priority date for domestic students. Applications are processed on a rolling basis. Application fee: $60. Electronic applications accepted. *Expenses:* Tuition: Full-time $16,128; part-time $8064 per credit hour. *Required fees:* $80; $80 per credit hour. $40 per semester. *Financial support:* Available to part-time students. Applicants required to submit FAFSA. *Unit head:* Jordan Holtzman, Program Director, Graduate Business Programs, 510-375-1348, E-mail: jholtzman@ndnu.edu.
Website: http://www.ndnu.edu/academics/schools-programs/school-business/

Notre Dame de Namur University, Division of Academic Affairs, School of Business and Management, Program in Public Administration, Belmont, CA 94002-1908. Offers human resource management (MPA); public affairs administration (MPA). *Program availability:* Part-time, evening/weekend, online learning. *Students:* 2 full-time (1 woman), 32 part-time (29 women). Average age 35. *Entrance requirements:* For master's, interview, minimum GPA of 2.5. Additional exam requirements/recommendations for international students: Required—TOEFL (minimum score 550 paper-based; 79 iBT). *Application deadline:* For fall admission, 8/1 priority date for domestic students; for spring admission, 12/1 priority date for domestic students. Applications are processed on a rolling basis. Application fee: $60. Electronic applications accepted. *Expenses:* Tuition: Full-time $16,128; part-time $8064 per credit hour. *Required fees:* $80; $80 per credit hour. $40 per semester. *Financial support:* Available to part-time students. Applicants required to submit FAFSA. *Unit head:* Jordan Holtzman, Program Director, Graduate Business Programs, 510-375-1348, E-mail: jholtzman@ndnu.edu.
Website: http://www.ndnu.edu/academics/schools-programs/school-business/graduate/mpa.aspx

Nova Southeastern University, H. Wayne Huizenga College of Business and Entrepreneurship, Fort Lauderdale, FL 33314-7796. Offers accounting (M Acc); business (MBA); business intelligence/analytics (MBA); complex health systems (MBA); enterprise informatics (MBA); entrepreneurship (MBA); finance (MBA); human resource management (MBA); international business (MBA); management (MBA); marketing (MBA); process improvement (MBA); public administration (MPA); real estate development (MS); sport revenue generation (MBA); supply chain management (MBA). *Accreditation:* NASPAA. *Program availability:* Part-time, evening/weekend, 100% online, blended/hybrid learning. *Faculty:* 85 full-time (37 women), 59 part-time/adjunct (19 women). *Students:* 1,999 full-time (1,225 women), 335 part-time (210 women); includes 1,516 minority (597 Black or African American, non-Hispanic/Latino; 4 American Indian or Alaska Native, non-Hispanic/Latino; 92 Asian, non-Hispanic/Latino; 789 Hispanic/Latino; 3 Native Hawaiian or other Pacific Islander, non-Hispanic/Latino; 31 Two or more races, non-Hispanic/Latino), 291 international. Average age 34. 1,269 applicants, 59% accepted, 551 enrolled. In 2017, 1,055 master's awarded. *Entrance requirements:* For master's, GMAT or GRE (depending on undergraduate GPA), official transcripts from all schools attended while in pursuit of bachelor's degree; minimum GPA of 2.5 from regionally-accredited institution. Additional exam requirements/recommendations for international students: Required—TOEFL (minimum score 550 paper-based; 79 iBT), IELTS (minimum score 6), PTE (minimum score 54). *Application deadline:* For fall admission, 8/5 priority date for domestic students, 7/29 priority date for international students; for winter admission, 12/16 priority date for domestic students, 12/9 priority date for international students; for summer admission, 4/21 priority date for domestic and international students. Applications are processed on a rolling basis. Application fee: $50. Electronic applications accepted. *Expenses:* $37,785 (online), $35,640 (in-classroom). *Financial support:* In 2017–18, 325 students received support. Federal Work-Study and scholarships/grants available. Support available to part-time students. Financial award application deadline: 4/15; financial award applicants required to submit FAFSA. *Faculty research:* Entrepreneurship and venture capital, ethics and social responsibility, global commerce and cultures, business process management. *Unit head:* Dr. J. Preston Jones, Dean, 954-262-5127, E-mail: prestonj@nova.edu. *Application contact:* Zeida Rodriguez, Associate Director of Enrollment Services, 954-262-5163, Fax: 954-262-3822, E-mail: zeida@nova.edu.
Website: http://www.huizenga.nova.edu

Oakland University, Graduate Study and Lifelong Learning, School of Business Administration, Department of Management and Marketing, Rochester, MI 48309-4401. Offers business administration (MBA); entrepreneurship (Certificate); general management (Certificate); human resource management (Certificate); international business (Certificate); management and marketing (EMBA); marketing (Certificate). *Expenses:* Tuition, state resident: full-time $16,950; part-time $706.25 per credit. Tuition, nonresident: full-time $24,648; part-time $1027 per credit.

Ohio Christian University, Graduate Programs, Circleville, OH 43113. Offers accounting (MBA); business administration (MBA); digital marketing (MBA); finance (MBA); healthcare management (MBA); human resources (MBA); management (MM); organizational leadership (MBA); pastoral care and counseling (MAM); practical theology (MAM).

The Ohio State University, Graduate School, Max M. Fisher College of Business, Program in Human Resource Management, Columbus, OH 43210. Offers human resource management (MHRM, PhD); labor and human resources (PhD). *Program availability:* Part-time. *Faculty:* 25. *Students:* 85 full-time (64 women), 23 part-time (15 women). Average age 26. In 2017, 54 master's, 3 doctorates awarded. *Degree requirements:* For doctorate, thesis/dissertation. *Entrance requirements:* For master's and doctorate, GRE General Test or GMAT. Additional exam requirements/recommendations for international students: Required—Michigan English Language Assessment Battery (minimum score 86); Recommended—TOEFL (minimum score 600 paper-based; 100 iBT), IELTS (minimum score 7). *Application deadline:* For fall

admission, 11/15 priority date for domestic and international students. Applications are processed on a rolling basis. Application fee: $60 ($70 for international students). Electronic applications accepted. *Financial support:* Fellowships with tuition reimbursements, research assistantships with tuition reimbursements, and teaching assistantships with tuition reimbursements available. *Unit head:* Dr. Bennett J. Tepper, Chair, 614-688-2129, E-mail: tepper.15@osu.edu. *Application contact:* Graduate and Professional Admissions, 614-292-9444, Fax: 614-292-3895, E-mail: gpadmissions@osu.edu.
Website: http://fisher.osu.edu/departments/management-and-hr/

Oklahoma Christian University, Graduate School of Business, Oklahoma City, OK 73136-1100. Offers accounting (M Acc, MBA); financial services (MBA); general business (MBA); health services management (MBA); human resources (MBA); international business (MBA); leadership and organizational development (MBA); marketing (MBA); nonprofit management (MBA); project management (MBA). *Accreditation:* ACBSP. *Program availability:* Part-time, 100% online. *Entrance requirements:* For master's, bachelor's degree. Additional exam requirements/recommendations for international students: Required—TOEFL (minimum score 550 paper-based). Electronic applications accepted. *Expenses:* Contact institution.

Ottawa University, Graduate Studies-Arizona, Programs in Business, Ottawa, KS 66067-3399. Offers business administration (MBA); finance (MBA); human resources (MA, MBA); leadership (MBA); marketing (MBA). Programs offered in Mesa, Phoenix, Tempe and West Valley, AZ. *Program availability:* Part-time, evening/weekend, online learning. *Degree requirements:* For master's, thesis or alternative. *Entrance requirements:* For master's, minimum undergraduate GPA of 3.0. Additional exam requirements/recommendations for international students: Required—TOEFL (minimum score 550 paper-based). Electronic applications accepted.

Pace University, Lubin School of Business, Program in Management, New York, NY 10038. Offers entrepreneurial studies (MBA); entrepreneurship (MS); human resource management (MBA, MS); strategic management (MBA, MS). *Program availability:* Part-time, evening/weekend. *Students:* 58 full-time (37 women), 72 part-time (40 women); includes 38 minority (15 Black or African American, non-Hispanic/Latino; 7 Asian, non-Hispanic/Latino; 12 Hispanic/Latino; 4 Two or more races, non-Hispanic/Latino), 40 international. Average age 30. 160 applicants, 56% accepted, 38 enrolled. In 2017, 47 master's awarded. *Entrance requirements:* For master's, GMAT, GRE (GMAT not required for MS with 3 years of HR experience in a management position), undergraduate degree, transcripts from all accredited colleges/universities attended, two letters of recommendation, resume, personal statement. Additional exam requirements/recommendations for international students: Required—TOEFL (minimum score 90 iBT), IELTS (minimum score 7) or PTE (minimum score 61). *Application deadline:* For fall admission, 8/1 priority date for domestic students, 6/1 for international students; for spring admission, 12/1 for domestic students, 10/1 for international students. Applications are processed on a rolling basis. Application fee: $70. Electronic applications accepted. *Financial support:* Research assistantships, career-related internships or fieldwork, Federal Work-Study, and unspecified assistantships available. Support available to part-time students. Financial award application deadline: 2/15; financial award applicants required to submit FAFSA. *Unit head:* Dr. John C. Byrne, Chairperson, 212-618-6581, E-mail: jbyrne@pace.edu. *Application contact:* Susan Ford-Goldschein, Director of Graduate Admissions, 212-346-1531, Fax: 212-346-1585, E-mail: graduateadmission@pace.edu.
Website: http://www.pace.edu/lubin/management-concentration-mba

Penn State Great Valley, Graduate Studies, Management Division, Malvern, PA 19355-1488. Offers business administration (MBA); cyber security (Certificate); data analytics (MPS, MS, Certificate); distributed energy and grid modernization (Certificate); finance (M Fin); health sector management (Certificate); human resource management (Certificate); information science (MSIS); leadership development (MLD); new ventures and entrepreneurship (Certificate); sustainable management practices (Certificate). *Accreditation:* AACSB. *Unit head:* Dr. James A. Nemes, Chancellor, 610-648-3202, Fax: 610-725-5296. *Application contact:* JoAnn Kelly, Director of Admissions, 610-648-3315, Fax: 610-725-5296, E-mail: jek2@psu.edu.
Website: http://greatvalley.psu.edu/academics/masters-degrees/engineering-management

Penn State Harrisburg, Graduate School, School of Public Affairs, Middletown, PA 17057. Offers criminal justice (MA); health administration (MHA); health administration: long term care (Certificate); homeland security (MPS, Certificate); public administration (MPA, PhD); public administration: non-profit administration (Certificate); public budgeting and financial management (Certificate); public sector human resource management (Certificate). *Accreditation:* NASPAA. *Unit head:* Dr. Mukund S. Kulkarni, Chancellor, 717-948-6105, Fax: 717-948-6452. *Application contact:* Robert W. Coffman, Jr., Director of Enrollment Management, Recruitment and Admissions, 717-948-6250, Fax: 717-948-6325, E-mail: hbgadmit@psu.edu.
Website: https://harrisburg.psu.edu/public-affairs

Penn State University Park, Graduate School, College of the Liberal Arts, School of Labor and Employment Relations, University Park, PA 16802. Offers human resources and employment relations (MS); labor and global workers' rights (MPS). *Unit head:* Dr. Susan Welch, Dean, 814-865-7691, Fax: 814-863-2085. *Application contact:* Lori Hawn, Director, Graduate Student Services, 814-865-1795, Fax: 814-863-4627, E-mail: l-gswww@lists.psu.edu.
Website: http://lser.la.psu.edu/

Pepperdine University, Graziadio Business School, Master of Science Programs, Malibu, CA 90263. Offers accounting (MS); applied analytics (MS); applied finance (MS); global business (MS); human resources (MS); management and leadership (MS); organization development (MS); real estate investment and finance (MS). *Accreditation:* AACSB. *Students:* 462 full-time (277 women), 104 part-time (68 women); includes 67 minority (23 Black or African American, non-Hispanic/Latino; 1 American Indian or Alaska Native, non-Hispanic/Latino; 41 Asian, non-Hispanic/Latino; 2 Hispanic/Latino), 380 international. Average age 27. 2,180 applicants, 63% accepted, 336 enrolled. In 2017, 291 master's awarded. *Entrance requirements:* For master's, GMAT or GRE, two letters of recommendation. Additional exam requirements/recommendations for international students: Required—TOEFL. *Application deadline:* For fall admission, 5/1 for domestic students, 4/1 for international students. Application fee: $75. Electronic applications accepted. *Financial support:* Applicants required to submit FAFSA. *Unit head:* Dr. Michael L. Williams, Associate Dean, 310-506-4112, Fax: 310-506-4126, E-mail: michael.williams@pepperdine.edu.
Website: http://bschool.pepperdine.edu/masters-degree/

Polytechnic University of Puerto Rico, Miami Campus, Graduate School, Miami, FL 33166. Offers accounting (MBA); business administration (MBA); construction management (MEM); environmental management (MEM); finance (MBA); human resources management (MBA); logistics and supply chain management (MBA); management of international enterprises (MBA); manufacturing management (MEM); marketing management (MBA); project management (MBA). *Program availability:* Part-time, evening/weekend, online learning. *Entrance requirements:* For master's, minimum GPA of 3.0. Electronic applications accepted.

Polytechnic University of Puerto Rico, Orlando Campus, Graduate School, Orlando, FL 32825. Offers accounting (MBA); business administration (MBA); construction management (MEM); engineering management (MEM); environmental management (MEM); finance (MBA); human resources management (MBA); management of international enterprises (MBA); management of technology (MBA); manufacturing management (MEM). *Program availability:* Part-time, evening/weekend, online learning. *Entrance requirements:* For master's, minimum GPA of 3.0. Additional exam requirements/recommendations for international students: Recommended—TOEFL. Electronic applications accepted.

Pontifical Catholic University of Puerto Rico, College of Business Administration, Program in Human Resources, Ponce, PR 00717-0777. Offers MBA, Professional Certificate. *Program availability:* Part-time, evening/weekend. *Degree requirements:* For master's, thesis. *Entrance requirements:* For master's, GRE, interview, minimum GPA of 2.75.

Pontificia Universidad Catolica Madre y Maestra, Graduate School, Faculty of Social and Administrative Sciences, Santiago, Dominican Republic. Offers business administration (MBA), including business development, finance, international business, management skills (M Mgmt, MBA), marketing, operations, strategic cost management, strategy, tourist destination planning and management; law (LL M), including civil law, corporate business law, criminal law, international relations, real estate law; management (M Mgmt), including higher financial management, insurance program administration, management skills (M Mgmt, MBA); psychology (MA), including clinical child and adolescent psychology, forensic psychology; strategic human resources (EMBA).

Portland State University, Graduate Studies, College of Urban and Public Affairs, Hatfield School of Government, Division of Public Administration, Portland, OR 97207-0751. Offers collaborative governance (Certificate); energy policy and management (Certificate); global management and leadership (MPA); health administration (MPA); human resource management (MPA); local government (MPA); natural resource policy and administration (MPA); nonprofit and public management (Certificate); nonprofit management (MPA); public administration (EMPA); public affairs and policy (PhD); sustainable food systems (Certificate). *Accreditation:* NASPAA (one or more programs are accredited). *Program availability:* Part-time, evening/weekend. *Faculty:* 15 full-time (6 women), 6 part-time/adjunct (4 women). *Students:* 84 full-time (54 women), 109 part-time (75 women); includes 40 minority (8 Black or African American, non-Hispanic/Latino; 5 American Indian or Alaska Native, non-Hispanic/Latino; 8 Asian, non-Hispanic/Latino; 12 Hispanic/Latino; 1 Native Hawaiian or other Pacific Islander, non-Hispanic/Latino; 6 Two or more races, non-Hispanic/Latino), 14 international. Average age 35. 118 applicants, 84% accepted, 56 enrolled. In 2017, 60 master's, 1 doctorate awarded. *Degree requirements:* For master's, integrative field experience (MPA), practicum (MPH); for doctorate, comprehensive exam, thesis/dissertation. *Entrance requirements:* For master's, GRE (minimum scores: verbal 150, quantitative 149, and analytic writing 4.5), minimum GPA of 3.0, 3 recommendation letters, resume, 500-word statement of intent; for doctorate, GRE, 3 recommendation letters, resume, 500-word personal essay. Additional exam requirements/recommendations for international students: Required—TOEFL (minimum score 550 paper-based; 80 iBT), IELTS (minimum score 7). *Application deadline:* For fall admission, 4/1 for domestic students, 3/1 for international students; for winter admission, 9/1 for domestic students, 8/1 for international students; for spring admission, 11/1 for domestic and international students. Application fee: $65. *Expenses:* Tuition, state resident: full-time $14,436; part-time $401 per credit. Tuition, nonresident: full-time $21,780; part-time $605 per credit. *Required fees:* $1380; $22 per credit. $119 per quarter. One-time fee: $325. Tuition and fees vary according to program. *Financial support:* In 2017-18, 39 students received support, including 5 research assistantships with full and partial tuition reimbursements available (averaging $8,341 per year), 4 teaching assistantships (averaging $5,292 per year); career-related internships or fieldwork, Federal Work-Study, scholarships/grants, and unspecified assistantships also available. Support available to part-time students. Financial award application deadline: 3/1; financial award applicants required to submit FAFSA. *Faculty research:* Public budgeting, program evaluation, nonprofit management, natural resources policy and administration. *Total annual research expenditures:* $679,077. *Unit head:* Dr. Masami Nishishiba, Chair, 503-725-5151, E-mail: nishism@pdx.edu. *Application contact:* Megan Heljeson, Office Coordinator, 503-725-3921, Fax: 503-725-8250, E-mail: publicad@pdx.edu.
Website: https://www.pdx.edu/hatfieldschool/public-administration

Purdue University, Graduate School, Krannert School of Management, Doctoral Program in Organizational Behavior and Human Resource Management, West Lafayette, IN 47907-2056. Offers PhD. *Students:* 6 full-time (3 women); includes 2 minority (1 Black or African American, non-Hispanic/Latino; 1 Asian, non-Hispanic/Latino). Average age 32. 56 applicants. In 2017, 3 doctorates awarded. *Degree requirements:* For doctorate, comprehensive exam, thesis/dissertation, dissertation proposal, dissertation defense. *Entrance requirements:* For doctorate, GMAT or GRE, bachelor's degree, two semesters of calculus, one semester each of linear algebra and statistics. Additional exam requirements/recommendations for international students: Required—TOEFL (minimum score 575 paper-based); Recommended—TWE. *Application deadline:* For fall admission, 1/15 priority date for domestic and international students. Application fee: $60 ($80 for international students). Electronic applications accepted. *Financial support:* In 2017-18, 1 fellowship with full tuition reimbursement (averaging $25,000 per year), research assistantships with partial tuition reimbursements (averaging $18,000 per year), teaching assistantships with partial tuition reimbursements (averaging $18,000 per year) were awarded; scholarships/grants, health care benefits, tuition waivers (full and partial), unspecified assistantships, and travel funds to present at a major conference also available. Support available to part-time students. Financial award application deadline: 1/15. *Faculty research:* Human resource management, organizational behavior. *Unit head:* Dr. David Hummels, Dean/Professor, 765-494-4366. *Application contact:* Kelly Felty, Associate Director, Krannert PhD Programs, 765-494-4375, E-mail: krannertphd@purdue.edu.
Website: http://www.krannert.purdue.edu/programs/phd/

Purdue University, Graduate School, Krannert School of Management, Master of Science in Human Resource Management Program, West Lafayette, IN 47907. Offers MSHRM. *Students:* 143 full-time (32 women), 6 part-time/adjunct (1 woman). *Students:* 51 full-time (25 women); includes 4 minority (3 Black or African American, non-Hispanic/Latino; 1 Asian, non-Hispanic/Latino), 26 international. Average age 24. 99 applicants, 57% accepted, 26 enrolled. In 2017, 26 master's awarded. *Entrance requirements:* For master's, GMAT or GRE, essays, recommendation letters, work experience/internship, minimum GPA of 3.0, four-year baccalaureate degree. Additional exam requirements/recommendations for international students: Required—TOEFL (minimum score 600 paper-based, 93 iBT), IELTS (minimum score 7.5), or PTE (minimum score 70). *Application deadline:* For fall admission, 11/15 for domestic and international students; for winter admission, 1/15 for domestic and international students; for spring admission, 3/1 for domestic and international students; for summer admission, 5/1 for domestic students. Applications are processed on a rolling basis. Application fee: $60 ($75 for international students). Electronic applications accepted. *Expenses:* Contact institution. *Financial support:* In 2017-18, 26 students received support. Scholarships/grants and unspecified assistantships available. Financial award applicants required to submit FAFSA. *Faculty research:* Performance periods and the dynamics of the performance-risk relationship, reactions to unfair events in computer-mediated groups: a test of uncertainty management theory, influences on job search self-efficacy of spouses of military personnel, cross-cultural social intelligence: an assessment for employees working in cross-national contexts. *Unit head:* Dr. David Hummels, Dean/Professor of Economics, 765-494-4366, E-mail: krannertdean@purdue.edu. *Application contact:* Thomas Bates, Associate Director of Admissions, 765-494-0773, Fax: 765-494-9841, E-mail: krannertmasters@purdue.edu.
Website: http://www.krannert.purdue.edu/masters/programs/mshrm/

Purdue University Global, School of Business, Davenport, IA 52807. Offers business administration (MBA); change leadership (MS); entrepreneurship (MBA); finance (MBA); health care management (MBA, MS); human resource (MBA); international business (MBA); management (MS); marketing (MBA); project management (MBA, MS); supply chain management and logistics (MBA, MS). *Accreditation:* ACBSP. *Program availability:* Part-time, evening/weekend, online learning. *Entrance requirements:* Additional exam requirements/recommendations for international students: Required—TOEFL (minimum score 550 paper-based; 80 iBT). Electronic applications accepted.

Regent's University London, Webster Graduate School, London, United Kingdom. Offers business (MBA); finance (MS); human resources (MA); information technology management (MA); international business (MA); international non-governmental organizations (MA); international relations (MA); management and leadership (MA); marketing (MA). *Program availability:* Part-time.

Regent University, Graduate School, School of Business and Leadership, Virginia Beach, VA 23464-9800. Offers business administration (MBA), including accounting, economics, entrepreneurship, finance and investing, general management, healthcare management (MA, MBA), human resource management (MA, MBA), innovation management, leadership, marketing, not-for-profit management (MA, MBA); business analytics (MS); business and design management (MA); church leadership (MA); leadership (Certificate); organizational leadership (MA, PhD), including ecclesial leadership (DSL, PhD), entrepreneurial leadership (PhD), healthcare management (MA, MBA), human resource development (PhD), human resource management (MA, MBA), individualized studies (DSL, PhD), interdisciplinary studies (MA), leadership coaching and mentoring (MA), not-for-profit management (MA, MBA), organizational development consulting (MA), servant leadership (MA, DSL); strategic leadership (DSL), including ecclesial leadership (DSL, PhD), global consulting, healthcare leadership, individualized studies (DSL, PhD), leadership coaching, servant leadership (MA, DSL), strategic foresight. *Program availability:* Part-time, evening/weekend, 100% online, blended/hybrid learning. *Faculty:* 9 full-time (2 women), 38 part-time/adjunct (11 women). *Students:* 129 full-time (80 women), 1,152 part-time (598 women); includes 685 minority (546 Black or African American, non-Hispanic/Latino; 10 American Indian or Alaska Native, non-Hispanic/Latino; 29 Asian, non-Hispanic/Latino; 65 Hispanic/Latino; 6 Native Hawaiian or other Pacific Islander, non-Hispanic/Latino; 29 Two or more races, non-Hispanic/Latino), 62 international. Average age 41. 1,721 applicants, 48% accepted, 624 enrolled. In 2017, 125 master's, 69 doctorates awarded. *Degree requirements:* For master's, thesis or alternative, 3-credit hour culminating experience; for doctorate, thesis/dissertation. *Entrance requirements:* For master's, college transcripts, resume, essay; for doctorate, college transcripts, resume, essay, writing sample; for Certificate, writing sample, resume, transcripts. Additional exam requirements/recommendations for international students: Required—TOEFL (minimum score 577 paper-based). *Application deadline:* For fall admission, 5/1 priority date for domestic students; for spring admission, 10/1 priority date for domestic students. Applications are processed on a rolling basis. Application fee: $50. Electronic applications accepted. *Expenses:* $650 per credit (MA, MS, MBA); $995 per credit (PhD); $300 per semester technology fee. *Financial support:* In 2017-18, 829 students received support. Career-related internships or fieldwork, scholarships/grants, and unspecified assistantships available. Support available to part-time students. *Faculty research:* Servant leadership, global business, team effectiveness, technology utilization, leadership development. *Unit head:* Dr. Doris Gomez, Dean, 757-352-4686, Fax: 757-352-4634, E-mail: dorigom@regent.edu. *Application contact:* Heidi Cece, Assistant Vice President of Enrollment Management, 800-373-5504, Fax: 757-352-4381, E-mail: admissions@regent.edu.
Website: http://www.regent.edu/school-of-business-and-leadership/

Regent University, Graduate School, School of Law, Virginia Beach, VA 23464. Offers American legal studies (LL M); human rights (LL M); law (MA, JD), including advanced paralegal studies (MA), alternative dispute resolution (MA), business (MA), criminal justice (MA), general legal studies (MA), human resources management (MA), human rights and rule of law (MA), national security (MA), non-profit organizational law (MA), regulatory compliance (MA), wealth management and financial planning (MA); JD/MA; JD/MBA. *Accreditation:* ABA. *Program availability:* Part-time, 100% online, blended/hybrid learning. *Faculty:* 16 full-time (5 women), 76 part-time/adjunct (22 women). *Students:* 313 full-time (181 women), 248 part-time (175 women); includes 240 minority (155 Black or African American, non-Hispanic/Latino; 3 American Indian or Alaska Native, non-Hispanic/Latino; 15 Asian, non-Hispanic/Latino; 45 Hispanic/Latino; 2 Native Hawaiian or other Pacific Islander, non-Hispanic/Latino; 20 Two or more races, non-Hispanic/Latino), 59 international. Average age 35. 923 applicants, 36% accepted, 188 enrolled. In 2017, 138 master's, 80 doctorates awarded. *Entrance requirements:* For master's, college transcripts, resume, personal statement; for doctorate, LSAT, minimum undergraduate GPA of 3.0, official transcripts, 2 letters of recommendation, resume, personal statement. Additional exam requirements/recommendations for international students: Required—TOEFL (minimum score 600 paper-based). *Application deadline:* For fall admission, 3/1 for domestic students. Applications are processed on a rolling basis. Application fee: $50. Electronic applications accepted. *Expenses:* $650 per credit (MA, LL M); $1,140 per credit (JD); $300 per semester technology fee. *Financial support:* In 2017-18, 459 students received support. Career-related internships or fieldwork, scholarships/grants, and unspecified assistantships available. Support available to part-time students. *Faculty research:* Family law, Constitutional law, law and culture, evidence and practice, intellectual property. *Unit head:* Michael Hernandez, Dean, 757-352-4040, Fax: 757-352-4595, E-mail: michher@regent.edu. *Application contact:* Ernie Walton, Assistant Dean of Admissions, 757-352-4315, E-mail: lawschool@regent.edu.
Website: https://www.regent.edu/school-of-law/

Regis University, College of Business and Economics, Denver, CO 80221-1099. Offers accounting (MS); executive leadership (Certificate); finance (MS); finance and accounting (MBA); health industry leadership (MBA); human resource management and leadership (MSOL); management (MBA); marketing (MBA); nonprofit leadership (Post-Graduate Certificate); nonprofit management (MNM); nonprofit organizational capacity building (Certificate); operations management (MBA); organizational leadership and management (MSOL); project leadership and management (MS, MSOL); strategic business management (Certificate); strategic human resource integration (Certificate); strategic management (MBA). Programs offered at Colorado Springs Campus, Northwest Denver Campus, Southeast Denver Campus, Fort Collins Campus, Broomfield Campus, Henderson (Nevada) Campus, and Summerlin (Nevada) Campus.

Human Resources Management

Program availability: Part-time, evening/weekend, 100% online, blended/hybrid learning. *Degree requirements:* For master's, thesis (for some programs), capstone or final research project. *Entrance requirements:* For master's, official transcript reflecting baccalaureate degree awarded from regionally-accredited college or university, interview, 2 years of full-time related work experience, resume, letters of recommendation. Additional exam requirements/recommendations for international students: Required—TOEFL (minimum score 550 paper-based; 82 iBT). Electronic applications accepted. *Expenses:* Contact institution. *Faculty research:* Impact of information technology on small business regulation of accounting, international project financing, mineral development, delivery of healthcare to rural indigenous communities.

Robert Morris University, School of Business, Moon Township, PA 15108-1189. Offers business administration (MBA); human resource management (MS); taxation (MS); MBA/MS. *Accreditation:* AACSB. *Program availability:* Part-time-only, evening/weekend, 100% online. *Faculty:* 12 full-time (4 women), 3 part-time/adjunct (2 women). *Students:* 163 part-time (61 women); includes 13 minority (6 Black or African American, non-Hispanic/Latino; 6 Asian, non-Hispanic/Latino; 1 Two or more races, non-Hispanic/Latino), 8 international. Average age 30. 167 applicants, 40% accepted, 32 enrolled. In 2017, 87 master's awarded. *Entrance requirements:* For master's, GMAT, letters of recommendation. Additional exam requirements/recommendations for international students: Required—TOEFL (minimum score 550 paper-based; 79 iBT). *Application deadline:* For fall admission, 7/1 priority date for domestic and international students; for spring admission, 11/1 priority date for domestic and international students. Applications are processed on a rolling basis. Application fee: $35. Electronic applications accepted. Application fee is waived when completed online. *Expenses:* $955 tuition per credit plus fees of $80 per credit. *Financial support:* Institutionally sponsored loans available. Support available to part-time students. Financial award application deadline: 5/1; financial award applicants required to submit FAFSA. *Unit head:* Dr. Michelle L. Patrick, Dean, 412-397-5445, Fax: 412-397-2585, E-mail: patrick@rmu.edu. *Application contact:* E-mail: graduateadmissions@rmu.edu.
Website: http://sbus.rmu.edu

Robert Morris University Illinois, Morris Graduate School of Management, Chicago, IL 60605. Offers accounting (MBA); accounting/finance (MBA); business analytics (MIS); health care administration (MM); higher education administration (MM); human performance (MS); human resource management (MBA); information security (MIS); information systems management (MIS); law enforcement administration (MM); management (MBA); management/finance (MBA); management/human resource management (MBA); sports administration (MM). *Program availability:* Part-time, evening/weekend. *Faculty:* 2 full-time (0 women), 26 part-time/adjunct (8 women). *Students:* 186 full-time (108 women), 114 part-time (57 women); includes 167 minority (88 Black or African American, non-Hispanic/Latino; 15 Asian, non-Hispanic/Latino; 62 Hispanic/Latino; 1 Native Hawaiian or other Pacific Islander, non-Hispanic/Latino; 1 Two or more races, non-Hispanic/Latino), 18 international. Average age 32. 157 applicants, 78% accepted, 72 enrolled. In 2017, 191 master's awarded. *Entrance requirements:* For master's, official transcripts and letters of recommendation (for some programs); written personal statement. Additional exam requirements/recommendations for international students: Required—TOEFL (minimum score 550 paper-based). *Application deadline:* Applications are processed on a rolling basis. Application fee: $20 ($100 for international students). Electronic applications accepted. *Expenses:* Tuition: Full-time $17,100; part-time $2850 per course. *Financial support:* In 2017–18, 381 students received support. Federal Work-Study, scholarships/grants, and unspecified assistantships available. Support available to part-time students. Financial award applicants required to submit FAFSA. *Unit head:* Kayed Akkawi, Dean, 312-935-6050, Fax: 312-935-6020, E-mail: kakkawi@robertmorris.edu. *Application contact:* Mark Daugherty, Director of Admissions, 312-935-4814, Fax: 312-935-6020, E-mail: mdaugherty@robertmorris.edu.

Rollins College, Hamilton Holt School, Master of Human Resources Program, Winter Park, FL 32789. Offers MHR. *Program availability:* Part-time, evening/weekend. *Faculty:* 4 full-time (0 women), 1 (woman) part-time/adjunct. *Students:* 9 full-time (6 women), 40 part-time (31 women); includes 16 minority (3 Black or African American, non-Hispanic/Latino; 2 American Indian or Alaska Native, non-Hispanic/Latino; 3 Asian, non-Hispanic/Latino; 6 Hispanic/Latino; 1 Two or more races, non-Hispanic/Latino), 8 international. Average age 31. In 2017, 21 master's awarded. *Degree requirements:* For master's, thesis optional. *Entrance requirements:* For master's, GMAT or GRE, official transcripts, two letters of recommendation, essay, current resume. Additional exam requirements/recommendations for international students: Required—TOEFL (minimum score 550 paper-based; 80 iBT). *Application deadline:* For fall admission, 4/1 for domestic students; for spring admission, 12/1 for domestic students. Application fee: $50. *Expenses:* $2,556 per course. *Financial support:* Scholarships/grants and unspecified assistantships available. Support available to part-time students. Financial award applicants required to submit FAFSA. *Unit head:* Dr. Donald Rogers, Faculty Director, 407-646-2348, E-mail: drogers@rollins.edu. *Application contact:* Graduate Coordinator, 407-646-2653, Fax: 407-646-1551, E-mail: eveningadmission@rollins.edu.
Website: http://www.rollins.edu/holt/graduate/mhr.html

Roosevelt University, Graduate Division, Walter E. Heller College of Business, Program in Human Resource Management, Chicago, IL 60605. Offers MSHRM. *Program availability:* Part-time, evening/weekend. *Students:* 15 full-time (12 women), 60 part-time (50 women); includes 38 minority (23 Black or African American, non-Hispanic/Latino; 1 American Indian or Alaska Native, non-Hispanic/Latino; 1 Asian, non-Hispanic/Latino; 13 Hispanic/Latino), 7 international. Average age 30. 46 applicants, 96% accepted, 24 enrolled. In 2017, 25 master's awarded. *Application deadline:* Applications are processed on a rolling basis. Application fee: $40. Electronic applications accepted. *Financial support:* Scholarships/grants available. *Application contact:* Michael Conwell, Graduate Admission Counselor, 312-281-3250, E-mail: mconwell@roosevelt.edu.
Website: https://www.roosevelt.edu/

Rutgers University–Newark, Graduate School, Program in Public Administration, Newark, NJ 07102. Offers health care administration (MPA); human resources administration (MPA); public administration (PhD); public management (MPA); public policy analysis (MPA); urban systems and issues (MPA). *Accreditation:* NASPAA (one or more programs are accredited). *Program availability:* Part-time, evening/weekend. *Degree requirements:* For master's, comprehensive exam, thesis or alternative; for doctorate, thesis/dissertation. *Entrance requirements:* For master's, GRE, minimum undergraduate B average; for doctorate, GRE, MPA, minimum B average. Electronic applications accepted. *Faculty research:* Government finance, municipal and state government, public productivity.

Rutgers University–New Brunswick, School of Management and Labor Relations, Program in Human Resource Management, Piscataway, NJ 08854-8097. Offers MHRM. *Program availability:* Part-time, evening/weekend. *Entrance requirements:* For master's, GMAT or GRE General Test, 3 letters of recommendation. Additional exam requirements/recommendations for international students: Required—TOEFL (minimum score 575 paper-based). Electronic applications accepted. *Expenses:* Contact institution. *Faculty research:* Human resource policy and planning, employee ownership and profit sharing, compensation and appraisal of performance, law and public policy, computers and decision making.

Rutgers University–New Brunswick, School of Management and Labor Relations, Program in Industrial Relations and Human Resources, Piscataway, NJ 08854-8097. Offers PhD. *Program availability:* Part-time. *Degree requirements:* For doctorate, comprehensive exam, thesis/dissertation. *Entrance requirements:* For doctorate, GRE or GMAT, 3 letters of recommendation. Additional exam requirements/recommendations for international students: Required—TOEFL (minimum score 575 paper-based; 91 iBT). Electronic applications accepted. *Faculty research:* Strategic human resources, labor relations, organizational change, worker representation.

Sacred Heart University, Graduate Programs, Jack Welch College of Business, Department of Management, Fairfield, CT 06825. Offers administration (MBA); human resource management (MS, Graduate Certificate); management (Graduate Certificate). *Program availability:* Part-time, evening/weekend. *Faculty:* 4 full-time (1 woman), 1 part-time/adjunct (0 women). *Students:* 72 full-time (38 women), 133 part-time (72 women); includes 44 minority (9 Black or African American, non-Hispanic/Latino; 1 American Indian or Alaska Native, non-Hispanic/Latino; 8 Asian, non-Hispanic/Latino; 24 Hispanic/Latino; 2 Two or more races, non-Hispanic/Latino), 45 international. Average age 31. 158 applicants, 89% accepted, 62 enrolled. In 2017, 85 master's awarded. *Degree requirements:* For master's, capstone project. *Entrance requirements:* For master's, GMAT/GRE, bachelor's degree. Additional exam requirements/recommendations for international students: Required—TOEFL (minimum score 570 paper-based, 80 iBT), TWE, or IELTS (6.5). *Application deadline:* Applications are processed on a rolling basis. Application fee: $75. Electronic applications accepted. *Expenses:* Contact institution. *Financial support:* Applicants required to submit FAFSA. *Unit head:* Nadene Koliopoulos, Director of Graduate Business Programs, 203-365-7660, E-mail: koliopoulosn@sacredheart.edu. *Application contact:* Pam Pillo, Executive Director of Graduate Admissions, 203-365-7619, E-mail: gradstudies@sacredheart.edu.

St. Ambrose University, College of Business, Program in Business Administration, Davenport, IA 52803-2898. Offers business administration (DBA); health care (MBA); human resources (MBA). *Accreditation:* ACBSP. *Program availability:* Part-time, evening/weekend. *Degree requirements:* For master's, comprehensive exam (for some programs), thesis or alternative, capstone seminar; for doctorate, comprehensive exam, thesis/dissertation, oral and written exams. *Entrance requirements:* For master's, GMAT; for doctorate, GMAT, master's degree. Additional exam requirements/recommendations for international students: Required—TOEFL. Electronic applications accepted. *Expenses:* Contact institution.

Saint Francis University, School of Business, Loretto, PA 15940-0600. Offers business administration (MBA); human resource management (MHRM). *Program availability:* Part-time, evening/weekend. *Faculty:* 10 full-time (4 women), 13 part-time/adjunct (9 women). *Students:* 52 full-time (17 women), 76 part-time (44 women); includes 10 minority (8 Black or African American, non-Hispanic/Latino; 1 Native Hawaiian or other Pacific Islander, non-Hispanic/Latino; 1 Two or more races, non-Hispanic/Latino), 1 international. Average age 30. 65 applicants, 77% accepted, 45 enrolled. In 2017, 67 master's awarded. *Degree requirements:* For master's, comprehensive exam (for some programs), thesis (for some programs). *Entrance requirements:* For master's, GMAT (waived if undergraduate QPA is 3.3 or above), 2 letters of recommendation, minimum GPA of 2.75, two essays. Additional exam requirements/recommendations for international students: Required—TOEFL (minimum score 550 paper-based; 57 iBT). *Application deadline:* For fall admission, 8/15 priority date for domestic and international students; for spring admission, 12/1 priority date for domestic students, 12/1 for international students. Applications are processed on a rolling basis. Application fee: $30. Electronic applications accepted. *Expenses:* Contact institution. *Financial support:* Fellowships with partial tuition reimbursements, career-related internships or fieldwork, and unspecified assistantships available. Financial award application deadline: 8/15; financial award applicants required to submit FAFSA. *Total annual research expenditures:* $425,000. *Unit head:* Dr. Randy L. Frye, Director, Graduate Business Programs, 814-472-3041, Fax: 814-472-3174, E-mail: rfrye@francis.edu. *Application contact:* Nicole Marie Bauman, Coordinator, Graduate Business Programs, 814-472-3026, Fax: 814-472-3369, E-mail: nbauman@francis.edu.
Website: http://francis.edu/school-of-business/

St. Joseph's College, Long Island Campus, Programs in Management, Field in Human Resources Management, Patchogue, NY 11772-2399. Offers MS. *Program availability:* Part-time, evening/weekend, 100% online, blended/hybrid learning. *Faculty:* 15 full-time (7 women), 22 part-time/adjunct (7 women). *Students:* 6 full-time (5 women), 20 part-time (16 women); includes 7 minority (3 Black or African American, non-Hispanic/Latino; 4 Hispanic/Latino). Average age 33. 25 applicants, 76% accepted, 10 enrolled. In 2017, 6 master's awarded. Application fee: $25. *Expenses: Tuition:* Full-time $17,550; part-time $975 per credit. *Required fees:* $362. *Financial support:* In 2017–18, 5 students received support. *Unit head:* Mary A. Chance, Assistant Professor/Interim Director of Graduate Management Studies, 631-687-1297, E-mail: mchance@sjcny.edu.

St. Joseph's College, New York, Programs in Management, Field in Human Resources Management, Brooklyn, NY 11205-3688. Offers MS. *Program availability:* Part-time, evening/weekend, 100% online, blended/hybrid learning. *Faculty:* 1 full-time (0 women), 6 part-time/adjunct (4 women). *Students:* 7 full-time (5 women), 16 part-time (13 women); includes 15 minority (11 Black or African American, non-Hispanic/Latino; 1 Asian, non-Hispanic/Latino; 2 Hispanic/Latino; 1 Two or more races, non-Hispanic/Latino). Average age 35. 10 applicants, 90% accepted, 5 enrolled. In 2017, 9 master's awarded. *Entrance requirements:* For master's, official transcripts, resume, two letters of reference, verification of employment. Additional exam requirements/recommendations for international students: Required—TOEFL (minimum score 80 iBT). *Application deadline:* Applications are processed on a rolling basis. Application fee: $25. Electronic applications accepted. *Expenses: Tuition:* Full-time $17,550; part-time $975 per credit. *Required fees:* $362. *Financial support:* In 2017–18, 5 students received support. *Unit head:* Sharon Didier, Assistant Chair/Co-Director of Graduate Management Studies/Associate Professor, 718-940-5790, E-mail: sdidier@sjcny.edu.
Website: https://www.sjcny.edu

Saint Joseph's University, Erivan K. Haub School of Business, Strategic Human Resource Management Program, Philadelphia, PA 19131-1395. Offers strategic human resources management (MS). *Program availability:* Part-time, online learning. *Faculty:* 8 full-time (2 women), 8 part-time/adjunct (2 women). *Students:* 33 part-time (27 women); includes 10 minority (6 Black or African American, non-Hispanic/Latino; 3 Asian, non-Hispanic/Latino; 1 Hispanic/Latino). Average age 34. 22 applicants, 73% accepted, 9 enrolled. In 2017, 5 master's awarded. *Degree requirements:* For master's, minimum GPA of 3.0. *Entrance requirements:* For master's, MAT, GRE, or GMAT, 2 letters of recommendation, resume, personal statement, official undergraduate and graduate transcripts. Additional exam requirements/recommendations for international students: Required—PTE, TOEFL, IELTS, or PTE. *Application deadline:* For fall admission, 7/15 priority date for domestic students; for spring admission, 11/15 priority date for domestic students; for summer admission, 4/15 priority date for domestic students. Applications are processed on a rolling basis. Application fee: $35. Electronic applications accepted. *Expenses:* Contact institution. *Financial support:* Scholarships/grants and unspecified assistantships available. Financial award application deadline: 5/1; financial award applicants required to submit FAFSA. *Unit head:* Jeannine Lajeunesse, Director, 610-

660-1626, E-mail: jlajeune@sju.edu. *Application contact:* Christine Anderson, Assistant Director, 610-660-2252, Fax: 610-660-1599, E-mail: chris.anderson@sju.edu. Website: https://www.sju.edu/majors-programs/graduate-business/master-degrees/strategic-human-resource-management-ms

Saint Leo University, Graduate Studies in Business, Saint Leo, FL 33574-6665. Offers accounting (M Acc, MBA); cybersecurity (MS); cybersecurity management (MBA); data analytics (MBA); health care management (MBA); human resource management (MBA); international and experiential business administration (MBA); management (MBA, DBA); marketing (MBA); marketing research and social media analytics (MBA); project management (MBA); social media marketing (MBA); sport business (MBA); supply chain global integration management (MBA). *Accreditation:* ACBSP. *Program availability:* Part-time, evening/weekend, 100% online, blended/hybrid learning. *Faculty:* 54 full-time (18 women), 52 part-time/adjunct (18 women). *Students:* 9 full-time (3 women), 1,867 part-time (1,079 women); includes 861 minority (598 Black or African American, non-Hispanic/Latino; 3 American Indian or Alaska Native, non-Hispanic/Latino; 38 Asian, non-Hispanic/Latino; 186 Hispanic/Latino; 3 Native Hawaiian or other Pacific Islander, non-Hispanic/Latino; 33 Two or more races, non-Hispanic/Latino), 68 international. Average age 37. 868 applicants, 63% accepted, 537 enrolled. In 2017, 859 master's, 3 doctorates awarded. *Degree requirements:* For doctorate, comprehensive exam, thesis/dissertation. *Entrance requirements:* For master's, GMAT with minimum score 500 (for M Acc), official transcripts, current resume, 2 professional recommendations, personal statement, bachelor's degree from regionally-accredited university; undergraduate degree in accounting and minimum undergraduate GPA of 3.0 (for M Acc); minimum undergraduate GPA of 3.0 in final 2 years of undergraduate study and 2 years' work experience (for MBA); for doctorate, GMAT (minimum score of 550) if master's GPA is under 3.25, official transcripts, current resume, 2 professional recommendations, personal statement, master's degree from regionally-accredited university with minimum GPA of 3.25, 3 years' work experience, interview. Additional exam requirements/recommendations for international students: Required—TOEFL (minimum score 550 paper-based; 78 iBT). *Application deadline:* For fall admission, 7/1 priority date for domestic and international students; for spring admission, 11/12 priority date for domestic students, 11/1 for international students. Applications are processed on a rolling basis. Application fee: $80. Electronic applications accepted. *Expenses:* Contact institution. *Financial support:* In 2017–18, 106 students received support. Career-related internships or fieldwork, health care benefits, and tuition remission for Saint Leo employees and their dependents available. Financial award application deadline: 3/1; financial award applicants required to submit FAFSA. *Faculty research:* Servant leadership, work/life balance, emotional intelligence, pricing, marketing. *Unit head:* Dr. Charles Hale, Dean, School of Business, 352-588-8599, Fax: 352-588-8912, E-mail: mbaslu@saintleo.edu. *Application contact:* Mark Russum, Assistant Vice President, Enrollment, 800-707-8846, Fax: 352-588-7873, E-mail: grad.admissions@saintleo.edu. Website: https://www.saintleo.edu/school-of-business

Saint Mary's University of Minnesota, Schools of Graduate and Professional Programs, Graduate School of Business and Technology, Human Resource Management Program, Winona, MN 55987-1399. Offers MA. *Unit head:* Holly Tapper, Director, 612-238-4547, E-mail: htapper@smumn.edu. *Application contact:* James Callinan, Director of Admissions for Graduate and Professional Programs, 612-728-5158, Fax: 612-728-5121, E-mail: jcallina@smumn.edu. Website: http://www.smumn.edu/graduate-home/areas-of-study/graduate-school-of-business-technology/ma-in-human-resource-management

Saint Peter's University, Graduate Business Programs, MBA Program, Jersey City, NJ 07306-5997. Offers finance (MBA); health care administration (MBA); human resource management (MBA); international business (MBA); management (MBA); management information systems (MBA); marketing (MBA); risk management (MBA); MBA/MS. *Program availability:* Part-time, evening/weekend. *Entrance requirements:* Additional exam requirements/recommendations for international students: Required—TOEFL. Electronic applications accepted. *Faculty research:* Finance, health care management, human resource management, international business, management, management information systems, marketing, risk management.

St. Thomas University, School of Business, Department of Management, Miami Gardens, FL 33054-6459. Offers accounting (MBA); general management (MSM, Certificate); health management (MBA, MSM, Certificate); human resource management (MBA, MSM, Certificate); international business (MBA, MIB, MSM, Certificate); justice administration (MSM, Certificate); management accounting (MSM, Certificate); public management (MSM, Certificate); sports administration (MSM). *Program availability:* Part-time, evening/weekend. *Degree requirements:* For master's, comprehensive exam. *Entrance requirements:* For master's, interview, minimum GPA of 3.0 or GMAT. Additional exam requirements/recommendations for international students: Required—TOEFL (minimum score 550 paper-based; 79 iBT). Electronic applications accepted.

Salve Regina University, Program in Management, Newport, RI 02840-4192. Offers business studies (CGS); human resource management (CGS); innovation and strategic management (MS); management (CGS); nonprofit management (CGS); social entrepreneurship (CGS). *Program availability:* Part-time, evening/weekend, online learning. *Entrance requirements:* For master's, GMAT, GRE General Test, or MAT. Additional exam requirements/recommendations for international students: Required—TOEFL (minimum score 600 paper-based; 100 iBT). Electronic applications accepted.

San Diego State University, Graduate and Research Affairs, College of Business Administration, Department of Management, San Diego, CA 92182. Offers entrepreneurship (MS); human resources management (MS); management science (MS). *Program availability:* Part-time, evening/weekend. *Degree requirements:* For master's, thesis or alternative. *Entrance requirements:* For master's, GMAT, resume, letters of reference. Additional exam requirements/recommendations for international students: Required—TOEFL. Electronic applications accepted.

San Ignacio University, Graduate Programs, Doral, FL 33178. Offers business administration (MBA), including human resources management, international business, marketing management; education (M Ed), including early childhood education, educational leadership, special education; hospitality management (MA), including gastronomy and restaurant management, tourism management.

Savannah State University, Master of Public Administration Program, Savannah, GA 31404. Offers city management (MPA); human resources (MPA). *Accreditation:* NASPAA. *Program availability:* Part-time. *Degree requirements:* For master's, comprehensive exam, thesis, public service internship, capstone seminar. *Entrance requirements:* For master's, GRE General Test, GMAT, or MAT, minimum cumulative GPA of 2.5, 3 letters of recommendation, essay, official transcripts, resume, essay of 500-1000 words detailing reasons for pursuing degree. Additional exam requirements/recommendations for international students: Required—TOEFL. Electronic applications accepted. *Expenses:* Contact institution. *Faculty research:* Community development, human resources, leadership, conflict resolution, city management, non-profit management.

Seattle Pacific University, Master of Arts in Management Program, Seattle, WA 98119-1997. Offers business intelligence and data analytics (MA); cybersecurity (MA);

faith and business (MA); human resources (MA); social and sustainable management (MA). *Students:* 4 full-time (all women), 12 part-time (8 women), 4 international. Average age 28. 15 applicants, 60% accepted, 7 enrolled. In 2017, 18 master's awarded. *Entrance requirements:* For master's, GMAT or GRE (waived with cumulative GPA of 3.3 or above), bachelor's degree from accredited college or university, resume, essay, official transcript. *Application deadline:* For fall admission, 8/1 for domestic students, 6/1 for international students; for winter admission, 11/1 for domestic students, 9/1 for international students; for spring admission, 2/1 for domestic students, 12/1 for international students; for summer admission, 5/1 for domestic students. Application fee: $50. *Application contact:* E-mail: drj@spu.edu. Website: http://spu.edu/academics/school-of-business-and-economics/graduate-programs/ma-management

Southern New Hampshire University, School of Business, Manchester, NH 03106-1045. Offers accounting (MBA, Graduate Certificate); accounting finance (MS); accounting/auditing (MS); accounting/forensic accounting (MS); accounting/management accounting (MS); accounting/taxation (MS); applied economics (MS); athletic administration (MBA, Graduate Certificate); business administration (IMBA, Certificate), including business information systems (Certificate), human resource management (Certificate); business analytics (MBA); business intelligence (MBA); communication (MA), including new media and marketing, public relations; community economic development (MBA); criminal justice (MBA); data analytics (MS); economics (MBA); engineering management (MBA); entrepreneurship (MBA); finance (MBA, MS, Graduate Certificate); finance/corporate finance (MS); finance/investments (MS); forensic accounting (MBA); forensic accounting and fraud examination (Graduate Certificate); healthcare informatics (MS); healthcare management (MBA); human resource management (MS); human resources (MBA); information technology (MS); information technology management (MBA); international business (PhD); Internet marketing (MBA); leadership (MBA); leadership of nonprofit organizations (Graduate Certificate); management (MS); marketing (MBA, MS, Graduate Certificate); music business (MBA); operations and project management (MS); operations and supply chain management (MBA, Graduate Certificate); organizational leadership (MS); project management (MBA, Graduate Certificate); public administration (MBA, Graduate Certificate); quantitative analysis (MBA); Six Sigma (Graduate Certificate); Six Sigma quality (MBA); social media marketing (MBA, Graduate Certificate); sport management (MBA, MS, Graduate Certificate); sustainability and environmental compliance (MBA); MBA/Certificate. *Accreditation:* ACBSP. *Program availability:* Part-time, evening/weekend, online learning. Terminal master's awarded for partial completion of doctoral program. *Degree requirements:* For master's, one foreign language, comprehensive exam (for some programs), thesis or alternative; for doctorate, one foreign language, comprehensive exam, thesis/dissertation. *Entrance requirements:* For master's, minimum GPA of 2.5; for doctorate, GMAT. Additional exam requirements/recommendations for international students: Required—TOEFL (minimum score 500 paper-based). *Application deadline:* Applications are processed on a rolling basis. Application fee: $40. Electronic applications accepted. *Expenses: Tuition:* Part-time $627 per credit hour. Part-time tuition and fees vary according to campus/location and program. *Financial support:* Career-related internships or fieldwork, Federal Work-Study, institutionally sponsored loans, scholarships/grants, tuition waivers (partial), and unspecified assistantships available. Support available to part-time students. Financial award applicants required to submit FAFSA. *Unit head:* Dr. Bill Lightfoot, Dean, 603-644-3102, Fax: 603-644-3144. *Application contact:* Office of Graduate Admission, 888-327-SNHU, Fax: 603-644-3144, E-mail: enroll@snhu.edu.

State University of New York Polytechnic Institute, MBA Program in Technology Management, Utica, NY 13502. Offers accounting and finance (MBA); business management (MBA); health informatics (MBA); human resource management (MBA); marketing management (MBA). *Program availability:* Part-time, online only, 100% online. *Faculty:* 8 full-time (2 women), 2 part-time/adjunct (1 woman). *Students:* 29 full-time (13 women), 85 part-time (41 women); includes 18 minority (4 Black or African American, non-Hispanic/Latino; 8 Asian, non-Hispanic/Latino; 6 Hispanic/Latino). Average age 32. 83 applicants, 55% accepted, 37 enrolled. In 2017, 41 master's awarded. *Degree requirements:* For master's, comprehensive exam, capstone project. *Entrance requirements:* For master's, GMAT, resume, letter of reference. Additional exam requirements/recommendations for international students: Required—TOEFL (minimum score 550 paper-based; 79 iBT), IELTS (minimum score 6.5). *Application deadline:* For fall admission, 7/1 priority date for domestic students, 7/1 for international students; for spring admission, 12/1 for domestic students, 11/1 for international students. Applications are processed on a rolling basis. Application fee: $60. Electronic applications accepted. *Expenses:* Contact institution. *Financial support:* Fellowships, research assistantships, and unspecified assistantships available. Financial award application deadline: 6/1; financial award applicants required to submit FAFSA. *Faculty research:* Economic development and design thinking, transfer of training, trade intensity and liquidity, enforcement and punishment, acculturation attitudes and consumption behavior. *Total annual research expenditures:* $20,000. *Unit head:* Dr. Rafael Romero, Program Coordinator, 315-792-7207, E-mail: rafael.romero@sunyit.edu. *Application contact:* Alicia Foster, Director of Graduate Admissions, E-mail: alicia.foster@sunyit.edu. Website: https://sunypoly.edu/academics/majors-and-programs/technology-management.html

Stevens Institute of Technology, Graduate School, School of Business, Program in Management, Hoboken, NJ 07030. Offers general management (MS); global innovation management (MS); human resource management (MS); information management (MS); project management (MS); technology commercialization (MS); technology management (MS). *Program availability:* Part-time, evening/weekend. *Students:* 56 full-time (18 women), 88 part-time (32 women); includes 18 minority (5 Black or African American, non-Hispanic/Latino; 12 Asian, non-Hispanic/Latino; 1 Hispanic/Latino), 87 international. Average age 30. 194 applicants, 78% accepted, 68 enrolled. In 2017, 87 master's awarded. *Degree requirements:* For master's, thesis optional, minimum B average in major field and overall. *Entrance requirements:* Additional exam requirements/recommendations for international students: Required—TOEFL (minimum score 74 iBT), IELTS (minimum score 6). *Application deadline:* For fall admission, 7/1 for domestic students, 4/15 for international students; for spring admission, 12/1 for domestic and international students. Applications are processed on a rolling basis. Application fee: $60. Electronic applications accepted. *Expenses: Tuition:* Full-time $34,494; part-time $1554 per credit. *Required fees:* $291 per semester. *Financial support:* Fellowships, research assistantships, teaching assistantships, career-related internships or fieldwork, Federal Work-Study, scholarships/grants, and unspecified assistantships available. Financial award application deadline: 2/15; financial award applicants required to submit FAFSA. *Unit head:* Brian Rothschild, Director, 201-216-3677, E-mail: brian.rothschild@stevens.edu. *Application contact:* Graduate Admissions, 888-783-8367, Fax: 888-511-1306, E-mail: graduate@stevens.edu. Website: https://www.stevens.edu/school-business/masters-programs/management

Stony Brook University, State University of New York, Graduate School, College of Business, Program in Business Administration, Stony Brook, NY 11794. Offers accounting (MBA); business administration (MBA); finance (MBA, Certificate); health care management (MBA); human resources (MBA); innovation (MBA); management

Human Resources Management

(MBA); marketing (MBA); operations management (MBA). *Faculty:* 39 full-time (13 women), 14 part-time/adjunct (5 women). *Students:* 181 full-time (98 women), 145 part-time (73 women); includes 68 minority (16 Black or African American, non-Hispanic/Latino; 1 American Indian or Alaska Native, non-Hispanic/Latino; 35 Asian, non-Hispanic/Latino; 11 Hispanic/Latino; 1 Native Hawaiian or other Pacific Islander, non-Hispanic/Latino; 4 Two or more races, non-Hispanic/Latino), 69 international. Average age 29. 154 applicants, 66% accepted, 58 enrolled. In 2017, 105 master's awarded. *Entrance requirements:* For master's, GMAT, 3 letters of recommendation from current or former employers or professors, transcripts, personal statement, resume. Additional exam requirements/recommendations for international students: Required—TOEFL (minimum score 550 paper-based; 90 iBT), IELTS (minimum score 6.5). *Application deadline:* For fall admission, 5/15 for domestic students, 3/15 for international students; for spring admission, 11/15 for domestic students, 10/15 for international students. Application fee: $100. *Expenses:* Contact institution. *Financial support:* Teaching assistantships available. *Total annual research expenditures:* $2,070. *Unit head:* Dr. Manuel London, Dean, 631-632-7159, E-mail: manuel.london@stonybrook.edu. *Application contact:* Dr. Dmytro Holod, Associate Dean for Academic Programs/ Graduate Director, 631-632-7183, Fax: 631-632-8181, E-mail: dmytro.holod@ stonybrook.edu.
Website: https://www.stonybrook.edu/commcms/business/

Stony Brook University, State University of New York, School of Professional Development, Stony Brook, NY 11794. Offers biology (MAT); chemistry (MAT); coaching (Graduate Certificate); earth science (MAT); educational computing (Graduate Certificate); educational leadership (Advanced Certificate); English (MAT); environmental management (MPS, Graduate Certificate); French (MAT); German (MAT); higher education administration (MA, Certificate); human resource management (MS, Graduate Certificate); industrial management (Graduate Certificate); information systems management (Graduate Certificate); Italian (MAT); liberal studies (MA); mathematics (MAT); operations research (Graduate Certificate); physics (MAT); school district business leadership (Advanced Certificate); social studies (MAT); Spanish (MAT). *Program availability:* Part-time, evening/weekend, online learning. *Faculty:* 3 full-time (2 women), 101 part-time/adjunct (45 women). *Students:* 190 full-time (126 women), 974 part-time (708 women); includes 255 minority (88 Black or African American, non-Hispanic/Latino; 2 American Indian or Alaska Native, non-Hispanic/Latino; 31 Asian, non-Hispanic/Latino; 113 Hispanic/Latino; 1 Native Hawaiian or other Pacific Islander, non-Hispanic/Latino; 20 Two or more races, non-Hispanic/Latino), 6 international. Average age 33. 411 applicants, 91% accepted, 288 enrolled. In 2017, 333 master's, 180 other advanced degrees awarded. *Entrance requirements:* Additional exam requirements/recommendations for international students: Required—TOEFL (minimum score 85 iBT). *Application deadline:* For fall admission, 1/15 for domestic students, 6/1 for international students; for spring admission, 10/1 for domestic and international students. Applications are processed on a rolling basis. Application fee: $100. *Expenses:* Contact institution. *Financial support:* Fellowships, research assistantships, teaching assistantships, and career-related internships or fieldwork available. Support available to part-time students. *Unit head:* Dr. Ken Lindblom, Dean, 631-632-7049, Fax: 631-632-9046, E-mail: kenneth.lindblom@stonybrook.edu. *Application contact:* Melissa Jordan, Assistant Dean, 631-632-7751, E-mail: melissa.jordan@stonybrook.edu.
Website: http://www.stonybrook.edu/spd/

Strayer University, Graduate Studies, Washington, DC 20005-2603. Offers accounting (MS); acquisition (MBA); business administration (MBA); communications technology (MS); educational management (M Ed); finance (MBA); health services administration (MHSA); hospitality and tourism management (MBA); human resource management (MBA); information systems (MS), including computer security management, decision support system management, enterprise resource management, network management, software engineering management, systems development management; management (MBA); management information systems (MS); marketing (MBA); professional accounting (MS), including accounting information systems, controllership, taxation; public administration (MPA); supply chain management (MBA); technology in education (M Ed). Programs also offered at campus locations in Birmingham, AL; Chamblee, GA; Cobb County, GA; Morrow, GA; White Marsh, MD; Charleston, SC; Columbia, SC; Greensboro, NC; Greenville, SC; Lexington, KY; Louisville, KY; Nashville, TN; North Raleigh, NC; Washington, DC. *Accreditation:* ACBSP. *Program availability:* Part-time, evening/weekend, online learning. *Degree requirements:* For master's, thesis. *Entrance requirements:* For master's, GMAT, GRE General Test, bachelor's degree from an accredited college or university, minimum undergraduate GPA of 2.75. Electronic applications accepted.

Tarleton State University, College of Graduate Studies, College of Business Administration, Department of Management, Stephenville, TX 76402. Offers human resources management (MS). *Program availability:* Part-time, evening/weekend, 100% online, blended/hybrid learning. *Faculty:* 11 full-time (3 women), 3 part-time/adjunct (1 woman). *Students:* 13 full-time (10 women), 99 part-time (75 women); includes 35 minority (11 Black or African American, non-Hispanic/Latino; 1 Asian, non-Hispanic/Latino; 18 Hispanic/Latino; 5 Two or more races, non-Hispanic/Latino). Average age 33. 52 applicants, 94% accepted, 39 enrolled. In 2017, 17 master's awarded. *Degree requirements:* For master's, comprehensive exam, thesis (for some programs). *Entrance requirements:* For master's, GRE, GMAT, minimum GPA of 3.0. Additional exam requirements/recommendations for international students: Required—TOEFL (minimum score 550 paper-based; 80 iBT), IELTS (minimum score 6). *Application deadline:* For fall admission, 8/15 priority date for domestic students; for spring admission, 1/7 for domestic students. Applications are processed on a rolling basis. Application fee: $45 ($145 for international students). Electronic applications accepted. *Expenses:* Contact institution. *Financial support:* Research assistantships, teaching assistantships, Federal Work-Study, scholarships/grants, and unspecified assistantships available. Financial award application deadline: 5/1; financial award applicants required to submit FAFSA. *Unit head:* Dr. Sue Joiner, Department Head, 254-968-9712, E-mail: sjoiner@ tarleton.edu. *Application contact:* Information Contact, 254-968-9104, Fax: 254-968-9670, E-mail: gradoffice@tarleton.edu.

Temple University, Fox School of Business, MBA Programs, Philadelphia, PA 19122-6096. Offers accounting (MBA); business management (MBA); financial management (MBA); healthcare and life sciences innovation (MBA); human resource management (MBA); international business (IMBA); IT management (MBA); marketing management (MBA); pharmaceutical management (MBA); strategic management (EMBA, MBA). EMBA offered in Philadelphia, PA and Tokyo, Japan. *Accreditation:* AACSB. *Program availability:* Part-time, evening/weekend, online learning. *Entrance requirements:* For master's, GMAT, minimum undergraduate GPA of 3.0. Additional exam requirements/ recommendations for international students: Required—TOEFL (minimum score 600 paper-based; 100 iBT), IELTS (minimum score 7.5). *Expenses:* Tuition, state resident: full-time $16,164; part-time $898 per credit hour. Tuition, nonresident: full-time $22,158; part-time $1231 per credit hour. *Required fees:* $890; $445 per semester. Full-time tuition and fees vary according to course load, degree level, campus/location and program.

Temple University, Fox School of Business, Specialized Master's Programs, Philadelphia, PA 19122-6096. Offers accountancy (MS); actuarial science (MS); finance (MS); financial engineering (MS); human resource management (MS); innovation management and entrepreneurship (MS); marketing (MS); statistics (MS). MS in innovation management and entrepreneurship delivered jointly with College of Engineering. *Accreditation:* AACSB. *Program availability:* Part-time. *Entrance requirements:* For master's, GRE General Test or GMAT, minimum undergraduate GPA of 3.0. Additional exam requirements/recommendations for international students: Required—TOEFL (minimum score 600 paper-based; 100 iBT), IELTS (minimum score 7.5). *Expenses:* Tuition, state resident: full-time $16,164; part-time $898 per credit hour. Tuition, nonresident: full-time $22,158; part-time $1231 per credit hour. *Required fees:* $890; $445 per semester. Full-time tuition and fees vary according to course load, degree level, campus/location and program.

Tennessee State University, The School of Graduate Studies and Research, College of Public Service, Nashville, TN 37209-1561. Offers human resource management (MPS); public administration (MPA, PhD); social work (MSW); strategic leadership (MPS); training and development (MPS). *Accreditation:* NASPAA (one or more programs are accredited). *Program availability:* Part-time, evening/weekend. *Degree requirements:* For master's, comprehensive exam, thesis optional; for doctorate, comprehensive exam, thesis/dissertation. *Entrance requirements:* For master's, GRE General Test, minimum GPA of 2.5, writing sample; for doctorate, GRE General Test, minimum GPA of 3.25, writing sample. *Faculty research:* Total quality management and process improvement, national health care policy and administration, starting non-profit ventures, public service ethics, state education financing across the U.S. public.

Tennessee Technological University, College of Graduate Studies, College of Business, MBA Program, Cookeville, TN 38505. Offers finance (MBA); human resource management (MBA); international business (MBA); management information systems (MBA). *Program availability:* Part-time, evening/weekend. In 2017, 77 master's awarded. *Entrance requirements:* For master's, GMAT or GRE. *Expenses:* Tuition, state resident: full-time $9925; part-time $565 per credit hour. Tuition, nonresident: full-time $22,993; part-time $1291 per credit hour. *Financial support:* In 2017–18, 2 research assistantships, 3 teaching assistantships were awarded; fellowships and unspecified assistantships also available. Financial award application deadline: 4/1; financial award applicants required to submit FAFSA. *Unit head:* Kate Nicewicz, Director, E-mail: knicewicz@tntech.edu. *Application contact:* Shelia K. Kendrick, Coordinator of Graduate Studies, 931-372-3808, Fax: 931-372-3497, E-mail: skendrick@tntech.edu.
Website: https://www.tntech.edu/cob/mba/

Tennessee Technological University, College of Graduate Studies, College of Interdisciplinary Studies, School of Professional Studies, Cookeville, TN 38505. Offers health care administration (MPS); human resources leadership (MPS); public safety (MPS); strategic leadership (MPS); teaching English to speakers of other languages (MPS); training and development (MPS). *Program availability:* Part-time, evening/ weekend, online learning. *Students:* 20 full-time (11 women), 74 part-time (46 women); includes 18 minority (11 Black or African American, non-Hispanic/Latino; 1 Hispanic/ Latino; 1 Native Hawaiian or other Pacific Islander, non-Hispanic/Latino; 5 Two or more races, non-Hispanic/Latino), 1 international. 50 applicants, 82% accepted, 29 enrolled. In 2017, 23 master's awarded. *Degree requirements:* For master's, comprehensive exam, thesis or alternative. *Entrance requirements:* For master's, GRE. Additional exam requirements/recommendations for international students: Required—TOEFL (minimum score 527 paper-based; 71 iBT), IELTS (minimum score 5.5), PTE (minimum score 48), or TOEIC (Test of English as an International Communication). *Application deadline:* For fall admission, 7/1 for domestic students, 5/1 for international students; for spring admission, 11/1 for domestic students, 10/1 for international students; for summer admission, 5/1 for domestic students, 2/1 for international students. Applications are processed on a rolling basis. Application fee: $35 ($40 for international students). Electronic applications accepted. *Expenses:* Tuition, state resident: full-time $9925; part-time $565 per credit hour. Tuition, nonresident: full-time $22,993; part-time $1291 per credit hour. *Financial support:* Application deadline: 4/1. *Unit head:* Dr. Joseph Roberts, Interim Director, School of Professional Studies, 931-372-6223, E-mail: jmroberts@tntech.edu. *Application contact:* Shelia K. Kendrick, Coordinator of Graduate Studies, 931-372-3808, Fax: 931-372-3497, E-mail: skendrick@tntech.edu.
Website: https://www.tntech.edu/is/sps/

Texas A&M University, Mays Business School, Department of Management, College Station, TX 77843. Offers entrepreneurial leadership (MS); human resource management (MS). *Faculty:* 32. *Students:* 90 full-time (63 women); includes 20 minority (3 Black or African American, non-Hispanic/Latino; 2 American Indian or Alaska Native, non-Hispanic/Latino; 2 Asian, non-Hispanic/Latino; 10 Hispanic/Latino; 3 Two or more races, non-Hispanic/Latino), 5 international. Average age 26. 163 applicants, 31% accepted, 40 enrolled. In 2017, 45 master's awarded. Terminal master's awarded for partial completion of doctoral program. *Degree requirements:* For master's, comprehensive exam. *Entrance requirements:* For master's, GMAT or GRE. Additional exam requirements/recommendations for international students: Required—TOEFL (minimum score 550 paper-based; 80 iBT), IELTS (minimum score 6), PTE (minimum score 53). *Application deadline:* For fall admission, 5/26 for domestic and international students. Applications are processed on a rolling basis. Application fee: $50 ($90 for international students). Electronic applications accepted. *Expenses:* Contact institution. *Financial support:* In 2017–18, 76 students received support, including 28 research assistantships with tuition reimbursements available (averaging $8,154 per year), 24 teaching assistantships with tuition reimbursements available (averaging $4,822 per year); career-related internships or fieldwork, institutionally sponsored loans, scholarships/grants, traineeships, health care benefits, tuition waivers (full and partial), and unspecified assistantships also available. Support available to part-time students. Financial award application deadline: 3/15; financial award applicants required to submit FAFSA. *Faculty research:* Strategic and human resource management, business and public policy, organizational behavior, organizational theory. *Unit head:* Dr. Wendy R. Boswell, Head, 979-845-4045, Fax: 979-845-9641, E-mail: wboswell@mays.tamu.edu. *Application contact:* Kristi R. Mora, Senior Academic Advisor II, 979-845-6127, Fax: 979-845-9641, E-mail: kmora@mays.tamu.edu.
Website: http://mays.tamu.edu/mgmt/

Texas A&M University–Central Texas, Graduate Studies and Research, Killeen, TX 76549. Offers accounting (MS); business administration (MBA); clinical mental health counseling (MS); criminal justice (MCJ); curriculum and instruction (M Ed); educational administration (M Ed); educational psychology - experimental psychology (MS); history (MA); human resource management (MS); information systems (MS); liberal studies (MS); management and leadership (MS); marriage and family therapy (MS); mathematics (MS); political science (MA); school counseling (M Ed); school psychology (Ed S).

Texas State University, The Graduate College, Emmett and Miriam McCoy College of Business Administration, Program in Human Resource Management, San Marcos, TX 78666. Offers MS. *Program availability:* Part-time. *Faculty:* 6 full-time (2 women). *Students:* 6 full-time (4 women), 11 part-time (10 women); includes 11 minority (1 Asian, non-Hispanic/Latino; 9 Hispanic/Latino; 1 Two or more races, non-Hispanic/Latino), 1 international. Average age 31. 28 applicants, 54% accepted, 7 enrolled. In 2017, 4 master's awarded. *Degree requirements:* For master's, comprehensive exam. *Entrance requirements:* For master's, GMAT or GRE, baccalaureate degree from regionally-accredited university (business administration or a related field preferred); knowledge of business functions (management, marketing, finance, accounting, MIS) through previous course work and/or work experience; 2 letters of recommendation; resume. Additional exam requirements/recommendations for international students: Required—TOEFL (minimum score 550 paper-based; 78 iBT), IELTS (minimum score 6.5). *Application deadline:* For fall admission, 2/1 priority date for domestic and international students; for spring admission, 10/1 for domestic and international students. Application fee: $40 ($90 for international students). Electronic applications accepted. *Expenses:* Tuition, state resident: full-time $7868; part-time $3934 per semester. Tuition, nonresident: full-time $17,828; part-time $8914 per semester. *Required fees:* $2092; $1435 per semester. Tuition and fees vary according to course load. *Financial support:* In 2017–18, 8 students received support, including 1 teaching assistantship (averaging $12,152 per year); research assistantships, Federal Work-Study, institutionally sponsored loans, scholarships/grants, health care benefits, and unspecified assistantships also available. Support available to part-time students. Financial award application deadline: 3/1; financial award applicants required to submit FAFSA. *Unit head:* Dr. William Chittenden, Graduate Advisor, 512-245-3591, Fax: 512-245-8365, E-mail: wc10@txstate.edu. *Application contact:* Dr. Andrea Golato, Dean of Graduate School, 512-245-2581, Fax: 512-245-8365, E-mail: gradcollege@txstate.edu. Website: http://graduate.mccoy.txstate.edu/grad_programs/MSHRM.html

Texas Woman's University, Graduate School, College of Business, Denton, TX 76204. Offers business administration (MBA), including accounting, business analytics, healthcare administration (MBA, MHA), human resources management, management; health systems management (MHSM); healthcare administration (MHA), including healthcare administration (MBA, MHA). *Accreditation:* ACBSP. *Program availability:* Part-time. *Faculty:* 32 full-time (12 women), 13 part-time/adjunct (9 women). *Students:* 373 full-time (312 women), 432 part-time (368 women); includes 569 minority (312 Black or African American, non-Hispanic/Latino; 1 American Indian or Alaska Native, non-Hispanic/Latino; 116 Asian, non-Hispanic/Latino; 118 Hispanic/Latino; 3 Native Hawaiian or other Pacific Islander, non-Hispanic/Latino; 19 Two or more races, non-Hispanic/Latino), 35 international. Average age 35. 314 applicants, 82% accepted, 184 enrolled. In 2017, 443 master's awarded. *Degree requirements:* For master's, thesis or alternative, capstone. *Entrance requirements:* For master's, minimum GPA of 3.0 in last 60 hours of undergraduate coursework and prior graduate coursework, 2 letters of reference, resume, 5 years of relevant experience (EMBA only). Additional exam requirements/recommendations for international students: Required—TOEFL (minimum score 550 paper-based; 79 iBT); Recommended—IELTS (minimum score 6.5), TSE (minimum score 53). *Application deadline:* For fall admission, 3/1 priority date for domestic students, 3/1 for international students; for spring admission, 11/1 priority date for domestic students, 7/1 for international students. Applications are processed on a rolling basis. Application fee: $50 ($75 for international students). Electronic applications accepted. *Expenses:* $7,520 per year full-time in-state; $16,820 per year full-time out-of-state. *Financial support:* In 2017–18, 198 students received support. Career-related internships or fieldwork, Federal Work-Study, institutionally sponsored loans, scholarships/grants, traineeships, health care benefits, and unspecified assistantships available. Support available to part-time students. Financial award application deadline: 3/1; financial award applicants required to submit FAFSA. *Faculty research:* Marketing and market research, economics, accounting, logistics and supply chain management, health systems. *Unit head:* Dr. Margaret A. Young, Director, 940-898-2458, Fax: 940-898-2120, E-mail: mba@twu.edu. *Application contact:* Korie Hawkins, Associate Director of Admissions, Graduate Recruitment, 940-898-3188, Fax: 940-898-3081, E-mail: admissions@twu.edu. Website: http://www.twu.edu/business/

Thomas College, Graduate School, Programs in Business, Waterville, ME 04901-5097. Offers business (MBA); computer technology education (MS); education (MS); human resource management (MBA). *Program availability:* Part-time, evening/weekend. *Entrance requirements:* For master's, GMAT, GRE, MAT or minimum GPA of 3.3 in first 3 graduate-level courses. Additional exam requirements/recommendations for international students: Recommended—TOEFL.

Thomas Edison State University, School of Business and Management, Program in Human Resources Management, Trenton, NJ 08608. Offers MSHRM. *Program availability:* Part-time, online learning. *Degree requirements:* For master's, final/capstone project. *Entrance requirements:* For master's, bachelor's degree from a regionally-accredited college or university; minimum 2 letters of recommendation; 3-5 years of related working experience; current resume. Additional exam requirements/recommendations for international students: Required—TOEFL (minimum score 550 paper-based; 79 iBT). Electronic applications accepted.

Tiffin University, Program in Business Administration, Tiffin, OH 44883-2161. Offers finance (MBA); general management (MBA); healthcare administration (MBA); human resource management (MBA); international business (MBA); leadership (MBA); marketing (MBA); non-profit management (MBA); sports management (MBA). *Accreditation:* ACBSP. *Program availability:* Part-time, evening/weekend, online learning. *Entrance requirements:* For master's, minimum undergraduate GPA of 2.5, work experience. Additional exam requirements/recommendations for international students: Required—TOEFL (minimum score 550 paper-based; 79 iBT), IELTS. Electronic applications accepted. Application fee is waived when completed online. *Faculty research:* Small business, executive development operations, research and statistical analysis, market research, management information systems.

Towson University, College of Liberal Arts, Program in Human Resource Development, Towson, MD 21252-0001. Offers education leadership (MS); general human resource management (MS). *Program availability:* Part-time, evening/weekend. *Students:* 23 full-time (19 women), 252 part-time (195 women); includes 63 minority (39 Black or African American, non-Hispanic/Latino; 11 Asian, non-Hispanic/Latino; 7 Hispanic/Latino; 6 Two or more races, non-Hispanic/Latino), 2 international. *Degree requirements:* For master's, comprehensive exam. *Entrance requirements:* For master's, bachelor's degree, 2 letters of recommendation, minimum GPA of 3.0, essay, resume. Additional exam requirements/recommendations for international students: Required—TOEFL. *Application deadline:* For fall admission, 1/17 for domestic students, 5/15 for international students; for spring admission, 10/15 for domestic students, 12/1 for international students. Applications are processed on a rolling basis. Application fee: $45. Electronic applications accepted. *Expenses:* Tuition, state resident: full-time $7960; part-time $398 per unit. Tuition, nonresident: full-time $16,480; part-time $824 per unit. *Required fees:* $2600; $130 per unit. $390 per term. *Financial support:* Application deadline: 4/1. *Unit head:* Dr. Abby Mello, Graduate Program Director, 410-704-3364, E-mail: amello@towson.edu. *Application contact:* Coverley Beidleman, Assistant Director of Graduate Admissions, 410-704-5630, Fax: 410-704-3030, E-mail: cbeidleman@towson.edu. Website: http://www.towson.edu/cla/departments/interdisciplinary/grad/hr/

Trident University International, College of Business Administration, Program in Business Administration, Cypress, CA 90630. Offers business administration (PhD); conflict and negotiation management (MBA); criminal justice administration (MBA);

entrepreneurship (MBA); finance (MBA); general management (MBA); government accounting (MBA); human resource management (MBA); information security and digital assurance management (MBA); information technology management (MBA); international business (MBA); logistics management (MBA); marketing (MBA); project management (MBA); public management (MBA); quality management (MBA); strategic leadership (MBA). *Program availability:* Part-time, evening/weekend, online learning. *Degree requirements:* For doctorate, comprehensive exam, thesis/dissertation, defense of dissertation. *Entrance requirements:* For master's, minimum GPA of 2.5 (students with GPA 3.0 or greater may transfer up to 30% of graduate level credits); for doctorate, minimum GPA of 3.4, curriculum vitae, course work in research methods or statistics. Additional exam requirements/recommendations for international students: Required—TOEFL. Electronic applications accepted.

Trinity International University, Trinity Law School, Santa Ana, CA 92705. Offers bioethics (MLS); church and ministry management (MLS); general legal studies (MLS); human resources management (MLS); human rights (MLS); law (JD); nonprofit organizations (MLS). *Program availability:* Part-time, evening/weekend. *Entrance requirements:* For doctorate, LSAT. Additional exam requirements/recommendations for international students: Required—TOEFL (minimum score 580 paper-based). *Expenses:* Contact institution.

Trinity Washington University, School of Business and Graduate Studies, Washington, DC 20017-1094. Offers business administration (MBA); communication (MA); international security studies (MA); organizational management (MSA), including federal program management, human resource management, nonprofit management, organizational development, public and community health. *Program availability:* Part-time, evening/weekend. *Degree requirements:* For master's, thesis (for some programs), capstone project (MSA). *Entrance requirements:* For master's, minimum GPA of 2.5. Additional exam requirements/recommendations for international students: Required—TOEFL (minimum score 550 paper-based).

Troy University, Graduate School, College of Business, Program in Human Resources Management, Troy, AL 36082. Offers MS. *Program availability:* Part-time, evening/weekend. *Faculty:* 8 full-time (2 women), 1 part-time/adjunct (0 women). *Students:* 58 full-time (48 women), 269 part-time (200 women); includes 121 minority (109 Black or African American, non-Hispanic/Latino; 1 American Indian or Alaska Native, non-Hispanic/Latino; 1 Asian, non-Hispanic/Latino; 5 Hispanic/Latino; 1 Native Hawaiian or other Pacific Islander, non-Hispanic/Latino; 4 Two or more races, non-Hispanic/Latino). Average age 33. 146 applicants, 95% accepted, 96 enrolled. In 2017, 93 master's awarded. *Degree requirements:* For master's, minimum GPA of 3.0; admission to candidacy. *Entrance requirements:* For master's, GRE (minimum score of 900 on old exam or 294 on new exam) or GMAT (minimum score of 500), bachelor's degree; minimum undergraduate GPA of 2.5 or 3.0 on last 30 semester hours, letter of recommendation. Additional exam requirements/recommendations for international students: Required—TOEFL (minimum score 523 paper-based; 70 iBT), IELTS (minimum score 6). *Application deadline:* Applications are processed on a rolling basis. Application fee: $50. Electronic applications accepted. *Expenses:* Tuition, state resident: part-time $417 per credit hour. Tuition, nonresident: part-time $834 per credit hour. *Required fees:* $42 per credit hour. $50 per semester. Tuition and fees vary according to campus/location. *Financial support:* Fellowships, career-related internships or fieldwork, and scholarships/grants available. Support available to part-time students. Financial award applicants required to submit FAFSA. *Unit head:* Dr. Bill Heisler, Director, 757-274-0474 Ext. 334, Fax: 241-241-0378, E-mail: wheisler@troy.edu. *Application contact:* Jessica A. Kimbro, Director of Graduate Admissions, 334-670-3178, E-mail: jacord@troy.edu.

United States International University–Africa, School of Business Administration, Nairobi, Kenya. Offers business administration (GEMBA); entrepreneurship (MBA); finance (MBA); human resource management (MBA); information technology management (MBA); integrated studies (MBA); international business administration (MBA); management and organizational development (MS); marketing (MBA); organizational development (EMS); strategic management (MBA). *Program availability:* Part-time, evening/weekend. *Degree requirements:* For master's, thesis. *Entrance requirements:* For master's, GMAT, 2 letters of reference, resume. Additional exam requirements/recommendations for international students: Required—TOEFL (minimum score 550 paper-based). *Faculty research:* Marketing in small business enterprises, total quality management in Kenya.

Universidad del Este, Graduate School, Carolina, PR 00984. Offers accounting (MBA); adult education (M Ed); agribusiness (MBA); criminal justice and criminology (MA); curriculum and instruction - early education (M Ed); curriculum and instruction - elementary (M Ed); curriculum and instruction - English (M Ed); curriculum and instruction - Spanish (M Ed); human resources (MBA); information security management (MBA); information technology and Web business development (MBA); management (MBA); public policy (MPA); social work (MA), including clinical social work; special education (M Ed); strategic leadership (MBA).

Universidad del Turabo, Graduate Programs, School of Business and Entrepreneurship, Program in Human Resources, Gurabo, PR 00778-3030. Offers MBA. *Entrance requirements:* For master's, GRE, EXADEP or GMAT, interview, essay, official transcript, recommendation letters. Electronic applications accepted.

Universidad Metropolitana, School of Business Administration, Program in Human Resources Management, San Juan, PR 00928-1150. Offers MBA. *Program availability:* Part-time.

University at Albany, State University of New York, Nelson A. Rockefeller College of Public Affairs and Policy, Department of Public Administration and Policy, Albany, NY 12222-0001. Offers financial management and public economics (MPA); financial market regulation (MPA); health policy (MPA); healthcare management (MPA); homeland security (MPA); human resources management (MPA); information strategy and management (MPA); local government management (MPA); nonprofit management (MPA); nonprofit management and leadership (Certificate); organizational behavior and theory (MPA, PhD); planning and policy analysis (CAS); policy analysis (MPA); politics and administration (PhD); public finance (PhD); public management (PhD); public policy (PhD); public sector management (Certificate); women and public policy (Certificate); JD/MPA. JD/MPA offered jointly with Albany Law School. *Accreditation:* NASPAA (one or more programs are accredited). *Faculty:* 21 full-time (7 women), 14 part-time/adjunct (7 women). *Students:* 115 full-time (59 women), 93 part-time (56 women); includes 41 minority (11 Black or African American, non-Hispanic/Latino; 9 Asian, non-Hispanic/Latino; 18 Hispanic/Latino; 3 Two or more races, non-Hispanic/Latino), 32 international. 236 applicants, 69% accepted, 86 enrolled. In 2017, 57 master's, 1 doctorate, 14 other advanced degrees awarded. *Degree requirements:* For doctorate, one foreign language, thesis/dissertation. *Entrance requirements:* For doctorate, GRE General Test. Additional exam requirements/recommendations for international students: Required—TOEFL (minimum score 550 paper-based). *Application deadline:* For fall admission, 2/1 priority date for domestic students, 5/1 for international students; for spring admission, 12/1 for domestic students. Applications are processed on a rolling basis. Application fee: $75. Electronic applications accepted. *Expenses:* Tuition, state resident: full-time $10,870; part-time $453 per credit hour. Tuition, nonresident: full-time $22,210; part-time $925

Human Resources Management

per credit hour. *Required fees:* $84.68 per credit hour. $508.06 per semester. Part-time tuition and fees vary according to course load and program. *Financial support:* Application deadline: 2/1. *Unit head:* Victor Asal, Chair, 518-591-8729, E-mail: vasal@albany.edu.
Website: http://www.albany.edu/rockefeller/pad.shtml

University at Albany, State University of New York, School of Business, MBA Programs, Albany, NY 12222. Offers business administration (MBA); cyber security (MBA); entrepreneurship (MBA); finance (MBA); human resource information systems (MBA); information systems and business analytics (MBA); marketing (MBA); JD/MBA. JD/MBA offered jointly with Albany Law School. *Program availability:* Part-time, evening/weekend. *Faculty:* 29 full-time (13 women), 9 part-time/adjunct (2 women). *Students:* 103 full-time (36 women), 188 part-time (69 women); includes 76 minority (27 Black or African American, non-Hispanic/Latino; 33 Asian, non-Hispanic/Latino; 16 Hispanic/Latino), 16 international. Average age 25. 181 applicants, 80% accepted, 114 enrolled. In 2017, 103 master's awarded. *Degree requirements:* For master's, thesis (for some programs), field or research project. *Entrance requirements:* For master's, GMAT, minimum undergraduate GPA of 3.0; 3 letters of recommendation; resume; statement of goals. Additional exam requirements/recommendations for international students: Required—TOEFL (minimum score 100 iBT); Recommended—IELTS (minimum score 7). *Application deadline:* For fall admission, 4/1 priority date for domestic students, 2/15 for international students; for spring admission, 12/1 for domestic students; for summer admission, 5/1 for domestic students. Applications are processed on a rolling basis. Application fee: $75. Electronic applications accepted. *Expenses:* $16,622.00 per year (for Full-Time MBA); $645 per credit hour (for Evening MBA). *Financial support:* In 2017–18, 25 students received support, including 7 fellowships with partial tuition reimbursements available (averaging $6,000 per year), 4 research assistantships with partial tuition reimbursements available, 21 teaching assistantships with partial tuition reimbursements available; unspecified assistantships also available. Financial award application deadline: 4/1; financial award applicants required to submit FAFSA. *Faculty research:* Social goods, information assurance, social computing, corporate entrepreneurship, asset pricing. *Total annual research expenditures:* $136,000. *Unit head:* Dr. Hany A. Shawky, Interim Dean, 518-956-8337, Fax: 518-442-3273, E-mail: hshawky@albany.edu. *Application contact:* Zina Mega Lawrence, Assistant Dean of Graduate Student Services, 518-956-8320, Fax: 518-442-4042, E-mail: zlawrence@albany.edu.
Website: https://graduatebusiness.albany.edu/

University at Buffalo, the State University of New York, Graduate School, Graduate School of Education, Department of Educational Leadership and Policy, Buffalo, NY 14260. Offers economics and education policy analysis (MA); education studies (Ed M); educational administration (Ed M, Ed D, PhD); educational culture, policy and society (PhD); higher education administration (Ed M, PhD); school building leadership (Certificate); school business and human resource administration (Certificate); school district business leadership (Certificate); school district leadership (Certificate). *Program availability:* Part-time, evening/weekend. *Faculty:* 16 full-time (10 women), 9 part-time/adjunct (6 women). *Students:* 65 full-time (44 women), 125 part-time (82 women); includes 29 minority (23 Black or African American, non-Hispanic/Latino; 3 Asian, non-Hispanic/Latino; 3 Hispanic/Latino), 19 international. Average age 35. 153 applicants, 75% accepted, 59 enrolled. In 2017, 45 master's, 4 doctorates, 23 other advanced degrees awarded. *Degree requirements:* For master's, comprehensive exam (for some programs), thesis optional; for doctorate, comprehensive exam, thesis/dissertation. *Entrance requirements:* For master's, interview, letters of reference; for doctorate, GRE General Test or MAT, writing sample, letters of reference. Additional exam requirements/recommendations for international students: Required—TOEFL (minimum score 550 paper-based; 79 iBT). *Application deadline:* For fall admission, 2/1 priority date for domestic students, 2/1 for international students; for spring admission, 11/15 priority date for domestic students, 10/1 for international students. Applications are processed on a rolling basis. Application fee: $50. Electronic applications accepted. *Financial support:* In 2017–18, 18 fellowships (averaging $5,673 per year), 34 research assistantships with tuition reimbursements (averaging $12,055 per year) were awarded; career-related internships or fieldwork, Federal Work-Study, institutionally sponsored loans, scholarships/grants, health care benefits, tuition waivers (full and partial), and unspecified assistantships also available. Financial award application deadline: 3/15; financial award applicants required to submit FAFSA. *Faculty research:* College access and choice, school leadership preparation and practice, public policy, curriculum and pedagogy, comparative and international education. *Total annual research expenditures:* $637,951. *Unit head:* Dr. Janina C. Brutt-Griffler, Chair, 716-645-2471, Fax: 716-645-2481, E-mail: bruttg@buffalo.edu. *Application contact:* Veronica Kase, Admission Assistant, 716-645-2110, Fax: 716-645-7937, E-mail: vakase@buffalo.edu.
Website: http://gse.buffalo.edu/elp

The University of Alabama in Huntsville, School of Graduate Studies, College of Business Administration, Programs in Business and Management, Huntsville, AL 35899. Offers business analytics (MSMS); federal contracting and procurement management (Certificate); human resource management (MSM); management (MBA), including acquisition management, entrepreneurship, federal contract accounting, finance, human resource management, logistics and supply chain management, marketing, project management; supply chain management (Certificate); technology and innovation management (Certificate). *Accreditation:* AACSB. *Program availability:* Part-time, evening/weekend. *Degree requirements:* For master's, comprehensive exam, thesis or alternative. *Entrance requirements:* For master's, GMAT (minimum score 500), minimum AACSB index of 1080. Additional exam requirements/recommendations for international students: Required—TOEFL (minimum score 550 paper-based; 80 iBT), IELTS (minimum score 6.5). Electronic applications accepted. *Faculty research:* Supply chain management, management of research and development, international marketing and branding, organizational behavior and human resource management, social networks and computational economics.

University of Bridgeport, School of Business, Bridgeport, CT 06604. Offers accounting (MBA); finance (MBA); general business (MBA); global financial services (MBA); human resource management (MBA); information systems and knowledge management (MBA); international business (MBA); management (MBA); marketing (MBA); operations management (MBA); small business and entrepreneurship (MBA); specialized business (MBA). *Accreditation:* ACBSP. *Program availability:* Part-time, evening/weekend. *Degree requirements:* For master's, thesis optional. *Entrance requirements:* For master's, GMAT. Additional exam requirements/recommendations for international students: Recommended—TOEFL (minimum score 550 paper-based; 80 iBT), IELTS (minimum score 6.5). Electronic applications accepted. *Expenses:* Contact institution.

University of California, Berkeley, UC Berkeley Extension, Certificate Programs in Business, Berkeley, CA 94720-1500. Offers accounting (Certificate); business administration (Certificate); finance (Certificate); human resource management (Certificate); management (Certificate); marketing (Certificate); project management (Certificate). *Accreditation:* AACSB. *Program availability:* Online learning.

University of Cincinnati, Carl H. Lindner College of Business, MA Program, Cincinnati, OH 45221. Offers human resources (MA). *Program availability:* Part-time, evening/weekend. *Faculty:* 14 full-time (4 women), 8 part-time/adjunct (3 women). *Students:* 8 full-time (all women), 12 part-time (10 women); includes 4 minority (2 Black or African American, non-Hispanic/Latino; 1 Asian, non-Hispanic/Latino; 1 Hispanic/Latino), 3 international. Average age 29. 29 applicants, 31% accepted, 6 enrolled. In 2017, 15 master's awarded. *Degree requirements:* For master's, capstone. *Entrance requirements:* For master's, GRE or GMAT. Additional exam requirements/recommendations for international students: Required—TOEFL (minimum score 577 paper-based; 90 iBT), IELTS (minimum score 6.5). *Application deadline:* For fall admission, 6/30 priority date for domestic students, 3/15 priority date for international students; for spring admission, 12/15 for domestic students, 9/15 for international students; for summer admission, 4/15 for domestic and international students. Applications are processed on a rolling basis. Application fee: $65 ($70 for international students). Electronic applications accepted. *Expenses:* $10,479 per term full-time resident, $14,398 per term full-time nonresident, $890 per credit hour part-time. *Financial support:* In 2017–18, 4 students received support. Scholarships/grants and tuition waivers (partial) available. Financial award application deadline: 3/15. *Unit head:* Dr. David Szymanski, Dean, 513-556-7001, Fax: 513-556-4891, E-mail: david.szymanski@uc.edu. *Application contact:* Dona Clary, Executive Director, Graduate Programs, 513-556-3645, E-mail: dona.clary@uc.edu.
Website: http://business.uc.edu/graduate/masters/ma-human-resources.html

University of Colorado Denver, Business School, Master of Business Administration Program, Denver, CO 80217. Offers bioinnovation and entrepreneurship (MBA); business intelligence (MBA); business strategy (MBA); business to business marketing (MBA); business to consumer marketing (MBA); change management (MBA); corporate financial management (MBA); enterprise technology management (MBA); entrepreneurship (MBA); health administration (MBA), including financial management, health administration, health information technologies, international health management and policy; human resources management (MBA); international business (MBA); investment management (MBA); managing for sustainability (MBA); sports and entertainment management (MBA). *Accreditation:* AACSB. *Program availability:* Part-time, evening/weekend, 100% online, blended/hybrid learning. *Degree requirements:* For master's, 48 semester hours, including 30 of core courses, 3 in international business, and 15 in electives from over 50 other business courses. *Entrance requirements:* For master's, GMAT, resume, official transcripts, essay, two letters of recommendation, financial statements (for international applicants). Additional exam requirements/recommendations for international students: Required—TOEFL (minimum score 560 paper-based; 83 iBT); Recommended—IELTS (minimum score 6.5). Electronic applications accepted. *Expenses:* Contact institution. *Faculty research:* Marketing, management, entrepreneurship, finance, health administration.

University of Colorado Denver, Business School, Program in Management and Organization, Denver, CO 80217. Offers business strategy (MS); change and innovation (MS); enterprise technology management (MS); entrepreneurship and innovation (MS); global management (MS); leadership (MS); managing for sustainability (MS); managing human resources (MS); sports and entertainment management (MS). *Accreditation:* AACSB. *Program availability:* Part-time, evening/weekend, online learning. *Degree requirements:* For master's, 30 semester hours (12 of required courses, 12 of management electives, and 6 of free electives). *Entrance requirements:* For master's, GMAT, resume, two letters of recommendation, essay, financial statements (for international applicants). Additional exam requirements/recommendations for international students: Required—TOEFL (minimum score 525 paper-based; 71 iBT); Recommended—IELTS (minimum score 6.5). Electronic applications accepted. *Expenses:* Contact institution. *Faculty research:* Human resource management, management of catastrophe, turnaround strategies.

University of Connecticut, Graduate School, eCampus, Program in Human Resource Management, Storrs, CT 06269. Offers MS.

University of Dallas, Satish and Yasmin Gupta College of Business, Irving, TX 75062-4736. Offers accounting (MBA, MS); business administration (DBA); business analytics (MS); business management (MBA); corporate finance (MBA); cybersecurity (MS); finance (MS); financial services (MBA); global business (MBA, MS); health services management (MBA); human resource management (MBA); information and technology management (MS); information assurance (MBA); information technology (MBA); information technology service management (MBA); marketing management (MBA); organization development (MBA); project management (MBA); sports and entertainment management (MBA); strategic leadership (MBA); supply chain management (MBA). *Accreditation:* AACSB. *Program availability:* Part-time, evening/weekend, online learning. *Entrance requirements:* Additional exam requirements/recommendations for international students: Required—TOEFL. *Application deadline:* Applications are processed on a rolling basis. Application fee: $50. Electronic applications accepted. *Expenses:* Contact institution. *Financial support:* Application deadline: 2/15; applicants required to submit FAFSA. *Unit head:* Brett J.L. Landry, Dean, 972-721-5356, E-mail: blandry@udallas.edu. *Application contact:* Dr. David Sweet, Dean, Braniff Graduate School, 972-721-5288, Fax: 972-721-5280, E-mail: dsweet@udallas.edu.
Website: http://www.udallas.edu/cob/

University of Denver, University College, Denver, CO 80208. Offers arts and culture (MA, Certificate); communication management (MS, Certificate), including translation studies (Certificate), world history and culture (Certificate); environmental policy and management (MS); geographic information systems (MS); global affairs (MA, Certificate), including human capital in organizations (Certificate), philanthropic leadership (Certificate), project management (Certificate), strategic innovation and change (Certificate); healthcare leadership (MS); information communications and technology (MS); leadership and organizations (MS); professional creative writing (MA, Certificate), including emergency planning and response (Certificate), organizational security (Certificate); security management (MS, Certificate); strategic human resources (Certificate). *Program availability:* Part-time, evening/weekend, online learning. *Faculty:* 118 part-time/adjunct (62 women). *Students:* 56 full-time (32 women), 1,287 part-time (707 women); includes 330 minority (99 Black or African American, non-Hispanic/Latino; 7 American Indian or Alaska Native, non-Hispanic/Latino; 43 Asian, non-Hispanic/Latino; 141 Hispanic/Latino; 3 Native Hawaiian or other Pacific Islander, non-Hispanic/Latino; 37 Two or more races, non-Hispanic/Latino), 84 international. Average age 34. 783 applicants, 86% accepted, 420 enrolled. In 2017, 461 master's, 173 other advanced degrees awarded. *Degree requirements:* For master's, capstone project. *Entrance requirements:* For master's, transcripts, two letters of recommendation, personal statement, resume. Additional exam requirements/recommendations for international students: Required—TOEFL (minimum score 550 paper-based; 80 iBT). *Application deadline:* For fall admission, 6/21 priority date for domestic students, 5/1 priority date for international students; for winter admission, 9/14 priority date for domestic students, 9/19 priority date for international students; for spring admission, 1/11 priority date for domestic students, 12/12 priority date for international students; for summer admission, 3/29 priority date for domestic students, 3/6 priority date for international students. Applications are processed on a rolling basis. Application fee: $75. Electronic applications accepted. *Expenses:* $7,968 per year half-time. *Financial support:* In 2017–18, 29 students received support. Teaching assistantships available. Financial award applicants required to submit FAFSA. *Unit head:* Dr. Michael McGuire, Dean, 303-871-3518, Fax: 303-871-3303, E-mail: mmcguire@du.edu. *Application contact:* Information Contact, 303-871-2291, E-mail: ucoladm@du.edu.
Website: http://universitycollege.du.edu/

University of Florida, Graduate School, Warrington College of Business Administration, Hough Graduate School of Business, Programs in Business Administration, Gainesville, FL 32611. Offers business administration (MA, MS, PhD); competitive strategy (MBA); finance (MBA); global management (MBA); Graham-Buffett security analysis (MBA); human resource management (MBA); information systems and operations management (MBA); international studies (MBA); management (MBA); real estate (MBA); JD/MBA; MBA/MS; MBA/PhD; MBA/Pharm D; MD/MBA. *Accreditation:* AACSB. *Program availability:* Part-time, evening/weekend, online learning. *Degree requirements:* For master's, capstone course. *Entrance requirements:* For master's and doctorate, GMAT (minimum score 465), minimum GPA of 3.0, interview. Additional exam requirements/recommendations for international students: Required—TOEFL (minimum score 550 paper-based; 80 iBT), IELTS (minimum score 6). Electronic applications accepted. *Faculty research:* Accounting, finance, insurance, management, real estate, urban analysis marketing.

University of Hawaii at Manoa, Office of Graduate Education, Shidler College of Business, Program in Business Administration, Honolulu, HI 96822. Offers Asian business studies (MBA); Chinese business studies (MBA); decision sciences (MBA); entrepreneurship (MBA); finance (MBA); finance and banking (MBA); human resources management (MBA); information management (MBA); information technology (MBA); international business (MBA); Japanese business studies (MBA); marketing (MBA); organizational behavior (MBA); organizational management (MBA); real estate (MBA); student-designed track (MBA). *Accreditation:* AACSB. *Program availability:* Part-time, evening/weekend. *Degree requirements:* For master's, thesis optional. *Entrance requirements:* For master's, GMAT, minimum GPA of 3.0. Additional exam requirements/recommendations for international students: Required—TOEFL (minimum score 600 paper-based; 100 iBT), IELTS (minimum score 7). *Expenses:* Contact institution.

University of Hawaii at Manoa, Office of Graduate Education, Shidler College of Business, Program in Human Resources Management, Honolulu, HI 96822. Offers MHRM. *Program availability:* Part-time. *Entrance requirements:* Additional exam requirements/recommendations for international students: Required—TOEFL (minimum score 600 paper-based; 100 iBT), IELTS (minimum score 7). *Expenses:* Contact institution.

University of Houston–Clear Lake, School of Business, Program in Administrative Science, Houston, TX 77058-1002. Offers environmental management (MS); human resource management (MBA). *Program availability:* Part-time, evening/weekend. *Degree requirements:* For master's, thesis optional. *Entrance requirements:* For master's, GMAT. Additional exam requirements/recommendations for international students: Required—TOEFL (minimum score 550 paper-based). Electronic applications accepted.

University of Houston–Downtown, Marilyn Davies College of Business, MBA Program, Houston, TX 77002. Offers accounting (MBA); finance (MBA); human resource management (MBA); international business (MBA); investment management (MBA); leadership (MBA); project management and process improvement (MBA); sales management and business development (MBA); supply chain management (MBA). *Accreditation:* AACSB. *Program availability:* Part-time, evening/weekend. *Faculty:* 36 full-time (13 women), 11 part-time/adjunct (6 women). *Students:* 4 full-time (2 women), 1,065 part-time (605 women); includes 821 minority (383 Black or African American, non-Hispanic/Latino; 3 American Indian or Alaska Native, non-Hispanic/Latino; 136 Asian, non-Hispanic/Latino; 299 Hispanic/Latino), 33 international. Average age 33. 418 applicants, 89% accepted, 308 enrolled. In 2017, 310 master's awarded. *Entrance requirements:* For master's, GMAT, two letters of recommendation from professional references, personal statement, resume. Additional exam requirements/recommendations for international students: Required—TOEFL (minimum score 81 iBT). *Application deadline:* For fall admission, 8/1 for domestic and international students. Application fee: $35 ($60 for international students). Electronic applications accepted. *Expenses:* $360 per credit resident; $725 per credit non-resident. *Financial support:* Federal Work-Study and scholarships/grants available. Financial award application deadline: 4/1; financial award applicants required to submit FAFSA. *Unit head:* Dr. Charles E. Gengler, Dean, 713-221-8179, Fax: 713-221-8675. *Application contact:* Ceshia Love, Director of Admissions, 713-221-8093, Fax: 713-223-7408, E-mail: gradadmissions@uhd.edu.
Website: http://mba.uhd.edu/

University of Illinois at Urbana–Champaign, Graduate College, College of Education, Department of Education Policy, Organization, and Leadership, Champaign, IL 61820. Offers educational organization and leadership (Ed M, MS, Ed D, PhD, CAS); educational policy studies (Ed M, MA, PhD); human resource education (Ed M, MS, Ed D, PhD, CAS). *Program availability:* Part-time, online learning.

University of Illinois at Urbana–Champaign, Graduate College, School of Labor and Employment Relations, Champaign, IL 61820. Offers human resources and industrial relations (MHRIR, PhD); MHRIR/JD; MHRIR/MBA. Terminal master's awarded for partial completion of doctoral program.

The University of Kansas, Graduate Studies, School of Business, Program in Business, Lawrence, KS 66045. Offers business and organizational leadership (MS); decision sciences and supply chain management (PhD); finance (PhD); human resources management (PhD); marketing (PhD); organizational behavior (PhD); strategic management (PhD); supply chain management and logistics (MS). *Accreditation:* AACSB. *Program availability:* Part-time. *Students:* 66 full-time (18 women), 227 part-time (76 women); includes 59 minority (21 Black or African American, non-Hispanic/Latino; 2 American Indian or Alaska Native, non-Hispanic/Latino; 13 Asian, non-Hispanic/Latino; 3 Hispanic/Latino; 20 Two or more races, non-Hispanic/Latino), 29 international. Average age 32. 329 applicants, 71% accepted, 185 enrolled. In 2017, 30 master's, 8 doctorates awarded. *Entrance requirements:* For master's, GMAT, official transcript, three letters of recommendation, resume, statement of purpose; for doctorate, GMAT or GRE, official transcript, three letters of recommendation, resume, statement of purpose. Additional exam requirements/recommendations for international students: Required—TOEFL (minimum score 600 paper-based; 100 iBT). *Application deadline:* For fall admission, 1/10 for domestic and international students. Application fee: $65 ($85 for international students). Electronic applications accepted. *Financial support:* Fellowships, research assistantships, teaching assistantships, scholarships/grants, health care benefits, tuition waivers (full), and unspecified assistantships available. Financial award application deadline: 1/10. *Faculty research:* Strategic human resource management, business ethics, organizational theory/behavior, corporate strategy, international business, supply chain management, Bayesian networks, game theory, decision analysis and time/series analysis, pricing, consumer effects, advertising and emotion. *Unit head:* Charly Edmonds, Director, 785-864-3841, E-mail: bschoolphd@ku.edu. *Application contact:* Graduate Admission Contact, 785-864-7500, E-mail: bschoolphd@ku.edu.
Website: http://www.business.ku.edu/

University of La Verne, College of Business and Public Management, Program in Leadership and Management, La Verne, CA 91750-4443. Offers human resource management (Certificate); leadership and management (MS), including human resource management, nonprofit management, organizational development; nonprofit management (Certificate); organizational leadership (Certificate). *Program availability:* Part-time. *Faculty:* 4 full-time (3 women), 5 part-time/adjunct (1 woman). *Students:* 49 full-time (25 women), 35 part-time (22 women); includes 47 minority (6 Black or African American, non-Hispanic/Latino; 4 Asian, non-Hispanic/Latino; 35 Hispanic/Latino; 2 Two or more races, non-Hispanic/Latino), 13 international. Average age 32. *Entrance requirements:* For master's, bachelor's degree, minimum undergraduate GPA of 2.75, 2 letters of recommendation, interview, resume. Additional exam requirements/recommendations for international students: Required—TOEFL (minimum score 550 paper-based). *Application deadline:* Applications are processed on a rolling basis. Application fee: $50. Tuition and fees vary according to program. *Financial support:* Federal Work-Study, institutionally sponsored loans, and scholarships/grants available. Financial award application deadline: 3/2; financial award applicants required to submit FAFSA. *Unit head:* Dr. Kathy Duncan, Program Director, 909-448-4415, E-mail: kduncan2@laverne.edu. *Application contact:* Barbara Cox, Associate Director of Graduate Admissions, 909-448-4004, E-mail: bcox@laverne.edu.
Website: https://business.laverne.edu/mslm/

University of La Verne, Regional and Online Campuses, Graduate Programs, Inland Empire Campus, Ontario, CA 91730. Offers business administration (MBA, MBA-EP), including accounting (MBA), finance (MBA), health services management (MBA-EP), information technology (MBA-EP), international business (MBA), managed care (MBA), management and leadership (MBA-EP), marketing (MBA-EP), supply chain management (MBA); leadership and management (MS), including human resource management, nonprofit management, organizational development. *Program availability:* Part-time, evening/weekend. *Faculty:* 5 part-time/adjunct (1 woman). *Students:* 24 full-time (13 women), 72 part-time (44 women); includes 64 minority (12 Black or African American, non-Hispanic/Latino; 13 Asian, non-Hispanic/Latino; 36 Hispanic/Latino; 3 Two or more races, non-Hispanic/Latino). Average age 38. In 2017, 42 master's awarded. *Application deadline:* Applications are processed on a rolling basis. Application fee: $50. *Expenses:* Contact institution. *Financial support:* Application deadline: 3/2; applicants required to submit FAFSA. *Unit head:* Juli Roberts, Campus Director, Inland Empire Regional Campus in Ontario, 760-955-6448, E-mail: jroberts@laverne.edu. *Application contact:* Admissions, 877-468-6858, E-mail: gradadmission@laverne.edu.
Website: https://laverne.edu/locations/

University of Lethbridge, School of Graduate Studies, Lethbridge, AB T1K 3M4, Canada. Offers addictions counseling (M Sc); agricultural biotechnology (M Sc); agricultural studies (M Sc, MA); anthropology (MA); archaeology (M Sc, MA); art (MA, MFA); biochemistry (M Sc); biological sciences (M Sc); biomolecular science (PhD); biosystems and biodiversity (PhD); Canadian studies (MA); chemistry (M Sc); computer science (M Sc); computer science and geographical information science (M Sc); counseling (MC); counseling psychology (M Ed); dramatic arts (MA); earth, space, and physical science (PhD); economics (MA); education (MA, PhD); educational leadership (M Ed); English (MA); environmental science (M Sc); evolution and behavior (PhD); exercise science (M Sc); French (MA); French/German (MA); French/Spanish (MA); general education (M Ed); geography (M Sc, MA); German (MA); health sciences (M Sc); individualized multidisciplinary (M Sc, MA); kinesiology (M Sc, MA); management (M Sc), including accounting, finance, human resource management and labor relations, information systems, international management, marketing, policy and strategy; mathematics (M Sc); music (M Mus, MA); Native American studies (MA); neuroscience (M Sc, PhD); new media (MA, MFA); nursing (M Sc, MN); philosophy (MA); physics (M Sc); political science (MA); psychology (M Sc, MA); religious studies (MA); sociology (MA); theatre and dramatic arts (MFA); theoretical and computational science (PhD); urban and regional studies (MA); women and gender studies (MA). *Program availability:* Part-time, evening/weekend. *Degree requirements:* For master's, thesis (for some programs); for doctorate, comprehensive exam, thesis/dissertation. *Entrance requirements:* For master's, GMAT (for M Sc in management), bachelor's degree in related field, minimum GPA of 3.0 during previous 20 graded semester courses, 2 years' teaching or related experience (M Ed); for doctorate, master's degree, minimum graduate GPA of 3.5. Additional exam requirements/recommendations for international students: Required—TOEFL (minimum score 580 paper-based; 93 iBT). Electronic applications accepted. *Faculty research:* Movement and brain plasticity, gibberellin physiology, photosynthesis, carbon cycling, molecular properties of main-group ring components.

University of Louisville, Graduate School, College of Arts and Sciences, Department of Urban and Public Affairs, Louisville, KY 40208. Offers public administration (MPA), including human resources management, non-profit management, public policy and administration; urban and public affairs (PhD), including urban planning and development, urban policy and administration; urban planning (MUP), including administration of planning organizations, housing and community development, land use and environmental planning, spatial analysis. *Program availability:* Part-time, evening/weekend. *Faculty:* 12 full-time (5 women), 4 part-time/adjunct (1 woman). *Students:* 50 full-time (19 women), 20 part-time (17 women); includes 17 minority (6 Black or African American, non-Hispanic/Latino; 1 Asian, non-Hispanic/Latino; 4 Hispanic/Latino; 6 Two or more races, non-Hispanic/Latino), 4 international. Average age 31. 47 applicants, 70% accepted, 22 enrolled. In 2017, 20 master's, 2 doctorates awarded. Terminal master's awarded for partial completion of doctoral program. *Degree requirements:* For master's, internship; for doctorate, comprehensive exam, thesis/dissertation. *Entrance requirements:* For master's, GRE General Test, minimum GPA of 3.0; for doctorate, GRE General Test, master's degree in appropriate field. Additional exam requirements/recommendations for international students: Required—TOEFL (minimum score 550 paper-based; 79 iBT). *Application deadline:* Applications are processed on a rolling basis. Application fee: $65. *Expenses:* Contact institution. *Financial support:* Fellowships, research assistantships, tuition waivers (full and partial), and unspecified assistantships available. Financial award application deadline: 2/1. *Faculty research:* Urban theory, sustainability, public administration, urban planning, urban management. *Total annual research expenditures:* $240,308. *Unit head:* Dr. David Simpson, Chair, 502-852-8019, Fax: 502-852-4558, E-mail: dave.simpson@louisville.edu. *Application contact:* Latonia Craig, Director of Graduate Recruitment and Diversity Retention, 502-852-5207, Fax: 502-852-4558, E-mail: gradadm@louisville.edu.
Website: http://supa.louisville.edu

University of Louisville, Graduate School, College of Education and Human Development, Department of Educational Leadership, Evaluation and Organizational Development, Louisville, KY 40292-0001. Offers educational leadership and organizational development (Ed D, PhD), including evaluation (PhD), human resource development (PhD), P-12 administration (PhD), post-secondary administration (PhD), sport administration (PhD); health professions education (Certificate); higher education administration (MA); human resources and organization development (MS), including health professions education, human resource leadership, workplace learning and performance; P-12 educational administration (Ed S), including principalship, supervisor of instruction. *Accreditation:* NCATE. *Program availability:* Part-time, evening/weekend, online learning. *Students:* 190 full-time (64 women), 516 part-time (298 women); includes 218 minority (131 Black or African American, non-Hispanic/Latino; 1 American Indian or Alaska Native, non-Hispanic/Latino; 16 Asian, non-Hispanic/Latino; 47 Hispanic/Latino; 2 Native Hawaiian or other Pacific Islander, non-Hispanic/Latino; 21

Human Resources Management

Two or more races, non-Hispanic/Latino), 3 international. Average age 36. 232 applicants, 84% accepted, 141 enrolled. In 2017, 68 master's, 2 doctorates, 17 other advanced degrees awarded. Application fee: $65. *Expenses:* Tuition, state resident: full-time $12,246; part-time $681 per credit hour. Tuition, nonresident: full-time $25,486; part-time $1417 per credit hour. *Required fees:* $196. Tuition and fees vary according to course load, program and reciprocity agreements. *Financial support:* Application deadline: 6/1; applicants required to submit FAFSA. *Faculty research:* Urban educational leadership and policy, human resource and organizational development, program evaluation, community and military partnerships, higher education, and economic education. *Total annual research expenditures:* $256,111. *Unit head:* Dr. Jeffrey Sun, Chair and Professor, 502-852-0618, E-mail: jeffrey.sun@louisville.edu. *Application contact:* Betty Hampton, Director of Graduate Student Services, 502-852-5597, Fax: 502-852-1465, E-mail: edadvise@louisville.edu. Website: http://louisville.edu/education/departments/eleod

University of Louisville, Graduate School, College of Education and Human Development, Departments of Early Childhood and Elementary Education, Middle and Secondary Education, and Special Education, Louisville, KY 40292-0001. Offers art education (MAT); autism and applied behavior analysis (Certificate); curriculum and instruction (PhD); early elementary education (MAT); exercise physiology (MS); health and physical education (MAT); health professions education (Certificate); higher education (MA); human resources and organization development (MS); instructional technology (M Ed); interdisciplinary early childhood education (MAT); middle school education (MAT); music education (MAT); secondary education (MAT); special education (MAT); sport administration (MS); teacher leadership (M Ed). *Program availability:* Part-time, evening/weekend. *Students:* 114 full-time (73 women), 173 part-time (114 women); includes 49 minority (19 Black or African American, non-Hispanic/Latino; 5 Asian, non-Hispanic/Latino; 13 Hispanic/Latino; 12 Two or more races, non-Hispanic/Latino), 7 international. Average age 29. 132 applicants, 73% accepted, 57 enrolled. In 2017, 70 master's, 2 doctorates, 2 other advanced degrees awarded. *Application deadline:* For spring admission, 1/1 priority date for international students. Application fee: $65. *Expenses:* Tuition, state resident: full-time $12,246; part-time $681 per credit hour. Tuition, nonresident: full-time $25,486; part-time $1417 per credit hour. *Required fees:* $196. Tuition and fees vary according to course load, program and reciprocity agreements. *Financial support:* Application deadline: 6/1; applicants required to submit FAFSA. *Faculty research:* STEM teaching and learning; content literacy for English language learners; social justice in teacher education; adolescent literacy; mathematics teacher development. *Total annual research expenditures:* $1.7 million. *Unit head:* Dr. Ann E. Larson, Dean, College of Education and Human Development, 502-852-6411, Fax: 502-852-1464, E-mail: ann@louisville.edu. *Application contact:* Betty Hampton, Director of Graduate Student Services, 502-852-5597, Fax: 502-852-1465, E-mail: edadvise@louisville.edu. Website: http://louisville.edu/delphi

The University of Manchester, Alliance Manchester Business School, M15 6PB, United Kingdom. Offers accounting and finance (M Sc); business (M Ent); business analysis and strategic management (M Sc); business analytics: operational research and risk analysis (M Sc); business psychology (M Sc); corporate communications and reputation management (M Sc); finance (M Sc); finance and business economics (M Sc); human resource management and industrial relations (M Sc); innovation management and entrepreneurship (M Sc); international business and management (M Sc); international human resource management and comparative industrial relations (M Sc); management (M Sc); marketing (M Sc); operations, project and supply chain management (M Sc); organizational psychology (M Sc); quantitative finance (M Sc). *Entrance requirements:* For master's, UK 2:1 honours degree or overseas equivalent. Additional exam requirements/recommendations for international students: Required—TOEFL (minimum score 100 iBT), IELTS (minimum score 7), PTE. Electronic applications accepted. *Faculty research:* Accounting and finance, management sciences and marketing, people management and organization, innovation management and policy, decision sciences.

University of Mary, Gary Tharaldson School of Business, Bismarck, ND 58504-9652. Offers business administration (MBA); energy management (MBA, MS); executive (MBA, MS); health care (MBA, MS); human resource management (MBA); project management (MBA, MPM); virtuous leadership (MBA, MPM, MS). *Program availability:* Part-time, evening/weekend. *Entrance requirements:* For master's, minimum GPA of 2.5. Additional exam requirements/recommendations for international students: Required—TOEFL (minimum score 550 paper-based; 80 iBT). Electronic applications accepted.

University of Memphis, Graduate School, University College, Memphis, TN 38152. Offers human resources leadership (MPS); liberal studies (MALS, Graduate Certificate); strategic leadership (MPS, Graduate Certificate); training and development (MPS). *Program availability:* Part-time, evening/weekend. *Faculty:* 3 full-time (1 woman), 1 part-time/adjunct (0 women). *Students:* 27 full-time (16 women), 105 part-time (79 women); includes 86 minority (78 Black or African American, non-Hispanic/Latino; 1 Asian, non-Hispanic/Latino; 2 Hispanic/Latino; 1 Native Hawaiian or other Pacific Islander, non-Hispanic/Latino; 4 Two or more races, non-Hispanic/Latino), 4 international. Average age 38. 70 applicants, 76% accepted, 39 enrolled. *Degree requirements:* For master's, comprehensive exam, thesis (for some programs). *Entrance requirements:* For master's, GRE (for MPS), resume, letters of recommendation, personal essay, interview, minimum undergraduate GPA of 2.75 (for MALS); portfolio in lieu of GRE for MPS applicants with substantial professional work experience; for Graduate Certificate, essay, letter of recommendation. Additional exam requirements/recommendations for international students: Required—TOEFL (minimum score 550 paper-based; 79 iBT). *Application deadline:* For fall admission, 7/1 for domestic students, 5/1 for international students; for spring admission, 11/1 for domestic students, 9/15 for international students. Applications are processed on a rolling basis. Application fee: $35 ($60 for international students). Electronic applications accepted. *Expenses:* Contact institution. *Financial support:* In 2017–18, 123 students received support, including 4 teaching assistantships with tuition reimbursements available (averaging $13,000 per year); research assistantships with full tuition reimbursements available, Federal Work-Study, scholarships/grants, and unspecified assistantships also available. Financial award application deadline: 2/3; financial award applicants required to submit FAFSA. *Faculty research:* Media ethics, history of psychiatry, public relations. *Unit head:* Dr. Joanne Gikas, Interim Dean, 901-678-2716, E-mail: jgikas@memphis.edu. *Application contact:* Dr. Colin Chapell, Graduate Studies Coordinator, 901-678-3066, Fax: 901-678-2971, E-mail: cbchpell@memphis.edu. Website: http://www.memphis.edu/univcoll/

University of Minnesota, Twin Cities Campus, Carlson School of Management, Master of Arts Program in Human Resources and Industrial Relations, Minneapolis, MN 55455. Offers MA. *Accreditation:* AACSB. *Program availability:* Part-time, evening/weekend. *Faculty:* 16 full-time (9 women), 14 part-time/adjunct (4 women). *Students:* 122 full-time (85 women), 38 part-time (32 women); includes 20 minority (8 Black or African American, non-Hispanic/Latino; 1 American Indian or Alaska Native, non-Hispanic/Latino; 7 Asian, non-Hispanic/Latino; 4 Hispanic/Latino), 60 international. Average age 25. 204 applicants, 61% accepted, 69 enrolled. In 2017, 70 master's

awarded. *Degree requirements:* For master's, thesis or alternative, 48 course credits. *Entrance requirements:* For master's, GMAT or GRE General Test, undergraduate degree from accredited institution, course in microeconomics. Additional exam requirements/recommendations for international students: Required—TOEFL (minimum score 550 paper-based; 79 iBT), IELTS (minimum score 6.5). *Application deadline:* For fall admission, 2/1 for domestic and international students. Applications are processed on a rolling basis. Application fee: $75 ($95 for international students). Electronic applications accepted. *Expenses:* $22,336 resident or reciprocity full-time per year; $33,556 nonresident full-time per year; $1,003 resident part-time per credit; $1,706 nonresident part-time per credit. *Financial support:* In 2017–18, 61 students received support, including 61 fellowships (averaging $7,500 per year), 1 research assistantship with partial tuition reimbursement available (averaging $16,225 per year), 5 teaching assistantships with partial tuition reimbursements available (averaging $9,000 per year); scholarships/grants, health care benefits, tuition waivers (partial), and unspecified assistantships also available. Financial award application deadline: 2/1; financial award applicants required to submit FAFSA. *Faculty research:* Staffing, training, and development; compensation and benefits; organization theory; collective bargaining. *Total annual research expenditures:* $27,000. *Unit head:* Stacy Doepner-Hove, Director, 612-625-8732, Fax: 612-624-8360, E-mail: doepn002@umn.edu. *Application contact:* Amy Danzeisen, Assistant Director for Admissions and Recruiting, 612-624-5704, Fax: 612-624-8360, E-mail: hrirgrad@umn.edu. Website: https://carlsonschool.umn.edu/degrees/master-arts-human-resources-industrial-relations

University of Missouri–St. Louis, College of Business Administration, St. Louis, MO 63121. Offers accounting (M Acc); business administration (MBA, DBA, PhD, Certificate), including logistics and supply chain management (PhD); business intelligence (Certificate); cybersecurity (Certificate); digital and social media marketing (Certificate); human resources management (Certificate); information systems (MS); logistics and supply chain management (Certificate); marketing management (Certificate). *Program availability:* Part-time, evening/weekend. *Faculty:* 51 full-time (21 women), 25 part-time/adjunct (5 women). *Students:* 146 full-time (77 women), 326 part-time (143 women); includes 82 minority (32 Black or African American, non-Hispanic/Latino; 1 American Indian or Alaska Native, non-Hispanic/Latino; 34 Asian, non-Hispanic/Latino; 11 Hispanic/Latino; 4 Two or more races, non-Hispanic/Latino), 89 international. 276 applicants, 83% accepted, 142 enrolled. *Degree requirements:* For doctorate, thesis/dissertation. *Entrance requirements:* For master's, GMAT, 2 letters of recommendation; for doctorate, GMAT or GRE, 3 letters of recommendation. Additional exam requirements/recommendations for international students: Recommended—TOEFL (minimum score 550 paper-based; 79 iBT), IELTS (minimum score 6.5). *Application deadline:* For fall admission, 7/1 priority date for domestic and international students; for spring admission, 12/1 priority date for domestic and international students. Applications are processed on a rolling basis. Application fee: $50 ($40 for international students). Electronic applications accepted. *Expenses:* Tuition, state resident: part-time $476.50 per credit hour. Tuition, nonresident: part-time $1169.70 per credit hour. *Financial support:* Research assistantships with tuition reimbursements, teaching assistantships with tuition reimbursements, career-related internships or fieldwork, Federal Work-Study, and institutionally sponsored loans available. Support available to part-time students. Financial award application deadline: 4/1; financial award applicants required to submit FAFSA. *Faculty research:* Statistical decision aids, commercial banking, corporate finance, operations management, information systems. *Unit head:* Charles E. Hoffman, Dean, 314-516-6109, Fax: 314-516-6420. *Application contact:* 314-516-5458, Fax: 314-516-6996, E-mail: gradadm@umsl.edu. Website: http://www.umsl.edu/divisions/business/

University of Nebraska at Kearney, College of Business and Technology, Department of Business, Kearney, NE 68849-0001. Offers accounting (MBA); generalist (MBA); human resources (MBA); human services (MBA); marketing (MBA). *Accreditation:* AACSB. *Program availability:* Part-time, evening/weekend. *Degree requirements:* For master's, thesis optional, capstone course. *Entrance requirements:* For master's, GRE or GMAT (if no significant managerial experience), letters of recommendation, essay, resume. Additional exam requirements/recommendations for international students: Recommended—TOEFL (minimum score 550 paper-based; 79 iBT), IELTS (minimum score 6.5). Electronic applications accepted. *Faculty research:* Small business financial management, employment law, expert systems, international trade and marketing, environmental economics.

University of New Haven, Graduate School, College of Arts and Sciences, Program in Industrial and Organizational Psychology, West Haven, CT 06516. Offers conflict management (MA); industrial organizational psychology (MA); industrial-human resources psychology (MA); organizational development and consultation (MA); psychology of conflict management (Graduate Certificate). *Program availability:* Part-time, evening/weekend. *Students:* 80 full-time (53 women), 10 part-time (6 women); includes 17 minority (8 Black or African American, non-Hispanic/Latino; 4 Asian, non-Hispanic/Latino; 5 Hispanic/Latino), 3 international. Average age 26. 116 applicants, 89% accepted, 47 enrolled. In 2017, 45 master's awarded. *Degree requirements:* For master's, thesis or alternative, internship or practicum. *Entrance requirements:* Additional exam requirements/recommendations for international students: Required—TOEFL (minimum score 80 iBT), IELTS, PTE. *Application deadline:* Applications are processed on a rolling basis. Application fee: $50. Electronic applications accepted. Application fee is waived when completed online. *Expenses:* Contact institution. *Financial support:* Research assistantships with partial tuition reimbursements, teaching assistantships with partial tuition reimbursements, career-related internships or fieldwork, Federal Work-Study, scholarships/grants, and unspecified assistantships available. Support available to part-time students. Financial award applicants required to submit FAFSA. *Unit head:* Dr. Eric Marcus, Coordinator, 203-932-1242, E-mail: emarcus@newhaven.edu. *Application contact:* Michelle Mason, Director of Graduate Enrollment, 203-932-7067. Website: http://www.newhaven.edu/4730/

University of New Haven, Graduate School, College of Business, Program in Business Administration, West Haven, CT 06516. Offers accounting (MBA); business administration (MBA); business intelligence (MBA); business policy and strategic leadership (MBA); finance (MBA), including chartered financial analyst; global marketing (MBA); human resources management (MBA); sport management (MBA). *Accreditation:* AACSB. *Program availability:* Part-time, evening/weekend. *Students:* 123 full-time (56 women), 67 part-time (28 women); includes 53 minority (27 Black or African American, non-Hispanic/Latino; 11 Asian, non-Hispanic/Latino; 12 Hispanic/Latino; 3 Two or more races, non-Hispanic/Latino), 50 international. Average age 28. 148 applicants, 89% accepted, 67 enrolled. In 2017, 106 master's awarded. *Entrance requirements:* For master's, GMAT. Additional exam requirements/recommendations for international students: Required—TOEFL (minimum score 80 iBT), IELTS, PTE. *Application deadline:* Applications are processed on a rolling basis. Application fee: $50. Electronic applications accepted. Application fee is waived when completed online. *Expenses:* Tuition: Full-time $16,020; part-time $890 per credit hour. *Required fees:* $220; $90 per term. *Financial support:* Research assistantships with partial tuition reimbursements, teaching assistantships with partial tuition reimbursements, career-related internships or fieldwork, Federal Work-Study, scholarships/grants, and unspecified assistantships

available. Support available to part-time students. Financial award applicants required to submit FAFSA. *Unit head:* Darell Singleterry, Director, 203-932-1085, E-mail: dsingleterry@newhaven.edu. *Application contact:* Michelle Mason, Director of Graduate Enrollment, 203-932-7067, E-mail: mmason@newhaven.edu.
Website: http://www.newhaven.edu/business/graduate-programs/mba/index.php

See Display on page 154 and Close-Up on page 185.

University of New Haven, Graduate School, College of Business, Program in Health Care Administration, West Haven, CT 06516. Offers health care administration (MS, Graduate Certificate); health care marketing (MS); health policy and finance (MS); human resource management (MS); long-term care (MS); long-term health care (Graduate Certificate); managed care (MS); medical group management (MS). *Program availability:* Part-time, evening/weekend. *Students:* 59 full-time (42 women), 78 part-time (58 women); includes 38 minority (28 Black or African American, non-Hispanic/Latino; 6 Asian, non-Hispanic/Latino; 4 Hispanic/Latino), 27 international. Average age 33. 127 applicants, 91% accepted, 53 enrolled. In 2017, 59 master's, 3 other advanced degrees awarded. *Entrance requirements:* Additional exam requirements/recommendations for international students: Required—TOEFL (minimum score 80 iBT), IELTS, PTE. *Application deadline:* Applications are processed on a rolling basis. Application fee: $50. Electronic applications accepted. Application fee is waived when completed online. *Expenses:* Tuition: Full-time $16,020; part-time $890 per credit hour. *Required fees:* $220; $90 per term. *Financial support:* Research assistantships with partial tuition reimbursements, teaching assistantships with partial tuition reimbursements, Federal Work-Study, scholarships/grants, and unspecified assistantships available. Support available to part-time students. Financial award applicants required to submit FAFSA. *Unit head:* Dr. Summer McGee, Associate Professor, 203-479-4104, E-mail: smcgee@newhaven.edu. *Application contact:* Michelle Mason, Director of Graduate Enrollment, 203-932-7067, E-mail: mmason@newhaven.edu.
Website: http://www.newhaven.edu/6848/

See Display on page 154 and Close-Up on page 185.

University of New Mexico, Anderson School of Management, Department of Organizational Studies, Albuquerque, NM 87131. Offers organizational behavior and human resources management (MBA); strategic management and policy (MBA). *Program availability:* Part-time. *Faculty:* 17 full-time (12 women), 17 part-time/adjunct (6 women). In 2017, 20 master's awarded. *Entrance requirements:* For master's, GMAT or GRE, minimum GPA of 3.0 on last 60 hours of coursework; bachelor's degree from regionally-accredited college or university in U.S. or its equivalent in another country. Additional exam requirements/recommendations for international students: Required—TOEFL (minimum score 550 paper-based; 79 iBT), IELTS (minimum score 6.5). *Application deadline:* For fall admission, 4/1 priority date for domestic and international students; for spring admission, 10/1 priority date for domestic and international students. Applications are processed on a rolling basis. Application fee: $50. Electronic applications accepted. *Expenses:* Contact institution. *Financial support:* In 2017–18, 14 students received support, including 4 fellowships (averaging $18,200 per year), 11 research assistantships with partial tuition reimbursements available (averaging $15,488 per year); career-related internships or fieldwork, Federal Work-Study, scholarships/grants, and unspecified assistantships also available. Support available to part-time students. Financial award application deadline: 6/1; financial award applicants required to submit FAFSA. *Faculty research:* Business ethics and social corporate responsibility, diversity, human resources, organizational strategy, organizational behavior. *Unit head:* Dr. Michelle Arthur, Chair, 505-277-6471, E-mail: arthurm@unm.edu. *Application contact:* Lisa Beauchene, Student Recruitment Specialist, 505-277-6471, E-mail: andersonadvising@unm.edu.
Website: https://www.mgt.unm.edu/dos/default.asp?mm-faculty

University of Northern Colorado, Graduate School, Monfort College of Business, Greeley, CO 80639. Offers accounting (MA); general business management (MBA); healthcare administration (MBA); human resources management (MBA). *Accreditation:* AACSB.

University of North Florida, Coggin College of Business, MBA Program, Jacksonville, FL 32224. Offers accounting (MBA); construction management (MBA); e-commerce (MBA); economics (MBA); finance (MBA); human resource management (MBA); international business (MBA); logistics (MBA); management applications (MBA). *Accreditation:* AACSB. *Program availability:* Part-time, evening/weekend. *Entrance requirements:* For master's, GMAT or GRE, U.S. bachelor's degree from regionally-accredited university or equivalent foreign degree. Additional exam requirements/recommendations for international students: Required—TOEFL (minimum score 550 paper-based; 79 iBT). *Faculty research:* Performance measures, costing, and inventory issues in logistics and supply chain management; inter-organizational systems; international management and marketing practices; e-commerce; organizational learning and socialization processes.

University of North Texas, Robert B. Toulouse School of Graduate Studies, Denton, TX 76203-5459. Offers accounting (MS); applied anthropology (MA, MS); applied behavior analysis (Certificate); applied geography (MA); applied technology and performance improvement (M Ed, MS); art education (MA); art history (MA); art museum education (Certificate); arts leadership (Certificate); audiology (Au D); behavior analysis (MS); behavioral science (PhD); biochemistry and molecular biology (MS); biology (MA, MS); biomedical engineering (MS); business analysis (MS); chemistry (MS); clinical health psychology (PhD); communication studies (MA, MS); computer engineering (MS); computer science (MS); counseling (M Ed, MS), including clinical mental health counseling (MS), college and university counseling, elementary school counseling, secondary school counseling; creative writing (MA); criminal justice (MS); curriculum and instruction (M Ed); decision sciences (MBA); design (MA, MFA), including fashion design (MFA), innovation studies, interior design (MFA); early childhood studies (MS); economics (MS); educational leadership (M Ed, Ed D); educational psychology (MS, PhD), including family studies (MS), gifted and talented (MS), human development (MS), learning and cognition (MS), research, measurement and evaluation (MS); electrical engineering (MS); emergency management (MPA); engineering technology (MS); English (MA); English as a second language (MS); environmental science (MS); finance (MBA, MS); financial management (MPA); French (MA); health services management (MBA); higher education (M Ed, Ed D); history (MA, MS); hospitality management (MS); human resources management (MPA); information science (MS); information systems (PhD); information technologies (MBA); interdisciplinary studies (MA, MS); international studies (MA); international sustainable tourism (MS); jazz studies (MM); journalism (MA, MJ, Graduate Certificate), including interactive and virtual digital communication (Graduate Certificate), narrative journalism (Graduate Certificate), public relations (Graduate Certificate); kinesiology (MS); linguistics (MA); local government management (MPA); logistics (PhD); logistics and supply chain management (MBA); long-term care, senior housing, and aging services (MA); management (PhD); marketing (MBA); mathematics (MA, MS); mechanical and energy engineering (MS, PhD); music (MA), including ethnomusicology, music theory, musicology, performance; music composition (PhD); music education (MM Ed, PhD); nonprofit management (MPA); operations and supply chain management (MBA); performance (MM, DMA); philosophy (MA); political science (MA); professional and technical communication (MA); radio,

television and film (MA, MFA); rehabilitation counseling (Certificate); sociology (MA); Spanish (MA); special education (M Ed); speech-language pathology (MA); strategic management (MBA); studio art (MFA); teaching (M Ed); MBA/MS. *Program availability:* Part-time, evening/weekend, online learning. Terminal master's awarded for partial completion of doctoral program. *Degree requirements:* For master's, variable foreign language requirement, comprehensive exam (for some programs), thesis (for some programs); for doctorate, variable foreign language requirement, comprehensive exam (for some programs), thesis/dissertation; for other advanced degree, variable foreign language requirement, comprehensive exam (for some programs). *Entrance requirements:* For master's and doctorate, GRE, GMAT. Additional exam requirements/recommendations for international students: Required—TOEFL (minimum score 550 paper-based; 79 iBT). Electronic applications accepted.

University of North Texas at Dallas, Graduate School, Dallas, TX 75241. Offers accounting (MBA); counseling (M Ed, MS); criminal justice (MS); curriculum and instruction (M Ed); educational administration (M Ed); human resources and organizational behavior (MBA); public administration (MS); strategic management (MBA).

University of Oklahoma, College of Arts and Sciences, Department of Human Relations, Norman, OK 73019. Offers clinical mental health (MHR); helping skills in human relations (Graduate Certificate); human relations (MHR); human resource diversity and development (Graduate Certificate); human resources (MHR); licensed professional counselor (MHR). *Program availability:* Part-time, evening/weekend. *Faculty:* 20 full-time (12 women), 9 part-time/adjunct (4 women). *Students:* 297 full-time (221 women), 335 part-time (227 women); includes 316 minority (159 Black or African American, non-Hispanic/Latino; 25 American Indian or Alaska Native, non-Hispanic/Latino; 21 Asian, non-Hispanic/Latino; 68 Hispanic/Latino; 3 Native Hawaiian or other Pacific Islander, non-Hispanic/Latino; 40 Two or more races, non-Hispanic/Latino), 13 international. Average age 35. 152 applicants, 89% accepted, 97 enrolled. In 2017, 255 master's, 95 other advanced degrees awarded. *Degree requirements:* For master's, comprehensive exam or thesis. *Entrance requirements:* For degree, minimum GPA of 3.0. Additional exam requirements/recommendations for international students: Required—TOEFL (minimum score 79 iBT) or IELTS (minimum score 6.5). *Application deadline:* For fall admission, 8/21 for domestic and international students; for spring admission, 1/23 for domestic and international students; for summer admission, 6/5 for domestic and international students. Application fee: $50 ($100 for international students). Electronic applications accepted. *Expenses:* Tuition, state resident: full-time $5119; part-time $213.30 per credit hour. Tuition, nonresident: full-time $19,778; part-time $824.10 per credit hour. *Required fees:* $3458; $133.55 per credit hour. $126.50 per semester. *Financial support:* In 2017–18, 101 students received support, including 6 research assistantships with full tuition reimbursements available (averaging $11,124 per year), 4 teaching assistantships with full tuition reimbursements available (averaging $12,468 per year); scholarships/grants also available. Financial award application deadline: 6/1; financial award applicants required to submit FAFSA. *Faculty research:* At-risk youth, strength model, women's health, adolescent addiction and recovery, group psychotherapy. *Unit head:* Dr. Wesley Long, Chair of Department of Human Relations, 405-325-1756, Fax: 405-325-4402, E-mail: wlong@ou.edu. *Application contact:* Lawana Miller, Admissions Coordinator, 405-325-1756, Fax: 405-325-4402, E-mail: lmiller@ou.edu.
Website: http://www.ou.edu/cas/humanrelations

University of Oklahoma, College of Arts and Sciences, Department of Psychology, Program in Organizational Dynamics, Tulsa, OK 74135. Offers human resource management (Graduate Certificate); organizational dynamics (MA), including human resource management, project management; project management (Graduate Certificate). *Program availability:* Part-time, evening/weekend. *Students:* 12 full-time (9 women), 45 part-time (27 women); includes 15 minority (4 Black or African American, non-Hispanic/Latino; 5 American Indian or Alaska Native, non-Hispanic/Latino; 2 Asian, non-Hispanic/Latino; 3 Hispanic/Latino; 1 Two or more races, non-Hispanic/Latino), 3 international. Average age 33. 16 applicants, 88% accepted, 12 enrolled. In 2017, 11 master's, 8 other advanced degrees awarded. Terminal master's awarded for partial completion of doctoral program. *Degree requirements:* For master's, comprehensive exam (for some programs), thesis (for some programs), capstone project, comprehensive exam, or thesis; 36 hours of coursework; for Graduate Certificate, 12 hours of coursework from approved list. *Entrance requirements:* For master's, GRE (for students who do not have requisite work experience), current resume showing at least 2 years of relevant work experience; 2 letters of recommendation; statement of career goals; transcripts; for Graduate Certificate, resume showing work experience; 2 letters of recommendation; statement of career goals; transcripts. Additional exam requirements/recommendations for international students: Required—TOEFL (minimum score 79 iBT) or IELTS (minimum score 6.5). *Application deadline:* For fall admission, 5/1 for domestic and international students; for spring admission, 11/1 for domestic and international students; for summer admission, 3/15 for domestic and international students. Application fee: $50 ($100 for international students). Electronic applications accepted. *Expenses:* Tuition, state resident: full-time $5119; part-time $213.30 per credit hour. Tuition, nonresident: full-time $19,778; part-time $824.10 per credit hour. *Required fees:* $3458; $133.55 per credit hour. $126.50 per semester. *Financial support:* In 2017–18, 12 students received support. Fellowships with full tuition reimbursements available, research assistantships with full tuition reimbursements available, and teaching assistantships with full tuition reimbursements available available. Financial award application deadline: 6/1; financial award applicants required to submit FAFSA. *Faculty research:* Organizational behavior, personality, organizational climate and culture, leadership, ethics. *Unit head:* Dr. Eric Day, Chair, 405-325-4511, Fax: 405-325-4737, E-mail: eday@ou.edu. *Application contact:* Jennifer Kisamore, Associate Professor of Psychology/Graduate Liaison for Organizational Dynamics, 918-660-3603, Fax: 918-660-3383, E-mail: odyn@ou.edu.
Website: http://odyn.ou.edu

University of Phoenix–Bay Area Campus, School of Business, San Jose, CA 95134-1805. Offers accountancy (MS); accounting (MBA); business administration (MBA, DBA); energy management (MBA); global management (MBA); health care management (MBA); human resource management (MBA); human resources management (MM); management (MM); marketing (MBA); organizational leadership (DM); project management (MBA); public administration (MPA); technology management (MBA). *Accreditation:* ACBSP. *Program availability:* Evening/weekend, online learning. *Degree requirements:* For master's, thesis (for some programs). *Entrance requirements:* For master's, minimum undergraduate GPA of 3.0, 3 years of work experience. Additional exam requirements/recommendations for international students: Required—TOEFL (minimum score 550 paper-based; 79 iBT). Electronic applications accepted.

University of Phoenix–Central Valley Campus, School of Business, Fresno, CA 93720-1552. Offers accounting (MBA); business administration (MBA); global management (MBA); human resources management (MBA, MM); management (MM); marketing (MBA); public administration (MBA, MM). *Accreditation:* ACBSP.

University of Phoenix–Dallas Campus, School of Business, Dallas, TX 75251. Offers accounting (MBA); business administration (MBA); global management (MBA); human resources management (MBA, MM); management (MM); marketing (MBA); public

Human Resources Management

administration (MBA, MM). *Accreditation:* ACBSP. *Program availability:* Evening/weekend, online learning. *Degree requirements:* For master's, thesis (for some programs). *Entrance requirements:* For master's, 3 years of work experience, minimum undergraduate GPA of 3.0. Additional exam requirements/recommendations for international students: Required—TOEFL (minimum score 550 paper-based; 79 iBT). Electronic applications accepted.

University of Phoenix–Hawaii Campus, School of Business, Honolulu, HI 96813-3800. Offers accounting (MBA); business administration (MBA); global management (MBA); human resources management (MBA, MM); management (MM); marketing (MBA); public administration (MBA, MM). *Accreditation:* ACBSP. *Program availability:* Evening/weekend. *Degree requirements:* For master's, thesis (for some programs). *Entrance requirements:* For master's, minimum undergraduate GPA of 3.0, 3 years of work experience. Additional exam requirements/recommendations for international students: Required—TOEFL (minimum score 550 paper-based; 79 iBT). Electronic applications accepted.

University of Phoenix–Houston Campus, School of Business, Houston, TX 77079-2004. Offers accounting (MBA); business administration (MBA); global management (MBA); human resources management (MBA, MM); management (MM); marketing (MBA); public administration (MBA, MM). *Accreditation:* ACBSP. *Program availability:* Evening/weekend, online learning. *Degree requirements:* For master's, thesis (for some programs). *Entrance requirements:* For master's, 3 years of work experience, minimum undergraduate GPA of 3.0. Additional exam requirements/recommendations for international students: Required—TOEFL (minimum score 550 paper-based; 79 iBT). Electronic applications accepted.

University of Phoenix–Las Vegas Campus, School of Business, Las Vegas, NV 89135. Offers accounting (MBA); business administration (MBA); global management (MBA); human resources management (MBA, MM); management (MM); marketing (MBA); public administration (MM). *Accreditation:* ACBSP. *Program availability:* Evening/weekend, online learning. *Degree requirements:* For master's, thesis (for some programs). *Entrance requirements:* For master's, minimum undergraduate GPA of 3.0, 3 years of work experience. Additional exam requirements/recommendations for international students: Required—TOEFL (minimum score 550 paper-based; 79 iBT). Electronic applications accepted.

University of Phoenix–Online Campus, School of Business, Phoenix, AZ 85034-7209. Offers accountancy (MS); accounting (MBA, Certificate); business administration (MBA); energy management (MBA); global management (MBA); health care management (MBA); human resource management (MBA, Certificate); human resources management (MM); management (MM); marketing (MBA, Certificate); project management (MBA, Certificate); public administration (MBA, MM); technology management (MBA). *Program availability:* Evening/weekend, online learning. *Entrance requirements:* Additional exam requirements/recommendations for international students: Required—TOEFL, TOEIC (Test of English as an International Communication), Berlitz Online English Proficiency Exam, PTE, or IELTS. Electronic applications accepted. *Expenses:* Contact institution.

University of Phoenix–Phoenix Campus, School of Business, Tempe, AZ 85282-2371. Offers accounting (MBA, MS, Certificate); business administration (MBA); energy management (MBA); global management (MBA); health care management (MBA); human resource management (MBA, Certificate); management (MM); marketing (MBA); project management (MBA); technology management (MBA). *Program availability:* Evening/weekend, online learning. *Entrance requirements:* Additional exam requirements/recommendations for international students: Required—TOEFL, TOEIC (Test of English as an International Communication), Berlitz Online English Proficiency Exam, PTE, or IELTS. Electronic applications accepted. *Expenses:* Contact institution.

University of Phoenix–Sacramento Valley Campus, School of Business, Sacramento, CA 95833-4334. Offers accounting (MBA); business administration (MBA); global management (MBA); human resources management (MBA, MM); management (MM); marketing (MBA); public administration (MBA, MM). *Accreditation:* ACBSP. *Program availability:* Evening/weekend. *Degree requirements:* For master's, thesis (for some programs). *Entrance requirements:* For master's, minimum undergraduate GPA of 3.0, 3 years work experience. Additional exam requirements/recommendations for international students: Required—TOEFL (minimum score 550 paper-based; 79 iBT). Electronic applications accepted.

University of Phoenix–San Antonio Campus, School of Business, San Antonio, TX 78230. Offers accounting (MBA); business administration (MBA); e-business (MBA); global management (MBA); human resources management (MBA, MM); management (MM); marketing (MBA); public administration (MBA, MM). *Accreditation:* ACBSP.

University of Phoenix–San Diego Campus, School of Business, San Diego, CA 92123. Offers accounting (MBA); business administration (MBA); global management (MBA); human resources management (MBA, MM); management (MM); marketing (MBA); public administration (MBA). *Accreditation:* ACBSP. *Program availability:* Evening/weekend. *Degree requirements:* For master's, thesis (for some programs). *Entrance requirements:* For master's, 3 years of work experience, minimum undergraduate GPA of 3.0. Additional exam requirements/recommendations for international students: Required—TOEFL (minimum score 550 paper-based; 79 iBT). Electronic applications accepted.

University of Pittsburgh, Katz Graduate School of Business, Doctoral Program in Business Administration, Pittsburgh, PA 15260. Offers accounting (PhD); business analytics and operations (PhD); finance (PhD); information systems and technology management (PhD); marketing (PhD); organizational behavior and human resources (PhD); strategic management (PhD). *Accreditation:* AACSB. *Program availability:* Evening/weekend. *Faculty:* 91 full-time (30 women), 14 part-time/adjunct (4 women). *Students:* 51 full-time (26 women), 1 (woman) part-time; includes 5 minority (1 Black or African American, non-Hispanic/Latino; 3 Asian, non-Hispanic/Latino; 1 Two or more races, non-Hispanic/Latino), 30 international. Average age 31. 337 applicants, 3% accepted, 10 enrolled. In 2017, 7 doctorates awarded. *Degree requirements:* For doctorate, comprehensive exam, thesis/dissertation, student teaching. *Entrance requirements:* For doctorate, GMAT or GRE, 3 recommendations, statement of purpose, transcripts of all previous course work and degrees. Additional exam requirements/recommendations for international students: Required—TOEFL (minimum score 100 iBT) or IELTS (minimum score 7.0). *Application deadline:* For fall admission, 1/1 for domestic and international students. Applications are processed on a rolling basis. Application fee: $50. Electronic applications accepted. *Financial support:* In 2017–18, 43 students received support, including 33 research assistantships with full tuition reimbursements available (averaging $26,500 per year), 10 teaching assistantships with full tuition reimbursements available (averaging $28,220 per year); Federal Work-Study, scholarships/grants, health care benefits, and unspecified assistantships also available. Financial award application deadline: 1/1; financial award applicants required to submit FAFSA. *Faculty research:* Accounting systems/financial reporting, corporate finance, shopper marketing/consumer behavior, management information systems, organizational behavior and entrepreneurship. *Total annual research expenditures:* $475,077. *Unit head:* Dr. Arjang A. Assad, Dean, 412-648-1556, Fax: 412-648-1552, E-mail: aassad@katz.pitt.edu. *Application contact:* Dr. Dennis Galletta, Director, 412-

648-1699, Fax: 412-648-3633, E-mail: galletta@katz.pitt.edu. Website: http://www.katz.business.pitt.edu/degrees/phd/

See Display on page 158 and Close-Up on page 187.

University of Pittsburgh, Katz Graduate School of Business, Master of Business Administration Programs, Pittsburgh, PA 15260. Offers finance (MBA); information systems (MBA); marketing (MBA); operations (MBA); organizational behavior and human resources (MBA); strategy, environment and organizations (MBA); MBA/JD; MBA/MID; MBA/MIS; MBA/MSE. *Accreditation:* AACSB. *Program availability:* Part-time, evening/weekend, blended/hybrid learning. *Faculty:* 91 full-time (30 women), 14 part-time/adjunct (4 women). *Students:* 139 full-time (49 women), 294 part-time (94 women); includes 65 minority (27 Black or African American, non-Hispanic/Latino; 20 Asian, non-Hispanic/Latino; 11 Hispanic/Latino; 7 Two or more races, non-Hispanic/Latino), 54 international. Average age 29. 651 applicants, 44% accepted, 158 enrolled. In 2017, 217 master's awarded. *Degree requirements:* For master's, minimum GPA of 3.0. *Entrance requirements:* For master's, GMAT, GRE. Additional exam requirements/recommendations for international students: Required—TOEFL (minimum score 100 iBT) or IELTS (minimum score 7.0). *Application deadline:* For fall admission, 4/1 priority date for domestic students, 2/1 priority date for international students. Application fee: $50. Electronic applications accepted. *Financial support:* In 2017–18, 136 students received support. Scholarships/grants available. Financial award application deadline: 6/1; financial award applicants required to submit FAFSA. *Faculty research:* Accounting systems/financial reporting, corporate finance, shopper marketing/consumer behavior, management information systems, organizational behavior and entrepreneurship. *Total annual research expenditures:* $475,077. *Unit head:* Dr. Arjang A. Assad, Dean, 412-648-1556, Fax: 412-648-1552, E-mail: aassad@katz.pitt.edu. *Application contact:* Thomas Keller, Director of MBA Admissions, 412-648-1700, Fax: 412-648-1659, E-mail: mba@katz.pitt.edu.
Website: http://www.business.pitt.edu/katz/mba/

See Display on page 158 and Close-Up on page 187.

University of Puerto Rico–Mayagüez, Graduate Studies, College of Business Administration, Mayagüez, PR 00681-9000. Offers business administration (MBA); finance (MBA); human resources (MBA); industrial management (MBA). *Program availability:* Part-time, evening/weekend. *Degree requirements:* For master's, one foreign language, comprehensive exam, thesis (for some programs). *Entrance requirements:* For master's, GMAT or EXADEP, bachelor's degree with courses in calculus, microeconomics, accounting and statistics. Additional exam requirements/recommendations for international students: Required—TOEFL (minimum score 500 paper-based), GMAT or EXADEP. Electronic applications accepted. *Faculty research:* Organizational studies, management, accounting, entrepreneurship, leadership and motivation.

University of Puerto Rico–Río Piedras, College of Business Administration, San Juan, PR 00931-3300. Offers accounting (MBA); finance (MBA, PhD); general business (MBA); human resources management (MBA); international trade and business (MBA, PhD); marketing (MBA); operations management (MBA); quantitative methods (MBA). *Accreditation:* AACSB. *Program availability:* Part-time. *Degree requirements:* For master's, comprehensive exam, thesis or alternative, research project. *Entrance requirements:* For master's, GMAT or PAEG, minimum GPA of 3.0, letter of recommendation; for doctorate, GMAT, PAEG, minimum GPA of 3.0, master degree. *Faculty research:* Management.

University of Regina, Faculty of Graduate Studies and Research, Kenneth Levene Graduate School of Business, Program in Human Resources Management, Regina, SK S4S 0A2, Canada. Offers MHRM, Master's Certificate. *Program availability:* Part-time. *Faculty:* 43 full-time (15 women), 6 part-time/adjunct (0 women). *Students:* 71 full-time (41 women), 35 part-time (26 women). 185 applicants, 35% accepted. In 2017, 46 master's awarded. *Degree requirements:* For master's, project. *Entrance requirements:* For master's, two years of relevant work experience. Additional exam requirements/recommendations for international students: Required—TOEFL (minimum score 580 paper-based; 80 iBT), IELTS (minimum score 6.5), PTE (minimum score 59). *Application deadline:* Applications are processed on a rolling basis. Application fee: $100. Electronic applications accepted. *Expenses:* CAD$20,150 per year. *Financial support:* In 2017–18, fellowships (averaging $6,000 per year), teaching assistantships (averaging $2,562 per year) were awarded; research assistantships, career-related internships or fieldwork, and scholarships/grants also available. Financial award application deadline: 6/15. *Faculty research:* Human behavior in organizations, labor relations and collective bargaining, organization theory, staffing organizations, human resources systems analysis. *Unit head:* Dr. David Senkow, Dean, 306-585-4162, Fax: 306-585-4719, E-mail: david.senkow@uregina.ca. *Application contact:* Lynn Barber, Graduate Programs, 306-337-8463, Fax: 306-585-5361, E-mail: lynn.barber@uregina.ca.
Website: http://www.uregina.ca/business/levene/

University of Rhode Island, Graduate School, College of Business, Schmidt Labor Research Center, Kingston, RI 02881. Offers labor relations and human resources (MS, Graduate Certificate); MS/JD. *Program availability:* Part-time, evening/weekend. *Faculty:* 1 (woman) full-time, 2 part-time/adjunct (1 woman). *Students:* 6 full-time (3 women), 19 part-time (15 women); includes 8 minority (4 Black or African American, non-Hispanic/Latino; 1 American Indian or Alaska Native, non-Hispanic/Latino; 3 Hispanic/Latino), 1 international. 24 applicants, 96% accepted, 10 enrolled. In 2017, 3 master's, 20 other advanced degrees awarded. *Entrance requirements:* Additional exam requirements/recommendations for international students: Required—TOEFL. *Application deadline:* For fall admission, 7/15 for domestic students, 2/1 for international students; for spring admission, 11/15 for domestic students, 7/15 for international students; for summer admission, 4/15 for domestic students. Application fee: $65. Electronic applications accepted. *Expenses:* Tuition, state resident: full-time $12,706; part-time $786 per credit. Tuition, nonresident: full-time $25,216; part-time $1401 per credit. *Required fees:* $1598; $45 per credit. One-time fee: $30 part-time. *Financial support:* In 2017–18, 2 teaching assistantships with tuition reimbursements (averaging $17,724 per year) were awarded; institutionally sponsored loans also available. Financial award application deadline: 2/1; financial award applicants required to submit FAFSA. *Unit head:* Dr. Aimee Phelps, Acting Director, 401-874-4693, E-mail: aimee@uri.edu.
Website: http://www.uri.edu/research/lrc/

University of Saint Mary, Graduate Programs, Program in Business Administration, Leavenworth, KS 66048-5082. Offers enterprise risk management (MBA); finance (MBA); general management (MBA); health care management (MBA); human resource management (MBA); marketing and advertising management (MBA). *Program availability:* Part-time, evening/weekend, 100% online, blended/hybrid learning. *Degree requirements:* For master's, thesis. *Entrance requirements:* For master's, minimum undergraduate GPA of 2.75, official transcripts, two letters of recommendation. Electronic applications accepted. *Expenses:* Contact institution.

University of South Carolina, The Graduate School, Darla Moore School of Business, Human Resources Program, Columbia, SC 29208. Offers MHR, JD/MHR. *Program availability:* Part-time. *Degree requirements:* For master's, internship. *Entrance* *requirements:* For master's, GMAT or GRE, minimum GPA of 3.0. Additional exam requirements/recommendations for international students: Required—TOEFL (minimum score 100 iBT); Recommended—IELTS. Electronic applications accepted. *Expenses:* Contact institution. *Faculty research:* Management and compensation, performance appraisal, work values, grievance systems, union formation, group behavior.

University of South Dakota, Graduate School, College of Arts and Sciences, Program in Administrative Studies, Vermillion, SD 57069. Offers addiction studies (MSA); criminal justice studies (MSA); health services administration (MSA); human resources (MSA); interdisciplinary studies (MSA); long term care administration (MSA); organizational leadership (MSA). *Program availability:* Part-time, evening/weekend, 100% online. *Degree requirements:* For master's, thesis or alternative. *Entrance requirements:* For master's, 3 years of work or experience, minimum GPA of 2.7, resume. Additional exam requirements/recommendations for international students: Required—TOEFL (minimum score 550 paper-based; 79 iBT). *Application deadline:* Applications are processed on a rolling basis. Application fee: $35. Electronic applications accepted. *Financial support:* Teaching assistantships with partial tuition reimbursements available. Financial award applicants required to submit FAFSA. *Application contact:* Graduate School, 605-658-6140, Fax: 605-677-6118, E-mail: grad@usd.edu.
Website: http://www.usd.edu/onlinemsa

University of Southern Indiana, Graduate Studies, Romain College of Business, Program in Business Administration, Evansville, IN 47712-3590. Offers accounting (MBA); data analytics (MBA); engineering management (MBA); general business administration (MBA); healthcare administration (MBA); human resource management (MBA). *Accreditation:* AACSB. *Program availability:* Part-time, evening/weekend, 100% online, blended/hybrid learning. *Faculty:* 22 full-time (4 women), 2 part-time/adjunct (0 women). *Students:* 312 full-time (167 women), 148 part-time (56 women); includes 72 minority (43 Black or African American, non-Hispanic/Latino; 8 Asian, non-Hispanic/Latino; 13 Hispanic/Latino; 8 Two or more races, non-Hispanic/Latino), 10 international. Average age 33. In 2017, 34 master's awarded. *Entrance requirements:* For master's, GMAT or GRE, minimum GPA of 2.5, resume, 3 professional references. Additional exam requirements/recommendations for international students: Required—TOEFL (minimum score 550 paper-based; 79 iBT), IELTS (minimum score 6). *Application deadline:* For fall admission, 8/1 for domestic students, 3/1 priority date for international students. Applications are processed on a rolling basis. Application fee: $40. Electronic applications accepted. *Expenses:* Tuition, state resident: full-time $9394. Tuition, nonresident: full-time $17,917. *Required fees:* $510. *Financial support:* In 2017–18, 18 students received support. Federal Work-Study, scholarships/grants, tuition waivers (full and partial), and unspecified assistantships available. Financial award application deadline: 3/1; financial award applicants required to submit FAFSA. *Unit head:* Dr. Jack E. Smothers, Program Director, 812-461-5248, E-mail: jesmothers@usi.edu. *Application contact:* Michelle Simmons, MBA Program Assistant, 812-464-1926, Fax: 812-465-1044, E-mail: masimmons3@usi.edu.
Website: http://www.usi.edu/business/mba

University of South Florida, Muma College of Business, Department of Management, Tampa, FL 33620-9951. Offers management (MS), including human resources, management information systems. *Accreditation:* AACSB. *Program availability:* Part-time, online learning. *Faculty:* 3 full-time (2 women). *Students:* 15 full-time (2 women), 26 part-time (13 women); includes 5 minority (3 Black or African American, non-Hispanic/Latino; 2 Hispanic/Latino), 26 international. Average age 27. 62 applicants, 56% accepted, 18 enrolled. In 2017, 35 master's awarded. Terminal master's awarded for partial completion of doctoral program. *Degree requirements:* For master's, comprehensive exam, thesis (for some programs). *Entrance requirements:* For master's, GMAT, letters of recommendation, resume, statement of purpose, relevant work experience. Additional exam requirements/recommendations for international students: Required—TOEFL (minimum score 550 paper-based; 79 iBT) or IELTS (minimum score 6.5). *Application deadline:* For fall admission, 6/1 for domestic students, 2/1 for international students; for spring admission, 10/15 for domestic students, 7/1 for international students. Application fee: $30. Electronic applications accepted. *Financial support:* In 2017–18, 1 student received support, including 1 research assistantship with tuition reimbursement available (averaging $9,002 per year), 3 teaching assistantships with tuition reimbursements available (averaging $9,002 per year); tuition waivers also available. Financial award applicants required to submit FAFSA. *Faculty research:* Leadership and employment relations, time management, personal motivation, crew resource management in aviation, psychology of gambling, organizational culture, issues of fairness, employment law, marketing strategy/implementation, organizational diversity, ethics, environmentally-friendly business practices, green business, sustainable business plans, institutional theory, social movement theory, diffusion of innovations, stakeholder human resources management, social responsibility. *Unit head:* Dr. Sally Fuller, Interim Department Chair/Associate Professor, 813-974-1766, Fax: 813-905-9964, E-mail: sfuller@usf.edu. *Application contact:* Stacee Bender, 813-974-4516, Fax: 813-974-9964, E-mail: staceebender@usf.edu.
Website: http://www.usf.edu/business/graduate/masters/management/

The University of Texas at Arlington, Graduate School, College of Business, Department of Management, Arlington, TX 76019. Offers human resources (MSHRM). *Program availability:* Part-time, evening/weekend. *Degree requirements:* For master's, thesis optional. *Entrance requirements:* For master's, GMAT/GRE. Additional exam requirements/recommendations for international students: Required—TOEFL (minimum score 550 paper-based; 79 iBT). *Faculty research:* Compensations, training, diversity, strategic human resources.

University of the Sacred Heart, Graduate Programs, Department of Business Administration, Program in Human Resource Management, San Juan, PR 00914-0383. Offers MBA. *Program availability:* Part-time, evening/weekend. *Degree requirements:* For master's, thesis. *Entrance requirements:* For master's, EXADEP, minimum undergraduate GPA of 2.75, interview.

University of Toronto, School of Graduate Studies, Faculty of Arts and Science, Centre for Industrial Relations and Human Resources, Toronto, ON M5S 1A1, Canada. Offers MIRHR, PhD. *Program availability:* Part-time. *Degree requirements:* For doctorate, thesis/dissertation. *Entrance requirements:* For master's, GRE or GMAT (for applicants who completed degree outside of Canada), minimum B+ in final 2 years of bachelor's degree completion, 2 letters of reference, resume; for doctorate, GRE or GMAT, MIR or equivalent, minimum B+ average, 3 letters of reference, resume. Additional exam requirements/recommendations for international students: Required—TOEFL (minimum score 600 paper-based; 100 iBT), IELTS, TWE (minimum score 5), Michigan English Language Assessment Battery, or COPE. Electronic applications accepted. *Expenses:* Contact institution.

University of Wisconsin–Madison, Graduate School, Wisconsin School of Business, Doctoral Program in Management and Human Resources, Madison, WI 53706-1380. Offers PhD. *Degree requirements:* For doctorate, comprehensive exam, thesis/dissertation. *Entrance requirements:* For doctorate, GMAT or GRE. Additional exam requirements/recommendations for international students: Recommended—TOEFL (minimum score 623 paper-based; 106 iBT), IELTS (minimum score 7.5), TSE. Electronic applications accepted. *Expenses:* Contact institution. *Faculty research:* Employee compensation, performance for work groups, small business management,

venture financing, arts industry, entrepreneurship, development economics, corporate finance, work motivation, diversity/discrimination, organizational justice.

University of Wisconsin–Madison, Graduate School, Wisconsin School of Business, Wisconsin Full-Time MBA Program, Madison, WI 53706. Offers applied security analysis (MBA); arts administration (MBA); brand and product management (MBA); corporate finance and investment banking (MBA); marketing research (MBA); operations and technology management (MBA); real estate (MBA); risk management and insurance (MBA); strategic human resource management (MBA); supply chain management (MBA). *Faculty:* 130 full-time (35 women), 42 part-time/adjunct (13 women). *Students:* 203 full-time (72 women); includes 34 minority (8 Black or African American, non-Hispanic/Latino; 10 Asian, non-Hispanic/Latino; 12 Hispanic/Latino; 4 Two or more races, non-Hispanic/Latino), 41 international. Average age 28. 556 applicants, 30% accepted, 104 enrolled. In 2017, 97 master's awarded. *Entrance requirements:* For master's, GMAT or GRE, bachelor's or equivalent degree, 2 years of work experience, essay, letter of recommendation, resume. Additional exam requirements/recommendations for international students: Required—TOEFL (minimum score 100 iBT), IELTS (minimum score 7.5). *Application deadline:* For fall admission, 11/2 for domestic and international students; for winter admission, 1/11 for domestic and international students; for spring admission, 3/1 for domestic and international students; for summer admission, 4/12 for domestic and international students. Applications are processed on a rolling basis. Application fee: $75 ($81 for international students). Electronic applications accepted. *Expenses:* $9,356 per semester resident, $18,288 non-resident. *Financial support:* In 2017–18, 183 students received support, including 14 fellowships with full tuition reimbursements available (averaging $25,420 per year), 7 research assistantships with full tuition reimbursements available (averaging $13,375 per year), 53 teaching assistantships with full tuition reimbursements available (averaging $13,375 per year); scholarships/grants, health care benefits, tuition waivers (full), and unspecified assistantships also available. Financial award application deadline: 4/11. *Faculty research:* Forms of competition and outcomes in dual distribution systems; explaining the accuracy of revised forecasts; supply chain planning for random demand surges; advanced demand information in a multi-product system; the effects of presentation salience and measurement subjectivity on nonprofessional investors' fair value judgments. *Unit head:* Dr. Don Hausch, Associate Dean, Full-time MBA Program, 608-262-9731, E-mail: don.hausch@wisc.edu. *Application contact:* Betsy Kacizak, Director of Admissions and Recruiting, Full-time MBA Program, 608-262-4000, E-mail: betsy.kacizak@wisc.edu.
Website: https://wsb.wisc.edu/

University of Wisconsin–Milwaukee, Graduate School, College of Letters and Science, Interdepartmental Program in Human Resources and Labor Relations, Milwaukee, WI 53201-0413. Offers human resources and labor relations (MHRLR); international human resources and labor relations (Graduate Certificate); mediation and negotiation (Graduate Certificate). *Program availability:* Part-time. *Students:* 14 full-time (10 women), 18 part-time (13 women); includes 8 minority (6 Black or African American, non-Hispanic/Latino; 1 Asian, non-Hispanic/Latino; 1 Two or more races, non-Hispanic/Latino), 1 international. Average age 31. 17 applicants, 65% accepted, 10 enrolled. In 2017, 13 master's awarded. *Entrance requirements:* For master's, GMAT or GRE General Test. Additional exam requirements/recommendations for international students: Required—TOEFL (minimum score 80 iBT), IELTS (minimum score 6.5). Application fee: $56 ($96 for international students). Electronic applications accepted. *Financial support:* Career-related internships or fieldwork available. Support available to part-time students. Financial award application deadline: 4/15; financial award applicants required to submit FAFSA. *Unit head:* Susan M. Donohue-Davies, Assistant Director, 414-299-4009, Fax: 414-229-5915, E-mail: suedono@uwm.edu.
Website: http://uwm.edu/human-resources-labor-relations/

University of Wisconsin–Platteville, School of Graduate Studies, Distance Learning Center, Platteville, WI 53818-3099. Offers criminal justice (MS); engineering (MS); integrated supply chain management (MS); organizational change leadership (MS); project management (MS). *Program availability:* Part-time, evening/weekend. *Students:* 16 full-time (8 women), 640 part-time (268 women); includes 114 minority (34 Black or African American, non-Hispanic/Latino; 5 American Indian or Alaska Native, non-Hispanic/Latino; 35 Asian, non-Hispanic/Latino; 40 Hispanic/Latino). 205 applicants, 73% accepted, 106 enrolled. In 2017, 201 master's awarded. *Degree requirements:* For master's, thesis or alternative. *Entrance requirements:* Additional exam requirements/recommendations for international students: Required—TOEFL (minimum score 550 paper-based; 79 iBT), IELTS (minimum score 6.5). *Application deadline:* For fall admission, 7/1 priority date for domestic students; for spring admission, 11/1 priority date for domestic students. Applications are processed on a rolling basis. Application fee: $56. Electronic applications accepted. *Expenses:* Contact institution. *Financial support:* Scholarships/grants available. Support available to part-time students. *Unit head:* Dawn Drake, Executive Director, 800-362-5460, Fax: 608-342-1071, E-mail: disted@uwplatt.edu.
Website: http://www.uwplatt.edu/disted/

Upper Iowa University, Online Master's Programs, Fayette, IA 52142-1857. Offers accounting (MBA); corporate financial management (MBA); emergency management and homeland security (MPA); general management (MPA); general studies (MPA); government administration (MPA); health and human services (MPA); human resources management (MBA); nonprofit organizational management (MPA); organizational development (MPA); public management (MPA); sport administration (MSA). MBA also available at Madison, WI campus. *Program availability:* Part-time, online learning. *Degree requirements:* For master's, research project. *Entrance requirements:* For master's, GMAT, GRE, or minimum GPA 2.7 during last 60 hours. Additional exam requirements/recommendations for international students: Required—TOEFL (minimum score 570 paper-based). Electronic applications accepted. *Faculty research:* Total quality management, teams, organization culture and climate, management.

Utah State University, School of Graduate Studies, Jon M. Huntsman School of Business, Program in Human Resources, Logan, UT 84322. Offers MHR. *Program availability:* Part-time, evening/weekend, online learning. *Entrance requirements:* For master's, GMAT or GRE, minimum GPA of 3.0. Additional exam requirements/recommendations for international students: Required—TOEFL. Electronic applications accepted. *Expenses:* Contact institution. *Faculty research:* International human resources, aging workforce.

Virginia Commonwealth University, Graduate School, L. Douglas Wilder School of Government and Public Affairs, Program in Public Administration, Richmond, VA 23284-9005. Offers financial management (MPA); human resource management (MPA); state and local government management (MPA). *Accreditation:* NASPAA. *Program availability:* Part-time. *Entrance requirements:* For master's, GRE, GMAT or LSAT. Additional exam requirements/recommendations for international students: Required—TOEFL (minimum score 600 paper-based; 100 iBT); Recommended—IELTS (minimum score 6.5). Electronic applications accepted. *Faculty research:* Environmental policy, executive leadership, human resource management, local government management, nonprofit management, public financial management, public policy analysis and evaluation.

Human Resources Management

Virginia International University, School of Business, Fairfax, VA 22030. Offers accounting (MBA, MS); entrepreneurship (MBA); executive management (Graduate Certificate); global logistics (MBA); health care management (MBA); hospitality and tourism management (MBA); human resources management (MBA); international business management (MBA); international finance (MBA); marketing management (MBA); mass media and public relations (MBA); project management (MBA, MS). *Program availability:* Part-time, online learning. *Entrance requirements:* For master's and Graduate Certificate, bachelor's degree. Additional exam requirements/recommendations for international students: Required—TOEFL (minimum score 550 paper-based; 80 iBT), IELTS (minimum score 6). Electronic applications accepted.

Walden University, Graduate Programs, School of Management, Minneapolis, MN 55401. Offers accounting (MBA, MS, DBA), including accounting for the professional (MS), accounting with CPA emphasis (MS), self-designed (MS); advanced project management (Graduate Certificate); applied project management (Graduate Certificate); auditing (Graduate Certificate); bridge to business administration (Post-Doctoral Certificate); bridge to management (Post-Doctoral Certificate); business management (Graduate Certificate); communication (MBA); corporate finance (MBA); digital marketing (Graduate Certificate); entrepreneurship (DBA); entrepreneurship and small business (MBA); finance (MS, DBA), including finance for the professional (MS), finance with CFA/investment (MS), finance with CPA emphasis (MS); global supply chain management (DBA); healthcare management (MBA, DBA); human resource management (MBA, MS, Graduate Certificate), including functional human resource management (MS), general program (MS), integrating functional and strategic human resource management (MS), organizational strategy (MS); human resources management (DBA); information systems management (DBA); international business (MBA, DBA); leadership (MBA, MS, DBA, Graduate Certificate), including general program (MS), human resource development (MS), leader development (MS), self-designed (MS); management (MS, PhD), including communications (MS), finance (PhD), general program (MS), healthcare management (MS), human resource management (MS), human resources management (PhD), information systems management (PhD), international business (MS), leadership (MS), leadership and organizational change (PhD), marketing (MS), project management (MS), strategy and operations (MS); managerial accounting (Graduate Certificate); marketing (MBA, MS, DBA); project management (MBA, MS, DBA); self-designed (MBA, DBA); social impact management (DBA); technology entrepreneurship (DBA). *Accreditation:* ACBSP. *Program availability:* Part-time, evening/weekend, online only, 100% online. *Degree requirements:* For master's, thesis (for some programs), residency (for EMBA); for doctorate, thesis/dissertation (for some programs), residency. *Entrance requirements:* For master's, bachelor's degree or higher; minimum GPA of 2.5; official transcripts; goal statement (for some programs); access to computer and Internet; for doctorate, master's degree or higher; three years of related professional or academic experience (preferred); minimum GPA of 3.0; goal statement and current resume (for select programs); official transcripts; access to computer and Internet; for other advanced degree, relevant work experience; access to computer and Internet. Additional exam requirements/recommendations for international students: Required—TOEFL (minimum score 550 paper-based, 79 iBT), IELTS (minimum score 6.5), Michigan English Language Assessment Battery (minimum score 82), or PTE (minimum score 53). Electronic applications accepted.

Walsh College of Accountancy and Business Administration, Graduate Programs, Program in Management, Troy, MI 48083. Offers human resources management (MS); international business (MS); strategic management (MS). *Program availability:* Part-time, evening/weekend, 100% online, blended/hybrid learning. *Faculty:* 10 full-time (6 women), 13 part-time/adjunct (6 women). *Students:* 49 (37 women); includes 18 minority (14 Black or African American, non-Hispanic/Latino; 2 Asian, non-Hispanic/Latino; 2 Hispanic/Latino), 2 international. Average age 33. 17 applicants, 76% accepted, 6 enrolled. In 2017, 15 master's awarded. *Entrance requirements:* For master's, minimum overall cumulative GPA of 2.75 from all colleges previously attended. Additional exam requirements/recommendations for international students: Required—TOEFL (minimum score 550 paper-based, 79 iBT), IELTS (6.5), Michigan English Language Assessment Battery, or MTELP (80). *Application deadline:* Applications are processed on a rolling basis. Application fee: $35. Electronic applications accepted. *Expenses:* $770 per semester credit hour plus $125 registration fee per semester. *Financial support:* In 2017–18, 1 student received support. Career-related internships or fieldwork and scholarships/grants available. Financial award application deadline: 6/30; financial award applicants required to submit FAFSA. *Faculty research:* Strategy practice and process, management learning and decision-making, human capital development, global leadership and citizenship, use of systems and complexity theory and management practice. *Unit head:* Dr. Ann Saurbier, Chair, Management, 248-823-1635, Fax: 248-689-0920, E-mail: asaurbie@walshcollege.edu. *Application contact:* Heather Rigby, Director, Admissions and Academic Advising, 248-823-1610, Fax: 248-823-1611, E-mail: hrigby@walshcollege.edu.

Warner University, School of Business, Lake Wales, FL 33859. Offers accounting (MBA); business administration (MBA); human resource management (MBA); international business (MBA); management (MSMC). *Program availability:* Part-time, evening/weekend, online learning. *Degree requirements:* For master's, comprehensive exam, thesis. *Entrance requirements:* For master's, minimum GPA of 3.0, 2 letters of recommendation. Additional exam requirements/recommendations for international students: Required—TOEFL. Electronic applications accepted.

Wayland Baptist University, Graduate Programs, Program in Education, Plainview, TX 79072-6998. Offers education administration (M Ed); education diagnostics (M Ed); education literacy (M Ed); elementary certification (M Ed); English (M Ed); English as a second language (M Ed); higher education administration (M Ed); human resources (M Ed); instructional leadership (M Ed); instructional technology (M Ed); leadership training and development (M Ed); science education (M Ed); secondary certification (M Ed); social studies (M Ed); special education (M Ed); sports administration and management (M Ed). *Program availability:* Part-time, evening/weekend, 100% online. *Faculty:* 33 full-time (17 women), 28 part-time/adjunct (17 women). *Students:* 16 full-time (13 women), 221 part-time (143 women); includes 97 minority (26 Black or African American, non-Hispanic/Latino; 1 American Indian or Alaska Native, non-Hispanic/Latino; 5 Asian, non-Hispanic/Latino; 54 Hispanic/Latino; 11 Two or more races, non-Hispanic/Latino), 1 international. Average age 39. 32 applicants, 97% accepted, 23 enrolled. In 2017, 78 master's awarded. *Degree requirements:* For master's, comprehensive exam, capstone course. *Entrance requirements:* For master's, GRE, GMAT or MAT. Additional exam requirements/recommendations for international students: Required—TOEFL (minimum score 500 paper-based; 61 iBT). *Application deadline:* Applications are processed on a rolling basis. Application fee: $50. Electronic applications accepted. *Expenses:* Tuition: Full-time $11,250; part-time $625 per credit hour. *Required fees:* $1200. *Financial support:* Federal Work-Study, institutionally sponsored loans, and scholarships/grants available. Support available to part-time students. Financial award application deadline: 5/1; financial award applicants required to submit FAFSA. *Unit head:* Dr. Gene Whitfill, Dean, 806-291-1047, Fax: 806-291-1951, E-mail: whitfillg@wbu.edu. *Application contact:* Amanda Stanton, Coordinator of Graduate Studies, 806-291-3423, Fax: 806-291-1950, E-mail: stanton@wbu.edu.

Wayland Baptist University, Graduate Programs, Programs in Business Administration/Management, Plainview, TX 79072-6998. Offers accounting (MBA); general business (MBA); health care administration (MAM, MBA); human resource management (MAM, MBA); international management (MBA); management (MBA, D Mgt); management information systems (MBA); organization management (MAM); project management (MBA). *Program availability:* Part-time, evening/weekend, online learning. *Faculty:* 30 full-time (5 women), 38 part-time/adjunct (9 women). *Students:* 42 full-time (20 women), 538 part-time (253 women); includes 311 minority (98 Black or African American, non-Hispanic/Latino; 4 American Indian or Alaska Native, non-Hispanic/Latino; 16 Asian, non-Hispanic/Latino; 153 Hispanic/Latino; 11 Native Hawaiian or other Pacific Islander, non-Hispanic/Latino; 29 Two or more races, non-Hispanic/Latino), 6 international. Average age 40. 100 applicants, 96% accepted, 60 enrolled. In 2017, 216 master's awarded. *Degree requirements:* For master's, capstone course. *Entrance requirements:* For master's, GMAT, GRE or MAT. Additional exam requirements/recommendations for international students: Required—TOEFL (minimum score 500 paper-based; 61 iBT). *Application deadline:* Applications are processed on a rolling basis. Application fee: $50. Electronic applications accepted. *Expenses:* Tuition: Full-time $11,250; part-time $625 per credit hour. *Required fees:* $1200. *Financial support:* Federal Work-Study, institutionally sponsored loans, and scholarships/grants available. Support available to part-time students. Financial award application deadline: 5/1; financial award applicants required to submit FAFSA. *Unit head:* Dr. Kelly Warren, Chairman, 806-291-1020, Fax: 806-291-1957, E-mail: warrenk@wbu.edu. *Application contact:* Amanda Stanton, Graduate Studies, 806-291-3423, Fax: 806-291-1950, E-mail: stanton@wbu.edu.

Waynesburg University, Graduate and Professional Studies, Canonsburg, PA 15370. Offers business (MBA), including energy management, finance, health systems, human resources, leadership, market development; counseling (MA), including addictions counseling, clinical mental health; counselor education and supervision (PhD); criminal investigation (MA); education (M Ed), including autism, curriculum and instruction, educational leadership, online teaching; nursing (MSN), including administration, education, informatics; nursing practice (DNP); special education (M Ed); technology (M Ed); MSN/MBA. *Accreditation:* AACN. *Program availability:* Part-time, evening/weekend. *Degree requirements:* For doctorate, thesis/dissertation. *Entrance requirements:* Additional exam requirements/recommendations for international students: Required—TOEFL. Electronic applications accepted.

Wayne State University, College of Liberal Arts and Sciences, Department of Political Science, Detroit, MI 48202. Offers political science (MA, PhD); public administration (MPA), including economic development policy and management, health and human services policy and management, human and fiscal resource management, nonprofit policy and management, organizational behavior and management, urban and metropolitan policy and management; JD/MA. *Accreditation:* NASPAA. *Faculty:* 18. *Students:* 48 full-time (20 women), 68 part-time (36 women); includes 37 minority (26 Black or African American, non-Hispanic/Latino; 3 Asian, non-Hispanic/Latino; 2 Hispanic/Latino; 6 Two or more races, non-Hispanic/Latino), 6 international. Average age 32. 105 applicants, 39% accepted, 20 enrolled. In 2017, 17 master's, 3 doctorates awarded. *Degree requirements:* For master's, comprehensive exam (for some programs), thesis (for some programs); for doctorate, thesis/dissertation. *Entrance requirements:* For master's, GRE General Test, substantial undergraduate preparation in the social sciences, minimum upper-division undergraduate GPA of 3.0, two letters of recommendation, personal statement; for doctorate, GRE General Test, 3 letters of recommendation, personal statement; interview. Additional exam requirements/recommendations for international students: Required—TOEFL (minimum score 550 paper-based; 79 iBT), TWE (minimum score 5.5), Michigan English Language Assessment Battery (minimum score 85); Recommended—IELTS (minimum score 6.5). *Application deadline:* For fall admission, 5/15 for domestic students, 5/1 priority date for international students; for winter admission, 10/15 for domestic students, 9/1 priority date for international students. Applications are processed on a rolling basis. Application fee: $50. Electronic applications accepted. *Expenses:* Contact institution. *Financial support:* In 2017–18, 44 students received support, including 6 fellowships with tuition reimbursements available (averaging $11,698 per year), 12 teaching assistantships with tuition reimbursements available (averaging $18,534 per year); research assistantships with tuition reimbursements available, scholarships/grants, health care benefits, and unspecified assistantships also available. Financial award applicants required to submit FAFSA. *Faculty research:* American government and politics, comparative politics, political methodology, political theory, public administration, public law, public policy, world politics/international relations, formal theory/modeling, gender and politics, international law, peace research, political economy, political psychology, politics of developing countries, race, religion, and ethnicity, urban politics. *Unit head:* Dr. Daniel Geller, Professor and Chair, 313-577-6328, E-mail: dgeller@wayne.edu. *Application contact:* Dr. Sharon Lean, Graduate Director, 313-577-2630, E-mail: gradpolisci@wayne.edu.
Website: http://clas.wayne.edu/politicalscience/

Wayne State University, College of Liberal Arts and Sciences, Program in Employment and Labor Relations, Detroit, MI 48202. Offers MA. *Program availability:* Part-time, evening/weekend. *Students:* 8 full-time (7 women), 17 part-time (12 women); includes 14 minority (11 Black or African American, non-Hispanic/Latino; 3 Hispanic/Latino), 3 international. Average age 35. 8 applicants, 63% accepted, 1 enrolled. In 2017, 9 master's awarded. *Entrance requirements:* For master's, GRE or GMAT, personal statement, three letters of recommendation written by former college or university professors and/or current employers, baccalaureate degree from accredited institution, writing sample. Additional exam requirements/recommendations for international students: Required—TOEFL (minimum score 550 paper-based; 79 iBT), IELTS (minimum score 6.5), Michigan English Language Assessment Battery (minimum score 85). *Application deadline:* For fall admission, 6/1 priority date for domestic students, 5/1 priority date for international students; for winter admission, 10/1 priority date for domestic students, 9/1 priority date for international students; for spring admission, 2/1 priority date for domestic students, 1/1 priority date for international students. Application fee: $50. Electronic applications accepted. *Expenses:* Tuition, state resident: full-time $10,224; part-time $638.98 per credit hour. Tuition, nonresident: full-time $22,145; part-time $1384.04 per credit hour. Tuition and fees vary according to course load and program. *Financial support:* In 2017–18, 15 students received support. Scholarships/grants available. Financial award applicants required to submit FAFSA. *Unit head:* Dr. Marick Masters, Director, 313-577-5358, E-mail: marickm@wayne.edu. *Application contact:* Linda Johnson, Academic Services Officer, 313-577-0175, E-mail: ab1232@wayne.edu.
Website: http://clas.wayne.edu/labor/maelr

Webster University, George Herbert Walker School of Business and Technology, Department of Business, St. Louis, MO 63119-3194. Offers business and organizational security management (MBA); decision support systems (MBA); environmental management (MBA); finance (MBA, MS); forensic accounting (MS); gerontology (MBA); human resources development (MBA); human resources management (MBA); information technology management (MBA); international business (MA, MBA); international relations (MBA); management and leadership (MBA); marketing (MBA); media communications (MBA); procurement and acquisitions management (MBA); Web services (MBA). *Accreditation:* ACBSP. *Program availability:* Part-time, evening/weekend, online learning. *Degree requirements:* For master's, comprehensive exam (for some programs), thesis (for some programs). *Entrance requirements:* Additional exam requirements/recommendations for international students: Required—TOEFL.

Webster University, George Herbert Walker School of Business and Technology, Department of Management, St. Louis, MO 63119-3194. Offers business and organizational security management (MA); digital marketing management (Graduate Certificate); government contracting (Graduate Certificate); health administration (MHA); health care management (MA); health services management (MA); human resources development (MA); human resources management (MA); information technology management (MA, MS); management (D Mgt); management and leadership (MA); marketing (MA); nonprofit leadership (MA); nonprofit revenue development (Graduate Certificate); organizational development (Graduate Certificate); procurement and acquisitions management (MA); public administration (MPA); space systems operations management (MS). *Program availability:* Part-time, evening/weekend, online learning. *Degree requirements:* For master's, thesis (for some programs); for doctorate, thesis/dissertation, written exam. *Entrance requirements:* For doctorate, GMAT, 3 years of work experience, MBA. Additional exam requirements/recommendations for international students: Required—TOEFL.

West Chester University of Pennsylvania, College of Business and Public Management, Department of Management, West Chester, PA 19383. Offers human resource management (MS, Certificate). *Program availability:* Part-time, evening/weekend, online only, 100% online. *Students:* 9 full-time (5 women), 21 part-time (16 women); includes 10 minority (4 Black or African American, non-Hispanic/Latino; 4 Asian, non-Hispanic/Latino; 2 Hispanic/Latino). Average age 32. 24 applicants, 92% accepted, 17 enrolled. *Degree requirements:* For master's, GMAT or GRE, bachelor's degree or above in any major/field from accredited institution; at least two years of professional experience in human resources (preferred). Additional exam requirements/recommendations for international students: Required—TOEFL or IELTS. *Application deadline:* For fall admission, 5/15 for international students; for spring admission, 10/15 for international students. Applications are processed on a rolling basis. Application fee: $50. Electronic applications accepted. *Expenses:* Tuition, state resident: full-time $9000; part-time $500 per credit. Tuition, nonresident: full-time $13,500; part-time $750 per credit. *Required fees:* $2959; $149.79 per credit. *Financial support:* Scholarships/grants and unspecified assistantships available. Financial award application deadline: 2/15; financial award applicants required to submit FAFSA. *Faculty research:* Organizational behavior, employment law, labor relations, compensation. *Unit head:* Dr. Evan Leach, Chair, 610-436-2305, E-mail: eleach@wcupa.edu. *Application contact:* Dr. Susan Fiorentino, Graduate Coordinator, 610-436-2019, E-mail: sfiorentino@wcupa.edu.
Website: http://www.wcupa.edu/business-publicManagement/management/default.aspx

Wilfrid Laurier University, Faculty of Graduate and Postdoctoral Studies, School of Business and Economics, Department of Business, Waterloo, ON N2L 3C5, Canada. Offers accounting (PhD); finance (M Fin); financial economics (PhD); marketing (PhD); operations and supply chain management (PhD); organizational behavior and human resource management (M Sc); organizational behaviour and human resource management (PhD); supply chain management (M Sc); technology management (EMTM). *Accreditation:* AACSB. *Program availability:* Part-time, evening/weekend. *Degree requirements:* For master's, thesis optional; for doctorate, comprehensive exam, thesis/dissertation. *Entrance requirements:* For master's, GMAT, 4-year honors degree with minimum B+ average; for doctorate, GMAT, master's degree, minimum B+ average. Additional exam requirements/recommendations for international students: Required—TOEFL (minimum score 89 iBT). Electronic applications accepted. *Faculty*

research: Financial economics, management and organizational behavior, operations and supply chain management.

Wilkes University, College of Graduate and Professional Studies, Jay S. Sidhu School of Business and Leadership, Wilkes-Barre, PA 18766-0002. Offers accounting (MBA); entrepreneurship (MBA); finance (MBA); health care administration (MBA); human resource management (MBA); international business (MBA); operations management (MBA); organizational leadership and development (MBA). *Accreditation:* ACBSP. *Program availability:* Part-time, evening/weekend. *Students:* 37 full-time (18 women), 87 part-time (45 women); includes 17 minority (4 Black or African American, non-Hispanic/Latino; 5 Asian, non-Hispanic/Latino; 6 Hispanic/Latino; 2 Two or more races, non-Hispanic/Latino), 14 international. Average age 30. In 2017, 77 master's awarded. *Entrance requirements:* For master's, GMAT. Additional exam requirements/recommendations for international students: Required—TOEFL (minimum score 550 paper-based; 79 iBT). *Application deadline:* Applications are processed on a rolling basis. Application fee: $45 ($65 for international students). Electronic applications accepted. *Expenses:* Contact institution. *Financial support:* Unspecified assistantships available. Financial award application required to submit FAFSA. *Unit head:* Dr. Abel Adekola, Dean, 570-408-4701, Fax: 570-408-7846, E-mail: abel.adekola@wilkes.edu. *Application contact:* Kristin Donati, Associate Director of Graduate Admissions, 570-408-3338, Fax: 570-408-7846, E-mail: kristin.donati@wilkes.edu.
Website: http://www.wilkes.edu/academics/colleges/sidhu-school-of-business-leadership/index.aspx

Wilmington University, College of Business, New Castle, DE 19720-6491. Offers accounting (MBA, MS); business administration (MBA, DBA); environmental stewardship (MBA); finance (MBA); health care administration (MBA, MSM); homeland security (MBA, MSM); human resource management (MSM); management information systems (MBA, MSN); marketing (MSM); marketing management (MBA); military leadership (MSM); organizational leadership (MBA, MSM); public administration (MSM). *Program availability:* Part-time, evening/weekend. *Faculty:* 16 full-time (8 women), 106 part-time/adjunct (49 women). *Students:* 525 full-time (294 women), 1,212 part-time (780 women); includes 557 minority (412 Black or African American, non-Hispanic/Latino; 14 American Indian or Alaska Native, non-Hispanic/Latino; 55 Asian, non-Hispanic/Latino; 25 Hispanic/Latino; 3 Native Hawaiian or other Pacific Islander, non-Hispanic/Latino; 48 Two or more races, non-Hispanic/Latino), 157 international. Average age 35. 1,484 applicants, 70% accepted, 685 enrolled. In 2017, 543 master's, 16 doctorates awarded. *Entrance requirements:* Additional exam requirements/recommendations for international students: Required—TOEFL (minimum score 500 paper-based). *Application deadline:* Applications are processed on a rolling basis. Application fee: $35. Electronic applications accepted. *Expenses: Tuition:* Part-time $466 per credit. *Required fees:* $25 per semester. Tuition and fees vary according to degree level and campus/location. *Financial support:* Applicants required to submit FAFSA. *Unit head:* Dr. Kathy S. Kennedy Ratajack, Dean, 302-356-2481. *Application contact:* Laura Morris, Director of Admissions, 877-967-5456, E-mail: infocenter@wilmu.edu.
Website: http://www.wilmu.edu/business/

York University, Faculty of Graduate Studies, Faculty of Liberal Arts and Professional Studies, Program in Human Resources Management, Toronto, ON M3J 1P3, Canada. Offers MHRM, PhD. *Program availability:* Part-time. *Degree requirements:* For master's, thesis or alternative. *Entrance requirements:* Additional exam requirements/recommendations for international students: Required—TOEFL (minimum score 600 paper-based). Electronic applications accepted.

Section 9
Industrial and Manufacturing Management

This section contains a directory of institutions offering graduate work in industrial and manufacturing management. Additional information about programs listed in the directory but not augmented by an in-depth entry may be obtained by writing directly to the dean of a graduate school or chair of a department at the address given in the directory.

For programs offering related work, see also in this book *Business Administration and Management* and *Human Resources*. In another guide in this series:

Graduate Programs in the Humanities, Arts & Social Sciences

See *Public, Regional, and Industrial Affairs* (*Industrial* and *Labor Relations*)

CONTENTS

Program Directory

Featured School: Display and Close-Up

See:

Industrial and Manufacturing Management

American InterContinental University Online, Program in Business Administration, Schaumburg, IL 60173. Offers accounting and finance (MBA); finance (MBA); healthcare management (MBA); human resource management (MBA); international business (MBA); management (MBA); marketing (MBA); operations management (MBA); organizational psychology and development (MBA); project management (MBA). *Accreditation:* ACBSP. *Program availability:* Evening/weekend, online learning. *Entrance requirements:* Additional exam requirements/recommendations for international students: Required—TOEFL (minimum score 550 paper-based). Electronic applications accepted.

Baruch College of the City University of New York, Zicklin School of Business, Department of Management, New York, NY 10010-5585. Offers entrepreneurship (MBA); management (PhD); operations management (MBA); organizational behavior/human resources management (MBA); sustainable business (MBA). PhD offered jointly with Graduate School and University Center of the City University of New York. *Program availability:* Part-time, evening/weekend. *Degree requirements:* For doctorate, comprehensive exam, thesis/dissertation. *Entrance requirements:* For master's, GMAT, 2 letters of recommendation, resume, 2 years of work experience; for doctorate, GMAT. Additional exam requirements/recommendations for international students: Required—TOEFL (minimum score 590 paper-based), TWE.

Bluffton University, Programs in Business, Bluffton, OH 45817. Offers accounting and financial management (MBA); health care management (MBA); leadership (MAOM, MBA); production and operations management (MBA); sustainability management (MBA). *Program availability:* Evening/weekend, blended/hybrid learning, videoconference. *Faculty:* 5 full-time (2 women), 8 part-time/adjunct (2 women). *Students:* 48 full-time (31 women); includes 11 minority (5 Black or African American, non-Hispanic/Latino; 1 Asian, non-Hispanic/Latino; 3 Hispanic/Latino; 2 Two or more races, non-Hispanic/Latino), 1 international. Average age 33. 44 applicants, 70% accepted, 26 enrolled. In 2017, 41 master's awarded. *Degree requirements:* For master's, integrated research project (for some programs). *Entrance requirements:* For master's, current resume, official transcript, bachelor's degree, minimum GPA of 3.0, personal essay. Additional exam requirements/recommendations for international students: Recommended—TOEFL (minimum score 550 paper-based). *Application deadline:* For fall admission, 7/31 priority date for domestic and international students. Applications are processed on a rolling basis. Application fee: $0. Electronic applications accepted. *Expenses:* $550 per credit hour, $150 per semester technology fee, $25 per semester payment plan fee. *Financial support:* Unspecified assistantships and faculty/staff grants available. Financial award applicants required to submit FAFSA. *Unit head:* Dr. Melissa Green, Director of Graduate Programs in Business, 419-358-3447, E-mail: greenm@bluffton.edu. *Application contact:* Carrie Mast, Administrative Assistant, Graduate Programs in Business, 419-358-3065, E-mail: mastc@bluffton.edu. Website: http://www.bluffton.edu/grad/

California State University, East Bay, Office of Graduate Studies, College of Business and Economics, MBA Program, Option in Operations and Supply Chain Management, Hayward, CA 94542-3000. Offers MBA. *Degree requirements:* For master's, comprehensive exam or thesis. *Entrance requirements:* For master's, GMAT, minimum GPA of 2.75. Additional exam requirements/recommendations for international students: Required—TOEFL (minimum score 550 paper-based). *Application deadline:* For fall admission, 6/1 for domestic and international students. Application fee: $55. Electronic applications accepted. *Financial support:* Fellowships, career-related internships or fieldwork, Federal Work-Study, institutionally sponsored loans, and scholarships/grants available. Support available to part-time students. Financial award application deadline: 3/1; financial award applicants required to submit FAFSA. *Unit head:* Dr. Zinovy Radovilsky, Program Advisor, 510-885-3307, E-mail: zinovy.radovilsky@csueastbay.edu. *Application contact:* Philip Cole-Regis, Administrative Support Coordinator, 510-885-3286, E-mail: philip.coleregis@csueastbay.edu. Website: http://www.csueastbay.edu/cbe/mba-options/operations-and-supply-chain-management-option.html

Carnegie Mellon University, Carnegie Institute of Technology and School of Design, Program in Product Development, Pittsburgh, PA 15213-3891. Offers MPD. *Entrance requirements:* For master's, GRE General Test, undergraduate degree in engineering, industrial design, or related fields, 3 letters of reference, 2 years of professional experience. Additional exam requirements/recommendations for international students: Required—TOEFL or TSE.

Carnegie Mellon University, College of Fine Arts, School of Design, Pittsburgh, PA 15213-3891. Offers design (MA, D Des, PhD); design for interaction (M Des); design theory (PhD); new product development (PhD); product development (MPD); typography and information design (PhD).

Carnegie Mellon University, Tepper School of Business, Program in Operations Management, Pittsburgh, PA 15213-3891. Offers PhD. *Degree requirements:* For doctorate, thesis/dissertation.

Case Western Reserve University, Weatherhead School of Management, Department of Operations, Cleveland, OH 44106. Offers operations and supply chain management (MSM); operations research (PhD); MBA/MSM. *Program availability:* Part-time. *Degree requirements:* For doctorate, thesis/dissertation. *Entrance requirements:* For master's, GRE General Test; for doctorate, GMAT, GRE General Test. *Expenses:* Tuition: Full-time $43,854; part-time $1827 per credit hour. *Required fees:* $50; $50 per credit hour. Tuition and fees vary according to course load and program. *Faculty research:* Mathematical finance, mathematical programming, scheduling, stochastic optimization, environmental/energy models.

Cedarville University, Graduate Programs, Cedarville, OH 45314. Offers business administration (MBA); family nurse practitioner (MSN); global ministry (M Div); global public health nursing (MSN); healthcare administration (MBA); ministry (M Min); nurse educator (MSN); operations management (MBA); pharmacy (Pharm D). *Program availability:* Part-time, evening/weekend, 100% online, blended/hybrid learning. *Faculty:* 23 full-time (9 women), 48 part-time/adjunct (21 women). *Students:* 202 full-time (123 women), 146 part-time (96 women); includes 63 minority (39 Black or African American, non-Hispanic/Latino; 3 American Indian or Alaska Native, non-Hispanic/Latino; 15 Asian, non-Hispanic/Latino; 2 Hispanic/Latino; 1 Native Hawaiian or other Pacific Islander, non-Hispanic/Latino; 3 Two or more races, non-Hispanic/Latino), 3 international. Average age 24. 345 applicants, 37% accepted, 91 enrolled. In 2017, 53 master's, 47 doctorates awarded. *Degree requirements:* For master's, portfolio; for doctorate, comprehensive exam. *Entrance requirements:* For master's, GRE, 2 professional recommendations; for doctorate, PCAT, professional recommendation from a practicing pharmacist or current employer/supervisor, resume, essay, interview. Additional exam requirements/recommendations for international students: Required—TOEFL (minimum score 550 paper-based; 80 iBT). *Application deadline:* For fall

admission, 5/1 priority date for domestic and international students; for spring admission, 11/1 priority date for domestic and international students. Applications are processed on a rolling basis. Application fee: $0. Electronic applications accepted. *Expenses: Tuition:* Full-time $12,594; part-time $566 per credit. One-time fee: $100 full-time. Tuition and fees vary according to degree level and program. *Financial support:* Scholarships/grants and unspecified assistantships available. Support available to part-time students. Financial award application deadline: 1/30; financial award applicants required to submit FAFSA. *Faculty research:* Establishing competencies of clinical reasoning for nursing students in Taiwan, social determinants of health in pediatric primary care, meeting needs of palliative care populations, natural product utility in cancer, monoclonal antibodies directed at angiogenesis regulation. *Total annual research expenditures:* $3,800. *Unit head:* Dr. Janice Supplee, Dean of Graduate Studies, 937-766-7700, E-mail: suppleej@cedarville.edu. *Application contact:* Jim Amstutz, Director of Graduate Admissions, 937-766-7878, Fax: 937-766-7575, E-mail: amstutzj@cedarville.edu. Website: https://www.cedarville.edu/Admissions/Graduate/Graduate-Programs.aspx

Central Connecticut State University, School of Graduate Studies, School of Engineering, Science and Technology, Department of Manufacturing and Construction Management, New Britain, CT 06050-4010. Offers construction management (MS, Certificate); environmental and occupational safety (Certificate); lean manufacturing and Six Sigma (Certificate); supply chain and logistics (Certificate); technology management (MS). *Program availability:* Part-time, evening/weekend. *Faculty:* 8 full-time (1 woman), 3 part-time/adjunct (0 women). *Students:* 25 full-time (10 women), 92 part-time (16 women); includes 31 minority (17 Black or African American, non-Hispanic/Latino; 5 Asian, non-Hispanic/Latino; 8 Hispanic/Latino; 1 Two or more races, non-Hispanic/Latino), 11 international. Average age 32. 77 applicants, 71% accepted, 37 enrolled. In 2017, 40 master's, 6 other advanced degrees awarded. *Degree requirements:* For master's, comprehensive exam, special project; for Certificate, qualifying exam. *Entrance requirements:* For master's, minimum undergraduate GPA of 2.7. Additional exam requirements/recommendations for international students: Required—TOEFL (minimum score 550 paper-based; 79 iBT); Recommended—IELTS (minimum score 6.5). *Application deadline:* For fall admission, 8/1 for domestic students, 5/1 for international students; for spring admission, 12/1 for domestic students, 11/1 for international students; for summer admission, 5/1 for domestic students. Applications are processed on a rolling basis. Application fee: $50. Electronic applications accepted. *Expenses: Tuition, area resident:* Full-time $6757. Tuition, state resident: full-time $9750; part-time $374 per credit. Tuition, nonresident: full-time $18,102; part-time $374 per credit. *Required fees:* $4635; $255 per credit. *Financial support:* In 2017–18, 17 students received support. Career-related internships or fieldwork, Federal Work-Study, scholarships/grants, and unspecified assistantships available. Support available to part-time students. Financial award application deadline: 3/1; financial award applicants required to submit FAFSA. *Faculty research:* All aspects of middle management, technical supervision in the workplace. *Unit head:* Dr. Ravindra Thamma, Chair, 860-832-1830, E-mail: thammarav@ccsu.edu. *Application contact:* Patricia Gardner, Associate Director of Graduate Studies, 860-832-2350, Fax: 860-832-2362. Website: http://www.ccsu.edu/mcm/

Central Michigan University, College of Graduate Studies, College of Science and Technology, School of Engineering and Technology, Mount Pleasant, MI 48859. Offers industrial management and technology (MA). *Program availability:* Part-time. *Degree requirements:* For master's, thesis or alternative. Electronic applications accepted. *Faculty research:* Computer applications, manufacturing process control, mechanical engineering automation, industrial technology.

Colorado Technical University Aurora, Programs in Business Administration and Management, Aurora, CO 80014. Offers accounting (MBA); business administration (MBA); business administration and management (EMBA); finance (MBA); human resource management (MBA); marketing (MBA); mediation and dispute resolution (MBA); operations management (MBA); project management (MBA); technology management (MBA). *Program availability:* Part-time, evening/weekend. *Degree requirements:* For master's, thesis or alternative. *Entrance requirements:* For master's, minimum undergraduate GPA of 3.0, resume.

Colorado Technical University Colorado Springs, Graduate Studies, Program in Management, Colorado Springs, CO 80907. Offers accounting (MBA, MSA); business administration (MBA); finance (MBA); human resources management (MBA); logistics/supply chain management (MBA); management (DM); marketing (MBA); mediation and dispute resolution (MBA); operations management (MBA); project management (MBA); technology management (MBA). *Accreditation:* ACBSP. *Program availability:* Part-time, evening/weekend, online learning. *Degree requirements:* For master's, thesis or alternative; for doctorate, thesis/dissertation. *Entrance requirements:* For doctorate, minimum graduate GPA of 3.0, 5 years of related work experience. *Faculty research:* Sexual harassment, performance evaluation, critical thinking.

Duke University, The Fuqua School of Business, The Duke MBA-Daytime Program, Durham, NC 27708-0586. Offers academic excellence in finance (Certificate); business administration (MBA); decision sciences (MBA); energy and environment (MBA); energy finance (MBA); entrepreneurship and innovation (MBA); finance (MBA); financial analysis (MBA); health sector management (Certificate); leadership and ethics (MBA); management (MBA); management science and technology management (Certificate); marketing (MBA); operations management (MBA); social entrepreneurship (MBA); strategy (MBA). *Faculty:* 96 full-time (19 women), 48 part-time/adjunct (15 women). *Students:* 876 full-time (297 women); includes 180 minority (39 Black or African American, non-Hispanic/Latino; 2 American Indian or Alaska Native, non-Hispanic/Latino; 83 Asian, non-Hispanic/Latino; 50 Hispanic/Latino; 6 Two or more races, non-Hispanic/Latino), 321 international. Average age 29. In 2017, 445 master's awarded. *Entrance requirements:* For master's, GMAT or GRE, transcripts, essays, resume, recommendation letters, interview. *Application deadline:* For fall admission, 9/12 for domestic and international students; for winter admission, 10/10 for domestic and international students; for spring admission, 1/3 for domestic and international students; for summer admission, 3/20 for domestic and international students. Application fee: $225. Electronic applications accepted. *Expenses:* $69,342 first-year tuition and fees. *Financial support:* In 2017–18, 423 students received support. Scholarships/grants available. Financial award applicants required to submit FAFSA. *Unit head:* Steve Misuraca, Assistant Dean, Daytime MBA Program. *Application contact:* Shari Hubert, Associate Dean, Office of Admissions, 919-660-7705, Fax: 919-681-8026, E-mail: admissions-info@fuqua.duke.edu. Website: https://www.fuqua.duke.edu/programs/daytime-mba

Duke University, The Fuqua School of Business, PhD Program, Durham, NC 27708-0586. Offers accounting (PhD); decision sciences (PhD); finance (PhD); management and organizations (PhD); marketing (PhD); operations management (PhD); strategy (PhD). *Faculty:* 96 full-time (19 women). *Students:* 64 full-time (25 women); includes 1 minority (Hispanic/Latino), 41 international. Average age 27. 617 applicants, 5% accepted, 14 enrolled. In 2017, 15 doctorates awarded. *Degree requirements:* For doctorate, thesis/dissertation, major field requirement (exam or major paper, depending upon the area). *Entrance requirements:* For doctorate, GMAT or GRE, transcripts, essays, recommendation letters, statement of purpose. Additional exam requirements/recommendations for international students: Required—TOEFL (minimum score 577 paper-based; 108 iBT), IELTS (minimum score 8). *Application deadline:* For fall admission, 12/31 priority date for domestic and international students. Application fee: $85. Electronic applications accepted. *Expenses:* $52,253. *Financial support:* In 2017–18, 66 students received support, including 66 fellowships with full tuition reimbursements available (averaging $29,200 per year), 63 research assistantships with full tuition reimbursements available (averaging $7,000 per year); institutionally sponsored loans, scholarships/grants, and tuition waivers (full) also available. Financial award applicants required to submit FAFSA. *Unit head:* William Boulding, Dean. *Application contact:* Qi Chen, Director of Graduate Studies, 919-660-7753, Fax: 919-660-7971, E-mail: qc2@duke.edu.

East Carolina University, Graduate School, College of Engineering and Technology, Department of Technology Systems, Greenville, NC 27858-4353. Offers computer network professional (Certificate); cyber security professional (Certificate); information assurance (Certificate); Lean Six Sigma Black Belt (Certificate); network technology (MS), including computer networking management, digital communications technology, information security, Web technologies; occupational safety (MS); technology management (MS, PhD), including industrial distribution and logistics (MS); Website developer (Certificate). *Students:* 19 full-time (4 women), 158 part-time (35 women); includes 43 minority (28 Black or African American, non-Hispanic/Latino; 2 American Indian or Alaska Native, non-Hispanic/Latino; 3 Asian, non-Hispanic/Latino; 6 Hispanic/Latino; 4 Two or more races, non-Hispanic/Latino), 6 international. Average age 39. 44 applicants, 91% accepted, 37 enrolled. In 2017, 30 master's, 29 other advanced degrees awarded. *Entrance requirements:* For master's and Certificate, GRE General Test or MAT, minimum GPA of 2.5; for doctorate, GRE General Test, related work experience. Additional exam requirements/recommendations for international students: Recommended—TOEFL (minimum score 78 iBT), IELTS (minimum score 6.5). *Application deadline:* For fall admission, 6/1 priority date for domestic students. Applications are processed on a rolling basis. Application fee: $75. *Expenses:* Tuition, state resident: full-time $4749; part-time $297 per credit hour. Tuition, nonresident: full-time $17,898; part-time $1119 per credit hour. *Required fees:* $2691; $224 per credit hour. Part-time tuition and fees vary according to course load and program. *Financial support:* Application deadline: 6/1. *Unit head:* Dr. Tijjani Mohammed, Chair, 252-328-9668, E-mail: mohammedt@ecu.edu.
Website: http://www.ecu.edu/cs-cet/techsystems/index.cfm

Embry-Riddle Aeronautical University–Worldwide, Department of Management, Daytona Beach, FL 32114-3900. Offers global management (MS); human resources management (MS); leadership (MS); operations management (MS); project management (MS). *Program availability:* Part-time, evening/weekend, EagleVision Classroom (between classrooms), EagleVision Home (faculty and students at home), and a blend of Classroom or Home. *Students:* 148 full-time (48 women), 192 part-time (52 women); includes 91 minority (46 Black or African American, non-Hispanic/Latino; 1 American Indian or Alaska Native, non-Hispanic/Latino; 11 Asian, non-Hispanic/Latino; 16 Hispanic/Latino; 17 Two or more races, non-Hispanic/Latino), 7 international. Average age 39. In 2017, 104 master's awarded. *Entrance requirements:* Additional exam requirements/recommendations for international students: Required—TOEFL (minimum score 550 paper-based, 79 iBT) or IELTS (6). *Application deadline:* Applications are processed on a rolling basis. Application fee: $50. Electronic applications accepted. *Expenses:* Contact institution. *Financial support:* Career-related internships or fieldwork and scholarships/grants available. Financial award applicants required to submit FAFSA. *Unit head:* Thomas Henkel, PhD, Department Chair, E-mail: thomas.henkel@erau.edu. *Application contact:* Worldwide Campus, 800-522-6787, E-mail: worldwide@erau.edu.

Emory University, Goizueta Business School, Full Time MBA Program, Atlanta, GA 30322. Offers accounting (MBA); alternative investments (MBA); business process consulting (MBA); business technology management (MBA); capital markets (MBA); corporate finance (MBA); customer relationship management (MBA); decision analytics (MBA); entrepreneurship (MBA); finance (MBA); global management (MBA); investment banking (MBA); management consulting (MBA); marketing (MBA); marketing analytics (MBA); marketing consulting (MBA); operations management (MBA); organization and management (MBA); product and brand management (MBA); real estate (MBA); social enterprise (MBA); strategy consulting (MBA). *Accreditation:* AACSB. *Faculty:* 74 full-time (18 women), 18 part-time/adjunct (6 women). *Students:* 353 full-time (96 women); includes 80 minority (18 Black or African American, non-Hispanic/Latino; 2 American Indian or Alaska Native, non-Hispanic/Latino; 39 Asian, non-Hispanic/Latino; 16 Hispanic/Latino; 1 Native Hawaiian or other Pacific Islander, non-Hispanic/Latino; 4 Two or more races, non-Hispanic/Latino), 104 international. Average age 29. 1,380 applicants, 34% accepted, 172 enrolled. In 2017, 179 master's awarded. *Degree requirements:* For master's, 1 leadership course; 2 mid-semester module programs; 2 global components. *Entrance requirements:* For master's, GMAT/GRE, essays, recommendation letters; undergraduate degree; interview. Additional exam requirements/recommendations for international students: Required—TOEFL (minimum score 100 iBT), IELTS (minimum score 7), PTE (minimum score 68). *Application deadline:* For fall admission, 10/6 for domestic and international students; for winter admission, 11/17 for domestic and international students; for spring admission, 1/3 priority date for domestic and international students; for summer admission, 3/9 for domestic and international students. Application fee: $150. Electronic applications accepted. *Expenses:* $59,616. *Financial support:* In 2017–18, 273 students received support. Career-related internships or fieldwork, institutionally sponsored loans, and scholarships/grants available. Financial award application deadline: 4/1; financial award applicants required to submit FAFSA. *Faculty research:* Corporate finance, information systems, digital marketing, asset pricing, sports management. *Unit head:* Brian Mitchell, Associate Dean, 404-727-4824, Fax: 404-712-9648, E-mail: brian.mitchell@emory.edu. *Application contact:* Julie Barefoot, Associate Dean, 404-727-6311, Fax: 404-727-4612, E-mail: mbaadmissions@emory.edu.
Website: http://www.goizueta.emory.edu

Everglades University, Graduate Programs, Program in Aviation Science, Boca Raton, FL 33431. Offers aviation operations management (MSA); aviation security (MSA); business administration (MSA). *Program availability:* Part-time, evening/weekend, 100% online. *Entrance requirements:* For master's, GMAT (minimum score of 400) or GRE (minimum score of 290), bachelor's or graduate degree from college accredited by an agency recognized by the U.S. Department of Education; minimum cumulative GPA of 2.0 at the baccalaureate level, 3.0 at the master's level. Additional exam requirements/recommendations for international students: Recommended—TOEFL (minimum score 500 paper-based). Electronic applications accepted. *Expenses:* Contact institution.

Georgetown University, Graduate School of Arts and Sciences, Department of Economics, Washington, DC 20057. Offers econometrics (PhD); economic development (PhD); economic theory (PhD); industrial organization (PhD); international macro and finance (PhD); international trade (PhD); labor economics (PhD); macroeconomics (PhD); public economics and political economy (PhD); MA/PhD; MS/MA. *Degree requirements:* For doctorate, comprehensive exam, thesis/dissertation. *Entrance requirements:* For doctorate, GRE General Test. Additional exam requirements/recommendations for international students: Required—TOEFL. *Faculty research:* International economics, economic development.

Harvard University, Harvard Business School, Doctoral Programs in Management, Boston, MA 02163. Offers accounting and management (DBA); business economics (PhD); health policy management (PhD); management (DBA); marketing (DBA); organizational behavior (PhD); science, technology and management (PhD); strategy (DBA); technology and operations management (DBA). *Degree requirements:* For doctorate, comprehensive exam (for some programs), thesis/dissertation. *Entrance requirements:* For doctorate, GRE General Test or GMAT. Additional exam requirements/recommendations for international students: Required—TOEFL.

HEC Montreal, School of Business Administration, Master of Science Programs in Administration, Program in Operations Management, Montréal, QC H3T 2A7, Canada. Offers M Sc. Program offered in French. *Students:* 57 full-time (29 women), 11 part-time (8 women). 40 applicants, 65% accepted, 18 enrolled. In 2017, 36 master's awarded. *Entrance requirements:* For master's, BBA, undergraduate degree in another field, degree deemed equivalent by program director and minimum GPA of 3.0 on 4.3 scale. Additional exam requirements/recommendations for international students: Required—TAGE MAGE (minimum recommended score of 283), GMAT (minimum recommended score of 630), or GRE. *Application deadline:* For fall admission, 3/15 for domestic and international students; for winter admission, 9/15 for domestic and international students. Application fee: $88 Canadian dollars ($184 Canadian dollars for international students). Electronic applications accepted. *Expenses:* Tuition, state resident: full-time $2869 Canadian dollars; part-time $79.70 Canadian dollars per credit. Tuition, nonresident: full-time $8883 Canadian dollars; part-time $246.76 Canadian dollars per credit. *International tuition:* $19,648 Canadian dollars full-time. *Required fees:* $41.20 Canadian dollars per credit. $67.94 Canadian dollars per term. Tuition and fees vary according to degree level and program. *Financial support:* Research assistantships, teaching assistantships, and scholarships/grants available. Financial award application deadline: 9/2. *Unit head:* Dr. Marie-Helene Jobin, Director, 514-340-6283, E-mail: anne.bourhis@hec.ca. *Application contact:* Marianne de Moura, Administrative Director, 514-340-6151, Fax: 514-340-6411, E-mail: aide@hec.ca.
Website: http://www.hec.ca/programmes/maitrises/maitrise-gestion-operations/index.html

Illinois Institute of Technology, Graduate College, School of Applied Technology, Department of Industrial Technology and Management, Wheaton, IL 60819. Offers MAS. *Program availability:* Part-time, evening/weekend, online learning. *Entrance requirements:* For master's, GRE (minimum score 900 verbal and quantitative; 2.5 analytical writing), bachelor's degree with minimum cumulative undergraduate GPA of 3.0 (or its equivalent) from accredited institution. Additional exam requirements/recommendations for international students: Required—TOEFL (minimum score 523 paper-based; 70 iBT), Recommended—IELTS (minimum score 5.5). Electronic applications accepted. *Faculty research:* Industrial logistics, industrial facilities, manufacturing technology, entrepreneurship, energy options.

Instituto Tecnologico de Santo Domingo, Graduate School, Area of Engineering, Santo Domingo, Dominican Republic. Offers construction administration (MS, Certificate); data telecommunications (M Eng, MS, Certificate); industrial engineering (M Eng, Certificate); industrial management (M Mgmt); information technology (Certificate); maintenance engineering (M Eng); occupational hazard prevention (M Mgmt); production management (Certificate); quantitative methods (Certificate); sanitary and environmental engineering (M Eng); structural engineering (M Eng); systems engineering and electronic data processing (Certificate); transportation systems engineering and electronic data processing (Certificate); transportation

Instituto Tecnológico y de Estudios Superiores de Monterrey, Campus Estado de México, Professional and Graduate Division, Estado de Mexico, Mexico. Offers administration of information technologies (MITA); architecture (M Arch); business administration (GMBA, MBA); computer sciences (MCS, PhD); education (M Ed); educational institution administration (MAD); educational technology and innovation (PhD); electronic commerce (MEC); environmental systems (MS); finance (MAF); humanistic studies (MHS); information sciences and knowledge management (MISKM); information systems (MS); manufacturing systems (MS); marketing (MEM); quality systems and productivity (MS); science and materials engineering (PhD); telecommunications management (MTM). *Program availability:* Part-time, online learning. *Degree requirements:* For master's, one foreign language, thesis (for some programs); for doctorate, one foreign language, thesis/dissertation. *Entrance requirements:* For master's, E-PAEP 500, interview; for doctorate, E-PAEP 500, research proposal. Additional exam requirements/recommendations for international students: Required—TOEFL (minimum score 550 paper-based). *Faculty research:* Surface treatments by plasmas, mechanical properties, robotics, graphical computing, mechatronics security protocols.

Instituto Tecnológico y de Estudios Superiores de Monterrey, Campus Irapuato, Graduate Programs, Irapuato, Mexico. Offers administration (MBA); administration of information technology (MAIT); administration of telecommunications (MAT); architecture (M Arch); computer science (MCS); education (M Ed); educational administration (MEA); educational innovation and technology (DEIT); educational technology (MET); electronic commerce (MBA); environmental administration and planning (MEAP); environmental systems (MES); finances (MBA); humanistic studies (MHS); international management for Latin American executives (MIMLAE); library and information science (MLIS); manufacturing quality management (MMQM); marketing research (MBA).

Inter American University of Puerto Rico, Metropolitan Campus, Graduate Programs, Program in Industrial Management, San Juan, PR 00919-1293. Offers MBA. *Degree requirements:* For master's, comprehensive exam. *Entrance requirements:* For master's, GRE or EXADEP, interview. Electronic applications accepted.

Inter American University of Puerto Rico, San Germán Campus, Graduate Studies Center, Program in Business Administration, San Germán, PR 00683-5008. Offers accounting (MBA); finance (MBA); general business administration (MBA); human resources (MBA, PhD); industrial relations (MBA); information systems (MBA); international and interregional business (PhD); management (MBA); marketing (MBA). *Program availability:* Part-time, evening/weekend. *Degree requirements:* For master's, comprehensive exam. *Entrance requirements:* For master's, GRE General Test or EXADEP, minimum GPA of 3.0.

Lawrence Technological University, College of Engineering, Southfield, MI 48075-1058. Offers architectural engineering (MS); automotive engineering (MS); biomedical engineering (MS); civil engineering (MA, MS, PhD), including environmental engineering (MS), geotechnical engineering (MS), structural engineering (MS), transportation

Industrial and Manufacturing Management

engineering (MS), water resource engineering (MS); construction engineering management (MA); electrical and computer engineering (MS); engineering management (MEM); engineering technology (MS); fire engineering (MS); industrial engineering (MS), including healthcare systems; manufacturing systems (ME); mechanical engineering (MS, DE, PhD), including automotive engineering (MS), energy engineering (MS), manufacturing (DE), solid mechanics (MS), thermal/fluid systems (MS); mechatronic systems engineering (MS). *Program availability:* Part-time, evening/weekend. *Faculty:* 27 full-time (5 women), 22 part-time/adjunct (2 women). *Students:* 20 full-time (8 women), 415 part-time (50 women); includes 24 minority (7 Black or African American, non-Hispanic/Latino; 8 Asian, non-Hispanic/Latino; 9 Hispanic/Latino), 299 international. Average age 27. 550 applicants, 24% accepted, 77 enrolled. In 2017, 269 master's, 10 doctorates awarded. Terminal master's awarded for partial completion of doctoral program. *Degree requirements:* For master's, thesis optional; for doctorate, comprehensive exam, thesis/dissertation optional. *Entrance requirements:* Additional exam requirements/recommendations for international students: Required—TOEFL (minimum score 550 paper-based; 79 iBT), IELTS (minimum score 6.5). *Application deadline:* For fall admission, 5/27 for international students; for spring admission, 10/8 for international students; for summer admission, 2/14 for international students. Applications are processed on a rolling basis. Application fee: $50. Electronic applications accepted. *Expenses:* Tuition: Full-time $15,274; part-time $1091 per credit. One-time fee: $150. *Financial support:* In 2017–18, 29 students received support, including 5 research assistantships with full tuition reimbursements available; unspecified assistantships also available. Financial award application deadline: 4/1; financial award applicants required to submit FAFSA. *Faculty research:* Innovative infrastructure and building structures and materials; connectivity and mobility; automotive systems modeling, simulation and testing; biomedical devices and materials; building mechanical/electrical systems. *Total annual research expenditures:* $1.4 million. *Unit head:* Dr. Nabil Grace, Dean, 248-204-2500, Fax: 248-204-2509, E-mail: engrdean@ltu.edu. *Application contact:* Jane Rohrback, Director of Admissions, 248-204-3160, Fax: 248-204-2228, E-mail: admissions@ltu.edu.
Website: http://www.ltu.edu/engineering/index.asp

Marquette University, Graduate School of Management, Executive MBA Program, Milwaukee, WI 53201-1881. Offers economics (MBA); finance (MBA); human resources (MBA); international business (MBA); management information systems (MBA); marketing (MBA); operations and supply chain management (MBA); sports business (MBA). *Accreditation:* AACSB. *Degree requirements:* For master's, international trip. *Entrance requirements:* For master's, GMAT or GRE, two letters of recommendation, official transcripts from current and previous colleges/universities. Additional exam requirements/recommendations for international students: Required—TOEFL (minimum score 550 paper-based; 88 iBT), IELTS (minimum score 6.5), PTE. Electronic applications accepted. *Expenses:* Contact institution. *Faculty research:* International trade and finance, customer relationship management, consumer satisfaction, customer service.

Marquette University, Graduate School of Management, Program in Business Administration, Milwaukee, WI 53201-1881. Offers business administration (MBA); economics (MBA); entrepreneurship (Certificate); finance (MBA); human resources (MBA); international business (MBA); management information systems (MBA); marketing (MBA); operations and supply chain management (MBA); sports business (MBA); JD/MBA; MBA/MA; MBA/MSN. *Accreditation:* AACSB. *Program availability:* Part-time, evening/weekend. *Degree requirements:* For Certificate, business plan. *Entrance requirements:* For master's, GMAT or GRE, letters of recommendation. Additional exam requirements/recommendations for international students: Required—TOEFL (minimum score 550 paper-based; 88 iBT), IELTS (minimum score 6.5), PTE. Electronic applications accepted. *Faculty research:* Ethics in the professions, services marketing, technology impact on decision-making, mentoring.

McGill University, Faculty of Graduate and Postdoctoral Studies, Desautels Faculty of Management, Montréal, QC H3A 2T5, Canada. Offers administration (PhD); entrepreneurial studies (MBA); finance (MBA); general management (Post Master's Certificate); information systems (MBA); international business (MBA); international practicing management (MM); management (MBA); management for development (MBA); manufacturing management (MMM); marketing (MBA); operations management (MBA); public accountancy (Diploma); strategic management (MBA); MBA/LL B; MD/MBA. MMM offered jointly with Faculty of Engineering; PhD with Concordia University, HEC Montreal, Université de Montréal, Université du Québec à Montréal.

McGill University, Faculty of Graduate and Postdoctoral Studies, Faculty of Engineering, Department of Mechanical Engineering and Desautels Faculty of Management, Master in Manufacturing Management, Montréal, QC H3A 2T5, Canada. Offers MMM.

Milligan College, Area of Business Administration, Milligan College, TN 37682. Offers health sector management (MBA, Graduate Certificate); leadership (MBA, Graduate Certificate); operations management (MBA, Graduate Certificate). *Program availability:* 100% online, blended/hybrid learning. *Faculty:* 4 full-time (1 woman), 3 part-time/adjunct (2 women). *Students:* 30 full-time (16 women), 1 international. Average age 38. 30 applicants, 83% accepted, 24 enrolled. In 2017, 27 master's awarded. *Degree requirements:* For master's, thesis or alternative. *Entrance requirements:* For master's, GMAT if undergraduate GPA less than 3.0, undergraduate degree and supporting transcripts, relevant full-time work experience, essay/personal statement, professional recommendations. Additional exam requirements/recommendations for international students: Required—TOEFL (minimum score 550 paper-based, 79 iBT) or IELTS (6.5). *Application deadline:* For fall admission, 8/1 for domestic students, 6/1 for international students; for spring admission, 1/15 for domestic students, 12/1 for international students. Applications are processed on a rolling basis. Application fee: $30. Electronic applications accepted. *Expenses:* Contact institution. *Financial support:* Scholarships/grants available. Financial award application deadline: 12/1; financial award applicants required to submit FAFSA. *Faculty research:* International microfinance; economic development in Appalachia; job satisfaction; business ethics; internal migration. *Unit head:* Dr. David Campbell, Area Chair of Business, 423-461-8674, Fax: 423-461-8677, E-mail: dacampbell@milligan.edu. *Application contact:* Rebecca Banton, Graduate Admissions Recruiter, Business Area, 423-461-8662, Fax: 423-461-8789, E-mail: rbbanton@milligan.edu.
Website: http://www.milligan.edu/GPS

Milwaukee School of Engineering, MS Program in New Product Management, Milwaukee, WI 53202-3109. Offers MS. *Program availability:* Part-time, evening/weekend. *Students:* 1 full-time (0 women), 7 part-time (4 women). Average age 30. 4 applicants, 100% accepted, 3 enrolled. In 2017, 3 master's awarded. *Degree requirements:* For master's, thesis or alternative, thesis defense or capstone project. *Entrance requirements:* For master's, GRE General Test or GMAT if undergraduate GPA less than 2.8, 2 letters of recommendation; bachelor's degree from accredited university; work experience (strongly recommended). Additional exam requirements/recommendations for international students: Required—TOEFL (minimum score 90 iBT), IELTS (minimum score 7). *Application deadline:* Applications are processed on a rolling basis. Application fee: $0. Electronic applications accepted. *Expenses: Tuition:* Part-time $814 per credit hour. *Required fees:* $12.50 per credit hour. *Financial support:*

Career-related internships or fieldwork, institutionally sponsored loans, and scholarships/grants available. Financial award application deadline: 3/15; financial award applicants required to submit FAFSA. *Faculty research:* New product development, product research and design, product development. *Unit head:* Gene Wright, Program Director, 414-277-2268, Fax: 414-277-2487, E-mail: wright@msoe.edu. *Application contact:* Brian Rutz, Graduate Admission Counselor, 414-277-7200, E-mail: dahlinghaus@msoe.edu.
Website: https://www.msoe.edu/academics/graduate-degrees/business/new-product-management/

Mississippi State University, Bagley College of Engineering, Department of Industrial and Systems Engineering, Mississippi State, MS 39762. Offers human factors and ergonomics (MS); industrial and systems engineering (PhD); industrial systems (MS); management systems (MS); manufacturing systems (MS); operations research (MS). *Program availability:* Part-time, blended/hybrid learning. *Faculty:* 13 full-time (2 women). *Students:* 33 full-time (10 women), 65 part-time (16 women); includes 22 minority (11 Black or African American, non-Hispanic/Latino; 5 Asian, non-Hispanic/Latino; 5 Hispanic/Latino; 1 Native Hawaiian or other Pacific Islander, non-Hispanic/Latino), 21 international. Average age 36. 64 applicants, 47% accepted, 19 enrolled. In 2017, 13 master's, 5 doctorates awarded. *Degree requirements:* For master's, comprehensive exam (for some programs), thesis optional, comprehensive oral or written exam; for doctorate, comprehensive exam, thesis/dissertation, candidacy exam. *Entrance requirements:* For master's, GRE (for graduates from program not accredited by EAC/ABET), minimum GPA of 3.0 on junior and senior years; for doctorate, GRE (for graduates from program not accredited by EAC/ABET), minimum GPA of 3.5 on master's degree and junior and senior years of BS. Additional exam requirements/recommendations for international students: Required—TOEFL (minimum score 550 paper-based; 79 iBT). Recommended—IELTS (minimum score 6.5). *Application deadline:* For fall admission, 7/1 for domestic students, 5/1 for international students; for spring admission, 11/1 for domestic students, 9/1 for international students. Applications are processed on a rolling basis. Application fee: $60 ($80 for international students). Electronic applications accepted. *Expenses:* Tuition, state resident: full-time $8318; part-time $462.12 per credit hour. Tuition, nonresident: full-time $22,358; part-time $1242.12 per credit hour. *Required fees:* $110; $12.24 per credit hour. $6.12 per semester. *Financial support:* In 2017–18, 20 research assistantships with full tuition reimbursements (averaging $16,589 per year), 1 teaching assistantship with full tuition reimbursement (averaging $17,669 per year) were awarded; Federal Work-Study, institutionally sponsored loans, and unspecified assistantships also available. Financial award application deadline: 4/1; financial award applicants required to submit FAFSA. *Faculty research:* Operations research, ergonomics, production systems, management systems, transportation. *Total annual research expenditures:* $2.2 million. *Unit head:* Dr. John Usher, Professor/Head, 662-325-8875, Fax: 662-325-7618, E-mail: usher@ise.msstate.edu. *Application contact:* Marina Hunt, Admissions and Enrollment Assistant, 662-325-5188, E-mail: mhunt@grad.msstate.edu.
Website: http://www.ise.msstate.edu/

Northern Illinois University, Graduate School, College of Engineering and Engineering Technology, Department of Technology, De Kalb, IL 60115-2854. Offers industrial management (MS). *Program availability:* Part-time, evening/weekend. *Faculty:* 14 full-time (1 woman), 1 part-time/adjunct (0 women). *Students:* 5 full-time (1 woman), 25 part-time (3 women); includes 10 minority (5 Black or African American, non-Hispanic/Latino; 1 Asian, non-Hispanic/Latino; 1 Hispanic/Latino; 3 Two or more races, non-Hispanic/Latino), 1 international. Average age 36. 11 applicants, 91% accepted, 5 enrolled. In 2017, 6 master's awarded. *Degree requirements:* For master's, thesis optional. *Entrance requirements:* For master's, GRE General Test, minimum GPA of 2.75. Additional exam requirements/recommendations for international students: Required—TOEFL (minimum score 550 paper-based). *Application deadline:* For fall admission, 6/1 for domestic students, 5/1 for international students; for spring admission, 11/1 for domestic students, 10/1 for international students. Applications are processed on a rolling basis. Application fee: $40. Electronic applications accepted. *Financial support:* In 2017–18, 3 research assistantships with full tuition reimbursements, 14 teaching assistantships with full tuition reimbursements were awarded; fellowships with full tuition reimbursements, career-related internships or fieldwork, Federal Work-Study, scholarships/grants, tuition waivers (full), and unspecified assistantships also available. Support available to part-time students. Financial award applicants required to submit FAFSA. *Faculty research:* Digital control, intelligent systems, engineering graphic design, occupational safety, ergonomics. *Unit head:* Dr. Abul Azad, Acting Associate Dean, 815-753-1349, Fax: 815-753-3702, E-mail: aazad@niu.edu. *Application contact:* Graduate School Office, 815-753-0395, E-mail: gradsch@niu.edu.
Website: http://www.niu.edu/tech/

Northwestern University, The Graduate School, Kellogg School of Management, Management Programs, Evanston, IL 60208. Offers accounting information and management (MBA, PhD); analytical finance (MBA); business administration (MBA); decision sciences (MBA); entrepreneurship and innovation (MBA); finance (MBA, PhD); health enterprise management (MBA); human resources management (MBA); international business (MBA); management and organizations (MBA, PhD); management and organizations and sociology (PhD); management and strategy (MBA); management studies (MS); managerial analytics (MBA); managerial economics (MBA); managerial economics and strategy (PhD); marketing (MBA, PhD); marketing management (MBA); media management (MBA); operations management (MBA, PhD); real estate (MBA); social enterprise at Kellogg (MBA); JD/MBA. *Program availability:* Part-time, evening/weekend. Terminal master's awarded for partial completion of doctoral program. *Degree requirements:* For doctorate, thesis/dissertation, 2 years of coursework, qualifying (field) exam and candidacy, summer research papers and presentations to faculty, proposal defense, final exam/defense. *Entrance requirements:* For master's, GMAT, GRE, interview, 2 letters of recommendation, college transcripts, resume, essays, Kellogg honor code; for doctorate, GMAT, GRE, statement of purpose, transcripts, 2 letters of recommendation, resume, interview. Additional exam requirements/recommendations for international students: Required—TOEFL, IELTS. Electronic applications accepted. *Expenses:* Contact institution. *Faculty research:* Business cycles and international finance, health policy, networks, non-market strategy, consumer psychology.

Oakland University, Graduate Study and Lifelong Learning, School of Business Administration, Department of Decision and Information Sciences, Rochester, MI 48309-4401. Offers information technology management (MS); management information systems (Certificate); production and operations management (Certificate). *Expenses:* Tuition, state resident: full-time $16,950; part-time $706.25 per credit. Tuition, nonresident: full-time $24,648; part-time $1027 per credit.

Penn State Erie, The Behrend College, Graduate School, Erie, PA 16563. Offers accounting (MPAC); applied clinical psychology (MA); business administration (MBA); quality and manufacturing management (MMM). *Accreditation:* AACSB. *Program availability:* Part-time. *Students:* 31 full-time (15 women), 126 part-time (39 women); includes 10 minority (4 Black or African American, non-Hispanic/Latino; 1 Hispanic/Latino; 5 Two or more races, non-Hispanic/Latino). Average age 31. 104 applicants, 75% accepted, 75 enrolled. In 2017, 72 master's awarded. *Entrance requirements:*

Additional exam requirements/recommendations for international students: Required—TOEFL (minimum score 550 paper-based; 80 iBT), IELTS. *Application deadline:* Applications are processed on a rolling basis. Application fee: $65. Electronic applications accepted. *Financial support:* Federal Work-Study available. Financial award application deadline: 2/15; financial award applicants required to submit FAFSA. *Unit head:* Dr. Ralph M. Ford, Chancellor, 814-898-6160, Fax: 814-898-6461. *Application contact:* Ann M. Burbules, Assistant Director, Graduate Admissions, 866-374-3378, Fax: 814-898-6044, E-mail: behrend.admissions@psu.edu. Website: http://behrend.psu.edu/

Polytechnic University of Puerto Rico, Graduate School, Hato Rey, PR 00918. Offers business administration (MBA), including computer information systems, general management, management of information systems, management of international enterprises; civil engineering (ME, MS); computer engineering (ME, MS); computer science (MCS, MS); electrical engineering (ME, MS); engineering management (MEM); environmental management (MEM); landscape architecture (M Land Arch); manufacturing competitiveness (MMC, MS); manufacturing engineering (ME, MS); mechanical engineering (M Mech E). *Program availability:* Part-time, evening/weekend. *Entrance requirements:* For master's, 3 letters of recommendation.

Polytechnic University of Puerto Rico, Miami Campus, Graduate School, Miami, FL 33166. Offers accounting (MBA); business administration (MBA); construction management (MEM); environmental management (MEM); finance (MBA); human resources management (MBA); logistics and supply chain management (MBA); management of international enterprises (MBA); manufacturing management (MEM); marketing management (MBA); project management (MBA). *Program availability:* Part-time, evening/weekend, online learning. *Entrance requirements:* For master's, minimum GPA of 3.0. Electronic applications accepted.

Polytechnic University of Puerto Rico, Orlando Campus, Graduate School, Orlando, FL 32825. Offers accounting (MBA); business administration (MBA); construction management (MEM); engineering management (MEM); environmental management (MEM); finance (MBA); human resources management (MBA); management of international enterprises (MBA); management of technology (MBA); manufacturing management (MEM). *Program availability:* Part-time, evening/weekend, online learning. *Entrance requirements:* For master's, minimum GPA of 3.0. Additional exam requirements/recommendations for international students: Recommended—TOEFL. Electronic applications accepted.

Regis University, College of Business and Economics, Denver, CO 80221-1099. Offers accounting (MS); executive leadership (Certificate); finance (MS); finance and accounting (MBA); health industry leadership (MBA); human resource management and leadership (MSOL); management (MBA); marketing (MBA); nonprofit leadership (Post-Graduate Certificate); nonprofit management (MNM); nonprofit organizational capacity building (Certificate); operations management (MBA); organizational leadership and management (MSOL); project leadership and management (MS, MSOL); strategic business management (Certificate); strategic human resource integration (Certificate); strategic management (MBA). Programs offered at Colorado Springs Campus, Northwest Denver Campus, Southeast Denver Campus, Fort Collins Campus, Broomfield Campus, Henderson (Nevada) Campus, and Summerlin (Nevada) Campus. *Program availability:* Part-time, evening/weekend, 100% online, blended/hybrid learning. *Degree requirements:* For master's, thesis (for some programs), capstone or final research project. *Entrance requirements:* For master's, official transcript reflecting baccalaureate degree awarded from regionally-accredited college or university, interview, 2 years of full-time related work experience, resume, letters of recommendation. Additional exam requirements/recommendations for international students: Required—TOEFL (minimum score 550 paper-based; 82 iBT). Electronic applications accepted. *Expenses:* Contact institution. *Faculty research:* Impact of information technology on small business regulation of accounting, international project financing, mineral development, delivery of healthcare to rural indigenous communities.

Rochester Institute of Technology, Graduate Enrollment Services, Kate Gleason College of Engineering, Design, Development and Manufacturing Department, MS Program in Manufacturing Leadership, Rochester, NY 14623. Offers MS. *Program availability:* Part-time, evening/weekend, 100% online. *Students:* 20 part-time (2 women); includes 4 minority (1 Black or African American, non-Hispanic/Latino; 1 Asian, non-Hispanic/Latino; 1 Hispanic/Latino; 1 Two or more races, non-Hispanic/Latino), 1 international. Average age 37. 9 applicants, 67% accepted, 4 enrolled. In 2017, 6 master's awarded. *Degree requirements:* For master's, thesis or alternative, capstone. *Entrance requirements:* For master's, minimum GPA of 3.0 (recommended). Additional exam requirements/recommendations for international students: Required—TOEFL (minimum score 550 paper-based; 79 iBT), IELTS (minimum score 6.5), PTE (minimum score 58). *Application deadline:* Applications are processed on a rolling basis. Application fee: $65. Electronic applications accepted. *Expenses:* $1,815 per credit hour (classroom and online rate). *Financial support:* Scholarships/grants available. Support available to part-time students. Financial award applicants required to submit FAFSA. *Faculty research:* Lean manufacturing, Lean Six Sigma, modeling and simulation, supply chain management, project management. *Unit head:* Mark Smith, Graduate Program Director, 585-475-7971, Fax: 585-475-4080, E-mail: mml@rit.edu. *Application contact:* Diane Ellison, Senior Associate Vice President, Graduate Enrollment Services, 585-475-2229, Fax: 585-475-7164, E-mail: gradinfo@rit.edu. Website: https://www.rit.edu/kgcoe/mml/

San Francisco State University, Division of Graduate Studies, College of Business, Program in Business Administration, San Francisco, CA 94132-1722. Offers decision sciences/operations research (MBA); ethics and compliance (MBA); finance (MBA); global business and innovation (MBA); healthcare administration (MBA); hospitality and tourism management (MBA); information systems (MBA); leadership (MBA); marketing (MBA); nonprofit and social enterprise leadership (MBA); sustainable business (MBA). *Accreditation:* AACSB. *Program availability:* Part-time, evening/weekend. *Degree requirements:* For master's, thesis, essay test. *Entrance requirements:* For master's, GMAT, minimum GPA of 2.7 in last 60 units. Additional exam requirements/recommendations for international students: Required—TOEFL (minimum score 550 paper-based). *Application deadline:* For fall admission, 5/1 priority date for domestic students, 4/1 for international students; for spring admission, 11/1 for domestic students, 10/15 for international students. Applications are processed on a rolling basis. Application fee: $55. *Financial support:* Application deadline: 3/1. *Unit head:* Dr. Sanjit Sengupta, Faculty Director, 415-817-4366, Fax: 415-817-4340, E-mail: sengupta@sfsu.edu. *Application contact:* Christopher Kingston, Director of Student Advising, 415-817-4322, Fax: 415-817-4340, E-mail: cak@sfsu.edu. Website: http://cob.sfsu.edu/graduate-programs/mba

Southern New Hampshire University, School of Business, Manchester, NH 03106-1045. Offers accounting (MBA, Graduate Certificate); accounting finance (MS); accounting/auditing (MS); accounting/forensic accounting (MS); accounting/management accounting (MS); accounting/taxation (MS); applied economics (MS); athletic administration (MBA, Graduate Certificate); business administration (IMBA, Certificate), including business information systems (Certificate), human resource management (Certificate); business analytics (MBA); business intelligence (MBA); communication (MA), including new media and marketing, public relations; community

economic development (MBA); criminal justice (MBA); data analytics (MS); economics (MBA); engineering management (MBA); entrepreneurship (MBA); finance (MBA, MS, Graduate Certificate); finance/corporate finance (MS); finance/investments (MS); forensic accounting (MBA); forensic accounting and fraud examination (Graduate Certificate); healthcare informatics (MBA); healthcare management (MBA); human resource management (MS); human resources (MS); information technology (MS); information technology management (MBA); international business (PhD); Internet marketing (MBA); leadership (MBA); leadership of nonprofit organizations (Graduate Certificate); management (MS); marketing (MBA, MS, Graduate Certificate); music business (MBA); operations and project management (MS); operations and supply chain management (MBA, Graduate Certificate); organizational leadership (MS); project management (MBA, Graduate Certificate); public administration (MBA, Graduate Certificate); quantitative analysis (MBA); Six Sigma (Graduate Certificate); Six Sigma quality (MBA); social media marketing (MBA, Graduate Certificate); sport management (MBA, MS, Graduate Certificate); sustainability and environmental compliance (MBA); MBA/Certificate. *Accreditation:* ACBSP. *Program availability:* Part-time, evening/weekend, online learning. Terminal master's awarded for partial completion of doctoral program. *Degree requirements:* For master's, one foreign language, comprehensive exam (for some programs), thesis or alternative; for doctorate, one foreign language, comprehensive exam, thesis/dissertation. *Entrance requirements:* For master's, minimum GPA of 2.5; for doctorate, GMAT. Additional exam requirements/recommendations for international students: Required—TOEFL (minimum score 500 paper-based). *Application deadline:* Applications are processed on a rolling basis. Application fee: $40. Electronic applications accepted. *Expenses: Tuition:* Part-time $627 per credit hour. Part-time tuition and fees vary according to campus/location and program. *Financial support:* Career-related internships or fieldwork, Federal Work-Study, institutionally sponsored loans, scholarships/grants, tuition waivers (partial), and unspecified assistantships available. Support available to part-time students. Financial award applicants required to submit FAFSA. *Unit head:* Dr. Bill Lightfoot, Dean, 603-644-3102, Fax: 603-644-3144. *Application contact:* Office of Graduate Admission, 888-327-SNHU, Fax: 603-644-3144, E-mail: enroll@snhu.edu.

Stevens Institute of Technology, Graduate School, Charles V. Schaefer Jr. School of Engineering and Science, Department of Mechanical Engineering, Program in Integrated Product Development, Hoboken, NJ 07030. Offers armament engineering (M Eng); computer and electrical engineering (M Eng); manufacturing technologies (M Eng); systems reliability and design (M Eng). *Program availability:* Part-time, evening/weekend. *Students:* 19 applicants. *Degree requirements:* For master's, thesis optional, minimum B average in major field and overall. *Entrance requirements:* Additional exam requirements/recommendations for international students: Required—TOEFL (minimum score 74 iBT), IELTS (minimum score 6). *Application deadline:* For fall admission, 7/1 for domestic students, 4/15 for international students; for spring admission, 12/1 for domestic and international students. Applications are processed on a rolling basis. Application fee: $60. Electronic applications accepted. *Expenses: Tuition:* Full-time $34,494; part-time $1554 per credit. *Required fees:* $291 per semester. *Financial support:* Fellowships, research assistantships, teaching assistantships, career-related internships or fieldwork, Federal Work-Study, scholarships/grants, and unspecified assistantships available. Financial award application deadline: 2/15; financial award applicants required to submit FAFSA. *Unit head:* Dr. Frank Fisher, Interim Department Director, 201-216-8913, Fax: 201-216-8315, E-mail: ffisher@stevens.edu. *Application contact:* Graduate Admissions, 888-783-8367, Fax: 888-511-1306, E-mail: graduate@stevens.edu.

Texas A&M University–Kingsville, College of Graduate Studies, Frank H. Dotterweich College of Engineering, Department of Industrial Management and Technology, Kingsville, TX 78363. Offers industrial management (MS). *Degree requirements:* For master's, variable foreign language requirement, comprehensive exam, thesis (for some programs). *Entrance requirements:* For master's, GRE, MAT, GMAT. Additional exam requirements/recommendations for international students: Required—TOEFL (minimum score 550 paper-based; 79 iBT). Electronic applications accepted.

Universidad de las Américas Puebla, Division of Graduate Studies, School of Engineering, Program in Industrial Engineering, Puebla, Mexico. Offers industrial engineering (MS); production management (M Adm). *Program availability:* Part-time, evening/weekend. *Degree requirements:* For master's, one foreign language, thesis. *Faculty research:* Textile industry, quality control.

Universidad de las Américas Puebla, Division of Graduate Studies, School of Engineering, Program in Manufacturing Administration, Puebla, Mexico. Offers MS. *Faculty research:* Operations research, construction.

The University of Alabama, Graduate School, Manderson Graduate School of Business, Department of Information Systems, Statistics, and Management Science, Program in Operations Management, Tuscaloosa, AL 35487. Offers MS, PhD. *Accreditation:* AACSB. *Program availability:* Online learning. *Students:* 23 full-time (12 women), 34 part-time (8 women); includes 8 minority (2 Black or African American, non-Hispanic/Latino; 3 Asian, non-Hispanic/Latino; 2 Hispanic/Latino; 1 Two or more races, non-Hispanic/Latino), 9 international. Average age 32. 47 applicants, 47% accepted, 14 enrolled. In 2017, 45 master's awarded. Terminal master's awarded for partial completion of doctoral program. *Degree requirements:* For master's, comprehensive exam, business calculus; for doctorate, comprehensive exam, thesis/dissertation. *Entrance requirements:* For master's, GMAT or GRE; for doctorate, GRE or GMAT. Additional exam requirements/recommendations for international students: Required—TOEFL (minimum score 94 iBT), IELTS (minimum score 7). *Application deadline:* For spring admission, 1/10 priority date for domestic and international students. Applications are processed on a rolling basis. Application fee: $50 ($60 for international students). Electronic applications accepted. *Financial support:* In 2017–18, teaching assistantships with full tuition reimbursements (averaging $13,500 per year) were awarded; scholarships/grants and health care benefits also available. Financial award application deadline: 1/10. *Faculty research:* Supply chain management, inventory, simulation, logistics. *Unit head:* Dr. John Mittenthal, Department Head, 205-348-6087, E-mail: jmittent@cba.ua.edu. *Application contact:* Paula Barrentine, Accounting Assistant, 205-348-8904, E-mail: pgbarrentine@cba.ua.edu.

University of Arkansas, Graduate School, College of Engineering, Department of Industrial Engineering, Operations Management Program, Fayetteville, AR 72701. Offers MS. *Program availability:* Part-time, evening/weekend, online learning. *Students:* 137 applicants, 94% accepted. In 2017, 214 master's awarded. *Degree requirements:* For master's, thesis optional. *Application deadline:* For fall admission, 8/1 for domestic students, 4/1 for international students; for spring admission, 12/1 for domestic students, 10/1 for international students; for summer admission, 4/15 for domestic students, 3/1 for international students. Applications are processed on a rolling basis. Application fee: $60. Electronic applications accepted. *Expenses:* Tuition, state resident: full-time $3782. Tuition, nonresident: full-time $10,238. *Financial support:* In 2017–18, 2 research assistantships were awarded; fellowships, teaching assistantships, and institutionally sponsored loans also available. *Unit head:* Gregory S. Parnell, Program Director, 479-575-3413, E-mail: msom@uark.edu. *Application contact:* Dr. Greg Parnell, Director/Chairman, 479-575-3156, Fax: 479-575-8431, E-mail: gparnell@uark.edu. Website: https://operations-management.uark.edu/

Industrial and Manufacturing Management

University of Bridgeport, School of Business, Bridgeport, CT 06604. Offers accounting (MBA); finance (MBA); general business (MBA); global financial services (MBA); human resource management (MBA); information systems and knowledge management (MBA); international business (MBA); management (MBA); marketing (MBA); operations management (MBA); small business and entrepreneurship (MBA); specialized business (MBA). *Accreditation:* ACBSP. *Program availability:* Part-time, evening/weekend. *Degree requirements:* For master's, thesis optional. *Entrance requirements:* For master's, GMAT. Additional exam requirements/recommendations for international students: Recommended—TOEFL (minimum score 550 paper-based; 80 iBT), IELTS (minimum score 6.5). Electronic applications accepted. *Expenses:* Contact institution.

University of Central Missouri, The Graduate School, Warrensburg, MO 64093. Offers accountancy (MA); accounting (MBA); applied mathematics (MS); aviation safety (MA); biology (MS); business administration (MBA); career and technical education leadership (MS); college student personnel administration (MS); communication (MA); computer science (MS); counseling (MS); criminal justice (MS); educational leadership (Ed D); educational technology (MS); elementary and early childhood education (MSE); English (MA); environmental studies (MA); finance (MBA); history (MA); human services/educational technology (Ed S); human services/learning resources (Ed S); human services/professional counseling (Ed S); industrial hygiene (MS); industrial management (MS); information systems (MBA); information technology (MS); kinesiology (MS); library science and information services (MS); literacy education (MSE); marketing (MBA); mathematics (MS); music (MA); occupational safety management (MS); psychology (MS); rural family nursing (MS); school administration (MSE); social gerontology (MS); sociology (MA); special education (MSE); speech language pathology (MS); superintendency (Ed S); teaching (MAT); teaching English as a second language (MA); technology (MS); technology management (PhD); theatre (MA). *Program availability:* Part-time, 100% online, blended/hybrid learning. *Faculty:* 337 full-time (145 women), 41 part-time/adjunct (28 women). *Students:* 785 full-time (398 women), 1,633 part-time (1,063 women); includes 231 minority (102 Black or African American, non-Hispanic/Latino; 4 American Indian or Alaska Native, non-Hispanic/Latino; 16 Asian, non-Hispanic/Latino; 52 Hispanic/Latino; 57 Two or more races, non-Hispanic/Latino), 692 international. Average age 30. In 2017, 2,605 master's, 122 other advanced degrees awarded. *Degree requirements:* For master's and Ed S, comprehensive exam (for some programs), thesis (for some programs). *Entrance requirements:* Additional exam requirements/recommendations for international students: Required—TOEFL (minimum score 550 paper-based; 79 iBT). *Application deadline:* For fall admission, 6/1 priority date for domestic and international students; for spring admission, 10/1 priority date for domestic and international students; for summer admission, 4/1 priority date for domestic and international students. Applications are processed on a rolling basis. Application fee: $30 ($75 for international students). Electronic applications accepted. *Expenses:* Tuition, state resident: full-time $8771; part-time $292.35 per credit hour. Tuition, nonresident: full-time $17,541; part-time $584.70 per credit hour. *Required fees:* $372; $24.78 per credit hour. *Financial support:* In 2017–18, 99 students received support. Research assistantships, teaching assistantships, career-related internships or fieldwork, Federal Work-Study, scholarships/grants, and administrative and laboratory assistantships available. Support available to part-time students. Financial award application deadline: 3/1; financial award applicants required to submit FAFSA. *Unit head:* Shellie Hewitt, Director of Graduate and International Student Services, 660-543-4621, Fax: 660-543-4778, E-mail: hewitt@ucmo.edu. *Application contact:* 660-543-4621, E-mail: admit_intl@ucmo.edu.
Website: http://www.ucmo.edu/graduate/

University of Chicago, Booth School of Business, Full-Time MBA Program, Chicago, IL 60637. Offers accounting (MBA); analytic finance (MBA); analytic management (MBA); econometrics and statistics (MBA); economics (MBA); entrepreneurship (MBA); finance (MBA); general management (MBA); health administration and policy (Certificate); international business (MBA); managerial and organizational behavior (MBA); marketing analytics (MBA); marketing management (MBA); operations management (MBA); strategic management (MBA); MBA/AM; MBA/JD; MBA/MA; MBA/MD; MBA/MPP. *Accreditation:* AACSB. *Faculty:* 154 full-time (26 women), 61 part-time/adjunct (12 women). *Students:* 1,176 full-time (481 women). In 2017, 586 master's awarded. *Entrance requirements:* For master's, GMAT or GRE, transcripts, resume, 2 letters of recommendation, essays, interview. Additional exam requirements/recommendations for international students: Required—TOEFL, IELTS, or PTE. *Application deadline:* For fall admission, 9/1 for domestic and international students; for winter admission, 1/1 for domestic and international students; for spring admission, 4/1 for domestic and international students. Application fee: $250. Electronic applications accepted. *Expenses:* Contact institution. *Unit head:* Stacey Kole, Deputy Dean for Alumni, Corporate Relations, and the Full-time MBA Program, 773-702-7121. *Application contact:* Kurt Ahlm, Associate Dean for Student Recruitment and Admissions, 773-702-7369, Fax: 773-702-9085, E-mail: admissions@chicagobooth.edu.
Website: https://www.chicagobooth.edu/programs/full-time

University of Cincinnati, Carl H. Lindner College of Business, PhD Programs, Cincinnati, OH 45221. Offers accounting (PhD); business analytics (PhD); economics (PhD); finance (PhD); information systems (PhD); management (PhD); marketing (PhD); operations and business analytics (PhD); operations research (PhD). *Faculty:* 37 full-time (13 women). *Students:* 29 full-time (12 women), 12 part-time (6 women); includes 5 minority (1 Black or African American, non-Hispanic/Latino; 4 Asian, non-Hispanic/Latino), 20 international. Average age 30. 123 applicants, 16% accepted, 11 enrolled. In 2017, 5 doctorates awarded. *Degree requirements:* For doctorate, comprehensive exam, thesis/dissertation. *Entrance requirements:* For doctorate, GMAT, GRE, transcripts, essays, resume, letters of recommendation. Additional exam requirements/recommendations for international students: Required—TOEFL (minimum score 600 paper-based; 100 iBT), IELTS (minimum score 7). *Application deadline:* For fall admission, 1/15 for domestic and international students. Application fee: $65 ($70 for international students). Electronic applications accepted. *Expenses:* $7,234 resident per term, $13,105 nonresident per term. *Financial support:* In 2017–18, 41 students received support, including 29 research assistantships with full tuition reimbursements available (averaging $23,250 per year); scholarships/grants, health care benefits, tuition waivers (full), and unspecified assistantships also available. Financial award application deadline: 1/15; financial award applicants required to submit FAFSA. *Faculty research:* Bayesian Prediction Theory, organizational fairness, consumer insight and market research, consumer insight and market research, density estimation from correlated data. *Unit head:* Dr. Suzanne Masterson, Director, 513-556-7125, Fax: 513-556-5499, E-mail: suzanne.masterson@uc.edu. *Application contact:* Angel Elvin, Assistant Director, 513-556-7190, Fax: 513-558-7006, E-mail: angel.elvin@uc.edu.
Website: http://business.uc.edu/graduate/phd.html

The University of Manchester, School of Mechanical, Aerospace and Civil Engineering, Manchester, United Kingdom. Offers advanced manufacturing technology (M Ent); aerospace engineering (M Phil, M Sc, PhD); civil engineering (M Phil, M Sc, PhD); environmental engineering (M Phil, PhD); management of projects (M Phil, M Sc, PhD); mechanical engineering (M Phil, M Sc, PhD); mechanical engineering design (M Ent); nuclear engineering (M Phil, D Eng, PhD).

University of Michigan–Flint, School of Management, Program in Business Administration, Flint, MI 48502-1950. Offers accounting (MBA); computer information systems (MBA); finance (MBA, Post-Master's Certificate); general business (Graduate Certificate); general business administration (MBA); health care management (MBA); international business (MBA, Post-Master's Certificate); lean manufacturing (MBA); marketing (Post-Master's Certificate); marketing and innovation management (MBA); organizational leadership (MBA). *Program availability:* Part-time, evening/weekend, mixed mode format. *Faculty:* 32 full-time (5 women), 8 part-time/adjunct (2 women). *Students:* 12 full-time (7 women), 147 part-time (51 women); includes 31 minority (15 Black or African American, non-Hispanic/Latino; 1 American Indian or Alaska Native, non-Hispanic/Latino; 9 Asian, non-Hispanic/Latino; 5 Hispanic/Latino; 1 Two or more races, non-Hispanic/Latino), 18 international. Average age 34. 110 applicants, 52% accepted, 29 enrolled. In 2017, 59 master's, 6 other advanced degrees awarded. *Entrance requirements:* For master's, GMAT or GRE, bachelor's degree in arts, sciences, engineering, or business administration from regionally-accredited college or university with minimum GPA of 3.0; for other advanced degree, bachelor's degree in arts, sciences, engineering, or business administration from regionally-accredited college or university with minimum GPA of 3.0, college-level math, statistics, or quantitative course (for Graduate Certificate); MBA or equivalent degree from regionally-accredited college or university (for Post Master's Certificate). Additional exam requirements/recommendations for international students: Required—TOEFL (minimum score 84 iBT), IELTS (minimum score 6.5). *Application deadline:* For fall admission, 8/1 for domestic students, 5/1 for international students; for winter admission, 11/15 for domestic students, 9/1 for international students; for spring admission, 3/15 for domestic students, 1/1 for international students; for summer admission, 5/15 for domestic students. Applications are processed on a rolling basis. Application fee: $55. Electronic applications accepted. *Expenses:* Contact institution. *Financial support:* Federal Work-Study, scholarships/grants, and unspecified assistantships available. Support available to part-time students. Financial award application deadline: 3/1; financial award applicants required to submit FAFSA. *Unit head:* Dr. Scott Johnson, Dean, School of Management, 810-762-3164, Fax: 810-237-6685, E-mail: scotjohn@umflint.edu. *Application contact:* Bradley T. Maki, Director of Graduate Admissions, 810-762-3171, E-mail: bmaki@umflint.edu.
Website: http://www.umflint.edu/graduateprograms/business-administration-mba

University of New Haven, Graduate School, Tagliatela College of Engineering, Program in Engineering and Operations Management, West Haven, CT 06516. Offers engineering and operations management (MS); engineering management (MS); Lean Six Sigma (Graduate Certificate). *Program availability:* Part-time. *Students:* 34 full-time (9 women), 49 part-time (7 women); includes 13 minority (7 Black or African American, non-Hispanic/Latino; 4 Asian, non-Hispanic/Latino; 2 Hispanic/Latino), 37 international. Average age 29. 84 applicants, 69% accepted, 18 enrolled. In 2017, 42 master's awarded. *Entrance requirements:* Additional exam requirements/recommendations for international students: Required—TOEFL (minimum score 75 iBT), IELTS, PTE (minimum score 50). *Application deadline:* Applications are processed on a rolling basis. Application fee: $50. Electronic applications accepted. Application fee is waived when completed online. *Expenses:* Tuition: Full-time $16,020; part-time $890 per credit hour. *Required fees:* $220; $90 per term. *Financial support:* Applicants required to submit FAFSA. *Unit head:* Dr. Ali Montazer, Program Director, 203-932-7050, E-mail: amontazer@newhaven.edu. *Application contact:* Michelle Mason, Director of Graduate Enrollment, 203-932-7067, E-mail: mmason@newhaven.edu.
Website: http://www.newhaven.edu/88389/

The University of North Carolina at Charlotte, College of Computing and Informatics, Program in Computing and Information Systems, Charlotte, NC 28223-0001. Offers computing and information systems (PhD), including bioinformatics, business information systems and operations management, computer science, interdisciplinary, software and information systems. *Faculty:* 2 full-time (0 women). *Students:* 103 full-time (33 women), 17 part-time (3 women); includes 6 minority (1 Black or African American, non-Hispanic/Latino; 3 Asian, non-Hispanic/Latino; 1 Hispanic/Latino; 1 Two or more races, non-Hispanic/Latino), 90 international. Average age 30. 86 applicants, 48% accepted, 23 enrolled. In 2017, 15 doctorates awarded. *Degree requirements:* For doctorate, comprehensive exam, thesis/dissertation. *Entrance requirements:* For doctorate, GRE or GMAT, baccalaureate degree, minimum GPA of 3.0 on courses related to the chosen field of PhD study, essay, reference letters. Additional exam requirements/recommendations for international students: Required—TOEFL (minimum score 523 paper-based, 70 iBT) or IELTS (6.5). *Application deadline:* For fall admission, 2/1 for domestic and international students; for spring admission, 9/1 for domestic and international students. Applications are processed on a rolling basis. Application fee: $75. Electronic applications accepted. *Expenses:* Tuition, state resident: full-time $4337. Tuition, nonresident: full-time $17,771. *Required fees:* $3211. Tuition and fees vary according to course load and program. *Financial support:* Career-related internships or fieldwork, institutionally sponsored loans, scholarships/grants, health care benefits, and unspecified assistantships available. Support available to part-time students. Financial award applicants required to submit FAFSA. *Unit head:* Dr. Fatma Mili, Dean. *Application contact:* Kathy B. Giddings, Director of Graduate Admissions, 704-687-5503, Fax: 704-687-1668, E-mail: gradadm@uncc.edu.

The University of North Carolina at Charlotte, William States Lee College of Engineering, Department of Systems Engineering and Engineering Management, Charlotte, NC 28223-0001. Offers energy analytics (Graduate Certificate); engineering management (MSEM); Lean Six Sigma (Graduate Certificate); logistics and supply chains (Graduate Certificate); systems analytics (Graduate Certificate). *Program availability:* Part-time, evening/weekend, 100% online, blended/hybrid learning. *Faculty:* 9 full-time (2 women), 1 part-time/adjunct (0 women). *Students:* 32 full-time (9 women), 54 part-time (11 women); includes 15 minority (8 Black or African American, non-Hispanic/Latino; 1 American Indian or Alaska Native, non-Hispanic/Latino; 2 Asian, non-Hispanic/Latino; 2 Hispanic/Latino; 2 Two or more races, non-Hispanic/Latino), 33 international. Average age 29. 156 applicants, 62% accepted, 25 enrolled. In 2017, 20 master's, 5 other advanced degrees awarded. *Degree requirements:* For master's, project or thesis. *Entrance requirements:* For master's, GRE or GMAT, bachelor's degree in engineering or a closely-related technical or scientific field, or in business, provided relevant technical course requirements have been met; undergraduate coursework in engineering economics, calculus, or statistics; minimum GPA of 3.0; for Graduate Certificate, bachelor's degree in engineering or closely-related technical or scientific field, or in business, provided relevant technical course requirements have been met; minimum GPA of 3.0; undergraduate coursework in engineering economics, calculus, and statistics; written description of work experience. Additional exam requirements/recommendations for international students: Required—TOEFL (minimum score 523 paper-based, 70 iBT) or IELTS (6.5). *Application deadline:* For fall admission, 3/1 priority date for domestic and international students; for spring admission, 10/1 priority date for domestic and international students; for summer admission, 4/1 priority date for domestic and international students. Applications are processed on a rolling basis. Application fee: $75. Electronic applications accepted. *Expenses:* Contact institution. *Financial support:* Career-related internships or fieldwork, institutionally sponsored loans, scholarships/grants, and unspecified assistantships available. Support available to part-time students. Financial award application deadline: 3/1; financial

award applicants required to submit FAFSA. *Total annual research expenditures:* $209,562. *Unit head:* Dr. Simon M. Hsiang, Chair, 704-687-1958, E-mail: shsiang1@uncc.edu. *Application contact:* Kathy B. Giddings, Director of Graduate Admissions, 704-687-5503, Fax: 704-687-1668, E-mail: gradadm@uncc.edu.
Website: http://seem.uncc.edu/

University of North Texas, Robert B. Toulouse School of Graduate Studies, Denton, TX 76203-5459. Offers accounting (MS); applied anthropology (MA, MS); applied behavior analysis (Certificate); applied geography (MA); applied technology and performance improvement (M Ed, MS); art education (MA); art history (MA); art museum education (Certificate); arts leadership (Certificate); audiology (Au D); behavior analysis (MS); behavioral science (PhD); biochemistry and molecular biology (MS); biology (MA, MS); biomedical engineering (MS); business analysis (MS); chemistry (MS); clinical health psychology (PhD); communication studies (MA, MS); computer engineering (MS); computer science (MS); counseling (M Ed, MS), including clinical mental health counseling (MS), college and university counseling, elementary school counseling, secondary school counseling; creative writing (MA); criminal justice (MS); curriculum and instruction (M Ed); decision sciences (MBA); design (MA, MFA), including fashion design (MFA), innovation studies, interior design (MFA); early childhood studies (MS); economics (MS); educational leadership (M Ed, Ed D); educational psychology (MS, PhD), including family studies (MS), gifted and talented (MS), human development (MS), learning and cognition (MS), research, measurement and evaluation (MS); electrical engineering (MS); emergency management (MPA); engineering technology (MS); English (MA); English as a second language (MA); environmental science (MS); finance (MBA, MS); financial management (MPA); French (MA); health services management (MBA); higher education (M Ed, Ed D); history (MA, MS); hospitality management (MS); human resources management (MPA); information science (MS); information systems (PhD); information technologies (MBA); interdisciplinary studies (MA, MS); international studies (MA); international sustainable tourism (MS); jazz studies (MM); journalism (MA, MJ, Graduate Certificate), including interactive and virtual digital communication (Graduate Certificate), narrative journalism (Graduate Certificate), public relations (Graduate Certificate); kinesiology (MS); linguistics (MA); local government management (MPA); logistics (PhD); logistics and supply chain management (MBA); long-term care, senior housing, and aging services (MA); management (PhD); marketing (MBA); mathematics (MA, MS); mechanical and energy engineering (MS, PhD); music (MA), including ethnomusicology, music theory, musicology, performance; music composition (PhD); music education (MM Ed, PhD); nonprofit management (MPA); operations and supply chain management (MBA); performance (MM, DMA); philosophy (MA); political science (MA); professional and technical communication (MA); radio, television and film (MA, MFA); rehabilitation counseling (Certificate); sociology (MA); Spanish (MA); special education (M Ed); speech-language pathology (MA); strategic management (MBA); studio art (MFA); teaching (M Ed); MBA/MS. *Program availability:* Part-time, evening/weekend, online learning. Terminal masters awarded for partial completion of doctoral program. *Degree requirements:* For master's, variable foreign language requirement, comprehensive exam (for some programs), thesis (for some programs); for doctorate, variable foreign language requirement, comprehensive exam (for some programs), thesis/dissertation; for other advanced degree, variable foreign language requirement, comprehensive exam (for some programs). *Entrance requirements:* For master's and doctorate, GRE, GMAT. Additional exam requirements/recommendations for international students: Required—TOEFL (minimum score 550 paper-based; 79 iBT). Electronic applications accepted.

University of Pittsburgh, Katz Graduate School of Business, Master of Business Administration Programs, Pittsburgh, PA 15260. Offers finance (MBA); information systems (MBA); marketing (MBA); operations (MBA); organizational behavior and human resources (MBA); strategy, environment and organizations (MBA); MBA/JD; MBA/MID; MBA/MIS; MBA/MSE. *Accreditation:* AACSB. *Program availability:* Part-time, evening/weekend, blended/hybrid learning. *Faculty:* 91 full-time (30 women), 14 part-time/adjunct (4 women). *Students:* 139 full-time (49 women), 294 part-time (94 women); includes 65 minority (27 Black or African American, non-Hispanic/Latino; 20 Asian, non-Hispanic/Latino; 11 Hispanic/Latino; 7 Two or more races, non-Hispanic/Latino), 54 international. Average age 29. 651 applicants, 44% accepted, 158 enrolled. In 2017, 217 master's awarded. *Degree requirements:* For master's, minimum GPA of 3.0. *Entrance requirements:* For master's, GMAT, GRE. Additional exam requirements/recommendations for international students: Required—TOEFL (minimum score 100 iBT) or IELTS (minimum score 7.0). *Application deadline:* For fall admission, 4/1 priority date for domestic students, 2/1 priority date for international students. Application fee: $50. Electronic applications accepted. *Financial support:* In 2017–18, 136 students received support. Scholarships/grants available. Financial award application deadline: 6/1; financial award applicants required to submit FAFSA. *Faculty research:* Accounting systems/financial reporting, corporate finance, shopper marketing/consumer behavior, management information systems, organizational behavior and entrepreneurship. *Total annual research expenditures:* $475,077. *Unit head:* Dr. Arjang A. Assad, Dean, 412-648-1556, Fax: 412-648-1552, E-mail: aassad@katz.pitt.edu. *Application contact:* Thomas Keller, Director of MBA Admissions, 412-648-1700, Fax: 412-648-1659, E-mail: mba@katz.pitt.edu.
Website: http://www.business.pitt.edu/katz/mba/

See Display on page 158 and Close-Up on page 187.

University of Portland, Dr. Robert B. Pamplin, Jr. School of Business, Portland, OR 97203-5798. Offers entrepreneurship (MBA); finance (MBA, MS); health care management (MBA); marketing (MBA); nonprofit management (EMBA); operations and technology management (MBA, MS); sustainability (MBA). *Accreditation:* AACSB. *Program availability:* Part-time, evening/weekend. *Entrance requirements:* For master's, GMAT, minimum GPA of 3.0, resume, 2 letters of recommendation. Additional exam requirements/recommendations for international students: Required—TOEFL (minimum score 570 paper-based; 89 iBT), IELTS (minimum score 7). *Expenses:* Contact institution.

University of Puerto Rico–Mayagüez, Graduate Studies, College of Business Administration, Mayagüez, PR 00681-9000. Offers business administration (MBA); finance (MBA); human resources (MBA); industrial management (MBA). *Program availability:* Part-time, evening/weekend. *Degree requirements:* For master's, one foreign language, comprehensive exam, thesis (for some programs). *Entrance requirements:* For master's, GMAT or EXADEP, bachelor's degree with courses in calculus, microeconomics, accounting and statistics. Additional exam requirements/recommendations for international students: Required—TOEFL (minimum score 500 paper-based), GMAT or EXADEP. Electronic applications accepted. *Faculty research:* Organizational studies, management, accounting, entrepreneurship, leadership and motivation.

University of Puerto Rico–Río Piedras, College of Business Administration, San Juan, PR 00931-3300. Offers accounting (MBA); finance (MBA, PhD); general business (MBA); human resources management (MBA); international trade and business (MBA, PhD); marketing (MBA); operations management (MBA); quantitative methods (MBA). *Accreditation:* AACSB. *Program availability:* Part-time. *Degree requirements:* For master's, comprehensive exam, thesis or alternative, research project. *Entrance requirements:* For master's, GMAT or PAEG, minimum GPA of 3.0, letter of

recommendation; for doctorate, GMAT, PAEG, minimum GPA of 3.0, master degree. *Faculty research:* Management.

University of Rochester, Simon Business School, Doctoral Program in Business Administration, Rochester, NY 14627. Offers accounting (PhD); computer information systems (PhD); finance (PhD); marketing (PhD); operations management (PhD). *Accreditation:* AACSB. *Faculty:* 70 full-time (12 women), 23 part-time/adjunct (6 women). *Students:* 50 full-time (17 women); includes 2 minority (both Asian, non-Hispanic/Latino), 41 international. Average age 28. 199 applicants, 10% accepted, 9 enrolled. In 2017, 8 doctorates awarded. *Degree requirements:* For doctorate, comprehensive exam, thesis/dissertation, qualifying exam. *Entrance requirements:* For doctorate, GMAT or GRE. Additional exam requirements/recommendations for international students: Required—TOEFL. *Application deadline:* For fall admission, 1/5 for domestic and international students. Application fee: $100. Electronic applications accepted. *Expenses:* Contact institution. *Financial support:* In 2017–18, 50 students received support. Fellowships, research assistantships, teaching assistantships, health care benefits, and tuition waivers (full) available. Financial award application deadline: 1/5. *Faculty research:* Empirical industrial organization, risk management, financial disclosure and regulation, social media, health care management. *Unit head:* Dr. Ron Kaniel, Committee Chair, 585-275-2959. *Application contact:* Sue Harris, PhD Administrator, 585-275-2959, E-mail: phdoffice@simon.rochester.edu.
Website: http://www.simon.rochester.edu/programs/phd/index.aspx

University of Southern Indiana, Graduate Studies, Pott College of Science, Engineering, and Education, Program in Industrial Management, Evansville, IN 47712-3590. Offers MSIM. *Program availability:* Part-time-only, evening/weekend. *Faculty:* 2 full-time (0 women). *Students:* 8 full-time (2 women), 6 part-time (2 women); includes 3 minority (2 Black or African American, non-Hispanic/Latino; 1 Hispanic/Latino), 3 international. Average age 31. In 2017, 4 master's awarded. *Degree requirements:* For master's, project. *Entrance requirements:* For master's, minimum GPA of 2.5, BS in engineering or engineering technology. Additional exam requirements/recommendations for international students: Required—TOEFL (minimum score 550 paper-based; 79 iBT), IELTS (minimum score 6). *Application deadline:* For fall admission, 8/15 priority date for domestic students, 3/1 priority date for international students. Applications are processed on a rolling basis. Application fee: $40. Electronic applications accepted. *Expenses:* Tuition, state resident: full-time $9394. Tuition, nonresident: full-time $17,917. *Required fees:* $510. *Financial support:* Federal Work-Study, scholarships/grants, tuition waivers (full and partial), and unspecified assistantships available. Financial award application deadline: 3/1; financial award applicants required to submit FAFSA. *Unit head:* Dr. Paul A. Kuban, Department Chair, 812-465-1090, E-mail: pkuban@usi.edu. *Application contact:* Dr. Mayola Rowser, Director, Graduate Studies, 812-465-7015, Fax: 812-464-1956, E-mail: mrowser@usi.edu.
Website: http://www.usi.edu/science/engineering/programs/master-of-science-in-industrial-management

The University of Tennessee, Graduate School, College of Business Administration, Program in Business Administration, Knoxville, TN 37996. Offers accounting (PhD); finance (MBA, PhD); logistics and transportation (MBA, PhD); management (PhD); marketing (MBA, PhD); operations management (MBA); professional business administration (MBA); statistics (PhD); JD/MBA; MS/MBA; Pharm D/MBA. Pharm D/MBA offered jointly with The University of Tennessee Health Science Center. *Accreditation:* AACSB. *Program availability:* Online learning. *Degree requirements:* For master's, thesis or alternative; for doctorate, thesis/dissertation. *Entrance requirements:* For master's and doctorate, GMAT, minimum GPA of 2.7. Additional exam requirements/recommendations for international students: Required—TOEFL. Electronic applications accepted.

The University of Texas at Austin, Graduate School, McCombs School of Business, Department of Information, Risk, and Operations Management, Austin, TX 78712-1111. Offers information management (MBA); information systems (PhD); information technology and management (MS); risk analysis and decision making (PhD); risk management (MBA); supply chain and operations management (MBA, PhD). *Degree requirements:* For doctorate, thesis/dissertation. *Entrance requirements:* For doctorate, GMAT or GRE. Electronic applications accepted. *Faculty research:* Stochastic processing and queuing, discrete nonlinear and large-scale optimization simulation, quality assurance logistics, distributed artificial intelligence, organizational modeling.

The University of Texas at Dallas, Naveen Jindal School of Management, Program in Organizations, Strategy and International Management, Richardson, TX 75080. Offers business administration (MBA); executive business administration (EMBA); global leadership (EMBA); healthcare leadership and management (MS); healthcare management (EMBA); innovation and entrepreneurship (MS); international management studies (MS, PhD); management science (MS, PhD); project management (EMBA); systems engineering and management (MS); MS/MBA. *Program availability:* Part-time, evening/weekend. *Faculty:* 18 full-time (6 women), 17 part-time/adjunct (2 women). *Students:* 608 full-time (232 women), 711 part-time (326 women); includes 446 minority (93 Black or African American, non-Hispanic/Latino; 3 American Indian or Alaska Native, non-Hispanic/Latino; 212 Asian, non-Hispanic/Latino; 107 Hispanic/Latino; 31 Two or more races, non-Hispanic/Latino), 339 international. Average age 32. 1,665 applicants, 36% accepted, 398 enrolled. In 2017, 473 master's, 14 doctorates awarded. *Degree requirements:* For doctorate, thesis/dissertation. *Entrance requirements:* For master's and doctorate, GMAT. Additional exam requirements/recommendations for international students: Required—TOEFL (minimum score 550 paper-based). *Application deadline:* For fall admission, 7/15 for domestic students, 5/1 priority date for international students; for spring admission, 11/15 for domestic students, 9/1 priority date for international students. Applications are processed on a rolling basis. Application fee: $50 ($100 for international students). Electronic applications accepted. *Expenses:* Tuition, state resident: full-time $12,916; part-time $718 per credit hour. Tuition, nonresident: full-time $25,252; part-time $1403 per credit hour. *Financial support:* In 2017–18, 369 students received support, including 22 research assistantships with partial tuition reimbursements available (averaging $36,554 per year), 88 teaching assistantships with partial tuition reimbursements available (averaging $25,176 per year); Federal Work-Study, institutionally sponsored loans, scholarships/grants, and unspecified assistantships also available. Support available to part-time students. Financial award application deadline: 4/30; financial award applicants required to submit FAFSA. *Faculty research:* International accounting, international trade and finance, economic development, international economics. *Unit head:* Dr. Erik W.K. Tsang, Area Coordinator, 972-883-4386, Fax: 972-883-5977, E-mail: ewktsang@utdallas.edu.
Website: http://jindal.utdallas.edu/osim/

The University of Texas at Tyler, College of Business and Technology, Program in Industrial Management, Tyler, TX 75799-0001. Offers MS. *Program availability:* Online learning. *Entrance requirements:* For master's, GMAT. Electronic applications accepted.

University of Utah, Graduate School, David Eccles School of Business, Business Administration Program, Salt Lake City, UT 84112. Offers accounting (PhD); business administration (EMBA, MBA, PMBA); finance (PhD); information systems (PhD); marketing (PhD); operations management (PhD); organizational behavior (PhD);

Industrial and Manufacturing Management

strategic management (PhD); MBA/JD; MBA/MHA; MBA/MS. *Program availability:* Part-time, evening/weekend, online learning. *Faculty:* 58 full-time (21 women), 37 part-time/adjunct (7 women). *Students:* 558 full-time (149 women), 103 part-time (21 women); includes 66 minority (1 Black or African American, non-Hispanic/Latino; 16 Asian, non-Hispanic/Latino; 41 Hispanic/Latino; 8 Two or more races, non-Hispanic/Latino; 50 international. Average age 27. 442 applicants, 70% accepted, 226 enrolled. In 2017, 298 master's, 7 doctorates awarded. *Entrance requirements:* For master's, GMAT or GRE; for doctorate, GMAT. Additional exam requirements/recommendations for international students: Required—TOEFL (minimum score 600 paper-based; 100 iBT), IELTS (minimum score 7). *Application deadline:* Applications are processed on a rolling basis. Application fee: $55 ($65 for international students). Electronic applications accepted. *Expenses:* Contact institution. *Financial support:* In 2017–18, 53 students received support. Fellowships, scholarships/grants, and unspecified assistantships available. Financial award application deadline: 2/1; financial award applicants required to submit FAFSA. *Faculty research:* Corporate finance, strategy services, consumer behavior, financial disclosures, operations. *Unit head:* Kristina Diekmann, Department Chair, 801-581-8524, Fax: 801-581-3380, E-mail: mastersinfo@business.utah.edu. *Application contact:* Christine Harris, Coordinator, 801-581-7785, Fax: 801-585-3962, E-mail: execch@business.utah.edu.
Website: http://www.business.utah.edu/

University of Utah, Graduate School, David Eccles School of Business, Master of Science in Information Systems Program, Salt Lake City, UT 84112-8939. Offers information systems (MS, Graduate Certificate), including business intelligence and analytics, IT security, product and process management, software and systems architecture. *Program availability:* Part-time, evening/weekend, 100% online, blended/hybrid learning. *Students:* 150 full-time (53 women), 121 part-time (38 women); includes 29 minority (2 Black or African American, non-Hispanic/Latino; 10 Asian, non-Hispanic/Latino; 12 Hispanic/Latino; 5 Two or more races, non-Hispanic/Latino), 124 international. Average age 28. In 2017, 155 master's awarded. *Degree requirements:* For master's, capstone project. *Entrance requirements:* For master's, GMAT/GRE, minimum undergraduate GPA of 3.0, 2 letters of recommendation, personal statement, professional resume. Additional exam requirements/recommendations for international students: Required—TOEFL (minimum score 550 paper-based; 80 iBT), IELTS (minimum score 6.5). *Application deadline:* For fall admission, 7/27 for domestic students, 3/30 for international students; for spring admission, 12/7 for domestic students, 9/7 priority date for international students; for summer admission, 4/12 for domestic students, 1/11 for international students. Applications are processed on a rolling basis. Application fee: $55 ($65 for international students). Electronic applications accepted. *Expenses:* Contact institution. *Financial support:* Fellowships with partial tuition reimbursements, teaching assistantships, tuition waivers (partial), and unspecified assistantships available. Financial award application deadline: 6/1; financial award applicants required to submit FAFSA. *Faculty research:* Business intelligence and analytics, software and system architecture, product and process management, IT security, Web and data mining, applications and management of IT in healthcare. *Unit head:* Dr. Bradden Blair, Director of the IS Programs, 801-587-9489, Fax: 801-581-3666, E-mail: b.blair@eccles.utah.edu. *Application contact:* Jan Bents, Admissions Coordinator, 801-587-5878, Fax: 801-581-3666, E-mail: jan.bents@eccles.utah.edu.
Website: http://msis.eccles.utah.edu

Wayne State University, College of Liberal Arts and Sciences, Department of Economics, Detroit, MI 48202. Offers applied macroeconomics (MA, PhD); health economics (MA, PhD); industrial organization (MA, PhD); international economics (MA, PhD); labor and human resources (MA, PhD); JD/MA. *Faculty:* 11. *Students:* 34 full-time (8 women), 9 part-time (3 women); includes 5 minority (4 Black or African American,

non-Hispanic/Latino; 1 Asian, non-Hispanic/Latino), 17 international. Average age 30. 90 applicants, 30% accepted, 13 enrolled. In 2017, 10 master's, 6 doctorates awarded. *Degree requirements:* For master's, comprehensive exam; for doctorate, comprehensive exam, thesis/dissertation, oral examination on research, completion of course work in quantitative methods, final lecture. *Entrance requirements:* For master's, minimum upper-division GPA of 3.0; prior coursework in intermediate microeconomic and macroeconomic theory, statistics, and elementary calculus; for doctorate, GRE, minimum upper-division GPA of 3.0, prior coursework in intermediate microeconomic and macroeconomic theory, statistics, two courses in calculus, three letters of recommendation from officials or teaching staff at institution(s) most recently attended, statement of purpose. Additional exam requirements/recommendations for international students: Required—TOEFL (minimum score 550 paper-based; 79 iBT), TWE (minimum score 5.5), Michigan English Language Assessment Battery (minimum score 85); Recommended—IELTS (minimum score 6.5). *Application deadline:* For fall admission, 5/1 for domestic and international students; for winter admission, 10/1 priority date for domestic students, 9/1 priority date for international students; for spring admission, 1/1 priority date for domestic and international students. Applications are processed on a rolling basis. Application fee: $50. Electronic applications accepted. *Expenses:* Tuition, state resident: full-time $10,224; part-time $638.98 per credit hour. Tuition, nonresident: full-time $22,145; part-time $1384.04 per credit hour. Tuition and fees vary according to course load and program. *Financial support:* In 2017–18, 25 students received support, including 2 fellowships with tuition reimbursements available (averaging $16,000 per year), 17 teaching assistantships with tuition reimbursements available (averaging $18,534 per year); research assistantships with tuition reimbursements available, scholarships/grants, health care benefits, and unspecified assistantships also available. Support available to part-time students. Financial award applicants required to submit FAFSA. *Faculty research:* Health economics, international economics, macro-economics, urban and labor economics, econometrics. *Unit head:* Dr. Kevin Cotter, Interim Chair, 313-577-3345, E-mail: kevin.cotter@wayne.edu. *Application contact:* Dr. Li Way Lee, Professor and Director of Graduate Studies, 313-577-3345, E-mail: aa1313@wayne.edu.
Website: http://clas.wayne.edu/economics/

Wilkes University, College of Graduate and Professional Studies, Jay S. Sidhu School of Business and Leadership, Wilkes-Barre, PA 18766-0002. Offers accounting (MBA); entrepreneurship (MBA); finance (MBA); health care administration (MBA); human resource management (MBA); international business (MBA); operations management (MBA); organizational leadership and development (MBA). *Accreditation:* ACBSP. *Program availability:* Part-time, evening/weekend. *Students:* 37 full-time (18 women), 87 part-time (45 women); includes 17 minority (4 Black or African American, non-Hispanic/Latino; 5 Asian, non-Hispanic/Latino; 6 Hispanic/Latino; 2 Two or more races, non-Hispanic/Latino), 14 international. Average age 30. In 2017, 77 master's awarded. *Entrance requirements:* For master's, GMAT. Additional exam requirements/recommendations for international students: Required—TOEFL (minimum score 550 paper-based; 79 iBT). *Application deadline:* Applications are processed on a rolling basis. Application fee: $45 ($65 for international students). Electronic applications accepted. *Expenses:* Contact institution. *Financial support:* Unspecified assistantships available. Financial award application deadline: 3/1; financial award applicants required to submit FAFSA. *Unit head:* Dr. Abel Adekola, Dean, 570-408-4701, Fax: 570-408-7846, E-mail: abel.adekola@wilkes.edu. *Application contact:* Kristin Donati, Associate Director of Graduate Admissions, 570-408-3338, Fax: 570-408-7846, E-mail: kristin.donati@wilkes.edu.
Website: http://www.wilkes.edu/academics/colleges/sidhu-school-of-business-leadership/index.aspx

Section 10
Insurance, Actuarial Science, and Risk Management

This section contains a directory of institutions offering graduate work in insurance and actuarial science. Additional information about programs listed in the directory but not augmented by an in-depth entry may be obtained by writing directly to the dean of a graduate school or chair of a department at the address given in the directory.

For programs offering related work, see also in this book *Business Administration and Management*.

CONTENTS

Program Directories

Actuarial Science

Ball State University, Graduate School, College of Sciences and Humanities, Department of Mathematical Sciences, Program in Actuarial Science, Muncie, IN 47306. Offers MA. *Program availability:* Part-time. *Students:* 14 full-time (5 women), 3 part-time (1 woman); includes 3 minority (2 Black or African American, non-Hispanic/Latino; 1 Asian, non-Hispanic/Latino), 11 international. Average age 26. 33 applicants, 82% accepted, 11 enrolled. In 2017, 14 master's awarded. *Entrance requirements:* For master's, minimum baccalaureate GPA of 2.75 or 3.0 in latter half of baccalaureate. Additional exam requirements/recommendations for international students: Required—TOEFL (minimum score 550 paper-based; 79 iBT), IELTS (minimum score 6.5). *Application deadline:* Applications are processed on a rolling basis. Application fee: $60. Electronic applications accepted. *Financial support:* Teaching assistantships with partial tuition reimbursements and unspecified assistantships available. Financial award application deadline: 3/1; financial award applicants required to submit FAFSA. *Unit head:* Dr. Michael Karls, Chairperson/Professor, 765-285-8640, Fax: 765-285-1721, E-mail: mkarls@bsu.edu. *Application contact:* Fax: 765-285-1721, E-mail: hfischer@bsu.edu.
Website: http://cms.bsu.edu/Academics/CollegesandDepartments/Math/AcademicsAdmissions/Programs/Masters/ActuarialScience.aspx

Boston University, Metropolitan College, Department of Actuarial Science, Boston, MA 02215. Offers MS. *Program availability:* Part-time, evening/weekend. *Faculty:* 2 full-time (1 woman), 11 part-time/adjunct (3 women). *Students:* 51 full-time (20 women), 29 part-time (17 women); includes 11 minority (2 Black or African American, non-Hispanic/Latino; 7 Asian, non-Hispanic/Latino; 2 Hispanic/Latino), 61 international. Average age 24. 332 applicants, 34% accepted, 41 enrolled. In 2017, 38 master's awarded. *Entrance requirements:* For master's, prerequisite coursework in calculus. Additional exam requirements/recommendations for international students: Required—TOEFL (minimum score 84 iBT). *Application deadline:* For fall admission, 5/15 priority date for international students; for spring admission, 10/15 priority date for international students. Applications are processed on a rolling basis. Application fee: $85. Electronic applications accepted. *Expenses:* Contact institution. *Financial support:* In 2017–18, 1 research assistantship with partial tuition reimbursement (averaging $8,400 per year), 8 teaching assistantships (averaging $8,400 per year) were awarded; career-related internships or fieldwork, scholarships/grants, and unspecified assistantships also available. *Faculty research:* Survival models, life contingencies, numerical analysis, operations research, compound interest. *Unit head:* Lois K. Horwitz, Chair, 617-353-8758, Fax: 617-353-8757, E-mail: lhorwitz@bu.edu. *Application contact:* Kris Weir, Administrative Coordinator, 617-353-8758, Fax: 617-353-8757, E-mail: actuary@bu.edu.
Website: http://www.bu.edu/actuary/

California State University, East Bay, Office of Graduate Studies, College of Science, Department of Statistics and Biostatistics, Statistics Program, Hayward, CA 94542-3000. Offers actuarial science (MS); applied statistics (MS); computational statistics (MS); mathematical statistics (MS). *Program availability:* Part-time, evening/weekend. *Students:* 19 full-time (8 women), 73 part-time (38 women); includes 36 minority (1 Black or African American, non-Hispanic/Latino; 26 Asian, non-Hispanic/Latino; 8 Hispanic/Latino; 1 Two or more races, non-Hispanic/Latino), 36 international. Average age 29. 79 applicants, 72% accepted, 42 enrolled. In 2017, 50 master's awarded. *Degree requirements:* For master's, comprehensive exam. *Entrance requirements:* For master's, letters of recommendation, minimum GPA of 3.0, math through lower-division calculus. Additional exam requirements/recommendations for international students: Required—TOEFL (minimum score 550 paper-based). *Application deadline:* For fall admission, 6/1 for domestic and international students. Application fee: $55. Electronic applications accepted. *Financial support:* Fellowships, career-related internships or fieldwork, Federal Work-Study, institutionally sponsored loans, scholarships/grants, and unspecified assistantships available. Support available to part-time students. Financial award application deadline: 3/2; financial award applicants required to submit FAFSA. *Unit head:* Dr. Lynn Eudey, Chair, 510-885-3617, E-mail: lynn.eudey@csueastbay.edu.
Website: http://www20.csueastbay.edu/csci/departments/statistics/

Central Connecticut State University, School of Graduate Studies, School of Engineering, Science and Technology, Department of Mathematical Sciences, New Britain, CT 06050-4010. Offers data mining (MS, Certificate); mathematics (MA, MS), including actuarial science (MA), computer science (MA), statistics (MA); mathematics education leadership (Sixth Year Certificate); mathematics for secondary education (Certificate). *Program availability:* Part-time, evening/weekend, 100% online. *Faculty:* 15 full-time (4 women). *Students:* 17 full-time (10 women), 65 part-time (36 women); includes 17 minority (8 Black or African American, non-Hispanic/Latino; 5 Asian, non-Hispanic/Latino; 3 Hispanic/Latino; 1 Two or more races, non-Hispanic/Latino), 2 international. Average age 35. 68 applicants, 81% accepted, 31 enrolled. In 2017, 21 master's, 5 other advanced degrees awarded. *Degree requirements:* For master's, comprehensive exam, thesis or alternative, special project; for other advanced degree, qualifying exam. *Entrance requirements:* For master's, minimum undergraduate GPA of 2.7; for other advanced degree, minimum undergraduate GPA of 3.0, essay, letters of recommendation. Additional exam requirements/recommendations for international students: Required—TOEFL (minimum score 550 paper-based; 79 iBT); Recommended—IELTS (minimum score 6.5). *Application deadline:* For fall admission, 8/1 for domestic students, 5/1 for international students; for spring admission, 11/1 for domestic and international students. Applications are processed on a rolling basis. Application fee: $50. Electronic applications accepted. *Expenses: Tuition, area resident:* Full-time $6757. Tuition, state resident: full-time $9750; part-time $374 per credit. Tuition, nonresident: full-time $18,102; part-time $374 per credit. *Required fees:* $4635; $255 per credit. *Financial support:* In 2017–18, 25 students received support. Career-related internships or fieldwork, Federal Work-Study, scholarships/grants, and unspecified assistantships available. Support available to part-time students. Financial award application deadline: 3/1; financial award applicants required to submit FAFSA. *Faculty research:* Statistics, actuarial mathematics, computer systems and engineering, computer programming techniques, operations research. *Unit head:* Dr. Philip Halloran, Chair, 860-832-2835, E-mail: halloranp@ccsu.edu. *Application contact:* Patricia Gardner, Associate Director of Graduate Studies, 860-832-2350, Fax: 860-832-2362.
Website: http://www.ccsu.edu/mathematics/

Columbia University, School of Professional Studies, Program in Actuarial Science, New York, NY 10027. Offers MS. *Program availability:* Part-time. *Degree requirements:* For master's, comprehensive exam. *Entrance requirements:* For master's, minimum GPA of 3.0, knowledge of economics, linear algebra, calculus. Additional exam requirements/recommendations for international students: Required—American Language Program placement test. Electronic applications accepted. *Expenses: Tuition:* Full-time $44,864; part-time $1704 per credit. *Required fees:* $2370 per semester. One-time fee: $105.

Florida State University, The Graduate School, College of Arts and Sciences, Department of Mathematics, Tallahassee, FL 32306-4510. Offers applied and computational mathematics (MS, PhD); biomathematics (MS, PhD); financial mathematics (MS, PhD), including actuarial science (MS); pure mathematics (MS, PhD). *Program availability:* Part-time (4 women). *Students:* 114 full-time (31 women); includes 8 minority (1 Black or African American, non-Hispanic/Latino; 1 Asian, non-Hispanic/Latino; 2 Hispanic/Latino; 4 Two or more races, non-Hispanic/Latino), 74 international. 160 applicants, 61% accepted, 43 enrolled. In 2017, 18 master's, 24 doctorates awarded. Terminal master's awarded for partial completion of doctoral program. *Degree requirements:* For master's, comprehensive exam (for some programs), thesis optional; for doctorate, comprehensive exam, thesis/dissertation, candidacy exam (including written qualifying examinations which differ by degree concentration). *Entrance requirements:* For master's and doctorate, GRE General Test, minimum upper-division GPA of 3.0, 4-year bachelor's degree. Additional exam requirements/recommendations for international students: Required—TOEFL (minimum score 550 paper-based; 80 iBT), IELTS (minimum score 6.5). *Application deadline:* For fall admission, 12/15 priority date for domestic and international students; for spring admission, 4/30 for domestic and international students. Application fee: $30. Electronic applications accepted. *Financial support:* In 2017–18, 104 students received support, including 2 fellowships with full tuition reimbursements available (averaging $24,053 per year), 10 research assistantships with full tuition reimbursements available (averaging $20,053 per year), 83 teaching assistantships with full tuition reimbursements available (averaging $20,053 per year); career-related internships or fieldwork, institutionally sponsored loans, scholarships/grants, health care benefits, tuition waivers (full and partial), and unspecified assistantships also available. Financial award application deadline: 12/15; financial award applicants required to submit FAFSA. *Faculty research:* Low-dimensional and geometric topology, mathematical modeling in neuroscience, computational stochastics and Monte Carlo methods, mathematical physics, applied analysis. *Total annual research expenditures:* $1.3 million. *Unit head:* Dr. Philip L. Bowers, Chairperson, 850-644-2202, Fax: 850-644-4053, E-mail: bowers@math.fsu.edu. *Application contact:* Elizabeth Scott, Graduate Advisor and Admissions Coordinator, 850-644-2278, Fax: 850-644-4053, E-mail: emscott2@fsu.edu.
Website: http://www.math.fsu.edu/

Georgia State University, J. Mack Robinson College of Business, Department of Risk Management and Insurance, Program in Actuarial Science, Atlanta, GA 30302-3083. Offers MAS. *Program availability:* Part-time, evening/weekend. *Entrance requirements:* For master's, GRE or GMAT, transcripts from all institutions attended, resume, essays. Additional exam requirements/recommendations for international students: Required—TOEFL (minimum score 610 paper-based; 101 iBT), IELTS (minimum score 7). *Application deadline:* Applications are processed on a rolling basis. Application fee: $50. Electronic applications accepted. *Expenses:* Tuition, state resident: full-time $7020. Tuition, nonresident: full-time $22,518. *Required fees:* $2128. Tuition and fees vary according to degree level and program. *Financial support:* Research assistantships, scholarships/grants, tuition waivers, and unspecified assistantships available. *Faculty research:* Quantification and pricing of risk, risk modeling, financial methods in insurance, economic theory, enterprise risk management. *Unit head:* Dr. Shaun Wang, Professor/Chair/Director, 404-413-7500, Fax: 404-413-7499. *Application contact:* Toby McChesney, Assistant Dean for Graduate Recruiting and Student Services, 404-413-7167, Fax: 404-413-7162, E-mail: rcbgradadmissions@gsu.edu.
Website: http://rmi.robinson.gsu.edu/academic-programs/mas/

Governors State University, College of Arts and Sciences, Program in Mathematics, University Park, IL 60484. Offers actuarial science (MS). *Program availability:* Part-time. *Faculty:* 41 full-time (14 women), 45 part-time/adjunct (18 women). *Students:* 4 full-time (2 women), 18 part-time (12 women); includes 5 minority (4 Black or African American, non-Hispanic/Latino; 1 Hispanic/Latino). Average age 34. 10 applicants, 70% accepted, 2 enrolled. In 2017, 12 master's awarded. *Application deadline:* For fall admission, 4/1 for domestic students. Applications are processed on a rolling basis. Application fee: $50. Electronic applications accepted. *Expenses:* Tuition, state resident: full-time $8472; part-time $353 per credit hour. Tuition, nonresident: full-time $16,944; part-time $706 per credit hour. *Required fees:* $1824; $76 per credit hour. $38 per term. Tuition and fees vary according to course load, degree level and program. *Financial support:* Application deadline: 5/1; applicants required to submit FAFSA. *Unit head:* Steve Shih, Chair, Division of Science, Mathematics, and Technology, 708-534-5000 Ext. 4547, E-mail: sshih@govst.edu.

Lock Haven University of Pennsylvania, College of Natural, Behavioral and Health Sciences, Lock Haven, PA 17745-2390. Offers actuarial science (PSM); athletic training (MS); health promotion/education (MHS); healthcare management (MHS); physician assistant (MHS). Program also offered at the Clearfield, Coudersport, and Harrisburg campuses. *Accreditation:* ARC-PA. *Entrance requirements:* For master's, minimum undergraduate GPA of 3.0. Additional exam requirements/recommendations for international students: Required—TOEFL. Electronic applications accepted.

Maryville University of Saint Louis, College of Arts and Sciences, St. Louis, MO 63141-7299. Offers actuarial science (MS); data science (MS); strategic communication and leadership (MA). *Program availability:* Part-time. *Faculty:* 7 full-time (4 women), 10 part-time/adjunct (4 women). *Students:* 57 full-time (30 women), 25 part-time (17 women); includes 10 minority (1 Black or African American, non-Hispanic/Latino; 1 American Indian or Alaska Native, non-Hispanic/Latino; 7 Asian, non-Hispanic/Latino; 1 Two or more races, non-Hispanic/Latino), 45 international. Average age 28. In 2017, 26 master's awarded. *Entrance requirements:* For master's, strong mathematics background, 2 letters of recommendation, and personal statement (MS). Additional exam requirements/recommendations for international students: Required—TOEFL (minimum score 550 paper-based; 80 iBT). *Application deadline:* Applications are processed on a rolling basis. Electronic applications accepted. *Expenses:* $797 per credit hour tuition; $1,200 per semester full-time fee. *Financial support:* Application deadline: 4/1; applicants required to submit FAFSA. *Unit head:* Cherie Fister, Dean, 314-529-9563, Fax: 314-529-9965, E-mail: cfister@maryville.edu. *Application contact:* Shani Lenore-Jenkins, Associate Vice President of Enrollment, 314-529-9359, E-mail: slenore@maryville.edu.
Website: https://www.maryville.edu/as/

Middle Tennessee State University, College of Graduate Studies, College of Basic and Applied Sciences, Program in Professional Science, Murfreesboro, TN 37132. Offers actuarial sciences (MS); biostatistics (MS); biotechnology (MS); engineering management (MS); health care informatics (MS). *Program availability:* Part-time, evening/weekend, online learning. *Degree requirements:* For master's, comprehensive exam. *Entrance requirements:* For master's, GRE. Additional exam requirements/recommendations for international students: Required—TOEFL (minimum score 525 paper-based; 71 iBT) or IELTS (minimum score 6).

The Ohio State University, Graduate School, College of Arts and Sciences, Division of Natural and Mathematical Sciences, Department of Mathematics, Columbus, OH 43210.

Offers actuarial and quantitative risk management (MAQRM); computational sciences (MMS); mathematical biosciences (MMS); mathematics (PhD); mathematics for educators (MMS). *Faculty:* 64. *Students:* 142 full-time (22 women); includes 7 minority (all Asian, non-Hispanic/Latino), 75 international. Average age 25. In 2017, 33 master's, 11 doctorates awarded. *Degree requirements:* For master's, thesis optional; for doctorate, one foreign language, thesis/dissertation. *Entrance requirements:* For master's, GRE General Test; for doctorate, GRE General Test (recommended); GRE Subject Test (mathematics). Additional exam requirements/recommendations for international students: Required—TOEFL (minimum score 550 paper-based; 79 iBT), Michigan English Language Assessment Battery (minimum score 82); Recommended—IELTS (minimum score 7). *Application deadline:* For fall admission, 12/15 priority date for domestic and international students. Applications are processed on a rolling basis. Application fee: $60 ($70 for international students). Electronic applications accepted. *Financial support:* Fellowships, research assistantships, teaching assistantships, Federal Work-Study, institutionally sponsored loans, and unspecified assistantships available. Support available to part-time students. *Unit head:* Dr. Luis Casian, Chair and Professor, 614-292-7173, E-mail: casian.1@osu.edu. *Application contact:* Erin Anthony, Graduate Studies Coordinator, 614-292-6274, Fax: 614-292-1479, E-mail: grad-info@math.osu.edu. Website: http://www.math.osu.edu/

Oregon State University, College of Science, Program in Mathematics, Corvallis, OR 97331. Offers differential geometry (MA, MS, PhD); financial and actuarial mathematics (MA, MS, PhD); mathematical biology (MA, MS, PhD); mathematics education (MS, PhD); number theory (MA, MS, PhD); numerical analysis (MA, MS, PhD); probability (MA). Terminal master's awarded for partial completion of doctoral program. *Degree requirements:* For master's, thesis or alternative; for doctorate, thesis/dissertation, qualifying exams. *Entrance requirements:* For master's and doctorate, GRE. Additional exam requirements/recommendations for international students: Required—TOEFL (minimum score 100 iBT). *Application deadline:* For fall admission, 1/15 for domestic and international students. Application fee: $75 ($85 for international students). Electronic applications accepted. *Financial support:* Application deadline: 1/15. *Unit head:* Malgorzata Peszynska, Graduate Chair, 541-737-9847, E-mail: mpesz@math.oregonstate.edu. *Application contact:* Mathematics Advisor, 541-737-4686, E-mail: gradinfo@math.oregonstate.edu. Website: http://www.math.oregonstate.edu/

Roosevelt University, Graduate Division, College of Arts and Sciences, Department of Math, Actuarial Science, and Economics, Chicago, IL 60605. Offers actuarial science (MS); mathematics (MS), including mathematical sciences. *Students:* 8 full-time (1 woman), 5 part-time (2 women); includes 4 minority (1 Black or African American, non-Hispanic/Latino; 3 Hispanic/Latino), 3 international. Average age 30. 24 applicants, 83% accepted, 2 enrolled. In 2017, 8 master's awarded. *Application deadline:* Applications are processed on a rolling basis. Application fee: $40. Electronic applications accepted. *Financial support:* Career-related internships or fieldwork, scholarships/grants, and unspecified assistantships available. *Application contact:* Sivling Lam, Graduate Admission Counselor, 312-281-3252, E-mail: slam02@roosevelt.edu.

St. John's University, The Peter J. Tobin College of Business, School of Risk Management, Insurance and Actuarial Science, Queens, NY 11439. Offers actuarial science (MS); business administration (MBA), including risk management and insurance; enterprise risk management (MBA, MS), including enterprise risk management (MS); risk management and insurance (MS). *Faculty:* 11 full-time (2 women), 7 part-time/adjunct (1 woman). *Students:* 51 full-time (24 women), 28 part-time (13 women); includes 15 minority (7 Black or African American, non-Hispanic/Latino; 4 Asian, non-Hispanic/Latino; 3 Hispanic/Latino; 1 Two or more races, non-Hispanic/Latino), 40 international. Average age 27. 58 applicants, 78% accepted, 27 enrolled. In 2017, 32 master's awarded. *Entrance requirements:* For master's, GMAT or GRE, 2 letters of recommendation, essay, resume, unofficial transcripts. Additional exam requirements/recommendations for international students: Required—TOEFL (minimum score 80 iBT), IELTS (minimum score 6.5). *Application deadline:* For fall admission, 11/1 for domestic and international students; for winter admission, 3/1 for domestic and international students; for spring admission, 6/1 for domestic and international students. Applications are processed on a rolling basis. Application fee: $70. Electronic applications accepted. *Expenses:* $22,410 per year. *Financial support:* Research assistantships, teaching assistantships, scholarships/grants, and unspecified assistantships available. Support available to part-time students. Financial award application deadline: 2/1; financial award applicants required to submit FAFSA. *Faculty research:* Insurance company operations and financial analysis, enterprise risk management, risk theory and modeling, credibility theory and actuarial price modeling, international insurance. *Unit head:* Dr. Mark J. Browne, Chair, 212-277-5175, E-mail: brownem1@stjohns.edu. *Application contact:* Amber Steiger, Associate Director of Enrollment Management, 718-990-1345, E-mail: steigera@stjohns.edu. Website: https://www.stjohns.edu/academics/schools-and-colleges/peter-j-tobin-college-business/school-risk-management-insurance-and-actuarial-science

Simon Fraser University, Office of Graduate Studies and Postdoctoral Fellows, Faculty of Science, Department of Statistics and Actuarial Science, Burnaby, BC V5A 1S6, Canada. Offers actuarial science (M Sc); statistics (M Sc, PhD). *Degree requirements:* For master's, participation in consulting, project; for doctorate, comprehensive exam, thesis/dissertation. *Entrance requirements:* For master's, minimum GPA of 3.0 (on scale of 4.33) or 3.33 based on last 60 credits of undergraduate courses; for doctorate, minimum GPA of 3.5 (on scale of 4.33). Additional exam requirements/recommendations for international students: Recommended—TOEFL (minimum score 580 paper-based; 93 iBT), IELTS (minimum score 7), TWE (minimum score 5). Electronic applications accepted. *Faculty research:* Biostatistics, experimental design, envirometrics, statistical computing, statistical theory.

Temple University, Fox School of Business, Specialized Master's Programs, Philadelphia, PA 19122-6096. Offers accountancy (MS); actuarial science (MS); finance (MS); financial engineering (MS); human resource management (MS); innovation management and entrepreneurship (MS); marketing (MS); statistics (MS). MS in innovation management and entrepreneurship delivered jointly with College of Engineering. *Accreditation:* AACSB. *Program availability:* Part-time. *Entrance requirements:* For master's, GRE General Test or GMAT, minimum undergraduate GPA of 3.0. Additional exam requirements/recommendations for international students: Required—TOEFL (minimum score 600 paper-based; 100 iBT), IELTS (minimum score 7.5). *Expenses:* Tuition, state resident: full-time $16,164; part-time $898 per credit hour. Tuition, nonresident: full-time $22,158; part-time $1231 per credit hour. *Required fees:* $890; $445 per semester. Full-time tuition and fees vary according to course load, degree level, campus/location and program.

Université du Québec à Montréal, Graduate Programs, Program in Actuarial Sciences, Montréal, QC H3C 3P8, Canada. Offers Diploma. *Program availability:* Part-time. *Entrance requirements:* For degree, appropriate bachelor's degree or equivalent and proficiency in French.

University of Illinois at Urbana–Champaign, Graduate College, College of Liberal Arts and Sciences, Department of Mathematics, Champaign, IL 61820. Offers applied mathematics (MS); applied mathematics: actuarial science (MS); mathematics (MS, PhD); teaching of mathematics (MS).

The University of Iowa, Graduate College, College of Liberal Arts and Sciences, Department of Statistics and Actuarial Science, Iowa City, IA 52242-1316. Offers actuarial science (MS); statistics (MS, PhD). *Degree requirements:* For master's, thesis optional, exam; for doctorate, comprehensive exam, thesis/dissertation. *Entrance requirements:* For master's and doctorate, GRE General Test, minimum GPA of 3.0. Additional exam requirements/recommendations for international students: Required—TOEFL (minimum score 550 paper-based; 81 iBT). Electronic applications accepted.

The University of Manchester, School of Mathematics, Manchester, United Kingdom. Offers actuarial science (PhD); applied mathematics (M Phil, PhD); applied numerical computing (M Phil, PhD); financial mathematics (M Phil, PhD); mathematical logic (M Phil); probability (M Phil, PhD); pure mathematics (M Phil, PhD); statistics (M Phil, PhD).

University of Nebraska–Lincoln, Graduate College, College of Business Administration, Interdepartmental Area of Actuarial Science, Lincoln, NE 68588. Offers MS. *Entrance requirements:* For master's, GRE. Additional exam requirements/recommendations for international students: Required—TOEFL (minimum score 550 paper-based). Electronic applications accepted. *Faculty research:* Risk theory, pensions, actuarial finance, decision theory, stochastic calculus.

The University of Texas at Austin, Graduate School, College of Natural Sciences, Department of Mathematics, Austin, TX 78712-1111. Offers MA, PhD. *Entrance requirements:* For master's and doctorate, GRE General Test. Electronic applications accepted.

The University of Texas at Dallas, School of Natural Sciences and Mathematics, Department of Mathematical Sciences, Richardson, TX 75080. Offers actuarial science (MS); mathematics (MS, PhD), including applied mathematics, data science (MS); engineering mathematics (MS), mathematics (MS); statistics (MS, PhD). *Program availability:* Part-time, evening/weekend. *Faculty:* 30 full-time (6 women), 3 part-time/adjunct (0 women). *Students:* 162 full-time (52 women), 41 part-time (16 women); includes 34 minority (7 Black or African American, non-Hispanic/Latino; 19 Asian, non-Hispanic/Latino; 6 Hispanic/Latino; 2 Two or more races, non-Hispanic/Latino), 123 international. Average age 29. 295 applicants, 36% accepted, 66 enrolled. In 2017, 34 master's, 9 doctorates awarded. *Degree requirements:* For master's, thesis optional; for doctorate, thesis/dissertation. *Entrance requirements:* For master's, GRE General Test, minimum GPA of 3.0 in upper-level course work in field; for doctorate, GRE General Test, minimum GPA of 3.5 in upper-level course work in field. Additional exam requirements/recommendations for international students: Required—TOEFL (minimum score 550 paper-based). *Application deadline:* For fall admission, 7/15 for domestic students, 5/1 priority date for international students; for spring admission, 11/15 for domestic students, 9/1 priority date for international students. Applications are processed on a rolling basis. Application fee: $50 ($100 for international students). Electronic applications accepted. *Expenses:* Tuition, state resident: full-time $12,916; part-time $718 per credit hour. Tuition, nonresident: full-time $25,252; part-time $1403 per credit hour. *Financial support:* In 2017–18, 116 students received support, including 9 research assistantships (averaging $26,200 per year), 87 teaching assistantships with partial tuition reimbursements available (averaging $17,403 per year); fellowships, career-related internships or fieldwork, Federal Work-Study, institutionally sponsored loans, scholarships/grants, and unspecified assistantships also available. Support available to part-time students. Financial award application deadline: 4/30; financial award applicants required to submit FAFSA. *Faculty research:* Sequential analysis, applications in semiconductor manufacturing, medical image analysis, computational anatomy, information theory, probability theory. *Unit head:* Dr. Vladimir Dragovic, Department Head, 972-883-6402, Fax: 972-883-6622, E-mail: mathdepthead@utdallas.edu. *Application contact:* Evangelina Bustamante, Graduate Student Coordinator, 972-883-2161, Fax: 972-883-6622, E-mail: utdmath@utdallas.edu. Website: http://www.utdallas.edu/math

University of Waterloo, Graduate Studies, Faculty of Mathematics, Department of Statistics and Actuarial Science, Waterloo, ON N2L 3G1, Canada. Offers actuarial science (M Math, MAS, PhD); biostatistics (PhD); statistics (M Math, PhD); statistics-biostatistics (M Math); statistics-computing (M Math); statistics-finance (M Math). *Degree requirements:* For master's, research paper or thesis; for doctorate, comprehensive exam, thesis/dissertation. *Entrance requirements:* For master's, honors degree in field, minimum B+ average; for doctorate, master's degree, minimum B+ average. Additional exam requirements/recommendations for international students: Required—TOEFL, IELTS, PTE. Electronic applications accepted. *Faculty research:* Data analysis, risk theory, inference, stochastic processes, quantitative finance.

University of Wisconsin–Madison, Graduate School, Wisconsin School of Business, Doctoral Program in Actuarial Science, Risk Management and Insurance, Madison, WI 53706-1380. Offers PhD. *Degree requirements:* For doctorate, comprehensive exam, thesis/dissertation. *Entrance requirements:* For doctorate, GMAT or GRE General Test. Additional exam requirements/recommendations for international students: Recommended—TOEFL (minimum score 623 paper-based; 106 iBT), IELTS (minimum score 7.5), TSE (minimum score 73). Electronic applications accepted. *Expenses:* Contact institution. *Faculty research:* Actuarial science, regression and business forecasting, panel data, economics of insurance markets, insurance regulation, public economics, behavioral economics, Bayesian methodology related to health insurance, tort reform and government programs, joint and several liability, superfund, predictive modeling, asymmetric information in insurance, psychology and economics, applied microeconomics, insurance markets, risk and decision making.

University of Wisconsin–Milwaukee, Graduate School, College of Letters and Science, Department of Mathematical Sciences, Milwaukee, WI 53201-0413. Offers mathematics (MS, PhD), including actuarial science, algebra (PhD), applied and computational mathematics (PhD), atmospheric science, foundations of advanced studies (MS), industrial mathematics, probability and statistics (PhD), standard mathematics (MS), statistics (MS), topology (PhD). *Students:* 70 full-time (15 women), 10 part-time (3 women); includes 2 minority (1 Black or African American, non-Hispanic/Latino; 1 Asian, non-Hispanic/Latino), 38 international. Average age 29. 154 applicants, 31% accepted, 25 enrolled. In 2017, 23 master's, 10 doctorates awarded. *Degree requirements:* For master's, comprehensive exam, thesis optional; for doctorate, 2 foreign languages, thesis/dissertation. *Entrance requirements:* Additional exam requirements/recommendations for international students: Required—TOEFL (minimum score 550 paper-based; 79 iBT), IELTS (minimum score 6.5). *Application deadline:* For fall admission, 1/1 priority date for domestic students; for spring admission, 9/1 for domestic students. Application fee: $56 ($96 for international students). Electronic applications accepted. *Financial support:* Fellowships, research assistantships, teaching assistantships, career-related internships or fieldwork, health care benefits, and unspecified assistantships available. Support available to part-time students. Financial award application deadline: 4/15; financial award applicants required to submit FAFSA. *Faculty research:* Algebra, applied mathematics, atmospheric science, probability and statistics, topology. *Unit head:* Richard Stockbridge, Department Chair, 414-229-4568, E-mail: stockbri@uwm.edu. *Application contact:* General Information Contact, 414-229-4982, Fax: 414-229-6967, E-mail: gradschool@uwm.edu. Website: http://www.uwm.edu/dept/math/

Insurance

California State University, Fullerton, Graduate Studies, College of Business and Economics, Program in Business Administration, Fullerton, CA 92831-3599. Offers business administration (MBA); business analytics (MBA); international business (MBA); organizational leadership (MBA); risk management and insurance (MBA). *Accreditation:* AACSB. *Program availability:* Part-time. *Faculty:* 12 full-time (5 women), 1 part-time/adjunct (0 women). *Students:* 64 full-time (35 women), 103 part-time (46 women); includes 81 minority (40 Asian, non-Hispanic/Latino; 36 Hispanic/Latino; 5 Two or more races, non-Hispanic/Latino), 36 international. Average age 29. 254 applicants, 47% accepted, 62 enrolled. *Entrance requirements:* For master's, GMAT. Application fee: $55. *Financial support:* Career-related internships or fieldwork, Federal Work-Study, institutionally sponsored loans, and scholarships/grants available. Support available to part-time students. Financial award application deadline: 3/1; financial award applicants required to submit FAFSA. *Unit head:* Shaun Pichler, Director, 657-278-7373, E-mail: spichler@fullerton.edu. *Application contact:* Admissions/Applications, 657-278-2371.

Florida State University, The Graduate School, College of Business, Tallahassee, FL 32306-1110. Offers accounting (M Acc), including assurance and advisory services, generalist, taxation; business administration (MBA, PhD), including accounting (PhD), finance (PhD), management information systems (PhD), marketing (PhD), organizational behavior and human resources (PhD), risk management and insurance (PhD), strategy (PhD); finance (MS); management information systems (MS); risk management and insurance (MS); JD/MBA; MSW/MBA. *Accreditation:* AACSB. *Program availability:* Part-time, 100% online. *Faculty:* 93 full-time (23 women), 2 part-time/adjunct (1 woman). *Students:* 229 full-time (96 women), 423 part-time (154 women); includes 159 minority (44 Black or African American, non-Hispanic/Latino; 24 Asian, non-Hispanic/Latino; 75 Hispanic/Latino; 1 Native Hawaiian or other Pacific Islander, non-Hispanic/Latino; 15 Two or more races, non-Hispanic/Latino), 48 international. Average age 31. 300 applicants, 61% accepted, 133 enrolled. In 2017, 268 master's, 9 doctorates awarded. Terminal master's awarded for partial completion of doctoral program. *Degree requirements:* For doctorate, comprehensive exam, thesis/dissertation. *Entrance requirements:* For master's, GMAT, GRE (for all except MS in finance), work experience (MBA, MS); minimum GPA of 3.0, letters of recommendation; for doctorate, GMAT, GRE (for marketing, organizational behavior, risk management and insurance, management information systems, and human resources only), minimum graduate GPA of 3.5, letters of recommendation. Additional exam requirements/recommendations for international students: Required—TOEFL (minimum score 600 paper-based; 85 iBT); Recommended—IELTS (minimum score 6). *Application deadline:* For fall admission, 6/1 for domestic and international students; for spring admission, 10/1 for domestic and international students; for summer admission, 3/1 for domestic and international students. Applications are processed on a rolling basis. Application fee: $30. Electronic applications accepted. *Expenses:* Contact institution. *Financial support:* In 2017–18, 146 students received support, including 26 fellowships (averaging $1,500 per year), 77 research assistantships with full tuition reimbursements available (averaging $20,000 per year), 43 teaching assistantships with full tuition reimbursements available (averaging $20,000 per year); career-related internships or fieldwork, scholarships/grants, health care benefits, tuition waivers (full and partial), and unspecified assistantships also available. Support available to part-time students. Financial award application deadline: 1/1; financial award applicants required to submit FAFSA. *Faculty research:* Business strategy, marketing, finance, accounting, business analytics. *Total annual research expenditures:* $1.4 million. *Unit head:* Dr. Michael Hartline, Dean, 850-644-4405, Fax: 850-644-0915, E-mail: mhartline@business.fsu.edu. *Application contact:* Jennifer Clark, Director, 850-644-6458, E-mail: gradprograms@business.fsu.edu.
Website: http://business.fsu.edu/

Georgia State University, J. Mack Robinson College of Business, Department of Risk Management and Insurance, Program in Risk Management and Insurance, Atlanta, GA 30302-3083. Offers enterprise risk management (MBA, Certificate); financial risk management (MBA); mathematical risk management (MS); risk and insurance (MS); risk management and insurance (MBA, PhD); MAS/MRM. *Program availability:* Part-time, evening/weekend. *Entrance requirements:* For master's, GRE or GMAT, transcripts from all institutions attended, resume, essays. Additional exam requirements/recommendations for international students: Required—TOEFL (minimum score 610 paper-based; 101 iBT), IELTS (minimum score 7). *Application deadline:* Applications are processed on a rolling basis. Application fee: $50. Electronic applications accepted. *Expenses:* Tuition, state resident: full-time $7020. Tuition, nonresident: full-time $22,518. *Required fees:* $2128. Tuition and fees vary according to degree level and program. *Financial support:* Research assistantships, scholarships/grants, tuition waivers, and unspecified assistantships available. *Faculty research:* Insurance economics, structure and performance of insurance markets, regulation and policy in insurance markets, asset pricing theory, financial econometrics. *Unit head:* Dr. Martin Grace, Professor of Risk Management and Legal Studies/Chair of the Department of Risk Management and Insurance, 404-413-7500, Fax: 404-413-7499. *Application contact:* Toby McChesney, Graduate Recruiting Contact, 404-413-7167, Fax: 404-413-7162, E-mail: rcbgradadmissions@gsu.edu.
Website: http://rmi.robinson.gsu.edu/academic-programs/ms-rmi/

Olivet College, Master of Business Administration in Insurance Program, Olivet, MI 49076-9701. Offers MBA. *Accreditation:* TEAC. *Program availability:* Part-time, online only, 100% online, blended/hybrid learning. *Degree requirements:* For master's, thesis optional. *Entrance requirements:* For master's, GMAT or CPCU designation, professional resume, official transcript, two letters of recommendation, 2 years of professional experience in field of insurance or risk management after earning undergraduate degree, minimum undergraduate GPA of 3.0. Electronic applications accepted. *Expenses:* Contact institution.

Pontificia Universidad Catolica Madre y Maestra, Graduate School, Faculty of Social and Administrative Sciences, Santiago, Dominican Republic. Offers business administration (MBA), including business development, finance, international business, management skills (M Mgmt, MBA), marketing, operations, strategic cost management, strategy, tourist destination planning and management; law (LL M), including civil law, corporate business law, criminal law, international relations, real estate law; management (M Mgmt), including higher financial management, insurance program administration, management skills (M Mgmt, MBA); psychology (MA), including clinical child and adolescent psychology, forensic psychology; strategic human resources (EMBA).

St. John's University, The Peter J. Tobin College of Business, School of Risk Management, Insurance and Actuarial Science, Queens, NY 11439. Offers actuarial science (MS); business administration (MBA), including risk management and insurance; enterprise risk management (MBA, MS), including enterprise risk management (MS); risk management and insurance (MS). *Faculty:* 11 full-time (2

women), 7 part-time/adjunct (1 woman). *Students:* 51 full-time (24 women), 28 part-time (13 women); includes 15 minority (7 Black or African American, non-Hispanic/Latino; 4 Asian, non-Hispanic/Latino; 3 Hispanic/Latino; 1 Two or more races, non-Hispanic/Latino), 40 international. Average age 27. 58 applicants, 78% accepted, 27 enrolled. In 2017, 32 master's awarded. *Entrance requirements:* For master's, GMAT or GRE, 2 letters of recommendation, essay, resume, unofficial transcripts. Additional exam requirements/recommendations for international students: Required—TOEFL (minimum score 80 iBT), IELTS (minimum score 6.5). *Application deadline:* For fall admission, 11/1 for domestic and international students; for winter admission, 3/1 for domestic and international students; for spring admission, 6/1 for domestic and international students. Applications are processed on a rolling basis. Application fee: $70. Electronic applications accepted. *Expenses:* $22,410 per year. *Financial support:* Research assistantships, teaching assistantships, scholarships/grants, and unspecified assistantships available. Support available to part-time students. Financial award application deadline: 2/1; financial award applicants required to submit FAFSA. *Faculty research:* Insurance company operations and financial analysis, enterprise risk management, risk theory and modeling, credibility theory and actuarial price modeling, international insurance. *Unit head:* Dr. Mark J. Browne, Chair, 212-277-5175, E-mail: brownem1@stjohns.edu. *Application contact:* Amber Steiger, Associate Director of Enrollment Management, 718-990-1345, E-mail: steigera@stjohns.edu.
Website: https://www.stjohns.edu/academics/schools-and-colleges/peter-j-tobin-college-business/school-risk-management-insurance-and-actuarial-science

Temple University, Fox School of Business, Doctoral Programs in Business, Philadelphia, PA 19122-6096. Offers accounting (PhD); entrepreneurship (PhD); finance (PhD); international business (PhD); management information systems (PhD); marketing (PhD); risk management and insurance (PhD); statistics (PhD); strategic management (PhD); tourism and sport (PhD). *Accreditation:* AACSB. *Degree requirements:* For doctorate, thesis/dissertation. *Entrance requirements:* For doctorate, GRE General Test, GMAT, minimum GPA of 3.0, master's degree. Additional exam requirements/recommendations for international students: Required—TOEFL (minimum score 600 paper-based; 100 iBT), IELTS (minimum score 7.5). Electronic applications accepted. *Expenses:* Tuition, state resident: full-time $16,164; part-time $898 per credit hour. Tuition, nonresident: full-time $22,158; part-time $1231 per credit hour. *Required fees:* $890; $445 per semester. Full-time tuition and fees vary according to course load, degree level, campus/location and program.

University of Colorado Denver, Business School, Program in Finance, Denver, CO 80217. Offers economics (MS); finance (MS); financial analysis and management (MS); financial and commodities risk management (MS); risk management and insurance (MS); MS/MA; MS/MBA. *Program availability:* Part-time, evening/weekend. *Degree requirements:* For master's, 30 semester hours (18 of required core courses, 9 of finance electives, and 3 of free elective). *Entrance requirements:* For master's, GMAT, essay, resume, two letters of recommendation; financial statements (for international students). Additional exam requirements/recommendations for international students: Required—TOEFL (minimum score 537 paper-based; 75 iBT); Recommended—IELTS (minimum score 6.5). Electronic applications accepted. *Expenses:* Contact institution. *Faculty research:* Corporate governance, debt maturity policies, regulation and financial markets, option management strategies.

University of Florida, Graduate School, Warrington College of Business Administration, Hough Graduate School of Business, Department of Finance, Insurance and Real Estate, Gainesville, FL 32611. Offers entrepreneurship (MS); finance (MS, PhD); financial services (Certificate); insurance (PhD); quantitative finance (PhD); real estate (MS); real estate and urban analysis (PhD); JD/MBA; JD/MS. Terminal master's awarded for partial completion of doctoral program. *Degree requirements:* For master's, comprehensive exam, thesis; for doctorate, comprehensive exam, thesis/dissertation. *Entrance requirements:* For master's, GMAT (minimum score of 465) or GRE General Test, minimum GPA of 3.0 for last 60 hours of undergraduate degree, work experience (preferred); for doctorate, GMAT (minimum score of 465) or GRE General Test, minimum GPA of 3.0. Additional exam requirements/recommendations for international students: Required—TOEFL (minimum score 550 paper-based; 80 iBT), IELTS (minimum score 6). Electronic applications accepted. *Faculty research:* Banking, empirical corporate finance, hedge funds.

University of Pennsylvania, Wharton School, Insurance and Risk Management Department, Philadelphia, PA 19104. Offers MBA, PhD. *Degree requirements:* For doctorate, thesis/dissertation. *Entrance requirements:* For master's, GMAT; for doctorate, GMAT or GRE. *Faculty research:* Fair rate of return in insurance economics of pension plans, insurance regulation, malpractice insurance, actuarial science, genetic testing and life insurance.

University of Wisconsin–Madison, Graduate School, Wisconsin School of Business, Doctoral Program in Actuarial Science, Risk Management and Insurance, Madison, WI 53706-1380. Offers PhD. *Degree requirements:* For doctorate, comprehensive exam, thesis/dissertation. *Entrance requirements:* For doctorate, GMAT or GRE General Test. Additional exam requirements/recommendations for international students: Recommended—TOEFL (minimum score 623 paper-based; 106 iBT), IELTS (minimum score 7.5), TSE (minimum score 73). Electronic applications accepted. *Expenses:* Contact institution. *Faculty research:* Actuarial science, regression and business forecasting, panel data, economics of insurance markets, insurance regulation, public economics, behavioral economics, Bayesian methodology related to health insurance, tort reform and government programs, joint and several liability, superfund, predictive modeling, asymmetric information in insurance, psychology and economics, applied microeconomics, insurance markets, risk and decision making.

University of Wisconsin–Madison, Graduate School, Wisconsin School of Business, Wisconsin Full-Time MBA Program, Madison, WI 53706. Offers applied security analysis (MBA); arts administration (MBA); brand and product management (MBA); corporate finance and investment banking (MBA); marketing research (MBA); operations and technology management (MBA); real estate (MBA); risk management and insurance (MBA); strategic human resource management (MBA); supply chain management (MBA). *Faculty:* 130 full-time (35 women), 42 part-time/adjunct (13 women). *Students:* 203 full-time (72 women); includes 34 minority (8 Black or African American, non-Hispanic/Latino; 10 Asian, non-Hispanic/Latino; 12 Hispanic/Latino; 4 Two or more races, non-Hispanic/Latino), 41 international. Average age 28. 556 applicants, 30% accepted, 104 enrolled. In 2017, 97 master's awarded. *Entrance requirements:* For master's, GMAT or GRE, bachelor's or equivalent degree, 2 years of work experience, essay, letter of recommendation, resume. Additional exam requirements/recommendations for international students: Required—TOEFL (minimum score 100 iBT), IELTS (minimum score 7.5). *Application deadline:* For fall admission, 11/2 for domestic and international students; for winter admission, 1/11 for domestic and

international students; for spring admission, 3/1 for domestic and international students; for summer admission, 4/12 for domestic and international students. Applications are processed on a rolling basis. Application fee: $75 ($81 for international students). Electronic applications accepted. *Expenses:* $9,356 per semester resident, $18,288 non-resident. *Financial support:* In 2017–18, 183 students received support, including 14 fellowships with full tuition reimbursements available (averaging $25,420 per year), 7 research assistantships with full tuition reimbursements available (averaging $13,375 per year), 53 teaching assistantships with full tuition reimbursements available (averaging $13,375 per year); scholarships/grants, health care benefits, tuition waivers (full), and unspecified assistantships also available. Financial award application deadline: 4/11. *Faculty research:* Forms of competition and outcomes in dual distribution systems; explaining the accuracy of revised forecasts; supply chain planning for random demand surges; advanced demand information in a multi-product system; the effects of presentation salience and measurement subjectivity on nonprofessional investors' fair value judgments. *Unit head:* Dr. Don Hausch, Associate Dean, Full-time MBA Program, 608-262-9731, E-mail: don.hausch@wisc.edu. *Application contact:* Betsy Kacizak, Director of Admissions and Recruiting, Full-time MBA Program, 608-262-4000, E-mail: betsy.kacizak@wisc.edu.
Website: https://wsb.wisc.edu/

Western Michigan University Thomas M. Cooley Law School, Graduate Programs, Lansing, MI 48901-3038. Offers administrative law (public law) (JD); business transactions (JD); Canadian law practice (JD); corporate law and finance (LL M); environmental law (public law) (JD); general practice (JD), including solo and small firm; general studies (LL M); homeland and national security law (LL M); insurance law (LL M); intellectual property (JD); intellectual property law (LL M); international law (JD); litigation (JD); taxation (LL M); U.S. legal studies for foreign attorneys (LL M); JD/LL M; JD/MBA; JD/MHA; JD/MPA; JD/MSW. *Program availability:* Part-time, evening/weekend, 100% online, blended/hybrid learning. *Degree requirements:* For master's, thesis (for some programs); for doctorate, minimum of 3 credits of clinical experience. *Entrance requirements:* For master's, JD or LL B; for doctorate, LSAT. Additional exam requirements/recommendations for international students: Required—TOEFL (for U.S. legal studies for foreign attorneys LL M program); Recommended—TOEFL. Electronic applications accepted. *Expenses:* Contact institution. *Faculty research:* Wrongful convictions, civil rights, environmental law, litigation techniques, data mining, intellectual property, practical and skills-based legal education.

Risk Management

Boston University, Metropolitan College, Department of Administrative Sciences, Boston, MA 02215. Offers applied business analytics (MS); economic development and tourism management (MSAS); enterprise risk management (MS); financial management (MS); global marketing management (MS); innovation and technology (MSAS); insurance management (MS); project management (MS); supply chain management (MS). *Accreditation:* AACSB. *Program availability:* Part-time, evening/weekend, 100% online, blended/hybrid learning. *Faculty:* 21 full-time (5 women), 34 part-time/adjunct (5 women). *Students:* 297 full-time (156 women), 597 part-time (298 women); includes 183 minority (58 Black or African American, non-Hispanic/Latino; 2 American Indian or Alaska Native, non-Hispanic/Latino; 56 Asian, non-Hispanic/Latino; 51 Hispanic/Latino; 2 Native Hawaiian or other Pacific Islander, non-Hispanic/Latino; 14 Two or more races, non-Hispanic/Latino), 391 international. Average age 30. 963 applicants, 4% accepted, 209 enrolled. In 2017, 372 master's awarded. *Degree requirements:* For master's, thesis optional. *Entrance requirements:* For master's, 1 year of work experience, minimum GPA of 3.0. Additional exam requirements/recommendations for international students: Required—TOEFL (minimum score 84 iBT). *Application deadline:* Applications are processed on a rolling basis. Application fee: $85. Electronic applications accepted. *Expenses:* Contact institution. *Financial support:* In 2017–18, 15 students received support, including 18 research assistantships (averaging $8,400 per year), 12 teaching assistantships (averaging $2,700 per year); career-related internships or fieldwork, Federal Work-Study, and unspecified assistantships also available. Financial award applicants required to submit FAFSA. *Faculty research:* International business, innovative process. *Unit head:* Dr. John Sullivan, Chair, 617-353-3016, E-mail: adminsc@bu.edu. *Application contact:* Fiona Niven, Administrative Sciences Department, 617-353-3016, E-mail: adminsc@bu.edu.
Website: http://www.bu.edu/met/academic-community/departments/administrative-sciences/

Brandeis University, International Business School (IBS), Master of Science in Finance Program, Waltham, MA 02454-9110. Offers asset management (MSF); corporate finance (MSF); risk management (MSF). *Faculty:* 40 full-time (16 women), 31 part-time/adjunct (7 women). *Students:* 115 full-time (66 women), 71 part-time (51 women); includes 1 minority (Asian, non-Hispanic/Latino), 180 international. Average age 22. 876 applicants, 36% accepted, 109 enrolled. In 2017, 33 master's awarded. *Entrance requirements:* For master's, GMAT or GRE. Additional exam requirements/recommendations for international students: Required—TOEFL (minimum score 600 paper-based; 100 iBT), IELTS (minimum score 7), PTE (minimum score 68). *Application deadline:* For fall admission, 11/1 priority date for domestic and international students; for winter admission, 1/15 priority date for domestic and international students; for spring admission, 3/15 priority date for domestic and international students; for summer admission, 4/15 for domestic and international students. Application fee: $100. Electronic applications accepted. *Expenses:* Contact institution. *Financial support:* In 2017–18, 75 students received support. Institutionally sponsored loans and scholarships (averaging $11,479 annually) available. Financial award application deadline: 4/15; financial award applicants required to submit FAFSA. *Faculty research:* Asset management, municipal finance, corporate finance, venture capital, international trade. *Unit head:* Peter Petri, Interim Dean, 781-736-2256. *Application contact:* Kelly Sugrue, Assistant Dean of Admissions, 781-736-2252, Fax: 781-736-2263, E-mail: admission@lemberg.brandeis.edu.
Website: https://www.brandeis.edu/global/msf

California State University, Fullerton, Graduate Studies, College of Business and Economics, Program in Business Administration, Fullerton, CA 92831-3599. Offers business administration (MBA); business analytics (MBA); international business (MBA); organizational leadership (MBA); risk management and insurance (MBA). *Accreditation:* AACSB. *Program availability:* Part-time. *Faculty:* 12 full-time (5 women), 1 part-time/adjunct (0 women). *Students:* 64 full-time (35 women), 103 part-time (46 women); includes 81 minority (40 Asian, non-Hispanic/Latino; 36 Hispanic/Latino; 5 Two or more races, non-Hispanic/Latino), 36 international. Average age 29. 254 applicants, 47% accepted, 62 enrolled. *Entrance requirements:* For master's, GMAT. Application fee: $55. *Financial support:* Career-related internships or fieldwork, Federal Work-Study, institutionally sponsored loans, and scholarships/grants available. Support available to part-time students. Financial award application deadline: 3/1; financial award applicants required to submit FAFSA. *Unit head:* Shaun Pichler, Director, 657-278-7373, E-mail: spichler@fullerton.edu. *Application contact:* Admissions/Applications, 657-278-2371.

Concordia University Wisconsin, Graduate Programs, School of Business Administration, MBA Program, Mequon, WI 53097-2402. Offers finance (MBA); health care administration (MBA); human resource management (MBA); international business (MBA); international business-bilingual English/Chinese (MBA); management (MBA); management information systems (MBA); managerial communications (MBA); marketing (MBA); public administration (MBA); risk management (MBA). *Program availability:* Online learning. *Degree requirements:* For master's, comprehensive exam, thesis or alternative. *Entrance requirements:* Additional exam requirements/recommendations for international students: Required—TOEFL. *Expenses:* Contact institution.

DePaul University, Kellstadt Graduate School of Business, Chicago, IL 60604. Offers accountancy (MBA, MSA); applied economics (MBA); audit and advisory services (MS); business administration (DBA); business analytics (MS); business strategy and decision-making (MBA); computational finance (MS); economics and policy analysis (MS); enterprise risk management (MS); entrepreneurship (MBA, MS); finance (MBA, MS); general business (MBA); hospitality leadership (MBA); hospitality leadership and operational performance (MS); human resources (MS); international business (MBA); management (MBA, MS); management information systems (MBA); marketing (MBA, MS); marketing analysis (MS); marketing strategy and planning (MBA); real estate (MS); real estate finance and investment (MBA); strategy, execution and valuation (MBA); supply chain management (MS); sustainable management (MS); taxation (MS); JD/MBA. *Accreditation:* AACSB. *Program availability:* Part-time, evening/weekend, online learning. *Entrance requirements:* For master's, GMAT/GRE, 2 letters of recommendation, resume, essay, official transcripts. Additional exam requirements/recommendations for international students: Required—TOEFL (minimum score 550 paper-based; 80 iBT). *Application deadline:* For fall admission, 7/1 for domestic students, 6/1 for international students; for winter admission, 10/1 for domestic students, 9/1 for international students; for spring admission, 2/1 for domestic students, 1/1 for international students. Applications are processed on a rolling basis. Application fee: $60. Electronic applications accepted. *Expenses:* Contact institution. *Financial support:* Application deadline: 4/1; applicants required to submit FAFSA. *Unit head:* Christa Hinton, Assistant Dean and Director, 312-362-8810, Fax: 312-362-6677, E-mail: chinton@depaul.edu. *Application contact:* Garry Cooke, Director of Recruitment and Admissions, 312-362-8810, Fax: 312-362-6677, E-mail: kgsb@depaul.edu.
Website: http://kellstadt.depaul.edu

Florida State University, The Graduate School, College of Business, Tallahassee, FL 32306-1110. Offers accounting (M Acc), including assurance and advisory services, generalist, taxation; business administration (MBA, PhD), including accounting (PhD), finance (PhD), management information systems (PhD), marketing (PhD), organizational behavior and human resources (PhD), risk management and insurance (PhD), strategy (PhD); finance (MS); management information systems (MS); risk management and insurance (MS); JD/MBA; MSW/MBA. *Accreditation:* AACSB. *Program availability:* Part-time, 100% online. *Faculty:* 93 full-time (23 women), 2 part-time/adjunct (1 woman). *Students:* 229 full-time (96 women), 423 part-time (154 women); includes 159 minority (44 Black or African American, non-Hispanic/Latino; 24 Asian, non-Hispanic/Latino; 75 Hispanic/Latino; 1 Native Hawaiian or other Pacific Islander, non-Hispanic/Latino; 15 Two or more races, non-Hispanic/Latino), 48 international. Average age 31. 300 applicants, 61% accepted, 133 enrolled. In 2017, 268 master's, 9 doctorates awarded. Terminal master's awarded for partial completion of doctoral program. *Degree requirements:* For doctorate, comprehensive exam, thesis/dissertation. *Entrance requirements:* For master's, GMAT, GRE (for all except MS in finance), work experience (MBA, MS); minimum GPA of 3.0, letters of recommendation; for doctorate, GMAT, GRE (for marketing, organizational behavior, risk management and insurance, management information systems, and human resources only), minimum graduate GPA of 3.5, letters of recommendation. Additional exam requirements/recommendations for international students: Required—TOEFL (minimum score 600 paper-based; 85 iBT); Recommended—IELTS (minimum score 6). *Application deadline:* For fall admission, 6/1 for domestic and international students; for spring admission, 10/1 for domestic and international students; for summer admission, 3/1 for domestic and international students. Applications are processed on a rolling basis. Application fee: $30. Electronic applications accepted. *Expenses:* Contact institution. *Financial support:* In 2017–18, 146 students received support, including 26 fellowships (averaging $1,500 per year), 77 research assistantships with full tuition reimbursements available (averaging $20,000 per year), 43 teaching assistantships with full tuition reimbursements available (averaging $20,000 per year); career-related internships or fieldwork, scholarships/grants, health care benefits, tuition waivers (full and partial), and unspecified assistantships also available. Support available to part-time students. Financial award application deadline: 1/1; financial award applicants required to submit FAFSA. *Faculty research:* Business strategy, marketing, finance, accounting, business analytics. *Total annual research expenditures:* $1.4 million. *Unit head:* Dr. Michael Hartline, Dean, 850-644-4405, Fax: 850-644-0915, E-mail: mhartline@business.fsu.edu. *Application contact:* Jennifer Clark, Director, 850-644-6458, E-mail: gradprograms@business.fsu.edu.
Website: http://business.fsu.edu/

Georgia State University, J. Mack Robinson College of Business, Department of Risk Management and Insurance, Program in Risk Management and Insurance, Atlanta, GA 30302-3083. Offers enterprise risk management (MBA, Certificate); financial risk management (MBA); mathematical risk management (MS); risk and insurance (MS); risk management and insurance (MBA, PhD); MAS/MRM. *Program availability:* Part-time, evening/weekend. *Entrance requirements:* For master's, GRE or GMAT, transcripts from all institutions attended, resume, essays. Additional exam requirements/recommendations for international students: Required—TOEFL (minimum score 610 paper-based; 101 iBT), IELTS (minimum score 7). *Application deadline:* Applications are processed on a rolling basis. Application fee: $50. Electronic applications accepted. *Expenses:* Tuition, state resident: full-time $7020. Tuition, nonresident: full-time $22,518. *Required fees:* $2128. Tuition and fees vary according to degree level and program. *Financial support:* Research assistantships, scholarships/grants, tuition waivers, and unspecified assistantships available. *Faculty research:* Insurance

Risk Management

economics, structure and performance of insurance markets, regulation and policy in insurance markets, asset pricing theory, financial econometrics. *Unit head:* Dr. Martin Grace, Professor of Risk Management and Legal Studies/Chair of the Department of Risk Management and Insurance, 404-413-7500, Fax: 404-413-7499. *Application contact:* Toby McChesney, Graduate Recruiting Contact, 404-413-7167, Fax: 404-413-7162, E-mail: rcbgradadmissions@gsu.edu.
Website: http://rmi.robinson.gsu.edu/academic-programs/ms-rmi/

Husson University, Master of Business Administration Program, Bangor, ME 04401-2999. Offers athletic administration (MBA); biotechnology and innovation (MBA); general business administration (MBA); healthcare management (MBA); hospitality and tourism management (MBA); organizational management (MBA); risk management (MBA). *Program availability:* Part-time, evening/weekend, 100% online, blended/hybrid learning. *Faculty:* 11 full-time (5 women), 19 part-time/adjunct (4 women). *Students:* 83 full-time (44 women), 287 part-time (176 women); includes 25 minority (7 Black or African American, non-Hispanic/Latino; 11 Asian, non-Hispanic/Latino; 4 Hispanic/Latino; 3 Two or more races, non-Hispanic/Latino), 16 international. Average age 35. 158 applicants, 77% accepted, 49 enrolled. In 2017, 120 master's awarded. *Degree requirements:* For master's, comprehensive exam (for some programs), thesis optional. *Entrance requirements:* For master's, minimum GPA of 3.0, letter of recommendation. Additional exam requirements/recommendations for international students: Required—TOEFL (minimum score 550 paper-based; 80 iBT), IELTS (minimum score 6.5). *Application deadline:* Applications are processed on a rolling basis. Application fee: $50. Electronic applications accepted. *Expenses:* $464 per credit. *Financial support:* In 2017–18, 13 students received support. Career-related internships or fieldwork, Federal Work-Study, scholarships/grants, and unspecified assistantships available. Financial award application deadline: 4/15; financial award applicants required to submit FAFSA. *Unit head:* Prof. Stephanie Shayne, Director, Graduate and Online Programs, 207-404-5632, Fax: 207-992-4987, E-mail: shaynes@husson.edu. *Application contact:* Kristen Card, Director of Graduate Admissions, 207-404-5660, Fax: 207-941-7935, E-mail: cardk@husson.edu.
Website: http://www.husson.edu/college-of-business/school-of-business-and-management/master-of-business-administration-mba

Iona College, School of Business, Department of Information Systems, New Rochelle, NY 10801-1890. Offers accounting and information systems (MS); business continuity and risk management (AC); information systems (MBA, MS, PMC); project management (MS). *Program availability:* Part-time, evening/weekend. *Faculty:* 7 full-time (1 woman), 1 part-time/adjunct (0 women). *Students:* 15 full-time (7 women), 8 part-time (3 women); includes 5 minority (3 Asian, non-Hispanic/Latino; 2 Hispanic/Latino), 3 international. Average age 26. 13 applicants, 92% accepted, 8 enrolled. In 2017, 15 master's, 1 other advanced degree awarded. *Entrance requirements:* For master's, GMAT, 2 letters of recommendation, minimum GPA of 3.0; for other advanced degree, GMAT, minimum GPA of 3.0. Additional exam requirements/recommendations for international students: Required—TOEFL (minimum score 550 paper-based; 80 iBT), IELTS (minimum score 6.5). *Application deadline:* For fall admission, 8/15 priority date for domestic students, 8/1 priority date for international students; for winter admission, 11/15 priority date for domestic students, 11/1 priority date for international students; for spring admission, 2/15 priority date for domestic students, 2/1 priority date for international students; for summer admission, 5/15 priority date for domestic students, 5/1 priority date for international students. Applications are processed on a rolling basis. Application fee: $50. Electronic applications accepted. *Expenses:* Contact institution. *Financial support:* In 2017–18, 4 students received support. Scholarships/grants, tuition waivers (partial), and unspecified assistantships available. Support available to part-time students. Financial award application deadline: 4/15; financial award applicants required to submit FAFSA. *Faculty research:* Fuzzy sets, risk management, computer security, competence set analysis, investment strategies. *Unit head:* Dr. Shoshana Altschuller, Department Chair, 914-637-7726, E-mail: saltschuller@iona.edu. *Application contact:* Katelyn Brunck, Director of MBA Admissions, 914-633-2451, Fax: 914-633-2277, E-mail: kbrunck@iona.edu.
Website: http://www.iona.edu/Academics/Hagan-School-of-Business/Departments/Information-Systems/Graduate-Programs.aspx

Johns Hopkins University, Carey Business School, MS in Business Analytics and Risk Management Program, Baltimore, MD 21218. Offers MS. *Program availability:* Part-time, evening/weekend. *Faculty:* 93 full-time (33 women), 45 part-time/adjunct (11 women). *Students:* 39 full-time (25 women), 11 part-time (4 women); includes 7 minority (4 Black or African American, non-Hispanic/Latino; 1 Asian, non-Hispanic/Latino; 2 Hispanic/Latino), 38 international. Average age 24. 158 applicants, 70% accepted, 42 enrolled. In 2017, 26 master's awarded. *Degree requirements:* For master's, 36 credits. *Entrance requirements:* For master's, GMAT or GRE. Additional exam requirements/recommendations for international students: Required—TOEFL, IELTS. *Application deadline:* For fall admission, 5/1 for domestic and international students. Applications are processed on a rolling basis. Application fee: $100. Electronic applications accepted. *Expenses:* $66,500 (full-time); $1,330 per credit (part-time). *Financial support:* In 2017–18, 7 students received support. Scholarships/grants available. Support available to part-time students. Financial award application deadline: 4/15; financial award applicants required to submit FAFSA. *Faculty research:* Emerging issues in risk management, health care/medical services, strategic options and simulation. *Unit head:* Dr. Kevin Frick, Vice Dean of Education, 410-234-9272, E-mail: kfrick@jhu.edu. *Application contact:* Office of Admissions, 410-234-9220, Fax: 443-529-1554, E-mail: carey.admissions@jhu.edu.

Loyola University Chicago, Quinlan School of Business, MBA Programs, Chicago, IL 60611. Offers accounting (MBA); business ethics (MBA); derivative markets (MBA); economics (MBA); entrepreneurship (MBA); finance (MBA); healthcare management (MBA); human resources management (MBA); information systems management (MBA); international business (MBA); management (MBA); marketing (MBA); risk management (MBA); supply chain management (MBA). *Program availability:* Part-time, evening/weekend. *Faculty:* 84 full-time (28 women), 12 part-time/adjunct (3 women). *Students:* 253 full-time (118 women), 76 part-time (35 women); includes 83 minority (21 Black or African American, non-Hispanic/Latino; 1 American Indian or Alaska Native, non-Hispanic/Latino; 33 Asian, non-Hispanic/Latino; 24 Hispanic/Latino; 4 Two or more races, non-Hispanic/Latino), 37 international. Average age 30. 334 applicants, 52% accepted, 80 enrolled. In 2017, 220 master's awarded. *Entrance requirements:* For master's, GMAT or GRE, official transcripts, two letters of recommendation, statement of purpose, resume. Additional exam requirements/recommendations for international students: Required—TOEFL (minimum score 90 iBT) or IELTS (minimum score 6.5). *Application deadline:* For fall admission, 7/15 for domestic and international students; for winter admission, 10/1 for domestic and international students; for spring admission, 1/15 for domestic and international students; for summer admission, 4/1 for domestic and international students. Applications are processed on a rolling basis. Application fee: $50. Electronic applications accepted. Application fee is waived when completed online. *Expenses:* $4,488 per course. *Financial support:* In 2017–18, 11 students received support. Research assistantships, career-related internships or fieldwork, Federal Work-Study, scholarships/grants, and health care benefits available. *Faculty research:* Social enterprise and responsibility, emerging markets, supply chain management, risk

management. *Unit head:* Katherine Acles, Assistant Dean for Graduate Programs, 312-915-6124, Fax: 312-915-7207, E-mail: kacles@luc.edu.

Metropolitan College of New York, Program in Business Administration, New York, NY 10006. Offers financial services (MBA); general management (MBA); healthcare systems and risk management (MBA); media management (MBA). *Accreditation:* ACBSP. *Program availability:* Evening/weekend. *Students:* 164 full-time (106 women), 37 part-time (31 women); includes 153 minority (112 Black or African American, non-Hispanic/Latino; 3 American Indian or Alaska Native, non-Hispanic/Latino; 10 Asian, non-Hispanic/Latino; 24 Hispanic/Latino; 1 Native Hawaiian or other Pacific Islander, non-Hispanic/Latino; 3 Two or more races, non-Hispanic/Latino), 31 international. Average age 37. 133 applicants, 62% accepted, 66 enrolled. In 2017, 100 master's awarded. *Degree requirements:* For master's, thesis, 10-day study abroad. *Entrance requirements:* For master's, GMAT. Additional exam requirements/recommendations for international students: Required—TOEFL (minimum score 600 paper-based). *Application deadline:* For fall admission, 7/15 priority date for domestic students; for winter admission, 11/15 priority date for domestic students; for spring admission, 3/30 priority date for domestic students. Applications are processed on a rolling basis. Application fee: $45. Electronic applications accepted. *Expenses:* $926 per credit, $395 fee per semester. *Financial support:* Scholarships/grants available. Financial award application deadline: 8/15; financial award applicants required to submit FAFSA. *Unit head:* Dr. Tilokie Depoo, Dean and Professor, School for Business, 212-343-1234 Ext. 2204. *Application contact:* Steebo Varghese, Assistant Director of Admissions, 212-343-1234 Ext. 2708, Fax: 212-343-8470.

New York University, School of Professional Studies, Division of Programs in Business, Program in Management and Systems, New York, NY 10012-1019. Offers management and systems (MS), including database technologies, enterprise risk management, strategy and leadership, systems management. *Program availability:* Part-time, evening/weekend, 100% online, blended/hybrid learning. *Students:* 257 full-time (153 women), 80 part-time (45 women); includes 44 minority (9 Black or African American, non-Hispanic/Latino; 1 American Indian or Alaska Native, non-Hispanic/Latino; 21 Asian, non-Hispanic/Latino; 11 Hispanic/Latino; 2 Two or more races, non-Hispanic/Latino), 272 international. Average age 27. 507 applicants, 63% accepted, 150 enrolled. In 2017, 170 master's awarded. *Degree requirements:* For master's, thesis, capstone project. *Entrance requirements:* For master's, GRE or GMAT (only upon request), bachelor's degree, resume with relevant professional work, internship or volunteer experience, two letters of recommendation, statement of purpose. Additional exam requirements/recommendations for international students: Required—TOEFL (minimum score 600 paper-based; 100 iBT), IELTS (minimum score 7). *Application deadline:* For fall admission, 2/1 priority date for domestic and international students; for spring admission, 10/15 priority date for domestic students, 8/15 priority date for international students; for summer admission, 5/1 priority date for domestic students, 1/15 priority date for international students. Applications are processed on a rolling basis. Application fee: $150. Electronic applications accepted. *Expenses:* $20,244 per term. *Financial support:* Fellowships, career-related internships or fieldwork, Federal Work-Study, scholarships/grants, and health care benefits available. Support available to part-time students. Financial award application deadline: 6/30; financial award applicants required to submit FAFSA. *Unit head:* Martin Ihrig, Associate Dean/Clinical Professor, 212-992-3288. *Application contact:* Admissions Office, 212-998-7100, E-mail: sps.gradadmissions@nyu.edu.
Website: http://www.sps.nyu.edu/academics/departments/information-technology.html

Ohio Dominican University, Division of Business, Program in Business Administration, Columbus, OH 43219-2099. Offers accounting (MBA); data analytics (MBA); finance (MBA); leadership (MBA); risk management (MBA); sport management (MBA). *Program availability:* Part-time, evening/weekend, 100% online, blended/hybrid learning. *Faculty:* 7 full-time (4 women), 9 part-time/adjunct (2 women). *Students:* 53 full-time (21 women), 112 part-time (49 women); includes 37 minority (20 Black or African American, non-Hispanic/Latino; 1 American Indian or Alaska Native, non-Hispanic/Latino; 6 Asian, non-Hispanic/Latino; 5 Hispanic/Latino; 5 Two or more races, non-Hispanic/Latino), 5 international. Average age 31. 110 applicants, 45% accepted, 40 enrolled. In 2017, 93 master's awarded. *Entrance requirements:* For master's, minimum overall GPA of 3.0 in undergraduate degree from regionally-accredited institution or 2.75 in last 60 semester hours of bachelor's degree. Additional exam requirements/recommendations for international students: Required—TOEFL (minimum score 550 paper-based), IELTS (minimum score 6.5). *Application deadline:* For fall admission, 8/15 for domestic students, 6/10 for international students; for spring admission, 1/4 for domestic students, 11/2 for international students; for summer admission, 5/30 for domestic students. Applications are processed on a rolling basis. Application fee: $25. Electronic applications accepted. *Expenses:* $600 per credit hour, $175 per semester technology fee, $50 per semester activity fee. *Financial support:* Applicants required to submit FAFSA. *Unit head:* Dr. Steve Vickner, Director of Master of Business Administration Program, 614-251-4569, E-mail: vickners@ohiodominican.edu. *Application contact:* John W. Naughton, Associate Vice President for Enrollment Management, 614-251-4721, Fax: 614-251-6654, E-mail: grad@ohiodominican.edu.
Website: http://www.ohiodominican.edu/academics/graduate/mba

Pace University, Lubin School of Business, Financial Management Program, New York, NY 10038. Offers financial management (MBA, MS); financial risk management (MS); international finance (MBA); investment management (MBA, MS). *Program availability:* Part-time, evening/weekend. *Students:* 103 full-time (41 women), 53 part-time (26 women); includes 24 minority (5 Black or African American, non-Hispanic/Latino; 11 Asian, non-Hispanic/Latino; 6 Hispanic/Latino; 1 Native Hawaiian or other Pacific Islander, non-Hispanic/Latino; 1 Two or more races, non-Hispanic/Latino), 103 international. Average age 26. 251 applicants, 61% accepted, 43 enrolled. In 2017, 108 master's awarded. *Entrance requirements:* For master's, GMAT, GRE (GMAT not required for MS with passing of Level 1 of Chartered Financial Analyst exam or Level 1 of Financial Risk Manager Exam), undergraduate degree, transcripts from all accredited colleges/universities attended, two letters of recommendation, resume, personal statement. Additional exam requirements/recommendations for international students: Required—TOEFL (minimum score 90 iBT), IELTS (minimum score 7) or PTE (minimum score 61). *Application deadline:* For fall admission, 8/1 priority date for domestic students, 6/1 for international students; for spring admission, 12/1 for domestic students, 10/1 for international students. Applications are processed on a rolling basis. Application fee: $70. Electronic applications accepted. *Financial support:* Research assistantships, career-related internships or fieldwork, Federal Work-Study, and tuition waivers (full and partial) available. Support available to part-time students. Financial award application deadline: 2/15; financial award applicants required to submit FAFSA. *Unit head:* Dr. P. V. Viswanath, Chairperson, 212-618-6518, E-mail: pviswanath@pace.edu. *Application contact:* Susan Ford-Goldschein, Director of Graduate Admissions, 212-346-1531, Fax: 212-346-1585, E-mail: graduateadmissions@pace.edu.
Website: http://www.pace.edu/lubin/financial-management-mba

Queens College of the City University of New York, Division of Social Sciences, Department of Economics, Queens, NY 11367-1597. Offers risk management: accounting (MS); risk management: dynamic financial analysis (MS); risk management: finance (MS). *Students:* 11 full-time (4 women), 38 part-time (21 women); includes 29 minority (6 Black or African American, non-Hispanic/Latino; 15 Asian, non-Hispanic/Latino; 5 Hispanic/Latino; 3 Two or more races, non-Hispanic/Latino), 12 international. Average age 31. *Degree requirements:* For master's, thesis. *Entrance requirements:* For master's, minimum GPA of 3.0. Additional exam requirements/recommendations for international students: Required—TOEFL (minimum score 100 iBT), IELTS (minimum score 7). *Financial support:* Federal Work-Study, institutionally sponsored loans, and tuition waivers (partial) available. Support available to part-time students. Financial award application deadline: 4/1; financial award applicants required to submit FAFSA. *Faculty research:* Business economics, urban economic problems, international economics, economics of nonprofit sector. *Unit head:* Dr. John Devereux, Chair, 718-997-5440, E-mail: john.devereux@qc.cuny.edu. *Application contact:* Elvira Casper, Program Coordinator, 718-997-5507, E-mail: elvira.casper@qc.cuny.edu.

St. John's University, The Peter J. Tobin College of Business, School of Risk Management, Insurance and Actuarial Science, Queens, NY 11439. Offers actuarial science (MS); business administration (MBA), including risk management and insurance; enterprise risk management (MBA, MS), including enterprise risk management (MS); risk management and insurance (MS). *Faculty:* 11 full-time (2 women), 7 part-time/adjunct (1 woman). *Students:* 51 full-time (24 women), 28 part-time (13 women); includes 15 minority (7 Black or African American, non-Hispanic/Latino; 4 Asian, non-Hispanic/Latino; 3 Hispanic/Latino; 1 Two or more races, non-Hispanic/Latino), 40 international. Average age 27. 58 applicants, 78% accepted, 27 enrolled. In 2017, 32 master's awarded. *Entrance requirements:* For master's, GMAT or GRE, 2 letters of recommendation, essay, resume, unofficial transcripts. Additional exam requirements/recommendations for international students: Required—TOEFL (minimum score 80 iBT), IELTS (minimum score 6.5). *Application deadline:* For fall admission, 11/1 for domestic and international students; for winter admission, 3/1 for domestic and international students; for spring admission, 6/1 for domestic and international students. Applications are processed on a rolling basis. Application fee: $70. Electronic applications accepted. *Expenses:* $22,410 per year. *Financial support:* Research assistantships, teaching assistantships, scholarships/grants, and unspecified assistantships available. Support available to part-time students. Financial award application deadline: 2/1; financial award applicants required to submit FAFSA. *Faculty research:* Insurance company operations and financial analysis, enterprise risk management, risk theory and modeling, credibility theory and actuarial price modeling, international insurance. *Unit head:* Dr. Mark J. Browne, Chair, 212-277-5175, E-mail: brownem1@stjohns.edu. *Application contact:* Amber Steiger, Associate Director of Enrollment Management, 718-990-1345, E-mail: steigera@stjohns.edu.
Website: https://www.stjohns.edu/academics/schools-and-colleges/peter-j-tobin-college-business/school-risk-management-insurance-and-actuarial-science

Saint Peter's University, Graduate Business Programs, MBA Program, Jersey City, NJ 07306-5997. Offers finance (MBA); health care administration (MBA); human resource management (MBA); international business (MBA); management (MBA); management information systems (MBA); marketing (MBA); risk management (MBA); MBA/MS. *Program availability:* Part-time, evening/weekend. *Entrance requirements:* Additional exam requirements/recommendations for international students: Required—TOEFL. Electronic applications accepted. *Faculty research:* Finance, health care management, human resource management, international business, management, management information systems, marketing, risk management.

Temple University, Fox School of Business, Doctoral Programs in Business, Philadelphia, PA 19122-6096. Offers accounting (PhD); entrepreneurship (PhD); finance (PhD); international business (PhD); management information systems (PhD); marketing (PhD); risk management and insurance (PhD); statistics (PhD); strategic management (PhD); tourism and sport (PhD). *Accreditation:* AACSB. *Degree requirements:* For doctorate, thesis/dissertation. *Entrance requirements:* For doctorate, GRE General Test, GMAT, minimum GPA of 3.0, master's degree. Additional exam requirements/recommendations for international students: Required—TOEFL (minimum score 600 paper-based; 100 iBT), IELTS (minimum score 7.5). Electronic applications accepted. *Expenses:* Tuition, state resident: full-time $16,164; part-time $898 per credit hour. Tuition, nonresident: full-time $22,158; part-time $1231 per credit hour. *Required fees:* $890; $445 per semester. Full-time tuition and fees vary according to course load, degree level, campus/location and program.

University of Colorado Denver, Business School, Program in Finance, Denver, CO 80217. Offers economics (MS); finance (MS); financial analysis and management (MS); financial and commodities risk management (MS); risk management and insurance (MS); MS/MA; MS/MBA. *Program availability:* Part-time, evening/weekend. *Entrance requirements:* For master's, 30 semester hours (18 of required core courses, 9 of finance electives, and 3 of free elective). *Entrance requirements:* For master's, GMAT, essay, resume, two letters of recommendation; financial statements (for international students). Additional exam requirements/recommendations for international students: Required—TOEFL (minimum score 537 paper-based; 75 iBT); Recommended—IELTS (minimum score 6.5). Electronic applications accepted. *Expenses:* Contact institution. *Faculty research:* Corporate governance, debt maturity policies, regulation and financial markets, option management strategies.

University of Michigan, Rackham Graduate School, College of Literature, Science, and the Arts, Department of Mathematics, Ann Arbor, MI 48109. Offers applied and interdisciplinary mathematics (AM, MS, PhD); mathematics (AM, MS, PhD); quantitative finance and risk management (MS). *Program availability:* Part-time. *Faculty:* 61 full-time (12 women). *Students:* 202 full-time (59 women), 6 part-time (2 women); includes 27 minority (4 Black or African American, non-Hispanic/Latino; 9 Asian, non-Hispanic/Latino; 9 Hispanic/Latino; 5 Two or more races, non-Hispanic/Latino), 134 international. Average age 26. 1,049 applicants, 22% accepted, 66 enrolled. In 2017, 53 master's, 16 doctorates awarded. *Degree requirements:* For doctorate, one foreign language, comprehensive exam, thesis/dissertation, oral defense of dissertation, preliminary exam. *Entrance requirements:* For master's and doctorate, GRE General Test, GRE Subject Test. Additional exam requirements/recommendations for international students: Required—TOEFL (minimum score 560 paper-based; 84 iBT). *Application deadline:* For fall admission, 12/15 for domestic and international students. Applications are processed on a rolling basis. Application fee: $75 ($90 for international students). Electronic applications accepted. *Expenses:* $11,184 resident, $22,578 non-resident per term; $164.19 per term fees. *Financial support:* In 2017–18, 138 students received support, including 36 fellowships with full tuition reimbursements available (averaging $25,000 per year), 36 research assistantships with full tuition reimbursements available (averaging $20,399 per year), 201 teaching assistantships with full tuition reimbursements available (averaging $20,399 per year). Financial award application deadline: 3/15. *Faculty research:* Algebra, analysis, topology, applied mathematics, geometry. *Unit head:* Prof. Anthony Bloch, Chair, 734-936-1310, Fax: 734-763-0937, E-mail: math-chair@umich.edu. *Application contact:* Prof. Kartik Prasanna, Admissions

Director, 734-615-3439, Fax: 734-763-0937, E-mail: math-admissionsdir@umich.edu. Website: http://www.lsa.umich.edu/math/

University of Pennsylvania, Wharton School, Insurance and Risk Management Department, Philadelphia, PA 19104. Offers MBA, PhD. *Degree requirements:* For doctorate, thesis/dissertation. *Entrance requirements:* For master's, GMAT; for doctorate, GMAT or GRE. *Faculty research:* Fair rate of return in insurance economics of pension plans, insurance regulation, malpractice insurance, actuarial science, genetic testing and life insurance.

University of Saint Mary, Graduate Programs, Program in Business Administration, Leavenworth, KS 66048-5082. Offers enterprise risk management (MBA); finance (MBA); general management (MBA); health care management (MBA); human resource management (MBA); marketing and advertising management (MBA). *Program availability:* Part-time, evening/weekend, 100% online, blended/hybrid learning. *Degree requirements:* For master's, thesis. *Entrance requirements:* For master's, minimum undergraduate GPA of 2.75, official transcripts, two letters of recommendation. Electronic applications accepted. *Expenses:* Contact institution.

The University of Texas at Austin, Graduate School, McCombs School of Business, Department of Information, Risk, and Operations Management, Austin, TX 78712-1111. Offers information management (MBA); information systems (PhD); information technology and management (MS); risk analysis and decision making (PhD); risk management (MBA); supply chain and operations management (MBA, PhD). *Degree requirements:* For doctorate, thesis/dissertation. *Entrance requirements:* For doctorate, GMAT or GRE. Electronic applications accepted. *Faculty research:* Stochastic processing and queuing, discrete nonlinear and large-scale optimization simulation, quality assurance logistics, distributed artificial intelligence, organizational modeling.

The University of Tulsa, Graduate School, Collins College of Business, Program in Finance, Tulsa, OK 74104-3189. Offers corporate finance (MS); risk management (MS); JD/MSF; MBA/MSF; MSF/MSAM. *Program availability:* Part-time, evening/weekend. *Faculty:* 9 full-time (1 woman). *Students:* 4 full-time (1 woman), 2 part-time (0 women); includes 2 minority (both Asian, non-Hispanic/Latino). Average age 26. 61 applicants, 44% accepted, 3 enrolled. In 2017, 7 master's awarded. *Degree requirements:* For master's, thesis optional. *Entrance requirements:* For master's, GMAT. Additional exam requirements/recommendations for international students: Required—TOEFL (minimum score 577 paper-based; 91 iBT), IELTS (minimum score 6.5). *Application deadline:* Applications are processed on a rolling basis. Application fee: $55. Electronic applications accepted. *Expenses:* Tuition: Full-time $22,230. *Required fees:* $2000. Tuition and fees vary according to course load and program. *Financial support:* In 2017–18, 3 students received support, including 3 teaching assistantships with full tuition reimbursements available (averaging $10,347 per year); fellowships with full tuition reimbursements available, research assistantships with full tuition reimbursements available, career-related internships or fieldwork, Federal Work-Study, institutionally sponsored loans, scholarships/grants, health care benefits, tuition waivers (full and partial), and unspecified assistantships also available. Support available to part-time students. Financial award application deadline: 2/1; financial award applicants required to submit FAFSA. *Unit head:* Dr. Ralph Jackson, Associate Dean, 918-631-2242, Fax: 918-631-2142, E-mail: ralph-jackson@utulsa.edu. *Application contact:* Information Contact, 918-631-2242, E-mail: graduate-business@utulsa.edu.

University of Wisconsin–Madison, Graduate School, Wisconsin School of Business, Doctoral Program in Actuarial Science, Risk Management and Insurance, Madison, WI 53706-1380. Offers PhD. *Degree requirements:* For doctorate, comprehensive exam, thesis/dissertation. *Entrance requirements:* For doctorate, GMAT or GRE General Test. Additional exam requirements/recommendations for international students: Recommended—TOEFL (minimum score 623 paper-based; 106 iBT), IELTS (minimum score 7.5), TSE (minimum score 73). Electronic applications accepted. *Expenses:* Contact institution. *Faculty research:* Actuarial science, regression and business forecasting, panel data, economics of insurance markets, insurance regulation, public economics, behavioral economics, Bayesian methodology related to health insurance, tort reform and government programs, joint and several liability, superfund, predictive modeling, asymmetric information in insurance, psychology and economics, applied microeconomics, insurance markets, risk and decision making.

University of Wisconsin–Madison, Graduate School, Wisconsin School of Business, Wisconsin Full-Time MBA Program, Madison, WI 53706. Offers applied security analysis (MBA); arts administration (MBA); brand and product management (MBA); corporate finance and investment banking (MBA); marketing research (MBA); operations and technology management (MBA); real estate (MBA); risk management and insurance (MBA); strategic human resource management (MBA); supply chain management (MBA). *Faculty:* 130 full-time (35 women), 42 part-time/adjunct (13 women). *Students:* 203 full-time (72 women); includes 34 minority (8 Black or African American, non-Hispanic/Latino; 10 Asian, non-Hispanic/Latino; 12 Hispanic/Latino; 4 Two or more races, non-Hispanic/Latino), 41 international. Average age 28. 556 applicants, 30% accepted, 104 enrolled. In 2017, 97 master's awarded. *Entrance requirements:* For master's, GMAT or GRE, bachelor's or equivalent degree, 2 years of work experience, essay, letter of recommendation, resume. Additional exam requirements/recommendations for international students: Required—TOEFL (minimum score 100 iBT), IELTS (minimum score 7.5). *Application deadline:* For fall admission, 11/2 for domestic and international students; for winter admission, 1/11 for domestic and international students; for spring admission, 3/1 for domestic and international students; for summer admission, 4/12 for domestic and international students. Applications are processed on a rolling basis. Application fee: $75 ($81 for international students). Electronic applications accepted. *Expenses:* $9,356 per semester resident, $18,288 non-resident. *Financial support:* In 2017–18, 183 students received support, including 14 fellowships with full tuition reimbursements available (averaging $25,420 per year), 7 research assistantships with full tuition reimbursements available (averaging $13,375 per year), 53 teaching assistantships with full tuition reimbursements available (averaging $13,375 per year); scholarships/grants, health care benefits, tuition waivers (full), and unspecified assistantships also available. Financial award application deadline: 4/11. *Faculty research:* Forms of competition and outcomes in dual distribution systems; explaining the accuracy of revised forecasts; supply chain planning for random demand surges; advanced demand information in a multi-product system; the effects of presentation salience and measurement subjectivity on nonprofessional investors' fair value judgments. *Unit head:* Dr. Don Hausch, Associate Dean, Full-time MBA Program, 608-262-9731, E-mail: don.hausch@wisc.edu. *Application contact:* Betsy Kacizak, Director of Admissions and Recruiting, Full-time MBA Program, 608-262-4000, E-mail: betsy.kacizak@wisc.edu.
Website: https://wsb.wisc.edu/

Yeshiva University, The Katz School, Program in Enterprise Risk Management, New York, NY 10033-3201. Offers MS. *Program availability:* Part-time, online learning.

Section 11
International Business

This section contains a directory of institutions offering graduate work in international business. Additional information about programs listed in the directory but not augmented by an in-depth entry may be obtained by writing directly to the dean of a graduate school or chair of a department at the address given in the directory.

For programs offering related work, see also in this book *Business Administration and Management, Entrepreneurship, Industrial and Manufacturing Management,* and *Organizational Behavior.* In another guide in this series:

Graduate Programs in the Humanities, Arts & Social Sciences

See *Political Science and International Affairs* and *Public, Regional, and Industrial Affairs*

CONTENTS

Program Directory

Featured Schools: Displays and Close-Ups

See:

International Business

Abilene Christian University, College of Graduate and Professional Studies, Program in Business Administration, Addison, TX 75001. Offers business analytics (MBA); corporate finance (MBA); general management (MBA); healthcare administration (MBA); human resource management (MBA); international business (MBA); management: business analytics (MS); management: healthcare administration (MS); management: international business (MS); management: marketing (MS); management: operations and supply chain management (MS); marketing (MBA); nonprofit leadership (MBA); operations and supply chain management (MBA). *Program availability:* Part-time, online only, 100% online. *Faculty:* 2 full-time (0 women), 6 part-time/adjunct (2 women). *Students:* 109 full-time (47 women), 51 part-time (22 women); includes 42 minority (33 Black or African American, non-Hispanic/Latino; 1 American Indian or Alaska Native, non-Hispanic/Latino; 2 Asian, non-Hispanic/Latino; 6 Hispanic/Latino). 125 applicants, 65% accepted, 58 enrolled. *Entrance requirements:* Additional exam requirements/recommendations for international students: Required—TOEFL (minimum score 80 iBT), IELTS (minimum score 6). *Application deadline:* For fall admission, 8/14 priority date for domestic students; for winter admission, 10/1 priority date for domestic students; for spring admission, 12/15 priority date for domestic students; for summer admission, 4/15 priority date for domestic students. Applications are processed on a rolling basis. Application fee: $50. Electronic applications accepted. *Expenses:* $700 per hour. *Financial support:* In 2017–18, 2 students received support. Application deadline: 4/1; applicants required to submit FAFSA. *Faculty research:* Organizational structure, financial management, cost accounting, unit analysis management. *Unit head:* Phil Vardiman, Program Director, 325-674-2153, E-mail: pxv02b@acu.edu. *Application contact:* Graduate Advisor, 817-219-7300, E-mail: gradonline@acu.edu. Website: http://www.acu.edu/online/academics/mba-business-administration.html

Amberton University, Graduate School, Department of Business Administration, Garland, TX 75041-5595. Offers agile project management (MS); general business (MBA); international business (MBA); management (MBA); project management (MBA); strategic leadership (MBA). *Program availability:* Part-time, evening/weekend. *Entrance requirements:* For master's, minimum GPA of 3.0. Applications are processed on a rolling basis. Application fee: $0. *Expenses: Tuition:* Part-time $795 per course. *Unit head:* Dr. Don Hebbard, Academic Dean, 972-635-8641 Ext. 157, Fax: 972-279-9773, E-mail: dhebbard@amberton.edu. *Application contact:* Adviser, 972-279-6511 Ext. 180, Fax: 972-279-9773, E-mail: advisor@amberton.edu.

American Business & Technology University, Programs in Business Administration, Saint Joseph, MO 64506. Offers business administration (MBA); financial management (MBA); global business management (MBA); information systems management (MBA); marketing and social media (MBA); project and operations management (MBA); public accounting (MBA). *Program availability:* Online learning.

American College Dublin, Graduate Programs, Dublin, Ireland. Offers business administration (MBA); creative writing (MFA); international business (MBA); oil and gas management (MBA); performance (MFA).

American InterContinental University Atlanta, Program in Global Technology Management, Atlanta, GA 30328. Offers MBA. *Program availability:* Part-time, evening/weekend, online learning. *Entrance requirements:* For master's, interview. Electronic applications accepted. *Faculty research:* E-commerce, service quality leadership, human resources management.

American InterContinental University Online, Program in Business Administration, Schaumburg, IL 60173. Offers accounting and finance (MBA); finance (MBA); healthcare management (MBA); human resource management (MBA); international business (MBA); management (MBA); marketing (MBA); operations management (MBA); organizational psychology and development (MBA); project management (MBA). *Accreditation:* ACBSP. *Program availability:* Evening/weekend, online learning. *Entrance requirements:* Additional exam requirements/recommendations for international students: Required—TOEFL (minimum score 550 paper-based). Electronic applications accepted.

The American University in Dubai, Graduate Programs, Dubai, United Arab Emirates. Offers construction management (MS); education (M Ed); finance (MBA); generalist (MBA); marketing (MBA). *Program availability:* Part-time, evening/weekend. *Degree requirements:* For master's, thesis optional. *Entrance requirements:* For master's, GMAT (for MBA); GRE (for M Ed and MS), minimum undergraduate GPA of 3.0, official transcripts, two reference forms, curriculum vitae/resume, statement of career objectives, work experience. Additional exam requirements/recommendations for international students: Required—TOEFL (minimum score 550 paper-based; 79 iBT). Electronic applications accepted.

The American University of Paris, Graduate Programs, Paris, France. Offers cross-cultural and sustainable business management (MA); cultural translation (MA); global communications (MA); global communications and civil society (MA); international affairs (MA); international affairs, conflict resolution and civil society development (MA); Middle East and Islamic studies (MA); Middle East and Islamic studies and international affairs (MA); public policy and international affairs (MA); public policy and international law (MA). *Degree requirements:* For master's, thesis (for some programs). *Entrance requirements:* For master's, minimum undergraduate GPA of 3.0. Additional exam requirements/recommendations for international students: Recommended—TOEFL, IELTS. Electronic applications accepted.

Anaheim University, Programs in Business Administration, Anaheim, CA 92806-5150. Offers entrepreneurship (ME, DBA); global sustainable management (MBA); international business (MBA, DBA, Certificate, Diploma); management (DBA); sustainable management (DBA, Certificate, Diploma). *Program availability:* Part-time, evening/weekend, online only, 100% online. Electronic applications accepted.

Argosy University, Atlanta, College of Business, Atlanta, GA 30328. Offers accounting (DBA); corporate compliance (MBA); customized professional concentration (MBA, DBA); finance (MBA); healthcare administration (MBA); information systems (DBA); information systems management (MBA); international business (MBA, DBA); management (MBA, MSM, DBA); marketing (MBA, DBA). *Accreditation:* ACBSP.

Argosy University, Chicago, College of Business, Chicago, IL 60601. Offers accounting (DBA); customized professional concentration (MBA, DBA); finance (MBA); fraud examination (MBA); global business sustainability (DBA); healthcare administration (MBA); information systems (DBA); information systems management (MBA); international business (MBA, DBA); management (MBA, MSM, DBA); marketing (MBA, DBA); organizational leadership (Ed D); public administration (MBA); sustainable management (MBA). *Accreditation:* ACBSP. *Program availability:* Online learning.

Argosy University, Hawai'i, College of Business, Honolulu, HI 96813. Offers accounting (DBA); corporate compliance (MBA); customized professional concentration (MBA, DBA); finance (MBA, Certificate); fraud examination (MBA); global business

sustainability (DBA); healthcare administration (MBA, Certificate); information systems (DBA); information systems management (MBA, Certificate); international business (MBA, DBA, Certificate); management (MBA, MSM, DBA); marketing (MBA, DBA, Certificate); organizational leadership (Ed D); public administration (MBA); sustainable management (MBA).

Argosy University, Los Angeles, College of Business, Los Angeles, CA 90045. Offers accounting (DBA); corporate compliance (MBA); customized professional concentration (MBA, DBA); finance (MBA); fraud examination (MBA); global business sustainability (DBA); healthcare administration (MBA); information systems (DBA); information systems management (MBA); international business (MBA, DBA); management (MBA, MSM, DBA); marketing (MBA, DBA); organizational leadership (Ed D); public administration (MBA); sustainable management (MBA).

Argosy University, Northern Virginia, College of Business, Arlington, VA 22209. Offers accounting (DBA); customized professional concentration (MBA, DBA); finance (MBA); fraud examination (MBA); global business sustainability (DBA); healthcare administration (MBA); information systems (DBA); information systems management (MBA); international business (MBA, DBA, Certificate); management (MBA, MSM, DBA); marketing (MBA, DBA, Certificate); organizational leadership (Ed D); public administration (MBA); sustainable management (MBA).

Argosy University, Orange County, College of Business, Orange, CA 92868. Offers accounting (DBA, Adv C); corporate compliance (MBA); customized professional concentration (MBA, DBA); finance (MBA, Certificate); fraud examination (MBA); global business sustainability (DBA); healthcare administration (MBA, Certificate); information systems (DBA, Adv C, Certificate); information systems management (MBA); international business (MBA, DBA, Adv C, Certificate); management (MBA, MSM, DBA, Adv C); marketing (MBA, DBA, Adv C, Certificate); organizational leadership (Ed D); public administration (MBA, Certificate); sustainable management (MBA).

Argosy University, Phoenix, College of Business, Phoenix, AZ 85021. Offers accounting (DBA); corporate compliance (MBA); customized professional concentration (MBA, DBA); finance (MBA); fraud examination (MBA); global business sustainability (DBA); healthcare administration (MBA); information systems (DBA); information systems management (MBA); international business (MBA, DBA); management (MBA, DBA); marketing (MBA, DBA); public administration (MBA); sustainable management (MBA).

Argosy University, Seattle, College of Business, Seattle, WA 98121. Offers accounting (DBA); corporate compliance (MBA); customized professional concentration (MBA, DBA); finance (MBA); fraud examination (MBA); global business sustainability (DBA); healthcare administration (MBA); information systems (DBA); information systems management (MBA); international business (MBA, DBA); management (MBA, MSM, DBA); marketing (MBA, DBA); organizational leadership (Ed D); public administration (MBA); sustainable management (MBA).

Argosy University, Tampa, College of Business, Tampa, FL 33607. Offers accounting (DBA); corporate compliance (MBA); customized professional concentration (MBA, DBA); finance (MBA); fraud examination (MBA); global business sustainability (DBA); healthcare administration (MBA); information systems (DBA); information systems management (MBA); international business (MBA, DBA); management (MBA, MSM, DBA); marketing (MBA, DBA); organizational leadership (Ed D); public administration (MBA); sustainable management (MBA).

Argosy University, Twin Cities, College of Business, Eagan, MN 55121. Offers accounting (DBA); customized professional concentration (MBA, DBA); finance (MBA); fraud examination (MBA); global business sustainability (DBA); healthcare administration (MBA); information systems (DBA); information systems management (MBA); international business (MBA, DBA); management (MBA, MSM, DBA); marketing (MBA, DBA); organizational leadership (Ed D); public administration (MBA); sustainable management (MBA).

Arizona State University at the Tempe campus, Thunderbird School of Global Management, Tempe, AZ 85287. Offers global affairs and management (MA); global management (MGM). *Accreditation:* AACSB. *Program availability:* Online learning. *Degree requirements:* For master's, one foreign language. *Entrance requirements:* For master's, GMAT. Additional exam requirements/recommendations for international students: Required—TOEFL.

Arizona State University at the Tempe campus, W. P. Carey School of Business, Program in Business Administration, Tempe, AZ 85287-4906. Offers entrepreneurship (MBA); finance (MBA); health sector management (MBA); international business (MBA); leadership (MBA); marketing (MBA); organizational behavior (PhD); strategic management (PhD); supply chain management (MBA, PhD); JD/MBA; MBA/M Acc; MBA/M Arch. *Accreditation:* AACSB. *Program availability:* Part-time, evening/weekend, online learning. Terminal master's awarded for partial completion of doctoral program. *Degree requirements:* For master's, thesis or alternative, internship, interactive Program of Study (iPOS) submitted before completing 50 percent of required credit hours; for doctorate, comprehensive exam, thesis/dissertation, interactive Program of Study (iPOS) submitted before completing 50 percent of required credit hours. *Entrance requirements:* For master's, GMAT, minimum GPA of 3.0 in last 2 years of work leading to bachelor's degree, 2 letters of recommendation, professional resume, official transcripts, 3 essays; for doctorate, GMAT or GRE, minimum GPA of 3.0 in last 2 years of work leading to bachelor's degree, 3 letters of recommendation, resume, personal statement/essay. Additional exam requirements/recommendations for international students: Required—TOEFL (minimum score 550 paper-based; 80 iBT), IELTS (minimum score 6.5). Electronic applications accepted. *Expenses:* Contact institution.

Ashland University, Dauch College of Business and Economics, Ashland, OH 44805-3702. Offers accounting (MBA); business analytics (MBA); entrepreneurship (MBA); financial management (MBA); global management (MBA); health care management and leadership (MBA); human resource management (MBA); human resources (MBA); management information systems (MBA); project management (MBA); sport management (MBA); supply chain management (MBA). *Accreditation:* ACBSP. *Program availability:* Part-time, evening/weekend, 100% online, blended/hybrid learning. *Faculty:* 20 full-time (8 women), 13 part-time/adjunct (2 women). *Students:* 458 full-time (210 women), 144 part-time (52 women); includes 88 minority (63 Black or African American, non-Hispanic/Latino; 1 American Indian or Alaska Native, non-Hispanic/Latino; 10 Asian, non-Hispanic/Latino; 14 Hispanic/Latino), 202 international. Average age 31. 216 applicants, 74% accepted, 115 enrolled. In 2017, 184 master's awarded. Terminal master's awarded for partial completion of doctoral program. *Degree requirements:* For master's, thesis optional, capstone course. *Entrance requirements:* For master's, 2 years of full-time work experience. Additional exam requirements/recommendations for international students: Required—TOEFL (minimum score 550 paper-based; 78 iBT).

Application deadline: For fall admission, 8/1 priority date for domestic students; for spring admission, 12/1 priority date for domestic students. Applications are processed on a rolling basis. Application fee: $30. Electronic applications accepted. *Expenses:* $815 per credit hour, $15 technology fee for online sections. *Financial support:* Scholarships/grants, tuition waivers (partial), and unspecified assistantships available. Financial award application deadline: 4/15; financial award applicants required to submit FAFSA. *Faculty research:* Relationship marketing strategy, executive compensation and company performance, online marketplaces in electronic commerce, diversity training in campus recreation departments, entrepreneurship in developing and emerging economies. *Unit head:* Dr. Elad Granot, Dean, 419-289-5932, E-mail: egranot@ashland.edu. *Application contact:* Stephen W. Krispinsky, Executive Director of MBA Program, 419-289-5236, Fax: 419-289-5910, E-mail: skrispin@ashland.edu. Website: http://www.mba.ashland.edu

Ashworth College, Graduate Programs, Norcross, GA 30092. Offers business administration (MBA); criminal justice (MS); health care administration (MBA, MS); human resource management (MBA, MS); international business (MBA); management (MS); marketing (MBA, MS).

Assumption College, Business Studies Program, Worcester, MA 01609-1296. Offers accounting (MBA); business studies (CAGS); finance/economics (MBA); human resources (MBA); international business (MBA); management (MBA); marketing (MBA); nonprofit leadership (MBA). *Program availability:* Part-time, evening/weekend. *Faculty:* 5 full-time (1 woman), 21 part-time/adjunct (6 women). *Students:* 29 full-time (13 women), 87 part-time (50 women); includes 15 minority (1 Black or African American, non-Hispanic/Latino; 4 Asian, non-Hispanic/Latino; 8 Hispanic/Latino; 2 Two or more races, non-Hispanic/Latino), 4 international. Average age 29. 34 applicants, 100% accepted, 26 enrolled. In 2017, 81 master's, 2 other advanced degrees awarded. *Degree requirements:* For master's, capstone. *Entrance requirements:* For master's, bachelor's degree, three letters of recommendation, official transcripts, personal statement, current resume; for CAGS, MBA or equivalent degree in a closely related field, three letters of recommendation, official transcripts, personal statement, current resume. Additional exam requirements/recommendations for international students: Required—TOEFL (minimum score 540 paper-based; 76 iBT), IELTS (minimum score 6). *Application deadline:* For fall admission, 8/10 priority date for domestic and international students; for spring admission, 1/4 priority date for domestic and international students; for summer admission, 5/10 priority date for domestic and international students. Application fee: $30. Electronic applications accepted. *Expenses:* Tuition: Full-time $11,952; part-time $664 per credit. *Required fees:* $70 per term. *Financial support:* In 2017–18, 19 students received support. Tuition waivers (full and partial), unspecified assistantships, and institutional discounts available. Financial award applicants required to submit FAFSA. *Faculty research:* Workplace diversity, dynamics of team interaction, utilization of leased employees, experiential learning project on due diligence market for prostheses. *Unit head:* Dr. Robin Frkal, Director, 508-767-7622, E-mail: ra.frkal@assumption.edu. *Application contact:* Karen Stoyanoff, Director of Recruitment for Graduate Enrollment, 508-767-7442, Fax: 508-799-4412, E-mail: graduate@assumption.edu. Website: http://graduate.assumption.edu/mba/assumption-mba

Avila University, School of Business, Kansas City, MO 64145-1698. Offers accounting (MBA); finance (MBA); health care administration (MBA); international business (MBA); management (MBA); management information systems (MBA); marketing (MBA). *Program availability:* Part-time, evening/weekend. *Faculty:* 6 full-time (2 women), 6 part-time/adjunct (2 women). *Students:* 49 full-time (19 women), 29 part-time (14 women); includes 16 minority (12 Black or African American, non-Hispanic/Latino; 1 Asian, non-Hispanic/Latino; 3 Hispanic/Latino), 19 international. Average age 32. 51 applicants, 47% accepted, 20 enrolled. In 2017, 31 master's awarded. *Degree requirements:* For master's, comprehensive exam, capstone course. *Entrance requirements:* For master's, GMAT (minimum score 420), minimum GPA of 3.0, interview. Additional exam requirements/recommendations for international students: Required—TOEFL (minimum score 550 paper-based). *Application deadline:* For fall admission, 7/30 priority date for domestic and international students; for winter admission, 11/30 priority date for domestic and international students; for spring admission, 2/28 priority date for domestic and international students; for summer admission, 6/1 priority date for domestic and international students. Applications are processed on a rolling basis. Application fee: $0. Electronic applications accepted. *Expenses:* Contact institution. *Financial support:* In 2017–18, 18 students received support. Career-related internships or fieldwork and scholarships/grants available. Support available to part-time students. Financial award applicants required to submit FAFSA. *Faculty research:* Leadership characteristics, financial hedging, group dynamics. *Unit head:* Dr. Wendy L. Acker, Interim Dean, 816-501-3720, Fax: 816-501-2463, E-mail: wendy.acker@avila.edu. *Application contact:* Brandon Black, MBA Admission Advisor, 816-501-3601, Fax: 816-501-2463, E-mail: brandon.black@avila.edu. Website: https://www.avila.edu/mrk/mba

Azusa Pacific University, School of Behavioral and Applied Sciences, Department of Leadership and Organizational Psychology, Program in Leadership, Azusa, CA 91702-7000. Offers executive leadership (MA); leadership development (MA); leadership studies (MA); sport management (MA). *Expenses:* Contact institution.

Azusa Pacific University, School of Business and Management, Azusa, CA 91702-7000. Offers accounting (MBA); business administration (MBA); entrepreneurship (MBA); finance (MBA); international business (MBA); marketing (MBA); organizational science (MBA); professional accountancy (M Acc); sport management (MBA). *Program availability:* Part-time, evening/weekend. *Degree requirements:* For master's, thesis (for some programs), final project. *Entrance requirements:* For master's, GMAT, minimum GPA of 3.0. Additional exam requirements/recommendations for international students: Required—TOEFL (minimum score 600 paper-based). *Expenses:* Contact institution. *Faculty research:* Gender issues, financial risk, leadership and ethics, marketing strategy.

Baldwin Wallace University, Graduate Programs, School of Business, Program in International Management, Berea, OH 44017-2088. Offers MBA. *Program availability:* Part-time, evening/weekend. *Students:* 2 full-time (both women), 6 part-time (2 women); includes 3 minority (2 Black or African American, non-Hispanic/Latino; 1 Hispanic/Latino), 1 international. Average age 34. 4 applicants, 75% accepted, 2 enrolled. In 2017, 4 master's awarded. *Degree requirements:* For master's, one foreign language, minimum overall GPA of 3.0. *Entrance requirements:* For master's, GMAT or minimum undergraduate GPA of 3.0, interview, work experience, bachelor's degree in any field. Additional exam requirements/recommendations for international students: Required—TOEFL (minimum score 550 paper-based; 79 iBT). *Application deadline:* For fall admission, 7/25 priority date for domestic students, 4/30 priority date for international students; for spring admission, 12/15 priority date for domestic students, 9/30 priority date for international students; for summer admission, 4/15 priority date for domestic students. Applications are processed on a rolling basis. Application fee: $25. Electronic applications accepted. Application fee is waived when completed online. *Expenses:* $948 per credit hour. *Financial support:* Unspecified assistantships available. Financial award applicants required to submit FAFSA. *Faculty research:* International finance, systems approach, international marketing. *Unit head:* Dale Kramer, Director, 440-826-3331, Fax: 440-826-3868, E-mail: dkramer@bw.edu. *Application contact:* Laura Spencer, Graduate

Application Specialist, 440-826-2191, Fax: 440-826-3868, E-mail: lspencer@bw.edu. Website: http://www.bw.edu/graduate/business/mba/

Barry University, Andreas School of Business, Graduate Certificate Programs, Miami Shores, FL 33161-6695. Offers finance (Certificate); health services administration (Certificate); international business (Certificate); management (Certificate); management information systems (Certificate); marketing (Certificate).

Baruch College of the City University of New York, Zicklin School of Business, Department of Marketing and International Business, New York, NY 10010-5585. Offers international business (MBA); marketing (MBA, MS, PhD). PhD offered jointly with Graduate School and University Center of the City University of New York. *Program availability:* Part-time, evening/weekend. *Degree requirements:* For doctorate, comprehensive exam, thesis/dissertation. *Entrance requirements:* For master's, GMAT, 2 letters of recommendation, resume, 2 years of work experience; for doctorate, GMAT. Additional exam requirements/recommendations for international students: Required—TOEFL (minimum score 590 paper-based), TWE (minimum score 5).

Baruch College of the City University of New York, Zicklin School of Business, International Executive MS Programs, New York, NY 10010-5585. Offers entrepreneurship (MS). *Program availability:* Part-time, evening/weekend. *Entrance requirements:* For master's, GMAT, 2 letters of recommendation, resume, 2 years of work experience. Additional exam requirements/recommendations for international students: Required—TOEFL (minimum score 590 paper-based), TWE (minimum score 5).

Benedictine University, Graduate Programs, Program in Business Administration, Lisle, IL 60532. Offers accounting (MBA); entrepreneurship and managing innovation (MBA); financial management (MBA); health administration (MBA); human resource management (MBA); information systems security (MBA); international business (MBA); management consulting (MBA); management information systems (MBA); marketing management (MBA); operations management and logistics (MBA); organizational leadership (MBA). *Program availability:* Part-time, evening/weekend, online learning. *Entrance requirements:* For master's, GMAT. Additional exam requirements/recommendations for international students: Required—TOEFL (minimum score 550 paper-based). Electronic applications accepted. *Faculty research:* Strategic leadership in professional organizations, sociology of professions, organizational change, social identity theory, applications to change management.

Boston University, Metropolitan College, Department of Administrative Sciences, Boston, MA 02215. Offers applied business analytics (MS); economic development and tourism management (MSAS); enterprise risk management (MS); financial management (MS); global marketing management (MS); innovation and technology (MSAS); insurance management (MS); project management (MS); supply chain management (MS). *Accreditation:* AACSB. *Program availability:* Part-time, evening/weekend, 100% online, blended/hybrid learning. *Faculty:* 21 full-time (5 women), 34 part-time/adjunct (5 women). *Students:* 297 full-time (156 women), 597 part-time (298 women); includes 183 minority (58 Black or African American, non-Hispanic/Latino; 2 American Indian or Alaska Native, non-Hispanic/Latino; 56 Asian, non-Hispanic/Latino; 51 Hispanic/Latino; 2 Native Hawaiian or other Pacific Islander, non-Hispanic/Latino; 14 Two or more races, non-Hispanic/Latino), 391 international. Average age 30. 963 applicants, 64% accepted, 209 enrolled. In 2017, 372 master's awarded. *Degree requirements:* For master's, thesis optional. *Entrance requirements:* For master's, 1 year of work experience, minimum GPA of 3.0. Additional exam requirements/recommendations for international students: Required—TOEFL (minimum score 84 iBT). *Application deadline:* Applications are processed on a rolling basis. Application fee: $85. Electronic applications accepted. *Expenses:* Contact institution. *Financial support:* In 2017–18, 15 students received support, including 18 research assistantships (averaging $8,400 per year), 12 teaching assistantships (averaging $2,700 per year); career-related internships or fieldwork, Federal Work-Study, and unspecified assistantships also available. Financial award applicants required to submit FAFSA. *Faculty research:* International business, innovative process. *Unit head:* Dr. John Sullivan, Chair, 617-353-3016, E-mail: adminsc@bu.edu. *Application contact:* Fiona Niven, Administrative Sciences Department, 617-353-3016, E-mail: adminsc@bu.edu. Website: http://www.bu.edu/met/academic-community/departments/administrative-sciences/

Brandeis University, International Business School (IBS), Waltham, MA 02454-9110. Offers MA, MBA, MSF, PhD. *Faculty:* 40 full-time (16 women), 31 part-time/adjunct (7 women). *Students:* 328 full-time (187 women), 72 part-time (52 women); includes 14 minority (1 Black or African American, non-Hispanic/Latino; 2 American Indian or Alaska Native, non-Hispanic/Latino; 9 Asian, non-Hispanic/Latino; 2 Hispanic/Latino), 360 international. 1,652 applicants, 39% accepted, 218 enrolled. In 2017, 171 master's, 3 doctorates awarded. *Degree requirements:* For doctorate, thesis/dissertation. *Entrance requirements:* For master's, GMAT or GRE, minimum two years of full-time work experience (for MBA); for doctorate, GRE, writing sample. Additional exam requirements/recommendations for international students: Required—TOEFL (minimum score 600 paper-based; 100 iBT), IELTS (minimum score 7), PTE (minimum score 68). *Application deadline:* For fall admission, 11/1 for domestic and international students; for winter admission, 1/15 for domestic and international students; for spring admission, 3/15 for domestic students, 3/15 priority date for international students; for summer admission, 4/15 for domestic and international students. Application fee: $100. Electronic applications accepted. *Expenses:* Contact institution. *Financial support:* In 2017–18, 188 students received support. Institutionally sponsored loans, health care benefits, and scholarships (averaging $17,578 annually) available. Financial award application deadline: 4/15. *Faculty research:* Corporate finance, fixed income, monetary policy, business strategy, cross-cultural interaction. *Unit head:* Peter Petri, Interim Dean, 781-736-2256. *Application contact:* Kelly Sugrue, Assistant Dean of Admissions, 781-736-2252, Fax: 781-736-2263, E-mail: globaladmissions@brandeis.edu. Website: http://www.brandeis.edu/global/

Brandman University, School of Business and Professional Studies, Irvine, CA 92618. Offers accounting (MBA); business administration (MBA); business intelligence and data analytics (MBA); e-business strategic management (MBA); entrepreneurship (MBA); finance (MBA); health administration (MBA); human resources (MBA, MS); international business (MBA); marketing (MBA); organizational leadership (MA, MBA, MPA); public administration (MPA). *Expenses:* Tuition: Part-time $640 per credit hour. Tuition and fees vary according to degree level and program. *Unit head:* Dr. Glenn Worthington, Dean, 253-861-1024, E-mail: gworthin@brandman.edu. *Application contact:* Dr. Glenn Worthington, Dean, 253-861-1024, E-mail: gworthin@brandman.edu. Website: https://www.brandman.edu/academic-programs/business-and-professional-studies

Brooklyn College of the City University of New York, School of Business, Brooklyn, NY 11210-2889. Offers accounting (MS); business administration (MS), including economic analysis, general business, global business and finance. *Program availability:* Part-time, evening/weekend. *Degree requirements:* For master's, comprehensive exam, thesis or alternative. *Entrance requirements:* For master's, GMAT, 2 letters of recommendation. Additional exam requirements/recommendations for international students: Required—TOEFL (minimum score 550 paper-based; 79 iBT). Electronic applications accepted. *Faculty research:* Econometrics, environmental economics, microeconomics, macroeconomics, taxation.

International Business

Bryant University, Graduate School of Business, Smithfield, RI 02917. Offers accounting (MPAC); business administration (MBA), including business analytics, general management, global finance, global supply chain management, international business; taxation (MST). *Program availability:* Part-time, 100% online. *Faculty:* 30 full-time (5 women), 7 part-time/adjunct (2 women). *Students:* 84 full-time (31 women), 91 part-time (35 women); includes 24 minority (4 Black or African American, non-Hispanic/Latino; 1 American Indian or Alaska Native, non-Hispanic/Latino; 6 Asian, non-Hispanic/Latino; 8 Hispanic/Latino; 5 Two or more races, non-Hispanic/Latino), 6 international. Average age 26. 215 applicants, 66% accepted, 96 enrolled. In 2017, 118 master's awarded. *Degree requirements:* For master's, comprehensive exam (for some programs). *Entrance requirements:* For master's, GMAT, resume, recommendation, college transcripts. Additional exam requirements/recommendations for international students: Required—TOEFL (minimum score 580 paper-based; 95 iBT). *Application deadline:* For fall admission, 7/15 for domestic and international students; for spring admission, 11/15 for domestic and international students; for summer admission, 4/15 for domestic and international students. Applications are processed on a rolling basis. Application fee: $80. Electronic applications accepted. *Expenses:* $45,102 total, $1,118 per credit hour, $1,500 study abroad fee (for full-time MBA); $40,248 total, $1,118 per credit hour (for part-time MBA); $30,280 total, $1,176 per credit hour (for MP Ac and MST); $13,146, $1,118 per credit hour (for CGS). *Financial support:* In 2017–18, 95 fellowships with full and partial tuition reimbursements (averaging $9,825 per year), 9 research assistantships with full and partial tuition reimbursements (averaging $7,100 per year) were awarded; scholarships/grants and unspecified assistantships also available. Support available to part-time students. Financial award application deadline: 2/15; financial award applicants required to submit FAFSA. *Faculty research:* International business, public sector auditing, taxation of partnerships, information systems security, financial markets microstructure. *Unit head:* Bjorn Carlsson, Graduate Program Director, 401-232-6707, E-mail: bcarlsson@bryant.edu. *Application contact:* Terri Rogers, Admissions Assistant, 401-232-6230, Fax: 401-232-6494, E-mail: graduateprograms@bryant.edu.
Website: http://gradschool.bryant.edu/business/

Butler University, Lacy School of Business, Indianapolis, IN 46208-3485. Offers entrepreneurship and innovation (MBA); finance (MBA); international business (MBA); leadership (MBA); marketing (MBA); professional accounting (MP Acc). *Accreditation:* AACSB. *Program availability:* Part-time. *Faculty:* 14 full-time (4 women), 9 part-time/adjunct (2 women). *Students:* 35 full-time (16 women), 111 part-time (38 women); includes 15 minority (2 Black or African American, non-Hispanic/Latino; 5 Asian, non-Hispanic/Latino; 8 Hispanic/Latino), 6 international. Average age 30. 149 applicants, 64% accepted, 43 enrolled. In 2017, 90 master's awarded. *Degree requirements:* For master's, comprehensive exam, thesis optional. *Entrance requirements:* For master's, GMAT, minimum AACSB index of 950, personal statement, two letters of recommendation, official transcripts, current resume. Additional exam requirements/recommendations for international students: Required—TOEFL (minimum score 550 paper-based; 79 iBT), IELTS (minimum score 6), Michigan English Language Assessment Battery (minimum score of 80). *Application deadline:* For fall admission, 8/1 for domestic and international students; for spring admission, 12/1 for domestic and international students; for summer admission, 4/1 for domestic and international students. Applications are processed on a rolling basis. Application fee: $0. Electronic applications accepted. *Expenses:* $820 per credit. *Financial support:* In 2017–18, 22 students received support. Scholarships/grants, tuition waivers (full and partial), and unspecified assistantships available. Financial award application deadline: 7/15; financial award applicants required to submit FAFSA. *Faculty research:* Higher education and pedagogy; ecotourism; healthcare issues and marketing public policy; domestic public policy, international finance and banking, international and management entrepreneurship, organizational management. *Unit head:* Dr. Stephen Standifird, Dean, 317-940-8407. *Application contact:* Diane Dubord, Graduate Student Service Specialist, 317-940-8107, Fax: 317-940-8250, E-mail: ddubord@butler.edu.
Website: https://www.butler.edu/lacyschool

California Intercontinental University, School of Business, Irvine, CA 92614. Offers banking and finance (MBA); entrepreneurship and business management (DBA); global business leadership (DBA); international management and marketing (MBA); organizational management and human resource management (MBA).

California Lutheran University, Graduate Studies, School of Management, Thousand Oaks, CA 91360-2787. Offers business (IMBA); entrepreneurship (MBA, Certificate); finance (MBA, Certificate); financial planning (MBA, MS, Certificate); human capital management (MBA, Certificate); information technology (MS); information technology management (MBA, Certificate); international business (MBA, Certificate); marketing (MBA, Certificate); public policy and administration (MPPA); quantitative economics (MS). *Program availability:* Part-time, evening/weekend, 100% online, blended/hybrid learning. *Faculty:* 17 full-time (4 women), 40 part-time/adjunct (9 women). *Students:* 423 full-time (168 women), 153 part-time (72 women); includes 124 minority (11 Black or African American, non-Hispanic/Latino; 1 American Indian or Alaska Native, non-Hispanic/Latino; 21 Asian, non-Hispanic/Latino; 75 Hispanic/Latino; 16 Two or more races, non-Hispanic/Latino), 294 international. Average age 31. 467 applicants, 72% accepted, 108 enrolled. In 2017, 306 master's awarded. *Degree requirements:* For master's, comprehensive exam (for some programs). *Entrance requirements:* For master's, GMAT, interview, minimum GPA of 3.0. *Application deadline:* Applications are processed on a rolling basis. Application fee: $50. Electronic applications accepted. *Expenses:* Contact institution. *Unit head:* Dr. Gerhard Apfelthaler, Dean, 805-493-3360. *Application contact:* 805-493-3325, Fax: 805-493-3861, E-mail: clugrad@callutheran.edu.
Website: http://www.callutheran.edu/management/

California State University, Fullerton, Graduate Studies, College of Business and Economics, Program in Business Administration, Fullerton, CA 92831-3599. Offers business administration (MBA); business analytics (MBA); international business (MBA); organizational leadership (MBA); risk management and insurance (MBA). *Accreditation:* AACSB. *Program availability:* Part-time. *Faculty:* 12 full-time (5 women), 1 part-time/adjunct (0 women). *Students:* 64 full-time (35 women), 103 part-time (46 women); includes 81 minority (40 Asian, non-Hispanic/Latino; 36 Hispanic/Latino; 5 Two or more races, non-Hispanic/Latino), 36 international. Average age 29. 254 applicants, 47% accepted, 62 enrolled. *Entrance requirements:* For master's, GMAT. Application fee: $55. *Financial support:* Career-related internships or fieldwork, Federal Work-Study, institutionally sponsored loans, and scholarships/grants available. Support available to part-time students. Financial award application deadline: 3/1; financial award applicants required to submit FAFSA. *Unit head:* Shaun Pichler, Director, 657-278-7373, E-mail: spichler@fullerton.edu. *Application contact:* Admissions/Applications, 657-278-2371.

California State University, Los Angeles, Graduate Division, College of Business and Economics, Department of Marketing, Los Angeles, CA 90032-8530. Offers international business (MBA, MS). *Program availability:* Part-time, evening/weekend. *Degree requirements:* For master's, comprehensive exam (MBA), thesis (MS). *Entrance requirements:* For master's, GMAT, minimum GPA of 2.5 during previous 2 years of course work. Additional exam requirements/recommendations for international students: Required—TOEFL (minimum score 550 paper-based). Electronic applications accepted.

California State University, San Bernardino, Graduate Studies, College of Business and Public Administration, Program in Business Administration, San Bernardino, CA 92407. Offers accounting (MBA); entrepreneurship (MBA); finance (MBA); global business (MBA); information management (MBA); information security (MBA); management (MBA); supply chain management (MBA). *Accreditation:* AACSB. *Program availability:* Part-time, evening/weekend, online learning. *Faculty:* 4 full-time (3 women), 6 part-time/adjunct (4 women). *Students:* 21 full-time (15 women), 122 part-time (30 women); includes 82 minority (15 Black or African American, non-Hispanic/Latino; 1 American Indian or Alaska Native, non-Hispanic/Latino; 19 Asian, non-Hispanic/Latino; 44 Hispanic/Latino; 3 Two or more races, non-Hispanic/Latino), 37 international. Average age 33. 258 applicants, 44% accepted, 50 enrolled. In 2017, 134 master's awarded. *Degree requirements:* For master's, comprehensive exam, thesis. *Entrance requirements:* Additional exam requirements/recommendations for international students: Required—TOEFL. *Application deadline:* For fall admission, 7/16 for domestic students, 7/20 for international students; for winter admission, 10/23 for domestic students, 10/20 for international students; for spring admission, 1/22 for domestic students, 1/20 for international students. Application fee: $55. *Expenses:* Contact institution. *Financial support:* Application deadline: 3/1. *Unit head:* Dr. Lawrence C. Rose, Dean, 909-537-3703, Fax: 909-537-7026, E-mail: lrose@csusb.edu. *Application contact:* Dr. Vipin Gupta, Associate Dean/MBA Director, 909-537-7380, Fax: 909-537-7026, E-mail: vgupta@csusb.edu.
Website: http://mba.csusb.edu/

California University of Management and Sciences, Graduate Programs, Anaheim, CA 92801. Offers business administration (MBA, DBA); computer information systems (MS); economics (MS); international business (MS); sports management (MS).

Canisius College, Graduate Division, Richard J. Wehle School of Business, Department of Management, Buffalo, NY 14208-1098. Offers business administration (MBA); international business (MS). *Accreditation:* AACSB. *Program availability:* Part-time, evening/weekend. *Faculty:* 8 full-time (4 women), 1 (woman) part-time/adjunct. *Students:* 104 full-time (49 women), 113 part-time (43 women); includes 25 minority (8 Black or African American, non-Hispanic/Latino; 2 American Indian or Alaska Native, non-Hispanic/Latino; 4 Asian, non-Hispanic/Latino; 6 Hispanic/Latino; 3 Native Hawaiian or other Pacific Islander, non-Hispanic/Latino; 2 Two or more races, non-Hispanic/Latino), 31 international. Average age 28. 140 applicants, 82% accepted, 72 enrolled. In 2017, 103 master's awarded. *Entrance requirements:* For master's, GMAT, GRE, official transcript from colleges attended, current resume. Additional exam requirements/recommendations for international students: Required—TOEFL (minimum score 550 paper-based, 80 iBT), IELTS (minimum score 6.5), or CAEL (minimum score 70). *Application deadline:* For fall admission, 7/1 priority date for domestic students; for spring admission, 11/1 priority date for domestic students. Applications are processed on a rolling basis. Application fee: $0. Electronic applications accepted. *Expenses:* Tuition: Full-time $22,860; part-time $820 per credit. *Required fees:* $720; $25 per credit. $65 per semester. One-time fee: $425. *Financial support:* Career-related internships or fieldwork, Federal Work-Study, scholarships/grants, tuition waivers (partial), and unspecified assistantships available. Support available to part-time students. Financial award application deadline: 4/30; financial award applicants required to submit FAFSA. *Faculty research:* Global leadership effectiveness, global supply chain management, quality management. *Unit head:* Dr. Lynn A. Fish, Chair of Management, Entrepreneurship and International Business, 716-888-2634, E-mail: fishl@canisius.edu.
Website: http://www.canisius.edu/graduate/

Central European University, Department of Legal Studies, Budapest, Hungary. Offers comparative Constitutional law (LL M); human rights (LL M, MA); international business law (LL M); juridical sciences (SJD). *Faculty:* 10 full-time (5 women), 9 part-time/adjunct (1 woman). *Students:* 90 full-time (52 women). Average age 28. 384 applicants, 33% accepted, 71 enrolled. In 2017, 53 master's, 3 doctorates awarded. Terminal master's awarded for partial completion of doctoral program. *Degree requirements:* For master's, one foreign language, thesis; for doctorate, one foreign language, comprehensive exam, thesis/dissertation. *Entrance requirements:* For master's and doctorate, LSAT. Additional exam requirements/recommendations for international students: Required—TOEFL (minimum score 570 paper-based); Recommended—IELTS (minimum score 6.5). *Application deadline:* For fall admission, 2/4 for domestic and international students. Application fee: $30. Electronic applications accepted. *Expenses:* Contact institution. *Financial support:* Fellowships, career-related internships or fieldwork, institutionally sponsored loans, scholarships/grants, and tuition waivers (full and partial) available. Financial award application deadline: 2/4. *Faculty research:* Institutional, Constitutional and human rights in European Union law; biomedical law and reproductive rights; data protection law; comparative and international business law and the regulation of business environments;. *Unit head:* Dr. Karoly Bard, Head of Department, 36 1 327-3294, Fax: 361-327-3198, E-mail: legalst@ceu.edu. *Application contact:* Zsuzsanna Jaszberenyi, Department Coordinator, 361-327-3272, Fax: 361-327-3198, E-mail: admissions@ceu.edu.
Website: http://legal.ceu.edu

Central Michigan University, College of Graduate Studies, College of Business Administration, MBA Program, Mount Pleasant, MI 48859. Offers accounting (MBA); business economics (MBA); consulting (MBA); finance (MBA); general business (MBA); human resource management (MBA); information systems (MBA); international business (MBA); logistics management (MBA); marketing (MBA); value-driven organization (MBA). *Program availability:* Part-time, evening/weekend, online learning. Electronic applications accepted. *Faculty research:* Accounting, consulting, international business, marketing, information systems.

Central Michigan University, College of Graduate Studies, Interdisciplinary Administration Programs, Mount Pleasant, MI 48859. Offers acquisitions administration (MSA, Graduate Certificate); general administration (MSA, Graduate Certificate); health services administration (MSA, Graduate Certificate); human resource administration (Graduate Certificate); human resources administration (MSA); information resource management (MSA, Graduate Certificate); international administration (MSA, Graduate Certificate); leadership (MSA, Graduate Certificate); public administration (MSA, Graduate Certificate); research administration (Graduate Certificate); sport administration (MSA). *Accreditation:* AACSB. *Program availability:* Part-time, evening/weekend, online learning. *Degree requirements:* For master's, thesis or alternative. *Entrance requirements:* For master's, bachelor's degree with minimum GPA of 2.7. Electronic applications accepted. *Faculty research:* Interdisciplinary studies in acquisitions administration, health services administration, sport administration, recreation and park administration, and international administration.

Christian Brothers University, School of Business, Memphis, TN 38104-5581. Offers accountancy (M Acc); business (MBA); international business (MIB); project management (Certificate); MBA/MIB. *Program availability:* Part-time, evening/weekend. *Entrance requirements:* For master's, GMAT, GRE. Additional exam requirements/recommendations for international students: Required—TOEFL.

City University of Seattle, Graduate Division, School of Management, Seattle, WA 98121. Offers accounting (Certificate); change leadership (MBA, Certificate); computer systems (MS); finance (Certificate); financial management (MBA); general management

(MBA); general management-Europe (MBA); global marketing (MBA); human resources management (Certificate); individualized study (MBA); information security (MS); information systems (MBA); leadership (MA); marketing (MBA, Certificate); project management (MBA, MS, Certificate); sustainable business (Certificate); technology management (MBA, Certificate). *Program availability:* Part-time, evening/weekend, online learning. *Degree requirements:* For master's, comprehensive exam (for some programs), thesis (for some programs). *Entrance requirements:* For master's, baccalaureate degree or equivalent from an accredited or otherwise recognized institution. Additional exam requirements/recommendations for international students: Required—TOEFL (minimum score 567 paper-based; 87 iBT); Recommended—IELTS. Electronic applications accepted.

Clarkson University, David D. Reh School of Business, Master's Program in Business Administration, Potsdam, NY 13699. Offers business fundamentals (Advanced Certificate); global supply chain management (Advanced Certificate); human resource management (Advanced Certificate); management and leadership (Advanced Certificate). *Accreditation:* AACSB. *Program availability:* Part-time, evening/weekend, 100% online, blended/hybrid learning. *Faculty:* 55 full-time (14 women), 38 part-time/adjunct (10 women). *Students:* 92 full-time (31 women), 50 part-time (24 women); includes 20 minority (5 Black or African American, non-Hispanic/Latino; 1 American Indian or Alaska Native, non-Hispanic/Latino; 8 Asian, non-Hispanic/Latino; 5 Hispanic/Latino; 1 Two or more races, non-Hispanic/Latino), 11 international. 174 applicants, 55% accepted, 67 enrolled. In 2017, 1 Advanced Certificate awarded. *Entrance requirements:* Additional exam requirements/recommendations for international students: Required—TOEFL (minimum score 550 paper-based, 80 iBT) or IELTS (6.5). *Application deadline:* Applications are processed on a rolling basis. Application fee: $50. Electronic applications accepted. *Expenses: Tuition:* Full-time $24,210; part-time $1345 per credit hour. Tuition and fees vary according to campus/location and program. *Financial support:* Scholarships/grants available. *Unit head:* Dr. Alan Bowman, Senior Associate Dean of Graduate Business Programs, 518-631-9887, E-mail: abowman@clarkson.edu. *Application contact:* Dan Capogna, Director of Graduate Admissions, 518-631-9910, E-mail: graduate@clarkson.edu.
Website: https://www.clarkson.edu/academics/graduate

Clayton State University, School of Graduate Studies, College of Business, Program in Business Administration, Morrow, GA 30260-0285. Offers accounting (MBA); human resource leadership (MBA); international business (MBA); sports and entertainment management (MBA); supply chain management (MBA). *Accreditation:* AACSB. *Program availability:* Part-time, evening/weekend. *Degree requirements:* For master's, thesis. *Entrance requirements:* For master's, GMAT, 3 letters of recommendation; statement of purpose; 2 official transcripts. Additional exam requirements/recommendations for international students: Required—TOEFL (minimum score 550 paper-based; 80 iBT). Electronic applications accepted. *Expenses:* Contact institution.

Colorado State University–Global Campus, Graduate Programs, Greenwood Village, CO 80111. Offers criminal justice and law enforcement administration (MS); education leadership (MS); finance (MS); healthcare administration and management (MS); human resource management (MHRM); information technology management (MITM); international management (MS); management (MS); organizational leadership (MS); professional accounting (MPA); project management (MS); teaching and learning (MS). *Accreditation:* ACBSP. *Program availability:* Online learning.

Columbia University, Graduate School of Business, Executive MBA Global Program, New York, NY 10027. Offers EMBA. Program offered jointly with London Business School. *Entrance requirements:* For master's, GMAT, 2 letters of reference, interview, minimum 5 years of work experience, curriculum vitae or resume, employer support. Additional exam requirements/recommendations for international students: Recommended—TOEFL, IELTS. Electronic applications accepted. *Expenses:* Contact institution.

Columbia University, Graduate School of Business, MBA Program, New York, NY 10027. Offers accounting (MBA); decision, risk, and operations (MBA); entrepreneurship (MBA); finance and economics (MBA); healthcare and pharmaceutical management (MBA); human resource management (MBA); international business (MBA); leadership and ethics (MBA); management (MBA); marketing (MBA); media (MBA); private equity (MBA); real estate (MBA); social enterprise (MBA); value investing (MBA); DDS/MBA; JD/MBA; MBA/MIA; MBA/MPH; MBA/MS; MD/MBA. *Entrance requirements:* For master's, GMAT, 2 letters of recommendation. Additional exam requirements/recommendations for international students: Required—TOEFL. Electronic applications accepted. *Expenses:* Contact institution. *Faculty research:* Human decision making and behavioral research; real estate market and mortgage defaults; financial crisis and corporate governance; international business; security analysis and accounting.

Concordia University Wisconsin, Graduate Programs, School of Business Administration, MBA Program, Mequon, WI 53097-2402. Offers finance (MBA); health care administration (MBA); human resource management (MBA); international business (MBA); international business-bilingual English/Chinese (MBA); management (MBA); management information systems (MBA); managerial communications (MBA); marketing (MBA); public administration (MBA); risk management (MBA). *Program availability:* Online learning. *Degree requirements:* For master's, comprehensive exam, thesis or alternative. *Entrance requirements:* Additional exam requirements/recommendations for international students: Required—TOEFL. *Expenses:* Contact institution.

Copenhagen Business School, Graduate Programs, Copenhagen, Denmark. Offers business administration (Exec MBA, MBA, PhD); business administration and information systems (M Sc); business, language and culture (M Sc); economics and business administration (M Sc); health management (MHM); international business and politics (M Sc); public administration (MPA); shipping and logistics (Exec MBA); technology, market and organization (MBA).

Daemen College, Department of Accounting/Information Systems, Amherst, NY 14226-3592. Offers global business (MS), including accounting, global business, management information systems, marketing. *Program availability:* Part-time, evening/weekend. *Degree requirements:* For master's, minimum GPA of 3.0. *Entrance requirements:* For master's, GMAT if undergraduate GPA is less than 3.0, 2 letters of recommendation; goal statement; transcripts; demonstration of satisfactory oral and written English. Additional exam requirements/recommendations for international students: Required—TOEFL (minimum score 500 paper-based; 63 iBT), IELTS (minimum score 5.5). Electronic applications accepted. *Faculty research:* Internationalization of small business, cultural influences on business practices, international human resource practices.

Dallas Baptist University, College of Business, Master of Business Administration Program, Dallas, TX 75211-9299. Offers accounting (MBA); business communication (MBA); conflict resolution management (MBA); entrepreneurship (MBA); finance (MBA); health care management (MBA); international business (MBA); leading the non-profit organization (MBA); management (MBA); management information systems (MBA); marketing (MBA); project management (MBA); technology and engineering management (MBA). *Accreditation:* ACBSP. *Program availability:* Part-time, evening/weekend, 100% online, blended/hybrid learning. *Application deadline:* Applications are processed on a rolling basis. Application fee: $25. Electronic applications accepted. Application fee is waived when completed online. *Expenses: Tuition:* Full-time $16,308; part-time $906 per credit hour. *Required fees:* $900; $450 per semester. Tuition and fees vary according to course load and degree level. *Unit head:* Dr. Sandra Reid, Chair of Graduate Business Programs, 214-333-5280, E-mail: sandra@dbu.edu. *Application contact:* Bobby Soto, Director of Admissions, 214-333-5242, E-mail: graduate@dbu.edu.
Website: http://www.dbu.edu/gsb/mba

Dallas Baptist University, Gary Cook School of Leadership, Program in International Studies, Dallas, TX 75211-9299. Offers East Asian studies (MA); European studies (MA); general international studies (MA); global business (MA); international immersion (MA); international ministry (MA); international relations (MA). *Program availability:* Part-time, evening/weekend. *Application deadline:* Applications are processed on a rolling basis. Application fee: $25. Electronic applications accepted. Application fee is waived when completed online. *Expenses: Tuition:* Full-time $16,308; part-time $906 per credit hour. *Required fees:* $900; $450 per semester. Tuition and fees vary according to course load and degree level. *Unit head:* Dr. Jack Goodyear, Dean, 214-333-5595, Fax: 214-333-6809, E-mail: jackg@dbu.edu. *Application contact:* Lee Bratcher, Program Director, 214-333-5808, E-mail: leeb@dbu.edu.
Website: http://www4.dbu.edu/leadership/mainternational

Dallas Baptist University, Graduate School of Ministry, Program in Global Leadership, Dallas, TX 75211-9299. Offers church planting (MA); East Asian Studies (MA); English as a second language (MA); general studies (MA); global communication (MA); global studies (MA); international business (MA); leading the nonprofit organization (MA); missions (MA); small group ministry (MA); urban ministry (MA). *Program availability:* Part-time, evening/weekend. *Application deadline:* Applications are processed on a rolling basis. Application fee: $25. Electronic applications accepted. Application fee is waived when completed online. *Expenses: Tuition:* Full-time $16,308; part-time $906 per credit hour. *Required fees:* $900; $450 per semester. Tuition and fees vary according to course load and degree level. *Unit head:* Dr. Robert R. Brooks, Dean, 214-333-5494, Fax: 214-333-5673, E-mail: bobb@dbu.edu. *Application contact:* Dr. Brent Thomason, Program Director, 214-333-5236, E-mail: brentt@dbu.edu.
Website: http://www.dbu.edu/ministry/degree-programs/m-a-in-global-leadership

Delaware Valley University, MBA Program, Doylestown, PA 18901-2697. Offers accounting (MBA); entrepreneurship (MBA); finance (MBA); food and agribusiness (MBA); general business (MBA); global executive leadership (MBA); human resource management (MBA); supply chain management (MBA). *Program availability:* Part-time, evening/weekend, online learning. *Entrance requirements:* For master's, minimum undergraduate GPA of 3.0. Electronic applications accepted. *Expenses:* Contact institution.

DePaul University, Kellstadt Graduate School of Business, Chicago, IL 60604. Offers accountancy (MBA, MSA); applied economics (MBA); audit and advisory services (MS); business administration (DBA); business analytics (MS); business strategy and decision-making (MBA); computational finance (MS); economics and policy analysis (MS); enterprise risk management (MS); entrepreneurship (MBA, MS); finance (MBA, MS); general business (MBA); hospitality leadership (MBA); hospitality leadership and operational performance (MS); human resources (MS); international business (MBA); management (MBA, MS); management information systems (MBA); marketing (MBA, MS); marketing analysis (MS); marketing strategy and planning (MBA); real estate (MS); real estate finance and investment (MBA); strategy, execution and valuation (MBA); supply chain management (MS); sustainable management (MS); taxation (MS); JD/MBA. *Accreditation:* AACSB. *Program availability:* Part-time, evening/weekend, online learning. *Entrance requirements:* For master's, GMAT/GRE, 2 letters of recommendation, resume, essay, official transcripts. Additional exam requirements/recommendations for international students: Required—TOEFL (minimum score 550 paper-based; 80 iBT). *Application deadline:* For fall admission, 7/1 for domestic students, 6/1 for international students; for winter admission, 10/1 for domestic students, 9/1 for international students; for spring admission, 2/1 for domestic students, 1/1 for international students. Applications are processed on a rolling basis. Application fee: $60. Electronic applications accepted. *Expenses:* Contact institution. *Financial support:* Application deadline: 4/1; applicants required to submit FAFSA. *Unit head:* Christa Hinton, Assistant Dean and Director, 312-362-8810, Fax: 312-362-6677, E-mail: chinton@depaul.edu. *Application contact:* Garry Cooke, Director of Recruitment and Admissions, 312-362-8810, Fax: 312-362-6677, E-mail: kgsb@depaul.edu.
Website: http://kellstadt.depaul.edu

Duke University, The Fuqua School of Business, The Duke MBA-Global Executive Program, Durham, NC 27708-0586. Offers business administration (MBA); energy and environment (MBA); entrepreneurship and innovation (MBA); finance (MBA); health sector management (Certificate); marketing (MBA); strategy (MBA). *Faculty:* 96 full-time (19 women), 48 part-time/adjunct (15 women). *Students:* 94 full-time (26 women); includes 34 minority (8 Black or African American, non-Hispanic/Latino; 21 Asian, non-Hispanic/Latino; 4 Hispanic/Latino; 1 Two or more races, non-Hispanic/Latino), 25 international. Average age 39. In 2017, 27 master's awarded. *Entrance requirements:* For master's, Executive Assessment, GMAT, or GRE, transcripts, essays, resume, recommendation letters, letter of company support, interview. *Application deadline:* For fall admission, 10/12 priority date for domestic and international students; for winter admission, 12/7 priority date for domestic and international students; for spring admission, 3/20 priority date for domestic and international students; for summer admission, 5/31 for domestic and international students. Applications are processed on a rolling basis. Application fee: $225. Electronic applications accepted. *Expenses:* Contact institution. *Financial support:* In 2017–18, 31 students received support. Scholarships/grants available. Financial award applicants required to submit FAFSA. *Unit head:* Karen Courtney, Associate Dean, Executive Programs. *Application contact:* Shari Hubert, Associate Dean, Office of Admissions, 919-660-7705, Fax: 919-681-8026, E-mail: admissions-info@fuqua.duke.edu.
Website: https://www.fuqua.duke.edu/programs/global-executive-mba

Duke University, The Fuqua School of Business, MMS: Duke Kunshan University Program, Durham, NC 27708-0586. Offers MMS. *Faculty:* 96 full-time (19 women), 48 part-time/adjunct (15 women). *Students:* 64 full-time (33 women), 57 international. Average age 23. In 2017, 49 master's awarded. *Entrance requirements:* For master's, GMAT or GRE, transcripts, essays, resume, recommendation letters, interview. *Application deadline:* For fall admission, 9/21 for domestic and international students; for winter admission, 1/24 for domestic and international students; for spring admission, 3/7 for domestic and international students; for summer admission, 4/11 for domestic and international students. Electronic applications accepted. *Financial support:* Applicants required to submit FAFSA. *Unit head:* Jeremy Petranka, Associate Dean. *Application contact:* Shari Hubert, Associate Dean, Office of Admissions, 919-660-7705, E-mail: mms-dku-info@fuqua.duke.edu.
Website: https://www.fuqua.duke.edu/programs/mms-duke-kunshan-university

D'Youville College, Department of Business, Buffalo, NY 14201-1084. Offers business administration (MBA); international business (MS). *Program availability:* Part-time, evening/weekend. *Degree requirements:* For master's, one foreign language, project or thesis. *Entrance requirements:* For master's, minimum GPA of 3.0. Additional exam

International Business

requirements/recommendations for international students: Required—TOEFL (minimum score 500 paper-based). Electronic applications accepted. *Faculty research:* Assessment, accreditation, supply chain, online learning, adult learning.

Eastern Michigan University, Graduate School, College of Arts and Sciences, Department of World Languages, Program in Language and International Trade, Ypsilanti, MI 48197. Offers MA. *Program availability:* Evening/weekend. In 2017, 1 master's awarded. *Degree requirements:* For master's, one foreign language. *Entrance requirements:* Additional exam requirements/recommendations for international students: Required—TOEFL. *Application deadline:* Applications are processed on a rolling basis. Application fee: $45. *Financial support:* Fellowships, research assistantships with full tuition reimbursements, teaching assistantships with full tuition reimbursements, career-related internships or fieldwork, Federal Work-Study, institutionally sponsored loans, scholarships/grants, tuition waivers (partial), and unspecified assistantships available. Support available to part-time students. Financial award applicants required to submit FAFSA. *Application contact:* Dr. Genevieve Peden, Program Advisor, 734-487-1498, Fax: 734-487-3411, E-mail: gpeden@emich.edu.

Eastern Michigan University, Graduate School, College of Business, Department of Marketing, Ypsilanti, MI 48197. Offers e-business (MBA); integrated marketing communications (MS, Postbaccalaureate Certificate); international business (MBA); marketing management (MBA); supply chain management (MBA). *Program availability:* Part-time, evening/weekend, online learning. *Faculty:* 21 full-time (8 women). *Students:* 24 full-time (20 women), 33 part-time (26 women); includes 15 minority (11 Black or African American, non-Hispanic/Latino; 3 Hispanic/Latino; 1 Two or more races, non-Hispanic/Latino). Average age 31. 41 applicants, 66% accepted, 23 enrolled. In 2017, 22 master's, 1 other advanced degree awarded. *Entrance requirements:* For master's, GMAT. Additional exam requirements/recommendations for international students: Required—TOEFL. *Application deadline:* For fall admission, 5/15 priority date for domestic students, 2/15 priority date for international students; for winter admission, 10/15 priority date for domestic students, 9/1 priority date for international students; for summer admission, 3/15 priority date for domestic students, 3/1 priority date for international students. Applications are processed on a rolling basis. Application fee: $45. *Financial support:* Fellowships, research assistantships with full tuition reimbursements, teaching assistantships with full tuition reimbursements, career-related internships or fieldwork, Federal Work-Study, institutionally sponsored loans, scholarships/grants, tuition waivers (partial), and unspecified assistantships available. Support available to part-time students. Financial award applicants required to submit FAFSA. *Unit head:* Dr. Lewis Hershey, Department Head, 734-487-3323, Fax: 734-487-7099, E-mail: lhershe1@emich.edu. *Application contact:* K. Michelle Henry, Director, Graduate Business Programs, 734-487-4444, Fax: 734-483-1316, E-mail: cob.graduate@emich.edu.
Website: http://www.mkt.emich.edu/index.html

Eastern Michigan University, Graduate School, College of Business, Programs in Business Administration, Ypsilanti, MI 48197. Offers business administration (MBA, Graduate Certificate); computer information systems (Graduate Certificate); e-business (MBA, Graduate Certificate); enterprise business intelligence (MBA); entrepreneurship (MBA, Graduate Certificate); finance (MBA, Graduate Certificate); human resources (MBA); human resources management (Graduate Certificate); information systems (MBA); internal auditing (MBA); international business (MBA, Graduate Certificate); marketing management (Graduate Certificate); nonprofit management (MBA); organizational development (Graduate Certificate); supply chain management (MBA, Graduate Certificate). *Accreditation:* AACSB. *Program availability:* Part-time, online learning. *Students:* 53 full-time (30 women), 297 part-time (170 women); includes 121 minority (72 Black or African American, non-Hispanic/Latino; 4 American Indian or Alaska Native, non-Hispanic/Latino; 15 Asian, non-Hispanic/Latino; 20 Hispanic/Latino; 10 Two or more races, non-Hispanic/Latino), 20 international. Average age 31. 247 applicants, 74% accepted, 94 enrolled. In 2017, 71 master's, 34 other advanced degrees awarded. *Entrance requirements:* For master's, GMAT (minimum score 450), minimum cumulative undergraduate GPA of 2.75. Additional exam requirements/recommendations for international students: Required—TOEFL. *Application deadline:* For fall admission, 5/15 priority date for domestic students, 2/15 priority date for international students; for winter admission, 10/15 priority date for domestic students, 9/1 priority date for international students; for summer admission, 3/15 priority date for domestic students, 3/1 priority date for international students. Applications are processed on a rolling basis. Application fee: $45. *Financial support:* Fellowships, research assistantships with full tuition reimbursements, teaching assistantships with full tuition reimbursements, career-related internships or fieldwork, Federal Work-Study, institutionally sponsored loans, scholarships/grants, tuition waivers (partial), and unspecified assistantships available. Support available to part-time students. Financial award applicants required to submit FAFSA. *Unit head:* K. Michelle Henry, Director, Graduate Business Programs, 734-487-4444, Fax: 734-483-1316, E-mail: cob.graduate@emich.edu.
Website: http://www.emich.edu/cob/mba/

Embry-Riddle Aeronautical University–Worldwide, Department of Decision Sciences, Daytona Beach, FL 32114-3900. Offers aviation and aerospace (MSPM); aviation/aerospace management (MSEM); financial management (MSEM, MSPM); general management (MSPM); global management (MSPM); human resources management (MSPM); information systems (MSPM); leadership (MSEM, MSPM); logistics and supply chain management (MSEM, MSLSCM, MSPM); management (MSEM, MSPM); project management (MSEM); systems engineering (MSEM, MSPM); technical management (MSPM). *Program availability:* Part-time, evening/weekend, EagleVision Classroom (between classrooms), EagleVision Home (faculty and students at home), and a blend of Classroom or Home. *Faculty:* 12 full-time (3 women), 53 part-time/adjunct (10 women). *Students:* 514 full-time (141 women), 476 part-time (111 women); includes 337 minority (136 Black or African American, non-Hispanic/Latino; 6 American Indian or Alaska Native, non-Hispanic/Latino; 39 Asian, non-Hispanic/Latino; 81 Hispanic/Latino; 4 Native Hawaiian or other Pacific Islander, non-Hispanic/Latino; 71 Two or more races, non-Hispanic/Latino), 21 international. Average age 36. 297 applicants, 72% accepted, 209 enrolled. In 2017, 292 master's awarded. *Degree requirements:* For master's, comprehensive exam (for some programs), thesis (for some programs). *Entrance requirements:* Additional exam requirements/recommendations for international students: Required—TOEFL (minimum score 550 paper-based; 79 iBT), IELTS (minimum score 6). *Application deadline:* Applications are processed on a rolling basis. Application fee: $50. Electronic applications accepted. *Expenses:* Contact institution. *Financial support:* Career-related internships or fieldwork and scholarships/grants available. Financial award applicants required to submit FAFSA. *Unit head:* Aman Gupta, PhD, Department Chair, E-mail: aman.gupta@erau.edu. *Application contact:* Worldwide Campus, 800-522-6787, E-mail: worldwide@erau.edu.

Embry-Riddle Aeronautical University–Worldwide, Department of Management, Daytona Beach, FL 32114-3900. Offers global management (MS); human resources management (MS); leadership (MS); operations management (MS); project management (MS). *Program availability:* Part-time, evening/weekend, EagleVision Classroom (between classrooms), EagleVision Home (faculty and students at home), and a blend of Classroom or Home. *Students:* 148 full-time (48 women), 192 part-time

(52 women); includes 91 minority (46 Black or African American, non-Hispanic/Latino; 1 American Indian or Alaska Native, non-Hispanic/Latino; 11 Asian, non-Hispanic/Latino; 16 Hispanic/Latino; 17 Two or more races, non-Hispanic/Latino), 7 international. Average age 39. In 2017, 104 master's awarded. *Entrance requirements:* Additional exam requirements/recommendations for international students: Required—TOEFL (minimum score 550 paper-based, 79 iBT) or IELTS (6). *Application deadline:* Applications are processed on a rolling basis. Application fee: $50. Electronic applications accepted. *Expenses:* Contact institution. *Financial support:* Career-related internships or fieldwork and scholarships/grants available. Financial award applicants required to submit FAFSA. *Unit head:* Thomas Henkel, PhD, Department Chair, E-mail: thomas.henkel@erau.edu. *Application contact:* Worldwide Campus, 800-522-6787, E-mail: worldwide@erau.edu.

Emory University, Goizueta Business School, Full Time MBA Program, Atlanta, GA 30322. Offers accounting (MBA); alternative investments (MBA); business process consulting (MBA); business technology management (MBA); capital markets (MBA); corporate finance (MBA); customer relationship management (MBA); decision analytics (MBA); entrepreneurship (MBA); finance (MBA); global management (MBA); investment banking (MBA); management consulting (MBA); marketing (MBA); marketing analytics (MBA); marketing consulting (MBA); operations management (MBA); organization and management (MBA); product and brand management (MBA); real estate (MBA); social enterprise (MBA); strategy consulting (MBA). *Accreditation:* AACSB. *Faculty:* 74 full-time (18 women), 18 part-time/adjunct (6 women). *Students:* 353 full-time (96 women); includes 80 minority (18 Black or African American, non-Hispanic/Latino; 2 American Indian or Alaska Native, non-Hispanic/Latino; 39 Asian, non-Hispanic/Latino; 16 Hispanic/Latino; 1 Native Hawaiian or other Pacific Islander, non-Hispanic/Latino; 4 Two or more races, non-Hispanic/Latino), 104 international. Average age 29. 1,380 applicants, 34% accepted, 172 enrolled. In 2017, 179 master's awarded. *Degree requirements:* For master's, 1 leadership course; 2 mid-semester module programs; 2 global components. *Entrance requirements:* For master's, GMAT/GRE, essays; recommendation letters; undergraduate degree; interview. Additional exam requirements/recommendations for international students: Required—TOEFL (minimum score 100 iBT), IELTS (minimum score 7), PTE (minimum score 68). *Application deadline:* For fall admission, 10/6 for domestic and international students; for winter admission, 11/17 for domestic and international students; for spring admission, 1/3 priority date for domestic and international students; for summer admission, 3/9 for domestic and international students. Application fee: $150. Electronic applications accepted. *Expenses:* $59,616. *Financial support:* In 2017–18, 273 students received support. Career-related internships or fieldwork, institutionally sponsored loans, and scholarships/grants available. Financial award application deadline: 4/1; financial award applicants required to submit FAFSA. *Faculty research:* Corporate finance, information systems, digital marketing, asset pricing, sports management. *Unit head:* Brian Mitchell, Associate Dean, 404-727-4824, Fax: 404-712-9648, E-mail: brian.mitchell@emory.edu. *Application contact:* Julie Barefoot, Associate Dean, 404-727-6311, Fax: 404-727-4612, E-mail: mbaadmissions@emory.edu.
Website: http://www.goizueta.emory.edu

ESSEC Business School, Graduate Programs, Paris, France. Offers business administration (PhD); executive business administration (MBA); global business administration (MBA); hospitality management (MBA); international luxury brand management (MBA); management (MSM).

Fairleigh Dickinson University, Florham Campus, Silberman College of Business, Department of Economics, Finance, and International Business, Program in International Business, Madison, NJ 07940-1099. Offers MBA, Certificate.

Fairleigh Dickinson University, Metropolitan Campus, Silberman College of Business, Department of Economics, Finance and International Business, Program in International Business, Teaneck, NJ 07666-1914. Offers MBA.

Florida Atlantic University, College of Business, Department of Management, Boca Raton, FL 33431-0991. Offers business administration (MBA); entrepreneurship (MBA); health management (MBA); international business (MBA); sport management (MBA). *Faculty:* 4 full-time (1 woman). *Students:* 122 full-time (86 women), 81 part-time (67 women); includes 117 minority (61 Black or African American, non-Hispanic/Latino; 12 Asian, non-Hispanic/Latino; 44 Hispanic/Latino), 3 international. Average age 35. 124 applicants, 73% accepted, 75 enrolled. In 2017, 70 master's awarded. *Entrance requirements:* For master's, GMAT or GRE General Test, minimum GPA of 3.0 in last 60 hours of course work. Additional exam requirements/recommendations for international students: Required—TOEFL (minimum score 600 paper-based; 61 iBT), IELTS (minimum score 6). *Application deadline:* For fall admission, 7/25 for domestic students, 2/15 for international students; for spring admission, 12/10 for domestic students, 7/15 for international students. Applications are processed on a rolling basis. Application fee: $30. Electronic applications accepted. *Expenses:* Tuition, state resident: full-time $7400; part-time $369.82 per credit. Tuition, nonresident: full-time $20,496; part-time $1042.81 per credit. *Financial support:* Research assistantships with full tuition reimbursements, career-related internships or fieldwork, tuition waivers (partial), and unspecified assistantships available. *Faculty research:* Sports administration, healthcare, policy, finance, real estate, senior living. *Unit head:* Dr. Roland Kidwell, Chair, 561-297-5634, E-mail: kidwellr@fau.edu.
Website: http://business.fau.edu/departments/management/index.aspx

Florida International University, Chapman Graduate School of Business, Department of Management and International Business, Miami, FL 33199. Offers human resources management (MSHRM); international business (MIB); management and international business (EMBA, IMBA, MBA, PhD). *Program availability:* Part-time, evening/weekend. *Faculty:* 28 full-time (10 women), 30 part-time/adjunct (10 women). *Students:* 970 full-time (565 women), 596 part-time (301 women); includes 1,119 minority (220 Black or African American, non-Hispanic/Latino; 45 Asian, non-Hispanic/Latino; 823 Hispanic/Latino; 5 Native Hawaiian or other Pacific Islander, non-Hispanic/Latino; 26 Two or more races, non-Hispanic/Latino), 180 international. Average age 32. 1,326 applicants, 45% accepted, 429 enrolled. In 2017, 795 master's, 13 doctorates awarded. *Degree requirements:* For doctorate, comprehensive exam, thesis/dissertation. *Entrance requirements:* For master's, GMAT or GRE (depending on program), minimum GPA of 3.0 in upper-level coursework; for doctorate, GMAT or GRE, letter of intent; 3 letters of recommendation; resume. Additional exam requirements/recommendations for international students: Required—TOEFL (minimum score 550 paper-based; 80 iBT) or IELTS (minimum score 6.5). *Application deadline:* For fall admission, 6/1 for domestic students, 4/1 for international students; for spring admission, 10/1 for domestic students, 9/1 for international students. Applications are processed on a rolling basis. Application fee: $30. Electronic applications accepted. *Expenses:* Contact institution. *Financial support:* Institutionally sponsored loans and scholarships/grants available. Financial award application deadline: 3/1; financial award applicants required to submit FAFSA. *Faculty research:* International business, strategy, entrepreneurship, human resource management. *Unit head:* Dr. Willam Newburry, Chair, 305-348-2791, E-mail: newburry@fiu.edu. *Application contact:* Jessica Aristizabal, Associate Director, Academic Support Services, 305-348-6880, E-mail: palger@fiu.edu.

Florida State University, The Graduate School, College of Human Sciences, Department of Retail, Merchandising and Product Development, Tallahassee, FL

32306-1492. Offers MS. *Program availability:* Part-time. *Faculty:* 5 full-time (4 women). *Students:* 3 full-time (all women); all minorities (1 Black or African American, non-Hispanic/Latino; 2 Two or more races, non-Hispanic/Latino). Average age 29. In 2017, 4 master's awarded. *Degree requirements:* For master's, thesis optional. *Entrance requirements:* For master's, GRE General Test, minimum upper-division GPA of 3.0. Additional exam requirements/recommendations for international students: Required—TOEFL (minimum score 550 paper-based; 80 iBT). *Application deadline:* For fall admission, 4/1 for domestic and international students; for spring admission, 10/1 for domestic and international students. Applications are processed on a rolling basis. Application fee: $30. Electronic applications accepted. *Expenses:* $480 per credit hour in-state; $1,111 per credit hour out-of-state. *Financial support:* In 2017–18, 3 students received support, including 2 research assistantships (averaging $9,332 per year), 1 teaching assistantship with full tuition reimbursement available (averaging $5,365 per year); career-related internships or fieldwork, institutionally sponsored loans, scholarships/grants, and unspecified assistantships also available. Financial award application deadline: 1/15; financial award applicants required to submit FAFSA. *Faculty research:* Global merchandising and product development. *Total annual research expenditures:* $19,383. *Unit head:* Dr. Robert C. Hickner, Interim Department Chair, 850-644-2498, Fax: 850-645-4673, E-mail: rhickner@fsu.edu.

Franklin University Switzerland, The Taylor Institute for Global Enterprise Management, 6924 Sorengo, Switzerland. Offers international management (MS).

George Mason University, College of Education and Human Development, School of Recreation, Health and Tourism, Manassas, VA 20110. Offers athletic training (MS); exercise, fitness, and health promotion (MS), including advanced practitioner, wellness practitioner; international sport management (Certificate); recreation, health and tourism (Certificate); sport management (MS), including sport and recreation studies. *Program availability:* Part-time, evening/weekend. *Faculty:* 14 full-time (13 women), 87 part-time/adjunct (48 women). *Students:* 62 full-time (24 women), 23 part-time (11 women); includes 27 minority (20 Black or African American, non-Hispanic/Latino; 1 Asian, non-Hispanic/Latino; 3 Hispanic/Latino; 1 Native Hawaiian or other Pacific Islander, non-Hispanic/Latino; 2 Two or more races, non-Hispanic/Latino), 8 international. Average age 26. 74 applicants, 93% accepted, 46 enrolled. In 2017, 20 master's awarded. *Degree requirements:* For master's, thesis optional. *Entrance requirements:* For master's, 3 letters of recommendation; official transcripts; expanded goals statement; undergraduate course in statistics and minimum GPA of 3.0 in last 60 credit hours overall (for MS in sport and recreation studies); baccalaureate degree related to kinesiology, exercise science or athletic training (for MS in exercise, fitness and health promotion). Additional exam requirements/recommendations for international students: Required—TOEFL (minimum score 575 paper-based; 88 iBT), IELTS (minimum score 6.5), PTE (minimum score 59). *Application deadline:* For fall admission, 4/2 priority date for domestic and international students; for spring admission, 11/1 for domestic and international students. Application fee: $75 ($80 for international students). Electronic applications accepted. *Expenses:* Tuition, state resident: full-time $11,228; part-time $459.50 per credit. Tuition, nonresident: full-time $30,932; part-time $1280.50 per credit. *Required fees:* $3252; $135.50 per credit. Part-time tuition and fees vary according to course load and program. *Financial support:* In 2017–18, 1 student received support, including 1 research assistantship with tuition reimbursement available; career-related internships or fieldwork, Federal Work-Study, scholarships/grants, unspecified assistantships, and health care benefits (for full-time research or teaching assistantship recipients) also available. Support available to part-time students. Financial award application deadline: 3/1; financial award applicants required to submit FAFSA. *Faculty research:* Sport for development and peace, sport analytics, leadership and coaching, diversity and inclusion in sport, sport communication. *Total annual research expenditures:* $826,386. *Unit head:* Martin Ford, Senior Associate Dean, 703-993-2004, E-mail: mford@gmu.edu. *Application contact:* Lindsey Olson, Office Assistant, 703-993-2098, Fax: 703-993-2025, E-mail: lolson7@gmu.edu.
Website: http://rht.gmu.edu/

Georgetown University, Graduate School of Arts and Sciences, Department of Economics, Washington, DC 20057. Offers econometrics (PhD); economic development (PhD); economic theory (PhD); industrial organization (PhD); international macro and finance (PhD); international trade (PhD); labor economics (PhD); macroeconomics (PhD); public economics and political economy (PhD); MA/PhD; MS/MA. *Degree requirements:* For doctorate, comprehensive exam, thesis/dissertation. *Entrance requirements:* For doctorate, GRE General Test. Additional exam requirements/recommendations for international students: Required—TOEFL. *Faculty research:* International economics, economic development.

Georgetown University, Law Center, Washington, DC 20001. Offers environmental law (LL M); global health law (LL M); global health law and international institutions (LL M); individualized study (LL M); international business and economic law (LL M); law (JD, SJD); national security law (LL M); securities and financial regulation (LL M); taxation (LL M); JD/LL M; JD/MA; JD/MBA; JD/MPH; JD/PhD. *Accreditation:* ABA. *Program availability:* Part-time, evening/weekend. *Degree requirements:* For master's, thesis; for doctorate, thesis/dissertation (for some programs). *Entrance requirements:* For master's, JD, LL B, or first law degree earned in country of origin; for doctorate, LSAT (for JD). Additional exam requirements/recommendations for international students: Required—TOEFL. *Expenses:* Contact institution. *Faculty research:* Constitutional law, legal history, jurisprudence.

The George Washington University, Elliott School of International Affairs, Program in International Trade and Investment Policy, Washington, DC 20052. Offers MA. *Program availability:* Part-time. *Students:* 27 full-time (10 women), 15 part-time (8 women); includes 14 minority (3 Black or African American, non-Hispanic/Latino; 2 Asian, non-Hispanic/Latino; 7 Hispanic/Latino; 2 Two or more races, non-Hispanic/Latino), 15 international. Average age 27. 57 applicants, 72% accepted, 13 enrolled. In 2017, 24 master's awarded. *Degree requirements:* For master's, one foreign language, capstone project. *Entrance requirements:* For master's, GRE General Test, 2 years of a modern foreign language, 2 semesters of introductory economics. Additional exam requirements/recommendations for international students: Required—TOEFL (minimum score 100 iBT), IELTS (minimum score 7). *Application deadline:* For fall admission, 1/15 priority date for domestic and international students; for spring admission, 10/1 for domestic students. Application fee: $75. Electronic applications accepted. *Expenses:* Tuition: Full-time $28,800; part-time $1655 per credit hour. *Required fees:* $45; $2.75 per credit hour. *Financial support:* In 2017–18, 11 students received support. Fellowships with partial tuition reimbursements available, Federal Work-Study, and scholarships/grants available. Financial award application deadline: 1/15. *Unit head:* Prof. Michael Moore, Director, 202-994-5230, E-mail: itip@gwu.edu. *Application contact:* Nicole A. Campbell, Director of Graduate Admissions, 202-994-7050, Fax: 202-994-9537, E-mail: esiagrad@gwu.edu.
Website: http://elliott.gwu.edu/international-trade-investment-policy

The George Washington University, School of Business, Department of International Business, Washington, DC 20052. Offers PhD. *Program availability:* Part-time, evening/weekend. *Students:* 2 applicants, 100% accepted. *Entrance requirements:* For doctorate, GMAT or GRE. Additional exam requirements/recommendations for international students: Required—TOEFL. *Application deadline:* For fall admission, 4/1

priority date for domestic students; for spring admission, 10/1 for domestic students. Applications are processed on a rolling basis. Application fee: $75. *Expenses: Tuition:* Full-time $28,800; part-time $1655 per credit hour. *Required fees:* $45; $2.75 per credit hour. *Financial support:* Fellowships, teaching assistantships, career-related internships or fieldwork, Federal Work-Study, and institutionally sponsored loans available. Financial award application deadline: 4/1. *Faculty research:* International trade, competitiveness, business management. *Unit head:* Robert Weiner, Chair, 202-994-5981, E-mail: rweiner@gwu.edu. *Application contact:* Christopher Storer, Executive Director, Graduate Admissions, 202-994-1212, E-mail: gwmba@gwu.edu.
Website: http://business.gwu.edu/about-us/departments/department-of-international-business/

Georgia Institute of Technology, Graduate Studies, Scheller College of Business, Program in Business Administration, Atlanta, GA 30332-0001. Offers business administration (MBA); global business (MBA); management of technology (MBA). *Accreditation:* AACSB. *Program availability:* Part-time, evening/weekend. *Entrance requirements:* For master's, GMAT, two essays, three letters of recommendation, transcript from each college/university attended. Additional exam requirements/recommendations for international students: Required—TOEFL (minimum score 600 paper-based; 100 iBT). Electronic applications accepted. *Expenses:* Contact institution.

Georgia State University, J. Mack Robinson College of Business, Institute of International Business, Atlanta, GA 30303. Offers international business (GMBA, MBA, MIB); international business and information technology (MBA); international entrepreneurship (MBA); MIB/MIA. *Program availability:* Part-time, evening/weekend. *Faculty:* 11 full-time (4 women). *Students:* 37 full-time (21 women); includes 19 minority (16 Black or African American, non-Hispanic/Latino; 1 Asian, non-Hispanic/Latino; 1 Hispanic/Latino; 1 Two or more races, non-Hispanic/Latino), 10 international. Average age 27. 44 applicants, 86% accepted, 18 enrolled. In 2017, 33 master's awarded. *Entrance requirements:* For master's, GRE or GMAT, transcripts from all institutions attended, resume, essays. Additional exam requirements/recommendations for international students: Required—TOEFL (minimum score 610 paper-based; 101 iBT), IELTS (minimum score 7). *Application deadline:* For fall admission, 5/1 priority date for domestic students, 2/1 priority date for international students; for spring admission, 9/15 priority date for domestic students, 5/1 priority date for international students. Applications are processed on a rolling basis. Application fee: $50. Electronic applications accepted. *Expenses:* Tuition, state resident: full-time $7020. Tuition, nonresident: full-time $22,518. *Required fees:* $2128. Tuition and fees vary according to degree level and program. *Financial support:* Research assistantships, teaching assistantships, scholarships/grants, tuition waivers (partial), and unspecified assistantships available. Financial award application deadline: 5/1. *Faculty research:* Business challenges in emerging markets (especially in India and China); interorganizational relationships in an international context, such as strategic alliances and global supply chain relations; globalization and entry mode strategy or new (or emerging) multinationals; emerging market development and business environments; cross-cultural effects on business processes and performance. *Unit head:* Dr. Daniel Bello, Professor/Director of the Institute of International Business, 404-413-7275, Fax: 404-413-7276. *Application contact:* Toby McChesney, Assistant Dean for Graduate Recruiting and Student Services, 404-413-7167, Fax: 404-413-7162, E-mail: rcbgradadmissions@gsu.edu.
Website: http://iib.gsu.edu/

Golden Gate University, Ageno School of Business, San Francisco, CA 94105-2968. Offers accounting (MBA); adaptive leadership (MBA); advanced financial planning (MS); business administration (EMBA, MBA, DBA); business analytics (MBA, MS); entrepreneurship (MBA); finance (MBA, MS, Certificate); financial life planning (Certificate); financial planning (MS, Certificate); global supply chain management (MBA, Certificate); human resource management (MBA, MS, Certificate); information technology management (MBA, MS, Certificate); international business (MBA); marketing (MBA, MS, Certificate); project management (MBA, MS, Certificate); psychology (MA, Certificate); public administration (EMPA, MBA); public administration leadership (Certificate); JD/MBA. *Program availability:* Part-time, evening/weekend. *Faculty:* 17 full-time (7 women), 280 part-time/adjunct (95 women). *Students:* 309 full-time (147 women), 527 part-time (266 women); includes 286 minority (56 Black or African American, non-Hispanic/Latino; 1 American Indian or Alaska Native, non-Hispanic/Latino; 131 Asian, non-Hispanic/Latino; 83 Hispanic/Latino; 4 Native Hawaiian or other Pacific Islander, non-Hispanic/Latino; 11 Two or more races, non-Hispanic/Latino), 209 international. Average age 35. 549 applicants, 66% accepted, 185 enrolled. *Degree requirements:* For doctorate, thesis/dissertation, qualifying examination. *Entrance requirements:* For master's, GMAT (for MBA), minimum GPA of 2.5 (MS). Additional exam requirements/recommendations for international students: Required—TOEFL (minimum score 550 paper-based; 79 iBT). *Application deadline:* For fall admission, 5/15 for domestic and international students; for winter admission, 1/15 for domestic and international students; for spring admission, 9/15 for domestic and international students. Applications are processed on a rolling basis. Application fee: $65 ($105 for international students). Electronic applications accepted. *Expenses:* $3,150 per 3-unit course. *Financial support:* Career-related internships or fieldwork, Federal Work-Study, institutionally sponsored loans, and scholarships/grants available. Support available to part-time students. Financial award applicants required to submit FAFSA. *Unit head:* Marianne Koch, Associate Dean, 415-442-6542, Fax: 415-442-6579, E-mail: mkoch@ggu.edu. *Application contact:* Angela Melero, Enrollment Services, 415-442-7800, Fax: 415-442-7807, E-mail: info@ggu.edu.
Website: http://www.ggu.edu/programs/business-and-management

Goldey-Beacom College, Graduate Program, Wilmington, DE 19808-1999. Offers business administration (MBA); finance (MS); financial management (MBA); health care management (MBA); human resource management (MBA); information technology (MBA); international business management (MBA); major finance (MBA); major taxation (MBA); management (MM); marketing management (MBA); taxation (MBA, MS). *Accreditation:* ACBSP. *Program availability:* Part-time, evening/weekend. *Entrance requirements:* For master's, GMAT, MAT, GRE, minimum GPA of 3.0. Additional exam requirements/recommendations for international students: Required—TOEFL (minimum score 65 iBT); Recommended—IELTS (minimum score 6). Electronic applications accepted.

Hallmark University, School of Business, San Antonio, TX 78230. Offers global management (MBA). *Degree requirements:* For master's, thesis (for some programs). *Entrance requirements:* For master's, bachelor's degree; minimum undergraduate GPA of 2.5; completion of one course each in college-level statistics, quanitative methods, and calculus or pre-calculus; official undergraduate transcripts; professional resume; personal statement; two letters of recommendation; two 200-word typed essays. Additional exam requirements/recommendations for international students: Required—TOEFL (minimum score 450 paper-based; 45 iBT). *Expenses:* Contact institution.

Harding University, Paul R. Carter College of Business Administration, Searcy, AR 72149-0001. Offers business (MBA); leadership and organizational management (MBA). *Accreditation:* ACBSP. *Program availability:* Part-time, evening/weekend, 100% online. *Faculty:* 26 part-time/adjunct (6 women). *Students:* 15 full-time (8 women), 90 part-time (36 women); includes 12 minority (8 Black or African American, non-

International Business

Hispanic/Latino; 2 Asian, non-Hispanic/Latino; 2 Hispanic/Latino), 2 international. Average age 34. 15 applicants, 100% accepted, 15 enrolled. In 2017, 66 master's awarded. *Degree requirements:* For master's, portfolio. *Entrance requirements:* For master's, GMAT (minimum score of 500) or GRE (minimum score of 300), minimum GPA of 3.0, 2 letters of recommendation, resume, 3 essays, all official transcripts. Additional exam requirements/recommendations for international students: Required—TOEFL (minimum score 550 paper-based; 79 iBT). *Application deadline:* For fall admission, 8/1 priority date for domestic and international students; for spring admission, 12/1 priority date for domestic and international students. Applications are processed on a rolling basis. Application fee: $40. Tuition and fees vary according to course load, degree level, campus/location and program. *Financial support:* Unspecified assistantships available. Financial award application deadline: 7/30; financial award applicants required to submit FAFSA. *Unit head:* 501-279-5789, Fax: 501-279-4805, E-mail: mba@harding.edu.
Website: http://www.harding.edu/mba

Hawai'i Pacific University, College of Business, Program in Business Administration, Honolulu, HI 96813. Offers finance (MBA); human resource management (MBA); information systems (MBA); international business (MBA); management (MBA); marketing (MBA); organizational change and development (MBA). *Program availability:* Part-time, evening/weekend, 100% online, blended/hybrid learning. *Faculty:* 7 full-time (3 women), 3 part-time/adjunct (0 women). *Students:* 88 full-time (34 women), 28 part-time (18 women); includes 63 minority (9 Black or African American, non-Hispanic/Latino; 17 Asian, non-Hispanic/Latino; 14 Hispanic/Latino; 1 Native Hawaiian or other Pacific Islander, non-Hispanic/Latino; 22 Two or more races, non-Hispanic/Latino), 29 international. Average age 32. 82 applicants, 78% accepted, 40 enrolled. In 2017, 87 master's awarded. *Entrance requirements:* For master's, GMAT or GRE. Additional exam requirements/recommendations for international students: Recommended—TOEFL (minimum score 550 paper-based; 80 iBT), IELTS (minimum score 6), TWE (minimum score 5). *Application deadline:* For fall admission, 1/15 priority date for domestic students; for spring admission, 10/15 priority date for domestic students. Applications are processed on a rolling basis. Application fee: $50. Electronic applications accepted. *Expenses:* Tuition: Full-time $18,000; part-time $1000 per credit. *Required fees:* $200; $26 per credit. Tuition and fees vary according to course load and program. *Financial support:* In 2017–18, 24 students received support. Research assistantships, career-related internships or fieldwork, Federal Work-Study, scholarships/grants, tuition waivers (partial), and unspecified assistantships available. Financial award application deadline: 3/1; financial award applicants required to submit FAFSA. *Unit head:* Dr. Daewoo Park, Department Chair, 808-544-1463, E-mail: dwpark@hpu.edu. *Application contact:* Danny Lam, Assistant Director of Graduate Admissions, 808-544-1135, E-mail: graduate@hpu.edu.
Website: https://www.hpu.edu/cob/grad-programs/mba.html

HEC Montreal, School of Business Administration, Doctoral Program in Administration, Montréal, QC H3T 2A7, Canada. Offers accounting (PhD); applied economics (PhD); data science (PhD); finance (PhD); financial engineering (PhD); information technology (PhD); international business (PhD); logistics and operations management (PhD); management science (PhD); management, strategy and organizations (PhD); marketing (PhD); organizational behaviour and human resources (PhD). Program offered jointly with Concordia University, McGill University, and Universite du Quebec a Montreal. *Accreditation:* AACSB. *Students:* 114 full-time (47 women). 78 applicants, 42% accepted, 24 enrolled. In 2017, 23 doctorates awarded. *Entrance requirements:* For doctorate, TAGE MAGE, GMAT, or GRE, master's degree in administration or related field. *Application deadline:* For fall admission, 1/15 for domestic and international students. Application fee: $88 ($187 for international students). Electronic applications accepted. *Expenses:* Tuition, state resident: full-time $2869 Canadian dollars; part-time $79.70 Canadian dollars per credit. Tuition, nonresident: full-time $8883 Canadian dollars; part-time $246.76 Canadian dollars per credit. *International tuition:* $19,648 Canadian dollars full-time. *Required fees:* $41.20 Canadian dollars per credit. $67.94 Canadian dollars per term. Tuition and fees vary according to degree level and program. *Financial support:* Research assistantships, teaching assistantships, and scholarships/grants available. Financial award application deadline: 9/2. *Faculty research:* Art management, business policy, entrepreneurship, new technologies, transportation. *Unit head:* Jacques Robert, Director, 514-340-6853, E-mail: jacques.robert@hec.ca. *Application contact:* Julie Bilodeau, PhD Program Analyst, 514-340-6151, Fax: 514-340-6411, E-mail: analyste.phd@hec.ca.
Website: http://www.hec.ca/en/programs/phd/index.html

HEC Montreal, School of Business Administration, Master of Science Programs in Administration, Program in International Business, Montréal, QC H3T 2A7, Canada. Offers M Sc. Program offered in French and also in English. *Students:* 82 full-time (53 women), 12 part-time (7 women). 127 applicants, 36% accepted, 33 enrolled. In 2017, 30 master's awarded. *Entrance requirements:* For master's, BBA, undergraduate degree in another field, degree deemed equivalent by program director and minimum GPA of 3.0 on 4.3 scale. Additional exam requirements/recommendations for international students: Required—TAGE MAGE (minimum recommended score of 283), GMAT (minimum recommended score of 630), or GRE. *Application deadline:* For fall admission, 3/15 for domestic and international students; for winter admission, 9/15 for domestic and international students. Application fee: $88 ($184 for international students). Electronic applications accepted. *Expenses:* Tuition, state resident: full-time $2869 Canadian dollars; part-time $79.70 Canadian dollars per credit. Tuition, nonresident: full-time $8883 Canadian dollars; part-time $246.76 Canadian dollars per credit. *International tuition:* $19,648 Canadian dollars full-time. *Required fees:* $41.20 Canadian dollars per credit. $67.94 Canadian dollars per term. Tuition and fees vary according to degree level and program. *Financial support:* Research assistantships, teaching assistantships, and scholarships/grants available. Financial award application deadline: 9/2. *Unit head:* Dr. Marie-Helene Jobin, Director, 514-340-6283, E-mail: marie-helene.jobin@hec.ca. *Application contact:* Marianne de Moura, Administrative Director, 514-340-6151, Fax: 514-340-6411, E-mail: aide@hec.ca.
Website: http://www.hec.ca/en/programs/masters/master-international-business/index.html

Hofstra University, Frank G. Zarb School of Business, Programs in Marketing and International Business, Hempstead, NY 11549. Offers business administration (MBA), including international business, marketing; international business (Advanced Certificate); marketing (MS, Advanced Certificate); marketing research (MS). *Program availability:* Part-time, evening/weekend, blended/hybrid learning. *Students:* 72 full-time (40 women), 20 part-time (11 women); includes 11 minority (2 Black or African American, non-Hispanic/Latino; 6 Asian, non-Hispanic/Latino; 2 Hispanic/Latino; 1 Two or more races, non-Hispanic/Latino), 58 international. Average age 25. 227 applicants, 74% accepted, 35 enrolled. In 2017, 51 master's awarded. *Degree requirements:* For master's, capstone course (for MBA), thesis (for MS), minimum GPA of 3.0. *Entrance requirements:* For master's, GMAT/GRE, 2 letters of recommendation, resume, essay. Additional exam requirements/recommendations for international students: Required—TOEFL (minimum score 550 paper-based; 80 iBT). Recommended—IELTS (minimum score 6). *Application deadline:* Applications are processed on a rolling basis. Application fee: $75. Electronic applications accepted. *Expenses:* $1,322 per credit. *Financial support:* In 2017–18, 28 students received support, including 24 fellowships with full and partial tuition reimbursements available (averaging $5,002 per year), 2 research

assistantships with full and partial tuition reimbursements available (averaging $7,390 per year); career-related internships or fieldwork, Federal Work-Study, institutionally sponsored loans, scholarships/grants, tuition waivers (full and partial), and unspecified assistantships also available. Support available to part-time students. Financial award applicants required to submit FAFSA. *Faculty research:* Cross-cultural consumer behavior; social, digital, global, and strategic issues in marketing; consumer health/well-being; ethnocentrism and animosity. *Unit head:* Dr. Anil Mathur, Chairperson, 516-463-5346, Fax: 516-463-4834, E-mail: anil.mathur@hofstra.edu. *Application contact:* Sunil Samuel, Assistant Vice President of Admissions, 516-463-4723, Fax: 516-463-4664, E-mail: graduateadmission@hofstra.edu.
Website: http://www.hofstra.edu/business/

Hope International University, School of Graduate and Professional Studies, Program in Business Administration, Fullerton, CA 92831-3138. Offers general management (MBA, MSM); international development (MBA, MSM); marketing management (MBA, MSM); non-profit management (MBA, MSM). *Program availability:* Part-time, online learning. *Degree requirements:* For master's, comprehensive exam (for some programs), thesis (for some programs), project. *Entrance requirements:* For master's, minimum GPA of 3.0; 2 references. Additional exam requirements/recommendations for international students: Required—TOEFL (minimum score 550 paper-based; 86 iBT); Recommended—IELTS (minimum score 6.5). Electronic applications accepted. *Expenses:* Contact institution.

Houston Baptist University, Archie W. Dunham College of Business, Program in International Business, Houston, TX 77074-3298. Offers MIB. *Program availability:* Part-time, evening/weekend. *Students:* 39 full-time (21 women), 7 part-time (4 women); includes 15 minority (7 Black or African American, non-Hispanic/Latino; 2 Asian, non-Hispanic/Latino; 6 Hispanic/Latino), 25 international. Average age 28. 53 applicants, 42% accepted, 10 enrolled. In 2017, 11 master's awarded. *Entrance requirements:* For master's, minimum GPA of 2.5, bachelor's degree conferred transcript, essay/personal statement, resume. Additional exam requirements/recommendations for international students: Required—TOEFL (minimum score 80 iBT), IELTS (minimum score 6.5). *Application deadline:* For fall admission, 8/1 for domestic students, 6/1 for international students; for spring admission, 1/1 for domestic students, 11/1 for international students; for summer admission, 5/1 for domestic students, 3/1 for international students. Applications are processed on a rolling basis. Application fee: $0 ($100 for international students). Electronic applications accepted. Application fee is waived when completed online. *Expenses:* Contact institution. *Financial support:* In 2017–18, 5 students received support. Federal Work-Study and scholarships/grants available. Support available to part-time students. Financial award application deadline: 4/1; financial award applicants required to submit FAFSA. *Unit head:* Dr. Michael Weeks, Dean, Archie W. Dunham College of Business, 281-649-3014, E-mail: mweeks@hbu.edu. *Application contact:* Laurel Motal, Graduate Student Services Coordinator, 281-649-3306, Fax: 281-649-3436, E-mail: lmotal@hbu.edu.
Website: http://www.hbu.edu/MIB

Howard University, School of Business, Graduate Programs in Business, Washington, DC 20059-0002. Offers accounting (MBA); entrepreneurship (MBA); finance (MBA); general management (MBA); human resources management (MBA); information systems (MBA); international business (MBA); marketing (MBA); supply chain management (MBA); JD/MBA. *Accreditation:* AACSB. *Program availability:* Part-time, evening/weekend, online learning. *Entrance requirements:* For master's, GMAT, minimum 1 year post undergraduate work experience, resume, 3 letters of recommendation, advanced college algebra. Additional exam requirements/recommendations for international students: Required—TOEFL. *Faculty research:* Marketing research in multi-ethnic populations, U.S. trade policies and international relations, risk management (finance).

Hult International Business School, Graduate Programs, Cambridge, MA 02141. Offers business administration (EMBA); business analytics (MBA, MIB); business statistics (MBS); disruptive innovation (MDI); entrepreneurship (MBA, MIB); family business (MBA, MIB); finance (MBA, MF, MIB); international marketing (MIM); marketing (MBA, MIB); project management (MBA, MIB). MDI and MBS offered in San Francisco; MBA also offered in Boston, San Francisco, Dubai, Shanghai, and New York. *Entrance requirements:* For master's, GMAT, 3 years of work experience. Additional exam requirements/recommendations for international students: Required—TOEFL. Electronic applications accepted. *Expenses:* Contact institution.

IGlobal University, Graduate Programs, Vienna, VA 22182. Offers accounting (MBA); data management and analytics (MSIT); entrepreneurship (MBA); finance (MBA); global business management (MBA); health care management (MBA); hospitality and tourism management (MBA); human resources management (MBA); information technology (MBA); information technology systems and management (MSIT); leadership and management (MBA); project management (MBA); public service and administration (MBA); software design and management (MSIT).

Indiana Tech, Program in Global Leadership, Fort Wayne, IN 46803-1297. Offers PhD. *Program availability:* Part-time, evening/weekend, online only, 100% online. *Entrance requirements:* For doctorate, GMAT, LSAT, GRE, or MAT, official transcripts of all previous undergraduate and graduate work including evidence of completion of a master's degree at regionally-accredited institution; original essay addressing the candidate's interest in the program and intended goals; current resume including educational record, employment history and relevant accomplishments; interview. Electronic applications accepted.

Instituto Tecnologico de Santo Domingo, Graduate School, Area of Business, Santo Domingo, Dominican Republic. Offers banking and securities markets (M Mgmt); corporate finance (M Mgmt); human resources management (M Mgmt, Certificate); international trade management (M Mgmt); marketing (M Mgmt); organizational development (M Mgmt); quality and productivity management (Certificate); tax management and planning (M Mgmt); upper management (M Mgmt).

Instituto Tecnologico de Santo Domingo, Graduate School, Area of Humanities and Social Sciences, Santo Domingo, Dominican Republic. Offers accounting (Certificate); adult education (Certificate); applied linguistics (MA); economics (MA); education (M Ed); educational psychology (MA, Certificate); gender and development (MA, Certificate); humanistic studies (MA); international marketing management (Certificate); international relations in the Caribbean basin (Certificate); intervention systems in family therapy (MA); linguistic and literary communication (Certificate); pedagogical support (MA); social science education (M Ed); sustainable human development (MA); terminal illness and death psychology (Certificate); youth and adult education (M Ed).

Instituto Tecnológico y de Estudios Superiores de Monterrey, Campus Central de Veracruz, Graduate Programs, Córdoba, Mexico. Offers administration (MA); administration of information technologies (MTI); computer sciences (MCC); education (MEE); educational institution administration (MAD); educational technology (MTE); electronic commerce (MCE); finance (MAF); humanistic studies (MEH); international business for Latin America (MNL); marketing (MMT); science (MCP). *Program availability:* Part-time, evening/weekend, online learning. *Degree requirements:* For master's, thesis (for some programs). *Entrance requirements:* For master's, PAEP College Board. Electronic applications accepted.

Instituto Tecnológico y de Estudios Superiores de Monterrey, Campus Chihuahua, Graduate Programs, Chihuahua, Mexico. Offers computer systems engineering (Ingeniero); electrical engineering (Ingeniero); electromechanical engineering (Ingeniero); electronic engineering (Ingeniero); engineering administration (MEA); industrial engineering (MIE, Ingeniero); international trade (MIT); mechanical engineering (Ingeniero).

Instituto Tecnológico y de Estudios Superiores de Monterrey, Campus Ciudad de México, Virtual University Division, Ciudad de Mexico, Mexico. Offers administration of information technologies (MA); computer sciences (MA); education (MA, PhD); educational technology (MA); environmental engineering (MA); environmental systems (MA); humanistic studies (MA); industrial engineering (MA); international business for Latin America (MA); quality systems (MA); quality systems and productivity (MA). *Program availability:* Part-time, evening/weekend, online learning. *Entrance requirements:* For master's and doctorate, Instituto entrance exam. Additional exam requirements/recommendations for international students: Required—TOEFL.

Instituto Tecnológico y de Estudios Superiores de Monterrey, Campus Cuernavaca, Programs in Business Administration, Temixco, Mexico. Offers finance (MA); human resources management (MA); international business (MA); marketing (MA).

Instituto Tecnológico y de Estudios Superiores de Monterrey, Campus Irapuato, Graduate Programs, Irapuato, Mexico. Offers administration (MBA); administration of information technology (MAIT); administration of telecommunications (MAT); architecture (M Arch); computer science (MCS); education (M Ed); educational administration (MEA); educational innovation and technology (DEIT); educational technology (MET); electronic commerce (MBA); environmental administration and planning (MEAP); environmental systems (MES); finances (MBA); humanistic studies (MHS); international management for Latin American executives (MIMLAE); library and information science (MLIS); manufacturing quality management (MMQM); marketing research (MBA).

Instituto Tecnológico y de Estudios Superiores de Monterrey, Campus Monterrey, Graduate School of Business Administration and Leadership, Program in Business Administration, Monterrey, Mexico. Offers business administration (MA, MBA); finance (M Sc); international business (M Sc); marketing (M Sc). *Program availability:* Part-time. *Degree requirements:* For master's, one foreign language, thesis. *Entrance requirements:* For master's, GMAT. Additional exam requirements/recommendations for international students: Required—TOEFL. *Faculty research:* Technology management, quality management, organizational theory and behavior.

Inter American University of Puerto Rico, Metropolitan Campus, Graduate Programs, Program in International Business, San Juan, PR 00919-1293. Offers international business (MIB); interregional and international business (PhD).

Inter American University of Puerto Rico, San Germán Campus, Graduate Studies Center, Program in Business Administration, San Germán, PR 00683-5008. Offers accounting (MBA); finance (MBA); general business administration (MBA); human resources (MBA, PhD); industrial relations (MBA); information systems (MBA); international and interregional business (PhD); management (MBA); marketing (MBA). *Program availability:* Part-time, evening/weekend. *Degree requirements:* For master's, comprehensive exam. *Entrance requirements:* For master's, GRE General Test or EXADEP, minimum GPA of 3.0.

International University in Geneva, Business Programs, Geneva, Switzerland. Offers business administration (MBA, DBA); entrepreneurship (MBA); international business (MIB); international trade (MIT); sales and marketing (MBA). *Accreditation:* ACBSP. *Program availability:* Part-time, evening/weekend. *Degree requirements:* For master's, comprehensive exam. *Entrance requirements:* For master's, GMAT. Additional exam requirements/recommendations for international students: Required—TOEFL. Electronic applications accepted.

The International University of Monaco, Graduate Programs, Monte Carlo, Monaco. Offers entrepreneurship (EMBA, MBA); financial engineering (M Sc); hedge fund and private equity (M Sc); international marketing (EMBA, MBA); international wealth management (M Sc); luxury goods and services (EMBA, M Sc, MBA); wealth and asset management (EMBA, MBA). *Program availability:* Part-time. *Degree requirements:* For master's, comprehensive exam (for some programs), applied research project. *Entrance requirements:* Additional exam requirements/recommendations for international students: Required—TOEFL (minimum score 550 paper-based), IELTS. Electronic applications accepted. *Faculty research:* Gaming, leadership, disintermediation.

Iona College, School of Business, Department of Finance, Business Economics and Legal Studies, New Rochelle, NY 10801-1890. Offers finance (MS); financial management (MBA, PMC); financial services (MS); international finance (MS). *Program availability:* Part-time, evening/weekend. *Faculty:* 7 full-time (3 women), 4 part-time/adjunct (1 woman). *Students:* 33 full-time (10 women), 31 part-time (15 women); includes 21 minority (8 Black or African American, non-Hispanic/Latino; 1 American Indian or Alaska Native, non-Hispanic/Latino; 3 Asian, non-Hispanic/Latino; 9 Hispanic/Latino), 6 international. Average age 27. 23 applicants, 91% accepted, 15 enrolled. In 2017, 88 master's awarded. *Entrance requirements:* For master's, GMAT, 2 letters of recommendation, minimum GPA of 3.0; for PMC, minimum GPA of 3.0. Additional exam requirements/recommendations for international students: Required—TOEFL (minimum score 550 paper-based; 80 iBT), IELTS (minimum score 6.5). *Application deadline:* For fall admission, 8/15 priority date for domestic students, 8/1 priority date for international students; for winter admission, 11/15 priority date for domestic students, 11/1 priority date for international students; for spring admission, 2/15 priority date for domestic students, 2/1 priority date for international students; for summer admission, 5/15 priority date for domestic students, 5/1 priority date for international students. Applications are processed on a rolling basis. Application fee: $50. Electronic applications accepted. *Expenses:* Contact institution. *Financial support:* In 2017–18, 15 students received support. Scholarships/grants, tuition waivers (partial), and unspecified assistantships available. Support available to part-time students. Financial award application deadline: 4/15; financial award applicants required to submit FAFSA. *Faculty research:* Options, insurance financing, asset depreciation ranges, international finance, emerging markets. *Unit head:* Dr. John F. Manley, Department Chair, 914-633-2284, E-mail: jmanley@iona.edu. *Application contact:* Katelyn Brunck, Director of MBA Admissions, 914-633-2451, Fax: 914-633-2277, E-mail: kbrunck@iona.edu.
Website: http://www.iona.edu/Academics/Hagan-School-of-Business/Departments/Finance-Business-Economics-Legal-Studies/Graduate-Programs.aspx

Iona College, School of Business, Department of Marketing and International Business, New Rochelle, NY 10801-1890. Offers international business (AC, PMC); marketing (MBA); sports and entertainment management (AC). *Program availability:* Part-time, evening/weekend. *Faculty:* 3 full-time (1 woman), 1 (woman) part-time/adjunct. *Students:* 13 full-time (8 women), 16 part-time (6 women); includes 10 minority (5 Black or African American, non-Hispanic/Latino; 1 Asian, non-Hispanic/Latino; 4 Hispanic/Latino), 2 international. Average age 24. 15 applicants, 100% accepted, 9 enrolled. In 2017, 21 master's, 65 other advanced degrees awarded. *Entrance requirements:* For master's, GMAT, 2 letters of recommendation, minimum GPA of 3.0; for other advanced degree, GMAT, minimum GPA of 3.0. Additional exam requirements/recommendations

for international students: Required—TOEFL (minimum score 550 paper-based; 80 iBT), IELTS (minimum score 6.5). *Application deadline:* For fall admission, 8/15 priority date for domestic students, 8/1 priority date for international students; for winter admission, 11/15 priority date for domestic students, 11/1 priority date for international students; for spring admission, 2/15 priority date for domestic students, 2/1 priority date for international students; for summer admission, 5/15 for domestic students, 5/1 priority date for international students. Applications are processed on a rolling basis. Application fee: $50. Electronic applications accepted. *Expenses:* Contact institution. *Financial support:* In 2017–18, 7 students received support. Scholarships/grants, tuition waivers (partial), and unspecified assistantships available. Support available to part-time students. Financial award application deadline: 4/15; financial award applicants required to submit FAFSA. *Faculty research:* Business ethics, international retailing, mega-marketing, consumer behavior and consumer confidence. *Unit head:* Dr. Susan G. Rozensher, Department Chair, 914-637-2748, E-mail: srozensher@iona.edu. *Application contact:* Katelyn Brunck, Director of MBA Admissions, 914-633-2451, Fax: 914-633-2277, E-mail: kbrunck@iona.edu.
Website: http://www.iona.edu/Academics/Hagan-School-of-Business/Departments/Marketing/Graduate-Programs.aspx

John Brown University, Soderquist College of Business, Siloam Springs, AR 72761-2121. Offers international business (MBA); leadership and ethics (MBA, MS). *Accreditation:* ACBSP. *Program availability:* Part-time, evening/weekend, online only, 100% online, blended/hybrid learning. *Entrance requirements:* For master's, MAT, GMAT or GRE if undergraduate GPA is less than 3.0, recommendation forms from three people, 200-word essay describing professional plans and reason for seeking acceptance. Additional exam requirements/recommendations for international students: Required—TOEFL (minimum score 550 paper-based; 79 iBT). Electronic applications accepted. *Faculty research:* Ethical leadership.

Kean University, College of Business and Public Management, Program in Global Management, Union, NJ 07083. Offers executive management (MBA); global management (MBA). *Program availability:* Part-time, evening/weekend. *Faculty:* 2 full-time (0 women). *Students:* 53 full-time (31 women), 21 part-time (14 women); includes 40 minority (14 Black or African American, non-Hispanic/Latino; 5 Asian, non-Hispanic/Latino; 20 Hispanic/Latino; 1 Native Hawaiian or other Pacific Islander, non-Hispanic/Latino), 18 international. Average age 33. 29 applicants, 100% accepted, 20 enrolled. In 2017, 30 master's awarded. *Degree requirements:* For master's, one foreign language, internship or consulting project. *Entrance requirements:* For master's, GMAT (minimum score of 500) or GRE (minimum Quantitative and Verbal scores of 152), minimum GPA of 3.0, 2 letters of recommendation, personal essay, resume; 5 years of experience (for executive management option). Additional exam requirements/recommendations for international students: Required—TOEFL (minimum score 550 paper-based; 79 iBT), IELTS (minimum score 6.5). *Application deadline:* For fall admission, 6/30 for domestic and international students; for spring admission, 12/1 for domestic and international students. Applications are processed on a rolling basis. Application fee: $75. Electronic applications accepted. *Expenses:* Tuition, state resident: full-time $13,419; part-time $653 per credit. Tuition, nonresident: full-time $18,188; part-time $801 per credit. *Required fees:* $3382; $154 per credit. Tuition and fees vary according to course level, course load, degree level and program. *Financial support:* Scholarships/grants and unspecified assistantships available. Financial award applicants required to submit FAFSA. *Unit head:* Dr. Veysel Yucetepe, Program Coordinator, 908-737-4762, E-mail: vyucetep@kean.edu. *Application contact:* Pedro Lopes, Admissions Counselor, 908-737-7100, E-mail: gradadmissions@kean.edu.
Website: http://grad.kean.edu/masters-programs/mba-global-management

Keiser University, Doctor of Business Administration Program, Fort Lauderdale, FL 33309. Offers global business (DBA); global management (DBA); marketing (DBA). Website: http://www.keiseruniversity.edu/graduateschool/business-administration-phd.php

Keiser University, Master of Business Administration Program, Fort Lauderdale, FL 33309. Offers accounting (MBA); health services administration (MBA); international business (MBA); management (MBA); marketing (MBA); technology management (MBA). All concentrations except technology management also offered in Mandarin. *Program availability:* Part-time, online learning. *Unit head:* Yan Luo-Beitler, Department Chair.
Website: http://www.keiseruniversity.edu/graduateschool/mba.php#accounting

Lake Forest Graduate School of Management, The Immersion MBA Program (iMBA), Lake Forest, IL 60045. Offers global business (MBA). *Program availability:* Online learning.

Lake Forest Graduate School of Management, The Leadership MBA Program, Lake Forest, IL 60045. Offers finance (MBA); global business (MBA); healthcare management (MBA); management (MBA); marketing (MBA); organizational behavior (MBA). *Program availability:* Part-time, evening/weekend. *Entrance requirements:* For master's, 4 years of work experience in field, interview, 2 letters of recommendation. Electronic applications accepted.

La Salle University, School of Business, Philadelphia, PA 19141-1199. Offers business administration (MBA, Post-MBA Certificate), including accounting, business systems and analytics, finance, general business administration, human resource management, management, marketing (Post-MBA Certificate); human capital development (MS, Certificate); international business (Post-MBA Certificate); nonprofit leadership (MS); MBA/MSN. *Accreditation:* AACSB. *Program availability:* Part-time, evening/weekend, 100% online, blended/hybrid learning. *Faculty:* 21 full-time (10 women), 19 part-time/adjunct (8 women). *Students:* 63 full-time (29 women), 282 part-time (172 women); includes 92 minority (58 Black or African American, non-Hispanic/Latino; 21 Asian, non-Hispanic/Latino; 10 Hispanic/Latino; 3 Two or more races, non-Hispanic/Latino), 23 international. Average age 33. 216 applicants, 57% accepted, 74 enrolled. In 2017, 146 master's awarded. *Entrance requirements:* Additional exam requirements/recommendations for international students: Required—TOEFL. *Application deadline:* For fall admission, 8/15 priority date for domestic students, 7/15 for international students; for spring admission, 12/15 priority date for domestic students, 11/15 for international students; for summer admission, 4/15 priority date for domestic students, 3/15 for international students. Applications are processed on a rolling basis. Application fee: $35. Electronic applications accepted. Application fee is waived when completed online. *Expenses:* Contact institution. *Financial support:* In 2017–18, 61 students received support. Scholarships/grants and unspecified assistantships available. Support available to part-time students. Financial award application deadline: 8/31; financial award applicants required to submit FAFSA. *Unit head:* Dr. MarySheila McDonald, Dean, 215-951-1040, Fax: 215-951-1886, E-mail: mcdonaldms@lasalle.edu. *Application contact:* Elizabeth Heenan, Director, Graduate and Adult Enrollment, 215-951-1100, Fax: 215-951-1462, E-mail: heenan@lasalle.edu.

Lenoir-Rhyne University, Graduate Programs, Charles M. Snipes School of Business, Hickory, NC 28601. Offers accounting (MBA); business analytics and information technology (MBA); entrepreneurship (MBA); global business (MBA); healthcare administration (MBA); innovation and change management (MBA); leadership development (MBA). *Accreditation:* ACBSP. *Program availability:* Part-time, evening/

International Business

weekend, online learning. *Degree requirements:* For master's, capstone course. *Entrance requirements:* For master's, GMAT, GRE, MAT, minimum undergraduate GPA of 2.7, graduate 3.0. Additional exam requirements/recommendations for international students: Required—TOEFL (minimum score 600 paper-based). Electronic applications accepted. *Expenses:* Contact institution.

Lewis University, College of Business, Program in Business Administration, Romeoville, IL 60446. Offers accounting (MBA); custom elective option (MBA); e-business (MBA); finance (MBA); healthcare management (MBA); human resources management (MBA); international business (MBA); management information systems (MBA); marketing (MBA); project management (MBA); technology and operations management (MBA). *Program availability:* Part-time, evening/weekend. *Students:* 130 full-time (77 women), 187 part-time (107 women); includes 83 minority (27 Black or African American, non-Hispanic/Latino; 3 American Indian or Alaska Native, non-Hispanic/Latino; 7 Asian, non-Hispanic/Latino; 40 Hispanic/Latino; 6 Two or more races, non-Hispanic/Latino), 31 international. Average age 31. In 2017, 99 master's awarded. *Degree requirements:* For master's, comprehensive exam. *Entrance requirements:* For master's, interview, bachelor's degree, resume, two recommendations. Additional exam requirements/recommendations for international students: Required—TOEFL (minimum score 550 paper-based), IELTS. *Application deadline:* For fall admission, 8/15 priority date for domestic students, 5/1 priority date for international students; for spring admission, 11/15 priority date for international students. Applications are processed on a rolling basis. Application fee: $40. Electronic applications accepted. Tuition and fees vary according to program. *Financial support:* Career-related internships or fieldwork, Federal Work-Study, scholarships/grants, and unspecified assistantships available. Financial award application deadline: 5/1; financial award applicants required to submit FAFSA. *Unit head:* Dr. Maureen Culleeney, Academic Program Director, 815-838-0500 Ext. 5631, E-mail: culleema@lewisu.edu. *Application contact:* Michele Ryan, Director of Admission, 815-838-0500 Ext. 5384, E-mail: ryanml@lewisu.edu.

Liberty University, School of Business, Lynchburg, VA 24515. Offers accounting (MBA, MS), including audit and financial reporting (MS), business (MS), financial services (MS), forensic accounting (MS), leadership (MS), taxation (MS); criminal justice (MBA); cyber security (MS); executive leadership (MA); information systems (MS), including information assurance, technology management; international business (MBA, DBA); leadership (DBA); marketing (MBA, MS, DBA), including digital marketing and advertising (MS), project management (MS), public relations (MS), sports marketing and media (MS); project management (MBA, DBA); public administration (MBA); public relations (MBA). *Program availability:* Part-time, online learning. *Students:* 1,887 full-time (1,003 women), 4,223 part-time (1,950 women); includes 1,570 minority (1,133 Black or African American, non-Hispanic/Latino; 30 American Indian or Alaska Native, non-Hispanic/Latino; 118 Asian, non-Hispanic/Latino; 149 Hispanic/Latino; 13 Native Hawaiian or other Pacific Islander, non-Hispanic/Latino; 127 Two or more races, non-Hispanic/Latino), 109 international. Average age 35. 5,680 applicants, 51% accepted, 1510 enrolled. In 2017, 1,290 master's, 17 doctorates awarded. *Entrance requirements:* For master's, minimum undergraduate GPA of 3.0, 15 hours of upper-level business courses. Additional exam requirements/recommendations for international students: Required—TOEFL (minimum score 600 paper-based; 100 iBT). *Application deadline:* Applications are processed on a rolling basis. Application fee: $50. Electronic applications accepted. *Expenses:* Contact institution. *Financial support:* Applicants required to submit FAFSA. *Unit head:* Dr. Scott Hicks, Dean, 434-592-4808, Fax: 434-582-2366, E-mail: smhicks@liberty.edu. *Application contact:* Jay Bridge, Director of Graduate Admissions, 800-424-9595, Fax: 800-628-7977, E-mail: gradadmissions@liberty.edu.
Website: http://www.liberty.edu/academics/business/index.cfm?PID=149

Lincoln University, Graduate Studies, Oakland, CA 94612. Offers finance and investments (DBA); finance management (MS); finance management and investments (MBA); general business (MBA); human resource management (MBA, DBA); international business (MBA, MS); management information systems (MBA). *Program availability:* Part-time. *Faculty:* 14 full-time (2 women), 20 part-time/adjunct (6 women). *Students:* 606 full-time (222 women), 31 part-time (14 women); includes 10 minority (8 Asian, non-Hispanic/Latino; 1 Hispanic/Latino; 1 Two or more races, non-Hispanic/Latino), 623 international. Average age 26. *Degree requirements:* For master's, research project (thesis), internship report, or comprehensive exam; for doctorate, comprehensive exam, thesis/dissertation. *Entrance requirements:* For master's, minimum GPA of 2.7; for doctorate, GMAT (minimum score: 550), GRE (minimum score: 1000), or equivalent test results (waived for master's degree with minimum cumulative GPA of 3.3). Additional exam requirements/recommendations for international students: Required—TOEFL minimum score 525 paper-based; 71 iBT or IELTS minimum score 5.5 (for MBA); TOEFL minimum score 550 paper-based; 79 iBT or IELTS minimum score 6 (for MS and DBA). *Application deadline:* For fall admission, 8/7 for domestic students, 7/14 for international students; for spring admission, 11/30 for domestic students, 10/31 for international students; for summer admission, 5/29 for domestic students, 5/5 for international students. Applications are processed on a rolling basis. Application fee: $75. Electronic applications accepted. *Expenses: Tuition:* Full-time $8100; part-time $450 per unit. *Required fees:* $360; $180 per semester. Tuition and fees vary according to course level, course load, degree level and program. *Financial support:* Teaching assistantships, career-related internships or fieldwork, and scholarships/grants available. Financial award applicants required to submit FAFSA. *Unit head:* Dr. Marshall Burak, Provost, 510-628-8016, Fax: 510-628-8012, E-mail: mburak@lincolnuca.edu. *Application contact:* Reenu Shrestha, Assistant to the President, 510-628-8017, Fax: 510-208-2826, E-mail: sreenu@lincolnuca.edu.

Lindenwood University, Graduate Programs, Plaster School of Business and Entrepreneurship, St. Charles, MO 63301-1695. Offers accountancy (M Acc); accounting (MBA); business administration (MBA); entrepreneurial studies (MBA); finance (MBA, MS); human resource management (MBA); international business (MBA); leadership (MA); management (MBA); marketing (MBA, MS); nonprofit administration (MA); public administration (MBA); sport management (MA); supply chain management (MBA). *Accreditation:* ACBSP. *Program availability:* Part-time, evening/weekend, 100% online. *Faculty:* 15 full-time (8 women), 26 part-time/adjunct (9 women). *Students:* 201 full-time (116 women), 253 part-time (153 women); includes 102 minority (80 Black or African American, non-Hispanic/Latino; 2 American Indian or Alaska Native, non-Hispanic/Latino; 6 Asian, non-Hispanic/Latino; 7 Hispanic/Latino; 7 Two or more races, non-Hispanic/Latino), 61 international. Average age 32. 370 applicants, 42% accepted, 134 enrolled. In 2017, 178 master's awarded. *Degree requirements:* For master's, comprehensive exam (for some programs), thesis (for some programs), minimum GPA of 3.0. *Entrance requirements:* For master's, interview, minimum undergraduate cumulative GPA of 3.0, letter of recommendation. Additional exam requirements/recommendations for international students: Required—TOEFL (minimum score 550 paper-based; 80 iBT); Recommended—IELTS (minimum score 6.5). *Application deadline:* For fall admission, 8/27 priority date for domestic and international students; for winter admission, 1/14 priority date for domestic and international students; for spring admission, 3/18 for domestic students, 3/18 priority date for international students; for summer admission, 6/3 priority date for domestic and international students. Applications are processed on a rolling basis. Application fee: $30 ($100 for international students). Electronic applications accepted. *Expenses:* Contact institution. *Financial*

support: In 2017–18, 439 students received support. Career-related internships or fieldwork, Federal Work-Study, institutionally sponsored loans, scholarships/grants, tuition waivers (partial), and unspecified assistantships available. Financial award application deadline: 6/30; financial award applicants required to submit FAFSA. *Unit head:* Roger Ellis, Dean, School of Business and Entrepreneurship, 636-949-4839, E-mail: rellis@lindenwood.edu. *Application contact:* Kara Schilli, Director, Evening and Graduate Admissions, 636-949-4349, Fax: 636-949-4109, E-mail: adultadmissions@lindenwood.edu.
Website: http://www.lindenwood.edu/academics/academic-schools/robert-w-plaster-school-of-business-entrepreneurship/

Long Island University–LIU Post, College of Management, Brookville, NY 11548-1300. Offers accountancy (MS); finance (MBA); information systems (MS); international business (MBA); management (MBA); management engineering (MS); marketing (MBA); taxation (MS); technical project management (MS); JD/MBA. *Accreditation:* AACSB. *Program availability:* Part-time, evening/weekend, blended/hybrid learning. *Faculty:* 23 full-time (7 women), 7 part-time/adjunct (1 woman). *Students:* 119 full-time (47 women), 62 part-time (23 women); includes 33 minority (11 Black or African American, non-Hispanic/Latino; 8 Asian, non-Hispanic/Latino; 13 Hispanic/Latino; 1 Two or more races, non-Hispanic/Latino), 56 international. Average age 28. 162 applicants, 62% accepted, 41 enrolled. In 2017, 91 master's awarded. *Entrance requirements:* For master's, GMAT, GRE, or LSAT. Additional exam requirements/recommendations for international students: Required—TOEFL (minimum score 550 paper-based, 75 iBT) or IELTS. *Application deadline:* Applications are processed on a rolling basis. Application fee: $50. Electronic applications accepted. *Expenses: Tuition:* Full-time $21,618; part-time $1201 per credit. *Required fees:* $1840; $920 per term. Tuition and fees vary according to course load. *Financial support:* In 2017–18, 47 students received support. Career-related internships or fieldwork, Federal Work-Study, and scholarships/grants available. Support available to part-time students. Financial award application deadline: 2/15; financial award applicants required to submit FAFSA. *Faculty research:* Innovation and property rights, knowledge sourcing, sustainability and firm performance, China and growth markets, corporate social responsibility, workforce compensation and issues. *Unit head:* Dr. Robert M. Valli, Dean, 516-299-3004, E-mail: rob.valli@liu.edu. *Application contact:* Rita Langdon, Graduate Admissions, 516-299-2900, Fax: 516-299-2137, E-mail: post-enroll@liu.edu.
Website: http://liu.edu/CWPost/Academics/Schools/COM

Loyola University Chicago, Quinlan School of Business, MBA Programs, Chicago, IL 60611. Offers accounting (MBA); business ethics (MBA); derivative markets (MBA); economics (MBA); entrepreneurship (MBA); finance (MBA); healthcare management (MBA); human resources management (MBA); information systems management (MBA); international business (MBA); management (MBA); marketing (MBA); risk management (MBA); supply chain management (MBA). *Program availability:* Part-time, evening/weekend. *Faculty:* 84 full-time (28 women), 12 part-time/adjunct (3 women). *Students:* 253 full-time (118 women), 76 part-time (35 women); includes 83 minority (21 Black or African American, non-Hispanic/Latino; 1 American Indian or Alaska Native, non-Hispanic/Latino; 33 Asian, non-Hispanic/Latino; 24 Hispanic/Latino; 4 Two or more races, non-Hispanic/Latino), 37 international. Average age 30. 334 applicants, 52% accepted, 80 enrolled. In 2017, 220 master's awarded. *Entrance requirements:* For master's, GMAT or GRE, official transcripts, two letters of recommendation, statement of purpose, resume. Additional exam requirements/recommendations for international students: Required—TOEFL (minimum score 90 iBT) or IELTS (minimum score 6.5). *Application deadline:* For fall admission, 7/15 for domestic and international students; for winter admission, 10/1 for domestic and international students; for spring admission, 1/15 for domestic and international students; for summer admission, 4/1 for domestic and international students. Applications are processed on a rolling basis. Application fee: $50. Electronic applications accepted. Application fee is waived when completed online. *Expenses:* $4,488 per course. *Financial support:* In 2017–18, 11 students received support. Research assistantships, career-related internships or fieldwork, Federal Work-Study, scholarships/grants, and health care benefits available. *Faculty research:* Social enterprise and responsibility, emerging markets, supply chain management, risk management. *Unit head:* Katherine Acles, Assistant Dean for Graduate Programs, 312-915-6124, Fax: 312-915-7207, E-mail: kacles@luc.edu.

Lynn University, College of Business and Management, Boca Raton, FL 33431-5598. Offers business administration (MBA), including aviation management, entrepreneurial management, financial valuation and investment management, hospitality management, human resource management, international business management, marketing, media management, social innovation management, sports management, Web development. *Program availability:* Part-time, evening/weekend, 100% online, blended/hybrid learning. *Faculty:* 29 full-time (11 women), 19 part-time/adjunct (7 women). *Students:* 287 full-time (124 women), 195 part-time (105 women); includes 110 minority (44 Black or African American, non-Hispanic/Latino; 2 American Indian or Alaska Native, non-Hispanic/Latino; 11 Asian, non-Hispanic/Latino; 47 Hispanic/Latino; 6 Two or more races, non-Hispanic/Latino), 135 international. Average age 28. 293 applicants, 94% accepted, 192 enrolled. In 2017, 236 master's awarded. *Degree requirements:* For master's, thesis, minimum GPA of 3.0, strategic management seminar, written presentation reflecting the integration and application of theory to practice. *Entrance requirements:* For master's, bachelor's degree from accredited institution, minimum undergraduate GPA of 2.5, official undergraduate transcripts, resume, personal statement, letter of recommendation from academic or professional sources, writing sample demonstrating capacity to perform at graduate level. Additional exam requirements/recommendations for international students: Required—TOEFL (minimum score 550 paper-based; 80 iBT), IELTS (minimum score 6.5). *Application deadline:* For fall admission, 8/18 for domestic students, 8/4 for international students; for spring admission, 12/15 for domestic students, 12/1 for international students; for summer admission, 4/17 for domestic students, 4/3 for international students. Applications are processed on a rolling basis. Application fee: $45. Electronic applications accepted. *Expenses:* $740 per credit. *Financial support:* Career-related internships or fieldwork, Federal Work-Study, scholarships/grants, tuition waivers (full and partial), and unspecified assistantships available. Support available to part-time students. Financial award application deadline: 3/1; financial award applicants required to submit FAFSA. *Faculty research:* Knowledge economy, urban economy, U.S. manufacturing industries, leadership personality, stock market reactions to terrorism, personality psychology, industrial/organizational psychology. *Unit head:* Dr. RT Good, Dean of the College of Business and Management, 561-237-7458, E-mail: rgood@lynn.edu. *Application contact:* Steven Pruitt, Director of Graduate and Undergraduate Evening Admission, 561-237-7834, Fax: 561-237-7100, E-mail: spruitt@lynn.edu.
Website: http://www.lynn.edu/academics/colleges/business-and-management

Madonna University, School of Business, Livonia, MI 48150-1173. Offers business administration (MBA); international business (MSBA); leadership studies (MSBA); leadership studies in criminal justice (MSBA); quality and operations management (MSBA). *Program availability:* Part-time, evening/weekend, online learning. *Degree requirements:* For master's, thesis (for some programs), foreign language proficiency (international business). *Entrance requirements:* For master's, GMAT, GRE General Test, minimum GPA of 3.0. Electronic applications accepted. *Faculty research:* Management, women in management, future studies.

Maine Maritime Academy, Loeb-Sullivan School of International Business and Logistics, Castine, ME 04420. Offers global logistics and maritime management (MS); international logistics management (MS). *Program availability:* Part-time, 100% online. *Faculty:* 6 full-time (1 woman), 5 part-time/adjunct (1 woman). *Students:* 8 full-time (2 women), 13 part-time (7 women). Average age 30. 26 applicants. In 2017, 17 master's awarded. *Degree requirements:* For master's, capstone course. *Entrance requirements:* For master's, GMAT or GRE, letter of recommendation. Additional exam requirements/recommendations for international students: Required—TOEFL, IELTS. *Application deadline:* For fall admission, 6/1 for domestic and international students; for spring admission, 3/15 for domestic and international students. Applications are processed on a rolling basis. Application fee: $40. Electronic applications accepted. Application fee is waived when completed online. *Financial support:* In 2017–18, 2 students received support, including teaching assistantships with full tuition reimbursements available (averaging $5,000 per year); career-related internships or fieldwork, Federal Work-Study, and institutionally sponsored loans also available. Support available to part-time students. Financial award application deadline: 4/15; financial award applicants required to submit FAFSA. *Faculty research:* Internet of things, trait intelligence, port operations, location theory. *Unit head:* Dr. Donald Maier, Dean, 207-326-2488, E-mail: donald.maier@mma.edu. *Application contact:* Debra Kingston, Program Coordinator, 207-326-2212, Fax: 207-326-2411, E-mail: debra.kingston@mma.edu. Website: http://ibl.mainemaritime.edu

Manhattanville College, School of Business, Master of Science in International Management Program, Purchase, NY 10577-2132. Offers international management (MS, Advanced Certificate), including business leadership (MS), finance (MS), human resource management (MS), marketing communication management (MS). *Program availability:* Part-time, evening/weekend. *Faculty:* 2 part-time/adjunct (0 women). *Students:* 6 full-time (3 women), 2 part-time (1 woman); includes 2 minority (1 Black or African American, non-Hispanic/Latino; 1 Two or more races, non-Hispanic/Latino), 2 international. Average age 34. 6 applicants, 67% accepted, 1 enrolled. In 2017, 2 master's awarded. *Degree requirements:* For master's, thesis (for some programs), final project. *Entrance requirements:* For master's, personal essay, transcripts, 2 letters of recommendation (academic or professional), resume, health form with proof of immunization (for those born after 1957). Additional exam requirements/recommendations for international students: Required—TOEFL (minimum score 563 paper-based, 85 iBT), IELTS (7), or iTEP (B2). *Application deadline:* Applications are processed on a rolling basis. Application fee: $75. Electronic applications accepted. *Expenses:* $915 per credit. *Financial support:* Federal Work-Study, institutionally sponsored loans, scholarships/grants, and unspecified assistantships available. Financial award application deadline: 3/15; financial award applicants required to submit FAFSA. *Unit head:* Laura Persky, Graduate Program Director, 914-323-5188, E-mail: laura.persky@mville.edu. *Application contact:* Monika Pottgen, Assistant Director, Recruitment and Admissions, 914-323-5150, E-mail: business@mville.edu. Website: https://www.mville.edu/programs/ms-international-management

Marconi International University, Graduate Programs, Pembroke Pines, FL 33028. Offers business administration (DBA); education leadership (Ed D); education leadership, management and emerging technologies (M Ed); international business administration (IMBA).

Marquette University, Graduate School of Management, Executive MBA Program, Milwaukee, WI 53201-1881. Offers economics (MBA); finance (MBA); human resources (MBA); international business (MBA); management information systems (MBA); marketing (MBA); operations and supply chain management (MBA); sports business (MBA). *Accreditation:* AACSB. *Degree requirements:* For master's, international trip. *Entrance requirements:* For master's, GMAT or GRE, two letters of recommendation, official transcripts from current and previous colleges/universities. Additional exam requirements/recommendations for international students: Required—TOEFL (minimum score 550 paper-based; 88 iBT), IELTS (minimum score 6.5), PTE. Electronic applications accepted. *Expenses:* Contact institution. *Faculty research:* International trade and finance, customer relationship management, consumer satisfaction, customer service.

Marquette University, Graduate School of Management, Program in Business Administration, Milwaukee, WI 53201-1881. Offers business administration (MBA); economics (MBA); entrepreneurship (Certificate); finance (MBA); human resources (MBA); international business (MBA); management information systems (MBA); marketing (MBA); operations and supply chain management (MBA); sports business (MBA); JD/MBA; MBA/MA; MBA/MSN. *Accreditation:* AACSB. *Program availability:* Part-time, evening/weekend. *Degree requirements:* For Certificate, business plan. *Entrance requirements:* For master's, GMAT or GRE, letters of recommendation. Additional exam requirements/recommendations for international students: Required—TOEFL (minimum score 550 paper-based; 88 iBT), IELTS (minimum score 6.5), PTE. Electronic applications accepted. *Faculty research:* Ethics in the professions, services marketing, technology impact on decision-making, mentoring.

McGill University, Faculty of Graduate and Postdoctoral Studies, Desautels Faculty of Management, Montréal, QC H3A 2T5, Canada. Offers administration (PhD); entrepreneurial studies (MBA); finance (MBA); general management (Post Master's Certificate); information systems (MBA); international business (MBA); international practicing management (MM); management (MBA); management for development (MBA); manufacturing management (MMM); marketing (MBA); operations management (MBA); public accountancy (Diploma); strategic management (MBA); MBA/LL B; MD/MBA. MMM offered jointly with Faculty of Engineering; PhD with Concordia University, HEC Montreal, Université de Montréal, Université du Québec à Montréal.

McKendree University, Graduate Programs, Master of Business Administration Program, Lebanon, IL 62254-1299. Offers business administration (MBA); human resource management (MBA); international business (MBA). *Program availability:* Part-time, evening/weekend, online learning. *Entrance requirements:* For master's, official transcripts from all institutions attended, essay, minimum GPA of 3.0, three references, resume. Additional exam requirements/recommendations for international students: Required—TOEFL. Electronic applications accepted.

Milwaukee School of Engineering, MS Program in Marketing and Export Management, Milwaukee, WI 53202-3109. Offers MS. *Program availability:* Part-time, evening/weekend. *Students:* 1 (woman) full-time, all international. 3 applicants, 33% accepted. In 2017, 2 master's awarded. *Degree requirements:* For master's, thesis or alternative, thesis defense or capstone project. *Entrance requirements:* For master's, GRE or GMAT if undergraduate GPA less than 2.8, 2 letters of recommendation; bachelor's degree from accredited university; work experience (strongly recommended). Additional exam requirements/recommendations for international students: Required—TOEFL (minimum score 90 iBT), IELTS (minimum score 7). *Application deadline:* Applications are processed on a rolling basis. Application fee: $0. Electronic applications accepted. *Expenses: Tuition:* Part-time $814 per credit hour. *Required fees:* $12.50 per credit hour. *Financial support:* Career-related internships or fieldwork, institutionally sponsored loans, scholarships/grants, and tuition waivers (full) available. Financial award application deadline: 3/15; financial award applicants required to submit FAFSA. *Unit head:* Gene Wright, Program Director, 414-277-2268, Fax: 414-277-2487, E-mail: wright@msoe.edu. *Application contact:* Brian Rutz, Graduate Admission Counselor, 414-277-7200, E-mail: rutz@msoe.edu. Website: https://www.msoe.edu/academics/graduate-degrees/business/marketing-export-management/

National American University, Roueche Graduate Center, Austin, TX 78731. Offers accounting (MBA); aviation management (MBA, MM); care coordination (MSN); community college leadership (Ed D); criminal justice (MM); e-marketing (MBA, MM); health care administration (MBA, MM); higher education (MM); human resources management (MBA, MM); information technology management (MBA, MM); international business (MBA); leadership (EMBA); management (MBA); nursing administration (MSN); nursing education (MSN); nursing (MSN); operations and configuration management (MBA, MM); project and process management (MBA, MM). Master's programs offered online through the Harold D. Buckingham Graduate School. *Program availability:* Part-time, evening/weekend, online learning. *Entrance requirements:* For master's, minimum undergraduate GPA of 2.75. Additional exam requirements/recommendations for international students: Required—TOEFL, TWE. Electronic applications accepted. *Faculty research:* Tourism, finance, marketing.

National University, Academic Affairs, School of Business and Management, La Jolla, CA 92037-1011. Offers accountancy (M Acc, Certificate); business administration (GMBA, MBA); business analytics (MS); cause leadership (MA); global management (MGM); human resource management (MA); management information systems (MS); marketing (MS); organizational leadership (MS). GMBA offered in Spanish. *Program availability:* Part-time, evening/weekend, 100% online, blended/hybrid learning. *Degree requirements:* For master's, thesis (for some programs). *Entrance requirements:* For master's, interview, minimum GPA of 2.5. Additional exam requirements/recommendations for international students: Required—TOEFL (minimum score 550 paper-based; 79 iBT), IELTS (minimum score 6). *Application deadline:* Applications are processed on a rolling basis. Application fee: $60 ($65 for international students). Electronic applications accepted. *Expenses: Tuition:* Part-time $430 per quarter hour. *Financial support:* Career-related internships or fieldwork, scholarships/grants, and tuition waivers (partial) available. Support available to part-time students. Financial award application deadline: 6/30; financial award applicants required to submit FAFSA. *Unit head:* Dr. Alfred Ntoko, Dean, 858-642-8400, Fax: 858-642-8719, E-mail: sobm@nu.edu. *Application contact:* Brandon Jouganatos, Vice President for Enrollment Services, 800-628-8648, E-mail: advisor@nu.edu. Website: http://www.nu.edu/OurPrograms/SchoolOfBusinessAndManagement.html

Newman University, MBA Program, Wichita, KS 67213-2097. Offers finance (MBA); international business (MBA); leadership (MBA); management (MBA); management information technology (MBA). *Program availability:* Part-time. *Degree requirements:* For master's, thesis optional. *Entrance requirements:* For master's, minimum GPA of 3.0; 2 letters of recommendation; course work in algebra, statistics, macroeconomics, and financial accounting. Additional exam requirements/recommendations for international students: Required—TOEFL (minimum score 600 paper-based; 100 iBT). Electronic applications accepted. *Expenses:* Contact institution.

New Mexico Highlands University, Graduate Studies, School of Business, Media and Technology, Las Vegas, NM 87701. Offers business administration (MBA), including human resource management, international business, management; media arts and technology (MA), including media arts and computer science. *Accreditation:* ACBSP. *Degree requirements:* For master's, comprehensive exam, thesis or alternative. *Entrance requirements:* For master's, minimum undergraduate GPA of 3.0. Additional exam requirements/recommendations for international students: Required—TOEFL (minimum score 540 paper-based). *Faculty research:* Real estate valuation, studying expert judgments in complex accounting, decision environments, green marketing, environmentalism, marketing research methodology.

New York University, Graduate School of Arts and Science, Department of Politics, New York, NY 10012-1019. Offers political campaign management (MA); politics (MA, PhD); JD/MA; MBA/MA. *Program availability:* Part-time. *Students:* Average age 27. 670 applicants, 45% accepted, 80 enrolled. In 2017, 101 master's, 13 doctorates awarded. Terminal master's awarded for partial completion of doctoral program. *Degree requirements:* For master's, one foreign language, thesis or alternative; for doctorate, 2 foreign languages, comprehensive exam, thesis/dissertation. *Entrance requirements:* For master's and doctorate, GRE General Test. Additional exam requirements/recommendations for international students: Required—TOEFL. *Application deadline:* For fall admission, 12/18 priority date for domestic students, 12/18 for international students. Application fee: $100. *Expenses: Tuition:* Full-time $41,352; part-time $19,968 per year. *Required fees:* $2496; $1628 per unit. $814 per term. Tuition and fees vary according to course load and program. *Financial support:* Fellowships, teaching assistantships, career-related internships or fieldwork, Federal Work-Study, and institutionally sponsored loans available. Financial award application deadline: 12/18; financial award applicants required to submit FAFSA. *Faculty research:* Comparative politics, democratic theory and practice, rational choice, political economy, international relations. *Unit head:* Sanford Gordon, Director of Graduate Studies, PhD Program, 212-998-8500, Fax: 212-995-4184, E-mail: politics.phd@nyu.edu. *Application contact:* Nicole Simonelli, Director of Graduate Studies, Master's Program, 212-998-8500, Fax: 212-995-4184, E-mail: politics.masters@nyu.edu. Website: http://www.nyu.edu/gsas/dept/politics/

Niagara University, Graduate Division of Business Administration, Niagara University, NY 14109. Offers accounting (MBA); business administration (MBA); finance (MBA, MS); financial planning (MBA); healthcare administration (MBA, MHA); human resources (MBA); international business (MBA); marketing (MBA); professional accountancy (MBA); strategic management (MBA); supply chain management (MBA). *Accreditation:* AACSB. *Program availability:* Part-time, evening/weekend. *Faculty:* 17 full-time, 11 part-time/adjunct. *Students:* 173 full-time (92 women), 77 part-time (39 women); includes 38 minority (8 Black or African American, non-Hispanic/Latino; 3 American Indian or Alaska Native, non-Hispanic/Latino; 8 Asian, non-Hispanic/Latino; 8 Hispanic/Latino; 11 Two or more races, non-Hispanic/Latino), 46 international. Average age 27. In 2017, 139 master's awarded. *Entrance requirements:* For master's, GMAT. Additional exam requirements/recommendations for international students: Required—TOEFL (minimum score 550 paper-based; 79 iBT), IELTS (minimum score 6). *Application deadline:* For fall admission, 8/1 for domestic students; for spring admission, 11/1 for domestic students. Applications are processed on a rolling basis. Electronic applications accepted. *Expenses:* Contact institution. *Financial support:* Fellowships, research assistantships, career-related internships or fieldwork, and Federal Work-Study available. Support available to part-time students. Financial award application deadline: 4/15; financial award applicants required to submit FAFSA. *Faculty research:* Capital flows, Federal Reserve policy, human resource management, public policy, issues in marketing, auctions, economics of information, risk and capital markets, management strategy, consumer behavior, Internet and social media marketing. *Unit head:* Dr. Paul Richardson, MBA Director/Chair of the Marketing Department, 716-286-8169, Fax: 716-286-8206, E-mail: psr@niagara.edu. *Application contact:* Evan Pierce, Associate Director for Graduate Recruitment, 716-286-8769, Fax: 716-286-8170, E-mail: epierce@niagara.edu. Website: http://mba.niagara.edu

International Business

Northeastern University, D'Amore-McKim School of Business, Boston, MA 02115-5096. Offers accounting (MS); business administration (EMBA, MBA); finance (MS); innovation (MS); international business (MS); international management (MS); taxation (MS); technological entrepreneurship (MS); JD/MBA; LL M/MBA; MBA/MSN; MS/MBA. *Accreditation:* AACSB. *Program availability:* Part-time, evening/weekend, online learning. *Faculty:* 184. *Students:* 1,489. In 2017, 800 master's awarded. *Entrance requirements:* For master's, GMAT or GRE. Application fee: $75. Electronic applications accepted. *Expenses:* Contact institution. *Financial support:* Scholarships/grants available. Financial award applicants required to submit FAFSA. *Unit head:* Dr. Raj Echambadi, Dean, D'Amore-McKim School of Business, 617-373-3232, Fax: 617-373-2056. *Application contact:* Evelyn Tate, Director, Graduate Recruitment and Admissions, 617-373-3258, E-mail: e.tate@northeastern.edu.
Website: http://damore-mckim.northeastern.edu/

Northern Arizona University, Office of the Provost, NAU-Yuma, Yuma, AZ 85365. Offers global business administration (MGBA). *Program availability:* Part-time, blended/hybrid learning. *Students:* 6 applicants, 100% accepted, 5 enrolled. *Degree requirements:* For master's, variable foreign language requirement, comprehensive exam (for some programs), thesis (for some programs). *Entrance requirements:* Additional exam requirements/recommendations for international students: Required—TOEFL (minimum score 80 iBT), IELTS (minimum score 6.5). *Application deadline:* Applications are processed on a rolling basis. Application fee: $65. Electronic applications accepted. *Expenses:* Tuition, state resident: full-time $9240; part-time $458 per credit hour. Tuition, nonresident: full-time $21,588; part-time $1199 per credit hour. *Required fees:* $1021; $14 per credit hour. $646 per semester. Tuition and fees vary according to course load, campus/location and program. *Financial support:* Application deadline: 2/1; applicants required to submit FAFSA. *Unit head:* Dr. Larry Gould, Associate Vice President/Campus Executive Officer, 928-317-6475, E-mail: larry.gould@nau.edu.
Website: http://yuma.nau.edu/

Northwestern University, The Graduate School, Kellogg School of Management, Management Programs, Evanston, IL 60208. Offers accounting information and management (MBA, PhD); analytical finance (MBA); business administration (MBA); decision sciences (MBA); entrepreneurship and innovation (MBA); finance (MBA, PhD); health enterprise management (MBA); human resources management (MBA); international business (MBA); management and organizations (MBA, PhD); management and organizations and sociology (PhD); management and strategy (MBA); management studies (MS); managerial analytics (MBA); managerial economics (MBA); managerial economics and strategy (PhD); marketing (MBA, PhD); marketing management (MBA); media management (MBA); operations management (MBA, PhD); real estate (MBA); social enterprise at Kellogg (MBA); JD/MBA. *Program availability:* Part-time, evening/weekend. Terminal master's awarded for partial completion of doctoral program. *Degree requirements:* For doctorate, thesis/dissertation, 2 years of coursework, qualifying (field) exam and candidacy, summer research papers and presentations to faculty, proposal defense, final exam/defense. *Entrance requirements:* For master's, GMAT, GRE, interview, 2 letters of recommendation, college transcripts, resume, essays, Kellogg honor code; for doctorate, GMAT, GRE, statement of purpose, transcripts, 2 letters of recommendation, resume, interview. Additional exam requirements/recommendations for international students: Required—TOEFL, IELTS. Electronic applications accepted. *Expenses:* Contact institution. *Faculty research:* Business cycles and international finance, health policy, networks, non-market strategy, consumer psychology.

Northwest University, College of Business, Kirkland, WA 98033. Offers business administration (MBA); international business (MBA); project management (MBA); social entrepreneurship (MBA). *Accreditation:* ACBSP. *Program availability:* Part-time, evening/weekend. *Degree requirements:* For master's, formalized research. *Entrance requirements:* For master's, GMAT. Additional exam requirements/recommendations for international students: Required—TOEFL (minimum score 550 paper-based; 75 iBT). Electronic applications accepted. *Expenses:* Contact institution.

Norwich University, College of Graduate and Continuing Studies, Master of Arts in Diplomacy Program, Northfield, VT 05663. Offers diplomacy (MA), including cyber diplomacy - policy, cyber diplomacy - technical, international commerce, international conflict management, international terrorism. *Program availability:* Evening/weekend, online only, mostly all online with a week-long residency requirement. *Degree requirements:* For master's, comprehensive exam, thesis optional. *Entrance requirements:* For master's, minimum undergraduate GPA of 2.75. Additional exam requirements/recommendations for international students: Required—TOEFL (minimum score 550 paper-based; 80 iBT), IELTS (minimum score 6.5). Electronic applications accepted. *Expenses:* Contact institution.

Nova Southeastern University, H. Wayne Huizenga College of Business and Entrepreneurship, Fort Lauderdale, FL 33314-7796. Offers accounting (M Acc); business (MBA); business intelligence/analytics (MBA); complex health systems (MBA); enterprise informatics (MBA); entrepreneurship (MBA); finance (MBA); human resource management (MBA); international business (MBA); management (MBA); marketing (MBA); process improvement (MBA); public administration (MPA); real estate development (MS); sport revenue generation (MBA); supply chain management (MBA). *Accreditation:* NASPAA. *Program availability:* Part-time, evening/weekend, 100% online, blended/hybrid learning. *Faculty:* 85 full-time (37 women), 59 part-time/adjunct (19 women). *Students:* 1,999 full-time (1,225 women), 335 part-time (210 women); includes 1,516 minority (597 Black or African American, non-Hispanic/Latino; 4 American Indian or Alaska Native, non-Hispanic/Latino; 92 Asian, non-Hispanic/Latino; 789 Hispanic/Latino; 3 Native Hawaiian or other Pacific Islander, non-Hispanic/Latino; 31 Two or more races, non-Hispanic/Latino), 291 international. Average age 34. 1,269 applicants, 59% accepted, 551 enrolled. In 2017, 1,055 master's awarded. *Entrance requirements:* For master's, GMAT or GRE (depending on undergraduate GPA), official transcripts from all schools attended while in pursuit of bachelor's degree; minimum GPA of 2.5 from regionally-accredited institution. Additional exam requirements/recommendations for international students: Required—TOEFL (minimum score 550 paper-based; 79 iBT), IELTS (minimum score 6), PTE (minimum score 54). *Application deadline:* For fall admission, 8/5 priority date for domestic students, 7/29 priority date for international students; for winter admission, 12/16 priority date for domestic students, 12/9 priority date for international students; for summer admission, 4/21 priority date for domestic and international students. Applications are processed on a rolling basis. Application fee: $50. Electronic applications accepted. *Expenses:* $37,785 (online), $35,640 (in-classroom). *Financial support:* In 2017–18, 325 students received support. Federal Work-Study and scholarships/grants available. Support available to part-time students. Financial award application deadline: 4/15; financial award applicants required to submit FAFSA. *Faculty research:* Entrepreneurship and venture capital, ethics and social responsibility, global commerce and cultures, business process management. *Unit head:* Dr. J. Preston Jones, Dean, 954-262-5127, E-mail: prestonj@nova.edu. *Application contact:* Zeida Rodriguez, Associate Director of Enrollment Services, 954-262-5163, Fax: 954-262-3822, E-mail: zeida@nova.edu.
Website: http://www.huizenga.nova.edu

Oakland University, Graduate Study and Lifelong Learning, School of Business Administration, Department of Management and Marketing, Rochester, MI 48309-4401. Offers business administration (MBA); entrepreneurship (Certificate); general management (Certificate); human resource management (Certificate); international business (Certificate); management and marketing (EMBA); marketing (Certificate). *Expenses:* Tuition, state resident: full-time $16,950; part-time $706.25 per credit. Tuition, nonresident: full-time $24,648; part-time $1027 per credit.

Oklahoma Christian University, Graduate School of Business, Oklahoma City, OK 73136-1100. Offers accounting (M Acc, MBA); financial services (MBA); general business (MBA); health services management (MBA); human resources (MBA); international business (MBA); leadership and organizational development (MBA); marketing (MBA); nonprofit management (MBA); project management (MBA). *Accreditation:* ACBSP. *Program availability:* Part-time, 100% online. *Entrance requirements:* For master's, bachelor's degree. Additional exam requirements/recommendations for international students: Required—TOEFL (minimum score 550 paper-based). Electronic applications accepted. *Expenses:* Contact institution.

Oklahoma State University, Spears School of Business, School of Marketing and International Business, Stillwater, OK 74078. Offers business administration (PhD), including marketing; marketing (MBA). *Program availability:* Part-time. *Faculty:* 21 full-time (5 women), 5 part-time/adjunct (2 women). *Students:* 63 full-time (19 women), 19 part-time (9 women); includes 5 minority (2 Asian, non-Hispanic/Latino; 2 Hispanic/Latino; 1 Two or more races, non-Hispanic/Latino), 65 international. Average age 27. 234 applicants, 20% accepted, 42 enrolled. In 2017, 41 master's, 1 doctorate awarded. *Entrance requirements:* For master's and doctorate, GRE or GMAT. Additional exam requirements/recommendations for international students: Required—TOEFL (minimum score 550 paper-based; 79 iBT). *Application deadline:* For fall admission, 3/1 priority date for international students; for spring admission, 8/1 priority date for international students. Applications are processed on a rolling basis. Application fee: $40 ($75 for international students). Electronic applications accepted. *Expenses:* Tuition, state resident: full-time $4019; part-time $2679.60 per year. Tuition, nonresident: full-time $15,286; part-time $10,190.40 per year. *Required fees:* $2129; $1419 per unit. Tuition and fees vary according to program. *Financial support:* Research assistantships, teaching assistantships, career-related internships or fieldwork, Federal Work-Study, scholarships/grants, health care benefits, tuition waivers (partial), and unspecified assistantships available. Support available to part-time students. Financial award application deadline: 3/1; financial award applicants required to submit FAFSA. *Faculty research:* Decision-making (consumer, managerial, cross-functional), communication effects, services marketing, public policy and marketing, corporate image. *Unit head:* Dr. Joshua L. Wiener, Department Head, 405-744-5192, Fax: 405-744-5180, E-mail: josh.wiener@okstate.edu. *Application contact:* Dr. Kevin Voss, PhD Coordinator, 405-744-5106, Fax: 405-744-5180, E-mail: kevin.voss@okstate.edu.
Website: https://business.okstate.edu/marketing/

Old Dominion University, Strome College of Business, Program in Maritime Trade and Supply Chain Management, Norfolk, VA 23529. Offers MS. *Program availability:* Part-time, evening/weekend. *Students:* 5 full-time (3 women), 13 part-time (5 women); includes 4 minority (3 Asian, non-Hispanic/Latino; 1 Hispanic/Latino), 4 international. Average age 33. In 2017, 1 master's awarded. *Degree requirements:* For master's, capstone course. *Entrance requirements:* For master's, GRE or GMAT, bachelor's degree, official transcripts, two letters of recommendation, current resume, statement of professional goals. Additional exam requirements/recommendations for international students: Required—TOEFL (minimum score 550 paper-based; 79 iBT), IELTS (minimum score 6.5). *Application deadline:* For fall admission, 6/1 for domestic students, 4/15 for international students; for spring admission, 11/1 for domestic students, 10/1 for international students. Applications are processed on a rolling basis. Electronic applications accepted. *Expenses:* Tuition, state resident: full-time $8928; part-time $496 per credit. Tuition, nonresident: full-time $22,482; part-time $1249 per credit. *Required fees:* $66 per semester. *Financial support:* In 2017–18, 2 students received support. Unspecified assistantships available. *Total annual research expenditures:* $400,000. *Unit head:* Dr. Wayne Talley, Director, 757-683-3534.

Oral Roberts University, School of Business, Tulsa, OK 74171. Offers accounting (MBA); entrepreneurship (MBA); finance (MBA); international business (MBA); management (MBA); marketing (MBA); not for profit management (MNM). *Accreditation:* ACBSP. *Program availability:* Part-time, online learning. *Faculty:* 7 full-time (0 women), 5 part-time/adjunct (4 women). *Students:* 71 applicants, 94% accepted, 56 enrolled. *Degree requirements:* For master's, thesis optional. *Entrance requirements:* For master's, minimum cumulative GPA of 3.0 from regionally-accredited institution. *Application deadline:* Applications are processed on a rolling basis. Application fee: $35. Electronic applications accepted. Application fee is waived when completed online. *Financial support:* In 2017–18, 39 students received support. Scholarships/grants and unspecified assistantships available. Financial award application deadline: 6/1. *Faculty research:* Social media, international business and marketing. *Unit head:* Dr. Marshal Wright, Chair of the Graduate School of Business, 918-495-6988, E-mail: mwright@oru.edu. *Application contact:* Sam Park, Enrollment Counselor, 918-495-7179, E-mail: sampark@oru.edu.
Website: http://www.oru.edu/university/departments/schools/bus

Pace University, Lubin School of Business, Advanced Professional Certificate Program, New York, NY 10038. Offers business economics (APC); e-business (APC); financial management (APC); international business (APC); international economics (APC); investment management (APC); marketing (APC); public accounting (APC). *Program availability:* Part-time, evening/weekend. *Students:* 1 applicant, 100% accepted. *Entrance requirements:* For degree, MBA or MS in business discipline, relevant professional experience. Additional exam requirements/recommendations for international students: Required—TOEFL (minimum score 90 iBT), IELTS (minimum score 7) or PTE (minimum score 61). *Application deadline:* For fall admission, 8/1 priority date for domestic students, 6/1 for international students; for spring admission, 12/1 for domestic students, 10/1 for international students. Applications are processed on a rolling basis. Application fee: $70. Electronic applications accepted. *Unit head:* Dr. Jack Yurkiewicz, Director, 212-618-6567, E-mail: jyurkiewicz@pace.edu. *Application contact:* Susan Ford-Goldschein, Director of Graduate Admissions, 212-346-1531, Fax: 212-346-1585, E-mail: graduateadmission@pace.edu.
Website: http://www.pace.edu/lubin/agc

Pace University, Lubin School of Business, Financial Management Program, New York, NY 10038. Offers financial management (MBA, MS); financial risk management (MS); international finance (MBA); investment management (MBA, MS). *Program availability:* Part-time, evening/weekend. *Students:* 103 full-time (41 women), 53 part-time (26 women); includes 24 minority (5 Black or African American, non-Hispanic/Latino; 11 Asian, non-Hispanic/Latino; 6 Hispanic/Latino; 1 Native Hawaiian or other Pacific Islander, non-Hispanic/Latino; 1 Two or more races, non-Hispanic/Latino), 103 international. Average age 26. 251 applicants, 61% accepted, 43 enrolled. In 2017, 108 master's awarded. *Entrance requirements:* For master's, GMAT, GRE (GMAT not required for MS with passing of Level 1 of Chartered Financial Analyst exam or Level 1 of Financial Risk Manager Exam), undergraduate degree, transcripts from all accredited colleges/universities attended, two letters of recommendation, resume, personal

statement. Additional exam requirements/recommendations for international students: Required—TOEFL (minimum score 90 iBT), IELTS (minimum score 7) or PTE (minimum score 61). *Application deadline:* For fall admission, 8/1 priority date for domestic students, 6/1 for international students; for spring admission, 12/1 for domestic students, 10/1 for international students. Applications are processed on a rolling basis. Application fee: $70. Electronic applications accepted. *Financial support:* Research assistantships, career-related internships or fieldwork, Federal Work-Study, and tuition waivers (full and partial) available. Support available to part-time students. Financial award application deadline: 2/15; financial award applicants required to submit FAFSA. *Unit head:* Dr. P. V. Viswanath, Chairperson, 212-618-6518, E-mail: pviswanath@pace.edu. *Application contact:* Susan Ford-Goldschein, Director of Graduate Admissions, 212-346-1531, Fax: 212-346-1585, E-mail: graduateadmissions@pace.edu.
Website: http://www.pace.edu/lubin/financial-management-mba

Pace University, Lubin School of Business, International Business Program, New York, NY 10038. Offers MBA. *Program availability:* Part-time, evening/weekend. *Students:* 6 full-time (4 women), 5 part-time (2 women); includes 2 minority (1 Asian, non-Hispanic/Latino; 1 Hispanic/Latino), 5 international. Average age 30. 24 applicants, 42% accepted, 3 enrolled. In 2017, 4 master's awarded. *Entrance requirements:* For master's, GMAT, GRE, undergraduate degree, transcripts from all accredited colleges/universities attended, two letters of recommendation, resume, personal statement. Additional exam requirements/recommendations for international students: Required—TOEFL (minimum score 90 iBT), IELTS (minimum score 7) or PTE (minimum score 61). *Application deadline:* For fall admission, 8/1 priority date for domestic students, 6/1 for international students; for spring admission, 12/1 for domestic students, 10/1 for international students. Applications are processed on a rolling basis. Application fee: $70. Electronic applications accepted. *Financial support:* Research assistantships, career-related internships or fieldwork, Federal Work-Study, and unspecified assistantships available. Support available to part-time students. Financial award application deadline: 2/15; financial award applicants required to submit FAFSA. *Unit head:* Lawrence G. Bridwell, Director, 914-773-3391, E-mail: lbridwell@pace.edu. *Application contact:* Susan Ford-Goldschein, Director of Graduate Admissions, 212-346-1531, Fax: 212-346-1585, E-mail: graduateadmission@pace.edu.
Website: http://www.pace.edu/lubin/mba-in-international-business

Pacific States University, College of Business, Los Angeles, CA 90010. Offers accounting (MBA, Certificate); beauty management (MBA); finance (MBA); international business (MBA); management of information technology (MBA); project management (Certificate); real estate management (MBA). *Program availability:* Part-time, evening/weekend, online learning. *Entrance requirements:* For master's, minimum undergraduate GPA of 2.5 during last 90 quarter units of course work, bachelor's degree in business administration or economics. Additional exam requirements/recommendations for international students: Required—TOEFL (minimum score 500 paper-based; 61 iBT), IELTS (minimum score 5.5). *Application deadline:* For fall admission, 9/1 priority date for domestic students, 8/1 priority date for international students; for winter admission, 12/1 priority date for domestic students, 11/1 priority date for international students; for spring admission, 3/1 priority date for domestic students, 2/1 priority date for international students; for summer admission, 6/1 priority date for domestic students, 5/1 priority date for international students. Applications are processed on a rolling basis. Application fee: $100. *Expenses:* Tuition: Part-time $380 per unit. *Financial support:* Scholarships/grants available. Financial award applicants required to submit FAFSA. *Unit head:* Chase C. Rhee, MBA Program Administrator, 323-731-2383 Ext. 208, Fax: 323-731-7276, E-mail: ccrhee@psuca.edu. *Application contact:* Maawiya Ayeva, Director of Admissions, 323-731-2383 Ext. 204, Fax: 323-731-7276, E-mail: admissions@psuca.edu.

Park University, School of Graduate and Professional Studies, Kansas City, MO 54105. Offers adult education (M Ed); business and government leadership (Graduate Certificate); business, government, and global society (MPA); communication and leadership (MA); creative and life writing (Graduate Certificate); disaster and emergency management (MPA, Graduate Certificate); educational leadership (M Ed); finance (MBA, Graduate Certificate); general business (MBA); global business (Graduate Certificate); healthcare administration (MHA); healthcare services management and leadership (Graduate Certificate); international business (MBA); language and literacy (M Ed), including English for speakers of other languages, special reading teacher/literacy coach; leadership of international healthcare organizations (Graduate Certificate); management information systems (MBA, Graduate Certificate); music performance (ADP, Graduate Certificate), including cello (MM, ADP), piano (MM, ADP), viola (MM, ADP), violin (MM, ADP); nonprofit and community services management (MPA); nonprofit leadership (Graduate Certificate); performance (MM), including cello (MM, ADP), piano (MM, ADP), viola (MM, ADP), violin (MM, ADP); public management (MPA); social work (MSW); teacher leadership (M Ed), including curriculum and assessment, instructional leader. *Program availability:* Part-time, evening/weekend, online learning. *Degree requirements:* For master's, comprehensive exam (for some programs), thesis (for some programs), internship (for some programs); exam (for some programs). *Entrance requirements:* For master's, GRE or GMAT (for some programs), teacher certification (for some M Ed programs), letters of recommendation, essay, resume (for some programs). Additional exam requirements/recommendations for international students: Required—TOEFL (minimum score 550 paper-based; 79 iBT), IELTS (minimum score 6). Electronic applications accepted.

Pepperdine University, Graziadio Business School, Full-Time MBA Programs, Malibu, CA 90263. Offers business administration (MBA); international business administration (MBA); JD/MBA; MBA/MPP. *Unit head:* Dr. Deryck J. Rensburg, Dean, 310-568-5689, Fax: 310-568-5500, E-mail: deryck.rensburg@pepperdine.edu. *Application contact:* Morag Knapp, Assistant Director of Admission, Graziadio School of Business and Management, 310-568-5527, E-mail: morag.knapp@pepperdine.edu.
Website: https://bschool.pepperdine.edu/mba-programs/full-time-mba/

Pepperdine University, Graziadio Business School, Master of Science Programs, Malibu, CA 90263. Offers accounting (MS); applied analytics (MS); applied finance (MS); global business (MS); human resources (MS); management and leadership (MS); organization development (MS); real estate investment and finance (MS). *Accreditation:* AACSB. *Students:* 462 full-time (277 women), 104 part-time (68 women); includes 67 minority (23 Black or African American, non-Hispanic/Latino; 1 American Indian or Alaska Native, non-Hispanic/Latino; 41 Asian, non-Hispanic/Latino; 2 Hispanic/Latino), 380 international. Average age 27. 2,180 applicants, 63% accepted, 336 enrolled. In 2017, 291 master's awarded. *Entrance requirements:* For master's, GMAT or GRE, two letters of recommendation. Additional exam requirements/recommendations for international students: Required—TOEFL. *Application deadline:* For fall admission, 5/1 for domestic students, 4/1 for international students. Application fee: $75. Electronic applications accepted. *Financial support:* Applicants required to submit FAFSA. *Unit head:* Dr. Michael L. Williams, Associate Dean, 310-506-4112, Fax: 310-506-4126, E-mail: michael.williams@pepperdine.edu.
Website: http://bschool.pepperdine.edu/masters-degree/

Pittsburg State University, Graduate School, Kelce College of Business, Department of Management and Marketing, Pittsburg, KS 66762. Offers general administration (MBA); international business (MBA). *Accreditation:* AACSB. *Program availability:* Part-time. *Students:* 80 (30 women). In 2017, 35 master's awarded. *Degree requirements:* For master's, thesis or alternative. *Entrance requirements:* For master's, GMAT or GRE. Additional exam requirements/recommendations for international students: Required—TOEFL (minimum score 550 paper-based; 79 iBT), IELTS (minimum score 6.5), PTE (minimum score 53). *Application deadline:* For fall admission, 7/15 for domestic students, 6/1 for international students; for spring admission, 12/15 for domestic students, 10/15 for international students; for summer admission, 5/15 for domestic students, 4/1 for international students. Applications are processed on a rolling basis. Application fee: $35 ($60 for international students). Electronic applications accepted. *Expenses:* Contact institution. *Financial support:* In 2017–18, 10 teaching assistantships with full tuition reimbursements (averaging $5,500 per year) were awarded; research assistantships, career-related internships or fieldwork, Federal Work-Study, and unspecified assistantships also available. Financial award application deadline: 2/1; financial award applicants required to submit FAFSA. *Faculty research:* Consumer behavior, productions management, forecasting interest rate swaps, strategy management. *Unit head:* Dr. Bienvenido Cortes, MBA Coordinator, 620-235-4594, E-mail: bcortes@pittstate.edu. *Application contact:* Lisa Allen, Assistant Director of Graduate and Continuing Studies, 620-235-4218, Fax: 620-235-4219, E-mail: lallen@pittstate.edu.
Website: http://www.pittstate.edu/mgmkt/

Point Park University, Rowland School of Business, Program in Business Administration, Pittsburgh, PA 15222-1984. Offers business analytics (MBA); global management and administration (MBA); health systems management (MBA); international business (MBA); management (MBA); management information systems (MBA); sports, arts and entertainment management (MBA). *Program availability:* Evening/weekend, 100% online.

Polytechnic University of Puerto Rico, Graduate School, Hato Rey, PR 00918. Offers business administration (MBA), including computer information systems, general management, management of information systems, management of international enterprises; civil engineering (ME, MS); computer engineering (ME, MS); computer science (MCS, MS); electrical engineering (ME, MS); engineering management (MEM); environmental management (MEM); landscape architecture (M Land Arch); manufacturing competitiveness (MMC, MS); manufacturing engineering (ME, MS); mechanical engineering (M Mech E). *Program availability:* Part-time, evening/weekend. *Entrance requirements:* For master's, 3 letters of recommendation.

Polytechnic University of Puerto Rico, Miami Campus, Graduate School, Miami, FL 33166. Offers accounting (MBA); business administration (MBA); construction management (MEM); environmental management (MEM); finance (MBA); human resources management (MBA); logistics and supply chain management (MBA); management of international enterprises (MBA); manufacturing management (MEM); marketing management (MBA); project management (MBA). *Program availability:* Part-time, evening/weekend, online learning. *Entrance requirements:* For master's, minimum GPA of 3.0. Electronic applications accepted.

Polytechnic University of Puerto Rico, Orlando Campus, Graduate School, Orlando, FL 32825. Offers accounting (MBA); business administration (MBA); construction management (MEM); engineering management (MEM); environmental management (MEM); finance (MBA); human resources management (MBA); management of international enterprises (MBA); management of technology (MBA); manufacturing management (MEM). *Program availability:* Part-time, evening/weekend, online learning. *Entrance requirements:* For master's, minimum GPA of 3.0. Additional exam requirements/recommendations for international students: Recommended—TOEFL. Electronic applications accepted.

Pontifical Catholic University of Puerto Rico, College of Business Administration, Program in International Business, Ponce, PR 00717-0777. Offers MBA. *Program availability:* Part-time, evening/weekend. *Entrance requirements:* For master's, GRE, interview, minimum GPA of 2.75.

Pontificia Universidad Catolica Madre y Maestra, Graduate School, Faculty of Social and Administrative Sciences, Santiago, Dominican Republic. Offers business administration (MBA), including business development, finance, international business, management skills (M Mgmt, MBA), marketing, operations, strategic cost management, strategy, tourist destination planning and management; law (LL M), including civil law, corporate business law, criminal law, international relations, real estate law; management (M Mgmt), including higher financial management, insurance program administration, management skills (M Mgmt, MBA); psychology (MA), including clinical child and adolescent psychology, forensic psychology; strategic human resources (EMBA).

Portland State University, Graduate Studies, The School of Business, Program in International Management, Portland, OR 97207-0751. Offers MIM. *Program availability:* Part-time, evening/weekend. *Faculty:* 2 full-time (1 woman). *Students:* 37 full-time (19 women), 2 part-time (both women); includes 12 minority (6 Asian, non-Hispanic/Latino; 3 Hispanic/Latino; 3 Two or more races, non-Hispanic/Latino), 23 international. Average age 26. 34 applicants, 85% accepted, 17 enrolled. In 2017, 33 master's awarded. *Degree requirements:* For master's, one foreign language, field study trip to China and Japan, international consulting project. *Entrance requirements:* For master's, GMAT, GRE General Test, minimum GPA of 2.75, resume, 2 letters of recommendation, essay. Additional exam requirements/recommendations for international students: Required—TOEFL (minimum score 550 paper-based; 80 iBT). *Application deadline:* For fall admission, 2/1 priority date for domestic and international students. Applications are processed on a rolling basis. Application fee: $65. Electronic applications accepted. *Expenses:* Contact institution. *Financial support:* In 2017–18, 4 students received support. Career-related internships or fieldwork, Federal Work-Study, institutionally sponsored loans, and scholarships/grants available. Support available to part-time students. Financial award application deadline: 3/1; financial award applicants required to submit FAFSA. *Unit head:* Tichelle Sorensen, Academic Director, 503-725-9936, E-mail: sorenset@pdx.edu. *Application contact:* 503-725-8001, E-mail: gradinfo.sba@pdx.edu.
Website: https://www.pdx.edu/sba/master-of-international-management

Providence College, School of Business, Providence, RI 02918. Offers accounting (MBA); finance (MBA); international business (MBA); management (MBA); marketing (MBA). *Accreditation:* AACSB. *Program availability:* Part-time, evening/weekend. *Entrance requirements:* For master's, GMAT. Additional exam requirements/recommendations for international students: Required—TOEFL (minimum score 577 paper-based; 90 iBT). *Expenses:* Contact institution.

Purdue University, Graduate School, Krannert School of Management, IMM Global Executive MBA Program, West Lafayette, IN 47906. Offers MBA. *Faculty:* 10 full-time (0 women), 10 part-time/adjunct (2 women). *Students:* 41 part-time (19 women); includes 14 minority (6 Black or African American, non-Hispanic/Latino; 5 Asian, non-Hispanic/Latino; 3 Hispanic/Latino), 13 international. Average age 39. 31 applicants, 97% accepted, 21 enrolled. In 2017, 2 master's awarded. *Entrance requirements:* For master's, GMAT or GRE, resume (minimum 5 years' work experience), official transcripts, two recommendations, interview. Additional exam requirements/recommendations for international students: Required—TOEFL, IELTS. *Application*

International Business

deadline: For spring admission, 2/1 for domestic and international students. Applications are processed on a rolling basis. Application fee: $60 ($75 for international students). Electronic applications accepted. *Expenses:* $51,000. *Financial support:* In 2017–18, 17 students received support. Scholarships/grants available. Financial award application deadline: 1/31; financial award applicants required to submit FAFSA. *Faculty research:* Dimensions of trust, communities of practice and networks, business in Latin America. *Unit head:* Dr. Aldas P. Kriauciunas, Executive Director, 765-496-1860, Fax: 765-494-0862, E-mail: akriauci@purdue.edu. *Application contact:* Nancy Smigiel, Assistant Director of Admissions, 765-494-4580, Fax: 765-494-0862, E-mail: nks@purdue.edu. Website: http://www.krannert.purdue.edu/executive/emba/IMM-Global-EMBA/home.php

Purdue University Global, School of Business, Davenport, IA 52807. Offers business administration (MBA); change leadership (MS); entrepreneurship (MBA); finance (MBA); health care management (MBA, MS); human resource (MBA); international business (MBA); management (MS); marketing (MBA); project management (MBA, MS); supply chain management and logistics (MBA, MS). *Accreditation:* ACBSP. *Program availability:* Part-time, evening/weekend, online learning. *Entrance requirements:* Additional exam requirements/recommendations for international students: Required—TOEFL (minimum score 550 paper-based; 80 iBT). Electronic applications accepted.

Regent's University London, Webster Graduate School, London, United Kingdom. Offers business (MBA); finance (MS); human resources (MA); information technology management (MA); international business (MA); international non-governmental organizations (MA); international relations (MA); management and leadership (MA); marketing (MA). *Program availability:* Part-time.

Rochester Institute of Technology, Graduate Enrollment Services, Saunders College of Business, Marketing and Management Department, MS Program in Management, Rochester, NY 14623. Offers MS. *Program availability:* Part-time. *Students:* 10 full-time (6 women), 10 part-time (4 women); includes 5 minority (3 Black or African American, non-Hispanic/Latino; 1 Hispanic/Latino; 1 Two or more races, non-Hispanic/Latino), 5 international. Average age 27. 89 applicants, 42% accepted, 10 enrolled. In 2017, 7 master's awarded. *Entrance requirements:* For master's, minimum GPA of 3.0 (recommended). Additional exam requirements/recommendations for international students: Required—TOEFL (minimum score 580 paper-based; 92 iBT), IELTS (minimum score 7), PTE (minimum score 63). *Application deadline:* Applications are processed on a rolling basis. Application fee: $65. Electronic applications accepted. *Expenses:* $1,815 per credit hour. *Financial support:* In 2017–18, 16 students received support. Research assistantships with partial tuition reimbursements available, teaching assistantships with partial tuition reimbursements available, career-related internships or fieldwork, scholarships/grants, and unspecified assistantships available. Support available to part-time students. Financial award applicants required to submit FAFSA. *Faculty research:* Impacts of clinical IT adoption in the U.S. healthcare system; social media and entrepreneurship; cybersecurity. *Unit head:* Matt Cornwell, Assistant Director of Student Services and Outreach, 585-475-6916, E-mail: mcornwell@saunders.rit.edu. *Application contact:* Diane Ellison, Senior Associate Vice President, Graduate Enrollment Services, 585-475-2229, Fax: 585-475-7164, E-mail: gradinfo@rit.edu. Website: http://saunders.rit.edu/programs/graduate/ms_management.php

Rockhurst University, Helzberg School of Management, Kansas City, MO 64110-2561. Offers accounting (MBA); business intelligence (MBA, Certificate); business intelligence and analytics (MS); data science (MBA, Certificate); entrepreneurship (MBA); finance (MBA); fundraising leadership (MBA, Certificate); healthcare management (MBA, Certificate); human capital (Certificate); international business (Certificate); management (MA, MBA, Certificate); nonprofit administration (Certificate); organizational development (Certificate); science leadership (Certificate). *Accreditation:* AACSB. *Program availability:* Part-time, evening/weekend. *Faculty:* 18 full-time (4 women), 20 part-time/adjunct (9 women). *Students:* 99 full-time (30 women), 355 part-time (132 women); includes 95 minority (30 Black or African American, non-Hispanic/Latino; 29 Asian, non-Hispanic/Latino; 25 Hispanic/Latino; 11 Two or more races, non-Hispanic/Latino), 8 international. Average age 32. 249 applicants, 81% accepted, 175 enrolled. In 2017, 145 master's, 17 other advanced degrees awarded. *Entrance requirements:* For master's, GMAT or GRE. Additional exam requirements/recommendations for international students: Required—TOEFL (minimum score 550 paper-based; 79 iBT). *Application deadline:* Applications are processed on a rolling basis. Application fee: $0. Electronic applications accepted. *Financial support:* Applicants required to submit FAFSA. *Faculty research:* Offshoring/outsourcing, systems analysis/synthesis, work teams, multilateral trade, path dependencies/creation. *Unit head:* Cheryl McConnell, Dean, 816-501-4201, Fax: 816-501-4650, E-mail: cheryl.mcconnell@rockhurst.edu. *Application contact:* Jonnae Hill, Director of Graduate Business Advising, 816-501-4823, E-mail: jonnae.hill@rockhurst.edu. Website: https://www.rockhurst.edu/helzberg

Rollins College, Crummer Graduate School of Business, Winter Park, FL 32789-4499. Offers entrepreneurship (MBA); finance (MBA); international business (MBA); management (MBA). *Accreditation:* AACSB. *Program availability:* Part-time, evening/weekend, online learning. *Faculty:* 20 full-time (4 women). *Students:* 261 full-time (119 women), 114 part-time (45 women); includes 86 minority (24 Black or African American, non-Hispanic/Latino; 13 Asian, non-Hispanic/Latino; 44 Hispanic/Latino; 5 Two or more races, non-Hispanic/Latino), 31 international. Average age 32. In 2017, 134 master's awarded. *Degree requirements:* For master's, minimum GPA of 2.85. *Entrance requirements:* For master's, GMAT or GRE, official transcripts, two letters of recommendation, essay, current resume/curriculum vitae, interview. Additional exam requirements/recommendations for international students: Required—TOEFL (minimum score 100 iBT) or IELTS (minimum score 7). *Application deadline:* Applications are processed on a rolling basis. Application fee: $50. Electronic applications accepted. *Expenses:* Contact institution. *Financial support:* Scholarships/grants available. Support available to part-time students. Financial award applicants required to submit FAFSA. *Faculty research:* Sustainability, world financial markets, international business, market research, strategic marketing. *Unit head:* Deborah Crown, Dean, 407-646-2249, Fax: 407-646-1550, E-mail: dcrown@rollins.edu. *Application contact:* Maralyn E. Graham, Admissions Coordinator, 407-646-2405, Fax: 407-646-1550, E-mail: mbaadmissions@rollins.edu. Website: http://www.rollins.edu/mba/

Rutgers University–Newark, Graduate School, Program in Management, Newark, NJ 07102. Offers accounting (PhD); accounting information systems (PhD); computer information systems (PhD); finance (PhD); information technology (PhD); international business (PhD); management science (PhD); marketing (PhD); organization management (PhD). Program offered jointly with New Jersey Institute of Technology. *Accreditation:* AACSB. *Degree requirements:* For doctorate, thesis/dissertation, cumulative exams. *Entrance requirements:* For doctorate, GMAT or GRE General Test, minimum undergraduate B average. Additional exam requirements/recommendations for international students: Required—TOEFL. Electronic applications accepted. *Faculty research:* Technology management, leadership and teams, consumer behavior, financial and markets, logistics.

Rutgers University–Newark, Rutgers Business School–Newark and New Brunswick, Doctoral Programs in Management, Newark, NJ 07102. Offers accounting (PhD); accounting information systems (PhD); economics (PhD); finance (PhD); individualized

study (PhD); information technology (PhD); international business (PhD); management science (PhD); marketing science (PhD); organizational management (PhD); science, technology and management (PhD); supply chain management (PhD). *Degree requirements:* For doctorate, comprehensive exam, thesis/dissertation. *Entrance requirements:* For doctorate, GRE or GMAT. Additional exam requirements/recommendations for international students: Required—TOEFL (minimum score 550 paper-based; 79 iBT). Electronic applications accepted.

St. John's University, The Peter J. Tobin College of Business, Program in International Business, Queens, NY 11439. Offers business administration (MBA), including international business. *Students:* 16 full-time (8 women), 6 part-time (2 women); includes 8 minority (3 Black or African American, non-Hispanic/Latino; 2 Asian, non-Hispanic/Latino; 3 Hispanic/Latino), 2 international. Average age 30. 21 applicants, 86% accepted, 15 enrolled. In 2017, 11 master's awarded. *Entrance requirements:* For master's, GMAT or GRE, 2 letters of recommendation, essay, resume, unofficial transcripts. Additional exam requirements/recommendations for international students: Required—TOEFL (minimum score 80 iBT), IELTS (minimum score 6.5). *Application deadline:* For fall admission, 11/1 for domestic and international students; for winter admission, 3/1 for domestic and international students; for spring admission, 6/1 for domestic and international students. Applications are processed on a rolling basis. Application fee: $70. Electronic applications accepted. *Expenses:* $22,410 per year. *Financial support:* Research assistantships, teaching assistantships, scholarships/grants, and unspecified assistantships available. Support available to part-time students. Financial award application deadline: 2/1; financial award applicants required to submit FAFSA. *Unit head:* Dr. John Angelidis, Chair, 718-990-6495, E-mail: angelidj@stjohns.edu. *Application contact:* Amber Steiger, Associate Director of Enrollment Management, 718-990-1345, E-mail: steigera@stjohns.edu.

Saint Joseph's University, Erivan K. Haub School of Business, MBA Program, Philadelphia, PA 19131-1395. Offers accounting (MBA); business intelligence analytics (MBA); finance (MBA); financial analysis reporting (Postbaccalaureate Certificate); general business (MBA); health and medical services administration (MBA); international business (MBA); international marketing (MBA); leading (MBA); marketing (MBA); DO/MBA. DO/MBA offered jointly with Philadelphia College of Osteopathic Medicine. *Program availability:* Part-time-only, evening/weekend, 100% online. *Students:* 85 full-time (36 women), 371 part-time (153 women); includes 74 minority (32 Black or African American, non-Hispanic/Latino; 15 Asian, non-Hispanic/Latino; 19 Hispanic/Latino; 1 Native Hawaiian or other Pacific Islander, non-Hispanic/Latino; 7 Two or more races, non-Hispanic/Latino), 36 international. Average age 30. 247 applicants, 76% accepted, 112 enrolled. In 2017, 163 master's awarded. *Degree requirements:* For master's, minimum GPA of 3.0. *Entrance requirements:* For master's, GMAT or GRE, 2 letters of recommendation, resume, personal statement, official undergraduate and graduate transcripts. Additional exam requirements/recommendations for international students: Required—PTE, TOEFL, IELTS, or PTE. *Application deadline:* For fall admission, 7/15 priority date for domestic students, 5/15 priority date for international students; for spring admission, 11/15 priority date for domestic students, 10/15 priority date for international students; for summer admission, 4/15 priority date for domestic students, 2/15 priority date for international students. Applications are processed on a rolling basis. Application fee: $35. Electronic applications accepted. *Expenses:* Contact institution. *Financial support:* Scholarships/grants and unspecified assistantships available. Financial award application deadline: 5/1; financial award applicants required to submit FAFSA. *Unit head:* Jeannine Lajeunesse, Director, 610-660-1626, Fax: 610-660-1599, E-mail: jlajeune@sju.edu. *Application contact:* Christine Anderson, Assistant Director, 610-660-2252, Fax: 610-660-1599, E-mail: chris.anderson@sju.edu. Website: http://www.sju.edu/haubmba

Saint Joseph's University, Erivan K. Haub School of Business, MS Program in Marketing, Philadelphia, PA 19131. Offers customer analytics and insights (MS); international marketing (MS). *Program availability:* Part-time, evening/weekend, 100% online. *Faculty:* 8 full-time (2 women), 4 part-time/adjunct (1 woman). *Students:* 30 full-time (18 women), 11 part-time (8 women); includes 4 minority (2 Black or African American, non-Hispanic/Latino; 1 Asian, non-Hispanic/Latino; 1 Hispanic/Latino), 26 international. Average age 27. 51 applicants, 55% accepted, 10 enrolled. In 2017, 10 master's awarded. *Degree requirements:* For master's, minimum GPA of 3.0. *Entrance requirements:* For master's, GMAT or GRE, 2 letters of recommendation, resume, personal statement, official undergraduate and graduate transcripts. Additional exam requirements/recommendations for international students: Required—PTE, TOEFL, IELTS, or PTE. *Application deadline:* For fall admission, 7/15 priority date for domestic students, 5/15 priority date for international students; for spring admission, 11/15 priority date for domestic students, 10/15 priority date for international students; for summer admission, 4/15 priority date for domestic students. Applications are processed on a rolling basis. Application fee: $35. Electronic applications accepted. *Financial support:* Scholarships/grants and unspecified assistantships available. Financial award application deadline: 5/1; financial award applicants required to submit FAFSA. *Unit head:* Jeannine Lajeunesse, Director, 610-660-1626, E-mail: jlajeune@sju.edu. *Application contact:* Christine Anderson, Assistant Director, 610-660-2252, Fax: 610-660-1599, E-mail: chris.anderson@sju.edu. Website: https://www.sju.edu/majors-programs/graduate-business/master-degrees/master-science-marketing

See Display on page 500 and Close-Up on page 519.

Saint Leo University, Graduate Studies in Business, Saint Leo, FL 33574-6665. Offers accounting (M Acc, MBA); cybersecurity (MS); cybersecurity management (MBA); data analytics (MBA); health care management (MBA); human resource management (MBA); international and experiential business administration (MBA); management (MBA, DBA); marketing (MBA); marketing research and social media analytics (MBA); project management (MBA); social media marketing (MBA); sport business (MBA); supply chain global integration management (MBA). *Accreditation:* ACBSP. *Program availability:* Part-time, evening/weekend, 100% online, blended/hybrid learning. *Faculty:* 54 full-time (18 women), 52 part-time/adjunct (18 women). *Students:* 9 full-time (3 women), 1,867 part-time (1,079 women); includes 861 minority (598 Black or African American, non-Hispanic/Latino; 3 American Indian or Alaska Native, non-Hispanic/Latino; 38 Asian, non-Hispanic/Latino; 186 Hispanic/Latino; 3 Native Hawaiian or other Pacific Islander, non-Hispanic/Latino; 33 Two or more races, non-Hispanic/Latino), 68 international. Average age 37. 868 applicants, 63% accepted, 537 enrolled. In 2017, 859 master's, 3 doctorates awarded. *Degree requirements:* For doctorate, comprehensive exam, thesis/dissertation. *Entrance requirements:* For master's, GMAT with minimum score 500 (for M Acc), official transcripts, current resume, 2 professional recommendations, personal statement, bachelor's degree from regionally-accredited university; undergraduate degree in accounting and minimum undergraduate GPA of 3.0 (for M Acc); minimum undergraduate GPA of 3.0 in final 2 years of undergraduate study and 2 years' work experience (for MBA); for doctorate, GMAT (minimum score of 550) if master's GPA is under 3.25, official transcripts, current resume, 2 professional recommendations, personal statement, master's degree from regionally-accredited university with minimum GPA of 3.25, 3 years' work experience, interview. Additional exam requirements/recommendations for international students: Required—TOEFL (minimum score 550 paper-based; 78 iBT). *Application deadline:* For fall admission, 7/1 priority date for domestic and international students; for spring admission, 11/12 priority date for domestic students, 11/1 for international students. Applications are processed on a rolling basis. Application fee: $80. Electronic applications accepted. *Expenses:* Contact institution. *Financial support:* In 2017–18, 106 students received support. Career-related internships or fieldwork, health care benefits, and tuition remission for Saint Leo employees and their dependents available. Financial award application deadline: 3/1; financial award applicants required to submit FAFSA. *Faculty research:* Servant leadership, work/life balance, emotional intelligence, pricing, marketing. *Unit head:* Dr. Charles Hale, Dean, School of Business, 352-588-8599, Fax: 352-588-8912, E-mail: mbaslu@saintleo.edu. *Application contact:* Mark Russum, Assistant Vice President, Enrollment, 800-707-8846, Fax: 352-588-7873, E-mail: grad.admissions@saintleo.edu. Website: https://www.saintleo.edu/school-of-business

Saint Louis University, Graduate Programs, John Cook School of Business, Boeing Institute of International Business, St. Louis, MO 63103. Offers business administration (PhD), including international business and marketing; executive international business (EMIB); international business (MBA). *Program availability:* Part-time, evening/weekend. *Degree requirements:* For master's, thesis, study abroad; for doctorate, comprehensive exam, thesis/dissertation. *Entrance requirements:* For master's, GMAT, work experience. Additional exam requirements/recommendations for international students: Required—TOEFL (minimum score 525 paper-based). *Expenses:* Contact institution. *Faculty research:* Foreign direct investment, technology transfer, emerging markets, Asian business, Latin American business.

Saint Peter's University, Graduate Business Programs, MBA Program, Jersey City, NJ 07306-5997. Offers finance (MBA); health care administration (MBA); human resource management (MBA); international business (MBA); management (MBA); management information systems (MBA); marketing (MBA); risk management (MBA); MBA/MS. *Program availability:* Part-time, evening/weekend. *Entrance requirements:* Additional exam requirements/recommendations for international students: Required—TOEFL. Electronic applications accepted. *Faculty research:* Finance, health care management, human resource management, international business, management, management information systems, marketing, risk management.

St. Thomas University, School of Business, Department of Management, Miami Gardens, FL 33054-6459. Offers accounting (MBA); general management (MSM, Certificate); health management (MBA, MSM, Certificate); human resource management (MBA, MSM, Certificate); international business (MBA, MIB, MSM, Certificate); justice administration (MSM, Certificate); management accounting (MSM, Certificate); public management (MSM, Certificate); sports administration (MS). *Program availability:* Part-time, evening/weekend. *Degree requirements:* For master's, comprehensive exam. *Entrance requirements:* For master's, interview, minimum GPA of 3.0 or GMAT. Additional exam requirements/recommendations for international students: Required—TOEFL (minimum score 550 paper-based; 79 iBT). Electronic applications accepted.

Salem International University, School of Business, Salem, WV 26426-0500. Offers information security (MBA); international business (MBA). *Program availability:* Part-time, online learning. *Entrance requirements:* For master's, minimum undergraduate GPA of 2.5, course work in business, resume. Additional exam requirements/recommendations for international students: Recommended—TOEFL (minimum score 550 paper-based), IELTS (minimum score 6.5). Electronic applications accepted. *Expenses:* Contact institution. *Faculty research:* Organizational behavior strategy, marketing services.

San Francisco State University, Division of Graduate Studies, College of Business, Program in Business Administration, San Francisco, CA 94132-1722. Offers decision sciences/operations research (MBA); ethics and compliance (MBA); finance (MBA); global business and innovation (MBA); healthcare administration (MBA); hospitality and tourism management (MBA); information systems (MBA); leadership (MBA); marketing (MBA); nonprofit and social enterprise leadership (MBA); sustainable business (MBA). *Accreditation:* AACSB. *Program availability:* Part-time, evening/weekend. *Degree requirements:* For master's, thesis, essay test. *Entrance requirements:* For master's, GMAT, minimum GPA of 2.7 in last 60 units. Additional exam requirements/recommendations for international students: Required—TOEFL (minimum score 550 paper-based). *Application deadline:* For fall admission, 5/1 priority date for domestic students, 4/1 for international students; for spring admission, 11/1 for domestic students, 10/15 for international students. Applications are processed on a rolling basis. Application fee: $55. *Financial support:* Application deadline: 3/1. *Unit head:* Dr. Sanjit Sengupta, Faculty Director, 415-817-4366, Fax: 415-817-4340, E-mail: sengupta@sfsu.edu. *Application contact:* Christopher Kingston, Director of Student Advising, 415-817-4322, Fax: 415-817-4340, E-mail: cak@sfsu.edu.
Website: http://cob.sfsu.edu/graduate-programs/mba

San Ignacio University, Graduate Programs, Doral, FL 33178. Offers business administration (MBA), including human resources management, international business, marketing management; education (M Ed), including early childhood education, educational leadership, special education; hospitality management (MA), including gastronomy and restaurant management, tourism management.

Schiller International University, MBA Program, Madrid, Spain, Madrid, Spain. Offers international business (MBA). *Program availability:* Part-time. *Degree requirements:* For master's, comprehensive exam, thesis optional. *Entrance requirements:* Additional exam requirements/recommendations for international students: Required—TOEFL (minimum score 550 paper-based).

Schiller International University, MBA Program Paris, France, Paris, France. Offers international business (MBA). Bilingual French/English MBA available for native French speakers. *Program availability:* Part-time, evening/weekend, online learning. *Degree requirements:* For master's, comprehensive exam, thesis or alternative. *Entrance requirements:* Additional exam requirements/recommendations for international students: Required—TOEFL (minimum score 550 paper-based).

Schiller International University, MBA Programs, Florida, Program in International Business, Largo, FL 33771. Offers MBA. *Program availability:* Part-time, evening/weekend, online learning. *Degree requirements:* For master's, thesis optional. *Entrance requirements:* Additional exam requirements/recommendations for international students: Required—TOEFL (minimum score 550 paper-based).

Schiller International University, MBA Programs, Heidelberg, Germany, Heidelberg, Germany. Offers international business (MBA, MIM); management of information technology (MBA). *Program availability:* Part-time, evening/weekend. *Degree requirements:* For master's, thesis optional. *Entrance requirements:* Additional exam requirements/recommendations for international students: Required—TOEFL (minimum score 550 paper-based). *Faculty research:* Leadership, international economy, foreign direct investment.

Seton Hall University, Stillman School of Business, Program in International Business, South Orange, NJ 07079-2697. Offers Certificate. *Program availability:* Part-time, evening/weekend. *Faculty:* 4 full-time (0 women), 1 part-time/adjunct (0 women). *Students:* 4 part-time (1 woman); includes 1 minority (Black or African American, non-Hispanic/Latino), 1 international. Average age 28. 14 applicants, 79% accepted, 4

enrolled. *Entrance requirements:* Additional exam requirements/recommendations for international students: Required—TOEFL (minimum score 607 paper-based; 80 iBT), IELTS (minimum score 6), PTE. *Application deadline:* For fall admission, 5/31 priority date for domestic students, 3/31 priority date for international students; for spring admission, 10/31 priority date for domestic students, 9/30 priority date for international students; for summer admission, 4/30 priority date for domestic students, 3/31 priority date for international students. Applications are processed on a rolling basis. Application fee: $75. Electronic applications accepted. *Expenses:* $1,305 per credit; $126 fees (fall and spring semester), $51 (summer semester). *Financial support:* In 2017–18, 2 students received support, including 2 research assistantships with full tuition reimbursements available (averaging $3,600 per year); career-related internships or fieldwork, scholarships/grants, and unspecified assistantships also available. Financial award application deadline: 6/30; financial award applicants required to submit FAFSA. *Faculty research:* Tariffs, international trade, polish economy, export-led growth, Chinese governance. *Unit head:* Dr. Laurence McCarthy, Director, 973-275-2957, Fax: 973-275-2465, E-mail: laurence.mccarthy@shu.edu. *Application contact:* Alfred Ayoub, Director of Graduate Admissions, 973-761-9262, Fax: 973-761-9208, E-mail: alfred.ayoub@shu.edu.
Website: http://www.shu.edu/academics/business/international-business

Seton Hall University, Stillman School of Business, Programs in Business Administration, South Orange, NJ 07079-2697. Offers accounting (MBA); entrepreneurial studies (Certificate); finance (MBA); financial decision making (Certificate); information technology management (MBA); international business (MBA); management (MBA); marketing (MBA); sport management (MBA); supply chain management (MBA, Certificate). *Program availability:* Part-time, evening/weekend. *Faculty:* 29 full-time (4 women), 18 part-time/adjunct (0 women). *Students:* 140 full-time (58 women), 154 part-time (49 women); includes 66 minority (25 Black or African American, non-Hispanic/Latino; 14 Asian, non-Hispanic/Latino; 23 Hispanic/Latino; 4 Two or more races, non-Hispanic/Latino), 88 international. Average age 32. 406 applicants, 75% accepted, 100 enrolled. In 2017, 132 master's awarded. *Degree requirements:* For master's, 20 hours of community service (Social Responsibility Project). *Entrance requirements:* For master's, GMAT or CPA, GRE (waived based on work experience or advanced degree from AACSB institution), MS in business discipline, professional degree or designation (MD, JD, PhD, DVM, DDS, CPA, etc.), minimum undergraduate GPA of 3.0. Additional exam requirements/recommendations for international students: Required—TOEFL (minimum score 607 paper-based; 80 iBT), IELTS (minimum score 6), PTE. *Application deadline:* For fall admission, 5/31 priority date for domestic students, 4/30 priority date for international students; for spring admission, 10/31 priority date for domestic students, 9/30 priority date for international students; for summer admission, 3/31 priority date for domestic students. Applications are processed on a rolling basis. Application fee: $75. Electronic applications accepted. *Expenses:* $1,305 per credit; $126 fees (fall and spring semester), $51 (summer semester). *Financial support:* In 2017–18, 41 students received support, including 25 research assistantships with full tuition reimbursements available (averaging $3,644 per year); career-related internships or fieldwork, scholarships/grants, and unspecified assistantships also available. Financial award application deadline: 6/30; financial award applicants required to submit FAFSA. *Faculty research:* Sport, hedge funds, executive compensation, social media, legal studies. *Unit head:* Dr. Joyce Strawser, Dean, 973-761-9013, Fax: 973-761-9217, E-mail: joyce.strawser@shu.edu. *Application contact:* Alfred Ayoub, Director of Graduate Admissions, 973-761-9262, Fax: 973-761-9208, E-mail: alfred.ayoub@shu.edu.
Website: http://www.shu.edu/business/mba-programs.cfm

SIT Graduate Institute, Graduate Programs, Master's Programs in Intercultural Service, Leadership, and Management, Brattleboro, VT 05302-0676. Offers intercultural service, leadership, and management (self-designed) (MA); international education (MA); peace and justice leadership (MA); sustainable development (MA). *Program availability:* Online learning. *Degree requirements:* For master's, one foreign language, thesis. *Entrance requirements:* For master's, 3 letters of reference. Additional exam requirements/recommendations for international students: Required—TOEFL, IELTS. *Faculty research:* Intercultural communication, conflict resolution, international education, world issues, international affairs.

Southeastern University, Jannetides College of Business and Entrepreneurial Leadership, Lakeland, FL 33801-6099. Offers executive leadership (MBA); global business administration (MBA); healthcare administration (MBA); missional leadership (MBA); organizational leadership (PhD); sport management (MBA); strategic leadership (DSL). *Accreditation:* ACBSP. *Program availability:* Evening/weekend, online learning. *Faculty:* 10 full-time (2 women), 8 part-time/adjunct (1 woman). *Students:* 80 full-time (38 women), 110 part-time (54 women); includes 51 minority (18 Black or African American, non-Hispanic/Latino; 5 Asian, non-Hispanic/Latino; 28 Hispanic/Latino), 7 international. Average age 31. *Entrance requirements:* For master's, GMAT, minimum cumulative GPA of 3.0, writing sample. Application fee: $50. Electronic applications accepted. *Unit head:* Lyle L. Bowlin, Dean, 863-667-5118, E-mail: llbowlin@seu.edu.
Website: http://www.seu.edu/business/

Southern New Hampshire University, School of Business, Manchester, NH 03106-1045. Offers accounting (MBA, Graduate Certificate); accounting finance (MS); accounting/auditing (MS); accounting/forensic accounting (MS); accounting/management accounting (MS); accounting/taxation (MS); applied economics (MS); athletic administration (MBA, Graduate Certificate); business administration (IMBA, Certificate), including business information systems (Certificate), human resource management (Certificate); business analytics (MBA); business intelligence (MBA); communication (MA), including new media and marketing, public relations; community economic development (MBA); criminal justice (MBA); data analytics (MS); economics (MBA); engineering management (MBA); entrepreneurship (MBA); finance (MBA, MS, Graduate Certificate); finance/corporate finance (MS); finance/investments (MS); forensic accounting (MBA); forensic accounting and fraud examination (Graduate Certificate); healthcare informatics (MBA); healthcare management (MBA); human resource management (MS); human resources (MBA); information technology (MS); information technology management (MBA); international business (PhD); Internet marketing (MBA); leadership (MBA); leadership of nonprofit organizations (Graduate Certificate); management (MS); marketing (MBA, MS, Graduate Certificate); music business (MBA); operations and project management (MS); operations and supply chain management (MBA, Graduate Certificate); organizational leadership (MS); project management (MBA, Graduate Certificate); public administration (MBA, Graduate Certificate); quantitative analysis (MBA); Six Sigma (Graduate Certificate); Six Sigma quality (MBA); social media marketing (MBA, Graduate Certificate); sport management (MBA, MS, Graduate Certificate); sustainability and environmental compliance (MBA); MBA/Certificate. *Accreditation:* ACBSP. *Program availability:* Part-time, evening/weekend, online learning. Terminal master's awarded for partial completion of doctoral program. *Degree requirements:* For master's, one foreign language, comprehensive exam (for some programs), thesis or alternative; for doctorate, one foreign language, comprehensive exam, thesis/dissertation. *Entrance requirements:* For master's, minimum GPA of 2.5; for doctorate, GMAT. Additional exam requirements/recommendations for international students: Required—TOEFL (minimum score 500 paper-based). *Application deadline:* Applications are processed on a rolling basis.

International Business

Application fee: $40. Electronic applications accepted. *Expenses: Tuition:* Part-time $627 per credit hour. Part-time tuition and fees vary according to campus/location and program. *Financial support:* Career-related internships or fieldwork, Federal Work-Study, institutionally sponsored loans, scholarships/grants, tuition waivers (partial), and unspecified assistantships available. Support available to part-time students. Financial award applicants required to submit FAFSA. *Unit head:* Dr. Bill Lightfoot, Dean, 603-644-3102, Fax: 603-644-3144. *Application contact:* Office of Graduate Admission, 888-327-SNHU, Fax: 603-644-3144, E-mail: enroll@snhu.edu.

Southern Oregon University, Graduate Studies, School of Business, Ashland, OR 97520. Offers accounting (Postbaccalaureate Certificate); business administration (MBA); international management (MIM). *Accreditation:* ACBSP. *Program availability:* Part-time, evening/weekend, online learning. *Degree requirements:* For master's, comprehensive exam. *Entrance requirements:* For master's, GMAT, minimum cumulative GPA of 3.0 in the last 90 quarter credits (60 semester credits) of undergraduate coursework. Additional exam requirements/recommendations for international students: Required—TOEFL (minimum score 540 paper-based; 76 iBT), IELTS (minimum score 6), ELPT (minimum score 964) or ELS (minimum score 112). Electronic applications accepted.

State University of New York Empire State College, School for Graduate Studies, Program in Business Administration, Saratoga Springs, NY 12866-4391. Offers global leadership (MBA); management (MBA). *Program availability:* Part-time, online learning. *Degree requirements:* For master's, thesis or alternative. *Entrance requirements:* For master's, previous course work in statistics, macroeconomics, microeconomics, and accounting. Additional exam requirements/recommendations for international students: Required—TOEFL (minimum score 600 paper-based). Electronic applications accepted. *Expenses:* Contact institution. *Faculty research:* Corporate strategy, managerial competencies, decision analysis, economics in transition, organizational communication.

Stevens Institute of Technology, Graduate School, School of Business, Program in Management, Hoboken, NJ 07030. Offers general management (MS); global innovation management (MS); human resource management (MS); information management (MS); project management (MS); technology commercialization (MS); technology management (MS). *Program availability:* Part-time, evening/weekend. *Students:* 56 full-time (18 women), 88 part-time (32 women); includes 18 minority (5 Black or African American, non-Hispanic/Latino; 12 Asian, non-Hispanic/Latino; 1 Hispanic/Latino), 87 international. Average age 30. 194 applicants, 78% accepted, 68 enrolled. In 2017, 87 master's awarded. *Degree requirements:* For master's, thesis optional, minimum B average in major field and overall. *Entrance requirements:* Additional exam requirements/recommendations for international students: Required—TOEFL (minimum score 74 iBT), IELTS (minimum score 6). *Application deadline:* For fall admission, 7/1 for domestic students, 4/15 for international students; for spring admission, 12/1 for domestic and international students. Applications are processed on a rolling basis. Application fee: $60. Electronic applications accepted. *Expenses: Tuition:* Full-time $34,494; part-time $1554 per credit. *Required fees:* $291 per semester. *Financial support:* Fellowships, research assistantships, teaching assistantships, career-related internships or fieldwork, Federal Work-Study, scholarships/grants, and unspecified assistantships available. Financial award application deadline: 2/15; financial award applicants required to submit FAFSA. *Unit head:* Brian Rothschild, Director, 201-216-3677, E-mail: brian.rothschild@stevens.edu. *Application contact:* Graduate Admissions, 888-783-8367, Fax: 888-511-1306, E-mail: graduate@stevens.edu.
Website: https://www.stevens.edu/school-business/masters-programs/management

Suffolk University, Sawyer Business School, Master of Business Administration Program, Boston, MA 02108-2770. Offers accounting (MBA); entrepreneurship (MBA); executive business administration (EMBA); finance (MBA); global business administration (GMBA); health administration (MBA); international business (MBA); marketing (MBA); nonprofit management (MBA); organizational behavior (MBA); strategic management (MBA); supply chain management (MBA); taxation (MBA); JD/MBA; MBA/MHA; MBA/MSA; MBA/MSF; MBA/MST. *Accreditation:* AACSB. *Program availability:* Part-time, evening/weekend, 100% online. *Faculty:* 16 full-time (6 women), 9 part-time/adjunct (1 woman). *Students:* 106 full-time (57 women), 236 part-time (135 women); includes 80 minority (23 Black or African American, non-Hispanic/Latino; 23 Asian, non-Hispanic/Latino; 28 Hispanic/Latino; 6 Two or more races, non-Hispanic/Latino), 41 international. Average age 30. 354 applicants, 69% accepted, 115 enrolled. In 2017, 170 master's awarded. *Entrance requirements:* For master's, GMAT, minimum undergraduate GPA of 2.75 (MBA), 5 years of managerial experience (EMBA). Additional exam requirements/recommendations for international students: Required—TOEFL (minimum score 550 paper-based; 80 iBT). *Application deadline:* For fall admission, 3/15 priority date for domestic students, 10/15 priority date for international students; for spring admission, 10/15 priority date for domestic and international students. Applications are processed on a rolling basis. Application fee: $50. Electronic applications accepted. *Expenses:* $43,980 per year full-time, $1,466 per credit part-time (for MBA); $1,794 per credit part-time (for Executive MBA). *Financial support:* In 2017-18, 198 students received support, including 1 fellowship (averaging $2,325 per year); career-related internships or fieldwork, Federal Work-Study, institutionally sponsored loans, and scholarships/grants also available. Support available to part-time students. Financial award application deadline: 4/1; financial award applicants required to submit FAFSA. *Faculty research:* Foreign investments; career strategies and boundaryless careers; corporate ethics codes; interest rates, inflation, and growth options; innovation and product development performance. *Unit head:* Jodi Detjen, Director of MBA Programs, 617-573-8306, E-mail: jdetjen@suffolk.edu. *Application contact:* Mara Marzocchi, Associate Director of Graduate Admissions, 617-573-8302, Fax: 617-305-1733, E-mail: grad.admission@suffolk.edu.
Website: http://www.suffolk.edu/mba

Temple University, Fox School of Business, Doctoral Programs in Business, Philadelphia, PA 19122-6096. Offers accounting (PhD); entrepreneurship (PhD); finance (PhD); international business (PhD); management information systems (PhD); marketing (PhD); risk management and insurance (PhD); statistics (PhD); strategic management (PhD); tourism and sport (PhD). *Accreditation:* AACSB. *Degree requirements:* For doctorate, thesis/dissertation. *Entrance requirements:* For doctorate, GRE General Test, GMAT, minimum GPA of 3.0, master's degree. Additional exam requirements/recommendations for international students: Required—TOEFL (minimum score 600 paper-based; 100 iBT), IELTS (minimum score 7.5). Electronic applications accepted. *Expenses:* Tuition, state resident: full-time $16,164; part-time $898 per credit hour. Tuition, nonresident: full-time $22,158; part-time $1231 per credit hour. *Required fees:* $890; $445 per semester. Full-time tuition and fees vary according to course load, degree level, campus/location and program.

Temple University, Fox School of Business, MBA Programs, Philadelphia, PA 19122-6096. Offers accounting (MBA); business management (MBA); financial management (MBA); healthcare and life sciences innovation (MBA); human resource management (MBA); international business (IMBA); IT management (MBA); marketing management (MBA); pharmaceutical management (MBA); strategic management (EMBA, MBA). EMBA offered in Philadelphia, PA and Tokyo, Japan. *Accreditation:* AACSB. *Program availability:* Part-time, evening/weekend, online learning. *Entrance requirements:* For

master's, GMAT, minimum undergraduate GPA of 3.0. Additional exam requirements/recommendations for international students: Required—TOEFL (minimum score 600 paper-based; 100 iBT), IELTS (minimum score 7.5). *Expenses:* Tuition, state resident: full-time $16,164; part-time $898 per credit hour. Tuition, nonresident: full-time $22,158; part-time $1231 per credit hour. *Required fees:* $890; $445 per semester. Full-time tuition and fees vary according to course load, degree level, campus/location and program.

Tennessee Technological University, College of Graduate Studies, College of Business, MBA Program, Cookeville, TN 38505. Offers finance (MBA); human resource management (MBA); international business (MBA); management information systems (MBA). *Program availability:* Part-time, evening/weekend. In 2017, 77 master's awarded. *Entrance requirements:* For master's, GMAT or GRE. *Expenses:* Tuition, state resident: full-time $9925; part-time $565 per credit hour. Tuition, nonresident: full-time $22,993; part-time $1291 per credit hour. *Financial support:* In 2017–18, 2 research assistantships, 3 teaching assistantships were awarded; fellowships and unspecified assistantships also available. Financial award application deadline: 4/1; financial award applicants required to submit FAFSA. *Unit head:* Kate Nicewicz, Director, E-mail: knicewicz@tntech.edu. *Application contact:* Shelia K. Kendrick, Coordinator of Graduate Studies, 931-372-3808, Fax: 931-372-3497, E-mail: skendrick@tntech.edu.
Website: https://www.tntech.edu/cob/mba/

Texas A&M International University, Office of Graduate Studies and Research, A.R. Sanchez, Jr. School of Business, Division of International Business and Technology Studies, Laredo, TX 78041. Offers information systems (MSIS); international business management (MBA, PhD). *Degree requirements:* For master's, thesis (for some programs). *Entrance requirements:* For master's, GMAT or GRE General Test. Additional exam requirements/recommendations for international students: Required—TOEFL (minimum score 550 paper-based; 79 iBT).

Texas A&M University–Corpus Christi, College of Graduate Studies, College of Business, Corpus Christi, TX 78412. Offers accounting (M Acc); business (MBA); finance (MBA); health care administration (MBA); international business (MBA). *Accreditation:* AACSB. *Program availability:* Part-time, evening/weekend, 100% online, blended/hybrid learning. *Faculty:* 31 full-time (11 women), 2 part-time/adjunct (0 women). *Students:* 107 full-time (50 women), 583 part-time (283 women); includes 259 minority (80 Black or African American, non-Hispanic/Latino; 85 Asian, non-Hispanic/Latino; 83 Hispanic/Latino; 11 Two or more races, non-Hispanic/Latino), 77 international. Average age 34. 485 applicants, 57% accepted, 236 enrolled. In 2017, 310 master's awarded. *Degree requirements:* For master's, 30 to 42 hours (for MBA; varies by concentration area, delivery format, and necessity for foundational courses for students with nonbusiness degrees). *Entrance requirements:* For master's, GMAT, GRE. Additional exam requirements/recommendations for international students: Required—TOEFL (minimum score 550 paper-based; 79 iBT), IELTS (minimum score 6.5). *Application deadline:* For fall admission, 7/15 priority date for domestic students, 5/1 priority date for international students; for spring admission, 11/15 priority date for domestic students, 9/1 priority date for international students; for summer admission, 4/15 priority date for domestic and international students. Applications are processed on a rolling basis. Application fee: $50 ($70 for international students). Electronic applications accepted. *Expenses:* Tuition, state resident: full-time $3568; part-time $198.24 per credit hour. Tuition, nonresident: full-time $11,038; part-time $613.24 per credit hour. *Required fees:* $2129; $1422.58 per semester. Tuition and fees vary according to program. *Financial support:* Research assistantships, teaching assistantships, career-related internships or fieldwork, Federal Work-Study, institutionally sponsored loans, scholarships/grants, health care benefits, and unspecified assistantships available. Support available to part-time students. Financial award application deadline: 3/15; financial award applicants required to submit FAFSA. *Unit head:* Dr. John Gamble, Dean, 361-825-6045, Fax: 361-825-2725, E-mail: john.gamble@tamucc.edu. *Application contact:* Sharon Polansky, Director of Master's Programs, 361-825-3448, Fax: 361-825-2755, E-mail: gradweb@tamucc.edu.
Website: http://cob.tamucc.edu

Thomas Edison State University, School of Business and Management, Program in International Business Finance, Trenton, NJ 08608. Offers MS. *Program availability:* Online learning. *Entrance requirements:* For master's, undergraduate coursework in financial accounting, microeconomics, finance and statistics.

Tiffin University, Program in Business Administration, Tiffin, OH 44883-2161. Offers finance (MBA); general management (MBA); healthcare administration (MBA); human resource management (MBA); international business (MBA); leadership (MBA); marketing (MBA); non-profit management (MBA); sports management (MBA). *Accreditation:* ACBSP. *Program availability:* Part-time, evening/weekend, online learning. *Entrance requirements:* For master's, minimum undergraduate GPA of 2.5, work experience. Additional exam requirements/recommendations for international students: Required—TOEFL (minimum score 550 paper-based; 79 iBT), IELTS. Electronic applications accepted. Application fee is waived when completed online. *Faculty research:* Small business, executive development operations, research and statistical analysis, market research, management information systems.

Trident University International, College of Business Administration, Program in Business Administration, Cypress, CA 90630. Offers business administration (PhD); conflict and negotiation management (MBA); criminal justice administration (MBA); entrepreneurship (MBA); finance (MBA); general management (MBA); government accounting (MBA); human resource management (MBA); information security and digital assurance management (MBA); information technology management (MBA); international business (MBA); logistics management (MBA); marketing (MBA); project management (MBA); public management (MBA); quality management (MBA); strategic leadership (MBA). *Program availability:* Part-time, evening/weekend, online learning. *Degree requirements:* For doctorate, comprehensive exam, thesis/dissertation, defense of dissertation. *Entrance requirements:* For master's, minimum GPA of 2.5 (students with GPA 3.0 or greater may transfer up to 30% of graduate level credits); for doctorate, minimum GPA of 3.4, curriculum vitae, course work in research methods or statistics. Additional exam requirements/recommendations for international students: Required—TOEFL. Electronic applications accepted.

Trinity Western University, School of Graduate Studies, Program in Business Administration, Langley, BC V2Y 1Y1, Canada. Offers international business (MBA); management of the growing enterprise (MBA); non-profit and charitable organization management (MBA). *Program availability:* Part-time, online learning. *Degree requirements:* For master's, thesis or alternative, applied project. *Entrance requirements:* For master's, GMAT (minimum score of 550 recommended). Additional exam requirements/recommendations for international students: Required—TOEFL (minimum score 600 paper-based; 100 iBT), IELTS. Electronic applications accepted.

Tufts University, The Fletcher School of Law and Diplomacy, Medford, MA 02155. Offers economics and public policy (PhD); international affairs (PhD); international business (MIB); international law (LL M); law and diplomacy (MA, MALD); transatlantic affairs (MA); DVM/MA; JD/MALD; MALD/MA; MALD/MBA; MALD/MS; MD/MA. MA in transatlantic affairs offered jointly with The College of Europe; PhD in economics and public policy with Tufts' Graduate School of Arts and Sciences. *Program availability:*

Online learning. *Degree requirements:* For master's, one foreign language, thesis; for doctorate, one foreign language, comprehensive exam, thesis/dissertation, dissertation defense. *Entrance requirements:* For master's and doctorate, GMAT or GRE General Test. Additional exam requirements/recommendations for international students: Required—TOEFL (minimum score 600 paper-based; 100 iBT), IELTS (minimum score 7). Electronic applications accepted. *Expenses:* Contact institution. *Faculty research:* Negotiation and conflict resolution, international organizations, international business and economic law, security studies, development economics.

Tulane University, A. B. Freeman School of Business, New Orleans, LA 70118-5669. Offers accounting (M Acct); analytics (MBA); banking and financial services (M Fin); energy (M Fin, MBA); entrepreneurship (MBA); finance (MBA, PhD); financial accounting (PhD); international business (MBA); international management (MBA); strategic management and leadership (MBA); JD/M Acct; JD/MBA; MBA/M Acc; MBA/MA; MBA/MD; MBA/ME; MBA/MPH. *Accreditation:* AACSB. *Program availability:* Part-time, evening/weekend. *Faculty:* 51 full-time (15 women), 38 part-time/adjunct (3 women). *Students:* 561 full-time (287 women), 297 part-time (151 women); includes 112 minority (43 Black or African American, non-Hispanic/Latino; 2 American Indian or Alaska Native, non-Hispanic/Latino; 24 Asian, non-Hispanic/Latino; 38 Hispanic/Latino; 5 Two or more races, non-Hispanic/Latino), 515 international. Average age 27. 2,021 applicants, 74% accepted, 476 enrolled. In 2017, 632 master's, 9 doctorates awarded. Terminal master's awarded for partial completion of doctoral program. *Degree requirements:* For master's, one foreign language, comprehensive exam (for some programs); for doctorate, one foreign language, comprehensive exam, thesis/dissertation. *Entrance requirements:* For master's and doctorate, GMAT or GRE, interview. Additional exam requirements/recommendations for international students: Required—TOEFL or IELTS. *Application deadline:* For fall admission, 11/1 priority date for domestic and international students; for winter admission, 1/6 for domestic and international students; for spring admission, 3/1 priority date for domestic and international students; for summer admission, 5/5 for domestic students. Applications are processed on a rolling basis. Application fee: $125. Electronic applications accepted. *Expenses:* Contact institution. *Financial support:* In 2017–18, 176 students received support. Fellowships with tuition reimbursements available, research assistantships, teaching assistantships, career-related internships or fieldwork, Federal Work-Study, tuition waivers (full and partial), and unspecified assistantships available. Support available to part-time students. Financial award application deadline: 4/15; financial award applicants required to submit FAFSA. *Faculty research:* Corporate finance, managerial accounting and financial reporting, strategic management and leadership, consumer behavior and decision making, organizational behavior and human resource management. *Unit head:* Ira Solomon, PhD, Dean, 504-865-5407, Fax: 504-865-5491, E-mail: businessdean@tulane.edu. *Application contact:* Melissa Booth, Assistant Dean for Graduate Admissions, 800-223-5402, E-mail: freeman.admissions@tulane.edu. Website: http://www.freeman.tulane.edu

United States International University–Africa, School of Business Administration, Nairobi, Kenya. Offers business administration (GEMBA); entrepreneurship (MBA); finance (MBA); human resource management (MBA); information technology management (MBA); integrated studies (MBA); international business administration (MBA); management and organizational development (MS); marketing (MBA); organizational development (EMS); strategic management (MBA). *Program availability:* Part-time, evening/weekend. *Degree requirements:* For master's, thesis. *Entrance requirements:* For master's, GMAT, 2 letters of reference, resume. Additional exam requirements/recommendations for international students: Required—TOEFL (minimum score 550 paper-based). *Faculty research:* Marketing in small business enterprises, total quality management in Kenya.

Universidad Autonoma de Guadalajara, Graduate Programs, Guadalajara, Mexico. Offers administrative law and justice (LL M); advertising and corporate communications (MA); architecture (M Arch); business (MBA); computational science (MCC); education (Ed M, Ed D); English-Spanish translation (MA); entrepreneurship and management (MBA); integrated management of digital animation (MA); international business (MIB); international corporate law (LL M); internet technologies (MS); manufacturing systems (MMS); occupational health (MS); philosophy (MA, PhD); power electronics (MS); quality systems (MQS); renewable energy (MS); social evaluation of projects (MBA); strategic market research (MBA); tax law (MA); teaching mathematics (MA).

Universidad Metropolitana, School of Business Administration, Program in International Business, San Juan, PR 00928-1150. Offers MBA.

Université de Sherbrooke, Faculty of Administration, Program in International Business, Sherbrooke, QC J1K 2R1, Canada. Offers M Sc. *Degree requirements:* For master's, one foreign language, thesis. *Entrance requirements:* For master's, bachelor's degree in related field, minimum GPA of 3.0 (on a 4.3 scale). Electronic applications accepted.

Université du Québec, École nationale d'administration publique, Graduate Programs in Public Administration, Program in International Administration, Quebec, QC G1K 9E5, Canada. Offers MAP, Diploma. *Program availability:* Part-time. *Entrance requirements:* For degree, appropriate bachelor's degree, proficiency in French.

Université Laval, Faculty of Administrative Sciences, Programs in Business Administration, Québec, QC G1K 7P4, Canada. Offers accounting (MBA); agri-food management (MBA); electronic business (MBA, Diploma); factory management and logistics (MBA); finance (MBA); firm management (MBA); geomatic management (MBA); information technology management (MBA); international management (MBA); management (MBA); management accounting (MBA, Diploma); marketing (MBA); modeling and organizational decision (MBA); occupational health and safety management (MBA); pharmacy management (MBA); social and environmental responsibility (MBA); technological entrepreneurship (Diploma). *Accreditation:* AACSB. *Program availability:* Part-time, evening/weekend, online learning. *Entrance requirements:* For master's and Diploma, knowledge of French and English. Electronic applications accepted.

University at Buffalo, the State University of New York, Graduate School, College of Arts and Sciences, Department of Geography, Buffalo, NY 14260. Offers earth systems science (MA, MS); economic geography and business geographics (MS); environmental modeling and analysis (MA); geographic information science (MA, MS); geography (MA, PhD); health geography (MS); international trade (MA); urban and regional analysis (MA). *Program availability:* Part-time. *Faculty:* 19 full-time (9 women), 1 part-time/adjunct (0 women). *Students:* 100 full-time (45 women); includes 66 minority (1 Black or African American, non-Hispanic/Latino; 64 Asian, non-Hispanic/Latino; 1 Hispanic/Latino). Average age 28. 140 applicants, 23% accepted, 29 enrolled. In 2017, 19 master's, 4 doctorates awarded. Terminal master's awarded for partial completion of doctoral program. *Degree requirements:* For master's, thesis (for some programs), project or portfolio; for doctorate, thesis/dissertation. *Entrance requirements:* For master's, GRE General Test, minimum GPA of 2.9; for doctorate, GRE General Test, minimum GPA of 3.0. Additional exam requirements/recommendations for international students: Required—TOEFL (minimum score 550 paper-based; 79 iBT). *Application deadline:* For fall admission, 5/1 priority date for domestic students, 3/10 priority date for international students; for spring admission, 11/1 priority date for domestic students, 9/1 priority date for international students. Applications are processed on a rolling basis. Application fee: $75. Electronic applications accepted. *Expenses:* Contact institution. *Financial support:* In 2017–18, 15 students received support, including 9 fellowships with full tuition reimbursements available (averaging $3,070 per year), 7 research assistantships with full tuition reimbursements available (averaging $14,000 per year), 15 teaching assistantships with full tuition reimbursements available (averaging $14,080 per year); career-related internships or fieldwork, Federal Work-Study, institutionally sponsored loans, traineeships, health care benefits, and unspecified assistantships also available. Financial award application deadline: 1/10. *Faculty research:* International business and world trade, geographic information systems and cartography, transportation, urban and regional analysis, physical and environmental geography. *Total annual research expenditures:* $2.6 million. *Unit head:* Dr. Sean Bennett, Chair, 716-645-0490, Fax: 716-645-2329, E-mail: seanb@buffalo.edu. *Application contact:* Wendy Zitzka, Graduate Secretary, 716-645-0471, Fax: 716-645-2329, E-mail: wzitzka@buffalo.edu. Website: http://www.geog.buffalo.edu/

University at Buffalo, the State University of New York, Graduate School, School of Management, Buffalo, NY 14260. Offers accounting (MS); analytics (MBA); business administration (PMBA); consulting (MBA); finance (MBA, MS), including financial risk management (MS), quantitative finance (MS); healthcare (MBA); information assurance (MBA); information systems (MBA); international management (MBA); management (EMBA, PhD); management information systems (MS); marketing (MBA); supply chain and operations (MBA); supply chains and operations management (MS); Au D/MBA; DDS/MBA; JD/MBA; M Arch/MBA; MD/MBA; MPH/MBA; MSW/MBA; Pharm D/MBA. *Accreditation:* AACSB. *Program availability:* Part-time, evening/weekend. *Faculty:* 80 full-time (26 women), 45 part-time/adjunct (12 women). *Students:* 597 full-time (251 women); includes 83 minority (19 Black or African American, non-Hispanic/Latino; 59 Asian, non-Hispanic/Latino; 5 Hispanic/Latino), 306 international. Average age 25. 2,109 applicants, 46% accepted, 376 enrolled. In 2017, 371 master's, 13 doctorates awarded. *Degree requirements:* For master's, capstone courses or projects; for doctorate, comprehensive exam, thesis/dissertation. *Entrance requirements:* For master's, GMAT (for MS in accounting, finance); GRE or GMAT (for MBA, MS in management information systems, supply chains and operations management), essays, letters of recommendation; for doctorate, GMAT or GRE, essays, writing sample, letters of recommendation. Additional exam requirements/recommendations for international students: Required—TOEFL (minimum score 95 iBT) or IELTS (minimum score 6.5). Recommended—TSE (minimum score 73). *Application deadline:* For fall admission, 10/15 priority date for domestic and international students; for winter admission, 2/1 priority date for domestic and international students; for spring admission, 4/15 for domestic students; for summer admission, 5/15 for domestic students. Application fee: $100. Electronic applications accepted. *Expenses:* Varies by program. *Financial support:* Fellowships with full and partial tuition reimbursements, research assistantships with full and partial tuition reimbursements, teaching assistantships with full and partial tuition reimbursements, career-related internships or fieldwork, Federal Work-Study, institutionally sponsored loans, scholarships/grants, health care benefits, and unspecified assistantships available. Financial award application deadline: 2/15. *Faculty research:* Data analytics, accounting and law, rate finance, consumer behavior, supply chain logistics, leadership and team effectiveness. *Total annual research expenditures:* $968,376. *Unit head:* Erin K. O'Brien, Assistant Dean and Director of Graduate Programs, 716-645-3204, Fax: 716-645-2341, E-mail: ekobrien@buffalo.edu. *Application contact:* Meghan Felser, Director of Admissions and Recruiting, 716-645-3204, Fax: 716-645-2341, E-mail: mpwood@buffalo.edu. Website: http://mgt.buffalo.edu/

The University of Akron, Graduate School, College of Business Administration, Program in International Business, Akron, OH 44325. Offers MBA, JD/MBA. *Program availability:* Part-time, evening/weekend. *Students:* 2 full-time (both women), 2 part-time (0 women), 1 international. Average age 26. 3 applicants, 67% accepted, 2 enrolled. In 2017, 2 master's awarded. *Entrance requirements:* For master's, GMAT, minimum GPA of 3.0 (preferred), two letters of recommendation, resume, statement of purpose. Additional exam requirements/recommendations for international students: Required—TOEFL (minimum score 550 paper-based; 79 iBT), IELTS (minimum score 6.5). *Application deadline:* For fall admission, 7/15 for domestic and international students; for spring admission, 11/15 for domestic and international students; for summer admission, 4/15 for domestic and international students. Application fee: $45 ($75 for international students). Electronic applications accepted. *Financial support:* Administrative assistantships available. *Unit head:* Dr. Terry Daugherty, Interim Chair, 330-972-8304, E-mail: td23@uakron.edu. *Application contact:* Dr. William Hauser, Director of Graduate Business Programs, 330-972-7043, Fax: 330-972-6588, E-mail: whauser@uakron.edu. Website: http://www.uakron.edu/cba/graduate/programs/mba/internationalbusiness.dot

University of Alberta, Faculty of Graduate Studies and Research, Program in Business Administration, Edmonton, AB T6G 2E1, Canada. Offers international business (MBA); leisure and sport management (MBA); natural resources and energy (MBA); technology commercialization (MBA); MBA/LL B; MBA/M Ag; MBA/M Eng; MBA/MF; MBA/PhD. *Accreditation:* AACSB. *Program availability:* Part-time, evening/weekend. *Degree requirements:* For master's, thesis or alternative. *Entrance requirements:* For master's, GMAT. Additional exam requirements/recommendations for international students: Required—TOEFL (minimum score 600 paper-based). Electronic applications accepted. *Faculty research:* Natural resources and energy/management and policy/family enterprise/international business/healthcare research management.

University of Baltimore, Graduate School, Merrick School of Business, Department of Management and International Business, Baltimore, MD 21201-5779. Offers global leadership (MS).

University of Bridgeport, School of Business, Bridgeport, CT 06604. Offers accounting (MBA); finance (MBA); general business (MBA); global financial services (MBA); human resource management (MBA); information systems and knowledge management (MBA); international business (MBA); management (MBA); marketing (MBA); operations management (MBA); small business and entrepreneurship (MBA); specialized business (MBA). *Accreditation:* ACBSP. *Program availability:* Part-time, evening/weekend. *Degree requirements:* For master's, thesis optional. *Entrance requirements:* For master's, GMAT. Additional exam requirements/recommendations for international students: Recommended—TOEFL (minimum score 550 paper-based; 80 iBT), IELTS (minimum score 6.5). Electronic applications accepted. *Expenses:* Contact institution.

University of California, Berkeley, UC Berkeley Extension, International Diploma Programs, Berkeley, CA 94720-1500. Offers business administration (Certificate); finance (Certificate); global business management (Certificate); marketing (Certificate); project management (Certificate). *Accreditation:* AACSB.

University of California, San Diego, Graduate Division, School of Global Policy and Strategy, Master of International Affairs Program, La Jolla, CA 92093. Offers international development and nonprofit management (MIA); international economics (MIA); international environmental policy (MIA); international management (MIA); international politics (MIA). Students will choose one of the following country/regional specializations: China, Japan, Korea, Latin America, or Southeast Asia. *Degree requirements:* For master's, one foreign language. *Entrance requirements:* For master's, GMAT or GRE General Test. Additional exam requirements/recommendations for international students: Required—TOEFL (minimum score 90 iBT), IELTS (minimum score 7). Electronic applications accepted.

International Business

University of Chicago, Booth School of Business, Executive MBA Program Asia (Hong Kong), 238466, Singapore. Offers MBA. *Program availability:* Part-time. *Students:* 135 part-time (31 women). In 2017, 70 master's awarded. *Entrance requirements:* For master's, GMAT, GRE, or Executive Assessment, letter of company support, letters of recommendation, essays, resume, interview. Electronic applications accepted. *Expenses:* Contact institution. *Unit head:* Richard Johnson, Associate Dean, Executive MBA Program, Europe and Asia, 852-2533-9520. *Application contact:* Executive MBA Program Asia, 852-2533-9500, E-mail: asia.inquiries@chicagobooth.edu.
Website: http://www.chicagobooth.edu/programs/exec-mba

University of Chicago, Booth School of Business, Executive MBA Program Europe (London), EC2V 5HA, United Kingdom. Offers MBA. *Program availability:* Part-time. *Students:* 181 part-time (34 women). In 2017, 82 master's awarded. *Entrance requirements:* For master's, GMAT, GRE, or Executive Assessment, letter of company support, letters of recommendation, essays, resume, interview. Electronic applications accepted. *Expenses:* Contact institution. *Unit head:* Richard Johnson, Associate Dean, Executive MBA Program, Europe and Asia, 852-2533-9520. *Application contact:* Executive MBA Program Europe, 44 20-7070-2200, Fax: 44 20-7070-2250, E-mail: europe.inquiries@chicagobooth.edu.
Website: http://www.chicagobooth.edu/programs/exec-mba

University of Chicago, Booth School of Business, Executive MBA Program North America, Chicago, IL 60611. Offers MBA. *Program availability:* Part-time. *Students:* 181 part-time (39 women). In 2017, 78 master's awarded. *Entrance requirements:* For master's, GMAT, GRE, or Executive Assessment, letter of company support, letters of recommendation, essays, resume, interview. Electronic applications accepted. *Expenses:* Contact institution. *Unit head:* Patty Keegan, Associate Dean, Executive MBA and Global Integration, 312-464-8751. *Application contact:* Executive MBA Program North America, 312-464-8750, E-mail: xp@chicagobooth.edu.
Website: http://www.chicagobooth.edu/programs/exec-mba

University of Chicago, Booth School of Business, Full-Time MBA Program, Chicago, IL 60637. Offers accounting (MBA); analytic finance (MBA); analytic management (MBA); econometrics and statistics (MBA); economics (MBA); entrepreneurship (MBA); finance (MBA); general management (MBA); health administration and policy (Certificate); international business (MBA); managerial and organizational behavior (MBA); marketing analytics (MBA); marketing management (MBA); operations management (MBA); strategic management (MBA); MBA/AM; MBA/JD; MBA/MA; MBA/MD; MBA/MPP. *Accreditation:* AACSB. *Faculty:* 154 full-time (26 women), 61 part-time/adjunct (12 women). *Students:* 1,176 full-time (481 women). In 2017, 586 master's awarded. *Entrance requirements:* For master's, GMAT or GRE, transcripts, resume, 2 letters of recommendation, essays, interview. Additional exam requirements/recommendations for international students: Required—TOEFL, IELTS, or PTE. *Application deadline:* For fall admission, 9/1 for domestic and international students; for winter admission, 1/1 for domestic and international students; for spring admission, 4/1 for domestic and international students. Application fee: $250. Electronic applications accepted. *Expenses:* Contact institution. *Unit head:* Stacey Kole, Deputy Dean for Alumni, Corporate Relations, and the Full-time MBA Program, 773-702-7121. *Application contact:* Kurt Ahlm, Associate Dean for Student Recruitment and Admissions, 773-702-7369, Fax: 773-702-9085, E-mail: admissions@chicagobooth.edu.
Website: https://www.chicagobooth.edu/programs/full-time

University of Colorado Denver, Business School, Master of Business Administration Program, Denver, CO 80217. Offers bioinnovation and entrepreneurship (MBA); business intelligence (MBA); business strategy (MBA); business to business marketing (MBA); business to consumer marketing (MBA); change management (MBA); corporate financial management (MBA); enterprise technology management (MBA); entrepreneurship (MBA); health administration (MBA), including financial management, health administration, health information technologies, international health management and policy; human resources management (MBA); international business (MBA); investment management (MBA); managing for sustainability (MBA); sports and entertainment management (MBA). *Accreditation:* AACSB. *Program availability:* Part-time, evening/weekend, 100% online, blended/hybrid learning. *Degree requirements:* For master's, 48 semester hours, including 30 of core courses, 3 in international business, and 15 in electives from over 50 other business courses. *Entrance requirements:* For master's, GMAT, resume, official transcripts, essay, two letters of recommendation, financial statements (for international applicants). Additional exam requirements/recommendations for international students: Required—TOEFL (minimum score 560 paper-based; 83 iBT); Recommended—IELTS (minimum score 6.5). Electronic applications accepted. *Expenses:* Contact institution. *Faculty research:* Marketing, management, entrepreneurship, finance, health administration.

University of Colorado Denver, Business School, Program in Global Energy Management, Denver, CO 80217. Offers MS. *Program availability:* Online learning. *Degree requirements:* For master's, 36 semester credit hours. *Entrance requirements:* For master's, GMAT if less than three years of experience in the energy industry (waived for students already holding a graduate degree), minimum of 5 years' experience in energy industry; resume; letters of recommendation; essays. Additional exam requirements/recommendations for international students: Required—TOEFL (minimum score 525 paper-based; 71 iBT); Recommended—IELTS (minimum score 6). Electronic applications accepted. *Expenses:* Contact institution.

University of Colorado Denver, Business School, Program in International Business, Denver, CO 80217. Offers MSIB. *Program availability:* Part-time, evening/weekend. *Degree requirements:* For master's, one foreign language, 42 credit hours; thesis, internship or international field study. *Entrance requirements:* For master's, GMAT, resume, essay, two letters of recommendation, financial statements (for international applicants). Additional exam requirements/recommendations for international students: Required—TOEFL (minimum score 525 paper-based; 71 iBT); Recommended—IELTS (minimum score 6.5). Electronic applications accepted. *Expenses:* Contact institution. *Faculty research:* Foreign direct investment, international business strategies, cross-cultural management, internationalization of research and development, global leadership development.

University of Colorado Denver, Business School, Program in Management and Organization, Denver, CO 80217. Offers business strategy (MS); change and innovation (MS); enterprise technology management (MS); entrepreneurship and innovation (MS); global management (MS); leadership (MS); managing for sustainability (MS); managing human resources (MS); sports and entertainment management (MS). *Accreditation:* AACSB. *Program availability:* Part-time, evening/weekend, online learning. *Degree requirements:* For master's, 30 semester hours (12 of required courses, 12 of management electives, and 6 of free electives). *Entrance requirements:* For master's, GMAT, resume, two letters of recommendation, essay, financial statements (for international applicants). Additional exam requirements/recommendations for international students: Required—TOEFL (minimum score 525 paper-based; 71 iBT); Recommended—IELTS (minimum score 6.5). Electronic applications accepted. *Expenses:* Contact institution. *Faculty research:* Human resource management, management of catastrophe, turnaround strategies.

University of Colorado Denver, Business School, Program in Marketing, Denver, CO 80217. Offers brand management and marketing communication (MS); global marketing (MS); high-tech and entrepreneurial marketing (MS); marketing for sustainability (MS); marketing research (MS); sports and entertainment marketing (MS). *Program availability:* Part-time, evening/weekend. *Degree requirements:* For master's, 30 semester hours (21 of marketing core courses, 9 of marketing electives). *Entrance requirements:* For master's, GMAT, resume, essay, two letters of recommendation, financial statements (for international applicants). Additional exam requirements/recommendations for international students: Required—TOEFL (minimum score 525 paper-based; 71 iBT); Recommended—IELTS (minimum score 6.5). Electronic applications accepted. *Expenses:* Contact institution. *Faculty research:* Marketing issues in the Chinese environment, impact of individual difference and contextual factors on the risk-taking behaviors of managers making new-business creation decisions, attribution theory perspective of conflict between marketers and engineers, organizational identity and identification, international market entry strategies.

University of Dallas, Satish and Yasmin Gupta College of Business, Irving, TX 75062-4736. Offers accounting (MBA, MS); business administration (DBA); business analytics (MS); business management (MBA); corporate finance (MBA); cybersecurity (MS); finance (MS); financial services (MBA); global business (MBA, MS); health services management (MBA); human resource management (MBA); information and technology management (MS); information assurance (MBA); information technology (MBA); information technology service management (MBA); marketing management (MBA); organization development (MBA); project management (MBA); sports and entertainment management (MBA); strategic leadership (MBA); supply chain management (MBA). *Accreditation:* AACSB. *Program availability:* Part-time, evening/weekend, online learning. *Entrance requirements:* Additional exam requirements/recommendations for international students: Required—TOEFL. *Application deadline:* Applications are processed on a rolling basis. Application fee: $50. Electronic applications accepted. *Expenses:* Contact institution. *Financial support:* Application deadline: 2/15; applicants required to submit FAFSA. *Unit head:* Brett J.L. Landry, Dean, 972-721-5356, E-mail: blandry@udallas.edu. *Application contact:* Dr. David Sweet, Dean, Braniff Graduate School, 972-721-5288, Fax: 972-721-5280, E-mail: dsweet@udallas.edu.
Website: http://www.udallas.edu/cob/

University of Florida, Graduate School, Warrington College of Business Administration, Hough Graduate School of Business, Department of Management, Gainesville, FL 32611. Offers health care risk management (MS); international business (MA); management (MS, PhD). *Accreditation:* AACSB. *Program availability:* Online learning. *Degree requirements:* For master's, comprehensive exam, thesis. *Entrance requirements:* For master's, GMAT (minimum score of 465) or GRE General Test, minimum GPA of 3.0. Additional exam requirements/recommendations for international students: Required—TOEFL (minimum score 550 paper-based; 80 iBT), IELTS (minimum score 6). Electronic applications accepted. *Faculty research:* Job attitudes, personality and individual differences, organizational entry and exit, knowledge management, competitive dynamics.

University of Florida, Graduate School, Warrington College of Business Administration, Hough Graduate School of Business, Programs in Business Administration, Gainesville, FL 32611. Offers business administration (MA, MS, PhD); competitive strategy (MBA); finance (MBA); global management (MBA); Graham-Buffett security analysis (MBA); human resource management (MBA); information systems and operations management (MBA); international studies (MBA); management (MBA); real estate (MBA); JD/MBA; MBA/MS; MBA/PhD; MBA/Pharm D; MD/MBA. *Accreditation:* AACSB. *Program availability:* Part-time, evening/weekend, online learning. *Degree requirements:* For master's, capstone course. *Entrance requirements:* For master's and doctorate, GMAT (minimum score 465), minimum GPA of 3.0, interview. Additional exam requirements/recommendations for international students: Required—TOEFL (minimum score 550 paper-based; 80 iBT), IELTS (minimum score 6). Electronic applications accepted. *Faculty research:* Accounting, finance, insurance, management, real estate, urban analysis marketing.

University of Florida, Levin College of Law, Gainesville, FL 32611. Offers comparative law (LL M), including tropical conservation and development; environmental and land use law (LL M); international taxation (LL M); law (JD); taxation (LL M, SJD). *Accreditation:* ABA. *Entrance requirements:* For doctorate, LSAT (for JD). Electronic applications accepted. *Faculty research:* Environmental and land use law, taxation, dispute resolution, family law, Constitutional law.

University of Hawaii at Manoa, Office of Graduate Education, Shidler College of Business, Program in Business Administration, Honolulu, HI 96822. Offers Asian business studies (MBA); Chinese business studies (MBA); decision sciences (MBA); entrepreneurship (MBA); finance (MBA); finance and banking (MBA); human resources management (MBA); information management (MBA); information technology (MBA); international business (MBA); Japanese business studies (MBA); marketing (MBA); organizational behavior (MBA); organizational management (MBA); real estate (MBA); student-designed track (MBA). *Accreditation:* AACSB. *Program availability:* Part-time, evening/weekend. *Degree requirements:* For master's, thesis optional. *Entrance requirements:* For master's, GMAT, minimum GPA of 3.0. Additional exam requirements/recommendations for international students: Required—TOEFL (minimum score 600 paper-based; 100 iBT), IELTS (minimum score 7). *Expenses:* Contact institution.

University of Hawaii at Manoa, Office of Graduate Education, Shidler College of Business, Program in International Management, Honolulu, HI 96822. Offers Asian finance (PhD); global information technology management (PhD); international accounting (PhD); international marketing (PhD); international organization and strategy (PhD). *Program availability:* Part-time. *Degree requirements:* For doctorate, comprehensive exam, thesis/dissertation. *Entrance requirements:* For doctorate, GMAT or GRE General Test, minimum GPA of 3.0. Additional exam requirements/recommendations for international students: Required—TOEFL (minimum score 600 paper-based; 100 iBT), IELTS (minimum score 7). *Expenses:* Contact institution.

University of Houston–Downtown, Marilyn Davies College of Business, MBA Program, Houston, TX 77002. Offers accounting (MBA); finance (MBA); human resource management (MBA); international business (MBA); investment management (MBA); leadership (MBA); project management and process improvement (MBA); sales management and business development (MBA); supply chain management (MBA). *Accreditation:* AACSB. *Program availability:* Part-time, evening/weekend. *Faculty:* 36 full-time (13 women), 11 part-time/adjunct (6 women). *Students:* 4 full-time (2 women), 1,065 part-time (605 women); includes 821 minority (383 Black or African American, non-Hispanic/Latino; 3 American Indian or Alaska Native, non-Hispanic/Latino; 136 Asian, non-Hispanic/Latino; 299 Hispanic/Latino), 33 international. Average age 33. 418 applicants, 89% accepted, 308 enrolled. In 2017, 310 master's awarded. *Entrance requirements:* For master's, GMAT, two letters of recommendation from professional references, personal statement, resume. Additional exam requirements/recommendations for international students: Required—TOEFL (minimum score 81 iBT). *Application deadline:* For fall admission, 8/1 for domestic and international students. Application fee: $35 ($60 for international students). Electronic applications accepted. *Expenses:* $360 per credit resident; $725 per credit non-resident. *Financial*

support: Federal Work-Study and scholarships/grants available. Financial award application deadline: 4/1; financial award applicants required to submit FAFSA. *Unit head:* Dr. Charles E. Gengler, Dean, 713-221-8179, Fax: 713-221-8675. *Application contact:* Ceshia Love, Director of Admissions, 713-221-8093, Fax: 713-223-7408, E-mail: gradadmissions@uhd.edu.
Website: http://mba.uhd.edu/

University of Houston–Victoria, School of Business Administration, Victoria, TX 77901-4450. Offers accounting (MBA); economic development and entrepreneurship (MS); finance (GMBA, MBA); general business (MBA); international business (MBA); management (GMBA, MBA); marketing (MBA). *Accreditation:* AACSB. *Program availability:* Part-time, evening/weekend, online learning. *Entrance requirements:* For master's, GMAT. Additional exam requirements/recommendations for international students: Required—TOEFL (minimum score 550 paper-based). Electronic applications accepted. *Faculty research:* Economic development, marketing, finance.

University of Kentucky, Graduate School, Patterson School of Diplomacy and International Commerce, Lexington, KY 40506-0027. Offers MA. *Degree requirements:* For master's, one foreign language, comprehensive exam, statistics. *Entrance requirements:* For master's, GRE General Test, minimum undergraduate GPA of 3.0. Additional exam requirements/recommendations for international students: Required—TOEFL (minimum score 550 paper-based; 79 iBT). Electronic applications accepted. *Faculty research:* International relations, foreign and defense policy, cross-cultural negotiation, international science and technology, diplomacy, international economics and development, geopolitical modeling.

University of La Verne, College of Business and Public Management, Graduate Programs in Business Administration, La Verne, CA 91750-4443. Offers accounting (MBA, MBA-EP); finance (MBA, MBA-EP); health services management (MBA); information technology (MBA, MBA-EP); international business (MBA, MBA-EP); management and leadership (MBA, MBA-EP); marketing (MBA, MBA-EP); supply chain management (MBA, MBA-EP). *Program availability:* Part-time, evening/weekend. *Faculty:* 24 full-time (11 women), 25 part-time/adjunct (6 women). *Students:* 390 full-time (193 women), 93 part-time (48 women); includes 96 minority (7 Black or African American, non-Hispanic/Latino; 1 American Indian or Alaska Native, non-Hispanic/Latino; 17 Asian, non-Hispanic/Latino; 67 Hispanic/Latino; 1 Native Hawaiian or other Pacific Islander, non-Hispanic/Latino; 3 Two or more races, non-Hispanic/Latino), 336 international. Average age 28. *Entrance requirements:* For master's, GMAT, MAT, or GRE, minimum undergraduate GPA of 3.0, 2 letters of recommendation, resume, statement of purpose. Additional exam requirements/recommendations for international students: Required—TOEFL (minimum score 550 paper-based; 85 iBT). *Application deadline:* Applications are processed on a rolling basis. Application fee: $50. Tuition and fees vary according to program. *Financial support:* Institutionally sponsored loans and scholarships/grants available. Financial award application deadline: 3/2; financial award applicants required to submit FAFSA. *Unit head:* Dr. Abe Helou, Chairperson, 909-448-4455, Fax: 909-392-2704, E-mail: ihelou@laverne.edu. *Application contact:* Rina Lazarian-Chehab, Senior Associate Director of Graduate Admissions, 909-448-4317, Fax: 909-971-2295, E-mail: rlazarian@laverne.edu.
Website: https://business.laverne.edu/mba/

University of La Verne, Regional and Online Campuses, Graduate Programs, Inland Empire Campus, Ontario, CA 91730. Offers business administration (MBA, MBA-EP), including accounting (MBA), finance (MBA), health services management (MBA-EP), information technology (MBA-EP), international business (MBA), managed care (MBA), management and leadership (MBA-EP), marketing (MBA-EP), supply chain management (MBA); leadership and management (MS), including human resource management, nonprofit management, organizational development. *Program availability:* Part-time, evening/weekend. *Faculty:* 5 part-time/adjunct (1 woman). *Students:* 24 full-time (13 women), 72 part-time (44 women); includes 64 minority (12 Black or African American, non-Hispanic/Latino; 13 Asian, non-Hispanic/Latino; 36 Hispanic/Latino; 3 Two or more races, non-Hispanic/Latino). Average age 38. In 2017, 42 master's awarded. *Application deadline:* Applications are processed on a rolling basis. Application fee: $50. *Expenses:* Contact institution. *Financial support:* Application deadline: 3/2; applicants required to submit FAFSA. *Unit head:* Juli Roberts, Campus Director, Inland Empire Regional Campus in Ontario, 760-955-6448, E-mail: jroberts@laverne.edu. *Application contact:* Admissions, 877-468-6858, E-mail: gradadmission@laverne.edu.
Website: https://laverne.edu/locations/

University of Lethbridge, School of Graduate Studies, Lethbridge, AB T1K 3M4, Canada. Offers addictions counseling (M Sc); agricultural biotechnology (M Sc); agricultural studies (M Sc, MA); anthropology (MA); archaeology (M Sc, MA); art (MA, MFA); biochemistry (M Sc); biological sciences (M Sc); biomolecular science (PhD); biosystems and biodiversity (PhD); Canadian studies (MA); chemistry (M Sc); computer science (M Sc); computer science and geographical information science (M Sc); counseling (MC); counseling psychology (M Ed); dramatic arts (MA); earth, space, and physical science (PhD); economics (MA); education (MA, PhD); educational leadership (M Ed); English (MA); environmental science (M Sc); evolution and behavior (PhD); exercise science (M Sc); French (MA); French/German (MA); French/Spanish (MA); general education (M Ed); geography (M Sc, MA); German (MA); health sciences (M Sc); individualized multidisciplinary (M Sc, MA); kinesiology (M Sc, MA); management (M Sc), including accounting, finance, human resource management and labor relations, information systems, international management, marketing, policy and strategy; mathematics (M Sc); music (M Mus, MA); Native American studies (MA); neuroscience (M Sc, PhD); new media (MA, MFA); nursing (M Sc, MN); philosophy (MA); physics (M Sc); political science (MA); psychology (M Sc, MA); religious studies (MA); sociology (MA); theatre and dramatic arts (MFA); theoretical and computational science (PhD); urban and regional studies (MA); women and gender studies (MA). *Program availability:* Part-time, evening/weekend. *Degree requirements:* For master's, thesis (for some programs). *Entrance requirements:* For master's, GMAT (for M Sc in management), bachelor's degree in related field, minimum GPA of 3.0 during previous 20 graded semester courses, 2 years' teaching or related experience (M Ed); for doctorate, master's degree, minimum graduate GPA of 3.5. Additional exam requirements/recommendations for international students: Required—TOEFL (minimum score 580 paper-based; 93 iBT). Electronic applications accepted. *Faculty research:* Movement and brain plasticity, gibberellin physiology, photosynthesis, carbon cycling, molecular properties of main-group ring components.

University of Louisville, Graduate School, College of Business, MBA Programs, Louisville, KY 40292-0001. Offers entrepreneurship (MBA); global business (MBA); health sector management (MBA). *Accreditation:* AACSB. *Program availability:* Part-time, evening/weekend. *Students:* 253 full-time (99 women), 21 part-time (6 women); includes 49 minority (25 Black or African American, non-Hispanic/Latino; 1 American Indian or Alaska Native, non-Hispanic/Latino; 10 Asian, non-Hispanic/Latino; 8 Hispanic/Latino; 5 Two or more races, non-Hispanic/Latino), 27 international. Average age 32. 295 applicants, 63% accepted, 155 enrolled. In 2017, 85 master's awarded. *Degree requirements:* For master's, international learning experience. *Entrance requirements:* For master's, GMAT, 2 letters of reference, personal interview, resume, personal

statement, college transcript(s). Additional exam requirements/recommendations for international students: Required—TOEFL (minimum score 83 iBT). *Application deadline:* For fall admission, 7/1 for domestic students; for spring admission, 12/1 for domestic students. Applications are processed on a rolling basis. Application fee: $65. *Expenses:* Tuition, state resident: full-time $12,246; part-time $681 per credit hour. Tuition, nonresident: full-time $25,486; part-time $1417 per credit hour. *Required fees:* $196. Tuition and fees vary according to course load, program and reciprocity agreements. *Financial support:* Fellowships with full tuition reimbursements, research assistantships with full tuition reimbursements, health care benefits, and unspecified assistantships available. Financial award application deadline: 3/31; financial award applicants required to submit FAFSA. *Faculty research:* Entrepreneurship, venture capital, retailing/franchising, corporate governance and leadership, supply chain management. *Total annual research expenditures:* $859,000. *Unit head:* Dr. Todd Mooradian, Dean, 502-852-6443, Fax: 502-852-7557, E-mail: todd.mooradian@louisville.edu. *Application contact:* Susan E. Hildebrand, Program Director, 502-852-7257, Fax: 502-852-4901, E-mail: s.hildebrand@louisville.edu.
Website: http://business.louisville.edu/mba

The University of Manchester, Alliance Manchester Business School, M15 6PB, United Kingdom. Offers accounting and finance (M Sc); business (M Ent); business analysis and strategic management (M Sc); business analytics: operational research and risk analysis (M Sc); business psychology (M Sc); corporate communications and reputation management (M Sc); finance (M Sc); finance and business economics (M Sc); human resource management and industrial relations (M Sc); innovation management and entrepreneurship (M Sc); international business and management (M Sc); international human resource management and comparative industrial relations (M Sc); management (M Sc); marketing (M Sc); operations, project and supply chain management (M Sc); organizational psychology (M Sc); quantitative finance (M Sc). *Entrance requirements:* For master's, UK 2:1 honours degree or overseas equivalent. Additional exam requirements/recommendations for international students: Required—TOEFL (minimum score 100 iBT), IELTS (minimum score 7), PTE. Electronic applications accepted. *Faculty research:* Accounting and finance, management sciences and marketing, people management and organization, innovation management and policy, decision sciences.

University of Mary Hardin-Baylor, Graduate Studies in Business Administration, Belton, TX 76513. Offers accounting (MBA); information systems management (MBA); international business (MBA); management (MBA). *Program availability:* Part-time, evening/weekend. *Faculty:* 12 full-time (5 women), 6 part-time/adjunct (4 women). *Students:* 16 full-time (10 women), 39 part-time (16 women); includes 15 minority (3 Black or African American, non-Hispanic/Latino; 1 Asian, non-Hispanic/Latino; 10 Hispanic/Latino; 1 Two or more races, non-Hispanic/Latino), 10 international. Average age 30. 72 applicants, 81% accepted, 16 enrolled. In 2017, 34 master's awarded. *Degree requirements:* For master's, comprehensive exam. *Entrance requirements:* For master's, minimum GPA of 3.0, interview. Additional exam requirements/recommendations for international students: Required—TOEFL (minimum score 60 iBT), IELTS (minimum score 4.5). *Application deadline:* For fall admission, 6/1 for domestic students, 4/30 priority date for international students; for spring admission, 11/1 for domestic students, 9/30 priority date for international students. Applications are processed on a rolling basis. Application fee: $35 ($135 for international students). Electronic applications accepted. *Expenses: Tuition:* Full-time $15,570; part-time $10,380 per credit hour. *Required fees:* $1350; $75 per credit hour. $50 per term. Tuition and fees vary according to course load and degree level. *Financial support:* In 2017–18, 32 students received support. Federal Work-Study, institutionally sponsored loans, unspecified assistantships, and scholarships for some active duty military personnel available. Support available to part-time students. Financial award applicants required to submit FAFSA. *Faculty research:* Financial management, financial markets, supply chain management. *Unit head:* Dr. Kirk Fischer, Assistant Dean, Graduate Programs in McLane College of Business, 254-295-4655, E-mail: kfischer@umhb.edu. *Application contact:* Sharon Aguilera, Assistant Director, Graduate Admissions, 254-295-4835, E-mail: saguilera@umhb.edu.
Website: http://www.graduate.umhb.edu/mba

University of Massachusetts Boston, College of Management, Program in International Management, Boston, MA 02125-3393. Offers MS. *Students:* 3 full-time (1 woman), 2 part-time (1 woman); includes 1 minority (Black or African American, non-Hispanic/Latino), 3 international. Average age 27. 1 applicant, 100% accepted, 1 enrolled. In 2017, 3 master's awarded. *Expenses:* Tuition, state resident: full-time $17,375. Tuition, nonresident: full-time $33,915. *Required fees:* $355. *Application contact:* Graduate Admissions Coordinator, 617-287-6400, Fax: 617-287-6236, E-mail: bos.gadm@dpc.umassp.edu.

University of Michigan–Flint, School of Management, Program in Business Administration, Flint, MI 48502-1950. Offers accounting (MBA); computer information systems (MBA); finance (MBA, Post-Master's Certificate); general business (Graduate Certificate); general business administration (MBA); health care management (MBA); international business (MBA, Post-Master's Certificate); lean manufacturing (MBA); marketing (Post-Master's Certificate); marketing and innovation management (MBA); organizational leadership (MBA). *Program availability:* Part-time, evening/weekend, mixed mode format. *Faculty:* 32 full-time (5 women), 8 part-time/adjunct (2 women). *Students:* 12 full-time (7 women), 147 part-time (51 women); includes 31 minority (15 Black or African American, non-Hispanic/Latino; 1 American Indian or Alaska Native, non-Hispanic/Latino; 9 Asian, non-Hispanic/Latino; 5 Hispanic/Latino; 1 Two or more races, non-Hispanic/Latino), 18 international. Average age 34. 110 applicants, 52% accepted, 29 enrolled. In 2017, 59 master's, 6 other advanced degrees awarded. *Entrance requirements:* For master's, GMAT or GRE, bachelor's degree in arts, sciences, engineering, or business administration from regionally-accredited college or university with minimum GPA of 3.0; for other advanced degree, bachelor's degree in arts, sciences, engineering, or business administration from regionally-accredited college or university with minimum GPA of 3.0, college-level math, statistics, or quantitative course (for Graduate Certificate); MBA or equivalent degree from regionally-accredited college or university (for Post Master's Certificate). Additional exam requirements/recommendations for international students: Required—TOEFL (minimum score 84 iBT), IELTS (minimum score 6.5). *Application deadline:* For fall admission, 8/1 for domestic students, 5/1 for international students; for winter admission, 11/15 for domestic students, 9/1 for international students; for spring admission, 3/15 for domestic students, 1/1 for international students; for summer admission, 5/15 for domestic students. Applications are processed on a rolling basis. Application fee: $55. Electronic applications accepted. *Expenses:* Contact institution. *Financial support:* Federal Work-Study, scholarships/grants, and unspecified assistantships available. Support available to part-time students. Financial award application deadline: 3/1; financial award applicants required to submit FAFSA. *Unit head:* Dr. Scott Johnson, Dean, School of Management, 810-762-3164, Fax: 810-237-6685, E-mail: scotjohn@umflint.edu. *Application contact:* Bradley T. Maki, Director of Graduate Admissions, 810-762-3171, E-mail: bmaki@umflint.edu.
Website: http://www.umflint.edu/graduateprograms/business-administration-mba

International Business

University of New Brunswick Saint John, Faculty of Business, Saint John, NB E2L 4L5, Canada. Offers administration (MBA); electronic commerce (MBA); international business (MBA); natural resource management (MBA). *Program availability:* Part-time. *Entrance requirements:* For master's, GMAT (minimum score of 550) or GRE (minimum 54th percentile), minimum GPA of 3.0. Additional exam requirements/recommendations for international students: Required—TOEFL (minimum score 580 paper-based; 93 iBT), TWE (minimum score 4.5). Electronic applications accepted. *Expenses:* Contact institution. *Faculty research:* International business, project management, innovation and technology management; business use of Weblogs and podcasts to communicate; corporate governance; high-involvement work systems; international competitiveness; supply chain management and logistics.

University of New Haven, Graduate School, College of Business, Program in Business Administration, West Haven, CT 06516. Offers accounting (MBA); business administration (MBA); business intelligence (MBA); business policy and strategic leadership (MBA); finance (MBA), including chartered financial analyst; global marketing (MBA); human resources management (MBA); sport management (MBA). *Accreditation:* AACSB. *Program availability:* Part-time, evening/weekend. *Students:* 123 full-time (56 women), 67 part-time (28 women); includes 53 minority (27 Black or African American, non-Hispanic/Latino; 11 Asian, non-Hispanic/Latino; 12 Hispanic/Latino; 3 Two or more races, non-Hispanic/Latino), 50 international. Average age 28. 148 applicants, 89% accepted, 67 enrolled. In 2017, 106 master's awarded. *Entrance requirements:* For master's, GMAT. Additional exam requirements/recommendations for international students: Required—TOEFL (minimum score 80 iBT), IELTS, PTE. *Application deadline:* Applications are processed on a rolling basis. Application fee: $50. Electronic applications accepted. Application fee is waived when completed online. *Expenses: Tuition:* Full-time $16,020; part-time $890 per credit hour. *Required fees:* $220; $90 per term. *Financial support:* Research assistantships with partial tuition reimbursements, teaching assistantships with partial tuition reimbursements, career-related internships or fieldwork, Federal Work-Study, scholarships/grants, and unspecified assistantships available. Support available to part-time students. Financial award applicants required to submit FAFSA. *Unit head:* Darell Singleterry, Director, 203-932-1085, E-mail: dsingleterry@newhaven.edu. *Application contact:* Michelle Mason, Director of Graduate Enrollment, 203-932-7067, E-mail: mmason@newhaven.edu. Website: http://www.newhaven.edu/business/graduate-programs/mba/index.php
See Display on page 154 and Close-Up on page 185.

University of New Mexico, Anderson School of Management, Department of Finance, International, Technology and Entrepreneurship, Albuquerque, NM 87131-1221. Offers entrepreneurship (MBA); finance (MBA); international management (MBA); international management in Latin America (MBA); management of technology (MBA). *Program availability:* Part-time. *Faculty:* 13 full-time (1 woman), 6 part-time/adjunct (1 woman). In 2017, 47 master's awarded. *Entrance requirements:* For master's, GMAT or GRE, minimum GPA of 3.0 on last 60 hours of coursework; bachelor's degree from regionally-accredited college or university in U.S. or its equivalent in another country. Additional exam requirements/recommendations for international students: Required—TOEFL (minimum score 550 paper-based; 79 iBT), IELTS (minimum score 6.5). *Application deadline:* For fall admission, 4/1 priority date for domestic and international students; for spring admission, 10/1 priority date for domestic and international students. Applications are processed on a rolling basis. Application fee: $50. Electronic applications accepted. *Expenses:* Contact institution. *Financial support:* In 2017–18, 17 students received support, including 9 fellowships (averaging $18,720 per year), 12 research assistantships with partial tuition reimbursements available (averaging $15,291 per year); career-related internships or fieldwork, Federal Work-Study, scholarships/grants, and unspecified assistantships also available. Support available to part-time students. Financial award application deadline: 6/1; financial award applicants required to submit FAFSA. *Faculty research:* Corporate finance, investments, management in Latin America, management of technology, entrepreneurship. *Unit head:* Dr. Raul Gouvea, Chair, 505-277-6471, E-mail: rauldg@unm.edu. *Application contact:* Lisa Beauchene, Student Recruitment Specialist, 505-277-6471, E-mail: andersonadvising@unm.edu. Website: https://www.mgt.unm.edu/fite/default.asp?mm-faculty

University of North Alabama, College of Business, Florence, AL 35632-0001. Offers business administration (MBA), including accounting, enterprise resource planning systems, executive, finance, health care management, information systems, international business, project management. *Accreditation:* AACSB; ACBSP. *Program availability:* Part-time, 100% online, blended/hybrid learning. *Faculty:* 26 full-time (1 woman), 4 part-time/adjunct (0 women). *Students:* 178 full-time (78 women), 498 part-time (237 women); includes 229 minority (92 Black or African American, non-Hispanic/Latino; 8 American Indian or Alaska Native, non-Hispanic/Latino; 104 Asian, non-Hispanic/Latino; 14 Hispanic/Latino; 11 Two or more races, non-Hispanic/Latino), 53 international. Average age 34. 354 applicants, 71% accepted, 190 enrolled. In 2017, 156 master's awarded. *Entrance requirements:* For master's, GMAT, GRE, minimum GPA of 2.75 in last 60 hours, 2.5 overall (on a 3.0 scale); 27 hours of course work in business and economics. Additional exam requirements/recommendations for international students: Required—TOEFL (minimum score 79 iBT), IELTS (minimum score 6), PTE (minimum score 54). *Application deadline:* Applications are processed on a rolling basis. Application fee: $50 ($100 for international students). Electronic applications accepted. *Expenses: Tuition:* Tuition, state resident: full-time $7824; part-time $5943 per year. Tuition, nonresident: full-time $15,648; part-time $11,736 per year. *Required fees:* $3064; $2298 per unit. Tuition and fees vary according to course load and reciprocity agreements. *Financial support:* In 2017–18, 114 students received support. Scholarships/grants available. Financial award application deadline: 2/1; financial award applicants required to submit FAFSA. *Total annual research expenditures:* $193,193. *Unit head:* Dr. Gregory A. Carnes, Dean, 256-765-4261, Fax: 256-765-4170, E-mail: gacarnes@una.edu. *Application contact:* Hillary N. Coats, Graduate Admissions Coordinator, 256-765-4447, E-mail: graduate@una.edu. Website: https://www.una.edu/mba/index.html

The University of North Carolina Wilmington, Cameron School of Business, Business Administration Program, Wilmington, NC 28403-3297. Offers business administration (MBA); business administration - international (MBA); business administration - professional (MBA). *Accreditation:* AACSB. *Program availability:* Part-time-only. *Faculty:* 37 full-time (10 women). *Students:* 104 full-time (35 women), 68 part-time (40 women); includes 28 minority (14 Black or African American, non-Hispanic/Latino; 3 Asian, non-Hispanic/Latino; 6 Hispanic/Latino; 5 Two or more races, non-Hispanic/Latino), 20 international. Average age 31. 109 applicants, 82% accepted, 78 enrolled. In 2017, 53 master's awarded. *Degree requirements:* For master's, thesis (for some programs), written case analysis and oral presentation (for professional), oral competency (for international). *Entrance requirements:* For master's, GMAT (for some programs), 2 years of appropriate work experience (for professional option), baccalaureate degree in the area of business and/or economics or six business prerequisite courses (for international option), resume, 3 letters of recommendation. Additional exam requirements/recommendations for international students: Required—TOEFL (minimum score 550 paper-based; 79 iBT), IELTS (minimum score 6.5). *Application deadline:* For fall admission, 6/1 for domestic students. Applications are processed on a rolling basis. Application fee: $75. Electronic applications accepted.

Expenses: $4,042 in-state full-time, $10,512 out-of-state full-time; $292.15 per credit hour in-state students; $926.49 out-of-state(online); $435.86 per credit hour in-state, $1,083.32 per credit hour out-of-state (for Executive MBA). *Financial support:* Scholarships/grants and unspecified assistantships available. Financial award application deadline: 1/1; financial award applicants required to submit FAFSA. *Unit head:* Dr. Thom Porter, Interim MBA Director, 910-962-7466, E-mail: portert@uncw.edu. *Application contact:* Candace Wilhelm, Graduate Programs Coordinator, 910-962-3903, Fax: 910-962-2184, E-mail: wilhelmc@uncw.edu. Website: https://csb.uncw.edu/MBA/index.html

University of North Florida, Coggin College of Business, MBA Program, Jacksonville, FL 32224. Offers accounting (MBA); construction management (MBA); e-commerce (MBA); economics (MBA); finance (MBA); human resource management (MBA); international business (MBA); logistics (MBA); management applications (MBA). *Accreditation:* AACSB. *Program availability:* Part-time, evening/weekend. *Entrance requirements:* For master's, GMAT or GRE, U.S. bachelor's degree from regionally-accredited university or equivalent foreign degree. Additional exam requirements/recommendations for international students: Required—TOEFL (minimum score 550 paper-based; 79 iBT). *Faculty research:* Performance measures, costing, and inventory issues in logistics and supply chain management; inter-organizational systems; international management and marketing practices; e-commerce; organizational learning and socialization processes.

University of Oklahoma, Price College of Business, Program in Business Administration, Oklahoma City, OK 73104. Offers business administration (MBA, PhD), including accounting (PhD), business administration, entrepreneurship and economic development (PhD), finance (PhD), management and international business (PhD), management of information systems (PhD), marketing/supply chain (PhD); JD/MBA; MBA/MS. *Accreditation:* AACSB. *Program availability:* Part-time, evening/weekend. *Students:* 100 full-time (27 women), 152 part-time (30 women); includes 36 minority (2 Black or African American, non-Hispanic/Latino; 4 American Indian or Alaska Native, non-Hispanic/Latino; 10 Asian, non-Hispanic/Latino; 13 Hispanic/Latino; 7 Two or more races, non-Hispanic/Latino), 32 international. Average age 31. 247 applicants, 29% accepted, 41 enrolled. In 2017, 118 master's, 9 doctorates awarded. *Degree requirements:* For doctorate, comprehensive exam, thesis/dissertation. *Entrance requirements:* For master's, GMAT or GRE, resume, 2 essays, interview; for doctorate, GMAT or GRE, resume, statement of goals, 3 letters of recommendation. Additional exam requirements/recommendations for international students: Required—TOEFL (minimum score 100 iBT) or IELTS (minimum score 7). *Application deadline:* For fall admission, 11/1 for domestic and international students; for summer admission, 11/1 for domestic and international students. Applications are processed on a rolling basis. Application fee: $50 ($100 for international students). Electronic applications accepted. *Expenses:* Contact institution. *Financial support:* In 2017–18, 107 students received support, including 6 fellowships with partial tuition reimbursements available (averaging $2,500 per year); research assistantships with full and partial tuition reimbursements available, teaching assistantships with full and partial tuition reimbursements available, career-related internships or fieldwork, scholarships/grants, health care benefits, and unspecified assistantships also available. Support available to part-time students. Financial award application deadline: 6/1; financial award applicants required to submit FAFSA. *Faculty research:* Energy finance; international accounting; organizational behavior and entrepreneurship; management information systems; supply chain. *Unit head:* Laku Chidambaram, Associate Dean for Academic Programs and Engagement, 405-325-8013. *Application contact:* Kate Hile, Associate Director of MBA Admissions, 405-325-4572, E-mail: khile@ou.edu. Website: http://www.ou.edu/price/divisions/graduate-programs/graduate.html

University of Pennsylvania, School of Arts and Sciences and Wharton School, Joseph H. Lauder Institute of Management and International Studies, Philadelphia, PA 19104. Offers international studies (MA); management and international studies (MBA); MBA/MA. Applications must be made concurrently and separately to the Wharton MBA program. *Degree requirements:* For master's, one foreign language, thesis. *Entrance requirements:* For master's, GMAT or GRE, advanced proficiency in a non-native language (Arabic, Chinese, French, German, Hindi, Japanese, Portuguese, Russian, or Spanish). Additional exam requirements/recommendations for international students: Required—TOEFL. Electronic applications accepted. *Expenses:* Contact institution. *Faculty research:* Finance, marketing, strategy, operations management, multinational management.

University of Phoenix–Bay Area Campus, School of Business, San Jose, CA 95134-1805. Offers accountancy (MS); accounting (MBA); business administration (MBA, DBA); energy management (MBA); global management (MBA); health care management (MBA); human resource management (MBA); human resources management (MM); management (MM); marketing (MBA); organizational leadership (DM); project management (MBA); public administration (MPA); technology management (MBA). *Accreditation:* ACBSP. *Program availability:* Evening/weekend, online learning. *Degree requirements:* For master's, thesis (for some programs). *Entrance requirements:* For master's, minimum undergraduate GPA of 3.0, 3 years of work experience. Additional exam requirements/recommendations for international students: Required—TOEFL (minimum score 550 paper-based; 79 iBT). Electronic applications accepted.

University of Phoenix–Central Valley Campus, School of Business, Fresno, CA 93720-1552. Offers accounting (MBA); business administration (MBA); global management (MBA); human resources management (MBA, MM); management (MM); marketing (MBA); public administration (MBA, MM). *Accreditation:* ACBSP.

University of Phoenix–Dallas Campus, School of Business, Dallas, TX 75251. Offers accounting (MBA); business administration (MBA); global management (MBA); human resources management (MBA, MM); management (MM); marketing (MBA); public administration (MBA, MM). *Accreditation:* ACBSP. *Program availability:* Evening/weekend, online learning. *Degree requirements:* For master's, thesis (for some programs). *Entrance requirements:* For master's, 3 years of work experience, minimum undergraduate GPA of 3.0. Additional exam requirements/recommendations for international students: Required—TOEFL (minimum score 550 paper-based; 79 iBT). Electronic applications accepted.

University of Phoenix–Hawaii Campus, School of Business, Honolulu, HI 96813-3800. Offers accounting (MBA); business administration (MBA); global management (MBA); human resources management (MBA, MM); management (MM); marketing (MBA); public administration (MBA, MM). *Accreditation:* ACBSP. *Program availability:* Evening/weekend. *Degree requirements:* For master's, thesis (for some programs). *Entrance requirements:* For master's, minimum undergraduate GPA of 3.0, 3 years of work experience. Additional exam requirements/recommendations for international students: Required—TOEFL (minimum score 550 paper-based; 79 iBT). Electronic applications accepted.

University of Phoenix–Houston Campus, School of Business, Houston, TX 77079-2004. Offers accounting (MBA); business administration (MBA, MM); global management (MBA); human resources management (MBA, MM); management (MM); marketing (MBA); public administration (MBA, MM). *Accreditation:* ACBSP. *Program availability:* Evening/weekend, online learning. *Degree requirements:* For master's, thesis (for some programs). *Entrance requirements:* For master's, 3 years of work experience, minimum undergraduate GPA of 3.0. Additional exam requirements/recommendations for international students: Required—TOEFL (minimum score 550 paper-based; 79 iBT). Electronic applications accepted.

University of Phoenix–Las Vegas Campus, School of Business, Las Vegas, NV 89135. Offers accounting (MBA); business administration (MBA); global management (MBA); human resources management (MBA, MM); management (MM); marketing (MBA); public administration (MM). *Accreditation:* ACBSP. *Program availability:* Evening/weekend, online learning. *Degree requirements:* For master's, thesis (for some programs). *Entrance requirements:* For master's, minimum undergraduate GPA of 3.0, 3 years of work experience. Additional exam requirements/recommendations for international students: Required—TOEFL (minimum score 550 paper-based; 79 iBT). Electronic applications accepted.

University of Phoenix–Online Campus, School of Business, Phoenix, AZ 85034-7209. Offers accountancy (MS); accounting (MBA, Certificate); business administration (MBA); energy management (MBA); global management (MBA); health care management (MBA); human resource management (MBA, Certificate); human resources management (MM); management (MM); marketing (MBA, Certificate); project management (MBA, Certificate); public administration (MBA, MM); technology management (MBA). *Program availability:* Evening/weekend, online learning. *Entrance requirements:* Additional exam requirements/recommendations for international students: Required—TOEFL, TOEIC (Test of English as an International Communication), Berlitz Online English Proficiency Exam, PTE, or IELTS. Electronic applications accepted. *Expenses:* Contact institution.

University of Phoenix–Phoenix Campus, School of Business, Tempe, AZ 85282-2371. Offers accounting (MBA, MS, Certificate); business administration (MBA); energy management (MBA); global management (MBA); health care management (MBA); human resource management (MBA, Certificate); management (MM); marketing (MBA); project management (MBA); technology management (MBA). *Program availability:* Evening/weekend, online learning. *Entrance requirements:* Additional exam requirements/recommendations for international students: Required—TOEFL, TOEIC (Test of English as an International Communication), Berlitz Online English Proficiency Exam, PTE, or IELTS. Electronic applications accepted. *Expenses:* Contact institution.

University of Phoenix–Sacramento Valley Campus, School of Business, Sacramento, CA 95833-4334. Offers accounting (MBA); business administration (MBA); global management (MBA); human resources management (MBA, MM); management (MM); marketing (MBA); public administration (MBA, MM). *Accreditation:* ACBSP. *Program availability:* Evening/weekend. *Degree requirements:* For master's, thesis (for some programs). *Entrance requirements:* For master's, minimum undergraduate GPA of 3.0, 3 years work experience. Additional exam requirements/recommendations for international students: Required—TOEFL (minimum score 550 paper-based; 79 iBT). Electronic applications accepted.

University of Phoenix–San Antonio Campus, School of Business, San Antonio, TX 78230. Offers accounting (MBA); business administration (MBA); e-business (MBA); global management (MBA); human resources management (MBA, MM); management (MM); marketing (MBA); public administration (MBA, MM). *Accreditation:* ACBSP.

University of Phoenix–San Diego Campus, School of Business, San Diego, CA 92123. Offers accounting (MBA); business administration (MBA); global management (MBA); human resources management (MBA, MM); management (MM); marketing (MBA); public administration (MBA, MM). *Accreditation:* ACBSP. *Program availability:* Evening/weekend. *Degree requirements:* For master's, thesis (for some programs). *Entrance requirements:* For master's, 3 years of work experience, minimum undergraduate GPA of 3.0. Additional exam requirements/recommendations for international students: Required—TOEFL (minimum score 550 paper-based; 79 iBT). Electronic applications accepted.

University of Pittsburgh, Katz Graduate School of Business, Augsburg Executive Fellows Program, Pittsburgh, PA 15260. Offers Certificate. Students nominated by Augsburg where they earn an MBA. *Faculty:* 91 full-time (30 women), 14 part-time/adjunct (4 women). *Students:* 15 full-time (3 women), all international. Average age 32. 15 applicants, 100% accepted, 15 enrolled. *Entrance requirements:* Additional exam requirements/recommendations for international students: Required—TOEFL (minimum score 100 iBT) or IELTS (minimum score 7.0). *Application deadline:* For fall admission, 2/1 priority date for international students. Application fee: $50. Electronic applications accepted. *Expenses:* Contact institution. *Financial support:* Applicants required to submit FAFSA. *Faculty research:* Accounting systems/financial reporting, corporate finance, shopper marketing/consumer behavior, management information systems, organizational behavior and entrepreneurship. *Total annual research expenditures:* $475,077. *Unit head:* Dr. Arjang A. Assad, Dean, 412-648-1556, Fax: 412-648-1552, E-mail: aassad@katz.pitt.edu. *Application contact:* Thomas Keller, Director of MBA Admissions, 412-648-1700, Fax: 412-648-1659, E-mail: mba@katz.pitt.edu.

University of Pittsburgh, Katz Graduate School of Business, MBA/Master of International Business Dual Degree Program, Pittsburgh, PA 15260. Offers MBA/MIB. *Program availability:* Part-time, evening/weekend. *Faculty:* 91 full-time (30 women), 14 part-time/adjunct (4 women). *Students:* 2 part-time (both women); includes 1 minority (Black or African American, non-Hispanic/Latino). Average age 32. 3 applicants. *Entrance requirements:* Additional exam requirements/recommendations for international students: Required—TOEFL (minimum score 100 iBT) or IELTS (minimum score 7.0). *Application deadline:* For fall admission, 4/1 priority date for domestic students, 2/1 priority date for international students. Application fee: $50. Electronic applications accepted. *Financial support:* Scholarships/grants available. Financial award application deadline: 6/1; financial award applicants required to submit FAFSA. *Faculty research:* Accounting systems/financial reporting, corporate finance, shopper marketing/consumer behavior, management information systems, organizational behavior and entrepreneurship. *Total annual research expenditures:* $475,077. *Unit head:* Dr. Arjang A. Assad, Dean, 412-648-1556, Fax: 412-648-1552, E-mail: aassad@katz.pitt.edu. *Application contact:* Thomas Keller, Director of MBA Admissions, 412-648-1700, Fax: 412-648-1659, E-mail: mba@katz.pitt.edu.
Website: https://www.katz.business.pitt.edu/mba/joint-and-dual/ib#section-1
See Display on page 158 and Close-Up on page 187.

University of Puerto Rico–Río Piedras, College of Business Administration, San Juan, PR 00931-3300. Offers accounting (MBA); finance (MBA, PhD); general business (MBA); human resources management (MBA); international trade and business (MBA, PhD); marketing (MBA); operations management (MBA); quantitative methods (MBA). *Accreditation:* AACSB. *Program availability:* Part-time. *Degree requirements:* For master's, comprehensive exam, thesis or alternative, research project. *Entrance requirements:* For master's, GMAT or PAEG, minimum GPA of 3.0, letter of recommendation; for doctorate, GMAT, PAEG, minimum GPA of 3.0, master degree. *Faculty research:* Management.

University of Regina, Faculty of Graduate Studies and Research, Kenneth Levene Graduate School of Business, Program in Business Administration, Regina, SK S4S 0A2, Canada. Offers business foundations (PGD); engineering management (MBA);

executive business administration (EMBA); international business (MBA); leadership (M Admin); organizational leadership (Master's Certificate); project management (Master's Certificate); public safety management (MBA). *Program availability:* Part-time, evening/weekend. *Faculty:* 43 full-time (15 women), 6 part-time/adjunct (0 women). *Students:* 35 full-time (15 women), 18 part-time (9 women). 172 applicants, 26% accepted. In 2017, 24 master's, 2 other advanced degrees awarded. *Degree requirements:* For master's, project (for some programs). *Entrance requirements:* For master's, GMAT, three years of relevant work experience, four-year undergraduate degree; for other advanced degree, GMAT (for PGD), four-year undergraduate degree and two years of relevant work experience (for Master's Certificate); three years' work experience (for PGD). Additional exam requirements/recommendations for international students: Required—TOEFL (minimum score 580 paper-based; 80 iBT), IELTS (minimum score 6.5), PTE (minimum score 59). *Application deadline:* Applications are processed on a rolling basis. Application fee: $100. Electronic applications accepted. *Expenses:* CAD$20,150 per year. *Financial support:* In 2017–18, fellowships (averaging $6,000 per year), teaching assistantships (averaging $2,562 per year) were awarded; research assistantships, career-related internships or fieldwork, and scholarships/grants also available. Financial award application deadline: 6/15. *Faculty research:* Business policy and strategy, production and operations management, human behavior in organizations, financial management, social issues in business. *Unit head:* Dr. David Senkow, Dean, 306-585-4719, Fax: 306-585-5361, E-mail: david.senkow@uregina.ca. *Application contact:* Ronald Camp, Graduate Programs, 306-337-2387, Fax: 306-585-5361, E-mail: ronald.camp@uregina.ca.
Website: http://www.uregina.ca/business/levene/

University of St. Thomas, Cameron School of Business, Houston, TX 77006-4696. Offers MBA, MCTM, MIB, MSA, MSF. *Program availability:* Part-time, evening/weekend. *Faculty:* 26 full-time (10 women), 7 part-time/adjunct (1 woman). *Students:* 136 full-time (73 women), 200 part-time (113 women); includes 155 minority (41 Black or African American, non-Hispanic/Latino; 1 American Indian or Alaska Native, non-Hispanic/Latino; 24 Asian, non-Hispanic/Latino; 81 Hispanic/Latino; 8 Two or more races, non-Hispanic/Latino; 99 international. Average age 31. 121 applicants, 97% accepted, 70 enrolled. In 2017, 186 master's awarded. *Degree requirements:* For master's, capstone (for some programs), additional course requirements for those sitting for state accountancy exam. *Entrance requirements:* For master's, minimum GPA of 2.5, 3 letters of recommendation. Additional exam requirements/recommendations for international students: Required—TOEFL (minimum score 550 paper-based; 79 iBT), IELTS (minimum score 6.5), PTE (minimum score 53). *Application deadline:* For fall admission, 7/15 for domestic and international students; for winter admission, 7/15 for domestic and international students; for spring admission, 11/15 for domestic students, 10/15 for international students. Applications are processed on a rolling basis. Application fee: $35. Electronic applications accepted. *Expenses:* Tuition: Full-time $20,934; part-time $1163 per credit hour. *Required fees:* $250; $210 per semester. *Financial support:* In 2017–18, 22 students received support, including research assistantships with partial tuition reimbursements available (averaging $3,000 per year); Federal Work-Study, scholarships/grants, unspecified assistantships, and state work-study, institutional employment also available. Support available to part-time students. Financial award application deadline: 4/15; financial award applicants required to submit FAFSA. *Unit head:* Dr. Beena George, Dean, 713-525-2100, Fax: 713-525-2110, E-mail: cameron@stthom.edu. *Application contact:* 713-525-2100, Fax: 713-525-2110, E-mail: cameron@stthom.edu.
Website: http://www.stthom.edu/Academics/Cameron_School_of_Business/Index.aqf

University of San Diego, School of Business, Program in Global Leadership, San Diego, CA 92110-2492. Offers MS. *Program availability:* Online learning. *Students:* 4 full-time (2 women), 35 part-time (11 women); includes 16 minority (4 Black or African American, non-Hispanic/Latino; 2 Asian, non-Hispanic/Latino; 5 Hispanic/Latino; 2 Native Hawaiian or other Pacific Islander, non-Hispanic/Latino; 3 Two or more races, non-Hispanic/Latino), 1 international. Average age 35. In 2017, 30 master's awarded. *Entrance requirements:* Additional exam requirements/recommendations for international students: Required—TOEFL (minimum score 580 paper-based; 92 iBT), TWE. *Application deadline:* For fall admission, 11/1 priority date for domestic students. Applications are processed on a rolling basis. Application fee: $80. Electronic applications accepted. *Financial support:* In 2017–18, 24 students received support. Career-related internships or fieldwork and scholarships/grants available. Financial award application deadline: 4/1; financial award applicants required to submit FAFSA. *Unit head:* E-mail: msgl@sandiego.edu. *Application contact:* Monica Mahon, Associate Director of Graduate Admissions, 619-260-4524, Fax: 619-260-4158, E-mail: grads@sandiego.edu.
Website: http://www.sandiego.edu/business/graduate/ms-global-leadership/

University of San Francisco, School of Law, Master of Law Programs, San Francisco, CA 94117-1080. Offers intellectual property and technology law (LL M); international transactions and comparative law (LL M). *Program availability:* Part-time. *Entrance requirements:* For master's, law degree from U.S. or foreign school (intellectual property and technology law); law degree from foreign school (international transactions and comparative law). Electronic applications accepted.

University of San Francisco, School of Management, Master in Global Entrepreneurial Management Program, San Francisco, CA 94117. Offers MGEM. Program offered jointly with IQS in Barcelona, Spain and Fu Jen Catholic University in Taipei, Taiwan. *Entrance requirements:* For master's, resume, transcripts from each college or university attended, two letters of recommendation, personal statement. Additional exam requirements/recommendations for international students: Required—TOEFL (minimum score 550 paper-based, 79 iBT), IELTS (minimum score 6), or PTE (minimum score 53). Electronic applications accepted. *Expenses:* Contact institution.

University of Saskatchewan, College of Graduate Studies and Research, Edwards School of Business, Program in Business Administration, Saskatoon, SK S7N 5A2, Canada. Offers agribusiness management (MBA); biotechnology management (MBA); health services management (MBA); indigenous management (MBA); international business management (MBA).

University of Saskatchewan, College of Graduate Studies and Research, School of Public Policy, Saskatoon, SK S7N 5A2, Canada. Offers MIT, MPA, MPP, PhD.

The University of Scranton, Kania School of Management, Program in Business Administration, Scranton, PA 18510. Offers accounting (MBA); finance (MBA); general business administration (MBA); health care management (MBA); international business (MBA); management information systems (MBA); marketing (MBA); operations management (MBA). *Accreditation:* AACSB. *Program availability:* Part-time, evening/weekend, 100% online. *Entrance requirements:* For master's, GMAT (for MBA). *Faculty research:* Financial markets, strategic impact of total quality management, internal accounting controls, consumer preference, information systems and the Internet.

University of South Carolina, The Graduate School, Darla Moore School of Business, International Business Administration Program, Columbia, SC 29208. Offers IMBA. *Degree requirements:* For master's, one foreign language, field consulting project/internship. *Entrance requirements:* For master's, GMAT or GRE, minimum two years of work experience. Additional exam requirements/recommendations for international students: Required—TOEFL (minimum score 100 iBT); Recommended—IELTS. Electronic applications accepted. *Expenses:* Contact institution.

International Business

The University of Tampa, Sykes College of Business, Tampa, FL 33606-1490. Offers accounting (MS); business analytics (MBA); cybersecurity (MBA, MS); entrepreneurship (MBA, MS); finance (MBA, MS); information systems management (MBA); innovation management (MBA); international business (MBA); marketing (MBA, MS); nonprofit management (MBA, Certificate). *Accreditation:* AACSB. *Program availability:* Part-time, evening/weekend. *Faculty:* 38 full-time (14 women), 6 part-time/adjunct (1 woman). *Students:* 229 full-time (1 woman), 115 part-time (51 women); includes 51 minority (26 Black or African American, non-Hispanic/Latino; 11 Asian, non-Hispanic/Latino; 1 Native Hawaiian or other Pacific Islander, non-Hispanic/Latino; 13 Two or more races, non-Hispanic/Latino), 182 international. Average age 28. 1,305 applicants, 39% accepted, 192 enrolled. In 2017, 266 master's awarded. *Degree requirements:* For master's, capstone. *Entrance requirements:* For master's, GMAT or GRE, official transcripts from all colleges and/or universities previously attended, resume, personal statement, letters of recommendation. Additional exam requirements/recommendations for international students: Required—TOEFL (minimum score 577 paper-based; 90 iBT), IELTS (minimum score 7.5). *Application deadline:* Applications are processed on a rolling basis. Application fee: $40. Electronic applications accepted. *Expenses:* Contact institution. *Financial support:* In 2017–18, 116 students received support. Career-related internships or fieldwork, scholarships/grants, and unspecified assistantships available. Financial award applicants required to submit FAFSA. *Faculty research:* Job market signaling, on-line shopping behaviors and social media, the Tampa Bay economy, digital literacy, entrepreneurship in small businesses. *Unit head:* Dr. Natasha F. Veltri, Associate Dean, 813-253-6289, E-mail: nveltri@ut.edu. *Application contact:* Chanelle Cox, Staff Assistant, Admissions for Graduate and Continuing Studies, 813-253-6249, E-mail: ccox@ut.edu.
Website: http://www.ut.edu/business/

The University of Texas at Dallas, Naveen Jindal School of Management, Program in Organizations, Strategy and International Management, Richardson, TX 75080. Offers business administration (MBA); executive business administration (EMBA); global leadership (EMBA); healthcare leadership and management (MS); healthcare management (EMBA); innovation and entrepreneurship (MS); international management studies (MS, PhD); management science (MS, PhD); project management (EMBA); systems engineering and management (MS); MS/MBA. *Program availability:* Part-time, evening/weekend. *Faculty:* 18 full-time (6 women), 17 part-time/adjunct (2 women). *Students:* 608 full-time (232 women), 711 part-time (326 women); includes 446 minority (93 Black or African American, non-Hispanic/Latino; 3 American Indian or Alaska Native, non-Hispanic/Latino; 212 Asian, non-Hispanic/Latino; 107 Hispanic/Latino; 31 Two or more races, non-Hispanic/Latino), 339 international. Average age 32. 1,665 applicants, 36% accepted, 398 enrolled. In 2017, 473 master's, 14 doctorates awarded. *Degree requirements:* For doctorate, thesis/dissertation. *Entrance requirements:* For master's and doctorate, GMAT. Additional exam requirements/recommendations for international students: Required—TOEFL (minimum score 550 paper-based). *Application deadline:* For fall admission, 7/15 for domestic students, 5/1 priority date for international students; for spring admission, 11/15 for domestic students, 9/1 priority date for international students. Applications are processed on a rolling basis. Application fee: $50 ($100 for international students). Electronic applications accepted. *Expenses:* Tuition, state resident: full-time $12,916; part-time $718 per credit hour. Tuition, nonresident: full-time $25,252; part-time $1403 per credit hour. *Financial support:* In 2017–18, 369 students received support, including 22 research assistantships with partial tuition reimbursements available (averaging $36,554 per year), 88 teaching assistantships with partial tuition reimbursements available (averaging $25,176 per year); Federal Work-Study, institutionally sponsored loans, scholarships/grants, and unspecified assistantships also available. Support available to part-time students. Financial award application deadline: 4/30; financial award applicants required to submit FAFSA. *Faculty research:* International accounting, international trade and finance, economic development, international economics. *Unit head:* Dr. Erik W.K. Tsang, Area Coordinator, 972-883-4386, Fax: 972-883-5977, E-mail: ewktsang@utdallas.edu.
Website: http://jindal.utdallas.edu/osim/

The University of Texas at El Paso, Graduate School, College of Business Administration, Programs in Business Administration, El Paso, TX 79968-0001. Offers business administration (MBA, Certificate); international business (PhD). *Accreditation:* AACSB. *Program availability:* Part-time, evening/weekend, online learning. *Degree requirements:* For master's, comprehensive exam. *Entrance requirements:* For master's and doctorate, GMAT. Additional exam requirements/recommendations for international students: Required—TOEFL. Electronic applications accepted. *Faculty research:* Cross-border modeling, human resources, and outsourcing and manufacturing; global information technology transfer; international investments and risk management.

University of the West, Department of Business Administration, Rosemead, CA 91770. Offers business administration (EMBA); computer information systems (MBA); finance (MBA); international business (MBA); nonprofit organization management (MBA). *Program availability:* Part-time, evening/weekend. *Entrance requirements:* Additional exam requirements/recommendations for international students: Required—TOEFL.

The University of Toledo, College of Graduate Studies, College of Business and Innovation, Department of Marketing and International Business, Toledo, OH 43606-3390. Offers MBA. *Program availability:* Part-time, evening/weekend. *Entrance requirements:* For master's, GMAT, GRE, or LSAT, minimum GPA of 2.7 for all prior academic work, three letters of recommendation, statement of purpose, transcripts from all prior institutions attended. Additional exam requirements/recommendations for international students: Required—TOEFL (minimum score 550 paper-based; 80 iBT). Electronic applications accepted.

University of Virginia, McIntire School of Commerce, MS Program in Global Commerce, Charlottesville, VA 22903. Offers global commerce (MS); global strategic management (MS); international management (Certificate). *Entrance requirements:* For master's, GMAT. Additional exam requirements/recommendations for international students: Required—TOEFL (minimum score 600 paper-based; 100 iBT), IELTS (minimum score 6.5).

University of Washington, Graduate School, Interdisciplinary Program in Global Trade, Transportation and Logistics Studies, Seattle, WA 98195. Offers Certificate.

University of Washington, Graduate School, Michael G. Foster School of Business, Seattle, WA 98195-3200. Offers auditing and assurance (MP Acc); business administration (MBA, PhD); entrepreneurship (MS); executive business administration (MBA); global executive business administration (MBA); information systems (MSIS); supply chain management (MSSCM); taxation (MP Acc); technology management (MBA); JD/MBA; MBA/MAIS; MBA/MHA. *Accreditation:* AACSB. *Program availability:* Part-time, evening/weekend, blended/hybrid learning. *Faculty:* 109 full-time (35 women), 54 part-time/adjunct (32 women). *Students:* 469 full-time (173 women), 638 part-time (216 women); includes 314 minority (15 Black or African American, non-Hispanic/Latino; 6 American Indian or Alaska Native, non-Hispanic/Latino; 246 Asian, non-Hispanic/Latino; 28 Hispanic/Latino; 5 Native Hawaiian or other Pacific Islander, non-Hispanic/Latino; 14 Two or more races, non-Hispanic/Latino), 125 international. Average age 32. 1,809 applicants, 84% accepted, 1107 enrolled. In 2017, 543 master's, 10 doctorates awarded. Terminal master's awarded for partial completion of doctoral program. *Degree*

requirements: For doctorate, comprehensive exam, thesis/dissertation. *Entrance requirements:* For master's and doctorate, GMAT, GRE. Additional exam requirements/recommendations for international students: Required—TOEFL (minimum score 600 paper-based; 100 iBT). *Application deadline:* For fall admission, 3/15 for domestic students, 1/15 for international students. Application fee: $85. Electronic applications accepted. *Expenses:* Contact institution. *Financial support:* Fellowships with partial tuition reimbursements, research assistantships with partial tuition reimbursements, teaching assistantships with partial tuition reimbursements, Federal Work-Study, institutionally sponsored loans, and scholarships/grants available. Financial award application deadline: 2/28; financial award applicants required to submit FAFSA. *Faculty research:* Finance, consumer behavior, marketing analytics, technology management, supply chain. *Unit head:* Dr. James Jiambalvo, Dean, 206-543-4750, E-mail: jjiambal@uw.edu. *Application contact:* Erin Town, Director of Admissions, 206-543-4661, Fax: 206-616-7351, E-mail: mba@uw.edu.
Website: http://www.foster.washington.edu/

The University of Western Ontario, Richard Ivey School of Business, London, ON N6A 3K7, Canada. Offers business (EMBA, PhD); corporate strategy and leadership elective (MBA); entrepreneurship elective (MBA); finance elective (MBA); health sector stream (MBA); international management elective (MBA); marketing elective (MBA); JD/MBA. *Degree requirements:* For master's, thesis (for some programs); for doctorate, thesis/dissertation. *Entrance requirements:* For master's, GMAT, 2 years of full-time work experience, interview. Additional exam requirements/recommendations for international students: Required—TOEFL (minimum score 100 iBT) or IELTS (minimum score 6). Electronic applications accepted. *Faculty research:* Strategy, organizational behavior, international business, finance, operations management.

University of Wisconsin–Oshkosh, Graduate Studies, College of Business, Program in Global Business Administration, Oshkosh, WI 54901. Offers GMBA. *Degree requirements:* For master's, integrative seminar, study abroad. *Entrance requirements:* For master's, GMAT, GRE, letters of recommendation. Additional exam requirements/recommendations for international students: Required—TOEFL (minimum score 79 iBT).

Vancouver Island University, Master of Business Administration Program, Nanaimo, BC V9R 5S5, Canada. Offers international business (MBA), including finance, marketing. Program offered jointly with University of Hertfordshire. *Accreditation:* ACBSP. *Program availability:* Part-time. *Degree requirements:* For master's, thesis. *Entrance requirements:* Additional exam requirements/recommendations for international students: Required—TOEFL (minimum score 88 iBT), IELTS (minimum score 6.5). Electronic applications accepted. *Expenses:* Contact institution. *Faculty research:* Tourism development, entrepreneurship, organizational development, strategic planning, international business strategy, intercultural team work.

Villanova University, Villanova School of Business, MBA - The Fast Track Program, Villanova, PA 19085. Offers finance (MBA); healthcare (MBA); international business (MBA); strategic management (MBA). *Accreditation:* AACSB. *Program availability:* Part-time, evening/weekend. *Faculty:* 68 full-time (22 women), 65 part-time/adjunct (11 women). *Students:* 128 part-time (55 women); includes 11 minority (3 Black or African American, non-Hispanic/Latino; 4 Asian, non-Hispanic/Latino; 4 Hispanic/Latino), 4 international. Average age 30. 79 applicants, 96% accepted, 64 enrolled. In 2017, 58 master's awarded. *Degree requirements:* For master's, minimum GPA of 3.0. *Entrance requirements:* For master's, GMAT or GRE, work experience, 2 letters of recommendation, 2 essays, resume, official transcripts, interview. Additional exam requirements/recommendations for international students: Required—TOEFL (minimum score 550 paper-based; 100 iBT). *Application deadline:* For fall admission, 6/30 for domestic and international students. Applications are processed on a rolling basis. Application fee: $65. Electronic applications accepted. *Expenses:* $56,016 per year tuition, $1,167 per credit; $50 semester fee. *Financial support:* Scholarships/grants available. Financial award application deadline: 6/30; financial award applicants required to submit FAFSA. *Faculty research:* Business analytics; creativity, innovation and entrepreneurship; global leadership; real estate; church management; business ethics; marketing and consumer insights. *Unit head:* Dr. Joyce Russell, Dean of Villanova School of Business, 610-519-5424, Fax: 610-519-6273, E-mail: joyce.russell@villanova.edu. *Application contact:* Kimberly Kane, Manager of Admissions, 610-519-3701, Fax: 610-519-6273, E-mail: kimberly.kane@villanova.edu.
Website: http://www1.villanova.edu/villanova/business/graduate/mba.html

Villanova University, Villanova School of Business, MBA - The Flex Track Program, Villanova, PA 19085. Offers healthcare (MBA); international business (MBA); marketing (MBA); real estate (MBA); strategic management (MBA); JD/MBA. *Accreditation:* AACSB. *Program availability:* Part-time, evening/weekend, online learning. *Faculty:* 68 full-time (22 women), 65 part-time/adjunct (11 women). *Students:* 13 full-time (4 women), 410 part-time (137 women); includes 105 minority (28 Black or African American, non-Hispanic/Latino; 1 American Indian or Alaska Native, non-Hispanic/Latino; 41 Asian, non-Hispanic/Latino; 29 Hispanic/Latino; 6 Two or more races, non-Hispanic/Latino), 13 international. Average age 31. 94 applicants, 94% accepted, 79 enrolled. In 2017, 201 master's awarded. *Degree requirements:* For master's, minimum GPA of 3.0. *Entrance requirements:* For master's, GMAT or GRE, work experience, 2 letters of recommendation, 2 essays, resume, official transcript. Additional exam requirements/recommendations for international students: Required—TOEFL (minimum score 550 paper-based; 100 iBT). *Application deadline:* For fall admission, 6/30 for domestic and international students; for spring admission, 11/15 for domestic and international students; for summer admission, 3/31 for domestic and international students. Applications are processed on a rolling basis. Application fee: $65. Electronic applications accepted. *Expenses:* $50,016 per year tuition, $1,167 per credit; $50 semester fee. *Financial support:* In 2017–18, 19 research assistantships with full tuition reimbursements (averaging $16,245 per year) were awarded; scholarships/grants also available. Financial award application deadline: 6/30; financial award applicants required to submit FAFSA. *Faculty research:* Business analytics; creativity, innovation and entrepreneurship; global leadership; real estate; church management; business ethics. *Unit head:* Dr. Joyce Russell, Dean of Villanova School of Business, 610-519-5424, Fax: 610-519-6273, E-mail: joyce.russell@villanova.edu. *Application contact:* Claire Bruno, Director of Recruitment and Enrollment Management, 610-519-4336, Fax: 610-519-6273, E-mail: claire.bruno@villanova.edu.
Website: http://www1.villanova.edu/villanova/business/graduate/mba.html

Virginia International University, School of Business, Fairfax, VA 22030. Offers accounting (MBA, MS); entrepreneurship (MBA); executive management (Graduate Certificate); global logistics (MBA); health care management (MBA); hospitality and tourism management (MBA); human resources management (MBA); international business management (MBA); international finance (MBA); marketing management (MBA); mass media and public relations (MBA); project management (MBA, MS). *Program availability:* Part-time, online learning. *Entrance requirements:* For master's and Graduate Certificate, bachelor's degree. Additional exam requirements/recommendations for international students: Required—TOEFL (minimum score 550 paper-based; 80 iBT), IELTS (minimum score 6). Electronic applications accepted.

Viterbo University, Master of Business Administration Program, La Crosse, WI 54601-4797. Offers general business administration (MBA); health care management (MBA);

international business (MBA); leadership (MBA); project management (MBA). *Accreditation:* ACBSP. *Program availability:* Part-time, evening/weekend. *Degree requirements:* For master's, 34 semester credits. *Entrance requirements:* For master's, bachelor's degree, transcripts, minimum undergraduate cumulative GPA of 3.0, 2 letters of reference, 3-5 page essay. Additional exam requirements/recommendations for international students: Recommended—TOEFL (minimum score 550 paper-based). Electronic applications accepted. *Expenses:* Contact institution.

Walden University, Graduate Programs, School of Management, Minneapolis, MN 55401. Offers accounting (MBA, MS, DBA), including accounting for the professional (MS), accounting with CPA emphasis (MS), self-designed (MS); advanced project management (Graduate Certificate); applied project management (Graduate Certificate); auditing (Graduate Certificate); bridge to business administration (Post-Doctoral Certificate); bridge to management (Post-Doctoral Certificate); business management (Graduate Certificate); communication (MBA); corporate finance (MBA); digital marketing (Graduate Certificate); entrepreneurship (DBA); entrepreneurship and small business (MBA); finance (MS, DBA), including finance for the professional (MS), finance with CFA/investment (MS), finance with CPA emphasis (MS); global supply chain management (DBA); healthcare management (MBA, DBA); human resource management (MBA, MS, Graduate Certificate), including functional human resource management (MS), general program (MS), integrating functional and strategic human resource management (MS), organizational strategy (MS); human resources management (DBA); information systems management (DBA); international business (MBA, DBA); leadership (MBA, MS, DBA, Graduate Certificate), including general program (MS), human resource leadership (MS), leader development (MS), self-designed (MS); management (MS, PhD), including communications (MS), finance (PhD), general program (MS), healthcare management (MS), human resource management (MS), human resources management (PhD), information systems management (PhD), international business (MS), leadership (MS), leadership and organizational change (PhD), marketing (MS), project management (MS), strategy and operations (MS); managerial accounting (Graduate Certificate); marketing (MBA, MS, DBA); project management (MBA, MS, DBA); self-designed (MBA, DBA); social impact management (DBA); technology entrepreneurship (DBA). *Accreditation:* ACBSP. *Program availability:* Part-time, evening/weekend, online only, 100% online. *Degree requirements:* For master's, thesis (for some programs), residency (for EMBA); for doctorate, thesis/dissertation (for some programs), residency. *Entrance requirements:* For master's, bachelor's degree or higher; minimum GPA of 2.5; official transcripts; goal statement (for some programs); access to computer and Internet; for doctorate, master's degree or higher; three years of related professional or academic experience (preferred); minimum GPA of 3.0; goal statement and current resume (for select programs); official transcripts; access to computer and Internet; for other advanced degree, relevant work experience; access to computer and Internet. Additional exam requirements/recommendations for international students: Required—TOEFL (minimum score 550 paper-based, 79 iBT), IELTS (minimum score 6.5), Michigan English Language Assessment Battery (minimum score 82), or PTE (minimum score 53). Electronic applications accepted.

Walsh College of Accountancy and Business Administration, Graduate Programs, Program in Management, Troy, MI 48083. Offers human resources management (MS); international business (MS); strategic management (MS). *Program availability:* Part-time, evening/weekend, 100% online, blended/hybrid learning. *Faculty:* 10 full-time (6 women), 13 part-time/adjunct (6 women). *Students:* 49 (37 women); includes 18 minority (14 Black or African American, non-Hispanic/Latino; 2 Asian, non-Hispanic/Latino; 2 Hispanic/Latino), 2 international. Average age 33. 17 applicants, 76% accepted, 6 enrolled. In 2017, 15 master's awarded. *Entrance requirements:* For master's, minimum overall cumulative GPA of 2.75 from all colleges previously attended. Additional exam requirements/recommendations for international students: Required—TOEFL (minimum score 550 paper-based, 79 iBT), IELTS (6.5), Michigan English Language Assessment Battery, or MTELP (80). *Application deadline:* Applications are processed on a rolling basis. Application fee: $35. Electronic applications accepted. *Expenses:* $770 per semester credit hour plus $125 registration fee per semester. *Financial support:* In 2017–18, 1 student received support. Career-related internships or fieldwork and scholarships/grants available. Financial award application deadline: 6/30; financial award applicants required to submit FAFSA. *Faculty research:* Strategy practice and process, management learning and decision-making, human capital development, global leadership and citizenship, use of systems and complexity theory and management practice. *Unit head:* Dr. Ann Saurbier, Chair, Management, 248-823-1635, Fax: 248-689-0920, E-mail: asaurbie@walshcollege.edu. *Application contact:* Heather Rigby, Director, Admissions and Academic Advising, 248-823-1610, Fax: 248-823-1611, E-mail: hrigby@walshcollege.edu.

Warner University, School of Business, Lake Wales, FL 33859. Offers accounting (MBA); business administration (MBA); human resource management (MBA); international business (MBA); management (MSMC). *Program availability:* Part-time, evening/weekend, online learning. *Degree requirements:* For master's, comprehensive exam, thesis. *Entrance requirements:* For master's, minimum GPA of 3.0, 2 letters of recommendation. Additional exam requirements/recommendations for international students: Required—TOEFL. Electronic applications accepted.

Wayland Baptist University, Graduate Programs, Programs in Business Administration/Management, Plainview, TX 79072-6998. Offers accounting (MBA); general business (MBA); health care administration (MAM, MBA); human resource management (MAM, MBA); international management (MBA); management (MBA, D Mgt); management information systems (MBA); organization management (MAM); project management (MBA). *Program availability:* Part-time, evening/weekend, online learning. *Faculty:* 30 full-time (5 women), 38 part-time/adjunct (9 women). *Students:* 42 full-time (20 women), 538 part-time (253 women); includes 311 minority (98 Black or African American, non-Hispanic/Latino; 4 American Indian or Alaska Native, non-Hispanic/Latino; 16 Asian, non-Hispanic/Latino; 153 Hispanic/Latino; 11 Native Hawaiian or other Pacific Islander, non-Hispanic/Latino; 29 Two or more races, non-Hispanic/Latino), 6 international. Average age 40. 100 applicants, 96% accepted, 60 enrolled. In 2017, 216 master's awarded. *Degree requirements:* For master's, capstone course. *Entrance requirements:* For master's, GMAT, GRE or MAT. Additional exam

requirements/recommendations for international students: Required—TOEFL (minimum score 500 paper-based; 61 iBT). *Application deadline:* Applications are processed on a rolling basis. Application fee: $50. Electronic applications accepted. *Expenses: Tuition:* Full-time $11,250; part-time $625 per credit hour. *Required fees:* $1200. *Financial support:* Federal Work-Study, institutionally sponsored loans, and scholarships/grants available. Support available to part-time students. Financial award application deadline: 5/1; financial award applicants required to submit FAFSA. *Unit head:* Dr. Kelly Warren, Chairman, 806-291-1020, Fax: 806-291-1957, E-mail: warrenk@wbu.edu. *Application contact:* Amanda Stanton, Graduate Studies, 806-291-3423, Fax: 806-291-1950, E-mail: stanton@wbu.edu.

Webber International University, Graduate School of Business, Babson Park, FL 33827-0096. Offers accounting (MBA); business (MBA); criminal justice management (MBA); international business (MBA); sport business management (MBA). *Program availability:* Part-time, evening/weekend, 100% online. *Faculty:* 10 full-time (4 women), 1 part-time/adjunct (0 women). *Students:* 50 full-time (29 women), 6 part-time (2 women); includes 19 minority (12 Black or African American, non-Hispanic/Latino; 6 Hispanic/Latino; 1 Two or more races, non-Hispanic/Latino), 6 international. Average age 24. 64 applicants, 61% accepted, 32 enrolled. In 2017, 29 master's awarded. *Degree requirements:* For master's, class trip (for international business); practicum (for criminal justice management). *Entrance requirements:* For master's, three recommendation letters, résumé, essay, official transcripts from all colleges and universities attended. Additional exam requirements/recommendations for international students: Recommended—TOEFL (minimum score 500 paper-based; 61 iBT), IELTS (minimum score 6). *Application deadline:* For fall admission, 7/1 for international students. Applications are processed on a rolling basis. Application fee: $50 ($75 for international students). Electronic applications accepted. *Expenses: Tuition:* Part-time $688 per hour. *Financial support:* In 2017–18, 11 students received support. Scholarships/grants and unspecified assistantships available. Financial award application deadline: 8/1; financial award applicants required to submit FAFSA. *Unit head:* Dr. Nikos Orphanoudakis, Dean, 863-638-2910, Fax: 863-638-1591, E-mail: orphanoudakisn@webber.edu. *Application contact:* Lacy Edwards, Admissions Counselor and MBA Coordinator, 863-638-2910, Fax: 863-638-1591, E-mail: admissions@webber.edu.

Webster University, George Herbert Walker School of Business and Technology, Department of Business, St. Louis, MO 63119-3194. Offers business and organizational security management (MBA); decision support systems (MBA); environmental management (MBA); finance (MBA, MS); forensic accounting (MS); gerontology (MBA); human resources development (MBA); human resources management (MBA); information technology management (MBA); international business (MA, MBA); international relations (MBA); management and leadership (MBA); marketing (MBA); media communications (MBA); procurement and acquisitions management (MBA); Web services (MBA). *Accreditation:* ACBSP. *Program availability:* Part-time, evening/weekend, online learning. *Degree requirements:* For master's, comprehensive exam (for some programs), thesis (for some programs). *Entrance requirements:* Additional exam requirements/recommendations for international students: Required—TOEFL.

Wilkes University, College of Graduate and Professional Studies, Jay S. Sidhu School of Business and Leadership, Wilkes-Barre, PA 18766-0002. Offers accounting (MBA); entrepreneurship (MBA); finance (MBA); health care administration (MBA); human resource management (MBA); international business (MBA); operations management (MBA); organizational leadership and development (MBA). *Accreditation:* ACBSP. *Program availability:* Part-time, evening/weekend. *Students:* 37 full-time (18 women), 87 part-time (45 women); includes 17 minority (4 Black or African American, non-Hispanic/Latino; 5 Asian, non-Hispanic/Latino; 6 Hispanic/Latino; 2 Two or more races, non-Hispanic/Latino), 14 international. Average age 30. In 2017, 77 master's awarded. *Entrance requirements:* For master's, GMAT. Additional exam requirements/recommendations for international students: Required—TOEFL (minimum score 550 paper-based; 79 iBT). *Application deadline:* Applications are processed on a rolling basis. Application fee: $45 ($65 for international students). Electronic applications accepted. *Expenses:* Contact institution. *Financial support:* Unspecified assistantships available. Financial award application deadline: 3/1; financial award applicants required to submit FAFSA. *Unit head:* Dr. Abel Adekola, Dean, 570-408-4701, Fax: 570-408-7846, E-mail: abel.adekola@wilkes.edu. *Application contact:* Kristin Donati, Associate Director of Graduate Admissions, 570-408-3338, Fax: 570-408-7846, E-mail: kristin.donati@wilkes.edu. Website: http://www.wilkes.edu/academics/colleges/sidhu-school-of-business-leadership/index.aspx

Xavier University, Williams College of Business, Master of Business Administration Program, Cincinnati, OH 45207. Offers business administration (Exec MBA, MBA); business intelligence (MBA); finance (MBA); health industry (MBA); international business (MBA); marketing (MBA); values-based leadership (MBA); MBA/MHSA; MSN/MBA. *Accreditation:* AACSB. *Program availability:* Part-time, evening/weekend. *Degree requirements:* For master's, capstone course. *Entrance requirements:* For master's, GMAT or GRE, official transcript; resume. Additional exam requirements/recommendations for international students: Required—TOEFL (minimum score 550 paper-based; 79 iBT). Electronic applications accepted. Application fee is waived when completed online. *Expenses:* Contact institution.

York University, Faculty of Graduate Studies, Schulich School of Business, Toronto, ON M3J 1P3, Canada. Offers accounting (M Acc); administration (PhD); business (MBA); business analytics (MBA); finance (MF); international business (IMBA); MBA/JD; MBA/MA; MBA/MFA. *Program availability:* Part-time, evening/weekend. *Degree requirements:* For master's, advanced proficiency in a second language, work term (IMBA); for doctorate, comprehensive exam, thesis/dissertation. *Entrance requirements:* For master's, GMAT or GRE, minimum GPA of 3.0 (3.3 for MF, MBA in business analytics, and IMBA); for doctorate, GMAT or GRE, minimum GPA of 3.3. Additional exam requirements/recommendations for international students: Required—TOEFL (minimum score 600 paper-based; 100 iBT), IELTS (minimum score 7), York English Language Test (minimum score 1); PearsonVUE (minimum score 64). Electronic applications accepted. *Faculty research:* Accounting, finance, marketing, operations management and information systems, organizational studies, strategic management.

Section 12
Management Information Systems

This section contains a directory of institutions offering graduate work in management information systems. Additional information about programs listed in the directory but not augmented by an in-depth entry may be obtained by writing directly to the dean of a graduate school or chair of a department at the address given in the directory.

For programs offering related work, see also in this book *Business Administration and Management.* In another guide in this series:

Graduate Programs in Engineering & Applied Sciences

See *Computer Science and Information Technology* and *Management of Engineering and Technology*

CONTENTS

Program Directory

Management Information Systems

Adelphi University, Robert B. Willumstad School of Business, MBA Program, Garden City, NY 11530-0701. Offers accounting (MBA); finance (MBA); health services administration (MBA); human resource management (MBA); management (MBA); management information systems (MBA); marketing (MBA); sport management (MBA). *Accreditation:* AACSB. *Program availability:* Part-time, evening/weekend. *Students:* 257 full-time (110 women), 78 part-time (38 women); includes 56 minority (18 Black or African American, non-Hispanic/Latino; 16 Asian, non-Hispanic/Latino; 19 Hispanic/Latino; 3 Two or more races, non-Hispanic/Latino), 181 international. Average age 28. 435 applicants, 61% accepted, 205 enrolled. In 2017, 130 master's awarded. *Degree requirements:* For master's, capstone course. *Entrance requirements:* For master's, GMAT, 2 letters of recommendation. Additional exam requirements/recommendations for international students: Required—TOEFL (minimum score 550 paper-based; 80 iBT), IELTS (minimum score 6.5). *Application deadline:* For fall admission, 4/1 for international students; for spring admission, 11/1 for international students. Applications are processed on a rolling basis. Application fee: $50. Electronic applications accepted. *Expenses:* Contact institution. *Financial support:* Research assistantships with partial tuition reimbursements, career-related internships or fieldwork, Federal Work-Study, institutionally sponsored loans, scholarships/grants, tuition waivers (partial), and unspecified assistantships available. Financial award application deadline: 3/1; financial award applicants required to submit FAFSA. *Faculty research:* Supply chain management, distribution channels, productivity benchmark analysis, data envelopment analysis, financial portfolio analysis. *Unit head:* Dr. Rakesh Gupta, Associate Dean, 516-877-4629. *Application contact:* E-mail: graduateadmissions@adelphi.edu.
Website: http://business.adelphi.edu/degree-programs/graduate-degree-programs/m-b-a/

Air Force Institute of Technology, Graduate School of Engineering and Management, Department of Systems and Engineering Management, Dayton, OH 45433-7765. Offers cost analysis (MS); environmental and engineering management (MS); environmental engineering science (MS); information resource/systems management (MS). *Accreditation:* ABET. *Program availability:* Part-time. *Degree requirements:* For master's, thesis. *Entrance requirements:* For master's, GRE, GMAT, minimum GPA of 3.0.

American Business & Technology University, Programs in Business Administration, Saint Joseph, MO 64506. Offers business administration (MBA); financial management (MBA); global business management (MBA); information systems management (MBA); marketing and social media (MBA); project and operations management (MBA); public accounting (MBA). *Program availability:* Online learning.

American InterContinental University Atlanta, Program in Information Technology, Atlanta, GA 30328. Offers MIT. *Program availability:* Part-time, evening/weekend. *Degree requirements:* For master's, technical proficiency demonstration. *Entrance requirements:* For master's, Computer Programmer Aptitude Battery Exam, interview. Electronic applications accepted. *Faculty research:* Operating systems, security issues, networks and routing, computer hardware.

American Sentinel University, Graduate Programs, Aurora, CO 80014. Offers business administration (MBA); business intelligence (MS); computer science (MSCS); health information management (MS); healthcare (MBA); information systems (MSIS); nursing (MSN). *Program availability:* Part-time, evening/weekend, online learning. *Entrance requirements:* Additional exam requirements/recommendations for international students: Required—TOEFL (minimum score 600 paper-based). Electronic applications accepted.

American University, Kogod School of Business, Department of Information Technology, Washington, DC 20016-8044. Offers analytics (MS). *Students:* 95 full-time (49 women), 91 part-time (38 women); includes 80 minority (32 Black or African American, non-Hispanic/Latino; 1 American Indian or Alaska Native, non-Hispanic/Latino; 18 Asian, non-Hispanic/Latino; 19 Hispanic/Latino; 10 Two or more races, non-Hispanic/Latino), 21 international. Average age 31. 210 applicants, 74% accepted, 88 enrolled. In 2017, 26 master's awarded. *Degree requirements:* For master's, comprehensive exam (for some programs). *Entrance requirements:* For master's, GMAT or GRE. Additional exam requirements/recommendations for international students: Required—TOEFL (minimum score 100 iBT). *Application deadline:* For fall admission, 1/15 priority date for domestic students, 3/15 for international students; for spring admission, 10/15 priority date for domestic students, 10/15 for international students. Application fee: $100. Electronic applications accepted. *Expenses:* Contact institution. *Financial support:* Scholarships/grants available. Financial award applicants required to submit FAFSA. *Unit head:* Edward Wasil, Chair, 202-885-1966, E-mail: ewasil@american.edu. *Application contact:* Jason Garner, Director of Admissions, 202-885-1926, E-mail: jgarner@american.edu.

American University, School of International Service, Washington, DC 20016-8071. Offers comparative and regional studies (Certificate); cross-cultural communication (Certificate); development management (MS); ethics, peace, and global affairs (MA); European studies (Certificate); global environmental policy (MA, Certificate); global information technology (Certificate); global media (MA); international affairs (MA), including comparative and regional studies, global governance, politics, and security, international economic relations, natural resources and sustainable development, U.S. foreign policy and national security; international arts management (Certificate); international communication (MA, Certificate); international development (MA); international economic policy (Certificate); international economic relations (Certificate); international economics (MA); international peace and conflict resolution (MA, Certificate); international politics (Certificate); international relations (MA, PhD); international service (MIS); peacebuilding (Certificate); social enterprise (MA); the Americas (Certificate); United States foreign policy (Certificate); JD/MA. *Program availability:* Part-time, evening/weekend, 100% online. *Faculty:* 112 full-time (50 women), 46 part-time/adjunct (19 women). *Students:* 495 full-time (333 women), 518 part-time (276 women); includes 360 minority (95 Black or African American, non-Hispanic/Latino; 2 American Indian or Alaska Native, non-Hispanic/Latino; 60 Asian, non-Hispanic/Latino; 164 Hispanic/Latino; 39 Two or more races, non-Hispanic/Latino), 98 international. Average age 30. 1,559 applicants, 81% accepted, 356 enrolled. In 2017, 427 master's, 9 doctorates, 5 other advanced degrees awarded. Terminal master's awarded for partial completion of doctoral program. *Degree requirements:* For master's, one foreign language, comprehensive exam; for doctorate, one foreign language, comprehensive exam, thesis/dissertation. *Entrance requirements:* For master's, GRE; GMAT or GRE (for MA in social enterprise), transcripts, resume, 2 letters of recommendation, statement of purpose; for doctorate, GRE, transcripts, resume, 3 letters of recommendation, statement of purpose. Additional exam requirements/recommendations for international students: Required—TOEFL (minimum score 600 paper-based; 100 iBT). *Application deadline:* For fall admission, 1/15 for domestic students, 1/1 for international students; for spring admission, 10/1 for

domestic students, 9/15 for international students. Application fee: $55. Electronic applications accepted. *Expenses:* Contact institution. *Financial support:* Research assistantships, teaching assistantships, institutionally sponsored loans, scholarships/grants, and unspecified assistantships available. Financial award application deadline: 1/15; financial award applicants required to submit FAFSA. *Application contact:* 202-885-1646, Fax: 202-885-1109, E-mail: sisgrad@american.edu.
Website: http://www.american.edu/sis/

American University of Armenia, Graduate Programs, Yerevan, Armenia. Offers business administration (MBA); computer and information science (MS), including business management, design and manufacturing, energy (ME, MS), industrial engineering and systems management; economics (MS); industrial engineering and systems management (ME), including business, computer aided design/manufacturing, energy (ME, MS), information technology; law (LL M); political science and international affairs (MPSIA); public health (MPH); teaching English as a foreign language (MA). *Program availability:* Part-time, evening/weekend. *Degree requirements:* For master's, thesis (for some programs), capstone/project. *Entrance requirements:* For master's, GRE, GMAT, or LSAT. Additional exam requirements/recommendations for international students: Recommended—TOEFL (minimum score 79 iBT), IELTS (minimum score 6.5). *Faculty research:* Microfinance, finance (rural/development, international, corporate), firm life cycle theory, TESOL, language proficiency testing, public policy, administrative law, economic development, cryptography, artificial intelligence, energy efficiency/renewable energy, computer-aided design/manufacturing, health financing, tuberculosis control, mother/child health, preventive ophthalmology, post-earthquake psychopathological investigations, tobacco control, environmental health risk assessments.

Argosy University, Atlanta, College of Business, Atlanta, GA 30328. Offers accounting (DBA); corporate compliance (MBA); customized professional concentration (MBA, DBA); finance (MBA); healthcare administration (MBA); information systems (DBA); information systems management (MBA); international business (MBA, DBA); management (MBA, MSM, DBA); marketing (MBA, DBA). *Accreditation:* ACBSP.

Argosy University, Chicago, College of Business, Chicago, IL 60601. Offers accounting (DBA); customized professional concentration (MBA, DBA); finance (MBA); fraud examination (MBA); global business sustainability (DBA); healthcare administration (MBA); information systems (DBA); information systems management (MBA); international business (MBA, DBA); management (MBA, MSM, DBA); marketing (MBA, DBA); organizational leadership (Ed D); public administration (MBA); sustainable management (MBA). *Accreditation:* ACBSP. *Program availability:* Online learning.

Argosy University, Hawai`i, College of Business, Honolulu, HI 96813. Offers accounting (DBA); corporate compliance (MBA); customized professional concentration (MBA, DBA); finance (MBA, Certificate); fraud examination (MBA); global business sustainability (DBA); healthcare administration (MBA, Certificate); information systems (DBA); information systems management (MBA, Certificate); international business (MBA, DBA, Certificate); management (MBA, MSM, DBA); marketing (MBA, DBA, Certificate); organizational leadership (Ed D); public administration (MBA); sustainable management (MBA).

Argosy University, Los Angeles, College of Business, Los Angeles, CA 90045. Offers accounting (DBA); corporate compliance (MBA); customized professional concentration (MBA, DBA); finance (MBA); fraud examination (MBA); global business sustainability (DBA); healthcare administration (MBA); information systems (DBA); information systems management (MBA); international business (MBA, DBA); management (MBA, MSM, DBA); marketing (MBA, DBA); organizational leadership (Ed D); public administration (MBA); sustainable management (MBA).

Argosy University, Northern Virginia, College of Business, Arlington, VA 22209. Offers accounting (DBA); customized professional concentration (MBA, DBA); finance (MBA); fraud examination (MBA); global business sustainability (DBA); healthcare administration (MBA); information systems (DBA); information systems management (MBA); international business (MBA, DBA, Certificate); management (MBA, MSM, DBA); marketing (MBA, DBA, Certificate); organizational leadership (Ed D); public administration (MBA); sustainable management (MBA).

Argosy University, Orange County, College of Business, Orange, CA 92868. Offers accounting (DBA, Adv C); corporate compliance (MBA); customized professional concentration (MBA, DBA); finance (MBA, Certificate); fraud examination (MBA); global business sustainability (DBA); healthcare administration (MBA, Certificate); information systems (DBA, Adv C, Certificate); information systems management (MBA); international business (MBA, DBA, Adv C, Certificate); management (MBA, MSM, DBA, Adv C); marketing (MBA, DBA, Adv C, Certificate); organizational leadership (Ed D); public administration (MBA, Certificate); sustainable management (MBA).

Argosy University, Phoenix, College of Business, Phoenix, AZ 85021. Offers accounting (DBA); corporate compliance (MBA); customized professional concentration (MBA, DBA); finance (MBA); fraud examination (MBA); global business sustainability (DBA); healthcare administration (MBA); information systems (DBA); information systems management (MBA); international business (MBA, DBA); management (MBA, DBA); marketing (MBA, DBA); public administration (MBA); sustainable management (MBA).

Argosy University, Seattle, College of Business, Seattle, WA 98121. Offers accounting (DBA); corporate compliance (MBA); customized professional concentration (MBA, DBA); finance (MBA); fraud examination (MBA); global business sustainability (DBA); healthcare administration (MBA); information systems (DBA); information systems management (MBA); international business (MBA, DBA); management (MBA, MSM, DBA); marketing (MBA, DBA); organizational leadership (Ed D); public administration (MBA); sustainable management (MBA).

Argosy University, Tampa, College of Business, Tampa, FL 33607. Offers accounting (DBA); corporate compliance (MBA); customized professional concentration (MBA, DBA); finance (MBA); fraud examination (MBA); global business sustainability (DBA); healthcare administration (MBA); information systems (DBA); information systems management (MBA); international business (MBA, DBA); management (MBA, MSM, DBA); marketing (MBA, DBA); organizational leadership (Ed D); public administration (MBA); sustainable management (MBA).

Argosy University, Twin Cities, College of Business, Eagan, MN 55121. Offers accounting (DBA); customized professional concentration (MBA, DBA); finance (MBA); fraud examination (MBA); global business sustainability (DBA); healthcare administration (MBA); information systems (DBA); information systems management (MBA); international business (MBA, DBA); management (MBA, MSM, DBA); marketing (MBA, DBA); organizational leadership (Ed D); public administration (MBA); sustainable management (MBA).

Arizona State University at the Tempe campus, Ira A. Fulton Schools of Engineering, The Polytechnic School, Programs in Technology Management, Mesa, AZ 85212. Offers aviation management and human factors (MS); environmental technology management (MS); global technology and development (MS); graphic information technology (MS); management of technology (MS). *Program availability:* Part-time, evening/weekend, online learning. *Degree requirements:* For master's, thesis or applied project and oral defense; interactive Program of Study (iPOS) submitted before completing 50 percent of required credit hours. *Entrance requirements:* For master's, GRE, minimum GPA of 3.0 or equivalent in last 2 years of work leading to bachelor's degree. Additional exam requirements/recommendations for international students: Required—TOEFL, IELTS, or PTE. Electronic applications accepted. *Faculty research:* Digital imaging, digital publishing, Internet development/e-commerce, information aviation human factors, pilot selection, databases, multimedia, commercial digital photography, digital workflow, computer graphics modeling and animation, information design, sociotechnology, visual and technical literacy, environmental management, quality management, project management, industrial ethics, hazardous materials, environmental chemistry.

Arizona State University at the Tempe campus, W. P. Carey School of Business, Department of Information Systems, Tempe, AZ 85287-4606. Offers business administration (PhD), including information systems; information management (MS); MBA/MS. *Program availability:* Evening/weekend, online learning. Terminal master's awarded for partial completion of doctoral program. *Degree requirements:* For master's, thesis or alternative, applied project, interactive Program of Study (iPOS) submitted before completing 50 percent of required credit hours; for doctorate, comprehensive exam, thesis/dissertation, interactive Program of Study (iPOS) submitted before completing 50 percent of required credit hours. *Entrance requirements:* For master's, 2 years of full-time related work experience, bachelor's degree in related field from accredited university, resume, essay, 2 letters of recommendation, official transcripts; for doctorate, GMAT, MBA, 2 years of full-time related work experience (recommended), bachelor's degree in related field from accredited university, 3 letters of recommendation, resume, personal statement. Additional exam requirements/recommendations for international students: Required—TOEFL (minimum score 550 paper-based; 80 iBT), IELTS (minimum score 6.5). Electronic applications accepted. *Expenses:* Contact institution. *Faculty research:* Strategy and technology, technology investments and firm valuation, Internet e-commerce, IT enablement for emergency preparedness and response, information supply chain, collaborative computing and security/privacy issues for e-health, enterprise information systems and their application to management control systems.

Arkansas State University, Graduate School, College of Business, Department of Computer and Information Technology, State University, AR 72467. Offers business administration education (SCCT); business technology education (SCCT). *Program availability:* Part-time. *Entrance requirements:* Additional exam requirements/recommendations for international students: Required—TOEFL (minimum score 550 paper-based; 79 iBT), IELTS (minimum score 6), PTE (minimum score 56). Electronic applications accepted. *Expenses:* Contact institution.

Ashland University, Dauch College of Business and Economics, Ashland, OH 44805-3702. Offers accounting (MBA); business analytics (MBA); entrepreneurship (MBA); financial management (MBA); global management (MBA); health care management and leadership (MBA); human resource management (MBA); human resources (MBA); management information systems (MBA); project management (MBA); sport management (MBA); supply chain management (MBA). *Accreditation:* ACBSP. *Program availability:* Part-time, evening/weekend, 100% online, blended/hybrid learning. *Faculty:* 20 full-time (8 women), 13 part-time/adjunct (2 women). *Students:* 458 full-time (210 women), 144 part-time (52 women); includes 88 minority (63 Black or African American, non-Hispanic/Latino; 1 American Indian or Alaska Native, non-Hispanic/Latino; 10 Asian, non-Hispanic/Latino; 14 Hispanic/Latino), 202 international. Average age 31. 216 applicants, 74% accepted, 115 enrolled. In 2017, 184 master's awarded. Terminal master's awarded for partial completion of doctoral program. *Degree requirements:* For master's, thesis optional, capstone course. *Entrance requirements:* For master's, 2 years of full-time work experience. Additional exam requirements/recommendations for international students: Required—TOEFL (minimum score 550 paper-based; 78 iBT). *Application deadline:* For fall admission, 8/1 priority date for domestic students; for spring admission, 12/1 priority date for domestic students. Applications are processed on a rolling basis. Application fee: $30. Electronic applications accepted. *Expenses:* $815 per credit hour, $15 technology fee for online sections. *Financial support:* Scholarships/grants, tuition waivers (partial), and unspecified assistantships available. Financial award application deadline: 4/15; financial award applicants required to submit FAFSA. *Faculty research:* Relationship marketing strategy, executive compensation and company performance, online marketplaces in electronic commerce, diversity training in campus recreation departments, entrepreneurship in developing and emerging economies. *Unit head:* Dr. Elad Granot, Dean, 419-289-5932, E-mail: egranot@ashland.edu. *Application contact:* Stephen W. Krispinsky, Executive Director of MBA Program, 419-289-5236, Fax: 419-289-5910, E-mail: skrispin@ashland.edu. Website: http://www.mba.ashland.edu

Aspen University, Programs in Information Management, Denver, CO 80246-1930. Offers information management (MS); information systems (Certificate). *Program availability:* Part-time, evening/weekend, online learning. Electronic applications accepted.

Auburn University at Montgomery, College of Business, Department of Information Systems, Montgomery, AL 36124-4023. Offers information systems management (MS). *Faculty:* 6 full-time (0 women). *Students:* 9 full-time (3 women), 6 part-time (3 women); includes 7 minority (5 Black or African American, non-Hispanic/Latino; 2 Asian, non-Hispanic/Latino), 5 international. Average age 30. 31 applicants, 71% accepted, 8 enrolled. In 2017, 11 master's awarded. *Degree requirements:* For master's, thesis optional. *Entrance requirements:* For master's, GMAT or GRE General Test. Additional exam requirements/recommendations for international students: Required—TOEFL (minimum score 500 paper-based; 61 iBT), IELTS (minimum score 5.5), PTE (minimum score 44). *Application deadline:* Applications are processed on a rolling basis. Application fee: $25 ($0 for international students). Electronic applications accepted. *Expenses:* Tuition, state resident: full-time $6930; part-time $385 per credit hour. Tuition, nonresident: full-time $15,588; part-time $866 per credit hour. *Required fees:* $640. *Financial support:* Application deadline: 3/1; applicants required to submit FAFSA. *Unit head:* Dr. David Ang, Head, 334-244-3455, Fax: 334-244-3792, E-mail: dang@aum.edu. *Application contact:* Dr. Joseph Newman, Associate Dean/Graduate Coordinator, 334-244-3905, Fax: 334-244-3792, E-mail: jnewman3@aum.edu. Website: http://business.aum.edu/academic-programs/undergraduate-programs/information-systems

Avila University, School of Business, Kansas City, MO 64145-1698. Offers accounting (MBA); finance (MBA); health care administration (MBA); international business (MBA); management (MBA); management information systems (MBA); marketing (MBA). *Program availability:* Part-time, evening/weekend. *Faculty:* 6 full-time (2 women), 6 part-time/adjunct (2 women). *Students:* 49 full-time (19 women), 29 part-time (14 women); includes 16 minority (12 Black or African American, non-Hispanic/Latino; 1 Asian, non-

Hispanic/Latino; 3 Hispanic/Latino), 19 international. Average age 32. 51 applicants, 47% accepted, 20 enrolled. In 2017, 31 master's awarded. *Degree requirements:* For master's, comprehensive exam, capstone course. *Entrance requirements:* For master's, GMAT (minimum score 420), minimum GPA of 3.0, interview. Additional exam requirements/recommendations for international students: Required—TOEFL (minimum score 550 paper-based). *Application deadline:* For fall admission, 7/30 priority date for domestic and international students; for winter admission, 11/30 priority date for domestic and international students; for spring admission, 2/28 priority date for domestic and international students; for summer admission, 6/1 priority date for domestic and international students. Applications are processed on a rolling basis. Application fee: $0. Electronic applications accepted. *Expenses:* Contact institution. *Financial support:* In 2017–18, 18 students received support. Career-related internships or fieldwork and scholarships/grants available. Support available to part-time students. Financial award applicants required to submit FAFSA. *Faculty research:* Leadership characteristics, financial hedging, group dynamics. *Unit head:* Dr. Wendy L. Acker, Interim Dean, 816-501-3720, Fax: 816-501-2463, E-mail: wendy.acker@avila.edu. *Application contact:* Brandon Black, MBA Admission Advisor, 816-501-3601, Fax: 816-501-2463, E-mail: brandon.black@avila.edu. Website: https://www.avila.edu/mrk/mba

Baker College Center for Graduate Studies–Online, Graduate Programs, Flint, MI 48507. Offers accounting (MBA); business administration (DBA); finance (MBA); general business (MBA); health care management (MBA); human resources management (MBA); information management (MBA); leadership studies (MBA); management information systems (MSIS); marketing (MBA). *Program availability:* Part-time, evening/weekend, online learning. *Degree requirements:* For master's, portfolio. *Entrance requirements:* For master's, 3 years of work experience, minimum undergraduate GPA of 2.5, writing sample, 3 letters of recommendation; for doctorate, MBA or acceptable related master's degree from accredited association, 5 years work experience, minimum graduate GPA of 3.25, writing sample, 3 professional references. Additional exam requirements/recommendations for international students: Required—TOEFL (minimum score 550 paper-based). Electronic applications accepted.

Ball State University, Graduate School, College of Communication, Information, and Media, Center for Information and Communication Sciences, Muncie, IN 47306. Offers information and communication sciences (MS); information and communication technologies (Certificate). *Program availability:* Part-time, 100% online. *Faculty:* 6 full-time (2 women). *Students:* 49 full-time (22 women), 20 part-time (5 women); includes 13 minority (6 Black or African American, non-Hispanic/Latino; 1 Asian, non-Hispanic/Latino; 3 Hispanic/Latino; 3 Two or more races, non-Hispanic/Latino), 5 international. Average age 26. 82 applicants, 72% accepted, 47 enrolled. In 2017, 52 master's awarded. *Entrance requirements:* For master's, minimum baccalaureate GPA of 2.75 or 3.0 in latter half of baccalaureate, statement of goals. Additional exam requirements/recommendations for international students: Required—TOEFL (minimum score 550 paper-based; 79 iBT), IELTS (minimum score 6.5). *Application deadline:* Applications are processed on a rolling basis. Application fee: $60. Electronic applications accepted. *Financial support:* In 2017–18, 14 students received support, including 14 research assistantships with partial tuition reimbursements available (averaging $7,904 per year); teaching assistantships with partial tuition reimbursements available and unspecified assistantships also available. Financial award application deadline: 3/1; financial award applicants required to submit FAFSA. *Unit head:* Dr. Dennis Trinkle, Director, 765-285-5942, E-mail: datrinkle@bsu.edu. Website: http://www.bsu.edu/cics

Ball State University, Graduate School, Miller College of Business, Department of Information Systems and Operations Management, Muncie, IN 47306. Offers business education (MA); information systems security management (Certificate). *Accreditation:* NCATE (one or more programs are accredited). *Program availability:* Part-time, online only, 100% online. *Faculty:* 4 full-time (0 women). *Students:* 6 full-time (4 women), 10 part-time (8 women); includes 3 minority (1 Hispanic/Latino; 2 Two or more races, non-Hispanic/Latino). Average age 31. 8 applicants, 88% accepted, 5 enrolled. In 2017, 6 master's awarded. *Entrance requirements:* For master's, minimum baccalaureate GPA of 2.75 or 3.0 in latter half of baccalaureate. Additional exam requirements/recommendations for international students: Required—TOEFL (minimum score 550 paper-based; 79 iBT), IELTS (minimum score 6.5). *Application deadline:* Applications are processed on a rolling basis. Application fee: $60. Electronic applications accepted. *Expenses:* Contact institution. *Financial support:* Application deadline: 3/1; applicants required to submit FAFSA. *Unit head:* Dr. John Ledbetter, Interim Chairperson, 765-285-5109, Fax: 765-285-5308, E-mail: jledbett@bsu.edu. Website: http://www.bsu.edu/isom

Barry University, Andreas School of Business, Graduate Certificate Programs, Miami Shores, FL 33161-6695. Offers finance (Certificate); health services administration (Certificate); international business (Certificate); management (Certificate); management information systems (Certificate); marketing (Certificate).

Baruch College of the City University of New York, Zicklin School of Business, Department of Statistics and Computer Information Systems, Program in Information Systems, New York, NY 10010-5585. Offers MBA, MS, PhD. *Program availability:* Part-time, evening/weekend. Terminal master's awarded for partial completion of doctoral program. *Degree requirements:* For master's, thesis or alternative; for doctorate, comprehensive exam, thesis/dissertation. *Entrance requirements:* For master's, GMAT, 2 letters of recommendation, resume, 2 years of work experience; for doctorate, GMAT. Additional exam requirements/recommendations for international students: Required—TOEFL (minimum score 590 paper-based), TWE (minimum score 5).

Baylor University, Graduate School, Hankamer School of Business, Department of Information Systems, Waco, TX 76798. Offers information systems (MSIS, PhD); information systems management (MBA); MBA/MSIS. *Students:* 34 full-time (17 women), 3 part-time (1 woman); includes 6 minority (1 Black or African American, non-Hispanic/Latino; 1 Asian, non-Hispanic/Latino; 2 Hispanic/Latino; 2 Two or more races, non-Hispanic/Latino), 22 international. In 2017, 13 master's, 2 doctorates awarded. *Entrance requirements:* For master's, GMAT; for doctorate, GMAT, GRE. Additional exam requirements/recommendations for international students: Required—TOEFL. *Application deadline:* Applications are processed on a rolling basis. Application fee: $25. *Financial support:* Research assistantships, career-related internships or fieldwork, and Federal Work-Study available. *Faculty research:* Computer personnel, group systems, information technology standards and infrastructure, international information systems, technology and the learning environment. *Unit head:* Dr. Gary Carini, Associate Dean, 254-710-4091, Fax: 254-710-1091, E-mail: gary_carini@baylor.edu. *Application contact:* Laurie Wilson, Director, Graduate Business Programs, 254-710-4163, Fax: 254-710-1066, E-mail: laurie_wilson@baylor.edu. Website: http://hsb.baylor.edu/isy/

Bay Path University, Program in Communications and Information Management, Longmeadow, MA 01106-2292. Offers MS. *Program availability:* Part-time, evening/weekend, 100% online. *Students:* 4 full-time (3 women), 18 part-time (13 women); includes 9 minority (4 Black or African American, non-Hispanic/Latino; 1 Asian, non-Hispanic/Latino; 3 Hispanic/Latino; 1 Two or more races, non-Hispanic/Latino). Average age 40. In 2017, 27 master's awarded. *Degree requirements:* For master's, twelve core

Management Information Systems

courses and four electives (each course is eight weeks long). *Application deadline:* Applications are processed on a rolling basis. Application fee: $45. Electronic applications accepted. Application fee is waived when completed online. *Expenses:* $815 per credit. *Financial support:* Unspecified assistantships available. Financial award applicants required to submit FAFSA. *Unit head:* Robin Saunders, Program Director, 413-565-1009. *Application contact:* Diane Ranaldi, Dean of Graduate Admissions, 413-565-1332, Fax: 413-565-1250, E-mail: dranaldi@baypath.edu.
Website: http://graduate.baypath.edu/Graduate-Programs/Programs-On-Campus/MS-Programs/Communications-And-Information-Management

Bay Path University, Program in Information Management, Longmeadow, MA 01106-2292. Offers MS. *Program availability:* Part-time, 100% online. *Students:* 4 full-time (1 woman), 2 part-time (both women); includes 1 minority (Black or African American, non-Hispanic/Latino). Average age 49. *Application deadline:* Applications are processed on a rolling basis. Application fee: $45. Electronic applications accepted. Application fee is waived when completed online. *Expenses:* $815 per credit. *Financial support:* Unspecified assistantships available. Financial award applicants required to submit FAFSA. *Unit head:* Robin Saunders, Director, 413-565-1009, E-mail: rsaunders@baypath.edu. *Application contact:* Diane Ranaldi, Dean of Graduate Admissions, 413-565-1332, Fax: 413-565-1250, E-mail: dranaldi@baypath.edu.
Website: http://www.baypath.edu/academics/graduate-programs/information-management-ms/

Bellevue University, Graduate School, College of Information Technology, Bellevue, NE 68005-3098. Offers computer information systems (MS); cybersecurity (MS); management of information systems (MS); project management (MPM).

Benedictine University, Graduate Programs, Program in Business Administration, Lisle, IL 60532. Offers accounting (MBA); entrepreneurship and managing innovation (MBA); financial management (MBA); health administration (MBA); human resource management (MBA); information systems security (MBA); international business (MBA); management consulting (MBA); management information systems (MBA); marketing management (MBA); operations management and logistics (MBA); organizational leadership (MBA). *Program availability:* Part-time, evening/weekend, online learning. *Entrance requirements:* For master's, GMAT. Additional exam requirements/recommendations for international students: Required—TOEFL (minimum score 550 paper-based). Electronic applications accepted. *Faculty research:* Strategic leadership in professional organizations, sociology of professions, organizational change, social identity theory, applications to change management.

Benedictine University, Graduate Programs, Program in Management Information Systems, Lisle, IL 60532. Offers MS, MBA/MS, MPH/MS. *Program availability:* Part-time. *Entrance requirements:* For master's, GMAT. Additional exam requirements/recommendations for international students: Required—TOEFL (minimum score 550 paper-based). Electronic applications accepted. *Faculty research:* Technology management, knowledge management, electronic commerce, information security.

Binghamton University, State University of New York, Graduate School, School of Management, Program in Management, Binghamton, NY 13902-6000. Offers finance (PhD); management information systems (PhD); marketing (PhD); organizational studies (PhD); supply chain management (PhD). *Students:* 8 full-time (5 women), 12 part-time (5 women), 19 international. Average age 30. 57 applicants, 21% accepted, 7 enrolled. In 2017, 3 doctorates awarded. *Degree requirements:* For doctorate, thesis/dissertation. *Entrance requirements:* For doctorate, GMAT. *Application deadline:* For fall admission, 2/1 for domestic students. *Financial support:* In 2017–18, 18 students received support. *Unit head:* Dr. Upinder Dhillon, Dean, 607-777-2314, E-mail: dhillon@binghamton.edu. *Application contact:* Marianne Ferry, Administrative Assistant, Executive Education and PhD Programs, 607-777-2342, E-mail: mferry@binghamton.edu.

Boston University, Metropolitan College, Department of Computer Science, Boston, MA 02215. Offers computer information systems (MS), including computer networks, data analytics, database management and business intelligence, health informatics, IT project management, security, Web application development; computer networks (Certificate); computer science (MS); data analytics (Certificate); digital forensics (Certificate); health informatics (Certificate); information technology project management (Certificate); software development (MS); software engineering in health care systems (Certificate); telecommunications (MS), including security. *Program availability:* Part-time, evening/weekend, online learning. *Faculty:* 10 full-time (2 women), 51 part-time/adjunct (5 women). *Students:* 109 full-time (39 women), 985 part-time (268 women); includes 286 minority (64 Black or African American, non-Hispanic/Latino; 3 American Indian or Alaska Native, non-Hispanic/Latino; 131 Asian, non-Hispanic/Latino; 73 Hispanic/Latino; 1 Native Hawaiian or other Pacific Islander, non-Hispanic/Latino; 14 Two or more races, non-Hispanic/Latino), 253 international. Average age 32. 952 applicants, 65% accepted, 230 enrolled. In 2017, 392 master's awarded. *Entrance requirements:* For master's and Certificate, official transcripts from regionally-accredited bachelor's degree program, 3 letters of recommendation, professional resume, personal statement. Additional exam requirements/recommendations for international students: Required—TOEFL (minimum score 84 iBT), IELTS. *Application deadline:* For fall admission, 6/1 priority date for international students; for spring admission, 10/1 priority date for international students. Applications are processed on a rolling basis. Application fee: $85. Electronic applications accepted. *Expenses:* Contact institution. *Financial support:* In 2017–18, 11 research assistantships (averaging $8,400 per year), 3 teaching assistantships (averaging $5,000 per year) were awarded; unspecified assistantships also available. Support available to part-time students. Financial award applicants required to submit FAFSA. *Faculty research:* Medical informatics, Web technologies, telecom and networks, security and forensics, software engineering, programming languages, multimedia and artificial intelligence (AI), information systems and IT project management. *Unit head:* Dr. Anatoly Temkin, Chair, 617-353-2566, Fax: 617-353-2367, E-mail: csinfo@bu.edu. *Application contact:* Lesley Moreau, Academic Program Coordinator, 617-353-2566, Fax: 617-353-2367, E-mail: metcs@bu.edu.
Website: http://www.bu.edu/csmet/

Bowie State University, Graduate Programs, Program in Management Information Systems, Bowie, MD 20715-9465. Offers information systems analyst (Certificate); management information systems (MS). *Program availability:* Part-time, evening/weekend. *Degree requirements:* For master's, comprehensive exam, thesis optional, research paper. *Entrance requirements:* For master's, minimum GPA of 2.5. Electronic applications accepted.

Brandeis University, Rabb School of Continuing Studies, Division of Graduate Professional Studies, Master of Science in Technology Management Program, Waltham, MA 02454-9110. Offers MS. *Program availability:* Part-time-only. *Faculty:* 55 part-time/adjunct (18 women). *Students:* 43 part-time (13 women); includes 9 minority (3 Black or African American, non-Hispanic/Latino; 3 Asian, non-Hispanic/Latino; 1 Hispanic/Latino; 2 Two or more races, non-Hispanic/Latino). Average age 40. 1 applicant, 100% accepted, 1 enrolled. In 2017, 18 master's awarded. *Entrance requirements:* For master's, four-year bachelor's degree from regionally-accredited U.S. institution or equivalent; official transcript(s) from every college or university attended; resume or curriculum vitae; statement of goals; letter of recommendation. Additional

exam requirements/recommendations for international students: Required—TWE (minimum score 4.5), TOEFL (minimum scores: 600 paper-based, 100 iBT), IELTS (7), or PTE (68). *Application deadline:* For fall admission, 6/20 priority date for domestic and international students; for winter admission, 9/12 priority date for domestic and international students; for spring admission, 12/19 priority date for domestic and international students; for summer admission, 3/13 priority date for domestic and international students. Applications are processed on a rolling basis. Application fee: $75. Electronic applications accepted. *Expenses:* $1,178 per credit. *Financial support:* Applicants required to submit FAFSA. *Unit head:* Dr. James La Creta, Chair, 781-736-8787, E-mail: jlacreta@brandeis.edu. *Application contact:* Frances Stearns, Director of Student and Faculty Operations, 781-736-8785, E-mail: fstearns@brandeis.edu.
Website: http://www.brandeis.edu/gps

Broadview University–West Jordan, Graduate Programs, West Jordan, UT 84088. Offers business administration (MBA); health care management (MSM); information technology (MSM); managerial leadership (MSM).

California Intercontinental University, School of Information Technology, Irvine, CA 92614. Offers information systems and enterprise resource management (DBA); information systems and knowledge management (MBA); project and quality management (MBA).

California Lutheran University, Graduate Studies, School of Management, Thousand Oaks, CA 91360-2787. Offers business (IMBA); entrepreneurship (MBA, Certificate); finance (MBA, Certificate); financial planning (MBA, MS, Certificate); human capital management (MBA, Certificate); information technology (MS); information technology management (MBA, Certificate); international business (MBA, Certificate); marketing (MBA, Certificate); public policy and administration (MPPA); quantitative economics (MS). *Program availability:* Part-time, evening/weekend, 100% online, blended/hybrid learning. *Faculty:* 17 full-time (4 women), 40 part-time/adjunct (9 women). *Students:* 423 full-time (168 women), 153 part-time (72 women); includes 124 minority (11 Black or African American, non-Hispanic/Latino; 1 American Indian or Alaska Native, non-Hispanic/Latino; 21 Asian, non-Hispanic/Latino; 75 Hispanic/Latino; 16 Two or more races, non-Hispanic/Latino), 294 international. Average age 31. 467 applicants, 72% accepted, 108 enrolled. In 2017, 306 master's awarded. *Degree requirements:* For master's, comprehensive exam (for some programs). *Entrance requirements:* For master's, GMAT, interview, minimum GPA of 3.0. *Application deadline:* Applications are processed on a rolling basis. Application fee: $50. Electronic applications accepted. *Expenses:* Contact institution. *Unit head:* Dr. Gerhard Apfelthaler, Dean, 805-493-3360. *Application contact:* 805-493-3325, Fax: 805-493-3861, E-mail: clugrad@callutheran.edu.
Website: http://www.callutheran.edu/management/

California State Polytechnic University, Pomona, Master of Science in Business Administration Program, Pomona, CA 91768-2557. Offers information systems auditing (MS). *Accreditation:* AACSB. *Program availability:* Part-time, evening/weekend. *Students:* 5 part-time (2 women); includes 3 minority (1 Asian, non-Hispanic/Latino; 2 Hispanic/Latino), 1 international. Average age 28. 24 applicants, 38% accepted, 5 enrolled. In 2017, 4 master's awarded. *Entrance requirements:* Additional exam requirements/recommendations for international students: Required—TOEFL (minimum score 550 paper-based). *Application deadline:* Applications are processed on a rolling basis. Application fee: $55. Electronic applications accepted. *Expenses:* Contact institution. *Financial support:* Application deadline: 3/2; applicants required to submit FAFSA. *Unit head:* Dr. Tarique Hossain, Associate Professor/Director of Graduate Programs, 909-869-2362, Fax: 909-869-4559, E-mail: tmhossain@cpp.edu. *Application contact:* Deborah L. Brandon, Executive Director of Admissions and Enrollment Planning, 909-869-3427, Fax: 909-869-5315, E-mail: dlbrandon@cpp.edu.
Website: http://www.cpp.edu/~cba/graduate-business-programs/programs/MSBA.shtml

California State University, Fullerton, Graduate Studies, College of Business and Economics, Department of Information Systems and Decision Sciences, Fullerton, CA 92831-3599. Offers decision science (MBA); information systems (MBA, MS); information systems and decision sciences (MS); information systems and e-commerce (MS); information technology (MS). *Program availability:* Part-time. *Faculty:* 14 full-time (4 women), 1 (woman) part-time/adjunct. *Students:* 164 full-time (81 women), 95 part-time (27 women); includes 63 minority (5 Black or African American, non-Hispanic/Latino; 33 Asian, non-Hispanic/Latino; 19 Hispanic/Latino; 6 Two or more races, non-Hispanic/Latino), 165 international. Average age 28. 589 applicants, 52% accepted, 93 enrolled. *Entrance requirements:* For master's, GMAT, minimum AACSB index of 950. Application fee: $55. *Financial support:* Career-related internships or fieldwork, Federal Work-Study, institutionally sponsored loans, and scholarships/grants available. Support available to part-time students. Financial award application deadline: 3/1; financial award applicants required to submit FAFSA. *Unit head:* Dr. Bhushan Kapoor, Chair, 657-278-2221. *Application contact:* Admissions/Applications, 657-278-2371.
Website: http://business.fullerton.edu/isds/

California State University, Los Angeles, Graduate Studies, College of Business and Economics, Department of Information Systems, Los Angeles, CA 90032-8530. Offers management (MS). *Program availability:* Part-time, evening/weekend. *Degree requirements:* For master's, comprehensive exam (MBA), thesis (MS). *Entrance requirements:* For master's, GMAT, minimum GPA of 2.5 during previous 2 years of course work. Additional exam requirements/recommendations for international students: Required—TOEFL (minimum score 550 paper-based). Electronic applications accepted.

California State University, Monterey Bay, College of Science, School of Computing and Design, Seaside, CA 93955-8001. Offers MS, MSMIT. MSMIT offered in conjunction with College of Business. *Degree requirements:* For master's, capstone or thesis. *Entrance requirements:* For master's, GRE, 2 letters of recommendation, minimum GPA of 3.0, technology screening assessment. Additional exam requirements/recommendations for international students: Required—TOEFL (minimum score 550 paper-based; 71 iBT). Electronic applications accepted. *Faculty research:* Electronic commerce, e-learning, knowledge management, international business, business and public policy.

California State University, San Bernardino, Graduate Studies, College of Business and Public Administration, Program in Business Administration, San Bernardino, CA 92407. Offers accounting (MBA); entrepreneurship (MBA); finance (MBA); global business (MBA); information management (MBA); information security (MBA); management (MBA); supply chain management (MBA). *Accreditation:* AACSB. *Program availability:* Part-time, evening/weekend, online learning. *Faculty:* 4 full-time (3 women), 6 part-time/adjunct (4 women). *Students:* 21 full-time (15 women), 122 part-time (30 women); includes 82 minority (15 Black or African American, non-Hispanic/Latino; 1 American Indian or Alaska Native, non-Hispanic/Latino; 19 Asian, non-Hispanic/Latino; 44 Hispanic/Latino; 3 Two or more races, non-Hispanic/Latino), 37 international. Average age 33. 258 applicants, 44% accepted, 50 enrolled. In 2017, 134 master's awarded. *Degree requirements:* For master's, comprehensive exam, thesis. *Entrance requirements:* Additional exam requirements/recommendations for international students: Required—TOEFL. *Application deadline:* For fall admission, 7/16 for domestic students, 7/20 for international students; for winter admission, 10/23 for domestic students, 10/20 for international students; for spring admission, 1/22 for domestic

students, 1/20 for international students. Application fee: $55. *Expenses:* Contact institution. *Financial support:* Application deadline: 3/1. *Unit head:* Dr. Lawrence C. Rose, Dean, 909-537-3703, Fax: 909-537-7026, E-mail: lrose@csusb.edu. *Application contact:* Dr. Vipin Gupta, Associate Dean/MBA Director, 909-537-7380, Fax: 909-537-7026, E-mail: vgupta@csusb.edu.
Website: http://mba.csusb.edu/

California University of Management and Sciences, Graduate Programs, Anaheim, CA 92801. Offers business administration (MBA, DBA); computer information systems (MS); economics (MS); international business (MS); sports management (MS).

Capella University, School of Business and Technology, Doctoral Programs in Technology, Minneapolis, MN 55402. Offers general information technology (PhD); global operations and supply chain management (DBA); information assurance and security (PhD); information technology education (PhD); information technology management (DBA, PhD).

Capella University, School of Business and Technology, Master's Programs in Technology, Minneapolis, MN 55402. Offers enterprise software architecture (MS); general information systems and technology management (MS); global operations and supply chain management (MBA); information assurance and security (MS); information technology management (MBA); network management (MS).

Capitol Technology University, Graduate Programs, Laurel, MD 20708-9759. Offers business administration (MBA); computer science (MS); electrical engineering (MS); information and telecommunications systems management (MS); information architecture (MS); network security (MS). *Program availability:* Part-time, evening/weekend, online learning. *Entrance requirements:* For master's, minimum GPA of 3.0. Electronic applications accepted.

Carnegie Mellon University, Heinz College Australia, Master of Science in Information Technology Program (Adelaide, South Australia), Adelaide SA 5000, Australia. Offers MSIT. *Entrance requirements:* For master's, GRE or GMAT, college-level course in advanced algebra/pre-calculus; college-level courses in economics and statistics (recommended). Additional exam requirements/recommendations for international students: Required—TOEFL or IELTS.

Carnegie Mellon University, Heinz College, School of Information Systems and Management, Master of Information Systems Management Program, Pittsburgh, PA 15213-3891. Offers MISM. *Entrance requirements:* For master's, GRE or GMAT, college-level course in advanced algebra/pre-calculus; college-level courses in economics and statistics (recommended). Additional exam requirements/recommendations for international students: Required—TOEFL or IELTS.

Carnegie Mellon University, Heinz College, School of Information Systems and Management, Master of Science in Information Security Policy and Management Program, Pittsburgh, PA 15213-3891. Offers MSISPM. *Entrance requirements:* For master's, GRE or GMAT, college-level course in advanced algebra/pre-calculus; college-level courses in economics and statistics (recommended). Additional exam requirements/recommendations for international students: Required—TOEFL or IELTS.

Carnegie Mellon University, Heinz College, School of Information Systems and Management, Program in Information Technology, Pittsburgh, PA 15213-3891. Offers MSIT.

Carnegie Mellon University, Tepper School of Business, Program in Business Technologies, Pittsburgh, PA 15213-3891. Offers PhD. *Degree requirements:* For doctorate, thesis/dissertation. *Entrance requirements:* For doctorate, GRE General Test.

The Catholic University of America, School of Engineering, Program in Engineering Management, Washington, DC 20064. Offers engineering management (MSE, Certificate), including engineering management and organization (MSE), project and systems engineering management (MSE), technology management (MSE); program management (Certificate); systems engineering and management of information technology (Certificate). *Program availability:* Part-time. *Faculty:* 4 part-time/adjunct (0 women). *Students:* 11 full-time (4 women), 9 part-time (4 women); includes 2 minority (1 Hispanic/Latino; 1 Two or more races, non-Hispanic/Latino), 11 international. Average age 31. 29 applicants, 66% accepted, 8 enrolled. In 2017, 17 master's awarded. *Degree requirements:* For master's, minimum GPA of 3.0. *Entrance requirements:* For master's and Certificate, statement of purpose, official copies of academic transcripts, two letters of recommendation. Additional exam requirements/recommendations for international students: Required—TOEFL (minimum score 550 paper-based; 80 iBT). *Application deadline:* For fall admission, 7/15 priority date for domestic students, 7/1 for international students; for spring admission, 11/15 priority date for domestic students, 11/1 for international students. Applications are processed on a rolling basis. Application fee: $55. Electronic applications accepted. *Expenses:* Contact institution. *Financial support:* Fellowships, research assistantships, teaching assistantships, Federal Work-Study, scholarships/grants, tuition waivers (full and partial), and unspecified assistantships available. Financial award application deadline: 2/1; financial award applicants required to submit FAFSA. *Faculty research:* Engineering management and organization, project and systems engineering management, technology management. *Unit head:* Melvin G. Williams, Jr., Director, 202-319-5191, Fax: 202-319-6860, E-mail: williamsme@cua.edu. *Application contact:* Dr. Steven Brown, Director of Graduate Admissions, 202-319-5057, Fax: 202-319-6533, E-mail: cua-admissions@cua.edu.
Website: https://engineering.catholic.edu/management/index.html

Central Michigan University, Central Michigan University Global Campus, Program in Administration, Mount Pleasant, MI 48859. Offers acquisitions administration (MSA, Certificate); engineering management administration (MSA, Certificate); general administration (MSA, Certificate); health services administration (MSA, Certificate); human resources administration (MSA, Certificate); information resource management (MSA); information resource management administration (Certificate); international administration (MSA, Certificate); leadership (MSA, Certificate); philanthropy and fundraising administration (MSA, Certificate); public administration (MSA, Certificate); recreation and park administration (MSA); research administration (MSA, Certificate). *Program availability:* Part-time, evening/weekend, online learning. *Entrance requirements:* For master's, minimum GPA of 2.7 in major. Electronic applications accepted.

Central Michigan University, College of Graduate Studies, College of Business Administration, Department of Business Information Systems, Mount Pleasant, MI 48859. Offers business computing (Graduate Certificate); information systems (MS), including accounting information systems, business informatics, enterprise systems using SAP software, information systems. *Program availability:* Part-time, evening/weekend. *Degree requirements:* For master's, thesis or alternative. Electronic applications accepted. *Faculty research:* Enterprise software, electronic commerce, decision support systems, ethical issues in information systems, information technology management and teaching issues.

Central Michigan University, College of Graduate Studies, College of Business Administration, MBA Program, Mount Pleasant, MI 48859. Offers accounting (MBA); business economics (MBA); consulting (MBA); finance (MBA); general business (MBA); human resource management (MBA); information systems (MBA); international business (MBA); logistics management (MBA); marketing (MBA); value-driven

organization (MBA). *Program availability:* Part-time, evening/weekend, online learning. Electronic applications accepted. *Faculty research:* Accounting, consulting, international business, marketing, information systems.

Central Michigan University, College of Graduate Studies, Interdisciplinary Administration Programs, Mount Pleasant, MI 48859. Offers acquisitions administration (MSA, Graduate Certificate); general administration (MSA, Graduate Certificate); health services administration (MSA, Graduate Certificate); human resource administration (Graduate Certificate); human resources administration (MSA); information resource management (MSA, Graduate Certificate); international administration (MSA, Graduate Certificate); leadership (MSA, Graduate Certificate); public administration (MSA, Graduate Certificate); research administration (Graduate Certificate); sport administration (MSA). *Accreditation:* AACSB. *Program availability:* Part-time, evening/weekend, online learning. *Degree requirements:* For master's, thesis or alternative. *Entrance requirements:* For master's, bachelor's degree with minimum GPA of 2.7. Electronic applications accepted. *Faculty research:* Interdisciplinary studies in acquisitions administration, health services administration, sport administration, recreation and park administration, and international administration.

Central Penn College, Graduate Programs, Summerdale, PA 17093-0309. Offers information systems management (MPS); organizational development (MPS). Programs offered in Harrisburg, PA. *Program availability:* Evening/weekend.

Charleston Southern University, College of Business, Charleston, SC 29423-8087. Offers accounting (MBA); finance (MBA); general management (MBA); human resource management (MS); leadership (MBA); management information systems (MBA); organizational leadership (MA). *Program availability:* Part-time, evening/weekend. *Degree requirements:* For master's, thesis optional. *Entrance requirements:* For master's, GMAT. Additional exam requirements/recommendations for international students: Required—TOEFL (minimum score 550 paper-based; 79 iBT). *Application deadline:* Applications are processed on a rolling basis. Application fee: $40. Electronic applications accepted. *Expenses:* Tuition: Part-time $500 per credit hour. One-time fee: $30. Tuition and fees vary according to program. *Financial support:* Research assistantships with full tuition reimbursements available. Financial award application deadline: 4/15; financial award applicants required to submit FAFSA. *Unit head:* Dr. David Palmer, Dean, 843-863-7025, Fax: 843-863-7922, E-mail: dpalmer@csuniv.edu. *Application contact:* Dr. Darin L. Gerdes, Associate Professor of Management, 843-863-7814, Fax: 843-863-7922, E-mail: dgerdes@csuniv.edu.
Website: http://www.csuniv.edu/business/

City College of the City University of New York, Graduate School, Grove School of Engineering, Department of Computer Science, New York, NY 10031-9198. Offers computer science (MS, PhD); information systems (MIS). PhD program offered jointly with Graduate School and University Center of the City University of New York. *Degree requirements:* For master's, thesis optional; for doctorate, one foreign language, comprehensive exam, thesis/dissertation. *Entrance requirements:* For master's and doctorate, GRE General Test. Additional exam requirements/recommendations for international students: Required—TOEFL (minimum score 500 paper-based; 61 iBT). *Faculty research:* Complexities of algebraic research, human issues in computer science, scientific computing, super compilers, parallel algorithms.

City University of Seattle, Graduate Division, School of Management, Seattle, WA 98121. Offers accounting (Certificate); change leadership (MBA, Certificate); computer systems (MS); finance (Certificate); financial management (MBA); general management (MBA); general management-Europe (MBA); global marketing (MBA); human resources management (Certificate); individualized study (MS); information security (MS); information systems (MBA); leadership (MA); marketing (MBA, Certificate); project management (MBA, MS, Certificate); sustainable business (Certificate); technology management (MBA, Certificate). *Program availability:* Part-time, evening/weekend, online learning. *Degree requirements:* For master's, comprehensive exam (for some programs), thesis (for some programs). *Entrance requirements:* For master's, baccalaureate degree or equivalent from an accredited or otherwise recognized institution. Additional exam requirements/recommendations for international students: Required—TOEFL (minimum score 567 paper-based; 87 iBT); Recommended—IELTS. Electronic applications accepted.

Claremont Graduate University, Graduate Programs, Center for Information Systems and Technology, Claremont, CA 91711-6160. Offers cybersecurity and networking (MS); data science and analytics (MS); electronic commerce (PhD); geographic information systems (MS); health informatics (MS); information systems (Certificate); IT strategy and innovation (MS); knowledge management (PhD); systems development (PhD); telecommunications and networking (PhD); MBA/MS. *Program availability:* Part-time. *Degree requirements:* For doctorate, comprehensive exam, thesis/dissertation, portfolio. *Entrance requirements:* For master's and doctorate, GMAT, GRE General Test. Additional exam requirements/recommendations for international students: Required—TOEFL (minimum score 75 iBT). Electronic applications accepted. *Faculty research:* Man-machine interaction, organizational aspects of computing, implementation of information systems, information systems practice.

Clark University, Graduate School, Graduate School of Management, Business Administration Program, Worcester, MA 01610-1477. Offers accounting (MBA); finance (MBA); information management and business analytics (MBA); management (MBA); marketing (MBA); social change (MBA); sustainability (MBA). *Accreditation:* AACSB. *Program availability:* Part-time, evening/weekend. *Students:* 87 full-time (41 women), 41 part-time (26 women); includes 19 minority (10 Black or African American, non-Hispanic/Latino; 4 Asian, non-Hispanic/Latino; 4 Hispanic/Latino; 1 Two or more races, non-Hispanic/Latino), 40 international. Average age 30. 242 applicants, 50% accepted, 54 enrolled. In 2017, 102 master's awarded. *Degree requirements:* For master's, thesis optional. *Entrance requirements:* For master's, GMAT or GRE, 2 references, resume or curriculum vitae, personal statement. Additional exam requirements/recommendations for international students: Required—TOEFL (minimum score 575 paper-based; 90 iBT), IELTS (minimum score 6.5). *Application deadline:* For fall admission, 4/15 priority date for domestic and international students; for spring admission, 12/1 priority date for domestic and international students. Application fee: $75. Electronic applications accepted. *Expenses:* $4,490 tuition per 14-week course; $2,245 per half-unit (7-week course); $40 activity fee (full-time students only); $80 miscellaneous one-time fee; $1,750 student services fee. *Financial support:* Fellowships, research assistantships, teaching assistantships, career-related internships or fieldwork, Federal Work-Study, institutionally sponsored loans, and tuition waivers (partial) available. Support available to part-time students. Financial award application deadline: 5/31. *Faculty research:* Marketing, accounting, human resource management, management information systems, business finance. *Unit head:* Dr. Priscilla Elsass, Dean, 508-793-7543, Fax: 508-793-8822, E-mail: pelsass@clarku.edu. *Application contact:* Yingying Chen, Assistant Director of Graduate Admissions, 508-793-7373, Fax: 508-798-4386, E-mail: graduateadmissions@clarku.edu.
Website: http://www.clarku.edu/programs/masters-business-administration

Clemson University, Graduate School, College of Business, Department of Management, Clemson, SC 29634. Offers business administration (PhD), including management information systems, strategy, entrepreneurship and organizational

Management Information Systems

behavior, supply chain and operations management; management (MS). *Accreditation:* AACSB. *Faculty:* 34 full-time (12 women), 1 part-time/adjunct (0 women). *Students:* 14 full-time (3 women), 1 part-time (0 women), 9 international. Average age 33. 30 applicants, 13% accepted. In 2017, 4 master's, 4 doctorates awarded. Terminal master's awarded for partial completion of doctoral program. *Degree requirements:* For master's, comprehensive exam, thesis optional; for doctorate, comprehensive exam, thesis/dissertation. *Entrance requirements:* For master's and doctorate, GMAT or GRE General Test, unofficial transcripts, two letters of reference, curriculum vitae. Additional exam requirements/recommendations for international students: Required—TOEFL (minimum score 94 iBT), IELTS (minimum score 7), PTE (minimum score 64). *Application deadline:* For fall admission, 1/15 priority date for domestic and international students. Application fee: $80 ($90 for international students). Electronic applications accepted. *Expenses:* $6,564 per semester full-time resident, $12,538 per semester full-time non-resident, $743 per credit hour part-time resident, $1,486 per credit hour part-time non-resident, $1,203 per credit hour online, other fees may apply per session. *Financial support:* In 2017–18, 10 students received support, including 1 fellowship with partial tuition reimbursement available (averaging $1,000 per year), 1 research assistantship with partial tuition reimbursement available (averaging $12,000 per year), 2 teaching assistantships with partial tuition reimbursements available (averaging $18,770 per year); unspecified assistantships also available. Financial award application deadline: 1/15. *Faculty research:* Effective use of information technology in business, manufacturing and service operations strategy, lean operations and quality management, healthcare operations, behavioral market design. *Total annual research expenditures:* $89,179. *Unit head:* Dr. V. Sridharan, Department Chair, 864-656-2624, E-mail: suhas@clemson.edu. *Application contact:* Dr. Janis Miller, Graduate Program Coordinator, 864-656-3757, E-mail: janism@clemson.edu.
Website: https://www.clemson.edu/business/departments/management/

Cleveland State University, College of Graduate Studies, Monte Ahuja College of Business, Doctor of Business Administration Program, Cleveland, OH 44115. Offers information systems (DBA); marketing (DBA). *Accreditation:* AACSB. *Program availability:* Part-time, evening/weekend. *Faculty:* 50 full-time (11 women). *Students:* 3 full-time (2 women), 16 part-time (8 women); includes 6 minority (3 Black or African American, non-Hispanic/Latino; 3 Asian, non-Hispanic/Latino), 2 international. Average age 40. In 2017, 7 doctorates awarded. *Degree requirements:* For doctorate, comprehensive exam, thesis/dissertation, oral dissertation defense. *Entrance requirements:* For doctorate, GMAT, MBA or equivalent. Additional exam requirements/recommendations for international students: Required—TOEFL (minimum score 550 paper-based; 78 iBT). *Application deadline:* For fall admission, 2/1 for domestic and international students. Application fee: $40. Electronic applications accepted. *Financial support:* In 2017–18, 5 research assistantships with full tuition reimbursements (averaging $12,700 per year), 4 teaching assistantships with full tuition reimbursements (averaging $12,700 per year) were awarded; tuition waivers (full) and unspecified assistantships also available. *Faculty research:* Supply chain management, international business, strategic management, risk analysis, consumer behavior. *Unit head:* Dr. Raj Shekhar G. Javalgi, Director, 216-687-3786, Fax: 216-687-9354, E-mail: r.javalgi@csuohio.edu. *Application contact:* Melinda J. Arnold, Administrative Secretary, 216-687-6952, Fax: 216-687-9257, E-mail: m.arnold@csuohio.edu.
Website: http://www.csuohio.edu/business/academics/mbajuris-doctor

Coastal Carolina University, College of Science, Conway, SC 29528-6054. Offers applied computing and information systems (Certificate); coastal marine and wetland studies (MS); information systems technology (MS); marine science (PhD); sports management (MS). *Program availability:* Part-time, evening/weekend, 100% online. *Faculty:* 29 full-time (7 women), 2 part-time/adjunct (1 woman). *Students:* 58 full-time (19 women), 38 part-time (19 women); includes 16 minority (14 Black or African American, non-Hispanic/Latino; 1 American Indian or Alaska Native, non-Hispanic/Latino; 2 Hispanic/Latino; 2 Two or more races, non-Hispanic/Latino), 8 international. Average age 27. 104 applicants, 62% accepted, 42 enrolled. In 2017, 9 master's awarded. *Degree requirements:* For master's, thesis or internship; for doctorate, comprehensive exam, thesis/dissertation. *Entrance requirements:* For master's, GRE, 3 letters of recommendation, resume, official transcripts, written statement of educational and career goals, baccalaureate degree; for doctorate, GRE, official transcripts; baccalaureate or master's degree; minimum GPA of 3.0 for all collegiate coursework; successful completion of at least two semesters of college-level calculus, physics, and chemistry; 3 letters of recommendation; written statement of educational and career goals; resume; for Certificate, 2 letters of reference, official transcripts, minimum GPA of 3.0 in all computing and information systems courses, documentation of graduation from accredited four-year college or university. Additional exam requirements/recommendations for international students: Required—TOEFL (minimum score 550 paper-based; 79 iBT), IELTS (minimum score 6.5). *Application deadline:* For fall admission, 1/15 priority date for domestic and international students; for spring admission, 11/1 priority date for domestic and international students. Applications are processed on a rolling basis. Application fee: $45. Electronic applications accepted. *Expenses:* Tuition, state resident: full-time $5184; part-time $576 per credit hour. Tuition, nonresident: full-time $9369; part-time $1041 per credit hour. *Required fees:* $90; $5 per credit hour. *Financial support:* Fellowships, research assistantships, teaching assistantships, and tuition waivers available. Financial award application deadline: 3/1; financial award applicants required to submit FAFSA. *Unit head:* Dr. Michael H. Roberts, Dean/Vice President for Research and Emerging Initiatives, 843-349-2282, Fax: 843-349-2545, E-mail: mroberts@coastal.edu. *Application contact:* Dr. James O. Luken, Associate Provost for Graduate Program/Vice-Dean of the Coastal Environment, 843-349-2235, Fax: 843-349-6444, E-mail: joluken@coastal.edu.
Website: https://www.coastal.edu/science/

College of Charleston, Graduate School, School of Sciences and Mathematics, Program in Computer and Information Sciences, Charleston, SC 29424-0001. Offers MS. Program offered jointly with The Citadel, The Military College of South Carolina. *Program availability:* Part-time, evening/weekend. *Degree requirements:* For master's, thesis optional. *Entrance requirements:* For master's, GRE. Additional exam requirements/recommendations for international students: Required—TOEFL (minimum score 81 iBT). Electronic applications accepted.

The College of St. Scholastica, Graduate Studies, Department of Computer Information Systems, Duluth, MN 55811-4199. Offers MA, Certificate. *Program availability:* Part-time, online learning. *Degree requirements:* For master's, thesis. *Entrance requirements:* Additional exam requirements/recommendations for international students: Required—TOEFL (minimum score 550 paper-based; 79 iBT). Electronic applications accepted. Application fee is waived when completed online. *Expenses:* Contact institution. *Faculty research:* Organization acceptance of software development methodologies.

Colorado State University, College of Business, Department of Computer Information Systems, Fort Collins, CO 80523-1277. Offers MCIS. *Program availability:* Part-time, evening/weekend, 100% online, blended/hybrid learning. *Faculty:* 9 full-time (6 women), 3 part-time/adjunct (0 women). *Students:* 56 full-time (18 women), 181 part-time (64 women); includes 45 minority (10 Black or African American, non-Hispanic/Latino; 18 Asian, non-Hispanic/Latino; 14 Hispanic/Latino; 3 Two or more races, non-Hispanic/

Latino), 62 international. Average age 34. 146 applicants, 64% accepted, 56 enrolled. In 2017, 85 master's awarded. *Entrance requirements:* For master's, GMAT (minimum score of 550) or GRE, minimum GPA of 3.0; bachelor's degree; letters of recommendation; resume; statement of purpose. Additional exam requirements/recommendations for international students: Required—TOEFL (minimum score 86 iBT), IELTS (minimum score 6.5), PTE (minimum score 58). *Application deadline:* For fall admission, 7/1 for domestic students, 5/1 for international students; for spring admission, 12/1 for domestic students, 10/1 for international students. Applications are processed on a rolling basis. Application fee: $60 ($70 for international students). Electronic applications accepted. *Expenses:* $313 per credit hour. *Financial support:* Scholarships/grants and unspecified assistantships available. *Faculty research:* Learning and effectively using information technology; predictors of programmer performance; he impact of information systems on identity and culture dynamics. *Total annual research expenditures:* $178,294. *Unit head:* Dr. Jon D. Clark, Chair, 970-491-1618, E-mail: jon.clark@colostate.edu. *Application contact:* Shirley Bennett, Program Assistant, 970-491-7929, E-mail: shirley.bennett@colostate.edu.
Website: https://biz.colostate.edu/Academics/Graduate-Programs/Master-of-Computer-Information-Systems

Colorado State University–Global Campus, Graduate Programs, Greenwood Village, CO 80111. Offers criminal justice and law enforcement administration (MS); education leadership (MS); finance (MS); healthcare administration and management (MS); human resource management (MHRM); information technology management (MITM); international management (MS); management (MS); organizational leadership (MS); professional accounting (MPA); project management (MS); teaching and learning (MS). *Accreditation:* ACBSP. *Program availability:* Online learning.

Concordia University Wisconsin, Graduate Programs, School of Business Administration, MBA Program, Mequon, WI 53097-2402. Offers finance (MBA); health care administration (MBA); human resource management (MBA); international business (MBA); international business-bilingual English/Chinese (MBA); management (MBA); management information systems (MBA); managerial communications (MBA); marketing (MBA); public administration (MBA); risk management (MBA). *Program availability:* Online learning. *Degree requirements:* For master's, comprehensive exam, thesis or alternative. *Entrance requirements:* Additional exam requirements/recommendations for international students: Required—TOEFL. *Expenses:* Contact institution.

Copenhagen Business School, Graduate Programs, Copenhagen, Denmark. Offers business administration (Exec MBA, MBA, PhD); business administration and information systems (M Sc); business, language and culture (M Sc); economics and business administration (M Sc); health management (MHM); international business and politics (M Sc); public administration (MPA); shipping and logistics (Exec MBA); technology, market and organization (MBA).

Daemen College, Department of Accounting/Information Systems, Amherst, NY 14226-3592. Offers global business (MS), including accounting, global business, management information systems, marketing. *Program availability:* Part-time, evening/weekend. *Degree requirements:* For master's, minimum GPA of 3.0. *Entrance requirements:* For master's, GMAT if undergraduate GPA is less than 3.0, 2 letters of recommendation; goal statement; transcripts; demonstration of satisfactory oral and written English. Additional exam requirements/recommendations for international students: Required—TOEFL (minimum score 500 paper-based; 63 iBT), IELTS (minimum score 5.5). Electronic applications accepted. *Faculty research:* Internationalization of small business, cultural influences on business practices, international human resource practices.

Dakota State University, College of Business and Information Systems, Madison, SD 57042-1799. Offers analytics (MSA); business analytics (Graduate Certificate); general management (MBA); health informatics (MSHI); information systems (MSIS, D Sc IS); information technology (Graduate Certificate). *Accreditation:* ACBSP. *Program availability:* Part-time, evening/weekend, 100% online, blended/hybrid learning. *Faculty:* 22 full-time (6 women), 1 (woman) part-time/adjunct. *Students:* 37 full-time (9 women), 168 part-time (52 women); includes 60 minority (29 Black or African American, non-Hispanic/Latino; 3 American Indian or Alaska Native, non-Hispanic/Latino; 15 Asian, non-Hispanic/Latino; 10 Hispanic/Latino; 1 Native Hawaiian or other Pacific Islander, non-Hispanic/Latino; 2 Two or more races, non-Hispanic/Latino), 40 international. Average age 38. 179 applicants, 57% accepted, 59 enrolled. In 2017, 49 master's, 8 doctorates, 5 other advanced degrees awarded. *Degree requirements:* For master's, comprehensive exam, thesis optional, integrative project; for doctorate, comprehensive exam, thesis/dissertation, portfolio. *Entrance requirements:* For master's, GRE General Test, demonstration of information systems skills, minimum GPA of 2.7; for doctorate, GRE General Test, demonstration of information systems skills; for Graduate Certificate, GMAT. Additional exam requirements/recommendations for international students: Required—TOEFL (minimum score 550 paper-based, 76 iBT) or IELTS (6.0). *Application deadline:* For fall admission, 6/15 for domestic students, 4/15 priority date for international students; for spring admission, 11/15 for domestic students, 10/15 priority date for international students; for summer admission, 4/15 for domestic students. Applications are processed on a rolling basis. Application fee: $35. Electronic applications accepted. *Expenses:* Tuition, state resident: full-time $5749. Tuition, nonresident: full-time $10,733. *Required fees:* $715. Tuition and fees vary according to campus/location and reciprocity agreements. *Financial support:* Research assistantships with partial tuition reimbursements, teaching assistantships with partial tuition reimbursements, and unspecified assistantships available. Financial award applicants required to submit FAFSA. *Faculty research:* Data mining and analytics, biometrics and information assurance, decision support systems, health informatics, STEM education for K-12 teachers/students and underrepresented populations. *Unit head:* Dr. Dorine Bennett, Dean of College of Business and Information Systems, 605-256-5165, E-mail: dorine.bennett@dsu.edu. *Application contact:* Erin Blankespoor, Senior Secretary, Office of Graduate Studies and Research, 605-256-5799, E-mail: erin.blankespoor@dsu.edu.
Website: http://dsu.edu/academics/colleges/college-of-business-and-information-systems

Dalhousie University, Faculty of Management, Centre for Advanced Management Education, Halifax, NS B3H 3J5, Canada. Offers financial services (MBA); information management (MIM); management (MPA); natural resources (MBA). *Program availability:* Part-time, online learning. *Entrance requirements:* For master's, GMAT, minimum GPA of 3.0, resume. Additional exam requirements/recommendations for international students: Required—TOEFL, IELTS, CANTEST, CAEL, or Michigan English Language Assessment Battery. Electronic applications accepted.

Dallas Baptist University, College of Business, Master of Business Administration Program, Dallas, TX 75211-9299. Offers accounting (MBA); business communication (MBA); conflict resolution management (MBA); entrepreneurship (MBA); finance (MBA); health care management (MBA); international business (MBA); leading the non-profit organization (MBA); management (MBA); management information systems (MBA); marketing (MBA); project management (MBA); technology and engineering management (MBA). *Accreditation:* ACBSP. *Program availability:* Part-time, evening/weekend, 100% online, blended/hybrid learning. *Application deadline:* Applications are

processed on a rolling basis. Application fee: $25. Electronic applications accepted. Application fee is waived when completed online. *Expenses: Tuition:* Full-time $16,308; part-time $906 per credit hour. *Required fees:* $900; $450 per semester. Tuition and fees vary according to course load and degree level. *Unit head:* Dr. Sandra Reid, Chair of Graduate Business Programs, 214-333-5280, E-mail: sandra@dbu.edu. *Application contact:* Bobby Soto, Director of Admissions, 214-333-5242, E-mail: graduate@dbu.edu.
Website: http://www.dbu.edu/gsb/mba

DePaul University, College of Computing and Digital Media, Chicago, IL 60604. Offers animation (MA, MFA); applied technology (MS); business information technology (MS); computational finance (MS); computer and information sciences (PhD); computer science (MS); creative producing (MFA); cybersecurity (MS); data science (MS); digital communication and media arts (MA); documentary (MS); e-commerce technology (MS); experience design (MA); film and television (MS); film and television directing (MFA); game design (MFA); game programming (MS); health informatics (MS); human centered design (PhD); human-computer interaction (MS); information systems (MS); network engineering and security (MS); product innovation and computing (MS); screenwriting (MFA); software engineering (MS); JD/MS. *Program availability:* Part-time, evening/weekend, online learning. *Degree requirements:* For master's, thesis (for some programs); for doctorate, comprehensive exam, thesis/dissertation. *Entrance requirements:* For master's, GRE or GMAT (for MS in computational finance only), bachelor's degree, resume (MS in predictive analytics only), IT experience (MS in information technology project management only), portfolio review (all MFA programs and MA in animation); for doctorate, GRE, master's degree in computer science. Additional exam requirements/recommendations for international students: Required—TOEFL (minimum score 590 paper-based; 80 iBT), IELTS (minimum score 6.5), PTE (minimum score 53). *Application deadline:* For fall admission, 8/1 priority date for domestic students, 6/15 priority date for international students; for winter admission, 12/1 priority date for domestic students, 10/15 priority date for international students; for spring admission, 3/1 priority date for domestic students, 1/15 priority date for international students; for summer admission, 5/1 for domestic students, 4/15 for international students. Applications are processed on a rolling basis. Application fee: $25. Electronic applications accepted. *Expenses:* Contact institution. *Financial support:* Fellowships with full tuition reimbursements, research assistantships with full and partial tuition reimbursements, teaching assistantships with full and partial tuition reimbursements, Federal Work-Study, scholarships/grants, tuition waivers (full and partial), and unspecified assistantships available. Support available to part-time students. Financial award application deadline: 4/20; financial award applicants required to submit FAFSA. *Faculty research:* Data mining, computer science, human-computer interaction, security, animation and film. *Unit head:* Elly Kafritsas-Wessels, Communications Manager, 312-362-5816, Fax: 312-362-5185, E-mail: ekafrits@cdm.depaul.edu. *Application contact:* Office of Admission, 312-362-8714, E-mail: admission@cdm.depaul.edu.
Website: http://cdm.depaul.edu

DePaul University, Kellstadt Graduate School of Business, Chicago, IL 60604. Offers accountancy (MBA, MSA); applied economics (MBA); audit and advisory services (MS); business administration (DBA); business analytics (MS); business strategy and decision-making (MBA); computational finance (MS); economics and policy analysis (MS); enterprise risk management (MS); entrepreneurship (MBA, MS); finance (MBA, MS); general business (MBA); hospitality leadership (MBA); hospitality leadership and operational performance (MS); human resources (MS); international business (MBA); management (MBA, MS); management information systems (MBA); marketing (MBA, MS); marketing analysis (MS); marketing strategy and planning (MBA); real estate (MS); real estate finance and investment (MBA); strategy, execution and valuation (MBA); supply chain management (MS); sustainable management (MS); taxation (MS); JD/MBA. *Accreditation:* AACSB. *Program availability:* Part-time, evening/weekend, online learning. *Entrance requirements:* For master's, GMAT/GRE, 2 letters of recommendation, resume, essay, official transcripts. Additional exam requirements/recommendations for international students: Required—TOEFL (minimum score 550 paper-based; 80 iBT). *Application deadline:* For fall admission, 7/1 for domestic students, 6/1 for international students; for winter admission, 10/1 for domestic students, 9/1 for international students; for spring admission, 2/1 for domestic students, 1/1 for international students. Applications are processed on a rolling basis. Application fee: $60. Electronic applications accepted. *Expenses:* Contact institution. *Financial support:* Application deadline: 4/1; applicants required to submit FAFSA. *Unit head:* Christa Hinton, Assistant Dean and Director, 312-362-8810, Fax: 312-362-6677, E-mail: chinton@depaul.edu. *Application contact:* Garry Cooke, Director of Recruitment and Admissions, 312-362-8810, Fax: 312-362-6677, E-mail: kgsb@depaul.edu.
Website: http://kellstadt.depaul.edu

DeSales University, Division of Business, Center Valley, PA 18034-9568. Offers accounting (MBA); computer information systems (MBA); finance (MBA); health care systems management (MBA); human resources management (MBA); management (MBA); marketing (MBA); project management (MBA); self-design (MBA); supply chain management (MBA); DNP/MBA; MSN/MBA. *Accreditation:* ACBSP. *Program availability:* Part-time, evening/weekend, 100% online, blended/hybrid learning. *Faculty:* 9 full-time (3 women), 32 part-time/adjunct (8 women). *Students:* 78 full-time (44 women), 323 part-time (164 women); includes 71 minority (22 Black or African American, non-Hispanic/Latino; 17 Asian, non-Hispanic/Latino; 24 Hispanic/Latino; 8 Two or more races, non-Hispanic/Latino; 1 international. Average age 34. 213 applicants, 40% accepted, 64 enrolled. In 2017, 123 master's awarded. *Entrance requirements:* For master's, GMAT (waived if undergraduate GPA is 3.0 or better), minimum GPA of 3.0 in undergraduate work, literacy in basic software, background or interest in the field of study, personal statement, 2 years of work experience. Additional exam requirements/recommendations for international students: Required—TOEFL. *Application deadline:* Applications are processed on a rolling basis. Application fee: $50. Electronic applications accepted. *Expenses:* Contact institution. *Financial support:* Applicants required to submit FAFSA. *Faculty research:* Quality improvement, executive development, productivity, cross-cultural managerial differences, leadership. *Unit head:* Dr. David M. Gilfoil, Director, MBA Program, 610-282-1100 Ext. 1828, Fax: 610-282-2869, E-mail: david.gilfoil@desales.edu. *Application contact:* Julia Ferraro, Director of Graduate Admissions, 610-282-1100 Ext. 1768, E-mail: gradadmissions@desales.edu.

DeSales University, Division of Science and Mathematics, Center Valley, PA 18034-9568. Offers cyber security (Postbaccalaureate Certificate); data analytics (Postbaccalaureate Certificate); information systems (MS), including cyber security, digital forensics, healthcare information management, project management. *Program availability:* Part-time, evening/weekend, 100% online, blended/hybrid learning. *Faculty:* 1 (woman) full-time, 2 part-time/adjunct (0 women). *Students:* 8 full-time (0 women), 12 part-time (6 women); includes 3 minority (1 Asian, non-Hispanic/Latino; 1 Hispanic/Latino; 1 Two or more races, non-Hispanic/Latino), 1 international. Average age 35. 35 applicants, 31% accepted, 5 enrolled. In 2017, 6 master's awarded. *Entrance requirements:* For master's, GRE or GMAT, bachelor's degree in computer-related discipline from accredited college or university, minimum undergraduate GPA of 3.0, personal statement, three letters of recommendation. Additional exam requirements/recommendations for international students: Required—TOEFL. *Application deadline:*

Applications are processed on a rolling basis. Application fee: $50. Electronic applications accepted. *Expenses:* Contact institution. *Financial support:* Applicants required to submit FAFSA. *Unit head:* Dr. Patricia Riola, Director/Assistant Professor of Computer Science, 610-282-1100 Ext. 1647, E-mail: patricia.riola@desales.edu. *Application contact:* Julia Ferraro, Director of Graduate Admissions, 610-282-1100 Ext. 1768, E-mail: gradadmissions@desales.edu.
Website: http://www.desales.edu/home/academics/graduate-studies/programs-of-study/msis—-master-of-science-in-information-systems

DeVry University–Folsom Campus, Graduate Programs, Folsom, CA 95630. Offers accounting (M Acc); accounting and financial management (MAFM); business administration (MBA); curriculum leadership (M Ed); educational leadership (M Ed); educational technology (M Ed); higher education leadership (M Ed); human resource management (MHRM); information systems management (MISM); network and communications management (MNCM); project management (MPM); public administration (MPA).

Dominican University, School of Information Studies, River Forest, IL 60305-1099. Offers information management (MSIM); knowledge management (Certificate); library and information science (MLIS, MPS, PhD); special studies (CSS); MBA/MLIS; MLIS/MA. MLIS/M Div offered jointly with McCormick Theological Seminary, MLIS/MA with Loyola University Chicago, MLIS/MM with Northwestern University. *Accreditation:* ALA (one or more programs are accredited). *Program availability:* Part-time, evening/weekend, 100% online, blended/hybrid learning. *Faculty:* 11 full-time (7 women), 16 part-time/adjunct (10 women). *Students:* 58 full-time (49 women), 184 part-time (145 women); includes 53 minority (29 Black or African American, non-Hispanic/Latino; 2 Asian, non-Hispanic/Latino; 21 Hispanic/Latino; 1 Two or more races, non-Hispanic/Latino), 5 international. Average age 34. 84 applicants, 94% accepted, 52 enrolled. In 2017, 86 master's awarded. *Degree requirements:* For doctorate, thesis/dissertation. *Entrance requirements:* For master's, minimum GPA of 3.0, GRE General Test, or MAT; for doctorate, MLIS or related MA, minimum GPA of 3.0, GRE General Test, or MAT. Additional exam requirements/recommendations for international students: Required—TOEFL. *Application deadline:* For fall admission, 6/1 priority date for domestic students; for winter admission, 3/1 priority date for domestic students; for spring admission, 10/1 priority date for domestic students. Applications are processed on a rolling basis. Application fee: $25. *Expenses:* Contact institution. *Financial support:* Fellowships, research assistantships, career-related internships or fieldwork, scholarships/grants, and unspecified assistantships available. Support available to part-time students. Financial award application deadline: 4/15; financial award applicants required to submit FAFSA. *Faculty research:* Productivity and the information environment, bibliometrics, library history, subject access, library materials and services for children. *Unit head:* Dr. Kate Marek, Director, 708-524-6648, Fax: 708-524-6657, E-mail: kmarek@dom.edu. *Application contact:* Catherine Galarza-Espino, Coordinator of Graduate Marketing and Recruiting, 708-524-6983, E-mail: cgalarza@dom.edu.
Website: http://sois.dom.edu

Drexel University, College of Computing and Informatics, Department of Information Science, Philadelphia, PA 19104-2875. Offers health informatics (MS); information science (PhD, Post-Master's Certificate, Postbaccalaureate Certificate); information systems (MS); library and information science (MS). *Program availability:* Part-time, evening/weekend, 100% online. *Faculty:* 21 full-time (11 women), 14 part-time/adjunct (7 women). *Students:* 168 full-time (98 women), 202 part-time (142 women); includes 75 minority (32 Black or African American, non-Hispanic/Latino; 13 Asian, non-Hispanic/Latino; 21 Hispanic/Latino; 9 Two or more races, non-Hispanic/Latino), 77 international. Average age 32. 453 applicants, 50% accepted, 101 enrolled. In 2017, 170 master's, 7 doctorates, 11 other advanced degrees awarded. *Degree requirements:* For doctorate, thesis/dissertation. *Entrance requirements:* For master's and doctorate, GRE General Test. Additional exam requirements/recommendations for international students: Required—TOEFL (minimum score 90 iBT), IELTS (minimum score 6.5). *Application deadline:* For fall admission, 8/15 for domestic students, 7/15 for international students; for spring admission, 3/1 for domestic students, 2/1 for international students. Applications are processed on a rolling basis. Application fee: $65. Electronic applications accepted. *Financial support:* In 2017–18, 81 students received support, including 2 fellowships with full tuition reimbursements available (averaging $32,667 per year), 19 research assistantships with full tuition reimbursements available (averaging $27,133 per year), 4 teaching assistantships with full tuition reimbursements available (averaging $27,657 per year); career-related internships or fieldwork, scholarships/grants, and tuition waivers (partial) also available. Support available to part-time students. Financial award application deadline: 3/1; financial award applicants required to submit FAFSA. *Total annual research expenditures:* $1.9 million. *Unit head:* Dr. Yi Deng, Dean/Professor, 215-895-2474, Fax: 215-895-2494, E-mail: yd362@drexel.edu. *Application contact:* Matthew Lechtenberg, Director, Recruitment, 215-895-2474, Fax: 215-895-2303, E-mail: cciinfo@drexel.edu.
Website: http://cci.drexel.edu/academics/graduate-programs/ms-in-health-informatics

Duquesne University, Palumbo-Donahue School of Business, Pittsburgh, PA 15282-0001. Offers accounting (M Acc); finance (MBA); information systems management (MSISM); management (MBA, MS); marketing (MBA); sports business (MS); supply chain management (MS); sustainability (MBA); JD/MBA; MBA/M Acc; MBA/MA; MBA/MES; MBA/MHMS; MSISM/MBA; Pharm D/MBA. *Accreditation:* AACSB. *Program availability:* Part-time, evening/weekend, minimal on-campus study. *Faculty:* 59 full-time (23 women), 25 part-time/adjunct (6 women). *Students:* 232 full-time (83 women), 46 part-time (18 women); includes 28 minority (14 Black or African American, non-Hispanic/Latino; 8 Asian, non-Hispanic/Latino; 4 Hispanic/Latino; 2 Two or more races, non-Hispanic/Latino), 24 international. Average age 29. 220 applicants, 83% accepted, 121 enrolled. In 2017, 113 master's awarded. *Entrance requirements:* For master's, GMAT or GRE, undergraduate transcripts, 2 letters of recommendation, current resume, personal statement. Additional exam requirements/recommendations for international students: Required—TOEFL (minimum score 577 paper-based; 90 iBT), IELTS (minimum score 7). *Application deadline:* For fall admission, 7/1 priority date for domestic and international students; for spring admission, 12/1 for domestic and international students; for summer admission, 4/1 for domestic and international students. Applications are processed on a rolling basis. Application fee: $0. Electronic applications accepted. *Expenses:* $934 per credit (MS in management, sports business); $1,259 per credit (MBA, MS in accountancy, information systems management). *Financial support:* In 2017–18, 211 students received support, including 12 fellowships with partial tuition reimbursements available (averaging $14,200 per year), 20 research assistantships with partial tuition reimbursements available (averaging $22,662 per year); career-related internships or fieldwork, scholarships/grants, and unspecified assistantships also available. Support available to part-time students. Financial award application deadline: 7/1; financial award applicants required to submit FAFSA. *Faculty research:* Investment management, business ethics, technology management, supply chain management, entrepreneurship. *Unit head:* Dr. Karen Donovan, Associate Dean of Graduate Programs and Executive Education, 412-396-6276, Fax: 412-396-1726, E-mail: donovan6@duq.edu. *Application contact:* Jeff Jewett, Director of Admissions and Enrollment Management, 412-396-6244, Fax: 412-396-1726, E-mail: decrostam@duq.edu.
Website: http://www.duq.edu/business/grad

Management Information Systems

East Carolina University, Graduate School, College of Engineering and Technology, Department of Technology Systems, Greenville, NC 27858-4353. Offers computer network professional (Certificate); cyber security professional (Certificate); information assurance (Certificate); Lean Six Sigma Black Belt (Certificate); network technology (MS), including computer networking management, digital communications technology, information security, Web technologies; occupational safety (MS); technology management (MS, PhD), including industrial distribution and logistics (MS); Website developer (Certificate). *Students:* 19 full-time (4 women), 158 part-time (35 women); includes 43 minority (28 Black or African American, non-Hispanic/Latino; 2 American Indian or Alaska Native, non-Hispanic/Latino; 3 Asian, non-Hispanic/Latino; 6 Hispanic/Latino; 4 Two or more races, non-Hispanic/Latino), 6 international. Average age 39. 44 applicants, 91% accepted, 37 enrolled. In 2017, 30 master's, 29 other advanced degrees awarded. *Entrance requirements:* For master's and Certificate, GRE General Test or MAT, minimum GPA of 2.5; for doctorate, GRE General Test, related work experience. Additional exam requirements/recommendations for international students: Recommended—TOEFL (minimum score 78 iBT), IELTS (minimum score 6.5). *Application deadline:* For fall admission, 6/1 priority date for domestic students. Applications are processed on a rolling basis. Application fee: $75. *Expenses:* Tuition, state resident: full-time $4749; part-time $297 per credit hour. Tuition, nonresident: full-time $17,898; part-time $1119 per credit hour. *Required fees:* $2691; $224 per credit hour. Part-time tuition and fees vary according to course load and program. *Financial support:* Application deadline: 6/1. *Unit head:* Dr. Tijjani Mohammed, Chair, 252-328-9668, E-mail: mohammedt@ecu.edu.
Website: http://www.ecu.edu/cs-cet/techsystems/index.cfm

Eastern Michigan University, Graduate School, College of Business, Department of Computer Information Systems, Ypsilanti, MI 48197. Offers MS. *Program availability:* Part-time, evening/weekend. *Faculty:* 7 full-time (0 women). *Students:* 19 full-time (12 women), 21 part-time (13 women); includes 6 minority (4 Asian, non-Hispanic/Latino; 1 Hispanic/Latino; 1 Two or more races, non-Hispanic/Latino), 27 international. Average age 30. 52 applicants, 44% accepted, 5 enrolled. In 2017, 20 master's awarded. *Entrance requirements:* Additional exam requirements/recommendations for international students: Required—TOEFL. *Application deadline:* For fall admission, 5/15 priority date for domestic students, 2/15 priority date for international students; for winter admission, 10/15 priority date for domestic students, 9/1 priority date for international students; for summer admission, 3/15 priority date for domestic students, 3/1 priority date for international students. Applications are processed on a rolling basis. Application fee: $45. *Financial support:* Fellowships, research assistantships with full tuition reimbursements, teaching assistantships with full tuition reimbursements, career-related internships or fieldwork, Federal Work-Study, institutionally sponsored loans, scholarships/grants, tuition waivers (partial), and unspecified assistantships available. Support available to part-time students. Financial award applicants required to submit FAFSA. *Unit head:* Dr. Zafar Khan, Interim Department Head, 734-487-2454, Fax: 734-487-1941, E-mail: zkhan@emich.edu.
Website: http://www.cis.emich.edu

Eastern Michigan University, Graduate School, College of Business, Programs in Business Administration, Ypsilanti, MI 48197. Offers business administration (MBA, Graduate Certificate); computer information systems (Graduate Certificate); e-business (MBA, Graduate Certificate); enterprise business intelligence (MBA); entrepreneurship (MBA, Graduate Certificate); finance (MBA, Graduate Certificate); human resources (MBA); human resources management (Graduate Certificate); information systems (MBA); internal auditing (MBA); international business (MBA, Graduate Certificate); marketing management (Graduate Certificate); nonprofit management (MBA); organizational development (Graduate Certificate); supply chain management (MBA, Graduate Certificate). *Accreditation:* AACSB. *Program availability:* Part-time, online learning. *Students:* 53 full-time (30 women), 297 part-time (170 women); includes 121 minority (72 Black or African American, non-Hispanic/Latino; 4 American Indian or Alaska Native, non-Hispanic/Latino; 15 Asian, non-Hispanic/Latino; 20 Hispanic/Latino; 10 Two or more races, non-Hispanic/Latino), 20 international. Average age 31. 247 applicants, 74% accepted, 94 enrolled. In 2017, 71 master's, 34 other advanced degrees awarded. *Entrance requirements:* For master's, GMAT (minimum score 450), minimum cumulative undergraduate GPA of 2.75. Additional exam requirements/recommendations for international students: Required—TOEFL. *Application deadline:* For fall admission, 5/15 priority date for domestic students, 2/15 priority date for international students; for winter admission, 10/15 priority date for domestic students, 9/1 priority date for international students; for summer admission, 3/15 priority date for domestic students, 3/1 priority date for international students. Applications are processed on a rolling basis. Application fee: $45. *Financial support:* Fellowships, research assistantships with full tuition reimbursements, teaching assistantships with full tuition reimbursements, career-related internships or fieldwork, Federal Work-Study, institutionally sponsored loans, scholarships/grants, tuition waivers (partial), and unspecified assistantships available. Support available to part-time students. Financial award applicants required to submit FAFSA. *Unit head:* K. Michelle Henry, Director, Graduate Business Programs, 734-487-4444, Fax: 734-483-1316, E-mail: cob.graduate@emich.edu.
Website: http://www.emich.edu/cob/mba/

Elmhurst College, Graduate Programs, Program in Computer Information Systems, Elmhurst, IL 60126-3296. Offers MS. *Program availability:* Part-time, evening/weekend, 100% online, blended/hybrid learning. *Faculty:* 2 full-time (0 women). *Students:* 3 full-time (1 woman), 17 part-time (3 women); includes 8 minority (4 Black or African American, non-Hispanic/Latino; 2 Hispanic/Latino; 2 Two or more races, non-Hispanic/Latino), 5 international. Average age 33. 14 applicants, 57% accepted, 5 enrolled. In 2017, 12 master's awarded. *Entrance requirements:* For master's, 3 recommendations, resume, statement of purpose. Additional exam requirements/recommendations for international students: Required—TOEFL (minimum score 550 paper-based; 79 iBT). *Application deadline:* Applications are processed on a rolling basis. Application fee: $0. Electronic applications accepted. *Expenses:* Contact institution. *Financial support:* In 2017–18, 8 students received support. Scholarships/grants available. Support available to part-time students. Financial award application deadline: 3/1; financial award applicants required to submit FAFSA. *Unit head:* Ali Ghane, Director, 630-617-3366, E-mail: alig@elmhurst.edu. *Application contact:* Timothy J. Panfil, Director of Enrollment Management, 630-617-3300 Ext. 3256, Fax: 630-617-6471, E-mail: panfilt@elmhurst.edu.
Website: http://www.elmhurst.edu/cis

Embry-Riddle Aeronautical University–Worldwide, Department of Decision Sciences, Daytona Beach, FL 32114-3900. Offers aviation and aerospace (MSPM); aviation/aerospace management (MSEM); financial management (MSEM, MSPM); general management (MSPM); global management (MSPM); human resources management (MSPM); information systems (MSPM); leadership (MSEM, MSPM); logistics and supply chain management (MSEM, MSLSCM, MSPM); management (MSEM, MSPM); project management (MSEM); systems engineering (MSEM, MSPM); technical management (MSPM). *Program availability:* Part-time, evening/weekend, EagleVision Classroom (between classrooms), EagleVision Home (faculty and students at home), and a blend of Classroom or Home. *Faculty:* 12 full-time (3 women), 53 part-time/adjunct (10 women). *Students:* 514 full-time (141 women), 476 part-time (111 women); includes 337 minority (136 Black or African American, non-Hispanic/Latino; 6 American Indian or Alaska Native, non-Hispanic/Latino; 39 Asian, non-Hispanic/Latino; 81 Hispanic/Latino; 4 Native Hawaiian or other Pacific Islander, non-Hispanic/Latino; 71 Two or more races, non-Hispanic/Latino), 21 international. Average age 36. 297 applicants, 72% accepted, 209 enrolled. In 2017, 292 master's awarded. *Degree requirements:* For master's, comprehensive exam (for some programs), thesis (for some programs). *Entrance requirements:* Additional exam requirements/recommendations for international students: Required—TOEFL (minimum score 550 paper-based; 79 iBT), IELTS (minimum score 6). *Application deadline:* Applications are processed on a rolling basis. Application fee: $50. Electronic applications accepted. *Expenses:* Contact institution. *Financial support:* Career-related internships or fieldwork and scholarships/grants available. Financial award applicants required to submit FAFSA. *Unit head:* Aman Gupta, PhD, Department Chair, E-mail: aman.gupta@erau.edu. *Application contact:* Worldwide Campus, 800-522-6787, E-mail: worldwide@erau.edu.

Embry-Riddle Aeronautical University–Worldwide, Department of Technology Management, Daytona Beach, FL 32114-3900. Offers information and security assurance (MS); management information systems (MS). *Program availability:* Part-time, evening/weekend, EagleVision Classroom (between classrooms), EagleVision Home (faculty and students at home), and a blend of Classroom or Home. *Faculty:* 2 full-time (1 woman), 20 part-time/adjunct (5 women). *Students:* 58 full-time (11 women), 51 part-time (18 women); includes 39 minority (15 Black or African American, non-Hispanic/Latino; 2 American Indian or Alaska Native, non-Hispanic/Latino; 5 Asian, non-Hispanic/Latino; 8 Hispanic/Latino; 9 Two or more races, non-Hispanic/Latino). Average age 38. 53 applicants, 68% accepted, 25 enrolled. In 2017, 12 master's awarded. *Entrance requirements:* Additional exam requirements/recommendations for international students: Required—TOEFL (minimum score 550 paper-based; 79 iBT), IELTS (minimum score 6). *Application deadline:* Applications are processed on a rolling basis. Application fee: $50. Electronic applications accepted. *Expenses: Tuition:* Full-time $7680; part-time $640 per credit hour. Tuition and fees vary according to program. *Financial support:* Career-related internships or fieldwork and scholarships/grants available. Financial award applicants required to submit FAFSA. *Unit head:* Dr. Aaron Glassman, Department Chair, E-mail: aaron.glassman@erau.edu. *Application contact:* Worldwide Campus, 800-522-6787, E-mail: worldwide@erau.edu.

Emory University, Goizueta Business School, Doctoral Program in Business, Atlanta, GA 30322. Offers accounting (PhD); finance (PhD); information systems and operations management (PhD); marketing (PhD); organization and management (PhD). *Students:* 250 applicants, 5% accepted. *Degree requirements:* For doctorate, comprehensive exam, thesis/dissertation. *Entrance requirements:* For doctorate, GMAT, interview. Additional exam requirements/recommendations for international students: Required—TOEFL (minimum score 600 paper-based; 100 iBT). *Application deadline:* For fall admission, 1/3 priority date for domestic and international students. Applications are processed on a rolling basis. Application fee: $75. Electronic applications accepted. *Expenses:* Contact institution. *Financial support:* Fellowships, scholarships/grants, and health care benefits available. Financial award application deadline: 1/3. *Faculty research:* Financial and managerial accounting, asset pricing strategy and organizational behavior, information technology marketing analytics and consumer behavior. *Unit head:* Kathryn Kadous, Associate Dean, 404-727-2306, Fax: 404-727-5337, E-mail: kathryn.kadous@emory.edu. *Application contact:* Allison Gilmore, Director of Admissions and Student Services, 404-727-6353, Fax: 404-727-5337, E-mail: allison.gilmore@emory.edu.
Website: https://goizueta.emory.edu/degree/phd/index.html

Emory University, Goizueta Business School, Full Time MBA Program, Atlanta, GA 30322. Offers accounting (MBA); alternative investments (MBA); business process consulting (MBA); business technology management (MBA); capital markets (MBA); corporate finance (MBA); customer relationship management (MBA); decision analytics (MBA); entrepreneurship (MBA); finance (MBA); global management (MBA); investment banking (MBA); management consulting (MBA); marketing (MBA); marketing analytics (MBA); marketing consulting (MBA); operations management (MBA); organization and management (MBA); product and brand management (MBA); real estate (MBA); social enterprise (MBA); strategy consulting (MBA). *Accreditation:* AACSB. *Faculty:* 74 full-time (18 women), 18 part-time/adjunct (6 women). *Students:* 353 full-time (96 women); includes 80 minority (18 Black or African American, non-Hispanic/Latino; 2 American Indian or Alaska Native, non-Hispanic/Latino; 39 Asian, non-Hispanic/Latino; 16 Hispanic/Latino; 1 Native Hawaiian or other Pacific Islander, non-Hispanic/Latino; 4 Two or more races, non-Hispanic/Latino), 104 international. Average age 29. 1,380 applicants, 34% accepted, 172 enrolled. In 2017, 179 master's awarded. *Degree requirements:* For master's, 1 leadership course; 2 mid-semester module programs; 2 global components. *Entrance requirements:* For master's, GMAT/GRE, essays; recommendation letters; undergraduate degree; interview. Additional exam requirements/recommendations for international students: Required—TOEFL (minimum score 100 iBT), IELTS (minimum score 7), PTE (minimum score 68). *Application deadline:* For fall admission, 10/6 for domestic and international students; for winter admission, 11/17 for domestic and international students; for spring admission, 1/3 priority date for domestic and international students; for summer admission, 3/9 for domestic and international students. Application fee: $150. Electronic applications accepted. *Expenses:* $59,616. *Financial support:* In 2017–18, 273 students received support. Career-related internships or fieldwork, institutionally sponsored loans, and scholarships/grants available. Financial award application deadline: 4/1; financial award applicants required to submit FAFSA. *Faculty research:* Corporate finance, information systems, digital marketing, asset pricing, sports management. *Unit head:* Brian Mitchell, Associate Dean, 404-727-4824, Fax: 404-712-9648, E-mail: brian.mitchell@emory.edu. *Application contact:* Julie Barefoot, Associate Dean, 404-727-6311, Fax: 404-727-4612, E-mail: mbaadmissions@emory.edu.
Website: http://www.goizueta.emory.edu

Endicott College, Van Loan School of Graduate and Professional Studies, Program in Information Technology, Beverly, MA 01915-2096. Offers MSIT. *Program availability:* Part-time, evening/weekend. *Faculty:* 4 part-time/adjunct (0 women). *Students:* 9 full-time (2 women), 4 part-time (2 women); includes 2 minority (both Asian, non-Hispanic/Latino), 6 international. Average age 29. 7 applicants, 100% accepted, 4 enrolled. In 2017, 9 master's awarded. *Degree requirements:* For master's, thesis. *Entrance requirements:* For master's, GRE or MAT, two letters of recommendation, undergraduate transcript. Additional exam requirements/recommendations for international students: Required—TOEFL. *Application deadline:* Applications are processed on a rolling basis. Application fee: $50. Electronic applications accepted. *Expenses:* Contact institution. *Financial support:* Applicants required to submit FAFSA. *Unit head:* TJ Hanratty, Associate Dean, 978-232-2832, Fax: 978-232-2832, E-mail: thanratt@endicott.edu. *Application contact:* Ian Menchini, Director, Graduate Enrollment and Advising, 978-232-5292, Fax: 978-232-3000, E-mail: imenchin@endicott.edu.
Website: https://vanloan.endicott.edu/programs-of-study/masters-programs/information-technology-program

Fairfield University, Dolan School of Business, Fairfield, CT 06824. Offers accounting (MBA, MS, CAS); business analytics (MS); finance (MBA, MS, CAS); information systems and business analytics (MBA); management (MBA, CAS); marketing (MBA,

CAS); taxation (CAS). *Accreditation:* AACSB. *Program availability:* Part-time, evening/weekend. *Faculty:* 18 full-time (6 women), 6 part-time/adjunct (2 women). *Students:* 120 full-time (57 women), 67 part-time (27 women); includes 20 minority (3 Black or African American, non-Hispanic/Latino; 1 American Indian or Alaska Native, non-Hispanic/Latino; 3 Asian, non-Hispanic/Latino; 11 Hispanic/Latino; 2 Two or more races, non-Hispanic/Latino), 33 international. Average age 26. 195 applicants, 87% accepted, 112 enrolled. In 2017, 93 master's awarded. *Degree requirements:* For master's, capstone course. *Entrance requirements:* For master's, GMAT (minimum score 500), 2 letters of reference, resume, minimum GPA of 3.0. Additional exam requirements/recommendations for international students: Required—TOEFL (minimum score 550 paper-based; 80 iBT) or IELTS (minimum score 6.5). *Application deadline:* For fall admission, 5/15 for international students; for spring admission, 10/15 for international students. Applications are processed on a rolling basis. Application fee: $60. Electronic applications accepted. *Expenses:* $925 per credit hour. *Financial support:* In 2017–18, 31 students received support. Scholarships/grants and unspecified assistantships available. Financial award applicants required to submit FAFSA. *Faculty research:* International finance, leadership and careers, ethics in accounting, emotions in consumer behavior and organizations, data analytics. *Unit head:* Dr. Mark Ligas, Interim Dean, 203-254-4070, Fax: 203-254-4105, E-mail: mligas@fairfield.edu. *Application contact:* Marianne Gumpper, Director of Graduate and Continuing Studies Admission, 203-254-4184, Fax: 203-254-4073, E-mail: gradadmis@fairfield.edu. Website: http://fairfield.edu/mba

Fairleigh Dickinson University, Metropolitan Campus, Silberman College of Business, Departments of Management, Marketing, and Entrepreneurial Studies, Program in Management, Teaneck, NJ 07666-1914. Offers management (MBA); management information systems (Certificate). *Accreditation:* AACSB.

Fairleigh Dickinson University, Metropolitan Campus, University College: Arts, Sciences, and Professional Studies, School of Computer Sciences and Engineering, Program in Management Information Systems, Teaneck, NJ 07666-1914. Offers MS.

Ferris State University, College of Business, Big Rapids, MI 49307. Offers business intelligence (MBA); design and innovation management (MBA); incident response (MBA); information security and intelligence (MS), including business intelligence, incident response, project management; lean systems and leadership (MBA); performance metrics (MBA); project management (MBA); supply chain management and lean logistics (MBA). *Accreditation:* ACBSP. *Program availability:* Part-time, evening/weekend, 100% online, blended/hybrid learning. *Faculty:* 18 full-time (7 women), 6 part-time/adjunct (3 women). *Students:* 19 full-time (10 women), 73 part-time (45 women); includes 8 minority (1 Black or African American, non-Hispanic/Latino; 2 Asian, non-Hispanic/Latino; 3 Hispanic/Latino; 2 Two or more races, non-Hispanic/Latino), 12 international. Average age 32. 52 applicants, 77% accepted, 16 enrolled. In 2017, 88 master's awarded. *Degree requirements:* For master's, comprehensive exam, thesis. *Entrance requirements:* For master's, GRE or GMAT, minimum GPA of 3.0 in junior-/senior-level classes and overall; statement of purpose; 3 letters of reference; resume; transcripts. Additional exam requirements/recommendations for international students: Required—TOEFL (minimum score 500 paper-based; 70 iBT), IELTS (minimum score 6.5). *Application deadline:* For fall admission, 7/1 priority date for domestic students, 6/15 for international students; for winter admission, 11/1 priority date for domestic students, 10/15 for international students; for spring admission, 3/1 priority date for domestic students, 2/15 for international students. Applications are processed on a rolling basis. Application fee: $0 ($30 for international students). Electronic applications accepted. *Expenses:* Contact institution. *Financial support:* Career-related internships or fieldwork, Federal Work-Study, scholarships/grants, and unspecified assistantships available. Support available to part-time students. Financial award application deadline: 3/15; financial award applicants required to submit FAFSA. *Faculty research:* Lifestyle medicine business models, lean systems value chain optimization, digital forensics/incident response, location-based services, passive data capture and analysis. *Unit head:* Dr. David Nicol, College of Business Dean, 231-591-2168, Fax: 231-591-3521, E-mail: davidnicol@ferris.edu. *Application contact:* Dr. Greg Gogolin, Professor, 231-591-3159, Fax: 231-591-3521, E-mail: greggogolin@ferris.edu. Website: http://cbgp.ferris.edu/

Florida Agricultural and Mechanical University, Division of Graduate Studies, Research, and Continuing Education, School of Business and Industry, Tallahassee, FL 32307-3200. Offers accounting (MBA); finance (MBA); management information systems (MBA); marketing (MBA). *Accreditation:* ACBSP. *Degree requirements:* For master's, residency. *Entrance requirements:* For master's, GMAT, minimum GPA of 3.0.

Florida Atlantic University, College of Business, Department of Information Technology and Operations Management, Boca Raton, FL 33431-0991. Offers information technology management (MS). *Faculty:* 14 full-time (4 women). *Students:* 29 full-time (13 women), 27 part-time (5 women); includes 30 minority (10 Black or African American, non-Hispanic/Latino; 2 Asian, non-Hispanic/Latino; 16 Hispanic/Latino; 2 Two or more races, non-Hispanic/Latino), 5 international. Average age 30. 30 applicants, 67% accepted, 18 enrolled. In 2017, 10 master's awarded. *Entrance requirements:* For master's, GMAT, minimum GPA of 3.0. Additional exam requirements/recommendations for international students: Required—TOEFL (minimum score 600 paper-based; 61 iBT), IELTS (minimum score 6). *Application deadline:* For fall admission, 7/1 priority date for domestic students, 2/15 priority date for international students; for spring admission, 4/1 priority date for domestic students, 1/15 priority date for international students. Applications are processed on a rolling basis. Application fee: $30. Electronic applications accepted. *Expenses:* Tuition, state resident: full-time $7400; part-time $369.82 per credit. Tuition, nonresident: full-time $20,496; part-time $1042.81 per credit. *Financial support:* Research assistantships, teaching assistantships, career-related internships or fieldwork, Federal Work-Study, institutionally sponsored loans, tuition waivers (partial), and unspecified assistantships available. Support available to part-time students. Financial award application deadline: 3/1; financial award applicants required to submit FAFSA. *Unit head:* Dr. Tamara Dinev, Chair, 561-297-2707. Website: http://business.fau.edu/departments/information-technology-operations-management/index.aspx

Florida Gulf Coast University, Lutgert College of Business, Program in Information Systems and Analytics, Fort Myers, FL 33965-6565. Offers MS. *Faculty:* 60 full-time (24 women), 31 part-time/adjunct (7 women). *Students:* 1 full-time (0 women), 2 part-time (0 women); includes 1 minority (Hispanic/Latino), 1 international. Average age 37. 3 applicants, 100% accepted, 3 enrolled. *Entrance requirements:* For master's, GMAT or GRE. Additional exam requirements/recommendations for international students: Required—TOEFL (minimum score 550 paper-based). *Application deadline:* For fall admission, 5/1 priority date for domestic students; for spring admission, 9/15 priority date for domestic students. Applications are processed on a rolling basis. Application fee: $30. Electronic applications accepted. *Expenses:* Tuition, state resident: part-time $290 per credit hour. Tuition, nonresident: part-time $1173 per credit hour. *Required fees:* $127 per credit hour. Tuition and fees vary according to course load. *Financial support:* Application deadline: 6/30; applicants required to submit FAFSA. *Unit head:* Robert Beatty, Dean, Lutgert College of Business, 239-590-7300, Fax: 239-590-7330, E-mail: rbeatty@fgcu.edu. *Application contact:* Judy Wynekoop, Associate Dean and

Professor of Computer Information Systems, 239-590-7387, Fax: 239-590-7330, E-mail: jwynekoo@fgcu.edu.

Florida Institute of Technology, Extended Studies Division, Melbourne, FL 32901-6975. Offers acquisition and contract management (MS); aerospace engineering (MS); business administration (MBA, DBA); computer information systems (MS); computer science (MS); electrical engineering (MS); engineering management (MS); human resources management (MS); logistics management (MS), including humanitarian and disaster relief logistics; management (MS), including acquisition and contract management, e-business, human resources management, information systems, logistics management, management, transportation management; material acquisition management (MS); mechanical engineering (MS); operations research (MS); project management (MS), including information systems, operations research; public administration (MPA); quality management (MS); software engineering (MS); space systems (MS); space systems management (MS); supply chain management (MS); systems management (MS), including information systems, operations research; technology management (MS). *Program availability:* Part-time, evening/weekend, online learning. *Students:* Average age 36. 962 applicants, 48% accepted, 323 enrolled. In 2017, 403 master's awarded. *Entrance requirements:* For master's, GMAT or resume showing 8 years of supervised experience, minimum GPA of 3.0, 2 letters of recommendation, resume. Additional exam requirements/recommendations for international students: Required—TOEFL (minimum score 550 paper-based; 79 iBT). *Application deadline:* For fall admission, 4/1 for international students; for spring admission, 9/30 for international students. Applications are processed on a rolling basis. Electronic applications accepted. *Expenses:* Contact institution. *Financial support:* Application deadline: 3/1; applicants required to submit FAFSA. *Unit head:* Dr. Theodore R. Richardson, III, Dean, 321-674-8123, Fax: 321-674-7597, E-mail: trichardson@fit.edu. *Application contact:* Carolyn Farrior, Director of Graduate Admissions, Online Learning and Off-Campus Programs, 321-674-7118, Fax: 321-674-8216, E-mail: cfarrior@fit.edu. Website: http://es.fit.edu

Florida International University, Chapman Graduate School of Business, Department of Decision Sciences and Information Systems, Miami, FL 33199. Offers decision sciences and information systems (PhD); health information management systems (MS); systems management (MS). *Program availability:* Part-time, evening/weekend. *Faculty:* 30 full-time (11 women), 11 part-time/adjunct (4 women). *Students:* 64 full-time (24 women), 65 part-time (26 women); includes 92 minority (25 Black or African American, non-Hispanic/Latino; 4 Asian, non-Hispanic/Latino; 59 Hispanic/Latino; 4 Two or more races, non-Hispanic/Latino), 28 international. Average age 33. 287 applicants, 44% accepted, 41 enrolled. In 2017, 84 master's awarded. *Entrance requirements:* For master's, GMAT or GRE, minimum GPA of 3.0 in upper-level coursework; letter of intent; resume. Additional exam requirements/recommendations for international students: Required—TOEFL (minimum score 550 paper-based; 80 iBT) or IELTS. *Application deadline:* For fall admission, 6/1 for domestic students, 4/1 for international students; for spring admission, 10/1 for domestic students, 9/1 for international students. Applications are processed on a rolling basis. Application fee: $30. Electronic applications accepted. *Expenses:* Contact institution. *Financial support:* Institutionally sponsored loans and scholarships/grants available. Financial award application deadline: 3/1; financial award applicants required to submit FAFSA. *Faculty research:* Artificial intelligence, data warehouses, operations management. *Unit head:* Dr. Richard Klein, Jr., Interim Chair, 305-348-2156, E-mail: rklein@fiu.edu. *Application contact:* Milza Rosales, Assistant Director of Admissions and Recruiting, Chapman Graduate School of Business, 305-348-7299, E-mail: mrosale@fiu.edu.

Florida International University, College of Engineering and Computing, School of Computing and Information Sciences, Miami, FL 33199. Offers computer science (MS, PhD); cybersecurity (MS); data science (MS); information technology (MS); telecommunications and networking (MS). *Program availability:* Part-time, evening/weekend. *Faculty:* 48 full-time (10 women), 29 part-time/adjunct (5 women). *Students:* 143 full-time (38 women), 127 part-time (20 women); includes 151 minority (16 Black or African American, non-Hispanic/Latino; 1 American Indian or Alaska Native, non-Hispanic/Latino; 7 Asian, non-Hispanic/Latino; 123 Hispanic/Latino; 4 Two or more races, non-Hispanic/Latino), 101 international. Average age 29. 403 applicants, 49% accepted, 84 enrolled. In 2017, 74 master's, 8 doctorates awarded. *Degree requirements:* For master's, thesis or alternative; for doctorate, comprehensive exam, thesis/dissertation. *Entrance requirements:* For master's and doctorate, GRE General Test, 3 letters of recommendation, minimum GPA of 3.0. Additional exam requirements/recommendations for international students: Required—TOEFL (minimum score 550 paper-based; 80 iBT). *Application deadline:* For fall admission, 6/1 for domestic students, 4/1 for international students; for spring admission, 10/1 for domestic students, 9/1 for international students. Applications are processed on a rolling basis. Application fee: $30. Electronic applications accepted. *Expenses:* Tuition, state resident: full-time $8912; part-time $446 per credit hour. Tuition, nonresident: full-time $21,393; part-time $992 per credit hour. *Required fees:* $390; $195 per semester. *Financial support:* Research assistantships, teaching assistantships, institutionally sponsored loans, scholarships/grants, and unspecified assistantships available. Financial award application deadline: 3/1; financial award applicants required to submit FAFSA. *Faculty research:* Database systems, software engineering, operating systems, networks. *Unit head:* Dr. S. S. Iyengar, Director, 305-348-3947, E-mail: iyengar@cis.fiu.edu. *Application contact:* Sara-Michelle Lemus, Engineering Admissions Officer, 305-348-1890, E-mail: grad_eng@fiu.edu.

Florida State University, The Graduate School, College of Business, Tallahassee, FL 32306-1110. Offers accounting (M Acc), including assurance and advisory services, generalist, taxation; business administration (MBA, PhD), including accounting (PhD), finance (PhD), management information systems (PhD), marketing (PhD), organizational behavior and human resources (PhD), risk management and insurance (PhD), strategy (PhD); finance (MS); management information systems (MS); risk management and insurance (MS); JD/MBA; MSW/MBA. *Accreditation:* AACSB. *Program availability:* Part-time, 100% online. *Faculty:* 93 full-time (23 women), 2 part-time/adjunct (1 woman). *Students:* 229 full-time (96 women), 423 part-time (154 women); includes 159 minority (44 Black or African American, non-Hispanic/Latino; 24 Asian, non-Hispanic/Latino; 75 Hispanic/Latino; 1 Native Hawaiian or other Pacific Islander, non-Hispanic/Latino; 15 Two or more races, non-Hispanic/Latino), 48 international. Average age 31. 300 applicants, 61% accepted, 133 enrolled. In 2017, 268 master's, 9 doctorates awarded. Terminal master's awarded for partial completion of doctoral program. *Degree requirements:* For doctorate, comprehensive exam, thesis/dissertation. *Entrance requirements:* For master's, GMAT, GRE (for all except MS in finance), work experience (MBA, MS); minimum GPA of 3.0, letters of recommendation; for doctorate, GMAT, GRE (for marketing, organizational behavior, risk management and insurance, management information systems, and human resources only), minimum graduate GPA of 3.5, letters of recommendation. Additional exam requirements/recommendations for international students: Required—TOEFL (minimum score 600 paper-based; 85 iBT); Recommended—IELTS (minimum score 6). *Application deadline:* For fall admission, 6/1 for domestic and international students; for spring admission, 10/1 for domestic and international students; for summer admission, 3/1 for domestic and international students. Applications are processed on a rolling

Management Information Systems

basis. Application fee: $30. Electronic applications accepted. *Expenses:* Contact institution. *Financial support:* In 2017–18, 146 students received support, including 26 fellowships (averaging $1,500 per year), 77 research assistantships with full tuition reimbursements available (averaging $20,000 per year), 43 teaching assistantships with full tuition reimbursements available (averaging $20,000 per year); career-related internships or fieldwork, scholarships/grants, health care benefits, tuition waivers (full and partial), and unspecified assistantships also available. Support available to part-time students. Financial award application deadline: 1/1; financial award applicants required to submit FAFSA. *Faculty research:* Business strategy, marketing, finance, accounting, business analytics. *Total annual research expenditures:* $1.4 million. *Unit head:* Dr. Michael Hartline, Dean, 850-644-4405, Fax: 850-644-0915, E-mail: mhartline@business.fsu.edu. *Application contact:* Jennifer Clark, Director, 850-644-6458, E-mail: gradprograms@business.fsu.edu.
Website: http://business.fsu.edu/

Florida State University, The Graduate School, College of Communication and Information, School of Information, Tallahassee, FL 32306-2100. Offers information (MA, MS, PhD, Specialist); information technology (MS). *Accreditation:* ALA (one or more programs are accredited). *Program availability:* Part-time, evening/weekend, 100% online, blended/hybrid learning. *Faculty:* 27 full-time (14 women), 4 part-time/adjunct (2 women). *Students:* 45 full-time (26 women), 264 part-time (197 women); includes 102 minority (31 Black or African American, non-Hispanic/Latino; 13 Asian, non-Hispanic/Latino; 46 Hispanic/Latino; 12 Two or more races, non-Hispanic/Latino), 16 international. Average age 34. 168 applicants, 62% accepted, 83 enrolled. In 2017, 108 master's, 7 doctorates, 2 other advanced degrees awarded. Terminal master's awarded for partial completion of doctoral program. *Degree requirements:* For master's, thesis optional, minimum GPA of 3.0, 36 hours (MSI); 32 hours (MSIT); for doctorate, comprehensive exam, thesis/dissertation, dissertation defense, manuscript clearance, minimum GPA of 3.0; for Specialist, minimum GPA of 3.0; 30 hours. *Entrance requirements:* For master's, GRE (recommended minimum percentile of 50 on each of the verbal and quantitative portions and writing score of 4.0), minimum GPA of 3.0 on last 2 years of baccalaureate degree, resume, statement of goals, two letters of recommendation, official transcripts from every college-level institution attended; for doctorate, GRE (recommended minimum percentile of 50 on each of the verbal and quantitative portions and writing score of 4.0), minimum GPA of 3.0 on last degree program, resume, 3 letters of recommendation, personal/goals statement, writing sample, brief digital video, official transcripts from all college-level institutions attended; for Specialist, GRE (recommended minimum percentile of 50 on each of the verbal and quantitative portions and writing score of 4.0), minimum graduate GPA of 3.2, resume, statement of goals, 2 letters of recommendation, writing sample, official transcripts from every college-level institution attended. Additional exam requirements/recommendations for international students: Required—TOEFL (minimum score 585 paper-based; 94 iBT), IELTS (minimum score 6.5). *Application deadline:* For fall admission, 7/1 for domestic and international students; for spring admission, 11/1 for domestic and international students. Applications are processed on a rolling basis. Application fee: $30. Electronic applications accepted. *Expenses:* Contact institution. *Financial support:* In 2017–18, 115 students received support, including 2 research assistantships with full tuition reimbursements available (averaging $18,310 per year), 24 teaching assistantships with full tuition reimbursements available (averaging $18,310 per year); career-related internships or fieldwork, Federal Work-Study, health care benefits, tuition waivers (full), and 4 assistantships (averaging $18,310) also available. Financial award application deadline: 3/1; financial award applicants required to submit FAFSA. *Faculty research:* Information technology, social informatics, health information, human information behavior, youth services. *Total annual research expenditures:* $296,509. *Unit head:* Dr. Lorri Mon, Director/Associate Professor, 850-644-5776, Fax: 850-644-9763, E-mail: lmon@fsu.edu. *Application contact:* Student Services, 850-645-3280, Fax: 850-644-9763, E-mail: ischooladvising@admin.fsu.edu.
Website: http://ischool.cci.fsu.edu

Fordham University, Gabelli School of Business, New York, NY 10023. Offers accounting (MBA, MS); applied statistics and decision-making (MS); business economics (DPS); capital markets (DPS); communications and media management (MBA); electronic business (MBA); entrepreneurship (MBA); finance (MBA, PhD); global finance (MS); global sustainability (MBA); health administration (MS); healthcare management (MBA); information systems (MBA, MS); investor relations (MS); management (EMBA, MBA, MS, PhD); marketing (MBA); marketing intelligence (MS); media management (MS); nonprofit leadership (MS); quantitative finance (MS); strategy and decision-making (DPS); taxation (MS); JD/MBA; MS/MBA. *Accreditation:* AACSB. *Program availability:* Part-time, evening/weekend. *Faculty:* 130 full-time (46 women), 42 part-time/adjunct (5 women). *Students:* 1,051 full-time (570 women), 563 part-time (313 women); includes 190 minority (48 Black or African American, non-Hispanic/Latino; 72 Asian, non-Hispanic/Latino; 69 Hispanic/Latino; 1 Native Hawaiian or other Pacific Islander, non-Hispanic/Latino), 1,106 international. Average age 27. 4,577 applicants, 58% accepted, 794 enrolled. In 2017, 937 master's awarded. Terminal master's awarded for partial completion of doctoral program. *Degree requirements:* For master's, internships (for some degrees); for doctorate, comprehensive exam (for some programs), thesis/dissertation. *Entrance requirements:* For master's, GMAT/GRE, 2 letters of recommendation, resume, 2 essays, transcripts, interview. Additional exam requirements/recommendations for international students: Required—TOEFL (minimum score 100 iBT), IELTS (minimum score 7). *Application deadline:* For fall admission, 11/15 priority date for domestic and international students; for winter admission, 1/19 priority date for domestic students, 1/1 priority date for international students; for spring admission, 4/15 for domestic students, 3/1 for international students; for summer admission, 6/1 for domestic students. Application fee: $130. Electronic applications accepted. *Expenses:* $1,495 per credit. *Financial support:* Career-related internships or fieldwork, institutionally sponsored loans, scholarships/grants, and unspecified assistantships available. Support available to part-time students. Financial award application deadline: 6/30; financial award applicants required to submit FAFSA. *Unit head:* Dr. Donna Rapaccioli, Dean, 212-636-6165, Fax: 212-307-1779, E-mail: rapaccioli@fordham.edu. *Application contact:* Lawrence Murray, Senior Assistant Dean of Graduate Admissions and Advising, 212-636-6200, Fax: 212-636-7076, E-mail: admissionsgb@fordham.edu.
Website: http://www.fordham.edu/gabelli

Franklin Pierce University, Graduate and Professional Studies, Rindge, NH 03461-0060. Offers curriculum and instruction (M Ed); elementary education (MS Ed); emerging network technologies (Graduate Certificate); energy and sustainability studies (MBA, Graduate Certificate); health administration (MBA, Graduate Certificate); human resource management (MBA, Graduate Certificate); information technology (MBA); leadership (MBA); nursing education (MS); nursing leadership (MS); physical therapy (DPT); physician assistant studies (MPAS); special education (M Ed); sports management (MBA). *Accreditation:* APTA. *Program availability:* Part-time, 100% online, blended/hybrid learning. *Degree requirements:* For master's, concentrated original research projects; student teaching; fieldwork and/or internship; leadership project; PRAXIS I and II (for M Ed); for doctorate, concentrated original research projects, clinical fieldwork and/or internship, leadership project. *Entrance requirements:* For master's, minimum GPA of 2.5, 3 letters of recommendation; competencies in accounting, economics, statistics, and computer skills through life experience or undergraduate coursework (for MBA); certification/e-portfolio, minimum C grade in all education courses (for M Ed); license to practice as RN (for MS); for doctorate, GRE, 80 hours of observation/work in PT settings; completion of anatomy, chemistry, physics, and statistics; minimum GPA of 3.0. Additional exam requirements/recommendations for international students: Required—TOEFL (minimum score 550 paper-based; 61 iBT). Electronic applications accepted. *Faculty research:* Evidence-based practice in sports physical therapy, human resource management in economic crisis, leadership in nursing, innovation in sports facility management, differentiated learning and understanding by design.

Friends University, Graduate School, Wichita, KS 67213. Offers family therapy (MSFT); global business administration (MBA), including accounting, business law, change management, health care leadership, management information systems, supply chain management and logistics; health care leadership (MHCL); management information systems (MMIS); professional business administration (MBA), including accounting, business law, change management, health care leadership, management information systems, supply chain management and logistics. *Program availability:* Part-time, evening/weekend, online learning. *Degree requirements:* For master's, research project. *Entrance requirements:* For master's, bachelor's degree from accredited institution, official transcripts, interview with program director, letter(s) of recommendation. Additional exam requirements/recommendations for international students: Required—TOEFL (minimum score 560 paper-based). Electronic applications accepted.

George Mason University, School of Business, Program in Management of Secure Information Systems, Fairfax, VA 22030. Offers MS. *Faculty:* 6 full-time (1 woman), 3 part-time/adjunct (1 woman). *Students:* 16 full-time (2 women), 1 (woman) part-time; includes 7 minority (1 Black or African American, non-Hispanic/Latino; 4 Asian, non-Hispanic/Latino; 1 Hispanic/Latino; 1 Two or more races, non-Hispanic/Latino). Average age 35. In 2017, 20 master's awarded. *Degree requirements:* For master's, thesis, capstone project. *Entrance requirements:* For master's, current resume; official copies of transcripts from all colleges or universities attended; two professional letters of recommendation; goal statement; interview. Additional exam requirements/recommendations for international students: Required—TOEFL (minimum score 650 paper-based; 93 iBT), IELTS, PTE. Application fee: $75 ($80 for international students). Electronic applications accepted. *Expenses:* $1,415.75 per credit tuition. *Financial support:* Career-related internships or fieldwork, Federal Work-Study, and scholarships/grants available. Support available to part-time students. Financial award applicants required to submit FAFSA. *Unit head:* Kumar Mehta, Director, 703-993-9412, Fax: 703-993-1809, E-mail: kmehta1@gmu.edu. *Application contact:* Jacky Buchy, Assistant Dean of Graduate Enrollment, 703-993-1856, Fax: 703-993-1778, E-mail: jbuchy@gmu.edu.
Website: http://business.gmu.edu/cyber-security-degree/

The George Washington University, School of Business, Department of Information Systems and Technology Management, Washington, DC 20052. Offers information and decision systems (PhD); information systems (MSIST); information systems development (MSIST); information systems management (MBA); information systems project management (MSIST); management information systems (MSIST); management of science, technology, and innovation (MBA, PhD). Programs also offered in Ashburn and Arlington, VA. *Program availability:* Part-time, evening/weekend, online learning. *Faculty:* 13 full-time (4 women), 3 part-time/adjunct (1 woman). *Students:* 108 full-time (49 women), 75 part-time (35 women); includes 48 minority (15 Black or African American, non-Hispanic/Latino; 28 Asian, non-Hispanic/Latino; 4 Hispanic/Latino; 1 Two or more races, non-Hispanic/Latino), 100 international. Average age 29. 425 applicants, 60% accepted, 68 enrolled. In 2017, 92 master's awarded. *Entrance requirements:* For master's, GMAT. Additional exam requirements/recommendations for international students: Required—TOEFL. *Application deadline:* For fall admission, 4/1 priority date for domestic students; for spring admission, 10/1 for domestic students. Applications are processed on a rolling basis. Application fee: $75. *Expenses:* Tuition: Full-time $28,800; part-time $1655 per credit hour. *Required fees:* $45; $2.75 per credit hour. *Financial support:* In 2017–18, 35 students received support. Fellowships, teaching assistantships, career-related internships or fieldwork, Federal Work-Study, institutionally sponsored loans, and tuition waivers available. Financial award application deadline: 4/1. *Faculty research:* Expert systems, decision support systems. *Unit head:* Richard Donnelly, Chair, 202-994-7155, E-mail: rgd@gwu.edu. *Application contact:* Christopher Storer, Executive Director, Graduate Admissions, 202-994-1212, E-mail: gwmba@gwu.edu.

Georgia College & State University, Graduate School, The J. Whitney Bunting School of Business, Program in Management Information Systems, Milledgeville, GA 31061. Offers MMIS. *Program availability:* Part-time-only, blended/hybrid learning. *Students:* 35 part-time (15 women); includes 9 minority (2 Black or African American, non-Hispanic/Latino; 4 Asian, non-Hispanic/Latino; 2 Hispanic/Latino; 1 Two or more races, non-Hispanic/Latino). Average age 38. 12 applicants, 83% accepted, 8 enrolled. In 2017, 11 master's awarded. *Degree requirements:* For master's, minimum GPA of 3.0, complete program within 7 years of start date. *Entrance requirements:* For master's, GRE or GMAT (not required for students who attended an AACSB accredited business school and maintained an overall undergraduate GPA of 3.2), transcript, certificate of immunization. *Application deadline:* For fall admission, 7/1 priority date for domestic students; for spring admission, 11/1 priority date for domestic students; for summer admission, 4/1 priority date for domestic students. Applications are processed on a rolling basis. Application fee: $40. Electronic applications accepted. *Expenses:* $2,592 per semester full-time tuition; $343 fees. *Financial support:* In 2017–18, 3 students received support. Unspecified assistantships available. Financial award application deadline: 3/1; financial award applicants required to submit FAFSA. *Unit head:* Dr. Dale Young, Dean, School of Business, 478-445-5497, E-mail: dale.young@gcsu.edu. *Application contact:* Lynn Hanson, Director of Graduate Programs, 478-445-5115, E-mail: lynn.hanson@gcsu.edu.
Website: http://www.gcsu.edu/business/graduateprograms/mmis.htm

Georgia Institute of Technology, Graduate Studies, Scheller College of Business, Program in Business Administration, Atlanta, GA 30332-0001. Offers business administration (MBA); global business (MBA); management of technology (MBA). *Accreditation:* AACSB. *Program availability:* Part-time, evening/weekend. *Entrance requirements:* For master's, GMAT, two essays, three letters of recommendation, transcript from each college/university attended. Additional exam requirements/recommendations for international students: Required—TOEFL (minimum score 600 paper-based; 100 iBT). Electronic applications accepted. *Expenses:* Contact institution.

Georgia Southern University, Jack N. Averitt College of Graduate Studies, Allen E. Paulson College of Engineering and Information Technology, Program in Information Technology, Statesboro, GA 30458. Offers MSAE. *Program availability:* Part-time. *Faculty:* 10 full-time (3 women). *Students:* 17 full-time (4 women), 14 part-time (6 women); includes 4 minority (3 Black or African American, non-Hispanic/Latino; 1 Hispanic/Latino), 15 international. Average age 31. In 2017, 3 master's awarded. *Degree requirements:* For master's, comprehensive exam, thesis (for some programs). *Entrance requirements:* For master's, undergraduate major or equivalent in proposed study area. Additional exam requirements/recommendations for international students: Required—TOEFL (minimum score 550 paper-based; 80 iBT), IELTS (minimum score 6). *Application deadline:* For fall admission, 3/1 priority date for domestic and international students; for spring admission, 11/1 priority date for domestic students, 10/1 for international students. Applications are processed on a rolling basis. Application fee: $50. Electronic applications accepted. *Expenses:* Tuition, state resident: full-time $4986; part-time $3324 per year. Tuition, nonresident: full-time $21,982; part-time $15,352 per year. *Required fees:* $2092; $1802 per credit hour. $901 per semester. Tuition and fees vary according to course load, campus/location and program. *Financial support:* In 2017–18, 12 students received support. Research assistantships, teaching assistantships, and unspecified assistantships available. Financial award application deadline: 4/20; financial award applicants required to submit FAFSA. *Faculty research:* Electrical systems, information technology, electromagnetics, digital control systems, applied engineering. *Total annual research expenditures:* $22,323. *Unit head:* Dr. Lei Chen, Interim Chair, 912-478-0334, E-mail: lchen@georgiasouthern.edu. Website: http://ceit.georgiasouthern.edu/it/

Georgia Southern University, Jack N. Averitt College of Graduate Studies, College of Business, Enterprise Resources Planning Certificate Program, Statesboro, GA 30458. Offers Graduate Certificate. *Program availability:* Part-time-only, online only, 100% online, blended/hybrid learning. *Faculty:* 11 full-time (2 women). *Students:* 3 part-time (1 woman); includes 1 minority (Black or African American, non-Hispanic/Latino). Average age 45. 5 applicants, 100% accepted, 3 enrolled. In 2017, 4 Graduate Certificates awarded. *Entrance requirements:* For degree, bachelor's degree or equivalent with minimum cumulative GPA of 2.7; official copies of all transcripts; resume with three references; personal statement. Additional exam requirements/recommendations for international students: Required—TOEFL (minimum score 550 paper-based), IELTS (minimum score 6). *Application deadline:* For fall admission, 6/15 for domestic students. Applications are processed on a rolling basis. Application fee: $50. Electronic applications accepted. *Expenses:* Contact institution. *Financial support:* In 2017–18, 1 student received support. Fellowships, research assistantships, teaching assistantships, scholarships/grants, and unspecified assistantships available. Financial award application deadline: 4/20; financial award applicants required to submit FAFSA. *Faculty research:* Enterprise resource planning (ERP) and business intelligence (BI) synergies, cloud-based and on-demand ERP solutions, IT artifact in ERP-centered supply chain information systems, impact of bring your own device (BYOD) policies on deployment of enterprise systems mobile applications, career readiness of SAP University Alliances students for positions in ERP user and consulting firms. *Unit head:* Dr. Camille Rogers, Program Coordinator, 912-478-0194, E-mail: cfrogers@georgiasouthern.edu. Website: http://cob.georgiasouthern.edu/is/degrees/online-erp-program/

Georgia Southern University, Jack N. Averitt College of Graduate Studies, College of Business, Program in Applied Economics, Statesboro, GA 30460. Offers applied economics (MS); information systems (Graduate Certificate). *Program availability:* Part-time-only, online only, 100% online. *Faculty:* 25 full-time (5 women). *Students:* 3 full-time (0 women), 28 part-time (10 women); includes 7 minority (2 Black or African American, non-Hispanic/Latino; 2 Asian, non-Hispanic/Latino; 1 Hispanic/Latino; 2 Two or more races, non-Hispanic/Latino), 4 international. Average age 34. 27 applicants, 100% accepted, 9 enrolled. In 2017, 5 master's, 1 other advanced degree awarded. *Entrance requirements:* For master's, GRE, minimum GPA of 3.0, current knowledge of calculus and statistics, introductory micro and macro courses. Additional exam requirements/recommendations for international students: Required—TOEFL (minimum score 550 paper-based; 80 iBT), IELTS (minimum score 6). *Application deadline:* For fall admission, 3/1 priority date for domestic students, 3/1 for international students; for spring admission, 10/1 priority date for domestic students, 10/1 for international students. Applications are processed on a rolling basis. Application fee: $50. Electronic applications accepted. *Expenses:* Tuition, state resident: full-time $4986; part-time $3324 per year. Tuition, nonresident: full-time $21,982; part-time $15,352 per year. *Required fees:* $2092; $1802 per credit hour. $901 per semester. Tuition and fees vary according to course load, campus/location and program. *Financial support:* In 2017–18, 1 student received support. Unspecified assistantships available. Financial award application deadline: 4/15; financial award applicants required to submit FAFSA. *Faculty research:* Analytical capabilities in economic development, financial economics, regulatory issues, market analysis, economic development. *Unit head:* 912-478-5767, Fax: 912-478-0710. Website: http://coba.georgiasouthern.edu/dfe/graduate/master-of-science-in-applied-economics/

Georgia Southwestern State University, School of Computing and Mathematics, Americus, GA 31709-4693. Offers computer information systems (Graduate Certificate); computer science (MS). *Program availability:* Part-time, 100% online, blended/hybrid learning. *Faculty:* 3 full-time (0 women), 1 part-time/adjunct (0 women). *Students:* 8 full-time (2 women), 10 part-time (3 women); includes 6 minority (3 Black or African American, non-Hispanic/Latino; 3 Asian, non-Hispanic/Latino), 7 international. Average age 35. 10 applicants, 50% accepted, 4 enrolled. In 2017, 10 master's awarded. *Degree requirements:* For master's, thesis optional, minimum cumulative GPA of 3.0; maximum of 6 credit hours with C grade; no courses with D grade; degree must be completed within 7 calendar years from date of initial enrollment in graduate course work; for Graduate Certificate, minimum cumulative GPA of 3.0; maximum of 6 credit hours with C grade; no courses with D grade; degree must be completed within 7 calendar years from date of initial enrollment in graduate course work. *Entrance requirements:* For master's and Graduate Certificate, GRE, bachelor's degree from regionally-accredited college; minimum undergraduate GPA of 2.5 as reported on official final transcripts from all institutions attended; letters of recommendation. Additional exam requirements/recommendations for international students: Required—TOEFL (minimum score 523 paper-based; 69 iBT), IELTS (minimum score 6.5). *Application deadline:* For fall admission, 5/31 for domestic students; for spring admission, 10/15 for domestic students; for summer admission, 3/15 for domestic students. Applications are processed on a rolling basis. Application fee: $25. Electronic applications accepted. *Expenses:* Contact institution. *Financial support:* Application deadline: 6/1; applicants required to submit FAFSA. *Unit head:* Dr. Boris V. Peltsverger, Dean, 229-931-2100. *Application contact:* Whitney Ford, Admissions Specialist, Office of Graduate Admission, 800-338-0082, Fax: 229-931-2983. Website: https://gsw.edu/Academics/Schools-and-Departments/School-of-Computing-and-Mathematics/index

Georgia State University, J. Mack Robinson College of Business, Department of Computer Information Systems, Atlanta, GA 30302-3083. Offers computer information systems (PhD); health informatics (MBA, MS); information systems (MSIS, Certificate); information systems development and project management (MBA); information systems management (MBA); managing information technology (Exec MS); the wireless organization (MBA). *Program availability:* Part-time, evening/weekend. *Faculty:* 24 full-time (2 women). *Students:* 173 full-time (70 women), 13 part-time (6 women); includes 28 minority (14 Black or African American, non-Hispanic/Latino; 11 Asian, non-Hispanic/Latino; 1 Hispanic/Latino; 2 Two or more races, non-Hispanic/Latino), 140 international. Average age 28. 551 applicants, 60% accepted, 94 enrolled. In 2017, 179 master's, 1 doctorate awarded. *Entrance requirements:* For master's, GRE or GMAT, transcripts from all institutions attended, resume, essays; for doctorate, GRE or GMAT, three letters

of recommendation, personal statement, transcripts from all institutions attended, resume. Additional exam requirements/recommendations for international students: Required—TOEFL (minimum score 610 paper-based; 101 iBT), IELTS (minimum score 7). *Application deadline:* For fall admission, 5/1 priority date for domestic students, 2/1 priority date for international students; for spring admission, 9/15 priority date for domestic students, 4/1 priority date for international students. Applications are processed on a rolling basis. Application fee: $50. Electronic applications accepted. *Expenses:* Tuition, state resident: full-time $7020. Tuition, nonresident: full-time $22,518. *Required fees:* $2128. Tuition and fees vary according to degree level and program. *Financial support:* Research assistantships, teaching assistantships, scholarships/grants, tuition waivers, and unspecified assistantships available. Financial award applicants required to submit FAFSA. *Faculty research:* Process and technological innovation, strategic IT management, intelligent systems, information systems security, software project risk. *Unit head:* Dr. Ephraim R. McLean, Professor/Chair, 404-413-7360, Fax: 404-413-7394. *Application contact:* Toby McChesney, Assistant Dean for Graduate Recruiting and Student Services, 404-413-7167, Fax: 404-413-7167, E-mail: rcbgradadmissions@gsu.edu. Website: http://cis.robinson.gsu.edu/

Georgia State University, J. Mack Robinson College of Business, Institute of International Business, Atlanta, GA 30303. Offers international business (GMBA, MBA, MIB); international business and information technology (MBA); international entrepreneurship (MBA); MIB/MIA. *Program availability:* Part-time, evening/weekend. *Faculty:* 11 full-time (4 women). *Students:* 37 full-time (21 women); includes 19 minority (16 Black or African American, non-Hispanic/Latino; 1 Asian, non-Hispanic/Latino; 1 Hispanic/Latino; 1 Two or more races, non-Hispanic/Latino), 10 international. Average age 27. 44 applicants, 86% accepted, 18 enrolled. In 2017, 33 master's awarded. *Entrance requirements:* For master's, GRE or GMAT, transcripts from all institutions attended, resume, essays. Additional exam requirements/recommendations for international students: Required—TOEFL (minimum score 610 paper-based; 101 iBT), IELTS (minimum score 7). *Application deadline:* For fall admission, 5/1 priority date for domestic students, 2/1 priority date for international students; for spring admission, 9/15 priority date for domestic students, 5/1 priority date for international students. Applications are processed on a rolling basis. Application fee: $50. Electronic applications accepted. *Expenses:* Tuition, state resident: full-time $7020. Tuition, nonresident: full-time $22,518. *Required fees:* $2128. Tuition and fees vary according to degree level and program. *Financial support:* Research assistantships, teaching assistantships, scholarships/grants, tuition waivers (partial), and unspecified assistantships available. Financial award application deadline: 5/1. *Faculty research:* Business challenges in emerging markets (especially in India and China); interorganizational relationships in an international context, such as strategic alliances and global supply chain relations; globalization and entry mode strategy or new (or emerging) multinationals; emerging market development and business environments; cross-cultural effects on business processes and performance. *Unit head:* Dr. Daniel Bello, Professor/Director of the Institute of International Business, 404-413-7275, Fax: 404-413-7276. *Application contact:* Toby McChesney, Assistant Dean for Graduate Recruiting and Student Services, 404-413-7167, Fax: 404-413-7162, E-mail: rcbgradadmissions@gsu.edu. Website: http://iib.gsu.edu/

Golden Gate University, Ageno School of Business, San Francisco, CA 94105-2968. Offers accounting (MBA); adaptive leadership (MBA); advanced financial planning (MS); business administration (EMBA, MBA, DBA); business analytics (MBA, MS); entrepreneurship (MBA); finance (MBA, MS, Certificate); financial life planning (Certificate); financial planning (MS, Certificate); global supply chain management (MBA, Certificate); human resource management (MBA, MS, Certificate); information technology management (MBA, MS, Certificate); international business (MBA); marketing (MBA, MS, Certificate); project management (MBA, MS, Certificate); psychology (MA, Certificate); public administration (EMPA, MBA); public administration leadership (Certificate); JD/MBA. *Program availability:* Part-time, evening/weekend. *Faculty:* 17 full-time (7 women), 280 part-time/adjunct (95 women). *Students:* 309 full-time (147 women), 527 part-time (266 women); includes 286 minority (56 Black or African American, non-Hispanic/Latino; 1 American Indian or Alaska Native, non-Hispanic/Latino; 131 Asian, non-Hispanic/Latino; 83 Hispanic/Latino; 4 Native Hawaiian or other Pacific Islander, non-Hispanic/Latino; 11 Two or more races, non-Hispanic/Latino), 209 international. Average age 35. 549 applicants, 66% accepted, 185 enrolled. *Degree requirements:* For doctorate, thesis/dissertation, qualifying examination. *Entrance requirements:* For master's, GMAT (for MBA), minimum GPA of 2.5 (MS). Additional exam requirements/recommendations for international students: Required—TOEFL (minimum score 550 paper-based; 79 iBT). *Application deadline:* For fall admission, 5/15 for domestic and international students; for winter admission, 1/15 for domestic and international students; for spring admission, 9/15 for domestic and international students. Applications are processed on a rolling basis. Application fee: $65 ($105 for international students). Electronic applications accepted. *Expenses:* $3,150 per 3-unit course. *Financial support:* Career-related internships or fieldwork, Federal Work-Study, institutionally sponsored loans, and scholarships/grants available. Support available to part-time students. Financial award applicants required to submit FAFSA. *Unit head:* Marianne Koch, Associate Dean, 415-442-6542, Fax: 415-442-6579, E-mail: mkoch@ggu.edu. *Application contact:* Angela Melero, Enrollment Services, 415-442-7800, Fax: 415-442-7807, E-mail: info@ggu.edu. Website: http://www.ggu.edu/programs/business-and-management

Goldey-Beacom College, Graduate Program, Wilmington, DE 19808-1999. Offers business administration (MBA); finance (MS); financial management (MBA); health care management (MBA); human resource management (MBA); information technology (MBA); international business management (MBA); major finance (MBA); major taxation (MBA); management (MM); marketing management (MBA); taxation (MBA, MS). *Accreditation:* ACBSP. *Program availability:* Part-time, evening/weekend. *Entrance requirements:* For master's, GMAT, MAT, GRE, minimum GPA of 3.0. Additional exam requirements/recommendations for international students: Required—TOEFL (minimum score 65 iBT); Recommended—IELTS (minimum score 6). Electronic applications accepted.

Governors State University, College of Business, Program in Management Information Systems, University Park, IL 60484. Offers MS. *Program availability:* Part-time. *Faculty:* 13 full-time (4 women), 15 part-time/adjunct (7 women). *Students:* 9 full-time (5 women), 8 part-time (3 women); includes 7 minority (5 Black or African American, non-Hispanic/Latino; 1 Asian, non-Hispanic/Latino; 1 Hispanic/Latino), 7 international. Average age 34. 22 applicants, 32% accepted, 1 enrolled. In 2017, 18 master's awarded. *Application deadline:* For fall admission, 4/1 for domestic students. Applications are processed on a rolling basis. Application fee: $50. Electronic applications accepted. *Expenses:* Contact institution. *Financial support:* Application deadline: 5/1; applicants required to submit FAFSA. *Unit head:* David Green, Chair, Division of Accounting, Finance, Management Information Systems, and Entrepreneurship, 708-534-5000 Ext. 4967, E-mail: dgreen@govst.edu.

The Graduate Center, City University of New York, Graduate Studies, Program in Business, New York, NY 10016-4039. Offers accounting (PhD); behavioral science

Management Information Systems

(PhD); finance (PhD); management planning systems (PhD). *Faculty:* 66 full-time (5 women). *Students:* 56 full-time (30 women); includes 6 minority (1 Black or African American, non-Hispanic/Latino; 1 American Indian or Alaska Native, non-Hispanic/Latino; 2 Asian, non-Hispanic/Latino; 2 Hispanic/Latino), 42 international. Average age 33. 177 applicants, 7% accepted, 10 enrolled. In 2017, 10 doctorates awarded. *Degree requirements:* For doctorate, thesis/dissertation. *Entrance requirements:* For doctorate, GMAT, writing sample (15 pages). Additional exam requirements/recommendations for international students: Required—TOEFL. *Application deadline:* For fall admission, 1/15 for domestic students. Application fee: $125. Electronic applications accepted. *Financial support:* In 2017–18, 50 students received support, including 54 fellowships, 5 teaching assistantships; research assistantships, career-related internships or fieldwork, Federal Work-Study, institutionally sponsored loans, and tuition waivers (full and partial) also available. Financial award application deadline: 2/1; financial award applicants required to submit FAFSA. *Unit head:* Dr. Joseph Weintrop, Executive Officer, 646-312-3092, Fax: 646-312-3031. *Application contact:* Les Gribben, Director of Admissions, 212-817-7470, Fax: 212-817-1624, E-mail: lgribben@gc.cuny.edu.

Grand Valley State University, Padnos College of Engineering and Computing, School of Computing and Information Systems, Allendale, MI 49401-9403. Offers computer information systems (MS), including databases, distributed systems, management of information systems, object-oriented systems, software engineering; data science and analytics (MS). *Program availability:* Part-time, evening/weekend. *Faculty:* 10 full-time (0 women). *Students:* 26 full-time (4 women), 59 part-time (13 women); includes 11 minority (2 Black or African American, non-Hispanic/Latino; 5 Asian, non-Hispanic/Latino; 3 Hispanic/Latino; 1 Two or more races, non-Hispanic/Latino), 27 international. Average age 30. 69 applicants, 83% accepted, 24 enrolled. In 2017, 20 master's awarded. *Degree requirements:* For master's, capstone course, project, or thesis. *Entrance requirements:* For master's, GRE (recommended with GPA below 3.0), minimum GPA of 3.0; knowledge of a programming language; coursework or experience in: computer architecture and/or organization, data structures and algorithms, databases, discrete math, networking, operating systems, and software engineering; minimum of 2 letters of recommendation; resume; personal statement. Additional exam requirements/recommendations for international students: Required—Michigan English Language Assessment Battery (minimum score 77), TOEFL (minimum iBT score of 80), or IELTS (6.5); GRE. *Application deadline:* For fall admission, 6/1 for international students; for winter admission, 9/1 for international students. Applications are processed on a rolling basis. Application fee: $30. Electronic applications accepted. *Expenses:* $686 per credit hour. *Financial support:* In 2017–18, 11 students received support, including 3 fellowships, 6 research assistantships with full and partial tuition reimbursements available (averaging $8,000 per year). *Faculty research:* Object technology, distributed computing, information systems management database, software engineering. *Unit head:* Dr. Paul Leidig, Director, 616-331-2060, Fax: 616-331-2144, E-mail: leidigp@gvsu.edu. *Application contact:* Dr. D. Robert Adams, Graduate Program Director, 616-331-3885, Fax: 616-331-2144, E-mail: adamsr@gvsu.edu. Website: http://www.cis.gvsu.edu/

Grantham University, College of Engineering and Computer Science, Lenexa, KS 66219. Offers information management (MS), including project management; information management technology (MS); information technology (MS). *Program availability:* Part-time, evening/weekend, online only, 100% online. *Faculty:* 1 full-time, 23 part-time/adjunct. *Students:* 167 full-time (52 women), 80 part-time (15 women); includes 131 minority (94 Black or African American, non-Hispanic/Latino; 2 American Indian or Alaska Native, non-Hispanic/Latino; 8 Asian, non-Hispanic/Latino; 16 Hispanic/Latino; 11 Two or more races, non-Hispanic/Latino). Average age 41. 56 applicants, 86% accepted, 42 enrolled. In 2017, 71 master's awarded. *Degree requirements:* For master's, comprehensive exam (for some programs), Project Management: PMP Prep Exam (for information management). *Entrance requirements:* For master's, baccalaureate or master's degree with minimum cumulative GPA of 2.5 from institution accredited by agency recognized by U.S. DOE or foreign equivalent; official transcripts showing proof of degree. Additional exam requirements/recommendations for international students: Required—TOEFL (minimum score 530 paper-based; 71 iBT), IELTS (minimum score 6.5), PTE (minimum score 50). *Application deadline:* Applications are processed on a rolling basis. Application fee: $0. Electronic applications accepted. *Expenses:* $325 per credit hour. *Financial support:* Scholarships/grants available. Financial award applicants required to submit FAFSA. *Faculty research:* Sensor networks and security, grid technologies, cloud computing. *Unit head:* Dr. Nancy Miller, Dean of the College of Engineering and Computer Science, 913-309-4738, Fax: 855-681-5201, E-mail: nmiller@grantham.edu. *Application contact:* Jared Parlette, Vice President of Student Enrollment, 800-955-2527 Ext. 803, Fax: 866-914-4557, E-mail: admissions@grantham.edu. Website: http://www.grantham.edu/engineering-and-computer-science/

Grantham University, Mark Skousen School of Business, Lenexa, KS 66219. Offers business administration (MBA); business intelligence (MS); human resources (Certificate); information management (MBA); performance improvement (MS); project management (MBA, Certificate). *Program availability:* Part-time, evening/weekend, online only, 100% online. *Faculty:* 1 full-time, 34 part-time/adjunct. *Students:* 610 full-time (231 women), 333 part-time (128 women); includes 466 minority (321 Black or African American, non-Hispanic/Latino; 12 American Indian or Alaska Native, non-Hispanic/Latino; 29 Asian, non-Hispanic/Latino; 71 Hispanic/Latino; 4 Native Hawaiian or other Pacific Islander, non-Hispanic/Latino; 29 Two or more races, non-Hispanic/Latino). Average age 40. 273 applicants, 87% accepted, 202 enrolled. In 2017, 362 master's awarded. *Degree requirements:* For master's, comprehensive exam (for some programs), PMP Prep Exams throughout the term (for MBA in project management); for Certificate, comprehensive exam (for some programs), PMP Prep Exam (for project management). *Entrance requirements:* For master's, baccalaureate or master's degree with minimum cumulative GPA of 2.5 from institution accredited by agency recognized by U.S. DOE or foreign equivalent; official transcripts showing proof of degree. Additional exam requirements/recommendations for international students: Required—TOEFL (minimum score 530 paper-based; 71 iBT), IELTS (minimum score 6.5), PTE (minimum score 50). *Application deadline:* Applications are processed on a rolling basis. Application fee: $0. Electronic applications accepted. *Expenses:* $325 per credit hour. *Financial support:* Scholarships/grants available. Financial award applicants required to submit FAFSA. *Faculty research:* How chronic diseases contribute to the rising costs of healthcare, marketing for entrepreneurs, managers' hiring practices of workers with disability, organizational structures, organizational change, online pedagogy, impact of instructor video tips in the online classroom, decision-making techniques. *Unit head:* Dr. David Marker, Dean of the Mark Skousen School of Business, 913-309-4747, Fax: 844-260-6287, E-mail: dmarker@grantham.edu. *Application contact:* Jared Parlette, Vice President of Student Enrollment, 800-955-2527 Ext. 803, Fax: 866-914-4557, E-mail: admissions@grantham.edu. Website: https://www.grantham.edu/school-of-business

Harrisburg University of Science and Technology, Program in Information Systems Engineering and Management, Harrisburg, PA 17101. Offers analytics (MS); digital government (MS); digital health (MS); entrepreneurship (MS); information security (MS); software engineering and systems development (MS). *Program availability:* Part-time, evening/weekend. *Degree requirements:* For master's, thesis optional. *Entrance*

requirements: For master's, baccalaureate degree. Additional exam requirements/recommendations for international students: Required—TOEFL (minimum score 520 paper-based; 80 iBT); Recommended—IELTS (minimum score 6). Electronic applications accepted. *Faculty research:* Healthcare Informatics, material analysis, enterprise systems, circuit design, enterprise architectures.

Hawai'i Pacific University, College of Business, Program in Business Administration, Honolulu, HI 96813. Offers finance (MBA); human resource management (MBA); information systems (MBA); international business (MBA); management (MBA); marketing (MBA); organizational change and development (MBA). *Program availability:* Part-time, evening/weekend, 100% online, blended/hybrid learning. *Faculty:* 7 full-time (3 women), 3 part-time/adjunct (0 women). *Students:* 88 full-time (34 women), 28 part-time (18 women); includes 63 minority (9 Black or African American, non-Hispanic/Latino; 17 Asian, non-Hispanic/Latino; 14 Hispanic/Latino; 1 Native Hawaiian or other Pacific Islander, non-Hispanic/Latino; 22 Two or more races, non-Hispanic/Latino), 29 international. Average age 32. 82 applicants, 78% accepted, 40 enrolled. In 2017, 87 master's awarded. *Entrance requirements:* For master's, GMAT or GRE. Additional exam requirements/recommendations for international students: Recommended—TOEFL (minimum score 550 paper-based; 80 iBT), IELTS (minimum score 6), TWE (minimum score 5). *Application deadline:* For fall admission, 1/15 priority date for domestic students; for spring admission, 10/15 priority date for domestic students. Applications are processed on a rolling basis. Application fee: $50. Electronic applications accepted. *Expenses:* Tuition: Full-time $18,000; part-time $1000 per credit. *Required fees:* $200; $26 per credit. Tuition and fees vary according to course load and program. *Financial support:* In 2017–18, 24 students received support. Research assistantships, career-related internships or fieldwork, Federal Work-Study, scholarships/grants, tuition waivers (partial), and unspecified assistantships available. Financial award application deadline: 3/1; financial award applicants required to submit FAFSA. *Unit head:* Dr. Daewoo Park, Department Chair, 808-544-1463, E-mail: dwpark@hpu.edu. *Application contact:* Danny Lam, Assistant Director of Graduate Admissions, 808-544-1135, E-mail: graduate@hpu.edu. Website: https://www.hpu.edu/cob/grad-programs/mba.html

Hawai'i Pacific University, College of Business, Program in Information Systems, Honolulu, HI 96813. Offers MSIS. *Program availability:* Part-time, evening/weekend. *Faculty:* 9 full-time (3 women), 3 part-time/adjunct (0 women). *Students:* 19 full-time (4 women), 13 part-time (4 women); includes 11 minority (4 Asian, non-Hispanic/Latino; 2 Hispanic/Latino; 5 Two or more races, non-Hispanic/Latino), 3 international. Average age 34. 20 applicants, 70% accepted, 11 enrolled. In 2017, 16 master's awarded. *Entrance requirements:* For master's, GMAT or GRE. Additional exam requirements/recommendations for international students: Recommended—TOEFL (minimum score 550 paper-based; 80 iBT), IELTS (minimum score 6), TWE (minimum score 5). *Application deadline:* For fall admission, 1/15 priority date for domestic students; for spring admission, 10/15 priority date for domestic students. Applications are processed on a rolling basis. Application fee: $50. Electronic applications accepted. *Expenses:* Tuition: Full-time $18,000; part-time $1000 per credit. *Required fees:* $200; $26 per credit. Tuition and fees vary according to course load and program. *Financial support:* In 2017–18, 2 students received support. Research assistantships, career-related internships or fieldwork, Federal Work-Study, scholarships/grants, tuition waivers (partial), and unspecified assistantships available. Financial award application deadline: 3/1; financial award applicants required to submit FAFSA. *Unit head:* Dr. Daewoo Park, Department Chair, 808-544-1463, E-mail: dwpark@hpu.edu. *Application contact:* Danny Lam, Assistant Director of Graduate Admissions, 808-544-1135, E-mail: graduate@hpu.edu. Website: https://www.hpu.edu/cob/grad-programs/msis.html

HEC Montreal, School of Business Administration, Graduate Diploma Programs in Administration, Montréal, QC H3T 2A7, Canada. Offers business administration (Graduate Diploma); business analysis - information technology (Graduate Diploma); e-business (Graduate Diploma); entrepreneurship (Graduate Diploma); financial professions (Graduate Diploma); human resources (Graduate Diploma); management (Graduate Diploma); management and sustainable development (Graduate Diploma); management of cultural organizations (Graduate Diploma); marketing communication (Graduate Diploma); organizational development (Graduate Diploma); professional accounting (Graduate Diploma); supply chain management (Graduate Diploma); taxation (Graduate Diploma). All courses are given in French. *Students:* 380 full-time (210 women), 819 part-time (501 women). 1,195 applicants, 72% accepted, 673 enrolled. In 2017, 629 Graduate Diplomas awarded. *Entrance requirements:* For degree, bachelor's degree. Application fee: $88 Canadian dollars ($184 Canadian dollars for international students). Electronic applications accepted. *Expenses:* Tuition, state resident: full-time $2869 Canadian dollars; part-time $79.70 Canadian dollars per credit. Tuition, nonresident: full-time $8883 Canadian dollars; part-time $246.76 Canadian dollars per credit. *International tuition:* $19,648 Canadian dollars full-time. *Required fees:* $41.20 Canadian dollars per credit. $67.94 Canadian dollars per term. Tuition and fees vary according to degree level and program. *Financial support:* Research assistantships, teaching assistantships, and scholarships/grants available. Financial award application deadline: 9/2. *Faculty research:* Art management, business policy, entrepreneurship, new technologies, transportation. *Unit head:* Renaud Lachance, Director, 514-340-7165, E-mail: renaud.lachance@hec.ca. *Application contact:* Anny Caron, Administrative Director, 514-340-6151, Fax: 514-340-6411, E-mail: aide@hec.ca. Website: http://www.hec.ca/programmes/dess/index.html

HEC Montreal, School of Business Administration, Master of Science Programs in Administration, Program in Business Analysis and Information Technologies, Montréal, QC H3T 2A7, Canada. Offers M Sc. All courses are given in French. *Students:* 21 full-time (3 women), 5 part-time (0 women). 2 applicants, 100% accepted, 2 enrolled. In 2017, 16 master's awarded. *Entrance requirements:* For master's, BBA, undergraduate degree in another field, degree deemed equivalent by program director and minimum GPA of 3.0 on 4.3 scale. Additional exam requirements/recommendations for international students: Required—TAGE MAGE (minimum recommended score of 283), GMAT (minimum recommended score of 630), or GRE. *Application deadline:* For fall admission, 3/15 for domestic and international students; for winter admission, 9/15 for domestic and international students. Application fee: $88 Canadian dollars ($184 Canadian dollars for international students). Electronic applications accepted. *Expenses:* Tuition, state resident: full-time $2869 Canadian dollars; part-time $79.70 Canadian dollars per credit. Tuition, nonresident: full-time $8883 Canadian dollars; part-time $246.76 Canadian dollars per credit. *International tuition:* $19,648 Canadian dollars full-time. *Required fees:* $41.20 Canadian dollars per credit. $67.94 Canadian dollars per term. Tuition and fees vary according to degree level and program. *Financial support:* Research assistantships, teaching assistantships, and scholarships/grants available. Financial award application deadline: 9/2. *Unit head:* Dr. Marie-Helene Jobin, Director, 514-340-6283, E-mail: marie-helene.jobin@hec.ca. *Application contact:* Marianne de Moura, Administrative Director, 514-340-6151, Fax: 514-340-6411, E-mail: aide@hec.ca. Website: http://www.hec.ca/programmes/maitrises/maitrise-technologies-information/index.html

Hodges University, Graduate Programs, Naples, FL 34119. Offers accounting (M Acc); business administration (MBA); clinical mental health counseling (MS); health services administration (MS); information systems management (MIS); legal studies (MS); management (MSM). *Program availability:* Part-time, evening/weekend, 100% online, blended/hybrid learning. *Degree requirements:* For master's, comprehensive exam (for some programs), thesis (for some programs). *Entrance requirements:* For master's, essay. Additional exam requirements/recommendations for international students: Recommended—TOEFL. Electronic applications accepted.

Hofstra University, Frank G. Zarb School of Business, Programs in Information Systems, Hempstead, NY 11549. Offers business administration (MBA), including business analytics, information systems, quality management; business analytics (MS); information systems (MS, Advanced Certificate). *Program availability:* Part-time, evening/weekend, blended/hybrid learning. *Students:* 85 full-time (38 women), 22 part-time (9 women); includes 12 minority (1 Black or African American, non-Hispanic/Latino; 8 Asian, non-Hispanic/Latino; 3 Hispanic/Latino), 78 international. Average age 27. 120 applicants, 63% accepted, 37 enrolled. In 2017, 40 master's awarded. *Degree requirements:* For master's, capstone course (for MBA), thesis (for MS), minimum GPA of 3.0. *Entrance requirements:* For master's, GMAT/GRE, 2 letters of recommendation, resume, essay; for Advanced Certificate, GMAT/GRE, 2 letters of recommendation, resume. Additional exam requirements/recommendations for international students: Required—TOEFL (minimum score 550 paper-based; 80 iBT); Recommended—IELTS (minimum score 6). *Application deadline:* Applications are processed on a rolling basis. Application fee: $75. Electronic applications accepted. *Expenses:* $1,322 per credit. *Financial support:* In 2017–18, 41 students received support, including 40 fellowships with full and partial tuition reimbursements available (averaging $5,921 per year), 2 research assistantships with full and partial tuition reimbursements available (averaging $5,483 per year); career-related internships or fieldwork, Federal Work-Study, institutionally sponsored loans, scholarships/grants, tuition waivers (full and partial), and unspecified assistantships also available. Support available to part-time students. Financial award applicants required to submit FAFSA. *Faculty research:* Big data and social media, healthcare IT and analytics, machine learning and artificial intelligence, inventory system and quality management, cybersecurity and information processing. *Unit head:* Dr. Hak Kim, Chairperson, 516-463-5716, Fax: 516-463-4834, E-mail: hak.j.kim@hofstra.edu. *Application contact:* Sunil Samuel, Assistant Vice President of Admissions, 516-463-4723, Fax: 516-463-4664, E-mail: graduateadmission@hofstra.edu.
Website: http://www.hofstra.edu/business/

Holy Family University, Graduate and Professional Programs, School of Business Administration, Philadelphia, PA 19114. Offers accountancy (MS); finance (MBA); health care administration (MBA); human resource management (MBA); information systems management (MBA). *Accreditation:* ACBSP. *Program availability:* Part-time, evening/weekend. *Degree requirements:* For master's, comprehensive exam, thesis optional. *Entrance requirements:* For master's, minimum GPA of 3.0, interview, essay/personal statement, current resume, official transcript of all college or university work. Additional exam requirements/recommendations for international students: Required—TOEFL (minimum score 550 paper-based; 79 iBT), IELTS (minimum score 6), PTE (minimum score 54). Electronic applications accepted. *Expenses: Tuition:* Full-time $13,518; part-time $9012 per credit hour. Tuition and fees vary according to degree level and program.

Hood College, Graduate School, Department of Economics and Business Administration, Frederick, MD 21701-8575. Offers accounting (MBA, Certificate); finance (MBA); financial management (Certificate); human resource management (MBA); information systems (MBA); marketing (MBA); organizational management (Certificate); public management (MBA). *Accreditation:* ACBSP. *Program availability:* Part-time, evening/weekend. *Faculty:* 4 full-time (2 women), 7 part-time/adjunct (1 woman). *Students:* 21 full-time (12 women), 91 part-time (47 women); includes 19 minority (8 Black or African American, non-Hispanic/Latino; 3 Asian, non-Hispanic/Latino; 8 Hispanic/Latino), 15 international. Average age 31. 34 applicants, 97% accepted, 23 enrolled. In 2017, 42 master's awarded. *Degree requirements:* For master's, capstone/final research project. *Entrance requirements:* For master's, minimum GPA of 3.0 (or resume and two letters of recommendation), copy of official transcripts, essay. Additional exam requirements/recommendations for international students: Required—TOEFL (minimum score 575 paper-based; 89 iBT), IELTS (minimum score 6.5). *Application deadline:* For fall admission, 8/15 for domestic students, 8/5 for international students; for spring admission, 12/1 for domestic and international students; for summer admission, 5/1 for domestic students, 4/15 for international students. Applications are processed on a rolling basis. Application fee: $35. Electronic applications accepted. *Expenses:* $550 per credit hour plus $110 per semester comprehensive fee. *Financial support:* Tuition waivers (partial) and unspecified assistantships available. Financial award applicants required to submit FAFSA. *Faculty research:* Corporate strategy and sustainable competitive advantages, business ethics, entrepreneurship, investments management, economic development. *Unit head:* Dr. April M. Boulton, Dean of the Graduate School, 301-696-3600, Fax: 301-696-3597, E-mail: gofurther@hood.edu. *Application contact:* Jan Marcus, Assistant Director of Graduate Admissions, 301-696-3603, E-mail: gofurther@hood.edu.

Howard University, School of Business, Graduate Programs in Business, Washington, DC 20059-0002. Offers accounting (MBA); entrepreneurship (MBA); finance (MBA); general management (MBA); human resources management (MBA); information systems (MBA); international business (MBA); marketing (MBA); supply chain management (MBA); JD/MBA. *Accreditation:* AACSB. *Program availability:* Part-time, evening/weekend, online learning. *Entrance requirements:* For master's, GMAT, minimum 1 year post undergraduate work experience, resume, 3 letters of recommendation, advanced college algebra. Additional exam requirements/recommendations for international students: Required—TOEFL. *Faculty research:* Marketing research in multi-ethnic populations, U.S. trade policies and international relations, risk management (finance).

Idaho State University, Office of Graduate Studies, College of Business, Pocatello, ID 83209-8020. Offers business administration (MBA, Postbaccalaureate Certificate); computer information systems (MS, Postbaccalaureate Certificate). *Accreditation:* AACSB. *Program availability:* Part-time. *Degree requirements:* For master's, comprehensive exam, thesis (for some programs), oral exam; for Postbaccalaureate Certificate, comprehensive exam, thesis (for some programs), 6 hours of clerkship. *Entrance requirements:* For master's, GMAT, GRE General Test, minimum GPA of 3.0, resume outlining work experience, 2 letters of reference; for Postbaccalaureate Certificate, GMAT, GRE General Test, minimum upper-level GPA of 3.0, resume of work experience. Additional exam requirements/recommendations for international students: Required—TOEFL (minimum score 550 paper-based; 80 iBT). Electronic applications accepted. *Faculty research:* Information assurance, computer information technology, finance management, marketing.

IGlobal University, Graduate Programs, Vienna, VA 22182. Offers accounting (MBA); data management and analytics (MSIT); entrepreneurship (MBA); finance (MBA); global business management (MBA); health care management (MBA); hospitality and tourism management (MBA); human resources management (MBA); information technology (MBA); information technology systems and management (MSIT); leadership and management (MBA); project management (MBA); public service and administration (MBA); software design and management (MSIT).

Illinois Institute of Technology, Graduate College, College of Science, Department of Computer Science, Chicago, IL 60616. Offers business (MCS); computational intelligence (MCS); computer science (MCS, MS, PhD); cyber-physical systems (MCS); data analytics (MCS); data science (MAS); database systems (MCS); distributed and cloud computing (MCS); education (MCS); finance (MCS); information security and assurance (MCS); networking and communications (MCS); software engineering (MCS); telecommunications and software engineering (MAS); MS/MAS. *Program availability:* Part-time, evening/weekend, online learning. Terminal master's awarded for partial completion of doctoral program. *Degree requirements:* For master's, thesis optional; for doctorate, comprehensive exam, thesis/dissertation. *Entrance requirements:* For master's, GRE General Test with minimum scores of 298 Quantitative and Verbal, 3.0 Analytical Writing (for MS); GRE General Test with minimum scores of 292 Quantitative and Verbal, 2.5 Analytical Writing (for MAS), minimum undergraduate GPA of 3.0; for doctorate, GRE General Test (minimum scores: 304 Quantitative and Verbal, 3.5 Analytical Writing), minimum undergraduate GPA of 3.0. Additional exam requirements/recommendations for international students: Required—TOEFL (minimum score 523 paper-based; 70 iBT). Electronic applications accepted. *Faculty research:* Parallel and distributed processing, high-performance computing, computational linguistics, information retrieval, data mining, grid computing.

Illinois Institute of Technology, Graduate College, Lewis College of Human Sciences, Department of Humanities, Chicago, IL 60616. Offers information architecture (MS); technical communication (PhD); technical communication and information design (MS). *Program availability:* Part-time. *Degree requirements:* For master's, comprehensive exam, thesis or alternative; for doctorate, comprehensive exam, thesis/dissertation. *Entrance requirements:* For master's, GRE General Test (minimum score 144 Quantitative, 153 Verbal, and 4.0 Analytical Writing), minimum undergraduate GPA of 3.0; 2 letters of recommendation from faculty or supervisors; professional statement discussing academic goals; for doctorate, GRE General Test (minimum score 144 Quantitative, 153 Verbal, and 4.0 Analytical Writing), bachelor's or master's degree in a field that, in combination with the 27-credit hour technical core, would provide a solid basis for advanced academic work leading to original research in the field; 3 letters of recommendation from faculty or supervisors; professional statement discussing academic goals. Additional exam requirements/recommendations for international students: Required—TOEFL (minimum score 95 iBT); Recommended—IELTS (minimum score 7). Electronic applications accepted. *Faculty research:* Linguistics, punishment theory, political communication, gender and technology, philosophical and ethical issues in neuroscience.

Illinois Institute of Technology, Graduate College, School of Applied Technology, Department of Information Technology and Management, Wheaton, IL 60189. Offers cyber forensics and security (MAS); information technology and management (MAS). *Program availability:* Part-time, evening/weekend, online learning. *Entrance requirements:* For master's, GRE (minimum score 300 Quantitative and Verbal, 2.5 Analytical Writing), bachelor's degree with minimum cumulative undergraduate GPA of 3.0 (or its equivalent) from accredited institution. Additional exam requirements/recommendations for international students: Required—TOEFL (minimum score 523 paper-based; 70 iBT); Recommended—IELTS (minimum score 5.5). Electronic applications accepted. *Faculty research:* Database design, voice over IP, process engineering, object-oriented programming, computer networking, online design, system administration.

Illinois State University, Graduate School, College of Applied Science and Technology, School of Information Technology, Normal, IL 61790. Offers MS. *Entrance requirements:* For master's, GRE General Test, minimum GPA of 3.0 in last 60 hours; proficiency in COBOL, FORTRAN, Pascal, or P12. *Faculty research:* Graduate practicum training in network support.

Indiana University Bloomington, School of Public and Environmental Affairs, Public Affairs Programs, Bloomington, IN 47405. Offers economic development (MPA); energy (MPA); environmental policy (PhD); environmental policy and natural resource management (MPA); information systems (MPA); international development (MPA); local government management (MPA); nonprofit management (MPA, Certificate); policy analysis (MPA); public budgeting and financial management (Certificate); public finance (PhD); public financial administration (MPA); public management (MPA, PhD, Certificate); public policy analysis (PhD); social entrepreneurship (Certificate); specialized public affairs (MPA); sustainability and sustainable development (MPA); JD/MPA; MPA/MA; MPA/MIS; MPA/MLS; MSES/MPA. *Accreditation:* NASPAA (one or more programs are accredited). *Program availability:* Part-time. *Degree requirements:* For master's, capstone, internship; for doctorate, comprehensive exam, thesis/dissertation. *Entrance requirements:* For master's, GRE General Test or GMAT, official transcripts, 3 letters of recommendation, resume, personal statement; for doctorate, GRE General Test, official transcripts, 3 letters of recommendation, statement of purpose. Additional exam requirements/recommendations for international students: Required—TOEFL (minimum score 600 paper-based; 96 iBT); Recommended—IELTS (minimum score 7). Electronic applications accepted. *Faculty research:* International development, environmental policy and resource management, policy analysis, public finance, public management, urban management, nonprofit management, energy policy, social policy, public finance.

Indiana University Northwest, College of Arts and Sciences, Gary, IN 46408. Offers clinical counseling (MS), including drug and alcohol counseling; community development/urban studies (Graduate Certificate); computer information systems (Graduate Certificate); liberal studies (MLS); race-ethnic studies (Graduate Certificate); women's and gender studies (Graduate Certificate). *Program availability:* Part-time, evening/weekend. *Entrance requirements:* For master's, GRE (recommended for MS), minimum undergraduate GPA of 3.0, bachelor's degree from accredited university (for MS). Electronic applications accepted. *Expenses:* Contact institution.

Instituto Tecnológico y de Estudios Superiores de Monterrey, Campus Central de Veracruz, Graduate Programs, Córdoba, Mexico. Offers administration (MA); administration of information technologies (MTI); computer sciences (MCC); education (MEE); educational institution administration (MAD); educational technology (MTE); electronic commerce (MCE); finance (MAF); humanistic studies (MEH); international business for Latin America (MNL); marketing (MMT); science (MCP). *Program availability:* Part-time, evening/weekend, online learning. *Degree requirements:* For master's, thesis (for some programs). *Entrance requirements:* For master's, PAEP College Board. Electronic applications accepted.

Instituto Tecnológico y de Estudios Superiores de Monterrey, Campus Ciudad de México, Virtual University Division, Ciudad de Mexico, Mexico. Offers administration of information technologies (MA); computer sciences (MA); education (MA, PhD); educational technology (MA); environmental engineering (MA); environmental systems (MA); humanistic studies (MA); industrial engineering (MA); international business for Latin America (MA); quality systems (MA); quality systems and productivity (MA). *Program availability:* Part-time, evening/weekend, online learning. *Entrance requirements:* For master's and doctorate, Instituto entrance exam. Additional exam requirements/recommendations for international students: Required—TOEFL.

Management Information Systems

Instituto Tecnológico y de Estudios Superiores de Monterrey, Campus Ciudad Juárez, Program in Administration of Information Technology, Ciudad Juárez, Mexico. Offers MAIT.

Instituto Tecnológico y de Estudios Superiores de Monterrey, Campus Ciudad Obregón, Program in Administration of Information Technology, Ciudad Obregón, Mexico. Offers MATI.

Instituto Tecnológico y de Estudios Superiores de Monterrey, Campus Estado de México, Professional and Graduate Division, Estado de Mexico, Mexico. Offers administration of information technologies (MITA); architecture (M Arch); business administration (GMBA, MBA); computer sciences (MCS, PhD); education (M Ed); educational institution administration (MAD); educational technology and innovation (PhD); electronic commerce (MEC); environmental systems (MS); finance (MAF); humanistic studies (MHS); information sciences and knowledge management (MISKM); information systems (MS); manufacturing systems (MS); marketing (MEM); quality systems and productivity (MS); science and materials engineering (PhD); telecommunications management (MTM). *Program availability:* Part-time, online learning. *Degree requirements:* For master's, one foreign language, thesis (for some programs); for doctorate, one foreign language, thesis/dissertation. *Entrance requirements:* For master's, E-PAEP 500, interview; for doctorate, E-PAEP 500, research proposal. Additional exam requirements/recommendations for international students: Required—TOEFL (minimum score 550 paper-based). *Faculty research:* Surface treatments by plasmas, mechanical properties, robotics, graphical computing, mechatronics security protocols.

Instituto Tecnológico y de Estudios Superiores de Monterrey, Campus Irapuato, Graduate Programs, Irapuato, Mexico. Offers administration (MBA); administration of information technology (MAIT); administration of telecommunications (MAT); architecture (M Arch); computer science (MCS); education (M Ed); educational administration (MEA); educational innovation and technology (DEIT); educational technology (MET); electronic commerce (MBA); environmental administration and planning (MEAP); environmental systems (MES); finances (MBA); humanistic studies (MHS); international management for Latin American executives (MIMLAE); library and information science (MLIS); manufacturing quality management (MMQM); marketing research (MBA).

Instituto Tecnológico y de Estudios Superiores de Monterrey, Campus Laguna, Graduate School, Torreón, Mexico. Offers business administration (MBA); industrial engineering (MIE); management information systems (MS). *Program availability:* Part-time. *Entrance requirements:* For master's, GMAT. *Faculty research:* Computer communications from home to the university.

Inter American University of Puerto Rico, Aguadilla Campus, Graduate School, Aguadilla, PR 00605. Offers accounting (MBA); counseling psychology specializing in family (MS); criminal justice (MA); educative management and leadership (MA); elementary education (M Ed); finance (MBA); human resources (MBA); industrial management (MBA); management information systems (MBA); marketing (MBA). *Program availability:* Part-time, evening/weekend. *Degree requirements:* For master's, comprehensive exam. *Entrance requirements:* For master's, EXADEP, 2 letters of recommendation, minimum GPA of 2.5. Electronic applications accepted.

Inter American University of Puerto Rico, Fajardo Campus, Graduate Programs, Fajardo, PR 00738-7003. Offers computer science (MS); educational management and leadership (MA Ed); general business (MBA); human resources (MBA); management information systems (MBA); marketing (MBA); special education (MA Ed). *Program availability:* Online learning. *Faculty:* 1 full-time (0 women), 25 part-time/adjunct (13 women). *Students:* 1 (woman) full-time, 126 part-time (81 women).

Inter American University of Puerto Rico, Metropolitan Campus, Graduate Programs, Program in Management Information Systems, San Juan, PR 00919-1293. Offers MBA.

Inter American University of Puerto Rico, San Germán Campus, Graduate Studies Center, Program in Business Administration, San Germán, PR 00683-5008. Offers accounting (MBA); finance (MBA); general business administration (MBA); human resources (MBA, PhD); industrial relations (MBA); information systems (MBA); international and interregional business (PhD); management (MBA); marketing (MBA). *Program availability:* Part-time, evening/weekend. *Degree requirements:* For master's, comprehensive exam. *Entrance requirements:* For master's, GRE General Test or EXADEP, minimum GPA of 3.0.

Iona College, School of Business, Department of Accounting, New Rochelle, NY 10801-1890. Offers accounting and information systems (MS); general accounting (MBA, AC); public accounting (MBA, MS, AC). *Program availability:* Part-time, evening/weekend. *Faculty:* 5 full-time (1 woman), 1 (woman) part-time/adjunct. *Students:* 25 full-time (13 women), 40 part-time (15 women); includes 26 minority (6 Black or African American, non-Hispanic/Latino; 1 American Indian or Alaska Native, non-Hispanic/Latino; 2 Asian, non-Hispanic/Latino; 16 Hispanic/Latino; 1 Two or more races, non-Hispanic/Latino), 4 international. Average age 28. 32 applicants, 100% accepted, 16 enrolled. In 2017, 59 master's, 6 other advanced degrees awarded. *Entrance requirements:* For master's and AC, minimum GPA of 3.0. Additional exam requirements/recommendations for international students: Required—TOEFL (minimum score 550 paper-based; 80 iBT), IELTS (minimum score 6.5). *Application deadline:* For fall admission, 8/15 priority date for domestic students, 8/1 priority date for international students; for winter admission, 11/15 priority date for domestic students, 11/1 priority date for international students; for spring admission, 2/15 priority date for domestic students, 2/1 priority date for international students; for summer admission, 5/15 priority date for domestic students, 5/1 priority date for international students. Applications are processed on a rolling basis. Application fee: $0. Electronic applications accepted. Tuition and fees vary according to program. *Financial support:* Scholarships/grants, tuition waivers (partial), and unspecified assistantships available. Support available to part-time students. Financial award application deadline: 4/15; financial award applicants required to submit FAFSA. *Faculty research:* Tax policy, investment returns, international accounting standards. *Unit head:* Dr. Jeffrey Haber, Chair, 914-633-2244, E-mail: jhaber@iona.edu. *Application contact:* Katelyn Brunck, Director of Graduate Admissions, 914-633-2451, Fax: 914-633-2277, E-mail: kbrunck@iona.edu. Website: https://www.iona.edu/academics/school-of-business/departments/accounting.aspx

Iowa State University of Science and Technology, Program in Business and Technology, Ames, IA 50011. Offers PhD. *Entrance requirements:* Additional exam requirements/recommendations for international students: Required—TOEFL (minimum score 600 paper-based; 100 iBT), IELTS (minimum score 7). Electronic applications accepted.

Iowa State University of Science and Technology, Program in Information Systems, Ames, IA 50011. Offers information systems (MS). *Degree requirements:* For master's, thesis or alternative. *Entrance requirements:* For master's, GMAT. Additional exam requirements/recommendations for international students: Recommended—TOEFL (minimum score 600 paper-based; 100 iBT), IELTS (minimum score 7). Electronic applications accepted. *Expenses:* Contact institution.

James Madison University, The Graduate School, College of Business, Program in Business Administration, Harrisonburg, VA 22801. Offers business (MBA), including executive leadership, information security, innovation. *Accreditation:* AACSB. *Program availability:* Part-time, evening/weekend, blended/hybrid learning. *Students:* 34 full-time (12 women), 96 part-time (33 women); includes 29 minority (10 Black or African American, non-Hispanic/Latino; 9 Asian, non-Hispanic/Latino; 8 Hispanic/Latino; 2 Two or more races, non-Hispanic/Latino), 3 international. Average age 30. In 2017, 39 master's awarded. Application fee: $55. Electronic applications accepted. *Expenses:* Tuition, state resident: full-time $10,512; part-time $438 per credit hour. Tuition, nonresident: full-time $28,358; part-time $1162 per credit hour. *Required fees:* $1128. *Financial support:* In 2017–18, 1 student received support. Federal Work-Study and 1 assistantship (averaging $7911) available. Financial award application deadline: 3/1; financial award applicants required to submit FAFSA. *Unit head:* Dr. Matthew A. Rutherford, Department Head, 540-568-8777, E-mail: rutherma@jmu.edu. *Application contact:* Lynette D. Michael, Director of Graduate Admissions, 540-568-6131 Ext. 6395, Fax: 540-568-7860, E-mail: michaeld@jmu.edu. Website: http://www.jmu.edu/cob/graduate/mba/index.shtml

Johns Hopkins University, Carey Business School, MS in Information Systems Program, Baltimore, MD 21218. Offers MS. *Program availability:* Part-time, evening/weekend. *Faculty:* 93 full-time (33 women), 45 part-time/adjunct (11 women). *Students:* 56 full-time (35 women), 40 part-time (10 women); includes 17 minority (7 Black or African American, non-Hispanic/Latino; 6 Asian, non-Hispanic/Latino; 2 Hispanic/Latino; 2 Two or more races, non-Hispanic/Latino), 68 international. Average age 24. 279 applicants, 59% accepted, 60 enrolled. In 2017, 25 master's awarded. *Degree requirements:* For master's, 36 credits. *Entrance requirements:* For master's, GMAT or GRE. Additional exam requirements/recommendations for international students: Required—TOEFL, IELTS. *Application deadline:* For fall admission, 5/1 for domestic and international students. Applications are processed on a rolling basis. Application fee: $100. Electronic applications accepted. *Expenses:* $66,500 (full-time); $1,330 per credit (part-time). *Financial support:* In 2017–18, 7 students received support. Scholarships/grants available. Support available to part-time students. Financial award application deadline: 4/15; financial award applicants required to submit FAFSA. *Faculty research:* Digital innovations in healthcare, digital marketplaces, healthcare information systems, information technology and strategy. *Unit head:* Dr. Kevin Frick, Vice Dean of Education, 410-234-9272, E-mail: kfrick@jhu.edu. *Application contact:* Office of Admissions, 410-234-9220, Fax: 443-529-1554, E-mail: carey.admissions@jhu.edu. Website: http://carey.jhu.edu/academics/master-of-science/ms-in-information-systems/

Johns Hopkins University, Engineering Program for Professionals, Part-time Program in Information Systems Engineering, Baltimore, MD 21218. Offers MS, Graduate Certificate, Post-Master's Certificate. *Program availability:* Part-time, evening/weekend, 100% online, blended/hybrid learning. *Entrance requirements:* Additional exam requirements/recommendations for international students: Required—TOEFL (minimum score 600 paper-based; 100 iBT). Electronic applications accepted.

Johnson & Wales University, Graduate Studies, MBA Program, Providence, RI 02903-3703. Offers accounting (MBA); business administration (MBA); finance (MBA); global fashion merchandising and management (MBA); hospitality (MBA); human resource management (MBA); information security/assurance (MBA); information technology (MBA); nonprofit management (MBA); operations and supply chain management (MBA); organizational leadership (MBA); organizational psychology (MBA); sport leadership (MBA). Program also offered on Denver campus. *Program availability:* Part-time, online learning. *Entrance requirements:* For master's, minimum GPA of 2.75. Additional exam requirements/recommendations for international students: Required—TOEFL (minimum score 550 paper-based); Recommended—IELTS, TWE. *Application deadline:* For fall admission, 8/15 priority date for domestic students, 6/28 priority date for international students; for winter admission, 11/10 priority date for domestic students, 9/20 priority date for international students; for spring admission, 2/5 priority date for domestic students, 12/20 priority date for international students. Applications are processed on a rolling basis. *Expenses: Tuition:* Full-time $12,636; part-time $702 per credit hour. *Financial support:* Tuition waivers (partial) and unspecified assistantships available. Support available to part-time students. Financial award application deadline: 5/1. *Faculty research:* International banking, global economy, international trade, cultural differences. *Unit head:* Dr. Karen Silva, Director, 401-598-2849, Fax: 401-598-1125. *Application contact:* Graduate School Admissions, 401-598-1015, Fax: 401-598-1286, E-mail: gradadm@jwu.edu.

Kean University, College of Natural, Applied and Health Sciences, Program in Computer Information Systems, Union, NJ 07083. Offers MS. *Program availability:* Part-time, 100% online. *Faculty:* 10 full-time (4 women). *Students:* 21 full-time (9 women), 6 part-time (1 woman); includes 8 minority (4 Black or African American, non-Hispanic/Latino; 4 Asian, non-Hispanic/Latino), 17 international. Average age 27. 23 applicants, 83% accepted, 11 enrolled. In 2017, 10 master's awarded. *Entrance requirements:* For master's, baccalaureate degree in computer science or closely-related field from accredited college or university; minimum cumulative GPA of 3.0; official transcripts from all institutions attended; two letters of recommendation; professional resume/curriculum vitae; personal statement. Additional exam requirements/recommendations for international students: Required—TOEFL (minimum score 550 paper-based; 79 iBT), IELTS (minimum score 6.5). *Application deadline:* For fall admission, 6/30 for domestic and international students; for spring admission, 12/1 for domestic and international students. Applications are processed on a rolling basis. Application fee: $75. Electronic applications accepted. *Expenses:* Tuition, state resident: full-time $13,419; part-time $653 per credit. Tuition, nonresident: full-time $18,188; part-time $801 per credit. *Required fees:* $3382; $154 per credit. Tuition and fees vary according to course level, course load, degree level and program. *Financial support:* Scholarships/grants and unspecified assistantships available. Financial award applicants required to submit FAFSA. *Unit head:* Dr. Jing-Chiou Liou, Program Coordinator, 908-737-3803, E-mail: jliou@kean.edu. *Application contact:* Pedro Lopes, Admissions Counselor, 908-737-7100, E-mail: gradadmissions@kean.edu. Website: http://grad.kean.edu/masters-programs/computer-information-systems

Keiser University, MS in Information Technology Leadership Program, Fort Lauderdale, FL 33309. Offers MS. Website: https://www.keiseruniversity.edu/information-technology-leadership-ms/

Kent State University, College of Business Administration, Doctoral Program in Management Systems, Kent, OH 44242. Offers PhD. *Faculty:* 18 full-time (6 women). *Students:* 9 full-time (7 women), 6 international. Average age 34. 12 applicants. In 2017, 1 doctorate awarded. *Degree requirements:* For doctorate, comprehensive exam, thesis/dissertation, oral defense. *Entrance requirements:* For doctorate, GMAT or GRE. Additional exam requirements/recommendations for international students: Required—TOEFL (minimum score 600 paper-based; 100 iBT), IELTS (minimum score 7). *Application deadline:* For fall admission, 1/1 for domestic students, 2/1 for international students. Application fee: $45 ($70 for international students). Electronic applications accepted. *Expenses:* $11,300 per academic year. *Financial support:* In 2017–18, 8 students received support, including 8 teaching assistantships with full tuition reimbursements available (averaging $23,000 per year); Federal Work-Study also available. Financial award application deadline: 2/1; financial award applicants required to submit FAFSA. *Unit head:* Dr. O. Felix Offodile, Chair and Professor, 330-672-2750, Fax: 330-672-2953, E-mail: foffodil@kent.edu. *Application contact:* Felecia A. Urbanek, Assistant Director, 330-672-2282, Fax: 330-672-7303, E-mail: gradbus@kent.edu. Website: http://www.kent.edu/business/phd

Lake Erie College, School of Business, Painesville, OH 44077-3389. Offers general management (MBA); health care administration (MBA); information technology management (MBA). *Program availability:* Part-time, evening/weekend. *Entrance requirements:* For master's, GMAT or minimum GPA of 3.0, resume, personal statement. Additional exam requirements/recommendations for international students: Required—TOEFL (minimum score 550 paper-based; 79 iBT), IELTS (minimum score 6), STEP Eiken 1st and pre-1st grade level (for Japanese students). Electronic applications accepted. Application fee is waived when completed online. *Expenses:* Contact institution.

Le Moyne College, Madden School of Business, Syracuse, NY 13214. Offers business administration (MBA); information systems (MS). *Accreditation:* AACSB. *Program availability:* Part-time, evening/weekend. *Faculty:* 13 full-time (4 women), 4 part-time/adjunct (2 women). *Students:* 55 full-time (19 women), 65 part-time (27 women); includes 11 minority (3 Black or African American, non-Hispanic/Latino; 1 American Indian or Alaska Native, non-Hispanic/Latino; 3 Asian, non-Hispanic/Latino; 4 Hispanic/Latino), 2 international. Average age 28. 75 applicants, 92% accepted, 66 enrolled. In 2017, 57 master's awarded. *Degree requirements:* For master's, capstone-level course. *Entrance requirements:* For master's, GMAT or GRE General Test, bachelor's degree with minimum GPA of 3.0, resume, 2 letters of recommendation, personal statement, transcripts, interview. Additional exam requirements/recommendations for international students: Required—TOEFL (minimum score 550 paper-based; 79 iBT); Recommended—IELTS (minimum score 6.5). *Application deadline:* For fall admission, 7/1 priority date for domestic and international students; for spring admission, 11/1 priority date for domestic and international students; for summer admission, 4/1 priority date for domestic and international students. Applications are processed on a rolling basis. Application fee: $0. Electronic applications accepted. *Expenses:* $797 per credit hour. *Financial support:* In 2017–18, 41 students received support. Career-related internships or fieldwork, scholarships/grants, health care benefits, and unspecified assistantships available. Support available to part-time students. Financial award applicants required to submit FAFSA. *Faculty research:* Performance evaluation outcomes assessment, technology outsourcing, international business, systems for Web-based information-seeking, non-profit business practices, business sustainability practices, management/leadership development, operations management optimization applications. *Unit head:* James Joseph, Dean of Madden School of Business, 315-445-4280, Fax: 315-445-4787, E-mail: josepjae@lemoyne.edu. *Application contact:* Kristen P. Richards, Senior Director of Enrollment Management, 315-445-5444, Fax: 315-445-6092, E-mail: trapaskp@lemoyne.edu. Website: http://www.lemoyne.edu/madden

Lenoir-Rhyne University, Graduate Programs, Charles M. Snipes School of Business, Hickory, NC 28601. Offers accounting (MBA); business analytics and information technology (MBA); entrepreneurship (MBA); global business (MBA); healthcare administration (MBA); innovation and change management (MBA); leadership development (MBA). *Accreditation:* ACBSP. *Program availability:* Part-time, evening/weekend, online learning. *Degree requirements:* For master's, capstone course. *Entrance requirements:* For master's, GMAT, GRE, MAT, minimum undergraduate GPA of 2.7, graduate 3.0. Additional exam requirements/recommendations for international students: Required—TOEFL (minimum score 600 paper-based). Electronic applications accepted. *Expenses:* Contact institution.

Lewis University, College of Business, Program in Business Administration, Romeoville, IL 60446. Offers accounting (MBA); custom elective option (MBA); e-business (MBA); finance (MBA); healthcare management (MBA); human resources management (MBA); international business (MBA); management information systems (MBA); marketing (MBA); project management (MBA); technology and operations management (MBA). *Program availability:* Part-time, evening/weekend. *Students:* 130 full-time (77 women), 187 part-time (107 women); includes 83 minority (27 Black or African American, non-Hispanic/Latino; 3 American Indian or Alaska Native, non-Hispanic/Latino; 7 Asian, non-Hispanic/Latino; 40 Hispanic/Latino; 6 Two or more races, non-Hispanic/Latino), 31 international. Average age 31. In 2017, 99 master's awarded. *Degree requirements:* For master's, comprehensive exam. *Entrance requirements:* For master's, interview, bachelor's degree, resume, two recommendations. Additional exam requirements/recommendations for international students: Required—TOEFL (minimum score 550 paper-based), IELTS. *Application deadline:* For fall admission, 8/15 priority date for domestic students, 5/1 priority date for international students; for spring admission, 11/15 priority date for international students. Applications are processed on a rolling basis. Application fee: $40. Electronic applications accepted. Tuition and fees vary according to program. *Financial support:* Career-related internships or fieldwork, Federal Work-Study, scholarships/grants, and unspecified assistantships available. Financial award application deadline: 5/1; financial award applicants required to submit FAFSA. *Unit head:* Dr. Maureen Culleeney, Academic Program Director, 815-838-0500 Ext. 5631, E-mail: culleema@lewisu.edu. *Application contact:* Michele Ryan, Director of Admission, 815-838-0500 Ext. 5384, E-mail: ryanml@lewisu.edu.

Liberty University, School of Business, Lynchburg, VA 24515. Offers accounting (MBA, MS), including audit and financial reporting (MS), business (MS), financial services (MS), forensic accounting (MS), leadership (MS), taxation (MS); criminal justice (MBA); cyber security (MS); executive leadership (MA); information systems (MS), including information assurance, technology management; international business (MBA, DBA); leadership (DBA); marketing (MBA, MS, DBA), including digital marketing and advertising (MS), project management (MS), public relations (MS), sports marketing and media (MS); project management (MBA, DBA); public administration (MBA); public relations (MBA). *Program availability:* Part-time, online learning. *Students:* 1,887 full-time (1,003 women), 4,223 part-time (1,950 women); includes 1,570 minority (1,133 Black or African American, non-Hispanic/Latino; 30 American Indian or Alaska Native, non-Hispanic/Latino; 118 Asian, non-Hispanic/Latino; 149 Hispanic/Latino; 13 Native Hawaiian or other Pacific Islander, non-Hispanic/Latino; 127 Two or more races, non-Hispanic/Latino), 109 international. Average age 35. 5,680 applicants, 51% accepted, 1510 enrolled. In 2017, 1,290 master's, 17 doctorates awarded. *Entrance requirements:* For master's, minimum undergraduate GPA of 3.0, 15 hours of upper-level business courses. Additional exam requirements/recommendations for international students: Required—TOEFL (minimum score 600 paper-based; 100 iBT). *Application deadline:* Applications are processed on a rolling basis. Application fee: $50. Electronic applications accepted. *Expenses:* Contact institution. *Financial support:* Applicants required to submit FAFSA. *Unit head:* Dr. Scott Hicks, Dean, 434-592-4808, Fax: 434-582-2366, E-mail: smhicks@liberty.edu. *Application contact:* Jay Bridge, Director of Graduate Admissions, 800-424-9595, Fax: 800-628-7977, E-mail: gradadmissions@liberty.edu. Website: http://www.liberty.edu/academics/business/index.cfm?PID-149

Lincoln University, Graduate Studies, Oakland, CA 94612. Offers finance and investments (DBA); finance management (MS); finance management and investments (MBA); general business (MBA); human resource management (MBA, DBA);

international business (MBA, MS); management information systems (MBA). *Program availability:* Part-time. *Faculty:* 14 full-time (2 women), 20 part-time/adjunct (6 women). *Students:* 606 full-time (222 women), 31 part-time (14 women); includes 10 minority (8 Asian, non-Hispanic/Latino; 1 Hispanic/Latino; 1 Two or more races, non-Hispanic/Latino), 623 international. Average age 26. *Degree requirements:* For master's, research project (thesis), internship report, or comprehensive exam; for doctorate, comprehensive exam, thesis/dissertation. *Entrance requirements:* For master's, minimum GPA of 2.7; for doctorate, GMAT (minimum score: 550), GRE (minimum score: 1000), or equivalent test results (waived for master's degree with minimum cumulative GPA of 3.3). Additional exam requirements/recommendations for international students: Required—TOEFL minimum score 525 paper-based; 71 iBT or IELTS minimum score 5.5 (for MBA); TOEFL minimum score 550 paper-based; 79 iBT or IELTS minimum score 6 (for MS and DBA). *Application deadline:* For fall admission, 8/7 for domestic students, 7/14 for international students; for spring admission, 11/30 for domestic students, 10/31 for international students; for summer admission, 5/29 for domestic students, 5/5 for international students. Applications are processed on a rolling basis. Application fee: $75. Electronic applications accepted. *Expenses: Tuition:* Full-time $8100; part-time $450 per unit. *Required fees:* $360; $180 per semester. Tuition and fees vary according to course level, course load, degree level and program. *Financial support:* Teaching assistantships, career-related internships or fieldwork, and scholarships/grants available. Financial award applicants required to submit FAFSA. *Unit head:* Dr. Marshall Burak, Provost, 510-628-8016, Fax: 510-628-8012, E-mail: mburak@lincolnuca.edu. *Application contact:* Reenu Shrestha, Assistant to the President, 510-628-8017, Fax: 510-208-2826, E-mail: sreenu@lincolnuca.edu.

Lincoln University, Graduate Studies, Jefferson City, MO 65101. Offers business administration (MBA), including accounting, management, management information systems, public administration/policy; elementary teaching (M Ed); environmental science (MS); guidance and counseling (M Ed), including community/agency counseling, elementary school, secondary school; higher education (MA); history (MA); integrated agricultural systems (MS); middle school (M Ed); natural sciences (MS); secondary teaching (M Ed); sociology (MA); sociology/criminal justice (MA). *Program availability:* Part-time, evening/weekend, 100% online, blended/hybrid learning. *Students:* 40 full-time (23 women), 64 part-time (32 women); includes 33 minority (30 Black or African American, non-Hispanic/Latino; 2 Hispanic/Latino; 1 Two or more races, non-Hispanic/Latino), 12 international. Average age 33. 48 applicants, 81% accepted, 22 enrolled. In 2017, 46 master's awarded. *Degree requirements:* For master's, comprehensive exam, thesis optional. *Entrance requirements:* For master's, GRE, MAT, or GMAT, minimum GPA of 2.75 overall, 3.0 in courses related to specialization; 3 letters of recommendation; minimum C average in English composition; personal statement of purpose. Additional exam requirements/recommendations for international students: Required—TOEFL (minimum score 500 paper-based; 61 iBT), IELTS (minimum score 5.5), Michigan English Language Assessment Battery (minimum score 80). *Application deadline:* For fall admission, 7/1 priority date for domestic students, 5/1 priority date for international students; for spring admission, 11/1 priority date for domestic students, 10/1 priority date for international students; for summer admission, 6/1 priority date for domestic students. Applications are processed on a rolling basis. Application fee: $30. Electronic applications accepted. *Expenses:* Tuition, state resident: part-time $291 per credit hour. Tuition, nonresident: part-time $541.50 per credit hour. *Financial support:* In 2017–18, 2 fellowships with tuition reimbursements, 3 research assistantships with tuition reimbursements were awarded; Federal Work-Study, scholarships/grants, and unspecified assistantships also available. Support available to part-time students. Financial award application deadline: 3/1; financial award applicants required to submit FAFSA. *Unit head:* Dr. Debra F. Greene, Interim Provost, 573-681-5247, Fax: 573-681-5106, E-mail: gradschool@lincolnu.edu. *Application contact:* Irasema Steck, Administrative Assistant, 573-681-5247, Fax: 573-681-5106, E-mail: gradschool@lincolnu.edu. Website: http://www.lincolnu.edu/web/graduate-studies/graduate-studies

Lindenwood University, Graduate Programs, School of Accelerated Degree Programs, St. Charles, MO 63301-1695. Offers administration (MSA), including management, marketing, project management; business administration (MBA); communications (MA), including digital and multimedia, media management, promotions, training and development; criminal justice and administration (MS); healthcare administration (MS); human resource management (MS); information technology (Certificate); managing information security (MS); managing information technology (MS); managing virtualization and cloud computing (MS); writing (MFA). *Program availability:* Part-time, evening/weekend, 100% online. *Faculty:* 12 full-time (5 women), 90 part-time/adjunct (37 women). *Students:* 597 full-time (383 women), 202 part-time (138 women); includes 248 minority (206 Black or African American, non-Hispanic/Latino; 3 American Indian or Alaska Native, non-Hispanic/Latino; 6 Asian, non-Hispanic/Latino; 21 Hispanic/Latino; 1 Native Hawaiian or other Pacific Islander, non-Hispanic/Latino; 11 Two or more races, non-Hispanic/Latino), 69 international. Average age 36. 526 applicants, 46% accepted, 204 enrolled. In 2017, 537 master's awarded. *Degree requirements:* For master's, thesis (for some programs), minimum cumulative GPA of 3.0; for Certificate, minimum cumulative GPA of 3.0. *Entrance requirements:* For master's, resume, personal statement, official undergraduate transcript, minimum undergraduate cumulative GPA of 3.0. Additional exam requirements/recommendations for international students: Required—TOEFL (minimum score 550 paper-based; 80 iBT); Recommended—IELTS (minimum score 6.5). *Application deadline:* For fall admission, 9/24 priority date for domestic and international students; for winter admission, 1/7 priority date for domestic and international students; for spring admission, 4/8 priority date for domestic and international students; for summer admission, 7/8 priority date for domestic and international students. Applications are processed on a rolling basis. Application fee: $30 ($100 for international students). Electronic applications accepted. *Expenses: Tuition:* Full-time $16,300; part-time $460 per credit. *Required fees:* $660; $330 per credit. Tuition and fees vary according to degree level and program. *Financial support:* In 2017–18, 738 students received support. Career-related internships or fieldwork, institutionally sponsored loans, scholarships/grants, tuition waivers (partial), and unspecified assistantships available. Financial award application deadline: 6/30; financial award applicants required to submit FAFSA. *Unit head:* Dr. Gina Ganahl, Dean, Accelerated Degree Programs, 636-949-4501, Fax: 636-949-4505, E-mail: gganahl@lindenwood.edu. *Application contact:* Kara Schilli, Director, Evening and Graduate Admissions, 636-949-4349, Fax: 636-949-4109, E-mail: adultadmissions@lindenwood.edu. Website: http://www.lindenwood.edu/academics/academic-schools/school-of-accelerated-degree-programs/

Lipscomb University, College of Computing and Technology, Nashville, TN 37204-3951. Offers data science (MS, Certificate); information technology (MS, Certificate), including data science (MS), information security (MS), information technology management (MS), software engineering (MS); software engineering (MS, Certificate). *Program availability:* Part-time, evening/weekend. *Faculty:* 6 full-time (0 women), 6 part-time/adjunct (1 woman). *Students:* 44 full-time (16 women), 10 part-time (1 woman); includes 18 minority (7 Black or African American, non-Hispanic/Latino; 1 American Indian or Alaska Native, non-Hispanic/Latino; 8 Asian, non-Hispanic/Latino; 2 Hispanic/Latino), 5 international. Average age 35. 54 applicants, 57% accepted, 24 enrolled. In

Management Information Systems

2017, 28 master's, 2 other advanced degrees awarded. *Degree requirements:* For master's, capstone project. *Entrance requirements:* For master's, GRE, 2 references, transcripts, resume, personal statement. Additional exam requirements/recommendations for international students: Required—TOEFL (minimum score 570 paper-based; 80 iBT). *Application deadline:* Applications are processed on a rolling basis. Application fee: $50 ($75 for international students). Electronic applications accepted. *Expenses:* $1,263. *Financial support:* Scholarships/grants and employer agreements available. Financial award applicants required to submit FAFSA. *Unit head:* Dr. Fortune S. Mhlanga, Dean, 615-966-5073, E-mail: fortune.mhlanga@lipscomb.edu. *Application contact:* Brett Ramsey, Enrollment Management Specialist, 615-966-1193, E-mail: brett.ramsey@lipscomb.edu.
Website: http://www.lipscomb.edu/technology/

London Metropolitan University, Graduate Programs, London, United Kingdom. Offers applied psychology (M Sc); architecture (MA); biomedical science (M Sc); blood science (M Sc); cancer pharmacology (M Sc); computer networking and cyber security (M Sc); computing and information systems (M Sc); conference interpreting (MA); counter-terrorism studies (M Sc); creative, digital and professional writing (MA); crime, violence and prevention (M Sc); criminology (M Sc); curating contemporary art (MA); data analytics (M Sc); digital media (MA); early childhood studies (MA); education (MA, Ed D); financial services law, regulation and compliance (LL M); food science (M Sc); forensic psychology (M Sc); health and social care management and policy (M Sc); human nutrition (M Sc); human resource management (MA); human rights and international conflict (MA); information technology (M Sc); intelligence and security studies (M Sc); international oil, gas and energy law (LL M); international relations (MA); interpreting (MA); learning and teaching in higher education (MA); legal practice (LL M); media and entertainment law (LL M); organizational and consumer psychology (M Sc); psychological therapy (M Sc); psychology of mental health (M Sc); public health (M Sc); public policy and management (MPA); security studies (M Sc); social work (M Sc); spatial planning and urban design (MA); sports therapy (M Sc); supporting older children and young people with dyslexia (MA); teaching languages (MA), including Arabic, English; translation (MA); woman and child abuse (MA).

Long Island University–LIU Post, College of Management, Brookville, NY 11548-1300. Offers accountancy (MS); finance (MBA); information systems (MS); international business (MBA); management (MBA); management engineering (MS); marketing (MBA); taxation (MS); technical project management (MS); JD/MBA. *Accreditation:* AACSB. *Program availability:* Part-time, evening/weekend, blended/hybrid learning. *Faculty:* 23 full-time (7 women), 7 part-time/adjunct (1 woman). *Students:* 119 full-time (47 women), 62 part-time (23 women); includes 33 minority (11 Black or African American, non-Hispanic/Latino; 8 Asian, non-Hispanic/Latino; 13 Hispanic/Latino; 1 Two or more races, non-Hispanic/Latino), 56 international. Average age 28. 162 applicants, 62% accepted, 41 enrolled. In 2017, 91 master's awarded. *Entrance requirements:* For master's, GMAT, GRE, or LSAT. Additional exam requirements/recommendations for international students: Required—TOEFL (minimum score 550 paper-based, 75 iBT) or IELTS. *Application deadline:* Applications are processed on a rolling basis. Application fee: $50. Electronic applications accepted. *Expenses:* Tuition: Full-time $21,618; part-time $1201 per credit. *Required fees:* $1840; $920 per term. Tuition and fees vary according to course load. *Financial support:* In 2017–18, 47 students received support. Career-related internships or fieldwork, Federal Work-Study, and scholarships/grants available. Support available to part-time students. Financial award application deadline: 2/15; financial award applicants required to submit FAFSA. *Faculty research:* Innovation and property rights, knowledge sourcing, sustainability and firm performance, China and growth markets, corporate social responsibility, workforce compensation and issues. *Unit head:* Dr. Robert M. Valli, Dean, 516-299-3004, E-mail: rob.valli@liu.edu. *Application contact:* Rita Langdon, Graduate Admissions, 516-299-2900, Fax: 516-299-2137, E-mail: post-enroll@liu.edu.
Website: http://liu.edu/CWPost/Academics/Schools/COM

Louisiana State University and Agricultural & Mechanical College, Graduate School, E. J. Ourso College of Business, Department of Information Systems and Decision Sciences, Baton Rouge, LA 70803. Offers MS, PhD. *Faculty:* 15 full-time (4 women), 1 part-time/adjunct (0 women). *Students:* 23 full-time (7 women), 12 part-time (3 women); includes 4 minority (2 Black or African American, non-Hispanic/Latino; 2 Asian, non-Hispanic/Latino), 10 international. Average age 30. 7 applicants, 86% accepted, 1 enrolled. In 2017, 19 master's awarded. *Financial support:* In 2017–18, 4 research assistantships (averaging $13,063 per year), 2 teaching assistantships (averaging $20,682 per year) were awarded. *Total annual research expenditures:* $76,567.

Louisiana Tech University, Graduate School, College of Business, Ruston, LA 71272. Offers accounting (M Acc, DBA); computer information systems (DBA); finance (MBA, DBA); information assurance (MBA); innovation (MBA); management (DBA); marketing (MBA, DBA). *Accreditation:* AACSB. *Program availability:* Part-time, evening/weekend, 100% online, blended/hybrid learning. *Faculty:* 36 full-time (7 women), 8 part-time/adjunct (3 women). *Students:* 104 full-time (43 women), 40 part-time (16 women); includes 22 minority (13 Black or African American, non-Hispanic/Latino; 2 Asian, non-Hispanic/Latino; 7 Two or more races, non-Hispanic/Latino), 32 international. Average age 29. 104 applicants, 58% accepted, 25 enrolled. In 2017, 71 master's, 4 doctorates awarded. *Degree requirements:* For doctorate, thesis/dissertation. *Entrance requirements:* For master's and doctorate, GMAT, transcript with bachelor's degree awarded. Additional exam requirements/recommendations for international students: Required—TOEFL (minimum score 550 paper-based; 80 iBT), IELTS (minimum score 6.5). *Application deadline:* For fall admission, 8/1 priority date for domestic students, 6/1 for international students; for winter admission, 11/1 priority date for domestic students, 9/1 for international students; for spring admission, 2/1 priority date for domestic students, 12/1 for international students; for summer admission, 5/1 priority date for domestic students, 3/1 for international students. Application fee: $40. Electronic applications accepted. *Expenses:* Tuition, state resident: full-time $5146. Tuition, nonresident: full-time $10,147. *International tuition:* $10,267 full-time. *Required fees:* $2273. *Financial support:* In 2017–18, 24 students received support, including 17 research assistantships with partial tuition reimbursements available (averaging $12,500 per year), 7 teaching assistantships with partial tuition reimbursements available (averaging $12,500 per year); scholarships/grants and unspecified assistantships also available. Financial award application deadline: 2/1. *Faculty research:* Consumer environmental behavior; identifying and analyzing current issues and future concerns in real estate; information assurance and related areas in business for Northwest Louisiana and the United States (business continuity, disaster recovery, accounting controls, auditing, computer forensics, and security attribution); value creation driven by the consumer and employee interface within exchange environments. *Unit head:* Dr. Christopher D. Martin, Dean, 318-257-4526, Fax: 318-257-4253. *Application contact:* Samantha J. Bailey, Graduate Management Admissions Specialist, 318-257-2924, Fax: 318-257-4487, E-mail: samantha@latech.edu.
Website: http://www.business.latech.edu/

Loyola University Chicago, Quinlan School of Business, MBA Programs, Chicago, IL 60611. Offers accounting (MBA); business ethics (MBA); derivative markets (MBA); economics (MBA); entrepreneurship (MBA); finance (MBA); healthcare management (MBA); human resources management (MBA); information systems management (MBA); international business (MBA); management (MBA); marketing (MBA); risk management (MBA); supply chain management (MBA). *Program availability:* Part-time, evening/weekend. *Faculty:* 84 full-time (28 women), 12 part-time/adjunct (3 women). *Students:* 253 full-time (118 women), 76 part-time (35 women); includes 83 minority (21 Black or African American, non-Hispanic/Latino; 1 American Indian or Alaska Native, non-Hispanic/Latino; 33 Asian, non-Hispanic/Latino; 24 Hispanic/Latino; 4 Two or more races, non-Hispanic/Latino), 37 international. Average age 30. 334 applicants, 52% accepted, 80 enrolled. In 2017, 220 master's awarded. *Entrance requirements:* For master's, GMAT or GRE, official transcripts, two letters of recommendation, statement of purpose, resume. Additional exam requirements/recommendations for international students: Required—TOEFL (minimum score 90 iBT) or IELTS (minimum score 6.5). *Application deadline:* For fall admission, 7/15 for domestic and international students; for winter admission, 10/1 for domestic and international students; for spring admission, 1/15 for domestic and international students; for summer admission, 4/1 for domestic and international students. Applications are processed on a rolling basis. Application fee: $50. Electronic applications accepted. Application fee is waived when completed online. *Expenses:* $4,488 per course. *Financial support:* In 2017–18, 11 students received support. Research assistantships, career-related internships or fieldwork, Federal Work-Study, scholarships/grants, and health care benefits available. *Faculty research:* Social enterprise and responsibility, emerging markets, supply chain management, risk management. *Unit head:* Katherine Acles, Assistant Dean for Graduate Programs, 312-915-6124, Fax: 312-915-7207, E-mail: kacles@luc.edu.

Loyola University Maryland, Graduate Programs, Sellinger School of Business, Professional MBA Program, Baltimore, MD 21210-2699. Offers finance (MBA); information systems (MBA); investments and applied portfolio management (MBA); management (MBA); marketing (MBA). *Accreditation:* AACSB. *Program availability:* Part-time, evening/weekend. *Entrance requirements:* For master's, GMAT, resume, essay, official transcripts, professional letter of recommendation. Additional exam requirements/recommendations for international students: Required—TOEFL (minimum score 550 paper-based, 80 iBT) or IELTS (minimum score 7). *Application deadline:* For fall admission, 8/1 priority date for domestic students, 4/1 for international students; for spring admission, 12/1 priority date for domestic students, 9/1 for international students; for summer admission, 5/1 priority date for domestic students. Applications are processed on a rolling basis. Application fee: $60. Electronic applications accepted. *Expenses:* Contact institution. *Financial support:* In 2017–18, 26 students received support. Scholarships/grants available. Financial award application deadline: 4/15; financial award applicants required to submit FAFSA. *Unit head:* Kelly Fader, Director of Graduate Cohort Program, 410-617-1617, E-mail: kgfader@loyola.edu. *Application contact:* Office of Graduate Business Programs, 410-617-5067, E-mail: mba@loyola.edu.

Marist College, Graduate Programs, School of Computer Science and Mathematics, Poughkeepsie, NY 12601-1387. Offers computer science/software development (MS); information systems (MS, Adv C); technology management (MS). *Program availability:* Part-time, evening/weekend, online learning. *Entrance requirements:* For master's, resume. Additional exam requirements/recommendations for international students: Required—TOEFL (minimum score 550 paper-based; 80 iBT); Recommended—IELTS (minimum score 6.5). Electronic applications accepted. *Faculty research:* Data quality, artificial intelligence, imaging, analysis of algorithms, distributed systems and applications.

Marquette University, Graduate School of Management, Executive MBA Program, Milwaukee, WI 53201-1881. Offers economics (MBA); finance (MBA); human resources (MBA); international business (MBA); management information systems (MBA); marketing (MBA); operations and supply chain management (MBA); sports business (MBA). *Accreditation:* AACSB. *Degree requirements:* For master's, international trip. *Entrance requirements:* For master's, GMAT or GRE, two letters of recommendation, official transcripts from current and previous colleges/universities. Additional exam requirements/recommendations for international students: Required—TOEFL (minimum score 550 paper-based; 88 iBT), IELTS (minimum score 6.5), PTE. Electronic applications accepted. *Expenses:* Contact institution. *Faculty research:* International trade and finance, customer relationship management, consumer satisfaction, customer service.

Marquette University, Graduate School of Management, Program in Business Administration, Milwaukee, WI 53201-1881. Offers business administration (MBA); economics (MBA); entrepreneurship (Certificate); finance (MBA); human resources (MBA); international business (MBA); management information systems (MBA); marketing (MBA); operations and supply chain management (MBA); sports business (MBA); JD/MBA; MBA/MA; MBA/MSN. *Accreditation:* AACSB. *Program availability:* Part-time, evening/weekend. *Degree requirements:* For Certificate, business plan. *Entrance requirements:* For master's, GMAT or GRE, letters of recommendation. Additional exam requirements/recommendations for international students: Required—TOEFL (minimum score 550 paper-based; 88 iBT), IELTS (minimum score 6.5), PTE. Electronic applications accepted. *Faculty research:* Ethics in the professions, services marketing, technology impact on decision-making, mentoring.

Marymount University, School of Business Administration, Program in Information Technology, Arlington, VA 22207-4299. Offers health care informatics (Certificate); information technology (MS, Certificate), including cybersecurity (MS), health care informatics (MS), project management and technology leadership (MS), software engineering (MS); information technology project management and technology leadership (Certificate); MS/MBA; MS/MS. *Program availability:* Part-time, evening/weekend. *Faculty:* 4 full-time (2 women), 12 part-time/adjunct (1 woman). *Students:* 40 full-time (18 women), 31 part-time (13 women); includes 28 minority (16 Black or African American, non-Hispanic/Latino; 4 Asian, non-Hispanic/Latino; 8 Hispanic/Latino), 29 international. Average age 31. 44 applicants, 98% accepted, 12 enrolled. In 2017, 25 master's, 10 other advanced degrees awarded. *Degree requirements:* For master's, thesis or alternative. *Entrance requirements:* For master's, resume, bachelor's degree in computer-related field or degree in another subject with certificate in computer-related field or related work experience; bachelor's degree in computer science or work in software development (for software engineering track). Additional exam requirements/recommendations for international students: Required—TOEFL (minimum score 600 paper-based; 96 iBT), IELTS (minimum score 6.5). *Application deadline:* For fall admission, 7/16 priority date for domestic and international students; for spring admission, 11/16 priority date for domestic and international students; for summer admission, 4/16 for domestic and international students. Applications are processed on a rolling basis. Application fee: $40. Electronic applications accepted. *Expenses:* $990 per credit. *Financial support:* In 2017–18, 5 students received support, including 4 research assistantships with full and partial tuition reimbursements available (averaging $7,425 per year); career-related internships or fieldwork, Federal Work-Study, scholarships/grants, and unspecified assistantships also available. Support available to part-time students. Financial award application deadline: 3/1; financial award applicants required to submit FAFSA. *Unit head:* Dr. Diane Murphy, Chair/Director, Information Technology, Management Sciences and Cybersecurity, 703-284-5958, Fax: 703-527-3830, E-mail: diane.murphy@marymount.edu. *Application contact:* Francesca Reed, Director, Graduate Admissions, 703-284-5901, Fax: 703-527-3815, E-mail: grad.admissions@marymount.edu.
Website: http://www.marymount.edu/Academics/School-of-Business-Administration/Graduate-Programs/Information-Technology-(M-S-)

Marywood University, Academic Affairs, Munley College of Liberal Arts and Sciences, School of Business and Global Innovation, Emphasis in Management Information Systems, Scranton, PA 18509-1598. Offers MBA, MS. *Program availability:* Part-time. Electronic applications accepted.

McGill University, Faculty of Graduate and Postdoctoral Studies, Desautels Faculty of Management, Montréal, QC H3A 2T5, Canada. Offers administration (PhD); entrepreneurial studies (MBA); finance (MBA); general management (Post Master's Certificate); information systems (MBA); international business (MBA); international practicing management (MM); management (MBA); management for development (MBA); manufacturing management (MMM); marketing (MBA); operations management (MBA); public accountancy (Diploma); strategic management (MBA); MBA/LL B; MD/MBA. MMM offered jointly with Faculty of Engineering; PhD with Concordia University, HEC Montreal, Université de Montréal, Université du Québec à Montréal.

McMaster University, School of Graduate Studies, DeGroote School of Business, Program in Information Systems, Hamilton, ON L8S 4M2, Canada. Offers PhD. *Program availability:* Part-time. *Degree requirements:* For doctorate, comprehensive exam, thesis/dissertation. *Entrance requirements:* For doctorate, GMAT or GRE General Test, master's degree, minimum B+ average. Additional exam requirements/recommendations for international students: Required—TOEFL (minimum score 580 paper-based). *Faculty research:* Information systems, operations management, web-based decision support systems, web-based agents, financial engineering.

Metropolitan State University, College of Management, St. Paul, MN 55106-5000. Offers business administration (MBA, DBA); business analytics (Graduate Certificate); database administration (Graduate Certificate); global supply chain management (Graduate Certificate); information assurance security (Graduate Certificate); management information systems (MMIS); MIS generalist (Graduate Certificate); MIS systems analysis and design (Graduate Certificate); project management (Graduate Certificate). *Program availability:* Part-time, evening/weekend. *Degree requirements:* For master's, thesis optional, computer language (MMIS). *Entrance requirements:* For master's, GMAT (for MBA), resume. Additional exam requirements/recommendations for international students: Required—TOEFL (minimum score 550 paper-based). *Application deadline:* For fall admission, 7/15 for international students; for winter admission, 11/15 for international students; for spring admission, 3/15 for international students. Applications are processed on a rolling basis. Application fee: $20. Electronic applications accepted. *Expenses:* Tuition, state resident: part-time $388.55 per credit. Tuition, nonresident: part-time $777.11 per credit. *Required fees:* $35.11 per credit. Part-time tuition and fees vary according to campus/location and program. *Financial support:* Research assistantships with partial tuition reimbursements, career-related internships or fieldwork, and Federal Work-Study available. Support available to part-time students. Financial award applicants required to submit FAFSA. *Faculty research:* Yugoslav economic system, workers' cooperatives, participative management and job enrichment, global business systems. *Unit head:* Allen Bellas, Interim Dean, 612-659-7272, Fax: 612-659-7268, E-mail: allen.bellas@metrostate.edu. *Application contact:* Allen Bellas, Interim Dean, 612-659-7272, Fax: 612-659-7268, E-mail: allen.bellas@metrostate.edu.
Website: https://www.metrostate.edu/academics/management

Michigan State University, The Graduate School, College of Communication Arts and Sciences, Department of Telecommunication, Information Studies, and Media, East Lansing, MI 48824. Offers digital media arts and technology (MA); information and telecommunication management (MA); information, policy and society (MA); serious game design (MA). *Entrance requirements:* Additional exam requirements/recommendations for international students: Required—TOEFL. Electronic applications accepted.

Michigan State University, The Graduate School, Eli Broad College of Business, Department of Accounting and Information Systems, East Lansing, MI 48224. Offers accounting (MS, PhD), including information systems (MS), public and corporate accounting (MS), taxation (MS); business information systems (PhD). *Accreditation:* AACSB. *Degree requirements:* For doctorate, comprehensive exam, thesis/dissertation. *Entrance requirements:* For master's, GMAT (minimum score 550), bachelor's degree in accounting; minimum cumulative GPA of 3.0 at any institution attended and in any junior-/senior-level accounting courses taken; 3 letters of recommendation (at least 1 from faculty); working knowledge of computers including word processing, spreadsheets, networking, and database management system; for doctorate, GMAT (minimum score 600), bachelor's degree; transcripts; 3 letters of recommendation; statement of purpose; resume; on-campus interview; personal qualifications of sound character, perseverance, intellectual curiosity, and interest in scholarly research. Additional exam requirements/recommendations for international students: Required—TOEFL (minimum score 600 paper-based; 100 iBT), IELTS (minimum score 7) accepted for MS only. Electronic applications accepted.

Middle Georgia State University, Office of Graduate Studies, Macon, GA 31206. Offers adult/gerontology acute care nurse practitioner (MSN); information technology (MS), including health informatics, information security and digital forensics, software development. *Entrance requirements:* For master's, GRE. Additional exam requirements/recommendations for international students: Required—TOEFL (minimum score 523 paper-based; 69 iBT). *Expenses:* Contact institution.

Middle Tennessee State University, College of Graduate Studies, Jennings A. Jones College of Business, Department of Computer Information Systems, Murfreesboro, TN 37132. Offers MS. *Program availability:* Part-time, evening/weekend, online learning. *Entrance requirements:* Additional exam requirements/recommendations for international students: Required—TOEFL (minimum score 525 paper-based; 71 iBT) or IELTS (minimum score 6). Electronic applications accepted. *Faculty research:* Safety and security, project management.

Minot State University, Graduate School, Information Systems Program, Minot, ND 58707-0002. Offers MSIS. *Program availability:* Part-time, online learning. *Entrance requirements:* Additional exam requirements/recommendations for international students: Required—TOEFL (minimum score 79 iBT), IELTS (minimum score 6).

Mississippi State University, Bagley College of Engineering, Department of Industrial and Systems Engineering, Mississippi State, MS 39762. Offers human factors and ergonomics (MS); industrial and systems engineering (PhD); industrial systems (MS); management systems (MS); manufacturing systems (MS); operations research (MS). *Program availability:* Part-time, blended/hybrid learning. *Faculty:* 13 full-time (2 women). *Students:* 33 full-time (10 women), 65 part-time (16 women); includes 22 minority (11 Black or African American, non-Hispanic/Latino; 5 Asian, non-Hispanic/Latino; 5 Hispanic/Latino; 1 Native Hawaiian or other Pacific Islander, non-Hispanic/Latino), 21 international. Average age 36. 64 applicants, 47% accepted, 19 enrolled. In 2017, 13 master's, 5 doctorates awarded. *Degree requirements:* For master's, comprehensive exam (for some programs), thesis optional, comprehensive oral or written exam; for doctorate, comprehensive exam, thesis/dissertation, candidacy exam. *Entrance requirements:* For master's, GRE (for graduates from program not accredited by EAC/ABET), minimum GPA of 3.0 on junior and senior years; for doctorate, GRE (for graduates from program not accredited by EAC/ABET), minimum GPA of 3.5 on master's degree and junior and senior years of BS. Additional exam requirements/

recommendations for international students: Required—TOEFL (minimum score 550 paper-based; 79 iBT); Recommended—IELTS (minimum score 6.5). *Application deadline:* For fall admission, 7/1 for domestic students, 5/1 for international students; for spring admission, 11/1 for domestic students, 9/1 for international students. Applications are processed on a rolling basis. Application fee: $60 ($80 for international students). Electronic applications accepted. *Expenses:* Tuition, state resident: full-time $8318; part-time $462.12 per credit hour. Tuition, nonresident: full-time $22,358; part-time $1242.12 per credit hour. *Required fees:* $110; $12.24 per credit hour. $6.12 per semester. *Financial support:* In 2017–18, 20 research assistantships with full tuition reimbursements (averaging $16,589 per year), 1 teaching assistantship with full tuition reimbursement (averaging $17,669 per year) were awarded; Federal Work-Study, institutionally sponsored loans, and unspecified assistantships also available. Financial award application deadline: 4/1; financial award applicants required to submit FAFSA. *Faculty research:* Operations research, ergonomics, production systems, management systems, transportation. *Total annual research expenditures:* $2.2 million. *Unit head:* Dr. John Usher, Professor/Head, 662-325-8875, Fax: 662-325-7618, E-mail: usher@ise.msstate.edu. *Application contact:* Marina Hunt, Admissions and Enrollment Assistant, 662-325-5188, E-mail: mhunt@grad.msstate.edu.
Website: http://www.ise.msstate.edu/

Mississippi State University, College of Business, Department of Management and Information Systems, Mississippi State, MS 39762. Offers business administration (MBA); information systems (MSIS, PhD); management (PhD); project management (MBA). *Program availability:* Part-time. *Faculty:* 19 full-time (5 women). *Students:* 63 full-time (21 women), 194 part-time (44 women); includes 21 minority (5 Black or African American, non-Hispanic/Latino; 4 Asian, non-Hispanic/Latino; 9 Hispanic/Latino; 3 Two or more races, non-Hispanic/Latino), 16 international. Average age 30. 163 applicants, 48% accepted, 63 enrolled. In 2017, 96 master's, 4 doctorates awarded. *Degree requirements:* For master's, comprehensive exam; for doctorate, comprehensive exam, thesis/dissertation. *Entrance requirements:* For master's, GMAT, minimum GPA of 3.0 in last 60 hours of undergraduate course work; for doctorate, GMAT (minimum score of 550), minimum GPA of 3.25 on all graduate work; BS with minimum GPA of 3.0 cumulative and last 60 hours. Additional exam requirements/recommendations for international students: Required—TOEFL (minimum score 575 paper-based; 84 iBT); Recommended—IELTS (minimum score 7). *Application deadline:* For fall admission, 7/1 for domestic students, 5/1 for international students; for spring admission, 11/1 for domestic students, 9/1 for international students. Applications are processed on a rolling basis. Application fee: $60 ($80 for international students). Electronic applications accepted. *Expenses:* Tuition, state resident: full-time $8318; part-time $462.12 per credit hour. Tuition, nonresident: full-time $22,358; part-time $1242.12 per credit hour. *Required fees:* $110; $12.24 per credit hour. $6.12 per semester. *Financial support:* Career-related internships or fieldwork, Federal Work-Study, institutionally sponsored loans, scholarships/grants, and unspecified assistantships available. Financial award applicants required to submit FAFSA. *Faculty research:* Electronic commerce, management of information technology. *Total annual research expenditures:* $1.3 million. *Unit head:* Dr. James J. Chrisman, Professor and Head, 662-325-1991, Fax: 662-325-8651, E-mail: jchrisman@business.msstate.edu. *Application contact:* Lakan Drinker, Admissions and Enrollment Assistant, 662-325-8951, E-mail: ldrinker@grad.msstate.edu.
Website: http://www.business.msstate.edu/programs/mis/index.php

Morehead State University, Graduate Programs, College of Business and Public Affairs, Department of Information Systems, Morehead, KY 40351. Offers MSIS. *Entrance requirements:* For master's, GRE, GMAT. Additional exam requirements/recommendations for international students: Required—TOEFL (minimum score 525 paper-based). Electronic applications accepted.

Morehead State University, Graduate Programs, College of Business and Public Affairs, School of Business Administration, Morehead, KY 40351. Offers business administration (MBA); information systems (MSIS); sport management (MA). *Program availability:* Part-time, evening/weekend. *Entrance requirements:* For master's, GRE or GMAT. Additional exam requirements/recommendations for international students: Required—TOEFL (minimum score 500 paper-based). Electronic applications accepted.

Morgan State University, School of Graduate Studies, Earl G. Graves School of Business and Management, PhD Program in Business Administration, Baltimore, MD 21251. Offers business administration (PhD), including accounting, information systems, management and marketing. *Accreditation:* AACSB. *Entrance requirements:* For doctorate, GMAT. Additional exam requirements/recommendations for international students: Required—TOEFL (minimum score 550 paper-based). *Application deadline:* For fall admission, 2/1 priority date for domestic students; for spring admission, 10/1 priority date for domestic students. Applications are processed on a rolling basis. Application fee: $0. *Expenses:* Tuition, state resident: part-time $433 per credit. Tuition, nonresident: part-time $851 per credit. *Required fees:* $81.50 per credit. *Financial support:* Application deadline: 2/1. *Unit head:* Dr. Augustus Abbey, Department Chair, 443-885-3285, E-mail: augustus.abbey@morgan.edu. *Application contact:* Dr. Dean Campbell, Graduate Recruitment Specialist, 443-885-3185, Fax: 443-885-8226, E-mail: dean.campbell@morgan.edu.

Murray State University, Arthur J. Bauernfeind College of Business, Department of Computer Science and Information Systems, Murray, KY 42071. Offers MSIS. *Program availability:* Part-time, evening/weekend, 100% online, blended/hybrid learning. *Faculty:* 9 full-time (1 woman). *Students:* 18 full-time (5 women), 9 part-time (1 woman); includes 2 minority (1 Asian, non-Hispanic/Latino; 1 Hispanic/Latino), 19 international. Average age 28. 89 applicants, 51% accepted, 6 enrolled. In 2017, 13 master's awarded. *Entrance requirements:* For master's, GRE or GMAT, minimum university GPA of 2.75. Additional exam requirements/recommendations for international students: Required—TOEFL (minimum score 527 paper-based; 71 iBT). *Application deadline:* Applications are processed on a rolling basis. Application fee: $40 ($50 for international students). Electronic applications accepted. *Expenses:* Tuition, state resident: full-time $9504. Tuition, nonresident: full-time $26,811. *International tuition:* $14,400 full-time. Tuition and fees vary according to course load, degree level and reciprocity agreements. *Financial support:* In 2017–18, 1 research assistantship was awarded; Federal Work-Study and unspecified assistantships also available. Financial award applicants required to submit FAFSA. *Unit head:* Dr. Victor Raj, Chair, Department of Computer Science and Information Systems, 270-809-6214, Fax: 270-809-3199, E-mail: vraj@murraystate.edu. *Application contact:* Kaitlyn Burzynski, Interim Assistant Director for Graduate Admission and Records, 270-809-5732, Fax: 270-809-3780, E-mail: msu.graduateadmissions@murraystate.edu.
Website: http://www.murraystate.edu/academics/CollegesDepartments/CollegeOfBusiness/Programs/CSIS/index.aspx

National American University, Roueche Graduate Center, Austin, TX 78731. Offers accounting (MBA); aviation management (MBA, MM); care coordination (MSN); community college leadership (Ed D); criminal justice (MM); e-marketing (MBA, MM); health care administration (MBA, MM); higher education (MM); human resources management (MBA, MM); information technology management (MBA, MM); international business (MBA); leadership (EMBA); management (MBA); nursing administration (MSN); nursing education (MSN); nursing informatics (MSN); operations

Management Information Systems

and configuration management (MBA, MM); project and process management (MBA, MM). Master's programs offered online through the Harold D. Buckingham Graduate School. *Program availability:* Part-time, evening/weekend, online learning. *Entrance requirements:* For master's, minimum undergraduate GPA of 2.75. Additional exam requirements/recommendations for international students: Required—TOEFL, TWE. Electronic applications accepted. *Faculty research:* Tourism, finance, marketing.

National University, Academic Affairs, School of Business and Management, La Jolla, CA 92037-1011. Offers accountancy (M Acc, Certificate); business administration (GMBA, MBA); business analytics (MS); cause leadership (MA); global management (MGM); human resource management (MA); management information systems (MS); marketing (MS); organizational leadership (MS). GMBA offered in Spanish. *Program availability:* Part-time, evening/weekend, 100% online, blended/hybrid learning. *Degree requirements:* For master's, thesis (for some programs). *Entrance requirements:* For master's, interview, minimum GPA of 2.5. Additional exam requirements/recommendations for international students: Required—TOEFL (minimum score 550 paper-based; 79 iBT), IELTS (minimum score 6). *Application deadline:* Applications are processed on a rolling basis. Application fee: $60 ($65 for international students). Electronic applications accepted. *Expenses: Tuition:* Part-time $430 per quarter hour. *Financial support:* Career-related internships or fieldwork, scholarships/grants, and tuition waivers (partial) available. Support available to part-time students. Financial award application deadline: 6/30; financial award applicants required to submit FAFSA. *Unit head:* Dr. Alfred Ntoko, Dean, 858-642-8400, Fax: 858-642-8719, E-mail: sobm@nu.edu. *Application contact:* Brandon Jouganatos, Vice President for Enrollment Services, 800-628-8648, E-mail: advisor@nu.edu.
Website: http://www.nu.edu/OurPrograms/SchoolOfBusinessAndManagement.html

National University, Academic Affairs, School of Engineering and Computing, La Jolla, CA 92037-1011. Offers computer science (MS), including advanced computing; cyber security and information assurance (MS); data analytics (MS); electrical engineering (MS); engineering management (MS); information technology management (MS); management information systems (MS); sustainability management (MS). *Program availability:* Part-time, evening/weekend, 100% online, blended/hybrid learning. *Degree requirements:* For master's, thesis (for some programs). *Entrance requirements:* For master's, interview, minimum GPA of 2.5. Additional exam requirements/recommendations for international students: Required—TOEFL (minimum score 550 paper-based; 79 iBT), IELTS (minimum score 6). *Application deadline:* Applications are processed on a rolling basis. Application fee: $60 ($65 for international students). Electronic applications accepted. *Expenses: Tuition:* Part-time $430 per quarter hour. *Financial support:* Career-related internships or fieldwork, institutionally sponsored loans, scholarships/grants, and tuition waivers (partial) available. Support available to part-time students. Financial award application deadline: 6/30; financial award applicants required to submit FAFSA. *Faculty research:* Educational technology, scholarships in science. *Unit head:* Dr. Jodi Reeves, Interim Dean, 858-309-3426, E-mail: jreeves@nu.edu. *Application contact:* Brandon Jouganatos, Vice President for Enrollment Services, 800-628-8648, E-mail: advisor@nu.edu.
Website: http://www.nu.edu/OurPrograms/SchoolOfEngineeringAndTechnology.html

Naval Postgraduate School, Departments and Academic Groups, Department of Information Sciences, Monterey, CA 93943. Offers electronic warfare systems engineering (MS); information sciences (PhD); information systems and operations (MS); information technology management (MS); information warfare systems engineering (MS); knowledge superiority (Certificate); remote sensing intelligence (MS); system technology (command, control and communications) (MS). Program open only to commissioned officers of the United States and friendly nations and selected United States federal civilian employees. *Program availability:* Part-time. *Degree requirements:* For master's, thesis (for some programs); for doctorate, thesis/dissertation. *Faculty research:* Designing inter-organisational collectivities for dynamic fit: stability, manoeuvrability and application in disaster relief endeavours; system self-awareness and related methods for Improving the use and understanding of data within DoD; evaluating a macrocognition model of team collaboration using real-world data from the Haiti relief effort; cyber distortion in command and control; performance and QoS in service-based systems.

Naval Postgraduate School, Departments and Academic Groups, Graduate School of Business and Public Policy, Monterey, CA 93943. Offers acquisition and contract management (MBA); business administration (EMBA, MBA); contract management (MS); defense business management (MBA); defense systems analysis (MS), including management; defense systems management (international) (MBA); financial management (MBA); information management (MBA); manpower systems analysis (MS); material logistics support management (MBA); program management (MS); resource planning and management for international defense (MBA); supply chain management (MBA); systems acquisition management (MBA); transportation management (MBA). Program only open to commissioned officers of the United States and friendly nations and selected United States federal civilian employees. *Accreditation:* AACSB; NASPAA. *Program availability:* Part-time, online learning. *Degree requirements:* For master's, thesis (for some programs), terminal project/capstone (for some programs). *Faculty research:* U.S. and European public procurement policies for small and medium-sized enterprises, examining external validity criticisms in the choice of students as subjects in accounting experiment studies, assurance of learning in contract management education, contracting for cloud computing: opportunities and risks, NPS, Apple App Store as a business model supporting U.S. Navy requirements.

New England Institute of Technology, Program in Information Technology, East Greenwich, RI 02818. Offers MS. *Program availability:* Part-time-only, evening/weekend, 100% online, blended/hybrid learning. *Entrance requirements:* For master's, minimum GPA of 2.5; bachelor's degree in related field from accredited institution. Additional exam requirements/recommendations for international students: Required—TOEFL. *Application deadline:* Applications are processed on a rolling basis. Application fee: $25. Electronic applications accepted. *Expenses:* $550 per credit. *Unit head:* Douglas H. Sherman, Senior Vice President and Provost, 401-739-5000 Ext. 3481, Fax: 401-886-0859, E-mail: dsherman@neit.edu. *Application contact:* Michael Caruso, Director of Admissions, 800-736-7744 Ext. 3411, Fax: 401-886-0868, E-mail: mcaruso@neit.edu.
Website: http://www.neit.edu/Programs/Masters-Degree/Information-Technology

New Jersey Institute of Technology, Ying Wu College of Computing, Newark, NJ 07102. Offers big data management and mining (Certificate); business and information systems (Certificate); computer science (MS, PhD), including bioinformatics (MS); computer science, computing and business (MS); cyber security and privacy (MS); software engineering (MS); data mining (Certificate); information security (Certificate); information systems (MS, PhD), including business and information systems (MS); emergency management and business continuity (MS); information systems; information technology administration and security (MS); IT administration (Certificate); network security and information assurance (Certificate); software engineering analysis/design (Certificate); Web systems development (Certificate). *Program availability:* Part-time, evening/weekend. *Faculty:* 64 full-time (10 women), 38 part-time/adjunct (4 women). *Students:* 818 full-time (241 women), 225 part-time (53 women); includes 162

minority (35 Black or African American, non-Hispanic/Latino; 77 Asian, non-Hispanic/Latino; 41 Hispanic/Latino; 9 Two or more races, non-Hispanic/Latino), 772 international. Average age 27. 2,666 applicants, 51% accepted, 377 enrolled. In 2017, 398 master's, 10 doctorates, 9 other advanced degrees awarded. Terminal master's awarded for partial completion of doctoral program. *Degree requirements:* For master's, thesis optional; for doctorate, thesis/dissertation. *Entrance requirements:* For master's, GRE General Test; for doctorate, GRE General Test, minimum graduate GPA of 3.5. Additional exam requirements/recommendations for international students: Required—TOEFL (minimum score 550 paper-based; 79 iBT). *Application deadline:* For fall admission, 6/1 priority date for domestic students, 5/1 priority date for international students; for spring admission, 11/15 priority date for domestic and international students. Applications are processed on a rolling basis. Application fee: $75. Electronic applications accepted. *Expenses:* Contact institution. *Financial support:* In 2017–18, 57 students received support, including 2 fellowships (averaging $23,254 per year), 47 research assistantships (averaging $24,412 per year), 44 teaching assistantships (averaging $23,528 per year); career-related internships or fieldwork, Federal Work-Study, institutionally sponsored loans, and unspecified assistantships also available. Financial award application deadline: 1/15. *Faculty research:* Computer systems, communications and networking, artificial intelligence, database engineering, systems analysis, analytics and optimization in crowdsourcing. *Total annual research expenditures:* $3 million. *Unit head:* Dr. Craig Gotsman, Dean, 973-542-5488, Fax: 973-596-5777, E-mail: marek.rusinkiewicz@njit.edu. *Application contact:* Stephen Eck, Director of Admissions, 973-596-3300, Fax: 973-596-3461, E-mail: admissions@njit.edu.
Website: http://computing.njit.edu/

Newman University, MBA Program, Wichita, KS 67213-2097. Offers finance (MBA); international business (MBA); leadership (MBA); management (MBA); management information technology (MBA). *Program availability:* Part-time. *Degree requirements:* For master's, thesis optional. *Entrance requirements:* For master's, minimum GPA of 3.0; 2 letters of recommendation; course work in algebra, statistics, macroeconomics, and financial accounting. Additional exam requirements/recommendations for international students: Required—TOEFL (minimum score 600 paper-based; 100 iBT). Electronic applications accepted. *Expenses:* Contact institution.

New Mexico State University, College of Business, MBA Program, Las Cruces, NM 88003. Offers agribusiness (MBA); finance (MBA); information systems (MBA). *Accreditation:* AACSB. *Program availability:* Part-time-only, evening/weekend, online with required 2-3 day orientation and 2-3 day concluding session in Las Cruces. *Students:* 47 full-time (24 women), 123 part-time (74 women); includes 98 minority (2 Black or African American, non-Hispanic/Latino; 3 American Indian or Alaska Native, non-Hispanic/Latino; 4 Asian, non-Hispanic/Latino; 85 Hispanic/Latino; 1 Native Hawaiian or other Pacific Islander, non-Hispanic/Latino; 3 Two or more races, non-Hispanic/Latino), 6 international. Average age 33. 166 applicants, 82% accepted, 19 enrolled. In 2017, 79 master's awarded. *Entrance requirements:* For master's, GMAT or GRE (depending upon undergraduate or graduate degree institution and GPA), minimum GPA of 3.5 from AACSB international or ACBSP-accredited institution or graduate degree from regionally-accredited U.S. university (without GMAT or GRE). Additional exam requirements/recommendations for international students: Required—TOEFL (minimum score 550 paper-based; 79 iBT), IELTS (minimum score 6.5). *Application deadline:* For fall admission, 7/15 priority date for domestic students, 4/15 priority date for international students; for spring admission, 4/15 priority date for domestic students, 9/15 priority date for international students; for summer admission, 4/15 for domestic students, 1/15 for international students. Applications are processed on a rolling basis. Application fee: $40 ($50 for international students). Electronic applications accepted. *Expenses:* Tuition, state resident: full-time $4390. Tuition, nonresident: full-time $15,309. *Required fees:* $853. *Financial support:* In 2017–18, 29 students received support. Fellowships, Federal Work-Study, institutionally sponsored loans, scholarships/grants, health care benefits, and unspecified assistantships available. Financial award application deadline: 3/1. *Unit head:* Dr. Kathy Brook, Associate Dean, 575-646-8003, Fax: 575-646-7977, E-mail: kbrook@nmsu.edu. *Application contact:* John Shonk, MBA Advisor, 575-646-8003, Fax: 575-646-7977, E-mail: mbaprog@nmsu.edu.
Website: http://business.nmsu.edu/mba

New York University, Leonard N. Stern School of Business, Department of Information, Operations and Management Sciences, New York, NY 10012-1019. Offers information systems (MBA, PhD); operations management (MBA, PhD); statistics (MBA, PhD). *Expenses: Tuition:* Full-time $41,352; part-time $19,968 per year. *Required fees:* $2496; $1628 per unit. $814 per term. Tuition and fees vary according to course load and program. *Faculty research:* Knowledge management, economics of information, computer-supported groups and communities financial information systems, data mining and business intelligence.

New York University, School of Professional Studies, Division of Programs in Business, Program in Management and Systems, New York, NY 10012-1019. Offers management and systems (MS), including database technologies, enterprise risk management, strategy and leadership, systems management. *Program availability:* Part-time, evening/weekend, 100% online, blended/hybrid learning. *Students:* 257 full-time (153 women), 80 part-time (45 women); includes 44 minority (9 Black or African American, non-Hispanic/Latino; 1 American Indian or Alaska Native, non-Hispanic/Latino; 21 Asian, non-Hispanic/Latino; 11 Hispanic/Latino; 2 Two or more races, non-Hispanic/Latino), 272 international. Average age 27. 507 applicants, 63% accepted, 150 enrolled. In 2017, 170 master's awarded. *Degree requirements:* For master's, thesis, capstone project. *Entrance requirements:* For master's, GRE or GMAT (only upon request), bachelor's degree, resume with relevant professional work, internship or volunteer experience, two letters of recommendation, statement of purpose. Additional exam requirements/recommendations for international students: Required—TOEFL (minimum score 600 paper-based; 100 iBT), IELTS (minimum score 7). *Application deadline:* For fall admission, 2/1 priority date for domestic and international students; for spring admission, 10/15 priority date for domestic students, 8/15 priority date for international students; for summer admission, 5/1 priority date for domestic students, 1/15 priority date for international students. Applications are processed on a rolling basis. Application fee: $150. Electronic applications accepted. *Expenses:* $20,244 per term. *Financial support:* Fellowships, career-related internships or fieldwork, Federal Work-Study, scholarships/grants, and health care benefits available. Support available to part-time students. Financial award application deadline: 6/30; financial award applicants required to submit FAFSA. *Unit head:* Martin Ihrig, Associate Dean/Clinical Professor, 212-992-3288. *Application contact:* Admissions Office, 212-998-7100, E-mail: sps.gradadmissions@nyu.edu.
Website: http://www.sps.nyu.edu/academics/departments/information-technology.html

North Carolina Agricultural and Technical State University, School of Graduate Studies, School of Technology, Department of Electronics, Computer, and Information Technology, Greensboro, NC 27411. Offers electronics and computer technology (MSIT, MSTM); information technology (MSIT, MSTM).

Northeastern University, College of Computer and Information Science, Boston, MA 02115-5096. Offers computer science (MS, PhD); data science (MS); game science and

design (MS); health informatics (MS); information assurance (MS); network science (PhD); personal health informatics (PhD). *Program availability:* Part-time, evening/weekend. *Faculty:* 93. *Students:* 1,451. In 2017, 322 master's, 8 doctorates awarded. Terminal master's awarded for partial completion of doctoral program. *Degree requirements:* For master's, thesis optional; for doctorate, comprehensive exam, thesis/dissertation. Application fee: $75. Electronic applications accepted. *Expenses:* Contact institution. *Financial support:* Research assistantships, teaching assistantships, scholarships/grants, health care benefits, and unspecified assistantships available. Financial award applicants required to submit FAFSA. *Unit head:* Dr. Carla E. Brodley, Professor and Dean, 617-373-5204, E-mail: c.brodley@northeastern.edu. *Application contact:* Dr. Rajmohan Rajaraman, Professor/Associate Dean/Director of the Graduate School, 617-373-2462, E-mail: ccis-gradschool@northeastern.edu.
Website: http://www.ccs.neu.edu/

Northeastern University, College of Engineering, Boston, MA 02115-5096. Offers bioengineering (MS, PhD); chemical engineering (MS, PhD); civil engineering (MS, PhD); computer engineering (MS); computer systems engineering (MS); electrical and computer engineering (MS); electrical and computer engineering leadership (MS); electrical engineering (PhD); energy systems (MS); engineering and public policy (MS); engineering management (MS, Certificate); environmental engineering (MS); industrial engineering (MS, PhD); information assurance (PhD); information systems (MS); interdisciplinary engineering (PhD); mechanical engineering (PhD); operations research (MS); telecommunication systems management (MS). *Program availability:* Part-time, online learning. *Faculty:* 225 full-time. *Students:* 3,720. In 2017, 851 master's, 74 doctorates awarded. Application fee: $75. Electronic applications accepted. *Expenses:* Contact institution. *Financial support:* Fellowships, research assistantships, teaching assistantships, career-related internships or fieldwork, scholarships/grants, health care benefits, tuition waivers, and unspecified assistantships available. Support available to part-time students. Financial award applicants required to submit FAFSA. *Unit head:* Dr. Nadine Aubry, Dean, College of Engineering, 617-373-5847, E-mail: n.aubry@neu.edu. *Application contact:* Jeffery Hengel, Director of Graduate Admissions, 617-373-2711, E-mail: j.hengel@northeastern.edu.
Website: http://www.coe.neu.edu/

Northern Illinois University, Graduate School, College of Business, Department of Operations Management and Information Systems, De Kalb, IL 60115-2854. Offers management information systems (MS). *Program availability:* Part-time. *Faculty:* 11 full-time (3 women), 3 part-time/adjunct (0 women). *Students:* 147 full-time (56 women), 47 part-time (11 women); includes 47 minority (7 Black or African American, non-Hispanic/Latino; 35 Asian, non-Hispanic/Latino; 3 Hispanic/Latino; 2 Two or more races, non-Hispanic/Latino), 128 international. Average age 26. 342 applicants, 65% accepted, 52 enrolled. In 2017, 130 master's awarded. *Entrance requirements:* For master's, GMAT, minimum GPA of 2.75. Additional exam requirements/recommendations for international students: Required—TOEFL (minimum score 550 paper-based). *Application deadline:* For fall admission, 6/1 for domestic students, 5/1 for international students; for spring admission, 11/1 for domestic students, 10/1 for international students. Applications are processed on a rolling basis. Application fee: $40. Electronic applications accepted. *Financial support:* In 2017–18, 9 research assistantships with full tuition reimbursements, 21 teaching assistantships with full tuition reimbursements were awarded; fellowships with full tuition reimbursements, career-related internships or fieldwork, Federal Work-Study, scholarships/grants, tuition waivers (full), and unspecified assistantships also available. Support available to part-time students. Financial award applicants required to submit FAFSA. *Faculty research:* Affordability of home ownership, Web portal competition intranet, electronic commerce, corporate-academic alliances. *Unit head:* Dr. Chang Liu, Chair, 815-753-3021, Fax: 815-753-7460. *Application contact:* Steve Kispert, Office of Graduate Studies in Business, 815-753-6372, E-mail: skispert@niu.edu.
Website: http://www.cob.niu.edu/omis/

Northwestern University, School of Professional Studies, Program in Information Systems, Evanston, IL 60208. Offers analytics and business intelligence (MS); database and Internet technologies (MS); information systems (MS); information systems management (MS); information systems security (MS); medical informatics (MS); software project management and development (MS). *Program availability:* Part-time, evening/weekend.
Website: https://sps.northwestern.edu/masters/information-systems/index.php

Northwest Missouri State University, Graduate School, School of Computer Science and Information Systems, Maryville, MO 64468-6001. Offers applied computer science (MS); information systems (MS); instructional technology (MS). *Program availability:* Part-time. *Faculty:* 19 full-time (5 women). *Students:* 211 full-time (74 women), 64 part-time (20 women), 264 international. Average age 24. 395 applicants, 70% accepted, 75 enrolled. In 2017, 267 master's awarded. *Degree requirements:* For master's, comprehensive exam. *Entrance requirements:* For master's, GRE General Test, minimum GPA of 3.0. Additional exam requirements/recommendations for international students: Required—TOEFL (minimum score 550 paper-based). *Application deadline:* Applications are processed on a rolling basis. Application fee: $0 ($50 for international students). *Expenses:* Tuition, state resident: full-time $4551; part-time $252.86 per credit hour. Tuition, nonresident: full-time $9103; part-time $505.72 per credit hour. *Required fees:* $2453; $136.25 per credit hour. Tuition and fees vary according to course load and program. *Financial support:* Research assistantships, teaching assistantships with full tuition reimbursements, and unspecified assistantships available. Financial award application deadline: 4/1; financial award applicants required to submit FAFSA. *Unit head:* Dr. Carol Spradling, Director of School of Computer Science and Information Systems, 660-562-1588, Fax: 660-562-1963, E-mail: c_sprad@nwmissouri.edu. *Application contact:* Dr. Gregory Haddock, Dean of Graduate School, 660-562-1145, Fax: 660-562-1096, E-mail: gradsch@nwmissouri.edu.
Website: http://www.nwmissouri.edu/csis/

Nova Southeastern University, College of Engineering and Computing, Fort Lauderdale, FL 33314-7796. Offers computer science (MS, PhD); information assurance (PhD); information assurance and cybersecurity (MS); information systems (PhD); information technology (MS); management information systems (MS). *Program availability:* Part-time, evening/weekend, blended/hybrid learning. *Faculty:* 19 full-time (5 women), 20 part-time/adjunct (3 women). *Students:* 244 full-time (75 women), 351 part-time (104 women); includes 282 minority (119 Black or African American, non-Hispanic/Latino; 1 American Indian or Alaska Native, non-Hispanic/Latino; 49 Asian, non-Hispanic/Latino; 98 Hispanic/Latino; 1 Native Hawaiian or other Pacific Islander, non-Hispanic/Latino; 14 Two or more races, non-Hispanic/Latino), 112 international. Average age 40. 148 applicants, 65% accepted. In 2017, 176 master's, 37 doctorates awarded. Terminal master's awarded for partial completion of doctoral program. *Degree requirements:* For master's, thesis optional; for doctorate, thesis/dissertation. *Entrance requirements:* For master's, minimum undergraduate GPA of 2.5; for doctorate, master's degree, minimum graduate GPA of 3.25. Additional exam requirements/recommendations for international students: Required—TOEFL (minimum score 80 iBT), IELTS (minimum score 6), PTE (minimum score 54). *Application deadline:* Applications are processed on a rolling basis. Application fee: $50. Electronic applications accepted. *Expenses:* $775 per credit hour tuition (master's); $1,115 per

credit hour tuition (doctoral). *Financial support:* Federal Work-Study, scholarships/grants, and corporate financial support available. Financial award application deadline: 4/15; financial award applicants required to submit FAFSA. *Faculty research:* Artificial intelligence, database management, human-computer interaction, business intelligence and data analytics, information assurance and cybersecurity. *Unit head:* Dr. Yong X. Tao, Dean, 954-262-2063, Fax: 954-262-2752, E-mail: ytao@nova.edu. *Application contact:* Nancy Azoulay, Director, Admissions, 954-262-2026, Fax: 954-262-2752, E-mail: azoulayn@nova.edu.
Website: http://scis.nova.edu

Oakland University, Graduate Study and Lifelong Learning, School of Business Administration, Department of Decision and Information Sciences, Rochester, MI 48309-4401. Offers information technology management (MS); management information systems (Certificate); production and operations management (Certificate). *Expenses:* Tuition, state resident: full-time $16,950; part-time $706.25 per credit. Tuition, nonresident: full-time $24,648; part-time $1027 per credit.

Oakland University, Graduate Study and Lifelong Learning, School of Engineering and Computer Science, Department of Computer Science and Engineering, Rochester, MI 48309-4401. Offers computer science (MS); computer science and informatics (PhD); software engineering and information technology (MS). *Program availability:* Part-time, evening/weekend. *Entrance requirements:* For master's, minimum GPA of 3.0. Electronic applications accepted. *Expenses:* Contact institution.

The Ohio State University, Graduate School, Max M. Fisher College of Business, Department of Accounting and Management Information Systems, Columbus, OH 43210. Offers accounting (M Acc); management information systems (PhD). *Accreditation:* AACSB. *Faculty:* 23. *Students:* 101 full-time (53 women). Average age 24. In 2017, 79 master's, 1 doctorate awarded. Terminal master's awarded for partial completion of doctoral program. *Degree requirements:* For doctorate, thesis/dissertation. *Entrance requirements:* For master's, GMAT (minimum score of 550 recommended, 600 preferred) or GRE; for doctorate, GMAT. Additional exam requirements/recommendations for international students: Required—TOEFL (minimum score 600 paper-based; 100 iBT), Michigan English Language Assessment Battery (minimum score 86); Recommended—IELTS (minimum score 7). *Application deadline:* For fall admission, 11/15 priority date for domestic and international students. Applications are processed on a rolling basis. Application fee: $60 ($70 for international students). Electronic applications accepted. *Financial support:* Fellowships with tuition reimbursements, research assistantships with tuition reimbursements, teaching assistantships with tuition reimbursements, career-related internships or fieldwork, Federal Work-Study, and institutionally sponsored loans available. Support available to part-time students. *Faculty research:* Artificial intelligence, protocol analysis, database design in decision-supporting systems. *Unit head:* Dr. Brian Mittendorf, Chair and Professor, 614-292-1720, E-mail: mittendorf.3@osu.edu. *Application contact:* Graduate and Professional Admissions, 614-292-6031, Fax: 614-292-3656, E-mail: gpadmissions@osu.edu.
Website: https://fisher.osu.edu/academic-departments/amis

Oklahoma State University, Spears School of Business, Department of Management Science and Information Systems, Stillwater, OK 74078. Offers management information systems (MS); management science and information systems (PhD); telecommunications management (MS). *Program availability:* Part-time, online learning. *Faculty:* 15 full-time (1 woman), 6 part-time/adjunct (3 women). *Students:* 84 full-time (25 women), 48 part-time (12 women); includes 13 minority (2 Black or African American, non-Hispanic/Latino; 2 American Indian or Alaska Native, non-Hispanic/Latino; 1 Asian, non-Hispanic/Latino; 4 Hispanic/Latino; 1 Native Hawaiian or other Pacific Islander, non-Hispanic/Latino; 3 Two or more races, non-Hispanic/Latino), 79 international. Average age 29. 391 applicants, 27% accepted, 65 enrolled. In 2017, 91 master's, 1 doctorate awarded. *Entrance requirements:* For master's and doctorate, GRE or GMAT. Additional exam requirements/recommendations for international students: Required—TOEFL (minimum score 550 paper-based; 79 iBT). *Application deadline:* For fall admission, 3/1 priority date for international students; for spring admission, 8/1 priority date for international students. Applications are processed on a rolling basis. Application fee: $40 ($75 for international students). Electronic applications accepted. *Expenses:* Tuition, state resident: full-time $4019; part-time $2679.60 per year. Tuition, nonresident: full-time $15,286; part-time $10,190.40 per year. *Required fees:* $2129; $1419 per unit. Tuition and fees vary according to program. *Financial support:* Research assistantships, teaching assistantships, career-related internships or fieldwork, Federal Work-Study, scholarships/grants, health care benefits, tuition waivers (partial), and unspecified assistantships available. Support available to part-time students. Financial award application deadline: 3/1; financial award applicants required to submit FAFSA. *Unit head:* Dr. Rick Wilson, Department Head, 405-744-3551, Fax: 405-744-5180, E-mail: rick.wilson@okstate.edu. *Application contact:* Dr. Rathin Sarathy, Graduate Coordinator, 405-744-8646, Fax: 405-744-5180, E-mail: rathin.sarathy@okstate.edu.
Website: https://business.okstate.edu/msis/

Old Dominion University, College of Sciences, Program in Computer Science, Norfolk, VA 23529. Offers computer information systems (MS); computer science (MS, PhD). *Program availability:* Part-time, 100% online. *Faculty:* 14 full-time (4 women), 3 part-time/adjunct (0 women). *Students:* 73 full-time (26 women), 68 part-time (13 women); includes 24 minority (7 Black or African American, non-Hispanic/Latino; 9 Asian, non-Hispanic/Latino; 4 Hispanic/Latino; 4 Two or more races, non-Hispanic/Latino), 76 international. Average age 30. 166 applicants, 54% accepted, 45 enrolled. In 2017, 38 master's, 7 doctorates awarded. Terminal master's awarded for partial completion of doctoral program. *Degree requirements:* For master's, comprehensive exam, thesis optional, 34 credit hours; for doctorate, comprehensive exam, thesis/dissertation, 48 credit hours beyond the MS. *Entrance requirements:* For master's, GRE General Test, minimum GPA of 3.0; for doctorate, GRE General Test, MS in computer science. Additional exam requirements/recommendations for international students: Required—TOEFL (minimum score 550 paper-based; 79 iBT), IELTS (minimum score 6.5). *Application deadline:* For fall admission, 6/1 for domestic students, 4/15 for international students; for spring admission, 11/1 for domestic students, 10/1 for international students; for summer admission, 3/1 for domestic students, 2/1 for international students. Applications are processed on a rolling basis. Application fee: $50. Electronic applications accepted. *Expenses:* Tuition, state resident: full-time $8928; part-time $496 per credit. Tuition, nonresident: full-time $22,482; part-time $1249 per credit. *Required fees:* $66 per semester. *Financial support:* In 2017–18, 80 students received support, including 5 fellowships with full tuition reimbursements available (averaging $19,000 per year), 32 research assistantships with partial tuition reimbursements available (averaging $18,000 per year), 55 teaching assistantships with partial tuition reimbursements available (averaging $10,000 per year); career-related internships or fieldwork and scholarships/grants also available. Financial award application deadline: 2/15; financial award applicants required to submit FAFSA. *Faculty research:* Machine intelligence and data science, Web science and digital libraries, cyber-physical systems, bioinformatics, scientific computing. *Total annual research expenditures:* $1.6 million. *Unit head:* Dr. Ravi Mukkamala, Department Chair, 757-683-6001, Fax: 757-683-4900, E-mail: mukka@cs.odu.edu. *Application contact:* Dr. Yaohang Li, Graduate Program Director, 757-683-6001, E-mail: yaohang@cs.odu.edu.
Website: http://www.cs.odu.edu/

Management Information Systems

Our Lady of the Lake University, School of Business and Leadership, Program in Information Systems and Security, San Antonio, TX 78207-4689. Offers MS. *Program availability:* Part-time, online only, 100% online. *Faculty:* 5 full-time (3 women), 2 part-time/adjunct (0 women). *Students:* 30 full-time (13 women), 7 part-time (2 women); includes 22 minority (3 Black or African American, non-Hispanic/Latino; 19 Hispanic/Latino). Average age 37. 23 applicants, 83% accepted, 11 enrolled. In 2017, 20 master's awarded. *Entrance requirements:* For master's, GRE or GMAT, official transcripts showing baccalaureate degree from regionally-accredited institution in technical discipline and minimum GPA of 3.0 for cumulative undergraduate work or 3.2 in the major field (technical discipline) of study. Additional exam requirements/recommendations for international students: Required—TOEFL. *Application deadline:* For fall admission, 6/15 for domestic and international students; for spring admission, 11/15 for domestic and international students; for summer admission, 4/15 for domestic and international students. Applications are processed on a rolling basis. Application fee: $40 ($50 for international students). Electronic applications accepted. Application fee is waived when completed online. *Expenses: Tuition:* Full-time $10,668; part-time $5334 per year. *Required fees:* $816; $816 per year. $408 per semester. *Financial support:* In 2017–18, 14 students received support. Federal Work-Study, scholarships/grants, unspecified assistantships, and tuition discounts available. Support available to part-time students. Financial award application deadline: 5/1; financial award applicants required to submit FAFSA. *Faculty research:* Computer information systems implementation and best practices, computer and network security, cyber security legal issues, information assurance, and information technology education. *Unit head:* Carol Jeffries-Horner, Chair, Computer Information Systems and Security Department, 210-528-6730, E-mail: cjeffries@ollusa.edu. *Application contact:* Office of Graduate Admissions, 210-431-3995, Fax: 210-431-3945, E-mail: gradadm@ollusa.edu. Website: http://www.ollusa.edu/s/1190/hybrid/default-hybrid-ollu.aspx?sid-1190&gid-1&pgid-7901

Pace University, Lubin School of Business, Information Systems Program, New York, NY 10038. Offers MBA. *Program availability:* Part-time, evening/weekend. *Students:* 4 full-time (all women), 10 part-time (4 women); includes 5 minority (1 Black or African American, non-Hispanic/Latino; 3 Asian, non-Hispanic/Latino; 1 Hispanic/Latino), 4 international. Average age 30. 5 applicants, 60% accepted, 2 enrolled. In 2017, 8 master's awarded. *Entrance requirements:* For master's, GMAT, GRE, undergraduate degree, transcripts from all accredited colleges/universities attended, two letters of recommendation, resume, personal statement. Additional exam requirements/recommendations for international students: Required—TOEFL (minimum score 90 iBT), IELTS (minimum score 7) or PTE (minimum score 61). *Application deadline:* For fall admission, 8/1 priority date for domestic students, 6/1 for international students; for spring admission, 12/1 for domestic students, 10/1 for international students. Applications are processed on a rolling basis. Application fee: $70. Electronic applications accepted. *Financial support:* Research assistantships, career-related internships or fieldwork, Federal Work-Study, and unspecified assistantships available. Support available to part-time students. Financial award application deadline: 2/15; financial award applicants required to submit FAFSA. *Unit head:* Dr. Li-Chiou Chen, Chairperson, 914-773-3907, E-mail: lchen@pace.edu. *Application contact:* Susan Ford-Goldschein, Director of Graduate Admissions, 212-346-1531, Fax: 212-346-1585, E-mail: graduateadmission@pace.edu. Website: http://www.pace.edu/lubin/mba-in-information-systems

Pace University, Seidenberg School of Computer Science and Information Systems, New York, NY 10038. Offers chief information security officer (APC); computer science (MS, PhD); enterprise analytics (MS); information and communication technology strategy and innovation (APC); information systems (MS, APC); Internet technology (MS); professional studies in computing (DPS); secure software and information engineering (APC); security and information assurance (Certificate); software development and engineering (MS, Certificate); telecommunications systems and networks (MS, Certificate). *Program availability:* Part-time, evening/weekend, online only, 100% online, blended/hybrid learning. *Faculty:* 26 full-time (7 women), 7 part-time/adjunct (2 women). *Students:* 569 full-time (203 women), 319 part-time (95 women); includes 186 minority (73 Black or African American, non-Hispanic/Latino; 3 American Indian or Alaska Native, non-Hispanic/Latino; 56 Asian, non-Hispanic/Latino; 43 Hispanic/Latino; 11 Two or more races, non-Hispanic/Latino), 541 international. Average age 30. 871 applicants, 90% accepted, 272 enrolled. In 2017, 311 master's, 10 doctorates, 2 other advanced degrees awarded. *Degree requirements:* For master's, thesis or alternative, capstone course; for doctorate, comprehensive exam (for some programs), thesis/dissertation. *Entrance requirements:* For master's, GRE General Test. Additional exam requirements/recommendations for international students: Required—TOEFL (minimum score 78 iBT), IELTS (minimum score 6.5) or PTE (minimum score 52). *Application deadline:* For fall admission, 8/1 priority date for domestic students, 6/1 for international students; for spring admission, 12/1 for domestic students, 10/1 for international students. Applications are processed on a rolling basis. Application fee: $70. Electronic applications accepted. *Expenses:* Contact institution. *Financial support:* In 2017–18, 45 students received support. Research assistantships, career-related internships or fieldwork, scholarships/grants, and unspecified assistantships available. Support available to part-time students. Financial award application deadline: 2/15; financial award applicants required to submit FAFSA. *Faculty research:* Cyber security/digital forensics; mobile app development; big data/enterprise analytics; artificial intelligence; software development. *Total annual research expenditures:* $314,545. *Unit head:* Dr. Jonathan Hill, Dean, Seidenberg School of Computer Science and Information Systems, 212-346-1864, E-mail: jhill@pace.edu. *Application contact:* Susan Ford-Goldschein, Director of Graduate Admissions, 914-422-4283, Fax: 212-346-1585, E-mail: graduateadmission@pace.edu. Website: http://www.pace.edu/seidenberg

Pacific States University, College of Business, Los Angeles, CA 90010. Offers accounting (MBA, Certificate); beauty management (MBA); finance (MBA); international business (MBA); management of information technology (MBA); project management (Certificate); real estate management (MBA). *Program availability:* Part-time, evening/weekend, online learning. *Entrance requirements:* For master's, minimum undergraduate GPA of 2.5 during last 90 quarter units of course work, bachelor's degree in business administration or economics. Additional exam requirements/recommendations for international students: Required—TOEFL (minimum score 500 paper-based; 61 iBT), IELTS (minimum score 5.5). *Application deadline:* For fall admission, 9/1 priority date for domestic students, 8/1 priority date for international students; for winter admission, 12/1 priority date for domestic students, 11/1 priority date for international students; for spring admission, 3/1 priority date for domestic students, 2/1 priority date for international students; for summer admission, 6/1 priority date for domestic students, 5/1 priority date for international students. Applications are processed on a rolling basis. Application fee: $100. *Expenses: Tuition:* Part-time $380 per unit. *Financial support:* Scholarships/grants available. Financial award applicants required to submit FAFSA. *Unit head:* Chase C. Rhee, MBA Program Administrator, 323-731-2383 Ext. 208, Fax: 323-731-7276, E-mail: ccrhee@psuca.edu. *Application contact:* Maawiya Ayeva, Director of Admissions, 323-731-2383 Ext. 204, Fax: 323-731-7276, E-mail: admissions@psuca.edu.

Pacific States University, College of Computer Science and Information Systems, Los Angeles, CA 90010. Offers computer science (MS); information systems (MS). *Program availability:* Part-time, evening/weekend. *Entrance requirements:* For master's, bachelor's degree in physics, engineering, computer science, information systems, or applied mathematics; minimum undergraduate GPA of 2.5 during last 90 quarter units of course work. Additional exam requirements/recommendations for international students: Required—TOEFL (minimum score 500 paper-based; 61 iBT), IELTS (minimum score 5.5). *Application deadline:* For fall admission, 9/1 priority date for domestic students, 8/1 priority date for international students; for winter admission, 12/1 priority date for domestic students, 11/1 priority date for international students; for spring admission, 3/1 priority date for domestic students, 2/1 priority date for international students; for summer admission, 6/1 priority date for domestic students, 5/1 priority date for international students. Applications are processed on a rolling basis. Application fee: $100. *Expenses: Tuition:* Part-time $380 per unit. *Financial support:* Scholarships/grants available. Financial award applicants required to submit FAFSA. *Application contact:* Maawiya Ayeva, Director of Admissions, 323-731-2383 Ext. 204, Fax: 323-731-7276, E-mail: admissions@psuca.edu.

Park University, School of Graduate and Professional Studies, Kansas City, MO 54105. Offers adult education (M Ed); business and government leadership (Graduate Certificate); business, government, and global society (MPA); communication and leadership (MA); creative and life writing (Graduate Certificate); disaster and emergency management (MPA, Graduate Certificate); educational leadership (M Ed); finance (MBA, Graduate Certificate); general business (MBA); global business (Graduate Certificate); healthcare administration (MHA); healthcare services management and leadership (Graduate Certificate); international business (MBA); language and literacy (M Ed), including English for speakers of other languages, special reading teacher/literacy coach; leadership of international healthcare organizations (Graduate Certificate); management information systems (MBA, Graduate Certificate); music performance (ADP, Graduate Certificate), including cello (MM, ADP), piano (MM, ADP), viola (MM, ADP), violin (MM, ADP); nonprofit and community services management (MPA); nonprofit leadership (Graduate Certificate); performance (MM), including cello (MM, ADP), piano (MM, ADP), viola (MM, ADP), violin (MM, ADP); public management (MPA); social work (MSW); teacher leadership (M Ed), including curriculum and assessment, instructional leader. *Program availability:* Part-time, evening/weekend, online learning. *Degree requirements:* For master's, comprehensive exam (for some programs), thesis (for some programs), internship (for some programs); exam (for some programs). *Entrance requirements:* For master's, GRE or GMAT (for some programs), teacher certification (for some M Ed programs), letters of recommendation, essay, resume (for some programs). Additional exam requirements/recommendations for international students: Required—TOEFL (minimum score 550 paper-based; 79 iBT), IELTS (minimum score 6). Electronic applications accepted.

Penn State Harrisburg, Graduate School, School of Business Administration, Middletown, PA 17057. Offers accounting (MPAC, Certificate); business administration (MBA); information systems (MS); operations and supply chain management (Certificate). *Program availability:* Part-time, evening/weekend. *Unit head:* Dr. Mukund S. Kulkarni, Chancellor, 717-948-6105, Fax: 717-948-6452. *Application contact:* Robert W. Coffman, Jr., Director of Enrollment Management, Recruitment and Admissions, 717-948-6250, Fax: 717-948-6325, E-mail: hbgadmit@psu.edu. Website: https://harrisburg.psu.edu/business-administration/

Penn State University Park, Graduate School, College of Information Sciences and Technology, University Park, PA 16802. Offers information sciences (MPS); information sciences and technology (MS, PhD). *Program availability:* Part-time, evening/weekend. *Students:* 108 full-time (36 women), 13 part-time (2 women). Average age 28. 203 applicants, 33% accepted, 38 enrolled. In 2017, 17 master's, 15 doctorates awarded. *Entrance requirements:* Additional exam requirements/recommendations for international students: Required—TOEFL (minimum score 550 paper-based; 80 iBT), IELTS. *Application deadline:* For fall admission, 12/15 for domestic and international students. Applications are processed on a rolling basis. Application fee: $65. Electronic applications accepted. *Expenses:* Contact institution. *Financial support:* Fellowships, research assistantships, teaching assistantships, career-related internships or fieldwork, Federal Work-Study, scholarships/grants, traineeships, health care benefits, and unspecified assistantships available. Support available to part-time students. Financial award application deadline: 2/15; financial award applicants required to submit FAFSA. *Unit head:* Dr. Andrew L. Sears, Dean, 814-865-3528, Fax: 814-865-7485. *Application contact:* Lori Hawn, Director, Graduate Student Services, 814-865-1795, Fax: 814-863-4627, E-mail: l-gswww@lists.psu.edu. Website: http://ist.psu.edu/

Point Park University, Rowland School of Business, Program in Business Administration, Pittsburgh, PA 15222-1984. Offers business analytics (MBA); global management and administration (MBA); health systems management (MBA); international business (MBA); management (MBA); management information systems (MBA); sports, arts and entertainment management (MBA). *Program availability:* Evening/weekend, 100% online.

Polytechnic University of Puerto Rico, Graduate School, Hato Rey, PR 00918. Offers business administration (MBA), including computer information systems, general management, management of information systems, management of international enterprises; civil engineering (ME, MS); computer engineering (ME, MS); computer science (MCS, MS); electrical engineering (ME, MS); engineering management (MEM); environmental management (MEM); landscape architecture (M Land Arch); manufacturing competitiveness (MMC, MS); manufacturing engineering (ME, MS); mechanical engineering (M Mech E). *Program availability:* Part-time, evening/weekend. *Entrance requirements:* For master's, 3 letters of recommendation.

Pontifical Catholic University of Puerto Rico, College of Business Administration, Program in Management Information Systems, Ponce, PR 00717-0777. Offers MBA, Professional Certificate. *Program availability:* Part-time, evening/weekend. *Degree requirements:* For master's, thesis. *Entrance requirements:* For master's, GRE, interview, minimum GPA of 2.75.

Prairie View A&M University, College of Engineering, Prairie View, TX 77446. Offers computer information systems (MSCIS); computer science (MSCS); electrical engineering (MSEE, PhDEE); general engineering (MS Engr). *Program availability:* Part-time, evening/weekend. *Faculty:* 27 full-time (7 women), 1 (woman) part-time/adjunct. *Students:* 165 full-time (45 women), 72 part-time (19 women); includes 87 minority (70 Black or African American, non-Hispanic/Latino; 14 Asian, non-Hispanic/Latino; 3 Hispanic/Latino), 128 international. Average age 31. 122 applicants, 86% accepted, 67 enrolled. In 2017, 66 master's awarded. *Degree requirements:* For master's, thesis optional; for doctorate, comprehensive exam, thesis/dissertation. *Entrance requirements:* For master's, GRE General Test (minimum score of 900), bachelor's degree in engineering from ABET-accredited institution; for doctorate, minimum GPA of 3.0. Additional exam requirements/recommendations for international students: Required—TOEFL (minimum score 550 paper-based; 79 iBT). *Application deadline:* For fall admission, 5/1 priority date for domestic and international students; for spring admission, 10/1 priority date for domestic students, 9/1 priority date for international students; for summer admission, 3/1 priority date for domestic students, 2/1 priority date for international students. Applications are processed on a rolling basis. Application fee: $50. Electronic applications accepted. *Expenses:* Tuition: state resident: part-time $242 per credit. Tuition, nonresident: part-time $695 per credit. *Required fees:* $149 per credit. *Financial support:* Fellowships, research assistantships, teaching assistantships, career-related internships or fieldwork, institutionally sponsored loans, scholarships/grants, health care benefits, tuition waivers (full), and unspecified assistantships available. Financial award application deadline: 4/1; financial award applicants required to submit FAFSA. *Faculty research:* Electrical and computer engineering: big data analysis, wireless communications, bioinformatics and computational biology, space radiation; computer science: cloud computing, cyber security; chemical engineering: thermochemical processing of biofuel, photochemical modeling; civil and environmental engineering: environmental sustainability, water resources, structure; mechanical engineering: thermal science, nanocomposites, computational fluid dynamics. *Unit head:* Dr. Shield Lin, Dean, 936-261-9958, Fax: 936-261-9868, E-mail: shlin@pvamu.edu. *Application contact:* Pauline Walker, Administrative Assistant II, Research and Graduate Studies, 936-261-3521, Fax: 936-261-3529, E-mail: gradadmissions@pvamu.edu.

Purdue University, Graduate School, College of Technology, Department of Computer and Information Technology, West Lafayette, IN 47907. Offers MS. *Faculty:* 28 full-time (11 women). *Students:* 52 full-time (29 women), 41 part-time (13 women); includes 10 minority (3 Black or African American, non-Hispanic/Latino; 2 Asian, non-Hispanic/Latino; 2 Hispanic/Latino; 3 Two or more races, non-Hispanic/Latino), 52 international. Average age 30. 157 applicants, 30% accepted, 29 enrolled. In 2017, 32 master's awarded. *Entrance requirements:* For master's, GRE, minimum GPA of 3.0 or equivalent. *Application deadline:* For fall admission, 4/1 for domestic and international students; for spring admission, 10/1 for domestic students, 9/1 for international students; for summer admission, 4/1 for domestic students, 2/15 for international students. Applications are processed on a rolling basis. Application fee: $60 ($75 for international students). Electronic applications accepted. *Unit head:* Marcus K. Rogers, Head of the Graduate Program, 765-494-2561, E-mail: rogersmk@purdue.edu. *Application contact:* Stacy Lane, Graduate Contact, 765-494-4545, E-mail: smlane@purdue.edu. Website: http://www.tech.purdue.edu/cit/

Purdue University Global, School of Information Technology, Davenport, IA 52807. Offers decision support systems (MS); information security and assurance (MS). *Program availability:* Part-time, evening/weekend, online learning. *Entrance requirements:* Additional exam requirements/recommendations for international students: Required—TOEFL (minimum score 550 paper-based; 80 iBT).

Radford University, College of Graduate Studies and Research, Program in Data and Information Management, Radford, VA 24142. Offers MS. *Program availability:* Part-time. *Faculty:* 4 full-time (0 women). *Students:* 9 full-time (1 woman), 2 part-time (0 women); includes 3 minority (2 Asian, non-Hispanic/Latino; 1 Hispanic/Latino), 3 international. Average age 30. 9 applicants, 89% accepted, 8 enrolled. *Entrance requirements:* For master's, GRE (minimum scores of 152 on quantitative portion and 148 on verbal portion, or 650 and 420, respectively, under old scoring system), minimum GPA of 3.0 overall from accredited educational institution, three letters of reference from faculty members familiar with academic performance in major coursework or from colleagues or supervisors familiar with work. Additional exam requirements/recommendations for international students: Required—TOEFL (minimum score 567 paper-based). *Application deadline:* Applications are processed on a rolling basis. Application fee: $50. Electronic applications accepted. *Expenses:* Tuition, state resident: full-time $8336; part-time $347 per credit hour. Tuition, nonresident: full-time $16,862; part-time $702 per credit hour. *Required fees:* $3220; $135 per credit hour. Tuition and fees vary according to course load and program. *Financial support:* In 2017–18, 4 students received support, including 4 teaching assistantships (averaging $11,000 per year); scholarships/grants and unspecified assistantships also available. Support available to part-time students. Financial award application deadline: 3/1; financial award applicants required to submit FAFSA. *Unit head:* Dr. Jeff Pittges, 540-831-5381, E-mail: jpittges@radford.edu.
Website: http://www.radford.edu/content/csat/home/daim.html

Regent's University London, Webster Graduate School, London, United Kingdom. Offers business (MBA); finance (MS); human resources (MA); information technology management (MA); international business (MA); international non-governmental organizations (MA); international relations (MA); management and leadership (MA); marketing (MA). *Program availability:* Part-time.

Regis University, College of Computer and Information Sciences, Denver, CO 80221-1099. Offers agile technologies (Certificate); cybersecurity (Certificate); data science (M Sc); database administration with Oracle (Certificate); database development (Certificate); database technologies (M Sc); enterprise Java software development (Certificate); enterprise resource planning (Certificate); executive information technology (Certificate); health care informatics (Certificate); health care informatics and information management (M Sc); information assurance (M Sc); information assurance policy management (Certificate); information technology management (M Sc); mobile software development (Certificate); software engineering (M Sc, Certificate); software engineering and database technology (M Sc); storage area networks (Certificate); systems engineering (M Sc, Certificate). *Program availability:* Part-time, evening/weekend, 100% online, blended/hybrid learning. *Degree requirements:* For master's, thesis (for some programs), final research project. *Entrance requirements:* For master's, official transcript reflecting baccalaureate degree awarded from regionally-accredited college or university, 2 years of related experience, resume, interview. Additional exam requirements/recommendations for international students: Required—TOEFL (minimum score 550 paper-based; 82 iBT). Electronic applications accepted. *Expenses:* Contact institution. *Faculty research:* Information policy, knowledge management, software architectures, data science.

Rivier University, School of Graduate Studies, Department of Computer Information Systems, Nashua, NH 03060. Offers MS. *Program availability:* Part-time.

Robert Morris University, School of Communications and Information Systems, Moon Township, PA 15108-1189. Offers communication and information systems (MS); cyber security (MS); data analytics (MS); information security and assurance (MS); information systems and communications (D Sc); information systems management (MS); information technology project management (MS); Internet information systems (MS); organizational leadership (MS). *Program availability:* Part-time, evening/weekend, online learning. *Faculty:* 23 full-time (10 women), 10 part-time/adjunct (3 women). *Students:* 258 part-time (99 women); includes 46 minority (22 Black or African American, non-Hispanic/Latino; 16 Asian, non-Hispanic/Latino; 5 Two or more races, non-Hispanic/Latino), 46 international. Average age 35. 226 applicants, 52% accepted, 79 enrolled. In 2017, 148 master's, 12 doctorates awarded. *Degree requirements:* For doctorate, thesis/dissertation. *Entrance requirements:* For doctorate, employer letter of endorsement, interview. Additional exam requirements/recommendations for international students: Required—TOEFL (minimum score 550 paper-based; 79 iBT). *Application deadline:* For fall admission, 7/1 priority date for domestic and international students; for spring admission, 11/1 priority date for domestic and international students. Applications are processed on a rolling basis. Application fee: $35. Electronic applications accepted. Application fee is waived when completed online. *Expenses:*

$920 per credit tuition plus university fees of $80 per credit. *Financial support:* Institutionally sponsored loans available. Support available to part-time students. Financial award application deadline: 5/1. *Unit head:* Ann Marie M. Le Blanc, Dean, 412-397-6433, Fax: 412-397-6469, E-mail: leblanc@rmu.edu. *Application contact:* E-mail: graduateadmissions@rmu.edu.
Website: http://www.rmu.edu/web/cms/schools/scis/Pages/default.aspx

Robert Morris University Illinois, Morris Graduate School of Management, Chicago, IL 60605. Offers accounting (MBA); accounting/finance (MBA); business analytics (MIS); health care administration (MM); higher education administration (MM); human performance (MS); human resource management (MBA); information security (MIS); information systems management (MIS); law enforcement administration (MM); management (MBA); management/finance (MBA); management/human resource management (MBA); sports administration (MM). *Program availability:* Part-time, evening/weekend. *Faculty:* 2 full-time (0 women), 26 part-time/adjunct (8 women). *Students:* 186 full-time (108 women), 114 part-time (57 women); includes 167 minority (88 Black or African American, non-Hispanic/Latino; 15 Asian, non-Hispanic/Latino; 62 Hispanic/Latino; 1 Native Hawaiian or other Pacific Islander, non-Hispanic/Latino; 1 Two or more races, non-Hispanic/Latino), 18 international. Average age 32. 157 applicants, 78% accepted, 72 enrolled. In 2017, 191 master's awarded. *Entrance requirements:* For master's, official transcripts and letters of recommendation (for some programs); written personal statement. Additional exam requirements/recommendations for international students: Required—TOEFL (minimum score 550 paper-based). *Application deadline:* Applications are processed on a rolling basis. Application fee: $20 ($100 for international students). Electronic applications accepted. *Expenses: Tuition:* Full-time $17,100; part-time $2850 per course. *Financial support:* In 2017–18, 381 students received support. Federal Work-Study, scholarships/grants, and unspecified assistantships available. Support available to part-time students. Financial award applicants required to submit FAFSA. *Unit head:* Kayed Akkawi, Dean, 312-935-6050, Fax: 312-935-6020, E-mail: kakkawi@robertmorris.edu. *Application contact:* Mark Daugherty, Director of Admissions, 312-935-4814, Fax: 312-935-6020, E-mail: mdaugherty@robertmorris.edu.

Rochester Institute of Technology, Graduate Enrollment Services, Golisano College of Computing and Information Sciences, Information Science and Technologies Department, Advanced Certificate Program in Networking, Planning and Design, Rochester, NY 14623. Offers Advanced Certificate. *Program availability:* Part-time, evening/weekend, 100% online. *Students:* 4 applicants. In 2017, 2 Advanced Certificates awarded. *Entrance requirements:* For degree, GRE, minimum GPA of 3.0 (recommended). Additional exam requirements/recommendations for international students: Required—TOEFL (minimum score 570 paper-based; 88 iBT), IELTS (minimum score 6.5), PTE (minimum score 61). *Application deadline:* Applications are processed on a rolling basis. Application fee: $65. Electronic applications accepted. *Expenses:* $1,815 per credit hour (classroom), $1,035 per credit hour (online study). *Financial support:* Available to part-time students. Applicants required to submit FAFSA. *Faculty research:* Enterprise network architectures and administration, emerging network technologies, the network design process, and project management. *Unit head:* Qi Yu, Graduate Program Director, 585-475-6929, E-mail: informaticsgrad@rit.edu. *Application contact:* Diane Ellison, Senior Associate Vice President, Graduate Enrollment Services, 585-475-2229, Fax: 585-475-7164, E-mail: gradinfo@rit.edu.
Website: http://www.ist.rit.edu/degrees/graduate/advanced-cert.php

Rose-Hulman Institute of Technology, Faculty of Engineering and Applied Sciences, Department of Electrical and Computer Engineering, Terre Haute, IN 47803-3999. Offers electrical and computer engineering (M Eng); electrical engineering (MS); systems engineering and management (MS). *Program availability:* Part-time. *Faculty:* 18 full-time (3 women), 1 (woman) part-time/adjunct. *Students:* 7 full-time (2 women), 5 part-time (2 women); includes 1 minority (Hispanic/Latino), 9 international. Average age 24. 19 applicants, 89% accepted, 4 enrolled. In 2017, 7 master's awarded. *Degree requirements:* For master's, thesis (for some programs). *Entrance requirements:* For master's, GRE, minimum GPA of 3.0. Additional exam requirements/recommendations for international students: Required—TOEFL (minimum score 580 paper-based; 92 iBT). *Application deadline:* For fall admission, 2/15 priority date for domestic and international students; for winter admission, 10/1 for domestic and international students; for spring admission, 1/15 for domestic and international students. Applications are processed on a rolling basis. Application fee: $0. Electronic applications accepted. *Expenses: Tuition:* Full-time $44,847. *Required fees:* $450. *Financial support:* In 2017–18, 12 students received support. Fellowships with tuition reimbursements available, research assistantships with tuition reimbursements available, institutionally sponsored loans, scholarships/grants, and tuition waivers (full and partial) available. *Faculty research:* VLSI, power systems, analog electronics, communications, electromagnetics. *Total annual research expenditures:* $55,933. *Unit head:* Dr. Mario Simoni, Chairman, 812-877-8341, Fax: 812-877-8895, E-mail: simoni@rose-hulman.edu. *Application contact:* Dr. Craig Downing, Associate Dean of the Faculty, 812-877-8822, Fax: 812-877-8061, E-mail: downing@rose-hulman.edu.
Website: http://www.rose-hulman.edu/academics/academic-departments/electrical-computer-engineering.aspx

Rutgers University–Newark, Graduate School, Program in Management, Newark, NJ 07102. Offers accounting (PhD); accounting information systems (PhD); computer information systems (PhD); finance (PhD); information technology (PhD); international business (PhD); management science (PhD); marketing (PhD); organization management (PhD). Program offered jointly with New Jersey Institute of Technology. *Accreditation:* AACSB. *Degree requirements:* For doctorate, thesis/dissertation, cumulative exams. *Entrance requirements:* For doctorate, GMAT or GRE General Test, minimum undergraduate B average. Additional exam requirements/recommendations for international students: Required—TOEFL. Electronic applications accepted. *Faculty research:* Technology management, leadership and teams, consumer behavior, financial and markets, logistics.

Rutgers University–Newark, Rutgers Business School–Newark and New Brunswick, Doctoral Programs in Management, Newark, NJ 07102. Offers accounting (PhD); accounting information systems (PhD); economics (PhD); finance (PhD); individualized study (PhD); information technology (PhD); international business (PhD); management science (PhD); marketing science (PhD); organizational management (PhD); science, technology and management (PhD); supply chain management (PhD). *Degree requirements:* For doctorate, comprehensive exam, thesis/dissertation. *Entrance requirements:* For doctorate, GRE or GMAT. Additional exam requirements/recommendations for international students: Required—TOEFL (minimum score 550 paper-based; 79 iBT). Electronic applications accepted.

Rutgers University–Newark, Rutgers Business School–Newark and New Brunswick, Program in Information Technology, Newark, NJ 07102. Offers MIT. *Entrance requirements:* For master's, GMAT. Additional exam requirements/recommendations for international students: Required—TOEFL.

St. John's University, The Peter J. Tobin College of Business, Department of Business Analytics and Information Systems, Queens, NY 11439. Offers MBA. *Faculty:* 9 full-time (0 women), 4 part-time/adjunct (3 women). *Students:* 24 full-time (10 women), 11 part-time (3 women); includes 17 minority (4 Black or African American, non-Hispanic/Latino; 9 Asian, non-Hispanic/Latino; 4 Hispanic/Latino), 10 international. Average age 28. 23

Management Information Systems

applicants, 83% accepted, 17 enrolled. In 2017, 10 master's awarded. *Entrance requirements:* For master's, GMAT or GRE, 2 letters of recommendation, essay, resume, unofficial transcripts. Additional exam requirements/recommendations for international students: Required—TOEFL (minimum score 80 iBT), IELTS (minimum score 6.5). *Application deadline:* For fall admission, 11/1 for domestic and international students; for winter admission, 3/1 for domestic and international students; for spring admission, 6/1 for domestic and international students. Applications are processed on a rolling basis. Application fee: $70. Electronic applications accepted. *Expenses:* $22,410 per year. *Financial support:* Research assistantships, teaching assistantships, scholarships/grants, and unspecified assistantships available. Support available to part-time students. Financial award application deadline: 2/1; financial award applicants required to submit FAFSA. *Unit head:* Dr. Manuel Russon, Chair, 718-990-7363, E-mail: russonm@stjohns.edu. *Application contact:* Amber Steiger, Associate Director of Enrollment Management, 718-990-1345, E-mail: steigera@stjohns.edu.
Website: https://www.stjohns.edu/academics/schools-and-colleges/peter-j-tobin-college-business/business-analytics-information-systems

Saint Peter's University, Graduate Business Programs, MBA Program, Jersey City, NJ 07306-5997. Offers finance (MBA); health care administration (MBA); human resource management (MBA); international business (MBA); management (MBA); management information systems (MBA); marketing (MBA); risk management (MBA); MBA/MS. *Program availability:* Part-time, evening/weekend. *Entrance requirements:* Additional exam requirements/recommendations for international students: Required—TOEFL. Electronic applications accepted. *Faculty research:* Finance, health care management, human resource management, international business, management, management information systems, marketing, risk management.

San Diego State University, Graduate and Research Affairs, College of Business Administration, Department of Management Information Systems, San Diego, CA 92182. Offers information systems (MS). *Program availability:* Evening/weekend. *Degree requirements:* For master's, thesis or alternative. *Entrance requirements:* For master's, GMAT, resume, letters of reference. Additional exam requirements/recommendations for international students: Required—TOEFL. Electronic applications accepted.

San Francisco State University, Division of Graduate Studies, College of Business, Program in Business Administration, San Francisco, CA 94132-1722. Offers decision sciences/operations research (MBA); ethics and compliance (MBA); finance (MBA); global business and innovation (MBA); healthcare administration (MBA); hospitality and tourism management (MBA); information systems (MBA); leadership (MBA); marketing (MBA); nonprofit and social enterprise leadership (MBA); sustainable business (MBA). *Accreditation:* AACSB. *Program availability:* Part-time, evening/weekend. *Degree requirements:* For master's, thesis, essay test. *Entrance requirements:* For master's, GMAT, minimum GPA of 2.7 in last 60 units. Additional exam requirements/recommendations for international students: Required—TOEFL (minimum score 550 paper-based). *Application deadline:* For fall admission, 5/1 priority date for domestic students, 4/1 for international students; for spring admission, 11/1 for domestic students, 10/15 for international students. Applications are processed on a rolling basis. Application fee: $55. *Financial support:* Application deadline: 3/1. *Unit head:* Dr. Sanjit Sengupta, Faculty Director, 415-817-4366, Fax: 415-817-4340, E-mail: sengupta@sfsu.edu. *Application contact:* Christopher Kingston, Director of Student Advising, 415-817-4322, Fax: 415-817-4340, E-mail: cak@sfsu.edu.
Website: http://cob.sfsu.edu/graduate-programs/mba

Santa Clara University, Leavey School of Business, Santa Clara, CA 95053. Offers business administration (MBA); business analytics (MS); finance (MS); information systems (MS); supply chain management and analytics (MS); JD/MBA. *Accreditation:* AACSB. *Program availability:* Part-time, evening/weekend, online curriculum with 2 on-campus intensives. *Faculty:* 100 full-time (30 women), 42 part-time/adjunct (16 women). *Students:* 413 full-time (226 women), 308 part-time (131 women); includes 246 minority (10 Black or African American, non-Hispanic/Latino; 175 Asian, non-Hispanic/Latino; 40 Hispanic/Latino; 2 Native Hawaiian or other Pacific Islander, non-Hispanic/Latino; 19 Two or more races, non-Hispanic/Latino), 256 international. Average age 31. 761 applicants, 63% accepted, 271 enrolled. In 2017, 267 master's awarded. *Entrance requirements:* For master's, GMAT, resume, essays, 2 letters of recommendation, 2 official transcripts. Additional exam requirements/recommendations for international students: Required—TOEFL (minimum score 100 iBT) or IELTS (7.0). Application fee: $100 ($150 for international students). Electronic applications accepted. *Expenses:* Contact institution. *Financial support:* In 2017–18, 192 students received support. Career-related internships or fieldwork, scholarships/grants, and unspecified assistantships available. Financial award applicants required to submit FAFSA. *Faculty research:* Digital marketing, database mining and retail, product innovation, industry disruption, entrepreneurship and cluster dynamics, innovation and temporary advantage, platform strategy, ethics and leadership, bank regulation, monetary policy, poverty alleviation, costs of financial crises, information technology and business intelligence, supply chain management, corporate social responsibility and institutional ownership, audits and financial reporting. *Unit head:* Caryn Beck-Dudley, Dean, 408-554-4523, E-mail: cbeckdudley@scu.edu. *Application contact:* Lenore Grant, Director, Graduate Business Recruitment and Admissions, 408-551-1633, E-mail: lgrant@scu.edu.
Website: http://www.scu.edu/business/

Schiller International University, MBA Programs, Florida, Program in Information Technology, Largo, FL 33771. Offers MBA. *Entrance requirements:* Additional exam requirements/recommendations for international students: Required—TOEFL.

Schiller International University, MBA Programs, Heidelberg, Germany, Heidelberg, Germany. Offers international business (MBA, MIM); management of information technology (MBA). *Program availability:* Part-time, evening/weekend. *Degree requirements:* For master's, thesis optional. *Entrance requirements:* Additional exam requirements/recommendations for international students: Required—TOEFL (minimum score 550 paper-based). *Faculty research:* Leadership, international economy, foreign direct investment.

Seattle Pacific University, Master of Science in Information Systems Management Program, Seattle, WA 98119-1997. Offers MS. *Students:* 1 (woman) full-time, 18 part-time (14 women); includes 2 minority (1 Black or African American, non-Hispanic/Latino; 1 Asian, non-Hispanic/Latino), 10 international. Average age 29. 12 applicants, 42% accepted, 2 enrolled. In 2017, 10 master's awarded. *Entrance requirements:* For master's, GMAT (minimum score of 500 preferred; 25 verbal, 30 quantitative, 4.4 analytical writing) GRE (minimum score of 295 preferred; 150 verbal/450 old scoring, 145 quantitative/525 old scoring), BA, resume as evidence of substantive work experience. Additional exam requirements/recommendations for international students: Required—TOEFL. *Application deadline:* For fall admission, 8/1 for domestic students, 6/1 for international students; for winter admission, 11/1 for domestic and international students; for spring admission, 2/1 for domestic students, 12/1 for international students; for summer admission, 5/1 for domestic students. Applications are processed on a rolling basis. Application fee: $50. Electronic applications accepted. *Financial support:* Applicants required to submit FAFSA. *Unit head:* Gary Karns, Associate Dean for Graduate Studies, 206-281-2948, Fax: 206-281-

2733. *Application contact:* 206-281-2091.
Website: http://spu.edu/academics/school-of-business-and-economics/graduate-programs/ms-ism

Shippensburg University of Pennsylvania, School of Graduate Studies, College of Arts and Sciences, Department of Computer Science and Engineering, Shippensburg, PA 17257-2299. Offers agile software engineering (Certificate); computer science (MS), including computer science, cybersecurity, IT leadership, management information systems, software engineering; IT leadership (Certificate). *Program availability:* Part-time, evening/weekend. *Faculty:* 7 full-time (3 women). *Students:* 3 full-time (2 women), 11 part-time (5 women), 10 international. Average age 29. 30 applicants, 53% accepted, 6 enrolled. In 2017, 15 master's awarded. *Entrance requirements:* For master's, GRE (if GPA less than 2.75), professional resume. Additional exam requirements/recommendations for international students: Required—TOEFL (minimum score 70 iBT) or IELTS (minimum score 6). *Application deadline:* For fall admission, 4/30 for international students; for spring admission, 9/30 for international students. Applications are processed on a rolling basis. Application fee: $45. Electronic applications accepted. *Expenses:* Tuition, state resident: part-time $500 per credit. Tuition, nonresident: part-time $750 per credit. *Required fees:* $145 per credit. *Financial support:* In 2017–18, 3 students received support. Career-related internships or fieldwork, scholarships/grants, unspecified assistantships, and resident hall director and student payroll positions available. Support available to part-time students. Financial award application deadline: 3/1; financial award applicants required to submit FAFSA. *Unit head:* Dr. Jeonghwa Lee, Professor and Director of Graduate Studies, 717-477-1178, Fax: 717-477-4002, E-mail: jlee@ship.edu. *Application contact:* Maya T. Mapp, Director of Admissions, 717-477-1231, Fax: 717-477-4016, E-mail: mtmapp@ship.edu.
Website: http://www.cs.ship.edu/

Shippensburg University of Pennsylvania, School of Graduate Studies, College of Arts and Sciences, Department of Sociology and Anthropology, Shippensburg, PA 17257-2299. Offers organizational development and leadership (MS), including business, higher education structure and policy, historical administration, leadership in society, management information systems, public organizations. *Program availability:* Part-time, evening/weekend. *Faculty:* 4 full-time (2 women). *Students:* 14 full-time (6 women), 19 part-time (11 women); includes 7 minority (4 Black or African American, non-Hispanic/Latino; 2 Hispanic/Latino; 1 Two or more races, non-Hispanic/Latino), 1 international. Average age 26. 31 applicants, 81% accepted, 15 enrolled. In 2017, 22 master's awarded. *Degree requirements:* For master's, capstone experience including internship. *Entrance requirements:* For master's, interview (if GPA less than 2.75), current resume, personal goals statement. Additional exam requirements/recommendations for international students: Required—TOEFL (minimum score 550 paper-based, 68 iBT) or IELTS (minimum score 6). *Application deadline:* For fall admission, 4/30 for international students; for spring admission, 9/30 for international students. Applications are processed on a rolling basis. Application fee: $45. Electronic applications accepted. *Expenses:* Tuition, state resident: part-time $500 per credit. Tuition, nonresident: part-time $750 per credit. *Required fees:* $145 per credit. *Financial support:* In 2017–18, 12 students received support. Career-related internships or fieldwork, scholarships/grants, unspecified assistantships, and resident hall director and student payroll positions available. Support available to part-time students. Financial award application deadline: 3/1; financial award applicants required to submit FAFSA. *Unit head:* Dr. Barbara J. Denison, Departmental Chair and Program Coordinator, 717-477-1735, Fax: 717-477-4011, E-mail: bjdeni@ship.edu. *Application contact:* Maya T. Mapp, Director of Admissions, 717-477-1231, Fax: 717-477-4016, E-mail: mtmapp@ship.edu.
Website: http://www.ship.edu/odl/

Shippensburg University of Pennsylvania, School of Graduate Studies, John L. Grove College of Business, Shippensburg, PA 17257-2299. Offers advanced studies in business (Certificate); advanced supply chain and logistics management (Certificate); business administration (MBA, DBA), including business administration (MBA), business analytics (MBA), finance (MBA), healthcare management (MBA), management information systems (MBA), supply chain management (MBA); finance (Certificate); health care management (Certificate); management information systems (Certificate). *Accreditation:* AACSB. *Program availability:* Part-time, evening/weekend, 100% online, blended/hybrid learning. *Faculty:* 23 full-time (5 women), 1 part-time/adjunct (0 women). *Students:* 46 full-time (14 women), 201 part-time (71 women); includes 35 minority (12 Black or African American, non-Hispanic/Latino; 10 Asian, non-Hispanic/Latino; 11 Hispanic/Latino; 2 Two or more races, non-Hispanic/Latino), 22 international. Average age 32. 169 applicants, 65% accepted, 77 enrolled. In 2017, 105 master's, 82 other advanced degrees awarded. *Degree requirements:* For master's, thesis optional, practicum; for doctorate, comprehensive exam, thesis/dissertation. *Entrance requirements:* For master's, GMAT (minimum score 450 if less than 5 years of mid-level experience, including management experience), current resume; relevant work/classroom experience; 500-word statement of purpose; prerequisites of quantitative analysis, computer usage, and oral and written communications; laptop computer; for doctorate, GMAT (minimum score of 600 if less than 5 years of substantive professional or teaching experience), 2 letters of recommendation from professionals in academia or industry; 2-3 page personal and professional statement; interview; resume. Additional exam requirements/recommendations for international students: Required—TOEFL (minimum score 550 paper-based, 68 iBT) or IELTS (minimum score 6). *Application deadline:* For fall admission, 4/30 for international students; for spring admission, 9/30 for international students. Applications are processed on a rolling basis. Application fee: $45. Electronic applications accepted. *Expenses:* Tuition, state resident: part-time $500 per credit. Tuition, nonresident: part-time $750 per credit. *Required fees:* $145 per credit. *Financial support:* In 2017–18, 14 students received support. Career-related internships or fieldwork, scholarships/grants, unspecified assistantships, and resident hall director and student payroll positions available. Support available to part-time students. Financial award application deadline: 3/1; financial award applicants required to submit FAFSA. *Unit head:* Dr. John G. Kooti, Dean of the College of Business, 717-477-1435, Fax: 717-477-4003, E-mail: jgkooti@ship.edu. *Application contact:* Maya T. Mapp, Director of Admissions, 717-477-1231, Fax: 717-477-4016, E-mail: mtmapp@ship.edu.
Website: http://www.ship.edu/business

Southeastern Oklahoma State University, School of Arts and Sciences, Durant, OK 74701-0609. Offers biology (MT); computer information systems (MT); occupational safety and health (MT). *Program availability:* Part-time, evening/weekend. *Degree requirements:* For master's, thesis optional. *Entrance requirements:* For master's, minimum GPA of 3.0 in last 60 hours or 2.75 overall. Additional exam requirements/recommendations for international students: Required—TOEFL (minimum score 550 paper-based; 79 iBT). Electronic applications accepted.

Southern Illinois University Edwardsville, Graduate School, School of Business, Department of Computer Management and Information Systems, Edwardsville, IL 62026. Offers MS. *Program availability:* Part-time, evening/weekend. *Degree requirements:* For master's, thesis or alternative, final exam. *Entrance requirements:* For master's, GMAT. Additional exam requirements/recommendations for international students: Required—TOEFL (minimum score 550 paper-based; 79 iBT), IELTS (minimum score 6.5). Electronic applications accepted.

Southern Illinois University Edwardsville, Graduate School, School of Business, Program in Business Administration, Edwardsville, IL 62026. Offers business analytics (MBA); management information systems (MBA); project management (MBA). *Accreditation:* AACSB. *Program availability:* Part-time, evening/weekend. *Degree requirements:* For master's, comprehensive exam. *Entrance requirements:* For master's, GMAT. Additional exam requirements/recommendations for international students: Required—TOEFL (minimum score 550 paper-based; 79 iBT), IELTS (minimum score 6.5). Electronic applications accepted.

Southern Methodist University, Cox School of Business, MBA Program, Dallas, TX 75275. Offers accounting (MBA, PMBA); business administration (EMBA); finance (MBA); financial statement analysis (PMBA); general business (MBA); information technology and operations management (MBA); management (MBA); marketing (MBA); real estate (MBA); strategy (MBA); strategy and entrepreneurship (MBA); JD/MBA; MA/MBA. *Program availability:* Part-time, evening/weekend. *Entrance requirements:* For master's, GMAT. Additional exam requirements/recommendations for international students: Required—TOEFL. Electronic applications accepted. *Expenses:* Contact institution. *Faculty research:* Corporate finance, financial reporting, modeling consumer decision-making, competition between national brands and store brands, institutional determinants of firms' strategy.

Southern New Hampshire University, School of Business, Manchester, NH 03106-1045. Offers accounting (MBA, Graduate Certificate); accounting finance (MS); accounting/auditing (MS); accounting/forensic accounting (MS); accounting/management accounting (MS); accounting/taxation (MS); applied economics (MS); athletic administration (MBA, Graduate Certificate); business administration (IMBA, Certificate), including business information systems (Certificate), human resource management (Certificate); business analytics (MBA); business intelligence (MBA); communication (MA), including new media and marketing, public relations; community economic development (MBA); criminal justice (MBA); data analytics (MS); economics (MBA); engineering management (MBA); entrepreneurship (MBA); finance (MBA, MS, Graduate Certificate); finance/corporate finance (MS); finance/investments (MS); forensic accounting (MBA); forensic accounting and fraud examination (Graduate Certificate); healthcare informatics (MBA); healthcare management (MBA); human resource management (MS); human resources (MBA); information technology (MS); information technology management (MBA); international business (PhD); Internet marketing (MBA); leadership (MBA); leadership of nonprofit organizations (Graduate Certificate); management (MS); marketing (MBA, MS, Graduate Certificate); music business (MBA); operations and project management (MBA); operations and supply chain management (MBA, Graduate Certificate); organizational leadership (MS); project management (MBA, Graduate Certificate); public administration (MBA, Graduate Certificate); quantitative analysis (MBA); Six Sigma (Graduate Certificate); Six Sigma quality (MBA); social media marketing (MBA, Graduate Certificate); sport management (MBA, MS, Graduate Certificate); sustainability and environmental compliance (MBA); MBA/Certificate. *Accreditation:* ACBSP. *Program availability:* Part-time, evening/weekend, online learning. Terminal master's awarded for partial completion of doctoral program. *Degree requirements:* For master's, one foreign language, comprehensive exam (for some programs), thesis or alternative; for doctorate, one foreign language, comprehensive exam, thesis/dissertation. *Entrance requirements:* For master's, minimum GPA of 2.5; for doctorate, GMAT. Additional exam requirements/recommendations for international students: Required—TOEFL (minimum score 500 paper-based). *Application deadline:* Applications are processed on a rolling basis. Application fee: $40. Electronic applications accepted. *Expenses: Tuition:* Part-time $627 per credit hour. Part-time tuition and fees vary according to campus/location and program. *Financial support:* Career-related internships or fieldwork, Federal Work-Study, institutionally sponsored loans, scholarships/grants, tuition waivers (partial), and unspecified assistantships available. Support available to part-time students. Financial award applicants required to submit FAFSA. *Unit head:* Dr. Bill Lightfoot, Dean, 603-644-3102, Fax: 603-644-3144. *Application contact:* Office of Graduate Admission, 888-327-SNHU, Fax: 603-644-3144, E-mail: enroll@snhu.edu.

Southern University at New Orleans, School of Graduate Studies, New Orleans, LA 70126-1009. Offers criminal justice (MA); management information systems (MS); museum studies (MA); social work (MSW). *Accreditation:* CSWE. *Program availability:* Part-time, evening/weekend. *Degree requirements:* For master's, thesis. *Entrance requirements:* For master's, GRE/GMAT. Additional exam requirements/recommendations for international students: Required—TOEFL.

South University, Program in Information Systems and Technology, Round Rock, TX 78681. Offers MS.

South University, Program in Information Systems and Technology, Montgomery, AL 36116-1120. Offers MS.

South University, Program in Information Systems and Technology, Tampa, FL 33614. Offers MS.

South University, Program in Information Systems and Technology, Virginia Beach, VA 23452. Offers MS.

South University, Program in Information Systems and Technology, Royal Palm Beach, FL 33411. Offers MS.

Stevens Institute of Technology, Graduate School, School of Business, Doctoral Program in Technology Management, Hoboken, NJ 07030. Offers information management (PhD); technology management (PhD); telecommunications management (PhD). *Program availability:* Part-time, evening/weekend, online learning. *Students:* 7 full-time (1 woman), 2 part-time (1 woman), 7 international. Average age 32. In 2017, 1 doctorate awarded. *Degree requirements:* For doctorate, comprehensive exam (for some programs), thesis/dissertation. *Entrance requirements:* Additional exam requirements/recommendations for international students: Required—TOEFL (minimum score 74 iBT), IELTS (minimum score 6). *Application deadline:* For fall admission, 2/1 for domestic and international students; for spring admission, 10/1 for domestic and international students. Applications are processed on a rolling basis. Application fee: $60. Electronic applications accepted. *Expenses: Tuition:* Full-time $34,494; part-time $1554 per credit. *Required fees:* $291 per semester. *Financial support:* Fellowships, research assistantships, teaching assistantships, career-related internships or fieldwork, Federal Work-Study, scholarships/grants, and unspecified assistantships available. Financial award application deadline: 2/15; financial award applicants required to submit FAFSA. *Unit head:* Dr. Thomas Lechler, Director, 201-216-8174, Fax: 201-216-5385, E-mail: tlechler@stevens.edu. *Application contact:* Graduate Admissions, 888-783-8367, Fax: 888-511-1306, E-mail: graduate@stevens.edu. Website: https://www.stevens.edu/school-business/phd-business-administration

Stevens Institute of Technology, Graduate School, School of Business, Program in Business Administration, Hoboken, NJ 07030. Offers business intelligence and analytics (MBA); engineering management (MBA); finance (MBA); information systems (MBA); innovation and entrepreneurship (MBA); marketing (MBA); pharmaceutical management (MBA); project management (MBA, Certificate); technology management (MBA); telecommunications management (MBA). *Accreditation:* AACSB. *Program availability:* Part-time, evening/weekend. *Students:* 46 full-time (19 women), 179 part-time (88 women); includes 46 minority (10 Black or African American, non-Hispanic/Latino; 2

American Indian or Alaska Native, non-Hispanic/Latino; 30 Asian, non-Hispanic/Latino; 4 Hispanic/Latino), 45 international. Average age 36. 218 applicants, 49% accepted, 53 enrolled. In 2017, 33 master's awarded. *Degree requirements:* For master's, thesis optional, minimum B average in major field and overall; for Certificate, minimum B average. *Entrance requirements:* Additional exam requirements/recommendations for international students: Required—TOEFL (minimum score 74 iBT), IELTS (minimum score 6). *Application deadline:* For fall admission, 7/1 for domestic students, 4/15 for international students; for spring admission, 12/1 for domestic and international students. Applications are processed on a rolling basis. Application fee: $60. Electronic applications accepted. *Expenses: Tuition:* Full-time $34,494; part-time $1554 per credit. *Required fees:* $291 per semester. *Financial support:* Fellowships, research assistantships, teaching assistantships, career-related internships or fieldwork, Federal Work-Study, scholarships/grants, and unspecified assistantships available. Financial award application deadline: 2/15; financial award applicants required to submit FAFSA. *Unit head:* Dr. Gregory Prastacos, Dean, 201-216-8366, E-mail: gprastac@stevens.edu. *Application contact:* Graduate Admissions, 888-783-8367, Fax: 888-511-1306, E-mail: graduate@stevens.edu. Website: https://www.stevens.edu/school-business/masters-programs/mbaemba

Stevens Institute of Technology, Graduate School, School of Business, Program in Information Systems, Hoboken, NJ 07030. Offers computer science (MS); e-commerce (MS); enterprise systems (MS); entrepreneurial information technology (MS); information architecture (MS); information management (MS, Certificate); information security (MS); information technology in financial services industry (MS); information technology in the pharmaceutical industry (MS); information technology outsourcing management (MS); project management (MS, Certificate); software engineering (MS); telecommunications (MS). *Program availability:* Part-time, evening/weekend. *Students:* 321 full-time (110 women), 58 part-time (18 women); includes 22 minority (7 Black or African American, non-Hispanic/Latino; 15 Asian, non-Hispanic/Latino; 321 international. Average age 26. 877 applicants, 67% accepted, 117 enrolled. In 2017, 168 master's, 2 other advanced degrees awarded. *Degree requirements:* For master's, thesis optional, minimum B average in major field and overall; for Certificate, minimum B average. *Entrance requirements:* Additional exam requirements/recommendations for international students: Required—TOEFL (minimum score 74 iBT), IELTS (minimum score 6). *Application deadline:* For fall admission, 7/1 for domestic students, 4/15 for international students; for spring admission, 12/1 for domestic and international students. Applications are processed on a rolling basis. Application fee: $60. Electronic applications accepted. *Expenses: Tuition:* Full-time $34,494; part-time $1554 per credit. *Required fees:* $291 per semester. *Financial support:* Fellowships, research assistantships, teaching assistantships, career-related internships or fieldwork, Federal Work-Study, scholarships/grants, and unspecified assistantships available. Financial award application deadline: 2/15; financial award applicants required to submit FAFSA. *Unit head:* Dr. Gregory Prastacos, Dean, 201-216-8366, E-mail: gprastac@stevens.edu. *Application contact:* Graduate Admissions, 888-783-8367, Fax: 888-511-1306, E-mail: graduate@stevens.edu. Website: https://www.stevens.edu/school-business/masters-programs/information-systems

Stevens Institute of Technology, Graduate School, School of Business, Program in Management, Hoboken, NJ 07030. Offers general management (MS); global innovation management (MS); human resource management (MS); information management (MS); project management (MS); technology commercialization (MS); technology management (MS). *Program availability:* Part-time, evening/weekend. *Students:* 56 full-time (18 women), 88 part-time (32 women); includes 18 minority (5 Black or African American, non-Hispanic/Latino; 12 Asian, non-Hispanic/Latino; 1 Hispanic/Latino), 87 international. Average age 30. 194 applicants, 78% accepted, 68 enrolled. In 2017, 87 master's awarded. *Degree requirements:* For master's, thesis optional, minimum B average in major field and overall. *Entrance requirements:* Additional exam requirements/recommendations for international students: Required—TOEFL (minimum score 74 iBT), IELTS (minimum score 6). *Application deadline:* For fall admission, 7/1 for domestic students, 4/15 for international students; for spring admission, 12/1 for domestic and international students. Applications are processed on a rolling basis. Application fee: $60. Electronic applications accepted. *Expenses: Tuition:* Full-time $34,494; part-time $1554 per credit. *Required fees:* $291 per semester. *Financial support:* Fellowships, research assistantships, teaching assistantships, career-related internships or fieldwork, Federal Work-Study, scholarships/grants, and unspecified assistantships available. Financial award application deadline: 2/15; financial award applicants required to submit FAFSA. *Unit head:* Brian Rothschild, Director, 201-216-3677, E-mail: brian.rothschild@stevens.edu. *Application contact:* Graduate Admissions, 888-783-8367, Fax: 888-511-1306, E-mail: graduate@stevens.edu. Website: https://www.stevens.edu/school-business/masters-programs/management

Stony Brook University, State University of New York, Graduate School, College of Engineering and Applied Sciences, Department of Computer Science, Stony Brook, NY 11794. Offers computer science (MS, PhD); information systems (Certificate); information systems engineering (MS); software engineering (Certificate). *Faculty:* 50 full-time (7 women), 3 part-time/adjunct (1 woman). *Students:* 489 full-time (114 women), 134 part-time (38 women); includes 28 minority (1 Black or African American, non-Hispanic/Latino; 19 Asian, non-Hispanic/Latino; 8 Hispanic/Latino), 565 international. Average age 26. 1,910 applicants, 35% accepted, 283 enrolled. In 2017, 181 master's, 12 doctorates awarded. Terminal master's awarded for partial completion of doctoral program. *Degree requirements:* For master's, thesis or alternative; for doctorate, comprehensive exam, thesis/dissertation. *Entrance requirements:* For master's and doctorate, GRE General Test. Additional exam requirements/recommendations for international students: Required—TOEFL (minimum score 90 iBT). *Application deadline:* For fall admission, 1/15 for domestic students; for spring admission, 10/1 for domestic students. Application fee: $100. *Expenses:* Contact institution. *Financial support:* In 2017–18, 1 fellowship, 84 research assistantships, 110 teaching assistantships were awarded. *Faculty research:* Cyber security, computer security, computer software, computer operating systems, computer and information sciences. *Total annual research expenditures:* $7.3 million. *Unit head:* Prof. Samir Das, Chair, 631-632-1807, E-mail: samir@cs.stonybrook.edu. *Application contact:* Cynthia Scalzo, Coordinator, 631-632-1521, E-mail: cscalzo@cs.stonybrook.edu. Website: http://www.cs.sunysb.edu/

Stony Brook University, State University of New York, School of Professional Development, Stony Brook, NY 11794. Offers biology (MAT); chemistry (MAT); coaching (Graduate Certificate); earth science (MAT); educational computing (Graduate Certificate); educational leadership (Advanced Certificate); English (MAT); environmental management (MPS, Graduate Certificate); French (MAT); German (MAT); higher education administration (MA, Certificate); human resource management (MS, Graduate Certificate); industrial management (Graduate Certificate); information systems management (Graduate Certificate); Italian (MAT); liberal studies (MA); mathematics (MAT); operations research (Graduate Certificate); physics (MAT); school district business leadership (Advanced Certificate); social studies (MAT); Spanish (MAT). *Program availability:* Part-time, evening/weekend, online learning. *Faculty:* 3 full-time (2 women), 101 part-time/adjunct (45 women). *Students:* 190 full-time (126 women), 974 part-time (708 women); includes 255 minority (88 Black or African

Management Information Systems

American, non-Hispanic/Latino; 2 American Indian or Alaska Native, non-Hispanic/Latino; 31 Asian, non-Hispanic/Latino; 113 Hispanic/Latino; 1 Native Hawaiian or other Pacific Islander, non-Hispanic/Latino; 20 Two or more races, non-Hispanic/Latino), 6 international. Average age 33. 411 applicants, 91% accepted, 288 enrolled. In 2017, 333 master's, 180 other advanced degrees awarded. *Entrance requirements:* Additional exam requirements/recommendations for international students: Required—TOEFL (minimum score 85 iBT). *Application deadline:* For fall admission, 1/15 for domestic students, 6/1 for international students; for spring admission, 10/1 for domestic and international students. Applications are processed on a rolling basis. Application fee: $100. *Expenses:* Contact institution. *Financial support:* Fellowships, research assistantships, teaching assistantships, and career-related internships or fieldwork available. Support available to part-time students. *Unit head:* Dr. Ken Lindblom, Dean, 631-632-7049, Fax: 631-632-9046, E-mail: kenneth.lindblom@stonybrook.edu. *Application contact:* Melissa Jordan, Assistant Dean, 631-632-7751, E-mail: melissa.jordan@stonybrook.edu.
Website: http://www.stonybrook.edu/spd/

Stratford University, School of Graduate Studies, Falls Church, VA 22043. Offers accounting (MS); business administration (MBA, DBA); cyber security (MS); cyber security leadership and policy (MS); digital forensics (MS); healthcare administration (MS); information systems (MS); information technology (DIT); networking and telecommunications (MS); software engineering (MS). *Program availability:* Part-time, evening/weekend, 100% online, blended/hybrid learning. *Students:* 272 full-time (110 women), 204 part-time (89 women). *Degree requirements:* For master's, comprehensive exam, capstone project. *Entrance requirements:* For master's, GRE or GMAT, baccalaureate degree. Additional exam requirements/recommendations for international students: Required—TOEFL (minimum score 79 iBT), IELTS (minimum score 6.5), PTE (minimum score 5). *Application deadline:* Applications are processed on a rolling basis. Application fee: $50. Electronic applications accepted. *Expenses: Tuition:* Full-time $33,405; part-time $11,135 per credit hour. One-time fee: $385 full-time. Tuition and fees vary according to degree level and program. *Financial support:* Federal Work-Study and scholarships/grants available. Financial award applicants required to submit FAFSA. *Unit head:* Dr. Valarie Trimarchi, Campus President, 703-539-6890, Fax: 703-539-6960. *Application contact:* Lori Smith, Admissions, 214-649-7113, E-mail: lasmith@stratford.edu.

Strayer University, Graduate Studies, Washington, DC 20005-2603. Offers accounting (MS); acquisition (MBA); business administration (MBA); communications technology (MS); educational management (M Ed); finance (MBA); health services administration (MHSA); hospitality and tourism management (MBA); human resource management (MBA); information systems (MS), including computer security management, decision support system management, enterprise resource management, network management, software engineering management, systems development management; management (MBA); management information systems (MBA); marketing (MBA); professional accounting (MS), including accounting information systems, controllership, taxation; public administration (MPA); supply chain management (MBA); technology in education (M Ed). Programs also offered at campus locations in Birmingham, AL; Chamblee, GA; Cobb County, GA; Morrow, GA; White Marsh, MD; Charleston, SC; Columbia, SC; Greensboro, NC; Greenville, SC; Lexington, KY; Louisville, KY; Nashville, TN; North Raleigh, NC; Washington, DC. *Accreditation:* ACBSP. *Program availability:* Part-time, evening/weekend, online learning. *Degree requirements:* For master's, thesis. *Entrance requirements:* For master's, GMAT, GRE General Test, bachelor's degree from an accredited college or university, minimum undergraduate GPA of 2.75. Electronic applications accepted.

Suffolk University, Sawyer Business School, Department of Public Administration, Boston, MA 02108-2770. Offers community health (MPA); information systems, performance management, and big data analytics (MPA); nonprofit management (MPA); state and local government (MPA); JD/MPA; MPA/MS; MPA/MSCJ; MPA/MSMHC; MPA/MSPS. *Accreditation:* NASPAA (one or more programs are accredited). *Program availability:* Part-time, evening/weekend. *Faculty:* 6 full-time (3 women), 8 part-time/adjunct (6 women). *Students:* 25 full-time (12 women), 90 part-time (56 women); includes 43 minority (20 Black or African American, non-Hispanic/Latino; 7 Asian, non-Hispanic/Latino; 14 Hispanic/Latino; 2 Two or more races, non-Hispanic/Latino), 2 international. Average age 34. 134 applicants, 38% accepted, 5 enrolled. In 2017, 44 master's awarded. *Entrance requirements:* Additional exam requirements/recommendations for international students: Required—TOEFL (minimum score 550 paper-based; 80 iBT). *Application deadline:* For fall admission, 3/15 priority date for domestic and international students; for spring admission, 10/15 priority date for domestic and international students. Applications are processed on a rolling basis. Application fee: $50. Electronic applications accepted. *Expenses:* $35,130 per year full-time tuition; $1,171 per credit part-time. *Financial support:* In 2017–18, 76 students received support, including 2 fellowships (averaging $4,650 per year); career-related internships or fieldwork, Federal Work-Study, institutionally sponsored loans, and scholarships/grants also available. Support available to part-time students. Financial award application deadline: 4/1; financial award applicants required to submit FAFSA. *Faculty research:* Local government, health care, federal policy, mental health, HIV/AIDS. *Unit head:* Brenda Bond, Director/Department Chair, 617-305-1768, E-mail: bbond@suffolk.edu. *Application contact:* Mara Marzocchi, Associate Director of Graduate Admissions, 617-573-8302, Fax: 617-305-1733, E-mail: grad.admission@suffolk.edu.
Website: http://www.suffolk.edu/mpa

Syracuse University, Martin J. Whitman School of Management, PhD Programs, Syracuse, NY 13244. Offers finance (PhD); management information systems (PhD). In 2017, 2 doctorates awarded. *Degree requirements:* For doctorate, comprehensive exam, thesis/dissertation, summer research paper. *Entrance requirements:* For doctorate, GMAT (preferred) or GRE, master's degree (preferred), transcripts, three recommendation letters, personal statement. Additional exam requirements/recommendations for international students: Required—TOEFL (minimum score 600 paper-based; 100 iBT). *Application deadline:* For fall admission, 1/15 for domestic and international students. Application fee: $75. Electronic applications accepted. *Financial support:* Fellowships with full tuition reimbursements, research assistantships with full tuition reimbursements, teaching assistantships with full tuition reimbursements, and scholarships/grants available. *Faculty research:* Marketing models, market microstructure, supply chain, auditing, corporate governance. *Unit head:* Dr. Michel Benaroch, Associate Dean for Research and PhD Programs, 315-443-3492, E-mail: mbenaroc@syr.edu. *Application contact:* Lisa Svegl, Executive Assistant for Development and PhD Programs, 315-443-9141, E-mail: lmsvegl@syr.edu.

Syracuse University, School of Information Studies, CAS Program in Information Security Management, Syracuse, NY 13244. Offers CAS. *Program availability:* Part-time, evening/weekend, online learning. *Students:* Average age 26. *Entrance requirements:* For degree, resume, personal statement, official transcripts. Additional exam requirements/recommendations for international students: Required—TOEFL (minimum score 100 iBT). *Application deadline:* For fall admission, 1/1 priority date for domestic and international students; for spring admission, 10/15 priority date for domestic and international students; for summer admission, 2/1 priority date for

domestic and international students. Applications are processed on a rolling basis. Application fee: $75. Electronic applications accepted. *Financial support:* Application deadline: 1/1. *Faculty research:* Information security, digital forensics, Internet security, risk management, security policy. *Unit head:* Carsten Oesterlund, Program Director, 315-443-2911, E-mail: igrad@syr.edu. *Application contact:* Susan Corieri, Director of Enrollment Management, 315-443-2575, E-mail: ischool@syr.edu.
Website: https://ischool.syr.edu/academics/graduate/cas/cas-information-security-management/

Syracuse University, School of Information Studies, MS Program in Enterprise Data Systems, Syracuse, NY 13244. Offers MS. *Program availability:* Part-time, evening/weekend, online learning. *Entrance requirements:* For master's, GRE General Test, official academic credentials, 500-word personal statement, two letters of recommendation, resume or curriculum vitae. Additional exam requirements/recommendations for international students: Required—TOEFL (minimum iBT score 100) or IELTS. *Application deadline:* For fall admission, 6/1 priority date for domestic and international students. Applications are processed on a rolling basis. Application fee: $75. Electronic applications accepted. *Financial support:* Research assistantships, teaching assistantships, career-related internships or fieldwork, institutionally sponsored loans, and scholarships/grants available. Financial award application deadline: 2/1. *Faculty research:* Information environments, telecommunications and enterprise network management, information architecture. *Unit head:* Carsten Oesterlund, Program Director, 315-443-2911, E-mail: igrad@syr.edu. *Application contact:* Susan Corieri, Assistant Dean for Enrollment Management, 315-443-2575, E-mail: igrad@syr.edu.
Website: https://ischool.syr.edu/academics/graduate/masters-degrees/ms-in-enterprise-data-systems/

Syracuse University, School of Information Studies, MS Program in Information Management, Syracuse, NY 13244. Offers MS. *Program availability:* Part-time, evening/weekend, online learning. *Entrance requirements:* For master's, GRE General Test, personal statement, two letters of recommendation, resume. Additional exam requirements/recommendations for international students: Required—TOEFL (minimum score 100 iBT). *Application deadline:* For fall admission, 2/1 priority date for domestic and international students; for spring admission, 10/15 priority date for domestic and international students. Applications are processed on a rolling basis. Application fee: $75. Electronic applications accepted. *Financial support:* Fellowships with full tuition reimbursements, research assistantships with partial tuition reimbursements, teaching assistantships with partial tuition reimbursements, and scholarships/grants available. Financial award application deadline: 1/1; financial award applicants required to submit FAFSA. *Faculty research:* Increasing the effectiveness of managers and executives who work with information resources, designing and managing mission-critical information technologies within organizations, developing corporate and government policies to maximize the benefits resulting from the widespread use of these technologies. *Unit head:* Carsten Oesterlund, Program Director, 315-443-2911, Fax: 315-443-6886, E-mail: igrad@syr.edu. *Application contact:* Susan Corieri, Assistant Dean for Enrollment Management, 315-443-2575, E-mail: igrad@syr.edu.
Website: https://ischool.syr.edu/academics/graduate/masters-degrees/ms-in-information-management/

Tarleton State University, College of Graduate Studies, College of Business Administration, Department of Marketing and Computer Information Systems, Stephenville, TX 76402. Offers information systems (MS). *Program availability:* Part-time, evening/weekend, 100% online, blended/hybrid learning. *Faculty:* 7 full-time (1 woman). *Students:* 5 full-time (2 women), 44 part-time (12 women); includes 18 minority (6 Black or African American, non-Hispanic/Latino; 6 Asian, non-Hispanic/Latino; 6 Hispanic/Latino), 1 international. Average age 32. 58 applicants, 88% accepted, 18 enrolled. In 2017, 1 master's awarded. *Degree requirements:* For master's, comprehensive exam, thesis (for some programs). *Entrance requirements:* For master's, GRE, minimum GPA of 3.0. Additional exam requirements/recommendations for international students: Required—TOEFL (minimum score 550 paper-based; 80 iBT), IELTS (minimum score 6). *Application deadline:* For fall admission, 8/15 priority date for domestic students; for spring admission, 1/7 for domestic students. Applications are processed on a rolling basis. Application fee: $45 ($145 for international students). Electronic applications accepted. *Expenses:* Contact institution. *Financial support:* Research assistantships and teaching assistantships available. Financial award application deadline: 5/1; financial award applicants required to submit FAFSA. *Unit head:* Dr. Joseph Schuessler, Department Head, 254-968-9893, E-mail: schuessler@tarleton.edu. *Application contact:* Information Contact, 254-968-9104, Fax: 254-968-9670, E-mail: gradoffice@tarleton.edu.
Website: http://www.tarleton.edu/cis/

Temple University, College of Education, Department of Teaching and Learning, Philadelphia, PA 19122-6096. Offers career and technical education (Ed M), including business, computing, and information technology, industrial education, marketing education; middle grades education (Ed M), including math and language arts, math and science, science and language arts; secondary education (Ed M), including English, math, social studies; teaching English to speakers of other languages (MS Ed); urban education (Ed M). *Program availability:* Part-time, evening/weekend. *Students:* 218 full-time (144 women), 296 part-time (183 women); includes 128 minority (74 Black or African American, non-Hispanic/Latino; 18 Asian, non-Hispanic/Latino; 25 Hispanic/Latino; 11 Two or more races, non-Hispanic/Latino), 13 international. 254 applicants, 54% accepted, 102 enrolled. In 2017, 128 master's awarded. Terminal master's awarded for partial completion of doctoral program. *Degree requirements:* For master's, thesis or alternative. *Entrance requirements:* Additional exam requirements/recommendations for international students: Required—TOEFL (minimum score 550 paper-based; 79 iBT). *Application deadline:* For fall admission, 4/1 for domestic students, 12/15 for international students; for spring admission, 10/1 for domestic students, 8/1 for international students. Application fee: $60. Electronic applications accepted. *Expenses:* Contact institution. *Financial support:* Fellowships, research assistantships, and teaching assistantships available. Financial award application deadline: 1/15; financial award applicants required to submit FAFSA. *Faculty research:* Workforce development, vocational education, technical education, industrial education, professional development, literacy, classroom management, school communities, curriculum development, instruction, applied linguistics, cross linguistic influence, bilingual education, oral proficiency, multilingualism. *Unit head:* Dr. Christine Woyshner, Chairperson, 215-204-6387, E-mail: christine.woyshner@temple.edu. *Application contact:* Sarah Stapleton, Assistant Director, Academic Operations, 215-204-8220, E-mail: sarah.stapleton@temple.edu.
Website: http://education.temple.edu/tl

Temple University, Fox School of Business, Doctoral Programs in Business, Philadelphia, PA 19122-6096. Offers accounting (PhD); entrepreneurship (PhD); finance (PhD); international business (PhD); management information systems (PhD); marketing (PhD); risk management and insurance (PhD); statistics (PhD); strategic management (PhD); tourism and sport (PhD). *Accreditation:* AACSB. *Degree requirements:* For doctorate, thesis/dissertation. *Entrance requirements:* For doctorate, GRE General Test, GMAT, minimum GPA of 3.0, master's degree. Additional exam requirements/recommendations for international students: Required—TOEFL (minimum score 600 paper-based; 100 iBT), IELTS (minimum score 7.5). Electronic applications accepted. *Expenses:* Tuition, state resident: full-time $16,164; part-time $898 per credit hour. Tuition, nonresident: full-time $22,158; part-time $1231 per credit hour. *Required fees:* $890; $445 per semester. Full-time tuition and fees vary according to course load, degree level, campus/location and program.

Tennessee Technological University, College of Graduate Studies, College of Business, MBA Program, Cookeville, TN 38505. Offers finance (MBA); human resource management (MBA); international business (MBA); management information systems (MBA). *Program availability:* Part-time, evening/weekend. In 2017, 77 master's awarded. *Entrance requirements:* For master's, GMAT or GRE. *Expenses:* Tuition, state resident: full-time $9925; part-time $565 per credit hour. Tuition, nonresident: full-time $22,993; part-time $1291 per credit hour. *Financial support:* In 2017–18, 2 research assistantships, 3 teaching assistantships were awarded; fellowships and unspecified assistantships also available. Financial award application deadline: 4/1; financial award applicants required to submit FAFSA. *Unit head:* Kate Nicewicz, Director, E-mail: knicewicz@tntech.edu. *Application contact:* Shelia K. Kendrick, Coordinator of Graduate Studies, 931-372-3808, Fax: 931-372-3497, E-mail: skendrick@tntech.edu.
Website: https://www.tntech.edu/cob/mba/

Texas A&M International University, Office of Graduate Studies and Research, A.R. Sanchez, Jr. School of Business, Division of International Business and Technology Studies, Laredo, TX 78041. Offers information systems (MSIS); international business management (MBA, PhD). *Degree requirements:* For master's, thesis (for some programs). *Entrance requirements:* For master's, GMAT or GRE General Test. Additional exam requirements/recommendations for international students: Required—TOEFL (minimum score 550 paper-based; 79 iBT).

Texas A&M University, Mays Business School, Department of Finance, College Station, TX 77843. Offers finance (MS); financial management (MFM); land economics and real estate (MRE); management information systems (MS). *Faculty:* 21. *Students:* 235 full-time (72 women), 10 part-time (4 women); includes 43 minority (2 Black or African American, non-Hispanic/Latino; 2 American Indian or Alaska Native, non-Hispanic/Latino; 11 Asian, non-Hispanic/Latino; 24 Hispanic/Latino; 4 Two or more races, non-Hispanic/Latino), 19 international. Average age 24. 179 applicants, 33% accepted, 50 enrolled. In 2017, 163 master's awarded. Terminal master's awarded for partial completion of doctoral program. *Degree requirements:* For master's, comprehensive exam. *Entrance requirements:* For master's, GMAT or GRE. Additional exam requirements/recommendations for international students: Required—TOEFL (minimum score 550 paper-based; 80 iBT), IELTS (minimum score 6), PTE (minimum score 53). *Application deadline:* For fall admission, 4/7 for domestic students. Applications are processed on a rolling basis. Application fee: $50 ($90 for international students). Electronic applications accepted. *Expenses:* Contact institution. *Financial support:* In 2017–18, 165 students received support, including 14 fellowships with tuition reimbursements available (averaging $2,232 per year), 23 research assistantships with tuition reimbursements available (averaging $10,754 per year), 12 teaching assistantships with tuition reimbursements available (averaging $3,926 per year); career-related internships or fieldwork, institutionally sponsored loans, scholarships/grants, traineeships, health care benefits, tuition waivers (full and partial), and unspecified assistantships also available. Support available to part-time students. Financial award application deadline: 3/15; financial award applicants required to submit FAFSA. *Unit head:* Dr. Sorin Sorescu, Head, 979-458-0380, Fax: 979-845-3884, E-mail: smsorescu@mays.tamu.edu. *Application contact:* Angela G. Degelman, Program Coordinator/Graduate Academic Advisor, 979-845-4858, Fax: 979-845-3884, E-mail: adegelman@mays.tamu.edu.
Website: http://mays.tamu.edu/finc/

Texas A&M University, Mays Business School, Department of Information and Operations Management, College Station, TX 77843. Offers management information systems (MS). *Faculty:* 15. *Students:* 260 full-time (103 women), 1 part-time (0 women); includes 14 minority (6 Asian, non-Hispanic/Latino; 7 Hispanic/Latino; 1 Two or more races, non-Hispanic/Latino), 200 international. Average age 26. 576 applicants, 11% accepted, 63 enrolled. In 2017, 157 master's awarded. Terminal master's awarded for partial completion of doctoral program. *Degree requirements:* For master's, comprehensive exam. *Entrance requirements:* For master's, GMAT. Additional exam requirements/recommendations for international students: Required—TOEFL (minimum score 550 paper-based; 80 iBT), IELTS (minimum score 6), PTE (minimum score 53). *Application deadline:* For fall admission, 12/1 priority date for domestic students, 2/15 for international students. Applications are processed on a rolling basis. Application fee: $50 ($90 for international students). Electronic applications accepted. *Expenses:* Contact institution. *Financial support:* In 2017–18, 207 students received support, including 1 fellowship with tuition reimbursement available (averaging $1,000 per year), 50 research assistantships with tuition reimbursements available (averaging $5,840 per year), 38 teaching assistantships with tuition reimbursements available (averaging $5,643 per year); career-related internships or fieldwork, institutionally sponsored loans, scholarships/grants, traineeships, health care benefits, tuition waivers, and unspecified assistantships also available. Support available to part-time students. Financial award application deadline: 3/15; financial award applicants required to submit FAFSA. *Unit head:* Dr. Rich Metters, Head, 979-845-1148, Fax: 979-845-1148, E-mail: rmetters@mays.tamu.edu. *Application contact:* Andre Araujo, Graduate Advisor, 979-845-0809, Fax: 979-845-1148, E-mail: aaraujo@mays.tamu.edu.
Website: http://mays.tamu.edu/info/

Texas A&M University–Central Texas, Graduate Studies and Research, Killeen, TX 76549. Offers accounting (MS); business administration (MBA); clinical mental health counseling (MS); criminal justice (MCJ); curriculum and instruction (M Ed); educational administration (M Ed); educational psychology - experimental psychology (MS); history (MA); human resource management (MS); information systems (MS); liberal studies (MS); management and leadership (MS); marriage and family therapy (MS); mathematics (MS); political science (MA); school counseling (M Ed); school psychology (Ed S).

Texas Southern University, Jesse H. Jones School of Business, Program in Management Information Systems, Houston, TX 77004-4584. Offers MS. Electronic applications accepted.

Texas State University, The Graduate College, Emmett and Miriam McCoy College of Business Administration, Program in Accounting and Information Technology, San Marcos, TX 78666. Offers MS. *Program availability:* Part-time. *Faculty:* 13 full-time (2 women), 2 part-time/adjunct (0 women). *Students:* 9 full-time (5 women), 6 part-time (4 women); includes 6 minority (1 Asian, non-Hispanic/Latino; 5 Hispanic/Latino), 4 international. Average age 36. 21 applicants, 43% accepted, 3 enrolled. In 2017, 6 master's awarded. *Degree requirements:* For master's, comprehensive exam. *Entrance requirements:* For master's, GMAT or GRE, baccalaureate degree from regionally-accredited university; two letters or forms of recommendation from persons best able to assess applicant's ability to succeed in graduate school; essay; resume showing work experience, extracurricular and community activities, and honors and achievements. Additional exam requirements/recommendations for international students: Required—TOEFL (minimum score 550 paper-based; 78 iBT), IELTS (minimum score 6.5).

Application deadline: For fall admission, 2/1 priority date for domestic and international students; for spring admission, 10/1 for domestic and international students. Application fee: $40 ($90 for international students). Electronic applications accepted. *Expenses:* Tuition, state resident: full-time $7868; part-time $3934 per semester. Tuition, nonresident: full-time $17,828; part-time $8914 per semester. *Required fees:* $2092; $1435 per semester. Tuition and fees vary according to course load. *Financial support:* In 2017–18, 7 students received support, including 4 teaching assistantships (averaging $12,407 per year); research assistantships, Federal Work-Study, institutionally sponsored loans, scholarships/grants, health care benefits, and unspecified assistantships also available. Support available to part-time students. Financial award application deadline: 3/1; financial award applicants required to submit FAFSA. *Unit head:* Dr. William Chittenden, Graduate Advisor, 512-245-3591, Fax: 512-245-8365, E-mail: wc10@txstate.edu. *Application contact:* Dr. Andrea Golato, Dean of Graduate School, 512-245-2581, Fax: 512-245-8365, E-mail: gradcollege@txstate.edu.
Website: http://www.gradcollege.txstate.edu/programs/msait.html

Texas Tech University, Rawls College of Business Administration, Lubbock, TX 79409-2101. Offers accounting (MSA, PhD), including audit/financial reporting (MSA), taxation (MSA); data science (MS); finance (PhD); general business (MBA); healthcare management (MS); information systems and operations management (PhD); management (PhD); marketing (PhD); STEM (MBA); JD/MBA; MBA/M Arch; MBA/MD; MBA/MS; MBA/Pharm D. *Accreditation:* AACSB. *Program availability:* Evening/weekend, 100% online, blended/hybrid learning. *Faculty:* 89 full-time (22 women). *Students:* 660 full-time (252 women); includes 174 minority (30 Black or African American, non-Hispanic/Latino; 3 American Indian or Alaska Native, non-Hispanic/Latino; 20 Asian, non-Hispanic/Latino; 104 Hispanic/Latino; 17 Two or more races, non-Hispanic/Latino), 99 international. Average age 29. 492 applicants, 51% accepted, 148 enrolled. In 2017, 439 master's, 6 doctorates awarded. *Degree requirements:* For master's, thesis (for MS); capstone course; for doctorate, comprehensive exam, thesis/dissertation, qualifying exams. *Entrance requirements:* For master's, GMAT, GRE, MCAT, PCAT, LSAT, or DAT, holistic review of academic credentials, resume, essay, letters of recommendation; for doctorate, GMAT, GRE, holistic review of academic credentials, resume, statement of purpose, letters of recommendation. Additional exam requirements/recommendations for international students: Required—TOEFL (minimum score 550 paper-based; 79 iBT), IELTS (minimum score 6.5), PTE (minimum score 60). *Application deadline:* For fall admission, 7/1 priority date for domestic students, 1/15 for international students; for spring admission, 12/1 priority date for domestic students, 6/15 for international students; for summer admission, 5/1 for domestic students. Applications are processed on a rolling basis. Application fee: $60. Electronic applications accepted. *Expenses:* $5,167.50 full-time; $9,000 per semester (for hybrid MBA). *Financial support:* In 2017–18, 81 students received support, including 1 research assistantship with full tuition reimbursement available (averaging $22,725 per year), 63 teaching assistantships with full tuition reimbursements available (averaging $22,725 per year); career-related internships or fieldwork, Federal Work-Study, scholarships/grants, health care benefits, and unspecified assistantships also available. Financial award application deadline: 3/1; financial award applicants required to submit FAFSA. *Faculty research:* Governmental and nonprofit accounting, securities and options futures, statistical analysis and design, leadership, consumer behavior. *Total annual research expenditures:* $230,000. *Unit head:* Dr. Margaret Williams, Dean, 806-834-2839, Fax: 806-742-1092, E-mail: margaret.l.williams@ttu.edu. *Application contact:* Jennifer Yack, Applications Manager, Graduate and Professional Programs, 806-742-3184, E-mail: rawlsgrad@ttu.edu.
Website: http://www.depts.ttu.edu/rawlsbusiness/graduate/

Touro College, Graduate School of Technology, New York, NY 10010. Offers information systems (MS); instructional technology (MS); Web and multimedia design (MA). *Faculty:* 18 part-time/adjunct (6 women). *Students:* 125 full-time (122 women), 177 part-time (163 women); includes 79 minority (39 Black or African American, non-Hispanic/Latino; 23 Asian, non-Hispanic/Latino; 14 Hispanic/Latino; 3 Two or more races, non-Hispanic/Latino), 150 international. Average age 34. *Entrance requirements:* Additional exam requirements/recommendations for international students: Required—TOEFL (minimum score 83 iBT), IELTS (minimum score 6.5), PTE (minimum score 58). Application fee: $50. *Unit head:* Dr. Issac Herskowitz, Dean of the Graduate School of Technology, 202-463-0400 Ext. 5231, E-mail: issac.herskowitz@touro.edu. *Application contact:* Jack Romano, Program Director, 212-463-0400 Ext. 5462.
Website: http://www.touro.edu/gst/

Trident University International, College of Business Administration, Program in Business Administration, Cypress, CA 90630. Offers business administration (PhD); conflict and negotiation management (MBA); criminal justice administration (MBA); entrepreneurship (MBA); finance (MBA); general management (MBA); government accounting (MBA); human resource management (MBA); information security and digital assurance management (MBA); information technology management (MBA); international business (MBA); logistics management (MBA); marketing (MBA); project management (MBA); public management (MBA); quality management (MBA); strategic leadership (MBA). *Program availability:* Part-time, evening/weekend, online learning. *Degree requirements:* For doctorate, comprehensive exam, thesis/dissertation, defense of dissertation. *Entrance requirements:* For master's, minimum GPA of 2.5 (students with GPA 3.0 or greater may transfer up to 30% of graduate level credits); for doctorate, minimum GPA of 3.4, curriculum vitae, course work in research methods or statistics. Additional exam requirements/recommendations for international students: Required—TOEFL. Electronic applications accepted.

Trident University International, College of Information Systems, Cypress, CA 90630. Offers business intelligence (Certificate); information technology management (MS). *Program availability:* Part-time, evening/weekend, online learning. *Entrance requirements:* For master's, minimum GPA of 2.5 (students with GPA 3.0 or greater may transfer up to 30% of graduate level credits); undergraduate degree completed within the past 5 years. Additional exam requirements/recommendations for international students: Required—TOEFL (minimum score 525 paper-based). Electronic applications accepted.

Troy University, Graduate School, College of Business, Program in Business Administration, Troy, AL 36082. Offers accounting (EMBA, MBA); criminal justice (EMBA); finance (MBA); general management (EMBA, MBA); healthcare management (EMBA); information systems (EMBA, MBA); international economic development (MBA). *Accreditation:* ACBSP. *Program availability:* Part-time, evening/weekend. *Faculty:* 6 full-time (2 women), 1 part-time/adjunct (0 women). *Students:* 43 full-time (22 women), 115 part-time (55 women); includes 50 minority (31 Black or African American, non-Hispanic/Latino; 12 Asian, non-Hispanic/Latino; 6 Hispanic/Latino; 1 Two or more races, non-Hispanic/Latino). Average age 30. 156 applicants, 76% accepted, 36 enrolled. In 2017, 95 master's awarded. *Degree requirements:* For master's, minimum GPA of 3.0, capstone course, research course. *Entrance requirements:* For master's, GMAT (minimum score 500) or GRE (minimum score 900 on old exam or 294 on new exam), bachelor's degree; minimum undergraduate GPA of 2.5 or 3.0 on last 30 semester hours, letter of recommendation. Additional exam requirements/recommendations for international students: Required—TOEFL (minimum score 523 paper-based; 70 iBT), IELTS (minimum score 6). *Application deadline:* Applications are

Management Information Systems

processed on a rolling basis. Application fee: $50. Electronic applications accepted. *Expenses:* Tuition, state resident: part-time $417 per credit hour. Tuition, nonresident: part-time $834 per credit hour. *Required fees:* $42 per credit hour. $50 per semester. Tuition and fees vary according to campus/location. *Financial support:* Fellowships, career-related internships or fieldwork, and scholarships/grants available. Support available to part-time students. Financial award applicants required to submit FAFSA. *Unit head:* Dr. Phillip Mixon, MBA Director, 334-670-3140, Fax: 334-670-3708, E-mail: pamixon@troy.edu. *Application contact:* Jessica A. Kimbro, Director of Graduate Admissions, 334-670-3178, E-mail: jacord@troy.edu.

Tulane University, School of Professional Advancement, New Orleans, LA 70118-5669. Offers health and wellness management (MPS); homeland security studies (MPS); information technology management (MPS); liberal arts (MLA). *Program availability:* Part-time. *Degree requirements:* For master's, thesis. *Entrance requirements:* For master's, GRE General Test, minimum B average in undergraduate course work. Additional exam requirements/recommendations for international students: Required—TOEFL. *Expenses: Tuition:* Full-time $50,920; part-time $2829 per credit hour. *Required fees:* $2040; $44.50 per credit hour. $580 per term. Tuition and fees vary according to course load, degree level and program.

Tuskegee University, Graduate Programs, Andrew F. Brimmer College of Business and Information Science, Tuskegee, AL 36088. Offers information systems and security management (MS). *Degree requirements:* For master's, thesis. *Entrance requirements:* For master's, GRE or GMAT, baccalaureate degree in computer science, management information systems, accounting, finance, management, information technology, or a closely-related field.

United States International University–Africa, School of Business Administration, Nairobi, Kenya. Offers business administration (GEMBA); entrepreneurship (MBA); finance (MBA); human resource management (MBA); information technology management (MBA); integrated studies (MBA); international business administration (MBA); management and organizational development (MS); marketing (MBA); organizational development (EMS); strategic management (MBA). *Program availability:* Part-time, evening/weekend. *Degree requirements:* For master's, thesis. *Entrance requirements:* For master's, GMAT, 2 letters of reference, resume. Additional exam requirements/recommendations for international students: Required—TOEFL (minimum score 550 paper-based). *Faculty research:* Marketing in small business enterprises, total quality management in Kenya.

Universidad del Este, Graduate School, Carolina, PR 00984. Offers accounting (MBA); adult education (M Ed); agribusiness (MBA); criminal justice and criminology (MA); curriculum and instruction - early education (M Ed); curriculum and instruction - elementary (M Ed); curriculum and instruction - English (M Ed); curriculum and instruction - Spanish (M Ed); human resources (MBA); information security management (MBA); information technology and Web business development (MBA); management (MBA); public policy (MPA); social work (MA), including clinical social work; special education (M Ed); strategic leadership (MBA).

Universidad del Turabo, Graduate Programs, School of Business and Entrepreneurship, Program in Management of Information Systems, Gurabo, PR 00778-3030. Offers DBA. *Entrance requirements:* For doctorate, GRE, EXADEP or GMAT, official transcript, recommendation letters, essay, curriculum vitae, interview. Electronic applications accepted.

Universidad Metropolitana, School of Business Administration, Program in Management Information Systems, San Juan, PR 00928-1150. Offers MBA.

Université de Sherbrooke, Faculty of Administration, Program in Governance, Audit and Security of Information Technology, Longueuil, QC J4K0A8, Canada. Offers M Adm. *Program availability:* Part-time, evening/weekend, online learning. *Degree requirements:* For master's, thesis. *Entrance requirements:* For master's, bachelor's degree, related work experience. Electronic applications accepted.

Université de Sherbrooke, Faculty of Administration, Program in Management Information Systems, Sherbrooke, QC J1K 2R1, Canada. Offers M Sc. *Degree requirements:* For master's, one foreign language, thesis. *Entrance requirements:* For master's, bachelor's degree in related field, minimum GPA of 3.0 (on 4.3 scale). Electronic applications accepted. *Faculty research:* Project management in IT, IT governance, business intelligence, IT performance.

Université de Sherbrooke, Faculty of Sciences, Centre de Formation en Technologies de L'information, Sherbrooke, QC J1K 2R1, Canada. Offers M Sc, Diploma. Electronic applications accepted.

Université du Québec à Montréal, Graduate Programs, Program in Management Information Systems, Montréal, QC H3C 3P8, Canada. Offers M Sc, M Sc A. *Program availability:* Part-time. *Entrance requirements:* For master's, appropriate bachelor's degree or equivalent and proficiency in French.

Université Laval, Faculty of Administrative Sciences, Programs in Business Administration, Québec, QC G1K 7P4, Canada. Offers accounting (MBA); agri-food management (MBA); electronic business (MBA, Diploma); factory management and logistics (MBA); finance (MBA); firm management (MBA); geomatic management (MBA); information technology management (MBA); international management (MBA); management (MBA); management accounting (MBA, Diploma); marketing (MBA); modeling and organizational decision (MBA); occupational health and safety management (MBA); pharmacy management (MBA); social and environmental responsibility (MBA); technological entrepreneurship (Diploma). *Accreditation:* AACSB. *Program availability:* Part-time, evening/weekend, online learning. *Entrance requirements:* For master's and Diploma, knowledge of French and English. Electronic applications accepted.

University at Albany, State University of New York, Nelson A. Rockefeller College of Public Affairs and Policy, Department of Public Administration and Policy, Albany, NY 12222-0001. Offers financial management and public economics (MPA); financial market regulation (MPA); health policy (MPA); healthcare management (MPA); homeland security (MPA); human resources management (MPA); information strategy and management (MPA); local government management (MPA); nonprofit management (MPA); nonprofit management and leadership (Certificate); organizational behavior and theory (MPA, PhD); planning and policy analysis (CAS); policy analysis (MPA); politics and administration (PhD); public finance (PhD); public management (PhD); public policy (PhD); public sector management (Certificate); women and public policy (Certificate); JD/MPA. JD/MPA offered jointly with Albany Law School. *Accreditation:* NASPAA (one or more programs are accredited). *Faculty:* 21 full-time (7 women), 14 part-time/adjunct (7 women). *Students:* 115 full-time (59 women), 93 part-time (56 women); includes 41 minority (11 Black or African American, non-Hispanic/Latino; 9 Asian, non-Hispanic/Latino; 18 Hispanic/Latino; 3 Two or more races, non-Hispanic/Latino), 32 international. 236 applicants, 69% accepted, 86 enrolled. In 2017, 57 master's, 1 doctorate, 14 other advanced degrees awarded. *Degree requirements:* For doctorate, one foreign language, thesis/dissertation. *Entrance requirements:* For doctorate, GRE General Test. Additional exam requirements/recommendations for international students: Required—TOEFL (minimum score 550 paper-based). *Application deadline:* For fall admission, 2/1 priority date for domestic students, 5/1 for international students; for spring admission, 12/1 for

domestic students. Applications are processed on a rolling basis. Application fee: $75. Electronic applications accepted. *Expenses:* Tuition, state resident: full-time $10,870; part-time $453 per credit hour. Tuition, nonresident: full-time $22,210; part-time $925 per credit hour. *Required fees:* $84.68 per credit hour. $508.06 per semester. Part-time tuition and fees vary according to course load and program. *Financial support:* Application deadline: 2/1. *Unit head:* Victor Asal, Chair, 518-591-8729, E-mail: vasal@albany.edu.
Website: http://www.albany.edu/rockefeller/pad.shtml

University at Albany, State University of New York, School of Business, MBA Programs, Albany, NY 12222. Offers business administration (MBA); cyber security (MBA); entrepreneurship (MBA); finance (MBA); human resource information systems (MBA); information systems and business analytics (MBA); marketing (MBA); JD/MBA. JD/MBA offered jointly with Albany Law School. *Program availability:* Part-time, evening/weekend. *Faculty:* 29 full-time (13 women), 9 part-time/adjunct (2 women). *Students:* 103 full-time (36 women), 188 part-time (69 women); includes 76 minority (27 Black or African American, non-Hispanic/Latino; 33 Asian, non-Hispanic/Latino; 16 Hispanic/Latino), 16 international. Average age 25. 181 applicants, 80% accepted, 114 enrolled. In 2017, 103 master's awarded. *Degree requirements:* For master's, thesis (for some programs), field or research project. *Entrance requirements:* For master's, GMAT, minimum undergraduate GPA of 3.0; 3 letters of recommendation; resume; statement of goals. Additional exam requirements/recommendations for international students: Required—TOEFL (minimum score 100 iBT); Recommended—IELTS (minimum score 7). *Application deadline:* For fall admission, 4/1 priority date for domestic students, 2/15 for international students; for spring admission, 12/1 for domestic students; for summer admission, 5/1 for domestic students. Applications are processed on a rolling basis. Application fee: $75. Electronic applications accepted. *Expenses:* $16,622.00 per year (for Full-Time MBA); $645 per credit hour (for Evening MBA). *Financial support:* In 2017–18, 25 students received support, including 7 fellowships with partial tuition reimbursements available (averaging $6,000 per year), 4 research assistantships with partial tuition reimbursements available, 21 teaching assistantships with partial tuition reimbursements available; unspecified assistantships also available. Financial award application deadline: 4/1; financial award applicants required to submit FAFSA. *Faculty research:* Social goods, information assurance, social computing, corporate entrepreneurship, asset pricing. *Total annual research expenditures:* $136,000. *Unit head:* Dr. Hany A. Shawky, Interim Dean, 518-956-8337, Fax: 518-442-3273, E-mail: hshawky@albany.edu. *Application contact:* Zina Mega Lawrence, Assistant Dean of Graduate Student Services, 518-956-8320, Fax: 518-442-4042, E-mail: zlawrence@albany.edu.
Website: https://graduatebusiness.albany.edu/

University at Buffalo, the State University of New York, Graduate School, School of Engineering and Applied Sciences, Department of Computer Science and Engineering, Buffalo, NY 14260. Offers computer science and engineering (MS, PhD); information assurance (Certificate). *Program availability:* Part-time. Terminal master's awarded for partial completion of doctoral program. *Degree requirements:* For master's, thesis or alternative; for doctorate, thesis/dissertation, comprehensive qualifying exam. *Entrance requirements:* For master's and doctorate, GRE General Test. Additional exam requirements/recommendations for international students: Required—TOEFL (minimum score 550 paper-based; 79 iBT). Electronic applications accepted. *Faculty research:* Theory and algorithms, databases and information retrieval, data mining and data science, artificial intelligence and machine learning, computer security and information assurance, computing education, cyber-physical systens (Internet of Things), distributed systems and networks, hardware and architecture, high-performance and computing and computational science, medical applications and bioinformatics, mobile systems, programming languages and software systems.

University at Buffalo, the State University of New York, Graduate School, School of Management, Buffalo, NY 14260. Offers accounting (MS); analytics (MBA); business administration (PMBA); consulting (MBA); finance (MBA, MS), including financial risk management (MS), quantitative finance (MS); healthcare (MBA); information assurance (MBA); information systems (MBA); international management (MBA); management (EMBA, PhD); management information systems (MS); marketing (MBA); supply chain and operations (MBA); supply chains and operations management (MS); Au D/MBA; DDS/MBA; JD/MBA; M Arch/MBA; MD/MBA; MPH/MBA; MSW/MBA; Pharm D/MBA. *Accreditation:* AACSB. *Program availability:* Part-time, evening/weekend. *Faculty:* 80 full-time (26 women), 45 part-time/adjunct (12 women). *Students:* 597 full-time (251 women); includes 83 minority (19 Black or African American, non-Hispanic/Latino; 59 Asian, non-Hispanic/Latino; 5 Hispanic/Latino), 306 international. Average age 25. 2,109 applicants, 46% accepted, 376 enrolled. In 2017, 371 master's, 13 doctorates awarded. *Degree requirements:* For master's, capstone courses or projects; for doctorate, comprehensive exam, thesis/dissertation. *Entrance requirements:* For master's, GMAT (for MS in accounting, finance); GRE or GMAT (for MBA, MS in management information systems, supply chains and operations management), essays, letters of recommendation; for doctorate, GMAT or GRE, essays, writing sample, letters of recommendation. Additional exam requirements/recommendations for international students: Required—TOEFL (minimum score 95 iBT) or IELTS (minimum score 6.5); Recommended—TSE (minimum score 73). *Application deadline:* For fall admission, 10/15 priority date for domestic and international students; for winter admission, 2/1 priority date for domestic and international students; for spring admission, 4/15 for domestic students; for summer admission, 5/15 for domestic students. Application fee: $100. Electronic applications accepted. *Expenses:* Varies by program. *Financial support:* Fellowships with full and partial tuition reimbursements, research assistantships with full and partial tuition reimbursements, teaching assistantships with full and partial tuition reimbursements, career-related internships or fieldwork, Federal Work-Study, institutionally sponsored loans, scholarships/grants, health care benefits, and unspecified assistantships available. Financial award application deadline: 2/15. *Faculty research:* Data analytics, accounting and law, rate finance, consumer behavior, supply chain logistics, leadership and team effectiveness. *Total annual research expenditures:* $968,376. *Unit head:* Erin K. O'Brien, Assistant Dean and Director of Graduate Programs, 716-645-3204, Fax: 716-645-2341, E-mail: ekobrien@buffalo.edu. *Application contact:* Meghan Felser, Director of Admissions and Recruiting, 716-645-3204, Fax: 716-645-2341, E-mail: mpwood@buffalo.edu.
Website: http://mgt.buffalo.edu/

The University of Akron, Graduate School, College of Business Administration, Department of Management, Program in Information Systems Management, Akron, OH 44325. Offers MSM. *Students:* 16 full-time (8 women), 16 part-time (7 women); includes 1 minority (Asian, non-Hispanic/Latino), 27 international. Average age 27. 31 applicants, 90% accepted, 8 enrolled. In 2017, 58 master's awarded. *Entrance requirements:* For master's, GMAT, GRE, MCAT, LSAT, PCAT, or CAT, undergraduate degree in information systems, minimum GPA of 3.0, two letters of recommendation, statement of purpose, resume. Additional exam requirements/recommendations for international students: Required—TOEFL (minimum score 79 iBT), IELTS (minimum score 6.5). *Application deadline:* For fall admission, 7/15 for domestic students, 7/1 for international students; for spring admission, 11/15 for domestic and international students; for summer admission, 4/15 for domestic and international students. Application fee: $45 ($70 for international students). Electronic applications accepted. *Unit head:* Dr. Steve

Ash, Chair, 330-972-6429, E-mail: ash@uakron.edu. *Application contact:* Dr. William Hauser, Director of Graduate Business Programs, 330-972-7043, Fax: 330-972-6588, E-mail: whauser@uakron.edu.
Website: http://www.uakron.edu/cba/graduate/programs/msm/

The University of Alabama at Birmingham, Collat School of Business, Program in Business Administration, Birmingham, AL 35294. Offers business administration (MBA), including finance, health care management, information technology management, marketing; MD/MBA. *Program availability:* Part-time, evening/weekend, 100% online, blended/hybrid learning. *Faculty:* 44 full-time (8 women), 11 part-time/adjunct (4 women). *Students:* 111 full-time (46 women), 308 part-time (136 women); includes 107 minority (73 Black or African American, non-Hispanic/Latino; 21 Asian, non-Hispanic/Latino; 8 Hispanic/Latino; 5 Two or more races, non-Hispanic/Latino), 56 international. Average age 33. 222 applicants, 89% accepted, 143 enrolled. In 2017, 114 master's awarded. *Entrance requirements:* For master's, GMAT. Additional exam requirements/recommendations for international students: Required—TOEFL (minimum score 80 iBT), IELTS (minimum score 6.5). *Application deadline:* For fall admission, 7/1 for domestic and international students; for spring admission, 11/1 for domestic and international students; for summer admission, 4/1 for domestic and international students. Applications are processed on a rolling basis. Application fee: $60 ($75 for international students). Electronic applications accepted. *Faculty research:* Open innovation, workplace issues, leadership, supply chain management, capital markets. *Total annual research expenditures:* $240,000. *Unit head:* Dr. Ken Miller, Executive Director, MBA Programs, 205-934-8855, E-mail: klmiller@uab.edu. *Application contact:* Christy Manning, Coordinator of Graduate Programs in Business, 205-934-8817, E-mail: cmanning@uab.edu.
Website: http://www.uab.edu/business/home/mba

The University of Alabama at Birmingham, Collat School of Business, Program in Management Information Systems, Birmingham, AL 35294. Offers management information systems (MS), including information security, information technology management. *Program availability:* Part-time, online only, 100% online. *Faculty:* 7 full-time (1 woman), 4 part-time/adjunct (2 women). *Students:* 8 full-time (0 women), 116 part-time (38 women); includes 49 minority (35 Black or African American, non-Hispanic/Latino; 1 American Indian or Alaska Native, non-Hispanic/Latino; 5 Asian, non-Hispanic/Latino; 3 Hispanic/Latino; 5 Two or more races, non-Hispanic/Latino), 1 international. Average age 37. 47 applicants, 94% accepted, 36 enrolled. In 2017, 35 master's awarded. *Entrance requirements:* For master's, GMAT. Additional exam requirements/recommendations for international students: Required—TOEFL (minimum score 80 iBT), IELTS (minimum score 6.5). *Application deadline:* For fall admission, 7/15 for domestic and international students; for spring admission, 11/15 for domestic students, 12/15 for international students; for summer admission, 4/15 for domestic and international students. Application fee: $50 ($60 for international students). *Faculty research:* Open innovation, information security, online communities. *Unit head:* Dr. Jack Howard, Department Chair, 205-934-8846, Fax: 205-934-8886, E-mail: jlhoward@uab.edu. *Application contact:* Wendy England, Online Program Coordinator, 205-934-8813, Fax: 205-975-4429.
Website: https://businessdegrees.uab.edu/mis-degree-masters/

The University of Alabama in Huntsville, School of Graduate Studies, College of Business Administration, Program in Accounting, Huntsville, AL 35899. Offers accounting (M Acc), including CPA preparatory with an emphasis in taxation, CPA preparatory with emphasis in assurance and financial reporting, general accounting, information systems audit and control (ISAC). *Accreditation:* AACSB. *Program availability:* Part-time, evening/weekend. *Degree requirements:* For master's, comprehensive exam, thesis or alternative. *Entrance requirements:* For master's, GMAT (minimum score 500), minimum AACSB index of 1080. Additional exam requirements/recommendations for international students: Required—TOEFL (minimum score 550 paper-based; 80 iBT), IELTS (minimum score 6.5). Electronic applications accepted. *Faculty research:* Accounting information systems, managerial accounting, behavioral accounting, state and local taxation, financial accounting.

The University of Alabama in Huntsville, School of Graduate Studies, College of Business Administration, Programs in Information Systems, Huntsville, AL 35899. Offers cybersecurity (MS, Certificate); enterprise resource planning (Certificate); information systems (MSIS); supply chain and logistics management (MS); supply chain management (Certificate). *Program availability:* Part-time, evening/weekend. *Degree requirements:* For master's, comprehensive exam, thesis or alternative. *Entrance requirements:* For master's, GMAT (minimum score 500), minimum AACSB index of 1080. Additional exam requirements/recommendations for international students: Required—TOEFL (minimum score 550 paper-based; 80 iBT), IELTS (minimum score 6.5). Electronic applications accepted. *Faculty research:* Supply chain information systems, information assurance and security, databases and conceptual schema, workflow management, inter-organizational information sharing.

The University of Arizona, Eller College of Management, Department of Management Information Systems, Tucson, AZ 85721. Offers MS, Graduate Certificate. *Degree requirements:* For master's, thesis or alternative. *Entrance requirements:* For master's, GMAT or GRE General Test, 2 letters of recommendation, resume. Additional exam requirements/recommendations for international students: Required—TOEFL (minimum score 550 paper-based; 80 iBT). Electronic applications accepted. *Faculty research:* Group decision support systems, domestic and international computing issues, expert systems, data management and structures.

University of Arkansas, Graduate School, Sam M. Walton College of Business Administration, Department of Information Systems, Fayetteville, AR 72701. Offers MIS. *Program availability:* Part-time, evening/weekend. In 2017, 25 master's awarded. *Entrance requirements:* For master's, GMAT. *Application deadline:* For fall admission, 8/1 for domestic students, 4/1 for international students; for spring admission, 12/1 for domestic students, 10/1 for international students; for summer admission, 4/15 for domestic students, 3/1 for international students. Application fee: $60. Electronic applications accepted. *Expenses:* Tuition, state resident: full-time $3782. Tuition, nonresident: full-time $10,238. *Financial support:* In 2017–18, 18 research assistantships, 7 teaching assistantships were awarded; fellowships with tuition reimbursements also available. Financial award application deadline: 4/1. *Unit head:* Dr. Rajiv Sabherwal, Department Chair, 479-575-2216, E-mail: rsabherwal@walton.uark.edu.
Website: https://information-systems.uark.edu/

University of Arkansas at Little Rock, Graduate School, College of Business, Little Rock, AR 72204-1099. Offers business administration (MBA); business information systems (MS, Graduate Certificate); management (Graduate Certificate). *Accreditation:* AACSB. *Program availability:* Part-time, evening/weekend. *Entrance requirements:* For master's, GMAT, minimum undergraduate GPA of 2.7. Additional exam requirements/recommendations for international students: Required—TOEFL (minimum score 525 paper-based).

University of Baltimore, Graduate School, Merrick School of Business, Department of Accounting, Baltimore, MD 21201-5779. Offers accounting and business advisory services (MS); accounting fundamentals (Graduate Certificate); forensic accounting

(Graduate Certificate); taxation (MS). *Program availability:* Part-time, evening/weekend. *Entrance requirements:* For master's, GMAT. Additional exam requirements/recommendations for international students: Required—TOEFL (minimum score 550 paper-based). Electronic applications accepted. *Faculty research:* Health care, accounting and administration, managerial accounting, financial accounting theory, accounting information.

University of Baltimore, Graduate School, Merrick School of Business, Department of Information Systems and Decision Science, Baltimore, MD 21201-5779. Offers accounting and business advisory services (MS).

University of Bridgeport, School of Business, Bridgeport, CT 06604. Offers accounting (MBA); finance (MBA); general business (MBA); global financial services (MBA); human resource management (MBA); information systems and knowledge management (MBA); international business (MBA); management (MBA); marketing (MBA); operations management (MBA); small business and entrepreneurship (MBA); specialized business (MBA). *Accreditation:* ACBSP. *Program availability:* Part-time, evening/weekend. *Degree requirements:* For master's, thesis optional. *Entrance requirements:* For master's, GMAT. Additional exam requirements/recommendations for international students: Recommended—TOEFL (minimum score 550 paper-based; 80 iBT), IELTS (minimum score 6.5). Electronic applications accepted. *Expenses:* Contact institution.

The University of British Columbia, Sauder School of Business, Doctoral Program in Business Administration, Vancouver, BC V6T 1Z2, Canada. Offers accounting (PhD); finance (PhD); management information systems (PhD); management science (PhD); marketing (PhD); organizational behavior (PhD); strategy and business economics (PhD); transportation and logistics (PhD); urban land economics (PhD). *Degree requirements:* For doctorate, comprehensive exam, thesis/dissertation. *Entrance requirements:* For doctorate, GMAT or GRE. Additional exam requirements/recommendations for international students: Required—TOEFL (minimum score 600 paper-based; 100 iBT). Electronic applications accepted. *Expenses:* Contact institution.

University of California, Berkeley, Graduate Division, School of Information, Program in Information Management and Systems, Berkeley, CA 94720-1500. Offers MIMS, PhD. Electronic applications accepted.

University of California, Berkeley, UC Berkeley Extension, Certificate Programs in Computer Technology and Information Management, Berkeley, CA 94720-1500. Offers information systems and management (Postbaccalaureate Certificate); UNIX/LINUX system administration (Certificate). *Program availability:* Online learning.

University of California, Santa Cruz, Jack Baskin School of Engineering, Department of Technology Management, Santa Cruz, CA 95064. Offers PhD. Terminal master's awarded for partial completion of doctoral program. *Degree requirements:* For doctorate, thesis/dissertation, 2 seminars. *Entrance requirements:* For doctorate, GRE General Test; GRE Subject Test preferably in computer science, engineering, physics, or mathematics (highly recommended). Additional exam requirements/recommendations for international students: Required—TOEFL (minimum score 570 paper-based; 89 iBT); Recommended—IELTS (minimum score 8). Electronic applications accepted. *Faculty research:* Integration of information systems, technology, and business management.

University of Central Missouri, The Graduate School, Warrensburg, MO 64093. Offers accountancy (MA); accounting (MBA); applied mathematics (MS); aviation safety (MA); biology (MS); business administration (MBA); career and technical education leadership (MS); college student personnel administration (MS); communication (MA); computer science (MS); counseling (MS); criminal justice (MS); educational leadership (Ed D); educational technology (MS); elementary and early childhood education (MSE); English (MA); environmental studies (MA); finance (MBA); history (MA); human services/educational technology (Ed S); human services/learning resources (Ed S); human services/professional counseling (Ed S); industrial hygiene (MS); industrial management (MS); information systems (MBA); information technology (MS); kinesiology (MS); library science and information services (MS); literacy education (MSE); marketing (MBA); mathematics (MS); music (MA); occupational safety management (MS); psychology (MS); rural family nursing (MS); school administration (MSE); social gerontology (MS); sociology (MA); special education (MSE); speech language pathology (MS); superintendency (Ed S); teaching (MAT); teaching English as a second language (MA); technology (MS); technology management (PhD); theatre (MA). *Program availability:* Part-time, 100% online, blended/hybrid learning. *Faculty:* 337 full-time (145 women), 41 part-time/adjunct (28 women). *Students:* 785 full-time (398 women), 1,633 part-time (1,063 women); includes 231 minority (102 Black or African American, non-Hispanic/Latino; 4 American Indian or Alaska Native, non-Hispanic/Latino; 16 Asian, non-Hispanic/Latino; 52 Hispanic/Latino; 57 Two or more races, non-Hispanic/Latino), 692 international. Average age 30. In 2017, 2,605 master's, 122 other advanced degrees awarded. *Degree requirements:* For master's and Ed S, comprehensive exam (for some programs), thesis (for some programs). *Entrance requirements:* Additional exam requirements/recommendations for international students: Required—TOEFL (minimum score 550 paper-based; 79 iBT). *Application deadline:* For fall admission, 6/1 priority date for domestic and international students; for spring admission, 10/1 priority date for domestic and international students; for summer admission, 4/1 priority date for domestic and international students. Applications are processed on a rolling basis. Application fee: $30 ($75 for international students). Electronic applications accepted. *Expenses:* Tuition, state resident: full-time $8771; part-time $292.35 per credit hour. Tuition, nonresident: full-time $17,541; part-time $584.70 per credit hour. *Required fees:* $372; $24.78 per credit hour. *Financial support:* In 2017–18, 99 students received support. Research assistantships, teaching assistantships, career-related internships or fieldwork, Federal Work-Study, scholarships/grants, and administrative and laboratory assistantships available. Support available to part-time students. Financial award application deadline: 3/1; financial award applicants required to submit FAFSA. *Unit head:* Shellie Hewitt, Director of Graduate and International Student Services, 660-543-4621, Fax: 660-543-4778, E-mail: hewitt@ucmo.edu. *Application contact:* 660-543-4621, E-mail: admit_intl@ucmo.edu.
Website: http://www.ucmo.edu/graduate/

University of Cincinnati, Carl H. Lindner College of Business, MS Program, Cincinnati, OH 45221. Offers accounting (MS); applied economics (MS); business analytics (MS); finance (MS); information systems (MS); marketing (MS); taxation (MS). *Program availability:* Part-time, evening/weekend. *Faculty:* 65 full-time (20 women), 27 part-time/adjunct (6 women). *Students:* 324 full-time (132 women), 204 part-time (77 women); includes 50 minority (18 Black or African American, non-Hispanic/Latino; 21 Asian, non-Hispanic/Latino; 5 Hispanic/Latino; 1 Native Hawaiian or other Pacific Islander, non-Hispanic/Latino; 5 Two or more races, non-Hispanic/Latino), 299 international. Average age 28. 1,756 applicants, 24% accepted, 351 enrolled. In 2017, 369 master's awarded. *Degree requirements:* For master's, thesis (for some programs), capstone. *Entrance requirements:* For master's, GMAT, GRE, resume, transcripts, essays, letters of recommendation. Additional exam requirements/recommendations for international students: Required—TOEFL (minimum score 577 paper-based; 90 iBT), IELTS (minimum score 6.5). *Application deadline:* For fall admission, 6/30 priority date for domestic students, 3/15 for international students; for spring admission, 12/15 for domestic students, 9/15 for international students; for summer admission, 4/15 for domestic and international students. Applications are processed on a rolling basis.

Management Information Systems

Application fee: $65 ($70 for international students). Electronic applications accepted. *Expenses:* $10,479 per term full-time resident, $14,398 per term full-time nonresident, $890 per credit hour part-time. *Financial support:* In 2017–18, 251 students received support, including 12 teaching assistantships with full and partial tuition reimbursements available (averaging $3,500 per year); scholarships/grants, tuition waivers (full and partial), and unspecified assistantships also available. Financial award application deadline: 2/1; financial award applicants required to submit FAFSA. *Faculty research:* Business analytics, financial management, organizational behavior, financial accounting, consumer insights. *Total annual research expenditures:* $24,842. *Unit head:* Dr. David Szymanski, Dean, 513-556-7001, Fax: 513-556-4891, E-mail: david.szymanski@uc.edu. *Application contact:* Dona Clary, Executive Director, Graduate Programs, 513-556-3546, Fax: 513-558-7006, E-mail: dona.clary@uc.edu. Website: http://business.uc.edu/graduate/masters.html

University of Cincinnati, Carl H. Lindner College of Business, PhD Programs, Cincinnati, OH 45221. Offers accounting (PhD); business analytics (PhD); economics (PhD); finance (PhD); information systems (PhD); management (PhD); marketing (PhD); operations and business analytics (PhD); operations research (PhD). *Faculty:* 37 full-time (13 women). *Students:* 29 full-time (12 women), 12 part-time (6 women); includes 5 minority (1 Black or African American, non-Hispanic/Latino; 4 Asian, non-Hispanic/Latino), 20 international. Average age 30. 123 applicants, 16% accepted, 11 enrolled. In 2017, 5 doctorates awarded. *Degree requirements:* For doctorate, comprehensive exam, thesis/dissertation. *Entrance requirements:* For doctorate, GMAT, GRE, transcripts, essays, resume, letters of recommendation. Additional exam requirements/recommendations for international students: Required—TOEFL (minimum score 600 paper-based; 100 iBT), IELTS (minimum score 7). *Application deadline:* For fall admission, 1/15 for domestic and international students. Application fee: $65 ($70 for international students). Electronic applications accepted. *Expenses:* $7,234 resident per term, $13,105 nonresident per term. *Financial support:* In 2017–18, 41 students received support, including 29 research assistantships with full tuition reimbursements available (averaging $23,250 per year); scholarships/grants, health care benefits, tuition waivers (full), and unspecified assistantships also available. Financial award application deadline: 1/15; financial award applicants required to submit FAFSA. *Faculty research:* Bayesian Prediction Theory, organizational fairness, consumer insight and market research, consumer insight and market research, density estimation from correlated data. *Unit head:* Dr. Suzanne Masterson, Director, 513-556-7125, Fax: 513-556-5499, E-mail: suzanne.masterson@uc.edu. *Application contact:* Angel Elvin, Assistant Director, 513-556-7190, Fax: 513-558-7006, E-mail: angel.elvin@uc.edu. Website: http://business.uc.edu/graduate/phd.html

University of Colorado Denver, Business School, Program in Computer Science and Information Systems, Denver, CO 80217. Offers PhD. *Degree requirements:* For doctorate, comprehensive exam, thesis/dissertation. *Entrance requirements:* For doctorate, GMAT or GRE General Test, letters of recommendation, portfolio, essay describing applicant's motivation and initial plan for doctoral study, resume. Additional exam requirements/recommendations for international students: Required—TOEFL (minimum score 525 paper-based; 71 iBT); Recommended—IELTS (minimum score 6.5). Electronic applications accepted. *Expenses:* Contact institution. *Faculty research:* Design science of information systems, information system economics, organizational impacts of information technology, high performance parallel and distributed systems, performance measurement and prediction.

University of Colorado Denver, Business School, Program in Information Systems, Denver, CO 80217. Offers accounting and information systems audit and control (MS); business intelligence systems (MS); digital health entrepreneurship (MS); enterprise risk management (MS); enterprise technology management (MS); geographic information systems (MS); health information technology (MS); technology innovation and entrepreneurship (MS); Web and mobile computing (MS). *Program availability:* Part-time, evening/weekend, online learning. *Degree requirements:* For master's, 30 credit hours. *Entrance requirements:* For master's, GMAT, resume, essay, two letters of recommendation, financial statements (for international applicants). Additional exam requirements/recommendations for international students: Required—TOEFL (minimum score 525 paper-based; 71 iBT); Recommended—IELTS (minimum score 6.5). Electronic applications accepted. *Expenses:* Contact institution. *Faculty research:* Human-computer interaction, expert systems, database management, electronic commerce, object-oriented software development.

University of Dallas, Satish and Yasmin Gupta College of Business, Irving, TX 75062-4736. Offers accounting (MBA, MS); business administration (DBA); business analytics (MS); business management (MBA); corporate finance (MBA); cybersecurity (MS); finance (MS); financial services (MBA); global business (MBA, MS); health services management (MBA); human resource management (MBA); information and technology management (MS); information assurance (MBA); information technology (MBA); information technology service management (MBA); marketing management (MBA); organization development (MBA); project management (MBA); sports and entertainment management (MBA); strategic leadership (MBA); supply chain management (MBA). *Accreditation:* AACSB. *Program availability:* Part-time, evening/weekend, online learning. *Entrance requirements:* Additional exam requirements/recommendations for international students: Required—TOEFL. *Application deadline:* Applications are processed on a rolling basis. Application fee: $50. Electronic applications accepted. *Expenses:* Contact institution. *Financial support:* Application deadline: 2/15; applicants required to submit FAFSA. *Unit head:* Brett J.L. Landry, Dean, 972-721-5356, E-mail: blandry@udallas.edu. *Application contact:* Dr. David Sweet, Dean, Braniff Graduate School, 972-721-5288, Fax: 972-721-5280, E-mail: dsweet@udallas.edu. Website: http://www.udallas.edu/cob/

University of Delaware, Alfred Lerner College of Business and Economics, Department of Accounting and Management Information Systems and Department of Electrical and Computer Engineering, Program in Information Systems and Technology Management, Newark, DE 19716. Offers MS. *Program availability:* Part-time, evening/weekend. *Entrance requirements:* For master's, GRE or GMAT, 2 letters of recommendation, resume, minimum GPA of 2.75. Additional exam requirements/recommendations for international students: Required—TOEFL (minimum score 600 paper-based). *Faculty research:* Security, developer trust, XML.

University of Delaware, Alfred Lerner College of Business and Economics, Program in Financial Service Analytics, Newark, DE 19716. Offers PhD. Program admits students every other year.

University of Detroit Mercy, College of Liberal Arts and Education, Detroit, MI 48221. Offers addiction counseling (MA); addiction studies (Certificate); clinical mental health counseling (MA); clinical psychology (MA, PhD); computer and information systems (MS); criminal justice (MA); curriculum and instruction (MA); economics (MA); educational administration (MA); financial economics (MA); industrial/organizational psychology (MA); information assurance (MS); intelligence analysis (MA); liberal studies (MALS); religious studies (MA); school counseling (MA, Certificate); school psychology (Spec); security administration (MS); special education: emotionally impaired/behaviorally disordered (MA); special education: learning disabilities (MA). *Program availability:* Part-time, evening/weekend. *Degree requirements:* For doctorate,

departmental qualifying exam. *Faculty research:* Psychology of aging, history of technology, Renaissance humanism, U.S. and Japanese economic relations.

University of Florida, Graduate School, Warrington College of Business Administration, Hough Graduate School of Business, Department of Information Systems and Operations Management, Gainesville, FL 32611. Offers information systems and operations management (PhD); supply chain management (Certificate). Terminal master's awarded for partial completion of doctoral program. *Degree requirements:* For doctorate, thesis/dissertation. *Entrance requirements:* For master's, GMAT or GRE General Test, minimum GPA of 3.0; for doctorate, GMAT (minimum score 650) or GRE General Test, minimum GPA of 3.0. Additional exam requirements/recommendations for international students: Required—TOEFL (minimum score 550 paper-based; 80 iBT), IELTS (minimum score 6). *Faculty research:* Expert systems, nonconvex optimization, manufacturing management, production and operation management, telecommunication.

University of Florida, Graduate School, Warrington College of Business Administration, Hough Graduate School of Business, Programs in Business Administration, Gainesville, FL 32611. Offers business administration (MA, MS, PhD); competitive strategy (MBA); finance (MBA); global management (MBA); Graham-Buffett security analysis (MBA); human resource management (MBA); information systems and operations management (MBA); international studies (MBA); management (MBA); real estate (MBA); JD/MBA; MBA/MS; MBA/PhD; MBA/Pharm D; MD/MBA. *Accreditation:* AACSB. *Program availability:* Part-time, evening/weekend, online learning. *Degree requirements:* For master's, capstone course. *Entrance requirements:* For master's and doctorate, GMAT (minimum score 465), minimum GPA of 3.0, interview. Additional exam requirements/recommendations for international students: Required—TOEFL (minimum score 550 paper-based; 80 iBT), IELTS (minimum score 6). Electronic applications accepted. *Faculty research:* Accounting, finance, insurance, management, real estate, urban analysis marketing.

University of Hawaii at Manoa, Office of Graduate Education, College of Social Sciences, School of Communications, Program in Telecommunication and Information Resource Management, Honolulu, HI 96822. Offers Graduate Certificate. *Program availability:* Part-time. *Entrance requirements:* Additional exam requirements/recommendations for international students: Required—TOEFL (minimum score 500 paper-based; 61 iBT), IELTS (minimum score 5).

University of Hawaii at Manoa, Office of Graduate Education, Shidler College of Business, Program in Accounting, Honolulu, HI 96822. Offers accounting (M Acc); accounting law (M Acc); information systems (M Acc); taxation (M Acc). *Program availability:* Part-time. *Entrance requirements:* For master's, GMAT, bachelor's degree in accounting, minimum GPA of 3.0. Additional exam requirements/recommendations for international students: Required—TOEFL (minimum score 550 paper-based; 79 iBT), IELTS (minimum score 5). *Faculty research:* International accounting, current tax topics, insurance industry financial reporting, behavioral accounting, auditing.

University of Hawaii at Manoa, Office of Graduate Education, Shidler College of Business, Program in Business Administration, Honolulu, HI 96822. Offers Asian business studies (MBA); Chinese business studies (MBA); decision sciences (MBA); entrepreneurship (MBA); finance (MBA); finance and banking (MBA); human resources management (MBA); information management (MBA); information technology (MBA); international business (MBA); Japanese business studies (MBA); marketing (MBA); organizational behavior (MBA); organizational management (MBA); real estate (MBA); student-designed track (MBA). *Accreditation:* AACSB. *Program availability:* Part-time, evening/weekend. *Degree requirements:* For master's, thesis optional. *Entrance requirements:* For master's, GMAT, minimum GPA of 3.0. Additional exam requirements/recommendations for international students: Required—TOEFL (minimum score 600 paper-based; 100 iBT), IELTS (minimum score 7). *Expenses:* Contact institution.

University of Hawaii at Manoa, Office of Graduate Education, Shidler College of Business, Program in International Management, Honolulu, HI 96822. Offers Asian finance (PhD); global information technology management (PhD); international accounting (PhD); international marketing (PhD); international organization and strategy (PhD). *Program availability:* Part-time. *Degree requirements:* For doctorate, comprehensive exam, thesis/dissertation. *Entrance requirements:* For doctorate, GMAT or GRE General Test, minimum GPA of 3.0. Additional exam requirements/recommendations for international students: Required—TOEFL (minimum score 600 paper-based; 100 iBT), IELTS (minimum score 7). *Expenses:* Contact institution.

University of Houston–Clear Lake, School of Business, Program in Management Information Systems, Houston, TX 77058-1002. Offers MS. *Program availability:* Part-time. *Entrance requirements:* For master's, GMAT. Additional exam requirements/recommendations for international students: Required—TOEFL (minimum score 550 paper-based).

University of Houston–Victoria, School of Arts and Sciences, Department of Computer Science, Victoria, TX 77901-4450. Offers computer information systems (MS); computer science (MS). *Program availability:* Part-time, evening/weekend, online learning. *Degree requirements:* For master's, comprehensive exam (for some programs), thesis (for some programs). *Entrance requirements:* For master's, GRE. Additional exam requirements/recommendations for international students: Required—TOEFL (minimum score 550 paper-based).

University of Illinois at Chicago, Liautaud Graduate School of Business, Department of Information and Decision Sciences, Chicago, IL 60607-7128. Offers management information systems (PhD). *Program availability:* Part-time, evening/weekend. *Degree requirements:* For doctorate, thesis/dissertation. *Entrance requirements:* For doctorate, GMAT, minimum GPA of 2.75. Additional exam requirements/recommendations for international students: Required—TOEFL. Electronic applications accepted. *Expenses:* Contact institution. *Faculty research:* Information management/technology and innovation, data and analytics, health informatics, risk management, business statistics and forecasting.

University of Illinois at Springfield, Graduate Programs, College of Business and Management, Program in Management Information Systems, Springfield, IL 62703-5407. Offers MS. *Program availability:* Part-time, evening/weekend, 100% online, blended/hybrid learning. *Faculty:* 10 full-time (2 women), 4 part-time/adjunct (2 women). *Students:* 121 full-time (50 women), 142 part-time (50 women); includes 47 minority (19 Black or African American, non-Hispanic/Latino; 15 Asian, non-Hispanic/Latino; 10 Hispanic/Latino; 3 Two or more races, non-Hispanic/Latino), 150 international. Average age 30. 402 applicants, 30% accepted, 52 enrolled. In 2017, 224 master's awarded. *Degree requirements:* For master's, thesis or alternative, thesis or closure seminar. *Entrance requirements:* For master's, GMAT or GRE General Test, courses in managerial and financial accounting, production/operations management, statistics, linear algebra or mathematics; competency in a structured, high-level programming language; minimum undergraduate GPA of 2.75. Additional exam requirements/recommendations for international students: Required—TOEFL (minimum score 550 paper-based; 61 iBT). *Application deadline:* Applications are processed on a rolling basis. Application fee: $60 ($75 for international students). Electronic applications accepted. *Expenses:* Contact institution. *Financial support:* In 2017–18, research assistantships with full tuition reimbursements (averaging $10,249 per year), teaching assistantships with full tuition reimbursements (averaging $10,303 per year) were awarded; fellowships, career-related internships or fieldwork, Federal Work-Study, scholarships/grants, health care benefits, and unspecified assistantships also available. Support available to part-time students. Financial award application deadline: 11/15; financial award applicants required to submit FAFSA. *Unit head:* Dr. Rassule Hadidi, Program Administrator, 217-206-6067, Fax: 217-206-7541, E-mail: rhadi1@uis.edu.

University of Illinois at Urbana–Champaign, Graduate College, School of Information Sciences, Champaign, IL 61820. Offers bioinformatics (MS); digital libraries (CAS); information management (MS); library and information science (MS, PhD, CAS). *Accreditation:* ALA (one or more programs are accredited). *Program availability:* Part-time, online learning. *Entrance requirements:* For degree, master's degree in library and information science or related field with minimum GPA of 3.0.

The University of Kansas, Graduate Studies, School of Engineering, Program in Information Technology, Lawrence, KS 66045. Offers MS. *Program availability:* Part-time, evening/weekend. *Students:* 3 full-time (all women), 16 part-time (2 women); includes 8 minority (6 Black or African American, non-Hispanic/Latino; 2 Asian, non-Hispanic/Latino), 2 international. Average age 38. 25 applicants, 60% accepted, 6 enrolled. In 2017, 3 master's awarded. *Entrance requirements:* For master's, GRE, official transcript, three recommendations, statement of academic objectives, resume. Additional exam requirements/recommendations for international students: Required—TOEFL (minimum score 600 paper-based; 100 iBT), IELTS (minimum score 6). *Application deadline:* For fall admission, 8/1 for domestic and international students; for spring admission, 1/1 for domestic and international students. Application fee: $65 ($85 for international students). Electronic applications accepted. *Faculty research:* Information security and privacy, game theory, graph theory, software process improvement, resilient and survivable networks, object orientation technology. *Unit head:* James Stiles, Associate Chair for Graduate Studies, 785-864-8803, E-mail: jstiles@eecs.ku.edu. *Application contact:* Pam Shadoin, Assistant to Graduate Director, 785-864-4487, Fax: 785-864-3226, E-mail: eecs_graduate@ku.edu. Website: http://eecs.ku.edu/prospective_students/graduate/masters#information_technology

University of La Verne, College of Business and Public Management, Graduate Programs in Business Administration, La Verne, CA 91750-4443. Offers accounting (MBA, MBA-EP); finance (MBA, MBA-EP); health services management (MBA); information technology (MBA, MBA-EP); international business (MBA, MBA-EP); management and leadership (MBA, MBA-EP); marketing (MBA, MBA-EP); supply chain management (MBA, MBA-EP). *Program availability:* Part-time, evening/weekend. *Faculty:* 24 full-time (11 women), 25 part-time/adjunct (6 women). *Students:* 390 full-time (193 women), 93 part-time (48 women); includes 96 minority (7 Black or African American, non-Hispanic/Latino; 1 American Indian or Alaska Native, non-Hispanic/Latino; 17 Asian, non-Hispanic/Latino; 67 Hispanic/Latino; 1 Native Hawaiian or other Pacific Islander, non-Hispanic/Latino; 3 Two or more races, non-Hispanic/Latino), 336 international. Average age 28. *Entrance requirements:* For master's, GMAT, MAT, or GRE, minimum undergraduate GPA of 3.0, 2 letters of recommendation, resume, statement of purpose. Additional exam requirements/recommendations for international students: Required—TOEFL (minimum score 550 paper-based; 85 iBT). *Application deadline:* Applications are processed on a rolling basis. Application fee: $50. Tuition and fees vary according to program. *Financial support:* Institutionally sponsored loans and scholarships/grants available. Financial award application deadline: 3/2; financial award applicants required to submit FAFSA. *Unit head:* Dr. Abe Helou, Chairperson, 909-448-4455, Fax: 909-392-2704, E-mail: ihelou@laverne.edu. *Application contact:* Rina Lazarian-Chehab, Senior Associate Director of Graduate Admissions, 909-448-4317, Fax: 909-971-2295, E-mail: rlazarian@laverne.edu. Website: https://business.laverne.edu/mba/

University of La Verne, Regional and Online Campuses, Graduate Programs, Central Coast/Vandenberg Air Force Base Campuses, La Verne, CA 91750-4443. Offers business administration for experienced professionals (MBA), including health services management, information technology; leadership and management (MS). *Program availability:* Part-time. *Students:* 6 full-time (1 woman), 37 part-time (20 women); includes 9 minority (1 Asian, non-Hispanic/Latino; 8 Hispanic/Latino). Average age 40. In 2017, 20 master's awarded. *Application deadline:* Applications are processed on a rolling basis. Application fee: $50. *Expenses:* Contact institution. *Financial support:* Application deadline: 3/2; applicants required to submit FAFSA. *Unit head:* Kitt Vincent, Director, Vandenberg AFB, 805-788-6202, Fax: 805-788-6201, E-mail: kvincent@laverne.edu. *Application contact:* Admissions, 805-734-6220, Fax: 805-734-6221, E-mail: vafb@laverne.edu. Website: http://www.laverne.edu/locations

University of La Verne, Regional and Online Campuses, Graduate Programs, Inland Empire Campus, Ontario, CA 91730. Offers business administration (MBA, MBA-EP), including accounting (MBA), finance (MBA), health services management (MBA-EP), information technology (MBA-EP), international business (MBA), managed care (MBA), management and leadership (MBA-EP), marketing (MBA-EP), supply chain management (MBA); leadership and management (MS), including human resource management, nonprofit management, organizational development. *Program availability:* Part-time, evening/weekend. *Faculty:* 5 part-time/adjunct (1 woman). *Students:* 24 full-time (13 women), 72 part-time (44 women); includes 64 minority (12 Black or African American, non-Hispanic/Latino; 13 Asian, non-Hispanic/Latino; 36 Hispanic/Latino; 3 Two or more races, non-Hispanic/Latino). Average age 38. In 2017, 42 master's awarded. *Application deadline:* Applications are processed on a rolling basis. Application fee: $50. *Expenses:* Contact institution. *Financial support:* Application deadline: 3/2; applicants required to submit FAFSA. *Unit head:* Juli Roberts, Campus Director, Inland Empire Regional Campus in Ontario, 760-955-6448, E-mail: jroberts@laverne.edu. *Application contact:* Admissions, 877-468-6858, E-mail: gradadmission@laverne.edu. Website: https://laverne.edu/locations/

University of Lethbridge, School of Graduate Studies, Lethbridge, AB T1K 3M4, Canada. Offers addictions counseling (M Sc); agricultural biotechnology (M Sc); agricultural studies (M Sc, MA); anthropology (MA); archaeology (M Sc, MA); art (MA, MFA); biochemistry (M Sc); biological sciences (M Sc); biomolecular science (PhD); biosystems and biodiversity (PhD); Canadian studies (MA); chemistry (M Sc); computer science (M Sc); computer science and geographical information science (M Sc); counseling (MC); counseling psychology (M Ed); dramatic arts (MA); earth, space, and physical science (PhD); economics (MA); education (MA, PhD); educational leadership (M Ed); English (MA); environmental science (M Sc); evolution and behavior (PhD); exercise science (M Sc); French (MA); French/German (MA); French/Spanish (MA); general education (M Ed); geography (M Sc, MA); German (MA); health sciences (M Sc); individualized multidisciplinary (M Sc, MA); kinesiology (M Sc, MA); management (M Sc), including accounting, finance, human resource management and labor relations, information systems, international management, marketing, policy and strategy; mathematics (M Sc); music (M Mus, MA); Native American studies (MA); neuroscience (M Sc, PhD); new media (MA, MFA); nursing (M Sc, MN); philosophy (MA); physics (M Sc); political science (MA); psychology (M Sc, MA); religious studies

(MA); sociology (MA); theatre and dramatic arts (MFA); theoretical and computational science (PhD); urban and regional studies (MA); women and gender studies (MA). *Program availability:* Part-time, evening/weekend. *Degree requirements:* For master's, thesis (for some programs); for doctorate, comprehensive exam, thesis/dissertation. *Entrance requirements:* For master's, GMAT (for M Sc in management), bachelor's degree in related field, minimum GPA of 3.0 during previous 20 graded semester courses, 2 years' teaching or related experience (M Ed); for doctorate, master's degree, minimum graduate GPA of 3.5. Additional exam requirements/recommendations for international students: Required—TOEFL (minimum score 580 paper-based; 93 iBT). Electronic applications accepted. *Faculty research:* Movement and brain plasticity, gibberellin physiology, photosynthesis, carbon cycling, molecular properties of main-group ring components.

University of Management and Technology, Program in Information Technology, Arlington, VA 22209-1609. Offers MS, Advanced Certificate.

University of Mary Hardin-Baylor, Graduate Studies in Business Administration, Belton, TX 76513. Offers accounting (MBA); information systems management (MBA); international business (MBA); management (MBA). *Program availability:* Part-time, evening/weekend. *Faculty:* 12 full-time (5 women), 6 part-time/adjunct (4 women). *Students:* 16 full-time (10 women), 39 part-time (16 women); includes 15 minority (3 Black or African American, non-Hispanic/Latino; 1 Asian, non-Hispanic/Latino; 10 Hispanic/Latino; 1 Two or more races, non-Hispanic/Latino), 10 international. Average age 30. 72 applicants, 81% accepted, 16 enrolled. In 2017, 34 master's awarded. *Degree requirements:* For master's, comprehensive exam. *Entrance requirements:* For master's, minimum GPA of 3.0, interview. Additional exam requirements/recommendations for international students: Required—TOEFL (minimum score 60 iBT), IELTS (minimum score 4.5). *Application deadline:* For fall admission, 6/1 for domestic students, 4/30 priority date for international students; for spring admission, 11/1 for domestic students, 9/30 priority date for international students. Applications are processed on a rolling basis. Application fee: $35 ($135 for international students). Electronic applications accepted. *Expenses:* Tuition: Full-time $15,570; part-time $10,380 per credit hour. *Required fees:* $1350; $75 per credit hour. $50 per term. Tuition and fees vary according to course load and degree level. *Financial support:* In 2017–18, 32 students received support. Federal Work-Study, institutionally sponsored loans, unspecified assistantships, and scholarships for some active duty military personnel available. Support available to part-time students. Financial award applicants required to submit FAFSA. *Faculty research:* Financial management, financial markets, supply chain management. *Unit head:* Dr. Kirk Fischer, Assistant Dean, Graduate Programs in McLane College of Business, 254-295-4655, E-mail: kfischer@umhb.edu. *Application contact:* Sharon Aguilera, Assistant Director, Graduate Admissions, 254-295-4835, E-mail: saguilera@umhb.edu. Website: http://www.graduate.umhb.edu/mba

University of Mary Hardin-Baylor, Graduate Studies in Information Systems, Belton, TX 76513. Offers MS. *Program availability:* Part-time, evening/weekend. *Faculty:* 5 full-time (1 woman), 2 part-time/adjunct (0 women). *Students:* 94 full-time (26 women), 23 part-time (5 women); includes 2 minority (1 Asian, non-Hispanic/Latino; 1 Hispanic/Latino), 113 international. Average age 24. 225 applicants, 98% accepted, 11 enrolled. In 2017, 131 master's awarded. *Degree requirements:* For master's, comprehensive exam. *Entrance requirements:* For master's, minimum GPA of 3.0, interview. Additional exam requirements/recommendations for international students: Required—TOEFL (minimum score 60 iBT), IELTS (minimum score 4.5). *Application deadline:* For fall admission, 6/1 for domestic students, 4/30 priority date for international students; for spring admission, 11/1 for domestic students, 9/30 priority date for international students. Applications are processed on a rolling basis. Application fee: $35 ($135 for international students). Electronic applications accepted. *Expenses:* Tuition: Full-time $15,570; part-time $10,380 per credit hour. *Required fees:* $1350; $75 per credit hour. $50 per term. Tuition and fees vary according to course load and degree level. *Financial support:* In 2017–18, 106 students received support. Federal Work-Study, unspecified assistantships, and scholarships for some active duty military personnel available. Support available to part-time students. Financial award applicants required to submit FAFSA. *Faculty research:* Sports statistical use, faith in the technology arena, ERP implementations. *Unit head:* Dr. Kirk Fischer, Associate Dean, Graduate Programs in McLane College of Business, 254-295-4655, E-mail: kfischer@umhb.edu. *Application contact:* Sharon Aguilera, Assistant Director, Graduate Admissions, 254-295-4835, E-mail: saguilera@umhb.edu. Website: https://go.umhb.edu/graduate/information-systems/home

University of Massachusetts Boston, College of Management, Program in Information Technology, Boston, MA 02125-3393. Offers MS. *Students:* 24 full-time (12 women), 22 part-time (10 women); includes 8 minority (4 Black or African American, non-Hispanic/Latino; 4 Asian, non-Hispanic/Latino), 29 international. Average age 30. 56 applicants, 48% accepted, 10 enrolled. In 2017, 20 master's awarded. *Expenses:* Tuition, state resident: full-time $17,375. Tuition, nonresident: full-time $33,915. *Required fees:* $355. *Unit head:* Dr. Jorge Haddock, Dean, 617-287-7702. *Application contact:* Graduate Admissions Coordinator, 617-287-6400, Fax: 617-287-6236, E-mail: bos.gadm@dpc.umassp.edu.

University of Memphis, Graduate School, Fogelman College of Business and Economics, Department of Business Information and Technology, Memphis, TN 38152. Offers MS, PhD, Graduate Certificate. *Students:* 20 applicants, 100% accepted, 8 enrolled. In 2017, 70 other advanced degrees awarded. *Financial support:* In 2017–18, 12 research assistantships (averaging $20,500 per year), 1 teaching assistantship (averaging $9,000 per year) were awarded. *Unit head:* Robin Poston, Chair, 901-678-5739, E-mail: rposton@memphis.edu. *Application contact:* Dr. Lloyd Brooks, Associate Dean, 901-678-4620, Fax: 901-678-3759, E-mail: lbrooks@memphis.edu. Website: http://www.memphis.edu/bitm/

University of Michigan–Dearborn, College of Business, MS Program in Information Systems, Dearborn, MI 48126. Offers MS. *Program availability:* Part-time, evening/weekend. *Faculty:* 45 full-time (19 women), 4 part-time/adjunct (2 women). *Students:* 4 full-time (1 woman), 19 part-time (5 women); includes 4 minority (1 Black or African American, non-Hispanic/Latino; 3 Asian, non-Hispanic/Latino), 4 international. Average age 30. 49 applicants, 35% accepted, 6 enrolled. In 2017, 20 master's awarded. *Entrance requirements:* For master's, GRE or GMAT, equivalent of four-year U.S. bachelor's degree from regionally-accredited institution, undergraduate course in finite math, pre-calculus, or calculus. Additional exam requirements/recommendations for international students: Required—TOEFL (minimum score 560 paper-based; 84 iBT), IELTS (minimum score 6.5). *Application deadline:* For fall admission, 8/1 for domestic students, 5/1 for international students; for winter admission, 12/1 for domestic students, 9/1 for international students; for spring admission, 4/1 for domestic students, 1/1 for international students. Applications are processed on a rolling basis. Application fee: $60. Electronic applications accepted. *Expenses:* $883 per credit hour in-state; $1,376 per credit hour out-state. *Financial support:* In 2017–18, 12 students received support. Scholarships/grants and non-resident tuition scholarships available. Financial award application deadline: 3/1; financial award applicants required to submit FAFSA. *Faculty research:* Business intelligence, behavioral finance, brand management and new media, management education, operations strategy. *Unit head:* Dr. Michael Kamen, Director,

Management Information Systems

Graduate Programs, 313-593-5460, E-mail: mkamen@umich.edu. *Application contact:* Joan Doherty, Academic Advisor/Counselor, 313-593-5460, Fax: 313-271-9838, E-mail: umd-gradbusiness@umich.edu.
Website: http://umdearborn.edu/cob/ms-information-systems/

University of Michigan–Dearborn, College of Education, Health, and Human Services, Master of Science Program in Health Information Technology, Dearborn, MI 48126. Offers MS. *Program availability:* Part-time, evening/weekend. *Faculty:* 2 part-time/adjunct (1 woman). *Students:* 6 full-time (5 women), 21 part-time (18 women); includes 10 minority (5 Black or African American, non-Hispanic/Latino; 3 Asian, non-Hispanic/Latino; 1 Hispanic/Latino; 1 Two or more races, non-Hispanic/Latino), 4 international. Average age 31. 19 applicants, 63% accepted, 8 enrolled. In 2017, 5 master's awarded. *Entrance requirements:* Additional exam requirements/recommendations for international students: Required—TOEFL (minimum score 560 paper-based; 84 iBT), IELTS (minimum score 6.5). *Application deadline:* For fall admission, 8/1 for domestic students, 5/1 for international students; for winter admission, 12/1 for domestic students, 9/1 for international students; for spring admission, 4/1 for domestic students, 1/1 for international students. Applications are processed on a rolling basis. Application fee: $60. Electronic applications accepted. *Expenses:* $683 per credit hour in-state; $1,176 per credit hour out-state. *Financial support:* In 2017–18, 8 students received support. Career-related internships or fieldwork and scholarships/grants available. Financial award application deadline: 3/1; financial award applicants required to submit FAFSA. *Faculty research:* Race and health, urban education, data analysis, economics. *Unit head:* Dr. Stein Brunvand, Director, Master's Programs, 313-583-6415, E-mail: sbrunvan@umich.edu. *Application contact:* Office of Graduate Studies, 313-583-6321, E-mail: umd-graduatestudies@umich.edu.
Website: http://umdearborn.edu/cehhs/cehhs_m_hit/

University of Michigan–Dearborn, College of Engineering and Computer Science, MS Program in Information Systems and Technology, Dearborn, MI 48128. Offers MS. *Program availability:* Part-time, evening/weekend, 100% online. *Faculty:* 13 full-time (3 women), 4 part-time/adjunct (0 women). *Students:* 10 full-time (7 women), 45 part-time (14 women); includes 14 minority (6 Black or African American, non-Hispanic/Latino; 5 Asian, non-Hispanic/Latino; 3 Two or more races, non-Hispanic/Latino), 17 international. Average age 35. 36 applicants, 64% accepted, 10 enrolled. In 2017, 8 master's awarded. *Entrance requirements:* For master's, bachelor's degree in engineering, a physical science, computer science, applied mathematics, business administration, or liberal arts with minimum cumulative GPA of 3.0. Additional exam requirements/recommendations for international students: Required—TOEFL (minimum score 560 paper-based; 84 iBT), IELTS (minimum score 6.5). *Application deadline:* For fall admission, 8/1 for domestic students, 5/1 for international students; for winter admission, 12/1 for domestic students, 9/1 for international students; for spring admission, 4/1 for domestic students, 1/1 for international students. Applications are processed on a rolling basis. Application fee: $60. Electronic applications accepted. *Expenses:* Tuition, state resident: full-time $13,602; part-time $788 per credit hour. Tuition, nonresident: full-time $22,234; part-time $1281 per credit hour. *Required fees:* $754; $754 per year. $377 per term. Tuition and fees vary according to course load, degree level, program and reciprocity agreements. *Financial support:* In 2017–18, 16 students received support. Scholarships/grants, unspecified assistantships, and non-resident tuition scholarships available. Support available to part-time students. Financial award application deadline: 3/1; financial award applicants required to submit FAFSA. *Faculty research:* Information security, enterprise information systems, data analytics, quality assurance. *Unit head:* Dr. Armen Zakarian, Chair, 313-593-5361, E-mail: zakarian@umich.edu. *Application contact:* Office of Graduate Studies, 313-583-6321, E-mail: umd-graduatestudies@umich.edu.
Website: https://umdearborn.edu/cecs/departments/industrial-and-manufacturing-systems-engineering/graduate-programs/ms-information-systems-and-technology

University of Michigan–Flint, College of Arts and Sciences, Program in Computer Science and Information Systems, Flint, MI 48502-1950. Offers computer science (MS); information systems (MS), including business information systems, health information systems. *Program availability:* Part-time, evening/weekend, 100% online. *Faculty:* 16 full-time (4 women), 11 part-time/adjunct (6 women). *Students:* 30 full-time (15 women), 59 part-time (20 women); includes 20 minority (6 Black or African American, non-Hispanic/Latino; 2 Asian, non-Hispanic/Latino; 9 Hispanic/Latino; 1 Native Hawaiian or other Pacific Islander, non-Hispanic/Latino; 2 Two or more races, non-Hispanic/Latino), 44 international. Average age 29. 285 applicants, 52% accepted, 32 enrolled. In 2017, 98 master's awarded. *Degree requirements:* For master's, thesis optional. *Entrance requirements:* For master's, BS from regionally-accredited institution in computer science, computer information systems, or computer engineering (preferred); minimum overall undergraduate GPA of 3.0. Additional exam requirements/recommendations for international students: Required—TOEFL (minimum score 84 iBT), IELTS (minimum score 6.5). *Application deadline:* For fall admission, 8/1 for domestic students, 5/1 for international students; for winter admission, 11/15 for domestic students, 10/1 for international students; for spring admission, 3/15 for domestic students. Applications are processed on a rolling basis. Application fee: $55. Electronic applications accepted. *Expenses:* Contact institution. *Financial support:* Federal Work-Study, scholarships/grants, and unspecified assistantships available. Financial award application deadline: 3/1; financial award applicants required to submit FAFSA. *Faculty research:* Computer network systems, database management systems, artificial intelligence and controlled systems. *Unit head:* Dr. Jeffrey Livermore, Director, 810-762-3131, Fax: 810-766-6780, E-mail: jefflive@umflint.edu. *Application contact:* Bradley T. Maki, Director of Graduate Admissions, 810-762-3171, Fax: 810-766-6789, E-mail: bmaki@umflint.edu.
Website: http://www.umflint.edu/graduateprograms/computer-science-information-systems-ms

University of Michigan–Flint, School of Management, Program in Business Administration, Flint, MI 48502-1950. Offers accounting (MBA); computer information systems (MBA); finance (MBA, Post-Master's Certificate); general business (Graduate Certificate); general business administration (MBA); health care management (MBA); international business (MBA, Post-Master's Certificate); lean manufacturing (MBA); marketing (Post-Master's Certificate); marketing and innovation management (MBA); organizational leadership (MBA). *Program availability:* Part-time, evening/weekend, mixed mode format. *Faculty:* 32 full-time (5 women), 8 part-time/adjunct (2 women). *Students:* 12 full-time (7 women), 147 part-time (51 women); includes 31 minority (15 Black or African American, non-Hispanic/Latino; 1 American Indian or Alaska Native, non-Hispanic/Latino; 9 Asian, non-Hispanic/Latino; 5 Hispanic/Latino; 1 Two or more races, non-Hispanic/Latino), 18 international. Average age 34. 110 applicants, 52% accepted, 29 enrolled. In 2017, 59 master's, 6 other advanced degrees awarded. *Entrance requirements:* For master's, GMAT or GRE, bachelor's degree in arts, sciences, engineering, or business administration from regionally-accredited college or university with minimum GPA of 3.0; for other advanced degree, bachelor's degree in arts, sciences, engineering, or business administration from regionally-accredited college or university with minimum GPA of 3.0, college-level math, statistics, or quantitative course (for Graduate Certificate); MBA or equivalent degree from regionally-accredited college or university (for Post Master's Certificate). Additional exam requirements/recommendations for international students: Required—TOEFL (minimum score 84 iBT), IELTS (minimum score 6.5). *Application deadline:* For fall admission, 8/1

for domestic students, 5/1 for international students; for winter admission, 11/15 for domestic students, 9/1 for international students; for spring admission, 3/15 for domestic students, 1/1 for international students; for summer admission, 5/15 for domestic students. Applications are processed on a rolling basis. Application fee: $55. Electronic applications accepted. *Expenses:* Contact institution. *Financial support:* Federal Work-Study, scholarships/grants, and unspecified assistantships available. Support available to part-time students. Financial award application deadline: 3/1; financial award applicants required to submit FAFSA. *Unit head:* Dr. Scott Johnson, Dean, School of Management, 810-762-3164, Fax: 810-237-6685, E-mail: scotjohn@umflint.edu. *Application contact:* Bradley T. Maki, Director of Graduate Admissions, 810-762-3171, E-mail: bmaki@umflint.edu.
Website: http://www.umflint.edu/graduateprograms/business-administration-mba

University of Minnesota, Twin Cities Campus, Carlson School of Management, Carlson Full-Time MBA Program, Minneapolis, MN 55455. Offers finance (MBA); information technology (MBA); management (MBA); marketing (MBA); medical industry orientation (MBA); supply chain and operations (MBA); JD/MBA; MBA/MPP; MBA/MSBA; MD/MBA; MHA/MBA; Pharm D/MBA. *Accreditation:* AACSB. *Faculty:* 143 full-time (42 women), 24 part-time/adjunct (6 women). *Students:* 200 full-time (63 women); includes 25 minority (4 Black or African American, non-Hispanic/Latino; 13 Asian, non-Hispanic/Latino; 5 Hispanic/Latino; 3 Two or more races, non-Hispanic/Latino), 41 international. Average age 29. 606 applicants, 45% accepted, 104 enrolled. In 2017, 85 master's awarded. *Entrance requirements:* For master's, GMAT or GRE. Additional exam requirements/recommendations for international students: Required—TOEFL (minimum score 580 paper-based; 84 iBT), IELTS (minimum score 7), PTE. *Application deadline:* For fall admission, 4/1 for domestic students, 2/1 for international students. Application fee: $75. Electronic applications accepted. *Expenses:* $19,104 per semester resident tuition, $24,468 per semester non-resident tuition; $1,138 per semester fees; $1,050 per semester student health plan; $179 per semester (for international students). *Financial support:* In 2017–18, 147 students received support, including 147 fellowships with tuition reimbursements available (averaging $23,479 per year); research assistantships with partial tuition reimbursements available, teaching assistantships with partial tuition reimbursements available, career-related internships or fieldwork, Federal Work-Study, institutionally sponsored loans, scholarships/grants, health care benefits, and unspecified assistantships also available. Financial award application deadline: 4/1; financial award applicants required to submit FAFSA. *Faculty research:* Market regulation and asset pricing, social networks and data analytics, consumer behavior, innovation and entrepreneurship, workplace wellbeing and labor relationships. *Total annual research expenditures:* $577,440. *Unit head:* Philip J. Miller, Assistant Dean, MBA and MS Programs, 612-625-5555, Fax: 612-625-1012, E-mail: mba@umn.edu. *Application contact:* Linh Gilles, Director of Admissions and Recruiting, 612-625-5555, Fax: 612-625-1012, E-mail: ftmba@umn.edu.
Website: http://www.csom.umn.edu/MBA/full-time/

University of Minnesota, Twin Cities Campus, Carlson School of Management, Carlson Part-Time MBA Program, Minneapolis, MN 55455. Offers finance (MBA); information technology (MBA); management (MBA); marketing (MBA); medical industry orientation (MBA); supply chain and operations (MBA). *Program availability:* Part-time-only, evening/weekend, 100% online, blended/hybrid learning. *Faculty:* 143 full-time (42 women), 26 part-time/adjunct (6 women). *Students:* 919 part-time (291 women); includes 120 minority (14 Black or African American, non-Hispanic/Latino; 2 American Indian or Alaska Native, non-Hispanic/Latino; 55 Asian, non-Hispanic/Latino; 26 Hispanic/Latino; 1 Native Hawaiian or other Pacific Islander, non-Hispanic/Latino; 22 Two or more races, non-Hispanic/Latino), 57 international. Average age 28. 226 applicants, 85% accepted, 167 enrolled. In 2017, 289 master's awarded. *Entrance requirements:* For master's, GMAT or GRE. Additional exam requirements/recommendations for international students: Required—TOEFL (minimum score 580 paper-based; 84 iBT), IELTS (minimum score 7), PTE. *Application deadline:* For fall admission, 5/15 priority date for domestic and international students; for spring admission, 10/15 priority date for domestic and international students. Applications are processed on a rolling basis. Application fee: $75. Electronic applications accepted. *Expenses:* $1,375 per credit tuition, $314 per semester fees. *Financial support:* Applicants required to submit FAFSA. *Faculty research:* Market regulation and asset pricing, social networks and data analytics, consumer behavior, innovation and entrepreneurship, workplace wellbeing and labor relationships. *Total annual research expenditures:* $577,440. *Unit head:* Philip J. Miller, Assistant Dean, MBA and MS Programs, 612-624-2039, Fax: 612-625-1012, E-mail: mba@umn.edu. *Application contact:* Linh Gilles, Director of Admissions and Recruiting, 612-625-5555, Fax: 612-625-1012, E-mail: ptmba@umn.edu.
Website: http://www.carlsonschool.umn.edu/ptmba

University of Minnesota, Twin Cities Campus, Carlson School of Management, Doctoral Program in Business Administration, Minneapolis, MN 55455. Offers accounting (PhD); finance (PhD); information and decision sciences (PhD); marketing (PhD); strategic management and entrepreneurship (PhD); supply chain and operations (PhD); work and organizations (PhD). *Faculty:* 102 full-time (32 women). *Students:* 95 full-time (32 women); includes 10 minority (2 Black or African American, non-Hispanic/Latino; 7 Asian, non-Hispanic/Latino; 1 Hispanic/Latino), 68 international. Average age 30. 357 applicants, 6% accepted, 17 enrolled. In 2017, 14 doctorates awarded. *Degree requirements:* For doctorate, comprehensive exam, thesis/dissertation, written and oral preliminary exams, proposal defense, final defense. *Entrance requirements:* For doctorate, GMAT, GRE General Test, minimum undergraduate GPA of 3.0, graduate 3.5 (recommended). Additional exam requirements/recommendations for international students: Required—TOEFL (minimum score 600 paper-based, 100 iBT) or IELTS (minimum score 7.0). *Application deadline:* For fall admission, 12/15 for domestic students, 12/15 priority date for international students. Applications are processed on a rolling basis. Application fee: $75 ($95 for international students). Electronic applications accepted. *Expenses:* Contact institution. *Financial support:* In 2017–18, 80 students received support, including 80 fellowships with full tuition reimbursements available (averaging $13,000 per year), 73 research assistantships with full tuition reimbursements available (averaging $7,520 per year), 73 teaching assistantships with full tuition reimbursements available (averaging $7,520 per year); institutionally sponsored loans, scholarships/grants, health care benefits, unspecified assistantships, and full student service fee waivers also available. Financial award application deadline: 12/15. *Faculty research:* Finance, strategy and entrepreneurship, marketing, information and decision science, operations, accounting, supply chain, human resources and industrial relations, organizational behavior. *Unit head:* Dr. Shawn P. Curley, Director, 612-624-6546, Fax: 612-624-8221, E-mail: curley@umn.edu. *Application contact:* Sandy Herzan, Associate Director, 612-624-0875, Fax: 612-624-8221, E-mail: herza002@umn.edu.
Website: http://carlsonschool.umn.edu/degrees/phd

University of Mississippi, Graduate School, School of Business Administration, University, MS 38677. Offers business administration (MBA, PhD); finance (PhD); management (PhD); management information systems (PhD); marketing (PhD); JD/MBA. *Accreditation:* AACSB. *Faculty:* 58 full-time (15 women), 8 part-time/adjunct (3 women). *Students:* 71 full-time (26 women), 112 part-time (27 women); includes 11 minority (4 Black or African American, non-Hispanic/Latino; 3 Asian, non-Hispanic/

Latino; 1 Hispanic/Latino; 3 Two or more races, non-Hispanic/Latino), 17 international. Average age 29. In 2017, 83 master's, 6 doctorates awarded. *Entrance requirements:* For master's, GMAT, minimum GPA of 3.0; for doctorate, GMAT. Additional exam requirements/recommendations for international students: Required—TOEFL. *Application deadline:* For fall admission, 2/1 priority date for domestic students; for spring admission, 11/1 for domestic students; for summer admission, 4/1 for domestic students. Applications are processed on a rolling basis. Application fee: $50. Electronic applications accepted. *Financial support:* Fellowships, career-related internships or fieldwork, scholarships/grants, tuition waivers (full), and unspecified assistantships available. Financial award application deadline: 3/1; financial award applicants required to submit FAFSA. *Unit head:* Dr. Ken Cyree, Dean, 662-915-5820, Fax: 662-915-5821, E-mail: info@bus.olemiss.edu. *Application contact:* Ashley Jones McGee, Director of MBA and MHA Administration, 662-915-5483, E-mail: ajones@olemiss.edu.
Website: http://www.olemissbusiness.com/

University of Missouri–St. Louis, College of Business Administration, St. Louis, MO 63121. Offers accounting (M Acc); business administration (MBA, DBA, PhD, Certificate), including logistics and supply chain management (PhD); business intelligence (Certificate); cybersecurity (Certificate); digital and social media marketing (Certificate); human resources management (Certificate); information systems (MS); logistics and supply chain management (Certificate); marketing management (Certificate). *Program availability:* Part-time, evening/weekend. *Faculty:* 51 full-time (21 women), 25 part-time/adjunct (5 women). *Students:* 146 full-time (77 women), 326 part-time (143 women); includes 82 minority (32 Black or African American, non-Hispanic/Latino; 1 American Indian or Alaska Native, non-Hispanic/Latino; 34 Asian, non-Hispanic/Latino; 11 Hispanic/Latino; 4 Two or more races, non-Hispanic/Latino), 89 international. 276 applicants, 83% accepted, 142 enrolled. *Degree requirements:* For doctorate, thesis/dissertation. *Entrance requirements:* For master's, GMAT, 2 letters of recommendation; for doctorate, GMAT or GRE, 3 letters of recommendation. Additional exam requirements/recommendations for international students: Recommended—TOEFL (minimum score 550 paper-based; 79 iBT), IELTS (minimum score 6.5). *Application deadline:* For fall admission, 7/1 priority date for domestic and international students; for spring admission, 12/1 priority date for domestic and international students. Applications are processed on a rolling basis. Application fee: $50 ($40 for international students). Electronic applications accepted. *Expenses:* Tuition, state resident: part-time $476.50 per credit hour. Tuition, nonresident: part-time $1169.70 per credit hour. *Financial support:* Research assistantships with tuition reimbursements, teaching assistantships with tuition reimbursements, career-related internships or fieldwork, Federal Work-Study, and institutionally sponsored loans available. Support available to part-time students. Financial award application deadline: 4/1; financial award applicants required to submit FAFSA. *Faculty research:* Statistical decision aids, commercial banking, corporate finance, operations management, information systems. *Unit head:* Charles E. Hoffman, Dean, 314-516-6109, Fax: 314-516-6420. *Application contact:* 314-516-5458, Fax: 314-516-6996, E-mail: gradadm@umsl.edu.
Website: http://www.umsl.edu/divisions/business/

University of Nebraska at Kearney, College of Education, Department of Teacher Education, Kearney, NE 68849-0001. Offers curriculum and instruction (MA Ed), including early childhood education, elementary education, English as a second language, instructional effectiveness, reading/special education, secondary education; instructional technology (MS Ed), including information technology, instructional technology, school librarian; reading PK-12 (MA Ed); special education (MA Ed), including advanced practitioner: assistive technology specialist, advanced practitioner: behavioral interventionist, advanced practitioner: inclusive collaboration specialist, gifted, teacher education. *Program availability:* Part-time, evening/weekend, online only, 100% online. *Degree requirements:* For master's, comprehensive exam, thesis optional. *Entrance requirements:* For master's, portfolio or GRE. Additional exam requirements/recommendations for international students: Recommended—TOEFL (minimum score 550 paper-based; 79 iBT), IELTS (minimum score 6.5). Electronic applications accepted. *Expenses:* Contact institution.

University of Nebraska at Omaha, Graduate Studies, College of Information Science and Technology, Department of Information Systems and Quantitative Analysis, Omaha, NE 68182. Offers data analytics (Certificate); information assurance (Certificate); information technology (MIT, PhD); management information systems (MS); project management (Certificate); systems analysis and design (Certificate). *Program availability:* Part-time, evening/weekend. *Degree requirements:* For master's, comprehensive exam, thesis (for some programs); for doctorate, comprehensive exam, thesis/dissertation. *Entrance requirements:* For master's, GRE General Test, minimum GPA of 3.0, 3 letters of recommendation, writing sample, resume, official transcripts; for doctorate, GMAT or GRE General Test, minimum GPA of 3.0, 3 letters of recommendation, writing sample, resume, official transcripts; for Certificate, minimum GPA of 3.0, official transcripts. Additional exam requirements/recommendations for international students: Required—TOEFL, IELTS, PTE. Electronic applications accepted.

University of Nebraska–Lincoln, Graduate College, College of Agricultural Sciences and Natural Resources, Program in Mechanized Systems Management, Lincoln, NE 68588. Offers MS. *Degree requirements:* For master's, thesis optional. *Entrance requirements:* For master's, GRE General Test. Additional exam requirements/recommendations for international students: Required—TOEFL (minimum score 550 paper-based). Electronic applications accepted. *Faculty research:* Irrigation management, agricultural power and machinery systems, sensors and controls, food/industrial materials handling and processing systems.

University of Nevada, Las Vegas, Graduate College, Lee Business School, Department of Management, Entrepreneurship and Technology, Las Vegas, NV 89154-6034. Offers data analytics (Certificate); data analytics and applied economics (MS); management (Certificate); management information systems (MS, Certificate); new venture management (Certificate); MS/MS. *Program availability:* Part-time, evening/weekend. *Faculty:* 11 full-time (2 women), 2 part-time/adjunct (0 women). *Students:* 35 full-time (13 women), 35 part-time (15 women); includes 22 minority (7 Black or African American, non-Hispanic/Latino; 3 Asian, non-Hispanic/Latino; 6 Hispanic/Latino; 6 Two or more races, non-Hispanic/Latino), 22 international. Average age 31. 57 applicants, 82% accepted, 29 enrolled. In 2017, 14 master's, 11 other advanced degrees awarded. *Degree requirements:* For master's, thesis optional. *Entrance requirements:* For master's, GMAT or GRE, bachelor's degree with minimum GPA 3.0; 2 letters of recommendation; for Certificate, GMAT or GRE. Additional exam requirements/recommendations for international students: Required—TOEFL (minimum score 550 paper-based; 80 iBT), IELTS (minimum score 7). *Application deadline:* For fall admission, 8/1 for domestic students, 5/1 for international students; for spring admission, 11/15 for domestic students, 10/1 for international students. Application fee: $60 ($95 for international students). Electronic applications accepted. *Expenses:* $275 per credit, $850 per course, $7,969 per year resident, $22,157 per year non-resident, $7,094 non-resident fee (7 credits or more), $1,307 annual health insurance fee. *Financial support:* In 2017–18, 10 students received support, including 7 research assistantships with partial tuition reimbursements available (averaging $11,429 per year), 3 teaching assistantships with partial tuition reimbursements available (averaging

$11,250 per year); institutionally sponsored loans, scholarships/grants, health care benefits, and unspecified assistantships also available. Financial award application deadline: 3/15; financial award applicants required to submit FAFSA. *Faculty research:* Decision-making, publish or perish, ethical issues in information systems, IT-enabled decision making, business ethics. *Unit head:* Dr. Sheng Wang, Chair/Associate Professor, 702-895-5394, E-mail: sheng.wang@unlv.edu. *Application contact:* Dr. Greg Moody, Graduate Coordinator, 702-895-1365, Fax: 702-895-4370, E-mail: gregory.moody@unlv.edu.
Website: https://www.unlv.edu/met

University of Nevada, Reno, Graduate School, College of Business Administration, Department of Information Systems, Reno, NV 89557. Offers MS. *Degree requirements:* For master's, thesis optional. *Entrance requirements:* For master's, GRE or GMAT, minimum GPA of 2.75. Additional exam requirements/recommendations for international students: Required—TOEFL (minimum score 500 paper-based; 61 iBT), IELTS (minimum score 6). Electronic applications accepted.

University of New Hampshire, Graduate School Manchester Campus, Manchester, NH 03101. Offers business administration (MBA); cybersecurity policy and risk management (MS); educational administration and supervision (Ed S); educational studies (M Ed); elementary education (M Ed); information technology (MS); public administration (MPA); public health (MPH, Certificate); secondary education (M Ed, MAT); social work (MSW); substance use disorders (Certificate). *Program availability:* Part-time, evening/weekend. *Students:* 13 full-time (6 women), 17 part-time (0 women); includes 7 minority (1 Black or African American, non-Hispanic/Latino; 4 Asian, non-Hispanic/Latino; 1 Hispanic/Latino; 1 Two or more races, non-Hispanic/Latino), 10 international. Average age 33. 42 applicants, 71% accepted, 8 enrolled. In 2017, 4 master's awarded. *Entrance requirements:* Additional exam requirements/recommendations for international students: Required—TOEFL (minimum score 550 paper-based; 80 iBT). *Application deadline:* For fall admission, 6/1 for domestic students, 4/1 for international students; for spring admission, 12/1 for domestic students. Application fee: $65. Electronic applications accepted. *Financial support:* Fellowships, research assistantships, teaching assistantships, Federal Work-Study, scholarships/grants, health care benefits, and unspecified assistantships available. Support available to part-time students. Financial award application deadline: 2/15; financial award applicants required to submit FAFSA. *Unit head:* Candice Morey, Educational Programs Coordinator, 603-641-4313, E-mail: unhm.gradcenter@unh.edu.
Website: http://www.gradschool.unh.edu/manchester/

University of New Mexico, Anderson School of Management, Department of Marketing, Information Systems, Information Assurance, and Operations Management, Albuquerque, NM 87131. Offers information assurance (MBA); information systems and assurance (MS); management information systems (MBA); marketing management (MBA); operations management (MBA). *Program availability:* Part-time. *Faculty:* 16 full-time (4 women), 12 part-time/adjunct (6 women). In 2017, 68 master's awarded. *Entrance requirements:* For master's, GMAT or GRE, minimum GPA of 3.0 on last 60 hours of coursework; bachelor's degree from regionally-accredited college or university in U.S. or its equivalent in another country. Additional exam requirements/recommendations for international students: Required—TOEFL (minimum score 550 paper-based; 79 iBT), IELTS (minimum score 6.5). *Application deadline:* For fall admission, 4/1 priority date for domestic and international students; for spring admission, 10/1 priority date for domestic and international students. Applications are processed on a rolling basis. Application fee: $50. Electronic applications accepted. *Expenses:* Contact institution. *Financial support:* In 2017–18, 23 students received support, including 13 fellowships (averaging $16,320 per year), 12 research assistantships with partial tuition reimbursements available (averaging $15,180 per year); career-related internships or fieldwork, Federal Work-Study, scholarships/grants, and unspecified assistantships also available. Support available to part-time students. Financial award application deadline: 6/1; financial award applicants required to submit FAFSA. *Faculty research:* Marketing, operations management, information systems, information assurance. *Unit head:* Dr. Mary Margaret Rogers, Chair, 505-277-6471, E-mail: mmrogers@unm.edu. *Application contact:* Lisa Beauchene, Student Recruitment Specialist, 505-277-6471, E-mail: andersonadvising@unm.edu.
Website: https://www.mgt.unm.edu/mids/default.asp?mm-faculty

University of North Alabama, College of Business, Florence, AL 35632-0001. Offers business administration (MBA), including accounting, enterprise resource planning systems, executive, finance, health care management, information systems, international business, project management. *Accreditation:* AACSB; ACBSP. *Program availability:* Part-time, 100% online, blended/hybrid learning. *Faculty:* 26 full-time (1 woman), 4 part-time/adjunct (0 women). *Students:* 178 full-time (78 women), 498 part-time (237 women); includes 229 minority (92 Black or African American, non-Hispanic/Latino; 8 American Indian or Alaska Native, non-Hispanic/Latino; 104 Asian, non-Hispanic/Latino; 14 Hispanic/Latino; 11 Two or more races, non-Hispanic/Latino), 53 international. Average age 34. 354 applicants, 71% accepted, 190 enrolled. In 2017, 156 master's awarded. *Entrance requirements:* For master's, GMAT, GRE, minimum GPA of 2.75 in last 60 hours, 2.5 overall (on a 3.0 scale); 27 hours of course work in business and economics. Additional exam requirements/recommendations for international students: Required—TOEFL (minimum score 79 iBT), IELTS (minimum score 6), PTE (minimum score 54). *Application deadline:* Applications are processed on a rolling basis. Application fee: $50 ($100 for international students). Electronic applications accepted. *Expenses:* Tuition, state resident: full-time $7824; part-time $5943 per year. Tuition, nonresident: full-time $15,648; part-time $11,736 per year. *Required fees:* $3064; $2298 per unit. Tuition and fees vary according to course load and reciprocity agreements. *Financial support:* In 2017–18, 114 students received support. Scholarships/grants available. Financial award application deadline: 2/1; financial award applicants required to submit FAFSA. *Total annual research expenditures:* $193,193. *Unit head:* Dr. Gregory A. Carnes, Dean, 256-765-4261, Fax: 256-765-4170, E-mail: gacarnes@una.edu. *Application contact:* Hillary N. Coats, Graduate Admissions Coordinator, 256-765-4447, E-mail: graduate@una.edu.
Website: https://www.una.edu/mba/index.html

The University of North Carolina at Chapel Hill, Kenan-Flagler Business School, Doctoral Program in Business Administration, Chapel Hill, NC 27599. Offers accounting (PhD); finance (PhD); marketing (PhD); operations management (PhD); organizational behavior (PhD); strategy (PhD). *Accreditation:* AACSB. *Degree requirements:* For doctorate, thesis/dissertation. *Entrance requirements:* For doctorate, GMAT or GRE General Test. Electronic applications accepted. *Expenses:* Contact institution.

The University of North Carolina at Charlotte, College of Computing and Informatics, Department of Software and Information Systems, Charlotte, NC 28223-0001. Offers advanced databases and knowledge discovery (Graduate Certificate); game design and development (Graduate Certificate); information security and privacy (Graduate Certificate); information technology (MS); management of information technology (Graduate Certificate); network security (Graduate Certificate); secure software development (Graduate Certificate). *Program availability:* Part-time, evening/weekend. *Faculty:* 19 full-time (7 women), 6 part-time/adjunct (0 women). *Students:* 109 full-time (50 women), 87 part-time (30 women); includes 36 minority (21 Black or African American, non-Hispanic/Latino; 8 Asian, non-Hispanic/Latino; 5 Hispanic/Latino; 2 Two

Management Information Systems

or more races, non-Hispanic/Latino), 121 international. Average age 27. 419 applicants, 64% accepted, 80 enrolled. In 2017, 120 master's, 13 other advanced degrees awarded. *Degree requirements:* For master's, project, internship, or thesis. *Entrance requirements:* For master's, GRE or GMAT, undergraduate or equivalent course work in data structures, object-oriented programming in C++, C#, or Java with minimum GPA of 3.0; for Graduate Certificate, bachelor's degree from accredited institution in computing, mathematical, engineering or business discipline with minimum overall GPA of 2.8, junior/senior 3.0; substantial knowledge of data structures and object-oriented programming in C++, C# or Java. Additional exam requirements/recommendations for international students: Required—TOEFL (minimum score 523 paper-based, 70 iBT) or IELTS (6.5). *Application deadline:* For fall admission, 3/1 for domestic and international students; for spring admission, 10/1 for domestic and international students. Applications are processed on a rolling basis. Application fee: $75. Electronic applications accepted. *Expenses:* Contact institution. *Financial support:* In 2017–18, 71 students received support, including 1 fellowship (averaging $70,000 per year), 28 research assistantships (averaging $12,983 per year), 42 teaching assistantships (averaging $10,671 per year); career-related internships or fieldwork, institutionally sponsored loans, scholarships/grants, and unspecified assistantships also available. Support available to part-time students. Financial award application deadline: 3/1; financial award applicants required to submit FAFSA. *Total annual research expenditures:* $2.5 million. *Unit head:* Dr. Mary Lou Maher, Chair, 704-687-1940, E-mail: mmaher9@uncc.edu. *Application contact:* Kathy B. Giddings, Director of Graduate Admissions, 704-687-5503, Fax: 704-687-1668, E-mail: gradadm@uncc.edu. Website: http://sis.uncc.edu/

The University of North Carolina at Charlotte, College of Computing and Informatics, Program in Computing and Information Systems, Charlotte, NC 28223-0001. Offers computing and information systems (PhD), including bioinformatics, business information systems and operations management, computer science, interdisciplinary, software and information systems. *Faculty:* 2 full-time (0 women). *Students:* 103 full-time (33 women), 17 part-time (3 women); includes 6 minority (1 Black or African American, non-Hispanic/Latino; 3 Asian, non-Hispanic/Latino; 1 Hispanic/Latino; 1 Two or more races, non-Hispanic/Latino), 90 international. Average age 30. 86 applicants, 48% accepted, 23 enrolled. In 2017, 15 doctorates awarded. *Degree requirements:* For doctorate, comprehensive exam, thesis/dissertation. *Entrance requirements:* For doctorate, GRE or GMAT, baccalaureate degree, minimum GPA of 3.0 on courses related to the chosen field of PhD study, essay, reference letters. Additional exam requirements/recommendations for international students: Required—TOEFL (minimum score 523 paper-based, 70 iBT) or IELTS (6.5). *Application deadline:* For fall admission, 2/1 for domestic and international students; for spring admission, 9/1 for domestic and international students. Applications are processed on a rolling basis. Application fee: $75. Electronic applications accepted. *Expenses:* Tuition, state resident: full-time $4337. Tuition, nonresident: full-time $17,771. *Required fees:* $3211. Tuition and fees vary according to course load and program. *Financial support:* Career-related internships or fieldwork, institutionally sponsored loans, scholarships/grants, health care benefits, and unspecified assistantships available. Support available to part-time students. Financial award applicants required to submit FAFSA. *Unit head:* Dr. Fatma Mili, Dean. *Application contact:* Kathy B. Giddings, Director of Graduate Admissions, 704-687-5503, Fax: 704-687-1668, E-mail: gradadm@uncc.edu.

The University of North Carolina at Greensboro, Graduate School, Bryan School of Business and Economics, Department of Information Systems and Supply Chain Management, Greensboro, NC 27412-5001. Offers information systems (PhD); information technology (Certificate); information technology and management (MS); supply chain management (Certificate). *Entrance requirements:* For master's, GMAT, GRE General Test. Additional exam requirements/recommendations for international students: Required—TOEFL. Electronic applications accepted.

The University of North Carolina Wilmington, Interdisciplinary Program in Computer Science and Information Systems, Wilmington, NC 28403-3297. Offers computer science and information systems (MS); data science (MS). *Faculty:* 11 full-time (3 women). *Students:* 32 full-time (15 women), 10 part-time (2 women); includes 4 minority (1 Black or African American, non-Hispanic/Latino; 3 Hispanic/Latino), 8 international. Average age 28. 45 applicants, 56% accepted, 23 enrolled. In 2017, 4 master's awarded. *Degree requirements:* For master's, thesis or alternative, research project. *Entrance requirements:* For master's, GMAT or GRE, 3 letters of recommendation, resume, statement of interest; baccalaureate degree in a computational field preferred (for data science). Additional exam requirements/recommendations for international students: Required—TOEFL (minimum score 550 paper-based; 79 iBT), IELTS (minimum score 6.5). *Application deadline:* For fall admission, 3/1 priority date for domestic students; for spring admission, 11/15 for domestic students. Applications are processed on a rolling basis. Application fee: $75. Electronic applications accepted. *Expenses:* $3,727 in-state full-time, $10,331 out-of-state full-time. *Financial support:* Scholarships/grants and unspecified assistantships available. Financial award application deadline: 1/1; financial award applicants required to submit FAFSA. *Unit head:* Dr. Clayton Ferner, Program Coordinator, 910-962-7552, E-mail: cferner@uncw.edu. *Application contact:* Candace Wilhelm, Graduate Coordinator, 910-962-3903, Fax: 910-962-7457, E-mail: wilhelmc@uncw.edu. Website: http://csb.uncw.edu/mscsis/

University of North Florida, College of Computing, Engineering, and Construction, School of Computing, Jacksonville, FL 32224. Offers computer science (MS); information systems (MS); software engineering (MS). *Program availability:* Part-time. *Degree requirements:* For master's, thesis. *Entrance requirements:* For master's, GRE General Test, minimum GPA of 3.0 in last 60 hours of course work. Additional exam requirements/recommendations for international students: Required—TOEFL (minimum score 500 paper-based; 61 iBT). Electronic applications accepted.

University of North Texas, Robert B. Toulouse School of Graduate Studies, Denton, TX 76203-5459. Offers accounting (MS); applied anthropology (MA, MS); applied behavior analysis (Certificate); applied geography (MA); applied technology and performance improvement (M Ed, MS); art education (MA); art history (MA); art museum education (Certificate); arts leadership (Certificate); audiology (Au D); behavior analysis (MS); behavioral science (PhD); biochemistry and molecular biology (MS); biology (MA, MS); biomedical engineering (MS); business analysis (MS); chemistry (MS); clinical health psychology (PhD); communication studies (MA, MS); computer engineering (MS); computer science (MS); counseling (M Ed, MS), including clinical mental health counseling (MS), college and university counseling, elementary school counseling, secondary school counseling; creative writing (MA); criminal justice (MS); curriculum and instruction (M Ed); decision sciences (MBA); design (MA, MFA), including fashion design (MFA), innovation studies, interior design (MFA); early childhood studies (MS); economics (MS); educational leadership (M Ed, Ed D); educational psychology (MS, PhD), including family studies (MS), gifted and talented (MS), human development (MS), learning and cognition (MS), research, measurement and evaluation (MS); electrical engineering (MS); emergency management (MPA); engineering technology (MS); English (MA); English as a second language (MA); environmental science (MS); finance (MBA, MS); financial management (MPA); French (MA); health services management (MBA); higher education (M Ed, Ed D); history (MA, MS); hospitality management (MS);

human resources management (MPA); information science (MS); information systems (PhD); information technologies (MBA); interdisciplinary studies (MA, MS); international studies (MA); international sustainable tourism (MS); jazz studies (MM); journalism (MA, MJ, Graduate Certificate), including interactive and virtual digital communication (Graduate Certificate), narrative journalism (Graduate Certificate), public relations (Graduate Certificate); kinesiology (MS); linguistics (MA); local government management (MPA); logistics (PhD); logistics and supply chain management (MBA); long-term care, senior housing, and aging services (MA); management (PhD); marketing (MBA); mathematics (MA, MS); mechanical and energy engineering (MS, PhD); music (MA), including ethnomusicology, music theory, musicology, performance; music composition (PhD); music education (MM Ed, PhD); nonprofit management (MPA); operations and supply chain management (MBA); performance (MM, DMA); philosophy (MA); political science (MA); professional and technical communication (MA); radio, television and film (MA, MFA); rehabilitation counseling (Certificate); sociology (MA); Spanish (MA); special education (M Ed); speech-language pathology (MA); strategic management (MBA); studio art (MFA); teaching (M Ed); MBA/MS. *Program availability:* Part-time, evening/weekend, online learning. Terminal master's awarded for partial completion of doctoral program. *Degree requirements:* For master's, variable foreign language requirement, comprehensive exam (for some programs), thesis (for some programs); for doctorate, variable foreign language requirement, comprehensive exam (for some programs), thesis/dissertation; for other advanced degree, variable foreign language requirement, comprehensive exam (for some programs). *Entrance requirements:* For master's and doctorate, GRE, GMAT. Additional exam requirements/recommendations for international students: Required—TOEFL (minimum score 550 paper-based; 79 iBT). Electronic applications accepted.

University of Oklahoma, Price College of Business, Division of Management Information Systems, Norman, OK 73019. Offers digital technologies (Graduate Certificate); management of information technology (MS), including business analytics. *Program availability:* Part-time, evening/weekend. *Faculty:* 11 full-time (5 women). *Students:* 35 full-time (15 women), 13 part-time (7 women); includes 12 minority (2 Black or African American, non-Hispanic/Latino; 1 American Indian or Alaska Native, non-Hispanic/Latino; 3 Asian, non-Hispanic/Latino; 4 Hispanic/Latino; 2 Two or more races, non-Hispanic/Latino), 13 international. Average age 28. 24 applicants, 38% accepted, 8 enrolled. In 2017, 23 master's, 2 other advanced degrees awarded. *Degree requirements:* For master's, thesis optional. *Entrance requirements:* For master's and Graduate Certificate, GMAT or GRE, resume, statement of goals, 3 letters of recommendation. Additional exam requirements/recommendations for international students: Required—TOEFL (minimum score 100 iBT) or IELTS (minimum score 7). *Application deadline:* For fall admission, 6/15 for domestic students, 3/1 for international students; for spring admission, 10/1 for domestic students, 8/1 for international students. Applications are processed on a rolling basis. Application fee: $50 ($100 for international students). Electronic applications accepted. *Expenses:* Tuition, state resident: full-time $5119; part-time $213.30 per credit hour. Tuition, nonresident: full-time $19,778; part-time $824.10 per credit hour. *Required fees:* $3458; $133.55 per credit hour. $126.50 per semester. *Financial support:* In 2017–18, 40 students received support, including 2 research assistantships with partial tuition reimbursements available (averaging $16,864 per year), 8 teaching assistantships with partial tuition reimbursements available (averaging $11,121 per year); career-related internships or fieldwork, scholarships/grants, and unspecified assistantships also available. Support available to part-time students. Financial award application deadline: 6/1; financial award applicants required to submit FAFSA. *Faculty research:* Human-computer interaction and cognition; deception detection in IT-mediated contexts; social media use; computer-mediated collaboration and communication; meaning in discourse about IT and discourse through IT. *Total annual research expenditures:* $208,471. *Unit head:* Radhika Santhanam, Chair/Division Director, 405-325-0791, E-mail: radhika@ou.edu. *Application contact:* Jennifer Aragon, Academic Advisor, 405-325-2074, Fax: 405-325-7118, E-mail: jhardman@ou.edu. Website: http://www.ou.edu/content/price/mis/mis_ms_in_mis.html

University of Oklahoma, Price College of Business, Program in Business Administration, Oklahoma City, OK 73104. Offers business administration (MBA, PhD), including accounting (PhD), business administration, entrepreneurship and economic development (PhD), finance (PhD), management and international business (PhD), management of information systems (PhD), marketing/supply chain (PhD); JD/MBA; MBA/MS. *Accreditation:* AACSB. *Program availability:* Part-time, evening/weekend. *Students:* 100 full-time (27 women), 152 part-time (30 women); includes 36 minority (2 Black or African American, non-Hispanic/Latino; 4 American Indian or Alaska Native, non-Hispanic/Latino; 10 Asian, non-Hispanic/Latino; 13 Hispanic/Latino; 7 Two or more races, non-Hispanic/Latino), 32 international. Average age 31. 247 applicants, 29% accepted, 41 enrolled. In 2017, 118 master's, 9 doctorates awarded. *Degree requirements:* For doctorate, comprehensive exam, thesis/dissertation. *Entrance requirements:* For master's, GMAT or GRE, resume, 2 essays, interview; for doctorate, GMAT or GRE, resume, statement of goals, 3 letters of recommendation. Additional exam requirements/recommendations for international students: Required—TOEFL (minimum score 100 iBT) or IELTS (minimum score 7). *Application deadline:* For fall admission, 11/1 for domestic and international students; for summer admission, 11/1 for domestic and international students. Applications are processed on a rolling basis. Application fee: $50 ($100 for international students). Electronic applications accepted. *Expenses:* Contact institution. *Financial support:* In 2017–18, 107 students received support, including 6 fellowships with partial tuition reimbursements available (averaging $2,500 per year); research assistantships with full and partial tuition reimbursements available, teaching assistantships with full and partial tuition reimbursements available, career-related internships or fieldwork, scholarships/grants, health care benefits, and unspecified assistantships also available. Support available to part-time students. Financial award application deadline: 6/1; financial award applicants required to submit FAFSA. *Faculty research:* Energy finance; international accounting; organizational behavior and entrepreneurship; management information systems; supply chain. *Unit head:* Laku Chidambaram, Associate Dean for Academic Programs and Engagement, 405-325-8013. *Application contact:* Kate Hile, Associate Director of MBA Admissions, 405-325-4572, E-mail: khile@ou.edu. Website: http://www.ou.edu/price/divisions/graduate-programs/graduate.html

University of Oregon, Graduate School, Interdisciplinary Program in Applied Information Management, Eugene, OR 97403. Offers MS. *Program availability:* Part-time, online learning. *Degree requirements:* For master's, project. *Entrance requirements:* Additional exam requirements/recommendations for international students: Required—TOEFL. Electronic applications accepted. *Expenses:* Contact institution. *Faculty research:* Business management, information design.

University of Pennsylvania, Wharton School, Operations and Information Management Department, Philadelphia, PA 19104. Offers MBA, PhD. Terminal master's awarded for partial completion of doctoral program. *Degree requirements:* For master's, thesis, preliminary exams; for doctorate, thesis/dissertation, preliminary exams. *Entrance requirements:* For master's, GMAT, GRE; for doctorate, GRE. Electronic applications accepted. *Faculty research:* Supply chain management, operations research, economics of information systems, risk analysis, electronic commerce.

University of Phoenix–Bay Area Campus, College of Information Systems and Technology, San Jose, CA 95134-1805. Offers information systems (MIS); organizational leadership/information systems and technology (DM). *Program availability:* Evening/weekend. *Degree requirements:* For master's, thesis (for some programs). *Entrance requirements:* For master's, minimum undergraduate GPA of 3.0, 3 years of work experience. Additional exam requirements/recommendations for international students: Required—TOEFL (minimum score 550 paper-based; 79 iBT). Electronic applications accepted.

University of Phoenix–Central Valley Campus, College of Information Systems and Technology, Fresno, CA 93720-1552. Offers information systems (MIS); technology management (MBA).

University of Phoenix–Dallas Campus, College of Information Systems and Technology, Dallas, TX 75251. Offers e-business (MBA); information systems (MIS); technology management (MBA). *Program availability:* Evening/weekend. *Degree requirements:* For master's, thesis (for some programs). *Entrance requirements:* For master's, minimum undergraduate GPA of 3.0, 3 years of work experience. Additional exam requirements/recommendations for international students: Required—TOEFL (minimum score 550 paper-based; 79 iBT). Electronic applications accepted.

University of Phoenix–Hawaii Campus, College of Information Systems and Technology, Honolulu, HI 96813-3800. Offers information systems (MIS); technology management (MBA). *Program availability:* Evening/weekend. *Degree requirements:* For master's, thesis (for some programs). *Entrance requirements:* For master's, minimum undergraduate GPA of 3.0, 3 years of work experience. Additional exam requirements/recommendations for international students: Required—TOEFL (minimum score 550 paper-based; 79 iBT). Electronic applications accepted.

University of Phoenix–Houston Campus, College of Information Systems and Technology, Houston, TX 77079-2004. Offers e-business (MBA); information systems (MIS); technology management (MBA). *Program availability:* Evening/weekend, online learning. *Degree requirements:* For master's, comprehensive exam (for some programs), thesis. *Entrance requirements:* For master's, minimum undergraduate GPA of 3.0, 3 years of work experience. Additional exam requirements/recommendations for international students: Required—TOEFL (minimum score 550 paper-based; 79 iBT). Electronic applications accepted.

University of Phoenix–Las Vegas Campus, College of Information Systems and Technology, Las Vegas, NV 89153. Offers information systems (MIS); technology management (MBA). *Program availability:* Evening/weekend. *Degree requirements:* For master's, thesis (for some programs). *Entrance requirements:* For master's, minimum undergraduate GPA of 3.0, 3 years of work experience. Additional exam requirements/recommendations for international students: Required—TOEFL (minimum score 550 paper-based; 79 iBT). Electronic applications accepted.

University of Phoenix–Online Campus, College of Information Systems and Technology, Phoenix, AZ 85034-7209. Offers MIS. *Program availability:* Evening/weekend, online learning. *Entrance requirements:* Additional exam requirements/recommendations for international students: Required—TOEFL, TOEIC (Test of English as an International Communication), Berlitz Online English Proficiency Exam, PTE, or IELTS. Electronic applications accepted. *Expenses:* Contact institution.

University of Phoenix–Sacramento Valley Campus, College of Information Systems and Technology, Sacramento, CA 95833-4334. Offers management (MIS); technology management (MBA). *Program availability:* Evening/weekend. *Degree requirements:* For master's, thesis (for some programs). *Entrance requirements:* For master's, minimum undergraduate GPA of 3.0, 3 years work experience. Additional exam requirements/recommendations for international students: Required—TOEFL (minimum score 550 paper-based; 79 iBT). Electronic applications accepted.

University of Phoenix–San Antonio Campus, College of Information Systems and Technology, San Antonio, TX 78230. Offers information systems (MIS); technology management (MBA).

University of Phoenix–San Diego Campus, College of Information Systems and Technology, San Diego, CA 92123. Offers management (MIS); technology management (MBA). *Program availability:* Evening/weekend. *Degree requirements:* For master's, thesis (for some programs). *Entrance requirements:* For master's, minimum undergraduate GPA of 3.0, 3 years work experience. Additional exam requirements/recommendations for international students: Required—TOEFL (minimum score 550 paper-based; 79 iBT). Electronic applications accepted.

University of Pittsburgh, Katz Graduate School of Business, Doctoral Program in Business Administration, Pittsburgh, PA 15260. Offers accounting (PhD); business analytics and operations (PhD); finance (PhD); information systems and technology management (PhD); marketing (PhD); organizational behavior and human resources (PhD); strategic management (PhD). *Accreditation:* AACSB. *Program availability:* Evening/weekend. *Faculty:* 91 full-time (30 women), 14 part-time/adjunct (4 women). *Students:* 51 full-time (26 women), 1 (woman) part-time; includes 5 minority (1 Black or African American, non-Hispanic/Latino; 3 Asian, non-Hispanic/Latino; 1 Two or more races, non-Hispanic/Latino), 30 international. Average age 31. 337 applicants, 3% accepted, 10 enrolled. In 2017, 7 doctorates awarded. *Degree requirements:* For doctorate, comprehensive exam, thesis/dissertation, student teaching. *Entrance requirements:* For doctorate, GMAT or GRE, 3 recommendations, statement of purpose, transcripts of all previous course work and degrees. Additional exam requirements/recommendations for international students: Required—TOEFL (minimum score 100 iBT) or IELTS (minimum score 7.0). *Application deadline:* For fall admission, 1/1 for domestic and international students. Applications are processed on a rolling basis. Application fee: $50. Electronic applications accepted. *Financial support:* In 2017–18, 43 students received support, including 33 research assistantships with full tuition reimbursements available (averaging $26,500 per year), 10 teaching assistantships with full tuition reimbursements available (averaging $28,220 per year); Federal Work-Study, scholarships/grants, health care benefits, and unspecified assistantships also available. Financial award application deadline: 1/1; financial award applicants required to submit FAFSA. *Faculty research:* Accounting systems/financial reporting, corporate finance, shopper marketing/consumer behavior, management information systems, organizational behavior and entrepreneurship. *Total annual research expenditures:* $475,077. *Unit head:* Dr. Arjang A. Assad, Dean, 412-648-1556, Fax: 412-648-1552, E-mail: aassad@katz.pitt.edu. *Application contact:* Dr. Dennis Galletta, Director, 412-648-1699, Fax: 412-648-3633, E-mail: galletta@katz.pitt.edu.
Website: http://www.katz.business.pitt.edu/degrees/phd/

See Display on page 158 and Close-Up on page 187.

University of Pittsburgh, Katz Graduate School of Business, Master of Business Administration Programs, Pittsburgh, PA 15260. Offers finance (MBA); information systems (MBA); marketing (MBA); operations (MBA); organizational behavior and human resources (MBA); strategy, environment and organizations (MBA); MBA/JD; MBA/MID; MBA/MIS; MBA/MSE. *Accreditation:* AACSB. *Program availability:* Part-time, evening/weekend, blended/hybrid learning. *Faculty:* 91 full-time (30 women), 14 part-time/adjunct (4 women). *Students:* 139 full-time (49 women), 294 part-time (94 women); includes 65 minority (27 Black or African American, non-Hispanic/Latino; 20 Asian, non-Hispanic/Latino; 11 Hispanic/Latino; 7 Two or more races, non-Hispanic/Latino), 54 international. Average age 29. 651 applicants, 44% accepted, 158 enrolled. In 2017, 217 master's awarded. *Degree requirements:* For master's, minimum GPA of 3.0. *Entrance requirements:* For master's, GMAT, GRE. Additional exam requirements/recommendations for international students: Required—TOEFL (minimum score 100 iBT) or IELTS (minimum score 7.0). *Application deadline:* For fall admission, 4/1 priority date for domestic students, 2/1 priority date for international students. Application fee: $50. Electronic applications accepted. *Financial support:* In 2017–18, 136 students received support. Scholarships/grants available. Financial award application deadline: 6/1; financial award applicants required to submit FAFSA. *Faculty research:* Accounting systems/financial reporting, corporate finance, shopper marketing/consumer behavior, management information systems, organizational behavior and entrepreneurship. *Total annual research expenditures:* $475,077. *Unit head:* Dr. Arjang A. Assad, Dean, 412-648-1556, Fax: 412-648-1552, E-mail: aassad@katz.pitt.edu. *Application contact:* Thomas Keller, Director of MBA Admissions, 412-648-1700, Fax: 412-648-1659, E-mail: mba@katz.pitt.edu.
Website: http://www.business.pitt.edu/katz/mba/

See Display on page 158 and Close-Up on page 187.

University of Pittsburgh, Katz Graduate School of Business, Master of Science in Management Information Systems Program, Pittsburgh, PA 15260. Offers MS. *Faculty:* 91 full-time (30 women), 14 part-time/adjunct (4 women). *Students:* 13 full-time (7 women), 1 part-time (0 women); includes 1 minority (Asian, non-Hispanic/Latino), 11 international. Average age 24. 168 applicants, 40% accepted, 13 enrolled. In 2017, 9 master's awarded. *Degree requirements:* For master's, minimum GPA of 3.0. *Entrance requirements:* For master's, GMAT, GRE. Additional exam requirements/recommendations for international students: Required—TOEFL (minimum score 100 iBT), IELTS (minimum score 7). *Application deadline:* For fall admission, 7/1 priority date for domestic students, 5/1 priority date for international students. Applications are processed on a rolling basis. Application fee: $50. Electronic applications accepted. *Financial support:* Scholarships/grants available. Financial award application deadline: 6/1; financial award applicants required to submit FAFSA. *Faculty research:* Accounting systems/financial reporting, corporate finance, shopper marketing/consumer behavior, management information systems, organizational behavior and entrepreneurship. *Total annual research expenditures:* $475,077. *Unit head:* Dr. Arjang A. Assad, Dean, 412-648-1556, Fax: 412-648-1552, E-mail: aassad@katz.pitt.edu. *Application contact:* Thomas Keller, Director of MBA Admissions, 412-648-1700, Fax: 412-648-1659, E-mail: mba@katz.pitt.edu.
Website: http://www.business.pitt.edu/katz/ms-programs/MIS

University of Pittsburgh, Katz Graduate School of Business, MBA/MS in Management of Information Systems Program, Pittsburgh, PA 15260. Offers MBA/MS. *Program availability:* Part-time, evening/weekend. *Faculty:* 91 full-time (30 women), 14 part-time/adjunct (4 women). *Students:* 15 full-time (5 women); includes 2 minority (1 Asian, non-Hispanic/Latino; 1 Hispanic/Latino), 9 international. Average age 28. 30 applicants, 30% accepted, 3 enrolled. *Entrance requirements:* Additional exam requirements/recommendations for international students: Required—TOEFL (minimum score 100 iBT) or IELTS (minimum score 7.0). *Application deadline:* For fall admission, 4/1 priority date for domestic students, 2/1 priority date for international students. Application fee: $50. Electronic applications accepted. *Financial support:* Scholarships/grants available. Financial award application deadline: 6/1; financial award applicants required to submit FAFSA. *Faculty research:* Accounting systems/financial reporting, corporate finance, shopper marketing/consumer behavior, management information systems, organizational behavior and entrepreneurship. *Total annual research expenditures:* $475,077. *Unit head:* Dr. Arjang A. Assad, Dean, 412-648-1556, Fax: 412-648-1552, E-mail: aassad@katz.pitt.edu. *Application contact:* Thomas Keller, Director, MBA Admissions, 412-648-1700, Fax: 412-648-1659, E-mail: mba@katz.pitt.edu.
Website: https://www.katz.business.pitt.edu/mba/joint-and-dual/mis#section-1

University of Redlands, School of Business, Redlands, CA 92373-0999. Offers business (MBA); information technology (MS); management (MA). *Program availability:* Evening/weekend. *Entrance requirements:* For master's, minimum GPA of 3.0, 2 letters of recommendation. *Faculty research:* Human resources management, educational leadership, humanities, teacher education.

University of Rochester, Simon Business School, Doctoral Program in Business Administration, Rochester, NY 14627. Offers accounting (PhD); computer information systems (PhD); finance (PhD); marketing (PhD); operations management (PhD). *Accreditation:* AACSB. *Faculty:* 70 full-time (12 women), 23 part-time/adjunct (6 women). *Students:* 50 full-time (17 women); includes 2 minority (both Asian, non-Hispanic/Latino), 41 international. Average age 28. 199 applicants, 10% accepted, 9 enrolled. In 2017, 8 doctorates awarded. *Degree requirements:* For doctorate, comprehensive exam, thesis/dissertation, qualifying exam. *Entrance requirements:* For doctorate, GMAT or GRE. Additional exam requirements/recommendations for international students: Required—TOEFL. *Application deadline:* For fall admission, 1/5 for domestic and international students. Application fee: $100. Electronic applications accepted. *Expenses:* Contact institution. *Financial support:* In 2017–18, 50 students received support. Fellowships, research assistantships, teaching assistantships, health care benefits, and tuition waivers (full) available. Financial award application deadline: 1/5. *Faculty research:* Empirical industrial organization, risk management, financial disclosure and regulation, social media, health care management. *Unit head:* Dr. Ron Kaniel, Committee Chair, 585-275-2959. *Application contact:* Sue Harris, PhD Administrator, 585-275-2959, E-mail: phdoffice@simon.rochester.edu.
Website: http://www.simon.rochester.edu/programs/phd/index.aspx

University of Rochester, Simon Business School, Full-Time Master's Program in Business Administration, Rochester, NY 14627. Offers business systems consulting (MBA); competitive and organizational strategy (MBA); computers and information systems (MBA); corporate accounting (MBA); entrepreneurship (MBA); finance (MBA); health sciences management (MBA); marketing (MBA); operations management (MBA); public accounting (MBA); strategy and organizations (MBA). *Accreditation:* AACSB. *Faculty:* 70 full-time (12 women), 23 part-time/adjunct (6 women). *Students:* 208 full-time (70 women). Average age 28. *Entrance requirements:* For master's, GMAT or GRE. *Application deadline:* For fall admission, 10/15 for domestic and international students; for winter admission, 1/5 for domestic and international students; for spring admission, 3/15 for domestic and international students; for summer admission, 5/15 for domestic and international students. Application fee: $150. *Financial support:* Fellowships, institutionally sponsored loans, scholarships/grants, and tuition waivers (full and partial) available. Financial award application deadline: 1/5; financial award applicants required to submit FAFSA. *Faculty research:* Empirical industrial organization, risk management, financial disclosure and regulation, social media, health care management. *Unit head:* Andrew Ainslie, Dean, 585-275-3316, E-mail: andrew.ainslie@simon.rochester.edu. *Application contact:* Rebekah S. Lewin, Assistant Dean of Admissions and Financial Aid, 585-275-3533, E-mail: admissions@simon.rochester.edu.
Website: http://www.simon.rochester.edu/programs/full-time-mba/index.aspx

University of Rochester, Simon Business School, Part-Time MBA Program, Rochester, NY 14627. Offers business systems consulting (MBA); competitive and

Management Information Systems

organizational strategy (MBA); computers and information systems (MBA); corporate accounting (MBA); entrepreneurship (MBA); finance (MBA); health sciences management (MBA); marketing (MBA), including brand management, marketing strategy, pricing; operations management (MBA); public accounting (MBA). *Program availability:* Part-time-only, evening/weekend. *Faculty:* 70 full-time (12 women), 23 part-time/adjunct (6 women). *Students:* 159 part-time (62 women); includes 25 minority (5 Black or African American, non-Hispanic/Latino; 9 Asian, non-Hispanic/Latino; 9 Hispanic/Latino; 2 Two or more races, non-Hispanic/Latino), 4 international. Average age 32. 39 applicants, 92% accepted, 35 enrolled. In 2017, 59 master's awarded. *Entrance requirements:* For master's, GRE or GMAT. *Application deadline:* For fall admission, 8/1 for domestic students; for spring admission, 2/15 for domestic students. Applications are processed on a rolling basis. Application fee: $150. Electronic applications accepted. *Expenses:* $1,875 per credit, $1,385 fees. *Financial support:* In 2017–18, 69 students received support. Tuition waivers (partial) available. Financial award application deadline: 8/1. *Unit head:* Andrew Ainslie, Dean, 585-275-3316, E-mail: andrew.ainslie@simon.rochester.edu. *Application contact:* Molly Mesko, Executive Director, EMBA and Part-Time Programs, 585-275-4277, E-mail: molly.mesko@simon.rochester.edu.
Website: http://www.simon.rochester.edu/programs/ptmba/index.aspx

University of San Francisco, School of Management, Master of Science in Information Systems Program, San Francisco, CA 94117. Offers MS. *Program availability:* Part-time, evening/weekend. *Degree requirements:* For master's, thesis. *Entrance requirements:* For master's, resume demonstrating minimum of two years of professional work experience, transcripts from each college or university attended, two letters of recommendation, personal statement. Additional exam requirements/recommendations for international students: Required—TOEFL (minimum score 600 paper-based, 100 iBT), IELTS (minimum score 7) or PTE (minimum score 68). Electronic applications accepted. *Expenses:* Contact institution.

The University of Scranton, Kania School of Management, Program in Business Administration, Scranton, PA 18510. Offers accounting (MBA); finance (MBA); general business administration (MBA); health care management (MBA); international business (MBA); management information systems (MBA); marketing (MBA); operations management (MBA). *Accreditation:* AACSB. *Program availability:* Part-time, evening/weekend, 100% online. *Entrance requirements:* For master's, GMAT (for MBA). *Faculty research:* Financial markets, strategic impact of total quality management, internal accounting controls, consumer preference, information systems and the Internet.

University of South Africa, College of Science, Engineering and Technology, Pretoria, South Africa. Offers chemical engineering (M Tech); information technology (M Tech).

University of South Alabama, School of Computing, Mobile, AL 36688. Offers computer science (MS); information systems (MS). *Program availability:* Part-time, evening/weekend. *Faculty:* 18 full-time (2 women). *Students:* 74 full-time (25 women), 20 part-time (7 women); includes 12 minority (2 Black or African American, non-Hispanic/Latino; 1 American Indian or Alaska Native, non-Hispanic/Latino; 6 Asian, non-Hispanic/Latino; 1 Native Hawaiian or other Pacific Islander, non-Hispanic/Latino; 2 Two or more races, non-Hispanic/Latino), 43 international. Average age 29. 124 applicants, 53% accepted, 17 enrolled. In 2017, 89 master's awarded. *Degree requirements:* For master's, comprehensive exam, project, thesis, or coursework only with additional credit hours earned; for doctorate, comprehensive exam, thesis/dissertation, minimum GPA of 3.0. *Entrance requirements:* For master's, GRE General Test, undergraduate degree, official transcripts, three letters of recommendation, statement of purpose; for doctorate, GRE, master's degree in related discipline, minimum graduate GPA of 3.5, statement of purpose, three letters of recommendation, curriculum vitae, official transcripts. Additional exam requirements/recommendations for international students: Required—TOEFL (minimum score 525 paper-based; 71 iBT). *Application deadline:* For fall admission, 7/15 priority date for domestic students, 6/15 priority date for international students; for spring admission, 12/1 priority date for domestic students, 11/1 priority date for international students; for summer admission, 5/1 priority date for domestic students, 4/1 priority date for international students. Applications are processed on a rolling basis. Application fee: $35. Electronic applications accepted. *Expenses:* Tuition, state resident: full-time $10,104; part-time $421 per semester hour. Tuition, nonresident: full-time $20,208; part-time $842 per semester hour. *Financial support:* Fellowships, research assistantships, teaching assistantships, Federal Work-Study, institutionally sponsored loans, scholarships/grants, and unspecified assistantships available. Support available to part-time students. Financial award application deadline: 3/31; financial award applicants required to submit FAFSA. *Faculty research:* Artificial intelligence, big data/data mining, STEM education, visual analytics. *Unit head:* Dr. Alec Yasinsac, Dean, School of Computing, 251-460-6390, Fax: 251-460-7274, E-mail: yasinsac@southalabama.edu. *Application contact:* Dr. Debra Chapman, Interim Graduate Director, 251-460-1599, Fax: 251-460-7274, E-mail: dchapman@southalabama.edu.
Website: http://www.southalabama.edu/colleges/soc/

University of South Florida, College of Engineering, Department of Industrial and Management Systems Engineering, Tampa, FL 33620-9951. Offers engineering management (MSEM); industrial engineering (MSIE, PhD); information technology (MSIT); materials science and engineering (MSMSE). *Program availability:* Part-time, online learning. *Faculty:* 14 full-time (3 women). *Students:* 117 full-time (25 women), 76 part-time (21 women); includes 19 minority (3 Black or African American, non-Hispanic/Latino; 4 Asian, non-Hispanic/Latino; 11 Hispanic/Latino; 1 Two or more races, non-Hispanic/Latino), 134 international. Average age 27. 417 applicants, 38% accepted, 58 enrolled. In 2017, 108 master's, 4 doctorates awarded. Terminal master's awarded for partial completion of doctoral program. *Degree requirements:* For master's, comprehensive exam, thesis (for some programs); for doctorate, comprehensive exam, thesis/dissertation, 2 tools of research as specified by dissertation committee. *Entrance requirements:* For master's, GRE General Test, BS in engineering (or equivalent) with minimum GPA of 3.0 in last 60 hours of coursework, letter of recommendation, resume; for doctorate, GRE General Test, minimum GPA of 3.0 in last 60 hours of undergraduate/graduate coursework, three letters of recommendation, statement of purpose, strong background in scientific and engineering principles. Additional exam requirements/recommendations for international students: Required—TOEFL (minimum score 550 paper-based; 79 iBT) or IELTS (minimum score 6.5). *Application deadline:* For fall admission, 2/15 for domestic and international students; for spring admission, 10/15 for domestic students, 9/15 for international students; for summer admission, 2/15 for domestic students, 1/15 for international students. Application fee: $30. Electronic applications accepted. *Financial support:* In 2017–18, 38 students received support, including 20 research assistantships with partial tuition reimbursements available (averaging $16,748 per year), 11 teaching assistantships with partial tuition reimbursements available (averaging $15,000 per year); tuition waivers (partial) also available. Financial award applicants required to submit FAFSA. *Faculty research:* Healthcare, healthcare systems, public health policies, energy and environment, manufacturing, logistics, transportation. *Total annual research expenditures:* $557,214. *Unit head:* Dr. Tapas K. Das, Professor and Department Chair, 813-974-5585, Fax: 813-974-5953, E-mail: das@usf.edu. *Application contact:* Dr. Alex Savachkin, Associate Professor and Graduate Director, 813-974-5577, Fax: 813-974-5953, E-mail: alexs@usf.edu.
Website: http://imse.eng.usf.edu

University of South Florida, Innovative Education, Tampa, FL 33620-9951. Offers adult, career and higher education (Graduate Certificate), including college teaching, leadership in developing human resources, leadership in higher education; Africana studies (Graduate Certificate), including diasporas and health disparities, genocide and human rights; aging studies (Graduate Certificate), including gerontology; art research (Graduate Certificate), including museum studies; business foundations (Graduate Certificate); chemical and biomedical engineering (Graduate Certificate), including materials science and engineering, water, health and sustainability; child and family studies (Graduate Certificate), including positive behavior support; civil and industrial engineering (Graduate Certificate), including transportation systems analysis; community and family health (Graduate Certificate), including maternal and child health, social marketing and public health, violence and injury: prevention and intervention, women's health; criminology (Graduate Certificate), including criminal justice administration; data science for public administration (Graduate Certificate); digital humanities (Graduate Certificate); educational measurement and research (Graduate Certificate), including evaluation; English (Graduate Certificate), including comparative literary studies, creative writing, professional and technical communication; entrepreneurship (Graduate Certificate); environmental health (Graduate Certificate), including safety management; epidemiology and biostatistics (Graduate Certificate), including applied biostatistics, biostatistics, concepts and tools of epidemiology, epidemiology, epidemiology of infectious diseases; geography, environment and planning (Graduate Certificate), including community development, environmental policy and management, geographical information systems; geology (Graduate Certificate), including hydrogeology; global health (Graduate Certificate), including disaster management, global health and Latin American and Caribbean studies, global health practice, humanitarian assistance, infection control; government and international affairs (Graduate Certificate), including Cuban studies, globalization studies; health policy and management (Graduate Certificate), including health management and leadership, public health policy and programs; hearing specialist: early intervention (Graduate Certificate); industrial and management systems engineering (Graduate Certificate), including systems engineering, technology management; information studies (Graduate Certificate), including school library media specialist; information systems/decision sciences (Graduate Certificate), including analytics and business intelligence; instructional technology (Graduate Certificate), including distance education, Florida digital/virtual educator, instructional design, multimedia design, Web design; internal medicine, bioethics and medical humanities (Graduate Certificate), including biomedical ethics; Latin American and Caribbean studies (Graduate Certificate); leadership for coastal resiliency planning (Graduate Certificate); mass communications (Graduate Certificate), including multimedia journalism; mathematics and statistics (Graduate Certificate), including mathematics; medicine (Graduate Certificate), including aging and neuroscience, bioinformatics, biotechnology, brain fitness and memory management, clinical investigation, hand and upper limb rehabilitation, health informatics, health sciences, integrative weight management, intellectual property, medicine and gender, metabolic and nutritional medicine, metabolic cardiology, pharmacy sciences; national and competitive intelligence (Graduate Certificate); nursing (Graduate Certificate), including simulation based academic fellowship in advanced pain management; psychological and social foundations (Graduate Certificate), including career counseling, college teaching, diversity in education, mental health counseling, school counseling; public affairs (Graduate Certificate), including nonprofit management, public management, research administration; public health (Graduate Certificate), including assessing chemical toxicity and public health risks, health equity, pharmacoepidemiology, public health generalist, toxicology, translational research in adolescent behavioral health; public health practices (Graduate Certificate), including planning for healthy communities; rehabilitation and mental health counseling (Graduate Certificate), including integrative mental health care, marriage and family therapy, rehabilitation technology; secondary education (Graduate Certificate), including ESOL, foreign language education: culture and content, foreign language education: professional; social work (Graduate Certificate), including geriatric social work/clinical gerontology; special education (Graduate Certificate), including autism spectrum disorder, disabilities education: severe/profound; world languages (Graduate Certificate), including teaching English as a second language (TESL) or foreign language. *Unit head:* Dr. Cynthia DeLuca, Associate Vice President and Assistant Vice Provost, 813-974-3077, Fax: 813-974-7061, E-mail: deluca@usf.edu. *Application contact:* Owen Hooper, Director, Summer and Alternative Calendar Programs, 813-974-6917, E-mail: hooper@usf.edu.
Website: http://www.usf.edu/innovative-education/

University of South Florida, Muma College of Business, Department of Information Systems and Decision Sciences, Tampa, FL 33620-9951. Offers business administration (PhD), including information systems; business analytics and information systems (MS), including analytics and business intelligence, information assurance. *Program availability:* Part-time. *Faculty:* 22 full-time (4 women). *Students:* 216 full-time (61 women), 110 part-time (43 women); includes 23 minority (8 Black or African American, non-Hispanic/Latino; 9 Asian, non-Hispanic/Latino; 4 Hispanic/Latino; 2 Two or more races, non-Hispanic/Latino), 269 international. Average age 27. 906 applicants, 62% accepted, 184 enrolled. In 2017, 137 master's awarded. Terminal master's awarded for partial completion of doctoral program. *Degree requirements:* For master's, comprehensive exam, thesis (for some programs), thesis or practicum project; for doctorate, comprehensive exam, thesis/dissertation. *Entrance requirements:* For master's, GMAT or GRE, letters of recommendation, statement of purpose, relevant work experience; for doctorate, GMAT or GRE, letters of recommendation, personal statement, interview. Additional exam requirements/recommendations for international students: Required—TOEFL (minimum score 550 paper-based; 79 iBT) or IELTS (minimum score 6.5). *Application deadline:* For fall admission, 6/1 for domestic students, 2/1 for international students; for spring admission, 10/15 for domestic students, 9/15 for international students. Applications are processed on a rolling basis. Application fee: $30. Electronic applications accepted. *Financial support:* In 2017–18, 40 students received support, including 8 research assistantships with tuition reimbursements available (averaging $11,972 per year), 22 teaching assistantships with tuition reimbursements available (averaging $9,002 per year); scholarships/grants, health care benefits, and unspecified assistantships also available. Financial award applicants required to submit FAFSA. *Faculty research:* Data mining, business intelligence, bioterrorism surveillance, health informatics/informatics, software engineering, agent-based modeling, distributed systems, statistics, electronic markets, e-commerce, business process improvement, operations management, supply chain, LEAN management, global information systems, organizational impacts of IT, enterprise resource planning, business intelligence, Web and mobile technologies, social networks, information security. *Total annual research expenditures:* $547,072. *Unit head:* Dr. Kaushal Chari, Chair and Professor, 813-974-6768, Fax: 813-974-6749, E-mail: kchari@usf.edu. *Application contact:* Barber Warner, 813-974-6776, Fax: 813-974-6749, E-mail: bwarner@usf.edu.
Website: http://business.usf.edu/departments/isds/

University of South Florida, Muma College of Business, Department of Management, Tampa, FL 33620-9951. Offers management (MS), including human resources, management information systems. *Accreditation:* AACSB. *Program availability:* Part-time, online learning. *Faculty:* 3 full-time (2 women). *Students:* 15 full-time (2 women), 26 part-time (13 women); includes 5 minority (3 Black or African American, non-

Hispanic/Latino; 2 Hispanic/Latino), 26 international. Average age 27. 62 applicants, 56% accepted, 18 enrolled. In 2017, 35 master's awarded. Terminal master's awarded for partial completion of doctoral program. *Degree requirements:* For master's, comprehensive exam, thesis (for some programs). *Entrance requirements:* For master's, GMAT, letters of recommendation, resume, statement of purpose, relevant work experience. Additional exam requirements/recommendations for international students: Required—TOEFL (minimum score 550 paper-based; 79 iBT) or IELTS (minimum score 6.5). *Application deadline:* For fall admission, 6/1 for domestic students, 2/1 for international students; for spring admission, 10/15 for domestic students, 7/1 for international students. Application fee: $30. Electronic applications accepted. *Financial support:* In 2017–18, 1 student received support, including 1 research assistantship with tuition reimbursement available (averaging $9,002 per year), 3 teaching assistantships with tuition reimbursements available (averaging $9,002 per year); tuition waivers also available. Financial award applicants required to submit FAFSA. *Faculty research:* Leadership and employment relations, time management, personal motivation, crew resource management in aviation, psychology of gambling, organizational culture, issues of fairness, employment law, marketing strategy/implementation, organizational diversity, ethics, environmentally-friendly business practices, green business, sustainable business plans, institutional theory, social movement theory, diffusion of innovations, stakeholder human resources management, social responsibility. *Unit head:* Dr. Sally Fuller, Interim Department Chair/Associate Professor, 813-974-1766, Fax: 813-905-9964, E-mail: sfuller@usf.edu. *Application contact:* Stacee Bender, 813-974-4516, Fax: 813-974-9964, E-mail: staceebender@usf.edu.
Website: http://www.usf.edu/business/graduate/masters/management/

The University of Tampa, Sykes College of Business, Tampa, FL 33606-1490. Offers accounting (MBA); business analytics (MBA); cybersecurity (MBA, MS); entrepreneurship (MBA, MS); finance (MBA, MS); information systems management (MBA); innovation management (MBA); international business (MBA); marketing (MBA, MS); nonprofit management (MBA, Certificate). *Accreditation:* AACSB. *Program availability:* Part-time, evening/weekend. *Faculty:* 38 full-time (14 women), 6 part-time/adjunct (1 woman). *Students:* 229 full-time (1 woman), 115 part-time (51 women); includes 51 minority (26 Black or African American, non-Hispanic/Latino; 11 Asian, non-Hispanic/Latino; 1 Native Hawaiian or other Pacific Islander, non-Hispanic/Latino; 13 Two or more races, non-Hispanic/Latino), 182 international. Average age 28. 1,305 applicants, 39% accepted, 192 enrolled. In 2017, 266 master's awarded. *Degree requirements:* For master's, capstone. *Entrance requirements:* For master's, GMAT or GRE, official transcripts from all colleges and/or universities previously attended, resume, personal statement, letters of recommendation. Additional exam requirements/recommendations for international students: Required—TOEFL (minimum score 577 paper-based; 90 iBT), IELTS (minimum score 7.5). *Application deadline:* Applications are processed on a rolling basis. Application fee: $40. Electronic applications accepted. *Expenses:* Contact institution. *Financial support:* In 2017–18, 116 students received support. Career-related internships or fieldwork, scholarships/grants, and unspecified assistantships available. Financial award applicants required to submit FAFSA. *Faculty research:* Job market signaling, on-line shopping behaviors and social media, the Tampa Bay economy, digital literacy, entrepreneurship in small businesses. *Unit head:* Dr. Natasha F. Veltri, Associate Dean, 813-253-6289, E-mail: nveltri@ut.edu. *Application contact:* Chanelle Cox, Staff Assistant, Admissions for Graduate and Continuing Studies, 813-253-6249, E-mail: ccox@ut.edu.
Website: http://www.ut.edu/business/

The University of Texas at Arlington, Graduate School, College of Business, Department of Information Systems and Operations Management, Arlington, TX 76019. Offers information systems (MS, PhD). *Program availability:* Part-time, evening/weekend. *Degree requirements:* For master's, thesis optional; for doctorate, comprehensive exam, thesis/dissertation. *Entrance requirements:* For master's, GMAT, minimum GPA of 3.0; for doctorate, GMAT/GRE. Additional exam requirements/recommendations for international students: Required—TOEFL (minimum score 550 paper-based; 79 iBT). *Faculty research:* Database modeling, strategic issues in information systems, simulations, production operations management.

The University of Texas at Austin, Graduate School, McCombs School of Business, Department of Information, Risk, and Operations Management, Austin, TX 78712-1111. Offers information management (MBA); information systems (PhD); information technology and management (MS); risk analysis and decision making (PhD); risk management (MBA); supply chain and operations management (MBA, PhD). *Degree requirements:* For doctorate, thesis/dissertation. *Entrance requirements:* For doctorate, GMAT or GRE. Electronic applications accepted. *Faculty research:* Stochastic processing and queuing, discrete nonlinear and large-scale optimization simulation, quality assurance logistics, distributed artificial intelligence, organizational modeling.

The University of Texas at Dallas, Naveen Jindal School of Management, Program in Information Systems, Richardson, TX 75080. Offers business analytics (MS); information technology and management (MS). *Program availability:* Part-time, evening/weekend. *Faculty:* 20 full-time (1 woman), 13 part-time/adjunct (3 women). *Students:* 1,290 full-time (496 women), 508 part-time (194 women); includes 147 minority (18 Black or African American, non-Hispanic/Latino; 100 Asian, non-Hispanic/Latino; 20 Hispanic/Latino; 1 Native Hawaiian or other Pacific Islander, non-Hispanic/Latino; 8 Two or more races, non-Hispanic/Latino), 1,551 international. Average age 26. 3,030 applicants, 39% accepted, 604 enrolled. In 2017, 736 master's awarded. *Degree requirements:* For master's, thesis optional. *Entrance requirements:* For master's, GMAT. Additional exam requirements/recommendations for international students: Required—TOEFL (minimum score 550 paper-based). *Application deadline:* For fall admission, 7/15 for domestic students, 5/1 priority date for international students; for spring admission, 11/15 for domestic students, 9/1 priority date for international students. Applications are processed on a rolling basis. Application fee: $50 ($100 for international students). Electronic applications accepted. *Expenses:* Tuition, state resident: full-time $12,916; part-time $718 per credit hour. Tuition, nonresident: full-time $25,252; part-time $1403 per credit hour. *Financial support:* In 2017–18, 536 students received support, including 4 research assistantships with partial tuition reimbursements available (averaging $14,400 per year), 44 teaching assistantships with partial tuition reimbursements available (averaging $10,210 per year); career-related internships or fieldwork, Federal Work-Study, institutionally sponsored loans, scholarships/grants, and unspecified assistantships also available. Support available to part-time students. Financial award application deadline: 4/30; financial award applicants required to submit FAFSA. *Faculty research:* Electronic commerce, decision support systems, data quality. *Unit head:* Dr. Syam Menon, Area Coordinator, 972-883-4779, E-mail: syam@utdallas.edu.
Website: http://jindal.utdallas.edu/isom/

The University of Texas Rio Grande Valley, College of Engineering and Computer Science, Department of Computer Science, Edinburg, TX 78541. Offers computer science (MS); information technology (MS). *Program availability:* Part-time, evening/weekend, online learning. *Degree requirements:* For master's, comprehensive exam, thesis optional. *Entrance requirements:* For master's, GRE General Test. Additional exam requirements/recommendations for international students: Required—TOEFL (minimum score 550 paper-based, 79 iBT) or IELTS (6.5). *Application deadline:* For fall admission, 4/15 priority date for domestic students; for spring admission, 10/15 priority date for domestic students; for summer admission, 3/1 priority date for domestic

students. Applications are processed on a rolling basis. Application fee: $50 ($100 for international students). Electronic applications accepted. *Expenses:* Tuition, state resident: full-time $5550; part-time $417 per credit hour. Tuition, nonresident: full-time $13,020; part-time $832 per credit hour. *Required fees:* $1169. *Financial support:* Research assistantships, teaching assistantships, career-related internships or fieldwork, Federal Work-Study, and scholarships/grants available. Support available to part-time students. Financial award applicants required to submit FAFSA. *Faculty research:* Artificial intelligence, distributed systems, Internet computing, theoretical computer sciences, information visualization. *Unit head:* Dr. Emmett Tomai, Chair, 956-665-2320, E-mail: emmett.tomai@utrgv.edu. *Application contact:* Dr. Zhixiang Chen, Graduate Coordinator, 956-665-2320, E-mail: zhixiang.chen@utrgv.edu.
Website: http://www.utrgv.edu/csci

University of the Sacred Heart, Graduate Programs, Department of Business Administration, Program in Information Systems Management, San Juan, PR 00914-0383. Offers MBA. *Program availability:* Part-time, evening/weekend. *Degree requirements:* For master's, thesis. *Entrance requirements:* For master's, EXADEP, minimum undergraduate GPA of 2.75, interview.

University of the West, Department of Business Administration, Rosemead, CA 91770. Offers business administration (EMBA); computer information systems (MBA); finance (MBA); international business (MBA); nonprofit organization management (MBA). *Program availability:* Part-time, evening/weekend. *Entrance requirements:* Additional exam requirements/recommendations for international students: Required—TOEFL.

University of Utah, Graduate School, David Eccles School of Business, Business Administration Program, Salt Lake City, UT 84112. Offers accounting (PhD); business administration (EMBA, MBA, PMBA); finance (PhD); information systems (PhD); marketing (PhD); operations management (PhD); organizational behavior (PhD); strategic management (PhD); MBA/JD; MBA/MHA; MBA/MS. *Program availability:* Part-time, evening/weekend, online learning. *Faculty:* 58 full-time (21 women), 37 part-time/adjunct (7 women). *Students:* 558 full-time (149 women), 103 part-time (21 women); includes 66 minority (1 Black or African American, non-Hispanic/Latino; 16 Asian, non-Hispanic/Latino; 41 Hispanic/Latino; 8 Two or more races, non-Hispanic/Latino), 50 international. Average age 27. 442 applicants, 70% accepted, 226 enrolled. In 2017, 298 master's, 7 doctorates awarded. *Entrance requirements:* For master's, GMAT or GRE; for doctorate, GMAT. Additional exam requirements/recommendations for international students: Required—TOEFL (minimum score 600 paper-based; 100 iBT), IELTS (minimum score 7). *Application deadline:* Applications are processed on a rolling basis. Application fee: $55 ($65 for international students). Electronic applications accepted. *Expenses:* Contact institution. *Financial support:* In 2017–18, 53 students received support. Fellowships, scholarships/grants, and unspecified assistantships available. Financial award application deadline: 2/1; financial award applicants required to submit FAFSA. *Faculty research:* Corporate finance, strategy services, consumer behavior, financial disclosures, operations. *Unit head:* Kristina Diekmann, Department Chair, 801-581-8524, Fax: 801-581-3380, E-mail: mastersinfo@business.utah.edu. *Application contact:* Christine Harris, Coordinator, 801-581-7785, Fax: 801-585-3962, E-mail: execch@business.utah.edu.
Website: http://www.business.utah.edu/

University of Utah, Graduate School, David Eccles School of Business, Master of Science in Information Systems Program, Salt Lake City, UT 84112-8939. Offers information systems (MS, Graduate Certificate), including business intelligence and analytics, IT security, product and process management, software and systems architecture. *Program availability:* Part-time, evening/weekend, 100% online, blended/hybrid learning. *Students:* 150 full-time (53 women), 121 part-time (38 women); includes 29 minority (2 Black or African American, non-Hispanic/Latino; 10 Asian, non-Hispanic/Latino; 12 Hispanic/Latino; 5 Two or more races, non-Hispanic/Latino), 124 international. Average age 28. In 2017, 155 master's awarded. *Degree requirements:* For master's, capstone project. *Entrance requirements:* For master's, GMAT/GRE, minimum undergraduate GPA of 3.0, 2 letters of recommendation, personal statement, professional resume. Additional exam requirements/recommendations for international students: Required—TOEFL (minimum score 550 paper-based; 80 iBT), IELTS (minimum score 6.5). *Application deadline:* For fall admission, 7/27 for domestic students, 3/30 for international students; for spring admission, 12/7 for domestic students, 9/7 priority date for international students; for summer admission, 4/12 for domestic students, 1/11 for international students. Applications are processed on a rolling basis. Application fee: $55 ($65 for international students). Electronic applications accepted. *Expenses:* Contact institution. *Financial support:* Fellowships with partial tuition reimbursements, teaching assistantships, tuition waivers (partial), and unspecified assistantships available. Financial award application deadline: 6/1; financial award applicants required to submit FAFSA. *Faculty research:* Business intelligence and analytics, software and system architecture, product and process management, IT security, Web and data mining, applications and management of IT in healthcare. *Unit head:* Dr. Bradden Blair, Director of the IS Programs, 801-587-9489, Fax: 801-581-3666, E-mail: b.blair@eccles.utah.edu. *Application contact:* Jan Bents, Admissions Coordinator, 801-587-5878, Fax: 801-581-3666, E-mail: jan.bents@eccles.utah.edu.
Website: http://msis.eccles.utah.edu

University of Washington, Graduate School, Michael G. Foster School of Business, Seattle, WA 98195-3200. Offers auditing and assurance (MP Acc); business administration (MBA, PhD); entrepreneurship (MS); executive business administration (MBA); global executive business administration (MBA); information systems (MSIS); supply chain management (MSSCM); taxation (MP Acc); technology management (MBA); JD/MBA; MBA/MAIS; MBA/MHA. *Accreditation:* AACSB. *Program availability:* Part-time, evening/weekend, blended/hybrid learning. *Faculty:* 109 full-time (35 women), 54 part-time/adjunct (32 women). *Students:* 469 full-time (173 women), 638 part-time (216 women); includes 314 minority (15 Black or African American, non-Hispanic/Latino; 6 American Indian or Alaska Native, non-Hispanic/Latino; 246 Asian, non-Hispanic/Latino; 28 Hispanic/Latino; 5 Native Hawaiian or other Pacific Islander, non-Hispanic/Latino; 14 Two or more races, non-Hispanic/Latino), 125 international. Average age 32. 1,809 applicants, 84% accepted, 1107 enrolled. In 2017, 543 master's, 10 doctorates awarded. Terminal master's awarded for partial completion of doctoral program. *Degree requirements:* For doctorate, comprehensive exam, thesis/dissertation. *Entrance requirements:* For master's and doctorate, GMAT, GRE. Additional exam requirements/recommendations for international students: Required—TOEFL (minimum score 600 paper-based; 100 iBT). *Application deadline:* For fall admission, 3/15 for domestic students, 1/15 for international students. Application fee: $85. Electronic applications accepted. *Expenses:* Contact institution. *Financial support:* Fellowships with partial tuition reimbursements, research assistantships with partial tuition reimbursements, teaching assistantships with partial tuition reimbursements, Federal Work-Study, institutionally sponsored loans, and scholarships/grants available. Financial award application deadline: 2/28; financial award applicants required to submit FAFSA. *Faculty research:* Finance, consumer behavior, marketing analytics, technology management, supply chain. *Unit head:* Dr. James Jiambalvo, Dean, 206-543-4750, E-mail: jjiambal@uw.edu. *Application contact:* Erin Town, Director of Admissions, 206-543-4661, Fax: 206-616-7351, E-mail: mba@uw.edu.
Website: http://www.foster.washington.edu/

Management Information Systems

University of Wisconsin–Madison, Graduate School, Wisconsin School of Business, Doctoral Program in Accounting and Information Systems, Madison, WI 53706-1380. Offers PhD. *Accreditation:* AACSB. *Degree requirements:* For doctorate, comprehensive exam, thesis/dissertation. *Entrance requirements:* For doctorate, GMAT or GRE. Additional exam requirements/recommendations for international students: Recommended—TOEFL (minimum score 623 paper-based; 106 iBT), IELTS (minimum score 7.5). Electronic applications accepted. *Expenses:* Contact institution. *Faculty research:* Auditing, financial reporting, economic theory, strategy, computer models, Internal audit and fraud, health care fiscal management, tax reporting, incentives used in nonprofit hospitals, CFO compensation, state and local taxation, audit quality, FASB pronouncements, financial statement analysis.

University of Wisconsin–Madison, Graduate School, Wisconsin School of Business, Doctoral Program in Operations and Information Management, Madison, WI 53706-1380. Offers information systems (PhD); operations management (PhD). *Degree requirements:* For doctorate, comprehensive exam, thesis/dissertation. *Entrance requirements:* For doctorate, GMAT or GRE General Test. Additional exam requirements/recommendations for international students: Recommended—TOEFL (minimum score 623 paper-based; 106 iBT), IELTS (minimum score 7.5), TSE (minimum score 73). Electronic applications accepted. *Expenses:* Contact institution. *Faculty research:* Supply chain management, reorganization of the factory, creating continuous innovation, transportation economics, organizational economics, health care operations management, econometric analysis, forecasting, project management.

Utah State University, School of Graduate Studies, Jon M. Huntsman School of Business, Department of Management Information Systems, Logan, UT 84322. Offers MMIS. *Program availability:* Part-time. *Degree requirements:* For master's, thesis optional. *Entrance requirements:* For master's, GMAT, minimum GPA of 3.2. Additional exam requirements/recommendations for international students: Required—TOEFL. *Faculty research:* Oral and written communication, methods of teaching, CASE tools, object-oriented programming, decision support systems.

Valparaiso University, Graduate School and Continuing Education, Program in Information Technology, Valparaiso, IN 46383. Offers computing (MS); management (MS); security8441 (MS). *Program availability:* Part-time, evening/weekend. *Entrance requirements:* For master's, minimum GPA of 3.0; minor or equivalent in computer science, information technology, or a related field. Additional exam requirements/recommendations for international students: Required—TOEFL (minimum score 550 paper-based; 80 iBT), IELTS (minimum score 6). Electronic applications accepted. *Expenses: Tuition:* Full-time $11,340; part-time $630 per credit hour. *Required fees:* $520; $250 per year. $125 per semester. Tuition and fees vary according to program and reciprocity agreements.

Virginia Commonwealth University, Graduate School, School of Business, Program in Information Systems, Richmond, VA 23284-9005. Offers MS. *Entrance requirements:* For master's, GMAT. Additional exam requirements/recommendations for international students: Required—TOEFL (minimum score 600 paper-based; 100 iBT); Recommended—IELTS (minimum score 6.5). Electronic applications accepted.

Virginia International University, School of Computer Information Systems, Fairfax, VA 22030. Offers business intelligence (Graduate Certificate); business intelligence and data analytics (MIS); computer science (MS), including computer animation and gaming, cybersecurity, data management networking, intelligent systems, software applications development, software engineering; cybersecurity (MIS); data management (MIS); enterprise project management (MIS); health informatics (MIS); information assurance (MIS); information systems (Graduate Certificate); information systems management (MS, Graduate Certificate); information technology (MS); information technology audit and compliance (Graduate Certificate); knowledge management (MIS); software engineering (MS). *Program availability:* Part-time, online learning. *Entrance requirements:* For master's, bachelor's degree. Additional exam requirements/recommendations for international students: Required—TOEFL (minimum score 550 paper-based; 80 iBT), IELTS. Electronic applications accepted.

Virginia Polytechnic Institute and State University, Graduate School, Intercollege, Blacksburg, VA 24061. Offers genetics, bioinformatics, and computational biology (PhD); information technology (MIT); macromolecular science and engineering (MS, PhD); translational biology, medicine, and health (PhD). *Students:* 167 full-time (86 women), 776 part-time (278 women); includes 252 minority (60 Black or African American, non-Hispanic/Latino; 113 Asian, non-Hispanic/Latino; 41 Hispanic/Latino; 1 Native Hawaiian or other Pacific Islander, non-Hispanic/Latino; 37 Two or more races, non-Hispanic/Latino), 81 international. Average age 33. 664 applicants, 65% accepted, 304 enrolled. In 2017, 93 master's, 13 doctorates awarded. *Degree requirements:* For master's, comprehensive exam (for some programs), thesis (for some programs); for doctorate, comprehensive exam (for some programs), thesis/dissertation (for some programs). *Entrance requirements:* For master's and doctorate, GRE/GMAT. Additional exam requirements/recommendations for international students: Required—TOEFL (minimum score 80 iBT). *Application deadline:* For fall admission, 8/1 for domestic students, 4/1 for international students; for spring admission, 1/1 for domestic students, 9/1 for international students. Applications are processed on a rolling basis. Application fee: $75. Electronic applications accepted. *Expenses:* Tuition, state resident: full-time $15,072; part-time $718.50 per credit hour. Tuition, nonresident: full-time $28,810; part-time $1448.25 per credit hour. *Required fees:* $2741; $502 per semester. Tuition and fees vary according to course load, campus/location and program. *Financial support:* In 2017–18, 39 fellowships with full and partial tuition reimbursements (averaging $17,696 per year), 119 research assistantships with full tuition reimbursements (averaging $24,500 per year), 20 teaching assistantships with full tuition reimbursements (averaging $24,663 per year) were awarded. Financial award application deadline: 3/1; financial award applicants required to submit FAFSA. *Unit head:* Dr. Karen P. DePauw, Vice President and Dean for Graduate Education, 540-231-7581, Fax: 540-231-1670, E-mail: kpdepauw@vt.edu.

Virginia Polytechnic Institute and State University, Graduate School, Pamplin College of Business, Blacksburg, VA 24061. Offers accounting and information systems (MACIS, PhD); business (PhD), including marketing (MS, PhD); business administration (MS), including business analytics, marketing (MS, PhD); business information technology (PhD); executive business research (PhD); finance (PhD); MS/MBA. *Faculty:* 131 full-time (42 women), 2 part-time/adjunct (1 woman). *Students:* 261 full-time (101 women), 189 part-time (76 women); includes 112 minority (32 Black or African American, non-Hispanic/Latino; 50 Asian, non-Hispanic/Latino; 15 Hispanic/Latino; 15 Two or more races, non-Hispanic/Latino), 80 international. Average age 32. 434 applicants, 57% accepted, 168 enrolled. In 2017, 142 master's, 11 doctorates awarded. *Degree requirements:* For master's, comprehensive exam (for some programs), thesis (for some programs); for doctorate, comprehensive exam (for some programs), thesis/dissertation (for some programs). *Entrance requirements:* For master's and doctorate, GRE/GMAT. Additional exam requirements/recommendations for international students: Required—TOEFL (minimum score 80 iBT). *Application deadline:* For fall admission, 8/1 for domestic students, 4/1 for international students; for spring admission, 1/1 for domestic students, 9/1 for international students. Applications are processed on a rolling basis. Application fee: $75. Electronic applications accepted. *Expenses:* Tuition, state resident: full-time $15,072; part-time $718.50 per credit hour. Tuition, nonresident: full-

time $28,810; part-time $1448.25 per credit hour. *Required fees:* $2741; $502 per semester. Tuition and fees vary according to course load, campus/location and program. *Financial support:* In 2017–18, 9 research assistantships with full tuition reimbursements (averaging $18,588 per year), 48 teaching assistantships with full tuition reimbursements (averaging $22,706 per year) were awarded. Financial award application deadline: 3/1; financial award applicants required to submit FAFSA. *Total annual research expenditures:* $3.4 million. *Unit head:* Dr. Robert T. Sumichrast, Dean, 540-231-6601, Fax: 540-231-4487, E-mail: busdean@vt.edu. *Application contact:* Kimberly Ridpath, Executive Assistant, 540-231-9647, Fax: 540-231-4487, E-mail: ridpathk@vt.edu.
Website: http://www.pamplin.vt.edu/

Virginia Polytechnic Institute and State University, VT Online, Blacksburg, VA 24061. Offers advanced transportation systems (Certificate); aerospace engineering (MS); agricultural and life sciences (MSLFS); business information systems (Graduate Certificate); career and technical education (MS); civil engineering (MS); computer engineering (M Eng, MS); decision support systems (Graduate Certificate); eLearning leadership (MA); electrical engineering (M Eng, MS); engineering administration (MEA); environmental engineering (Certificate); environmental politics and policy (Graduate Certificate); environmental sciences and engineering (MS); foundations of political analysis (Graduate Certificate); health product risk management (Graduate Certificate); industrial and systems engineering (MS); information policy and society (Graduate Certificate); information security (Graduate Certificate); information technology (MIT); instructional technology (MA); integrative STEM education (MA Ed); liberal arts (Graduate Certificate); life sciences: health product risk management (MS); natural resources (MNR, Graduate Certificate); networking (Graduate Certificate); nonprofit and nongovernmental organization management (Graduate Certificate); ocean engineering (MS); political science (MA); security studies (Graduate Certificate); software development (Graduate Certificate). *Expenses:* Tuition, state resident: full-time $15,072; part-time $718.50 per credit hour. Tuition, nonresident: full-time $28,810; part-time $1448.25 per credit hour. *Required fees:* $2741; $502 per semester. Tuition and fees vary according to course load, campus/location and program.

Walden University, Graduate Programs, School of Information Systems and Technology, Minneapolis, MN 55401. Offers information systems (Graduate Certificate); information systems management (MISM); information technology (MS, DIT), including health informatics (MS), information assurance and cyber security (MS), information systems (MS), software engineering (MS). *Program availability:* Part-time, evening/weekend, online only, 100% online. *Degree requirements:* For doctorate, thesis/dissertation (for some programs), residency. *Entrance requirements:* For master's, bachelor's degree or higher; minimum GPA of 2.5; official transcripts; goal statement (for some programs); access to computer and Internet; for doctorate, master's degree or higher; three years of related professional or academic experience (preferred); minimum GPA of 3.0; goal statement and current resume (for select programs); official transcripts; access to computer and Internet; for Graduate Certificate, relevant work experience; access to computer and Internet. Additional exam requirements/recommendations for international students: Required—TOEFL (minimum score 550 paper-based, 79 iBT), IELTS (minimum score 6.5), Michigan English Language Assessment Battery (minimum score 82), or PTE (minimum score 53). Electronic applications accepted.

Walden University, Graduate Programs, School of Management, Minneapolis, MN 55401. Offers accounting (MBA, MS, DBA), including accounting for the professional (MS), accounting with CPA emphasis (MS), self-designed (MS); advanced project management (Graduate Certificate); applied project management (Graduate Certificate); auditing (Graduate Certificate); bridge to business administration (Post-Doctoral Certificate); bridge to management (Post-Doctoral Certificate); business management (Graduate Certificate); communication (MBA); corporate finance (MBA); digital marketing (Graduate Certificate); entrepreneurship (DBA); entrepreneurship and small business (MBA); finance (MS, DBA), including finance for the professional (MS), finance with CFA/investment (MS), finance with CPA emphasis (MS); global supply chain management (DBA); healthcare management (MBA, DBA); human resource management (MBA, MS, Graduate Certificate), including functional human resource management (MS), general program (MS), integrating functional and strategic human resource management (MS), organizational strategy (MS); human resources management (DBA); information systems management (DBA); international business (MBA, DBA); leadership (MBA, MS, DBA, Graduate Certificate), including general program (MS), human resource leadership (MS), leader development (MS), self-designed (MS); management (MS, PhD), including communications (MS), finance (PhD), general program (MS), healthcare management (MS), human resource management (MS), human resources management (PhD), information systems management (PhD), international business (MS), leadership (MS), leadership and organizational change (PhD), marketing (MS), project management (MS), strategy and operations (MS); managerial accounting (Graduate Certificate); marketing (MBA, MS, DBA); project management (MBA, MS, DBA); self-designed (MBA, DBA); social impact management (DBA); technology entrepreneurship (DBA). *Accreditation:* ACBSP. *Program availability:* Part-time, evening/weekend, online only, 100% online. *Degree requirements:* For master's, thesis (for some programs), residency (for EMBA); for doctorate, thesis/dissertation (for some programs), residency. *Entrance requirements:* For master's, bachelor's degree or higher; minimum GPA of 2.5; official transcripts; goal statement (for some programs); access to computer and Internet; for doctorate, master's degree or higher; three years of related professional or academic experience (preferred); minimum GPA of 3.0; goal statement and current resume (for select programs); official transcripts; access to computer and Internet; for other advanced degree, relevant work experience; access to computer and Internet. Additional exam requirements/recommendations for international students: Required—TOEFL (minimum score 550 paper-based, 79 iBT), IELTS (minimum score 6.5), Michigan English Language Assessment Battery (minimum score 82), or PTE (minimum score 53). Electronic applications accepted.

Walsh College of Accountancy and Business Administration, Graduate Programs, Program in Information Technology, Troy, MI 48083. Offers chief information officer (MSIT); cybersecurity (MSIT); data science (MSIT); global project and program management (MSIT). *Program availability:* Part-time, evening/weekend. *Faculty:* 2 full-time (1 woman), 5 part-time/adjunct (2 women). *Students:* 72 (25 women); includes 24 minority (15 Black or African American, non-Hispanic/Latino; 4 Asian, non-Hispanic/Latino; 2 Hispanic/Latino; 3 Two or more races, non-Hispanic/Latino), 12 international. Average age 36. 44 applicants, 82% accepted, 27 enrolled. In 2017, 14 master's awarded. *Entrance requirements:* For master's, minimum overall cumulative GPA of 2.75 from all colleges previously attended. Additional exam requirements/recommendations for international students: Required—TOEFL (minimum score 550 paper-based, 79 iBT), IELTS (6.5), Michigan English Language Assessment Battery, or MTELP (80). *Application deadline:* Applications are processed on a rolling basis. Application fee: $35. Electronic applications accepted. *Expenses:* $770 per semester credit hour plus $125 registration fee per semester. *Financial support:* In 2017–18, 3 students received support. Career-related internships or fieldwork and scholarships/grants available. Financial award application deadline: 6/30; financial award applicants required to submit FAFSA. *Faculty research:* Business intelligence, data and decision-making, cyber security, project management, mobile technologies. *Unit head:* David

Schippers, Chair, Information Technology and Decision Sciences, 248-823-1635, Fax: 248-689-0920, E-mail: dschippe@walshcollege.edu. *Application contact:* Heather Rigby, Director, Admissions and Academic Advising, 248-823-1600, Fax: 248-823-1611, E-mail: hrigby@walshcollege.edu.

Wayland Baptist University, Graduate Programs, Programs in Business Administration/Management, Plainview, TX 79072-6998. Offers accounting (MBA); general business (MBA); health care administration (MAM, MBA); human resource management (MAM, MBA); international management (MBA); management (MBA, D Mgt); management information systems (MBA); organization management (MAM); project management (MBA). *Program availability:* Part-time, evening/weekend, online learning. *Faculty:* 30 full-time (5 women), 38 part-time/adjunct (9 women). *Students:* 42 full-time (20 women), 538 part-time (253 women); includes 311 minority (98 Black or African American, non-Hispanic/Latino; 4 American Indian or Alaska Native, non-Hispanic/Latino; 16 Asian, non-Hispanic/Latino; 153 Hispanic/Latino; 11 Native Hawaiian or other Pacific Islander, non-Hispanic/Latino; 29 Two or more races, non-Hispanic/Latino), 6 international. Average age 40. 100 applicants, 96% accepted, 60 enrolled. In 2017, 216 master's awarded. *Degree requirements:* For master's, capstone course. *Entrance requirements:* For master's, GMAT, GRE or MAT. Additional exam requirements/recommendations for international students: Required—TOEFL (minimum score 500 paper-based; 61 iBT). *Application deadline:* Applications are processed on a rolling basis. Application fee: $50. Electronic applications accepted. *Expenses: Tuition:* Full-time $11,250; part-time $625 per credit hour. *Required fees:* $1200. *Financial support:* Federal Work-Study, institutionally sponsored loans, and scholarships/grants available. Support available to part-time students. Financial award application deadline: 5/1; financial award applicants required to submit FAFSA. *Unit head:* Dr. Kelly Warren, Chairman, 806-291-1020, Fax: 806-291-1957, E-mail: warrenk@wbu.edu. *Application contact:* Amanda Stanton, Graduate Studies, 806-291-3423, Fax: 806-291-1950, E-mail: stanton@wbu.edu.

Wayne State University, Mike Ilitch School of Business, Detroit, MI 48202. Offers accounting (MS, MSA, Postbaccalaureate Certificate); business (EMS, Graduate Certificate); business administration (MBA, PhD); data science (MS), including business analytics; entrepreneurship and innovation (Postbaccalaureate Certificate); finance (MS); information systems management (Postbaccalaureate Certificate); taxation (MST); JD/MBA. Application deadline for PhD is February 15. *Accreditation:* AACSB. *Program availability:* Part-time, evening/weekend. *Faculty:* 32. *Students:* 235 full-time (121 women), 1,082 part-time (480 women); includes 356 minority (202 Black or African American, non-Hispanic/Latino; 2 American Indian or Alaska Native, non-Hispanic/Latino; 79 Asian, non-Hispanic/Latino; 47 Hispanic/Latino; 26 Two or more races, non-Hispanic/Latino), 87 international. Average age 30. 1,285 applicants, 43% accepted, 308 enrolled. In 2017, 200 master's, 2 doctorates, 9 other advanced degrees awarded. *Degree requirements:* For doctorate, thesis/dissertation. *Entrance requirements:* For master's, GMAT, GRE, LSAT, MCAT, at least three years of relevant work experience that shows increased responsibility, or minimum GPA of 3.0 from AACSB-accredited program or 3.2 from regionally-accredited program, undergraduate degree from accredited institution; undergraduate degree in accounting, business administration, or area of business administration (for MS and MST); for doctorate, GMAT (minimum score of 600), minimum undergraduate GPA of 3.0, 3.5 upper-division or graduate; three letters of recommendation; brief essay; undergraduate degree from accredited institution; personal statement; for other advanced degree, bachelor's degree from accredited institution. Additional exam requirements/recommendations for international students: Required—TOEFL (minimum score 550 paper-based; 79 iBT), Michigan English Language Assessment Battery (minimum score 85); Recommended—IELTS (minimum score 6.5), TWE (minimum score 5.5). *Application deadline:* For fall admission, 7/1 for domestic students, 5/1 for international students; for winter admission, 11/1 for domestic students, 9/1 priority date for international students; for spring admission, 3/1 for domestic students, 1/1 priority date for international students. Applications are processed on a rolling basis. Application fee: $50. Electronic applications accepted. *Expenses:* Contact institution. *Financial support:* In 2017–18, 165 students received support, including 1 fellowship with tuition reimbursement available (averaging $18,534 per year), 1 teaching assistantship with tuition reimbursement available (averaging $18,534 per year); research assistantships with tuition reimbursements available, scholarships/grants, health care benefits, and unspecified assistantships also available. Support available to part-time students. Financial award applicants required to submit FAFSA. *Faculty research:* Executive compensation and stock performance, consumer reactions to pricing strategies, communication across the automotive supply chain, performance of firms in sub-Saharan Africa, implementation issues with ERP software. *Unit head:* Dr. Robert Forsythe, Dean, School of Business Administration, 313-577-4501, E-mail: robert.forsythe@wayne.edu. *Application contact:* Kiantee N. Rupert-Jones, Director, 313-577-4511, Fax: 313-577-9442, E-mail: gradbusiness@wayne.edu.
Website: http://ilitchbusiness.wayne.edu/

Wayne State University, School of Information Sciences, Detroit, MI 48202. Offers archival administration (Graduate Certificate); information management (MS, Graduate Certificate); library and information science (MLIS, Graduate Certificate, Spec); public library services to children and young adults (Graduate Certificate); MLIS/MA. *Accreditation:* ALA (one or more programs are accredited). *Program availability:* Part-time, evening/weekend, 100% online, blended/hybrid learning. *Faculty:* 12 full-time (9 women), 17 part-time/adjunct (12 women). *Students:* 100 full-time (80 women), 359 part-time (290 women); includes 77 minority (42 Black or African American, non-Hispanic/Latino; 2 American Indian or Alaska Native, non-Hispanic/Latino; 3 Asian, non-Hispanic/Latino; 19 Hispanic/Latino; 1 Native Hawaiian or other Pacific Islander, non-Hispanic/Latino; 10 Two or more races, non-Hispanic/Latino), 1 international. Average age 33. 258 applicants, 60% accepted, 100 enrolled. In 2017, 149 master's, 34 other advanced degrees awarded. *Degree requirements:* For master's and other advanced degree, e-portfolio. *Entrance requirements:* For master's, GRE or MAT (if undergraduate GPA is between 2.5 and 2.99), minimum undergraduate GPA of 3.0 or graduate degree, personal statement, resume or curriculum vitae; for other advanced degree, GRE or MAT (if undergraduate GPA is between 2.5 and 2.99), minimum undergraduate GPA of 3.0 or graduate degree, personal statement, resume or curriculum vitae, MLIS (for specialist certificate). Additional exam requirements/recommendations for international students: Required—TOEFL (minimum score 550 paper-based; 79 iBT); Recommended—IELTS (minimum score 6.5), TWE (minimum score 5.5). *Application deadline:* For fall admission, 7/1 for domestic students, 5/1 priority date for international students; for winter admission, 10/1 priority date for domestic students, 9/1 priority date for international students; for spring admission, 2/1 priority date for domestic students, 1/1 priority date for international students. Applications are processed on a rolling basis. Application fee: $50. Electronic applications accepted. *Expenses:* Contact institution. *Financial support:* In 2017–18, 133 students received support. Fellowships with tuition reimbursements available, scholarships/grants, health care benefits, and unspecified assistantships available. Support available to part-time students. Financial award applicants required to submit FAFSA. *Faculty research:* Library services, information management issues, digital content management, library/community engagement, archives and preservation. *Unit head:* Dr. Jon Cawthorne, Dean, 313-577-4020, E-mail: jon.cawthorne@wayne.edu. *Application contact:* Academic Services Officer II, 313-577-1825, E-mail: asklis@wayne.edu.
Website: http://slis.wayne.edu/

Webster University, George Herbert Walker School of Business and Technology, Department of Business, St. Louis, MO 63119-3194. Offers business and organizational security management (MBA); decision support systems (MBA); environmental management (MBA); finance (MBA, MS); forensic accounting (MS); gerontology (MBA); human resources development (MBA); human resources management (MBA); information technology management (MBA); international business (MA, MBA); international relations (MBA); management and leadership (MBA); marketing (MBA); media communications (MBA); procurement and acquisitions management (MBA); Web services (MBA). *Accreditation:* ACBSP. *Program availability:* Part-time, evening/weekend, online learning. *Degree requirements:* For master's, comprehensive exam (for some programs), thesis (for some programs). *Entrance requirements:* Additional exam requirements/recommendations for international students: Required—TOEFL.

Webster University, George Herbert Walker School of Business and Technology, Department of Management, St. Louis, MO 63119-3194. Offers business and organizational security management (MA); digital marketing management (Graduate Certificate); government contracting (Graduate Certificate); health administration (MHA); health care management (MA); health services management (MA); human resources development (MA); human resources management (MA); information technology management (MA, MS); management (D Mgt); management and leadership (MA); marketing (MA); nonprofit leadership (MA); nonprofit revenue development (Graduate Certificate); organizational development (Graduate Certificate); procurement and acquisitions management (MA); public administration (MPA); space systems operations management (MS). *Program availability:* Part-time, evening/weekend, online learning. *Degree requirements:* For master's, thesis (for some programs); for doctorate, thesis/dissertation, written exam. *Entrance requirements:* For doctorate, GMAT, 3 years of work experience, MBA. Additional exam requirements/recommendations for international students: Required—TOEFL.

West Chester University of Pennsylvania, College of the Sciences and Mathematics, Department of Computer Science, West Chester, PA 19383. Offers computer science (MS); computer security (information assurance) (Certificate); information systems (Certificate); Web technology (Certificate). *Program availability:* Part-time, evening/weekend. *Students:* 13 full-time (5 women), 13 part-time (5 women); includes 7 minority (3 Black or African American, non-Hispanic/Latino; 4 Asian, non-Hispanic/Latino), 7 international. Average age 35. 27 applicants, 89% accepted, 13 enrolled. In 2017, 17 master's, 9 other advanced degrees awarded. *Degree requirements:* For master's, thesis optional, 33 credits; for Certificate, 12 credits. *Entrance requirements:* For master's, GRE, two letters of reference; for Certificate, BS. Additional exam requirements/recommendations for international students: Required—TOEFL or IELTS. *Application deadline:* For fall admission, 5/15 for international students; for spring admission, 10/15 for international students. Applications are processed on a rolling basis. Application fee: $50. Electronic applications accepted. *Expenses:* Tuition, state resident: full-time $9000; part-time $500 per credit. Tuition, nonresident: full-time $13,500; part-time $750 per credit. *Required fees:* $2959; $149.79 per credit. *Financial support:* Scholarships/grants and unspecified assistantships available. Financial award application deadline: 2/15; financial award applicants required to submit FAFSA. *Faculty research:* Security in mobile ad-hoc networks, intrusion detection, security and trust in pervasive computing, cloud computing, wireless sensor networks, cloud computing and data mining. *Unit head:* Dr. James Fabrey, Chair, 610-436-2204, E-mail: jfabrey@wcupa.edu. *Application contact:* Dr. Afrand Agah, Graduate Coordinator, 610-430-4419, E-mail: aagah@wcupa.edu.
Website: http://www.cs.wcupa.edu/

Western Governors University, College of Business, Salt Lake City, UT 84107. Offers information technology management (MBA); integrated healthcare management (MS); management and strategy (MBA); strategic leadership (MBA). *Program availability:* Evening/weekend. *Degree requirements:* For master's, capstone project. *Entrance requirements:* For master's, Readiness Assessment, transcripts. Additional exam requirements/recommendations for international students: Required—TOEFL (minimum score 450 paper-based; 80 iBT). Electronic applications accepted.

Wichita State University, Graduate School, W. Frank Barton School of Business, School of Accountancy, Wichita, KS 67260. Offers accounting information systems (M Acc); taxation (M Acc). *Accreditation:* AACSB. *Program availability:* Part-time, evening/weekend. *Unit head:* Dr. Paul D. Harrison, Director, 316-978-3215, Fax: 316-978-3660, E-mail: paul.harrison@wichita.edu. *Application contact:* Jordan Oleson, Admissions Coordinator, 316-978-3095, Fax: 316-978-3253, E-mail: jordan.oleson@wichita.edu.
Website: http://www.wichita.edu/acct

Wilmington University, College of Business, New Castle, DE 19720-6491. Offers accounting (MBA, MS); business administration (MBA, DBA); environmental stewardship (MBA); finance (MBA); health care administration (MBA, MSM); homeland security (MBA, MSM); human resource management (MSM); management information systems (MBA, MSN); marketing (MSM); marketing management (MBA); military leadership (MSM); organizational leadership (MBA, MSM); public administration (MSM). *Program availability:* Part-time, evening/weekend. *Faculty:* 16 full-time (8 women), 106 part-time/adjunct (49 women). *Students:* 525 full-time (294 women), 1,212 part-time (780 women); includes 557 minority (412 Black or African American, non-Hispanic/Latino; 14 American Indian or Alaska Native, non-Hispanic/Latino; 55 Asian, non-Hispanic/Latino; 25 Hispanic/Latino; 3 Native Hawaiian or other Pacific Islander, non-Hispanic/Latino; 48 Two or more races, non-Hispanic/Latino), 157 international. Average age 35. 1,484 applicants, 70% accepted, 685 enrolled. In 2017, 543 master's, 16 doctorates awarded. *Entrance requirements:* Additional exam requirements/recommendations for international students: Required—TOEFL (minimum score 500 paper-based). *Application deadline:* Applications are processed on a rolling basis. Application fee: $35. Electronic applications accepted. *Expenses: Tuition:* Part-time $466 per credit. *Required fees:* $25 per semester. Tuition and fees vary according to degree level and campus/location. *Financial support:* Applicants required to submit FAFSA. *Unit head:* Dr. Kathy S. Kennedy Ratajack, Dean, 302-356-2481. *Application contact:* Laura Morris, Director of Admissions, 877-967-5456, E-mail: infocenter@wilmu.edu.
Website: http://www.wilmu.edu/business/

Wilmington University, College of Technology, New Castle, DE 19720-6491. Offers cybersecurity (MS); information assurance (MS); information systems technologies (MS); management and management information systems (MS); technology project management (MS); Web design (MS). *Program availability:* Part-time, evening/weekend. *Faculty:* 5 full-time (2 women), 99 part-time/adjunct (31 women). *Students:* 631 full-time (159 women), 486 part-time (141 women); includes 91 minority (53 Black or African American, non-Hispanic/Latino; 3 American Indian or Alaska Native, non-Hispanic/Latino; 22 Asian, non-Hispanic/Latino; 5 Hispanic/Latino; 2 Native Hawaiian or other Pacific Islander, non-Hispanic/Latino; 6 Two or more races, non-Hispanic/Latino), 917 international. Average age 26. 774 applicants, 45% accepted, 307 enrolled. In 2017, 965 master's awarded. *Entrance requirements:* Additional exam requirements/recommendations for international students: Required—TOEFL (minimum score 500 paper-based). *Application deadline:* Applications are processed on a rolling basis. Application fee: $35. Electronic applications accepted. *Expenses: Tuition:* Part-time

Management Information Systems

$466 per credit. *Required fees:* $25 per semester. Tuition and fees vary according to degree level and campus/location. *Unit head:* Dr. Mary Ann K. Westerfield, Dean. *Application contact:* Laura Morris, Director of Admissions, 877-967-5464, E-mail: infocenter@wilmu.edu.
Website: http://www.wilmu.edu/technology/

Winston-Salem State University, Program in Computer Science and Information Technology, Winston-Salem, NC 27110-0003. Offers MS. *Program availability:* Part-time. *Degree requirements:* For master's, thesis optional. *Entrance requirements:* For master's, GRE, resume. Electronic applications accepted. *Faculty research:* Artificial intelligence, network protocols, software engineering.

Worcester Polytechnic Institute, Graduate Admissions, Foisie Business School, Worcester, MA 01609-2280. Offers business administration (PhD); information technology (MS), including information security management; management (Graduate Certificate); marketing and technological innovation (MS); operations design and leadership (MS); supply chain management (MS); technology (MS). *Accreditation:* AACSB. *Program availability:* Part-time, evening/weekend, 100% online, blended/hybrid learning. *Faculty:* 26 full-time (12 women), 9 part-time/adjunct (0 women). *Students:* 254 full-time (153 women), 150 part-time (52 women); includes 34 minority (3 Black or African American, non-Hispanic/Latino; 10 Asian, non-Hispanic/Latino; 14 Hispanic/Latino; 7 Two or more races, non-Hispanic/Latino), 230 international. Average age 29. 677 applicants, 71% accepted, 146 enrolled. In 2017, 188 master's, 14 doctorates awarded. *Degree requirements:* For master's, thesis optional. *Entrance requirements:* For master's and Graduate Certificate, GMAT or GRE General Test, 3 letters of recommendation, statement of purpose, resume. Additional exam requirements/recommendations for international students: Required—TOEFL (minimum score 563 paper-based; 84 iBT), IELTS (minimum score 7). *Application deadline:* For fall admission, 6/1 priority date for domestic and international students; for spring admission, 11/1 priority date for domestic students, 10/1 priority date for international students. Applications are processed on a rolling basis. Application fee: $70. Electronic applications accepted. *Expenses: Tuition:* Full-time $26,226; part-time $1457 per credit. *Required fees:* $60; $30 per credit. One-time fee: $15. Tuition and fees vary according to course load. *Financial support:* Career-related internships or fieldwork, institutionally sponsored loans, scholarships/grants, and unspecified assistantships available. Financial award application deadline: 6/1. *Unit head:* Melissa Terrio, Executive Director, 508-831-4665, Fax: 508-831-4665, E-mail: biz@wpi.edu. *Application contact:* Margaret Clancey, Recruiting Operations Coordinator, 508-831-4980, Fax: 508-831-5720, E-mail: maclancey@wpi.edu.
Website: https://www.wpi.edu/academics/business

Wright State University, Graduate School, Raj Soin College of Business, Department of Information Systems and Operations Management, Information Systems Program, Dayton, OH 45435. Offers MIS.

Section 13
Management Strategy and Policy

This section contains a directory of institutions offering graduate work in management strategy and policy. Additional information about programs listed in the directory but not augmented by an in-depth entry may be obtained by writing directly to the dean of a graduate school or chair of a department at the address given in the directory.

For programs offering related work, see also in this book *Business Administration and Management*. In another guide in this series: **Graduate Programs in the Humanities, Arts & Social Sciences**

See *Public, Regional, and Industrial Affairs (Industrial and Labor Relations)*

CONTENTS

Program Directories

Featured Schools: Displays and Close-Ups

See:

Management Strategy and Policy

Amberton University, Graduate School, Department of Business Administration, Garland, TX 75041-5595. Offers agile project management (MS); general business (MBA); international business (MBA); management (MBA); project management (MBA); strategic leadership (MBA). *Program availability:* Part-time, evening/weekend. *Entrance requirements:* For master's, minimum GPA of 3.0. *Application deadline:* Applications are processed on a rolling basis. Application fee: $0. *Expenses: Tuition:* Part-time $795 per course. *Unit head:* Dr. Don Hebbard, Academic Dean, 972-635-8641 Ext. 157, Fax: 972-279-9773, E-mail: dhebbard@amberton.edu. *Application contact:* Adviser, 972-279-6511 Ext. 180, Fax: 972-279-9773, E-mail: advisor@amberton.edu.

Antioch University Santa Barbara, Program in Business Administration, Santa Barbara, CA 93101-1581. Offers non-profit management (MBA); social business (MBA); strategic leadership (MBA).

Arizona State University at the Tempe campus, W. P. Carey School of Business, Program in Business Administration, Tempe, AZ 85287-4906. Offers entrepreneurship (MBA); finance (MBA); health sector management (MBA); international business (MBA); leadership (MBA); marketing (MBA); organizational behavior (PhD); strategic management (PhD); supply chain management (MBA, PhD); MBA; MBA/M Acc; MBA/M Arch. *Accreditation:* AACSB. *Program availability:* Part-time, evening/weekend, online learning. Terminal master's awarded for partial completion of doctoral program. *Degree requirements:* For master's, thesis or alternative, internship, interactive Program of Study (iPOS) submitted before completing 50 percent of required credit hours; for doctorate, comprehensive exam, thesis/dissertation, interactive Program of Study (iPOS) submitted before completing 50 percent of required credit hours. *Entrance requirements:* For master's, GMAT, minimum GPA of 3.0 in last 2 years of work leading to bachelor's degree, 2 letters of recommendation, professional resume, official transcripts, 3 essays; for doctorate, GMAT or GRE, minimum GPA of 3.0 in last 2 years of work leading to bachelor's degree, 3 letters of recommendation, resume, personal statement/essay. Additional exam requirements/recommendations for international students: Required—TOEFL (minimum score 550 paper-based; 80 iBT), IELTS (minimum score 6.5). Electronic applications accepted. *Expenses:* Contact institution.

Bay Path University, Program in Leadership and Negotiation, Longmeadow, MA 01106-2292. Offers MS. *Program availability:* Part-time, 100% online, blended/hybrid learning. *Students:* 3 full-time (all women), 26 part-time (23 women); includes 5 minority (4 Black or African American, non-Hispanic/Latino; 1 Hispanic/Latino). Average age 42. *Entrance requirements:* For master's, minimum GPA of 3.0. *Application deadline:* Applications are processed on a rolling basis. Application fee: $45. Electronic applications accepted. Application fee is waived when completed online. *Expenses:* $785 per credit. *Financial support:* Unspecified assistantships available. Financial award applicants required to submit FAFSA. *Unit head:* Dr. Joshua Weiss, Director, E-mail: joweiss@baypath.edu. *Application contact:* Diane Ranaldi, Dean of Graduate Admissions, 413-565-1332, Fax: 413-565-1250, E-mail: dranaldi@baypath.edu. Website: http://graduate.baypath.edu/graduate-programs/programs-online/ms-programs/leadership-and-negotiation

Black Hills State University, Graduate Studies, Program in Strategic Leadership, Spearfish, SD 57799. Offers MS. *Program availability:* Part-time, evening/weekend. *Entrance requirements:* Additional exam requirements/recommendations for international students: Required—TOEFL (minimum score 500 paper-based; 60 iBT).

Boston University, Metropolitan College, Department of Computer Science, Boston, MA 02215. Offers computer information systems (MS), including computer networks, data analytics, database management and business intelligence, health informatics, IT project management, security, Web application development; computer networks (Certificate); computer science (MS); data analytics (Certificate); digital forensics (Certificate); health informatics (Certificate); information technology project management (Certificate); software development (MS); software engineering in health care systems (Certificate); telecommunications (MS), including security. *Program availability:* Part-time, evening/weekend, online learning. *Faculty:* 10 full-time (2 women), 51 part-time/adjunct (5 women). *Students:* 109 full-time (39 women), 985 part-time (268 women); includes 286 minority (64 Black or African American, non-Hispanic/Latino; 3 American Indian or Alaska Native, non-Hispanic/Latino; 131 Asian, non-Hispanic/Latino; 73 Hispanic/Latino; 1 Native Hawaiian or other Pacific Islander, non-Hispanic/Latino; 14 Two or more races, non-Hispanic/Latino), 253 international. Average age 32. 952 applicants, 65% accepted, 230 enrolled. In 2017, 392 master's awarded. *Entrance requirements:* For master's and Certificate, official transcripts from regionally-accredited bachelor's degree program, 3 letters of recommendation, professional resume, personal statement. Additional exam requirements/recommendations for international students: Required—TOEFL (minimum score 84 iBT), IELTS. *Application deadline:* For fall admission, 6/1 priority date for international students; for spring admission, 10/1 priority date for international students. Applications are processed on a rolling basis. Application fee: $85. Electronic applications accepted. *Expenses:* Contact institution. *Financial support:* In 2017–18, 11 research assistantships (averaging $8,400 per year), 3 teaching assistantships (averaging $5,000 per year) were awarded; unspecified assistantships also available. Support available to part-time students. Financial award applicants required to submit FAFSA. *Faculty research:* Medical informatics, Web technologies, telecom and networks, security and forensics, software engineering, programming languages, multimedia and artificial intelligence (AI), information systems and IT project management. *Unit head:* Dr. Anatoly Temkin, Chair, 617-353-2566, Fax: 617-353-2367, E-mail: csinfo@bu.edu. *Application contact:* Lesley Moreau, Academic Program Coordinator, 617-353-2566, Fax: 617-353-2367, E-mail: metcs@bu.edu. Website: http://www.bu.edu/csmet/

Brandeis University, Rabb School of Continuing Studies, Division of Graduate Professional Studies, Master of Science in Strategic Analytics Program, Waltham, MA 02454-9110. Offers MS. *Program availability:* Part-time-only. *Faculty:* 55 part-time/adjunct (18 women). *Students:* 85 part-time (42 women); includes 22 minority (4 Black or African American, non-Hispanic/Latino; 14 Asian, non-Hispanic/Latino; 2 Hispanic/Latino; 2 Two or more races, non-Hispanic/Latino). Average age 37. 12 applicants, 100% accepted, 6 enrolled. In 2017, 16 master's awarded. *Entrance requirements:* For master's, four-year bachelor's degree from regionally-accredited U.S. institution or equivalent; official transcript(s) from every college or university attended; resume or curriculum vitae; statement of goals; letter of recommendation. Additional exam requirements/recommendations for international students: Required—TWE (minimum score 4.5), TOEFL (minimum scores: 600 paper-based, 100 iBT), IELTS (7), or PTE (68). *Application deadline:* For fall admission, 6/20 priority date for domestic students, 6/19 priority date for international students; for winter admission, 9/12 priority date for domestic and international students; for spring admission, 12/19 priority date for domestic and international students; for summer admission, 3/13 priority date for domestic and international students. Applications are processed on a rolling basis.

Application fee: $75. Electronic applications accepted. *Expenses:* $1,178 per credit. *Financial support:* Applicants required to submit FAFSA. *Unit head:* Gregory Block, Program Chair, 781-736-8787, E-mail: gblock@brandeis.edu. *Application contact:* Frances Stearns, Director of Student and Faculty Operations, 781-736-8785, E-mail: fstearns@brandeis.edu. Website: http://www.brandeis.edu/gps/

California Miramar University, Program in Strategic Leadership, San Diego, CA 92108. Offers MS. *Degree requirements:* For master's, capstone project.

California State University, East Bay, Office of Graduate Studies, College of Business and Economics, MBA Program, Option in Strategy and Innovation, Hayward, CA 94542-3000. Offers MBA. *Program availability:* Part-time, evening/weekend. *Degree requirements:* For master's, comprehensive exam or thesis. *Entrance requirements:* For master's, GMAT, minimum GPA of 2.75. Additional exam requirements/recommendations for international students: Required—TOEFL (minimum score 550 paper-based). *Application deadline:* For fall admission, 6/1 for domestic and international students. Application fee: $55. *Financial support:* Career-related internships or fieldwork, Federal Work-Study, institutionally sponsored loans, and scholarships/grants available. Support available to part-time students. Financial award application deadline: 3/2. *Unit head:* Dr. Yi Jiang-Karnes, Program Advisor, 510-885-3290, E-mail: yi.jiang@csueastbay.edu. *Application contact:* Philip Cole-Regis, Administrative Support Coordinator, 510-885-3286, E-mail: philip.coleregis@csueastbay.edu. Website: http://www.csueastbay.edu/cbe/mba-options/strategy-and-international-business-option.html

Capella University, School of Business and Technology, Doctoral Programs in Business, Minneapolis, MN 55402. Offers accounting (DBA, PhD); business intelligence (DBA); finance (DBA, PhD); general business management (PhD); human resource management (DBA, PhD); leadership (DBA, PhD); management education (PhD); marketing (DBA, PhD); project management (DBA, PhD); strategy and innovation (DBA, PhD). *Accreditation:* ACBSP.

Capella University, School of Business and Technology, Master's Programs in Business, Minneapolis, MN 55402. Offers accounting (MBA); business analysis (MS); business intelligence (MBA); entrepreneurship (MBA); finance (MBA); general business administration (MBA); general human resource management (MS); general leadership (MS); health care management (MBA); human resource management (MBA); marketing (MBA); project management (MBA, MS). *Accreditation:* ACBSP.

Claremont Graduate University, Graduate Programs, Peter F. Drucker and Masatoshi Ito Graduate School of Management, Program in Executive Management, Claremont, CA 91711-6160. Offers advanced management (MS); executive management (EMBA); leadership (Certificate); management (MA, PhD, Certificate); strategy (Certificate). *Accreditation:* AACSB. *Program availability:* Part-time. *Entrance requirements:* Additional exam requirements/recommendations for international students: Required—TOEFL (minimum score 75 iBT). Electronic applications accepted. *Expenses:* Contact institution. *Faculty research:* Strategy and leadership, brand management, cost management and control, organizational transformation, general management.

Cleary University, Online Program in Business Administration, Howell, MI 48843. Offers analytics, technology, and innovation (MBA, Graduate Certificate); financial planning (Graduate Certificate); global leadership (MBA, Graduate Certificate); health care leadership (MBA, Graduate Certificate). *Program availability:* Part-time, evening/weekend, online learning. *Degree requirements:* For master's, thesis. *Entrance requirements:* For master's, bachelor's degree; minimum GPA of 2.5; professional resume indicating minimum of 2 years of management or related experience; undergraduate degree from accredited college or university with at least 18 quarter hours (or 12 semester hours) of accounting study (for MBA in accounting). Additional exam requirements/recommendations for international students: Required—TOEFL (minimum score 550 paper-based; 79 iBT), Michigan English Language Assessment Battery (minimum score 75). Electronic applications accepted.

College of Staten Island of the City University of New York, Graduate Programs, School of Business, Program in Business Management, Staten Island, NY 10314-6600. Offers large scale data analysis (MS); strategic management (MS). *Program availability:* Part-time, evening/weekend. *Faculty:* 2 full-time (0 women), 2 part-time/adjunct (0 women). *Students:* 25. 57 applicants, 35% accepted, 15 enrolled. In 2017, 11 master's awarded. *Degree requirements:* For master's, 30 credit hours, or ten courses at three credits each. *Entrance requirements:* For master's, GMAT or GRE, baccalaureate degree in business or related field; minimum overall GPA of 3.0; letter of intent; two letters of recommendation; 2 courses each in accounting, economics, and quantitative methods; 1 course each in communications, computer fundamentals, management, and marketing. Additional exam requirements/recommendations for international students: Required—TOEFL (minimum score 550 paper-based; 79 iBT), IELTS (minimum score 6.5). *Application deadline:* For fall admission, 6/30 priority date for domestic and international students. Applications are processed on a rolling basis. Application fee: $125. Electronic applications accepted. *Expenses:* Tuition, state resident: full-time $10,450; part-time $440 per credit. Tuition, nonresident: full-time $19,320; part-time $440 per credit. *Required fees:* $181.10 per semester. Tuition and fees vary according to program. *Faculty research:* Knowledge integration, management innovation, organizational decision-making, strategic alliances. *Unit head:* Dr. Heidi Bertels, 718-982-2924, E-mail: heidi.bertels@csi.cuny.edu. *Application contact:* Sasha Spence, Associate Director for Graduate Admissions, 718-982-2019, Fax: 718-982-2500, E-mail: sasha.spence@csi.cuny.edu. Website: https://www.csi.cuny.edu/sites/default/files/pdf/admissions/grad/pdf/Business%20Management%20Fact%20Sheet.pdf

Davenport University, Sneden Graduate School, Grand Rapids, MI 49512. Offers accounting (MBA); business administration (EMBA); finance (MBA); health care management (MBA); human resources (MBA); information assurance (MS); public health (MPH); strategic management (MBA). *Program availability:* Evening/weekend. *Entrance requirements:* For master's, GMAT, minimum undergraduate GPA of 2.75. Additional exam requirements/recommendations for international students: Required—TOEFL. Electronic applications accepted. *Faculty research:* Leadership, management, marketing, organizational culture.

Defiance College, Program in Business Administration, Defiance, OH 43512-1610. Offers leadership (MBA). *Program availability:* Part-time, evening/weekend. *Degree requirements:* For master's, thesis. *Entrance requirements:* For master's, minimum GPA of 2.75. Additional exam requirements/recommendations for international students: Recommended—TOEFL. *Application deadline:* For fall admission, 8/1 for domestic and international students. Applications are processed on a rolling basis. Application fee:

$25. Electronic applications accepted. *Unit head:* William Sholl, Assistant Professor, 419-783-2441, Fax: 419-784-0426, E-mail: wsholl@definance.edu. *Application contact:* William Sholl, Assistant Professor, 419-783-2441, Fax: 419-784-0426, E-mail: wsholl@definance.edu.
Website: http://www.definance.edu/graduate-programs/mba-home.html

DePaul University, Kellstadt Graduate School of Business, Chicago, IL 60604. Offers accountancy (MBA, MSA); applied economics (MBA); audit and advisory services (MS); business administration (DBA); business analytics (MS); business strategy and decision-making (MBA); computational finance (MS); economics and policy analysis (MS); enterprise risk management (MS); entrepreneurship (MBA, MS); finance (MBA, MS); general business (MBA); hospitality leadership (MBA); hospitality leadership and operational performance (MS); human resources (MS); international business (MBA); management (MBA, MS); management information systems (MBA); marketing (MBA, MS); marketing analysis (MS); marketing strategy and planning (MBA); real estate (MS); real estate finance and investment (MBA); strategy, execution and valuation (MBA); supply chain management (MS); sustainable management (MBA); taxation (MS); JD/MBA. *Accreditation:* AACSB. *Program availability:* Part-time, evening/weekend, online learning. *Entrance requirements:* For master's, GMAT/GRE, 2 letters of recommendation, resume, essay, official transcripts. Additional exam requirements/recommendations for international students: Required—TOEFL (minimum score 550 paper-based; 80 iBT). *Application deadline:* For fall admission, 7/1 for domestic students, 6/1 for international students; for winter admission, 10/1 for domestic students, 9/1 for international students; for spring admission, 2/1 for domestic students, 1/1 for international students. Applications are processed on a rolling basis. Application fee: $60. Electronic applications accepted. *Expenses:* Contact institution. *Financial support:* Application deadline: 4/1; applicants required to submit FAFSA. *Unit head:* Christa Hinton, Assistant Dean and Director, 312-362-8810, Fax: 312-362-6677, E-mail: chinton@depaul.edu. *Application contact:* Garry Cooke, Director of Recruitment and Admissions, 312-362-8810, Fax: 312-362-6677, E-mail: kgsb@depaul.edu.
Website: http://kellstadt.depaul.edu

Drexel University, LeBow College of Business, Program in Business Administration, Philadelphia, PA 19104-2875. Offers business administration (MBA, PhD, APC), including accounting (MBA, PhD), decision sciences (PhD), economics (MBA, PhD), finance (MBA, PhD), legal studies (MBA), management (MBA), marketing (MBA, PhD), organizational sciences (PhD), quantitative methods (MBA), strategic management (PhD). *Accreditation:* AACSB. *Program availability:* Part-time, evening/weekend, online learning. Terminal master's awarded for partial completion of doctoral program. *Entrance requirements:* For master's, GMAT, minimum GPA of 2.75; for doctorate, GMAT. Additional exam requirements/recommendations for international students: Required—TOEFL. Electronic applications accepted. *Faculty research:* Decision support systems, individual and group behavior, operations research, techniques and strategy.

Duke University, The Fuqua School of Business, The Duke MBA-Daytime Program, Durham, NC 27708-0586. Offers academic excellence in finance (Certificate); business administration (MBA); decision sciences (MBA); energy and environment (MBA); energy finance (MBA); entrepreneurship and innovation (MBA); finance (MBA); financial analysis (MBA); health sector management (Certificate); leadership and ethics (MBA); management (MBA); management science and technology management (Certificate); marketing (MBA); operations management (MBA); social entrepreneurship (MBA); strategy (MBA). *Faculty:* 96 full-time (19 women), 48 part-time/adjunct (15 women). *Students:* 876 full-time (297 women); includes 180 minority (39 Black or African American, non-Hispanic/Latino; 2 American Indian or Alaska Native, non-Hispanic/Latino; 83 Asian, non-Hispanic/Latino; 50 Hispanic/Latino; 6 Two or more races, non-Hispanic/Latino), 321 international. Average age 29. In 2017, 445 master's awarded. *Entrance requirements:* For master's, GMAT or GRE, transcripts, essays, resume, recommendation letters, interview. *Application deadline:* For fall admission, 9/12 for domestic and international students; for winter admission, 10/10 for domestic and international students; for spring admission, 1/3 for domestic and international students; for summer admission, 3/20 for domestic and international students. Application fee: $225. Electronic applications accepted. *Expenses:* $69,342 first-year tuition and fees. *Financial support:* In 2017–18, 423 students received support. Scholarships/grants available. Financial award applicants required to submit FAFSA. *Unit head:* Steve Misuraca, Assistant Dean, Daytime MBA Program. *Application contact:* Shari Hubert, Associate Dean, Office of Admissions, 919-660-7705, Fax: 919-681-8026, E-mail: admissions-info@fuqua.duke.edu.
Website: https://www.fuqua.duke.edu/programs/daytime-mba

Duke University, The Fuqua School of Business, The Duke MBA-Global Executive Program, Durham, NC 27708-0586. Offers business administration (MBA); energy and environment (MBA); entrepreneurship and innovation (MBA); finance (MBA); health sector management (Certificate); marketing (MBA); strategy (MBA). *Faculty:* 96 full-time (19 women), 48 part-time/adjunct (15 women). *Students:* 94 full-time (26 women); includes 34 minority (8 Black or African American, non-Hispanic/Latino; 21 Asian, non-Hispanic/Latino; 4 Hispanic/Latino; 1 Two or more races, non-Hispanic/Latino), 25 international. Average age 39. In 2017, 27 master's awarded. *Entrance requirements:* For master's, Executive Assessment, GMAT, or GRE, transcripts, essays, resume, recommendation letters, letter of company support, interview. *Application deadline:* For fall admission, 10/12 priority date for domestic and international students; for winter admission, 12/7 priority date for domestic and international students; for spring admission, 3/20 priority date for domestic and international students; for summer admission, 5/31 for domestic and international students. Applications are processed on a rolling basis. Application fee: $225. Electronic applications accepted. *Expenses:* Contact institution. *Financial support:* In 2017–18, 31 students received support. Scholarships/grants available. Financial award applicants required to submit FAFSA. *Unit head:* Karen Courtney, Associate Dean, Executive Programs. *Application contact:* Shari Hubert, Associate Dean, Office of Admissions, 919-660-7705, Fax: 919-681-8026, E-mail: admissions-info@fuqua.duke.edu.
Website: https://www.fuqua.duke.edu/programs/global-executive-mba

Duke University, The Fuqua School of Business, The Duke MBA-Weekend Executive Program, Durham, NC 27708-0586. Offers business administration (MBA); energy and environment (MBA); entrepreneurship and innovation (MBA); finance (MBA); health sector management (Certificate); marketing (MBA); strategy (MBA). *Faculty:* 96 full-time (19 women), 48 part-time/adjunct (15 women). *Students:* 219 full-time (59 women); includes 80 minority (13 Black or African American, non-Hispanic/Latino; 3 American Indian or Alaska Native, non-Hispanic/Latino; 45 Asian, non-Hispanic/Latino; 13 Hispanic/Latino; 6 Two or more races, non-Hispanic/Latino), 32 international. Average age 35. In 2017, 92 master's awarded. *Entrance requirements:* For master's, Executive Assessment, GMAT or GRE, transcripts, essays, resume, recommendation letters, letter of company support, interview. *Application deadline:* For fall admission, 10/12 priority date for domestic and international students; for winter admission, 12/7 priority date for domestic and international students; for spring admission, 2/7 priority date for domestic and international students; for summer admission, 3/20 for domestic and international students. Applications are processed on a rolling basis. Application fee: $225. Electronic applications accepted. *Expenses:* Contact institution. *Financial support:* In 2017–18, 44

students received support. Scholarships/grants available. Financial award applicants required to submit FAFSA. *Unit head:* Karen Courtney, Associate Dean, Executive Programs. *Application contact:* Shari Hubert, Associate Dean, Office of Admissions, 919-660-7705, Fax: 919-681-8026, E-mail: admissions-info@fuqua.duke.edu.
Website: https://www.fuqua.duke.edu/programs/weekend-executive-mba

Duke University, The Fuqua School of Business, Master of Quantitative Management Program: Business Analytics, Durham, NC 27708-0586. Offers finance (MQM); forensics (MQM); marketing (MQM); strategy (MQM). *Faculty:* 96 full-time (19 women), 48 part-time/adjunct (15 women). *Students:* 140 full-time (81 women); includes 11 minority (9 Asian, non-Hispanic/Latino; 2 Hispanic/Latino), 118 international. Average age 24. *Entrance requirements:* For master's, GMAT/GRE, transcripts, essays, resume, recommendation letters. *Application deadline:* For fall admission, 9/13 for domestic and international students; for winter admission, 1/17 for domestic and international students; for spring admission, 2/28 for domestic and international students; for summer admission, 4/4 for domestic and international students. Application fee: $125. Electronic applications accepted. *Expenses:* $66,907 tuition and fees. *Financial support:* In 2017–18, 46 students received support. Scholarships/grants available. Financial award applicants required to submit FAFSA. *Unit head:* Jeremy Petranka, Associate Dean. *Application contact:* Shari Hubert, Associate Dean, Office of Admissions, 919-660-7705, Fax: 919-681-8026, E-mail: admissions-info@fuqua.duke.edu.
Website: https://www.fuqua.duke.edu/programs/mqm-business-analytics

Duke University, The Fuqua School of Business, PhD Program, Durham, NC 27708-0586. Offers accounting (PhD); decision sciences (PhD); finance (PhD); management and organizations (PhD); marketing (PhD); operations management (PhD); strategy (PhD). *Faculty:* 96 full-time (19 women). *Students:* 64 full-time (25 women); includes 1 minority (Hispanic/Latino), 41 international. Average age 27. 617 applicants, 5% accepted, 14 enrolled. In 2017, 15 doctorates awarded. *Degree requirements:* For doctorate, thesis/dissertation, major field requirement (exam or major paper, depending upon the area). *Entrance requirements:* For doctorate, GMAT or GRE, transcripts, essays, recommendation letters, statement of purpose. Additional exam requirements/recommendations for international students: Required—TOEFL (minimum score 577 paper-based; 108 iBT), IELTS (minimum score 8). *Application deadline:* For fall admission, 12/31 priority date for domestic and international students. Application fee: $85. Electronic applications accepted. *Expenses:* $52,253. *Financial support:* In 2017–18, 66 students received support, including 66 fellowships with full tuition reimbursements available (averaging $29,200 per year), 63 research assistantships with full tuition reimbursements available (averaging $7,000 per year); institutionally sponsored loans, scholarships/grants, and tuition waivers (full) also available. Financial award applicants required to submit FAFSA. *Unit head:* William Boulding, Dean. *Application contact:* Qi Chen, Director of Graduate Studies, 919-660-7753, Fax: 919-660-7971, E-mail: qc2@duke.edu.

East Tennessee State University, School of Graduate Studies, School of Continuing Studies and Academic Outreach, Johnson City, TN 37614. Offers archival studies (Postbaccalaureate Certificate); liberal studies (MALS); reinforcing education through artistic learning (Postbaccalaureate Certificate); strategic leadership (MPS); training and development (MPS). *Program availability:* Part-time, online learning. In 2017, 9 master's, 1 other advanced degree awarded. *Degree requirements:* For master's, comprehensive exam, thesis (for some programs), professional project. *Entrance requirements:* For master's, GRE General Test, minimum GPA of 2.75, professional portfolio, three letters of recommendation, interview, writing sample; for Postbaccalaureate Certificate, minimum GPA of 2.5, three letters of recommendation, interview. Additional exam requirements/recommendations for international students: Required—TOEFL (minimum score 550 paper-based; 79 iBT). *Application deadline:* For fall admission, 6/1 for domestic students, 4/29 for international students; for spring admission, 11/1 for domestic students, 9/29 for international students. Application fee: $55 ($65 for international students). Electronic applications accepted. *Financial support:* Research assistantships with full tuition reimbursements, teaching assistantships with full tuition reimbursements, institutionally sponsored loans, scholarships/grants, tuition waivers, and unspecified assistantships available. Financial award application deadline: 7/1; financial award applicants required to submit FAFSA. *Faculty research:* Appalachian studies, women's and gender studies, interdisciplinary theory, regional and Southern cultures. *Unit head:* Dr. Rick E. Osborn, Dean, 423-439-4223, Fax: 423-439-7091, E-mail: osbornr@etsu.edu. *Application contact:* Dr. Rick E. Osborn, Dean, 423-439-4223, Fax: 423-439-7091, E-mail: osbornr@etsu.edu.
Website: http://www.etsu.edu/academicaffairs/scs/

Fisher College, Master of Business Administration Program, Boston, MA 02116-1500. Offers strategic leadership (MBA). *Program availability:* Part-time, evening/weekend, online only, 100% online. *Faculty:* 5 full-time (1 woman), 6 part-time/adjunct (1 woman). *Students:* 12 full-time (6 women), 29 part-time (16 women); includes 13 minority (2 Black or African American, non-Hispanic/Latino; 1 Asian, non-Hispanic/Latino; 9 Hispanic/Latino; 1 Two or more races, non-Hispanic/Latino), 5 international. Average age 31. 57 applicants, 56% accepted, 19 enrolled. In 2017, 8 master's awarded. *Degree requirements:* For master's, comprehensive exam. *Entrance requirements:* Additional exam requirements/recommendations for international students: Required—TOEFL (minimum score 80 iBT), IELTS (minimum score 6.5). *Application deadline:* For fall admission, 8/1 for domestic and international students; for winter admission, 11/1 for domestic and international students. Applications are processed on a rolling basis. Electronic applications accepted. *Expenses: Tuition:* Full-time $28,512; part-time $14,256 per semester. *Required fees:* $4800. Tuition and fees vary according to class time. *Financial support:* In 2017–18, 2 students received support. Scholarships/grants and unspecified assistantships available. Financial award applicants required to submit FAFSA. *Faculty research:* Humanistic management, the role of human resources in employee engagement. *Unit head:* Neil Trotta, Assistant Dean, School of Graduate Studies/MBA Program Director, 617-236-8867, Fax: 617-236-5462, E-mail: ntrotta@fisher.edu.
Website: http://www.fisher.edu/mba

Florida State University, The Graduate School, College of Business, Tallahassee, FL 32306-1110. Offers accounting (M Acc), including assurance and advisory services, generalist, taxation; business administration (MBA), including accounting (PhD), finance (PhD), management information systems (PhD), marketing (PhD), organizational behavior and human resources (PhD), risk management and insurance (PhD), strategy (PhD); finance (MS); management information systems (MS); risk management and insurance (MS); JD/MBA; MSW/MBA. *Accreditation:* AACSB. *Program availability:* Part-time, 100% online. *Faculty:* 93 full-time (23 women), 2 part-time/adjunct (1 woman). *Students:* 229 full-time (96 women), 423 part-time (154 women); includes 159 minority (44 Black or African American, non-Hispanic/Latino; 24 Asian, non-Hispanic/Latino; 75 Hispanic/Latino; 1 Native Hawaiian or other Pacific Islander, non-Hispanic/Latino; 15 Two or more races, non-Hispanic/Latino), 48 international. Average age 31. 300 applicants, 61% accepted, 133 enrolled. In 2017, 268 master's, 9 doctorates awarded. Terminal master's awarded for partial completion of doctoral program. *Degree requirements:* For doctorate, comprehensive exam, thesis/dissertation. *Entrance requirements:* For master's, GMAT, GRE (for all except MS in finance), work experience (MBA, MS); minimum GPA of 3.0, letters of recommendation;

Management Strategy and Policy

for doctorate, GMAT, GRE (for marketing, organizational behavior, risk management and insurance, management information systems, and human resources only), minimum graduate GPA of 3.5, letters of recommendation. Additional exam requirements/recommendations for international students: Required—TOEFL (minimum score 600 paper-based; 85 iBT); Recommended—IELTS (minimum score 6). *Application deadline:* For fall admission, 6/1 for domestic and international students; for spring admission, 10/1 for domestic and international students; for summer admission, 3/1 for domestic and international students. Applications are processed on a rolling basis. Application fee: $30. Electronic applications accepted. *Expenses:* Contact institution. *Financial support:* In 2017–18, 146 students received support, including 26 fellowships (averaging $1,500 per year), 77 research assistantships with full tuition reimbursements available (averaging $20,000 per year), 43 teaching assistantships with full tuition reimbursements available (averaging $20,000 per year); career-related internships or fieldwork, scholarships/grants, health care benefits, tuition waivers (full and partial), and unspecified assistantships also available. Support available to part-time students. Financial award application deadline: 1/1; financial award applicants required to submit FAFSA. *Faculty research:* Business strategy, marketing, finance, accounting, business analytics. *Total annual research expenditures:* $1.4 million. *Unit head:* Dr. Michael Hartline, Dean, 850-644-4405, Fax: 850-644-0915, E-mail: mhartline@business.fsu.edu. *Application contact:* Jennifer Clark, Director, 850-644-6458, E-mail: gradprograms@business.fsu.edu.
Website: http://business.fsu.edu/

Freed-Hardeman University, Program in Business Administration, Henderson, TN 38340-2399. Offers accounting (MBA); corporate responsibility (MBA); leadership (MBA). *Accreditation:* ACBSP. *Program availability:* Part-time, evening/weekend, online learning. *Entrance requirements:* For master's, GMAT. Additional exam requirements/ recommendations for international students: Required—TOEFL (minimum score 500 paper-based).

Friends University, Graduate School, Wichita, KS 67213. Offers family therapy (MSFT); global business administration (MBA), including accounting, business law, change management, health care leadership, management information systems, supply chain management and logistics; health care leadership (MHCL); management information systems (MMIS); professional business administration (MBA), including accounting, business law, change management, health care leadership, management information systems, supply chain management and logistics. *Program availability:* Part-time, evening/weekend, online learning. *Degree requirements:* For master's, research project. *Entrance requirements:* For master's, bachelor's degree from accredited institution, official transcripts, interview with program director, letter(s) of recommendation. Additional exam requirements/recommendations for international students: Required—TOEFL (minimum score 560 paper-based). Electronic applications accepted.

The George Washington University, School of Business, Department of Decision Sciences, Washington, DC 20052. Offers business analytics (MS, Certificate); project management (MS). *Program availability:* Online learning. *Faculty:* 17 full-time (1 woman), 4 part-time/adjunct (1 woman). *Students:* 84 full-time (44 women), 131 part-time (65 women); includes 57 minority (30 Black or African American, non-Hispanic/Latino; 1 American Indian or Alaska Native, non-Hispanic/Latino; 13 Asian, non-Hispanic/Latino; 8 Hispanic/Latino; 5 Two or more races, non-Hispanic/Latino), 105 international. Average age 33. 914 applicants, 44% accepted, 80 enrolled. In 2017, 97 master's, 65 other advanced degrees awarded. Application fee: $75. *Expenses:* Tuition: Full-time $28,800; part-time $1655 per credit hour. *Required fees:* $45; $2.75 per credit hour. *Financial support:* Tuition waivers available. *Unit head:* Prof. Refik Soyer, Chair, 202-994-6445, E-mail: soyer@gwu.edu. *Application contact:* Christopher Storer, Executive Director, Graduate Admissions, 202-994-1212, E-mail: gwmba@gwu.edu.
Website: http://business.gwu.edu/decisionsciences/

The George Washington University, School of Business, Department of Strategic Management and Public Policy, Washington, DC 20052. Offers MBA, PhD. *Accreditation:* NASPAA. *Program availability:* Part-time, evening/weekend. *Faculty:* 13 full-time (3 women). *Students:* 170 full-time (74 women); includes 35 minority (7 Black or African American, non-Hispanic/Latino; 13 Asian, non-Hispanic/Latino; 9 Hispanic/Latino; 6 Two or more races, non-Hispanic/Latino), 73 international. Average age 28. 452 applicants, 54% accepted, 82 enrolled. In 2017, 87 master's awarded. *Entrance requirements:* For master's, GMAT; for doctorate, GMAT or GRE. Additional exam requirements/recommendations for international students: Required—TOEFL. *Application deadline:* For fall admission, 4/1 priority date for domestic students; for spring admission, 10/1 for domestic students. Applications are processed on a rolling basis. Application fee: $75. *Expenses: Tuition:* Full-time $28,800; part-time $1655 per credit hour. *Required fees:* $45; $2.75 per credit hour. *Financial support:* In 2017–18, 1 student received support. Fellowships, teaching assistantships, career-related internships or fieldwork, Federal Work-Study, and institutionally sponsored loans available. Financial award application deadline: 4/1. *Unit head:* Dr. Jennifer Griffin, Chair, 202-994-2536, E-mail: jgriffin@gwu.edu. *Application contact:* Christopher Storer, Executive Director, Graduate Admissions, 202-994-1212, E-mail: gwmba@gwu.edu.
Website: http://business.gwu.edu/smpp/

Georgia State University, J. Mack Robinson College of Business, Department of Managerial Sciences, Atlanta, GA 30302-3083. Offers business analysis (MBA, MS); entrepreneurship (MBA); human resources management (MBA, MS); operations management (MBA, MS); organization behavior/human resource management (PhD); organization management (MBA); organizational change (MS); strategic management (PhD). *Accreditation:* AACSB. *Program availability:* Part-time, evening/weekend. *Faculty:* 25 full-time (11 women). *Students:* 20 full-time (12 women); includes 7 minority (4 Black or African American, non-Hispanic/Latino; 2 Hispanic/Latino; 1 Two or more races, non-Hispanic/Latino), 6 international. Average age 33. 77 applicants, 18% accepted, 10 enrolled. In 2017, 25 master's, 1 doctorate awarded. *Entrance requirements:* For master's, GRE or GMAT, transcripts from all institutions attended, resume, essays; for doctorate, GMAT, three letters of recommendation, personal statement, transcripts from all institutions attended, resume. Additional exam requirements/recommendations for international students: Required—TOEFL (minimum score 610 paper-based; 101 iBT), IELTS (minimum score 7). *Application deadline:* For fall admission, 5/1 priority date for domestic students, 2/1 priority date for international students; for spring admission, 9/15 priority date for domestic students, 4/1 priority date for international students. Applications are processed on a rolling basis. Application fee: $50. Electronic applications accepted. *Expenses:* Tuition, state resident: full-time $7020. Tuition, nonresident: full-time $22,518. *Required fees:* $2128. Tuition and fees vary according to degree level and program. *Financial support:* Research assistantships, teaching assistantships, scholarships/grants, tuition waivers, and unspecified assistantships available. Financial award applicants required to submit FAFSA. *Faculty research:* Entrepreneurship and innovation; strategy process; workplace interactions, relationships, and processes; leadership and culture; supply chain management. *Unit head:* Dr. Pamela S. Barr, Interim Chair, 404-413-7525, Fax: 404-413-7571. *Application contact:* Toby McChesney, Assistant Dean for Graduate Recruiting and Student Services, 404-413-7167, Fax: 404-413-7162, E-mail: rcbgradadmissions@gsu.edu.
Website: http://mgmt.robinson.gsu.edu/

Grantham University, Mark Skousen School of Business, Lenexa, KS 66219. Offers business administration (MBA); business intelligence (MS); human resources (Certificate); information management (MBA); performance improvement (MS); project management (MBA, Certificate). *Program availability:* Part-time, evening/weekend, online only, 100% online. *Faculty:* 1 full-time, 34 part-time/adjunct. *Students:* 610 full-time (231 women), 333 part-time (128 women); includes 466 minority (321 Black or African American, non-Hispanic/Latino; 12 American Indian or Alaska Native, non-Hispanic/Latino; 29 Asian, non-Hispanic/Latino; 71 Hispanic/Latino; 4 Native Hawaiian or other Pacific Islander, non-Hispanic/Latino; 29 Two or more races, non-Hispanic/Latino). Average age 40. 273 applicants, 87% accepted, 202 enrolled. In 2017, 362 master's awarded. *Degree requirements:* For master's, comprehensive exam (for some programs), PMP Prep Exams throughout the term (for MBA in project management); for Certificate, comprehensive exam (for some programs), PMP Prep Exam (for project management). *Entrance requirements:* For master's, baccalaureate or master's degree with minimum cumulative GPA of 2.5 from institution accredited by agency recognized by U.S. DOE or foreign equivalent; official transcripts showing proof of degree. Additional exam requirements/recommendations for international students: Required—TOEFL (minimum score 530 paper-based; 71 iBT), IELTS (minimum score 6.5), PTE (minimum score 50). *Application deadline:* Applications are processed on a rolling basis. Application fee: $0. Electronic applications accepted. *Expenses:* $325 per credit hour. *Financial support:* Scholarships/grants available. Financial award applicants required to submit FAFSA. *Faculty research:* How chronic diseases contribute to the rising costs of healthcare, marketing for entrepreneurs, managers' hiring practices of workers with disability, organizational structures, organizational change, online pedagogy, impact of instructor video tips in the online classroom, decision-making techniques. *Unit head:* Dr. David Marker, Dean of the Mark Skousen School of Business, 913-309-4747, Fax: 844-260-6287, E-mail: dmarker@grantham.edu. *Application contact:* Jared Parlette, Vice President of Student Enrollment, 800-955-2527 Ext. 803, Fax: 866-914-4557, E-mail: admissions@grantham.edu.
Website: https://www.grantham.edu/school-of-business/

Gwynedd Mercy University, School of Graduate and Professional Studies, Gwynedd Valley, PA 19437-0901. Offers health care administration (MBA); management (MSM); strategic management and leadership (MBA). *Program availability:* Part-time, evening/weekend. *Faculty:* 5 full-time (all women), 22 part-time/adjunct (8 women). *Students:* 63 full-time (37 women); includes 20 minority (16 Black or African American, non-Hispanic/Latino; 2 Asian, non-Hispanic/Latino; 2 Hispanic/Latino). Average age 39. In 2017, 56 master's awarded. *Degree requirements:* For master's, thesis. *Entrance requirements:* For master's, minimum GPA of 3.0. *Application deadline:* Applications are processed on a rolling basis. *Expenses:* $640 per credit, $17 per credit part-time fee, $165 graduation fee. *Financial support:* Career-related internships or fieldwork, Federal Work-Study, tuition waivers (full and partial), and unspecified assistantships available. Financial award application deadline: 8/31; financial award applicants required to submit FAFSA. *Unit head:* Dr. Mary Sortino, Dean, 215-646-7300, E-mail: sortino.m@gmercyu.edu. *Application contact:* Information Contact, 800-342-5462, Fax: 215-641-5556.

Harrisburg University of Science and Technology, Program in Information Systems Engineering and Management, Harrisburg, PA 17101. Offers analytics (MS); digital government (MS); digital health (MS); entrepreneurship (MS); information security (MS); software engineering and systems development (MS). *Program availability:* Part-time, evening/weekend. *Degree requirements:* For master's, thesis optional. *Entrance requirements:* For master's, baccalaureate degree. Additional exam requirements/recommendations for international students: Required—TOEFL (minimum score 520 paper-based; 80 iBT); Recommended—IELTS (minimum score 6). Electronic applications accepted. *Faculty research:* Healthcare Informatics, material analysis, enterprise systems, circuit design, enterprise architectures.

Harvard University, Harvard Business School, Doctoral Programs in Management, Boston, MA 02163. Offers accounting and management (DBA); business economics (PhD); health policy management (PhD); management (DBA); marketing (DBA); organizational behavior (PhD); science, technology and management (PhD); strategy (DBA); technology and operations management (DBA). *Degree requirements:* For doctorate, comprehensive exam (for some programs), thesis/dissertation. *Entrance requirements:* For doctorate, GRE General Test or GMAT. Additional exam requirements/recommendations for international students: Required—TOEFL.

HEC Montreal, School of Business Administration, Master of Science Programs in Administration, Program in Business Intelligence, Montréal, QC H3T 2A7, Canada. Offers M Sc. All courses are given in French. *Students:* 59 full-time (22 women), 39 part-time (13 women). 62 applicants, 79% accepted, 37 enrolled. In 2017, 35 master's awarded. *Degree requirements:* For master's, thesis. *Entrance requirements:* For master's, BBA, undergraduate degree in another field, degree deemed equivalent by program director and minimum GPA of 3.0 on 4.3 scale. Additional exam requirements/recommendations for international students: Required—TAGE MAGE (minimum recommended score of 283), GMAT (minimum recommended score of 630), or GRE. *Application deadline:* For fall admission, 3/15 for domestic and international students; for winter admission, 9/15 for domestic and international students. Application fee: $88 Canadian dollars ($184 Canadian dollars for international students). Electronic applications accepted. *Expenses:* Tuition, state resident: full-time $2869 Canadian dollars; part-time $79.70 Canadian dollars per credit. Tuition, nonresident: full-time $8883 Canadian dollars; part-time $246.76 Canadian dollars per credit. *International tuition:* $19,648 Canadian dollars full-time. *Required fees:* $41.20 Canadian dollars per credit. $67.94 Canadian dollars per term. Tuition and fees vary according to degree level and program. *Financial support:* Research assistantships, teaching assistantships, and scholarships/grants available. Financial award application deadline: 9/2. *Unit head:* Dr. Marie-Helene Jobin, Director, 514-340-6283, E-mail: marie-helene.jobin@hec.ca. *Application contact:* Marianne de Moura, Administrative Director, 514-340-6151, Fax: 514-340-6411, E-mail: aide@hec.ca.
Website: http://www.hec.ca/programmes/maitrises/maitrise-intelligence-affaires/index.html

HEC Montreal, School of Business Administration, Master of Science Programs in Administration, Program in Strategy, Montréal, QC H3T 2A7, Canada. Offers M Sc. Program offered in French. *Students:* 79 full-time (35 women), 7 part-time (5 women). 56 applicants, 80% accepted, 33 enrolled. In 2017, 40 master's awarded. *Entrance requirements:* For master's, BBA, undergraduate degree in another field, degree deemed equivalent by program director and minimum GPA of 3.0 on 4.3 scale. Additional exam requirements/recommendations for international students: Required—TAGE MAGE (minimum recommended score of 283), GMAT (minimum recommended score of 630), or GRE. *Application deadline:* For fall admission, 3/15 for domestic and international students; for winter admission, 9/15 for domestic and international students. Application fee: $88 ($184 for international students). Electronic applications accepted. *Expenses:* Tuition, state resident: full-time $2869 Canadian dollars; part-time $79.70 Canadian dollars per credit. Tuition, nonresident: full-time $8883 Canadian dollars; part-time $246.76 Canadian dollars per credit. *International tuition:* $19,648 Canadian dollars full-time. *Required fees:* $41.20 Canadian dollars per credit. $67.94 Canadian dollars per term. Tuition and fees vary according to degree level and program. *Financial support:* Research assistantships, teaching assistantships, and scholarships/

grants available. Financial award application deadline: 9/2. *Unit head:* Dr. Marie-Helene Jobin, Director, 514-340-6283, E-mail: marie-helene.jobin@hec.ca. *Application contact:* Marianne de Moura, Administrative Director, 514-340-6151, Fax: 514-340-6411, E-mail: aide@hec.ca.
Website: http://www.hec.ca/programmes/maitrises/maitrise-strategie/index.html

Hofstra University, Frank G. Zarb School of Business, Programs in Information Systems, Hempstead, NY 11549. Offers business administration (MBA), including business analytics, information systems, quality management; business analytics (MS); information systems (MS, Advanced Certificate). *Program availability:* Part-time, evening/weekend, blended/hybrid learning. *Students:* 85 full-time (38 women), 22 part-time (9 women); includes 12 minority (1 Black or African American, non-Hispanic/Latino; 8 Asian, non-Hispanic/Latino; 3 Hispanic/Latino), 78 international. Average age 27. 120 applicants, 63% accepted, 37 enrolled. In 2017, 40 master's awarded. *Degree requirements:* For master's, capstone course (for MBA), thesis (for MS), minimum GPA of 3.0. *Entrance requirements:* For master's, GMAT/GRE, 2 letters of recommendation, resume, essay; for Advanced Certificate, GMAT/GRE, 2 letters of recommendation, resume. Additional exam requirements/recommendations for international students: Required—TOEFL (minimum score 550 paper-based; 80 iBT); Recommended—IELTS (minimum score 6). *Application deadline:* Applications are processed on a rolling basis. Application fee: $75. Electronic applications accepted. *Expenses:* $1,322 per credit. *Financial support:* In 2017–18, 41 students received support, including 40 fellowships with full and partial tuition reimbursements available (averaging $5,921 per year), 2 research assistantships with full and partial tuition reimbursements available (averaging $5,483 per year); career-related internships or fieldwork, Federal Work-Study, institutionally sponsored loans, scholarships/grants, tuition waivers (full and partial), and unspecified assistantships also available. Support available to part-time students. Financial award applicants required to submit FAFSA. *Faculty research:* Big data and social media, healthcare IT and analytics, machine learning and artificial intelligence, inventory system and quality management, cybersecurity and information processing. *Unit head:* Dr. Hak Kim, Chairperson, 516-463-5716, Fax: 516-463-4834, E-mail: hak.j.kim@hofstra.edu. *Application contact:* Sunil Samuel, Assistant Vice President of Admissions, 516-463-4723, Fax: 516-463-4664, E-mail: graduateadmission@hofstra.edu.
Website: http://www.hofstra.edu/business/

Hofstra University, Frank G. Zarb School of Business, Programs in Management and General Business, Hempstead, NY 11549. Offers business administration (MBA), including health services management, management, sports and entertainment management, strategic business management, strategic healthcare management; general management (Advanced Certificate); human resource management (MS, Advanced Certificate). *Program availability:* Part-time, evening/weekend, blended/hybrid learning. *Students:* 131 full-time (58 women), 145 part-time (65 women); includes 102 minority (23 Black or African American, non-Hispanic/Latino; 39 Asian, non-Hispanic/Latino; 37 Hispanic/Latino; 3 Two or more races, non-Hispanic/Latino), 25 international. Average age 33. 327 applicants, 72% accepted, 104 enrolled. In 2017, 116 master's awarded. *Degree requirements:* For master's, thesis optional, capstone course (for MBA), thesis (for MS), minimum GPA of 3.0. *Entrance requirements:* For master's, GMAT/GRE, 2 letters of recommendation, resume, essay. Additional exam requirements/recommendations for international students: Required—TOEFL (minimum score 550 paper-based; 80 iBT); Recommended—IELTS (minimum score 6). *Application deadline:* Applications are processed on a rolling basis. Application fee: $75. Electronic applications accepted. *Expenses:* $1,322 per credit. *Financial support:* In 2017–18, 78 students received support, including 75 fellowships with full and partial tuition reimbursements available (averaging $4,785 per year); research assistantships with full and partial tuition reimbursements available, career-related internships or fieldwork, Federal Work-Study, institutionally sponsored loans, scholarships/grants, tuition waivers (full and partial), and unspecified assistantships also available. Support available to part-time students. Financial award applicants required to submit FAFSA. *Faculty research:* Organizational change; sustainability; entrepreneurial spawning; family business; global supply chain strategies. *Unit head:* Dr. Kaushik Sengupta, Chairperson, 516-463-7825, Fax: 516-463-4834, E-mail: kaushik.sengupta@hofstra.edu. *Application contact:* Sunil Samuel, Assistant Vice President of Admissions, 516-463-4723, Fax: 516-463-4664, E-mail: graduateadmission@hofstra.edu.
Website: http://www.hofstra.edu/business/

James Madison University, The Graduate School, College of Business, Program in Strategic Leadership, Harrisonburg, VA 22801. Offers postsecondary analysis and leadership (PhD), including nonprofit and community leadership, organizational science and leadership, postsecondary analysis and leadership. *Program availability:* Part-time, evening/weekend, online learning. *Students:* 8 full-time (3 women), 34 part-time (16 women); includes 4 minority (2 Black or African American, non-Hispanic/Latino; 1 Asian, non-Hispanic/Latino; 1 Hispanic/Latino), 4 international. Average age 30. In 2017, 3 doctorates awarded. Application fee: $55. Electronic applications accepted. *Expenses:* Tuition, state resident: full-time $10,512; part-time $438 per credit hour. Tuition, nonresident: full-time $28,358; part-time $1162 per credit hour. *Required fees:* $1128. *Financial support:* In 2017–18, 6 students received support. Fellowships, career-related internships or fieldwork, Federal Work-Study, unspecified assistantships, and 6 doctoral assistantships (stipend varies) available. Financial award application deadline: 3/1; financial award applicants required to submit FAFSA. *Unit head:* Dr. Karen A. Ford, Director of Strategic Leadership Studies, 540-568-7020, Fax: 540-568-7117, E-mail: fordka@jmu.edu. *Application contact:* Lynette D. Michael, Director of Graduate Admissions, 540-568-6131 Ext. 6395, Fax: 540-568-7860, E-mail: michaeld@jmu.edu.
Website: http://www.jmu.edu/leadership/

Lawrence Technological University, College of Management, Southfield, MI 48075-1058. Offers business administration (MBA, DBA), including business analytics (MBA, MS), cybersecurity (MBA, MS), finance (MBA), information systems (MBA), information technology (MBA), marketing (MBA), project management (MBA, MS); cybersecurity (Graduate Certificate); health IT management (Graduate Certificate); information assurance mangement (Graduate Certificate); information systems (MS), including enterprise resource planning, enterprise security management, project management (MBA, MS); information technology (MS, DM), including business analytics (MBA, MS), cybersecurity (MBA, MS), information assurance (MS), project management (MBA, MS); management (PhD); nonprofit management and leadership (Graduate Certificate); operations management (MS), including manufacturing operations, service operations; project management (Graduate Certificate). *Accreditation:* ACBSP. *Program availability:* Part-time, evening/weekend, 100% online. *Faculty:* 13 full-time (6 women), 7 part-time/adjunct (1 woman). *Students:* 8 full-time (3 women), 280 part-time (102 women); includes 70 minority (34 Black or African American, non-Hispanic/Latino; 2 American Indian or Alaska Native, non-Hispanic/Latino; 18 Asian, non-Hispanic/Latino; 11 Hispanic/Latino; 5 Two or more races, non-Hispanic/Latino), 73 international. Average age 34. 143 applicants, 50% accepted, 68 enrolled. In 2017, 114 master's, 7 doctorates, 10 other advanced degrees awarded. Terminal master's awarded for partial completion of doctoral program. *Degree requirements:* For master's, thesis (for some programs); for doctorate, comprehensive exam, thesis/dissertation. *Entrance requirements:* Additional exam requirements/recommendations for international students: Required—TOEFL (minimum score 550 paper-based; 79 iBT), IELTS (minimum score 6.5). *Application deadline:* For fall admission, 5/27 for international students; for spring admission, 10/8

for international students; for summer admission, 2/14 for international students. Applications are processed on a rolling basis. Application fee: $50. Electronic applications accepted. *Expenses: Tuition:* Full-time $15,274; part-time $1091 per credit. One-time fee: $150. *Financial support:* In 2017–18, 35 students received support, including 8 research assistantships with partial tuition reimbursements available (averaging $3,360 per year); career-related internships or fieldwork, unspecified assistantships, and corporate tuition incentives also available. Financial award application deadline: 4/1; financial award applicants required to submit FAFSA. *Faculty research:* Cybersecurity; risk management; IT governance; security controls and countermeasures; threat modeling cyber resilience; autonomous cars; natural language processing; text mining; machine learning; reflective leadership; emerging leadership theories and practice; motivational studies; teaching effectiveness strategies; teamwork; organization development; strategic planning; strengths-based and positive organizational scholarship; global leadership; globalization; corporate governance. *Unit head:* Dr. Bahman Mirshab, Dean, 248-204-3050, E-mail: mgtdean@ltu.edu. *Application contact:* Jane Rohrback, Director of Admissions, 248-204-3160, Fax: 248-204-2228, E-mail: admissions@ltu.edu.
Website: http://www.ltu.edu/management/index.asp

Lenoir-Rhyne University, Graduate Programs, Charles M. Snipes School of Business, Hickory, NC 28601. Offers accounting (MBA); business analytics and information technology (MBA); entrepreneurship (MBA); global business (MBA); healthcare administration (MBA); innovation and change management (MBA); leadership development (MBA). *Accreditation:* ACBSP. *Program availability:* Part-time, evening/weekend, online learning. *Degree requirements:* For master's, capstone course. *Entrance requirements:* For master's, GMAT, GRE, MAT, minimum undergraduate GPA of 2.7, graduate 3.0. Additional exam requirements/recommendations for international students: Required—TOEFL (minimum score 600 paper-based). Electronic applications accepted. *Expenses:* Contact institution.

LeTourneau University, Graduate Programs, Longview, TX 75607-7001. Offers business (MBA); counseling (MA), including licensed professional counselor, marriage and family therapy, school counseling; curriculum and instruction (M Ed); educational administration (M Ed); engineering (ME, MS); engineering management (MEM); health care administration (MS); marriage and family therapy (MA); psychology (MA); strategic leadership (MSL); teacher leadership (M Ed); teaching and learning (M Ed). *Program availability:* Part-time, 100% online, blended/hybrid learning. *Students:* 55 full-time (35 women), 337 part-time (266 women); includes 218 minority (140 Black or African American, non-Hispanic/Latino; 2 American Indian or Alaska Native, non-Hispanic/Latino; 5 Asian, non-Hispanic/Latino; 32 Hispanic/Latino; 39 Two or more races, non-Hispanic/Latino), 3 international. Average age 37. *Entrance requirements:* Additional exam requirements/recommendations for international students: Required—TOEFL. *Application deadline:* For fall admission, 8/22 for domestic students, 8/29 for international students; for winter admission, 10/10 for domestic students; for spring admission, 1/2 for domestic students, 1/10 for international students; for summer admission, 5/1 for domestic and international students. Applications are processed on a rolling basis. Electronic applications accepted. *Expenses:* Contact institution. *Financial support:* Research assistantships, institutionally sponsored loans, and unspecified assistantships available. Financial award applicants required to submit FAFSA.
Website: http://www.letu.edu

Lipscomb University, Program in Organizational Leadership, Nashville, TN 37204-3951. Offers aging services leadership (Certificate); global leadership (Certificate); organizational leadership (MPS); performance coaching (Certificate); strategic leadership (Certificate). *Program availability:* Part-time, online only, blended/hybrid learning. *Faculty:* 1 (woman) full-time, 3 part-time/adjunct (1 woman). *Students:* 27 full-time (14 women), 6 part-time (4 women); includes 8 minority (4 Black or African American, non-Hispanic/Latino; 4 Hispanic/Latino), 1 international. Average age 43. 34 applicants, 68% accepted, 15 enrolled. In 2017, 7 master's, 17 Certificates awarded. *Entrance requirements:* For master's, GRE or GMAT, two references, resume, interview. Additional exam requirements/recommendations for international students: Required—TOEFL (minimum score 550 paper-based). *Application deadline:* For fall admission, 8/1 for domestic students. Applications are processed on a rolling basis. Application fee: $50 ($75 for international students). Electronic applications accepted. *Expenses:* Contact institution. *Unit head:* Dr. Hope Nordstrom, Director, 615-966-1107, E-mail: hope.nordstrom@lipscomb.edu. *Application contact:* Barbara Blackman, Coordinator of Graduate Studies, 615-966-6287, Fax: 615-966-7619, E-mail: graduatestudies@lipscomb.edu.

Manhattanville College, School of Business, Master of Science in Business Leadership Program, Purchase, NY 10577-2132. Offers MS, Advanced Certificate. *Program availability:* Part-time, evening/weekend. *Faculty:* 6 part-time/adjunct (4 women). *Students:* 2 full-time (1 woman), 5 part-time (3 women); includes 4 minority (1 Black or African American, non-Hispanic/Latino; 1 Asian, non-Hispanic/Latino; 2 Hispanic/Latino). Average age 39. 11 applicants, 18% accepted. In 2017, 3 master's awarded. *Degree requirements:* For master's, thesis (for some programs), final project. *Entrance requirements:* For master's, personal essay, transcripts, 2 letters of recommendation (academic or professional), resume, health form with proof of immunization (for those born after 1957). Additional exam requirements/recommendations for international students: Required—TOEFL (minimum score 563 paper-based, 85 iBT), IELTS (7), or iTEP (B2). *Application deadline:* Applications are processed on a rolling basis. Application fee: $75. Electronic applications accepted. *Expenses:* $915 per credit. *Financial support:* Federal Work-Study, institutionally sponsored loans, scholarships/grants, and unspecified assistantships available. Financial award application deadline: 3/15; financial award applicants required to submit FAFSA. *Unit head:* Laura Persky, Graduate Program Director, 914-323-5188, E-mail: laura.persky@mville.edu. *Application contact:* Monika Pottgen, Assistant Director of Recruitment and Admissions, 914-323-5150, E-mail: business@mville.edu.
Website: https://www.mville.edu/programs/ms-business-leadership

McGill University, Faculty of Graduate and Postdoctoral Studies, Desautels Faculty of Management, Montréal, QC H3A 2T5, Canada. Offers administration (PhD); entrepreneurial studies (MBA); finance (MBA); general management (Post Master's Certificate); information systems (MBA); international business (MBA); international practicing management (MM); management (MBA); management for development (MBA); manufacturing management (MMM); marketing (MBA); operations management (MBA); public accountancy (Diploma); strategic management (MBA); MBA/LL B; MD/MBA. MMM offered jointly with Faculty of Engineering; PhD with Concordia University, HEC Montreal, Université de Montréal, Université du Québec à Montréal.

Mercyhurst University, Graduate Studies, Program in Organizational Leadership, Erie, PA 16546. Offers accounting (MS); higher education administration (MS); human resources (MS); organizational leadership (MS, Certificate); sports leadership (MS); strategy and innovation (MS). *Program availability:* Part-time, evening/weekend. *Degree requirements:* For master's, thesis. *Entrance requirements:* For master's, GRE General Test or MAT, interview, resume, essay, three professional references, transcripts. Additional exam requirements/recommendations for international students: Required—TOEFL (minimum score 80 iBT), IELTS (minimum score 6.5). Electronic applications accepted. *Faculty research:* Leadership training, organizational communication, leadership pedagogy.

Management Strategy and Policy

Messiah College, Program in Business and Leadership, Mechanicsburg, PA 17055. Offers leadership (MBA, Certificate); management (Certificate); strategic leadership (MA). *Program availability:* Online learning.

Michigan State University, The Graduate School, Eli Broad College of Business, Department of Management, East Lansing, MI 48224. Offers management (PhD); management, strategy, and leadership (MS). *Program availability:* Part-time, online learning. *Degree requirements:* For doctorate, comprehensive exam, thesis/dissertation. *Entrance requirements:* For master's, full-time managerial experience in a supervisory role; for doctorate, GMAT or GRE, letters of recommendation, experience in teaching and conducting research, work experience in business contexts, personal essay. Additional exam requirements/recommendations for international students: Required—TOEFL (minimum score 600 paper-based). Electronic applications accepted.

Middle Tennessee State University, College of Graduate Studies, University College, Murfreesboro, TN 37132. Offers advanced studies in teaching and learning (M Ed); human resources leadership (MPS); nursing administration (MSN); nursing education (MSN); strategic leadership (MPS); training and development (MPS). *Program availability:* Part-time, evening/weekend, online learning. *Entrance requirements:* Additional exam requirements/recommendations for international students: Required—TOEFL (minimum score 525 paper-based; 71 iBT) or IELTS (minimum score 6).

Mount Mercy University, Program in Strategic Leadership, Cedar Rapids, IA 52402-4797. Offers MSL. *Program availability:* Evening/weekend.

Neumann University, Program in Organizational and Strategic Leadership, Aston, PA 19014-1298. Offers MS. *Program availability:* Part-time, evening/weekend, 100% online, blended/hybrid learning. *Faculty:* 7 part-time/adjunct (3 women). *Students:* 55 part-time (31 women); includes 9 minority (7 Black or African American, non-Hispanic/Latino; 1 Asian, non-Hispanic/Latino; 1 Hispanic/Latino), 2 international. Average age 38. 34 applicants, 76% accepted, 22 enrolled. In 2017, 50 master's awarded. *Degree requirements:* For master's, project. *Entrance requirements:* For master's, official transcripts from all institutions attended, current resume, letter of intent, letter of recommendation. Additional exam requirements/recommendations for international students: Required—TOEFL (minimum score 70 iBT). *Application deadline:* Applications are processed on a rolling basis. Application fee: $0. Electronic applications accepted. *Expenses:* $615 per credit hour. *Financial support:* Scholarships/grants and health care benefits available. Support available to part-time students. Financial award application deadline: 3/15; financial award applicants required to submit FAFSA. *Unit head:* Dr. Samuel M. Lemon, Program Director, Master of Science in Organizational and Strategic Leadership, 610-361-5239, Fax: 610-361-5235, E-mail: lemons@neumann.edu. *Application contact:* Janice Sackawicz, Coordinator of Student Services, Division of Continuing Adult and Professional Studies, 610-558-5629, Fax: 610-361-5235, E-mail: caps@neumann.edu.

New England College, Program in Management, Henniker, NH 03242-3293. Offers accounting (MSA); healthcare administration (MS); international relations (MA); marketing management (MS); nonprofit leadership (MS); project management (MS); strategic leadership (MS). *Program availability:* Part-time, evening/weekend. *Degree requirements:* For master's, independent research project. Electronic applications accepted.

The New School, Parsons School of Design, Program in Strategic Design and Management, New York, NY 10011. Offers business of design (Advanced Certificate); strategic design and management (MS). *Program availability:* Part-time, 100% online. *Faculty:* 6 full-time (2 women), 26 part-time/adjunct (9 women). *Students:* 218 full-time (164 women), 6 part-time (5 women); includes 38 minority (10 Black or African American, non-Hispanic/Latino; 13 Asian, non-Hispanic/Latino; 11 Hispanic/Latino; 4 Two or more races, non-Hispanic/Latino), 143 international. Average age 27. 267 applicants, 78% accepted, 117 enrolled. In 2017, 103 master's, 6 other advanced degrees awarded. *Degree requirements:* For master's, thesis or alternative, integrative studio. *Entrance requirements:* For master's, transcripts, resume, statement of purpose, recommendation letters, essay, interview. Additional exam requirements/recommendations for international students: Required—TOEFL (minimum score 92 iBT), IELTS (minimum score 7), PTE (minimum score 63). *Application deadline:* For fall admission, 1/1 priority date for domestic and international students; for summer admission, 1/5 priority date for domestic and international students. Applications are processed on a rolling basis. Application fee: $50. Electronic applications accepted. *Expenses:* $1,744 per credit. *Financial support:* In 2017–18, 125 students received support, including 1 teaching assistantship (averaging $8,931 per year); career-related internships or fieldwork, Federal Work-Study, scholarships/grants, and unspecified assistantships also available. Support available to part-time students. Financial award application deadline: 2/1; financial award applicants required to submit FAFSA. *Unit head:* Rhea Alexander, Program Director, E-mail: alexanrc@newschool.edu. *Application contact:* Courtney Malenius, Director of Graduate Admission, 212-229-5150 Ext. 4011, E-mail: maleniuc@newschool.edu.
Website: http://www.newschool.edu/parsons/masters-design-management/

New York University, Leonard N. Stern School of Business, Department of Management and Organizations, New York, NY 10012-1019. Offers management organizations (MBA); organization theory (PhD); organizational behavior (PhD); strategy (PhD). *Expenses: Tuition:* Full-time $41,352; part-time $19,968 per year. *Required fees:* $2496; $1628 per unit. $814 per term. Tuition and fees vary according to course load and program. *Faculty research:* Strategic management, managerial cognition, interpersonal processes, conflict and negotiation.

Niagara University, Graduate Division of Business Administration, Niagara University, NY 14109. Offers accounting (MBA); business administration (MBA, MS); financial planning (MBA); healthcare administration (MBA, MHA); human resources (MBA); international business (MBA); marketing (MBA); professional accountancy (MBA); strategic management (MBA); supply chain management (MBA). *Accreditation:* AACSB. *Program availability:* Part-time, evening/weekend. *Faculty:* 17 full-time, 11 part-time/adjunct. *Students:* 173 full-time (92 women), 77 part-time (39 women); includes 38 minority (8 Black or African American, non-Hispanic/Latino; 3 American Indian or Alaska Native, non-Hispanic/Latino; 8 Asian, non-Hispanic/Latino; 8 Hispanic/Latino; 11 Two or more races, non-Hispanic/Latino), 46 international. Average age 27. In 2017, 139 master's awarded. *Entrance requirements:* For master's, GMAT. Additional exam requirements/recommendations for international students: Required—TOEFL (minimum score 550 paper-based; 79 iBT), IELTS (minimum score 6). *Application deadline:* For fall admission, 8/1 for domestic students; for spring admission, 11/1 for domestic students. Applications are processed on a rolling basis. Electronic applications accepted. *Expenses:* Contact institution. *Financial support:* Fellowships, research assistantships, career-related internships or fieldwork, and Federal Work-Study available. Support available to part-time students. Financial award application deadline: 4/15; financial award applicants required to submit FAFSA. *Faculty research:* Capital flows, Federal Reserve policy, human resource management, public policy, issues in marketing, auctions, economics of information, risk and capital markets, management strategy, consumer behavior, Internet and social media marketing. *Unit head:* Dr. Paul Richardson, MBA Director/Chair of the Marketing Department, 716-286-8169, Fax: 716-286-8206, E-mail: psr@niagara.edu. *Application contact:* Evan Pierce,

Associate Director for Graduate Recruitment, 716-286-8769, Fax: 716-286-8170, E-mail: epierce@niagara.edu.
Website: http://mba.niagara.edu

North Central College, School of Graduate and Professional Studies, Program in Business Administration, Naperville, IL 60566-7063. Offers change management (MBA); finance (MBA); human resource management (MBA); management (MBA). *Program availability:* Part-time, evening/weekend. *Degree requirements:* For master's, thesis optional, project. *Entrance requirements:* For master's, interview. Additional exam requirements/recommendations for international students: Required—TOEFL (minimum score 550 paper-based; 80 iBT), IELTS (minimum score 6.5). Electronic applications accepted. Application fee is waived when completed online. *Expenses:* Contact institution.

Northwestern University, The Graduate School, Kellogg School of Management, Department of Management and Strategy, Evanston, IL 60208. Offers PhD.

Northwestern University, The Graduate School, Kellogg School of Management, Department of Managerial Economics and Decision Sciences, Evanston, IL 60208. Offers PhD. Admissions and degree offered through The Graduate School. *Degree requirements:* For doctorate, comprehensive exam, thesis/dissertation. *Entrance requirements:* For doctorate, GMAT or GRE General Test. Additional exam requirements/recommendations for international students: Required—TOEFL. Electronic applications accepted. *Faculty research:* Competitive strategy and organization, managerial economics, decision sciences, game theory, operations management.

Northwestern University, The Graduate School, Kellogg School of Management, Management Programs, Evanston, IL 60208. Offers accounting information and management (MBA, PhD); analytical finance (MBA); business administration (MBA); decision sciences (MBA); entrepreneurship and innovation (MBA); finance (MBA, PhD); health enterprise management (MBA); human resources management (MBA); international business (MBA); management and organizations (MBA, PhD); management and organizations and sociology (PhD); management and strategy (MBA); management studies (MS); managerial analytics (MBA); managerial economics (MBA); managerial economics and strategy (PhD); marketing (MBA, PhD); marketing management (MBA); media management (MBA); operations management (MBA, PhD); real estate (MBA); social enterprise at Kellogg (MBA); JD/MBA. *Program availability:* Part-time, evening/weekend. Terminal master's awarded for partial completion of doctoral program. *Degree requirements:* For doctorate, thesis/dissertation, 2 years of coursework, qualifying (field) exam and candidacy, summer research papers and presentations to faculty, proposal defense, final exam/defense. *Entrance requirements:* For master's, GMAT, GRE, interview, 2 letters of recommendation, college transcripts, resume, essays, Kellogg honor code; for doctorate, GMAT, GRE, statement of purpose, transcripts, 2 letters of recommendation, resume, interview. Additional exam requirements/recommendations for international students: Required—TOEFL, IELTS. Electronic applications accepted. *Expenses:* Contact institution. *Faculty research:* Business cycles and international finance, health policy, networks, non-market policy, consumer psychology.

Northwestern University, School of Professional Studies, Program in Information Systems, Evanston, IL 60208. Offers analytics and business intelligence (MS); database and Internet technologies (MS); information systems (MS); information systems management (MS); information systems security (MS); medical informatics (MS); software project management and development (MS). *Program availability:* Part-time, evening/weekend.
Website: https://sps.northwestern.edu/masters/information-systems/index.php

Norwich University, College of Graduate and Continuing Studies, Master of Science in Leadership Program, Northfield, VT 05663. Offers leadership (MS), including human resources leadership, leading change management consulting, organizational leadership, public sector/government/military leadership. *Program availability:* Evening/weekend, online only, mostly all online with a week-long residency requirement. *Degree requirements:* For master's, capstone. *Entrance requirements:* For master's, minimum undergraduate GPA of 2.75. Additional exam requirements/recommendations for international students: Required—TOEFL (minimum score 550 paper-based; 80 iBT), IELTS (minimum score 6.5). Electronic applications accepted. *Expenses:* Contact institution.

Nova Southeastern University, H. Wayne Huizenga College of Business and Entrepreneurship, Fort Lauderdale, FL 33314-7796. Offers accounting (M Acc); business (MBA); business intelligence/analytics (MBA); complex health systems (MBA); enterprise informatics (MBA); entrepreneurship (MBA); finance (MBA); human resource management (MBA); international business (MBA); management (MBA); marketing (MBA); process improvement (MBA); public administration (MPA); real estate development (MS); sport revenue generation (MBA); supply chain management (MBA). *Accreditation:* NASPAA. *Program availability:* Part-time, evening/weekend, 100% online, blended/hybrid learning. *Faculty:* 85 full-time (37 women), 59 part-time/adjunct (19 women). *Students:* 1,999 full-time (1,225 women), 335 part-time (210 women); includes 1,516 minority (597 Black or African American, non-Hispanic/Latino; 4 American Indian or Alaska Native, non-Hispanic/Latino; 92 Asian, non-Hispanic/Latino; 789 Hispanic/Latino; 3 Native Hawaiian or other Pacific Islander, non-Hispanic/Latino; 31 Two or more races, non-Hispanic/Latino), 291 international. Average age 34. 1,269 applicants, 59% accepted, 551 enrolled. In 2017, 1,055 master's awarded. *Entrance requirements:* For master's, GMAT or GRE (depending on undergraduate GPA), official transcripts from all schools attended while in pursuit of bachelor's degree; minimum GPA of 2.5 from regionally-accredited institution. Additional exam requirements/recommendations for international students: Required—TOEFL (minimum score 550 paper-based; 79 iBT), IELTS (minimum score 6), PTE (minimum score 54). *Application deadline:* For fall admission, 8/5 priority date for domestic students, 7/29 priority date for international students; for winter admission, 12/16 priority date for domestic students, 12/9 priority date for international students; for summer admission, 4/21 priority date for domestic and international students. Applications are processed on a rolling basis. Application fee: $50. Electronic applications accepted. *Expenses:* $37,785 (online), $35,640 (in-classroom). *Financial support:* In 2017–18, 325 students received support. Federal Work-Study and scholarships/grants available. Support available to part-time students. Financial award application deadline: 4/15; financial award applicants required to submit FAFSA. *Faculty research:* Entrepreneurship and venture capital, ethics and social responsibility, global commerce and cultures, business process management. *Unit head:* Dr. J. Preston Jones, Dean, 954-262-5127, E-mail: prestonj@nova.edu. *Application contact:* Zeida Rodriguez, Associate Director of Enrollment Services, 954-262-5163, Fax: 954-262-3822, E-mail: zeida@nova.edu.
Website: http://www.huizenga.nova.edu

Ohio Dominican University, Division of Business, Columbus, OH 43219-2099. Offers business administration (MBA), including accounting, data analytics, finance, leadership, risk management, sport management; healthcare administration (MS); sport management (MS). *Accreditation:* ACBSP. *Program availability:* Part-time, evening/weekend, 100% online, blended/hybrid learning. *Faculty:* 9 full-time (4 women), 14 part-time/adjunct (5 women). *Students:* 65 full-time (26 women), 130 part-time (57 women);

includes 48 minority (30 Black or African American, non-Hispanic/Latino; 1 American Indian or Alaska Native, non-Hispanic/Latino; 6 Asian, non-Hispanic/Latino; 6 Hispanic/Latino; 5 Two or more races, non-Hispanic/Latino), 9 international. Average age 30. 148 applicants, 45% accepted, 53 enrolled. *Degree requirements:* For master's, thesis or alternative. *Entrance requirements:* Additional exam requirements/recommendations for international students: Required—TOEFL (minimum score 550 paper-based), IELTS (minimum score 6.5). *Application deadline:* For fall admission, 8/15 for domestic students, 6/10 for international students; for spring admission, 1/4 for domestic students, 11/2 for international students. Applications are processed on a rolling basis. Application fee: $25. Electronic applications accepted. *Financial support:* Applicants required to submit FAFSA. *Unit head:* Dr. Kenneth C. Fah, Chair, 614-251-4566, E-mail: fahk@ohiodominican.edu. *Application contact:* John W. Naughton, Director for Graduate Admissions, 614-251-4721, Fax: 614-251-6654, E-mail: grad@ohiodominican.edu. Website: http://www.ohiodominican.edu/academics/graduate/mba

Oklahoma Wesleyan University, Professional Studies Division, Bartlesville, OK 74006-6299. Offers nursing administration (MSN); nursing education (MSN); strategic leadership (MS); theology and apologetics (MA).

Pace University, Lubin School of Business, Program in Management, New York, NY 10038. Offers entrepreneurial studies (MBA); entrepreneurship (MS); human resource management (MBA, MS); strategic management (MBA, MS). *Program availability:* Part-time, evening/weekend. *Students:* 58 full-time (37 women), 72 part-time (40 women); includes 38 minority (15 Black or African American, non-Hispanic/Latino; 7 Asian, non-Hispanic/Latino; 12 Hispanic/Latino; 4 Two or more races, non-Hispanic/Latino), 40 international. Average age 30. 160 applicants, 56% accepted, 38 enrolled. In 2017, 47 master's awarded. *Entrance requirements:* For master's, GMAT, GRE (GMAT not required for MS with 3 years of HR experience in a management position), undergraduate degree, transcripts from all accredited colleges/universities attended, two letters of recommendation, resume, personal statement. Additional exam requirements/recommendations for international students: Required—TOEFL (minimum score 90 iBT), IELTS (minimum score 7) or PTE (minimum score 61). *Application deadline:* For fall admission, 8/1 priority date for domestic students, 6/1 for international students; for spring admission, 12/1 for domestic students, 10/1 for international students. Applications are processed on a rolling basis. Application fee: $70. Electronic applications accepted. *Financial support:* Research assistantships, career-related internships or fieldwork, Federal Work-Study, and unspecified assistantships available. Support available to part-time students. Financial award application deadline: 2/15; financial award applicants required to submit FAFSA. *Unit head:* Dr. John C. Byrne, Chairperson, 212-618-6581, E-mail: jbyrne@pace.edu. *Application contact:* Susan Ford-Goldschein, Director of Graduate Admissions, 212-346-1531, Fax: 212-346-1585, E-mail: graduateadmission@pace.edu. Website: http://www.pace.edu/lubin/management-concentration-mba

Pontificia Universidad Catolica Madre y Maestra, Graduate School, Faculty of Social and Administrative Sciences, Santiago, Dominican Republic. Offers business administration (MBA), including business development, finance, international business, management skills (M Mgmt, MBA), marketing, operations, strategic cost management, strategy, tourist destination planning and management; law (LL M), including civil law, corporate business law, criminal law, international relations, real estate law; management (M Mgmt), including higher financial management, insurance program administration, management skills (M Mgmt, MBA); psychology (MA), including clinical child and adolescent psychology, forensic psychology; strategic human resources (EMBA).

Regent University, Graduate School, School of Business and Leadership, Virginia Beach, VA 23464-9800. Offers business administration (MBA), including accounting, economics, entrepreneurship, finance and investing, general management, healthcare management (MA, MBA), human resource management (MA, MBA), innovation management, leadership, marketing, not-for-profit management (MA, MBA); business analytics (MS); business and design management (MA); church leadership (MA); leadership (Certificate); organizational leadership (MA, PhD), including ecclesial leadership (DSL, PhD), entrepreneurial leadership (PhD), healthcare management (MA, MBA), human resource development (PhD), human resource management (MA, MBA), individualized studies (DSL, PhD), interdisciplinary studies (MA), leadership coaching and mentoring (MA), not-for-profit management (MA, MBA), organizational development consulting (MA), servant leadership (MA, DSL); strategic leadership (DSL), including ecclesial leadership (DSL, PhD), global consulting, healthcare leadership, individualized studies (DSL, PhD), leadership coaching, servant leadership (MA, DSL), strategic foresight. *Program availability:* Part-time, evening/weekend, 100% online, blended/hybrid learning. *Faculty:* 9 full-time (2 women), 38 part-time/adjunct (11 women). *Students:* 129 full-time (80 women), 1,152 part-time (598 women); includes 685 minority (546 Black or African American, non-Hispanic/Latino; 10 American Indian or Alaska Native, non-Hispanic/Latino; 29 Asian, non-Hispanic/Latino; 65 Hispanic/Latino; 6 Native Hawaiian or other Pacific Islander, non-Hispanic/Latino; 29 Two or more races, non-Hispanic/Latino), 62 international. Average age 41. 1,721 applicants, 48% accepted, 624 enrolled. In 2017, 125 master's, 69 doctorates awarded. *Degree requirements:* For master's, thesis or alternative, 3-credit hour culminating experience; for doctorate, thesis/dissertation. *Entrance requirements:* For master's, college transcripts, resume, essay; for doctorate, college transcripts, resume, essay, writing sample; for Certificate, writing sample, resume, transcripts. Additional exam requirements/recommendations for international students: Required—TOEFL (minimum score 577 paper-based). *Application deadline:* For fall admission, 5/1 priority date for domestic students; for spring admission, 10/1 priority date for domestic students. Applications are processed on a rolling basis. Application fee: $50. Electronic applications accepted. *Expenses:* $650 per credit (MA, MS, MBA); $995 per credit (PhD); $300 per semester technology fee. *Financial support:* In 2017–18, 829 students received support. Career-related internships or fieldwork, scholarships/grants, and unspecified assistantships available. Support available to part-time students. *Faculty research:* Servant leadership, global business, team effectiveness, technology utilization, leadership development. *Unit head:* Dr. Doris Gomez, Dean, 757-352-4686, Fax: 757-352-4634, E-mail: dorigom@regent.edu. *Application contact:* Heidi Cece, Assistant Vice President of Enrollment Management, 800-373-5504, Fax: 757-352-4381, E-mail: admissions@regent.edu. Website: https://www.regent.edu/school-of-business-and-leadership/

Regis University, College of Business and Economics, Denver, CO 80221-1099. Offers accounting (MS); executive leadership (Certificate); finance (MS); finance and accounting (MBA); health industry leadership (MBA); human resource management and leadership (MSOL); management (MBA); marketing (MBA); nonprofit leadership (Post-Graduate Certificate); nonprofit management (MNM); nonprofit organizational capacity building (Certificate); operations management (MBA); organizational leadership and management (MSOL); project leadership and management (MS, MSOL); strategic business management (Certificate); strategic human resource integration (Certificate); strategic management (MBA). Programs offered at Colorado Springs Campus, Northwest Denver Campus, Southeast Denver Campus, Fort Collins Campus, Broomfield Campus, Henderson (Nevada) Campus, and Summerlin (Nevada) Campus. *Program availability:* Part-time, evening/weekend, 100% online, blended/hybrid learning.

Degree requirements: For master's, thesis (for some programs), capstone or final research project. *Entrance requirements:* For master's, official transcript reflecting baccalaureate degree awarded from regionally-accredited college or university, interview, 2 years of full-time related work experience, resume, letters of recommendation. Additional exam requirements/recommendations for international students: Required—TOEFL (minimum score 550 paper-based; 82 iBT). Electronic applications accepted. *Expenses:* Contact institution. *Faculty research:* Impact of information technology on small business regulation of accounting, international project financing, mineral development, delivery of healthcare to rural indigenous communities.

Roberts Wesleyan College, Graduate Business Programs, Rochester, NY 14624-1997. Offers strategic leadership (MS); strategic marketing (MS). *Program availability:* Evening/weekend. *Degree requirements:* For master's, thesis or alternative. *Entrance requirements:* For master's, GMAT, minimum GPA of 2.75, verifiable work experience. *Expenses:* Contact institution.

Rockhurst University, Helzberg School of Management, Kansas City, MO 64110-2561. Offers accounting (MBA); business intelligence (MBA, Certificate); business intelligence and analytics (MS); data science (MBA, Certificate); entrepreneurship (MBA); finance (MBA); fundraising leadership (MBA, Certificate); healthcare management (MBA, Certificate); human capital (Certificate); international business (Certificate); management (MA, MBA, Certificate); nonprofit administration (Certificate); organizational development (Certificate); science leadership (Certificate). *Accreditation:* AACSB. *Program availability:* Part-time, evening/weekend. *Faculty:* 18 full-time (4 women), 20 part-time/adjunct (9 women). *Students:* 99 full-time (30 women), 355 part-time (132 women); includes 95 minority (30 Black or African American, non-Hispanic/Latino; 29 Asian, non-Hispanic/Latino; 25 Hispanic/Latino; 11 Two or more races, non-Hispanic/Latino), 8 international. Average age 32. 249 applicants, 81% accepted, 175 enrolled. In 2017, 145 master's, 17 other advanced degrees awarded. *Entrance requirements:* For master's, GMAT or GRE. Additional exam requirements/recommendations for international students: Required—TOEFL (minimum score 550 paper-based; 79 iBT). *Application deadline:* Applications are processed on a rolling basis. Application fee: $0. Electronic applications accepted. *Financial support:* Applicants required to submit FAFSA. *Faculty research:* Offshoring/outsourcing, systems analysis/synthesis, work teams, multilateral trade, path dependencies/creation. *Unit head:* Cheryl McConnell, Dean, 816-501-4201, Fax: 816-501-4650, E-mail: cheryl.mcconnell@rockhurst.edu. *Application contact:* Jonnae Hill, Director of Graduate Business Advising, 816-501-4823, E-mail: jonnae.hill@rockhurst.edu. Website: https://www.rockhurst.edu/helzberg

St. John's University, The Peter J. Tobin College of Business, Department of Management, Queens, NY 11439. Offers business administration (MBA), including strategic management. *Faculty:* 15 full-time (5 women), 9 part-time/adjunct (4 women). *Students:* 31 full-time (13 women), 21 part-time (7 women); includes 24 minority (8 Black or African American, non-Hispanic/Latino; 3 Asian, non-Hispanic/Latino; 10 Hispanic/Latino; 1 Native Hawaiian or other Pacific Islander, non-Hispanic/Latino; 2 Two or more races, non-Hispanic/Latino), 2 international. Average age 26. 37 applicants, 86% accepted, 30 enrolled. In 2017, 17 master's awarded. *Entrance requirements:* For master's, GMAT or GRE, 2 letters of recommendation, essay, resume, unofficial transcripts. Additional exam requirements/recommendations for international students: Required—TOEFL (minimum score 80 iBT), IELTS (minimum score 6.5). *Application deadline:* For fall admission, 11/1 for domestic and international students; for winter admission, 3/1 for domestic and international students; for spring admission, 6/1 for domestic and international students. Applications are processed on a rolling basis. Application fee: $70. Electronic applications accepted. *Expenses:* $22,410 per year. *Financial support:* Research assistantships, teaching assistantships, scholarships/grants, and unspecified assistantships available. Support available to part-time students. Financial award application deadline: 2/1; financial award applicants required to submit FAFSA. *Total annual research expenditures:* $27,189. *Unit head:* Dr. John Angelidis, Chair, 718-990-6495, E-mail: angelidj@stjohns.edu. *Application contact:* Amber Steiger, Associate Director of Enrollment Management, 718-990-1345, E-mail: steigera@stjohns.edu. Website: http://www.stjohns.edu/academics/schools-and-colleges/peter-j-tobin-college-business/management

Saint Mary-of-the-Woods College, Master of Leadership Development Program, Saint Mary of the Woods, IN 47876. Offers not-for-profit leadership (MLD); organizational leadership (MLD). *Program availability:* Part-time. *Students:* 47 full-time (41 women); includes 4 minority (all Black or African American, non-Hispanic/Latino). Average age 35. 26 applicants, 81% accepted, 19 enrolled. In 2017, 24 master's awarded. *Degree requirements:* For master's, thesis. *Application deadline:* Applications are processed on a rolling basis. Application fee: $0. Electronic applications accepted. *Expenses:* $565 per credit hour. *Financial support:* In 2017–18, 28 students received support. Scholarships/grants available. Financial award applicants required to submit FAFSA. *Application contact:* Office of Graduate Admissions, 800-926-7692, E-mail: graduate@smwc.edu. Website: http://www.smwc.edu

Salve Regina University, Program in Management, Newport, RI 02840-4192. Offers business studies (CGS); human resource management (CGS); innovation and strategic management (MS); management (CGS); nonprofit management (CGS); social entrepreneurship (CGS). *Program availability:* Part-time, evening/weekend, online learning. *Entrance requirements:* For master's, GMAT, GRE General Test, or MAT. Additional exam requirements/recommendations for international students: Required—TOEFL (minimum score 600 paper-based; 100 iBT). Electronic applications accepted.

Southeastern University, Jannetides College of Business and Entrepreneurial Leadership, Lakeland, FL 33801-6099. Offers executive leadership (MBA); global business administration (MBA); healthcare administration (MBA); missional leadership (MBA); organizational leadership (PhD); sport management (MBA); strategic leadership (DSL). *Accreditation:* ACBSP. *Program availability:* Evening/weekend, online learning. *Faculty:* 10 full-time (2 women), 8 part-time/adjunct (1 woman). *Students:* 80 full-time (38 women), 110 part-time (54 women); includes 51 minority (18 Black or African American, non-Hispanic/Latino; 5 Asian, non-Hispanic/Latino; 28 Hispanic/Latino), 7 international. Average age 31. *Entrance requirements:* For master's, GMAT, minimum cumulative GPA of 3.0, writing sample. Application fee: $50. Electronic applications accepted. *Unit head:* Lyle L. Bowlin, Dean, 863-667-5118, E-mail: llbowlin@seu.edu. Website: http://www.seu.edu/business/

Southern Methodist University, Cox School of Business, MBA Program, Dallas, TX 75275. Offers accounting (MBA, PMBA); business administration (EMBA); finance (MBA); financial statement analysis (PMBA); general business (MBA); information technology and operations management (MBA); management (MBA); marketing (MBA); real estate (MBA); strategy (MBA); strategy and entrepreneurship (MBA); JD/MBA; MA/MBA. *Program availability:* Part-time, evening/weekend. *Entrance requirements:* For master's, GMAT. Additional exam requirements/recommendations for international students: Required—TOEFL. Electronic applications accepted. *Expenses:* Contact institution. *Faculty research:* Corporate finance, financial reporting, modeling consumer decision-making, competition between national brands and store brands, institutional determinants of firms' strategy.

Management Strategy and Policy

Stevens Institute of Technology, Graduate School, School of Business, Program in Management, Hoboken, NJ 07030. Offers general management (MS); global innovation management (MS); human resource management (MS); information management (MS); project management (MS); technology commercialization (MS); technology management (MS). *Program availability:* Part-time, evening/weekend. *Students:* 56 full-time (18 women), 88 part-time (32 women); includes 18 minority (3 Black or African American, non-Hispanic/Latino; 12 Asian, non-Hispanic/Latino; 1 Hispanic/Latino), 87 international. Average age 30. 194 applicants, 78% accepted, 68 enrolled. In 2017, 87 master's awarded. *Degree requirements:* For master's, thesis optional, minimum B average in major field and overall. *Entrance requirements:* Additional exam requirements/recommendations for international students: Required—TOEFL (minimum score 74 iBT), IELTS (minimum score 6). *Application deadline:* For fall admission, 7/1 for domestic students, 4/15 for international students; for spring admission, 12/1 for domestic and international students. Applications are processed on a rolling basis. Application fee: $60. Electronic applications accepted. *Expenses: Tuition:* Full-time $34,494; part-time $1554 per credit. *Required fees:* $291 per semester. *Financial support:* Fellowships, research assistantships, teaching assistantships, career-related internships or fieldwork, Federal Work-Study, scholarships/grants, and unspecified assistantships available. Financial award application deadline: 2/15; financial award applicants required to submit FAFSA. *Unit head:* Brian Rothschild, Director, 201-216-3677, E-mail: brian.rothschild@stevens.edu. *Application contact:* Graduate Admissions, 888-783-8367, Fax: 888-511-1306, E-mail: graduate@stevens.edu.
Website: https://www.stevens.edu/school-business/masters-programs/management

Stockton University, Office of Graduate Studies, Program in Data Science and Strategic Analytics, Galloway, NJ 08205-9441. Offers MS. *Program availability:* Part-time, online learning. *Faculty:* 1 full-time (0 women), 2 part-time/adjunct (0 women). *Students:* 10 full-time (2 women), 3 part-time (2 women); includes 3 minority (1 Asian, non-Hispanic/Latino; 2 Hispanic/Latino). Average age 32. 22 applicants, 73% accepted, 13 enrolled. *Unit head:* Dr. J. Russell Manson, Director. *Application contact:* Tara Williams, Assistant Director of Graduate Enrollment, 609-626-3640, Fax: 609-626-6050, E-mail: gradschool@stockton.edu.
Website: https://stockton.edu/graduate/data-science_strategic-analytics.html

Suffolk University, Sawyer Business School, Master of Business Administration Program, Boston, MA 02108-2770. Offers accounting (MBA); entrepreneurship (MBA); executive business administration (EMBA); finance (MBA); global business administration (GMBA); health administration (MBA); international business (MBA); marketing (MBA); nonprofit management (MBA); organizational behavior (MBA); strategic management (MBA); supply chain management (MBA); taxation (MBA); JD/MBA; MBA/MHA; MBA/MSA; MBA/MSF; MBA/MST. *Accreditation:* AACSB. *Program availability:* Part-time, evening/weekend, 100% online. *Faculty:* 16 full-time (6 women), 9 part-time/adjunct (1 woman). *Students:* 106 full-time (57 women), 236 part-time (135 women); includes 80 minority (23 Black or African American, non-Hispanic/Latino; 23 Asian, non-Hispanic/Latino; 28 Hispanic/Latino; 6 Two or more races, non-Hispanic/Latino), 41 international. Average age 30. 354 applicants, 69% accepted, 115 enrolled. In 2017, 170 master's awarded. *Entrance requirements:* For master's, GMAT, minimum undergraduate GPA of 2.75 (MBA), 5 years of managerial experience (EMBA). Additional exam requirements/recommendations for international students: Required—TOEFL (minimum score 550 paper-based; 80 iBT). *Application deadline:* For fall admission, 3/15 priority date for domestic students, 10/15 priority date for international students; for spring admission, 10/15 priority date for domestic and international students. Applications are processed on a rolling basis. Application fee: $50. Electronic applications accepted. *Expenses:* $43,980 per year full-time, $1,466 per credit part-time (for MBA); $1,794 per credit part-time (for Executive MBA). *Financial support:* In 2017-18, 198 students received support, including 1 fellowship (averaging $2,325 per year); career-related internships or fieldwork, Federal Work-Study, institutionally sponsored loans, and scholarships/grants also available. Support available to part-time students. Financial award application deadline: 4/1; financial award applicants required to submit FAFSA. *Faculty research:* Foreign investments; career strategies and boundaryless careers; corporate ethics codes; interest rates, inflation, and growth options; innovation and product development performance. *Unit head:* Jodi Detjen, Director of MBA Programs, 617-573-8306, E-mail: jdetjen@suffolk.edu. *Application contact:* Mara Marzocchi, Associate Director of Graduate Admissions, 617-573-8302, Fax: 617-305-1733, E-mail: grad.admission@suffolk.edu.
Website: http://www.suffolk.edu/mba

Temple University, Fox School of Business, Doctoral Programs in Business, Philadelphia, PA 19122-6096. Offers accounting (PhD); entrepreneurship (PhD); finance (PhD); international business (PhD); management information systems (PhD); marketing (PhD); risk management and insurance (PhD); statistics (PhD); strategic management (PhD); tourism and sport (PhD). *Accreditation:* AACSB. *Degree requirements:* For doctorate, thesis/dissertation. *Entrance requirements:* For doctorate, GRE General Test, GMAT, minimum GPA of 3.0, master's degree. Additional exam requirements/recommendations for international students: Required—TOEFL (minimum score 600 paper-based; 100 iBT), IELTS (minimum score 7.5). Electronic applications accepted. *Expenses:* Tuition, state resident: full-time $16,164; part-time $898 per credit hour. Tuition, nonresident: full-time $22,158; part-time $1231 per credit hour. *Required fees:* $890; $445 per semester. Full-time tuition and fees vary according to course load, degree level, campus/location and program.

Tennessee State University, The School of Graduate Studies and Research, College of Public Service, Nashville, TN 37209-1561. Offers human resource management (MPS); public administration (MPA, PhD); social work (MSW); strategic leadership (MPS); training and development (MPS). *Accreditation:* NASPAA (one or more programs are accredited). *Program availability:* Part-time, evening/weekend. *Degree requirements:* For master's, comprehensive exam, thesis optional; for doctorate, comprehensive exam, thesis/dissertation. *Entrance requirements:* For master's, GRE General Test, minimum GPA of 2.5, writing sample; for doctorate, GRE General Test, minimum GPA of 3.25, writing sample. *Faculty research:* Total quality management and process improvement, national health care policy and administration, starting non-profit ventures, public service ethics, state education financing across the U.S. public.

Tennessee Technological University, College of Graduate Studies, College of Interdisciplinary Studies, School of Professional Studies, Cookeville, TN 38505. Offers health care administration (MPS); human resources leadership (MPS); public safety (MPS); strategic leadership (MPS); teaching English to speakers of other languages (MPS); training and development (MPS). *Program availability:* Part-time, evening/weekend, online learning. *Students:* 20 full-time (11 women), 74 part-time (46 women); includes 18 minority (11 Black or African American, non-Hispanic/Latino; 1 Hispanic/Latino; 1 Native Hawaiian or other Pacific Islander, non-Hispanic/Latino; 5 Two or more races, non-Hispanic/Latino), 1 international. 50 applicants, 82% accepted, 29 enrolled. In 2017, 23 master's awarded. *Degree requirements:* For master's, comprehensive exam, thesis or alternative. *Entrance requirements:* For master's, GRE. Additional exam requirements/recommendations for international students: Required—TOEFL (minimum score 527 paper-based; 71 iBT), IELTS (minimum score 5.5), PTE (minimum score 48), or TOEIC (Test of English as an International Communication). *Application deadline:* For fall admission, 7/1 for domestic students, 5/1 for international students; for spring

admission, 11/1 for domestic students, 10/1 for international students; for summer admission, 5/1 for domestic students, 2/1 for international students. Applications are processed on a rolling basis. Application fee: $35 ($40 for international students). Electronic applications accepted. *Expenses:* Tuition, state resident: full-time $9925; part-time $565 per credit hour. Tuition, nonresident: full-time $22,993; part-time $1291 per credit hour. *Financial support:* Application deadline: 4/1. *Unit head:* Dr. Joseph Roberts, Interim Director, School of Professional Studies, 931-372-6223, E-mail: jmroberts@tntech.edu. *Application contact:* Shelia K. Kendrick, Coordinator of Graduate Studies, 931-372-3808, Fax: 931-372-3497, E-mail: skendrick@tntech.edu. Website: https://www.tntech.edu/is/sps/

Thomas Jefferson University, Kanbar College of Design, Engineering and Commerce, Innovation MBA Program, Philadelphia, PA 19107. Offers business analytics (MBA); general business (MBA); management (MBA); marketing (MBA); strategy and design thinking (MBA); MBA/MS. *Program availability:* Part-time, evening/weekend, online learning. *Entrance requirements:* For master's, GMAT. Additional exam requirements/recommendations for international students: Required—TOEFL (minimum score 550 paper-based; 79 iBT).

Thomas Jefferson University, School of Continuing and Professional Studies, Philadelphia, PA 19107. Offers strategic leadership (D Mgt).

Tufts University, Graduate School of Arts and Sciences, Graduate Certificate Programs, Program Evaluation Program, Medford, MA 02155. Offers Certificate. *Program availability:* Part-time, evening/weekend. Electronic applications accepted. *Expenses:* Contact institution.

Tulane University, A. B. Freeman School of Business, New Orleans, LA 70118-5669. Offers accounting (M Acct); analytics (MBA); banking and financial services (M Fin); energy (M Fin, MBA); entrepreneurship (MBA); finance (MBA, PhD); financial accounting (PhD); international business (MBA); international management (MBA); strategic management and leadership (MBA); JD/M Acct; JD/MBA; MBA/M Acc; MBA/MA; MBA/MD; MBA/ME; MBA/MPH. *Accreditation:* AACSB. *Program availability:* Part-time, evening/weekend. *Faculty:* 51 full-time (15 women), 38 part-time/adjunct (3 women). *Students:* 561 full-time (287 women), 297 part-time (151 women); includes 112 minority (43 Black or African American, non-Hispanic/Latino; 2 American Indian or Alaska Native, non-Hispanic/Latino; 24 Asian, non-Hispanic/Latino; 38 Hispanic/Latino; 5 Two or more races, non-Hispanic/Latino), 515 international. Average age 27. 2,021 applicants, 74% accepted, 476 enrolled. In 2017, 632 master's, 9 doctorates awarded. Terminal master's awarded for partial completion of doctoral program. *Degree requirements:* For master's, one foreign language, comprehensive exam (for some programs); for doctorate, one foreign language, comprehensive exam, thesis/dissertation. *Entrance requirements:* For master's and doctorate, GMAT or GRE, interview. Additional exam requirements/recommendations for international students: Required—TOEFL or IELTS. *Application deadline:* For fall admission, 11/1 priority date for domestic and international students; for winter admission, 1/6 for domestic and international students; for spring admission, 3/1 priority date for domestic and international students; for summer admission, 5/5 for domestic students. Applications are processed on a rolling basis. Application fee: $125. Electronic applications accepted. *Expenses:* Contact institution. *Financial support:* In 2017–18, 176 students received support. Fellowships with tuition reimbursements available, research assistantships, teaching assistantships, career-related internships or fieldwork, Federal Work-Study, tuition waivers (full and partial), and unspecified assistantships available. Support available to part-time students. Financial award application deadline: 4/15; financial award applicants required to submit FAFSA. *Faculty research:* Corporate finance, managerial accounting and financial reporting, strategic management and leadership, consumer behavior and decision making, organizational behavior and human resource management. *Unit head:* Ira Solomon, PhD, Dean, 504-865-5407, Fax: 504-865-5491, E-mail: businessdean@tulane.edu. *Application contact:* Melissa Booth, Assistant Dean for Graduate Admissions, 800-223-5402, E-mail: freeman.admissions@tulane.edu.
Website: http://www.freeman.tulane.edu

United States International University–Africa, School of Business Administration, Nairobi, Kenya. Offers business administration (GEMBA); entrepreneurship (MBA); finance (MBA); human resource management (MBA); information technology management (MBA); integrated studies (MBA); international business administration (MBA); management and organizational development (MS); marketing (MBA); organizational development (EMS); strategic management (MBA). *Program availability:* Part-time, evening/weekend. *Degree requirements:* For master's, thesis. *Entrance requirements:* For master's, GMAT, 2 letters of reference, resume. Additional exam requirements/recommendations for international students: Required—TOEFL (minimum score 550 paper-based). *Faculty research:* Marketing in small business enterprises, total quality management in Kenya.

Universidad del Este, Graduate School, Carolina, PR 00984. Offers accounting (MBA); adult education (M Ed); agribusiness (MBA); criminal justice and criminology (MA); curriculum and instruction - early education (M Ed); curriculum and instruction - elementary (M Ed); curriculum and instruction - English (M Ed); curriculum and instruction - Spanish (M Ed); human resources (MBA); information security management (MBA); information technology and Web business development (MBA); management (MBA); public policy (MPA); social work (MA), including clinical social work; special education (M Ed); strategic leadership (MBA).

The University of Arizona, Eller College of Management, Department of Management and Organizations, Tucson, AZ 85721. Offers MS, PhD. *Program availability:* Evening/weekend. *Entrance requirements:* Additional exam requirements/recommendations for international students: Required—TOEFL (minimum score 550 paper-based; 79 iBT). Electronic applications accepted. *Faculty research:* Organizational behavior, human resources, decision-making, health economics and finance, immigration.

The University of British Columbia, Sauder School of Business, Doctoral Program in Business Administration, Vancouver, BC V6T 1Z2, Canada. Offers accounting (PhD); finance (PhD); management information systems (PhD); management science (PhD); marketing (PhD); organizational behavior (PhD); strategy and business economics (PhD); transportation and logistics (PhD); urban land economics (PhD). *Degree requirements:* For doctorate, comprehensive exam, thesis/dissertation. *Entrance requirements:* For doctorate, GMAT or GRE. Additional exam requirements/recommendations for international students: Required—TOEFL (minimum score 600 paper-based; 100 iBT). Electronic applications accepted. *Expenses:* Contact institution.

University of Calgary, Faculty of Graduate Studies, Centre for Military and Strategic Studies, Calgary, AB T2N 1N4, Canada. Offers MSS, PhD. PhD offered in special cases only. *Program availability:* Part-time. *Degree requirements:* For master's, thesis; for doctorate, comprehensive exam, thesis/dissertation. *Entrance requirements:* For master's, minimum GPA of 3.4. Additional exam requirements/recommendations for international students: Recommended—TOEFL (minimum score 550 paper-based). *Faculty research:* Military history, Israeli studies, strategic studies, int'l relations, Arctic security.

University of California, Davis, Graduate School of Management, Full-Time MBA Program, Davis, CA 95616. Offers business analytics and technologies (MBA); entrepreneurship and innovation (MBA); finance and accounting (MBA); general

management (MBA); marketing (MBA); organizational behavior (MBA); public health management (MBA); strategy (MBA); technology management (MBA); DVM/MBA; JD/MBA; M Engr/MBA; MBA/MPH; MBA/MS; MD/MBA; MSN/MBA; PhD/MBA. *Faculty:* 52 full-time (15 women). *Students:* 96 full-time (42 women); includes 31 minority (1 Black or African American, non-Hispanic/Latino; 17 Asian, non-Hispanic/Latino; 5 Hispanic/Latino; 8 Two or more races, non-Hispanic/Latino), 36 international. Average age 29. 290 applicants, 37% accepted, 45 enrolled. In 2017, 44 master's awarded. *Degree requirements:* For master's, integrated management project. *Entrance requirements:* For master's, GMAT or GRE, letters of recommendation, resume, essays, equivalent of a 4-year U.S. undergraduate degree, transcript. Additional exam requirements/recommendations for international students: Required—TOEFL (minimum score 600 paper-based; 100 iBT), IELTS (minimum score 7). *Application deadline:* For fall admission, 5/18 priority date for domestic and international students. Application fee: $125. Electronic applications accepted. *Expenses:* Contact institution. *Financial support:* In 2017–18, 90 students received support. Fellowships, research assistantships, teaching assistantships with partial tuition reimbursements available, institutionally sponsored loans, scholarships/grants, health care benefits, tuition waivers (partial), and unspecified assistantships available. Financial award application deadline: 3/1; financial award applicants required to submit FAFSA. *Faculty research:* Finance, marketing, management, business analytics, accounting. *Unit head:* James Stevens, Senior Assistant Dean of Student Affairs, 530-752-7658, Fax: 530-754-9355, E-mail: admissions@gsm.ucdavis.edu. *Application contact:* Kristy Bird MaKieve, Interim Director of Admissions, 530-754-5476, Fax: 530-754-9355, E-mail: admissions@gsm.ucdavis.edu.
Website: http://gsm.ucdavis.edu/daytime-mba-program

University of California, Davis, Graduate School of Management, MBA Programs in Sacramento and San Francisco Bay Area, Davis, CA 95616. Offers business analytics and technologies (MBA); entrepreneurship and innovation (MBA); finance and accounting (MBA); general management (MBA); marketing (MBA); organizational behavior (MBA); public health management (MBA); strategy (MBA); technology management (MBA). *Program availability:* Part-time-only, evening/weekend. *Faculty:* 99 part-time/adjunct (30 women). *Students:* 323 part-time (133 women); includes 148 minority (7 Black or African American, non-Hispanic/Latino; 96 Asian, non-Hispanic/Latino; 26 Hispanic/Latino; 1 Native Hawaiian or other Pacific Islander, non-Hispanic/Latino; 18 Two or more races, non-Hispanic/Latino), 37 international. Average age 30. 202 applicants, 75% accepted, 111 enrolled. In 2017, 112 master's awarded. *Degree requirements:* For master's, integrated management project. *Entrance requirements:* For master's, GMAT or GRE, letters of recommendation, resume, equivalent of a 4-year undergraduate degree. Additional exam requirements/recommendations for international students: Required—TOEFL (minimum score 600 paper-based; 100 iBT), IELTS (minimum score 7). *Application deadline:* For fall admission, 5/18 priority date for domestic and international students. Application fee: $125. Electronic applications accepted. *Expenses:* Contact institution. *Financial support:* In 2017–18, 67 students received support. Fellowships, teaching assistantships with partial tuition reimbursements available, scholarships/grants, and unspecified assistantships available. Support available to part-time students. Financial award application deadline: 3/1; financial award applicants required to submit FAFSA. *Faculty research:* Accounting, finance, marketing, management, business analytics. *Unit head:* James Stevens, Senior Assistant Dean of Student Affairs, 530-752-7658, Fax: 530-754-9355, E-mail: admissions@gsm.ucdavis.edu. *Application contact:* Kristy Bird MaKieve, Interim Director of Admissions, 530-754-5476, Fax: 530-754-9355, E-mail: admissions@gsm.ucdavis.edu.
Website: http://gsm.ucdavis.edu/mba-programs

University of California, Los Angeles, Graduate Division, UCLA Anderson School of Management, Los Angeles, CA 90095-1481. Offers accounting (PhD); behavioral decision making (PhD); business administration (EMBA, MBA); business analytics (MSBA); decisions, operations, and technology management (PhD); finance (PhD); financial engineering (MFE); global economics and management (PhD); management and organizations (PhD); marketing (PhD); strategy and policy (PhD); DDS/MBA; MBA/JD; MBA/MD; MBA/MLAS; MBA/MLIS; MBA/MN; MBA/MPH; MBA/MPP; MBA/MSCS; MBA/MURP. *Accreditation:* AACSB. *Program availability:* Part-time, evening/weekend. *Faculty:* 88 full-time (20 women), 107 part-time/adjunct (21 women). *Students:* 918 full-time (314 women), 1,269 part-time (399 women); includes 743 minority (38 Black or African American, non-Hispanic/Latino; 3 American Indian or Alaska Native, non-Hispanic/Latino; 531 Asian, non-Hispanic/Latino; 115 Hispanic/Latino; 4 Native Hawaiian or other Pacific Islander, non-Hispanic/Latino; 52 Two or more races, non-Hispanic/Latino), 544 international. Average age 31. 5,842 applicants, 29% accepted, 1015 enrolled. In 2017, 855 master's, 14 doctorates awarded. Terminal master's awarded for partial completion of doctoral program. *Degree requirements:* For master's, comprehensive exam, field consulting project (for MBA, FEMBA, EMBA and GEMBA); internship (for MBA only); thesis/dissertation (for MFE); 10 capstone (for MSBA); for doctorate, comprehensive exam, thesis/dissertation, oral and written qualifying exams. *Entrance requirements:* For master's, GMAT or GRE, 4-year bachelor's degree or equivalent; 2 letters of recommendation; interview (by invitation only); 2 essays; 4-8 years of full-time work experience (for FEMBA only); minimum eight years of work experience with at least three years at management level (for EMBA only); for doctorate, GMAT or GRE, bachelor's degree from college or university of fully-recognized standing, minimum B average during junior and senior undergraduate years, 3 letters of recommendation, statement of purpose. Additional exam requirements/recommendations for international students: Required—TOEFL (minimum score 560 paper-based; 87 iBT), IELTS (minimum score 7), TOEFL with minimum iBT score of 100 (for MSBA). *Application deadline:* For fall admission, 10/2 for domestic and international students; for winter admission, 1/8 for domestic and international students; for spring admission, 4/16 for domestic and international students. Applications are processed on a rolling basis. Application fee: $200. Electronic applications accepted. *Expenses:* Contact institution. *Financial support:* In 2017–18, 649 students received support, including 440 fellowships (averaging $29,273 per year); research assistantships with partial tuition reimbursements available, teaching assistantships with partial tuition reimbursements available, career-related internships or fieldwork, institutionally sponsored loans, and scholarships/grants also available. Support available to part-time students. *Faculty research:* Finance/global economics, entrepreneurship, accounting, human resources/organizational behavior, marketing and behavioral decision-making. *Total annual research expenditures:* $1.3 million. *Unit head:* Dean, 310-825-7982, Fax: 310-206-2073. *Application contact:* Alex Lawrence, Assistant Dean and Director of MBA Admissions, 310-825-6944, Fax: 310-825-8582, E-mail: mba.admissions@anderson.ucla.edu.
Website: http://www.anderson.ucla.edu/

University of Charleston, Master of Science in Strategic Leadership Program, Charleston, WV 25304-1099. Offers MS. *Entrance requirements:* For master's, bachelor's degree from regionally-accredited college or university with minimum GPA of 3.0. Electronic applications accepted.

University of Chicago, Booth School of Business, Full-Time MBA Program, Chicago, IL 60637. Offers accounting (MBA); analytic finance (MBA); analytic management (MBA); econometrics and statistics (MBA); economics (MBA); entrepreneurship (MBA); finance

(MBA); general management (MBA); health administration and policy (Certificate); international business (MBA); managerial and organizational behavior (MBA); marketing analytics (MBA); marketing management (MBA); operations management (MBA); strategic management (MBA); MBA/AM; MBA/JD; MBA/MA; MBA/MD; MBA/MPP. *Accreditation:* AACSB. *Faculty:* 154 full-time (26 women), 61 part-time/adjunct (12 women). *Students:* 1,176 full-time (481 women). In 2017, 586 master's awarded. *Entrance requirements:* For master's, GMAT or GRE, transcripts, resume, 2 letters of recommendation, essays, interview. Additional exam requirements/recommendations for international students: Required—TOEFL, IELTS, or PTE. *Application deadline:* For fall admission, 9/1 for domestic and international students; for winter admission, 1/1 for domestic and international students; for spring admission, 4/1 for domestic and international students. Application fee: $250. Electronic applications accepted. *Expenses:* Contact institution. *Unit head:* Stacey Kole, Deputy Dean for Alumni, Corporate Relations, and the Full-time MBA Program, 773-702-7121. *Application contact:* Kurt Ahlm, Associate Dean for Student Recruitment and Admissions, 773-702-7369, Fax: 773-702-9085, E-mail: admissions@chicagobooth.edu.
Website: https://www.chicagobooth.edu/programs/full-time

University of Colorado Denver, Business School, Master of Business Administration Program, Denver, CO 80217. Offers bioinnovation and entrepreneurship (MBA); business intelligence (MBA); business strategy (MBA); business to business marketing (MBA); business to consumer marketing (MBA); change management (MBA); corporate financial management (MBA); enterprise technology management (MBA); entrepreneurship (MBA); health administration (MBA), including financial management, health administration, health information technologies, international health management and policy; human resources management (MBA); international business (MBA); investment management (MBA); managing for sustainability (MBA); sports and entertainment management (MBA). *Accreditation:* AACSB. *Program availability:* Part-time, evening/weekend, 100% online, blended/hybrid learning. *Degree requirements:* For master's, 48 semester hours, including 30 of core courses, 3 in international business, and 15 in electives from over 50 other business courses. *Entrance requirements:* For master's, GMAT, resume, official transcripts, essay, two letters of recommendation, financial statements (for international applicants). Additional exam requirements/recommendations for international students: Required—TOEFL (minimum score 560 paper-based; 83 iBT); Recommended—IELTS (minimum score 6.5). Electronic applications accepted. *Expenses:* Contact institution. *Faculty research:* Marketing, management, entrepreneurship, finance, health administration.

University of Colorado Denver, Business School, Program in Management and Organization, Denver, CO 80217. Offers business strategy (MS); change and innovation (MS); enterprise technology management (MS); entrepreneurship and innovation (MS); global management (MS); leadership (MS); managing for sustainability (MS); managing human resources (MS); sports and entertainment management (MS). *Accreditation:* AACSB. *Program availability:* Part-time, evening/weekend, online learning. *Degree requirements:* For master's, 30 semester hours (12 of required courses, 12 of management electives, and 6 of free electives). *Entrance requirements:* For master's, GMAT, resume, two letters of recommendation, essay, financial statements (for international applicants). Additional exam requirements/recommendations for international students: Required—TOEFL (minimum score 525 paper-based; 71 iBT); Recommended—IELTS (minimum score 6.5). Electronic applications accepted. *Expenses:* Contact institution. *Faculty research:* Human resource management, management of catastrophe, turnaround strategies.

University of Dallas, Satish and Yasmin Gupta College of Business, Irving, TX 75062-4736. Offers accounting (MBA, MS); business administration (DBA); business analytics (MS); business management (MBA); corporate finance (MBA); cybersecurity (MS); finance (MS); financial services (MBA); global business (MBA, MS); health services management (MBA); human resource management (MBA); information and technology management (MS); information assurance (MBA); information technology (MBA); information technology service management (MBA); marketing management (MBA); organization development (MBA); project management (MBA); sports and entertainment management (MBA); strategic leadership (MBA); supply chain management (MBA). *Accreditation:* AACSB. *Program availability:* Part-time, evening/weekend, online learning. *Entrance requirements:* Additional exam requirements/recommendations for international students: Required—TOEFL. *Application deadline:* Applications are processed on a rolling basis. Application fee: $50. Electronic applications accepted. *Expenses:* Contact institution. *Financial support:* Application deadline: 2/15; applicants required to submit FAFSA. *Unit head:* Brett J.L. Landry, Dean, 972-721-5356, E-mail: blandry@udallas.edu. *Application contact:* Dr. David Sweet, Dean, Braniff Graduate School, 972-721-5288, Fax: 972-721-5280, E-mail: dsweet@udallas.edu.
Website: http://www.udallas.edu/cob/

University of Detroit Mercy, College of Business Administration, Detroit, MI 48221. Offers business administration (MBA); business fundamentals (Certificate); business turnaround management (Certificate); ethical leadership and change management (Certificate); finance (Certificate); forensic accounting (Certificate); JD/MBA; MBA/MHSA. *Program availability:* Part-time, evening/weekend, 100% online, blended/hybrid learning. *Entrance requirements:* For master's, GMAT, resume, letter of recommendation, transcripts; for Certificate, resume, letter of recommendation, transcripts. Electronic applications accepted. Application fee is waived when completed online. *Expenses:* Contact institution. *Faculty research:* Ethics, international finance, trade policy, leadership, information technology.

University of Illinois at Urbana–Champaign, Graduate College, College of Education, Department of Education Policy, Organization, and Leadership, Champaign, IL 61820. Offers educational organization and leadership (Ed M, MS, Ed D, PhD, CAS); educational policy studies (Ed M, MA, PhD); human resource education (Ed M, MS, Ed D, PhD, CAS). *Program availability:* Part-time, online learning.

The University of Kansas, Graduate Studies, School of Business, Program in Business, Lawrence, KS 66045. Offers business and organizational leadership (MS); decision sciences and supply chain management (PhD); finance (PhD); human resources management (PhD); marketing (PhD); organizational behavior (PhD); strategic management (PhD); supply chain management and logistics (MS). *Accreditation:* AACSB. *Program availability:* Part-time. *Students:* 66 full-time (18 women), 227 part-time (76 women); includes 59 minority (21 Black or African American, non-Hispanic/Latino; 2 American Indian or Alaska Native, non-Hispanic/Latino; 13 Asian, non-Hispanic/Latino; 3 Hispanic/Latino; 20 Two or more races, non-Hispanic/Latino), 29 international. Average age 32. 329 applicants, 71% accepted, 185 enrolled. In 2017, 30 master's, 8 doctorates awarded. *Entrance requirements:* For master's, GMAT, official transcript, three letters of recommendation, resume, statement of purpose; for doctorate, GMAT or GRE, official transcript, three letters of recommendation, resume, statement of purpose. Additional exam requirements/recommendations for international students: Required—TOEFL (minimum score 600 paper-based; 100 iBT). *Application deadline:* For fall admission, 1/10 for domestic and international students. Application fee: $65 ($85 for international students). Electronic applications accepted. *Financial support:* Fellowships, research assistantships, teaching assistantships, scholarships/grants, health care benefits, tuition waivers (full), and unspecified assistantships available. Financial award application deadline: 1/10.

Management Strategy and Policy

Faculty research: Strategic human resource management, business ethics, organizational theory/behavior, corporate strategy, international business, supply chain management, Bayesian networks, game theory, decision analysis and time/series analysis, pricing, consumer effects, advertising and emotion. *Unit head:* Charly Edmonds, Director, 785-864-3841, E-mail: bschoolphd@ku.edu. *Application contact:* Graduate Admission Contact, 785-864-7500, E-mail: bschoolphd@ku.edu. Website: http://www.business.ku.edu/

University of Lethbridge, School of Graduate Studies, Lethbridge, AB T1K 3M4, Canada. Offers addictions counseling (M Sc); agricultural biotechnology (M Sc); agricultural studies (M Sc, MA); anthropology (MA); archaeology (M Sc, MA); art (MA, MFA); biochemistry (M Sc); biological sciences (M Sc); biomolecular science (PhD); biosystems and biodiversity (PhD); Canadian studies (MA); chemistry (M Sc); computer science (M Sc); computer science and geographical information science (M Sc); counseling (MC); counseling psychology (M Ed); dramatic arts (MA); earth, space, and physical science (PhD); economics (MA); education (MA, PhD); educational leadership (M Ed); English (MA); environmental science (M Sc); evolution and behavior (PhD); exercise science (M Sc); French (MA); French/German (MA); French/Spanish (MA); general education (M Ed); geography (M Sc, MA); German (MA); health sciences (M Sc); individualized multidisciplinary (M Sc, MA); kinesiology (M Sc, MA); management (M Sc), including accounting, finance, human resource management and labor relations, information systems, international management, marketing, policy and strategy; mathematics (M Sc); music (M Mus, MA); Native American studies (MA); neuroscience (M Sc, PhD); new media (MA, MFA); nursing (M Sc, MN); philosophy (MA); physics (M Sc); political science (MA); psychology (M Sc, MA); religious studies (MA); sociology (MA); theatre and dramatic arts (MFA); theoretical and computational science (PhD); urban and regional studies (MA); women and gender studies (MA). *Program availability:* Part-time, evening/weekend. *Degree requirements:* For master's, thesis (for some programs); for doctorate, comprehensive exam, thesis/dissertation. *Entrance requirements:* For master's, GMAT (for M Sc in management), bachelor's degree in related field, minimum GPA of 3.0 during previous 20 graded semester courses, 2 years' teaching or related experience (M Ed); for doctorate, master's degree, minimum graduate GPA of 3.5. Additional exam requirements/recommendations for international students: Required—TOEFL (minimum score 580 paper-based; 93 iBT). Electronic applications accepted. *Faculty research:* Movement and brain plasticity, gibberellin physiology, photosynthesis, carbon cycling, molecular properties of main-group ring components.

The University of Manchester, Alliance Manchester Business School, M15 6PB, United Kingdom. Offers accounting and finance (M Sc); business (M Ent); business analysis and strategic management (M Sc); business analytics: operational research and risk analysis (M Sc); business psychology (M Sc); corporate communications and reputation management (M Sc); finance (M Sc); finance and business economics (M Sc); human resource management and industrial relations (M Sc); innovation management and entrepreneurship (M Sc); international business and management (M Sc); international human resource management and comparative industrial relations (M Sc); management (M Sc); marketing (M Sc); operations, project and supply chain management (M Sc); organizational psychology (M Sc); quantitative finance (M Sc). *Entrance requirements:* For master's, UK 2:1 honours degree or overseas equivalent. Additional exam requirements/recommendations for international students: Required—TOEFL (minimum score 100 iBT), IELTS (minimum score 7), PTE. Electronic applications accepted. *Faculty research:* Accounting and finance, management sciences and marketing, people management and organization, innovation management and policy, decision sciences.

University of Massachusetts Amherst, Graduate School, Isenberg School of Management, Program in Management, Amherst, MA 01003. Offers accounting (PhD); business administration (MBA); entrepreneurship (MBA); finance (MBA, PhD); healthcare administration (MBA); hospitality and tourism management (PhD); management science (PhD); marketing (MBA, PhD); organization studies (PhD); sport management (PhD); strategic management (PhD); MBA/MS. *Accreditation:* AACSB. *Program availability:* Part-time, evening/weekend, online learning. Terminal master's awarded for partial completion of doctoral program. *Degree requirements:* For doctorate, comprehensive exam, thesis/dissertation. *Entrance requirements:* For master's and doctorate, GMAT or GRE General Test. Additional exam requirements/recommendations for international students: Required—TOEFL (minimum score 550 paper-based; 80 iBT), IELTS (minimum score 6.5). Electronic applications accepted.

University of Memphis, Graduate School, University College, Memphis, TN 38152. Offers human resources leadership (MPS); liberal studies (MALS, Graduate Certificate); strategic leadership (MPS, Graduate Certificate); training and development (MPS). *Program availability:* Part-time, evening/weekend. *Faculty:* 3 full-time (1 woman), 1 part-time/adjunct (0 women). *Students:* 27 full-time (16 women), 105 part-time (79 women); includes 86 minority (78 Black or African American, non-Hispanic/Latino; 1 Asian, non-Hispanic/Latino; 2 Hispanic/Latino; 1 Native Hawaiian or other Pacific Islander, non-Hispanic/Latino; 4 Two or more races, non-Hispanic/Latino), 4 international. Average age 38. 70 applicants, 76% accepted, 39 enrolled. *Degree requirements:* For master's, comprehensive exam, thesis (for some programs). *Entrance requirements:* For master's, GRE (for MPS), resume, letters of recommendation, personal essay, interview, minimum undergraduate GPA of 2.75 (for MALS); portfolio in lieu of GRE (for MPS applicants with substantial professional work experience); for Graduate Certificate, essay, letter of recommendation. Additional exam requirements/recommendations for international students: Required—TOEFL (minimum score 550 paper-based; 79 iBT). *Application deadline:* For fall admission, 7/1 for domestic students, 5/1 for international students; for spring admission, 11/1 for domestic students, 9/15 for international students. Applications are processed on a rolling basis. Application fee: $35 ($60 for international students). Electronic applications accepted. *Expenses:* Contact institution. *Financial support:* In 2017–18, 123 students received support, including 4 teaching assistantships with tuition reimbursements available (averaging $13,000 per year); research assistantships with full tuition reimbursements available, Federal Work-Study, scholarships/grants, and unspecified assistantships also available. Financial award application deadline: 2/3; financial award applicants required to submit FAFSA. *Faculty research:* Media ethics, history of psychiatry, public relations. *Unit head:* Dr. Joanne Gikas, Interim Dean, 901-678-2716, E-mail: jgikas@memphis.edu. *Application contact:* Dr. Colin Chapell, Graduate Studies Coordinator, 901-678-3066, Fax: 901-678-2971, E-mail: cbchpell@memphis.edu.
Website: http://www.memphis.edu/univcoll/

University of Minnesota, Twin Cities Campus, Carlson School of Management, Doctoral Program in Business Administration, Minneapolis, MN 55455. Offers accounting (PhD); finance (PhD); information and decision sciences (PhD); marketing (PhD); strategic management and entrepreneurship (PhD); supply chain and operations (PhD); work and organizations (PhD). *Faculty:* 102 full-time (32 women). *Students:* 95 full-time (32 women); includes 10 minority (2 Black or African American, non-Hispanic/Latino; 7 Asian, non-Hispanic/Latino; 1 Hispanic/Latino), 68 international. Average age 30. 357 applicants, 6% accepted, 17 enrolled. In 2017, 14 doctorates awarded. *Degree requirements:* For doctorate, comprehensive exam, thesis/dissertation, written and oral preliminary exams, proposal defense, final defense. *Entrance requirements:* For

doctorate, GMAT, GRE General Test, minimum undergraduate GPA of 3.0, graduate 3.5 (recommended). Additional exam requirements/recommendations for international students: Required—TOEFL (minimum score 600 paper-based, 100 iBT) or IELTS (minimum score 7.0). *Application deadline:* For fall admission, 12/15 for domestic students, 12/15 priority date for international students. Applications are processed on a rolling basis. Application fee: $75 ($95 for international students). Electronic applications accepted. *Expenses:* Contact institution. *Financial support:* In 2017–18, 80 students received support, including 80 fellowships with full tuition reimbursements available (averaging $13,000 per year), 73 research assistantships with full tuition reimbursements available (averaging $7,520 per year), 73 teaching assistantships with full tuition reimbursements available (averaging $7,520 per year); institutionally sponsored loans, scholarships/grants, health care benefits, unspecified assistantships, and full student service fee waivers also available. Financial award application deadline: 12/15. *Faculty research:* Finance, strategy and entrepreneurship, marketing, information and decision science, operations, accounting, supply chain, human resources and industrial relations, organizational behavior. *Unit head:* Dr. Shawn P. Curley, Director, 612-624-6546, Fax: 612-624-8221, E-mail: curley@umn.edu. *Application contact:* Sandy Herzan, Associate Director, 612-624-0875, Fax: 612-624-8221, E-mail: herza002@umn.edu.
Website: http://carlsonschool.umn.edu/degrees/phd

University of New Haven, Graduate School, College of Business, Program in Business Administration, West Haven, CT 06516. Offers accounting (MBA); business administration (MBA); business intelligence (MBA); business policy and strategic leadership (MBA); finance (MBA), including chartered financial analyst; global marketing (MBA); human resources management (MBA); sport management (MBA). *Accreditation:* AACSB. *Program availability:* Part-time, evening/weekend. *Students:* 123 full-time (56 women), 67 part-time (28 women); includes 53 minority (27 Black or African American, non-Hispanic/Latino; 11 Asian, non-Hispanic/Latino; 12 Hispanic/Latino; 3 Two or more races, non-Hispanic/Latino), 50 international. Average age 28. 148 applicants, 89% accepted, 67 enrolled. In 2017, 106 master's awarded. *Entrance requirements:* For master's, GMAT. Additional exam requirements/recommendations for international students: Required—TOEFL (minimum score 80 iBT), IELTS, PTE. *Application deadline:* Applications are processed on a rolling basis. Application fee: $50. Electronic applications accepted. Application fee is waived when completed online. *Expenses: Tuition:* Full-time $16,020; part-time $890 per credit hour. *Required fees:* $220; $90 per term. *Financial support:* Research assistantships with partial tuition reimbursements, teaching assistantships with partial tuition reimbursements, career-related internships or fieldwork, Federal Work-Study, scholarships/grants, and unspecified assistantships available. Support available to part-time students. Financial award applicants required to submit FAFSA. *Unit head:* Darell Singleterry, Director, 203-932-1085, E-mail: dsingleterry@newhaven.edu. *Application contact:* Michelle Mason, Director of Graduate Enrollment, 203-932-7067, E-mail: mmason@newhaven.edu.
Website: http://www.newhaven.edu/business/graduate-programs/mba/index.php
See Display on page 154 and Close-Up on page 185.

University of New Mexico, Anderson School of Management, Department of Marketing, Information Systems, Information Assurance, and Operations Management, Albuquerque, NM 87131. Offers information assurance (MBA); information systems and assurance (MS); management information systems (MBA); marketing management (MBA); operations management (MBA). *Program availability:* Part-time. *Faculty:* 16 full-time (4 women), 12 part-time/adjunct (6 women). In 2017, 68 master's awarded. *Entrance requirements:* For master's, GMAT or GRE, minimum GPA of 3.0 on last 60 hours of coursework; bachelor's degree from regionally-accredited college or university in U.S. or its equivalent in another country. Additional exam requirements/recommendations for international students: Required—TOEFL (minimum score 550 paper-based; 79 iBT), IELTS (minimum score 6.5). *Application deadline:* For fall admission, 4/1 priority date for domestic and international students; for spring admission, 10/1 priority date for domestic and international students. Applications are processed on a rolling basis. Application fee: $50. Electronic applications accepted. *Expenses:* Contact institution. *Financial support:* In 2017–18, 23 students received support, including 13 fellowships (averaging $16,320 per year), 12 research assistantships with partial tuition reimbursements available (averaging $15,180 per year); career-related internships or fieldwork, Federal Work-Study, scholarships/grants, and unspecified assistantships also available. Support available to part-time students. Financial award application deadline: 6/1; financial award applicants required to submit FAFSA. *Faculty research:* Marketing, operations management, information systems, information assurance. *Unit head:* Dr. Mary Margaret Rogers, Chair, 505-277-6471, E-mail: mmrogers@unm.edu. *Application contact:* Lisa Beauchene, Student Recruitment Specialist, 505-277-6471, E-mail: andersonadvising@unm.edu.
Website: https://www.mgt.unm.edu/mids/default.asp?mm-faculty

University of New Mexico, Anderson School of Management, Department of Organizational Studies, Albuquerque, NM 87131. Offers organizational behavior and human resources management (MBA); strategic management and policy (MBA). *Program availability:* Part-time. *Faculty:* 17 full-time (12 women), 17 part-time/adjunct (6 women). In 2017, 20 master's awarded. *Entrance requirements:* For master's, GMAT or GRE, minimum GPA of 3.0 on last 60 hours of coursework; bachelor's degree from regionally-accredited college or university in U.S. or its equivalent in another country. Additional exam requirements/recommendations for international students: Required—TOEFL (minimum score 550 paper-based; 79 iBT), IELTS (minimum score 6.5). *Application deadline:* For fall admission, 4/1 priority date for domestic and international students; for spring admission, 10/1 priority date for domestic and international students. Applications are processed on a rolling basis. Application fee: $50. Electronic applications accepted. *Expenses:* Contact institution. *Financial support:* In 2017–18, 14 students received support, including 4 fellowships (averaging $18,200 per year), 11 research assistantships with partial tuition reimbursements available (averaging $15,488 per year); career-related internships or fieldwork, Federal Work-Study, scholarships/grants, and unspecified assistantships also available. Support available to part-time students. Financial award application deadline: 6/1; financial award applicants required to submit FAFSA. *Faculty research:* Business ethics and social corporate responsibility, diversity, human resources, organizational strategy, organizational behavior. *Unit head:* Dr. Michelle Arthur, Chair, 505-277-6471, E-mail: arthurm@unm.edu. *Application contact:* Lisa Beauchene, Student Recruitment Specialist, 505-277-6471, E-mail: andersonadvising@unm.edu.
Website: https://www.mgt.unm.edu/dos/default.asp?mm-faculty

The University of North Carolina at Chapel Hill, Kenan-Flagler Business School, Doctoral Program in Business Administration, Chapel Hill, NC 27599. Offers accounting (PhD); finance (PhD); marketing (PhD); operations management (PhD); organizational behavior (PhD); strategy (PhD). *Accreditation:* AACSB. *Degree requirements:* For doctorate, thesis/dissertation. *Entrance requirements:* For doctorate, GMAT or GRE General Test. Electronic applications accepted. *Expenses:* Contact institution.

University of North Texas, Robert B. Toulouse School of Graduate Studies, Denton, TX 76203-5459. Offers accounting (MS); applied anthropology (MA, MS); applied behavior analysis (Certificate); applied geography (MA); applied technology and performance improvement (M Ed, MS); art education (MA); art history (MA); art museum education (Certificate); arts leadership (Certificate); audiology (Au D); behavior analysis (MS); behavioral science (PhD); biochemistry and molecular biology (MS); biology (MA, MS); biomedical engineering (MS); business analysis (MS); chemistry (MS); clinical health psychology (PhD); communication studies (MA, MS); computer engineering (MS); computer science (MS); counseling (M Ed, MS), including clinical mental health counseling (MS), college and university counseling, elementary school counseling, secondary school counseling; creative writing (MA); criminal justice (MS); curriculum and instruction (M Ed); decision sciences (MBA); design (MA, MFA), including fashion design (MFA), innovation studies, interior design (MFA); early childhood studies (MS); economics (MS); educational leadership (M Ed, Ed D); educational psychology (MS, PhD), including family studies (MS), gifted and talented (MS), human development (MS), learning and cognition (MS), research, measurement and evaluation (MS); electrical engineering (MS); emergency management (MPA); engineering technology (MS); English (MA); English as a second language (MA); environmental science (MS); finance (MBA, MS); financial management (MPA); French (MA); health services management (MBA); higher education (M Ed, Ed D); history (MA, MS); hospitality management (MS); human resources management (MPA); information science (MS); information systems (PhD); information technologies (MBA); interdisciplinary studies (MA, MS); international studies (MA); international sustainable tourism (MS); jazz studies (MM); journalism (MA, MJ, Graduate Certificate), including interactive and virtual digital communication (Graduate Certificate), narrative journalism (Graduate Certificate), public relations (Graduate Certificate); kinesiology (MS); linguistics (MA); local government management (MPA); logistics (PhD); logistics and supply chain management (MBA); long-term care, senior housing, and aging services (MA); management (PhD); marketing (MBA); mathematics (MA, MS); mechanical and energy engineering (MS, PhD); music (MA), including ethnomusicology, music theory, musicology, performance; music composition (PhD); music education (MM Ed, PhD); nonprofit management (MPA); operations and supply chain management (MBA); performance (MM, DMA); philosophy (MA); political science (MA); professional and technical communication (MA); radio, television and film (MA, MFA); rehabilitation counseling (Certificate); sociology (MA); Spanish (MA); special education (M Ed); speech-language pathology (MA); strategic management (MBA); studio art (MFA); teaching (M Ed); MBA/MS. *Program availability:* Part-time, evening/weekend, online learning. Terminal master's awarded for partial completion of doctoral program. *Degree requirements:* For master's, variable foreign language requirement, comprehensive exam (for some programs), thesis (for some programs); for doctorate, variable foreign language requirement, comprehensive exam (for some programs), thesis/dissertation; for other advanced degree, variable foreign language requirement, comprehensive exam (for some programs). *Entrance requirements:* For master's and doctorate, GRE, GMAT. Additional exam requirements/recommendations for international students: Required—TOEFL (minimum score 550 paper-based; 79 iBT). Electronic applications accepted.

University of North Texas at Dallas, Graduate School, Dallas, TX 75241. Offers accounting (MBA); counseling (M Ed, MS); criminal justice (MS); curriculum and instruction (M Ed); educational administration (M Ed); human resources and organizational behavior (MBA); public leadership (MS); strategic management (MBA).

University of Pittsburgh, Katz Graduate School of Business, Doctoral Program in Business Administration, Pittsburgh, PA 15260. Offers accounting (PhD); business analytics and operations (PhD); finance (PhD); information systems and technology management (PhD); marketing (PhD); organizational behavior and human resources (PhD); strategic management (PhD). *Accreditation:* AACSB. *Program availability:* Evening/weekend. *Faculty:* 91 full-time (30 women), 14 part-time/adjunct (4 women). *Students:* 51 full-time (26 women), 1 (woman) part-time; includes 5 minority (1 Black or African American, non-Hispanic/Latino; 3 Asian, non-Hispanic/Latino; 1 Two or more races, non-Hispanic/Latino), 30 international. Average age 31. 337 applicants, 3% accepted, 10 enrolled. In 2017, 7 doctorates awarded. *Degree requirements:* For doctorate, comprehensive exam, thesis/dissertation, student teaching. *Entrance requirements:* For doctorate, GMAT or GRE, 3 recommendations, statement of purpose, transcripts of all previous course work and degrees. Additional exam requirements/recommendations for international students: Required—TOEFL (minimum score 100 iBT) or IELTS (minimum score 7.0). *Application deadline:* For fall admission, 1/1 for domestic and international students. Applications are processed on a rolling basis. Application fee: $50. Electronic applications accepted. *Financial support:* In 2017–18, 43 students received support, including 33 research assistantships with full tuition reimbursements available (averaging $26,500 per year), 10 teaching assistantships with full tuition reimbursements available (averaging $28,220 per year); Federal Work-Study, scholarships/grants, health care benefits, and unspecified assistantships also available. Financial award application deadline: 1/1; financial award applicants required to submit FAFSA. *Faculty research:* Accounting systems/financial reporting, corporate finance, shopper marketing/consumer behavior, management information systems, organizational behavior and entrepreneurship. *Total annual research expenditures:* $475,077. *Unit head:* Dr. Arjang A. Assad, Dean, 412-648-1556, Fax: 412-648-1552, E-mail: aassad@katz.pitt.edu. *Application contact:* Dr. Dennis Galletta, Director, 412-648-1699, Fax: 412-648-3633, E-mail: galletta@katz.pitt.edu.
Website: http://www.katz.business.pitt.edu/degrees/phd/

See Display on page 158 and Close-Up on page 187.

University of Pittsburgh, Katz Graduate School of Business, Master of Business Administration Programs, Pittsburgh, PA 15260. Offers finance (MBA); information systems (MBA); marketing (MBA); operations (MBA); organizational behavior and human resources (MBA); strategy, environment and organizations (MBA); MBA/JD; MBA/MID; MBA/MIS; MBA/MSE. *Accreditation:* AACSB. *Program availability:* Part-time, evening/weekend, blended/hybrid learning. *Faculty:* 91 full-time (30 women), 14 part-time/adjunct (4 women). *Students:* 139 full-time (49 women), 294 part-time (94 women); includes 65 minority (27 Black or African American, non-Hispanic/Latino; 20 Asian, non-Hispanic/Latino; 11 Hispanic/Latino; 7 Two or more races, non-Hispanic/Latino), 54 international. Average age 29. 651 applicants, 44% accepted, 158 enrolled. In 2017, 217 master's awarded. *Degree requirements:* For master's, minimum GPA of 3.0. *Entrance requirements:* For master's, GMAT, GRE. Additional exam requirements/recommendations for international students: Required—TOEFL (minimum score 100 iBT) or IELTS (minimum score 7.0). *Application deadline:* For fall admission, 4/1 priority date for domestic students, 2/1 priority date for international students. Application fee: $50. Electronic applications accepted. *Financial support:* In 2017–18, 136 students received support. Scholarships/grants available. Financial award application deadline: 6/1; financial award applicants required to submit FAFSA. *Faculty research:* Accounting systems/financial reporting, corporate finance, shopper marketing/consumer behavior, management information systems, organizational behavior and entrepreneurship. *Total annual research expenditures:* $475,077. *Unit head:* Dr. Arjang A. Assad, Dean, 412-648-1556, Fax: 412-648-1552, E-mail: aassad@katz.pitt.edu. *Application contact:* Thomas Keller, Director of MBA Admissions, 412-648-1700, Fax: 412-648-1659, E-mail: mba@katz.pitt.edu.
Website: http://www.business.pitt.edu/katz/mba/

See Display on page 158 and Close-Up on page 187.

University of Rhode Island, Graduate School, College of Business, Kingston, RI 02881. Offers accounting (MS); business administration (MBA, PhD), including finance (MBA), general business (MBA), management (MBA), marketing, operations and supply chain management (PhD), supply chain management (MBA); finance (MBA, MS, PhD); general business (MBA); health care management (MBA); labor research (MS, Graduate Certificate), including labor relations and human resources; management (MBA); marketing (MBA); strategic innovation (MBA); supply chain management (MBA); textiles, fashion merchandising and design (MS, Certificate), including fashion merchandising (Certificate), master seamstress (Certificate), textiles, fashion merchandising and design (MS); MS/JD; Pharm D/MBA. *Accreditation:* AACSB. *Program availability:* Part-time, evening/weekend. *Faculty:* 61 full-time (28 women), 2 part-time/adjunct (1 woman). *Students:* 88 full-time (37 women), 180 part-time (94 women); includes 36 minority (9 Black or African American, non-Hispanic/Latino; 2 American Indian or Alaska Native, non-Hispanic/Latino; 13 Asian, non-Hispanic/Latino; 10 Hispanic/Latino; 2 Two or more races, non-Hispanic/Latino), 20 international. 205 applicants, 68% accepted, 97 enrolled. In 2017, 128 master's, 1 doctorate, 20 other advanced degrees awarded. *Entrance requirements:* Additional exam requirements/recommendations for international students: Required—TOEFL. Application fee: $65. Electronic applications accepted. *Expenses:* Tuition, state resident: full-time $12,706; part-time $786 per credit. Tuition, nonresident: full-time $25,216; part-time $1401 per credit. *Required fees:* $1598; $45 per credit. One-time fee: $30 part-time. *Financial support:* In 2017–18, 19 teaching assistantships with tuition reimbursements (averaging $14,589 per year) were awarded; research assistantships also available. Financial award applicants required to submit FAFSA. *Unit head:* Dr. Maling Ebrahimpour, Dean, 401-874-4348, Fax: 401-874-4312, E-mail: mebrahimpour@uri.edu. *Application contact:* Lisa Lancellotta, Coordinator, MBA Programs, 401-874-4241, Fax: 401-874-4312, E-mail: mba@uri.edu.
Website: https://web.uri.edu/business/

See Display on page 159 and Close-Up on page 189.

University of Rochester, Simon Business School, Full-Time Master's Program in Business Administration, Rochester, NY 14627. Offers business systems consulting (MBA); competitive and organizational strategy (MBA); computers and information systems (MBA); corporate accounting (MBA); entrepreneurship (MBA); finance (MBA); health sciences management (MBA); marketing (MBA); operations management (MBA); public accounting (MBA); strategy and organizations (MBA). *Accreditation:* AACSB. *Faculty:* 70 full-time (12 women), 23 part-time/adjunct (6 women). *Students:* 208 full-time (70 women). Average age 28. *Entrance requirements:* For master's, GMAT or GRE. *Application deadline:* For fall admission, 10/15 for domestic and international students; for winter admission, 1/5 for domestic and international students; for spring admission, 3/15 for domestic and international students; for summer admission, 5/15 for domestic and international students. Application fee: $150. *Financial support:* Fellowships, institutionally sponsored loans, scholarships/grants, and tuition waivers (full and partial) available. Financial award application deadline: 1/5; financial award applicants required to submit FAFSA. *Faculty research:* Empirical industrial organization, risk management, financial disclosure and regulation, social media, health care management. *Unit head:* Andrew Ainslie, Dean, 585-275-3316, E-mail: andrew.ainslie@simon.rochester.edu. *Application contact:* Rebekah S. Lewin, Assistant Dean of Admissions and Financial Aid, 585-275-3533, E-mail: admissions@simon.rochester.edu.
Website: http://www.simon.rochester.edu/programs/full-time-mba/index.aspx

University of Rochester, Simon Business School, Part-Time MBA Program, Rochester, NY 14627. Offers business systems consulting (MBA); competitive and organizational strategy (MBA); computers and information systems (MBA); corporate accounting (MBA); entrepreneurship (MBA); finance (MBA); health sciences management (MBA); marketing (MBA), including brand management, marketing strategy, pricing; operations management (MBA); public accounting (MBA). *Program availability:* Part-time-only, evening/weekend. *Faculty:* 70 full-time (12 women), 23 part-time/adjunct (6 women). *Students:* 159 part-time (62 women); includes 25 minority (5 Black or African American, non-Hispanic/Latino; 9 Asian, non-Hispanic/Latino; 9 Hispanic/Latino; 2 Two or more races, non-Hispanic/Latino), 4 international. Average age 32. 39 applicants, 92% accepted, 35 enrolled. In 2017, 59 master's awarded. *Entrance requirements:* For master's, GRE or GMAT. *Application deadline:* For fall admission, 8/1 for domestic students; for spring admission, 2/15 for domestic students. Applications are processed on a rolling basis. Application fee: $150. Electronic applications accepted. *Expenses:* $1,875 per credit, $1,385 fees. *Financial support:* In 2017–18, 69 students received support. Tuition waivers (partial) available. Financial award application deadline: 8/1. *Unit head:* Andrew Ainslie, Dean, 585-275-3316, E-mail: andrew.ainslie@simon.rochester.edu. *Application contact:* Molly Mesko, Executive Director, EMBA and Part-Time Programs, 585-275-4277, E-mail: molly.mesko@simon.rochester.edu.
Website: http://www.simon.rochester.edu/programs/ptmba/index.aspx

University of South Florida, Innovative Education, Tampa, FL 33620-9951. Offers adult, career and higher education (Graduate Certificate), including college teaching, leadership in developing human resources, leadership in higher education; Africana studies (Graduate Certificate), including diasporas and health disparities, genocide and human rights; aging studies (Graduate Certificate), including gerontology; art research (Graduate Certificate), including museum studies; business foundations (Graduate Certificate); chemical and biomedical engineering (Graduate Certificate), including materials science and engineering, water, health and sustainability; child and family studies (Graduate Certificate), including positive behavior support; civil and industrial engineering (Graduate Certificate), including transportation systems analysis; community and family health (Graduate Certificate), including maternal and child health, social marketing and public health, violence and injury: prevention and intervention, women's health; criminology (Graduate Certificate), including criminal justice administration; data science for public administration (Graduate Certificate); digital humanities (Graduate Certificate); educational measurement and research (Graduate Certificate), including evaluation; English (Graduate Certificate), including comparative literary studies, creative writing, professional and technical communication; entrepreneurship (Graduate Certificate); environmental health (Graduate Certificate), including safety management; epidemiology and biostatistics (Graduate Certificate), including applied biostatistics, biostatistics, concepts and tools of epidemiology, epidemiology, epidemiology of infectious diseases; geography, environment and planning (Graduate Certificate), including community development, environmental policy and management, geographical information systems; geology (Graduate Certificate), including hydrogeology; global health (Graduate Certificate), including disaster management, global health and Latin American and Caribbean studies, global health practice, humanitarian assistance, infection control; government and international affairs (Graduate Certificate), including Cuban studies, globalization studies; health policy and management (Graduate Certificate), including health management and leadership, public health policy and programs; hearing specialist: early intervention (Graduate Certificate); industrial and management systems engineering (Graduate Certificate), including systems engineering, technology management; information studies (Graduate Certificate), including school library media specialist; information systems/decision sciences (Graduate Certificate), including analytics and business intelligence;

Management Strategy and Policy

instructional technology (Graduate Certificate), including distance education, Florida digital/virtual educator, instructional design, multimedia design, Web design; internal medicine, bioethics and medical humanities (Graduate Certificate), including biomedical ethics; Latin American and Caribbean studies (Graduate Certificate); leadership for coastal resiliency planning (Graduate Certificate); mass communications (Graduate Certificate), including multimedia journalism; mathematics and statistics (Graduate Certificate), including mathematics; medicine (Graduate Certificate), including aging and neuroscience, bioinformatics, biotechnology, brain fitness and memory management, clinical investigation, hand and upper limb rehabilitation, health informatics, health sciences, integrative weight management, intellectual property, medicine and gender, metabolic and nutritional medicine, metabolic cardiology, pharmacy sciences; national and competitive intelligence (Graduate Certificate); nursing (Graduate Certificate), including simulation based academic fellowship in advanced pain management; psychological and social foundations (Graduate Certificate), including career counseling, college teaching, diversity in education, mental health counseling, school counseling; public affairs (Graduate Certificate), including nonprofit management, public management, research administration; public health (Graduate Certificate), including assessing chemical toxicity and public health risks, health equity, pharmacoepidemiology, public health generalist, toxicology, translational research in adolescent behavioral health; public health practices (Graduate Certificate), including planning for healthy communities; rehabilitation and mental health counseling (Graduate Certificate), including integrative mental health care, marriage and family therapy, rehabilitation technology; secondary education (Graduate Certificate), including ESOL, foreign language education: culture and content, foreign language education: professional; social work (Graduate Certificate), including geriatric social work/clinical gerontology; special education (Graduate Certificate), including autism spectrum disorder, disabilities education: severe/profound; world languages (Graduate Certificate), including teaching English as a second language (TESL) or foreign language. *Unit head:* Dr. Cynthia DeLuca, Associate Vice President and Assistant Vice Provost, 813-974-3077, Fax: 813-974-7061, E-mail: deluca@usf.edu. *Application contact:* Owen Hooper, Director, Summer and Alternative Calendar Programs, 813-974-6917, E-mail: hooper@usf.edu.
Website: http://www.usf.edu/innovative-education/

University of South Florida, Muma College of Business, Department of Information Systems and Decision Sciences, Tampa, FL 33620-9951. Offers business administration (PhD), including information systems; business analytics and information systems (MS), including analytics and business intelligence, information assurance. *Program availability:* Part-time. *Faculty:* 22 full-time (4 women). *Students:* 216 full-time (61 women), 110 part-time (43 women); includes 23 minority (8 Black or African American, non-Hispanic/Latino; 9 Asian, non-Hispanic/Latino; 4 Hispanic/Latino; 2 Two or more races, non-Hispanic/Latino), 269 international. Average age 27. 906 applicants, 62% accepted, 184 enrolled. In 2017, 137 master's awarded. Terminal master's awarded for partial completion of doctoral program. *Degree requirements:* For master's, comprehensive exam, thesis (for some programs), thesis or practicum project; for doctorate, comprehensive exam, thesis/dissertation. *Entrance requirements:* For master's, GMAT or GRE, letters of recommendation, statement of purpose, relevant work experience; for doctorate, GMAT or GRE, letters of recommendation, personal statement, interview. Additional exam requirements/recommendations for international students: Required—TOEFL (minimum score 550 paper-based; 79 iBT) or IELTS (minimum score 6.5). *Application deadline:* For fall admission, 6/1 for domestic students, 2/1 for international students; for spring admission, 10/15 for domestic students, 9/15 for international students. Applications are processed on a rolling basis. Application fee: $30. Electronic applications accepted. *Financial support:* In 2017–18, 40 students received support, including 8 research assistantships with tuition reimbursements available (averaging $11,972 per year), 22 teaching assistantships with tuition reimbursements available (averaging $9,002 per year); scholarships/grants, health care benefits, and unspecified assistantships also available. Financial award applicants required to submit FAFSA. *Faculty research:* Data mining, business intelligence, bioterrorism surveillance, health informatics/informatics, software engineering, agent-based modeling, distributed systems, statistics, electronic markets, e-commerce, business process improvement, operations management, supply chain, LEAN management, global information systems, organizational impacts of IT, enterprise resource planning, business intelligence, Web and mobile technologies, social networks, information security. *Total annual research expenditures:* $547,072. *Unit head:* Dr. Kaushal Chari, Chair and Professor, 813-974-6768, Fax: 813-974-6749, E-mail: kchari@usf.edu. *Application contact:* Barber Warner, 813-974-6776, Fax: 813-974-6749, E-mail: bwarner@usf.edu.
Website: http://business.usf.edu/departments/isds/

The University of Texas at Dallas, Naveen Jindal School of Management, Program in Information Systems, Richardson, TX 75080. Offers business analytics (MS); information technology and management (MS). *Program availability:* Part-time, evening/weekend. *Faculty:* 20 full-time (1 woman), 13 part-time/adjunct (3 women). *Students:* 1,290 full-time (496 women), 508 part-time (194 women); includes 147 minority (18 Black or African American, non-Hispanic/Latino; 100 Asian, non-Hispanic/Latino; 20 Hispanic/Latino; 1 Native Hawaiian or other Pacific Islander, non-Hispanic/Latino; 8 Two or more races, non-Hispanic/Latino), 1,551 international. Average age 26. 3,030 applicants, 39% accepted, 604 enrolled. In 2017, 736 master's awarded. *Degree requirements:* For master's, thesis optional. *Entrance requirements:* For master's, GMAT. Additional exam requirements/recommendations for international students: Required—TOEFL (minimum score 550 paper-based). *Application deadline:* For fall admission, 7/15 for domestic students, 5/1 priority date for international students; for spring admission, 11/15 for domestic students, 9/1 priority date for international students. Applications are processed on a rolling basis. Application fee: $50 ($100 for international students). Electronic applications accepted. *Expenses:* Tuition, state resident: full-time $12,916; part-time $718 per credit hour. Tuition, nonresident: full-time $25,252; part-time $1403 per credit hour. *Financial support:* In 2017–18, 536 students received support, including 4 research assistantships with partial tuition reimbursements available (averaging $14,400 per year), 44 teaching assistantships with partial tuition reimbursements available (averaging $10,210 per year); career-related internships or fieldwork, Federal Work-Study, institutionally sponsored loans, scholarships/grants, and unspecified assistantships also available. Support available to part-time students. Financial award application deadline: 4/30; financial award applicants required to submit FAFSA. *Faculty research:* Electronic commerce, decision support systems, data quality. *Unit head:* Dr. Syam Menon, Area Coordinator, 972-883-4779, E-mail: syam@utdallas.edu.
Website: http://jindal.utdallas.edu/isom/

University of Utah, Graduate School, David Eccles School of Business, Business Administration Program, Salt Lake City, UT 84112. Offers accounting (PhD); business administration (EMBA, MBA, PMBA); finance (PhD); information systems (PhD); marketing (PhD); operations management (PhD); organizational behavior (PhD); strategic management (PhD); MBA/JD; MBA/MHA; MBA/MS. *Program availability:* Part-time, evening/weekend, online learning. *Faculty:* 58 full-time (21 women), 37 part-time/adjunct (7 women). *Students:* 558 full-time (149 women), 103 part-time (21 women); includes 66 minority (1 Black or African American, non-Hispanic/Latino; 16 Asian, non-Hispanic/Latino; 41 Hispanic/Latino; 8 Two or more races, non-Hispanic/Latino), 50 international. Average age 27. 442 applicants, 70% accepted, 226 enrolled. In 2017, 298 master's, 7 doctorates awarded. *Entrance requirements:* For master's, GMAT or GRE; for doctorate, GMAT. Additional exam requirements/recommendations for international students: Required—TOEFL (minimum score 600 paper-based; 100 iBT), IELTS (minimum score 7). *Application deadline:* Applications are processed on a rolling basis. Application fee: $55 ($65 for international students). Electronic applications accepted. *Expenses:* Contact institution. *Financial support:* In 2017–18, 53 students received support. Fellowships, scholarships/grants, and unspecified assistantships available. Financial award application deadline: 2/1; financial award applicants required to submit FAFSA. *Faculty research:* Corporate finance, strategy services, consumer behavior, financial disclosures, operations. *Unit head:* Kristina Diekmann, Department Chair, 801-581-8524, Fax: 801-581-3380, E-mail: mastersinfo@business.utah.edu. *Application contact:* Christine Harris, Coordinator, 801-581-7785, Fax: 801-585-3962, E-mail: execch@business.utah.edu.
Website: http://www.business.utah.edu/

University of Utah, Graduate School, David Eccles School of Business, Master of Science in Information Systems Program, Salt Lake City, UT 84112-8939. Offers information systems (MS, Graduate Certificate), including business intelligence and analytics, IT security, product and process management, software and systems architecture. *Program availability:* Part-time, evening/weekend, 100% online, blended/hybrid learning. *Students:* 150 full-time (53 women), 121 part-time (38 women); includes 29 minority (2 Black or African American, non-Hispanic/Latino; 10 Asian, non-Hispanic/Latino; 12 Hispanic/Latino; 5 Two or more races, non-Hispanic/Latino), 124 international. Average age 28. In 2017, 155 master's awarded. *Degree requirements:* For master's, capstone project. *Entrance requirements:* For master's, GMAT/GRE, minimum undergraduate GPA of 3.0, 2 letters of recommendation, personal statement, professional resume. Additional exam requirements/recommendations for international students: Required—TOEFL (minimum score 550 paper-based; 80 iBT), IELTS (minimum score 6.5). *Application deadline:* For fall admission, 7/27 for domestic students, 3/30 for international students; for spring admission, 12/7 for domestic students, 9/7 priority date for international students; for summer admission, 4/12 for domestic students, 1/11 for international students. Applications are processed on a rolling basis. Application fee: $55 ($65 for international students). Electronic applications accepted. *Expenses:* Contact institution. *Financial support:* Fellowships with partial tuition reimbursements, teaching assistantships, tuition waivers (partial), and unspecified assistantships available. Financial award application deadline: 6/1; financial award applicants required to submit FAFSA. *Faculty research:* Business intelligence and analytics, software and system architecture, product and process management, IT security, Web and data mining, applications and management of IT in healthcare. *Unit head:* Dr. Bradden Blair, Director of the IS Programs, 801-587-9489, Fax: 801-581-3666, E-mail: b.blair@eccles.utah.edu. *Application contact:* Jan Bents, Admissions Coordinator, 801-587-5878, Fax: 801-581-3666, E-mail: jan.bents@eccles.utah.edu.
Website: http://msis.eccles.utah.edu

University of Virginia, McIntire School of Commerce, MS Program in Global Commerce, Charlottesville, VA 22903. Offers global commerce (MS); global strategic management (MS); international management (Certificate). *Entrance requirements:* For master's, GMAT. Additional exam requirements/recommendations for international students: Required—TOEFL (minimum score 600 paper-based; 100 iBT), IELTS (minimum score 6.5).

The University of Western Ontario, Richard Ivey School of Business, London, ON N6A 3K7, Canada. Offers business (EMBA, PhD); corporate strategy and leadership elective (MBA); entrepreneurship elective (MBA); finance elective (MBA); health sector stream (MBA); international management elective (MBA); marketing elective (MBA); JD/MBA. *Degree requirements:* For master's, thesis (for some programs); for doctorate, thesis/dissertation. *Entrance requirements:* For master's, GMAT, 2 years of full-time work experience, interview. Additional exam requirements/recommendations for international students: Required—TOEFL (minimum score 100 iBT) or IELTS (minimium score 6). Electronic applications accepted. *Faculty research:* Strategy, organizational behavior, international business, finance, operations management.

University of Wisconsin–Madison, Graduate School, College of Engineering, Department of Industrial and Systems Engineering, Madison, WI 53706. Offers industrial engineering (MS, PhD), including human factors and health systems engineering (MS), systems engineering and analytics (MS). *Program availability:* Part-time. *Faculty:* 19 full-time (5 women). *Students:* 97 full-time (40 women), 17 part-time (8 women); includes 6 minority (1 Black or African American, non-Hispanic/Latino; 4 Asian, non-Hispanic/Latino; 1 Hispanic/Latino), 77 international. Average age 26. 421 applicants, 25% accepted, 38 enrolled. In 2017, 28 master's, 12 doctorates awarded. Terminal master's awarded for partial completion of doctoral program. *Degree requirements:* For master's, thesis optional, 30 credits; minimum GPA of 3.0; for doctorate, comprehensive exam, thesis/dissertation, minimum of 51 credits; minimum GPA of 3.0. *Entrance requirements:* For master's and doctorate, GRE General Test, minimum GPA of 3.0, BS in engineering or equivalent, course work in computer programming and statistics. Additional exam requirements/recommendations for international students: Required—TOEFL (minimum score 580 paper-based; 92 iBT), IELTS (minimum score 7). *Application deadline:* For fall admission, 1/1 for domestic and international students; for spring admission, 10/1 for domestic and international students; for summer admission, 1/1 for domestic and international students. Application fee: $75 ($81 for international students). Electronic applications accepted. *Expenses:* $11,987 resident; $25,314 non-resident; $17,988 MN resident. *Financial support:* In 2017–18, 58 students received support, including 1 fellowship with full tuition reimbursement available (averaging $27,336 per year), 34 research assistantships with full tuition reimbursements available (averaging $24,996 per year), 17 teaching assistantships with full tuition reimbursements available (averaging $17,196 per year); career-related internships or fieldwork, Federal Work-Study, institutionally sponsored loans, scholarships/grants, traineeships, health care benefits, and unspecified assistantships also available. Financial award application deadline: 12/1; financial award applicants required to submit FAFSA. *Faculty research:* Operations research; human factors and ergonomics; health systems engineering; manufacturing and production systems. *Total annual research expenditures:* $13.6 million. *Unit head:* Dr. Jeff Lindroth, Chair, 608-262-2686, E-mail: ie@engr.wisc.edu. *Application contact:* Pam Peterson, Student Services Coordinator, 608-263-4025, Fax: 608-890-2204, E-mail: prpeterson@wisc.edu.
Website: http://www.engr.wisc.edu/department/industrial-systems-engineering/

University of Wisconsin–Milwaukee, Graduate School, Lubar School of Business, Milwaukee, WI 53201. Offers business administration (MBA); executive business administration (EMBA); management science (MS, PhD, Graduate Certificate), including business analytics (Graduate Certificate), enterprise resource planning (Graduate Certificate), information technology management (MS), investment management (Graduate Certificate), nonprofit management (Graduate Certificate), nonprofit management and leadership (MS), state and local taxation (Graduate Certificate), technology entrepreneurship (Graduate Certificate). *Accreditation:* AACSB. *Program availability:* Part-time, evening/weekend. *Students:* 321 full-time (137 women), 252 part-time (93 women); includes 94 minority (25 Black or African American, non-Hispanic/Latino; 1 American Indian or Alaska Native, non-Hispanic/Latino; 28 Asian, non-

Hispanic/Latino; 6 Hispanic/Latino; 34 Two or more races, non-Hispanic/Latino), 66 international. Average age 32. 426 applicants, 61% accepted, 191 enrolled. In 2017, 266 master's, 8 doctorates, 21 other advanced degrees awarded. *Degree requirements:* For master's, comprehensive exam (for some programs); for doctorate, comprehensive exam, thesis/dissertation. *Entrance requirements:* For master's and doctorate, GMAT or GRE General Test. Additional exam requirements/recommendations for international students: Required—TOEFL (minimum score 550 paper-based; 79 iBT), IELTS (minimum score 6.5). *Application deadline:* For fall admission, 1/1 priority date for domestic students; for spring admission, 9/1 for domestic students. Application fee: $56 ($96 for international students). Electronic applications accepted. *Expenses:* Contact institution. *Financial support:* Fellowships with full tuition reimbursements, research assistantships with full tuition reimbursements, teaching assistantships with full tuition reimbursements, career-related internships or fieldwork, Federal Work-Study, health care benefits, unspecified assistantships, and project assistantships available. Support available to part-time students. Financial award application deadline: 4/15; financial award applicants required to submit FAFSA. *Faculty research:* Applied management research in finance, management information systems, marketing, operations research, organizational sciences. *Unit head:* V. Kanti Prasad, Dean, 414-229-6256, E-mail: deanprasad@uwm.edu. *Application contact:* Business Graduate Student Services, 414-229-5403, E-mail: mba-ms@uwm.edu.
Website: https://uwm.edu/business/

Valparaiso University, Graduate School and Continuing Education, College of Business, Valparaiso, IN 46383. Offers business administration (MBA); business decision-making (Certificate); business intelligence (Certificate); engineering management (Certificate); finance (Certificate); general business (Certificate); leading the global enterprise (Certificate); management (Certificate); JD/MBA; MSN/MBA. *Accreditation:* AACSB. *Program availability:* Part-time, evening/weekend, online learning. *Entrance requirements:* For master's, GMAT, GRE, minimum GPA of 3.0. Additional exam requirements/recommendations for international students: Required—TOEFL (minimum score 550 paper-based; 80 iBT), IELTS (minimum score 6). Electronic applications accepted. *Expenses:* Contact institution.

Vanderbilt University, Vanderbilt University Owen Graduate School of Management, Vanderbilt MBA Program, Nashville, TN 37203. Offers accounting (MBA); finance (MBA); general management (MBA); health care (MBA); human and organizational performance (MBA); marketing (MBA); operations (MBA); strategy (MBA); MBA/JD; MBA/M Div; MBA/MD; MBA/MSN; MBA/MTS; MBA/PhD. *Accreditation:* AACSB. *Degree requirements:* For master's, 62 credit hours of coursework; completion of ethics course; minimum GPA of 3.0. *Entrance requirements:* For master's, GMAT (preferred) or GRE, 2 years of work experience (recommended). Additional exam requirements/ recommendations for international students: Required—TOEFL (minimum score 100 iBT). Electronic applications accepted. *Expenses:* Contact institution. *Faculty research:* Accounting and finance, business strategy and economics, marketing, operations management, organization studies.

Villanova University, Villanova School of Business, MBA - The Fast Track Program, Villanova, PA 19085. Offers finance (MBA); healthcare (MBA); international business (MBA); strategic management (MBA). *Accreditation:* AACSB. *Program availability:* Part-time, evening/weekend. *Faculty:* 68 full-time (22 women), 65 part-time/adjunct (11 women). *Students:* 128 part-time (55 women); includes 11 minority (3 Black or African American, non-Hispanic/Latino; 4 Asian, non-Hispanic/Latino; 4 Hispanic/Latino), 4 international. Average age 30. 79 applicants, 96% accepted, 64 enrolled. In 2017, 58 master's awarded. *Degree requirements:* For master's, minimum GPA of 3.0. *Entrance requirements:* For master's, GMAT or GRE, work experience, 2 letters of recommendation, 2 essays, resume, official transcripts, interview. Additional exam requirements/recommendations for international students: Required—TOEFL (minimum score 550 paper-based; 100 iBT). *Application deadline:* For fall admission, 6/30 for domestic and international students. Applications are processed on a rolling basis. Application fee: $65. Electronic applications accepted. *Expenses:* $56,016 per year tuition, $1,167 per credit; $50 semester fee. *Financial support:* Scholarships/grants available. Financial award application deadline: 6/30; financial award applicants required to submit FAFSA. *Faculty research:* Business analytics; creativity, innovation and entrepreneurship; global leadership; real estate; church management; business ethics; marketing and consumer insights. *Unit head:* Dr. Joyce Russell, Dean of Villanova School of Business, 610-519-5424, Fax: 610-519-6273, E-mail: joyce.russell@villanova.edu. *Application contact:* Kimberly Kane, Manager of Admissions, 610-519-3701, Fax: 610-519-6273, E-mail: kimberly.kane@villanova.edu.
Website: http://www1.villanova.edu/villanova/business/graduate/mba.html

Villanova University, Villanova School of Business, MBA - The Flex Track Program, Villanova, PA 19085. Offers healthcare (MBA); international business (MBA); marketing (MBA); real estate (MBA); strategic management (MBA); JD/MBA. *Accreditation:* AACSB. *Program availability:* Part-time, evening/weekend, online learning. *Faculty:* 68 full-time (22 women), 65 part-time/adjunct (11 women). *Students:* 13 full-time (4 women), 410 part-time (137 women); includes 105 minority (28 Black or African American, non-Hispanic/Latino; 1 American Indian or Alaska Native, non-Hispanic/Latino; 41 Asian, non-Hispanic/Latino; 29 Hispanic/Latino; 6 Two or more races, non-Hispanic/Latino), 13 international. Average age 31. 94 applicants, 94% accepted, 79 enrolled. In 2017, 201 master's awarded. *Degree requirements:* For master's, minimum GPA of 3.0. *Entrance requirements:* For master's, GMAT or GRE, work experience, 2 letters of recommendation, 2 essays, resume, official transcript. Additional exam requirements/recommendations for international students: Required—TOEFL (minimum score 550 paper-based; 100 iBT). *Application deadline:* For fall admission, 6/30 for domestic and international students; for spring admission, 11/15 for domestic and international students; for summer admission, 3/31 for domestic and international students. Applications are processed on a rolling basis. Application fee: $65. Electronic applications accepted. *Expenses:* $50,016 per year tuition, $1,167 per credit; $50 semester fee. *Financial support:* In 2017–18, 19 research assistantships with full tuition reimbursements (averaging $16,245 per year) were awarded; scholarships/grants also available. Financial award application deadline: 6/30; financial award applicants required to submit FAFSA. *Faculty research:* Business analytics; creativity, innovation and entrepreneurship; global leadership; real estate; church management; business ethics. *Unit head:* Dr. Joyce Russell, Dean of Villanova School of Business, 610-519-5424, Fax: 610-519-6273, E-mail: joyce.russell@villanova.edu. *Application contact:* Claire Bruno, Director of Recruitment and Enrollment Management, 610-519-4336, Fax: 610-519-6273, E-mail: claire.bruno@villanova.edu.
Website: http://www1.villanova.edu/villanova/business/graduate/mba.html

Walsh College of Accountancy and Business Administration, Graduate Programs, Program in Management, Troy, MI 48083. Offers human resources management (MS); international business (MS); strategic management (MS). *Program availability:* Part-time, evening/weekend, 100% online, blended/hybrid learning. *Faculty:* 10 full-time (6 women), 13 part-time/adjunct (6 women). *Students:* 49 (37 women); includes 18 minority (14 Black or African American, non-Hispanic/Latino; 2 Asian, non-Hispanic/Latino; 2 Hispanic/Latino), 2 international. Average age 33. 17 applicants, 76% accepted, 6 enrolled. In 2017, 15 master's awarded. *Entrance requirements:* For master's, minimum overall cumulative GPA of 2.75 from all colleges previously attended. Additional exam

requirements/recommendations for international students: Required—TOEFL (minimum score 550 paper-based, 79 iBT), IELTS (6.5), Michigan English Language Assessment Battery, or MTELP (80). *Application deadline:* Applications are processed on a rolling basis. Application fee: $35. Electronic applications accepted. *Expenses:* $770 per semester credit hour plus $125 registration fee per semester. *Financial support:* In 2017–18, 1 student received support. Career-related internships or fieldwork and scholarships/grants available. Financial award application deadline: 6/30; financial award applicants required to submit FAFSA. *Faculty research:* Strategy practice and process, management learning and decision-making, human capital development, global leadership and citizenship, use of systems and complexity theory and management practice. *Unit head:* Dr. Ann Saurbier, Chair, Management, 248-823-1635, Fax: 248-689-0920, E-mail: asaurbie@walshcollege.edu. *Application contact:* Heather Rigby, Director, Admissions and Academic Advising, 248-823-1610, Fax: 248-823-1611, E-mail: hrigby@walshcollege.edu.

Wayne State University, College of Engineering, Department of Computer Science, Detroit, MI 48202. Offers computer science (MS, PhD), including bioinformatics and computational biology (PhD); data science and business analytics (MS). Application deadline for PhD is February 17. *Faculty:* 19. *Students:* 96 full-time (40 women), 28 part-time (6 women); includes 11 minority (2 Black or African American, non-Hispanic/Latino; 7 Asian, non-Hispanic/Latino; 2 Two or more races, non-Hispanic/Latino), 86 international. Average age 29. 283 applicants, 31% accepted, 19 enrolled. In 2017, 58 master's, 6 doctorates awarded. *Degree requirements:* For master's, thesis (for some programs), practicum (for MS in data science and business analytics); for doctorate, thesis/dissertation. *Entrance requirements:* For master's, GRE (GMAT accepted for MS in data science and business analytics), minimum GPA of 3.0, three letters of recommendation, adequate preparation in computer science and mathematics courses, personal statement, resume (for MS in data science and business analytics); for doctorate, GRE, bachelor's or master's degree in computer science or related field; minimum GPA of 3.3 in most recent degree; three letters of recommendation; personal statement; adequate preparation in computer science and mathematics courses. Additional exam requirements/recommendations for international students: Required—TOEFL (minimum score 550 paper-based; 79 iBT), TWE (minimum score 5.5); Recommended—IELTS (minimum score 6.5). *Application deadline:* For fall admission, 6/1 priority date for domestic students, 5/1 priority date for international students; for winter admission, 10/1 priority date for domestic students, 9/1 priority date for international students; for spring admission, 2/1 priority date for domestic students, 1/2 priority date for international students. Applications are processed on a rolling basis. Application fee: $50. Electronic applications accepted. *Expenses:* Contact institution. *Financial support:* In 2017–18, 68 students received support, including 5 fellowships with tuition reimbursements available (averaging $17,200 per year), 14 research assistantships with tuition reimbursements available (averaging $19,553 per year), 31 teaching assistantships with tuition reimbursements available (averaging $19,560 per year); scholarships/grants, health care benefits, and unspecified assistantships also available. Financial award application deadline: 2/17; financial award applicants required to submit FAFSA. *Faculty research:* Software engineering, databases, bioinformatics, artificial intelligence, networking, distributed and parallel computing, security, graphics, visualizations. *Total annual research expenditures:* $1.1 million. *Unit head:* Dr. Loren Schwiebert, Chair, 313-577-5474, E-mail: loren@wayne.edu. *Application contact:* Areej Salaymeh, Graduate Advisor, 313-577-2477, E-mail: csgradadvisor@cs.wayne.edu.
Website: http://engineering.wayne.edu/cs/

Wayne State University, College of Engineering, Department of Industrial and Systems Engineering, Detroit, MI 48202. Offers data science and business analytics (MS); engineering management (MS); industrial engineering (MS, PhD); manufacturing engineering (MS); systems engineering (Certificate). *Program availability:* Online learning. *Faculty:* 10. *Students:* 238 full-time (34 women), 128 part-time (39 women); includes 39 minority (14 Black or African American, non-Hispanic/Latino; 19 Asian, non-Hispanic/Latino; 6 Hispanic/Latino), 249 international. Average age 29. 712 applicants, 34% accepted, 69 enrolled. In 2017, 211 master's, 3 doctorates awarded. *Degree requirements:* For master's, thesis (for some programs); for doctorate, thesis/dissertation. *Entrance requirements:* For master's, GRE or GMAT (for applicants to MS in data science and business analytics), BS from ABET-accredited institution; for doctorate, GRE, graduate degree in engineering or related discipline with minimum graduate GPA of 3.5, statement of purpose, resume/curriculum vitae, three letters of recommendation; for Certificate, GRE (for applicants from non-ABET institutions), BS in engineering or other technical field from ABET-accredited institution with minimum GPA of 3.0 in upper-division course work, at least one year of full-time work experience as practicing engineer or technical leader. Additional exam requirements/recommendations for international students: Required—TOEFL (minimum score 550 paper-based; 79 iBT), TWE (minimum score 5.5), Michigan English Language Assessment Battery (minimum score 85); GRE; Recommended—IELTS (minimum score 6.5). *Application deadline:* Applications are processed on a rolling basis. Application fee: $50. Electronic applications accepted. *Expenses:* Contact institution. *Financial support:* In 2017–18, 118 students received support, including 2 fellowships with tuition reimbursements available (averaging $19,588 per year), 5 research assistantships with tuition reimbursements available (averaging $20,012 per year), 13 teaching assistantships with tuition reimbursements available (averaging $19,560 per year); scholarships/grants, tuition waivers (full), and unspecified assistantships also available. Financial award applicants required to submit FAFSA. *Faculty research:* Manufacturing systems, infrastructure, and management. *Total annual research expenditures:* $320,400. *Unit head:* Dr. Leslie Monplaisir, Associate Professor/Chair, 313-577-3821, Fax: 313-577-8833, E-mail: leslie.monplaisir@wayne.edu. *Application contact:* Eric Scimeca, Graduate Program Coordinator, 313-577-0412, E-mail: eric.scimeca@wayne.edu.
Website: http://engineering.wayne.edu/ise/

Wayne State University, Mike Ilitch School of Business, Detroit, MI 48202. Offers accounting (MS, MSA, Postbaccalaureate Certificate); business (EMS, Graduate Certificate); business administration (MBA, PhD); business science (MS), including business analytics; entrepreneurship and innovation (Postbaccalaureate Certificate); finance (MS); information systems management (Postbaccalaureate Certificate); taxation (MST); JD/MBA. Application deadline for PhD is February 15. *Accreditation:* AACSB. *Program availability:* Part-time, evening/weekend. *Faculty:* 32. *Students:* 235 full-time (121 women), 1,082 part-time (480 women); includes 356 minority (202 Black or African American, non-Hispanic/Latino; 2 American Indian or Alaska Native, non-Hispanic/Latino; 79 Asian, non-Hispanic/Latino; 47 Hispanic/Latino; 26 Two or more races, non-Hispanic/Latino), 87 international. Average age 30. 1,285 applicants, 43% accepted, 308 enrolled. In 2017, 200 master's, 2 doctorates, 9 other advanced degrees awarded. *Degree requirements:* For doctorate, thesis/dissertation. *Entrance requirements:* For master's, GMAT, GRE, LSAT, MCAT, at least three years of relevant work experience that shows increased responsibility, or minimum GPA of 3.0 from AACSB-accredited program or 3.2 from regionally-accredited program, undergraduate degree from accredited institution, undergraduate degree in accounting, business administration, or area of business administration (for MS and MST); for doctorate, GMAT (minimum score of 600), minimum undergraduate GPA of 3.0, 3.5 upper-division or graduate; three letters of recommendation; brief essay; undergraduate degree from accredited institution; personal statement; for other advanced degree, bachelor's degree from accredited institution. Additional exam requirements/recommendations for international students: Required—TOEFL (minimum score 550 paper-based; 79 iBT), Michigan English Language Assessment Battery (minimum score 85); Recommended—IELTS (minimum score 6.5), TWE (minimum score 5.5). *Application deadline:* For fall admission, 7/1 for domestic students, 5/1 priority date for international students; for winter admission, 11/1 for domestic students, 9/1 priority date for international students; for spring admission, 3/1 for domestic students, 1/1 priority date for international students. Applications are processed on a rolling basis. Application fee: $50. Electronic applications accepted. *Expenses:* Contact institution. *Financial support:* In 2017–18, 165 students received support, including 1 fellowship with tuition reimbursement available (averaging $18,534 per year), 1 teaching assistantship with tuition reimbursement available (averaging $18,534 per year); research assistantships with tuition reimbursements available, scholarships/grants, health care benefits, and unspecified assistantships also available. Support available to part-time students. Financial award applicants required to submit FAFSA. *Faculty research:* Executive compensation and stock performance, consumer reactions to pricing strategies, communication across the automotive supply chain, performance of firms in sub-Saharan Africa, implementation issues with ERP software. *Unit head:* Dr. Robert Forsythe, Dean, School of Business Administration, 313-577-4501, E-mail: robert.forsythe@wayne.edu. *Application contact:* Kiantee N. Rupert-Jones, Director,

313-577-4511, Fax: 313-577-9442, E-mail: gradbusiness@wayne.edu. Website: http://ilitchbusiness.wayne.edu/

Western Governors University, College of Business, Salt Lake City, UT 84107. Offers information technology management (MBA); integrated healthcare management (MS); management and strategy (MBA); strategic leadership (MBA). *Program availability:* Evening/weekend. *Degree requirements:* For master's, capstone project. *Entrance requirements:* For master's, Readiness Assessment, transcripts. Additional exam requirements/recommendations for international students: Required—TOEFL (minimum score 450 paper-based; 80 iBT). Electronic applications accepted.

Xavier University, Williams College of Business, Master of Business Administration Program, Cincinnati, OH 45207. Offers business administration (Exec MBA, MBA); business intelligence (MBA); finance (MBA); health industry (MBA); international business (MBA); marketing (MBA); values-based leadership (MBA); MBA/MHSA; MSN/MBA. *Accreditation:* AACSB. *Program availability:* Part-time, evening/weekend. *Degree requirements:* For master's, capstone course. *Entrance requirements:* For master's, GMAT or GRE, official transcript, resume. Additional exam requirements/recommendations for international students: Required—TOEFL (minimum score 550 paper-based; 79 iBT). Electronic applications accepted. Application fee is waived when completed online. *Expenses:* Contact institution.

Sustainability Management

Adler University, Graduate Programs, Master of Public Administration Program, Chicago, IL 60602. Offers criminal justice (MPA); sustainable communities (MPA). *Program availability:* Part-time, evening/weekend.

American University, Kogod School of Business, Program in Sustainability Management, Washington, DC 20016-8044. Offers MS. *Students:* 16 full-time (12 women), 18 part-time (9 women); includes 8 minority (3 Black or African American, non-Hispanic/Latino; 2 Asian, non-Hispanic/Latino; 2 Hispanic/Latino; 1 Two or more races, non-Hispanic/Latino), 4 international. Average age 29. 49 applicants, 100% accepted, 24 enrolled. In 2017, 8 master's awarded. *Entrance requirements:* For master's, GMAT/GRE, resume, personal statement, 2 letters of recommendation, transcripts. Additional exam requirements/recommendations for international students: Required—TOEFL (minimum score 100 iBT). *Application deadline:* For fall admission, 1/15 priority date for domestic students, 1/15 for international students; for spring admission, 10/15 priority date for domestic students, 10/15 for international students. Application fee: $100. *Expenses:* Contact institution. *Financial support:* Application deadline: 2/1; applicants required to submit FAFSA. *Application contact:* Jason Garner, Director of Admissions, 202-885-1926, E-mail: jgarner@american.edu. Website: http://www.kogod.american.edu

Anaheim University, Programs in Business Administration, Anaheim, CA 92806-5150. Offers entrepreneurship (ME, DBA); global sustainable management (MBA); international business (MBA, DBA, Certificate, Diploma); management (DBA); sustainable management (DBA, Certificate, Diploma). *Program availability:* Part-time, evening/weekend, online only, 100% online. Electronic applications accepted.

Antioch University New England, Graduate School, Department of Management, Program in Sustainability (Green MBA), Keene, NH 03431-3552. Offers MBA. *Program availability:* Part-time. *Entrance requirements:* For master's, GRE, resume, 3 letters of recommendation. Additional exam requirements/recommendations for international students: Required—TOEFL (minimum score 600 paper-based).

Aquinas College, School of Management, Grand Rapids, MI 49506. Offers marketing management (MM); organizational leadership (MM); sustainable business (MM). *Program availability:* Part-time, evening/weekend. *Students:* 11 full-time (6 women), 30 part-time (20 women); includes 7 minority (2 Black or African American, non-Hispanic/Latino; 1 Asian, non-Hispanic/Latino; 4 Hispanic/Latino). *Entrance requirements:* For master's, GMAT, minimum undergraduate GPA of 2.75, 2 years of work experience. Additional exam requirements/recommendations for international students: Required—TOEFL (minimum score 550 paper-based). *Application deadline:* Applications are processed on a rolling basis. Application fee: $0. *Expenses:* Contact institution. *Financial support:* Scholarships/grants available. Support available to part-time students. Financial award application deadline: 3/15; financial award applicants required to submit FAFSA. *Unit head:* Cynthia G. VanGelderen, Interim Director, 616-632-2922, Fax: 616-732-4489. *Application contact:* Lynn Atkins-Rykert, Program Coordinator, 616-632-2925, Fax: 616-732-4489, E-mail: atkinlyn@aquinas.edu.

Argosy University, Chicago, College of Business, Chicago, IL 60601. Offers accounting (DBA); customized professional concentration (MBA, DBA); finance (MBA); fraud examination (MBA); global business sustainability (DBA); healthcare administration (MBA); information systems (DBA); information systems management (MBA); international business (MBA, DBA); management (MBA, MSM, DBA); marketing (MBA, DBA); organizational leadership (Ed D); public administration (MBA); sustainable management (MBA). *Accreditation:* ACBSP. *Program availability:* Online learning.

Argosy University, Hawai`i, College of Business, Honolulu, HI 96813. Offers accounting (DBA); corporate compliance (MBA); customized professional concentration (MBA, DBA); finance (MBA, Certificate); fraud examination (MBA); global business sustainability (DBA); healthcare administration (MBA, Certificate); information systems (DBA); information systems management (MBA, Certificate); international business (MBA, DBA, Certificate); management (MBA, MSM, DBA); marketing (MBA, DBA, Certificate); organizational leadership (Ed D); public administration (MBA); sustainable management (MBA).

Argosy University, Los Angeles, College of Business, Los Angeles, CA 90045. Offers accounting (DBA); corporate compliance (MBA); customized professional concentration (MBA, DBA); finance (MBA); fraud examination (MBA); global business sustainability (DBA); healthcare administration (MBA); information systems (DBA); information systems management (MBA); international business (MBA, DBA); management (MBA, MSM, DBA); marketing (MBA, DBA); organizational leadership (Ed D); public administration (MBA); sustainable management (MBA).

Argosy University, Northern Virginia, College of Business, Arlington, VA 22209. Offers accounting (DBA); customized professional concentration (MBA, DBA); finance (MBA); fraud examination (MBA); global business sustainability (DBA); healthcare administration (MBA); information systems (DBA); information systems management (MBA); international business (MBA, DBA, Certificate); management (MBA, MSM, DBA); marketing (MBA, DBA, Certificate); organizational leadership (Ed D); public administration (MBA); sustainable management (MBA).

Argosy University, Orange County, College of Business, Orange, CA 92868. Offers accounting (DBA, Adv C); corporate compliance (MBA); customized professional concentration (MBA, DBA); finance (MBA, Certificate); fraud examination (MBA); global business sustainability (DBA); healthcare administration (MBA, Certificate); information systems (DBA, Adv C, Certificate); information systems management (MBA); international business (MBA, DBA, Adv C, Certificate); management (MBA, MSM, DBA, Adv C); marketing (MBA, DBA, Adv C, Certificate); organizational leadership (Ed D); public administration (MBA, Certificate); sustainable management (MBA).

Argosy University, Phoenix, College of Business, Phoenix, AZ 85021. Offers accounting (DBA); corporate compliance (MBA); customized professional concentration (MBA, DBA); finance (MBA); fraud examination (MBA); global business sustainability (DBA); healthcare administration (MBA); information systems (DBA); information systems management (MBA); international business (MBA, DBA); management (MBA, DBA); marketing (MBA, DBA); public administration (MBA); sustainable management (MBA).

Argosy University, Seattle, College of Business, Seattle, WA 98121. Offers accounting (DBA); corporate compliance (MBA); customized professional concentration (MBA, DBA); finance (MBA); fraud examination (MBA); global business sustainability (DBA); healthcare administration (MBA); information systems (DBA); information systems management (MBA); international business (MBA, DBA); management (MBA, MSM, DBA); marketing (MBA, DBA); organizational leadership (Ed D); public administration (MBA); sustainable management (MBA).

Argosy University, Tampa, College of Business, Tampa, FL 33607. Offers accounting (DBA); corporate compliance (MBA); customized professional concentration (MBA, DBA); finance (MBA); fraud examination (MBA); global business sustainability (DBA); healthcare administration (MBA); information systems (DBA); information systems management (MBA); international business (MBA, DBA); management (MBA, MSM, DBA); marketing (MBA, DBA); organizational leadership (Ed D); public administration (MBA); sustainable management (MBA).

Argosy University, Twin Cities, College of Business, Eagan, MN 55121. Offers accounting (DBA); customized professional concentration (MBA, DBA); finance (MBA); fraud examination (MBA); global business sustainability (DBA); healthcare administration (MBA); information systems (DBA); information systems management (MBA); international business (MBA, DBA); management (MBA, MSM, DBA); marketing (MBA, DBA); organizational leadership (Ed D); public administration (MBA); sustainable management (MBA).

Bard College, Bard Center for Environmental Policy, Annandale-on-Hudson, NY 12504. Offers climate science and policy (MS, Professional Certificate), including agriculture (MS), ecosystems (MS); environmental policy (MS, Professional Certificate); sustainability (MBA); MS/JD; MS/MAT. *Program availability:* Part-time. *Degree requirements:* For master's, thesis, 4-month, full-time internship. *Entrance requirements:* For master's, GRE, coursework in statistics, chemistry and one other semester of college science; personal statement; curriculum vitae; 3 letters of recommendation; sample of written work. Additional exam requirements/recommendations for international students: Required—TOEFL (minimum score 600 paper-based; 100 iBT). Electronic applications accepted. *Expenses:* Contact institution. *Faculty research:* Climate and agriculture, alternative energy, environmental economics, environmental toxicology, EPA law, sustainable development, international relations, literature and composition, human rights, agronomy, advocacy, leadership.

Baruch College of the City University of New York, Zicklin School of Business, Department of Management, New York, NY 10010-5585. Offers entrepreneurship (MBA); management (PhD); operations management (MBA); organizational behavior/human resources management (MBA); sustainable business (MBA). PhD offered jointly with Graduate School and University Center of the City University of New York. *Program availability:* Part-time, evening/weekend. *Degree requirements:* For doctorate, comprehensive exam, thesis/dissertation. *Entrance requirements:* For master's, GMAT, 2 letters of recommendation, resume, 2 years of work experience; for doctorate, GMAT. Additional exam requirements/recommendations for international students: Required—TOEFL (minimum score 590 paper-based), TWE.

Bluffton University, Programs in Business, Bluffton, OH 45817. Offers accounting and financial management (MBA); health care management (MBA); leadership (MAOM, MBA); production and operations management (MBA); sustainability management (MBA). *Program availability:* Evening/weekend, blended/hybrid learning, videoconference. *Faculty:* 5 full-time (2 women), 8 part-time/adjunct (2 women). *Students:* 48 full-time (31 women); includes 11 minority (5 Black or African American, non-Hispanic/Latino; 1 Asian, non-Hispanic/Latino; 3 Hispanic/Latino; 2 Two or more races, non-Hispanic/Latino), 1 international. Average age 33. 44 applicants, 70% accepted, 26 enrolled. In 2017, 41 master's awarded. *Degree requirements:* For master's, integrated research project (for some programs). *Entrance requirements:* For master's, current resume, official transcript, bachelor's degree, minimum GPA of 3.0, personal essay. Additional exam requirements/recommendations for international students: Recommended—TOEFL (minimum score 550 paper-based). *Application* *deadline:* For fall admission, 7/31 priority date for domestic and international students. Applications are processed on a rolling basis. Application fee: $0. Electronic applications accepted. *Expenses:* $550 per credit hour, $150 per semester technology fee, $25 per semester payment plan fee. *Financial support:* Unspecified assistantships and faculty/staff grants available. Financial award applicants required to submit FAFSA. *Unit head:* Dr. Melissa Green, Director of Graduate Programs in Business, 419-358-3447, E-mail: greenm@bluffton.edu. *Application contact:* Carrie Mast, Administrative Assistant, Graduate Programs in Business, 419-358-3065, E-mail: mastc@bluffton.edu. Website: http://www.bluffton.edu/grad/

Case Western Reserve University, Weatherhead School of Management, Department of Design and Innovation, Cleveland, OH 44106. Offers designing sustainable systems (PhD). *Program availability:* Part-time, evening/weekend. *Degree requirements:* For doctorate, thesis/dissertation. *Entrance requirements:* For doctorate, GMAT. *Expenses: Tuition:* Full-time $43,854; part-time $1827 per credit hour. *Required fees:* $50; $50 per credit hour. Tuition and fees vary according to course load and program. *Faculty research:* Decision support, business forecasting systems, design and use of information systems, artificial intelligence, executive information systems.

Chatham University, Program in Business Administration, Pittsburgh, PA 15232-2826. Offers business administration (MBA); healthcare management (MBA); sustainability (MBA); women's leadership (MBA). *Program availability:* Part-time, evening/weekend. *Faculty:* 6 part-time/adjunct (2 women). *Students:* 19 full-time (12 women), 36 part-time (20 women); includes 8 minority (4 Black or African American, non-Hispanic/Latino; 3 Asian, non-Hispanic/Latino; 1 Hispanic/Latino), 5 international. Average age 31. 57 applicants, 56% accepted, 24 enrolled. In 2017, 20 master's awarded. *Entrance requirements:* For master's, minimum GPA of 3.0, letters of recommendation. Additional exam requirements/recommendations for international students: Required—TOEFL (minimum score 600 paper-based; 100 iBT), IELTS (minimum score 7), TWE. *Application deadline:* For fall admission, 4/1 for domestic and international students; for spring admission, 11/1 for domestic students, 10/1 for international students. Applications are processed on a rolling basis. Application fee: $45. Electronic applications accepted. Application fee is waived when completed online. *Expenses:* Contact institution. *Financial support:* Applicants required to submit FAFSA. *Unit head:* Dr. Rachel Chung, Director of Business and Entrepreneurship Program, 412-365-2433. *Application contact:* Katie Noel, Assistant Director of Graduate Admission, 412-365-2758, Fax: 412-365-1609, E-mail: gradadmissions@chatham.edu. Website: http://www.chatham.edu/mba

City University of Seattle, Graduate Division, School of Management, Seattle, WA 98121. Offers accounting (Certificate); change leadership (MBA, Certificate); computer systems (MS); finance (Certificate); financial management (MBA); general management (MBA); general management-Europe (MBA); global marketing (MBA); human resources management (Certificate); individualized study (MBA); information security (MS); information systems (MBA); leadership (MA); marketing (MBA, Certificate); project management (MBA, MS, Certificate); sustainable business (Certificate); technology management (MBA, Certificate). *Program availability:* Part-time, evening/weekend, online learning. *Degree requirements:* For master's, comprehensive exam (for some programs), thesis (for some programs). *Entrance requirements:* For master's, baccalaureate degree or equivalent from an accredited or otherwise recognized institution. Additional exam requirements/recommendations for international students: Required—TOEFL (minimum score 567 paper-based; 87 iBT); Recommended—IELTS. Electronic applications accepted.

Clark University, Graduate School, Graduate School of Management, Business Administration Program, Worcester, MA 01610-1477. Offers accounting (MBA); finance (MBA); information management and business analytics (MBA); management (MBA); marketing (MBA); social change (MBA); sustainability (MBA). *Accreditation:* AACSB. *Program availability:* Part-time, evening/weekend. *Students:* 87 full-time (41 women), 41 part-time (26 women); includes 19 minority (10 Black or African American, non-Hispanic/Latino; 4 Asian, non-Hispanic/Latino; 4 Hispanic/Latino; 1 Two or more races, non-Hispanic/Latino), 40 international. Average age 30. 242 applicants, 50% accepted, 54 enrolled. In 2017, 102 master's awarded. *Degree requirements:* For master's, thesis optional. *Entrance requirements:* For master's, GMAT or GRE, 2 references, resume or curriculum vitae, personal statement. Additional exam requirements/recommendations for international students: Required—TOEFL (minimum score 575 paper-based; 90 iBT), IELTS (minimum score 6.5). *Application deadline:* For fall admission, 4/15 priority date for domestic and international students; for spring admission, 12/1 priority date for domestic and international students. Application fee: $75. Electronic applications accepted. *Expenses:* $4,490 tuition per 14-week course, $2,245 per half-unit (7-week course); $40 activity fee (full-time students only); $80 miscellaneous one-time fee; $1,750 student services fee. *Financial support:* Fellowships, research assistantships, teaching assistantships, career-related internships or fieldwork, Federal Work-Study, institutionally sponsored loans, and tuition waivers (partial) available. Support available to part-time students. Financial award application deadline: 5/31. *Faculty research:* Marketing, accounting, human resource management, management information systems, business finance. *Unit head:* Dr. Priscilla Elsass, Dean, 508-793-7543, Fax: 508-793-8822, E-mail: pelsass@clarku.edu. *Application contact:* Yingying Chen, Assistant Director of Graduate Admissions, 508-793-7373, Fax: 508-798-4386, E-mail: graduateadmissions@clarku.edu. Website: http://www.clarku.edu/programs/masters-business-administration

Colorado State University, Warner College of Natural Resources, Department of Ecosystem Science and Sustainability, Fort Collins, CO 80523-1476. Offers greenhouse gas management and accounting (MGMA); watershed science (MS). *Faculty:* 10 full-time (3 women), 3 part-time/adjunct (2 women). *Students:* 14 full-time (5 women), 18 part-time (12 women); includes 5 minority (4 Hispanic/Latino; 1 Two or more races, non-Hispanic/Latino), 4 international. Average age 30. 34 applicants, 62% accepted, 12 enrolled. In 2017, 9 master's awarded. *Degree requirements:* For master's, thesis (for some programs). *Entrance requirements:* For master's, GRE (70th percentile or higher), minimum GPA of 3.0; resume; transcript; letters of recommendation; statement of purpose; undergraduate degree in a related field. Additional exam requirements/recommendations for international students: Required—TOEFL (minimum score 550 paper-based; 80 iBT), IELTS (minimum score 6.5). *Application deadline:* For fall admission, 2/1 priority date for domestic and international students. Application fee: $60 ($70 for international students). Electronic applications accepted. *Expenses:* $1,250 per semester (for MGMA). *Financial support:* In 2017–18, 9 research assistantships (averaging $23,945 per year), 8 teaching assistantships (averaging $11,583 per year) were awarded; scholarships/grants and unspecified assistantships also available. *Faculty research:* Animal-habitat relationships; pastoral ecology and simulation; solving applied problems in ecosystem science and sustainable ecosystem management; intersections and boundaries of human activities, physical processes, and ecosystems; theoretical and applied ecology. *Total annual research expenditures:* $2.1 million. *Unit head:* Dr. John Moore, Department Head, 970-491-5589, Fax: 970-491-1965, E-mail: john.moore@colostate.edu. *Application contact:* Nikki Foxley, ESS Department and Academic Success Coordinator, 970-491-5589, Fax: 970-491-1965, E-mail: nikki.foxley@colostate.edu. Website: http://warnercnr.colostate.edu/departments/ess

Columbia University, School of Professional Studies, Program in Sustainability Management, New York, NY 10027. Offers MS. Program offered in collaboration with Columbia University's Earth Institute. *Program availability:* Part-time. Electronic applications accepted. *Expenses: Tuition:* Full-time $44,864; part-time $1704 per credit. *Required fees:* $2370 per semester. One-time fee: $105.

DePaul University, Kellstadt Graduate School of Business, Chicago, IL 60604. Offers accountancy (MBA, MSA); applied economics (MBA); audit and advisory services (MS); business administration (DBA); business analytics (MS); business strategy and decision-making (MBA); computational finance (MS); economics and policy analysis (MS); enterprise risk management (MS); entrepreneurship (MBA, MS); finance (MBA, MS); general business (MBA); hospitality leadership (MBA); hospitality leadership and operational performance (MS); human resources (MS); international business (MBA); management (MBA, MS); management information systems (MBA); marketing (MBA, MS); marketing analysis (MS); marketing strategy and planning (MBA); real estate (MS); real estate finance and investment (MBA); strategy, execution and valuation (MBA); supply chain management (MS); sustainable management (MS); taxation (MS); JD/MBA. *Accreditation:* AACSB. *Program availability:* Part-time, evening/weekend, online learning. *Entrance requirements:* For master's, GMAT/GRE, 2 letters of recommendation, resume, essay, official transcripts. Additional exam requirements/recommendations for international students: Required—TOEFL (minimum score 550 paper-based; 80 iBT). *Application deadline:* For fall admission, 7/1 for domestic students, 6/1 for international students; for winter admission, 10/1 for domestic students, 9/1 for international students; for spring admission, 2/1 for domestic students, 1/1 for international students. Applications are processed on a rolling basis. Application fee: $60. Electronic applications accepted. *Expenses:* Contact institution. *Financial support:* Application deadline: 4/1; applicants required to submit FAFSA. *Unit head:* Christa Hinton, Assistant Dean and Director, 312-362-8810, Fax: 312-362-6677, E-mail: chinton@depaul.edu. *Application contact:* Garry Cooke, Director of Recruitment and Admissions, 312-362-8810, Fax: 312-362-6677, E-mail: kgsb@depaul.edu. Website: http://kellstadt.depaul.edu

Duquesne University, Palumbo-Donahue School of Business, Pittsburgh, PA 15282-0001. Offers accounting (M Acc); finance (MBA); information systems management (MSISM); management (MBA, MS); marketing (MBA); sports business (MS); supply chain management (MS); sustainability (MBA); JD/MBA; MBA/M Acc; MBA/MA; MBA/MES; MBA/MHMS; MSISM/MBA; Pharm D/MBA. *Accreditation:* AACSB. *Program availability:* Part-time, evening/weekend, minimal on-campus study. *Faculty:* 59 full-time (23 women), 25 part-time/adjunct (6 women). *Students:* 232 full-time (83 women), 46 part-time (18 women); includes 28 minority (14 Black or African American, non-Hispanic/Latino; 8 Asian, non-Hispanic/Latino; 4 Hispanic/Latino; 2 Two or more races, non-Hispanic/Latino), 24 international. Average age 29. 220 applicants, 83% accepted, 121 enrolled. In 2017, 113 master's awarded. *Entrance requirements:* For master's, GMAT or GRE, undergraduate transcripts, 2 letters of recommendation, current resume, personal statement. Additional exam requirements/recommendations for international students: Required—TOEFL (minimum score 577 paper-based; 90 iBT), IELTS (minimum score 7). *Application deadline:* For fall admission, 7/1 priority date for domestic and international students; for spring admission, 12/1 for domestic and international students; for summer admission, 4/1 for domestic and international students. Applications are processed on a rolling basis. Application fee: $0. Electronic applications accepted. *Expenses:* $934 per credit (MS in management, sports business); $1,259 per credit (MBA, MS in accountancy, information systems management). *Financial support:* In 2017–18, 211 students received support, including 12 fellowships with partial tuition reimbursements available (averaging $14,200 per year), 20 research assistantships with partial tuition reimbursements available (averaging $22,662 per year); career-related internships or fieldwork, scholarships/grants, and unspecified assistantships also available. Support available to part-time students. Financial award application deadline: 7/1; financial award applicants required to submit FAFSA. *Faculty research:* Investment management, business ethics, technology management, supply chain management, entrepreneurship. *Unit head:* Dr. Karen Donovan, Associate Dean of Graduate Programs and Executive Education, 412-396-6276, Fax: 412-396-1726, E-mail: donovan6@duq.edu. *Application contact:* Jeff Jewett, Director of Admissions and Enrollment Management, 412-396-6244, Fax: 412-396-1726, E-mail: decrostam@duq.edu. Website: http://www.duq.edu/business/grad

Edgewood College, Program in Business, Madison, WI 53711-1997. Offers accountancy (MS); sustainability leadership (MBA). *Accreditation:* ACBSP. *Program availability:* Part-time, evening/weekend. *Students:* 19 full-time (12 women), 107 part-time (63 women); includes 16 minority (3 Black or African American, non-Hispanic/Latino; 5 Asian, non-Hispanic/Latino; 4 Hispanic/Latino; 4 Two or more races, non-Hispanic/Latino), 13 international. Average age 34. In 2017, 47 master's awarded. *Entrance requirements:* For master's, GMAT (minimum score 430), minimum GPA of 2.75, 2 letters of recommendation. Additional exam requirements/recommendations for international students: Required—TOEFL. *Application deadline:* For fall admission, 8/15 for domestic students, 5/1 for international students; for spring admission, 1/8 for domestic students, 11/1 for international students. Applications are processed on a rolling basis. Application fee: $30. Electronic applications accepted. *Expenses: Tuition:* Part-time $930 per credit. *Financial support:* Career-related internships or fieldwork and scholarships/grants available. *Unit head:* Dr. Stevie Watson, Dean, 608-663-2224, Fax: 608-663-3291, E-mail: swatson@edgewood.edu. *Application contact:* Joann Eastman, Admissions Counselor, 608-663-3250, Fax: 608-663-2214, E-mail: gps@edgewood.edu. Website: https://www.edgewood.edu/academics/schools/school-of-business

Edgewood College, Program in Social Innovation and Sustainability Leadership, Madison, WI 53711-1997. Offers MA. *Program availability:* Part-time, evening/weekend. *Faculty:* 1 full-time (0 women), 2 part-time/adjunct (1 woman). *Students:* 5 full-time (4 women), 7 part-time (4 women); includes 2 minority (1 Hispanic/Latino; 1 Two or more races, non-Hispanic/Latino). Average age 37. 15 applicants, 100% accepted, 12 enrolled. In 2017, 5 master's awarded. *Application deadline:* For fall admission, 7/1 for domestic students. Application fee: $30. *Expenses:* Contact institution. *Financial support:* In 2017–18, 14 students received support. Scholarships/grants available. Support available to part-time students. Financial award application deadline: 5/1; financial award applicants required to submit FAFSA. *Faculty research:* Community development, collaborative decision-making, leadership, community well-being, organizational change. *Unit head:* Dr. Stephan Gilchrist, Director, 608-663-6991, E-mail: sgilchrist@edgewood.edu. Website: https://www.edgewood.edu/academics/programs/details/social-innovation-and-sustainability-leadership/graduate

Fairleigh Dickinson University, Florham Campus, Silberman College of Business, Certificate Program in Managing Sustainability, Madison, NJ 07940-1099. Offers Certificate.

Franklin Pierce University, Graduate and Professional Studies, Rindge, NH 03461-0060. Offers curriculum and instruction (M Ed); elementary education (MS Ed); emerging network technologies (Graduate Certificate); energy and sustainability studies (MBA, Graduate Certificate); health administration (MBA, Graduate Certificate); human

Sustainability Management

resource management (MBA, Graduate Certificate); information technology (MBA); leadership (MBA); nursing education (MS); nursing leadership (MS); physical therapy (DPT); physician assistant studies (MPAS); special education (M Ed); sports management (MBA). *Accreditation:* APTA. *Program availability:* Part-time, 100% online, blended/hybrid learning. *Degree requirements:* For master's, concentrated original research projects; student teaching; fieldwork and/or internship; leadership project; PRAXIS I and II (for M Ed); for doctorate, concentrated original research projects, clinical fieldwork and/or internship, leadership project. *Entrance requirements:* For master's, minimum GPA of 2.5, 3 letters of recommendation; competencies in accounting, economics, statistics, and computer skills through life experience or undergraduate coursework (for MBA); certification/e-portfolio, minimum C grade in all education courses (for M Ed); license to practice as RN (for MS); for doctorate, GRE, 80 hours of observation/work in PT settings; completion of anatomy, chemistry, physics, and statistics; minimum GPA of 3.0. Additional exam requirements/recommendations for international students: Required—TOEFL (minimum score 550 paper-based; 61 iBT). Electronic applications accepted. *Faculty research:* Evidence-based practice in sports physical therapy, human resource management in economic crisis, leadership in nursing, innovation in sports facility management, differentiated learning and understanding by design.

Goddard College, Graduate Division, Master of Arts in Social Innovation and Sustainability Program, Plainfield, VT 05667-9432. Offers MA. *Program availability:* Part-time, online learning. *Degree requirements:* For master's, thesis. *Entrance requirements:* For master's, 3 letters of recommendation, relevant prior training or experience, interview. Electronic applications accepted.

Illinois Institute of Technology, Stuart School of Business, Program in Business Administration, Chicago, IL 60661. Offers sustainability (MBA); JD/MBA; M Des/MBA; MBA/MS. *Accreditation:* AACSB. *Program availability:* Part-time, evening/weekend. *Entrance requirements:* For master's, GRE (minimum score 298) or GMAT (500). Additional exam requirements/recommendations for international students: Required—TOEFL (minimum score 600 paper-based; 85 iBT); Recommended—IELTS (minimum score 7). Electronic applications accepted. *Expenses:* Contact institution. *Faculty research:* Global management and marketing strategy, technological innovation, management science, financial management, knowledge management.

Indiana University Bloomington, School of Public and Environmental Affairs, Public Affairs Programs, Bloomington, IN 47405. Offers economic development (MPA); energy (MPA); environmental policy (PhD); environmental policy and natural resource management (MPA); information systems (MPA); international development (MPA); local government management (MPA); nonprofit management (MPA, Certificate); policy analysis (MPA); public budgeting and financial management (Certificate); public finance (PhD); public financial administration (MPA); public management (MPA, PhD, Certificate); public policy analysis (PhD); social entrepreneurship (Certificate); specialized public affairs (MPA); sustainability and sustainable development (MPA); JD/MPA; MPA/MA; MPA/MIS; MPA/MLS; MSES/MPA. *Accreditation:* NASPAA (one or more programs are accredited). *Program availability:* Part-time. *Degree requirements:* For master's, capstone, internship; for doctorate, comprehensive exam, thesis/dissertation. *Entrance requirements:* For master's, GRE General Test or GMAT, official transcripts, 3 letters of recommendation, resume, personal statement; for doctorate, GRE General Test, official transcripts, 3 letters of recommendation, statement of purpose. Additional exam requirements/recommendations for international students: Required—TOEFL (minimum score 600 paper-based; 96 iBT); Recommended—IELTS (minimum score 7). Electronic applications accepted. *Faculty research:* International development, environmental policy and resource management, policy analysis, public finance, public management, urban management, nonprofit management, energy policy, social policy, public finance.

James Madison University, The Graduate School, College of Integrated Science and Engineering, Program in Environmental Management and Sustainability, Harrisonburg, VA 22801. Offers MS. *Students:* 17 full-time (9 women), 5 part-time (4 women); includes 2 minority (1 Black or African American, non-Hispanic/Latino; 1 Hispanic/Latino), 6 international. Average age 30. In 2017, 21 master's awarded. Application fee: $55. Electronic applications accepted. *Expenses:* Tuition, state resident: full-time $10,512; part-time $438 per credit hour. Tuition, nonresident: full-time $28,358; part-time $1162 per credit hour. *Required fees:* $1128. *Financial support:* Fellowships, Federal Work-Study, and unspecified assistantships available. Financial award application deadline: 3/1; financial award applicants required to submit FAFSA. *Unit head:* Dr. Eric H. Maslen, Department Head, 540-568-2740, E-mail: masleneh@jmu.edu. *Application contact:* Lynette D. Michael, Director of Graduate Admissions, 540-568-6131 Ext. 6395, Fax: 540-567-7860, E-mail: michaeld@jmu.edu.
Website: http://www.jmu.edu/mems-malta/index.shtml

Maastricht School of Management, Graduate Programs, Maastricht, Netherlands. Offers business administration (MBA, DBA, PhD); facility management (Exec MBA); management (M Sc); sustainability (Exec MBA).

Maharishi University of Management, Graduate Studies, Program in Business Administration, Fairfield, IA 52557. Offers accounting (MBA); management (PhD); sustainability (MBA). *Program availability:* Evening/weekend, online learning. *Degree requirements:* For doctorate, thesis/dissertation. *Entrance requirements:* For master's, GMAT, minimum GPA of 3.0; for doctorate, minimum GPA of 3.0. Additional exam requirements/recommendations for international students: Required—TOEFL. *Faculty research:* Leadership, effects of the group dynamics of consciousness on the economy, innovation, employee development, cooperative strategy.

Michigan Technological University, Graduate School, Interdisciplinary Programs, Houghton, MI 49931. Offers atmospheric sciences (PhD); automotive systems and controls (Graduate Certificate); biochemistry and molecular biology (PhD); computational science and engineering (PhD); data science (MS, Graduate Certificate); engineering-environmental (PhD); international profile (Graduate Certificate); nanotechnology (Graduate Certificate); sustainability (Graduate Certificate); sustainable water resources systems (Graduate Certificate). *Program availability:* Part-time. *Faculty:* 115 full-time (26 women), 9 part-time/adjunct (2 women). *Students:* 58 full-time (18 women), 17 part-time (5 women). Average age 28. 508 applicants, 28% accepted, 27 enrolled. In 2017, 10 master's, 7 doctorates, 11 other advanced degrees awarded. Terminal master's awarded for partial completion of doctoral program. *Degree requirements:* For master's, comprehensive exam (for some programs), thesis (for some programs); for doctorate, comprehensive exam, thesis/dissertation. *Entrance requirements:* For master's, doctorate, and Graduate Certificate, GRE, statement of purpose, personal statement, official transcripts, 2-3 letters of recommendation. Additional exam requirements/recommendations for international students: Required—TOEFL or IELTS. *Application deadline:* Applications are processed on a rolling basis. Electronic applications accepted. *Expenses:* Tuition, state resident: full-time $17,100; part-time $950 per credit. Tuition, nonresident: full-time $17,100; part-time $950 per credit. *Required fees:* $248; $124 per term. Tuition and fees vary according to course load and program. *Financial support:* In 2017–18, 67 students received support, including 9 fellowships with tuition reimbursements available (averaging $15,790 per year), 17 research assistantships with tuition reimbursements available (averaging $15,790 per year), 7 teaching assistantships with tuition reimbursements available (averaging $15,790 per year); career-related internships or fieldwork, Federal Work-Study, scholarships/grants, health care benefits, unspecified assistantships, and cooperative program also available. Financial award applicants required to submit FAFSA. *Faculty research:* Big data, atmospheric sciences, bioinformatics and systems biology, molecular dynamics, environmental studies. *Unit head:* Dr. Pushpalatha Murthy, Dean of the Graduate School/Associate Provost for Graduate Education, 906-487-3007, Fax: 906-487-2284, E-mail: ppmurthy@mtu.edu. *Application contact:* Carol T. Wingerson, Administrative Aide, 906-487-2328, Fax: 906-487-2284, E-mail: gradadms@mtu.edu.

Naropa University, Graduate Programs, Program in Resilient Leadership, Boulder, CO 80302-6697. Offers MA. *Faculty:* 2 full-time (both women), 3 part-time/adjunct (2 women). *Students:* 11 full-time (9 women); includes 4 minority (1 Black or African American, non-Hispanic/Latino; 3 Hispanic/Latino). Average age 30. 8 applicants, 100% accepted, 6 enrolled. In 2017, 5 master's awarded. *Degree requirements:* For master's, applied leadership project. *Entrance requirements:* For master's, interview; letter of interest; resume/curriculum vitae with pertinent academic, employment and volunteer activity; 2 letters of recommendation; transcripts. Additional exam requirements/recommendations for international students: Required—TOEFL (minimum score 550 paper-based; 80 iBT). *Application deadline:* For fall admission, 1/15 priority date for domestic and international students. Applications are processed on a rolling basis. Application fee: $60. Electronic applications accepted. *Expenses:* $995 per credit. *Financial support:* In 2017–18, 11 students received support. Research assistantships with partial tuition reimbursements available, career-related internships or fieldwork, Federal Work-Study, scholarships/grants, tuition waivers (partial), and unspecified assistantships available. Support available to part-time students. Financial award application deadline: 3/1; financial award applicants required to submit FAFSA. *Unit head:* Dr. Jeanine Canty, Chair, Environmental Studies, 303-245-4735, E-mail: jcanty@naropa.edu. *Application contact:* Office of Admissions, 303-546-3572, Fax: 303-546-3583, E-mail: rregnery@naropa.edu.
Website: http://www.naropa.edu/academics/masters/resilient-leadership/index.php

National University, Academic Affairs, School of Engineering and Computing, La Jolla, CA 92037-1011. Offers computer science (MS), including advanced computing; cyber security and information assurance (MS); data analytics (MS); electrical engineering (MS); engineering management (MS); information technology management (MS); management information systems (MS); sustainability management (MS). *Program availability:* Part-time, evening/weekend, 100% online, blended/hybrid learning. *Degree requirements:* For master's, thesis (for some programs). *Entrance requirements:* For master's, interview, minimum GPA of 2.5. Additional exam requirements/recommendations for international students: Required—TOEFL (minimum score 550 paper-based; 79 iBT), IELTS (minimum score 6). *Application deadline:* Applications are processed on a rolling basis. Application fee: $60 ($65 for international students). Electronic applications accepted. *Expenses: Tuition:* Part-time $430 per quarter hour. *Financial support:* Career-related internships or fieldwork, institutionally sponsored loans, scholarships/grants, and tuition waivers (partial) available. Support available to part-time students. Financial award application deadline: 6/30; financial award applicants required to submit FAFSA. *Faculty research:* Educational technology, scholarships in science. *Unit head:* Dr. Jodi Reeves, Interim Dean, 858-309-3426, E-mail: jreeves@nu.edu. *Application contact:* Brandon Jouganatos, Vice President for Enrollment Services, 800-628-8648, E-mail: advisor@nu.edu.
Website: http://www.nu.edu/OurPrograms/SchoolOfEngineeringAndTechnology.html

The New School, Schools of Public Engagement, Program in Environmental Policy and Sustainability Management, New York, NY 10011. Offers environmental policy and sustainability management (MS). *Program availability:* Part-time, evening/weekend. *Faculty:* 3 full-time (1 woman), 4 part-time/adjunct (3 women). *Students:* 32 full-time (22 women), 15 part-time (7 women); includes 14 minority (4 Black or African American, non-Hispanic/Latino; 1 Asian, non-Hispanic/Latino; 5 Hispanic/Latino; 4 Two or more races, non-Hispanic/Latino), 7 international. Average age 29. 76 applicants, 92% accepted, 22 enrolled. In 2017, 22 master's awarded. *Degree requirements:* For master's, thesis. *Entrance requirements:* For master's, two letters of recommendation, statement of purpose, resume, transcripts. Additional exam requirements/recommendations for international students: Required—TOEFL (minimum score 92 iBT), IELTS (minimum score 7), PTE (minimum score 68). *Application deadline:* For fall admission, 1/15 priority date for domestic and international students; for spring admission, 10/15 priority date for domestic and international students. Applications are processed on a rolling basis. Application fee: $50. Electronic applications accepted. *Expenses:* $1,650 per credit. *Financial support:* Teaching assistantships, career-related internships or fieldwork, Federal Work-Study, scholarships/grants, and unspecified assistantships available. Support available to part-time students. Financial award application deadline: 2/1; financial award applicants required to submit FAFSA. *Unit head:* Suzanne Bostwick, Associate Director, 212-229-5400 Ext. 1601, E-mail: bostwics@newschool.edu. *Application contact:* Gabriela Garcia Juarez, Assistant Director, Graduate Admission, 212-229-5150 Ext. 1666, E-mail: garciajg@newschool.edu.
Website: https://www.newschool.edu/public-engagement/ms-environmental-policy-sustainability-management/

Oklahoma State University, Graduate College, Stillwater, OK 74078. Offers aerospace security (Graduate Certificate); bioenergy and sustainable technology (Graduate Certificate); business data mining (Graduate Certificate); business sustainability (Graduate Certificate); environmental science (MS); international studies (MS); non-profit management (Graduate Certificate); teaching English to speakers of other languages (Graduate Certificate); telecommunications management (MS). Programs are interdisciplinary. *Students:* 31 full-time (21 women), 55 part-time (32 women); includes 15 minority (5 Black or African American, non-Hispanic/Latino; 3 Asian, non-Hispanic/Latino; 5 Hispanic/Latino; 2 Two or more races, non-Hispanic/Latino), 44 international. Average age 29. 334 applicants, 84% accepted, 73 enrolled. In 2017, 29 master's, 5 doctorates awarded. *Degree requirements:* For master's, thesis (for some programs); for doctorate, comprehensive exam, thesis/dissertation. *Entrance requirements:* For master's and doctorate, GRE or GMAT. Additional exam requirements/recommendations for international students: Required—TOEFL (minimum score 550 paper-based; 79 iBT). *Application deadline:* For fall admission, 3/1 priority date for domestic and international students; for spring admission, 8/1 priority date for domestic and international students. Applications are processed on a rolling basis. Application fee: $40 ($75 for international students). Electronic applications accepted. *Expenses:* Tuition, state resident: full-time $4019; part-time $2679.60 per year. Tuition, nonresident: full-time $15,286; part-time $10,190.40 per year. *Required fees:* $2129; $1419 per unit. Tuition and fees vary according to program. *Financial support:* Research assistantships, career-related internships or fieldwork, Federal Work-Study, scholarships/grants, health care benefits, tuition waivers (partial), and unspecified assistantships available. Support available to part-time students. Financial award application deadline: 3/1; financial award applicants required to submit FAFSA. *Unit head:* Dr. Sheryl Tucker, Dean, 405-744-6368, Fax: 405-744-0355, E-mail: gradi@okstate.edu. *Application contact:* Dr. Susan Mathew, Assistant Director of Graduate Admissions, 405-744-6368, Fax: 405-744-0355, E-mail: gradi@okstate.edu.
Website: http://gradcollege.okstate.edu/

Oregon State University, College of Forestry, Program in Forest Ecosystems and Society, Corvallis, OR 97331. Offers forest biology (MF); forest, wildlife and landscape ecology (MS, PhD); genetics and physiology (MS, PhD); integrated social and ecological systems (MS, PhD); science of conservation, restoration and sustainable management (MS, PhD); silviculture (MF); social science, policy, and natural resources (MS, PhD); soil-plant-atmosphere continuum (MS, PhD); sustainable recreation and tourism (MS). *Program availability:* Part-time. *Entrance requirements:* For master's and doctorate, GRE. Additional exam requirements/recommendations for international students: Required—TOEFL (minimum score 80 iBT), IELTS (minimum score 6.5). *Application deadline:* For fall admission, 8/1 for domestic students, 4/1 for international students; for winter admission, 12/1 for domestic students, 7/1 for international students; for spring admission, 2/1 for domestic students, 10/1 for international students; for summer admission, 5/1 for domestic students, 1/1 for international students. Application fee: $75 ($85 for international students). *Faculty research:* Ecosystem structure and function, nutrient cycling, biotechnology, vegetation management, integrated forest protection. *Unit head:* Jessica Bagley, Advisor, 541-737-6556, E-mail: jessica.bagley@oregonstate.edu. *Application contact:* Jessica Bagley, Advisor, 541-737-6556, E-mail: jessica.bagley@oregonstate.edu.
Website: http://fes.forestry.oregonstate.edu/

Oregon State University, College of Forestry, Program in Sustainable Forest Management, Corvallis, OR 97331. Offers engineering for sustainable forestry (MF, MS, PhD). *Program availability:* Part-time. *Entrance requirements:* For master's and doctorate, GRE. Additional exam requirements/recommendations for international students: Required—TOEFL (minimum score 80 iBT), IELTS (minimum score 6.5). *Application deadline:* For fall admission, 8/1 for domestic students, 4/1 for international students; for winter admission, 12/1 for domestic students, 7/1 for international students; for spring admission, 2/1 for domestic students, 10/1 for international students; for summer admission, 5/1 for domestic students, 1/1 for international students. Application fee: $75 ($85 for international students). *Unit head:* John Session, Sustainable Forest Management Advisor, 541-737-2818, E-mail: john.sessions@oregonstate.edu. *Application contact:* Madison Dudley, Sustainable Forest Management Graduate Program Coordinator, 541-737-2818, E-mail: madison.dudley@oregonstate.edu.
Website: http://ferm.forestry.oregonstate.edu/academic-programs/graduate-degree

Penn State Great Valley, Graduate Studies, Management Division, Malvern, PA 19355-1488. Offers business administration (MBA); cyber security (Certificate); data analytics (MPS, MS, Certificate); distributed energy and grid modernization (Certificate); finance (M Fin); health sector management (Certificate); human resource management (Certificate); information science (MSIS); leadership development (MLD); new ventures and entrepreneurship (Certificate); sustainable management practices (Certificate). *Accreditation:* AACSB. *Unit head:* Dr. James A. Nemes, Chancellor, 610-648-3202, Fax: 610-725-5296. *Application contact:* JoAnn Kelly, Director of Admissions, 610-648-3315, Fax: 610-725-5296, E-mail: jek2@psu.edu.
Website: http://greatvalley.psu.edu/academics/masters-degrees/engineering-management

Presidio Graduate School, Graduate Programs - San Francisco, San Francisco, CA 94129. Offers sustainable energy management (Certificate); sustainable management (MBA, MPA, Certificate); MBA/JD; MBA/MPA. MBA/JD offered in conjunction with the University of California, Hastings College of the Law. Application fee: $75.

Presidio Graduate School, MBA Programs - Seattle, San Francisco, CA 94129. Offers cooperative management (Certificate); sustainable business (MBA); sustainable systems (MBA). *Program availability:* Part-time, evening/weekend, blended/hybrid learning. *Entrance requirements:* For master's and Certificate, Quantitative Assessment Summary, GRE, or GMAT, resume, two letters of recommendation, essay, transcripts. Additional exam requirements/recommendations for international students: Required—TOEFL (minimum score 90 iBT), IELTS (minimum score 6.5). *Application deadline:* For fall admission, 6/1 priority date for domestic and international students. Applications are processed on a rolling basis. Application fee: $75. Electronic applications accepted. *Financial support:* Scholarships/grants available. Financial award application deadline: 6/15; financial award applicants required to submit FAFSA. *Unit head:* Dariush Rafinejad, Provost, 415-651-6555, E-mail: info@presidio.edu. *Application contact:* Kari Dorth, Director of Admissions, 415-655-8912, E-mail: admissions@presidio.edu.
Website: https://www.presidio.edu/seattle-mba-overview/

Rochester Institute of Technology, Graduate Enrollment Services, Golisano Institute for Sustainability, Rochester, NY 14623. Offers M Arch, MS, PhD. *Program availability:* Part-time. *Students:* 64 full-time (36 women), 20 part-time (7 women); includes 1 minority (Two or more races, non-Hispanic/Latino), 50 international. Average age 29. 164 applicants, 55% accepted, 22 enrolled. In 2017, 12 master's, 1 doctorate awarded. *Entrance requirements:* For master's and doctorate, GRE, minimum GPA of 3.0 (recommended). *Application deadline:* For fall admission, 2/15 priority date for domestic and international students; for spring admission, 12/15 priority date for domestic and international students. Applications are processed on a rolling basis. Application fee: $65. Electronic applications accepted. *Expenses:* $1,815 per credit hour. *Financial support:* In 2017–18, 74 students received support. Research assistantships with tuition reimbursements available, teaching assistantships with tuition reimbursements available, career-related internships or fieldwork, scholarships/grants, unspecified assistantships, and health care benefits (for PhD program only) available. Support available to part-time students. Financial award applicants required to submit FAFSA. *Faculty research:* Environmentally responsive architecture and passive/natural building design and systems; renewable energy; advanced manufacturing technology; built environments; eco-friendly electronics and e-waste; energy generation, storage, and systems; pollution prevention; transportation and interconnected smart city systems. *Unit head:* Dr. Nabil Nasr, Associate Provost and Director, 585-475-5101, E-mail: info@sustainability.rit.edu. *Application contact:* Diane Ellison, Senior Associate Vice President, Graduate Enrollment Services, 585-475-2229, Fax: 585-475-7164, E-mail: gradinfo@rit.edu.
Website: http://www.rit.edu/gis/

Royal Roads University, Graduate Studies, Environment and Sustainability Program, Victoria, BC V9B 5Y2, Canada. Offers environment and management (M Sc, MA); environment and sustainability (MAIS); environmental education and communication (MA, G Dip, Graduate Certificate); MA/MS. *Program availability:* Blended/hybrid learning. *Faculty:* 6 full-time (2 women), 22 part-time/adjunct (13 women). *Degree requirements:* For master's, thesis. *Entrance requirements:* For master's, 5-7 years of related work experience. *Application deadline:* Applications are processed on a rolling basis. Application fee: $120 ($240 for international students). Electronic applications accepted. *Financial support:* Federal Work-Study, institutionally sponsored loans, scholarships/grants, and bursaries available. Support available to part-time students. *Faculty research:* Sustainable development, atmospheric processes, sustainable communities, chemical fate and transport of persistent organic pollutants, educational technology. *Total annual research expenditures:* $40,000. *Unit head:* Dr. Brigitte Harris, Dean, 250-391-2511. *Application contact:* 250-391-2511, E-mail: admissions@royalroads.ca.

San Francisco State University, Division of Graduate Studies, College of Business, Program in Business Administration, San Francisco, CA 94132-1722. Offers decision sciences/operations research (MBA); ethics and compliance (MBA); finance (MBA); global business and innovation (MBA); healthcare administration (MBA); hospitality and tourism management (MBA); information systems (MBA); leadership (MBA); marketing (MBA); nonprofit and social enterprise leadership (MBA); sustainable business (MBA). *Accreditation:* AACSB. *Program availability:* Part-time, evening/weekend. *Degree requirements:* For master's, thesis, essay test. *Entrance requirements:* For master's, GMAT, minimum GPA of 2.7 in last 60 units. Additional exam requirements/recommendations for international students: Required—TOEFL (minimum score 550 paper-based). *Application deadline:* For fall admission, 5/1 priority date for domestic students, 4/1 for international students; for spring admission, 11/1 for domestic students, 10/15 for international students. Applications are processed on a rolling basis. Application fee: $55. *Financial support:* Application deadline: 3/1. *Unit head:* Dr. Sanjit Sengupta, Faculty Director, 415-817-4366, Fax: 415-817-4340, E-mail: sengupta@sfsu.edu. *Application contact:* Christopher Kingston, Director of Student Advising, 415-817-4322, Fax: 415-817-4340, E-mail: cak@sfsu.edu.
Website: http://cob.sfsu.edu/graduate-programs/mba

Seattle Pacific University, Master of Arts in Management Program, Seattle, WA 98119-1997. Offers business intelligence and data analytics (MA); cybersecurity (MA); faith and business (MA); human resources (MA); social and sustainable management (MA). *Students:* 4 full-time (all women), 12 part-time (8 women), 4 international. Average age 28. 15 applicants, 60% accepted, 7 enrolled. In 2017, 18 master's awarded. *Entrance requirements:* For master's, GMAT or GRE (waived with cumulative GPA of 3.3 or above), bachelor's degree from accredited college or university, resume, essay, official transcript. *Application deadline:* For fall admission, 8/1 for domestic students, 6/1 for international students; for winter admission, 11/1 for domestic students, 9/1 for international students; for spring admission, 2/1 for domestic students, 12/1 for international students; for summer admission, 5/1 for domestic students. Application fee: $50. *Application contact:* E-mail: drj@spu.edu.
Website: http://spu.edu/academics/school-of-business-and-economics/graduate-programs/ma-management

Seattle Pacific University, Master of Business Administration Program, Seattle, WA 98119-1997. Offers business administration (MBA); social and sustainable enterprise (MBA). *Accreditation:* AACSB. *Program availability:* Part-time. *Students:* 3 full-time (1 woman), 25 part-time (16 women); includes 6 minority (1 Black or African American, non-Hispanic/Latino; 1 Asian, non-Hispanic/Latino; 3 Hispanic/Latino; 1 Two or more races, non-Hispanic/Latino), 4 international. Average age 34. 26 applicants, 38% accepted, 7 enrolled. In 2017, 12 master's awarded. *Entrance requirements:* For master's, GMAT (minimum preferred scores of 500; 25 verbal; 30 quantitative; 4.4 analytical writing), BA, resume as evidence of substantive work experience. Additional exam requirements/recommendations for international students: Required—TOEFL (minimum score 90 iBT), IELTS (minimum score 7). *Application deadline:* For fall admission, 8/1 for domestic and international students; for winter admission, 11/1 for domestic and international students; for spring admission, 2/1 for domestic and international students. Applications are processed on a rolling basis. Application fee: $50. Electronic applications accepted. *Financial support:* Scholarships/grants available. Financial award applicants required to submit FAFSA. *Unit head:* Gary Karns, Associate Dean for Graduate Studies, 206-281-2948, Fax: 206-281-2733. *Application contact:* 206-281-2091.
Website: http://spu.edu/academics/school-of-business-and-economics/graduate-programs/mba

SIT Graduate Institute, Graduate Programs, Master's Program in Climate Change and Global Sustainability, Brattleboro, VT 05302-0676. Offers MA.

Southeastern Louisiana University, College of Arts, Humanities and Social Sciences, Department of Sociology and Criminal Justice, Hammond, LA 70402. Offers criminal justice (MS); globalization and sustainability (MS). *Program availability:* Part-time, evening/weekend. *Faculty:* 5 full-time (0 women). *Students:* 14 full-time (9 women), 4 part-time (0 women); includes 5 minority (2 Black or African American, non-Hispanic/Latino; 1 Hispanic/Latino; 2 Two or more races, non-Hispanic/Latino), 1 international. Average age 26. 13 applicants, 46% accepted, 5 enrolled. In 2017, 12 master's awarded. *Degree requirements:* For master's, comprehensive exam, thesis (for some programs), internship research (for those who select an internship track). *Entrance requirements:* For master's, GRE General Test (verbal and quantitative). Additional exam requirements/recommendations for international students: Required—TOEFL (minimum score 500 paper-based; 61 iBT). *Application deadline:* For fall admission, 7/15 priority date for domestic students, 6/1 priority date for international students; for spring admission, 12/1 priority date for domestic students, 10/1 priority date for international students. Applications are processed on a rolling basis. Application fee: $20 ($30 for international students). Electronic applications accepted. *Expenses:* Tuition, state resident: full-time $6684. Tuition, nonresident: full-time $19,162. *Required fees:* $2088. *Financial support:* In 2017–18, 8 students received support, including 7 research assistantships (averaging $6,506 per year); teaching assistantships, career-related internships or fieldwork, Federal Work-Study, institutionally sponsored loans, scholarships/grants, and unspecified assistantships also available. Support available to part-time students. Financial award application deadline: 5/1; financial award applicants required to submit FAFSA. *Faculty research:* Criminology, environmental sociology, globalization, sociology of disasters, sociology of religion. *Unit head:* Dr. Kenneth Bolton, Department Head, 985-549-2110, Fax: 985-549-5961, E-mail: kbolton@southeastern.edu. *Application contact:* Amanda Harper, Graduate Admissions Analyst, 985-549-5620, Fax: 985-549-5632, E-mail: admissions@southeastern.edu.
Website: http://www.southeastern.edu/acad_research/depts/soc_cj/grad_degree/index.html

Southern New Hampshire University, School of Business, Manchester, NH 03106-1045. Offers accounting (MBA, Graduate Certificate); accounting finance (MS); accounting/auditing (MS); accounting/forensic accounting (MS); accounting/management accounting (MS); accounting/taxation (MS); applied economics (MS); athletic administration (MBA, Graduate Certificate); business administration (IMBA, Certificate), including business information systems (Certificate), human resource management (Certificate); business analytics (MBA); business intelligence (MBA); communication (MA), including new media and marketing, public relations; community economic development (MBA); criminal justice (MBA); data analytics (MS); economics (MBA); engineering management (MBA); entrepreneurship (MBA); finance (MBA, MS, Graduate Certificate); finance/corporate finance (MS); finance/investments (MS); forensic accounting (MBA); forensic accounting and fraud examination (Graduate Certificate); healthcare informatics (MS); healthcare management (MBA); human resource management (MS); human resources (MBA); information technology (MS); information technology management (MBA); international business (PhD); Internet marketing (MBA); leadership (MBA); leadership of nonprofit organizations (Graduate Certificate); management (MS); marketing (MBA, MS, Graduate Certificate); music business (MBA); operations and project management (MS); operations and supply chain management (MBA, Graduate Certificate); organizational leadership (MS); project management (MBA, Graduate Certificate); public administration (MBA, Graduate Certificate); quantitative analysis (MBA); Six Sigma (Graduate Certificate); Six Sigma quality (MBA); social media marketing (MBA, Graduate Certificate); sport management

Sustainability Management

(MBA, MS, Graduate Certificate); sustainability and environmental compliance (MBA); MBA/Certificate. *Accreditation:* ACBSP. *Program availability:* Part-time, evening/weekend, online learning. Terminal master's awarded for partial completion of doctoral program. *Degree requirements:* For master's, one foreign language, comprehensive exam (for some programs), thesis or alternative; for doctorate, one foreign language, comprehensive exam, thesis/dissertation. *Entrance requirements:* For master's, minimum GPA of 2.5; for doctorate, GMAT. Additional exam requirements/recommendations for international students: Required—TOEFL (minimum score 500 paper-based). *Application deadline:* Applications are processed on a rolling basis. Application fee: $40. Electronic applications accepted. *Expenses: Tuition:* Part-time $627 per credit hour. Part-time tuition and fees vary according to campus/location and program. *Financial support:* Career-related internships or fieldwork, Federal Work-Study, institutionally sponsored loans, scholarships/grants, tuition waivers (partial), and unspecified assistantships available. Support available to part-time students. Financial award applicants required to submit FAFSA. *Unit head:* Dr. Bill Lightfoot, Dean, 603-644-3102, Fax: 603-644-3144. *Application contact:* Office of Graduate Admission, 888-327-SNHU, Fax: 603-644-3144, E-mail: enroll@snhu.edu.

South University, Graduate Programs, College of Business, Savannah, GA 31406. Offers corrections (MBA); entrepreneurship and small business (MBA); healthcare administration (MBA); hospitality management (MBA); leadership (MS); public administration (MPA); sustainability (MBA).

State University of New York College of Environmental Science and Forestry, Department of Paper and Bioprocess Engineering, Syracuse, NY 13210-2779. Offers biomaterials engineering (MS, PhD); bioprocess engineering (MPS, MS, PhD); bioprocessing (Advanced Certificate); paper science and engineering (MPS, MS, PhD); sustainable engineering management (MPS). *Program availability:* Part-time. *Faculty:* 13 full-time (2 women), 1 part-time/adjunct (0 women). *Students:* 25 full-time (12 women), 2 part-time (1 woman), 17 international. Average age 28. 23 applicants, 87% accepted, 13 enrolled. In 2017, 7 master's, 3 doctorates awarded. Terminal master's awarded for partial completion of doctoral program. *Degree requirements:* For master's, thesis; for doctorate, comprehensive exam, thesis/dissertation; for Advanced Certificate, 15 credit hours. *Entrance requirements:* For master's and doctorate, GRE General Test, minimum GPA of 3.0; for Advanced Certificate, BS, calculus plus science major. Additional exam requirements/recommendations for international students: Required—TOEFL (minimum score 550 paper-based; 80 iBT), IELTS (minimum score 6). *Application deadline:* For fall admission, 2/1 priority date for domestic and international students; for spring admission, 11/1 priority date for domestic and international students. Applications are processed on a rolling basis. Application fee: $60. Electronic applications accepted. *Expenses:* Tuition, state resident: full-time $10,870; part-time $453 per credit. Tuition, nonresident: full-time $22,210; part-time $925 per credit. *Required fees:* $1435; $70.85 per credit. One-time fee: $25 full-time. Part-time tuition and fees vary according to course load. *Financial support:* In 2017–18, 12 students received support. Unspecified assistantships available. Financial award application deadline: 6/30; financial award applicants required to submit FAFSA. *Faculty research:* Sustainable products and processes, biorefinery, pulping and papermaking, nanocellulose, bioconversions, process control and modeling. *Total annual research expenditures:* $1.2 million. *Unit head:* Dr. Bandaru Ramarao, Interim Chair, 315-470-6502, Fax: 315-470-6945, E-mail: bvramara@esf.edu. *Application contact:* Scott Shannon, Associate Provost and Dean, Instruction and Graduate Studies, 315-470-6599, Fax: 315-470-6978, E-mail: esfgrad@esf.edu.
Website: http://www.esf.edu/pbe/

Syracuse University, College of Engineering and Computer Science, CAS Program in Sustainable Enterprise, Syracuse, NY 13244. Offers CAS. *Unit head:* Dr. Todd Moss, Faculty Director, Sustainable Enterprise Partnership, 315-443-9215, E-mail: tmoss@syr.edu. *Application contact:* Kathleen Joyce, Assistant Dean, 315-443-2219, E-mail: topgrads@syr.edu.
Website: http://eng-cs.syr.edu/our-departments/mechanical-and-aerospace-engineering/graduate/academic-programs/?programID=1549&degree=graduate_certificate

The University of British Columbia, Faculty of Forestry, Program in Sustainable Forest Management, Vancouver, BC V6T 1Z1, Canada. Offers MSFM.

The University of British Columbia, Faculty of Science, Institute for Resources, Environment and Sustainability, Vancouver, BC V6T 1Z4, Canada. Offers M Sc, MA, PhD. *Degree requirements:* For master's, thesis; for doctorate, comprehensive exam, thesis/dissertation. *Entrance requirements:* Additional exam requirements/recommendations for international students: Required—TOEFL. Electronic applications accepted. *Expenses:* Contact institution. *Faculty research:* Land management, water resources, energy, environmental assessment, risk evaluation.

University of California, Berkeley, UC Berkeley Extension, Certificate Programs in Sustainability Studies, Berkeley, CA 94720-1500. Offers leadership in sustainability and environmental management (Professional Certificate); solar energy and green building (Professional Certificate); sustainable design (Professional Certificate).

University of California, Merced, Graduate Division, School of Engineering, Merced, CA 95343. Offers biological engineering and small scale technologies (MS, PhD); electrical engineering and computer science (MS, PhD); environmental systems (MS, PhD); management of innovation, sustainability, and technology (MM); mechanical engineering (MS); mechanical engineering and applied mechanics (PhD). *Faculty:* 55 full-time (13 women), 2 part-time/adjunct (1 woman). *Students:* 184 full-time (66 women), 1 part-time (0 women); includes 41 minority (2 Black or African American, non-Hispanic/Latino; 16 Asian, non-Hispanic/Latino; 18 Hispanic/Latino; 1 Native Hawaiian or other Pacific Islander, non-Hispanic/Latino; 4 Two or more races, non-Hispanic/Latino), 112 international. Average age 28. 348 applicants, 35% accepted, 55 enrolled. In 2017, 13 master's, 15 doctorates awarded. Terminal master's awarded for partial completion of doctoral program. *Degree requirements:* For master's, variable foreign language requirement, comprehensive exam, thesis or alternative; for doctorate, variable foreign language requirement, comprehensive exam, thesis/dissertation. *Entrance requirements:* For master's and doctorate, GRE. Additional exam requirements/recommendations for international students: Required—TOEFL (minimum score 550 paper-based; 80 iBT); Recommended—IELTS (minimum score 7). *Application deadline:* For fall admission, 1/15 priority date for domestic and international students. Applications are processed on a rolling basis. Application fee: $90 ($110 for international students). Electronic applications accepted. *Expenses:* Contact institution. *Financial support:* In 2017–18, 150 students received support, including 16 fellowships with full tuition reimbursements available (averaging $19,088 per year), 45 research assistantships with full tuition reimbursements available (averaging $18,389 per year), 89 teaching assistantships with full tuition reimbursements available (averaging $19,249 per year); scholarships/grants, traineeships, and health care benefits also available. Financial award application deadline: 1/15. *Faculty research:* Water resources, biotechnology, renewable energy, big data, cyber-physical systems. *Total annual research expenditures:* $3.3 million. *Unit head:* Dr. Mark Matsumoto, Dean, 209-228-4047, Fax: 209-228-4047, E-mail: mmatsumoto@ucmerced.edu. *Application contact:* Tsu Ya, Director of Admissions and Academic Services, 209-228-4521, Fax: 209-228-6906, E-mail: tya@ucmerced.edu.

University of Colorado Denver, Business School, Master of Business Administration Program, Denver, CO 80217. Offers bioinnovation and entrepreneurship (MBA); business intelligence (MBA); business strategy (MBA); business to business marketing (MBA); business to consumer marketing (MBA); change management (MBA); corporate financial management (MBA); enterprise technology management (MBA); entrepreneurship (MBA); health administration (MBA), including financial management, health administration, health information technologies, international health management and policy; human resources management (MBA); international business (MBA); investment management (MBA); managing for sustainability (MBA); sports and entertainment management (MBA). *Accreditation:* AACSB. *Program availability:* Part-time, evening/weekend, 100% online, blended/hybrid learning. *Degree requirements:* For master's, 48 semester hours, including 30 of core courses, 3 in international business, and 15 in electives from over 50 other business courses. *Entrance requirements:* For master's, GMAT, resume, official transcripts, essay, two letters of recommendation, financial statements (for international applicants). Additional exam requirements/recommendations for international students: Required—TOEFL (minimum score 560 paper-based; 83 iBT); Recommended—IELTS (minimum score 6.5). Electronic applications accepted. *Expenses:* Contact institution. *Faculty research:* Marketing, management, entrepreneurship, finance, health administration.

University of Colorado Denver, Business School, Program in Management and Organization, Denver, CO 80217. Offers business strategy (MS); change and innovation (MS); enterprise technology management (MS); entrepreneurship and innovation (MS); global management (MS); leadership (MS); managing for sustainability (MS); managing human resources (MS); sports and entertainment management (MS). *Accreditation:* AACSB. *Program availability:* Part-time, evening/weekend, online learning. *Degree requirements:* For master's, 30 semester hours (12 of required courses, 12 of management electives, and 6 of free electives). *Entrance requirements:* For master's, GMAT, resume, two letters of recommendation, essay, financial statements (for international applicants). Additional exam requirements/recommendations for international students: Required—TOEFL (minimum score 525 paper-based; 71 iBT); Recommended—IELTS (minimum score 6.5). Electronic applications accepted. *Expenses:* Contact institution. *Faculty research:* Human resource management, management of catastrophe, turnaround strategies.

University of Louisville, School of Interdisciplinary and Graduate Studies, Louisville, KY 40292. Offers interdisciplinary studies (MA, MS, PhD), including bioethics and medical humanities (MA), bioinformatics (PhD), sustainability (MA, MS), translational bioengineering (PhD), translational neuroscience (PhD). *Program availability:* Part-time. *Students:* 26 full-time (17 women), 12 part-time (6 women); includes 5 minority (1 Black or African American, non-Hispanic/Latino; 2 Two or more races, non-Hispanic/Latino), 9 international. Average age 31. 29 applicants, 38% accepted, 11 enrolled. *Degree requirements:* For master's, variable foreign language requirement, comprehensive exam (for some programs), thesis (for some programs); for doctorate, variable foreign language requirement, comprehensive exam, thesis/dissertation. *Entrance requirements:* For master's and doctorate, GRE General Test, 3 letters of recommendation, transcripts from previous post-secondary educational institutions. Additional exam requirements/recommendations for international students: Required—TOEFL (minimum score 550 paper-based; 79 iBT), IELTS (minimum score 6.5). *Application deadline:* For fall admission, 12/1 priority date for domestic and international students; for winter admission, 11/1 for domestic students, 6/1 for international students; for spring admission, 11/1 for domestic students, 6/1 for international students; for summer admission, 4/1 for domestic students, 1/1 for international students. Applications are processed on a rolling basis. Application fee: $65. Electronic applications accepted. *Expenses:* Tuition, state resident: full-time $12,246; part-time $681 per credit hour. Tuition, nonresident: full-time $25,486; part-time $1417 per credit hour. *Required fees:* $196. Tuition and fees vary according to course load, program and reciprocity agreements. *Financial support:* In 2017–18, 120 fellowships with full tuition reimbursements (averaging $20,000 per year) were awarded. Financial award application deadline: 1/15. *Unit head:* Dr. Beth A. Boehm, Dean and Vice Provost for Graduate Affairs, 502-852-6495, E-mail: beth.boehm@louisville.edu. *Application contact:* Dr. Paul DeMarco, Associate Dean, 502-852-6490, E-mail: gradadm@louisville.edu.
Website: http://www.graduate.louisville.edu

University of New Hampshire, Graduate School, College of Liberal Arts, Department of Political Science, Durham, NH 03824. Offers political science (MA, Postbaccalaureate Certificate), including political science (MA), sustainability politics and policy (Postbaccalaureate Certificate). *Program availability:* Part-time. *Students:* 12 full-time (7 women), 30 part-time (16 women); includes 5 minority (2 Black or African American, non-Hispanic/Latino; 1 Asian, non-Hispanic/Latino; 1 Hispanic/Latino; 1 Two or more races, non-Hispanic/Latino), 1 international. Average age 30. 27 applicants, 70% accepted, 13 enrolled. In 2017, 13 master's awarded. *Entrance requirements:* For master's, GRE General Test. Additional exam requirements/recommendations for international students: Required—TOEFL (minimum score 550 paper-based; 80 iBT). *Application deadline:* For fall admission, 4/1 for domestic and international students; for spring admission, 11/1 for domestic students. Application fee: $65. Electronic applications accepted. *Financial support:* In 2017–18, 4 students received support, including 3 teaching assistantships; fellowships, research assistantships, career-related internships or fieldwork, Federal Work-Study, scholarships/grants, and tuition waivers (full and partial) also available. Support available to part-time students. Financial award application deadline: 2/15. *Unit head:* Mary Malone, Chair, 603-862-1406. *Application contact:* Tama Andrews, Graduate Program Coordinator, 603-862-2321.
Website: http://cola.unh.edu/political-science

University of Portland, Dr. Robert B. Pamplin, Jr. School of Business, Portland, OR 97203-5798. Offers entrepreneurship (MBA); finance (MBA, MS); health care management (MBA); marketing (MBA); nonprofit management (EMBA); operations and technology management (MBA, MS); sustainability (MBA). *Accreditation:* AACSB. *Program availability:* Part-time, evening/weekend. *Entrance requirements:* For master's, GMAT, minimum GPA of 3.0, resume, 2 letters of recommendation. Additional exam requirements/recommendations for international students: Required—TOEFL (minimum score 570 paper-based; 89 iBT), IELTS (minimum score 7). *Expenses:* Contact institution.

University of Saint Francis, Graduate School, Keith Busse School of Business and Entrepreneurial Leadership, Fort Wayne, IN 46808-3994. Offers business administration (MBA), including sustainability; environmental health (MEH); healthcare administration (MHA); organizational leadership (MOL). *Accreditation:* ACBSP. *Program availability:* Part-time, evening/weekend, online only, 100% online. *Faculty:* 4 full-time (3 women), 11 part-time/adjunct (1 woman). *Students:* 75 full-time (43 women), 108 part-time (59 women); includes 37 minority (21 Black or African American, non-Hispanic/Latino; 1 Asian, non-Hispanic/Latino; 11 Hispanic/Latino; 1 Native Hawaiian or other Pacific Islander, non-Hispanic/Latino; 3 Two or more races, non-Hispanic/Latino). Average age 34. 101 applicants, 98% accepted, 75 enrolled. In 2017, 133 master's awarded. *Entrance requirements:* For master's, GMAT (if cumulative GPA is below 2.75 with less than five years' professional work experience), minimum undergraduate GPA of 2.75; statement of professional goals; resume. Additional exam requirements/

recommendations for international students: Required—TOEFL (minimum score 550 paper-based) or IELTS (minimum score 6.5). *Application deadline:* For fall admission, 7/1 for international students; for spring admission, 11/1 for international students; for summer admission, 3/1 for international students. Applications are processed on a rolling basis. Application fee: $0. Electronic applications accepted. *Expenses:* $475 per hour. *Financial support:* Application deadline: 4/15; applicants required to submit FAFSA. *Unit head:* Dr. Robert Lee, Dean, 260-399-7700 Ext. 8304, Fax: 260-399-8174, E-mail: rlee@sf.edu. *Application contact:* Kyle Richardson, Associate Director of Enrollment Services for Adult Learning, 260-399-7700 Ext. 6310, Fax: 260-399-8152, E-mail: krichardson@sf.edu.
Website: https://business.sf.edu/graduate/

University of Saskatchewan, College of Graduate Studies and Research, School of Environment and Sustainability, Saskatoon, SK S7N 5A2, Canada. Offers MES.

University of Southern Maine, College of Management and Human Service, School of Business, Portland, ME 04104-9300. Offers accounting (MBA); business administration (MBA); finance (MBA); health management and policy (MBA); sustainability (MBA); JD/MBA; MBA/MSA; MBA/MSN; MS/MBA. *Accreditation:* AACSB. *Program availability:* Part-time, evening/weekend. *Entrance requirements:* For master's, GMAT or GRE, minimum AACSB index of 1100. Additional exam requirements/recommendations for international students: Required—TOEFL (minimum score 550 paper-based; 79 iBT). Electronic applications accepted. *Faculty research:* Economic development, management information systems, real options, system dynamics, simulation.

University of South Florida, College of Global Sustainability, Tampa, FL 33620-9951. Offers energy, global, water and sustainable tourism (Graduate Certificate); global sustainability (MA), including building sustainable enterprise, climate change and sustainability, coastal sustainability, entrepreneurship, food sustainability and security, sustainability policy, sustainable energy, sustainable tourism, water. *Faculty:* 2 full-time (0 women). *Students:* 124 full-time (64 women), 77 part-time (45 women); includes 33 minority (12 Black or African American, non-Hispanic/Latino; 1 American Indian or Alaska Native, non-Hispanic/Latino; 1 Asian, non-Hispanic/Latino; 14 Hispanic/Latino; 5 Two or more races, non-Hispanic/Latino; 87 international. Average age 28. 220 applicants, 65% accepted, 101 enrolled. In 2017, 50 master's awarded. *Degree requirements:* For master's, comprehensive exam (for some programs), thesis or alternative, internship. *Entrance requirements:* For master's, minimum GPA of 3.0 in undergraduate coursework; at least two letters of recommendation (one must be academic); 200-250 word essay on student's background, professional goals, and reasons for seeking degree. Additional exam requirements/recommendations for international students: Required—TOEFL (minimum score 550 paper-based; 79 iBT). *Application deadline:* For fall admission, 6/1 for domestic students, 5/1 for international students; for spring admission, 10/15 for domestic students, 9/15 for international students. Electronic applications accepted. *Financial support:* In 2017–18, 22 students received support. *Faculty research:* Global sustainability, integrated resource management, systems thinking, green communities, entrepreneurship, ecotourism. *Total annual research expenditures:* $107,829. *Unit head:* Dr. Govindan Parayil, Dean, 813-974-9694, E-mail: gparayil@usf.edu.
Website: http://psgs.usf.edu/

University of Vermont, Graduate College, Grossman School of Business, Program in Sustainable Innovation, Burlington, VT 05405. Offers MBA, MBA/JD. MBA/JD offered in collaboration with Vermont Law School. *Students:* 31 (14 women). 61 applicants, 84% accepted, 31 enrolled. In 2017, 16 master's awarded. *Entrance requirements:* For master's, GMAT or GRE, resume. Additional exam requirements/recommendations for international students: Required—TOEFL (minimum iBT score of 90) or IELTS (6.5). *Application deadline:* For summer admission, 2/15 priority date for domestic and international students. Applications are processed on a rolling basis. Electronic applications accepted. *Expenses:* $646 per credit in-state, $1,100 per credit out-of-state. *Financial support:* Scholarships/grants available. *Unit head:* David Jones, Director, 802-656-4611, E-mail: si-mba@uvm.edu.
Website: https://www.uvm.edu/business/simba_sustainable_innovation_mba

University of Wisconsin–Green Bay, Graduate Studies, Program in Sustainable Management, Green Bay, WI 54311-7001. Offers MS. Program held jointly with four other University of Wisconsin System campuses: Oshkosh, Parkside, Stout, and Superior. *Program availability:* Part-time, evening/weekend, online only, 100% online. *Degree requirements:* For master's, capstone project. *Entrance requirements:* For master's, bachelor's degree from nationally-accredited university with minimum cumulative GPA of 3.0. Additional exam requirements/recommendations for international students: Required—TOEFL. Electronic applications accepted.

University of Wisconsin–Parkside, College of Natural and Health Sciences, Program in Sustainable Management, Kenosha, WI 53141-2000. Offers MS. *Program availability:* Online learning.

University of Wisconsin–Stout, Graduate School, College of Management, Program in Sustainable Management, Menomonie, WI 54751. Offers MS. Program offered in collaboration with University of Wisconsin-Parkside, University of Wisconsin-River Falls and University of Wisconisn-Superior. *Program availability:* Online learning.

University of Wisconsin–Superior, Graduate Division, Department of Business and Economics, Superior, WI 54880-4500. Offers sustainable management (MS). Electronic applications accepted.

Section 14
Marketing

This section contains a directory of institutions offering graduate work in marketing, followed by an in-depth entry submitted by an institution that chose to prepare a detailed program description. Additional information about programs listed in the directory but not augmented by an in-depth entry may be obtained by writing directly to the dean of a graduate school or chair of a department at the address given in the directory.

For programs offering related work, see also in this book *Advertising and Public Relations, Business Administration and Management,* and *Hospitality Management.* In another guide in this series:

Graduate Programs in the Humanities, Arts & Social Sciences

See *Communication and Media* and *Public, Regional, and Industrial Affairs*

CONTENTS

Program Directories

Featured Schools: Displays and Close-Ups

See also:

Marketing

Abilene Christian University, College of Graduate and Professional Studies, Program in Business Administration, Addison, TX 75001. Offers business analytics (MBA); corporate finance (MBA); general management (MBA); healthcare administration (MBA); human resource management (MBA); international business (MBA); management: business analytics (MS); management: healthcare administration (MS); management: international business (MS); management: marketing (MS); management: operations and supply chain management (MS); marketing (MBA); nonprofit leadership (MBA); operations and supply chain management (MBA). *Program availability:* Part-time, online only, 100% online. *Faculty:* 2 full-time (0 women), 6 part-time/adjunct (2 women). *Students:* 109 full-time (47 women), 51 part-time (22 women); includes 42 minority (33 Black or African American, non-Hispanic/Latino; 1 American Indian or Alaska Native, non-Hispanic/Latino; 2 Asian, non-Hispanic/Latino; 6 Hispanic/Latino). 125 applicants, 65% accepted, 58 enrolled. *Entrance requirements:* Additional exam requirements/recommendations for international students: Required—TOEFL (minimum score 80 iBT), IELTS (minimum score 6). *Application deadline:* For fall admission, 8/14 priority date for domestic students; for winter admission, 10/1 priority date for domestic students; for spring admission, 12/15 priority date for domestic students; for summer admission, 4/15 priority date for domestic students. Applications are processed on a rolling basis. Application fee: $50. Electronic applications accepted. *Expenses:* $700 per hour. *Financial support:* In 2017–18, 2 students received support. Application deadline: 4/1; applicants required to submit FAFSA. *Faculty research:* Organizational structure, financial management, cost accounting, unit analysis management. *Unit head:* Phil Vardiman, Program Director, 325-674-2153, E-mail: pxv02b@acu.edu. *Application contact:* Graduate Advisor, 817-219-7300, E-mail: gradonline@acu.edu.
Website: http://www.acu.edu/online/academics/mba-business-administration.html

Adelphi University, Robert B. Willumstad School of Business, MBA Program, Garden City, NY 11530-0701. Offers accounting (MBA); finance (MBA); health services administration (MBA); human resource management (MBA); management (MBA); management information systems (MBA); marketing (MBA); sport management (MBA). *Accreditation:* AACSB. *Program availability:* Part-time, evening/weekend. *Students:* 257 full-time (110 women), 78 part-time (38 women); includes 56 minority (18 Black or African American, non-Hispanic/Latino; 16 Asian, non-Hispanic/Latino; 19 Hispanic/Latino; 3 Two or more races, non-Hispanic/Latino), 181 international. Average age 28. 435 applicants, 61% accepted, 205 enrolled. In 2017, 130 master's awarded. *Degree requirements:* For master's, capstone course. *Entrance requirements:* For master's, GMAT, 2 letters of recommendation. Additional exam requirements/recommendations for international students: Required—TOEFL (minimum score 550 paper-based; 80 iBT), IELTS (minimum score 6.5). *Application deadline:* For fall admission, 4/1 for international students; for spring admission, 11/1 for international students. Applications are processed on a rolling basis. Application fee: $50. Electronic applications accepted. *Expenses:* Contact institution. *Financial support:* Research assistantships with partial tuition reimbursements, career-related internships or fieldwork, Federal Work-Study, institutionally sponsored loans, scholarships/grants, tuition waivers (partial), and unspecified assistantships available. Financial award application deadline: 3/1; financial award applicants required to submit FAFSA. *Faculty research:* Supply chain management, distribution channels, productivity benchmark analysis, data envelopment analysis, financial portfolio analysis. *Unit head:* Dr. Rakesh Gupta, Associate Dean, 516-877-4629. *Application contact:* E-mail: graduateadmissions@adelphi.edu.
Website: http://business.adelphi.edu/degree-programs/graduate-degree-programs/m-b-a/

American Business & Technology University, Programs in Business Administration, Saint Joseph, MO 64506. Offers business administration (MBA); financial management (MBA); global business management (MBA); information systems management (MBA); marketing and social media (MBA); project and operations management (MBA); public accounting (MBA). *Program availability:* Online learning.

American College of Thessaloniki, Department of Business Administration, Pylea, Greece. Offers banking and finance (MBA); entrepreneurship (MBA, Certificate); finance (Certificate); management (MBA, Certificate); marketing (MBA, Certificate). *Program availability:* Part-time, evening/weekend. *Degree requirements:* For master's, thesis. *Entrance requirements:* For master's, bachelor's degree. Additional exam requirements/recommendations for international students: Recommended—TOEFL. Electronic applications accepted.

American InterContinental University Online, Program in Business Administration, Schaumburg, IL 60173. Offers accounting and finance (MBA); finance (MBA); healthcare management (MBA); human resource management (MBA); international business (MBA); management (MBA); marketing (MBA); operations management (MBA); organizational psychology and development (MBA); project management (MBA). *Accreditation:* ACBSP. *Program availability:* Evening/weekend, online learning. *Entrance requirements:* Additional exam requirements/recommendations for international students: Required—TOEFL (minimum score 550 paper-based). Electronic applications accepted.

American University, Kogod School of Business, Department of Marketing, Washington, DC 20016-8044. Offers MS. *Program availability:* Part-time, evening/weekend. *Students:* 20 full-time (18 women); includes 6 minority (2 Black or African American, non-Hispanic/Latino; 1 Hispanic/Latino; 3 Two or more races, non-Hispanic/Latino), 7 international. Average age 25. 74 applicants, 54% accepted, 19 enrolled. In 2017, 15 master's awarded. *Entrance requirements:* For master's, GMAT/GRE, resume, personal statement, 2 letters of recommendation, transcripts, interview. Additional exam requirements/recommendations for international students: Required—TOEFL (minimum score 550 paper-based; 100 iBT). *Application deadline:* For fall admission, 1/15 priority date for domestic students, 1/15 for international students; for spring admission, 10/15 priority date for domestic students, 10/15 for international students. Application fee: $100. *Expenses:* Contact institution. *Financial support:* Application deadline: 2/1; applicants required to submit FAFSA. *Faculty research:* Internet marketing, database marketing, consumer behavior, advertising research, public policy in marketing. *Unit head:* Dr. Sonya Grier, Department Chair, 202-885-1971, E-mail: sonya.grier@american.edu. *Application contact:* Jason Garner, Director, Graduate Admissions, 202-885-1922, E-mail: jgarner@american.edu.
Website: http://www.american.edu/kogod/graduate/index.cfm

The American University in Dubai, Graduate Programs, Dubai, United Arab Emirates. Offers construction management (MS); education (M Ed); finance (MBA); generalist (MBA); marketing (MBA). *Program availability:* Part-time, evening/weekend. *Degree requirements:* For master's, thesis optional. *Entrance requirements:* For master's, GMAT (for MBA); GRE (for M Ed and MS), minimum undergraduate GPA of 3.0, official transcripts, two reference forms, curriculum vitae/resume, statement of career objectives, work experience. Additional exam requirements/recommendations for

international students: Required—TOEFL (minimum score 550 paper-based; 79 iBT). Electronic applications accepted.

Anderson University, College of Business, Anderson, SC 29621-4035. Offers business administration (MBA); healthcare leadership (MBA); human resources (MBA); marketing (MBA); organizational leadership (MOL); supply chain management (MBA). *Accreditation:* ACBSP. *Expenses:* Contact institution. *Financial support:* Tuition waivers available. Financial award application deadline: 3/1; financial award applicants required to submit FAFSA. *Unit head:* Steve Nail, Dean, 864-MBA-6000. *Application contact:* Mallory Knight, Graduate Admission Counselor, 864-231-2182, Fax: 864-231-2115, E-mail: malloryknight@andersonuniversity.edu.
Website: http://www.andersonuniversity.edu/business

Aquinas College, School of Management, Grand Rapids, MI 49506. Offers marketing management (MM); organizational leadership (MM); sustainable business (MM). *Program availability:* Part-time, evening/weekend. *Students:* 11 full-time (6 women), 30 part-time (20 women); includes 7 minority (2 Black or African American, non-Hispanic/Latino; 4 Hispanic/Latino). *Entrance requirements:* For master's, GMAT, minimum undergraduate GPA of 2.75, 2 years of work experience. Additional exam requirements/recommendations for international students: Required—TOEFL (minimum score 550 paper-based). *Application deadline:* Applications are processed on a rolling basis. Application fee: $0. *Expenses:* Contact institution. *Financial support:* Scholarships/grants available. Support available to part-time students. Financial award application deadline: 3/15; financial award applicants required to submit FAFSA. *Unit head:* Cynthia G. VanGelderen, Interim Director, 616-632-2922, Fax: 616-732-4489. *Application contact:* Lynn Atkins-Rykert, Program Coordinator, 616-632-2925, Fax: 616-732-4489, E-mail: atkinlyn@aquinas.edu.

Argosy University, Atlanta, College of Business, Atlanta, GA 30328. Offers accounting (DBA); corporate compliance (MBA); customized professional concentration (MBA, DBA); finance (MBA); healthcare administration (MBA); information systems (DBA); information systems management (MBA); international business (MBA, DBA); management (MBA, MSM, DBA); marketing (MBA, DBA). *Accreditation:* ACBSP.

Argosy University, Chicago, College of Business, Chicago, IL 60601. Offers accounting (DBA); customized professional concentration (MBA, DBA); finance (MBA); fraud examination (MBA); global business sustainability (DBA); healthcare administration (MBA); information systems (DBA); information systems management (MBA); international business (MBA, DBA); management (MBA, MSM, DBA); marketing (MBA, DBA); organizational leadership (Ed D); public administration (MBA); sustainable management (MBA). *Accreditation:* ACBSP. *Program availability:* Online learning.

Argosy University, Hawai`i, College of Business, Honolulu, HI 96813. Offers accounting (DBA); corporate compliance (MBA); customized professional concentration (MBA, DBA); finance (MBA, Certificate); fraud examination (MBA); global business sustainability (DBA); healthcare administration (MBA, Certificate); information systems (DBA); information systems management (MBA, Certificate); international business (MBA, DBA, Certificate); management (MBA, MSM, DBA); marketing (MBA, DBA, Certificate); organizational leadership (Ed D); public administration (MBA); sustainable management (MBA).

Argosy University, Los Angeles, College of Business, Los Angeles, CA 90045. Offers accounting (DBA); corporate compliance (MBA); customized professional concentration (MBA, DBA); finance (MBA); fraud examination (MBA); global business sustainability (DBA); healthcare administration (MBA); information systems (DBA); information systems management (MBA); international business (MBA, DBA); management (MBA, MSM, DBA); marketing (MBA, DBA); organizational leadership (Ed D); public administration (MBA); sustainable management (MBA).

Argosy University, Northern Virginia, College of Business, Arlington, VA 22209. Offers accounting (DBA); customized professional concentration (MBA, DBA); finance (MBA); fraud examination (MBA); global business sustainability (DBA); healthcare administration (MBA); information systems (DBA); information systems management (MBA); international business (MBA, DBA, Certificate); management (MBA, MSM, DBA); marketing (MBA, DBA, Certificate); organizational leadership (Ed D); public administration (MBA); sustainable management (MBA).

Argosy University, Orange County, College of Business, Orange, CA 92868. Offers accounting (DBA, Adv C); corporate compliance (MBA); customized professional concentration (MBA, DBA); finance (MBA, Certificate); fraud examination (MBA); global business sustainability (DBA); healthcare administration (MBA, Certificate); information systems (DBA, Adv C, Certificate); information systems management (MBA); international business (MBA, DBA, Adv C, Certificate); management (MBA, MSM, DBA, Adv C); marketing (MBA, DBA, Adv C, Certificate); organizational leadership (Ed D); public administration (MBA, Certificate); sustainable management (MBA).

Argosy University, Phoenix, College of Business, Phoenix, AZ 85021. Offers accounting (DBA); corporate compliance (MBA); customized professional concentration (MBA, DBA); finance (MBA); fraud examination (MBA); global business sustainability (DBA); healthcare administration (MBA); information systems (DBA); information systems management (MBA); international business (MBA, DBA); management (MBA, DBA); marketing (MBA, DBA); public administration (MBA); sustainable management (MBA).

Argosy University, Seattle, College of Business, Seattle, WA 98121. Offers accounting (DBA); corporate compliance (MBA); customized professional concentration (MBA, DBA); finance (MBA); fraud examination (MBA); global business sustainability (DBA); healthcare administration (MBA); information systems (DBA); information systems management (MBA); international business (MBA, DBA); management (MBA, MSM, DBA); marketing (MBA, DBA); organizational leadership (Ed D); public administration (MBA); sustainable management (MBA).

Argosy University, Tampa, College of Business, Tampa, FL 33607. Offers accounting (DBA); corporate compliance (MBA); customized professional concentration (MBA, DBA); finance (MBA); fraud examination (MBA); global business sustainability (DBA); healthcare administration (MBA); information systems (DBA); information systems management (MBA); international business (MBA, DBA); management (MBA, MSM, DBA); marketing (MBA, DBA); organizational leadership (Ed D); public administration (MBA); sustainable management (MBA).

Argosy University, Twin Cities, College of Business, Eagan, MN 55121. Offers accounting (DBA); customized professional concentration (MBA, DBA); finance (MBA); fraud examination (MBA); global business sustainability (DBA); healthcare administration (MBA); information systems (DBA); information systems management (MBA); international business (MBA, DBA); management (MBA, MSM, DBA); marketing (MBA, DBA); organizational leadership (Ed D); public administration (MBA); sustainable management (MBA).

Arizona State University at the Tempe campus, W. P. Carey School of Business, Department of Marketing, Tempe, AZ 85287-4106. Offers business administration (PhD), including marketing; real estate development (MRED). *Program availability:* Part-time, evening/weekend, online learning. *Degree requirements:* For master's, thesis or alternative, capstone project, interactive Program of Study (iPOS) submitted before completing 50 percent of required credit hours; for doctorate, comprehensive exam, thesis/dissertation, interactive Program of Study (iPOS) submitted before completing 50 percent of required credit hours. *Entrance requirements:* For master's, GMAT, GRE, or LSAT, minimum GPA of 3.0 in last 2 years of work leading to bachelor's degree, 3 personal references, resume, official transcripts, personal statement; for doctorate, GMAT, minimum GPA of 3.0 in last 2 years of work leading to bachelor's degree, 3 letters of recommendation, personal statement/essay. Additional exam requirements/ recommendations for international students: Required—TOEFL (minimum score 550 paper-based; 80 iBT), IELTS (minimum score 6.5). Electronic applications accepted. *Expenses:* Contact institution. *Faculty research:* Service marketing and management, strategic marketing, customer portfolio management, characteristics and skills of high-performing managers, market orientation, market segmentation, consumer behavior, marketing strategy, new product development, management of innovation, social influences on consumption, e-commerce, market research methodology.

Arizona State University at the Tempe campus, W. P. Carey School of Business, Program in Business Administration, Tempe, AZ 85287-4906. Offers entrepreneurship (MBA); finance (MBA); health sector management (MBA); international business (MBA); leadership (MBA); marketing (MBA); organizational behavior (PhD); strategic management (MBA, PhD); supply chain management (MBA, PhD); JD/MBA; MBA/M Acc; MBA/M Arch. *Accreditation:* AACSB. *Program availability:* Part-time, evening/weekend, online learning. Terminal master's awarded for partial completion of doctoral program. *Degree requirements:* For master's, thesis or alternative, internship, interactive Program of Study (iPOS) submitted before completing 50 percent of required credit hours; for doctorate, comprehensive exam, thesis/dissertation, interactive Program of Study (iPOS) submitted before completing 50 percent of required credit hours. *Entrance requirements:* For master's, GMAT, minimum GPA of 3.0 in last 2 years of work leading to bachelor's degree, 2 letters of recommendation, professional resume, official transcripts, 3 essays; for doctorate, GMAT or GRE, minimum GPA of 3.0 in last 2 years of work leading to bachelor's degree, 3 letters of recommendation, resume, personal statement/essay. Additional exam requirements/recommendations for international students: Required—TOEFL (minimum score 550 paper-based; 80 iBT), IELTS (minimum score 6.5). Electronic applications accepted. *Expenses:* Contact institution.

Ashworth College, Graduate Programs, Norcross, GA 30092. Offers business administration (MBA); criminal justice (MS); health care administration (MBA, MS); human resource management (MBA, MS); international business (MBA); management (MS); marketing (MBA, MS).

Assumption College, Business Studies Program, Worcester, MA 01609-1296. Offers accounting (MBA); business studies (CAGS); finance/economics (MBA); human resources (MBA); international business (MBA); management (MBA); marketing (MBA); nonprofit leadership (MBA). *Program availability:* Part-time, evening/weekend. *Faculty:* 5 full-time (1 woman), 21 part-time/adjunct (6 women). *Students:* 29 full-time (13 women), 87 part-time (50 women); includes 15 minority (1 Black or African American, non-Hispanic/Latino; 4 Asian, non-Hispanic/Latino; 8 Hispanic/Latino; 2 Two or more races, non-Hispanic/Latino), 4 international. Average age 29. 34 applicants, 100% accepted, 26 enrolled. In 2017, 81 master's, 2 other advanced degrees awarded. *Degree requirements:* For master's, capstone. *Entrance requirements:* For master's, bachelor's degree, three letters of recommendation, official transcripts, personal statement, current resume; for CAGS, MBA or equivalent degree in a closely related field, three letters of recommendation, official transcripts, personal statement, current resume. Additional exam requirements/recommendations for international students: Required—TOEFL (minimum score 540 paper-based; 76 iBT), IELTS (minimum score 6). *Application deadline:* For fall admission, 8/10 priority date for domestic and international students; for spring admission, 1/4 priority date for domestic and international students; for summer admission, 5/10 priority date for domestic and international students. Application fee: $30. Electronic applications accepted. *Expenses:* Tuition: Full-time $11,952; part-time $664 per credit. *Required fees:* $70 per term. *Financial support:* In 2017–18, 19 students received support. Tuition waivers (full and partial), unspecified assistantships, and institutional discounts available. Financial award applicants required to submit FAFSA. *Faculty research:* Workplace diversity, dynamics of team interaction, utilization of leased employees, experiential learning project on due diligence market for prostheses. *Unit head:* Dr. Robin Frkal, Director, 508-767-7622, E-mail: ra.frkal@ assumption.edu. *Application contact:* Karen Stoyanoff, Director of Recruitment for Graduate Enrollment, 508-767-7442, Fax: 508-799-4412, E-mail: graduate@ assumption.edu.
Website: http://graduate.assumption.edu/mba/assumption-mba

Averett University, Master of Business Administration Program, Danville, VA 24541. Offers business administration (MBA); human resources management (MBA); leadership (MBA); marketing (MBA). *Program availability:* Part-time, evening/weekend, 100% online, blended/hybrid learning. *Faculty:* 7 full-time (0 women), 12 part-time/ adjunct (4 women). *Students:* 53 full-time (28 women), 129 part-time (83 women); includes 82 minority (65 Black or African American, non-Hispanic/Latino; 1 American Indian or Alaska Native, non-Hispanic/Latino; 5 Asian, non-Hispanic/Latino; 4 Hispanic/Latino; 7 Two or more races, non-Hispanic/Latino). Average age 38. 88 applicants, 81% accepted, 65 enrolled. In 2017, 129 master's awarded. *Degree requirements:* For master's, 41-credit core curriculum, minimum GPA of 3.0 throughout program, no more than 2 grades of C, completion of degree requirements within six years from start of program. *Entrance requirements:* For master's, minimum cumulative GPA of 3.0 over the last 60 semester hours of undergraduate study toward a baccalaureate degree, official transcripts, three years of full-time work experience, three letters of recommendation, current resume. Additional exam requirements/recommendations for international students: Required—TOEFL (minimum score 600 paper-based; 100 iBT). *Application deadline:* Applications are processed on a rolling basis. Electronic applications accepted. *Expenses:* $11,790. *Financial support:* Application deadline: 3/1; applicants required to submit FAFSA. *Unit head:* Dr. Peggy C. Wright, Chair, Business Department, 434-791-7118, E-mail: pwright@averett.edu. *Application contact:* Melissa Anderson, Director of Admissions, Graduate and Professional Studies, 804-729-8285, E-mail: manderson@averett.edu.
Website: http://gps.averett.edu/programs/master-degrees/

Avila University, School of Business, Kansas City, MO 64145-1698. Offers accounting (MBA); finance (MBA); health care administration (MBA); international business (MBA); management (MBA); management information systems (MBA); marketing (MBA). *Program availability:* Part-time, evening/weekend. *Faculty:* 6 full-time (2 women), 6 part-time/adjunct (2 women). *Students:* 49 full-time (19 women), 29 part-time (14 women); includes 16 minority (12 Black or African American, non-Hispanic/Latino; 1 Asian, non-Hispanic/Latino; 3 Hispanic/Latino), 19 international. Average age 32. 51 applicants, 47% accepted, 20 enrolled. In 2017, 31 master's awarded. *Degree requirements:* For master's, comprehensive exam, capstone course. *Entrance requirements:* For master's, GMAT (minimum score 420), minimum GPA of 3.0, interview. Additional exam

requirements/recommendations for international students: Required—TOEFL (minimum score 550 paper-based). *Application deadline:* For fall admission, 7/30 priority date for domestic and international students; for winter admission, 11/30 priority date for domestic and international students; for spring admission, 2/28 priority date for domestic and international students; for summer admission, 6/1 priority date for domestic and international students. Applications are processed on a rolling basis. Application fee: $0. Electronic applications accepted. *Expenses:* Contact institution. *Financial support:* In 2017–18, 18 students received support. Career-related internships or fieldwork and scholarships/grants available. Support available to part-time students. Financial award applicants required to submit FAFSA. *Faculty research:* Leadership characteristics, financial hedging, group dynamics. *Unit head:* Dr. Wendy L. Acker, Interim Dean, 816-501-3720, Fax: 816-501-2463, E-mail: wendy.acker@avila.edu. *Application contact:* Brandon Black, MBA Admission Advisor, 816-501-3601, Fax: 816-501-2463, E-mail: brandon.black@avila.edu.
Website: https://www.avila.edu/mrk/mba

Azusa Pacific University, School of Business and Management, Azusa, CA 91702-7000. Offers accounting (MBA); business administration (MBA); entrepreneurship (MBA); finance (MBA); international business (MBA); marketing (MBA); organizational science (MBA); professional accountancy (M Acc); sport management (MBA). *Program availability:* Part-time, evening/weekend. *Degree requirements:* For master's, thesis (for some programs), final project. *Entrance requirements:* For master's, GMAT, minimum GPA of 3.0. Additional exam requirements/recommendations for international students: Required—TOEFL (minimum score 600 paper-based). *Expenses:* Contact institution. *Faculty research:* Gender issues, financial risk, leadership and ethics, marketing strategy.

Baker College Center for Graduate Studies–Online, Graduate Programs, Flint, MI 48507. Offers accounting (MBA); business administration (DBA); finance (MBA); general business (MBA); health care management (MBA); human resources management (MBA); information management (MBA); leadership studies (MBA); management information systems (MSIS); marketing (MBA). *Program availability:* Part-time, evening/ weekend, online learning. *Degree requirements:* For master's, portfolio. *Entrance requirements:* For master's, 3 years of work experience, minimum undergraduate GPA of 2.5, writing sample, 3 letters of recommendation; for doctorate, MBA or acceptable related master's degree from accredited association, 5 years work experience, minimum graduate GPA of 3.25, writing sample, 3 professional references. Additional exam requirements/recommendations for international students: Required—TOEFL (minimum score 550 paper-based). Electronic applications accepted.

Barry University, Andreas School of Business, Graduate Certificate Programs, Miami Shores, FL 33161-6695. Offers finance (Certificate); health services administration (Certificate); international business (Certificate); management (Certificate); management information systems (Certificate); marketing (Certificate).

Baruch College of the City University of New York, Zicklin School of Business, Department of Marketing and International Business, New York, NY 10010-5585. Offers international business (MBA); marketing (MBA, MS, PhD). PhD offered jointly with Graduate School and University Center of the City University of New York. *Program availability:* Part-time, evening/weekend. *Degree requirements:* For doctorate, comprehensive exam, thesis/dissertation. *Entrance requirements:* For master's, GMAT, 2 letters of recommendation, resume, 2 years of work experience; for doctorate, GMAT. Additional exam requirements/recommendations for international students: Required—TOEFL (minimum score 590 paper-based), TWE (minimum score 5).

Bayamón Central University, Graduate Programs, Program in Business Administration, Bayamón, PR 00960-1725. Offers accounting (MBA); finance (MBA); general business (MBA); management (MBA); marketing (MBA). *Program availability:* Part-time, evening/weekend. *Degree requirements:* For master's, comprehensive exam (for some programs). *Entrance requirements:* For master's, EXADEP, bachelor's degree in business or related field.

Benedictine University, Graduate Programs, Program in Business Administration, Lisle, IL 60532. Offers accounting (MBA); entrepreneurship and managing innovation (MBA); financial management (MBA); health administration (MBA); human resource management (MBA); information systems security (MBA); international business (MBA); management consulting (MBA); management information systems (MBA); marketing management (MBA); operations management and logistics (MBA); organizational leadership (MBA). *Program availability:* Part-time, evening/weekend, online learning. *Entrance requirements:* For master's, GMAT. Additional exam requirements/ recommendations for international students: Required—TOEFL (minimum score 550 paper-based). Electronic applications accepted. *Faculty research:* Strategic leadership in professional organizations, sociology of professions, organizational change, social identity theory, applications to change management.

Bentley University, McCallum Graduate School of Business, Master's Program in Marketing Analytics, Waltham, MA 02452-4705. Offers MSMA. *Program availability:* Part-time, evening/weekend. *Faculty:* 71 full-time (25 women), 33 part-time/adjunct (15 women). *Students:* 66 full-time (48 women), 31 part-time (16 women); includes 7 minority (1 Black or African American, non-Hispanic/Latino; 3 Asian, non-Hispanic/ Latino; 3 Hispanic/Latino), 67 international. Average age 26. 183 applicants, 73% accepted, 47 enrolled. In 2017, 46 master's awarded. *Entrance requirements:* For master's, GMAT or GRE General Test, current resume; two letters of recommendation; official copies of all university-level transcripts; 2 essays. Additional exam requirements/ recommendations for international students: Required—TOEFL (minimum score 100) or IELTS (minimum score 7). *Application deadline:* Applications are processed on a rolling basis. Application fee: $75. Electronic applications accepted. *Expenses:* Tuition: Part-time $4445 per course. *Required fees:* $170 per unit. *Financial support:* In 2017–18, 30 students received support. Scholarships/grants available. Financial award application deadline: 6/1; financial award applicants required to submit FAFSA. *Faculty research:* Marketing information processing; blogging and social media; customer lifetime value and customer relationship management; measuring and improving productivity; online consumer behavior. *Unit head:* Dr. Paul D. Berger, Visiting Professor/MS Director, 781-891-2746, E-mail: pberger@bentley.edu. *Application contact:* Graduate Admissions, 781-891-2108, Fax: 781-891-2464, E-mail: applygrad@bentley.edu.
Website: https://admissions.bentley.edu/graduate/masters-in-analytics

Binghamton University, State University of New York, Graduate School, School of Management, Program in Management, Binghamton, NY 13902-6000. Offers finance (PhD); management information systems (PhD); marketing (PhD); organizational studies (PhD); supply chain management (PhD). *Students:* 8 full-time (5 women), 12 part-time (5 women), 19 international. Average age 30. 57 applicants, 21% accepted, 7 enrolled. In 2017, 3 doctorates awarded. *Degree requirements:* For doctorate, thesis/ dissertation. *Entrance requirements:* For doctorate, GMAT. *Application deadline:* For fall admission, 2/1 for domestic students. *Financial support:* In 2017–18, 18 students received support. *Unit head:* Dr. Upinder Dhillon, Dean, 607-777-2314, E-mail: dhillon@ binghamton.edu. *Application contact:* Marianne Ferry, Administrative Assistant, Executive Education and PhD Programs, 607-777-2342, E-mail: mferry@ binghamton.edu.

Marketing

Brandeis University, International Business School (IBS), Master of Business Administration Program, Waltham, MA 02454-9110. Offers data analytics (MBA); finance (MBA); marketing (MBA); real estate (MBA). *Faculty:* 40 full-time (16 women), 31 part-time/adjunct (7 women). *Students:* 35 full-time (18 women), 1 (woman) part-time; includes 3 minority (1 Black or African American, non-Hispanic/Latino; 2 Asian, non-Hispanic/Latino), 30 international. Average age 27. 75 applicants, 49% accepted, 17 enrolled. In 2017, 21 master's awarded. *Entrance requirements:* For master's, GMAT or GRE, minimum two years of full-time work experience. Additional exam requirements/recommendations for international students: Required—TOEFL (minimum score 600 paper-based; 100 iBT), IELTS (minimum score 7), PTE (minimum score 68). *Application deadline:* For fall admission, 11/1 priority date for domestic and international students; for winter admission, 1/15 priority date for domestic and international students; for spring admission, 3/15 priority date for domestic and international students; for summer admission, 4/15 for domestic and international students. Application fee: $100. Electronic applications accepted. *Expenses:* Contact institution. *Financial support:* In 2017–18, 32 students received support. Institutionally sponsored loans and scholarships (averaging $29,641 annually) available. Financial award application deadline: 4/15; financial award applicants required to submit FAFSA. *Faculty research:* Strategic alliances, IPO and venture capital financing, real estate, risk management, data analytics. *Unit head:* Peter Petri, Interim Dean, 781-736-2256. *Application contact:* Kelly Sugrue, Assistant Dean of Admissions, 781-736-2252, Fax: 781-736-2263, E-mail: globaladmissions@brandeis.edu.

Brandman University, School of Business and Professional Studies, Irvine, CA 92618. Offers accounting (MBA); business administration (MBA); business intelligence and data analytics (MBA); e-business strategic management (MBA); entrepreneurship (MBA); finance (MBA); health administration (MBA); human resources (MBA, MS); international business (MBA); marketing (MBA); organizational leadership (MA, MBA, MPA); public administration (MPA). *Expenses:* Tuition: Part-time $640 per credit hour. Tuition and fees vary according to degree level and program. *Unit head:* Dr. Glenn Worthington, Dean, 253-861-1024, E-mail: gworthin@brandman.edu. *Application contact:* Dr. Glenn Worthington, Dean, 253-861-1024, E-mail: gworthin@brandman.edu. Website: https://www.brandman.edu/academic-programs/business-and-professional-studies

Brigham Young University, Graduate Studies, BYU Marriott School of Business, MBA Program, Provo, UT 84602. Offers entrepreneurship (MBA); finance (MBA); global supply chain management (MBA); marketing (MBA); strategic human resources (MBA); JD/MBA; MBA/MS. *Accreditation:* AACSB. *Faculty:* 134 full-time (15 women), 65 part-time/adjunct (16 women). *Students:* 303 full-time (65 women); includes 26 minority (3 American Indian or Alaska Native, non-Hispanic/Latino; 8 Asian, non-Hispanic/Latino; 11 Hispanic/Latino; 4 Native Hawaiian or other Pacific Islander, non-Hispanic/Latino), 58 international. Average age 30. 339 applicants, 52% accepted, 136 enrolled. In 2017, 163 master's awarded. *Entrance requirements:* For master's, GMAT or GRE, commitment to BYU Honor Code, undergraduate degree. Additional exam requirements/recommendations for international students: Required—TOEFL (minimum score 590 paper-based; 100 iBT), IELTS (minimum score 7). *Application deadline:* For fall admission, 5/1 for domestic students, 3/1 for international students. Applications are processed on a rolling basis. Application fee: $50. Electronic applications accepted. *Expenses:* Contact institution. *Financial support:* Research assistantships, teaching assistantships, career-related internships or fieldwork, institutionally sponsored loans, and scholarships/grants available. Financial award application deadline: 3/1; financial award applicants required to submit FAFSA. *Faculty research:* Finance, marketing, supply chain management, entrepreneurship, strategic human resources. *Unit head:* Dr. Grant McQueen, Director, 801-422-3500, E-mail: mba@byu.edu. *Application contact:* Yvette Anderson, MBA Program Admissions Director, 801-422-3500, Fax: 801-422-0513, E-mail: mba@byu.edu.
Website: http://mba.byu.edu

Bryan College, MBA Program, Dayton, TN 37321. Offers business administration (MBA); healthcare administration (MBA); human resources (MBA); marketing (MBA); ministry (MBA); sports management (MBA). *Program availability:* Online only, 100% online. *Entrance requirements:* For master's, resume, 2 letters of recommendation. Additional exam requirements/recommendations for international students: Required—TOEFL. *Application deadline:* For fall admission, 7/1 for domestic and international students; for winter admission, 11/15 for domestic and international students; for spring admission, 12/1 for domestic and international students; for summer admission, 5/1 for domestic and international students. Applications are processed on a rolling basis. Application fee: $50. Electronic applications accepted. *Expenses:* Contact institution. *Financial support:* Scholarships/grants available. Financial award applicants required to submit FAFSA. *Unit head:* Dr. Adina Scruggs, Dean of Adult and Graduate Studies, 423-634-2057, E-mail: adina.scruggs@bryan.edu. *Application contact:* Mandi K Sullivan, Director of Academic Programs, 423-634-9880, E-mail: mandi.sullivan@bryan.edu. Website: http://www.bryan.edu/academics/adult-education/graduate/online-mba/

Butler University, Lacy School of Business, Indianapolis, IN 46208-3485. Offers entrepreneurship and innovation (MBA); finance (MBA); international business (MBA); leadership (MBA); marketing (MBA); professional accounting (MP Acc). *Accreditation:* AACSB. *Program availability:* Part-time. *Faculty:* 14 full-time (4 women), 9 part-time/adjunct (2 women). *Students:* 35 full-time (16 women), 111 part-time (38 women); includes 15 minority (2 Black or African American, non-Hispanic/Latino; 5 Asian, non-Hispanic/Latino; 8 Hispanic/Latino), 6 international. Average age 30. 149 applicants, 64% accepted, 43 enrolled. In 2017, 90 master's awarded. *Degree requirements:* For master's, comprehensive exam, thesis optional. *Entrance requirements:* For master's, GMAT, minimum AACSB index of 950, personal statement, two letters of recommendation, official transcripts, current resume. Additional exam requirements/recommendations for international students: Required—TOEFL (minimum score 550 paper-based; 79 iBT), IELTS (minimum score 6), Michigan English Language Assessment Battery (minimum score of 80). *Application deadline:* For fall admission, 8/1 for domestic and international students; for spring admission, 12/1 for domestic and international students; for summer admission, 4/1 for domestic and international students. Applications are processed on a rolling basis. Application fee: $0. Electronic applications accepted. *Expenses:* $820 per credit. *Financial support:* In 2017–18, 22 students received support. Scholarships/grants, tuition waivers (full and partial), and unspecified assistantships available. Financial award application deadline: 7/15; financial award applicants required to submit FAFSA. *Faculty research:* Higher education and pedagogy; ecotourism; healthcare issues and marketing public policy; domestic public policy, international finance and banking, international and management entrepreneurship, organizational management. *Unit head:* Dr. Stephen Standifird, Dean, 317-940-6307. *Application contact:* Diane Dubord, Graduate Student Service Specialist, 317-940-8107, Fax: 317-940-8250, E-mail: ddubord@butler.edu. Website: https://www.butler.edu/lacyschool

California Coast University, School of Administration and Management, Santa Ana, CA 92701. Offers business marketing (MBA); health care management (MBA); human resource management (MBA); management (MBA, MS). *Program availability:* Online learning. Electronic applications accepted.

California Intercontinental University, School of Business, Irvine, CA 92614. Offers banking and finance (MBA); entrepreneurship and business management (DBA); global business leadership (DBA); international management and marketing (MBA); organizational management and human resource management (MBA).

California Lutheran University, Graduate Studies, School of Management, Thousand Oaks, CA 91360-2787. Offers business (IMBA); entrepreneurship (MBA, Certificate); finance (MBA, Certificate); financial planning (MBA, MS, Certificate); human capital management (MBA, Certificate); information technology (MS); information technology management (MBA, Certificate); international business (MBA, Certificate); marketing (MBA, Certificate); public policy and administration (MPPA); quantitative economics (MS). *Program availability:* Part-time, evening/weekend, 100% online, blended/hybrid learning. *Faculty:* 17 full-time (4 women), 40 part-time/adjunct (9 women). *Students:* 423 full-time (168 women), 153 part-time (72 women); includes 124 minority (11 Black or African American, non-Hispanic/Latino; 1 American Indian or Alaska Native, non-Hispanic/Latino; 21 Asian, non-Hispanic/Latino; 75 Hispanic/Latino; 16 Two or more races, non-Hispanic/Latino), 294 international. Average age 31. 467 applicants, 72% accepted, 108 enrolled. In 2017, 306 master's awarded. *Degree requirements:* For master's, comprehensive exam (for some programs). *Entrance requirements:* For master's, GMAT, interview, minimum GPA of 3.0. *Application deadline:* Applications are processed on a rolling basis. Application fee: $50. Electronic applications accepted. *Expenses:* Contact institution. *Unit head:* Dr. Gerhard Apfelthaler, Dean, 805-493-3360. *Application contact:* 805-493-3325, Fax: 805-493-3861, E-mail: clugrad@callutheran.edu. Website: http://www.callutheran.edu/management/

California State University, East Bay, Office of Graduate Studies, College of Business and Economics, MBA Program, Option in Marketing Management, Hayward, CA 94542-3000. Offers MBA. *Program availability:* Part-time, evening/weekend. *Students:* 10 full-time (5 women), 9 part-time (7 women); includes 8 minority (3 Asian, non-Hispanic/Latino; 4 Hispanic/Latino; 1 Two or more races, non-Hispanic/Latino), 5 international. Average age 31. 25 applicants, 40% accepted, 4 enrolled. In 2017, 10 master's awarded. *Degree requirements:* For master's, comprehensive exam or thesis. *Entrance requirements:* For master's, GMAT, minimum GPA of 2.75. Additional exam requirements/recommendations for international students: Required—TOEFL (minimum score 550 paper-based). *Application deadline:* For fall admission, 6/1 for domestic and international students. Application fee: $55. Electronic applications accepted. *Financial support:* Fellowships, teaching assistantships, career-related internships or fieldwork, Federal Work-Study, institutionally sponsored loans, and scholarships/grants available. Support available to part-time students. Financial award application deadline: 3/2; financial award applicants required to submit FAFSA. *Unit head:* Dr. Lan Wu, Program Advisor, 510-885-3290, E-mail: lan.wu@csueastbay.edu. *Application contact:* Philip Cole-Regis, Administrative Support Coordinator, 510-885-3286, E-mail: philip.coleregis@csueastbay.edu. Website: http://www20.csueastbay.edu/cbe/mba-options/marketing-option.html

California State University, Los Angeles, Graduate Studies, College of Business and Economics, Department of Marketing, Los Angeles, CA 90032-8530. Offers international business (MBA, MS). *Program availability:* Part-time, evening/weekend. *Degree requirements:* For master's, comprehensive exam (MBA), thesis (MS). *Entrance requirements:* For master's, GMAT, minimum GPA of 2.5 during previous 2 years of course work. Additional exam requirements/recommendations for international students: Required—TOEFL (minimum score 550 paper-based). Electronic applications accepted.

California State University, San Bernardino, Graduate Studies, College of Arts and Letters, Program in Communication Studies, San Bernardino, CA 92407. Offers communication studies (MA); integrated marketing communication (MA). *Faculty:* 6 full-time (3 women). *Students:* 7 full-time (all women), 30 part-time (19 women); includes 19 minority (4 Black or African American, non-Hispanic/Latino; 2 Asian, non-Hispanic/Latino; 12 Hispanic/Latino; 1 Two or more races, non-Hispanic/Latino), 3 international. Average age 31. 33 applicants, 52% accepted, 12 enrolled. In 2017, 3 master's awarded. *Degree requirements:* For master's, comprehensive exam. *Entrance requirements:* Additional exam requirements/recommendations for international students: Required—TOEFL. *Application deadline:* For fall admission, 5/15 for domestic students. Application fee: $55. *Unit head:* Ahlam Muhtaseb, Graduate Coordinator, 909-537-5897, Fax: 909-537-7585, E-mail: amuhtase@csusb.edu. *Application contact:* Dr. Dorota Huizinga, Dean of Graduate Studies, 909-537-3064, Fax: 909-537-7034, E-mail: dorota.huizinga@csusb.edu.

Capella University, School of Business and Technology, Doctoral Programs in Business, Minneapolis, MN 55402. Offers accounting (DBA, PhD); business intelligence (DBA); finance (DBA, PhD); general business management (PhD); human resource management (DBA, PhD); leadership (DBA, PhD); management education (PhD); marketing (DBA, PhD); project management (DBA, PhD); strategy and innovation (DBA, PhD). *Accreditation:* ACBSP.

Capella University, School of Business and Technology, Master's Programs in Business, Minneapolis, MN 55402. Offers accounting (MBA); business analysis (MS); business intelligence (MBA); entrepreneurship (MBA); finance (MBA); general business administration (MBA); general human resource management (MS); general leadership (MS); health care management (MBA); human resource management (MBA); marketing (MBA); project management (MBA, MS). *Accreditation:* ACBSP.

Cardinal Stritch University, College of Business and Management, Milwaukee, WI 53217-3985. Offers cyber security (MBA); healthcare management (MBA); justice administration (MBA); marketing (MBA). *Accreditation:* ACBSP. *Program availability:* Part-time, evening/weekend, 100% online, blended/hybrid learning. *Students:* 133 full-time (72 women), 98 part-time (54 women); includes 88 minority (64 Black or African American, non-Hispanic/Latino; 1 American Indian or Alaska Native, non-Hispanic/Latino; 12 Asian, non-Hispanic/Latino; 10 Hispanic/Latino; 1 Two or more races, non-Hispanic/Latino), 8 international. Average age 36. 144 applicants, 100% accepted, 57 enrolled. In 2017, 118 master's awarded. *Degree requirements:* For master's, thesis. *Entrance requirements:* For master's, 3 years of management or related experience, minimum GPA of 2.5. Additional exam requirements/recommendations for international students: Required—TOEFL (minimum score 79 iBT), IELTS (minimum score 6.5). *Application deadline:* Applications are processed on a rolling basis. Application fee: $0. Electronic applications accepted. *Expenses:* $665 per credit. *Financial support:* Career-related internships or fieldwork, Federal Work-Study, and scholarships/grants available. Financial award applicants required to submit FAFSA. *Unit head:* Janette Braverman, Dean, 414-410-4004, E-mail: jmbraverman1@stritch.edu. *Application contact:* Graduate Admissions, 414-410-4042, E-mail: admissions@stritch.edu. Website: http://www.stritch.edu/cbm

Carnegie Mellon University, Tepper School of Business, Program in Marketing, Pittsburgh, PA 15213-3891. Offers PhD. *Degree requirements:* For doctorate, thesis/dissertation.

Central Michigan University, Central Michigan University Global Campus, Program in Business Administration, Mount Pleasant, MI 48859. Offers enterprise resource planning (MBA, Certificate); human resource management (MBA); logistics management (MBA, Certificate); marketing (MBA); value-driven organization (MBA). *Program availability:* Part-time, evening/weekend. *Entrance requirements:* For master's, GMAT.

Central Michigan University, College of Graduate Studies, College of Business Administration, MBA Program, Mount Pleasant, MI 48859. Offers accounting (MBA); business economics (MBA); consulting (MBA); finance (MBA); general business (MBA); human resource management (MBA); information systems (MBA); international business (MBA); logistics management (MBA); marketing (MBA); value-driven organization (MBA). *Program availability:* Part-time, evening/weekend, online learning. Electronic applications accepted. *Faculty research:* Accounting, consulting, international business, marketing, information systems.

City College of the City University of New York, Graduate School, Division of Humanities and the Arts, Department of Media and Communication Arts, Program in Branding and Integrated Communications, New York, NY 10031. Offers MPS. *Entrance requirements:* Additional exam requirements/recommendations for international students: Required—TOEFL (minimum score 90 iBT).

City University of Seattle, Graduate Division, School of Management, Seattle, WA 98121. Offers accounting (Certificate); change leadership (MBA, Certificate); computer systems (MS); finance (Certificate); financial management (MBA); general management (MBA); general management-Europe (MBA); global marketing (MBA); human resources management (Certificate); individualized study (MBA); information security (MS); information systems (MBA); leadership (MA); marketing (MBA, Certificate); project management (MBA, MS, Certificate); sustainable business (Certificate); technology management (MBA, Certificate). *Program availability:* Part-time, evening/weekend, online learning. *Degree requirements:* For master's, comprehensive exam (for some programs), thesis (for some programs). *Entrance requirements:* For master's, baccalaureate degree or equivalent from an accredited or otherwise recognized institution. Additional exam requirements/recommendations for international students: Required—TOEFL (minimum score 567 paper-based; 87 iBT); Recommended—IELTS. Electronic applications accepted.

Clark University, Graduate School, Graduate School of Management, Business Administration Program, Worcester, MA 01610-1477. Offers accounting (MBA); finance (MBA); information management and business analytics (MBA); management (MBA); marketing (MBA); social change (MBA); sustainability (MBA). *Accreditation:* AACSB. *Program availability:* Part-time, evening/weekend. *Students:* 87 full-time (41 women), 41 part-time (26 women); includes 19 minority (10 Black or African American, non-Hispanic/Latino; 4 Asian, non-Hispanic/Latino; 4 Hispanic/Latino; 1 Two or more races, non-Hispanic/Latino), 40 international. Average age 30. 242 applicants, 50% accepted, 54 enrolled. In 2017, 102 master's awarded. *Degree requirements:* For master's, thesis optional. *Entrance requirements:* For master's, GMAT or GRE, 2 references, resume or curriculum vitae, personal statement. Additional exam requirements/recommendations for international students: Required—TOEFL (minimum score 575 paper-based; 90 iBT), IELTS (minimum score 6.5). *Application deadline:* For fall admission, 4/15 priority date for domestic and international students; for spring admission, 12/1 priority date for domestic and international students. Application fee: $75. Electronic applications accepted. *Expenses:* $4,490 tuition per 14-week course, $2,245 per half-unit (7-week course); $40 activity fee (full-time students only); $80 miscellaneous one-time fee; $1,750 student services fee. *Financial support:* Fellowships, research assistantships, teaching assistantships, career-related internships or fieldwork, Federal Work-Study, institutionally sponsored loans, and tuition waivers (partial) available. Support available to part-time students. Financial award application deadline: 5/31. *Faculty research:* Marketing, accounting, human resource management, management information systems, business finance. *Unit head:* Dr. Priscilla Elsass, Dean, 508-793-7543, Fax: 508-793-8822, E-mail: pelsass@clarku.edu. *Application contact:* Yingying Chen, Assistant Director of Graduate Admissions, 508-793-7373, Fax: 508-798-4386, E-mail: graduateadmissions@clarku.edu.
Website: http://www.clarku.edu/programs/masters-business-administration

Clemson University, Graduate School, College of Business, Department of Marketing, Clemson, SC 29634. Offers MS. *Program availability:* Part-time, evening/weekend. *Faculty:* 15 full-time (6 women), 1 part-time/adjunct (0 women). *Students:* 18 full-time (8 women), 4 part-time (2 women); includes 2 minority (both Black or African American, non-Hispanic/Latino), 14 international. Average age 27. 110 applicants, 64% accepted, 8 enrolled. In 2017, 26 master's awarded. *Degree requirements:* For master's, research project. *Entrance requirements:* For master's, GRE General Test or GMAT, unofficial transcripts, letters of recommendation. Additional exam requirements/recommendations for international students: Required—TOEFL (minimum score 90 iBT), IELTS (minimum score 6), PTE (minimum score 54). *Application deadline:* For fall admission, 4/15 for international students. Application fee: $80 ($90 for international students). Electronic applications accepted. *Expenses:* $6,564 per semester full-time resident, $12,538 per semester full-time non-resident, $743 per credit hour part-time resident, $1,486 per credit hour part-time non-resident, $1,203 per credit hour online, other fees may apply per session. *Financial support:* In 2017–18, 2 students received support. Unspecified assistantships available. *Faculty research:* Consumer behavior, sales, relationship marketing, research methodology, services. *Unit head:* Dr. Jesse Moore, Interim Department Chair, 864-656-1086, E-mail: jessem@clemson.edu. *Application contact:* Dr. Michael Dorsch, Graduate Program Coordinator, 864-656-5288, E-mail: mdorsch@clemson.edu.
Website: https://www.clemson.edu/business/departments/marketing/

Cleveland State University, College of Graduate Studies, Monte Ahuja College of Business, Doctor of Business Administration Program, Cleveland, OH 44115. Offers information systems (DBA); marketing (DBA). *Accreditation:* AACSB. *Program availability:* Part-time, evening/weekend. *Faculty:* 50 full-time (11 women). *Students:* 3 full-time (2 women), 16 part-time (8 women); includes 6 minority (3 Black or African American, non-Hispanic/Latino; 3 Asian, non-Hispanic/Latino), 2 international. Average age 40. In 2017, 7 doctorates awarded. *Degree requirements:* For doctorate, comprehensive exam, thesis/dissertation, oral dissertation defense. *Entrance requirements:* For doctorate, GMAT, MBA or equivalent. Additional exam requirements/recommendations for international students: Required—TOEFL (minimum score 550 paper-based; 78 iBT). *Application deadline:* For fall admission, 2/1 for domestic and international students. Application fee: $40. Electronic applications accepted. *Financial support:* In 2017–18, 5 research assistantships with full tuition reimbursements (averaging $12,700 per year), 4 teaching assistantships with full tuition reimbursements (averaging $12,700 per year) were awarded; tuition waivers (full) and unspecified assistantships also available. *Faculty research:* Supply chain management, international business, strategic management, risk analysis, consumer behavior. *Unit head:* Dr. Raj Shekhar G. Javalgi, Director, 216-687-3786, Fax: 216-687-9354, E-mail: r.javalgi@csuohio.edu. *Application contact:* Melinda J. Arnold, Administrative Secretary, 216-687-6952, Fax: 216-687-9257, E-mail: m.arnold@csuohio.edu.
Website: http://www.csuohio.edu/business/academics/mbajuris-doctor

Colorado Technical University Aurora, Programs in Business Administration and Management, Aurora, CO 80014. Offers accounting (MBA); business administration (MBA); business administration and management (EMBA); finance (MBA); human resource management (MBA); marketing (MBA); mediation and dispute resolution (MBA); operations management (MBA); project management (MBA); technology management (MBA). *Program availability:* Part-time, evening/weekend. *Degree requirements:* For master's, thesis or alternative. *Entrance requirements:* For master's, minimum undergraduate GPA of 3.0, resume.

Colorado Technical University Colorado Springs, Graduate Studies, Program in Management, Colorado Springs, CO 80907. Offers accounting (MBA, MSA); business administration (MBA); finance (MBA); human resources management (MBA); logistics/supply chain management (MBA); management (DM); marketing (MBA); mediation and dispute resolution (MBA); operations management (MBA); project management (MBA); technology management (MBA). *Accreditation:* ACBSP. *Program availability:* Part-time, evening/weekend, online learning. *Degree requirements:* For master's, thesis or alternative; for doctorate, thesis/dissertation. *Entrance requirements:* For doctorate, minimum graduate GPA of 3.0, 5 years of related work experience. *Faculty research:* Sexual harassment, performance evaluation, critical thinking.

Columbia Southern University, MBA Program, Orange Beach, AL 36561. Offers finance (MBA); health care management (MBA); human resource management (MBA); marketing (MBA); project management (MBA); public administration (MBA). *Program availability:* Part-time, evening/weekend, online learning. *Entrance requirements:* For master's, bachelor's degree from accredited/approved institution. Additional exam requirements/recommendations for international students: Required—TOEFL. Electronic applications accepted.

Columbia University, Graduate School of Business, Doctoral Program in Business, New York, NY 10027. Offers business (PhD), including accounting, decision, risk, and operations, finance and economics, management, marketing. *Accreditation:* AACSB. *Degree requirements:* For doctorate, comprehensive exam, thesis/dissertation, major field exam, research paper, thesis proposal. *Entrance requirements:* For doctorate, GMAT or GRE (finance), 2 letters of reference, resume. Additional exam requirements/recommendations for international students: Required—TOEFL. Electronic applications accepted. *Expenses:* Contact institution. *Faculty research:* Human decision making and behavioral research; real estate market and mortgage defaults; financial crisis and corporate governance; international business; security analysis and accounting.

Columbia University, Graduate School of Business, MBA Program, New York, NY 10027. Offers accounting (MBA); decision, risk, and operations (MBA); entrepreneurship (MBA); finance and economics (MBA); healthcare and pharmaceutical management (MBA); human resource management (MBA); international business (MBA); leadership and ethics (MBA); management (MBA); marketing (MBA); media (MBA); private equity (MBA); real estate (MBA); social enterprise (MBA); value investing (MBA); DDS/MBA; JD/MBA; MBA/MIA; MBA/MPH; MBA/MS; MD/MBA. *Entrance requirements:* For master's, GMAT, 2 letters of recommendation. Additional exam requirements/recommendations for international students: Required—TOEFL. Electronic applications accepted. *Expenses:* Contact institution. *Faculty research:* Human decision making and behavioral research; real estate market and mortgage defaults; financial crisis and corporate governance; international business; security analysis and accounting.

Concordia University, School of Graduate Studies, John Molson School of Business, Montreal, QC H3H 0A1, Canada. Offers administration (M Sc), including finance, management, marketing; business administration (MBA, PhD, Certificate, Diploma); executive business administration (EMBA); supply chain management (MSCM). PhD program offered jointly with HEC Montreal, McGill University, and Université du Québec à Montréal. *Program availability:* Part-time, evening/weekend. *Degree requirements:* For master's, one foreign language, thesis (for some programs), research project; for doctorate, one foreign language, thesis/dissertation; for other advanced degree, one foreign language. *Entrance requirements:* For master's, GMAT, minimum 2 years of work experience (for MBA); letters of recommendation, bachelor's degree from recognized university with minimum GPA of 3.0, curriculum vitae; for doctorate, GMAT (minimum score of 600), official transcripts, curriculum vitae, 3 letters of reference, statement of purpose; for other advanced degree, minimum GPA of 2.7, 2 letters of reference, statement of purpose, resume. Additional exam requirements/recommendations for international students: Required—TOEFL (minimum score 90 iBT), IELTS (minimum score 7). Electronic applications accepted. *Expenses:* Contact institution. *Faculty research:* General business, capital markets, international business.

Concordia University Wisconsin, Graduate Programs, School of Business Administration, MBA Program, Mequon, WI 53097-2402. Offers finance (MBA); health care administration (MBA); human resource management (MBA); international business (MBA); international business-bilingual English/Chinese (MBA); management (MBA); management information systems (MBA); managerial communications (MBA); marketing (MBA); public administration (MBA); risk management (MBA). *Program availability:* Online learning. *Degree requirements:* For master's, comprehensive exam, thesis or alternative. *Entrance requirements:* Additional exam requirements/recommendations for international students: Required—TOEFL. *Expenses:* Contact institution.

Cornell University, Graduate School, Graduate Field of Management, Ithaca, NY 14853. Offers accounting (PhD); finance (PhD); marketing (PhD); organizational behavior (PhD); production and operations management (PhD). *Accreditation:* AACSB. *Degree requirements:* For doctorate, comprehensive exam, thesis/dissertation. *Entrance requirements:* For doctorate, GMAT or GRE General Test. Additional exam requirements/recommendations for international students: Required—TOEFL (minimum score 600 paper-based; 77 iBT). Electronic applications accepted. *Expenses:* Contact institution. *Faculty research:* Operations and manufacturing.

Daemen College, Department of Accounting/Information Systems, Amherst, NY 14226-3592. Offers global business (MS), including accounting, global business, management information systems, marketing. *Program availability:* Part-time, evening/weekend. *Degree requirements:* For master's, minimum GPA of 3.0. *Entrance requirements:* For master's, GMAT if undergraduate GPA is less than 3.0, 2 letters of recommendation; goal statement; transcripts; demonstration of satisfactory oral and written English. Additional exam requirements/recommendations for international students: Required—TOEFL (minimum score 500 paper-based; 63 iBT), IELTS (minimum score 5.5). Electronic applications accepted. *Faculty research:* Internationalization of small business, cultural influences on business practices, international human resource practices.

Dallas Baptist University, College of Business, Master of Business Administration Program, Dallas, TX 75211-9299. Offers accounting (MBA); business communication (MBA); conflict resolution management (MBA); entrepreneurship (MBA); finance (MBA); health care management (MBA); international business (MBA); leading the non-profit organization (MBA); management (MBA); management information systems (MBA); marketing (MBA); project management (MBA); technology and engineering management (MBA). *Accreditation:* ACBSP. *Program availability:* Part-time, evening/weekend, 100% online, blended/hybrid learning. *Application deadline:* Applications are processed on a rolling basis. Application fee: $25. Electronic applications accepted. Application fee is waived when completed online. *Expenses:* Tuition: Full-time $16,308; part-time $906 per credit hour. *Required fees:* $900; $450 per semester. Tuition and fees vary according to course load and degree level. *Unit head:* Dr. Sandra Reid, Chair of Graduate Business Programs, 214-333-5280, E-mail: sandra@dbu.edu. *Application contact:* Bobby Soto, Director of Admissions, 214-333-5242, E-mail: graduate@dbu.edu.
Website: http://www.dbu.edu/gsb/mba

Marketing

DePaul University, Kellstadt Graduate School of Business, Chicago, IL 60604. Offers accountancy (MBA, MSA); applied economics (MBA); audit and advisory services (MS); business administration (DBA); business analytics (MS); business strategy and decision-making (MBA); computational finance (MS); economics and policy analysis (MS); enterprise risk management (MS); entrepreneurship (MBA, MS); finance (MBA, MS); general business (MBA); hospitality leadership (MBA); hospitality leadership and operational performance (MS); human resources (MS); international business (MBA); management (MBA, MS); management information systems (MBA); marketing (MBA, MS); marketing analysis (MS); marketing strategy and planning (MBA); real estate (MS); real estate finance and investment (MBA); strategy, execution and valuation (MBA); supply chain management (MS); sustainable management (MS); taxation (MS); JD/MBA. *Accreditation:* AACSB. *Program availability:* Part-time, evening/weekend, online learning. *Entrance requirements:* For master's, GMAT/GRE, 2 letters of recommendation, resume, essay, official transcripts. Additional exam requirements/recommendations for international students: Required—TOEFL (minimum score 550 paper-based; 80 iBT). *Application deadline:* For fall admission, 7/1 for domestic students, 6/1 for international students; for winter admission, 10/1 for domestic students, 9/1 for international students; for spring admission, 2/1 for domestic students, 1/1 for international students. Applications are processed on a rolling basis. Application fee: $60. Electronic applications accepted. *Expenses:* Contact institution. *Financial support:* Application deadline: 4/1; applicants required to submit FAFSA. *Unit head:* Christa Hinton, Assistant Dean and Director, 312-362-8810, Fax: 312-362-6677, E-mail: chinton@depaul.edu. *Application contact:* Garry Cooke, Director of Recruitment and Admissions, 312-362-8810, Fax: 312-362-6677, E-mail: kgsb@depaul.edu. Website: http://kellstadt.depaul.edu

DEREE - The American College of Greece, Graduate Programs, Athens, Greece. Offers applied psychology (MS); communication (MA); leadership (MS); marketing (MS).

DeSales University, Division of Business, Center Valley, PA 18034-9568. Offers accounting (MBA); computer information systems (MBA); finance (MBA); health care systems management (MBA); human resources management (MBA); management (MBA); marketing (MBA); project management (MBA); self-design (MBA); supply chain management (MBA); DNP/MBA; MSN/MBA. *Accreditation:* ACBSP. *Program availability:* Part-time, evening/weekend, 100% online, blended/hybrid learning. *Faculty:* 9 full-time (3 women), 32 part-time/adjunct (8 women). *Students:* 78 full-time (44 women), 323 part-time (164 women); includes 71 minority (22 Black or African American, non-Hispanic/Latino; 17 Asian, non-Hispanic/Latino; 24 Hispanic/Latino; 8 Two or more races, non-Hispanic/Latino), 1 international. Average age 34. 213 applicants, 40% accepted, 64 enrolled. In 2017, 123 master's awarded. *Entrance requirements:* For master's, GMAT (waived if undergraduate GPA is 3.0 or better), minimum GPA of 3.0 in undergraduate work, literacy in basic software, background or interest in the field of study, personal statement, 2 years of work experience. Additional exam requirements/recommendations for international students: Required—TOEFL. *Application deadline:* Applications are processed on a rolling basis. Application fee: $50. Electronic applications accepted. *Expenses:* Contact institution. *Financial support:* Applicants required to submit FAFSA. *Faculty research:* Quality improvement, executive development, productivity, cross-cultural managerial differences, leadership. *Unit head:* Dr. David M. Gilfoil, Director, MBA Program, 610-282-1100 Ext. 1828, Fax: 610-282-2869, E-mail: david.gilfoil@desales.edu. *Application contact:* Julia Ferraro, Director of Graduate Admissions, 610-282-1100 Ext. 1768, E-mail: gradadmissions@desales.edu.

Drexel University, LeBow College of Business, Program in Business Administration, Philadelphia, PA 19104-2875. Offers business administration (MBA, PhD, APC), including accounting (MBA, PhD), decision sciences (PhD), economics (MBA, PhD), finance (MBA, PhD), legal studies (MBA), management (MBA), marketing (MBA, PhD), organizational sciences (PhD), quantitative methods (MBA), strategic management (PhD). *Accreditation:* AACSB. *Program availability:* Part-time, evening/weekend, online learning. Terminal master's awarded for partial completion of doctoral program. *Entrance requirements:* For master's, GMAT, minimum GPA of 2.75; for doctorate, GMAT. Additional exam requirements/recommendations for international students: Required—TOEFL. Electronic applications accepted. *Faculty research:* Decision support systems, individual and group behavior, operations research, techniques and strategy.

Duke University, The Fuqua School of Business, The Duke MBA-Daytime Program, Durham, NC 27708-0586. Offers academic excellence in finance (Certificate); business administration (MBA); decision sciences (MBA); energy and environment (MBA); energy finance (MBA); entrepreneurship and innovation (MBA); finance (MBA); financial analysis (MBA); health sector management (Certificate); leadership and ethics (MBA); management (MBA); management science and technology management (Certificate); marketing (MBA); operations management (MBA); social entrepreneurship (MBA); strategy (MBA). *Faculty:* 96 full-time (19 women), 48 part-time/adjunct (15 women). *Students:* 876 full-time (297 women); includes 180 minority (39 Black or African American, non-Hispanic/Latino; 2 American Indian or Alaska Native, non-Hispanic/Latino; 83 Asian, non-Hispanic/Latino; 50 Hispanic/Latino; 6 Two or more races, non-Hispanic/Latino), 321 international. Average age 29. In 2017, 445 master's awarded. *Entrance requirements:* For master's, GMAT or GRE, transcripts, essays, resume, recommendation letters, interview. *Application deadline:* For fall admission, 9/12 for domestic and international students; for winter admission, 10/10 for domestic and international students; for spring admission, 1/3 for domestic and international students; for summer admission, 3/20 for domestic and international students. Application fee: $225. Electronic applications accepted. *Expenses:* $69,342 first-year tuition and fees. *Financial support:* In 2017–18, 423 students received support. Scholarships/grants available. Financial award applicants required to submit FAFSA. *Unit head:* Steve Misuraca, Assistant Dean, Daytime MBA Program. *Application contact:* Shari Hubert, Associate Dean, Office of Admissions, 919-660-7705, Fax: 919-681-8026, E-mail: admissions-info@fuqua.duke.edu. Website: https://www.fuqua.duke.edu/programs/daytime-mba

Duke University, The Fuqua School of Business, The Duke MBA-Global Executive Program, Durham, NC 27708-0586. Offers business administration (MBA); energy and environment (MBA); entrepreneurship and innovation (MBA); finance (MBA); health sector management (Certificate); marketing (MBA); strategy (MBA). *Faculty:* 96 full-time (19 women), 48 part-time/adjunct (15 women). *Students:* 94 full-time (26 women); includes 34 minority (8 Black or African American, non-Hispanic/Latino; 21 Asian, non-Hispanic/Latino; 4 Hispanic/Latino; 1 Two or more races, non-Hispanic/Latino), 25 international. Average age 39. In 2017, 27 master's awarded. *Entrance requirements:* For master's, Executive Assessment, GMAT, or GRE, transcripts, essays, resume, recommendation letters, letter of company support, interview. *Application deadline:* For fall admission, 10/12 priority date for domestic and international students; for winter admission, 12/7 priority date for domestic and international students; for spring admission, 3/20 priority date for domestic and international students; for summer admission, 5/31 for domestic and international students. Applications are processed on a rolling basis. Application fee: $225. Electronic applications accepted. *Expenses:* Contact institution. *Financial support:* In 2017–18, 31 students received support. Scholarships/grants available. Financial award applicants required to submit FAFSA. *Unit head:* Karen Courtney, Associate Dean, Executive Programs. *Application contact:*

Shari Hubert, Associate Dean, Office of Admissions, 919-660-7705, Fax: 919-681-8026, E-mail: admissions-info@fuqua.duke.edu. Website: https://www.fuqua.duke.edu/programs/global-executive-mba

Duke University, The Fuqua School of Business, The Duke MBA-Weekend Executive Program, Durham, NC 27708-0586. Offers business administration (MBA); energy and environment (MBA); entrepreneurship and innovation (MBA); finance (MBA); health sector management (Certificate); marketing (MBA); strategy (MBA). *Faculty:* 96 full-time (19 women), 48 part-time/adjunct (15 women). *Students:* 219 full-time (59 women); includes 80 minority (13 Black or African American, non-Hispanic/Latino; 3 American Indian or Alaska Native, non-Hispanic/Latino; 45 Asian, non-Hispanic/Latino; 13 Hispanic/Latino; 6 Two or more races, non-Hispanic/Latino), 32 international. Average age 35. In 2017, 92 master's awarded. *Entrance requirements:* For master's, Executive Assessment, GMAT or GRE, transcripts, essays, resume, recommendation letters, letter of company support, interview. *Application deadline:* For fall admission, 10/12 priority date for domestic and international students; for winter admission, 12/7 priority date for domestic and international students; for spring admission, 2/7 priority date for domestic and international students; for summer admission, 3/20 for domestic and international students. Applications are processed on a rolling basis. Application fee: $225. Electronic applications accepted. *Expenses:* Contact institution. *Financial support:* In 2017–18, 44 students received support. Scholarships/grants available. Financial award applicants required to submit FAFSA. *Unit head:* Karen Courtney, Associate Dean, Executive Programs. *Application contact:* Shari Hubert, Associate Dean, Office of Admissions, 919-660-7705, Fax: 919-681-8026, E-mail: admissions-info@fuqua.duke.edu. Website: https://www.fuqua.duke.edu/programs/weekend-executive-mba

Duke University, The Fuqua School of Business, Master of Quantitative Management Program: Business Analytics, Durham, NC 27708-0586. Offers finance (MQM); forensics (MQM); marketing (MQM); strategy (MQM). *Faculty:* 96 full-time (19 women), 48 part-time/adjunct (15 women). *Students:* 140 full-time (81 women); includes 11 minority (9 Asian, non-Hispanic/Latino; 2 Hispanic/Latino), 118 international. Average age 24. *Entrance requirements:* For master's, GMAT/GRE, transcripts, essays, resume, recommendation letters. *Application deadline:* For fall admission, 9/13 for domestic and international students; for winter admission, 1/17 for domestic and international students; for spring admission, 2/28 for domestic and international students; for summer admission, 4/4 for domestic and international students. Application fee: $125. Electronic applications accepted. *Expenses:* $66,907 tuition and fees. *Financial support:* In 2017–18, 46 students received support. Scholarships/grants available. Financial award applicants required to submit FAFSA. *Unit head:* Jeremy Petranka, Associate Dean. *Application contact:* Shari Hubert, Associate Dean, Office of Admissions, 919-660-7705, Fax: 919-681-8026, E-mail: admissions-info@fuqua.duke.edu. Website: https://www.fuqua.duke.edu/programs/mqm-business-analytics

Duke University, The Fuqua School of Business, PhD Program, Durham, NC 27708-0586. Offers accounting (PhD); decision sciences (PhD); finance (PhD); management and organizations (PhD); marketing (PhD); operations management (PhD); strategy (PhD). *Faculty:* 96 full-time (19 women). *Students:* 64 full-time (25 women); includes 1 minority (Hispanic/Latino), 41 international. Average age 27. 617 applicants, 5% accepted, 14 enrolled. In 2017, 15 doctorates awarded. *Degree requirements:* For doctorate, thesis/dissertation, major field requirement (exam or major paper, depending upon the area). *Entrance requirements:* For doctorate, GMAT or GRE, transcripts, essays, recommendation letters, statement of purpose. Additional exam requirements/recommendations for international students: Required—TOEFL (minimum score 577 paper-based; 108 iBT), IELTS (minimum score 8). *Application deadline:* For fall admission, 12/31 priority date for domestic and international students. Application fee: $85. Electronic applications accepted. *Expenses:* $52,253. *Financial support:* In 2017–18, 66 students received support, including 66 fellowships with full tuition reimbursements available (averaging $29,200 per year), 63 research assistantships with full tuition reimbursements available (averaging $7,000 per year); institutionally sponsored loans, scholarships/grants, and tuition waivers (full) also available. Financial award applicants required to submit FAFSA. *Unit head:* William Boulding, Dean. *Application contact:* Qi Chen, Director of Graduate Studies, 919-660-7753, Fax: 919-660-7971, E-mail: qc2@duke.edu.

Duquesne University, Palumbo-Donahue School of Business, Pittsburgh, PA 15282-0001. Offers accounting (M Acc); finance (MBA); information systems management (MSISM); management (MBA, MS); marketing (MBA); sports business (MS); supply chain management (MS); sustainability (MBA); JD/MBA; MBA/M Acc; MBA/MA; MBA/MES; MBA/MHMS; MSISM/MBA; Pharm D/MBA. *Accreditation:* AACSB. *Program availability:* Part-time, evening/weekend, minimal on-campus study. *Faculty:* 59 full-time (23 women), 25 part-time/adjunct (6 women). *Students:* 232 full-time (83 women), 46 part-time (18 women); includes 28 minority (14 Black or African American, non-Hispanic/Latino; 8 Asian, non-Hispanic/Latino; 4 Hispanic/Latino; 2 Two or more races, non-Hispanic/Latino), 24 international. Average age 29. 220 applicants, 83% accepted, 121 enrolled. In 2017, 113 master's awarded. *Entrance requirements:* For master's, GMAT or GRE, undergraduate transcripts, 2 letters of recommendation, current resume, personal statement. Additional exam requirements/recommendations for international students: Required—TOEFL (minimum score 577 paper-based; 90 iBT), IELTS (minimum score 7). *Application deadline:* For fall admission, 7/1 priority date for domestic and international students; for spring admission, 12/1 for domestic and international students; for summer admission, 4/1 for domestic and international students. Applications are processed on a rolling basis. Application fee: $0. Electronic applications accepted. *Expenses:* $934 per credit (MS in management, sports business); $1,259 per credit (MBA, MS in accountancy, information systems management). *Financial support:* In 2017–18, 211 students received support, including 12 fellowships with partial tuition reimbursements available (averaging $14,200 per year), 20 research assistantships with partial tuition reimbursements available (averaging $22,662 per year); career-related internships or fieldwork, scholarships/grants, and unspecified assistantships also available. Support available to part-time students. Financial award application deadline: 7/1; financial award applicants required to submit FAFSA. *Faculty research:* Investment management, business ethics, technology management, supply chain management, entrepreneurship. *Unit head:* Dr. Karen Donovan, Associate Dean of Graduate Programs and Executive Education, 412-396-6276, Fax: 412-396-1726, E-mail: donovan6@duq.edu. *Application contact:* Jeff Jewett, Director of Admissions and Enrollment Management, 412-396-6244, Fax: 412-396-1726, E-mail: decrostam@duq.edu. Website: http://www.duq.edu/business/grad

Eastern Michigan University, Graduate School, Academic and Student Affairs Division, Ypsilanti, MI 48197. Offers individualized studies (MA, MS); integrated marketing communications (MS). *Students:* 4 full-time (2 women), 36 part-time (25 women); includes 6 minority (2 Asian, non-Hispanic/Latino; 1 Hispanic/Latino; 3 Two or more races, non-Hispanic/Latino). Average age 35. 64 applicants, 84% accepted, 26 enrolled. In 2017, 1 master's awarded. *Entrance requirements:* Additional exam requirements/recommendations for international students: Required—TOEFL. Application fee: $45. *Unit head:* Dr. Wade Tornquist, Interim Dean, 734-487-0042, Fax: 734-487-0050, E-mail: wade.tornquist@emich.edu. *Application contact:* Graduate Admissions, 734-487-2400, Fax: 734-487-6559, E-mail: graduate.admissions@emich.edu.

Eastern Michigan University, Graduate School, College of Business, Department of Marketing, Program in Integrated Marketing Communications, Ypsilanti, MI 48197. Offers MS, Postbaccalaureate Certificate. *Students:* 24 full-time (20 women), 33 part-time (26 women); includes 15 minority (11 Black or African American, non-Hispanic/Latino; 3 Hispanic/Latino; 1 Two or more races, non-Hispanic/Latino). Average age 31. 41 applicants, 66% accepted, 23 enrolled. In 2017, 22 master's, 1 other advanced degree awarded. Application fee: $45. *Application contact:* K. Michelle Henry, Director, Graduate Business Programs, 734-487-4444, Fax: 734-478-1316, E-mail: cob.graduate@emich.edu.

Eastern Michigan University, Graduate School, College of Business, Programs in Business Administration, Ypsilanti, MI 48197. Offers business administration (MBA, Graduate Certificate); computer information systems (Graduate Certificate); e-business (MBA, Graduate Certificate); enterprise business intelligence (MBA); entrepreneurship (MBA, Graduate Certificate); finance (MBA, Graduate Certificate); human resources (MBA); human resources management (Graduate Certificate); information systems (MBA); internal auditing (MBA); international business (MBA, Graduate Certificate); marketing management (Graduate Certificate); nonprofit management (MBA); organizational development (Graduate Certificate); supply chain management (MBA, Graduate Certificate). *Accreditation:* AACSB. *Program availability:* Part-time, online learning. *Students:* 53 full-time (30 women), 297 part-time (170 women); includes 121 minority (72 Black or African American, non-Hispanic/Latino; 4 American Indian or Alaska Native, non-Hispanic/Latino; 15 Asian, non-Hispanic/Latino; 20 Hispanic/Latino; 10 Two or more races, non-Hispanic/Latino), 20 international. Average age 31. 247 applicants, 74% accepted, 94 enrolled. In 2017, 71 master's, 34 other advanced degrees awarded. *Entrance requirements:* For master's, GMAT (minimum score 450), minimum cumulative undergraduate GPA of 2.75. Additional exam requirements/recommendations for international students: Required—TOEFL. *Application deadline:* For fall admission, 5/15 priority date for domestic students, 2/15 priority date for international students; for winter admission, 10/15 priority date for domestic students, 9/1 priority date for international students; for summer admission, 3/15 priority date for domestic students, 3/1 priority date for international students. Applications are processed on a rolling basis. Application fee: $45. *Financial support:* Fellowships, research assistantships with full tuition reimbursements, teaching assistantships with full tuition reimbursements, career-related internships or fieldwork, Federal Work-Study, institutionally sponsored loans, scholarships/grants, tuition waivers (partial), and unspecified assistantships available. Support available to part-time students. Financial award applicants required to submit FAFSA. *Unit head:* K. Michelle Henry, Director, Graduate Business Programs, 734-487-4444, Fax: 734-483-1316, E-mail: cob.graduate@emich.edu.
Website: http://www.emich.edu/cob/mba/

East Tennessee State University, School of Graduate Studies, College of Business and Technology, Department of Management and Marketing, Johnson City, TN 37614. Offers business administration (MBA, Postbaccalaureate Certificate); digital marketing (MS); entrepreneurial leadership (Postbaccalaureate Certificate); health care management (Postbaccalaureate Certificate). *Program availability:* Part-time, evening/weekend. *Degree requirements:* For master's, comprehensive exam, capstone. *Entrance requirements:* For master's, GMAT, minimum GPA of 2.5 (for MBA), 3.0 (for MS); current resume; three letters of recommendation; for Postbaccalaureate Certificate, minimum GPA of 2.5, undergraduate degree. Additional exam requirements/recommendations for international students: Required—TOEFL (minimum score 550 paper-based; 79 iBT). *Application deadline:* For fall admission, 6/1 for domestic students, 4/29 for international students; for spring admission, 11/1 for domestic students, 9/29 for international students. Application fee: $55 ($65 for international students). Electronic applications accepted. *Financial support:* Research assistantships with full tuition reimbursements, teaching assistantships with full tuition reimbursements, career-related internships or fieldwork, institutionally sponsored loans, scholarships/grants, and unspecified assistantships available. Financial award application deadline: 7/1; financial award applicants required to submit FAFSA. *Faculty research:* Sustainability, healthcare effectiveness, consumer behavior, merchandising trends, organizational management issues. *Unit head:* Charles Gorman, Chair, 423-439-4433, Fax: 423-439-5661, E-mail: gormanc@etsu.edu. *Application contact:* Charles Gorman, Chair, 423-439-4433, Fax: 423-439-5661, E-mail: gormanc@etsu.edu.
Website: http://www.etsu.edu/cbat/mgmtmkt/

Emory University, Goizueta Business School, Doctoral Program in Business, Atlanta, GA 30322. Offers accounting (PhD); finance (PhD); information systems and operations management (PhD); marketing (PhD); organization and management (PhD). *Students:* 250 applicants, 5% accepted. *Degree requirements:* For doctorate, comprehensive exam, thesis/dissertation. *Entrance requirements:* For doctorate, GMAT, interview. Additional exam requirements/recommendations for international students: Required—TOEFL (minimum score 600 paper-based; 100 iBT). *Application deadline:* For fall admission, 1/3 priority date for domestic and international students. Applications are processed on a rolling basis. Application fee: $75. Electronic applications accepted. *Expenses:* Contact institution. *Financial support:* Fellowships, scholarships/grants, and health care benefits available. Financial award application deadline: 1/3. *Faculty research:* Financial and managerial accounting, asset pricing strategy and organizational behavior, information technology marketing analytics and consumer behavior. *Unit head:* Kathryn Kadous, Associate Dean, 404-727-2306, Fax: 404-727-5337, E-mail: kathryn.kadous@emory.edu. *Application contact:* Allison Gilmore, Director of Admissions and Student Services, 404-727-6353, Fax: 404-727-5337, E-mail: allison.gilmore@emory.edu.
Website: https://goizueta.emory.edu/degree/phd/index.html

Emory University, Goizueta Business School, Full Time MBA Program, Atlanta, GA 30322. Offers accounting (MBA); alternative investments (MBA); business process consulting (MBA); business technology management (MBA); capital markets (MBA); corporate finance (MBA); customer relationship management (MBA); decision analytics (MBA); entrepreneurship (MBA); finance (MBA); global management (MBA); investment banking (MBA); management consulting (MBA); marketing (MBA); marketing analytics (MBA); marketing consulting (MBA); operations management (MBA); organization and management (MBA); product and brand management (MBA); real estate (MBA); social enterprise (MBA); strategy consulting (MBA). *Accreditation:* AACSB. *Faculty:* 74 full-time (18 women), 18 part-time/adjunct (6 women). *Students:* 353 full-time (96 women); includes 80 minority (18 Black or African American, non-Hispanic/Latino; 2 American Indian or Alaska Native, non-Hispanic/Latino; 39 Asian, non-Hispanic/Latino; 16 Hispanic/Latino; 1 Native Hawaiian or other Pacific Islander, non-Hispanic/Latino; 4 Two or more races, non-Hispanic/Latino), 104 international. Average age 29. 1,380 applicants, 34% accepted, 172 enrolled. In 2017, 179 master's awarded. *Degree requirements:* For master's, 1 leadership course; 2 mid-semester module programs; 2 global components. *Entrance requirements:* For master's, GMAT/GRE, essays; recommendation letters; undergraduate degree; interview. Additional exam requirements/recommendations for international students: Required—TOEFL (minimum score 100 iBT), IELTS (minimum score 7), PTE (minimum score 68). *Application deadline:* For fall admission, 10/6 for domestic and international students; for winter admission, 11/17 for domestic and international students; for spring admission, 1/3 priority date for domestic and international students; for summer admission, 3/9 for

domestic and international students. Application fee: $150. Electronic applications accepted. *Expenses:* $59,616. *Financial support:* In 2017–18, 273 students received support. Career-related internships or fieldwork, institutionally sponsored loans, and scholarships/grants available. Financial award application deadline: 4/1; financial award applicants required to submit FAFSA. *Faculty research:* Corporate finance, information systems, digital marketing, asset pricing, sports management. *Unit head:* Brian Mitchell, Associate Dean, 404-727-4824, Fax: 404-712-9648, E-mail: brian.mitchell@emory.edu. *Application contact:* Julie Barefoot, Associate Dean, 404-727-6311, Fax: 404-727-4612, E-mail: mbaadmissions@emory.edu.
Website: http://www.goizueta.emory.edu

Fairfield University, Dolan School of Business, Fairfield, CT 06824. Offers accounting (MBA, MS, CAS); business analytics (MS); finance (MBA, MS, CAS); information systems and business analytics (MBA); management (MBA, CAS); marketing (MBA, CAS); taxation (CAS). *Accreditation:* AACSB. *Program availability:* Part-time, evening/weekend. *Faculty:* 18 full-time (6 women), 6 part-time/adjunct (2 women). *Students:* 120 full-time (57 women), 67 part-time (27 women); includes 20 minority (3 Black or African American, non-Hispanic/Latino; 1 American Indian or Alaska Native, non-Hispanic/Latino; 3 Asian, non-Hispanic/Latino; 11 Hispanic/Latino; 2 Two or more races, non-Hispanic/Latino), 33 international. Average age 26. 195 applicants, 87% accepted, 112 enrolled. In 2017, 93 master's awarded. *Degree requirements:* For master's, capstone course. *Entrance requirements:* For master's, GMAT (minimum score 500), 2 letters of reference, resume, minimum GPA of 3.0. Additional exam requirements/recommendations for international students: Required—TOEFL (minimum score 550 paper-based; 80 iBT) or IELTS (minimum score 6.5). *Application deadline:* For fall admission, 5/15 for international students; for spring admission, 10/15 for international students. Applications are processed on a rolling basis. Application fee: $60. Electronic applications accepted. *Expenses:* $925 per credit hour. *Financial support:* In 2017–18, 31 students received support. Scholarships/grants and unspecified assistantships available. Financial award applicants required to submit FAFSA. *Faculty research:* International finance, leadership and careers, ethics in accounting, emotions in consumer behavior and organizations, data analytics. *Unit head:* Dr. Mark Ligas, Interim Dean, 203-254-4070, Fax: 203-254-4105, E-mail: mligas@fairfield.edu. *Application contact:* Marianne Gumpper, Director of Graduate and Continuing Studies Admission, 203-254-4184, Fax: 203-254-4073, E-mail: gradadmis@fairfield.edu.
Website: http://fairfield.edu/mba

Fairleigh Dickinson University, Florham Campus, Silberman College of Business, Departments of Management, Marketing, and Entrepreneurial Studies, Program in Marketing, Madison, NJ 07940-1099. Offers MBA, Certificate. *Entrance requirements:* For master's, GMAT.

Fairleigh Dickinson University, Metropolitan Campus, Silberman College of Business, Departments of Management, Marketing, and Entrepreneurial Studies, Program in Marketing, Teaneck, NJ 07666-1914. Offers MBA, Certificate.

Fashion Institute of Technology, School of Graduate Studies, Program in Cosmetics and Fragrance Marketing and Management, New York, NY 10001-5992. Offers MPS. *Degree requirements:* For master's, capstone seminar. *Entrance requirements:* Additional exam requirements/recommendations for international students: Required—TOEFL (minimum score 550 paper-based). Electronic applications accepted.

Florida Agricultural and Mechanical University, Division of Graduate Studies, Research, and Continuing Education, School of Business and Industry, Tallahassee, FL 32307-3200. Offers accounting (MBA); finance (MBA); management information systems (MBA); marketing (MBA). *Accreditation:* ACBSP. *Degree requirements:* For master's, residency. *Entrance requirements:* For master's, GMAT, minimum GPA of 3.0.

Florida International University, Chapman Graduate School of Business, Department of Marketing and Logistics, Miami, FL 33199. Offers marketing (MS). *Program availability:* Evening/weekend. *Faculty:* 23 full-time (11 women), 19 part-time/adjunct (7 women). *Students:* 128 full-time (96 women), 1 part-time (0 women); includes 110 minority (8 Black or African American, non-Hispanic/Latino; 3 Asian, non-Hispanic/Latino; 94 Hispanic/Latino; 5 Two or more races, non-Hispanic/Latino), 12 international. Average age 28. 174 applicants, 60% accepted, 87 enrolled. In 2017, 43 master's awarded. *Entrance requirements:* For master's, GMAT/GRE or 3 years of work experience, minimum AACSB index of 1000, minimum GPA of 3.0. Application fee: $20. *Expenses:* Tuition, state resident: full-time $8912; part-time $446 per credit hour. Tuition, nonresident: full-time $21,393; part-time $992 per credit hour. *Required fees:* $390; $195 per semester. *Unit head:* Anthony Miyazaki, Chair, 305-348-2571, Fax: 305-348-3792, E-mail: anthony.miyazaki@fiu.edu. *Application contact:* Nanett Rojas, Manager, Admissions Operations, 305-348-7464, Fax: 305-348-7441, E-mail: gradadm@fiu.edu.

Florida National University, Program in Business Administration, Hialeah, FL 33012. Offers accounting (MBA); finance (MBA); general management (MBA); health services administration (MBA); marketing (MBA); public management and leadership (MBA). *Program availability:* Part-time, blended/hybrid learning. *Degree requirements:* For master's, capstone. *Entrance requirements:* For master's, writing assessment, bachelor's degree from accredited institution; official undergraduate transcripts; minimum undergraduate GPA of 2.5, GMAT (minimum score of 400), or GRE (minimum score of 900); two letters of recommendation; resume. Additional exam requirements/recommendations for international students: Required—TOEFL (minimum score 500 paper-based; 62 iBT), IELTS (minimum score 5.5). *Application deadline:* Applications are processed on a rolling basis. Electronic applications accepted. *Expenses:* Contact institution. *Financial support:* Federal Work-Study, institutionally sponsored loans, scholarships/grants, and tuition waivers available. Financial award applicants required to submit FAFSA. *Unit head:* Dr. Ernesto Gonzalez, Business and Economics Department Head, 305-821-3333 Ext. 1070, Fax: 305-362-0595, E-mail: egonzalez@fnu.edu.
Website: https://www.fnu.edu/prospective-students/our-programs/select-a-program/master-of-business-administration-mba-masters/

Florida State University, The Graduate School, College of Business, Tallahassee, FL 32306-1110. Offers accounting (M Acc), including assurance and advisory services, generalist, taxation; business administration (MBA, PhD), including accounting (PhD), finance (PhD), management information systems (PhD), marketing (PhD), organizational behavior and human resources (PhD), risk management and insurance (PhD), strategy (PhD); finance (MS); management information systems (MS); risk management and insurance (MS); JD/MBA; MSW/MBA. *Accreditation:* AACSB. *Program availability:* Part-time, 100% online. *Faculty:* 93 full-time (23 women), 2 part-time/adjunct (1 woman). *Students:* 229 full-time (96 women), 423 part-time (154 women); includes 159 minority (44 Black or African American, non-Hispanic/Latino; 24 Asian, non-Hispanic/Latino; 75 Hispanic/Latino; 1 Native Hawaiian or other Pacific Islander, non-Hispanic/Latino; 15 Two or more races, non-Hispanic/Latino), 48 international. Average age 31. 300 applicants, 61% accepted, 133 enrolled. In 2017, 268 master's, 9 doctorates awarded. Terminal master's awarded for partial completion of doctoral program. *Degree requirements:* For doctorate, comprehensive exam, thesis/dissertation. *Entrance requirements:* For master's, GMAT, GRE (for all except MS in finance), work experience (MBA, MS); minimum GPA of 3.0, letters of recommendation; for doctorate, GMAT, GRE (for marketing, organizational behavior, risk management

and insurance, management information systems, and human resources only), minimum graduate GPA of 3.5, letters of recommendation. Additional exam requirements/recommendations for international students: Required—TOEFL (minimum score 600 paper-based; 85 iBT); Recommended—IELTS (minimum score 6). *Application deadline:* For fall admission, 6/1 for domestic and international students; for spring admission, 10/1 for domestic and international students; for summer admission, 3/1 for domestic and international students. Applications are processed on a rolling basis. Application fee: $30. Electronic applications accepted. *Expenses:* Contact institution. *Financial support:* In 2017–18, 146 students received support, including 26 fellowships (averaging $1,500 per year), 77 research assistantships with full tuition reimbursements available (averaging $20,000 per year), 43 teaching assistantships with full tuition reimbursements available (averaging $20,000 per year); career-related internships or fieldwork, scholarships/grants, health care benefits, tuition waivers (full and partial), and unspecified assistantships also available. Support available to part-time students. Financial award application deadline: 1/1; financial award applicants required to submit FAFSA. *Faculty research:* Business strategy, marketing, finance, accounting, business analytics. *Total annual research expenditures:* $1.4 million. *Unit head:* Dr. Michael Hartline, Dean, 850-644-4405, Fax: 850-644-0915, E-mail: mhartline@business.fsu.edu. *Application contact:* Jennifer Clark, Director, 850-644-6458, E-mail: gradprograms@business.fsu.edu.
Website: http://business.fsu.edu/

Florida State University, The Graduate School, College of Communication and Information, School of Communication, Tallahassee, FL 32306. Offers communication theory and research (PhD); integrated marketing communication (MA, MS); media and communication studies (MA, MS); public interest media and communication (MA, MS). *Program availability:* Part-time. *Faculty:* 20 full-time (11 women), 1 part-time/adjunct (0 women). *Students:* 104 full-time (74 women), 38 part-time (27 women); includes 81 minority (20 Black or African American, non-Hispanic/Latino; 24 Asian, non-Hispanic/Latino; 26 Hispanic/Latino; 1 Native Hawaiian or other Pacific Islander, non-Hispanic/Latino; 10 Two or more races, non-Hispanic/Latino). Average age 24. 184 applicants, 59% accepted, 46 enrolled. In 2017, 59 master's, 5 doctorates awarded. *Degree requirements:* For master's, thesis (for some programs); for doctorate, comprehensive exam, thesis/dissertation. *Entrance requirements:* For master's, GRE General Test, minimum GPA of 3.0; for doctorate, GRE General Test, minimum GPA of 3.3 in graduate course work. Additional exam requirements/recommendations for international students: Required—TOEFL (minimum score 600 paper-based; 100 iBT), IELTS (minimum score 7). *Application deadline:* For fall admission, 7/1 priority date for domestic students, 5/1 priority date for international students; for spring admission, 11/1 priority date for domestic and international students; for summer admission, 3/1 priority date for domestic and international students. Applications are processed on a rolling basis. Application fee: $30. Electronic applications accepted. *Expenses:* Contact institution. *Financial support:* In 2017–18, 112 students received support, including 28 research assistantships with full tuition reimbursements available (averaging $11,752 per year), 81 teaching assistantships with full tuition reimbursements available (averaging $10,109 per year); scholarships/grants, tuition waivers (full and partial), and unspecified assistantships also available. Financial award application deadline: 11/1; financial award applicants required to submit FAFSA. *Faculty research:* Communication in the public interest; strategic communication; media and technology; multicultural, intercultural, and international communication. *Total annual research expenditures:* $41,657. *Unit head:* Dr. Jennifer Proffitt, Director, 850-644-5034, Fax: 850-644-8642, E-mail: jennifer.proffitt@cci.fsu.edu. *Application contact:* Natashia Hinson-Turner, Graduate Coordinator, 850-644-5034, Fax: 850-644-8642, E-mail: comgradadvising@cci.fsu.edu.
Website: http://www.cci.fsu.edu

Fordham University, Gabelli School of Business, New York, NY 10023. Offers accounting (MBA, MS); applied statistics and decision-making (MS); business economics (DPS); capital markets (DPS); communications and media management (MBA); electronic business (MBA); entrepreneurship (MBA); finance (MBA, PhD); global finance (MS); global sustainability (MBA); health administration (MS); healthcare management (MBA); information systems (MBA, MS); investor relations (MS); management (EMBA, MBA, MS, PhD); marketing (MBA); marketing intelligence (MS); media management (MS); nonprofit leadership (MS); quantitative finance (MS); strategy and decision-making (DPS); taxation (MS); JD/MBA; MS/MBA. *Accreditation:* AACSB. *Program availability:* Part-time, evening/weekend. *Faculty:* 130 full-time (46 women), 42 part-time/adjunct (5 women). *Students:* 1,051 full-time (570 women), 563 part-time (313 women); includes 190 minority (48 Black or African American, non-Hispanic/Latino; 72 Asian, non-Hispanic/Latino; 69 Hispanic/Latino; 1 Native Hawaiian or other Pacific Islander, non-Hispanic/Latino), 1,106 international. Average age 27. 4,597 applicants, 58% accepted, 794 enrolled. In 2017, 937 master's awarded. Terminal master's awarded for partial completion of doctoral program. *Degree requirements:* For master's, internships (for some degrees); for doctorate, comprehensive exam (for some programs), thesis/dissertation. *Entrance requirements:* For master's, GMAT/GRE, 2 letters of recommendation, resume, 2 essays, transcripts, interview. Additional exam requirements/recommendations for international students: Required—TOEFL (minimum score 100 iBT), IELTS (minimum score 7). *Application deadline:* For fall admission, 11/15 priority date for domestic and international students; for winter admission, 1/19 priority date for domestic students, 1/1 priority date for international students; for spring admission, 4/15 for domestic students, 3/1 for international students; for summer admission, 6/1 for domestic students. Application fee: $130. Electronic applications accepted. *Expenses:* $1,495 per credit. *Financial support:* Career-related internships or fieldwork, institutionally sponsored loans, scholarships/grants, and unspecified assistantships available. Support available to part-time students. Financial award application deadline: 6/30; financial award applicants required to submit FAFSA. *Unit head:* Dr. Donna Rapaccioli, Dean, 212-636-6165, Fax: 212-307-1779, E-mail: rapaccioli@fordham.edu. *Application contact:* Lawrence Murray, Senior Assistant Dean of Graduate Admissions and Advising, 212-636-6200, Fax: 212-636-7076, E-mail: admissionsgb@fordham.edu.
Website: http://www.fordham.edu/gabelli

Franklin University, Marketing and Communication Program, Columbus, OH 43215-5399. Offers MS. *Program availability:* Part-time, evening/weekend. *Entrance requirements:* For master's, minimum undergraduate GPA of 2.75. Additional exam requirements/recommendations for international students: Required—TOEFL (minimum score 550 paper-based). Electronic applications accepted.

Full Sail University, Internet Marketing Master of Science Program - Online, Winter Park, FL 32792-7437. Offers MS. *Program availability:* Online learning.

Gannon University, School of Graduate Studies, College of Engineering and Business, Dahlkemper School of Business, Program in Business Administration, Erie, PA 16541-0001. Offers business administration (MBA); finance (MBA); human resources management (MBA); marketing (MBA). *Accreditation:* ACBSP. *Program availability:* Part-time, evening/weekend, 100% online, blended/hybrid learning. *Entrance requirements:* For master's, GMAT, bachelor's degree in any discipline from any accredited college or university, resume, transcripts, 3 letters of recommendation. Additional exam requirements/recommendations for international students: Required—

TOEFL (minimum score 79 iBT). Electronic applications accepted. Application fee is waived when completed online.

Geneva College, Program in Business Administration, Beaver Falls, PA 15010-3599. Offers business administration (MBA); finance (MBA); marketing (MBA); operations (MBA). *Accreditation:* ACBSP. *Program availability:* Part-time, evening/weekend. *Faculty:* 5 full-time (1 woman), 3 part-time/adjunct (0 women). *Students:* 33 full-time (13 women), 8 part-time (2 women); includes 6 minority (4 Black or African American, non-Hispanic/Latino; 1 American Indian or Alaska Native, non-Hispanic/Latino; 1 Asian, non-Hispanic/Latino). Average age 37. 25 applicants, 52% accepted, 10 enrolled. In 2017, 14 master's awarded. *Degree requirements:* For master's, 36 credit hours of course work (30 of which are required of all students). *Entrance requirements:* For master's, GMAT (if college GPA less than 2.5), undergraduate transcript, 2 letters of recommendation, resume, goals statement. Additional exam requirements/recommendations for international students: Required—TOEFL. *Application deadline:* For fall admission, 3/1 priority date for domestic students; for spring admission, 11/1 priority date for domestic students. Applications are processed on a rolling basis. Electronic applications accepted. *Expenses:* $710 per credit. *Financial support:* In 2017–18, 1 student received support. Scholarships/grants available. Financial award application deadline: 8/1; financial award applicants required to submit FAFSA. *Unit head:* Dr. Gary Vander Plaats, Director of the MBA Program, 724-847-6619, E-mail: gpvander@geneva.edu. *Application contact:* Marina Frazier, Director of Graduate Enrollment, 724-847-6697, E-mail: mba@geneva.edu.
Website: http://www.geneva.edu/page/masters_business

George Fox University, College of Business, Newberg, OR 97132-2697. Offers accounting (DBA); finance (MBA); management (DBA); management and leadership (MBA); marketing (DBA); organizational strategy (MBA); strategic human resource management (MBA). MBA offered in Newberg, OR and in Portland, OR. *Accreditation:* ACBSP. *Program availability:* Part-time, evening/weekend, online learning. *Degree requirements:* For master's, capstone project; for doctorate, credit-applied research project. *Entrance requirements:* For master's, resume (5 years of professional experience); 3 professional references; interview; financial e-learning course; official transcripts; for doctorate, GRE or GMAT, resume; personal mission statement; academic research writing sample; official transcript from each college/university attended; three professional references. Additional exam requirements/recommendations for international students: Required—TOEFL (minimum score 577 paper-based; 90 iBT) or IELTS (minimum score 7). Electronic applications accepted. *Expenses:* Contact institution.

The George Washington University, School of Business, Department of Marketing, Washington, DC 20052. Offers MBA, PhD. *Program availability:* Part-time, evening/weekend. *Students:* 1 (woman) part-time; minority (Hispanic/Latino). Average age 25. 7 applicants, 100% accepted, 1 enrolled. *Entrance requirements:* For master's, GMAT; for doctorate, GMAT or GRE. Additional exam requirements/recommendations for international students: Required—TOEFL. *Application deadline:* For fall admission, 4/1 priority date for domestic students; for spring admission, 10/1 for domestic students. Applications are processed on a rolling basis. Application fee: $60. *Expenses:* Tuition: Full-time $28,800; part-time $1655 per credit hour. *Required fees:* $45; $2.75 per credit hour. *Financial support:* Fellowships, teaching assistantships, career-related internships or fieldwork, Federal Work-Study, and institutionally sponsored loans available. Financial award application deadline: 4/1. *Faculty research:* Strategic marketing, marketing and public policy, marketing management. *Unit head:* Pradeep Rau, Chairman, 202-994-4989, E-mail: prau@gwu.edu. *Application contact:* Christopher Storer, Executive Director, Graduate Admissions, 202-994-1212, E-mail: gwmba@gwu.edu.
Website: http://business.gwu.edu/marketing/

Georgia State University, J. Mack Robinson College of Business, Department of Marketing, Atlanta, GA 30302-3083. Offers MBA, MS, PhD. *Program availability:* Part-time, evening/weekend. *Faculty:* 28 full-time (10 women). *Students:* 51 full-time (31 women), 1 part-time (0 women); includes 22 minority (19 Black or African American, non-Hispanic/Latino; 1 Hispanic/Latino; 2 Two or more races, non-Hispanic/Latino), 20 international. Average age 30. 33 applicants, 12% accepted, 3 enrolled. In 2017, 30 master's, 1 doctorate awarded. *Entrance requirements:* For master's, GRE or GMAT, transcripts from all institutions attended, resume, essays; for doctorate, GRE or GMAT, three letters of recommendation, personal statement, transcripts from all institutions attended, resume. Additional exam requirements/recommendations for international students: Required—TOEFL (minimum score 610 paper-based; 101 iBT), IELTS (minimum score 7). *Application deadline:* For fall admission, 5/1 priority date for domestic students, 2/1 priority date for international students; for spring admission, 9/15 priority date for domestic students, 4/1 priority date for international students. Applications are processed on a rolling basis. Application fee: $50. Electronic applications accepted. *Expenses:* Tuition, state resident: full-time $7020. Tuition, nonresident: full-time $22,518. *Required fees:* $2128. Tuition and fees vary according to degree level and program. *Financial support:* Research assistantships, teaching assistantships, scholarships/grants, tuition waivers (partial), and unspecified assistantships available. Financial award applicants required to submit FAFSA. *Faculty research:* Marketing strategy, market in science, brand and customer management, digital and social media marketing, global marketing. *Unit head:* Dr. Naveen Donthu, Professor/Chair of the Department of Marketing, 404-413-7650, Fax: 404-413-7699. *Application contact:* Toby McChesney, Assistant Dean for Graduate Recruiting and Student Services, 404-413-7167, Fax: 404-413-7162, E-mail: rcbgradadmissions@gsu.edu.
Website: http://robinson.gsu.edu/marketing/

Golden Gate University, Ageno School of Business, San Francisco, CA 94105-2968. Offers accounting (MBA); adaptive leadership (MBA); advanced financial planning (MS); business administration (EMBA, MBA, DBA); business analytics (MBA, MS); entrepreneurship (MBA); finance (MBA, MS, Certificate); financial life planning (Certificate); financial planning (MS, Certificate); global supply chain management (MBA, Certificate); human resource management (MBA, MS, Certificate); information technology management (MBA, MS, Certificate); international business (MBA); marketing (MBA, MS, Certificate); project management (MBA, MS, Certificate); psychology (MA, Certificate); public administration (EMPA, MBA); public administration leadership (Certificate); JD/MBA. *Program availability:* Part-time, evening/weekend. *Faculty:* 17 full-time (7 women), 280 part-time/adjunct (95 women). *Students:* 309 full-time (147 women), 527 part-time (266 women); includes 286 minority (56 Black or African American, non-Hispanic/Latino; 1 American Indian or Alaska Native, non-Hispanic/Latino; 131 Asian, non-Hispanic/Latino; 83 Hispanic/Latino; 4 Native Hawaiian or other Pacific Islander, non-Hispanic/Latino; 11 Two or more races, non-Hispanic/Latino), 209 international. Average age 35. 549 applicants, 66% accepted, 185 enrolled. *Degree requirements:* For doctorate, thesis/dissertation, qualifying examination. *Entrance requirements:* For master's, GMAT (for MBA), minimum GPA of 2.5 (MS). Additional exam requirements/recommendations for international students: Required—TOEFL (minimum score 550 paper-based; 79 iBT). *Application deadline:* For fall admission, 5/15 for domestic and international students; for winter admission, 1/15 for domestic and international students; for spring admission, 9/15 for domestic and

international students. Applications are processed on a rolling basis. Application fee: $65 ($105 for international students). Electronic applications accepted. *Expenses:* $3,150 per 3-unit course. *Financial support:* Career-related internships or fieldwork, Federal Work-Study, institutionally sponsored loans, and scholarships/grants available. Support available to part-time students. Financial award applicants required to submit FAFSA. *Unit head:* Marianne Koch, Associate Dean, 415-442-6542, Fax: 415-442-6579, E-mail: mkoch@ggu.edu. *Application contact:* Angela Melero, Enrollment Services, 415-442-7800, Fax: 415-442-7807, E-mail: info@ggu.edu.
Website: http://www.ggu.edu/programs/business-and-management

Goldey-Beacom College, Graduate Program, Wilmington, DE 19808-1999. Offers business administration (MBA); finance (MS); financial management (MBA); health care management (MBA); human resource management (MBA); information technology (MBA); international business management (MBA); major finance (MBA); major taxation (MBA); management (MM); marketing management (MBA); taxation (MBA, MS). *Accreditation:* ACBSP. *Program availability:* Part-time, evening/weekend. *Entrance requirements:* For master's, GMAT, MAT, GRE, minimum GPA of 3.0. Additional exam requirements/recommendations for international students: Required—TOEFL (minimum score 65 iBT); Recommended—IELTS (minimum score 6). Electronic applications accepted.

Grand Canyon University, Colangelo College of Business, Phoenix, AZ 85017-1097. Offers accounting (MBA, MS); business analytics (MS); disaster preparedness and executive fire service leadership (MS); finance (MBA); general management (MBA); health systems management (MBA); information technology management (MS); leadership (MBA, MS); marketing (MBA); organizational leadership and entrepreneurship (MS); project management (MBA); sports business (MBA); strategic human resource management (MBA). *Accreditation:* ACBSP. *Program availability:* Part-time, evening/weekend, online learning. *Entrance requirements:* For master's, equivalent of two years' full-time professional work experience. Additional exam requirements/recommendations for international students: Required—TOEFL (minimum score 575 paper-based; 90 iBT), IELTS (minimum score 7). Electronic applications accepted.

Grand Canyon University, College of Doctoral Studies, Phoenix, AZ 85017-1097. Offers data analytics (DBA); general psychology (PhD), including cognition and instruction, industrial and organizational psychology, integrating technology, learning, and psychology, performance psychology; management (DBA); marketing (DBA); organizational leadership (Ed D), including behavioral health, Christian ministry, health care administration, organizational development. *Degree requirements:* For doctorate, comprehensive exam, thesis/dissertation. *Entrance requirements:* For doctorate, minimum GPA of 3.4 on earned advanced degree from regionally-accredited institution; transcripts; goals statement.

Harvard University, Harvard Business School, Doctoral Programs in Management, Boston, MA 02163. Offers accounting and management (DBA); business economics (PhD); health policy management (PhD); management (DBA); marketing (DBA); organizational behavior (PhD); science, technology and management (PhD); strategy (DBA); technology and operations management (DBA). *Degree requirements:* For doctorate, comprehensive exam (for some programs), thesis/dissertation. *Entrance requirements:* For doctorate, GRE General Test or GMAT. Additional exam requirements/recommendations for international students: Required—TOEFL.

Hawai'i Pacific University, College of Business, Program in Business Administration, Honolulu, HI 96813. Offers finance (MBA); human resource management (MBA); information systems (MBA); international business (MBA); management (MBA); marketing (MBA); organizational change and development (MBA). *Program availability:* Part-time, evening/weekend, 100% online, blended/hybrid learning. *Faculty:* 7 full-time (3 women), 3 part-time/adjunct (0 women). *Students:* 88 full-time (34 women), 28 part-time (18 women); includes 63 minority (9 Black or African American, non-Hispanic/Latino; 17 Asian, non-Hispanic/Latino; 14 Hispanic/Latino; 1 Native Hawaiian or other Pacific Islander, non-Hispanic/Latino; 22 Two or more races, non-Hispanic/Latino), 29 international. Average age 32. 82 applicants, 78% accepted, 40 enrolled. In 2017, 87 master's awarded. *Entrance requirements:* For master's, GMAT or GRE. Additional exam requirements/recommendations for international students: Recommended—TOEFL (minimum score 550 paper-based; 80 iBT), IELTS (minimum score 6), TWE (minimum score 5). *Application deadline:* For fall admission, 1/15 priority date for domestic students; for spring admission, 10/15 priority date for domestic students. Applications are processed on a rolling basis. Application fee: $50. Electronic applications accepted. *Expenses: Tuition:* Full-time $18,000; part-time $1000 per credit. *Required fees:* $200; $26 per credit. Tuition and fees vary according to course load and program. *Financial support:* In 2017–18, 24 students received support. Research assistantships, career-related internships or fieldwork, Federal Work-Study, scholarships/grants, tuition waivers (partial), and unspecified assistantships available. Financial award application deadline: 3/1; financial award applicants required to submit FAFSA. *Unit head:* Dr. Daewoo Park, Department Chair, 808-544-1463, E-mail: dwpark@hpu.edu. *Application contact:* Danny Lam, Assistant Director of Graduate Admissions, 808-544-1135, E-mail: graduate@hpu.edu.
Website: https://www.hpu.edu/cob/grad-programs/mba.html

HEC Montreal, School of Business Administration, Doctoral Program in Administration, Montréal, QC H3T 2A7, Canada. Offers accounting (PhD); applied economics (PhD); data science (PhD); finance (PhD); financial engineering (PhD); information technology (PhD); international business (PhD); logistics and operations management (PhD); management science (PhD); management, strategy and organizations (PhD); marketing (PhD); organizational behaviour and human resources (PhD). Program offered jointly with Concordia University, McGill University, and Universite du Quebec a Montreal. *Accreditation:* AACSB. *Students:* 114 full-time (47 women). 78 applicants, 42% accepted, 24 enrolled. In 2017, 23 doctorates awarded. *Entrance requirements:* For doctorate, TAGE MAGE, GMAT, or GRE, master's degree in administration or related field. *Application deadline:* For fall admission, 1/15 for domestic and international students. Application fee: $88 ($187 for international students). Electronic applications accepted. *Expenses:* Tuition, state resident: full-time $2869 Canadian dollars; part-time $79.70 Canadian dollars per credit. Tuition, nonresident: full-time $8883 Canadian dollars; part-time $246.76 Canadian dollars per credit. *International tuition:* $19,648 Canadian dollars full-time. *Required fees:* $41.20 Canadian dollars per credit. $67.94 Canadian dollars per term. Tuition and fees vary according to degree level and program. *Financial support:* Research assistantships, teaching assistantships, and scholarships/ grants available. Financial award application deadline: 9/2. *Faculty research:* Art management, business policy, entrepreneurship, new technologies, transportation. *Unit head:* Jacques Robert, Director, 514-340-6853, E-mail: jacques.robert@hec.ca. *Application contact:* Julie Bilodeau, PhD Program Analyst, 514-340-6151, Fax: 514-340-6411, E-mail: analyste.phd@hec.ca.
Website: http://www.hec.ca/en/programs/phd/index.html

HEC Montreal, School of Business Administration, Master of Science Programs in Administration, Program in Marketing, Montréal, QC H3T 2A7, Canada. Offers M Sc. Program offered in French. *Students:* 82 full-time (63 women), 22 part-time (18 women). 85 applicants, 53% accepted, 27 enrolled. In 2017, 55 master's awarded. *Entrance requirements:* For master's, BBA, undergraduate degree in another field, degree deemed equivalent by program director and minimum GPA of 3.0 on 4.3 scale. Additional exam requirements/recommendations for international students: Required—TAGE MAGE (minimum recommended score of 283), GMAT (minimum recommended score of 630), or GRE. *Application deadline:* For fall admission, 3/15 for domestic and international students; for winter admission, 9/15 for domestic and international students. Application fee: $88 Canadian dollars ($184 Canadian dollars for international students). Electronic applications accepted. *Expenses:* Tuition, state resident: full-time $2869 Canadian dollars; part-time $79.70 Canadian dollars per credit. Tuition, nonresident: full-time $8883 Canadian dollars; part-time $246.76 Canadian dollars per credit. *International tuition:* $19,648 Canadian dollars full-time. *Required fees:* $41.20 Canadian dollars per credit. $67.94 Canadian dollars per term. Tuition and fees vary according to degree level and program. *Financial support:* Research assistantships, teaching assistantships, and scholarships/grants available. Financial award application deadline: 9/2. *Unit head:* Dr. Marie-Helene Jobin, Director, 514-340-6283, E-mail: marie-helene.jobin@hec.ca. *Application contact:* Marianne de Moura, Administrative Director, 514-340-6151, Fax: 514-340-6411, E-mail: aide@hec.ca.
Website: http://www.hec.ca/programmes/maitrises/maitrise-marketing/index.html

Herzing University Online, Program in Business Administration, Menomonee Falls, WI 53051. Offers accounting (MBA); business administration (MBA); business management (MBA); healthcare management (MBA); human resources (MBA); marketing (MBA); project management (MBA); technology management (MBA). *Program availability:* Online learning.

Hofstra University, Frank G. Zarb School of Business, Programs in Marketing and International Business, Hempstead, NY 11549. Offers business administration (MBA), including international business, marketing; international business (Advanced Certificate); marketing (MS, Advanced Certificate); marketing research (MS). *Program availability:* Part-time, evening/weekend, blended/hybrid learning. *Students:* 72 full-time (40 women), 20 part-time (11 women); includes 11 minority (2 Black or African American, non-Hispanic/Latino; 6 Asian, non-Hispanic/Latino; 2 Hispanic/Latino; 1 Two or more races, non-Hispanic/Latino), 58 international. Average age 25. 227 applicants, 74% accepted, 35 enrolled. In 2017, 51 master's awarded. *Degree requirements:* For master's, capstone course (for MBA), thesis (for MS), minimum GPA of 3.0. *Entrance requirements:* For master's, GMAT/GRE, 2 letters of recommendation, resume, essay. Additional exam requirements/recommendations for international students: Required—TOEFL (minimum score 550 paper-based; 80 iBT); Recommended—IELTS (minimum score 6). *Application deadline:* Applications are processed on a rolling basis. Application fee: $75. Electronic applications accepted. *Expenses:* $1,322 per credit. *Financial support:* In 2017–18, 28 students received support, including 24 fellowships with full and partial tuition reimbursements available (averaging $5,002 per year), 2 research assistantships with full and partial tuition reimbursements available (averaging $7,390 per year); career-related internships or fieldwork, Federal Work-Study, institutionally sponsored loans, scholarships/grants, tuition waivers (full and partial), and unspecified assistantships also available. Support available to part-time students. Financial award applicants required to submit FAFSA. *Faculty research:* Cross-cultural consumer behavior; social, digital, global, and strategic issues in marketing; consumer health/well-being; ethnocentrism and animosity. *Unit head:* Dr. Anil Mathur, Chairperson, 516-463-5346, Fax: 516-463-4834, E-mail: anil.mathur@hofstra.edu. *Application contact:* Sunil Samuel, Assistant Vice President of Admissions, 516-463-4723, Fax: 516-463-4664, E-mail: graduateadmission@hofstra.edu.
Website: http://www.hofstra.edu/business/

Holy Names University, Graduate Division, Department of Business, Oakland, CA 94619-1699. Offers finance (MBA); management and leadership (MBA); marketing (MBA). *Program availability:* Part-time, evening/weekend. *Entrance requirements:* For master's, minimum undergraduate GPA of 2.6 overall, 3.0 in major; two recommendations (letter or form) from previous professors or current or previous work supervisors; 1-3 page personal statement; resume. Additional exam requirements/recommendations for international students: Required—TOEFL (minimum score 550 paper-based; 79 iBT). Electronic applications accepted. Application fee is waived when completed online. *Expenses:* Contact institution. *Faculty research:* Business ethics, sustainable economics, accounting models, cross-cultural management, diversity in organizations.

Hood College, Graduate School, Department of Economics and Business Administration, Frederick, MD 21701-8575. Offers accounting (MBA, Certificate); finance (MBA); financial management (Certificate); human resource management (MBA); information systems (MBA); marketing (MBA); organizational management (Certificate); public management (MBA). *Accreditation:* ACBSP. *Program availability:* Part-time, evening/weekend. *Faculty:* 4 full-time (2 women), 7 part-time/adjunct (1 woman). *Students:* 21 full-time (12 women), 91 part-time (47 women); includes 19 minority (8 Black or African American, non-Hispanic/Latino; 3 Asian, non-Hispanic/Latino; 8 Hispanic/Latino), 15 international. Average age 31. 34 applicants, 97% accepted, 23 enrolled. In 2017, 42 master's awarded. *Degree requirements:* For master's, capstone/final research project. *Entrance requirements:* For master's, minimum GPA of 3.0 (or resume and two letters of recommendation), copy of official transcripts, essay. Additional exam requirements/recommendations for international students: Required—TOEFL (minimum score 575 paper-based; 89 iBT), IELTS (minimum score 6.5). *Application deadline:* For fall admission, 8/15 for domestic students, 8/5 for international students; for spring admission, 12/1 for domestic and international students; for summer admission, 5/1 for domestic students, 4/15 for international students. Applications are processed on a rolling basis. Application fee: $35. Electronic applications accepted. *Expenses:* $550 per credit hour plus $110 per semester comprehensive fee. *Financial support:* Tuition waivers (partial) and unspecified assistantships available. Financial award applicants required to submit FAFSA. *Faculty research:* Corporate strategy and sustainable competitive advantages, business ethics, entrepreneurship, investments management, economic development. *Unit head:* Dr. April M. Boulton, Dean of the Graduate School, 301-696-3600, Fax: 301-696-3597, E-mail: gofurther@hood.edu. *Application contact:* Jan Marcus, Assistant Director of Graduate Admissions, 301-696-3603, E-mail: gofurther@hood.edu.

Hope International University, School of Graduate and Professional Studies, Program in Business Administration, Fullerton, CA 92831-3138. Offers general management (MBA, MSM); international development (MBA, MSM); marketing management (MBA, MSM); non-profit management (MBA, MSM). *Program availability:* Part-time, online learning. *Degree requirements:* For master's, comprehensive exam (for some programs), thesis (for some programs), project. *Entrance requirements:* For master's, minimum GPA of 3.0; 2 references. Additional exam requirements/recommendations for international students: Required—TOEFL (minimum score 550 paper-based; 86 iBT); Recommended—IELTS (minimum score 6.5). Electronic applications accepted. *Expenses:* Contact institution.

Howard University, School of Business, Graduate Programs in Business, Washington, DC 20059-0002. Offers accounting (MBA); entrepreneurship (MBA); finance (MBA); general management (MBA); human resources management (MBA); information systems (MBA); international business (MBA); marketing (MBA); supply chain management (MBA); JD/MBA. *Accreditation:* AACSB. *Program availability:* Part-time, evening/weekend, online learning. *Entrance requirements:* For master's, GMAT,

Marketing

minimum 1 year post undergraduate work experience, resume, 3 letters of recommendation, advanced college algebra. Additional exam requirements/recommendations for international students: Required—TOEFL. *Faculty research:* Marketing research in multi-ethnic populations, U.S. trade policies and international relations, risk management (finance).

Hult International Business School, Graduate Programs, Cambridge, MA 02141. Offers business administration (EMBA); business analytics (MBA, MIB); business statistics (MBS); disruptive innovation (MDI); entrepreneurship (MBA, MIB); family business (MBA, MIB); finance (MBA, MF, MIB); international marketing (MIM); marketing (MBA, MIB); project management (MBA, MIB). MDI and MBS offered in San Francisco; MBA also offered in Boston, San Francisco, Dubai, Shanghai, and New York. *Entrance requirements:* For master's, GMAT, 3 years of work experience. Additional exam requirements/recommendations for international students: Required—TOEFL. Electronic applications accepted. *Expenses:* Contact institution.

Illinois Institute of Technology, Stuart School of Business, Program in Marketing Analytics and Communication, Chicago, IL 60661. Offers MS, MBA/MS. *Program availability:* Part-time, evening/weekend. *Entrance requirements:* For master's, GRE (minimum score 1000) or GMAT (500). Additional exam requirements/recommendations for international students: Required—TOEFL (minimum score 600 paper-based; 85 iBT); Recommended—IELTS (minimum score 7). Electronic applications accepted. *Expenses:* Contact institution.

Indiana Tech, Program in Business Administration, Fort Wayne, IN 46803-1297. Offers accounting (MBA); health care management (MBA); human resources (MBA); management (MBA); marketing (MBA). *Program availability:* Part-time, evening/weekend, online learning. *Entrance requirements:* For master's, GMAT, bachelor's degree from regionally-accredited university; minimum undergraduate GPA of 2.5; 2 years of significant work experience; 3 letters of recommendation. Electronic applications accepted.

Indiana University–Purdue University Indianapolis, Kelley School of Business, Evening MBA Program, Indianapolis, IN 46202-5151. Offers accounting (MBA); entrepreneurship (MBA); finance (MBA); general administration (MBA); marketing (MBA); supply chain management (MBA); MBA/JD; MBA/MD; MBA/MHA; MBA/MS; MBA/MSA; MBA/MSE. *Program availability:* Part-time-only, evening/weekend, online learning. *Entrance requirements:* For master's, GMAT or GRE, 2 years of professional work experience. Additional exam requirements/recommendations for international students: Required—TOEFL or IELTS. Electronic applications accepted. *Expenses:* Contact institution. *Faculty research:* Entrepreneurship; corporate finance; international business; consumer behavior; supply chain; business law.

Indiana University South Bend, Judd Leighton School of Business and Economics, South Bend, IN 46615. Offers accounting (MSA); business (Graduate Certificate); business administration (MBA), including finance, human resource management, marketing; MBA/MSA. *Program availability:* Part-time, evening/weekend. *Entrance requirements:* For master's, GMAT. Additional exam requirements/recommendations for international students: Required—TOEFL (minimum score 550 paper-based; 79 iBT). Electronic applications accepted. *Expenses:* Contact institution. *Faculty research:* Financial accounting, consumer research, capital budgeting research, business strategy research.

Instituto Tecnologico de Santo Domingo, Graduate School, Area of Business, Santo Domingo, Dominican Republic. Offers banking and securities markets (M Mgmt); corporate finance (M Mgmt); human resources management (M Mgmt, Certificate); international trade management (M Mgmt); marketing (M Mgmt); organizational development (M Mgmt); quality and productivity management (Certificate); tax management and planning (M Mgmt); upper management (M Mgmt).

Instituto Tecnologico de Santo Domingo, Graduate School, Area of Humanities and Social Sciences, Santo Domingo, Dominican Republic. Offers accounting (Certificate); adult education (Certificate); applied linguistics (MA); economics (MA); education (M Ed); educational psychology (MA, Certificate); gender and development (MA, Certificate); humanistic studies (MA); international marketing management (Certificate); international relations in the Caribbean basin (Certificate); intervention systems in family therapy (MA); linguistic and literary communication (Certificate); pedagogical support (MA); social science education (M Ed); sustainable human development (MA); terminal illness and death psychology (Certificate); youth and adult education (M Ed).

Instituto Tecnológico y de Estudios Superiores de Monterrey, Campus Central de Veracruz, Graduate Programs, Córdoba, Mexico. Offers administration (MA); administration of information technologies (MTI); computer sciences (MCC); education (MEE); educational institution administration (MAD); educational technology (MTE); electronic commerce (MCE); finance (MAF); humanistic studies (MEH); international business for Latin America (MNL); marketing (MMT); science (MCP). *Program availability:* Part-time, evening/weekend, online learning. *Degree requirements:* For master's, thesis (for some programs). *Entrance requirements:* For master's, PAEP College Board. Electronic applications accepted.

Instituto Tecnológico y de Estudios Superiores de Monterrey, Campus Ciudad Obregón, Program in Marketing Technology, Ciudad Obregón, Mexico. Offers MMT.

Instituto Tecnológico y de Estudios Superiores de Monterrey, Campus Cuernavaca, Programs in Business Administration, Temixco, Mexico. Offers finance (MA); human resources management (MA); international business (MA); marketing (MA).

Instituto Tecnológico y de Estudios Superiores de Monterrey, Campus Estado de México, Professional and Graduate Division, Estado de Mexico, Mexico. Offers administration of information technologies (MITA); architecture (M Arch); business administration (GMBA, MBA); computer sciences (MCS, PhD); education (M Ed); educational institution administration (MAD); educational technology and innovation (PhD); electronic commerce (MEC); environmental systems (MS); finance (MAF); humanistic studies (MHS); information sciences and knowledge management (MISKM); information systems (MS); manufacturing systems (MS); marketing (MEM); quality systems and productivity (MS); science and materials engineering (PhD); telecommunications management (MTM). *Program availability:* Part-time, online learning. *Degree requirements:* For master's, one foreign language, thesis (for some programs); for doctorate, one foreign language, thesis/dissertation. *Entrance requirements:* For master's, E-PAEP 500, interview; for doctorate, E-PAEP 500, research proposal. Additional exam requirements/recommendations for international students: Required—TOEFL (minimum score 550 paper-based). *Faculty research:* Surface treatments by plasmas, mechanical properties, robotics, graphical computing, mechatronics security protocols.

Instituto Tecnológico y de Estudios Superiores de Monterrey, Campus Monterrey, Graduate School of Business Administration and Leadership, Program in Business Administration, Monterrey, Mexico. Offers business administration (MA, MBA); finance (M Sc); international business (M Sc); marketing (M Sc). *Program availability:* Part-time. *Degree requirements:* For master's, one foreign language, thesis. *Entrance requirements:* For master's, GMAT. Additional exam requirements/recommendations for international students: Required—TOEFL. *Faculty research:* Technology management, quality management, organizational theory and behavior.

Inter American University of Puerto Rico, Aguadilla Campus, Graduate School, Aguadilla, PR 00605. Offers accounting (MBA); counseling psychology specializing in family (MS); criminal justice (MA); educative management and leadership (MA); elementary education (M Ed); finance (MBA); human resources (MBA); industrial management (MBA); management information systems (MBA); marketing (MBA). *Program availability:* Part-time, evening/weekend. *Degree requirements:* For master's, comprehensive exam. *Entrance requirements:* For master's, EXADEP, 2 letters of recommendation, minimum GPA of 2.5. Electronic applications accepted.

Inter American University of Puerto Rico, Fajardo Campus, Graduate Programs, Fajardo, PR 00738-7003. Offers computer science (MS); educational management and leadership (MA Ed); general business (MBA); human resources (MBA); management information systems (MBA); marketing (MBA); special education (MA Ed). *Program availability:* Online learning. *Faculty:* 1 full-time (0 women), 25 part-time/adjunct (13 women). *Students:* 1 (woman) full-time, 126 part-time (81 women).

Inter American University of Puerto Rico, Guayama Campus, Department of Business Administration, Guayama, PR 00785. Offers marketing (MBA).

Inter American University of Puerto Rico, Metropolitan Campus, Graduate Programs, Program in Marketing, San Juan, PR 00919-1293. Offers MBA. *Degree requirements:* For master's, comprehensive exam. *Entrance requirements:* For master's, GRE or EXADEP, interview. Electronic applications accepted.

Inter American University of Puerto Rico, Ponce Campus, Graduate School, Mercedita, PR 00715-1602. Offers accounting (MBA); biology (M Ed); chemistry (M Ed); criminal justice (MA); elementary education (M Ed); English as a Second Language (M Ed); finance (MBA); history (M Ed); human resources (MBA); marketing (MBA); mathematics (M Ed); Spanish (M Ed). *Entrance requirements:* For master's, minimum GPA of 2.5.

Inter American University of Puerto Rico, San Germán Campus, Graduate Studies Center, Program in Business Administration, San Germán, PR 00683-5008. Offers accounting (MBA); finance (MBA); general business administration (MBA); human resources (MBA, PhD); industrial relations (MBA); information systems (MBA); international and interregional business (PhD); management (MBA); marketing (MBA). *Program availability:* Part-time, evening/weekend. *Degree requirements:* For master's, comprehensive exam. *Entrance requirements:* For master's, GRE General Test or EXADEP, minimum GPA of 3.0.

International University in Geneva, Business Programs, Geneva, Switzerland. Offers business administration (MBA, DBA); entrepreneurship (MBA); international business (MIB); international trade (MIT); sales and marketing (MBA). *Accreditation:* ACBSP. *Program availability:* Part-time, evening/weekend. *Degree requirements:* For master's, comprehensive exam. *Entrance requirements:* For master's, GMAT. Additional exam requirements/recommendations for international students: Required—TOEFL. Electronic applications accepted.

The International University of Monaco, Graduate Programs, Monte Carlo, Monaco. Offers entrepreneurship (EMBA, MBA); financial engineering (M Sc); hedge fund and private equity (M Sc); international marketing (EMBA, MBA); international wealth management (M Sc); luxury goods and services (EMBA, M Sc, MBA); wealth and asset management (EMBA, MBA). *Program availability:* Part-time. *Degree requirements:* For master's, comprehensive exam (for some programs), applied research project. *Entrance requirements:* Additional exam requirements/recommendations for international students: Required—TOEFL (minimum score 550 paper-based), IELTS. Electronic applications accepted. *Faculty research:* Gaming, leadership, disintermediation.

Iona College, School of Business, Department of Marketing and International Business, New Rochelle, NY 10801-1890. Offers international business (AC, PMC); marketing (MBA); sports and entertainment management (AC). *Program availability:* Part-time, evening/weekend. *Faculty:* 3 full-time (1 woman), 1 (woman) part-time/adjunct. *Students:* 13 full-time (8 women), 16 part-time (6 women); includes 10 minority (5 Black or African American, non-Hispanic/Latino; 1 Asian, non-Hispanic/Latino; 4 Hispanic/Latino), 2 international. Average age 24. 15 applicants, 100% accepted, 9 enrolled. In 2017, 21 master's, 65 other advanced degrees awarded. *Entrance requirements:* For master's, GMAT, 2 letters of recommendation, minimum GPA of 3.0; for other advanced degree, GMAT, minimum GPA of 3.0. Additional exam requirements/recommendations for international students: Required—TOEFL (minimum score 550 paper-based; 80 iBT), IELTS (minimum score 6.5). *Application deadline:* For fall admission, 8/15 priority date for domestic students, 8/1 priority date for international students; for winter admission, 11/15 priority date for domestic students, 11/1 priority date for international students; for spring admission, 2/15 priority date for domestic students, 2/1 priority date for international students; for summer admission, 5/15 for domestic students, 5/1 priority date for international students. Applications are processed on a rolling basis. Application fee: $50. Electronic applications accepted. *Expenses:* Contact institution. *Financial support:* In 2017–18, 7 students received support. Scholarships/grants, tuition waivers (partial), and unspecified assistantships available. Support available to part-time students. Financial award application deadline: 4/15; financial award applicants required to submit FAFSA. *Faculty research:* Business ethics, international retailing, mega-marketing, consumer behavior and consumer confidence. *Unit head:* Dr. Susan G. Rozensher, Department Chair, 914-637-2748, E-mail: srozensher@iona.edu. *Application contact:* Katelyn Brunck, Director of MBA Admissions, 914-633-2451, Fax: 914-633-2277, E-mail: kbrunck@iona.edu.
Website: http://www.iona.edu/Academics/Hagan-School-of-Business/Departments/Marketing/Graduate-Programs.aspx

Jacksonville University, Davis College of Business, Accelerated Day-time MBA Program, Jacksonville, FL 32211. Offers accounting and finance (MBA); business administration (MBA); consumer goods and services marketing (MBA); management (MBA); management accounting (MBA). *Faculty:* 5 full-time (2 women). *Students:* 43 full-time (17 women), 7 part-time (2 women); includes 9 minority (4 Black or African American, non-Hispanic/Latino; 4 Hispanic/Latino; 1 Two or more races, non-Hispanic/Latino), 18 international. Average age 26. 70 applicants, 90% accepted, 44 enrolled. In 2017, 42 master's awarded. *Entrance requirements:* For master's, GMAT or GRE, bachelor's degree from regionally-accredited institution, original transcripts of academic work, statement of intent, resume, 3 letters of recommendation; 3 years of work experience (recommended); interview with program advisor. Additional exam requirements/recommendations for international students: Required—TOEFL (minimum score 550 paper-based; 79 iBT), IELTS (minimum score 6), PTE (minimum score 53). *Application deadline:* For fall admission, 7/1 priority date for domestic students, 6/15 priority date for international students; for spring admission, 12/1 priority date for domestic students, 11/15 priority date for international students; for summer admission, 4/1 for domestic students, 3/15 for international students. Applications are processed on a rolling basis. Application fee: $50. Electronic applications accepted. *Expenses:* $793 per credit hour; $150-$250 books per course (estimated). *Financial support:* Scholarships/grants, health care benefits, and unspecified assistantships available. Financial award application deadline: 6/30; financial award applicants required to submit FAFSA. *Faculty research:* Behavioral finance, game theory, regional economic integration, information sabotage, public choice and public finance. *Unit head:* Dr. Douglas Johansen, Associate Dean and Graduate Programs Director, 904-256-7763, Fax: 904-256-7168, E-mail: djohans@ju.edu. *Application contact:* AnnaMaria Murphy, Assistant Director of Graduate Admissions, 904-256-7426, Fax: 904-256-7012, E-mail: mba@ju.edu.

See Display on page 104 and Close-Up on page 175.

Jacksonville University, Davis College of Business, Executive Master of Business Administration Program, Jacksonville, FL 32211. Offers consumer goods and services marketing (MBA); leadership development (MBA). *Accreditation:* AACSB. *Program availability:* Evening/weekend. *Faculty:* 23 full-time (8 women), 4 part-time/adjunct (2 women). *Students:* 25 full-time (10 women), 13 part-time (7 women); includes 6 minority (5 Black or African American, non-Hispanic/Latino; 1 Two or more races, non-Hispanic/Latino). Average age 39. 43 applicants, 91% accepted, 32 enrolled. In 2017, 10 master's awarded. *Entrance requirements:* For master's, resume, 5-7 years of professional experience, 3 letters of recommendation, corporate letter of support, statement of purpose, interview. Additional exam requirements/recommendations for international students: Required—TOEFL (minimum score 550 paper-based; 79 iBT), IELTS (minimum score 6), PTE (minimum score 53). *Application deadline:* For fall admission, 7/1 priority date for domestic students, 6/15 priority date for international students; for spring admission, 12/1 priority date for domestic students, 11/15 for international students; for summer admission, 4/1 priority date for domestic students, 3/15 for international students. Applications are processed on a rolling basis. Application fee: $50. Electronic applications accepted. *Expenses:* $61,360 tuition (includes books, international trip, executive physical at Mayo Clinic, software, fees and meals while on campus). *Financial support:* In 2017-18, 2 students received support. Scholarships/grants, health care benefits, and unspecified assistantships available. Financial award application deadline: 6/30; financial award applicants required to submit FAFSA. *Faculty research:* Data analytics, emerging markets and economic development, high-performing teams, government deficit, learning from corporate failure. *Unit head:* Dr. Douglas Johansen, Associate Dean and Director of Graduate Studies, 904-256-7763, Fax: 904-256-7168, E-mail: djohans@ju.edu. *Application contact:* AnnaMaria Murphy, Assistant Director of Graduate Admissions, 904-256-7426, Fax: 904-256-7012, E-mail: mba@ju.edu.
See Display on page 104 and Close-Up on page 175.

Jacksonville University, Davis College of Business, FLEX Master of Business Administration Program, Jacksonville, FL 32211. Offers accounting and finance (MBA); business management (MBA); consumer goods and services marketing (MBA); management (MBA); management accounting (MBA); JD/MBA; MBA/MPP; MSN/MBA. MBA/JD offered jointly with Florida School of Law; MSN/MBA offered jointly with JU's Keigwin School of Nursing; MBA/MPP offered jointly with JU's Public Policy Institute. *Accreditation:* AACSB. *Program availability:* Part-time, evening/weekend, blended/hybrid learning. *Faculty:* 23 full-time (8 women), 4 part-time/adjunct (2 women). *Students:* 32 full-time (7 women), 80 part-time (30 women); includes 34 minority (15 Black or African American, non-Hispanic/Latino; 1 American Indian or Alaska Native, non-Hispanic/Latino; 6 Asian, non-Hispanic/Latino; 10 Hispanic/Latino; 2 Two or more races, non-Hispanic/Latino), 2 international. Average age 33. 43 applicants, 91% accepted, 32 enrolled. In 2017, 56 master's awarded. *Entrance requirements:* For master's, GMAT or GRE, bachelor's degree from regionally-accredited institution, 3 years of full-time work experience (recommended), resume, statement of intent, 3 letters of recommendation, interview with program advisor. Additional exam requirements/recommendations for international students: Required—TOEFL (minimum score 550 paper-based; 79 iBT), IELTS (minimum score 6), PTE (minimum score 53). *Application deadline:* For fall admission, 7/1 priority date for domestic students, 6/15 priority date for international students; for spring admission, 12/1 priority date for domestic students, 11/15 priority date for international students; for summer admission, 4/1 priority date for domestic students, 3/15 priority date for international students. Applications are processed on a rolling basis. Application fee: $50. Electronic applications accepted. *Expenses:* $793 per credit hour; $150-$250 books per course (estimated). *Financial support:* Scholarships/grants and health care benefits available. Financial award application deadline: 6/30; financial award applicants required to submit FAFSA. *Faculty research:* Downsizing with integrity; impact of YouTube videos; game theory; analysis of effective tax rates; creativity innovation and change. *Unit head:* Dr. Douglas Johansen, Associate Dean and Director of Graduate Studies, 904-256-7763, Fax: 904-256-7168, E-mail: djohans@ju.edu. *Application contact:* AnnaMaria Murphy, Assistant Director of Graduate Admissions, 904-256-7426, Fax: 904-256-7012, E-mail: mba@ju.edu.
See Display on page 104 and Close-Up on page 175.

Johns Hopkins University, Carey Business School, MS in Marketing Program, Baltimore, MD 21218. Offers MS. *Program availability:* Part-time, evening/weekend. *Faculty:* 93 full-time (33 women), 45 part-time/adjunct (11 women). *Students:* 151 full-time (105 women), 13 part-time (12 women); includes 6 minority (3 Black or African American, non-Hispanic/Latino; 1 Asian, non-Hispanic/Latino; 2 Hispanic/Latino), 150 international. Average age 23. 639 applicants, 71% accepted, 152 enrolled. In 2017, 130 master's awarded. *Degree requirements:* For master's, 36 credits. *Entrance requirements:* For master's, GMAT or GRE. Additional exam requirements/recommendations for international students: Required—TOEFL, IELTS. *Application deadline:* For fall admission, 4/3 for domestic and international students. Applications are processed on a rolling basis. Application fee: $100. Electronic applications accepted. *Expenses:* $66,500 (full-time); $1,330 per credit (part-time). *Financial support:* In 2017-18, 22 students received support. Scholarships/grants available. Support available to part-time students. Financial award application deadline: 4/15; financial award applicants required to submit FAFSA. *Faculty research:* Decision making, marketing management, marketing strategy. *Unit head:* Dr. Kevin Frick, Vice Dean of Education, 410-234-9272, E-mail: kfrick@jhu.edu. *Application contact:* Office of Admissions, 410-234-9220, Fax: 443-529-1554, E-mail: carey.admissions@jhu.edu. Website: http://carey.jhu.edu/academics/master-of-science/ms-in-marketing/

Kansas State University, Graduate School, College of Business, Program in Business Administration, Manhattan, KS 66506. Offers data analytics (MBA); finance (MBA); management (MBA); marketing (MBA); technology entrepreneurship (MBA). *Accreditation:* AACSB. *Program availability:* Part-time, 100% online. *Entrance requirements:* For master's, GMAT (minimum score of 500), minimum undergraduate GPA of 3.0. Additional exam requirements/recommendations for international students: Required—TOEFL (minimum score 550 paper-based; 79 iBT); Recommended—IELTS (minimum score 7). Electronic applications accepted. *Expenses:* Contact institution. *Faculty research:* Organizational citizenship behavior, service marketing, impression management, human resources management, lean manufacturing and supply chain management, financial market behavior and investment management, data analytics, corporate responsibility, technology entrepreneurship.

Keiser University, Doctor of Business Administration Program, Fort Lauderdale, FL 33309. Offers global business (DBA); global management (DBA); marketing (DBA). Website: http://www.keiseruniversity.edu/graduateschool/business-administration-phd.php

Keiser University, Master of Business Administration Program, Fort Lauderdale, FL 33309. Offers accounting (MBA); health services administration (MBA); international business (MBA); management (MBA); marketing (MBA); technology management (MBA). All concentrations except technology management also offered in Mandarin. *Program availability:* Part-time, online learning. *Unit head:* Yan Luo-Beitler, Department Chair. Website: http://www.keiseruniversity.edu/graduateschool/mba.php#accounting

Kent State University, College of Business Administration, Doctoral Program in Marketing, Kent, OH 44242. Offers PhD. *Faculty:* 18 full-time (8 women). *Students:* 7 full-time (5 women), 5 international. Average age 32. 10 applicants, 20% accepted. In 2017, 2 doctorates awarded. *Degree requirements:* For doctorate, comprehensive exam, thesis/dissertation, oral defense. *Entrance requirements:* For doctorate, GMAT or GRE. Additional exam requirements/recommendations for international students: Required—TOEFL (minimum score 600 paper-based; 100 iBT), IELTS (minimum score 7). *Application deadline:* For fall admission, 1/1 for domestic students, 2/1 for international students. Application fee: $45 ($70 for international students). Electronic applications accepted. *Expenses:* $11,300 per academic year. *Financial support:* In 2017-18, 8 students received support, including 8 teaching assistantships with full tuition reimbursements available (averaging $23,000 per year); Federal Work-Study also available. Financial award application deadline: 2/1; financial award applicants required to submit FAFSA. *Faculty research:* Advertising effects, satisfaction, international marketing, high-tech marketing, personality and consumer behavior. *Unit head:* Dr. Robert Jewell, Chair and Professor, 330-672-2170, Fax: 330-672-5006, E-mail: rjewell1@kent.edu. *Application contact:* Felecia A. Urbanek, Assistant Director, 330-672-2282, Fax: 330-672-7303, E-mail: gradbus@kent.edu.
Website: http://www.kent.edu/business/phd

King University, School of Business and Economics, Bristol, TN 37620-2699. Offers accounting (MBA); finance (MBA); healthcare management (MBA); human resources management (MBA); leadership (MBA); management (MBA); marketing (MBA); project management (MBA). *Program availability:* Part-time, evening/weekend, online learning. *Degree requirements:* For master's, comprehensive exam, thesis optional. *Entrance requirements:* For master's, GMAT, 2 years of work experience. Additional exam requirements/recommendations for international students: Required—TOEFL (minimum score 550 paper-based). Electronic applications accepted. *Faculty research:* International monetary policy.

Lake Forest Graduate School of Management, The Leadership MBA Program, Lake Forest, IL 60045. Offers finance (MBA); global business (MBA); healthcare management (MBA); management (MBA); marketing (MBA); organizational behavior (MBA). *Program availability:* Part-time, evening/weekend. *Entrance requirements:* For master's, 4 years of work experience in field, interview, 2 letters of recommendation. Electronic applications accepted.

La Salle University, School of Business, Master of Business Administration Program, Philadelphia, PA 19141-1199. Offers accounting (MBA, Post-MBA Certificate); business systems and analytics (MBA, Post-MBA Certificate); finance (MBA, Post-MBA Certificate); general business administration (MBA, Post-MBA Certificate); human resource management (MBA, Post-MBA Certificate); management (MBA, Post-MBA Certificate); marketing (Post-MBA Certificate); MBA/MSN. Program also offered in Switzerland. *Accreditation:* AACSB. *Program availability:* Part-time, evening/weekend, online learning. *Faculty:* 22 full-time (10 women), 10 part-time/adjunct (3 women). *Students:* 59 full-time (25 women), 200 part-time (109 women); includes 66 minority (36 Black or African American, non-Hispanic/Latino; 21 Asian, non-Hispanic/Latino; 7 Hispanic/Latino; 2 Two or more races, non-Hispanic/Latino), 22 international. Average age 31. 216 applicants, 57% accepted, 74 enrolled. In 2017, 146 master's awarded. *Entrance requirements:* For master's, GMAT or GRE, two letters of reference; resume; for Post-MBA Certificate, MBA with minimum GPA of 3.0. Additional exam requirements/recommendations for international students: Required—TOEFL. *Application deadline:* For fall admission, 8/15 priority date for domestic students, 7/15 for international students; for spring admission, 12/15 priority date for domestic students, 11/15 for international students; for summer admission, 4/15 priority date for domestic students, 3/15 for international students. Applications are processed on a rolling basis. Application fee: $35. Electronic applications accepted. Application fee is waived when completed online. *Expenses:* Contact institution. *Financial support:* In 2017-18, 51 students received support. Scholarships/grants available. Support available to part-time students. Financial award application deadline: 8/31; financial award applicants required to submit FAFSA. *Unit head:* Dr. MarySheila McDonald, Interim Dean, 215-951-1040, Fax: 215-951-1886, E-mail: mcdonaldms@lasalle.edu. *Application contact:* Elizabeth Heenan, Director, Graduate and Adult Enrollment, 215-951-1100, Fax: 215-951-1462, E-mail: heenan@lasalle.edu.

Lasell College, Graduate and Professional Studies in Communication, Newton, MA 02466-2709. Offers health communication (MSC, Graduate Certificate); integrated marketing communication (MSC, Graduate Certificate); public relations (MSC, Graduate Certificate). *Program availability:* Part-time, evening/weekend, 100% online, blended/hybrid learning. *Faculty:* 3 full-time (2 women), 7 part-time/adjunct (5 women). *Students:* 25 full-time (16 women), 35 part-time (28 women); includes 12 minority (6 Black or African American, non-Hispanic/Latino; 1 Asian, non-Hispanic/Latino; 4 Hispanic/Latino; 1 Two or more races, non-Hispanic/Latino), 16 international. Average age 30. 53 applicants, 45% accepted, 22 enrolled. In 2017, 28 master's awarded. *Degree requirements:* For master's, comprehensive exam, thesis or alternative, minimum GPA of 3.0; special project or internship. *Entrance requirements:* For master's, one-page personal statement, 2 letters of recommendation, resume, bachelor's degree transcript; for Graduate Certificate, bachelor's degree transcript, 2 letters of recommendation, 1-page personal statement, resume. Additional exam requirements/recommendations for international students: Required—TOEFL (minimum score 550 paper-based, 79 iBT) or IELTS (minimum score 6). *Application deadline:* For fall admission, 8/31 priority date for domestic students, 6/30 priority date for international students; for spring admission, 12/31 priority date for domestic students, 10/31 priority date for international students. Applications are processed on a rolling basis. Electronic applications accepted. *Expenses:* $600 per credit. *Financial support:* Federal Work-Study, scholarships/grants, and tuition discounts available. Support available to part-time students. Financial award application deadline: 8/31; financial award applicants required to submit FAFSA. *Faculty research:* Terrorists' use of the Internet; refugees' use of cell phones as means of communication in Jordan and Germany; political communication; analysis of the media coverage of the conflict and peace process in northern Ireland; interpersonal communication; strategies to address bullying in online communities, in schools and in the workplace. *Unit head:* Eric Turner, Vice President of Graduate and Professional Studies, 617-243-2071, Fax: 617-243-2450, E-mail: gradinfo@lasell.edu. *Application contact:* Adrienne Franciosi, Director of Graduate Enrollment, 617-243-2214, Fax: 617-243-2450, E-mail: gradinfo@lasell.edu.
Website: http://www.lasell.edu/academics/graduate-and-professional-studies/programs-of-study/master-of-science-in-communication.html

Lasell College, Graduate and Professional Studies in Management, Newton, MA 02466-2709. Offers business administration (MBA); elder care management (MSM); hospitality and event management (MSM); human resources management (MSM, Graduate Certificate); management (MSM, Graduate Certificate); marketing (MS, Graduate Certificate); project management (MSM, Graduate Certificate). *Accreditation:* ACBSP. *Program availability:* Part-time, evening/weekend, 100% online, blended/hybrid learning. *Faculty:* 1 full-time (0 women), 15 part-time/adjunct (11 women). *Students:* 41 full-time (25 women), 102 part-time (70 women); includes 34 minority (19 Black or African American, non-Hispanic/Latino; 5 Asian, non-Hispanic/Latino; 8 Hispanic/Latino; 2 Two or more races, non-Hispanic/Latino), 29 international. Average age 32. 128

Marketing

applicants, 46% accepted, 38 enrolled. In 2017, 66 master's, 3 other advanced degrees awarded. *Degree requirements:* For master's, minimum GPA of 3.0; internship or research paper (for MSM). *Entrance requirements:* For master's, one-page personal statement, 2 letters of recommendation, resume, bachelor's degree transcript; proof of microeconomics and statistics (for MBA); for Graduate Certificate, bachelor's degree transcript, 2 letters of recommendation, 1-page personal statement, resume. Additional exam requirements/recommendations for international students: Required—TOEFL (minimum score 550 paper-based, 79 iBT) or IELTS (minimum score 6). *Application deadline:* For fall admission, 8/31 priority date for domestic students, 6/30 priority date for international students; for spring admission, 12/31 priority date for domestic students, 10/31 priority date for international students. Applications are processed on a rolling basis. Electronic applications accepted. *Expenses:* $600 per credit. *Financial support:* Federal Work-Study, scholarships/grants, and tuition discounts available. Support available to part-time students. Financial award application deadline: 8/31; financial award applicants required to submit FAFSA. *Unit head:* Eric Turner, Vice President of Graduate and Professional Studies, 617-243-2071, Fax: 617-243-2450, E-mail: gradinfo@lasell.edu. *Application contact:* Adrienne Franciosi, Director of Graduate Enrollment, 617-243-2214, Fax: 617-243-2450, E-mail: gradinfo@lasell.edu.
Website: http://www.lasell.edu/academics/graduate-and-professional-studies/programs-of-study/master-of-science-in-management.html

La Sierra University, School of Business and Management, Riverside, CA 92505. Offers accounting (MBA); finance (MBA); general management (MBA); human resources management (MBA); leadership, values, and ethics for business and management (Certificate); marketing (MBA). *Degree requirements:* For master's, research project. *Entrance requirements:* For master's, GMAT, minimum GPA of 3.0. Additional exam requirements/recommendations for international students: Required—TOEFL. *Faculty research:* Financial econometrics, institutional assessment and strategic planning, legal issues in management, behavioral finance, content of financial reports.

Lawrence Technological University, College of Management, Southfield, MI 48075-1058. Offers business administration (MBA, DBA), including business analytics (MBA, MS), cybersecurity (MBA, MS), finance (MBA), information systems (MBA), information technology (MBA), marketing (MBA), project management (MBA, MS); cybersecurity (Graduate Certificate); health IT management (Graduate Certificate); information assurance mangement (Graduate Certificate); information systems (MS), including enterprise resource planning, enterprise security management, project management (MBA, MS); information technology (MS, DM), including business analytics (MBA, MS), cybersecurity (MBA, MS), information assurance (MS), project management (MBA, MS); management (PhD); nonprofit management and leadership (Graduate Certificate); operations management (MS), including manufacturing operations, service operations; project management (Graduate Certificate). *Accreditation:* ACBSP. *Program availability:* Part-time, evening/weekend, 100% online. *Faculty:* 13 full-time (6 women), 7 part-time/adjunct (1 woman). *Students:* 8 full-time (3 women), 280 part-time (102 women); includes 70 minority (34 Black or African American, non-Hispanic/Latino; 2 American Indian or Alaska Native, non-Hispanic/Latino; 18 Asian, non-Hispanic/Latino; 11 Hispanic/Latino; 5 Two or more races, non-Hispanic/Latino), 73 international. Average age 34. 143 applicants, 50% accepted, 68 enrolled. In 2017, 114 master's, 7 doctorates, 10 other advanced degrees awarded. Terminal master's awarded for partial completion of doctoral program. *Degree requirements:* For master's, thesis (for some programs); for doctorate, comprehensive exam, thesis/dissertation. *Entrance requirements:* Additional exam requirements/recommendations for international students: Required—TOEFL (minimum score 550 paper-based; 79 iBT), IELTS (minimum score 6.5). *Application deadline:* For fall admission, 5/27 for international students; for spring admission, 10/8 for international students; for summer admission, 2/14 for international students. Applications are processed on a rolling basis. Application fee: $50. Electronic applications accepted. *Expenses: Tuition:* Full-time $15,274; part-time $1091 per credit. One-time fee: $150. *Financial support:* In 2017–18, 35 students received support, including 8 research assistantships with partial tuition reimbursements available (averaging $3,360 per year); career-related internships or fieldwork, unspecified assistantships, and corporate tuition incentives also available. Financial award application deadline: 4/1; financial award applicants required to submit FAFSA. *Faculty research:* Cybersecurity; risk management; IT governance; security controls and countermeasures; threat modeling cyber resilience; autonomous cars; natural language processing; text mining; machine learning; reflective leadership; emerging leadership theories and practice; motivational studies; teaching effectiveness strategies; teamwork; organization development; strategic planning; strengths-based and positive organizational scholarship; global leadership; globalization; corporate governance. *Unit head:* Dr. Bahman Mirshab, Dean, 248-204-3050, E-mail: mgtdean@ltu.edu. *Application contact:* Jane Rohrback, Director of Admissions, 248-204-3160, Fax: 248-204-2228, E-mail: admissions@ltu.edu.
Website: http://www.ltu.edu/management/index.asp

Lewis University, College of Business, Program in Business Administration, Romeoville, IL 60446. Offers accounting (MBA); custom elective option (MBA); e-business (MBA); finance (MBA); healthcare management (MBA); human resources management (MBA); international business (MBA); management information systems (MBA); marketing (MBA); project management (MBA); technology and operations management (MBA). *Program availability:* Part-time, evening/weekend. *Students:* 130 full-time (77 women), 187 part-time (107 women); includes 83 minority (27 Black or African American, non-Hispanic/Latino; 3 American Indian or Alaska Native, non-Hispanic/Latino; 7 Asian, non-Hispanic/Latino; 40 Hispanic/Latino; 6 Two or more races, non-Hispanic/Latino), 31 international. Average age 31. In 2017, 99 master's awarded. *Degree requirements:* For master's, comprehensive exam. *Entrance requirements:* For master's, interview, bachelor's degree, resume, two recommendations. Additional exam requirements/recommendations for international students: Required—TOEFL (minimum score 550 paper-based), IELTS. *Application deadline:* For fall admission, 8/15 priority date for domestic students, 5/1 priority date for international students; for spring admission, 11/15 priority date for international students. Applications are processed on a rolling basis. Application fee: $40. Electronic applications accepted. Tuition and fees vary according to program. *Financial support:* Career-related internships or fieldwork, Federal Work-Study, scholarships/grants, and unspecified assistantships available. Financial award application deadline: 5/1; financial award applicants required to submit FAFSA. *Unit head:* Dr. Maureen Culleeney, Academic Program Director, 815-838-0500 Ext. 5631, E-mail: culleema@lewisu.edu. *Application contact:* Michele Ryan, Director of Admission, 815-838-0500 Ext. 5384, E-mail: ryanml@lewisu.edu.

Liberty University, School of Business, Lynchburg, VA 24515. Offers accounting (MBA, MS), including audit and financial reporting (MS), business (MS), financial services (MS), forensic accounting (MS), leadership (MS), taxation (MS); criminal justice (MBA); cyber security (MS); executive leadership (MA); information systems (MS), including information assurance, technology management; international business (MBA, DBA); leadership (DBA); marketing (MBA, MS, DBA), including digital marketing and advertising (MS), project management (MS), public relations (MS), sports marketing and media (MS); project management (MBA, DBA); public administration (MBA); public relations (MBA). *Program availability:* Part-time, online learning. *Students:* 1,887 full-time (1,003 women), 4,223 part-time (1,950 women); includes 1,570 minority (1,133

Black or African American, non-Hispanic/Latino; 30 American Indian or Alaska Native, non-Hispanic/Latino; 118 Asian, non-Hispanic/Latino; 149 Hispanic/Latino; 13 Native Hawaiian or other Pacific Islander, non-Hispanic/Latino; 127 Two or more races, non-Hispanic/Latino), 109 international. Average age 35. 5,680 applicants, 51% accepted, 1510 enrolled. In 2017, 1,290 master's, 17 doctorates awarded. *Entrance requirements:* For master's, minimum undergraduate GPA of 3.0, 15 hours of upper-level business courses. Additional exam requirements/recommendations for international students: Required—TOEFL (minimum score 600 paper-based; 100 iBT). *Application deadline:* Applications are processed on a rolling basis. Application fee: $50. Electronic applications accepted. *Expenses:* Contact institution. *Financial support:* Applicants required to submit FAFSA. *Unit head:* Dr. Scott Hicks, Dean, 434-592-4808, Fax: 434-582-2366, E-mail: smhicks@liberty.edu. *Application contact:* Jay Bridge, Director of Graduate Admissions, 800-424-9595, Fax: 800-628-7977, E-mail: gradadmissions@liberty.edu.
Website: http://www.liberty.edu/academics/business/index.cfm?PID=149

LIM College, MPS Program, New York, NY 10022-5268. Offers business of fashion (MPS); fashion marketing (MPS); fashion merchandising and retail management (MPS); global fashion supply chain management (MPS). *Accreditation:* ACBSP. *Program availability:* Part-time, 100% online. *Faculty:* 1 full-time, 28 part-time/adjunct. *Students:* 113 full-time (111 women), 48 part-time (44 women). Average age 24. 285 applicants, 71% accepted, 114 enrolled. *Entrance requirements:* Additional exam requirements/recommendations for international students: Required—TOEFL (minimum score 550 paper-based), IELTS (minimum score 6.5), PTE (minimum score 55). *Application deadline:* Applications are processed on a rolling basis. Application fee: $40. Electronic applications accepted. *Expenses: Tuition:* Full-time $27,750; part-time $925 per credit. *Required fees:* $100 per term. *Unit head:* Dr. Susan Baxter, Dean of Graduate Studies, E-mail: graduatestudies@limcollege.edu. *Application contact:* Haley Drogus, Assistant Director of Graduate Admissions, 212-310-0639, E-mail: graduateadmissions@limcollege.edu.
Website: http://www.limcollege.edu/academics/graduate

Lindenwood University, Graduate Programs, Plaster School of Business and Entrepreneurship, St. Charles, MO 63301-1695. Offers accountancy (M Acc); accounting (MBA); business administration (MBA); entrepreneurial studies (MBA); finance (MBA, MS); human resource management (MBA); international business (MBA); leadership (MA); management (MBA); marketing (MBA, MS); nonprofit administration (MA); public administration (MBA); sport management (MA); supply chain management (MBA). *Accreditation:* ACBSP. *Program availability:* Part-time, evening/weekend, 100% online. *Faculty:* 15 full-time (8 women), 26 part-time/adjunct (9 women). *Students:* 201 full-time (116 women), 253 part-time (153 women); includes 102 minority (80 Black or African American, non-Hispanic/Latino; 2 American Indian or Alaska Native, non-Hispanic/Latino; 6 Asian, non-Hispanic/Latino; 7 Hispanic/Latino; 7 Two or more races, non-Hispanic/Latino), 61 international. Average age 32. 370 applicants, 42% accepted, 134 enrolled. In 2017, 178 master's awarded. *Degree requirements:* For master's, comprehensive exam (for some programs), thesis (for some programs), minimum GPA of 3.0. *Entrance requirements:* For master's, interview, minimum undergraduate cumulative GPA of 3.0, letter of recommendation. Additional exam requirements/recommendations for international students: Required—TOEFL (minimum score 550 paper-based; 80 iBT); Recommended—IELTS (minimum score 6.5). *Application deadline:* For fall admission, 8/27 priority date for domestic and international students; for winter admission, 1/14 priority date for domestic and international students; for spring admission, 3/18 for domestic students, 3/18 priority date for international students; for summer admission, 6/3 priority date for domestic and international students. Applications are processed on a rolling basis. Application fee: $30 ($100 for international students). Electronic applications accepted. *Expenses:* Contact institution. *Financial support:* In 2017–18, 439 students received support. Career-related internships or fieldwork, Federal Work-Study, institutionally sponsored loans, scholarships/grants, tuition waivers (partial), and unspecified assistantships available. Financial award application deadline: 6/30; financial award applicants required to submit FAFSA. *Unit head:* Roger Ellis, Dean, School of Business and Entrepreneurship, 636-949-4839, E-mail: rellis@lindenwood.edu. *Application contact:* Kara Schilli, Director, Evening and Graduate Admissions, 636-949-4349, Fax: 636-949-4109, E-mail: adultadmissions@lindenwood.edu.
Website: http://www.lindenwood.edu/academics/academic-schools/robert-w-plaster-school-of-business-entrepreneurship/

Lindenwood University, Graduate Programs, School of Accelerated Degree Programs, St. Charles, MO 63301-1695. Offers administration (MSA), including management, marketing, project management; business administration (MBA); communications (MA), including digital and multimedia, media management, promotions, training and development; criminal justice and administration (MS); healthcare administration (MS); human resource management (MS); information technology (Certificate); managing information security (MS); managing information technology (MS); managing virtualization and cloud computing (MS); writing (MFA). *Program availability:* Part-time, evening/weekend, 100% online. *Faculty:* 12 full-time (5 women), 90 part-time/adjunct (37 women). *Students:* 597 full-time (383 women), 202 part-time (138 women); includes 248 minority (206 Black or African American, non-Hispanic/Latino; 3 American Indian or Alaska Native, non-Hispanic/Latino; 6 Asian, non-Hispanic/Latino; 21 Hispanic/Latino; 1 Native Hawaiian or other Pacific Islander, non-Hispanic/Latino; 11 Two or more races, non-Hispanic/Latino), 69 international. Average age 36. 526 applicants, 46% accepted, 204 enrolled. In 2017, 537 master's awarded. *Degree requirements:* For master's, thesis (for some programs), minimum cumulative GPA of 3.0; for Certificate, minimum cumulative GPA of 3.0. *Entrance requirements:* For master's, resume, personal statement, official undergraduate transcript, minimum undergraduate cumulative GPA of 3.0. Additional exam requirements/recommendations for international students: Required—TOEFL (minimum score 550 paper-based; 80 iBT); Recommended—IELTS (minimum score 6.5). *Application deadline:* For fall admission, 9/24 priority date for domestic and international students; for winter admission, 1/7 priority date for domestic and international students; for spring admission, 4/8 priority date for domestic and international students; for summer admission, 7/8 priority date for domestic and international students. Applications are processed on a rolling basis. Application fee: $30 ($100 for international students). Electronic applications accepted. *Expenses: Tuition:* Full-time $16,300; part-time $460 per credit. *Required fees:* $660; $330 per credit. Tuition and fees vary according to degree level and program. *Financial support:* In 2017–18, 738 students received support. Career-related internships or fieldwork, institutionally sponsored loans, scholarships/grants, tuition waivers (partial), and unspecified assistantships available. Financial award application deadline: 6/30; financial award applicants required to submit FAFSA. *Unit head:* Dr. Gina Ganahl, Dean, Accelerated Degree Programs, 636-949-4501, Fax: 636-949-4505, E-mail: gganahl@lindenwood.edu. *Application contact:* Kara Schilli, Director, Evening and Graduate Admissions, 636-949-4349, Fax: 636-949-4109, E-mail: adultadmissions@lindenwood.edu.
Website: http://www.lindenwood.edu/academics/academic-schools/school-of-accelerated-degree-programs/

Long Island University–LIU Post, College of Management, Brookville, NY 11548-1300. Offers accountancy (MS); finance (MBA); information systems (MS); international

business (MBA); management (MBA); management engineering (MS); marketing (MBA); taxation (MS); technical project management (MS); JD/MBA. *Accreditation:* AACSB. *Program availability:* Part-time, evening/weekend, blended/hybrid learning. *Faculty:* 23 full-time (7 women), 7 part-time/adjunct (1 woman). *Students:* 119 full-time (47 women), 62 part-time (23 women); includes 33 minority (11 Black or African American, non-Hispanic/Latino; 8 Asian, non-Hispanic/Latino; 13 Hispanic/Latino; 1 Two or more races, non-Hispanic/Latino), 56 international. Average age 28. 162 applicants, 62% accepted, 41 enrolled. In 2017, 91 master's awarded. *Entrance requirements:* For master's, GMAT, GRE, or LSAT. Additional exam requirements/recommendations for international students: Required—TOEFL (minimum score 550 paper-based, 75 iBT) or IELTS. *Application deadline:* Applications are processed on a rolling basis. Application fee: $50. Electronic applications accepted. *Expenses: Tuition:* Full-time $21,618; part-time $1201 per credit. *Required fees:* $1840; $920 per term. Tuition and fees vary according to course load. *Financial support:* In 2017–18, 47 students received support. Career-related internships or fieldwork, Federal Work-Study, and scholarships/grants available. Support available to part-time students. Financial award application deadline: 2/15; financial award applicants required to submit FAFSA. *Faculty research:* Innovation and property rights, knowledge sourcing, sustainability and firm performance, China and growth markets, corporate social responsibility, workforce compensation and issues. *Unit head:* Dr. Robert M. Valli, Dean, 516-299-3004, E-mail: rob.valli@liu.edu. *Application contact:* Rita Langdon, Graduate Admissions, 516-299-2900, Fax: 516-299-2137, E-mail: post-enroll@liu.edu.
Website: http://liu.edu/CWPost/Academics/Schools/COM

Louisiana Tech University, Graduate School, College of Business, Ruston, LA 71272. Offers accounting (M Acc, DBA); computer information systems (DBA); finance (MBA, DBA); information assurance (MBA); innovation (MBA); management (DBA); marketing (MBA, DBA). *Accreditation:* AACSB. *Program availability:* Part-time, evening/weekend, 100% online, blended/hybrid learning. *Faculty:* 36 full-time (7 women), 8 part-time/adjunct (3 women). *Students:* 104 full-time (43 women), 40 part-time (16 women); includes 22 minority (13 Black or African American, non-Hispanic/Latino; 2 Asian, non-Hispanic/Latino; 7 Two or more races, non-Hispanic/Latino), 32 international. Average age 29. 104 applicants, 58% accepted, 25 enrolled. In 2017, 71 master's, 4 doctorates awarded. *Degree requirements:* For doctorate, thesis/dissertation. *Entrance requirements:* For master's and doctorate, GMAT, transcript with bachelor's degree awarded. Additional exam requirements/recommendations for international students: Required—TOEFL (minimum score 550 paper-based; 80 iBT), IELTS (minimum score 6.5). *Application deadline:* For fall admission, 8/1 priority date for domestic students, 6/1 for international students; for winter admission, 11/1 priority date for domestic students, 9/1 for international students; for spring admission, 2/1 priority date for domestic students, 12/1 for international students; for summer admission, 5/1 priority date for domestic students, 3/1 for international students. Application fee: $40. Electronic applications accepted. *Expenses:* Tuition, state resident: full-time $5146. Tuition, nonresident: full-time $10,147. *International tuition:* $10,267 full-time. *Required fees:* $2273. *Financial support:* In 2017–18, 24 students received support, including 17 research assistantships with partial tuition reimbursements available (averaging $12,500 per year), 7 teaching assistantships with partial tuition reimbursements available (averaging $12,500 per year); scholarships/grants and unspecified assistantships also available. Financial award application deadline: 2/1. *Faculty research:* Consumer environmental behavior; identifying and analyzing current issues and future concerns in real estate; information assurance and related areas in business for Northwest Louisiana and the United States (business continuity, disaster recovery, accounting controls, auditing, computer forensics, and security attribution); value creation driven by the consumer and employee interface within exchange environments. *Unit head:* Dr. Christopher D. Martin, Dean, 318-257-4526, Fax: 318-257-4253. *Application contact:* Samantha J. Bailey, Graduate Management Admissions Specialist, 318-257-2924, Fax: 318-257-4487, E-mail: samantha@latech.edu.
Website: http://www.business.latech.edu/

Loyola University Chicago, Quinlan School of Business, Master of Science in Integrated Marketing Communications Program, Chicago, IL 60611. Offers MS. *Program availability:* Part-time, evening/weekend. *Faculty:* 13 full-time (11 women), 5 part-time/adjunct (1 woman). *Students:* 24 full-time (20 women), 3 part-time (1 woman); includes 6 minority (3 Black or African American, non-Hispanic/Latino; 1 Asian, non-Hispanic/Latino; 2 Hispanic/Latino), 14 international. Average age 27. 93 applicants, 68% accepted, 12 enrolled. In 2017, 23 master's awarded. *Entrance requirements:* For master's, GMAT or GRE, official transcripts, two letters of recommendation, statement of purpose, resume. Additional exam requirements/recommendations for international students: Required—TOEFL (minimum score 90 iBT) or IELTS (minimum score 6.5). *Application deadline:* For fall admission, 7/15 for domestic and international students; for winter admission, 10/1 for domestic and international students; for spring admission, 1/15 for domestic and international students; for summer admission, 4/1 for domestic and international students. Applications are processed on a rolling basis. Application fee: $50. Electronic applications accepted. *Expenses:* $4,488 per course. *Financial support:* In 2017–18, 2 students received support. Research assistantships, career-related internships or fieldwork, Federal Work-Study, scholarships/grants, and health care benefits available. *Faculty research:* Brand strategy, consumer behavior, digital/interactive marketing, international marketing. *Unit head:* Dr. Mary Ann McGrath, Chair, 312-915-6136, E-mail: mmcgrat@luc.edu.
Website: http://luc.edu/quinlan/mba/masters-in-marketing/

Loyola University Chicago, Quinlan School of Business, MBA Programs, Chicago, IL 60611. Offers accounting (MBA); business ethics (MBA); derivative markets (MBA); economics (MBA); entrepreneurship (MBA); finance (MBA); healthcare management (MBA); human resources management (MBA); information systems management (MBA); international business (MBA); management (MBA); marketing (MBA); risk management (MBA); supply chain management (MBA). *Program availability:* Part-time, evening/weekend. *Faculty:* 84 full-time (28 women), 12 part-time/adjunct (3 women). *Students:* 253 full-time (118 women), 76 part-time (35 women); includes 83 minority (21 Black or African American, non-Hispanic/Latino; 1 American Indian or Alaska Native, non-Hispanic/Latino; 33 Asian, non-Hispanic/Latino; 24 Hispanic/Latino; 4 Two or more races, non-Hispanic/Latino), 37 international. Average age 30. 334 applicants, 52% accepted, 80 enrolled. In 2017, 220 master's awarded. *Entrance requirements:* For master's, GMAT or GRE, official transcripts, two letters of recommendation, statement of purpose, resume. Additional exam requirements/recommendations for international students: Required—TOEFL (minimum score 90 iBT) or IELTS (minimum score 6.5). *Application deadline:* For fall admission, 7/15 for domestic and international students; for winter admission, 10/1 for domestic and international students; for spring admission, 1/15 for domestic and international students; for summer admission, 4/1 for domestic and international students. Applications are processed on a rolling basis. Application fee: $50. Electronic applications accepted. Application fee is waived when completed online. *Expenses:* $4,488 per course. *Financial support:* In 2017–18, 11 students received support. Research assistantships, career-related internships or fieldwork, Federal Work-Study, scholarships/grants, and health care benefits available. *Faculty research:* Social enterprise and responsibility, emerging markets, supply chain management, risk management. *Unit head:* Katherine Acles, Assistant Dean for Graduate Programs, 312-915-6124, Fax: 312-915-7207, E-mail: kacles@luc.edu.

Loyola University Maryland, Graduate Programs, Sellinger School of Business, Professional MBA Program, Baltimore, MD 21210-2699. Offers finance (MBA); information systems (MBA); investments and applied portfolio management (MBA); management (MBA); marketing (MBA). *Accreditation:* AACSB. *Program availability:* Part-time, evening/weekend. *Entrance requirements:* For master's, GMAT, resume, essay, official transcripts, professional letter of recommendation. Additional exam requirements/recommendations for international students: Required—TOEFL (minimum score 550 paper-based, 80 iBT) or IELTS (minimum score 7). *Application deadline:* For fall admission, 8/1 priority date for domestic students, 4/1 for international students; for spring admission, 12/1 priority date for domestic students, 9/1 for international students; for summer admission, 5/1 priority date for domestic students. Applications are processed on a rolling basis. Application fee: $60. Electronic applications accepted. *Expenses:* Contact institution. *Financial support:* In 2017–18, 26 students received support. Scholarships/grants available. Financial award application deadline: 4/15; financial award applicants required to submit FAFSA. *Unit head:* Kelly Fader, Director of Graduate Cohort Program, 410-617-1617, E-mail: kgfader@loyola.edu. *Application contact:* Office of Graduate Business Programs, 410-617-5067, E-mail: mba@loyola.edu.

Lynn University, College of Business and Management, Boca Raton, FL 33431-5598. Offers business administration (MBA), including aviation management, entrepreneurial management, financial valuation and investment management, hospitality management, human resource management, international business management, marketing, media management, social innovation management, sports management, Web development. *Program availability:* Part-time, evening/weekend, 100% online, blended/hybrid learning. *Faculty:* 29 full-time (11 women), 19 part-time/adjunct (7 women). *Students:* 287 full-time (124 women), 195 part-time (105 women); includes 110 minority (44 Black or African American, non-Hispanic/Latino; 2 American Indian or Alaska Native, non-Hispanic/Latino; 11 Asian, non-Hispanic/Latino; 47 Hispanic/Latino; 6 Two or more races, non-Hispanic/Latino), 135 international. Average age 28. 293 applicants, 94% accepted, 192 enrolled. In 2017, 236 master's awarded. *Degree requirements:* For master's, thesis, minimum GPA of 3.0, strategic management seminar, written presentation reflecting the integration and application of theory to practice. *Entrance requirements:* For master's, bachelor's degree from accredited institution, minimum undergraduate GPA of 2.5, official undergraduate transcripts, resume, personal statement, letter of recommendation from academic or professional sources, writing sample demonstrating capacity to perform at graduate level. Additional exam requirements/recommendations for international students: Required—TOEFL (minimum score 550 paper-based; 80 iBT), IELTS (minimum score 6.5). *Application deadline:* For fall admission, 8/18 for domestic students, 8/4 for international students; for spring admission, 12/15 for domestic students, 12/1 for international students; for summer admission, 4/17 for domestic students, 4/3 for international students. Applications are processed on a rolling basis. Application fee: $45. Electronic applications accepted. *Expenses:* $740 per credit. *Financial support:* Career-related internships or fieldwork, Federal Work-Study, scholarships/grants, tuition waivers (full and partial), and unspecified assistantships available. Support available to part-time students. Financial award application deadline: 3/1; financial award applicants required to submit FAFSA. *Faculty research:* Knowledge economy, urban economy, U.S. manufacturing industries, leadership personality, stock market reactions to terrorism, personality psychology, industrial/organizational psychology. *Unit head:* Dr. RT Good, Dean of the College of Business and Management, 561-237-7458, E-mail: rgood@lynn.edu. *Application contact:* Steven Pruitt, Director of Graduate and Undergraduate Evening Admission, 561-237-7834, Fax: 561-237-7100, E-mail: spruitt@lynn.edu.
Website: http://www.lynn.edu/academics/colleges/business-and-management

Manhattanville College, School of Business, Master of Science in Marketing Communication Management Program, Purchase, NY 10577-2132. Offers MS, Advanced Certificate. *Program availability:* Part-time, evening/weekend. *Faculty:* 3 part-time/adjunct (1 woman). *Students:* 13 full-time (8 women), 6 part-time (4 women); includes 6 minority (1 Asian, non-Hispanic/Latino; 5 Hispanic/Latino), 2 international. Average age 30. 20 applicants, 30% accepted, 5 enrolled. In 2017, 4 master's awarded. *Degree requirements:* For master's, thesis (for some programs), final project. *Entrance requirements:* For master's, personal essay, transcripts, 2 letters of recommendation (academic or professional), resume, health form with proof of immunization (for those born after 1957). Additional exam requirements/recommendations for international students: Required—TOEFL (minimum score 563 paper-based, 85 iBT), IELTS (7), or iTEP (B2). *Application deadline:* Applications are processed on a rolling basis. Application fee: $75. Electronic applications accepted. *Expenses:* $915 per credit. *Financial support:* Federal Work-Study, institutionally sponsored loans, scholarships/grants, and unspecified assistantships available. Financial award application deadline: 3/15; financial award applicants required to submit FAFSA. *Unit head:* Laura Persky, Graduate Program Director, 914-323-5188, E-mail: laura.persky@mville.edu. *Application contact:* Monika Pottgen, Assistant Director, Recruitment and Admissions, 914-323-5150, E-mail: business@mville.edu.
Website: https://www.mville.edu/programs/ms-marketing-communication-management

Marist College, Graduate Programs, School of Communication and the Arts, Program in Integrated Marketing Communication, Poughkeepsie, NY 12601-1387. Offers MA. *Entrance requirements:* For master's, GRE or GMAT, official undergraduate/graduate transcripts from all institutions attended; current resume; completed recommendation forms for three references; personal statement.

Marquette University, Graduate School of Management, Executive MBA Program, Milwaukee, WI 53201-1881. Offers economics (MBA); finance (MBA); human resources (MBA); international business (MBA); management information systems (MBA); marketing (MBA); operations and supply chain management (MBA); sports business (MBA). *Accreditation:* AACSB. *Degree requirements:* For master's, international trip. *Entrance requirements:* For master's, GMAT or GRE, two letters of recommendation, official transcripts from current and previous colleges/universities. Additional exam requirements/recommendations for international students: Required—TOEFL (minimum score 550 paper-based; 88 iBT), IELTS (minimum score 6.5), PTE. Electronic applications accepted. *Expenses:* Contact institution. *Faculty research:* International trade and finance, customer relationship management, consumer satisfaction, customer service.

Marquette University, Graduate School of Management, Program in Business Administration, Milwaukee, WI 53201-1881. Offers business administration (MBA); economics (MBA); entrepreneurship (Certificate); finance (MBA); human resources (MBA); international business (MBA); management information systems (MBA); marketing (MBA); operations and supply chain management (MBA); sports business (MBA); JD/MBA; MBA/MA; MBA/MSN. *Accreditation:* AACSB. *Program availability:* Part-time, evening/weekend. *Degree requirements:* For Certificate, business plan. *Entrance requirements:* For master's, GMAT or GRE, letters of recommendation. Additional exam requirements/recommendations for international students: Required—TOEFL (minimum score 550 paper-based; 88 iBT), IELTS (minimum score 6.5), PTE. Electronic applications accepted. *Faculty research:* Ethics in the professions, services marketing, technology impact on decision-making, mentoring.

Marketing

Maryville University of Saint Louis, The John E. Simon School of Business, St. Louis, MO 63141-7299. Offers accounting (MBA, MS, Certificate); business studies (Certificate); cybersecurity (MBA, MS, Certificate); financial services (MBA, Certificate); healthcare practice management (MBA, Certificate); human resource management (MBA, Certificate); information technology (MBA, Certificate); management (MBA, Certificate); management and leadership (MA); marketing (MBA, Certificate); project management (MBA, Certificate); sport business management (MBA); supply chain management (Certificate); supply chain management/logistics (MBA). *Accreditation:* ACBSP. *Program availability:* Part-time, 100% online, blended/hybrid learning. *Faculty:* 5 full-time (3 women), 51 part-time/adjunct (16 women). *Students:* 222 full-time (96 women), 498 part-time (222 women); includes 185 minority (104 Black or African American, non-Hispanic/Latino; 5 American Indian or Alaska Native, non-Hispanic/Latino; 30 Asian, non-Hispanic/Latino; 37 Hispanic/Latino; 9 Two or more races, non-Hispanic/Latino), 26 international. Average age 33. In 2017, 106 master's awarded. *Degree requirements:* For master's, capstone course (for MBA). *Entrance requirements:* Additional exam requirements/recommendations for international students: Required—TOEFL (minimum score 563 paper-based; 85 iBT). *Application deadline:* Applications are processed on a rolling basis. Electronic applications accepted. *Expenses:* Contact institution. *Financial support:* Career-related internships or fieldwork, Federal Work-Study, tuition waivers (partial), and campus employment available. Financial award application deadline: 4/1; financial award applicants required to submit FAFSA. *Unit head:* Pam Horwitz, Interim Dean, 314-529-9680, Fax: 314-529-9975. *Application contact:* Dustin Loeffler, Director for Graduate Studies in Business, 314-529-9571, Fax: 314-529-9975, E-mail: dloeffler@maryville.edu.
Website: http://www.maryville.edu/bu/business-administration-masters/

McGill University, Faculty of Graduate and Postdoctoral Studies, Desautels Faculty of Management, Montréal, QC H3A 2T5, Canada. Offers administration (PhD); entrepreneurial studies (MBA); finance (MBA); general management (Post Master's Certificate); information systems (MBA); international business (MBA); international practicing management (MM); management (MBA); management for development (MBA); manufacturing management (MMM); marketing (MBA); operations management (MBA); public accountancy (Diploma); strategic management (MBA); MBA/LL B; MD/MBA. MMM offered jointly with Faculty of Engineering; PhD with Concordia University, HEC Montreal, Université de Montréal, Université du Québec à Montréal.

Melbourne Business School, Graduate Programs, Carlton, Australia. Offers business administration (Exec MBA, MBA); management (PhD); management science (PhD); marketing (PhD); social impact (Graduate Certificate); JD/MBA.

Michigan State University, The Graduate School, Eli Broad College of Business, Department of Marketing, East Lansing, MI 48224. Offers marketing (PhD); marketing research (MS). *Degree requirements:* For doctorate, comprehensive exam, thesis/dissertation. *Entrance requirements:* For master's, GMAT, bachelor's degree with minimum GPA of 3.0 in last 2 years of undergraduate work; transcripts; 3 letters of recommendation; statement of purpose; resume; working knowledge of computers; basic understanding of accounting, finance, marketing, and the management of people; laptop capable of running Windows software; for doctorate, GMAT (taken within past 5 years), bachelor's degree; letters of recommendation; statement of purpose; previous work experience; personal qualifications of sound character, perseverance, intellectual curiosity, and an interest in scholarly research. Additional exam requirements/recommendations for international students: Required—TOEFL (minimum score 100 iBT), PTE (minimum score 70), IELTS (minimum score 7) accepted for MS only.

Michigan State University, The Graduate School, Eli Broad College of Business, Program in Business Administration, East Lansing, MI 48224. Offers finance (MBA); human resource management (MBA); integrative management (MBA); marketing (MBA); supply chain management (MBA). MBA in integrative management is through Weekend MBA Program; other 4 concentrations are through Full-Time MBA Program. *Program availability:* Evening/weekend. *Degree requirements:* For master's, enrichment experience. *Entrance requirements:* For master's, GMAT or GRE, 4-year bachelor's degree; resume; work experience (minimum of 5 years for Weekend MBA); 2-3 personal essays; 2 letters of recommendation; personal interview. Additional exam requirements/recommendations for international students: Required—PTE (minimum score 70), TOEFL (minimum score 100 iBT) or IELTS (minimum score 7) for full-time MBA applicants. Electronic applications accepted. *Expenses:* Contact institution.

Milwaukee School of Engineering, MS Program in Marketing and Export Management, Milwaukee, WI 53202-3109. Offers MS. *Program availability:* Part-time, evening/weekend. *Students:* 1 (woman) full-time, all international. 3 applicants, 33% accepted. In 2017, 2 master's awarded. *Degree requirements:* For master's, thesis or alternative, thesis defense or capstone project. *Entrance requirements:* For master's, GRE or GMAT if undergraduate GPA less than 2.8, 2 letters of recommendation; bachelor's degree from accredited university; work experience (strongly recommended). Additional exam requirements/recommendations for international students: Required—TOEFL (minimum score 90 iBT), IELTS (minimum score 7). *Application deadline:* Applications are processed on a rolling basis. Application fee: $0. Electronic applications accepted. *Expenses: Tuition:* Part-time $814 per credit hour. *Required fees:* $12.50 per credit hour. *Financial support:* Career-related internships or fieldwork, institutionally sponsored loans, scholarships/grants, and tuition waivers (full) available. Financial award application deadline: 3/15; financial award applicants required to submit FAFSA. *Unit head:* Gene Wright, Program Director, 414-277-2268, Fax: 414-277-2487, E-mail: wright@msoe.edu. *Application contact:* Brian Rutz, Graduate Admission Counselor, 414-277-7200, E-mail: rutz@msoe.edu.
Website: https://www.msoe.edu/academics/graduate-degrees/business/marketing-export-management/

Mississippi State University, College of Business, Department of Marketing, Quantitative Analysis and Business Law, Mississippi State, MS 39762. Offers business administration (PhD), including marketing. *Program availability:* Part-time, evening/weekend. *Faculty:* 13 full-time (3 women). *Students:* 5 full-time (3 women), 2 part-time (1 woman); includes 1 minority (Black or African American, non-Hispanic/Latino), 1 international. Average age 30. 16 applicants, 6% accepted, 1 enrolled. In 2017, 1 doctorate awarded. *Degree requirements:* For doctorate, comprehensive exam, thesis/dissertation. *Entrance requirements:* For doctorate, GMAT (taken within last five years with minimum score of 550), minimum GPA of 3.25 on all prior graduate work. Additional exam requirements/recommendations for international students: Required—TOEFL (minimum score 575 paper-based; 84 iBT). Recommended—IELTS (minimum score 6.5). *Application deadline:* For fall admission, 7/1 for domestic students, 5/1 for international students; for spring admission, 11/1 for domestic students, 9/1 for international students. Applications are processed on a rolling basis. Application fee: $60 ($80 for international students). Electronic applications accepted. *Expenses:* Tuition, state resident: full-time $8318; part-time $462.12 per credit hour. Tuition, nonresident: full-time $22,358; part-time $1242.12 per credit hour. *Required fees:* $110; $12.24 per credit hour. $6.12 per semester. *Financial support:* Federal Work-Study, institutionally sponsored loans, and scholarships/grants available. Financial award application deadline: 4/1; financial award applicants required to submit FAFSA. *Unit head:* Dr. Melissa Moore, Professor and Head, 662-325-8556, Fax: 662-325-7012, E-mail: mmoore@business.msstate.edu. *Application contact:* Lakan Drinker, Admissions and Enrollment Assistant, 662-325-8951, E-mail: ldrinker@grad.msstate.edu.
Website: http://www.business.msstate.edu/programs/marketing/index.php

Molloy College, Graduate Business Program, Rockville Centre, NY 11571-5002. Offers accounting (MBA); finance (MBA, Post-Master's Certificate, Postbaccalaureate Certificate); healthcare (MBA, Post-Master's Certificate, Postbaccalaureate Certificate); management (MBA); marketing (MBA, Post-Master's Certificate, Postbaccalaureate Certificate); personal financial planning (MBA). *Program availability:* Part-time, evening/weekend. *Faculty:* 8 full-time (3 women), 7 part-time/adjunct (2 women). *Students:* 53 full-time (29 women), 175 part-time (89 women); includes 88 minority (38 Black or African American, non-Hispanic/Latino; 18 Asian, non-Hispanic/Latino; 30 Hispanic/Latino; 2 Two or more races, non-Hispanic/Latino), 3 international. Average age 39. 128 applicants, 68% accepted, 81 enrolled. In 2017, 125 master's awarded. *Entrance requirements:* Additional exam requirements/recommendations for international students: Required—TOEFL (minimum score 550 paper-based; 79 iBT). *Application deadline:* Applications are processed on a rolling basis. Application fee: $60. Electronic applications accepted. *Expenses: Tuition:* Full-time $19,980; part-time $1110 per credit. *Required fees:* $1040. Tuition and fees vary according to course load and degree level. *Financial support:* Application deadline: 3/1; applicants required to submit FAFSA. *Faculty research:* Graduate education - pedagogy and the capstone experience; Freedom of Speech in the workplace; employer liability for sexual harassment in the workplace; educational economics and industrial organization; corporate governance and distressed debt analysis; social network analysis; market segmentation. *Unit head:* Dr. Maureen Mackenzie, Dean, Division of Business/Director of Graduate Programs, 516-323-3080, E-mail: mmackenzie@molloy.edu. *Application contact:* Jaclyn Machowicz, Assistant Director for Admissions, 516-323-4010, E-mail: jmachowicz@molloy.edu.
Website: http://www.molloy.edu/academics/graduate-programs/graduate-business

Monmouth University, Graduate Studies, Leon Hess Business School, West Long Branch, NJ 07764-1898. Offers accounting (MBA, Certificate); business administration (MBA); finance (MBA); management (MBA); marketing (MBA); real estate (MBA). *Accreditation:* AACSB. *Program availability:* Part-time, evening/weekend. *Faculty:* 20 full-time (4 women), 8 part-time/adjunct (0 women). *Students:* 101 full-time (55 women), 107 part-time (44 women); includes 19 minority (3 Black or African American, non-Hispanic/Latino; 6 Asian, non-Hispanic/Latino; 6 Hispanic/Latino; 1 Native Hawaiian or other Pacific Islander, non-Hispanic/Latino; 3 Two or more races, non-Hispanic/Latino), 13 international. Average age 30. In 2017, 61 master's, 1 other advanced degree awarded. *Degree requirements:* For master's, capstone course. *Entrance requirements:* For master's, GMAT or GRE, current resume; essay (500 words or less). Additional exam requirements/recommendations for international students: Required—TOEFL (minimum score 550 paper-based; 79 iBT), IELTS (minimum score 6), Michigan English Language Assessment Battery (minimum score 77) or Certificate of Advanced English (minimum score 160). *Application deadline:* For fall admission, 7/15 priority date for domestic students, 6/1 for international students; for spring admission, 12/1 priority date for domestic students, 11/1 for international students; for summer admission, 5/1 for domestic students. Applications are processed on a rolling basis. Application fee: $50. Electronic applications accepted. *Expenses: Tuition:* Full-time $21,366; part-time $7122 per credit. *Required fees:* $700; $175 per term. *Financial support:* In 2017–18, 42 students received support. Institutionally sponsored loans, scholarships/grants, and unspecified assistantships available. Support available to part-time students. Financial award applicants required to submit FAFSA. *Faculty research:* Information technology and marketing, behavioral research in accounting, human resources, management of technology. *Unit head:* Dr. Susan Gupta, MBA Program Director, 732-571-3639, Fax: 732-263-5517, E-mail: sgupta@monmouth.edu. *Application contact:* Laurie Kuhn, Associate Director of Graduate Admission, 732-571-3452, Fax: 732-263-5123, E-mail: gradadm@monmouth.edu.
Website: https://www.monmouth.edu/business-school/leon-hess-business-school.aspx

See Display on page 115 and Close-Up on page 177.

Monroe College, King Graduate School, Bronx, NY 10468. Offers accounting (MS); business administration (MBA), including entrepreneurship, finance, general business administration, healthcare management, human resources, information technology, marketing; computer science (MS); criminal justice (MS); hospitality management (MS); public health (MPH), including biostatistics and epidemiology, community health, health administration and leadership. *Program availability:* Online learning. Application fee: $50.
Website: https://www.monroecollege.edu/Degrees/King-Graduate-School/

Morgan State University, School of Graduate Studies, Earl G. Graves School of Business and Management, PhD Program in Business Administration, Baltimore, MD 21251. Offers business administration (PhD), including accounting, information systems, management and marketing. *Accreditation:* AACSB. *Entrance requirements:* For doctorate, GMAT. Additional exam requirements/recommendations for international students: Required—TOEFL (minimum score 550 paper-based). *Application deadline:* For fall admission, 2/1 priority date for domestic students; for spring admission, 10/1 priority date for domestic students. Applications are processed on a rolling basis. Application fee: $0. *Expenses:* Tuition, state resident: part-time $433 per credit. Tuition, nonresident: part-time $851 per credit. *Required fees:* $81.50 per credit. *Financial support:* Application deadline: 2/1. *Unit head:* Dr. Augustus Abbey, Department Chair, 443-885-3285, E-mail: augustus.abbey@morgan.edu. *Application contact:* Dr. Dean Campbell, Graduate Recruitment Specialist, 443-885-3185, Fax: 443-885-8226, E-mail: dean.campbell@morgan.edu.

Murray State University, Arthur J. Bauernfeind College of Business, MBA Program, Murray, KY 42071. Offers accounting (MBA); finance (MBA); global communications (MBA); human resource management (MBA); marketing (MBA). *Accreditation:* AACSB. *Program availability:* Part-time, evening/weekend, 100% online, blended/hybrid learning. *Faculty:* 49 full-time (18 women), 3 part-time/adjunct (0 women). *Students:* 54 full-time (22 women), 79 part-time (37 women); includes 13 minority (6 Black or African American, non-Hispanic/Latino; 1 American Indian or Alaska Native, non-Hispanic/Latino; 2 Asian, non-Hispanic/Latino; 2 Hispanic/Latino; 2 Two or more races, non-Hispanic/Latino), 30 international. Average age 29. 70 applicants, 81% accepted, 34 enrolled. In 2017, 61 master's awarded. *Entrance requirements:* For master's, GRE or GMAT, minimum university GPA of 2.75. Additional exam requirements/recommendations for international students: Required—TOEFL (minimum score 527 paper-based; 71 iBT). *Application deadline:* Applications are processed on a rolling basis. Application fee: $40 ($50 for international students). *Expenses:* Tuition, state resident: full-time $9504. Tuition, nonresident: full-time $26,811. *International tuition:* $14,400 full-time. Tuition and fees vary according to course load, degree level and reciprocity agreements. *Financial support:* In 2017–18, 5 research assistantships, 5 teaching assistantships were awarded; Federal Work-Study also available. Financial award applicants required to submit FAFSA. *Faculty research:* Human resource management, e-commerce, supply-chain management, investment management, accounting. *Unit head:* Dr. Joy Humphreys, Assistant Dean and MBA Director, 270-809-4259, Fax: 270-809-3482, E-mail: jumphreys4@murraystate.edu. *Application contact:* Kaitlyn Burzynski, Interim Assistant Director for Graduate Admission and Records, 270-809-5732, Fax: 270-809-3780, E-mail: msu.graduateadmissions@murraystate.edu.
Website: http://www.murraystate.edu/academics/CollegesDepartments/CollegeOfBusiness/Programs/mba/index.aspx

National American University, Roueche Graduate Center, Austin, TX 78731. Offers accounting (MBA); aviation management (MBA, MM); care coordination (MSN); community college leadership (Ed D); criminal justice (MM); e-marketing (MBA, MM); health care administration (MBA, MM); higher education (MM); human resources management (MBA, MM); information technology management (MBA, MM); international business (MBA); leadership (EMBA); management (MBA); nursing administration (MSN); nursing education (MSN); nursing informatics (MSN); operations and configuration management (MBA, MM); project and process management (MBA, MM). Master's programs offered online through the Harold D. Buckingham Graduate School. *Program availability:* Part-time, evening/weekend, online learning. *Entrance requirements:* For master's, minimum undergraduate GPA of 2.75. Additional exam requirements/recommendations for international students: Required—TOEFL, TWE. Electronic applications accepted. *Faculty research:* Tourism, finance, marketing.

National University, Academic Affairs, School of Business and Management, La Jolla, CA 92037-1011. Offers accountancy (M Acc, Certificate); business administration (GMBA, MBA); business analytics (MS); cause leadership (MA); global management (MGM); human resource management (MA); management information systems (MS); marketing (MS); organizational leadership (MS). GMBA offered in Spanish. *Program availability:* Part-time, evening/weekend, 100% online, blended/hybrid learning. *Degree requirements:* For master's, thesis (for some programs). *Entrance requirements:* For master's, interview, minimum GPA of 2.5. Additional exam requirements/recommendations for international students: Required—TOEFL (minimum score 550 paper-based; 79 iBT), IELTS (minimum score 6). *Application deadline:* Applications are processed on a rolling basis. Application fee: $60 ($65 for international students). Electronic applications accepted. *Expenses: Tuition:* Part-time $430 per quarter hour. *Financial support:* Career-related internships or fieldwork, scholarships/grants, and tuition waivers (partial) available. Support available to part-time students. Financial award application deadline: 6/30; financial award applicants required to submit FAFSA. *Unit head:* Dr. Alfred Ntoko, Dean, 858-642-8400, Fax: 858-642-8719, E-mail: sobm@nu.edu. *Application contact:* Brandon Jouganatos, Vice President for Enrollment Services, 800-628-8648, E-mail: advisor@nu.edu.
Website: http://www.nu.edu/OurPrograms/SchoolOfBusinessAndManagement.html

National University College, Graduate Programs, Bayamón, PR 00960. Offers digital marketing (MBA); general business (MBA); special education (M Ed).

New England College, Program in Management, Henniker, NH 03242-3293. Offers accounting (MSA); healthcare administration (MS); international relations (MA); marketing management (MS); nonprofit leadership (MS); project management (MS); strategic leadership (MS). *Program availability:* Part-time, evening/weekend. *Degree requirements:* For master's, independent research project. Electronic applications accepted.

New Jersey City University, School of Business, Program in Marketing, Jersey City, NJ 07305-1597. Offers MBA.

New Mexico State University, College of Business, Department of Marketing, Las Cruces, NM 88003. Offers business administration (PhD), including marketing. *Program availability:* Part-time. *Faculty:* 5 full-time (1 woman). *Students:* 9 full-time (6 women), 3 part-time (2 women); includes 3 minority (2 Hispanic/Latino; 1 Two or more races, non-Hispanic/Latino), 6 international. Average age 35. 18 applicants, 44% accepted, 4 enrolled. In 2017, 1 doctorate awarded. *Entrance requirements:* For doctorate, GMAT or GRE, graduate degree, work experience. Additional exam requirements/recommendations for international students: Required—TOEFL (minimum score 550 paper-based; 79 iBT), IELTS (minimum score 6.5). *Application deadline:* For fall admission, 2/1 for domestic and international students. Application fee: $40 ($50 for international students). Electronic applications accepted. *Expenses:* Tuition, state resident: full-time $4390. Tuition, nonresident: full-time $15,309. *Required fees:* $853. *Financial support:* In 2017–18, 9 students received support, including 2 fellowships (averaging $4,390 per year), 8 teaching assistantships (averaging $21,775 per year); career-related internships or fieldwork, Federal Work-Study, scholarships/grants, traineeships, health care benefits, and unspecified assistantships also available. Support available to part-time students. Financial award application deadline: 3/1. *Faculty research:* Consumer behavior, social media marketing, ethics in marketing, advertising, public policy. *Unit head:* Dr. Nancy Oretskin, Interim Department Head, 575-646-3341, Fax: 575-646-1498, E-mail: noretski@nmsu.edu.
Website: http://business.nmsu.edu/departments/marketing

New York Institute of Technology, School of Management, Department of Business Administration, Old Westbury, NY 11568-8000. Offers executive management (MBA), including finance, marketing, operations and supply chain management. *Accreditation:* AACSB. *Program availability:* Part-time. *Faculty:* 25 full-time (4 women), 20 part-time/adjunct (6 women). *Students:* 398 full-time (187 women), 138 part-time (63 women); includes 43 minority (9 Black or African American, non-Hispanic/Latino; 1 American Indian or Alaska Native, non-Hispanic/Latino; 22 Asian, non-Hispanic/Latino; 9 Hispanic/Latino; 2 Two or more races, non-Hispanic/Latino), 432 international. Average age 26. 635 applicants, 75% accepted, 196 enrolled. In 2017, 230 master's awarded. *Entrance requirements:* For master's, bachelor's degree; minimum undergraduate GPA of 3.0. Additional exam requirements/recommendations for international students: Required—TOEFL (minimum score 79 iBT), IELTS (minimum score 6). *Application deadline:* Applications are processed on a rolling basis. Application fee: $50. Electronic applications accepted. *Expenses:* $1,285 per credit plus fees. *Financial support:* Career-related internships or fieldwork, Federal Work-Study, scholarships/grants, tuition waivers (full and partial), and unspecified assistantships available. Support available to part-time students. Financial award application deadline: 2/15; financial award applicants required to submit FAFSA. *Faculty research:* Accounting, economics, finance, management, marketing. *Unit head:* Dr. Jess Boronico, Dean, 516-686-7838, E-mail: som@nyit.edu. *Application contact:* Alice Dolitsky, Director, Graduate Admissions, 516-686-7520, Fax: 516-686-1116, E-mail: nyitgrad@nyit.edu.
Website: http://www.nyit.edu/degrees/management_mba

New York University, Leonard N. Stern School of Business, Department of Marketing, New York, NY 10012-1019. Offers entertainment, media and technology (MBA); general marketing (MBA); marketing (PhD); product management (MBA). *Expenses: Tuition:* Full-time $41,352; part-time $19,968 per year. *Required fees:* $2496; $1628 per unit. $814 per term. Tuition and fees vary according to course load and program.

New York University, School of Professional Studies, Division of Programs in Business, Program in Integrated Marketing, New York, NY 10012-1019. Offers integrated marketing (MS), including brand management, digital marketing, marketing analytics. *Program availability:* Part-time, evening/weekend. *Students:* 821 full-time (611 women), 176 part-time (134 women); includes 70 minority (12 Black or African American, non-Hispanic/Latino; 1 American Indian or Alaska Native, non-Hispanic/Latino; 38 Asian, non-Hispanic/Latino; 17 Hispanic/Latino; 2 Two or more races, non-Hispanic/Latino), 865 international. Average age 25. 1,688 applicants, 61% accepted, 416 enrolled. In 2017, 744 master's awarded. *Degree requirements:* For master's, thesis, capstone project. *Entrance requirements:* For master's, GRE or GMAT (only upon request), bachelor's degree, resume with relevant professional work, internship or volunteer experience, two letters of recommendation, statement of purpose. Additional

exam requirements/recommendations for international students: Required—TOEFL (minimum score 600 paper-based; 100 iBT), IELTS (minimum score 7). *Application deadline:* For fall admission, 2/1 priority date for domestic and international students; for spring admission, 10/15 priority date for domestic students, 8/15 priority date for international students. Applications are processed on a rolling basis. Application fee: $150. Electronic applications accepted. *Expenses:* $20,244 per term. *Financial support:* Fellowships, career-related internships or fieldwork, Federal Work-Study, scholarships/grants, and health care benefits available. Support available to part-time students. Financial award application deadline: 6/30; financial award applicants required to submit FAFSA. *Unit head:* Martin Ihrig, Associate Dean/Clinical Professor, 212-992-3228. *Application contact:* Admissions Office, 212-998-7100, E-mail: scps.gradadmissions@nyu.edu.
Website: http://www.sps.nyu.edu/academics/departments/marketing-and-pr.html

New York University, School of Professional Studies, Division of Programs in Business, Programs in Marketing and Public Relations, New York, NY 10012-1019. Offers public relations and corporate communication (MS), including corporate and organizational communication, public relations management. *Program availability:* Part-time, evening/weekend. *Students:* 224 full-time (197 women), 62 part-time (56 women); includes 40 minority (18 Black or African American, non-Hispanic/Latino; 1 American Indian or Alaska Native, non-Hispanic/Latino; 7 Asian, non-Hispanic/Latino; 11 Hispanic/Latino; 3 Two or more races, non-Hispanic/Latino), 219 international. Average age 25. 355 applicants, 69% accepted, 110 enrolled. In 2017, 316 master's awarded. *Degree requirements:* For master's, thesis. *Entrance requirements:* For master's, GRE or GMAT (only upon request), bachelor's degree, resume with relevant professional work, internship or volunteer experience, two letters of recommendation, statement of purpose. Additional exam requirements/recommendations for international students: Required—TOEFL (minimum score 600 paper-based; 100 iBT), IELTS (minimum score 7). *Application deadline:* For fall admission, 2/1 priority date for domestic and international students; for spring admission, 10/15 priority date for domestic students, 8/15 priority date for international students. Applications are processed on a rolling basis. Application fee: $150. Electronic applications accepted. *Expenses:* $20,244 per term. *Financial support:* Fellowships, career-related internships or fieldwork, Federal Work-Study, scholarships/grants, and health care benefits available. Support available to part-time students. Financial award application deadline: 6/30; financial award applicants required to submit FAFSA. *Unit head:* Martin Ihrig, Associate Dean/Clinical Professor, 212-992-3288. *Application contact:* Admissions Office, 212-998-7100, E-mail: sps.gradadmissions@nyu.edu.
Website: http://www.sps.nyu.edu/academics/departments/marketing-and-pr.html

New York University, School of Professional Studies, Preston Robert Tisch Institute for Global Sport, New York, NY 10012-1019. Offers sports business (MS), including global sports media, professional and collegiate sports operations, sports law, sports marketing and sales. *Program availability:* Part-time, evening/weekend. *Students:* 70 full-time (21 women), 38 part-time (13 women); includes 21 minority (6 Black or African American, non-Hispanic/Latino; 7 Asian, non-Hispanic/Latino; 5 Hispanic/Latino; 1 Native Hawaiian or other Pacific Islander, non-Hispanic/Latino; 2 Two or more races, non-Hispanic/Latino), 52 international. Average age 26. 145 applicants, 67% accepted, 46 enrolled. In 2017, 78 master's awarded. *Degree requirements:* For master's, thesis. *Entrance requirements:* For master's, GRE or GMAT (only upon request), bachelor's degree, resume with relevant professional work, internship or volunteer experience, two letters of recommendation, statement of purpose. Additional exam requirements/recommendations for international students: Required—TOEFL (minimum score 600 paper-based; 100 iBT), IELTS (minimum score 7). *Application deadline:* For fall admission, 2/1 priority date for domestic and international students; for spring admission, 10/15 priority date for domestic students, 8/15 priority date for international students. Applications are processed on a rolling basis. Application fee: $150. Electronic applications accepted. *Expenses:* $20,244 per term. *Financial support:* Fellowships, career-related internships or fieldwork, Federal Work-Study, scholarships/grants, and health care benefits available. Support available to part-time students. Financial award application deadline: 6/30; financial award applicants required to submit FAFSA. *Unit head:* Vince Gennaro, Associate Dean/Clinical Associate Professor, 212-995-4676. *Application contact:* Admissions Office, 212-998-7100, E-mail: sps.gradadmissions@nyu.edu.
Website: http://www.sps.nyu.edu/content/scps/academics/departments/tisch-institute.html

Niagara University, Graduate Division of Business Administration, Niagara University, NY 14109. Offers accounting (MBA); business administration (MBA); finance (MBA, MS); financial planning (MBA); healthcare administration (MBA, MHA); human resources (MBA); international business (MBA); marketing (MBA); professional accountancy (MBA); strategic management (MBA); supply chain management (MBA). *Accreditation:* AACSB. *Program availability:* Part-time, evening/weekend. *Faculty:* 17 full-time, 11 part-time/adjunct. *Students:* 173 full-time (92 women), 77 part-time (39 women); includes 38 minority (8 Black or African American, non-Hispanic/Latino; 3 American Indian or Alaska Native, non-Hispanic/Latino; 8 Asian, non-Hispanic/Latino; 8 Hispanic/Latino; 11 Two or more races, non-Hispanic/Latino), 46 international. Average age 27. In 2017, 139 master's awarded. *Entrance requirements:* For master's, GMAT. Additional exam requirements/recommendations for international students: Required—TOEFL (minimum score 550 paper-based; 79 iBT), IELTS (minimum score 6). *Application deadline:* For fall admission, 8/1 for domestic students; for spring admission, 11/1 for domestic students. Applications are processed on a rolling basis. Electronic applications accepted. *Expenses:* Contact institution. *Financial support:* Fellowships, research assistantships, career-related internships or fieldwork, and Federal Work-Study available. Support available to part-time students. Financial award application deadline: 4/15; financial award applicants required to submit FAFSA. *Faculty research:* Capital flows, Federal Reserve policy, human resource management, public policy, issues in marketing, auctions, economics of information, risk and capital markets, management strategy, consumer behavior, Internet and social media marketing. *Unit head:* Dr. Paul Richardson, MBA Director/Chair of the Marketing Department, 716-286-8169, Fax: 716-286-8206, E-mail: psr@niagara.edu. *Application contact:* Evan Pierce, Associate Director for Graduate Recruitment, 716-286-8769, Fax: 716-286-8170, E-mail: epierce@niagara.edu.
Website: http://mba.niagara.edu

Northwestern University, The Graduate School, Kellogg School of Management, Department of Marketing, Evanston, IL 60208. Offers PhD. Admissions and degree offered through The Graduate School. *Degree requirements:* For doctorate, comprehensive exam, thesis/dissertation. *Entrance requirements:* For doctorate, GMAT or GRE General Test. Additional exam requirements/recommendations for international students: Required—TOEFL. Electronic applications accepted. *Faculty research:* Choice models, database and high-tech marketing, consumer information processing, ethnographic analysis of consumption, psychometric analysis of consumer behavior.

Northwestern University, The Graduate School, Kellogg School of Management, Management Programs, Evanston, IL 60208. Offers accounting information and management (MBA, PhD); analytical finance (MBA); business administration (MBA); decision sciences (MBA); entrepreneurship and innovation (MBA); finance (MBA, PhD);

Marketing

health enterprise management (MBA); human resources management (MBA); international business (MBA); management and organizations (MBA, PhD); management and organizations and sociology (PhD); management and strategy (MBA); management studies (MS); managerial analytics (MBA); managerial economics (MBA); managerial economics and strategy (PhD); marketing (MBA, PhD); marketing management (MBA); media management (MBA); operations management (MBA, PhD); real estate (MBA); social enterprise at Kellogg (MBA); JD/MBA. *Program availability:* Part-time, evening/weekend. Terminal master's awarded for partial completion of doctoral program. *Degree requirements:* For doctorate, thesis/dissertation, 2 years of coursework, qualifying (field) exam and candidacy, summer research papers and presentations to faculty, proposal defense, final exam/defense. *Entrance requirements:* For master's, GMAT, GRE, interview, 2 letters of recommendation, college transcripts, resume, essays, Kellogg honor code; for doctorate, GMAT, GRE, statement of purpose, transcripts, 2 letters of recommendation, resume, interview. Additional exam requirements/recommendations for international students: Required—TOEFL, IELTS. Electronic applications accepted. *Expenses:* Contact institution. *Faculty research:* Business cycles and international finance, health policy, networks, non-market strategy, consumer psychology.

Northwestern University, Medill School of Journalism, Media, and Integrated Marketing Communications, Integrated Marketing Communications Program, Evanston, IL 60208. Offers brand strategy (MSIMC); content marketing (MSIMC); direct and interactive marketing (MSIMC); marketing analytics (MSIMC); strategic communications (MSIMC). *Program availability:* Part-time. *Entrance requirements:* For master's, GRE General Test or GMAT, full-time work experience (preferred). Additional exam requirements/recommendations for international students: Required—TOEFL. Electronic applications accepted. *Faculty research:* Data mining, business to business marketing, values in advertising, political advertising.

Northwest Missouri State University, Graduate School, Melvin and Valorie Booth College of Business and Professional Studies, Maryville, MO 64468-6001. Offers agricultural economics (MBA); business decision and analytics (MBA); general management (MBA); human resource management (MBA); marketing (MBA). *Program availability:* Part-time. *Faculty:* 17 full-time (6 women). *Students:* 40 full-time (13 women), 95 part-time (48 women); includes 16 minority (8 Black or African American, non-Hispanic/Latino; 1 American Indian or Alaska Native, non-Hispanic/Latino; 2 Asian, non-Hispanic/Latino; 3 Hispanic/Latino; 2 Two or more races, non-Hispanic/Latino), 15 international. Average age 31. 142 applicants, 66% accepted, 70 enrolled. In 2017, 53 master's awarded. *Degree requirements:* For master's, comprehensive exam. *Entrance requirements:* For master's, GMAT, GRE, minimum GPA of 2.5. Additional exam requirements/recommendations for international students: Required—TOEFL (minimum score 550 paper-based). *Application deadline:* For fall admission, 7/1 for domestic and international students; for spring admission, 11/15 for domestic and international students; for summer admission, 4/1 for domestic and international students. Applications are processed on a rolling basis. Application fee: $0 ($50 for international students). Electronic applications accepted. *Expenses:* $389.11 per credit in-state tuition; $641.97 per credit out-of-state tuition. *Financial support:* Research assistantships with full tuition reimbursements, teaching assistantships with full tuition reimbursements, career-related internships or fieldwork, and administrative assistantships, tutorial assistantships available. Financial award application deadline: 4/1; financial award applicants required to submit FAFSA. *Unit head:* Dr. Steve Ludwig, Director of the Melvin And Valorie Booth School of Business, 660-562-1749, Fax: 660-562-1096, E-mail: sludwig@nwmissouri.edu.
Website: https://www.nwmissouri.edu/business/index.htm

Notre Dame de Namur University, Division of Academic Affairs, School of Business and Management, Program in Business Administration, Belmont, CA 94002-1908. Offers finance (MBA); human resource management (MBA); marketing (MBA); media and promotion (MBA). *Accreditation:* ACBSP. *Program availability:* Part-time, evening/weekend. *Students:* 28 full-time (24 women), 93 part-time (56 women). Average age 35. *Entrance requirements:* For master's, minimum GPA of 2.5. Additional exam requirements/recommendations for international students: Required—TOEFL (minimum score 550 paper-based; 79 iBT). *Application deadline:* For fall admission, 8/1 priority date for domestic students; for spring admission, 12/1 priority date for domestic students. Applications are processed on a rolling basis. Application fee: $60. Electronic applications accepted. *Expenses: Tuition:* Full-time $16,128; part-time $8064 per credit hour. *Required fees:* $80; $80 per credit hour. $40 per semester. *Financial support:* Available to part-time students. Applicants required to submit FAFSA. *Unit head:* Jordan Holtzman, Program Director, Graduate Business Programs, 510-375-1348, E-mail: jholtzman@ndnu.edu.
Website: http://www.ndnu.edu/academics/schools-programs/school-business/

Nova Southeastern University, H. Wayne Huizenga College of Business and Entrepreneurship, Fort Lauderdale, FL 33314-7796. Offers accounting (M Acc); business (MBA); business intelligence/analytics (MBA); complex health systems (MBA); enterprise informatics (MBA); entrepreneurship (MBA); finance (MBA); human resource management (MBA); international business (MBA); management (MBA); marketing (MBA); process improvement (MBA); public administration (MPA); real estate development (MS); sport revenue generation (MBA); supply chain management (MBA). *Accreditation:* NASPAA. *Program availability:* Part-time, evening/weekend, 100% online, blended/hybrid learning. *Faculty:* 85 full-time (37 women), 59 part-time/adjunct (19 women). *Students:* 1,999 full-time (1,225 women), 335 part-time (210 women); includes 1,516 minority (597 Black or African American, non-Hispanic/Latino; 4 American Indian or Alaska Native, non-Hispanic/Latino; 92 Asian, non-Hispanic/Latino; 789 Hispanic/Latino; 3 Native Hawaiian or other Pacific Islander, non-Hispanic/Latino; 31 Two or more races, non-Hispanic/Latino), 291 international. Average age 34. 1,269 applicants, 59% accepted, 551 enrolled. In 2017, 1,055 master's awarded. *Entrance requirements:* For master's, GMAT or GRE (depending on undergraduate GPA), official transcripts from all schools attended while in pursuit of bachelor's degree; minimum GPA of 2.5 from regionally-accredited institution. Additional exam requirements/recommendations for international students: Required—TOEFL (minimum score 550 paper-based; 79 iBT), IELTS (minimum score 6), PTE (minimum score 54). *Application deadline:* For fall admission, 8/5 priority date for domestic students, 7/29 priority date for international students; for winter admission, 12/16 priority date for domestic students, 12/9 priority date for international students; for summer admission, 4/21 priority date for domestic and international students. Applications are processed on a rolling basis. Application fee: $50. Electronic applications accepted. *Expenses:* $37,785 (online), $35,640 (in-classroom). *Financial support:* In 2017–18, 325 students received support. Federal Work-Study and scholarships/grants available. Support available to part-time students. Financial award application deadline: 4/15; financial award applicants required to submit FAFSA. *Faculty research:* Entrepreneurship and venture capital, ethics and social responsibility, global commerce and cultures, business process management. *Unit head:* Dr. J. Preston Jones, Dean, 954-262-5127, E-mail: prestonj@nova.edu. *Application contact:* Zeida Rodriguez, Associate Director of Enrollment Services, 954-262-5163, Fax: 954-262-3822, E-mail: zeida@nova.edu.
Website: http://www.huizenga.nova.edu

Oakland University, Graduate Study and Lifelong Learning, School of Business Administration, Department of Management and Marketing, Rochester, MI 48309-4401. Offers business administration (MBA); entrepreneurship (Certificate); general management (Certificate); human resource management (Certificate); international business (Certificate); management and marketing (EMBA); marketing (Certificate). *Expenses:* Tuition, state resident: full-time $16,950; part-time $706.25 per credit. Tuition, nonresident: full-time $24,648; part-time $1027 per credit.

Ohio Christian University, Graduate Programs, Circleville, OH 43113. Offers accounting (MBA); business administration (MBA); digital marketing (MBA); finance (MBA); healthcare management (MBA); human resources (MBA); management (MM); organizational leadership (MBA); pastoral care and counseling (MAM); practical theology (MAM).

Oklahoma Christian University, Graduate School of Business, Oklahoma City, OK 73136-1100. Offers accounting (M Acc, MBA); financial services (MBA); general business (MBA); health services management (MBA); human resources (MBA); international business (MBA); leadership and organizational development (MBA); marketing (MBA); nonprofit management (MBA); project management (MBA). *Accreditation:* ACBSP. *Program availability:* Part-time, 100% online. *Entrance requirements:* For master's, bachelor's degree. Additional exam requirements/recommendations for international students: Required—TOEFL (minimum score 550 paper-based). Electronic applications accepted. *Expenses:* Contact institution.

Oklahoma State University, Spears School of Business, School of Marketing and International Business, Stillwater, OK 74078. Offers business administration (PhD), including marketing; marketing (MBA). *Program availability:* Part-time. *Faculty:* 21 full-time (5 women), 5 part-time/adjunct (2 women). *Students:* 63 full-time (19 women), 19 part-time (9 women); includes 5 minority (2 Asian, non-Hispanic/Latino; 2 Hispanic/Latino; 1 Two or more races, non-Hispanic/Latino), 65 international. Average age 27. 234 applicants, 20% accepted, 42 enrolled. In 2017, 41 master's, 1 doctorate awarded. *Entrance requirements:* For master's and doctorate, GRE or GMAT. Additional exam requirements/recommendations for international students: Required—TOEFL (minimum score 550 paper-based; 79 iBT). *Application deadline:* For fall admission, 3/1 priority date for international students; for spring admission, 8/1 priority date for international students. Applications are processed on a rolling basis. Application fee: $40 ($75 for international students). Electronic applications accepted. *Expenses:* Tuition, state resident: full-time $4019; part-time $2679.60 per year. Tuition, nonresident: full-time $15,286; part-time $10,190.40 per year. *Required fees:* $2129; $1419 per unit. Tuition and fees vary according to program. *Financial support:* Research assistantships, teaching assistantships, career-related internships or fieldwork, Federal Work-Study, scholarships/grants, health care benefits, tuition waivers (partial), and unspecified assistantships available. Support available to part-time students. Financial award application deadline: 3/1; financial award applicants required to submit FAFSA. *Faculty research:* Decision-making (consumer, managerial, cross-functional), communication effects, services marketing, public policy and marketing, corporate image. *Unit head:* Dr. Joshua L. Wiener, Department Head, 405-744-5192, Fax: 405-744-5180, E-mail: josh.wiener@okstate.edu. *Application contact:* Dr. Kevin Voss, PhD Coordinator, 405-744-5106, Fax: 405-744-5180, E-mail: kevin.voss@okstate.edu.
Website: https://business.okstate.edu/marketing/

Old Dominion University, College of Health Sciences, School of Dental Hygiene, Norfolk, VA 23529. Offers dental hygiene (MS), including community/public health, education, generalist, global health, marketing, modeling and simulation, research. *Program availability:* Part-time, evening/weekend, blended/hybrid learning. *Faculty:* 10 full-time (9 women). *Students:* 3 full-time (1 woman), 22 part-time (21 women); includes 5 minority (3 Black or African American, non-Hispanic/Latino; 1 Asian, non-Hispanic/Latino; 1 Hispanic/Latino), 3 international. Average age 38. 12 applicants, 25% accepted, 2 enrolled. In 2017, 8 master's awarded. *Degree requirements:* For master's, comprehensive exam, thesis optional, writing proficiency exam, responsible conduct of research training. *Entrance requirements:* For master's, Dental Hygiene National Board Examination or copy of license to practice dental hygiene, BS or certificate in dental hygiene or related area, minimum GPA of 2.8 (3.0 in major), 4 letters of recommendation. Additional exam requirements/recommendations for international students: Required—TOEFL (minimum score 550 paper-based, 79 iBT) or IELTS (minimum score 6.5). *Application deadline:* For fall admission, 7/1 for domestic students, 4/15 for international students; for spring admission, 12/1 for domestic students, 10/1 for international students; for summer admission, 3/1 for domestic students, 2/1 for international students. Applications are processed on a rolling basis. Application fee: $50. Electronic applications accepted. *Expenses:* Contact institution. *Financial support:* In 2017–18, 4 students received support, including 4 teaching assistantships with partial tuition reimbursements available (averaging $13,000 per year); scholarships/grants and health care benefits also available. Support available to part-time students. Financial award application deadline: 2/15; financial award applicants required to submit CSS PROFILE or FAFSA. *Faculty research:* Clinical dental hygiene, dental hygiene client health behaviors, dental hygiene education interventions, oral product testing, cold plasma. *Total annual research expenditures:* $43,581. *Unit head:* Dr. Denise M. Claiborne, Assistant Professor/Graduate Program Director, 757-683-5949, Fax: 757-683-5239, E-mail: dclaibor@odu.edu. *Application contact:* William Heffelfinger, Director of Graduate Admissions, 757-683-5554, Fax: 757-683-3255, E-mail: gradadmit@odu.edu.
Website: http://www.odu.edu/academics/programs/masters/dental-hygiene

Old Dominion University, Strome College of Business, Doctoral Program in Business Administration, Norfolk, VA 23529. Offers business administration (PhD), including finance, IT and supply chain management, marketing, strategic management. *Accreditation:* AACSB. *Faculty:* 35 full-time (6 women). *Students:* 27 full-time (8 women), 25 part-time (6 women); includes 1 minority (Asian, non-Hispanic/Latino), 41 international. Average age 35. 63 applicants, 30% accepted, 8 enrolled. In 2017, 9 doctorates awarded. *Degree requirements:* For doctorate, comprehensive exam, thesis/dissertation. *Entrance requirements:* For doctorate, GMAT or GRE. Additional exam requirements/recommendations for international students: Required—TOEFL (minimum score 550 paper-based; 79 iBT). *Application deadline:* For fall admission, 3/1 priority date for domestic and international students. Application fee: $50. Electronic applications accepted. *Expenses:* Tuition, state resident: full-time $8928; part-time $496 per credit. Tuition, nonresident: full-time $22,482; part-time $1249 per credit. *Required fees:* $66 per semester. *Financial support:* In 2017–18, 36 students received support, including 15 research assistantships with full tuition reimbursements available (averaging $18,500 per year), 13 teaching assistantships with full tuition reimbursements available (averaging $18,500 per year); unspecified assistantships and tuition grants (for fourth-year students) also available. Financial award application deadline: 3/1; financial award applicants required to submit FAFSA. *Faculty research:* International business, buyer behavior, financial markets, strategy, operations research. *Unit head:* Dr. John B. Ford, Graduate Program Director, 757-683-3587, Fax: 757-683-4076, E-mail: jbford@odu.edu. *Application contact:* Katrina Davenport, Program Coordinator, 757-683-5138, Fax: 757-683-4076, E-mail: kdavenpo@odu.edu.
Website: http://www.odu.edu/business/academics/graduate/scb-phd

Oral Roberts University, School of Business, Tulsa, OK 74171. Offers accounting (MBA); entrepreneurship (MBA); finance (MBA); international business (MBA); management (MBA); marketing (MBA); not for profit management (MNM). *Accreditation:* ACBSP. *Program availability:* Part-time, online learning. *Faculty:* 7 full-time (0 women), 5 part-time/adjunct (4 women). *Students:* 71 applicants, 94% accepted, 56 enrolled. *Degree requirements:* For master's, thesis optional. *Entrance requirements:* For master's, minimum cumulative GPA of 3.0 from regionally-accredited institution. *Application deadline:* Applications are processed on a rolling basis. Application fee: $35. Electronic applications accepted. Application fee is waived when completed online. *Financial support:* In 2017–18, 39 students received support. Scholarships/grants and unspecified assistantships available. Financial award application deadline: 6/1. *Faculty research:* Social media, international business and marketing. *Unit head:* Dr. Marshal Wright, Chair of the Graduate School of Business, 918-495-6988, E-mail: mwright@oru.edu. *Application contact:* Sam Park, Enrollment Counselor, 918-495-7179, E-mail: sampark@oru.edu.
Website: http://www.oru.edu/university/departments/schools/bus

Ottawa University, Graduate Studies-Arizona, Programs in Business, Ottawa, KS 66067-3399. Offers business administration (MBA); finance (MBA); human resources (MA, MBA); leadership (MBA); marketing (MBA). Programs offered in Mesa, Phoenix, Tempe and West Valley, AZ. *Program availability:* Part-time, evening/weekend, online learning. *Degree requirements:* For master's, thesis or alternative. *Entrance requirements:* For master's, minimum undergraduate GPA of 3.0. Additional exam requirements/recommendations for international students: Required—TOEFL (minimum score 550 paper-based). Electronic applications accepted.

Pace University, Lubin School of Business, Advanced Professional Certificate Program, New York, NY 10038. Offers business economics (APC); e-business (APC); financial management (APC); international business (APC); international economics (APC); investment management (APC); marketing (APC); public accounting (APC). *Program availability:* Part-time, evening/weekend. *Students:* 1 applicant, 100% accepted. *Entrance requirements:* For degree, MBA or MS in business discipline, relevant professional experience. Additional exam requirements/recommendations for international students: Required—TOEFL (minimum score 90 iBT), IELTS (minimum score 7) or PTE (minimum score 61). *Application deadline:* For fall admission, 8/1 priority date for domestic students, 6/1 for international students; for spring admission, 12/1 for domestic students, 10/1 for international students. Applications are processed on a rolling basis. Application fee: $70. Electronic applications accepted. *Unit head:* Dr. Jack Yurkiewicz, Director, 212-618-6567, E-mail: jyurkiewicz@pace.edu. *Application contact:* Susan Ford-Goldschein, Director of Graduate Admissions, 212-346-1531, Fax: 212-346-1585, E-mail: graduateadmission@pace.edu.
Website: http://www.pace.edu/lubin/agc

Pace University, Lubin School of Business, Doctor of Professional Studies Program, New York, NY 10038. Offers finance (DPS); management (DPS); marketing (DPS). *Program availability:* Part-time. *Students:* 12 full-time (5 women), 67 part-time (29 women); includes 22 minority (12 Black or African American, non-Hispanic/Latino; 5 Asian, non-Hispanic/Latino; 4 Hispanic/Latino; 1 Two or more races, non-Hispanic/Latino), 3 international. Average age 50. 31 applicants, 81% accepted, 13 enrolled. In 2017, 4 doctorates awarded. *Degree requirements:* For doctorate, thesis/dissertation, oral and written exam. *Entrance requirements:* For doctorate, MBA or similar master's degree, 10 years of experience in business, transcripts from all accredited colleges/universities attended, 4 letters of recommendation, interview. Additional exam requirements/recommendations for international students: Required—TOEFL (minimum score 90 iBT), IELTS (minimum score 7) or PTE (minimum score 61). *Application deadline:* For fall admission, 6/1 priority date for domestic students, 6/1 for international students. Applications are processed on a rolling basis. Application fee: $70. Electronic applications accepted. *Unit head:* Dr. John P. Dory, Director, Doctoral Program in Business, 212-618-6660, E-mail: jdory@pace.edu. *Application contact:* Margaret Hanson, Program Coordinator for Doctoral Programs, 212-618-6660, E-mail: dps.bus@pace.edu.
Website: http://www.pace.edu/lubin/dps/

Pace University, Lubin School of Business, Marketing Program, New York, NY 10038. Offers analytics and customer intelligence (MS); marketing management (MBA); social media and mobile marketing (MS). *Program availability:* Part-time, evening/weekend. *Students:* 31 full-time (22 women), 19 part-time (15 women); includes 8 minority (1 Black or African American, non-Hispanic/Latino; 2 Asian, non-Hispanic/Latino; 4 Hispanic/Latino; 1 Two or more races, non-Hispanic/Latino), 24 international. Average age 26. 84 applicants, 60% accepted, 18 enrolled. In 2017, 34 master's awarded. *Entrance requirements:* For master's, GMAT, GRE, undergraduate degree, transcripts from all accredited colleges/universities attended, two letters of recommendation, resume, personal statement. Additional exam requirements/recommendations for international students: Required—TOEFL (minimum score 90 iBT), IELTS (minimum score 7) or PTE (minimum score 61). *Application deadline:* For fall admission, 8/1 priority date for domestic students, 6/1 for international students; for spring admission, 12/1 for domestic students, 10/1 for international students. Applications are processed on a rolling basis. Application fee: $70. Electronic applications accepted. *Financial support:* Research assistantships, career-related internships or fieldwork, and Federal Work-Study available. Support available to part-time students. Financial award application deadline: 2/15; financial award applicants required to submit FAFSA. *Unit head:* Dr. Ipshita Ray, Chairperson, 212-618-6505, E-mail: iray@pace.edu. *Application contact:* Susan Ford-Goldschein, Director of Graduate Admissions, 212-346-1531, Fax: 212-346-1585, E-mail: graduateadmission@pace.edu.
Website: http://www.pace.edu/lubin/mba-in-marketing-management

Polytechnic University of Puerto Rico, Miami Campus, Graduate School, Miami, FL 33166. Offers accounting (MBA); business administration (MBA); construction management (MEM); environmental management (MEM); finance (MBA); human resources management (MBA); logistics and supply chain management (MBA); management of international enterprises (MBA); manufacturing management (MEM); marketing management (MBA); project management (MBA). *Program availability:* Part-time, evening/weekend, online learning. *Entrance requirements:* For master's, minimum GPA of 3.0. Electronic applications accepted.

Pontifical Catholic University of Puerto Rico, College of Business Administration, Program in Marketing, Ponce, PR 00717-0777. Offers MBA. *Program availability:* Part-time, evening/weekend. *Degree requirements:* For master's, thesis. *Entrance requirements:* For master's, GRE, interview, minimum GPA of 2.75.

Pontificia Universidad Catolica Madre y Maestra, Graduate School, Faculty of Social and Administrative Sciences, Santiago, Dominican Republic. Offers business administration (MBA), including business development, finance, international business, management skills (M Mgmt, MBA), marketing, operations, strategic cost management, strategy, tourist destination planning and management; law (LL M), including civil law, corporate business law, criminal law, international relations, real estate law; management (M Mgmt), including higher financial management, insurance program administration, management skills (M Mgmt, MBA); psychology (MA), including clinical child and adolescent psychology, forensic psychology; strategic human resources (EMBA).

Post University, Program in Business Administration, Waterbury, CT 06723-2540. Offers accounting (MSA); business administration (MBA); corporate finance (MBA); corporate innovation (MBA); healthcare systems leadership (MBA); leadership (MBA); marketing (MBA); project management (MBA, MS). *Accreditation:* ACBSP. *Program availability:* Online learning. *Entrance requirements:* For master's, resume. *Expenses: Tuition:* Part-time $730 per credit hour. Part-time tuition and fees vary according to degree level and program. *Application contact:* Veronica Montalvo, Vice President, Online Education Enrollment Management and Admissions, 203-596-6164, E-mail: vmontalvo@post.edu.

Providence College, School of Business, Providence, RI 02918. Offers accounting (MBA); finance (MBA); international business (MBA); management (MBA); marketing (MBA). *Accreditation:* AACSB. *Program availability:* Part-time, evening/weekend. *Entrance requirements:* For master's, GMAT. Additional exam requirements/recommendations for international students: Required—TOEFL (minimum score 577 paper-based; 90 iBT). *Expenses:* Contact institution.

Purdue University Global, School of Business, Davenport, IA 52807. Offers business administration (MBA); change management (MS); entrepreneurship (MBA); finance (MBA); health care management (MBA, MS); human resource (MBA); international business (MBA); management (MS); marketing (MBA); project management (MBA, MS); supply chain management and logistics (MBA, MS). *Accreditation:* ACBSP. *Program availability:* Part-time, evening/weekend, online learning. *Entrance requirements:* Additional exam requirements/recommendations for international students: Required—TOEFL (minimum score 550 paper-based; 80 iBT). Electronic applications accepted.

Queen's University at Kingston, Queens School of Business, Program in Business Administration, Kingston, ON K7L 3N6, Canada. Offers consulting and project management (MBA); finance (MBA); innovation and entrepreneurship (MBA); marketing (MBA). *Degree requirements:* For master's, thesis optional, research project. *Entrance requirements:* For master's, GMAT, minimum B+ average. Additional exam requirements/recommendations for international students: Required—TOEFL. Electronic applications accepted. *Faculty research:* Management fundamentals, strategic thinking, global business, innovation and change, leadership.

Regent's University London, Webster Graduate School, London, United Kingdom. Offers business (MBA); finance (MS); human resources (MA); information technology management (MA); international business (MA); international non-governmental organizations (MA); international relations (MA); management and leadership (MA); marketing (MA). *Program availability:* Part-time.

Regent University, Graduate School, School of Business and Leadership, Virginia Beach, VA 23464-9800. Offers business administration (MBA), including accounting, economics, entrepreneurship, finance and investing, general management, healthcare management (MA, MBA), human resource management (MA, MBA), innovation management, leadership, marketing, not-for-profit management (MA, MBA); business analytics (MS); business and design management (MA); church leadership (MA); leadership (Certificate); organizational leadership (MA, PhD), including ecclesial leadership (DSL, PhD), entrepreneurial leadership (PhD), healthcare management (MA, MBA), human resource development (PhD), human resource management (MA, MBA), individualized studies (DSL, PhD), interdisciplinary studies (MA), leadership coaching and mentoring (MA), not-for-profit management (MA, MBA), organizational development consulting (MA), servant leadership (MA, DSL); strategic leadership (DSL), including ecclesial leadership (DSL, PhD), global consulting, healthcare leadership, individualized studies (DSL, PhD), leadership coaching, servant leadership (MA, DSL), strategic foresight. *Program availability:* Part-time, evening/weekend, 100% online, blended/hybrid learning. *Faculty:* 9 full-time (2 women), 38 part-time/adjunct (11 women). *Students:* 129 full-time (80 women), 1,152 part-time (598 women); includes 685 minority (546 Black or African American, non-Hispanic/Latino; 10 American Indian or Alaska Native, non-Hispanic/Latino; 29 Asian, non-Hispanic/Latino; 65 Hispanic/Latino; 6 Native Hawaiian or other Pacific Islander, non-Hispanic/Latino; 29 Two or more races, non-Hispanic/Latino), 62 international. Average age 41. 1,721 applicants, 48% accepted, 624 enrolled. In 2017, 125 master's, 69 doctorates awarded. *Degree requirements:* For master's, thesis or alternative, 3-credit hour culminating experience; for doctorate, thesis/dissertation. *Entrance requirements:* For master's, college transcripts, resume, essay; for doctorate, college transcripts, resume, essay, writing sample; for Certificate, writing sample, resume, transcripts. Additional exam requirements/recommendations for international students: Required—TOEFL (minimum score 577 paper-based). *Application deadline:* For fall admission, 5/1 priority date for domestic students; for spring admission, 10/1 priority date for domestic students. Applications are processed on a rolling basis. Application fee: $50. Electronic applications accepted. *Expenses:* $650 per credit (MA, MS, MBA); $995 per credit (PhD); $300 per semester technology fee. *Financial support:* In 2017–18, 829 students received support. Career-related internships or fieldwork, scholarships/grants, and unspecified assistantships available. Support available to part-time students. *Faculty research:* Servant leadership, global business, team effectiveness, technology utilization, leadership development. *Unit head:* Dr. Doris Gomez, Dean, 757-352-4686, Fax: 757-352-4634, E-mail: dorigom@regent.edu. *Application contact:* Heidi Cece, Assistant Vice President of Enrollment Management, 800-373-5504, Fax: 757-352-4381, E-mail: admissions@regent.edu.
Website: https://www.regent.edu/school-of-business-and-leadership/

Regis University, College of Business and Economics, Denver, CO 80221-1099. Offers accounting (MS); executive leadership (Certificate); finance (MS); finance and accounting (MBA); health industry leadership (MBA); human resource management and leadership (MSOL); management (MBA); marketing (MBA); nonprofit leadership (Post-Graduate Certificate); nonprofit management (MNM); nonprofit organizational capacity building (Certificate); operations management (MBA); organizational leadership and management (MSOL); project leadership and management (MS, MSOL); strategic business management (Certificate); strategic human resource integration (Certificate); strategic management (Certificate). Programs offered at Colorado Springs Campus, Northwest Denver Campus, Southeast Denver Campus, Fort Collins Campus, Broomfield Campus, Henderson (Nevada) Campus, and Summerlin (Nevada) Campus. *Program availability:* Part-time, evening/weekend, 100% online, blended/hybrid learning. *Degree requirements:* For master's, thesis (for some programs), capstone or final research project. *Entrance requirements:* For master's, official transcript reflecting baccalaureate degree awarded from regionally-accredited college or university, interview, 2 years of full-time related work experience, resume, letters of recommendation. Additional exam requirements/recommendations for international students: Required—TOEFL (minimum score 550 paper-based; 82 iBT). Electronic applications accepted. *Expenses:* Contact institution. *Faculty research:* Impact of information technology on small business regulation of accounting, international project financing, mineral development, delivery of healthcare to rural indigenous communities.

Roberts Wesleyan College, Graduate Business Programs, Rochester, NY 14624-1997. Offers strategic leadership (MS); strategic marketing (MS). *Program availability:* Evening/weekend. *Degree requirements:* For master's, thesis or alternative. *Entrance requirements:* For master's, GMAT, minimum GPA of 2.75, verifiable work experience. *Expenses:* Contact institution.

Marketing

Roosevelt University, Graduate Division, College of Arts and Sciences, Department of Communication, Chicago, IL 60605. Offers integrated marketing communications (MSIMC). *Program availability:* Part-time, evening/weekend. *Students:* 38 full-time (28 women), 25 part-time (19 women); includes 28 minority (19 Black or African American, non-Hispanic/Latino; 3 Asian, non-Hispanic/Latino; 5 Hispanic/Latino; 1 Two or more races, non-Hispanic/Latino), 24 international. Average age 27. 43 applicants, 95% accepted, 15 enrolled. In 2017, 38 master's awarded. *Application deadline:* Applications are processed on a rolling basis. Application fee: $40. Electronic applications accepted. *Financial support:* Career-related internships or fieldwork, scholarships/grants, and unspecified assistantships available. *Unit head:* Marian Azzaro, Chair, 312-281-3239. *Application contact:* Sivling Lam, Graduate Admission Counselor, 312-281-3252, E-mail: slam02@roosevelt.edu.

Rowan University, Graduate School, College of Communication and Creative Arts, Integrated Marketing Communication and New Media Certificate of Graduate Study Program, Glassboro, NJ 08028-1701. Offers CGS. Electronic applications accepted. *Expenses:* Tuition, state resident: full-time $15,020; part-time $751 per semester hour. Tuition, nonresident: full-time $15,020; part-time $751 per semester hour. *Required fees:* $3158; $157.90 per semester hour. Tuition and fees vary according to course load, campus/location and program.

Rutgers University–Newark, Graduate School, Program in Management, Newark, NJ 07102. Offers accounting (PhD); accounting information systems (PhD); computer information systems (PhD); finance (PhD); information technology (PhD); international business (PhD); management science (PhD); marketing (PhD); organization management (PhD). Program offered jointly with New Jersey Institute of Technology. *Accreditation:* AACSB. *Degree requirements:* For doctorate, thesis/dissertation, cumulative exams. *Entrance requirements:* For doctorate, GMAT or GRE General Test, minimum undergraduate B average. Additional exam requirements/recommendations for international students: Required—TOEFL. Electronic applications accepted. *Faculty research:* Technology management, leadership and teams, consumer behavior, financial and markets, logistics.

Rutgers University–Newark, Rutgers Business School–Newark and New Brunswick, Doctoral Programs in Management, Newark, NJ 07102. Offers accounting (PhD); accounting information systems (PhD); economics (PhD); finance (PhD); individualized study (PhD); information technology (PhD); international business (PhD); management science (PhD); marketing science (PhD); organizational management (PhD); science, technology and management (PhD); supply chain management (PhD). *Degree requirements:* For doctorate, comprehensive exam, thesis/dissertation. *Entrance requirements:* For doctorate, GRE or GMAT. Additional exam requirements/recommendations for international students: Required—TOEFL (minimum score 550 paper-based; 79 iBT). Electronic applications accepted.

Sacred Heart University, Graduate Programs, Jack Welch College of Business, Department of Marketing, Fairfield, CT 06825. Offers digital marketing (MS); marketing (MBA, Graduate Certificate). *Program availability:* Part-time, evening/weekend. *Faculty:* 4 full-time (1 woman), 1 part-time/adjunct (0 women). *Students:* 21 full-time (16 women), 23 part-time (15 women); includes 6 minority (2 Black or African American, non-Hispanic/Latino; 4 Hispanic/Latino), 18 international. Average age 28. 29 applicants, 100% accepted, 17 enrolled. In 2017, 8 master's awarded. *Degree requirements:* For master's, capstone project. *Entrance requirements:* For master's, GMAT, bachelor's degree from accredited institution with minimum GPA of 3.0. Additional exam requirements/recommendations for international students: Required—TOEFL (minimum score 570 paper-based, 80 iBT), TWE, or IELTS (6.5); Recommended—TSE. *Application deadline:* Applications are processed on a rolling basis. Application fee: $75. Electronic applications accepted. *Expenses:* Contact institution. *Financial support:* Unspecified assistantships available. Financial award applicants required to submit FAFSA. *Unit head:* Dr. Anca Micu, Associate Dean/Director of MS in Marketing, 203-371-7813, Fax: 203-365-7538, E-mail: marketing@sacredheart.edu. *Application contact:* Pam Pillo, Executive Director of Graduate Admissions, 203-365-7619, E-mail: gradstudies@sacredheart.edu.
Website: http://www.sacredheart.edu/academics/johnfwelchcollegeofbusiness/graduateprogramscertificates/msindigitalmarketing/

St. Bonaventure University, School of Graduate Studies, Jandoli School of Communication, Program in Integrated Marketing Communications, St. Bonaventure, NY 14778-2284. Offers MA. *Program availability:* Part-time, evening/weekend, 100% online. *Faculty:* 5 full-time (3 women), 6 part-time/adjunct (4 women). *Students:* 31 full-time (17 women), 45 part-time (33 women); includes 14 minority (4 Black or African American, non-Hispanic/Latino; 1 American Indian or Alaska Native, non-Hispanic/Latino; 7 Hispanic/Latino; 2 Two or more races, non-Hispanic/Latino), 4 international. Average age 27. 32 applicants, 91% accepted, 20 enrolled. In 2017, 17 master's awarded. *Degree requirements:* For master's, campaign project. *Entrance requirements:* For master's, transcripts, personal statement describing desire to pursue the IMC program. Additional exam requirements/recommendations for international students: Required—TOEFL (minimum score 550 paper-based; 79 iBT). *Application deadline:* For fall admission, 6/5 for domestic students, 2/1 for international students; for spring admission, 10/15 for domestic students, 7/1 for international students. Applications are processed on a rolling basis. Application fee: $0. Electronic applications accepted. *Expenses:* $733 per credit hour, $100 graduation fee. *Financial support:* Federal Work-Study, scholarships/grants, health care benefits, and unspecified assistantships available. Support available to part-time students. Financial award application deadline: 4/15; financial award applicants required to submit FAFSA. *Faculty research:* Network analysis of internal and external communication networks in organizations, organizational behavior, student engagement in active learning. *Unit head:* Dr. Richard Lee, Director, 716-375-2563, Fax: 716-375-2588, E-mail: rlee@sbu.edu. *Application contact:* Bruce Campbell, Director of Graduate Admissions, 716-375-2429, Fax: 716-375-4015, E-mail: gradsch@sbu.edu.
Website: http://www.sbu.edu/academics/schools/journalism-and-mass-communications/graduate-degrees/ma-integrated-marketing-communications

St. Catherine University, Graduate Programs, Program in Business Administration, St. Paul, MN 55105. Offers healthcare (MBA); integrated marketing communications (MBA); management (MBA). *Program availability:* Part-time, evening/weekend. *Students:* 62 part-time (54 women); includes 8 minority (4 Black or African American, non-Hispanic/Latino; 2 Asian, non-Hispanic/Latino; 2 Two or more races, non-Hispanic/Latino), 1 international. Average age 33. 28 applicants, 71% accepted, 18 enrolled. In 2017, 31 master's awarded. *Entrance requirements:* For master's, GMAT (if undergraduate GPA is less than 3.0), 2+ years' work or volunteer experience in professional setting(s). Additional exam requirements/recommendations for international students: Required—TOEFL. *Application deadline:* For fall admission, 8/1 priority date for domestic students; for spring admission, 12/15 priority date for domestic students. Application fee: $35. *Expenses:* Contact institution. *Unit head:* Michelle Wieser, Director, 651-690-6355, E-mail: mawieser@stkate.edu.

St. John's University, The Peter J. Tobin College of Business, Department of Marketing, Queens, NY 11439. Offers business administration (MBA), including marketing management. *Faculty:* 12 full-time (5 women), 5 part-time/adjunct (1 woman). *Students:* 40 full-time (27 women), 17 part-time (10 women); includes 16 minority (7 Black or African American, non-Hispanic/Latino; 2 Asian, non-Hispanic/Latino; 5 Hispanic/Latino; 2 Two or more races, non-Hispanic/Latino), 14 international. Average age 25. 41 applicants, 88% accepted, 26 enrolled. In 2017, 22 master's awarded. *Entrance requirements:* For master's, GMAT or GRE, 2 letters of recommendation, essay, resume, unofficial transcripts. Additional exam requirements/recommendations for international students: Required—TOEFL (minimum score 80 iBT), IELTS (minimum score 6.5). *Application deadline:* For fall admission, 11/1 for domestic and international students; for winter admission, 3/1 for domestic students; for spring admission, 6/1 for domestic and international students. Applications are processed on a rolling basis. Application fee: $70. Electronic applications accepted. *Expenses:* $22,410 per year. *Financial support:* Research assistantships, teaching assistantships, scholarships/grants, and unspecified assistantships available. Support available to part-time students. Financial award application deadline: 2/1; financial award applicants required to submit FAFSA. *Unit head:* Dr. Iris Mohr, Chair, 718-990-7307, E-mail: mohri@stjohns.edu. *Application contact:* Amber Steiger, Associate Director of Enrollment Management, 718-990-1345, E-mail: steigera@stjohns.edu.
Website: http://www.stjohns.edu/academics/schools-and-colleges/peter-j-tobin-college-business/marketing

Saint Joseph's University, Erivan K. Haub School of Business, Graduate Food Marketing Program, Philadelphia, PA 19131-1395. Offers MBA, MS. *Program availability:* Part-time, evening/weekend, online learning. *Faculty:* 7 full-time (1 woman), 1 part-time/adjunct (0 women). *Students:* 1 full-time (0 women), 39 part-time (23 women); includes 6 minority (2 Black or African American, non-Hispanic/Latino; 1 Asian, non-Hispanic/Latino; 2 Hispanic/Latino; 1 Two or more races, non-Hispanic/Latino), 1 international. Average age 35. 15 applicants, 87% accepted, 8 enrolled. In 2017, 10 master's awarded. *Degree requirements:* For master's, minimum GPA of 3.0. *Entrance requirements:* For master's, 4 years of industry experience, interview or GMAT/GRE, letter of recommendation, resume, official transcripts, personal statement. Additional exam requirements/recommendations for international students: Required—TOEFL, IELTS or PTE. *Application deadline:* Applications are processed on a rolling basis. Application fee: $0. Electronic applications accepted. *Expenses:* Contact institution. *Financial support:* Scholarships/grants and unspecified assistantships available. Financial award application deadline: 5/1; financial award applicants required to submit FAFSA. *Unit head:* Terese W. Waldron, Director, 610-660-3150, Fax: 610-660-3153, E-mail: twaldron@sju.edu. *Application contact:* Kathleen Klarich, Program Manager, 610-660-3155, Fax: 610-660-3160, E-mail: kklarich@sju.edu.
Website: https://www.sju.edu/majors-programs/graduate-business/master-degrees/food-marketing-mba-or-ms

Saint Joseph's University, Erivan K. Haub School of Business, MBA Program, Philadelphia, PA 19131-1395. Offers accounting (MBA); business intelligence analytics (MBA); finance (MBA); financial analysis reporting (Postbaccalaureate Certificate); general business (MBA); health and medical services administration (MBA); international business (MBA); international marketing (MBA); leading (MBA); marketing (MBA); DO/MBA. DO/MBA offered jointly with Philadelphia College of Osteopathic Medicine. *Program availability:* Part-time-only, evening/weekend, 100% online. *Students:* 85 full-time (36 women), 371 part-time (153 women); includes 74 minority (32 Black or African American, non-Hispanic/Latino; 15 Asian, non-Hispanic/Latino; 19 Hispanic/Latino; 1 Native Hawaiian or other Pacific Islander, non-Hispanic/Latino; 7 Two or more races, non-Hispanic/Latino), 36 international. Average age 30. 247 applicants, 76% accepted, 112 enrolled. In 2017, 163 master's awarded. *Degree requirements:* For master's, minimum GPA of 3.0. *Entrance requirements:* For master's, GMAT or GRE, 2 letters of recommendation, resume, personal statement, official undergraduate and graduate transcripts. Additional exam requirements/recommendations for international students: Required—PTE, TOEFL, IELTS, or PTE. *Application deadline:* For fall admission, 7/15 priority date for domestic students, 5/15 priority date for international students; for spring admission, 11/15 priority date for domestic students, 10/15 priority date for international students; for summer admission, 4/15 priority date for domestic students, 2/15 priority date for international students. Applications are processed on a rolling basis. Application fee: $35. Electronic applications accepted. *Expenses:* Contact institution. *Financial support:* Scholarships/grants and unspecified assistantships available. Financial award application deadline: 5/1; financial award applicants required to submit FAFSA. *Unit head:* Jeannine Lajeunesse, Director, 610-660-1626, Fax: 610-660-1599, E-mail: jlajeune@sju.edu. *Application contact:* Christine Anderson, Assistant Director, 610-660-2252, Fax: 610-660-1599, E-mail: chris.anderson@sju.edu.
Website: http://www.sju.edu/haubmba

 Saint Joseph's University, Erivan K. Haub School of Business, MS Program in Marketing, Philadelphia, PA 19131. Offers customer analytics and insights (MS); international marketing (MS). *Program availability:* Part-time, evening/weekend, 100% online. *Faculty:* 8 full-time (2 women), 4 part-time/adjunct (1 woman). *Students:* 30 full-time (18 women), 11 part-time (8 women); includes 4 minority (2 Black or African American, non-Hispanic/Latino; 1 Asian, non-Hispanic/Latino; 1 Hispanic/Latino), 26 international. Average age 27. 51 applicants, 55% accepted, 10 enrolled. In 2017, 10 master's awarded. *Degree requirements:* For master's, minimum GPA of 3.0. *Entrance requirements:* For master's, GMAT or GRE, 2 letters of recommendation, resume, personal statement, official undergraduate and graduate transcripts. Additional exam requirements/recommendations for international students: Required—PTE, TOEFL, IELTS, or PTE. *Application deadline:* For fall admission, 7/15 priority date for domestic students, 5/15 priority date for international students; for spring admission, 11/15 priority date for domestic students, 10/15 priority date for international students; for summer admission, 4/15 priority date for domestic students. Applications are processed on a rolling basis. Application fee: $35. Electronic applications accepted. *Financial support:* Scholarships/grants and unspecified assistantships available. Financial award application deadline: 5/1; financial award applicants required to submit FAFSA. *Unit head:* Jeannine Lajeunesse, Director, 610-660-1626, E-mail: jlajeune@sju.edu. *Application contact:* Christine Anderson, Assistant Director, 610-660-2252, Fax: 610-660-1599, E-mail: chris.anderson@sju.edu.
Website: https://www.sju.edu/majors-programs/graduate-business/master-degrees/master-science-marketing

See Display on the next page and Close-Up on page 519.

Saint Joseph's University, Erivan K. Haub School of Business, Pharmaceutical and Healthcare Marketing MBA Program, Philadelphia, PA 19131-1395. Offers MBA, Post Master's Certificate. *Program availability:* Part-time, evening/weekend, 100% online. *Faculty:* 2 full-time (0 women), 9 part-time/adjunct (1 woman). *Students:* 4 full-time (2 women), 109 part-time (57 women); includes 38 minority (15 Black or African American, non-Hispanic/Latino; 13 Asian, non-Hispanic/Latino; 8 Hispanic/Latino; 2 Two or more races, non-Hispanic/Latino), 2 international. Average age 43. 39 applicants, 77% accepted, 24 enrolled. In 2017, 22 master's, 1 other advanced degree awarded. *Degree requirements:* For master's, minimum GPA of 3.0. *Entrance requirements:* For master's, 4 years of industry experience, letter of recommendation, resume, interview, official transcripts; for Post Master's Certificate, MBA, 4 years of industry experience, resume. Additional exam requirements/recommendations for international students: Required—PTE, TOEFL, IELTS, or PTE. *Application deadline:* For fall admission, 7/15 for domestic students, 4/15 for international students; for spring admission, 11/15 for domestic

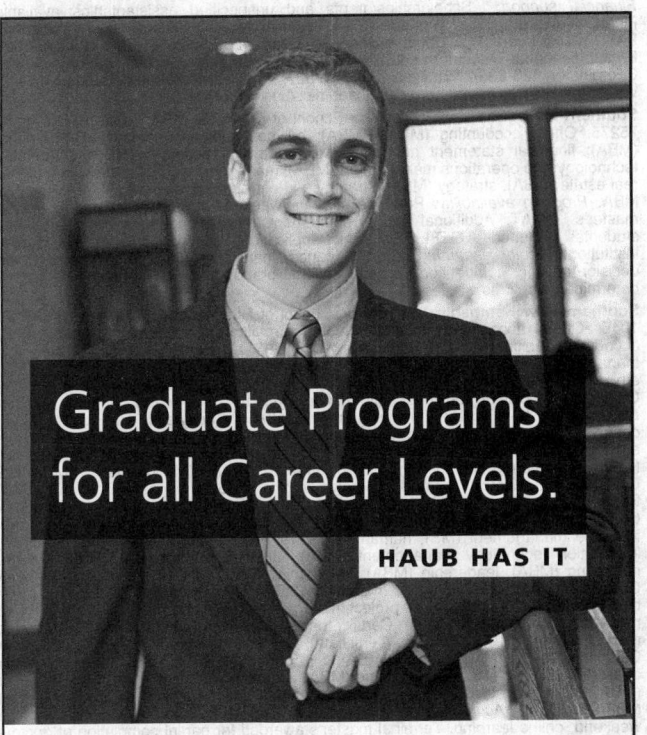
students, 10/15 for international students. Applications are processed on a rolling basis. Electronic applications accepted. *Expenses:* Contact institution. *Financial support:* Scholarships/grants and unspecified assistantships available. Financial award application deadline: 5/1; financial award applicants required to submit FAFSA. *Unit head:* Terese W. Waldron, Director, 610-660-3150, Fax: 610-660-5160, E-mail: twaldron@sju.edu. *Application contact:* Jon Dart, Senior Manager, 610-660-3149, Fax: 610-660-3160, E-mail: jdart@sju.edu.
Website: http://www.sju.edu/epharma

Saint Leo University, Graduate Studies in Business, Saint Leo, FL 33574-6665. Offers accounting (M Acc, MBA); cybersecurity (MS); cybersecurity management (MBA); data analytics (MBA); health care management (MBA); human resource management (MBA); international and experiential business administration (MBA); management (MBA, DBA); marketing (MBA); marketing research and social media analytics (MBA); project management (MBA); social media marketing (MBA); sport business (MBA); supply chain global integration management (MBA). *Accreditation:* ACBSP. *Program availability:* Part-time, evening/weekend, 100% online, blended/hybrid learning. *Faculty:* 54 full-time (18 women), 52 part-time/adjunct (18 women). *Students:* 9 full-time (3 women), 1,867 part-time (1,079 women); includes 861 minority (598 Black or African American, non-Hispanic/Latino; 3 American Indian or Alaska Native, non-Hispanic/Latino; 38 Asian, non-Hispanic/Latino; 186 Hispanic/Latino; 3 Native Hawaiian or other Pacific Islander, non-Hispanic/Latino; 33 Two or more races, non-Hispanic/Latino), 68 international. Average age 37. 868 applicants, 63% accepted, 537 enrolled. In 2017, 859 master's, 3 doctorates awarded. *Degree requirements:* For doctorate, comprehensive exam, thesis/dissertation. *Entrance requirements:* For master's, GMAT with minimum score 500 (for M Acc), official transcripts, current resume, 2 professional recommendations, personal statement, bachelor's degree from regionally-accredited university; undergraduate degree in accounting and minimum undergraduate GPA of 3.0 (for M Acc); minimum undergraduate GPA of 3.0 in final 2 years of undergraduate study and 2 years' work experience (for MBA); for doctorate, GMAT (minimum score of 550) if master's GPA is under 3.25, official transcripts, current resume, 2 professional recommendations, personal statement, master's degree from regionally-accredited university with minimum GPA of 3.25, 3 years' work experience, interview. Additional exam requirements/recommendations for international students: Required—TOEFL (minimum score 550 paper-based; 78 iBT). *Application deadline:* For fall admission, 7/1 priority date for domestic and international students; for spring admission, 11/12 priority date for domestic students, 11/1 for international students. Applications are processed on a rolling basis. Application fee: $80. Electronic applications accepted. *Expenses:* Contact institution. *Financial support:* In 2017–18, 106 students received support. Career-related internships or fieldwork, health care benefits, and tuition remission for Saint Leo employees and their dependents available. Financial award application deadline: 3/1; financial award applicants required to submit FAFSA. *Faculty research:* Servant leadership, work/life balance, emotional intelligence, pricing, marketing. *Unit head:* Dr. Charles Hale, Dean, School of Business, 352-588-8599, Fax: 352-588-8912, E-mail: mbaslu@saintleo.edu. *Application contact:* Mark Russum, Assistant Vice President, Enrollment, 800-707-8846, Fax: 352-588-7873, E-mail: grad.admissions@saintleo.edu.
Website: https://www.saintleo.edu/school-of-business

Saint Peter's University, Graduate Business Programs, MBA Program, Jersey City, NJ 07306-5997. Offers finance (MBA); health care administration (MBA); human resource management (MBA); international business (MBA); management (MBA); management information systems (MBA); marketing (MBA); risk management (MBA); MBA/MS. *Program availability:* Part-time, evening/weekend. *Entrance requirements:* Additional exam requirements/recommendations for international students: Required—TOEFL. Electronic applications accepted. *Faculty research:* Finance, health care management, human resource management, international business, management, management information systems, marketing, risk management.

St. Thomas Aquinas College, Division of Business Administration, Sparkill, NY 10976. Offers business administration (MBA); finance (MBA); management (MBA); marketing (MBA). *Program availability:* Part-time, evening/weekend. *Entrance requirements:* For master's, GMAT. Additional exam requirements/recommendations for international students: Required—TOEFL. Electronic applications accepted.

Saint Xavier University, Graduate Studies, Graham School of Management, Chicago, IL 60655-3105. Offers employee health benefits (Certificate); finance (MBA); financial fraud examination and management (MBA, Certificate); financial planning (MBA, Certificate); generalist/individualized (MBA); health administration (MBA); managed care (Certificate); management (MBA); marketing (MBA); project management (MBA, Certificate); MBA/MS. *Accreditation:* AACSB. *Program availability:* Part-time, evening/weekend. *Entrance requirements:* For master's, GMAT, minimum GPA of 3.0, 2 years of work experience. Electronic applications accepted. *Expenses:* Contact institution.

Samford University, Brock School of Business, Birmingham, AL 35229. Offers accountancy (M Acc); entrepreneurship (MBA); finance (MBA); marketing (MBA); JD/M Acc; JD/MBA; MBA/M Acc; MBA/M Div; MBA/MSEM; MBA/Pharm D. Programs offered jointly with Cumberland School of Law, Beeson School of Divinity, Howard College of Arts and Sciences, and McWhorter School of Pharmacy. *Accreditation:* AACSB. *Program availability:* Part-time, 100% online, blended/hybrid learning. *Faculty:* 8 full-time (1 woman), 5 part-time/adjunct (0 women). *Students:* 79 full-time (31 women), 18 part-time (8 women); includes 7 minority (2 Black or African American, non-Hispanic/Latino; 1 Asian, non-Hispanic/Latino; 3 Hispanic/Latino; 1 Two or more races, non-Hispanic/Latino), 8 international. Average age 28. 46 applicants, 78% accepted, 16 enrolled. In 2017, 78 master's awarded. *Degree requirements:* For master's, capstone course. *Entrance requirements:* For master's, GMAT or GRE, resume, transcripts; essay (international applicants only). Additional exam requirements/recommendations for international students: Required—TOEFL (minimum score 90 iBT), IELTS (minimum score 6.5). *Application deadline:* For fall admission, 8/1 for domestic and international students; for spring admission, 12/1 for domestic and international students; for summer admission, 5/1 for domestic and international students. Applications are processed on a rolling basis. Application fee: $35. Electronic applications accepted. Application fee is waived when completed online. *Expenses:* $813 per credit hour tuition; $425 per semester fees. *Financial support:* In 2017–18, 59 students received support. Scholarships/grants available. Financial award application deadline: 2/15; financial award applicants required to submit FAFSA. *Unit head:* Dr. Barbara Cartledge, Assistant Dean, 205-726-2935, Fax: 205-726-2540, E-mail: bhcartle@samford.edu. *Application contact:* Elizabeth Anne Gambrell, Associate Director, 205-726-2040, Fax: 205-726-2540, E-mail: eagambre@samford.edu.
Website: http://www.samford.edu/business

San Diego State University, Graduate and Research Affairs, College of Business Administration, Department of Marketing, San Diego, CA 92182. Offers MS. *Program availability:* Part-time, evening/weekend. *Degree requirements:* For master's, thesis or alternative. *Entrance requirements:* For master's, GMAT, resume, letters of reference. Additional exam requirements/recommendations for international students: Required—TOEFL. Electronic applications accepted.

San Francisco State University, Division of Graduate Studies, College of Business, Program in Business Administration, San Francisco, CA 94132-1722. Offers decision sciences/operations research (MBA); ethics and compliance (MBA); finance (MBA);

Marketing

global business and innovation (MBA); healthcare administration (MBA); hospitality and tourism management (MBA); information systems (MBA); leadership (MBA); marketing (MBA); nonprofit and social enterprise leadership (MBA); sustainable business (MBA). *Accreditation:* AACSB. *Program availability:* Part-time, evening/weekend. *Degree requirements:* For master's, thesis, essay test. *Entrance requirements:* For master's, GMAT, minimum GPA of 2.7 in last 60 units. Additional exam requirements/recommendations for international students: Required—TOEFL (minimum score 550 paper-based). *Application deadline:* For fall admission, 5/1 priority date for domestic students, 4/1 for international students; for spring admission, 11/1 for domestic students, 10/15 for international students. Applications are processed on a rolling basis. Application fee: $55. *Financial support:* Application deadline: 3/1. *Unit head:* Dr. Sanjit Sengupta, Faculty Director, 415-817-4366, Fax: 415-817-4340, E-mail: sengupta@sfsu.edu. *Application contact:* Christopher Kingston, Director of Student Advising, 415-817-4322, Fax: 415-817-4340, E-mail: cak@sfsu.edu.
Website: http://cob.sfsu.edu/graduate-programs/mba

San Ignacio University, Graduate Programs, Doral, FL 33178. Offers business administration (MBA), including human resources management, international business, marketing management; education (M Ed), including early childhood education, educational leadership, special education; hospitality management (MA), including gastronomy and restaurant management, tourism management.

Seton Hall University, Stillman School of Business, Programs in Business Administration, South Orange, NJ 07079-2697. Offers accounting (MBA); entrepreneurial studies (Certificate); finance (MBA); financial decision making (Certificate); information technology management (MBA); international business (MBA); management (MBA); marketing (MBA); sport management (MBA); supply chain management (MBA, Certificate). *Program availability:* Part-time, evening/weekend. *Faculty:* 29 full-time (4 women), 18 part-time/adjunct (0 women). *Students:* 140 full-time (58 women), 154 part-time (49 women); includes 66 minority (25 Black or African American, non-Hispanic/Latino; 14 Asian, non-Hispanic/Latino; 23 Hispanic/Latino; 4 Two or more races, non-Hispanic/Latino), 88 international. Average age 32. 406 applicants, 75% accepted, 100 enrolled. In 2017, 132 master's awarded. *Degree requirements:* For master's, 20 hours of community service (Social Responsibility Project). *Entrance requirements:* For master's, GMAT or CPA, GRE (waived based on work experience or advanced degree from AACSB institution), MS in business discipline, professional degree or designation (MD, JD, PhD, DVM, DDS, CPA, etc.), minimum undergraduate GPA of 3.0. Additional exam requirements/recommendations for international students: Required—TOEFL (minimum score 607 paper-based; 80 iBT), IELTS (minimum score 6), PTE. *Application deadline:* For fall admission, 5/31 priority date for domestic students, 4/30 priority date for international students; for spring admission, 10/31 priority date for domestic students, 9/30 priority date for international students; for summer admission, 3/31 priority date for domestic students. Applications are processed on a rolling basis. Application fee: $75. Electronic applications accepted. *Expenses:* $1,305 per credit; $126 fees (fall and spring semester), $51 (summer semester). *Financial support:* In 2017–18, 41 students received support, including 25 research assistantships with full tuition reimbursements available (averaging $3,644 per year); career-related internships or fieldwork, scholarships/grants, and unspecified assistantships also available. Financial award application deadline: 6/30; financial award applicants required to submit FAFSA. *Faculty research:* Sport, hedge funds, executive compensation, social media, legal studies. *Unit head:* Dr. Joyce Strawser, Dean, 973-761-9013, Fax: 973-761-9217, E-mail: joyce.strawser@shu.edu. *Application contact:* Alfred Ayoub, Director of Graduate Admissions, 973-761-9262, Fax: 973-761-9208, E-mail: alfred.ayoub@shu.edu.
Website: http://www.shu.edu/business/mba-programs.cfm

Slippery Rock University of Pennsylvania, Graduate Studies (Recruitment), College of Business, School of Business, Slippery Rock, PA 16057-1383. Offers accounting/finance (MBA); general (MBA); marketing/management (MBA). *Program availability:* Part-time, evening/weekend. *Degree requirements:* For master's, comprehensive exam (for some programs), thesis (for some programs). *Entrance requirements:* For master's, minimum cumulative GPA of 3.0, official transcripts, three references. Additional exam requirements/recommendations for international students: Required—TOEFL (minimum score 550 paper-based; 80 iBT). Electronic applications accepted. *Expenses:* Contact institution.

Southeastern Louisiana University, College of Arts, Humanities and Social Sciences, Department of Languages and Communication, Hammond, LA 70402. Offers health communications (MA); journalism (MA); marketing (MA); public relations (MA); sociology (MA). *Program availability:* Part-time, evening/weekend. *Faculty:* 5 full-time (3 women). *Students:* 7 full-time (6 women), 11 part-time (7 women); includes 10 minority (5 Black or African American, non-Hispanic/Latino; 3 Hispanic/Latino; 2 Two or more races, non-Hispanic/Latino). Average age 28. 133 applicants, 51% accepted, 10 enrolled. In 2017, 36 master's awarded. *Degree requirements:* For master's, comprehensive exam. *Entrance requirements:* For master's, GRE (minimum score 148 on Verbal section, 3.5 Written). Additional exam requirements/recommendations for international students: Required—TOEFL (minimum score 525 paper-based; 75 iBT). *Application deadline:* For fall admission, 7/15 priority date for domestic students, 6/1 priority date for international students; for spring admission, 12/1 priority date for domestic students, 10/1 priority date for international students. Applications are processed on a rolling basis. Application fee: $20 ($30 for international students). Electronic applications accepted. *Expenses:* Tuition, state resident: full-time $6684. Tuition, nonresident: full-time $19,162. *Required fees:* $2088. *Financial support:* In 2017–18, 12 students received support, including 7 research assistantships (averaging $6,082 per year); career-related internships or fieldwork, Federal Work-Study, institutionally sponsored loans, scholarships/grants, traineeships, health care benefits, tuition waivers, and unspecified assistantships also available. Financial award application deadline: 5/1; financial award applicants required to submit FAFSA. *Faculty research:* Communicate with the millennial generation to enhance organizational effectiveness, conflict resolution and mediation among nations, journalism history, media law, media writing, media convergence, external compliances accreditation and strategic planning. *Unit head:* Dr. Lucia Harrison, Department Head, 985-549-2105, Fax: 985-549-5014, E-mail: lharrison@southeastern.edu. *Application contact:* Amanda Harper, Graduate Admissions Analyst, 985-549-5620, Fax: 985-549-5632, E-mail: admissions@southeastern.edu.
Website: http://www.southeastern.edu/acad_research/depts/lang_comm/index.html

Southern Adventist University, School of Business, Collegedale, TN 37315-0370. Offers accounting (MBA); finance (MBA); healthcare administration (MBA); management (MBA); marketing management (MBA). *Program availability:* Part-time, evening/weekend, 100% online. *Entrance requirements:* For master's, GMAT, minimum cumulative undergraduate GPA of 3.0. Additional exam requirements/recommendations for international students: Required—TOEFL (minimum score 600 paper-based; 100 iBT). *Application deadline:* For fall admission, 7/1 for domestic students, 5/1 for international students; for winter admission, 11/1 for domestic students, 9/1 for international students; for summer admission, 4/1 for domestic students, 2/1 for international students. Applications are processed on a rolling basis. Application fee: $40. Electronic applications accepted. *Expenses: Tuition:* Full-time $11,430; part-time $635 per credit hour. Tuition and fees vary according to degree level and program.

Financial support: Scholarships/grants and unspecified assistantships available. Financial award application deadline: 9/1; financial award applicants required to submit FAFSA. *Unit head:* Dr. Stephanie Sheehan, Dean, 423-236-2659, Fax: 423-236-1527, E-mail: ssheehan@southern.edu. *Application contact:* Teshia Price, Graduate Studies Coordinator, 423-236-2751, Fax: 423-236-1527, E-mail: tprice@southern.edu.
Website: https://www.southern.edu/academics/business.html

Southern Methodist University, Cox School of Business, MBA Program, Dallas, TX 75275. Offers accounting (MBA, PMBA); business administration (EMBA); finance (MBA); financial statement analysis (PMBA); general business (MBA); information technology and operations management (MBA); management (MBA); marketing (MBA); real estate (MBA); strategy (MBA); strategy and entrepreneurship (MBA); JD/MBA; MA/MBA. *Program availability:* Part-time, evening/weekend. *Entrance requirements:* For master's, GMAT. Additional exam requirements/recommendations for international students: Required—TOEFL. Electronic applications accepted. *Expenses:* Contact institution. *Faculty research:* Corporate finance, financial reporting, modeling consumer decision-making, competition between national brands and store brands, institutional determinants of firms' strategy.

Southern New Hampshire University, School of Business, Manchester, NH 03106-1045. Offers accounting (MBA, Graduate Certificate); accounting finance (MS); accounting/auditing (MS); accounting/forensic accounting (MS); accounting/management accounting (MS); accounting/taxation (MS); applied economics (MS); athletic administration (MBA, Graduate Certificate); business administration (IMBA, Certificate), including business information systems (Certificate), human resource management (Certificate); business analytics (MBA); business intelligence (MBA); communication (MA), including new media and marketing, public relations; community economic development (MBA); criminal justice (MBA); data analytics (MS); economics (MBA); engineering management (MBA); entrepreneurship (MBA); finance (MBA, MS, Graduate Certificate); finance/corporate finance (MS); finance/investments (MS); forensic accounting (MBA); forensic accounting and fraud examination (Graduate Certificate); healthcare informatics (MBA); healthcare management (MBA); human resource management (MS); human resources (MBA); information technology (MS); information technology management (MBA); international business (PhD); Internet marketing (MBA); leadership (MBA); leadership of nonprofit organizations (Graduate Certificate); management (MS); marketing (MBA, MS, Graduate Certificate); music business (MBA); operations and project management (MS); operations and supply chain management (MBA, Graduate Certificate); organizational leadership (MS); project management (MBA, Graduate Certificate); public administration (MBA, Graduate Certificate); quantitative analysis (MBA); Six Sigma (Graduate Certificate); Six Sigma quality (MBA); social media marketing (MBA, Graduate Certificate); sport management (MBA, MS, Graduate Certificate); sustainability and environmental compliance (MBA); MBA/Certificate. *Accreditation:* ACBSP. *Program availability:* Part-time, evening/weekend, online learning. Terminal master's awarded for partial completion of doctoral program. *Degree requirements:* For master's, one foreign language, comprehensive exam (for some programs), thesis or alternative; for doctorate, one foreign language, comprehensive exam, thesis/dissertation. *Entrance requirements:* For master's, minimum GPA of 2.5; for doctorate, GMAT. Additional exam requirements/recommendations for international students: Required—TOEFL (minimum score 500 paper-based). *Application deadline:* Applications are processed on a rolling basis. Application fee: $40. Electronic applications accepted. *Expenses: Tuition:* Part-time $627 per credit hour. Part-time tuition and fees vary according to campus/location and program. *Financial support:* Career-related internships or fieldwork, Federal Work-Study, institutionally sponsored loans, scholarships/grants, tuition waivers (partial), and unspecified assistantships available. Support available to part-time students. Financial award applicants required to submit FAFSA. *Unit head:* Dr. Bill Lightfoot, Dean, 603-644-3102, Fax: 603-644-3144. *Application contact:* Office of Graduate Admission, 888-327-SNHU, Fax: 603-644-3144, E-mail: enroll@snhu.edu.

Southwest Minnesota State University, Department of Business and Public Affairs, Marshall, MN 56258. Offers leadership (MBA); management (MBA); marketing (MBA). *Program availability:* Part-time, evening/weekend, online learning. *Degree requirements:* For master's, thesis. *Entrance requirements:* For master's, GMAT (minimum score: 450). Additional exam requirements/recommendations for international students: Recommended—TOEFL (minimum score 550 paper-based; 79 iBT), IELTS. Electronic applications accepted.

State University of New York Polytechnic Institute, MBA Program in Technology Management, Utica, NY 13502. Offers accounting and finance (MBA); business management (MBA); health informatics (MBA); human resource management (MBA); marketing management (MBA). *Program availability:* Part-time, online only, 100% online. *Faculty:* 8 full-time (2 women), 2 part-time/adjunct (1 woman). *Students:* 29 full-time (13 women), 85 part-time (41 women); includes 18 minority (4 Black or African American, non-Hispanic/Latino; 8 Asian, non-Hispanic/Latino; 6 Hispanic/Latino). Average age 32. 83 applicants, 55% accepted, 37 enrolled. In 2017, 41 master's awarded. *Degree requirements:* For master's, comprehensive exam, capstone project. *Entrance requirements:* For master's, GMAT, resume, letter of reference. Additional exam requirements/recommendations for international students: Required—TOEFL (minimum score 550 paper-based; 79 iBT), IELTS (minimum score 6.5). *Application deadline:* For fall admission, 7/1 priority date for domestic students, 7/1 for international students; for spring admission, 12/1 for domestic students, 11/1 for international students. Applications are processed on a rolling basis. Application fee: $60. Electronic applications accepted. *Expenses:* Contact institution. *Financial support:* Fellowships, research assistantships, and unspecified assistantships available. Financial award application deadline: 6/1; financial award applicants required to submit FAFSA. *Faculty research:* Economic development and design thinking, transfer of training, trade intensity and liquidity, enforcement and punishment, acculturation attitudes and consumption behavior. Total annual research expenditures: $20,000. *Unit head:* Dr. Rafael Romero, Program Coordinator, 315-792-7207, E-mail: rafael.romero@sunyit.edu. *Application contact:* Alicia Foster, Director of Graduate Admissions, E-mail: alicia.foster@sunyit.edu.
Website: https://sunypoly.edu/academics/majors-and-programs/technology-management.html

Stephen F. Austin State University, Graduate School, College of Business, Program in Business Administration, Nacogdoches, TX 75962. Offers business (MBA); management and marketing (MBA). *Accreditation:* AACSB. *Program availability:* Part-time, evening/weekend. *Degree requirements:* For master's, comprehensive exam. *Entrance requirements:* For master's, GMAT, minimum AACSB index of 1000. Additional exam requirements/recommendations for international students: Required—TOEFL (minimum score 550 paper-based). *Faculty research:* Strategic implications, information search, multinational firms, philosophical guidance.

Stevens Institute of Technology, Graduate School, School of Business, Program in Business Administration, Hoboken, NJ 07030. Offers business intelligence and analytics (MBA); engineering management (MBA); finance (MBA); information systems (MBA); innovation and entrepreneurship (MBA); marketing (MBA); pharmaceutical management (MBA); project management (MBA, Certificate); technology management (MBA); telecommunications management (MBA). *Accreditation:* AACSB. *Program availability:*

Part-time, evening/weekend. *Students:* 46 full-time (19 women), 179 part-time (88 women); includes 46 minority (10 Black or African American, non-Hispanic/Latino; 2 American Indian or Alaska Native, non-Hispanic/Latino; 30 Asian, non-Hispanic/Latino; 4 Hispanic/Latino), 45 international. Average age 36. 218 applicants, 49% accepted, 53 enrolled. In 2017, 33 master's awarded. *Degree requirements:* For master's, thesis optional, minimum B average in major field and overall; for Certificate, minimum B average. *Entrance requirements:* Additional exam requirements/recommendations for international students: Required—TOEFL (minimum score 74 iBT), IELTS (minimum score 6). *Application deadline:* For fall admission, 7/1 for domestic students, 4/15 for international students; for spring admission, 12/1 for domestic and international students. Applications are processed on a rolling basis. Application fee: $60. Electronic applications accepted. *Expenses: Tuition:* Full-time $34,494; part-time $1554 per credit. *Required fees:* $291 per semester. *Financial support:* Fellowships, research assistantships, teaching assistantships, career-related internships or fieldwork, Federal Work-Study, scholarships/grants, and unspecified assistantships available. Financial award application deadline: 2/15; financial award applicants required to submit FAFSA. *Unit head:* Dr. Gregory Prastacos, Dean, 201-216-8366, E-mail: gprastac@stevens.edu. *Application contact:* Graduate Admissions, 888-783-8367, Fax: 888-511-1306, E-mail: graduate@stevens.edu.
Website: https://www.stevens.edu/school-business/masters-programs/mbaemba

Stony Brook University, State University of New York, Graduate School, College of Business, Program in Business Administration, Stony Brook, NY 11794. Offers accounting (MBA); business administration (MBA); finance (MBA, Certificate); health care management (MBA); human resources (MBA); innovation (MBA); management (MBA); marketing (MBA); operations management (MBA). *Faculty:* 39 full-time (13 women), 14 part-time/adjunct (5 women). *Students:* 181 full-time (98 women), 145 part-time (73 women); includes 68 minority (16 Black or African American, non-Hispanic/Latino; 1 American Indian or Alaska Native, non-Hispanic/Latino; 35 Asian, non-Hispanic/Latino; 11 Hispanic/Latino; 1 Native Hawaiian or other Pacific Islander, non-Hispanic/Latino; 4 Two or more races, non-Hispanic/Latino), 69 international. Average age 29. 154 applicants, 66% accepted, 58 enrolled. In 2017, 105 master's awarded. *Entrance requirements:* For master's, GMAT, 3 letters of recommendation from current or former employers or professors, transcripts, personal statement, resume. Additional exam requirements/recommendations for international students: Required—TOEFL (minimum score 550 paper-based; 90 iBT), IELTS (minimum score 6.5). *Application deadline:* For fall admission, 5/15 for domestic students, 3/15 for international students; for spring admission, 11/15 for domestic students, 10/15 for international students. Application fee: $100. *Expenses:* Contact institution. *Financial support:* Teaching assistantships available. *Total annual research expenditures:* $2,070. *Unit head:* Dr. Manuel London, Dean, 631-632-7159, E-mail: manuel.london@stonybrook.edu. *Application contact:* Dr. Dmytro Holod, Associate Dean for Academic Programs/Graduate Director, 631-632-7183, Fax: 631-632-8181, E-mail: dmytro.holod@stonybrook.edu.
Website: https://www.stonybrook.edu/commcms/business/

Strayer University, Graduate Studies, Washington, DC 20005-2603. Offers accounting (MS); acquisition (MBA); business administration (MBA); communications technology (MS); educational management (M Ed); finance (MBA); health services administration (MHSA); hospitality and tourism management (MBA); human resource management (MBA); information systems (MS), including computer security management, decision support system management, enterprise resource management, network management, software engineering management, systems development management; management (MBA); management information systems (MS); marketing (MBA); professional accounting (MS), including accounting information systems, controllership, taxation; public administration (MPA); supply chain management (MBA); technology in education (M Ed). Programs also offered at campus locations in Birmingham, AL; Chamblee, GA; Cobb County, GA; Morrow, GA; White Marsh, MD; Charleston, SC; Columbia, SC; Greensboro, NC; Greenville, SC; Lexington, KY; Louisville, KY; Nashville, TN; North Raleigh, NC; Washington, DC. *Accreditation:* ACBSP. *Program availability:* Part-time, evening/weekend, online learning. *Degree requirements:* For master's, thesis. *Entrance requirements:* For master's, GMAT, GRE General Test, bachelor's degree from an accredited college or university, minimum undergraduate GPA of 2.75. Electronic applications accepted.

Suffolk University, College of Arts and Sciences, Advertising and Public Relations Department, Boston, MA 02108-2770. Offers communication studies (MAC); integrated marketing communication (MAC); public relations and advertising (MAC). *Program availability:* Part-time, evening/weekend. *Faculty:* 4 full-time (3 women). *Students:* 25 full-time (18 women), 14 part-time (13 women); includes 10 minority (4 Black or African American, non-Hispanic/Latino; 5 Hispanic/Latino; 1 Two or more races, non-Hispanic/Latino), 9 international. Average age 26. 41 applicants, 71% accepted, 2 enrolled. In 2017, 10 master's awarded. *Degree requirements:* For master's, thesis optional. *Entrance requirements:* For master's, GRE General Test, MAT, or GMAT, 2 letters of recommendation, resume. Additional exam requirements/recommendations for international students: Required—TOEFL (minimum score 550 paper-based; 80 iBT). *Application deadline:* For fall admission, 3/15 priority date for domestic and international students; for spring admission, 10/15 priority date for domestic and international students. Applications are processed on a rolling basis. Application fee: $50. Electronic applications accepted. *Expenses:* $29,520 per year full-time tuition; $1,230 per credit part-time. *Financial support:* In 2017-18, 31 students received support, including 4 fellowships (averaging $6,200 per year); career-related internships or fieldwork, Federal Work-Study, institutionally sponsored loans, and scholarships/grants also available. Support available to part-time students. Financial award application deadline: 4/1; financial award applicants required to submit FAFSA. *Faculty research:* Branding law and management, health care communication, gender roles and violence in video games, new media, political communication. *Unit head:* Robert Rosenthal, Chair, 617-573-8502, E-mail: rrosenthal@suffolk.edu. *Application contact:* Mara Marzocchi, Associate Director of Graduate Admissions, 617-573-8302, Fax: 617-305-1733, E-mail: grad.admission@suffolk.edu.
Website: http://www.suffolk.edu/college/graduate/69298.php

Suffolk University, Sawyer Business School, Master of Business Administration Program, Boston, MA 02108-2770. Offers accounting (MBA); entrepreneurship (MBA); executive business administration (EMBA); finance (MBA); global business administration (GMBA); health administration (MBA); international business (MBA); marketing (MBA); nonprofit management (MBA); organizational behavior (MBA); strategic management (MBA); supply chain management (MBA); taxation (MBA); JD/MBA; MBA/MHA; MBA/MSA; MBA/MSF; MBA/MST. *Accreditation:* AACSB. *Program availability:* Part-time, evening/weekend, 100% online. *Faculty:* 16 full-time (6 women), 9 part-time/adjunct (1 woman). *Students:* 106 full-time (57 women), 236 part-time (135 women); includes 80 minority (23 Black or African American, non-Hispanic/Latino; 23 Asian, non-Hispanic/Latino; 28 Hispanic/Latino; 6 Two or more races, non-Hispanic/Latino), 41 international. Average age 30. 354 applicants, 69% accepted, 115 enrolled. In 2017, 170 master's awarded. *Entrance requirements:* For master's, GMAT, minimum undergraduate GPA of 2.75 (MBA), 5 years of managerial experience (EMBA). Additional exam requirements/recommendations for international students: Required—TOEFL (minimum score 550 paper-based; 80 iBT). *Application deadline:* For fall

admission, 3/15 priority date for domestic students, 10/15 priority date for international students; for spring admission, 10/15 priority date for domestic and international students. Applications are processed on a rolling basis. Application fee: $50. Electronic applications accepted. *Expenses:* $43,980 per year full-time, $1,466 per credit part-time (for MBA); $1,794 per credit part-time (for Executive MBA). *Financial support:* In 2017-18, 198 students received support, including 1 fellowship (averaging $2,325 per year); career-related internships or fieldwork, Federal Work-Study, institutionally sponsored loans, and scholarships/grants also available. Support available to part-time students. Financial award application deadline: 4/1; financial award applicants required to submit FAFSA. *Faculty research:* Foreign investments; career strategies and boundaryless careers; corporate ethics codes; interest rates, inflation, and growth options; innovation and product development performance. *Unit head:* Jodi Detjen, Director of MBA Programs, 617-573-8306, E-mail: jdetjen@suffolk.edu. *Application contact:* Mara Marzocchi, Associate Director of Graduate Admissions, 617-573-8302, Fax: 617-305-1733, E-mail: grad.admission@suffolk.edu.
Website: http://www.suffolk.edu/mba

Syracuse University, Martin J. Whitman School of Management, Master of Business Administration Program, Syracuse, NY 13244. Offers accounting (MBA); business analytics (MBA); entrepreneurship (MBA); marketing management (MBA); real estate (MBA); supply chain management (MBA); JD/MBA. *Program availability:* Part-time, 100% online. *Students:* 22 full-time (9 women), 495 part-time (147 women); includes 182 minority (81 Black or African American, non-Hispanic/Latino; 3 American Indian or Alaska Native, non-Hispanic/Latino; 42 Asian, non-Hispanic/Latino; 52 Hispanic/Latino; 4 Native Hawaiian or other Pacific Islander, non-Hispanic/Latino). Average age 32. 1,086 applicants, 73% accepted, 516 enrolled. In 2017, 84 master's awarded. *Entrance requirements:* For master's, GMAT or GRE, resume, essay, 5-minute video interview, two letters of recommendation, transcripts (unofficial). Additional exam requirements/recommendations for international students: Required—TOEFL (minimum score 100 iBT), IELTS (minimum score 7), PTE (minimum score 68). *Application deadline:* For fall admission, 11/30 for domestic students, 11/30 priority date for international students; for winter admission, 1/1 for domestic students, 1/1 priority date for international students; for spring admission, 2/15 for domestic and international students; for summer admission, 4/19 for domestic students. Application fee: $75. Electronic applications accepted. *Expenses:* Contact institution. *Financial support:* In 2017-18, 22 students received support. Merit scholarships available. Financial award application deadline: 2/15. *Faculty research:* Data analysis, economics of international business, financial markets and institutions, operations management, supply chain management. *Unit head:* Dr. Alexander McKelvie, Associate Dean for Undergraduate and Full-time Master's Education, 315-443-7252, E-mail: mckelvie@syr.edu. *Application contact:* Shri Ramakrishnan, Assistant Director, Graduate Recruitment, 315-443-3497, Fax: 315-443-9517, E-mail: busgrad@syr.edu.
Website: http://whitman.syr.edu/ftmba/

Tarleton State University, College of Graduate Studies, College of Business Administration, Department of Marketing and Computer Information Systems, Stephenville, TX 76402. Offers information systems (MS). *Program availability:* Part-time, evening/weekend, online, blended/hybrid learning. *Faculty:* 7 full-time (1 woman). *Students:* 5 full-time (2 women), 44 part-time (12 women); includes 18 minority (6 Black or African American, non-Hispanic/Latino; 6 Asian, non-Hispanic/Latino; 6 Hispanic/Latino), 1 international. Average age 32. 58 applicants, 88% accepted, 18 enrolled. In 2017, 1 master's awarded. *Degree requirements:* For master's, comprehensive exam, thesis (for some programs). *Entrance requirements:* For master's, GRE, minimum GPA of 3.0. Additional exam requirements/recommendations for international students: Required—TOEFL (minimum score 550 paper-based; 80 iBT), IELTS (minimum score 6). *Application deadline:* For fall admission, 8/15 priority date for domestic students; for spring admission, 1/7 for domestic students. Applications are processed on a rolling basis. Application fee: $45 ($145 for international students). Electronic applications accepted. *Expenses:* Contact institution. *Financial support:* Research assistantships and teaching assistantships available. Financial award application deadline: 5/1; financial award applicants required to submit FAFSA. *Unit head:* Dr. Joseph Schuessler, Department Head, 254-968-9893, E-mail: schuessler@tarleton.edu. *Application contact:* Information Contact, 254-968-9104, Fax: 254-968-9670, E-mail: gradoffice@tarleton.edu.
Website: http://www.tarleton.edu/cis/

Temple University, Fox School of Business, Doctoral Programs in Business, Philadelphia, PA 19122-6096. Offers accounting (PhD); entrepreneurship (PhD); finance (PhD); international business (PhD); management information systems (PhD); marketing (PhD); risk management and insurance (PhD); statistics (PhD); strategic management (PhD); tourism and sport (PhD). *Accreditation:* AACSB. *Degree requirements:* For doctorate, thesis/dissertation. *Entrance requirements:* For doctorate, GRE General Test, GMAT, minimum GPA of 3.0, master's degree. Additional exam requirements/recommendations for international students: Required—TOEFL (minimum score 600 paper-based; 100 iBT), IELTS (minimum score 7.5). Electronic applications accepted. *Expenses:* Tuition, state resident: full-time $16,164; part-time $898 per credit hour. Tuition, nonresident: full-time $22,158; part-time $1231 per credit hour. *Required fees:* $890; $445 per semester. Full-time tuition and fees vary according to course load, degree level, campus/location and program.

Temple University, Fox School of Business, MBA Programs, Philadelphia, PA 19122-6096. Offers accounting (MBA); business management (MBA); financial management (MBA); healthcare and life sciences innovation (MBA); human resource management (MBA); international business (IMBA); IT management (MBA); marketing management (MBA); pharmaceutical management (MBA); strategic management (EMBA, MBA). EMBA offered in Philadelphia, PA and Tokyo, Japan. *Accreditation:* AACSB. *Program availability:* Part-time, evening/weekend, online learning. *Entrance requirements:* For master's, GMAT, minimum undergraduate GPA of 3.0. Additional exam requirements/recommendations for international students: Required—TOEFL (minimum score 600 paper-based; 100 iBT), IELTS (minimum score 7.5). *Expenses:* Tuition, state resident: full-time $16,164; part-time $898 per credit hour. Tuition, nonresident: full-time $22,158; part-time $1231 per credit hour. *Required fees:* $890; $445 per semester. Full-time tuition and fees vary according to course load, degree level, campus/location and program.

Temple University, Fox School of Business, Specialized Master's Programs, Philadelphia, PA 19122-6096. Offers accountancy (MS); actuarial science (MS); finance (MS); financial engineering (MS); human resource management (MS); innovation management and entrepreneurship (MS); marketing (MS); statistics (MS). MS in innovation management and entrepreneurship delivered jointly with College of Engineering. *Accreditation:* AACSB. *Program availability:* Part-time. *Entrance requirements:* For master's, GRE General Test or GMAT, minimum undergraduate GPA of 3.0. Additional exam requirements/recommendations for international students: Required—TOEFL (minimum score 600 paper-based; 100 iBT), IELTS (minimum score 7.5). *Expenses:* Tuition, state resident: full-time $16,164; part-time $898 per credit hour. Tuition, nonresident: full-time $22,158; part-time $1231 per credit hour. *Required fees:* $890; $445 per semester. Full-time tuition and fees vary according to course load, degree level, campus/location and program.

Marketing

Texas A&M University, Mays Business School, Department of Marketing, College Station, TX 77843. Offers MS. *Faculty:* 10. *Students:* 74 full-time (54 women), 2 part-time (1 woman); includes 7 minority (1 Black or African American, non-Hispanic/Latino; 5 Hispanic/Latino; 1 Two or more races, non-Hispanic/Latino), 20 international. Average age 25. 152 applicants, 18% accepted, 19 enrolled. In 2017, 47 master's awarded. Terminal master's awarded for partial completion of doctoral program. *Degree requirements:* For master's, comprehensive exam. *Entrance requirements:* For master's, GMAT or GRE. Additional exam requirements/recommendations for international students: Required—TOEFL (minimum score 550 paper-based; 80 iBT), IELTS (minimum score 6), PTE (minimum score 53). *Application deadline:* Applications are processed on a rolling basis. Application fee: $50 ($90 for international students). Electronic applications accepted. *Expenses:* Contact institution. *Financial support:* In 2017–18, 60 students received support, including 1 fellowship with tuition reimbursement available (averaging $19,568 per year), 13 research assistantships with tuition reimbursements available (averaging $12,241 per year), 33 teaching assistantships with tuition reimbursements available (averaging $4,331 per year); career-related internships or fieldwork, institutionally sponsored loans, scholarships/grants, traineeships, health care benefits, tuition waivers (full and partial), and unspecified assistantships also available. Support available to part-time students. Financial award application deadline: 3/15; financial award applicants required to submit FAFSA. *Faculty research:* Consumer behavior, innovation and product management, international marketing, marketing management and strategy, services marketing. *Unit head:* Dr. Mark B. Houston, Head, 979-845-7257, E-mail: mhouston@mays.tamu.edu. *Application contact:* Stephen W. McDaniel, Master's Advisor, 979-845-5801, E-mail: smcdaniel@mays.tamu.edu.
Website: http://mays.tamu.edu/mktg/

Texas A&M University–Commerce, College of Business, Commerce, TX 75429. Offers accounting (MSA); business administration (MBA); business analytics (MS); finance (MSF); management (MS); marketing (MS). *Accreditation:* AACSB. *Program availability:* Part-time, evening/weekend, 100% online, blended/hybrid learning. *Faculty:* 50 full-time (19 women), 7 part-time/adjunct (0 women). *Students:* 479 full-time (248 women), 1,056 part-time (556 women); includes 660 minority (281 Black or African American, non-Hispanic/Latino; 4 American Indian or Alaska Native, non-Hispanic/Latino; 120 Asian, non-Hispanic/Latino; 222 Hispanic/Latino; 33 Two or more races, non-Hispanic/Latino), 224 international. Average age 33. 930 applicants, 61% accepted, 363 enrolled. In 2017, 686 master's awarded. *Degree requirements:* For master's, comprehensive exam. *Entrance requirements:* For master's, GRE General Test, GMAT, letter of recommendation. Additional exam requirements/recommendations for international students: Required—TOEFL (minimum score 550 paper-based; 79 iBT), IELTS (minimum score 6). *Application deadline:* For fall admission, 6/1 priority date for international students; for spring admission, 10/15 priority date for international students; for summer admission, 3/15 priority date for international students. Applications are processed on a rolling basis. Application fee: $50 ($75 for international students). Electronic applications accepted. *Expenses:* Contact institution. *Financial support:* In 2017–18, 46 students received support, including 20 research assistantships with partial tuition reimbursements available (averaging $8,000 per year); Federal Work-Study, institutionally sponsored loans, scholarships/grants, health care benefits, and unspecified assistantships also available. Financial award application deadline: 5/1; financial award applicants required to submit FAFSA. *Faculty research:* Applied economics with emphasis on industries that are important to the region including health, energy and agriculture; finance research on banking, investments, financial institutions and risk management; marketing and big data decisions of product choice behavior and channel behavior of consumers; strategic management and organizational behavior phenomena; international accounting in governmental sectors. *Total annual research expenditures:* $1,920. *Unit head:* Dr. Shanan Gwaltney Gibson, Dean of College of Business, 903-886-5191, Fax: 903-886-5650, E-mail: shanan.gibson@tamuc.edu. *Application contact:* Vicky Turner, Doctoral Degree and Special Programs Coordinator, 903-886-5167, E-mail: vicky.turner@tamuc.edu.
Website: http://www.tamuc.edu/academics/graduateSchool/programs/businessEntrepreneurship/default.aspx

Texas Tech University, Rawls College of Business Administration, Lubbock, TX 79409-2101. Offers accounting (MSA, PhD), including audit/financial reporting (MSA), taxation (MSA); data science (MS); finance (PhD); general business (MBA); healthcare management (MS); information systems and operations management (PhD); management (PhD); marketing (PhD); STEM (MBA); JD/MBA; JD/MSA; MBA/M Arch; MBA/MD; MBA/MS; MBA/Pharm D. *Accreditation:* AACSB. *Program availability:* Evening/weekend, 100% online, blended/hybrid learning. *Faculty:* 89 full-time (22 women). *Students:* 660 full-time (252 women); includes 174 minority (30 Black or African American, non-Hispanic/Latino; 3 American Indian or Alaska Native, non-Hispanic/Latino; 20 Asian, non-Hispanic/Latino; 104 Hispanic/Latino; 17 Two or more races, non-Hispanic/Latino), 99 international. Average age 29. 492 applicants, 51% accepted, 148 enrolled. In 2017, 439 master's, 6 doctorates awarded. *Degree requirements:* For master's, thesis (for MS); capstone course; for doctorate, comprehensive exam, thesis/dissertation, qualifying exams. *Entrance requirements:* For master's, GMAT, GRE, MCAT, PCAT, LSAT, or DAT, holistic review of academic credentials, resume, essay, letters of recommendation; for doctorate, GMAT, GRE, holistic review of academic credentials, resume, statement of purpose, letters of recommendation. Additional exam requirements/recommendations for international students: Required—TOEFL (minimum score 550 paper-based; 79 iBT), IELTS (minimum score 6.5), PTE (minimum score 60). *Application deadline:* For fall admission, 7/1 priority date for domestic students, 1/15 for international students; for spring admission, 12/1 priority date for domestic students, 6/15 for international students; for summer admission, 5/1 for domestic students. Applications are processed on a rolling basis. Application fee: $60. Electronic applications accepted. *Expenses:* $5,167.50 full-time; $9,000 per semester (for hybrid MBA). *Financial support:* In 2017–18, 81 students received support, including 1 research assistantship with full tuition reimbursement available (averaging $22,725 per year), 63 teaching assistantships with full tuition reimbursements available (averaging $22,725 per year); career-related internships or fieldwork, Federal Work-Study, scholarships/grants, health care benefits, and unspecified assistantships also available. Financial award application deadline: 3/1; financial award applicants required to submit FAFSA. *Faculty research:* Governmental and nonprofit accounting, securities and options futures, statistical analysis and design, leadership, consumer behavior. *Total annual research expenditures:* $230,000. *Unit head:* Dr. Margaret Williams, Dean, 806-834-2839, Fax: 806-742-1092, E-mail: margaret.l.williams@ttu.edu. *Application contact:* Jennifer Yack, Admissions Manager, Graduate and Professional Programs, 806-742-3184, E-mail: rawlsgrad@ttu.edu.
Website: http://www.depts.ttu.edu/rawlsbusiness/graduate/

Thomas Jefferson University, Kanbar College of Design, Engineering and Commerce, Innovation MBA Program, Philadelphia, PA 19107. Offers business analytics (MBA); general business (MBA); management (MBA); marketing (MBA); strategy and design thinking (MBA); MBA/MS. *Program availability:* Part-time, evening/weekend, online learning. *Entrance requirements:* For master's, GMAT. Additional exam requirements/recommendations for international students: Required—TOEFL (minimum score 550 paper-based; 79 iBT).

Tiffin University, Program in Business Administration, Tiffin, OH 44883-2161. Offers finance (MBA); general management (MBA); healthcare administration (MBA); human resource management (MBA); international business (MBA); leadership (MBA); marketing (MBA); non-profit management (MBA); sports management (MBA). *Accreditation:* ACBSP. *Program availability:* Part-time, evening/weekend, online learning. *Entrance requirements:* For master's, minimum undergraduate GPA of 2.5, work experience. Additional exam requirements/recommendations for international students: Required—TOEFL (minimum score 550 paper-based; 79 iBT), IELTS. Electronic applications accepted. Application fee is waived when completed online. *Faculty research:* Small business, executive development operations, research and statistical analysis, market research, management information systems.

Trident University International, College of Business Administration, Program in Business Administration, Cypress, CA 90630. Offers business administration (PhD); conflict and negotiation management (MBA); criminal justice administration (MBA); entrepreneurship (MBA); finance (MBA); general management (MBA); government accounting (MBA); human resource management (MBA); information security and digital assurance management (MBA); information technology management (MBA); international business (MBA); logistics management (MBA); marketing (MBA); project management (MBA); public management (MBA); quality management (MBA); strategic leadership (MBA). *Program availability:* Part-time, evening/weekend, online learning. *Degree requirements:* For doctorate, comprehensive exam, thesis/dissertation, defense of dissertation. *Entrance requirements:* For master's, minimum GPA of 2.5 (students with GPA 3.0 or greater may transfer up to 30% of graduate level credits); for doctorate, minimum GPA of 3.4, curriculum vitae, course work in research methods or statistics. Additional exam requirements/recommendations for international students: Required—TOEFL. Electronic applications accepted.

United States International University–Africa, School of Business Administration, Nairobi, Kenya. Offers business administration (GEMBA); entrepreneurship (MBA); finance (MBA); human resource management (MBA); information technology management (MBA); integrated studies (MBA); international business administration (MBA); management and organizational development (MS); marketing (MBA); organizational development (EMS); strategic management (MBA). *Program availability:* Part-time, evening/weekend. *Degree requirements:* For master's, thesis. *Entrance requirements:* For master's, GMAT, 2 letters of reference, resume. Additional exam requirements/recommendations for international students: Required—TOEFL (minimum score 550 paper-based). *Faculty research:* Marketing in small business enterprises, total quality management in Kenya.

Universidad del Turabo, Graduate Programs, School of Business and Entrepreneurship, Program in Marketing, Gurabo, PR 00778-3030. Offers MBA. *Program availability:* Part-time, evening/weekend. *Entrance requirements:* For master's, GRE, EXADEP or GMAT, interview, essay, official transcript, recommendation letters. Electronic applications accepted.

Universidad Iberoamericana, Graduate School, Santo Domingo D.N., Dominican Republic. Offers business administration (MBA, PMBA); constitutional law (LL M); dentistry (DMD); educational management (MA); integrated marketing communication (MA); psychopedagogical intervention (M Ed); real estate law (LL M); strategic management of human talent (MM).

Universidad Metropolitana, School of Business Administration, Program in Marketing, San Juan, PR 00928-1150. Offers MBA. *Program availability:* Part-time. *Degree requirements:* For master's, thesis or alternative. *Entrance requirements:* For master's, GMAT, PAEG, interview. Electronic applications accepted.

Université de Sherbrooke, Faculty of Administration, Program in Marketing, Sherbrooke, QC J1K 2R1, Canada. Offers M Sc. *Degree requirements:* For master's, one foreign language, thesis. *Entrance requirements:* For master's, bachelor's degree in related field, minimum GPA of 3.0 (on 4.3 scale). Electronic applications accepted. *Faculty research:* Consumer behavior, sales force, branding, prices management.

Université Laval, Faculty of Administrative Sciences, Programs in Business Administration, Québec, QC G1K 7P4, Canada. Offers accounting (MBA); agri-food management (MBA); electronic business (MBA, Diploma); factory management and logistics (MBA); finance (MBA); firm management (MBA); geomatic management (MBA); information technology management (MBA); international management (MBA); management (MBA); management accounting (MBA, Diploma); marketing (MBA); modeling and organizational decision (MBA); occupational health and safety management (MBA); pharmacy management (MBA); social and environmental responsibility (MBA); technological entrepreneurship (Diploma). *Accreditation:* AACSB. *Program availability:* Part-time, evening/weekend, online learning. *Entrance requirements:* For master's and Diploma, knowledge of French and English. Electronic applications accepted.

University at Albany, State University of New York, School of Business, MBA Programs, Albany, NY 12222. Offers business administration (MBA); cyber security (MBA); entrepreneurship (MBA); finance (MBA); human resource information systems (MBA); information systems and business analytics (MBA); marketing (MBA); JD/MBA. JD/MBA offered jointly with Albany Law School. *Program availability:* Part-time, evening/weekend. *Faculty:* 29 full-time (13 women), 9 part-time/adjunct (2 women). *Students:* 103 full-time (36 women), 188 part-time (69 women); includes 76 minority (27 Black or African American, non-Hispanic/Latino; 33 Asian, non-Hispanic/Latino; 16 Hispanic/Latino), 16 international. Average age 25. 181 applicants, 80% accepted, 114 enrolled. In 2017, 103 master's awarded. *Degree requirements:* For master's, thesis (for some programs), field or research project. *Entrance requirements:* For master's, GMAT, minimum undergraduate GPA of 3.0; 3 letters of recommendation; resume; statement of goals. Additional exam requirements/recommendations for international students: Required—TOEFL (minimum score 100 iBT). Recommended—IELTS (minimum score 7). *Application deadline:* For fall admission, 4/1 priority date for domestic students, 2/15 for international students; for spring admission, 12/1 for domestic students; for summer admission, 5/1 for domestic students. Applications are processed on a rolling basis. Application fee: $75. Electronic applications accepted. *Expenses:* $16,622.00 per year (for Full-Time MBA); $645 per credit hour (for Evening MBA). *Financial support:* In 2017–18, 25 students received support, including 7 fellowships with partial tuition reimbursements available (averaging $6,000 per year), 4 research assistantships with partial tuition reimbursements available, 21 teaching assistantships with partial tuition reimbursements available; unspecified assistantships also available. Financial award application deadline: 4/1; financial award applicants required to submit FAFSA. *Faculty research:* Social goods, information assurance, social computing, corporate entrepreneurship, asset pricing. *Total annual research expenditures:* $136,000. *Unit head:* Dr. Hany A. Shawky, Interim Dean, 518-956-8337, Fax: 518-442-3273, E-mail: hshawky@albany.edu. *Application contact:* Zina Mega Lawrence, Assistant Dean of Graduate Student Services, 518-956-8320, Fax: 518-442-4042, E-mail: zlawrence@albany.edu.
Website: https://graduatebusiness.albany.edu/

University at Buffalo, the State University of New York, Graduate School, School of Management, Buffalo, NY 14260. Offers accounting (MS); analytics (MBA); business administration (PMBA); consulting (MBA); finance (MBA, MS), including financial risk

management (MS), quantitative finance (MS); healthcare (MBA); information assurance (MBA); information systems (MBA); international management (MBA); management (EMBA, PhD); management information systems (MS); marketing (MBA); supply chain and operations (MBA); supply chains and operations management (MS); Au D/MBA; DDS/MBA; JD/MBA; M Arch/MBA; MD/MBA; MPH/MBA; MSW/MBA; Pharm D/MBA. *Accreditation:* AACSB. *Program availability:* Part-time, evening/weekend. *Faculty:* 80 full-time (26 women), 45 part-time/adjunct (12 women). *Students:* 597 full-time (251 women); includes 83 minority (19 Black or African American, non-Hispanic/Latino; 59 Asian, non-Hispanic/Latino; 5 Hispanic/Latino), 306 international. Average age 25. 2,109 applicants, 46% accepted, 376 enrolled. In 2017, 371 master's, 13 doctorates awarded. *Degree requirements:* For master's, capstone courses or projects; for doctorate, comprehensive exam, thesis/dissertation. *Entrance requirements:* For master's, GMAT (for MS in accounting, finance); GRE or GMAT (for MBA, MS in management information systems, supply chains and operations management), essays, letters of recommendation; for doctorate, GMAT or GRE, essays, writing sample, letters of recommendation. Additional exam requirements/recommendations for international students: Required—TOEFL (minimum score 95 iBT) or IELTS (minimum score 6.5); Recommended—TSE (minimum score 73). *Application deadline:* For fall admission, 10/15 priority date for domestic and international students; for winter admission, 2/1 priority date for domestic and international students; for spring admission, 4/15 for domestic students; for summer admission, 5/15 for domestic students. Application fee: $100. Electronic applications accepted. *Expenses:* Varies by program. *Financial support:* Fellowships with full and partial tuition reimbursements, research assistantships with full and partial tuition reimbursements, teaching assistantships with full and partial tuition reimbursements, career-related internships or fieldwork, Federal Work-Study, institutionally sponsored loans, scholarships/grants, health care benefits, and unspecified assistantships available. Financial award application deadline: 2/15. *Faculty research:* Data analytics, accounting and law, rate finance, consumer behavior, supply chain logistics, leadership and team effectiveness. *Total annual research expenditures:* $968,376. *Unit head:* Erin K. O'Brien, Assistant Dean and Director of Graduate Programs, 716-645-3204, Fax: 716-645-2341, E-mail: ekobrien@buffalo.edu. *Application contact:* Meghan Felser, Director of Admissions and Recruiting, 716-645-3204, Fax: 716-645-2341, E-mail: mpwood@buffalo.edu.
Website: http://mgt.buffalo.edu/

The University of Akron, Graduate School, College of Business Administration, Department of Marketing, Akron, OH 44325. Offers MBA. *Program availability:* Part-time, evening/weekend. *Faculty:* 8 full-time (2 women), 2 part-time/adjunct (1 woman). *Students:* 6 full-time (3 women), 7 part-time (3 women), 1 international. Average age 25. 14 applicants, 64% accepted, 6 enrolled. In 2017, 13 master's awarded. *Entrance requirements:* For master's, GMAT, GRE, MCAT, LSAT, PCAT, or CAT, minimum GPA of 3.0 (preferred), two letters of recommendation, resume, statement of purpose. Additional exam requirements/recommendations for international students: Required—TOEFL (minimum score 79 iBT), IELTS (minimum score 6.5). *Application deadline:* For fall admission, 7/15 for domestic and international students; for spring admission, 11/15 for domestic and international students; for summer admission, 4/15 for domestic and international students. Application fee: $45 ($75 for international students). Electronic applications accepted. *Financial support:* In 2017–18, 1 teaching assistantship with full and partial tuition reimbursement was awarded. *Faculty research:* Multi-channel marketing, direct interactive marketing, strategic retailing, marketing strategy and telemarketing. *Total annual research expenditures:* $11,700. *Unit head:* Dr. Terry Daugherty, Chair, 330-972-8304, E-mail: td23@uakron.edu. *Application contact:* Dr. William Hauser, Director of Graduate Business Programs, 330-972-7043, Fax: 330-972-6588, E-mail: whauser@uakron.edu.
Website: http://www.uakron.edu/cba/departments/marketing/

The University of Alabama, Graduate School, Manderson Graduate School of Business, Department of Marketing, Tuscaloosa, AL 35487. Offers MS, PhD. *Accreditation:* AACSB. *Faculty:* 20 full-time (6 women), 2 part-time/adjunct (0 women). *Students:* 64 full-time (30 women), 28 part-time (16 women); includes 16 minority (10 Black or African American, non-Hispanic/Latino; 2 Asian, non-Hispanic/Latino; 3 Hispanic/Latino; 1 Two or more races, non-Hispanic/Latino), 11 international. Average age 28. 130 applicants, 63% accepted, 60 enrolled. In 2017, 58 master's, 2 doctorates awarded. Terminal master's awarded for partial completion of doctoral program. *Degree requirements:* For master's, internship; for doctorate, comprehensive exam, thesis/dissertation. *Entrance requirements:* For master's, GRE or GMAT; for doctorate, GRE or GMAT, minimum GPA of 3.0. *Application deadline:* For fall admission, 4/1 priority date for domestic and international students; for spring admission, 2/1 priority date for domestic and international students. Applications are processed on a rolling basis. Application fee: $50 ($60 for international students). Electronic applications accepted. *Financial support:* In 2017–18, 25 students received support, including fellowships with full tuition reimbursements available (averaging $15,000 per year), research assistantships with full tuition reimbursements available (averaging $25,000 per year), teaching assistantships with full tuition reimbursements available (averaging $25,000 per year); scholarships/grants, health care benefits, and unspecified assistantships also available. *Faculty research:* Relationship marketing, consumer behavior, services marketing, professional selling, supply chain management. *Unit head:* Dr. David Mothersbaugh, Department Head, 205-348-2871, E-mail: dmothers@culverhouse.ua.edu. *Application contact:* Courtney Cox, Office Associate II, 205-348-6183, Fax: 205-348-6695, E-mail: crhodes@cba.ua.edu.
Website: http://cba.ua.edu/mkt

The University of Alabama at Birmingham, Collat School of Business, Program in Business Administration, Birmingham, AL 35294. Offers business administration (MBA), including finance, health care management, information technology management, marketing; MD/MBA. *Program availability:* Part-time, evening/weekend, 100% online, blended/hybrid learning. *Faculty:* 44 full-time (8 women), 11 part-time/adjunct (4 women). *Students:* 111 full-time (46 women), 308 part-time (136 women); includes 107 minority (73 Black or African American, non-Hispanic/Latino; 21 Asian, non-Hispanic/Latino; 8 Hispanic/Latino; 5 Two or more races, non-Hispanic/Latino), 56 international. Average age 33. 222 applicants, 89% accepted, 143 enrolled. In 2017, 114 master's awarded. *Entrance requirements:* For master's, GMAT. Additional exam requirements/recommendations for international students: Required—TOEFL (minimum score 80 iBT), IELTS (minimum score 6.5). *Application deadline:* For fall admission, 7/1 for domestic and international students; for spring admission, 11/1 for domestic and international students; for summer admission, 4/1 for domestic and international students. Applications are processed on a rolling basis. Application fee: $60 ($75 for international students). Electronic applications accepted. *Faculty research:* Open innovation, workplace issues, leadership, supply chain management, capital markets. *Total annual research expenditures:* $240,000. *Unit head:* Dr. Ken Miller, Executive Director, MBA Programs, 205-934-8855, E-mail: klmiller@uab.edu. *Application contact:* Christy Manning, Coordinator of Graduate Programs in Business, 205-934-8817, E-mail: cmanning@uab.edu.
Website: http://www.uab.edu/business/home/mba

The University of Alabama in Huntsville, School of Graduate Studies, College of Business Administration, Programs in Business and Management, Huntsville, AL 35899. Offers business analytics (MSMS); federal contracting and procurement management

(Certificate); human resource management (MSM); management (MBA), including acquisition management, entrepreneurship, federal contract accounting, finance, human resource management, logistics and supply chain management, marketing, project management; supply chain management (Certificate); technology and innovation management (Certificate). *Accreditation:* AACSB. *Program availability:* Part-time, evening/weekend. *Degree requirements:* For master's, comprehensive exam, thesis or alternative. *Entrance requirements:* For master's, GMAT (minimum score 500), minimum AACSB index of 1080. Additional exam requirements/recommendations for international students: Required—TOEFL (minimum score 550 paper-based; 80 iBT), IELTS (minimum score 6.5). Electronic applications accepted. *Faculty research:* Supply chain management, management of research and development, international marketing and branding, organizational behavior and human resource management, social networks and computational economics.

University of Alberta, Faculty of Graduate Studies and Research, Doctoral Program in Business, Edmonton, AB T6G 2E1, Canada. Offers accounting (PhD); finance (PhD); human resources/industrial relations (PhD); management science (PhD); marketing (PhD); organizational analysis (PhD); MBA/PhD. *Accreditation:* AACSB. *Program availability:* Part-time. *Degree requirements:* For doctorate, comprehensive exam, thesis/dissertation. *Entrance requirements:* For doctorate, GMAT. Additional exam requirements/recommendations for international students: Required—TOEFL (minimum score 550 paper-based). Electronic applications accepted. *Faculty research:* Accounting, capital markets and corporate finance, organizational change and human resource management, marketing, strategic management.

The University of Arizona, Eller College of Management, Department of Marketing, Tucson, AZ 85721. Offers MBA, MS, PhD. *Degree requirements:* For doctorate, comprehensive exam, thesis/dissertation. *Entrance requirements:* For doctorate, GMAT (minimum score 600). Additional exam requirements/recommendations for international students: Required—TOEFL (minimum score 600 paper-based). Electronic applications accepted. *Faculty research:* Consumer behavior, customer relationship management, research methods, brand strategy, public policy.

University of Baltimore, Graduate School, Merrick School of Business, Department of Marketing and Entrepreneurship, Baltimore, MD 21201-5779. Offers innovation management and technology commercialization (MS). *Program availability:* Part-time, evening/weekend. *Entrance requirements:* For master's, GMAT. Additional exam requirements/recommendations for international students: Required—TOEFL (minimum score 550 paper-based). Electronic applications accepted.

University of Bridgeport, School of Business, Bridgeport, CT 06604. Offers accounting (MBA); finance (MBA); general business (MBA); global financial services (MBA); human resource management (MBA); information systems and knowledge management (MBA); international business (MBA); management (MBA); marketing (MBA); operations management (MBA); small business and entrepreneurship (MBA); specialized business (MBA). *Accreditation:* ACBSP. *Program availability:* Part-time, evening/weekend. *Degree requirements:* For master's, thesis optional. *Entrance requirements:* For master's, GMAT. Additional exam requirements/recommendations for international students: Recommended—TOEFL (minimum score 550 paper-based; 80 iBT), IELTS (minimum score 6.5). Electronic applications accepted. *Expenses:* Contact institution.

The University of British Columbia, Sauder School of Business, Doctoral Program in Business Administration, Vancouver, BC V6T 1Z2, Canada. Offers accounting (PhD); finance (PhD); management information systems (PhD); management science (PhD); marketing (PhD); organizational behavior (PhD); strategy and business economics (PhD); transportation and logistics (PhD); urban land economics (PhD). *Degree requirements:* For doctorate, comprehensive exam, thesis/dissertation. *Entrance requirements:* For doctorate, GMAT or GRE. Additional exam requirements/recommendations for international students: Required—TOEFL (minimum score 600 paper-based; 100 iBT). Electronic applications accepted. *Expenses:* Contact institution.

University of California, Berkeley, Graduate Division, Haas School of Business, PhD in Business Administration Program, Berkeley, CA 94720-1500. Offers accounting (PhD); business and public policy (PhD); finance (PhD); management of organizations (PhD); marketing (PhD); real estate (PhD). *Accreditation:* AACSB. *Students:* 72 full-time (20 women); includes 30 minority (26 Asian, non-Hispanic/Latino; 4 Hispanic/Latino). Average age 27. *Degree requirements:* For doctorate, comprehensive exam, thesis/dissertation, written preliminary exams, oral qualifying exam. *Entrance requirements:* For doctorate, GMAT or GRE, minimum GPA of 3.0 in undergraduate and graduate coursework. Additional exam requirements/recommendations for international students: Required—TOEFL (minimum score 570 paper-based; 70 iBT), IELTS (minimum score 7). *Application deadline:* For fall admission, 12/1 for domestic and international students. Application fee: $105 ($125 for international students). Electronic applications accepted. *Expenses:* Contact institution. *Financial support:* Fellowships with tuition reimbursements, research assistantships with tuition reimbursements, teaching assistantships with tuition reimbursements, scholarships/grants, health care benefits, tuition waivers (full), unspecified assistantships, and transit passes, travel grants available. Financial award application deadline: 12/1. *Faculty research:* Accounting, business and public policy, entrepreneurship, finance, management of organizations, marketing, operations and information technology management, real estate. *Unit head:* Dr. Nicolae Garleanu, Director, 510-643-6349, Fax: 510-643-4255. *Application contact:* Melissa Hacker, Director, Student Affairs, 510-642-3944, Fax: 510-643-4255, E-mail: melhacker@haas.berkeley.edu.
Website: http://www.haas.berkeley.edu/Phd/

University of California, Berkeley, UC Berkeley Extension, Certificate Programs in Business, Berkeley, CA 94720-1500. Offers accounting (Certificate); business administration (Certificate); finance (Certificate); human resource management (Certificate); management (Certificate); marketing (Certificate); project management (Certificate). *Accreditation:* AACSB. *Program availability:* Online learning.

University of California, Berkeley, UC Berkeley Extension, International Diploma Programs, Berkeley, CA 94720-1500. Offers business administration (Certificate); finance (Certificate); global business management (Certificate); marketing (Certificate); project management (Certificate). *Accreditation:* AACSB.

University of California, Davis, Graduate School of Management, Full-Time MBA Program, Davis, CA 95616. Offers business analytics and technologies (MBA); entrepreneurship and innovation (MBA); finance and accounting (MBA); general management (MBA); marketing (MBA); organizational behavior (MBA); public health management (MBA); strategy (MBA); technology management (MBA); DVM/MBA; JD/MBA; M Engr/MBA; MBA/MPH; MBA/MS; MD/MBA; MSN/MBA; PhD/MBA. *Faculty:* 52 full-time (15 women). *Students:* 96 full-time (42 women); includes 31 minority (1 Black or African American, non-Hispanic/Latino; 17 Asian, non-Hispanic/Latino; 5 Hispanic/Latino; 8 Two or more races, non-Hispanic/Latino), 36 international. Average age 29. 290 applicants, 37% accepted, 45 enrolled. In 2017, 44 master's awarded. *Degree requirements:* For master's, integrated management project. *Entrance requirements:* For master's, GMAT or GRE, letters of recommendation, resume, essays, equivalent of a 4-year U.S. undergraduate degree, transcript. Additional exam requirements/recommendations for international students: Required—TOEFL (minimum score 600 paper-based; 100 iBT), IELTS (minimum score 7). *Application deadline:* For fall

Marketing

admission, 5/18 priority date for domestic and international students. Application fee: $125. Electronic applications accepted. *Expenses:* Contact institution. *Financial support:* In 2017–18, 90 students received support. Fellowships, research assistantships, teaching assistantships with partial tuition reimbursements available, institutionally sponsored loans, scholarships/grants, health care benefits, tuition waivers (partial), and unspecified assistantships available. Financial award application deadline: 3/1; financial award applicants required to submit FAFSA. *Faculty research:* Finance, marketing, management, business analytics, accounting. *Unit head:* James Stevens, Senior Assistant Dean of Student Affairs, 530-752-7658, Fax: 530-754-9355, E-mail: admissions@gsm.ucdavis.edu. *Application contact:* Kristy Bird MaKieve, Interim Director of Admissions, 530-754-5476, Fax: 530-754-9355, E-mail: admissions@gsm.ucdavis.edu.
Website: http://gsm.ucdavis.edu/daytime-mba-program

University of California, Davis, Graduate School of Management, MBA Programs in Sacramento and San Francisco Bay Area, Davis, CA 95616. Offers business analytics and technologies (MBA); entrepreneurship and innovation (MBA); finance and accounting (MBA); general management (MBA); marketing (MBA); organizational behavior (MBA); public health management (MBA); strategy (MBA); technology management (MBA). *Program availability:* Part-time-only, evening/weekend. *Faculty:* 99 part-time/adjunct (30 women). *Students:* 323 part-time (133 women); includes 148 minority (7 Black or African American, non-Hispanic/Latino; 96 Asian, non-Hispanic/Latino; 26 Hispanic/Latino; 1 Native Hawaiian or other Pacific Islander, non-Hispanic/Latino; 18 Two or more races, non-Hispanic/Latino), 37 international. Average age 30. 202 applicants, 75% accepted, 111 enrolled. In 2017, 112 master's awarded. *Degree requirements:* For master's, integrated management project. *Entrance requirements:* For master's, GMAT or GRE, letters of recommendation, resume, equivalent of a 4-year undergraduate degree. Additional exam requirements/recommendations for international students: Required—TOEFL (minimum score 600 paper-based; 100 iBT), IELTS (minimum score 7). *Application deadline:* For fall admission, 5/18 priority date for domestic and international students. Application fee: $125. Electronic applications accepted. *Expenses:* Contact institution. *Financial support:* In 2017–18, 67 students received support. Fellowships, teaching assistantships with partial tuition reimbursements available, scholarships/grants, and unspecified assistantships available. Support available to part-time students. Financial award application deadline: 3/1; financial award applicants required to submit FAFSA. *Faculty research:* Accounting, finance, marketing, management, business analytics. *Unit head:* James Stevens, Senior Assistant Dean of Student Affairs, 530-752-7658, Fax: 530-754-9355, E-mail: admissions@gsm.ucdavis.edu. *Application contact:* Kristy Bird MaKieve, Interim Director of Admissions, 530-754-5476, Fax: 530-754-9355, E-mail: admissions@gsm.ucdavis.edu.
Website: http://gsm.ucdavis.edu/mba-programs

University of California, Los Angeles, Graduate Division, UCLA Anderson School of Management, Los Angeles, CA 90095-1481. Offers accounting (PhD); behavioral decision making (PhD); business administration (EMBA, MBA); business analytics (MSBA); decisions, operations, and technology management (PhD); finance (PhD); financial engineering (MFE); global economics and management (PhD); management and organizations (PhD); marketing (PhD); strategy and policy (PhD); DDS/MBA; MBA/JD; MBA/MD; MBA/MLAS; MBA/MLIS; MBA/MN; MBA/MPH; MBA/MPP; MBA/MSCS; MBA/MURP. *Accreditation:* AACSB. *Program availability:* Part-time, evening/weekend. *Faculty:* 88 full-time (20 women), 107 part-time/adjunct (21 women). *Students:* 918 full-time (314 women), 1,269 part-time (399 women); includes 743 minority (38 Black or African American, non-Hispanic/Latino; 3 American Indian or Alaska Native, non-Hispanic/Latino; 531 Asian, non-Hispanic/Latino; 115 Hispanic/Latino; 4 Native Hawaiian or other Pacific Islander, non-Hispanic/Latino; 52 Two or more races, non-Hispanic/Latino), 544 international. Average age 31. 5,842 applicants, 29% accepted, 1015 enrolled. In 2017, 855 master's, 14 doctorates awarded. Terminal master's awarded for partial completion of doctoral program. *Degree requirements:* For master's, comprehensive exam, field consulting project (for MBA, FEMBA, EMBA and GEMBA); internship (for MBA only); thesis/dissertation (for MFE); 10 capstone (for MSBA); for doctorate, comprehensive exam, thesis/dissertation, oral and written qualifying exams. *Entrance requirements:* For master's, GMAT or GRE, 4-year bachelor's degree or equivalent; 2 letters of recommendation; interview (by invitation only); 2 essays; 4-8 years of full-time work experience (for FEMBA only); minimum eight years of work experience with at least three years at management level (for EMBA only); for doctorate, GMAT or GRE, bachelor's degree from college or university of fully-recognized standing, minimum B average during junior and senior undergraduate years, 3 letters of recommendation, statement of purpose. Additional exam requirements/recommendations for international students: Required—TOEFL (minimum score 560 paper-based; 87 iBT), IELTS (minimum score 7), TOEFL with minimum iBT score of 100 (for MSBA). *Application deadline:* For fall admission, 10/2 for domestic and international students; for winter admission, 1/8 for domestic and international students; for spring admission, 4/16 for domestic and international students. Applications are processed on a rolling basis. Application fee: $200. Electronic applications accepted. *Expenses:* Contact institution. *Financial support:* In 2017–18, 649 students received support, including 440 fellowships (averaging $29,273 per year); research assistantships with partial tuition reimbursements available, teaching assistantships with partial tuition reimbursements available, career-related internships or fieldwork, institutionally sponsored loans, and scholarships/grants also available. Support available to part-time students. *Faculty research:* Finance/global economics, entrepreneurship, accounting, human resources/organizational behavior, marketing and behavioral decision-making. *Total annual research expenditures:* $1.3 million. *Unit head:* Dean, 310-825-7982, Fax: 310-206-2073. *Application contact:* Alex Lawrence, Assistant Dean and Director of MBA Admissions, 310-825-6944, Fax: 310-825-8582, E-mail: mba.admissions@anderson.ucla.edu.
Website: http://www.anderson.ucla.edu/

University of Central Missouri, The Graduate School, Warrensburg, MO 64093. Offers accountancy (MA); accounting (MBA); applied mathematics (MS); aviation safety (MA); biology (MS); business administration (MBA); career and technical education leadership (MS); college student personnel administration (MS); communication (MA); computer science (MS); counseling (MS); criminal justice (MS); educational leadership (Ed D); educational technology (MS); elementary and early childhood education (MSE); English (MA); environmental studies (MA); finance (MBA); history (MA); human services/educational technology (Ed S); human services/learning resources (Ed S); human services/professional counseling (Ed S); industrial hygiene (MS); industrial management (MS); information systems (MBA); information technology (MS); kinesiology (MS); library science and information services (MS); literacy education (MSE); marketing (MBA); mathematics (MS); music (MA); occupational safety management (MS); psychology (MS); rural family nursing (MS); school administration (MSE); social gerontology (MS); sociology (MA); special education (MSE); speech language pathology (MS); superintendency (Ed S); teaching (MAT); teaching English as a second language (MA); technology (MS); technology management (PhD); theatre (MA). *Program availability:* Part-time, 100% online, blended/hybrid learning. *Faculty:* 337 full-time (145 women), 41 part-time/adjunct (28 women). *Students:* 785 full-time (398 women), 1,633 part-time (1,063 women); includes 231 minority (102 Black or African American, non-Hispanic/

Latino; 4 American Indian or Alaska Native, non-Hispanic/Latino; 16 Asian, non-Hispanic/Latino; 52 Hispanic/Latino; 57 Two or more races, non-Hispanic/Latino), 692 international. Average age 30. In 2017, 2,605 master's, 122 other advanced degrees awarded. *Degree requirements:* For master's and Ed S, comprehensive exam (for some programs), thesis (for some programs). *Entrance requirements:* Additional exam requirements/recommendations for international students: Required—TOEFL (minimum score 550 paper-based; 79 iBT). *Application deadline:* For fall admission, 6/1 priority date for domestic and international students; for spring admission, 10/1 priority date for domestic and international students; for summer admission, 4/1 priority date for domestic and international students. Applications are processed on a rolling basis. Application fee: $30 ($75 for international students). Electronic applications accepted. *Expenses:* Tuition, state resident: full-time $8771; part-time $292.35 per credit hour. Tuition, nonresident: full-time $17,541; part-time $584.70 per credit hour. *Required fees:* $372; $24.78 per credit hour. *Financial support:* In 2017–18, 99 students received support. Research assistantships, teaching assistantships, career-related internships or fieldwork, Federal Work-Study, scholarships/grants, and administrative and laboratory assistantships available. Support available to part-time students. Financial award application deadline: 3/1; financial award applicants required to submit FAFSA. *Unit head:* Shellie Hewitt, Director of Graduate and International Student Services, 660-543-4621, Fax: 660-543-4778, E-mail: hewitt@ucmo.edu. *Application contact:* 660-543-4621, E-mail: admit_intl@ucmo.edu.
Website: http://www.ucmo.edu/graduate/

University of Chicago, Booth School of Business, Full-Time MBA Program, Chicago, IL 60637. Offers accounting (MBA); analytic finance (MBA); analytic management (MBA); econometrics and statistics (MBA); economics (MBA); entrepreneurship (MBA); finance (MBA); general management (MBA); health administration and policy (Certificate); international business (MBA); managerial and organizational behavior (MBA); marketing analytics (MBA); marketing management (MBA); operations management (MBA); strategic management (MBA); MBA/AM; MBA/JD; MBA/MA; MBA/MD; MBA/MPP. *Accreditation:* AACSB. *Faculty:* 154 full-time (26 women), 61 part-time/adjunct (12 women). *Students:* 1,176 full-time (481 women). In 2017, 586 master's awarded. *Entrance requirements:* For master's, GMAT or GRE, transcripts, resume, 2 letters of recommendation, essays, interview. Additional exam requirements/recommendations for international students: Required—TOEFL, IELTS, or PTE. *Application deadline:* For fall admission, 9/1 for domestic and international students; for winter admission, 1/1 for domestic and international students; for spring admission, 4/1 for domestic and international students. Application fee: $250. Electronic applications accepted. *Expenses:* Contact institution. *Unit head:* Stacey Kole, Deputy Dean for Alumni, Corporate Relations, and the Full-time MBA Program, 773-702-7121. *Application contact:* Kurt Ahlm, Associate Dean for Student Recruitment and Admissions, 773-702-7369, Fax: 773-702-9085, E-mail: admissions@chicagobooth.edu.
Website: https://www.chicagobooth.edu/programs/full-time

University of Cincinnati, Carl H. Lindner College of Business, MS Program, Cincinnati, OH 45221. Offers accounting (MS); applied economics (MS); business analytics (MS); finance (MS); information systems (MS); marketing (MS); taxation (MS). *Program availability:* Part-time, evening/weekend. *Faculty:* 65 full-time (20 women), 27 part-time/adjunct (6 women). *Students:* 324 full-time (132 women), 204 part-time (77 women); includes 50 minority (18 Black or African American, non-Hispanic/Latino; 21 Asian, non-Hispanic/Latino; 5 Hispanic/Latino; 1 Native Hawaiian or other Pacific Islander, non-Hispanic/Latino; 5 Two or more races, non-Hispanic/Latino), 299 international. Average age 28. 1,756 applicants, 24% accepted, 351 enrolled. In 2017, 369 master's awarded. *Degree requirements:* For master's, thesis (for some programs), capstone. *Entrance requirements:* For master's, GMAT, GRE, resume, transcripts, essays, letters of recommendation. Additional exam requirements/recommendations for international students: Required—TOEFL (minimum score 577 paper-based; 90 iBT), IELTS (minimum score 6.5). *Application deadline:* For fall admission, 6/30 priority date for domestic students, 3/15 for international students; for spring admission, 12/15 for domestic students, 9/15 for international students; for summer admission, 4/15 for domestic and international students. Applications are processed on a rolling basis. Application fee: $65 ($70 for international students). Electronic applications accepted. *Expenses:* $10,479 per term full-time resident, $14,398 per term full-time nonresident, $890 per credit hour part-time. *Financial support:* In 2017–18, 251 students received support, including 12 teaching assistantships with full and partial tuition reimbursements available (averaging $3,500 per year); scholarships/grants, tuition waivers (full and partial), and unspecified assistantships also available. Financial award application deadline: 2/1; financial award applicants required to submit FAFSA. *Faculty research:* Business analytics, financial management, organizational behavior, financial accounting, consumer insights. *Total annual research expenditures:* $24,842. *Unit head:* Dr. David Szymanski, Dean, 513-556-7001, Fax: 513-556-4891, E-mail: david.szymanski@uc.edu. *Application contact:* Dona Clary, Executive Director, Graduate Programs, 513-556-3546, Fax: 513-558-7006, E-mail: dona.clary@uc.edu.
Website: http://business.uc.edu/graduate/masters.html

University of Cincinnati, Carl H. Lindner College of Business, PhD Programs, Cincinnati, OH 45221. Offers accounting (PhD); business analytics (PhD); economics (PhD); finance (PhD); information systems (PhD); management (PhD); marketing (PhD); operations and business analytics (PhD); operations research (PhD). *Faculty:* 37 full-time (13 women). *Students:* 29 full-time (12 women), 12 part-time (6 women); includes 5 minority (1 Black or African American, non-Hispanic/Latino; 4 Asian, non-Hispanic/Latino), 20 international. Average age 30. 123 applicants, 16% accepted, 11 enrolled. In 2017, 5 doctorates awarded. *Degree requirements:* For doctorate, comprehensive exam, thesis/dissertation. *Entrance requirements:* For doctorate, GMAT, GRE, transcripts, essays, resume, letters of recommendation. Additional exam requirements/recommendations for international students: Required—TOEFL (minimum score 600 paper-based; 100 iBT), IELTS (minimum score 7). *Application deadline:* For fall admission, 1/15 for domestic and international students. Application fee: $65 ($70 for international students). Electronic applications accepted. *Expenses:* $7,234 resident per term, $13,105 nonresident per term. *Financial support:* In 2017–18, 41 students received support, including 29 research assistantships with full tuition reimbursements available (averaging $23,250 per year); scholarships/grants, health care benefits, tuition waivers (full), and unspecified assistantships also available. Financial award application deadline: 1/15; financial award applicants required to submit FAFSA. *Faculty research:* Bayesian Prediction Theory, organizational fairness, consumer insight and market research, consumer insight and market research, density estimation from correlated data. *Unit head:* Dr. Suzanne Masterson, Director, 513-556-7125, Fax: 513-556-5499, E-mail: suzanne.masterson@uc.edu. *Application contact:* Angel Elvin, Assistant Director, 513-556-7190, Fax: 513-558-7006, E-mail: angel.elvin@uc.edu.
Website: http://business.uc.edu/graduate/phd.html

University of Colorado Denver, Business School, Master of Business Administration Program, Denver, CO 80217. Offers bioinnovation and entrepreneurship (MBA); business intelligence (MBA); business strategy (MBA); business to business marketing (MBA); business to consumer marketing (MBA); change management (MBA); corporate financial management (MBA); enterprise technology management (MBA); entrepreneurship (MBA); health administration (MBA), including financial management, health administration, health information technologies, international health management and policy; human resources management (MBA); international business (MBA); investment management (MBA); managing for sustainability (MBA); sports and entertainment management (MBA). *Accreditation:* AACSB. *Program availability:* Part-time, evening/weekend, 100% online, blended/hybrid learning. *Degree requirements:* For master's, 48 semester hours, including 30 of core courses, 3 in international business, and 15 in electives from over 50 other business courses. *Entrance requirements:* For master's, GMAT, resume, official transcripts, essay, two letters of recommendation, financial statements (for international applicants). Additional exam requirements/recommendations for international students: Required—TOEFL (minimum score 560 paper-based; 83 iBT); Recommended—IELTS (minimum score 6.5). Electronic applications accepted. *Expenses:* Contact institution. *Faculty research:* Marketing, management, entrepreneurship, finance, health administration.

University of Colorado Denver, Business School, Program in Marketing, Denver, CO 80217. Offers brand management and marketing communication (MS); global marketing (MS); high-tech and entrepreneurial marketing (MS); marketing for sustainability (MS); marketing research (MS); sports and entertainment marketing (MS). *Program availability:* Part-time, evening/weekend. *Degree requirements:* For master's, 30 semester hours (21 of marketing core courses, 9 of marketing electives). *Entrance requirements:* For master's, GMAT, resume, essay, two letters of recommendation, financial statements (for international applicants). Additional exam requirements/ recommendations for international students: Required—TOEFL (minimum score 525 paper-based; 71 iBT); Recommended—IELTS (minimum score 6.5). Electronic applications accepted. *Expenses:* Contact institution. *Faculty research:* Marketing issues in the Chinese environment, impact of individual difference and contextual factors on the risk-taking behaviors of managers making new-business creation decisions, attribution theory perspective of conflict between marketers and engineers, organizational identity and identification, international market entry strategies.

University of Connecticut, Graduate School, School of Business, Storrs, CT 06269. Offers accounting (MS, PhD); business administration (MBA, PhD); finance (PhD); health care management and insurance studies (MBA); management (PhD); management consulting (MBA); marketing (PhD); marketing intelligence (MBA). *Accreditation:* AACSB. *Degree requirements:* For master's, comprehensive exam; for doctorate, thesis/dissertation. *Entrance requirements:* For master's and doctorate, GMAT. Additional exam requirements/recommendations for international students: Required—TOEFL (minimum score 550 paper-based). Electronic applications accepted.
See Display on page 146 and Close-Up on page 183.

University of Dallas, Satish and Yasmin Gupta College of Business, Irving, TX 75062-4736. Offers accounting (MBA, MS); business administration (DBA); business analytics (MS); business management (MBA); corporate finance (MBA); cybersecurity (MS); finance (MS); financial services (MBA); global business (MBA, MS); health services management (MBA); human resource management (MBA); information and technology management (MS); information assurance (MBA); information technology (MBA); information technology service management (MBA); marketing management (MBA); organization development (MBA); project management (MBA); sports and entertainment management (MBA); strategic leadership (MBA); supply chain management (MBA). *Accreditation:* AACSB. *Program availability:* Part-time, evening/weekend, online learning. *Entrance requirements:* Additional exam requirements/recommendations for international students: Required—TOEFL. *Application deadline:* Applications are processed on a rolling basis. Application fee: $50. Electronic applications accepted. *Expenses:* Contact institution. *Financial support:* Application deadline: 2/15; applicants required to submit FAFSA. *Unit head:* Brett J.L. Landry, Dean, 972-721-5356, E-mail: blandry@udallas.edu. *Application contact:* Dr. David Sweet, Dean, Braniff Graduate School, 972-721-5288, Fax: 972-721-5280, E-mail: dsweet@udallas.edu.
Website: http://www.udallas.edu/cob/

University of Dayton, School of Business Administration, Dayton, OH 45469. Offers accounting (MBA); cyber security (MBA); finance (MBA); marketing (MBA); JD/MBA. *Accreditation:* AACSB. *Program availability:* Part-time, evening/weekend, blended/hybrid learning. *Faculty:* 23 full-time (8 women), 12 part-time/adjunct (2 women). *Students:* 57 full-time (24 women), 82 part-time (32 women); includes 10 minority (5 Black or African American, non-Hispanic/Latino; 2 Asian, non-Hispanic/Latino; 3 Hispanic/Latino), 18 international. Average age 31. 269 applicants, 31% accepted. In 2017, 88 master's awarded. *Entrance requirements:* For master's, GMAT (minimum score of 500 total, 19 verbal); GRE (minimum score of 149 verbal, 146 quantitative), minimum GPA of 3.0, current resume. Additional exam requirements/recommendations for international students: Required—TOEFL (minimum score 550 paper-based; 80 iBT); Recommended—IELTS (minimum score 6.5). *Application deadline:* For fall admission, 5/1 for international students; for spring admission, 11/1 for international students. Applications are processed on a rolling basis. Application fee: $0 ($50 for international students). Electronic applications accepted. *Expenses:* Contact institution. *Financial support:* In 2017–18, 10 research assistantships with partial tuition reimbursements (averaging $9,295 per year) were awarded; teaching assistantships, career-related internships or fieldwork, institutionally sponsored loans, scholarships/grants, traineeships, tuition waivers, and unspecified assistantships also available. Financial award application deadline: 3/1; financial award applicants required to submit FAFSA. *Faculty research:* Management information systems, economics, finance, marketing, entrepreneurship, accounting, cyber security, analytics. *Unit head:* Scott MacDonald, Director, MBA Program, 937-229-3733, Fax: 937-229-3882, E-mail: smacdonald1@udayton.edu. *Application contact:* Mandy Bingaman, MBA Program Manager, 937-229-3733, Fax: 937-229-3882, E-mail: mbingaman1@udayton.edu.
Website: https://www.udayton.edu/business/academics/master_of_business_administration/index.php

University of Denver, Daniels College of Business, Department of Marketing, Denver, CO 80208. Offers MBA, MS. *Program availability:* Part-time, evening/weekend. *Faculty:* 15 full-time (8 women), 5 part-time/adjunct (2 women). *Students:* 41 full-time (30 women), 17 part-time (12 women); includes 13 minority (3 Black or African American, non-Hispanic/Latino; 1 Asian, non-Hispanic/Latino; 8 Hispanic/Latino; 1 Two or more races, non-Hispanic/Latino), 11 international. Average age 25. 178 applicants, 36% accepted, 30 enrolled. In 2017, 18 master's awarded. *Entrance requirements:* For master's, GRE General Test or GMAT, bachelor's degree, transcripts, essays, resume, interview. Additional exam requirements/recommendations for international students: Required—TOEFL (minimum score 570 paper-based; 88 iBT). *Application deadline:* For fall admission, 11/15 priority date for domestic and international students; for spring admission, 10/1 priority date for domestic and international students. Applications are processed on a rolling basis. Application fee: $100. Electronic applications accepted. *Expenses:* $47,823 per year full-time; $1,320 per credit. *Financial support:* In 2017–18, 54 students received support. Teaching assistantships with tuition reimbursements available, career-related internships or fieldwork, Federal Work-Study, institutionally sponsored loans, scholarships/grants, and unspecified assistantships available. Support available to part-time students. Financial award application deadline: 2/15; financial award applicants required to submit FAFSA. *Faculty research:* Consumer behavior, co-creating the customer experience, marketing education and pedagogy, new-product/service innovation, marketing strategy. *Unit head:* Dr. Donald Bacon, Professor and Co-Chair, 303-871-3317, E-mail: dbacon@du.edu. *Application contact:* Karen Gross,

Assistant to the Chair, 303-871-3317, E-mail: karen.gross@du.edu.
Website: https://daniels.du.edu/marketing

University of Florida, Graduate School, Warrington College of Business Administration, Hough Graduate School of Business, Department of Marketing, Gainesville, FL 32611. Offers MA, MS, PhD. Terminal master's awarded for partial completion of doctoral program. *Degree requirements:* For master's, comprehensive exam, thesis optional; for doctorate, comprehensive exam, thesis/dissertation. *Entrance requirements:* For master's and doctorate, GMAT (minimum score of 465) or GRE General Test, minimum GPA of 3.0. Additional exam requirements/recommendations for international students: Required—TOEFL (minimum score 550 paper-based; 80 iBT), IELTS (minimum score 6). Electronic applications accepted. *Faculty research:* Consumer behavior, decision-making, behavioral decision theory, marketing models, marketing strategy.

University of Hawaii at Manoa, Office of Graduate Education, Shidler College of Business, Program in Business Administration, Honolulu, HI 96822. Offers Asian business studies (MBA); Chinese business studies (MBA); decision sciences (MBA); entrepreneurship (MBA); finance (MBA); finance and banking (MBA); human resources management (MBA); information management (MBA); information technology (MBA); international business (MBA); Japanese business studies (MBA); marketing (MBA); organizational behavior (MBA); organizational management (MBA); real estate (MBA); student-designed track (MBA). *Accreditation:* AACSB. *Program availability:* Part-time, evening/weekend. *Degree requirements:* For master's, thesis optional. *Entrance requirements:* For master's, GMAT, minimum GPA of 3.0. Additional exam requirements/recommendations for international students: Required—TOEFL (minimum score 600 paper-based; 100 iBT), IELTS (minimum score 7). *Expenses:* Contact institution.

University of Hawaii at Manoa, Office of Graduate Education, Shidler College of Business, Program in International Management, Honolulu, HI 96822. Offers Asian finance (PhD); global information technology management (PhD); international accounting (PhD); international marketing (PhD); international organization and strategy (PhD). *Program availability:* Part-time. *Degree requirements:* For doctorate, comprehensive exam, thesis/dissertation. *Entrance requirements:* For doctorate, GMAT or GRE General Test, minimum GPA of 3.0. Additional exam requirements/recommendations for international students: Required—TOEFL (minimum score 600 paper-based; 100 iBT), IELTS (minimum score 7). *Expenses:* Contact institution.

University of Houston, Bauer College of Business, Marketing Program, Houston, TX 77204. Offers PhD. *Program availability:* Part-time, evening/weekend. *Degree requirements:* For doctorate, comprehensive exam, thesis/dissertation. *Entrance requirements:* For doctorate, GMAT or GRE. *Faculty research:* Accountancy and taxation, finance, international business, management.

University of Houston–Victoria, School of Business Administration, Victoria, TX 77901-4450. Offers accounting (MBA); economic development and entrepreneurship (MS); finance (GMBA, MBA); general business (MBA); international business (MBA); management (GMBA, MBA); marketing (MBA). *Accreditation:* AACSB. *Program availability:* Part-time, evening/weekend, online learning. *Entrance requirements:* For master's, GMAT. Additional exam requirements/recommendations for international students: Required—TOEFL (minimum score 550 paper-based). Electronic applications accepted. *Faculty research:* Economic development, marketing, finance.

The University of Iowa, Tippie College of Business, Department of Marketing, Iowa City, IA 52242-1316. Offers PhD. *Faculty:* 10 full-time (3 women), 8 part-time/adjunct (1 woman). *Students:* 11 full-time (6 women); includes 1 minority (Asian, non-Hispanic/Latino), 9 international. Average age 32. 23 applicants, 22% accepted, 3 enrolled. In 2017, 2 doctorates awarded. *Degree requirements:* For doctorate, comprehensive exam, thesis/dissertation. *Entrance requirements:* Additional exam requirements/recommendations for international students: Required—TOEFL (minimum iBT score 100) or IELTS (minimum score 7.0). *Application deadline:* For fall admission, 1/15 priority date for domestic and international students. Application fee: $60 ($100 for international students). Electronic applications accepted. *Financial support:* In 2017–18, 11 students received support, including 11 fellowships (averaging $4,200 per year), 11 teaching assistantships with full tuition reimbursements available (averaging $19,016 per year); health care benefits and unspecified assistantships also available. Financial award application deadline: 1/15. *Faculty research:* Judgments and decision-making under certainty; consumer behavior: cognitive neuroscience, attitudes and evaluation; hierarchical Bayesian estimation; marketing-finance interface; advertising effects. *Unit head:* Prof. Dhananjay Nayakankuppam, Department Executive Officer, 319-335-1013, Fax: 319-335-1956, E-mail: dhananjay-nayakankuppam@uiowa.edu. *Application contact:* Renea L. Jay, Associate Director, Non-MBA Graduate Programs, 319-335-0830, Fax: 319-335-0860, E-mail: renea-jay@uiowa.edu.
Website: https://tippie.uiowa.edu/marketing

The University of Iowa, Tippie College of Business, Professional MBA Program, Iowa City, IA 52242-1316. Offers business administration (MBA); business analytics (MBA); finance (MBA); leadership (MBA); marketing (MBA). *Program availability:* Part-time-only, evening/weekend. *Faculty:* 50 full-time (11 women), 22 part-time/adjunct (2 women). *Students:* 873 part-time (325 women); includes 102 minority (16 Black or African American, non-Hispanic/Latino; 1 American Indian or Alaska Native, non-Hispanic/Latino; 54 Asian, non-Hispanic/Latino; 22 Hispanic/Latino; 9 Two or more races, non-Hispanic/Latino), 44 international. Average age 33. 155 applicants, 94% accepted, 137 enrolled. In 2017, 176 master's awarded. *Degree requirements:* For master's, successful completion of nine required courses and six electives totaling 45 credits, minimum GPA of 2.75. *Entrance requirements:* For master's, GMAT or GRE. Additional exam requirements/recommendations for international students: Required—TOEFL (minimum score 600 paper-based; 100 iBT), IELTS (minimum score 7). *Application deadline:* For fall admission, 7/30 for domestic and international students; for spring admission, 12/15 for domestic and international students; for summer admission, 4/30 for domestic and international students. Applications are processed on a rolling basis. Application fee: $60 ($100 for international students). Electronic applications accepted. *Expenses:* Contact institution. *Faculty research:* Capital markets; analytics techniques and applications; organizational and market systems analysis; applied econometrics; talent effectiveness. *Unit head:* Prof. Sarah Fisher Gardial, Dean, 319-335-0862, Fax: 319-335-0860, E-mail: sarah-gardial@uiowa.edu.
Website: https://tippie.uiowa.edu/future-graduate-students/mba-programs/professional-mba

The University of Kansas, Graduate Studies, School of Business, Program in Business, Lawrence, KS 66045. Offers business and organizational leadership (MS); decision sciences and supply chain management (PhD); finance (PhD); human resources management (PhD); marketing (PhD); organizational behavior (PhD); strategic management (PhD); supply chain management and logistics (MS). *Accreditation:* AACSB. *Program availability:* Part-time. *Students:* 66 full-time (18 women), 227 part-time (76 women); includes 59 minority (21 Black or African American, non-Hispanic/Latino; 2 American Indian or Alaska Native, non-Hispanic/Latino; 13 Asian, non-Hispanic/Latino; 3 Hispanic/Latino; 20 Two or more races, non-Hispanic/Latino), 29 international. Average age 32. 329 applicants, 71% accepted, 185 enrolled.

Marketing

In 2017, 30 master's, 8 doctorates awarded. *Entrance requirements:* For master's, GMAT, official transcript, three letters of recommendation, resume, statement of purpose; for doctorate, GMAT or GRE, official transcript, three letters of recommendation, resume, statement of purpose. Additional exam requirements/recommendations for international students: Required—TOEFL (minimum score 600 paper-based; 100 iBT). *Application deadline:* For fall admission, 1/10 for domestic and international students. Application fee: $65 ($85 for international students). Electronic applications accepted. *Financial support:* Fellowships, research assistantships, teaching assistantships, scholarships/grants, health care benefits, tuition waivers (full), and unspecified assistantships available. Financial award application deadline: 1/10. *Faculty research:* Strategic human resource management, business ethics, organizational theory/behavior, corporate strategy, international business, supply chain management, Bayesian networks, game theory, decision analysis and time/series analysis, pricing, consumer effects, advertising and emotion. *Unit head:* Charly Edmonds, Director, 785-864-3841, E-mail: bschoolphd@ku.edu. *Application contact:* Graduate Admission Contact, 785-864-7500, E-mail: bschoolphd@ku.edu. Website: http://www.business.ku.edu/

University of La Verne, College of Business and Public Management, Graduate Programs in Business Administration, La Verne, CA 91750-4443. Offers accounting (MBA, MBA-EP); finance (MBA, MBA-EP); health services management (MBA); information technology (MBA, MBA-EP); international business (MBA, MBA-EP); management and leadership (MBA, MBA-EP); marketing (MBA, MBA-EP); supply chain management (MBA, MBA-EP). *Program availability:* Part-time, evening/weekend. *Faculty:* 24 full-time (11 women), 25 part-time/adjunct (6 women). *Students:* 390 full-time (193 women), 93 part-time (48 women); includes 96 minority (7 Black or African American, non-Hispanic/Latino; 1 American Indian or Alaska Native, non-Hispanic/Latino; 17 Asian, non-Hispanic/Latino; 67 Hispanic/Latino; 1 Native Hawaiian or other Pacific Islander, non-Hispanic/Latino; 3 Two or more races, non-Hispanic/Latino), 336 international. Average age 28. *Entrance requirements:* For master's, GMAT, MAT, or GRE, minimum undergraduate GPA of 3.0, 2 letters of recommendation, resume, statement of purpose. Additional exam requirements/recommendations for international students: Required—TOEFL (minimum score 550 paper-based; 85 iBT). *Application deadline:* Applications are processed on a rolling basis. Application fee: $50. Tuition and fees vary according to program. *Financial support:* Institutionally sponsored loans and scholarships/grants available. Financial award application deadline: 3/2; financial award applicants required to submit FAFSA. *Unit head:* Dr. Abe Helou, Chairperson, 909-448-4455, Fax: 909-392-2704, E-mail: ihelou@laverne.edu. *Application contact:* Rina Lazarian-Chehab, Senior Associate Director of Graduate Admissions, 909-448-4317, Fax: 909-971-2295, E-mail: rlazarian@laverne.edu. Website: https://business.laverne.edu/mba/

University of La Verne, Regional and Online Campuses, Graduate Programs, Inland Empire Campus, Ontario, CA 91730. Offers business administration (MBA, MBA-EP), including accounting (MBA), finance (MBA), health services management (MBA-EP), information technology (MBA-EP), international business (MBA), managed care (MBA), management and leadership (MBA-EP), marketing (MBA-EP), supply chain management (MBA); leadership and management (MS), including human resource management, nonprofit management, organizational development. *Program availability:* Part-time, evening/weekend. *Faculty:* 5 part-time/adjunct (1 woman). *Students:* 24 full-time (13 women), 72 part-time (44 women); includes 64 minority (12 Black or African American, non-Hispanic/Latino; 13 Asian, non-Hispanic/Latino; 36 Hispanic/Latino; 3 Two or more races, non-Hispanic/Latino). Average age 38. In 2017, 42 master's awarded. *Application deadline:* Applications are processed on a rolling basis. Application fee: $50. *Expenses:* Contact institution. *Financial support:* Application deadline: 3/2; applicants required to submit FAFSA. *Unit head:* Juli Roberts, Campus Director, Inland Empire Regional Campus in Ontario, 760-955-6448, E-mail: jroberts@laverne.edu. *Application contact:* Admissions, 877-468-6858, E-mail: gradadmission@laverne.edu. Website: https://laverne.edu/locations/

University of Lethbridge, School of Graduate Studies, Lethbridge, AB T1K 3M4, Canada. Offers addictions counseling (M Sc); agricultural biotechnology (M Sc); agricultural studies (M Sc, MA); anthropology (MA); archaeology (M Sc, MA); art (MA, MFA); biochemistry (M Sc); biological sciences (M Sc); biomolecular science (PhD); biosystems and biodiversity (PhD); Canadian studies (MA); chemistry (M Sc); computer science (M Sc); computer science and geographical information science (M Sc); counseling (MC); counseling psychology (M Ed); dramatic arts (MA); earth, space, and physical science (PhD); economics (MA); education (MA, PhD); educational leadership (M Ed); English (MA); environmental science (M Sc); evolution and behavior (PhD); exercise science (M Sc); French (MA); French/German (MA); French/Spanish (MA); general education (M Ed); geography (M Sc, MA); German (MA); health sciences (M Sc); individualized multidisciplinary (M Sc, MA); kinesiology (M Sc, MA); management (M Sc), including accounting, finance, human resource management and labor relations, information systems, international management, marketing, policy and strategy; mathematics (M Sc); music (M Mus, MA); Native American studies (MA); neuroscience (M Sc, PhD); new media (MA, MFA); nursing (M Sc, MN); philosophy (MA); physics (M Sc); political science (MA); psychology (M Sc, MA); religious studies (MA); sociology (MA); theatre and dramatic arts (MFA); theoretical and computational science (PhD); urban and regional studies (MA); women and gender studies (MA). *Program availability:* Part-time, evening/weekend. *Degree requirements:* For master's, thesis (for some programs); for doctorate, comprehensive exam, thesis/dissertation. *Entrance requirements:* For master's, GMAT (for M Sc in management), bachelor's degree in related field, minimum GPA of 3.0 during previous 20 graded semester courses, 2 years' teaching or related experience (M Ed); for doctorate, master's degree, minimum graduate GPA of 3.5. Additional exam requirements/recommendations for international students: Required—TOEFL (minimum score 580 paper-based; 93 iBT). Electronic applications accepted. *Faculty research:* Movement and brain plasticity, gibberellin physiology, photosynthesis, carbon cycling, molecular properties of main-group ring compounds.

The University of Manchester, Alliance Manchester Business School, M15 6PB, United Kingdom. Offers accounting and finance (M Sc); business (M Ent); business analysis and strategic management (M Sc); business analytics: operational research and risk analysis (M Sc); business psychology (M Sc); corporate communications and reputation management (M Sc); finance (M Sc); finance and business economics (M Sc); human resource management and industrial relations (M Sc); innovation management and entrepreneurship (M Sc); international business and management (M Sc); international human resource management and comparative industrial relations (M Sc); management (M Sc); marketing (M Sc); operations, project and supply chain management (M Sc); organizational psychology (M Sc); quantitative finance (M Sc). *Entrance requirements:* For master's, UK 2:1 honours degree or overseas equivalent. Additional exam requirements/recommendations for international students: Required—TOEFL (minimum score 100 iBT), IELTS (minimum score 7), PTE. Electronic applications accepted. *Faculty research:* Accounting and finance, management sciences and marketing, people management and organization, innovation management and policy, decision sciences.

University of Massachusetts Amherst, Graduate School, Isenberg School of Management, Program in Management, Amherst, MA 01003. Offers accounting (PhD);

business administration (MBA); entrepreneurship (MBA); finance (MBA, PhD); healthcare administration (MBA); hospitality and tourism management (PhD); management science (PhD); marketing (MBA, PhD); organization studies (PhD); sport management (PhD); strategic management (PhD); MBA/MS. *Accreditation:* AACSB. *Program availability:* Part-time, evening/weekend, online learning. Terminal master's awarded for partial completion of doctoral program. *Degree requirements:* For doctorate, comprehensive exam, thesis/dissertation. *Entrance requirements:* For master's and doctorate, GMAT or GRE General Test. Additional exam requirements/recommendations for international students: Required—TOEFL (minimum score 550 paper-based; 80 iBT), IELTS (minimum score 6.5). Electronic applications accepted.

University of Memphis, Graduate School, Fogelman College of Business and Economics, Program in Business Administration, Memphis, TN 38152. Offers accounting (MBA, PhD); business administration (IMBA); economics (PhD); executive business administration (MBA); finance (PhD); management (MS); marketing and supply chain management (PhD); real estate development (MS); JD/MBA. *Accreditation:* AACSB. *Faculty:* 2 part-time/adjunct (0 women). *Students:* 166 full-time (76 women), 361 part-time (142 women); includes 161 minority (91 Black or African American, non-Hispanic/Latino; 51 Asian, non-Hispanic/Latino; 10 Hispanic/Latino; 9 Two or more races, non-Hispanic/Latino), 89 international. Average age 32. 263 applicants, 83% accepted, 157 enrolled. In 2017, 186 master's, 14 doctorates awarded. *Degree requirements:* For master's, comprehensive exam; for doctorate, comprehensive exam, thesis/dissertation. *Entrance requirements:* For master's, GMAT, resume; for doctorate, GMAT, interview, minimum GPA of 3.4, resume, letter of recommendation. Additional exam requirements/recommendations for international students: Required—TOEFL (minimum score 550 paper-based). *Application deadline:* For fall admission, 8/1 for domestic students; for spring admission, 12/1 for domestic students. Application fee: $35 ($60 for international students). *Financial support:* In 2017–18, 164 students received support, including 17 research assistantships with full tuition reimbursements available (averaging $53,750 per year), 13 teaching assistantships with full tuition reimbursements available (averaging $20,798 per year); career-related internships or fieldwork, Federal Work-Study, scholarships/grants, and unspecified assistantships also available. Financial award application deadline: 2/15; financial award applicants required to submit FAFSA. *Faculty research:* Competitive business strategy, finance microstructures, supply chain management innovations, health care economics, litigation risks and corporate audits. *Unit head:* Dr. Rajiv Grover, Dean, 901-678-3759, E-mail: rgrover@memphis.edu. *Application contact:* Dr. Carol V. Danehower, Associate Dean, 901-678-5402, Fax: 901-678-3579, E-mail: fcbegp@memphis.edu. Website: https://web0.memphis.edu/gradcatalog/degreeprog/fcbe/fcbe.php

University of Michigan–Flint, School of Management, Program in Business Administration, Flint, MI 48502-1950. Offers accounting (MBA); computer information systems (MBA); finance (MBA, Post-Master's Certificate); general business (Graduate Certificate); general business administration (MBA); health care management (MBA); international business (MBA, Post-Master's Certificate); lean manufacturing (MBA); marketing (Post-Master's Certificate); marketing and innovation management (MBA); organizational leadership (MBA). *Program availability:* Part-time, evening/weekend, mixed mode format. *Faculty:* 32 full-time (5 women), 8 part-time/adjunct (2 women). *Students:* 12 full-time (7 women), 147 part-time (51 women); includes 31 minority (15 Black or African American, non-Hispanic/Latino; 1 American Indian or Alaska Native, non-Hispanic/Latino; 9 Asian, non-Hispanic/Latino; 5 Hispanic/Latino; 1 Two or more races, non-Hispanic/Latino), 18 international. Average age 34. 110 applicants, 52% accepted, 29 enrolled. In 2017, 59 master's, 6 other advanced degrees awarded. *Entrance requirements:* For master's, GMAT or GRE, bachelor's degree in arts, sciences, engineering, or business administration from regionally-accredited college or university with minimum GPA of 3.0; for other advanced degree, bachelor's degree in arts, sciences, engineering, or business administration from regionally-accredited college or university with minimum GPA of 3.0, college-level math, statistics, or quantitative course (for Graduate Certificate); MBA or equivalent degree from regionally-accredited college or university (for Post Master's Certificate). Additional exam requirements/recommendations for international students: Required—TOEFL (minimum score 84 iBT), IELTS (minimum score 6.5). *Application deadline:* For fall admission, 8/1 for domestic students, 5/1 for international students; for winter admission, 11/15 for domestic students, 9/1 for international students; for spring admission, 3/15 for domestic students, 1/1 for international students; for summer admission, 5/15 for domestic students. Applications are processed on a rolling basis. Application fee: $55. Electronic applications accepted. *Expenses:* Contact institution. *Financial support:* Federal Work-Study, scholarships/grants, and unspecified assistantships available. Support available to part-time students. Financial award application deadline: 3/1; financial award applicants required to submit FAFSA. *Unit head:* Dr. Scott Johnson, Dean, School of Management, 810-762-3164, Fax: 810-237-6685, E-mail: scotjohn@umflint.edu. *Application contact:* Bradley T. Maki, Director of Graduate Admissions, 810-762-3171, E-mail: bmaki@umflint.edu. Website: http://www.umflint.edu/graduateprograms/business-administration-mba

University of Minnesota, Twin Cities Campus, Carlson School of Management, Carlson Full-Time MBA Program, Minneapolis, MN 55455. Offers finance (MBA); information technology (MBA); management (MBA); marketing (MBA); medical industry orientation (MBA); supply chain and operations (MBA); JD/MBA; MBA/MPP; MBA/MSBA; MD/MBA; MHA/MBA; Pharm D/MBA. *Accreditation:* AACSB. *Faculty:* 143 full-time (42 women), 24 part-time/adjunct (6 women). *Students:* 200 full-time (63 women); includes 25 minority (4 Black or African American, non-Hispanic/Latino; 13 Asian, non-Hispanic/Latino; 5 Hispanic/Latino; 3 Two or more races, non-Hispanic/Latino), 41 international. Average age 29. 606 applicants, 45% accepted, 104 enrolled. In 2017, 85 master's awarded. *Entrance requirements:* For master's, GMAT or GRE. Additional exam requirements/recommendations for international students: Required—TOEFL (minimum score 580 paper-based; 84 iBT), IELTS (minimum score 7), PTE. *Application deadline:* For fall admission, 4/1 for domestic students, 2/1 for international students. Application fee: $75. Electronic applications accepted. *Expenses:* $19,104 per semester resident tuition; $24,468 per semester non-resident tuition; $1,138 per semester fees; $1,050 per semester student health plan; $179 per semester (for international students). *Financial support:* In 2017–18, 147 students received support, including 147 fellowships with tuition reimbursements available (averaging $23,479 per year); research assistantships with partial tuition reimbursements available, teaching assistantships with partial tuition reimbursements available, career-related internships or fieldwork, Federal Work-Study, institutionally sponsored loans, scholarships/grants, health care benefits, and unspecified assistantships also available. Financial award application deadline: 4/1; financial award applicants required to submit FAFSA. *Faculty research:* Market regulation and asset pricing, social networks and data analytics, consumer behavior, innovation and entrepreneurship, workplace wellbeing and labor relationships. *Total annual research expenditures:* $577,440. *Unit head:* Philip J. Miller, Assistant Dean, MBA and MS Programs, 612-625-5555, Fax: 612-625-1012, E-mail: mba@umn.edu. *Application contact:* Linh Gilles, Director of Admissions and Recruiting, 612-625-5555, Fax: 612-625-1012, E-mail: ftmba@umn.edu. Website: http://www.csom.umn.edu/MBA/full-time/

University of Minnesota, Twin Cities Campus, Carlson School of Management, Carlson Part-Time MBA Program, Minneapolis, MN 55455. Offers finance (MBA); information technology (MBA); management (MBA); marketing (MBA); medical industry orientation (MBA); supply chain and operations (MBA). *Program availability:* Part-time-only, evening/weekend, 100% online, blended/hybrid learning. *Faculty:* 143 full-time (42 women), 26 part-time/adjunct (6 women). *Students:* 919 part-time (291 women); includes 120 minority (14 Black or African American, non-Hispanic/Latino; 2 American Indian or Alaska Native, non-Hispanic/Latino; 55 Asian, non-Hispanic/Latino; 26 Hispanic/Latino; 1 Native Hawaiian or other Pacific Islander, non-Hispanic/Latino; 22 Two or more races, non-Hispanic/Latino), 57 international. Average age 28. 226 applicants, 85% accepted, 167 enrolled. In 2017, 289 master's awarded. *Entrance requirements:* For master's, GMAT or GRE. Additional exam requirements/recommendations for international students: Required—TOEFL (minimum score 580 paper-based; 84 iBT), IELTS (minimum score 7), PTE. *Application deadline:* For fall admission, 5/15 priority date for domestic and international students; for spring admission, 10/15 priority date for domestic and international students. Applications are processed on a rolling basis. Application fee: $75. Electronic applications accepted. *Expenses:* $1,375 per credit tuition, $314 per semester fees. *Financial support:* Applicants required to submit FAFSA. *Faculty research:* Market regulation and asset pricing, social networks and data analytics, consumer behavior, innovation and entrepreneurship, workplace wellbeing and labor relationships. *Total annual research expenditures:* $577,440. *Unit head:* Philip J. Miller, Assistant Dean, MBA and MS Programs, 612-624-2039, Fax: 612-625-1012, E-mail: mba@umn.edu. *Application contact:* Linh Gilles, Director of Admissions and Recruiting, 612-625-5555, Fax: 612-625-1012, E-mail: ptmba@umn.edu.
Website: http://www.carlsonschool.umn.edu/ptmba

University of Minnesota, Twin Cities Campus, Carlson School of Management, Doctoral Program in Business Administration, Minneapolis, MN 55455. Offers accounting (PhD); finance (PhD); information and decision sciences (PhD); marketing (PhD); strategic management and entrepreneurship (PhD); supply chain and operations (PhD); work and organizations (PhD). *Faculty:* 102 full-time (32 women). *Students:* 95 full-time (32 women); includes 10 minority (2 Black or African American, non-Hispanic/Latino; 7 Asian, non-Hispanic/Latino; 1 Hispanic/Latino), 68 international. Average age 30. 357 applicants, 6% accepted, 17 enrolled. In 2017, 14 doctorates awarded. *Degree requirements:* For doctorate, comprehensive exam, thesis/dissertation, written and oral preliminary exams, proposal defense, final defense. *Entrance requirements:* For doctorate, GMAT, GRE General Test, minimum undergraduate GPA of 3.0, graduate 3.5 (recommended). Additional exam requirements/recommendations for international students: Required—TOEFL (minimum score 600 paper-based, 100 iBT) or IELTS (minimum score 7.0). *Application deadline:* For fall admission, 12/15 for domestic students, 12/15 priority date for international students. Applications are processed on a rolling basis. Application fee: $75 ($95 for international students). Electronic applications accepted. *Expenses:* Contact institution. *Financial support:* In 2017–18, 80 students received support, including 80 fellowships with full tuition reimbursements available (averaging $13,000 per year), 73 research assistantships with full tuition reimbursements available (averaging $7,520 per year), 73 teaching assistantships with full tuition reimbursements available (averaging $7,520 per year), institutionally sponsored loans, scholarships/grants, health care benefits, unspecified assistantships, and full student service fee waivers also available. Financial award application deadline: 12/15. *Faculty research:* Finance, strategy and entrepreneurship, marketing, information and decision science, operations, accounting, supply chain, human resources and industrial relations, organizational behavior. *Unit head:* Dr. Shawn P. Curley, Director, 612-624-6546, Fax: 612-624-8221, E-mail: curley@umn.edu. *Application contact:* Sandy Herzan, Associate Director, 612-624-0875, Fax: 612-624-8221, E-mail: herza002@umn.edu.
Website: http://carlsonschool.umn.edu/degrees/phd

University of Mississippi, Graduate School, School of Business Administration, University, MS 38677. Offers business administration (MBA, PhD); finance (PhD); management (PhD); management information systems (PhD); marketing (PhD); JD/MBA. *Accreditation:* AACSB. *Faculty:* 58 full-time (15 women), 8 part-time/adjunct (3 women). *Students:* 71 full-time (26 women), 112 part-time (27 women); includes 11 minority (4 Black or African American, non-Hispanic/Latino; 3 Asian, non-Hispanic/Latino; 1 Hispanic/Latino; 3 Two or more races, non-Hispanic/Latino), 17 international. Average age 29. In 2017, 83 master's, 6 doctorates awarded. *Entrance requirements:* For master's, GMAT, minimum GPA of 3.0; for doctorate, GMAT. Additional exam requirements/recommendations for international students: Required—TOEFL. *Application deadline:* For fall admission, 2/1 priority date for domestic students; for spring admission, 11/1 for domestic students; for summer admission, 4/1 for domestic students. Applications are processed on a rolling basis. Application fee: $50. Electronic applications accepted. *Financial support:* Fellowships, career-related internships or fieldwork, scholarships/grants, tuition waivers (full), and unspecified assistantships available. Financial award application deadline: 3/1; financial award applicants required to submit FAFSA. *Unit head:* Dr. Ken Cyree, Dean, 662-915-5820, Fax: 662-915-5821, E-mail: info@bus.olemiss.edu. *Application contact:* Ashley Jones McGee, Director of MBA and MHA Administration, 662-915-5483, E-mail: ajones@olemiss.edu.
Website: http://www.olemissbusiness.com/

University of Missouri, Office of Research and Graduate Studies, Robert J. Trulaske, Sr. College of Business, Program in Business Administration, Columbia, MO 65211. Offers business administration (MBA); executive business administration (MBA); finance (PhD); management (PhD); marketing (PhD); MBA/JD; MBA/MHA; MBA/MSIE. *Accreditation:* AACSB. *Degree requirements:* For doctorate, thesis/dissertation. *Entrance requirements:* For master's and doctorate, GMAT, minimum GPA of 3.0. Additional exam requirements/recommendations for international students: Required—TOEFL (minimum score 500 paper-based; 61 iBT). Electronic applications accepted.

University of Missouri–St. Louis, College of Business Administration, St. Louis, MO 63121. Offers accounting (M Acc); business administration (MBA, DBA, PhD, Certificate), including logistics and supply chain management (PhD); business intelligence (Certificate); cybersecurity (Certificate); digital and social media marketing (Certificate); human resources management (Certificate); information systems (MS); logistics and supply chain management (Certificate); marketing management (Certificate). *Program availability:* Part-time, evening/weekend. *Faculty:* 51 full-time (21 women), 25 part-time/adjunct (5 women). *Students:* 146 full-time (77 women), 326 part-time (143 women); includes 82 minority (32 Black or African American, non-Hispanic/Latino; 1 American Indian or Alaska Native, non-Hispanic/Latino; 34 Asian, non-Hispanic/Latino; 11 Hispanic/Latino; 4 Two or more races, non-Hispanic/Latino), 89 international. 276 applicants, 83% accepted, 142 enrolled. *Degree requirements:* For doctorate, thesis/dissertation. *Entrance requirements:* For master's, GMAT, 2 letters of recommendation; for doctorate, GMAT or GRE, 3 letters of recommendation. Additional exam requirements/recommendations for international students: Recommended—TOEFL (minimum score 550 paper-based; 79 iBT), IELTS (minimum score 6.5). *Application deadline:* For fall admission, 7/1 priority date for domestic and international students; for spring admission, 12/1 priority date for domestic and international students. Applications are processed on a rolling basis. Application fee: $50 ($40 for international students). Electronic applications accepted. *Expenses:* Tuition, state resident: part-time

$476.50 per credit hour. Tuition, nonresident: part-time $1169.70 per credit hour. *Financial support:* Research assistantships with tuition reimbursements, teaching assistantships with tuition reimbursements, career-related internships or fieldwork, Federal Work-Study, and institutionally sponsored loans available. Support available to part-time students. Financial award application deadline: 4/1; financial award applicants required to submit FAFSA. *Faculty research:* Statistical decision aids, commercial banking, corporate finance, operations management, information systems. *Unit head:* Charles E. Hoffman, Dean, 314-516-6109, Fax: 314-516-6420. *Application contact:* 314-516-5458, Fax: 314-516-6996, E-mail: gradadm@umsl.edu.
Website: http://www.umsl.edu/divisions/business/

University of Nebraska at Kearney, College of Business and Technology, Department of Business, Kearney, NE 68849-0001. Offers accounting (MBA); generalist (MBA); human resources (MBA); human services (MBA); marketing (MBA). *Accreditation:* AACSB. *Program availability:* Part-time, evening/weekend. *Degree requirements:* For master's, thesis optional, capstone course. *Entrance requirements:* For master's, GRE or GMAT (if no significant managerial experience), letters of recommendation, essay, resume. Additional exam requirements/recommendations for international students: Recommended—TOEFL (minimum score 550 paper-based; 79 iBT), IELTS (minimum score 6.5). Electronic applications accepted. *Faculty research:* Small business financial management, employment law, expert systems, international trade and marketing, environmental economics.

University of Nebraska–Lincoln, Graduate College, College of Arts and Sciences, Department of Communication Studies, Lincoln, NE 68588. Offers instructional communication (MA, PhD); interpersonal communication (MA, PhD); marketing, communication studies, and advertising (MA, PhD); organizational communication (MA, PhD); rhetoric and culture (MA, PhD). *Degree requirements:* For master's, thesis optional; for doctorate, comprehensive exam, thesis/dissertation. *Entrance requirements:* For master's and doctorate, GRE General Test, writing sample. Additional exam requirements/recommendations for international students: Required—TOEFL (minimum score 600 paper-based). Electronic applications accepted. *Faculty research:* Message strategies, gender communication, political communication, organizational communication, instructional communication.

University of Nebraska–Lincoln, Graduate College, College of Business Administration, Interdepartmental Area of Business, Department of Marketing, Lincoln, NE 68588. Offers business (MA, PhD). *Degree requirements:* For doctorate, comprehensive exam, thesis/dissertation. *Entrance requirements:* For master's and doctorate, GMAT. Additional exam requirements/recommendations for international students: Required—TOEFL. Electronic applications accepted. *Faculty research:* Channel information, marketing research methodology, sales management, cross-cultural marketing, impact of new technology.

University of Nebraska–Lincoln, Graduate College, College of Journalism and Mass Communications, Lincoln, NE 68588. Offers marketing, communication and advertising (MA); professional journalism (MA). *Program availability:* Online learning. *Degree requirements:* For master's, thesis. *Entrance requirements:* For master's, samples of work. Additional exam requirements/recommendations for international students: Required—TOEFL (minimum score 600 paper-based). Electronic applications accepted. *Faculty research:* Interactive media and the Internet, community newspapers, children's radio, advertising involvement, telecommunications policy.

University of New Brunswick Fredericton, School of Graduate Studies, Faculty of Forestry and Environmental Management, Fredericton, NB E3B 5A3, Canada. Offers ecological foundations of forest management (PhD); environmental management (MEM); forest engineering (M Sc FE, MFE); forest products marketing (MBA); forest resources (M Sc F, MF, PhD). *Program availability:* Part-time. *Degree requirements:* For master's, thesis; for doctorate, thesis/dissertation. *Entrance requirements:* For master's and doctorate, minimum GPA of 3.0. Additional exam requirements/recommendations for international students: Required—TOEFL (minimum score 550 paper-based; 80 iBT), IELTS (minimum score 7), TWE (minimum score 4). Electronic applications accepted. *Faculty research:* Forest machines, soils, and ecosystems; integrated forest management; forest meteorology; wood engineering; stream ecosystems dynamics; forest and natural resources policy; forest operations planning; wood technology and mechanics; forest road construction and engineering; forest, wildlife, insect, bird, and fire ecology; remote sensing; insect impacts; silviculture; LiDAR analytics; integrated pest management; forest tree genetics; genetic resource conservation and sustainable management.

University of New Haven, Graduate School, College of Business, Program in Business Administration, West Haven, CT 06516. Offers accounting (MBA); business administration (MBA); business intelligence (MBA); business policy and strategic leadership (MBA); finance (MBA), including chartered financial analyst; global marketing (MBA); human resources management (MBA); sport management (MBA). *Accreditation:* AACSB. *Program availability:* Part-time, evening/weekend. *Students:* 123 full-time (56 women), 67 part-time (28 women); includes 53 minority (27 Black or African American, non-Hispanic/Latino; 11 Asian, non-Hispanic/Latino; 12 Hispanic/Latino; 3 Two or more races, non-Hispanic/Latino), 50 international. Average age 28. 148 applicants, 89% accepted, 67 enrolled. In 2017, 106 master's awarded. *Entrance requirements:* For master's, GMAT. Additional exam requirements/recommendations for international students: Required—TOEFL (minimum score 80 iBT), IELTS, PTE. *Application deadline:* Applications are processed on a rolling basis. Application fee: $50. Electronic applications accepted. Application fee is waived when completed online. *Expenses:* Tuition: Full-time $16,020; part-time $890 per credit hour. Required fees: $220; $90 per term. *Financial support:* Research assistantships with partial tuition reimbursements, teaching assistantships with partial tuition reimbursements, career-related internships or fieldwork, Federal Work-Study, scholarships/grants, and unspecified assistantships available. Support available to part-time students. Financial award applicants required to submit FAFSA. *Unit head:* Darell Singleterry, Director, 203-932-1085, E-mail: dsingleterry@newhaven.edu. *Application contact:* Michelle Mason, Director of Graduate Enrollment, 203-932-7067, E-mail: mmason@newhaven.edu.
Website: http://www.newhaven.edu/business/graduate-programs/mba/index.php
See Display on page 154 and Close-Up on page 185.

University of New Mexico, Anderson School of Management, Department of Marketing, Information Systems, Information Assurance, and Operations Management, Albuquerque, NM 87131. Offers information assurance (MBA); information systems and assurance (MS); management information systems (MBA); marketing management (MBA); operations management (MBA). *Program availability:* Part-time. *Faculty:* 16 full-time (4 women), 12 part-time/adjunct (6 women). In 2017, 68 master's awarded. *Entrance requirements:* For master's, GMAT or GRE, minimum GPA of 3.0 on last 60 hours of coursework; bachelor's degree from regionally-accredited college or university in U.S. or its equivalent in another country. Additional exam requirements/recommendations for international students: Required—TOEFL (minimum score 550 paper-based; 79 iBT), IELTS (minimum score 6.5). *Application deadline:* For fall admission, 4/1 priority date for domestic and international students; for spring admission, 10/1 priority date for domestic and international students. Applications are processed on a rolling basis. Application fee: $50. Electronic applications accepted.

Marketing

Expenses: Contact institution. *Financial support:* In 2017–18, 23 students received support, including 13 fellowships (averaging $16,320 per year), 12 research assistantships with partial tuition reimbursements available (averaging $15,180 per year); career-related internships or fieldwork, Federal Work-Study, scholarships/grants, and unspecified assistantships also available. Support available to part-time students. Financial award application deadline: 6/1; financial aid applicants required to submit FAFSA. *Faculty research:* Marketing, operations management, information systems, information assurance. *Unit head:* Dr. Mary Margaret Rogers, Chair, 505-277-6471, E-mail: mmrogers@unm.edu. *Application contact:* Lisa Beauchene, Student Recruitment Specialist, 505-277-6471, E-mail: andersonadvising@unm.edu. Website: https://www.mgt.unm.edu/mids/default.asp?mm-faculty

The University of North Carolina at Chapel Hill, Kenan-Flagler Business School, Doctoral Program in Business Administration, Chapel Hill, NC 27599. Offers accounting (PhD); finance (PhD); marketing (PhD); operations management (PhD); organizational behavior (PhD); strategy (PhD). *Accreditation:* AACSB. *Degree requirements:* For doctorate, thesis/dissertation. *Entrance requirements:* For doctorate, GMAT or GRE General Test. Electronic applications accepted. *Expenses:* Contact institution.

The University of North Carolina at Greensboro, Graduate School, Bryan School of Business and Economics, Department of Consumer, Apparel, and Retail Studies, Greensboro, NC 27412-5001. Offers MS, PhD. *Degree requirements:* For master's, one foreign language; for doctorate, one foreign language, thesis/dissertation. *Entrance requirements:* For master's and doctorate, GRE General Test. Additional exam requirements/recommendations for international students: Required—TOEFL. Electronic applications accepted. *Faculty research:* Impact of phosphate removal, protective clothing for pesticide workers, fabric hand: subjective and objective measurements.

University of North Texas, Robert B. Toulouse School of Graduate Studies, Denton, TX 76203-5459. Offers accounting (MS); applied anthropology (MA, MS); applied behavior analysis (Certificate); applied geography (MA); applied technology and performance improvement (M Ed, MS); art education (MA); art history (MA); art museum education (Certificate); arts leadership (Certificate); audiology (Au D); behavior analysis (MS); behavioral science (PhD); biochemistry and molecular biology (MS); biology (MA, MS); biomedical engineering (MS); business analysis (MS); chemistry (MS); clinical health psychology (PhD); communication studies (MA, MS); computer engineering (MS); computer science (MS); counseling (M Ed, MS), including clinical mental health counseling (MS), college and university counseling, elementary school counseling, secondary school counseling; creative writing (MA); criminal justice (MS); curriculum and instruction (M Ed); decision sciences (MBA); design (MA, MFA), including fashion design (MFA), innovation studies, interior design (MFA); early childhood studies (MS); economics (MS); educational leadership (M Ed, Ed D); educational psychology (MS, PhD), including family studies (MS), gifted and talented (MS), human development (MS), learning and cognition (MS), research, measurement and evaluation (MS); electrical engineering (MS); emergency management (MPA); engineering technology (MS); English (MA); English as a second language (MA); environmental science (MS); finance (MBA, MS); financial management (MPA); French (MA); health services management (MBA); higher education (M Ed, Ed D); history (MA, MS); hospitality management (MS); human resources management (MPA); information science (MS); information systems (PhD); information technologies (MBA); interdisciplinary studies (MA, MS); international studies (MA); international sustainable tourism (MS); jazz studies (MM); journalism (MA, MJ, Graduate Certificate), including interactive and virtual digital communication (Graduate Certificate), narrative journalism (Graduate Certificate), public relations (Graduate Certificate); kinesiology (MS); linguistics (MA); local government management (MPA); logistics (PhD); logistics and supply chain management (MBA); long-term care, senior housing, and aging services (MA); management (PhD); marketing (MBA); mathematics (MA, MS); mechanical and energy engineering (MS, PhD); music (MA), including ethnomusicology, music theory, musicology, performance; music composition (PhD); music education (MM Ed, PhD); nonprofit management (MPA); operations and supply chain management (MBA); performance (MM, DMA); philosophy (MA); political science (MA); professional and technical communication (MA); radio, television and film (MA, MFA); rehabilitation counseling (Certificate); sociology (MA); Spanish (MA); special education (M Ed); speech-language pathology (MA); strategic management (MBA); studio art (MFA); teaching (M Ed); MBA/MS. *Program availability:* Part-time, evening/weekend, online learning. Terminal master's awarded for partial completion of doctoral program. *Degree requirements:* For master's, variable foreign language requirement, comprehensive exam (for some programs), thesis (for some programs); for doctorate, variable foreign language requirement, comprehensive exam (for some programs), thesis/dissertation; for other advanced degree, variable foreign language requirement, comprehensive exam (for some programs). *Entrance requirements:* For master's and doctorate, GRE, GMAT. Additional exam requirements/recommendations for international students: Required—TOEFL (minimum score 550 paper-based; 79 iBT). Electronic applications accepted.

University of Notre Dame, Mendoza College of Business, Master of Business Administration Program, Notre Dame, IN 46556. Offers business analytics (MBA); business leadership (MBA); consulting (MBA); corporate finance (MBA); innovation and entrepreneurship (MBA); investments (MBA); marketing (MBA); MBA/MSBA. *Accreditation:* AACSB. *Faculty:* 60 full-time (10 women), 14 part-time/adjunct (1 woman). *Students:* 294 full-time (70 women); includes 46 minority (8 Black or African American, non-Hispanic/Latino; 3 American Indian or Alaska Native, non-Hispanic/Latino; 12 Asian, non-Hispanic/Latino; 20 Hispanic/Latino; 1 Native Hawaiian or other Pacific Islander, non-Hispanic/Latino; 2 Two or more races, non-Hispanic/Latino), 74 international. Average age 29. 633 applicants, 42% accepted, 131 enrolled. In 2017, 182 master's awarded. *Entrance requirements:* For master's, GMAT or GRE, work experience, essay, four-slide presentation, two recommendations, transcripts from all colleges and/or universities attended, interview. Additional exam requirements/recommendations for international students: Required—PTE (minimum score 68), TOEFL (minimum iBT score of 109), IELTS (7.5), or documentation of at least six semesters of full-time university education in English. *Application deadline:* For fall admission, 10/17 for domestic and international students; for winter admission, 1/9 for domestic and international students; for spring admission, 2/20 for domestic and international students; for summer admission, 3/17 for domestic students. Application fee: $175. Electronic applications accepted. *Expenses:* $74,133 (for one-year MBA); $106,526 (two-year MBA); $113,050 (for MBA/MSBA). *Financial support:* In 2017–18, 251 students received support, including 247 fellowships (averaging $27,748 per year); unspecified assistantships also available. Financial award application deadline: 2/28; financial aid applicants required to submit FAFSA. *Faculty research:* Market microstructure; marketing and public policy; corporate finance and accounting; corporate governance and ethical behavior; high performing organizations. *Unit head:* Dr. Katherine Spiess, Associate Dean, Graduate Business Programs, 574-631-7236, E-mail: spiess.1@nd.edu. *Application contact:* Kristin McAndrew, Director of Admissions, Graduate Business Programs, 574-631-8488, E-mail: kmcandre@nd.edu. Website: http://mendoza.nd.edu/programs/mba-programs/

University of Oklahoma, Price College of Business, Program in Business Administration, Oklahoma City, OK 73104. Offers business administration (MBA, PhD), including accounting (PhD), business administration, entrepreneurship and economic development (PhD), finance (PhD), management and international business (PhD), management of information systems (PhD), marketing/supply chain (PhD); JD/MBA; MBA/MS. *Accreditation:* AACSB. *Program availability:* Evening/weekend. *Students:* 100 full-time (27 women), 152 part-time (30 women); includes 36 minority (2 Black or African American, non-Hispanic/Latino; 4 American Indian or Alaska Native, non-Hispanic/Latino; 10 Asian, non-Hispanic/Latino; 13 Hispanic/Latino; 7 Two or more races, non-Hispanic/Latino), 32 international. Average age 31. 247 applicants, 29% accepted, 41 enrolled. In 2017, 118 master's, 9 doctorates awarded. *Degree requirements:* For doctorate, comprehensive exam, thesis/dissertation. *Entrance requirements:* For master's, GMAT or GRE, resume, 2 essays, interview; for doctorate, GMAT or GRE, resume, statement of goals, 3 letters of recommendation. Additional exam requirements/recommendations for international students: Required—TOEFL (minimum score 100 iBT) or IELTS (minimum score 7). *Application deadline:* For fall admission, 11/1 for domestic and international students; for summer admission, 11/1 for domestic and international students. Applications are processed on a rolling basis. Application fee: $50 ($100 for international students). Electronic applications accepted. *Expenses:* Contact institution. *Financial support:* In 2017–18, 107 students received support, including 6 fellowships with partial tuition reimbursements available (averaging $2,500 per year); research assistantships with full and partial tuition reimbursements available, teaching assistantships with full and partial tuition reimbursements available, career-related internships or fieldwork, scholarships/grants, health care benefits, and unspecified assistantships also available. Support available to part-time students. Financial award application deadline: 6/1; financial aid applicants required to submit FAFSA. *Faculty research:* Energy finance; international accounting; organizational behavior and entrepreneurship; management information systems; supply chain. *Unit head:* Laku Chidambaram, Associate Dean for Academic Programs and Engagement, 405-325-8013. *Application contact:* Kate Hile, Associate Director of MBA Admissions, 405-325-4572, E-mail: khile@ou.edu. Website: http://www.ou.edu/price/divisions/graduate-programs/graduate.html

University of Oregon, Graduate School, Charles H. Lundquist College of Business, Department of Marketing, Eugene, OR 97403. Offers PhD. *Program availability:* Part-time. *Degree requirements:* For doctorate, thesis/dissertation, 2 comprehensive exams. *Entrance requirements:* For doctorate, GMAT. Additional exam requirements/recommendations for international students: Required—TOEFL. *Faculty research:* Consumer behavior, marketing research, international marketing, marketing management, price quality.

University of Pennsylvania, Wharton School, Marketing Department, Philadelphia, PA 19104. Offers MBA, PhD. Terminal master's awarded for partial completion of doctoral program. *Degree requirements:* For master's, thesis optional; for doctorate, thesis/dissertation. *Entrance requirements:* For doctorate, GMAT or GRE. *Faculty research:* Scanner data, consumer preferences, decision-making theory, modeling for marketing and e-business.

University of Phoenix–Bay Area Campus, School of Business, San Jose, CA 95134-1805. Offers accountancy (MS); accounting (MBA); business administration (MBA, DBA); energy management (MBA); global management (MBA); health care management (MBA); human resource management (MBA); human resources management (MM); management (MM); marketing (MBA); organizational leadership (DM); project management (MBA); public administration (MPA); technology management (MBA). *Accreditation:* ACBSP. *Program availability:* Evening/weekend, online learning. *Degree requirements:* For master's, thesis (for some programs). *Entrance requirements:* For master's, minimum undergraduate GPA of 3.0, 3 years of work experience. Additional exam requirements/recommendations for international students: Required—TOEFL (minimum score 550 paper-based; 79 iBT). Electronic applications accepted.

University of Phoenix–Central Valley Campus, School of Business, Fresno, CA 93720-1552. Offers accounting (MBA); business administration (MBA); global management (MBA); human resources management (MBA, MM); management (MM); marketing (MBA); public administration (MBA, MM). *Accreditation:* ACBSP.

University of Phoenix–Dallas Campus, School of Business, Dallas, TX 75251. Offers accounting (MBA); business administration (MBA); global management (MBA); human resources management (MBA, MM); management (MM); marketing (MBA); public administration (MBA, MM). *Accreditation:* ACBSP. *Program availability:* Evening/weekend, online learning. *Degree requirements:* For master's, thesis (for some programs). *Entrance requirements:* For master's, 3 years of work experience, minimum undergraduate GPA of 3.0. Additional exam requirements/recommendations for international students: Required—TOEFL (minimum score 550 paper-based; 79 iBT). Electronic applications accepted.

University of Phoenix–Hawaii Campus, School of Business, Honolulu, HI 96813-3800. Offers accounting (MBA); business administration (MBA); global management (MBA); human resources management (MBA, MM); management (MM); marketing (MBA); public administration (MBA, MM). *Accreditation:* ACBSP. *Program availability:* Evening/weekend. *Degree requirements:* For master's, thesis (for some programs). *Entrance requirements:* For master's, minimum undergraduate GPA of 3.0, 3 years of work experience. Additional exam requirements/recommendations for international students: Required—TOEFL (minimum score 550 paper-based; 79 iBT). Electronic applications accepted.

University of Phoenix–Houston Campus, School of Business, Houston, TX 77079-2004. Offers accounting (MBA); business administration (MBA); global management (MBA); human resources management (MBA, MM); management (MM); marketing (MBA); public administration (MBA, MM). *Accreditation:* ACBSP. *Program availability:* Evening/weekend, online learning. *Degree requirements:* For master's, thesis (for some programs). *Entrance requirements:* For master's, 3 years of work experience, minimum undergraduate GPA of 3.0. Additional exam requirements/recommendations for international students: Required—TOEFL (minimum score 550 paper-based; 79 iBT). Electronic applications accepted.

University of Phoenix–Las Vegas Campus, School of Business, Las Vegas, NV 89135. Offers accounting (MBA); business administration (MBA); global management (MBA); human resources management (MBA, MM); management (MM); marketing (MBA); public administration (MM). *Accreditation:* ACBSP. *Program availability:* Evening/weekend, online learning. *Degree requirements:* For master's, thesis (for some programs). *Entrance requirements:* For master's, minimum undergraduate GPA of 3.0, 3 years of work experience. Additional exam requirements/recommendations for international students: Required—TOEFL (minimum score 550 paper-based; 79 iBT). Electronic applications accepted.

University of Phoenix–Online Campus, School of Business, Phoenix, AZ 85034-7209. Offers accountancy (MS); accounting (MBA, Certificate); business administration (MBA); energy management (MBA); global management (MBA); health care management (MBA); human resource management (MBA, Certificate); human resources management (MM); management (MM); marketing (MBA, Certificate); project management (MBA, Certificate); public administration (MBA, MM); technology management (MBA). *Program availability:* Evening/weekend, online learning. *Entrance* *requirements:* Additional exam requirements/recommendations for international students: Required—TOEFL, TOEIC (Test of English as an International Communication), Berlitz Online English Proficiency Exam, PTE, or IELTS. Electronic applications accepted. *Expenses:* Contact institution.

University of Phoenix–Phoenix Campus, School of Business, Tempe, AZ 85282-2371. Offers accounting (MBA, MS, Certificate); business administration (MBA); energy management (MBA); global management (MBA); health care management (MBA); human resource management (MBA, Certificate); management (MM); marketing (MBA); project management (MBA); technology management (MBA). *Program availability:* Evening/weekend, online learning. *Entrance requirements:* Additional exam requirements/recommendations for international students: Required—TOEFL, TOEIC (Test of English as an International Communication), Berlitz Online English Proficiency Exam, PTE, or IELTS. Electronic applications accepted. *Expenses:* Contact institution.

University of Phoenix–Sacramento Valley Campus, School of Business, Sacramento, CA 95833-4334. Offers accounting (MBA); business administration (MBA); global management (MBA); human resources management (MBA, MM); management (MM); marketing (MBA); public administration (MBA, MM). *Accreditation:* ACBSP. *Program availability:* Evening/weekend. *Degree requirements:* For master's, thesis (for some programs). *Entrance requirements:* For master's, minimum undergraduate GPA of 3.0, 3 years work experience. Additional exam requirements/recommendations for international students: Required—TOEFL (minimum score 550 paper-based; 79 iBT). Electronic applications accepted.

University of Phoenix–San Antonio Campus, School of Business, San Antonio, TX 78230. Offers accounting (MBA); business administration (MBA); e-business (MBA); global management (MBA); human resources management (MBA, MM); management (MM); marketing (MBA); public administration (MBA, MM). *Accreditation:* ACBSP.

University of Phoenix–San Diego Campus, School of Business, San Diego, CA 92123. Offers accounting (MBA); business administration (MBA); global management (MBA); human resources management (MBA, MM); management (MM); marketing (MBA); public administration (MBA). *Accreditation:* ACBSP. *Program availability:* Evening/weekend. *Degree requirements:* For master's, thesis (for some programs). *Entrance requirements:* For master's, 3 years of work experience, minimum undergraduate GPA of 3.0. Additional exam requirements/recommendations for international students: Required—TOEFL (minimum score 550 paper-based; 79 iBT). Electronic applications accepted.

University of Pittsburgh, Katz Graduate School of Business, Doctoral Program in Business Administration, Pittsburgh, PA 15260. Offers accounting (PhD); business analytics and operations (PhD); finance (PhD); information systems and technology management (PhD); marketing (PhD); organizational behavior and human resources (PhD); strategic management (PhD). *Accreditation:* AACSB. *Program availability:* Evening/weekend. *Faculty:* 91 full-time (30 women), 14 part-time/adjunct (4 women). *Students:* 51 full-time (26 women), 1 (woman) part-time; includes 5 minority (1 Black or African American, non-Hispanic/Latino; 3 Asian, non-Hispanic/Latino; 1 Two or more races, non-Hispanic/Latino), 30 international. Average age 31. 337 applicants, 3% accepted, 10 enrolled. In 2017, 7 doctorates awarded. *Degree requirements:* For doctorate, comprehensive exam, thesis/dissertation, student teaching. *Entrance requirements:* For doctorate, GMAT or GRE, 3 recommendations, statement of purpose, transcripts of all previous course work and degrees. Additional exam requirements/recommendations for international students: Required—TOEFL (minimum score 100 iBT) or IELTS (minimum score 7.0). *Application deadline:* For fall admission, 1/1 for domestic and international students. Applications are processed on a rolling basis. Application fee: $50. Electronic applications accepted. *Financial support:* In 2017–18, 43 students received support, including 33 research assistantships with full tuition reimbursements available (averaging $26,500 per year), 10 teaching assistantships with full tuition reimbursements available (averaging $28,220 per year); Federal Work-Study, scholarships/grants, health care benefits, and unspecified assistantships also available. Financial award application deadline: 1/1; financial award applicants required to submit FAFSA. *Faculty research:* Accounting systems/financial reporting, corporate finance, shopper marketing/consumer behavior, management information systems, organizational behavior and entrepreneurship. *Total annual research expenditures:* $475,077. *Unit head:* Dr. Arjang A. Assad, Dean, 412-648-1556, Fax: 412-648-1552, E-mail: aassad@katz.pitt.edu. *Application contact:* Dr. Dennis Galletta, Director, 412-648-1699, Fax: 412-648-3633, E-mail: galletta@katz.pitt.edu.
Website: http://www.katz.business.pitt.edu/degrees/phd/.
See Display on page 158 and Close-Up on page 187.

University of Pittsburgh, Katz Graduate School of Business, Master of Business Administration Programs, Pittsburgh, PA 15260. Offers finance (MBA); information systems (MBA); marketing (MBA); operations (MBA); organizational behavior and human resources (MBA); strategy, environment and organizations (MBA); MBA/JD; MBA/MID; MBA/MIS; MBA/MSE. *Accreditation:* AACSB. *Program availability:* Part-time, evening/weekend, blended/hybrid learning. *Faculty:* 91 full-time (30 women), 14 part-time/adjunct (4 women). *Students:* 139 full-time (49 women), 294 part-time (94 women); includes 65 minority (27 Black or African American, non-Hispanic/Latino; 20 Asian, non-Hispanic/Latino; 11 Hispanic/Latino; 7 Two or more races, non-Hispanic/Latino), 54 international. Average age 29. 651 applicants, 44% accepted, 158 enrolled. In 2017, 217 master's awarded. *Degree requirements:* For master's, minimum GPA of 3.0. *Entrance requirements:* For master's, GMAT, GRE. Additional exam requirements/recommendations for international students: Required—TOEFL (minimum score 100 iBT) or IELTS (minimum score 7.0). *Application deadline:* For fall admission, 4/1 priority date for domestic students, 2/1 priority date for international students. Application fee: $50. Electronic applications accepted. *Financial support:* In 2017–18, 136 students received support. Scholarships/grants available. Financial award application deadline: 6/1; financial award applicants required to submit FAFSA. *Faculty research:* Accounting systems/financial reporting, corporate finance, shopper marketing/consumer behavior, management information systems, organizational behavior and entrepreneurship. *Total annual research expenditures:* $475,077. *Unit head:* Dr. Arjang A. Assad, Dean, 412-648-1556, Fax: 412-648-1552, E-mail: aassad@katz.pitt.edu. *Application contact:* Thomas Keller, Director of MBA Admissions, 412-648-1700, Fax: 412-648-1659, E-mail: mba@katz.pitt.edu.
Website: http://www.business.pitt.edu/katz/mba/
See Display on page 158 and Close-Up on page 187.

University of Pittsburgh, Katz Graduate School of Business, Master of Science in Marketing Science Program, Pittsburgh, PA 15260. Offers MS. *Program availability:* Part-time, evening/weekend. *Faculty:* 91 full-time (30 women), 14 part-time/adjunct (4 women). *Students:* 7 full-time (5 women), 1 part-time (0 women), 5 international. Average age 24. 109 applicants, 33% accepted, 7 enrolled. In 2017, 2 master's awarded. *Degree requirements:* For master's, minimum GPA of 3.0. *Entrance requirements:* For master's, GMAT, GRE. Additional exam requirements/recommendations for international students: Required—TOEFL (minimum score 100 iBT), IELTS (minimum score 7). *Application deadline:* For fall admission, 7/1 priority date for domestic students, 5/1 priority date for international students. Applications are processed on a rolling basis. Application fee: $50. Electronic applications accepted.

Expenses: Contact institution. *Financial support:* Scholarships/grants available. Financial award application deadline: 6/1; financial award applicants required to submit FAFSA. *Faculty research:* Accounting systems/financial reporting, corporate finance, shopper marketing/consumer behavior, management information systems, organizational behavior and entrepreneurship. *Total annual research expenditures:* $475,077. *Unit head:* Dr. Arjang A. Assad, Dean, 412-648-1556, Fax: 412-648-1552, E-mail: aassad@katz.pitt.edu. *Application contact:* Thomas Keller, Director of MBA Admissions, 412-648-1700, Fax: 412-648-1659, E-mail: mba@katz.pitt.edu.
Website: https://www.katz.business.pitt.edu/degrees/ms/marketing-science

University of Portland, Dr. Robert B. Pamplin, Jr. School of Business, Portland, OR 97203-5798. Offers entrepreneurship (MBA); finance (MBA, MS); health care management (MBA); marketing (MBA); nonprofit management (EMBA); operations and technology management (MBA, MS); sustainability (MBA). *Accreditation:* AACSB. *Program availability:* Part-time, evening/weekend. *Entrance requirements:* For master's, GMAT, minimum GPA of 3.0, resume, 2 letters of recommendation. Additional exam requirements/recommendations for international students: Required—TOEFL (minimum score 570 paper-based; 89 iBT), IELTS (minimum score 7). *Expenses:* Contact institution.

University of Puerto Rico–Río Piedras, College of Business Administration, San Juan, PR 00931-3300. Offers accounting (MBA); finance (MBA, PhD); general business (MBA); human resources management (MBA); international trade and business (MBA, PhD); marketing (MBA); operations management (MBA); quantitative methods (MBA). *Accreditation:* AACSB. *Program availability:* Part-time. *Degree requirements:* For master's, comprehensive exam, thesis or alternative, research project. *Entrance requirements:* For master's, GMAT or PAEG, minimum GPA of 3.0, letter of recommendation; for doctorate, GMAT, PAEG, minimum GPA of 3.0, master degree. *Faculty research:* Management.

University of Rhode Island, Graduate School, College of Business, Program in Business Administration, Kingston, RI 02881. Offers finance (MBA); general business (MBA); management (MBA); marketing (MBA, PhD); operations and supply chain management (PhD); supply chain management (MBA); Pharm D/MBA. *Faculty:* 34 full-time (13 women). *Students:* 47 full-time (13 women), 146 part-time (72 women); includes 22 minority (3 Black or African American, non-Hispanic/Latino; 1 American Indian or Alaska Native, non-Hispanic/Latino; 11 Asian, non-Hispanic/Latino; 6 Hispanic/Latino; 1 Two or more races, non-Hispanic/Latino), 16 international. 131 applicants, 59% accepted, 58 enrolled. In 2017, 94 master's, 1 doctorate awarded. *Entrance requirements:* Additional exam requirements/recommendations for international students: Required—TOEFL. *Application deadline:* For fall admission, 6/30 for domestic students; for spring admission, 10/31 for domestic students; for summer admission, 3/31 for domestic students. Electronic applications accepted. *Expenses:* Tuition, state resident: full-time $12,706; part-time $786 per credit. Tuition, nonresident: full-time $25,216; part-time $1401 per credit. *Required fees:* $1598; $45 per credit. One-time fee: $30 part-time. *Financial support:* In 2017–18, 15 teaching assistantships (averaging $16,541 per year) were awarded. Financial award application deadline: 2/1. *Unit head:* Lisa Lancellotta, Coordinator, MBA Programs, 401-874-4241, E-mail: mba@uri.edu.

University of Rochester, Simon Business School, Doctoral Program in Business Administration, Rochester, NY 14627. Offers accounting (PhD); computer information systems (PhD); finance (PhD); marketing (PhD); operations management (PhD). *Accreditation:* AACSB. *Faculty:* 70 full-time (12 women), 23 part-time/adjunct (6 women). *Students:* 50 full-time (17 women); includes 2 minority (both Asian, non-Hispanic/Latino), 41 international. Average age 28. 199 applicants, 10% accepted, 9 enrolled. In 2017, 8 doctorates awarded. *Degree requirements:* For doctorate, comprehensive exam, thesis/dissertation, qualifying exam. *Entrance requirements:* For doctorate, GMAT or GRE. Additional exam requirements/recommendations for international students: Required—TOEFL. *Application deadline:* For fall admission, 1/5 for domestic and international students. Application fee: $100. Electronic applications accepted. *Expenses:* Contact institution. *Financial support:* In 2017–18, 50 students received support. Fellowships, research assistantships, teaching assistantships, health care benefits, and tuition waivers (full) available. Financial award application deadline: 1/5. *Faculty research:* Empirical industrial organization, risk management, financial disclosure and regulation, social media, health care management. *Unit head:* Dr. Ron Kaniel, Committee Chair, 585-275-2959. *Application contact:* Sue Harris, PhD Administrator, 585-275-2959, E-mail: phdoffice@simon.rochester.edu.
Website: http://www.simon.rochester.edu/programs/phd/index.aspx

University of Rochester, Simon Business School, Full-Time Master's Program in Business Administration, Rochester, NY 14627. Offers business systems consulting (MBA); competitive and organizational strategy (MBA); computers and information systems (MBA); corporate accounting (MBA); entrepreneurship (MBA); finance (MBA); health sciences management (MBA); marketing (MBA); operations management (MBA); public accounting (MBA); strategy and organizations (MBA). *Accreditation:* AACSB. *Faculty:* 70 full-time (12 women), 23 part-time/adjunct (6 women). *Students:* 208 full-time (70 women). Average age 28. *Entrance requirements:* For master's, GMAT or GRE. *Application deadline:* For fall admission, 10/15 for domestic and international students; for winter admission, 1/5 for domestic and international students; for spring admission, 3/15 for domestic and international students; for summer admission, 5/15 for domestic and international students. Application fee: $150. *Financial support:* Fellowships, institutionally sponsored loans, scholarships/grants, and tuition waivers (full and partial) available. Financial award application deadline: 1/5; financial award applicants required to submit FAFSA. *Faculty research:* Empirical industrial organization, risk management, financial disclosure and regulation, social media, health care management. *Unit head:* Andrew Ainslie, Dean, 585-275-3316, E-mail: andrew.ainslie@simon.rochester.edu. *Application contact:* Rebekah S. Lewin, Assistant Dean of Admissions and Financial Aid, 585-275-3533, E-mail: admissions@simon.rochester.edu.
Website: http://www.simon.rochester.edu/programs/full-time-mba/index.aspx

University of Rochester, Simon Business School, Part-Time MBA Program, Rochester, NY 14627. Offers business systems consulting (MBA); competitive and organizational strategy (MBA); computers and information systems (MBA); corporate accounting (MBA); entrepreneurship (MBA); finance (MBA); health sciences management (MBA); marketing (MBA), including brand management, marketing strategy, pricing; operations management (MBA); public accounting (MBA). *Program availability:* Part-time-only, evening/weekend. *Faculty:* 70 full-time (12 women), 23 part-time/adjunct (6 women). *Students:* 159 part-time (62 women); includes 25 minority (5 Black or African American, non-Hispanic/Latino; 9 Asian, non-Hispanic/Latino; 9 Hispanic/Latino; 2 Two or more races, non-Hispanic/Latino), 4 international. Average age 32. 39 applicants, 92% accepted, 35 enrolled. In 2017, 59 master's awarded. *Entrance requirements:* For master's, GRE or GMAT. *Application deadline:* For fall admission, 8/1 for domestic students; for spring admission, 2/15 for domestic students. Applications are processed on a rolling basis. Application fee: $150. Electronic applications accepted. *Expenses:* $1,875 per credit, $1,385 fees. *Financial support:* In 2017–18, 69 students received support. Tuition waivers (partial) available. Financial award application deadline: 8/1. *Unit head:* Andrew Ainslie, Dean, 585-275-3316, E-mail: andrew.ainslie@simon.rochester.edu. *Application contact:* Molly Mesko, Executive Director, EMBA and Part-Time Programs, 585-275-4277, E-mail: molly.mesko@simon.rochester.edu.
Website: http://www.simon.rochester.edu/programs/ptmba/index.aspx

Marketing

University of Saint Mary, Graduate Programs, Program in Business Administration, Leavenworth, KS 66048-5082. Offers enterprise risk management (MBA); finance (MBA); general management (MBA); health care management (MBA); human resource management (MBA); marketing and advertising management (MBA). *Program availability:* Part-time, evening/weekend, 100% online, blended/hybrid learning. *Degree requirements:* For master's, thesis. *Entrance requirements:* For master's, minimum undergraduate GPA of 2.75, official transcripts, two letters of recommendation. Electronic applications accepted. *Expenses:* Contact institution.

University of San Francisco, School of Management, Master of Business Administration Program, San Francisco, CA 94117. Offers entrepreneurship and innovation (MBA); finance (MBA); marketing (MBA); organization development (MBA); DDS/MBA; JD/MBA; MBA/MAPS. *Accreditation:* AACSB. *Program availability:* Part-time, evening/weekend. *Entrance requirements:* For master's, GMAT or GRE, resume (two years of professional work experience required for part-time students, preferred for full-time), transcripts from each college or university attended, two letters of recommendation, personal statement, interview. Additional exam requirements/recommendations for international students: Required—TOEFL (minimum score 600 paper-based, 100 iBT), IELTS (minimum score 7) or PTE (minimum score 68). Electronic applications accepted. *Expenses:* Contact institution. *Faculty research:* International financial markets, technology transfer licensing, international marketing, strategic planning.

University of Saskatchewan, College of Graduate Studies and Research, Edwards School of Business, Department of Management and Marketing, Saskatoon, SK S7N 5A2, Canada. Offers marketing (M Sc). *Program availability:* Part-time. *Degree requirements:* For master's, thesis. *Entrance requirements:* For master's, GMAT. Additional exam requirements/recommendations for international students: Required—TOEFL.

The University of Scranton, Kania School of Management, Program in Business Administration, Scranton, PA 18510. Offers accounting (MBA); finance (MBA); general business administration (MBA); health care management (MBA); international business (MBA); management information systems (MBA); marketing (MBA); operations management (MBA). *Accreditation:* AACSB. *Program availability:* Part-time, evening/weekend, 100% online. *Entrance requirements:* For master's, GMAT (for MBA). *Faculty research:* Financial markets, strategic impact of total quality management, internal accounting controls, consumer preference, information systems and the Internet.

University of Sioux Falls, Vucurevich School of Business, Sioux Falls, SD 57105-1699. Offers entrepreneurial leadership (MBA); general management (MBA); health care management (MBA); marketing (MBA). *Program availability:* Part-time, evening/weekend. *Degree requirements:* For master's, project. *Entrance requirements:* For master's, minimum GPA of 3.0. Additional exam requirements/recommendations for international students: Required—TOEFL. *Expenses:* Contact institution.

University of South Africa, College of Economic and Management Sciences, Pretoria, South Africa. Offers accounting (D Admin, D Com); accounting science (DA); auditing (D Admin, D Com); business administration (M Tech); business economics (D Admin); business leadership (DBL); business management (D Admin, D Com); economic management analysis (M Tech); economics (D Admin, D Com, PhD); human resource development (M Tech); industrial psychology (D Admin, D Com, PhD); logistics (D Com); marketing (M Tech); public administration (D Admin, D Com, DPA, PhD); public management (M Tech); quantitative management (D Admin, D Com); real estate (M Tech); statistics (D Admin, PhD); tourism management (D Admin, D Com); transport economics (D Admin, D Com).

University of South Alabama, Mitchell College of Business, Program in Business Administration, Mobile, AL 36688. Offers business administration (MBA); management (DBA); marketing (DBA). *Accreditation:* AACSB. *Program availability:* Part-time, evening/weekend. *Faculty:* 9 full-time (2 women). *Students:* 67 full-time (35 women), 8 part-time (1 woman); includes 15 minority (7 Black or African American, non-Hispanic/Latino; 1 American Indian or Alaska Native, non-Hispanic/Latino; 5 Asian, non-Hispanic/Latino; 2 Hispanic/Latino), 8 international. Average age 34. 74 applicants, 43% accepted, 26 enrolled. In 2017, 18 master's, 2 doctorates awarded. *Degree requirements:* For master's, comprehensive exam; for doctorate, comprehensive exam, thesis/dissertation. *Entrance requirements:* For master's, GMAT (minimum score of 450, 3.0 in Analytical Writing section), minimum undergraduate GPA of 3.0; for doctorate, MBA/specialized master's degree, 5 years of professional experience, 3 letters of reference, curriculum vitae, interview. Additional exam requirements/recommendations for international students: Required—TOEFL (minimum score 525 paper-based; 71 iBT). *Application deadline:* For fall admission, 7/15 for domestic students, 6/15 for international students; for spring admission, 12/1 for domestic students; for summer admission, 1/31 for domestic students. Application fee: $35. Electronic applications accepted. *Expenses:* Contact institution. *Financial support:* Research assistantships and unspecified assistantships available. Support available to part-time students. Financial award application deadline: 3/31; financial award applicants required to submit FAFSA. *Unit head:* Dr. Bob Wood, Dean of Business, 251-460-7167, Fax: 251-460-6529, E-mail: bgwood@southalabama.edu. *Application contact:* Dr. Alex Sharland, Assistant Dean and Director of Graduate Studies, 251-460-6418, Fax: 251-460-6529, E-mail: mcobgraduate@southalabama.edu.

University of South Dakota, Graduate School, Beacom School of Business, Department of Business Administration, Vermillion, SD 57069. Offers business administration (MBA); business analytics (MBA, Graduate Certificate); health services administration (MBA); long term care management (Graduate Certificate); marketing (MBA, Graduate Certificate); operations and supply chain management (MBA, Graduate Certificate); JD/MBA. *Accreditation:* AACSB. *Program availability:* Part-time, blended/hybrid learning. *Degree requirements:* For master's, thesis or alternative. *Entrance requirements:* For master's, GMAT, minimum GPA of 2.7, resume. Additional exam requirements/recommendations for international students: Required—TOEFL (minimum score 550 paper-based; 79 iBT), IELTS (minimum score 6). *Application deadline:* For fall admission, 6/1 priority date for domestic students, 5/1 priority date for international students; for spring admission, 10/1 priority date for domestic students, 9/1 priority date for international students; for summer admission, 3/1 priority date for domestic students. Applications are processed on a rolling basis. Application fee: $35. Electronic applications accepted. *Expenses:* Contact institution. *Financial support:* Research assistantships with partial tuition reimbursements, teaching assistantships with partial tuition reimbursements, career-related internships or fieldwork, Federal Work-Study, and unspecified assistantships available. Financial award applicants required to submit FAFSA. *Application contact:* Graduate School, 605-658-6140, Fax: 605-677-6118, E-mail: grad@usd.edu.
Website: http://www.usd.edu/business/business-administration/graduate

University of South Florida, Muma College of Business, Department of Marketing, Tampa, FL 33620-9951. Offers business administration (PhD), including marketing; marketing (MSM); sport and entertainment management (MS). *Program availability:* Part-time, evening/weekend. *Faculty:* 15 full-time (3 women). *Students:* 55 full-time (23 women), 17 part-time (10 women); includes 5 minority (1 Asian, non-Hispanic/Latino; 3 Hispanic/Latino; 1 Two or more races, non-Hispanic/Latino), 44 international. Average

age 25. 89 applicants, 66% accepted, 39 enrolled. In 2017, 41 master's, 3 doctorates awarded. Terminal master's awarded for partial completion of doctoral program. *Degree requirements:* For master's, comprehensive exam, thesis or alternative; for doctorate, comprehensive exam, thesis/dissertation. *Entrance requirements:* For master's, GMAT or GRE, minimum GPA of 3.0 in upper-division undergraduate and marketing coursework, two letters of recommendation; for doctorate, GMAT or GRE, personal statement, recommendations, interview. Additional exam requirements/recommendations for international students: Required—TOEFL (minimum score 550 paper-based; 79 iBT) or IELTS (minimum score 6.5). *Application deadline:* For fall admission, 1/2 for domestic and international students; for spring admission, 10/15 for domestic students, 7/1 for international students. Applications are processed on a rolling basis. Application fee: $30. Electronic applications accepted. *Financial support:* In 2017–18, 6 students received support, including 5 research assistantships (averaging $14,943 per year), 6 teaching assistantships (averaging $11,972 per year); health care benefits and unspecified assistantships also available. *Faculty research:* Branding; consumer behavior; marketing communications' effectiveness; customer satisfaction; customer delight; consumer reactions to new technology, products and services; consumer emotions; brand strategies; communications; advertising effectiveness; green alliances; strategic marketing; international business; international marketing; consumer research; customer service branding; focus group research; market surveys; market research; promotion; services marketing; strategic planning. *Total annual research expenditures:* $17,504. *Unit head:* Dr. Anand Kumar, Interim Department Chair/Associate Professor, 813-974-6205, Fax: 813-974-6175, E-mail: akumar@usf.edu. *Application contact:* Stacee Bender, 813-974-4516, Fax: 813-974-6175, E-mail: staceebender@usf.edu.
Website: http://business.usf.edu/departments/marketing/

The University of Tampa, Sykes College of Business, Tampa, FL 33606-1490. Offers accounting (MS); business analytics (MBA); cybersecurity (MBA, MS); entrepreneurship (MBA, MS); finance (MBA, MS); information systems management (MBA); innovation management (MBA); international business (MBA); marketing (MBA, MS); nonprofit management (MBA, Certificate). *Accreditation:* AACSB. *Program availability:* Part-time, evening/weekend. *Faculty:* 38 full-time (14 women), 6 part-time/adjunct (1 woman). *Students:* 229 full-time (1 woman), 115 part-time (51 women); includes 51 minority (26 Black or African American, non-Hispanic/Latino; 11 Asian, non-Hispanic/Latino; 1 Native Hawaiian or other Pacific Islander, non-Hispanic/Latino; 13 Two or more races, non-Hispanic/Latino), 182 international. Average age 28. 1,305 applicants, 39% accepted, 192 enrolled. In 2017, 266 master's awarded. *Degree requirements:* For master's, capstone. *Entrance requirements:* For master's, GMAT or GRE, official transcripts from all colleges and/or universities previously attended, resume, personal statement, letters of recommendation. Additional exam requirements/recommendations for international students: Required—TOEFL (minimum score 577 paper-based; 90 iBT), IELTS (minimum score 7.5). *Application deadline:* Applications are processed on a rolling basis. Application fee: $40. Electronic applications accepted. *Expenses:* Contact institution. *Financial support:* In 2017–18, 116 students received support. Career-related internships or fieldwork, scholarships/grants, and unspecified assistantships available. Financial award applicants required to submit FAFSA. *Faculty research:* Job market signaling, on-line shopping behaviors and social media, the Tampa Bay economy, digital literacy, entrepreneurship in small businesses. *Unit head:* Dr. Natasha F. Veltri, Associate Dean, 813-253-6289, E-mail: nveltri@ut.edu. *Application contact:* Chanelle Cox, Staff Assistant, Admissions for Graduate and Continuing Studies, 813-253-6249, E-mail: ccox@ut.edu.
Website: http://www.ut.edu/business/

The University of Tennessee, Graduate School, College of Business Administration, Program in Business Administration, Knoxville, TN 37996. Offers accounting (PhD); finance (MBA, PhD); logistics and transportation (MBA, PhD); management (PhD); marketing (MBA, PhD); operations management (MBA); professional business administration (MBA); statistics (PhD); JD/MBA; MS/MBA; Pharm D/MBA. Pharm D/MBA offered jointly with The University of Tennessee Health Science Center. *Accreditation:* AACSB. *Program availability:* Online learning. *Degree requirements:* For master's, thesis or alternative; for doctorate, thesis/dissertation. *Entrance requirements:* For master's and doctorate, GMAT, minimum GPA of 2.7. Additional exam requirements/recommendations for international students: Required—TOEFL. Electronic applications accepted.

The University of Texas at Arlington, Graduate School, College of Business, Department of Marketing, Arlington, TX 76019. Offers marketing (MBA); marketing research (MS). *Program availability:* Part-time, evening/weekend. *Degree requirements:* For master's, thesis optional. *Entrance requirements:* For master's, GMAT, GRE. Additional exam requirements/recommendations for international students: Required—TOEFL (minimum score 550 paper-based; 79 iBT). Electronic applications accepted. *Faculty research:* Marketing strategy, marketing research, international marketing.

The University of Texas at Austin, Graduate School, McCombs School of Business, Department of Marketing, Austin, TX 78712-1111. Offers MBA, MS, PhD. *Degree requirements:* For doctorate, comprehensive exam, thesis/dissertation. *Entrance requirements:* For doctorate, GMAT or GRE. Electronic applications accepted. *Faculty research:* Internet marketing, strategic marketing, buy behavior.

The University of Texas at Dallas, Naveen Jindal School of Management, Program in Marketing, Richardson, TX 75080. Offers marketing (MS). *Program availability:* Part-time, evening/weekend. *Faculty:* 14 full-time (2 women), 5 part-time/adjunct (2 women). *Students:* 100 full-time (63 women), 35 part-time (23 women); includes 29 minority (3 Black or African American, non-Hispanic/Latino; 1 American Indian or Alaska Native, non-Hispanic/Latino; 14 Asian, non-Hispanic/Latino; 9 Hispanic/Latino; 2 Two or more races, non-Hispanic/Latino), 75 international. Average age 26. 283 applicants, 54% accepted, 60 enrolled. In 2017, 67 master's awarded. *Degree requirements:* For master's, thesis optional. *Entrance requirements:* For master's, GMAT, minimum GPA of 3.0 in upper-level coursework in field. Additional exam requirements/recommendations for international students: Required—TOEFL (minimum score 550 paper-based). *Application deadline:* For fall admission, 7/15 for domestic students, 5/1 priority date for international students; for spring admission, 11/15 for domestic students, 9/1 priority date for international students. Applications are processed on a rolling basis. Application fee: $50 ($100 for international students). Electronic applications accepted. *Expenses:* Tuition, state resident: full-time $12,916; part-time $718 per credit hour. Tuition, nonresident: full-time $25,252; part-time $1403 per credit hour. *Financial support:* In 2017–18, 34 students received support, including 1 fellowship (averaging $1,000 per year), 7 teaching assistantships with partial tuition reimbursements available (averaging $10,050 per year); research assistantships with partial tuition reimbursements available, career-related internships or fieldwork, Federal Work-Study, institutionally sponsored loans, scholarships/grants, and unspecified assistantships also available. Support available to part-time students. Financial award application deadline: 4/30; financial award applicants required to submit FAFSA. *Faculty research:* Inventory control and risk management. *Unit head:* Dr. Sanjay Jain, Area Coordinator, 972-883-5059, E-mail: sxj164830@utdallas.edu.
Website: http://jindal.utdallas.edu/marketing/

The University of Texas at San Antonio, College of Business, Department of Marketing, San Antonio, TX 78249-0617. Offers marketing (PhD); marketing management (MBA); tourism destination development (MBA). *Program availability:* Part-time, evening/weekend. *Faculty:* 10 full-time (1 woman), 1 part-time/adjunct (0 women). *Students:* 20 full-time (9 women), 8 part-time (4 women); includes 15 minority (1 Black or African American, non-Hispanic/Latino; 2 Asian, non-Hispanic/Latino; 12 Hispanic/Latino), 7 international. Average age 28. 53 applicants, 26% accepted, 11 enrolled. In 2017, 2 master's, 4 doctorates awarded. *Degree requirements:* For master's, comprehensive exam (for some programs), thesis (for some programs). *Entrance requirements:* For master's, GMAT, minimum GPA of 3.0. Additional exam requirements/recommendations for international students: Required—TOEFL (minimum score 550 paper-based; 79 iBT). *Application deadline:* For fall admission, 7/31 for domestic students, 3/1 for international students; for spring admission, 10/15 for domestic students, 9/15 for international students. Applications are processed on a rolling basis. Application fee: $50 ($90 for international students). Electronic applications accepted. *Expenses:* Tuition, state resident: full-time $5495. Tuition, nonresident: full-time $21,938. *Required fees:* $1915. Tuition and fees vary according to program. *Financial support:* Career-related internships or fieldwork, Federal Work-Study, scholarships/grants, and unspecified assistantships available. Support available to part-time students. *Faculty research:* Consumer behavior, cross-cultural research, psycholinguistics, pricing, mass media and materialism. *Total annual research expenditures:* $28,111. *Unit head:* Dr. Suman Basuroy, Department Chair, 210-458-6330, Fax: 210-458-5783, E-mail: suman.barusoy@utsa.edu. Website: http://business.utsa.edu/marketing/

The University of Texas at Tyler, College of Business and Technology, Program in Business Administration, Tyler, TX 75799-0001. Offers cyber security (MBA); engineering management (MBA); general management (MBA); healthcare management (MBA); internal assurance and consulting (MBA); marketing (MBA); oil, gas and energy (MBA); organizational development (MBA); quality management (MBA). *Accreditation:* AACSB. *Program availability:* Part-time, online learning. *Entrance requirements:* Additional exam requirements/recommendations for international students: Required—TOEFL (minimum score 550 paper-based). *Faculty research:* General business, inventory control, institutional markets, service marketing, product distribution, accounting fraud, financial reporting and recognition.

The University of Texas Rio Grande Valley, Robert C. Vackar College of Business and Entrepreneurship, Program in Business Administration, Edinburg, TX 78539. Offers business administration (MBA); finance (PhD); management (PhD); marketing (PhD). *Program availability:* Part-time, evening/weekend, online learning. *Degree requirements:* For master's, thesis optional. *Entrance requirements:* For master's, GMAT, minimum GPA of 3.0. Additional exam requirements/recommendations for international students: Required—TOEFL (minimum score 500 paper-based). Electronic applications accepted. *Expenses:* Tuition, state resident: full-time $5550; part-time $417 per credit hour. Tuition, nonresident: full-time $13,020; part-time $832 per credit hour. *Required fees:* $1169. *Faculty research:* Human resources, border region, entrepreneurship, marketing.

University of the Cumberlands, Graduate Programs in Education, Williamsburg, KY 40769-1372. Offers all grades (P-12) (M Ed); business and marketing (MA Ed, MAT); counselor education and supervision (Ed D); director of pupil personnel (Certificate); director of special education (Certificate); educational administration and supervision (Ed S); educational leadership (Ed D); elementary education (MA Ed, MAT); instructional leadership - principalship (MA Ed); instructional leadership - school principal (Certificate); middle school education (MA Ed, MAT); reading and writing (MA Ed); school counseling (MA Ed); school superintendent (Certificate); secondary education (MA Ed, MAT); special education (MAT); supervisor of instruction (Certificate); teacher leader (MA Ed). *Program availability:* Part-time, evening/weekend, online learning. *Degree requirements:* For master's, comprehensive exam. Electronic applications accepted.

University of the Sacred Heart, Graduate Programs, Department of Business Administration, Program in International Marketing, San Juan, PR 00914-0383. Offers MBA. *Program availability:* Part-time, evening/weekend. *Degree requirements:* For master's, thesis. *Entrance requirements:* For master's, EXADEP, minimum undergraduate GPA of 2.75, interview.

The University of Toledo, College of Graduate Studies, College of Business and Innovation, Department of Marketing and International Business, Toledo, OH 43606-3390. Offers MBA. *Program availability:* Part-time, evening/weekend. *Entrance requirements:* For master's, GMAT, GRE, or LSAT, minimum GPA of 2.7 for all prior academic work, three letters of recommendation, statement of purpose, transcripts from all prior institutions attended. Additional exam requirements/recommendations for international students: Required—TOEFL (minimum score 550 paper-based; 80 iBT). Electronic applications accepted.

University of Utah, Graduate School, David Eccles School of Business, Business Administration Program, Salt Lake City, UT 84112. Offers accounting (PhD); business administration (EMBA, MBA, PMBA); finance (PhD); information systems (PhD); marketing (PhD); operations management (PhD); organizational behavior (PhD); strategic management (PhD); MBA/JD; MBA/MHA; MBA/MS. *Program availability:* Part-time, evening/weekend, online learning. *Faculty:* 58 full-time (21 women), 37 part-time/adjunct (7 women). *Students:* 558 full-time (149 women), 103 part-time (21 women); includes 66 minority (1 Black or African American, non-Hispanic/Latino; 16 Asian, non-Hispanic/Latino; 41 Hispanic/Latino; 8 Two or more races, non-Hispanic/Latino), 50 international. Average age 27. 442 applicants, 70% accepted, 226 enrolled. In 2017, 298 master's, 7 doctorates awarded. *Entrance requirements:* For master's, GMAT or GRE; for doctorate, GMAT. Additional exam requirements/recommendations for international students: Required—TOEFL (minimum score 600 paper-based; 100 iBT), IELTS (minimum score 7). *Application deadline:* Applications are processed on a rolling basis. Application fee: $55 ($65 for international students). Electronic applications accepted. *Expenses:* Contact institution. *Financial support:* In 2017–18, 53 students received support. Fellowships, scholarships/grants, and unspecified assistantships available. Financial award application deadline: 2/1; financial award applicants required to submit FAFSA. *Faculty research:* Corporate finance, strategy services, consumer behavior, financial disclosures, operations. *Unit head:* Kristina Diekmann, Department Chair, 801-581-8524, Fax: 801-581-3380, E-mail: mastersinfo@business.utah.edu. *Application contact:* Christine Harris, Coordinator, 801-581-7785, Fax: 801-585-3962, E-mail: execch@business.utah.edu. Website: http://www.business.utah.edu/

University of Virginia, McIntire School of Commerce, Master's Program in Commerce, Charlottesville, VA 22903. Offers business analytics (MSC); finance (MSC); marketing and management (MSC). *Entrance requirements:* For master's, GMAT, 2 letters of recommendation; prerequisite course work in financial accounting, microeconomics, and introduction to statistics. Additional exam requirements/recommendations for international students: Required—TOEFL (minimum score 600 paper-based; 100 iBT), IELTS (minimum score 7.5). Electronic applications accepted. *Expenses:* Contact institution.

The University of Western Ontario, Richard Ivey School of Business, London, ON N6A 3K7, Canada. Offers business (EMBA, PhD); corporate strategy and leadership

elective (MBA); entrepreneurship elective (MBA); finance elective (MBA); health sector stream (MBA); international management elective (MBA); marketing elective (MBA); JD/MBA. *Degree requirements:* For master's, thesis (for some programs); for doctorate, thesis/dissertation. *Entrance requirements:* For master's, GMAT, 2 years of full-time work experience, interview. Additional exam requirements/recommendations for international students: Required—TOEFL (minimum score 100 iBT) or IELTS (minimium score 6). Electronic applications accepted. *Faculty research:* Strategy, organizational behavior, international business, finance, operations management.

University of Wisconsin–Madison, Graduate School, Wisconsin School of Business, Doctoral Program in Marketing, Madison, WI 53706-1380. Offers PhD. *Degree requirements:* For doctorate, comprehensive exam, thesis/dissertation. *Entrance requirements:* For doctorate, GMAT or GRE. Additional exam requirements/recommendations for international students: Recommended—TOEFL (minimum score 623 paper-based; 106 iBT), IELTS (minimum score 7.5), TSE (minimum score 73). Electronic applications accepted. *Expenses:* Contact institution. *Faculty research:* Marketing strategy, consumer behavior, channels of distribution, advertising, price promotions, behavioral and experimental economics, creativity and design, extensions of research involving the sense of touch, ethics.

University of Wisconsin–Whitewater, School of Graduate Studies, College of Business and Economics, Program in Business and Marketing Education, Whitewater, WI 53190-1790. Offers MS. *Accreditation:* NCATE. *Program availability:* Part-time, evening/weekend, online learning. *Degree requirements:* For master's, thesis or alternative. *Entrance requirements:* For master's, interview, teaching license. Additional exam requirements/recommendations for international students: Required—TOEFL (minimum score 550 paper-based; 80 iBT), IELTS (minimum score 6). Electronic applications accepted.

Ursuline College, School of Graduate and Professional Studies, Program in Business Administration, Pepper Pike, OH 44124-4398. Offers ethical and entrepreneurial leadership (MBA); financial planning and accounting (MBA); health services management (MBA); management (MBA); management and leadership (MBA); marketing and communications management (MBA). *Program availability:* Part-time. *Faculty:* 3 full-time (2 women), 3 part-time/adjunct (2 women). *Students:* 3 full-time (all women), 26 part-time (23 women); includes 13 minority (12 Black or African American, non-Hispanic/Latino; 1 Two or more races, non-Hispanic/Latino). Average age 38. 13 applicants, 85% accepted, 6 enrolled. In 2017, 11 master's awarded. *Degree requirements:* For master's, comprehensive exam (for some programs). *Entrance requirements:* For master's, GRE. Additional exam requirements/recommendations for international students: Required—TOEFL (minimum score 500 paper-based) or GRE. *Application deadline:* Applications are processed on a rolling basis. Application fee: $25. Electronic applications accepted. *Expenses:* $842 per credit hour. *Financial support:* In 2017–18, 3 students received support. Scholarships/grants available. Financial award application deadline: 8/1; financial award applicants required to submit FAFSA. *Faculty research:* Gift economy; sharing economy; cooperative business models; collaborative leadership; corporate social responsibility and the triple bottom line, defined as the three P's: people, planet and profit. *Unit head:* Dr. Anthony Caffarelli, Associate Professor, 440-646-8134, Fax: 440-684-6088, E-mail: tcafarelli@ursuline.edu. *Application contact:* Melanie Steele, Director of Graduate Admission, 440-646-8146, Fax: 440-684-6138, E-mail: graduateadmissions@ursuline.edu.

Vancouver Island University, Master of Business Administration Program, Nanaimo, BC V9R 5S5, Canada. Offers international business (MBA), including finance, marketing. Program offered jointly with University of Hertfordshire. *Accreditation:* ACBSP. *Program availability:* Part-time. *Degree requirements:* For master's, thesis. *Entrance requirements:* Additional exam requirements/recommendations for international students: Required—TOEFL (minimum score 88 iBT), IELTS (minimum score 6.5). Electronic applications accepted. *Expenses:* Contact institution. *Faculty research:* Tourism development, entrepreneurship, organizational development, strategic planning, international business strategy, intercultural team work.

Vanderbilt University, Vanderbilt University Owen Graduate School of Management, Master of Marketing Program, Nashville, TN 37240-1001. Offers M Mark. *Entrance requirements:* For master's, GMAT, resume, two essays, two letters of recommendation, interview. Additional exam requirements/recommendations for international students: Required—TOEFL or IELTS. Electronic applications accepted.

Vanderbilt University, Vanderbilt University Owen Graduate School of Management, Vanderbilt MBA Program, Nashville, TN 37203. Offers accounting (MBA); finance (MBA); general management (MBA); health care (MBA); human and organizational performance (MBA); marketing (MBA); operations (MBA); strategy (MBA); MBA/JD; MBA/M Div; MBA/MD; MBA/MSN; MBA/MTS; MBA/PhD. *Accreditation:* AACSB. *Degree requirements:* For master's, 62 credit hours of coursework; completion of ethics course; minimum GPA of 3.0. *Entrance requirements:* For master's, GMAT (preferred) or GRE, 2 years of work experience (recommended). Additional exam requirements/recommendations for international students: Required—TOEFL (minimum score 100 iBT). Electronic applications accepted. *Expenses:* Contact institution. *Faculty research:* Accounting and finance, business strategy and economics, marketing, operations management, organization studies.

Villanova University, Villanova School of Business, MBA - The Flex Track Program, Villanova, PA 19085. Offers healthcare (MBA); international business (MBA); marketing (MBA); real estate (MBA); strategic management (MBA); JD/MBA. *Accreditation:* AACSB. *Program availability:* Part-time, evening/weekend, online learning. *Faculty:* 68 full-time (22 women), 65 part-time/adjunct (11 women). *Students:* 13 full-time (4 women), 410 part-time (137 women); includes 105 minority (28 Black or African American, non-Hispanic/Latino; 1 American Indian or Alaska Native, non-Hispanic/Latino; 41 Asian, non-Hispanic/Latino; 29 Hispanic/Latino; 6 Two or more races, non-Hispanic/Latino), 13 international. Average age 31. 94 applicants, 94% accepted, 79 enrolled. In 2017, 201 master's awarded. *Degree requirements:* For master's, minimum GPA of 3.0. *Entrance requirements:* For master's, GMAT or GRE, work experience, 2 letters of recommendation, 2 essays, resume, official transcript. Additional exam requirements/recommendations for international students: Required—TOEFL (minimum score 550 paper-based; 100 iBT). *Application deadline:* For fall admission, 6/30 for domestic and international students; for spring admission, 11/15 for domestic and international students; for summer admission, 3/31 for domestic and international students. Applications are processed on a rolling basis. Application fee: $65. Electronic applications accepted. *Expenses:* $50,016 per year tuition, $1,167 per credit; $50 semester fee. *Financial support:* In 2017–18, 19 research assistantships with full tuition reimbursements (averaging $16,245 per year) were awarded; scholarships/grants also available. Financial award application deadline: 6/30; financial award applicants required to submit FAFSA. *Faculty research:* Business analytics; creativity, innovation and entrepreneurship; global leadership; real estate; church management; business ethics. *Unit head:* Dr. Joyce Russell, Dean of Villanova School of Business, 610-519-5424, Fax: 610-519-6273, E-mail: joyce.russell@villanova.edu. *Application contact:* Claire Bruno, Director of Recruitment and Enrollment Management, 610-519-4336, Fax: 610-519-6273, E-mail: claire.bruno@villanova.edu. Website: http://www1.villanova.edu/villanova/business/graduate/mba.html

Marketing

Virginia International University, School of Business, Fairfax, VA 22030. Offers accounting (MBA, MS); entrepreneurship (MBA); executive management (Graduate Certificate); global logistics (MBA); health care management (MBA); hospitality and tourism management (MBA); human resources management (MBA); international business management (MBA); international finance (MBA); marketing management (MBA); mass media and public relations (MBA); project management (MBA, MS). *Program availability:* Part-time, online learning. *Entrance requirements:* For master's and Graduate Certificate, bachelor's degree. Additional exam requirements/recommendations for international students: Required—TOEFL (minimum score 550 paper-based; 80 iBT), IELTS (minimum score 6). Electronic applications accepted.

Virginia Polytechnic Institute and State University, Graduate School, Pamplin College of Business, Blacksburg, VA 24061. Offers accounting and information systems (MACIS, PhD); business (PhD), including marketing (MS, PhD); business administration (MS), including business analytics, marketing (MS, PhD); business information technology (PhD); executive business research (PhD); finance (PhD); MS/MBA. *Faculty:* 131 full-time (42 women), 2 part-time/adjunct (1 woman). *Students:* 261 full-time (101 women), 189 part-time (76 women); includes 112 minority (32 Black or African American, non-Hispanic/Latino; 50 Asian, non-Hispanic/Latino; 15 Hispanic/Latino; 15 Two or more races, non-Hispanic/Latino), 80 international. Average age 32. 434 applicants, 57% accepted, 168 enrolled. In 2017, 142 master's, 11 doctorates awarded. *Degree requirements:* For master's, comprehensive exam (for some programs), thesis (for some programs); for doctorate, comprehensive exam (for some programs), thesis/dissertation (for some programs). *Entrance requirements:* For master's and doctorate, GRE/GMAT. Additional exam requirements/recommendations for international students: Required—TOEFL (minimum score 80 iBT). *Application deadline:* For fall admission, 8/1 for domestic students, 4/1 for international students; for spring admission, 1/1 for domestic students, 9/1 for international students. Applications are processed on a rolling basis. Application fee: $75. Electronic applications accepted. *Expenses:* Tuition, state resident: full-time $15,072; part-time $718.50 per credit hour. Tuition, nonresident: full-time $28,810; part-time $1448.25 per credit hour. *Required fees:* $2741; $502 per semester. Tuition and fees vary according to course load, campus/location and program. *Financial support:* In 2017–18, 9 research assistantships with full tuition reimbursements (averaging $18,588 per year), 48 teaching assistantships with full tuition reimbursements (averaging $22,706 per year) were awarded. Financial award application deadline: 3/1; financial award applicants required to submit FAFSA. *Total annual research expenditures:* $3.4 million. *Unit head:* Dr. Robert T. Sumichrast, Dean, 540-231-6601, Fax: 540-231-4487, E-mail: busdean@vt.edu. *Application contact:* Kimberly Ridpath, Executive Assistant, 540-231-9647, Fax: 540-231-4487, E-mail: ridpathk@vt.edu.
Website: http://www.pamplin.vt.edu/

Wagner College, Division of Graduate Studies, Nicolais School of Business, Staten Island, NY 10301-4495. Offers accounting (MS); business administration (MBA); finance (MBA); management (Exec MBA); marketing (MBA); media management (MS). *Accreditation:* ACBSP. *Program availability:* Part-time, evening/weekend. *Faculty:* 8 full-time (3 women), 17 part-time/adjunct (5 women). *Students:* 90 full-time (41 women), 27 part-time (9 women); includes 18 minority (10 Black or African American, non-Hispanic/Latino; 2 Asian, non-Hispanic/Latino; 4 Hispanic/Latino; 2 Two or more races, non-Hispanic/Latino), 14 international. Average age 27. 85 applicants, 92% accepted, 58 enrolled. In 2017, 72 master's awarded. *Degree requirements:* For master's, thesis optional. *Entrance requirements:* For master's, minimum GPA of 2.75, proficiency in computers and math. Additional exam requirements/recommendations for international students: Required—TOEFL (minimum score 550 paper-based; 79 iBT), IELTS (minimum score 6.5). *Application deadline:* For fall admission, 5/1 priority date for domestic students, 3/1 priority date for international students; for spring admission, 12/1 for domestic students, 11/1 for international students. Applications are processed on a rolling basis. Application fee: $60. *Financial support:* In 2017–18, 93 students received support. Career-related internships or fieldwork, unspecified assistantships, and alumni fellowship grants available. Financial award application deadline: 4/1; financial award applicants required to submit FAFSA. *Unit head:* Dr. Donald Crooks, Director, 718-390-3429, Fax: 718-390-3429, E-mail: dcrooks@wagner.edu. *Application contact:* Patricia Clancy, Assistant Director for Enrollment, 718-420-4464, Fax: 718-390-3105, E-mail: patricia.clancy@wagner.edu.

Walden University, Graduate Programs, School of Management, Minneapolis, MN 55401. Offers accounting (MBA, MS, DBA), including accounting for the professional (MS), accounting with CPA emphasis (MS), self-designed (MS); advanced project management (Graduate Certificate); applied project management (Graduate Certificate); auditing (Graduate Certificate); bridge to business administration (Post-Doctoral Certificate); bridge to management (Post-Doctoral Certificate); business management (Graduate Certificate); communication (MBA); corporate finance (MBA); digital marketing (Graduate Certificate); entrepreneurship (DBA); entrepreneurship and small business (MBA); finance (MS, DBA), including finance for the professional (MS), finance with CFA/investment (MS), finance with CPA emphasis (MS); global supply chain management (DBA); healthcare management (MBA, DBA); human resource management (MBA, MS, Graduate Certificate), including functional human resource management (MS), general program (MS), integrating functional and strategic human resource management (MS), organizational strategy (MS); human resources management (DBA); information systems management (DBA); international business (MBA, DBA); leadership (MBA, MS, DBA, Graduate Certificate), including general program (MS), human resource leadership (MS), leader development (MS), self-designed (MS); management (MS, PhD), including communications (MS), finance (PhD), general program (MS), healthcare management (MS), human resource management (MS), human resources management (PhD), information systems management (PhD), international business (MS), leadership (MS), leadership and organizational change (PhD), marketing (MS), project management (MS), strategy and operations (MS); managerial accounting (Graduate Certificate); marketing (MBA, MS, DBA); project management (MBA, MS, DBA); self-designed (MBA, DBA); social impact management (DBA); technology entrepreneurship (DBA). *Accreditation:* ACBSP. *Program availability:* Part-time, evening/weekend, online only, 100% online. *Degree requirements:* For master's, thesis (for some programs), residency (for EMBA); for doctorate, thesis/dissertation (for some programs), residency. *Entrance requirements:* For master's, bachelor's degree or higher; minimum GPA of 2.5; official transcripts; goal statement (for some programs); access to computer and Internet; for doctorate, master's degree or higher; three years of related professional or academic experience (preferred); minimum GPA of 3.0; goal statement and current resume (for select programs); official transcripts; access to computer and Internet; for other advanced degree, relevant work experience; access to computer and Internet. Additional exam requirements/recommendations for international students: Required—TOEFL (minimum score 550 paper-based, 79 iBT), IELTS (minimum score 6.5), Michigan English Language Assessment Battery (minimum score 82), or PTE (minimum score 53). Electronic applications accepted.

Walsh College of Accountancy and Business Administration, Graduate Programs, Program in Marketing, Troy, MI 48083. Offers MS. *Program availability:* Part-time, evening/weekend. *Faculty:* 6 full-time (4 women), 9 part-time/adjunct (3 women). *Students:* 39 (21 women); includes 8 minority (6 Black or African American, non-Hispanic/Latino; 1 American Indian or Alaska Native, non-Hispanic/Latino; 1 Asian, non-Hispanic/Latino), 1 international. Average age 33. 20 applicants, 75% accepted, 13

enrolled. In 2017, 7 master's awarded. *Degree requirements:* For master's, internship or project. *Entrance requirements:* For master's, minimum overall cumulative GPA of 2.75 from all colleges previously attended. Additional exam requirements/recommendations for international students: Required—TOEFL (minimum score 550 paper-based, 79 iBT), IELTS (6.5), Michigan English Language Assessment Battery, or MTELP (80). *Application deadline:* Applications are processed on a rolling basis. Application fee: $35. Electronic applications accepted. *Expenses:* $770 per semester credit hour plus $125 registration fee per semester. *Financial support:* In 2017–18, 3 students received support. Career-related internships or fieldwork and scholarships/grants available. Financial award application deadline: 6/30; financial award applicants required to submit FAFSA. *Faculty research:* Consumer behavior, advertising research, brand management, innovation and strategy, philanthropic initiatives within a value proposition. *Unit head:* Dr. Michael Levens, Chair, Marketing, 248-823-1635, Fax: 248-689-0920, E-mail: mlevens@walshcollege.edu. *Application contact:* Heather Rigby, Director, Admissions and Academic Advising, 248-823-1610, Fax: 248-823-1611, E-mail: hrigby@walshcollege.edu.

Walsh University, Graduate Programs, MBA Program, North Canton, OH 44720-3396. Offers healthcare management (MBA); management (MBA); marketing (MBA). *Program availability:* Part-time, evening/weekend, online only, 100% online. *Degree requirements:* For master's, capstone course in strategic management. *Entrance requirements:* For master's, GMAT (minimum score of 490), minimum GPA of 3.0. Additional exam requirements/recommendations for international students: Required—TOEFL (minimum score 500 paper-based; 61 iBT). Electronic applications accepted. Application fee is waived when completed online. *Expenses:* Contact institution. *Faculty research:* Medical tourism, familial influence in financial fitness, pedagogy in finance courses, sociocultural aspects of women entrepreneurs, patient satisfaction.

Webster University, George Herbert Walker School of Business and Technology, Department of Business, St. Louis, MO 63119-3194. Offers business and organizational security management (MBA); decision support systems (MBA); environmental management (MBA); finance (MBA, MS); forensic accounting (MS); gerontology (MBA); human resources development (MBA); human resources management (MBA); information technology management (MBA); international business (MA, MBA); international relations (MBA); management and leadership (MBA); marketing (MBA); media communications (MBA); procurement and acquisitions management (MBA); Web services (MBA). *Accreditation:* ACBSP. *Program availability:* Part-time, evening/weekend, online learning. *Degree requirements:* For master's, comprehensive exam (for some programs), thesis (for some programs). *Entrance requirements:* Additional exam requirements/recommendations for international students: Required—TOEFL.

Webster University, George Herbert Walker School of Business and Technology, Department of Management, St. Louis, MO 63119-3194. Offers business and organizational security management (MA); digital marketing management (Graduate Certificate); government contracting (Graduate Certificate); health administration (MHA); health care management (MA); health services management (MA); human resources development (MA); human resources management (MA); information technology management (MA, MS); management (D Mgt); management and leadership (MA); marketing (MA); nonprofit leadership (MA); nonprofit revenue development (Graduate Certificate); organizational development (Graduate Certificate); procurement and acquisitions management (MA); public administration (MPA); space systems operations management (MS). *Program availability:* Part-time, evening/weekend, online learning. *Degree requirements:* For master's, thesis (for some programs); for doctorate, thesis/dissertation, written exam. *Entrance requirements:* For doctorate, GMAT, 3 years of work experience, MBA. Additional exam requirements/recommendations for international students: Required—TOEFL.

West Virginia University, College of Business and Economics, Morgantown, WV 26506. Offers accountancy (M Acc); accounting (PhD); business administration (MBA); business cyber security management (MS); business data analytics (MS); economics (MA, PhD); finance (MS, PhD); forensic and fraud examination (MS); industrial relations (MS); management (PhD); marketing (PhD). *Program availability:* Part-time, online learning. *Students:* 343 full-time (141 women), 43 part-time (12 women); includes 59 minority (22 Black or African American, non-Hispanic/Latino; 11 Asian, non-Hispanic/Latino; 12 Hispanic/Latino; 14 Two or more races, non-Hispanic/Latino), 54 international. Terminal master's awarded for partial completion of doctoral program. *Degree requirements:* For master's, thesis optional; for doctorate, comprehensive exam, thesis/dissertation. *Entrance requirements:* For doctorate, GRE General Test, minimum GPA of 3.0. Additional exam requirements/recommendations for international students: Required—TOEFL (minimum score 550 paper-based; 92 iBT). *Application deadline:* For fall admission, 10/15 priority date for domestic and international students; for spring admission, 3/1 priority date for domestic and international students. Applications are processed on a rolling basis. Application fee: $60. Electronic applications accepted. *Expenses:* Contact institution. *Financial support:* Fellowships, research assistantships, teaching assistantships, career-related internships or fieldwork, Federal Work-Study, institutionally sponsored loans, scholarships/grants, health care benefits, tuition waivers (full and partial), unspecified assistantships, and administrative assistantships available. Financial award application deadline: 2/1; financial award applicants required to submit FAFSA. *Faculty research:* Regional labor market studies, economic development, market research, economic forecasting, energy analysis. *Unit head:* Dr. Javier Reyes, Dean, 304-293-7800, Fax: 304-293-4056, E-mail: javier.reyes@mail.wvu.edu. *Application contact:* Dr. Mark Gavin, Associate Dean for Graduate Programs, 304-293-7952, Fax: 304-293-7188, E-mail: mark.gavin@mail.wvu.edu.
Website: http://www.be.wvu.edu

West Virginia University, Reed College of Media, Morgantown, WV 26506-6010. Offers data marketing communications (MS); integrated marketing communications (MS, Graduate Certificate); journalism (MSJ); media solutions and innovation (MSJ). *Program availability:* Part-time, online learning. *Students:* 165 full-time (122 women), 232 part-time (167 women); includes 81 minority (46 Black or African American, non-Hispanic/Latino; 5 Asian, non-Hispanic/Latino; 20 Hispanic/Latino; 10 Two or more races, non-Hispanic/Latino), 6 international. *Degree requirements:* For master's, thesis or alternative. *Entrance requirements:* For master's, GRE General Test, minimum GPA of 3.0, writing samples. Additional exam requirements/recommendations for international students: Required—TOEFL (minimum score 550 paper-based). *Application deadline:* For fall admission, 3/1 priority date for domestic students, 3/1 for international students. Application fee: $60. Electronic applications accepted. *Expenses:* Tuition, state resident: full-time $9450. Tuition, nonresident: full-time $24,390. *Financial support:* Research assistantships, teaching assistantships, career-related internships or fieldwork, Federal Work-Study, institutionally sponsored loans, health care benefits, tuition waivers (full and partial), and administrative assistantships available. Financial award application deadline: 2/1; financial award applicants required to submit FAFSA. *Faculty research:* History, law, and women in media; press management; public opinion; advertising effectiveness; international advertising. *Unit head:* Dr. Maryann Reed, Dean, 304-293-3505 Ext. 5409, Fax: 304-293-3072, E-mail: maryann.reed@mail.wvu.edu. *Application contact:* Dr. Steve Urbanski, Director of Graduate Studies/Associate Professor, 304-293-6797, Fax: 304-293-3072, E-mail: steve.urbanski@mail.wvu.edu.
Website: http://reedcollegeofmedia.wvu.edu/

Peterson's Graduate Programs in Business, Education, Information Studies, Law & Social Work 2019

Wilfrid Laurier University, Faculty of Graduate and Postdoctoral Studies, School of Business and Economics, Department of Business, Waterloo, ON N2L 3C5, Canada. Offers accounting (PhD); finance (M Fin); financial economics (PhD); marketing (PhD); operations and supply chain management (PhD); organizational behavior and human resource management (M Sc); organizational behaviour and human resource management (PhD); supply chain management (M Sc); technology management (EMTM). *Accreditation:* AACSB. *Program availability:* Part-time, evening/weekend. *Degree requirements:* For master's, thesis optional; for doctorate, comprehensive exam, thesis/dissertation. *Entrance requirements:* For master's, GMAT, 4-year honors degree with minimum B+ average; for doctorate, GMAT, master's degree, minimum B+ average. Additional exam requirements/recommendations for international students: Required—TOEFL (minimum score 89 iBT). Electronic applications accepted. *Faculty research:* Financial economics, management and organizational behavior, operations and supply chain management.

William Woods University, Graduate and Adult Studies, Fulton, MO 65251-1098. Offers administration (M Ed, Ed S); athletic/activities administration (M Ed); curriculum and instruction (M Ed, Ed S); educational leadership (Ed D); equestrian education (M Ed); health management (MBA); human resources (MBA); leadership (MBA); marketing, advertising, and public relations (MBA); teaching and technology (M Ed). *Program availability:* Part-time, evening/weekend. *Degree requirements:* For master's, capstone course (MBA), action research (M Ed); for Ed S, field experience. *Entrance requirements:* Additional exam requirements/recommendations for international students: Required—TOEFL (minimum score 550 paper-based). Electronic applications accepted. *Expenses:* Contact institution.

Wilmington University, College of Business, New Castle, DE 19720-6491. Offers accounting (MBA, MS); business administration (MBA, DBA); environmental stewardship (MBA); finance (MBA); health care administration (MBA, MSM); homeland security (MBA, MSM); human resource management (MSM); management information systems (MBA, MSN); marketing (MSM); marketing management (MBA); military leadership (MSM); organizational leadership (MBA, MSM); public administration (MSM). *Program availability:* Part-time, evening/weekend. *Faculty:* 16 full-time (8 women), 106 part-time/adjunct (49 women). *Students:* 525 full-time (294 women), 1,212 part-time (780 women); includes 557 minority (412 Black or African American, non-Hispanic/Latino; 14 American Indian or Alaska Native, non-Hispanic/Latino; 55 Asian, non-Hispanic/Latino; 25 Hispanic/Latino; 3 Native Hawaiian or other Pacific Islander, non-Hispanic/Latino; 48 Two or more races, non-Hispanic/Latino), 157 international. Average age 35. 1,484 applicants, 70% accepted, 685 enrolled. In 2017, 543 master's, 16 doctorates awarded. *Entrance requirements:* Additional exam requirements/recommendations for international students: Required—TOEFL (minimum score 500 paper-based). *Application deadline:* Applications are processed on a rolling basis. Application fee: $35. Electronic applications accepted. *Expenses: Tuition:* Part-time $466 per credit. *Required fees:* $25 per semester. Tuition and fees vary according to degree level and campus/location. *Financial support:* Applicants required to submit FAFSA. *Unit head:* Dr. Kathy S. Kennedy Ratajack, Dean, 302-356-2481. *Application contact:* Laura Morris, Director of Admissions, 877-967-5456, E-mail: infocenter@wilmu.edu.
Website: http://www.wilmu.edu/business/

Wingate University, Porter B. Byrum School of Business, Wingate, NC 28174. Offers accounting (MAC); corporate innovation (MBA); finance (MBA); general management (MBA); healthcare management (MBA); marketing (MBA); project management (MBA). *Accreditation:* ACBSP. *Program availability:* Part-time, evening/weekend. *Entrance requirements:* For master's, GMAT, work experience, 2 letters of recommendation. Electronic applications accepted. *Expenses:* Contact institution. *Faculty research:* Stochastic processes, business ethics, regional economic development, municipal finance, consumer behavior.

Worcester Polytechnic Institute, Graduate Admissions, Foisie Business School, Worcester, MA 01609-2280. Offers business administration (PhD); information technology (MS), including information security management; management (Graduate Certificate); marketing and technological innovation (MS); operations design and leadership (MS); supply chain management (MS); technology (MS). *Accreditation:* AACSB. *Program availability:* Part-time, evening/weekend, 100% online, blended/hybrid learning. *Faculty:* 26 full-time (12 women), 9 part-time/adjunct (0 women). *Students:* 254 full-time (153 women), 150 part-time (52 women); includes 34 minority (3 Black or African American, non-Hispanic/Latino; 10 Asian, non-Hispanic/Latino; 14 Hispanic/Latino; 7 Two or more races, non-Hispanic/Latino), 230 international. Average age 29. 677 applicants, 71% accepted, 146 enrolled. In 2017, 188 master's, 14 doctorates awarded. *Degree requirements:* For master's, thesis optional. *Entrance requirements:* For master's and Graduate Certificate, GMAT or GRE General Test, 3 letters of recommendation, statement of purpose, resume. Additional exam requirements/recommendations for international students: Required—TOEFL (minimum score 563 paper-based; 84 iBT), IELTS (minimum score 7). *Application deadline:* For fall admission, 6/1 priority date for domestic and international students; for spring admission, 11/1 priority date for domestic students, 10/1 priority date for international students. Applications are processed on a rolling basis. Application fee: $70. Electronic applications accepted. *Expenses: Tuition:* Full-time $26,226; part-time $1457 per credit. *Required fees:* $60; $30 per credit. One-time fee: $15. Tuition and fees vary according to course load. *Financial support:* Career-related internships or fieldwork, institutionally sponsored loans, scholarships/grants, and unspecified assistantships available. Financial award application deadline: 6/1. *Unit head:* Melissa Terrio, Executive Director, 508-831-4665, Fax: 508-831-4665, E-mail: biz@wpi.edu. *Application contact:* Margaret Clancey, Recruiting Operations Coordinator, 508-831-4980, Fax: 508-831-5720, E-mail: maclancey@wpi.edu.
Website: https://www.wpi.edu/academics/business

Worcester State University, Graduate School, Program in Management, Worcester, MA 01602-2597. Offers accounting (MS); managerial leadership (MS); marketing (MS). *Program availability:* Part-time, evening/weekend. *Faculty:* 6 full-time, 1 part-time/adjunct. *Students:* 12 full-time (7 women), 44 part-time (26 women); includes 14 minority (7 Black or African American, non-Hispanic/Latino; 2 Asian, non-Hispanic/Latino; 5 Hispanic/Latino), 3 international. Average age 32. 50 applicants, 80% accepted, 21 enrolled. In 2017, 10 master's awarded. *Degree requirements:* For master's, comprehensive exam (for some programs), thesis optional. *Entrance requirements:* For master's, GMAT, 3 letters of recommendation from professors and/or supervisors. Additional exam requirements/recommendations for international students: Required—TOEFL (minimum score 550 paper-based; 79 iBT). *Application deadline:* For fall admission, 6/15 for domestic and international students; for spring admission, 11/1 for domestic and international students; for summer admission, 4/1 for domestic and international students. Applications are processed on a rolling basis. Application fee: $50. Electronic applications accepted. *Expenses: Tuition,* state resident: full-time $3042; part-time $169 per credit hour. Tuition, nonresident: full-time $3042; part-time $169 per credit hour. *Required fees:* $2754; $153 per credit hour. *Financial support:* Career-related internships or fieldwork, scholarships/grants, and unspecified assistantships available. Financial award application deadline: 3/1; financial award applicants required to submit FAFSA. *Unit head:* Dr. Elizabeth Wark, Program Coordinator, 508-929-8743, E-mail: ewark@worcester.edu. *Application contact:* Sara Grady, Associate Dean, Graduate Studies and Professional Development, 508-929-8130, E-mail: sara.grady@worcester.edu.

Xavier University, Williams College of Business, Master of Business Administration Program, Cincinnati, OH 45207. Offers business administration (Exec MBA, MBA); business intelligence (MBA); finance (MBA); health industry (MBA); international business (MBA); marketing (MBA); values-based leadership (MBA); MBA/MHSA; MSN/MBA. *Accreditation:* AACSB. *Program availability:* Part-time, evening/weekend. *Degree requirements:* For master's, capstone course. *Entrance requirements:* For master's, GMAT or GRE, official transcript; resume. Additional exam requirements/recommendations for international students: Required—TOEFL (minimum score 550 paper-based; 79 iBT). Electronic applications accepted. Application fee is waived when completed online. *Expenses:* Contact institution.

Yale University, Yale School of Management and Graduate School of Arts and Sciences, Doctoral Program in Management, New Haven, CT 06520. Offers accounting (PhD); financial economics (PhD); marketing (PhD); organizations and management (PhD). *Accreditation:* AACSB. *Degree requirements:* For doctorate, comprehensive exam, thesis/dissertation. *Entrance requirements:* For doctorate, GMAT or GRE General Test. Additional exam requirements/recommendations for international students: Required—TOEFL or IELTS. Electronic applications accepted. *Expenses:* Contact institution. *Faculty research:* Pricing of options and futures, term structure of interest rates, use of accounting numbers in debt contracts, product differentiation, e-commerce and marketing, behavioral finance.

Yeshiva University, The Katz School, Program in Marketing, New York, NY 10033-3201. Offers MS. *Program availability:* Part-time, online learning.

Yeshiva University, Sy Syms School of Business, New York, NY 10016. Offers accounting (MS); business (EMBA); marketing (MS); taxation (MS). *Program availability:* Part-time. *Entrance requirements:* For master's, minimum GPA of 3.5 or GMAT.

York College of Pennsylvania, Graham School of Business, York, PA 17403-3651. Offers accounting (M Acc); business (MBA); continuous improvement (MBA); financial management (MBA); health care management (MBA); management (MBA); marketing (MBA); self-designed (MBA). *Accreditation:* ACBSP. *Program availability:* Part-time, evening/weekend. *Faculty:* 9 full-time (2 women), 3 part-time/adjunct (0 women). *Students:* 3 full-time (2 women), 72 part-time (33 women); includes 14 minority (7 Black or African American, non-Hispanic/Latino; 3 Asian, non-Hispanic/Latino; 1 Hispanic/Latino; 3 Two or more races, non-Hispanic/Latino). Average age 35. 68 applicants, 76% accepted, 28 enrolled. In 2017, 17 master's awarded. *Degree requirements:* For master's, directed study. *Entrance requirements:* For master's, GMAT. Additional exam requirements/recommendations for international students: Required—TOEFL (minimum score 530 paper-based; 72 iBT), IELTS (minimum score 6). *Application deadline:* For fall admission, 7/15 priority date for domestic students, 5/1 for international students; for spring admission, 11/15 priority date for domestic students, 9/1 for international students; for summer admission, 4/15 priority date for domestic students. Applications are processed on a rolling basis. Application fee: $0. Electronic applications accepted. *Expenses:* $795 per credit. *Financial support:* In 2017–18, 3 students received support. Scholarships/grants available. Financial award applicants required to submit FAFSA. *Unit head:* Nicole Cornell Sadowski, MBA Director, 717-815-1491, Fax: 717-600-3999, E-mail: ncornell@ycp.edu. *Application contact:* MBA Office, 717-815-1491, Fax: 717-600-3999, E-mail: mba@ycp.edu.
Website: http://www.ycp.edu/mba

Youngstown State University, Graduate School, Williamson College of Business Administration, Department of Marketing, Youngstown, OH 44555-0001. Offers MBA. *Program availability:* Part-time, evening/weekend. *Degree requirements:* For master's, thesis optional. *Entrance requirements:* For master's, GMAT, minimum GPA of 2.7. Additional exam requirements/recommendations for international students: Required—TOEFL. *Faculty research:* Media, international marketing, advanced marketing simulations, ethics in business.

Marketing Research

Baldwin Wallace University, Graduate Programs, School of Business, Program in Analytics, Berea, OH 44017-2088. Offers MBA. *Program availability:* Part-time, evening/weekend. *Students:* 11 full-time (3 women), 12 part-time (7 women); includes 1 minority (Black or African American, non-Hispanic/Latino), 2 international. Average age 33. 8 applicants, 88% accepted, 4 enrolled. In 2017, 6 master's awarded. *Entrance requirements:* For master's, GMAT or minimum GPA of 3.0, bachelor's degree in any field, work experience. Additional exam requirements/recommendations for international students: Required—TOEFL (minimum score 550 paper-based; 79 iBT). *Application deadline:* For fall admission, 7/25 for domestic students; for spring admission, 12/15 for domestic students; for summer admission, 4/15 for domestic students. Applications are processed on a rolling basis. Electronic applications accepted. *Expenses:* $948 per credit hour. *Unit head:* Dale Kramer, MBA Program Director, 440-826-3331, Fax: 440-826-3868, E-mail: dkramer@bw.edu. *Application contact:* Laura Spencer, Graduate Application Specialist, 440-826-2191, Fax: 440-826-3868, E-mail: lspencer@bw.edu.
Website: http://www.bw.edu/graduate/business/mba/

Hofstra University, Frank G. Zarb School of Business, Programs in Marketing and International Business, Hempstead, NY 11549. Offers business administration (MBA), including international business, marketing; international business (Advanced Certificate); marketing (MS, Advanced Certificate); marketing research (MS). *Program availability:* Part-time, evening/weekend, blended/hybrid learning. *Students:* 72 full-time (40 women), 20 part-time (11 women); includes 11 minority (2 Black or African American, non-Hispanic/Latino; 6 Asian, non-Hispanic/Latino; 2 Hispanic/Latino; 1 Two or more races, non-Hispanic/Latino), 58 international. Average age 25. 227 applicants, 74% accepted, 35 enrolled. In 2017, 51 master's awarded. *Degree requirements:* For

master's, capstone course (for MBA), thesis, (for MS), minimum GPA of 3.0. *Entrance requirements:* For master's, GMAT/GRE, 2 letters of recommendation, resume, essay. Additional exam requirements/recommendations for international students: Required—TOEFL (minimum score 550 paper-based; 80 iBT); Recommended—IELTS (minimum score 6). *Application deadline:* Applications are processed on a rolling basis. Application fee: $75. Electronic applications accepted. *Expenses:* $1,322 per credit. *Financial support:* In 2017–18, 28 students received support, including 24 fellowships with full and partial tuition reimbursements available (averaging $5,002 per year), 2 research assistantships with full and partial tuition reimbursements available (averaging $7,390 per year); career-related internships or fieldwork, Federal Work-Study, institutionally sponsored loans, scholarships/grants, tuition waivers (full and partial), and unspecified assistantships also available. Support available to part-time students. Financial award applicants required to submit FAFSA. *Faculty research:* Cross-cultural consumer behavior; social, digital, global, and strategic issues in marketing; consumer health/well-being; ethnocentrism and animosity. *Unit head:* Dr. Anil Mathur, Chairperson, 516-463-5346, Fax: 516-463-4834, E-mail: anil.mathur@hofstra.edu. *Application contact:* Sunil Samuel, Assistant Vice President of Admissions, 516-463-4723, Fax: 516-463-4664, E-mail: graduateadmission@hofstra.edu.
Website: http://www.hofstra.edu/business/

Instituto Tecnológico y de Estudios Superiores de Monterrey, Campus Irapuato, Graduate Programs, Irapuato, Mexico. Offers administration (MBA); administration of information technology (MAIT); administration of telecommunications (MAT); architecture (M Arch); computer science (MCS); education (M Ed); educational administration (MEA); educational innovation and technology (DEIT); educational technology (MET); electronic commerce (MBA); environmental administration and planning (MEAP); environmental systems (MES); finances (MBA); humanistic studies (MHS); international management for Latin American executives (MIMLAE); library and information science (MLIS); manufacturing quality management (MMQM); marketing research (MBA).

Marquette University, Graduate School of Management, Department of Economics, Milwaukee, WI 53201-1881. Offers business economics (MSAE); financial economics (MSAE); international economics (MSAE); marketing research (MSAE); real estate economics (MSAE). *Program availability:* Part-time, evening/weekend. *Degree requirements:* For master's, comprehensive exam, professional project. *Entrance requirements:* For master's, GMAT or GRE General Test. Additional exam requirements/recommendations for international students: Required—TOEFL, IELTS, PTE. Electronic applications accepted. *Faculty research:* Monetary and fiscal policy in open economy, housing and regional migration, political economy of taxation and state/local government.

Michigan State University, The Graduate School, Eli Broad College of Business, Department of Marketing, East Lansing, MI 48224. Offers marketing (PhD); marketing research (MS). *Degree requirements:* For doctorate, comprehensive exam, thesis/dissertation. *Entrance requirements:* For master's, GMAT, bachelor's degree with minimum GPA of 3.0 in last 2 years of undergraduate work; transcripts; 3 letters of recommendation; statement of purpose; resume; working knowledge of computers; basic understanding of accounting, finance, marketing, and the management of people; laptop capable of running Windows software; for doctorate, GMAT (taken within past 5 years), bachelor's degree; letters of recommendation; statement of purpose; previous work experience; personal qualifications of sound character, perseverance, intellectual curiosity, and an interest in scholarly research. Additional exam requirements/recommendations for international students: Required—TOEFL (minimum score 100 iBT), PTE (minimum score 70), IELTS (minimum score 7) accepted for MS only.

Pacific Lutheran University, School of Business, Master of Science in Market Research Program, Tacoma, WA 98447. Offers MS. *Entrance requirements:* For master's, GRE or GMAT, two references, official transcripts, resume, statement of professional goals and quantitative skills. Additional exam requirements/recommendations for international students: Required—TOEFL (minimum score 88 iBT) or IELTS (minimum score 6.5).

Saint Leo University, Graduate Studies in Business, Saint Leo, FL 33574-6665. Offers accounting (M Acc, MBA); cybersecurity (MS); cybersecurity management (MBA); data analytics (MBA); health care management (MBA); human resource management (MBA); international and experiential business administration (MBA); management (MBA, DBA); marketing (MBA); marketing research and social media analytics (MBA); project management (MBA); social media marketing (MBA); sport business (MBA); supply chain global integration management (MBA). *Accreditation:* ACBSP. *Program availability:* Part-time, evening/weekend, 100% online, blended/hybrid learning. *Faculty:* 54 full-time (18 women), 52 part-time/adjunct (18 women). *Students:* 9 full-time (3 women), 1,867 part-time (1,079 women); includes 861 minority (598 Black or African American, non-Hispanic/Latino; 3 American Indian or Alaska Native, non-Hispanic/Latino; 38 Asian, non-Hispanic/Latino; 186 Hispanic/Latino; 3 Native Hawaiian or other Pacific Islander, non-Hispanic/Latino; 33 Two or more races, non-Hispanic/Latino), 68 international. Average age 37. 868 applicants, 63% accepted, 537 enrolled. In 2017, 859 master's, 3 doctorates awarded. *Degree requirements:* For doctorate, comprehensive exam, thesis/dissertation. *Entrance requirements:* For master's, GMAT with minimum score 500 (for M Acc), official transcripts, current resume, 2 professional recommendations, personal statement, bachelor's degree from regionally-accredited university; undergraduate degree in accounting and minimum undergraduate GPA of 3.0 (for M Acc); minimum undergraduate GPA of 3.0 in final 2 years of undergraduate study and 2 years' work experience (for MBA); for doctorate, GMAT (minimum score of 550) if master's GPA is under 3.25, official transcripts, current resume, 2 professional recommendations, personal statement, master's degree from regionally-accredited university with minimum GPA of 3.25, 3 years' work experience, interview. Additional exam requirements/recommendations for international students: Required—TOEFL (minimum score 550 paper-based; 78 iBT). *Application deadline:* For fall admission, 7/1 priority date for domestic and international students; for spring admission, 11/12 priority date for domestic students, 11/1 for international students. Applications are processed on a rolling basis. Application fee: $80. Electronic applications accepted. *Expenses:* Contact institution. *Financial support:* In 2017–18, 106 students received support. Career-related internships or fieldwork, health care benefits, and tuition remission for Saint Leo employees and their dependents available. Financial award application deadline: 3/1; financial award applicants required to submit FAFSA. *Faculty research:* Servant leadership, work/life balance, emotional intelligence, pricing, marketing. *Unit head:* Dr. Charles Hale, Dean, School of Business, 352-588-8599, Fax: 352-588-8912, E-mail: mbaslu@saintleo.edu. *Application contact:* Mark Russum, Assistant Vice President, Enrollment, 800-707-8846, Fax: 352-588-7873, E-mail: grad.admissions@saintleo.edu.
Website: https://www.saintleo.edu/school-of-business

Southern Illinois University Edwardsville, Graduate School, School of Business, Department of Management and Marketing, Edwardsville, IL 62026. Offers marketing research (MMR). *Program availability:* Part-time, evening/weekend. *Degree requirements:* For master's, comprehensive exam, final exam. *Entrance requirements:* For master's, GMAT. Additional exam requirements/recommendations for international students: Required—TOEFL (minimum score 550 paper-based; 79 iBT), IELTS (minimum score 6.5). Electronic applications accepted.

Towson University, College of Business and Economics, Program in Marketing Intelligence, Towson, MD 21252-0001. Offers MS, Postbaccalaureate Certificate. *Students:* 11 full-time (7 women), 18 part-time (12 women); includes 9 minority (5 Black or African American, non-Hispanic/Latino; 2 Asian, non-Hispanic/Latino; 1 Hispanic/Latino; 1 Two or more races, non-Hispanic/Latino), 9 international. *Expenses:* Tuition, state resident: full-time $7960; part-time $398 per unit. Tuition, nonresident: full-time $16,480; part-time $824 per unit. *Required fees:* $2600; $130 per year. $390 per term. *Unit head:* Dr. Philippe Duverger, Program Director, 410-704-3538, E-mail: pduverger@towson.edu. *Application contact:* Coverley Beidleman, Assistant Director of Graduate Admissions, 410-704-5630, Fax: 410-704-3030, E-mail: cbeidleman@towson.edu.
Website: http://www.towson.edu/cbe/departments/marketing/grad/

Universidad Autonoma de Guadalajara, Graduate Programs, Guadalajara, Mexico. Offers administrative law and justice (LL M); advertising and corporate communications (MA); architecture (M Arch); business (MBA); computational science (MCC); education (Ed M, Ed D); English-Spanish translation (MA); entrepreneurship and management (MBA); integrated management of digital animation (MA); international business (MIB); international corporate law (LL M); internet technologies (MS); manufacturing systems (MMS); occupational health (MS); philosophy (MA, PhD); power electronics (MS); quality systems (MQS); renewable energy (MS); social evaluation of projects (MBA); strategic market research (MBA); tax law (MA); teaching mathematics (MA).

Universidad de las Americas, A.C., Program in Business Administration, Mexico City, Mexico. Offers finance (MBA); marketing research (MBA); production and quality (MBA).

University of Colorado Denver, Business School, Program in Marketing, Denver, CO 80217. Offers brand management and marketing communication (MS); global marketing (MS); high-tech and entrepreneurial marketing (MS); marketing for sustainability (MS); marketing research (MS); sports and entertainment marketing (MS). *Program availability:* Part-time, evening/weekend. *Degree requirements:* For master's, 30 semester hours (21 of marketing core courses, 9 of marketing electives). *Entrance requirements:* For master's, GMAT, resume, essay, two letters of recommendation, financial statements (for international applicants). Additional exam requirements/recommendations for international students: Required—TOEFL (minimum score 525 paper-based; 71 iBT); Recommended—IELTS (minimum score 6.5). Electronic applications accepted. *Expenses:* Contact institution. *Faculty research:* Marketing issues in the Chinese environment, impact of individual difference and contextual factors on the risk-taking behaviors of managers making new-business creation decisions, attribution theory perspective of conflict between marketers and engineers, organizational identity and identification, international market entry strategies.

University of Missouri–St. Louis, College of Business Administration, St. Louis, MO 63121. Offers accounting (M Acc); business administration (MBA, DBA, PhD, Certificate), including logistics and supply chain management (PhD); business intelligence (Certificate); cybersecurity (Certificate); digital and social media marketing (Certificate); human resources management (Certificate); information systems (MS); logistics and supply chain management (Certificate); marketing management (Certificate). *Program availability:* Part-time, evening/weekend. *Faculty:* 51 full-time (21 women), 25 part-time/adjunct (5 women). *Students:* 146 full-time (77 women), 326 part-time (143 women); includes 82 minority (32 Black or African American, non-Hispanic/Latino; 1 American Indian or Alaska Native, non-Hispanic/Latino; 34 Asian, non-Hispanic/Latino; 11 Hispanic/Latino; 4 Two or more races, non-Hispanic/Latino), 89 international. 276 applicants, 83% accepted, 142 enrolled. *Degree requirements:* For doctorate, thesis/dissertation. *Entrance requirements:* For master's, GMAT, 2 letters of recommendation; for doctorate, GMAT or GRE, 3 letters of recommendation. Additional exam requirements/recommendations for international students: Recommended—TOEFL (minimum score 550 paper-based; 79 iBT), IELTS (minimum score 6.5). *Application deadline:* For fall admission, 7/1 priority date for domestic and international students; for spring admission, 12/1 priority date for domestic and international students. Applications are processed on a rolling basis. Application fee: $50 ($40 for international students). Electronic applications accepted. *Expenses:* Tuition, state resident: part-time $476.50 per credit hour. Tuition, nonresident: part-time $1169.70 per credit hour. *Financial support:* Research assistantships with tuition reimbursements, teaching assistantships with tuition reimbursements, career-related internships or fieldwork, Federal Work-Study, and institutionally sponsored loans available. Support available to part-time students. Financial award application deadline: 4/1; financial award applicants required to submit FAFSA. *Faculty research:* Statistical decision aids, commercial banking, corporate finance, operations management, information systems. *Unit head:* Charles E. Hoffman, Dean, 314-516-6109, Fax: 314-516-6420. *Application contact:* 314-516-5458, Fax: 314-516-6996, E-mail: gradadm@umsl.edu.
Website: http://www.umsl.edu/divisions/business/

University of Rochester, Simon Business School, Master of Science Program in Marketing Analytics, Rochester, NY 14627. Offers MS. *Faculty:* 70 full-time (12 women), 23 part-time/adjunct (6 women). *Students:* 60 full-time (47 women). Average age 22. *Entrance requirements:* For master's, GMAT or GRE. *Application deadline:* For fall admission, 10/15 for domestic and international students; for winter admission, 1/5 for domestic and international students; for spring admission, 3/15 for domestic and international students; for summer admission, 5/15 for domestic and international students. Application fee: $150. *Financial support:* Scholarships/grants available. Financial award application deadline: 1/1. *Unit head:* Andrew Ainslie, Dean, 585-275-3316, E-mail: andrew.ainslie@simon.rochester.edu. *Application contact:* Rebekah S. Lewin, Assistant Dean for Admissions and Financial Aid, 585-275-3533, E-mail: admissions@simon.rochester.edu.
Website: http://www.simon.rochester.edu/programs/full-time-ms-in-marketing-analytics/index.aspx

The University of Texas at Arlington, Graduate School, College of Business, Department of Marketing, Arlington, TX 76019. Offers marketing (MBA); marketing research (MS). *Program availability:* Part-time, evening/weekend. *Degree requirements:* For master's, thesis optional. *Entrance requirements:* For master's, GMAT, GRE. Additional exam requirements/recommendations for international students: Required—TOEFL (minimum score 550 paper-based; 79 iBT). Electronic applications accepted. *Faculty research:* Marketing strategy, marketing research, international marketing.

University of Wisconsin–Madison, Graduate School, Wisconsin School of Business, Wisconsin Full-Time MBA Program, Madison, WI 53706. Offers applied security analysis (MBA); arts administration (MBA); brand and product management (MBA); corporate finance and investment banking (MBA); marketing research (MBA); operations and technology management (MBA); real estate (MBA); risk management and insurance (MBA); strategic human resource management (MBA); supply chain management (MBA). *Faculty:* 130 full-time (35 women), 42 part-time/adjunct (13 women). *Students:* 203 full-time (72 women); includes 34 minority (8 Black or African American, non-Hispanic/Latino; 10 Asian, non-Hispanic/Latino; 12 Hispanic/Latino; 4 Two or more races, non-Hispanic/Latino), 41 international. Average age 28. 556 applicants, 30% accepted, 104 enrolled. In 2017, 97 master's awarded. *Entrance requirements:* For master's, GMAT or GRE, bachelor's or equivalent degree, 2 years of work experience, essay, letter of recommendation, resume. Additional exam requirements/recommendations for international students: Required—TOEFL (minimum score 100 iBT), IELTS (minimum score 7.5). *Application deadline:* For fall admission, 11/

2 for domestic and international students; for winter admission, 1/11 for domestic and international students; for spring admission, 3/1 for domestic and international students; for summer admission, 4/12 for domestic and international students. Applications are processed on a rolling basis. Application fee: $75 ($81 for international students). Electronic applications accepted. *Expenses:* $9,356 per semester resident, $18,288 non-resident. *Financial support:* In 2017–18, 183 students received support, including 14 fellowships with full tuition reimbursements available (averaging $25,420 per year), 7 research assistantships with full tuition reimbursements available (averaging $13,375 per year), 53 teaching assistantships with full tuition reimbursements available (averaging $13,375 per year); scholarships/grants, health care benefits, tuition waivers (full), and unspecified assistantships also available. Financial award application deadline: 4/11. *Faculty research:* Forms of competition and outcomes in dual distribution systems; explaining the accuracy of revised forecasts; supply chain planning for random demand surges; advanced demand information in a multi-product system; the effects of presentation salience and measurement subjectivity on nonprofessional investors' fair value judgments. *Unit head:* Dr. Don Hausch, Associate Dean, Full-time MBA Program, 608-262-9731, E-mail: don.hausch@wisc.edu. *Application contact:* Betsy Kacizak, Director of Admissions and Recruiting, Full-time MBA Program, 608-262-4000, E-mail: betsy.kacizak@wisc.edu.
Website: https://wsb.wisc.edu/

SAINT JOSEPH'S UNIVERSITY
Marketing

 For more information, visit http://petersons.to/sjuintlmarketing

Programs of Study

The Master of Science in Marketing (M.S.M.) program at Saint Joseph's University' Haub School of Business (HSB) is designed to provide students with the technological savvy, global orientation, and advanced business skills to market products and services anywhere in the world. Students develop competencies in core marketing concepts, and then focus their degree with one of two in-demand specializations: Customer Analytics and Insights or International Marketing. From consumer behavior and research, to analytics and strategy, students gain practical, immediately applicable expertise that sets them apart from their peers.

The M.S.M. program is designed for marketing professionals who want to deepen their knowledge and advance their career or recent college graduates or early careerists who want to prepare for their next professional opportunity.

Offered in a variety of formats, students can attend full- or part-time and take courses online, on campus, or both. Classes are offered in the fall, spring, and summer terms, and students can begin any semester. Students can pace the program according to their needs, and can graduate in one year or take up to six years to complete the degree. Online courses include synchronous and asynchronous sessions along with other collaborative learning tools.

The M.S.M. curriculum consists of 10 upper level courses (30 credits) which provide students with advanced learning in core marketing concepts, as well as allowing students to specialize in a chosen track. An international study tour complements the classroom experience.

Students come from all majors and backgrounds. For those whose undergraduate degree is in a non-business major, four foundations courses (12 credits) are offered to prepare them for success in the program. Opportunities for foundation course waivers are determined for every applicant.

The Haub School of Business has more than 80 full-time faculty who contribute scholarly research to the classroom along with part-time faculty who are senior executives in their field. Small classes allow for in-depth discussions, reflection, experiential exercises, writing assignments, and team projects, as well as facilitate interactions with fellow students, faculty, and guest lecturers.

Students in the M.S.M. program graduate prepared to create solutions, introduce new capabilities, influence marketing strategy and ultimately, contribute to their organization's bottom line.

Graduates of the program can connect with more than 67,000 SJU alumni around the globe. Numerous formal and informal events and activities allow students to network with their peers, alumni, lecturers, and business representatives. With lifetime access to the Career Development Center, students receive guidance on vital techniques including resume writing, interviewing, networking, and job search.

A recent survey of those who have earned a graduate business degree at Saint Joseph's University has shown that 73 percent report receiving a raise after completing their program; 76 percent say the program significantly helped them advance their career; 70 percent indicate that their degree from the Haub School provided them with more opportunities to increase their salary and gain professional recognition; and 86 percent say the program provided them with the strategic business acumen they needed to succeed in their chosen field.

Research Facilities

The Post Learning Commons and Drexel Library make up the Post Academic Center and support the academic programs of Saint Joseph's University with books and periodicals in both print and electronic formats, research databases, audio-visual materials, and microforms. Research resources and support are available on campus and fully online.

The Wall Street Trading Room at SJU's Haub School of Business supports the financial education programs and provides students with the knowledge and skills required for competing in a global job market. The room provides access to electronic sources of financial and investment data, analytical tools, and trading simulations. The room allows hands-on learning, curriculum enhancements, and more effective class projects. Trading simulations provide opportunities for real trading experiences. Continuous access to financial data and software provides an integrated learning environment to focus on analysis, synthesis, and evaluation.

Financial Aid

Financial aid is available and includes federal loans, university scholarships, graduate assistantships, employer tuition deferral programs, and loans from private lenders. SJU also offers tuition benefits to eligible military personnel and veterans through the Yellow Ribbon Program.

Cost of Study

Tuition for the 2018–19 academic year is $1,043 per credit for domestic and international students. Tuition is charged on a per credit basis, per semester, and is the same for online and on-campus courses. There are no additional fees for domestic students; international students may incur additional fees in regard to their visa, as well as a university health plan. Tuition is subject to change by the order of the Saint Joseph's University Board of Trustees.

Living and Housing Costs

The Office of Residence Life offers limited on-campus housing options for graduate students; availability is not guaranteed. The 2018–19 rates range from $5,120 to $6,120 per person per semester. Residence Life also assists students with off-campus housing recommendations. More information can be found at https://offcampushousing.sju.edu/.

Student Life

Students in the M.S.M. program may choose to participate in SJU's Graduate Business Student Association (GBSA). The GBSA enhances the graduate experience by promoting professional development and a sense of community among graduate business students, faculty, and administration. All students are automatically members of the GBSA and no registration is required. This student-run organization aims to build strategic relationships by providing networking opportunities through social and service activities.

The Office of Adult Student Life assists graduate students by providing support in overcoming obstacles and resources to foster success. The ASL Office seeks to help adult students develop a personalized plan for success, coordinate adult student groups, organize programs to meet adult student needs, and provide adult student advocacy as needed.

Location

Located in Philadelphia, Pennsylvania, SJU's community enjoys the surroundings of one of America's first major cities. Widely known as "The City of Brotherly Love" Philadelphia's historical importance and vibrant communities create a charming and unique culture. The city is the fifth-largest metropolis in the U.S. and is home to historical landmarks and world-class museums, a number of professional sports teams and dining options, and major events that enrich its cultural life. There are also opportunities to explore Philadelphia's outdoors with a wealth of year-round festivals and cultural events, parks, zoos, and aquariums. With eight Fortune 500

Saint Joseph's University

companies, Philadelphia offers numerous internship, networking, and post-graduation job opportunities.

The SJU campus is just a train ride away from Center City Philadelphia, allowing students to easily access the culture, art, nightlife, and opportunity that Philadelphia has to offer. The city is also conveniently located between New York City and Washington D.C., providing convenient access to additional cultural and employment opportunities.

The University and the School

For over 160 years, Saint Joseph's University has been engaging students in a rigorous Jesuit education that empowers them to become leaders in their industries and communities. Built upon the Ignatian credo of *cura personalis*, the Saint Joseph's education encompasses all aspects of personal growth and development: high achievement, deepening understanding, strengthening reasoning and communication skills, and developing moral character.

The university offers approximately 8,086 students 55 majors, 50 minors, 30-plus degree completion and certificate programs, and 52 graduate programs through two schools. The College of Arts and Sciences offers programs in the humanities, natural sciences, and social sciences.

The Erivan K. Haub School of Business provides a wide-range of programs including STEM master's degrees and graduate programs in analytics. It is an international AACSB-accredited institution in business and accounting, offering programs at the bachelor's, master's, and executive master's levels. *U.S. News & World Report* has ranked the school's part-time MBA, risk-management and insurance, marketing, management, and finance programs among the top in the nation. The Haub School was recently named one of the nation's top business schools in the Princeton Review's "The Best 294 Business Schools," and the undergraduate program was recently recognized by Bloomberg's Businessweek.

It is the largest Jesuit business school in the country with 3,600 students, 84 full-time faculty and more than 22,000 alumni.

Faculty

The professors in the Master of Science in Marketing program are full-time faculty engaged in cutting-edge research and part-time faculty who are senior executives in their fields. All instructors infuse their classes with relevant, real-world learning and scholarship, providing students with practical business knowledge that they can apply immediately in their careers.

Additional information regarding members of the M.S.M. faculty can be found online at https://www.sju.edu/majors-programs/graduate-business/master-degrees/master-science-marketing/meet-faculty.

Applying

Applications are reviewed on a rolling basis. Students may apply to start the M.S.M. program in the fall, spring, or summer terms. The priority application deadline is July 15 for fall semester, November 15 for spring semester, and March 15 for summer semester.

Applicants must have a baccalaureate degree from an accredited university and complete the official application. Required application materials include: official transcripts for all credits earned (undergraduate and graduate),

two letters of recommendation, a current resume, a $35 application fee, a personal statement (specifics available online), and official GMAT or GRE scores from within the past seven years (GMAT may be waived under certain circumstances; more details are available online).

Additional requirements and details for international students are available at https://www.sju.edu/majors-programs/graduate-business/master-degrees/ /master-science-marketing/admission-requirements.

Correspondence and Information

Graduate Business Office
Master of Science in Marketing
Saint Joseph's University
5600 City Avenue, MV 280
Philadelphia, Pennsylvania 19131
Phone: 610-660-1690
E-mail: sjumba@sju.edu
Website: sju.edu/ms/marketing

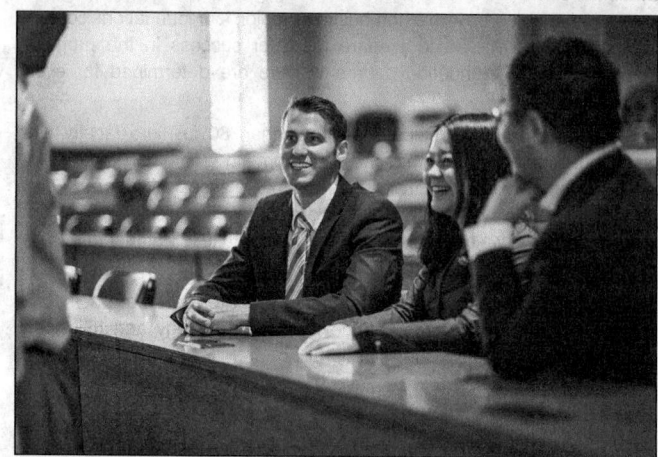

Section 15
Nonprofit Management

This section contains a directory of institutions offering graduate work in nonprofit management. Additional information about programs listed in the directory may be obtained by writing directly to the dean of a graduate school or chair of a department at the address given in the directory.

For programs offering related work, see also in this book *Accounting and Finance* and *Business Administration and Management*. In another guide in this series:

Graduate Programs in the Humanities, Arts & Social Sciences

See *Public, Regional, and Industrial Affairs*

CONTENTS

Program Directory

Nonprofit Management

Abilene Christian University, College of Graduate and Professional Studies, Program in Business Administration, Addison, TX 75001. Offers business analytics (MBA); corporate finance (MBA); general management (MBA); healthcare administration (MBA); human resource management (MBA); international business (MBA); management: business analytics (MS); management: healthcare administration (MS); management: international business (MS); management: marketing (MS); management: operations and supply chain management (MS); marketing (MBA); nonprofit leadership (MBA); operations and supply chain management (MBA). *Program availability:* Part-time, online only, 100% online. *Faculty:* 2 full-time (0 women), 6 part-time/adjunct (2 women). *Students:* 109 full-time (47 women), 51 part-time (22 women); includes 42 minority (33 Black or African American, non-Hispanic/Latino; 1 American Indian or Alaska Native, non-Hispanic/Latino; 2 Asian, non-Hispanic/Latino; 6 Hispanic/Latino). 125 applicants, 65% accepted, 58 enrolled. *Entrance requirements:* Additional exam requirements/recommendations for international students: Required—TOEFL (minimum score 80 iBT), IELTS (minimum score 6). *Application deadline:* For fall admission, 8/14 priority date for domestic students; for winter admission, 10/1 priority date for domestic students; for spring admission, 12/15 priority date for domestic students; for summer admission, 4/15 priority date for domestic students. Applications are processed on a rolling basis. Application fee: $50. Electronic applications accepted. *Expenses:* $700 per hour. *Financial support:* In 2017–18, 2 students received support. Application deadline: 4/1; applicants required to submit FAFSA. *Faculty research:* Organizational structure, financial management, cost accounting, unit analysis management. *Unit head:* Phil Vardiman, Program Director, 325-674-2153, E-mail: pxv02b@acu.edu. *Application contact:* Graduate Advisor, 817-219-7300, E-mail: gradonline@acu.edu.
Website: http://www.acu.edu/online/academics/mba-business-administration.html

Adler University, Graduate Programs, MA in Nonprofit Management Program, Chicago, IL 60602. Offers MA. *Program availability:* Online learning.

American Jewish University, Graduate School of Nonprofit Management, Program in Business Administration, Bel Air, CA 90077-1599. Offers general nonprofit administration (MBA); Jewish nonprofit administration (MBA). *Program availability:* Part-time, evening/weekend. *Degree requirements:* For master's, thesis, internship. *Entrance requirements:* For master's, GMAT or GRE General Test, interview, minimum undergraduate GPA of 3.0. Additional exam requirements/recommendations for international students: Required—TOEFL (minimum score 550 paper-based).

American University, School of Public Affairs, Department of Public Administration and Policy, Washington, DC 20016-8070. Offers organization development (MSOD, Certificate, including leadership for organizational change (Certificate), organization development (MSOD); public administration (MPA, PhD, Certificate, including nonprofit management (Certificate), public financial management (Certificate), public management (Certificate); public administration and policy (MPAP), including public administration policy; public policy (MPP), including public policy; public policy (Certificate), including public policy analysis; LL M/MPA; MPA/JD; MPP/JD; MPP/LL M. *Program availability:* Part-time, evening/weekend, online learning. *Faculty:* 31 full-time (12 women), 36 part-time/adjunct (13 women). *Students:* 211 full-time (129 women), 305 part-time (202 women); includes 132 minority (84 Black or African American, non-Hispanic/Latino; 4 American Indian or Alaska Native, non-Hispanic/Latino; 24 Asian, non-Hispanic/Latino; 10 Hispanic/Latino; 10 Two or more races, non-Hispanic/Latino), 34 international. Average age 31. 658 applicants, 86% accepted, 230 enrolled. In 2017, 178 master's, 6 doctorates, 7 other advanced degrees awarded. *Degree requirements:* For master's, comprehensive exam; for doctorate, comprehensive exam, thesis/dissertation. *Entrance requirements:* For master's, GRE, statement of purpose, 2 recommendations, resume, transcript; for doctorate, GRE, 3 recommendations, statement of purpose, resume, writing sample, transcript; for Certificate, bachelor's degree. Additional exam requirements/recommendations for international students: Required—TOEFL (minimum score 600 paper-based; 100 iBT). *Application deadline:* For fall admission, 2/15 priority date for domestic students, 5/1 for international students; for spring admission, 11/1 for domestic students, 9/15 for international students. Application fee: $55. *Expenses:* Contact institution. *Financial support:* Research assistantships, teaching assistantships, institutionally sponsored loans, scholarships/grants, and unspecified assistantships available. Financial award applicants required to submit FAFSA. *Unit head:* Dr. Dave Marcotte, Department Chair, 202-885-3108, E-mail: marcotte@american.edu. *Application contact:* Jennifer Forney, Assistant Dean, Graduate Enrollment, E-mail: forney@american.edu.
Website: http://www.american.edu/spa/dpap/

Antioch University Santa Barbara, Program in Business Administration, Santa Barbara, CA 93101-1581. Offers non-profit management (MBA); social business (MBA); strategic leadership (MBA).

Arizona State University at the Tempe campus, College of Public Programs, School of Community Resources and Development, Phoenix, AZ 85004-0685. Offers community resources and development (MS, PhD); nonprofit leadership and management (Graduate Certificate); nonprofit studies (MNpS); sustainable tourism (MAS). *Program availability:* Part-time, evening/weekend. Terminal master's awarded for partial completion of doctoral program. *Degree requirements:* For master's, thesis or alternative, interactive Program of Study (iPOS) submitted before completing 50 percent of required credit hours; for doctorate, comprehensive exam, thesis/dissertation, interactive Program of Study (iPOS) submitted before completing 50 percent of required credit hours. *Entrance requirements:* For master's and doctorate, GRE, minimum GPA of 3.0 or equivalent in last 2 years of work leading to bachelor's degree. Additional exam requirements/recommendations for international students: Required—TOEFL, IELTS, or PTE. Electronic applications accepted. *Expenses:* Contact institution.

Arizona State University at the Tempe campus, College of Public Programs, School of Public Affairs, Phoenix, AZ 85004-0687. Offers emergency management and homeland security (MA); program evaluation (MS); public administration (MPA, PhD), including nonprofit administration (MPA), urban management (MPA); public policy (MPP); MPA/MSW. *Accreditation:* NASPAA (one or more programs are accredited). *Program availability:* Part-time, evening/weekend. Terminal master's awarded for partial completion of doctoral program. *Degree requirements:* For master's, thesis or alternative, policy analysis or capstone project; interactive Program of Study (iPOS) submitted before completing 50 percent of required credit hours; for doctorate, comprehensive exam, thesis/dissertation, interactive Program of Study (iPOS) submitted before completing 50 percent of required credit hours. *Entrance requirements:* For master's, GRE, minimum GPA of 3.0 or equivalent in last 2 years of work leading to bachelor's degree; for doctorate, GRE, minimum GPA of 3.0 or equivalent in last 2 years of work leading to bachelor's degree, 3 letters of recommendation, resume, statement of goals, samples of research reports. Additional exam requirements/recommendations for international students:

Required—TOEFL (minimum score 600 paper-based; 100 iBT), IELTS (minimum score 6.5). Electronic applications accepted. *Expenses:* Contact institution.

Assumption College, Business Studies Program, Worcester, MA 01609-1296. Offers accounting (MBA); business studies (CAGS); finance/economics (MBA); human resources (MBA); international business (MBA); management (MBA); marketing (MBA); nonprofit leadership (MBA). *Program availability:* Part-time, evening/weekend. *Faculty:* 5 full-time (1 woman), 21 part-time/adjunct (6 women). *Students:* 29 full-time (13 women), 87 part-time (50 women); includes 15 minority (1 Black or African American, non-Hispanic/Latino; 4 Asian, non-Hispanic/Latino; 8 Hispanic/Latino; 2 Two or more races, non-Hispanic/Latino), 4 international. Average age 29. 34 applicants, 100% accepted, 26 enrolled. In 2017, 81 master's, 2 other advanced degrees awarded. *Degree requirements:* For master's, capstone. *Entrance requirements:* For master's, bachelor's degree, three letters of recommendation, official transcripts, personal statement, current resume; for CAGS, MBA or equivalent degree in a closely related field, three letters of recommendation, official transcripts, personal statement, current resume. Additional exam requirements/recommendations for international students: Required—TOEFL (minimum score 540 paper-based; 76 iBT), IELTS (minimum score 6). *Application deadline:* For fall admission, 8/10 priority date for domestic and international students; for spring admission, 1/4 priority date for domestic and international students; for summer admission, 5/10 priority date for domestic and international students. Application fee: $30. Electronic applications accepted. *Expenses:* Tuition: Full-time $11,952; part-time $664 per credit. *Required fees:* $70 per term. *Financial support:* In 2017–18, 19 students received support. Tuition waivers (full and partial), unspecified assistantships, and institutional discounts available. Financial award applicants required to submit FAFSA. *Faculty research:* Workplace diversity, dynamics of team interaction, utilization of leased employees, experiential learning project on due diligence market for prostheses. *Unit head:* Dr. Robin Frkal, Director, 508-767-7622, E-mail: ra.frkal@assumption.edu. *Application contact:* Karen Stoyanoff, Director of Recruitment for Graduate Enrollment, 508-767-7442, Fax: 508-799-4412, E-mail: graduate@assumption.edu.
Website: http://graduate.assumption.edu/mba/assumption-mba

Avila University, School of Professional Studies, Kansas City, MO 64145-1698. Offers executive leadership (MS); fundraising (MA); instructional design and technology (MA, MS); leadership coaching (MS); project management (MS); strategic human resources (MS). *Program availability:* Part-time-only, evening/weekend, 100% online, blended/hybrid learning. *Faculty:* 14 part-time/adjunct (8 women). *Students:* 85 full-time (61 women), 45 part-time (33 women); includes 42 minority (35 Black or African American, non-Hispanic/Latino; 2 Asian, non-Hispanic/Latino; 4 Hispanic/Latino; 1 Two or more races, non-Hispanic/Latino), 3 international. Average age 37. 63 applicants, 60% accepted, 29 enrolled. In 2017, 39 master's awarded. *Degree requirements:* For master's, thesis optional. *Entrance requirements:* For master's, 2 letters of recommendation, minimum GPA of 3.0 during last 60 hours, resume, statement of intent. Additional exam requirements/recommendations for international students: Required—TOEFL (minimum score 550 paper-based; 79 iBT). *Application deadline:* Applications are processed on a rolling basis. Application fee: $0. Electronic applications accepted. *Expenses:* Contact institution. *Financial support:* In 2017–18, 14 students received support. Unspecified assistantships available. Support available to part-time students. Financial award applicants required to submit FAFSA. *Unit head:* Kari Clevenger, Associate Dean/Director, 816-501-3675, Fax: 816-941-4650, E-mail: advantage@avila.edu. *Application contact:* Jessica Burson, Graduate Admission Advisor, 816-501-2482, Fax: 816-941-4650, E-mail: advantage@avila.edu.
Website: https://www.avila.edu/mrk/advantage-3

Baruch College of the City University of New York, Austin W. Marxe School of Public and International Affairs, Program in Public Administration, New York, NY 10010-5585. Offers general public administration (MPA); health care policy (MPA); nonprofit administration (MPA); policy analysis and evaluation (MPA); public management (MPA); urban development and sustainability (MPA); MS/MPA. *Accreditation:* NASPAA. *Program availability:* Part-time, evening/weekend. *Degree requirements:* For master's, thesis, capstone. *Entrance requirements:* For master's, GRE General Test. Additional exam requirements/recommendations for international students: Required—TOEFL. Electronic applications accepted. *Expenses:* Contact institution. *Faculty research:* Urbanization, population and poverty in the developing world, housing and community development, labor unions and housing, government-nongovernment relations, immigration policy, social network analysis, cross-sectoral governance, comparative healthcare systems, program evaluation, social welfare policy, health outcomes, educational policy and leadership, transnationalism, infant health, welfare reform, racial/ethnic disparities in health, urban politics, homelessness, race and ethnic relations.

Bay Path University, Program in Nonprofit Management and Philanthropy, Longmeadow, MA 01106-2292. Offers MS. *Program availability:* Part-time, 100% online. *Students:* 2 full-time (1 woman), 43 part-time (42 women); includes 16 minority (8 Black or African American, non-Hispanic/Latino; 6 Hispanic/Latino; 2 Two or more races, non-Hispanic/Latino). Average age 35. In 2017, 13 master's awarded. *Degree requirements:* For master's, eight courses (24 credits) and four electives (12 credits) for a total of 36 credits; capstone paper. *Application deadline:* Applications are processed on a rolling basis. Application fee: $45. Electronic applications accepted. Application fee is waived when completed online. *Expenses:* $675 per credit. *Financial support:* Unspecified assistantships available. Financial award applicants required to submit FAFSA. *Unit head:* Silvia de Haas-Phillips, Program Director, E-mail: sdphillips@baypath.edu. *Application contact:* Diane Ranaldi, Dean of Graduate Admissions, 413-565-1332, Fax: 413-565-1250, E-mail: dranaldi@baypath.edu.
Website: http://graduate.baypath.edu/Graduate-Programs/Programs-On-Campus/MS-Programs/Nonprofit-Management-and-Philanthropy

Bay Path University, Program in Strategic Fundraising and Philanthropy, Longmeadow, MA 01106-2292. Offers higher education fundraising (MS); nonprofit fundraising (MS). *Program availability:* Part-time, 100% online. *Students:* 2 full-time (both women), 9 part-time (7 women); includes 2 minority (1 Black or African American, non-Hispanic/Latino; 1 Native Hawaiian or other Pacific Islander, non-Hispanic/Latino). Average age 36. In 2017, 4 master's awarded. *Degree requirements:* For master's, 36 hours of coursework including portfolio. *Application deadline:* Applications are processed on a rolling basis. Application fee: $45. Electronic applications accepted. Application fee is waived when completed online. *Expenses:* $675 per credit. *Financial support:* Unspecified assistantships available. Financial award applicants required to submit FAFSA. *Unit head:* Silvia de Haas-Phillips, Program Director, E-mail: sdphillips@baypath.edu. *Application contact:* Diane Ranaldi, Dean of Graduate Admissions, 413-565-1332, Fax: 413-565-1250, E-mail: dranaldi@baypath.edu.
Website: http://graduate.baypath.edu/Graduate-Programs/Programs-On-Campus/MS-Programs/Strategic-Fundraising-and-Philanthropy

Bradley University, The Graduate School, College of Education and Health Sciences, Department of Leadership in Education, Nonprofits and Counseling, Peoria, IL 61625-0002. Offers counseling (MA), including clinical mental health counseling, professional school counseling; leadership in educational administration (MA); nonprofit leadership (MA). *Accreditation:* ACA; NCATE. *Program availability:* Part-time, evening/weekend. *Degree requirements:* For master's, comprehensive exam, thesis optional. *Entrance requirements:* For master's, GRE General Test or MAT, interview, 3 letters of recommendation. Additional exam requirements/recommendations for international students: Required—TOEFL (minimum score 550 paper-based; 79 iBT), IELTS (minimum score 6.5). Electronic applications accepted.

Brandeis University, The Heller School for Social Policy and Management, Program in Nonprofit Management, Waltham, MA 02454-9110. Offers child, youth, and family management (MBA); health care management (MBA); social impact management (MBA); social policy and management (MBA); sustainable development (MBA); MBA/MA; MBA/MD. MBA/MD program offered in conjunction with Tufts University School of Medicine. *Accreditation:* AACSB. *Program availability:* Part-time. *Degree requirements:* For master's, team consulting project. *Entrance requirements:* For master's, GMAT (preferred) or GRE, 2 letters of recommendation, problem statement analysis, 3-5 years of professional experience. Additional exam requirements/recommendations for international students: Required—TOEFL (minimum score 600 paper-based; 100 iBT). Electronic applications accepted. *Expenses:* Contact institution. *Faculty research:* Health care; children and families; elder and disabled services; social impact management; organizations in the non-profit, for-profit, or public sector.

Brigham Young University, Graduate Studies, BYU Marriott School of Business, Master of Public Administration Program, Provo, UT 84602. Offers healthcare (MPA); local government (MPA); nonprofit management (MPA); state and federal government (MPA); JD/MPA. *Accreditation:* NASPAA. *Faculty:* 134 full-time (15 women), 65 part-time/adjunct (16 women). *Students:* 105 full-time (50 women); includes 10 minority (3 Black or African American, non-Hispanic/Latino; 3 Asian, non-Hispanic/Latino; 3 Hispanic/Latino; 1 Native Hawaiian or other Pacific Islander, non-Hispanic/Latino), 14 international. Average age 27. 95 applicants, 73% accepted, 50 enrolled. In 2017, 41 master's awarded. *Entrance requirements:* For master's, GMAT or GRE, commitment to BYU Honor Code. Additional exam requirements/recommendations for international students: Required—TOEFL (minimum score 580 paper-based; 85 iBT). *Application deadline:* For fall admission, 1/15 for domestic and international students. Application fee: $50. Electronic applications accepted. *Expenses:* Contact institution. *Financial support:* Research assistantships, teaching assistantships, career-related internships or fieldwork, institutionally sponsored loans, and scholarships/grants available. Financial award application deadline: 4/15; financial award applicants required to submit FAFSA. *Faculty research:* Taxes, budgeting, nonprofit, ethics, decision modeling, work balance, organizational behavior. *Unit head:* Dr. Lori Wadsworth, Director, 801-422-5956, E-mail: mpa@byu.edu. *Application contact:* Catherine Cooper, Associate Director, 801-422-9173, E-mail: mpa@byu.edu.
Website: https://marriottschool.byu.edu/mpa/

Cairn University, School of Business, Langhorne, PA 19047-2990. Offers accounting (MBA); business administration (MBA); international entrepreneurship (MBA); nonprofit leadership (MBA); organizational leadership (MSOL, Postbaccalaureate Certificate). *Program availability:* Part-time, evening/weekend, 100% online, blended/hybrid learning. *Entrance requirements:* Additional exam requirements/recommendations for international students: Required—TOEFL (minimum score 550 paper-based). Electronic applications accepted. Application fee is waived when completed online. *Expenses:* Contact institution.

California Baptist University, Program in Leadership and Community Development, Riverside, CA 92504-3206. Offers MA. *Program availability:* Part-time, evening/weekend. *Students:* 1 applicant, 100% accepted. In 2017, 2 master's awarded. *Entrance requirements:* For master's, minimum cumulative GPA of 2.75, three letters of recommendation, current resume, 500-word comprehensive essay. Additional exam requirements/recommendations for international students: Required—TOEFL (minimum score 80 iBT). *Application deadline:* For fall admission, 8/1 priority date for domestic students, 7/1 priority date for international students; for spring admission, 12/1 for domestic students, 11/1 priority date for international students. Applications are processed on a rolling basis. Application fee: $45. Electronic applications accepted. *Expenses:* Contact institution. *Financial support:* In 2017–18, 1 student received support. Applicants required to submit CSS PROFILE or FAFSA. *Faculty research:* Educational leadership, curriculum and instruction, sociology of education, K-12 education, global education. *Unit head:* Dr. John Shoup, Dean, School of Education, 951-343-4205, E-mail: jshoup@calbaptist.edu.
Website: http://www.calbaptist.edu/academics/schools-colleges/school-education/programs/graduate/master-arts-leadership-and-community-development/

California State University, Northridge, Graduate Studies, Tseng College, Program in Nonprofit-Sector Management, Northridge, CA 91330. Offers Graduate Certificate. Offered in collaboration with College of Social and Behavioral Sciences. *Entrance requirements:* For degree, bachelor's degree from accredited college or university with minimum GPA of 2.5 in last 60 semester units or 90 quarter units; at least one year of work experience in the public or non-profit sector. *Unit head:* Pat Lyon, Program Manager, 818-677-3332.
Website: http://tsengcollege.csun.edu/programs/NSM

Cambridge College, School of Management, Boston, MA 02129. Offers business negotiation and conflict resolution (M Mgt); general business (M Mgt); health care informatics (M Mgt); health care management (M Mgt); leadership in human and organizational dynamics (M Mgt); non-profit and public organization management (M Mgt); small business development (M Mgt); technology management (M Mgt). *Program availability:* Part-time, evening/weekend. *Degree requirements:* For master's, thesis, seminars. *Entrance requirements:* For master's, resume, 2 professional references. Additional exam requirements/recommendations for international students: Required—TOEFL (minimum score 550 paper-based; 79 iBT), Michigan English Language Assessment Battery (minimum score 85); Recommended—IELTS (minimum score 6). Electronic applications accepted. *Expenses:* Contact institution. *Faculty research:* Negotiation, mediation and conflict resolution; leadership; management of diverse organizations; case studies and simulation methodologies for management education, digital as a second language; social networking for digital immigrants, non-profit and public management.

Capella University, School of Public Service Leadership, Doctoral Programs in Healthcare, Minneapolis, MN 55402. Offers criminal justice (PhD); emergency management (PhD); epidemiology (Dr PH); general health administration (DHA); general public administration (DPA); health advocacy and leadership (Dr PH); health care administration (PhD); health care leadership (DHA); health policy advocacy (DHA); multidisciplinary human services (PhD); nonprofit management and leadership (PhD); public safety leadership (PhD); social and community services (PhD).

Carlos Albizu University, Miami Campus, Graduate Programs, Miami, FL 33172-2209. Offers clinical psychology (PhD, Psy D); entrepreneurship (MBA); exceptional student education (MS); human services (PhD); industrial/organizational psychology

(MS); marriage and family therapy (MS); mental health counseling (MS); nonprofit management (MBA); organizational management (MBA); psychology (MS); speech and language pathology (MS); teaching English for speakers of other languages (MS). *Accreditation:* APA. *Program availability:* Part-time, evening/weekend, 100% online, blended/hybrid learning. *Faculty:* 32 full-time (24 women), 27 part-time/adjunct (15 women). *Students:* 411 full-time (345 women), 248 part-time (215 women); includes 562 minority (53 Black or African American, non-Hispanic/Latino; 4 Asian, non-Hispanic/Latino; 498 Hispanic/Latino; 7 Two or more races, non-Hispanic/Latino), 23 international. Average age 34. 391 applicants, 42% accepted, 154 enrolled. In 2017, 96 master's, 54 doctorates awarded. Terminal master's awarded for partial completion of doctoral program. *Degree requirements:* For master's, comprehensive exam (for some programs), integrative project (for MBA); research project (for exceptional student education, teaching English as a second language); for doctorate, comprehensive examinations, internship, project/dissertation. *Entrance requirements:* For master's, GRE/EXADEP, bachelor's degree from accredited institution, minimum GPA of 3.0, 3 letters of recommendation, interview, resume, statement of purpose, official transcripts; for doctorate, GRE (for Psy D), 3 letters of recommendation, resume, interview, statement of purpose, official transcripts; bachelor's degree and minimum GPA of 3.25 (for Psy D); master's degree and minimum GPA of 3.0 (for PhD). Additional exam requirements/recommendations for international students: Required—Michigan Test of English Language Proficiency. *Application deadline:* For fall admission, 4/1 priority date for domestic students, 5/1 priority date for international students; for spring admission, 11/1 priority date for domestic students, 9/1 priority date for international students. Applications are processed on a rolling basis. Application fee: $50. Electronic applications accepted. Application fee is waived when completed online. *Expenses:* Contact institution. *Financial support:* In 2017–18, 145 students received support. Federal Work-Study, scholarships/grants, unspecified assistantships, and tuition discounts available. Financial award application deadline: 6/1; financial award applicants required to submit FAFSA. *Faculty research:* Psychotherapy, forensic psychology, neuropsychology, special education, speech-language pathology, criminal justice. *Unit head:* Dr. Etiony Aldarondo, Provost, 305-593-1223 Ext. 3138, Fax: 305-592-7930, E-mail: ealdarondo@albizu.edu. *Application contact:* Sonia Feliciano, Institutional Director of Student Recruitment, 305-593-1223 Ext. 3108, Fax: 305-477-8983, E-mail: sfeliciano@albizu.edu.

Case Western Reserve University, Jack, Joseph and Morton Mandel School of Applied Social Sciences, Cleveland, OH 44087. Offers nonprofit management (MNO); social welfare (PhD); social work (MSSA); JD/MSSA; MSSA/MA; MSSA/MBA; MSSA/MNO. *Accreditation:* CSWE (one or more programs are accredited). *Program availability:* Part-time, evening/weekend, 100% online. *Students:* 630 full-time (544 women), 61 part-time (54 women); includes 253 minority (187 Black or African American, non-Hispanic/Latino; 2 American Indian or Alaska Native, non-Hispanic/Latino; 10 Asian, non-Hispanic/Latino; 34 Hispanic/Latino; 1 Native Hawaiian or other Pacific Islander, non-Hispanic/Latino; 19 Two or more races, non-Hispanic/Latino), 34 international. Average age 32. 848 applicants, 78% accepted, 320 enrolled. In 2017, 184 master's, 3 doctorates awarded. *Degree requirements:* For master's, fieldwork; for doctorate, thesis/dissertation. *Entrance requirements:* For master's, minimum undergraduate GPA of 2.7 or GRE/MAT; for doctorate, GRE General Test. Additional exam requirements/recommendations for international students: Required—TOEFL (minimum score 557 paper-based, 90 iBT) or IELTS (minimum score 7). *Application deadline:* For fall admission, 4/15 for domestic and international students; for spring admission, 11/2 for domestic students; for summer admission, 3/1 for domestic students. Applications are processed on a rolling basis. Application fee: $0. Electronic applications accepted. *Financial support:* In 2017–18, 650 students received support, including 650 fellowships with full tuition reimbursements available (averaging $10,000 per year); career-related internships or fieldwork, Federal Work-Study, institutionally sponsored loans, scholarships/grants, tuition waivers (partial), and paid field placements (for MSSA students) also available. Support available to part-time students. Financial award application deadline: 4/15; financial award applicants required to submit FAFSA. *Faculty research:* Urban poverty, community social development, substance abuse, health, child welfare, aging, mental health, behavioral health, policy, mixed income communities, trauma, school social work, adoption. *Total annual research expenditures:* $9.1 million. *Unit head:* Dr. Grover Cleveland Gilmore, Dean, 216-368-2256, E-mail: msassdean@case.edu. *Application contact:* Richard Sigg, Director of Recruitment and Enrollment, 216-368-1655, E-mail: richard.sigg@case.edu.
Website: http://msass.case.edu/

Case Western Reserve University, Weatherhead School of Management, Mandel Center for Nonprofit Organizations, Cleveland, OH 44106-7167. Offers MNO, CNM, JD/MNO, MNO/MSSA, MSSA/MNO. *Entrance requirements:* For master's, GMAT or GRE. Additional exam requirements/recommendations for international students: Required—TOEFL. *Expenses:* Contact institution. *Faculty research:* Leadership management of non-profit organizations, strategic alliances, economic analysis of non-profit organizations.

Central Michigan University, Central Michigan University Global Campus, Program in Administration, Mount Pleasant, MI 48859. Offers acquisitions administration (MSA, Certificate); engineering management administration (MSA, Certificate); general administration (MSA, Certificate); health services administration (MSA, Certificate); human resources administration (MSA, Certificate); information resource management (MSA); information resource management administration (Certificate); international administration (MSA, Certificate); leadership (MSA, Certificate); philanthropy and fundraising administration (MSA, Certificate); public administration (MSA, Certificate); recreation and park administration (MSA); research administration (MSA, Certificate). *Program availability:* Part-time, evening/weekend, online learning. *Entrance requirements:* For master's, minimum GPA of 2.7 in major. Electronic applications accepted.

Chaminade University of Honolulu, Office of Professional and Continuing Education, Program in Business Administration, Honolulu, HI 96816-1578. Offers accounting (MBA); business (MBA); island business (MBA); not-for-profit (MBA). *Program availability:* Part-time, evening/weekend, 100% online, blended/hybrid learning. *Faculty:* 5 full-time (2 women), 8 part-time/adjunct (2 women). *Students:* 80 full-time (44 women), 54 part-time (37 women); includes 95 minority (6 Black or African American, non-Hispanic/Latino; 2 American Indian or Alaska Native, non-Hispanic/Latino; 42 Asian, non-Hispanic/Latino; 8 Hispanic/Latino; 34 Native Hawaiian or other Pacific Islander, non-Hispanic/Latino; 3 Two or more races, non-Hispanic/Latino), 5 international. Average age 32. 36 applicants, 94% accepted, 24 enrolled. In 2017, 39 master's awarded. *Entrance requirements:* For master's, minimum GPA of 3.0, resume, two years or more of work experience. Additional exam requirements/recommendations for international students: Required—TOEFL (minimum score 550 paper-based; 79 iBT). *Application deadline:* Applications are processed on a rolling basis. Application fee: $40. Electronic applications accepted. *Expenses:* $900 per credit hour with $93 fee per online course. *Financial support:* Applicants required to submit FAFSA. *Unit head:* Dr. Scott J. Schroeder, Dean, 808-739-4612, Fax: 808-735-4734, E-mail: mba@chaminade.edu. *Application contact:* 808-735-4755, E-mail: gradserv@chaminade.edu.
Website: https://pace.chaminade.edu/graduate-programs/mba-program/

Nonprofit Management

Cleveland State University, College of Graduate Studies, Maxine Goodman Levin College of Urban Affairs, Program in Environmental Studies, Cleveland, OH 44115. Offers environmental nonprofit management (MAES); environmental planning (MAES); policy and administration (MAES); sustainable economic development (MAES); urban economic development (Certificate); JD/MAES. *Program availability:* Part-time, evening/weekend. *Faculty:* 16 full-time (8 women), 13 part-time/adjunct (5 women). *Students:* 11 full-time (7 women), 8 part-time (4 women); includes 6 minority (5 Black or African American, non-Hispanic/Latino; 1 Hispanic/Latino). Average age 29. 10 applicants, 100% accepted, 5 enrolled. In 2017, 3 master's awarded. *Degree requirements:* For master's, thesis or alternative, exit project. *Entrance requirements:* For master's, GRE General Test (minimum score: verbal and quantitative combined 40th percentile, analytical writing 4.0), minimum GPA of 3.0. Additional exam requirements/recommendations for international students: Required—TOEFL (minimum score 550 paper-based; 78 iBT), IELTS (6.0), or International Test of English Proficiency (iTEP). *Application deadline:* For fall admission, 7/1 priority date for domestic students, 5/15 for international students; for spring admission, 11/15 for domestic students, 11/1 for international students; for summer admission, 4/1 for domestic students, 3/15 for international students. Applications are processed on a rolling basis. Application fee: $40. Electronic applications accepted. *Expenses:* Contact institution. *Financial support:* In 2017–18, 4 students received support. Research assistantships with tuition reimbursements available, teaching assistantships with partial tuition reimbursements available, scholarships/grants, tuition waivers (full and partial), and unspecified assistantships available. Support available to part-time students. Financial award application deadline: 3/1; financial award applicants required to submit FAFSA. *Faculty research:* Environmental policy and administration, environmental planning, geographic information systems (GIS), urban sustainability planning and management, energy policy, land re-use. *Unit head:* Dr. Sanda Kaufman, Professor/Program Director, 216-687-2367, Fax: 216-687-9239, E-mail: s.kaufman@csuohio.edu. *Application contact:* David Arrighi, Graduate Academic Advisor, 216-523-7522, Fax: 216-687-5398, E-mail: d.arrighi@csuohio.edu.
Website: http://urban.csuohio.edu/academics/graduate/maes/

Cleveland State University, College of Graduate Studies, Maxine Goodman Levin College of Urban Affairs, Program in Nonprofit Administration and Leadership, Cleveland, OH 44115. Offers local and urban management (Certificate); nonprofit administration and leadership (MNAL); nonprofit management (Certificate). *Program availability:* Part-time, evening/weekend. *Faculty:* 16 full-time (8 women), 13 part-time/adjunct (5 women). *Students:* 4 full-time (3 women), 15 part-time (12 women); includes 6 minority (3 Black or African American, non-Hispanic/Latino; 3 Hispanic/Latino). Average age 34. 23 applicants, 52% accepted, 3 enrolled. In 2017, 5 master's awarded. *Degree requirements:* For master's, thesis or alternative, capstone course. *Entrance requirements:* For master's, GRE (minimum score: verbal and quantitative combined 40th percentile, analytical writing 4.0), minimum GPA of 3.0. Additional exam requirements/recommendations for international students: Required—TOEFL (minimum score 550 paper-based; 78 iBT), IELTS (6.0), or International Test of English Proficiency (iTEP). *Application deadline:* For fall admission, 7/15 priority date for domestic students, 5/15 for international students; for spring admission, 11/15 for domestic students, 11/1 for international students; for summer admission, 4/1 for domestic students, 3/15 for international students. Applications are processed on a rolling basis. Application fee: $40. Electronic applications accepted. *Expenses:* Contact institution. *Financial support:* In 2017–18, 3 students received support, including 2 research assistantships with full tuition reimbursements available (averaging $7,200 per year), 3 teaching assistantships with partial tuition reimbursements available (averaging $2,400 per year); career-related internships or fieldwork, scholarships/grants, and unspecified assistantships also available. Support available to part-time students. Financial award application deadline: 3/1; financial award applicants required to submit FAFSA. *Faculty research:* Human resource management, volunteerism, performance measurement in nonprofits, government-nonprofit partnerships. *Unit head:* Dr. Mittie Davis Jones, Associate Professor and Department Chairperson, 216-687-3861, Fax: 216-687-9342, E-mail: m.d.jones97@csuohio.edu. *Application contact:* David Arrighi, Graduate Academic Advisor, 216-523-7522, Fax: 216-687-5398, E-mail: urbanprograms@csuohio.edu.
Website: http://urban.csuohio.edu/academics/graduate/mnal/

Cleveland State University, College of Graduate Studies, Maxine Goodman Levin College of Urban Affairs, Program in Public Administration, Cleveland, OH 44115. Offers economic development (MPA); non-profit management (MPA); public management (MPA); JD/MPA. *Accreditation:* NASPAA. *Program availability:* Part-time, evening/weekend. *Faculty:* 16 full-time (8 women), 13 part-time/adjunct (5 women). *Students:* 23 full-time (15 women), 45 part-time (24 women); includes 19 minority (14 Black or African American, non-Hispanic/Latino; 1 Asian, non-Hispanic/Latino; 1 Hispanic/Latino; 3 Two or more races, non-Hispanic/Latino), 3 international. Average age 32. 79 applicants, 77% accepted, 12 enrolled. In 2017, 35 master's awarded. *Degree requirements:* For master's, thesis or alternative, exit project. *Entrance requirements:* For master's, GRE General Test (minimum scores in 40th percentile verbal and quantitative, 4.0 writing), minimum GPA of 3.0. Additional exam requirements/recommendations for international students: Required—TOEFL (minimum score 550 paper-based; 78 iBT), IELTS (6.0), or International Test of English Proficiency (iTEP). *Application deadline:* For fall admission, 7/1 priority date for domestic students, 5/15 for international students; for spring admission, 11/15 for domestic students, 11/1 for international students; for summer admission, 4/1 for domestic students, 3/15 for international students. Applications are processed on a rolling basis. Application fee: $40. Electronic applications accepted. *Expenses:* Contact institution. *Financial support:* In 2017–18, 16 students received support, including 5 research assistantships with full tuition reimbursements available (averaging $7,200 per year), 1 teaching assistantship with partial tuition reimbursement available (averaging $2,400 per year); scholarships/grants, tuition waivers (full and partial), and unspecified assistantships also available. Support available to part-time students. Financial award application deadline: 3/1; financial award applicants required to submit FAFSA. *Faculty research:* City management, nonprofit management, health care administration, public management, economic development. *Unit head:* Dr. Nicholas Zingale, Director, 216-802-3389, Fax: 216-687-9342, E-mail: n.zingale@csuohio.edu. *Application contact:* David Arrighi, Graduate Academic Advisor, 216-523-7522, Fax: 216-687-5398, E-mail: d.arrighi@csuohio.edu.
Website: http://urban.csuohio.edu/academics/graduate/mpa/

The College at Brockport, State University of New York, School of Business and Management, Department of Public Administration, Brockport, NY 14420-2997. Offers arts administration (AGC); nonprofit management (AGC); public administration (MPA), including health care management, nonprofit management, poverty studies, public management, public safety. *Accreditation:* NASPAA. *Program availability:* Part-time, evening/weekend. *Faculty:* 5 full-time (3 women), 5 part-time/adjunct (1 woman). *Students:* 54 full-time (38 women), 95 part-time (57 women); includes 38 minority (19 Black or African American, non-Hispanic/Latino; 3 Asian, non-Hispanic/Latino; 11 Hispanic/Latino; 5 Two or more races, non-Hispanic/Latino), 4 international. 53 applicants, 91% accepted, 31 enrolled. In 2017, 59 master's, 6 other advanced degrees awarded. *Degree requirements:* For master's, thesis or alternative. *Entrance requirements:* For master's, GRE or minimum GPA of 3.0, letters of recommendation, statement of objectives, current resume. Additional exam requirements/

recommendations for international students: Required—TOEFL (minimum score 550 paper-based; 79 iBT), IELTS (minimum score 6.5). *Application deadline:* For fall admission, 8/15 priority date for domestic and international students; for spring admission, 1/15 priority date for domestic and international students; for summer admission, 4/15 priority date for domestic and international students. Application fee: $50. Electronic applications accepted. *Expenses:* Tuition, state resident: full-time $10,870; part-time $453 per credit hour. Tuition, nonresident: full-time $22,210. *Required fees:* $988; $246 per semester. *Financial support:* In 2017–18, 1 fellowship with full tuition reimbursement (averaging $7,500 per year), 1 teaching assistantship with full tuition reimbursement (averaging $6,000 per year) were awarded; Federal Work-Study, scholarships/grants, and unspecified assistantships also available. Support available to part-time students. Financial award application deadline: 3/15; financial award applicants required to submit FAFSA. *Faculty research:* E-government, performance management, nonprofits and policy implementation, Medicaid and disabilities. *Unit head:* Dr. Celia Watt, Graduate Director, 585-395-5538, Fax: 585-395-2172, E-mail: cwatt@brockport.edu. *Application contact:* Danielle A. Welch, Graduate Admissions Counselor, 585-395-2525, Fax: 585-395-2515.
Website: https://www.brockport.edu/academics/public_administration/graduate/masters.html

Columbia University, School of Professional Studies, Program in Fundraising Management, New York, NY 10027. Offers MS. *Program availability:* Part-time, evening/weekend. *Degree requirements:* For master's, internship. *Entrance requirements:* For master's, BA with minimum GPA of 3.0. Additional exam requirements/recommendations for international students: Required—American Language Program placement test; Recommended—TOEFL. Electronic applications accepted. *Expenses:* Tuition: Full-time $44,864; part-time $1704 per credit. *Required fees:* $2370 per semester. One-time fee: $105. *Faculty research:* Fundraising for annual campaigns, capital campaigns, nonprofit financial management, research for fundraising and planned giving.

Corban University, Graduate School, The Corban MBA, Salem, OR 97301-9392. Offers management (MBA); non-profit management (MBA). *Program availability:* Online learning.

Daemen College, Program in Executive Leadership and Change, Amherst, NY 14226-3592. Offers business (MS); health professions (MS); not-for-profit organizations (MS). *Program availability:* Part-time, evening/weekend. *Degree requirements:* For master's, thesis, cohort learning sequence (2 years for weekend cohort; 3 years for weeknight cohort). *Entrance requirements:* For master's, 2 letters of recommendation, interview, goal statement, official transcripts, resume. Additional exam requirements/recommendations for international students: Required—TOEFL (minimum score 500 paper-based; 63 iBT), IELTS (minimum score 5.5). Electronic applications accepted.

Dallas Baptist University, College of Business, Master of Business Administration Program, Dallas, TX 75211-9299. Offers accounting (MBA); business communication (MBA); conflict resolution management (MBA); entrepreneurship (MBA); finance (MBA); health care management (MBA); international business (MBA); leading the non-profit organization (MBA); management (MBA); management information systems (MBA); marketing (MBA); project management (MBA); technology and engineering management (MBA). *Accreditation:* ACBSP. *Program availability:* Part-time, evening/weekend, 100% online, blended/hybrid learning. *Application deadline:* Applications are processed on a rolling basis. Application fee: $25. Electronic applications accepted. Application fee is waived when completed online. *Expenses: Tuition:* Full-time $16,308; part-time $906 per credit hour. *Required fees:* $900; $450 per semester. Tuition and fees vary according to course load and degree level. *Unit head:* Dr. Sandra Reid, Chair of Graduate Business Programs, 214-333-5280, E-mail: sandra@dbu.edu. *Application contact:* Bobby Soto, Director of Admissions, 214-333-5242, E-mail: graduate@dbu.edu.
Website: http://www.dbu.edu/gsb/mba

Dallas Baptist University, Graduate School of Ministry, Program in Christian Ministry, Dallas, TX 75211-9299. Offers chaplaincy (MA); counseling ministry (MA); family ministry (MA); general ministry (MA); leading the nonprofit organization (MA); ministry leadership (MA); professional life coaching (MA); urban ministry (MA). *Program availability:* Part-time, evening/weekend. *Application deadline:* Applications are processed on a rolling basis. Application fee: $25. Electronic applications accepted. Application fee is waived when completed online. *Expenses: Tuition:* Full-time $16,308; part-time $906 per credit hour. *Required fees:* $900; $450 per semester. Tuition and fees vary according to course load and degree level. *Unit head:* Dr. Robert R. Brooks, Dean, 214-333-5494, Fax: 214-333-5673, E-mail: bobb@dbu.edu. *Application contact:* Dr. Jon Choi, Program Director, 214-333-5375, Fax: 214-333-5689, E-mail: jon@dbu.edu.
Website: http://www.dbu.edu/ministry/degree-programs/m-a-in-christian-ministry

Dallas Baptist University, Graduate School of Ministry, Program in Global Leadership, Dallas, TX 75211-9299. Offers church planting (MA); East Asian Studies (MA); English as a second language (MA); general studies (MA); global communication (MA); global studies (MA); international business (MA); leading the nonprofit organization (MA); missions (MA); small group ministry (MA); urban ministry (MA). *Program availability:* Part-time, evening/weekend. *Application deadline:* Applications are processed on a rolling basis. Application fee: $25. Electronic applications accepted. Application fee is waived when completed online. *Expenses: Tuition:* Full-time $16,308; part-time $906 per credit hour. *Required fees:* $900; $450 per semester. Tuition and fees vary according to course load and degree level. *Unit head:* Dr. Robert R. Brooks, Dean, 214-333-5494, Fax: 214-333-5673, E-mail: bobb@dbu.edu. *Application contact:* Dr. Brent Thomason, Program Director, 214-333-5236, E-mail: brentt@dbu.edu.
Website: http://www.dbu.edu/ministry/degree-programs/m-a-in-global-leadership

DePaul University, College of Liberal Arts and Social Sciences, Chicago, IL 60614. Offers Arabic (MA); Chinese (MA); critical ethnic studies (MA); English (MA); French (MA); German (MA); history (MA); interdisciplinary studies (MA, MS); international public service (MS); international studies (MA); Italian (MA); Japanese (MA); liberal studies (MA); nonprofit management (MNM); public administration (MPA); public health (MPH); public policy (MPP); public service management (MS); refugee and forced migration studies (MS); social work (MSW); sociology (MA); Spanish (MA); sustainable urban development (MA); women's and gender studies (MA); writing and publishing (MA); writing, rhetoric and discourse (MA); MA/PhD. *Program availability:* Part-time, evening/weekend, online learning. Terminal master's awarded for partial completion of doctoral program. *Degree requirements:* For master's, variable foreign language requirement, comprehensive exam (for some programs), thesis (for some programs). *Application deadline:* Applications are processed on a rolling basis. Application fee: $40. Electronic applications accepted. *Financial support:* Applicants required to submit FAFSA. *Unit head:* Dr. Guillermo Vasquez de Velasco, Dean, 773-325-7305. *Application contact:* Ann Spittle, Director of Graduate Admission, 773-325-8369, Fax: 312-476-3244, E-mail: graddepaul@depaul.edu.
Website: http://las.depaul.edu/

Drury University, Master of Nonprofit and Civic Leadership Program, Springfield, MO 65802. Offers MNCL. *Program availability:* Part-time, evening/weekend. *Entrance* *requirements:* For master's, GRE, bachelor's degree, minimum GPA of 3.0. Additional exam requirements/recommendations for international students: Recommended—TOEFL (minimum score 80 iBT), IELTS (minimum score 6.5). Electronic applications accepted. *Expenses:* Contact institution. *Faculty research:* Nonprofit leadership, organizational change, leadership accountability, digital media, health communication.

Eastern Mennonite University, Program in Business Administration, Harrisonburg, VA 22802-2462. Offers general management (MBA); health services administration (MBA); non-profit leadership (MBA). *Program availability:* Part-time, evening/weekend. *Degree requirements:* For master's, final capstone course. *Entrance requirements:* For master's, GMAT, minimum GPA of 2.5, 2 years of work experience, 2 letters of reference. Additional exam requirements/recommendations for international students: Required—TOEFL (minimum score 500 paper-based). *Application deadline:* For fall admission, 3/1 priority date for domestic and international students. Applications are processed on a rolling basis. Application fee: $25. Electronic applications accepted. *Expenses:* Contact institution. *Financial support:* Application deadline: 6/30; applicants required to submit FAFSA. *Faculty research:* Information security, Anabaptist/Mennonite experiences and perspectives, limits of multi-cultural education, international development performance criteria. *Unit head:* Dr. James M. Leaman, Department Chair, 540-432-4152, Fax: 540-432-4071, E-mail: james.leaman@emu.edu. *Application contact:* Patricia S. Eckard, Administrative Coordinator, 540-432-4150, Fax: 540-432-4071, E-mail: eckardp@emu.edu.
Website: http://www.emu.edu/mba/

Eastern Michigan University, Graduate School, College of Arts and Sciences, Department of Political Science, Programs in Public Administration, Ypsilanti, MI 48197. Offers general public management (Graduate Certificate); local government management (Graduate Certificate); management of public healthcare services (Graduate Certificate); nonprofit management (Graduate Certificate); public administration (MPA); public budget management (Graduate Certificate); public land planning and development management (Graduate Certificate); public personnel management (Graduate Certificate); public policy analysis (Graduate Certificate). *Accreditation:* NASPAA. *Students:* 11 full-time (6 women), 41 part-time (19 women); includes 18 minority (13 Black or African American, non-Hispanic/Latino; 1 Hispanic/Latino; 4 Two or more races, non-Hispanic/Latino). Average age 34. 42 applicants, 79% accepted, 14 enrolled. In 2017, 23 master's, 4 other advanced degrees awarded. Application fee: $45. *Application contact:* Dr. Jeffrey L. Bernstein, Program Advisor, 734-487-6970, Fax: 734-487-3340, E-mail: jeffrey.bernstein@emich.edu.
Website: http://www.emich.edu/polisci

Eastern Michigan University, Graduate School, College of Business, Programs in Business Administration, Ypsilanti, MI 48197. Offers business administration (MBA, Graduate Certificate); computer information systems (Graduate Certificate); e-business (MBA, Graduate Certificate); enterprise business intelligence (MBA); entrepreneurship (MBA, Graduate Certificate); finance (MBA, Graduate Certificate); human resources (MBA); human resources management (Graduate Certificate); information systems (MBA); internal auditing (MBA); international business (MBA, Graduate Certificate); marketing management (Graduate Certificate); nonprofit management (MBA); organizational development (Graduate Certificate); supply chain management (MBA, Graduate Certificate). *Accreditation:* AACSB. *Program availability:* Part-time, online learning. *Students:* 53 full-time (30 women), 297 part-time (170 women); includes 121 minority (72 Black or African American, non-Hispanic/Latino; 4 American Indian or Alaska Native, non-Hispanic/Latino; 15 Asian, non-Hispanic/Latino; 20 Hispanic/Latino; 10 Two or more races, non-Hispanic/Latino), 20 international. Average age 31. 247 applicants, 74% accepted, 94 enrolled. In 2017, 71 master's, 34 other advanced degrees awarded. *Entrance requirements:* For master's, GMAT (minimum score 450), minimum cumulative undergraduate GPA of 2.75. Additional exam requirements/recommendations for international students: Required—TOEFL. *Application deadline:* For fall admission, 5/15 priority date for domestic students, 2/15 priority date for international students; for winter admission, 10/15 priority date for domestic students, 9/1 priority date for international students; for summer admission, 3/15 priority date for domestic students, 3/1 priority date for international students. Applications are processed on a rolling basis. Application fee: $45. *Financial support:* Fellowships, research assistantships with full tuition reimbursements, teaching assistantships with full tuition reimbursements, career-related internships or fieldwork, Federal Work-Study, institutionally sponsored loans, scholarships/grants, tuition waivers (partial), and unspecified assistantships available. Support available to part-time students. Financial award applicants required to submit FAFSA. *Unit head:* K. Michelle Henry, Director, Graduate Business Programs, 734-487-4444, Fax: 734-483-1316, E-mail: cob.graduate@emich.edu.
Website: http://www.emich.edu/cob/mba/

Eastern Michigan University, Graduate School, College of Health and Human Services, Interdisciplinary Program in Non-Profit Management, Ypsilanti, MI 48197. Offers Graduate Certificate. *Unit head:* Dr. Marcia Bombyk, Program Coordinator, 734-487-0393, Fax: 734-487-8536, E-mail: mbombyk@emich.edu.

Eastern University, Program in Organizational Leadership, St. Davids, PA 19087-3696. Offers leadership studies (CAGS); organizational leadership (PhD), including business management, educational administration, public and nonprofit administration. *Students:* 98 full-time (60 women); includes 31 minority (26 Black or African American, non-Hispanic/Latino; 2 Asian, non-Hispanic/Latino; 2 Hispanic/Latino; 1 Two or more races, non-Hispanic/Latino), 4 international. Average age 47. In 2017, 8 doctorates, 10 other advanced degrees awarded. *Application deadline:* Applications are processed on a rolling basis. Application fee: $75. Electronic applications accepted. *Expenses:* Contact institution. *Unit head:* Michael Dziedziak, Executive Director of Enrollment, 800-452-0996, E-mail: gpsadmissions@eastern.edu.
Website: https://www.eastern.edu/academics/programs/phd-organizational-leadership/phd-organizational-leadership-0

East Tennessee State University, School of Graduate Studies, College of Arts and Sciences, Department of Political Science, International Affairs and Public Administration, Johnson City, TN 37614. Offers economic development (Postbaccalaureate Certificate); economic development and planning (MPA); local government management (MPA); nonprofit and public financial management (MPA); urban planning (Postbaccalaureate Certificate). *Program availability:* Part-time. *Degree requirements:* For master's, internship, capstone. *Entrance requirements:* For master's, GRE General Test, three letters of recommendation. Additional exam requirements/recommendations for international students: Required—TOEFL (minimum score 550 paper-based; 79 iBT). *Application deadline:* For fall admission, 6/1 for domestic students, 4/29 for international students; for spring admission, 11/1 for domestic students, 9/29 for international students. Application fee: $55 ($65 for international students). Electronic applications accepted. *Financial support:* Research assistantships with full tuition reimbursements, teaching assistantships with full tuition reimbursements, career-related internships or fieldwork, institutionally sponsored loans, scholarships/grants, and unspecified assistantships available. Financial award application deadline: 7/1; financial award applicants required to submit FAFSA. *Faculty research:* Labor issues, presidency, public law in American politics, East Asian politics, European politics, Middle Eastern politics, development in comparative politics, international

political economy, international relations, world politics in international affairs. *Unit head:* Dr. Andrew Battista, Chair, 423-439-6628, Fax: 423-439-4348, E-mail: battista@etsu.edu. *Application contact:* Dr. Andrew Battista, Chair, 423-439-6628, Fax: 423-439-4348, E-mail: battista@etsu.edu.
Website: http://www.etsu.edu/cas/polisci/

Fairleigh Dickinson University, Metropolitan Campus, Anthony J. Petrocelli College of Continuing Studies, Public Administration Institute, Teaneck, NJ 07666-1914. Offers public administration (MPA, Certificate); public non-profit management (Certificate).

Florida Atlantic University, College for Design and Social Inquiry, School of Public Administration, Boca Raton, FL 33431-0991. Offers MPA, PhD. *Accreditation:* NASPAA (one or more programs are accredited). *Program availability:* Part-time, evening/weekend. *Faculty:* 12 full-time (4 women), 1 part-time/adjunct (0 women). *Students:* 28 full-time (14 women), 77 part-time (44 women); includes 48 minority (24 Black or African American, non-Hispanic/Latino; 3 Asian, non-Hispanic/Latino; 19 Hispanic/Latino; 2 Two or more races, non-Hispanic/Latino), 5 international. Average age 34. 80 applicants, 31% accepted, 16 enrolled. In 2017, 56 master's, 6 doctorates awarded. *Degree requirements:* For master's, thesis optional; for doctorate, comprehensive exam, thesis/dissertation. *Entrance requirements:* For master's, GRE General Test, minimum GPA of 3.0; for doctorate, GRE General Test, faculty reference, scholarly writing samples, letters of recommendation. Additional exam requirements/recommendations for international students: Required—TOEFL (minimum score 500 paper-based; 61 iBT), IELTS (minimum score 6). *Application deadline:* For fall admission, 5/1 priority date for domestic students, 2/15 for international students; for spring admission, 11/1 for domestic students, 7/15 for international students. Applications are processed on a rolling basis. Application fee: $30. *Expenses:* Tuition, state resident: full-time $7400; part-time $369.82 per credit. Tuition, nonresident: full-time $20,496; part-time $1042.81 per credit. *Financial support:* Fellowships with full tuition reimbursements, research assistantships with partial tuition reimbursements, teaching assistantships with partial tuition reimbursements, career-related internships or fieldwork, Federal Work-Study, institutionally sponsored loans, and tuition waivers (partial) available. Support available to part-time students. Financial award application deadline: 4/1. *Faculty research:* Public finance and budgeting, public management, evaluation, criminal justice, postmodern public administration. *Unit head:* Leslie Leip, Program Coordinator, 954-924-8818, E-mail: lleip@fau.edu.
Website: http://www.fau.edu/spa/

Fordham University, Gabelli School of Business, New York, NY 10023. Offers accounting (MBA, MS); applied statistics and decision-making (MS); business economics (DPS); capital markets (DPS); communications and media management (MBA); electronic business (MBA); entrepreneurship (MBA); finance (MBA, PhD); global finance (MS); global sustainability (MBA); health administration (MS); healthcare management (MBA); information systems (MBA, MS); investor relations (MS); management (EMBA, MBA, MS, PhD); marketing (MBA); marketing intelligence (MS); media management (MS); nonprofit leadership (MS); quantitative finance (MS); strategy and decision-making (DPS); taxation (MS); JD/MBA; MS/MBA. *Accreditation:* AACSB. *Program availability:* Part-time, evening/weekend. *Faculty:* 130 full-time (46 women), 42 part-time/adjunct (5 women). *Students:* 1,051 full-time (570 women), 563 part-time (313 women); includes 190 minority (48 Black or African American, non-Hispanic/Latino; 72 Asian, non-Hispanic/Latino; 69 Hispanic/Latino; 1 Native Hawaiian or other Pacific Islander, non-Hispanic/Latino), 1,106 international. Average age 27. 4,577 applicants, 58% accepted, 794 enrolled. In 2017, 937 master's awarded. Terminal master's awarded for partial completion of doctoral program. *Degree requirements:* For master's, internships (for some degrees); for doctorate, comprehensive exam (for some programs), thesis/dissertation. *Entrance requirements:* For master's, GMAT/GRE, 2 letters of recommendation, resume, 2 essays, transcripts, interview. Additional exam requirements/recommendations for international students: Required—TOEFL (minimum score 100 iBT), IELTS (minimum score 7). *Application deadline:* For fall admission, 11/15 priority date for domestic and international students; for winter admission, 1/19 priority date for domestic students, 1/1 priority date for international students; for spring admission, 4/15 for domestic students, 3/1 for international students; for summer admission, 6/1 for domestic students. Application fee: $130. Electronic applications accepted. *Expenses:* $1,495 per credit. *Financial support:* Career-related internships or fieldwork, institutionally sponsored loans, scholarships/grants, and unspecified assistantships available. Support available to part-time students. Financial award application deadline: 6/30; financial award applicants required to submit FAFSA. *Unit head:* Dr. Donna Rapaccioli, Dean, 212-636-6165, Fax: 212-307-1779, E-mail: rapaccioli@fordham.edu. *Application contact:* Lawrence Murray, Senior Assistant Dean of Graduate Admissions and Advising, 212-636-6200, Fax: 212-636-7076, E-mail: admissionsgb@fordham.edu.
Website: http://www.fordham.edu/gabelli

Fordham University, Graduate School of Social Service, New York, NY 10023. Offers nonprofit leadership (MS); social work (MSW, PhD); JD/MSW; MSW/MPH. MS program jointly sponsored with Graduate School of Business and conducted through the Fordham Center for Nonprofit Leaders; MSW/MPH offered with Ichan School of Public Health at Mount Sinai. *Accreditation:* CSWE (one or more programs are accredited). *Program availability:* Part-time, evening/weekend, 100% online, blended/hybrid learning. *Faculty:* 37 full-time (25 women), 106 part-time/adjunct (29 women). *Students:* 1,026 full-time (891 women), 636 part-time (560 women); includes 881 minority (377 Black or African American, non-Hispanic/Latino; 3 American Indian or Alaska Native, non-Hispanic/Latino; 52 Asian, non-Hispanic/Latino; 411 Hispanic/Latino; 7 Native Hawaiian or other Pacific Islander, non-Hispanic/Latino; 31 Two or more races, non-Hispanic/Latino), 24 international. Average age 32. In 2017, 697 master's, 5 doctorates awarded. *Degree requirements:* For master's, 1200 hours of field placement; for doctorate, comprehensive exam, thesis/dissertation. *Entrance requirements:* For master's, BA in liberal arts; for doctorate, GRE, master's degree in social work or related field. Additional exam requirements/recommendations for international students: Required—TOEFL (minimum score 600 paper-based; 100 iBT), IELTS. *Application deadline:* For fall admission, 2/1 priority date for domestic students; for spring admission, 11/1 priority date for domestic students. Applications are processed on a rolling basis. Application fee: $60. Electronic applications accepted. *Expenses:* Contact institution. *Financial support:* In 2017–18, 838 students received support, including 39 research assistantships with partial tuition reimbursements available (averaging $1,980 per year); fellowships with partial tuition reimbursements available, career-related internships or fieldwork, Federal Work-Study, scholarships/grants, tuition waivers (partial), and unspecified assistantships also available. Support available to part-time students. Financial award application deadline: 2/1. *Faculty research:* Aging, children and family, healthcare, domestic violence, substance abuse. *Unit head:* Dr. Debra McPhee, Dean, 212-636-6616, E-mail: dmcphee1@fordham.edu. *Application contact:* Melba Remice, Assistant Dean of Admissions, 212-636-6600, Fax: 212-636-6613, E-mail: gssadmission@fordham.edu.
Website: http://www.fordham.edu/gss/

Geneva College, Program in Leadership Studies, Beaver Falls, PA 15010-3599. Offers business management (MS); ministry leadership (MS); non-profit leadership (MS); organizational management (MS); project management (MS). *Program availability:*

Nonprofit Management

Online only, 100% online. *Faculty:* 4 part-time/adjunct (1 woman). *Students:* 32 full-time (22 women); includes 10 minority (8 Black or African American, non-Hispanic/Latino; 1 Asian, non-Hispanic/Latino; 1 Hispanic/Latino). Average age 43. 25 applicants, 60% accepted, 11 enrolled. In 2017, 35 master's awarded. *Degree requirements:* For master's, thesis or alternative, capstone leadership studies project. *Entrance requirements:* For master's, undergraduate degree from regionally-accredited college or university, one to three years of experience in the workplace, minimum GPA of 3.0 (preferred), resume, essay, two recommendations. Additional exam requirements/recommendations for international students: Required—TOEFL. *Application deadline:* For fall admission, 9/21 for domestic students; for spring admission, 2/23 for domestic students; for summer admission, 7/22 for domestic students. Applications are processed on a rolling basis. Electronic applications accepted. *Expenses:* $640 per credit. *Financial support:* Scholarships/grants available. Financial award application deadline: 8/1; financial award applicants required to submit FAFSA. *Faculty research:* Servant leadership, leadership essentials. *Unit head:* John D. Gallo, Dean of Graduate, Adult and Online Programs, 800-576-3111, Fax: 724-847-6839, E-mail: msls@geneva.edu. *Application contact:* Graduate Enrollment Representative, 800-576-3111, Fax: 724-847-6839, E-mail: msls@geneva.edu.
Website: http://www.geneva.edu/graduate/leadership-studies/

The George Washington University, Columbian College of Arts and Sciences, Department of Organizational Sciences and Communication, Washington, DC 20052. Offers human resources management (MA); non-profit management (Graduate Certificate); organizational management (Graduate Certificate). *Program availability:* Part-time, evening/weekend. *Faculty:* 10 full-time (6 women), 6 part-time/adjunct (4 women). *Students:* 50 full-time (26 women), 26 part-time (20 women); includes 25 minority (8 Black or African American, non-Hispanic/Latino; 6 Asian, non-Hispanic/Latino; 6 Hispanic/Latino; 1 Native Hawaiian or other Pacific Islander, non-Hispanic/Latino; 4 Two or more races, non-Hispanic/Latino), 8 international. Average age 27. 138 applicants, 67% accepted, 39 enrolled. In 2017, 31 master's, 19 other advanced degrees awarded. *Degree requirements:* For master's, comprehensive exam. *Entrance requirements:* For master's, GRE General Test, minimum GPA of 3.0; for Graduate Certificate, minimum GPA of 3.0. Additional exam requirements/recommendations for international students: Required—TOEFL (minimum score 500 paper-based; 80 iBT). *Application deadline:* For fall admission, 1/15 priority date for domestic and international students; for spring admission, 10/1 priority date for domestic students, 9/1 priority date for international students. Applications are processed on a rolling basis. Application fee: $75. Electronic applications accepted. *Expenses: Tuition:* Full-time $28,800; part-time $1655 per credit hour. *Required fees:* $45; $2.75 per credit hour. *Financial support:* Federal Work-Study and institutionally sponsored loans available. *Unit head:* Dr. Lynn Offermann, Chair, 202-994-8507, E-mail: lro@gwu.edu. *Application contact:* Information Contact, 202-994-1878, Fax: 202-994-1881.
Website: http://www.gwu.edu/~orgsci/

Georgian Court University, School of Business and Digital Media, Lakewood, NJ 08701-2697. Offers business (MBA); business essentials (Certificate); nonprofit management (Certificate). *Program availability:* Part-time, evening/weekend. *Faculty:* 6 full-time (3 women), 11 part-time/adjunct (3 women). *Students:* 29 full-time (19 women), 31 part-time (24 women); includes 17 minority (7 Black or African American, non-Hispanic/Latino; 3 Asian, non-Hispanic/Latino; 4 Hispanic/Latino; 3 Two or more races, non-Hispanic/Latino), 2 international. Average age 31. 54 applicants, 65% accepted, 21 enrolled. In 2017, 33 master's, 7 other advanced degrees awarded. *Entrance requirements:* For master's, GMAT or CPA exam, 3 letters of recommendation. Additional exam requirements/recommendations for international students: Required—TOEFL (minimum score 550 paper-based). *Application deadline:* For fall admission, 8/15 priority date for domestic students, 5/1 for international students; for spring admission, 1/15 priority date for domestic students, 10/1 for international students. Applications are processed on a rolling basis. Application fee: $40. Electronic applications accepted. *Expenses: Tuition:* Part-time $839 per credit. *Required fees:* $248 per semester. Tuition and fees vary according to campus/location and program. *Financial support:* Scholarships/grants, health care benefits, and unspecified assistantships available. Financial award application deadline: 4/15; financial award applicants required to submit FAFSA. *Unit head:* Dr. Cathleen McQuillen, Dean, 732-987-2623, Fax: 732-987-2024, E-mail: cmcquillen@georgian.edu. *Application contact:* Patrick Givens, Director of Graduate and Professional Studies Admissions, 732-987-2736, Fax: 732-987-2000, E-mail: gps@georgian.edu.
Website: http://georgian.edu/academics/school-of-business/

Georgia Southern University, Jack N. Averitt College of Graduate Studies, College of Liberal Arts and Social Sciences, Institute for Public and Nonprofit Studies, Program in Public and Nonprofit Management, Statesboro, GA 30458. Offers Graduate Certificate. *Program availability:* Part-time, blended/hybrid learning. *Students:* 2 part-time (1 woman); includes 1 minority (Black or African American, non-Hispanic/Latino). Average age 31. 3 applicants, 100% accepted, 2 enrolled. *Entrance requirements:* For degree, GRE, three years of work experience in the public or nonprofit sector, bachelor's degree, minimum cumulative undergraduate GPA of 2.75, three letters of recommendation, statement of career goals and objectives. Additional exam requirements/recommendations for international students: Required—TOEFL (minimum score 550 paper-based; 80 iBT), IELTS (minimum score 6). *Application deadline:* For fall admission, 3/1 for domestic students; for spring admission, 10/1 for domestic students. Application fee: $50. Electronic applications accepted. *Expenses:* Tuition, state resident: full-time $4986; part-time $3324 per year. Tuition, nonresident: full-time $21,982; part-time $15,352 per year. *Required fees:* $2092; $1802 per credit hour. $901 per semester. Tuition and fees vary according to course load, campus/location and program. *Financial support:* In 2017–18, 3 fellowships with full tuition reimbursements (averaging $7,750 per year) were awarded. Financial award application deadline: 4/20; financial award applicants required to submit FAFSA. *Faculty research:* Human resource management, ethics in administration, nonprofit budgeting. *Unit head:* Dr. Trenton Davis, Director, 912-478-5430, Fax: 912-478-8029, E-mail: tjdavis@georgiasouthern.edu.
Website: http://class.georgiasouthern.edu/ipns/online-certificate/

Georgia State University, Andrew Young School of Policy Studies, Department of Public Management and Policy, Atlanta, GA 30303. Offers criminal justice (MPA); disaster management (Certificate); disaster policy (MPA); environmental policy (PhD); health policy (PhD); management and finance (MPA); nonprofit management (MPA, Certificate); nonprofit policy (MPA); planning and economic development (MPP, Certificate); policy analysis and evaluation (MPA), including planning and economic development; public and nonprofit management (PhD); public finance and budgeting (PhD), including science and technology policy, urban and regional economic development; public finance policy (MPA), including social policy; public health (MPA). *Accreditation:* NASPAA (one or more programs are accredited). *Program availability:* Part-time. *Faculty:* 17 full-time (9 women). *Students:* 125 full-time (75 women), 78 part-time (51 women); includes 90 minority (67 Black or African American, non-Hispanic/Latino; 5 Asian, non-Hispanic/Latino; 9 Hispanic/Latino; 9 Two or more races, non-Hispanic/Latino), 34 international. Average age 30. 275 applicants, 62% accepted, 88 enrolled. In 2017, 71 master's, 5 doctorates, 12 other advanced degrees awarded. Terminal master's awarded for partial completion of doctoral program. *Degree*

requirements: For master's, thesis optional; for doctorate, comprehensive exam, thesis/dissertation. *Entrance requirements:* For master's and doctorate, GRE. Additional exam requirements/recommendations for international students: Required—TOEFL (minimum score 603 paper-based; 100 iBT) or IELTS (minimum score 7). *Application deadline:* For fall admission, 1/15 for domestic and international students. Application fee: $50. Electronic applications accepted. *Expenses:* Tuition, state resident: full-time $7020. Tuition, nonresident: full-time $22,518. *Required fees:* $2128. Tuition and fees vary according to degree level and program. *Financial support:* In 2017–18, fellowships (averaging $8,194 per year), research assistantships (averaging $8,068 per year), teaching assistantships (averaging $3,600 per year) were awarded; institutionally sponsored loans, scholarships/grants, health care benefits, and unspecified assistantships also available. Financial award application deadline: 2/1. *Faculty research:* Public budgeting and finance, public management, nonprofit management, performance measurement and management, urban development. *Unit head:* Dr. Carolyn Bourdeaux, Chair and Professor, 404-413-0013, Fax: 404-413-0104, E-mail: cbourdeaux@gsu.edu.
Website: http://aysps.gsu.edu/pmap/

Grand Valley State University, College of Community and Public Service, School of Public, Nonprofit and Health Administration, Program in Philanthropy and Nonprofit Leadership, Allendale, MI 49401-9403. Offers MPNL. *Program availability:* Part-time, evening/weekend. *Students:* 1 (woman) full-time, 19 part-time (all women); includes 2 minority (1 Black or African American, non-Hispanic/Latino; 1 Two or more races, non-Hispanic/Latino). Average age 41. 8 applicants, 88% accepted, 6 enrolled. In 2017, 1 master's awarded. *Degree requirements:* For master's, capstone. *Entrance requirements:* For master's, 3 years of full-time work experience, 3 letters of reference, 250-750 word essay on career and educational objectives, resume. Additional exam requirements/recommendations for international students: Required—TOEFL (minimum iBT score of 80), IELTS (6.5), or Michigan English Language Assessment Battery (77). *Application deadline:* For fall admission, 6/1 for domestic students; for winter admission, 11/1 for domestic students; for spring admission, 4/1 for domestic students. Applications are processed on a rolling basis. Electronic applications accepted. *Expenses:* $627 per credit hour. *Financial support:* In 2017–18, 5 students received support, including 4 fellowships, 2 research assistantships with full and partial tuition reimbursements available (averaging $4,000 per year). *Unit head:* Dr. Richard Jelier, Director, 616-331-6575, Fax: 616-331-7120, E-mail: jelierr@gvsu.edu. *Application contact:* Dr. Michelle Wooddell, Graduate Program Director/Recruiting Contact, 616-331-6495, Fax: 616-331-7120, E-mail: wooddelm@gvsu.edu.

Gratz College, Graduate Programs, Program in Nonprofit Management, Melrose Park, PA 19027. Offers MS.

Hamline University, School of Business, St. Paul, MN 55104-1284. Offers business administration (MBA); nonprofit management (MNM); public administration (MPA, DPA); MBA/MNM; MBA/MPA; MPA/MNM. *Program availability:* Part-time, evening/weekend, blended/hybrid learning. *Faculty:* 16 full-time (6 women), 15 part-time/adjunct (4 women). *Students:* 18 full-time (8 women), 309 part-time (165 women); includes 89 minority (43 Black or African American, non-Hispanic/Latino; 3 American Indian or Alaska Native, non-Hispanic/Latino; 22 Asian, non-Hispanic/Latino; 12 Hispanic/Latino; 9 Two or more races, non-Hispanic/Latino), 15 international. Average age 34. 174 applicants, 61% accepted, 68 enrolled. In 2017, 152 master's, 4 doctorates awarded. *Degree requirements:* For master's, thesis (for some programs); for doctorate, comprehensive exam, thesis/dissertation. *Entrance requirements:* For master's and doctorate, personal statement, official transcripts, resume or curriculum vitae, letters of recommendation, writing sample. Additional exam requirements/recommendations for international students: Required—TOEFL (minimum score 550 paper-based; 80 iBT), IELTS (minimum score 6.5). *Application deadline:* For fall admission, 6/1 for domestic and international students; for spring admission, 11/1 for domestic students, 10/1 for international students; for summer admission, 3/1 for domestic students, 2/1 for international students. Applications are processed on a rolling basis. Application fee: $0 ($100 fee for international students). Electronic applications accepted. *Expenses:* $530 per credit (for MPA), $495 per credit (for MNM), $775 per credit plus fees (for DPA). *Financial support:* Career-related internships or fieldwork, Federal Work-Study, scholarships/grants, and unspecified assistantships available. Support available to part-time students. Financial award application deadline: 4/20; financial award applicants required to submit FAFSA. *Faculty research:* Experiential learning, organizational process/politics, gender differences, social equity, pyramid schemes. *Unit head:* Dr. Anne McCarthy, Dean, 651-523-2284, Fax: 651-523-3098, E-mail: hsb@hamline.edu. *Application contact:* Shawn Skoog, Director of Graduate Recruitment and Admission, 651-523-2900, Fax: 651-523-3058, E-mail: gradprog@hamline.edu.
Website: http://www.hamline.edu/business

Hebrew Union College–Jewish Institute of Religion, School of Jewish Nonprofit Management, Los Angeles, CA 90007. Offers MA.

Hope International University, School of Graduate and Professional Studies, Program in Business Administration, Fullerton, CA 92831-3138. Offers general management (MBA, MSM); international development (MBA, MSM); marketing management (MBA, MSM); non-profit management (MBA, MSM). *Program availability:* Part-time, online learning. *Degree requirements:* For master's, comprehensive exam (for some programs), thesis (for some programs), project. *Entrance requirements:* For master's, minimum GPA of 3.0; 2 references. Additional exam requirements/recommendations for international students: Required—TOEFL (minimum score 550 paper-based; 86 iBT); Recommended—IELTS (minimum score 6.5). Electronic applications accepted. *Expenses:* Contact institution.

Indiana University Bloomington, School of Public and Environmental Affairs, Public Affairs Programs, Bloomington, IN 47405. Offers economic development (MPA); energy (MPA); environmental policy (PhD); environmental policy and natural resource management (MPA); information systems (MPA); international development (MPA); local government management (MPA); nonprofit management (MPA, Certificate); policy analysis (MPA); public budgeting and financial management (Certificate); public finance (PhD); public financial administration (MPA); public management (MPA, PhD, Certificate); public policy analysis (PhD); social entrepreneurship (Certificate); specialized public affairs (MPA); sustainability and sustainable development (MPA); JD/MPA; MPA/MA; MPA/MIS; MPA/MLS; MSES/MPA. *Accreditation:* NASPAA (one or more programs are accredited). *Program availability:* Part-time. *Degree requirements:* For master's, capstone, internship; for doctorate, comprehensive exam, thesis/dissertation. *Entrance requirements:* For master's, GRE General Test or GMAT, official transcripts, 3 letters of recommendation, resume, personal statement; for doctorate, GRE General Test, official transcripts, 3 letters of recommendation, statement of purpose. Additional exam requirements/recommendations for international students: Required—TOEFL (minimum score 600 paper-based; 96 iBT); Recommended—IELTS (minimum score 7). Electronic applications accepted. *Faculty research:* International development, environmental policy and resource management, policy analysis, public finance, public management, urban management, nonprofit management, energy policy, social policy, public finance.

Indiana University Bloomington, University Graduate School, College of Arts and Sciences, Robert A. and Sandra S. Borns Jewish Studies Program, Bloomington, IN

47405. Offers Jewish studies (MA), including nonprofit management; Jewish studies and history (MA). *Degree requirements:* For master's, one foreign language, thesis. *Entrance requirements:* Additional exam requirements/recommendations for international students: Required—TOEFL. Electronic applications accepted. *Faculty research:* Jewish studies, religious studies, history, Holocaust study.

Indiana University Northwest, School of Public and Environmental Affairs, Gary, IN 46408. Offers criminal justice (MPA); environmental affairs (Graduate Certificate); health services (MPA); nonprofit management (Certificate); public management (MPA, Graduate Certificate). *Accreditation:* NASPAA (one or more programs are accredited). *Program availability:* Part-time. *Entrance requirements:* For master's, GRE General Test (minimum combined verbal and quantitative score of 280), GMAT, or LSAT, letters of recommendation. Electronic applications accepted. *Faculty research:* Employment in income security policies, evidence in criminal justice, equal employment law, social welfare policy and welfare reform, public finance in developing countries.

Indiana University of Pennsylvania, School of Graduate Studies and Research, College of Humanities and Social Sciences, Department of Sociology, Program in Administration and Leadership Studies, Indiana, PA 15705. Offers PhD. *Program availability:* Part-time, evening/weekend. *Faculty:* 14 full-time (11 women). *Students:* 2 full-time (0 women), 87 part-time (45 women); includes 19 minority (12 Black or African American, non-Hispanic/Latino; 4 Hispanic/Latino; 3 Two or more races, non-Hispanic/Latino), 1 international. Average age 44. 28 applicants, 79% accepted, 15 enrolled. In 2017, 8 doctorates awarded. *Degree requirements:* For doctorate, comprehensive exam, thesis/dissertation. *Entrance requirements:* For doctorate, GRE, resume, writing sample, 3 letters of recommendation. Additional exam requirements/recommendations for international students: Required—TOEFL (minimum score 540 paper-based). *Application deadline:* For fall admission, 2/15 priority date for domestic students. Applications are processed on a rolling basis. Application fee: $50. Electronic applications accepted. *Expenses:* Contact institution. *Financial support:* In 2017–18, 2 fellowships with full tuition reimbursements (averaging $2,500 per year), 4 research assistantships with tuition reimbursements (averaging $5,764 per year), 1 teaching assistantship with partial tuition reimbursement (averaging $23,305 per year) were awarded; career-related internships or fieldwork, Federal Work-Study, scholarships/grants, and unspecified assistantships also available. Support available to part-time students. Financial award application deadline: 4/15; financial award applicants required to submit FAFSA. *Unit head:* Dr. Robert Millward, Graduate Coordinator, 724-357-5593, E-mail: millward@iup.edu.
Website: http://www.iup.edu/grad/ALS/default.aspx

Indiana University–Purdue University Indianapolis, School of Public and Environmental Affairs, Indianapolis, IN 46202. Offers criminal justice and public safety (MS); homeland security and emergency management (Graduate Certificate); library management (Graduate Certificate); nonprofit management (Graduate Certificate); public affairs (MPA); public management (Graduate Certificate); social entrepreneurship and nonprofit public benefit organizations (Graduate Certificate); JD/MPA; MLS/NMC; MLS/PMC; MPA/MA. *Accreditation:* CAHME (one or more programs are accredited); NASPAA. *Program availability:* Part-time, evening/weekend, online learning. *Entrance requirements:* For master's, GRE General Test, GMAT or LSAT, minimum GPA of 3.0 (preferred). Additional exam requirements/recommendations for international students: Required—TOEFL (minimum score 93 iBT), IELTS (minimum score 6.5). Electronic applications accepted. *Faculty research:* Nonprofit and public management, public policy, urban policy, sustainability policy, disaster preparedness and recovery, vehicular safety, homicide, offender rehabilitation and re-entry.

Indiana University South Bend, College of Liberal Arts and Sciences, South Bend, IN 46615. Offers advanced computer programming (Graduate Certificate); applied informatics (Graduate Certificate); applied mathematics and computer science (MS); behavior modification (Graduate Certificate); computer applications (Graduate Certificate); computer programming (Graduate Certificate); correctional management and supervision (Graduate Certificate); English (MA); health systems management (Graduate Certificate); international studies (Graduate Certificate); liberal studies (MLS); nonprofit management (Graduate Certificate); paralegal studies (Graduate Certificate); professional writing (Graduate Certificate); public affairs (MPA); public management (Graduate Certificate); social and cultural diversity (Graduate Certificate); strategic sustainability leadership (Graduate Certificate); technology for administration (Graduate Certificate). *Program availability:* Part-time, evening/weekend. *Degree requirements:* For master's, variable foreign language requirement, thesis (for some programs). *Entrance requirements:* For master's, minimum GPA of 3.0. Additional exam requirements/recommendations for international students: Required—TOEFL (minimum score 550 paper-based; 80 iBT). *Expenses:* Contact institution. *Faculty research:* Artificial intelligence, bioinformatics, English language and literature, creative writing, computer networks.

Iona College, School of Arts and Science, Department of Mass Communication, New Rochelle, NY 10801-1890. Offers non-profit public relations (Certificate); public relations (MA); sports communication and media (MA). *Accreditation:* ACEJMC (one or more programs are accredited). *Program availability:* Part-time, evening/weekend. *Faculty:* 4 full-time (1 woman), 5 part-time/adjunct (0 women). *Students:* 21 full-time (12 women), 13 part-time (8 women); includes 16 minority (11 Black or African American, non-Hispanic/Latino; 1 Asian, non-Hispanic/Latino; 4 Hispanic/Latino), 1 international. Average age 27. 18 applicants, 100% accepted, 11 enrolled. In 2017, 18 master's, 3 other advanced degrees awarded. *Degree requirements:* For master's, comprehensive exam (for some programs), thesis or alternative. *Entrance requirements:* For master's, GRE General Test if undergraduate GPA is below 3.0. Additional exam requirements/recommendations for international students: Required—TOEFL (minimum score 550 paper-based; 80 iBT), IELTS (minimum score 6). *Application deadline:* For fall admission, 8/1 for domestic students, 5/1 for international students; for spring admission, 1/1 for domestic students, 9/1 for international students. Applications are processed on a rolling basis. Electronic applications accepted. *Expenses:* Contact institution. *Financial support:* In 2017–18, 8 students received support. Scholarships/grants, tuition waivers (partial), and unspecified assistantships available. Support available to part-time students. Financial award application deadline: 4/15; financial award applicants required to submit FAFSA. *Faculty research:* Media ecology, new media, corporate communication, media images, organizational learning in public relations, media law, medicine ethics. *Unit head:* Anthony Kelso, PhD, Chair, 914-633-7795, E-mail: akelso@iona.edu. *Application contact:* Katelyn Brunck, Assistant Director of Graduate Admissions, 914-633-2492, Fax: 914-633-2277, E-mail: kbrunck@iona.edu. Website: http://www.iona.edu/Academics/School-of-Arts-Science/Departments/Mass-Communication/Graduate-Programs.aspx

James Madison University, The Graduate School, College of Arts and Letters, Program in Public Administration, Harrisonburg, VA 22801. Offers individualized (MPA); public management (MPA), including international stabilization and recovery, management in international non-governmental organizations, nonprofit management, public management. Public and nonprofit management program offered in Roanoke. *Accreditation:* NASPAA. *Program availability:* Part-time. *Students:* 23 full-time (11 women), 16 part-time (7 women); includes 7 minority (4 Black or African American, non-Hispanic/Latino; 1 Hispanic/Latino; 2 Two or more races, non-Hispanic/Latino). Average age 30. In 2017, 19 master's awarded. Application fee: $55. Electronic applications accepted. *Expenses:* Tuition, state resident: full-time $10,512; part-time $438 per credit hour. Tuition, nonresident: full-time $28,358; part-time $1162 per credit hour. *Required fees:* $1128. *Financial support:* In 2017–18, 14 students received support, including 14 fellowships; Federal Work-Study and assistantships (averaging $7911) also available. Financial award application deadline: 3/1; financial award applicants required to submit FAFSA. *Unit head:* Dr. Charles Blake, Department Head, 540-568-6149, E-mail: blakech@jmu.edu. *Application contact:* Lynette D. Michael, Director of Graduate Admissions, 540-568-6131, Fax: 540-568-7860, E-mail: michaeld@jmu.edu.
Website: http://www.jmu.edu/mpa

James Madison University, The Graduate School, College of Business, Program in Strategic Leadership, Harrisonburg, VA 22801. Offers postsecondary analysis and leadership (PhD), including nonprofit and community leadership, organizational science and leadership, postsecondary analysis and leadership. *Program availability:* Part-time, evening/weekend, online learning. *Students:* 8 full-time (3 women), 34 part-time (16 women); includes 4 minority (2 Black or African American, non-Hispanic/Latino; 1 Asian, non-Hispanic/Latino; 1 Hispanic/Latino), 4 international. Average age 30. In 2017, 3 doctorates awarded. Application fee: $55. Electronic applications accepted. *Expenses:* Tuition, state resident: full-time $10,512; part-time $438 per credit hour. Tuition, nonresident: full-time $28,358; part-time $1162 per credit hour. *Required fees:* $1128. *Financial support:* In 2017–18, 6 students received support. Fellowships, career-related internships or fieldwork, Federal Work-Study, unspecified assistantships, and 6 doctoral assistantships (stipend varies) available. Financial award application deadline: 3/1; financial award applicants required to submit FAFSA. *Unit head:* Dr. Karen A. Ford, Director of Strategic Leadership Studies, 540-568-7020, Fax: 540-568-7117, E-mail: fordka@jmu.edu. *Application contact:* Lynette D. Michael, Director of Graduate Admissions, 540-568-6131 Ext. 6395, Fax: 540-568-7860, E-mail: michaeld@jmu.edu.
Website: http://www.jmu.edu/leadership/

John Carroll University, Graduate Studies, Program in Nonprofit Administration, University Heights, OH 44118. Offers MA. *Program availability:* Part-time, evening/weekend. *Faculty:* 1 (woman) full-time, 3 part-time/adjunct (2 women). *Students:* 9 full-time (3 women), 36 part-time (20 women); includes 6 minority (5 Black or African American, non-Hispanic/Latino; 1 Hispanic/Latino), 11 international. Average age 33. In 2017, 21 master's awarded. *Degree requirements:* For master's, thesis optional. *Entrance requirements:* For master's, minimum GPA of 3.0, interview. Additional exam requirements/recommendations for international students: Required—TOEFL. *Application deadline:* For fall admission, 7/15 priority date for domestic students; for winter admission, 11/1 priority date for domestic students; for spring admission, 5/1 priority date for domestic students. Applications are processed on a rolling basis. Application fee: $25 ($35 for international students). Electronic applications accepted. *Expenses:* Tuition: Full-time $16,238; part-time $788 per credit hour. One-time fee: $200. Part-time tuition and fees vary according to course load and program. *Financial support:* Research assistantships with full tuition reimbursements and scholarships/grants available. *Unit head:* Dani Robbins, Director, 216-397-1568, E-mail: nonprofit@jcu.edu. *Application contact:* Jennifer L. Tucker, Records Management Assistant, 216-397-1925, Fax: 216-397-1835, E-mail: jtucker@jcu.edu.

Johns Hopkins University, Zanvyl Krieger School of Arts and Sciences, Advanced Academic Programs, Program in Government, Washington, DC 20036. Offers global security studies (MA); government (MA); national securities study (Certificate); nonprofit management (Certificate); public management (MA); research administration (MS); MA/MBA. *Program availability:* Part-time, evening/weekend, online learning. *Degree requirements:* For master's, thesis. *Entrance requirements:* For master's, minimum GPA of 3.0. Additional exam requirements/recommendations for international students: Required—TOEFL (minimum score 100 iBT). Electronic applications accepted.

Johnson & Wales University, Graduate Studies, MBA Program, Providence, RI 02903-3703. Offers accounting (MBA); business administration (MBA); finance (MBA); global fashion merchandising and management (MBA); hospitality (MBA); human resource management (MBA); information security/assurance (MBA); information technology (MBA); nonprofit management (MBA); operations and supply chain management (MBA); organizational leadership (MBA); organizational psychology (MBA); sport leadership (MBA). Program also offered on Denver campus. *Program availability:* Part-time, online learning. *Entrance requirements:* For master's, minimum GPA of 2.75. Additional exam requirements/recommendations for international students: Required—TOEFL (minimum score 550 paper-based); Recommended—IELTS, TWE. *Application deadline:* For fall admission, 8/15 priority date for domestic students, 6/28 priority date for international students; for winter admission, 11/10 priority date for domestic students, 9/20 priority date for international students; for spring admission, 2/5 priority date for domestic students, 12/20 priority date for international students. Applications are processed on a rolling basis. *Expenses:* Tuition: Full-time $12,636; part-time $702 per credit hour. *Financial support:* Tuition waivers (partial) and unspecified assistantships available. Support available to part-time students. Financial award application deadline: 5/1. *Faculty research:* International banking, global economy, international trade, cultural differences. *Unit head:* Dr. Karen Silva, Director, 401-598-2849, Fax: 401-598-1125. *Application contact:* Graduate School Admissions, 401-598-1015, Fax: 401-598-1286, E-mail: gradadm@jwu.edu.

Johnson & Wales University, Graduate Studies, MS Program in Nonprofit Management, Providence, RI 02903-3703. Offers MS. *Program availability:* Online only, 100% online. *Expenses:* Tuition: Full-time $12,636; part-time $702 per credit hour. *Application contact:* Graduate School Admissions, 401-598-1015, Fax: 401-598-1286, E-mail: pvdgrad@admissions.jwu.edu.

Johnson University, Graduate and Professional Programs, Knoxville, TN 37998-1001. Offers biblical interpretation (Graduate Certificate); business administration (MBA); Christian ministries (Graduate Certificate); clinical mental health counseling (MA); educational technology (MA); intercultural studies (MA); leadership (MBA); leadership studies (PhD); New Testament (MA); nonprofit management (MBA); school counseling (MA); spiritual formation and leadership (Graduate Certificate); strategic ministry (MA); teacher education (MA). *Program availability:* Part-time, evening/weekend, 100% online, blended/hybrid learning. *Degree requirements:* For master's, variable foreign language requirement, comprehensive exam, thesis (for some programs), internships; for doctorate, variable foreign language requirement, comprehensive exam, thesis/dissertation, internships. *Entrance requirements:* For master's, PRAXIS (for MA in teacher education); MAT (for counseling); GRE or GMAT (for MBA), interview, 3 references, transcripts, essay, minimum GPA of 2.5 or 3.0 (depending on program); for doctorate, GRE or MAT (taken not less than 5 years prior), interview, 3 references, transcripts, essay, minimum GPA of 3.0; for Graduate Certificate, interview, 3 references, transcripts, essay, minimum GPA of 3.0. Additional exam requirements/recommendations for international students: Required—TOEFL (minimum score 527 paper-based; 71 iBT). Electronic applications accepted. *Expenses:* Contact institution.

Kean University, College of Business and Public Management, Program in Public Administration, Union, NJ 07083. Offers health services administration (MPA); non-profit management (MPA); public administration (MPA). *Accreditation:* NASPAA. *Program availability:* Part-time. *Faculty:* 14 full-time (4 women). *Students:* 55 full-time (40 women), 47 part-time (35 women); includes 86 minority (51 Black or African American,

Nonprofit Management

non-Hispanic/Latino; 10 Asian, non-Hispanic/Latino; 22 Hispanic/Latino; 3 Two or more races, non-Hispanic/Latino), 3 international. Average age 31. 62 applicants, 94% accepted, 33 enrolled. In 2017, 57 master's awarded. *Degree requirements:* For master's, thesis, internship, research seminar. *Entrance requirements:* For master's, minimum cumulative GPA of 3.0, official transcripts from all institutions attended, two letters of recommendation, personal statement, writing sample, professional resume/curriculum vitae. Additional exam requirements/recommendations for international students: Required—TOEFL (minimum score 550 paper-based; 79 iBT), IELTS (minimum score 6.5). *Application deadline:* For fall admission, 6/30 for domestic and international students; for spring admission, 12/1 for domestic and international students. Applications are processed on a rolling basis. Application fee: $75. Electronic applications accepted. *Expenses:* Tuition, state resident: full-time $13,419; part-time $653 per credit. Tuition, nonresident: full-time $18,188; part-time $801 per credit. *Required fees:* $3382; $154 per credit. Tuition and fees vary according to course level, course load, degree level and program. *Financial support:* Scholarships/grants and unspecified assistantships available. Financial award applicants required to submit FAFSA. *Unit head:* Dr. Patricia Moore, Program Coordinator, 908-737-4314, E-mail: pmoore@kean.edu. *Application contact:* Pedro Lopes, Admissions Counselor, 908-737-7100, E-mail: gradadmissions@kean.edu.
Website: http://grad.kean.edu/masters-programs/public-administration

La Salle University, School of Business, Program in Nonprofit Leadership, Philadelphia, PA 19141-1199. Offers MS. *Program availability:* Part-time, evening/weekend, online only, 100% online. *Faculty:* 6 part-time/adjunct (3 women). *Students:* 3 full-time (all women), 61 part-time (46 women); includes 14 minority (11 Black or African American, non-Hispanic/Latino; 3 Hispanic/Latino). Average age 37. 12 applicants, 100% accepted, 12 enrolled. In 2017, 5 master's awarded. *Degree requirements:* For master's, completion of all required courses within seven-year period; minimum cumulative GPA of 3.0. *Entrance requirements:* For master's, professional resume; personal statement explaining the applicant's interest in and goals for pursuit of this degree; 2 letters of recommendation. Additional exam requirements/recommendations for international students: Required—TOEFL. *Application deadline:* For fall admission, 8/15 priority date for domestic students, 7/15 for international students; for spring admission, 12/15 priority date for domestic students, 11/15 for international students; for summer admission, 4/15 priority date for domestic students, 3/15 for international students. Applications are processed on a rolling basis. Application fee: $35. Electronic applications accepted. Application fee is waived when completed online. *Expenses:* Contact institution. *Financial support:* In 2017–18, 7 students received support. Federal Work-Study, scholarships/grants, and unspecified assistantships available. Support available to part-time students. Financial award application deadline: 8/31; financial award applicants required to submit FAFSA. *Unit head:* Laura Otten, Director, 215-991-3682, Fax: 215-951-1960, E-mail: npl@lasalle.edu. *Application contact:* Lynnette Clement, Online Program Coordinator, Nonprofit Leadership, 215-991-3682, Fax: 215-951-1960, E-mail: clementl@lasalle.edu.
Website: http://www.lasalle.edu/nonprofit-leadership/

Lawrence Technological University, College of Management, Southfield, MI 48075-1058. Offers business administration (MBA, DBA), including business analytics (MBA, MS), cybersecurity (MBA, MS), finance (MBA), information systems (MBA), information technology (MBA), marketing (MBA), project management (MBA, MS); cybersecurity (Graduate Certificate); health IT management (Graduate Certificate); information assurance mangement (Graduate Certificate); information systems (MS), including enterprise resource planning, enterprise security management, project management (MBA, MS); information technology (MS, DM), including business analytics (MBA, MS), cybersecurity (MBA, MS), information assurance (MS), project management (MBA, MS); management (PhD); nonprofit management and leadership (Graduate Certificate); operations management (MS), including manufacturing operations, service operations; project management (Graduate Certificate). *Accreditation:* ACBSP. *Program availability:* Part-time, evening/weekend, 100% online. *Faculty:* 13 full-time (6 women), 7 part-time/adjunct (1 woman). *Students:* 8 full-time (3 women), 280 part-time (102 women); includes 70 minority (34 Black or African American, non-Hispanic/Latino; 2 American Indian or Alaska Native, non-Hispanic/Latino; 18 Asian, non-Hispanic/Latino; 11 Hispanic/Latino; 5 Two or more races, non-Hispanic/Latino), 73 international. Average age 34. 143 applicants, 50% accepted, 68 enrolled. In 2017, 114 master's, 7 doctorates, 10 other advanced degrees awarded. Terminal master's awarded for partial completion of doctoral program. *Degree requirements:* For master's (for some programs); for doctorate, comprehensive exam, thesis/dissertation. *Entrance requirements:* Additional exam requirements/recommendations for international students: Required—TOEFL (minimum score 550 paper-based; 79 iBT), IELTS (minimum score 6.5). *Application deadline:* For fall admission, 5/27 for international students; for spring admission, 10/8 for international students; for summer admission, 2/14 for international students. Applications are processed on a rolling basis. Application fee: $50. Electronic applications accepted. *Expenses: Tuition:* Full-time $15,274; part-time $1091 per credit. One-time fee: $150. *Financial support:* In 2017–18, 35 students received support, including 8 research assistantships with partial tuition reimbursements available (averaging $3,360 per year); career-related internships or fieldwork, unspecified assistantships, and corporate tuition incentives also available. Financial award application deadline: 4/1; financial award applicants required to submit FAFSA. *Faculty research:* Cybersecurity; risk management; IT governance; security controls and countermeasures; threat modeling cyber resilience; autonomous cars; natural language processing; text mining; machine learning; reflective leadership; emerging leadership theories and practice; motivational studies; teaching effectiveness strategies; teamwork; organization development; strategic planning; strengths-based and positive organizational scholarship; global leadership; globalization; corporate governance. *Unit head:* Dr. Bahman Mirshab, Dean, 248-204-3050, E-mail: mgtdean@ltu.edu. *Application contact:* Jane Rohrback, Director of Admissions, 248-204-3160, Fax: 248-204-2228, E-mail: admissions@ltu.edu.
Website: http://www.ltu.edu/management/index.asp

Lewis University, College of Arts and Sciences, Program in Organizational Leadership, Romeoville, IL 60446. Offers higher education/student services (MA); non-profit management (MA); organizational and leadership coaching (MA); organizational management (MA); training and development (MA). *Program availability:* Part-time, evening/weekend, 100% online, blended/hybrid learning. *Students:* 16 full-time (11 women), 154 part-time (115 women); includes 49 minority (27 Black or African American, non-Hispanic/Latino; 1 American Indian or Alaska Native, non-Hispanic/Latino; 4 Asian, non-Hispanic/Latino; 12 Hispanic/Latino; 5 Two or more races, non-Hispanic/Latino), 4 international. Average age 37. *Entrance requirements:* For master's, bachelor's degree, personal statement, minimum GPA of 3.0, letters of recommendation. Additional exam requirements/recommendations for international students: Required—TOEFL (minimum score 550 paper-based; 79 iBT), IELTS (minimum score 6). *Application deadline:* For fall admission, 5/1 priority date for international students; for spring admission, 11/15 priority date for international students. Applications are processed on a rolling basis. Application fee: $40. Electronic applications accepted. Tuition and fees vary according to program. *Financial support:* Federal Work-Study, tuition waivers, and unspecified assistantships available. Financial award application deadline: 5/1; financial award applicants required to submit FAFSA.

Unit head: Dr. Lesley Page, Chair of Organizational Leadership, 815-838-0500, E-mail: pagele@lewisu.edu. *Application contact:* Kathy Lisak, Graduate Admission Counselor, 815-836-5610, E-mail: grad@lewisu.edu.

Liberty University, Helms School of Government, Lynchburg, VA 24515. Offers criminal justice (MS), including forensic psychology, homeland security, public administration (MA, MS); international relations (MS); political science (MS); public administration (MPA), including business and government, healthcare, law and public policy, public and non-profit management; public policy (MA), including campaigns and elections, international affairs, Middle East affairs, public administration (MA, MS). *Program availability:* Part-time, online learning. *Students:* 287 full-time (148 women), 639 part-time (248 women); includes 231 minority (173 Black or African American, non-Hispanic/Latino; 4 American Indian or Alaska Native, non-Hispanic/Latino; 8 Asian, non-Hispanic/Latino; 20 Hispanic/Latino; 1 Native Hawaiian or other Pacific Islander, non-Hispanic/Latino; 25 Two or more races, non-Hispanic/Latino), 7 international. Average age 35. 876 applicants, 64% accepted, 277 enrolled. In 2017, 211 master's awarded. *Entrance requirements:* For master's, minimum undergraduate GPA of 3.0. Additional exam requirements/recommendations for international students: Required—TOEFL (minimum score 600 paper-based; 100 iBT). *Application deadline:* Applications are processed on a rolling basis. Application fee: $50. Electronic applications accepted. *Unit head:* Shawn D. Akers, Dean, 434-592-4986. *Application contact:* Jay Bridge, Director of Admissions, 800-424-9595, Fax: 800-628-7977, E-mail: gradadmissions@liberty.edu.

Lindenwood University, Graduate Programs, Plaster School of Business and Entrepreneurship, St. Charles, MO 63301-1695. Offers accountancy (M Acc); accounting (MBA); business administration (MBA); entrepreneurial studies (MBA); finance (MBA, MS); human resource management (MBA); international business (MBA); leadership (MA); management (MBA); marketing (MBA, MS); nonprofit administration (MA); public administration (MBA); sport management (MA); supply chain management (MBA). *Accreditation:* ACBSP. *Program availability:* Part-time, evening/weekend, 100% online. *Faculty:* 15 full-time (8 women), 26 part-time/adjunct (9 women). *Students:* 201 full-time (116 women), 253 part-time (153 women); includes 102 minority (80 Black or African American, non-Hispanic/Latino; 2 American Indian or Alaska Native, non-Hispanic/Latino; 6 Asian, non-Hispanic/Latino; 7 Hispanic/Latino; 7 Two or more races, non-Hispanic/Latino), 61 international. Average age 32. 370 applicants, 42% accepted, 134 enrolled. In 2017, 178 master's awarded. *Degree requirements:* For master's, comprehensive exam (for some programs), thesis (for some programs), minimum GPA of 3.0. *Entrance requirements:* For master's, interview, minimum undergraduate cumulative GPA of 3.0, letter of recommendation. Additional exam requirements/recommendations for international students: Required—TOEFL (minimum score 550 paper-based; 80 iBT); Recommended—IELTS (minimum score 6.5). *Application deadline:* For fall admission, 8/27 priority date for domestic and international students; for winter admission, 1/14 priority date for domestic and international students; for spring admission, 3/18 for domestic students, 3/18 priority date for international students; for summer admission, 6/3 priority date for domestic and international students. Applications are processed on a rolling basis. Application fee: $30 ($100 for international students). Electronic applications accepted. *Expenses:* Contact institution. *Financial support:* In 2017–18, 439 students received support. Career-related internships or fieldwork, Federal Work-Study, institutionally sponsored loans, scholarships/grants, tuition waivers (partial), and unspecified assistantships available. Financial award application deadline: 6/30; financial award applicants required to submit FAFSA. *Unit head:* Roger Ellis, Dean, School of Business and Entrepreneurship, 636-949-4839, E-mail: rellis@lindenwood.edu. *Application contact:* Kara Schilli, Director, Evening and Graduate Admissions, 636-949-4349, Fax: 636-949-4109, E-mail: adultadmissions@lindenwood.edu.
Website: http://www.lindenwood.edu/academics/academic-schools/robert-w-plaster-school-of-business-entrepreneurship/

Lipscomb University, Nelson and Sue Andrews Institute for Civic Leadership, Nashville, TN 37204-3951. Offers civic leadership (MA, Graduate Certificate); cross sector collaboration (MA); non-profit leadership (MA). *Program availability:* Part-time, evening/weekend. *Faculty:* 3 full-time (2 women). *Students:* 18 full-time (13 women); includes 11 minority (9 Black or African American, non-Hispanic/Latino; 1 Hispanic/Latino; 1 Two or more races, non-Hispanic/Latino). Average age 33. 30 applicants, 37% accepted, 7 enrolled. In 2017, 11 master's awarded. *Degree requirements:* For master's, project, externship. *Entrance requirements:* For master's, GRE, GMAT or MAT, transcripts, 2 references, essay, resume. Additional exam requirements/recommendations for international students: Required—TOEFL (minimum score 570 paper-based; 80 iBT). *Application deadline:* Applications are processed on a rolling basis. Application fee: $50 ($75 for international students). Electronic applications accepted. *Expenses:* $1,290. *Financial support:* Applicants required to submit FAFSA. *Unit head:* Linda Peek Schacht, Executive Director, 615-966-1341, E-mail: linda.schacht@lipscomb.edu. *Application contact:* Dr. MIchelle Steele, Academic Director, 615-966-5181, E-mail: michelle.steele@lipscomb.edu.
Website: http://www.lipscomb.edu/civicleadership

Long Island University–LIU Brooklyn, School of Business, Public Administration and Information Sciences, Brooklyn, NY 11201-8423. Offers accounting (MBA); accounting (MS); business administration (MBA); computer science (MS); gerontology (Advanced Certificate); health administration (MPA); human resources management (MS); not-for-profit management (Advanced Certificate); public administration (MPA); taxation (MS). *Program availability:* Part-time, evening/weekend. *Faculty:* 18 full-time (7 women), 28 part-time/adjunct (8 women). *Students:* 226 full-time (140 women), 232 part-time (150 women); includes 272 minority (192 Black or African American, non-Hispanic/Latino; 2 American Indian or Alaska Native, non-Hispanic/Latino; 35 Asian, non-Hispanic/Latino; 40 Hispanic/Latino; 3 Two or more races, non-Hispanic/Latino), 88 international. Average age 32. 495 applicants, 64% accepted, 149 enrolled. In 2017, 189 master's, 13 other advanced degrees awarded. *Entrance requirements:* Additional exam requirements/recommendations for international students: Required—TOEFL (minimum score 550 paper-based; 75 iBT). *Application deadline:* Applications are processed on a rolling basis. Application fee: $50. Electronic applications accepted. *Expenses: Tuition:* Full-time $21,618; part-time $1201 per credit. *Required fees:* $1840; $920 per term. Tuition and fees vary according to course load. *Financial support:* In 2017–18, 78 students received support. Career-related internships or fieldwork, Federal Work-Study, scholarships/grants, and unspecified assistantships available. Support available to part-time students. Financial award application deadline: 2/15; financial award applicants required to submit FAFSA. *Faculty research:* Tax policy; public sector budgeting and gender inequities; technology and innovation; game theory; knowledge management. *Unit head:* Dr. Edward Rogoff, Dean, 718-488-1159, E-mail: edward.rogoff@liu.edu. *Application contact:* Luis Santiago, Dean of Enrollment, 718-488-1011, Fax: 718-780-6110, E-mail: bkln-admissions@liu.edu.
Website: http://liu.edu/Brooklyn/Academics/School-of-Business-Public-Administration-and-Information-Sciences

Long Island University–LIU Post, School of Health Professions and Nursing, Brookville, NY 11548-1300. Offers biomedical science (MS); cardiovascular perfusion (MS); clinical lab sciences (MS); clinical laboratory management (MS); dietetic internship (Advanced Certificate); family nurse practitioner (MS, Advanced Certificate); forensic social work (Advanced Certificate); gerontology (Advanced Certificate); health administration (MPA); non-profit management (Advanced Certificate); nursing education

(MS); nutrition (MS); public administration (MPA); social work (MSW). *Program availability:* Part-time, blended/hybrid learning. *Faculty:* 23 full-time (17 women), 33 part-time/adjunct (19 women). *Students:* 228 full-time (174 women), 227 part-time (185 women); includes 172 minority (76 Black or African American, non-Hispanic/Latino; 1 American Indian or Alaska Native, non-Hispanic/Latino; 44 Asian, non-Hispanic/Latino; 48 Hispanic/Latino; 3 Two or more races, non-Hispanic/Latino), 60 international. Average age 31. 392 applicants, 67% accepted, 138 enrolled. In 2017, 180 master's, 26 other advanced degrees awarded. *Degree requirements:* For master's, comprehensive exam (for some programs), thesis (for some programs). *Entrance requirements:* Additional exam requirements/recommendations for international students: Required— TOEFL (minimum score 85 iBT) or IELTS (7.5). *Application deadline:* Applications are processed on a rolling basis. Application fee: $50. Electronic applications accepted. *Expenses: Tuition:* Full-time $21,618; part-time $1201 per credit. *Required fees:* $1840; $920 per term. Tuition and fees vary according to course load. *Financial support:* In 2017–18, 102 students received support. Research assistantships, teaching assistantships, career-related internships or fieldwork, Federal Work-Study, scholarships/grants, and unspecified assistantships available. Support available to part-time students. Financial award application deadline: 2/15; financial award applicants required to submit FAFSA. *Faculty research:* Antibiotic resistance, evidence-based practice, family care, interprofessional learning, simulation learning. *Unit head:* Dr. Stacy Gropack, Dean, 516-299-2485, Fax: 516-299-2527, E-mail: post-shpn@liu.edu. *Application contact:* Kathy Riley, Associate Director of Graduate Admissions, 516-299-2900, Fax: 516-299-2137, E-mail: post-enroll@liu.edu.
Website: http://liu.edu/post/health

Louisiana State University in Shreveport, College of Arts and Sciences, Program in Nonprofit Administration, Shreveport, LA 71115-2399. Offers MS. *Program availability:* Part-time, evening/weekend, online learning. *Students:* 95 full-time (89 women), 51 part-time (33 women); includes 50 minority (38 Black or African American, non-Hispanic/Latino; 1 Asian, non-Hispanic/Latino; 3 Hispanic/Latino; 8 Two or more races, non-Hispanic/Latino), 1 international. Average age 38. 163 applicants, 90% accepted, 69 enrolled. In 2017, 1 master's awarded. *Degree requirements:* For master's, final project. *Entrance requirements:* For master's, GRE, minimum GPA of 3.0 in last 2 undergraduate years, interview, recommendations. Additional exam requirements/recommendations for international students: Required—TOEFL (minimum score 550 paper-based; 61 iBT). *Application deadline:* For fall admission, 6/30 for domestic and international students; for spring admission, 11/30 for domestic and international students; for summer admission, 4/30 for domestic and international students. Applications are processed on a rolling basis. Application fee: $20 ($30 for international students). Electronic applications accepted. *Expenses:* Tuition, state resident: full-time $3098; part-time $344 per credit hour. Tuition, nonresident: full-time $9923; part-time $1103 per credit hour. *Required fees:* $384 per semester. Tuition and fees vary according to program. *Financial support:* In 2017–18, 2 research assistantships (averaging $3,780 per year) were awarded. Financial award applicants required to submit FAFSA. *Unit head:* Stacey Hargis, Interim Program Director, 318-795-4245, Fax: 318-797-5358, E-mail: stacey.hargis@lsus.edu. *Application contact:* Mary Catherine Harvison, Director of Admissions, 318-797-2400, Fax: 318-797-5286, E-mail: mary.harvison@lsus.edu.

Marymount University, School of Business Administration, Program in Leadership and Management, Arlington, VA 22207-4299. Offers association and nonprofit management (Certificate); leadership and management (MS); management studies (Certificate). *Program availability:* Part-time, evening/weekend. *Faculty:* 2 full-time (1 woman). *Students:* 1 (woman) full-time, 13 part-time (8 women); includes 4 minority (3 Black or African American, non-Hispanic/Latino; 1 Two or more races, non-Hispanic/Latino). Average age 40. 5 applicants, 100% accepted, 2 enrolled. In 2017, 4 master's awarded. *Degree requirements:* For master's, thesis or alternative. *Entrance requirements:* For master's, GMAT or GRE General Test, resume, interview, at least 3 years of managerial experience, essay on a topic provided by School of Business Administration; for Certificate, resume, at least 3 years of managerial experience. Additional exam requirements/recommendations for international students: Required—TOEFL (minimum score 600 paper-based; 96 iBT), IELTS (minimum score 6.5). *Application deadline:* For fall admission, 7/16 priority date for domestic and international students; for spring admission, 11/16 priority date for domestic and international students; for summer admission, 4/16 for domestic and international students. Applications are processed on a rolling basis. Application fee: $40. Electronic applications accepted. *Expenses:* $990 per credit. *Financial support:* Career-related internships or fieldwork, Federal Work-Study, scholarships/grants, and unspecified assistantships available. Support available to part-time students. Financial award application deadline: 3/1; financial award applicants required to submit FAFSA. *Unit head:* Dr. Lorri Cooper, Chair, Management and Marketing/Director, 703-284-5950, Fax: 703-527-3830, E-mail: lorri.cooper@marymount.edu. *Application contact:* Francesca Reed, Director, Graduate Admissions, 703-284-5901, Fax: 703-527-3815, E-mail: grad.admissions@marymount.edu.
Website: http://www.marymount.edu/Academics/School-of-Business-Administration/Graduate-Programs/Leadership-Management-(M-S-)

Mercer University, Graduate Studies, Cecil B. Day Campus, Penfield College, Atlanta, GA 30341. Offers certified rehabilitation counseling (MS); clinical mental health (MS); counselor education and supervision (PhD); criminal justice and public safety leadership (MS); health informatics (MS); human services (MS), including child and adolescent services, gerontology services; organizational leadership (MS), including leadership for the health care professional, leadership for the nonprofit organization, organizational development and change; school counseling (MS). *Program availability:* Part-time, evening/weekend, 100% online, blended/hybrid learning. *Faculty:* 17 full-time (10 women), 27 part-time/adjunct (24 women). *Students:* 199 full-time (165 women), 266 part-time (218 women); includes 268 minority (226 Black or African American, non-Hispanic/Latino; 1 American Indian or Alaska Native, non-Hispanic/Latino; 19 Asian, non-Hispanic/Latino; 19 Hispanic/Latino; 3 Two or more races, non-Hispanic/Latino). Average age 32. 300 applicants, 45% accepted, 114 enrolled. In 2017, 101 master's, 5 doctorates awarded. *Degree requirements:* For master's, comprehensive exam (for some programs), thesis (for some programs); for doctorate, thesis/dissertation. *Entrance requirements:* For master's, GRE or MAT, Georgia Professional Standards Commission (GPSC) Certification at the SC-5 level; for doctorate, GRE or MAT. Additional exam requirements/recommendations for international students: Recommended—TOEFL (minimum score 550 paper-based; 80 iBT), IELTS (minimum score 6.5). *Application deadline:* For fall admission, 7/1 priority date for domestic and international students; for spring admission, 11/1 priority date for domestic and international students; for summer admission, 4/1 priority date for domestic and international students. Application fee: $35. Electronic applications accepted. Application fee is waived when completed online. *Expenses:* $637 per credit. *Financial support:* In 2017–18, 32 students received support. Federal Work-Study, scholarships/grants, and unspecified assistantships available. Financial award applicants required to submit FAFSA. *Faculty research:* Marriage and families issues, leadership and ethics, cyber-bullying, trauma, narrative counseling and theory. *Total annual research expenditures:* $85,000. *Unit head:* Dr. Priscilla R. Danheiser, Dean, 678-547-6028, Fax: 678-547-6008, E-mail: danheiser_p@mercer.edu. *Application contact:* Dr. Melissa McCants Cruz, Director of Graduate Admissions, 678-547-6024, E-mail: penfield.admissions@mercer.edu.
Website: http://penfield.mercer.edu/programs/graduate-professional/

Minnesota State University Mankato, College of Graduate Studies and Research, College of Social and Behavioral Sciences, Urban and Regional Studies Institute, Mankato, MN 56001. Offers local government management (Certificate); non-profit leadership (Certificate); urban and regional studies (MA); urban planning (MA, Certificate). *Degree requirements:* For master's, one foreign language, comprehensive exam, thesis or alternative. *Entrance requirements:* For master's, minimum GPA of 3.0 during previous 2 years, 2 letters of recommendation. Additional exam requirements/recommendations for international students: Required—TOEFL. Electronic applications accepted.

Mount Aloysius College, Program in Business Administration, Cresson, PA 16630. Offers accounting (MBA); health and human services administration (MBA); non-profit management (MBA); project management (MBA). *Program availability:* Part-time, evening/weekend. *Entrance requirements:* Additional exam requirements/recommendations for international students: Required—IELTS (minimum score 5.5); Recommended—TOEFL. *Application deadline:* For fall admission, 8/1 for domestic students; for spring admission, 12/1 for domestic students. Applications are processed on a rolling basis. Application fee: $30. Electronic applications accepted. Application fee is waived when completed online. *Expenses: Tuition:* Full-time $14,000; part-time $790 per credit hour. *Financial support:* Unspecified assistantships available. Financial award applicants required to submit FAFSA. *Application contact:* Matthew P. Bodenschatz, Director of Graduate and Continuing Education Admissions, 814-886-6556, Fax: 814-886-6441, E-mail: mbodenschatz@mtaloy.edu.
Website: http://www.mtaloy.edu

Murray State University, College of Education and Human Services, Department of Community Leadership and Human Services, Murray, KY 42071. Offers nonprofit leadership studies (MS, Certificate). *Program availability:* Part-time, evening/weekend, 100% online, blended/hybrid learning. *Faculty:* 6 full-time (2 women), 1 part-time/adjunct (0 women). *Students:* 4 full-time (all women), 14 part-time (12 women); includes 3 minority (2 Black or African American, non-Hispanic/Latino; 1 American Indian or Alaska Native, non-Hispanic/Latino), 1 international. Average age 41. 7 applicants, 57% accepted, 2 enrolled. In 2017, 3 master's awarded. *Entrance requirements:* For master's, GRE or GMAT, minimum university GPA of 2.75. Additional exam requirements/recommendations for international students: Required—TOEFL (minimum score 527 paper-based; 71 iBT). *Application deadline:* Applications are processed on a rolling basis. Application fee: $40 ($50 for international students). Electronic applications accepted. *Expenses:* Tuition, state resident: full-time $9504. Tuition, nonresident: full-time $26,811. *International tuition:* $14,400 full-time. Tuition and fees vary according to course load, degree level and reciprocity agreements. *Financial support:* Federal Work-Study and unspecified assistantships available. Financial award applicants required to submit FAFSA. *Faculty research:* Service learning, engaged citizenship, volunteer development, youth programming, philanthropy. *Unit head:* Dr. Paul Lucko, Chair, Community Leadership and Human Services, 270-809-2785, E-mail: plucko@murraystate.edu. *Application contact:* Kaitlyn Burzynski, Interim Assistant Director for Graduate Admission and Records, 270-809-5732, Fax: 270-809-3780, E-mail: msu.graduateadmissions@murraystate.edu.
Website: https://www.murraystate.edu/academics/CollegesDepartments/CollegeOfEducationandHumanServices/coehsacademicunits/CLHS/index.aspx

New England College, Program in Management, Henniker, NH 03242-3293. Offers accounting (MSA); healthcare administration (MS); international relations (MA); marketing management (MS); nonprofit leadership (MS); project management (MS); strategic leadership (MS). *Program availability:* Part-time, evening/weekend. *Degree requirements:* For master's, independent research project. Electronic applications accepted.

The New School, Schools of Public Engagement, Program in Nonprofit Management, New York, NY 10011. Offers MS. *Program availability:* Part-time, evening/weekend. *Faculty:* 3 full-time (0 women), 6 part-time/adjunct (4 women). *Students:* 23 full-time (19 women), 29 part-time (24 women); includes 19 minority (9 Black or African American, non-Hispanic/Latino; 3 Asian, non-Hispanic/Latino; 7 Hispanic/Latino), 4 international. Average age 30. 52 applicants, 90% accepted, 13 enrolled. In 2017, 23 master's awarded. *Degree requirements:* For master's, capstone project: Paper of Publishable Quality (PPQ), Professional Decision Report (PDR), or thesis. *Entrance requirements:* For master's, two letters of recommendation, statement of purpose, resume, transcripts. Additional exam requirements/recommendations for international students: Required— TOEFL (minimum score 92 iBT), IELTS (minimum score 7), PTE (minimum score 68). *Application deadline:* For fall admission, 1/15 priority date for domestic and international students; for spring admission, 10/15 priority date for domestic and international students. Applications are processed on a rolling basis. Application fee: $50. Electronic applications accepted. *Expenses:* $1,650 per credit. *Financial support:* In 2017–18, 34 students received support, including 1 teaching assistantship (averaging $6,028 per year); career-related internships or fieldwork, Federal Work-Study, institutionally sponsored loans, scholarships/grants, and unspecified assistantships also available. Support available to part-time students. Financial award application deadline: 2/1; financial award applicants required to submit FAFSA. *Unit head:* Suzanne Bostwick, Chair, 212-229-5400 Ext. 1601, E-mail: bostwics@newschool.edu. *Application contact:* Gabriela Garcia Juarez, Assistant Director, Graduate Admission, 212-229-5150 Ext. 1666, E-mail: garciajg@newschool.edu.
Website: https://www.newschool.edu/public-engagement/ms-nonprofit-management/

New York University, Wagner Graduate School of Public Service, Program in Public Administration, New York, NY 10012. Offers public administration (PhD); public and nonprofit management and policy (MPA, Advanced Certificate), including financial management and public finance (MPA), international policy and management (MPA), management for public and nonprofit organizations, public policy analysis, social impact, innovation, and investment (MPA); JD/MPA; MBA/MPA; MPA/MA. *Accreditation:* NASPAA (one or more programs are accredited). *Program availability:* Part-time. *Students:* Average age 27. 951 applicants, 63% accepted, 238 enrolled. In 2017, 233 master's, 6 doctorates, 1 other advanced degree awarded. *Degree requirements:* For master's, thesis or alternative, capstone end event; for doctorate, one foreign language, comprehensive exam, thesis/dissertation, preliminary qualifying examination. *Entrance requirements:* Additional exam requirements/recommendations for international students: Required—TOEFL (minimum score 100 iBT), IELTS (minimum score 7.5), TWE. *Application deadline:* For fall admission, 1/5 for domestic and international students; for spring admission, 10/1 for domestic and international students. Application fee: $85. Electronic applications accepted. *Expenses:* Contact institution. *Financial support:* In 2017–18, 152 students received support, including 137 fellowships with full and partial tuition reimbursements available (averaging $16,683 per year), 2 research assistantships with full tuition reimbursements available (averaging $56,524 per year); career-related internships or fieldwork, Federal Work-Study, scholarships/grants, health care benefits, and unspecified assistantships also available. Support available to part-time students. Financial award application deadline: 1/5; financial award applicants required to submit FAFSA. *Unit head:* Prof. Katherine O'Regan, Associate Professor of Public Policy, 212-998-7498, E-mail: katherine.oregan@nyu.edu. *Application contact:* Sandra Oliveira, Admissions Officer, 212-998-7414, Fax: 212-995-4611, E-mail: wagner.admissions@nyu.edu.
Website: http://wagner.nyu.edu/

Nonprofit Management

North Carolina State University, Graduate School, College of Humanities and Social Sciences, School of Public and International Affairs, Raleigh, NC 27695. Offers international studies (MIS); nonprofit management (Certificate); public administration (MPA, PhD). *Accreditation:* NASPAA (one or more programs are accredited). *Program availability:* Part-time, evening/weekend. *Entrance requirements:* For master's, GRE General Test, minimum GPA of 3.0 during previous 2 years. Electronic applications accepted. *Faculty research:* Public sector leadership and ethics, financial management, management systems evaluation, computer applications, service delivery.

Northeastern University, College of Professional Studies, Boston, MA 02115-5096. Offers applied nutrition (MS); college athletics administration (MSL); commerce and economic development (MS); corporate and organizational communication (MS); criminal justice (MS); digital media (MPS); elearning and instructional design (M Ed); elementary education (MAT); geographic information technology (MPS); global studies and international relations (MS); higher education administration (M Ed); homeland security (MA); human services (MS); informatics (MPS); leadership (MS); learning analytics (M Ed); learning and instruction (M Ed); nonprofit management (MS); professional sports administration (MSL); project management (MS); regulatory affairs for drugs, biologics, and medical devices (MS); respiratory care leadership (MS); special education (M Ed); technical communication (MS). *Program availability:* Part-time, evening/weekend, 100% online, blended/hybrid learning. *Faculty:* 82 full-time (51 women), 853 part-time/adjunct (366 women). *Students:* 5,278 part-time (3,230 women). In 2017, 1,586 master's awarded. *Application deadline:* Applications are processed on a rolling basis. Application fee: $0. Electronic applications accepted. *Expenses:* Contact institution. *Financial support:* Applicants required to submit FAFSA. *Unit head:* Dr. Mary Loeffelholz, Dean of the College of Professional Studies. *Application contact:* E-mail: cpsadmissions@northeastern.edu.
Website: https://cps.northeastern.edu/

Northern Kentucky University, Office of Graduate Programs, College of Arts and Sciences, Program in Public Administration, Highland Heights, KY 41099. Offers non-profit management (Certificate); public administration (MPA). *Accreditation:* NASPAA. *Program availability:* Part-time. *Degree requirements:* For master's, 39 semester hours, including completion of the capstone course. *Entrance requirements:* For master's, GRE, minimum GPA of 2.5, letters of references, portfolios; for Certificate, minimum GPA of 2.0. Additional exam requirements/recommendations for international students: Required—TOEFL (minimum score 79 iBT); Recommended—IELTS (minimum score 6.5). Electronic applications accepted. *Faculty research:* Nonprofit management, human resource management, urban planning, service-learning, homeland security.

North Park University, School of Business and Nonprofit Management, Chicago, IL 60625-4895. Offers MBA, MHEA, MHRM, MM, MNA. *Program availability:* Part-time, evening/weekend, online learning. *Entrance requirements:* For master's, GMAT, GRE. Additional exam requirements/recommendations for international students: Required—TOEFL. *Expenses:* Contact institution.

Norwich University, College of Graduate and Continuing Studies, Master of Public Administration Program, Northfield, VT 05663. Offers criminal justice and public safety (MPA); fiscal management (MPA); international development and influence (MPA); municipal governance (MPA); nonprofit management (MPA); policy analysis and analytics (MPA); public administration leadership and crisis management (MPA); public works and sustainability (MPA). *Program availability:* Evening/weekend, online only, mostly all online with a week-long residency requirement. *Degree requirements:* For master's, capstone. *Entrance requirements:* For master's, minimum undergraduate GPA of 2.75. Additional exam requirements/recommendations for international students: Required—TOEFL (minimum score 550 paper-based; 80 iBT), IELTS (minimum score 6.5). Electronic applications accepted. *Expenses:* Contact institution.

Notre Dame of Maryland University, Graduate Studies, Program in Nonprofit Management, Baltimore, MD 21210-2476. Offers MA. *Program availability:* Part-time, evening/weekend. *Degree requirements:* For master's, thesis optional. *Entrance requirements:* For master's, minimum GPA of 3.0. Additional exam requirements/recommendations for international students: Required—TOEFL (minimum score 500 paper-based; 61 iBT). Electronic applications accepted.

Oakland University, Graduate Study and Lifelong Learning, College of Arts and Sciences, Department of Political Science, Rochester, MI 48309-4401. Offers local government management (Graduate Certificate); non-profit and organizational management (PMC); public administration (MPA). *Accreditation:* NASPAA. *Program availability:* Part-time, evening/weekend. *Entrance requirements:* For master's, minimum GPA of 3.0. Additional exam requirements/recommendations for international students: Required—TOEFL (minimum score 550 paper-based). Electronic applications accepted. *Expenses:* Tuition, state resident: full-time $16,950; part-time $706.25 per credit. Tuition, nonresident: full-time $24,648; part-time $1027 per credit.

Oklahoma Christian University, Graduate School of Business, Oklahoma City, OK 73136-1100. Offers accounting (M Acc, MBA); financial services (MBA); general business (MBA); health services management (MBA); human resources (MBA); international business (MBA); leadership and organizational development (MBA); marketing (MBA); nonprofit management (MBA); project management (MBA). *Accreditation:* ACBSP. *Program availability:* Part-time, 100% online. *Entrance requirements:* For master's, bachelor's degree. Additional exam requirements/recommendations for international students: Required—TOEFL (minimum score 550 paper-based). Electronic applications accepted. *Expenses:* Contact institution.

Oklahoma State University, Graduate College, Stillwater, OK 74078. Offers aerospace security (Graduate Certificate); bioenergy and sustainable technology (Graduate Certificate); business data mining (Graduate Certificate); business sustainability (Graduate Certificate); environmental science (MS); international studies (MS); non-profit management (Graduate Certificate); teaching English to speakers of other languages (Graduate Certificate); telecommunications management (MS). Programs are interdisciplinary. *Students:* 31 full-time (21 women), 55 part-time (32 women); includes 15 minority (5 Black or African American, non-Hispanic/Latino; 3 Asian, non-Hispanic/Latino; 5 Hispanic/Latino; 2 Two or more races, non-Hispanic/Latino), 44 international. Average age 29. 334 applicants, 84% accepted, 73 enrolled. In 2017, 29 master's, 5 doctorates awarded. *Degree requirements:* For master's, thesis (for some programs); for doctorate, comprehensive exam, thesis/dissertation. *Entrance requirements:* For master's and doctorate, GRE or GMAT. Additional exam requirements/recommendations for international students: Required—TOEFL (minimum score 550 paper-based; 79 iBT). *Application deadline:* For fall admission, 3/1 priority date for domestic and international students; for spring admission, 8/1 priority date for domestic and international students. Applications are processed on a rolling basis. Application fee: $40 ($75 for international students). Electronic applications accepted. *Expenses:* Tuition, state resident: full-time $4019; part-time $2679.60 per year. Tuition, nonresident: full-time $15,286; part-time $10,190.40 per year. *Required fees:* $2129; $1419 per unit. Tuition and fees vary according to program. *Financial support:* Research assistantships, career-related internships or fieldwork, Federal Work-Study, scholarships/grants, health care benefits, tuition waivers (partial), and unspecified assistantships available. Support available to part-time students. Financial award application deadline: 3/1; financial award applicants required to submit FAFSA. *Unit*

head: Dr. Sheryl Tucker, Dean, 405-744-6368, Fax: 405-744-0355, E-mail: gradi@okstate.edu. *Application contact:* Dr. Susan Mathew, Assistant Director of Graduate Admissions, 405-744-6368, Fax: 405-744-0355, E-mail: gradi@okstate.edu.
Website: http://gradcollege.okstate.edu/

Oral Roberts University, School of Business, Tulsa, OK 74171. Offers accounting (MBA); entrepreneurship (MBA); finance (MBA); international business (MBA); management (MBA); marketing (MBA); not for profit management (MNM). *Accreditation:* ACBSP. *Program availability:* Part-time, online learning. *Faculty:* 7 full-time (0 women), 5 part-time/adjunct (4 women). *Students:* 71 applicants, 94% accepted, 56 enrolled. *Degree requirements:* For master's, thesis optional. *Entrance requirements:* For master's, minimum cumulative GPA of 3.0 from regionally-accredited institution. *Application deadline:* Applications are processed on a rolling basis. Application fee: $35. Electronic applications accepted. Application fee is waived when completed online. *Financial support:* In 2017–18, 39 students received support. Scholarships/grants and unspecified assistantships available. Financial award application deadline: 6/1. *Faculty research:* Social media, international business and marketing. *Unit head:* Dr. Marshal Wright, Chair of the Graduate School of Business, 918-495-6988, E-mail: mwright@oru.edu. *Application contact:* Sam Park, Enrollment Counselor, 918-495-7179, E-mail: sampark@oru.edu.
Website: http://www.oru.edu/university/departments/schools/bus

Our Lady of the Lake University, School of Business and Leadership, Program in Nonprofit Management, San Antonio, TX 78207-4689. Offers MS. *Program availability:* Part-time, evening/weekend, online only, 100% online. *Faculty:* 2 full-time (0 women), 2 part-time/adjunct (0 women). *Students:* 25 full-time (20 women), 4 part-time (3 women); includes 12 minority (1 Black or African American, non-Hispanic/Latino; 11 Hispanic/Latino). Average age 35. 38 applicants, 82% accepted, 19 enrolled. In 2017, 9 master's awarded. *Entrance requirements:* For master's, official transcripts showing minimum cumulative GPA of 2.5, 2 letters of recommendation, resume. Additional exam requirements/recommendations for international students: Required—TOEFL. *Application deadline:* For fall admission, 6/15 for domestic and international students. Application fee: $40 ($50 for international students). Electronic applications accepted. *Expenses:* Contact institution. *Financial support:* In 2017–18, 1 student received support. Federal Work-Study, scholarships/grants, unspecified assistantships, and tuition discounts available. Support available to part-time students. Financial award application deadline: 5/1; financial award applicants required to submit FAFSA. *Unit head:* Dr. Ronald Crowe, Chair of Business Programs, 210-434-6711 Ext. 2713, E-mail: rcrowe@ollusa.edu. *Application contact:* Office of Graduate Admissions, 210-431-3995, Fax: 210-431-3945, E-mail: gradadm@ollusa.edu.
Website: http://www.ollusa.edu/s/1190/hybrid/default-hybrid-ollu.aspx?sid-1190&gid-1&pgid-7921

Pace University, Dyson College of Arts and Sciences, Department of Public Administration, New York, NY 10038. Offers government management (MPA); health care administration (MPA); not-for-profit management (MPA); JD/MPA. *Program availability:* Part-time, evening/weekend. *Faculty:* 6 full-time (4 women), 4 part-time/adjunct (1 woman). *Students:* 34 full-time (18 women), 66 part-time (45 women); includes 59 minority (38 Black or African American, non-Hispanic/Latino; 9 Asian, non-Hispanic/Latino; 11 Hispanic/Latino; 1 Two or more races, non-Hispanic/Latino), 8 international. Average age 31. In 2017, 53 master's awarded. *Degree requirements:* For master's, comprehensive exam, thesis (for some programs), capstone project. *Entrance requirements:* For master's, 2 letters of recommendation, resume, personal statement, official transcripts, essay. Additional exam requirements/recommendations for international students: Required—TOEFL (minimum score 88 iBT), IELTS (minimum score 7) or PTE (minimum score 60). *Application deadline:* For fall admission, 8/1 priority date for domestic students, 6/1 for international students; for spring admission, 12/1 priority date for domestic students, 10/1 for international students. Applications are processed on a rolling basis. Application fee: $70. Electronic applications accepted. *Financial support:* Research assistantships, career-related internships or fieldwork, Federal Work-Study, and tuition waivers (partial) available. Support available to part-time students. Financial award application deadline: 2/15; financial award applicants required to submit FAFSA. *Unit head:* Dr. Hillary Knepper, Chairperson, 914-773-3140, E-mail: hknepper@pace.edu. *Application contact:* Susan Ford-Goldschein, Director of Admissions, 914-422-4283, Fax: 212-346-1585, E-mail: graduateadmission@pace.edu.
Website: http://www.pace.edu/dyson/academic-departments-and-programs/public-admin

Park University, School of Graduate and Professional Studies, Kansas City, MO 54105. Offers adult education (M Ed); business and government leadership (Graduate Certificate); business, government, and global society (MPA); communication and leadership (MA); creative and life writing (Graduate Certificate); disaster and emergency management (MPA, Graduate Certificate); educational leadership (M Ed); finance (MBA, Graduate Certificate); general business (MBA); global business (Graduate Certificate); healthcare administration (MHA); healthcare services management and leadership (Graduate Certificate); international business (MBA); language and literacy (M Ed), including English for speakers of other languages, special reading teacher/literacy coach; leadership of international healthcare organizations (Graduate Certificate); management information systems (MBA, Graduate Certificate); music performance (ADP, Graduate Certificate), including cello (MM, ADP), piano (MM, ADP), viola (MM, ADP), violin (MM, ADP); nonprofit and community services management (MPA); nonprofit leadership (Graduate Certificate); performance (MM), including cello (MM, ADP), piano (MM, ADP), viola (MM, ADP), violin (MM, ADP); public management (MPA); social work (MSW); teacher leadership (M Ed), including curriculum and assessment, instructional leader. *Program availability:* Part-time, evening/weekend, online learning. *Degree requirements:* For master's, comprehensive exam (for some programs), thesis (for some programs), internship (for some programs); exam (for some programs). *Entrance requirements:* For master's, GRE or GMAT (for some programs), teacher certification (for some M Ed programs), letters of recommendation, essay, resume (for some programs). Additional exam requirements/recommendations for international students: Required—TOEFL (minimum score 550 paper-based; 79 iBT), IELTS (minimum score 6). Electronic applications accepted.

Penn State Harrisburg, Graduate School, School of Public Affairs, Middletown, PA 17057. Offers criminal justice (MA); health administration (MHA); health administration: long term care (Certificate); homeland security (MPS, Certificate); public administration (MPA, PhD); public administration: non-profit administration (Certificate); public budgeting and financial management (Certificate); public sector human resource management (Certificate). *Accreditation:* NASPAA. *Unit head:* Dr. Mukund S. Kulkarni, Chancellor, 717-948-6105, Fax: 717-948-6452. *Application contact:* Robert W. Coffman, Jr., Director of Enrollment Management, Recruitment and Admissions, 717-948-6250, Fax: 717-948-6325, E-mail: hbgadmit@psu.edu.
Website: https://harrisburg.psu.edu/public-affairs

Portland State University, Graduate Studies, College of Urban and Public Affairs, Hatfield School of Government, Division of Public Administration, Portland, OR 97207-0751. Offers collaborative governance (Certificate); energy policy and management (Certificate); global management and leadership (MPA); health administration (MPA); human resource management (MPA); local government (MPA); natural resource policy and administration (MPA); nonprofit and public management (Certificate); nonprofit management (MPA);

public administration (EMPA); public affairs and policy (PhD); sustainable food systems (Certificate). *Accreditation:* NASPAA (one or more programs are accredited). *Program availability:* Part-time, evening/weekend. *Faculty:* 15 full-time (6 women), 6 part-time/adjunct (4 women). *Students:* 84 full-time (54 women), 109 part-time (75 women); includes 40 minority (8 Black or African American, non-Hispanic/Latino; 5 American Indian or Alaska Native, non-Hispanic/Latino; 8 Asian, non-Hispanic/Latino; 12 Hispanic/Latino; 1 Native Hawaiian or other Pacific Islander, non-Hispanic/Latino; 6 Two or more races, non-Hispanic/Latino), 14 international. Average age 35. 118 applicants, 84% accepted, 56 enrolled. In 2017, 60 master's, 1 doctorate awarded. *Degree requirements:* For master's, integrative field experience (MPA), practicum (MPH); for doctorate, comprehensive exam, thesis/dissertation. *Entrance requirements:* For master's, GRE (minimum scores: verbal 150, quantitative 149, and analytic writing 4.5), minimum GPA of 3.0, 3 recommendation letters, resume, 500-word statement of intent; for doctorate, GRE, 3 recommendation letters, resume, 500-word personal essay. Additional exam requirements/recommendations for international students: Required—TOEFL (minimum score 550 paper-based; 80 iBT), IELTS (minimum score 7). *Application deadline:* For fall admission, 4/1 for domestic students, 3/1 for international students; for winter admission, 9/1 for domestic students, 8/1 for international students; for spring admission, 11/1 for domestic and international students. Application fee: $65. *Expenses:* Tuition, state resident: full-time $14,436; part-time $401 per credit. Tuition, nonresident: full-time $21,780; part-time $605 per credit. *Required fees:* $1380; $22 per credit. $119 per quarter. One-time fee: $325. Tuition and fees vary according to program. *Financial support:* In 2017–18, 39 students received support, including 5 research assistantships with full and partial tuition reimbursements available (averaging $8,341 per year), 4 teaching assistantships (averaging $5,292 per year); career-related internships or fieldwork, Federal Work-Study, scholarships/grants, and unspecified assistantships also available. Support available to part-time students. Financial award application deadline: 3/1; financial award applicants required to submit FAFSA. *Faculty research:* Public budgeting, program evaluation, nonprofit management, natural resources policy and administration. *Total annual research expenditures:* $679,077. *Unit head:* Dr. Masami Nishishiba, Chair, 503-725-5151, E-mail: nishism@pdx.edu. *Application contact:* Megan Heljeson, Office Coordinator, 503-725-3921, Fax: 503-725-8250, E-mail: publicad@pdx.edu.
Website: https://www.pdx.edu/hatfieldschool/public-administration

Post University, Program in Counseling and Human Services, Waterbury, CT 06723-2540. Offers counseling and human services (MS); counseling and human services/alcohol and drug counseling (MS); counseling and human services/clinical mental health counseling (MS); counseling and human services/forensic mental health counseling (MS); counseling and human services/non-profit management (MS). *Program availability:* Part-time, evening/weekend, online learning. *Entrance requirements:* For master's, resume. *Expenses: Tuition:* Part-time $730 per credit hour. Part-time tuition and fees vary according to degree level and program. *Application contact:* Veronica Montalvo, Vice President, Online Education Enrollment Management and Admissions, 203-596-6164, E-mail: vmontalvo@post.edu.
Website: https://post.edu/academics/online-master-of-science-in-counseling-and-human-services

Regent University, Graduate School, Robertson School of Government, Virginia Beach, VA 23464. Offers government (MA), including American government, healthcare policy and ethics (MA, MPA), international relations, law and public policy, national security studies, political communication, political theory, religion and politics; national security studies (MA), including cybersecurity, homeland security, international security, Middle East politics; public administration (MPA), including emergency management and homeland security, federal government, general public administration, healthcare policy and ethics (MA, MPA), law, nonprofit administration and faith-based organizations, public leadership and management, servant leadership. *Program availability:* Part-time, evening/weekend, 100% online, blended/hybrid learning. *Faculty:* 8 full-time (1 woman), 20 part-time/adjunct (3 women). *Students:* 39 full-time (23 women), 137 part-time (78 women); includes 83 minority (49 Black or African American, non-Hispanic/Latino; 1 American Indian or Alaska Native, non-Hispanic/Latino; 7 Asian, non-Hispanic/Latino; 15 Hispanic/Latino; 11 Two or more races, non-Hispanic/Latino). Average age 35. 345 applicants, 31% accepted, 57 enrolled. In 2017, 38 master's awarded. *Degree requirements:* For master's, thesis optional, internship. *Entrance requirements:* For master's, GRE General Test or LSAT, personal essay, writing sample, resume, college transcripts. Additional exam requirements/recommendations for international students: Required—TOEFL (minimum score 577 paper-based). *Application deadline:* For fall admission, 5/1 priority date for domestic students; for spring admission, 11/1 priority date for domestic students. Applications are processed on a rolling basis. Application fee: $50. Electronic applications accepted. *Expenses:* $650 per credit; $300 technology fee per semester. *Financial support:* In 2017–18, 116 students received support. Career-related internships or fieldwork, scholarships/grants, and unspecified assistantships available. Support available to part-time students. *Faculty research:* International relations and politics, public administration, leadership and ethics, Biblical law, Constitutional law and Supreme Court. *Unit head:* Dr. Eric Patterson, Dean, 757-352-4616, Fax: 757-352-4735, E-mail: epatterson@regent.edu. *Application contact:* Heidi Cece, Assistant Vice President of Enrollment Management, 800-373-5504, Fax: 757-352-4381, E-mail: admissions@regent.edu.
Website: https://www.regent.edu/robertson-school-of-government/

Regent University, Graduate School, School of Business and Leadership, Virginia Beach, VA 23464-9800. Offers business administration (MBA), including accounting, economics, entrepreneurship, finance and investing, general management, healthcare management (MA, MBA), human resource management (MA, MBA), innovation management, leadership, marketing, not-for-profit management (MA, MBA); business analytics (MS); business and design management (MA); church leadership (MA); leadership (Certificate); organizational leadership (MA, PhD), including ecclesial leadership (DSL, PhD), entrepreneurial leadership (PhD), healthcare management (MA, MBA), human resource development (PhD), human resource management (MA, MBA), individualized studies (DSL, PhD), interdisciplinary studies (MA), leadership coaching and mentoring (MA), not-for-profit management (MA, MBA), organizational development consulting (MA), servant leadership (MA, DSL); strategic leadership (DSL), including ecclesial leadership (DSL, PhD), global consulting, healthcare leadership, individualized studies (DSL, PhD), leadership coaching, servant leadership (MA, DSL), strategic foresight. *Program availability:* Part-time, evening/weekend, 100% online, blended/hybrid learning. *Faculty:* 9 full-time (2 women), 38 part-time/adjunct (11 women). *Students:* 129 full-time (80 women), 1,152 part-time (598 women); includes 685 minority (546 Black or African American, non-Hispanic/Latino; 10 American Indian or Alaska Native, non-Hispanic/Latino; 29 Asian, non-Hispanic/Latino; 65 Hispanic/Latino; 6 Native Hawaiian or other Pacific Islander, non-Hispanic/Latino; 29 Two or more races, non-Hispanic/Latino), 62 international. Average age 41. 1,721 applicants, 48% accepted, 624 enrolled. In 2017, 125 master's, 69 doctorates awarded. *Degree requirements:* For master's, thesis or alternative, 3-credit hour culminating experience; for doctorate, thesis/dissertation. *Entrance requirements:* For master's, college transcripts, resume, essay; for doctorate, college transcripts, resume, essay, writing sample; for Certificate, writing sample, resume, transcripts. Additional exam requirements/recommendations for international students: Required—TOEFL (minimum score 577 paper-based). *Application deadline:* For fall admission, 5/1 priority date for domestic students; for spring admission, 10/1 priority date

for domestic students. Applications are processed on a rolling basis. Application fee: $50. Electronic applications accepted. *Expenses:* $650 per credit (MA, MS, MBA); $995 per credit (PhD); $300 per semester technology fee. *Financial support:* In 2017–18, 829 students received support. Career-related internships or fieldwork, scholarships/grants, and unspecified assistantships available. Support available to part-time students. *Faculty research:* Servant leadership, global business, team effectiveness, technology utilization, leadership development. *Unit head:* Dr. Doris Gomez, Dean, 757-352-4686, Fax: 757-352-4634, E-mail: dorigom@regent.edu. *Application contact:* Heidi Cece, Assistant Vice President of Enrollment Management, 800-373-5504, Fax: 757-352-4381, E-mail: admissions@regent.edu.
Website: https://www.regent.edu/school-of-business-and-leadership/

Regent University, Graduate School, School of Law, Virginia Beach, VA 23464. Offers American legal studies (LL M); human rights (LL M); law (MA, JD), including advanced paralegal studies (MA), alternative dispute resolution (MA), business (MA), criminal justice (MA), general legal studies (MA), human resources management (MA), human rights and rule of law (MA), national security (MA), non-profit organizational law (MA), regulatory compliance (MA), wealth management and financial planning (MA); JD/MA; JD/MBA. *Accreditation:* ABA. *Program availability:* Part-time, 100% online, blended/hybrid learning. *Faculty:* 16 full-time (5 women), 76 part-time/adjunct (22 women). *Students:* 313 full-time (181 women), 248 part-time (175 women); includes 240 minority (155 Black or African American, non-Hispanic/Latino; 3 American Indian or Alaska Native, non-Hispanic/Latino; 15 Asian, non-Hispanic/Latino; 45 Hispanic/Latino; 2 Native Hawaiian or other Pacific Islander, non-Hispanic/Latino; 20 Two or more races, non-Hispanic/Latino), 59 international. Average age 35. 923 applicants, 36% accepted, 188 enrolled. In 2017, 138 master's, 80 doctorates awarded. *Entrance requirements:* For master's, college transcripts, resume, personal statement; for doctorate, LSAT, minimum undergraduate GPA of 3.0, official transcripts, 2 letters of recommendation, resume, personal statement. Additional exam requirements/recommendations for international students: Required—TOEFL (minimum score 600 paper-based). *Application deadline:* For fall admission, 3/1 for domestic students. Applications are processed on a rolling basis. Application fee: $50. Electronic applications accepted. *Expenses:* $650 per credit (MA, LL M); $1,140 per credit (JD); $300 per semester technology fee. *Financial support:* In 2017–18, 459 students received support. Career-related internships or fieldwork, scholarships/grants, and unspecified assistantships available. Support available to part-time students. *Faculty research:* Family law, Constitutional law, law and culture, evidence and practice, intellectual property. *Unit head:* Michael Hernandez, Dean, 757-352-4040, Fax: 757-352-4595, E-mail: michher@regent.edu. *Application contact:* Ernie Walton, Assistant Dean of Admissions, 757-352-4315, E-mail: lawschool@regent.edu.
Website: https://www.regent.edu/school-of-law/

Regis University, College of Business and Economics, Denver, CO 80221-1099. Offers accounting (MS); executive leadership (Certificate); finance (MS); finance and accounting (MBA); health industry leadership (MBA); human resource management and leadership (MSOL); management (MBA); marketing (MBA); nonprofit leadership (Post-Graduate Certificate); nonprofit management (MNM); nonprofit organizational capacity building (Certificate); operations management (MBA); organizational leadership and management (MSOL); project leadership and management (MS, MSOL); strategic business management (Certificate); strategic human resource integration (Certificate); strategic management (MBA). Programs offered at Colorado Springs Campus, Northwest Denver Campus, Southeast Denver Campus, Fort Collins Campus, Broomfield Campus, Henderson (Nevada) Campus, and Summerlin (Nevada) Campus. *Program availability:* Part-time, evening/weekend, 100% online, blended/hybrid learning. *Degree requirements:* For master's, thesis (for some programs), capstone or final research project. *Entrance requirements:* For master's, official transcript reflecting baccalaureate degree awarded from regionally-accredited college or university, interview, 2 years of full-time related work experience, resume, letters of recommendation. Additional exam requirements/recommendations for international students: Required—TOEFL (minimum score 550 paper-based; 82 iBT). Electronic applications accepted. *Expenses:* Contact institution. *Faculty research:* Impact of information technology on small business regulation of accounting, international project financing, mineral development, delivery of healthcare to rural indigenous communities.

Rockhurst University, Helzberg School of Management, Kansas City, MO 64110-2561. Offers accounting (MBA); business intelligence (MBA, Certificate); business intelligence and analytics (MS); data science (MBA, Certificate); entrepreneurship (MBA); finance (MBA); fundraising leadership (MBA, Certificate); healthcare management (MBA, Certificate); human capital (Certificate); international business (Certificate); management (MA, MBA, Certificate); nonprofit administration (Certificate); organizational development (Certificate); science leadership (Certificate). *Accreditation:* AACSB. *Program availability:* Part-time, evening/weekend. *Faculty:* 18 full-time (4 women), 20 part-time/adjunct (9 women). *Students:* 99 full-time (30 women), 355 part-time (132 women); includes 95 minority (30 Black or African American, non-Hispanic/Latino; 29 Asian, non-Hispanic/Latino; 25 Hispanic/Latino; 11 Two or more races, non-Hispanic/Latino), 8 international. Average age 32. 249 applicants, 81% accepted, 175 enrolled. In 2017, 145 master's, 17 other advanced degrees awarded. *Entrance requirements:* For master's, GMAT or GRE. Additional exam requirements/recommendations for international students: Required—TOEFL (minimum score 550 paper-based; 79 iBT). *Application deadline:* Applications are processed on a rolling basis. Application fee: $0. Electronic applications accepted. *Financial support:* Applicants required to submit FAFSA. *Faculty research:* Offshoring/outsourcing, systems analysis/synthesis, work teams, multilateral trade, path dependencies/creation. *Unit head:* Cheryl McConnell, Dean, 816-501-4201, Fax: 816-501-4650, E-mail: cheryl.mcconnell@rockhurst.edu. *Application contact:* Jonnae Hill, Director of Graduate Business Advising, 816-501-4823, E-mail: jonnae.hill@rockhurst.edu.
Website: https://www.rockhurst.edu/helzberg

St. Cloud State University, School of Graduate Studies, College of Social Sciences, Department of Economics, Program in Public and Nonprofit Institutions, St. Cloud, MN 56301-4498. Offers MS. *Program availability:* Part-time. *Degree requirements:* For master's, thesis or alternative. *Entrance requirements:* For master's, GRE General Test, minimum GPA of 2.75. Additional exam requirements/recommendations for international students: Required—Michigan English Language Assessment Battery; Recommended—TOEFL (minimum score 550 paper-based), IELTS (minimum score 6.5). Electronic applications accepted.

Saint Mary-of-the-Woods College, Master of Leadership Development Program, Saint Mary of the Woods, IN 47876. Offers not-for-profit leadership (MLD); organizational leadership (MLD). *Program availability:* Part-time. *Students:* 47 full-time (41 women); includes 4 minority (all Black or African American, non-Hispanic/Latino). Average age 35. 26 applicants, 81% accepted, 19 enrolled. In 2017, 24 master's awarded. *Degree requirements:* For master's, thesis. *Application deadline:* Applications are processed on a rolling basis. Application fee: $0. Electronic applications accepted. *Expenses:* $565 per credit hour. *Financial support:* In 2017–18, 28 students received support. Scholarships/grants available. Financial award applicants required to submit FAFSA. *Application contact:* Office of Graduate Admissions, 800-926-7692, E-mail: graduate@smwc.edu.
Website: http://www.smwc.edu

Nonprofit Management

Salve Regina University, Program in Business Administration, Newport, RI 02840-4192. Offers cybersecurity issues in business (MBA); entrepreneurial enterprise (MBA); health care administration and management (MBA); nonprofit management (MBA); social ventures (MBA). *Program availability:* Part-time, evening/weekend, online learning. *Entrance requirements:* For master's, GMAT, GRE General Test, or MAT, 6 undergraduate credits each in accounting, economics, quantitative analysis and calculus or statistics. Additional exam requirements/recommendations for international students: Required—TOEFL (minimum score 600 paper-based; 100 iBT) or IELTS. Electronic applications accepted.

Salve Regina University, Program in Management, Newport, RI 02840-4192. Offers business studies (CGS); human resource management (CGS); innovation and strategic management (MS); management (CGS); nonprofit management (CGS); social entrepreneurship (CGS). *Program availability:* Part-time, evening/weekend, online learning. *Entrance requirements:* For master's, GMAT, GRE General Test, or MAT. Additional exam requirements/recommendations for international students: Required—TOEFL (minimum score 600 paper-based; 100 iBT). Electronic applications accepted.

San Francisco State University, Division of Graduate Studies, College of Business, Program in Business Administration, San Francisco, CA 94132-1722. Offers decision sciences/operations research (MBA); ethics and compliance (MBA); finance (MBA); global business and innovation (MBA); healthcare administration (MBA); hospitality and tourism management (MBA); information systems (MBA); leadership (MBA); marketing (MBA); nonprofit and social enterprise leadership (MBA); sustainable business (MBA). *Accreditation:* AACSB. *Program availability:* Part-time, evening/weekend. *Degree requirements:* For master's, thesis, essay test. *Entrance requirements:* For master's, GMAT, minimum GPA of 2.7 in last 60 units. Additional exam requirements/recommendations for international students: Required—TOEFL (minimum score 550 paper-based). *Application deadline:* For fall admission, 5/1 priority date for domestic students, 4/1 for international students; for spring admission, 11/1 for domestic students, 10/15 for international students. Applications are processed on a rolling basis. Application fee: $55. *Financial support:* Application deadline: 3/1. *Unit head:* Dr. Sanjit Sengupta, Faculty Director, 415-817-4366, Fax: 415-817-4340, E-mail: sengupta@sfsu.edu. *Application contact:* Christopher Kingston, Director of Student Advising, 415-817-4322, Fax: 415-817-4340, E-mail: cak@sfsu.edu.
Website: http://cob.sfsu.edu/graduate-programs/mba

San Francisco State University, Division of Graduate Studies, College of Health and Social Sciences, Public Administration Program, San Francisco, CA 94132-1722. Offers criminal justice administration (MPA); environmental administration and policy (MPA); gerontology (MPA); nonprofit administration (MPA); public management (MPA); public policy (MPA); urban administration (MPA). *Accreditation:* NASPAA. *Unit head:* Dr. Jennifer Shea, Graduate Coordinator, 415-817-4462, Fax: 415-817-4464, E-mail: jshea@sfsu.edu.
Website: http://mpa.sfsu.edu/

Seton Hall University, College of Arts and Sciences, Department of Political Science and Public Affairs, South Orange, NJ 07079-2697. Offers nonprofit organization management (Graduate Certificate); public administration (MPA), including health policy and management, nonprofit organization management, public service: leadership, governance, and policy. *Accreditation:* CAHME; NASPAA. *Program availability:* Part-time, evening/weekend. *Degree requirements:* For master's, thesis or alternative, internship or practicum. *Entrance requirements:* Additional exam requirements/recommendations for international students: Required—TOEFL. Electronic applications accepted.

Simmons College, School of Management, Boston, MA 02115. Offers business administration (MBA); health care (MBA); management (MS, MSM), including communications management (MS), non-profit management (MS); MBA/MSW; MS/MA. *Accreditation:* AACSB. *Program availability:* Part-time, evening/weekend, 100% online, blended/hybrid learning. *Faculty:* 23 full-time (15 women), 5 part-time/adjunct (all women). *Students:* 7 full-time (all women), 130 part-time (118 women); includes 34 minority (14 Black or African American, non-Hispanic/Latino; 8 Asian, non-Hispanic/Latino; 10 Hispanic/Latino; 2 Two or more races, non-Hispanic/Latino), 1 international. Average age 32. 53 applicants, 68% accepted, 19 enrolled. In 2017, 77 master's awarded. *Entrance requirements:* For master's, GMAT or GRE. Additional exam requirements/recommendations for international students: Required—TOEFL. *Application deadline:* For fall admission, 7/18 priority date for domestic students; for summer admission, 4/24 priority date for domestic students. Applications are processed on a rolling basis. Application fee: $75. Electronic applications accepted. *Expenses:* $1,295 per credit hour, $3,885 per course, $123 activity fee per semester. *Financial support:* Scholarships/grants and unspecified assistantships available. Financial award applicants required to submit FAFSA. *Faculty research:* Gender and organizations, leadership, health care management. *Unit head:* Patricia Deyton, Associate Dean for Graduate Programs, 617-521-3876.
Website: http://www.simmons.edu/som

Southern New Hampshire University, School of Business, Manchester, NH 03106-1045. Offers accounting (MBA, Graduate Certificate); accounting finance (MS); accounting/auditing (MS); accounting/forensic accounting (MS); accounting/management accounting (MS); accounting/taxation (MS); applied economics (MS); athletic administration (MBA, Graduate Certificate); business administration (IMBA, Certificate), including business information systems (Certificate), human resource management (Certificate); business analytics (MBA); business intelligence (MBA); communication (MA), including new media and marketing, public relations; community economic development (MBA); criminal justice (MBA); data analytics (MS); economics (MBA); engineering management (MBA); entrepreneurship (MBA); finance (MBA, MS, Graduate Certificate); finance/corporate finance (MS); finance/investments (MS); forensic accounting (MBA); forensic accounting and fraud examination (Graduate Certificate); healthcare informatics (MBA); healthcare management (MBA); human resource management (MS); human resources (MBA); information technology (MS); information technology management (MBA); international business (PhD); Internet marketing (MBA); leadership (MBA); leadership of nonprofit organizations (Graduate Certificate); management (MS); marketing (MBA, MS, Graduate Certificate); music business (MBA); operations and project management (MS); operations and supply chain management (MBA, Graduate Certificate); organizational leadership (MS); project management (MBA, Graduate Certificate); public administration (MBA, Graduate Certificate); quantitative analysis (MBA); Six Sigma (Graduate Certificate); Six Sigma quality (MBA); social media marketing (MBA, Graduate Certificate); sport management (MBA, MS, Graduate Certificate); sustainability and environmental compliance (MBA); MBA/Certificate. *Accreditation:* ACBSP. *Program availability:* Part-time, evening/weekend, online learning. Terminal master's awarded for partial completion of doctoral program. *Degree requirements:* For master's, one foreign language, comprehensive exam (for some programs), thesis or alternative; for doctorate, one foreign language, comprehensive exam, thesis/dissertation. *Entrance requirements:* For master's, minimum GPA of 2.5; for doctorate, GMAT. Additional exam requirements/recommendations for international students: Required—TOEFL (minimum score 500 paper-based). *Application deadline:* Applications are processed on a rolling basis. Application fee: $40. Electronic applications accepted. *Expenses: Tuition:* Part-time

$627 per credit hour. Part-time tuition and fees vary according to campus/location and program. *Financial support:* Career-related internships or fieldwork, Federal Work-Study, institutionally sponsored loans, scholarships/grants, tuition waivers (partial), and unspecified assistantships available. Support available to part-time students. Financial award applicants required to submit FAFSA. *Unit head:* Dr. Bill Lightfoot, Dean, 603-644-3102, Fax: 603-644-3144. *Application contact:* Office of Graduate Admission, 888-327-SNHU, Fax: 603-644-3144, E-mail: enroll@snhu.edu.

Suffolk University, Sawyer Business School, Department of Public Administration, Boston, MA 02108-2770. Offers community health (MPA); information systems, performance management, and big data analytics (MPA); nonprofit management (MPA); state and local government (MPA); JD/MPA; MPA/MS; MPA/MSCJ; MPA/MSMHC; MPA/MSPS. *Accreditation:* NASPAA (one or more programs are accredited). *Program availability:* Part-time, evening/weekend. *Faculty:* 6 full-time (3 women), 8 part-time/adjunct (6 women). *Students:* 25 full-time (12 women), 90 part-time (56 women); includes 43 minority (20 Black or African American, non-Hispanic/Latino; 7 Asian, non-Hispanic/Latino; 14 Hispanic/Latino; 2 Two or more races, non-Hispanic/Latino), 2 international. Average age 34. 134 applicants, 38% accepted, 5 enrolled. In 2017, 44 master's awarded. *Entrance requirements:* Additional exam requirements/recommendations for international students: Required—TOEFL (minimum score 550 paper-based; 80 iBT). *Application deadline:* For fall admission, 3/15 priority date for domestic and international students; for spring admission, 10/15 priority date for domestic and international students. Applications are processed on a rolling basis. Application fee: $50. Electronic applications accepted. *Expenses:* $35,130 per year full-time tuition; $1,171 per credit part-time. *Financial support:* In 2017–18, 76 students received support, including 2 fellowships (averaging $4,650 per year); career-related internships or fieldwork, Federal Work-Study, institutionally sponsored loans, and scholarships/grants also available. Support available to part-time students. Financial award application deadline: 4/1; financial award applicants required to submit FAFSA. *Faculty research:* Local government, health care, federal policy, mental health, HIV/AIDS. *Unit head:* Brenda Bond, Director/Department Chair, 617-305-1768, E-mail: bbond@suffolk.edu. *Application contact:* Mara Marzocchi, Associate Director of Graduate Admissions, 617-573-8302, Fax: 617-305-1733, E-mail: grad.admission@suffolk.edu.
Website: http://www.suffolk.edu/mpa

Suffolk University, Sawyer Business School, Master of Business Administration Program, Boston, MA 02108-2770. Offers accounting (MBA); entrepreneurship (MBA); executive business administration (EMBA); finance (MBA); global business administration (GMBA); health administration (MBA); international business (MBA); marketing (MBA); nonprofit management (MBA); organizational behavior (MBA); strategic management (MBA); supply chain management (MBA); taxation (MBA); JD/MBA; MBA/MHA; MBA/MSA; MBA/MSF; MBA/MST. *Accreditation:* AACSB. *Program availability:* Part-time, evening/weekend, 100% online. *Faculty:* 16 full-time (6 women), 9 part-time/adjunct (1 woman). *Students:* 106 full-time (57 women), 236 part-time (135 women); includes 80 minority (23 Black or African American, non-Hispanic/Latino; 23 Asian, non-Hispanic/Latino; 28 Hispanic/Latino; 6 Two or more races, non-Hispanic/Latino), 41 international. Average age 30. 354 applicants, 69% accepted, 115 enrolled. In 2017, 170 master's awarded. *Entrance requirements:* For master's, GMAT, minimum undergraduate GPA of 2.75 (MBA), 5 years of managerial experience (EMBA). Additional exam requirements/recommendations for international students: Required—TOEFL (minimum score 550 paper-based; 80 iBT). *Application deadline:* For fall admission, 3/15 priority date for domestic students, 10/15 priority date for international students; for spring admission, 10/15 priority date for domestic and international students. Applications are processed on a rolling basis. Application fee: $50. Electronic applications accepted. *Expenses:* $43,980 per year full-time, $1,466 per credit part-time (for MBA); $1,794 per credit part-time (for Executive MBA). *Financial support:* In 2017–18, 198 students received support, including 1 fellowship (averaging $2,325 per year); career-related internships or fieldwork, Federal Work-Study, institutionally sponsored loans, and scholarships/grants also available. Support available to part-time students. Financial award application deadline: 4/1; financial award applicants required to submit FAFSA. *Faculty research:* Foreign investments; career strategies and boundaryless careers; corporate ethics codes; interest rates, inflation, and growth options; innovation and product development performance. *Unit head:* Jodi Detjen, Director of MBA Programs, 617-573-8306, E-mail: jdetjen@suffolk.edu. *Application contact:* Mara Marzocchi, Associate Director of Graduate Admissions, 617-573-8302, Fax: 617-305-1733, E-mail: grad.admission@suffolk.edu.
Website: http://www.suffolk.edu/mba

Texas A&M University, Bush School of Government and Public Service, College Station, TX 77845. Offers homeland security (Certificate); international affairs (MIA, Certificate); national security affairs (Certificate); non-profit management (Certificate); public service and administration (MPSA). *Accreditation:* NASPAA. *Faculty:* 66. *Students:* 332 full-time (182 women), 54 part-time (16 women); includes 94 minority (19 Black or African American, non-Hispanic/Latino; 10 Asian, non-Hispanic/Latino; 56 Hispanic/Latino; 9 Two or more races, non-Hispanic/Latino), 41 international. Average age 29. 297 applicants, 94% accepted, 164 enrolled. In 2017, 154 master's awarded. *Degree requirements:* For master's, summer internship. *Entrance requirements:* For master's, GRE (preferred) or GMAT. Additional exam requirements/recommendations for international students: Required—TOEFL (minimum score 550 paper-based; 80 iBT), IELTS (minimum score 6), PTE (minimum score 53). *Application deadline:* For fall admission, 1/15 for domestic and international students. Application fee: $50 ($90 for international students). Electronic applications accepted. *Expenses:* Contact institution. *Financial support:* In 2017–18, 417 students received support, including 29 fellowships with tuition reimbursements available (averaging $20,966 per year), 71 research assistantships with tuition reimbursements available (averaging $9,778 per year); teaching assistantships, career-related internships or fieldwork, institutionally sponsored loans, scholarships/grants, traineeships, health care benefits, tuition waivers (full and partial), and unspecified assistantships also available. Support available to part-time students. Financial award application deadline: 3/15; financial award applicants required to submit FAFSA. *Faculty research:* Public policy, Presidential studies, public leadership, economic policy, social policy. *Unit head:* Dr. Mark Welsh, Dean, 979-862-8007, E-mail: mwelsh@tamu.edu. *Application contact:* Kathryn Meyer, Director of Recruitment and Admissions, 979-458-4767, Fax: 979-845-4155, E-mail: bushschooladmissions@tamu.edu.
Website: http://bush.tamu.edu/

Thomas Edison State University, John S. Watson School of Public Service and Continuing Studies, Trenton, NJ 08608. Offers community and economic development (MSM); environmental policy/environmental justice (MSM); homeland security (MSHS, MSM); information and technology for public service (MSM); nonprofit management (MSM); public and municipal finance (MSM); public health (MSM); public service administration and leadership (MSM); public service leadership (MPSL). *Program availability:* Part-time, online learning. *Entrance requirements:* Additional exam requirements/recommendations for international students: Required—TOEFL (minimum score 550 paper-based; 79 iBT). Electronic applications accepted.

Tiffin University, Program in Business Administration, Tiffin, OH 44883-2161. Offers finance (MBA); general management (MBA); healthcare administration (MBA); human resource management (MBA); international business (MBA); leadership (MBA); marketing (MBA); non-profit management (MBA); sports management (MBA). *Accreditation:* ACBSP. *Program availability:* Part-time, evening/weekend, online learning. *Entrance requirements:* For master's, minimum undergraduate GPA of 2.5, work experience. Additional exam requirements/recommendations for international students: Required—TOEFL (minimum score 550 paper-based; 79 iBT), IELTS. Electronic applications accepted. Application fee is waived when completed online. *Faculty research:* Small business, executive development operations, research and statistical analysis, market research, management information systems.

Trinity Washington University, School of Business and Graduate Studies, Washington, DC 20017-1094. Offers business administration (MBA); communication (MA); international security studies (MA); organizational management (MSA), including federal program management, human resource management, nonprofit management, organizational development, public and community health. *Program availability:* Part-time, evening/weekend. *Degree requirements:* For master's, thesis (for some programs), capstone project (MSA). *Entrance requirements:* For master's, minimum GPA of 2.5. Additional exam requirements/recommendations for international students: Required—TOEFL (minimum score 550 paper-based).

Trinity Western University, School of Graduate Studies, Program in Business Administration, Langley, BC V2Y 1Y1, Canada. Offers international business (MBA); management of the growing enterprise (MBA); non-profit and charitable organization management (MBA). *Program availability:* Part-time, online learning. *Degree requirements:* For master's, thesis or alternative, applied project. *Entrance requirements:* For master's, GMAT (minimum score of 550 recommended). Additional exam requirements/recommendations for international students: Required—TOEFL (minimum score 600 paper-based; 100 iBT), IELTS. Electronic applications accepted.

Trinity Western University, School of Graduate Studies, Program in Leadership, Langley, BC V2Y 1Y1, Canada. Offers business (MA, Certificate); Christian ministry (MA); education (MA, Certificate); healthcare (MA, Certificate); non-profit (MA, Certificate). *Program availability:* Online learning. *Degree requirements:* For master's, major project. *Entrance requirements:* For master's, minimum GPA of 2.7. Additional exam requirements/recommendations for international students: Required—TOEFL (minimum score 620 paper-based; 105 iBT). Electronic applications accepted. *Expenses:* Contact institution. *Faculty research:* Servant leadership.

Tufts University, Graduate School of Arts and Sciences, Graduate Certificate Programs, Management of Community Organizations Program, Medford, MA 02155. Offers Certificate. *Program availability:* Part-time, evening/weekend. Electronic applications accepted. *Expenses:* Contact institution.

University at Albany, State University of New York, Nelson A. Rockefeller College of Public Affairs and Policy, Department of Public Administration and Policy, Albany, NY 12222-0001. Offers financial management and public economics (MPA); financial market regulation (MPA); health policy (MPA); healthcare management (MPA); homeland security (MPA); human resources management (MPA); information strategy and management (MPA); local government management (MPA); nonprofit management (MPA); nonprofit management and leadership (Certificate); organizational behavior and theory (MPA, PhD); planning and policy analysis (CAS); policy analysis (MPA); politics and administration (PhD); public finance (PhD); public management (PhD); public policy (PhD); public sector management (Certificate); women and public policy (Certificate); JD/MPA. JD/MPA offered jointly with Albany Law School. *Accreditation:* NASPAA (one or more programs are accredited). *Faculty:* 21 full-time (7 women), 14 part-time/adjunct (7 women). *Students:* 115 full-time (59 women), 93 part-time (56 women); includes 41 minority (11 Black or African American, non-Hispanic/Latino; 9 Asian, non-Hispanic/Latino; 18 Hispanic/Latino; 3 Two or more races, non-Hispanic/Latino), 32 international. 236 applicants, 69% accepted, 86 enrolled. In 2017, 57 master's, 1 doctorate, 14 other advanced degrees awarded. *Degree requirements:* For doctorate, one foreign language, thesis/dissertation. *Entrance requirements:* For doctorate, GRE General Test. Additional exam requirements/recommendations for international students: Required—TOEFL (minimum score 550 paper-based). *Application deadline:* For fall admission, 2/1 priority date for domestic students, 5/1 for international students; for spring admission, 12/1 for domestic students. Applications are processed on a rolling basis. Application fee: $75. Electronic applications accepted. *Expenses:* Tuition, state resident: full-time $10,870; part-time $453 per credit hour. Tuition, nonresident: full-time $22,210; part-time $925 per credit hour. *Required fees:* $84.68 per credit hour. $508.06 per semester. Part-time tuition and fees vary according to course load and program. *Financial support:* Application deadline: 2/1. *Unit head:* Victor Asal, Chair, 518-591-8729, E-mail: vasal@albany.edu.
Website: http://www.albany.edu/rockefeller/pad.shtml

University of Arkansas at Little Rock, Graduate School, College of Social Sciences and Communication, Program in Nonprofit Management, Little Rock, AR 72204-1099. Offers Graduate Certificate. *Entrance requirements:* For degree, baccalaureate degree, essay, two letters of reference.

University of California, San Diego, Graduate Division, School of Global Policy and Strategy, Master of International Affairs Program, La Jolla, CA 92093. Offers international development and nonprofit management (MIA); international economics (MIA); international environmental policy (MIA); international management (MIA); international politics (MIA). Students will choose one of the following country/regional specializations: China, Japan, Korea, Latin America, or Southeast Asia. *Degree requirements:* For master's, one foreign language. *Entrance requirements:* For master's, GMAT or GRE General Test. Additional exam requirements/recommendations for international students: Required—TOEFL (minimum score 90 iBT), IELTS (minimum score 7). Electronic applications accepted.

University of Central Florida, College of Community Innovation and Education, School of Public Administration, Orlando, FL 32816. Offers emergency management and homeland security (Certificate); fundraising (Certificate); nonprofit management (MNM, Certificate); public administration (MPA); research administration (MRA); urban and regional planning (MS). *Accreditation:* NASPAA. *Program availability:* Part-time, evening/weekend. *Students:* 110 full-time (76 women), 290 part-time (215 women); includes 193 minority (96 Black or African American, non-Hispanic/Latino; 2 American Indian or Alaska Native, non-Hispanic/Latino; 13 Asian, non-Hispanic/Latino; 74 Hispanic/Latino; 8 Two or more races, non-Hispanic/Latino), 6 international. Average age 32. 255 applicants, 78% accepted, 152 enrolled. In 2017, 95 master's, 34 other advanced degrees awarded. *Degree requirements:* For master's, comprehensive exam, thesis or alternative, research report. *Entrance requirements:* For master's, letters of recommendation, goal statement, resume. Additional exam requirements/recommendations for international students: Required—TOEFL. *Application deadline:* For fall admission, 6/15 for domestic students; for spring admission, 11/1 for domestic students. Application fee: $30. Electronic applications accepted. *Expenses:* Tuition, state resident: part-time $288.16 per credit hour. Tuition, nonresident: part-time $1073.31 per credit hour. Tuition and fees vary according to program. *Financial support:* In 2017–18, 11 students received support, including 2 fellowships with partial tuition reimbursements available (averaging $5,300 per year), 6 research assistantships with partial tuition reimbursements available (averaging $9,637 per year), 3 teaching assistantships with partial tuition reimbursements available (averaging $9,390 per year); career-related internships or fieldwork, Federal Work-Study, institutionally sponsored loans, health care benefits, tuition waivers (partial), and unspecified assistantships also available. Financial award application deadline: 3/1; financial award applicants required to submit FAFSA. *Unit head:* Dr. Naim Kapucu, Director, 407-823-6096, Fax: 407-823-5651, E-mail: kapucu@ucf.edu. *Application contact:* Associate Director, Graduate Admissions, 407-823-2766, Fax: 407-823-6442, E-mail: gradadmissions@ucf.edu. Website: https://www.cohpa.ucf.edu/publicadmin/

University of Central Oklahoma, The Jackson College of Graduate Studies, College of Liberal Arts, Department of Political Science, Edmond, OK 73034-5209. Offers political science (MA), including international affairs; public administration (MPA), including public and nonprofit management, urban management. *Program availability:* Part-time. *Faculty:* 11 full-time (4 women), 1 part-time/adjunct (0 women). *Students:* 42 full-time (21 women), 58 part-time (26 women); includes 33 minority (14 Black or African American, non-Hispanic/Latino; 3 American Indian or Alaska Native, non-Hispanic/Latino; 10 Hispanic/Latino; 6 Two or more races, non-Hispanic/Latino), 18 international. Average age 32. 127 applicants, 84% accepted, 29 enrolled. In 2017, 32 master's awarded. *Degree requirements:* For master's, comprehensive exam (for some programs), thesis (for some programs). *Entrance requirements:* For master's, 18 undergraduate hours in political science. Additional exam requirements/recommendations for international students: Required—TOEFL (minimum score 550 paper-based; 79 iBT), IELTS (minimum score 6.5). *Application deadline:* For fall admission, 7/15 for international students; for spring admission, 11/15 for international students. Applications are processed on a rolling basis. Application fee: $60. Electronic applications accepted. *Expenses:* Tuition, state resident: full-time $5375; part-time $268.75 per credit hour. Tuition, nonresident: full-time $13,295; part-time $664.75 per credit hour. *Required fees:* $626; $31.30 per credit hour. One-time fee: $50. Tuition and fees vary according to program. *Financial support:* In 2017–18, 20 students received support, including 3 research assistantships with partial tuition reimbursements available (averaging $3,943 per year), 4 teaching assistantships with partial tuition reimbursements available (averaging $7,394 per year); career-related internships or fieldwork, scholarships/grants, tuition waivers (partial), and unspecified assistantships also available. Financial award application deadline: 3/31; financial award applicants required to submit FAFSA. *Unit head:* Dr. Lou Furmanski, Department Chair, 405-974-5540, Fax: 405-974-3823. *Application contact:* Dr. Jan Hardt, Graduate Advisor, 405-974-5840, Fax: 405-974-3823, E-mail: gradcoll@uco.edu.
Website: http://sites.uco.edu/la/political-science/index.asp

University of Colorado Denver, School of Public Affairs, Program in Public Affairs and Administration, Denver, CO 80127. Offers public administration (MPA), including domestic violence, emergency management and homeland security, environmental policy, management and law, homeland security and defense, local government, nonprofit management, public administration; public affairs (PhD). *Accreditation:* NASPAA. *Program availability:* Part-time, evening/weekend, online learning. *Degree requirements:* For master's, thesis or alternative, 36-39 credit hours; for doctorate, comprehensive exam, thesis/dissertation, minimum of 66 semester hours, including at least 30 hours of dissertation. *Entrance requirements:* For master's, GRE, GMAT or LSAT, resume, essay, transcripts, recommendations; for doctorate, GRE, resume, essay, transcripts, recommendations. Additional exam requirements/recommendations for international students: Required—TOEFL (minimum score 550 paper-based; 80 iBT); Recommended—IELTS (minimum score 6.5). Electronic applications accepted. *Expenses:* Contact institution. *Faculty research:* Housing, education and the social and economic issues of vulnerable populations; nonprofit governance and management; education finance, effectiveness and reform; P-20 education initiatives; municipal government accountability.

University of Connecticut, Graduate School, College of Liberal Arts and Sciences, Department of Public Policy, Storrs, CT 06269. Offers public administration (MPA, Graduate Certificate), including nonprofit management (Graduate Certificate), public financial management (Graduate Certificate); survey research (MA, Graduate Certificate), including quantitative research methods (Graduate Certificate), survey research (MA); JD/MPA; MPA/MSW. *Degree requirements:* For master's, comprehensive exam. *Entrance requirements:* For master's, GRE General Test. Additional exam requirements/recommendations for international students: Required—TOEFL (minimum score 550 paper-based). Electronic applications accepted.

University of Florida, Graduate School, College of Agricultural and Life Sciences, Department of Family, Youth, and Community Sciences, Gainesville, FL 32611. Offers community studies (MS); family and youth development (MS); family, youth and community sciences (MS); nonprofit organization development (MS). *Program availability:* Part-time, online learning. *Degree requirements:* For master's, comprehensive exam (for some programs), thesis (for some programs). *Entrance requirements:* For master's, GRE General Test, minimum GPA of 3.0. Additional exam requirements/recommendations for international students: Required—TOEFL (minimum score 550 paper-based; 80 iBT), IELTS (minimum score 6). Electronic applications accepted. *Faculty research:* Adolescent risk behaviors, family risk and resilience, family financial management, community-based organizations/interventions, nutrition and wellness.

University of Georgia, School of Social Work, Athens, GA 30602. Offers MA, MSW, PhD, Certificate, MSW/JD. *Accreditation:* CSWE (one or more programs are accredited). *Program availability:* Part-time, evening/weekend. *Degree requirements:* For master's, thesis or alternative; for doctorate, one foreign language, thesis/dissertation. *Entrance requirements:* For master's and doctorate, GRE General Test. Electronic applications accepted. *Faculty research:* Juvenile justice, substance abuse, civil rights and social justice, gerontology, social policy.

University of Houston–Downtown, College of Humanities and Social Sciences, Department of Social Sciences, Houston, TX 77002. Offers non-profit management (MA). *Program availability:* Part-time, evening/weekend, online only, 100% online. *Faculty:* 5 full-time (1 woman), 3 part-time/adjunct (0 women). *Students:* 20 full-time (13 women), 62 part-time (49 women); includes 64 minority (46 Black or African American, non-Hispanic/Latino; 1 American Indian or Alaska Native, non-Hispanic/Latino; 1 Asian, non-Hispanic/Latino; 16 Hispanic/Latino), 1 international. Average age 38. 45 applicants, 96% accepted, 34 enrolled. In 2017, 21 master's awarded. *Degree requirements:* For master's, thesis or capstone project, internship which will include capstone assignments. *Entrance requirements:* For master's, GRE, essay, resume, 3 letters of recommendation, transcripts. Additional exam requirements/recommendations for international students: Required—TOEFL (minimum score 550 paper-based; 50 iBT). *Application deadline:* For fall admission, 7/15 for domestic and international students; for spring admission, 11/15 for domestic and international students. Application fee: $35 ($60 for international students). Electronic applications accepted. *Expenses:* $335 per credit resident; $700 per credit non-resident. *Financial support:* Federal Work-Study and scholarships/grants available. Financial award application deadline: 4/1; financial award applicants required to submit FAFSA. *Unit head:* Dr. David Branham, Chair, 713-221-8208, Fax: 713-226-5205, E-mail: branhamd@uhd.edu. *Application contact:* Ceshia Love, Director of Admissions, 713-221-8093, Fax: 713-223-7408, E-mail: gradadmissions@uhd.edu.
Website: https://www.uhd.edu/academics/humanities/graduate-programs/master-arts-non-profit-management/Pages/ma-index.aspx

Nonprofit Management

University of La Verne, College of Business and Public Management, Master's Program in Public Administration, La Verne, CA 91750-4443. Offers gerontology (MPA); nonprofit (MPA); public health (MPA); urban management and affairs (MPA). *Accreditation:* NASPAA. *Program availability:* Part-time. *Faculty:* 11 full-time (5 women), 1 part-time/adjunct (0 women). *Students:* 33 full-time (18 women), 21 part-time (15 women); includes 40 minority (3 Black or African American, non-Hispanic/Latino; 2 Asian, non-Hispanic/Latino; 35 Hispanic/Latino), 1 international. Average age 33. *Entrance requirements:* For master's, minimum undergraduate GPA of 3.0, statement of purpose, 2 letters of recommendation, resume. Additional exam requirements/recommendations for international students: Required—TOEFL (minimum score 550 paper-based). *Application deadline:* Applications are processed on a rolling basis. Application fee: $50. *Expenses:* Contact institution. *Financial support:* Institutionally sponsored loans and scholarships/grants available. Financial award application deadline: 3/2; financial award applicants required to submit FAFSA. *Unit head:* Marcia Godwin, Chairperson, 909-448-4103, E-mail: mgodwin@laverne.edu. *Application contact:* Cathy Cook, Associate Director of Graduate Admissions, 909-448-4719, Fax: 909-971-2295, E-mail: ccook2@laverne.edu.
Website: https://business.laverne.edu/mpa/

University of La Verne, College of Business and Public Management, Program in Leadership and Management, La Verne, CA 91750-4443. Offers human resource management (Certificate); leadership and management (MS), including human resource management, nonprofit management, organizational development; nonprofit management (Certificate); organizational leadership (Certificate). *Program availability:* Part-time. *Faculty:* 4 full-time (3 women), 5 part-time/adjunct (1 woman). *Students:* 49 full-time (25 women), 35 part-time (22 women); includes 47 minority (6 Black or African American, non-Hispanic/Latino; 4 Asian, non-Hispanic/Latino; 35 Hispanic/Latino; 2 Two or more races, non-Hispanic/Latino), 13 international. Average age 32. *Entrance requirements:* For master's, bachelor's degree, minimum undergraduate GPA of 2.75, 2 letters of recommendation, interview, resume. Additional exam requirements/recommendations for international students: Required—TOEFL (minimum score 550 paper-based). *Application deadline:* Applications are processed on a rolling basis. Application fee: $50. Tuition and fees vary according to program. *Financial support:* Federal Work-Study, institutionally sponsored loans, and scholarships/grants available. Financial award application deadline: 3/2; financial award applicants required to submit FAFSA. *Unit head:* Dr. Kathy Duncan, Program Director, 909-448-4415, E-mail: kduncan2@laverne.edu. *Application contact:* Barbara Cox, Associate Director of Graduate Admissions, 909-448-4004, E-mail: bcox@laverne.edu.
Website: https://business.laverne.edu/mslm/

University of La Verne, Regional and Online Campuses, Graduate Programs, Inland Empire Campus, Ontario, CA 91730. Offers business administration (MBA, MBA-EP), including accounting (MBA), finance (MBA), health services management (MBA-EP), information technology (MBA-EP), international business (MBA), managed care (MBA), management and leadership (MBA-EP), marketing (MBA-EP), supply chain management (MBA); leadership and management (MS), including human resource management, nonprofit management, organizational development. *Program availability:* Part-time, evening/weekend. *Faculty:* 5 part-time/adjunct (1 woman). *Students:* 24 full-time (13 women), 72 part-time (44 women); includes 64 minority (12 Black or African American, non-Hispanic/Latino; 13 Asian, non-Hispanic/Latino; 36 Hispanic/Latino; 3 Two or more races, non-Hispanic/Latino). Average age 38. In 2017, 42 master's awarded. *Application deadline:* Applications are processed on a rolling basis. Application fee: $50. *Expenses:* Contact institution. *Financial support:* Application deadline: 3/2; applicants required to submit FAFSA. *Unit head:* Juli Roberts, Campus Director, Inland Empire Regional Campus in Ontario, 760-955-6448, E-mail: jroberts@laverne.edu. *Application contact:* Admissions, 877-468-6858, E-mail: gradadmission@laverne.edu.
Website: https://laverne.edu/locations/

University of Louisville, Graduate School, College of Arts and Sciences, Department of Urban and Public Affairs, Louisville, KY 40208. Offers public administration (MPA), including human resources management, non-profit management, public policy and administration; urban and public affairs (PhD), including urban planning and development, urban policy and administration; urban planning (MUP), including administration of planning organizations, housing and community development, land use and environmental planning, spatial analysis. *Program availability:* Part-time, evening/weekend. *Faculty:* 12 full-time (5 women), 4 part-time/adjunct (1 woman). *Students:* 50 full-time (19 women), 20 part-time (17 women); includes 17 minority (6 Black or African American, non-Hispanic/Latino; 1 Asian, non-Hispanic/Latino; 4 Hispanic/Latino; 6 Two or more races, non-Hispanic/Latino), 4 international. Average age 31. 47 applicants, 70% accepted, 22 enrolled. In 2017, 20 master's, 2 doctorates awarded. Terminal master's awarded for partial completion of doctoral program. *Degree requirements:* For master's, internship; for doctorate, comprehensive exam, thesis/dissertation. *Entrance requirements:* For master's, GRE General Test, minimum GPA of 3.0; for doctorate, GRE General Test, master's degree in appropriate field. Additional exam requirements/recommendations for international students: Required—TOEFL (minimum score 550 paper-based; 79 iBT). *Application deadline:* Applications are processed on a rolling basis. Application fee: $65. *Expenses:* Contact institution. *Financial support:* Fellowships, research assistantships, tuition waivers (full and partial), and unspecified assistantships available. Financial award application deadline: 2/1. *Faculty research:* Urban theory, sustainability, public administration, urban planning, urban management. *Total annual research expenditures:* $240,308. *Unit head:* Dr. David Simpson, Chair, 502-852-8019, Fax: 502-852-4558, E-mail: dave.simpson@louisville.edu. *Application contact:* Latonia Craig, Director of Graduate Recruitment and Diversity Retention, 502-852-5207, Fax: 502-852-4558, E-mail: gradadm@louisville.edu.
Website: http://supa.louisville.edu/

University of Lynchburg, Graduate Studies, MA Program in Nonprofit Leadership Studies, Lynchburg, VA 24501-3199. Offers non profit leadership (MA). *Program availability:* Part-time, evening/weekend, 100% online, blended/hybrid learning. *Students:* 12 full-time (10 women), 18 part-time (12 women); includes 7 minority (5 Black or African American, non-Hispanic/Latino; 2 Hispanic/Latino), 5 international. Average age 31. 17 applicants, 100% accepted, 11 enrolled. *Degree requirements:* For master's, capstone project. *Entrance requirements:* For master's, GRE. Additional exam requirements/recommendations for international students: Required—TOEFL (minimum score 550 paper-based; 80 iBT), IELTS (minimum score 6). *Application deadline:* For fall admission, 7/31 for domestic and international students; for spring admission, 11/30 for domestic and international students. Applications are processed on a rolling basis. Application fee: $30. Electronic applications accepted. Application fee is waived when completed online. *Expenses:* $510 per credit tuition, $100 fees. *Financial support:* Scholarships/grants and unspecified assistantships available. Financial award applicants required to submit FAFSA. *Unit head:* Dr. Jimmy Roux, Program Director, Nonprofit Leadership, 434-544-8648, E-mail: roux@lynchburg.edu. *Application contact:* Ellen Thompson, Graduate Admission Counselor, 434-544-8841, E-mail: thompson_e@lynchburg.edu.
Website: https://www.lynchburg.edu/graduate/master-of-nonprofit-leadership-studies/

University of Maryland, Baltimore County, The Graduate School, College of Arts, Humanities and Social Sciences, Department of Sociology, Anthropology, and Health Administration and Policy, Baltimore, MD 21250. Offers applied sociology (MA); nonprofit sector (Postbaccalaureate Certificate). *Program availability:* Part-time, evening/weekend. *Faculty:* 18 full-time (13 women), 1 (woman) part-time/adjunct. *Students:* 13 full-time (10 women), 16 part-time (9 women); includes 10 minority (4 Black or African American, non-Hispanic/Latino; 3 Asian, non-Hispanic/Latino; 2 Hispanic/Latino; 1 Two or more races, non-Hispanic/Latino). Average age 27. 19 applicants, 63% accepted, 8 enrolled. In 2017, 9 master's, 4 other advanced degrees awarded. *Degree requirements:* For master's, thesis or alternative. *Entrance requirements:* For master's, minimum GPA of 3.0. Additional exam requirements/recommendations for international students: Required—TOEFL. *Application deadline:* For fall admission, 3/15 for domestic students, 1/1 for international students; for spring admission, 11/15 for domestic students, 9/1 for international students. Application fee: $70. Electronic applications accepted. *Expenses: Required fees:* $132. *Financial support:* In 2017–18, 10 students received support, including 1 research assistantship with tuition reimbursement available, 9 teaching assistantships with tuition reimbursements available; scholarships/grants, health care benefits, unspecified assistantships, and tuition remission also available. *Faculty research:* Health, illness, and medicine; aging and the life course; diversity, gender, and culture; applied research methods. *Unit head:* Dr. J. Kevin Eckert, Department Chair, 410-455-5698, Fax: 410-455-1154, E-mail: eckert@umbc.edu. *Application contact:* Dr. Marina Adler, Graduate Program Director, 410-455-3155, Fax: 410-455-1154, E-mail: adler@umbc.edu.
Website: http://sociology.umbc.edu/

University of Memphis, Graduate School, College of Arts and Sciences, Division of Public and Nonprofit Administration, Memphis, TN 38152. Offers local government management (Graduate Certificate); philanthropy and nonprofit leadership (Graduate Certificate). *Accreditation:* NASPAA. *Program availability:* Part-time, evening/weekend, blended/hybrid learning. *Faculty:* 6 full-time (3 women), 1 part-time/adjunct (0 women). *Students:* 13 full-time (5 women), 28 part-time (19 women); includes 22 minority (21 Black or African American, non-Hispanic/Latino; 1 Two or more races, non-Hispanic/Latino), 1 international. Average age 36. 26 applicants, 96% accepted, 14 enrolled. In 2017, 16 master's, 13 other advanced degrees awarded. *Degree requirements:* For master's, comprehensive exam, thesis or alternative, internship. *Entrance requirements:* For master's, GRE General Test, GMAT, MAT, or LSAT, minimum GPA of 3.0, resume, two references, statement of interest. Additional exam requirements/recommendations for international students: Required—TOEFL. *Application deadline:* For fall admission, 7/1 for domestic students, 5/1 for international students; for spring admission, 12/1 for domestic students, 9/15 for international students; for summer admission, 5/1 for domestic students, 2/1 for international students. Applications are processed on a rolling basis. Application fee: $35 ($60 for international students). Electronic applications accepted. *Expenses:* Contact institution. *Financial support:* In 2017–18, 37 students received support, including 5 fellowships (averaging $11,200 per year); research assistantships with full tuition reimbursements available, career-related internships or fieldwork, Federal Work-Study, scholarships/grants, health care benefits, and unspecified assistantships also available. Support available to part-time students. Financial award application deadline: 2/1; financial award applicants required to submit FAFSA. *Faculty research:* Nonprofit organization governance, local government management, community collaboration, urban problems, accountability. *Unit head:* Dr. Michael Howell-Moroney, Chair, 901-678-3360, Fax: 901-678-2981, E-mail: mhwllmrn@memphis.edu. *Application contact:* Dr. Sharon Wrobel, MPA Coordinator, 901-678-4720, Fax: 901-678-2981, E-mail: swrobel@memphis.edu.
Website: http://www.memphis.edu/padm/

University of Michigan–Flint, Graduate Programs, Program in Public Administration, Flint, MI 48502-1950. Offers administration of non-profit agencies (MPA); criminal justice administration (MPA); educational administration (MPA); general public administration (MPA); healthcare administration (MPA). *Program availability:* Part-time. *Faculty:* 1 full-time (0 women), 2 part-time/adjunct (both women). *Students:* 13 full-time (6 women), 88 part-time (59 women); includes 38 minority (29 Black or African American, non-Hispanic/Latino; 3 American Indian or Alaska Native, non-Hispanic/Latino; 2 Asian, non-Hispanic/Latino; 4 Two or more races, non-Hispanic/Latino), 3 international. Average age 37. 63 applicants, 81% accepted, 37 enrolled. In 2017, 55 master's awarded. *Degree requirements:* For master's, thesis or alternative, internship. *Entrance requirements:* For master's, bachelor's degree from regionally-accredited institution, minimum overall undergraduate GPA of 3.0. Additional exam requirements/recommendations for international students: Required—TOEFL (minimum score 84 iBT), IELTS (minimum score 6.5). *Application deadline:* For fall admission, 8/1 for domestic students, 5/1 for international students; for winter admission, 11/15 for domestic students, 9/1 for international students; for spring admission, 3/15 for domestic students, 1/1 for international students; for summer admission, 5/15 for domestic students. Applications are processed on a rolling basis. Application fee: $55. Electronic applications accepted. *Expenses:* Contact institution. *Financial support:* Career-related internships or fieldwork, Federal Work-Study, and scholarships/grants available. Support available to part-time students. Financial award application deadline: 3/1; financial award applicants required to submit FAFSA. *Unit head:* Dr. Kathryn Schellenberg, Director, 810-762-3340, E-mail: kathsch@umflint.edu. *Application contact:* Bradley T. Maki, Director of Graduate Admissions, 810-762-3171, Fax: 810-766-6789, E-mail: bmaki@umflint.edu.
Website: http://www.umflint.edu/graduateprograms/public-administration-mpa

University of Missouri, Office of Research and Graduate Studies, Harry S Truman School of Public Affairs, Columbia, MO 65211. Offers grantsmanship (Graduate Certificate); nonprofit management (Graduate Certificate); organizational change (Graduate Certificate); public affairs (MPA, PhD); public management (Graduate Certificate); science and public policy (Graduate Certificate). *Accreditation:* NASPAA. *Entrance requirements:* For master's, GRE General Test, minimum GPA of 3.0. Additional exam requirements/recommendations for international students: Required—TOEFL (minimum score 550 paper-based; 80 iBT), IELTS (minimum score 6.5). Electronic applications accepted.

University of Missouri–St. Louis, Graduate School, Program in Public Policy Administration, St. Louis, MO 63121. Offers local government management (MPPA, Certificate); nonprofit management and leadership (MPPA, Certificate); policy and program evaluation (MPPA, Certificate). *Accreditation:* NASPAA. *Program availability:* Part-time, evening/weekend. *Faculty:* 2 full-time (1 woman), 4 part-time/adjunct (3 women). *Students:* 9 full-time (5 women), 34 part-time (19 women); includes 10 minority (6 Black or African American, non-Hispanic/Latino; 2 Asian, non-Hispanic/Latino; 1 Hispanic/Latino; 1 Two or more races, non-Hispanic/Latino). 34 applicants, 79% accepted, 14 enrolled. *Degree requirements:* For master's, exit project. *Entrance requirements:* For master's, 3 letters of recommendation, personal statement. Additional exam requirements/recommendations for international students: Recommended—TOEFL (minimum score 550 paper-based), IELTS (minimum score 6.5). *Application deadline:* For fall admission, 7/1 priority date for domestic and international students; for spring admission, 12/1 priority date for domestic and international students. Applications are processed on a rolling basis. Application fee: $50 ($40 for international students). Electronic applications accepted. *Expenses:* Tuition, state resident: part-time $476.50 per credit hour. Tuition, nonresident: part-time $1169.70 per credit hour. *Financial*

support: Research assistantships with tuition reimbursements and career-related internships or fieldwork available. Financial award application deadline: 4/1; financial award applicants required to submit FAFSA. *Faculty research:* Urban policy, public finance, evaluation. *Unit head:* Daniel Sise, Interim Director, 314-516-6378, Fax: 314-516-5210, E-mail: sised@umsl.edu. *Application contact:* 314-516-5458, Fax: 314-516-6996, E-mail: gradadm@umsl.edu.
Website: http://www.umsl.edu/gradschool/ppa/

University of Nevada, Las Vegas, Graduate College, Greenspun College of Urban Affairs, School of Public Policy and Leadership, Las Vegas, NV 89154-4030. Offers crisis and emergency management (MS); emergency crisis management cybersecurity (Certificate); environmental science (MS, PhD); non-profit management (Certificate); public administration (MPA); public affairs (PhD); public management (Certificate); urban leadership (MA). *Program availability:* Part-time. *Faculty:* 13 full-time (5 women), 10 part-time/adjunct (3 women). *Students:* 76 full-time (40 women), 107 part-time (66 women); includes 79 minority (19 Black or African American, non-Hispanic/Latino; 1 American Indian or Alaska Native, non-Hispanic/Latino; 6 Asian, non-Hispanic/Latino; 40 Hispanic/Latino; 3 Native Hawaiian or other Pacific Islander, non-Hispanic/Latino; 10 Two or more races, non-Hispanic/Latino), 1 international. Average age 37. 86 applicants, 80% accepted, 47 enrolled. In 2017, 61 master's, 6 doctorates, 14 other advanced degrees awarded. *Degree requirements:* For master's, comprehensive exam (for some programs), thesis (for some programs), oral exam; for doctorate, comprehensive exam, thesis/dissertation; for Certificate, portfolio. *Entrance requirements:* For master's, GRE General Test or GMAT, bachelor's degree with minimum GPA 2.75; statement of purpose; 3 letters of recommendation; for doctorate, GRE General Test, master's degree with minimum GPA of 3.5; 3 letters of recommendation; statement of purpose; writing sample; personal interview; for Certificate, bachelor's degree; 2 letters of recommendation; writing sample. Additional exam requirements/recommendations for international students: Required—TOEFL (minimum score 550 paper-based; 80 iBT), IELTS (minimum score 7). *Application deadline:* For fall admission, 6/1 for domestic and international students; for spring admission, 11/1 for domestic and international students; for summer admission, 3/1 for domestic students. Application fee: $60 ($95 for international students). Electronic applications accepted. *Expenses:* $275 per credit, $850 per course, $7,969 per year resident, $22,157 per year non-resident, $7,094 non-resident fee (7 credits or more), $1,307 annual health insurance fee. *Financial support:* In 2017–18, 23 students received support, including 7 research assistantships with partial tuition reimbursements available (averaging $15,995 per year), 16 teaching assistantships with partial tuition reimbursements available (averaging $15,547 per year); institutionally sponsored loans, scholarships/grants, health care benefits, and unspecified assistantships also available. Financial award application deadline: 3/15; financial award applicants required to submit FAFSA. *Total annual research expenditures:* $63,202. *Unit head:* Dr. Christopher Stream, Director, 702-895-5120, Fax: 702-895-4436, E-mail: chris.stream@unlv.edu. *Application contact:* Dr. Jayce Farmer, Graduate Coordinator, 702-895-4828, E-mail: jayce.farmer@unlv.edu.
Website: https://www.unlv.edu/publicpolicy

University of New Haven, Graduate School, Henry C. Lee College of Criminal Justice and Forensic Sciences, Program in Public Administration, West Haven, CT 06516. Offers fire and emergency medical services (MPA); municipal management (MPA); nonprofit organization management (MPA); public administration (MPA, Graduate Certificate); public finance (MPA); public safety (MPA). *Program availability:* Part-time, evening/weekend. *Students:* 36 full-time (20 women), 25 part-time (10 women); includes 21 minority (15 Black or African American, non-Hispanic/Latino; 1 American Indian or Alaska Native, non-Hispanic/Latino; 1 Asian, non-Hispanic/Latino; 3 Hispanic/Latino; 1 Two or more races, non-Hispanic/Latino), 3 international. Average age 37. 46 applicants, 91% accepted, 21 enrolled. In 2017, 15 master's, 1 other advanced degree awarded. *Entrance requirements:* Additional exam requirements/recommendations for international students: Required—TOEFL (minimum score 80 iBT), IELTS, PTE. *Application deadline:* Applications are processed on a rolling basis. Application fee: $50. Electronic applications accepted. Application fee is waived when completed online. *Expenses: Tuition:* Full-time $16,020; part-time $890 per credit hour. *Required fees:* $220; $90 per term. *Financial support:* Research assistantships with partial tuition reimbursements, teaching assistantships with partial tuition reimbursements, career-related internships or fieldwork, Federal Work-Study, scholarships/grants, and unspecified assistantships available. Support available to part-time students. Financial award application deadline: 5/1; financial award applicants required to submit FAFSA. *Unit head:* Dr. Cynthia Conrad, Associate Professor, 203-932-7486, E-mail: cconrad@newhaven.edu. *Application contact:* Michelle Mason, Director of Graduate Enrollment, 203-932-7067, E-mail: mmason@newhaven.edu.
Website: http://www.newhaven.edu/lee-college/graduate-programs/public-administration/

The University of North Carolina at Charlotte, College of Liberal Arts and Sciences, Department of Political Science and Public Administration, Charlotte, NC 28223-0001. Offers emergency management (Graduate Certificate); non-profit management (Graduate Certificate); public administration (MPA), including arts administration, emergency management, non-profit management, public budgeting and finance, urban management and policy; public budgeting and finance (Graduate Certificate); urban management and policy (Graduate Certificate). *Accreditation:* NASPAA. *Program availability:* Part-time, evening/weekend. *Faculty:* 19 full-time (9 women), 4 part-time/adjunct (1 woman). *Students:* 20 full-time (11 women), 61 part-time (41 women); includes 21 minority (12 Black or African American, non-Hispanic/Latino; 2 American Indian or Alaska Native, non-Hispanic/Latino; 1 Asian, non-Hispanic/Latino; 4 Hispanic/Latino; 2 Two or more races, non-Hispanic/Latino), 1 international. Average age 28. 48 applicants, 67% accepted, 22 enrolled. In 2017, 25 master's, 15 other advanced degrees awarded. *Degree requirements:* For master's, research project or thesis. *Entrance requirements:* For master's, GRE General Test, bachelor's degree, or its equivalent, from accredited college or university; minimum undergraduate GPA of 3.0; 3 letters of recommendation; statement of purpose; for Graduate Certificate, statement of purpose (1-2 pages in length) explaining applicant's career goals, how the Graduate Certificate fits into achieving those goals, and any relevant work experience; official transcripts; letters of recommendation. Additional exam requirements/recommendations for international students: Required—TOEFL (minimum score 523 paper-based, 70 iBT) or IELTS (6.5). *Application deadline:* For fall admission, 8/1 for domestic and international students; for spring admission, 12/1 for domestic and international students. Applications are processed on a rolling basis. Application fee: $75. Electronic applications accepted. *Expenses:* Tuition, state resident: full-time $4337. Tuition, nonresident: full-time $17,771. *Required fees:* $3211. Tuition and fees vary according to course load and program. *Financial support:* In 2017–18, 14 students received support, including 13 research assistantships (averaging $9,015 per year), 1 teaching assistantship (averaging $19,500 per year); career-related internships or fieldwork, Federal Work-Study, institutionally sponsored loans, scholarships/grants, and unspecified assistantships also available. Support available to part-time students. Financial award application deadline: 3/1; financial award applicants required to submit FAFSA. *Total annual research expenditures:* $419,411. *Unit head:* Dr. Greg Weeks, Chair, 704-687-7574, E-mail: gbweeks@uncc.edu. *Application contact:* Kathy B. Giddings, Director of Graduate Admissions, 704-687-5503, Fax: 704-687-1668, E-mail: gradadm@uncc.edu.
Website: http://politicalscience.uncc.edu/

The University of North Carolina at Greensboro, Graduate School, College of Arts and Sciences, Department of Political Science, Greensboro, NC 27412-5001. Offers nonprofit management (Certificate); public affairs (MPA); urban and economic development (Certificate). *Accreditation:* NASPAA. *Degree requirements:* For master's, comprehensive exam. *Entrance requirements:* For master's, GRE General Test. Additional exam requirements/recommendations for international students: Required—TOEFL. Electronic applications accepted. *Faculty research:* U.S. Constitution, Canadian parliament, public management, ethical challenge of public service.

University of Northern Iowa, Graduate College, MA Program in Philanthropy and Nonprofit Development, Cedar Falls, IA 50614. Offers MA. *Entrance requirements:* For master's, minimum GPA of 3.0; 3 letters of recommendation; experience in the philanthropy and/or nonprofit areas. Additional exam requirements/recommendations for international students: Required—TOEFL (minimum score 500 paper-based; 61 iBT). Electronic applications accepted.

University of North Florida, College of Arts and Sciences, Department of Political Science and Public Administration, Jacksonville, FL 32224. Offers nonprofit management (Graduate Certificate); public administration (MPA). *Accreditation:* NASPAA. *Program availability:* Part-time. *Degree requirements:* For master's, thesis or alternative, internship. *Entrance requirements:* For master's, GRE General Test, minimum GPA of 3.0 in last 60 hours, 2 letters of recommendation, interview. Additional exam requirements/recommendations for international students: Required—TOEFL (minimum score 500 paper-based; 61 iBT). Electronic applications accepted. *Faculty research:* America's usage of the Internet, use of information communication technologies by educators and children.

University of North Texas, Robert B. Toulouse School of Graduate Studies, Denton, TX 76203-5459. Offers accounting (MS); applied anthropology (MA, MS); applied behavior analysis (Certificate); applied geography (MA); applied technology and performance improvement (M Ed, MS); art education (Certificate); art history (MA); art museum education (Certificate); arts leadership (Certificate); audiology (Au D); behavior analysis (MS); behavioral science (PhD); biochemistry and molecular biology (MS); biology (MA, MS); biomedical engineering (MS); business analysis (MS); chemistry (MS); clinical health psychology (PhD); communication studies (MA, MS); computer engineering (MS); computer science (MS); counseling (M Ed, MS), including clinical mental health counseling (MS), college and university counseling, elementary school counseling, secondary school counseling; creative writing (MA); criminal justice (MS); curriculum and instruction (M Ed); decision sciences (MBA); design (MA, MFA), including fashion design (MFA), innovation studies, interior design (MFA); early childhood studies (MS); economics (MS); educational leadership (M Ed, Ed D); educational psychology (MS, PhD), including family studies (MS), gifted and talented (MS), human development (MS), learning and cognition (MS), research, measurement and evaluation (MS); electrical engineering (MS); emergency management (MPA); engineering technology (MS); English (MA); English as a second language (MA); environmental science (MS); finance (MBA, MS); financial management (MPA); French (MA); health services management (MBA); higher education (M Ed, Ed D); history (MA, MS); hospitality management (MS); human resources management (MPA); information science (MS); information systems (PhD); information technologies (MBA); interdisciplinary studies (MA, MS); international studies (MA); international sustainable tourism (MS); jazz studies (MM); journalism (MA, MJ, Graduate Certificate), including interactive and virtual digital communication (Graduate Certificate), narrative journalism (Graduate Certificate), public relations (Graduate Certificate); kinesiology (MS); linguistics (MA); local government management (MPA); logistics (PhD); logistics and supply chain management (MBA); long-term care, senior housing, and aging services (MA); management (PhD); marketing (MBA); mathematics (MA, MS); mechanical and energy engineering (MS, PhD); music (MA), including ethnomusicology, music theory, musicology, performance; music composition (PhD); music education (MM Ed, PhD); nonprofit management (MPA); operations and supply chain management (MBA); performance (MM, DMA); philosophy (MA); political science (MA); professional and technical communication (MA); radio, television and film (MA, MFA); rehabilitation counseling (Certificate); sociology (MS); Spanish (MA); special education (M Ed); speech-language pathology (MS); strategic management (MBA); studio art (MFA); teaching (M Ed); MBA/MS. *Program availability:* Part-time, evening/weekend, online learning. Terminal master's awarded for partial completion of doctoral program. *Degree requirements:* For master's, variable foreign language requirement, comprehensive exam (for some programs), thesis (for some programs); for doctorate, variable foreign language requirement, comprehensive exam (for some programs), thesis/dissertation; for other advanced degree, variable foreign language requirement, comprehensive exam (for some programs). *Entrance requirements:* For master's and doctorate, GRE, GMAT. Additional exam requirements/recommendations for international students: Required—TOEFL (minimum score 550 paper-based; 79 iBT). Electronic applications accepted.

University of Notre Dame, Mendoza College of Business, Master in Nonprofit Administration Program, Notre Dame, IN 46556. Offers MNA. *Accreditation:* AACSB. *Program availability:* Part-time-only, blended/hybrid learning. *Faculty:* 9 full-time (1 woman), 5 part-time/adjunct (3 women). *Students:* 63 part-time (34 women); includes 11 minority (5 Black or African American, non-Hispanic/Latino; 4 Hispanic/Latino; 2 Two or more races, non-Hispanic/Latino), 9 international. Average age 35. 41 applicants, 95% accepted, 25 enrolled. In 2017, 24 master's awarded. *Degree requirements:* For master's, thesis. *Entrance requirements:* For master's, GRE General Test or GMAT (waiver available to qualifying applicants), minimum of two years' nonprofit work experience. Additional exam requirements/recommendations for international students: Required—TOEFL (minimum score 600 paper-based; 100 iBT), IELTS (minimum score 7). *Application deadline:* Applications are processed on a rolling basis. Application fee: $150. Electronic applications accepted. *Expenses:* Contact institution. *Financial support:* Application deadline: 4/30. *Unit head:* Dr. Angela R. Logan, Director of Nonprofit Professional Development, 574-631-7793, Fax: 574-631-6532, E-mail: alogan2@nd.edu.
Website: http://mendoza.nd.edu/programs/specialized-masters/master-of-nonprofit-administration/

University of Oklahoma, College of Arts and Sciences, Department of Political Science, Program in Public Administration, Norman, OK 73019. Offers general (MPA); nonprofit management (MPA); public management (MPA); public policy (MPA). *Program availability:* Part-time, evening/weekend. *Students:* 36 full-time (22 women), 60 part-time (35 women); includes 27 minority (7 Black or African American, non-Hispanic/Latino; 5 American Indian or Alaska Native, non-Hispanic/Latino; 3 Asian, non-Hispanic/Latino; 7 Hispanic/Latino; 1 Native Hawaiian or other Pacific Islander, non-Hispanic/Latino; 4 Two or more races, non-Hispanic/Latino), 2 international. Average age 31. 30 applicants, 77% accepted, 20 enrolled. In 2017, 18 master's awarded. Terminal master's awarded for partial completion of doctoral program. *Degree requirements:* For master's, comprehensive exam, thesis or alternative, 36 hours. *Entrance requirements:* For master's, GRE, purpose statement, resume, two letters of recommendation. Additional exam requirements/recommendations for international students: Required—TOEFL

Nonprofit Management

(minimum score 100 iBT) or IELTS (minimum score 7.0). *Application deadline:* Applications are processed on a rolling basis. Application fee: $50 ($100 for international students). Electronic applications accepted. *Expenses:* Tuition, state resident: full-time $5119; part-time $213.30 per credit hour. Tuition, nonresident: full-time $19,778; part-time $824.10 per credit hour. *Required fees:* $3458; $133.55 per credit hour. $126.50 per semester. *Financial support:* In 2017–18, 44 students received support. Research assistantships with full tuition reimbursements available, teaching assistantships with full tuition reimbursements available, career-related internships or fieldwork, scholarships/grants, health care benefits, unspecified assistantships, and travel and conference attendance funding available. Financial award application deadline: 6/1; financial award applicants required to submit FAFSA. *Faculty research:* Public and nonprofit management, public policy analysis, program evaluation, public finance and budgeting. *Unit head:* Prof. Scott Robinson, Chair, 405-325-2061, Fax: 405-325-0718, E-mail: pscgradprog@ou.edu. *Application contact:* Jeff Alexander, Graduate Programs Coordinator, 405-325-1845, Fax: 405-325-0718, E-mail: pscgradprog@ou.edu. Website: http://www.ou.edu/content/cas/psc/graduate/mpa.html

University of Oklahoma, College of Professional and Continuing Studies, Norman, OK 73019. Offers administrative leadership (MA, Graduate Certificate), including government and military leadership (MA), organizational leadership (MA), volunteer and non-profit leadership (MA); corrections management (Graduate Certificate); criminal justice (MS); integrated studies (MA), including human and health services administration, integrated studies; museum studies (MA); prevention science (MPS); restorative justice administration (Graduate Certificate). *Program availability:* Part-time, 100% online, blended/hybrid learning. *Faculty:* 16 full-time (8 women). *Students:* 64 full-time (39 women), 558 part-time (278 women); includes 191 minority (42 Black or African American, non-Hispanic/Latino; 42 American Indian or Alaska Native, non-Hispanic/Latino; 16 Asian, non-Hispanic/Latino; 46 Hispanic/Latino; 1 Native Hawaiian or other Pacific Islander, non-Hispanic/Latino; 44 Two or more races, non-Hispanic/Latino), 4 international. Average age 35. 151 applicants, 95% accepted, 97 enrolled. In 2017, 202 master's, 11 other advanced degrees awarded. *Degree requirements:* For master's, comprehensive exam, thesis optional, 33 credit hours; project/internship (for museum studies program only); for Graduate Certificate, 12 graduate credit hours (for Graduate Certificate). *Entrance requirements:* For master's and Graduate Certificate, minimum GPA of 3.0 in last 60 undergraduate hours; statement of goals; resume. Additional exam requirements/recommendations for international students: Required—TOEFL (minimum score 79 iBT) or IELTS (minimum score 6.5). *Application deadline:* For fall admission, 7/15 for domestic and international students; for winter admission, 12/1 for domestic and international students; for spring admission, 5/1 for domestic and international students. Applications are processed on a rolling basis. Application fee: $50 ($100 for international students). Electronic applications accepted. *Expenses:* Tuition, state resident: full-time $5119; part-time $213.30 per credit hour. Tuition, nonresident: full-time $19,778; part-time $824.10 per credit hour. *Required fees:* $3458; $133.55 per credit hour. $126.50 per semester. *Financial support:* In 2017–18, 92 students received support. Career-related internships or fieldwork, institutionally sponsored loans, scholarships/grants, health care benefits, and tuition waivers available. Support available to part-time students. Financial award application deadline: 6/1; financial award applicants required to submit FAFSA. *Faculty research:* Change management and leadership; policing and corrections management; neuro-psychology of addiction; disproportionate minority contact; ethnic identity and nationalism. *Unit head:* Dr. Martha L. Banz, Associate Provost for Continuing Education/Interim Dean, College of Professional and Continuing Studies, 405-325-4414, Fax: 405-325-7132, E-mail: mlbanz@ou.edu. *Application contact:* Lindsey Gunderson, Graduate Academic Advisor, 405-325-5827, Fax: 405-325-7132, E-mail: lindsey.gunderson@ou.edu. Website: https://pacs.ou.edu/

University of Oregon, Graduate School, College of Design, School of Planning, Public Policy and Management, Program in Nonprofit Management, Eugene, OR 97403. Offers MNM, Graduate Certificate. *Degree requirements:* For master's, internship, project.

University of Pennsylvania, School of Arts and Sciences, Fels Institute of Government, Philadelphia, PA 19104. Offers economic development and growth (Certificate); government administration (MGA); nonprofit administration (Certificate); organization dynamics (MS); politics (Certificate); public administration (MPA); public finance (Certificate). *Program availability:* Part-time, evening/weekend. *Students:* 44 full-time (27 women), 78 part-time (41 women); includes 30 minority (9 Black or African American, non-Hispanic/Latino; 8 Asian, non-Hispanic/Latino; 10 Hispanic/Latino; 3 Two or more races, non-Hispanic/Latino), 10 international. Average age 31. 333 applicants, 47% accepted, 88 enrolled. In 2017, 57 master's, 9 other advanced degrees awarded. *Financial support:* Application deadline: 1/1. Website: http://www.fels.upenn.edu/

University of Pittsburgh, Graduate School of Public and International Affairs, Master of Public Administration Program, Pittsburgh, PA 15260. Offers energy and environment (MPA); governance and international public management (MPA); policy research and analysis (MPA); public and nonprofit management (MPA); urban affairs and planning (MPA); JD/MPA; MPH/MPA; MSIS/MPA; MSW/MPA. *Accreditation:* NASPAA. *Program availability:* Part-time, evening/weekend. *Faculty:* 30 full-time (11 women), 14 part-time/adjunct (5 women). *Students:* 100 full-time (75 women), 18 part-time (12 women); includes 13 minority (6 Black or African American, non-Hispanic/Latino; 3 Asian, non-Hispanic/Latino; 4 Hispanic/Latino), 54 international. Average age 26. 220 applicants, 87% accepted, 44 enrolled. In 2017, 54 master's awarded. *Degree requirements:* For master's, thesis optional, capstone seminar. *Entrance requirements:* For master's, GRE General Test or GMAT, 2 letters of recommendation, resume, undergraduate transcripts, personal statement. Additional exam requirements/recommendations for international students: Required—TOEFL (minimum score 80 iBT); Recommended—IELTS (minimum score 7). *Application deadline:* For fall admission, 2/1 priority date for domestic students, 1/15 priority date for international students; for spring admission, 11/1 priority date for domestic students, 8/1 priority date for international students. Application fee: $50. Electronic applications accepted. *Expenses:* $23,140 per year in-state, $37,830 out-of-state. *Financial support:* In 2017–18, 23 students received support, including 1 fellowship with full tuition reimbursement available (averaging $37,000 per year), 1 research assistantship with full tuition reimbursement available (averaging $37,000 per year); career-related internships or fieldwork and scholarships/grants also available. Financial award application deadline: 2/1; financial award applicants required to submit FAFSA. *Faculty research:* Urban affairs and planning, governance and international public management, public and nonprofit management, policy research and analysis, energy and environment. *Total annual research expenditures:* $1.6 million. *Unit head:* Dr. John Keeler, Dean, 412-648-7605, Fax: 412-648-7601, E-mail: gspia@pitt.edu. *Application contact:* Dr. Michael Rizzi, Director of Student Services, 412-648-7643, Fax: 412-648-7641, E-mail: rizzim@pitt.edu. Website: http://www.gspia.pitt.edu

University of Portland, Dr. Robert B. Pamplin, Jr. School of Business, Portland, OR 97203-5798. Offers entrepreneurship (MBA); finance (MBA, MS); health care management (MBA); marketing (MBA); nonprofit management (EMBA); operations and technology management (MBA, MS); sustainability (MBA). *Accreditation:* AACSB. *Program availability:* Part-time, evening/weekend. *Entrance requirements:* For master's,

GMAT, minimum GPA of 3.0, resume, 2 letters of recommendation. Additional exam requirements/recommendations for international students: Required—TOEFL (minimum score 570 paper-based; 89 iBT), IELTS (minimum score 7). *Expenses:* Contact institution.

University of San Diego, School of Leadership and Education Sciences, Department of Leadership Studies, San Diego, CA 92110-2492. Offers higher education leadership (MA); leadership studies (MA, PhD, Certificate); nonprofit leadership and management (MA). *Program availability:* Part-time, evening/weekend. *Faculty:* 10 full-time (5 women), 18 part-time/adjunct (7 women). *Students:* 53 full-time (34 women), 202 part-time (140 women); includes 118 minority (24 Black or African American, non-Hispanic/Latino; 16 Asian, non-Hispanic/Latino; 64 Hispanic/Latino; 1 Native Hawaiian or other Pacific Islander, non-Hispanic/Latino; 13 Two or more races, non-Hispanic/Latino), 23 international. Average age 34. 243 applicants, 73% accepted, 77 enrolled. In 2017, 53 master's, 15 doctorates awarded. *Degree requirements:* For master's, thesis (for some programs), international experience; for doctorate, comprehensive exam, thesis/dissertation, international experience. *Entrance requirements:* For master's, GRE (recommended with GPA less than 3.25); for doctorate, GRE (less than 5 years old), master's degree, minimum GPA of 3.5 (recommended), resume. Additional exam requirements/recommendations for international students: Required—TOEFL (minimum score 580 paper-based; 83 iBT), TWE. Application fee: $45. Electronic applications accepted. *Financial support:* In 2017–18, 204 students received support. Career-related internships or fieldwork, Federal Work-Study, institutionally sponsored loans, unspecified assistantships, and stipends available. Support available to part-time students. Financial award application deadline: 4/1; financial award applicants required to submit FAFSA. *Faculty research:* Higher education administration policy and relations, organizational leadership, nonprofits and philanthropy, student affairs leadership. *Unit head:* Dr. Lea Hubbard, Graduate Program Director, 619-260-7818, E-mail: lhubbard@sandiego.edu. *Application contact:* Monica Mahon, Associate Director of Graduate Admissions, 619-260-4524, Fax: 619-260-4158, E-mail: grads@sandiego.edu. Website: https://www.sandiego.edu/soles/leadership-studies/

University of San Francisco, School of Management, Master of Nonprofit Administration Program, San Francisco, CA 94117. Offers MNA. *Program availability:* Part-time, evening/weekend. *Degree requirements:* For master's, thesis optional. *Entrance requirements:* For master's, resume demonstrating minimum of two years of professional work experience, transcripts from each college or university attended, two letters of recommendation, personal statement. Additional exam requirements/recommendations for international students: Required—TOEFL (minimum score 600 paper-based, 100 iBT), IELTS (minimum score 7) or PTE (minimum score 68). Electronic applications accepted. *Expenses:* Contact institution. *Faculty research:* Philanthropy in ethnic communities.

University of Southern California, Graduate School, Sol Price School of Public Policy, Master of Public Administration Program, Los Angeles, CA 90089. Offers nonprofit management and policy (Graduate Certificate); political management (Graduate Certificate); public administration (MPA); public management (Graduate Certificate); MPA/JD; MPA/M PI; MPA/MA; MPA/MAJCS; MPA/MS; MPA/MSW. *Accreditation:* NASPAA (one or more programs are accredited). *Program availability:* Part-time, evening/weekend, online learning. Terminal master's awarded for partial completion of doctoral program. *Degree requirements:* For master's, capstone, internship. *Entrance requirements:* For master's, GRE, GMAT. Additional exam requirements/recommendations for international students: Required—TOEFL (minimum score 600 paper-based; 100 iBT). Electronic applications accepted. *Faculty research:* Collaborative governance and decision-making, nonprofit management, environmental management, institutional analysis, local government, civic engagement.

University of Southern Indiana, Graduate Studies, College of Liberal Arts, Program in Public Administration, Evansville, IN 47712-3590. Offers nonprofit administration (MPA); public sector administration (MPA). *Program availability:* Part-time, evening/weekend. *Faculty:* 5 full-time (2 women). *Students:* 22 full-time (13 women), 8 part-time (6 women); includes 6 minority (5 Black or African American, non-Hispanic/Latino; 1 Hispanic/Latino), 2 international. Average age 32. In 2017, 6 master's awarded. *Entrance requirements:* For master's, resume, 2 letters of reference, personal statement, minimum GPA of 3.0. Additional exam requirements/recommendations for international students: Required—TOEFL (minimum score 550 paper-based; 79 iBT), IELTS (minimum score 6). *Application deadline:* For fall admission, 8/15 priority date for domestic students, 3/1 priority date for international students; for spring admission, 1/5 for domestic students, 11/15 for international students. Applications are processed on a rolling basis. Application fee: $40. Electronic applications accepted. *Expenses:* Tuition, state resident: full-time $9394. Tuition, nonresident: full-time $17,917. *Required fees:* $510. *Financial support:* In 2017–18, 4 students received support. Federal Work-Study, scholarships/grants, tuition waivers (full and partial), and unspecified assistantships available. Financial award application deadline: 3/1; financial award applicants required to submit FAFSA. *Unit head:* Dr. Matthew J. Hanka, Director, 812-461-5204, E-mail: mjhanka@usi.edu. *Application contact:* Dr. Mayola Rowser, Director, Graduate Studies, 812-465-7015, E-mail: mrowser@usi.edu. Website: http://www.usi.edu/liberal-arts/master-of-public-administration

University of South Florida, Innovative Education, Tampa, FL 33620-9951. Offers adult, career and higher education (Graduate Certificate), including college teaching, leadership in developing human resources, leadership in higher education; Africana studies (Graduate Certificate), including diasporas and health disparities, genocide and human rights; aging studies (Graduate Certificate), including gerontology; art research (Graduate Certificate), including museum studies; business foundations (Graduate Certificate); chemical and biomedical engineering (Graduate Certificate), including materials science and engineering, water, health and sustainability; child and family studies (Graduate Certificate), including positive behavior support; civil and industrial engineering (Graduate Certificate), including transportation systems analysis; community and family health (Graduate Certificate), including maternal and child health, social marketing and public health, violence and injury: prevention and intervention, women's health; criminology (Graduate Certificate), including criminal justice administration; data science for public administration (Graduate Certificate); digital humanities (Graduate Certificate); educational measurement and research (Graduate Certificate), including evaluation; English (Graduate Certificate), including comparative literary studies, creative writing, professional and technical communication; entrepreneurship (Graduate Certificate); environmental health (Graduate Certificate), including safety management; epidemiology and biostatistics (Graduate Certificate), including applied biostatistics, biostatistics, concepts and tools of epidemiology, epidemiology, epidemiology of infectious diseases; geography, environment and planning (Graduate Certificate), including community development, environmental policy and management, geographical information systems; geology (Graduate Certificate), including hydrogeology; global health (Graduate Certificate), including disaster management, global health and Latin American and Caribbean studies, global health practice, humanitarian assistance, infection control; government and international affairs (Graduate Certificate), including Cuban studies, globalization studies; health policy and management (Graduate Certificate), including health management and leadership,

public health policy and programs; hearing specialist: early intervention (Graduate Certificate); industrial and management systems engineering (Graduate Certificate), including systems engineering, technology management; information studies (Graduate Certificate), including school library media specialist; information systems/decision sciences (Graduate Certificate), including analytics and business intelligence; instructional technology (Graduate Certificate), including distance education, Florida digital/virtual educator, instructional design, multimedia design, Web design; internal medicine, bioethics and medical humanities (Graduate Certificate), including biomedical ethics; Latin American and Caribbean studies (Graduate Certificate); leadership for coastal resiliency planning (Graduate Certificate); mass communications (Graduate Certificate), including multimedia journalism; mathematics and statistics (Graduate Certificate), including mathematics; medicine (Graduate Certificate), including aging and neuroscience, bioinformatics, biotechnology, brain fitness and memory management, clinical investigation, hand and upper limb rehabilitation, health informatics, health sciences, integrative weight management, intellectual property, medicine and gender, metabolic and nutritional medicine, metabolic cardiology, pharmacy sciences; national and competitive intelligence (Graduate Certificate); nursing (Graduate Certificate), including simulation based academic fellowship in advanced pain management; psychological and social foundations (Graduate Certificate), including career counseling, college teaching, diversity in education, mental health counseling, school counseling; public affairs (Graduate Certificate), including nonprofit management, public management, research administration; public health (Graduate Certificate), including assessing chemical toxicity and public health risks, health equity, pharmacoepidemiology, public health generalist, toxicology, translational research in adolescent behavioral health; public health practices (Graduate Certificate), including planning for healthy communities; rehabilitation and mental health counseling (Graduate Certificate), including integrative mental health care, marriage and family therapy, rehabilitation technology; secondary education (Graduate Certificate), including ESOL, foreign language education: culture and content, foreign language education: professional; social work (Graduate Certificate), including geriatric social work/clinical gerontology; special education (Graduate Certificate), including autism spectrum disorder, disabilities education: severe/profound; world languages (Graduate Certificate), including teaching English as a second language (TESL) or foreign language. *Unit head:* Dr. Cynthia DeLuca, Associate Vice President and Assistant Vice Provost, 813-974-3077, Fax: 813-974-7061, E-mail: deluca@usf.edu. *Application contact:* Owen Hooper, Director, Summer and Alternative Calendar Programs, 813-974-6917, E-mail: hooper@usf.edu.
Website: http://www.usf.edu/innovative-education/

The University of Tampa, Sykes College of Business, Tampa, FL 33606-1490. Offers accounting (MS); business analytics (MBA); cybersecurity (MBA, MS); entrepreneurship (MBA, MS); finance (MBA, MS); information systems management (MBA); innovation management (MBA); international business (MBA); marketing (MBA, MS); nonprofit management (MBA, Certificate). *Accreditation:* AACSB. *Program availability:* Part-time, evening/weekend. *Faculty:* 38 full-time (14 women), 6 part-time/adjunct (1 woman). *Students:* 229 full-time (1 woman), 115 part-time (51 women); includes 51 minority (26 Black or African American, non-Hispanic/Latino; 11 Asian, non-Hispanic/Latino; 1 Native Hawaiian or other Pacific Islander, non-Hispanic/Latino; 13 Two or more races, non-Hispanic/Latino), 182 international. Average age 28. 1,305 applicants, 39% accepted, 192 enrolled. In 2017, 266 master's awarded. *Degree requirements:* For master's, capstone. *Entrance requirements:* For master's, GMAT or GRE, official transcripts from all colleges and/or universities previously attended, resume, personal statement, letters of recommendation. Additional exam requirements/recommendations for international students: Required—TOEFL (minimum score 577 paper-based; 90 iBT), IELTS (minimum score 7.5). *Application deadline:* Applications are processed on a rolling basis. Application fee: $40. Electronic applications accepted. *Expenses:* Contact institution. *Financial support:* In 2017–18, 116 students received support. Career-related internships or fieldwork, scholarships/grants, and unspecified assistantships available. Financial award applicants required to submit FAFSA. *Faculty research:* Job market signaling, on-line shopping behaviors and social media, the Tampa Bay economy, digital literacy, entrepreneurship in small businesses. *Unit head:* Dr. Natasha F. Veltri, Associate Dean, 813-253-6289, E-mail: nveltri@ut.edu. *Application contact:* Chanelle Cox, Staff Assistant, Admissions for Graduate and Continuing Studies, 813-253-6249, E-mail: ccox@ut.edu.
Website: http://www.ut.edu/business/

The University of Tennessee at Chattanooga, Department of Political Science and Public Service, Chattanooga, TN 37403. Offers local government management (MPA); non profit management (MPA); public administration (MPA); public administration and non-profit management (Postbaccalaureate Certificate). *Program availability:* Part-time, evening/weekend. *Students:* 14 full-time (7 women), 12 part-time (9 women); includes 8 minority (5 Black or African American, non-Hispanic/Latino; 2 Asian, non-Hispanic/Latino; 1 Two or more races, non-Hispanic/Latino). Average age 30. 18 applicants, 100% accepted, 11 enrolled. In 2017, 7 master's, 1 other advanced degree awarded. *Degree requirements:* For master's, comprehensive exam, thesis or alternative, internship. *Entrance requirements:* For master's, GRE General Test; for Postbaccalaureate Certificate, bachelor's degree with related experience or master's degree. Additional exam requirements/recommendations for international students: Required—TOEFL (minimum score 550 paper-based; 79 iBT), IELTS (minimum score 6). *Application deadline:* For fall admission, 6/15 priority date for domestic students, 7/1 for international students; for spring admission, 11/1 priority date for domestic students, 11/1 for international students. Applications are processed on a rolling basis. Application fee: $35 ($40 for international students). Electronic applications accepted. *Expenses:* Contact institution. *Financial support:* Research assistantships, career-related internships or fieldwork, scholarships/grants, and unspecified assistantships available. Support available to part-time students. Financial award application deadline: 7/1; financial award applicants required to submit FAFSA. *Faculty research:* Organizational cultures and renewal, management theory, public policy, policy analysis, nonprofit organization. *Unit head:* Dr. Michelle D. Deardorf, Department Head, 423-425-4231, Fax: 423-425-2373, E-mail: michelle-deardorff@utc.edu. *Application contact:* Dr. Joanne Romagni, Dean of the Graduate School, 423-425-4478, Fax: 423-425-5223, E-mail: joanne-romagni@utc.edu.
Website: http://www.utc.edu/political-science-public-service/

The University of Texas at Dallas, School of Economic, Political and Policy Sciences, Program in Public and Nonprofit Management, Richardson, TX 75080. Offers applied sociology (MS); public affairs (MPA, PhD). *Accreditation:* NASPAA. *Program availability:* Part-time, evening/weekend. *Faculty:* 12 full-time (5 women), 3 part-time/adjunct (1 woman). *Students:* 37 full-time (27 women), 81 part-time (53 women); includes 48 minority (17 Black or African American, non-Hispanic/Latino; 1 American Indian or Alaska Native, non-Hispanic/Latino; 6 Asian, non-Hispanic/Latino; 17 Hispanic/Latino; 7 Two or more races, non-Hispanic/Latino), 19 international. Average age 37. 60 applicants, 62% accepted, 21 enrolled. In 2017, 14 master's, 4 doctorates awarded. *Degree requirements:* For master's, internship; for doctorate, thesis/dissertation. *Entrance requirements:* For master's and doctorate, GRE (minimum combined score of 1000 on verbal and quantitative), minimum GPA of 3.0 in upper-level course work in field. Additional exam requirements/recommendations for international students:

Required—TOEFL (minimum score 550 paper-based). *Application deadline:* For fall admission, 7/15 for domestic students, 5/1 priority date for international students; for spring admission, 11/15 for domestic students, 9/1 priority date for international students. Applications are processed on a rolling basis. Application fee: $50 ($100 for international students). Electronic applications accepted. *Expenses:* Tuition, state resident: full-time $12,916; part-time $718 per credit hour. Tuition, nonresident: full-time $25,252; part-time $1403 per credit hour. *Financial support:* In 2017–18, 68 students received support, including 10 teaching assistantships with partial tuition reimbursements available (averaging $13,100 per year); research assistantships with partial tuition reimbursements available, career-related internships or fieldwork, Federal Work-Study, institutionally sponsored loans, and scholarships/grants also available. Support available to part-time students. Financial award application deadline: 4/30; financial award applicants required to submit FAFSA. *Faculty research:* Corporate citizenship and urban problem solving, policy analysis, presidential decision-making, hazardous material safety, emergency management. *Unit head:* Dr. Doug Goodman, Program Head, 972-883-4969, Fax: 972-883-2735, E-mail: doug.goodman@utdallas.edu. *Application contact:* Rita Medford, Graduate Program Administrator, 972-883-4932, Fax: 972-883-2735, E-mail: medford@utdallas.edu.
Website: http://www.utdallas.edu/epps/public-affairs/

University of the Sacred Heart, Graduate Programs, Program in Nonprofit Organization Administration, San Juan, PR 00914-0383. Offers MBA.

University of the West, Department of Business Administration, Rosemead, CA 91770. Offers business administration (EMBA); computer information systems (MBA); finance (MBA); international business (MBA); nonprofit organization management (MBA). *Program availability:* Part-time, evening/weekend. *Entrance requirements:* Additional exam requirements/recommendations for international students: Required—TOEFL.

The University of Toledo, College of Graduate Studies, College of Languages, Literature and Social Sciences, Department of Political Science and Public Administration, Toledo, OH 43606-3390. Offers health care policy and administration (Certificate); management of non-profit organizations (Certificate); municipal administration (Certificate); political science (MA); public administration (MPA); JD/MPA. *Program availability:* Part-time. *Degree requirements:* For master's, comprehensive exam (for some programs), thesis. *Entrance requirements:* For master's, GRE General Test, minimum cumulative point-hour ratio of 2.7 (3.0 for MPA) for all previous academic work, three letters of recommendation, statement of purpose, transcripts from all prior institutions attended; for Certificate, minimum cumulative point-hour ratio of 2.7 for all previous academic work, three letters of recommendation, statement of purpose, transcripts from all prior institutions attended. Additional exam requirements/recommendations for international students: Required—TOEFL (minimum score 550 paper-based; 80 iBT). Electronic applications accepted. *Faculty research:* Economic development, health care, Third World, criminal justice, Eastern Europe.

University of West Georgia, College of Social Sciences, Carrollton, GA 30118. Offers criminology (MA); data analysis and evaluation methods (Postbaccalaureate Certificate); European Union studies (Postbaccalaureate Certificate); integrative health systems (Postbaccalaureate Certificate); nonprofit management and community development (Postbaccalaureate Certificate); psychology (MA, PhD), including consciousness and society (PhD); public administration (MPA); public management (Postbaccalaureate Certificate); sociology (MA). *Program availability:* Part-time, evening/weekend, 100% online, blended/hybrid learning. *Faculty:* 48 full-time (22 women). *Students:* 124 full-time (84 women), 73 part-time (46 women); includes 69 minority (56 Black or African American, non-Hispanic/Latino; 4 Asian, non-Hispanic/Latino; 6 Hispanic/Latino; 3 Two or more races, non-Hispanic/Latino), 10 international. Average age 32. 95 applicants, 89% accepted, 63 enrolled. In 2017, 44 master's, 2 doctorates, 4 other advanced degrees awarded. *Entrance requirements:* Additional exam requirements/recommendations for international students: Required—TOEFL (minimum score 523 paper-based; 69 iBT); Recommended—IELTS (minimum score 6.5). *Application deadline:* For fall admission, 7/15 for domestic students, 6/1 for international students; for spring admission, 11/30 for domestic students, 10/15 for international students; for summer admission, 5/15 for domestic students, 3/30 for international students. Applications are processed on a rolling basis. Application fee: $40. Electronic applications accepted. Tuition and fees vary according to degree level and program. *Financial support:* Fellowships, research assistantships, teaching assistantships, career-related internships or fieldwork, Federal Work-Study, institutionally sponsored loans, scholarships/grants, and unspecified assistantships available. Support available to part-time students. Financial award application deadline: 4/1; financial award applicants required to submit FAFSA. *Unit head:* Dr. N. Jane McCandless, Dean of Social Sciences, 678-839-5170, Fax: 678-839-5171, E-mail: jmccandl@westga.edu. *Application contact:* Dr. Toby Ziglar, Assistant Dean of the Graduate School, 678-839-1394, Fax: 678-839-1395, E-mail: graduate@westga.edu.
Website: https://www.westga.edu/coss

University of Wisconsin–Milwaukee, Graduate School, College of Letters and Science, Department of Public and Nonprofit Administration, Milwaukee, WI 53201-0413. Offers public administration (MPA), including general public administration, municipal management, non-profit management. *Program availability:* Part-time. *Students:* 15 full-time (8 women), 10 part-time (5 women); includes 9 minority (1 Black or African American, non-Hispanic/Latino; 8 Two or more races, non-Hispanic/Latino). Average age 31. 17 applicants, 76% accepted, 9 enrolled. In 2017, 12 master's awarded. *Entrance requirements:* For master's, GRE General Test, minimum GPA of 3.0. Additional exam requirements/recommendations for international students: Required—TOEFL (minimum score 550 paper-based; 79 iBT), IELTS (minimum score 6.5). *Application deadline:* For fall admission, 1/1 priority date for domestic students; for spring admission, 9/1 for domestic students. Application fee: $56 ($96 for international students). Electronic applications accepted. *Financial support:* Fellowships, research assistantships, teaching assistantships, career-related internships or fieldwork, health care benefits, and unspecified assistantships available. Support available to part-time students. Financial award application deadline: 4/15; financial award applicants required to submit FAFSA. *Unit head:* Douglas Ihrke, Department Chair, 414-229-4732, E-mail: dihrke@uwm.edu. *Application contact:* General Information Contact, 414-229-4982, Fax: 414-229-6967, E-mail: gradschool@uwm.edu.
Website: https://uwm.edu/public-nonprofit-administration/

University of Wisconsin–Milwaukee, Graduate School, Helen Bader School of Social Welfare, Department of Social Work, Milwaukee, WI 53201-0413. Offers applied gerontology (Graduate Certificate); nonprofit management (Graduate Certificate); social welfare (PhD); social work (MSW, PhD). *Accreditation:* CSWE. *Program availability:* Part-time. *Students:* 194 full-time (169 women), 111 part-time (97 women); includes 83 minority (36 Black or African American, non-Hispanic/Latino; 1 American Indian or Alaska Native, non-Hispanic/Latino; 9 Asian, non-Hispanic/Latino; 1 Hispanic/Latino; 36 Two or more races, non-Hispanic/Latino), 3 international. Average age 31. 361 applicants, 61% accepted, 128 enrolled. In 2017, 156 master's, 68 other advanced degrees awarded. *Entrance requirements:* For doctorate, GRE, bachelor's degree. Additional exam requirements/recommendations for international students: Required—TOEFL (minimum score 550 paper-based; 79 iBT), IELTS (minimum score 6.5). *Application deadline:* For fall admission, 1/1 priority date for domestic students; for

Nonprofit Management

spring admission, 9/1 for domestic students. Application fee: $56 ($96 for international students). Electronic applications accepted. *Financial support:* Fellowships, research assistantships, teaching assistantships, career-related internships or fieldwork, health care benefits, unspecified assistantships, and project assistantships available. Support available to part-time students. Financial award application deadline: 4/15; financial award applicants required to submit FAFSA. *Application contact:* Deb Padgett, Associate Professor, Social Work, 414-229-6452, E-mail: dpadgett@uwm.edu. Website: http://uwm.edu/socialwelfare/academics/

University of Wisconsin–Milwaukee, Graduate School, Lubar School of Business, MS and Certificate Business Programs, Milwaukee, WI 53201-0413. Offers business analytics (Graduate Certificate); enterprise resource planning (Graduate Certificate); information technology management (MS); investment management (Graduate Certificate); nonprofit management (Graduate Certificate); nonprofit management and leadership (MS); state and local taxation (Graduate Certificate). *Students:* 164 full-time (87 women), 120 part-time (51 women); includes 51 minority (15 Black or African American, non-Hispanic/Latino; 18 Asian, non-Hispanic/Latino; 3 Hispanic/Latino; 15 Two or more races, non-Hispanic/Latino), 55 international. Average age 31. 227 applicants, 54% accepted, 74 enrolled. In 2017, 157 master's, 21 other advanced degrees awarded. *Entrance requirements:* Additional exam requirements/recommendations for international students: Required—TOEFL (minimum score 550 paper-based; 79 iBT), IELTS (minimum score 6.5). Application fee: $56 ($96 for international students). Electronic applications accepted. *Financial support:* Fellowships, research assistantships, teaching assistantships, health care benefits, unspecified assistantships, and project assistantships available. Financial award applicants required to submit FAFSA. *Application contact:* General Information Contact, 414-229-4982, Fax: 414-229-6967, E-mail: gradschool@uwm.edu.

Upper Iowa University, Online Master's Programs, Fayette, IA 52142-1857. Offers accounting (MBA); corporate financial management (MBA); emergency management and homeland security (MPA); general management (MBA); general studies (MPA); government administration (MPA); health and human services (MPA); human resources management (MBA); nonprofit organizational management (MPA); organizational development (MBA); public management (MPA); sport administration (MSA). MBA also available at Madison, WI campus. *Program availability:* Part-time, online learning. *Degree requirements:* For master's, research project. *Entrance requirements:* For master's, GMAT, GRE, or minimum GPA of 2.7 during last 60 hours. Additional exam requirements/recommendations for international students: Required—TOEFL (minimum score 570 paper-based). Electronic applications accepted. *Faculty research:* Total quality management, teams, organization culture and climate, management.

Villanova University, Graduate School of Liberal Arts and Sciences, Department of Public Administration, Villanova, PA 19085-1699. Offers city management (Certificate); nonprofit management (Certificate); public administration (MPA, Certificate). *Accreditation:* NASPAA. *Program availability:* Part-time, evening/weekend, 100% online. *Faculty:* 19. *Students:* 136 full-time (71 women), 64 part-time (30 women); includes 57 minority (29 Black or African American, non-Hispanic/Latino; 2 American Indian or Alaska Native, non-Hispanic/Latino; 6 Asian, non-Hispanic/Latino; 16 Hispanic/Latino; 4 Two or more races, non-Hispanic/Latino), 4 international. Average age 35. 66 applicants, 100% accepted, 22 enrolled. In 2017, 79 master's, 29 other advanced degrees awarded. *Degree requirements:* For master's, comprehensive exam. *Entrance requirements:* For master's, GRE General Test, minimum GPA of 3.0, statement of goals, 3 letters of recommendation. Additional exam requirements/recommendations for international students: Required—TOEFL. *Application deadline:* For fall admission, 5/1 for international students; for spring admission, 10/15 for international students. Applications are processed on a rolling basis. Application fee: $50. Electronic applications accepted. *Financial support:* Career-related internships or fieldwork, scholarships/grants, and unspecified assistantships available. Financial award application deadline: 3/15; financial award applicants required to submit FAFSA. *Unit head:* Dr. Catherine Wilson, Program Director, 610-519-7851. Website: http://www1.villanova.edu/villanova/artsci/publicadmin.html

Virginia Commonwealth University, Graduate School, College of Humanities and Sciences, Program in Nonprofit Management, Richmond, VA 23284-9005. Offers Graduate Certificate. *Program availability:* Part-time. *Entrance requirements:* Additional exam requirements/recommendations for international students: Required—TOEFL (minimum score 600 paper-based; 100 iBT); Recommended—IELTS (minimum score 6.5). Electronic applications accepted.

Virginia Polytechnic Institute and State University, VT Online, Blacksburg, VA 24061. Offers advanced transportation systems (Certificate); aerospace engineering (MS); agricultural and life sciences (MSLFS); business information systems (Graduate Certificate); career and technical education (MS); civil engineering (MS); computer engineering (M Eng, MS); decision support systems (Graduate Certificate); eLearning leadership (MA); electrical engineering (M Eng, MS); engineering administration (MEA); environmental engineering (Certificate); environmental politics and policy (Graduate Certificate); environmental sciences and engineering (MS); foundations of political analysis (Graduate Certificate); health product risk management (Graduate Certificate); industrial and systems engineering (MS); information policy and society (Graduate Certificate); information security (Graduate Certificate); information technology (MIT); instructional technology (MA); integrative STEM education (MA Ed); liberal arts (Graduate Certificate); life sciences: health product risk management (MS); natural resources (MNR, Graduate Certificate); networking (Graduate Certificate); nonprofit and nongovernmental organization management (Graduate Certificate); ocean engineering (MS); political science (MA); security studies (Graduate Certificate); software development (Graduate Certificate). *Expenses:* Tuition, state resident: full-time $15,072; part-time $718.50 per credit hour. Tuition, nonresident: full-time $28,810; part-time $1448.25 per credit hour. *Required fees:* $2741; $502 per semester. Tuition and fees vary according to course load, campus/location and program.

Walden University, Graduate Programs, School of Public Policy and Administration, Minneapolis, MN 55401. Offers criminal justice (MPA, MPP, MS, Graduate Certificate), including emergency management (MS, PhD), general program (MS), global leadership (MS, PhD), homeland security and policy coordination (MS, PhD), law and public policy (MS, PhD), policy analysis (MS, PhD), public management and leadership (MS, PhD), self-designed (MS), terrorism, mediation, and peace (MS, PhD); criminal justice and executive management (MS), including global leadership (MS, PhD); criminal justice leadership and executive management (MS), including emergency management (MS, PhD), general program, homeland security and policy coordination (MS, PhD), law and public policy (MS, PhD), policy analysis (MS, PhD), public management and leadership (MS, PhD), self-designed, terrorism, mediation, and peace (MS, PhD); emergency management (MPA, MPP, MS), including criminal justice (MS, PhD), general program (MS), homeland security (MS), public management and leadership (MS, PhD), terrorism and emergency management (MS); general program (MPA, MPP); global leadership (MPA, MPP); government management (Graduate Certificate); health policy (MPA, MPP); homeland security (Graduate Certificate); homeland security and policy coordination (MPA, MPP); international nongovernmental organizations (MPA, MPP); law and public policy (MPA, MPP); local government management for sustainable communities (MPA, MPP); nonprofit management (Graduate Certificate); nonprofit

management and leadership (MPA, MPP, MS), including global leadership (MS, PhD), international nongovernmental organization (MS), local government for sustainable communities (MS), self designed (MS); online teaching in higher education (Post-Master's Certificate); policy analysis (MPA); public management and leadership (MPA, MPP, Graduate Certificate); public policy (Graduate Certificate); public policy and administration (PhD), including criminal justice (MS, PhD), emergency management (MS, PhD), global leadership (MS, PhD), health policy, homeland security and policy coordination (MS, PhD), international nongovernmental organizations, law and public policy (MS, PhD), local government management for sustainable communities, nonprofit management and leadership, policy analysis (MS, PhD), public management and leadership (MS, PhD), terrorism, mediation, and peace (MS, PhD); strategic planning and public policy (Graduate Certificate); terrorism, mediation, and peace (MPA, MPP). *Program availability:* Part-time, evening/weekend, online only, 100% online. *Degree requirements:* For doctorate, thesis/dissertation, residency. *Entrance requirements:* For master's, bachelor's degree or higher; minimum GPA of 2.5; official transcripts; goal statement (for some programs); access to computer and Internet; for doctorate, master's degree or higher; three years of related professional or academic experience (preferred); minimum GPA of 3.0; goal statement and current resume (for select programs); official transcripts; access to computer and Internet; for other advanced degree, relevant work experience; access to computer and Internet. Additional exam requirements/recommendations for international students: Required—TOEFL (minimum score 550 paper-based, 79 iBT), IELTS (minimum score 6.5), Michigan English Language Assessment Battery (minimum score 82), or PTE (minimum score 53). Electronic applications accepted.

Walden University, Graduate Programs, School of Social Work and Human Services, Minneapolis, MN 55401. Offers addictions and social work (DSW); advanced clinical practice (MSW); clinical expertise (DSW); criminal justice (DSW); disaster, crisis, and intervention (DSW); family studies and interventions (DSW); human and social services (PhD), including advanced research, community and social services, community intervention and leadership, conflict management, criminal justice, disaster crisis and intervention, family studies and intervention, gerontology, global social services, higher education, human services and nonprofit administration, mental health facilitation; medical social work (DSW); military social work (MSW); policy practice (DSW); social work (PhD), including addictions and social work, clinical expertise, criminal justice, disaster, crisis and intervention, family studies and interventions, medical social work, policy practice, social work administration; social work administration (DSW); social work in healthcare (MSW); social work with children and families (MSW). *Accreditation:* CSWE. *Program availability:* Part-time, evening/weekend, online only, 100% online. *Degree requirements:* For master's, residency (for some programs); for doctorate, thesis/dissertation, residency. *Entrance requirements:* For master's, bachelor's degree or higher; minimum GPA of 2.5; official transcripts; goal statement (for some programs); access to computer and Internet; for doctorate, master's degree or higher; three years of related professional or academic experience (preferred); minimum GPA of 3.0; goal statement and current resume (for select programs); official transcripts; access to computer and Internet. Additional exam requirements/recommendations for international students: Required—TOEFL (minimum score 550 paper-based, 79 iBT), IELTS (minimum score 6.5), Michigan English Language Assessment Battery (minimum score 82), or PTE (minimum score 53). Electronic applications accepted.

Warner Pacific University, Graduate Programs, Portland, OR 97215-4099. Offers human services (MA); not-for-profit leadership (MS); organizational leadership (MS); teaching (MAT). *Program availability:* Part-time, evening/weekend. *Degree requirements:* For master's, thesis or alternative, presentation of defense. *Entrance requirements:* For master's, interview, minimum GPA of 2.5, letters of recommendation. *Faculty research:* New Testament studies, nineteenth-century Wesleyan theology, preaching and church growth, Christian ethics.

Wayne State University, College of Liberal Arts and Sciences, Department of Political Science, Detroit, MI 48202. Offers political science (MA, PhD); public administration (MPA), including economic development policy and management, health and human services policy and management, human and fiscal resource management, nonprofit policy and management, organizational behavior and management, urban and metropolitan policy and management; JD/MA. *Accreditation:* NASPAA. *Faculty:* 18. *Students:* 48 full-time (20 women), 68 part-time (36 women); includes 37 minority (26 Black or African American, non-Hispanic/Latino; 3 Asian, non-Hispanic/Latino; 2 Hispanic/Latino; 6 Two or more races, non-Hispanic/Latino), 6 international. Average age 32. 105 applicants, 39% accepted, 20 enrolled. In 2017, 17 master's, 3 doctorates awarded. *Degree requirements:* For master's, comprehensive exam (for some programs), thesis (for some programs); for doctorate, thesis/dissertation. *Entrance requirements:* For master's, GRE General Test, substantial undergraduate preparation in the social sciences, minimum upper-division undergraduate GPA of 3.0, two letters of recommendation, personal statement; for doctorate, GRE General Test, 3 letters of recommendation, personal statement; interview. Additional exam requirements/recommendations for international students: Required—TOEFL (minimum score 550 paper-based; 79 iBT), TWE (minimum score 5.5), Michigan English Language Assessment Battery (minimum score 85); Recommended—IELTS (minimum score 6.5). *Application deadline:* For fall admission, 5/15 for domestic students, 5/1 priority date for international students; for winter admission, 10/15 for domestic students, 9/1 priority date for international students. Applications are processed on a rolling basis. Application fee: $50. Electronic applications accepted. *Expenses:* Contact institution. *Financial support:* In 2017–18, 44 students received support, including 6 fellowships with tuition reimbursements available (averaging $11,698 per year), 12 teaching assistantships with tuition reimbursements available (averaging $18,534 per year); research assistantships with tuition reimbursements available, scholarships/grants, health care benefits, and unspecified assistantships also available. Financial award applicants required to submit FAFSA. *Faculty research:* American government and politics, comparative politics, political methodology, political theory, public administration, public law, public policy, world politics/international relations, formal theory/modeling, gender and politics, international law, peace research, political economy, political psychology, politics of developing countries, race, religion, and ethnicity, urban politics. *Unit head:* Dr. Daniel Geller, Professor and Chair, 313-577-6328, E-mail: dgeller@wayne.edu. *Application contact:* Dr. Sharon Lean, Graduate Director, 313-577-2630, E-mail: gradpolisci@wayne.edu. Website: http://clas.wayne.edu/politicalscience/

Webster University, George Herbert Walker School of Business and Technology, Department of Management, St. Louis, MO 63119-3194. Offers business and organizational security management (MA); digital marketing management (Graduate Certificate); government contracting (Graduate Certificate); health administration (MHA); health care management (MA); health services management (MA); human resources development (MA); human resources management (MA); information technology management (MA, MS); management (D Mgt); management and leadership (MA); marketing (MA); nonprofit leadership (MA); nonprofit revenue development (Graduate Certificate); organizational development (Graduate Certificate); procurement and acquisitions management (MA); public administration (MPA); space systems operations management (MS). *Program availability:* Part-time, evening/weekend, online learning. *Degree requirements:* For master's, thesis (for some programs); for doctorate, thesis/

dissertation, written exam. *Entrance requirements:* For doctorate, GMAT, 3 years of work experience, MBA. Additional exam requirements/recommendations for international students: Required—TOEFL.

West Chester University of Pennsylvania, College of Business and Public Management, Department of Public Policy and Administration, West Chester, PA 19383. Offers administration (Certificate); non profit administration (Certificate); nonprofit administration (MPA); public administration (MPA); public policy and administration (MPA, DPA). *Accreditation:* NASPAA. *Program availability:* Part-time, evening/weekend, 100% online. *Students:* 69 full-time (32 women), 149 part-time (77 women); includes 82 minority (67 Black or African American, non-Hispanic/Latino; 1 Asian, non-Hispanic/Latino; 11 Hispanic/Latino; 3 Two or more races, non-Hispanic/Latino), 8 international. Average age 34. 117 applicants, 86% accepted, 67 enrolled. In 2017, 32 master's, 12 other advanced degrees awarded. Terminal master's awarded for partial completion of doctoral program. *Degree requirements:* For master's, capstone project. *Entrance requirements:* For master's, statement of professional goals, resume, two letters of reference, academic transcripts. Additional exam requirements/recommendations for international students: Required—TOEFL or IELTS. *Application deadline:* For fall admission, 5/15 for international students; for spring admission, 10/15 for international students. Applications are processed on a rolling basis. Application fee: $50. Electronic applications accepted. *Expenses:* Tuition, state resident: full-time $9000; part-time $500 per credit. Tuition, nonresident: full-time $13,500; part-time $750 per credit. *Required fees:* $2959; $149.79 per credit. *Financial support:* Scholarships/grants and unspecified assistantships available. Financial award application deadline: 2/15; financial award applicants required to submit FAFSA. *Faculty research:* Public policy, economic development, research methodology, public administration, nonprofit administration. *Unit head:* Dr. Jeremy Phillips, Department Chair/Director of DPA Program, 610-436-2016, E-mail: jphillips@wcupa.edu. *Application contact:* Dr. Alison Turner, MPA Graduate Coordinator, 610-436-2438, E-mail: aturner@wcupa.edu.
Website: http://www.wcupa.edu/business-publicManagement/mpa/

Western Michigan University, Graduate College, College of Arts and Sciences, School of Public Affairs and Administration, Kalamazoo, MI 49008. Offers health care administration (MPA, Graduate Certificate); nonprofit leadership and administration (Graduate Certificate); public administration (PhD). *Accreditation:* NASPAA (one or more programs are accredited). *Degree requirements:* For doctorate, thesis/dissertation.

Westfield State University, College of Graduate and Continuing Education, Department of Political Science, Westfield, MA 01086. Offers criminal justice administration (MPA); non-profit management (MPA); public management (MPA). *Program availability:* Part-time, evening/weekend. *Faculty:* 3 full-time (1 woman), 3 part-time/adjunct (2 women). *Students:* 9 full-time (2 women), 40 part-time (17 women); includes 13 minority (2 Black or African American, non-Hispanic/Latino; 2 American Indian or Alaska Native, non-Hispanic/Latino; 8 Hispanic/Latino; 1 Two or more races, non-Hispanic/Latino). Average age 33. 19 applicants, 100% accepted, 14 enrolled. In 2017, 16 master's awarded. *Degree requirements:* For master's, comprehensive exam, thesis (for some programs). *Entrance requirements:* For master's, GRE General Test or MAT, minimum undergraduate GPA of 2.8. Additional exam requirements/recommendations for international students: Recommended—TOEFL (minimum score 550 paper-based; 79 iBT). *Application deadline:* For fall admission, 7/1 for domestic students; for spring admission, 11/1 for domestic students; for summer admission, 4/1 for domestic students. Applications are processed on a rolling basis. Application fee: $50. *Expenses:* Tuition, state resident: part-time $332 per credit. Tuition, nonresident: part-time $332 per credit. *Required fees:* $75 per semester. Tuition and fees vary according to program. *Financial support:* Unspecified assistantships available. Financial award application deadline: 3/1; financial award applicants required to submit FAFSA. *Unit head:* Dr. Hugh Jo, Chair, 413-572-8806, Fax: 413-572-8168, E-mail: hjo@westfield.ma.edu. *Application contact:* Shelly Henrichon, Admissions Coordinator, 413-572-8022, Fax: 413-572-5227, E-mail: mhenrichon@westfield.ma.edu.

Worcester State University, Graduate School, Program in Non-Profit Management, Worcester, MA 01602-2597. Offers MS. *Program availability:* Part-time, evening/weekend. *Faculty:* 3 full-time, 1 part-time/adjunct. *Students:* 1 (woman) full-time, 8 part-time (6 women); includes 1 minority (Black or African American, non-Hispanic/Latino), 1 international. Average age 38. 9 applicants, 67% accepted, 2 enrolled. In 2017, 7 master's awarded. *Degree requirements:* For master's, comprehensive exam (for some programs), thesis. *Entrance requirements:* For master's, GRE General Test or MAT. Additional exam requirements/recommendations for international students: Required—TOEFL (minimum score 550 paper-based; 79 iBT). *Application deadline:* For fall admission, 6/15 for domestic and international students; for spring admission, 11/1 for domestic and international students; for summer admission, 4/1 for domestic and international students. Applications are processed on a rolling basis. Application fee: $50. Electronic applications accepted. *Expenses:* Tuition, state resident: full-time $3042; part-time $169 per credit hour. Tuition, nonresident: full-time $3042; part-time $169 per credit hour. *Required fees:* $2754; $153 per credit hour. *Financial support:* Career-related internships or fieldwork, scholarships/grants, and unspecified assistantships available. Financial award application deadline: 3/1; financial award applicants required to submit FAFSA. *Unit head:* Dr. Shiko Gathuo, Coordinator, 508-929-8892, E-mail: agathuo@worcester.edu. *Application contact:* Sara Grady, Associate Dean, Graduate Studies and Professional Development, 508-929-8130, E-mail: sara.grady@worcester.edu.

Section 16
Organizational Studies

This section contains a directory of institutions offering graduate work in organizational studies. Additional information about programs listed in the directory but not augmented by an in-depth entry may be obtained by writing directly to the dean of a graduate school or chair of a department at the address given in the directory.

For programs offering related work, see also in this book *Business Administration and Management, Human Resources,* and *Industrial and Manufacturing Management.* In another guide in this series:

Graduate Programs in the Humanities, Arts & Social Sciences

See *Communication and Media* and *Public, Regional, and Industrial Affairs*

CONTENTS

Organizational Behavior

Argosy University, Chicago, Illinois School of Professional Psychology, Doctoral Program in Clinical Psychology, Chicago, IL 60601. Offers child and adolescent psychology (Psy D); client-centered and experiential psychotherapies (Psy D); diversity and multicultural psychology (Psy D); family psychology (Psy D); forensic psychology (Psy D); health psychology (Psy D); neuropsychology (Psy D); organizational consulting (Psy D); psychoanalytic psychology (Psy D); psychology and spirituality (Psy D). *Accreditation:* APA.

Arizona State University at the Tempe campus, W. P. Carey School of Business, Program in Business Administration, Tempe, AZ 85287-4906. Offers entrepreneurship (MBA); finance (MBA); health sector management (MBA); international business (MBA); leadership (MBA); marketing (MBA); organizational behavior (PhD); strategic management (PhD); supply chain management (MBA, PhD); JD/MBA; MBA/M Acc; MBA/M Arch. *Accreditation:* AACSB. *Program availability:* Part-time, evening/weekend, online learning. Terminal master's awarded for partial completion of doctoral program. *Degree requirements:* For master's, thesis or alternative, internship, interactive Program of Study (iPOS) submitted before completing 50 percent of required credit hours; for doctorate, comprehensive exam, thesis/dissertation, interactive Program of Study (iPOS) submitted before completing 50 percent of required credit hours. *Entrance requirements:* For master's, GMAT, minimum GPA of 3.0 in last 2 years of work leading to bachelor's degree, 2 letters of recommendation, professional resume, official transcripts, 3 essays; for doctorate, GMAT or GRE, minimum GPA of 3.0 in last 2 years of work leading to bachelor's degree, 3 letters of recommendation, resume, personal statement/essay. Additional exam requirements/recommendations for international students: Required—TOEFL (minimum score 550 paper-based; 80 iBT), IELTS (minimum score 6.5). Electronic applications accepted. *Expenses:* Contact institution.

A.T. Still University, College of Graduate Health Studies, Kirksville, MO 63501. Offers dental public health (MPH); exercise and sport psychology (Certificate); fundamentals of education (Certificate); geriatric exercise science (Certificate); global health (Certificate); health administration (MHA, DHA); health professions (Ed D); health sciences (DH Sc); kinesiology (MS); leadership and organizational behavior (Certificate); public health (MPH); sports conditioning (Certificate). *Program availability:* Part-time, evening/weekend, online, 100% online, blended/hybrid learning. *Faculty:* 28 full-time (18 women), 83 part-time/adjunct (43 women). *Students:* 537 full-time (334 women), 516 part-time (316 women); includes 397 minority (171 Black or African American, non-Hispanic/Latino; 14 American Indian or Alaska Native, non-Hispanic/Latino; 84 Asian, non-Hispanic/Latino; 106 Hispanic/Latino; 1 Native Hawaiian or other Pacific Islander, non-Hispanic/Latino; 21 Two or more races, non-Hispanic/Latino), 43 international. Average age 36. 392 applicants, 84% accepted, 270 enrolled. In 2017, 138 master's, 102 doctorates, 116 other advanced degrees awarded. *Degree requirements:* For master's, thesis, integrated terminal project, practicum; for doctorate, thesis/dissertation. *Entrance requirements:* For master's, minimum GPA of 2.5, bachelor's degree or equivalent, essay, resume, English proficiency; for doctorate, minimum GPA of 2.5, master's or terminal degree, essay, past experience in relevant field, resume, English proficiency. Additional exam requirements/recommendations for international students: Required—TOEFL (minimum score 550 paper-based; 80 iBT). *Application deadline:* For fall admission, 6/26 for domestic students, 5/20 for international students; for winter admission, 9/11 for domestic students, 9/12 for international students; for spring admission, 12/11 for domestic students, 12/12 for international students; for summer admission, 3/5 for domestic students, 3/6 for international students. Applications are processed on a rolling basis. Application fee: $70. Electronic applications accepted. *Financial support:* In 2017–18, 18 students received support. Scholarships/grants available. Financial award applicants required to submit FAFSA. *Faculty research:* Public health: influence of availability of comprehensive wellness resources online, student wellness, oral health care needs assessment of community, oral health knowledge and behaviors of Medicaid-eligible pregnant women and mothers of young children in relations to early childhood caries and tooth decay, alcohol use and alcohol related problems among college students. *Unit head:* Dr. Donald Altman, Dean, 480-219-6008, Fax: 660-626-2826, E-mail: daltman@atsu.edu. *Application contact:* Amie Waldemer, Associate Director, Online Admissions, 480-219-6146, E-mail: awaldemer@atsu.edu.
Website: http://www.atsu.edu/college-of-graduate-health-studies

Baruch College of the City University of New York, Zicklin School of Business, Department of Management, New York, NY 10010-5585. Offers entrepreneurship (MBA); management (PhD); operations management (MBA); organizational behavior/human resources management (MBA); sustainable business (MBA). PhD offered jointly with Graduate School and University Center of the City University of New York. *Program availability:* Part-time, evening/weekend. *Degree requirements:* For doctorate, comprehensive exam, thesis/dissertation. *Entrance requirements:* For master's, GMAT, 2 letters of recommendation, resume, 2 years of work experience; for doctorate, GMAT. Additional exam requirements/recommendations for international students: Required—TOEFL (minimum score 590 paper-based), TWE.

Benedictine University, Graduate Programs, Program in Management and Organizational Behavior, Lisle, IL 60532. Offers MS, PhD, MBA/MS, MPH/MS. *Program availability:* Part-time, evening/weekend. *Entrance requirements:* For master's, GMAT. Additional exam requirements/recommendations for international students: Required—TOEFL (minimum score 550 paper-based). Electronic applications accepted. *Faculty research:* Organizational change, transformation, development, learning organizations, career transitions for academics.

Boston College, Carroll School of Management, Department of Management and Organization, Chestnut Hill, MA 02467-3800. Offers PhD. *Degree requirements:* For doctorate, comprehensive exam, thesis/dissertation, teaching experience. *Entrance requirements:* For doctorate, GMAT or GRE, letters of recommendation, resume, transcripts. Additional exam requirements/recommendations for international students: Required—TOEFL (minimum score 100 iBT), IELTS (minimum score 7.5), or PTE (minimum score 68). Electronic applications accepted. *Faculty research:* Organizational transformation, mergers and acquisitions, managerial effectiveness, organizational change, organizational structure.

Brooklyn College of the City University of New York, School of Natural and Behavioral Sciences, Department of Psychology, Brooklyn, NY 11210-2889. Offers experimental psychology (MA); industrial and organizational psychology (MA), including human relations, organizational behavior; mental health counseling (MA); psychology (PhD). *Program availability:* Part-time. *Degree requirements:* For master's, comprehensive exam, thesis (for some programs). *Entrance requirements:* For master's, minimum GPA of 3.0, 2 letters of recommendation, essay; for doctorate, GRE. Additional exam requirements/recommendations for international students: Required—TOEFL (minimum score 520 paper-based; 69 iBT). Electronic applications accepted.

California State University, East Bay, Office of Graduate Studies, College of Business and Economics, MBA Program, Option in Human Resources and Organizational Behavior, Hayward, CA 94542-3000. Offers MBA. *Program availability:* Part-time, evening/weekend. *Students:* 5 full-time (4 women), 17 part-time (15 women); includes 18 minority (4 Black or African American, non-Hispanic/Latino; 6 Asian, non-Hispanic/Latino; 5 Hispanic/Latino; 3 Two or more races, non-Hispanic/Latino), 2 international. Average age 33. 20 applicants, 35% accepted, 6 enrolled. In 2017, 10 master's awarded. *Degree requirements:* For master's, comprehensive exam or thesis. *Entrance requirements:* For master's, GMAT, minimum GPA of 2.75. Additional exam requirements/recommendations for international students: Required—TOEFL (minimum score 550 paper-based). *Application deadline:* For fall admission, 6/1 for domestic and international students. Application fee: $55. Electronic applications accepted. *Financial support:* Fellowships, career-related internships or fieldwork, Federal Work-Study, institutionally sponsored loans, and scholarships/grants available. Support available to part-time students. Financial award application deadline: 3/2; financial award applicants required to submit FAFSA. *Unit head:* Dr. Asha Rao, Program Advisor, 510-885-3290, E-mail: asha.rao@csueastbay.edu. *Application contact:* Philip Wiley, Administrative Support Coordinator, 510-885-3286, E-mail: philip.coleregis@csueastbay.edu.
Website: http://www20.csueastbay.edu/cbe/mba-options/Human-Resources-Management-Option.html

Carnegie Mellon University, Dietrich College of Humanities and Social Sciences, Department of Social and Decision Sciences, Pittsburgh, PA 15213-3891. Offers behavioral decision research (PhD); social and decision science (PhD); strategy, entrepreneurship, and technological change (PhD). Terminal master's awarded for partial completion of doctoral program. *Degree requirements:* For doctorate, comprehensive exam, thesis/dissertation, research paper. *Entrance requirements:* For doctorate, GRE General Test. Additional exam requirements/recommendations for international students: Required—TOEFL. Electronic applications accepted. *Faculty research:* Organization theory, political science, sociology, technology studies.

Carnegie Mellon University, Tepper School of Business, Organizational Behavior and Theory Program, Pittsburgh, PA 15213-3891. Offers PhD. *Degree requirements:* For doctorate, thesis/dissertation. *Entrance requirements:* For doctorate, GMAT or GRE General Test. Additional exam requirements/recommendations for international students: Required—TOEFL. *Faculty research:* Negotiation, organizational learning, interorganizational relations and strategy, group process and performance, communication process and electronic media, group goal setting, uncertainty in organizations, creation and effect of institutions and psychological contracts.

Case Western Reserve University, Weatherhead School of Management, Department of Organizational Behavior, Cleveland, OH 44106. Offers organizational behavior (PhD); positive organization development and change (MS). *Program availability:* Part-time, evening/weekend. *Degree requirements:* For doctorate, thesis/dissertation. *Entrance requirements:* For master's and doctorate, GMAT. *Expenses:* Tuition: Full-time $43,854; part-time $1827 per credit hour. *Required fees:* $50; $50 per credit hour. Tuition and fees vary according to course load and program. *Faculty research:* Social innovation in global management, competency-based learning, life-long learning, organizational theory, organizational change.

Clemson University, Graduate School, College of Business, Department of Management, Clemson, SC 29634. Offers business administration (PhD), including management information systems, strategy, entrepreneurship and organizational behavior, supply chain and operations management; management (MS). *Accreditation:* AACSB. *Faculty:* 34 full-time (12 women), 1 part-time/adjunct (0 women). *Students:* 14 full-time (3 women), 1 part-time (0 women), 9 international. Average age 33. 30 applicants, 13% accepted. In 2017, 4 master's, 4 doctorates awarded. Terminal master's awarded for partial completion of doctoral program. *Degree requirements:* For master's, comprehensive exam, thesis optional; for doctorate, comprehensive exam, thesis/dissertation. *Entrance requirements:* For master's and doctorate, GMAT or GRE General Test, unofficial transcripts, two letters of reference, curriculum vitae. Additional exam requirements/recommendations for international students: Required—TOEFL (minimum score 94 iBT), IELTS (minimum score 7), PTE (minimum score 64). *Application deadline:* For fall admission, 1/15 priority date for domestic and international students. Application fee: $80 ($90 for international students). Electronic applications accepted. *Expenses:* $6,564 per semester full-time resident, $12,538 per semester full-time non-resident, $743 per credit hour part-time resident, $1,486 per credit hour part-time non-resident, $1,203 per credit hour online, other fees may apply per session. *Financial support:* In 2017–18, 10 students received support, including 1 fellowship with partial tuition reimbursement available (averaging $1,000 per year), 1 research assistantship with partial tuition reimbursement available (averaging $12,000 per year), 2 teaching assistantships with partial tuition reimbursements available (averaging $18,770 per year); unspecified assistantships also available. Financial award application deadline: 1/15. *Faculty research:* Effective use of information technology in business, manufacturing and service operations strategy, lean operations and quality management, healthcare operations, behavioral market design. *Total annual research expenditures:* $89,179. *Unit head:* Dr. V. Sridharan, Department Chair, 864-656-2624, E-mail: suhas@clemson.edu. *Application contact:* Dr. Janis Miller, Graduate Program Coordinator, 864-656-3757, E-mail: janism@clemson.edu.
Website: https://www.clemson.edu/business/departments/management/

Cornell University, Graduate School, Graduate Field of Management, Ithaca, NY 14853. Offers accounting (PhD); finance (PhD); marketing (PhD); organizational behavior (PhD); production and operations management (PhD). *Accreditation:* AACSB. *Degree requirements:* For doctorate, comprehensive exam, thesis/dissertation. *Entrance requirements:* For doctorate, GMAT or GRE General Test. Additional exam requirements/recommendations for international students: Required—TOEFL (minimum score 600 paper-based; 77 iBT). Electronic applications accepted. *Expenses:* Contact institution. *Faculty research:* Operations and manufacturing.

Cornell University, Graduate School, Graduate Fields of Industrial and Labor Relations, Ithaca, NY 14853. Offers collective bargaining, labor law and labor history (MILR, MPS, MS, PhD); economic and social statistics (MILR); human resource studies (MILR, MPS, MS, PhD); industrial and labor relations problems (MILR, MPS, MS, PhD); international and comparative labor (MILR, MPS, MS, PhD); labor economics (MILR, MPS, MS, PhD); organizational behavior (MILR, MPS, MS, PhD). *Degree requirements:* For master's, thesis (MS); for doctorate, comprehensive exam, thesis/dissertation, teaching experience. *Entrance requirements:* For master's and doctorate, GMAT or GRE General Test, 2 academic recommendations. Additional exam requirements/recommendations for international students: Required—TOEFL (minimum score 550 paper-based; 77 iBT). Electronic applications accepted. *Expenses:* Contact institution.

Drexel University, LeBow College of Business, Program in Business Administration, Philadelphia, PA 19104-2875. Offers business administration (MBA, PhD, APC), including accounting (MBA, PhD), decision sciences (PhD), economics (MBA, PhD), finance (MBA, PhD), legal studies (MBA), management (MBA), marketing (MBA, PhD), organizational sciences (PhD), quantitative methods (MBA), strategic management (PhD). *Accreditation:* AACSB. *Program availability:* Part-time, evening/weekend, online learning. Terminal master's awarded for partial completion of doctoral program. *Entrance requirements:* For master's, GMAT, minimum GPA of 2.75; for doctorate, GMAT. Additional exam requirements/recommendations for international students: Required—TOEFL. Electronic applications accepted. *Faculty research:* Decision support systems, individual and group behavior, operations research, techniques and strategy.

Fairleigh Dickinson University, Florham Campus, Maxwell Becton College of Arts and Sciences, Department of Psychology, Program in Organizational Behavior, Madison, NJ 07940-1099. Offers organizational behavior (MA); organizational leadership (Certificate).

Florida Institute of Technology, College of Psychology and Liberal Arts, Program in Applied Behavior Analysis and Organizational Behavior Management, Melbourne, FL 32901-6975. Offers MS. *Program availability:* Part-time. *Students:* Average age 25. 36 applicants, 39% accepted, 7 enrolled. In 2017, 5 master's awarded. *Degree requirements:* For master's, comprehensive exam, thesis or alternative, minimum of 50 credits, all course grades of B or higher. *Entrance requirements:* For master's, GRE General Test, 3 letters of recommendation, resume, statement of objectives. Additional exam requirements/recommendations for international students: Required—TOEFL (minimum score 550 paper-based; 79 iBT). *Application deadline:* Applications are processed on a rolling basis. Electronic applications accepted. *Expenses: Tuition:* Part-time $1241 per credit hour. Part-time tuition and fees vary according to campus/location. *Unit head:* Dr. David Wilder, Program Chair, 321-674-7516, E-mail: dawilder@fit.edu. *Application contact:* Cheryl A. Brown, Associate Director of Graduate Admissions, 321-674-7581, Fax: 321-723-9468, E-mail: cbrown@fit.edu. Website: http://cpla.fit.edu/programs.php

Florida Institute of Technology, College of Psychology and Liberal Arts, Program in Organizational Behavior Management, Melbourne, FL 32901-6975. Offers MS. *Students:* Average age 24. 10 applicants, 20% accepted, 2 enrolled. *Degree requirements:* For master's, comprehensive exam, thesis optional, minimum of 42 credit hours, all course grades of B or higher. *Entrance requirements:* For master's, GRE General Test, 3 letters of recommendation, resume, statement of objectives. Additional exam requirements/recommendations for international students: Required—TOEFL (minimum score 550 paper-based; 79 iBT). *Expenses: Tuition:* Part-time $1241 per credit hour. Part-time tuition and fees vary according to campus/location. *Financial support:* Applicants required to submit FAFSA. *Unit head:* Dr. David Wilder, Program Chair, Campus Behavior Analysis Programs, 321-674-7516, E-mail: dawilder@fit.edu. *Application contact:* Cheryl A. Brown, Associate Director of Graduate Admissions, 321-674-7581, Fax: 321-723-9468, E-mail: cbrown@fit.edu. Website: http://www.fit.edu/programs/

Florida State University, The Graduate School, College of Business, Tallahassee, FL 32306-1110. Offers accounting (M Acc), including assurance and advisory services, generalist, taxation; business administration (MBA, PhD), including accounting (PhD), finance (PhD), management information systems (PhD), marketing (PhD), organizational behavior and human resources (PhD), risk management and insurance (PhD), strategy (PhD); finance (MS); management information systems (MS); risk management and insurance (MS); JD/MBA; MSW/MBA. *Accreditation:* AACSB. *Program availability:* Part-time, 100% online. *Faculty:* 93 full-time (23 women), 2 part-time/adjunct (1 woman). *Students:* 229 full-time (96 women), 423 part-time (154 women); includes 159 minority (44 Black or African American, non-Hispanic/Latino; 24 Asian, non-Hispanic/Latino; 75 Hispanic/Latino; 1 Native Hawaiian or other Pacific Islander, non-Hispanic/Latino; 15 Two or more races, non-Hispanic/Latino), 48 international. Average age 31. 300 applicants, 61% accepted, 133 enrolled. In 2017, 268 master's, 9 doctorates awarded. Terminal master's awarded for partial completion of doctoral program. *Degree requirements:* For doctorate, comprehensive exam, thesis/dissertation. *Entrance requirements:* For master's, GMAT, GRE (for all except MS in finance), work experience (MBA, MS); minimum GPA of 3.0, letters of recommendation; for doctorate, GMAT, GRE (for marketing, organizational behavior, risk management and insurance, management information systems, and human resources only), minimum graduate GPA of 3.5, letters of recommendation. Additional exam requirements/recommendations for international students: Required—TOEFL (minimum score 600 paper-based; 85 iBT); Recommended—IELTS (minimum score 6). *Application deadline:* For fall admission, 6/1 for domestic and international students; for spring admission, 10/1 for domestic and international students; for summer admission, 3/1 for domestic and international students. Applications are processed on a rolling basis. Application fee: $30. Electronic applications accepted. *Expenses:* Contact institution. *Financial support:* In 2017–18, 146 students received support, including 26 fellowships (averaging $1,500 per year), 77 research assistantships with full tuition reimbursements available (averaging $20,000 per year), 43 teaching assistantships with full tuition reimbursements available (averaging $20,000 per year); career-related internships or fieldwork, scholarships/grants, health care benefits, tuition waivers (full and partial), and unspecified assistantships also available. Support available to part-time students. Financial award application deadline: 1/1; financial award applicants required to submit FAFSA. *Faculty research:* Business strategy, marketing, finance, accounting, business analytics. *Total annual research expenditures:* $1.4 million. *Unit head:* Dr. Michael Hartline, Dean, 850-644-4405, Fax: 850-644-0915, E-mail: mhartline@business.fsu.edu. *Application contact:* Jennifer Clark, Director, 850-644-6458, E-mail: gradprograms@business.fsu.edu. Website: http://business.fsu.edu/

The Graduate Center, City University of New York, Graduate Studies, Program in Business, New York, NY 10016-4039. Offers accounting (PhD); behavioral science (PhD); finance (PhD); management planning systems (PhD). *Faculty:* 66 full-time (5 women). *Students:* 56 full-time (30 women); includes 6 minority (1 Black or African American, non-Hispanic/Latino; 1 American Indian or Alaska Native, non-Hispanic/Latino; 2 Asian, non-Hispanic/Latino; 2 Hispanic/Latino), 42 international. Average age 33. 177 applicants, 7% accepted, 10 enrolled. In 2017, 10 doctorates awarded. *Degree requirements:* For doctorate, thesis/dissertation. *Entrance requirements:* For doctorate, GMAT, writing sample (15 pages). Additional exam requirements/recommendations for international students: Required—TOEFL. *Application deadline:* For fall admission, 1/15 for domestic students. Application fee: $125. Electronic applications accepted. *Financial support:* In 2017–18, 50 students received support, including 54 fellowships, 5 teaching assistantships; research assistantships, career-related internships or fieldwork, Federal Work-Study, institutionally sponsored loans, and tuition waivers (full and partial) also available. Financial award application deadline: 2/1; financial award applicants required to submit FAFSA. *Unit head:* Dr. Joseph Weintrop, Executive Officer, 646-312-3092, Fax: 646-312-3031. *Application contact:* Les Gribben, Director of Admissions, 212-817-7470, Fax: 212-817-1624, E-mail: lgribben@gc.cuny.edu.

Hampton University, School of Liberal Arts and Education, Program in Sport Administration, Hampton, VA 23668. Offers intercollegiate athletics (MS); international sports (MS); organizational behavior and sport business leadership (MS). *Program availability:* Part-time, evening/weekend. *Students:* 29 full-time (6 women), 21 part-time (7 women); includes 46 minority (all Black or African American, non-Hispanic/Latino). Average age 26. 34 applicants, 53% accepted, 1 enrolled. In 2017, 14 master's awarded. *Degree requirements:* For master's, thesis (for some programs). *Entrance requirements:* For master's, GRE. Additional exam requirements/recommendations for international students: Required—TOEFL (minimum score 525 paper-based) or IELTS (6.5). *Application deadline:* For fall admission, 6/1 priority date for domestic students, 4/1 priority date for international students; for spring admission, 11/1 priority date for domestic students, 9/1 priority date for international students; for summer admission, 4/1 priority date for domestic students, 2/1 priority date for international students. Applications are processed on a rolling basis. Application fee: $35. Electronic applications accepted. *Expenses:* Contact institution. *Financial support:* Fellowships, research assistantships, teaching assistantships, and career-related internships or fieldwork available. Financial award application deadline: 6/30; financial award applicants required to submit FAFSA. *Faculty research:* International sport, intercollegiate sport, sport leadership, professional sport, event management. *Unit head:* Dr. Aaron Livingston, Program Coordinator, 757-637-2278, E-mail: aaron.livingston@hamptonu.edu.

Harvard University, Graduate School of Arts and Sciences and Doctoral Programs in Management, Committee on Organizational Behavior, Cambridge, MA 02138. Offers PhD. *Entrance requirements:* For doctorate, GRE General Test or GMAT, major in psychology or sociology, course work in statistics or mathematics. Additional exam requirements/recommendations for international students: Required—TOEFL.

Harvard University, Harvard Business School, Doctoral Programs in Management, Boston, MA 02163. Offers accounting and management (DBA); business economics (PhD); health policy management (PhD); management (DBA); marketing (DBA); organizational behavior (PhD); science, technology and management (PhD); strategy (DBA); technology and operations management (DBA). *Degree requirements:* For doctorate, comprehensive exam (for some programs), thesis/dissertation. *Entrance requirements:* For doctorate, GRE General Test or GMAT. Additional exam requirements/recommendations for international students: Required—TOEFL.

International Institute for Restorative Practices, Graduate Programs, Bethlehem, PA 18018. Offers MS, Certificate. *Program availability:* Online learning. *Expenses:* Contact institution.

John Jay College of Criminal Justice of the City University of New York, Graduate Studies, Programs in Criminal Justice, New York, NY 10019. Offers criminal justice (MA, PhD); criminology and deviance (PhD); forensic psychology (PhD); forensic science (PhD); international crime and justice (MA); law and philosophy (PhD); organizational behavior (PhD); public policy (PhD). *Program availability:* Part-time, evening/weekend. Terminal master's awarded for partial completion of doctoral program. *Degree requirements:* For master's, thesis or alternative; for doctorate, one foreign language, thesis/dissertation. *Entrance requirements:* For master's, GRE General Test, minimum B average; for doctorate, GRE General Test. Additional exam requirements/recommendations for international students: Required—TOEFL (minimum score 500 paper-based).

Lake Forest Graduate School of Management, The Leadership MBA Program, Lake Forest, IL 60045. Offers finance (MBA); global business (MBA); healthcare management (MBA); management (MBA); marketing (MBA); organizational behavior (MBA). *Program availability:* Part-time, evening/weekend. *Entrance requirements:* For master's, 4 years of work experience in field, interview, 2 letters of recommendation. Electronic applications accepted.

New York University, Leonard N. Stern School of Business, Department of Management and Organizations, New York, NY 10012-1019. Offers management organizations (MBA); organization theory (PhD); organizational behavior (PhD); strategy (PhD). *Expenses: Tuition:* Full-time $41,352; part-time $19,968 per year. *Required fees:* $2496; $1628 per unit. $814 per term. Tuition and fees vary according to course load and program. *Faculty research:* Strategic management, managerial cognition, interpersonal processes, conflict and negotiation.

New York University, Tandon School of Engineering, Department of Technology Management, Major in Organizational Behavior, New York, NY 10012-1019. Offers MS. *Program availability:* Part-time, evening/weekend. *Faculty:* 10 full-time (2 women), 36 part-time/adjunct (4 women). *Students:* 3 full-time (all women), 10 part-time (6 women); includes 5 minority (3 Asian, non-Hispanic/Latino; 2 Hispanic/Latino), 3 international. Average age 32. In 2017, 16 master's awarded. *Entrance requirements:* For master's, GMAT, minimum B average in undergraduate course work. Additional exam requirements/recommendations for international students: Required—TOEFL (minimum score 550 paper-based; 80 iBT); Recommended—IELTS (minimum score 6.5). *Application deadline:* For fall admission, 2/15 priority date for domestic and international students; for spring admission, 11/1 priority date for domestic and international students. Applications are processed on a rolling basis. Application fee: $75. Electronic applications accepted. *Expenses: Tuition:* Full-time $41,352; part-time $19,968 per year. *Required fees:* $2496; $1628 per unit. $814 per term. Tuition and fees vary according to course load and program. *Financial support:* Applicants required to submit FAFSA. *Total annual research expenditures:* $2.9 million. *Unit head:* Dr. Harold G. Kaufman, Program Director, 718-260-3485, E-mail: hgk224@nyu.edu. *Application contact:* Raymond Lutzky, Director of Graduate Enrollment Management, 718-637-5984, Fax: 718-260-3624, E-mail: rlutzky@poly.edu.

Northwestern University, The Graduate School, School of Education and Social Policy, Program in Learning and Organizational Change, Evanston, IL 60208. Offers MS. *Program availability:* Part-time, evening/weekend, online learning. *Degree requirements:* For master's, thesis, practicum. *Entrance requirements:* For master's, GRE or GMAT (recommended), letters of recommendation. Additional exam requirements/recommendations for international students: Required—TOEFL (minimum score 600 paper-based; 100 iBT); Recommended—IELTS (minimum score 7). Electronic applications accepted. *Faculty research:* Strategic change, learning and performance, workplace learning, leadership development, cognitive design, knowledge management.

Phillips Graduate University, Doctoral Program in Organizational Management and Consulting, Chatsworth, CA 91311. Offers Psy D. *Program availability:* Evening/weekend. *Degree requirements:* For doctorate, thesis/dissertation. *Entrance requirements:* For doctorate, minimum GPA of 3.0, interview. *Application deadline:* For fall admission, 1/29 priority date for domestic students. Applications are processed on a rolling basis. Application fee: $80. Electronic applications accepted. *Expenses: Tuition:* Part-time $897 per unit. *Required fees:* $375 per semester. Part-time tuition and fees vary according to degree level and program. *Financial support:* Tuition waivers (full and partial) available. *Application contact:* Christine Montagna, Admissions Advisor, 818-600-4945, Fax: 818-386-5699, E-mail: cmontagna@pgu.edu. Website: https://www.pgu.edu/organizational-management-consulting-doctoral-psyd.html

Organizational Behavior

Purdue University, Graduate School, Krannert School of Management, Doctoral Program in Organizational Behavior and Human Resource Management, West Lafayette, IN 47907-2056. Offers PhD. *Students:* 6 full-time (3 women); includes 2 minority (1 Black or African American, non-Hispanic/Latino; 1 Asian, non-Hispanic/Latino). Average age 32. 56 applicants. In 2017, 3 doctorates awarded. *Degree requirements:* For doctorate, comprehensive exam, thesis/dissertation, dissertation proposal, dissertation defense. *Entrance requirements:* For doctorate, GMAT or GRE, bachelor's degree, two semesters of calculus, one semester each of linear algebra and statistics. Additional exam requirements/recommendations for international students: Required—TOEFL (minimum score 575 paper-based); Recommended—TWE. *Application deadline:* For fall admission, 1/15 priority date for domestic and international students. Application fee: $60 ($80 for international students). Electronic applications accepted. *Financial support:* In 2017–18, 1 fellowship with full tuition reimbursement (averaging $25,000 per year), research assistantships with partial tuition reimbursements (averaging $18,000 per year), teaching assistantships with partial tuition reimbursements (averaging $18,000 per year) were awarded; scholarships/grants, health care benefits, tuition waivers (full and partial), unspecified assistantships, and travel funds to present at a major conference also available. Support available to part-time students. Financial award application deadline: 1/15. *Faculty research:* Human resource management, organizational behavior. *Unit head:* Dr. David Hummels, Dean/Professor, 765-494-4366. *Application contact:* Kelly Felty, Associate Director, Krannert PhD Programs, 765-494-4375, E-mail: krannertphd@purdue.edu.
Website: http://www.krannert.purdue.edu/programs/phd/

Saybrook University, School of Organizational Leadership and Transformation, San Francisco, CA 94612. Offers MA. Program offered jointly with Bastyr University. *Degree requirements:* For master's, thesis (for some programs), oral exams. *Entrance requirements:* For master's, bachelor's degree from an accredited college or university. *Faculty research:* Cross-functional work teams, communication, management authority, employee influence, systems theory.

Saybrook University, School of Psychology and Interdisciplinary Inquiry, San Francisco, CA 94612. Offers human science (MA, PhD), including consciousness and spirituality, humanistic and transpersonal psychology, integrative health studies, organizational systems, social transformation; organizational systems (MA, PhD), including consciousness and spirituality, humanistic and transpersonal psychology, integrative health studies, leadership of sustainable systems (MA), organizational systems, social transformation; psychology (MA, PhD), including consciousness and spirituality, creativity studies (MA), humanistic and transpersonal psychology, integrative health studies, Jungian studies, marriage and family therapy (MA), organizational systems, social transformation. *Program availability:* Online learning. Terminal master's awarded for partial completion of doctoral program. *Degree requirements:* For master's, thesis or alternative; for doctorate, thesis/dissertation. *Entrance requirements:* Additional exam requirements/recommendations for international students: Required—TOEFL (minimum score 580 paper-based; 93 iBT). Electronic applications accepted. *Faculty research:* Humanistic theory, health studies, organizational systems, consciousness and spirituality, social transformation.

Suffolk University, Sawyer Business School, Master of Business Administration Program, Boston, MA 02108-2770. Offers accounting (MBA); entrepreneurship (MBA); executive business administration (EMBA); finance (MBA); global business administration (GMBA); health administration (MBA); international business (MBA); marketing (MBA); nonprofit management (MBA); organizational behavior (MBA); strategic management (MBA); supply chain management (MBA); taxation (MBA); JD/MBA; MBA/MHA; MBA/MSA; MBA/MSF; MBA/MST. *Accreditation:* AACSB. *Program availability:* Part-time, evening/weekend, 100% online. *Faculty:* 16 full-time (6 women), 9 part-time/adjunct (1 woman). *Students:* 106 full-time (57 women), 236 part-time (135 women); includes 80 minority (23 Black or African American, non-Hispanic/Latino; 23 Asian, non-Hispanic/Latino; 28 Hispanic/Latino; 6 Two or more races, non-Hispanic/Latino), 41 international. Average age 30. 354 applicants, 69% accepted, 115 enrolled. In 2017, 170 master's awarded. *Entrance requirements:* For master's, GMAT, minimum undergraduate GPA of 2.75 (MBA), 5 years of managerial experience (EMBA). Additional exam requirements/recommendations for international students: Required—TOEFL (minimum score 550 paper-based; 80 iBT). *Application deadline:* For fall admission, 3/15 priority date for domestic students, 10/15 priority date for international students; for spring admission, 10/15 priority date for domestic and international students. Applications are processed on a rolling basis. Application fee: $50. Electronic applications accepted. *Expenses:* $43,980 per year full-time, $1,466 per credit part-time (for MBA); $1,794 per credit part-time (for Executive MBA). *Financial support:* In 2017–18, 198 students received support, including 1 fellowship (averaging $2,325 per year); career-related internships or fieldwork, Federal Work-Study, institutionally sponsored loans, and scholarships/grants also available. Support available to part-time students. Financial award application deadline: 4/1; financial award applicants required to submit FAFSA. *Faculty research:* Foreign investments; career strategies and boundaryless careers; corporate ethics codes; interest rates, inflation, and growth options; innovation and product development performance. *Unit head:* Jodi Detjen, Director of MBA Programs, 617-573-8306, E-mail: jdetjen@suffolk.edu. *Application contact:* Mara Marzocchi, Associate Director of Graduate Admissions, 617-573-8302, Fax: 617-305-1733, E-mail: grad.admission@suffolk.edu.
Website: http://www.suffolk.edu/mba

Universidad de las Americas, A.C., Program in International Organizations and Institutions, Mexico City, Mexico. Offers MA.

Université de Sherbrooke, Faculty of Administration, Program in Organizational Change and Intervention, Sherbrooke, QC J1K 2R1, Canada. Offers M Sc. *Degree requirements:* For master's, one foreign language, thesis. *Entrance requirements:* For master's, bachelor's degree in related field, minimum GPA of 3.0 (on 4.3 scale). Electronic applications accepted. *Faculty research:* Organizational change, organizational communication, process approaches and qualitative research, organizational behavior.

University at Albany, State University of New York, Nelson A. Rockefeller College of Public Affairs and Policy, Department of Public Administration and Policy, Albany, NY 12222-0001. Offers financial management and public economics (MPA); financial market regulation (MPA); health policy (MPA); healthcare management (MPA); homeland security (MPA); human resources management (MPA); information strategy and management (MPA); local government management (MPA); nonprofit management (MPA); nonprofit management and leadership (Certificate); organizational behavior and theory (MPA, PhD); planning and policy analysis (CAS); policy analysis (MPA); politics and administration (PhD); public finance (PhD); public management (PhD); public policy (PhD); public sector management (Certificate); women and public policy (Certificate); JD/MPA. JD/MPA offered jointly with Albany Law School. *Accreditation:* NASPAA (one or more programs are accredited). *Faculty:* 21 full-time (7 women), 14 part-time/adjunct (7 women). *Students:* 115 full-time (59 women), 93 part-time (56 women); includes 41 minority (11 Black or African American, non-Hispanic/Latino; 9 Asian, non-Hispanic/Latino; 18 Hispanic/Latino; 3 Two or more races, non-Hispanic/Latino), 32 international. 236 applicants, 69% accepted, 86 enrolled. In 2017, 57 master's, 1 doctorate, 14 other advanced degrees awarded. *Degree requirements:* For doctorate, one foreign language, thesis/dissertation. *Entrance requirements:* For doctorate, GRE General Test. Additional exam requirements/recommendations for international students: Required—TOEFL (minimum score 550 paper-based). *Application deadline:* For fall admission, 2/1 priority date for domestic students, 5/1 for international students; for spring admission, 12/1 for domestic students. Applications are processed on a rolling basis. Application fee: $75. Electronic applications accepted. *Expenses:* Tuition, state resident: full-time $453 per credit hour. Tuition, nonresident: full-time $22,210; part-time $925 per credit hour. *Required fees:* $84.68 per credit hour. $508.06 per semester. Part-time tuition and fees vary according to course load and program. *Financial support:* Application deadline: 2/1. *Unit head:* Victor Asal, Chair, 518-591-8729, E-mail: vasal@albany.edu.
Website: http://www.albany.edu/rockefeller/pad.shtml

The University of British Columbia, Sauder School of Business, Doctoral Program in Business Administration, Vancouver, BC V6T 1Z2, Canada. Offers accounting (PhD); finance (PhD); management information systems (PhD); management science (PhD); marketing (PhD); organizational behavior (PhD); strategy and business economics (PhD); transportation and logistics (PhD); urban land economics (PhD). *Degree requirements:* For doctorate, comprehensive exam, thesis/dissertation. *Entrance requirements:* For doctorate, GMAT or GRE. Additional exam requirements/recommendations for international students: Required—TOEFL (minimum score 600 paper-based; 100 iBT). Electronic applications accepted. *Expenses:* Contact institution.

University of California, Berkeley, Graduate Division, Haas School of Business, PhD in Business Administration Program, Berkeley, CA 94720-1500. Offers accounting (PhD); business and public policy (PhD); finance (PhD); management of organizations (PhD); marketing (PhD); real estate (PhD). *Accreditation:* AACSB. *Students:* 72 full-time (20 women); includes 30 minority (26 Asian, non-Hispanic/Latino; 4 Hispanic/Latino). Average age 27. *Degree requirements:* For doctorate, comprehensive exam, thesis/dissertation, written preliminary exams, oral qualifying exam. *Entrance requirements:* For doctorate, GMAT or GRE, minimum GPA of 3.0 in undergraduate and graduate coursework. Additional exam requirements/recommendations for international students: Required—TOEFL (minimum score 570 paper-based; 70 iBT), IELTS (minimum score 7). *Application deadline:* For fall admission, 12/1 for domestic and international students. Application fee: $105 ($125 for international students). Electronic applications accepted. *Expenses:* Contact institution. *Financial support:* Fellowships with tuition reimbursements, research assistantships with tuition reimbursements, teaching assistantships with tuition reimbursements, scholarships/grants, health care benefits, tuition waivers (full), unspecified assistantships, and transit passes, travel grants available. Financial award application deadline: 12/1. *Faculty research:* Accounting, business and public policy, entrepreneurship, finance, management of organizations, marketing, operations and information technology management, real estate. *Unit head:* Dr. Nicolae Garleanu, Director, 510-643-6349, Fax: 510-643-4255. *Application contact:* Melissa Hacker, Director, Student Affairs, 510-642-3944, Fax: 510-643-4255, E-mail: melhacker@haas.berkeley.edu.
Website: http://www.haas.berkeley.edu/Phd/

University of California, Davis, Graduate School of Management, Full-Time MBA Program, Davis, CA 95616. Offers business analytics and technologies (MBA); entrepreneurship and innovation (MBA); finance and accounting (MBA); general management (MBA); marketing (MBA); organizational behavior (MBA); public health management (MBA); strategy (MBA); technology management (MBA); DVM/MBA; JD/MBA; M Engr/MBA; MBA/MPH; MBA/MS; MD/MBA; MSN/MBA; PhD/MBA. *Faculty:* 52 full-time (15 women). *Students:* 96 full-time (42 women); includes 31 minority (1 Black or African American, non-Hispanic/Latino; 17 Asian, non-Hispanic/Latino; 5 Hispanic/Latino; 8 Two or more races, non-Hispanic/Latino), 36 international. Average age 29. 290 applicants, 37% accepted, 45 enrolled. In 2017, 44 master's awarded. *Degree requirements:* For master's, integrated management project. *Entrance requirements:* For master's, GMAT or GRE, letters of recommendation, resume, essays, equivalent of a 4-year U.S. undergraduate degree, transcript. Additional exam requirements/recommendations for international students: Required—TOEFL (minimum score 600 paper-based; 100 iBT), IELTS (minimum score 7). *Application deadline:* For fall admission, 5/18 priority date for domestic and international students. Application fee: $125. Electronic applications accepted. *Expenses:* Contact institution. *Financial support:* In 2017–18, 90 students received support. Fellowships, research assistantships, teaching assistantships with partial tuition reimbursements available, institutionally sponsored loans, scholarships/grants, health care benefits, tuition waivers (partial), and unspecified assistantships available. Financial award application deadline: 3/1; financial award applicants required to submit FAFSA. *Faculty research:* Finance, marketing, management, business analytics, accounting. *Unit head:* James Stevens, Senior Assistant Dean of Student Affairs, 530-752-7658, Fax: 530-754-9355, E-mail: admissions@gsm.ucdavis.edu. *Application contact:* Kristy Bird MaKieve, Interim Director of Admissions, 530-754-5476, Fax: 530-754-9355, E-mail: admissions@gsm.ucdavis.edu.
Website: http://gsm.ucdavis.edu/daytime-mba-program

University of California, Davis, Graduate School of Management, MBA Programs in Sacramento and San Francisco Bay Area, Davis, CA 95616. Offers business analytics and technologies (MBA); entrepreneurship and innovation (MBA); finance and accounting (MBA); general management (MBA); marketing (MBA); organizational behavior (MBA); public health management (MBA); strategy (MBA); technology management (MBA). *Program availability:* Part-time-only, evening/weekend. *Faculty:* 99 part-time/adjunct (30 women). *Students:* 323 part-time (133 women); includes 148 minority (7 Black or African American, non-Hispanic/Latino; 96 Asian, non-Hispanic/Latino; 26 Hispanic/Latino; 1 Native Hawaiian or other Pacific Islander, non-Hispanic/Latino; 18 Two or more races, non-Hispanic/Latino), 37 international. Average age 30. 202 applicants, 75% accepted, 111 enrolled. In 2017, 112 master's awarded. *Degree requirements:* For master's, integrated management project. *Entrance requirements:* For master's, GMAT or GRE, letters of recommendation, resume, equivalent of a 4-year undergraduate degree. Additional exam requirements/recommendations for international students: Required—TOEFL (minimum score 600 paper-based; 100 iBT), IELTS (minimum score 7). *Application deadline:* For fall admission, 5/18 priority date for domestic and international students. Application fee: $125. Electronic applications accepted. *Expenses:* Contact institution. *Financial support:* In 2017–18, 67 students received support. Fellowships, teaching assistantships with partial tuition reimbursements available, scholarships/grants, and unspecified assistantships available. Support available to part-time students. Financial award application deadline: 3/1; financial award applicants required to submit FAFSA. *Faculty research:* Accounting, finance, marketing, management, business analytics. *Unit head:* James Stevens, Senior Assistant Dean of Student Affairs, 530-752-7658, Fax: 530-754-9355, E-mail: admissions@gsm.ucdavis.edu. *Application contact:* Kristy Bird MaKieve, Interim Director of Admissions, 530-754-5476, Fax: 530-754-9355, E-mail: admissions@gsm.ucdavis.edu.
Website: http://gsm.ucdavis.edu/mba-programs

University of Chicago, Booth School of Business, Full-Time MBA Program, Chicago, IL 60637. Offers accounting (MBA); analytic finance (MBA); analytic management (MBA); econometrics and statistics (MBA); economics (MBA); entrepreneurship (MBA); finance

(MBA); general management (MBA); health administration and policy (Certificate); international business (MBA); managerial and organizational behavior (MBA); marketing analytics (MBA); marketing management (MBA); operations management (MBA); strategic management (MBA); MBA/AM; MBA/JD; MBA/MA; MBA/MD; MBA/MPP. *Accreditation:* AACSB. *Faculty:* 154 full-time (26 women), 61 part-time/adjunct (12 women). *Students:* 1,176 full-time (481 women). In 2017, 586 master's awarded. *Entrance requirements:* For master's, GMAT or GRE, transcripts, resume, 2 letters of recommendation, essays, interview. Additional exam requirements/recommendations for international students: Required—TOEFL, IELTS, or PTE. *Application deadline:* For fall admission, 9/1 for domestic and international students; for winter admission, 1/1 for domestic and international students; for spring admission, 4/1 for domestic and international students. Application fee: $250. Electronic applications accepted. *Expenses:* Contact institution. *Unit head:* Stacey Kole, Deputy Dean for Alumni, Corporate Relations, and the Full-time MBA Program, 773-702-7121. *Application contact:* Kurt Ahlm, Associate Dean for Student Recruitment and Admissions, 773-702-7369, Fax: 773-702-9085, E-mail: admissions@chicagobooth.edu.
Website: https://www.chicagobooth.edu/programs/full-time

University of Hartford, College of Arts and Sciences, Department of Psychology, Program in Organizational Behavior, West Hartford, CT 06117-1599. Offers MS. *Program availability:* Part-time, evening/weekend. *Entrance requirements:* Additional exam requirements/recommendations for international students: Required—TOEFL (minimum score 550 paper-based). Electronic applications accepted.

University of Hawaii at Manoa, Office of Graduate Education, Shidler College of Business, Program in Business Administration, Honolulu, HI 96822. Offers Asian business studies (MBA); Chinese business studies (MBA); decision sciences (MBA); entrepreneurship (MBA); finance (MBA); finance and banking (MBA); human resources management (MBA); information management (MBA); information technology (MBA); international business (MBA); Japanese business studies (MBA); marketing (MBA); organizational behavior (MBA); organizational management (MBA); real estate (MBA); student-designed track (MBA). *Accreditation:* AACSB. *Program availability:* Part-time, evening/weekend. *Degree requirements:* For master's, thesis optional. *Entrance requirements:* For master's, GMAT, minimum GPA of 3.0. Additional exam requirements/recommendations for international students: Required—TOEFL (minimum score 600 paper-based; 100 iBT), IELTS (minimum score 7). *Expenses:* Contact institution.

The University of Kansas, Graduate Studies, School of Business, Program in Business, Lawrence, KS 66045. Offers business and organizational leadership (MS); decision sciences and supply chain management (PhD); finance (PhD); human resources management (PhD); marketing (PhD); organizational behavior (PhD); strategic management (PhD); supply chain management and logistics (MS). *Accreditation:* AACSB. *Program availability:* Part-time. *Students:* 66 full-time (18 women), 227 part-time (76 women); includes 59 minority (21 Black or African American, non-Hispanic/Latino; 2 American Indian or Alaska Native, non-Hispanic/Latino; 13 Asian, non-Hispanic/Latino; 3 Hispanic/Latino; 20 Two or more races, non-Hispanic/Latino), 29 international. Average age 32. 329 applicants, 71% accepted, 185 enrolled. In 2017, 30 master's, 8 doctorates awarded. *Entrance requirements:* For master's, GMAT, official transcript, three letters of recommendation, resume, statement of purpose; for doctorate, GMAT or GRE, official transcript, three letters of recommendation, resume, statement of purpose. Additional exam requirements/recommendations for international students: Required—TOEFL (minimum score 600 paper-based; 100 iBT). *Application deadline:* For fall admission, 1/10 for domestic and international students. Application fee: $65 ($85 for international students). Electronic applications accepted. *Financial support:* Fellowships, research assistantships, teaching assistantships, scholarships/grants, health care benefits, tuition waivers (full), and unspecified assistantships available. Financial award application deadline: 1/10. *Faculty research:* Strategic human resource management, business ethics, organizational theory/behavior, corporate strategy, international business, supply chain management, Bayesian networks, game theory, decision analysis and time/series analysis, pricing, consumer effects, advertising and emotion. *Unit head:* Charly Edmonds, Director, 785-864-3841, E-mail: bschoolphd@ku.edu. *Application contact:* Graduate Admission Contact, 785-864-7500, E-mail: bschoolphd@ku.edu.
Website: http://www.business.ku.edu/

University of New Mexico, Anderson School of Management, Department of Organizational Studies, Albuquerque, NM 87131. Offers organizational behavior and human resources management (MBA); strategic management and policy (MBA). *Program availability:* Part-time. *Faculty:* 17 full-time (12 women), 17 part-time/adjunct (6 women). In 2017, 20 master's awarded. *Entrance requirements:* For master's, GMAT or GRE, minimum GPA of 3.0 on last 60 hours of coursework; bachelor's degree from regionally-accredited college or university in U.S. or its equivalent in another country. Additional exam requirements/recommendations for international students: Required—TOEFL (minimum score 550 paper-based; 79 iBT), IELTS (minimum score 6.5). *Application deadline:* For fall admission, 4/1 priority date for domestic and international students; for spring admission, 10/1 priority date for domestic and international students. Applications are processed on a rolling basis. Application fee: $50. Electronic applications accepted. *Expenses:* Contact institution. *Financial support:* In 2017–18, 14 students received support, including 4 fellowships (averaging $18,200 per year), 11 research assistantships with partial tuition reimbursements available (averaging $15,488 per year); career-related internships or fieldwork, Federal Work-Study, scholarships/grants, and unspecified assistantships also available. Support available to part-time students. Financial award application deadline: 6/1; financial award applicants required to submit FAFSA. *Faculty research:* Business ethics and social corporate responsibility, diversity, human resources, organizational strategy, organizational behavior. *Unit head:* Dr. Michelle Arthur, Chair, 505-277-6471, E-mail: arthurm@unm.edu. *Application contact:* Lisa Beauchene, Student Recruitment Specialist, 505-277-6471, E-mail: andersonadvising@unm.edu.
Website: https://www.mgt.unm.edu/dos/default.asp?mm-faculty

The University of North Carolina at Chapel Hill, Kenan-Flagler Business School, Doctoral Program in Business Administration, Chapel Hill, NC 27599. Offers accounting (PhD); finance (PhD); marketing (PhD); operations management (PhD); organizational behavior (PhD); strategy (PhD). *Accreditation:* AACSB. *Degree requirements:* For doctorate, thesis/dissertation. *Entrance requirements:* For doctorate, GMAT or GRE General Test. Electronic applications accepted. *Expenses:* Contact institution.

University of North Texas at Dallas, Graduate School, Dallas, TX 75241. Offers accounting (MBA); counseling (M Ed, MS); criminal justice (MS); curriculum and instruction (M Ed); educational administration (M Ed); human resources and organizational behavior (MBA); public leadership (MS); strategic management (MBA).

University of Oklahoma, College of Arts and Sciences, Department of Psychology, Program in Organizational Dynamics, Tulsa, OK 74135. Offers human resource management (Graduate Certificate); organizational dynamics (MA), including human resource management, project management; project management (Graduate Certificate). *Program availability:* Part-time, evening/weekend. *Students:* 12 full-time (9 women), 45 part-time (27 women); includes 15 minority (4 Black or African American, non-Hispanic/Latino; 5 American Indian or Alaska Native, non-Hispanic/Latino; 2 Asian,

non-Hispanic/Latino; 3 Hispanic/Latino; 1 Two or more races, non-Hispanic/Latino), 3 international. Average age 33. 16 applicants, 88% accepted, 12 enrolled. In 2017, 11 master's, 8 other advanced degrees awarded. Terminal master's awarded for partial completion of doctoral program. *Degree requirements:* For master's, comprehensive exam (for some programs), thesis (for some programs), capstone project, comprehensive exam, or thesis; 36 hours of coursework; for Graduate Certificate, 12 hours of coursework from approved list. *Entrance requirements:* For master's, GRE (for students who do not have requisite work experience), current resume showing at least 2 years of relevant work experience; 2 letters of recommendation; statement of career goals; transcripts; for Graduate Certificate, resume showing work experience; 2 letters of recommendation; statement of career goals; transcripts. Additional exam requirements/recommendations for international students: Required—TOEFL (minimum score 79 iBT) or IELTS (minimum score 6.5). *Application deadline:* For fall admission, 5/1 for domestic and international students; for spring admission, 11/1 for domestic and international students; for summer admission, 3/15 for domestic and international students. Application fee: $50 ($100 for international students). Electronic applications accepted. *Expenses:* Tuition, state resident: full-time $5119; part-time $213.30 per credit hour. Tuition, nonresident: full-time $19,778; part-time $824.10 per credit hour. *Required fees:* $3458; $133.55 per credit hour. $126.50 per semester. *Financial support:* In 2017–18, 12 students received support. Fellowships with full tuition reimbursements available, research assistantships with full tuition reimbursements available, and teaching assistantships with full tuition reimbursements available available. Financial award application deadline: 6/1; financial award applicants required to submit FAFSA. *Faculty research:* Organizational behavior, personality, organizational climate and culture, leadership, ethics. *Unit head:* Dr. Eric Day, Chair, 405-325-4511, Fax: 405-325-4737, E-mail: eday@ou.edu. *Application contact:* Jennifer Kisamore, Associate Professor of Psychology/Graduate Liaison for Organizational Dynamics, 918-660-3603, Fax: 918-660-3383, E-mail: odyn@ou.edu.
Website: http://odyn.ou.edu

University of Pittsburgh, Katz Graduate School of Business, Doctoral Program in Business Administration, Pittsburgh, PA 15260. Offers accounting (PhD); business analytics and operations (PhD); finance (PhD); information systems and technology management (PhD); marketing (PhD); organizational behavior and human resources (PhD); strategic management (PhD). *Accreditation:* AACSB. *Program availability:* Evening/weekend. *Faculty:* 91 full-time (30 women), 14 part-time/adjunct (4 women). *Students:* 51 full-time (26 women), 1 (woman) part-time; includes 5 minority (1 Black or African American, non-Hispanic/Latino; 3 Asian, non-Hispanic/Latino; 1 Two or more races, non-Hispanic/Latino), 30 international. Average age 31. 337 applicants, 3% accepted, 10 enrolled. In 2017, 7 doctorates awarded. *Degree requirements:* For doctorate, comprehensive exam, thesis/dissertation, student teaching. *Entrance requirements:* For doctorate, GMAT or GRE, 3 recommendations, statement of purpose, transcripts of all previous course work and degrees. Additional exam requirements/recommendations for international students: Required—TOEFL (minimum score 100 iBT) or IELTS (minimum score 7.0). *Application deadline:* For fall admission, 1/1 for domestic and international students. Applications are processed on a rolling basis. Application fee: $50. Electronic applications accepted. *Financial support:* In 2017–18, 43 students received support, including 33 research assistantships with full tuition reimbursements available (averaging $26,500 per year), 10 teaching assistantships with full tuition reimbursements available (averaging $28,220 per year); Federal Work-Study, scholarships/grants, health care benefits, and unspecified assistantships also available. Financial award application deadline: 1/1; financial award applicants required to submit FAFSA. *Faculty research:* Accounting systems/financial reporting, corporate finance, shopper marketing/consumer behavior, management information systems, organizational behavior and entrepreneurship. *Total annual research expenditures:* $475,077. *Unit head:* Dr. Arjang A. Assad, Dean, 412-648-1556, Fax: 412-648-1552, E-mail: aassad@katz.pitt.edu. *Application contact:* Dr. Dennis Galletta, Director, 412-648-1699, Fax: 412-648-3633, E-mail: galletta@katz.pitt.edu.
Website: http://www.katz.business.pitt.edu/degrees/phd/

See Display on page 158 and Close-Up on page 187.

University of Pittsburgh, Katz Graduate School of Business, Master of Business Administration Programs, Pittsburgh, PA 15260. Offers finance (MBA); information systems (MBA); marketing (MBA); operations (MBA); organizational behavior and human resources (MBA); strategy, environment and organizations (MBA); MBA/JD; MBA/MID; MBA/MIS; MBA/MSE. *Accreditation:* AACSB. *Program availability:* Part-time, evening/weekend, blended/hybrid learning. *Faculty:* 91 full-time (30 women), 14 part-time/adjunct (4 women). *Students:* 139 full-time (49 women), 294 part-time (94 women); includes 65 minority (27 Black or African American, non-Hispanic/Latino; 20 Asian, non-Hispanic/Latino; 11 Hispanic/Latino; 7 Two or more races, non-Hispanic/Latino), 54 international. Average age 29. 651 applicants, 44% accepted, 158 enrolled. In 2017, 217 master's awarded. *Degree requirements:* For master's, minimum GPA of 3.0. *Entrance requirements:* For master's, GMAT, GRE. Additional exam requirements/recommendations for international students: Required—TOEFL (minimum score 100 iBT) or IELTS (minimum score 7.0). *Application deadline:* For fall admission, 4/1 priority date for domestic students, 2/1 priority date for international students. Application fee: $50. Electronic applications accepted. *Financial support:* In 2017–18, 136 students received support. Scholarships/grants available. Financial award application deadline: 6/1; financial award applicants required to submit FAFSA. *Faculty research:* Accounting systems/financial reporting, corporate finance, shopper marketing/consumer behavior, management information systems, organizational behavior and entrepreneurship. *Total annual research expenditures:* $475,077. *Unit head:* Dr. Arjang A. Assad, Dean, 412-648-1556, Fax: 412-648-1552, E-mail: aassad@katz.pitt.edu. *Application contact:* Thomas Keller, Director of MBA Admissions, 412-648-1700, Fax: 412-648-1659, E-mail: mba@katz.pitt.edu.
Website: http://www.business.pitt.edu/katz/mba/

See Display on page 158 and Close-Up on page 187.

The University of Texas at Austin, Graduate School, College of Liberal Arts, Program in Human Dimensions of Organizations, Austin, TX 78712-1111. Offers MA. *Program availability:* Evening/weekend, online learning. *Degree requirements:* For master's, capstone project.

University of Utah, Graduate School, David Eccles School of Business, Business Administration Program, Salt Lake City, UT 84112. Offers accounting (PhD); business administration (EMBA, MBA, PMBA); finance (PhD); information systems (PhD); marketing (PhD); operations management (PhD); organizational behavior (PhD); strategic management (PhD); MBA/JD; MBA/MHA; MBA/MS. *Program availability:* Part-time, evening/weekend, online learning. *Faculty:* 58 full-time (21 women), 37 part-time/adjunct (7 women). *Students:* 558 full-time (149 women), 103 part-time (21 women); includes 66 minority (1 Black or African American, non-Hispanic/Latino; 16 Asian, non-Hispanic/Latino; 41 Hispanic/Latino; 8 Two or more races, non-Hispanic/Latino), 50 international. Average age 27. 442 applicants, 70% accepted, 226 enrolled. In 2017, 298 master's, 7 doctorates awarded. *Entrance requirements:* For master's, GMAT or GRE; for doctorate, GMAT. Additional exam requirements/recommendations for international students: Required—TOEFL (minimum score 600 paper-based; 100 iBT), IELTS (minimum score 7).

Organizational Behavior

Application deadline: Applications are processed on a rolling basis. Application fee: $55 ($65 for international students). Electronic applications accepted. *Expenses:* Contact institution. *Financial support:* In 2017–18, 53 students received support. Fellowships, scholarships/grants, and unspecified assistantships available. Financial award application deadline: 2/1; financial award applicants required to submit FAFSA. *Faculty research:* Corporate finance, strategy services, consumer behavior, financial disclosures, operations. *Unit head:* Kristina Diekmann, Department Chair, 801-581-8524, Fax: 801-581-3380, E-mail: mastersinfo@business.utah.edu. *Application contact:* Christine Harris, Coordinator, 801-581-7785, Fax: 801-585-3962, E-mail: execch@business.utah.edu. Website: http://www.business.utah.edu/

Wayne State University, College of Liberal Arts and Sciences, Department of Political Science, Detroit, MI 48202. Offers political science (MA, PhD); public administration (MPA), including economic development policy and management, health and human services policy and management, human and fiscal resource management, nonprofit policy and management, organizational behavior and management, urban and metropolitan policy and management; JD/MA. *Accreditation:* NASPAA. *Faculty:* 18. *Students:* 48 full-time (20 women), 68 part-time (36 women); includes 37 minority (26 Black or African American, non-Hispanic/Latino; 3 Asian, non-Hispanic/Latino; 2 Hispanic/Latino; 6 Two or more races, non-Hispanic/Latino), 6 international. Average age 32. 105 applicants, 39% accepted. In 2017, 17 master's, 3 doctorates awarded. *Degree requirements:* For master's, comprehensive exam (for some programs), thesis (for some programs); for doctorate, thesis/dissertation. *Entrance requirements:* For master's, GRE General Test, substantial undergraduate preparation in the social sciences, minimum upper-division undergraduate GPA of 3.0, two letters of recommendation, personal statement; for doctorate, GRE General Test, 3 letters of recommendation; personal statement; interview. Additional exam requirements/recommendations for international students: Required—TOEFL (minimum score 550 paper-based; 79 iBT), TWE (minimum score 5.5), Michigan English Language Assessment Battery (minimum score 85); Recommended—IELTS (minimum score 6.5). *Application deadline:* For fall admission, 5/15 for domestic students, 5/1 priority date for international students; for winter admission, 10/15 for domestic students, 9/1 priority date for international students. Applications are processed on a rolling basis. Application fee: $50. Electronic applications accepted. *Expenses:* Contact institution. *Financial support:* In 2017–18, 44 students received support, including 6 fellowships with tuition reimbursements available (averaging $11,698 per year), 12 teaching assistantships with tuition reimbursements available (averaging $18,534 per year); research assistantships with tuition reimbursements available, scholarships/grants, health care benefits, and unspecified assistantships also available. Financial award applicants required to submit FAFSA. *Faculty research:* American government and politics, comparative politics, political methodology, political theory, public administration, public law, public policy, world politics/international relations, formal theory/modeling, gender and politics, international law, peace research, political economy, political psychology, politics of developing countries, race, religion, and ethnicity, urban politics. *Unit head:* Dr. Daniel Geller, Professor and Chair, 313-577-6328, E-mail: dgeller@wayne.edu. *Application contact:* Dr. Sharon Lean, Graduate Director, 313-577-2630, E-mail: gradpolisci@wayne.edu. Website: http://clas.wayne.edu/politicalscience/

Wilfrid Laurier University, Faculty of Graduate and Postdoctoral Studies, School of Business and Economics, Department of Business, Waterloo, ON N2L 3C5, Canada. Offers accounting (PhD); finance (M Fin); financial economics (PhD); marketing (PhD); operations and supply chain management (PhD); organizational behavior and human resource management (M Sc); organizational behaviour and human resource management (PhD); supply chain management (M Sc); technology management (EMTM). *Accreditation:* AACSB. *Program availability:* Part-time, evening/weekend. *Degree requirements:* For master's, thesis optional; for doctorate, comprehensive exam, thesis/dissertation. *Entrance requirements:* For master's, GMAT, 4-year honors degree with minimum B+ average; for doctorate, GMAT, master's degree, minimum B+ average. Additional exam requirements/recommendations for international students: Required—TOEFL (minimum score 89 iBT). Electronic applications accepted. *Faculty research:* Financial economics, management and organizational behavior, operations and supply chain management.

Organizational Management

Albertus Magnus College, Master of Science in Management and Organizational Leadership Program, New Haven, CT 06511-1189. Offers MS. *Program availability:* Part-time, evening/weekend, blended/hybrid learning. *Degree requirements:* For master's, thesis optional, project. *Entrance requirements:* For master's, bachelor's degree from regionally-accredited college or university, minimum GPA of 2.8, three years of professional and/or related experience, official transcripts, essay. Additional exam requirements/recommendations for international students: Recommended—TOEFL (minimum score 550 paper-based; 80 iBT). *Application deadline:* For fall admission, 8/14 for domestic students; for spring admission, 1/15 for domestic students. Applications are processed on a rolling basis. Application fee: $50. Electronic applications accepted. *Expenses:* Contact institution. *Financial support:* Federal Work-Study and unspecified assistantships available. Support available to part-time students. Financial award applicants required to submit FAFSA. *Faculty research:* Quantitative analysis of decision-making, conflict resolution, scientific method, information literacy, leadership management, principles of organizational management, quality management, business ethics, organizational behavior, human resources, international and global business, critical thinking skills in conducting research including developing hypothesis, evaluating research methods, conducting research, analyzing data, interpreting and presenting findings creative thinking skills. *Unit head:* Dr. Howard Fero, Director of Leadership Programs, 203-773-4424, E-mail: hfero@albertus.edu. *Application contact:* Anthony Reich, Director of Admission, Division of Professional and Graduate Studies, 203-773-5032, E-mail: arreich@albertus.edu. Website: http://www.albertus.edu/graduate-degrees/graduate-degree-programs/management-and-organizational-leadership/

Alvernia University, School of Graduate Studies, Program in Leadership, Reading, PA 19607-1799. Offers PhD. *Degree requirements:* For doctorate, comprehensive exam, thesis/dissertation (for some programs). *Entrance requirements:* For doctorate, GRE, GMAT, or MAT, minimum GPA of 3.3, 3 letters of recommendation, resume, interview.

The American College of Financial Services, Graduate Programs, Bryn Mawr, PA 19010-2105. Offers financial services (MSFS); leadership (MSM). *Program availability:* Part-time, evening/weekend, online learning. Electronic applications accepted. *Faculty research:* Retirement counseling, social security, aging, family composition, inflation.

American University, School of Public Affairs, Department of Public Administration and Policy, Washington, DC 20016-8070. Offers organization development (MSOD, Certificate), including leadership for organizational change (Certificate), organization development (MSOD); public administration (MPA, PhD, Certificate), including nonprofit management (Certificate), public financial management (Certificate), public management (Certificate); public administration and policy (MPAP), including public administration policy; public policy (MPP), including public policy; public policy (Certificate), including public policy analysis; LL M/MPA; MPA/JD; MPP/JD; MPP/LL M. *Program availability:* Part-time, evening/weekend, online learning. *Faculty:* 31 full-time (12 women), 36 part-time/adjunct (13 women). *Students:* 211 full-time (129 women), 305 part-time (202 women); includes 132 minority (84 Black or African American, non-Hispanic/Latino; 4 American Indian or Alaska Native, non-Hispanic/Latino; 24 Asian, non-Hispanic/Latino; 10 Hispanic/Latino; 10 Two or more races, non-Hispanic/Latino), 34 international. Average age 34. 658 applicants, 86% accepted, 230 enrolled. In 2017, 178 master's, 6 doctorates, 7 other advanced degrees awarded. *Degree requirements:* For master's, comprehensive exam; for doctorate, comprehensive exam, thesis/dissertation. *Entrance requirements:* For master's, GRE, statement of purpose, 2 recommendations, resume, transcript; for doctorate, GRE, 3 recommendations, statement of purpose, resume, writing sample, transcript; for Certificate, bachelor's degree. Additional exam requirements/recommendations for international students: Required—TOEFL (minimum score 600 paper-based; 100 iBT). *Application deadline:* For fall admission, 2/15 priority date for domestic students, 5/1 for international students; for spring admission, 11/1 for domestic students, 9/15 for international students. Application fee: $55. *Expenses:* Contact institution. *Financial support:* Research assistantships, teaching assistantships, institutionally sponsored loans, scholarships/grants, and unspecified assistantships available. Financial award application deadline: 2/1; financial award applicants required to submit FAFSA. *Unit head:* Dr. Dave Marcotte, Department Chair, 202-885-3108, E-mail: marcotte@american.edu. *Application contact:* Jennifer Forney, Assistant Dean, Graduate Enrollment, E-mail: forney@american.edu. Website: http://www.american.edu/spa/dpap/

Anderson University, College of Business, Anderson, SC 29621-4035. Offers business administration (MBA); healthcare leadership (MBA); human resources (MBA); marketing (MBA); organizational leadership (MOL); supply chain management (MBA). *Accreditation:* ACBSP. *Expenses:* Contact institution. *Financial support:* Tuition waivers available. Financial award application deadline: 3/1; financial award applicants required to submit FAFSA. *Unit head:* Steve Nail, Dean, 864-MBA-6000. *Application contact:* Mallory Knight, Graduate Admission Counselor, 864-231-2182, Fax: 864-231-2115, E-mail: malloryknight@andersonuniversity.edu. Website: http://www.andersonuniversity.edu/business

Antioch University Los Angeles, Program in Leadership, Management and Business, Culver City, CA 90230. Offers human resource development (MA); leadership (MA); organizational development (MA). *Program availability:* Part-time, evening/weekend. *Faculty:* 7. *Students:* 25 full-time (20 women); includes 16 minority (5 Black or African American, non-Hispanic/Latino; 2 Asian, non-Hispanic/Latino; 7 Hispanic/Latino; 2 Two or more races, non-Hispanic/Latino), 1 international. Average age 33. In 2017, 8 master's awarded. *Entrance requirements:* For master's, interview. Additional exam requirements/recommendations for international students: Required—TOEFL. *Application deadline:* For fall admission, 8/4 for domestic students; for winter admission, 11/3 for domestic students; for spring admission, 2/2 for domestic students. *Financial support:* In 2017–18, 23 students received support. Career-related internships or fieldwork, Federal Work-Study, and scholarships/grants available. Support available to part-time students. Financial award application deadline: 3/24; financial award applicants required to submit CSS PROFILE or FAFSA. *Faculty research:* Systems thinking and chaos theory, technology and organizational structure, nonprofit management, power and empowerment. *Unit head:* Dr. Susan Nero, Chair, 310-578-1080 Ext. 226, Fax: 310-882-4824, E-mail: susan_nero@antiochla.edu. *Application contact:* Information Contact, 310-578-1090, Fax: 310-822-4824, E-mail: admissions@antiochla.edu. Website: http://www.antiochla.edu

Apollos University, School of Business and Management, Great Falls, MT 59401. Offers business administration (MBA, DBA); organizational management (MS).

Aquinas College, School of Management, Grand Rapids, MI 49506. Offers marketing management (MM); organizational leadership (MM); sustainable business (MM). *Program availability:* Part-time, evening/weekend. *Students:* 11 full-time (6 women), 30 part-time (20 women); includes 7 minority (2 Black or African American, non-Hispanic/Latino; 1 Asian, non-Hispanic/Latino; 4 Hispanic/Latino). *Entrance requirements:* For master's, GMAT, minimum undergraduate GPA of 2.75, 2 years of work experience. Additional exam requirements/recommendations for international students: Required—TOEFL (minimum score 550 paper-based). *Application deadline:* Applications are processed on a rolling basis. Application fee: $0. *Expenses:* Contact institution. *Financial support:* Scholarships/grants available. Support available to part-time students. Financial award application deadline: 3/15; financial award applicants required to submit FAFSA. *Unit head:* Cynthia G. VanGelderen, Interim Director, 616-632-2922, Fax: 616-732-4489. *Application contact:* Lynn Atkins-Rykert, Program Coordinator, 616-632-2925, Fax: 616-732-4489, E-mail: atkinlyn@aquinas.edu.

Argosy University, Chicago, College of Business, Program in Organizational Leadership, Chicago, IL 60601. Offers Ed D.

Argosy University, Hawai′i, College of Business, Program in Organizational Leadership, Honolulu, HI 96813. Offers Ed D.

Argosy University, Los Angeles, College of Business, Los Angeles, CA 90045. Offers accounting (DBA); corporate compliance (MBA); customized professional concentration (MBA, DBA); finance (MBA); fraud examination (MBA); global business sustainability (DBA); healthcare administration (MBA); information systems (DBA); information systems management (MBA); international business (MBA, DBA); management (MBA, MSM, DBA); marketing (MBA, DBA); organizational leadership (Ed D); public administration (MBA); sustainable management (MBA).

Argosy University, Northern Virginia, College of Business, Arlington, VA 22209. Offers accounting (DBA); customized professional concentration (MBA, DBA); finance (MBA); fraud examination (MBA); global business sustainability (DBA); healthcare administration (MBA); information systems (DBA); information systems management (MBA); international business (MBA, DBA, Certificate); management (MBA, MSM, DBA); marketing (MBA, DBA, Certificate); organizational leadership (Ed D); public administration (MBA); sustainable management (MBA).

Argosy University, Orange County, College of Business, Program in Organizational Leadership, Orange, CA 92868. Offers Ed D.

Argosy University, Seattle, College of Business, Seattle, WA 98121. Offers accounting (DBA); corporate compliance (MBA); customized professional concentration (MBA, DBA); finance (MBA); fraud examination (MBA); global business sustainability (DBA); healthcare administration (MBA); information systems (DBA); information systems management (MBA); international business (MBA, DBA); management (MBA, MSM, DBA); marketing (MBA, DBA); organizational leadership (Ed D); public administration (MBA); sustainable management (MBA).

Argosy University, Tampa, College of Business, Tampa, FL 33607. Offers accounting (DBA); corporate compliance (MBA); customized professional concentration (MBA, DBA); finance (MBA); fraud examination (MBA); global business sustainability (DBA); healthcare administration (MBA); information systems (DBA); information systems management (MBA); international business (MBA, DBA); management (MBA, MSM, DBA); marketing (MBA, DBA); organizational leadership (Ed D); public administration (MBA); sustainable management (MBA).

Argosy University, Twin Cities, College of Business, Eagan, MN 55121. Offers accounting (DBA); customized professional concentration (MBA, DBA); finance (MBA); fraud examination (MBA); global business sustainability (DBA); healthcare administration (MBA); information systems (DBA); information systems management (MBA); international business (MBA, DBA); management (MBA, MSM, DBA); marketing (MBA, DBA); organizational leadership (Ed D); public administration (MBA); sustainable management (MBA).

Athabasca University, Centre for Interdisciplinary Studies, Athabasca, AB T9S 3A3, Canada. Offers adult education (MA); community studies (MA); cultural studies (MA); educational studies (MA); global change (MA); heritage resource management (Postbaccalaureate Certificate); legislative drafting (Postbaccalaureate Certificate); work, organization, and leadership (MA). *Program availability:* Part-time, evening/weekend, online learning. *Degree requirements:* For master's, project. *Entrance requirements:* Additional exam requirements/recommendations for international students: Required—TOEFL (minimum score 560 paper-based). Electronic applications accepted. *Faculty research:* Women's history, literature and culture studies, sustainable development, labor and education.

Atlantic University, Program in Mindful Leadership, Virginia Beach, VA 23451-2061. Offers global leadership (MA). *Program availability:* Online learning. *Degree requirements:* For master's, capstone project. *Entrance requirements:* For master's, bachelor's degree, official transcripts, minimum undergraduate GPA of 3.0, essay, current resume, interview. Application fee: $50. *Expenses:* $360 per credit. *Application contact:* Rachel Alvidrez, Associate Vice President of Enrollment Management Services, 757-631-8101, Fax: 757-631-8096, E-mail: rachel.alvidrez@atlanticuniv.edu.
Website: https://www.atlanticuniv.edu/academics/programs/mindful-leadership-m-a-and-grad-certificate/

Auburn University at Montgomery, College of Public Policy and Justice, Department of Justice and Public Safety, Montgomery, AL 36124-4023. Offers criminal studies (MSJPS); homeland security (MSJPS); homeland security and emergency management (MS); legal studies (MSJPS); organizational leadership (MSJPS). *Program availability:* Part-time, evening/weekend. *Faculty:* 5 full-time (2 women). *Students:* 9 full-time (3 women), 33 part-time (20 women); includes 23 minority (22 Black or African American, non-Hispanic/Latino; 1 Asian, non-Hispanic/Latino). Average age 30. 24 applicants, 75% accepted, 9 enrolled. In 2017, 23 master's awarded. *Degree requirements:* For master's, comprehensive exam, thesis optional. *Entrance requirements:* For master's, GRE General Test or MAT. Additional exam requirements/recommendations for international students: Recommended—TOEFL (minimum score 500 paper-based; 61 iBT), IELTS (minimum score 5.5), TSE (minimum score 44). *Application deadline:* For fall admission, 7/15 for international students; for spring admission, 11/15 for international students; for summer admission, 4/15 for international students. Applications are processed on a rolling basis. Application fee: $25. Electronic applications accepted. *Expenses:* Tuition, state resident: full-time $6930; part-time $385 per credit hour. Tuition, nonresident: full-time $15,588; part-time $866 per credit hour. *Required fees:* $640. *Financial support:* Career-related internships or fieldwork and scholarships/grants available. Support available to part-time students. Financial award application deadline: 3/1; financial award applicants required to submit FAFSA. *Faculty research:* Law enforcement, corrections, juvenile justice. *Unit head:* Dr. Ralph Ioimo, Head, 334-244-3691, Fax: 334-244-3244, E-mail: rioimo@aum.edu.
Website: http://cppj.aum.edu/departments/justice-and-public-safety

Augsburg University, Program in Leadership, Minneapolis, MN 55454-1351. Offers MA. *Program availability:* Part-time, evening/weekend. *Degree requirements:* For master's, thesis or alternative. *Entrance requirements:* For master's, MAT, minimum GPA of 3.0. Additional exam requirements/recommendations for international students: Required—TOEFL (minimum score 600 paper-based). *Faculty research:* Soviet leaders, artificial intelligence, homelessness.

Austin Peay State University, College of Graduate Studies, College of Behavioral and Health Sciences, Department of Leadership and Organizational Administration, Clarksville, TN 37044. Offers strategic leadership (MPS). *Program availability:* Part-time, online learning. *Faculty:* 3 full-time (all women), 1 (woman) part-time/adjunct. *Students:* 11 full-time (4 women), 29 part-time (19 women); includes 15 minority (10 Black or African American, non-Hispanic/Latino; 4 Hispanic/Latino; 1 Two or more races, non-Hispanic/Latino). Average age 39. 24 applicants, 92% accepted, 22 enrolled. In 2017, 18 master's awarded. *Degree requirements:* For master's, project. *Entrance requirements:* For master's, GRE General Test, minimum GPA of 2.75. Additional exam requirements/recommendations for international students: Required—TOEFL (minimum score 500 paper-based). *Application deadline:* For fall admission, 8/8 priority date for domestic students. Applications are processed on a rolling basis. Application fee: $45 ($55 for international students). Electronic applications accepted. *Expenses:* Tuition, state resident: full-time $7686; part-time $427 per credit hour. Tuition, nonresident: full-time $20,268; part-time $1126 per credit hour. *Required fees:* $1529; $76.45 per credit hour. *Financial support:* Career-related internships or fieldwork, Federal Work-Study, institutionally sponsored loans, scholarships/grants, and unspecified assistantships available. Support available to part-time students. Financial award application deadline: 4/1; financial award applicants required to submit FAFSA. *Unit head:* Dr. William Rayburn, Department Chair, 931-221-6377, E-mail: rayburnw@apsu.edu. *Application contact:* Megan Mitchell, Coordinator of Graduate Admissions, 931-221-6189, Fax: 931-221-7641, E-mail: mitchellm@apsu.edu.
Website: http://www.apsu.edu/leadership

Avila University, School of Professional Studies, Kansas City, MO 64145-1698. Offers executive leadership (MS); fundraising (MA); instructional design and technology (MA, MS); leadership coaching (MS); project management (MA); strategic human resources (MS). *Program availability:* Part-time-only, evening/weekend, 100% online, blended/hybrid learning. *Faculty:* 14 part-time/adjunct (8 women). *Students:* 85 full-time (61 women), 45 part-time (33 women); includes 42 minority (35 Black or African American, non-Hispanic/Latino; 2 Asian, non-Hispanic/Latino; 4 Hispanic/Latino; 1 Two or more races, non-Hispanic/Latino), 3 international. Average age 37. 63 applicants, 60%

accepted, 29 enrolled. In 2017, 39 master's awarded. *Degree requirements:* For master's, thesis optional. *Entrance requirements:* For master's, 2 letters of recommendation, minimum GPA of 3.0 during last 60 hours, resume, statement of intent. Additional exam requirements/recommendations for international students: Required—TOEFL (minimum score 550 paper-based; 79 iBT). *Application deadline:* Applications are processed on a rolling basis. Application fee: $0. Electronic applications accepted. *Expenses:* Contact institution. *Financial support:* In 2017–18, 14 students received support. Unspecified assistantships available. Support available to part-time students. Financial award applicants required to submit FAFSA. *Unit head:* Kari Clevenger, Associate Dean/Director, 816-501-3675, Fax: 816-941-4650, E-mail: advantage@avila.edu. *Application contact:* Jessica Burson, Graduate Admission Advisor, 816-501-2482, Fax: 816-941-4650, E-mail: advantage@avila.edu.
Website: https://www.avila.edu/mrk/advantage-3

Azusa Pacific University, University College, Azusa, CA 91702-7000. Offers leadership and organizational studies (MA); public health (MPH). *Program availability:* Online learning.

Baker University, School of Professional and Graduate Studies, Programs in Business, Baldwin City, KS 66006-0065. Offers MAOL, MBA, MSM, MSSM. Programs also offered in Overland Park, KS; Topeka, KS; and Wichita, KS. *Program availability:* Part-time, evening/weekend, online learning. *Students:* 23 full-time (14 women), 346 part-time (160 women); includes 106 minority (40 Black or African American, non-Hispanic/Latino; 19 American Indian or Alaska Native, non-Hispanic/Latino; 10 Asian, non-Hispanic/Latino; 24 Hispanic/Latino; 13 Two or more races, non-Hispanic/Latino), 1 international. Average age 34. In 2017, 192 master's awarded. *Entrance requirements:* For master's, 2 years of full-time work experience. Additional exam requirements/recommendations for international students: Required—TOEFL (minimum score 600 paper-based; 100 iBT). *Application deadline:* Applications are processed on a rolling basis. *Financial support:* Applicants required to submit FAFSA. *Unit head:* Dr. Emily Ford, Interim Dean of the School of Professional and Graduate Studies, 785-594-8475, E-mail: emily.ford@bakeru.edu. *Application contact:* Kelly Belk, Vice President of Enrollment Management, 913-491-4432, E-mail: kelly.belk@learn.bakeru.edu.
Website: https://www.bakeru.edu/spgs/

Bellevue University, Graduate School, College of Professional Studies, Bellevue, NE 68005-3098. Offers instructional design and development (MS); justice administration and criminal management (MS); leadership (MA); organizational performance (MS); public administration (MPA); security management (MS).

Benedictine University, Graduate Programs, Doctoral Program in Values-Driven Leadership, Lisle, IL 60532. Offers DBA, PhD. Electronic applications accepted.

Benedictine University, Graduate Programs, Program in Business Administration, Lisle, IL 60532. Offers accounting (MBA); entrepreneurship and managing innovation (MBA); financial management (MBA); health administration (MBA); human resource management (MBA); information systems security (MBA); international business (MBA); management consulting (MBA); management information systems (MBA); marketing management (MBA); operations management and logistics (MBA); organizational leadership (MBA). *Program availability:* Part-time, evening/weekend, online learning. *Entrance requirements:* For master's, GMAT. Additional exam requirements/recommendations for international students: Required—TOEFL (minimum score 550 paper-based). Electronic applications accepted. *Faculty research:* Strategic leadership in professional organizations, sociology of professions, organizational change, social identity theory, applications to change management.

Benedictine University, Graduate Programs, Program in Organization Development, Lisle, IL 60532. Offers PhD. *Program availability:* Evening/weekend. *Degree requirements:* For doctorate, thesis/dissertation. *Entrance requirements:* Additional exam requirements/recommendations for international students: Required—TOEFL (minimum score 550 paper-based). Electronic applications accepted. *Faculty research:* Change management, appreciative inquiry, innovation and organization design, global and international organization development, organization renewal.

Bethel University, Graduate School, St. Paul, MN 55112-6999. Offers business administration (MBA); classroom management (Certificate); counseling (MA); K-12 education (MA); leadership (Ed D); leadership foundations (Certificate); nurse educator (MS, Certificate); nurse-midwifery (MS); physician assistant (MS); special education (MA); strategic leadership (MA); teaching (MA); teaching and learning (Certificate). *Program availability:* Part-time, evening/weekend, 100% online, blended/hybrid learning. *Faculty:* 22 full-time (16 women), 70 part-time/adjunct (44 women). *Students:* 611 full-time (431 women), 393 part-time (249 women); includes 176 minority (82 Black or African American, non-Hispanic/Latino; 4 American Indian or Alaska Native, non-Hispanic/Latino; 31 Asian, non-Hispanic/Latino; 39 Hispanic/Latino; 2 Native Hawaiian or other Pacific Islander, non-Hispanic/Latino; 18 Two or more races, non-Hispanic/Latino), 9 international. Average age 36. 668 applicants, 42% accepted, 223 enrolled. In 2017, 287 master's, 30 doctorates, 172 other advanced degrees awarded. *Degree requirements:* For master's, comprehensive exam (for some programs), thesis (for some programs); for doctorate, comprehensive exam, thesis/dissertation. *Entrance requirements:* Additional exam requirements/recommendations for international students: Required—TOEFL (minimum score 550 paper-based, 80 iBT) or IELTS. *Application deadline:* Applications are processed on a rolling basis. Application fee: $0. Electronic applications accepted. *Expenses:* Contact institution. *Financial support:* Teaching assistantships, career-related internships or fieldwork, and scholarships/grants available. Support available to part-time students. Financial award applicants required to submit FAFSA. *Unit head:* Dr. Randy Bergen, Associate Provost, 651-635-8000, Fax: 651-635-8004, E-mail: r-bergen@bethel.edu. *Application contact:* Director of Admissions, 651-635-8000, Fax: 651-635-8004, E-mail: gs@bethel.edu.
Website: https://www.bethel.edu/graduate/

Binghamton University, State University of New York, Graduate School, School of Management, Program in Management, Binghamton, NY 13902-6000. Offers finance (PhD); management information systems (PhD); marketing (PhD); organizational studies (PhD); supply chain management (PhD). *Students:* 8 full-time (5 women), 12 part-time (5 women), 19 international. Average age 30. 57 applicants, 21% accepted, 7 enrolled. In 2017, 3 doctorates awarded. *Degree requirements:* For doctorate, thesis/dissertation. *Entrance requirements:* For doctorate, GMAT. *Application deadline:* For fall admission, 2/1 for domestic students. *Financial support:* In 2017–18, 18 students received support. *Unit head:* Dr. Upinder Dhillon, Dean, 607-777-2314, E-mail: dhillon@binghamton.edu. *Application contact:* Marianne Ferry, Administrative Assistant, Executive Education and PhD Programs, 607-777-2342, E-mail: mferry@binghamton.edu.

Boise State University, College of Engineering, Department of Organizational Performance and Workplace Learning, Boise, ID 83725-0399. Offers organizational performance and workplace learning (MS); workplace e-learning and performance support (Graduate Certificate); workplace instructional design (Graduate Certificate); workplace performance improvement (Graduate Certificate). *Program availability:* Part-time, 100% online. *Faculty:* 16. *Students:* 13 full-time (6 women), 158 part-time (100 women); includes 30 minority (14 Black or African American, non-Hispanic/Latino; 4 Asian, non-Hispanic/Latino; 10 Hispanic/Latino; 2 Two or more races, non-Hispanic/

Organizational Management

Latino), 12 international. Average age 39. 65 applicants, 83% accepted, 37 enrolled. In 2017, 32 master's, 25 other advanced degrees awarded. *Degree requirements:* For master's, thesis optional. *Entrance requirements:* Additional exam requirements/recommendations for international students: Required—TOEFL (minimum score 550 paper-based; 80 iBT), IELTS (minimum score 6). Application fee: $65 ($95 for international students). Electronic applications accepted. *Expenses:* Tuition, state resident: full-time $6471; part-time $390 per credit. Tuition, nonresident: full-time $21,787; part-time $685 per credit. *Required fees:* $2283; $100 per term. Part-time tuition and fees vary according to course load and program. *Financial support:* Scholarships/grants and unspecified assistantships available. Financial award applicants required to submit FAFSA. *Unit head:* Dr. Tony Marker, Department Chair, 208-426-1015, E-mail: anthonymarker@boisestate.edu. *Application contact:* Jo Ann Fenner, Program Coordinator, 208-426-2489, E-mail: jfenner@boisestate.edu. Website: http://opwl.boisestate.edu/

Boston College, Carroll School of Management, Department of Management and Organization, Chestnut Hill, MA 02467-3800. Offers PhD. *Degree requirements:* For doctorate, comprehensive exam, thesis/dissertation, teaching experience. *Entrance requirements:* For doctorate, GMAT or GRE, letters of recommendation, resume, transcripts. Additional exam requirements/recommendations for international students: Required—TOEFL (minimum score 100 iBT), IELTS (minimum score 7.5), or PTE (minimum score 68). Electronic applications accepted. *Faculty research:* Organizational transformation, mergers and acquisitions, managerial effectiveness, organizational change, organizational structure.

Boston University, Metropolitan College, Program in Leadership, Boston, MA 02215. Offers MS. Program offered at military locations in Massachusetts and North Carolina. *Faculty:* 2 full-time (0 women), 7 part-time/adjunct (2 women). *Students:* 25 part-time (4 women); includes 3 minority (all Black or African American, non-Hispanic/Latino). Average age 36. 12 applicants, 83% accepted, 5 enrolled. In 2017, 20 master's awarded. *Application deadline:* Applications are processed on a rolling basis. *Expenses:* Contact institution. *Unit head:* Dr. Lou Chitkushev, Associate Dean, 617-353-3010, Fax: 617-353-6066. *Application contact:* Larry Watson, Director of Military Programs, Virginia and North Carolina, 910-451-5574, E-mail: lwatson@bu.edu. Website: http://www.bu.edu/met/subject/leadership/

Bowling Green State University, Graduate College, College of Business, Program in Organization Development, Bowling Green, OH 43403. Offers MOD. *Program availability:* Part-time, evening/weekend. *Degree requirements:* For master's, thesis or alternative, internship. *Entrance requirements:* For master's, GMAT or GRE General Test. Additional exam requirements/recommendations for international students: Required—TOEFL. Electronic applications accepted. *Faculty research:* Charismatic leadership, self-managing work teams, knowledge workers, stress, effects of change processes.

Brandman University, School of Business and Professional Studies, Irvine, CA 92618. Offers accounting (MBA); business administration (MBA); business intelligence and data analytics (MBA); e-business strategic management (MBA); entrepreneurship (MBA); finance (MBA); health administration (MBA); human resources (MBA, MS); international business (MBA); marketing (MBA); organizational leadership (MA, MBA, MPA); public administration (MPA). *Expenses: Tuition:* Part-time $640 per credit hour. Tuition and fees vary according to degree level and program. *Unit head:* Dr. Glenn Worthington, Dean, 253-861-1024, E-mail: gworthin@brandman.edu. *Application contact:* Dr. Glenn Worthington, Dean, 253-861-1024, E-mail: gworthin@brandman.edu. Website: https://www.brandman.edu/academic-programs/business-and-professional-studies

Brenau University, Sydney O. Smith Graduate School, College of Business and Mass Communication, Gainesville, GA 30501. Offers accounting (MBA); business administration (MBA); healthcare management (MBA); organizational leadership (MS); project management (MBA). *Accreditation:* ACBSP. *Program availability:* Part-time, evening/weekend, online learning. *Degree requirements:* For master's, comprehensive exam (for some programs). *Entrance requirements:* For master's, resume, minimum undergraduate GPA of 2.5. Additional exam requirements/recommendations for international students: Required—TOEFL (minimum score 500 paper-based; 61 iBT); Recommended—IELTS (minimum score 5). Electronic applications accepted. *Expenses:* Contact institution.

Briercrest Seminary, Graduate Programs, Program in Leadership and Management, Caronport, SK S0H 0S0, Canada. Offers organizational leadership (MA). *Program availability:* Part-time. *Degree requirements:* For master's, comprehensive exam, thesis optional. *Entrance requirements:* Additional exam requirements/recommendations for international students: Required—TOEFL (minimum score 550 paper-based).

Cabrini University, Academic Affairs, Radnor, PA 19087. Offers accounting (M Acc); autism spectrum disorder (M Ed); biological sciences (MS), including civic leadership; criminology and criminal justice (MA); curriculum, instruction, and assessment (M Ed); educational leadership (M Ed, Ed D), including curriculum and instructional leadership (Ed D), preK-12 leadership (Ed D); English as a second language (M Ed); organizational leadership (DBA, PhD); preK to 4 (M Ed); reading specialist (M Ed); secondary education (M Ed), including biology, chemistry, English, English/communication, mathematics, social studies; special education grades 7-12 (M Ed); special education preK-8 (M Ed); teaching and learning (M Ed). *Program availability:* Part-time, evening/weekend. *Faculty:* 23 full-time (17 women), 46 part-time/adjunct (38 women). *Students:* 60 full-time (35 women), 559 part-time (435 women); includes 93 minority (66 Black or African American, non-Hispanic/Latino; 1 American Indian or Alaska Native, non-Hispanic/Latino; 8 Asian, non-Hispanic/Latino; 15 Hispanic/Latino; 3 Two or more races, non-Hispanic/Latino), 4 international. Average age 33. 290 applicants, 82% accepted, 154 enrolled. In 2017, 283 master's awarded. *Degree requirements:* For master's, comprehensive exam (for some programs), thesis (for some programs); for doctorate, comprehensive exam (for some programs), thesis/dissertation. *Entrance requirements:* For master's, professional resume, personal statement, two recommendations, official transcripts; for doctorate, official transcripts, minimum master's GPA of 3.0, two recommendations, interview with admissions committee. Additional exam requirements/recommendations for international students: Required—TOEFL (minimum score 80 iBT). *Application deadline:* For fall admission, 8/26 for domestic students, 8/1 for international students; for winter admission, 1/13 for domestic students, 12/20 for international students; for spring admission, 1/13 for domestic students, 12/20 for international students; for summer admission, 5/20 for domestic students, 4/30 for international students. Applications are processed on a rolling basis. Application fee: $50. Electronic applications accepted. Application fee is waived when completed online. *Expenses:* Contact institution. *Financial support:* In 2017–18, 1,459 students received support. Tuition waivers and unspecified assistantships available. Financial award application deadline: 5/1; financial award applicants required to submit FAFSA. *Unit head:* Dr. Maliha Zaman, 610-902-8502, Fax: 610-902-8797, E-mail: msz37@cabrini.edu. *Application contact:* Diane Greenwood, Director of Graduate Admissions, 610-902-8291, E-mail: diane.l.greenwood@cabrini.edu. Website: http://cabrini.edu/graduate

Cairn University, School of Business, Langhorne, PA 19047-2990. Offers accounting (MBA); business administration (MBA); international entrepreneurship (MBA); nonprofit leadership (MBA); organizational leadership (MSOL, Postbaccalaureate Certificate). *Program availability:* Part-time, evening/weekend, 100% online, blended/hybrid learning. *Entrance requirements:* Additional exam requirements/recommendations for international students: Required—TOEFL (minimum score 550 paper-based). Electronic applications accepted. Application fee is waived when completed online. *Expenses:* Contact institution.

California Baptist University, Program in Leadership and Organizational Studies, Riverside, CA 92504-3206. Offers MA. *Program availability:* Part-time, evening/weekend. *Faculty:* 3 full-time (0 women), 3 part-time/adjunct (0 women). *Students:* 1 full-time (0 women), 22 part-time (14 women); includes 13 minority (3 Black or African American, non-Hispanic/Latino; 1 Asian, non-Hispanic/Latino; 7 Hispanic/Latino; 2 Two or more races, non-Hispanic/Latino), 1 international. Average age 39. 33 applicants, 55% accepted, 12 enrolled. In 2017, 7 master's awarded. *Entrance requirements:* For master's, minimum undergraduate GPA of 2.75; three recommendations; resume; 500-word essay. Additional exam requirements/recommendations for international students: Required—TOEFL (minimum score 80 iBT). *Application deadline:* For fall admission, 8/1 priority date for domestic students, 7/1 for international students; for spring admission, 11/1 priority date for domestic students, 11/1 for international students. Applications are processed on a rolling basis. Application fee: $45. Electronic applications accepted. *Expenses:* Contact institution. *Financial support:* In 2017–18, 7 students received support. Federal Work-Study and scholarships/grants available. Financial award applicants required to submit CSS PROFILE or FAFSA. *Faculty research:* Leadership, educational history, assessment. *Unit head:* Dr. John Shoup, Dean, School of Education, 951-343-4205, E-mail: jshoup@calbaptist.edu. *Application contact:* David Little, Graduate Admissions Counselor, 951-552-8093, E-mail: dlittle@calbaptist.edu. Website: http://www.calbaptist.edu/academics/schools-colleges/school-education/programs/graduate/master-arts-leadership-and-organizational-studies

California Baptist University, Program in Organizational Leadership, Riverside, CA 92503. Offers MA. *Program availability:* Part-time, evening/weekend. *Faculty:* 5 full-time (2 women), 2 part-time/adjunct (1 woman). *Students:* 49 full-time (34 women), 29 part-time (22 women); includes 35 minority (11 Black or African American, non-Hispanic/Latino; 2 Asian, non-Hispanic/Latino; 21 Hispanic/Latino; 1 Two or more races, non-Hispanic/Latino). Average age 37. 34 applicants, 88% accepted, 25 enrolled. In 2017, 52 master's awarded. *Degree requirements:* For master's, capstone project. *Entrance requirements:* For master's, minimum cumulative GPA of 2.25, current resume, two letters of recommendation, comprehensive 500-word essay. Additional exam requirements/recommendations for international students: Required—TOEFL (minimum score 80 iBT). *Application deadline:* For fall admission, 8/1 priority date for domestic students, 7/1 for international students; for spring admission, 12/1 priority date for domestic students, 11/1 for international students. Applications are processed on a rolling basis. Application fee: $45. Electronic applications accepted. *Expenses:* Contact institution. *Financial support:* In 2017–18, 36 students received support. Federal Work-Study and scholarships/grants available. Financial award applicants required to submit CSS PROFILE or FAFSA. *Faculty research:* Organizational development, public administration, public service motivation, networked governance, finance. *Unit head:* Dr. Alfred Greg Bowden, Director, MA in Organizational Leadership, 951-343-5560, E-mail: abowden@calbaptist.edu. *Application contact:* Ted Meyer, Dean of Enrollment Services, Online and Professional Studies, 951-343-3909, E-mail: tmeyer@calbaptist.edu. Website: http://www.cbuonline.edu/programs/program/master-of-arts-in-organizational-leadership

California Coast University, School of Education, Santa Ana, CA 92701. Offers administration (M Ed); curriculum and instruction (M Ed); educational administration (Ed D); educational psychology (Ed D); organizational leadership (Ed D). *Program availability:* Online learning.

California College of the Arts, Graduate Programs, MBA in Design Strategy Program, San Francisco, CA 94107. Offers MBA. *Accreditation:* NASAD. *Faculty:* 1 (woman) full-time, 16 part-time/adjunct (5 women). *Students:* 88 full-time (62 women); includes 24 minority (3 Black or African American, non-Hispanic/Latino; 14 Asian, non-Hispanic/Latino; 6 Hispanic/Latino; 1 Native Hawaiian or other Pacific Islander, non-Hispanic/Latino), 26 international. Average age 30. 187 applicants, 68% accepted, 49 enrolled. In 2017, 53 master's awarded. *Degree requirements:* For master's, thesis. *Entrance requirements:* Additional exam requirements/recommendations for international students: Required—TOEFL, IELTS, or PTE. *Application deadline:* For fall admission, 1/31 priority date for domestic and international students. Applications are processed on a rolling basis. Application fee: $70. Electronic applications accepted. *Expenses:* $49,230 per year full-time tuition, $490 per year fees; $1,641 per unit part-time tuition. *Financial support:* Federal Work-Study and scholarships/grants available. Financial award application deadline: 7/31; financial award applicants required to submit FAFSA. *Unit head:* Andy Dong, Program Chair, 800-447-1ART, E-mail: andy@cca.edu. *Application contact:* Wes Fanelli, Assistant Director of Graduate Admissions, 415-703-9533, Fax: 415-703-9539, E-mail: wfanelli@cca.edu.

California Intercontinental University, School of Business, Irvine, CA 92614. Offers banking and finance (MBA); entrepreneurship and business management (DBA); global business leadership (DBA); international management and marketing (MBA); organizational management and human resource management (MBA).

California State University, Fullerton, Graduate Studies, College of Business and Economics, Program in Business Administration, Fullerton, CA 92831-3599. Offers business administration (MBA); business analytics (MBA); international business (MBA); organizational leadership (MBA); risk management and insurance (MBA). *Accreditation:* AACSB. *Program availability:* Part-time. *Faculty:* 12 full-time (5 women), 1 part-time/adjunct (0 women). *Students:* 64 full-time (35 women), 103 part-time (46 women); includes 81 minority (40 Asian, non-Hispanic/Latino; 36 Hispanic/Latino; 5 Two or more races, non-Hispanic/Latino), 36 international. Average age 29. 254 applicants, 47% accepted, 62 enrolled. *Entrance requirements:* For master's, GMAT. Application fee: $55. *Financial support:* Career-related internships or fieldwork, Federal Work-Study, institutionally sponsored loans, and scholarships/grants available. Support available to part-time students. Financial award application deadline: 3/1; financial award applicants required to submit FAFSA. *Unit head:* Shaun Pichler, Director, 657-278-7373, E-mail: spichler@fullerton.edu. *Application contact:* Admissions/Applications, 657-278-2371.

Calvary University, Graduate School and Seminary, Kansas City, MO 64147. Offers Bible and theology (MS); Biblical counseling (MA); education (MS), including administration and leadership, Christian education, curriculum and instruction, elementary education; organizational development (MS); pastoral studies (M Div); worship arts (MS). *Program availability:* Part-time, evening/weekend. *Faculty:* 6 full-time (2 women), 2 part-time/adjunct (1 woman). *Students:* 11 full-time (3 women), 29 part-time (15 women); includes 12 minority (4 Black or African American, non-Hispanic/Latino; 1 American Indian or Alaska Native, non-Hispanic/Latino; 6 Asian, non-Hispanic/Latino; 1 Native Hawaiian or other Pacific Islander, non-Hispanic/Latino). Average age 39. *Degree requirements:* For master's, variable foreign language requirement, comprehensive exam, thesis or alternative. *Entrance requirements:* For master's, minimum GPA of 2.5, BA or BS, doctrine agreement. Additional exam requirements/

recommendations for international students: Required—TOEFL (minimum score 550 paper-based). *Application deadline:* Applications are processed on a rolling basis. Application fee: $0. Electronic applications accepted. *Expenses:* Contact institution. *Financial support:* Scholarships/grants available. Financial award application deadline: 11/5; financial award applicants required to submit FAFSA. *Unit head:* Dr. Thomas Baurain, Director of Seminary, 816-322-0110 Ext. 1502, Fax: 816-331-4474, E-mail: thomas.baurain@calvary.edu. *Application contact:* Ann Rogers, Admissions Office Assistant, 800-326-3960 Ext. 1321, Fax: 816-331-4474, E-mail: admissions@calvary.edu.
Website: http://www.calvary.edu

Cambridge College, School of Management, Boston, MA 02129. Offers business negotiation and conflict resolution (M Mgt); general business (M Mgt); health care informatics (M Mgt); health care management (M Mgt); leadership in human and organizational dynamics (M Mgt); non-profit and public organization management (M Mgt); small business development (M Mgt); technology management (M Mgt). *Program availability:* Part-time, evening/weekend. *Degree requirements:* For master's, thesis, seminars. *Entrance requirements:* For master's, resume, 2 professional references. Additional exam requirements/recommendations for international students: Required—TOEFL (minimum score 550 paper-based; 79 iBT), Michigan English Language Assessment Battery (minimum score 85); Recommended—IELTS (minimum score 6). Electronic applications accepted. *Expenses:* Contact institution. *Faculty research:* Negotiation, mediation and conflict resolution; leadership; management of diverse organizations; case studies and simulation methodologies for management education, digital as a second language: social networking for digital immigrants, non-profit and public management.

Capella University, School of Business and Technology, Doctoral Programs in Business, Minneapolis, MN 55402. Offers accounting (DBA, PhD); business intelligence (DBA); finance (DBA, PhD); general business management (PhD); human resource management (DBA, PhD); leadership (DBA, PhD); management education (PhD); marketing (DBA, PhD); project management (DBA, PhD); strategy and innovation (DBA, PhD). *Accreditation:* ACBSP.

Capella University, School of Business and Technology, Master's Programs in Business, Minneapolis, MN 55402. Offers accounting (MBA); business analysis (MS); business intelligence (MBA); entrepreneurship (MBA); finance (MBA); general business administration (MBA); general human resource management (MS); general leadership (MS); health care management (MBA); human resource management (MBA); marketing (MBA); project management (MBA, MS). *Accreditation:* ACBSP.

Carlos Albizu University, Miami Campus, Graduate Programs, Miami, FL 33172-2209. Offers clinical psychology (PhD, Psy D); entrepreneurship (MBA); exceptional student education (MS); human services (PhD); industrial/organizational psychology (MS); marriage and family therapy (MS); mental health counseling (MS); nonprofit management (MBA); organizational management (MBA); psychology (MS); speech and language pathology (MS); teaching English for speakers of other languages (MS). *Accreditation:* APA. *Program availability:* Part-time, evening/weekend, 100% online, blended/hybrid learning. *Faculty:* 32 full-time (24 women), 27 part-time/adjunct (15 women). *Students:* 411 full-time (345 women), 248 part-time (215 women); includes 562 minority (53 Black or African American, non-Hispanic/Latino; 4 Asian, non-Hispanic/Latino; 498 Hispanic/Latino; 7 Two or more races, non-Hispanic/Latino), 23 international. Average age 34. 391 applicants, 42% accepted, 154 enrolled. In 2017, 96 master's, 54 doctorates awarded. Terminal master's awarded for partial completion of doctoral program. *Degree requirements:* For master's, comprehensive exam (for some programs), integrative project (for MBA); research project (for exceptional student education, teaching English as a second language); for doctorate, comprehensive examinations, internship, project/dissertation. *Entrance requirements:* For master's, GRE/EXADEP, bachelor's degree from accredited institution, minimum GPA of 3.0, 3 letters of recommendation, interview, resume, statement of purpose, official transcripts; for doctorate, GRE (for Psy D), 3 letters of recommendation, resume, interview, statement of purpose, official transcripts; bachelor's degree and minimum GPA of 3.25 (for Psy D); master's degree and minimum GPA of 3.0 (for PhD). Additional exam requirements/recommendations for international students: Required—Michigan Test of English Language Proficiency. *Application deadline:* For fall admission, 4/1 priority date for domestic students, 5/1 priority date for international students; for spring admission, 11/1 priority date for domestic students, 9/1 priority date for international students. Applications are processed on a rolling basis. Application fee: $50. Electronic applications accepted. Application fee is waived when completed online. *Expenses:* Contact institution. *Financial support:* In 2017–18, 145 students received support. Federal Work-Study, scholarships/grants, unspecified assistantships, and tuition discounts available. Financial award application deadline: 6/1; financial award applicants required to submit FAFSA. *Faculty research:* Psychotherapy, forensic psychology, neuropsychology, special education, speech-language pathology, criminal justice. *Unit head:* Dr. Etiony Aldarondo, Provost, 305-593-1223 Ext. 3138, Fax: 305-592-7930, E-mail: ealdarondo@albizu.edu. *Application contact:* Sonia Feliciano, Institutional Director of Student Recruitment, 305-593-1223 Ext. 3108, Fax: 305-477-8983, E-mail: sfeliciano@albizu.edu.

Carlow University, College of Leadership and Social Change, Pittsburgh, PA 15213-3165. Offers MA, MBA, MS, MSW, Psy D, Certificate, MA/MS. *Program availability:* Part-time, evening/weekend, 100% online, blended/hybrid learning. *Students:* 273 full-time (225 women), 70 part-time (51 women); includes 98 minority (75 Black or African American, non-Hispanic/Latino; 1 American Indian or Alaska Native, non-Hispanic/Latino; 6 Asian, non-Hispanic/Latino; 8 Hispanic/Latino; 8 Two or more races, non-Hispanic/Latino), 1 international. Average age 36. 210 applicants, 87% accepted, 109 enrolled. In 2017, 130 master's, 6 doctorates, 1 other advanced degree awarded. *Degree requirements:* For doctorate, thesis/dissertation, internship. *Entrance requirements:* For master's, personal essay; resume or curriculum vitae; three recommendations; official transcripts; interview; minimum undergraduate GPA of 3.0; for doctorate, GRE, resume or curriculum vitae; personal essay; reflective essay; official transcripts from all previous undergraduate and graduate institutions; three letters of recommendation; master's degree in closely-related field. Additional exam requirements/recommendations for international students: Required—TOEFL (minimum score 550 paper-based). *Application deadline:* For fall admission, 6/15 priority date for domestic and international students; for spring admission, 11/15 priority date for domestic and international students. Applications are processed on a rolling basis. Application fee: $0. Electronic applications accepted. *Expenses:* Contact institution. *Financial support:* Application deadline: 4/1; applicants required to submit FAFSA. *Unit head:* Dr. Allyson M. Lowe, Dean, 412-578-6663, Fax: 412-578-6357, E-mail: amlowe@carlow.edu. *Application contact:* 412-578-6059, Fax: 412-578-6321, E-mail: gradstudies@carlow.edu.
Website: http://www.carlow.edu/College_of_Leadership_and_Social_Change.aspx

Carson-Newman University, Program in Social Entrepreneurship, Jefferson City, TN 37760. Offers MAASJ. *Program availability:* Part-time, evening/weekend, 100% online, blended/hybrid learning. *Faculty:* 1 part-time/adjunct (0 women). *Students:* 2 full-time (0 women), 6 part-time (2 women); includes 1 minority (Two or more races, non-Hispanic/Latino), 2 international. Average age 27. 3 applicants, 100% accepted, 3 enrolled. In

2017, 3 master's awarded. *Degree requirements:* For master's, completion of degree within five years of admissions into program. *Entrance requirements:* For master's, GRE (minimum score of 290), minimum GPA of 3.0. Additional exam requirements/recommendations for international students: Recommended—TOEFL (minimum score 79 iBT), IELTS (minimum score 6.5), TSE (minimum score 53). *Application deadline:* For fall admission, 7/15 for domestic students. Applications are processed on a rolling basis. Application fee: $50. *Expenses:* Tuition: Full-time $10,516; part-time $478 per credit hour. *Required fees:* $240; $120 per semester. One-time fee: $150. *Financial support:* Federal Work-Study and tuition waivers (full and partial) available. Financial award applicants required to submit FAFSA. *Unit head:* Dr. Laura Wadlington, Department Chair, 865-471-3270. *Application contact:* Nilma Stewart, Graduate Admissions and Services Adviser, 865-471-3223, Fax: 865-471-3875, E-mail: adults@cn.edu.
Website: http://www.cn.edu/graduate-adult-studies/programs/applied-social-justice

Central Penn College, Graduate Programs, Summerdale, PA 17093-0309. Offers information systems management (MPS); organizational development (MPS). Programs offered in Harrisburg, PA. *Program availability:* Evening/weekend.

Charleston Southern University, College of Business, Charleston, SC 29423-8087. Offers accounting (MBA); finance (MBA); general management (MBA); human resource management (MS); leadership (MBA); management information systems (MBA); organizational leadership (MA). *Program availability:* Part-time, evening/weekend. *Degree requirements:* For master's, thesis optional. *Entrance requirements:* For master's, GMAT. Additional exam requirements/recommendations for international students: Required—TOEFL (minimum score 550 paper-based; 79 iBT). *Application deadline:* Applications are processed on a rolling basis. Application fee: $40. Electronic applications accepted. *Expenses:* Tuition: Part-time $500 per credit hour. One-time fee: $30. Tuition and fees vary according to program. *Financial support:* Research assistantships with full tuition reimbursements available. Financial award application deadline: 4/15; financial award applicants required to submit FAFSA. *Unit head:* Dr. David Palmer, Dean, 843-863-7025, Fax: 843-863-7922, E-mail: dpalmer@csuniv.edu. *Application contact:* Dr. Darin L. Gerdes, Associate Professor of Management, 843-863-7814, Fax: 843-863-7922, E-mail: dgerdes@csuniv.edu.
Website: http://www.csuniv.edu/business/

Charter Oak State College, Program in Organizational Effectiveness and Leadership, New Britain, CT 06053-2142. Offers MS. *Program availability:* Part-time, evening/weekend, online only, 100% online. *Faculty:* 7 part-time/adjunct (3 women). *Students:* 6 full-time (2 women), 78 part-time (47 women); includes 29 minority (19 Black or African American, non-Hispanic/Latino; 3 Asian, non-Hispanic/Latino; 7 Hispanic/Latino). *Degree requirements:* For master's, capstone seminar. *Entrance requirements:* For master's, bachelor's degree with minimum GPA of 3.0, transcripts from all colleges attended, two references, three years of relevant work experience, personal statement, resume or curriculum vitae. *Application deadline:* Applications are processed on a rolling basis. Application fee: $75. Electronic applications accepted. *Expenses:* Contact institution. *Financial support:* Scholarships/grants available. Financial award applicants required to submit FAFSA. *Unit head:* Dr. Thomas Barron, Director of Organizational Effectiveness and Leadership Program, 860-515-3838, E-mail: tbarron@charteroak.edu.
Website: http://www.charteroak.edu/masters/

The Chicago School of Professional Psychology, Program in Business Psychology, Chicago, IL 60610. Offers business psychology (PhD); industrial and organizational business psychology (Psy D); industrial and organizational psychology (MA); organizational leadership (MA, PhD). *Degree requirements:* For doctorate, thesis/dissertation optional. *Entrance requirements:* For doctorate, GRE. Additional exam requirements/recommendations for international students: Required—TOEFL.

City University of Seattle, Graduate Division, School of Management, Seattle, WA 98121. Offers accounting (Certificate); change leadership (MBA, Certificate); computer systems (MS); finance (Certificate); financial management (MBA); general management (MBA); general management-Europe (MBA); global marketing (MBA); human resources management (Certificate); individualized study (MBA); information security (MS); information systems (MBA); leadership (MA); marketing (MBA, Certificate); project management (MBA, MS, Certificate); sustainable business (Certificate); technology management (MBA, Certificate). *Program availability:* Part-time, evening/weekend, online learning. *Degree requirements:* For master's, comprehensive exam (for some programs), thesis (for some programs). *Entrance requirements:* For master's, baccalaureate degree or equivalent from an accredited or otherwise recognized institution. Additional exam requirements/recommendations for international students: Required—TOEFL (minimum score 567 paper-based; 87 iBT); Recommended—IELTS. Electronic applications accepted.

Clarks Summit University, Baptist Bible Seminary, South Abington Township, PA 18411. Offers Biblical apologetics (MA); Biblical studies (MA); church education (M Min); church planting (M Div, M Min); communication (D Min); counseling and spiritual development (D Min); global ministry (M Min, D Min); ministry (PhD); missions (M Min); organizational leadership (M Min); outreach pastor (M Min); pastoral counseling (M Min); pastoral leadership (M Div, M Min); pastoral ministry (D Min); theological studies (D Min); theology (Th M); youth pastor (M Min). M Min in missions available only for Association of Baptists for World Evangelism missionary personnel. *Program availability:* Part-time, evening/weekend, online learning. Terminal master's awarded for partial completion of doctoral program. *Degree requirements:* For master's, 2 foreign languages, thesis, oral exam (for M Div); for doctorate, 2 foreign languages, comprehensive exam (for some programs), thesis/dissertation, oral exam. *Entrance requirements:* For doctorate, Greek and Hebrew entrance exams (for PhD). *Application deadline:* Applications are processed on a rolling basis. Application fee: $30. Electronic applications accepted. *Financial support:* Career-related internships or fieldwork and scholarships/grants available. Support available to part-time students. *Unit head:* Dr. Wayne Slusser, Dean, 570-585-9348, Fax: 570-585-4057, E-mail: wslusser@clarkssummitu.edu. *Application contact:* Dr. Wayne Slusser, Dean, 570-585-9348, Fax: 570-585-4057, E-mail: wslusser@clarkssummitu.edu.
Website: https://www.clarkssummitu.edu/seminary/

Clarks Summit University, Online Master's Programs, South Abington Township, PA 18411. Offers Bible (MA); counseling (MA, MS); curriculum and instruction (M Ed); educational administration (M Ed); literature (MA); organizational leadership (MA). *Program availability:* Part-time, evening/weekend, online learning. *Entrance requirements:* Additional exam requirements/recommendations for international students: Required—TOEFL (minimum score 500 paper-based). *Application deadline:* Applications are processed on a rolling basis. Application fee: $30. *Financial support:* Institutionally sponsored loans and scholarships/grants available. Financial award application deadline: 8/20; financial award applicants required to submit FAFSA. *Unit head:* Dr. James Lytle, President, 570-586-2400 Ext. 9222, Fax: 570-586-1753. *Application contact:* Drew Whipple, Vice President for Enrollment Management, 570-585-9370, Fax: 570-585-9299, E-mail: awhipple@clarkssummitu.edu.
Website: https://www.clarkssummitu.edu/online-masters-degrees/

College of Saint Elizabeth, Department of Business Administration and Management, Morristown, NJ 07960-6989. Offers human resource management (MS); organizational

Organizational Management

change (MS). *Program availability:* Part-time. *Faculty:* 1 (woman) full-time, 5 part-time/adjunct (3 women). *Students:* 5 full-time (all women), 19 part-time (14 women); includes 8 minority (4 Black or African American, non-Hispanic/Latino; 1 Asian, non-Hispanic/Latino; 2 Hispanic/Latino; 1 Two or more races, non-Hispanic/Latino), 3 international. Average age 37. 11 applicants, 100% accepted, 5 enrolled. In 2017, 5 master's awarded. *Degree requirements:* For master's, thesis. *Entrance requirements:* Additional exam requirements/recommendations for international students: Required—TOEFL (minimum score 550 paper-based; 79 iBT), IELTS (minimum score 6.5). *Application deadline:* For fall admission, 5/1 for international students. Applications are processed on a rolling basis. Application fee: $35. Electronic applications accepted. Application fee is waived when completed online. *Financial support:* Career-related internships or fieldwork, scholarships/grants, tuition waivers (partial), and unspecified assistantships available. Financial award applicants required to submit FAFSA. *Unit head:* Dr. Regina Riccioni, Program Chair and Director, 973-290-4271, E-mail: rriccioni@cse.edu. *Application contact:* Lori J. Fragoso, Director of Graduate and Continuing Studies Admissions, 973-290-4413, Fax: 973-290-4710, E-mail: apply@cse.edu. Website: http://www.cse.edu/academics/prof-studies/

College of Saint Mary, Program in Organizational Leadership, Omaha, NE 68106. Offers MOL. *Program availability:* Part-time, evening/weekend. *Entrance requirements:* For master's, resume. Electronic applications accepted.

The College of Saint Rose, Graduate Studies, Huether School of Business, Program in Organizational Leadership and Change Management, Albany, NY 12203-1419. Offers Advanced Certificate. *Program availability:* Part-time, evening/weekend. *Students:* 1 applicant. In 2017, 1 Advanced Certificate awarded. *Entrance requirements:* Additional exam requirements/recommendations for international students: Required—TOEFL (minimum score 550 paper-based; 80 iBT), IELTS (minimum score 6), PTE (minimum score 56). *Application deadline:* For fall admission, 4/1 priority date for domestic and international students; for spring admission, 10/15 priority date for domestic and international students; for summer admission, 3/15 priority date for domestic and international students. Applications are processed on a rolling basis. Application fee: $40. Electronic applications accepted. *Expenses: Tuition:* Full-time $7191; part-time $799 per credit hour. *Required fees:* $924; $462 per credit hour. Tuition and fees vary according to course load. *Financial support:* Career-related internships or fieldwork and scholarships/grants available. Support available to part-time students. Financial award application deadline: 4/15. *Unit head:* John F. Dion, Program Coordinator, 518-458-5488, E-mail: dionj@strose.edu. *Application contact:* Cris Murray, Assistant Vice President for Graduate Recruitment and Enrollment, 518-485-3390, Fax: 518-458-5479, E-mail: grad@strose.edu.
Website: https://www.strose.edu/academics/graduate-programs/graduate-studies/organizational-leadership-and-change-management-certificate/

Colorado State University–Global Campus, Graduate Programs, Greenwood Village, CO 80111. Offers criminal justice and law enforcement administration (MS); education leadership (MS); finance (MS); healthcare administration and management (MS); human resource management (MHRM); information technology management (MITM); international management (MS); management (MS); organizational leadership (MS); professional accounting (MPA); project management (MS); teaching and learning (MS). *Accreditation:* ACBSP. *Program availability:* Online learning.

Columbia College, Graduate Programs, Program in Organizational Leadership, Columbia, SC 29203-5998. Offers organizational change and leadership (MA). *Program availability:* Part-time, evening/weekend, online learning. *Degree requirements:* For master's, thesis, practicum. *Entrance requirements:* For master's, GRE General Test, MAT, 2 letters of recommendation, minimum GPA of 3.2. Additional exam requirements/recommendations for international students: Required—TOEFL. *Application deadline:* For fall admission, 7/15 priority date for domestic students, 7/15 for international students. Applications are processed on a rolling basis. Application fee: $50. Electronic applications accepted. *Expenses:* Contact institution. *Financial support:* Available to part-time students. Application deadline: 7/1; applicants required to submit FAFSA. *Faculty research:* Envisioning and the resolution of conflict, environmental conflict resolution, crisis negotiation. *Unit head:* Dr. Katrina Spigner, Director, 803-786-3871, Fax: 803-786-3790, E-mail: kspigner@columbiasc.edu.
Website: https://www.columbiasc.edu/program/organizational-leadership

Columbia Southern University, Program in Organizational Leadership, Orange Beach, AL 36561. Offers MS.

Columbus State University, Graduate Studies, Turner College of Business, Columbus, GA 31907-5645. Offers applied computer science (MS), including informational assurance, modeling and simulation, software development; business administration (MBA); cyber security (MS); human resource management (Certificate); information systems security (Certificate); modeling and simulation (Certificate); organizational leadership (MS), including human resource management, leader development, servant leadership; servant leadership (Certificate). *Accreditation:* AACSB. *Program availability:* Part-time, evening/weekend, 100% online, blended/hybrid learning. *Faculty:* 20 full-time (5 women), 1 (woman) part-time/adjunct. *Students:* 70 full-time (20 women), 134 part-time (44 women); includes 76 minority (34 Black or African American, non-Hispanic/Latino; 2 American Indian or Alaska Native, non-Hispanic/Latino; 11 Asian, non-Hispanic/Latino; 20 Hispanic/Latino; 9 Two or more races, non-Hispanic/Latino), 30 international. Average age 30. 218 applicants, 56% accepted, 73 enrolled. In 2017, 110 master's, 1 other advanced degree awarded. *Entrance requirements:* For master's, GMAT, GRE, minimum undergraduate GPA of 2.75, letters of recommendation. Additional exam requirements/recommendations for international students: Required—TOEFL (minimum score 550 paper-based; 79 iBT). *Application deadline:* For fall admission, 6/30 for domestic students, 5/1 for international students; for spring admission, 11/1 for domestic and international students; for summer admission, 3/1 for domestic and international students. Applications are processed on a rolling basis. Application fee: $50. Electronic applications accepted. *Expenses:* Contact institution. *Financial support:* In 2017–18, 20 students received support, including 18 research assistantships (averaging $3,000 per year); Federal Work-Study also available. Financial award application deadline: 5/1; financial award applicants required to submit FAFSA. *Unit head:* Dr. Linda U. Hadley, Dean, 706-507-8153, Fax: 706-568-2184, E-mail: hadley_linda@columbusstate.edu. *Application contact:* Catrina Smith-Edmond, Assistant Director for Graduate and Global Admission, 706-507-8824, Fax: 706-568-5091, E-mail: smithedmond_catrina@columbusstate.edu.
Website: http://turner.columbusstate.edu/

Concordia College–New York, Program in Business Leadership, Bronxville, NY 10708-1998. Offers MS. *Degree requirements:* For master's, capstone seminar.

Concordia University, School of Graduate Studies, Faculty of Arts and Science, Department of Applied Human Sciences, Montréal, QC H3G 1M8, Canada. Offers human systems intervention (MA); youth work (Graduate Diploma). *Degree requirements:* For master's, 2-week residential laboratory. *Entrance requirements:* For master's, 1 week residential laboratory, 2 full years of work experience. *Faculty research:* Health promotion, adult learning and transitions, applications of group development and small group leadership, adolescent development, generational issues in immigrant families.

Concordia University Ann Arbor, Graduate Programs, Ann Arbor, MI 48105-2797. Offers curriculum and instruction (MS); educational leadership (MS); organizational leadership and administration (MS). *Program availability:* Part-time, evening/weekend. *Degree requirements:* For master's, thesis. *Entrance requirements:* Additional exam requirements/recommendations for international students: Required—TOEFL (minimum score 80 iBT); Recommended—IELTS (minimum score 6.5). Electronic applications accepted.

Concordia University, St. Paul, College of Business and Technology, St. Paul, MN 55104-5494. Offers business administration (MBA), including cyber-security leadership; health care management (MBA); human resource management (MA); information technology (MBA); leadership and management (MA); strategic communication management (MA). *Accreditation:* ACBSP. *Program availability:* Part-time, evening/weekend, 100% online, blended/hybrid learning. *Faculty:* 12 full-time (5 women), 33 part-time/adjunct (16 women). *Students:* 475 full-time (293 women), 35 part-time (17 women); includes 122 minority (57 Black or African American, non-Hispanic/Latino; 1 American Indian or Alaska Native, non-Hispanic/Latino; 34 Asian, non-Hispanic/Latino; 12 Hispanic/Latino; 1 Native Hawaiian or other Pacific Islander, non-Hispanic/Latino; 17 Two or more races, non-Hispanic/Latino), 47 international. Average age 33. 203 applicants, 70% accepted, 136 enrolled. In 2017, 172 master's awarded. *Degree requirements:* For master's, thesis (for some programs). *Entrance requirements:* For master's, official transcripts from regionally-accredited institution stating the conferral of a bachelor's degree with minimum cumulative GPA of 3.0; personal statement; professional resume. Additional exam requirements/recommendations for international students: Recommended—TOEFL (minimum score 547 paper-based; 78 iBT), IELTS (minimum score 6). *Application deadline:* For fall admission, 8/1 for domestic and international students; for spring admission, 12/1 for domestic and international students; for summer admission, 5/1 for domestic and international students. Applications are processed on a rolling basis. Application fee: $0. Electronic applications accepted. *Expenses:* $625 per credit (for MBA); $475 per credit (for MA). *Financial support:* In 2017–18, 292 students received support. Scholarships/grants and unspecified assistantships available. Financial award applicants required to submit FAFSA. *Faculty research:* Alternative dispute resolution, franchising, entrepreneurship, applied business ethics, strategic leadership development. *Unit head:* Dr. Kevin Hall, Dean, 651-603-6165, Fax: 651-641-8807, E-mail: khall@csp.edu. *Application contact:* Amber Faletti, Director of Enrollment Management, 651-641-8838, Fax: 651-603-6320, E-mail: faletti@csp.edu.

Concordia University Wisconsin, Graduate Programs, School of Business Administration, Program in Organizational Leadership Administration, Mequon, WI 53097-2402. Offers MS. *Degree requirements:* For master's, comprehensive exam, thesis or alternative. *Entrance requirements:* Additional exam requirements/recommendations for international students: Required—TOEFL.

Crandall University, Graduate Programs, Moncton, NB E1C 9L7, Canada. Offers literacy education (M Ed); organizational management (MOM); resource education (M Ed).

Creighton University, Graduate School, Department of Interdisciplinary Studies, MS Program in Organizational Leadership, Omaha, NE 68178-0001. Offers MS. *Program availability:* Part-time, online only, 100% online. *Faculty:* 1 (woman) full-time. *Students:* 5 full-time (2 women), 34 part-time (22 women); includes 4 minority (2 Black or African American, non-Hispanic/Latino; 2 American Indian or Alaska Native, non-Hispanic/Latino). Average age 34. 23 applicants, 74% accepted, 14 enrolled. In 2017, 15 master's awarded. *Degree requirements:* For master's, project-based capstone. *Entrance requirements:* For master's, two years of work experience, minimum undergraduate GPA of 3.0, two letters of recommendation, personal statement. Additional exam requirements/recommendations for international students: Required—TOEFL (minimum score 90 iBT), IELTS (minimum score 6.6). *Application deadline:* For fall admission, 7/1 for domestic and international students; for spring admission, 11/1 for domestic and international students; for summer admission, 3/1 for domestic and international students. Applications are processed on a rolling basis. Application fee: $50. Electronic applications accepted. *Expenses:* Contact institution. *Financial support:* Scholarships/grants available. *Unit head:* Dr. Gretchen Oltman, Director, 402-280-3418, Fax: 402-280-2423, E-mail: gretchenoltman@creighton.edu. *Application contact:* Lindsay Johnson, Director of Graduate and Adult Recruitment, 402-280-2703, Fax: 402-280-2423, E-mail: gradschool@creighton.edu.

Dallas Baptist University, College of Business, Management Program, Dallas, TX 75211-9299. Offers conflict resolution management (MA); general management (MA, MS); health care management (MA); human resource management (MA); organizational communication (MA); performance management (MA); professional sales and management optimization (MA). *Program availability:* Part-time, evening/weekend, online learning. *Application deadline:* Applications are processed on a rolling basis. Application fee: $25. Electronic applications accepted. Application fee is waived when completed online. *Expenses: Tuition:* Full-time $16,308; part-time $906 per credit hour. *Required fees:* $900; $450 per semester. Tuition and fees vary according to course load and degree level. *Unit head:* Dr. Sandra Reid, Chair, Graduate School of Business, 214-333-6860, E-mail: sandra@dbu.edu. *Application contact:* Richard Nassar, Director, 214-333-6801, E-mail: richardn@dbu.edu.
Website: http://www.dbu.edu/gsb/ma-in-management

Dallas Baptist University, Gary Cook School of Leadership, Program in Educational Leadership, Dallas, TX 75211-9299. Offers higher education leadership (Ed D), including educational ministry leadership, general leadership, higher education leadership. *Program availability:* Part-time. *Degree requirements:* For doctorate, thesis/dissertation. *Application deadline:* Applications are processed on a rolling basis. Application fee: $25. Electronic applications accepted. Application fee is waived when completed online. *Expenses: Tuition:* Full-time $16,308; part-time $906 per credit hour. *Required fees:* $900; $450 per semester. Tuition and fees vary according to course load and degree level. *Unit head:* Dr. Jack Goodyear, Dean, 214-333-5595, E-mail: jackg@dbu.edu. *Application contact:* Dr. Ozzie Ingram, Program Director, 214-333-6875, E-mail: ozzie@dbu.edu.
Website: http://www4.dbu.edu/leadership/education-leadership-ed-d

Dallas Baptist University, Gary Cook School of Leadership, Program in Leadership, Dallas, TX 75211-9299. Offers MA. *Program availability:* Part-time, evening/weekend. *Application deadline:* Applications are processed on a rolling basis. Application fee: $25. Electronic applications accepted. Application fee is waived when completed online. *Expenses: Tuition:* Full-time $16,308; part-time $906 per credit hour. *Required fees:* $900; $450 per semester. Tuition and fees vary according to course load and degree level. *Unit head:* Dr. Jack Goodyear, Dean, 214-333-5595, Fax: 214-333-6809, E-mail: jackg@dbu.edu. *Application contact:* Dr. Dale Meinecke, Program Director, 214-333-7169, E-mail: dalem@dbu.edu.
Website: http://www4.dbu.edu/leadership/maleadership

Drury University, Master of Arts in Communication Program, Springfield, MO 65802. Offers integrated marketing communications (MA); organizational leadership and change (MA). *Program availability:* Part-time, evening/weekend. *Entrance requirements:* For master's, GRE. Additional exam requirements/recommendations for international students: Required—TOEFL (minimum score 80 iBT); Recommended—IELTS (minimum score 6.5). Electronic applications accepted. *Expenses:* Contact institution. *Faculty research:* Nonprofit leadership, organizational change, leadership accountability, digital media, health communication.

Duke University, The Fuqua School of Business, The Duke MBA-Daytime Program, Durham, NC 27708-0586. Offers academic excellence in finance (Certificate); business administration (MBA); decision sciences (MBA); energy and environment (MBA); energy finance (MBA); entrepreneurship and innovation (MBA); finance (MBA); financial analysis (MBA); health sector management (Certificate); leadership and ethics (MBA); management (MBA); management science and technology management (Certificate); marketing (MBA); operations management (MBA); social entrepreneurship (MBA); strategy (MBA). *Faculty:* 96 full-time (19 women), 48 part-time/adjunct (15 women). *Students:* 876 full-time (297 women); includes 180 minority (39 Black or African American, non-Hispanic/Latino; 2 American Indian or Alaska Native, non-Hispanic/Latino; 83 Asian, non-Hispanic/Latino; 50 Hispanic/Latino; 6 Two or more races, non-Hispanic/Latino), 321 international. Average age 29. In 2017, 445 master's awarded. *Entrance requirements:* For master's, GMAT or GRE, transcripts, essays, resume, recommendation letters, interview. *Application deadline:* For fall admission, 9/12 for domestic and international students; for winter admission, 10/10 for domestic and international students; for spring admission, 1/3 for domestic and international students; for summer admission, 3/20 for domestic and international students. Application fee: $225. Electronic applications accepted. *Expenses:* $69,342 first-year tuition and fees. *Financial support:* In 2017–18, 423 students received support. Scholarships/grants available. Financial award applicants required to submit FAFSA. *Unit head:* Steve Misuraca, Assistant Dean, Daytime MBA Program. *Application contact:* Shari Hubert, Associate Dean, Office of Admissions, 919-660-7705, Fax: 919-681-8026, E-mail: admissions-info@fuqua.duke.edu.
Website: https://www.fuqua.duke.edu/programs/daytime-mba

Duke University, The Fuqua School of Business, PhD Program, Durham, NC 27708-0586. Offers accounting (PhD); decision sciences (PhD); finance (PhD); management and organizations (PhD); marketing (PhD); operations management (PhD); strategy (PhD). *Faculty:* 96 full-time (19 women). *Students:* 64 full-time (25 women); includes 1 minority (Hispanic/Latino), 41 international. Average age 27. 617 applicants, 5% accepted, 14 enrolled. In 2017, 15 doctorates awarded. *Degree requirements:* For doctorate, thesis/dissertation, major field requirement (exam or major paper, depending upon the area). *Entrance requirements:* For doctorate, GMAT or GRE, transcripts, essays, recommendation letters, statement of purpose. Additional exam requirements/recommendations for international students: Required—TOEFL (minimum score 577 paper-based; 108 iBT), IELTS (minimum score 8). *Application deadline:* For fall admission, 12/31 priority date for domestic and international students. Application fee: $85. Electronic applications accepted. *Expenses:* $52,253. *Financial support:* In 2017–18, 66 students received support, including 66 fellowships with full tuition reimbursements available (averaging $29,200 per year), 63 research assistantships with full tuition reimbursements available (averaging $7,000 per year); institutionally sponsored loans, scholarships/grants, and tuition waivers (full) also available. Financial award applicants required to submit FAFSA. *Unit head:* William Boulding, Dean. *Application contact:* Qi Chen, Director of Graduate Studies, 919-660-7753, Fax: 919-660-7971, E-mail: qc2@duke.edu.

Duquesne University, Graduate School of Liberal Arts, Master of Science in Leadership Program, Pittsburgh, PA 15282-0001. Offers MS. *Program availability:* Part-time, evening/weekend, online only, 100% online. *Students:* 29 full-time (12 women), 45 part-time (25 women); includes 18 minority (13 Black or African American, non-Hispanic/Latino; 2 Asian, non-Hispanic/Latino; 1 Hispanic/Latino; 2 Two or more races, non-Hispanic/Latino), 1 international. Average age 37. 25 applicants, 100% accepted, 19 enrolled. In 2017, 96 master's awarded. *Entrance requirements:* Additional exam requirements/recommendations for international students: Required—TOEFL. *Application deadline:* For fall admission, 8/1 for domestic students; for spring admission, 11/15 priority date for domestic students; for summer admission, 4/15 for domestic students. Applications are processed on a rolling basis. Application fee: $0. Electronic applications accepted. *Expenses:* $988 per credit. *Financial support:* Available to part-time students. Application deadline: 5/1. *Unit head:* Dr. Magali Michael, Director, 412-396-6389, E-mail: michael@duq.edu. *Application contact:* Linda Rendulic, Assistant to the Dean, 412-396-6400, Fax: 412-396-5265, E-mail: rendulic@duq.edu.
Website: http://duq.edu/academics/schools/liberal-arts/academic-programs/leadership

Eastern Connecticut State University, School of Education and Professional Studies/Graduate Division, Program in Organizational Management, Willimantic, CT 06226-2295. Offers MS. *Program availability:* Part-time, evening/weekend. *Faculty:* 6 full-time (3 women), 2 part-time/adjunct (1 woman). *Students:* 6 full-time (2 women), 27 part-time (19 women); includes 12 minority (4 Black or African American, non-Hispanic/Latino; 1 American Indian or Alaska Native, non-Hispanic/Latino; 3 Asian, non-Hispanic/Latino; 4 Hispanic/Latino). Average age 36. 12 applicants, 83% accepted, 9 enrolled. In 2017, 11 master's awarded. *Degree requirements:* For master's, comprehensive exam or thesis. *Entrance requirements:* For master's, minimum GPA of 2.7, bachelor's degree from accredited institution. Additional exam requirements/recommendations for international students: Required—TOEFL (minimum score 550 paper-based; 79 iBT); Recommended—IELTS (minimum score 6). *Application deadline:* For fall admission, 7/6 priority date for domestic and international students; for spring admission, 11/3 priority date for domestic and international students. Applications are processed on a rolling basis. Application fee: $50. Electronic applications accepted. *Expenses: Tuition, area resident:* Full-time $12,252. Tuition, state resident: full-time $15,245; part-time $582 per credit hour. Tuition, nonresident: full-time $24,828; part-time $582 per credit hour. *Required fees:* $40 per semester. Full-time tuition and fees vary according to reciprocity agreements. *Financial support:* Research assistantships, career-related internships or fieldwork, institutionally sponsored loans, and unspecified assistantships available. Financial award application deadline: 3/1; financial award applicants required to submit FAFSA. *Unit head:* Dr. Elizabeth Scott, Advisor, 860-465-5366, Fax: 860-465-4459, E-mail: scotte@easternct.edu. *Application contact:* Paula Goyette, Graduate Division, School of Education and Professional Studies, 860-465-5292, E-mail: graduateadmissions@easternct.edu.

Eastern Mennonite University, Program in Organizational Leadership, Harrisonburg, VA 22802-2462. Offers MA. Application fee: $50. *Unit head:* David Brubaker, Director, 540-432-4423, E-mail: mol@emu.edu. *Application contact:* Lois Shank, Assistant to the Provost, 540-432-4105, Fax: 540-432-4444, E-mail: graduate@emu.edu.
Website: http://www.emu.edu/ma-in-organizational-leadership/

Eastern Michigan University, Graduate School, College of Business, Department of Management, Program in Human Resources Management and Organizational Development, Ypsilanti, MI 48197. Offers MSHROD. *Program availability:* Part-time, evening/weekend, online learning. *Students:* 10 full-time (4 women), 58 part-time (40 women); includes 19 minority (11 Black or African American, non-Hispanic/Latino; 2 Asian, non-Hispanic/Latino; 3 Hispanic/Latino; 3 Two or more races, non-Hispanic/Latino), 4 international. Average age 31. 41 applicants, 76% accepted, 18 enrolled. In 2017, 92 master's awarded. *Degree requirements:* For master's, thesis optional. *Entrance requirements:* For master's, GMAT. Additional exam requirements/

recommendations for international students: Required—TOEFL. *Application deadline:* Applications are processed on a rolling basis. Application fee: $45. *Financial support:* Fellowships, research assistantships with full tuition reimbursements, teaching assistantships with full tuition reimbursements, career-related internships or fieldwork, Federal Work-Study, institutionally sponsored loans, scholarships/grants, tuition waivers (partial), and unspecified assistantships available. Support available to part-time students. Financial award applicants required to submit FAFSA. *Unit head:* Dr. Fraya Wagner-Marsh, Department Head, 734-487-3240, Fax: 734-487-4100, E-mail: fraya.wagner@emich.edu.
Website: http://www.emich.edu/cob/departments_centers/management/mshrod.php

Eastern Michigan University, Graduate School, College of Business, Programs in Business Administration, Ypsilanti, MI 48197. Offers business administration (MBA, Graduate Certificate); computer information systems (Graduate Certificate); e-business (MBA, Graduate Certificate); enterprise business intelligence (MBA); entrepreneurship (MBA, Graduate Certificate); finance (MBA, Graduate Certificate); human resources (MBA); human resources management (Graduate Certificate); information systems (MBA); internal auditing (MBA); international business (MBA, Graduate Certificate); marketing management (Graduate Certificate); nonprofit management (MBA); organizational development (Graduate Certificate); supply chain management (MBA, Graduate Certificate). *Accreditation:* AACSB. *Program availability:* Part-time, online learning. *Students:* 53 full-time (30 women), 297 part-time (170 women); includes 121 minority (72 Black or African American, non-Hispanic/Latino; 4 American Indian or Alaska Native, non-Hispanic/Latino; 15 Asian, non-Hispanic/Latino; 20 Hispanic/Latino; 10 Two or more races, non-Hispanic/Latino), 20 international. Average age 31. 247 applicants, 74% accepted, 94 enrolled. In 2017, 71 master's, 34 other advanced degrees awarded. *Entrance requirements:* For master's, GMAT (minimum score 450), minimum cumulative undergraduate GPA of 2.75. Additional exam requirements/recommendations for international students: Required—TOEFL. *Application deadline:* For fall admission, 5/15 priority date for domestic students, 2/15 priority date for international students; for winter admission, 10/15 priority date for domestic students, 9/1 priority date for international students; for summer admission, 3/15 priority date for domestic students, 3/1 priority date for international students. Applications are processed on a rolling basis. Application fee: $45. *Financial support:* Fellowships, research assistantships with full tuition reimbursements, teaching assistantships with full tuition reimbursements, career-related internships or fieldwork, Federal Work-Study, institutionally sponsored loans, scholarships/grants, tuition waivers (partial), and unspecified assistantships available. Support available to part-time students. Financial award applicants required to submit FAFSA. *Unit head:* K. Michelle Henry, Director, Graduate Business Programs, 734-487-4444, Fax: 734-483-1316, E-mail: cob.graduate@emich.edu.
Website: http://www.emich.edu/cob/mba/

Eastern University, Graduate Programs in Business and Leadership, St. Davids, PA 19087-3696. Offers health administration (MBA); health services management (MS); management (MBA); organizational leadership (MA); social impact (MBA). *Program availability:* Part-time, evening/weekend, online learning. *Students:* 55 full-time (34 women), 195 part-time (126 women); includes 123 minority (93 Black or African American, non-Hispanic/Latino; 1 American Indian or Alaska Native, non-Hispanic/Latino; 12 Asian, non-Hispanic/Latino; 12 Hispanic/Latino; 5 Two or more races, non-Hispanic/Latino), 23 international. Average age 34. In 2017, 123 master's awarded. *Application deadline:* Applications are processed on a rolling basis. Application fee: $35. Electronic applications accepted. Application fee is waived when completed online. *Expenses:* Contact institution. *Financial support:* Applicants required to submit FAFSA. *Unit head:* Michael Dziedziak, Executive Director of Enrollment, 800-452-0996, E-mail: gpsadmissions@eastern.edu.
Website: https://www.eastern.edu/academics/programs/graduate-business

Eastern University, Program in Organizational Leadership, St. Davids, PA 19087-3696. Offers leadership studies (CAGS); organizational leadership (PhD), including business management, educational administration, public and nonprofit administration. *Students:* 98 full-time (60 women); includes 31 minority (26 Black or African American, non-Hispanic/Latino; 2 Asian, non-Hispanic/Latino; 2 Hispanic/Latino; 1 Two or more races, non-Hispanic/Latino), 4 international. Average age 47. In 2017, 8 doctorates, 10 other advanced degrees awarded. *Application deadline:* Applications are processed on a rolling basis. Application fee: $75. Electronic applications accepted. *Expenses:* Contact institution. *Unit head:* Michael Dziedziak, Executive Director of Enrollment, 800-452-0996, E-mail: gpsadmissions@eastern.edu.
Website: https://www.eastern.edu/academics/programs/phd-organizational-leadership/phd-organizational-leadership-0

Embry-Riddle Aeronautical University–Worldwide, Department of Organizational Leadership, Daytona Beach, FL 32114-3900. Offers leadership (MS). *Program availability:* Part-time, evening/weekend, EagleVision Classroom (between classrooms), EagleVision Home (faculty and students at home), and a blend of Classroom or Home. *Faculty:* 4 full-time (2 women), 33 part-time/adjunct (12 women). *Students:* 64 full-time (27 women), 70 part-time (35 women); includes 25 minority (10 Black or African American, non-Hispanic/Latino; 3 Asian, non-Hispanic/Latino; 6 Hispanic/Latino; 6 Two or more races, non-Hispanic/Latino), 1 international. Average age 38. 38 applicants, 66% accepted, 20 enrolled. In 2017, 44 master's awarded. *Entrance requirements:* Additional exam requirements/recommendations for international students: Required—TOEFL (minimum score 550 paper-based; 79 iBT), IELTS (minimum score 6). *Application deadline:* Applications are processed on a rolling basis. Application fee: $50. Electronic applications accepted. *Expenses:* Contact institution. *Financial support:* Career-related internships or fieldwork and scholarships/grants available. Financial award applicants required to submit FAFSA. *Unit head:* Matt P. Earnhardt, PhD, Department Chair, E-mail: matthew.earnhardt@erau.edu. *Application contact:* Worldwide Campus, 800-522-6787, E-mail: worldwide@erau.edu.

Emory & Henry College, Graduate Programs, Emory, VA 24327. Offers American history (MA Ed); education professional studies (M Ed); occupational therapy (MOT); organizational leadership (MCOL); physical therapy (DPT); physician assistant studies (MPAS); reading specialist (MA Ed). *Program availability:* Part-time. *Faculty:* 7 full-time (3 women). *Students:* 194 full-time (128 women), 4 part-time (2 women); includes 6 minority (2 Black or African American, non-Hispanic/Latino; 1 American Indian or Alaska Native, non-Hispanic/Latino; 1 Asian, non-Hispanic/Latino; 2 Hispanic/Latino). Average age 25. 525 applicants, 21% accepted, 74 enrolled. In 2017, 24 master's awarded. *Degree requirements:* For master's, thesis optional; for doctorate, thesis/dissertation optional. *Entrance requirements:* For master's, GRE or PRAXIS I, official transcripts from all colleges previously attended, three professional recommendations, essay. Additional exam requirements/recommendations for international students: Recommended—TOEFL, IELTS (minimum score 6). *Application deadline:* Applications are processed on a rolling basis. Electronic applications accepted. *Expenses:* Contact institution. *Financial support:* Application deadline: 10/15; applicants required to submit FAFSA. *Unit head:* Dr. Michael Puglisi, Associate Dean for Academic Affairs, 276-944-6662, E-mail: mpuglisi@ehc.edu. *Application contact:* Mary Bolt, Director of Transfer and Graduate Admission, 276-944-6135, E-mail: mbolt@ehc.edu.

Organizational Management

Emory University, Goizueta Business School, Doctoral Program in Business, Atlanta, GA 30322. Offers accounting (PhD); finance (PhD); information systems and operations management (PhD); marketing (PhD); organization and management (PhD). *Students:* 250 applicants, 5% accepted. *Degree requirements:* For doctorate, comprehensive exam, thesis/dissertation. *Entrance requirements:* For doctorate, GMAT, interview. Additional exam requirements/recommendations for international students: Required— TOEFL (minimum score 600 paper-based; 100 iBT). *Application deadline:* For fall admission, 1/3 priority date for domestic and international students. Applications are processed on a rolling basis. Application fee: $75. Electronic applications accepted. *Expenses:* Contact institution. *Financial support:* Fellowships, scholarships/grants, and health care benefits available. Financial award application deadline: 1/3. *Faculty research:* Financial and managerial accounting, asset pricing strategy and organizational behavior, information technology marketing analytics and consumer behavior. *Unit head:* Kathryn Kadous, Associate Dean, 404-727-2306, Fax: 404-727-5337, E-mail: kathryn.kadous@emory.edu. *Application contact:* Allison Gilmore, Director of Admissions and Student Services, 404-727-6353, Fax: 404-727-5337, E-mail: allison.gilmore@emory.edu.
Website: https://goizueta.emory.edu/degree/phd/index.html

Emory University, Goizueta Business School, Full Time MBA Program, Atlanta, GA 30322. Offers accounting (MBA); alternative investments (MBA); business process consulting (MBA); business technology management (MBA); capital markets (MBA); corporate finance (MBA); customer relationship management (MBA); decision analytics (MBA); entrepreneurship (MBA); finance (MBA); global management (MBA); investment banking (MBA); management consulting (MBA); marketing (MBA); marketing analytics (MBA); marketing consulting (MBA); operations management (MBA); organization and management (MBA); product and brand management (MBA); real estate (MBA); social enterprise (MBA); strategy consulting (MBA). *Accreditation:* AACSB. *Faculty:* 74 full-time (18 women), 18 part-time/adjunct (6 women). *Students:* 353 full-time (96 women); includes 80 minority (18 Black or African American, non-Hispanic/Latino; 2 American Indian or Alaska Native, non-Hispanic/Latino; 39 Asian, non-Hispanic/Latino; 16 Hispanic/Latino; 1 Native Hawaiian or other Pacific Islander, non-Hispanic/Latino; 4 Two or more races, non-Hispanic/Latino), 104 international. Average age 29. 1,380 applicants, 34% accepted, 172 enrolled. In 2017, 179 master's awarded. *Degree requirements:* For master's, 1 leadership course; 2 mid-semester module programs; 2 global components. *Entrance requirements:* For master's, GMAT/GRE, essays; recommendation letters; undergraduate degree; interview. Additional exam requirements/recommendations for international students: Required—TOEFL (minimum score 100 iBT), IELTS (minimum score 7), PTE (minimum score 68). *Application deadline:* For fall admission, 10/6 for domestic and international students; for winter admission, 11/17 for domestic and international students; for spring admission, 1/3 priority date for domestic and international students; for summer admission, 3/9 for domestic and international students. Application fee: $150. Electronic applications accepted. *Expenses:* $59,616. *Financial support:* In 2017–18, 273 students received support. Career-related internships or fieldwork, institutionally sponsored loans, and scholarships/grants available. Financial award application deadline: 4/1; financial award applicants required to submit FAFSA. *Faculty research:* Corporate finance, information systems, digital marketing, asset pricing, sports management. *Unit head:* Brian Mitchell, Associate Dean, 404-727-4824, Fax: 404-712-9648, E-mail: brian.mitchell@emory.edu. *Application contact:* Julie Barefoot, Associate Dean, 404-727-6311, Fax: 404-727-4612, E-mail: mbaadmissions@emory.edu.
Website: http://www.goizueta.emory.edu

Endicott College, Van Loan School of Graduate and Professional Studies, Program in Business Administration, Beverly, MA 01915-2096. Offers business administration (MBA); organizational leadership (MBA). *Program availability:* Part-time, evening/weekend, 100% online, blended/hybrid learning. *Faculty:* 3 full-time (1 woman), 39 part-time/adjunct (11 women). *Students:* 149 full-time (66 women), 79 part-time (38 women); includes 39 minority (13 Black or African American, non-Hispanic/Latino; 7 Asian, non-Hispanic/Latino; 12 Hispanic/Latino; 7 Two or more races, non-Hispanic/Latino), 9 international. Average age 31. 98 applicants, 100% accepted, 82 enrolled. In 2017, 135 master's awarded. *Degree requirements:* For master's, thesis, project. *Entrance requirements:* For master's, two recommendations, undergraduate transcript, essay. Additional exam requirements/recommendations for international students: Required— TOEFL. *Application deadline:* Applications are processed on a rolling basis. Application fee: $50. Electronic applications accepted. *Expenses:* Tuition varies by track. *Financial support:* Scholarships/grants available. Financial award applicants required to submit FAFSA. *Faculty research:* Adult learning and development, supply chain management, marketing, ethics. *Unit head:* Richard Maybury, Dean, MBA Programs, 978-232-2764, Fax: 978-232-3000, E-mail: rmaybury@endicott.edu. *Application contact:* Ian Menchini, Director, Graduate Enrollment and Advising, 978-232-5292, Fax: 978-232-3000, E-mail: imenchin@endicott.edu.
Website: https://vanloan.endicott.edu/programs-of-study/masters-programs/master-of-business-administration-mba-programs

Endicott College, Van Loan School of Graduate and Professional Studies, Program in Organizational Management, Beverly, MA 01915-2096. Offers M Ed. *Program availability:* Part-time, evening/weekend, 100% online. *Faculty:* 2 full-time (1 woman), 4 part-time/adjunct (2 women). *Students:* 45 full-time (38 women), 4 part-time (3 women); includes 4 minority (1 Black or African American, non-Hispanic/Latino; 3 Hispanic/Latino). Average age 39. 1 applicant, 100% accepted, 1 enrolled. In 2017, 49 master's awarded. *Degree requirements:* For master's, thesis. *Entrance requirements:* For master's, GRE or MAT, two letters of recommendation, personal interview, 250-500 word essay, official transcripts of undergraduate and graduate course work. Additional exam requirements/recommendations for international students: Required—TOEFL. *Application deadline:* Applications are processed on a rolling basis. Application fee: $50. Electronic applications accepted. *Expenses:* Contact institution. *Financial support:* Applicants required to submit FAFSA. *Unit head:* Richard Weissman, Director, 978-232-2269, Fax: 978-232-3000, E-mail: rweissma@endicott.edu. *Application contact:* Ian Menchini, Director, Graduate Enrollment and Advising, 978-232-5292, Fax: 978-232-3000, E-mail: imenchin@endicott.edu.
Website: https://vanloan.endicott.edu/programs-of-study/masters-programs/organizational-management-program

Evangel University, Organizational Leadership Program, Springfield, MO 65802. Offers MOL. *Program availability:* Part-time, evening/weekend, 100% online, blended/hybrid learning. *Faculty:* 2 full-time (0 women), 2 part-time/adjunct (1 woman). *Students:* 32 full-time (15 women); includes 2 minority (1 American Indian or Alaska Native, non-Hispanic/Latino; 1 Hispanic/Latino). Average age 38. 14 applicants, 93% accepted, 13 enrolled. In 2017, 16 master's awarded. *Entrance requirements:* Additional exam requirements/recommendations for international students: Required—TOEFL (minimum score 550 paper-based). *Application deadline:* For fall admission, 7/15 priority date for domestic students, 8/1 for international students; for spring admission, 11/15 priority date for domestic students, 12/1 for international students. Applications are processed on a rolling basis. Application fee: $25. Electronic applications accepted. *Expenses:* Tuition: Full-time $7200; part-time $4800 per credit hour. *Required fees:* $210; $155 per semester. *Financial support:* In 2017–18, 13 students received support. Scholarships/grants available. Financial award application deadline: 4/1; financial award applicants

required to submit FAFSA. *Unit head:* Dr. Jeff Fulks, Program Coordinator, 417-865-2815 Ext. 8212, Fax: 417-575-5484, E-mail: fulksj@evangel.edu. *Application contact:* Michael Mann, Enrollment Coordinator, Graduate Studies, 417-865-2815 Ext. 8276, Fax: 417-575-5484, E-mail: mannm@evangel.edu.
Website: http://www.evangel.edu/academics/graduate-studies/graduate-programs

Excelsior College, School of Health Sciences, Albany, NY 12203-5159. Offers health care administration (MS); health professions education (MSHS); healthcare informatics (MS); organizational development (MS); public health (MSHS). *Program availability:* Part-time, evening/weekend, online learning. *Faculty:* 4 part-time/adjunct (all women). *Students:* 133 part-time (92 women); includes 84 minority (49 Black or African American, non-Hispanic/Latino; 4 American Indian or Alaska Native, non-Hispanic/Latino; 8 Asian, non-Hispanic/Latino; 13 Hispanic/Latino; 2 Native Hawaiian or other Pacific Islander, non-Hispanic/Latino; 8 Two or more races, non-Hispanic/Latino). Average age 40. In 2017, 38 master's awarded. *Application deadline:* Applications are processed on a rolling basis. Application fee: $50. Electronic applications accepted. *Expenses:* Tuition: Part-time $645 per credit. *Required fees:* $265 per credit. *Financial support:* Scholarships/grants available. *Unit head:* Dr. Barbara Pieper, Dean, 518-464-8500, Fax: 518-464-8777. *Application contact:* Admissions Counselor, 518-464-8500, Fax: 518-464-8777, E-mail: gradadmissions@excelsior.edu.

Fairleigh Dickinson University, Florham Campus, Maxwell Becton College of Arts and Sciences, Department of Psychology, Program in Organizational Behavior, Madison, NJ 07940-1099. Offers organizational behavior (MA); organizational leadership (Certificate).

Fielding Graduate University, Graduate Programs, School of Leadership Studies, Programs in Evidence Based Coaching, Santa Barbara, CA 93105-3814. Offers comprehensive evidence based coaching (Graduate Certificate); evidence based coaching for organizational leadership (Graduate Certificate). *Program availability:* Part-time, evening/weekend, blended/hybrid learning. *Faculty:* 20 part-time/adjunct (13 women). *Students:* 34 part-time (26 women); includes 9 minority (2 Black or African American, non-Hispanic/Latino; 1 American Indian or Alaska Native, non-Hispanic/Latino; 1 Asian, non-Hispanic/Latino; 5 Hispanic/Latino). Average age 49. 16 applicants, 100% accepted, 13 enrolled. In 2017, 47 Graduate Certificates awarded. *Entrance requirements:* For degree, bachelor's degree from regionally-accredited U.S. institution or equivalent, resume, official transcript. *Application deadline:* For fall admission, 7/1 for domestic and international students; for spring admission, 11/1 for domestic and international students; for summer admission, 3/1 for domestic and international students. Application fee: $75. Electronic applications accepted. *Expenses:* Contact institution. *Financial support:* Scholarships/grants available. Support available to part-time students. Financial award applicants required to submit FAFSA. *Unit head:* Terry Hilderbrand, PhD, Program Faculty Lead, E-mail: admissions@fielding.edu. *Application contact:* Enrollment Coordinator, 800-340-1099 Ext. 4098, Fax: 805-687-9793, E-mail: hodadmission@fielding.edu.
Website: http://www.fielding.edu/our-programs/school-of-leadership-studies/comprehensive-evidence-based-coaching-certificate/

Florida Institute of Technology, College of Psychology and Liberal Arts, Program in Applied Behavior Analysis and Organizational Behavior Management, Melbourne, FL 32901-6975. Offers MS. *Program availability:* Part-time. *Students:* Average age 25. 36 applicants, 39% accepted, 7 enrolled. In 2017, 5 master's awarded. *Degree requirements:* For master's, comprehensive exam, thesis or alternative, minimum of 50 credits, all course grades of B or higher. *Entrance requirements:* For master's, GRE General Test, 3 letters of recommendation, resume, statement of objectives. Additional exam requirements/recommendations for international students: Required—TOEFL (minimum score 550 paper-based; 79 iBT). *Application deadline:* Applications are processed on a rolling basis. Electronic applications accepted. *Expenses:* Tuition: Part-time $1241 per credit hour. Part-time tuition and fees vary according to campus/location. *Unit head:* Dr. David Wilder, Program Chair, 321-674-7516, E-mail: dawilder@fit.edu. *Application contact:* Cheryl A. Brown, Associate Director of Graduate Admissions, 321-674-7581, Fax: 321-723-9468, E-mail: cbrown@fit.edu.
Website: http://cpla.fit.edu/programs.php

Florida Institute of Technology, College of Psychology and Liberal Arts, Program in Organizational Behavior Management, Melbourne, FL 32901-6975. Offers MS. *Students:* Average age 24. 10 applicants, 20% accepted, 2 enrolled. *Degree requirements:* For master's, comprehensive exam, thesis optional, minimum of 42 credit hours, all course grades of B or higher. *Entrance requirements:* For master's, GRE General Test, 3 letters of recommendation, resume, statement of objectives. Additional exam requirements/recommendations for international students: Required—TOEFL (minimum score 550 paper-based; 79 iBT). *Expenses:* Tuition: Part-time $1241 per credit hour. Part-time tuition and fees vary according to campus/location. *Financial support:* Applicants required to submit FAFSA. *Unit head:* Dr. David Wilder, Program Chair, Campus Behavior Analysis Programs, 321-674-7516, E-mail: dawilder@fit.edu. *Application contact:* Cheryl A. Brown, Associate Director of Graduate Admissions, 321-674-7581, Fax: 321-723-9468, E-mail: cbrown@fit.edu.
Website: http://www.fit.edu/programs/

Gannon University, School of Graduate Studies, College of Humanities, Education, and Social Sciences, School of Humanities, Program in Organizational Learning and Leadership, Erie, PA 16541-0001. Offers PhD. *Program availability:* Part-time, evening/weekend. *Degree requirements:* For doctorate, thesis/dissertation. *Entrance requirements:* For doctorate, GRE, master's or other post-baccalaureate professional graduate-level degree from regionally-accredited institution of higher education with minimum GPA of 3.5; 2 years of post-baccalaureate work experience; 3 letters of recommendation; transcripts; resume; statement of purpose. Additional exam requirements/recommendations for international students: Required—TOEFL (minimum score 79 iBT). Electronic applications accepted. Application fee is waived when completed online.

Gardner-Webb University, Graduate School, School of Education, Boiling Springs, NC 28017. Offers curriculum and instruction (Ed D); educational leadership (Ed D); executive leadership studies (MA, Ed S); organizational leadership (Ed D); school administration (MA). *Accreditation:* NCATE. *Program availability:* Part-time, evening/weekend. *Faculty:* 15 full-time (7 women), 33 part-time/adjunct (20 women). *Students:* 13 full-time (10 women), 736 part-time (567 women); includes 332 minority (306 Black or African American, non-Hispanic/Latino; 6 American Indian or Alaska Native, non-Hispanic/Latino; 4 Asian, non-Hispanic/Latino; 9 Hispanic/Latino; 1 Native Hawaiian or other Pacific Islander, non-Hispanic/Latino; 6 Two or more races, non-Hispanic/Latino). Average age 33. *Degree requirements:* For master's, comprehensive exam. *Entrance requirements:* For master's, GRE General Test or NTE, PRAXIS, minimum GPA of 2.5. *Application deadline:* For fall admission, 8/1 priority date for domestic students. Applications are processed on a rolling basis. Electronic applications accepted. *Expenses:* Contact institution. *Financial support:* Unspecified assistantships available. *Application contact:* Office of Graduate Admissions, 877-498-4723, Fax: 704-406-3895, E-mail: gradinfo@gardner-webb.edu.

Geneva College, Program in Leadership Studies, Beaver Falls, PA 15010-3599. Offers business management (MS); ministry leadership (MS); non-profit leadership (MS);

organizational management (MS); project management (MS). *Program availability:* Online only, 100% online. *Faculty:* 4 part-time/adjunct (1 woman). *Students:* 32 full-time (22 women); includes 10 minority (8 Black or African American, non-Hispanic/Latino; 1 Asian, non-Hispanic/Latino; 1 Hispanic/Latino). Average age 43. 25 applicants, 60% accepted, 11 enrolled. In 2017, 35 master's awarded. *Degree requirements:* For master's, thesis or alternative, capstone leadership studies project. *Entrance requirements:* For master's, undergraduate degree from regionally-accredited college or university, one to three years of experience in the workplace, minimum GPA of 3.0 (preferred), resume, essay, two recommendations. Additional exam requirements/recommendations for international students: Required—TOEFL. *Application deadline:* For fall admission, 9/21 for domestic students; for spring admission, 2/23 for domestic students; for summer admission, 7/22 for domestic students. Applications are processed on a rolling basis. Electronic applications accepted. *Expenses:* $640 per credit. *Financial support:* Scholarships/grants available. Financial award application deadline: 8/1; financial award applicants required to submit FAFSA. *Faculty research:* Servant leadership, leadership essentials. *Unit head:* John D. Gallo, Dean of Graduate, Adult and Online Programs, 800-576-3111, Fax: 724-847-6839, E-mail: msls@geneva.edu. *Application contact:* Graduate Enrollment Representative, 800-576-3111, Fax: 724-847-6839, E-mail: msls@geneva.edu.
Website: http://www.geneva.edu/graduate/leadership-studies/

George Fox University, College of Business, Newberg, OR 97132-2697. Offers accounting (DBA); finance (MBA); management (DBA); management and leadership (MBA); marketing (DBA); organizational strategy (MBA); strategic human resource management (MBA). MBA offered in Newberg, OR and in Portland, OR. *Accreditation:* ACBSP. *Program availability:* Part-time, evening/weekend, online learning. *Degree requirements:* For master's, capstone project; for doctorate, credit-applied research project. *Entrance requirements:* For master's, resume (5 years of professional experience); 3 professional references; interview; financial e-learning course; official transcripts; for doctorate, GRE or GMAT, resume; personal mission statement; academic research writing sample; official transcript from each college/university attended; three professional references. Additional exam requirements/recommendations for international students: Required—TOEFL (minimum score 577 paper-based; 90 iBT) or IELTS (minimum score 7). Electronic applications accepted. *Expenses:* Contact institution.

George Mason University, Schar School of Policy and Government, Program in Organization Development and Knowledge Management, Arlington, VA 22201. Offers MS. *Faculty:* 3 full-time (1 woman), 3 part-time/adjunct (1 woman). *Students:* 1 (woman) full-time, 47 part-time (38 women); includes 20 minority (10 Black or African American, non-Hispanic/Latino; 3 Asian, non-Hispanic/Latino; 4 Hispanic/Latino; 1 Native Hawaiian or other Pacific Islander, non-Hispanic/Latino; 2 Two or more races, non-Hispanic/Latino). Average age 35. 37 applicants, 95% accepted, 24 enrolled. In 2017, 23 master's awarded. *Degree requirements:* For master's, thesis or alternative, internship. *Entrance requirements:* For master's, GRE (for students seeking merit-based scholarships), bachelor's degree with minimum GPA of 3.0, current resume, 2 letters of recommendation, expanded goals statement, 2 copies of official transcripts. Additional exam requirements/recommendations for international students: Required—TOEFL (minimum score 575 paper-based; 88 iBT), IELTS (minimum score 6.5), PTE (minimum score 59). *Application deadline:* For fall admission, 2/1 priority date for domestic and international students. Applications are processed on a rolling basis. Application fee: $75 ($80 for international students). Electronic applications accepted. *Expenses:* $795 per credit in-state tuition, $1,516 out-of-state. *Financial support:* Career-related internships or fieldwork, Federal Work-Study, scholarships/grants, unspecified assistantships, and health care benefits (for full-time research or teaching assistantship recipients) available. Financial award application deadline: 3/1; financial award applicants required to submit FAFSA. *Faculty research:* Organization development; appreciative intelligence; leadership; collaborative learning; knowledge management. *Unit head:* Tojo Joseph Thatchenkery, Director, 703-993-3808, Fax: 703-993-8215, E-mail: thatchen@gmu.edu. *Application contact:* Stephanie Ellis, Graduate Admissions Coordinator, 703-993-4478, E-mail: sellis11@gmu.edu.
Website: http://spgia.gmu.edu/programs/graduate-degrees/organization-development-knowledge-management-odkm/

The George Washington University, Columbian College of Arts and Sciences, Department of Organizational Sciences and Communication, Washington, DC 20052. Offers human resources management (MA); non-profit management (Graduate Certificate); organizational management (Graduate Certificate). *Program availability:* Part-time, evening/weekend. *Faculty:* 10 full-time (6 women), 6 part-time/adjunct (4 women). *Students:* 50 full-time (26 women), 26 part-time (20 women); includes 25 minority (8 Black or African American, non-Hispanic/Latino; 6 Asian, non-Hispanic/Latino; 6 Hispanic/Latino; 1 Native Hawaiian or other Pacific Islander, non-Hispanic/Latino; 4 Two or more races, non-Hispanic/Latino), 8 international. Average age 27. 138 applicants, 67% accepted, 39 enrolled. In 2017, 31 master's, 19 other advanced degrees awarded. *Degree requirements:* For master's, comprehensive exam. *Entrance requirements:* For master's, GRE General Test, minimum GPA of 3.0; for Graduate Certificate, minimum GPA of 3.0. Additional exam requirements/recommendations for international students: Required—TOEFL (minimum score 500 paper-based; 80 iBT). *Application deadline:* For fall admission, 1/15 priority date for domestic and international students; for spring admission, 10/1 priority date for domestic students, 9/1 priority date for international students. Applications are processed on a rolling basis. Application fee: $75. Electronic applications accepted. *Expenses:* Tuition: Full-time $28,800; part-time $1655 per credit hour. *Required fees:* $45; $2.75 per credit hour. *Financial support:* Federal Work-Study and institutionally sponsored loans available. *Unit head:* Dr. Lynn Offermann, Chair, 202-994-8507, E-mail: lro@gwu.edu. *Application contact:* Information Contact, 202-994-1878, Fax: 202-994-1881.
Website: http://www.gwu.edu/~orgsci/

The George Washington University, Graduate School of Education and Human Development, Department of Human and Organizational Learning, Program in Organizational Learning and Change, Washington, DC 20052. Offers Graduate Certificate. In 2017, 1 Graduate Certificate awarded. *Entrance requirements:* For degree, two letters of recommendation, resume, statement of purpose. *Expenses:* Tuition: Full-time $28,800; part-time $1655 per credit hour. *Required fees:* $45; $2.75 per credit hour. *Unit head:* Michael Feuer, Dean, 202-994-6161, E-mail: mjfeuer@gwu.edu. *Application contact:* Sarah Lang, Director of Graduate Admissions, 202-994-1447, Fax: 202-994-7207, E-mail: slang@gwu.edu.
Website: http://gsehd.gwu.edu/programs/organizational-learning-change

Georgia State University, J. Mack Robinson College of Business, Department of Managerial Sciences, Atlanta, GA 30302-3083. Offers business analysis (MBA, MS); entrepreneurship (MBA); human resources management (MBA, MS); operations management (MBA, MS); organization behavior/human resource management (PhD); organization management (MBA); organizational change (MS); strategic management (PhD). *Accreditation:* AACSB. *Program availability:* Part-time, evening/weekend. *Faculty:* 25 full-time (11 women). *Students:* 20 full-time (12 women); includes 7 minority (4 Black or African American, non-Hispanic/Latino; 2 Hispanic/Latino; 1 Two or more races, non-Hispanic/Latino), 6 international. Average age 33. 77 applicants, 18%

accepted, 10 enrolled. In 2017, 25 master's, 1 doctorate awarded. *Entrance requirements:* For master's, GRE or GMAT, transcripts from all institutions attended, resume, essays; for doctorate, GMAT, three letters of recommendation, personal statement, transcripts from all institutions attended, resume. Additional exam requirements/recommendations for international students: Required—TOEFL (minimum score 610 paper-based; 101 iBT), IELTS (minimum score 7). *Application deadline:* For fall admission, 2/1 priority date for domestic students, 2/1 priority date for international students; for spring admission, 9/15 priority date for domestic students, 4/1 priority date for international students. Applications are processed on a rolling basis. Application fee: $50. Electronic applications accepted. *Expenses:* Tuition, state resident: full-time $7020. Tuition, nonresident: full-time $22,518. *Required fees:* $2128. Tuition and fees vary according to degree level and program. *Financial support:* Research assistantships, teaching assistantships, scholarships/grants, tuition waivers, and unspecified assistantships available. Financial award applicants required to submit FAFSA. *Faculty research:* Entrepreneurship and innovation; strategy process; workplace interactions, relationships, and processes; leadership and culture; supply chain management. *Unit head:* Dr. Pamela S. Barr, Interim Chair, 404-413-7525, Fax: 404-413-7571. *Application contact:* Toby McChesney, Assistant Dean for Graduate Recruiting and Student Services, 404-413-7167, Fax: 404-413-7162, E-mail: rcbgradadmissions@gsu.edu.
Website: http://mgmt.robinson.gsu.edu/

Gonzaga University, School of Leadership Studies, Spokane, WA 99258. Offers communication and leadership (MA); leadership studies (PhD); organizational leadership (MA). *Program availability:* Part-time, evening/weekend, 100% online, blended/hybrid learning, immersion weekends. *Faculty:* 17 full-time (6 women), 22 part-time/adjunct (8 women). *Students:* 46 full-time (29 women), 600 part-time (368 women); includes 125 minority (31 Black or African American, non-Hispanic/Latino; 11 American Indian or Alaska Native, non-Hispanic/Latino; 16 Asian, non-Hispanic/Latino; 43 Hispanic/Latino; 3 Native Hawaiian or other Pacific Islander, non-Hispanic/Latino; 21 Two or more races, non-Hispanic/Latino), 24 international. Average age 38. 298 applicants, 91% accepted, 199 enrolled. In 2017, 405 master's, 11 doctorates awarded. *Degree requirements:* For master's, leadership seminar; for doctorate, thesis/dissertation. *Entrance requirements:* For master's, MAT or GRE, official transcripts, minimum GPA of 3.0 or MAT/GRE, letter of recommendation, statement of purpose, resume; for doctorate, MAT, GRE, 500-word narrative, short sample of writing, current resume/curriculum vitae, two official transcripts from each college attended, three letters of recommendation, master's degree with minimum GPA of 3.5, interview with department chair and faculty. Additional exam requirements/recommendations for international students: Required—TOEFL (minimum score 88 iBT) or IELTS (minimum score 6.5). *Application deadline:* For fall admission, 7/16 for domestic students; for spring admission, 11/16 for domestic students; for summer admission, 4/16 for domestic students. Applications are processed on a rolling basis. Application fee: $50. Electronic applications accepted. *Expenses:* $995 per credit. *Financial support:* In 2017–18, 70 students received support. Scholarships/grants and unspecified assistantships available. Support available to part-time students. Financial award applicants required to submit FAFSA. *Unit head:* Dr. Jolanta Weber, Interim Dean, 509-313-6595, E-mail: weberj@gonzaga.edu. *Application contact:* Teresa Crane, Assistant to the Dean, 509-313-6645, E-mail: guonlinestudentservices@gonzaga.edu.
Website: https://www.gonzaga.edu/school-of-professional-studies

Graceland University, School of Nursing, Independence, MO 64050-3434. Offers adult and gerontology acute care (MSN, PMC); family nurse practitioner (MSN, PMC); nurse educator (MSN, PMC); organizational leadership (DNP). *Accreditation:* AACN. *Program availability:* Part-time, online learning. *Faculty:* 13 full-time (11 women), 24 part-time/adjunct (all women). *Students:* 338 full-time (294 women), 311 part-time (282 women); includes 102 minority (33 Black or African American, non-Hispanic/Latino; 8 American Indian or Alaska Native, non-Hispanic/Latino; 18 Asian, non-Hispanic/Latino; 29 Hispanic/Latino; 1 Native Hawaiian or other Pacific Islander, non-Hispanic/Latino; 13 Two or more races, non-Hispanic/Latino), 2 international. Average age 36. 119 applicants, 86% accepted, 95 enrolled. In 2017, 158 master's, 2 doctorates awarded. *Degree requirements:* For master's, comprehensive exam (for some programs), thesis optional, scholarly project; for doctorate, capstone project. *Entrance requirements:* For master's, BSN from nationally-accredited program, RN license, minimum GPA of 3.0, satisfactory criminal background check, three professional reference letters, professional goals statement of 150 words or less; for doctorate, MSN from nationally-accredited program, RN license, minimum GPA of 3.2, criminal background check. Additional exam requirements/recommendations for international students: Required—TOEFL (minimum score 550 paper-based; 79 iBT). *Application deadline:* For fall admission, 6/1 priority date for domestic students; for winter admission, 10/1 priority date for domestic students; for spring admission, 10/1 priority date for domestic students; for summer admission, 2/1 for domestic students. Application fee: $50. Electronic applications accepted. *Expenses:* $775 per credit hour tuition, $1,800 practicum fees, $480 research fees, $846 university technology fees, $655 lab fees, $300 program support fees. *Financial support:* In 2017–18, 14 students received support. Institutionally sponsored loans available. Support available to part-time students. Financial award application deadline: 6/1; financial award applicants required to submit FAFSA. *Faculty research:* International nursing, family care-giving, health promotion, mental health nursing. *Unit head:* Dr. Claudia D. Horton, Interim Vice President for Independence Campus/Dean, 816-423-4670, Fax: 816-423-4753, E-mail: horton@graceland.edu. *Application contact:* Admissions Representative, 816-423-4717, Fax: 816-833-2990, E-mail: distancelearning@graceland.edu.
Website: http://www.graceland.edu/nursing

Grand Canyon University, Colangelo College of Business, Phoenix, AZ 85017-1097. Offers accounting (MBA, MS); business analytics (MS); disaster preparedness and executive fire service leadership (MS); finance (MBA); general management (MBA); health systems management (MBA); information technology management (MS); leadership (MBA, MS); marketing (MBA); organizational leadership and entrepreneurship (MS); project management (MBA); sports business (MBA); strategic human resource management (MBA). *Accreditation:* ACBSP. *Program availability:* Part-time, evening/weekend, online learning. *Entrance requirements:* For master's, equivalent of two years' full-time professional work experience. Additional exam requirements/recommendations for international students: Required—TOEFL (minimum score 575 paper-based; 90 iBT), IELTS (minimum score 7). Electronic applications accepted.

Grand Canyon University, College of Doctoral Studies, Phoenix, AZ 85017-1097. Offers data analytics (DBA); general psychology (PhD), including cognition and instruction, industrial and organizational psychology, integrating technology, learning, and psychology, performance psychology; management (DBA); marketing (DBA); organizational leadership (Ed D), including behavioral health, Christian ministry, health care administration, organizational development. *Degree requirements:* For doctorate, comprehensive exam, thesis/dissertation. *Entrance requirements:* For doctorate, minimum GPA of 3.4 on earned advanced degree from regionally-accredited institution; transcripts; goals statement.

Organizational Management

Grand View University, Graduate Studies, Des Moines, IA 50316-1599. Offers athletic training (MS); clinical nurse leader (MSN, Post Master's Certificate); nursing education (MSN, Post Master's Certificate); organizational leadership (MS); sport management (MS); teacher leadership (M Ed); urban education (M Ed). *Program availability:* Part-time, evening/weekend. *Degree requirements:* For master's, completion of all required coursework in common core and selected track with minimum cumulative GPA of 3.0 and no more than two grades of C. *Entrance requirements:* For master's, GRE, GMAT, or essay, minimum undergraduate GPA of 3.0, professional resume, 3 letters of recommendation, interview. *Additional exam requirements/recommendations for international students:* Required—TOEFL (minimum score 550 paper-based). Electronic applications accepted.

Granite State College, MS in Leadership Program, Concord, NH 03301. Offers MS. *Program availability:* Part-time, evening/weekend, 100% online, blended/hybrid learning. *Faculty:* 1 (woman) full-time, 10 part-time/adjunct (4 women). *Students:* 14 full-time (6 women), 30 part-time (27 women); includes 2 minority (1 American Indian or Alaska Native, non-Hispanic/Latino; 1 Hispanic/Latino). Average age 36. 10 applicants, 90% accepted, 9 enrolled. In 2017, 32 master's awarded. *Degree requirements:* For master's, capstone. *Entrance requirements:* For master's, bachelor's degree with minimum GPA of 3.0 on last 60 credit hours, 500-1000 word statement of purpose, two letters of professional or academic reference, resume, official transcripts. *Additional exam requirements/recommendations for international students:* Required—TOEFL (minimum score 80 iBT), IELTS (minimum score 6.5). *Application deadline:* Applications are processed on a rolling basis. Application fee: $0. Electronic applications accepted. *Expenses:* Tuition, state resident: full-time $9450; part-time $525 per credit. Tuition, nonresident: full-time $10,080; part-time $560 per credit. *Financial support:* Federal Work-Study and National Guard course waivers available. Financial award applicants required to submit FAFSA. *Unit head:* Dr. Johnna Herrick-Phelps, Vice Provost of Academic Affairs, 603-228-3000, E-mail: johnna.herrick-phelps@granite.edu. *Application contact:* Ana Gonzalez, Administrative Assistant, Office of Graduate Studies, 603-822-5433, Fax: 603-513-1387, E-mail: gsc.graduatestudies@granite.edu. Website: https://www.granite.edu/degree-programs/masters-degrees/leadership/

Harding University, Paul R. Carter College of Business Administration, Searcy, AR 72149-0001. Offers international business (MBA); leadership and organizational management (MBA). *Accreditation:* ACBSP. *Program availability:* Part-time, evening/weekend, 100% online. *Faculty:* 26 part-time/adjunct (6 women). *Students:* 15 full-time (8 women), 90 part-time (36 women); includes 12 minority (8 Black or African American, non-Hispanic/Latino; 2 Asian, non-Hispanic/Latino; 2 Hispanic/Latino), 2 international. Average age 34. 15 applicants, 100% accepted, 15 enrolled. In 2017, 66 master's awarded. *Degree requirements:* For master's, portfolio. *Entrance requirements:* For master's, GMAT (minimum score of 500) or GRE (minimum score of 300), minimum GPA of 3.0, 2 letters of recommendation, resume, 3 essays, all official transcripts. *Additional exam requirements/recommendations for international students:* Required—TOEFL (minimum score 550 paper-based; 79 iBT). *Application deadline:* For fall admission, 8/1 priority date for domestic and international students; for spring admission, 12/1 priority date for domestic and international students. Applications are processed on a rolling basis. Application fee: $40. Tuition and fees vary according to course load, degree level, campus/location and program. *Financial support:* Unspecified assistantships available. Financial award application deadline: 7/30; financial award applicants required to submit FAFSA. *Unit head:* 501-279-5789, Fax: 501-279-4805, E-mail: mba@harding.edu. Website: http://www.harding.edu/mba

Hawai`i Pacific University, College of Business, Program in Business Administration, Honolulu, HI 96813. Offers finance (MBA); human resource management (MBA); information systems (MBA); international business (MBA); management (MBA); marketing (MBA); organizational change and development (MBA). *Program availability:* Part-time, evening/weekend, 100% online, blended/hybrid learning. *Faculty:* 7 full-time (3 women), 3 part-time/adjunct (0 women). *Students:* 88 full-time (34 women), 28 part-time (18 women); includes 63 minority (9 Black or African American, non-Hispanic/Latino; 17 Asian, non-Hispanic/Latino; 14 Hispanic/Latino; 1 Native Hawaiian or other Pacific Islander, non-Hispanic/Latino; 22 Two or more races, non-Hispanic/Latino), 29 international. Average age 32. 82 applicants, 78% accepted, 40 enrolled. In 2017, 87 master's awarded. *Entrance requirements:* For master's, GMAT or GRE. *Additional exam requirements/recommendations for international students:* Recommended—TOEFL (minimum score 550 paper-based; 80 iBT), IELTS (minimum score 6), TWE (minimum score 5). *Application deadline:* For fall admission, 1/15 priority date for domestic students; for spring admission, 10/15 priority date for domestic students. Applications are processed on a rolling basis. Application fee: $50. Electronic applications accepted. *Expenses:* Tuition: Full-time $18,000; part-time $1000 per credit. *Required fees:* $200; $26 per credit. Tuition and fees vary according to course load and program. *Financial support:* In 2017–18, 24 students received support. Research assistantships, career-related internships or fieldwork, Federal Work-Study, scholarships/grants, tuition waivers (partial), and unspecified assistantships available. Financial award application deadline: 3/1; financial award applicants required to submit FAFSA. *Unit head:* Dr. Daewoo Park, Department Chair, 808-544-1463, E-mail: dwpark@hpu.edu. *Application contact:* Danny Lam, Assistant Director of Graduate Admissions, 808-544-1135, E-mail: graduate@hpu.edu. Website: https://www.hpu.edu/cob/grad-programs/mba.html

Hawai`i Pacific University, College of Business, Program in Organizational Change, Honolulu, HI 96813. Offers MA. *Program availability:* Part-time, evening/weekend, 100% online, blended/hybrid learning. *Faculty:* 7 full-time (3 women), 3 part-time/adjunct (0 women). *Students:* 14 full-time (9 women), 10 part-time (5 women); includes 17 minority (1 Black or African American, non-Hispanic/Latino; 6 Hispanic/Latino; 2 Native Hawaiian or other Pacific Islander, non-Hispanic/Latino; 8 Two or more races, non-Hispanic/Latino), 1 international. Average age 37. 16 applicants, 81% accepted, 10 enrolled. In 2017, 12 master's awarded. *Entrance requirements:* Additional exam requirements/recommendations for international students: Recommended—TOEFL (minimum score 550 paper-based; 80 iBT), IELTS (minimum score 6), TWE (minimum score 5). *Application deadline:* For fall admission, 1/15 priority date for domestic students; for spring admission, 10/15 priority date for domestic students. Applications are processed on a rolling basis. Application fee: $50. Electronic applications accepted. *Expenses:* Tuition: Full-time $18,000; part-time $1000 per credit. *Required fees:* $200; $26 per credit. Tuition and fees vary according to course load and program. *Financial support:* In 2017–18, 3 students received support. Research assistantships, career-related internships or fieldwork, Federal Work-Study, scholarships/grants, tuition waivers (partial), and unspecified assistantships available. Financial award application deadline: 3/1; financial award applicants required to submit FAFSA. *Unit head:* Dr. Daewoo Park, Department Chair, 808-544-1463, E-mail: dwpark@hpu.edu. *Application contact:* Danny Lam, Assistant Director of Graduate Admissions, 808-544-1135, E-mail: graduate@hpu.edu. Website: https://www.hpu.edu/cob/grad-programs/maodc.html

HEC Montreal, School of Business Administration, Master in Management in Cultural Enterprises Program, Montréal, QC H3T 2A7, Canada. Offers MM. All courses are given in French. *Program availability:* Part-time. *Students:* 16 full-time (12 women), 29 part-time (25 women). 23 applicants, 91% accepted, 17 enrolled. In 2017, 41 master's awarded. *Entrance requirements:* For master's, bachelor's degree in cultural field, work experience in cultural or artistic organization. *Application deadline:* For fall admission, 4/15 for domestic and international students; for winter admission, 9/15 for domestic and international students. Application fee: $88 ($184 for international students). Electronic applications accepted. *Expenses:* Tuition, state resident: full-time $2869 Canadian dollars; part-time $79.70 Canadian dollars per credit. Tuition, nonresident: full-time $8883 Canadian dollars; part-time $246.76 Canadian dollars per credit. *International tuition:* $19,648 Canadian dollars full-time. *Required fees:* $41.20 Canadian dollars per credit. $67.94 Canadian dollars per term. Tuition and fees vary according to degree level and program. *Financial support:* Research assistantships, teaching assistantships, and scholarships/grants available. Financial award application deadline: 9/2. *Unit head:* Renaud Lachance, Director, 514-340-7165, E-mail: renaud.lachance@hec.ca. *Application contact:* Anny Caron, Administrative Director, 514-340-6151, Fax: 514-340-6411, E-mail: aide@hec.ca. Website: http://www.hec.ca/programmes/maitrises/maitrise-management-entreprises-culturelles/index.html

HEC Montreal, School of Business Administration, Master of Science Programs in Administration, Program in Management and Social Innovations, Montréal, QC H3T 2A7, Canada. Offers M Sc. Program offered in French. *Students:* 41 full-time (30 women), 7 part-time (4 women). 17 applicants, 82% accepted, 12 enrolled. In 2017, 14 master's awarded. *Degree requirements:* For master's, thesis. *Entrance requirements:* For master's, BBA, undergraduate degree in another field, degree deemed equivalent by program director and minimum GPA of 3.0 on 4.3 scale. *Additional exam requirements/recommendations for international students:* Required—TAGE MAGE (minimum recommended score of 283), GMAT (minimum recommended score of 630), or GRE. *Application deadline:* For fall admission, 3/15 for domestic and international students; for winter admission, 9/15 for domestic and international students. Application fee: $88 ($184 for international students). Electronic applications accepted. *Expenses:* Tuition, state resident: full-time $2869 Canadian dollars; part-time $79.70 Canadian dollars per credit. Tuition, nonresident: full-time $8883 Canadian dollars; part-time $246.76 Canadian dollars per credit. *International tuition:* $19,648 Canadian dollars full-time. *Required fees:* $41.20 Canadian dollars per credit. $67.94 Canadian dollars per term. Tuition and fees vary according to degree level and program. *Financial support:* Research assistantships, teaching assistantships, and scholarships/grants available. Financial award application deadline: 9/2. *Unit head:* Dr. Marie-Helene Jobin, Director, 514-340-6283, E-mail: marie-helene.jobin@hec.ca. *Application contact:* Marianne de Moura, Administrative Director, 514-340-6151, Fax: 514-340-6411, E-mail: aide@hec.ca. Website: http://www.hec.ca/programmes/maitrises/maitrise-gestions-en-contexte-innovations-sociales/index.html

HEC Montreal, School of Business Administration, Master of Science Programs in Administration, Program in Organizational Development, Montréal, QC H3T 2A7, Canada. Offers M Sc. Program offered in French. *Students:* 54 full-time (38 women), 22 part-time (19 women). 60 applicants, 67% accepted, 26 enrolled. In 2017, 24 master's awarded. *Entrance requirements:* For master's, BBA, undergraduate degree in another field, degree deemed equivalent by program director and minimum GPA of 3.0 on 4.3 scale. *Additional exam requirements/recommendations for international students:* Required—TAGE MAGE (minimum recommended score of 283), GMAT (minimum recommended score of 630), or GRE. *Application deadline:* For fall admission, 3/15 for domestic and international students; for winter admission, 9/15 for domestic and international students. Application fee: $88 ($184 for international students). Electronic applications accepted. *Expenses:* Tuition, state resident: full-time $2869 Canadian dollars; part-time $79.70 Canadian dollars per credit. Tuition, nonresident: full-time $8883 Canadian dollars; part-time $246.76 Canadian dollars per credit. *International tuition:* $19,648 Canadian dollars full-time. *Required fees:* $41.20 Canadian dollars per credit. $67.94 Canadian dollars per term. Tuition and fees vary according to degree level and program. *Financial support:* Research assistantships, teaching assistantships, and scholarships/grants available. Financial award application deadline: 9/2. *Unit head:* Dr. Marie-Helene Jobin, Director, 514-340-6283, E-mail: marie-helene.jobin@hec.ca. *Application contact:* Marianne de Moura, Administrative Director, 514-340-6151, Fax: 514-340-6411, E-mail: aide@hec.ca. Website: http://www.hec.ca/programmes/maitrises/maitrise-developpement-organisationnel/index.html

Hood College, Graduate School, Department of Economics and Business Administration, Frederick, MD 21701-8575. Offers accounting (MBA, Certificate); finance (MBA); financial management (Certificate); human resource management (MBA); information systems (MBA); marketing (MBA); organizational management (Certificate); public management (MBA). *Accreditation:* ACBSP. *Program availability:* Part-time, evening/weekend. *Faculty:* 4 full-time (2 women), 7 part-time/adjunct (1 woman). *Students:* 21 full-time (12 women), 91 part-time (47 women); includes 19 minority (8 Black or African American, non-Hispanic/Latino; 3 Asian, non-Hispanic/Latino; 8 Hispanic/Latino), 15 international. Average age 31. 34 applicants, 97% accepted, 23 enrolled. In 2017, 42 master's awarded. *Degree requirements:* For master's, capstone/final research project. *Entrance requirements:* For master's, minimum GPA of 3.0 (or resume and two letters of recommendation), copy of official transcripts, essay. *Additional exam requirements/recommendations for international students:* Required—TOEFL (minimum score 575 paper-based; 89 iBT), IELTS (minimum score 6.5). *Application deadline:* For fall admission, 8/15 for domestic students, 8/5 for international students; for spring admission, 12/1 for domestic and international students; for summer admission, 5/1 for domestic students, 4/15 for international students. Applications are processed on a rolling basis. Application fee: $35. Electronic applications accepted. *Expenses:* $550 per credit hour plus $110 per semester comprehensive fee. *Financial support:* Tuition waivers (partial) and unspecified assistantships available. Financial award applicants required to submit FAFSA. *Faculty research:* Corporate strategy and sustainable competitive advantages, business ethics, entrepreneurship, investments management, economic development. *Unit head:* Dr. April M. Boulton, Dean of the Graduate School, 301-696-3600, Fax: 301-696-3597, E-mail: gofurther@hood.edu. *Application contact:* Jan Marcus, Assistant Director of Graduate Admissions, 301-696-3603, E-mail: gofurther@hood.edu.

Hood College, Graduate School, Program in Organizational Leadership, Frederick, MD 21701-8575. Offers DBA, DOL. *Program availability:* Part-time-only, evening/weekend. *Faculty:* 3 full-time (2 women). *Students:* 35 part-time (20 women); includes 13 minority (8 Black or African American, non-Hispanic/Latino; 2 Asian, non-Hispanic/Latino; 1 Hispanic/Latino; 2 Two or more races, non-Hispanic/Latino). Average age 45. 27 applicants, 81% accepted, 18 enrolled. *Degree requirements:* For doctorate, research-based capstone project. *Entrance requirements:* For doctorate, master's degree; minimum GPA of 3.25; one course in statistics; resume; two letters of recommendation; two essays; standardized test scores (SLLA, GRE, GMAT, or MAT) or evidence of master's-level culminating research experience. *Application deadline:* For fall admission, 4/15 priority date for domestic and international students. Application fee: $35. Electronic applications accepted. *Expenses:* $890 per credit hour (for DOL); $1,020 per credit hour (for DBA); $525 comprehensive fee per semester. *Financial support:* Applicants required to submit FAFSA. *Unit head:* Dr. Kathleen C. Bands, Director, 301-696-3818, E-mail: bands@hood.edu. *Application contact:* E-mail: gofurther@hood.edu.

Huntington University, Graduate School, Huntington, IN 46750-1299. Offers adolescent and young adult education (M Ed); business administration (MBA); counseling (MA), including licensed mental health counselor; early adolescent education (M Ed); elementary education (M Ed); global youth ministry (MA); occupational therapy (OTD); organizational leadership (MA); pastoral leadership (MA); TESOL education (M Ed). *Program availability:* Part-time, online learning. *Faculty:* 17 full-time (10 women), 14 part-time/adjunct (4 women). *Students:* 221 full-time (163 women), 22 part-time (13 women). *Degree requirements:* For master's, comprehensive exam (for some programs), thesis (for some programs). *Entrance requirements:* For master's, GRE (for counseling and education students only); for doctorate, GRE (for occupational therapy students). Additional exam requirements/recommendations for international students: Required—TOEFL (minimum score 85 iBT), IELTS (minimum score 6.5). *Application deadline:* For fall admission, 7/1 for domestic students, 5/1 for international students; for winter admission, 10/1 for domestic students, 9/1 for international students; for spring admission, 11/30 for domestic students, 10/30 for international students. Applications are processed on a rolling basis. Application fee: $30. Electronic applications accepted. *Expenses:* Contact institution. *Financial support:* Scholarships/grants and unspecified assistantships available. Support available to part-time students. Financial award application deadline: 8/1; financial award applicants required to submit FAFSA. *Faculty research:* Leadership, educational technology trends, evangelism, youth ministry, mental health. *Unit head:* Michael Wanous, Vice President for Academic Affairs, 260-359-4008, Fax: 260-359-4126, E-mail: mwanous@huntington.edu. *Application contact:* Evan Bennett, Assistant Director of Graduate Admissions, 260-359-4111, Fax: 260-359-4126, E-mail: graduate@huntington.edu.
Website: http://www.huntington.edu/graduate

Husson University, Master of Business Administration Program, Bangor, ME 04401-2999. Offers athletic administration (MBA); biotechnology and innovation (MBA); general business administration (MBA); healthcare management (MBA); hospitality and tourism management (MBA); organizational management (MBA); risk management (MBA). *Program availability:* Part-time, evening/weekend, 100% online, blended/hybrid learning. *Faculty:* 11 full-time (5 women), 19 part-time/adjunct (4 women). *Students:* 83 full-time (44 women), 287 part-time (176 women); includes 25 minority (7 Black or African American, non-Hispanic/Latino; 11 Asian, non-Hispanic/Latino; 4 Hispanic/Latino; 3 Two or more races, non-Hispanic/Latino), 16 international. Average age 35. 158 applicants, 77% accepted, 49 enrolled. In 2017, 120 master's awarded. *Degree requirements:* For master's, comprehensive exam (for some programs), thesis optional. *Entrance requirements:* For master's, minimum GPA of 3.0, letter of recommendation. Additional exam requirements/recommendations for international students: Required—TOEFL (minimum score 550 paper-based; 80 iBT), IELTS (minimum score 6.5). *Application deadline:* Applications are processed on a rolling basis. Application fee: $50. Electronic applications accepted. *Expenses:* $464 per credit. *Financial support:* In 2017–18, 13 students received support. Career-related internships or fieldwork, Federal Work-Study, scholarships/grants, and unspecified assistantships available. Financial award application deadline: 4/15; financial award applicants required to submit FAFSA. *Unit head:* Prof. Stephanie Shayne, Director, Graduate and Online Programs, 207-404-5632, Fax: 207-992-4987, E-mail: shaynes@husson.edu. *Application contact:* Kristen Card, Director of Graduate Admissions, 207-404-5660, Fax: 207-941-7935, E-mail: cardk@husson.edu.
Website: http://www.husson.edu/college-of-business/school-of-business-and-management/master-of-business-administration-mba/

Immaculata University, College of Graduate Studies, Program in Organization Leadership, Immaculata, PA 19345. Offers MA. *Program availability:* Part-time, evening/weekend. *Degree requirements:* For master's, comprehensive exam, thesis optional. *Entrance requirements:* For master's, GMAT, GRE General Test, MAT. Additional exam requirements/recommendations for international students: Required—TOEFL, IELTS. Electronic applications accepted.

Indiana Tech, Program in Organizational Leadership, Fort Wayne, IN 46803-1297. Offers MS. *Program availability:* Part-time, evening/weekend, online only, 100% online. *Entrance requirements:* For master's, minimum GPA of 2.5, bachelor's degree from regionally-accredited university, minimum three years of work experience, three letters of recommendation, essay, current resume. Electronic applications accepted.

Indiana University Bloomington, School of Public and Environmental Affairs, Public Affairs Programs, Bloomington, IN 47405. Offers economic development (MPA); energy (MPA); environmental policy (PhD); environmental policy and natural resource management (MPA); information systems (MPA); international development (MPA); local government management (MPA); nonprofit management (MPA, Certificate); policy analysis (MPA); public budgeting and financial management (Certificate); public finance (PhD); public financial administration (MPA); public management (MPA, PhD, Certificate); public policy analysis (PhD); social entrepreneurship (Certificate); specialized public affairs (MPA); sustainability and sustainable development (MPA); JD/MPA; MPA/MA; MPA/MIS; MPA/MLS; MSES/MPA. *Accreditation:* NASPAA (one or more programs are accredited). *Program availability:* Part-time. *Degree requirements:* For master's, capstone, internship; for doctorate, comprehensive exam, thesis/dissertation. *Entrance requirements:* For master's, GRE General Test or GMAT, official transcripts, 3 letters of recommendation, resume, personal statement; for doctorate, GRE General Test, official transcripts, 3 letters of recommendation, statement of purpose. Additional exam requirements/recommendations for international students: Required—TOEFL (minimum score 600 paper-based; 96 iBT); Recommended—IELTS (minimum score 7). Electronic applications accepted. *Faculty research:* International development, environmental policy and resource management, policy analysis, public finance, public management, urban management, nonprofit management, energy policy, social policy, public finance.

Indiana University–Purdue University Fort Wayne, College of Engineering, Technology, and Computer Science, Department of Organizational Leadership and Supervision, Fort Wayne, IN 46805-1499. Offers human resources (MS); leadership (MS); organizational leadership and supervision (Certificate). *Program availability:* Part-time. *Entrance requirements:* For master's, GRE or GMAT (if undergraduate GPA is below 3.0), current resume, 2 recent letters of recommendation, essay. Additional exam requirements/recommendations for international students: Required—TOEFL (minimum score 550 paper-based; 79 iBT); Recommended—TWE. Electronic applications accepted. *Faculty research:* Replication problem and psychology, virtual leadership.

Indiana University–Purdue University Indianapolis, School of Engineering and Technology, MS in Technology Program, Indianapolis, IN 46202. Offers applied data management and analytics (MS); facilities management (MS); information security and assurance (MS); motorsports (MS); organizational leadership (MS); technical communication (MS). *Program availability:* Online learning.

Indiana University–Purdue University Indianapolis, School of Public and Environmental Affairs, Indianapolis, IN 46202. Offers criminal justice and public safety (MS); homeland security and emergency management (Graduate Certificate); library management (Graduate Certificate); nonprofit management (Graduate Certificate); public affairs (MPA); public management (Graduate Certificate); social entrepreneurship: nonprofit and public benefit organizations (Graduate Certificate); JD/MPA; MLS/NMC; MLS/PMC; MPA/MA. *Accreditation:* CAHME (one or more programs

are accredited); NASPAA. *Program availability:* Part-time, evening/weekend, online learning. *Entrance requirements:* For master's, GRE General Test, GMAT or LSAT, minimum GPA of 3.0 (preferred). Additional exam requirements/recommendations for international students: Required—TOEFL (minimum score 93 iBT), IELTS (minimum score 6.5). Electronic applications accepted. *Faculty research:* Nonprofit and public management, public policy, urban policy, sustainability policy, disaster preparedness and recovery, vehicular safety, homicide, offender rehabilitation and re-entry.

Indiana Wesleyan University, College of Adult and Professional Studies, Graduate Studies in Business, Marion, IN 46953. Offers accounting (MBA, Graduate Certificate); applied management (MBA); business administration (MBA); health care (MBA, Graduate Certificate); human resources (MBA, Graduate Certificate); management (MS); organizational leadership (MA). *Program availability:* Part-time, evening/weekend, online learning. *Degree requirements:* For master's, applied business or management project. *Entrance requirements:* For master's, minimum GPA of 2.5, 2 years of related work experience. Additional exam requirements/recommendations for international students: Required—TOEFL (minimum score 550 paper-based). Electronic applications accepted.

Indiana Wesleyan University, College of Adult and Professional Studies, Program in Organizational Leadership, Marion, IN 46953. Offers Ed D. *Program availability:* Part-time, online learning. *Degree requirements:* For doctorate, comprehensive exam, thesis/dissertation, applied field project. *Entrance requirements:* For doctorate, GRE, GMAT. Additional exam requirements/recommendations for international students: Required—TOEFL. *Faculty research:* Organizational leadership as a new structural model for research and teaching, wisdom and its application for leaders, stewardship and its application for leaders, followership and its application for leaders, the importance of a world view in establishing authenticity for leaders.

Instituto Tecnologico de Santo Domingo, Graduate School, Area of Business, Santo Domingo, Dominican Republic. Offers banking and securities markets (M Mgmt); corporate finance (M Mgmt); human resources management (M Mgmt, Certificate); international trade management (M Mgmt); marketing (M Mgmt); organizational development (M Mgmt); quality and productivity management (Certificate); tax management and planning (M Mgmt); upper management (M Mgmt).

Jacksonville University, Davis College of Business, Master of Science in Organizational Leadership Program, Jacksonville, FL 32211. Offers MS. *Program availability:* Part-time-only, evening/weekend, 100% online, blended/hybrid learning. *Faculty:* 9 full-time (2 women). *Students:* 5 full-time (2 women), 35 part-time (23 women); includes 18 minority (11 Black or African American, non-Hispanic/Latino; 1 Asian, non-Hispanic/Latino; 6 Hispanic/Latino), 1 international. Average age 36. 26 applicants, 100% accepted, 18 enrolled. In 2017, 7 master's awarded. *Entrance requirements:* For master's, GMAT or GRE, bachelor's degree from regionally-accredited institution, 3 years of full-time work experience (recommended), resume, statement of intent, 3 letters of recommendation, interview with program advisor. Additional exam requirements/recommendations for international students: Required—TOEFL (minimum score 550 paper-based; 79 iBT), IELTS (minimum score 6), PTE (minimum score 53). *Application deadline:* For fall admission, 7/1 priority date for domestic students, 6/15 priority date for international students; for spring admission, 12/1 priority date for domestic students, 11/15 priority date for international students; for summer admission, 4/1 priority date for domestic students, 3/15 priority date for international students. Applications are processed on a rolling basis. Application fee: $50. Electronic applications accepted. *Expenses:* $793 per credit hour; $150-$250 books per course (estimated). *Financial support:* Scholarships/grants and health care benefits available. Financial award application deadline: 6/30; financial award applicants required to submit FAFSA. *Faculty research:* Ethics; science of a start-up culture; organizational culture; sustainability. *Unit head:* Dr. Douglas Johansen, Associate Dean and Graduate Programs Director, 904-256-7763, Fax: 904-256-7168, E-mail: djohans@ju.edu. *Application contact:* AnnaMaria Murphy, Assistant Director of Graduate Admissions, 904-256-7426, Fax: 904-256-7012, E-mail: mba@ju.edu.
See Display on page 104 and Close-Up on page 175.

James Madison University, The Graduate School, College of Business, Program in Strategic Leadership, Harrisonburg, VA 22801. Offers postsecondary analysis and leadership (PhD), including nonprofit and community leadership, organizational science and leadership, postsecondary analysis and leadership. *Program availability:* Part-time, evening/weekend, online learning. *Students:* 8 full-time (3 women), 34 part-time (16 women); includes 4 minority (2 Black or African American, non-Hispanic/Latino; 1 Asian, non-Hispanic/Latino; 1 Hispanic/Latino), 4 international. Average age 30. In 2017, 3 doctorates awarded. Application fee: $55. Electronic applications accepted. *Expenses:* Tuition, state resident: full-time $10,512; part-time $438 per credit hour. Tuition, nonresident: full-time $28,358; part-time $1162 per credit hour. *Required fees:* $1128. *Financial support:* In 2017–18, 6 students received support. Fellowships, career-related internships or fieldwork, Federal Work-Study, unspecified assistantships, and 6 doctoral assistantships (stipend varies) available. Financial award application deadline: 3/1; financial award applicants required to submit FAFSA. *Unit head:* Dr. Karen A. Ford, Director of Strategic Leadership Studies, 540-568-7020, Fax: 540-568-7117, E-mail: fordka@jmu.edu. *Application contact:* Lynette D. Michael, Director of Graduate Admissions, 540-568-6131 Ext. 6395, Fax: 540-568-7860, E-mail: michaeld@jmu.edu. Website: http://www.jmu.edu/leadership/

John F. Kennedy University, School of Management, Program in Business Administration, Pleasant Hill, CA 94523-4817. Offers business administration (MBA); organizational leadership (Certificate). *Program availability:* Part-time, evening/weekend. *Degree requirements:* For master's, thesis or alternative. *Entrance requirements:* For master's, interview. Additional exam requirements/recommendations for international students: Required—TOEFL.

Johns Hopkins University, School of Education, Master's Programs in Education, Baltimore, MD 21218. Offers counseling (MS), including clinical mental health counseling, school counseling; education (MS), including educational studies, gifted education, reading, school administration and supervision, technology for educators; elementary education (MAT); health professions (M Ed); intelligence analysis (MS); organizational leadership (MS); secondary education (MAT), including biology, chemistry, earth/space science, English, physics, social studies; special education (MS), including early childhood special education, general special education studies, mild to moderate disabilities, severe disabilities. *Program availability:* Part-time, evening/weekend, 100% online, blended/hybrid learning. *Degree requirements:* For master's, comprehensive exam (for some programs), portfolio, capstone project and/or internship; PRAXIS II (subject area assessments) for initial teacher preparation programs that lead to licensure. *Entrance requirements:* For master's, GRE (for full-time programs only); PRAXIS I/core or state-approved alternative (for initial teacher preparation programs that lead to licensure), minimum of bachelor's degree from regionally- or nationally-accredited institution; minimum GPA of 3.0 in all previous programs of study; official transcripts from all post-secondary institutions attended; essay; curriculum vitae/resume; letters of recommendation (3 for full-time programs, 2 for part-time programs); dispositions survey. Additional exam requirements/recommendations for international students: Required—TOEFL (minimum score 600 paper-based; 100 iBT), IELTS (minimum score 7). Electronic applications accepted. *Expenses:* Contact institution.

Organizational Management

Johnson & Wales University, Graduate Studies, MBA Program, Providence, RI 02903-3703. Offers accounting (MBA); business administration (MBA); finance (MBA); global fashion merchandising and management (MBA); hospitality (MBA); human resource management (MBA); information security/assurance (MBA); information technology (MBA); nonprofit management (MBA); operations and supply chain management (MBA); organizational leadership (MBA); organizational psychology (MBA); sport leadership (MBA). Program also offered on Denver campus. *Program availability:* Part-time, online learning. *Entrance requirements:* For master's, minimum GPA of 2.75. Additional exam requirements/recommendations for international students: Required—TOEFL (minimum score 550 paper-based); Recommended—IELTS, TWE. *Application deadline:* For fall admission, 8/15 priority date for domestic students, 6/28 priority date for international students; for winter admission, 11/10 priority date for domestic students, 9/20 priority date for international students; for spring admission, 2/5 priority date for domestic students, 12/20 priority date for international students. Applications are processed on a rolling basis. *Expenses: Tuition:* Full-time $12,636; part-time $702 per credit hour. *Financial support:* Tuition waivers (partial) and unspecified assistantships available. Support available to part-time students. Financial award application deadline: 5/1. *Faculty research:* International banking, global economy, international trade, cultural differences. *Unit head:* Dr. Karen Silva, Director, 401-598-2849, Fax: 401-598-1125. *Application contact:* Graduate School Admissions, 401-598-1015, Fax: 401-598-1286, E-mail: gradadm@jwu.edu.

Judson University, Master of Arts in Organizational Leadership Program, Elgin, IL 60123-1498. Offers MA. *Program availability:* Part-time, evening/weekend, 100% online, blended/hybrid learning. *Faculty:* 4 full-time (2 women), 7 part-time/adjunct (1 woman). *Students:* 13 full-time (7 women), 9 part-time (6 women); includes 9 minority (3 Black or African American, non-Hispanic/Latino; 5 Hispanic/Latino; 1 Two or more races, non-Hispanic/Latino), 1 international. Average age 34. 12 applicants, 58% accepted, 7 enrolled. In 2017, 21 master's awarded. *Degree requirements:* For master's, thesis optional. *Entrance requirements:* For master's, bachelor's degree with minimum GPA of 2.5; official transcripts; two years of work experience; two letters of reference; professional resume. Additional exam requirements/recommendations for international students: Required—TOEFL (minimum score 550 paper-based). *Application deadline:* Applications are processed on a rolling basis. Application fee: $35. Electronic applications accepted. Tuition and fees vary according to course load, degree level and program. *Financial support:* Institutionally sponsored loans and unspecified assistantships available. Financial award applicants required to submit FAFSA. *Faculty research:* Human resource management, public affairs, international marketing, intergenerational leadership. *Unit head:* Dr. Teri Stein, Chair, 847-628-1524, E-mail: tstein@judsonu.edu. *Application contact:* Dr. Teri Stein, Chair, 847-628-1524, E-mail: tstein@judsonu.edu.
Website: http://www.judsonu.edu/maol/

Keiser University, MS in Organizational Leadership Program, Fort Lauderdale, FL 33309. Offers MSOL.

LaGrange College, Graduate Programs, Program in Organizational Leadership, LaGrange, GA 30240-2999. Offers MA. Program is held on Albany campus. *Program availability:* Evening/weekend. *Entrance requirements:* For master's, GRE or MAT, minimum GPA of 2.5, 3 letters of reference. Additional exam requirements/recommendations for international students: Required—TOEFL (minimum score 500 paper-based; 61 iBT). Electronic applications accepted.

Lenoir-Rhyne University, Graduate Programs, School of Education, Program in Leadership, Hickory, NC 28601. Offers community and nonprofit leadership (MA); general management (MA); higher education leadership (MA); second language community services (MA). *Program availability:* Online learning. *Entrance requirements:* Additional exam requirements/recommendations for international students: Required—TOEFL (minimum score 600 paper-based). Electronic applications accepted. *Expenses:* Contact institution.

Lewis University, College of Arts and Sciences, Program in Organizational Leadership, Romeoville, IL 60446. Offers higher education/student services (MA); non-profit management (MA); organizational and leadership coaching (MA); organizational management (MA); training and development (MA). *Program availability:* Part-time, evening/weekend, 100% online, blended/hybrid learning. *Students:* 16 full-time (11 women), 154 part-time (115 women); includes 49 minority (27 Black or African American, non-Hispanic/Latino; 1 American Indian or Alaska Native, non-Hispanic/Latino; 4 Asian, non-Hispanic/Latino; 12 Hispanic/Latino; 5 Two or more races, non-Hispanic/Latino), 4 international. Average age 37. *Entrance requirements:* For master's, bachelor's degree, personal statement, minimum GPA of 3.0, letters of recommendation. Additional exam requirements/recommendations for international students: Required—TOEFL (minimum score 550 paper-based; 79 iBT), IELTS (minimum score 6). *Application deadline:* For fall admission, 5/1 priority date for international students; for spring admission, 11/15 priority date for international students. Applications are processed on a rolling basis. Application fee: $40. Electronic applications accepted. Tuition and fees vary according to program. *Financial support:* Federal Work-Study, tuition waivers, and unspecified assistantships available. Financial award application deadline: 5/1; financial award applicants required to submit FAFSA. *Unit head:* Dr. Lesley Page, Chair of Organizational Leadership, 815-838-0500, E-mail: pagele@lewisu.edu. *Application contact:* Kathy Lisak, Graduate Admission Counselor, 815-836-5610, E-mail: grad@lewisu.edu.

Lincoln Christian University, Graduate Programs, Lincoln, IL 62656-2167. Offers Bible and theology (MA); Biblical studies (MA); church history/historical theology (MA); counseling (MA); formative worship (MA); intercultural studies (MA); ministry (MA); organizational leadership (MA); philosophy and apologetics (MA); spiritual formation (MA); theology (MA). MA in spiritual formation offered in Normal, IL. *Program availability:* Online learning. *Faculty:* 21 full-time (3 women), 29 part-time/adjunct (7 women). *Students:* 97 full-time (42 women), 226 part-time (81 women). Average age 39. *Entrance requirements:* For master's, minimum cumulative GPA of 2.5 in undergraduate degree studies. Additional exam requirements/recommendations for international students: Required—TOEFL (minimum score 550 paper-based); Recommended—IELTS (minimum score 6). *Application deadline:* For fall admission, 8/1 for domestic students, 3/1 for international students; for spring admission, 11/15 for domestic students, 11/1 for international students. Application fee: $25 ($50 for international students). Application fee is waived when completed online. *Expenses: Tuition:* Full-time $7920; part-time $5280 per credit hour. *Required fees:* $150; $150 per course. *Financial support:* Applicants required to submit FAFSA. *Application contact:* Lindsey Clark, Associate Director of Graduate Enrollment, 217-732-3168 Ext. 2398, E-mail: lclark@lincolnchristian.edu.
Website: https://lincolnchristian.edu/academics/programs/masters/

Lipscomb University, Nelson and Sue Andrews Institute for Civic Leadership, Nashville, TN 37204-3951. Offers civic leadership (MA, Graduate Certificate); cross sector collaboration (MA); non-profit leadership (MA). *Program availability:* Part-time, evening/weekend. *Faculty:* 3 full-time (2 women). *Students:* 18 full-time (13 women); includes 11 minority (9 Black or African American, non-Hispanic/Latino; 1 Hispanic/Latino; 1 Two or more races, non-Hispanic/Latino). Average age 33. 30 applicants, 37% accepted, 7 enrolled. In 2017, 11 master's awarded. *Degree requirements:* For master's, project, externship. *Entrance requirements:* For master's, GRE, GMAT or MAT, transcripts, 2 references, essay, resume. Additional exam requirements/recommendations for international students: Required—TOEFL (minimum score 570 paper-based; 80 iBT). *Application deadline:* Applications are processed on a rolling basis. Application fee: $50 ($75 for international students). Electronic applications accepted. *Expenses:* $1,290. *Financial support:* Applicants required to submit FAFSA. *Unit head:* Linda Peek Schacht, Executive Director, 615-966-1341, E-mail: linda.schacht@lipscomb.edu. *Application contact:* Dr. Michelle Steele, Academic Director, 615-966-5181, E-mail: michelle.steele@lipscomb.edu.
Website: http://www.lipscomb.edu/civicleadership

Lipscomb University, Program in Organizational Leadership, Nashville, TN 37204-3951. Offers aging services leadership (Certificate); global leadership (Certificate); organizational leadership (MPS); performance coaching (Certificate); strategic leadership (Certificate). *Program availability:* Part-time, online only, blended/hybrid learning. *Faculty:* 1 (woman) full-time, 3 part-time/adjunct (1 woman). *Students:* 27 full-time (14 women), 6 part-time (4 women); includes 8 minority (4 Black or African American, non-Hispanic/Latino; 4 Hispanic/Latino), 1 international. Average age 43. 34 applicants, 68% accepted, 15 enrolled. In 2017, 7 master's, 17 Certificates awarded. *Entrance requirements:* For master's, GRE or GMAT, two references, resume, interview. Additional exam requirements/recommendations for international students: Required—TOEFL (minimum score 550 paper-based). *Application deadline:* For fall admission, 8/1 for domestic students. Applications are processed on a rolling basis. Application fee: $50 ($75 for international students). Electronic applications accepted. *Expenses:* Contact institution. *Unit head:* Dr. Hope Nordstrom, Director, 615-966-1107, E-mail: hope.nordstrom@lipscomb.edu. *Application contact:* Barbara Blackman, Coordinator of Graduate Studies, 615-966-6287, Fax: 615-966-7619, E-mail: graduatestudies@lipscomb.edu.

Lourdes University, Graduate School, Sylvania, OH 43560-2898. Offers business (MBA); leadership (M Ed); nurse anesthesia (MSN); nurse educator (MSN); nurse leader (MSN); organizational leadership (MOL); reading (M Ed); teaching and curriculum (M Ed); theology (MA). *Program availability:* Evening/weekend. *Entrance requirements:* Additional exam requirements/recommendations for international students: Required—TOEFL.

Loyola University New Orleans, Joseph A. Butt, S.J., College of Business, Program in Business Administration, New Orleans, LA 70118-6195. Offers organizational performance excellence (MBA); JD/MBA; MBA/MPS. *Accreditation:* AACSB. *Program availability:* Part-time, evening/weekend, online learning. *Faculty:* 6 full-time (3 women), 7 part-time/adjunct (0 women). *Students:* 22 full-time (10 women), 61 part-time (36 women); includes 23 minority (13 Black or African American, non-Hispanic/Latino; 2 Asian, non-Hispanic/Latino; 8 Hispanic/Latino), 8 international. Average age 31. 51 applicants, 92% accepted, 37 enrolled. In 2017, 42 master's awarded. *Degree requirements:* For master's, capstone project. *Entrance requirements:* For master's, GMAT or GRE, minimum GPA of 3.0, transcript, resume, 2 letters of recommendation, work experience in field, personal statement. Additional exam requirements/recommendations for international students: Required—TOEFL (minimum score 580 paper-based; 92 iBT). *Application deadline:* For fall admission, 6/15 priority date for domestic students, 5/15 priority date for international students; for spring admission, 11/15 priority date for domestic students, 10/15 priority date for international students. Applications are processed on a rolling basis. Application fee: $50. Electronic applications accepted. *Expenses:* $1,005 per hour tuition; $733 per semester full-time fees, $376.50 part-time. *Financial support:* Research assistantships, scholarships/grants, tuition waivers (partial), and unspecified assistantships available. Financial award application deadline: 5/1; financial award applicants required to submit FAFSA. *Faculty research:* Ethics, international business, entrepreneurship, quality management, risk management. *Unit head:* Dr. J. Patrick O'Brien, Interim Dean, 504-864-7979, Fax: 504-864-7970, E-mail: mba@loyno.edu. *Application contact:* Ashley Francis, Director of Graduate Programs, 504-864-7979, Fax: 504-864-7970, E-mail: mba@loyno.edu.
Website: http://www.business.loyno.edu/mba/programs

Malone University, Graduate Program in Organizational Leadership, Canton, OH 44709. Offers MAOL. *Program availability:* Part-time, evening/weekend. *Entrance requirements:* For master's, minimum GPA of 3.0. Additional exam requirements/recommendations for international students: Required—TOEFL (minimum score 550 paper-based; 79 iBT). *Expenses:* Contact institution. *Faculty research:* Graduates' perceptions of the impact of a Christian higher education.

Manhattan College, Graduate Programs, School of Continuing and Professional Studies, Riverdale, NY 10471. Offers organizational leadership (MS). *Program availability:* Part-time, evening/weekend. *Faculty:* 13 part-time/adjunct (10 women). *Students:* 64 full-time, 22 part-time; includes 41 minority (17 Black or African American, non-Hispanic/Latino; 4 Asian, non-Hispanic/Latino; 18 Hispanic/Latino; 2 Two or more races, non-Hispanic/Latino). Average age 33. In 2017, 46 master's awarded. *Entrance requirements:* For master's, bachelor's degree, minimum cumulative GPA of 2.75, at least three years of work experience. Additional exam requirements/recommendations for international students: Required—TOEFL, IELTS. *Application deadline:* For fall admission, 8/1 for domestic students; for spring admission, 11/15 for domestic students. Applications are processed on a rolling basis. Application fee: $75. Electronic applications accepted. *Expenses:* Contact institution. *Unit head:* Cheryl Harrison, Dean, 718-862-7862, Fax: 718-862-8049, E-mail: cheryl.harrison@manhattan.edu. *Application contact:* William Bisset, Vice President for Enrollment Management, 718-862-7199, Fax: 718-862-8019, E-mail: william.bisset@manhattan.edu.
Website: https://manhattan.edu/academics/schools-and-departments/scps/

Manhattanville College, School of Business, Master of Science in Human Resource Management and Organizational Effectiveness Program, Purchase, NY 10577-2132. Offers human resource management (Advanced Certificate); human resource management and organizational effectiveness (MS), including human resource management, organizational effectiveness. *Program availability:* Part-time, evening/weekend. *Faculty:* 8 part-time/adjunct (2 women). *Students:* 14 full-time (11 women), 7 part-time (all women); includes 7 minority (2 Asian, non-Hispanic/Latino; 5 Hispanic/Latino), 1 international. Average age 33. 23 applicants, 39% accepted, 7 enrolled. In 2017, 15 master's awarded. *Degree requirements:* For master's, thesis (for some programs), final project. *Entrance requirements:* For master's, personal essay, transcripts, 2 letters of recommendation (academic or professional), resume, health form with proof of immunization (for those born after 1957). Additional exam requirements/recommendations for international students: Required—TOEFL (minimum score 563 paper-based, 85 iBT), IELTS (7), or iTEP (B2). *Application deadline:* Applications are processed on a rolling basis. Application fee: $75. Electronic applications accepted. *Expenses:* $915 per credit. *Financial support:* Federal Work-Study, institutionally sponsored loans, scholarships/grants, and unspecified assistantships available. Financial award application deadline: 3/15; financial award applicants required to submit FAFSA. *Unit head:* Laura Persky, Graduate Program Director, 914-323-5188, E-mail: laura.persky@mville.edu. *Application contact:* Monika Pottgen, Assistant Director, Recruitment and Admissions, 914-323-5150, E-mail: business@mville.edu.
Website: https://www.mville.edu/programs/ms-human-resource-management

Mansfield University of Pennsylvania, Graduate Studies, Program in Organizational Leadership, Mansfield, PA 16933. Offers MA. *Program availability:* Online learning.

Maranatha Baptist University, Program in Organizational Leadership, Watertown, WI 53094. Offers MOL. *Degree requirements:* For master's, capstone project.

Marian University, School of Business and Public Safety, Fond du Lac, WI 54935-4699. Offers organizational leadership (MS). *Program availability:* Part-time, evening/weekend. *Degree requirements:* For master's, comprehensive group project. *Entrance requirements:* For master's, 3 years of managerial experience, minimum GPA of 2.75, letters of professional reference. Additional exam requirements/recommendations for international students: Required—TOEFL (minimum score 525 paper-based; 70 iBT). Electronic applications accepted. *Expenses:* Contact institution. *Faculty research:* Organizational values, statistical decision-making, learning organization, quality planning, customer research.

Marlboro College, Graduate and Professional Studies, Program in Business Administration, Marlboro, VT 05344. Offers mission-driven organizations (MBA); project management (MBA); social innovation (MBA). *Program availability:* Part-time, evening/weekend, blended/hybrid learning. *Degree requirements:* For master's, 45 credits including a Master Workshop. *Entrance requirements:* For master's, letter of intent, essay, transcripts, 2 letters of recommendation. *Application deadline:* For fall admission, 7/1 priority date for domestic students; for winter admission, 11/1 priority date for domestic students. Applications are processed on a rolling basis. Application fee: $0. Electronic applications accepted. *Expenses:* $794 per credit. *Financial support:* Scholarships/grants available. Financial award applicants required to submit FAFSA. *Unit head:* Tristan Toleno, Co-Chair, 802-258-9200, Fax: 802-258-9201, E-mail: tristant@gradschool.marlboro.edu. *Application contact:* Amanda Mehegan, Assistant Director of Graduate Admissions, 802-258-9209, Fax: 802-258-9201, E-mail: graduateadmissions@marlboro.edu.
Website: https://www.marlboro.edu/academics/graduate/management

Marlboro College, Graduate and Professional Studies, Program in Management, Marlboro, VT 05344. Offers mission-driven organizations (MS); project management (MS); social innovation (MS). *Program availability:* Part-time, evening/weekend, blended/hybrid learning. *Degree requirements:* For master's, capstone project. *Entrance requirements:* For master's, statement of intent, 2 letters of recommendation. Additional exam requirements/recommendations for international students: Recommended—TOEFL (minimum score 577 paper-based; 90 iBT), IELTS (minimum score 7). *Application deadline:* For fall admission, 8/5 for domestic students; for winter admission, 12/5 for domestic students; for spring admission, 4/5 for domestic students. Applications are processed on a rolling basis. Application fee: $0. Electronic applications accepted. *Expenses:* $794 per credit. *Financial support:* Scholarships/grants available. Financial award applicants required to submit FAFSA. *Unit head:* Tristan Toleno, Co-Chair, 802-258-9200, Fax: 802-258-9201, E-mail: tristant@gradschool.marlboro.edu. *Application contact:* Amanda Mehegan, Assistant Director of Graduate Admissions, 802-258-9209, Fax: 802-258-9201, E-mail: graduateadmissions@marlboro.edu.
Website: https://www.marlboro.edu/academics/graduate/management

Medaille College, Program in Business Administration - Amherst, Amherst, NY 14221. Offers business administration (MBA); organizational leadership (MA). *Program availability:* Evening/weekend. *Degree requirements:* For master's, thesis or alternative. *Entrance requirements:* For master's, GMAT, minimum undergraduate GPA of 2.7, 3 years of work experience. Additional exam requirements/recommendations for international students: Required—TOEFL (minimum score 550 paper-based). Electronic applications accepted. *Expenses:* Contact institution.

Medaille College, Program in Business Administration - Rochester, Rochester, NY 14623. Offers business administration (MBA); organizational leadership (MA). *Program availability:* Evening/weekend. *Degree requirements:* For master's, thesis or alternative. *Entrance requirements:* For master's, GMAT, 3 years of work experience, minimum undergraduate GPA of 2.7. Additional exam requirements/recommendations for international students: Required—TOEFL (minimum score 550 paper-based). *Expenses:* Contact institution.

Mercer University, Graduate Studies, Cecil B. Day Campus, Penfield College, Atlanta, GA 30341. Offers certified rehabilitation counseling (MS); clinical mental health (MS); counselor education and supervision (PhD); criminal justice and public safety leadership (MS); health informatics (MS); human services (MS), including child and adolescent services, gerontology services; organizational leadership (MS), including leadership for the health care professional, leadership for the nonprofit organization, organizational development and change; school counseling (MS). *Program availability:* Part-time, evening/weekend, 100% online, blended/hybrid learning. *Faculty:* 17 full-time (10 women), 27 part-time/adjunct (24 women). *Students:* 199 full-time (165 women), 266 part-time (218 women); includes 268 minority (226 Black or African American, non-Hispanic/Latino; 1 American Indian or Alaska Native, non-Hispanic/Latino; 19 Asian, non-Hispanic/Latino; 19 Hispanic/Latino; 3 Two or more races, non-Hispanic/Latino). Average age 32. 300 applicants, 45% accepted, 114 enrolled. In 2017, 101 master's, 5 doctorates awarded. *Degree requirements:* For master's, comprehensive exam (for some programs), thesis (for some programs); for doctorate, thesis/dissertation. *Entrance requirements:* For master's, GRE or MAT, Georgia Professional Standards Commission (GPSC) Certification at the SC-5 level; for doctorate, GRE or MAT. Additional exam requirements/recommendations for international students: Recommended—TOEFL (minimum score 550 paper-based; 80 iBT), IELTS (minimum score 6.5). *Application deadline:* For fall admission, 7/1 priority date for domestic and international students; for spring admission, 11/1 priority date for domestic and international students; for summer admission, 4/1 priority date for domestic and international students. Application fee: $35. Electronic applications accepted. Application fee is waived when completed online. *Expenses:* $637 per credit. *Financial support:* In 2017–18, 32 students received support. Federal Work-Study, scholarships/grants, and unspecified assistantships available. Financial award applicants required to submit FAFSA. *Faculty research:* Marriage and families issues, leadership and ethics, cyber-bullying, trauma, narrative counseling and theory. *Total annual research expenditures:* $85,000. *Unit head:* Dr. Priscilla R. Danheiser, Dean, 678-547-6028, Fax: 678-547-6008, E-mail: danheiser_p@mercer.edu. *Application contact:* Dr. Melissa McCants Cruz, Director of Graduate Admissions, 678-547-6024, E-mail: penfield.admissions@mercer.edu.
Website: http://penfield.mercer.edu/programs/graduate-professional/

Mercy College, School of Business, Program in Organizational Leadership, Dobbs Ferry, NY 10522-1189. Offers MS. *Program availability:* Part-time, evening/weekend, 100% online, blended/hybrid learning. *Students:* 37 full-time (29 women), 25 part-time (21 women); includes 41 minority (21 Black or African American, non-Hispanic/Latino; 1 Asian, non-Hispanic/Latino; 18 Hispanic/Latino; 1 Two or more races, non-Hispanic/Latino), 5 international. Average age 32. 61 applicants, 84% accepted, 30 enrolled. In 2017, 34 master's awarded. *Degree requirements:* For master's, thesis or alternative. *Entrance requirements:* For master's, interview by program director, resume, 2 letters of reference. Additional exam requirements/recommendations for international students: Required—TOEFL (minimum score 600 paper-based; 100 iBT), IELTS (minimum score 8). *Application deadline:* For fall admission, 8/1 for international students. Applications are processed on a rolling basis. Application fee: $40. Electronic applications accepted.

Expenses: Contact institution. *Financial support:* Career-related internships or fieldwork, Federal Work-Study, scholarships/grants, and unspecified assistantships available. Support available to part-time students. Financial award applicants required to submit FAFSA. *Unit head:* Ed Weis, Dean, School of Business, 914-674-7490, E-mail: eweis@mercy.edu. *Application contact:* Allison Gurdineer, Senior Director of Admissions, 877-637-2946, E-mail: admissions@mercy.edu.
Website: https://www.mercy.edu/degrees-programs/ms-organizational-leadership

Mercyhurst University, Graduate Studies, Program in Organizational Leadership, Erie, PA 16546. Offers accounting (MS); higher education administration (MS); human resources (MS); organizational leadership (MS, Certificate); sports leadership (MS); strategy and innovation (MS). *Program availability:* Part-time, evening/weekend. *Degree requirements:* For master's, thesis. *Entrance requirements:* For master's, GRE General Test or MAT, interview, resume, essay, three professional references, transcripts. Additional exam requirements/recommendations for international students: Required—TOEFL (minimum score 80 iBT), IELTS (minimum score 6.5). Electronic applications accepted. *Faculty research:* Leadership training, organizational communication, leadership pedagogy.

Messiah College, Program in Business and Leadership, Mechanicsburg, PA 17055. Offers leadership (MBA, Certificate); management (Certificate); strategic leadership (MA). *Program availability:* Online learning.

Mid-America Christian University, Program in Leadership, Oklahoma City, OK 73170-4504. Offers MA. *Entrance requirements:* For master's, bachelor's degree from a regionally accredited college or university, minimum overall cumulative GPA of 2.75 of bachelor course work. Additional exam requirements/recommendations for international students: Required—TOEFL (minimum score 550 paper-based).

Midway University, Graduate Programs, Midway, KY 40347-1120. Offers education (MAT); leadership (MBA). *Degree requirements:* For master's, capstone course. *Entrance requirements:* For master's, GMAT (for MBA); GRE or PRAXIS I (for MAT), bachelor's degree; interview; minimum GPA of 3.0 (for MBA), 2.75 (for MAT); 3 years of professional work experience (for MBA). Additional exam requirements/recommendations for international students: Required—TOEFL (minimum score 550 paper-based; 80 iBT).

Misericordia University, College of Business, Program in Organizational Management, Dallas, PA 18612-1098. Offers healthcare management (MS); human resource management (MS); management (MS). *Program availability:* Part-time, evening/weekend, online learning. *Entrance requirements:* For master's, GRE General Test, MAT (35th percentile or higher), or minimum undergraduate GPA of 3.0. Additional exam requirements/recommendations for international students: Required—TOEFL. Electronic applications accepted. Application fee is waived when completed online. *Expenses:* Contact institution.

Mount St. Joseph University, Master of Science in Organizational Leadership Program, Cincinnati, OH 45233-1670. Offers MS. *Program availability:* Part-time, evening/weekend. *Faculty:* 1 (woman) full-time. *Students:* 59 part-time (41 women); includes 12 minority (9 Black or African American, non-Hispanic/Latino; 1 Hispanic/Latino; 2 Two or more races, non-Hispanic/Latino). Average age 41. In 2017, 31 master's awarded. *Degree requirements:* For master's, 36 credit hours. *Entrance requirements:* For master's, minimum GPA of 3.0, interview, 3 years of work experience, 2 letters of reference, resume, letter of intent, essay, official transcript. Additional exam requirements/recommendations for international students: Required—TOEFL (minimum score 560 paper-based; 83 iBT). *Application deadline:* Applications are processed on a rolling basis. Application fee: $50. Electronic applications accepted. *Expenses:* $635 per credit hour. *Financial support:* Applicants required to submit FAFSA. *Faculty research:* Gender and cultural effects on management education, group identity formation, leadership skill development, methods for improving instructional effectiveness, technology-based productivity improvement. *Unit head:* Dr. Anna Goldhahn, Assistant Dean/Director of Graduate Programs, 513-244-4924, Fax: 513-244-4270, E-mail: anna.goldhahn@msj.edu. *Application contact:* Mary Brigham, Assistant Director of Graduate Recruitment, 513-244-4233, Fax: 513-244-4629, E-mail: mary.brigham@msj.edu.
Website: http://www.msj.edu/academics/graduate-programs/master-of-science-in-organizational-leadership-program/

National University, Academic Affairs, School of Business and Management, La Jolla, CA 92037-1011. Offers accountancy (M Acc, Certificate); business administration (GMBA, MBA); business analytics (MS); cause leadership (MA); global management (MGM); human resource management (MA); management information systems (MS); marketing (MS); organizational leadership (MS). GMBA offered in Spanish. *Program availability:* Part-time, evening/weekend, 100% online, blended/hybrid learning. *Degree requirements:* For master's, thesis (for some programs). *Entrance requirements:* For master's, interview, minimum GPA of 2.5. Additional exam requirements/recommendations for international students: Required—TOEFL (minimum score 550 paper-based; 79 iBT), IELTS (minimum score 6). *Application deadline:* Applications are processed on a rolling basis. Application fee: $60 ($65 for international students). Electronic applications accepted. *Expenses:* Tuition: Part-time $430 per quarter hour. *Financial support:* Career-related internships or fieldwork, scholarships/grants, and tuition waivers (partial) available. Support available to part-time students. Financial award application deadline: 6/30; financial award applicants required to submit FAFSA. *Unit head:* Dr. Alfred Ntoko, Dean, 858-642-8400, Fax: 858-642-8719, E-mail: sobm@nu.edu. *Application contact:* Brandon Jouganatos, Vice President for Enrollment Services, 800-628-8648, E-mail: advisor@nu.edu.
Website: http://www.nu.edu/OurPrograms/SchoolOfBusinessAndManagement.html

National University, Academic Affairs, School of Professional Studies, La Jolla, CA 92037-1011. Offers criminal justice (MCJ); digital cinema production (MFA); digital journalism (MA); homeland security and emergency management (MS); juvenile justice (MS); professional screenwriting (MFA); public administration (MPA), including human resource management, organizational leadership. *Program availability:* Part-time, evening/weekend, 100% online, blended/hybrid learning. *Degree requirements:* For master's, thesis (for some programs). *Entrance requirements:* For master's, interview, minimum GPA of 2.5. Additional exam requirements/recommendations for international students: Required—TOEFL (minimum score 550 paper-based; 79 iBT), IELTS (minimum score 6). *Application deadline:* Applications are processed on a rolling basis. Application fee: $60 ($65 for international students). Electronic applications accepted. *Expenses:* Tuition: Part-time $430 per quarter hour. *Financial support:* Career-related internships or fieldwork, institutionally sponsored loans, scholarships/grants, and tuition waivers (partial) available. Support available to part-time students. Financial award application deadline: 6/30; financial award applicants required to submit FAFSA. *Unit head:* Dr. Daniel Donaldson, Dean, 858-642-8480, E-mail: sops@nu.edu. *Application contact:* Brandon Jouganatos, Vice President for Enrollment Services, 800-628-8648, E-mail: advisor@nu.edu.
Website: http://www.nu.edu/OurPrograms/School-of-Professional-Studies.html

Neumann University, Program in Organizational and Strategic Leadership, Aston, PA 19014-1298. Offers MS. *Program availability:* Part-time, evening/weekend, 100% online, blended/hybrid learning. *Faculty:* 7 part-time/adjunct (3 women). *Students:* 55 part-time

Organizational Management

(31 women); includes 9 minority (7 Black or African American, non-Hispanic/Latino; 1 Asian, non-Hispanic/Latino; 1 Hispanic/Latino), 2 international. Average age 38. 34 applicants, 76% accepted, 22 enrolled. In 2017, 50 master's awarded. *Degree requirements:* For master's, project. *Entrance requirements:* For master's, official transcripts from all institutions attended, current resume, letter of intent, letter of recommendation. Additional exam requirements/recommendations for international students: Required—TOEFL (minimum score 70 iBT). *Application deadline:* Applications are processed on a rolling basis. Application fee: $0. Electronic applications accepted. *Expenses:* $615 per credit hour. *Financial support:* Scholarships/grants and health care benefits available. Support available to part-time students. Financial award application deadline: 3/15; financial award applicants required to submit FAFSA. *Unit head:* Dr. Samuel M. Lemon, Program Director, Master of Science in Organizational and Strategic Leadership, 610-361-5239, Fax: 610-361-5235, E-mail: lemons@neumann.edu. *Application contact:* Janice Sackawicz, Coordinator of Student Services, Division of Continuing Adult and Professional Studies, 610-558-5629, Fax: 610-361-5235, E-mail: caps@neumann.edu.

New Jersey City University, School of Business, Program in Organizational Management and Leadership, Jersey City, NJ 07305-1597. Offers MBA.

Newman University, Master of Science in Education Program, Wichita, KS 67213-2097. Offers building leadership (MS Ed); curriculum and instruction (MS Ed), including English as a second language, reading specialist; organizational leadership (MS Ed). *Accreditation:* NCATE. *Program availability:* Part-time, evening/weekend, online learning. *Degree requirements:* For master's, thesis optional. *Entrance requirements:* For master's, 3 years' full-time teaching experience, minimum GPA of 3.0, writing sample, 2 letters of recommendation, evidence of teaching certification. Additional exam requirements/recommendations for international students: Required—TOEFL (minimum score 600 paper-based; 100 iBT). Electronic applications accepted. *Expenses:* Contact institution. *Faculty research:* Online course design and deliver, staff engagement, classroom action.

Newman University, MBA Program, Wichita, KS 67213-2097. Offers finance (MBA); international business (MBA); leadership (MBA); management (MBA); management information technology (MBA). *Program availability:* Part-time. *Degree requirements:* For master's, thesis optional. *Entrance requirements:* For master's, minimum GPA of 3.0; 2 letters of recommendation; course work in algebra, statistics, macroeconomics, and financial accounting. Additional exam requirements/recommendations for international students: Required—TOEFL (minimum score 600 paper-based; 100 iBT). Electronic applications accepted. *Expenses:* Contact institution.

The New School, Schools of Public Engagement, Program in Organizational Change Management, New York, NY 10011. Offers leadership and change (Graduate Certificate); organizational change management (MS); organizational development (Graduate Certificate). *Program availability:* Part-time, evening/weekend. *Faculty:* 3 full-time (1 woman), 6 part-time/adjunct (4 women). *Students:* 20 full-time (15 women), 24 part-time (22 women); includes 22 minority (8 Black or African American, non-Hispanic/Latino; 2 Asian, non-Hispanic/Latino; 10 Hispanic/Latino; 2 Two or more races, non-Hispanic/Latino), 3 international. Average age 34. 25 applicants, 80% accepted, 6 enrolled. In 2017, 15 master's, 5 other advanced degrees awarded. *Degree requirements:* For master's, thesis or alternative, capstone project: Paper of Publishable Quality (PPQ). *Entrance requirements:* For master's, minimum of three years' full-time organizational work experience, two letters of recommendation, statement of purpose, resume, transcripts. Additional exam requirements/recommendations for international students: Required—TOEFL (minimum score 92 iBT), IELTS (minimum score 7), PTE (minimum score 68). *Application deadline:* For fall admission, 1/15 priority date for domestic and international students; for spring admission, 10/15 priority date for domestic and international students. Applications are processed on a rolling basis. Application fee: $50. Electronic applications accepted. *Expenses:* $1,650 per credit. *Financial support:* In 2017–18, 28 students received support. Career-related internships or fieldwork, Federal Work-Study, scholarships/grants, and unspecified assistantships available. Support available to part-time students. Financial award application deadline: 2/1; financial award applicants required to submit FAFSA. *Unit head:* Suzanne Bostwick, Chair, 212-229-5400 Ext. 1601, E-mail: bostwics@newschool.edu. *Application contact:* Gabriela Garcia Juarez, Assistant Director, Graduate Admission, 212-229-5150 Ext. 1666, E-mail: garciajg@newschool.edu.
Website: https://www.newschool.edu/public-engagement/ms-organizational-change-management/

New York University, Leonard N. Stern School of Business, Department of Management and Organizations, New York, NY 10012-1019. Offers management organizations (MBA); organization theory (PhD); organizational behavior (PhD); strategy (PhD). *Expenses: Tuition:* Full-time $41,352; part-time $19,968 per year. *Required fees:* $2496; $1628 per unit. $814 per term. Tuition and fees vary according to course load and program. *Faculty research:* Strategic management, managerial cognition, interpersonal processes, conflict and negotiation.

New York University, School of Professional Studies, Division of Programs in Business, Program in Leadership and Human Capital Management, New York, NY 10012-1019. Offers human resource management and development (MS), including global talent management, human resource management, learning, development, and executive coaching, organizational effectiveness. *Program availability:* Part-time, evening/weekend, 100% online, blended/hybrid learning. *Students:* 101 full-time (88 women), 107 part-time (93 women); includes 68 minority (19 Black or African American, non-Hispanic/Latino; 25 Asian, non-Hispanic/Latino; 21 Hispanic/Latino; 3 Two or more races, non-Hispanic/Latino), 93 international. Average age 29. 251 applicants, 52% accepted, 60 enrolled. In 2017, 180 master's awarded. *Degree requirements:* For master's, thesis. *Entrance requirements:* For master's, GRE or GMAT (only upon request), bachelor's degree, resume with relevant professional work, internship or volunteer experience, two letters of recommendation, statement of purpose. Additional exam requirements/recommendations for international students: Required—TOEFL (minimum score 600 paper-based; 100 iBT), IELTS (minimum score 7). *Application deadline:* For fall admission, 2/1 priority date for domestic and international students; for spring admission, 10/15 priority date for domestic students, 8/15 priority date for international students; for summer admission, 5/1 priority date for domestic students, 1/15 priority date for international students. Applications are processed on a rolling basis. Application fee: $150. Electronic applications accepted. *Expenses:* $20,244 per term. *Financial support:* Fellowships, career-related internships or fieldwork, Federal Work-Study, scholarships/grants, and health care benefits available. Support available to part-time students. Financial award application deadline: 6/30; financial award applicants required to submit FAFSA. *Unit head:* Martin Ihrig, Associate Dean/Clinical Professor, 212-992-3288. *Application contact:* Admissions Office, 212-998-7100, E-mail: sps.gradadmissions@nyu.edu.
Website: http://www.sps.nyu.edu/academics/departments/leadership.html

Nichols College, Graduate and Professional Studies, Dudley, MA 01571-5000. Offers business administration (MBA); counterterrorism (MS); organizational leadership (MSOL). *Program availability:* Part-time, evening/weekend, online learning. *Degree requirements:* For master's, project (for MOL). *Entrance requirements:* For master's, 2 letters of recommendation, current resume, official transcripts, 800-word personal

statement. Additional exam requirements/recommendations for international students: Required—TOEFL (minimum score 500 paper-based). Electronic applications accepted.

Northern Arizona University, Office of the Provost, Master of Administration Program, Flagstaff, AZ 86011. Offers organizational leadership (M Adm). *Program availability:* Part-time, online learning. *Students:* 58 applicants, 98% accepted, 57 enrolled. *Degree requirements:* For master's, projects. *Entrance requirements:* For master's, five years' related work experience, minimum GPA of 3.0. Additional exam requirements/recommendations for international students: Required—TOEFL (minimum score 550 paper-based; 80 iBT), IELTS (minimum score 7). *Application deadline:* For fall admission, 3/1 priority date for international students; for spring admission, 9/15 priority date for international students. Applications are processed on a rolling basis. Application fee: $65. Electronic applications accepted. *Expenses:* Tuition, state resident: full-time $9240; part-time $458 per credit hour. Tuition, nonresident: full-time $21,588; part-time $1199 per credit hour. *Required fees:* $1021; $14 per credit hour. $646 per semester. Tuition and fees vary according to course load, campus/location and program. *Financial support:* In 2017–18, 1 student received support, including 1 teaching assistantship with partial tuition reimbursement available (averaging $6,000 per year); health care benefits and unspecified assistantships also available. Financial award application deadline: 2/1; financial award applicants required to submit FAFSA. *Unit head:* Dr. Alex Steenstra, Chair, 928-317-6083, E-mail: alex.steenstra@nau.edu. *Application contact:* Pam Torbico, Coordinator, 928-523-6694, E-mail: m.admin@nau.edu.
Website: http://extended.nau.edu/madmin/

Northern Kentucky University, Office of Graduate Programs, College of Business, Program in Executive Leadership and Organizational Change, Highland Heights, KY 41099. Offers MS. *Program availability:* Part-time, evening/weekend. *Entrance requirements:* For master's, resume, current career essay, future career objectives essay, personal statement, 3 letters of recommendation with cover forms, transcripts. Additional exam requirements/recommendations for international students: Required—TOEFL (minimum score 79 iBT); Recommended—IELTS (minimum score 6.5). Electronic applications accepted. *Expenses:* Contact institution. *Faculty research:* Leadership assessment and development, teams and conflict management, organizational strategy development and systems thinking, organizational consultation.

Northwestern University, The Graduate School, Kellogg School of Management, Department of Management and Organizations, Evanston, IL 60208. Offers PhD. Admissions and degree offered through The Graduate School. *Degree requirements:* For doctorate, comprehensive exam, thesis/dissertation. *Entrance requirements:* For doctorate, GMAT or GRE General Test. Additional exam requirements/recommendations for international students: Required—TOEFL. Electronic applications accepted. *Faculty research:* Bargaining and negotiation, organizational design, decision-making, organizational change, strategic alliances.

Northwestern University, The Graduate School, Kellogg School of Management, Management Programs, Evanston, IL 60208. Offers accounting information and management (MBA, PhD); analytical finance (MBA); business administration (MBA); decision sciences (MBA); entrepreneurship and innovation (MBA); finance (MBA, PhD); health enterprise management (MBA); human resources management (MBA); international business (MBA); management and organizations (MBA, PhD); management and organizations and sociology (PhD); management and strategy (MBA); management studies (MS); managerial analytics (MBA); managerial economics (MBA); managerial economics and strategy (PhD); marketing (MBA, PhD); marketing management (MBA); media management (MBA); operations management (MBA, PhD); real estate (MBA); social enterprise at Kellogg (MBA); JD/MBA. *Program availability:* Part-time, evening/weekend. Terminal master's awarded for partial completion of doctoral program. *Degree requirements:* For doctorate, thesis/dissertation, 2 years of coursework, qualifying (field) exam and candidacy, summer research papers and presentations to faculty, proposal defense, final exam/defense. *Entrance requirements:* For master's, GMAT, GRE, interview, 2 letters of recommendation, college transcripts, resume, essays, Kellogg honor code; for doctorate, GMAT, GRE, statement of purpose, transcripts, 2 letters of recommendation, resume, interview. Additional exam requirements/recommendations for international students: Required—TOEFL, IELTS. Electronic applications accepted. *Expenses:* Contact institution. *Faculty research:* Business cycles and international finance, health policy, networks, non-market strategy, consumer psychology.

Northwestern University, The Graduate School, School of Education and Social Policy, Program in Learning and Organizational Change, Evanston, IL 60208. Offers MS. *Program availability:* Part-time, evening/weekend, online learning. *Degree requirements:* For master's, thesis, practicum. *Entrance requirements:* For master's, GRE or GMAT (recommended), letters of recommendation. Additional exam requirements/recommendations for international students: Required—TOEFL (minimum score 600 paper-based; 100 iBT); Recommended—IELTS (minimum score 7). Electronic applications accepted. *Faculty research:* Strategic change, learning and performance, workplace learning, leadership development, cognitive design, knowledge management.

Northwest University, College of Business, Kirkland, WA 98033. Offers business administration (MBA); international business (MBA); project management (MBA); social entrepreneurship (MBA). *Accreditation:* ACBSP. *Program availability:* Part-time, evening/weekend. *Degree requirements:* For master's, formalized research. *Entrance requirements:* For master's, GMAT. Additional exam requirements/recommendations for international students: Required—TOEFL (minimum score 550 paper-based; 75 iBT). Electronic applications accepted. *Expenses:* Contact institution.

Norwich University, College of Graduate and Continuing Studies, Master of Business Administration Program, Northfield, VT 05663. Offers construction management (MBA); energy management (MBA); finance (MBA); logistics (MBA); organizational leadership (MBA); project management (MBA); supply chain management (MBA). *Accreditation:* ACBSP. *Program availability:* Evening/weekend, online only, mostly all online with a week-long residency requirement. *Degree requirements:* For master's, comprehensive exam. *Entrance requirements:* For master's, minimum undergraduate GPA of 2.75. Additional exam requirements/recommendations for international students: Required—TOEFL (minimum score 550 paper-based; 80 iBT), IELTS (minimum score 6.5). Electronic applications accepted. *Expenses:* Contact institution.

Norwich University, College of Graduate and Continuing Studies, Master of Science in Executive Leadership Program, Northfield, VT 05663. Offers MS. *Program availability:* Evening/weekend, online only, mostly all online with a week-long residency requirement. *Degree requirements:* For master's, capstone. *Entrance requirements:* For master's, minimum of eight years of formal leadership experience, minimum GPA of 2.75. Additional exam requirements/recommendations for international students: Required—TOEFL (minimum score 550 paper-based; 80 iBT), IELTS (minimum score 6.5). Electronic applications accepted. *Expenses:* Contact institution.

Norwich University, College of Graduate and Continuing Studies, Master of Science in Leadership Program, Northfield, VT 05663. Offers leadership (MS), including human resources leadership, leading change management consulting, organizational leadership, public sector/government/military leadership. *Program availability:* Evening/weekend, online only, mostly all online with a week-long residency requirement. *Degree* *requirements:* For master's, capstone. *Entrance requirements:* For master's, minimum undergraduate GPA of 2.75. Additional exam requirements/recommendations for international students: Required—TOEFL (minimum score 550 paper-based; 80 iBT), IELTS (minimum score 6.5). Electronic applications accepted. *Expenses:* Contact institution.

Nyack College, School of Business and Leadership, Nyack, NY 10960. Offers business administration (MBA); organizational leadership (MS). *Program availability:* Part-time, evening/weekend, 100% online, blended/hybrid learning. *Students:* 33 full-time (22 women), 10 part-time (7 women); includes 31 minority (23 Black or African American, non-Hispanic/Latino; 7 Hispanic/Latino; 1 Two or more races, non-Hispanic/Latino), 3 international. Average age 38. In 2017, 33 master's awarded. *Degree requirements:* For master's, thesis (for some programs), capstone project (for MBA). *Entrance requirements:* For master's, transcripts, personal goals statement, recommendations, resume, interview. Additional exam requirements/recommendations for international students: Required—TOEFL (minimum score 550 paper-based; 80 iBT), IELTS (minimum score 6.5). *Application deadline:* Applications are processed on a rolling basis. Application fee: $50. Electronic applications accepted. *Expenses:* $725 per credit (for MS); $800 per credit (for MBA). *Financial support:* Scholarships/grants available. Financial award applicants required to submit FAFSA. *Unit head:* Dr. Anita Underwood, Dean, 845-675-4511. *Application contact:* Joseph M. Williams, Graduate Admissions Associate, 845-770-5711, E-mail: admissions.grad@nyack.edu.
Website: http://www.nyack.edu/sbl

Nyack College, School of Social Work, Nyack, NY 10960. Offers clinical social work practice (MSW); leadership in organizations and communities (MSW). *Program availability:* Part-time, evening/weekend. *Students:* 58 full-time (50 women), 27 part-time (21 women); includes 77 minority (50 Black or African American, non-Hispanic/Latino; 5 Asian, non-Hispanic/Latino; 21 Hispanic/Latino; 1 Two or more races, non-Hispanic/Latino), 3 international. Average age 36. In 2017, 15 master's awarded. *Degree requirements:* For master's, field work. *Entrance requirements:* For master's, official transcripts, academic and professional references, personal statement, essay or case reflection. Additional exam requirements/recommendations for international students: Required—TOEFL (minimum score 550 paper-based; 80 iBT). *Application deadline:* Applications are processed on a rolling basis. Application fee: $45. Electronic applications accepted. *Expenses:* $800 per credit. *Financial support:* Scholarships/grants available. Financial award applicants required to submit FAFSA. *Unit head:* Dr. Janet Furness, Director of MSW Program, 646-378-6169. *Application contact:* DeLissa Dixon, Admissions Associate, 646-378-6105, E-mail: admissions.grad@nyack.edu.
Website: https://www.nyack.edu/msw

Oakland University, Graduate Study and Lifelong Learning, School of Education and Human Services, Department of Organizational Leadership, Rochester, MI 48309-4401. Offers educational leadership (M Ed, PhD); higher education (Certificate); school administration (Ed S). *Entrance requirements:* Additional exam requirements/recommendations for international students: Required—TOEFL (minimum score 550 paper-based). *Expenses:* Tuition, state resident: full-time $16,950; part-time $706.25 per credit. Tuition, nonresident: full-time $24,648; part-time $1027 per credit.

Ohio Christian University, Graduate Programs, Circleville, OH 43113. Offers accounting (MBA); business administration (MBA); digital marketing (MBA); finance (MBA); healthcare management (MBA); human resources (MBA); management (MM); organizational leadership (MBA); pastoral care and counseling (MAM); practical theology (MAM).

Oklahoma Christian University, Graduate School of Business, Oklahoma City, OK 73136-1100. Offers accounting (M Acc, MBA); financial services (MBA); general business (MBA); health services management (MBA); human resources (MBA); international business (MBA); leadership and organizational development (MBA); marketing (MBA); nonprofit management (MBA); project management (MBA). *Accreditation:* ACBSP. *Program availability:* Part-time, 100% online. *Entrance requirements:* For master's, bachelor's degree. Additional exam requirements/recommendations for international students: Required—TOEFL (minimum score 550 paper-based). Electronic applications accepted. *Expenses:* Contact institution.

Olivet Nazarene University, Program in Organizational Leadership, Bourbonnais, IL 60914. Offers MOL.

Our Lady of the Lake University, School of Business and Leadership, Program in Leadership Studies, San Antonio, TX 78207-4689. Offers PhD. *Program availability:* Part-time, evening/weekend. *Faculty:* 9 full-time (6 women), 9 part-time/adjunct (3 women). *Students:* 284 full-time (163 women), 6 part-time (4 women); includes 223 minority (29 Black or African American, non-Hispanic/Latino; 194 Hispanic/Latino). Average age 45. 69 applicants, 99% accepted, 52 enrolled. In 2017, 39 doctorates awarded. *Degree requirements:* For doctorate, comprehensive exam, thesis/dissertation. *Entrance requirements:* For doctorate, GRE or MAT, master's degree with minimum of 36 credit hours in appropriate field from regionally-accredited college or university; minimum GPA of 3.3 in all previous master's degree work (preferred); résumé; personal statement. Additional exam requirements/recommendations for international students: Required—TOEFL. *Application deadline:* For fall admission, 5/15 for domestic and international students. Application fee: $40 ($50 for international students). Electronic applications accepted. Application fee is waived when completed online. *Expenses:* Contact institution. *Financial support:* In 2017–18, 6 students received support. Federal Work-Study, scholarships/grants, unspecified assistantships, and tuition discounts available. Support available to part-time students. Financial award application deadline: 5/1; financial award applicants required to submit FAFSA. *Unit head:* Dr. Esther Chavez Gergen, Chair of Leadership Department, 210-434-6711 Ext. 2287, E-mail: esgergen@lake.ollusa.edu. *Application contact:* Office of Graduate Admissions, 210-434-3995, Fax: 210-431-3945, E-mail: gradadm@ollusa.edu.
Website: http://www.ollusa.edu/s/1190/hybrid/default-hybrid-ollu.aspx?sid-1190&gid-1&pgid-7956

Our Lady of the Lake University, School of Business and Leadership, Program in Organizational Leadership, San Antonio, TX 78207-4689. Offers MS. *Program availability:* Part-time, evening/weekend. *Faculty:* 4 full-time (2 women), 13 part-time/adjunct (4 women). *Students:* 63 full-time (39 women), 3 part-time (all women); includes 50 minority (4 Black or African American, non-Hispanic/Latino; 46 Hispanic/Latino). Average age 34. 35 applicants, 97% accepted, 26 enrolled. In 2017, 29 master's awarded. *Entrance requirements:* For master's, official transcripts showing minimum cumulative GPA of 2.5, 2 letters of recommendation, resume, personal statement. Additional exam requirements/recommendations for international students: Required—TOEFL. *Application deadline:* For fall admission, 6/15 for domestic and international students; for spring admission, 11/15 for domestic and international students. Application fee: $40 ($50 for international students). Electronic applications accepted. *Expenses:* Tuition: Full-time $10,668; part-time $5334 per year. *Required fees:* $816; $816 per year. $408 per semester. *Financial support:* In 2017–18, 33 students received support. Federal Work-Study, scholarships/grants, unspecified assistantships, and tuition discounts available. Support available to part-time students. Financial award application deadline: 5/1; financial award applicants required to submit FAFSA. *Unit head:* Dr. Esther Chavez Gergen, Leadership Studies Program Chair, 210-434-6711,

E-mail: esgergen@ollusa.edu. *Application contact:* Graduate Admission, 210-431-3995, Fax: 210-431-3945, E-mail: gradadm@ollusa.edu.
Website: http://www.ollusa.edu/s/1190/hybrid/default-hybrid-ollu.aspx?sid-1190&gid-1&pgid-7906

Oxford Graduate School, Graduate Programs, Dayton, TN 37321-6736. Offers family life education (M Litt); integration of religion and society (D Phil); organizational leadership (M Litt). *Entrance requirements:* For master's, official transcripts, three letters of recommendation, bachelor's degree or its equivalent, minimum undergraduate GPA of 3.0, minimum of 3 years of professional experience; for doctorate, official transcripts, three letters of recommendation, master's degree with minimum GPA of 3.0, minimum of 5 years of professional experience. *Expenses:* Contact institution.

Palm Beach Atlantic University, MacArthur School of Leadership, West Palm Beach, FL 33416-4708. Offers MS. *Program availability:* Part-time, evening/weekend, blended/hybrid learning. *Entrance requirements:* For master's, minimum GPA of 3.0; essay. Additional exam requirements/recommendations for international students: Required—TOEFL (minimum score 550 paper-based; 79 iBT). Electronic applications accepted. *Faculty research:* Ethics, business strategies, organizational leadership.

Peirce College, Program in Organizational Leadership and Management, Philadelphia, PA 19102-4699. Offers MS. *Degree requirements:* For master's, capstone project. *Entrance requirements:* For master's, official transcripts, current resume, statement of intent, two letters of recommendation.

Penn State University Park, Graduate School, Smeal College of Business, University Park, PA 16802. Offers accounting (M Acc); business administration (MBA, MS, PhD); management and organizational leadership (MPS). *Accreditation:* AACSB. *Program availability:* Part-time, evening/weekend. *Students:* 290 full-time (97 women), 7 part-time (2 women). Average age 29. 1,125 applicants, 27% accepted, 236 enrolled. In 2017, 235 master's, 10 doctorates awarded. *Entrance requirements:* Additional exam requirements/recommendations for international students: Required—TOEFL (minimum score 550 paper-based; 80 iBT), IELTS. *Application deadline:* Applications are processed on a rolling basis. Application fee: $65. Electronic applications accepted. *Expenses:* Contact institution. *Financial support:* Fellowships, research assistantships, teaching assistantships, career-related internships or fieldwork, Federal Work-Study, scholarships/grants, traineeships, health care benefits, and unspecified assistantships available. Support available to part-time students. Financial award application deadline: 2/15; financial award applicants required to submit FAFSA. *Unit head:* Dr. Charles H. Whiteman, Dean, 814-863-0448, Fax: 814-865-7064. *Application contact:* Lori Hawn, Graduate Student Services, 814-865-1795, Fax: 814-863-4627, E-mail: l-gswww@lists.psu.edu.
Website: http://smeal.psu.edu/

Pepperdine University, Graduate School of Education and Psychology, Division of Education, Los Angeles, CA 90263. Offers administration and preliminary administrative services (MS); education (MA); educational leadership, administration, and policy (Ed D); global leadership and change (PhD); learning technologies (MA, Ed D); organizational leadership (Ed D); social entrepreneurship and change (MA); teaching (MA); teaching: TESOL (MA). *Program availability:* Part-time, evening/weekend, blended/hybrid learning. *Students:* 214 full-time (139 women), 327 part-time (216 women); includes 248 minority (113 Black or African American, non-Hispanic/Latino; 2 American Indian or Alaska Native, non-Hispanic/Latino; 48 Asian, non-Hispanic/Latino; 61 Hispanic/Latino; 6 Native Hawaiian or other Pacific Islander, non-Hispanic/Latino; 18 Two or more races, non-Hispanic/Latino), 49 international. Average age 39. 410 applicants, 91% accepted, 160 enrolled. In 2017, 151 master's, 88 doctorates awarded. *Degree requirements:* For doctorate, thesis/dissertation. *Entrance requirements:* For master's, GRE General Test; for doctorate, GRE General Test, MAT. Additional exam requirements/recommendations for international students: Required—TOEFL. *Application deadline:* Applications are processed on a rolling basis. Application fee: $55. Electronic applications accepted. *Expenses:* Contact institution. *Financial support:* Research assistantships, teaching assistantships, career-related internships or fieldwork, institutionally sponsored loans, and scholarships/grants available. Support available to part-time students. Financial award application deadline: 7/1; financial award applicants required to submit FAFSA. *Unit head:* Dr. Martine Jago, Associate Dean, Education Division, 310-568-2828, E-mail: martine.jago@pepperdine.edu. *Application contact:* Chris Costa, Director of Enrollment, 310-568-2850, E-mail: chris.costa@pepperdine.edu.
Website: http://gsep.pepperdine.edu/masters-education/

Peru State College, Graduate Programs, Program in Organizational Management, Peru, NE 68421. Offers MS. Program offered online only. *Program availability:* Part-time, online learning. *Degree requirements:* For master's, thesis (for some programs). *Expenses:* Contact institution. *Faculty research:* Emotional intelligence.

Pfeiffer University, Program in Leadership and Organizational Change, Misenheimer, NC 28109-0960. Offers MS, MBA/MS. *Entrance requirements:* For master's, GRE or GMAT.

Point Loma Nazarene University, College of Extended Learning, Program in Organizational Leadership, San Diego, CA 92106-2899. Offers MA. *Program availability:* Online learning. *Faculty:* 11 part-time/adjunct (3 women). *Students:* 7 full-time (all women), 80 part-time (54 women); includes 41 minority (8 Black or African American, non-Hispanic/Latino; 1 American Indian or Alaska Native, non-Hispanic/Latino; 2 Asian, non-Hispanic/Latino; 25 Hispanic/Latino; 5 Two or more races, non-Hispanic/Latino), 1 international. Average age 35. 38 applicants, 97% accepted, 28 enrolled. In 2017, 34 master's awarded. *Application deadline:* For fall admission, 8/8 priority date for domestic students. *Expenses:* Contact institution. *Unit head:* Dave Phillips, Dean, 619-619-2771, E-mail: davidphillips@pointloma.edu. *Application contact:* Joanie Joy, Senior Director of Enrollment Management, 619-329-6785, E-mail: gradinfo@pointloma.edu.
Website: https://www.pointloma.edu/graduate-studies/programs/organizational-leadership-ma

Point Loma Nazarene University, Fermanian School of Business, San Diego, CA 92106-2899. Offers general business (MBA); healthcare management (MBA); innovation and entrepreneurship (MBA); organizational leadership (MBA); project management (MBA). *Accreditation:* ACBSP. *Program availability:* Part-time, evening/weekend. *Faculty:* 7 full-time (0 women), 5 part-time/adjunct (3 women). *Students:* 27 full-time (8 women), 94 part-time (45 women); includes 52 minority (6 Black or African American, non-Hispanic/Latino; 1 American Indian or Alaska Native, non-Hispanic/Latino; 7 Asian, non-Hispanic/Latino; 33 Hispanic/Latino; 5 Two or more races, non-Hispanic/Latino), 11 international. Average age 31. 74 applicants, 99% accepted, 56 enrolled. In 2017, 45 master's awarded. *Entrance requirements:* For master's, GMAT, letters of recommendation, essay, interview. Additional exam requirements/recommendations for international students: Required—TOEFL. *Application deadline:* For fall admission, 7/26 priority date for domestic students; for spring admission, 11/29 priority date for domestic students; for summer admission, 4/2 priority date for domestic students. Applications are processed on a rolling basis. Application fee: $50. Electronic applications accepted. *Expenses:* Contact institution. *Financial support:* Applicants required to submit FAFSA. *Unit head:* Jamie McIlwaine, Associate Dean, Graduate Business, 619-849-2721, E-mail: jmcilwai@pointloma.edu. *Application contact:* Joanie Joy, Senior Director of Enrollment Management, 619-329-6785, E-mail: gradinfo@pointloma.edu.
Website: https://www.pointloma.edu/schools-departments-colleges/fermanian-school-business

Organizational Management

Point Park University, Rowland School of Business, Program in Management, Pittsburgh, PA 15222-1984. Offers health care administration and management (MS); leadership (MA). *Program availability:* 100% online.

Purdue University Global, School of Business, Davenport, IA 52807. Offers business administration (MBA); change leadership (MS); entrepreneurship (MBA); finance (MBA); health care management (MBA, MS); human resource (MBA); international business (MBA); management (MS); marketing (MBA); project management (MBA, MS); supply chain management and logistics (MBA, MS). *Accreditation:* ACBSP. *Program availability:* Part-time, evening/weekend, online learning. *Entrance requirements:* Additional exam requirements/recommendations for international students: Required—TOEFL (minimum score 550 paper-based; 80 iBT). Electronic applications accepted.

Queens University of Charlotte, McColl School of Business, Charlotte, NC 28274-0002. Offers business administration (EMBA, MBA, PMBA); organization development (MSOD). *Accreditation:* AACSB. *Program availability:* Part-time, evening/weekend, online learning. *Degree requirements:* For master's, capstone course. *Entrance requirements:* For master's, GMAT, minimum GPA of 2.5. Additional exam requirements/recommendations for international students: Required—TOEFL. Electronic applications accepted. *Expenses:* Contact institution.

Quinnipiac University, School of Business, Program in Organizational Leadership, Hamden, CT 06518-1940. Offers MS. *Program availability:* Part-time, evening/weekend, online only, 100% online. *Faculty:* 5 full-time (3 women). *Students:* 9 full-time (8 women), 228 part-time (153 women); includes 62 minority (31 Black or African American, non-Hispanic/Latino; 5 Asian, non-Hispanic/Latino; 20 Hispanic/Latino; 6 Two or more races, non-Hispanic/Latino). 96 applicants, 93% accepted, 75 enrolled. In 2017, 83 master's awarded. *Entrance requirements:* For master's, four years of work experience. Additional exam requirements/recommendations for international students: Required—TOEFL (minimum score 575 paper-based; 90 iBT), IELTS (minimum score 6.5). *Application deadline:* For fall admission, 7/30 priority date for domestic students, 4/30 for international students; for spring admission, 12/31 priority date for domestic students, 4/30 for international students; for summer admission, 4/30 priority date for domestic students. Applications are processed on a rolling basis. Application fee: $45. Electronic applications accepted. *Expenses:* Contact institution. *Financial support:* Federal Work-Study and unspecified assistantships available. Financial award application deadline: 6/1; financial award applicants required to submit FAFSA. *Faculty research:* Virtual teams, women and leadership, virtual human resources applications and practices, emotional intelligence and its application in the workplace. *Application contact:* Quinnipiac University Online Admissions, 203-582-3918, Fax: 203-582-3443, E-mail: quonlineadmissions@qu.edu.
Website: https://quonline.quinnipiac.edu/online-programs/online-graduate-programs/ms-in-organizational-leadership/

Regent University, Graduate School, School of Business and Leadership, Virginia Beach, VA 23464-9800. Offers business administration (MBA), including accounting, economics, entrepreneurship, finance and investing, general management, healthcare management (MA, MBA), human resource management (MA, MBA), innovation management, leadership, marketing, not-for-profit management (MA, MBA); business analytics (MS); business and design management (MA); church leadership (MA); leadership (Certificate); organizational leadership (MA, PhD), including ecclesial leadership (DSL, PhD), entrepreneurial leadership (PhD), healthcare management (MA, MBA), human resource development (PhD), human resource management (MA, MBA), individualized studies (DSL, PhD), interdisciplinary studies (MA), leadership coaching and mentoring (MA), not-for-profit management (MA, MBA), organizational development consulting (MA), servant leadership (MA, DSL); strategic leadership (DSL), including ecclesia leadership (DSL, PhD), global consulting, healthcare leadership, individualized studies (DSL, PhD), leadership coaching, servant leadership (MA, DSL), strategic foresight. *Program availability:* Part-time, evening/weekend, 100% online, blended/hybrid learning. *Faculty:* 9 full-time (2 women), 38 part-time/adjunct (11 women). *Students:* 129 full-time (80 women), 1,152 part-time (598 women); includes 685 minority (546 Black or African American, non-Hispanic/Latino; 10 American Indian or Alaska Native, non-Hispanic/Latino; 29 Asian, non-Hispanic/Latino; 65 Hispanic/Latino; 6 Native Hawaiian or other Pacific Islander, non-Hispanic/Latino; 29 Two or more races, non-Hispanic/Latino), 62 international. Average age 41. 1,721 applicants, 48% accepted, 624 enrolled. In 2017, 125 master's, 69 doctorates awarded. *Degree requirements:* For master's, thesis or alternative, 3-credit hour culminating experience; for doctorate, thesis/dissertation. *Entrance requirements:* For master's, college transcripts, resume, essay; for doctorate, college transcripts, resume, essay, writing sample; for Certificate, writing sample, resume, transcripts. Additional exam requirements/recommendations for international students: Required—TOEFL (minimum score 577 paper-based). *Application deadline:* For fall admission, 5/1 priority date for domestic students; for spring admission, 10/1 priority date for domestic students. Applications are processed on a rolling basis. Application fee: $50. Electronic applications accepted. *Expenses:* $650 per credit (MA, MS, MBA); $995 per credit (PhD); $300 per semester technology fee. *Financial support:* In 2017–18, 829 students received support. Career-related internships or fieldwork, scholarships/grants, and unspecified assistantships available. Support available to part-time students. *Faculty research:* Servant leadership, global business, team effectiveness, technology utilization, leadership development. *Unit head:* Dr. Doris Gomez, Dean, 757-352-4686, Fax: 757-352-4634, E-mail: dorigom@regent.edu. *Application contact:* Heidi Cece, Assistant Vice President of Enrollment Management, 800-373-5504, Fax: 757-352-4381, E-mail: admissions@regent.edu.
Website: https://www.regent.edu/school-of-business-and-leadership/

Regis University, College of Business and Economics, Denver, CO 80221-1099. Offers accounting (MS); executive leadership (Certificate); finance (MS); finance and accounting (MBA); health industry leadership (MBA); human resource management and leadership (MSOL); management (MBA); marketing (MBA); nonprofit leadership (Post-Graduate Certificate); nonprofit management (MNM); nonprofit organizational capacity building (Certificate); operations management (MBA); organizational leadership and management (MSOL); project leadership and management (MS, MSOL); strategic business management (Certificate); strategic human resource integration (Certificate); strategic management (MBA). Programs offered at Colorado Springs Campus, Northwest Denver Campus, Southeast Denver Campus, Fort Collins Campus, Broomfield Campus, Henderson (Nevada) Campus, and Summerlin (Nevada) Campus. *Program availability:* Part-time, evening/weekend, 100% online, blended/hybrid learning. *Degree requirements:* For master's, thesis (for some programs), capstone or final research project. *Entrance requirements:* For master's, official transcript reflecting baccalaureate degree awarded from regionally-accredited college or university, interview, 2 years of full-time related work experience, resume, letters of recommendation. Additional exam requirements/recommendations for international students: Required—TOEFL (minimum score 550 paper-based; 82 iBT). Electronic applications accepted. *Expenses:* Contact institution. *Faculty research:* Impact of information technology on small business regulation of accounting, international project financing, mineral development, delivery of healthcare to rural indigenous communities.

Rider University, College of Education and Human Services, Program in Organizational Leadership, Lawrenceville, NJ 08648-3001. Offers MA. *Program availability:* Online learning. *Entrance requirements:* For master's, resume.

Robert Morris University, School of Communications and Information Systems, Moon Township, PA 15108-1189. Offers communication and information systems (MS); cyber security (MS); data analytics (MS); information security and assurance (MS); information systems and communications (D Sc); information systems management (MS); information technology project management (MS); Internet information systems (MS); organizational leadership (MS). *Program availability:* Part-time, evening/weekend, online learning. *Faculty:* 23 full-time (10 women), 10 part-time/adjunct (3 women). *Students:* 258 full-time (99 women); includes 46 minority (22 Black or African American, non-Hispanic/Latino; 16 Asian, non-Hispanic/Latino; 5 Hispanic/Latino; 3 Two or more races, non-Hispanic/Latino), 46 international. Average age 35. 226 applicants, 52% accepted, 79 enrolled. In 2017, 148 master's, 12 doctorates awarded. *Degree requirements:* For doctorate, thesis/dissertation. *Entrance requirements:* For doctorate, employer letter of endorsement, interview. Additional exam requirements/recommendations for international students: Required—TOEFL (minimum score 550 paper-based; 79 iBT). *Application deadline:* For fall admission, 7/1 priority date for domestic and international students; for spring admission, 11/1 priority date for domestic and international students. Applications are processed on a rolling basis. Application fee: $35. Electronic applications accepted. Application fee is waived when completed online. *Expenses:* $920 per credit tuition plus university fees of $80 per credit. *Financial support:* Institutionally sponsored loans available. Support available to part-time students. Financial award application deadline: 5/1. *Unit head:* Ann Marie M. Le Blanc, Dean, 412-397-6433, Fax: 412-397-6469, E-mail: leblanc@rmu.edu. *Application contact:* E-mail: graduateadmissions@rmu.edu.
Website: http://www.rmu.edu/web/cms/schools/scis/Pages/default.aspx

Rochester Institute of Technology, Graduate Enrollment Services, College of Applied Science and Technology, School of International Hospitality and Service Innovation, Advanced Certificate Program in Organizational Learning, Rochester, NY 14623. Offers Advanced Certificate. *Program availability:* Part-time, evening/weekend, online only, 100% online. *Students:* 2 applicants, 50% accepted. *Entrance requirements:* For degree, minimum GPA of 3.0 (recommended). Additional exam requirements/recommendations for international students: Required—TOEFL (minimum score 570 paper-based; 88 iBT), IELTS (minimum score 6.5), PTE (minimum score 62). *Application deadline:* Applications are processed on a rolling basis. Application fee: $65. Electronic applications accepted. *Expenses:* $1,035 per credit hour (online study). *Financial support:* Scholarships/grants available. Support available to part-time students. Financial award applicants required to submit FAFSA. *Unit head:* Dr. Linda Underhill, Department Chair, 585-475-4399, Fax: 585-475-7080, E-mail: cast@rit.edu. *Application contact:* Diane Ellison, Senior Associate Vice President, Graduate Enrollment Services, 585-475-2229, Fax: 585-475-7164, E-mail: gradinfo@rit.edu.
Website: http://www.rit.edu/cast/servicesystems/organizational-learning

Roosevelt University, Graduate Division, Walter E. Heller College of Business, Program in Organization Development, Chicago, IL 60605. Offers MA. *Program availability:* Part-time, evening/weekend. *Students:* 3 full-time (0 women), 33 part-time (22 women); includes 21 minority (19 Black or African American, non-Hispanic/Latino; 1 Hispanic/Latino; 1 Two or more races, non-Hispanic/Latino). Average age 39. 11 applicants, 100% accepted, 7 enrolled. In 2017, 4 master's awarded. *Application deadline:* Applications are processed on a rolling basis. Application fee: $40. Electronic applications accepted. *Financial support:* Scholarships/grants and unspecified assistantships available. *Application contact:* Michael Conwell, Graduate Admission Counselor, 312-281-3250, E-mail: mconwell@roosevelt.edu.

Rutgers University–Newark, Rutgers Business School–Newark and New Brunswick, Doctoral Programs in Management, Newark, NJ 07102. Offers accounting (PhD); accounting information systems (PhD); economics (PhD); finance (PhD); individualized study (PhD); information technology (PhD); international business (PhD); management science (PhD); marketing science (PhD); organizational management (PhD); science, technology and management (PhD); supply chain management (PhD). *Degree requirements:* For doctorate, comprehensive exam, thesis/dissertation. *Entrance requirements:* For doctorate, GRE or GMAT. Additional exam requirements/recommendations for international students: Required—TOEFL (minimum score 550 paper-based; 79 iBT). Electronic applications accepted.

Sage Graduate School, School of Management, Program in Organization Management, Troy, NY 12180-4115. Offers MS. *Program availability:* Part-time, evening/weekend. *Faculty:* 5 full-time (3 women), 5 part-time/adjunct (1 woman). *Students:* 3 full-time (all women), 26 part-time (23 women); includes 6 minority (4 Black or African American, non-Hispanic/Latino; 1 Asian, non-Hispanic/Latino; 1 Hispanic/Latino), 1 international. Average age 34. 23 applicants, 61% accepted, 8 enrolled. In 2017, 16 master's awarded. *Degree requirements:* For master's, capstone seminar. *Entrance requirements:* For master's, minimum GPA of 2.75. Additional exam requirements/recommendations for international students: Required—TOEFL (minimum score 550 paper-based). *Application deadline:* Applications are processed on a rolling basis. Application fee: $30. Electronic applications accepted. Tuition and fees vary according to degree level and program. *Financial support:* Fellowships, research assistantships, and unspecified assistantships available. Financial award application deadline: 3/1; financial award applicants required to submit FAFSA. *Unit head:* Dr. Kimberly Fredericks, Dean, School of Management, 518-292-1782, Fax: 518-292-1964, E-mail: fredek1@sage.edu. *Application contact:* Wendy D. Diefendorf, Director of Graduate and Adult Admission, 518-244-2443, Fax: 518-244-6880, E-mail: diefew@sage.edu.
Website: http://www.sage.edu/academics/management/programs/organization_management/

St. Ambrose University, College of Business, Program in Organizational Leadership, Davenport, IA 52801. Offers MOL. *Program availability:* Part-time, evening/weekend. *Degree requirements:* For master's, comprehensive exam (for some programs), thesis or alternative, integration projects. *Entrance requirements:* Additional exam requirements/recommendations for international students: Required—TOEFL. Electronic applications accepted. *Expenses:* Contact institution.

St. Catherine University, Graduate Programs, Program in Organizational Leadership, St. Paul, MN 55105. Offers MA. *Program availability:* Part-time, evening/weekend. *Degree requirements:* For master's, thesis. *Entrance requirements:* For master's, GMAT, GRE General Test or MAT, 2 years of work experience, minimum GPA of 3.0. Additional exam requirements/recommendations for international students: Required—TOEFL (minimum score 600 paper-based; 100 iBT). *Application deadline:* For fall admission, 8/1 priority date for domestic students; for winter admission, 12/1 priority date for domestic students; for spring admission, 3/1 priority date for domestic students. Applications are processed on a rolling basis. Application fee: $35. *Expenses:* Contact institution. *Financial support:* Research assistantships, career-related internships or fieldwork, and institutionally sponsored loans available. Support available to part-time students. Financial award application deadline: 4/1; financial award applicants required to submit FAFSA. *Faculty research:* Ethics. *Unit head:* Amy Ihlan, Interim Director, 651-690-6887, Fax: 651-690-6024.
Website: https://www.stkate.edu/academics/graduate-degrees/academic-programs/maol

St. Edward's University, Bill Munday School of Business, Program in Leadership and Change, Austin, TX 78704. Offers MS. *Program availability:* Part-time-only, evening/weekend. *Students:* 9 full-time (5 women), 54 part-time (35 women); includes 29 minority (10 Black or African American, non-Hispanic/Latino; 1 Asian, non-Hispanic/Latino; 15 Hispanic/Latino; 3 Two or more races, non-Hispanic/Latino), 3 international. Average age 33. 31 applicants, 68% accepted, 15 enrolled. In 2017, 27 master's awarded. *Entrance requirements:* Additional exam requirements/recommendations for international students: Required—TOEFL, IELTS. *Application deadline:* For fall admission, 6/1 priority date for domestic and international students; for spring admission, 10/1 priority date for domestic and international students. Applications are processed on a rolling basis. Application fee: $50. Electronic applications accepted. *Expenses: Tuition:* Full-time $26,406; part-time $1467 per hour. *Required fees:* $75 per trimester. Full-time tuition and fees vary according to course load and program. *Unit head:* Dr. Tom Sechrest, Program Director/Associate Professor of Management, 512-637-1954, E-mail: thomasls@stedwards.edu. *Application contact:* Mike Leveriza, Graduate Admissions Advisor, 512-448-8745, E-mail: mleveriz@stedwards.edu.

St. Joseph's College, Long Island Campus, Programs in Management, Field in Organizational Management, Patchogue, NY 11772-2399. Offers MS. *Program availability:* Part-time, evening/weekend, 100% online, blended/hybrid learning. *Faculty:* 15 full-time (7 women), 22 part-time/adjunct (7 women). *Students:* 2 full-time (both women), 19 part-time (12 women); includes 9 minority (3 Black or African American, non-Hispanic/Latino; 1 Asian, non-Hispanic/Latino; 5 Hispanic/Latino). Average age 32. 20 applicants, 70% accepted, 5 enrolled. In 2017, 7 master's awarded. Application fee: $25. *Expenses: Tuition:* Full-time $17,550; part-time $975 per credit. *Required fees:* $362. *Financial support:* In 2017–18, 5 students received support. *Unit head:* Mary A. Chance, Assistant Professor/Interim Director of Graduate Management Studies, 631-687-1297, E-mail: mchance@sjcny.edu.

St. Joseph's College, New York, Programs in Management, Field in Organizational Management, Brooklyn, NY 11205-3688. Offers MS. *Program availability:* Part-time, evening/weekend, 100% online, blended/hybrid learning. *Faculty:* 1 full-time (0 women), 6 part-time/adjunct (4 women). *Students:* 8 full-time (7 women); all minorities (5 Black or African American, non-Hispanic/Latino; 3 Hispanic/Latino). Average age 42. 11 applicants, 45% accepted, 4 enrolled. In 2017, 5 master's awarded. *Entrance requirements:* For master's, official transcripts, resume, two letters of reference, verification of employment. Additional exam requirements/recommendations for international students: Required—TOEFL (minimum score 80 iBT). *Application deadline:* Applications are processed on a rolling basis. Application fee: $25. Electronic applications accepted. *Expenses: Tuition:* Full-time $17,550; part-time $975 per credit. *Required fees:* $362. *Financial support:* In 2017–18, 1 student received support. *Unit head:* Sharon Didier, Assistant Chair/Co-Director of Graduate Management Studies/Associate Professor, 718-940-5790, E-mail: sdidier@sjcny.edu.

Saint Mary-of-the-Woods College, Master of Leadership Development Program, Saint Mary of the Woods, IN 47876. Offers not-for-profit leadership (MLD); organizational leadership (MLD). *Program availability:* Part-time. *Students:* 47 full-time (41 women); includes 4 minority (all Black or African American, non-Hispanic/Latino). Average age 35. 26 applicants, 81% accepted, 19 enrolled. In 2017, 24 master's awarded. *Degree requirements:* For master's, thesis. *Application deadline:* Applications are processed on a rolling basis. Application fee: $0. Electronic applications accepted. *Expenses:* $565 per credit hour. *Financial support:* In 2017–18, 28 students received support. Scholarships/grants available. Financial award applicants required to submit FAFSA. *Application contact:* Office of Graduate Admissions, 800-926-7692, E-mail: graduate@smwc.edu. Website: http://www.smwc.edu

Saint Mary's College of California, Kalmanovitz School of Education, Leadership Programs, Moraga, CA 94556. Offers coaching and facilitation (MA); organizational leadership and change (MA); peacebuilding and conflict transformation (MA); social justice (MA). *Accreditation:* AACSB. *Program availability:* Part-time, evening/weekend, online learning. *Degree requirements:* For master's, research project. *Entrance requirements:* For master's, letters of recommendation, interview. Electronic applications accepted. *Expenses:* Contact institution. *Faculty research:* Leadership, organizational change, values, adult learning, transformative learning.

Saint Mary's University of Minnesota, Schools of Graduate and Professional Programs, Graduate School of Business and Technology, Organizational Leadership Program, Winona, MN 55987-1399. Offers MA. *Program availability:* Online learning. *Unit head:* George Diaz, Director, 612-238-4510, E-mail: gdiaz@smumn.edu. *Application contact:* James Callinan, Director of Admissions for Graduate and Professional Programs, 612-728-5158, Fax: 612-728-5121, E-mail: jcallina@smumn.edu. Website: http://www.smumn.edu/graduate-home/areas-of-study/graduate-school-of-business-technology/ma-in-organizational-leadership

Salve Regina University, Program in Management, Newport, RI 02840-4192. Offers business studies (CGS); human resource management (CGS); innovation and strategic management (MS); management (CGS); nonprofit management (CGS); social entrepreneurship (CGS). *Program availability:* Part-time, evening/weekend, online learning. *Entrance requirements:* For master's, GMAT, GRE General Test, or MAT. Additional exam requirements/recommendations for international students: Required—TOEFL (minimum score 600 paper-based; 100 iBT). Electronic applications accepted.

San Diego Christian College, Graduate Programs, Santee, CA 92071. Offers education (MAT); organization (MSL).

Saybrook University, LIOS MA Residential Programs, Kirkland, WA 98033. Offers leadership and organization development (MA); psychology counseling (MA). *Degree requirements:* For master's, thesis (for some programs), oral exams. *Entrance requirements:* For master's, bachelor's degree from an accredited university or college. Additional exam requirements/recommendations for international students: Recommended—TOEFL, IELTS, TWE.

Saybrook University, School of Organizational Leadership and Transformation, San Francisco, CA 94612. Offers MA. Program offered jointly with Bastyr University. *Degree requirements:* For master's, thesis (for some programs), oral exams. *Entrance requirements:* For master's, bachelor's degree from an accredited college or university. *Faculty research:* Cross-functional work teams, communication, management authority, employee influence, systems theory.

Saybrook University, School of Psychology and Interdisciplinary Inquiry, San Francisco, CA 94612. Offers human science (MA, PhD), including consciousness and spirituality, humanistic and transpersonal psychology, integrative health studies, organizational systems, social transformation; organizational systems (MA, PhD), including consciousness and spirituality, humanistic and transpersonal psychology, integrative health studies, leadership of sustainable systems (MA), organizational systems, social transformation; psychology (MA, PhD), including consciousness and spirituality, creativity studies (MA), humanistic and transpersonal psychology, integrative health studies, Jungian studies, marriage and family therapy (MA), organizational systems, social transformation. *Program availability:* Online learning. Terminal master's awarded for partial completion of doctoral program. *Degree requirements:* For master's, thesis or alternative; for doctorate, thesis/dissertation. *Entrance requirements:*

Additional exam requirements/recommendations for international students: Required—TOEFL (minimum score 580 paper-based; 93 iBT). Electronic applications accepted. *Faculty research:* Humanistic theory, health studies, organizational systems, consciousness and spirituality, social transformation.

Seattle University, Albers School of Business and Economics, Center for Leadership Formation, Seattle, WA 98122-1090. Offers leadership (EMBA, Certificate). *Program availability:* Evening/weekend. *Faculty:* 13 full-time (5 women), 3 part-time/adjunct (2 women). *Students:* 62 full-time (28 women); includes 6 minority (1 Black or African American, non-Hispanic/Latino; 4 Asian, non-Hispanic/Latino; 1 Native Hawaiian or other Pacific Islander, non-Hispanic/Latino), 1 international. Average age 45. 47 applicants, 96% accepted, 38 enrolled. In 2017, 31 master's, 42 other advanced degrees awarded. *Entrance requirements:* For master's, GMAT or three online courses, 7 years of continuous professional experience, undergraduate degree with minimum GPA of 3.0, resume, statement of intent/interest, three letters of recommendation; for Certificate, 7 years of continuous professional experience, undergraduate degree with minimum GPA of 3.0, resume, statement of intent/interest, three letters of recommendation. Additional exam requirements/recommendations for international students: Required—TOEFL (minimum score 580 paper-based; 92 iBT), IELTS (minimum score 7), PTE (minimum score 62). *Application deadline:* Applications are processed on a rolling basis. Application fee: $55. Electronic applications accepted. *Expenses:* Contact institution. *Financial support:* In 2017–18, 8 students received support. Scholarships/grants available. Financial award applicants required to submit FAFSA. *Unit head:* Dr. Marilyn Gist, Associate Dean of Executive Education, 206-296-5413, E-mail: gistm@seattleu.edu. *Application contact:* Sommer Harrison, Manager, Graduate Programs Outreach, 206-296-2529, E-mail: emba@seattleu.edu. Website: https://www.seattleu.edu/albers/executive/

Shippensburg University of Pennsylvania, School of Graduate Studies, College of Arts and Sciences, Department of Sociology and Anthropology, Shippensburg, PA 17257-2299. Offers organizational development and leadership (MS), including business, higher education structure and policy, historical administration, leadership in society, management information systems, public organizations. *Program availability:* Part-time, evening/weekend. *Faculty:* 4 full-time (2 women). *Students:* 14 full-time (6 women), 19 part-time (11 women); includes 7 minority (4 Black or African American, non-Hispanic/Latino; 2 Hispanic/Latino; 1 Two or more races, non-Hispanic/Latino), 1 international. Average age 26. 31 applicants, 81% accepted, 15 enrolled. In 2017, 22 master's awarded. *Degree requirements:* For master's, capstone experience including internship. *Entrance requirements:* For master's, interview (if GPA less than 2.75), current resume, personal goals statement. Additional exam requirements/recommendations for international students: Required—TOEFL (minimum score 550 paper-based, 68 iBT) or IELTS (minimum score 6). *Application deadline:* For fall admission, 4/30 for international students; for spring admission, 9/30 for international students. Applications are processed on a rolling basis. Application fee: $45. Electronic applications accepted. *Expenses:* Tuition, state resident: part-time $500 per credit. Tuition, nonresident: part-time $750 per credit. *Required fees:* $145 per credit. *Financial support:* In 2017–18, 12 students received support. Career-related internships or fieldwork, scholarships/grants, unspecified assistantships, and resident hall director and student payroll positions available. Support available to part-time students. Financial award application deadline: 3/1; financial award applicants required to submit FAFSA. *Unit head:* Dr. Barbara J. Denison, Departmental Chair and Program Coordinator, 717-477-1735, Fax: 717-477-4011, E-mail: bjdeni@ship.edu. *Application contact:* Maya T. Mapp, Director of Admissions, 717-477-1231, Fax: 717-477-4016, E-mail: mtmapp@ship.edu. Website: http://www.ship.edu/odl/

Siena Heights University, Graduate College, Adrian, MI 49221-1796. Offers clinical mental health counseling (MA); educational leadership (Specialist); leadership (MA), including health care leadership, organizational leadership; teacher education (MA), including early childhood education, early childhood education: Montessori, education leadership: principal, elementary education: reading K-12, leadership: higher education, secondary education: reading K-12, special education: cognitive impairment, special education: learning disabilities. *Program availability:* Part-time, evening/weekend. *Degree requirements:* For master's, thesis, presentation. *Entrance requirements:* For master's, minimum GPA of 3.0, current resume, essay, all post-secondary transcripts, 3 letters of reference, conviction disclosure form; copy of teaching certificate (for some education programs); for Specialist, master's degree, minimum GPA of 3.0, current resume, essay, all post-secondary transcripts, 3 letters of reference, conviction disclosure form; copy of teaching certificate (for some education programs). Electronic applications accepted.

Simpson University, School of Graduate Studies, Redding, CA 96003-8606. Offers counseling psychology (MA); organizational leadership (MA). *Program availability:* Evening/weekend, 100% online, blended/hybrid learning. *Degree requirements:* For master's, thesis optional, portfolio capstone, integrative essay. *Entrance requirements:* For master's, three letters of recommendation, personal statement, resume, transcripts, personal interview, bachelor's degree in psychology or related field with minimum GPA of 3.0 in final 60 credits (for counseling psychology); two references (for organizational leadership). Additional exam requirements/recommendations for international students: Required—TOEFL (minimum score 550 paper-based; 79 iBT). Electronic applications accepted. *Expenses:* Contact institution. *Faculty research:* Development of executive functioning in young children, cognitive neuropsychology, historical issues in the neurosciences, neurotheology.

SIT Graduate Institute, Graduate Programs, Master's Programs in Intercultural Service, Leadership, and Management, Master's Program in Intercultural Service, Leadership, and Management (Self-Designed), Brattleboro, VT 05302-0676. Offers MA.

Southeastern University, College of Education, Lakeland, FL 33801-6099. Offers curriculum and instruction (Ed D); educational leadership (M Ed); elementary education (M Ed); exceptional student education (M Ed); exceptional student education/educational therapy (M Ed); kinesiology (M Ed); organizational leadership (Ed D); reading education (M Ed); teaching English to speakers of other languages (M Ed). *Faculty:* 8 full-time (5 women), 12 part-time/adjunct (7 women). *Students:* 139 full-time (109 women), 225 part-time (172 women); includes 107 minority (57 Black or African American, non-Hispanic/Latino; 2 Asian, non-Hispanic/Latino; 48 Hispanic/Latino), 4 international. Average age 40. Application fee: $50. Electronic applications accepted. *Unit head:* James A. Anderson, Dean, 863-667-5366, E-mail: jaanderson2@seu.edu. Website: http://www.seu.edu/education/

Southeastern University, Jannetides College of Business and Entrepreneurial Leadership, Lakeland, FL 33801-6099. Offers executive leadership (MBA); global business administration (MBA); healthcare administration (MBA); missional leadership (MBA); organizational leadership (PhD); sport management (MBA); strategic leadership (DSL). *Accreditation:* ACBSP. *Program availability:* Evening/weekend, online learning. *Faculty:* 10 full-time (2 women), 8 part-time/adjunct (1 woman). *Students:* 80 full-time (38 women), 110 part-time (54 women); includes 51 minority (18 Black or African American, non-Hispanic/Latino; 5 Asian, non-Hispanic/Latino; 28 Hispanic/Latino), 7 international. Average age 31. *Entrance requirements:* For master's, GMAT, minimum cumulative GPA of 3.0, writing sample. Application fee: $50. Electronic applications accepted. *Unit head:* Lyle L. Bowlin, Dean, 863-667-5118, E-mail: llbowlin@seu.edu. Website: http://www.seu.edu/business/

Organizational Management

Southern Arkansas University–Magnolia, School of Graduate Studies, Magnolia, AR 71753. Offers agriculture (MS); business administration (MBA), including agribusiness, social entrepreneurship, supply chain management; clinical and mental health counseling (MS); computer and information sciences (MS), including cyber security and privacy, data science, information technology; gifted and talented (M Ed), including curriculum and instruction, educational administration and supervision, gifted and talented P-8/7-12, instructional specialist P-4; higher, adult and lifelong education (M Ed); kinesiology (M Ed), including coaching; library media and information specialist (M Ed); public administration (MPA); school counseling K-12 (M Ed); student affairs and college counseling (M Ed); teaching (MAT). *Accreditation:* NCATE. *Program availability:* Part-time, 100% online, blended/hybrid learning. *Faculty:* 36 full-time (20 women), 31 part-time/adjunct (12 women). *Students:* 242 full-time (89 women), 889 part-time (459 women); includes 167 minority (143 Black or African American, non-Hispanic/Latino; 7 American Indian or Alaska Native, non-Hispanic/Latino; 7 Asian, non-Hispanic/Latino; 3 Hispanic/Latino; 7 Two or more races, non-Hispanic/Latino), 562 international. Average age 28. 400 applicants, 100% accepted, 239 enrolled. In 2017, 875 master's awarded. *Degree requirements:* For master's, comprehensive exam (for some programs), thesis optional. *Entrance requirements:* For master's, GRE, MAT or GMAT, minimum GPA of 2.5. Additional exam requirements/recommendations for international students: Required—TOEFL (minimum score 550 paper-based), IELTS (minimum score 6). *Application deadline:* For fall admission, 7/20 for domestic students, 7/10 for international students; for spring admission, 12/1 for domestic students, 11/15 for international students; for summer admission, 4/1 for domestic students, 5/1 for international students. Applications are processed on a rolling basis. Application fee: $25 ($50 for international students). Electronic applications accepted. *Expenses:* Tuition, state resident: full-time $6038. Tuition, nonresident: full-time $8558. *Required fees:* $804. One-time fee: $110 full-time. Tuition and fees vary according to course load. *Financial support:* Career-related internships or fieldwork, Federal Work-Study, scholarships/grants, tuition waivers (full), and unspecified assistantships available. Financial award applicants required to submit FAFSA. *Faculty research:* Alternative certification for teachers, supervision of instruction, instructional leadership, counseling. *Unit head:* Dr. Kim Bloss, Dean, School of Graduate Studies, 870-235-4150, Fax: 870-235-5227, E-mail: kkbloss@saumag.edu. *Application contact:* Shrijana Malakar, Admissions Specialist, 870-235-4150, Fax: 870-235-5227, E-mail: smalakar@saumag.edu.
Website: http://www.saumag.edu/graduate

Southern New Hampshire University, School of Business, Manchester, NH 03106-1045. Offers accounting (MBA, Graduate Certificate); accounting finance (MS); accounting/auditing (MS); accounting/forensic accounting (MS); accounting/management accounting (MS); accounting/taxation (MS); applied economics (MS); athletic administration (MBA, Graduate Certificate); business administration (IMBA, Certificate), including business information systems (Certificate), human resource management (Certificate); business analytics (MBA); business intelligence (MBA); communication (MA), including new media and marketing, public relations; community economic development (MBA); criminal justice (MBA); data analytics (MS); economics (MBA); engineering management (MBA); entrepreneurship (MBA); finance (MBA, MS, Graduate Certificate); finance/corporate finance (MS); finance/investments (MS); forensic accounting (MBA); forensic accounting and fraud examination (Graduate Certificate); healthcare informatics (MBA); healthcare management (MBA); human resource management (MS); human resources (MBA); information technology (MS); information technology management (MBA); international business (PhD); Internet marketing (MBA); leadership (MBA); leadership of nonprofit organizations (Graduate Certificate); management (MS); marketing (MBA, MS, Graduate Certificate); music business (MBA); operations and project management (MS); operations and supply chain management (MBA, Graduate Certificate); organizational leadership (MS); project management (MBA, Graduate Certificate); public administration (MBA, Graduate Certificate); quantitative analysis (MBA); Six Sigma (Graduate Certificate); Six Sigma quality (MBA); social media marketing (MBA, Graduate Certificate); sport management (MBA, MS, Graduate Certificate); sustainability and environmental compliance (MBA); MBA/Certificate. *Accreditation:* ACBSP. *Program availability:* Part-time, evening/weekend, online learning. Terminal master's awarded for partial completion of doctoral program. *Degree requirements:* For master's, one foreign language, comprehensive exam (for some programs), thesis or alternative; for doctorate, one foreign language, comprehensive exam, thesis/dissertation. *Entrance requirements:* For master's, minimum GPA of 2.5; for doctorate, GMAT. Additional exam requirements/recommendations for international students: Required—TOEFL (minimum score 500 paper-based). *Application deadline:* Applications are processed on a rolling basis. Application fee: $40. Electronic applications accepted. *Expenses:* Tuition: Part-time $627 per credit hour. Part-time tuition and fees vary according to campus/location and program. *Financial support:* Career-related internships or fieldwork, Federal Work-Study, institutionally sponsored loans, scholarships/grants, tuition waivers (partial), and unspecified assistantships available. Support available to part-time students. Financial award applicants required to submit FAFSA. *Unit head:* Dr. Bill Lightfoot, Dean, 603-644-3102, Fax: 603-644-3144. *Application contact:* Office of Graduate Admission, 888-327-SNHU, Fax: 603-644-3144, E-mail: enroll@snhu.edu.

South University, Graduate Programs, College of Business, Program in Leadership, Savannah, GA 31406. Offers MS.

South University, Program in Leadership, Virginia Beach, VA 23452. Offers MS.

South University, Program in Leadership, Columbia, SC 29203. Offers MS.

Southwest University, MBA Program, Kenner, LA 70062. Offers business administration (MBA); management (MBA); organizational management (MBA).

Southwest University, Program in Organizational Management, Kenner, LA 70062. Offers MA.

Springfield College, Graduate Programs, Program in Human Services, Springfield, MA 01109-3797. Offers mental health counseling (MS); organizational management and leadership (MS). *Program availability:* Part-time, evening/weekend, blended/hybrid learning. *Degree requirements:* For master's, comprehensive exam, thesis (for some programs), Community Action Research Project. *Entrance requirements:* Additional exam requirements/recommendations for international students: Required—TOEFL (minimum score 550 paper-based). *Application deadline:* For fall admission, 8/31 for domestic and international students; for winter admission, 11/1 for domestic and international students; for spring admission, 12/31 for domestic and international students; for summer admission, 4/30 for domestic and international students. Applications are processed on a rolling basis. Application fee: $40. Electronic applications accepted. *Expenses:* Contact institution. *Financial support:* Application deadline: 3/1; applicants required to submit FAFSA. *Unit head:* Dr. John Eisler, Dean, 413-748-3982, E-mail: jeisler@springfieldcollege.edu. *Application contact:* Marisol Guevara, Assistant Director of Recruitment and Outreach, 413-748-3624, E-mail: mguevara@springfieldcollege.edu.
Website: https://springfield.edu/school-of-professional-and-continuing-studies/degrees-and-programs/master-of-science

State University of New York College at Potsdam, School of Education and Professional Studies, Program in Information and Communication Technology, Potsdam, NY 13676. Offers educational technology specialist (MS Ed); organizational performance, leadership and technology (MS Ed). *Program availability:* Part-time, evening/weekend. *Degree requirements:* For master's, culminating experience. *Entrance requirements:* For master's, minimum GPA of 3.0 in last 60 hours of course work. Additional exam requirements/recommendations for international students: Required—TOEFL (minimum score 550 paper-based; 80 iBT), IELTS (minimum score 6). Electronic applications accepted.

Stockton University, Office of Graduate Studies, Program in Organizational Leadership, Galloway, NJ 08205-9441. Offers Ed D. *Program availability:* Evening/weekend. *Faculty:* 3 full-time (1 woman). *Students:* 2 full-time (1 woman), 68 part-time (45 women); includes 25 minority (21 Black or African American, non-Hispanic/Latino; 1 American Indian or Alaska Native, non-Hispanic/Latino; 3 Hispanic/Latino), 1 international. Average age 43. 45 applicants, 71% accepted, 24 enrolled. *Degree requirements:* For doctorate, thesis/dissertation. *Entrance requirements:* For doctorate, minimum overall GPA of 3.0, three letters of recommendation, essay, resume, official transcripts, personal interview. *Application deadline:* For fall admission, 6/1 for domestic students; for spring admission, 11/16 for domestic students. Application fee: $50. *Expenses:* Contact institution. *Unit head:* Dr. Joseph Marchetti, Director, 609-652-4642. *Application contact:* Tara Williams, Assistant Director of Enrollment Management, 609-626-3640, Fax: 609-626-6050, E-mail: gradschool@stockton.edu.

Syracuse University, Maxwell School of Citizenship and Public Affairs, CAS Program in Leadership of International and Non-Governmental Organizations, Syracuse, NY 13244. Offers CAS. *Program availability:* Part-time. In 2017, 35 CASs awarded. *Entrance requirements:* For degree, resume, three letters of recommendation, personal statement, official transcripts. Additional exam requirements/recommendations for international students: Required—TOEFL (minimum score 100 iBT). *Application deadline:* For fall admission, 2/1 priority date for domestic and international students; for spring admission, 8/15 priority date for domestic and international students. Applications are processed on a rolling basis. Application fee: $75. Electronic applications accepted. *Financial support:* Application deadline: 1/1. *Faculty research:* Managing nongovernment organizations in transitional and development countries, public budgeting, fundamentals of public policy, humanitarian action. *Unit head:* Steven Lux, Director, Executive Education, 315-443-3759, E-mail: sjlux@maxwell.syr.edu. *Application contact:* Margaret Lane, Assistant Director, Executive Education Programs, 315-443-8708, E-mail: melane02@maxwell.syr.edu.
Website: http://www.maxwell.syr.edu/

Thomas Edison State University, School of Business and Management, Program in Management, Trenton, NJ 08608. Offers accounting (MSM); organizational leadership (MSM); project management (MSM). *Program availability:* Part-time, 100% online. *Degree requirements:* For master's, final capstone project. *Entrance requirements:* For master's, bachelor's degree from a regionally-accredited college or university; minimum 2 letters of recommendation; 3-5 years of related working experience; current resume. Additional exam requirements/recommendations for international students: Required—TOEFL (minimum score 550 paper-based; 79 iBT). Electronic applications accepted.

Trevecca Nazarene University, Graduate Business Programs, Nashville, TN 37210-2877. Offers business administration (MBA); health care leadership and innovation (MS); management (MSM). *Program availability:* Evening/weekend, online learning. *Faculty:* 12 full-time (1 woman), 15 part-time/adjunct (8 women). *Students:* 236 full-time (145 women), 50 part-time (29 women); includes 154 minority (128 Black or African American, non-Hispanic/Latino; 1 American Indian or Alaska Native, non-Hispanic/Latino; 4 Asian, non-Hispanic/Latino; 18 Hispanic/Latino; 3 Two or more races, non-Hispanic/Latino), 4 international. Average age 33. In 2017, 55 master's awarded. *Entrance requirements:* For master's, minimum GPA of 2.75, resume, official transcript from regionally accredited institution, minimum math grade of C, minimum English composition grade of C. Additional exam requirements/recommendations for international students: Required—TOEFL (minimum score 550 paper-based; 80 iBT). *Application deadline:* Applications are processed on a rolling basis. Application fee: $0. Electronic applications accepted. *Expenses:* $520 per credit hour. *Financial support:* Applicants required to submit FAFSA. *Unit head:* Dr. Rick Mann, Director of Graduate and Professional Programs for School of Business, 615-248-1529, E-mail: management@trevecca.edu. *Application contact:* 615-248-1529, E-mail: sgcsadmissions@trevecca.edu.
Website: http://www.trevecca.edu/mba

Trevecca Nazarene University, Graduate Leadership Programs, Nashville, TN 37210-2877. Offers leadership and professional practice (Ed D); organizational leadership (MOL). *Program availability:* Online learning. *Faculty:* 9 full-time (5 women), 27 part-time/adjunct (12 women). *Students:* 282 full-time (205 women), 214 part-time (141 women); includes 302 minority (254 Black or African American, non-Hispanic/Latino; 4 American Indian or Alaska Native, non-Hispanic/Latino; 1 Asian, non-Hispanic/Latino; 25 Hispanic/Latino; 1 Native Hawaiian or other Pacific Islander, non-Hispanic/Latino; 17 Two or more races, non-Hispanic/Latino), 1 international. Average age 40. In 2017, 68 master's, 75 doctorates awarded. *Degree requirements:* For master's, capstone course; for doctorate, thesis/dissertation, proposal study, symposium presentation. *Entrance requirements:* For master's, minimum GPA of 2.5, official transcript from regionally accredited institution; for doctorate, minimum GPA of 3.4, official transcript from regionally accredited institution, resume, writing sample, references. Additional exam requirements/recommendations for international students: Required—TOEFL (minimum score 550 paper-based; 80 iBT). *Application deadline:* Applications are processed on a rolling basis. Application fee: $0. Electronic applications accepted. *Expenses:* $420 per credit hour (MOL); $699 per credit hour (EdD). *Financial support:* Applicants required to submit FAFSA. *Unit head:* Dr. Ricky Christman, Associate Vice President and Dean, Graduate and Continuing Studies/Director of Master of Organizational Leadership, 615-248-1529, E-mail: sgcsadmissions@trevecca.edu. *Application contact:* 844-TNU-GRAD, E-mail: sgcsadmissions@trevecca.edu.

Trinity Washington University, School of Business and Graduate Studies, Washington, DC 20017-1094. Offers business administration (MBA); communication (MA); international security studies (MA); organizational management (MSA), including federal program management, human resource management, nonprofit management, organizational development, public and community health. *Program availability:* Part-time, evening/weekend. *Degree requirements:* For master's, thesis (for some programs), capstone project (MSA). *Entrance requirements:* For master's, minimum GPA of 2.5. Additional exam requirements/recommendations for international students: Required—TOEFL (minimum score 550 paper-based).

Trinity Western University, School of Graduate Studies, Program in Leadership, Langley, BC V2Y 1Y1, Canada. Offers business (MA, Certificate); Christian ministry (MA); education (MA, Certificate); healthcare (MA, Certificate); non-profit (MA, Certificate). *Program availability:* Online learning. *Degree requirements:* For master's, major project. *Entrance requirements:* For master's, minimum GPA of 2.7. Additional exam requirements/recommendations for international students: Required—TOEFL (minimum score 620 paper-based; 105 iBT). Electronic applications accepted. *Expenses:* Contact institution. *Faculty research:* Servant leadership.

Tufts University, Graduate School of Arts and Sciences, Program in Diversity and Inclusion Leadership, Medford, MA 02155. Offers MA. *Program availability:* Part-time. *Students:* 4 part-time (2 women); includes 2 minority (1 Black or African American, non-Hispanic/Latino; 1 Hispanic/Latino). Average age 27. 9 applicants, 78% accepted, 4 enrolled. *Degree requirements:* For master's, thesis or capstone project. *Entrance requirements:* Additional exam requirements/recommendations for international students: Required—TOEFL, IELTS. *Application deadline:* For fall admission, 2/15 for domestic and international students; for spring admission, 10/15 for domestic and international students. Application fee: $85. Electronic applications accepted. *Expenses:* Contact institution. *Financial support:* Tuition waivers (full and partial) and unspecified assistantships available. Financial award application deadline: 2/15. *Unit head:* Dr. Robert Cook, Program Director, 617-627-4191, E-mail: dean.gsas@tufts.edu. *Application contact:* Office of Graduate Admissions, 617-627-3395, E-mail: gradadmissions@tufts.edu.
Website: https://asegrad.tufts.edu/academics/explore-graduate-programs/diversity-and-inclusion-leadership

Union Institute & University, Master of Science Program in Organizational Leadership, Cincinnati, OH 45206-1925. Offers MS. *Program availability:* Part-time, online only, 100% online. *Degree requirements:* For master's, capstone project. *Entrance requirements:* For master's, recommendations, transcripts, essay. Additional exam requirements/recommendations for international students: Required—TOEFL. *Application deadline:* Applications are processed on a rolling basis. Application fee: $50. Electronic applications accepted. *Expenses:* Contact institution. *Financial support:* Federal Work-Study available. *Faculty research:* Leadership. *Application contact:* Admissions Office, 513-861-6400, E-mail: admissions@myunion.edu.
Website: https://myunion.edu/academics/masters/organizational-leadership/

United States International University–Africa, School of Business Administration, Nairobi, Kenya. Offers business administration (GEMBA); entrepreneurship (MBA); finance (MBA); human resource management (MBA); information technology management (MBA); integrated studies (MBA); international business administration (MBA); management and organizational development (MS); marketing (MBA); organizational development (EMS); strategic management (MBA). *Program availability:* Part-time, evening/weekend. *Degree requirements:* For master's, thesis. *Entrance requirements:* For master's, GMAT, 2 letters of reference, resume. Additional exam requirements/recommendations for international students: Required—TOEFL (minimum score 550 paper-based). *Faculty research:* Marketing in small business enterprises, total quality management in Kenya.

Université Laval, Faculty of Administrative Sciences, Programs in Business Administration, Québec, QC G1K 7P4, Canada. Offers accounting (MBA); agri-food management (MBA); electronic business (MBA, Diploma); factory management and logistics (MBA); finance (MBA); firm management (MBA); geomatic management (MBA); information technology management (MBA); international management (MBA); management (MBA); management accounting (MBA, Diploma); marketing (MBA); modeling and organizational decision (MBA); occupational health and safety management (MBA); pharmacy management (MBA); social and environmental responsibility (MBA); technological entrepreneurship (Diploma). *Accreditation:* AACSB. *Program availability:* Part-time, evening/weekend, online learning. *Entrance requirements:* For master's and Diploma, knowledge of French and English. Electronic applications accepted.

University of Alberta, Faculty of Graduate Studies and Research, Doctoral Program in Business, Edmonton, AB T6G 2E1, Canada. Offers accounting (PhD); finance (PhD); human resources/industrial relations (PhD); management science (PhD); marketing (PhD); organizational analysis (PhD); MBA/PhD. *Accreditation:* AACSB. *Program availability:* Part-time. *Degree requirements:* For doctorate, comprehensive exam, thesis/dissertation. *Entrance requirements:* For doctorate, GMAT. Additional exam requirements/recommendations for international students: Required—TOEFL (minimum score 550 paper-based). Electronic applications accepted. *Faculty research:* Accounting, capital markets and corporate finance, organizational change and human resource management, marketing, strategic management.

The University of Arizona, Eller College of Management, Department of Management and Organizations, Tucson, AZ 85721. Offers MS, PhD. *Program availability:* Evening/weekend. *Entrance requirements:* Additional exam requirements/recommendations for international students: Required—TOEFL (minimum score 550 paper-based; 79 iBT). Electronic applications accepted. *Faculty research:* Organizational behavior, human resources, decision-making, health economics and finance, immigration.

University of Central Arkansas, Graduate School, Interdisciplinary PhD Program in Leadership Studies, Conway, AR 72035-0001. Offers PhD. *Program availability:* Part-time. *Degree requirements:* For doctorate, thesis/dissertation. *Entrance requirements:* For doctorate, GRE. Additional exam requirements/recommendations for international students: Required—TOEFL. Electronic applications accepted.

University of Charleston, Doctor of Executive Leadership Program, Charleston, WV 25304-1099. Offers DEL. *Entrance requirements:* Additional exam requirements/recommendations for international students: Required—TOEFL. Electronic applications accepted.

University of Cincinnati, Graduate School, McMicken College of Arts and Sciences, Center for Organizational Leadership, Cincinnati, OH 45221. Offers MALER. *Program availability:* Part-time, evening/weekend. *Entrance requirements:* For master's, GRE or GMAT. Additional exam requirements/recommendations for international students: Required—TOEFL (minimum score 520 paper-based; 68 iBT). Electronic applications accepted. *Expenses: Tuition, area resident:* Full-time $14,468. *Tuition, state resident:* full-time $14,968; part-time $754 per credit hour. *Tuition, nonresident:* full-time $24,210; part-time $1311 per credit hour. *International tuition:* $26,460 full-time. *Required fees:* $3958; $84 per credit hour. One-time fee: $85 full-time. Tuition and fees vary according to course load, degree level and program. *Faculty research:* Leadership and diversity.

University of Colorado Boulder, Graduate School, Master of Science Program in Organizational Leadership, Boulder, CO 80309. *Students:* 40 full-time (26 women), 2 part-time (both women); includes 8 minority (1 Black or African American, non-Hispanic/Latino; 2 Asian, non-Hispanic/Latino; 4 Hispanic/Latino; 1 Two or more races, non-Hispanic/Latino), 1 international. Average age 39. 57 applicants, 86% accepted. *Application deadline:* For fall admission, 7/23 for domestic students; for spring admission, 7/23 for domestic students. Application fee: $60 ($80 for international students). Electronic applications accepted. *Financial support:* In 2017–18, 11 students received support. Scholarships/grants, health care benefits, and unspecified assistantships available. Financial award application deadline: 2/15; financial award applicants required to submit FAFSA. *Application contact:* E-mail: gradinfo@colorado.edu.
Website: https://www.colorado.edu/graduateschool/organizational-leadership

University of Dallas, Braniff Graduate School of Liberal Arts, Program in Leadership, Irving, TX 75062-4736. Offers MA. *Expenses: Tuition:* Full-time $33,750; part-time $22,500 per year. Tuition and fees vary according to program. *Unit head:* Dr. Brett Bourbon, Director, 972-265-5829, E-mail: bourbon@udallas.edu.
Website: http://udallas.edu/braniff/academics/ma/leadership/index.php

University of Dallas, Satish and Yasmin Gupta College of Business, Irving, TX 75062-4736. Offers accounting (MBA, MS); business administration (DBA); business analytics (MS); business management (MBA); corporate finance (MBA); cybersecurity (MS); finance (MS); financial services (MBA); global business (MBA, MS); health services management (MBA); human resource management (MBA); information and technology management (MS); information assurance (MBA); information technology (MBA); information technology service management (MBA); marketing management (MBA); organization development (MBA); project management (MBA); sports and entertainment management (MBA); strategic leadership (MBA); supply chain management (MBA). *Accreditation:* AACSB. *Program availability:* Part-time, evening/weekend, online learning. *Entrance requirements:* Additional exam requirements/recommendations for international students: Required—TOEFL. *Application deadline:* Applications are processed on a rolling basis. Application fee: $50. Electronic applications accepted. *Expenses:* Contact institution. *Financial support:* Application deadline: 2/15; applicants required to submit FAFSA. *Unit head:* Brett J.L. Landry, Dean, 972-721-5356, E-mail: blandry@udallas.edu. *Application contact:* Dr. David Sweet, Dean, Braniff Graduate School, 972-721-5288, Fax: 972-721-5280, E-mail: dsweet@udallas.edu.
Website: http://www.udallas.edu/cob/

University of Denver, University College, Denver, CO 80208. Offers arts and culture (MA, Certificate); communication management (MS, Certificate), including translation studies (Certificate); world history and culture (Certificate); environmental policy and management (MS); geographic information systems (MS); global affairs (MA, Certificate), including human capital in organizations (Certificate), philanthropic leadership (Certificate), project management (Certificate), strategic innovation and change (Certificate); healthcare leadership (MS); information communications and technology (MS); leadership and organizations (MS); professional creative writing (MA, Certificate), including emergency planning and response (Certificate), organizational security (Certificate); security management (MS, Certificate); strategic human resources (Certificate). *Program availability:* Part-time, evening/weekend, online learning. *Faculty:* 118 part-time/adjunct (62 women). *Students:* 56 full-time (32 women), 1,287 part-time (707 women); includes 330 minority (99 Black or African American, non-Hispanic/Latino; 7 American Indian or Alaska Native, non-Hispanic/Latino; 43 Asian, non-Hispanic/Latino; 141 Hispanic/Latino; 3 Native Hawaiian or other Pacific Islander, non-Hispanic/Latino; 37 Two or more races, non-Hispanic/Latino), 84 international. Average age 34. 783 applicants, 86% accepted, 420 enrolled. In 2017, 461 master's, 173 other advanced degrees awarded. *Degree requirements:* For master's, capstone project. *Entrance requirements:* For master's, transcripts, two letters of recommendation, personal statement, resume. Additional exam requirements/recommendations for international students: Required—TOEFL (minimum score 550 paper-based; 80 iBT). *Application deadline:* For fall admission, 6/21 priority date for domestic students, 5/1 priority date for international students; for winter admission, 9/14 priority date for domestic students, 9/19 priority date for international students; for spring admission, 1/11 priority date for domestic students, 12/12 priority date for international students; for summer admission, 3/29 priority date for domestic students, 3/6 priority date for international students. Applications are processed on a rolling basis. Application fee: $75. Electronic applications accepted. *Expenses:* $7,968 per year half-time. *Financial support:* In 2017–18, 29 students received support. Teaching assistantships available. Financial award applicants required to submit FAFSA. *Unit head:* Dr. Michael McGuire, Dean, 303-871-3518, Fax: 303-871-3303, E-mail: mmcguire@du.edu. *Application contact:* Information Contact, 303-871-2291, E-mail: ucoladm@du.edu.
Website: http://universitycollege.du.edu/

University of Guelph, Graduate Studies, College of Management and Economics, MA (Leadership) Program, Guelph, ON N1G 2W1, Canada. Offers MA. *Program availability:* Part-time, evening/weekend, online learning. *Entrance requirements:* For master's, minimum B-average, minimum 5 years of relevant work experience. Additional exam requirements/recommendations for international students: Required—TOEFL (minimum score 550 paper-based). Electronic applications accepted. *Faculty research:* Theories of leadership, organizational change, ethics in leadership, decision making, politics of organizations.

University of Hawaii at Manoa, Office of Graduate Education, Shidler College of Business, Program in Business Administration, Honolulu, HI 96822. Offers Asian business studies (MBA); Chinese business studies (MBA); decision sciences (MBA); entrepreneurship (MBA); finance (MBA); finance and banking (MBA); human resources management (MBA); information management (MBA); information technology (MBA); international business (MBA); Japanese business studies (MBA); marketing (MBA); organizational behavior (MBA); organizational management (MBA); real estate (MBA); student-designed track (MBA). *Accreditation:* AACSB. *Program availability:* Part-time, evening/weekend. *Degree requirements:* For master's, thesis optional. *Entrance requirements:* For master's, GMAT, minimum GPA of 3.0. Additional exam requirements/recommendations for international students: Required—TOEFL (minimum score 600 paper-based; 100 iBT), IELTS (minimum score 7). *Expenses:* Contact institution.

University of Hawaii at Manoa, Office of Graduate Education, Shidler College of Business, Program in International Management, Honolulu, HI 96822. Offers Asian finance (PhD); global information technology management (PhD); international accounting (PhD); international marketing (PhD); international organization and strategy (PhD). *Program availability:* Part-time. *Degree requirements:* For doctorate, comprehensive exam, thesis/dissertation. *Entrance requirements:* For doctorate, GMAT or GRE General Test, minimum GPA of 3.0. Additional exam requirements/recommendations for international students: Required—TOEFL (minimum score 600 paper-based; 100 iBT), IELTS (minimum score 7). *Expenses:* Contact institution.

The University of Kansas, Graduate Studies, School of Business, Program in Business, Lawrence, KS 66045. Offers business and organizational leadership (MS); decision sciences and supply chain management (PhD); finance (PhD); human resources management (PhD); marketing (PhD); organizational behavior (PhD); strategic management (PhD); supply chain management and logistics (MS). *Accreditation:* AACSB. *Program availability:* Part-time. *Students:* 66 full-time (18 women), 227 part-time (76 women); includes 59 minority (21 Black or African American, non-Hispanic/Latino; 2 American Indian or Alaska Native, non-Hispanic/Latino; 13 Asian, non-Hispanic/Latino; 3 Hispanic/Latino; 20 Two or more races, non-Hispanic/Latino), 29 international. Average age 32. 329 applicants, 71% accepted, 185 enrolled. In 2017, 30 master's, 8 doctorates awarded. *Entrance requirements:* For master's, GMAT, official transcript, three letters of recommendation, resume, statement of purpose; for doctorate, GMAT or GRE, official transcript, three letters of recommendation, resume, statement of purpose. Additional exam requirements/recommendations for international students: Required—TOEFL (minimum score 600 paper-based; 100 iBT). *Application deadline:* For fall admission, 1/10 for domestic and international students. Application fee: $65 ($85 for international students). Electronic applications accepted. *Financial support:* Fellowships, research assistantships, teaching assistantships, scholarships/grants, health care benefits, tuition waivers (full), and unspecified assistantships available. Financial award application deadline: 1/10. *Faculty research:* Strategic human resource management, business ethics, organizational theory/behavior, corporate strategy, international business, supply chain

Organizational Management

management, Bayesian networks, game theory, decision analysis and time/series analysis, pricing, consumer effects, advertising and emotion. *Unit head:* Charly Edmonds, Director, 785-864-3841, E-mail: bschoolphd@ku.edu. *Application contact:* Graduate Admission Contact, 785-864-7500, E-mail: bschoolphd@ku.edu. Website: http://www.business.ku.edu/

The University of Kansas, University of Kansas Medical Center, School of Nursing, Kansas City, KS 66160. Offers adult/gerontological clinical nurse specialist (PMC); adult/gerontological nurse practitioner (PMC); health care informatics (PMC); health professions educator (PMC); nurse midwife (PMC); nursing (MS, DNP, PhD); organizational leadership (PMC); psychiatric/mental health nurse practitioner (PMC); public health nursing (PMC). *Accreditation:* AACN; ACNM/ACME. *Program availability:* Part-time, 100% online, blended/hybrid learning. *Faculty:* 56. *Students:* 48 full-time (44 women), 260 part-time (235 women); includes 50 minority (12 Black or African American, non-Hispanic/Latino; 2 American Indian or Alaska Native, non-Hispanic/Latino; 16 Asian, non-Hispanic/Latino; 8 Hispanic/Latino; 12 Two or more races, non-Hispanic/Latino). Average age 36. 87 applicants, 95% accepted, 61 enrolled. In 2017, 37 master's, 18 doctorates, 3 other advanced degrees awarded. Terminal master's awarded for partial completion of doctoral program. *Degree requirements:* For master's, comprehensive exam, thesis (for some programs), general oral exam; for doctorate, thesis/dissertation or alternative, comprehensive oral exam (for DNP); comprehensive written and oral exam, or three publications (for PhD). *Entrance requirements:* For master's, bachelor's degree in nursing, minimum GPA of 3.0, 1 year of clinical experience, RN license in KS and MO; for doctorate, GRE General Test (for PhD only), bachelor's degree in nursing, minimum GPA of 3.5, RN license in KS and MO. Additional exam requirements/recommendations for international students: Required—TOEFL. *Application deadline:* For fall admission, 4/1 for domestic and international students; for spring admission, 9/1 for domestic and international students. Application fee: $75. Electronic applications accepted. *Financial support:* In 2017–18, 5 research assistantships with tuition reimbursements (averaging $20,000 per year), 30 teaching assistantships with tuition reimbursements (averaging $20,000 per year) were awarded; scholarships/grants and traineeships also available. Financial award application deadline: 3/1; financial award applicants required to submit FAFSA. *Faculty research:* Breastfeeding practices of teen mothers, national database of nursing quality indicators, caregiving of families of patients using technology in the home, simulation in nursing education, diaphragm fatigue. *Total annual research expenditures:* $1.4 million. *Unit head:* Dr. Sally Maliski, Dean, 913-588-1601, Fax: 913-588-1660, E-mail: smaliski@kumc.edu. *Application contact:* Dr. Pamela K. Barnes, Associate Dean, Student Affairs, 913-588-1619, Fax: 913-588-1615, E-mail: pbarnes2@kumc.edu. Website: http://nursing.kumc.edu

University of La Verne, College of Business and Public Management, Program in Leadership and Management, La Verne, CA 91750-4443. Offers human resource management (Certificate); leadership and management (MS), including human resource management, nonprofit management, organizational development; nonprofit management (Certificate); organizational leadership (Certificate). *Program availability:* Part-time. *Faculty:* 4 full-time (3 women), 5 part-time/adjunct (1 woman). *Students:* 49 full-time (25 women), 35 part-time (22 women); includes 47 minority (6 Black or African American, non-Hispanic/Latino; 4 Asian, non-Hispanic/Latino; 35 Hispanic/Latino; 2 Two or more races, non-Hispanic/Latino), 13 international. Average age 32. *Entrance requirements:* For master's, bachelor's degree, minimum undergraduate GPA of 2.75, 2 letters of recommendation, interview, resume. Additional exam requirements/recommendations for international students: Required—TOEFL (minimum score 550 paper-based). *Application deadline:* Applications are processed on a rolling basis. Application fee: $50. Tuition and fees vary according to program. *Financial support:* Federal Work-Study, institutionally sponsored loans, and scholarships/grants available. Financial award application deadline: 3/2; financial award applicants required to submit FAFSA. *Unit head:* Dr. Kathy Duncan, Program Director, 909-448-4415, E-mail: kduncan2@laverne.edu. *Application contact:* Barbara Cox, Associate Director of Graduate Admissions, 909-448-4004, E-mail: bcox@laverne.edu. Website: https://business.laverne.edu/mslm/

University of La Verne, LaFetra College of Education, Doctoral Program in Organizational Leadership, La Verne, CA 91750-4443. Offers Ed D. *Program availability:* Part-time. *Faculty:* 8 full-time (5 women). *Students:* 103 full-time (75 women), 40 part-time (23 women); includes 77 minority (19 Black or African American, non-Hispanic/Latino; 6 Asian, non-Hispanic/Latino; 48 Hispanic/Latino; 4 Two or more races, non-Hispanic/Latino), 1 international. Average age 45. *Entrance requirements:* For doctorate, GRE or MAT, minimum graduate GPA of 3.0, resume or curriculum vitae, 2 endorsement forms. Additional exam requirements/recommendations for international students: Required—TOEFL (minimum score 550 paper-based). *Application deadline:* Applications are processed on a rolling basis. Application fee: $75. *Expenses:* Contact institution. *Financial support:* Institutionally sponsored loans and scholarships/grants available. Financial award application deadline: 3/2; financial award applicants required to submit FAFSA. *Unit head:* Dr. Rich Whitney, Assistant Professor, Organizational Leadership, 909-448-4790, E-mail: rwhitney@laverne.edu. *Application contact:* Christy Ranells, Associate Director of Graduate Admission, 909-448-4644, Fax: 909-971-2295, E-mail: cranells@laverne.edu. Website: https://education.laverne.edu/edd/

University of La Verne, Regional and Online Campuses, Graduate Programs, Inland Empire Campus, Ontario, CA 91730. Offers business administration (MBA, MBA-EP), including accounting (MBA), finance (MBA), health services management (MBA-EP), information technology (MBA-EP), international business (MBA), managed care (MBA), management and leadership (MBA-EP), marketing (MBA-EP), supply chain management (MBA); leadership and management (MS), including human resource management, nonprofit management, organizational development. *Program availability:* Part-time, evening/weekend. *Faculty:* 5 part-time/adjunct (1 woman). *Students:* 24 full-time (13 women), 72 part-time (44 women); includes 64 minority (12 Black or African American, non-Hispanic/Latino; 13 Asian, non-Hispanic/Latino; 36 Hispanic/Latino; 3 Two or more races, non-Hispanic/Latino). Average age 38. In 2017, 42 master's awarded. *Application deadline:* Applications are processed on a rolling basis. Application fee: $50. *Expenses:* Contact institution. *Financial support:* Application deadline: 3/2; applicants required to submit FAFSA. *Unit head:* Juli Roberts, Campus Director, Inland Empire Regional Campus in Ontario, 760-955-6448, E-mail: jroberts@laverne.edu. *Application contact:* Admissions, 877-468-6858, E-mail: gradadmission@laverne.edu. Website: https://laverne.edu/locations/

University of La Verne, Regional and Online Campuses, Graduate Programs, Kern County Campus, Bakersfield, CA 93301. Offers business administration for experienced professionals (MBA-EP); education (special emphasis) (M Ed); educational counseling (MS); educational leadership (M Ed); health administration (MHA); leadership and management (MS); mild/moderate education specialist (Credential); multiple subject (elementary) (Credential); organizational leadership (Ed D); preliminary administrative services (Credential); single subject (secondary) (Credential); special education studies (MS). *Program availability:* Part-time, evening/weekend. *Students:* Average age 36. In 2017, 3 master's awarded. *Application deadline:* Applications are processed on a rolling

basis. Application fee: $50. *Expenses:* Contact institution. *Financial support:* Institutionally sponsored loans available. Financial award application deadline: 3/2; financial award applicants required to submit FAFSA. *Unit head:* Nora Dominguez, Regional Campus Director, 661-861-6802, E-mail: ndominguez@laverne.edu. *Application contact:* Rebecca Murillo, Associate Director of Admissions, 661-861-6807, E-mail: rmurillo@laverne.edu. Website: https://laverne.edu/locations/

University of Maryland Eastern Shore, Graduate Programs, Program in Organizational Leadership, Princess Anne, MD 21853. Offers PhD. *Program availability:* Evening/weekend. *Degree requirements:* For doctorate, comprehensive exam, thesis/dissertation, internship. *Entrance requirements:* For doctorate, interview, writing sample, successful record of employment or career in organization/profession. Additional exam requirements/recommendations for international students: Required—TOEFL (minimum score 80 iBT). Electronic applications accepted.

University of Massachusetts Amherst, Graduate School, Isenberg School of Management, Program in Management, Amherst, MA 01003. Offers accounting (PhD); business administration (MBA); entrepreneurship (MBA); finance (MBA, PhD); healthcare administration (MBA); hospitality and tourism management (PhD); management science (PhD); marketing (MBA, PhD); organization studies (PhD); sport management (PhD); strategic management (PhD); MBA/MS. *Accreditation:* AACSB. *Program availability:* Part-time, evening/weekend, online learning. Terminal master's awarded for partial completion of doctoral program. *Degree requirements:* For doctorate, comprehensive exam, thesis/dissertation. *Entrance requirements:* For master's and doctorate, GMAT or GRE General Test. Additional exam requirements/recommendations for international students: Required—TOEFL (minimum score 550 paper-based; 80 iBT), IELTS (minimum score 6.5). Electronic applications accepted.

University of Michigan–Flint, School of Management, Program in Business Administration, Flint, MI 48502-1950. Offers accounting (MBA); computer information systems (MBA); finance (MBA, Post-Master's Certificate); general business (Graduate Certificate); general business administration (MBA); health care management (MBA); international business (MBA, Post-Master's Certificate); lean manufacturing (MBA); marketing (Post-Master's Certificate); marketing and innovation management (MBA); organizational leadership (MBA). *Program availability:* Part-time, evening/weekend, mixed mode format. *Faculty:* 32 full-time (5 women), 8 part-time/adjunct (2 women). *Students:* 12 full-time (7 women), 147 part-time (51 women); includes 31 minority (15 Black or African American, non-Hispanic/Latino; 1 American Indian or Alaska Native, non-Hispanic/Latino; 9 Asian, non-Hispanic/Latino; 5 Hispanic/Latino; 1 Two or more races, non-Hispanic/Latino), 18 international. Average age 34. 110 applicants, 52% accepted, 29 enrolled. In 2017, 59 master's, 6 other advanced degrees awarded. *Entrance requirements:* For master's, GMAT or GRE, bachelor's degree in arts, sciences, engineering, or business administration from regionally-accredited college or university with minimum GPA of 3.0; for other advanced degree, bachelor's degree in arts, sciences, engineering, or business administration from regionally-accredited college or university with minimum GPA of 3.0, college-level math, statistics, or quantitative course (for Graduate Certificate); MBA or equivalent degree from regionally-accredited college or university (for Post Master's Certificate). Additional exam requirements/recommendations for international students: Required—TOEFL (minimum score 84 iBT), IELTS (minimum score 6.5). *Application deadline:* For fall admission, 8/1 for domestic students, 5/1 for international students; for winter admission, 11/15 for domestic students, 9/1 for international students; for spring admission, 3/15 for domestic students, 1/1 for international students; for summer admission, 5/15 for domestic students. Applications are processed on a rolling basis. Application fee: $55. Electronic applications accepted. *Expenses:* Contact institution. *Financial support:* Federal Work-Study, scholarships/grants, and unspecified assistantships available. Support available to part-time students. Financial award application deadline: 3/1; financial award applicants required to submit FAFSA. *Unit head:* Dr. Scott Johnson, Dean, School of Management, 810-762-3164, Fax: 810-237-6685, E-mail: scotjohn@umflint.edu. *Application contact:* Bradley T. Maki, Director of Graduate Admissions, 810-762-3171, E-mail: bmaki@umflint.edu. Website: http://www.umflint.edu/graduateprograms/business-administration-mba

University of Michigan–Flint, School of Management, Program in Leadership and Organizational Dynamics, Flint, MI 48502-1950. Offers leadership and organizational dynamics (MS); organizational leadership (Post-Master's Certificate). *Program availability:* Part-time, evening/weekend, mixed mode format. *Faculty:* 32 full-time (5 women), 8 part-time/adjunct (2 women). *Students:* 4 part-time (1 woman). Average age 35. 13 applicants, 85% accepted, 4 enrolled. *Entrance requirements:* For master's, GMAT or GRE, bachelor's degree in arts, sciences, engineering, or business administration from regionally-accredited college or university with minimum GPA of 3.0; minimum of three years of supervisory experience described through resume; for Post-Master's Certificate, MBA or equivalent degree from regionally-accredited college or university (for Post-Master's Certificate). Additional exam requirements/recommendations for international students: Required—TOEFL (minimum score 84 iBT), IELTS (minimum score 6.5). *Application deadline:* For fall admission, 8/1 for domestic students, 5/1 for international students; for winter admission, 11/15 for domestic students, 9/1 for international students; for spring admission, 3/15 for domestic students, 1/1 for international students; for summer admission, 5/15 for domestic students, 3/1 for international students. Applications are processed on a rolling basis. Application fee: $55. Electronic applications accepted. *Expenses:* Contact institution. *Financial support:* Federal Work-Study, scholarships/grants, and unspecified assistantships available. Support available to part-time students. Financial award application deadline: 3/1; financial award applicants required to submit FAFSA. *Unit head:* Dr. Scott Johnson, Dean, School of Management, 810-762-6579, Fax: 810-237-6685, E-mail: scotjohn@umflint.edu. *Application contact:* Bradley T. Maki, Director of Graduate Admissions, 810-762-3171, Fax: 810-766-6789, E-mail: bmaki@umflint.edu. Website: https://www.umflint.edu/graduateprograms/leadership-organizational-dynamics-ms

University of Missouri, Office of Research and Graduate Studies, Harry S Truman School of Public Affairs, Columbia, MO 65211. Offers grantsmanship (Graduate Certificate); nonprofit management (Graduate Certificate); organizational change (Graduate Certificate); public affairs (MPA, PhD); public management (Graduate Certificate); science and public policy (Graduate Certificate). *Accreditation:* NASPAA. *Entrance requirements:* For master's, GRE General Test, minimum GPA of 3.0. Additional exam requirements/recommendations for international students: Required—TOEFL (minimum score 550 paper-based; 80 iBT), IELTS (minimum score 6.5). Electronic applications accepted.

University of Nebraska at Omaha, Graduate Studies, College of Arts and Sciences, Program in Critical and Creative Thinking, Omaha, NE 68182. Offers MA. *Program availability:* Part-time, online learning. *Entrance requirements:* For master's, undergraduate degree with minimum GPA of 3.0. Additional exam requirements/recommendations for international students: Required—TOEFL, IELTS, or PTE. Electronic applications accepted.

University of New Haven, Graduate School, College of Arts and Sciences, Program in Industrial and Organizational Psychology, West Haven, CT 06516. Offers conflict

management (MA); industrial organizational psychology (MA); industrial-human resources psychology (MA); organizational development and consultation (MA); psychology of conflict management (Graduate Certificate). *Program availability:* Part-time, evening/weekend. *Students:* 80 full-time (53 women), 10 part-time (6 women); includes 17 minority (8 Black or African American, non-Hispanic/Latino; 4 Asian, non-Hispanic/Latino; 5 Hispanic/Latino), 3 international. Average age 26. 116 applicants, 89% accepted, 47 enrolled. In 2017, 45 master's awarded. *Degree requirements:* For master's, thesis or alternative, internship or practicum. *Entrance requirements:* Additional exam requirements/recommendations for international students: Required—TOEFL (minimum score 80 iBT), IELTS, PTE. *Application deadline:* Applications are processed on a rolling basis. Application fee: $50. Electronic applications accepted. Application fee is waived when completed online. *Expenses:* Contact institution. *Financial support:* Research assistantships with partial tuition reimbursements, teaching assistantships with partial tuition reimbursements, career-related internships or fieldwork, Federal Work-Study, scholarships/grants, and unspecified assistantships available. Support available to part-time students. Financial award required to submit FAFSA. *Unit head:* Dr. Eric Marcus, Coordinator, 203-932-1242, E-mail: emarcus@newhaven.edu. *Application contact:* Michelle Mason, Director of Graduate Enrollment, 203-932-7067.
Website: http://www.newhaven.edu/4730/

University of New Mexico, Anderson School of Management, Department of Organizational Studies, Albuquerque, NM 87131. Offers organizational behavior and human resources management (MBA); strategic management and policy (MBA). *Program availability:* Part-time. *Faculty:* 17 full-time (12 women), 17 part-time/adjunct (6 women). In 2017, 20 master's awarded. *Entrance requirements:* For master's, GMAT or GRE, minimum GPA of 3.0 on last 60 hours of coursework; bachelor's degree from regionally-accredited college or university in U.S. or its equivalent in another country. Additional exam requirements/recommendations for international students: Required—TOEFL (minimum score 550 paper-based; 79 iBT), IELTS (minimum score 6.5). *Application deadline:* For fall admission, 4/1 priority date for domestic and international students; for spring admission, 10/1 priority date for domestic and international students. Applications are processed on a rolling basis. Application fee: $50. Electronic applications accepted. *Expenses:* Contact institution. *Financial support:* In 2017–18, 14 students received support, including 4 fellowships (averaging $18,200 per year), 11 research assistantships with partial tuition reimbursements available (averaging $15,488 per year); career-related internships or fieldwork, Federal Work-Study, scholarships/grants, and unspecified assistantships also available. Support available to part-time students. Financial award application deadline: 6/1; financial award applicants required to submit FAFSA. *Faculty research:* Business ethics and social corporate responsibility, diversity, human resources, organizational strategy, organizational behavior. *Unit head:* Dr. Michelle Arthur, Chair, 505-277-6471, E-mail: arthurm@unm.edu. *Application contact:* Lisa Beauchene, Student Recruitment Specialist, 505-277-6471, E-mail: andersonadvising@unm.edu.
Website: https://www.mgt.unm.edu/dos/default.asp?mm-faculty

University of Northwestern–St. Paul, Master of Organizational Leadership Program, St. Paul, MN 55113-1598. Offers MOL. *Program availability:* Part-time, evening/weekend, online learning. *Application deadline:* Applications are processed on a rolling basis. Electronic applications accepted. *Application contact:* Graduate Studies Admissions, 651-631-5200, E-mail: gradstudies@unwsp.edu.
Website: https://www.unwsp.edu/web/graduate-studies/master-of-organizational-leadership

University of Oklahoma, College of Professional and Continuing Studies, Norman, OK 73019. Offers administrative leadership (MA, Graduate Certificate), including government and military leadership (MA), organizational leadership (MA), volunteer and non-profit leadership (MA); corrections management (Graduate Certificate); criminal justice (MS); integrated studies (MA), including human and health services administration, integrated studies; museum studies (MA); prevention science (MPS); restorative justice administration (Graduate Certificate). *Program availability:* Part-time, 100% online, blended/hybrid learning. *Faculty:* 16 full-time (8 women). *Students:* 64 full-time (39 women), 558 part-time (278 women); includes 191 minority (42 Black or African American, non-Hispanic/Latino; 42 American Indian or Alaska Native, non-Hispanic/Latino; 16 Asian, non-Hispanic/Latino; 46 Hispanic/Latino; 1 Native Hawaiian or other Pacific Islander, non-Hispanic/Latino; 44 Two or more races, non-Hispanic/Latino), 4 international. Average age 35. 151 applicants, 95% accepted, 97 enrolled. In 2017, 202 master's, 11 other advanced degrees awarded. *Degree requirements:* For master's, comprehensive exam, thesis optional, 33 credit hours; project/internship (for museum studies program only); for Graduate Certificate, 12 graduate credit hours (for Graduate Certificate. *Entrance requirements:* For master's and Graduate Certificate, minimum GPA of 3.0 in last 60 undergraduate hours; statement of goals; resume. Additional exam requirements/recommendations for international students: Required—TOEFL (minimum score 79 iBT) or IELTS (minimum score 6.5). *Application deadline:* For fall admission, 7/15 for domestic and international students; for winter admission, 12/1 for domestic and international students; for spring admission, 5/1 for domestic and international students. Applications are processed on a rolling basis. Application fee: $50 ($100 for international students). Electronic applications accepted. *Expenses:* Tuition, state resident: full-time $5119; part-time $213.30 per credit hour. Tuition, nonresident: full-time $19,778; part-time $824.10 per credit hour. *Required fees:* $3458; $133.55 per credit hour. $126.50 per semester. *Financial support:* In 2017–18, 92 students received support. Career-related internships or fieldwork, institutionally sponsored loans, scholarships/grants, health care benefits, and tuition waivers available. Support available to part-time students. Financial award application deadline: 6/1; financial award applicants required to submit FAFSA. *Faculty research:* Change management and leadership; policing and corrections management; neuro-psychology of addiction; disproportionate minority contact; ethnic identity and nationalism. *Unit head:* Dr. Martha L. Banz, Associate Provost for Continuing Education/Interim Dean, College of Professional and Continuing Studies, 405-325-4414, Fax: 405-325-7132, E-mail: mlbanz@ou.edu. *Application contact:* Lindsey Gunderson, Graduate Academic Advisor, 405-325-5827, Fax: 405-325-7132, E-mail: lindsey.gunderson@ou.edu.
Website: https://pacs.ou.edu/

University of Pennsylvania, School of Arts and Sciences, College of Liberal and Professional Studies, Philadelphia, PA 19104. Offers applied geosciences (MSAG); applied positive psychology (MAP); chemical sciences (MCS); environmental studies (MES); individualized study (MLA); liberal arts (M Phil); medical physics (MMP); organization dynamics (M Phil). *Students:* 191 full-time (112 women), 311 part-time (178 women); includes 99 minority (34 Black or African American, non-Hispanic/Latino; 2 American Indian or Alaska Native, non-Hispanic/Latino; 28 Asian, non-Hispanic/Latino; 24 Hispanic/Latino; 11 Two or more races, non-Hispanic/Latino), 83 international. Average age 34. 633 applicants, 52% accepted, 249 enrolled. In 2017, 141 master's awarded. *Unit head:* Nora Lewis, Vice Dean, Professional and Liberal Education, 215-898-7326, E-mail: nlewis@sas.upenn.edu.
Website: http://www.sas.upenn.edu/lps/graduate

University of Pennsylvania, School of Arts and Sciences, Fels Institute of Government, Philadelphia, PA 19104. Offers economic development and growth (Certificate); government administration (MGA); nonprofit administration (Certificate); organization dynamics (MS); politics (Certificate); public administration (MPA); public finance (Certificate). *Program availability:* Part-time, evening/weekend. *Students:* 44 full-time (27 women), 78 part-time (41 women); includes 30 minority (9 Black or African American, non-Hispanic/Latino; 8 Asian, non-Hispanic/Latino; 10 Hispanic/Latino; 3 Two or more races, non-Hispanic/Latino), 10 international. Average age 31. 333 applicants, 47% accepted, 88 enrolled. In 2017, 57 master's, 9 other advanced degrees awarded. *Financial support:* Application deadline: 1/1.
Website: http://www.fels.upenn.edu/

University of Phoenix–Bay Area Campus, College of Information Systems and Technology, San Jose, CA 95134-1805. Offers information systems (MIS); organizational leadership/information systems and technology (DM). *Program availability:* Evening/weekend. *Degree requirements:* For master's, thesis (for some programs). *Entrance requirements:* For master's, minimum undergraduate GPA of 3.0, 3 years of work experience. Additional exam requirements/recommendations for international students: Required—TOEFL (minimum score 550 paper-based; 79 iBT). Electronic applications accepted.

University of Phoenix–Bay Area Campus, School of Business, San Jose, CA 95134-1805. Offers accountancy (MS); accounting (MBA); business administration (MBA, DBA); energy management (MBA); global management (MBA); health care management (MBA); human resource management (MBA); human resources management (MM); management (MM); marketing (MBA); organizational leadership (DM); project management (MBA); public administration (MPA); technology management (MBA). *Accreditation:* ACBSP. *Program availability:* Evening/weekend, online learning. *Degree requirements:* For master's, thesis (for some programs). *Entrance requirements:* For master's, minimum undergraduate GPA of 3.0, 3 years of work experience. Additional exam requirements/recommendations for international students: Required—TOEFL (minimum score 550 paper-based; 79 iBT). Electronic applications accepted.

University of Phoenix–Online Campus, School of Advanced Studies, Phoenix, AZ 85034-7209. Offers business administration (DBA); education (Ed S); educational leadership (Ed D), including curriculum and instruction, education technology, educational leadership; health administration (DHA); higher education administration (PhD); industrial/organizational psychology (PhD); nursing (PhD); organizational leadership (DM), including information systems and technology, organizational leadership. *Program availability:* Evening/weekend, online learning. *Degree requirements:* For doctorate, thesis/dissertation. *Entrance requirements:* Additional exam requirements/recommendations for international students: Required—TOEFL, TOEIC (Test of English as an International Communication), Berlitz Online English Proficiency Exam, PTE, or IELTS. Electronic applications accepted. *Expenses:* Contact institution.

University of Portland, School of Education, Portland, OR 97203-5798. Offers education (MA, MAT); educational leadership (M Ed); English for speakers of other languages (M Ed); initial administrator licensure (M Ed); neuroeducation (M Ed, Ed D); organizational leadership and development (Ed D); reading (M Ed); school leadership and development (Ed D); special education (M Ed). M Ed also available through the Graduate Outreach Program for teachers residing in the Oregon and Washington state areas. *Accreditation:* NCATE. *Program availability:* Part-time, evening/weekend. *Entrance requirements:* For master's, minimum GPA of 3.0, teaching certificate, letters of recommendation, resume, statement of goals, official transcripts. Additional exam requirements/recommendations for international students: Required—TOEFL (minimum score 550 paper-based; 80 iBT), IELTS (minimum score 7). *Faculty research:* Multicultural education, supervision/leadership.

University of Regina, Faculty of Graduate Studies and Research, Kenneth Levene Graduate School of Business, Program in Business Administration, Regina, SK S4S 0A2, Canada. Offers business foundations (PGD); engineering management (MBA); executive business administration (EMBA); international business (MBA); leadership (M Admin); organizational leadership (Master's Certificate); project management (Master's Certificate); public safety management (MBA). *Program availability:* Part-time, evening/weekend. *Faculty:* 43 full-time (15 women), 6 part-time/adjunct (0 women). *Students:* 35 full-time (15 women), 18 part-time (9 women). 172 applicants, 26% accepted. In 2017, 24 master's, 2 other advanced degrees awarded. *Degree requirements:* For master's, project (for some programs). *Entrance requirements:* For master's, GMAT, three years of relevant work experience, four-year undergraduate degree; for other advanced degree, GMAT (for PGD), four-year undergraduate degree and two years of relevant work experience (for Master's Certificate); three years' work experience (for PGD). Additional exam requirements/recommendations for international students: Required—TOEFL (minimum score 580 paper-based; 80 iBT), IELTS (minimum score 6.5), PTE (minimum score 59). *Application deadline:* Applications are processed on a rolling basis. Application fee: $100. Electronic applications accepted. *Expenses:* CAD$20,150 per year. *Financial support:* In 2017–18, fellowships (averaging $6,000 per year), teaching assistantships (averaging $2,562 per year) were awarded; research assistantships, career-related internships or fieldwork, and scholarships/grants also available. Financial award application deadline: 6/15. *Faculty research:* Business policy and strategy, production and operations management, human behavior in organizations, financial management, social issues in business. *Unit head:* Dr. David Senkow, Dean, 306-585-4719, Fax: 306-585-5361, E-mail: david.senkow@uregina.ca. *Application contact:* Ronald Camp, Graduate Programs, 306-337-2387, Fax: 306-585-5361, E-mail: ronald.camp@uregina.ca.
Website: http://www.uregina.ca/business/levene/

University of Saint Francis, Graduate School, Keith Busse School of Business and Entrepreneurial Leadership, Fort Wayne, IN 46808-3994. Offers business administration (MBA), including sustainability; environmental health (MEH); healthcare administration (MHA); organizational leadership (MOL). *Accreditation:* ACBSP. *Program availability:* Part-time, evening/weekend, online only, 100% online. *Faculty:* 4 full-time (3 women), 11 part-time/adjunct (1 woman). *Students:* 75 full-time (43 women), 108 part-time (59 women); includes 37 minority (21 Black or African American, non-Hispanic/Latino; 1 Asian, non-Hispanic/Latino; 11 Hispanic/Latino; 1 Native Hawaiian or other Pacific Islander, non-Hispanic/Latino; 3 Two or more races, non-Hispanic/Latino). Average age 34. 101 applicants, 98% accepted, 75 enrolled. In 2017, 133 master's awarded. *Entrance requirements:* For master's, GMAT (if cumulative GPA is below 2.75 with less than five years' professional work experience), minimum undergraduate GPA of 2.75; statement of professional goals; resume. Additional exam requirements/recommendations for international students: Required—TOEFL (minimum score 550 paper-based) or IELTS (minimum score 6.5). *Application deadline:* For fall admission, 7/1 for international students; for spring admission, 11/1 for international students; for summer admission, 3/1 for international students. Applications are processed on a rolling basis. Application fee: $0. Electronic applications accepted. *Expenses:* $475 per hour. *Financial support:* Application deadline: 4/15; applicants required to submit FAFSA. *Unit head:* Dr. Robert Lee, Dean, 260-399-7700 Ext. 8304, Fax: 260-399-8174, E-mail: rlee@sf.edu. *Application contact:* Kyle Richardson, Associate Director of Enrollment Services for Adult Learning, 260-399-7700 Ext. 6310, Fax: 260-399-8152, E-mail: krichardson@sf.edu.
Website: https://business.sf.edu/graduate/

Organizational Management

University of St. Thomas, College of Education, Leadership and Counseling, Department of Organization Learning and Development, St. Paul, MN 55105-1096. Offers organization development and change (Ed D). *Program availability:* Part-time, evening/weekend. *Degree requirements:* For doctorate, comprehensive exam, thesis/dissertation. *Entrance requirements:* For doctorate, minimum GPA of 3.5, interview, 5-7 years of organization development or leadership experience. Additional exam requirements/recommendations for international students: Required—TOEFL (minimum score 550 paper-based). *Application deadline:* For fall admission, 7/15 priority date for domestic and international students; for spring admission, 12/9 priority date for domestic and international students; for summer admission, 4/3 priority date for domestic students, 4/3 for international students. Applications are processed on a rolling basis. Electronic applications accepted. *Expenses:* Contact institution. *Financial support:* Fellowships, research assistantships, institutionally sponsored loans, and scholarships/grants available. Support available to part-time students. Financial award application deadline: 8/1; financial award applicants required to submit FAFSA. *Faculty research:* Workplace conflict, physician leaders, virtual teams, technology use in schools/workplace, developing masterful practitioners. *Application contact:* Liz G. Knight, Program Manager, 651-962-4459, Fax: 651-962-4169, E-mail: egknight@stthomas.edu.

University of San Francisco, School of Management, Master of Business Administration Program, San Francisco, CA 94117. Offers entrepreneurship and innovation (MBA); finance (MBA); marketing (MBA); organization development (MBA); DDS/MBA; JD/MBA; MBA/MAPS. *Accreditation:* AACSB. *Program availability:* Part-time, evening/weekend. *Entrance requirements:* For master's, GMAT or GRE, resume (two years of professional work experience required for part-time students, preferred for full-time), transcripts from each college or university attended, two letters of recommendation, personal statement, interview. Additional exam requirements/recommendations for international students: Required—TOEFL (minimum score 600 paper-based, 100 iBT), IELTS (minimum score 7) or PTE (minimum score 68). Electronic applications accepted. *Expenses:* Contact institution. *Faculty research:* International financial markets, technology transfer licensing, international marketing, strategic planning.

University of San Francisco, School of Management, Master of Science in Organization Development Program, San Fransisco, CA 94117. Offers MSOD. *Program availability:* Part-time, evening/weekend. *Degree requirements:* For master's, thesis. *Entrance requirements:* For master's, resume demonstrating minimum of two years of professional work experience, transcripts from each college or university attended, two letters of recommendation, personal statement. Additional exam requirements/recommendations for international students: Required—TOEFL (minimum score 600 paper-based, 100 iBT), IELTS (minimum score 7) or PTE. Electronic applications accepted. *Expenses:* Contact institution.

University of South Dakota, Graduate School, College of Arts and Sciences, Program in Administrative Studies, Vermillion, SD 57069. Offers addiction studies (MSA); criminal justice studies (MSA); health services administration (MSA); human resources (MSA); interdisciplinary studies (MSA); long term care administration (MSA); organizational leadership (MSA). *Program availability:* Part-time, evening/weekend, 100% online. *Degree requirements:* For master's, thesis or alternative. *Entrance requirements:* For master's, 3 years of work or experience, minimum GPA of 2.7, resume. Additional exam requirements/recommendations for international students: Required—TOEFL (minimum score 550 paper-based; 79 iBT). *Application deadline:* Applications are processed on a rolling basis. Application fee: $35. Electronic applications accepted. *Financial support:* Teaching assistantships with partial tuition reimbursements available. Financial award applicants required to submit FAFSA. *Application contact:* Graduate School, 605-658-6140, Fax: 605-677-6118, E-mail: grad@usd.edu. Website: http://www.usd.edu/onlinemsa

University of Southern California, Graduate School, Sol Price School of Public Policy, Executive Master of Leadership Program, Los Angeles, CA 90089. Offers EML. *Program availability:* Part-time, evening/weekend. *Entrance requirements:* Additional exam requirements/recommendations for international students: Required—TOEFL (minimum score 600 paper-based; 100 iBT). Electronic applications accepted. *Expenses:* Contact institution. *Faculty research:* Strategic planning, organizational transformation, strategic management, leadership.

The University of Texas at San Antonio, College of Business, Department of Management, San Antonio, TX 78249-0617. Offers management and organization studies (PhD). *Faculty:* 13 full-time (3 women). *Students:* 162 full-time (69 women), 79 part-time (31 women); includes 121 minority (17 Black or African American, non-Hispanic/Latino; 1 American Indian or Alaska Native, non-Hispanic/Latino; 18 Asian, non-Hispanic/Latino; 79 Hispanic/Latino; 1 Native Hawaiian or other Pacific Islander, non-Hispanic/Latino; 5 Two or more races, non-Hispanic/Latino), 9 international. Average age 32. 180 applicants, 64% accepted, 84 enrolled. In 2017, 1 doctorate awarded. Terminal master's awarded for partial completion of doctoral program. *Degree requirements:* For doctorate, comprehensive exam, thesis/dissertation. *Entrance requirements:* For doctorate, GMAT, GRE. Additional exam requirements/recommendations for international students: Required—TOEFL (minimum score 550 paper-based; 79 iBT), IELTS (minimum score 6.5). *Application deadline:* For fall admission, 7/31 for domestic students, 3/1 for international students; for spring admission, 10/15 for domestic students, 9/15 for international students. Application fee: $50 ($90 for international students). Electronic applications accepted. *Expenses:* Tuition, state resident: full-time $5495. Tuition, nonresident: full-time $21,938. *Required fees:* $1915. Tuition and fees vary according to program. *Unit head:* Dr. Robert L. Cardy, Chair, 210-458-4310, Fax: 210-458-5783, E-mail: robert.cardy@utsa.edu. *Application contact:* Caron Kiley, Assistant Director of Graduate Fiscal Services/PhD Program Manager, 210-458-7324, E-mail: caron.kiley@utsa.edu. Website: https://business.utsa.edu/management/

The University of Texas at Tyler, College of Business and Technology, Program in Business Administration, Tyler, TX 75799-0001. Offers cyber security (MBA); engineering management (MBA); general management (MBA); healthcare management (MBA); internal assurance and consulting (MBA); marketing (MBA); oil, gas and energy (MBA); organizational development (MBA); quality management (MBA). *Accreditation:* AACSB. *Program availability:* Part-time, online learning. *Entrance requirements:* Additional exam requirements/recommendations for international students: Required—TOEFL (minimum score 550 paper-based). *Faculty research:* General business, inventory control, institutional markets, service marketing, product distribution, accounting fraud, financial reporting and recognition.

University of the Incarnate Word, School of Professional Studies, San Antonio, TX 78209-6397. Offers communication arts (MAA), including applied administration, communication arts, healthcare administration, industrial and organizational psychology, organizational development; organizational development and leadership (MS); professional studies (DBA). *Program availability:* Part-time, evening/weekend, 100% online, blended/hybrid learning. *Faculty:* 9 full-time (3 women), 25 part-time/adjunct (10 women). *Students:* 528 full-time (263 women), 348 part-time (141 women); includes 543 minority (122 Black or African American, non-Hispanic/Latino; 3 American Indian or Alaska Native, non-Hispanic/Latino; 26 Asian, non-Hispanic/Latino; 365 Hispanic/Latino; 6 Native Hawaiian or other Pacific Islander, non-Hispanic/Latino; 21 Two or more races,

non-Hispanic/Latino). In 2017, 377 master's, 10 doctorates awarded. *Degree requirements:* For master's, comprehensive exam (for some programs), thesis or alternative. *Entrance requirements:* For master's, GMAT, GRE, official transcripts from all other colleges attended. Additional exam requirements/recommendations for international students: Required—TOEFL (minimum score 560 paper-based; 83 iBT). *Application deadline:* Applications are processed on a rolling basis. Electronic applications accepted. *Expenses:* $915 per credit hour (for master's programs); $940 per credit hour (for doctoral program). *Financial support:* Scholarships/grants and unspecified assistantships available. Financial award applicants required to submit FAFSA. *Unit head:* Dr. Cyndi Porter, Vice President, 877-603-1130, E-mail: porter@uiwtx.edu. *Application contact:* Julie Weber, Director of Marketing and Recruitment, 210-318-1876, Fax: 210-829-2756, E-mail: eapadmission@uiwtx.edu. Website: http://sps.uiw.edu/

University of Wisconsin–Platteville, School of Graduate Studies, Distance Learning Center, Online Master of Science in Organizational Change Leadership Program, Platteville, WI 53818-3099. Offers MS. *Program availability:* Part-time. *Students:* 2 full-time (1 woman), 92 part-time (56 women); includes 19 minority (4 Black or African American, non-Hispanic/Latino; 2 American Indian or Alaska Native, non-Hispanic/Latino; 4 Asian, non-Hispanic/Latino; 9 Hispanic/Latino). 26 applicants, 85% accepted, 15 enrolled. In 2017, 17 master's awarded. *Degree requirements:* For master's, capstone, research paper, or thesis research. *Entrance requirements:* Additional exam requirements/recommendations for international students: Required—TOEFL (minimum score 550 paper-based; 79 iBT), IELTS (minimum score 6.5). *Application deadline:* Applications are processed on a rolling basis. Application fee: $56. Electronic applications accepted. *Unit head:* Dawn Drake, Executive Director, 800-362-5460, Fax: 608-342-1071, E-mail: disted@uwplatt.edu.

Upper Iowa University, Online Master's Programs, Fayette, IA 52142-1857. Offers accounting (MBA); corporate financial management (MBA); emergency management and homeland security (MPA); general management (MBA); general studies (MPA); government administration (MPA); health and human services (MPA); human resources management (MBA); nonprofit organizational management (MPA); organizational development (MBA); public management (MPA); sport administration (MSA). MBA also available at Madison, WI campus. *Program availability:* Part-time, online learning. *Degree requirements:* For master's, research project. *Entrance requirements:* For master's, GMAT, GRE, or minimum GPA of 2.7 during last 60 hours. Additional exam requirements/recommendations for international students: Required—TOEFL (minimum score 570 paper-based). Electronic applications accepted. *Faculty research:* Total quality management, teams, organization culture and climate, management.

Vanderbilt University, Peabody College, Department of Leadership, Policy, and Organizations, Nashville, TN 37240-1001. Offers education policy (MPP); educational leadership and policy (Ed D); higher education (M Ed); higher education leadership and policy (Ed D); independent school leadership (M Ed); international education policy and management (M Ed); leadership and learning in organizations (Ed D); leadership and organizational performance (M Ed). *Program availability:* Part-time, on-campus immersion once every semester. *Faculty:* 30 full-time (15 women), 19 part-time/adjunct (6 women). *Students:* 141 full-time (105 women), 139 part-time (84 women); includes 66 minority (32 Black or African American, non-Hispanic/Latino; 13 Asian, non-Hispanic/Latino; 14 Hispanic/Latino; 1 Native Hawaiian or other Pacific Islander, non-Hispanic/Latino; 6 Two or more races, non-Hispanic/Latino), 25 international. Average age 30. 525 applicants, 66% accepted, 139 enrolled. In 2017, 109 master's, 22 doctorates awarded. *Degree requirements:* For master's, comprehensive exam, thesis optional; for doctorate, thesis/dissertation, qualifying exams, residency. *Entrance requirements:* For master's and doctorate, GRE General Test. Additional exam requirements/recommendations for international students: Required—TOEFL (minimum score 550 paper-based; 80 iBT). *Application deadline:* For fall admission, 12/31 priority date for domestic and international students; for spring admission, 11/1 priority date for domestic and international students. Applications are processed on a rolling basis. Application fee: $0. Electronic applications accepted. *Financial support:* Fellowships with partial tuition reimbursements, research assistantships with partial tuition reimbursements, teaching assistantships with partial tuition reimbursements, Federal Work-Study, institutionally sponsored loans, scholarships/grants, tuition waivers (partial), and unspecified assistantships available. Support available to part-time students. Financial award application deadline: 1/15; financial award applicants required to submit FAFSA. *Faculty research:* Financial aid policies, teacher labor markets, school choice, educational leadership, higher education access and equity. *Unit head:* Dr. Ellen B. Goldring, Chair, 615-322-8000, Fax: 615-343-7094, E-mail: ellen.b.goldring@vanderbilt.edu. *Application contact:* Rosie Moody, Educational Coordinator, 615-322-8019, Fax: 615-343-7094, E-mail: rosie.moody@vanderbilt.edu. Website: http://peabody.vanderbilt.edu/departments/lpo/index.php

Vanderbilt University, Vanderbilt University Owen Graduate School of Management, Vanderbilt MBA Program, Nashville, TN 37203. Offers accounting (MBA); finance (MBA); general management (MBA); health care (MBA); human and organizational performance (MBA); marketing (MBA); operations (MBA); strategy (MBA); MBA/JD; MBA/M Div; MBA/MD; MBA/MSN; MBA/MTS; MBA/PhD. *Accreditation:* AACSB. *Degree requirements:* For master's, 62 credit hours of coursework; completion of ethics course; minimum GPA of 3.0. *Entrance requirements:* For master's, GMAT (preferred) or GRE, 2 years of work experience (recommended). Additional exam requirements/recommendations for international students: Required—TOEFL (minimum score 100 iBT). Electronic applications accepted. *Expenses:* Contact institution. *Faculty research:* Accounting and finance, business strategy and economics, marketing, operations management, organization studies.

Viterbo University, Master of Arts in Servant Leadership Program, La Crosse, WI 54601-4797. Offers ethical leadership in organizations (Certificate); servant leadership (MA). *Program availability:* Part-time, evening/weekend. *Degree requirements:* For master's, 30 credits (15 credits of Servant Leadership core courses and any combination of 15 elective credits). *Entrance requirements:* For master's, letter of reference, statement of goals, baccalaureate degree, transcript, interview. Additional exam requirements/recommendations for international students: Required—TOEFL (minimum score 525 paper-based). Electronic applications accepted. *Expenses:* Contact institution. *Faculty research:* Organizational culture, community building, ethical decision-making, leadership theory and practice.

Walden University, Graduate Programs, School of Management, Minneapolis, MN 55401. Offers accounting (MBA, MS, DBA), including accounting for the professional (MS), accounting with CPA emphasis (MS), self-designed (MS); advanced project management (Graduate Certificate); applied project management (Graduate Certificate); auditing (Graduate Certificate); bridge to business administration (Post-Doctoral Certificate); bridge to management (Post-Doctoral Certificate); business management (Graduate Certificate); communication (MBA); corporate finance (MBA); digital marketing (Graduate Certificate); entrepreneurship (DBA); entrepreneurship and small business (MBA); finance (MS, DBA), including finance for the professional (MS), finance with CFA/investment (MS), finance with CPA emphasis (MS); global supply chain management (DBA); healthcare management (MBA, DBA); human resource management (MBA, MS, Graduate Certificate), including functional human resource management (MS), general program (MS), integrating functional and strategic human resource management (MS), organizational strategy (MS); human resources management (DBA); information systems management (DBA); international business (MBA, DBA); leadership (MBA, MS, DBA, Graduate Certificate), including general program (MS), human resource leadership (MS), leader development (MS), self-designed (MS); management (MS, PhD), including communications (MS), finance (PhD), general program (MS), healthcare management (MS), human resource management (MS), human resources management (PhD), information systems management (PhD), international business (MS), leadership (MS), leadership and organizational change (PhD), marketing (MS), project management (MS), strategy and operations (MS); managerial accounting (Graduate Certificate); marketing (MBA, MS, DBA); project management (MBA, MS, DBA); self-designed (MBA, DBA); social impact management (DBA); technology entrepreneurship (DBA). *Accreditation:* ACBSP. *Program availability:* Part-time, evening/weekend, online only, 100% online. *Degree requirements:* For master's, thesis (for some programs), residency (for EMBA); for doctorate, thesis/dissertation (for some programs), residency. *Entrance requirements:* For master's, bachelor's degree or higher; minimum GPA of 2.5; official transcripts; goal statement (for some programs); access to computer and Internet; for doctorate, master's degree or higher; three years of related professional or academic experience (preferred); minimum GPA of 3.0; goal statement and current resume (for select programs); official transcripts; access to computer and Internet; for other advanced degree, relevant work experience; access to computer and Internet. Additional exam requirements/recommendations for international students: Required—TOEFL (minimum score 550 paper-based, 79 iBT), IELTS (minimum score 6.5), Michigan English Language Assessment Battery (minimum score 82), or PTE (minimum score 53). Electronic applications accepted.

Walden University, Graduate Programs, School of Public Policy and Administration, Minneapolis, MN 55401. Offers criminal justice (MPA, MPP, MS, Graduate Certificate), including emergency management (MS, PhD), general program (MS), global leadership (MS, PhD), homeland security and policy coordination (MS, PhD), law and public policy (MS, PhD), policy analysis (MS, PhD), public management and leadership (MS, PhD), self-designed (MS), terrorism, mediation, and peace (MS, PhD); criminal justice and executive management (MS), including global leadership (MS, PhD); criminal justice leadership and executive management (MS), including emergency management (MS, PhD), general program, homeland security and policy coordination (MS, PhD), law and public policy (MS, PhD), policy analysis (MS, PhD), public management and leadership (MS, PhD), self-designed, terrorism, mediation, and peace (MS, PhD); emergency management (MPA, MPP, MS), including criminal justice (MS, PhD), general program (MS), homeland security (MS), public management and leadership (MS, PhD), terrorism and emergency management (MS); general program (MPA, MPP); global leadership (MPA, MPP); government management (Graduate Certificate); health policy (MPA, MPP); homeland security (Graduate Certificate); homeland security and policy coordination (MPA, MPP); international nongovernmental organizations (MPA, MPP); law and public policy (MPA, MPP); local government management for sustainable communities (MPA, MPP); nonprofit management (Graduate Certificate); nonprofit management and leadership (MPA, MPP, MS), including global leadership (MS, PhD), international nongovernmental organization (MS), local government for sustainable communities (MS), self designed (MS); online teaching in higher education (Post-Master's Certificate); policy analysis (MPA); public management and leadership (MPA, MPP, Graduate Certificate); public policy (Graduate Certificate); public policy and administration (PhD), including criminal justice (MS, PhD), emergency management (MS, PhD), global leadership (MS, PhD), health policy, homeland security and policy coordination (MS, PhD), international nongovernmental organizations, law and public policy (MS, PhD), local government management for sustainable communities, nonprofit management and leadership, policy analysis (MS, PhD), public management and leadership (MS, PhD), terrorism, mediation, and peace (MS, PhD); strategic planning and public policy (Graduate Certificate); terrorism, mediation, and peace (MPA, MPP). *Program availability:* Part-time, evening/weekend, online only, 100% online. *Degree requirements:* For doctorate, thesis/dissertation, residency. *Entrance requirements:* For master's, bachelor's degree or higher; minimum GPA of 2.5; official transcripts; goal statement (for some programs); access to computer and Internet; for doctorate, master's degree or higher; three years of related professional or academic experience (preferred); minimum GPA of 3.0; goal statement and current resume (for select programs); official transcripts; access to computer and Internet; for other advanced degree, relevant work experience; access to computer and Internet. Additional exam requirements/recommendations for international students: Required—TOEFL (minimum score 550 paper-based, 79 iBT), IELTS (minimum score 6.5), Michigan English Language Assessment Battery (minimum score 82), or PTE (minimum score 53). Electronic applications accepted.

Waldorf University, Program in Organizational Leadership, Forest City, IA 50436. Offers criminal justice leadership (MA); emergency management leadership (MA); fire/rescue executive leadership (MA); human resource development (MA); public administration (MA); sport management (MA); teacher leader (MA).

Warner Pacific University, Graduate Programs, Portland, OR 97215-4099. Offers human services (MA); not-for-profit leadership (MS); organizational leadership (MS); teaching (MAT). *Program availability:* Part-time, evening/weekend. *Degree requirements:* For master's, thesis or alternative, presentation of defense. *Entrance requirements:* For master's, interview, minimum GPA of 2.5, letters of recommendation. *Faculty research:* New Testament studies, nineteenth-century Wesleyan theology, preaching and church growth, Christian ethics.

Washington University in St. Louis, Olin Business School, Master of Science in Leadership Program, Washington, DC 20036. Offers MS. Program offered in partnership with the Brookings Institution. *Program availability:* Part-time. *Faculty:* 98 full-time (25 women), 54 part-time/adjunct (12 women). *Students:* 78 part-time (32 women); includes 26 minority (13 Black or African American, non-Hispanic/Latino; 1 Asian, non-Hispanic/Latino; 2 Hispanic/Latino; 1 Native Hawaiian or other Pacific Islander, non-Hispanic/Latino; 9 Two or more races, non-Hispanic/Latino). 28 applicants, 54% accepted, 14 enrolled. *Degree requirements:* For master's, 30 credit hours, eighteen of those in leadership courses (including five core courses and two residential courses at Washington University in St. Louis). *Entrance requirements:* For master's, bachelor's degree. *Application deadline:* Applications are processed on a rolling basis. Application fee: $50. Electronic applications accepted. *Unit head:* Dr. Mark Taylor, Dean, 314-935-5000, E-mail: mark.p.taylor@wustl.edu. *Application contact:* Autumn Clarke, Associate Registrar, 202-238-3558, E-mail: auclarke@brookings.edu. Website: http://www.olin.wustl.edu/EN-US/academic-programs/Pages/MS-Leadership.aspx

Wayland Baptist University, Graduate Programs, Programs in Business Administration/Management, Plainview, TX 79072-6998. Offers accounting (MBA); general business (MBA); health care administration (MAM, MBA); human resource management (MAM, MBA); international management (MBA); management (MBA, D Mgt); management information systems (MBA); organization management (MAM); project management (MBA). *Program availability:* Part-time, evening/weekend, online learning. *Faculty:* 30 full-time (5 women), 38 part-time/adjunct (9 women). *Students:* 42

full-time (20 women), 538 part-time (253 women); includes 311 minority (98 Black or African American, non-Hispanic/Latino; 4 American Indian or Alaska Native, non-Hispanic/Latino; 16 Asian, non-Hispanic/Latino; 153 Hispanic/Latino; 11 Native Hawaiian or other Pacific Islander, non-Hispanic/Latino; 29 Two or more races, non-Hispanic/Latino), 6 international. Average age 40. 100 applicants, 96% accepted, 60 enrolled. In 2017, 216 master's awarded. *Degree requirements:* For master's, capstone course. *Entrance requirements:* For master's, GMAT, GRE or MAT. Additional exam requirements/recommendations for international students: Required—TOEFL (minimum score 500 paper-based; 61 iBT). *Application deadline:* Applications are processed on a rolling basis. Application fee: $50. Electronic applications accepted. *Expenses: Tuition:* Full-time $11,250; part-time $625 per credit hour. *Required fees:* $1200. *Financial support:* Federal Work-Study, institutionally sponsored loans, and scholarships/grants available. Support available to part-time students. Financial award application deadline: 5/1; financial award applicants required to submit FAFSA. *Unit head:* Dr. Kelly Warren, Chairman, 806-291-1020, Fax: 806-291-1957, E-mail: warrenk@wbu.edu. *Application contact:* Amanda Stanton, Graduate Studies, 806-291-3423, Fax: 806-291-1950, E-mail: stanton@wbu.edu.

Waynesburg University, Graduate and Professional Studies, Canonsburg, PA 15370. Offers business (MBA), including energy management, finance, health systems, human resources, leadership, market development; counseling (MA), including addictions counseling, clinical mental health; counselor education and supervision (PhD); criminal investigation (MA); education (M Ed), including autism, curriculum and instruction, educational leadership, online teaching; nursing (MSN), including administration, education, informatics; nursing practice (DNP); special education (M Ed); technology (M Ed); MSN/MBA. *Accreditation:* AACN. *Program availability:* Part-time, evening/weekend. *Degree requirements:* For doctorate, thesis/dissertation. *Entrance requirements:* Additional exam requirements/recommendations for international students: Required—TOEFL. Electronic applications accepted.

Wayne State College, Department of Health, Human Performance and Sport, Wayne, NE 68787. Offers exercise science (MSE); organizational management (MS), including sport management. *Program availability:* Part-time, evening/weekend. *Degree requirements:* For master's, comprehensive exam, thesis optional. *Entrance requirements:* For master's, GRE General Test, minimum GPA of 3.0. Additional exam requirements/recommendations for international students: Required—TOEFL (minimum score 550 paper-based). Electronic applications accepted.

Wayne State University, College of Liberal Arts and Sciences, Department of Political Science, Detroit, MI 48202. Offers political science (MA, PhD); public administration (MPA), including economic development policy and management, health and human services policy and management, human and fiscal resource management, nonprofit policy and management, organizational behavior and management, urban and metropolitan policy and management; JD/MA. *Accreditation:* NASPAA. *Faculty:* 18. *Students:* 48 full-time (20 women), 68 part-time (36 women); includes 37 minority (26 Black or African American, non-Hispanic/Latino; 3 Asian, non-Hispanic/Latino; 2 Hispanic/Latino; 6 Two or more races, non-Hispanic/Latino), 6 international. Average age 32. 105 applicants, 39% accepted, 20 enrolled. In 2017, 17 master's, 3 doctorates awarded. *Degree requirements:* For master's, comprehensive exam (for some programs), thesis (for some programs); for doctorate, thesis/dissertation. *Entrance requirements:* For master's, GRE General Test, substantial undergraduate preparation in the social sciences, minimum upper-division undergraduate GPA of 3.0, two letters of recommendation, personal statement; for doctorate, GRE General Test, 3 letters of recommendation; personal statement; interview. Additional exam requirements/recommendations for international students: Required—TOEFL (minimum score 550 paper-based; 79 iBT), TWE (minimum score 5.5), Michigan English Language Assessment Battery (minimum score 85); Recommended—IELTS (minimum score 6.5). *Application deadline:* For fall admission, 5/15 for domestic students, 5/1 priority date for international students; for winter admission, 10/15 for domestic students, 9/1 priority date for international students. Applications are processed on a rolling basis. Application fee: $50. Electronic applications accepted. *Expenses:* Contact institution. *Financial support:* In 2017–18, 44 students received support, including 6 fellowships with tuition reimbursements available (averaging $11,698 per year), 12 teaching assistantships with tuition reimbursements available (averaging $18,534 per year); research assistantships with tuition reimbursements available, scholarships/grants, health care benefits, and unspecified assistantships also available. Financial award applicants required to submit FAFSA. *Faculty research:* American government and politics, comparative politics, political methodology, political theory, public administration, public law, public policy, world politics/international relations, formal theory/modeling, gender and politics, international law, peace research, political economy, political psychology, politics of developing countries, race, religion, and ethnicity, urban politics. *Unit head:* Dr. Daniel Geller, Professor and Chair, 313-577-6328, E-mail: dgeller@wayne.edu. *Application contact:* Dr. Sharon Lean, Graduate Director, 313-577-2630, E-mail: gradpolisci@wayne.edu.

Website: http://clas.wayne.edu/politicalscience/

Western New England University, College of Business, Program in Organizational Leadership, Springfield, MA 01119. Offers MS, Pharm D/MS. *Program availability:* Part-time, evening/weekend. *Faculty:* 8 full-time (6 women). *Students:* 13 part-time (9 women). Average age 38. 12 applicants, 83% accepted, 9 enrolled. In 2017, 3 master's awarded. *Entrance requirements:* For master's, GMAT, transcript, two letters of recommendation, two essays, resume. Additional exam requirements/recommendations for international students: Required—TOEFL (minimum score 79 iBT). *Application deadline:* Applications are processed on a rolling basis. Application fee: $30. Electronic applications accepted. *Expenses:* Contact institution. *Financial support:* Application deadline: 4/15; applicants required to submit FAFSA. *Unit head:* Dr. Rob Kleine, Dean, 413-782-1395, E-mail: rob.kleine@wne.edu. *Application contact:* Matthew Fox, Director of Admissions for Graduate Students and Adult Learners, 413-782-1410, Fax: 413-782-1777, E-mail: study@wne.edu.

Website: http://www1.wne.edu/academics/graduate/organizational-leadership.cfm

West Liberty University, School of Professional Studies, Triadelphia, WV 26059. Offers organizational leadership (MPS). *Entrance requirements:* For master's, bachelor's degree from accredited institution, minimum GPA of 2.5. Additional exam requirements/recommendations for international students: Required—TOEFL. *Application deadline:* Applications are processed on a rolling basis. Tuition and fees vary according to course load and program. *Unit head:* Dr. Thomas Michaud, Dean, 304-217-2800, E-mail: tmichaud@westliberty.edu.

Website: http://www.westliberty.edu/highlands/ps/

Wheeling Jesuit University, Department of Social Sciences, Wheeling, WV 26003-6295. Offers MSOL. *Program availability:* Part-time, evening/weekend. *Degree requirements:* For master's, thesis. *Entrance requirements:* For master's, MAT, minimum GPA of 2.75, minimum of three years full-time professional work experience. Additional exam requirements/recommendations for international students: Required—TOEFL (minimum score 600 paper-based; 100 iBT). Electronic applications accepted. Application fee is waived when completed online. *Faculty research:* History, theory and philosophy of leadership; gender roles and leadership; spirituality and leadership.

Organizational Management

Wilfrid Laurier University, Faculty of Graduate and Postdoctoral Studies, Lyle S. Hallman Faculty of Social Work, Waterloo, ON N2L 3C5, Canada. Offers Aboriginal studies (MSW); community, policy, planning and organizations (MSW); critical social policy and organizational studies (PhD); individuals, families and groups (MSW); social work practice (individuals, families, groups and communities) (PhD); social work practice: individuals, families, groups and communities (PhD). *Program availability:* Part-time. *Degree requirements:* For master's, thesis optional; for doctorate, thesis/dissertation. *Entrance requirements:* For master's, course work in social science, research methodology, and statistics; honors BA with a minimum B average; for doctorate, master's degree in social work, minimum A- average. Additional exam requirements/recommendations for international students: Required—TOEFL (minimum score 89 iBT). Electronic applications accepted. *Expenses:* Contact institution.

Wilkes University, College of Graduate and Professional Studies, Jay S. Sidhu School of Business and Leadership, Wilkes-Barre, PA 18766-0002. Offers accounting (MBA); entrepreneurship (MBA); finance (MBA); health care administration (MBA); human resource management (MBA); international business (MBA); operations management (MBA); organizational leadership and development (MBA). *Accreditation:* ACBSP. *Program availability:* Part-time, evening/weekend. *Students:* 37 full-time (18 women), 87 part-time (45 women); includes 17 minority (4 Black or African American, non-Hispanic/Latino; 5 Asian, non-Hispanic/Latino; 6 Hispanic/Latino; 2 Two or more races, non-Hispanic/Latino), 14 international. Average age 30. In 2017, 77 master's awarded. *Entrance requirements:* For master's, GMAT. Additional exam requirements/recommendations for international students: Required—TOEFL (minimum score 550 paper-based; 79 iBT). *Application deadline:* Applications are processed on a rolling basis. Application fee: $45 ($65 for international students). Electronic applications accepted. *Expenses:* Contact institution. *Financial support:* Unspecified assistantships available. Financial award application deadline: 3/1; financial award applicants required to submit FAFSA. *Unit head:* Dr. Abel Adekola, Dean, 570-408-4701, Fax: 570-408-7846, E-mail: abel.adekola@wilkes.edu. *Application contact:* Kristin Donati, Associate Director of Graduate Admissions, 570-408-3338, Fax: 570-408-7846, E-mail: kristin.donati@wilkes.edu.
Website: http://www.wilkes.edu/academics/colleges/sidhu-school-of-business-leadership/index.aspx

William Penn University, College for Working Adults, Oskaloosa, IA 52577-1799. Offers business leadership (MBL). *Program availability:* Online learning.

Williamson College, Program in Organizational Leadership, Franklin, TN 37067. Offers MA. *Program availability:* Evening/weekend. *Degree requirements:* For master's, capstone project. *Entrance requirements:* For master's, essay, official transcripts, minimum overall GPA of 2.5.

Wilmington University, College of Business, New Castle, DE 19720-6491. Offers accounting (MBA, MS); business administration (MBA, DBA); environmental stewardship (MBA); finance (MBA); health care administration (MBA, MSM); homeland security (MBA, MSM); human resource management (MSM); management information systems (MBA, MSN); marketing (MSM); marketing management (MBA); military leadership (MSM); organizational leadership (MBA, MSM); public administration (MSM). *Program availability:* Part-time, evening/weekend. *Faculty:* 16 full-time (8 women), 106 part-time/adjunct (49 women). *Students:* 525 full-time (294 women), 1,212 part-time (780 women); includes 557 minority (412 Black or African American, non-Hispanic/Latino; 14 American Indian or Alaska Native, non-Hispanic/Latino; 55 Asian, non-Hispanic/Latino; 25 Hispanic/Latino; 3 Native Hawaiian or other Pacific Islander, non-Hispanic/Latino; 48 Two or more races, non-Hispanic/Latino), 157 international. Average age 35. 1,484 applicants, 70% accepted, 685 enrolled. In 2017, 543 master's, 16 doctorates awarded. *Entrance requirements:* Additional exam requirements/recommendations for international students: Required—TOEFL (minimum score 500 paper-based). *Application deadline:* Applications are processed on a rolling basis. Application fee: $35. Electronic applications accepted. *Expenses: Tuition:* Part-time $466 per credit. *Required fees:* $25 per semester. Tuition and fees vary according to degree level and campus/location. *Financial support:* Applicants required to submit FAFSA. *Unit head:* Dr. Kathy S. Kennedy Ratajack, Dean, 302-356-2481. *Application contact:* Laura Morris, Director of Admissions, 877-967-5456, E-mail: infocenter@wilmu.edu.
Website: http://www.wilmu.edu/business/

Winona State University, College of Education, Department of Leadership Education, Winona, MN 55987. Offers education leadership (MS, Ed S), including k-12 principal (Ed S), superintendent (Ed S); organizational leadership (MS); professional leadership (MS); sport management (MS). MS in sport management offered in cooperation with Department of Physical Education and Sport Science. *Accreditation:* NCATE. *Program availability:* Part-time, evening/weekend. *Degree requirements:* For master's, comprehensive exam, thesis optional; for Ed S, thesis optional.

Winona State University, College of Nursing and Health Sciences, Winona, MN 55987. Offers adult-gerontology acute care nurse practitioner (MS, DNP, Post Master's Certificate); adult-gerontology clinical nurse specialist (MS, DNP, Post Master's Certificate); adult-gerontology primary care nurse practitioner (MS, DNP, Post Master's Certificate); family nurse practitioner (MS, DNP, Post Master's Certificate); nurse educator (MS); nursing and organizational leadership (MS, DNP, Post Master's Certificate); practice and leadership innovations (DNP, Post Master's Certificate). *Accreditation:* AACN. *Program availability:* Part-time, online learning. *Degree requirements:* For master's, thesis; for doctorate, capstone. *Entrance requirements:* For master's, GRE (if GPA less than 3.0). Additional exam requirements/recommendations for international students: Required—TOEFL (minimum score 550 paper-based).

Woodbury University, School of Business, Program in Organizational Leadership, Burbank, CA 91504. Offers MA. *Program availability:* Evening/weekend. *Entrance requirements:* For master's, GRE General Test (if GPA less than 2.5), 3 recommendations, essay, resume, academic transcripts. Additional exam requirements/recommendations for international students: Required—TOEFL (minimum score 550 paper-based; 83 iBT), IELTS (minimum score 6.5).

Worcester Polytechnic Institute, Graduate Admissions, Foisie Business School, Worcester, MA 01609-2280. Offers business administration (PhD); information technology (MS), including information security management; management (Graduate Certificate); marketing and technological innovation (MS); operations design and leadership (MS); supply chain management (MS); technology (MS). *Accreditation:* AACSB. *Program availability:* Part-time, evening/weekend, 100% online, blended/hybrid learning. *Faculty:* 26 full-time (12 women), 9 part-time/adjunct (0 women). *Students:* 254 full-time (153 women), 150 part-time (52 women); includes 34 minority (3 Black or African American, non-Hispanic/Latino; 10 Asian, non-Hispanic/Latino; 14 Hispanic/Latino; 7 Two or more races, non-Hispanic/Latino), 230 international. Average age 29. 677 applicants, 71% accepted, 146 enrolled. In 2017, 188 master's, 14 doctorates awarded. *Degree requirements:* For master's, thesis optional. *Entrance requirements:* For master's and Graduate Certificate, GMAT or GRE General Test, 3 letters of recommendation, statement of purpose, resume. Additional exam requirements/recommendations for international students: Required—TOEFL (minimum score 563 paper-based; 84 iBT), IELTS (minimum score 7). *Application deadline:* For fall admission, 6/1 priority date for domestic and international students; for spring admission, 11/1 priority date for domestic students, 10/1 priority date for international students. Applications are processed on a rolling basis. Application fee: $70. Electronic applications accepted. *Expenses: Tuition:* Full-time $26,226; part-time $1457 per credit. *Required fees:* $60; $30 per credit. One-time fee: $15. Tuition and fees vary according to course load. *Financial support:* Career-related internships or fieldwork, institutionally sponsored loans, scholarships/grants, and unspecified assistantships available. Financial award application deadline: 6/1. *Unit head:* Melissa Terrio, Executive Director, 508-831-4665, Fax: 508-831-4665, E-mail: biz@wpi.edu. *Application contact:* Margaret Clancey, Recruiting Operations Coordinator, 508-831-4980, Fax: 508-831-5720, E-mail: maclancey@wpi.edu.
Website: https://www.wpi.edu/academics/business

Worcester State University, Graduate School, Program in Management, Worcester, MA 01602-2597. Offers accounting (MS); managerial leadership (MS); marketing (MS). *Program availability:* Part-time, evening/weekend. *Faculty:* 6 full-time, 1 part-time/adjunct. *Students:* 12 full-time (7 women), 44 part-time (26 women); includes 14 minority (7 Black or African American, non-Hispanic/Latino; 2 Asian, non-Hispanic/Latino; 5 Hispanic/Latino), 3 international. Average age 32. 50 applicants, 80% accepted, 21 enrolled. In 2017, 10 master's awarded. *Degree requirements:* For master's, comprehensive exam (for some programs), thesis optional. *Entrance requirements:* For master's, GMAT, 3 letters of recommendation from professors and/or supervisors. Additional exam requirements/recommendations for international students: Required—TOEFL (minimum score 550 paper-based; 79 iBT). *Application deadline:* For fall admission, 6/15 for domestic and international students; for spring admission, 11/1 for domestic and international students; for summer admission, 4/1 for domestic and international students. Applications are processed on a rolling basis. Application fee: $50. Electronic applications accepted. *Expenses:* Tuition, state resident: full-time $3042; part-time $169 per credit hour. Tuition, nonresident: full-time $3042; part-time $169 per credit hour. *Required fees:* $2754; $153 per credit hour. *Financial support:* Career-related internships or fieldwork, scholarships/grants, and unspecified assistantships available. Financial award application deadline: 3/1; financial award applicants required to submit FAFSA. *Unit head:* Dr. Elizabeth Wark, Program Coordinator, 508-929-8743, E-mail: ewark@worcester.edu. *Application contact:* Sara Grady, Associate Dean, Graduate Studies and Professional Development, 508-929-8130, E-mail: sara.grady@worcester.edu.

Yale University, Yale School of Management and Graduate School of Arts and Sciences, Doctoral Program in Management, New Haven, CT 06520. Offers accounting (PhD); financial economics (PhD); marketing (PhD); organizations and management (PhD). *Accreditation:* AACSB. *Degree requirements:* For doctorate, comprehensive exam, thesis/dissertation. *Entrance requirements:* For doctorate, GMAT or GRE General Test. Additional exam requirements/recommendations for international students: Required—TOEFL or IELTS. Electronic applications accepted. *Expenses:* Contact institution. *Faculty research:* Pricing of options and futures, term structure of interest rates, use of accounting numbers in debt contracts, product differentiation, e-commerce and marketing, behavioral finance.

Section 17
Project Management

This section contains a directory of institutions offering graduate work in project management. Additional information about programs listed in the directory but not augmented by an in-depth entry may be obtained by writing directly to the dean of a graduate school or chair of a department at the address given in the directory.

For programs offering related work, see also in this book *Business Administration and Management.*

CONTENTS

Program Directory

Project Management

Albertus Magnus College, Master of Business Administration Program, New Haven, CT 06511-1189. Offers accounting (MBA); general management (MBA); health care management (MBA); human resource management (MBA); leadership (MBA); project management (MBA). Program also offered in East Hartford, CT. *Program availability:* Part-time, evening/weekend, 100% online, blended/hybrid learning. *Degree requirements:* For master's, thesis, capstone project, business plan, minimum cumulative GPA of 3.0, completion of all requirements within seven years of matriculation. *Entrance requirements:* For master's, 3 years of management or related experience, minimum GPA of 2.5, 2 letters of recommendation, official transcripts. Additional exam requirements/recommendations for international students: Recommended—TOEFL (minimum score 550 paper-based; 80 iBT). *Application deadline:* Applications are processed on a rolling basis. Application fee: $50. Electronic applications accepted. *Expenses:* Contact institution. *Financial support:* Federal Work-Study and unspecified assistantships available. Support available to part-time students. Financial award applicants required to submit FAFSA. *Faculty research:* Finance, project management, accounting, business administration, generalist. *Unit head:* Dr. Wayne Gineo, Director, 203-672-6670, E-mail: wgineo@albertus.edu. *Application contact:* Anthony Reich, Director of Admission, Division of Professional and Graduate Studies, 203-773-5302, E-mail: arreich@albertus.edu.
Website: http://www.albertus.edu/business-administration/ms/

Amberton University, Graduate School, Department of Business Administration, Garland, TX 75041-5595. Offers agile project management (MS); general business (MBA); international business (MBA); management (MBA); project management (MBA); strategic leadership (MBA). *Program availability:* Part-time, evening/weekend. *Entrance requirements:* For master's, minimum GPA of 3.0. *Application deadline:* Applications are processed on a rolling basis. Application fee: $0. *Expenses:* Tuition: Part-time $795 per course. *Unit head:* Dr. Don Hebbard, Academic Dean, 972-635-8641 Ext. 157, Fax: 972-279-9773, E-mail: dhebbard@amberton.edu. *Application contact:* Adviser, 972-279-6511 Ext. 180, Fax: 972-279-9773, E-mail: advisor@amberton.edu.

American Business & Technology University, Programs in Business Administration, Saint Joseph, MO 64506. Offers business administration (MBA); financial management (MBA); global business management (MBA); information systems management (MBA); marketing and social media (MBA); project and operations management (MBA); public accounting (MBA). *Program availability:* Online learning.

American InterContinental University Online, Program in Business Administration, Schaumburg, IL 60173. Offers accounting and finance (MBA); finance (MBA); healthcare management (MBA); human resource management (MBA); international business (MBA); management (MBA); marketing (MBA); operations management (MBA); organizational psychology and development (MBA); project management (MBA). *Accreditation:* ACBSP. *Program availability:* Evening/weekend, online learning. *Entrance requirements:* Additional exam requirements/recommendations for international students: Required—TOEFL (minimum score 550 paper-based). Electronic applications accepted.

American InterContinental University Online, Program in Information Technology, Schaumburg, IL 60173. Offers Internet security (MIT); IT project management (MIT). *Program availability:* Evening/weekend, online learning. *Entrance requirements:* Additional exam requirements/recommendations for international students: Required—TOEFL (minimum score 550 paper-based). Electronic applications accepted.

American University, School of Professional and Extended Studies, Washington, DC 20016-8030. Offers agile project management (MS); healthcare management (MS, Graduate Certificate); human resource analytics and management (MS, Graduate Certificate); instructional design and learning analytics (MS); measurement and evaluation (MS); project monitoring and evaluation (Graduate Certificate); sports analytics and management (MS, Graduate Certificate). *Program availability:* Part-time, evening/weekend, 100% online. *Faculty:* 27 full-time (13 women), 21 part-time/adjunct (10 women). *Students:* 17 full-time (8 women), 59 part-time (34 women); includes 9 minority (5 Black or African American, non-Hispanic/Latino; 2 Asian, non-Hispanic/Latino; 1 Two or more races, non-Hispanic/Latino), 5 international. Average age 31. 55 applicants, 89% accepted, 38 enrolled. In 2017, 8 other advanced degrees awarded. *Entrance requirements:* For master's, official transcript(s), resume. Additional exam requirements/recommendations for international students: Required—TOEFL (minimum score 600 paper-based; 100 iBT). *Application deadline:* Applications are processed on a rolling basis. Application fee: $55. Electronic applications accepted. *Expenses:* Contact institution. *Financial support:* Applicants required to submit FAFSA. *Unit head:* Carola Weil, Dean, 202-885-5990, Fax: 202-895-4960, E-mail: weil@american.edu. *Application contact:* Emily Aronoff, Assistant Director for Recruitment and Admission, 202-895-4953, E-mail: aronoff@american.edu.
Website: http://www.american.edu/spexs/

Ashland University, Dauch College of Business and Economics, Ashland, OH 44805-3702. Offers accounting (MBA); business analytics (MBA); entrepreneurship (MBA); financial management (MBA); global management (MBA); health care management and leadership (MBA); human resource management (MBA); human resources (MBA); management information systems (MBA); project management (MBA); sport management (MBA); supply chain management (MBA). *Accreditation:* ACBSP. *Program availability:* Part-time, evening/weekend, 100% online, blended/hybrid learning. *Faculty:* 20 full-time (8 women), 13 part-time/adjunct (2 women). *Students:* 458 full-time (210 women), 144 part-time (52 women); includes 88 minority (63 Black or African American, non-Hispanic/Latino; 1 American Indian or Alaska Native, non-Hispanic/Latino; 10 Asian, non-Hispanic/Latino; 14 Hispanic/Latino), 202 international. Average age 31. 216 applicants, 74% accepted, 115 enrolled. In 2017, 184 master's awarded. Terminal master's awarded for partial completion of doctoral program. *Degree requirements:* For master's, thesis optional, capstone course. *Entrance requirements:* For master's, 2 years of full-time work experience. Additional exam requirements/recommendations for international students: Required—TOEFL (minimum score 550 paper-based; 78 iBT). *Application deadline:* For fall admission, 8/1 priority date for domestic students; for spring admission, 12/1 priority date for domestic students. Applications are processed on a rolling basis. Application fee: $30. Electronic applications accepted. *Expenses:* $815 per credit hour, $15 technology fee for online sections. *Financial support:* Scholarships/grants, tuition waivers (partial), and unspecified assistantships available. Financial award application deadline: 4/15; financial award applicants required to submit FAFSA. *Faculty research:* Relationship marketing strategy, executive compensation and company performance, online marketplaces in electronic commerce, diversity training in campus recreation departments, entrepreneurship in developing and emerging economies. *Unit head:* Dr. Elad Granot, Dean, 419-289-5932, E-mail: egranot@ashland.edu. *Application contact:* Stephen W. Krispinsky, Executive Director of MBA Program, 419-289-5236, Fax: 419-289-5910, E-mail: skrispin@ashland.edu.
Website: http://www.mba.ashland.edu

Aspen University, Program in Business Administration, Denver, CO 80246-1930. Offers business administration (MBA); finance (MBA); information management (MBA); project management (MBA, Certificate). *Program availability:* Part-time, evening/weekend, online learning. *Entrance requirements:* Additional exam requirements/recommendations for international students: Required—TOEFL (minimum score 530 paper-based). Electronic applications accepted.

Athabasca University, Faculty of Business, Edmonton, AB T5L 4W1, Canada. Offers business administration (MBA); information technology management (MBA), including policing concentration; innovative management (DBA); management (GDM); project management (MBA, GDM). *Program availability:* Part-time, evening/weekend, online learning. *Degree requirements:* For master's, thesis or alternative, applied project. *Entrance requirements:* For master's, 3-8 years of managerial experience, 3 years with undergraduate degree, 5 years' managerial experience with professional designation, 8-10 years' management experience (on exception). Electronic applications accepted. *Expenses:* Contact institution. *Faculty research:* Human resources, project management, operations research, information technology management, corporate stewardship, energy management.

Avila University, School of Professional Studies, Kansas City, MO 64145-1698. Offers executive leadership (MS); fundraising (MA); instructional design and technology (MA, MS); leadership coaching (MS); project management (MA); strategic human resources (MS). *Program availability:* Part-time-only, evening/weekend, 100% online, blended/hybrid learning. *Faculty:* 14 part-time/adjunct (8 women). *Students:* 85 full-time (61 women), 45 part-time (33 women); includes 42 minority (35 Black or African American, non-Hispanic/Latino; 2 Asian, non-Hispanic/Latino; 4 Hispanic/Latino; 1 Two or more races, non-Hispanic/Latino), 3 international. Average age 37. 63 applicants, 60% accepted, 29 enrolled. In 2017, 39 master's awarded. *Degree requirements:* For master's, thesis optional. *Entrance requirements:* For master's, 2 letters of recommendation, minimum GPA of 3.0 during last 60 hours, resume, statement of intent. Additional exam requirements/recommendations for international students: Required—TOEFL (minimum score 550 paper-based; 79 iBT). *Application deadline:* Applications are processed on a rolling basis. Application fee: $0. Electronic applications accepted. *Expenses:* Contact institution. *Financial support:* In 2017–18, 14 students received support. Unspecified assistantships available. Support available to part-time students. Financial award applicants required to submit FAFSA. *Unit head:* Kari Clevenger, Associate Dean/Director, 816-501-3675, Fax: 816-941-4650, E-mail: advantage@avila.edu. *Application contact:* Jessica Burson, Graduate Admission Advisor, 816-501-2482, Fax: 816-941-4650, E-mail: advantage@avila.edu.
Website: https://www.avila.edu/mrk/advantage-3

Bellevue University, Graduate School, College of Information Technology, Bellevue, NE 68005-3098. Offers computer information systems (MS); cybersecurity (MS); management of information systems (MS); project management (MPM).

Boston University, Metropolitan College, Department of Administrative Sciences, Boston, MA 02215. Offers applied business analytics (MS); economic development and tourism management (MSAS); enterprise risk management (MS); financial management (MS); global marketing management (MS); innovation and technology (MSAS); insurance management (MS); project management (MS); supply chain management (MS). *Accreditation:* AACSB. *Program availability:* Part-time, evening/weekend, 100% online, blended/hybrid learning. *Faculty:* 21 full-time (5 women), 34 part-time/adjunct (5 women). *Students:* 297 full-time (156 women), 597 part-time (298 women); includes 183 minority (58 Black or African American, non-Hispanic/Latino; 2 American Indian or Alaska Native, non-Hispanic/Latino; 56 Asian, non-Hispanic/Latino; 51 Hispanic/Latino; 2 Native Hawaiian or other Pacific Islander, non-Hispanic/Latino; 14 Two or more races, non-Hispanic/Latino), 391 international. Average age 30. 963 applicants, 64% accepted, 209 enrolled. In 2017, 372 master's awarded. *Degree requirements:* For master's, thesis optional. *Entrance requirements:* For master's, 1 year of work experience, minimum GPA of 3.0. Additional exam requirements/recommendations for international students: Required—TOEFL (minimum score 84 iBT). *Application deadline:* Applications are processed on a rolling basis. Application fee: $85. Electronic applications accepted. *Expenses:* Contact institution. *Financial support:* In 2017–18, 15 students received support, including 18 research assistantships (averaging $8,400 per year), 12 teaching assistantships (averaging $2,700 per year); career-related internships or fieldwork, Federal Work-Study, and unspecified assistantships also available. Financial award applicants required to submit FAFSA. *Faculty research:* International business, innovative process. *Unit head:* Dr. John Sullivan, Chair, 617-353-3016, E-mail: adminsc@bu.edu. *Application contact:* Fiona Niven, Administrative Sciences Department, 617-353-3016, E-mail: adminsc@bu.edu.
Website: http://www.bu.edu/met/academic-community/departments/administrative-sciences/

Boston University, Metropolitan College, Department of Computer Science, Boston, MA 02215. Offers computer information systems (MS), including computer networks, data analytics, database management and business intelligence, health informatics, IT project management, security, Web application development; computer networks (Certificate); computer science (MS); data analytics (Certificate); digital forensics (Certificate); health informatics (Certificate); information technology project management (Certificate); software development (MS); software engineering in health care systems (Certificate); telecommunications (MS), including security. *Program availability:* Part-time, evening/weekend, online learning. *Faculty:* 10 full-time (2 women), 51 part-time/adjunct (5 women). *Students:* 109 full-time (39 women), 985 part-time (268 women); includes 286 minority (64 Black or African American, non-Hispanic/Latino; 3 American Indian or Alaska Native, non-Hispanic/Latino; 131 Asian, non-Hispanic/Latino; 73 Hispanic/Latino; 1 Native Hawaiian or other Pacific Islander, non-Hispanic/Latino; 14 Two or more races, non-Hispanic/Latino), 253 international. Average age 32. 952 applicants, 65% accepted, 230 enrolled. In 2017, 392 master's awarded. *Entrance requirements:* For master's and Certificate, official transcripts from regionally-accredited bachelor's degree program, 3 letters of recommendation, professional resume, personal statement. Additional exam requirements/recommendations for international students: Required—TOEFL (minimum score 84 iBT), IELTS. *Application deadline:* For fall admission, 6/1 priority date for international students; for spring admission, 10/1 priority date for international students. Applications are processed on a rolling basis. Application fee: $85. Electronic applications accepted. *Expenses:* Contact institution. *Financial support:* In 2017–18, 11 research assistantships (averaging $8,400 per year), 3 teaching assistantships (averaging $5,000 per year) were awarded; unspecified assistantships also available. Support available to part-time students. Financial award applicants required to submit FAFSA. *Faculty research:* Medical informatics, Web technologies, telecom and networks, security and forensics, software engineering, programming languages, multimedia and artificial intelligence (AI), information systems and IT project management. *Unit head:* Dr. Anatoly Temkin, Chair, 617-353-2566, Fax: 617-353-2367, E-mail: csinfo@bu.edu. *Application contact:* Lesley Moreau, Academic Program Coordinator, 617-353-2566, Fax: 617-353-2367, E-mail: metcs@bu.edu. Website: http://www.bu.edu/csmet/

Brandeis University, Rabb School of Continuing Studies, Division of Graduate Professional Studies, Master of Science Program in Project and Program Management, Waltham, MA 02454-9110. Offers MS. *Program availability:* Part-time-only. *Faculty:* 55 part-time/adjunct (18 women). *Students:* 138 part-time (84 women); includes 43 minority (25 Black or African American, non-Hispanic/Latino; 12 Asian, non-Hispanic/Latino; 6 Hispanic/Latino). Average age 38. 18 applicants, 89% accepted, 15 enrolled. In 2017, 32 master's awarded. *Entrance requirements:* For master's, four-year bachelor's degree from regionally-accredited U.S. institution or equivalent; official transcript(s) from every college or university attended; resume or curriculum vitae; statement of goals; letter of recommendation. Additional exam requirements/recommendations for international students: Required—TWE (minimum score 4.5), TOEFL (minimum scores: 600 paper-based, 100 iBT), IELTS (7), or PTE (68). *Application deadline:* For fall admission, 6/20 priority date for domestic and international students; for winter admission, 9/12 priority date for domestic and international students; for spring admission, 12/19 priority date for domestic and international students; for summer admission, 3/13 priority date for domestic and international students. Applications are processed on a rolling basis. Application fee: $75. Electronic applications accepted. *Expenses:* $1,178 per credit. *Financial support:* Applicants required to submit FAFSA. *Unit head:* Leanne Bateman, Program Chair, 781-736-8787, E-mail: lbateman@brandeis.edu. *Application contact:* Frances Stearns, Director of Student and Faculty Operations, 781-736-8785, E-mail: fstearns@brandeis.edu. Website: http://www.brandeis.edu/gps

Brenau University, Sydney O. Smith Graduate School, College of Business and Mass Communication, Gainesville, GA 30501. Offers accounting (MBA); business administration (MBA); healthcare management (MBA); organizational leadership (MBA); project management (MBA). *Accreditation:* ACBSP. *Program availability:* Part-time, evening/weekend, online learning. *Degree requirements:* For master's, comprehensive exam (for some programs). *Entrance requirements:* For master's, resume, minimum undergraduate GPA of 2.5. Additional exam requirements/recommendations for international students: Required—TOEFL (minimum score 500 paper-based; 61 iBT); Recommended—IELTS (minimum score 5). Electronic applications accepted. *Expenses:* Contact institution.

California Intercontinental University, School of Information Technology, Irvine, CA 92614. Offers information systems and enterprise resource management (DBA); information systems and knowledge management (MBA); project and quality management (MBA).

Capella University, School of Business and Technology, Doctoral Programs in Business, Minneapolis, MN 55402. Offers accounting (DBA, PhD); business intelligence (DBA); finance (DBA, PhD); general business management (PhD); human resource management (DBA, PhD); leadership (DBA, PhD); management education (PhD); marketing (DBA, PhD); project management (DBA, PhD); strategy and innovation (DBA, PhD). *Accreditation:* ACBSP.

Capella University, School of Business and Technology, Master's Programs in Business, Minneapolis, MN 55402. Offers accounting (MBA); business analysis (MS); business intelligence (MBA); entrepreneurship (MBA); finance (MBA); general business administration (MBA); general human resource management (MS); general leadership (MS); health care management (MBA); human resource management (MBA); marketing (MBA); project management (MBA, MS). *Accreditation:* ACBSP.

Carlow University, College of Leadership and Social Change, MBA Program, Pittsburgh, PA 15213-3165. Offers fraud and forensics (MBA); healthcare management (MBA); human resource management (MBA); leadership and management (MBA); project management (MBA). *Program availability:* Part-time, evening/weekend, 100% online, blended/hybrid learning. *Students:* 81 full-time (62 women), 28 part-time (18 women); includes 32 minority (26 Black or African American, non-Hispanic/Latino; 2 Asian, non-Hispanic/Latino; 1 Hispanic/Latino; 3 Two or more races, non-Hispanic/Latino). Average age 32. 46 applicants, 98% accepted, 32 enrolled. In 2017, 97 master's awarded. *Entrance requirements:* For master's, minimum undergraduate GPA of 3.0 (preferred); personal essay; resume; official transcripts; two professional recommendations. Additional exam requirements/recommendations for international students: Required—TOEFL (minimum score 550 paper-based). *Application deadline:* Applications are processed on a rolling basis. Electronic applications accepted. *Expenses: Tuition:* Full-time $12,103; part-time $825 per credit hour. Tuition and fees vary according to program. *Financial support:* Application deadline: 4/1; applicants required to submit FAFSA. *Unit head:* Dr. Howard Stern, Chair, MBA Program, 412-578-8828, E-mail: hastern@carlow.edu. *Application contact:* 412-578-6059, Fax: 412-578-6321, E-mail: gradstudies@carlow.edu. Website: http://www.carlow.edu/Business_Administration.aspx

The Catholic University of America, Busch School of Business and Economics, Washington, DC 20064. Offers accounting (MS); business analysis (MSBA); integral economic development management (MA); integral economic development policy (MA); management (MS), including Federal contract management, human resource management, leadership and management, project management, sales management. *Program availability:* Part-time. *Faculty:* 27 full-time (6 women), 45 part-time/adjunct (15 women). *Students:* 74 full-time (50 women), 9 part-time (3 women); includes 26 minority (5 Black or African American, non-Hispanic/Latino; 1 American Indian or Alaska Native, non-Hispanic/Latino; 3 Asian, non-Hispanic/Latino; 8 Two or more races, non-Hispanic/Latino), 18 international. Average age 31. 99 applicants, 86% accepted, 61 enrolled. In 2017, 46 master's awarded. *Degree requirements:* For master's, comprehensive exam (for some programs). *Entrance requirements:* For master's, GRE General Test, statement of purpose, official copies of academic transcripts, three letters of recommendation. Additional exam requirements/recommendations for international students: Required—TOEFL (minimum score 550 paper-based; 80 iBT). *Application deadline:* For fall admission, 7/15 priority date for domestic students, 7/1 for international students; for spring admission, 11/15 priority date for domestic students, 11/1 for international students. Applications are processed on a rolling basis. Application fee: $55. Electronic applications accepted. *Expenses:* Contact institution. *Financial support:* Fellowships, research assistantships, teaching assistantships, Federal Work-Study, scholarships/grants, tuition waivers (full and partial), and unspecified assistantships available. Financial award application deadline: 2/1; financial award applicants required to submit FAFSA. *Faculty research:* Integrity of the marketing process, economics of energy and the environment, emerging markets, social change, international finance and economic development. *Total annual research expenditures:* $31,390. *Unit head:* Dr. William Bowman, Dean, 202-319-5290, Fax: 202-319-4426, E-mail: otey@cua.edu. *Application contact:* Dr. Steven Brown, Director of Graduate Admissions, 202-319-5057, Fax: 202-319-6533, E-mail: cua-admissions@cua.edu. Website: https://business.catholic.edu/

The Catholic University of America, School of Engineering, Program in Engineering Management, Washington, DC 20064. Offers engineering management (MSE, Certificate),

including engineering management and organization (MSE), project and systems engineering management (MSE), technology management (MSE); program management (Certificate); systems engineering and management of information technology (Certificate). *Program availability:* Part-time. *Faculty:* 4 part-time/adjunct (0 women). *Students:* 11 full-time (4 women), 9 part-time (4 women); includes 2 minority (1 Hispanic/Latino; 1 Two or more races, non-Hispanic/Latino), 11 international. Average age 31. 29 applicants, 66% accepted, 8 enrolled. In 2017, 17 master's awarded. *Degree requirements:* For master's, minimum GPA of 3.0. *Entrance requirements:* For master's and Certificate, statement of purpose, official copies of academic transcripts, two letters of recommendation. Additional exam requirements/recommendations for international students: Required—TOEFL (minimum score 550 paper-based; 80 iBT). *Application deadline:* For fall admission, 7/15 priority date for domestic students, 7/1 for international students; for spring admission, 11/15 priority date for domestic students, 11/1 for international students. Applications are processed on a rolling basis. Application fee: $55. Electronic applications accepted. *Expenses:* Contact institution. *Financial support:* Fellowships, research assistantships, teaching assistantships, Federal Work-Study, scholarships/grants, tuition waivers (full and partial), and unspecified assistantships available. Financial award application deadline: 2/1; financial award applicants required to submit FAFSA. *Faculty research:* Engineering management and organization, project and systems engineering management, technology management. *Unit head:* Melvin G. Williams, Jr., Director, 202-319-5191, Fax: 202-319-6860, E-mail: williamsme@cua.edu. *Application contact:* Dr. Steven Brown, Director of Graduate Admissions, 202-319-5057, Fax: 202-319-6533, E-mail: cua-admissions@cua.edu. Website: https://engineering.catholic.edu/management/index.html

Christian Brothers University, School of Business, Memphis, TN 38104-5581. Offers accountancy (M Acc); business (MBA); international business (MIB); project management (Certificate); MBA/MIB. *Program availability:* Part-time, evening/weekend. *Entrance requirements:* For master's, GMAT, GRE. Additional exam requirements/recommendations for international students: Required—TOEFL.

The Citadel, The Military College of South Carolina, Citadel Graduate College, School of Engineering, Department of Engineering Leadership and Program Management, Charleston, SC 29409. Offers project management (MS); systems engineering management (Graduate Certificate); technical program management (Graduate Certificate); technical project management (Graduate Certificate). *Program availability:* Part-time, evening/weekend. *Entrance requirements:* For master's, GRE or GMAT, minimum of one year of professional experience or permission from department head; two letters of reference; resume detailing previous work; for Graduate Certificate, one-page letter of intent; resume detailing previous work. Additional exam requirements/recommendations for international students: Required—TOEFL (minimum score 550 paper-based; 79 iBT). Electronic applications accepted. *Expenses:* Tuition, state resident: part-time $587 per credit hour. Tuition, nonresident: part-time $988 per credit hour. *Required fees:* $90 per term.

City University of Seattle, Graduate Division, School of Management, Seattle, WA 98121. Offers accounting (Certificate); change leadership (MBA, Certificate); computer systems (MS); finance (Certificate); financial management (MBA); general management (MBA); general management-Europe (MBA); global marketing (MBA); human resources management (Certificate); individualized study (MBA); information security (MS); information systems (MBA); leadership (MA); marketing (MBA, Certificate); project management (MBA, MS, Certificate); sustainable business (Certificate); technology management (MBA, Certificate). *Program availability:* Part-time, evening/weekend, online learning. *Degree requirements:* For master's, comprehensive exam (for some programs), thesis (for some programs). *Entrance requirements:* For master's, baccalaureate degree or equivalent from an accredited or otherwise recognized institution. Additional exam requirements/recommendations for international students: Required—TOEFL (minimum score 567 paper-based; 87 iBT); Recommended—IELTS. Electronic applications accepted.

Colorado Christian University, Program in Business Administration, Lakewood, CO 80226. Offers corporate training (MA); information security (MA); leadership (MBA); project management (MBA). *Program availability:* Part-time, evening/weekend, online learning. *Degree requirements:* For master's, thesis optional. *Entrance requirements:* For master's, GMAT, 2 letters of recommendation, resume. Additional exam requirements/recommendations for international students: Required—TOEFL. Electronic applications accepted. *Expenses:* Contact institution.

Colorado State University–Global Campus, Graduate Programs, Greenwood Village, CO 80111. Offers criminal justice and law enforcement administration (MS); education leadership (MS); finance (MS); healthcare administration and management (MS); human resource management (MHRM); information technology management (MITM); international management (MS); management (MS); organizational leadership (MS); professional accounting (MPA); project management (MS); teaching and learning (MS). *Accreditation:* ACBSP. *Program availability:* Online learning.

Colorado Technical University Aurora, Programs in Business Administration and Management, Aurora, CO 80014. Offers accounting (MBA); business administration (MBA); business administration and management (EMBA); finance (MBA); human resource management (MBA); marketing (MBA); mediation and dispute resolution (MBA); operations management (MBA); project management (MBA); technology management (MBA). *Program availability:* Part-time, evening/weekend. *Degree requirements:* For master's, thesis or alternative. *Entrance requirements:* For master's, minimum undergraduate GPA of 3.0, resume.

Colorado Technical University Colorado Springs, Graduate Studies, Program in Management, Colorado Springs, CO 80907. Offers accounting (MBA, MSA); business administration (MBA); finance (MBA); human resources management (MBA); logistics/supply chain management (MBA); management (DM); marketing (MBA); mediation and dispute resolution (MBA); operations management (MBA); project management (MBA); technology management (MBA). *Accreditation:* ACBSP. *Program availability:* Part-time, evening/weekend, online learning. *Degree requirements:* For master's, thesis or alternative; for doctorate, thesis/dissertation. *Entrance requirements:* For doctorate, minimum graduate GPA of 3.0, 5 years of related work experience. *Faculty research:* Sexual harassment, performance evaluation, critical thinking.

Dallas Baptist University, College of Business, Master of Business Administration Program, Dallas, TX 75211-9299. Offers accounting (MBA); business communication (MBA); conflict resolution management (MBA); entrepreneurship (MBA); finance (MBA); health care management (MBA); international business (MBA); leading the non-profit organization (MBA); management (MBA); management information systems (MBA); marketing (MBA); project management (MBA); technology and engineering management (MBA). *Accreditation:* ACBSP. *Program availability:* Part-time, evening/weekend, 100% online, blended/hybrid learning. *Application deadline:* Applications are processed on a rolling basis. Application fee: $25. Electronic applications accepted. Application fee is waived when completed online. *Expenses: Tuition:* Full-time $16,308; part-time $906 per credit hour. *Required fees:* $900; $450 per semester. Tuition and fees vary according to course load and degree level. *Unit head:* Dr. Sandra Reid, Chair of Graduate Business Programs, 214-333-5280, E-mail: sandra@dbu.edu. *Application contact:* Bobby Soto, Director of Admissions, 214-333-5242, E-mail: graduate@dbu.edu. Website: http://www.dbu.edu/gsb/mba

Project Management

DeSales University, Division of Business, Center Valley, PA 18034-9568. Offers accounting (MBA); computer information systems (MBA); finance (MBA); health care systems management (MBA); human resources management (MBA); management (MBA); marketing (MBA); project management (MBA); self-design (MBA); supply chain management (MBA); DNP/MBA; MSN/MBA. *Accreditation:* ACBSP. *Program availability:* Part-time, evening/weekend, 100% online, blended/hybrid learning. *Faculty:* 9 full-time (3 women), 32 part-time/adjunct (8 women). *Students:* 78 full-time (44 women), 323 part-time (164 women); includes 71 minority (22 Black or African American, non-Hispanic/Latino; 17 Asian, non-Hispanic/Latino; 24 Hispanic/Latino; 8 Two or more races, non-Hispanic/Latino), 1 international. Average age 34. 213 applicants, 40% accepted, 64 enrolled. In 2017, 123 master's awarded. *Entrance requirements:* For master's, GMAT (waived if undergraduate GPA is 3.0 or better), minimum GPA of 3.0 in undergraduate work, literacy in basic software, background or interest in the field of study, personal statement, 2 years of work experience. Additional exam requirements/recommendations for international students: Required—TOEFL. *Application deadline:* Applications are processed on a rolling basis. Application fee: $50. Electronic applications accepted. *Expenses:* Contact institution. *Financial support:* Applicants required to submit FAFSA. *Faculty research:* Quality improvement, executive development, productivity, cross-cultural managerial differences, leadership. *Unit head:* Dr. David M. Gilfoil, Director, MBA Program, 610-282-1100 Ext. 1828, Fax: 610-282-2869, E-mail: david.gilfoil@desales.edu. *Application contact:* Julia Ferraro, Director of Graduate Admissions, 610-282-1100 Ext. 1768, E-mail: gradadmissions@desales.edu.

DeSales University, Division of Science and Mathematics, Center Valley, PA 18034-9568. Offers cyber security (Postbaccalaureate Certificate); data analytics (Postbaccalaureate Certificate); information systems (MS), including cyber security, digital forensics, healthcare information management, project management. *Program availability:* Part-time, evening/weekend, 100% online, blended/hybrid learning. *Faculty:* 1 (woman) full-time, 2 part-time/adjunct (0 women). *Students:* 8 full-time (0 women), 12 part-time (6 women); includes 3 minority (1 Asian, non-Hispanic/Latino; 1 Hispanic/Latino; 1 Two or more races, non-Hispanic/Latino), 1 international. Average age 35. 35 applicants, 31% accepted, 5 enrolled. In 2017, 6 master's awarded. *Entrance requirements:* For master's, GRE or GMAT, bachelor's degree in computer-related discipline from accredited college or university, minimum undergraduate GPA of 3.0, personal statement, three letters of recommendation. Additional exam requirements/recommendations for international students: Required—TOEFL. *Application deadline:* Applications are processed on a rolling basis. Application fee: $50. Electronic applications accepted. *Expenses:* Contact institution. *Financial support:* Applicants required to submit FAFSA. *Unit head:* Dr. Patricia Riola, Director/Assistant Professor of Computer Science, 610-282-1100 Ext. 1647, E-mail: patricia.riola@desales.edu. *Application contact:* Julia Ferraro, Director of Graduate Admissions, 610-282-1100 Ext. 1768, E-mail: gradadmissions@desales.edu.
Website: http://www.desales.edu/home/academics/graduate-studies/programs-of-study/msis—master-of-science-in-information-systems

DeVry University–Folsom Campus, Graduate Programs, Folsom, CA 95630. Offers accounting (M Acc); accounting and financial management (MAFM); business administration (MBA); curriculum leadership (M Ed); educational leadership (M Ed); educational technology (M Ed); higher education leadership (M Ed); human resource management (MHRM); information systems management (MISM); network and communications management (MNCM); project management (MPM); public administration (MPA).

Drexel University, Goodwin College of Professional Studies, School of Technology and Professional Studies, Philadelphia, PA 19104-2875. Offers construction management (MS); creativity and innovation (MS); engineering technology (MS); food science (MS); hospitality management (MS); professional studies: creativity studies (MS); professional studies: e-learning leadership (MS); professional studies: homeland security management (MS); project management (MS); property management (MS); sport management (MS). *Program availability:* Part-time, evening/weekend. *Entrance requirements:* Additional exam requirements/recommendations for international students: Required—TOEFL, IELTS. Electronic applications accepted. Application fee is waived when completed online.

Elmhurst College, Graduate Programs, Program in Project Management, Elmhurst, IL 60126-3296. Offers MPM. *Program availability:* Part-time, evening/weekend, online learning. *Faculty:* 1 (woman) full-time, 6 part-time/adjunct (2 women). *Students:* 4 part-time (1 woman). Average age 40. In 2017, 1 master's awarded. *Entrance requirements:* For master's, 3 recommendations, resume, statement of purpose. Additional exam requirements/recommendations for international students: Required—TOEFL (minimum score 550 paper-based; 79 iBT). *Application deadline:* Applications are processed on a rolling basis. Application fee: $0. Electronic applications accepted. *Expenses:* Contact institution. *Financial support:* In 2017–18, 2 students received support. Scholarships/grants available. Support available to part-time students. Financial award application deadline: 3/1; financial award applicants required to submit FAFSA. *Unit head:* Dr. Bruce Fischer, Director, 630-617-3408, E-mail: brucef@elmhurst.edu. *Application contact:* Timothy J. Panfil, Director of Enrollment Management, 630-617-3300 Ext. 3256, Fax: 630-617-6471, E-mail: panfilt@elmhurst.edu.
Website: http://www.elmhurst.edu/master_project_management

Embry-Riddle Aeronautical University–Worldwide, Department of Decision Sciences, Daytona Beach, FL 32114-3900. Offers aviation and aerospace (MSPM); aviation/aerospace management (MSEM); financial management (MSEM, MSPM); general management (MSPM); global management (MSPM); human resources management (MSPM); information systems (MSPM); leadership (MSEM, MSPM); logistics and supply chain management (MSEM, MSLSCM, MSPM); management (MSEM, MSPM); project management (MSEM); systems engineering (MSEM, MSPM); technical management (MSPM). *Program availability:* Part-time, evening/weekend, EagleVision Classroom (between classrooms), EagleVision Home (faculty and students at home), and a blend of Classroom or Home. *Faculty:* 12 full-time (3 women), 53 part-time/adjunct (10 women). *Students:* 514 full-time (141 women), 476 part-time (111 women); includes 337 minority (136 Black or African American, non-Hispanic/Latino; 6 American Indian or Alaska Native, non-Hispanic/Latino; 39 Asian, non-Hispanic/Latino; 81 Hispanic/Latino; 4 Native Hawaiian or other Pacific Islander, non-Hispanic/Latino; 71 Two or more races, non-Hispanic/Latino), 21 international. Average age 36. 297 applicants, 72% accepted, 209 enrolled. In 2017, 292 master's awarded. *Degree requirements:* For master's, comprehensive exam (for some programs), thesis (for some programs). *Entrance requirements:* Additional exam requirements/recommendations for international students: Required—TOEFL (minimum score 550 paper-based; 79 iBT), IELTS (minimum score 6). *Application deadline:* Applications are processed on a rolling basis. Application fee: $50. Electronic applications accepted. *Expenses:* Contact institution. *Financial support:* Career-related internships or fieldwork and scholarships/grants available. Financial award applicants required to submit FAFSA. *Unit head:* Aman Gupta, PhD, Department Chair, E-mail: aman.gupta@erau.edu. *Application contact:* Worldwide Campus, 800-522-6787, E-mail: worldwide@erau.edu.

Embry-Riddle Aeronautical University–Worldwide, Department of Management, Daytona Beach, FL 32114-3900. Offers global management (MS); human resources management (MS); leadership (MS); operations management (MS); project management (MS). *Program availability:* Part-time, evening/weekend, EagleVision Classroom (between classrooms), EagleVision Home (faculty and students at home), and a blend of Classroom or Home. *Students:* 148 full-time (48 women), 192 part-time (52 women); includes 91 minority (46 Black or African American, non-Hispanic/Latino; 1 American Indian or Alaska Native, non-Hispanic/Latino; 11 Asian, non-Hispanic/Latino; 16 Hispanic/Latino; 17 Two or more races, non-Hispanic/Latino), 7 international. Average age 39. In 2017, 104 master's awarded. *Entrance requirements:* Additional exam requirements/recommendations for international students: Required—TOEFL (minimum score 550 paper-based, 79 iBT) or IELTS (6). *Application deadline:* Applications are processed on a rolling basis. Application fee: $50. Electronic applications accepted. *Expenses:* Contact institution. *Financial support:* Career-related internships or fieldwork and scholarships/grants available. Financial award applicants required to submit FAFSA. *Unit head:* Thomas Henkel, PhD, Department Chair, E-mail: thomas.henkel@erau.edu. *Application contact:* Worldwide Campus, 800-522-6787, E-mail: worldwide@erau.edu.

Everglades University, Graduate Programs, Program in Business Administration, Boca Raton, FL 33431. Offers accounting for managers (MBA); aviation management (MBA); human resource management (MBA); project management (MBA). *Program availability:* Part-time, evening/weekend, 100% online. *Entrance requirements:* For master's, GMAT (minimum score of 400) or GRE (minimum score of 290), bachelor's or graduate degree from college accredited by an agency recognized by the U.S. Department of Education; minimum cumulative GPA of 2.0 at the baccalaureate level, 3.0 at the master's level. Additional exam requirements/recommendations for international students: Recommended—TOEFL (minimum score 500 paper-based). Electronic applications accepted. *Expenses:* Contact institution.

Ferris State University, College of Business, Big Rapids, MI 49307. Offers business intelligence (MBA); design and innovation management (MBA); incident response (MBA); information security and intelligence (MS), including business intelligence, incident response, project management; lean systems and leadership (MBA); performance metrics (MBA); project management (MBA); supply chain management and lean logistics (MBA). *Accreditation:* ACBSP. *Program availability:* Part-time, evening/weekend, 100% online, blended/hybrid learning. *Faculty:* 18 full-time (7 women), 6 part-time/adjunct (3 women). *Students:* 19 full-time (10 women), 73 part-time (45 women); includes 8 minority (1 Black or African American, non-Hispanic/Latino; 2 Asian, non-Hispanic/Latino; 3 Hispanic/Latino; 2 Two or more races, non-Hispanic/Latino), 12 international. Average age 32. 52 applicants, 77% accepted, 16 enrolled. In 2017, 88 master's awarded. *Degree requirements:* For master's, comprehensive exam, thesis. *Entrance requirements:* For master's, GRE or GMAT, minimum GPA of 3.0 in junior-/senior-level classes and overall; statement of purpose; 3 letters of reference; resume; transcripts. Additional exam requirements/recommendations for international students: Required—TOEFL (minimum score 500 paper-based; 70 iBT), IELTS (minimum score 6.5). *Application deadline:* For fall admission, 7/1 priority date for domestic students, 6/15 for international students; for winter admission, 11/1 priority date for domestic students, 10/15 for international students; for spring admission, 3/1 priority date for domestic students, 2/15 for international students. Applications are processed on a rolling basis. Application fee: $0 ($30 for international students). Electronic applications accepted. *Expenses:* Contact institution. *Financial support:* Career-related internships or fieldwork, Federal Work-Study, scholarships/grants, and unspecified assistantships available. Support available to part-time students. Financial award application deadline: 3/15; financial award applicants required to submit FAFSA. *Faculty research:* Lifestyle medicine business models, lean systems value chain optimization, digital forensics/incident response, location-based services, passive data capture and analysis. *Unit head:* Dr. David Nicol, College of Business Dean, 231-591-2168, Fax: 231-591-3521, E-mail: davidnicol@ferris.edu. *Application contact:* Dr. Greg Gogolin, Professor, 231-591-3159, Fax: 231-591-3521, E-mail: greggogolin@ferris.edu.
Website: http://cbgp.ferris.edu/

Florida Institute of Technology, Extended Studies Division, Melbourne, FL 32901-6975. Offers acquisition and contract management (MS); aerospace engineering (MS); business administration (MBA, DBA); computer information systems (MS); computer science (MS); electrical engineering (MS); engineering management (MS); human resources management (MS); logistics management (MS), including humanitarian and disaster relief logistics; management (MS), including acquisition and contract management, e-business, human resources management, information systems, logistics management, management, transportation management; material acquisition management (MS); mechanical engineering (MS); operations research (MS); project management (MS), including information systems, operations research; public administration (MPA); quality management (MS); software engineering (MS); space systems (MS); space systems management (MS); supply chain management (MS); systems management (MS), including information systems, operations research; technology management (MS). *Program availability:* Part-time, evening/weekend, online learning. *Students:* Average age 36. 962 applicants, 48% accepted, 323 enrolled. In 2017, 403 master's awarded. *Entrance requirements:* For master's, GMAT or resume showing 8 years of supervised experience, minimum GPA of 3.0, 2 letters of recommendation, resume. Additional exam requirements/recommendations for international students: Required—TOEFL (minimum score 550 paper-based; 79 iBT). *Application deadline:* For fall admission, 4/1 for international students; for spring admission, 9/30 for international students. Applications are processed on a rolling basis. Electronic applications accepted. *Expenses:* Contact institution. *Financial support:* Application deadline: 3/1; applicants required to submit FAFSA. *Unit head:* Dr. Theodore R. Richardson, III, Dean, 321-674-8123, Fax: 321-674-7597, E-mail: trichardson@fit.edu. *Application contact:* Carolyn Farrior, Director of Graduate Admissions, Online Learning and Off-Campus Programs, 321-674-7118, Fax: 321-674-8216, E-mail: cfarrior@fit.edu.
Website: http://es.fit.edu/

Geneva College, Program in Leadership Studies, Beaver Falls, PA 15010-3599. Offers business management (MS); ministry leadership (MS); non-profit leadership (MS); organizational management (MS); project management (MS). *Program availability:* Online only, 100% online. *Faculty:* 4 part-time/adjunct (1 woman). *Students:* 32 full-time (22 women); includes 10 minority (8 Black or African American, non-Hispanic/Latino; 1 Asian, non-Hispanic/Latino; 1 Hispanic/Latino). Average age 43. 25 applicants, 60% accepted, 11 enrolled. In 2017, 35 master's awarded. *Degree requirements:* For master's, thesis or alternative, capstone leadership studies project. *Entrance requirements:* For master's, undergraduate degree from regionally-accredited college or university, one to three years of experience in the workplace, minimum GPA of 3.0 (preferred), resume, essay, two recommendations. Additional exam requirements/recommendations for international students: Required—TOEFL. *Application deadline:* For fall admission, 9/21 for domestic students; for spring admission, 2/23 for domestic students; for summer admission, 7/22 for domestic students. Applications are processed on a rolling basis. Electronic applications accepted. *Expenses:* $640 per credit. *Financial support:* Scholarships/grants available. Financial award application deadline: 8/1; financial award applicants required to submit FAFSA. *Faculty research:* Servant leadership, leadership essentials. *Unit head:* John D. Gallo, Dean of Graduate, Adult and Online Programs, 800-576-3111, Fax: 724-847-6839, E-mail: msls@geneva.edu. *Application contact:* Graduate Enrollment Representative, 800-576-3111, Fax: 724-847-6839, E-mail: msls@geneva.edu.
Website: http://www.geneva.edu/graduate/leadership-studies/

George Mason University, Volgenau School of Engineering, Sid and Reva Dewberry Department of Civil, Environmental, and Infrastructure Engineering, Fairfax, VA 22030. Offers construction project management (MS); transportation engineering (PhD). *Faculty:* 14 full-time (4 women), 18 part-time/adjunct (7 women). *Students:* 55 full-time (20 women), 68 part-time (18 women); includes 26 minority (4 Black or African American, non-Hispanic/Latino; 10 Asian, non-Hispanic/Latino; 12 Hispanic/Latino), 42 international. Average age 29. 117 applicants, 67% accepted, 32 enrolled. In 2017, 30 master's, 1 doctorate awarded. *Degree requirements:* For master's, thesis (for some programs), 30 credits, departmental seminars; for doctorate, thesis/dissertation, qualifying exams. *Entrance requirements:* For master's, GRE, photocopy of passport; 2 official college transcripts; resume; official bank statement; proof of financial support; expanded goals statement; self-evaluation form; BS in engineering or other related science; 3 letters of recommendation; for doctorate, GRE (for those who received degree outside of the U.S.), photocopy of passport; 2 official college transcripts; resume; official bank statement; proof of financial support; expanded goals statement; self-evaluation form; baccalaureate degree in engineering or related science; master's degree (preferred); 3 letters of recommendation. Additional exam requirements/recommendations for international students: Required—TOEFL (minimum score 575 paper-based; 88 iBT), IELTS (minimum score 6.5), PTE (minimum score 59). *Application deadline:* For fall admission, 12/15 priority date for domestic and international students; for spring admission, 8/15 priority date for domestic and international students. Application fee: $75 ($80 for international students). Electronic applications accepted. *Expenses:* $695 per credit in-state tuition. *Financial support:* In 2017–18, 28 students received support, including 17 research assistantships with tuition reimbursements available (averaging $20,618 per year), 11 teaching assistantships with tuition reimbursements available (averaging $19,110 per year); career-related internships or fieldwork, Federal Work-Study, scholarships/grants, unspecified assistantships, and health care benefits (for full-time research or teaching assistantship recipients) also available. Support available to part-time students. Financial award application deadline: 3/1; financial award applicants required to submit FAFSA. *Faculty research:* Evolutionary design, infrastructure security, intelligent transportation systems, national transportation networks, water quality modeling. *Total annual research expenditures:* $1.6 million. *Unit head:* LIza Wilson Durant, Acting Chair, 703-993-1687, Fax: 703-993-9790, E-mail: ldurant2@gmu.edu. *Application contact:* Laura Kosoglu, Director, Graduate Program, 703-993-1675, Fax: 703-993-9790, E-mail: ceiegrad@gmu.edu.
Website: http://civil.gmu.edu/

The George Washington University, School of Business, Department of Decision Sciences, Washington, DC 20052. Offers business analytics (MS, Certificate); project management (MS). *Program availability:* Online learning. *Faculty:* 17 full-time (1 woman), 4 part-time/adjunct (1 woman). *Students:* 84 full-time (44 women), 131 part-time (65 women); includes 57 minority (30 Black or African American, non-Hispanic/Latino; 1 American Indian or Alaska Native, non-Hispanic/Latino; 13 Asian, non-Hispanic/Latino; 8 Hispanic/Latino; 5 Two or more races, non-Hispanic/Latino), 105 international. Average age 33. 914 applicants, 44% accepted, 80 enrolled. In 2017, 97 master's, 65 other advanced degrees awarded. Application fee: $75. *Expenses:* Tuition: Full-time $28,800; part-time $1655 per credit hour. *Required fees:* $45; $2.75 per credit hour. *Financial support:* Tuition waivers available. *Unit head:* Prof. Refik Soyer, Chair, 202-994-6445, E-mail: soyer@gwu.edu. *Application contact:* Christopher Storer, Executive Director, Graduate Admissions, 202-994-1212, E-mail: gwmba@gwu.edu.
Website: http://business.gwu.edu/decisionsciences/

The George Washington University, School of Business, Department of Information Systems and Technology Management, Washington, DC 20052. Offers information and decision systems (PhD); information systems (MSIST); information systems development (MSIST); information systems management (MBA); information systems project management (MSIST); management information systems (MSIST); management of science, technology, and innovation (MBA, PhD). Programs also offered in Ashburn and Arlington, VA. *Program availability:* Part-time, evening/weekend, online learning. *Faculty:* 13 full-time (4 women), 3 part-time/adjunct (1 woman). *Students:* 108 full-time (49 women), 75 part-time (35 women); includes 48 minority (15 Black or African American, non-Hispanic/Latino; 28 Asian, non-Hispanic/Latino; 4 Hispanic/Latino; 1 Two or more races, non-Hispanic/Latino), 100 international. Average age 29. 425 applicants, 60% accepted, 68 enrolled. In 2017, 92 master's awarded. *Entrance requirements:* For master's, GMAT. Additional exam requirements/recommendations for international students: Required—TOEFL. *Application deadline:* For fall admission, 4/1 priority date for domestic students; for spring admission, 10/1 for domestic students. Applications are processed on a rolling basis. Application fee: $75. *Expenses:* Tuition: Full-time $28,800; part-time $1655 per credit hour. *Required fees:* $45; $2.75 per credit hour. *Financial support:* In 2017–18, 35 students received support. Fellowships, teaching assistantships, career-related internships or fieldwork, Federal Work-Study, institutionally sponsored loans, and tuition waivers available. Financial award application deadline: 4/1. *Faculty research:* Expert systems, decision support systems. *Unit head:* Richard Donnelly, Chair, 202-994-7155, E-mail: rgd@gwu.edu. *Application contact:* Christopher Storer, Executive Director, Graduate Admissions, 202-994-1212, E-mail: gwmba@gwu.edu.

Golden Gate University, Ageno School of Business, San Francisco, CA 94105-2968. Offers accounting (MBA); adaptive leadership (MBA); advanced financial planning (MS); business administration (EMBA, MBA, DBA); business analytics (MBA, MS); entrepreneurship (MBA); finance (MBA, MS, Certificate); financial life planning (Certificate); financial planning (MS, Certificate); global supply chain management (MBA, Certificate); human resource management (MBA, MS, Certificate); information technology management (MBA, MS, Certificate); international business (MBA); marketing (MBA, MS, Certificate); project management (MBA, MS, Certificate); psychology (MA, Certificate); public administration (EMPA, MBA); public administration leadership (Certificate); JD/MBA. *Program availability:* Part-time, evening/weekend. *Faculty:* 17 full-time (7 women), 280 part-time/adjunct (95 women). *Students:* 309 full-time (147 women), 527 part-time (266 women); includes 286 minority (56 Black or African American, non-Hispanic/Latino; 1 American Indian or Alaska Native, non-Hispanic/Latino; 131 Asian, non-Hispanic/Latino; 83 Hispanic/Latino; 4 Native Hawaiian or other Pacific Islander, non-Hispanic/Latino; 11 Two or more races, non-Hispanic/Latino), 209 international. Average age 35. 549 applicants, 66% accepted, 185 enrolled. *Degree requirements:* For doctorate, thesis/dissertation, qualifying examination. *Entrance requirements:* For master's, GMAT (for MBA), minimum GPA of 2.5 (MS). Additional exam requirements/recommendations for international students: Required—TOEFL (minimum score 550 paper-based; 79 iBT). *Application deadline:* For fall admission, 5/15 for domestic and international students; for winter admission, 1/15 for domestic and international students; for spring admission, 9/15 for domestic and international students. Applications are processed on a rolling basis. Application fee: $65 ($105 for international students). Electronic applications accepted. *Expenses:* $3,150 per 3-unit course. *Financial support:* Career-related internships or fieldwork, Federal Work-Study, institutionally sponsored loans, and scholarships/grants available. Support available to part-time students. Financial award applicants required to submit FAFSA. *Unit head:* Marianne Koch, Associate Dean, 415-442-6542, Fax: 415-442-6579, E-mail: mkoch@ggu.edu. *Application contact:* Angela Melero, Enrollment Services, 415-442-7800, Fax: 415-442-7807, E-mail: info@ggu.edu.
Website: http://www.ggu.edu/programs/business-and-management

Grand Canyon University, Colangelo College of Business, Phoenix, AZ 85017-1097. Offers accounting (MBA, MS); business analytics (MS); disaster preparedness and executive fire service leadership (MS); finance (MBA); general management (MBA); health systems management (MBA); information technology management (MS); leadership (MBA, MS); marketing (MBA); organizational leadership and entrepreneurship (MS); project management (MBA); sports business (MBA); strategic human resource management (MBA). *Accreditation:* ACBSP. *Program availability:* Part-time, evening/weekend, online learning. *Entrance requirements:* For master's, equivalent of two years' full-time professional work experience. Additional exam requirements/recommendations for international students: Required—TOEFL (minimum score 575 paper-based; 90 iBT), IELTS (minimum score 7). Electronic applications accepted.

Granite State College, MS in Project Management Program, Concord, NH 03301. Offers MS. *Program availability:* Part-time, 100% online, blended/hybrid learning. *Faculty:* 1 (woman) full-time, 7 part-time/adjunct (4 women). *Students:* 9 full-time (5 women), 22 part-time (10 women); includes 2 minority (1 Black or African American, non-Hispanic/Latino; 1 American Indian or Alaska Native, non-Hispanic/Latino). Average age 38. 9 applicants, 100% accepted, 9 enrolled. In 2017, 23 master's awarded. *Degree requirements:* For master's, capstone. *Entrance requirements:* For master's, bachelor's degree with minimum GPA of 3.0 on last 60 credit hours, 500-1000 word statement of purpose, two letters of professional or academic reference, resume, official transcripts. Additional exam requirements/recommendations for international students: Required—TOEFL (minimum score 80 iBT), IELTS (minimum score 6.5). *Application deadline:* Applications are processed on a rolling basis. Application fee: $0. Electronic applications accepted. *Expenses:* Tuition, state resident: full-time $9450; part-time $525 per credit. Tuition, nonresident: full-time $10,080; part-time $560 per credit. *Financial support:* Federal Work-Study and National Guard course waivers available. Financial award applicants required to submit FAFSA. *Unit head:* Dr. Johnna Herrick-Phelps, Vice Provost for Academic Affairs, 855-228-3000, E-mail: johnna.herrick-phelps@granite.edu. *Application contact:* Ana Gonzalez, Administrative Assistant, Office of Graduate Studies, 603-513-1334, Fax: 603-513-1387, E-mail: gsc.graduatestudies@granite.edu.
Website: https://www.granite.edu/degree-programs/masters-degrees/project-management/

Grantham University, College of Engineering and Computer Science, Lenexa, KS 66219. Offers information management (MS), including project management; information management technology (MS); information technology (MS). *Program availability:* Part-time, evening/weekend, online only, 100% online. *Faculty:* 1 full-time, 23 part-time/adjunct. *Students:* 167 full-time (52 women), 80 part-time (15 women); includes 131 minority (94 Black or African American, non-Hispanic/Latino; 2 American Indian or Alaska Native, non-Hispanic/Latino; 8 Asian, non-Hispanic/Latino; 16 Hispanic/Latino; 11 Two or more races, non-Hispanic/Latino). Average age 41. 56 applicants, 86% accepted, 42 enrolled. In 2017, 71 master's awarded. *Degree requirements:* For master's, comprehensive exam (for some programs), Project Management: PMP Prep Exam (for information management). *Entrance requirements:* For master's, baccalaureate or master's degree with minimum cumulative GPA of 2.5 from institution accredited by agency recognized by U.S. DOE or foreign equivalent; official transcripts showing proof of degree. Additional exam requirements/recommendations for international students: Required—TOEFL (minimum score 530 paper-based; 71 iBT), IELTS (minimum score 6.5), PTE (minimum score 50). *Application deadline:* Applications are processed on a rolling basis. Application fee: $0. Electronic applications accepted. *Expenses:* $325 per credit hour. *Financial support:* Scholarships/grants available. Financial award applicants required to submit FAFSA. *Faculty research:* Sensor networks and security, grid technologies, cloud computing. *Unit head:* Dr. Nancy Miller, Dean of the College of Engineering and Computer Science, 913-309-4738, Fax: 855-681-5201, E-mail: nmiller@grantham.edu. *Application contact:* Jared Parlette, Vice President of Student Enrollment, 800-955-2527 Ext. 803, Fax: 866-914-4557, E-mail: admissions@grantham.edu.
Website: http://www.grantham.edu/engineering-and-computer-science/

Grantham University, Mark Skousen School of Business, Lenexa, KS 66219. Offers business administration (MBA); business intelligence (MS); human resources (Certificate); information management (MBA); performance improvement (MS); project management (MBA, Certificate). *Program availability:* Part-time, evening/weekend, online only, 100% online. *Faculty:* 1 full-time, 34 part-time/adjunct. *Students:* 610 full-time (231 women), 333 part-time (128 women); includes 466 minority (321 Black or African American, non-Hispanic/Latino; 12 American Indian or Alaska Native, non-Hispanic/Latino; 29 Asian, non-Hispanic/Latino; 71 Hispanic/Latino; 4 Native Hawaiian or other Pacific Islander, non-Hispanic/Latino; 29 Two or more races, non-Hispanic/Latino). Average age 40. 273 applicants, 87% accepted, 202 enrolled. In 2017, 362 master's awarded. *Degree requirements:* For master's, comprehensive exam (for some programs), PMP Prep Exams throughout the term (for MBA in project management); for Certificate, comprehensive exam (for some programs), PMP Prep Exam (for project management). *Entrance requirements:* For master's, baccalaureate or master's degree with minimum cumulative GPA of 2.5 from institution accredited by agency recognized by U.S. DOE or foreign equivalent; official transcripts showing proof of degree. Additional exam requirements/recommendations for international students: Required—TOEFL (minimum score 530 paper-based; 71 iBT), IELTS (minimum score 6.5), PTE (minimum score 50). *Application deadline:* Applications are processed on a rolling basis. Application fee: $0. Electronic applications accepted. *Expenses:* $325 per credit hour. *Financial support:* Scholarships/grants available. Financial award applicants required to submit FAFSA. *Faculty research:* How chronic diseases contribute to the rising costs of healthcare, marketing for entrepreneurs, managers' hiring practices of workers with disability, organizational structures, organizational change, online pedagogy, impact of instructor video tips in the online classroom, decision-making techniques. *Unit head:* Dr. David Marker, Dean of the Mark Skousen School of Business, 913-309-4747, Fax: 844-260-6287, E-mail: dmarker@grantham.edu. *Application contact:* Jared Parlette, Vice President of Student Enrollment, 800-955-2527 Ext. 803, Fax: 866-914-4557, E-mail: admissions@grantham.edu.
Website: https://www.grantham.edu/school-of-business/

Harrisburg University of Science and Technology, Program in Project Management, Harrisburg, PA 17101. Offers information technology (MS). *Program availability:* Part-time, evening/weekend. *Degree requirements:* For master's, thesis optional. *Entrance requirements:* For master's, baccalaureate degree. Additional exam requirements/recommendations for international students: Required—TOEFL (minimum score 520 paper-based; 80 iBT); Recommended—IELTS (minimum score 6). Electronic applications accepted. *Faculty research:* Strategic planning, organizational development.

Herzing University Online, Program in Business Administration, Menomonee Falls, WI 53051. Offers accounting (MBA); business administration (MBA); business management (MBA); healthcare management (MBA); human resources (MBA); marketing (MBA); project management (MBA); technology management (MBA). *Program availability:* Online learning.

Project Management

Hult International Business School, Graduate Programs, Cambridge, MA 02141. Offers business administration (EMBA); business analytics (MBA, MIB); business statistics (MBS); disruptive innovation (MDI); entrepreneurship (MBA, MIB); family business (MBA, MIB); finance (MBA, MF, MIB); international marketing (MIM); marketing (MBA, MIB); project management (MBA, MIB). MDI and MBS offered in San Francisco; MBA also offered in Boston, San Francisco, Dubai, Shanghai, and New York. *Entrance requirements:* For master's, GMAT, 3 years of work experience. Additional exam requirements/recommendations for international students: Required—TOEFL. Electronic applications accepted. *Expenses:* Contact institution.

IGlobal University, Graduate Programs, Vienna, VA 22182. Offers accounting (MBA); data management and analytics (MSIT); entrepreneurship (MBA); finance (MBA); global business management (MBA); health care management (MBA); hospitality and tourism management (MBA); human resources management (MBA); information technology (MBA); information technology systems and management (MSIT); leadership and management (MBA); project management (MBA); public service and administration (MBA); software design and management (MSIT).

Iona College, School of Business, Department of Information Systems, New Rochelle, NY 10801-1890. Offers accounting and information systems (MS); business continuity and risk management (AC); information systems (MBA, MS, PMC); project management (MS). *Program availability:* Part-time, evening/weekend. *Faculty:* 7 full-time (1 woman), 1 part-time/adjunct (0 women). *Students:* 15 full-time (7 women), 8 part-time (3 women); includes 5 minority (3 Asian, non-Hispanic/Latino; 2 Hispanic/Latino), 3 international. Average age 26. 13 applicants, 92% accepted, 8 enrolled. In 2017, 15 master's, 1 other advanced degree awarded. *Entrance requirements:* For master's, GMAT, 2 letters of recommendation, minimum GPA of 3.0; for other advanced degree, GMAT, minimum GPA of 3.0. Additional exam requirements/recommendations for international students: Required—TOEFL (minimum score 550 paper-based; 80 iBT), IELTS (minimum score 6.5). *Application deadline:* For fall admission, 8/15 priority date for domestic students, 8/1 priority date for international students; for winter admission, 11/15 priority date for domestic students, 11/1 priority date for international students; for spring admission, 2/15 priority date for domestic students, 2/1 priority date for international students; for summer admission, 5/15 priority date for domestic students, 5/1 priority date for international students. Applications are processed on a rolling basis. Application fee: $50. Electronic applications accepted. *Expenses:* Contact institution. *Financial support:* In 2017–18, 4 students received support. Scholarships/grants, tuition waivers (partial), and unspecified assistantships available. Support available to part-time students. Financial award application deadline: 4/15; financial award applicants required to submit FAFSA. *Faculty research:* Fuzzy sets, risk management, computer security, competence set analysis, investment strategies. *Unit head:* Dr. Shoshana Altschuller, Department Chair, 914-637-7726, E-mail: saltschuller@iona.edu. *Application contact:* Katelyn Brunck, Director of MBA Admissions, 914-633-2451, Fax: 914-633-2277, E-mail: kbrunck@iona.edu.
Website: http://www.iona.edu/Academics/Hagan-School-of-Business/Departments/Information-Systems/Graduate-Programs.aspx

King University, School of Business and Economics, Bristol, TN 37620-2699. Offers accounting (MBA); finance (MBA); healthcare management (MBA); human resources management (MBA); leadership (MBA); management (MBA); marketing (MBA); project management (MBA). *Program availability:* Part-time, evening/weekend, online learning. *Degree requirements:* For master's, comprehensive exam, thesis optional. *Entrance requirements:* For master's, GMAT, 2 years of work experience. Additional exam requirements/recommendations for international students: Required—TOEFL (minimum score 550 paper-based). Electronic applications accepted. *Faculty research:* International monetary policy.

Lakeland University, Graduate Studies Division, Program in Business Administration, Plymouth, WI 53073. Offers accounting (MBA); finance (MBA); healthcare management (MBA); project management (MBA). *Entrance requirements:* For master's, GMAT. *Expenses:* Contact institution.

Lasell College, Graduate and Professional Studies in Management, Newton, MA 02466-2709. Offers business administration (MBA); elder care management (MSM); hospitality and event management (MSM); human resources management (MSM, Graduate Certificate); management (MSM, Graduate Certificate); marketing (MS, Graduate Certificate); project management (MSM, Graduate Certificate). *Accreditation:* ACBSP. *Program availability:* Part-time, evening/weekend, 100% online, blended/hybrid learning. *Faculty:* 1 full-time (0 women), 15 part-time/adjunct (11 women). *Students:* 41 full-time (25 women), 102 part-time (70 women); includes 34 minority (19 Black or African American, non-Hispanic/Latino; 5 Asian, non-Hispanic/Latino; 8 Hispanic/Latino; 2 Two or more races, non-Hispanic/Latino), 29 international. Average age 32. 128 applicants, 46% accepted, 38 enrolled. In 2017, 66 master's, 3 other advanced degrees awarded. *Degree requirements:* For master's, minimum GPA of 3.0; internship or research paper (for MSM). *Entrance requirements:* For master's, one-page personal statement, 2 letters of recommendation, resume, bachelor's degree transcript; proof of microeconomics and statistics (for MBA); for Graduate Certificate, bachelor's degree transcript, 2 letters of recommendation, 1-page personal statement, resume. Additional exam requirements/recommendations for international students: Required—TOEFL (minimum score 550 paper-based, 79 iBT) or IELTS (minimum score 6). *Application deadline:* For fall admission, 8/31 priority date for domestic students, 6/30 priority date for international students; for spring admission, 12/31 priority date for domestic students, 10/31 priority date for international students. Applications are processed on a rolling basis. Electronic applications accepted. *Expenses:* $600 per credit. *Financial support:* Federal Work-Study, scholarships/grants, and tuition discounts available. Support available to part-time students. Financial award application deadline: 8/31; financial award applicants required to submit FAFSA. *Unit head:* Eric Turner, Vice President of Graduate and Professional Studies, 617-243-2071, Fax: 617-243-2450, E-mail: gradinfo@lasell.edu. *Application contact:* Adrienne Franciosi, Director of Graduate Enrollment, 617-243-2214, Fax: 617-243-2450, E-mail: gradinfo@lasell.edu.
Website: http://www.lasell.edu/academics/graduate-and-professional-studies/programs-of-study/master-of-science-in-management.html

Lawrence Technological University, College of Management, Southfield, MI 48075-1058. Offers business administration (MBA, DBA), including business analytics (MBA, MS), cybersecurity (MBA, MS), finance (MBA), information systems (MBA), information technology (MBA), marketing (MBA), project management (MBA, MS); cybersecurity (Graduate Certificate); health IT management (Graduate Certificate); information assurance mangement (Graduate Certificate); information systems (MS), including enterprise resource planning, enterprise security management, project management (MBA, MS); information technology (MS, DM), including business analytics (MBA, MS), cybersecurity (MBA, MS), information assurance (MS), project management (MBA, MS); management (PhD); nonprofit management and leadership (Graduate Certificate); operations management (MS), including manufacturing operations, service operations; project management (Graduate Certificate). *Accreditation:* ACBSP. *Program availability:* Part-time, evening/weekend, 100% online. *Faculty:* 13 full-time (6 women), 7 part-time/adjunct (1 woman). *Students:* 8 full-time (3 women), 280 part-time (102 women); includes 70 minority (34 Black or African American, non-Hispanic/Latino; 2 American Indian or Alaska Native, non-Hispanic/Latino; 18 Asian, non-Hispanic/Latino; 11

Hispanic/Latino; 5 Two or more races, non-Hispanic/Latino), 73 international. Average age 34. 143 applicants, 50% accepted, 68 enrolled. In 2017, 114 master's, 7 doctorates, 10 other advanced degrees awarded. Terminal master's awarded for partial completion of doctoral program. *Degree requirements:* For master's, thesis (for some programs); for doctorate, comprehensive exam, thesis/dissertation. *Entrance requirements:* Additional exam requirements/recommendations for international students: Required—TOEFL (minimum score 550 paper-based; 79 iBT), IELTS (minimum score 6.5). *Application deadline:* For fall admission, 5/27 for international students; for spring admission, 10/8 for international students; for summer admission, 2/14 for international students. Applications are processed on a rolling basis. Application fee: $50. Electronic applications accepted. *Expenses: Tuition:* Full-time $15,274; part-time $1091 per credit. One-time fee: $150. *Financial support:* In 2017–18, 35 students received support, including 8 research assistantships with partial tuition reimbursements available (averaging $3,360 per year); career-related internships or fieldwork, unspecified assistantships, and corporate tuition incentives also available. Financial award application deadline: 4/1; financial award applicants required to submit FAFSA. *Faculty research:* Cybersecurity; risk management; IT governance; security controls and countermeasures; threat modeling cyber resilience; autonomous cars; natural language processing; text mining; machine learning; reflective leadership; emerging leadership theories and practice; motivational studies; teaching effectiveness strategies; teamwork; organization development; strategic planning; strengths-based and positive organizational scholarship; global leadership; globalization; corporate governance. *Unit head:* Dr. Bahman Mirshab, Dean, 248-204-3050, E-mail: mgtdean@ltu.edu. *Application contact:* Jane Rohrback, Director of Admissions, 248-204-3160, Fax: 248-204-2228, E-mail: admissions@ltu.edu.
Website: http://www.ltu.edu/management/index.asp

Lebanon Valley College, Program in Business Administration, Annville, PA 17003-1400. Offers business administration (MBA); healthcare management (MBA); human resources (MBA); leadership and ethics (MBA); project management (MBA). *Program availability:* Part-time, evening/weekend. *Faculty:* 7 full-time (1 woman), 8 part-time/adjunct (1 woman). *Students:* 11 full-time (5 women), 66 part-time (28 women); includes 11 minority (3 Black or African American, non-Hispanic/Latino; 4 Asian, non-Hispanic/Latino; 4 Hispanic/Latino), 3 international. Average age 34. 21 applicants, 81% accepted, 16 enrolled. In 2017, 32 master's awarded. *Degree requirements:* For master's, capstone course. *Entrance requirements:* For master's, GMAT, 3 years of work experience, resume, professional statement (application form, resume, personal statement, transcripts). Additional exam requirements/recommendations for international students: Required—TOEFL (minimum score 80 iBT), IELTS (minimum score 6.5) or STEP Eiken (grade 1). *Application deadline:* Applications are processed on a rolling basis. Application fee: $0. Electronic applications accepted. *Expenses:* $660 per credit hour. *Financial support:* Career-related internships or fieldwork and scholarships/grants available. Financial award application deadline: 3/1; financial award applicants required to submit FAFSA. *Faculty research:* Leadership, motivation, BI, information systems strategies, emerging market development, the role of informational business education, economic growth. *Unit head:* Dr. David Setley, Associate Professor/Chair of Business Administration/Director of the MBA Program, 717-867-6104, Fax: 717-867-6018, E-mail: setley@lvc.edu. *Application contact:* Christine M. Martin, Enrollment and Operations Specialist, 717-867-6486, Fax: 717-867-6013, E-mail: cmartin@lvc.edu.
Website: http://www.lvc.edu/mba

Lehigh University, College of Business and Economics, Department of Management, Bethlehem, PA 18015. Offers business administration (MBA); project management (MBA); MBA/E; MBA/M Ed. *Accreditation:* AACSB. *Program availability:* Part-time, evening/weekend, synchronous with live class. *Faculty:* 11 full-time (2 women), 1 part-time/adjunct (0 women). *Students:* 42 full-time (20 women), 158 part-time (40 women); includes 35 minority (6 Black or African American, non-Hispanic/Latino; 15 Asian, non-Hispanic/Latino; 10 Hispanic/Latino; 4 Two or more races, non-Hispanic/Latino), 20 international. Average age 33. 194 applicants, 68% accepted, 40 enrolled. In 2017, 70 master's awarded. *Entrance requirements:* For master's, GMAT or GRE. Additional exam requirements/recommendations for international students: Required—TOEFL (minimum score 600 paper-based; 94 iBT), IELTS (minimum score 7). *Application deadline:* For fall admission, 7/15 for domestic students, 5/1 for international students; for spring admission, 12/1 for domestic students. Application fee: $75. Electronic applications accepted. *Financial support:* In 2017–18, 33 students received support, including 10 fellowships (averaging $5,250 per year); teaching assistantships, scholarships/grants, health care benefits, tuition waivers (partial), and unspecified assistantships also available. Support available to part-time students. Financial award application deadline: 1/15. *Faculty research:* Information systems, organizational behavior, supply chain management, strategic management, entrepreneurship. *Unit head:* Dr. Yuliang Yao, Department Chair, 610-758-6726, Fax: 610-758-6941, E-mail: yuy3@lehigh.edu. *Application contact:* Michael Tarantino, Director of Recruitment and Admissions, 610-758-3418, Fax: 610-758-5283, E-mail: mgt215@lehigh.edu.
Website: http://www4.lehigh.edu/business/academics/depts/management

Lewis University, College of Business, Program in Business Administration, Romeoville, IL 60446. Offers accounting (MBA); custom elective option (MBA); e-business (MBA); finance (MBA); healthcare management (MBA); human resources management (MBA); international business (MBA); management information systems (MBA); marketing (MBA); project management (MBA); technology and operations management (MBA). *Program availability:* Part-time, evening/weekend. *Students:* 130 full-time (77 women), 187 part-time (107 women); includes 83 minority (27 Black or African American, non-Hispanic/Latino; 3 American Indian or Alaska Native, non-Hispanic/Latino; 7 Asian, non-Hispanic/Latino; 40 Hispanic/Latino; 6 Two or more races, non-Hispanic/Latino), 31 international. Average age 31. In 2017, 99 master's awarded. *Degree requirements:* For master's, comprehensive exam. *Entrance requirements:* For master's, interview, bachelor's degree, resume, two recommendations. Additional exam requirements/recommendations for international students: Required—TOEFL (minimum score 550 paper-based), IELTS. *Application deadline:* For fall admission, 8/15 priority date for domestic students, 5/1 priority date for international students; for spring admission, 11/15 priority date for international students. Applications are processed on a rolling basis. Application fee: $40. Electronic applications accepted. Tuition and fees vary according to program. *Financial support:* Career-related internships or fieldwork, Federal Work-Study, scholarships/grants, and unspecified assistantships available. Financial award application deadline: 5/1; financial award applicants required to submit FAFSA. *Unit head:* Dr. Maureen Culleeney, Academic Program Director, 815-838-0500 Ext. 5631, E-mail: culleema@lewisu.edu. *Application contact:* Michele Ryan, Director of Admission, 815-838-0500 Ext. 5384, E-mail: ryanml@lewisu.edu.

Lewis University, College of Business, Program in Project Management, Romeoville, IL 60446. Offers MS. *Program availability:* Part-time, evening/weekend, 100% online, blended/hybrid learning. *Students:* 5 full-time (3 women), 18 part-time (9 women); includes 6 minority (3 Black or African American, non-Hispanic/Latino; 3 Hispanic/Latino). Average age 34. *Entrance requirements:* For master's, bachelor's degree, interview, resume, statement of purpose, 2 letters of recommendation, minimum GPA of 2.75. Additional exam requirements/recommendations for international students: Required—TOEFL (minimum score 550 paper-based; 80 iBT). *Application deadline:* For fall admission, 5/1 priority date for international students; for spring admission, 11/15 priority date for international students. Applications are processed on a rolling basis. Application fee: $40. Electronic applications accepted. Tuition and fees vary according to program. *Financial support:* Career-related internships or fieldwork, Federal Work-Study, and unspecified assistantships available. Support available to part-time students. Financial award application deadline: 5/1; financial award applicants required to submit FAFSA. *Unit head:* Rev. Dr. Kevin Spiess, Academic Program Director, 815-838-0500 Ext. 5399, E-mail: spiesske@lewisu.edu. *Application contact:* Michele Ryan, Director of Admission, 815-838-0500 Ext. 5384, E-mail: gsm@lewisu.edu.

Liberty University, School of Business, Lynchburg, VA 24515. Offers accounting (MBA, MS), including audit and financial reporting (MS), business (MS), financial services (MS), forensic accounting (MS), leadership (MS), taxation (MS); criminal justice (MBA); cyber security (MS); executive leadership (MA); information systems (MS), including information assurance, technology management; international business (MBA, DBA); leadership (DBA); marketing (MBA, MS, DBA), including digital marketing and advertising (MS), project management (MS), public relations (MS), sports marketing and media (MS); project management (MBA, DBA); public administration (MBA); public relations (MBA). *Program availability:* Part-time, online learning. *Students:* 1,887 full-time (1,003 women), 4,223 part-time (1,950 women); includes 1,570 minority (1,133 Black or African American, non-Hispanic/Latino; 30 American Indian or Alaska Native, non-Hispanic/Latino; 118 Asian, non-Hispanic/Latino; 149 Hispanic/Latino; 13 Native Hawaiian or other Pacific Islander, non-Hispanic/Latino; 127 Two or more races, non-Hispanic/Latino), 109 international. Average age 35. 5,680 applicants, 51% accepted, 1510 enrolled. In 2017, 1,290 master's, 17 doctorates awarded. *Entrance requirements:* For master's, minimum undergraduate GPA of 3.0, 15 hours of upper-level business courses. Additional exam requirements/recommendations for international students: Required—TOEFL (minimum score 600 paper-based; 100 iBT). *Application deadline:* Applications are processed on a rolling basis. Application fee: $50. Electronic applications accepted. *Expenses:* Contact institution. *Financial support:* Applicants required to submit FAFSA. *Unit head:* Dr. Scott Hicks, Dean, 434-592-4808, Fax: 434-582-2366, E-mail: smhicks@liberty.edu. *Application contact:* Jay Bridge, Director of Graduate Admissions, 800-424-9595, Fax: 800-628-7977, E-mail: gradadmissions@liberty.edu.
Website: http://www.liberty.edu/academics/business/index.cfm?PID-149

Lindenwood University, Graduate Programs, School of Accelerated Degree Programs, St. Charles, MO 63301-1695. Offers administration (MSA), including management, marketing, project management; business administration (MBA); communications (MA), including digital and multimedia, media management, promotions, training and development; criminal justice and administration (MS); healthcare administration (MS); human resource management (MS); information technology (Certificate); managing information security (MS); managing information technology (MS); managing virtualization and cloud computing (MS); writing (MFA). *Program availability:* Part-time, evening/weekend, 100% online. *Faculty:* 12 full-time (5 women), 90 part-time/adjunct (37 women). *Students:* 597 full-time (383 women), 202 part-time (138 women); includes 248 minority (206 Black or African American, non-Hispanic/Latino; 3 American Indian or Alaska Native, non-Hispanic/Latino; 6 Asian, non-Hispanic/Latino; 21 Hispanic/Latino; 1 Native Hawaiian or other Pacific Islander, non-Hispanic/Latino; 11 Two or more races, non-Hispanic/Latino), 69 international. Average age 36. 526 applicants, 46% accepted, 204 enrolled. In 2017, 537 master's awarded. *Degree requirements:* For master's, thesis (for some programs), minimum cumulative GPA of 3.0; for Certificate, minimum cumulative GPA of 3.0. *Entrance requirements:* For master's, resume, personal statement, official undergraduate transcript, minimum undergraduate cumulative GPA of 3.0. Additional exam requirements/recommendations for international students: Required—TOEFL (minimum score 550 paper-based; 80 iBT); Recommended—IELTS (minimum score 6.5). *Application deadline:* For fall admission, 9/24 priority date for domestic and international students; for winter admission, 1/7 priority date for domestic and international students; for spring admission, 4/8 priority date for domestic and international students; for summer admission, 7/8 priority date for domestic and international students. Applications are processed on a rolling basis. Application fee: $30 ($100 for international students). Electronic applications accepted. *Expenses: Tuition:* Full-time $16,300; part-time $460 per credit. *Required fees:* $660; $330 per credit. Tuition and fees vary according to degree level and program. *Financial support:* In 2017–18, 738 students received support. Career-related internships or fieldwork, institutionally sponsored loans, scholarships/grants, tuition waivers (partial), and unspecified assistantships available. Financial award application deadline: 6/30; financial award applicants required to submit FAFSA. *Unit head:* Dr. Gina Ganahl, Dean, Accelerated Degree Programs, 636-949-4501, Fax: 636-949-4505, E-mail: gganahl@lindenwood.edu. *Application contact:* Kara Schilli, Director, Evening and Graduate Admissions, 636-949-4349, Fax: 636-949-4109, E-mail: adultadmissions@lindenwood.edu.
Website: http://www.lindenwood.edu/academics/academic-schools/school-of-accelerated-degree-programs/

Marlboro College, Graduate and Professional Studies, Program in Business Administration, Marlboro, VT 05344. Offers mission-driven organizations (MBA); project management (MBA); social innovation (MBA). *Program availability:* Part-time, evening/weekend, blended/hybrid learning. *Degree requirements:* For master's, 45 credits including a Master Workshop. *Entrance requirements:* For master's, letter of intent, essay, transcripts, 2 letters of recommendation. *Application deadline:* For fall admission, 7/1 priority date for domestic students; for winter admission, 11/1 priority date for domestic students. Applications are processed on a rolling basis. Application fee: $0. Electronic applications accepted. *Expenses:* $794 per credit. *Financial support:* Scholarships/grants available. Financial award applicants required to submit FAFSA. *Unit head:* Tristan Toleno, Co-Chair, 802-258-9200, Fax: 802-258-9201, E-mail: tristant@gradschool.marlboro.edu. *Application contact:* Amanda Mehegan, Assistant Director of Graduate Admissions, 802-258-9209, Fax: 802-258-9201, E-mail: graduateadmissions@marlboro.edu.
Website: https://www.marlboro.edu/academics/graduate/management

Marlboro College, Graduate and Professional Studies, Program in Management, Marlboro, VT 05344. Offers mission-driven organizations (MS); project management (MS); social innovation (MS). *Program availability:* Part-time, evening/weekend, blended/hybrid learning. *Degree requirements:* For master's, capstone project. *Entrance requirements:* For master's, statement of intent, 2 letters of recommendation. Additional exam requirements/recommendations for international students: Recommended—TOEFL (minimum score 577 paper-based; 90 iBT), IELTS (minimum score 7). *Application deadline:* For fall admission, 8/5 for domestic students; for winter admission, 12/5 for domestic students; for spring admission, 4/5 for domestic students. Applications are processed on a rolling basis. Application fee: $0. Electronic applications accepted. *Expenses:* $794 per credit. *Financial support:* Scholarships/grants available. Financial award applicants required to submit FAFSA. *Unit head:* Tristan Toleno, Co-Chair, 802-258-9200, Fax: 802-258-9201, E-mail: tristant@gradschool.marlboro.edu. *Application contact:* Amanda Mehegan, Assistant Director of Graduate Admissions, 802-258-9209, Fax: 802-258-9201, E-mail: graduateadmissions@marlboro.edu.
Website: https://www.marlboro.edu/academics/graduate/management

Marymount University, School of Business Administration, Program in Information Technology, Arlington, VA 22207-4299. Offers health care informatics (Certificate); information technology (MS, Certificate), including cybersecurity (MS), health care informatics (MS), project management and technology leadership (MS), software engineering (MS); information technology project management and technology leadership (Certificate); MS/MBA; MS/MS. *Program availability:* Part-time, evening/weekend. *Faculty:* 4 full-time (2 women), 12 part-time/adjunct (1 woman). *Students:* 40 full-time (18 women), 31 part-time (13 women); includes 28 minority (16 Black or African American, non-Hispanic/Latino; 4 Asian, non-Hispanic/Latino; 8 Hispanic/Latino), 29 international. Average age 31. 44 applicants, 98% accepted, 12 enrolled. In 2017, 25 master's, 10 other advanced degrees awarded. *Degree requirements:* For master's, thesis or alternative. *Entrance requirements:* For master's, resume, bachelor's degree in computer-related field or degree in another subject with certificate in computer-related field or related work experience; bachelor's degree in computer science or work in software development (for software engineering track). Additional exam requirements/recommendations for international students: Required—TOEFL (minimum score 600 paper-based; 96 iBT), IELTS (minimum score 6.5). *Application deadline:* For fall admission, 7/16 priority date for domestic and international students; for spring admission, 11/16 priority date for domestic and international students; for summer admission, 4/16 for domestic and international students. Applications are processed on a rolling basis. Application fee: $40. Electronic applications accepted. *Expenses:* $990 per credit. *Financial support:* In 2017–18, 5 students received support, including 4 research assistantships with full and partial tuition reimbursements available (averaging $7,425 per year); career-related internships or fieldwork, Federal Work-Study, scholarships/grants, and unspecified assistantships also available. Support available to part-time students. Financial award application deadline: 3/1; financial award applicants required to submit FAFSA. *Unit head:* Dr. Diane Murphy, Chair/Director, Information Technology, Management Sciences and Cybersecurity, 703-284-5958, Fax: 703-527-3830, E-mail: diane.murphy@marymount.edu. *Application contact:* Francesca Reed, Director, Graduate Admissions, 703-284-5901, Fax: 703-527-3815, E-mail: grad.admissions@marymount.edu.
Website: http://www.marymount.edu/Academics/School-of-Business-Administration/Graduate-Programs/Information-Technology-(M-S-)

Maryville University of Saint Louis, The John E. Simon School of Business, St. Louis, MO 63141-7299. Offers accounting (MBA, MS, Certificate); business studies (Certificate); cybersecurity (MBA, MS, Certificate); financial services (MBA, Certificate); healthcare practice management (MBA, Certificate); human resource management (MBA, Certificate); information technology (MBA, Certificate); management (MBA, Certificate); management and leadership (MA); marketing (MBA, Certificate); project management (MBA, Certificate); sport business management (MBA); supply chain management (Certificate); supply chain management/logistics (MBA). *Accreditation:* ACBSP. *Program availability:* Part-time, 100% online, blended/hybrid learning. *Faculty:* 5 full-time (3 women), 51 part-time/adjunct (16 women). *Students:* 222 full-time (96 women), 498 part-time (222 women); includes 185 minority (104 Black or African American, non-Hispanic/Latino; 5 American Indian or Alaska Native, non-Hispanic/Latino; 30 Asian, non-Hispanic/Latino; 37 Hispanic/Latino; 9 Two or more races, non-Hispanic/Latino), 26 international. Average age 33. In 2017, 106 master's awarded. *Degree requirements:* For master's, capstone course (for MBA). *Entrance requirements:* Additional exam requirements/recommendations for international students: Required—TOEFL (minimum score 563 paper-based; 85 iBT). *Application deadline:* Applications are processed on a rolling basis. Electronic applications accepted. *Expenses:* Contact institution. *Financial support:* Career-related internships or fieldwork, Federal Work-Study, tuition waivers (partial), and campus employment available. Financial award application deadline: 4/1; financial award applicants required to submit FAFSA. *Unit head:* Pam Horwitz, Interim Dean, 314-529-9680, Fax: 314-529-9975. *Application contact:* Dustin Loeffler, Director for Graduate Studies in Business, 314-529-9571, Fax: 314-529-9975, E-mail: dloeffler@maryville.edu.
Website: http://www.maryville.edu/bu/business-administration-masters/

Meredith College, School of Business, Raleigh, NC 27607-5298. Offers entrepreneurship and family business (MBA); human resource management (MBA); project management (MBA). *Accreditation:* AACSB. *Program availability:* Part-time, evening/weekend. *Students:* 5 full-time (all women), 88 part-time (73 women); includes 33 minority (24 Black or African American, non-Hispanic/Latino; 1 Asian, non-Hispanic/Latino; 6 Hispanic/Latino; 2 Two or more races, non-Hispanic/Latino), 4 international. Average age 34. 62 applicants, 63% accepted, 29 enrolled. In 2017, 18 master's awarded. *Degree requirements:* For master's, thesis optional. *Entrance requirements:* For master's, GMAT, interview, minimum GPA of 2.5, letters of recommendation. Additional exam requirements/recommendations for international students: Required—TOEFL. *Application deadline:* For fall admission, 7/1 priority date for domestic and international students; for spring admission, 11/1 priority date for domestic and international students. Applications are processed on a rolling basis. Application fee: $50. Electronic applications accepted. *Expenses:* Contact institution. *Financial support:* Career-related internships or fieldwork, institutionally sponsored loans, scholarships/grants, and tuition waivers (partial) available. Support available to part-time students. Financial award application deadline: 2/15; financial award applicants required to submit FAFSA. *Unit head:* Kristie Ogilvie, Dean, 919-760-8432, Fax: 919-760-8470.
Website: https://www.meredith.edu/school-of-business

Metropolitan State University, College of Management, St. Paul, MN 55106-5000. Offers business administration (MBA, DBA); business analytics (Graduate Certificate); database administration (Graduate Certificate); global supply chain management (Graduate Certificate); information assurance security (Graduate Certificate); management information systems (MMIS); MIS generalist (Graduate Certificate); MIS systems analysis and design (Graduate Certificate); project management (Graduate Certificate). *Program availability:* Part-time, evening/weekend. *Degree requirements:* For master's, thesis optional, computer language (MMIS). *Entrance requirements:* For master's, GMAT (for MBA), resume. Additional exam requirements/recommendations for international students: Required—TOEFL (minimum score 550 paper-based). *Application deadline:* For fall admission, 7/15 for international students; for winter admission, 11/15 for international students; for spring admission, 3/15 for international students. Applications are processed on a rolling basis. Application fee: $20. Electronic applications accepted. *Expenses:* Tuition, state resident: part-time $388.55 per credit. Tuition, nonresident: part-time $777.11 per credit. *Required fees:* $35.11 per credit. Part-time tuition and fees vary according to campus/location and program. *Financial support:* Research assistantships with partial tuition reimbursements, career-related internships or fieldwork, and Federal Work-Study available. Support available to part-time students. Financial award applicants required to submit FAFSA. *Faculty research:* Yugoslav economic system, workers' cooperatives, participative management and job enrichment, global business systems. *Unit head:* Allen Bellas, Interim Dean, 612-659-7272, Fax: 612-659-7268, E-mail: allen.bellas@metrostate.edu. *Application contact:* Allen Bellas, Interim Dean, 612-659-7272, Fax: 612-659-7268, E-mail: allen.bellas@metrostate.edu.
Website: https://www.metrostate.edu/academics/management

Mississippi State University, College of Business, Department of Management and Information Systems, Mississippi State, MS 39762. Offers business administration

Project Management

(MBA); information systems (MSIS, PhD); management (PhD); project management (MBA). *Program availability:* Part-time. *Faculty:* 19 full-time (5 women). *Students:* 63 full-time (21 women), 194 part-time (44 women); includes 21 minority (5 Black or African American, non-Hispanic/Latino; 4 Asian, non-Hispanic/Latino; 9 Hispanic/Latino; 3 Two or more races, non-Hispanic/Latino), 16 international. Average age 30. 163 applicants, 48% accepted, 63 enrolled. In 2017, 96 master's, 4 doctorates awarded. *Degree requirements:* For master's, comprehensive exam; for doctorate, comprehensive exam, thesis/dissertation. *Entrance requirements:* For master's, GMAT, minimum GPA of 3.0 in last 60 hours of undergraduate course work; for doctorate, GMAT (minimum score of 550), minimum GPA of 3.25 on all graduate work; BS with minimum GPA of 3.0 cumulative and last 60 hours. Additional exam requirements/recommendations for international students: Required—TOEFL (minimum score 575 paper-based; 84 iBT); Recommended—IELTS (minimum score 7). *Application deadline:* For fall admission, 7/1 for domestic students, 5/1 for international students; for spring admission, 11/1 for domestic students, 9/1 for international students. Applications are processed on a rolling basis. Application fee: $60 ($80 for international students). Electronic applications accepted. *Expenses:* Tuition, state resident: full-time $8318; part-time $462.12 per credit hour. Tuition, nonresident: full-time $22,358; part-time $1242.12 per credit hour. *Required fees:* $110; $12.24 per credit hour. $6.12 per semester. *Financial support:* Career-related internships or fieldwork, Federal Work-Study, institutionally sponsored loans, scholarships/grants, and unspecified assistantships available. Financial award applicants required to submit FAFSA. *Faculty research:* Electronic commerce, management of information technology. *Total annual research expenditures:* $1.3 million. *Unit head:* Dr. James J. Chrisman, Professor and Head, 662-325-1991, Fax: 662-325-8651, E-mail: jchrisman@business.msstate.edu. *Application contact:* Lakan Drinker, Admissions and Enrollment Assistant, 662-325-8951, E-mail: ldrinker@grad.msstate.edu.
Website: http://www.business.msstate.edu/programs/mis/index.php

Missouri State University, Graduate College, College of Business, Department of Technology and Construction Management, Springfield, MO 65897. Offers project management (MS). *Program availability:* Part-time. *Faculty:* 4 full-time (0 women), 2 part-time/adjunct (1 woman). *Students:* 20 full-time (9 women), 42 part-time (12 women); includes 8 minority (3 Black or African American, non-Hispanic/Latino; 1 American Indian or Alaska Native, non-Hispanic/Latino; 1 Asian, non-Hispanic/Latino; 1 Hispanic/Latino; 2 Two or more races, non-Hispanic/Latino), 8 international. Average age 31. 44 applicants, 68% accepted, 17 enrolled. In 2017, 41 master's awarded. *Degree requirements:* For master's, thesis or alternative. *Entrance requirements:* For master's, GRE or GMAT, minimum GPA of 2.75. Additional exam requirements/recommendations for international students: Required—TOEFL (minimum score 550 paper-based; 79 iBT), IELTS (minimum score 6). *Application deadline:* For fall admission, 7/20 priority date for domestic students, 5/1 for international students; for spring admission, 12/20 priority date for domestic students, 9/1 for international students; for summer admission, 5/20 priority date for domestic students. Applications are processed on a rolling basis. Application fee: $35 ($50 for international students). Electronic applications accepted. *Expenses:* Tuition, state resident: full-time $2915; part-time $2021 per credit hour. Tuition, nonresident: full-time $5354; part-time $3647 per credit hour. *International tuition:* $11,992 full-time. *Required fees:* $173; $173 per credit hour. Tuition and fees vary according to class time, course level, course load, degree level, campus/location and program. *Financial support:* Federal Work-Study, institutionally sponsored loans, scholarships/grants, and unspecified assistantships available. Financial award application deadline: 3/31; financial award applicants required to submit FAFSA. *Unit head:* Dr. Richard N. Callahan, Department Head, 417-836-5121, Fax: 417-836-8556, E-mail: indmgt@missouristate.edu. *Application contact:* Stephanie Praschan, Director, Graduate Enrollment Management, 417-836-5330, Fax: 417-836-6200, E-mail: stephaniepraschan@missouristate.edu.
Website: http://tcm.missouristate.edu/

Montana Tech of The University of Montana, Project Engineering and Management Program, Butte, MT 59701-8997. Offers MPEM. *Program availability:* Part-time, evening/weekend, online learning. *Degree requirements:* For master's, comprehensive exam, final project presentation. *Entrance requirements:* For master's, minimum GPA of 3.0. Additional exam requirements/recommendations for international students: Required—TOEFL (minimum score 550 paper-based; 80 iBT), IELTS (minimum score 7). Electronic applications accepted.

Morgan State University, School of Graduate Studies, Earl G. Graves School of Business and Management, Program in Project Management, Baltimore, MD 21251. Offers MS. *Expenses:* Tuition, state resident: part-time $433 per credit. Tuition, nonresident: part-time $851 per credit. *Required fees:* $81.50 per credit.

Mount Aloysius College, Program in Business Administration, Cresson, PA 16630. Offers accounting (MBA); health and human services administration (MBA); non-profit management (MBA); project management (MBA). *Program availability:* Part-time, evening/weekend. *Entrance requirements:* Additional exam requirements/recommendations for international students: Required—IELTS (minimum score 5.5); Recommended—TOEFL. *Application deadline:* For fall admission, 8/1 for domestic students; for spring admission, 12/1 for domestic students. Applications are processed on a rolling basis. Application fee: $30. Electronic applications accepted. Application fee is waived when completed online. *Expenses:* Tuition: Full-time $14,000; part-time $790 per credit hour. *Financial support:* Unspecified assistantships available. Financial award applicants required to submit FAFSA. *Application contact:* Matthew P. Bodenschatz, Director of Graduate and Continuing Education Admissions, 814-886-6556, Fax: 814-886-6441, E-mail: mbodenschatz@mtaloy.edu.
Website: http://www.mtaloy.edu

National American University, Roueche Graduate Center, Austin, TX 78731. Offers accounting (MBA); aviation management (MBA, MM); care coordination (MSN); community college leadership (Ed D); criminal justice (MM); e-marketing (MBA, MM); health care administration (MBA, MM); higher education (MM); human resources management (MBA, MM); information technology management (MBA, MM); international business (MBA); leadership (EMBA); management (MBA); nursing administration (MSN); nursing education (MSN); nursing informatics (MSN); operations and configuration management (MBA, MM); project and process management (MBA, MM). Master's programs offered online through the Harold D. Buckingham Graduate School. *Program availability:* Part-time, evening/weekend, online learning. *Entrance requirements:* For master's, minimum undergraduate GPA of 2.75. Additional exam requirements/recommendations for international students: Required—TOEFL, TWE. Electronic applications accepted. *Faculty research:* Tourism, finance, marketing.

New England College, Program in Management, Henniker, NH 03242-3293. Offers accounting (MSA); healthcare administration (MS); international relations (MA); marketing management (MS); nonprofit leadership (MS); project management (MS); strategic leadership (MS). *Program availability:* Part-time, evening/weekend. *Degree requirements:* For master's, independent research project. Electronic applications accepted.

New York University, School of Professional Studies, Division of Programs in Business, Program in Project Management, New York, NY 10012-1019. Offers MS. *Program availability:* Part-time, evening/weekend. *Students:* 64 full-time (31 women), 21

part-time (14 women); includes 18 minority (7 Black or African American, non-Hispanic/Latino; 5 Asian, non-Hispanic/Latino; 4 Hispanic/Latino; 1 Native Hawaiian or other Pacific Islander, non-Hispanic/Latino; 1 Two or more races, non-Hispanic/Latino), 61 international. Average age 27. 188 applicants, 61% accepted, 49 enrolled. In 2017, 44 master's awarded. *Degree requirements:* For master's, thesis. *Entrance requirements:* For master's, GRE or GMAT (only upon request), bachelor's degree, resume with relevant professional work, internship or volunteer experience, two letters of recommendation, statement of purpose. Additional exam requirements/recommendations for international students: Required—TOEFL (minimum score 600 paper-based; 100 iBT), IELTS (minimum score 7). *Application deadline:* For fall admission, 2/1 priority date for domestic and international students; for spring admission, 10/15 priority date for domestic students, 8/15 priority date for international students; for summer admission, 5/1 priority date for domestic students, 1/15 priority date for international students. Applications are processed on a rolling basis. Application fee: $150. Electronic applications accepted. *Expenses:* $20,244 per term. *Financial support:* Fellowships, career-related internships or fieldwork, Federal Work-Study, scholarships/grants, and health care benefits available. Support available to part-time students. Financial award application deadline: 6/30; financial award applicants required to submit FAFSA. *Unit head:* Martin Ihrig, Associate Dean and Clinical Assistant Professor, 212-992-3288. *Application contact:* Office of Admissions, 212-998-7100, E-mail: sps.gradadmissions@nyu.edu.
Website: http://www.sps.nyu.edu/content/scps/academics/departments/information-technology/academic-offerings/graduate/ms-in-project-management.html

Northeastern University, College of Professional Studies, Boston, MA 02115-5096. Offers applied nutrition (MS); college athletics administration (MSL); commerce and economic development (MS); corporate and organizational communication (MS); criminal justice (MS); digital media (MPS); elearning and instructional design (M Ed); elementary education (MAT); geographic information technology (MPS); global studies and international relations (MS); higher education administration (M Ed); homeland security (MA); human services (MS); informatics (MPS); leadership (MS); learning analytics (M Ed); learning and instruction (M Ed); nonprofit management (MS); professional sports administration (MSL); project management (MS); regulatory affairs for drugs, biologics, and medical devices (MS); respiratory care leadership (MS); special education (M Ed); technical communication (MS). *Program availability:* Part-time, evening/weekend, 100% online, blended/hybrid learning. *Faculty:* 82 full-time (51 women), 853 part-time/adjunct (366 women). *Students:* 5,278 part-time (3,230 women). In 2017, 1,586 master's awarded. *Application deadline:* Applications are processed on a rolling basis. Application fee: $0. Electronic applications accepted. *Expenses:* Contact institution. *Financial support:* Applicants required to submit FAFSA. *Unit head:* Dr. Mary Loeffelholz, Dean of the College of Professional Studies. *Application contact:* E-mail: cpsadmissions@northeastern.edu.
Website: https://cps.northeastern.edu/

Northwestern University, McCormick School of Engineering and Applied Science, Department of Civil and Environmental Engineering, Master of Project Management Program, Evanston, IL 60208. Offers MS. *Program availability:* Part-time, evening/weekend. *Degree requirements:* For master's, capstone report. *Entrance requirements:* Additional exam requirements/recommendations for international students: Required—TOEFL (minimum score 560 paper-based; 83 iBT), IELTS. Electronic applications accepted. *Faculty research:* Construction management, real estate development, sustainability, and transportation management.

Northwestern University, School of Professional Studies, Program in Information Systems, Evanston, IL 60208. Offers analytics and business intelligence (MS); database and Internet technologies (MS); information systems (MS); information systems management (MS); information systems security (MS); medical informatics (MS); software project management and development (MS). *Program availability:* Part-time, evening/weekend.
Website: https://sps.northwestern.edu/masters/information-systems/index.php

Northwest University, College of Business, Kirkland, WA 98033. Offers business administration (MBA); international business (MBA); project management (MBA); social entrepreneurship (MBA). *Accreditation:* ACBSP. *Program availability:* Part-time, evening/weekend. *Degree requirements:* For master's, formalized research. *Entrance requirements:* For master's, GMAT. Additional exam requirements/recommendations for international students: Required—TOEFL (minimum score 550 paper-based; 75 iBT). Electronic applications accepted. *Expenses:* Contact institution.

Norwich University, College of Graduate and Continuing Studies, Master of Business Administration Program, Northfield, VT 05663. Offers construction management (MBA); energy management (MBA); finance (MBA); logistics (MBA); organizational leadership (MBA); project management (MBA); supply chain management (MBA). *Accreditation:* ACBSP. *Program availability:* Evening/weekend, online only, mostly all online with a week-long residency requirement. *Degree requirements:* For master's, comprehensive exam. *Entrance requirements:* For master's, minimum undergraduate GPA of 2.75. Additional exam requirements/recommendations for international students: Required—TOEFL (minimum score 550 paper-based; 80 iBT), IELTS (minimum score 6.5). Electronic applications accepted. *Expenses:* Contact institution.

Norwich University, College of Graduate and Continuing Studies, Master of Science in Information Security and Assurance Program, Northfield, VT 05663. Offers information security and assurance (MS), including computer forensic investigation/incident response team management, critical infrastructure protection and cyber crime, cyber law and international perspectives on cyberspace, project management, vulnerability management. *Program availability:* Evening/weekend, online only, mostly all online with a week-long residency requirement. *Entrance requirements:* For master's, minimum undergraduate GPA of 2.75. Additional exam requirements/recommendations for international students: Required—TOEFL (minimum score 550 paper-based; 80 iBT), IELTS (minimum score 6.5). Electronic applications accepted. *Expenses:* Contact institution.

Oklahoma Christian University, Graduate School of Business, Oklahoma City, OK 73136-1100. Offers accounting (M Acc, MBA); financial services (MBA); general business (MBA); health services management (MBA); human resources (MBA); international business (MBA); leadership and organizational development (MBA); marketing (MBA); nonprofit management (MBA); project management (MBA). *Accreditation:* ACBSP. *Program availability:* Part-time, 100% online. *Entrance requirements:* For master's, bachelor's degree. Additional exam requirements/recommendations for international students: Required—TOEFL (minimum score 550 paper-based). Electronic applications accepted. *Expenses:* Contact institution.

Pacific States University, College of Business, Los Angeles, CA 90010. Offers accounting (MBA, Certificate); beauty management (MBA); finance (MBA); international business (MBA); management of information technology (MBA); project management (Certificate); real estate management (MBA). *Program availability:* Part-time, evening/weekend, online learning. *Entrance requirements:* For master's, minimum undergraduate GPA of 2.5 during last 90 quarter units of course work, bachelor's degree in business administration or economics. Additional exam requirements/recommendations for international students: Required—TOEFL (minimum score 500 paper-based; 61 iBT), IELTS (minimum score 5.5). *Application deadline:* For fall admission, 9/1 priority date for domestic students, 8/1 priority date for international students; for winter admission, 12/1 priority date for domestic students, 11/1 priority date for international students; for spring admission, 3/1 priority date for domestic students, 2/1 priority date for international students; for summer admission, 6/1 priority date for domestic students, 5/1 priority date for international students. Applications are processed on a rolling basis. Application fee: $100. *Expenses:* Tuition: Part-time $380 per unit. *Financial support:* Scholarships/grants available. Financial award applicants required to submit FAFSA. *Unit head:* Chase C. Rhee, MBA Program Administrator, 323-731-2383 Ext. 208, Fax: 323-731-7276, E-mail: ccrhee@psuca.edu. *Application contact:* Maawiya Ayeva, Director of Admissions, 323-731-2383 Ext. 204, Fax: 323-731-7276, E-mail: admissions@psuca.edu.

Point Loma Nazarene University, Fermanian School of Business, San Diego, CA 92106-2899. Offers general business (MBA); healthcare management (MBA); innovation and entrepreneurship (MBA); organizational leadership (MBA); project management (MBA). *Accreditation:* ACBSP. *Program availability:* Part-time, evening/weekend. *Faculty:* 7 full-time (0 women), 5 part-time/adjunct (3 women). *Students:* 27 full-time (8 women), 94 part-time (45 women); includes 52 minority (6 Black or African American, non-Hispanic/Latino; 1 American Indian or Alaska Native, non-Hispanic/Latino; 7 Asian, non-Hispanic/Latino; 33 Hispanic/Latino; 5 Two or more races, non-Hispanic/Latino), 11 international. Average age 31. 74 applicants, 99% accepted, 56 enrolled. In 2017, 45 master's awarded. *Entrance requirements:* For master's, GMAT, letters of recommendation, essay, interview. Additional exam requirements/recommendations for international students: Required—TOEFL. *Application deadline:* For fall admission, 7/26 priority date for domestic students; for spring admission, 11/29 priority date for domestic students; for summer admission, 4/2 priority date for domestic students. Applications are processed on a rolling basis. Application fee: $50. Electronic applications accepted. *Expenses:* Contact institution. *Financial support:* Applicants required to submit FAFSA. *Unit head:* Jamie McIlwaine, Associate Dean, Graduate Business, 619-849-2721, E-mail: jmcilwai@pointloma.edu. *Application contact:* Joanie Joy, Senior Director of Enrollment Management, 619-329-6785, E-mail: gradinfo@pointloma.edu.
Website: https://www.pointloma.edu/schools-departments-colleges/fermanian-school-business

Polytechnic University of Puerto Rico, Miami Campus, Graduate School, Miami, FL 33166. Offers accounting (MBA); business administration (MBA); construction management (MEM); environmental management (MEM); finance (MBA); human resources management (MBA); logistics and supply chain management (MBA); management of international enterprises (MBA); manufacturing management (MEM); marketing management (MBA); project management (MBA). *Program availability:* Part-time, evening/weekend, online learning. *Entrance requirements:* For master's, minimum GPA of 3.0. Electronic applications accepted.

Post University, Program in Business Administration, Waterbury, CT 06723-2540. Offers accounting (MSA); business administration (MBA); corporate finance (MBA); corporate innovation (MBA); healthcare systems leadership (MBA); leadership (MBA); marketing (MBA); project management (MBA, MS). *Accreditation:* ACBSP. *Program availability:* Online learning. *Entrance requirements:* For master's, resume. *Expenses:* Tuition: Part-time $730 per credit hour. Part-time tuition and fees vary according to degree level and program. *Application contact:* Veronica Montalvo, Vice President, Online Education Enrollment Management and Admissions, 203-596-6164, E-mail: vmontalvo@post.edu.

Purdue University Global, School of Business, Davenport, IA 52807. Offers business administration (MBA); change leadership (MS); entrepreneurship (MBA); finance (MBA); health care management (MBA, MS); human resource (MBA); international business (MBA); management (MS); marketing (MBA); project management (MBA, MS); supply chain management and logistics (MBA, MS). *Accreditation:* ACBSP. *Program availability:* Part-time, evening/weekend, online learning. *Entrance requirements:* Additional exam requirements/recommendations for international students: Required—TOEFL (minimum score 550 paper-based; 80 iBT). Electronic applications accepted.

Queen's University at Kingston, Queens School of Business, Program in Business Administration, Kingston, ON K7L 3N6, Canada. Offers consulting and project management (MBA); finance (MBA); innovation and entrepreneurship (MBA); marketing (MBA). *Degree requirements:* For master's, thesis optional, research project. *Entrance requirements:* For master's, GMAT, minimum B+ average. Additional exam requirements/recommendations for international students: Required—TOEFL. Electronic applications accepted. *Faculty research:* Management fundamentals, strategic thinking, global business, innovation and change, leadership.

Regis University, College of Business and Economics, Denver, CO 80221-1099. Offers accounting (MS); executive leadership (Certificate); finance (MS); finance and accounting (MBA); health industry leadership (MBA); human resource management and leadership (MSOL); management (MBA); marketing (MBA); nonprofit leadership (Post-Graduate Certificate); nonprofit management (MNM); nonprofit organizational capacity building (Certificate); operations management (MBA); organizational leadership and management (MSOL); project leadership and management (MS, MSOL); strategic business management (Certificate); strategic human resource integration (Certificate); strategic management (MBA). Programs offered at Colorado Springs Campus, Northwest Denver Campus, Southeast Denver Campus, Fort Collins Campus, Broomfield Campus, Henderson (Nevada) Campus, and Summerlin (Nevada) Campus. *Program availability:* Part-time, evening/weekend, 100% online, blended/hybrid learning. *Degree requirements:* For master's, thesis (for some programs), capstone or final research project. *Entrance requirements:* For master's, official transcript reflecting baccalaureate degree awarded from regionally-accredited college or university, interview, 2 years of full-time related work experience, resume, letters of recommendation. Additional exam requirements/recommendations for international students: Required—TOEFL (minimum score 550 paper-based; 82 iBT). Electronic applications accepted. *Expenses:* Contact institution. *Faculty research:* Impact of information technology on small business regulation of accounting, international project financing, mineral development, delivery of healthcare to rural indigenous communities.

Robert Morris University, School of Communications and Information Systems, Moon Township, PA 15108-1189. Offers communication and information systems (MS); cyber security (MS); data analytics (MS); information security and assurance (MS); information systems and communications (D Sc); information systems management (MS); information technology project management (MS); Internet information systems (MS); organizational leadership (MS). *Program availability:* Part-time, evening/weekend, online learning. *Faculty:* 23 full-time (10 women), 10 part-time/adjunct (3 women). *Students:* 258 part-time (99 women); includes 46 minority (22 Black or African American, non-Hispanic/Latino; 16 Asian, non-Hispanic/Latino; 5 Hispanic/Latino; 3 Two or more races, non-Hispanic/Latino), 46 international. Average age 35. 226 applicants, 52% accepted, 79 enrolled. In 2017, 148 master's, 12 doctorates awarded. *Degree requirements:* For doctorate, thesis/dissertation. *Entrance requirements:* For doctorate, employer letter of endorsement, interview. Additional exam requirements/recommendations for international students: Required—TOEFL (minimum score 550 paper-based; 79 iBT). *Application deadline:* For fall admission, 7/1 priority date for domestic and international

students; for spring admission, 11/1 priority date for domestic and international students. Applications are processed on a rolling basis. Application fee: $35. Electronic applications accepted. Application fee is waived when completed online. *Expenses:* $920 per credit tuition plus university fees of $80 per credit. *Financial support:* Institutionally sponsored loans available. Support available to part-time students. Financial award application deadline: 5/1. *Unit head:* Ann Marie M. Le Blanc, Dean, 412-397-6433, Fax: 412-397-6469, E-mail: leblanc@rmu.edu. *Application contact:* E-mail: graduateadmissions@rmu.edu.
Website: http://www.rmu.edu/web/cms/schools/scis/Pages/default.aspx

Rochester Institute of Technology, Graduate Enrollment Services, School of Individualized Study, Graduate Programs Department, Advanced Certificate Program in Project Management, Rochester, NY 14623. Offers Advanced Certificate. *Program availability:* Part-time, evening/weekend, 100% online, blended/hybrid learning. *Students:* 1 full-time (0 women), 3 part-time (all women), 1 international. Average age 31. 7 applicants, 14% accepted. In 2017, 12 Advanced Certificates awarded. *Entrance requirements:* For degree, minimum GPA of 3.0 (recommended). Additional exam requirements/recommendations for international students: Required—TOEFL (minimum score 550 paper-based; 79 iBT), IELTS (minimum score 6.5), PTE (minimum score 58). *Application deadline:* Applications are processed on a rolling basis. Application fee: $65. Electronic applications accepted. *Expenses:* $1,815 per credit hour (classroom), $1,035 per credit hour (online study). *Financial support:* Available to part-time students. Applicants required to submit FAFSA. *Faculty research:* Risk management; cross-cultural teams; automation of management process; non-traditional management tools; human performance and emotional intelligence. *Unit head:* Peter Boyd, Graduate Program Director, 585-475-6320, E-mail: plbcms@rit.edu. *Application contact:* Diane Ellison, Senior Associate Vice President, Graduate Enrollment Services, 585-475-2229, Fax: 585-475-7164, E-mail: gradinfo@rit.edu.
Website: http://www.rit.edu/academicaffairs/sois/getting-started/graduate/advanced-certificates

Saint Leo University, Graduate Studies in Business, Saint Leo, FL 33574-6665. Offers accounting (M Acc, MBA); cybersecurity (MS); cybersecurity management (MBA); data analytics (MBA); health care management (MBA); human resource management (MBA); international and experiential business administration (MBA); management (MBA, DBA); marketing (MBA); marketing research and social media analytics (MBA); project management (MBA); social media marketing (MBA); sport business (MBA); supply chain global integration management (MBA). *Accreditation:* ACBSP. *Program availability:* Part-time, evening/weekend, 100% online, blended/hybrid learning. *Faculty:* 54 full-time (18 women), 52 part-time/adjunct (18 women). *Students:* 9 full-time (3 women), 1,867 part-time (1,079 women); includes 861 minority (598 Black or African American, non-Hispanic/Latino; 3 American Indian or Alaska Native, non-Hispanic/Latino; 38 Asian, non-Hispanic/Latino; 186 Hispanic/Latino; 3 Native Hawaiian or other Pacific Islander, non-Hispanic/Latino; 33 Two or more races, non-Hispanic/Latino), 68 international. Average age 37. 868 applicants, 63% accepted, 537 enrolled. In 2017, 859 master's, 3 doctorates awarded. *Degree requirements:* For doctorate, comprehensive exam, thesis/dissertation. *Entrance requirements:* For master's, GMAT with minimum score 500 (for M Acc), official transcripts, current resume, 2 professional recommendations, personal statement, bachelor's degree from regionally-accredited university; undergraduate degree in accounting and minimum undergraduate GPA of 3.0 (for M Acc); minimum undergraduate GPA of 3.0 in final 2 years of undergraduate study and 2 years' work experience (for MBA); for doctorate, GMAT (minimum score of 550) if master's GPA is under 3.25, official transcripts, current resume, 2 professional recommendations, personal statement, master's degree from regionally-accredited university with minimum GPA of 3.25, 3 years' work experience, interview. Additional exam requirements/recommendations for international students: Required—TOEFL (minimum score 550 paper-based; 78 iBT). *Application deadline:* For fall admission, 7/1 priority date for domestic and international students; for spring admission, 11/12 priority date for domestic students, 11/1 for international students. Applications are processed on a rolling basis. Application fee: $80. Electronic applications accepted. *Expenses:* Contact institution. *Financial support:* In 2017–18, 106 students received support. Career-related internships or fieldwork, health care benefits, and tuition remission for Saint Leo employees and their dependents available. Financial award application deadline: 3/1; financial award applicants required to submit FAFSA. *Faculty research:* Servant leadership, work/life balance, emotional intelligence, pricing, marketing. *Unit head:* Dr. Charles Hale, Dean, School of Business, 352-588-8599, Fax: 352-588-8912, E-mail: mbaslu@saintleo.edu. *Application contact:* Mark Russum, Assistant Vice President, Enrollment, 800-707-8846, Fax: 352-588-7873, E-mail: grad.admissions@saintleo.edu.
Website: https://www.saintleo.edu/school-of-business

Saint Mary's University of Minnesota, Schools of Graduate and Professional Programs, Graduate School of Business and Technology, Project Management Program, Winona, MN 55987-1399. Offers MS, Certificate. *Program availability:* Part-time, evening/weekend, online learning. *Unit head:* William Johnson, Director, 612-728-5178, E-mail: wcjohn06@smumn.edu. *Application contact:* James Callinan, Director of Admissions for Graduate and Professional Programs, 612-728-5158, Fax: 612-728-5121, E-mail: jcallina@smumn.edu.
Website: http://www.smumn.edu/graduate-home/areas-of-study/graduate-school-of-business-technology/ms-in-project-management

Saint Xavier University, Graduate Studies, Graham School of Management, Chicago, IL 60655-3105. Offers employee health benefits (Certificate); finance (MBA); financial fraud examination and management (MBA, Certificate); financial planning (MBA, Certificate); generalist/individualized (MBA); health administration (MBA); managed care (Certificate); management (MBA); marketing (MBA); project management (MBA, Certificate); MBA/MS. *Accreditation:* AACSB. *Program availability:* Part-time, evening/weekend. *Entrance requirements:* For master's, GMAT, minimum GPA of 3.0, 2 years of work experience. Electronic applications accepted. *Expenses:* Contact institution.

Sam Houston State University, College of Business Administration, Department of Management and Marketing, Huntsville, TX 77341. Offers project management (MS). *Program availability:* Part-time, online learning. *Entrance requirements:* For master's, GMAT, official transcripts, current resume, essay. Additional exam requirements/recommendations for international students: Required—TOEFL (minimum score 79 iBT), IELTS (minimum score 6.5). Electronic applications accepted.

Southern Illinois University Edwardsville, Graduate School, School of Business, Program in Business Administration, Edwardsville, IL 62026. Offers business analytics (MBA); management information systems (MBA); project management (MBA). *Accreditation:* AACSB. *Program availability:* Part-time, evening/weekend. *Degree requirements:* For master's, comprehensive exam. *Entrance requirements:* For master's, GMAT. Additional exam requirements/recommendations for international students: Required—TOEFL (minimum score 550 paper-based; 79 iBT), IELTS (minimum score 6.5). Electronic applications accepted.

Southern New Hampshire University, School of Business, Manchester, NH 03106-1045. Offers accounting (MBA, Graduate Certificate); accounting finance (MS); accounting/auditing (MS); accounting/forensic accounting (MS); accounting/management accounting (MS); accounting/taxation (MS); applied economics (MS); athletic administration (MBA, Graduate Certificate); business administration (IMBA,

Project Management

Certificate), including business information systems (Certificate), human resource management (Certificate); business analytics (MBA); business intelligence (MBA); communication (MA), including new media and marketing, public relations; community economic development (MBA); criminal justice (MBA); data analytics (MS); economics (MBA); engineering management (MBA); entrepreneurship (MBA); finance (MBA, MS, Graduate Certificate); finance/corporate finance (MS); finance/investments (MS); forensic accounting (MBA); forensic accounting and fraud examination (Graduate Certificate); healthcare informatics (MBA); healthcare management (MBA); human resource management (MS); human resources (MBA); information technology (MS); information technology management (MBA); international business (PhD); Internet marketing (MBA); leadership (MBA); leadership of nonprofit organizations (Graduate Certificate); management (MS); marketing (MBA, MS, Graduate Certificate); music business (MBA); operations and project management (MS); operations and supply chain management (MBA, Graduate Certificate); organizational leadership (MS); project management (MBA, Graduate Certificate); public administration (MBA, Graduate Certificate); quantitative analysis (MBA); Six Sigma (Graduate Certificate); Six Sigma quality (MBA); social media marketing (MBA, Graduate Certificate); sport management (MBA, MS, Graduate Certificate); sustainability and environmental compliance (MBA); MBA/Certificate. *Accreditation:* ACBSP. *Program availability:* Part-time, evening/weekend, online learning. Terminal master's awarded for partial completion of doctoral program. *Degree requirements:* For master's, one foreign language, comprehensive exam (for some programs), thesis or alternative; for doctorate, one foreign language, comprehensive exam, thesis/dissertation. *Entrance requirements:* For master's, minimum GPA of 2.5; for doctorate, GMAT. Additional exam requirements/recommendations for international students: Required—TOEFL (minimum score 500 paper-based). *Application deadline:* Applications are processed on a rolling basis. Application fee: $40. Electronic applications accepted. *Expenses: Tuition:* Part-time $627 per credit hour. Part-time tuition and fees vary according to campus/location and program. *Financial support:* Career-related internships or fieldwork, Federal Work-Study, institutionally sponsored loans, scholarships/grants, tuition waivers (partial), and unspecified assistantships available. Support available to part-time students. Financial award applicants required to submit FAFSA. *Unit head:* Dr. Bill Lightfoot, Dean, 603-644-3102, Fax: 603-644-3144. *Application contact:* Office of Graduate Admission, 888-327-SNHU, Fax: 603-644-3144, E-mail: enroll@snhu.edu.

Stevens Institute of Technology, Graduate School, School of Business, Program in Business Administration, Hoboken, NJ 07030. Offers business intelligence and analytics (MBA); engineering management (MBA); finance (MBA); information systems (MBA); innovation and entrepreneurship (MBA); marketing (MBA); pharmaceutical management (MBA); project management (MBA, Certificate); technology management (MBA); telecommunications management (MBA). *Accreditation:* AACSB. *Program availability:* Part-time, evening/weekend. *Students:* 46 full-time (19 women), 179 part-time (88 women); includes 46 minority (10 Black or African American, non-Hispanic/Latino; 2 American Indian or Alaska Native, non-Hispanic/Latino; 30 Asian, non-Hispanic/Latino; 4 Hispanic/Latino), 45 international. Average age 36. 218 applicants, 49% accepted, 53 enrolled. In 2017, 33 master's awarded. *Degree requirements:* For master's, thesis optional, minimum B average in major field and overall; for Certificate, minimum B average. *Entrance requirements:* Additional exam requirements/recommendations for international students: Required—TOEFL (minimum score 74 iBT), IELTS (minimum score 6). *Application deadline:* For fall admission, 7/1 for domestic students, 4/15 for international students; for spring admission, 12/1 for domestic and international students. Applications are processed on a rolling basis. Application fee: $60. Electronic applications accepted. *Expenses: Tuition:* Full-time $34,494; part-time $1554 per credit. *Required fees:* $291 per semester. *Financial support:* Fellowships, research assistantships, teaching assistantships, career-related internships or fieldwork, Federal Work-Study, scholarships/grants, and unspecified assistantships available. Financial award application deadline: 2/15; financial award applicants required to submit FAFSA. *Unit head:* Dr. Gregory Prastacos, Dean, 201-216-8366, E-mail: gprastac@stevens.edu. *Application contact:* Graduate Admissions, 888-783-8367, Fax: 888-511-1306, E-mail: graduate@stevens.edu. Website: https://www.stevens.edu/school-business/masters-programs/mbaemba

Stevens Institute of Technology, Graduate School, School of Business, Program in Information Systems, Hoboken, NJ 07030. Offers computer science (MS); e-commerce (MS); enterprise systems (MS); entrepreneurial information technology (MS); information architecture (MS); information management (MS, Certificate); information security (MS); information technology in financial services industry (MS); information technology in the pharmaceutical industry (MS); information technology outsourcing management (MS); project management (MS, Certificate); software engineering (MS); telecommunications (MS). *Program availability:* Part-time, evening/weekend. *Students:* 321 full-time (110 women), 58 part-time (18 women); includes 22 minority (7 Black or African American, non-Hispanic/Latino; 15 Asian, non-Hispanic/Latino), 321 international. Average age 26. 877 applicants, 67% accepted, 117 enrolled. In 2017, 168 master's, 2 other advanced degrees awarded. *Degree requirements:* For master's, thesis optional, minimum B average in major field and overall; for Certificate, minimum B average. *Entrance requirements:* Additional exam requirements/recommendations for international students: Required—TOEFL (minimum score 74 iBT), IELTS (minimum score 6). *Application deadline:* For fall admission, 7/1 for domestic students, 4/15 for international students; for spring admission, 12/1 for domestic and international students. Applications are processed on a rolling basis. Application fee: $60. Electronic applications accepted. *Expenses: Tuition:* Full-time $34,494; part-time $1554 per credit. *Required fees:* $291 per semester. *Financial support:* Fellowships, research assistantships, teaching assistantships, career-related internships or fieldwork, Federal Work-Study, scholarships/grants, and unspecified assistantships available. Financial award application deadline: 2/15; financial award applicants required to submit FAFSA. *Unit head:* Dr. Gregory Prastacos, Dean, 201-216-8366, E-mail: gprastac@stevens.edu. *Application contact:* Graduate Admissions, 888-783-8367, Fax: 888-511-1306, E-mail: graduate@stevens.edu. Website: https://www.stevens.edu/school-business/masters-programs/information-systems

Stevens Institute of Technology, Graduate School, School of Business, Program in Management, Hoboken, NJ 07030. Offers general management (MS); global innovation management (MS); human resource management (MS); information management (MS); project management (MS); technology commercialization (MS); technology management (MS). *Program availability:* Part-time, evening/weekend. *Students:* 56 full-time (18 women), 88 part-time (32 women); includes 18 minority (5 Black or African American, non-Hispanic/Latino; 12 Asian, non-Hispanic/Latino; 1 Hispanic/Latino), 87 international. Average age 30. 194 applicants, 78% accepted, 68 enrolled. In 2017, 87 master's awarded. *Degree requirements:* For master's, thesis optional, minimum B average in major field and overall. *Entrance requirements:* Additional exam requirements/recommendations for international students: Required—TOEFL (minimum score 74 iBT), IELTS (minimum score 6). *Application deadline:* For fall admission, 7/1 for domestic students, 4/15 for international students; for spring admission, 12/1 for domestic and international students. Applications are processed on a rolling basis. Application fee: $60. Electronic applications accepted. *Expenses: Tuition:* Full-time $34,494; part-time $1554 per credit. *Required fees:* $291 per semester. *Financial support:* Fellowships, research assistantships, teaching assistantships, career-related internships or fieldwork, Federal Work-Study, scholarships/grants, and unspecified assistantships available. Financial award application deadline: 2/15; financial award applicants required to submit FAFSA. *Unit head:* Brian Rothschild, Director, 201-216-3677, E-mail: brian.rothschild@stevens.edu. *Application contact:* Graduate Admissions, 888-783-8367, Fax: 888-511-1306, E-mail: graduate@stevens.edu. Website: https://www.stevens.edu/school-business/masters-programs/management

Stevenson University, Program in Healthcare Management, Owings Mills, MD 21153. Offers project management (MS); quality management and patient safety (MS). *Program availability:* Part-time, online only, 100% online. *Faculty:* 2 full-time (both women), 7 part-time/adjunct (4 women). *Students:* 4 full-time (2 women), 35 part-time (28 women); includes 11 minority (9 Black or African American, non-Hispanic/Latino; 2 Asian, non-Hispanic/Latino). Average age 30. 24 applicants, 71% accepted, 13 enrolled. In 2017, 10 master's awarded. *Degree requirements:* For master's, capstone course. *Entrance requirements:* For master's, official college transcripts from all previous academic work, minimum cumulative GPA of 3.0 in past academic work, minimum grade of B in statistics or an upper-level math and English composition, two professional letters of recommendation with at least one from a current or past supervisor, 250-word personal statement. *Application deadline:* Applications are processed on a rolling basis. Electronic applications accepted. *Expenses:* Contact institution. *Financial support:* Unspecified assistantships available. Financial award applicants required to submit FAFSA. *Unit head:* Sharon Buchbinder, PhD, Coordinator, 443-394-9290, Fax: 443-394-0538, E-mail: sbuchbinder@stevenson.edu. *Application contact:* Amanda Courter, Enrollment Counselor, 443-352-4243, Fax: 443-394-0538, E-mail: acourter@stevenson.edu. Website: http://www.stevenson.edu

Thomas Edison State University, School of Business and Management, Program in Management, Trenton, NJ 08608. Offers accounting (MSM); organizational leadership (MSM); project management (MSM). *Program availability:* Part-time, 100% online. *Degree requirements:* For master's, final capstone project. *Entrance requirements:* For master's, bachelor's degree from a regionally-accredited college or university; minimum 2 letters of recommendation; 3-5 years of related working experience; current resume. Additional exam requirements/recommendations for international students: Required—TOEFL (minimum score 550 paper-based; 79 iBT). Electronic applications accepted.

Trident University International, College of Business Administration, Program in Business Administration, Cypress, CA 90630. Offers business administration (PhD); conflict and negotiation management (MBA); criminal justice administration (MBA); entrepreneurship (MBA); finance (MBA); general management (MBA); government accounting (MBA); human resource management (MBA); information security and digital assurance management (MBA); information technology management (MBA); international business (MBA); logistics management (MBA); marketing (MBA); project management (MBA); public management (MBA); quality management (MBA); strategic leadership (MBA). *Program availability:* Part-time, evening/weekend, online learning. *Degree requirements:* For doctorate, comprehensive exam, thesis/dissertation, defense of dissertation. *Entrance requirements:* For master's, minimum GPA of 2.5 (students with GPA 3.0 or greater may transfer up to 30% of graduate level credits); for doctorate, minimum GPA of 3.4, curriculum vitae, course work in research methods or statistics. Additional exam requirements/recommendations for international students: Required—TOEFL. Electronic applications accepted.

Universidad del Turabo, Graduate Programs, School of Business and Entrepreneurship, Program in Project Management, Gurabo, PR 00778-3030. Offers MBA. *Entrance requirements:* For master's, GRE, EXADEP or GMAT, interview, essay, official transcript, recommendation letters. Electronic applications accepted.

Universidad Nacional Pedro Henriquez Urena, Graduate School, Santo Domingo, Dominican Republic. Offers agricultural diversity (MS), including horticultural/fruit production, tropical animal production; conservation of monuments and cultural assets (M Arch); ecology and environment (MS); environmental engineering (MEE); international relations (MA); natural resource management (MS); political science (MA); project optimization (MPM); project feasibility (MPM); project management (MPM); sanitation engineering (ME); science for teachers (MS); tropical Caribbean architecture (M Arch).

Université du Québec à Chicoutimi, Graduate Programs, Program in Project Management, Chicoutimi, QC G7H 2B1, Canada. Offers M Sc. *Program availability:* Part-time. *Entrance requirements:* For master's, appropriate bachelor's degree, proficiency in French.

Université du Québec à Montréal, Graduate Programs, Program in Project Management, Montréal, QC H3C 3P8, Canada. Offers MGP, Diploma. *Program availability:* Part-time. *Entrance requirements:* For master's and Diploma, appropriate bachelor's degree or equivalent, proficiency in French.

Université du Québec à Rimouski, Graduate Programs, Program in Project Management, Rimouski, QC G5L 3A1, Canada. Offers M Sc, Diploma. Programs offered jointly with Université du Québec à Chicoutimi, Université du Québec à Trois-Rivières, Université du Québec en Outaouais, Université du Québec en Abitibi-Témiscamingue, and Université du Québec à Montréal. *Program availability:* Part-time. *Entrance requirements:* For master's, proficiency in French, appropriate bachelor's degree.

Université du Québec en Abitibi-Témiscamingue, Graduate Programs, Program in Project Management, Rouyn-Noranda, QC J9X 5E4, Canada. Offers M Sc, DESS. M Sc offered jointly with Université du Québec à Chicoutimi, Université du Québec à Rimouski, Université du Québec à Trois-Rivières, Université du Québec en Outaouais, and Université du Québec à Montréal. *Program availability:* Part-time. *Entrance requirements:* For master's, appropriate bachelor's degree, proficiency in French.

Université du Québec en Outaouais, Graduate Programs, Program in Project Management, Gatineau, QC J8X 3X7, Canada. Offers M Sc, MA, DESS, Diploma. Programs offered jointly with Universite du Quebec a Chicoutimi, Universite du Quebec a Rimouski, Universite du Quebec a Trois-Rivieres, Universite du Quebec en Abitibi-T'miscamingue, and Universite du Quebec a Montreal. *Program availability:* Part-time, evening/weekend. *Degree requirements:* For master's, thesis (for some programs). *Entrance requirements:* For master's, appropriate bachelor's degree, proficiency in French.

The University of Alabama in Huntsville, School of Graduate Studies, College of Business Administration, Programs in Business and Management, Huntsville, AL 35899. Offers business analytics (MSMS); federal contracting and procurement management (Certificate); human resource management (MSM); management (MBA), including acquisition management, entrepreneurship, federal contract accounting, finance, human resource management, logistics and supply chain management, marketing, project management; supply chain management (Certificate); technology and innovation management (Certificate). *Accreditation:* AACSB. *Program availability:* Part-time, evening/weekend. *Degree requirements:* For master's, comprehensive exam, thesis or alternative. *Entrance requirements:* For master's, GMAT (minimum score 500), minimum AACSB index of 1080. Additional exam requirements/recommendations for international students: Required—TOEFL (minimum score 550 paper-based; 80 iBT), IELTS (minimum score 6.5). Electronic applications accepted. *Faculty research:* Supply chain management, management of research and development, international marketing and branding, organizational behavior and human resource management, social networks and computational economics.

University of Alaska Anchorage, School of Engineering, Program in Project Management, Anchorage, AK 99508. Offers MS. *Program availability:* Part-time, evening/weekend, online learning. *Degree requirements:* For master's, thesis or alternative, case study and research project. *Entrance requirements:* For master's, two years of project management experience. Additional exam requirements/recommendations for international students: Required—TOEFL (minimum score 550 paper-based). *Expenses:* Contact institution.

University of Calgary, Faculty of Graduate Studies, Schulich School of Engineering, Department of Civil Engineering, Calgary, AB T2N 1N4, Canada. Offers avalanche mechanics (M Sc, PhD); civil engineering (M Eng, M Sc, PhD); energy and environment engineering (M Eng, M Sc, PhD); environmental engineering (M Eng, M Sc, PhD); geotechnical engineering (M Eng, M Sc, PhD); materials science (M Eng, M Sc, PhD); project management (M Eng, M Sc, PhD); structures and solid mechanics (M Eng, M Sc, PhD); transportation engineering (M Eng, M Sc, PhD); water resources (M Eng, M Sc, PhD). *Program availability:* Part-time. *Degree requirements:* For master's, thesis; for doctorate, thesis/dissertation, written and oral candidacy exam. *Entrance requirements:* For master's, minimum GPA of 3.0; for doctorate, minimum GPA of 3.5. Additional exam requirements/recommendations for international students: Required—TOEFL (minimum score 580 paper-based; 93 iBT), IELTS (minimum score 7). Electronic applications accepted. *Faculty research:* Geotechnical engineering, energy and environment, transportation, project management, structures and solid mechanics.

University of California, Berkeley, UC Berkeley Extension, Certificate Programs in Business, Berkeley, CA 94720-1500. Offers accounting (Certificate); business administration (Certificate); finance (Certificate); human resource management (Certificate); management (Certificate); marketing (Certificate); project management (Certificate). *Accreditation:* AACSB. *Program availability:* Online learning.

University of California, Berkeley, UC Berkeley Extension, International Diploma Programs, Berkeley, CA 94720-1500. Offers business administration (Certificate); finance (Certificate); global business management (Certificate); marketing (Certificate); project management (Certificate). *Accreditation:* AACSB.

University of Dallas, Satish and Yasmin Gupta College of Business, Irving, TX 75062-4736. Offers accounting (MBA, MS); business administration (DBA); business analytics (MS); business management (MBA); corporate finance (MBA); cybersecurity (MS); finance (MS); financial services (MBA); global business (MBA, MS); health services management (MBA); human resource management (MBA); information and technology management (MS); information assurance (MBA); information technology (MBA); information technology service management (MBA); marketing management (MBA); organization development (MBA); project management (MBA); sports and entertainment management (MBA); strategic leadership (MBA); supply chain management (MBA). *Accreditation:* AACSB. *Program availability:* Part-time, evening/weekend, online learning. *Entrance requirements:* Additional exam requirements/recommendations for international students: Required—TOEFL. *Application deadline:* Applications are processed on a rolling basis. Application fee: $50. Electronic applications accepted. *Expenses:* Contact institution. *Financial support:* Application deadline: 2/15; applicants required to submit FAFSA. *Unit head:* Brett J.L. Landry, Dean, 972-721-5356, E-mail: blandry@udallas.edu. *Application contact:* Dr. David Sweet, Dean, Braniff Graduate School, 972-721-5288, Fax: 972-721-5280, E-mail: dsweet@udallas.edu. Website: http://www.udallas.edu/cob/

University of Denver, University College, Denver, CO 80208. Offers arts and culture (MA, Certificate); communication management (MS, Certificate), including translation studies (Certificate), world history and culture (Certificate); environmental policy and management (MS); geographic information systems (MS); global affairs (MA, Certificate), including human capital in organizations (Certificate), philanthropic leadership (Certificate), project management (Certificate), strategic innovation and change (Certificate); healthcare leadership (MS); information communications and technology (MS); leadership and organizations (MS); professional creative writing (MA, Certificate), including emergency planning and response (Certificate), organizational security (Certificate); security management (MS, Certificate); strategic human resources (Certificate). *Program availability:* Part-time, evening/weekend, online learning. *Faculty:* 118 part-time/adjunct (62 women). *Students:* 56 full-time (32 women), 1,287 part-time (707 women); includes 330 minority (99 Black or African American, non-Hispanic/Latino; 7 American Indian or Alaska Native, non-Hispanic/Latino; 43 Asian, non-Hispanic/Latino; 141 Hispanic/Latino; 3 Native Hawaiian or other Pacific Islander, non-Hispanic/Latino; 37 Two or more races, non-Hispanic/Latino), 84 international. Average age 34. 783 applicants, 86% accepted, 420 enrolled. In 2017, 461 master's, 173 other advanced degrees awarded. *Degree requirements:* For master's, capstone project. *Entrance requirements:* For master's, transcripts, two letters of recommendation, personal statement, resume. Additional exam requirements/recommendations for international students: Required—TOEFL (minimum score 550 paper-based; 80 iBT). *Application deadline:* For fall admission, 6/21 priority date for domestic students, 5/1 priority date for international students; for winter admission, 9/14 priority date for domestic students, 9/19 priority date for international students; for spring admission, 1/11 priority date for domestic students, 12/12 priority date for international students; for summer admission, 3/29 priority date for domestic students, 3/6 priority date for international students. Applications are processed on a rolling basis. Application fee: $75. Electronic applications accepted. *Expenses:* $7,968 per year half-time. *Financial support:* In 2017–18, 29 students received support. Teaching assistantships available. Financial award applicants required to submit FAFSA. *Unit head:* Dr. Michael McGuire, Dean, 303-871-3518, Fax: 303-871-3303, E-mail: mmcguire@du.edu. *Application contact:* Information Contact, 303-871-2291, E-mail: ucoladm@du.edu. Website: http://universitycollege.du.edu/

University of Houston, College of Technology, Department of Information and Logistics Technology, Houston, TX 77204. Offers information security (MS); supply chain and logistics management (MS); technology project management (MS). *Program availability:* Part-time. *Degree requirements:* For master's, project or thesis (most programs). *Entrance requirements:* For master's, GMAT. Additional exam requirements/recommendations for international students: Required—TOEFL (minimum score 550 paper-based; 79 iBT). Electronic applications accepted.

University of Houston–Downtown, Marilyn Davies College of Business, MBA Program, Houston, TX 77002. Offers accounting (MBA); finance (MBA); human resource management (MBA); international business (MBA); investment management (MBA); leadership (MBA); project management and process improvement (MBA); sales management and business development (MBA); supply chain management (MBA). *Accreditation:* AACSB. *Program availability:* Part-time, evening/weekend. *Faculty:* 36 full-time (13 women), 11 part-time/adjunct (6 women). *Students:* 4 full-time (2 women), 1,065 part-time (605 women); includes 821 minority (383 Black or African American, non-Hispanic/Latino; 3 American Indian or Alaska Native, non-Hispanic/Latino; 136

Asian, non-Hispanic/Latino; 299 Hispanic/Latino), 33 international. Average age 33. 418 applicants, 89% accepted, 308 enrolled. In 2017, 310 master's awarded. *Entrance requirements:* For master's, GMAT, two letters of recommendation from professional references, personal statement, resume. Additional exam requirements/recommendations for international students: Required—TOEFL (minimum score 81 iBT). *Application deadline:* For fall admission, 8/1 for domestic and international students. Application fee: $35 ($60 for international students). Electronic applications accepted. *Expenses:* $360 per credit resident; $725 per credit non-resident. *Financial support:* Federal Work-Study and scholarships/grants available. Financial award application deadline: 4/1; financial award applicants required to submit FAFSA. *Unit head:* Dr. Charles E. Gengler, Dean, 713-221-8179, Fax: 713-221-8675. *Application contact:* Ceshia Love, Director of Admissions, 713-221-8093, Fax: 713-223-7408, E-mail: gradadmissions@uhd.edu. Website: http://mba.uhd.edu/

The University of Kansas, Graduate Studies, School of Engineering, Program in Project Management, Overland Park, KS 66045. Offers ME, MS. *Program availability:* Part-time. *Students:* 7 full-time (0 women), 29 part-time (11 women); includes 12 minority (5 Black or African American, non-Hispanic/Latino; 5 Asian, non-Hispanic/Latino; 1 Hispanic/Latino; 1 Two or more races, non-Hispanic/Latino), 1 international. Average age 37. 35 applicants, 69% accepted, 15 enrolled. In 2017, 17 master's awarded. *Entrance requirements:* For master's, undergraduate degree in engineering or closely-related science, minimum undergraduate GPA of 3.0, two years' full-time work experience in engineering or technology-based company (for ME), current resume, official transcript, 3 letters of recommendation. Application fee: $65 ($85 for international students). Electronic applications accepted. *Unit head:* Herbert R. Tuttle, Assistant Dean, 913-897-8561, E-mail: htuttle@ku.edu. *Application contact:* Jennifer Keleher-Price, Graduate Admissions Contact, 913-867-8635, E-mail: jkeleher-price@ku.edu. Website: https://pmgt.ku.edu/ms-pm

University of Management and Technology, Program in Business Administration, Arlington, VA 22209-1609. Offers general management (MBA, DBA); project management (MBA). *Program availability:* Part-time, evening/weekend, online learning. *Degree requirements:* For master's, comprehensive exam; for doctorate, thesis/dissertation. *Entrance requirements:* For master's, 3 recommendations, resume. Additional exam requirements/recommendations for international students: Required—TOEFL (minimum score 530 paper-based; 71 iBT). Electronic applications accepted.

University of Management and Technology, Program in Computer Science, Arlington, VA 22209-1609. Offers computer science (MS); information technology (AC); project management (AC); software engineering (MS). *Program availability:* Part-time, evening/weekend, online learning. *Entrance requirements:* For master's, 3 recommendations, resume. Additional exam requirements/recommendations for international students: Required—TOEFL (minimum score 530 paper-based; 71 iBT). Electronic applications accepted.

University of Management and Technology, Program in Management, Arlington, VA 22209-1609. Offers acquisition management (MS, AC); criminal justice administration (MS); general management (MS); project management (MS, AC). *Program availability:* Part-time, evening/weekend, online learning. *Entrance requirements:* For master's, 3 recommendations, resume. Additional exam requirements/recommendations for international students: Required—TOEFL (minimum score 530 paper-based; 71 iBT). Electronic applications accepted.

The University of Manchester, Alliance Manchester Business School, M15 6PB, United Kingdom. Offers accounting and finance (M Sc); business (M Ent); business analysis and strategic management (M Sc); business analytics: operational research and risk analysis (M Sc); business psychology (M Sc); corporate communications and reputation management (M Sc); finance (M Sc); finance and business economics (M Sc); human resource management and industrial relations (M Sc); innovation management and entrepreneurship (M Sc); international business and management (M Sc); international human resource management and comparative industrial relations (M Sc); management (M Sc); marketing (M Sc); operations, project and supply chain management (M Sc); organizational psychology (M Sc); quantitative finance (M Sc). *Entrance requirements:* For master's, UK 2:1 honours degree or overseas equivalent. Additional exam requirements/recommendations for international students: Required—TOEFL (minimum score 100 iBT), IELTS (minimum score 7), PTE. Electronic applications accepted. *Faculty research:* Accounting and finance, management sciences and marketing, people management and organization, innovation management and policy, decision sciences.

University of Mary, Gary Tharaldson School of Business, Bismarck, ND 58504-9652. Offers business administration (MBA); energy management (MBA, MS); executive (MBA, MS); health care (MBA, MS); human resource management (MBA); project management (MBA, MPM); virtuous leadership (MBA, MPM, MS). *Program availability:* Part-time, evening/weekend. *Entrance requirements:* For master's, minimum GPA of 2.5. Additional exam requirements/recommendations for international students: Required—TOEFL (minimum score 550 paper-based; 80 iBT). Electronic applications accepted.

University of Michigan–Dearborn, College of Engineering and Computer Science, MS Program in Program and Project Management, Dearborn, MI 48128. Offers MS. *Program availability:* Part-time, evening/weekend, 100% online. *Faculty:* 6 full-time (1 woman), 2 part-time/adjunct (1 woman). *Students:* 9 full-time (5 women), 40 part-time (13 women); includes 10 minority (3 Black or African American, non-Hispanic/Latino; 1 American Indian or Alaska Native, non-Hispanic/Latino; 5 Asian, non-Hispanic/Latino; 1 Hispanic/Latino), 12 international. Average age 36. 29 applicants, 83% accepted, 14 enrolled. In 2017, 19 master's awarded. *Entrance requirements:* For master's, regionally-accredited (or international equivalent) undergraduate degree in engineering, business, economics, math, computer science or other physical sciences; at least two years of practical work experience. Additional exam requirements/recommendations for international students: Required—TOEFL (minimum score 560 paper-based; 84 iBT), IELTS (minimum score 6.5). *Application deadline:* For fall admission, 8/1 for domestic students, 5/1 for international students; for winter admission, 12/1 for domestic students, 9/1 for international students; for spring admission, 4/1 for domestic students, 1/1 for international students. Applications are processed on a rolling basis. Application fee: $60. Electronic applications accepted. *Expenses:* Tuition, state resident: full-time $13,602; part-time $788 per credit hour. Tuition, nonresident: full-time $22,234; part-time $1281 per credit hour. *Required fees:* $754; $754 per year. $377 per term. Tuition and fees vary according to course load, degree level, program and reciprocity agreements. *Financial support:* In 2017–18, 9 students received support. Scholarships/grants, unspecified assistantships, and non-resident tuition scholarships available. Support available to part-time students. Financial award application deadline: 3/1; financial award applicants required to submit FAFSA. *Faculty research:* Risk analysis, decision sciences, project scheduling, project optimization, agile project management. *Unit head:* Dr. Armen Zakarian, Chair, 313-593-5361, E-mail: zakarian@umich.edu. *Application contact:* Office of Graduate Studies, 313-583-6321, E-mail: umd-graduatestudies@umich.edu. Website: https://umdearborn.edu/cecs/departments/industrial-and-manufacturing-systems-engineering/graduate-programs/ms-program-and-project-management

Project Management

University of Nebraska at Omaha, Graduate Studies, College of Information Science and Technology, Department of Information Systems and Quantitative Analysis, Omaha, NE 68182. Offers data analytics (Certificate); information assurance (Certificate); information technology (MIT, PhD); management information systems (MS); project management (Certificate); systems analysis and design (Certificate). *Program availability:* Part-time, evening/weekend. *Degree requirements:* For master's, comprehensive exam, thesis (for some programs); for doctorate, comprehensive exam, thesis/dissertation. *Entrance requirements:* For master's, GRE General Test, minimum GPA of 3.0, 3 letters of recommendation, writing sample, resume, official transcripts; for doctorate, GMAT or GRE General Test, minimum GPA of 3.0, 3 letters of recommendation, writing sample, resume, official transcripts; for Certificate, minimum GPA of 3.0, official transcripts. Additional exam requirements/recommendations for international students: Required—TOEFL, IELTS, PTE. Electronic applications accepted.

University of North Alabama, College of Business, Florence, AL 35632-0001. Offers business administration (MBA), including accounting, enterprise resource planning systems, executive, finance, health care management, information systems, international business, project management. *Accreditation:* AACSB; ACBSP. *Program availability:* Part-time, 100% online, blended/hybrid learning. *Faculty:* 26 full-time (1 woman), 4 part-time/adjunct (0 women). *Students:* 178 full-time (78 women), 498 part-time (237 women); includes 229 minority (92 Black or African American, non-Hispanic/Latino; 8 American Indian or Alaska Native, non-Hispanic/Latino; 104 Asian, non-Hispanic/Latino; 14 Hispanic/Latino; 11 Two or more races, non-Hispanic/Latino), 53 international. Average age 34. 354 applicants, 71% accepted, 190 enrolled. In 2017, 156 master's awarded. *Entrance requirements:* For master's, GMAT, GRE, minimum GPA of 2.75 in last 60 hours, 2.5 overall (on a 3.0 scale); 27 hours of course work in business and economics. Additional exam requirements/recommendations for international students: Required—TOEFL (minimum score 79 iBT), IELTS (minimum score 6), PTE (minimum score 54). *Application deadline:* Applications are processed on a rolling basis. Application fee: $50 ($100 for international students). Electronic applications accepted. *Expenses:* Tuition, state resident: full-time $7824; part-time $5943 per year. Tuition, nonresident: full-time $15,648; part-time $11,736 per year. *Required fees:* $3064; $2298 per unit. Tuition and fees vary according to course load and reciprocity agreements. *Financial support:* In 2017–18, 114 students received support. Scholarships/grants available. Financial award application deadline: 2/1; financial award applicants required to submit FAFSA. *Total annual research expenditures:* $193,193. *Unit head:* Dr. Gregory A. Carnes, Dean, 256-765-4261, Fax: 256-765-4170, E-mail: gacarnes@una.edu. *Application contact:* Hillary N. Coats, Graduate Admissions Coordinator, 256-765-4447, E-mail: graduate@una.edu.
Website: https://www.una.edu/mba/index.html

University of Oklahoma, College of Arts and Sciences, Department of Psychology, Program in Organizational Dynamics, Tulsa, OK 74135. Offers human resource management (Graduate Certificate); organizational dynamics (MA), including human resource management, project management; project management (Graduate Certificate). *Program availability:* Part-time, evening/weekend. *Students:* 12 full-time (9 women), 45 part-time (27 women); includes 15 minority (4 Black or African American, non-Hispanic/Latino; 5 American Indian or Alaska Native, non-Hispanic/Latino; 2 Asian, non-Hispanic/Latino; 3 Hispanic/Latino; 1 Two or more races, non-Hispanic/Latino), 3 international. Average age 33. 16 applicants, 88% accepted, 12 enrolled. In 2017, 11 master's, 8 other advanced degrees awarded. Terminal master's awarded for partial completion of doctoral program. *Degree requirements:* For master's, comprehensive exam (for some programs), thesis (for some programs), capstone project, comprehensive exam, or thesis; 36 hours of coursework; for Graduate Certificate, 12 hours of coursework from approved list. *Entrance requirements:* For master's, GRE (for students who do not have requisite work experience), current resume showing at least 2 years of relevant work experience; 2 letters of recommendation; statement of career goals; transcripts; for Graduate Certificate, resume showing work experience; 2 letters of recommendation; statement of career goals; transcripts. Additional exam requirements/recommendations for international students: Required—TOEFL (minimum score 79 iBT) or IELTS (minimum score 6.5). *Application deadline:* For fall admission, 5/1 for domestic and international students; for spring admission, 11/1 for domestic and international students; for summer admission, 3/15 for domestic and international students. Application fee: $50 ($100 for international students). Electronic applications accepted. *Expenses:* Tuition, state resident: full-time $5119; part-time $213.30 per credit hour. Tuition, nonresident: full-time $19,778; part-time $824.10 per credit hour. *Required fees:* $3458; $133.55 per credit hour. $126.50 per semester. *Financial support:* In 2017–18, 12 students received support. Fellowships with full tuition reimbursements available, research assistantships with full tuition reimbursements available, and teaching assistantships with full tuition reimbursements available available. Financial award application deadline: 6/1; financial award applicants required to submit FAFSA. *Faculty research:* Organizational behavior, personality, organizational climate and culture, leadership, ethics. *Unit head:* Dr. Eric Day, 405-325-4511, Fax: 405-325-4737, E-mail: eday@ou.edu. *Application contact:* Jennifer Kisamore, Associate Professor of Psychology/Graduate Liaison for Organizational Dynamics, 918-660-3603, Fax: 918-660-3383, E-mail: odyn@ou.edu.
Website: http://odyn.ou.edu

University of Ottawa, Faculty of Graduate and Postdoctoral Studies, Faculty of Engineering, Engineering Management Program, Ottawa, ON K1N 6N5, Canada. Offers engineering management (M Eng); information technology (Certificate); project management (Certificate). *Degree requirements:* For master's, thesis or alternative. *Entrance requirements:* For master's and Certificate, honors degree or equivalent, minimum B average. Electronic applications accepted.

University of Phoenix–Bay Area Campus, School of Business, San Jose, CA 95134-1805. Offers accountancy (MS); accounting (MBA); business administration (MBA, DBA); energy management (MBA); global management (MBA); health care management (MBA); human resource management (MBA); human resources management (MM); management (MM); marketing (MBA); organizational leadership (DM); project management (MBA); public administration (MPA); technology management (MBA). *Accreditation:* ACBSP. *Program availability:* Evening/weekend, online learning. *Degree requirements:* For master's, thesis (for some programs). *Entrance requirements:* For master's, minimum undergraduate GPA of 3.0, 3 years of work experience. Additional exam requirements/recommendations for international students: Required—TOEFL (minimum score 550 paper-based; 79 iBT). Electronic applications accepted.

University of Phoenix–Online Campus, School of Business, Phoenix, AZ 85034-7209. Offers accountancy (MS); accounting (MBA, Certificate); business administration (MBA); energy management (MBA); global management (MBA); health care management (MBA); human resource management (MBA, Certificate); human resources management (MM); management (MM); marketing (MBA, Certificate); project management (MBA, Certificate); public administration (MBA, MM); technology management (MBA). *Program availability:* Evening/weekend, online learning. *Entrance requirements:* Additional exam requirements/recommendations for international students: Required—TOEFL, TOEIC (Test of English as an International Communication), Berlitz Online English Proficiency Exam, PTE, or IELTS. Electronic applications accepted. *Expenses:* Contact institution.

University of Phoenix–Phoenix Campus, School of Business, Tempe, AZ 85282-2371. Offers accounting (MBA, MS, Certificate); business administration (MBA); energy management (MBA); global management (MBA); health care management (MBA); human resource management (MBA, Certificate); management (MM); marketing (MBA); project management (MBA); technology management (MBA). *Program availability:* Evening/weekend, online learning. *Entrance requirements:* Additional exam requirements/recommendations for international students: Required—TOEFL, TOEIC (Test of English as an International Communication), Berlitz Online English Proficiency Exam, PTE, or IELTS. Electronic applications accepted. *Expenses:* Contact institution.

University of Regina, Faculty of Graduate Studies and Research, Kenneth Levene Graduate School of Business, Program in Business Administration, Regina, SK S4S 0A2, Canada. Offers business foundations (PGD); engineering management (MBA); executive business administration (EMBA); international business (MBA); leadership (M Admin); organizational leadership (Master's Certificate); project management (Master's Certificate); public safety management (MBA). *Program availability:* Part-time, evening/weekend. *Faculty:* 43 full-time (15 women), 6 part-time/adjunct (0 women). *Students:* 35 full-time (15 women), 18 part-time (9 women). 172 applicants, 26% accepted. In 2017, 24 master's, 2 other advanced degrees awarded. *Degree requirements:* For master's, project (for some programs). *Entrance requirements:* For master's, GMAT, three years of relevant work experience, four-year undergraduate degree; for other advanced degree, GMAT (for PGD), four-year undergraduate degree and two years of relevant work experience (for Master's Certificate); three years' work experience (for PGD). Additional exam requirements/recommendations for international students: Required—TOEFL (minimum score 580 paper-based; 80 iBT), IELTS (minimum score 6.5), PTE (minimum score 59). *Application deadline:* Applications are processed on a rolling basis. Application fee: $100. Electronic applications accepted. *Expenses:* CAD$20,150 per year. *Financial support:* In 2017–18, fellowships (averaging $6,000 per year), teaching assistantships (averaging $2,562 per year) were awarded; research assistantships, career-related internships or fieldwork, and scholarships/grants also available. Financial award application deadline: 6/15. *Faculty research:* Business policy and strategy, production and operations management, human behavior in organizations, financial management, social issues in business. *Unit head:* Dr. David Senkow, Dean, 306-585-4719, Fax: 306-585-5361, E-mail: david.senkow@uregina.ca. *Application contact:* Ronald Camp, Graduate Programs, 306-337-2387, Fax: 306-585-5361, E-mail: ronald.camp@uregina.ca.
Website: http://www.uregina.ca/business/levene/

The University of Tennessee at Chattanooga, Engineering Management and Technology Program, Chattanooga, TN 37403. Offers construction management (Graduate Certificate); engineering management (MS); fundamentals of engineering management (Graduate Certificate); leadership and ethics (Graduate Certificate); logistics and supply chain management (Graduate Certificate); power systems management (Graduate Certificate); project and technology management (Graduate Certificate); quality management (Graduate Certificate). *Program availability:* 100% online, blended/hybrid learning. *Students:* 14 full-time (3 women), 50 part-time (11 women); includes 17 minority (10 Black or African American, non-Hispanic/Latino; 1 Asian, non-Hispanic/Latino; 6 Hispanic/Latino), 5 international. Average age 33. 34 applicants, 94% accepted, 20 enrolled. In 2017, 18 master's, 6 other advanced degrees awarded. *Degree requirements:* For master's, thesis. *Entrance requirements:* For master's, GRE General Test, letters of recommendation; minimum undergraduate GPA of 2.7 overall or 3.0 in final two years; for Graduate Certificate, baccalaureate degree and professional experience or have already been admitted to engineering/engineering management graduate program. Additional exam requirements/recommendations for international students: Required—TOEFL (minimum score 550 paper-based; 79 iBT), IELTS (minimum score 6). *Application deadline:* For fall admission, 6/15 priority date for domestic students, 7/1 for international students; for spring admission, 11/1 priority date for domestic students, 11/1 for international students. Applications are processed on a rolling basis. Application fee: $35 ($40 for international students). Electronic applications accepted. *Expenses:* Contact institution. *Financial support:* Research assistantships, teaching assistantships, career-related internships or fieldwork, scholarships/grants, and unspecified assistantships available. Support available to part-time students. Financial award application deadline: 7/1; financial award applicants required to submit FAFSA. *Faculty research:* Plant layout design, lean manufacturing, Six Sigma, value management, product development. *Total annual research expenditures:* $108,577. *Unit head:* Dr. Neslihan Alp, Department Head, 423-425-4032, Fax: 423-425-5818, E-mail: neslihan-alp@utc.edu. *Application contact:* Dr. Joanne Romagni, Dean of the Graduate School, 423-425-4478, Fax: 423-425-5223, E-mail: joanne-romagni@utc.edu.
Website: https://www.utc.edu/college-engineering-computer-science/programs/engineering-management-and-technology/index.php

The University of Texas at Dallas, Naveen Jindal School of Management, Program in Organizations, Strategy and International Management, Richardson, TX 75080. Offers business administration (MBA); executive business administration (EMBA); global leadership (EMBA); healthcare leadership and management (MS); healthcare management (EMBA); innovation and entrepreneurship (MS); international management studies (MS, PhD); management science (MS, PhD); project management (EMBA); systems engineering and management (MS); MS/MBA. *Program availability:* Part-time, evening/weekend. *Faculty:* 18 full-time (6 women), 17 part-time/adjunct (2 women). *Students:* 608 full-time (232 women), 711 part-time (326 women); includes 446 minority (93 Black or African American, non-Hispanic/Latino; 3 American Indian or Alaska Native, non-Hispanic/Latino; 212 Asian, non-Hispanic/Latino; 107 Hispanic/Latino; 31 Two or more races, non-Hispanic/Latino), 339 international. Average age 32. 1,665 applicants, 36% accepted, 398 enrolled. In 2017, 473 master's, 14 doctorates awarded. *Degree requirements:* For doctorate, thesis/dissertation. *Entrance requirements:* For master's and doctorate, GMAT. Additional exam requirements/recommendations for international students: Required—TOEFL (minimum score 550 paper-based). *Application deadline:* For fall admission, 7/15 for domestic students, 5/1 priority date for international students; for spring admission, 11/15 for domestic students, 9/1 priority date for international students. Applications are processed on a rolling basis. Application fee: $50 ($100 for international students). Electronic applications accepted. *Expenses:* Tuition, state resident: full-time $12,916; part-time $718 per credit hour. Tuition, nonresident: full-time $25,252; part-time $1403 per credit hour. *Financial support:* In 2017–18, 369 students received support, including 22 research assistantships with partial tuition reimbursements available (averaging $36,554 per year), 88 teaching assistantships with partial tuition reimbursements available (averaging $25,176 per year); Federal Work-Study, institutionally sponsored loans, scholarships/grants, and unspecified assistantships also available. Support available to part-time students. Financial award application deadline: 4/30; financial award applicants required to submit FAFSA. *Faculty research:* International accounting, international trade and finance, economic development, international economics. *Unit head:* Dr. Erik W.K. Tsang, Area Coordinator, 972-883-4386, Fax: 972-883-5977, E-mail: ewktsang@utdallas.edu.
Website: http://jindal.utdallas.edu/osim/

University of Wisconsin–Platteville, School of Graduate Studies, Distance Learning Center, Online Master of Science in Project Management Program, Platteville, WI 53818-3099. Offers MS. *Program availability:* Part-time. *Students:* 3 full-time (all women), 230 part-time (99 women); includes 52 minority (21 Black or African American, non-Hispanic/Latino; 1 American Indian or Alaska Native, non-Hispanic/Latino; 18 Asian, non-Hispanic/Latino; 12 Hispanic/Latino). 74 applicants, 68% accepted, 34 enrolled. In 2017, 71 master's awarded. *Degree requirements:* For master's, thesis or alternative. *Entrance requirements:* Additional exam requirements/recommendations for international students: Required—TOEFL (minimum score 550 paper-based; 79 iBT), IELTS (minimum score 6.5). *Application deadline:* For fall admission, 7/1 priority date for domestic students; for spring admission, 11/1 priority date for domestic students. Applications are processed on a rolling basis. Application fee: $56. Electronic applications accepted. *Unit head:* William Haskins, Coordinator, 608-342-1961, Fax: 608-342-1466, E-mail: disted@uwplatt.edu.
Website: http://www.uwplatt.edu/disted/project-management.html

University of Wisconsin–Stout, Graduate School, College of Management, Program in Operations and Supply Management, Menomonie, WI 54751. Offers operations management (MS); project management (MS); quality management (MS); supply chain management (MS).

Virginia International University, School of Business, Fairfax, VA 22030. Offers accounting (MBA, MS); entrepreneurship (MBA); executive management (Graduate Certificate); global logistics (MBA); health care management (MBA); hospitality and tourism management (MBA); human resources management (MBA); international business management (MBA); international finance (MBA); marketing management (MBA); mass media and public relations (MBA); project management (MBA, MS). *Program availability:* Part-time, online learning. *Entrance requirements:* For master's and Graduate Certificate, bachelor's degree. Additional exam requirements/recommendations for international students: Required—TOEFL (minimum score 550 paper-based; 80 iBT), IELTS (minimum score 6). Electronic applications accepted.

Virginia International University, School of Computer Information Systems, Fairfax, VA 22030. Offers business intelligence (Graduate Certificate); business intelligence and data analytics (MIS); computer science (MS), including computer animation and gaming, cybersecurity, data management networking, intelligent systems, software applications development, software engineering; cybersecurity (MIS); data management (MIS); enterprise project management (MIS); health informatics (MIS); information assurance (MIS); information systems (Graduate Certificate); information systems management (MS, Graduate Certificate); information technology (MS); information technology audit and compliance (Graduate Certificate); knowledge management (MIS); software engineering (MS). *Program availability:* Part-time, online learning. *Entrance requirements:* For master's, bachelor's degree. Additional exam requirements/recommendations for international students: Required—TOEFL (minimum score 550 paper-based; 80 iBT), IELTS. Electronic applications accepted.

Viterbo University, Master of Business Administration Program, La Crosse, WI 54601-4797. Offers general business administration (MBA); health care management (MBA); international business (MBA); leadership (MBA); project management (MBA). *Accreditation:* ACBSP. *Program availability:* Part-time, evening/weekend. *Degree requirements:* For master's, 34 semester credits. *Entrance requirements:* For master's, bachelor's degree, transcripts, minimum undergraduate cumulative GPA of 3.0, 2 letters of reference, 3-5 page essay. Additional exam requirements/recommendations for international students: Recommended—TOEFL (minimum score 550 paper-based). Electronic applications accepted. *Expenses:* Contact institution.

Walden University, Graduate Programs, School of Management, Minneapolis, MN 55401. Offers accounting (MBA, MS, DBA), including accounting for the professional (MS), accounting with CPA emphasis (MS), self-designed (MS); advanced project management (Graduate Certificate); applied project management (Graduate Certificate); auditing (Graduate Certificate); bridge to business administration (Post-Doctoral Certificate); bridge to management (Post-Doctoral Certificate); business management (Graduate Certificate); communication (MBA); corporate finance (MBA); digital marketing (Graduate Certificate); entrepreneurship (DBA); entrepreneurship and small business (MBA); finance (MS, DBA), including finance for the professional (MS), finance with CFA/investment (MS), finance with CPA emphasis (MS); global supply chain management (DBA); healthcare management (MBA, DBA); human resource management (MBA, MS, Graduate Certificate), including functional human resource management (MS), general program (MS), integrating functional and strategic human resource management (MS), organizational strategy (MS); human resources management (DBA); information systems management (DBA); international business (MBA, DBA); leadership (MBA, MS, DBA, Graduate Certificate), including general program (MS), human resource leadership (MS), leader development (MS), self-designed (MS); management (MS, PhD), including communications (MS), finance (PhD), general program (MS), healthcare management (MS), human resource management (MS), human resources management (PhD), information systems management (PhD), international business (MS), leadership (MS), leadership and organizational change (PhD), marketing (MS), project management (MS), strategy and operations (MS); managerial accounting (Graduate Certificate); marketing (MBA, MS, DBA); project management (MBA, MS, DBA); self-designed (MBA, DBA); social impact management (DBA); technology entrepreneurship (DBA). *Accreditation:* ACBSP. *Program availability:* Part-time, evening/weekend, online only, 100% online. *Degree requirements:* For master's, thesis (for some programs), residency (for EMBA); for doctorate, thesis/dissertation (for some programs), residency. *Entrance requirements:* For master's, bachelor's degree or higher; minimum GPA of 2.5; official transcripts; goal statement (for some programs); access to computer and Internet; for doctorate, master's degree or higher; three years of related professional or academic experience (preferred); minimum GPA of 3.0; goal statement and current resume (for select programs); official transcripts; access to computer and Internet; for other advanced degree, relevant work experience; access to computer and Internet. Additional exam requirements/recommendations for international students: Required—TOEFL (minimum

score 550 paper-based, 79 iBT), IELTS (minimum score 6.5), Michigan English Language Assessment Battery (minimum score 82), or PTE (minimum score 53). Electronic applications accepted.

Walsh College of Accountancy and Business Administration, Graduate Programs, Program in Information Technology, Troy, MI 48083. Offers chief information officer (MSIT); cybersecurity (MSIT); data science (MSIT); global project and program management (MSIT). *Program availability:* Part-time, evening/weekend. *Faculty:* 2 full-time (1 woman), 5 part-time/adjunct (2 women). *Students:* 72 (25 women); includes 24 minority (15 Black or African American, non-Hispanic/Latino; 4 Asian, non-Hispanic/Latino; 2 Hispanic/Latino; 3 Two or more races, non-Hispanic/Latino), 12 international. Average age 36. 44 applicants, 82% accepted, 27 enrolled. In 2017, 14 master's awarded. *Entrance requirements:* For master's, minimum overall cumulative GPA of 2.75 from all colleges previously attended. Additional exam requirements/recommendations for international students: Required—TOEFL (minimum score 550 paper-based, 79 iBT), IELTS (6.5), Michigan English Language Assessment Battery, or MTELP (80). *Application deadline:* Applications are processed on a rolling basis. Application fee: $35. Electronic applications accepted. *Expenses:* $770 per semester credit hour plus $125 registration fee per semester. *Financial support:* In 2017–18, 3 students received support. Career-related internships or fieldwork and scholarships/grants available. Financial award application deadline: 6/30; financial award applicants required to submit FAFSA. *Faculty research:* Business intelligence, data and decision-making, cyber security, project management, mobile technologies. *Unit head:* David Schippers, Chair, Information Technology and Decision Sciences, 248-823-1635, Fax: 248-689-0920, E-mail: dschippe@walshcollege.edu. *Application contact:* Heather Rigby, Director, Admissions and Academic Advising, 248-823-1600, Fax: 248-823-1611, E-mail: hrigby@walshcollege.edu.

Wayland Baptist University, Graduate Programs, Programs in Business Administration/Management, Plainview, TX 79072-6998. Offers accounting (MBA); general business (MBA); health care administration (MAM, MBA); human resource management (MAM, MBA); international management (MBA); management (MBA, D Mgt); management information systems (MBA); organization management (MAM); project management (MBA). *Program availability:* Part-time, evening/weekend, online learning. *Faculty:* 30 full-time (5 women), 38 part-time/adjunct (9 women). *Students:* 42 full-time (20 women), 538 part-time (253 women); includes 311 minority (98 Black or African American, non-Hispanic/Latino; 4 American Indian or Alaska Native, non-Hispanic/Latino; 16 Asian, non-Hispanic/Latino; 153 Hispanic/Latino; 11 Native Hawaiian or other Pacific Islander, non-Hispanic/Latino; 29 Two or more races, non-Hispanic/Latino), 6 international. Average age 40. 100 applicants, 96% accepted, 60 enrolled. In 2017, 216 master's awarded. *Degree requirements:* For master's, capstone course. *Entrance requirements:* For master's, GMAT, GRE or MAT. Additional exam requirements/recommendations for international students: Required—TOEFL (minimum score 500 paper-based; 61 iBT). *Application deadline:* Applications are processed on a rolling basis. Application fee: $50. Electronic applications accepted. *Expenses: Tuition:* Full-time $11,250; part-time $625 per credit hour. *Required fees:* $1200. *Financial support:* Federal Work-Study, institutionally sponsored loans, and scholarships/grants available. Support available to part-time students. Financial award application deadline: 5/1; financial award applicants required to submit FAFSA. *Unit head:* Dr. Kelly Warren, Chairman, 806-291-1020, Fax: 806-291-1957, E-mail: warrenk@wbu.edu. *Application contact:* Amanda Stanton, Graduate Studies, 806-291-3423, Fax: 806-291-1950, E-mail: stanton@wbu.edu.

Western Carolina University, Graduate School, College of Business, Program in Project Management, Cullowhee, NC 28723. Offers MPM, Graduate Certificate. *Program availability:* Part-time, evening/weekend, online learning. *Entrance requirements:* For master's, GMAT or GRE, work experience in project management, appropriate undergraduate degree with minimum GPA of 3.0, employer recommendation, resume. Additional exam requirements/recommendations for international students: Required—TOEFL (minimum score 550 paper-based; 79 iBT). *Expenses:* Tuition, state resident: full-time $4436. Tuition, nonresident: full-time $14,842. *Required fees:* $2926.

Wilmington University, College of Technology, New Castle, DE 19720-6491. Offers cybersecurity (MS); information assurance (MS); information systems technologies (MS); management and management information systems (MS); technology project management (MS); Web design (MS). *Program availability:* Part-time, evening/weekend. *Faculty:* 5 full-time (2 women), 99 part-time/adjunct (31 women). *Students:* 631 full-time (159 women), 486 part-time (141 women); includes 91 minority (53 Black or African American, non-Hispanic/Latino; 3 American Indian or Alaska Native, non-Hispanic/Latino; 22 Asian, non-Hispanic/Latino; 5 Hispanic/Latino; 2 Native Hawaiian or other Pacific Islander, non-Hispanic/Latino; 6 Two or more races, non-Hispanic/Latino), 917 international. Average age 26. 774 applicants, 45% accepted, 307 enrolled. In 2017, 965 master's awarded. *Entrance requirements:* Additional exam requirements/recommendations for international students: Required—TOEFL (minimum score 500 paper-based). *Application deadline:* Applications are processed on a rolling basis. Application fee: $35. Electronic applications accepted. *Expenses: Tuition:* Part-time $466 per credit. *Required fees:* $25 per semester. Tuition and fees vary according to degree level and campus/location. *Unit head:* Dr. Mary Ann K. Westerfield, Dean. *Application contact:* Laura Morris, Director of Admissions, 877-967-5464, E-mail: infocenter@wilmu.edu.
Website: http://www.wilmu.edu/technology/

Wingate University, Porter B. Byrum School of Business, Wingate, NC 28174. Offers accounting (MAC); corporate innovation (MBA); finance (MBA); general management (MBA); healthcare management (MBA); marketing (MBA); project management (MBA). *Accreditation:* ACBSP. *Program availability:* Part-time, evening/weekend. *Entrance requirements:* For master's, GMAT, work experience, 2 letters of recommendation. Electronic applications accepted. *Expenses:* Contact institution. *Faculty research:* Stochastic processes, business ethics, regional economic development, municipal finance, consumer behavior.

Section 18
Quality Management

This section contains a directory of institutions offering graduate work in quality management. Additional information about programs listed in the directory may be obtained by writing directly to the dean of a graduate school or chair of a department at the address given in the directory.

For programs offering related work, see also in this book *Business Administration and Management*.

CONTENTS

Program Directory

Quality Management

California Intercontinental University, School of Information Technology, Irvine, CA 92614. Offers information systems and enterprise resource management (DBA); information systems and knowledge management (MBA); project and quality management (MBA).

California State University, Dominguez Hills, College of Extended and International Education, Program in Quality Assurance, Carson, CA 90747-0001. Offers MS. *Program availability:* Part-time, evening/weekend, 100% online. *Degree requirements:* For master's, thesis. *Entrance requirements:* For master's, minimum GPA of 2.75. Additional exam requirements/recommendations for international students: Required—TOEFL. Electronic applications accepted. *Expenses:* Contact institution. *Faculty research:* Six Sigma, lean thinking, risk management, quality management.

Calumet College of Saint Joseph, Program in Quality Assurance, Whiting, IN 46394-2195. Offers MS.

Eastern Michigan University, Graduate School, College of Technology, School of Engineering Technology, Programs in Quality Management, Ypsilanti, MI 48197. Offers MS, Graduate Certificate. *Program availability:* Part-time, evening/weekend, online learning. *Students:* 4 full-time (2 women), 45 part-time (15 women); includes 15 minority (9 Black or African American, non-Hispanic/Latino; 2 Asian, non-Hispanic/Latino; 3 Hispanic/Latino; 1 Two or more races, non-Hispanic/Latino), 1 international. Average age 44. 24 applicants, 88% accepted, 12 enrolled. In 2017, 12 master's, 1 other advanced degree awarded. *Entrance requirements:* Additional exam requirements/recommendations for international students: Required—TOEFL. *Application deadline:* Applications are processed on a rolling basis. Application fee: $45. *Financial support:* Fellowships, research assistantships with full tuition reimbursements, teaching assistantships with full tuition reimbursements, career-related internships or fieldwork, Federal Work-Study, institutionally sponsored loans, scholarships/grants, tuition waivers (partial), and unspecified assistantships available. Support available to part-time students. Financial award applicants required to submit FAFSA. *Application contact:* Dr. Herman Tang, Program Coordinator, 734-487-2040, Fax: 734-487-8755, E-mail: htang2@emich.edu.

Florida Institute of Technology, Extended Studies Division, Melbourne, FL 32901-6975. Offers acquisition and contract management (MS); aerospace engineering (MS); business administration (MBA, DBA); computer information systems (MS); computer science (MS); electrical engineering (MS); engineering management (MS); human resources management (MS); logistics management (MS), including humanitarian and disaster relief logistics; management (MS), including acquisition and contract management, e-business, human resources management, information systems, logistics management, management, transportation management; material acquisition management (MS); mechanical engineering (MS); operations research (MS); project management (MS), including information systems, operations research; public administration (MPA); quality management (MS); software engineering (MS); space systems (MS); space systems management (MS); supply chain management (MS); systems management (MS), including information systems, operations research; technology management (MS). *Program availability:* Part-time, evening/weekend, online learning. *Students:* Average age 36. 962 applicants, 48% accepted, 323 enrolled. In 2017, 403 master's awarded. *Entrance requirements:* For master's, GMAT or resume showing 8 years of supervised experience, minimum GPA of 3.0, 2 letters of recommendation, resume. Additional exam requirements/recommendations for international students: Required—TOEFL (minimum score 550 paper-based; 79 iBT). *Application deadline:* For fall admission, 4/1 for international students; for spring admission, 9/30 for international students. Applications are processed on a rolling basis. Electronic applications accepted. *Expenses:* Contact institution. *Financial support:* Application deadline: 3/1; applicants required to submit FAFSA. *Unit head:* Dr. Theodore R. Richardson, III, Dean, 321-674-8123, Fax: 321-674-7597, E-mail: trichardson@fit.edu. *Application contact:* Carolyn Farrior, Director of Graduate Admissions, Online Learning and Off-Campus Programs, 321-674-7118, Fax: 321-674-8216, E-mail: cfarrior@fit.edu.
Website: http://es.fit.edu

Hofstra University, Frank G. Zarb School of Business, Programs in Information Systems, Hempstead, NY 11549. Offers business administration (MBA), including business analytics, information systems, quality management; business analytics (MS); information systems (MS, Advanced Certificate). *Program availability:* Part-time, evening/weekend, blended/hybrid learning. *Students:* 85 full-time (38 women), 22 part-time (9 women); includes 12 minority (1 Black or African American, non-Hispanic/Latino; 8 Asian, non-Hispanic/Latino; 3 Hispanic/Latino), 78 international. Average age 27. 120 applicants, 63% accepted, 37 enrolled. In 2017, 49 master's awarded. *Degree requirements:* For master's, capstone course (for MBA), thesis (for MS), minimum GPA of 3.0. *Entrance requirements:* For master's, GMAT/GRE, 2 letters of recommendation, resume, essay; for Advanced Certificate, GMAT/GRE, 2 letters of recommendation, resume. Additional exam requirements/recommendations for international students: Required—TOEFL (minimum score 550 paper-based; 80 iBT); Recommended—IELTS (minimum score 6). *Application deadline:* Applications are processed on a rolling basis. Application fee: $75. Electronic applications accepted. *Expenses:* $1,322 per credit. *Financial support:* In 2017–18, 41 students received support, including 40 fellowships with full and partial tuition reimbursements available (averaging $5,921 per year), 2 research assistantships with full and partial tuition reimbursements available (averaging $5,483 per year); career-related internships or fieldwork, Federal Work-Study, institutionally sponsored loans, scholarships/grants, tuition waivers (full and partial), and unspecified assistantships also available. Support available to part-time students. Financial award applicants required to submit FAFSA. *Faculty research:* Big data and social media, healthcare IT and analytics, machine learning and artificial intelligence, inventory system and quality management, cybersecurity and information processing. *Unit head:* Dr. Hak Kim, Chairperson, 516-463-5716, Fax: 516-463-4834, E-mail: hak.j.kim@hofstra.edu. *Application contact:* Sunil Samuel, Assistant Vice President of Admissions, 516-463-4723, Fax: 516-463-4664, E-mail: graduateadmission@hofstra.edu.
Website: http://www.hofstra.edu/business/

Instituto Tecnologico de Santo Domingo, Graduate School, Area of Business, Santo Domingo, Dominican Republic. Offers banking and securities markets (M Mgmt); corporate finance (M Mgmt); human resources management (M Mgmt, Certificate); international trade management (M Mgmt); marketing (M Mgmt); organizational development (M Mgmt); quality and productivity management (Certificate); tax management and planning (M Mgmt); upper management (M Mgmt).

Instituto Tecnológico y de Estudios Superiores de Monterrey, Campus Ciudad de México, Virtual University Division, Ciudad de Mexico, Mexico. Offers administration of information technologies (MA); computer sciences (MA); education (MA, PhD); educational technology (MA); environmental engineering (MA); environmental systems (MA); humanistic studies (MA); industrial engineering (MA); international business for Latin America (MA); quality systems (MA); quality systems and productivity (MA). *Program availability:* Part-time, evening/weekend, online learning. *Entrance requirements:* For master's and doctorate, Instituto entrance exam. Additional exam requirements/recommendations for international students: Required—TOEFL.

Instituto Tecnológico y de Estudios Superiores de Monterrey, Campus Ciudad Juárez, Program in Quality Management, Ciudad Juárez, Mexico. Offers MQM.

Instituto Tecnológico y de Estudios Superiores de Monterrey, Campus Estado de México, Professional and Graduate Division, Estado de Mexico, Mexico. Offers administration of information technologies (MITA); architecture (M Arch); business administration (GMBA, MBA); computer sciences (MCS, PhD); education (M Ed); educational institution administration (MAD); educational technology and innovation (PhD); electronic commerce (MEC); environmental systems (MS); finance (MAF); humanistic studies (MHS); information sciences and knowledge management (MISKM); information systems (MS); manufacturing systems (MS); marketing (MEM); quality systems and productivity (MS); science and materials engineering (PhD); telecommunications management (MTM). *Program availability:* Part-time, online learning. *Degree requirements:* For master's, one foreign language, thesis (for some programs); for doctorate, one foreign language, thesis/dissertation. *Entrance requirements:* For master's, E-PAEP 500, interview; for doctorate, E-PAEP 500, research proposal. Additional exam requirements/recommendations for international students: Required—TOEFL (minimum score 550 paper-based). *Faculty research:* Surface treatments by plasmas, mechanical properties, robotics, graphical computing, mechatronics security protocols.

Instituto Tecnológico y de Estudios Superiores de Monterrey, Campus Irapuato, Graduate Programs, Irapuato, Mexico. Offers administration (MBA); administration of information technology (MAIT); administration of telecommunications (MAT); architecture (M Arch); computer science (MCS); education (M Ed); educational administration (MEA); educational innovation and technology (DEIT); educational technology (MET); electronic commerce (MBA); environmental administration and planning (MEAP); environmental systems (MES); finances (MBA); humanistic studies (MHS); international management for Latin American executives (MIMLAE); library and information science (MLIS); manufacturing quality management (MMQM); marketing research (MBA).

Madonna University, School of Business, Livonia, MI 48150-1173. Offers business administration (MBA); international business (MSBA); leadership studies (MSBA); leadership studies in criminal justice (MSBA); quality and operations management (MSBA). *Program availability:* Part-time, evening/weekend, online learning. *Degree requirements:* For master's, thesis (for some programs), foreign language proficiency (international business). *Entrance requirements:* For master's, GMAT, GRE General Test, minimum GPA of 3.0. Electronic applications accepted. *Faculty research:* Management, women in management, future studies.

Mount Mercy University, Program in Business Administration, Cedar Rapids, IA 52402-4797. Offers human resource (MBA); quality management (MBA). *Program availability:* Evening/weekend. *Entrance requirements:* For master's, minimum cumulative GPA of 3.0, 2 letters of recommendation, resume. Additional exam requirements/recommendations for international students: Required—TOEFL (minimum score 570 paper-based; 88 iBT). Electronic applications accepted.

The National Graduate School of Quality Management, Graduate Programs, Falmouth, MA 02541. Offers homeland security (MS); quality systems management (MS, DBA).

Northwestern University, School of Professional Studies, Program in Regulatory Compliance, Evanston, IL 60208. Offers clinical research (MS); healthcare compliance (MS); quality systems (MS). Offered in partnership with Northwestern Univesity's Clinical and Translational Sciences Institute. *Program availability:* Part-time, evening/weekend.
Website: https://sps.northwestern.edu/masters/regulatory-compliance/index.php

Penn State Erie, The Behrend College, Graduate School, Erie, PA 16563. Offers accounting (MPAC); applied clinical psychology (MA); business administration (MBA); quality and manufacturing management (MMM). *Accreditation:* AACSB. *Program availability:* Part-time. *Students:* 31 full-time (15 women), 126 part-time (39 women); includes 10 minority (4 Black or African American, non-Hispanic/Latino; 1 Hispanic/Latino; 5 Two or more races, non-Hispanic/Latino). Average age 31. 104 applicants, 75% accepted, 75 enrolled. In 2017, 72 master's awarded. *Entrance requirements:* Additional exam requirements/recommendations for international students: Required—TOEFL (minimum score 550 paper-based; 80 iBT), IELTS. *Application deadline:* Applications are processed on a rolling basis. Application fee: $65. Electronic applications accepted. *Financial support:* Federal Work-Study available. Financial award application deadline: 2/15; financial award applicants required to submit FAFSA. *Unit head:* Dr. Ralph M. Ford, Chancellor, 814-898-6160, Fax: 814-898-6461. *Application contact:* Ann M. Burbules, Assistant Director, Graduate Admissions, 866-374-3378, Fax: 814-898-6044, E-mail: behrend.admissions@psu.edu.
Website: http://behrend.psu.edu/

Regis College, Program in Regulatory and Clinical Research Management, Weston, MA 02493. Offers MS. *Program availability:* Part-time, evening/weekend, blended/hybrid learning. *Degree requirements:* For master's, thesis optional, internship/field experience. *Entrance requirements:* For master's, GRE or MAT, official transcripts, 2 recommendations, personal statement, resume, interview. Additional exam requirements/recommendations for international students: Required—TOEFL (minimum score 560 paper-based; 79 iBT); Recommended—IELTS (minimum score 6.5). *Application deadline:* Applications are processed on a rolling basis. Application fee: $65. Electronic applications accepted. *Financial support:* Career-related internships or fieldwork, scholarships/grants, and unspecified assistantships available. Financial award applicants required to submit FAFSA. *Faculty research:* FDA regulatory affairs medical device. *Unit head:* Dr. Joni Beshansky, Director, 781-768-7008, E-mail: joni.beshansky@regiscollege.edu.

Rutgers University–New Brunswick, Graduate School-New Brunswick, Program in Statistics, Piscataway, NJ 08854-8097. Offers applied statistics (MS); biostatistics (MS); data mining (MS); quality and productivity management (MS); statistics (MS, PhD). *Program availability:* Part-time. Terminal master's awarded for partial completion of doctoral program. *Degree requirements:* For master's, comprehensive exam, essay, exam, non-thesis essay paper; for doctorate, one foreign language, thesis/dissertation, qualifying oral and written exams. *Entrance requirements:* For master's, GRE General Test; for doctorate, GRE General Test, GRE Subject Test (recommended). Additional exam requirements/recommendations for international students: Required—TOEFL (minimum score 550 paper-based). Electronic applications accepted. *Faculty research:* Probability, decision theory, linear models, multivariate statistics, statistical computing.

Southern New Hampshire University, School of Business, Manchester, NH 03106-1045. Offers accounting (MBA, Graduate Certificate); accounting finance (MS); accounting/auditing (MS); accounting/forensic accounting (MS); accounting/management accounting (MS); accounting/taxation (MS); applied economics (MS); athletic administration (MBA, Graduate Certificate); business administration (IMBA, Certificate), including business information systems (Certificate), human resource management (Certificate); business analytics (MBA); business intelligence (MBA); communication (MA), including new media and marketing, public relations; community economic development (MBA); criminal justice (MBA); data analytics (MS); economics (MBA); engineering management (MBA); entrepreneurship (MBA); finance (MBA, MS, Graduate Certificate); finance/corporate finance (MS); finance/investments (MS); forensic accounting (MBA); forensic accounting and fraud examination (Graduate Certificate); healthcare informatics (MBA); healthcare management (MBA); human resource management (MS); human resources (MBA); information technology (MS); information technology management (MBA); international business (PhD); Internet marketing (MBA); leadership (MBA); leadership of nonprofit organizations (Graduate Certificate); management (MS); marketing (MBA, MS, Graduate Certificate); music business (MBA); operations and project management (MS); operations and supply chain management (MBA, Graduate Certificate); organizational leadership (MS); project management (MBA, Graduate Certificate); public administration (MBA, Graduate Certificate); quantitative analysis (MBA); Six Sigma (Graduate Certificate); Six Sigma quality (MBA); social media marketing (MBA, Graduate Certificate); sport management (MBA, MS, Graduate Certificate); sustainability and environmental compliance (MBA); MBA/Certificate. *Accreditation:* ACBSP. *Program availability:* Part-time, evening/weekend, online learning. Terminal master's awarded for partial completion of doctoral program. *Degree requirements:* For master's, one foreign language, comprehensive exam (for some programs), thesis or alternative; for doctorate, one foreign language, comprehensive exam, thesis/dissertation. *Entrance requirements:* For master's, minimum GPA of 2.5; for doctorate, GMAT. Additional exam requirements/recommendations for international students: Required—TOEFL (minimum score 500 paper-based). *Application deadline:* Applications are processed on a rolling basis. Application fee: $40. Electronic applications accepted. *Expenses: Tuition:* Part-time $627 per credit hour. Part-time tuition and fees vary according to campus/location and program. *Financial support:* Career-related internships or fieldwork, Federal Work-Study, institutionally sponsored loans, scholarships/grants, tuition waivers (partial), and unspecified assistantships available. Support available to part-time students. Financial award applicants required to submit FAFSA. *Unit head:* Dr. Bill Lightfoot, Dean, 603-644-3102, Fax: 603-644-3144. *Application contact:* Office of Graduate Admission, 888-327-SNHU, Fax: 603-644-3144, E-mail: enroll@snhu.edu.

Stevens Institute of Technology, Graduate School, Charles V. Schaefer Jr. School of Engineering and Science, Department of Civil, Environmental, and Ocean Engineering, Program in Construction Management, Hoboken, NJ 07030. Offers construction management (MS, Certificate), including construction accounting/estimating (Certificate), construction engineering (Certificate), construction law/disputes (Certificate), construction/quality management (Certificate). *Program availability:* Part-time, evening/weekend. *Students:* 91 full-time (18 women), 19 part-time (4 women); includes 7 minority (4 Black or African American, non-Hispanic/Latino; 1 American Indian or Alaska Native, non-Hispanic/Latino; 2 Asian, non-Hispanic/Latino), 88 international. Average age 24. 187 applicants, 88% accepted, 52 enrolled. In 2017, 37 master's, 7 other advanced degrees awarded. *Degree requirements:* For master's, thesis optional, minimum B average in major field and overall; for Certificate, minimum B average. *Entrance requirements:* Additional exam requirements/recommendations for international students: Required—TOEFL (minimum score 74 iBT), IELTS (minimum score 6). *Application deadline:* For fall admission, 7/1 for domestic students, 4/15 for international students; for spring admission, 12/1 for domestic and international students. Applications are processed on a rolling basis. Application fee: $60. Electronic applications accepted. *Expenses: Tuition:* Full-time $34,494; part-time $1554 per credit. *Required fees:* $291 per semester. *Financial support:* Fellowships, research assistantships, teaching assistantships, career-related internships or fieldwork, Federal Work-Study, scholarships/grants, and unspecified assistantships available. Financial award application deadline: 2/15; financial award applicants required to submit FAFSA. *Unit head:* Dr. Linda Thomas, Director, 201-216-5681, E-mail: lthomas2@stevens.edu. *Application contact:* Graduate Admission, 888-783-8367, Fax: 888-511-1306, E-mail: graduate@stevens.edu.

Stevenson University, Program in Healthcare Management, Owings Mills, MD 21153. Offers project management (MS); quality management and patient safety (MS). *Program availability:* Part-time, online only, 100% online. *Faculty:* 2 full-time (both women), 7 part-time/adjunct (4 women). *Students:* 4 full-time (2 women), 35 part-time (28 women); includes 11 minority (9 Black or African American, non-Hispanic/Latino; 2 Asian, non-Hispanic/Latino). Average age 30. 24 applicants, 71% accepted, 13 enrolled. In 2017, 10 master's awarded. *Degree requirements:* For master's, capstone course. *Entrance requirements:* For master's, official college transcripts from all previous academic work, minimum cumulative GPA of 3.0 in past academic work, minimum grade of B in statistics or an upper-level math and English composition, two professional letters of recommendation with at least one from a current or past supervisor, 250-word personal statement. *Application deadline:* Applications are processed on a rolling basis. Electronic applications accepted. *Expenses:* Contact institution. *Financial support:* Unspecified assistantships available. Financial award applicants required to submit FAFSA. *Unit head:* Sharon Buchbinder, PhD, Coordinator, 443-394-9290, Fax: 443-394-0538, E-mail: sbuchbinder@stevenson.edu. *Application contact:* Amanda Courter, Enrollment Counselor, 443-352-4243, Fax: 443-394-0538, E-mail: acourter@stevenson.edu.
Website: http://www.stevenson.edu

Trident University International, College of Business Administration, Program in Business Administration, Cypress, CA 90630. Offers business administration (PhD); conflict and negotiation management (MBA); criminal justice administration (MBA); entrepreneurship (MBA); finance (MBA); general management (MBA); government accounting (MBA); human resource management (MBA); information security and digital assurance management (MBA); information technology management (MBA); international business (MBA); logistics management (MBA); marketing (MBA); project management (MBA); public management (MBA); quality management (MBA); strategic leadership (MBA). *Program availability:* Part-time, evening/weekend, online learning. *Degree requirements:* For doctorate, comprehensive exam, thesis/dissertation, defense of dissertation. *Entrance requirements:* For master's, minimum GPA of 2.5 (students with GPA 3.0 or greater may transfer up to 30% of graduate level credits); for doctorate, minimum GPA of 3.4, curriculum vitae, course work in research methods or statistics. Additional exam requirements/recommendations for international students: Required—TOEFL. Electronic applications accepted.

Trident University International, College of Health Sciences, Program in Health Sciences, Cypress, CA 90630. Offers clinical research administration (MS, Certificate); emergency and disaster management (MS, Certificate); environmental health science (Certificate); health care administration (PhD); health care management (MS), including health informatics; health education (MS, Certificate); health informatics (Certificate); health sciences (PhD); international health (MS); international health: educator or researcher option (PhD); international health: practitioner option (PhD); law and expert witness studies (MS, Certificate); public health (MS); quality assurance (Certificate). *Program availability:* Part-time, evening/weekend, online learning. *Degree requirements:* For doctorate, comprehensive exam, thesis/dissertation, defense of dissertation. *Entrance requirements:* For master's, minimum GPA of 2.5 (students with GPA 3.0 or greater may transfer up to 30% of graduate level credits); for doctorate, minimum GPA of 3.4, curriculum vitae, course work in research methods or statistics. Additional exam requirements/recommendations for international students: Required—TOEFL. Electronic applications accepted.

Universidad de las Americas, A.C., Program in Business Administration, Mexico City, Mexico. Offers finance (MBA); marketing research (MBA); production and quality (MBA).

Universidad del Turabo, Graduate Programs, School of Business and Entrepreneurship, Program in Quality Management, Gurabo, PR 00778-3030. Offers MBA. *Entrance requirements:* For master's, GRE, EXADEP or GMAT, interview, essay, official transcript, recommendation letters. Electronic applications accepted.

The University of Alabama, Graduate School, College of Human Environmental Sciences, Program in Human Environmental Science, Tuscaloosa, AL 35487. Offers interactive technology (MS); quality management (MS); restaurant and meeting management (MS); rural community health (MS); sport management (MS). *Program availability:* Part-time, evening/weekend, online learning. *Students:* 90 full-time (44 women), 158 part-time (86 women); includes 60 minority (42 Black or African American, non-Hispanic/Latino; 1 American Indian or Alaska Native, non-Hispanic/Latino; 2 Asian, non-Hispanic/Latino; 7 Hispanic/Latino; 3 Native Hawaiian or other Pacific Islander, non-Hispanic/Latino; 5 Two or more races, non-Hispanic/Latino). Average age 34. 147 applicants, 84% accepted, 110 enrolled. In 2017, 108 master's awarded. *Degree requirements:* For master's, comprehensive exam. *Entrance requirements:* For master's, GRE (for some specializations), minimum GPA of 3.0. Additional exam requirements/recommendations for international students: Required—TOEFL. *Application deadline:* For fall admission, 7/1 for domestic students; for spring admission, 11/1 for domestic students; for summer admission, 4/15 for domestic students. Applications are processed on a rolling basis. Application fee: $50 ($60 for international students). Electronic applications accepted. *Financial support:* Teaching assistantships with full tuition reimbursements available. Financial award application deadline: 7/1. *Faculty research:* Rural health, hospitality management, sport management, interactive technology, consumer quality management, environmental health and safety. *Unit head:* Dr. Milla D. Boschung, Dean, 205-348-6250, Fax: 205-348-1786, E-mail: mboschun@ches.ua.edu. *Application contact:* Dr. Stuart Usdan, Associate Dean, 205-348-6150, Fax: 205-348-3789, E-mail: susdan@ches.ua.edu.
Website: http://www.ches.ua.edu/programs-of-study.html

University of Central Florida, College of Engineering and Computer Science, Department of Industrial Engineering and Management Systems, Orlando, FL 32816. Offers engineering management (MSEM); industrial engineering (MS, MSIE, PhD); project engineering (Certificate); quality assurance (Certificate); systems engineering (Certificate); training simulation (Certificate). *Program availability:* Part-time, evening/weekend. *Students:* 93 full-time (26 women), 222 part-time (80 women); includes 122 minority (36 Black or African American, non-Hispanic/Latino; 1 American Indian or Alaska Native, non-Hispanic/Latino; 19 Asian, non-Hispanic/Latino; 62 Hispanic/Latino; 4 Two or more races, non-Hispanic/Latino), 57 international. Average age 32. 275 applicants, 81% accepted, 134 enrolled. In 2017, 46 master's, 12 doctorates, 22 other advanced degrees awarded. *Degree requirements:* For master's, thesis or alternative; for doctorate, thesis/dissertation, departmental qualifying exam, candidacy exam. *Entrance requirements:* For master's, minimum GPA of 3.0 in last 60 hours of course work, letters of recommendation, goal statement, resume; for doctorate, GRE, minimum GPA of 3.0 in last 60 hours of course work, letters of recommendation, goal statement, resume. Additional exam requirements/recommendations for international students: Required—TOEFL. *Application deadline:* For fall admission, 7/15 for domestic students; for spring admission, 12/1 for domestic students. Application fee: $30. Electronic applications accepted. *Expenses: Tuition,* state resident: part-time $288.16 per credit hour. Tuition, nonresident: part-time $1073.31 per credit hour. Tuition and fees vary according to program. *Financial support:* In 2017–18, 29 students received support, including 8 fellowships with partial tuition reimbursements available (averaging $6,028 per year), 15 research assistantships with partial tuition reimbursements available (averaging $10,697 per year), 12 teaching assistantships with partial tuition reimbursements available (averaging $11,602 per year); career-related internships or fieldwork, Federal Work-Study, institutionally sponsored loans, health care benefits, tuition waivers (partial), and unspecified assistantships also available. Financial award application deadline: 3/1; financial award applicants required to submit FAFSA. *Unit head:* Dr. Waldemar Karwowski, Chair, 407-823-0042, E-mail: wkar@ucf.edu. *Application contact:* Associate Director, Graduate Admissions, 407-823-2766, Fax: 407-823-6442, E-mail: gradadmissions@ucf.edu.
Website: http://iems.ucf.edu

University of Massachusetts Boston, College of Advancing and Professional Studies, Program in Critical and Creative Thinking, Boston, MA 02125-3393. Offers MA, Certificate. *Program availability:* Part-time, evening/weekend. *Faculty:* 1 part-time/adjunct (0 women). *Students:* 3 full-time (2 women), 30 part-time (19 women); includes 9 minority (5 Black or African American, non-Hispanic/Latino; 1 Asian, non-Hispanic/Latino; 2 Hispanic/Latino; 1 Two or more races, non-Hispanic/Latino), 4 international. Average age 35. 15 applicants, 100% accepted, 11 enrolled. In 2017, 8 master's, 9 other advanced degrees awarded. *Entrance requirements:* For master's, GRE General Test or MAT, minimum GPA of 3.0; for Certificate, minimum GPA of 2.75. *Application deadline:* For fall admission, 3/1 for domestic students; for spring admission, 11/1 for domestic students. *Expenses: Tuition,* state resident: full-time $17,375. Tuition, nonresident: full-time $33,915. *Required fees:* $355. *Financial support:* Research assistantships, teaching assistantships, career-related internships or fieldwork, Federal Work-Study, and unspecified assistantships available. Support available to part-time students. Financial award application deadline: 3/1; financial award applicants required to submit FAFSA. *Unit head:* Dr. Peter Taylor, Director, 617-287-7636, E-mail: peter.taylor@umb.edu. *Application contact:* Graduate Admissions Coordinator, 617-287-6400, Fax: 617-287-6236, E-mail: bos.gadm@dpc.umassp.edu.

The University of Tennessee at Chattanooga, Engineering Management and Technology Program, Chattanooga, TN 37403. Offers construction management (Graduate Certificate); engineering management (MS); fundamentals of engineering management (Graduate Certificate); leadership and ethics (Graduate Certificate); logistics and supply chain management (Graduate Certificate); power systems management (Graduate Certificate); project and technology management (Graduate Certificate); quality management (Graduate Certificate). *Program availability:* 100% online, blended/hybrid learning. *Students:* 14 full-time (3 women), 50 part-time (11 women); includes 17 minority (10 Black or African American, non-Hispanic/Latino; 1 Asian, non-Hispanic/Latino; 6 Hispanic/Latino), 5 international. Average age 33. 34 applicants, 94% accepted, 20 enrolled. In 2017, 18 master's, 6 other advanced degrees awarded. *Degree requirements:* For master's, thesis. *Entrance requirements:* For master's, GRE General Test, letters of recommendation; minimum undergraduate GPA of 2.7 overall or 3.0 in final two years; for Graduate Certificate, baccalaureate degree and professional experience or have already been admitted to engineering/engineering management graduate program. Additional exam requirements/recommendations for international students: Required—TOEFL (minimum score 550 paper-based; 79 iBT), IELTS (minimum score 6). *Application deadline:* For fall admission, 6/15 priority date for domestic students, 7/1 for international students; for spring admission, 11/1 priority date for domestic students, 11/1 for international students. Applications are processed on a rolling basis. Application fee: $35 ($40 for international students). Electronic applications accepted. *Expenses:* Contact institution. *Financial support:* Research assistantships, teaching assistantships, career-related internships or fieldwork, scholarships/grants, and unspecified assistantships available. Support available to part-time students. Financial award application deadline: 7/1; financial award applicants required to submit FAFSA. *Faculty research:* Plant layout design, lean manufacturing, Six Sigma, value management, product development. *Total annual research expenditures:* $108,577. *Unit head:* Dr. Neslihan Alp, Department Head, 423-425-4032, Fax: 423-425-5818, E-mail: neslihan-alp@utc.edu. *Application contact:* Dr. Joanne Romagni, Dean of the Graduate School, 423-425-4478, Fax: 423-425-5223, E-mail: joanne-romagni@utc.edu.

Website: https://www.utc.edu/college-engineering-computer-science/programs/engineering-management-and-technology/index.php

The University of Texas at Tyler, College of Business and Technology, Program in Business Administration, Tyler, TX 75799-0001. Offers cyber security (MBA); engineering management (MBA); general management (MBA); healthcare management (MBA); internal assurance and consulting (MBA); marketing (MBA); oil, gas and energy (MBA); organizational development (MBA); quality management (MBA). *Accreditation:* AACSB. *Program availability:* Part-time, online learning. *Entrance requirements:* Additional exam requirements/recommendations for international students: Required—TOEFL (minimum score 550 paper-based). *Faculty research:* General business, inventory control, institutional markets, service marketing, product distribution, accounting fraud, financial reporting and recognition.

University of Wisconsin–Stout, Graduate School, College of Management, Program in Operations and Supply Management, Menomonie, WI 54751. Offers operations management (MS); project management (MS); quality management (MS); supply chain management (MS).

Section 19
Quantitative Analysis and Business Analytics

This section contains a directory of institutions offering graduate work in quantitative analysis. Additional information about programs listed in the directory may be obtained by writing directly to the dean of a graduate school or chair of a department at the address given in the directory.

For programs offering related work, see also in this book *Business Administration and Management*.

CONTENTS

Business Analytics

Abilene Christian University, College of Graduate and Professional Studies, Program in Business Administration, Addison, TX 75001. Offers business analytics (MBA); corporate finance (MBA); general management (MBA); healthcare administration (MBA); human resource management (MBA); international business (MBA); management: business analytics (MS); management: healthcare administration (MS); management: international business (MS); management: marketing (MS); management: operations and supply chain management (MS); marketing (MBA); nonprofit leadership (MBA); operations and supply chain management (MBA). *Program availability:* Part-time, online only, 100% online. *Faculty:* 2 full-time (0 women), 6 part-time/adjunct (2 women). *Students:* 109 full-time (47 women), 51 part-time (22 women); includes 42 minority (33 Black or African American, non-Hispanic/Latino; 1 American Indian or Alaska Native, non-Hispanic/Latino; 2 Asian, non-Hispanic/Latino; 6 Hispanic/Latino). 125 applicants, 65% accepted, 58 enrolled. *Entrance requirements:* Additional exam requirements/recommendations for international students: Required—TOEFL (minimum score 80 iBT), IELTS (minimum score 6). *Application deadline:* For fall admission, 8/14 priority date for domestic students; for winter admission, 10/1 priority date for domestic students; for spring admission, 12/15 priority date for domestic students; for summer admission, 4/15 priority date for domestic students. Applications are processed on a rolling basis. Application fee: $50. Electronic applications accepted. *Expenses:* $700 per hour. *Financial support:* In 2017–18, 2 students received support. Application deadline: 4/1; applicants required to submit FAFSA. *Faculty research:* Organizational structure, financial management, cost accounting, unit analysis management. *Unit head:* Phil Vardiman, Program Director, 325-674-2153, E-mail: pxv02b@acu.edu. *Application contact:* Graduate Advisor, 817-219-7300, E-mail: gradonline@acu.edu.
Website: http://www.acu.edu/online/academics/mba-business-administration.html

American Public University System, AMU/APU Graduate Programs, Charles Town, WV 25414. Offers accounting (MS); applied business analytics (MS); business administration (MBA); criminal justice (MA); cybersecurity studies (MS); educational leadership (M Ed); environmental policy and management (MS); global security (DGS); health information management (MS); history (MA), including American military history, American Revolution, civil war, war since 1945, World War II; information technology (MS); international relations and conflict resolution (MA), including American politics and government, comparative government and development, general, international relations, public policy; national security studies (MA); nursing (MSN); political science (MA); public policy (MPP); reverse logistics management (MA), including comparative and security issues, conflict resolution, international and transnational security issues, peacekeeping; space studies (MS); sports management (MS); strategic intelligence (DSI); teaching (M Ed), including secondary social studies; transportation and logistics management (MA). *Program availability:* Part-time, evening/weekend, online only, 100% online. *Students:* 455 full-time (227 women), 7,939 part-time (3,353 women); includes 2,793 minority (1,429 Black or African American, non-Hispanic/Latino; 48 American Indian or Alaska Native, non-Hispanic/Latino; 205 Asian, non-Hispanic/Latino; 766 Hispanic/Latino; 62 Native Hawaiian or other Pacific Islander, non-Hispanic/Latino; 283 Two or more races, non-Hispanic/Latino), 101 international. Average age 37. In 2017, 2,977 master's awarded. *Degree requirements:* For master's, comprehensive exam or practicum. *Entrance requirements:* For master's, official transcript showing earned bachelor's degree from institution accredited by recognized accrediting body. Additional exam requirements/recommendations for international students: Required—TOEFL (minimum score 550 paper-based), IELTS (minimum score 6.5). *Application deadline:* Applications are processed on a rolling basis. Application fee: $0. Electronic applications accepted. *Expenses:* Tuition: Full-time $6300; part-time $350 per credit. *Required fees:* $300; $50 per course. *Financial support:* Scholarships/grants available. Financial award applicants required to submit FAFSA. *Unit head:* Dr. Wallace Boston, President, 877-468-6268, Fax: 304-728-2348, E-mail: president@apus.edu. *Application contact:* Yoci Deal, Associate Vice President, Graduate and International Admissions, 877-468-6268, Fax: 304-724-3764, E-mail: info@apus.edu.
Website: http://www.apus.edu

Ashland University, Dauch College of Business and Economics, Ashland, OH 44805-3702. Offers accounting (MBA); business analytics (MBA); entrepreneurship (MBA); financial management (MBA); global management (MBA); health care management and leadership (MBA); human resource management (MBA); human resources (MBA); management information systems (MBA); project management (MBA); sport management (MBA); supply chain management (MBA). *Accreditation:* ACBSP. *Program availability:* Part-time, evening/weekend, 100% online, blended/hybrid learning. *Faculty:* 20 full-time (4 women), 13 part-time/adjunct (2 women). *Students:* 458 full-time (210 women), 144 part-time (52 women); includes 88 minority (63 Black or African American, non-Hispanic/Latino; 1 American Indian or Alaska Native, non-Hispanic/Latino; 10 Asian, non-Hispanic/Latino; 14 Hispanic/Latino), 202 international. Average age 31. 216 applicants, 74% accepted, 115 enrolled. In 2017, 184 master's awarded. Terminal master's awarded for partial completion of doctoral program. *Degree requirements:* For master's, thesis optional, capstone course. *Entrance requirements:* For master's, 2 years of full-time work experience. Additional exam requirements/recommendations for international students: Required—TOEFL (minimum score 550 paper-based; 78 iBT). *Application deadline:* For fall admission, 8/1 priority date for domestic students; for spring admission, 12/1 priority date for domestic students. Applications are processed on a rolling basis. Application fee: $30. Electronic applications accepted. *Expenses:* $815 per credit hour, $15 technology fee for online sections. *Financial support:* Scholarships/grants, tuition waivers (partial), and unspecified assistantships available. Financial award application deadline: 4/15; financial award applicants required to submit FAFSA. *Faculty research:* Relationship marketing strategy, executive compensation and company performance, online marketplaces in electronic commerce, diversity training in campus recreation departments, entrepreneurship in developing and emerging economies. *Unit head:* Dr. Elad Granot, Dean, 419-289-5932, E-mail: egranot@ashland.edu. *Application contact:* Stephen W. Krispinsky, Executive Director of MBA Program, 419-289-5236, Fax: 419-289-5910, E-mail: skrispin@ashland.edu.
Website: http://www.mba.ashland.edu

Babson College, F. W. Olin Graduate School of Business, Babson Park, MA 02457-0310. Offers accounting (MSA); advanced management (Certificate); business administration (MBA); business analytics (MS); finance (MS); global entrepreneurship (MS); technological entrepreneurship (MS). *Accreditation:* AACSB. *Program availability:* Part-time, evening/weekend, online learning. *Entrance requirements:* For master's, GMAT, 2 years of work experience, resume, letters of recommendation. Additional exam requirements/recommendations for international students: Required—TOEFL (minimum score 100 iBT), IELTS (minimum score 6.5). Electronic applications accepted. *Faculty research:* Entrepreneurship, sustainability, global markets, process of innovation, social media and advertising.

Baldwin Wallace University, Graduate Programs, School of Business, Berea, OH 44017-2088. Offers accounting (MBA); analytics (MBA); health care (MBA); human resources (MBA); international management (MBA); management (MAM, MBA). *Program availability:* Part-time, evening/weekend, blended/hybrid learning. *Faculty:* 21 full-time (8 women), 24 part-time/adjunct (6 women). *Students:* 198 full-time (98 women), 114 part-time (61 women); includes 65 minority (33 Black or African American, non-Hispanic/Latino; 12 Asian, non-Hispanic/Latino; 15 Hispanic/Latino; 5 Two or more races, non-Hispanic/Latino), 4 international. Average age 34. 161 applicants, 64% accepted, 59 enrolled. In 2017, 135 master's awarded. *Degree requirements:* For master's, minimum overall GPA of 3.0. *Entrance requirements:* For master's, GMAT or minimum GPA of 3.0, bachelor's degree in any field, work experience. Additional exam requirements/recommendations for international students: Required—TOEFL (minimum score 550 paper-based; 79 iBT). *Application deadline:* For fall admission, 7/25 priority date for domestic students, 4/30 priority date for international students; for spring admission, 12/15 priority date for domestic students, 9/30 priority date for international students; for summer admission, 4/15 for domestic students. Applications are processed on a rolling basis. Electronic applications accepted. *Expenses:* Contact institution. *Financial support:* Applicants required to submit FAFSA. *Unit head:* John Lanigan, Dean of School of Business, 440-826-3566, Fax: 440-826-3868, E-mail: jlanigan@bw.edu. *Application contact:* Laura Spencer, Graduate Application Specialist, 440-826-2191, Fax: 440-826-3868, E-mail: lspencer@bw.edu.
Website: http://www.bw.edu/graduate/business/

Bentley University, McCallum Graduate School of Business, Graduate Business Certificate Program, Waltham, MA 02452-4705. Offers accounting (GBC); business analytics (GBC); business ethics (GBC); financial planning (GBC); fraud and forensic accounting (GBC); marketing analytics (GBC); taxation (GBC). *Accreditation:* AACSB. *Program availability:* Part-time, evening/weekend. *Faculty:* 71 full-time (25 women), 33 part-time/adjunct (15 women). *Students:* 7 part-time (3 women); includes 2 minority (1 Black or African American, non-Hispanic/Latino; 1 Asian, non-Hispanic/Latino). Average age 42. 9 applicants, 100% accepted, 6 enrolled. In 2017, 58 GBCs awarded. *Entrance requirements:* For degree, GMAT or GRE General Test, current resume; two letters of recommendation; official copies of all university-level transcripts; 2 essays. Additional exam requirements/recommendations for international students: Required—TOEFL (minimum score 100) or IELTS (minimum score 7). *Application deadline:* Applications are processed on a rolling basis. Application fee: $75. Electronic applications accepted. *Expenses:* Contact institution. *Financial support:* Application deadline: 6/1; applicants required to submit FAFSA. *Unit head:* Dr. Roy A. Wiggins, III, Acting Co-Provost, Dean of Business, 781-891-3166. *Application contact:* Graduate Admissions, 781-891-2108, Fax: 781-891-2464, E-mail: applygrad@bentley.edu.
Website: https://www.bentley.edu/current-graduate-students/programs-certificates#certificates

Bentley University, McCallum Graduate School of Business, Master's Program in Business Analytics, Waltham, MA 02452-4705. Offers MS. *Program availability:* Part-time, evening/weekend. *Faculty:* 71 full-time (25 women), 33 part-time/adjunct (15 women). *Students:* 105 full-time (67 women), 44 part-time (21 women); includes 12 minority (9 Asian, non-Hispanic/Latino; 2 Hispanic/Latino; 1 Two or more races, non-Hispanic/Latino), 102 international. Average age 27. 367 applicants, 65% accepted, 75 enrolled. In 2017, 57 master's awarded. *Entrance requirements:* For master's, GMAT or GRE General Test, current resume; two letters of recommendation; official copies of all university-level transcripts; 2 essays. Additional exam requirements/recommendations for international students: Required—TOEFL (minimum score 100) or IELTS (minimum score 7). *Application deadline:* Applications are processed on a rolling basis. Application fee: $75. Electronic applications accepted. *Expenses:* Tuition: Part-time $4445 per course. *Required fees:* $170 per unit. *Financial support:* In 2017–18, 74 students received support. Scholarships/grants and unspecified assistantships available. Financial award application deadline: 6/1; financial award applicants required to submit FAFSA. *Application contact:* Graduate Admissions, 781-891-2108, Fax: 781-891-2464, E-mail: applygrad@bentley.edu.
Website: https://admissions.bentley.edu/graduate/masters-in-analytics

Boston University, Metropolitan College, Department of Administrative Sciences, Boston, MA 02215. Offers applied business analytics (MS); economic development and tourism management (MSAS); enterprise risk management (MS); financial management (MS); global marketing management (MS); innovation and technology (MSAS); insurance management (MS); project management (MS); supply chain management (MS). *Accreditation:* AACSB. *Program availability:* Part-time, evening/weekend, 100% online, blended/hybrid learning. *Faculty:* 21 full-time (5 women), 34 part-time/adjunct (5 women). *Students:* 297 full-time (156 women), 597 part-time (298 women); includes 183 minority (58 Black or African American, non-Hispanic/Latino; 2 American Indian or Alaska Native, non-Hispanic/Latino; 56 Asian, non-Hispanic/Latino; 51 Hispanic/Latino; 2 Native Hawaiian or other Pacific Islander, non-Hispanic/Latino; 14 Two or more races, non-Hispanic/Latino), 391 international. Average age 30. 963 applicants, 64% accepted, 209 enrolled. In 2017, 372 master's awarded. *Degree requirements:* For master's, thesis optional. *Entrance requirements:* For master's, 1 year of work experience, minimum GPA of 3.0. Additional exam requirements/recommendations for international students: Required—TOEFL (minimum score 84 iBT). *Application deadline:* Applications are processed on a rolling basis. Application fee: $85. Electronic applications accepted. *Expenses:* Contact institution. *Financial support:* In 2017–18, 15 students received support, including 18 research assistantships (averaging $8,400 per year), 12 teaching assistantships (averaging $2,700 per year); career-related internships or fieldwork, Federal Work-Study, and unspecified assistantships also available. Financial award applicants required to submit FAFSA. *Faculty research:* International business, innovative process. *Unit head:* Dr. John Sullivan, Chair, 617-353-3016, E-mail: adminsc@bu.edu. *Application contact:* Fiona Niven, Administrative Sciences Department, 617-353-3016, E-mail: adminsc@bu.edu.
Website: http://www.bu.edu/met/academic-community/departments/administrative-sciences/

Bryant University, Graduate School of Business, Smithfield, RI 02917. Offers accounting (MPAC); business administration (MBA), including business analytics, general management, global finance, global supply chain management, international business; taxation (MST). *Program availability:* Part-time, 100% online. *Faculty:* 30 full-time (5 women), 7 part-time/adjunct (2 women). *Students:* 84 full-time (31 women), 91 part-time (35 women); includes 24 minority (4 Black or African American, non-Hispanic/Latino; 1 American Indian or Alaska Native, non-Hispanic/Latino; 6 Asian, non-Hispanic/Latino; 8 Hispanic/Latino; 5 Two or more races, non-Hispanic/Latino), 6 international. Average age 26. 215 applicants, 66% accepted, 96 enrolled. In 2017, 118 master's awarded. *Degree requirements:* For master's, comprehensive exam (for some programs). *Entrance requirements:* For master's, GMAT, resume, recommendation,

college transcripts. Additional exam requirements/recommendations for international students: Required—TOEFL (minimum score 580 paper-based; 95 iBT). *Application deadline:* For fall admission, 7/15 for domestic and international students; for spring admission, 11/15 for domestic and international students; for summer admission, 4/15 for domestic and international students. Applications are processed on a rolling basis. Application fee: $80. Electronic applications accepted. *Expenses:* $45,102 total, $1,118 per credit hour, $1,500 study abroad fee (for full-time MBA); $40,248 total, $1,118 per credit hour (for part-time MBA); $30,280 total, $1,176 per credit hour (for MP Ac and MST); $13,146, $1,118 per credit hour (for CGS). *Financial support:* In 2017–18, 95 fellowships with full and partial tuition reimbursements (averaging $9,825 per year), 9 research assistantships with full and partial tuition reimbursements (averaging $7,100 per year) were awarded; scholarships/grants and unspecified assistantships also available. Support available to part-time students. Financial award application deadline: 2/15; financial award applicants required to submit FAFSA. *Faculty research:* International business, public sector auditing, taxation of partnerships, information systems security, financial markets microstructure. *Unit head:* Bjorn Carlsson, Graduate Program Director, 401-232-6707, E-mail: bcarlsson@bryant.edu. *Application contact:* Terri Rogers, Admissions Assistant, 401-232-6230, Fax: 401-232-6494, E-mail: graduateprograms@bryant.edu.
Website: http://gradschool.bryant.edu/business/

California Polytechnic State University, San Luis Obispo, Orfalea College of Business, Program in Business Analytics, San Luis Obispo, CA 93407. Offers MS. *Students:* 28 full-time (13 women), 1 (woman) part-time; includes 7 minority (5 Asian, non-Hispanic/Latino; 1 Hispanic/Latino; 1 Two or more races, non-Hispanic/Latino), 7 international. Average age 24. In 2017, 24 master's awarded. *Degree requirements:* For master's, comprehensive exam (for some programs), thesis (for some programs). *Entrance requirements:* For master's, GMAT. Additional exam requirements/recommendations for international students: Required—TOEFL (minimum score 80 iBT). *Application deadline:* Applications are processed on a rolling basis. Application fee: $55. Electronic applications accepted. *Expenses:* Tuition, state resident: full-time $7176; part-time $4164 per year. *Required fees:* $3690; $3219 per year. $1073 per trimester. *Financial support:* Fellowships, career-related internships or fieldwork, Federal Work-Study, institutionally sponsored loans, scholarships/grants, and unspecified assistantships available. Support available to part-time students. Financial award application deadline: 3/2; financial award applicants required to submit FAFSA. *Faculty research:* Management of high-tech firms, Pacific Rim, capital market structures, economics of environmental policy, marketing of services. *Unit head:* Dr. Scott Dawson, Dean, 805-756-2705, E-mail: scdawson@calpoly.edu. *Application contact:* Dr. Sanjiv Jaggia, Associate Dean, Graduate Programs, 805-756-7519, E-mail: sjaggia@calpoly.edu.
Website: http://www.cob.calpoly.edu/gradbusiness/degree-programs/ms-business-analytics/

California State University, Fullerton, Graduate Studies, College of Business and Economics, Program in Business Administration, Fullerton, CA 92831-3599. Offers business administration (MBA); business analytics (MBA); international business (MBA); organizational leadership (MBA); risk management and insurance (MBA). *Accreditation:* AACSB. *Program availability:* Part-time. *Faculty:* 12 full-time (5 women), 1 part-time/adjunct (0 women). *Students:* 64 full-time (35 women), 103 part-time (46 women); includes 81 minority (40 Asian, non-Hispanic/Latino; 36 Hispanic/Latino; 5 Two or more races, non-Hispanic/Latino), 36 international. Average age 29. 254 applicants, 47% accepted, 62 enrolled. *Entrance requirements:* For master's, GMAT. Application fee: $55. *Financial support:* Career-related internships or fieldwork, Federal Work-Study, institutionally sponsored loans, and scholarships/grants available. Support available to part-time students. Financial award application deadline: 3/1; financial award applicants required to submit FAFSA. *Unit head:* Shaun Pichler, Director, 657-278-7373, E-mail: spichler@fullerton.edu. *Application contact:* Admissions/Applications, 657-278-2371.

California University of Pennsylvania, School of Graduate Studies and Research, Eberly College of Science and Technology, Program in Business Administration, California, PA 15419-1394. Offers business analytics (MBA); entrepreneurship (MBA); healthcare management (MBA). *Program availability:* Part-time, evening/weekend. *Degree requirements:* For master's, comprehensive exam. *Entrance requirements:* For master's, minimum GPA of 3.0, official transcripts. Additional exam requirements/recommendations for international students: Required—TOEFL (minimum score 550 paper-based). *Application deadline:* For fall admission, 8/1 priority date for domestic and international students; for winter admission, 12/1 priority date for domestic and international students; for spring admission, 5/1 priority date for domestic and international students. Applications are processed on a rolling basis. Application fee: $25. Electronic applications accepted. *Financial support:* Applicants required to submit FAFSA. *Faculty research:* Economics, applied economics, consumer behavior, technology and business, impact of technology. *Unit head:* Dr. Arshad Chawdhry, Graduate Coordinator, 724-938-5990, Fax: 724-938-5908, E-mail: chawdhry@cup.edu. *Application contact:* Suzanne C. Powers, Director of Graduate Admissions and Recruitment, 724-938-4029, Fax: 724-938-5712, E-mail: powers_s@cup.edu.

Case Western Reserve University, Weatherhead School of Management, Program in Business Analytics, Cleveland, OH 44106. Offers MSM. *Expenses:* Tuition: Full-time $43,854; part-time $1827 per credit hour. *Required fees:* $50; $50 per credit hour. Tuition and fees vary according to course load and program.

Central European University, Department of Economics, 1051, Hungary. Offers business administration (PhD); business analytics (M Sc); economic policy in global markets (MA); economics (MA, PhD); finance (MS); global economic relations (MA); technology management and innovation (MS). *Program availability:* Part-time. *Faculty:* 23 full-time (2 women), 25 part-time/adjunct (4 women). *Students:* 177 full-time (77 women), 125 part-time (39 women). Average age 31. 530 applicants, 49% accepted, 144 enrolled. In 2017, 150 master's, 6 doctorates awarded. *Degree requirements:* For master's, one foreign language, thesis; for doctorate, one foreign language, comprehensive exam, thesis/dissertation. *Entrance requirements:* For master's and doctorate, interview. Additional exam requirements/recommendations for international students: Required—TOEFL (minimum score 570 paper-based); Recommended—IELTS (minimum score 6.5). *Application deadline:* For fall admission, 2/4 for domestic and international students. Application fee: $30. Electronic applications accepted. *Expenses: Tuition:* Full-time 12,000 euros. *Required fees:* 230 euros. One-time fee: 30 euros full-time. Tuition and fees vary according to course level, course load, degree level and program. *Financial support:* Fellowships, teaching assistantships, career-related internships or fieldwork, institutionally sponsored loans, scholarships/grants, health care benefits, and tuition waivers (full and partial) available. *Faculty research:* Economic theory (microeconomics and macroeconomics) and econometrics, as well as study of many applied fields, including labor economics, health economics and economics of education, industrial organization, monetary economics, international economics, law and economics, comparative institutional economics, corporate governance, and economics of transition. *Unit head:* Miklos Koren, Head of Department, 36 1 327-3000 Ext. 2212, E-mail: econbusi@ceu.edu. *Application contact:* Zsuzsanna Jaszberenyi, Admissions Officer, 361-324-3009, Fax: 367-327-3211, E-mail: admissions@ceu.edu.
Website: http://economics.ceu.edu/

Clark University, Graduate School, Graduate School of Management, Business Administration Program, Worcester, MA 01610-1477. Offers accounting (MBA); finance (MBA); information management and business analytics (MBA); management (MBA); marketing (MBA); social change (MBA); sustainability (MBA). *Accreditation:* AACSB. *Program availability:* Part-time, evening/weekend. *Students:* 87 full-time (41 women), 41 part-time (26 women); includes 19 minority (10 Black or African American, non-Hispanic/Latino; 4 Asian, non-Hispanic/Latino; 4 Hispanic/Latino; 1 Two or more races, non-Hispanic/Latino), 40 international. Average age 30. 242 applicants, 50% accepted, 54 enrolled. In 2017, 102 master's awarded. *Degree requirements:* For master's, thesis optional. *Entrance requirements:* For master's, GMAT or GRE, 2 references, resume or curriculum vitae, personal statement. Additional exam requirements/recommendations for international students: Required—TOEFL (minimum score 575 paper-based; 90 iBT), IELTS (minimum score 6.5). *Application deadline:* For fall admission, 4/15 priority date for domestic and international students; for spring admission, 12/1 priority date for domestic and international students. Application fee: $75. Electronic applications accepted. *Expenses:* $4,490 tuition per 14-week course, $2,245 per half-unit (7-week course); $40 activity fee (full-time students only); $80 miscellaneous one-time fee; $1,750 student services fee. *Financial support:* Fellowships, research assistantships, teaching assistantships, career-related internships or fieldwork, Federal Work-Study, institutionally sponsored loans, and tuition waivers (partial) available. Support available to part-time students. Financial award application deadline: 5/31. *Faculty research:* Marketing, accounting, human resource management, management information systems, business finance. *Unit head:* Dr. Priscilla Elsass, Dean, 508-793-7543, Fax: 508-793-8822, E-mail: pelsass@clarku.edu. *Application contact:* Yingying Chen, Assistant Director of Graduate Admissions, 508-793-7373, Fax: 508-798-4386, E-mail: graduateadmissions@clarku.edu.
Website: http://www.clarku.edu/programs/masters-business-administration

Cleary University, Online Program in Business Administration, Howell, MI 48843. Offers analytics, technology, and innovation (MBA, Graduate Certificate); financial planning (Graduate Certificate); global leadership (MBA, Graduate Certificate); health care leadership (MBA, Graduate Certificate). *Program availability:* Part-time, evening/weekend, online learning. *Degree requirements:* For master's, thesis. *Entrance requirements:* For master's, bachelor's degree; minimum GPA 2.5; professional resume indicating minimum of 2 years of management or related experience; undergraduate degree from accredited college or university with at least 18 quarter hours (or 12 semester hours) of accounting study (for MBA in accounting). Additional exam requirements/recommendations for international students: Required—TOEFL (minimum score 550 paper-based; 79 iBT), Michigan English Language Assessment Battery (minimum score 75). Electronic applications accepted.

Clemson University, Graduate School, College of Business, Master of Business Administration Program, Greenville, SC 29634. Offers business administration (MBA); business analytics (MBA); entrepreneurship and innovation (MBA). *Accreditation:* AACSB. *Program availability:* Part-time, evening/weekend. *Faculty:* 2 full-time (1 woman), 8 part-time/adjunct (1 woman). *Students:* 242 full-time (96 women), 736 part-time (222 women); includes 81 minority (46 Black or African American, non-Hispanic/Latino; 13 Asian, non-Hispanic/Latino; 17 Hispanic/Latino; 1 Native Hawaiian or other Pacific Islander, non-Hispanic/Latino; 4 Two or more races, non-Hispanic/Latino), 35 international. Average age 31. 413 applicants, 82% accepted, 233 enrolled. In 2017, 364 master's awarded. *Entrance requirements:* For master's, GMAT, resume, unofficial transcripts, personal statement, letters of recommendation. Additional exam requirements/recommendations for international students: Required—TOEFL (minimum score 80 iBT), IELTS (minimum score 6.5), PTE (minimum score 54). *Application deadline:* For fall admission, 7/15 for domestic students, 4/15 for international students; for spring admission, 12/1 for domestic students. Applications are processed on a rolling basis. Application fee: $80 ($90 for international students). Electronic applications accepted. *Expenses:* Contact institution. *Unit head:* Dr. Gregory Pickett, Senior Associate Dean, 864-656-3975, E-mail: pgregor@clemson.edu. *Application contact:* Laura Fischman, Assistant Director of Admissions, 864-365-0604, E-mail: ann6@clemson.edu.
Website: https://www.clemson.edu/business/departments/mba/

The College of Saint Rose, Graduate Studies, Huether School of Business, Program in Business Analytics, Albany, NY 12203-1419. Offers MS. *Program availability:* Part-time, evening/weekend. *Students:* 4 full-time (2 women), 5 part-time (4 women); includes 3 minority (1 Black or African American, non-Hispanic/Latino; 2 Two or more races, non-Hispanic/Latino). Average age 31. 15 applicants, 87% accepted, 8 enrolled. *Entrance requirements:* Additional exam requirements/recommendations for international students: Required—TOEFL (minimum score 550 paper-based; 80 iBT), IELTS (minimum score 6), PTE (minimum score 56). *Application deadline:* For fall admission, 4/1 priority date for domestic students, 4/1 for international students; for spring admission, 10/15 priority date for domestic students, 10/15 for international students; for summer admission, 3/15 priority date for domestic and international students. Application fee: $40. *Expenses: Tuition:* Full-time $7191; part-time $799 per credit hour. *Required fees:* $924; $462 per credit hour. Tuition and fees vary according to course load. *Financial support:* Career-related internships or fieldwork, scholarships/grants, health care benefits, tuition waivers (partial), and unspecified assistantships available. Support available to part-time students. Financial award application deadline: 4/15. *Unit head:* Eyyub Kibis, Assistant Professor, 518-485-3024, E-mail: kibise@strose.edu. *Application contact:* Cris Murray, Assistant Vice President for Graduate Recruitment and Enrollment, 518-485-3390, Fax: 518-458-5479, E-mail: grad@strose.edu.
Website: https://www.strose.edu/business-analytics-ms/

The College of William and Mary, Raymond A. Mason School of Business, Master of Science in Business Analytics Program, Williamsburg, VA 23185. Offers MS. *Faculty:* 7 full-time (1 woman). *Students:* 84 full-time (35 women); includes 15 minority (1 Black or African American, non-Hispanic/Latino; 9 Asian, non-Hispanic/Latino; 2 Hispanic/Latino; 3 Two or more races, non-Hispanic/Latino), 21 international. Average age 22. 233 applicants, 58% accepted, 84 enrolled. In 2017, 45 master's awarded. *Entrance requirements:* For master's, GRE or GMAT (recommended). Additional exam requirements/recommendations for international students: Required—TOEFL (minimum iBT score of 100), IELTS (7), or 4 years of studies in the U.S. *Application deadline:* For fall admission, 12/1 priority date for domestic and international students; for winter admission, 2/1 for domestic and international students; for spring admission, 4/1 for domestic and international students; for summer admission, 6/1 for domestic and international students. Application fee: $100. Electronic applications accepted. *Expenses:* Contact institution. *Financial support:* Fellowships, research assistantships, teaching assistantships, scholarships/grants, and tuition waivers available. Financial award application deadline: 8/1. *Faculty research:* Artificial intelligence, natural language processing, bot and anomaly detection, optimization, machine learning. *Unit head:* Dr. James R. Bradley, Director, 757-221-2802, E-mail: james.bradley@mason.wm.edu. *Application contact:* Brian Nigg, Program Director, 757-221-1763, Fax: 757-221-2884, E-mail: brian.nigg@mason.wm.edu.
Website: http://mason.wm.edu/programs/msba/index.php

Creighton University, Graduate School, Heider College of Business, Omaha, NE 68178-0001. Offers accounting (MAC); business administration (MBA, DBA); business

Business Analytics

intelligence and analytics (MS); finance (M Fin); investment management and financial analysis (MIMFA); JD/MBA; MBA/MIMFA; MD/MBA; Pharm D/MBA. *Accreditation:* AACSB. *Program availability:* Part-time, evening/weekend, 100% online, blended/hybrid learning. *Faculty:* 33 full-time (10 women), 22 part-time/adjunct (3 women). *Students:* 60 full-time (24 women), 308 part-time (95 women); includes 31 minority (14 Black or African American, non-Hispanic/Latino; 1 American Indian or Alaska Native, non-Hispanic/Latino; 9 Asian, non-Hispanic/Latino; 3 Hispanic/Latino; 2 Native Hawaiian or other Pacific Islander, non-Hispanic/Latino; 2 Two or more races, non-Hispanic/Latino), 28 international. Average age 32. 253 applicants, 74% accepted, 123 enrolled. In 2017, 139 master's awarded. *Degree requirements:* For master's, thesis optional; for doctorate, thesis/dissertation optional. *Entrance requirements:* For master's, GMAT, resume, 2 letters of recommendation. Additional exam requirements/recommendations for international students: Required—TOEFL (minimum score 90 iBT). *Application deadline:* For fall admission, 7/1 priority date for domestic students, 3/1 for international students; for winter admission, 10/1 priority date for domestic students, 7/1 for international students; for spring admission, 4/1 priority date for domestic students, 10/1 for international students; for summer admission, 5/1 for domestic and international students. Applications are processed on a rolling basis. Application fee: $50. Electronic applications accepted. *Expenses:* Contact institution. *Financial support:* In 2017–18, 10 fellowships with partial tuition reimbursements (averaging $8,448 per year) were awarded; career-related internships or fieldwork, tuition waivers (partial), and unspecified assistantships also available. Financial award application deadline: 3/1. *Faculty research:* Small business issues, economics, business analytics. *Unit head:* Dr. Deborah Wells, Associate Dean for Graduate Programs, 402-280-2841, E-mail: deborahwells@creighton.edu. *Application contact:* Chris Karasek, Assistant Dean, 402-280-2829, Fax: 402-280-2172, E-mail: chriskarasek@creighton.edu.
Website: http://business.creighton.edu.

Dakota State University, College of Business and Information Systems, Madison, SD 57042-1799. Offers analytics (MSA); business analytics (Graduate Certificate); general management (MBA); health informatics (MSHI); information systems (MSIS, D Sc IS); information technology (Graduate Certificate). *Accreditation:* ACBSP. *Program availability:* Part-time, evening/weekend, 100% online, blended/hybrid learning. *Faculty:* 22 full-time (6 women), 1 (woman) part-time/adjunct. *Students:* 37 full-time (9 women), 168 part-time (52 women); includes 60 minority (29 Black or African American, non-Hispanic/Latino; 3 American Indian or Alaska Native, non-Hispanic/Latino; 15 Asian, non-Hispanic/Latino; 10 Hispanic/Latino; 1 Native Hawaiian or other Pacific Islander, non-Hispanic/Latino; 2 Two or more races, non-Hispanic/Latino), 40 international. Average age 38. 179 applicants, 57% accepted, 59 enrolled. In 2017, 49 master's, 8 doctorates, 5 other advanced degrees awarded. *Degree requirements:* For master's, comprehensive exam, thesis optional, integrative project; for doctorate, comprehensive exam, thesis/dissertation, portfolio. *Entrance requirements:* For master's, GRE General Test, demonstration of information systems skills, minimum GPA of 2.7; for doctorate, GRE General Test, demonstration of information systems skills; for Graduate Certificate, GMAT. Additional exam requirements/recommendations for international students: Required—TOEFL (minimum score 550 paper-based, 76 iBT) or IELTS (6.0). *Application deadline:* For fall admission, 6/15 for domestic students, 4/15 priority date for international students; for spring admission, 11/15 for domestic students, 10/15 priority date for international students; for summer admission, 4/15 for domestic students. Applications are processed on a rolling basis. Application fee: $35. Electronic applications accepted. *Expenses:* Tuition, state resident: full-time $5749. Tuition, nonresident: full-time $10,733. *Required fees:* $715. Tuition and fees vary according to campus/location and reciprocity agreements. *Financial support:* Research assistantships with partial tuition reimbursements, teaching assistantships with partial tuition reimbursements, and unspecified assistantships available. Financial award applicants required to submit FAFSA. *Faculty research:* Data mining and analytics, biometrics and information assurance, decision support systems, health informatics, STEM education for K-12 teachers/students and underrepresented populations. *Unit head:* Dr. Dorine Bennett, Dean of College of Business and Information Systems, 605-256-5165, E-mail: dorine.bennett@dsu.edu. *Application contact:* Erin Blankespoor, Senior Secretary, Office of Graduate Studies and Research, 605-256-5799, E-mail: erin.blankespoor@dsu.edu.
Website: http://dsu.edu/academics/colleges/college-of-business-and-information-systems

DePaul University, Kellstadt Graduate School of Business, Chicago, IL 60604. Offers accountancy (MBA, MSA); applied economics (MBA); audit and advisory services (MS); business administration (DBA); business analytics (MS); business strategy and decision-making (MBA); computational finance (MS); economics and policy analysis (MS); enterprise risk management (MS); entrepreneurship (MBA, MS); finance (MBA, MS); general business (MBA); hospitality leadership (MBA); hospitality leadership and operational performance (MS); human resources (MS); international business (MBA); management (MBA, MS); management information systems (MBA); marketing (MBA, MS); marketing analysis (MS); marketing strategy and planning (MBA); real estate (MBA); real estate finance and investment (MBA); strategy, execution and valuation (MBA); supply chain management (MS); sustainable management (MS); taxation (MS); JD/MBA. *Accreditation:* AACSB. *Program availability:* Part-time, evening/weekend, online learning. *Entrance requirements:* For master's, GMAT/GRE, 2 letters of recommendation, resume, essay, official transcripts. Additional exam requirements/recommendations for international students: Required—TOEFL (minimum score 550 paper-based; 80 iBT). *Application deadline:* For fall admission, 7/1 for domestic students, 6/1 for international students; for winter admission, 10/1 for domestic students, 9/1 for international students; for spring admission, 2/1 for domestic students, 1/1 for international students. Applications are processed on a rolling basis. Application fee: $60. Electronic applications accepted. *Expenses:* Contact institution. *Financial support:* Application deadline: 4/1; applicants required to submit FAFSA. *Unit head:* Christa Hinton, Assistant Dean and Director, 312-362-8810, Fax: 312-362-6677, E-mail: chinton@depaul.edu. *Application contact:* Garry Cooke, Director of Recruitment and Admissions, 312-362-8810, Fax: 312-362-6677, E-mail: kgsb@depaul.edu.
Website: http://kellstadt.depaul.edu.

Duke University, The Fuqua School of Business, Master of Quantitative Management Program: Business Analytics, Durham, NC 27708-0586. Offers finance (MQM); forensics (MQM); marketing (MQM); strategy (MQM). *Faculty:* 96 full-time (19 women), 48 part-time/adjunct (15 women). *Students:* 140 full-time (81 women); includes 11 minority (9 Asian, non-Hispanic/Latino; 2 Hispanic/Latino), 118 international. Average age 24. *Entrance requirements:* For master's, GMAT/GRE, transcripts, essays, resume, recommendation letters. *Application deadline:* For fall admission, 9/13 for domestic and international students; for winter admission, 1/17 for domestic and international students; for spring admission, 2/28 for domestic and international students; for summer admission, 4/4 for domestic and international students. Application fee: $125. Electronic applications accepted. *Expenses:* $66,907 tuition and fees. *Financial support:* In 2017–18, 46 students received support. Scholarships/grants available. Financial award applicants required to submit FAFSA. *Unit head:* Jeremy Petranka, Associate Dean. *Application contact:* Shari Hubert, Associate Dean, Office of Admissions, 919-660-7705, Fax: 919-681-8026, E-mail: admissions-info@fuqua.duke.edu.
Website: https://www.fuqua.duke.edu/programs/mqm-business-analytics

Fairfield University, Dolan School of Business, Fairfield, CT 06824. Offers accounting (MBA, MS, CAS); business analytics (MS); finance (MBA, MS, CAS); information systems and business analytics (MBA); management (MBA, CAS); marketing (MBA, CAS); taxation (CAS). *Accreditation:* AACSB. *Program availability:* Part-time, evening/weekend. *Faculty:* 18 full-time (6 women), 6 part-time/adjunct (2 women). *Students:* 120 full-time (57 women), 67 part-time (27 women); includes 20 minority (3 Black or African American, non-Hispanic/Latino; 1 American Indian or Alaska Native, non-Hispanic/Latino; 3 Asian, non-Hispanic/Latino; 11 Hispanic/Latino; 2 Two or more races, non-Hispanic/Latino), 33 international. Average age 26. 195 applicants, 87% accepted, 112 enrolled. In 2017, 93 master's awarded. *Degree requirements:* For master's, capstone course. *Entrance requirements:* For master's, GMAT (minimum score 500), 2 letters of reference, resume, minimum GPA of 3.0. Additional exam requirements/recommendations for international students: Required—TOEFL (minimum score 550 paper-based; 80 iBT) or IELTS (minimum score 6.5). *Application deadline:* For fall admission, 5/15 for international students; for spring admission, 10/15 for international students. Applications are processed on a rolling basis. Application fee: $60. Electronic applications accepted. *Expenses:* $925 per credit hour. *Financial support:* In 2017–18, 31 students received support. Scholarships/grants and unspecified assistantships available. Financial award applicants required to submit FAFSA. *Faculty research:* International finance, leadership and careers, ethics in accounting, emotions in consumer behavior and organizations, data analytics. *Unit head:* Dr. Mark Ligas, Interim Dean, 203-254-4070, Fax: 203-254-4105, E-mail: mligas@fairfield.edu. *Application contact:* Marianne Gumpper, Director of Graduate and Continuing Studies Admission, 203-254-4184, Fax: 203-254-4073, E-mail: gradadmis@fairfield.edu.
Website: http://fairfield.edu/mba

The George Washington University, School of Business, Department of Decision Sciences, Washington, DC 20052. Offers business analytics (MS, Certificate); project management (MS). *Program availability:* Online learning. *Faculty:* 17 full-time (1 woman), 4 part-time/adjunct (1 woman). *Students:* 84 full-time (44 women), 131 part-time (65 women); includes 57 minority (30 Black or African American, non-Hispanic/Latino; 1 American Indian or Alaska Native, non-Hispanic/Latino; 13 Asian, non-Hispanic/Latino; 8 Hispanic/Latino; 5 Two or more races, non-Hispanic/Latino), 105 international. Average age 33. 914 applicants, 44% accepted, 80 enrolled. In 2017, 97 master's, 65 other advanced degrees awarded. Application fee: $75. *Expenses:* Tuition: Full-time $28,800; part-time $1655 per credit hour. *Required fees:* $45; $2.75 per credit hour. *Financial support:* Tuition waivers available. *Unit head:* Prof. Refik Soyer, Chair, 202-994-6445, E-mail: soyer@gwu.edu. *Application contact:* Christopher Storer, Executive Director, Graduate Admissions, 202-994-1212, E-mail: gwmba@gwu.edu.
Website: http://business.gwu.edu/decisionsciences/

Golden Gate University, Ageno School of Business, San Francisco, CA 94105-2968. Offers accounting (MBA); adaptive leadership (MBA); advanced financial planning (MS); business administration (EMBA, MBA, DBA); business analytics (MBA, MS); entrepreneurship (MBA); finance (MBA, MS, Certificate); financial life planning (Certificate); financial planning (MS, Certificate); global supply chain management (MBA, Certificate); human resource management (MBA, MS, Certificate); information technology management (MBA, MS, Certificate); international business (MBA); marketing (MBA, MS, Certificate); project management (MBA, MS, Certificate); psychology (MA, Certificate); public administration (EMPA, MBA); public administration leadership (Certificate); JD/MBA. *Program availability:* Part-time, evening/weekend. *Faculty:* 17 full-time (7 women), 280 part-time/adjunct (95 women). *Students:* 309 full-time (147 women), 527 part-time (266 women); includes 286 minority (56 Black or African American, non-Hispanic/Latino; 1 American Indian or Alaska Native, non-Hispanic/Latino; 131 Asian, non-Hispanic/Latino; 83 Hispanic/Latino; 4 Native Hawaiian or other Pacific Islander, non-Hispanic/Latino; 11 Two or more races, non-Hispanic/Latino), 209 international. Average age 35. 549 applicants, 66% accepted, 185 enrolled. *Degree requirements:* For doctorate, thesis/dissertation, qualifying examination. *Entrance requirements:* For master's, GMAT (for MBA), minimum GPA of 2.5 (MS). Additional exam requirements/recommendations for international students: Required—TOEFL (minimum score 550 paper-based; 79 iBT). *Application deadline:* For fall admission, 5/15 for domestic and international students; for winter admission, 1/15 for domestic and international students; for spring admission, 9/15 for domestic and international students. Applications are processed on a rolling basis. Application fee: $65 ($105 for international students). Electronic applications accepted. *Expenses:* $3,150 per 3-unit course. *Financial support:* Career-related internships or fieldwork, Federal Work-Study, institutionally sponsored loans, and scholarships/grants available. Support available to part-time students. Financial award applicants required to submit FAFSA. *Unit head:* Marianne Koch, Associate Dean, 415-442-6542, Fax: 415-442-6579, E-mail: mkoch@ggu.edu. *Application contact:* Angela Melero, Enrollment Services, 415-442-7800, Fax: 415-442-7807, E-mail: info@ggu.edu.
Website: http://www.ggu.edu/programs/business-and-management

Grand Canyon University, Colangelo College of Business, Phoenix, AZ 85017-1097. Offers accounting (MBA, MS); business analytics (MS); disaster preparedness and executive fire service leadership (MS); finance (MBA); general management (MBA); health systems management (MBA); information technology management (MS); leadership (MBA, MS); marketing (MBA); organizational leadership and entrepreneurship (MS); project management (MBA); sports business (MBA); strategic human resource management (MBA). *Accreditation:* ACBSP. *Program availability:* Part-time, evening/weekend, online learning. *Entrance requirements:* For master's, equivalent of two years' full-time professional work experience. Additional exam requirements/recommendations for international students: Required—TOEFL (minimum score 575 paper-based; 90 iBT), IELTS (minimum score 7). Electronic applications accepted.

HEC Montreal, School of Business Administration, Master of Science Programs in Administration, Program in Business Analytics, Montréal, QC H3T 2A7, Canada. Offers M Sc. Program offered in French and also in English. *Students:* 35 full-time (6 women), 14 part-time (3 women). 31 applicants, 84% accepted, 22 enrolled. In 2017, 13 master's awarded. *Entrance requirements:* For master's, BBA, undergraduate degree in another field, degree deemed equivalent by program director and minimum GPA of 3.0 on 4.3 scale. Additional exam requirements/recommendations for international students: Required—TAGE MAGE (minimum recommended score of 283), GMAT (minimum recommended score of 630), or GRE. *Application deadline:* For fall admission, 3/15 for domestic and international students; for winter admission, 9/15 for domestic and international students. Application fee: $88 ($184 for international students). Electronic applications accepted. *Expenses:* Tuition, state resident: full-time $2869 Canadian dollars; part-time $79.70 Canadian dollars per credit. Tuition, nonresident: full-time $8883 Canadian dollars; part-time $246.76 Canadian dollars per credit. *International tuition:* $19,648 Canadian dollars full-time. *Required fees:* $41.20 Canadian dollars per credit. $67.94 Canadian dollars per term. Tuition and fees vary according to degree level and program. *Financial support:* Research assistantships, teaching assistantships, and scholarships/grants available. Financial award application deadline: 9/2. *Unit head:* Dr. Marie-Helene Jobin, Director, 514-340-6283, E-mail: marie-helene.jobin@hec.ca. *Application contact:* Marianne de Moura, Administrative Director, 514-340-6151, Fax: 514-340-6411, E-mail: aide@hec.ca.
Website: http://www.hec.ca/en/programs/masters/master-business-analytics/index.html

Hult International Business School, Graduate Programs, Cambridge, MA 02141. Offers business administration (EMBA); business analytics (MBA, MIB); business statistics (MBS); disruptive innovation (MDI); entrepreneurship (MBA, MIB); family business (MBA, MIB); finance (MBA, MF, MIB); international marketing (MIM); marketing (MBA, MIB); project management (MBA, MIB). MDI and MBS offered in San Francisco; MBA also offered in Boston, San Francisco, Dubai, Shanghai, and New York. *Entrance requirements:* For master's, GMAT, 3 years of work experience. Additional exam requirements/recommendations for international students: Required—TOEFL. Electronic applications accepted. *Expenses:* Contact institution.

Iowa State University of Science and Technology, Program in Business Analytics, Ames, IA 50011. Offers MS. *Program availability:* Online learning.

Johns Hopkins University, Carey Business School, MS in Business Analytics and Risk Management Program, Baltimore, MD 21218. Offers MS. *Program availability:* Part-time, evening/weekend. *Faculty:* 93 full-time (33 women), 45 part-time/adjunct (11 women). *Students:* 39 full-time (25 women), 11 part-time (4 women); includes 7 minority (4 Black or African American, non-Hispanic/Latino; 1 Asian, non-Hispanic/Latino; 2 Hispanic/Latino), 38 international. Average age 24. 158 applicants, 70% accepted, 42 enrolled. In 2017, 26 master's awarded. *Degree requirements:* For master's, 36 credits. *Entrance requirements:* For master's, GMAT or GRE. Additional exam requirements/recommendations for international students: Required—TOEFL, IELTS. *Application deadline:* For fall admission, 5/1 for domestic and international students. Applications are processed on a rolling basis. Application fee: $100. Electronic applications accepted. *Expenses:* $66,500 (full-time); $1,330 per credit (part-time). *Financial support:* In 2017–18, 7 students received support. Scholarships/grants available. Support available to part-time students. Financial award application deadline: 4/15; financial award applicants required to submit FAFSA. *Faculty research:* Emerging issues in risk management, health care/medical services, strategic options and simulation. *Unit head:* Dr. Kevin Frick, Vice Dean of Education, 410-234-9272, E-mail: kfrick@jhu.edu. *Application contact:* Office of Admissions, 410-234-9220, Fax: 443-529-1554, E-mail: carey.admissions@jhu.edu.

La Salle University, School of Business, Master of Business Administration Program, Philadelphia, PA 19141-1199. Offers accounting (MBA, Post-MBA Certificate); business systems and analytics (MBA, Post-MBA Certificate); finance (MBA, Post-MBA Certificate); general business administration (MBA, Post-MBA Certificate); human resource management (MBA, Post-MBA Certificate); management (MBA, Post-MBA Certificate); marketing (Post-MBA Certificate); MBA/MSN. Program also offered in Switzerland. *Accreditation:* AACSB. *Program availability:* Part-time, evening/weekend, online learning. *Faculty:* 22 full-time (10 women), 10 part-time/adjunct (3 women). *Students:* 59 full-time (25 women), 200 part-time (109 women); includes 66 minority (36 Black or African American, non-Hispanic/Latino; 21 Asian, non-Hispanic/Latino; 7 Hispanic/Latino; 2 Two or more races, non-Hispanic/Latino), 22 international. Average age 31. 216 applicants, 57% accepted, 74 enrolled. In 2017, 146 master's awarded. *Entrance requirements:* For master's, GMAT or GRE, two letters of reference; resume; for Post-MBA Certificate, MBA with minimum GPA of 3.0. Additional exam requirements/recommendations for international students: Required—TOEFL. *Application deadline:* For fall admission, 8/15 priority date for domestic students, 7/15 for international students; for spring admission, 12/15 priority date for domestic students, 11/15 for international students; for summer admission, 4/15 priority date for domestic students, 3/15 for international students. Applications are processed on a rolling basis. Application fee: $35. Electronic applications accepted. Application fee is waived when completed online. *Expenses:* Contact institution. *Financial support:* In 2017–18, 51 students received support. Scholarships/grants available. Support available to part-time students. Financial award application deadline: 8/31; financial award applicants required to submit FAFSA. *Unit head:* Dr. MarySheila McDonald, Interim Dean, 215-951-1040, Fax: 215-951-1886, E-mail: mcdonaldms@lasalle.edu. *Application contact:* Elizabeth Heenan, Director, Graduate and Adult Enrollment, 215-951-1100, Fax: 215-951-1462, E-mail: heenan@lasalle.edu.

Lenoir-Rhyne University, Graduate Programs, Charles M. Snipes School of Business, Hickory, NC 28601. Offers accounting (MBA); business analytics and information technology (MBA); entrepreneurship (MBA); global business (MBA); healthcare administration (MBA); innovation and change management (MBA); leadership development (MBA). *Accreditation:* ACBSP. *Program availability:* Part-time, evening/weekend, online learning. *Degree requirements:* For master's, capstone course. *Entrance requirements:* For master's, GMAT, GRE, MAT, minimum undergraduate GPA of 2.7, graduate 3.0. Additional exam requirements/recommendations for international students: Required—TOEFL (minimum score 600 paper-based). Electronic applications accepted. *Expenses:* Contact institution.

Lewis University, College of Business, Program in Business Analytics, Romeoville, IL 60446. Offers financial analytics (MS); healthcare analytics (MS); marketing analytics (MS); operations analytics (MS). *Program availability:* Part-time, evening/weekend, 100% online, blended/hybrid learning. *Students:* 19 full-time (9 women), 37 part-time (26 women); includes 12 minority (6 Black or African American, non-Hispanic/Latino; 5 Hispanic/Latino; 1 Two or more races, non-Hispanic/Latino), 6 international. Average age 34. *Degree requirements:* For master's, comprehensive exam. *Entrance requirements:* For master's, bachelor's degree, transcripts from each college/university attended, letters of recommendation, resume. Additional exam requirements/recommendations for international students: Required—TOEFL, IELTS. *Application deadline:* Applications are processed on a rolling basis. Electronic applications accepted. Tuition and fees vary according to program. *Financial support:* Career-related internships or fieldwork, Federal Work-Study, and unspecified assistantships available. Financial award applicants required to submit FAFSA. *Unit head:* Dr. Ryan Butt, Dean, 800-888-0500, E-mail: buttry@lewisu.edu. *Application contact:* Michele Ryan, Director of Admission, 815-836-5384, E-mail: ryanml@lewisu.edu.
Website: http://www.lewisu.edu/academics/business-analytics/

Loyola University Chicago, Quinlan School of Business, Master of Science in Business Data Analytics Program, Chicago, IL 60611. Offers MS, Certificate. *Program availability:* Evening/weekend. *Faculty:* 15 full-time (2 women), 7 part-time/adjunct (0 women). *Students:* 21 full-time (11 women), 7 part-time (1 woman); includes 7 minority (2 Black or African American, non-Hispanic/Latino; 1 Asian, non-Hispanic/Latino; 3 Hispanic/Latino; 1 Two or more races, non-Hispanic/Latino), 9 international. Average age 32. 53 applicants, 68% accepted, 19 enrolled. In 2017, 28 other advanced degrees awarded. *Entrance requirements:* For master's, GMAT or GRE, official transcripts, two letters of recommendation, statement of purpose, resume. Additional exam requirements/recommendations for international students: Required—TOEFL (minimum score 90 iBT), IELTS (minimum score 6.5). *Application deadline:* For fall admission, 7/15 for domestic students. Application fee: $50. Electronic applications accepted. *Expenses:* $4,488 per course. *Financial support:* In 2017–18, 2 students received support. Research assistantships, career-related internships or fieldwork, Federal Work-Study, scholarships/grants, and health care benefits available. *Unit head:* Dr. Steven Todd, Director, 312-915-7218, E-mail: stodd@luc.edu.
Website: https://www.luc.edu/quinlan/masters/business-data-analytics/

Merrimack College, Girard School of Business, North Andover, MA 01845-5800. Offers accounting (MS); business analytics (MS); management (MS). *Program availability:* Part-time, evening/weekend, 100% online. *Faculty:* 13 full-time, 19 part-time/adjunct. *Students:* 86 full-time (33 women), 31 part-time (11 women); includes 10 minority (2 Black or African American, non-Hispanic/Latino; 2 Asian, non-Hispanic/Latino; 6 Hispanic/Latino), 34 international. Average age 27. 139 applicants, 78% accepted, 61 enrolled. In 2017, 74 master's awarded. *Degree requirements:* For master's, comprehensive exam (for some programs), thesis optional, capstone. *Entrance requirements:* For master's, official college transcripts, resume, personal statement, 2 recommendations. Additional exam requirements/recommendations for international students: Required—TOEFL (minimum score 84 iBT), IELTS (minimum score 6.5), PTE (minimum score 56). *Application deadline:* For fall admission, 8/24 for domestic students, 7/30 for international students; for spring admission, 1/10 for domestic and international students; for summer admission, 5/10 for domestic students, 4/10 for international students. Applications are processed on a rolling basis. Application fee: $0. Electronic applications accepted. *Expenses:* Contact institution. *Financial support:* Career-related internships or fieldwork, scholarships/grants, health care benefits, and unspecified assistantships available. Support available to part-time students. Financial award application deadline: 5/1; financial award applicants required to submit FAFSA. *Application contact:* Jennifer Greenwood, Graduate Admission Counselor, 978-837-3563, E-mail: graduate@merrimack.edu.
Website: http://www.merrimack.edu/academics/graduate/

Metropolitan State University, College of Management, St. Paul, MN 55106-5000. Offers business administration (MBA, DBA); business analytics (Graduate Certificate); database administration (Graduate Certificate); global supply chain management (Graduate Certificate); information assurance security (Graduate Certificate); management information systems (MMIS); MIS generalist (Graduate Certificate); MIS systems analysis and design (Graduate Certificate); project management (Graduate Certificate). *Program availability:* Part-time, evening/weekend. *Degree requirements:* For master's, thesis optional, computer language (MMIS). *Entrance requirements:* For master's, GMAT (for MBA), resume. Additional exam requirements/recommendations for international students: Required—TOEFL (minimum score 550 paper-based). *Application deadline:* For fall admission, 7/15 for international students; for winter admission, 11/15 for international students; for spring admission, 3/15 for international students. Applications are processed on a rolling basis. Application fee: $20. Electronic applications accepted. *Expenses:* Tuition, state resident: part-time $388.55 per credit. Tuition, nonresident: part-time $777.11 per credit. *Required fees:* $35.11 per credit. Part-time tuition and fees vary according to campus/location and program. *Financial support:* Research assistantships with partial tuition reimbursements, career-related internships or fieldwork, and Federal Work-Study available. Support available to part-time students. Financial award applicants required to submit FAFSA. *Faculty research:* Yugoslav economic system, workers' cooperatives, participative management and job enrichment, global business systems. *Unit head:* Allen Bellas, Interim Dean, 612-659-7272, Fax: 612-659-7268, E-mail: allen.bellas@metrostate.edu. *Application contact:* Allen Bellas, Interim Dean, 612-659-7272, Fax: 612-659-7268, E-mail: allen.bellas@metrostate.edu.
Website: https://www.metrostate.edu/academics/management

Michigan State University, The Graduate School, Eli Broad College of Business, Program in Business Analytics, East Lansing, MI 48224. Offers MS. Program offered in collaboration with MSU's College of Engineering and College of Natural Science. *Entrance requirements:* For master's, GMAT or GRE, bachelor's degree; minimum cumulative GPA of 3.0 in undergraduate course work and in college-level courses in introductory calculus and statistics; working knowledge of personal computers; knowledge of programming languages; experience in using statistical software program packages; recent laptop computer with MS Office. Additional exam requirements/recommendations for international students: Required—PTE (minimum score 70), TOEFL or IELTS. Electronic applications accepted. *Faculty research:* Artificial intelligence, evolution, and game theory, computational modeling using high performance computing.

Moravian College, Graduate and Continuing Studies, Business and Management Programs, Bethlehem, PA 18018-6650. Offers accounting (MBA); business analytics (MBA); business management (MBA); health administration (MHA); healthcare management (MBA); HR leadership (MSHRM); human resource management (MBA); learning and performance management (MSHRM); supply chain management (MBA). *Program availability:* Part-time, evening/weekend. *Faculty:* 5 full-time (2 women), 9 part-time/adjunct (3 women). *Students:* 13 full-time (10 women), 80 part-time (45 women); includes 13 minority (6 Black or African American, non-Hispanic/Latino; 6 Hispanic/Latino; 1 Two or more races, non-Hispanic/Latino). Average age 31. 55 applicants, 91% accepted, 31 enrolled. In 2017, 29 master's awarded. *Entrance requirements:* For master's, current resume, official transcripts, 2 letters of recommendation. Additional exam requirements/recommendations for international students: Required—TOEFL (minimum score 550 paper-based), IELTS (minimum score 6.5). *Application deadline:* For fall admission, 8/1 priority date for domestic and international students; for spring admission, 1/1 priority date for domestic and international students; for summer admission, 5/1 priority date for domestic and international students. Applications are processed on a rolling basis. Electronic applications accepted. *Expenses:* Tuition: Full-time $15,714; part-time $2619 per course. *Required fees:* $45 per semester. Tuition and fees vary according to program. *Financial support:* In 2017–18, 3 students received support, including 2 research assistantships with full tuition reimbursements available. Financial award applicants required to submit FAFSA. *Faculty research:* Leadership, change management, human resources. *Unit head:* Dr. Liz Kleintop, Associate Chair of Graduate Business, 610-861-1400, Fax: 610-861-1466, E-mail: graduate@moravian.edu. *Application contact:* Sean Rossi, Student Experience Mentor, 610-861-1400, Fax: 610-861-1466, E-mail: graduate@moravian.edu.
Website: https://www.moravian.edu/graduate

National University, Academic Affairs, School of Business and Management, La Jolla, CA 92037-1011. Offers accountancy (M Acc, Certificate); business administration (GMBA, MBA); business analytics (MS); cause leadership (MA); global management (MGM); human resource management (MA); management information systems (MS); marketing (MS); organizational leadership (MS). GMBA offered in Spanish. *Program availability:* Part-time, evening/weekend, 100% online, blended/hybrid learning. *Degree requirements:* For master's, thesis (for some programs). *Entrance requirements:* For master's, interview, minimum GPA of 2.5. Additional exam requirements/recommendations for international students: Required—TOEFL (minimum score 550 paper-based; 79 iBT), IELTS (minimum score 6). *Application deadline:* Applications are processed on a rolling basis. Application fee: $60 ($65 for international students). Electronic applications accepted. *Expenses:* Tuition: Part-time $430 per quarter hour. *Financial support:* Career-related internships or fieldwork, scholarships/grants, and tuition waivers (partial) available. Support available to part-time students. Financial award application deadline: 6/30; financial award applicants required to submit FAFSA. *Unit head:* Dr. Alfred Ntoko, Dean, 858-642-8400, Fax: 858-642-8719, E-mail: sobm@nu.edu. *Application contact:* Brandon Jouganatos, Vice President for Enrollment Services, 800-628-8648, E-mail: advisor@nu.edu.
Website: http://www.nu.edu/OurPrograms/SchoolOfBusinessAndManagement.html

Business Analytics

Northwestern University, The Graduate School, Kellogg School of Management, Management Programs, Evanston, IL 60208. Offers accounting information and management (MBA, PhD); analytical finance (MBA); business administration (MBA); decision sciences (MBA); entrepreneurship and innovation (MBA); finance (MBA, PhD); health enterprise management (MBA); human resources management (MBA); international business (MBA); management and organizations (MBA, PhD); management and organizations and sociology (PhD); management and strategy (MBA); management studies (MS); managerial analytics (MBA); managerial economics (MBA); managerial economics and strategy (PhD); marketing (MBA, PhD); marketing management (MBA); media management (MBA); operations management (MBA, PhD); real estate (MBA); social enterprise at Kellogg (MBA); JD/MBA. *Program availability:* Part-time, evening/weekend. Terminal master's awarded for partial completion of doctoral program. *Degree requirements:* For doctorate, thesis/dissertation, 2 years of coursework, qualifying (field) exam and candidacy, summer research papers and presentations to faculty, proposal defense, final exam/defense. *Entrance requirements:* For master's, GMAT, GRE, interview, 2 letters of recommendation, college transcripts, resume, essays, Kellogg honor code; for doctorate, GMAT, GRE, statement of purpose, transcripts, 2 letters of recommendation, resume, interview. Additional exam requirements/recommendations for international students: Required—TOEFL, IELTS. Electronic applications accepted. *Expenses:* Contact institution. *Faculty research:* Business cycles and international finance, health policy, networks, non-market strategy, consumer psychology.

Northwest Missouri State University, Graduate School, Melvin and Valorie Booth College of Business and Professional Studies, Maryville, MO 64468-6001. Offers agricultural economics (MBA); business decision and analytics (MBA); general management (MBA); human resource management (MBA); marketing (MBA). *Program availability:* Part-time. *Faculty:* 17 full-time (6 women). *Students:* 40 full-time (13 women), 95 part-time (48 women); includes 16 minority (8 Black or African American, non-Hispanic/Latino; 1 American Indian or Alaska Native, non-Hispanic/Latino; 2 Asian, non-Hispanic/Latino; 3 Hispanic/Latino; 2 Two or more races, non-Hispanic/Latino), 15 international. Average age 31. 142 applicants, 66% accepted, 70 enrolled. In 2017, 53 master's awarded. *Degree requirements:* For master's, comprehensive exam. *Entrance requirements:* For master's, GMAT, GRE, minimum GPA of 2.5. Additional exam requirements/recommendations for international students: Required—TOEFL (minimum score 550 paper-based). *Application deadline:* For fall admission, 7/1 for domestic and international students; for spring admission, 11/15 for domestic and international students; for summer admission, 4/1 for domestic and international students. Applications are processed on a rolling basis. Application fee: $0 ($50 for international students). Electronic applications accepted. *Expenses:* $389.11 per credit in-state tuition; $641.97 per credit out-of-state tuition. *Financial support:* Research assistantships with full tuition reimbursements, teaching assistantships with full tuition reimbursements, career-related internships or fieldwork, and administrative assistantships, tutorial assistantships available. Financial award application deadline: 4/1; financial award applicants required to submit FAFSA. *Unit head:* Dr. Steve Ludwig, Director of the Melvin And Valorie Booth School of Business, 660-562-1749, Fax: 660-562-1096, E-mail: sludwig@nwmissouri.edu.
Website: https://www.nwmissouri.edu/business/index.htm

Nova Southeastern University, H. Wayne Huizenga College of Business and Entrepreneurship, Fort Lauderdale, FL 33314-7796. Offers accounting (M Acc); business (MBA); business intelligence/analytics (MBA); complex health systems (MBA); enterprise informatics (MBA); entrepreneurship (MBA); finance (MBA); human resource management (MBA); international business (MBA); management (MBA); marketing (MBA); process improvement (MBA); public administration (MPA); real estate development (MS); sport revenue generation (MBA); supply chain management (MBA). *Accreditation:* NASPAA. *Program availability:* Part-time, evening/weekend, 100% online, blended/hybrid learning. *Faculty:* 85 full-time (37 women), 59 part-time/adjunct (19 women). *Students:* 1,999 full-time (1,225 women), 335 part-time (210 women); includes 1,516 minority (597 Black or African American, non-Hispanic/Latino; 4 American Indian or Alaska Native, non-Hispanic/Latino; 92 Asian, non-Hispanic/Latino; 789 Hispanic/Latino; 3 Native Hawaiian or other Pacific Islander, non-Hispanic/Latino; 31 Two or more races, non-Hispanic/Latino), 291 international. Average age 34. 1,269 applicants, 59% accepted, 551 enrolled. In 2017, 1,055 master's awarded. *Entrance requirements:* For master's, GMAT or GRE (depending on undergraduate GPA), official transcripts from all schools attended while in pursuit of bachelor's degree; minimum GPA of 2.5 from regionally-accredited institution. Additional exam requirements/recommendations for international students: Required—TOEFL (minimum score 550 paper-based; 79 iBT), IELTS (minimum score 6), PTE (minimum score 54). *Application deadline:* For fall admission, 8/5 priority date for domestic students, 7/29 priority date for international students; for winter admission, 12/16 priority date for domestic students, 12/9 priority date for international students; for summer admission, 4/21 priority date for domestic and international students. Applications are processed on a rolling basis. Application fee: $50. Electronic applications accepted. *Expenses:* $37,785 (online), $35,640 (in-classroom). *Financial support:* In 2017–18, 325 students received support. Federal Work-Study and scholarships/grants available. Support available to part-time students. Financial award application deadline: 4/15; financial award applicants required to submit FAFSA. *Faculty research:* Entrepreneurship and venture capital, ethics and social responsibility, global commerce and cultures, business process management. *Unit head:* Dr. J. Preston Jones, Dean, 954-262-5127, E-mail: prestonj@nova.edu. *Application contact:* Zeida Rodriguez, Associate Director of Enrollment Services, 954-262-5163, Fax: 954-262-3822, E-mail: zeida@nova.edu.
Website: http://www.huizenga.nova.edu

Point Park University, Rowland School of Business, Program in Business Administration, Pittsburgh, PA 15222-1984. Offers business analytics (MBA); global management and administration (MBA); health systems management (MBA); international business (MBA); management (MBA); management information systems (MBA); sports, arts and entertainment management (MBA). *Program availability:* Evening/weekend, 100% online.

Regent University, Graduate School, School of Business and Leadership, Virginia Beach, VA 23464-9800. Offers business administration (MBA), including accounting, economics, entrepreneurship, finance and investing, general management, healthcare management (MA, MBA), human resource management (MA, MBA), innovation management, leadership, marketing, not-for-profit management (MA, MBA); business analytics (MS); business and design management (MA); church leadership (MA); leadership (Certificate); organizational leadership (MA, PhD), including ecclesial leadership (DSL, PhD), entrepreneurial leadership (PhD), healthcare management (MA, MBA), human resource development (PhD), human resource management (MA, MBA), individualized studies (DSL, PhD), interdisciplinary studies (MA), leadership coaching and mentoring (MA), not-for-profit management (MA, MBA), organizational development consulting (MA), servant leadership (MA, DSL); strategic leadership (DSL), including ecclesial leadership (DSL, PhD), global consulting, healthcare leadership, individualized studies (DSL, PhD), leadership coaching, servant leadership (MA, DSL), strategic foresight. *Program availability:* Part-time, evening/weekend, 100% online, blended/hybrid learning. *Faculty:* 9 full-time (2 women), 38 part-time/adjunct (11 women). *Students:* 129 full-time (80 women), 1,152 part-time (598 women); includes 685 minority (546 Black or African American, non-Hispanic/Latino; 10 American Indian or Alaska Native, non-Hispanic/Latino; 29 Asian, non-Hispanic/Latino; 65 Hispanic/Latino; 6 Native Hawaiian or other Pacific Islander, non-Hispanic/Latino; 29 Two or more races, non-Hispanic/Latino), 62 international. Average age 41. 1,721 applicants, 48% accepted, 624 enrolled. In 2017, 125 master's, 69 doctorates awarded. *Degree requirements:* For master's, thesis or alternative, 3-credit hour culminating experience; for doctorate, thesis/dissertation. *Entrance requirements:* For master's, college transcripts, resume, essay; for doctorate, college transcripts, resume, essay, writing sample; for Certificate, writing sample, resume, transcripts. Additional exam requirements/recommendations for international students: Required—TOEFL (minimum score 577 paper-based). *Application deadline:* For fall admission, 5/1 priority date for domestic students; for spring admission, 10/1 priority date for domestic students. Applications are processed on a rolling basis. Application fee: $50. Electronic applications accepted. *Expenses:* $650 per credit (MA, MS, MBA); $995 per credit (PhD); $300 per semester technology fee. *Financial support:* In 2017–18, 829 students received support. Career-related internships or fieldwork, scholarships/grants, and unspecified assistantships available. Support available to part-time students. *Faculty research:* Servant leadership, global business, team effectiveness, technology utilization, leadership development. *Unit head:* Dr. Doris Gomez, Dean, 757-352-4686, Fax: 757-352-4634, E-mail: dorigom@regent.edu. *Application contact:* Heidi Cece, Assistant Vice President of Enrollment Management, 800-373-5504, Fax: 757-352-4381, E-mail: admissions@regent.edu.
Website: https://www.regent.edu/school-of-business-and-leadership/

Rensselaer Polytechnic Institute, Graduate School, Lally School of Management, Program in Business Analytics, Troy, NY 12180-3590. Offers MS. *Program availability:* Part-time. *Faculty:* 36 full-time (9 women), 5 part-time/adjunct (0 women). *Students:* 35 full-time (17 women), 4 part-time (3 women); includes 4 minority (3 Asian, non-Hispanic/Latino; 1 Two or more races, non-Hispanic/Latino), 30 international. Average age 27. 506 applicants, 26% accepted, 25 enrolled. In 2017, 20 master's awarded. *Entrance requirements:* For master's, GMAT or GRE, personal statement. Additional exam requirements/recommendations for international students: Required—PTE, TOEFL (minimum score 570 paper-based; 88 iBT), IELTS (minimum score 6.5), or PTE (minimum score 60). *Application deadline:* For fall admission, 1/1 for domestic and international students. Applications are processed on a rolling basis. Application fee: $75. Electronic applications accepted. *Expenses:* Tuition: Full-time $52,550; part-time $2125 per credit hour. *Required fees:* $2890. *Financial support:* Scholarships/grants available. Financial award application deadline: 1/1. *Total annual research expenditures:* $60,850. *Unit head:* Pindaro Demertzoglou, Graduate Program Director, 518-276-2753, E-mail: demerp@rpi.edu.
Website: https://lallyschool.rpi.edu/ms-business-analytics

Robert Morris University Illinois, Morris Graduate School of Management, Chicago, IL 60605. Offers accounting (MBA); accounting/finance (MBA); business analytics (MIS); health care administration (MM); higher education administration (MM); human performance (MS); human resource management (MBA); information security (MIS); information systems management (MIS); law enforcement administration (MM); management (MBA); management/finance (MBA); management/human resource management (MBA); sports administration (MM). *Program availability:* Part-time, evening/weekend. *Faculty:* 2 full-time (0 women), 26 part-time/adjunct (8 women). *Students:* 186 full-time (108 women), 114 part-time (57 women); includes 167 minority (88 Black or African American, non-Hispanic/Latino; 15 Asian, non-Hispanic/Latino; 62 Hispanic/Latino; 1 Native Hawaiian or other Pacific Islander, non-Hispanic/Latino; 1 Two or more races, non-Hispanic/Latino), 18 international. Average age 32. 157 applicants, 78% accepted, 72 enrolled. In 2017, 191 master's awarded. *Entrance requirements:* For master's, official transcripts and letters of recommendation (for some programs); written personal statement. Additional exam requirements/recommendations for international students: Required—TOEFL (minimum score 550 paper-based). *Application deadline:* Applications are processed on a rolling basis. Application fee: $20 ($100 for international students). Electronic applications accepted. *Expenses:* Tuition: Full-time $17,100; part-time $2850 per course. *Financial support:* In 2017–18, 381 students received support. Federal Work-Study, scholarships/grants, and unspecified assistantships available. Support available to part-time students. Financial award applicants required to submit FAFSA. *Unit head:* Kayed Akkawi, Dean, 312-935-6050, Fax: 312-935-6020, E-mail: kakkawi@robertmorris.edu. *Application contact:* Mark Daugherty, Director of Admissions, 312-935-4814, Fax: 312-935-6020, E-mail: mdaugherty@robertmorris.edu.

Rockhurst University, Helzberg School of Management, Kansas City, MO 64110-2561. Offers accounting (MBA); business intelligence (MBA, Certificate); business intelligence and analytics (MS); data science (MBA, Certificate); entrepreneurship (MBA); finance (MBA); fundraising leadership (MBA, Certificate); healthcare management (MBA, Certificate); human capital (Certificate); international business (Certificate); management (MA, MBA, Certificate); nonprofit administration (Certificate); organizational development (Certificate); science leadership (Certificate). *Accreditation:* AACSB. *Program availability:* Part-time, evening/weekend. *Faculty:* 18 full-time (4 women), 20 part-time/adjunct (9 women). *Students:* 99 full-time (30 women), 355 part-time (132 women); includes 95 minority (30 Black or African American, non-Hispanic/Latino; 29 Asian, non-Hispanic/Latino; 25 Hispanic/Latino; 11 Two or more races, non-Hispanic/Latino), 8 international. Average age 32. 249 applicants, 81% accepted, 175 enrolled. In 2017, 145 master's, 17 other advanced degrees awarded. *Entrance requirements:* For master's, GMAT or GRE. Additional exam requirements/recommendations for international students: Required—TOEFL (minimum score 550 paper-based; 79 iBT). *Application deadline:* Applications are processed on a rolling basis. Application fee: $0. Electronic applications accepted. *Financial support:* Applicants required to submit FAFSA. *Faculty research:* Offshoring/outsourcing, systems analysis/synthesis, work teams, multilateral trade, path dependencies/creation. *Unit head:* Cheryl McConnell, Dean, 816-501-4201, Fax: 816-501-4650, E-mail: cheryl.mcconnell@rockhurst.edu. *Application contact:* Jonnae Hill, Director of Graduate Business Advising, 816-501-4823, E-mail: jonnae.hill@rockhurst.edu.
Website: https://www.rockhurst.edu/helzberg

St. John's University, The Peter J. Tobin College of Business, Department of Business Analytics and Information Systems, Queens, NY 11439. Offers MBA. *Faculty:* 9 full-time (0 women), 4 part-time/adjunct (3 women). *Students:* 24 full-time (10 women), 11 part-time (3 women); includes 17 minority (4 Black or African American, non-Hispanic/Latino; 9 Asian, non-Hispanic/Latino; 4 Hispanic/Latino), 10 international. Average age 28. 23 applicants, 83% accepted, 17 enrolled. In 2017, 10 master's awarded. *Entrance requirements:* For master's, GMAT or GRE, 2 letters of recommendation, essay, resume, unofficial transcripts. Additional exam requirements/recommendations for international students: Required—TOEFL (minimum score 80 iBT), IELTS (minimum score 6.5). *Application deadline:* For fall admission, 11/1 for domestic and international students; for winter admission, 3/1 for domestic and international students; for spring admission, 6/1 for domestic and international students. Applications are processed on a rolling basis. Application fee: $70. Electronic applications accepted. *Expenses:* $22,410 per year. *Financial support:* Research assistantships, teaching assistantships, scholarships/grants, and unspecified assistantships available. Support available to part-time students. Financial award application deadline: 2/1; financial award applicants required to submit FAFSA. *Unit head:* Dr. Manuel Russon, Chair, 718-990-7363, E-mail:

russonm@stjohns.edu. *Application contact:* Amber Steiger, Associate Director of Enrollment Management, 718-990-1345, E-mail: steigera@stjohns.edu. Website: https://www.stjohns.edu/academics/schools-and-colleges/peter-j-tobin-college-business/business-analytics-information-systems

Saint Joseph's University, Erivan K. Haub School of Business, MS Program in Business Intelligence and Analytics, Philadelphia, PA 19131-1395. Offers MS. *Program availability:* Part-time, evening/weekend, 100% online. *Faculty:* 8 full-time (4 women), 23 part-time/adjunct (4 women). *Students:* 64 full-time (21 women), 242 part-time (93 women); includes 78 minority (35 Black or African American, non-Hispanic/Latino; 30 Asian, non-Hispanic/Latino; 10 Hispanic/Latino; 3 Two or more races, non-Hispanic/Latino), 64 international. Average age 33. 207 applicants, 76% accepted, 77 enrolled. In 2017, 116 master's awarded. *Degree requirements:* For master's, minimum GPA of 3.0. *Entrance requirements:* For master's, GMAT or GRE, 2 letters of recommendation, resume, personal statement, official undergraduate and graduate transcripts. Additional exam requirements/recommendations for international students: Required—PTE, TOEFL, IELTS, or PTE. *Application deadline:* For fall admission, 7/15 priority date for domestic students, 5/15 priority date for international students; for spring admission, 11/15 priority date for domestic students, 10/15 priority date for international students; for summer admission, 4/15 priority date for domestic students. Applications are processed on a rolling basis. Application fee: $35. Electronic applications accepted. *Financial support:* Scholarships/grants and unspecified assistantships available. Financial award application deadline: 5/1; financial award applicants required to submit FAFSA. *Unit head:* Jeannine Lajeunesse, Director, 610-660-1626, Fax: 610-660-1229, E-mail: jlajeune@sju.edu. *Application contact:* Christine Anderson, Assistant Director, 610-660-2252, Fax: 610-660-1599, E-mail: chris.anderson@sju.edu. Website: http://www.sju.edu/hsb/bi/

See Display on this page and Close-Up on page 603.

Saint Mary's College of California, School of Economics and Business Administration, MS in Business Analytics Program, Moraga, CA 94575. Offers MS.

Santa Clara University, Leavey School of Business, Santa Clara, CA 95053. Offers business administration (MBA); business analytics (MS); finance (MS); information systems (MS); supply chain management and analytics (MS); JD/MBA. *Accreditation:* AACSB. *Program availability:* Part-time, evening/weekend, online curriculum with 2 on-campus intensives. *Faculty:* 100 full-time (30 women), 42 part-time/adjunct (16 women). *Students:* 413 full-time (226 women), 308 part-time (131 women); includes 246 minority (10 Black or African American, non-Hispanic/Latino; 175 Asian, non-Hispanic/Latino; 40 Hispanic/Latino; 2 Native Hawaiian or other Pacific Islander, non-Hispanic/Latino; 19 Two or more races, non-Hispanic/Latino), 256 international. Average age 31. 761 applicants, 63% accepted, 271 enrolled. In 2017, 267 master's awarded. *Entrance requirements:* For master's, GMAT, resume, essays, 2 letters of recommendation, 2 official transcripts. Additional exam requirements/recommendations for international students: Required—TOEFL (minimum score 100 iBT) or IELTS (7.0). Application fee: $100 ($150 for international students). Electronic applications accepted. *Expenses:* Contact institution. *Financial support:* In 2017–18, 192 students received support. Career-related internships or fieldwork, scholarships/grants, and unspecified assistantships available. Financial award applicants required to submit FAFSA. *Faculty research:* Digital marketing, database mining and retail, product innovation, industry disruption, entrepreneurship and cluster dynamics, innovation and temporary advantage, platform strategy, ethics and leadership, bank regulation, monetary policy, poverty alleviation, costs of financial crises, information technology and business intelligence, supply chain management, corporate social responsibility and institutional ownership, audits and financial reporting. *Unit head:* Caryn Beck-Dudley, Dean, 408-554-4523, E-mail: cbeckdudley@scu.edu. *Application contact:* Lenore Grant, Director, Graduate Business Recruitment and Admissions, 408-551-1633, E-mail: lgrant@scu.edu. Website: http://www.scu.edu/business/

Shippensburg University of Pennsylvania, School of Graduate Studies, John L. Grove College of Business, Shippensburg, PA 17257-2299. Offers advanced studies in business (Certificate); advanced supply chain and logistics management (Certificate); business administration (MBA, DBA), including business administration (MBA), business analytics (MBA), finance (MBA), healthcare management (MBA), management information systems (MBA), supply chain management (MBA); finance (Certificate); health care management (Certificate); management information systems (Certificate). *Accreditation:* AACSB. *Program availability:* Part-time, evening/weekend, 100% online, blended/hybrid learning. *Faculty:* 23 full-time (5 women), 1 part-time/adjunct (0 women). *Students:* 46 full-time (14 women), 201 part-time (71 women); includes 35 minority (12 Black or African American, non-Hispanic/Latino; 10 Asian, non-Hispanic/Latino; 11 Hispanic/Latino; 2 Two or more races, non-Hispanic/Latino), 22 international. Average age 32. 169 applicants, 65% accepted, 77 enrolled. In 2017, 105 master's, 82 other advanced degrees awarded. *Degree requirements:* For master's, thesis optional, practicum; for doctorate, comprehensive exam, thesis/dissertation. *Entrance requirements:* For master's, GMAT (minimum score 450 if less than 5 years of mid-level experience, including management experience), current resume; relevant work/classroom experience; 500-word statement of purpose; prerequisites of quantitative analysis, computer usage, and oral and written communications; laptop computer; for doctorate, GMAT (minimum score of 600 if less than 5 years of substantive professional or teaching experience), 2 letters of recommendation from professionals in academia or industry; 2-3 page personal and professional statement; interview; resume. Additional exam requirements/recommendations for international students: Required—TOEFL (minimum score 550 paper-based, 68 iBT) or IELTS (minimum score 6). *Application deadline:* For fall admission, 4/30 for international students; for spring admission, 9/30 for international students. Applications are processed on a rolling basis. Application fee: $45. Electronic applications accepted. *Expenses:* Tuition, state resident: part-time $500 per credit. Tuition, nonresident: part-time $750 per credit. *Required fees:* $145 per credit. *Financial support:* In 2017–18, 14 students received support. Career-related internships or fieldwork, scholarships/grants, unspecified assistantships, and resident hall director and student payroll positions available. Support available to part-time students. Financial award application deadline: 3/1; financial award applicants required to submit FAFSA. *Unit head:* Dr. John G. Kooti, Dean of the College of Business, 717-477-1435, Fax: 717-477-4003, E-mail: jgkooti@ship.edu. *Application contact:* Maya T. Mapp, Director of Admissions, 717-477-1231, Fax: 717-477-4016, E-mail: mtmapp@ship.edu. Website: http://www.ship.edu/business

Southern Illinois University Edwardsville, Graduate School, School of Business, Program in Business Administration, Edwardsville, IL 62026. Offers business analytics (MBA); management information systems (MBA); project management (MBA). *Accreditation:* AACSB. *Program availability:* Part-time, evening/weekend. *Degree requirements:* For master's, comprehensive exam. *Entrance requirements:* For master's, GMAT. Additional exam requirements/recommendations for international students: Required—TOEFL (minimum score 550 paper-based; 79 iBT), IELTS (minimum score 6.5). Electronic applications accepted.

Business Analytics

Southern New Hampshire University, School of Business, Manchester, NH 03106-1045. Offers accounting (MBA, Graduate Certificate); accounting finance (MS); accounting/auditing (MS); accounting/forensic accounting (MS); accounting/management accounting (MS); accounting/taxation (MS); applied economics (MS); athletic administration (MBA, Graduate Certificate); business administration (IMBA, Certificate), including business information systems (Certificate), human resource management (Certificate); business analytics (MBA); business intelligence (MBA); communication (MA), including new media and marketing, public relations; community economic development (MBA); criminal justice (MBA); data analytics (MS); economics (MBA); engineering management (MBA); entrepreneurship (MBA); finance (MBA, MS, Graduate Certificate); finance/corporate finance (MS); finance/investments (MS); forensic accounting (MBA); forensic accounting and fraud examination (Graduate Certificate); healthcare informatics (MBA); healthcare management (MBA); human resource management (MS); human resources (MBA); information technology (MS); information technology management (MBA); international business (PhD); Internet marketing (MBA); leadership (MBA); leadership of nonprofit organizations (Graduate Certificate); management (MS); marketing (MBA, MS, Graduate Certificate); music business (MBA); operations and project management (MS); operations and supply chain management (MBA, Graduate Certificate); organizational leadership (MS); project management (MBA, Graduate Certificate); public administration (MBA, Graduate Certificate); quantitative analysis (MBA); Six Sigma (Graduate Certificate); Six Sigma quality (MBA); social media marketing (MBA, Graduate Certificate); sport management (MBA, MS, Graduate Certificate); sustainability and environmental compliance (MBA); MBA/Certificate. *Accreditation:* ACBSP. *Program availability:* Part-time, evening/weekend, online learning. Terminal master's awarded for partial completion of doctoral program. *Degree requirements:* For master's, one foreign language, comprehensive exam (for some programs), thesis or alternative; for doctorate, one foreign language, comprehensive exam, thesis/dissertation. *Entrance requirements:* For master's, minimum GPA of 2.5; for doctorate, GMAT. Additional exam requirements/recommendations for international students: Required—TOEFL (minimum score 500 paper-based). *Application deadline:* Applications are processed on a rolling basis. Application fee: $40. Electronic applications accepted. *Expenses: Tuition:* Part-time $627 per credit hour. Part-time tuition and fees vary according to campus/location and program. *Financial support:* Career-related internships or fieldwork, Federal Work-Study, institutionally sponsored loans, scholarships/grants, tuition waivers (partial), and unspecified assistantships available. Support available to part-time students. Financial award applicants required to submit FAFSA. *Unit head:* Dr. Bill Lightfoot, Dean, 603-644-3102, Fax: 603-644-3144. *Application contact:* Office of Graduate Admission, 888-327-SNHU, Fax: 603-644-3144, E-mail: enroll@snhu.edu.

Stevens Institute of Technology, Graduate School, School of Business, Program in Business Administration, Hoboken, NJ 07030. Offers business intelligence and analytics (MBA); engineering management (MBA); finance (MBA); information systems (MBA); innovation and entrepreneurship (MBA); marketing (MBA); pharmaceutical management (MBA); project management (MBA, Certificate); technology management (MBA); telecommunications management (MBA). *Accreditation:* AACSB. *Program availability:* Part-time, evening/weekend. *Students:* 46 full-time (19 women), 179 part-time (88 women); includes 46 minority (10 Black or African American, non-Hispanic/Latino; 2 American Indian or Alaska Native, non-Hispanic/Latino; 30 Asian, non-Hispanic/Latino; 4 Hispanic/Latino), 45 international. Average age 36. 218 applicants, 49% accepted, 53 enrolled. In 2017, 33 master's awarded. *Degree requirements:* For master's, thesis optional, minimum B average in major field and overall; for Certificate, minimum B average. *Entrance requirements:* Additional exam requirements/recommendations for international students: Required—TOEFL (minimum score 74 iBT), IELTS (minimum score 6). *Application deadline:* For fall admission, 7/1 for domestic students, 4/15 for international students; for spring admission, 12/1 for domestic and international students. Applications are processed on a rolling basis. Application fee: $60. Electronic applications accepted. *Expenses: Tuition:* Full-time $34,494; part-time $1554 per credit. *Required fees:* $291 per semester. *Financial support:* Fellowships, research assistantships, teaching assistantships, career-related internships or fieldwork, Federal Work-Study, scholarships/grants, and unspecified assistantships available. Financial award application deadline: 2/15; financial award applicants required to submit FAFSA. *Unit head:* Dr. Gregory Prastacos, Dean, 201-216-8366, E-mail: gprastac@stevens.edu. *Application contact:* Graduate Admissions, 888-783-8367, Fax: 888-511-1306, E-mail: graduate@stevens.edu.
Website: https://www.stevens.edu/school-business/masters-programs/mbaemba

Syracuse University, Martin J. Whitman School of Management, Master of Business Administration Program, Syracuse, NY 13244. Offers accounting (MBA); business analytics (MBA); entrepreneurship (MBA); marketing management (MBA); real estate (MBA); supply chain management (MBA); JD/MBA. *Program availability:* Part-time, 100% online. *Students:* 22 full-time (9 women), 495 part-time (147 women); includes 182 minority (81 Black or African American, non-Hispanic/Latino; 3 American Indian or Alaska Native, non-Hispanic/Latino; 42 Asian, non-Hispanic/Latino; 52 Hispanic/Latino; 4 Native Hawaiian or other Pacific Islander, non-Hispanic/Latino). Average age 32. 1,086 applicants, 73% accepted, 516 enrolled. In 2017, 84 master's awarded. *Entrance requirements:* For master's, GMAT or GRE, resume, essay, 5-minute video interview, two letters of recommendation, transcripts (unofficial). Additional exam requirements/recommendations for international students: Required—TOEFL (minimum score 100 iBT), IELTS (minimum score 7), PTE (minimum score 68). *Application deadline:* For fall admission, 11/30 for domestic students, 11/30 priority date for international students; for winter admission, 1/1 for domestic students, 1/1 priority date for international students; for spring admission, 2/15 for domestic and international students; for summer admission, 4/19 for domestic students. Application fee: $75. Electronic applications accepted. *Expenses:* Contact institution. *Financial support:* In 2017–18, 22 students received support. Merit scholarships available. Financial award application deadline: 2/15. *Faculty research:* Data analysis, economics of international business, financial markets and institutions, operations management, supply chain management. *Unit head:* Dr. Alexander McKelvie, Associate Dean for Undergraduate and Full-time Master's Education, 315-443-7252, E-mail: mckelvie@syr.edu. *Application contact:* Shri Ramakrishnan, Assistant Director, Graduate Recruitment, 315-443-3497, Fax: 315-443-9517, E-mail: busgrad@syr.edu.
Website: http://whitman.syr.edu/ftmba/

Syracuse University, Martin J. Whitman School of Management, MS in Business Analytics Program, Syracuse, NY 13244. Offers MS. *Program availability:* Part-time, evening/weekend, 100% online. *Students:* 27 part-time (10 women); includes 11 minority (4 Black or African American, non-Hispanic/Latino; 4 Asian, non-Hispanic/Latino; 2 Hispanic/Latino; 1 Native Hawaiian or other Pacific Islander, non-Hispanic/Latino). Average age 38. 45 applicants, 82% accepted, 27 enrolled. *Entrance requirements:* For master's, GMAT or GRE, resume, essay, 5-minute video interview, two letters of recommendation, transcripts (unofficial). Additional exam requirements/recommendations for international students: Required—TOEFL (minimum score 100 iBT), IELTS (minimum score 7), PTE (minimum score 68). *Application deadline:* For fall admission, 11/30 for domestic and international students; for winter admission, 1/1 for domestic and international students; for spring admission, 2/15 for domestic and international students; for summer admission, 4/19 for domestic students. Application

fee: $75. Electronic applications accepted. *Expenses:* Contact institution. *Financial support:* Merit-based scholarships available. Financial award application deadline: 2/15. *Faculty research:* Data analysis and decision making, business analytics, accounting analytics, financial services analytics, marketing analytics. *Unit head:* Dr. Alexander McKelvie, Associate Dean for Undergraduate and Full-time Master's Education, 315-443-7252, Fax: 315-443-9517, E-mail: mckelvie@syr.edu. *Application contact:* Shri Ramakrishnan, Assistant Director, Graduate Recruitment, 315-443-3497, Fax: 315-443-9517, E-mail: sramak01@syr.edu.

Texas A&M University–Commerce, College of Business, Commerce, TX 75429. Offers accounting (MSA); business administration (MBA); business analytics (MS); finance (MSF); management (MS); marketing (MS). *Accreditation:* AACSB. *Program availability:* Part-time, evening/weekend, 100% online, blended/hybrid learning. *Faculty:* 50 full-time (19 women), 7 part-time/adjunct (0 women). *Students:* 479 full-time (248 women), 1,056 part-time (556 women); includes 660 minority (281 Black or African American, non-Hispanic/Latino; 4 American Indian or Alaska Native, non-Hispanic/Latino; 120 Asian, non-Hispanic/Latino; 222 Hispanic/Latino; 33 Two or more races, non-Hispanic/Latino), 224 international. Average age 33. 930 applicants, 61% accepted, 363 enrolled. In 2017, 686 master's awarded. *Degree requirements:* For master's, comprehensive exam. *Entrance requirements:* For master's, GRE General Test, GMAT, letter of recommendation. Additional exam requirements/recommendations for international students: Required—TOEFL (minimum score 550 paper-based; 79 iBT), IELTS (minimum score 6). *Application deadline:* For fall admission, 6/1 priority date for international students; for spring admission, 10/15 priority date for international students; for summer admission, 3/15 priority date for international students. Applications are processed on a rolling basis. Application fee: $50 ($75 for international students). Electronic applications accepted. *Expenses:* Contact institution. *Financial support:* In 2017–18, 46 students received support, including 20 research assistantships with partial tuition reimbursements available (averaging $8,000 per year); Federal Work-Study, institutionally sponsored loans, scholarships/grants, health care benefits, and unspecified assistantships also available. Financial award application deadline: 5/1; financial award applicants required to submit FAFSA. *Faculty research:* Applied economics with emphasis on industries that are important to the region including health, energy and agriculture; finance research on banking, investments, financial institutions and risk management; marketing and big data decisions of product choice behavior and channel behavior of consumers; strategic management and organizational behavior phenomena; international accounting in governmental sectors. *Total annual research expenditures:* $1,920. *Unit head:* Dr. Shanan Gwaltney Gibson, Dean of College of Business, 903-886-5191, Fax: 903-886-5650, E-mail: shanan.gibson@tamuc.edu. *Application contact:* Vicky Turner, Doctoral Degree and Special Programs Coordinator, 903-886-5167, E-mail: vicky.turner@tamuc.edu.
Website: http://www.tamuc.edu/academics/graduateSchool/programs/businessEntrepreneurship/default.aspx

Texas Woman's University, Graduate School, College of Business, Program in Health Care Administration, Houston, TX 77030. Offers healthcare administration (MHA), including business analytics. Program offered at Texas Medical Center in Houston. *Accreditation:* CAHME. *Program availability:* Part-time, evening/weekend, blended/hybrid learning. *Faculty:* 5 full-time (2 women), 4 part-time/adjunct (all women). *Students:* 93 full-time (81 women), 62 part-time (52 women); includes 120 minority (48 Black or African American, non-Hispanic/Latino; 2 American Indian or Alaska Native, non-Hispanic/Latino; 43 Asian, non-Hispanic/Latino; 19 Hispanic/Latino; 8 Two or more races, non-Hispanic/Latino), 5 international. Average age 30. 72 applicants, 81% accepted, 36 enrolled. In 2017, 24 master's awarded. *Degree requirements:* For master's, comprehensive exam, thesis or alternative, capstone, portfolio. *Entrance requirements:* For master's, GMAT (preferred minimum score 450) or GRE General Test (preferred minimum scores 150 [450 old version] Verbal, 141 [450 old version] Quantitative), interview, resume, 3 letters of reference, essay, minimum GPA of 3.0 in last 60 hours of undergraduate degree and in all graduate course work. Additional exam requirements/recommendations for international students: Required—TOEFL (minimum score 550 paper-based; 79 iBT); Recommended—IELTS (minimum score 6.5), TSE (minimum score 53). *Application deadline:* For fall admission, 5/30 for domestic students, 3/1 priority date for international students; for spring admission, 9/30 for domestic students, 7/1 priority date for international students; for summer admission, 3/1 for domestic students, 2/1 priority date for international students. Applications are processed on a rolling basis. Application fee: $50 ($75 for international students). Electronic applications accepted. *Expenses:* $7,520 per year full-time in-state; $16,829 per year full-time out-of-state. *Financial support:* In 2017–18, 38 students received support. Career-related internships or fieldwork, Federal Work-Study, institutionally sponsored loans, scholarships/grants, traineeships, health care benefits, and unspecified assistantships available. Support available to part-time students. Financial award application deadline: 3/1; financial award applicants required to submit FAFSA. *Faculty research:* Patient safety and health policy, competition and market structure on health care quality, performance measurement and promotion. *Unit head:* Dr. Gerald Goodman, Director, 940-898-2458, Fax: 940-898-2120, E-mail: mba@twu.edu. *Application contact:* Korie Hawkins, Associate Director of Admissions, Graduate Recruitment, 940-898-3188, Fax: 940-898-3081, E-mail: admissions@twu.edu.
Website: http://www.twu.edu/health-care-administration/

Thomas Jefferson University, Kanbar College of Design, Engineering and Commerce, Innovation MBA Program, Philadelphia, PA 19107. Offers business analytics (MBA); general business (MBA); management (MBA); marketing (MBA); strategy and design thinking (MBA); MBA/MS. *Program availability:* Part-time, evening/weekend, online learning. *Entrance requirements:* For master's, GMAT. Additional exam requirements/recommendations for international students: Required—TOEFL (minimum score 550 paper-based; 79 iBT).

Tulane University, A. B. Freeman School of Business, New Orleans, LA 70118-5669. Offers accounting (M Acct); analytics (MBA); banking and financial services (M Fin); energy (M Fin, MBA); entrepreneurship (MBA); finance (MBA, PhD); financial accounting (PhD); international business (MBA); international management (MBA); strategic management and leadership (MBA); JD/M Acct; JD/MBA; MBA/M Acc; MBA/MA; MBA/MD; MBA/ME; MBA/MPH. *Accreditation:* AACSB. *Program availability:* Part-time, evening/weekend. *Faculty:* 51 full-time (15 women), 18 part-time/adjunct (3 women). *Students:* 561 full-time (287 women), 297 part-time (151 women); includes 112 minority (43 Black or African American, non-Hispanic/Latino; 2 American Indian or Alaska Native, non-Hispanic/Latino; 24 Asian, non-Hispanic/Latino; 38 Hispanic/Latino; 5 Two or more races, non-Hispanic/Latino), 515 international. Average age 27. 2,021 applicants, 74% accepted, 476 enrolled. In 2017, 632 master's, 9 doctorates awarded. Terminal master's awarded for partial completion of doctoral program. *Degree requirements:* For master's, one foreign language, comprehensive exam (for some programs); for doctorate, one foreign language, comprehensive exam, thesis/dissertation. *Entrance requirements:* For master's and doctorate, GMAT or GRE, interview. Additional exam requirements/recommendations for international students: Required—TOEFL or IELTS. *Application deadline:* For fall admission, 11/1 priority date for domestic and international students; for winter admission, 1/6 for domestic and international students; for spring admission, 3/1 priority date for domestic and international students; for summer admission, 5/5 for domestic students. Applications are processed on a rolling basis. Application fee: $125. Electronic applications accepted. *Expenses:* Contact institution. *Financial support:* In 2017–18, 176 students received support. Fellowships with tuition reimbursements available, research assistantships, teaching assistantships, career-related internships or fieldwork, Federal Work-Study, tuition waivers (full and partial), and unspecified assistantships available. Support available to part-time students. Financial award application deadline: 4/15; financial award applicants required to submit FAFSA. *Faculty research:* Corporate finance, managerial accounting and financial reporting, strategic management and leadership, consumer behavior and decision making, organizational behavior and human resource management. *Unit head:* Ira Solomon, PhD, Dean, 504-865-5407, Fax: 504-865-5491, E-mail: businessdean@tulane.edu. *Application contact:* Melissa Booth, Assistant Dean for Graduate Admissions, 800-223-5402, E-mail: freeman.admissions@tulane.edu. Website: http://www.freeman.tulane.edu

University at Albany, State University of New York, School of Business, MBA Programs, Albany, NY 12222. Offers business administration (MBA); cyber security (MBA); entrepreneurship (MBA); finance (MBA); human resource information systems (MBA); information systems and business analytics (MBA); marketing (MBA); JD/MBA. JD/MBA offered jointly with Albany Law School. *Program availability:* Part-time, evening/weekend. *Faculty:* 29 full-time (13 women), 9 part-time/adjunct (2 women). *Students:* 103 full-time (36 women), 188 part-time (69 women); includes 76 minority (27 Black or African American, non-Hispanic/Latino; 33 Asian, non-Hispanic/Latino; 16 Hispanic/Latino), 16 international. Average age 25. 181 applicants, 80% accepted, 114 enrolled. In 2017, 103 master's awarded. *Degree requirements:* For master's, thesis (for some programs), field or research project. *Entrance requirements:* For master's, GMAT, minimum undergraduate GPA of 3.0; 3 letters of recommendation; resume; statement of goals. Additional exam requirements/recommendations for international students: Required—TOEFL (minimum score 100 iBT); Recommended—IELTS (minimum score 7). *Application deadline:* For fall admission, 4/1 priority date for domestic students, 2/15 for international students; for spring admission, 12/1 for domestic students; for summer admission, 5/1 for domestic students. Applications are processed on a rolling basis. Application fee: $75. Electronic applications accepted. *Expenses:* $16,622.00 per year (for Full-Time MBA); $645 per credit hour (for Evening MBA). *Financial support:* In 2017–18, 25 students received support, including 7 fellowships with partial tuition reimbursements available (averaging $6,000 per year), 4 research assistantships with partial tuition reimbursements available, 21 teaching assistantships with partial tuition reimbursements available; unspecified assistantships also available. Financial award application deadline: 4/1; financial award applicants required to submit FAFSA. *Faculty research:* Social goods, information assurance, social computing, corporate entrepreneurship, asset pricing. *Total annual research expenditures:* $136,000. *Unit head:* Dr. Hany A. Shawky, Interim Dean, 518-956-8337, Fax: 518-442-3273, E-mail: hshawky@albany.edu. *Application contact:* Zina Mega Lawrence, Assistant Dean of Graduate Student Services, 518-956-8320, Fax: 518-442-4042, E-mail: zlawrence@albany.edu.
Website: https://graduatebusiness.albany.edu/

University at Buffalo, the State University of New York, Graduate School, School of Management, Buffalo, NY 14260. Offers accounting (MS); analytics (MBA); business administration (PMBA); consulting (MBA); finance (MBA, MS), including financial risk management (MS), quantitative finance (MS); healthcare (MBA); information assurance (MBA); information systems (MBA); international management (MBA); management (EMBA, PhD); management information systems (MS); marketing (MBA); supply chain and operations (MBA); supply chains and operations management (MS); Au D/MBA; DDS/MBA; JD/MBA; M Arch/MBA; MD/MBA; MPH/MBA; MSW/MBA; Pharm D/MBA. *Accreditation:* AACSB. *Program availability:* Part-time, evening/weekend. *Faculty:* 80 full-time (26 women), 45 part-time/adjunct (12 women). *Students:* 597 full-time (251 women); includes 83 minority (19 Black or African American, non-Hispanic/Latino; 59 Asian, non-Hispanic/Latino; 5 Hispanic/Latino), 306 international. Average age 25. 2,109 applicants, 46% accepted, 376 enrolled. In 2017, 345 master's, 13 doctorates awarded. *Degree requirements:* For master's, capstone courses or projects; for doctorate, comprehensive exam, thesis/dissertation. *Entrance requirements:* For master's, GMAT (for MS in accounting, finance); GRE or GMAT (for MBA, MS in management information systems, supply chains and operations management), essays, letters of recommendation; for doctorate, GMAT or GRE, essays, writing sample, letters of recommendation. Additional exam requirements/recommendations for international students: Required—TOEFL (minimum score 95 iBT) or IELTS (minimum score 6.5); Recommended—TSE (minimum score 73). *Application deadline:* For fall admission, 10/15 priority date for domestic and international students; for winter admission, 2/1 priority date for domestic and international students; for spring admission, 4/15 for domestic students; for summer admission, 5/15 for domestic students. Application fee: $100. Electronic applications accepted. *Expenses:* Varies by program. *Financial support:* Fellowships with full and partial tuition reimbursements, research assistantships with full and partial tuition reimbursements, teaching assistantships with full and partial tuition reimbursements, career-related internships or fieldwork, Federal Work-Study, institutionally sponsored loans, scholarships/grants, health care benefits, and unspecified assistantships available. Financial award application deadline: 2/15. *Faculty research:* Data analytics, accounting and law, rate finance, consumer behavior, supply chain logistics, leadership and team effectiveness. *Total annual research expenditures:* $968,376. *Unit head:* Erin K. O'Brien, Assistant Dean and Director of Graduate Programs, 716-645-3204, Fax: 716-645-2341, E-mail: ekobrien@buffalo.edu. *Application contact:* Meghan Felser, Director of Admissions and Recruiting, 716-645-3204, Fax: 716-645-2341, E-mail: mpwood@buffalo.edu.
Website: http://mgt.buffalo.edu/

The University of Alabama in Huntsville, School of Graduate Studies, College of Business Administration, Programs in Business and Management, Huntsville, AL 35899. Offers business analytics (MSMS); federal contracting and procurement management (Certificate); human resource management (MSM); management (MBA), including acquisition management, entrepreneurship, federal contract accounting, finance, human resource management, logistics and supply chain management, marketing, project management; supply chain management (Certificate); technology and innovation management (Certificate). *Accreditation:* AACSB. *Program availability:* Part-time, evening/weekend. *Degree requirements:* For master's, comprehensive exam, thesis or alternative. *Entrance requirements:* For master's, GMAT (minimum score 500), minimum AACSB index of 1080. Additional exam requirements/recommendations for international students: Required—TOEFL (minimum score 550 paper-based; 80 iBT), IELTS (minimum score 6.5). Electronic applications accepted. *Faculty research:* Supply chain management, management of research and development, international marketing and branding, organizational behavior and human resource management, social networks and computational economics.

The University of British Columbia, Sauder School of Business, Master of Business Analytics Program, Vancouver, BC V6T 1Z2, Canada. Offers MSBA. *Degree requirements:* For master's, industry project. *Entrance requirements:* For master's, GMAT or GRE, strong quantitative or analytical background, bachelor's degree or recognized equivalent from accredited university-level institution, minimum B+ average in undergraduate upper-level course work. Additional exam requirements/recommendations for international students: Required—TOEFL, IELTS or Michigan

English Language Assessment Battery. Electronic applications accepted. *Expenses:* Contact institution. *Faculty research:* Operations and logistics.

University of California, Davis, Graduate School of Management, Full-Time MBA Program, Davis, CA 95616. Offers business analytics and technologies (MBA); entrepreneurship and innovation (MBA); finance and accounting (MBA); general management (MBA); marketing (MBA); organizational behavior (MBA); public health management (MBA); strategy (MBA); technology management (MBA); DVM/MBA; JD/MBA; M Engr/MBA; MBA/MPH; MBA/MS; MD/MBA; MSN/MBA; PhD/MBA. *Faculty:* 52 full-time (15 women). *Students:* 96 full-time (42 women); includes 31 minority (1 Black or African American, non-Hispanic/Latino; 17 Asian, non-Hispanic/Latino; 5 Hispanic/Latino; 8 Two or more races, non-Hispanic/Latino), 36 international. Average age 29. 290 applicants, 37% accepted, 45 enrolled. In 2017, 44 master's awarded. *Degree requirements:* For master's, integrated management project. *Entrance requirements:* For master's, GMAT or GRE, letters of recommendation, resume, essays, equivalent of a 4-year U.S. undergraduate degree, transcript. Additional exam requirements/recommendations for international students: Required—TOEFL (minimum score 600 paper-based; 100 iBT), IELTS (minimum score 7). *Application deadline:* For fall admission, 5/18 priority date for domestic and international students. Application fee: $125. Electronic applications accepted. *Expenses:* Contact institution. *Financial support:* In 2017–18, 90 students received support. Fellowships, research assistantships, teaching assistantships with partial tuition reimbursements available, institutionally sponsored loans, scholarships/grants, health care benefits, tuition waivers (partial), and unspecified assistantships available. Financial award application deadline: 3/1; financial award applicants required to submit FAFSA. *Faculty research:* Finance, marketing, management, business analytics, accounting. *Unit head:* James Stevens, Senior Assistant Dean of Student Affairs, 530-752-7658, Fax: 530-754-9355, E-mail: admissions@gsm.ucdavis.edu. *Application contact:* Kristy Bird MaKieve, Interim Director of Admissions, 530-754-5476, Fax: 530-754-9355, E-mail: admissions@gsm.ucdavis.edu.
Website: http://gsm.ucdavis.edu/daytime-mba-program

University of California, Davis, Graduate School of Management, Master of Science in Business Analytics Program, San Francisco, CA 94102. Offers MSBA. *Faculty:* 16 full-time (4 women). *Students:* 43 full-time (24 women); includes 7 minority (all American Indian or Alaska Native, non-Hispanic/Latino), 32 international. Average age 27. 608 applicants, 15% accepted, 43 enrolled. *Degree requirements:* For master's, comprehensive exam. *Entrance requirements:* For master's, GMAT or GRE, resume; equivalent of undergraduate 4-year U.S. degree; essays; coursework in statistics, computer science, and math; letters of recommendation. Additional exam requirements/recommendations for international students: Required—TOEFL (minimum score 600 paper-based; 100 iBT), IELTS (minimum score 7). *Application deadline:* For fall admission, 5/18 priority date for domestic and international students. Application fee: $125. Electronic applications accepted. *Financial support:* In 2017–18, 39 students received support. Fellowships, research assistantships, teaching assistantships with partial tuition reimbursements available, and tuition waivers (partial) available. Financial award application deadline: 3/1; financial award applicants required to submit FAFSA. *Faculty research:* Business analytics, market research, competitive strategy, optimization, network effects. *Unit head:* James Stevens, Senior Assistant Dean of Student Affairs, 530-752-7658, Fax: 530-754-9355, E-mail: admissions@gsm.ucdavis.edu. *Application contact:* Kristy Bird MaKieve, Interim Director of Admissions, 530-754-5476, Fax: 530-754-9355, E-mail: admissions@gsm.ucdavis.edu.
Website: https://gsm.ucdavis.edu/msba-masters-science-business-analytics

University of California, Davis, Graduate School of Management, MBA Programs in Sacramento and San Francisco Bay Area, Davis, CA 95616. Offers business analytics and technologies (MBA); entrepreneurship and innovation (MBA); finance and accounting (MBA); general management (MBA); marketing (MBA); organizational behavior (MBA); public health management (MBA); strategy (MBA); technology management (MBA). *Program availability:* Part-time-only, evening/weekend. *Faculty:* 99 part-time/adjunct (30 women). *Students:* 323 part-time (133 women); includes 148 minority (7 Black or African American, non-Hispanic/Latino; 96 Asian, non-Hispanic/Latino; 26 Hispanic/Latino; 1 Native Hawaiian or other Pacific Islander, non-Hispanic/Latino; 18 Two or more races, non-Hispanic/Latino), 37 international. Average age 30. 202 applicants, 75% accepted, 111 enrolled. In 2017, 112 master's awarded. *Degree requirements:* For master's, integrated management project. *Entrance requirements:* For master's, GMAT or GRE, letters of recommendation, resume, equivalent of a 4-year undergraduate degree. Additional exam requirements/recommendations for international students: Required—TOEFL (minimum score 600 paper-based; 100 iBT), IELTS (minimum score 7). *Application deadline:* For fall admission, 5/18 priority date for domestic and international students. Application fee: $125. Electronic applications accepted. *Expenses:* Contact institution. *Financial support:* In 2017–18, 67 students received support. Fellowships, teaching assistantships with partial tuition reimbursements available, scholarships/grants, and unspecified assistantships available. Support available to part-time students. Financial award application deadline: 3/1; financial award applicants required to submit FAFSA. *Faculty research:* Accounting, finance, marketing, management, business analytics. *Unit head:* James Stevens, Senior Assistant Dean of Student Affairs, 530-752-7658, Fax: 530-754-9355, E-mail: admissions@gsm.ucdavis.edu. *Application contact:* Kristy Bird MaKieve, Interim Director of Admissions, 530-754-5476, Fax: 530-754-9355, E-mail: admissions@gsm.ucdavis.edu.
Website: http://gsm.ucdavis.edu/mba-programs

University of California, Los Angeles, Graduate Division, UCLA Anderson School of Management, Los Angeles, CA 90095-1481. Offers accounting (PhD); behavioral decision making (PhD); business administration (EMBA, MBA); business analytics (MSBA); decisions, operations, and technology management (PhD); finance (PhD); financial engineering (MFE); global economics and management (PhD); management and organizations (PhD); marketing (PhD); strategy and policy (PhD); DDS/MBA; MBA/JD; MBA/MD; MBA/MLAS; MBA/MLIS; MBA/MN; MBA/MPH; MBA/MPP; MBA/MSCS; MBA/MURP. *Accreditation:* AACSB. *Program availability:* Part-time, evening/weekend. *Faculty:* 88 full-time (20 women), 107 part-time/adjunct (21 women). *Students:* 918 full-time (314 women), 1,269 part-time (399 women); includes 743 minority (38 Black or African American, non-Hispanic/Latino; 3 American Indian or Alaska Native, non-Hispanic/Latino; 531 Asian, non-Hispanic/Latino; 115 Hispanic/Latino; 4 Native Hawaiian or other Pacific Islander, non-Hispanic/Latino; 52 Two or more races, non-Hispanic/Latino), 544 international. Average age 31. 5,842 applicants, 29% accepted, 1015 enrolled. In 2017, 855 master's, 14 doctorates awarded. Terminal master's awarded for partial completion of doctoral program. *Degree requirements:* For master's, comprehensive exam, field consulting project (for MBA, FEMBA, EMBA and GEMBA); internship (for MBA only); thesis/dissertation (for MFE); 10 capstone (for MSBA); for doctorate, comprehensive exam, thesis/dissertation, oral and written qualifying exams. *Entrance requirements:* For master's, GMAT or GRE, 4-year bachelor's degree or equivalent; 2 letters of recommendation; interview (by invitation only); 2 essays; 4-8 years of full-time work experience (for FEMBA only); minimum eight years of work experience with at least three years at management level (for EMBA only); for doctorate, GMAT or GRE, bachelor's degree from college or university of fully-recognized standing, minimum B average during junior and senior undergraduate years, 3 letters of recommendation, statement of

Business Analytics

purpose. Additional exam requirements/recommendations for international students: Required—TOEFL (minimum score 560 paper-based; 87 iBT), IELTS (minimum score 7), TOEFL with minimum iBT score of 100 (for MSBA). *Application deadline:* For fall admission, 10/2 for domestic and international students; for winter admission, 1/8 for domestic and international students; for spring admission, 4/16 for domestic and international students. Applications are processed on a rolling basis. Application fee: $200. Electronic applications accepted. *Expenses:* Contact institution. *Financial support:* In 2017–18, 649 students received support, including 440 fellowships (averaging $29,273 per year); research assistantships with partial tuition reimbursements available, teaching assistantships with partial tuition reimbursements available, career-related internships or fieldwork, institutionally sponsored loans, and scholarships/grants also available. Support available to part-time students. *Faculty research:* Finance/global economics, entrepreneurship, accounting, human resources/organizational behavior, marketing and behavioral decision-making. *Total annual research expenditures:* $1.3 million. *Unit head:* Dean, 310-825-7982, Fax: 310-206-2073. *Application contact:* Alex Lawrence, Assistant Dean and Director of MBA Admissions, 310-825-6944, Fax: 310-825-8582, E-mail: mba.admissions@anderson.ucla.edu.
Website: http://www.anderson.ucla.edu/

University of California, San Diego, Graduate Division, Rady School of Management, La Jolla, CA 92093. Offers business administration (MBA); business analytics (MS); finance (MF); management (PhD). *Accreditation:* AACSB. *Program availability:* Part-time, evening/weekend. *Faculty:* 28 full-time (5 women), 5 part-time/adjunct (1 woman). *Students:* 436 full-time (201 women), 119 part-time (60 women). 2,265 applicants, 33% accepted, 307 enrolled. In 2017, 193 master's, 2 doctorates awarded. *Degree requirements:* For master's, capstone project; for doctorate, comprehensive exam, thesis/dissertation. *Entrance requirements:* For master's, GMAT (for MBA); GMAT or GRE General Test (for MF); for doctorate, GMAT or GRE General Test. Additional exam requirements/recommendations for international students: Required—TOEFL (minimum score 550 paper-based; 80 iBT), IELTS (minimum score 7). *Application deadline:* Applications are processed on a rolling basis. Application fee: $200. Electronic applications accepted. *Expenses:* Contact institution. *Financial support:* Fellowships, teaching assistantships, and scholarships/grants available. Financial award applicants required to submit FAFSA. *Faculty research:* Innovation technology, operations management, finance, behavioral economics, organizational strategy, marketing, business analytics. *Unit head:* Robert Sullivan, Dean, 858-822-0830, E-mail: rssullivan@ucsd.edu. *Application contact:* Jay Bryant, Director of Graduate Recruitment and Admissions, 858-534-0864, E-mail: radygradadmissions@ucsd.edu.
Website: http://rady.ucsd.edu/

University of Central Oklahoma, The Jackson College of Graduate Studies, College of Business, Edmond, OK 73034-5209. Offers business administration (MBA); business analytics (MS). *Program availability:* Part-time. *Faculty:* 17 full-time (6 women), 2 part-time/adjunct (0 women). *Students:* 76 full-time (32 women), 29 part-time (16 women); includes 28 minority (8 Black or African American, non-Hispanic/Latino; 7 American Indian or Alaska Native, non-Hispanic/Latino; 5 Asian, non-Hispanic/Latino; 2 Hispanic/Latino; 6 Two or more races, non-Hispanic/Latino), 13 international. Average age 30. 161 applicants, 58% accepted, 66 enrolled. In 2017, 45 master's awarded. *Degree requirements:* For master's, comprehensive exam (for some programs), thesis optional. *Entrance requirements:* For master's, GMAT, GRE. Additional exam requirements/recommendations for international students: Required—TOEFL (minimum score 550 paper-based; 79 iBT), IELTS (minimum score 6.5). *Application deadline:* For fall admission, 7/15 for international students; for spring admission, 11/15 for international students. Applications are processed on a rolling basis. Application fee: $60. Electronic applications accepted. *Expenses:* Contact institution. *Financial support:* In 2017–18, 12 students received support, including 2 teaching assistantships (averaging $8,873 per year); research assistantships, career-related internships or fieldwork, Federal Work-Study, scholarships/grants, tuition waivers (partial), and unspecified assistantships also available. Financial award application deadline: 3/31; financial award applicants required to submit FAFSA. *Unit head:* Dr. Randal Ice, Interim Dean, 405-974-2810. *Application contact:* Jeffrey Hicks, Director of MBA Enrollment, 405-974-5445, E-mail: mba@uco.edu.

University of Cincinnati, Carl H. Lindner College of Business, MS Program, Cincinnati, OH 45221. Offers accounting (MS); applied economics (MS); business analytics (MS); finance (MS); information systems (MS); marketing (MS); taxation (MS). *Program availability:* Part-time, evening/weekend. *Faculty:* 65 full-time (20 women), 27 part-time/adjunct (6 women). *Students:* 324 full-time (132 women), 204 part-time (77 women); includes 50 minority (18 Black or African American, non-Hispanic/Latino; 21 Asian, non-Hispanic/Latino; 5 Hispanic/Latino; 1 Native Hawaiian or other Pacific Islander, non-Hispanic/Latino; 5 Two or more races, non-Hispanic/Latino), 299 international. Average age 28. 1,756 applicants, 24% accepted, 351 enrolled. In 2017, 369 master's awarded. *Degree requirements:* For master's, thesis (for some programs), capstone. *Entrance requirements:* For master's, GMAT, GRE, resume, transcripts, essays, letters of recommendation. Additional exam requirements/recommendations for international students: Required—TOEFL (minimum score 577 paper-based; 90 iBT), IELTS (minimum score 6.5). *Application deadline:* For fall admission, 6/30 priority date for domestic students, 3/15 for international students; for spring admission, 12/15 for domestic students, 9/15 for international students; for summer admission, 4/15 for domestic and international students. Applications are processed on a rolling basis. Application fee: $65 ($70 for international students). Electronic applications accepted. *Expenses:* $10,479 per term full-time resident, $14,398 per term full-time nonresident, $890 per credit hour part-time. *Financial support:* In 2017–18, 251 students received support, including 12 teaching assistantships with full and partial tuition reimbursements available (averaging $3,500 per year); scholarships/grants, tuition waivers (full and partial), and unspecified assistantships also available. Financial award application deadline: 2/1; financial award applicants required to submit FAFSA. *Faculty research:* Business analytics, financial management, organizational behavior, financial accounting, consumer insights. *Total annual research expenditures:* $24,842. *Unit head:* Dr. David Szymanski, Dean, 513-556-7001, Fax: 513-556-4891, E-mail: david.szymanski@uc.edu. *Application contact:* Dona Clary, Executive Director, Graduate Programs, 513-556-3546, Fax: 513-558-7006, E-mail: dona.clary@uc.edu.
Website: http://business.uc.edu/graduate/masters.html

University of Cincinnati, Carl H. Lindner College of Business, PhD Programs, Cincinnati, OH 45221. Offers accounting (PhD); business analytics (PhD); economics (PhD); finance (PhD); information systems (PhD); management (PhD); marketing (PhD); operations and business analytics (PhD); operations research (PhD). *Faculty:* 37 full-time (13 women). *Students:* 29 full-time (12 women), 12 part-time (6 women); includes 5 minority (1 Black or African American, non-Hispanic/Latino; 4 Asian, non-Hispanic/Latino), 20 international. Average age 30. 123 applicants, 16% accepted, 11 enrolled. In 2017, 5 doctorates awarded. *Degree requirements:* For doctorate, comprehensive exam, thesis/dissertation. *Entrance requirements:* For doctorate, GMAT, GRE, transcripts, essays, resume, letters of recommendation. Additional exam requirements/recommendations for international students: Required—TOEFL (minimum score 600 paper-based; 100 iBT), IELTS (minimum score 7). *Application deadline:* For fall admission, 1/15 for domestic and international students. Electronic applications accepted. *Expenses:* $7,234 resident per term, $13,105 nonresident per term. *Financial support:* In 2017–18, 41 students

received support, including 29 research assistantships with full tuition reimbursements available (averaging $23,250 per year); scholarships/grants, health care benefits, tuition waivers (full), and unspecified assistantships also available. Financial award application deadline: 1/15; financial award applicants required to submit FAFSA. *Faculty research:* Bayesian Prediction Theory, organizational fairness, consumer insight and market research, consumer insight and market research, density estimation from correlated data. *Unit head:* Dr. Suzanne Masterson, Director, 513-556-7125, Fax: 513-556-5499, E-mail: suzanne.masterson@uc.edu. *Application contact:* Angel Elvin, Assistant Director, 513-556-7190, Fax: 513-558-7006, E-mail: angel.elvin@uc.edu.
Website: http://business.uc.edu/graduate/phd.html

University of Dallas, Satish and Yasmin Gupta College of Business, Irving, TX 75062-4736. Offers accounting (MBA, MS); business administration (DBA); business analytics (MS); business management (MBA); corporate finance (MBA); cybersecurity (MS); finance (MS); financial services (MBA); global business (MBA, MS); health services management (MBA); human resource management (MBA); information and technology management (MS); information assurance (MBA); information technology (MBA); information technology service management (MBA); marketing management (MBA); organization development (MBA); project management (MBA); sports and entertainment management (MBA); strategic leadership (MBA); supply chain management (MBA). *Accreditation:* AACSB. *Program availability:* Part-time, evening/weekend, online learning. *Entrance requirements:* Additional exam requirements/recommendations for international students: Required—TOEFL. *Application deadline:* Applications are processed on a rolling basis. Application fee: $50. Electronic applications accepted. *Expenses:* Contact institution. *Financial support:* Application deadline: 2/15; applicants required to submit FAFSA. *Unit head:* Brett J.L. Landry, Dean, 972-721-5356, E-mail: blandry@udallas.edu. *Application contact:* Dr. David Sweet, Dean, Braniff Graduate School, 972-721-5288, Fax: 972-721-5280, E-mail: dsweet@udallas.edu.
Website: http://www.udallas.edu/cob/

The University of Iowa, Tippie College of Business, MS Program in Business Analytics, Iowa City, IA 52242-1316. Offers MS. Program offered at the Cedar Rapids, Des Moines and Quad City locations. *Program availability:* Part-time-only, evening/weekend. *Faculty:* 8 full-time (2 women), 3 part-time/adjunct (0 women). *Students:* 171 part-time (55 women); includes 17 minority (2 Black or African American, non-Hispanic/Latino; 8 Asian, non-Hispanic/Latino; 4 Hispanic/Latino; 3 Two or more races, non-Hispanic/Latino), 21 international. Average age 37. 194 applicants, 72% accepted, 110 enrolled. In 2017, 12 master's awarded. *Degree requirements:* For master's, 30 hours. *Entrance requirements:* Additional exam requirements/recommendations for international students: Required—TOEFL (minimum score 100 iBT). *Application deadline:* For fall admission, 7/30 priority date for domestic and international students; for spring admission, 12/30 priority date for domestic and international students; for summer admission, 4/30 priority date for domestic and international students. Application fee: $60 ($100 for international students). Electronic applications accepted. *Unit head:* Prof. Nick Street, Department Executive Officer, 319-335-0858, Fax: 319-335-1956, E-mail: nick-street@uiowa.edu. *Application contact:* Renea L. Jay, Associate Director, Non-MBA Graduate Programs, 319-335-0830, Fax: 319-335-0860, E-mail: renea-jay@uiowa.edu.
Website: https://tippie.uiowa.edu/future-graduate-students/masters-programs/business-analytics

The University of Iowa, Tippie College of Business, Professional MBA Program, Iowa City, IA 52242-1316. Offers business administration (MBA); business analytics (MBA); finance (MBA); leadership (MBA); marketing (MBA). *Program availability:* Part-time-only, evening/weekend. *Faculty:* 50 full-time (11 women), 22 part-time/adjunct (2 women). *Students:* 873 part-time (325 women); includes 102 minority (16 Black or African American, non-Hispanic/Latino; 1 American Indian or Alaska Native, non-Hispanic/Latino; 54 Asian, non-Hispanic/Latino; 22 Hispanic/Latino; 9 Two or more races, non-Hispanic/Latino), 44 international. Average age 33. 155 applicants, 94% accepted, 137 enrolled. In 2017, 176 master's awarded. *Degree requirements:* For master's, successful completion of nine required courses and six electives totaling 45 credits, minimum GPA of 2.75. *Entrance requirements:* For master's, GMAT or GRE. Additional exam requirements/recommendations for international students: Required—TOEFL (minimum score 600 paper-based; 100 iBT), IELTS (minimum score 7). *Application deadline:* For fall admission, 7/30 for domestic and international students; for spring admission, 12/15 for domestic and international students; for summer admission, 4/30 for domestic and international students. Applications are processed on a rolling basis. Application fee: $60 ($100 for international students). Electronic applications accepted. *Expenses:* Contact institution. *Faculty research:* Capital markets; analytics techniques and applications; organizational and market systems analysis; applied econometrics; talent effectiveness. *Unit head:* Prof. Sarah Fisher Gardial, Dean, 319-335-0862, Fax: 319-335-0860, E-mail: sarah-gardial@uiowa.edu.
Website: https://tippie.uiowa.edu/future-graduate-students/mba-programs/professional-mba

The University of Manchester, Alliance Manchester Business School, M15 6PB, United Kingdom. Offers accounting and finance (M Sc); business (M Ent); business analysis and strategic management (M Sc); business analytics: operational research and risk analysis (M Sc); business psychology (M Sc); corporate communications and reputation management (M Sc); finance (M Sc); finance and business economics (M Sc); human resource management and industrial relations (M Sc); innovation management and entrepreneurship (M Sc); international business and management (M Sc); international human resource management and comparative industrial relations (M Sc); management (M Sc); marketing (M Sc); operations, project and supply chain management (M Sc); organizational psychology (M Sc); quantitative finance (M Sc). *Entrance requirements:* For master's, UK 2:1 honours degree or overseas equivalent. Additional exam requirements/recommendations for international students: Required—TOEFL (minimum score 100 iBT), IELTS (minimum score 7), PTE. Electronic applications accepted. *Faculty research:* Accounting and finance, management sciences and marketing, people management and organization, innovation management and policy, decision sciences.

University of Massachusetts Boston, College of Management, Program in Business Analytics, Boston, MA 02125-3393. Offers MS. *Students:* 4 full-time (2 women), 2 part-time (1 woman); includes 1 minority (Asian, non-Hispanic/Latino), 3 international. Average age 37. 8 applicants, 75% accepted, 4 enrolled. *Expenses:* Tuition, state resident: full-time $17,375. Tuition, nonresident: full-time $33,915. *Required fees:* $355. *Unit head:* Dr. Philip Quaglieri, Dean, 617-287-7700, E-mail: philip.quaglieri@umb.edu. *Application contact:* Graduate Admissions Coordinator, 617-287-6400, Fax: 617-287-6236, E-mail: bos.gadm@dpc.umassp.edu.
Website: https://www.umb.edu/academics/cm/masters_programs/degrees/master_of_science_in_business_analytics_msba

The University of North Carolina at Charlotte, Belk College of Business, Department of Management, Charlotte, NC 28223-0001. Offers business administration (MBA, DBA, PhD); business analytics (Graduate Certificate); management (MS). *Program availability:* Part-time, evening/weekend. *Faculty:* 13 full-time (5 women). *Students:* 85 full-time (38 women), 286 part-time (91 women); includes 69 minority (24 Black or African American, non-Hispanic/Latino; 1 American Indian or Alaska Native, non-Hispanic/Latino; 18 Asian, non-Hispanic/Latino; 18 Hispanic/Latino; 8 Two or more races, non-Hispanic/Latino), 127 international. Average age 33. 237 applicants, 58% accepted, 90 enrolled. In 2017, 128 master's, 1 doctorate awarded. Terminal master's

awarded for partial completion of doctoral program. *Degree requirements:* For doctorate, comprehensive exam (for some programs), thesis/dissertation. *Entrance requirements:* For master's, GMAT or GRE, bachelor's degree from regionally-accredited college or university; at least three evaluations from persons familiar with applicant's personal and professional qualifications; essay describing applicant's experience and objectives; resume; for doctorate, GMAT (minimum score of 650) or GRE (minimum 700 on quantitative section, 500 on verbal), baccalaureate or master's degree in business, economics, or related field such as mathematical finance, mathematics, or physics with minimum undergraduate GPA of 3.5 (3.25 graduate); three letters of recommendation; statement of purpose; for Graduate Certificate, transcripts, minimum undergraduate GPA of 2.75, essay describing experience and objectives. Additional exam requirements/recommendations for international students: Required—TOEFL (minimum score 523 paper-based, 70 iBT) or IELTS (6.5). *Application deadline:* For fall admission, 1/15 for domestic and international students; for spring admission, 10/1 priority date for domestic and international students; for summer admission, 4/1 priority date for domestic and international students. Applications are processed on a rolling basis. Application fee: $75. Electronic applications accepted. *Expenses:* Contact institution. *Financial support:* Research assistantships, teaching assistantships, career-related internships or fieldwork, institutionally sponsored loans, scholarships/grants, and unspecified assistantships available. Support available to part-time students. Financial award application deadline: 3/1; financial award applicants required to submit FAFSA. *Total annual research expenditures:* $122,929. *Unit head:* Dr. David J. Woehr, Department Chair, 704-687-7684, Fax: 704-687-1380, E-mail: dwoehr@uncc.edu. *Application contact:* Kathy B. Giddings, Director of Graduate Admissions, 704-687-5503, Fax: 704-687-1668, E-mail: gradadm@uncc.edu.
Website: https://belkcollege.uncc.edu/departments/management

University of Notre Dame, Mendoza College of Business, Master of Business Administration Program, Notre Dame, IN 46556. Offers business analytics (MBA); business leadership (MBA); consulting (MBA); corporate finance (MBA); innovation and entrepreneurship (MBA); investments (MBA); marketing (MBA); MBA/MSBA. *Accreditation:* AACSB. *Faculty:* 60 full-time (10 women), 14 part-time/adjunct (1 woman). *Students:* 294 full-time (70 women); includes 46 minority (8 Black or African American, non-Hispanic/Latino; 3 American Indian or Alaska Native, non-Hispanic/Latino; 12 Asian, non-Hispanic/Latino; 20 Hispanic/Latino; 1 Native Hawaiian or other Pacific Islander, non-Hispanic/Latino; 2 Two or more races, non-Hispanic/Latino), 74 international. Average age 29. 633 applicants, 42% accepted, 131 enrolled. In 2017, 182 master's awarded. *Entrance requirements:* For master's, GMAT or GRE, work experience, essay, four-slide presentation, two recommendations, transcripts from all colleges and/or universities attended, interview. Additional exam requirements/recommendations for international students: Required—PTE (minimum score 68), TOEFL (minimum iBT score of 109), IELTS (7.5), or documentation of at least six semesters of full-time university education in English. *Application deadline:* For fall admission, 10/17 for domestic and international students; for winter admission, 1/9 for domestic and international students; for spring admission, 2/20 for domestic and international students; for summer admission, 3/17 for domestic students. Application fee: $175. Electronic applications accepted. *Expenses:* $74,133 (for one-year MBA); $106,526 (two-year MBA) $113,050 (for MBA/MSBA). *Financial support:* In 2017–18, 251 students received support, including 247 fellowships (averaging $27,748 per year); unspecified assistantships also available. Financial award application deadline: 2/28; financial award applicants required to submit FAFSA. *Faculty research:* Market microstructure; marketing and public policy; corporate finance and accounting; corporate governance and ethical behavior; high performing organizations. *Unit head:* Dr. Katherine Spiess, Associate Dean, Graduate Business Programs, 574-631-7236, E-mail: spiess.1@nd.edu. *Application contact:* Kristin McAndrew, Director of Admissions, Graduate Business Programs, 574-631-8488, E-mail: kmcandre@nd.edu.
Website: http://mendoza.nd.edu/programs/mba-programs/

University of Notre Dame, Mendoza College of Business, Master of Science in Business Analytics Program, Notre Dame, IN 46556. Offers MSBA. *Faculty:* 6 full-time (1 woman), 3 part-time/adjunct (0 women). *Students:* 23 full-time (3 women); includes 7 minority (1 Asian, non-Hispanic/Latino; 5 Hispanic/Latino; 1 Native Hawaiian or other Pacific Islander, non-Hispanic/Latino). Average age 34. In 2017, 25 master's awarded. *Entrance requirements:* For master's, minimum of two years of work experience, evidence of quantitative capabilities to complete a rigorous analytical curriculum. Additional exam requirements/recommendations for international students: Required—TOEFL, IELTS. *Application deadline:* For fall admission, 10/15 for domestic students; for summer admission, 7/15 for domestic students. Applications are processed on a rolling basis. Application fee: $50. Electronic applications accepted. *Expenses:* Contact institution. *Financial support:* In 2017–18, 22 students received support, including 22 fellowships (averaging $6,706 per year). Financial award application deadline: 10/15; financial award applicants required to submit FAFSA. *Faculty research:* Methods and approaches for improving decision making, applied work on decision-making models and processes for accounting; financial management; resource allocation; risk management; the development, improvement and evaluation of statistical methods and measurement issues; supply chain management and integration; design of lean service processes; and adoption of lean manufacturing systems. *Unit head:* Mike Chapple, Academic Director, Master of Science in Business Analytics, 574-631-5863, E-mail: mchapple@nd.edu. *Application contact:* Kaitlyn Reeves, Admissions Coordinator, 574-631-1593, Fax: 574-631-6783, E-mail: kreeves@nd.edu.
Website: http://mendoza.nd.edu/programs/specialized-masters/ms-in-business-analytics/

University of Oklahoma, Price College of Business, Division of Management Information Systems, Norman, OK 73019. Offers digital technologies (Graduate Certificate); management of information technology (MS), including business analytics. *Program availability:* Part-time, evening/weekend. *Faculty:* 11 full-time (5 women). *Students:* 35 full-time (15 women), 13 part-time (7 women); includes 12 minority (2 Black or African American, non-Hispanic/Latino; 1 American Indian or Alaska Native, non-Hispanic/Latino; 3 Asian, non-Hispanic/Latino; 4 Hispanic/Latino; 2 Two or more races, non-Hispanic/Latino), 13 international. Average age 28. 24 applicants, 38% accepted, 8 enrolled. In 2017, 23 master's, 2 other advanced degrees awarded. *Degree requirements:* For master's, thesis optional. *Entrance requirements:* For master's and Graduate Certificate, GMAT or GRE, resume, statement of goals, 3 letters of recommendation. Additional exam requirements/recommendations for international students: Required—TOEFL (minimum score 100 iBT) or IELTS (minimum score 7). *Application deadline:* For fall admission, 6/15 for domestic students, 3/1 for international students; for spring admission, 10/1 for domestic students, 8/1 for international students. Applications are processed on a rolling basis. Application fee: $50 ($100 for international students). Electronic applications accepted. *Expenses:* Tuition, state resident: full-time $5119; part-time $213.30 per credit hour. Tuition, nonresident: full-time $19,778; part-time $824.10 per credit hour. *Required fees:* $3458; $133.55 per credit hour. $126.50 per semester. *Financial support:* In 2017–18, 40 students received support, including 2 research assistantships with partial tuition reimbursements available (averaging $16,864 per year), 8 teaching assistantships with partial tuition reimbursements available (averaging $11,121 per year); career-related internships or fieldwork, scholarships/grants, and unspecified assistantships also available. Support available to part-time students. Financial award application deadline: 6/1; financial award applicants required to submit FAFSA. *Faculty research:* Human-

computer interaction and cognition; deception detection in IT-mediated contexts; social media use; computer-mediated collaboration and communication; meaning in discourse about IT and discourse through IT. *Total annual research expenditures:* $208,471. *Unit head:* Radhika Santhanam, Chair/Division Director, 405-325-0791, E-mail: radhika@ou.edu. *Application contact:* Jennifer Aragon, Academic Advisor, 405-325-2074, Fax: 405-325-7118, E-mail: jhardman@ou.edu.
Website: http://www.ou.edu/content/price/mis/mis_ms_in_mis.html

University of Pittsburgh, Katz Graduate School of Business, Doctoral Program in Business Administration, Pittsburgh, PA 15260. Offers accounting (PhD); business analytics and operations (PhD); finance (PhD); information systems and technology management (PhD); marketing (PhD); organizational behavior and human resources (PhD); strategic management (PhD). *Accreditation:* AACSB. *Program availability:* Evening/weekend. *Faculty:* 91 full-time (30 women), 14 part-time/adjunct (4 women). *Students:* 51 full-time (26 women), 1 (woman) part-time; includes 5 minority (1 Black or African American, non-Hispanic/Latino; 3 Asian, non-Hispanic/Latino; 1 Two or more races, non-Hispanic/Latino), 30 international. Average age 31. 337 applicants, 3% accepted, 10 enrolled. In 2017, 7 doctorates awarded. *Degree requirements:* For doctorate, comprehensive exam, thesis/dissertation, student teaching. *Entrance requirements:* For doctorate, GMAT or GRE, 3 recommendations, statement of purpose, transcripts of all previous course work and degrees. Additional exam requirements/recommendations for international students: Required—TOEFL (minimum score 100 iBT) or IELTS (minimum score 7.0). *Application deadline:* For fall admission, 1/1 for domestic and international students. Applications are processed on a rolling basis. Application fee: $50. Electronic applications accepted. *Financial support:* In 2017–18, 43 students received support, including 33 research assistantships with full tuition reimbursements available (averaging $26,500 per year), 10 teaching assistantships with full tuition reimbursements available (averaging $28,220 per year); Federal Work-Study, scholarships/grants, health care benefits, and unspecified assistantships also available. Financial award application deadline: 1/1; financial award applicants required to submit FAFSA. *Faculty research:* Accounting systems/financial reporting, corporate finance, shopper marketing/consumer behavior, management information systems, organizational behavior and entrepreneurship. *Total annual research expenditures:* $475,077. *Unit head:* Dr. Arjang A. Assad, Dean, 412-648-1556, Fax: 412-648-1552, E-mail: aassad@katz.pitt.edu. *Application contact:* Dr. Dennis Galletta, Director, 412-648-1699, Fax: 412-648-3633, E-mail: galletta@katz.pitt.edu.
Website: http://www.katz.business.pitt.edu/degrees/phd/

See Display on page 158 and Close-Up on page 187.

University of South Dakota, Graduate School, Beacom School of Business, Department of Business Administration, Vermillion, SD 57069. Offers business administration (MBA); business analytics (MBA, Graduate Certificate); health services administration (MBA); long term care management (Graduate Certificate); marketing (MBA, Graduate Certificate); operations and supply chain management (MBA, Graduate Certificate); JD/MBA. *Accreditation:* AACSB. *Program availability:* Part-time, blended/hybrid learning. *Degree requirements:* For master's, thesis or alternative. *Entrance requirements:* For master's, GMAT, minimum GPA of 2.7, resume. Additional exam requirements/recommendations for international students: Required—TOEFL (minimum score 550 paper-based; 79 iBT), IELTS (minimum score 6). *Application deadline:* For fall admission, 6/1 priority date for domestic students, 5/1 priority date for international students; for spring admission, 10/1 priority date for domestic students, 9/1 priority date for international students; for summer admission, 3/1 priority date for domestic students. Applications are processed on a rolling basis. Application fee: $35. Electronic applications accepted. *Expenses:* Contact institution. *Financial support:* Research assistantships with partial tuition reimbursements, teaching assistantships with partial tuition reimbursements, career-related internships or fieldwork, Federal Work-Study, and unspecified assistantships available. Financial award applicants required to submit FAFSA. *Application contact:* Graduate School, 605-658-6140, Fax: 605-677-6118, E-mail: grad@usd.edu.
Website: http://www.usd.edu/business/business-administration/graduate

The University of Tampa, Sykes College of Business, Tampa, FL 33606-1490. Offers accounting (MS); business analytics (MBA); cybersecurity (MBA, MS); entrepreneurship (MBA, MS); finance (MBA, MS); information systems management (MBA); innovation management (MBA); international business (MBA); marketing (MBA, MS); nonprofit management (MBA, Certificate). *Accreditation:* AACSB. *Program availability:* Part-time, evening/weekend. *Faculty:* 38 full-time (14 women), 6 part-time/adjunct (1 woman). *Students:* 229 full-time (1 woman), 115 part-time (51 women); includes 51 minority (26 Black or African American, non-Hispanic/Latino; 11 Asian, non-Hispanic/Latino; 1 Native Hawaiian or other Pacific Islander, non-Hispanic/Latino; 13 Two or more races, non-Hispanic/Latino), 182 international. Average age 28. 1,305 applicants, 39% accepted, 192 enrolled. In 2017, 266 master's awarded. *Degree requirements:* For master's, capstone. *Entrance requirements:* For master's, GMAT or GRE, official transcripts from all colleges and/or universities previously attended, resume, personal statement, letters of recommendation. Additional exam requirements/recommendations for international students: Required—TOEFL (minimum score 577 paper-based; 90 iBT), IELTS (minimum score 7.5). *Application deadline:* Applications are processed on a rolling basis. Application fee: $40. Electronic applications accepted. *Expenses:* Contact institution. *Financial support:* In 2017–18, 116 students received support. Career-related internships or fieldwork, scholarships/grants, and unspecified assistantships available. Financial award applicants required to submit FAFSA. *Faculty research:* Job market signaling, on-line shopping behaviors and social media, the Tampa Bay economy, digital literacy, entrepreneurship in small businesses. *Unit head:* Dr. Natasha F. Veltri, Associate Dean, 813-253-6289, E-mail: nveltri@ut.edu. *Application contact:* Chanelle Cox, Staff Assistant, Admissions for Graduate and Continuing Studies, 813-253-6249, E-mail: ccox@ut.edu.
Website: http://www.ut.edu/business/

The University of Tulsa, Graduate School, Collins College of Business, Program in Business Analytics, Tulsa, OK 74104-3189. Offers MS. *Program availability:* Part-time. *Students:* 6 full-time (3 women), 6 part-time (0 women); includes 1 minority (Asian, non-Hispanic/Latino), 4 international. Average age 26. 20 applicants, 75% accepted, 12 enrolled. *Entrance requirements:* Additional exam requirements/recommendations for international students: Required—TOEFL (minimum score 90 iBT), IELTS. *Application deadline:* Applications are processed on a rolling basis. Application fee: $55. Electronic applications accepted. *Expenses: Tuition:* Full-time $22,230. *Required fees:* $2000. Tuition and fees vary according to course load and program. *Financial support:* Applicants required to submit FAFSA. *Unit head:* Dr. Ralph Jackson, Associate Dean, 918-631-2213, E-mail: ralph-jackson@utulsa.edu. *Application contact:* Information Contact, 918-631-2242, E-mail: graduate-business@utulsa.edu.
Website: https://business.utulsa.edu/academics/master-science-business-analytics/

University of Wisconsin–Milwaukee, Graduate School, Lubar School of Business, MS and Certificate Business Programs, Milwaukee, WI 53201-0413. Offers business analytics (Graduate Certificate); enterprise resource planning (Graduate Certificate); information technology management (MS); investment management (Graduate Certificate); nonprofit management (Graduate Certificate); nonprofit management and leadership (MS); state and local taxation (Graduate Certificate). *Students:* 164 full-time (87 women), 120 part-time (51 women); includes 51 minority (15 Black or African American, non-Hispanic/Latino; 18 Asian, non-Hispanic/Latino; 3 Hispanic/Latino; 15

Business Analytics

Two or more races, non-Hispanic/Latino), 55 international. Average age 31. 227 applicants, 54% accepted, 74 enrolled. In 2017, 157 master's, 21 other advanced degrees awarded. *Entrance requirements:* Additional exam requirements/recommendations for international students: Required—TOEFL (minimum score 550 paper-based; 79 iBT), IELTS (minimum score 6.5). Application fee: $56 ($96 for international students). Electronic applications accepted. *Financial support:* Fellowships, research assistantships, teaching assistantships, health care benefits, unspecified assistantships, and project assistantships available. Financial award applicants required to submit FAFSA. *Application contact:* General Information Contact, 414-229-4982, Fax: 414-229-6967, E-mail: gradschool@uwm.edu.

Virginia Polytechnic Institute and State University, Graduate School, Pamplin College of Business, Blacksburg, VA 24061. Offers accounting and information systems (MACIS, PhD); business (PhD), including marketing (MS, PhD); business administration (MS), including business analytics, marketing (MS, PhD); business information technology (PhD); executive business research (PhD); finance (PhD); MS/MBA. *Faculty:* 131 full-time (42 women), 2 part-time/adjunct (1 woman). *Students:* 261 full-time (101 women), 189 part-time (76 women); includes 112 minority (32 Black or African American, non-Hispanic/Latino; 50 Asian, non-Hispanic/Latino; 15 Hispanic/Latino; 15 Two or more races, non-Hispanic/Latino), 80 international. Average age 32. 434 applicants, 57% accepted, 168 enrolled. In 2017, 142 master's, 11 doctorates awarded. *Degree requirements:* For master's, comprehensive exam (for some programs), thesis (for some programs); for doctorate, comprehensive exam (for some programs), thesis/dissertation (for some programs). *Entrance requirements:* For master's and doctorate, GRE/GMAT. Additional exam requirements/recommendations for international students: Required—TOEFL (minimum score 80 iBT). *Application deadline:* For fall admission, 8/1 for domestic students, 4/1 for international students; for spring admission, 1/1 for domestic students, 9/1 for international students. Applications are processed on a rolling basis. Application fee: $75. Electronic applications accepted. *Expenses:* Tuition, state resident: full-time $15,072; part-time $718.50 per credit hour. Tuition, nonresident: full-time $28,810; part-time $1448.25 per credit hour. *Required fees:* $2741; $502 per semester. Tuition and fees vary according to course load, campus/location and program. *Financial support:* In 2017–18, 9 research assistantships with full tuition reimbursements (averaging $18,588 per year), 48 teaching assistantships with full tuition reimbursements (averaging $22,706 per year) were awarded. Financial award application deadline: 3/1; financial award applicants required to submit FAFSA. *Total annual research expenditures:* $3.4 million. *Unit head:* Dr. Robert T. Sumichrast, Dean, 540-231-6601, Fax: 540-231-4487, E-mail: busdean@vt.edu. *Application contact:* Kimberly Ridpath, Executive Assistant, 540-231-9647, Fax: 540-231-4487, E-mail: ridpathk@vt.edu.
Website: http://www.pamplin.vt.edu/

Wake Forest University, School of Business, MS in Business Analytics Program, Winston-Salem, NC 27106. Offers MSBA. *Faculty:* 10 full-time (2 women), 3 part-time/adjunct (2 women). *Students:* 67 full-time (37 women); includes 9 minority (4 Black or African American, non-Hispanic/Latino; 1 Asian, non-Hispanic/Latino; 2 Hispanic/Latino; 2 Two or more races, non-Hispanic/Latino), 28 international. Average age 24. 304 applicants, 50% accepted, 67 enrolled. In 2017, 37 master's awarded. *Degree requirements:* For master's, 37 credit hours. *Entrance requirements:* For master's, GMAT, bachelor's degree in business, engineering, mathematics, economics, computer science or liberal arts; coursework in calculus and statistics. Additional exam requirements/recommendations for international students: Required—TOEFL (minimum score 600 paper-based). *Application deadline:* For fall admission, 5/1 for domestic students, 2/2 for international students. Applications are processed on a rolling basis. Application fee: $100. Electronic applications accepted. *Expenses:* Contact institution. *Financial support:* Scholarships/grants available. Financial award application deadline: 4/15; financial award applicants required to submit FAFSA. *Unit head:* Jeffrey Camm, Associate Dean, Business Analytics, 336-758-5422, Fax: 336-758-5830, E-mail: busadmissions@wfu.edu. *Application contact:* Denise Kelly, Administrative Assistant, 336-758-5422, Fax: 336-758-5830, E-mail: busadmissions@wfu.edu.
Website: http://business.wfu.edu/ms-analytics/

Walsh College of Accountancy and Business Administration, Graduate Programs, Program in Accountancy, Troy, MI 48083. Offers data analytics (MAC); finance (MAC); taxation (MAC). *Program availability:* Part-time, evening/weekend. *Students:* 252 (139 women); includes 64 minority (22 Black or African American, non-Hispanic/Latino; 9 Asian, non-Hispanic/Latino; 11 Hispanic/Latino; 1 Two or more races, non-Hispanic/Latino), 21 international. Average age 32. 94 applicants, 76% accepted, 71 enrolled. In 2017, 93 master's awarded. *Degree requirements:* For master's, thesis optional. *Entrance requirements:* For master's, minimum overall cumulative GPA of 2.75 from all colleges previously attended. Additional exam requirements/recommendations for international students: Required—TOEFL (minimum score 550 paper-based, 79 iBT), IELTS (6.5), Michigan English Language Assessment Battery, or MTELP (80). *Application deadline:* Applications are processed on a rolling basis. Application fee: $35. Electronic applications accepted. *Expenses:* $770 per semester credit hour plus $125 registration fee per semester. *Financial support:* In 2017–18, 19 students received support. Career-related internships or fieldwork and scholarships/grants available. Financial award application deadline: 6/30; financial award applicants required to submit FAFSA. *Unit head:* John Black, Chair, Accounting, Tax and Business Law, 248-823-1635, Fax: 248-689-0920, E-mail: jblack@walshcollege.edu. *Application contact:* Heather Rigby, Director, Admissions and Academic Advising, 248-823-1600, Fax: 248-823-1611, E-mail: hrigby@walshcollege.edu.

West Chester University of Pennsylvania, College of Business and Public Management, School of Business, West Chester, PA 19383. Offers business analytics (Certificate); business education (MBA). *Accreditation:* AACSB. *Program availability:* Part-time, evening/weekend, online only, 100% online. *Students:* 41 full-time (17 women), 388 part-time (150 women); includes 69 minority (33 Black or African American, non-Hispanic/Latino; 19 Asian, non-Hispanic/Latino; 14 Hispanic/Latino; 3 Two or more races, non-Hispanic/Latino). Average age 32. 268 applicants, 68%

accepted, 153 enrolled. In 2017, 78 master's, 21 other advanced degrees awarded. *Degree requirements:* For master's, minimum GPA of 3.0. *Entrance requirements:* For master's, GMAT or GRE, statement of professional goals, resume, three letters of recommendation, transcripts. Additional exam requirements/recommendations for international students: Required—TOEFL or IELTS. *Application deadline:* For fall admission, 5/15 for international students; for spring admission, 10/15 for international students. Applications are processed on a rolling basis. Application fee: $50. Electronic applications accepted. *Expenses:* Tuition, state resident: full-time $9000; part-time $500 per credit. Tuition, nonresident: full-time $13,500; part-time $750 per credit. *Required fees:* $2959; $149.79 per credit. *Financial support:* Scholarships/grants and unspecified assistantships available. Financial award application deadline: 2/15; financial award applicants required to submit FAFSA. *Unit head:* Dr. Brian Halsey, MBA Director/Graduate Coordinator, 610-425-5000 Ext. 4444, E-mail: mba@wcupa.edu. *Application contact:* Office of Graduate Studies and Extended Education, 610-436-2943, Fax: 610-436-2763, E-mail: gradstudy@wcupa.edu.
Website: http://www.wcupa.edu/mba

West Virginia University, College of Business and Economics, Morgantown, WV 26506. Offers accountancy (M Acc); accounting (PhD); business administration (MBA); business cyber security management (MS); business data analytics (MS); economics (MA, PhD); finance (MS, PhD); forensic and fraud examination (MS); industrial relations (MS); management (PhD); marketing (PhD). *Program availability:* Part-time, online learning. *Students:* 343 full-time (141 women), 43 part-time (12 women); includes 59 minority (22 Black or African American, non-Hispanic/Latino; 11 Asian, non-Hispanic/Latino; 12 Hispanic/Latino; 14 Two or more races, non-Hispanic/Latino), 54 international. Terminal master's awarded for partial completion of doctoral program. *Degree requirements:* For master's, thesis optional; for doctorate, comprehensive exam, thesis/dissertation. *Entrance requirements:* For doctorate, GRE General Test, minimum GPA of 3.0. Additional exam requirements/recommendations for international students: Required—TOEFL (minimum score 550 paper-based; 92 iBT). *Application deadline:* For fall admission, 10/15 priority date for domestic and international students; for spring admission, 3/1 priority date for domestic and international students. Applications are processed on a rolling basis. Application fee: $60. Electronic applications accepted. *Expenses:* Contact institution. *Financial support:* Fellowships, research assistantships, teaching assistantships, career-related internships or fieldwork, Federal Work-Study, institutionally sponsored loans, scholarships/grants, health care benefits, tuition waivers (full and partial), unspecified assistantships, and administrative assistantships available. Financial award application deadline: 2/1; financial award applicants required to submit FAFSA. *Faculty research:* Regional labor market studies, economic development, market research, economic forecasting, energy analysis. *Unit head:* Dr. Javier Reyes, Dean, 304-293-7800, Fax: 304-293-4056, E-mail: javier.reyes@mail.wvu.edu. *Application contact:* Dr. Mark Gavin, Associate Dean for Graduate Programs, 304-293-7952, Fax: 304-293-7188, E-mail: mark.gavin@mail.wvu.edu.
Website: http://www.be.wvu.edu

William Paterson University of New Jersey, Cotsakos College of Business, Wayne, NJ 07470-8420. Offers applied business analytics (MS); business administration (MBA, Certificate); sales leadership (MS). *Accreditation:* AACSB. *Program availability:* Part-time, evening/weekend. *Faculty:* 16 full-time (3 women), 3 part-time/adjunct (1 woman). *Students:* 69 full-time (37 women), 194 part-time (96 women); includes 109 minority (27 Black or African American, non-Hispanic/Latino; 13 Asian, non-Hispanic/Latino; 57 Hispanic/Latino; 12 Two or more races, non-Hispanic/Latino), 26 international. Average age 31. 164 applicants, 87% accepted, 96 enrolled. In 2017, 73 master's awarded. *Entrance requirements:* For master's, GMAT (minimum score 500) or GRE (minimum 152 Verbal, 152 Quantitative), minimum GPA of 3.0, professional resume. Additional exam requirements/recommendations for international students: Required—TOEFL (minimum score 550 paper-based; 79 iBT), IELTS (minimum score 6). *Application deadline:* For fall admission, 6/1 for domestic students, 3/1 for international students; for spring admission, 11/1 for domestic students, 10/1 for international students. Applications are processed on a rolling basis. Application fee: $50. Electronic applications accepted. *Expenses:* Tuition, state resident: full-time $13,920; part-time $6264 per year. Tuition, nonresident: full-time $21,700; part-time $9765 per year. *Required fees:* $80; $36 per year. Tuition and fees vary according to course load, degree level and program. *Financial support:* In 2017–18, 5,300 students received support. Career-related internships or fieldwork, Federal Work-Study, scholarships/grants, and unspecified assistantships available. Support available to part-time students. Financial award application deadline: 3/15; financial award applicants required to submit FAFSA. *Faculty research:* Labor markets, job characteristics and ethical behavior, institutional trading of stocks and bonds, education funding, and pricing strategies in business to business markets. *Unit head:* Dr. Siamack Shojai, Dean, 973-720-2964, Fax: 973-720-2809, E-mail: shojais@wpunj.edu. *Application contact:* Tinu Adeniran, Assistant Director, Graduate Admissions, 973-720-2764, Fax: 973-720-2035, E-mail: adenirant@wpunj.edu.
Website: http://www.wpunj.edu/ccob

York University, Faculty of Graduate Studies, Schulich School of Business, Toronto, ON M3J 1P3, Canada. Offers accounting (M Acc); administration (PhD); business (MBA); business analytics (MBA); finance (MF); international business (IMBA); MBA/JD; MBA/MA; MBA/MFA. *Program availability:* Part-time, evening/weekend. *Degree requirements:* For master's, advanced proficiency in a second language, work term (IMBA); for doctorate, comprehensive exam, thesis/dissertation. *Entrance requirements:* For master's, GMAT or GRE, minimum GPA of 3.0 (3.3 for MF, MBA in business analytics, and IMBA); for doctorate, GMAT or GRE, minimum GPA of 3.3. Additional exam requirements/recommendations for international students: Required—TOEFL (minimum score 600 paper-based; 100 iBT), IELTS (minimum score 7), York English Language Test (minimum score 1); PearsonVUE (minimum score 64). Electronic applications accepted. *Faculty research:* Accounting, finance, marketing, operations management and information systems, organizational studies, strategic management.

Quantitative Analysis

Baruch College of the City University of New York, Zicklin School of Business, Department of Operations Research and Quantitative Methods, New York, NY 10010-5585. Offers quantitative methods and modeling (MBA, MS). *Program availability:* Part-time.

Baruch College of the City University of New York, Zicklin School of Business, Department of Statistics and Computer Information Systems, Program in Decision Sciences, New York, NY 10010-5585. Offers MBA. *Program availability:* Part-time, evening/weekend. *Entrance requirements:* For master's, GMAT, 2 letters of

recommendation, resume, 2 years of work experience. Additional exam requirements/recommendations for international students: Required—TOEFL (minimum score 590 paper-based), TWE (minimum score 5).

Columbia University, Graduate School of Arts and Sciences, New York, NY 10027. Offers African-American studies (MA); American studies (MA); anthropology (MA, PhD); art history and archaeology (MA, PhD); astronomy (PhD); biological sciences (PhD); biotechnology (MA); chemical physics (PhD); chemistry (PhD); classical studies (MA, PhD); classics (MA, PhD); climate and society (MA); conservation biology (MA); earth and environmental sciences (PhD); East Asia: regional studies (MA); East Asian languages and cultures (MA, PhD); ecology, evolution and environmental biology (MA), including conservation biology; ecology, evolution, and environmental biology (PhD), including ecology and evolutionary biology, evolutionary primatology; economics (MA, PhD); English and comparative literature (MA, PhD); French and Romance philology (MA, PhD); Germanic languages (MA, PhD); global French studies (MA); global thought (MA); Hispanic cultural studies (MA); history (PhD); history and literature (MA); human rights studies (MA); Islamic studies (MA); Italian (MA, PhD); Japanese pedagogy (MA); Jewish studies (MA); Latin America and the Caribbean: regional studies (MA); Latin American and Iberian cultures (PhD); mathematics (MA, PhD), including finance (MA); medieval and Renaissance studies (MA); Middle Eastern, South Asian, and African studies (MA, PhD); modern art: critical and curatorial studies (MA); modern European studies (MA); museum anthropology (MA); music (DMA, PhD); oral history (MA); philosophical foundations of physics (MA); philosophy (MA, PhD); physics (PhD); political science (MA, PhD); psychology (PhD); quantitative methods in the social sciences (MA); religion (MA, PhD); Russia, Eurasia and East Europe: regional studies (MA); Russian translation (MA); Slavic cultures (MA); Slavic languages (MA, PhD); sociology (MA, PhD); South Asian studies (MA); statistics (MA, PhD); theatre (PhD). Dual-degree programs require admission to both Graduate School of Arts and Sciences and another Columbia school. *Program availability:* Part-time. Terminal master's awarded for partial completion of doctoral program. *Degree requirements:* For master's, variable foreign language requirement, comprehensive exam (for some programs); thesis (for some programs); for doctorate, variable foreign language requirement, comprehensive exam (for some programs), thesis/dissertation. *Entrance requirements:* For master's and doctorate, GRE General Test, GRE Subject Test (for some programs). Additional exam requirements/recommendations for international students: Required—TOEFL, IELTS. Electronic applications accepted. *Expenses: Tuition:* Full-time $44,864; part-time $1704 per credit. *Required fees:* $2370 per semester. One-time fee: $105.

Drexel University, LeBow College of Business, Program in Business Administration, Philadelphia, PA 19104-2875. Offers business administration (MBA, PhD, APC), including accounting (MBA, PhD); decision sciences (PhD); economics (MBA, PhD); finance (MBA, PhD); legal studies (MBA); management (MBA); marketing (MBA, PhD); organizational sciences (PhD); quantitative methods (MBA); strategic management (PhD). *Accreditation:* AACSB. *Program availability:* Part-time, evening/weekend, online learning. Terminal master's awarded for partial completion of doctoral program. *Entrance requirements:* For master's, GMAT, minimum GPA of 2.75; for doctorate, GMAT. Additional exam requirements/recommendations for international students: Required—TOEFL. Electronic applications accepted. *Faculty research:* Decision support systems, individual and group behavior, operations research, techniques and strategy.

Duke University, The Fuqua School of Business, The Duke MBA-Daytime Program, Durham, NC 27708-0586. Offers academic excellence in finance (Certificate); business administration (MBA); decision sciences (MBA); energy and environment (MBA); energy finance (MBA); entrepreneurship and innovation (MBA); finance (MBA); financial analysis (MBA); health sector management (Certificate); leadership and ethics (MBA); management (MBA); management science and technology management (Certificate); marketing (MBA); operations management (MBA); social entrepreneurship (MBA); strategy (MBA). *Faculty:* 96 full-time (19 women), 48 part-time/adjunct (15 women). *Students:* 876 full-time (297 women); includes 180 minority (39 Black or African American, non-Hispanic/Latino; 2 American Indian or Alaska Native, non-Hispanic/Latino; 83 Asian, non-Hispanic/Latino; 50 Hispanic/Latino; 6 Two or more races, non-Hispanic/Latino; 321 international. Average age 29. In 2017, 445 master's awarded. *Entrance requirements:* For master's, GMAT or GRE, transcripts, essays, resume, recommendation letters, interview. *Application deadline:* For fall admission, 9/12 for domestic and international students; for winter admission, 10/10 for domestic and international students; for spring admission, 1/3 for domestic and international students; for summer admission, 3/20 for domestic and international students. Application fee: $225. Electronic applications accepted. *Expenses:* $69,342 first-year tuition and fees. *Financial support:* In 2017–18, 423 students received support. Scholarships/grants available. Financial award applicants required to submit FAFSA. *Unit head:* Steve Misuraca, Assistant Dean, Daytime MBA Program. *Application contact:* Shari Hubert, Associate Dean, Office of Admissions, 919-660-7705, Fax: 919-681-8026, E-mail: admissions-info@fuqua.duke.edu.
Website: https://www.fuqua.duke.edu/programs/daytime-mba

Duke University, The Fuqua School of Business, Master of Quantitative Management Program: Business Analytics, Durham, NC 27708-0586. Offers finance (MQM); forensics (MQM); marketing (MQM); strategy (MQM). *Faculty:* 96 full-time (19 women), 48 part-time/adjunct (15 women). *Students:* 140 full-time (81 women); includes 11 minority (9 Asian, non-Hispanic/Latino; 2 Hispanic/Latino), 118 international. Average age 24. *Entrance requirements:* For master's, GMAT/GRE, transcripts, essays, resume, recommendation letters. *Application deadline:* For fall admission, 9/13 for domestic and international students; for winter admission, 1/17 for domestic and international students; for spring admission, 2/28 for domestic and international students; for summer admission, 4/4 for domestic and international students. Application fee: $125. Electronic applications accepted. *Expenses:* $66,907 tuition and fees. *Financial support:* In 2017–18, 46 students received support. Scholarships/grants available. Financial award applicants required to submit FAFSA. *Unit head:* Jeremy Petranka, Associate Dean. *Application contact:* Shari Hubert, Associate Dean, Office of Admissions, 919-660-7705, Fax: 919-681-8026, E-mail: admissions-info@fuqua.duke.edu.
Website: https://www.fuqua.duke.edu/programs/mqm-business-analytics

Duke University, The Fuqua School of Business, PhD Program, Durham, NC 27708-0586. Offers accounting (PhD); decision sciences (PhD); finance (PhD); management and organizations (PhD); marketing (PhD); operations management (PhD); strategy (PhD). *Faculty:* 96 full-time (19 women). *Students:* 64 full-time (25 women); includes 1 minority (Hispanic/Latino), 41 international. Average age 27. 617 applicants, 5% accepted, 14 enrolled. In 2017, 15 doctorates awarded. *Degree requirements:* For doctorate, thesis/dissertation, major field requirement (exam or major paper, depending upon the area). *Entrance requirements:* For doctorate, GMAT or GRE, transcripts, essays, recommendation letters, statement of purpose. Additional exam requirements/recommendations for international students: Required—TOEFL (minimum score 577 paper-based; 108 iBT), IELTS (minimum score 8). *Application deadline:* For fall admission, 12/31 priority date for domestic and international students. Application fee: $85. Electronic applications accepted. *Expenses:* $52,253. *Financial support:* In 2017–18, 66 students received support, including 66 fellowships with full tuition reimbursements available (averaging $29,200 per year), 63 research assistantships with full tuition reimbursements available (averaging $7,000 per year); institutionally sponsored loans, scholarships/grants, and tuition waivers (full) also available. Financial award applicants required to submit FAFSA. *Unit head:* William Boulding, Dean. *Application contact:* Qi Chen, Director of Graduate Studies, 919-660-7753, Fax: 919-660-7971, E-mail: qc2@duke.edu.

Fordham University, Gabelli School of Business, New York, NY 10023. Offers accounting (MBA, MS); applied statistics and decision-making (MS); business economics (DPS); capital markets (DPS); communications and media management (MBA); electronic business (MBA); entrepreneurship (MBA); finance (MBA, PhD); global finance (MS); global sustainability (MBA); health administration (MS); healthcare management (MBA); information systems (MBA, MS); investor relations (MS); management (EMBA, MBA, MS, PhD); marketing (MBA); marketing intelligence (MS); media management (MS); nonprofit leadership (MS); quantitative finance (MS); strategy and decision-making (DPS); taxation (MS); JD/MBA; MS/MBA. *Accreditation:* AACSB. *Program availability:* Part-time, evening/weekend. *Faculty:* 130 full-time (46 women), 42 part-time/adjunct (5 women). *Students:* 1,051 full-time (570 women), 563 part-time (313 women); includes 190 minority (48 Black or African American, non-Hispanic/Latino; 72 Asian, non-Hispanic/Latino; 69 Hispanic/Latino; 1 Native Hawaiian or other Pacific Islander, non-Hispanic/Latino), 1,106 international. Average age 27. 4,577 applicants, 58% accepted, 794 enrolled. In 2017, 937 master's awarded. Terminal master's awarded for partial completion of doctoral program. *Degree requirements:* For master's, internships (for some degrees); for doctorate, comprehensive exam (for some programs), thesis/dissertation. *Entrance requirements:* For master's, GMAT/GRE, 2 letters of recommendation, resume, 2 essays, transcripts, interview. Additional exam requirements/recommendations for international students: Required—TOEFL (minimum score 100 iBT), IELTS (minimum score 7). *Application deadline:* For fall admission, 11/15 priority date for domestic and international students; for winter admission, 1/19 priority date for domestic students, 1/1 priority date for international students; for spring admission, 4/15 for domestic students, 3/1 for international students; for summer admission, 6/1 for domestic students. Application fee: $130. Electronic applications accepted. *Expenses:* $1,495 per credit. *Financial support:* Career-related internships or fieldwork, institutionally sponsored loans, scholarships/grants, and unspecified assistantships available. Support available to part-time students. Financial award application deadline: 6/30; financial award applicants required to submit FAFSA. *Unit head:* Dr. Donna Rapaccioli, Dean, 212-636-6165, Fax: 212-307-1779, E-mail: rapaccioli@fordham.edu. *Application contact:* Lawrence Murray, Senior Assistant Dean of Graduate Admissions and Advising, 212-636-6200, Fax: 212-636-7076, E-mail: admissionsgb@fordham.edu.
Website: http://www.fordham.edu/gabelli

Harvard University, Graduate School of Arts and Sciences, Harvard John A. Paulson School of Engineering and Applied Sciences, Cambridge, MA 02138. Offers applied mathematics (PhD); applied physics (PhD); computational science and engineering (ME, SM); computer science (PhD); data science (SM); design engineering (MDE); engineering science (ME), including electrical engineering (ME, SM, PhD); engineering sciences (SM, PhD), including bioengineering (PhD), electrical engineering (ME, SM, PhD), environmental science and engineering (PhD), materials science and mechanical engineering (PhD). MDE offered in collaboration with Graduate School of Design. *Program availability:* Part-time. *Faculty:* 86 full-time (16 women), 51 part-time/adjunct (13 women). *Students:* 502 full-time (156 women), 22 part-time (15 women); includes 90 minority (1 Black or African American, non-Hispanic/Latino; 61 Asian, non-Hispanic/Latino; 17 Hispanic/Latino; 1 Native Hawaiian or other Pacific Islander, non-Hispanic/Latino; 10 Two or more races, non-Hispanic/Latino), 277 international. Average age 27. 2,707 applicants, 10% accepted, 142 enrolled. In 2017, 34 master's, 64 doctorates awarded. Terminal master's awarded for partial completion of doctoral program. *Degree requirements:* For master's, thesis (for ME); for doctorate, comprehensive exam, thesis/dissertation. *Entrance requirements:* For master's and doctorate, GRE General Test, GRE Subject Test (recommended), 3 letters of recommendation. Additional exam requirements/recommendations for international students: Required—TOEFL (minimum score 80 iBT). *Application deadline:* For fall admission, 12/15 priority date for domestic and international students. Application fee: $105. Electronic applications accepted. *Expenses:* Contact institution. *Financial support:* In 2017–18, 413 students received support, including 122 fellowships with full tuition reimbursements available (averaging $26,424 per year), 277 research assistantships with tuition reimbursements available (averaging $35,232 per year), 76 teaching assistantships with tuition reimbursements available (averaging $6,313 per year); health care benefits also available. *Faculty research:* Applied mathematics, applied physics, computer science and electrical engineering, environmental engineering, mechanical and biomedical engineering. *Total annual research expenditures:* $56.3 million. *Unit head:* Francis J. Doyle, III, Dean, 617-495-5829, Fax: 617-495-5264, E-mail: dean@seas.harvard.edu. *Application contact:* Office of Admissions and Financial Aid, 617-495-5315, E-mail: admissions@seas.harvard.edu.
Website: http://www.seas.harvard.edu/

Hofstra University, Frank G. Zarb School of Business, Programs in Finance, Hempstead, NY 11549. Offers business administration (MBA), including finance; corporate finance (Advanced Certificate); finance (MS), including financial and risk management, investment analysis; investment management (Advanced Certificate); quantitative finance (MS). *Program availability:* Part-time, evening/weekend, blended/hybrid learning. *Students:* 157 full-time (55 women), 44 part-time (11 women); includes 23 minority (6 Black or African American, non-Hispanic/Latino; 7 Asian, non-Hispanic/Latino; 8 Hispanic/Latino; 1 American Indian or Alaska Native, non-Hispanic/Latino; 1 Two or more races, non-Hispanic/Latino), 134 international. Average age 25. 530 applicants, 75% accepted, 71 enrolled. In 2017, 103 master's awarded. *Degree requirements:* For master's, capstone course (for MBA), thesis (for MS), minimum GPA of 3.0. *Entrance requirements:* For master's, GMAT/GRE, 2 letters of recommendation, resume, essay. Additional exam requirements/recommendations for international students: Required—TOEFL (minimum score 550 paper-based; 80 iBT); Recommended—IELTS (minimum score 6). *Application deadline:* Applications are processed on a rolling basis. Application fee: $75. Electronic applications accepted. *Expenses:* $1,322 per credit. *Financial support:* In 2017–18, 57 students received support, including 51 fellowships with full and partial tuition reimbursements available (averaging $5,604 per year); research assistantships with full and partial tuition reimbursements available, career-related internships or fieldwork, Federal Work-Study, institutionally sponsored loans, scholarships/grants, tuition waivers (full and partial), and unspecified assistantships also available. Support available to part-time students. Financial award applicants required to submit FAFSA. *Faculty research:* Individual investors and financial crisis; short-sale constraints and futures trading; social media and sentiment in financial markets; external monitoring of firms; CEO inside debt and insider trading. *Unit head:* Dr. K. G. Viswanathan, Chairperson, 516-463-5699, Fax: 516-463-4834, E-mail: k.g.viswanathan@hofstra.edu. *Application contact:* Sunil Samuel, Assistant Vice President of Admissions, 516-463-4723, Fax: 516-463-4664, E-mail: graduateadmission@hofstra.edu.
Website: http://www.hofstra.edu/business/

Instituto Tecnologico de Santo Domingo, Graduate School, Area of Engineering, Santo Domingo, Dominican Republic. Offers construction administration (MS, Certificate); data telecommunications (M Eng, MS, Certificate); industrial engineering (M Eng, Certificate); industrial management (M Mgmt); information technology (Certificate); maintenance engineering (M Eng); occupational hazard prevention (M Mgmt); production management (Certificate); quantitative methods (Certificate); sanitary and environmental engineering (M Eng); structural engineering (M Eng); systems engineering and electronic data processing (Certificate); transportation (Certificate).

Quantitative Analysis

Lehigh University, College of Business and Economics, Department of Finance, Bethlehem, PA 18015. Offers analytical finance (MS). *Faculty:* 6 full-time (1 woman). *Students:* 60 full-time (30 women), 1 (woman) part-time, 59 international. Average age 23. 278 applicants, 42% accepted, 24 enrolled. In 2017, 41 master's awarded. *Degree requirements:* For master's, capstone project. *Entrance requirements:* For master's, GMAT or GRE, bachelor's degree from a mathematically rigorous program, minimum GPA of 3.0. Additional exam requirements/recommendations for international students: Required—TOEFL (minimum score 600 paper-based; 94 iBT), IELTS (minimum score 7). *Application deadline:* For fall admission, 7/15 for domestic students, 4/15 for international students. Application fee: $75. Electronic applications accepted. *Financial support:* Fellowships, research assistantships, teaching assistantships, and health care benefits available. *Total annual research expenditures:* $334,916. *Unit head:* Nandu Nayar, Department Chair, 610-758-4161, E-mail: nan2@lehigh.edu. *Application contact:* Michael Tarantino, Director of Recruitment and Admissions, 610-758-3418, Fax: 610-758-5283, E-mail: mgt215@lehigh.edu.
Website: http://www4.lehigh.edu/business/academics/depts/finance

Rutgers University–Newark, School of Public Health, Newark, NJ 07107-1709. Offers clinical epidemiology (Certificate); dental public health (MPH); general public health (Certificate); public policy and oral health services administration (Certificate); quantitative methods (MPH); urban health (MPH); DMD/MPH; MD/MPH; MS/MPH. *Program availability:* Part-time, evening/weekend. *Degree requirements:* For master's, thesis, internship. *Entrance requirements:* For master's, GRE General Test. Additional exam requirements/recommendations for international students: Required—TOEFL. Electronic applications accepted.

San Francisco State University, Division of Graduate Studies, College of Business, Program in Business Administration, San Francisco, CA 94132-1722. Offers decision sciences/operations research (MBA); ethics and compliance (MBA); finance (MBA); global business and innovation (MBA); healthcare administration (MBA); hospitality and tourism management (MBA); information systems (MBA); leadership (MBA); marketing (MBA); nonprofit and social enterprise leadership (MBA); sustainable business (MBA). *Accreditation:* AACSB. *Program availability:* Part-time, evening/weekend. *Degree requirements:* For master's, thesis, essay test. *Entrance requirements:* For master's, GMAT, minimum GPA of 2.7 in last 60 units. Additional exam requirements/recommendations for international students: Required—TOEFL (minimum score 550 paper-based). *Application deadline:* For fall admission, 5/1 priority date for domestic students, 4/1 for international students; for spring admission, 11/1 for domestic students, 10/15 for international students. Applications are processed on a rolling basis. Application fee: $55. *Financial support:* Application deadline: 3/1. *Unit head:* Dr. Sanjit Sengupta, Faculty Director, 415-817-4366, Fax: 415-817-4340, E-mail: sengupta@sfsu.edu. *Application contact:* Christopher Kingston, Director of Student Advising, 415-817-4322, Fax: 415-817-4340, E-mail: cak@sfsu.edu.
Website: http://cob.sfsu.edu/graduate-programs/mba

Southern New Hampshire University, School of Business, Manchester, NH 03106-1045. Offers accounting (MBA, Graduate Certificate); accounting finance (MS); accounting/auditing (MS); accounting/forensic accounting (MS); accounting/management accounting (MS); accounting/taxation (MS); applied economics (MS); athletic administration (MBA, Graduate Certificate); business administration (IMBA, Certificate), including business information systems (Certificate), human resource management (Certificate); business analytics (MBA); business intelligence (MBA); communication (MA), including new media and marketing, public relations; community economic development (MBA); criminal justice (MBA); data analytics (MS); economics (MBA); engineering management (MBA); entrepreneurship (MBA); finance (MBA, MS, Graduate Certificate); finance/corporate finance (MS); finance/investments (MS); forensic accounting (MBA); forensic accounting and fraud examination (Graduate Certificate); healthcare informatics (MBA); healthcare management (MBA); human resource management (MS); human resources (MBA); information technology (MS); information technology management (MBA); international business (PhD); Internet marketing (MBA); leadership (MBA); leadership of nonprofit organizations (Graduate Certificate); management (MS); marketing (MBA, MS, Graduate Certificate); music business (MBA); operations and project management (MS); operations and supply chain management (MBA, Graduate Certificate); organizational leadership (MS); project management (MBA, Graduate Certificate); public administration (MBA, Graduate Certificate); quantitative analysis (MBA); Six Sigma (Graduate Certificate); Six Sigma quality (MBA); social media marketing (MBA, Graduate Certificate); sport management (MBA, MS, Graduate Certificate); sustainability and environmental compliance (MBA); MBA/Certificate. *Accreditation:* ACBSP. *Program availability:* Part-time, evening/weekend, online learning. Terminal master's awarded for partial completion of doctoral program. *Degree requirements:* For master's, one foreign language, comprehensive exam (for some programs), thesis or alternative; for doctorate, one foreign language, comprehensive exam, thesis/dissertation. *Entrance requirements:* For master's, minimum GPA of 2.5; for doctorate, GMAT. Additional exam requirements/recommendations for international students: Required—TOEFL (minimum score 500 paper-based). *Application deadline:* Applications are processed on a rolling basis. Application fee: $40. Electronic applications accepted. *Expenses: Tuition:* Part-time $627 per credit hour. Part-time tuition and fees vary according to campus/location and program. *Financial support:* Career-related internships or fieldwork, Federal Work-Study, institutionally sponsored loans, scholarships/grants, tuition waivers (partial), and unspecified assistantships available. Support available to part-time students. Financial award applicants required to submit FAFSA. *Unit head:* Dr. Bill Lightfoot, Dean, 603-644-3102, Fax: 603-644-3144. *Application contact:* Office of Graduate Admission, 888-327-SNHU, Fax: 603-644-3144, E-mail: enroll@snhu.edu.

Stockton University, Office of Graduate Studies, Program in Data Science and Strategic Analytics, Galloway, NJ 08205-9441. Offers MS. *Program availability:* Part-time, online learning. *Faculty:* 1 full-time (0 women), 2 part-time/adjunct (0 women). *Students:* 10 full-time (2 women), 3 part-time (2 women); includes 3 minority (1 Asian, non-Hispanic/Latino; 2 Hispanic/Latino). Average age 32. 22 applicants, 73% accepted, 13 enrolled. *Unit head:* Dr. J. Russell Manson, Director. *Application contact:* Tara Williams, Assistant Director of Graduate Enrollment, 609-626-3640, Fax: 609-626-6050, E-mail: gradschool@stockton.edu.
Website: https://stockton.edu/graduate/data-science_strategic-analytics.html

University at Buffalo, the State University of New York, Graduate School, School of Management, Buffalo, NY 14260. Offers accounting (MS); analytics (MBA); business administration (PMBA); consulting (MBA); finance (MBA, MS), including financial risk management (MS), quantitative finance (MS); healthcare (MBA); information assurance (MBA); information systems (MBA); international management (MBA); management (EMBA, PhD); management information systems (MS); marketing (MBA); supply chain and operations (MBA); supply chains and operations management (MS); Au D/MBA; DDS/MBA; JD/MBA; M Arch/MBA; MD/MBA; MPH/MBA; MSW/MBA; Pharm D/MBA. *Accreditation:* AACSB. *Program availability:* Part-time, evening/weekend. *Faculty:* 80 full-time (26 women), 45 part-time/adjunct (12 women). *Students:* 597 full-time (251 women); includes 83 minority (19 Black or African American, non-Hispanic/Latino; 59 Asian, non-Hispanic/Latino; 5 Hispanic/Latino), 306 international. Average age 25.2, 2,109 applicants, 46% accepted, 376 enrolled. In 2017, 371 master's, 13 doctorates awarded.

Degree requirements: For master's, capstone courses or projects; for doctorate, comprehensive exam, thesis/dissertation. *Entrance requirements:* For master's, GMAT (for MS in accounting, finance); GRE or GMAT (for MBA, MS in management information systems, supply chains and operations management), essays, letters of recommendation; for doctorate, GMAT or GRE, essays, writing sample, letters of recommendation. Additional exam requirements/recommendations for international students: Required—TOEFL (minimum score 95 iBT) or IELTS (minimum score 6.5); Recommended—TSE (minimum score 73). *Application deadline:* For fall admission, 10/15 priority date for domestic and international students; for winter admission, 2/1 priority date for domestic and international students; for spring admission, 4/15 for domestic students; for summer admission, 5/15 for domestic students. Application fee: $100. Electronic applications accepted. *Expenses:* Varies by program. *Financial support:* Fellowships with full and partial tuition reimbursements, research assistantships with full and partial tuition reimbursements, teaching assistantships with full and partial tuition reimbursements, career-related internships or fieldwork, Federal Work-Study, institutionally sponsored loans, scholarships/grants, health care benefits, and unspecified assistantships available. Financial award application deadline: 2/15. *Faculty research:* Data analytics, accounting and law, rate finance, consumer behavior, supply chain logistics, leadership and team effectiveness. *Total annual research expenditures:* $968,376. *Unit head:* Erin K. O'Brien, Assistant Dean and Director of Graduate Programs, 716-645-3204, Fax: 716-645-2341, E-mail: ekobrien@buffalo.edu. *Application contact:* Meghan Felser, Director of Admissions and Recruiting, 716-645-3204, Fax: 716-645-2341, E-mail: mpwood@buffalo.edu.
Website: http://mgt.buffalo.edu/

The University of Alabama at Birmingham, School of Public Health, Program in Public Health, Birmingham, AL 35294. Offers applied epidemiology and pharmacoepidemiology (MSPH); biostatistics (MPH); clinical and translational science (MSPH); environmental health (MPH); environmental health and toxicology (MSPH); epidemiology (MPH); general theory and practice (MPH); health behavior (MPH); health care organization (MPH); health policy quantitative policy analysis (MPH); industrial hygiene (MPH, MSPH); maternal and child health policy (Dr PH); maternal and child health policy and leadership (MPH); occupational health and safety (MPH); outcomes research (MSPH, Dr PH); public health (PhD); public health management (Dr PH); public health preparedness management (MPH). *Program availability:* Part-time, online learning. *Degree requirements:* For doctorate, comprehensive exam, thesis/dissertation. *Entrance requirements:* For master's and doctorate, GRE. Additional exam requirements/recommendations for international students: Recommended—TOEFL (minimum score 550 paper-based; 79 iBT), IELTS (minimum score 6.5). Electronic applications accepted.

The University of British Columbia, Faculty of Arts and Faculty of Graduate Studies, Department of Psychology, Vancouver, BC V6T 1Z4, Canada. Offers behavioral neuroscience (MA, PhD); clinical psychology (MA, PhD); cognitive science (MA, PhD); developmental psychology (MA, PhD); health psychology (MA, PhD); quantitative methods (MA, PhD); social/personality psychology (MA, PhD). *Accreditation:* APA (one or more programs are accredited). Terminal master's awarded for partial completion of doctoral program. *Degree requirements:* For master's, thesis; for doctorate, comprehensive exam, thesis/dissertation. *Entrance requirements:* For master's and doctorate, GRE General Test. Additional exam requirements/recommendations for international students: Required—TOEFL. Electronic applications accepted. *Expenses:* Contact institution. *Faculty research:* Clinical, developmental, social/personality, cognition, behavioral neuroscience.

University of California, Santa Barbara, Graduate Division, College of Letters and Sciences, Division of Mathematics, Life, and Physical Sciences, Department of Geography, Santa Barbara, CA 93106-4060. Offers cognitive science (PhD); geography (MA, PhD); global studies (PhD); quantitative methods in the social sciences (PhD); technology and society (PhD); transportation (PhD); MA/PhD. Terminal master's awarded for partial completion of doctoral program. *Degree requirements:* For master's, comprehensive exam (for some programs), thesis or alternative; for doctorate, comprehensive exam, thesis/dissertation, 1 quarter of teaching assistantship. *Entrance requirements:* For master's and doctorate, GRE (minimum combined verbal and quantitative scores above 1100 in old scoring system or 301 in new scoring system). Additional exam requirements/recommendations for international students: Required—TOEFL (minimum score 550 paper-based; 80 iBT), IELTS (minimum score 7). Electronic applications accepted. *Faculty research:* Earth system science; human environment relations; modeling, measurement, and computation.

University of California, Santa Barbara, Graduate Division, College of Letters and Sciences, Division of Mathematics, Life, and Physical Sciences, Department of Statistics and Applied Probability, Santa Barbara, CA 93106-3110. Offers bioengineering (PhD); financial mathematics and statistics (PhD); quantitative methods in the social sciences (PhD); statistics (MA), including applied statistics, mathematical statistics; statistics and applied probability (PhD); MA/PhD. Terminal master's awarded for partial completion of doctoral program. *Degree requirements:* For master's, comprehensive exam, thesis optional; for doctorate, comprehensive exam, thesis/dissertation. *Entrance requirements:* For master's and doctorate, GRE General Test. Additional exam requirements/recommendations for international students: Required—TOEFL (minimum score 550 paper-based; 80 iBT), IELTS (minimum score 7). Electronic applications accepted. *Faculty research:* Bayesian inference, financial mathematics, stochastic processes, environmental statistics, biostatistical modeling.

University of California, Santa Barbara, Graduate Division, College of Letters and Sciences, Division of Social Sciences, Department of Communication, Santa Barbara, CA 93106-4020. Offers cognitive science (PhD); communication (PhD); feminist studies (PhD); language, interaction and social organization (PhD); quantitative methods in the social sciences (PhD); society and technology (PhD); MA/PhD. Terminal master's awarded for partial completion of doctoral program. *Degree requirements:* For doctorate, comprehensive exam, thesis/dissertation. *Entrance requirements:* For doctorate, GRE. Additional exam requirements/recommendations for international students: Required—TOEFL (minimum score 80 iBT), IELTS (minimum score 7). Electronic applications accepted. *Faculty research:* Interpersonal, intergroup, intercultural, organizational, health, media.

University of California, Santa Barbara, Graduate Division, College of Letters and Sciences, Division of Social Sciences, Department of Sociology, Santa Barbara, CA 93106-9430. Offers interdisciplinary emphasis: Black studies (PhD); interdisciplinary emphasis: environment and society (PhD); interdisciplinary emphasis: feminist studies (PhD); interdisciplinary emphasis: global studies (PhD); interdisciplinary emphasis: language, interaction and social organization (PhD); interdisciplinary emphasis: quantitative methods in the social sciences (PhD); interdisciplinary emphasis: technology and society (PhD); sociology (PhD); MA/PhD. Terminal master's awarded for partial completion of doctoral program. *Degree requirements:* For doctorate, comprehensive exam, thesis/dissertation. *Entrance requirements:* For doctorate, GRE General Test. Additional exam requirements/recommendations for international students: Required—TOEFL (minimum score 550 paper-based; 80 iBT), IELTS (minimum score 7). Electronic applications accepted. *Faculty research:* Gender and sexualities, race/ethnicity, social movements, conversation analysis, global sociology.

University of Colorado Denver, Business School, Program in Decision Sciences, Denver, CO 80217. Offers MS, MS/MBA. *Program availability:* Part-time, evening/weekend. *Degree requirements:* For master's, 30 semester hours (18 of required courses and 12 of electives). *Entrance requirements:* For master's, GMAT, essay, resume, two letters of recommendation; financial statements (for international students). Additional exam requirements/recommendations for international students: Required—TOEFL (minimum score 537 paper-based; 75 iBT); Recommended—IELTS (minimum score 6.5). Electronic applications accepted. *Expenses:* Contact institution. *Faculty research:* Quantitative business analysis, quantitative methods and modeling, business intelligence, forecasting, quality and Six Sigma, optimization, project management, data mining, supply chain management.

University of Connecticut, Graduate School, College of Liberal Arts and Sciences, Department of Public Policy, Field of Survey Research, Storrs, CT 06269. Offers quantitative research methods (Graduate Certificate); survey research (MA). *Degree requirements:* For master's, comprehensive exam. *Entrance requirements:* For master's, GRE General Test. Additional exam requirements/recommendations for international students: Required—TOEFL (minimum score 550 paper-based). Electronic applications accepted.

University of Florida, Graduate School, College of Liberal Arts and Sciences, Department of Mathematics, Gainesville, FL 32611. Offers mathematics (MAT, MS, MST, PhD), including imaging science and technology (PhD), mathematics (PhD), quantitative finance (PhD). *Program availability:* Part-time. Terminal master's awarded for partial completion of doctoral program. *Degree requirements:* For master's, comprehensive exam, thesis optional, first-year exam; for doctorate, one foreign language, comprehensive exam, thesis/dissertation. *Entrance requirements:* For master's and doctorate, GRE General Test, GRE Subject Test (math), minimum GPA of 3.0. Additional exam requirements/recommendations for international students: Required—TOEFL (minimum score 550 paper-based; 80 iBT), IELTS (minimum score 6). Electronic applications accepted. *Faculty research:* Applied mathematics, including imaging, optimization and biomathematics; analysis and probability; combinatorics and number theory; topology and foundations; group theory.

University of Florida, Graduate School, College of Liberal Arts and Sciences, Department of Statistics, Gainesville, FL 32611. Offers quantitative finance (PhD); statistics (M Stat, MS Stat, PhD). *Program availability:* Part-time. Terminal master's awarded for partial completion of doctoral program. *Degree requirements:* For master's, variable foreign language requirement, comprehensive exam, final oral exam; thesis (for MS Stat); for doctorate, comprehensive exam, thesis/dissertation. *Entrance requirements:* For master's and doctorate, GRE General Test, minimum GPA of 3.0. Additional exam requirements/recommendations for international students: Required—TOEFL (minimum score 550 paper-based; 80 iBT), IELTS (minimum score 6). Electronic applications accepted. *Faculty research:* Bayesian statistics, biostatistics, Markov Chain Monte Carlo (MCMC), nonparametric statistics, statistical genetics/genomics.

University of Florida, Graduate School, Warrington College of Business Administration, Hough Graduate School of Business, Department of Finance, Insurance and Real Estate, Gainesville, FL 32611. Offers entrepreneurship (MS); finance (MS, PhD); financial services (Certificate); insurance (PhD); quantitative finance (PhD); real estate (MS); real estate and urban analysis (PhD); JD/MBA; JD/MS. Terminal master's awarded for partial completion of doctoral program. *Degree requirements:* For master's, comprehensive exam, thesis; for doctorate, comprehensive exam, thesis/dissertation. *Entrance requirements:* For master's, GMAT (minimum score of 465) or GRE General Test, minimum GPA of 3.0 for last 60 hours of undergraduate degree, work experience (preferred); for doctorate, GMAT (minimum score of 465) or GRE General Test, minimum GPA of 3.0. Additional exam requirements/recommendations for international students: Required—TOEFL (minimum score 550 paper-based; 80 iBT), IELTS (minimum score 6). Electronic applications accepted. *Faculty research:* Banking, empirical corporate finance, hedge funds.

The University of Iowa, Graduate College, College of Public Health, Department of Biostatistics, Iowa City, IA 52242-1316. Offers biostatistics (MS, PhD, Certificate); quantitative methods (MPH). *Degree requirements:* For master's, thesis optional, exam; for doctorate, comprehensive exam, thesis/dissertation. *Entrance requirements:* For master's and doctorate, GRE General Test, minimum GPA of 3.0. Additional exam requirements/recommendations for international students: Required—TOEFL (minimum score 600 paper-based; 100 iBT). Electronic applications accepted.

University of Maryland, College Park, Academic Affairs, College of Education, Department of Human Development and Quantitative Methodology, College Park, MD 20742. Offers MA, Ed D, PhD. *Entrance requirements:* Additional exam requirements/recommendations for international students: Required—TOEFL.

University of Michigan, Rackham Graduate School, College of Literature, Science, and the Arts, Department of Mathematics, Ann Arbor, MI 48109. Offers applied and interdisciplinary mathematics (AM, MS, PhD); mathematics (AM, MS, PhD); quantitative finance and risk management (MS). *Program availability:* Part-time. *Faculty:* 61 full-time (12 women). *Students:* 202 full-time (59 women), 6 part-time (2 women); includes 27 minority (4 Black or African American, non-Hispanic/Latino; 9 Asian, non-Hispanic/Latino; 9 Hispanic/Latino; 5 Two or more races, non-Hispanic/Latino), 134 international. Average age 26. 1,049 applicants, 22% accepted, 66 enrolled. In 2017, 53 master's, 16 doctorates awarded. *Degree requirements:* For doctorate, one foreign language, comprehensive exam, thesis/dissertation, oral defense of dissertation, preliminary exam. *Entrance requirements:* For master's and doctorate, GRE General Test, GRE Subject Test. Additional exam requirements/recommendations for international students: Required—TOEFL (minimum score 560 paper-based; 84 iBT). *Application deadline:* For fall admission, 12/15 for domestic and international students. Applications are processed on a rolling basis. Application fee: $75 ($90 for international students). Electronic applications accepted. *Expenses:* $11,184 resident, $22,578 non-resident per term; $164.19 per term fees. *Financial support:* In 2017–18, 138 students received support, including 36 fellowships with full tuition reimbursements available (averaging $25,000 per year), 36 research assistantships with full tuition reimbursements available (averaging $20,399 per year), 201 teaching assistantships with full tuition reimbursements available (averaging $20,399 per year). Financial award application deadline: 3/15. *Faculty research:* Algebra, analysis, topology, applied mathematics, geometry. *Unit head:* Prof. Anthony Bloch, Chair, 734-763-0937, E-mail: math-chair@umich.edu. *Application contact:* Prof. Kartik Prasanna, Admissions Director, 734-615-3439, Fax: 734-763-0937, E-mail: math-admissionsdir@umich.edu. Website: http://www.lsa.umich.edu/math/

University of Minnesota, Twin Cities Campus, College of Science and Engineering, School of Mathematics, Minneapolis, MN 55455-0213. Offers mathematics (MS, PhD); quantitative finance (Certificate). *Program availability:* Part-time. Terminal master's awarded for partial completion of doctoral program. *Degree requirements:* For master's, thesis (for some programs); for doctorate, 2 foreign languages, thesis/dissertation. *Entrance requirements:* For master's, GRE Subject Test (recommended); for doctorate, GRE Subject Test. Additional exam requirements/recommendations for international students: Required—TOEFL. Electronic applications accepted. *Faculty research:* Partial

and ordinary differential equations, algebra and number theory, geometry, combinatorics, numerical analysis, probability, financial mathematics.

University of New Hampshire, Graduate School, Interdisciplinary Programs, Program in Analytics, Durham, NH 03824. Offers MS, Postbaccalaureate Certificate, MS/MPP. *Students:* 27 full-time (14 women), 1 part-time (0 women); includes 2 minority (1 Black or African American, non-Hispanic/Latino; 1 Hispanic/Latino), 5 international. Average age 31. 16 applicants, 25% accepted, 1 enrolled. In 2017, 25 master's, 3 other advanced degrees awarded. *Entrance requirements:* For master's, minimum GPA of 3.0, statistics course, interview. Additional exam requirements/recommendations for international students: Required—TOEFL (minimum score 550 paper-based; 80 iBT). *Application deadline:* For summer admission, 4/30 for domestic and international students. Application fee: $65. Electronic applications accepted. *Financial support:* Scholarships/grants available. Financial award application deadline: 2/15. *Unit head:* Robert McGrath, Director, 603-862-0688. *Application contact:* Lyin Schramm, Program Coordinator, 603-862-0803.
Website: http://www.unh.edu/analytics/master-science-analytics

University of New Mexico, Graduate Studies, College of Arts and Sciences, Program in Psychology, Albuquerque, NM 87131-2039. Offers behavioral neuroscience (PhD); clinical psychology (PhD); cognitive neuroimaging (PhD); developmental psychology (PhD); evolution (PhD); health psychology (PhD); quantitative methodology (PhD). *Accreditation:* APA. *Students:* Average age 30. 227 applicants, 11% accepted, 16 enrolled. In 2017, 10 doctorates awarded. *Degree requirements:* For doctorate, comprehensive exam, thesis/dissertation. *Entrance requirements:* For doctorate, GRE General Test, GRE Subject Test (psychology), minimum GPA of 3.0. Additional exam requirements/recommendations for international students: Required—TOEFL (minimum score 550 paper-based; 79 iBT), IELTS (minimum score 6.5). *Application deadline:* For fall admission, 12/15 priority date for domestic and international students. Applications are processed on a rolling basis. Application fee: $50. Electronic applications accepted. *Financial support:* Fellowships, research assistantships, teaching assistantships, career-related internships or fieldwork, Federal Work-Study, institutionally sponsored loans, scholarships/grants, health care benefits, tuition waivers (partial), and unspecified assistantships available. Financial award application deadline: 3/1; financial award applicants required to submit FAFSA. *Faculty research:* Addiction, cognition, brain and behavior, developmental, evolutionary, functioning neuroimaging, health psychology, learning and memory, neuroscience. *Total annual research expenditures:* $727,970. *Unit head:* Dr. Jane Ellen Smith, Department Chair, 505-277-4121, Fax: 505-277-1394. *Application contact:* Rikk Murphy, Graduate Program Coordinator, 505-277-5009, Fax: 505-277-1394, E-mail: advising@unm.edu.
Website: http://psych.unm.edu

University of North Texas, Robert B. Toulouse School of Graduate Studies, Denton, TX 76203-5459. Offers accounting (MS); applied anthropology (MA, MS); applied behavior analysis (Certificate); applied geography (MA); applied technology and performance improvement (M Ed, MS); art education (MA); art history (MA); art museum education (Certificate); arts leadership (Certificate); audiology (Au D); behavior analysis (MS); behavioral science (PhD); biochemistry and molecular biology (MS); biology (MA, MS); biomedical engineering (MS); business analysis (MS); chemistry (MS); clinical health psychology (PhD); communication studies (MA, MS); computer engineering (MS); computer science (MS); counseling (M Ed, MS), including clinical mental health counseling (MS), college and university counseling, elementary school counseling, secondary school counseling; creative writing (MA); criminal justice (MS); curriculum and instruction (M Ed); decision sciences (MBA); design (MA, MFA), including fashion design (MFA), innovation studies, interior design (MFA); early childhood studies (MS); economics (MS); educational leadership (M Ed, Ed D); educational psychology (MS, PhD), including family studies (MS), gifted and talented (MS), human development (MS); learning and cognition (MS), research, measurement and evaluation (MS); electrical engineering (MS); emergency management (MPA); engineering technology (MS); English (MA); English as a second language (MA); environmental science (MS); finance (MBA, MS); financial management (MPA); French (MA); health services management (MBA); higher education (M Ed, Ed D); history (MA, MS); hospitality management (MS); human resources management (MPA); information science (MS); information systems (PhD); information technologies (MBA); interdisciplinary studies (MA, MS); international studies (MA); international sustainable tourism (MS); jazz studies (MM); journalism (MA, MJ, Graduate Certificate), including interactive and virtual digital communication (Graduate Certificate), narrative journalism (Graduate Certificate), public relations (Graduate Certificate); kinesiology (MS); linguistics (MA); local government management (MPA); logistics (PhD); logistics and supply chain management (MBA); long-term care, senior housing, and aging services (MA); management (PhD); marketing (MBA); mathematics (MS); mechanical and energy engineering (MS, PhD); music (MA), including ethnomusicology, music theory, musicology, performance; music composition (PhD); music education (MM Ed, PhD); nonprofit management (MPA); operations and supply chain management (MBA); performance (MM, DMA); philosophy (MA); political science (MA); professional and technical communication (MA); radio, television and film (MA, MFA); rehabilitation counseling (Certificate); sociology (MA); Spanish (MA); special education (M Ed); speech-language pathology (MA); strategic management (MBA); studio art (MFA); teaching (M Ed); MBA/MS. *Program availability:* Part-time, evening/weekend, online learning. Terminal master's awarded for partial completion of doctoral program. *Degree requirements:* For master's, variable foreign language requirement, comprehensive exam, thesis (for some programs); for doctorate, variable foreign language requirement, comprehensive exam (for some programs), thesis/dissertation; for other advanced degree, variable foreign language requirement, comprehensive exam (for some programs). *Entrance requirements:* For master's and doctorate, GRE, GMAT. Additional exam requirements/recommendations for international students: Required—TOEFL (minimum score 550 paper-based; 79 iBT). Electronic applications accepted.

University of Oregon, Graduate School, Charles H. Lundquist College of Business, Department of Decision Sciences, Eugene, OR 97403. Offers MA, MS. *Entrance requirements:* For master's, GMAT. *Faculty research:* Time-series analysis, production scheduling, nonparametric methods, decision theory.

University of Puerto Rico–Río Piedras, College of Business Administration, San Juan, PR 00931-3300. Offers accounting (MBA); finance (MBA, PhD); general business (MBA); human resources management (MBA); international trade and business (MBA, PhD); marketing (MBA); operations management (MBA); quantitative methods (MBA). *Accreditation:* AACSB. *Program availability:* Part-time. *Degree requirements:* For master's, comprehensive exam, thesis or alternative, research project. *Entrance requirements:* For master's, GMAT or PAEG, minimum GPA of 3.0, letter of recommendation; for doctorate, GMAT, PAEG, minimum GPA of 3.0, master degree. *Faculty research:* Management.

University of South Africa, College of Economic and Management Sciences, Pretoria, South Africa. Offers accounting (D Admin, D Com); accounting science (DA); auditing (D Admin, D Com); business administration (M Tech); business economics (D Admin); business leadership (DBL); business management (D Admin, D Com); economic management analysis (M Tech); economics (D Admin, D Com, PhD); human resource development (M Tech); industrial psychology (D Admin, D Com, PhD); logistics

Quantitative Analysis

(D Com); marketing (M Tech); public administration (D Admin, D Com, DPA, PhD); public management (M Tech); quantitative management (D Admin, D Com); real estate (M Tech); statistics (D Admin, PhD); tourism management (D Admin, D Com); transport economics (D Admin, D Com).

University of Southern California, Graduate School, Dana and David Dornsife College of Letters, Arts and Sciences, Department of Psychology, Los Angeles, CA 90089. Offers brain and cognitive science (PhD); clinical science (PhD); developmental psychology (PhD); human behavior (MHB); quantitative methods (PhD); social psychology (PhD). *Accreditation:* APA. *Degree requirements:* For doctorate, comprehensive exam, thesis/dissertation, one-year internship (for clinical science students). *Entrance requirements:* For doctorate, GRE. Additional exam requirements/recommendations for international students: Recommended—TOEFL (minimum score 600 paper-based; 100 iBT). Electronic applications accepted. *Faculty research:* Affective neuroscience; children and families; vision, culture and ethnicity; intergroup relations; aggression and violence; language and reading development; substance abuse.

The University of Texas at Arlington, Graduate School, College of Business, Department of Finance and Real Estate, Arlington, TX 76019. Offers finance (PhD); quantitative finance (MS); real estate (MS). *Program availability:* Part-time, evening/weekend. *Degree requirements:* For master's, thesis optional; for doctorate, comprehensive exam, thesis/dissertation. *Entrance requirements:* For master's, GMAT/GRE, minimum GPA of 3.0; for doctorate, GMAT/GRE. Additional exam requirements/recommendations for international students: Required—TOEFL (minimum score 550 paper-based; 79 iBT).

The University of Texas at Austin, Graduate School, College of Education, Department of Educational Psychology, Austin, TX 78712-1111. Offers academic educational psychology (M Ed, MA); counseling psychology (PhD); counselor education (M Ed); human development, culture and learning sciences (PhD); program evaluation (MA); quantitative methods (M Ed, MA, PhD); school psychology (MA, PhD). *Accreditation:* APA (one or more programs are accredited). *Degree requirements:* For master's, thesis optional; for doctorate, thesis/dissertation. *Entrance requirements:* For master's and doctorate, GRE General Test, 3 letters of recommendation. Additional exam requirements/recommendations for international students: Required—TOEFL.

The University of Texas Health Science Center at Houston, MD Anderson UTHealth Graduate School, Houston, TX 77225-0036. Offers biochemistry and cell biology (PhD); biomedical sciences (MS); cancer biology (PhD); genetic counseling (MS); genetics and epigenetics (PhD); immunology (PhD); medical physics (MS, PhD); microbiology and infectious diseases (PhD); neuroscience (PhD); quantitative sciences (PhD); therapeutics and pharmacology (PhD); MD/PhD. Terminal master's awarded for partial completion of doctoral program. *Degree requirements:* For master's, thesis; for doctorate, thesis/dissertation. *Entrance requirements:* For master's and doctorate, GRE General Test. Additional exam requirements/recommendations for international students: Required—TOEFL. Electronic applications accepted. *Faculty research:* Biomedical sciences.

Vanderbilt University, Peabody College, Department of Psychology and Human Development, Nashville, TN 37240-1001. Offers child studies (M Ed); clinical psychological assessment (M Ed); quantitative methods (M Ed). *Accreditation:* APA. *Program availability:* Part-time. *Faculty:* 36 full-time (22 women), 7 part-time/adjunct (3 women). *Students:* 38 full-time (35 women), 12 part-time (all women); includes 7 minority (1 Black or African American, non-Hispanic/Latino; 1 Asian, non-Hispanic/Latino; 5 Hispanic/Latino), 7 international. Average age 25. 140 applicants, 36% accepted, 19 enrolled. In 2017, 24 master's awarded. *Degree requirements:* For master's, comprehensive exam (for some programs), thesis optional. *Entrance requirements:* For master's, GRE General Test. Additional exam requirements/recommendations for international students: Required—TOEFL (minimum score 550 paper-based; 80 iBT). *Application deadline:* For fall admission, 12/31 for domestic and international students; for spring admission, 11/1 for domestic and international students. Applications are processed on a rolling basis. Application fee: $0. Electronic applications accepted. *Financial support:* Fellowships with partial tuition reimbursements, research assistantships with partial tuition reimbursements, teaching assistantships with partial tuition reimbursements, Federal Work-Study, institutionally sponsored loans, scholarships/grants, tuition waivers (partial), and unspecified assistantships available. Financial award application deadline: 1/15; financial award applicants required to submit FAFSA. *Faculty research:* Cognitive development, quantitative methods, educational neuroscience, depression in adolescence, educational psychology. *Unit head:* Dr. Amy Needham, Chair, 615-322-8141, Fax: 615-343-9494, E-mail: amy.needham@vanderbilt.edu. *Application contact:* Ally Armstead, Educational Coordinator, 615-343-4963, Fax: 615-343-9494, E-mail: ally.armstead@vanderbilt.edu.
Website: http://peabody.vanderbilt.edu/departments/psych/index.php

Virginia Polytechnic Institute and State University, VT Online, Blacksburg, VA 24061. Offers advanced transportation systems (Certificate); aerospace engineering (MS); agricultural and life sciences (MSLFS); business information systems (Graduate Certificate); career and technical education (MS); civil engineering (MS); computer engineering (M Eng, MS); decision support systems (Graduate Certificate); eLearning leadership (MA); electrical engineering (M Eng, MS); engineering administration (MEA); environmental engineering (Certificate); environmental politics and policy (Graduate Certificate); environmental sciences and engineering (MS); foundations of political analysis (Graduate Certificate); health product risk management (Graduate Certificate); industrial and systems engineering (MS); information policy and society (Graduate Certificate); information security (Graduate Certificate); information technology (MIT); instructional technology (MA Ed); integrative STEM education (MA Ed); liberal arts (Graduate Certificate); life sciences: health product risk management (MS); natural resources (MNR, Graduate Certificate); networking (Graduate Certificate); nonprofit and nongovernmental organization management (Graduate Certificate); ocean engineering (MS); political science (MA); security studies (Graduate Certificate); software development (Graduate Certificate). *Expenses:* Tuition, state resident: full-time $15,072; part-time $718.50 per credit hour. Tuition, nonresident: full-time $28,810; part-time $1448.25 per credit hour. *Required fees:* $2741; $502 per semester. Tuition and fees vary according to course load, campus/location and program.

SAINT JOSEPH'S UNIVERSITY

Business Intelligence and Analytics

 For more information, visit http://petersons.to/sjubusintel

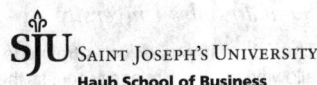

Programs of Study

For more than a decade, the Master of Science in Business Intelligence and Analytics program at Saint Joseph's University (SJU) has trained professionals to maximize organizational knowledge and find success in their data. This STEM-designated program trains students to drive organizational performance in all functional areas. They learn how to use data to create new opportunities, identify effective strategies, and improve decision-making.

Business intelligence and analytics is one of the fastest growing fields in the world. As such, it provides robust professional opportunities for both early careerists and experienced professionals. Data has never been more important to organizations as it is today. Students in this program develop the expertise and advanced business credentials to succeed in data-driven environments.

The Master of Science in Business Intelligence and Analytics (M.S.B.I.A.) program has 30 credits of coursework including two core and eight elective courses. Core courses include prerequisites or co-requisites that are met through the scheduled course sequence. Specializations in cyber analytics, data analytics, general business intelligence, or programming languages allow students to create customized programs of study.

Students can earn their degrees on a full-time or part-time basis either online or on campus. On average, the full-time program takes 1 to 1.5 years to complete and the part-time option takes 2 years. Students have up to 6 years to complete their degree. On-campus classes are offered in 15-week sessions, with each class meeting one night per week. Online classes are normally offered in 8-week accelerated sessions, with most classes meeting live online one evening per week.

Students will work with real data and case studies to develop analytical skills that are immediately applicable and relevant across diverse industries, creating value for themselves and their organizations.

Because this is one of only a few business intelligence and analytics programs taught within a business context, students graduate with a competitive advantage. The SAS Institute, a leader in business analytics services and software and the largest independent vendor in the market, endorses the program. This endorsement enables students to earn an SAS-endorsed Business Intelligence Certificate.

The business intelligence master's program also has two certificate options: Cyber Analytics and Data Analytics.

The M.S.B.I.A. program at Saint Joseph's University equips students with the advanced business credentials, SAS-endorsed certificate, and skill set to become leaders in departments, organizations, and teams. These attributes set them apart from peers and attract the interest of senior leadership in the data-driven environment in which businesses now operate.

The Haub School of Business holds dual accreditation from AACSB, which places it among the top 5 percent of business programs in the world. According to *U.S. News & World Report* and *The Princeton Review*, the Haub School of Business is one of the nation's top business schools.

With over 67,000 graduates across the globe, Saint Joseph's University has an especially strong alumni network. All alumni and students have lifetime access to the Career Development Center, offering a host of resources such resume review, interview prep, on-campus career fairs and interviews, workshops, and networking events.

A recent survey of those who have earned a graduate business degree at Saint Joseph's University has shown that 73 percent report receiving a raise after completing their program; 76 percent say the program significantly helped them advance their career; 70 percent indicate that their degree from the Haub School provided them with more opportunities to increase their salary and gain professional recognition; and 86 percent say the program provided them with the strategic business acumen they needed to succeed in their chosen field.

Research Facilities

The Post Learning Commons and Drexel Library make up the Post Academic Center and support the academic programs of Saint Joseph's University with books and periodicals in both print and electronic formats, research databases, audio-visual materials, and microforms. Research resources and support are available on campus and fully online.

Financial Aid

Saint Joseph's University is committed to providing information and resources to help students manage the costs of graduate education, including need- and non-need-based loans and tuition financing options. Potential resources include scholarships, graduate assistantships that provide a stipend and tuition remission, and Federal loans. SJU offers tuition benefits to eligible military personnel, veterans and their families through the Yellow Ribbon Program.

Students applying for financial assistance through Saint Joseph's must complete the Free Application for Federal Student Aid (FAFSA).

The university also offers an employer tuition-deferral program for students who receive tuition reimbursement from their employers.

Cost of Study

For the 2018–19 academic year, tuition for the M.S.B.I.A. program is $1,043 per credit. Tuition is subject to change by the order of the Saint Joseph's University Board of Trustees.

Living and Housing Costs

The Office of Residence Life offers limited on-campus housing options for graduate students; availability is not guaranteed. The 2018–19 rates range from $5,120 to $6,120 per person per semester. Residence Life also assists students with off-campus housing recommendations. More information can be found at https://offcampushousing.sju.edu/.

Student Life

Students in the MSBIA program may choose to participate in SJU's Graduate Business Student Association (GBSA). The GBSA enhances the graduate experience by promoting professional development and a sense of community among graduate business students, faculty, and administration. All students are automatically members of the GBSA and no registration is required. This student-run organization aims to build strategic relationships by providing networking opportunities through social and service activities.

The Office of Adult Student Life assists graduate students by providing support in overcoming obstacles and resources to foster success. The ASL Office seeks to help adult students develop a personalized plan for success, coordinate adult student groups, organize programs to meet adult student needs, and provide adult student advocacy as needed.

Location

Located in Philadelphia, Pennsylvania, SJU's community enjoys the surroundings of one of America's first major cities. Widely known as "The City of Brotherly Love" Philadelphia's historical importance and vibrant communities create a charming and unique culture. The city is the fifth-largest metropolis in the U.S. and is home to historical landmarks and world-class museums, a number of professional sports teams and dining options, and major events that enrich its cultural life. There are also opportunities to explore Philadelphia's outdoors with a wealth of year-round festivals and cultural events, parks, zoos, and aquariums. With eight Fortune 500 companies, Philadelphia offers numerous internship, networking, and post-graduation job opportunities.

Saint Joseph's University

The SJU campus is just a train ride away from Center City Philadelphia, allowing students to easily access the culture, art, nightlife, and opportunity that Philadelphia has to offer. The city is also conveniently located between New York City and Washington D.C., providing convenient access to additional cultural and employment opportunities.

The University and the School

Founded in 1851, St. Joseph's University prepares students for engaged citizenship, personal excellence, and professional success. Its rigorous Jesuit education integrates a liberal arts foundation with program-specific curricula that meet the needs of complex and changing fields.

The university offers approximately 8,086 students 55 majors, 50 minors, 30-plus degree completion and certificate programs, and 52 graduate programs through two schools. The College of Arts and Sciences offers programs in the humanities, natural sciences, and social sciences.

The Erivan K. Haub School of Business provides a wide-range of programs including STEM master's degrees and graduate programs in analytics. It is an international AACSB-accredited institution in business and accounting, offering programs at the bachelor's, master's, and executive master's levels. *U.S. News & World Report* has ranked the school's part-time MBA, risk-management and insurance, marketing, management, and finance programs among the top in the nation. The Haub School was recently named one of the nation's top business schools in the Princeton Review's "The Best 294 Business Schools," and the undergraduate program was recently recognized by Bloomberg's Businessweek.

It is the largest Jesuit business school in the country with 3,600 students, 84 full-time faculty and more than 22,000 alumni.

Faculty

Highly-qualified faculty members lead the data analytics master's program. They develop and teach the curriculum and create vibrant learning environments. They are successful researchers and practitioners who have in-depth knowledge about industry best practices.

Assistant Professor Nicolle Clements, Ph.D., the academic coordinator of the M.S.B.I.A. program, is an experienced researcher and practitioner. Her research interests include environmental and spatial applications of multiple testing procedures, multiplicative time series modeling, and statistical analysis procedures associated with substance abuse treatment. In addition to her academic work, Dr. Clements has been a statistical consultant since 2010.

Ronald (Ron) K. Klimberg, Ph.D. is a Professor in the Decision and System Sciences Department of the Haub School of Business at Saint Joseph's. Before joining the faculty of Saint Joseph's in 1997, he was a professor at Boston University, an operations research analyst for the Food and Drug Administration, and a consultant. Ron was the 2007 recipient of the Tengelmann Award for his excellence in scholarship, teaching, and research. His research has been directed toward the development and application of quantitative methods, e.g., statistics, forecasting, data mining, and management science techniques, such that the results add value to the organization and the results are effectively communicated.

Additional information about the M.S.B.I.A. faculty can be found online at https://www.sju.edu/majors-programs/graduate-business/master-degrees/business-intelligence-and-analytics-ms/meet-faculty.

Applying

MSBIA students come from all majors and backgrounds. Applicants must have a baccalaureate degree from an accredited university and complete the official application. Required application materials include: official transcripts for all credits earned (undergraduate and graduate), two letters of recommendation, a current resume, a$35 application fee, a personal statement (specifics available online), and official GMAT or GRE scores from within the past seven years (GMAT may be waived under certain circumstances; more details are available online).

Applications are reviewed on a rolling basis. Students may apply to start the program in the fall, spring, or summer terms. The priority application deadline is July 15 for fall semester, November 15 for spring semester, and April 15

for summer semesters. Additional requirements and details for international students are available at https://www.sju.edu/majors-programs/graduate-business/master-degrees/business-intelligence-and-analytics-ms/admission-0.

Correspondence and Information

MSBIA Program
St. Joseph's University Erivan K. Haub School of Business
5600 City Avenue, MV 280
Philadelphia, Pennsylvania 19131
Phone: 610-660-1690
E-mail: sjums@sju.edu
Website: https://sites.sju.edu/hsb/bi
    https://www.sju.edu/majors-programs/graduate-business/master-degrees/business-intelligence-and-analytics-ms

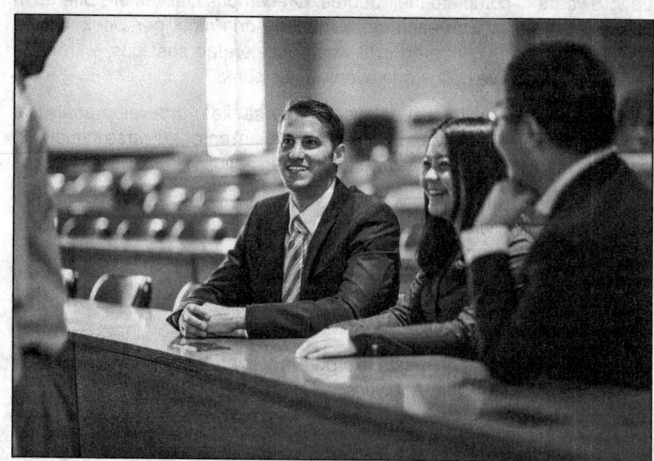

Section 20
Real Estate

This section contains a directory of institutions offering graduate work in real estate. Additional information about programs listed in the directory but not augmented by an in-depth entry may be obtained by writing directly to the dean of a graduate school or chair of a department at the address given in the directory.

For programs offering related work, see also in this book *Business Administration and Management*.

CONTENTS

Program Directory

Displays and Close-Ups

Real Estate

American University, Kogod School of Business, Department of Finance, Washington, DC 20016-8044. Offers finance (MS, Certificate); real estate (MS, Certificate). *Program availability:* Part-time, evening/weekend. *Students:* 40 full-time (16 women), 24 part-time (10 women); includes 13 minority (8 Black or African American, non-Hispanic/Latino; 4 Asian, non-Hispanic/Latino; 1 Two or more races, non-Hispanic/Latino), 32 international. Average age 28. 130 applicants, 72% accepted, 36 enrolled. In 2017, 49 master's, 2 other advanced degrees awarded. *Degree requirements:* For master's, comprehensive exam (for some programs). *Entrance requirements:* For master's, GMAT/GRE, resume, personal statement, interview, 2 letters of recommendation. Additional exam requirements/recommendations for international students: Required—TOEFL (minimum score 100 iBT). *Application deadline:* For fall admission, 1/15 priority date for domestic students, 1/15 for international students; for spring admission, 10/15 priority date for domestic students, 10/15 for international students. Applications are processed on a rolling basis. Application fee: $100. *Expenses:* Contact institution. *Financial support:* Application deadline: 2/1; applicants required to submit FAFSA. *Unit head:* Dr. Jeffrey Harris, Department Chair, Finance and Real Estate, 202-885-6669, Fax: 202-885-1946, E-mail: jharris@american.edu. *Application contact:* Jason Garner, Director of Admissions, 202-885-1926, E-mail: jgarner@american.edu. Website: http://www.american.edu/kogod/

Arizona State University at the Tempe campus, W. P. Carey School of Business, Department of Marketing, Tempe, AZ 85287-4106. Offers business administration (PhD), including marketing; real estate development (MRED). *Program availability:* Part-time, evening/weekend, online learning. *Degree requirements:* For master's, thesis or alternative, capstone project, interactive Program of Study (iPOS) submitted before completing 50 percent of required credit hours; for doctorate, comprehensive exam, thesis/dissertation, interactive Program of Study (iPOS) submitted before completing 50 percent of required credit hours. *Entrance requirements:* For master's, GMAT, GRE, or LSAT, minimum GPA of 3.0 in last 2 years of work leading to bachelor's degree, 3 personal references, resume, official transcripts, personal statement; for doctorate, GMAT, minimum GPA of 3.0 in last 2 years of work leading to bachelor's degree, 3 letters of recommendation, personal statement/essay. Additional exam requirements/recommendations for international students: Required—TOEFL (minimum score 550 paper-based; 80 iBT), IELTS (minimum score 6.5). Electronic applications accepted. *Expenses:* Contact institution. *Faculty research:* Service marketing and management, strategic marketing, customer portfolio management, characteristics and skills of high-performing managers, market orientation, market segmentation, consumer behavior, marketing strategy, new product development, management of innovation, social influences on consumption, e-commerce, market research methodology.

Auburn University, Graduate School, Interdepartmental Programs, Program in Real Estate Development, Auburn University, AL 36849. Offers MRED. *Students:* 36 part-time (7 women); includes 12 minority (8 Black or African American, non-Hispanic/Latino; 1 Asian, non-Hispanic/Latino; 2 Hispanic/Latino; 1 Two or more races, non-Hispanic/Latino), 1 international. Average age 38. 29 applicants, 86% accepted, 20 enrolled. In 2017, 14 master's awarded. Application fee: $50 ($60 for international students). *Expenses:* Tuition, state resident: full-time $10,974; part-time $519 per credit hour. Tuition, nonresident: full-time $29,658; part-time $1557 per credit hour. *Required fees:* $816 per semester. Tuition and fees vary according to degree level and program. *Unit head:* Joe Collazo, Assistant Director, 334-844-5078, E-mail: mred@business.auburn.edu. *Application contact:* Dr. George Flowers, Dean of the Graduate School, 334-844-2125. Website: http://mred.auburn.edu/

Baruch College of the City University of New York, Zicklin School of Business, Department of Real Estate, New York, NY 10010-5585. Offers MBA, MS.

Brandeis University, International Business School (IBS), Master of Business Administration Program, Waltham, MA 02454-9110. Offers data analytics (MBA); finance (MBA); marketing (MBA); real estate (MBA). *Faculty:* 40 full-time (16 women), 31 part-time/adjunct (7 women). *Students:* 35 full-time (18 women), 1 (woman) part-time; includes 3 minority (1 Black or African American, non-Hispanic/Latino; 2 Asian, non-Hispanic/Latino), 30 international. Average age 27. 75 applicants, 49% accepted, 17 enrolled. In 2017, 21 master's awarded. *Entrance requirements:* For master's, GMAT or GRE, minimum two years of full-time work experience. Additional exam requirements/recommendations for international students: Required—TOEFL (minimum score 600 paper-based; 100 iBT), IELTS (minimum score 7), PTE (minimum score 68). *Application deadline:* For fall admission, 11/1 priority date for domestic and international students; for winter admission, 1/15 priority date for domestic and international students; for spring admission, 3/15 priority date for domestic and international students; for summer admission, 4/15 for domestic and international students. Application fee: $100. Electronic applications accepted. *Expenses:* Contact institution. *Financial support:* In 2017–18, 32 students received support. Institutionally sponsored loans and scholarships (averaging $29,641 annually) available. Financial award application deadline: 4/15; financial award applicants required to submit FAFSA. *Faculty research:* Strategic alliances, IPO and venture capital financing, real estate, risk management, data analytics. *Unit head:* Peter Petri, Interim Dean, 781-736-2256. *Application contact:* Kelly Sugrue, Assistant Dean of Admissions, 781-736-2252, Fax: 781-736-2263, E-mail: globaladmissions@brandeis.edu.

California State University, Sacramento, College of Business Administration, Sacramento, CA 95819. Offers accountancy (MS); business administration (IMBA, MBA); human resources (MBA); urban land development (MBA). *Accreditation:* AACSB. *Program availability:* Part-time, evening/weekend, 100% online, blended/hybrid learning. *Students:* 122 full-time (62 women), 153 part-time (75 women); includes 114 minority (10 Black or African American, non-Hispanic/Latino; 2 American Indian or Alaska Native, non-Hispanic/Latino; 73 Asian, non-Hispanic/Latino; 25 Hispanic/Latino; 4 Native Hawaiian or other Pacific Islander, non-Hispanic/Latino), 6 international. Average age 34. 230 applicants, 75% accepted, 134 enrolled. In 2017, 123 master's awarded. *Degree requirements:* For master's, comprehensive exam, project, thesis, or writing proficiency exam. *Entrance requirements:* For master's, GMAT. Additional exam requirements/recommendations for international students: Required—TOEFL (minimum score 550 paper-based; 80 iBT). *Application deadline:* For fall admission, 2/1 for domestic students, 3/1 for international students; for spring admission, 9/15 for domestic students, 9/30 for international students. Applications are processed on a rolling basis. Application fee: $55. Electronic applications accepted. *Expenses:* Contact institution. *Financial support:* Teaching assistantships, career-related internships or fieldwork, Federal Work-Study, and scholarships/grants available. Support available to part-time students. Financial award application deadline: 3/1; financial award applicants required to submit FAFSA. *Unit head:* Dr. Pierre A. Balthazard, Dean, 916-278-6578, Fax: 916-278-5793, E-mail: cba@csus.edu. *Application contact:* Jose Martinez, Graduate Admissions Supervisor, 916-278-7871, E-mail: martinj@skymail.csus.edu. Website: http://www.cba.csus.edu

Clemson University, Graduate School, College of Architecture, Arts, and Humanities, Department of City Planning and Real Estate Development and College of Business, Master of Real Estate Development Program, Greenville, SC 29601. Offers MRED. *Faculty:* 3 full-time (0 women), 10 part-time/adjunct (1 woman). *Students:* 80 full-time (12 women); includes 8 minority (4 Black or African American, non-Hispanic/Latino; 4 Hispanic/Latino), 6 international. Average age 26. 48 applicants, 94% accepted, 27 enrolled. In 2017, 28 master's awarded. *Degree requirements:* For master's, practicum. *Entrance requirements:* For master's, GRE General Test or GMAT, 3 letters of recommendation, resume, personal statement, unofficial transcripts, portfolio for 12-month program. Additional exam requirements/recommendations for international students: Required—TOEFL (minimum score 80 iBT), IELTS (minimum score 6.5), PTE (minimum score 54). *Application deadline:* For fall admission, 1/15 priority date for domestic and international students. Applications are processed on a rolling basis. Application fee: $80 ($90 for international students). Electronic applications accepted. *Expenses:* Contact institution. *Financial support:* In 2017–18, 11 students received support, including 10 fellowships (averaging $2,023 per year); career-related internships or fieldwork also available. Financial award application deadline: 2/15. *Faculty research:* Real estate education, real estate investment/finance, sustainability, public-private partnership. *Unit head:* Dr. John Gaber, Department Chair, 864-656-1208, E-mail: jgaber@clemson.edu. *Application contact:* Dr. Robert Benedict, Program Director, 864-656-2476, E-mail: benedic@clemson.edu. Website: http://www.clemson.edu/caah/departments/real-estate-development/

Cleveland State University, College of Graduate Studies, Maxine Goodman Levin College of Urban Affairs, Program in Urban Planning and Development, Cleveland, OH 44115. Offers economic development (MUPD); environmental sustainability (MUPD); historic preservation (MUPD); housing and neighborhood development (MUPD); real estate development and finance (MUPD); urban economic development (Certificate); urban geographic information systems (MUPD); JD/MUPD. *Accreditation:* ACSP. *Program availability:* Part-time, evening/weekend. *Faculty:* 16 full-time (8 women), 13 part-time/adjunct (5 women). *Students:* 20 full-time (7 women), 15 part-time (5 women); includes 1 minority (Black or African American, non-Hispanic/Latino), 2 international. Average age 28. 48 applicants, 56% accepted, 14 enrolled. In 2017, 24 master's awarded. *Degree requirements:* For master's, thesis or alternative, exit project. *Entrance requirements:* For master's, GRE General Test (minimum score: 50th percentile combined verbal and quantitative, 4.0 analytical writing), minimum GPA of 3.0. Additional exam requirements/recommendations for international students: Required—TOEFL (minimum score 550 paper-based; 78 iBT), IELTS (6.0), or International Test of English Proficiency (iTEP). *Application deadline:* For fall admission, 7/1 priority date for domestic students, 5/15 for international students; for spring admission, 11/15 for domestic students, 11/1 for international students; for summer admission, 4/1 for domestic students, 3/15 for international students. Applications are processed on a rolling basis. Application fee: $40. Electronic applications accepted. *Expenses:* Contact institution. *Financial support:* In 2017–18, 10 students received support, including 5 research assistantships with full tuition reimbursements available (averaging $7,200 per year), 3 teaching assistantships with partial tuition reimbursements available (averaging $2,400 per year); scholarships/grants, tuition waivers (full and partial), and unspecified assistantships also available. Support available to part-time students. Financial award application deadline: 3/1; financial award applicants required to submit FAFSA. *Faculty research:* Housing and neighborhood development, urban housing policy, environmental sustainability, economic development, GIS and planning decision support. *Unit head:* Dr. Stephanie Ryberg-Webster, Assistant Professor/Program Director, 216-802-3386, Fax: 216-687-2013, E-mail: s.ryberg@csuohio.edu. *Application contact:* David Arrighi, Graduate Academic Advisor, 216-523-7522, Fax: 216-687-5398, E-mail: d.arrighi@csuohio.edu. Website: http://www.csuohio.edu/urban/mupd/mupd

Columbia University, Graduate School of Architecture, Planning, and Preservation, Program in Real Estate Development, New York, NY 10027. Offers MS. *Degree requirements:* For master's, thesis. *Entrance requirements:* For master's, GRE General Test. *Expenses: Tuition:* Full-time $44,864; part-time $1704 per credit. *Required fees:* $2370 per semester. One-time fee: $105.

Columbia University, Graduate School of Business, MBA Program, New York, NY 10027. Offers accounting (MBA); decision, risk, and operations (MBA); entrepreneurship (MBA); finance and economics (MBA); healthcare and pharmaceutical management (MBA); human resource management (MBA); international business (MBA); leadership and ethics (MBA); management (MBA); marketing (MBA); media (MBA); private equity (MBA); real estate (MBA); social enterprise (MBA); value investing (MBA); DDS/MBA; JD/MBA; MBA/MIA; MBA/MPH; MBA/MS; MD/MBA. *Entrance requirements:* For master's, GMAT, 2 letters of recommendation. Additional exam requirements/recommendations for international students: Required—TOEFL. Electronic applications accepted. *Expenses:* Contact institution. *Faculty research:* Human decision making and behavioral research; real estate market and mortgage defaults; financial crisis and corporate governance; international business; security analysis and accounting.

Cornell University, Graduate School, Graduate Fields of Architecture, Art and Planning, Field of Real Estate, Ithaca, NY 14853. Offers MPS. *Degree requirements:* For master's, project paper. *Entrance requirements:* For master's, GMAT, 2 letters of recommendation, resume. Additional exam requirements/recommendations for international students: Required—TOEFL (minimum score 600 paper-based; 77 iBT). Electronic applications accepted. *Faculty research:* Smart growth, economic development, urban redevelopment, development financing, securitization of real estate.

DePaul University, Kellstadt Graduate School of Business, Chicago, IL 60604. Offers accountancy (MBA, MSA); applied economics (MBA); audit and advisory services (MS); business administration (DBA); business analytics (MS); business strategy and decision-making (MBA); computational finance (MS); economics and policy analysis (MS); enterprise risk management (MS); entrepreneurship (MBA, MS); finance (MBA, MS); general business (MBA); hospitality leadership (MBA); hospitality leadership and operational performance (MS); human resources (MS); international business (MBA); management (MBA, MS); management information systems (MBA); marketing (MBA, MS); marketing analysis (MS); marketing strategy and planning (MBA); real estate (MBA); real estate finance and investment (MBA); strategy, execution and valuation (MBA); supply chain management (MS); sustainable management (MS); taxation (MS); JD/MBA. *Accreditation:* AACSB. *Program availability:* Part-time, evening/weekend, online learning. *Entrance requirements:* For master's, GMAT/GRE, 2 letters of recommendation, resume, essay, official transcripts. Additional exam requirements/recommendations for international students: Required—TOEFL (minimum score 550 paper-based; 80 iBT). *Application deadline:* For fall admission, 7/1 for domestic students, 6/1 for international students; for winter admission, 10/1 for domestic students, 9/1 for international students; for spring admission, 2/1 for domestic students, 1/1 for

international students. Applications are processed on a rolling basis. Application fee: $60. Electronic applications accepted. *Expenses:* Contact institution. *Financial support:* Application deadline: 4/1; applicants required to submit FAFSA. *Unit head:* Christa Hinton, Assistant Dean and Director, 312-362-8810, Fax: 312-362-6677, E-mail: chinton@depaul.edu. *Application contact:* Garry Cooke, Director of Recruitment and Admissions, 312-362-8810, Fax: 312-362-6677, E-mail: kgsb@depaul.edu.
Website: http://kellstadt.depaul.edu

Drexel University, Goodwin College of Professional Studies, School of Technology and Professional Studies, Philadelphia, PA 19104-2875. Offers construction management (MS); creativity and innovation (MS); engineering technology (MS); food science (MS); hospitality management (MS); professional studies: creativity studies (MS); professional studies: e-learning leadership (MS); professional studies: homeland security management (MS); project management (MS); property management (MS); sport management (MS). *Program availability:* Part-time, evening/weekend. *Entrance requirements:* Additional exam requirements/recommendations for international students: Required—TOEFL, IELTS. Electronic applications accepted. Application fee is waived when completed online.

Emory University, Goizueta Business School, Full Time MBA Program, Atlanta, GA 30322. Offers accounting (MBA); alternative investments (MBA); business process consulting (MBA); business technology management (MBA); capital markets (MBA); corporate finance (MBA); customer relationship management (MBA); decision analytics (MBA); entrepreneurship (MBA); finance (MBA); global management (MBA); investment banking (MBA); management consulting (MBA); marketing (MBA); marketing analytics (MBA); marketing consulting (MBA); operations management (MBA); organization and management (MBA); product and brand management (MBA); real estate (MBA); social enterprise (MBA); strategy consulting (MBA). *Accreditation:* AACSB. *Faculty:* 74 full-time (18 women), 18 part-time/adjunct (6 women). *Students:* 353 full-time (96 women); includes 80 minority (18 Black or African American, non-Hispanic/Latino; 2 American Indian or Alaska Native, non-Hispanic/Latino; 39 Asian, non-Hispanic/Latino; 16 Hispanic/Latino; 1 Native Hawaiian or other Pacific Islander, non-Hispanic/Latino; 4 Two or more races, non-Hispanic/Latino), 104 international. Average age 29. 1,380 applicants, 34% accepted, 172 enrolled. In 2017, 179 master's awarded. *Degree requirements:* For master's, 1 leadership course; 2 mid-semester module programs; 2 global components. *Entrance requirements:* For master's, GMAT/GRE, essays; recommendation letters; undergraduate degree; interview. Additional exam requirements/recommendations for international students: Required—TOEFL (minimum score 100 iBT), IELTS (minimum score 7), PTE (minimum score 68). *Application deadline:* For fall admission, 10/6 for domestic and international students; for winter admission, 11/17 for domestic and international students; for spring admission, 1/3 priority date for domestic and international students; for summer admission, 3/9 for domestic and international students. Application fee: $150. Electronic applications accepted. *Expenses:* $59,616. *Financial support:* In 2017–18, 273 students received support. Career-related internships or fieldwork, institutionally sponsored loans, and scholarships/grants available. Financial award application deadline: 4/1; financial award applicants required to submit FAFSA. *Faculty research:* Corporate finance, information systems, digital marketing, asset pricing, sports management. *Unit head:* Brian Mitchell, Associate Dean, 404-727-4824, Fax: 404-712-9648, E-mail: brian.mitchell@emory.edu. *Application contact:* Julie Barefoot, Associate Dean, 404-727-6311, Fax: 404-727-4612, E-mail: mbaadmissions@emory.edu.
Website: http://www.goizueta.emory.edu

Florida International University, Chapman Graduate School of Business, Hollo School of Real Estate, Miami, FL 33199. Offers international real estate (MS). *Program availability:* Part-time, evening/weekend. *Faculty:* 5 full-time (1 woman), 4 part-time/adjunct (2 women). *Students:* 82 full-time (32 women), 7 part-time (3 women); includes 56 minority (10 Black or African American, non-Hispanic/Latino; 2 Asian, non-Hispanic/Latino; 42 Hispanic/Latino; 2 Two or more races, non-Hispanic/Latino), 15 international. Average age 33. 138 applicants, 60% accepted, 56 enrolled. In 2017, 83 master's awarded. *Entrance requirements:* For master's, GMAT or GRE, letter of intent; resume. Additional exam requirements/recommendations for international students: Required—TOEFL (minimum score 550 paper-based; 80 iBT) or IELTS (minimum score 6.5). *Application deadline:* For fall admission, 4/1 for domestic and international students. Application fee: $30. Electronic applications accepted. *Expenses:* Contact institution. *Financial support:* Institutionally sponsored loans and scholarships/grants available. Financial award application deadline: 3/1; financial award applicants required to submit FAFSA. *Faculty research:* International real estate, real estate investments, commercial real estate. *Unit head:* Eli Beracha, Director, 305-779-7898, E-mail: eli.beracha@fiu.edu. *Application contact:* Isabel Lopez, Associate Director for Academic Support Services, 305-348-4198, E-mail: isabel.lopez@fiu.edu.

Georgetown University, Graduate School of Arts and Sciences, School of Continuing Studies, Washington, DC 20057. Offers American studies (MALS); applied intelligence (MPS); Catholic studies (MALS); classical civilizations (MALS); emergency and disaster management (MPS); ethics and the professions (MALS); global strategic communications (MPS); hospitality management (MPS); human resources management (MPS); humanities (MALS); individualized study (MALS); integrated marketing communications (MPS); international affairs (MALS); Islam and Muslim-Christian relations (MALS); journalism (MPS); liberal studies (DLS); literature and society (MALS); medieval and early modern European studies (MALS); public relations and corporate communications (MPS); real estate (MPS); religious studies (MALS); social and public policy (MALS); sports industry management (MPS); systems engineering management (MPS); technology management (MPS); the theory and practice of American democracy (MALS); urban and regional planning (MPS); visual culture (MALS). MPS in systems engineering management offered jointly with Stevens Institute of Technology. *Entrance requirements:* Additional exam requirements/recommendations for international students: Required—TOEFL.

The George Washington University, School of Business, Program in Walkable Urban Real Estate Development, Washington, DC 20052. Offers Professional Certificate. *Students:* 2 applicants, 100% accepted. In 2017, 2 Professional Certificates awarded. *Expenses:* Tuition: Full-time $28,800; part-time $1655 per credit hour. *Required fees:* $45; $2.75 per credit hour. *Unit head:* Robert Valero, Executive Director, 202-994-0920, Fax: 202-994-5966, E-mail: rjvalero@gwu.edu. *Application contact:* Christopher Storer, Executive Director, Graduate Admissions, 202-994-1212, E-mail: gwmba@gwu.edu.

Georgia State University, J. Mack Robinson College of Business, Department of Real Estate, Atlanta, GA 30302-3083. Offers hotel real estate (MBA); real estate (MBA, MS, PhD, Certificate). *Program availability:* Part-time, evening/weekend. *Faculty:* 2 full-time (1 woman). *Students:* 11 full-time (3 women); includes 6 minority (4 Black or African American, non-Hispanic/Latino; 1 Asian, non-Hispanic/Latino; 1 Two or more races, non-Hispanic/Latino), 2 international. Average age 31. 29 applicants, 45% accepted, 3 enrolled. In 2017, 18 master's awarded. *Entrance requirements:* For master's, GRE or GMAT, transcripts from all institutions attended, resume, essays; for doctorate, GRE or GMAT, three letters of recommendation, personal statement, transcripts from all institutions attended, resume. Additional exam requirements/recommendations for international students: Required—TOEFL (minimum score 610 paper-based; 101 iBT), IELTS (minimum score 7). *Application deadline:* For fall admission, 5/1 priority date for

domestic students, 2/1 priority date for international students; for spring admission, 9/15 priority date for domestic students, 4/1 priority date for international students. Applications are processed on a rolling basis. Application fee: $50. Electronic applications accepted. *Expenses:* Tuition, state resident: full-time $7020. Tuition, nonresident: full-time $22,518. *Required fees:* $2128. Tuition and fees vary according to degree level and program. *Financial support:* Research assistantships, teaching assistantships, scholarships/grants, and unspecified assistantships available. *Faculty research:* International real estate investments, corporate real estate, capital formation, consumer behavior applied to real estate, real estate development. *Unit head:* Dr. Gerald D. Gay, Professor of Finance/Interim Chair of the Department of Real Estate, 404-413-7720, Fax: 404-413-7736. *Application contact:* Toby McChesney, Assistant Dean for Graduate Recruiting and Student Services, 404-413-7167, Fax: 404-413-7162, E-mail: rcbgradadmissions@gsu.edu.
Website: http://realestate.robinson.gsu.edu/

Instituto Centroamericano de Administración de Empresas, Graduate Programs, La Garita, Costa Rica. Offers agribusiness management (MIAM); business administration (EMBA); finance (MBA); real estate management (MGREM); sustainable development (MBA); technology (MBA). *Degree requirements:* For master's, comprehensive exam, essay. *Entrance requirements:* For master's, GMAT or GRE General Test, fluency in Spanish, interview, letters of recommendation, minimum 1 year of work experience. Additional exam requirements/recommendations for international students: Recommended—TOEFL. Electronic applications accepted. *Faculty research:* Competitiveness, production.

Johns Hopkins University, Carey Business School, MS in Real Estate and Infrastructure Program, Baltimore, MD 21218. Offers MS. *Program availability:* Part-time, evening/weekend. *Faculty:* 93 full-time (33 women), 45 part-time/adjunct (11 women). *Students:* 19 full-time (5 women), 53 part-time (15 women); includes 20 minority (11 Black or African American, non-Hispanic/Latino; 6 Asian, non-Hispanic/Latino; 2 Hispanic/Latino; 1 Two or more races, non-Hispanic/Latino), 15 international. Average age 30. 84 applicants, 89% accepted, 35 enrolled. In 2017, 66 master's awarded. *Degree requirements:* For master's, 36 credits. *Entrance requirements:* For master's, GMAT or GRE. Additional exam requirements/recommendations for international students: Required—TOEFL, IELTS. *Application deadline:* For fall admission, 5/1 for domestic and international students. Applications are processed on a rolling basis. Application fee: $100. Electronic applications accepted. *Expenses:* $66,500 (full-time); $1,330 per credit (part-time). *Financial support:* In 2017–18, 37 students received support. Scholarships/grants available. Support available to part-time students. Financial award application deadline: 4/15; financial award applicants required to submit FAFSA. *Faculty research:* Real estate markets and investment, retail businesses and product differentiation, spatial competition in cities, structural modeling and estimation. *Unit head:* Dr. Kevin Frick, Vice Dean of Education, 410-234-9272, E-mail: kfrick@jhu.edu. *Application contact:* Office of Admissions, 410-234-9220, Fax: 443-529-1554, E-mail: carey.admissions@jhu.edu.
Website: http://carey.jhu.edu/academics/master-of-science/ms-in-real-estate-infrastructure/

Longwood University, College of Graduate and Professional Studies, College of Business and Economics, Farmville, VA 23909. Offers general business (MBA); real estate (MBA); retail management (MBA). *Accreditation:* AACSB. *Program availability:* Part-time, online only, 100% online. *Degree requirements:* For master's, internship. *Entrance requirements:* For master's, GMAT or GRE, personal essay, 3 recommendations, official transcripts from all colleges and universities attended. Additional exam requirements/recommendations for international students: Required—TOEFL (minimum score 570 paper-based), IELTS (minimum score 6.5). Electronic applications accepted. *Expenses:* Contact institution.

Marquette University, Graduate School of Management, Department of Economics, Milwaukee, WI 53201-1881. Offers business economics (MSAE); financial economics (MSAE); international economics (MSAE); marketing research (MSAE); real estate economics (MSAE). *Program availability:* Part-time, evening/weekend. *Degree requirements:* For master's, comprehensive exam, professional project. *Entrance requirements:* For master's, GMAT or GRE General Test. Additional exam requirements/recommendations for international students: Required—TOEFL, IELTS, PTE. Electronic applications accepted. *Faculty research:* Monetary and fiscal policy in open economy, housing and regional migration, political economy of taxation and state/local government.

Massachusetts Institute of Technology, School of Architecture and Planning, Center for Real Estate, Cambridge, MA 02139. Offers real estate development (MSRED). *Degree requirements:* For master's, thesis. *Entrance requirements:* For master's, GMAT or GRE General Test. Additional exam requirements/recommendations for international students: Required—TOEFL, IELTS. Electronic applications accepted. *Faculty research:* Methods, urban economics, entrepreneurship, strategic planning, housing, leadership development, international housing economics and finance, mortgage securitization, innovation, big data, the local tax implications of inefficient land use, post-war neighborhood decline, the supply of workplace flexibility, LinkedIn economic graph.

Monmouth University, Graduate Studies, Leon Hess Business School, West Long Branch, NJ 07764-1898. Offers accounting (MBA, Certificate); business administration (MBA); finance (MBA); management (MBA); marketing (MBA); real estate (MBA). *Accreditation:* AACSB. *Program availability:* Part-time, evening/weekend. *Faculty:* 20 full-time (4 women), 8 part-time/adjunct (0 women). *Students:* 101 full-time (55 women), 107 part-time (44 women); includes 19 minority (3 Black or African American, non-Hispanic/Latino; 6 Asian, non-Hispanic/Latino; 6 Hispanic/Latino; 1 Native Hawaiian or other Pacific Islander, non-Hispanic/Latino; 3 Two or more races, non-Hispanic/Latino), 13 international. Average age 30. In 2017, 61 master's, 1 other advanced degree awarded. *Degree requirements:* For master's, capstone course. *Entrance requirements:* For master's, GMAT or GRE, current resume; essay (500 words or less). Additional exam requirements/recommendations for international students: Required—TOEFL (minimum score 550 paper-based; 79 iBT), IELTS (minimum score 6), Michigan English Language Assessment Battery (minimum score 77) or Certificate of Advanced English (minimum score 160). *Application deadline:* For fall admission, 7/15 priority date for domestic students, 6/1 for international students; for spring admission, 12/1 priority date for domestic students, 11/1 for international students; for summer admission, 5/1 for domestic students. Applications are processed on a rolling basis. Application fee: $50. Electronic applications accepted. *Expenses:* Tuition: Full-time $21,366; part-time $7122 per credit. *Required fees:* $700; $175 per term. *Financial support:* In 2017–18, 42 students received support. Institutionally sponsored loans, scholarships/grants, and unspecified assistantships available. Support available to part-time students. Financial award applicants required to submit FAFSA. *Faculty research:* Information technology and marketing, behavioral research in accounting, human resources, management of technology. *Unit head:* Dr. Susan Gupta, MBA Program Director, 732-571-3639, Fax: 732-263-5517, E-mail: sgupta@monmouth.edu. *Application contact:* Laurie Kuhn, Associate Director of Graduate Admission, 732-571-3452, Fax: 732-263-5123, E-mail: gradadm@monmouth.edu.
Website: https://www.monmouth.edu/business-school/leon-hess-business-school.aspx
See Display on page 115 and Close-Up on page 177.

Real Estate

New York University, School of Professional Studies, Schack Institute of Real Estate, Program in Real Estate, New York, NY 10012-1019. Offers real estate (MS), including finance and investment, real estate asset management. *Program availability:* Part-time, evening/weekend. *Students:* 182 full-time (72 women), 297 part-time (60 women); includes 67 minority (5 Black or African American, non-Hispanic/Latino; 37 Asian, non-Hispanic/Latino; 21 Hispanic/Latino; 1 Native Hawaiian or other Pacific Islander, non-Hispanic/Latino; 3 Two or more races, non-Hispanic/Latino), 158 international. Average age 28. 267 applicants, 67% accepted, 96 enrolled. In 2017, 330 master's awarded. *Degree requirements:* For master's, thesis, capstone project. *Entrance requirements:* For master's, GRE or GMAT (only upon request), bachelor's degree, resume with relevant professional work, internship or volunteer experience, two letters of recommendation, statement of purpose. Additional exam requirements/recommendations for international students: Required—TOEFL (minimum score 600 paper-based; 100 iBT), IELTS (minimum score 7). *Application deadline:* For fall admission, 2/1 priority date for domestic and international students; for spring admission, 10/15 priority date for domestic students, 8/15 priority date for international students; for summer admission, 5/1 priority date for domestic students, 1/15 priority date for international students. Applications are processed on a rolling basis. Application fee: $150. Electronic applications accepted. *Expenses:* $20,244 per term. *Financial support:* Fellowships, career-related internships or fieldwork, Federal Work-Study, scholarships/grants, and health care benefits available. Support available to part-time students. Financial award application deadline: 6/30; financial award applicants required to submit FAFSA. *Unit head:* Sam Chandan, Associate Dean/Chair/Clinical Professor, 212-992-3335. *Application contact:* Office of Admissions, 212-998-7100, E-mail: sps.gradadmissions@nyu.edu.
Website: http://www.sps.nyu.edu/content/scps/academics/departments/schack/academic-offerings/graduate.html

New York University, School of Professional Studies, Schack Institute of Real Estate, Program in Real Estate Development, New York, NY 10012-1019. Offers real estate development (MS), including global real estate, sustainable development, the business of development. *Program availability:* Part-time, evening/weekend. *Students:* 78 full-time (26 women), 140 part-time (35 women); includes 34 minority (8 Black or African American, non-Hispanic/Latino; 1 American Indian or Alaska Native, non-Hispanic/Latino; 7 Asian, non-Hispanic/Latino; 14 Hispanic/Latino; 1 Native Hawaiian or other Pacific Islander, non-Hispanic/Latino; 3 Two or more races, non-Hispanic/Latino), 51 international. Average age 28. 176 applicants, 67% accepted, 68 enrolled. In 2017, 126 master's awarded. *Degree requirements:* For master's, thesis, capstone project. *Entrance requirements:* For master's, GRE or GMAT (only upon request), bachelor's degree, resume with relevant professional work, internship or volunteer experience, two letters of recommendation, statement of purpose. Additional exam requirements/recommendations for international students: Required—TOEFL (minimum score 600 paper-based; 100 iBT), IELTS (minimum score 7). *Application deadline:* For fall admission, 2/1 priority date for domestic and international students; for spring admission, 10/15 priority date for domestic students, 8/15 priority date for international students; for summer admission, 5/1 priority date for domestic students, 1/15 priority date for international students. Applications are processed on a rolling basis. Application fee: $150. Electronic applications accepted. *Expenses:* $20,244 per term. *Financial support:* Fellowships, career-related internships or fieldwork, Federal Work-Study, scholarships/grants, and health care benefits available. Support available to part-time students. Financial award application deadline: 6/30; financial award applicants required to submit FAFSA. *Unit head:* Sam Chandan, Associate Dean/Chair/Clinical Professor, 212-992-3335. *Application contact:* Office of Admissions, 212-998-7100, E-mail: sps.gradadmissions@nyu.edu.
Website: http://www.sps.nyu.edu/academics/departments/schack/academic-offerings/graduate/ms-in-real-estate-development.html

Northwestern University, The Graduate School, Kellogg School of Management, Management Programs, Evanston, IL 60208. Offers accounting information and management (MBA, PhD); analytical finance (MBA); business administration (MBA); decision sciences (MBA); entrepreneurship and innovation (MBA); finance (MBA, PhD); health enterprise management (MBA); human resources management (MBA); international business (MBA); management and organizations (MBA, PhD); management and organizations and sociology (PhD); management and strategy (MBA); management studies (MS); managerial analytics (MBA); managerial economics (MBA); managerial economics and strategy (PhD); marketing (MBA, PhD); marketing management (MBA); media management (MBA); operations management (MBA, PhD); real estate (MBA); social enterprise at Kellogg (MBA); JD/MBA. *Program availability:* Part-time, evening/weekend. Terminal master's awarded for partial completion of doctoral program. *Degree requirements:* For doctorate, thesis/dissertation, 2 years of coursework, qualifying (field) exam and candidacy, summer research papers and presentations to faculty, proposal defense, final exam/defense. *Entrance requirements:* For master's, GMAT, GRE, interview, 2 letters of recommendation, college transcripts, resume, essays, Kellogg honor code; for doctorate, GMAT, GRE, statement of purpose, transcripts, 2 letters of recommendation, resume, interview. Additional exam requirements/recommendations for international students: Required—TOEFL, IELTS. Electronic applications accepted. *Expenses:* Contact institution. *Faculty research:* Business cycles and international finance, health policy, networks, non-market strategy, consumer psychology.

Pacific States University, College of Business, Los Angeles, CA 90010. Offers accounting (MBA, Certificate); beauty management (MBA); finance (MBA); international business (MBA); management of information technology (MBA); project management (Certificate); real estate management (MBA). *Program availability:* Part-time, evening/weekend, online learning. *Entrance requirements:* For master's, minimum undergraduate GPA of 2.5 during last 90 quarter units of course work, bachelor's degree in business administration or economics. Additional exam requirements/recommendations for international students: Required—TOEFL (minimum score 500 paper-based; 61 iBT), IELTS (minimum score 5.5). *Application deadline:* For fall admission, 9/1 priority date for domestic students, 8/1 priority date for international students; for winter admission, 12/1 priority date for domestic students, 11/1 priority date for international students; for spring admission, 3/1 priority date for domestic students, 2/1 priority date for international students; for summer admission, 6/1 priority date for domestic students, 5/1 priority date for international students. Applications are processed on a rolling basis. Application fee: $100. *Expenses: Tuition:* Part-time $380 per unit. *Financial support:* Scholarships/grants available. Financial award applicants required to submit FAFSA. *Unit head:* Chase C. Rhee, MBA Program Administrator, 323-731-2383 Ext. 208, Fax: 323-731-7276, E-mail: ccrhee@psuca.edu. *Application contact:* Maawiya Ayeva, Director of Admissions, 323-731-2383 Ext. 204, Fax: 323-731-7276, E-mail: admissions@psuca.edu.

Pontificia Universidad Catolica Madre y Maestra, Graduate School, Faculty of Social and Administrative Sciences, Santiago, Dominican Republic. Offers business administration (MBA), including business development, finance, international business, management skills (M Mgmt, MBA), marketing, operations, strategic cost management, strategy, tourist destination planning and management; law (LL M), including civil law, corporate business law, criminal law, international relations, real estate law; management (M Mgmt), including higher financial management, insurance program

administration, management skills (M Mgmt, MBA); psychology (MA), including clinical child and adolescent psychology, forensic psychology; strategic human resources (EMBA).

Portland State University, Graduate Studies, College of Urban and Public Affairs, Nohad A. Toulan School of Urban Studies and Planning, Portland, OR 97207-0751. Offers applied social demography (Certificate); energy policy and management (Certificate); real estate development (Certificate); sustainable food systems (Certificate); transportation (Certificate); urban design (Certificate); urban studies (PhD); urban studies and planning (MRED, MURP, MUS); urban studies: regional science (PhD). *Program availability:* Part-time, evening/weekend. *Faculty:* 16 full-time (8 women), 10 part-time/adjunct (3 women). *Students:* 93 full-time (46 women), 53 part-time (24 women); includes 28 minority (4 Black or African American, non-Hispanic/Latino; 6 Asian, non-Hispanic/Latino; 11 Hispanic/Latino; 7 Two or more races, non-Hispanic/Latino), 15 international. Average age 33. 163 applicants, 60% accepted, 56 enrolled. In 2017, 35 master's, 7 doctorates awarded. *Degree requirements:* For doctorate, comprehensive exam, thesis/dissertation, residency. *Entrance requirements:* For doctorate, GRE General Test, minimum GPA of 2.75, statement of purpose, 3 letters of recommendation, resume/curriculum vitae. Additional exam requirements/recommendations for international students: Required—TOEFL (minimum score 550 paper-based; 80 iBT). *Application deadline:* For fall admission, 1/15 for domestic and international students. Application fee: $65. Electronic applications accepted. *Expenses:* Tuition, state resident: full-time $14,436; part-time $401 per credit. Tuition, nonresident: full-time $21,780; part-time $605 per credit. *Required fees:* $1380; $22 per credit. $119 per quarter. One-time fee: $325. Tuition and fees vary according to program. *Financial support:* In 2017–18, 44 students received support, including 26 research assistantships with full and partial tuition reimbursements available (averaging $10,070 per year); career-related internships or fieldwork, Federal Work-Study, scholarships/grants, and unspecified assistantships also available. Support available to part-time students. Financial award application deadline: 3/1; financial award applicants required to submit FAFSA. *Total annual research expenditures:* $5.1 million. *Unit head:* Dr. Connie Ozawa, Director, 503-725-5126, E-mail: ozawac@pdx.edu. *Application contact:* Erin Looney, Office Coordinator, 503-725-4045, Fax: 503-725-8770, E-mail: bmangan@pdx.edu.
Website: https://www.pdx.edu/cupa/

Portland State University, Graduate Studies, The School of Business, Master of Real Estate Development Program, Portland, OR 97207-0751. Offers MRED. *Students:* 21 full-time (7 women), 25 part-time (10 women); includes 6 minority (1 Black or African American, non-Hispanic/Latino; 3 Asian, non-Hispanic/Latino; 2 Hispanic/Latino), 3 international. Average age 32. 37 applicants, 89% accepted, 24 enrolled. In 2017, 21 master's awarded. *Degree requirements:* For master's, real estate development workshop. *Entrance requirements:* For master's, GMAT or GRE, resume, statement of purpose, 2 professional references, transcripts. Additional exam requirements/recommendations for international students: Required—TOEFL (minimum score 550 paper-based; 80 iBT). *Application deadline:* For fall admission, 5/1 priority date for domestic and international students; for spring admission, 1/15 priority date for domestic and international students. Application fee: $65. Electronic applications accepted. *Expenses:* Contact institution. *Financial support:* Career-related internships or fieldwork, Federal Work-Study, scholarships/grants, and unspecified assistantships available. *Unit head:* Julie Gibson, Executive Director, 503-725-5109, E-mail: jcgibson@pdx.edu. *Application contact:* Gerard Mildner, Academic Director, 503-725-5175, E-mail: mildnerg@pdx.edu.
Website: https://www.pdx.edu/realestate/

Pratt Institute, School of Architecture, Program in Real Estate Practice, Brooklyn, NY 11205-3899. Offers MS. *Program availability:* Part-time, evening/weekend. *Students:* 10 full-time (7 women); includes 2 minority (1 Black or African American, non-Hispanic/Latino; 1 Two or more races, non-Hispanic/Latino), 6 international. Average age 28. 27 applicants, 89% accepted, 9 enrolled. *Degree requirements:* For master's, thesis optional. *Entrance requirements:* For master's, bachelor's degree in architecture, business, construction management, engineering, or interior design; 500-word statement of purpose. Additional exam requirements/recommendations for international students: Required—TOEFL (minimum score 550 paper-based; 79 iBT), IELTS (minimum score 6.5), PTE. *Application deadline:* For fall admission, 1/5 for domestic students. Application fee: $50 ($90 for international students). Electronic applications accepted. *Expenses: Tuition:* Full-time $30,834. *Required fees:* $1974. *Financial support:* Career-related internships or fieldwork, Federal Work-Study, institutionally sponsored loans, scholarships/grants, health care benefits, and unspecified assistantships available. Support available to part-time students. Financial award application deadline: 2/1; financial award applicants required to submit FAFSA. *Unit head:* Thomas Hanrahan, Dean, 718-399-4304, Fax: 718-399-4315, E-mail: hanrahan@pratt.edu. *Application contact:* Natalie Capannelli, Director of Graduate Admissions, 718-636-3551, Fax: 718-399-4242, E-mail: ncapanne@pratt.edu.
Website: http://www.pratt.edu/academics/architecture/real-estate-practice/

Roosevelt University, Graduate Division, Walter E. Heller College of Business, School of Real Estate, Chicago, IL 60605. Offers real estate (MS). *Program availability:* Part-time, evening/weekend. *Students:* 3 full-time (1 woman), 41 part-time (19 women); includes 25 minority (20 Black or African American, non-Hispanic/Latino; 1 Asian, non-Hispanic/Latino; 2 Hispanic/Latino; 2 Two or more races, non-Hispanic/Latino), 3 international. Average age 36. 24 applicants, 100% accepted, 16 enrolled. In 2017, 17 master's awarded. *Application deadline:* Applications are processed on a rolling basis. Application fee: $40. Electronic applications accepted. *Financial support:* Career-related internships or fieldwork, scholarships/grants, and unspecified assistantships available. *Unit head:* Collette English Dixon, Program Director, 312-341-3767, E-mail: cenglishdixon@roosevelt.edu. *Application contact:* Michael Conwell, Graduate Admission Counselor, 312-281-3250, E-mail: mconwell@roosevelt.edu.
Website: https://www.roosevelt.edu/

Rutgers University–Newark, Rutgers Business School–Newark and New Brunswick, Program in Real Estate and Logistics, Newark, NJ 07102. Offers MRE.

Southern Methodist University, Cox School of Business, MBA Program, Dallas, TX 75275. Offers accounting (MBA, PMBA); business administration (EMBA); finance (MBA); financial statement analysis (PMBA); general business (MBA); information technology and operations management (MBA); management (MBA); marketing (MBA); real estate (MBA); strategy (MBA); strategy and entrepreneurship (MBA); JD/MBA; MA/MBA. *Program availability:* Part-time, evening/weekend. *Entrance requirements:* For master's, GMAT. Additional exam requirements/recommendations for international students: Required—TOEFL. Electronic applications accepted. *Expenses:* Contact institution. *Faculty research:* Corporate finance, financial reporting, modeling consumer decision-making, competition between national brands and store brands, institutional determinants of firms' strategy.

Syracuse University, Martin J. Whitman School of Management, Master of Business Administration Program, Syracuse, NY 13244. Offers accounting (MBA); business analytics (MBA); entrepreneurship (MBA); marketing management (MBA); real estate (MBA); supply chain management (MBA); JD/MBA. *Program availability:* Part-time, 100% online. *Students:* 22 full-time (9 women), 495 part-time (147 women); includes

182 minority (81 Black or African American, non-Hispanic/Latino; 3 American Indian or Alaska Native, non-Hispanic/Latino; 42 Asian, non-Hispanic/Latino; 52 Hispanic/Latino; 4 Native Hawaiian or other Pacific Islander, non-Hispanic/Latino). Average age 32. 1,086 applicants, 73% accepted, 516 enrolled. In 2017, 84 master's awarded. *Entrance requirements:* For master's, GMAT or GRE, resume, essay, 5-minute video interview, two letters of recommendation, transcripts (unofficial). Additional exam requirements/recommendations for international students: Required—TOEFL (minimum score 100 iBT), IELTS (minimum score 7), PTE (minimum score 68). *Application deadline:* For fall admission, 11/30 for domestic students, 11/30 priority date for international students; for winter admission, 1/1 for domestic students, 1/1 priority date for international students; for spring admission, 2/15 for domestic and international students; for summer admission, 4/19 for domestic students. Application fee: $75. Electronic applications accepted. *Expenses:* Contact institution. *Financial support:* In 2017–18, 22 students received support. Merit scholarships available. Financial award application deadline: 2/15. *Faculty research:* Data analysis, economics of international business, financial markets and institutions, operations management, supply chain management. *Unit head:* Dr. Alexander McKelvie, Associate Dean for Undergraduate and Full-time Master's Education, 315-443-7252, E-mail: mckelvie@syr.edu. *Application contact:* Shri Ramakrishnan, Assistant Director, Graduate Recruitment, 315-443-3497, Fax: 315-443-9517, E-mail: busgrad@syr.edu.
Website: http://whitman.syr.edu/ftmba/

Texas A&M University, Mays Business School, Department of Finance, College Station, TX 77843. Offers finance (MS); financial management (MFM); land economics and real estate (MRE); management information systems (MS). *Faculty:* 21. *Students:* 235 full-time (72 women), 10 part-time (4 women); includes 43 minority (2 Black or African American, non-Hispanic/Latino; 2 American Indian or Alaska Native, non-Hispanic/Latino; 11 Asian, non-Hispanic/Latino; 24 Hispanic/Latino; 4 Two or more races, non-Hispanic/Latino), 19 international. Average age 24. 179 applicants, 33% accepted, 50 enrolled. In 2017, 163 master's awarded. Terminal master's awarded for partial completion of doctoral program. *Degree requirements:* For master's, comprehensive exam. *Entrance requirements:* For master's, GMAT or GRE. Additional exam requirements/recommendations for international students: Required—TOEFL (minimum score 550 paper-based; 80 iBT), IELTS (minimum score 6), PTE (minimum score 53). *Application deadline:* For fall admission, 4/7 for domestic students. Applications are processed on a rolling basis. Application fee: $50 ($90 for international students). Electronic applications accepted. *Expenses:* Contact institution. *Financial support:* In 2017–18, 165 students received support, including 14 fellowships with tuition reimbursements available (averaging $2,232 per year), 23 research assistantships with tuition reimbursements available (averaging $10,754 per year), 12 teaching assistantships with tuition reimbursements available (averaging $3,926 per year); career-related internships or fieldwork, institutionally sponsored loans, scholarships/grants, traineeships, health care benefits, tuition waivers (full and partial), and unspecified assistantships also available. Support available to part-time students. Financial award application deadline: 3/15; financial award applicants required to submit FAFSA. *Unit head:* Dr. Sorin Sorescu, Head, 979-458-0380, Fax: 979-845-3884, E-mail: smsorescu@mays.tamu.edu. *Application contact:* Angela G. Degelman, Program Coordinator/Graduate Academic Advisor, 979-845-4858, Fax: 979-845-3884, E-mail: adegelman@mays.tamu.edu.
Website: http://mays.tamu.edu/finc/

Thomas Jefferson University, College of Architecture and the Built Environment, Program in Real Estate Development, Philadelphia, PA 19107. Offers MS.

Universidad Iberoamericana, Graduate School, Santo Domingo D.N., Dominican Republic. Offers business administration (MBA, PMBA); constitutional law (LL M); dentistry (DMD); educational management (MA); integrated marketing communication (MA); psychopedagogical intervention (M Ed); real estate law (LL M); strategic management of human talent (MM).

University at Buffalo, the State University of New York, Graduate School, School of Architecture and Planning, Department of Urban and Regional Planning, Buffalo, NY 12414. Offers community health and food systems (MUP); economic development (MUP); environment/land use (MUP); historic preservation (MUP, Certificate); neighborhood/community development (MUP); real estate development (MSRED); urban and regional planning (PhD); urban design (MUP); JD/MUP; M Arch/MUP. *Accreditation:* ACSP. *Program availability:* Part-time. *Faculty:* 13 full-time (6 women), 12 part-time/adjunct (3 women). *Students:* 76 full-time (27 women), 20 part-time (9 women); includes 17 minority (9 Black or African American, non-Hispanic/Latino; 5 Hispanic/Latino; 3 Two or more races, non-Hispanic/Latino), 20 international. Average age 27. 196 applicants, 20% accepted, 32 enrolled. In 2017, 35 master's, 1 doctorate, 5 other advanced degrees awarded. *Degree requirements:* For master's, thesis or alternative, project; for doctorate, comprehensive exam, thesis/dissertation. *Entrance requirements:* For master's, resume, three letters of recommendation, personal statement, transcripts; for doctorate, GRE, transcripts, three letters of recommendation, resume, research statement, writing sample. Additional exam requirements/recommendations for international students: Required—TOEFL (minimum score 79 iBT), IELTS (minimum score 6.5). *Application deadline:* For fall admission, 3/1 priority date for domestic and international students; for spring admission, 10/31 priority date for domestic students, 10/1 priority date for international students. Applications are processed on a rolling basis. Application fee: $75. Electronic applications accepted. *Expenses:* $13,382. *Financial support:* In 2017–18, 45 students received support, including 3 fellowships with full tuition reimbursements available (averaging $15,600 per year), 2 research assistantships with partial tuition reimbursements available (averaging $13,390 per year), 15 teaching assistantships with partial tuition reimbursements available (averaging $4,800 per year); career-related internships or fieldwork, Federal Work-Study, institutionally sponsored loans, scholarships/grants, health care benefits, and unspecified assistantships also available. Financial award application deadline: 3/1; financial award applicants required to submit FAFSA. *Faculty research:* Economic and international development, environmental and land use planning, GIS and spatial analysis, urban design and physical planning, neighborhood planning and community development, historic preservation. *Total annual research expenditures:* $1.3 million. *Unit head:* Dr. Daniel B. Hess, Professor and Chair, 716-829-3671 Ext. 109, Fax: 716-829-3256, E-mail: dbhess@buffalo.edu. *Application contact:* Donna Rogalski, Department Secretary, 716-829-3671, Fax: 716-829-3256, E-mail: dmr1@buffalo.edu.
Website: http://www.ap.buffalo.edu/planning/

University of California, Berkeley, Graduate Division, Haas School of Business, PhD in Business Administration Program, Berkeley, CA 94720-1500. Offers accounting (PhD); business and public policy (PhD); finance (PhD); management of organizations (PhD); marketing (PhD); real estate (PhD). *Accreditation:* AACSB. *Students:* 72 full-time (20 women); includes 30 minority (26 Asian, non-Hispanic/Latino; 4 Hispanic/Latino). Average age 27. *Degree requirements:* For doctorate, comprehensive exam, thesis/dissertation, written preliminary exams, oral qualifying exam. *Entrance requirements:* For doctorate, GMAT or GRE, minimum GPA of 3.0 in undergraduate and graduate coursework. Additional exam requirements/recommendations for international students: Required—TOEFL (minimum score 570 paper-based; 70 iBT), IELTS (minimum score 7). *Application deadline:* For fall admission, 12/1 for domestic and international students.

Application fee: $105 ($125 for international students). Electronic applications accepted. *Expenses:* Contact institution. *Financial support:* Fellowships with tuition reimbursements, research assistantships with tuition reimbursements, teaching assistantships with tuition reimbursements, scholarships/grants, health care benefits, tuition waivers (full), unspecified assistantships, and transit passes, travel grants available. Financial award application deadline: 12/1. *Faculty research:* Accounting, business and public policy, entrepreneurship, finance, management of organizations, marketing, operations and information technology management, real estate. *Unit head:* Dr. Nicolae Garleanu, Director, 510-643-6349, Fax: 510-643-4255. *Application contact:* Melissa Hacker, Director, Student Affairs, 510-642-3944, Fax: 510-643-4255, E-mail: melhacker@haas.berkeley.edu.
Website: http://www.haas.berkeley.edu/Phd/

University of Central Florida, College of Business Administration, Dr. P. Phillips School of Real Estate, Orlando, FL 32816. Offers MSRE. *Program availability:* Part-time. *Students:* 13 part-time (3 women); includes 8 minority (2 Black or African American, non-Hispanic/Latino; 3 Asian, non-Hispanic/Latino; 2 Hispanic/Latino; 1 Two or more races, non-Hispanic/Latino). Average age 31. 25 applicants, 84% accepted, 13 enrolled. In 2017, 19 master's awarded. *Degree requirements:* For master's, capstone course. *Entrance requirements:* For master's, letters of recommendation, resume. Additional exam requirements/recommendations for international students: Required—TOEFL. *Application deadline:* For fall admission, 7/1 for domestic students. Application fee: $30. Electronic applications accepted. *Expenses:* Tuition, state resident: part-time $288.16 per credit hour. Tuition, nonresident: part-time $1073.31 per credit hour. Tuition and fees vary according to program. *Financial support:* Application deadline: 3/1; applicants required to submit FAFSA. *Unit head:* Dr. Ajai Singh, Chair and Director, 407-823-5756, Fax: 407-823-6676, E-mail: ajai.singh@ucf.edu. *Application contact:* Associate Director, Graduate Admissions, 407-823-2766, Fax: 407-823-6442, E-mail: gradadmissions@ucf.edu.
Website: http://business.ucf.edu/degree/professional-ms-real-estate/

University of Denver, Daniels College of Business, Franklin L. Burns School of Real Estate and Construction Management, Denver, CO 80208. Offers real estate and the built environment (MBA, MS). *Program availability:* Part-time, evening/weekend. *Faculty:* 7 full-time (1 woman), 7 part-time/adjunct (1 woman). *Students:* 21 full-time (6 women), 54 part-time (12 women); includes 16 minority (2 Black or African American, non-Hispanic/Latino; 2 Asian, non-Hispanic/Latino; 8 Hispanic/Latino; 4 Two or more races, non-Hispanic/Latino), 4 international. Average age 33. 43 applicants, 79% accepted, 19 enrolled. In 2017, 39 master's awarded. *Entrance requirements:* For master's, GRE General Test or GMAT, bachelor's degree, transcripts, essays, resume, interview. Additional exam requirements/recommendations for international students: Required—TOEFL (minimum score 570 paper-based; 88 iBT), TWE. *Application deadline:* For fall admission, 11/15 priority date for domestic and international students; for spring admission, 10/1 priority date for domestic and international students. Applications are processed on a rolling basis. Application fee: $100. Electronic applications accepted. *Expenses:* $47,823 per year full-time; $1,320 per credit. *Financial support:* In 2017–18, 57 students received support, including 1 teaching assistantship with tuition reimbursement available (averaging $748 per year); Federal Work-Study, institutionally sponsored loans, scholarships/grants, and unspecified assistantships also available. Support available to part-time students. Financial award application deadline: 2/15; financial award applicants required to submit FAFSA. *Unit head:* Dr. Barbara Jackson, Associate Professor and Director, 303-871-3470, Fax: 303-871-2971, E-mail: barbara.jackson@du.edu. *Application contact:* Ceci Smith, Assistant to the Director, 303-871-2145, E-mail: ceci.smith@du.edu.
Website: https://daniels.du.edu/burns-school/

University of Florida, Graduate School, Warrington College of Business Administration, Hough Graduate School of Business, Department of Finance, Insurance and Real Estate, Gainesville, FL 32611. Offers entrepreneurship (MS); finance (MS, PhD); financial services (Certificate); insurance (PhD); quantitative finance (PhD); real estate (MS); real estate and urban analysis (PhD); JD/MBA; JD/MS. Terminal master's awarded for partial completion of doctoral program. *Degree requirements:* For master's, comprehensive exam, thesis; for doctorate, comprehensive exam, thesis/dissertation. *Entrance requirements:* For master's, GMAT (minimum score of 465) or GRE General Test, minimum GPA of 3.0 for last 60 hours of undergraduate degree, work experience (preferred); for doctorate, GMAT (minimum score of 465) or GRE General Test, minimum GPA of 3.0. Additional exam requirements/recommendations for international students: Required—TOEFL (minimum score 550 paper-based; 80 iBT), IELTS (minimum score 6). Electronic applications accepted. *Faculty research:* Banking, empirical corporate finance, hedge funds.

University of Florida, Graduate School, Warrington College of Business Administration, Hough Graduate School of Business, Programs in Business Administration, Gainesville, FL 32611. Offers business administration (MA, MS, PhD); competitive strategy (MBA); finance (MBA); global management (MBA); Graham-Buffett security analysis (MBA); human resource management (MBA); information systems and operations management (MBA); international studies (MBA); management (MBA); real estate (MBA); JD/MBA; MBA/MS; MBA/PhD; MBA/Pharm D; MD/MBA. *Accreditation:* AACSB. *Program availability:* Part-time, evening/weekend, online learning. *Degree requirements:* For master's, capstone course. *Entrance requirements:* For master's and doctorate, GMAT (minimum score 465), minimum GPA of 3.0, interview. Additional exam requirements/recommendations for international students: Required—TOEFL (minimum score 550 paper-based; 80 iBT), IELTS (minimum score 6). Electronic applications accepted. *Faculty research:* Accounting, finance, insurance, management, real estate, urban analysis marketing.

University of Hawaii at Manoa, Office of Graduate Education, Shidler College of Business, Program in Business Administration, Honolulu, HI 96822. Offers Asian business studies (MBA); Chinese business studies (MBA); decision sciences (MBA); entrepreneurship (MBA); finance (MBA); finance and banking (MBA); human resources management (MBA); information management (MBA); information technology (MBA); international business (MBA); Japanese business studies (MBA); marketing (MBA); organizational behavior (MBA); organizational management (MBA); real estate (MBA); student-designed track (MBA). *Accreditation:* AACSB. *Program availability:* Part-time, evening/weekend. *Degree requirements:* For master's, thesis optional. *Entrance requirements:* For master's, GMAT, minimum GPA of 3.0. Additional exam requirements/recommendations for international students: Required—TOEFL (minimum score 600 paper-based; 100 iBT), IELTS (minimum score 7). *Expenses:* Contact institution.

University of Illinois at Chicago, Liautaud Graduate School of Business, Program in Real Estate, Chicago, IL 60607-7128. Offers MA.

University of Maryland, College Park, Academic Affairs, School of Architecture, Planning and Preservation, Program in Real Estate Development, College Park, MD 20742. Offers MRED.

University of Memphis, Graduate School, Fogelman College of Business and Economics, Program in Business Administration, Memphis, TN 38152. Offers accounting (MBA, PhD); business administration (IMBA); economics (PhD); executive

Real Estate

business administration (MBA); finance (PhD); management (PhD); marketing (MS); marketing and supply chain management (PhD); real estate development (MS); JD/MBA. *Accreditation:* AACSB. *Faculty:* 2 part-time/adjunct (0 women). *Students:* 166 full-time (76 women), 361 part-time (142 women); includes 161 minority (91 Black or African American, non-Hispanic/Latino; 51 Asian, non-Hispanic/Latino; 10 Hispanic/Latino; 9 Two or more races, non-Hispanic/Latino), 89 international. Average age 32. 263 applicants, 83% accepted, 157 enrolled. In 2017, 186 master's, 14 doctorates awarded. *Degree requirements:* For master's, comprehensive exam; for doctorate, comprehensive exam, thesis/dissertation. *Entrance requirements:* For master's, GMAT, resume; for doctorate, GMAT, interview, minimum GPA of 3.4, resume, letter of recommendation. Additional exam requirements/recommendations for international students: Required—TOEFL (minimum score 550 paper-based). *Application deadline:* For fall admission, 8/1 for domestic students; for spring admission, 12/1 for domestic students. Application fee: $35 ($60 for international students). *Financial support:* In 2017–18, 164 students received support, including 17 research assistantships with full tuition reimbursements available (averaging $53,750 per year), 13 teaching assistantships with full tuition reimbursements available (averaging $20,798 per year); career-related internships or fieldwork, Federal Work-Study, scholarships/grants, and unspecified assistantships also available. Financial award application deadline: 2/15; financial award applicants required to submit FAFSA. *Faculty research:* Competitive business strategy, finance microstructures, supply chain management innovations, health care economics, litigation risks and corporate audits. *Unit head:* Dr. Rajiv Grover, Dean, 901-678-3759, E-mail: rgrover@memphis.edu. *Application contact:* Dr. Carol V. Danehower, Associate Dean, 901-678-5402, Fax: 901-678-3579, E-mail: fcbegp@memphis.edu.
Website: https://web0.memphis.edu/gradcatalog/degreeprog/fcbe/fcbe.php

University of Miami, Graduate School, University of Miami School of Law, Coral Gables, FL 33146. Offers entertainment, arts, and sports law (LL M); estate planning (LL M); intensive English (LL M); international arbitration (LL M); international law (LL M), including general international law, inter-American law; law (JD); maritime law (LL M); real estate/property development (LL M); taxation (LL M); taxation of cross-border investment (LL M); the business of innovation, law and technology (BILT) (JD); U.S. and transnational law for foreign-trained lawyers (LL M); JD/LL M; JD/MA; JD/MBA; JD/MBA/LL M; JD/MD; JD/MM; JD/MPA; JD/MPH; JD/MPS; JD/MS Ed; JD/PhD. *Accreditation:* ABA. *Faculty:* 89 full-time (45 women), 115 part-time/adjunct (27 women). *Students:* 1,099 full-time (534 women), 93 part-time (48 women); includes 455 minority (63 Black or African American, non-Hispanic/Latino; 3 American Indian or Alaska Native, non-Hispanic/Latino; 25 Asian, non-Hispanic/Latino; 330 Hispanic/Latino; 1 Native Hawaiian or other Pacific Islander, non-Hispanic/Latino; 33 Two or more races, non-Hispanic/Latino), 53 international. 2,356 applicants, 59% accepted, 316 enrolled. *Entrance requirements:* For doctorate, LSAT, 2 letters of recommendation. Additional exam requirements/recommendations for international students: Required—TOEFL (minimum score 580 paper-based; 92 iBT), IELTS (minimum score 7). *Application deadline:* For fall admission, 7/31 for domestic and international students. Applications are processed on a rolling basis. Application fee: $60. Electronic applications accepted. *Expenses:* Contact institution. *Financial support:* Fellowships, research assistantships, career-related internships or fieldwork, Federal Work-Study, institutionally sponsored loans, scholarships/grants, and unspecified assistantships available. Financial award application deadline: 3/1; financial award applicants required to submit FAFSA. *Faculty research:* Energy/climate change, international finance, Internet law/law of electronic commerce, race/social justice, art law/cultural heritage law. *Unit head:* Michael Goodnight, Associate Dean of Admissions and Enrollment Management, 305-284-2527, Fax: 305-284-3084, E-mail: mgoodnig@law.miami.edu. *Application contact:* Therese Lambert, Director of Student Recruitment, 305-284-6746, Fax: 305-284-3084, E-mail: tlambert@law.miami.edu.
Website: http://www.law.miami.edu/

See Display on page 1510 and Close-Up on page 1527.

The University of North Carolina at Charlotte, Belk College of Business, Interdisciplinary Business Programs, Charlotte, NC 28223-0001. Offers mathematical finance (MS); real estate (MS, Graduate Certificate). *Program availability:* Part-time, evening/weekend. *Faculty:* 15 full-time (3 women), 2 part-time/adjunct (0 women). *Students:* 72 full-time (19 women), 61 part-time (17 women); includes 23 minority (8 Black or African American, non-Hispanic/Latino; 8 Asian, non-Hispanic/Latino; 5 Hispanic/Latino; 2 Two or more races, non-Hispanic/Latino), 59 international. Average age 26. 172 applicants, 73% accepted, 72 enrolled. In 2017, 49 master's awarded. *Degree requirements:* For master's, comprehensive exam (for some programs). *Entrance requirements:* For master's, GRE or GMAT, baccalaureate degree in related field with minimum GPA of 3.0 overall and in junior and senior years; transcript of all previous academic work; resume; recommendations; for Graduate Certificate, basic proficiency in using spreadsheet computer software, to be demonstrated by past project or certificate from completion of training course in Excel; previous coursework in financial management. Additional exam requirements/recommendations for international students: Required—TOEFL (minimum score 523 paper-based, 70 iBT) or IELTS (6.5). *Application deadline:* For fall admission, 3/1 priority date for domestic and international students; for spring admission, 10/1 priority date for domestic and international students; for summer admission, 4/1 priority date for domestic and international students. Applications are processed on a rolling basis. Application fee: $75. Electronic applications accepted. *Expenses:* Contact institution. *Financial support:* Research assistantships, teaching assistantships, career-related internships or fieldwork, scholarships/grants, and unspecified assistantships available. Support available to part-time students. Financial award application deadline: 3/1; financial award applicants required to submit FAFSA. *Unit head:* Dr. Steven Ott, Dean, 704-687-7577, Fax: 704-687-1393, E-mail: cob-dean@uncc.edu. *Application contact:* Kathy B. Giddings, Director of Graduate Admissions, 704-687-5503, Fax: 704-687-1668, E-mail: gradadm@uncc.edu.
Website: http://belkcollege.uncc.edu/

University of Pennsylvania, Wharton School, Real Estate Department, Philadelphia, PA 19104. Offers MBA, PhD. Terminal master's awarded for partial completion of doctoral program. *Degree requirements:* For doctorate, thesis/dissertation. *Entrance requirements:* For master's, GMAT; for doctorate, GRE General Test. *Faculty research:* Public economics and taxation economics and finance of real estate markets, economics of housing markets, real estate development.

University of San Diego, School of Business, Program in Real Estate, San Diego, CA 92110-2492. Offers MS, MBA/MSRE. *Program availability:* Part-time, evening/weekend. *Students:* 19 full-time (4 women), 7 part-time (0 women); includes 6 minority (1 Asian, non-Hispanic/Latino; 5 Hispanic/Latino). Average age 31. In 2017, 11 master's awarded. *Degree requirements:* For master's, capstone course. *Entrance requirements:* For master's, GMAT (minimum score of 550), minimum GPA of 3.0. Additional exam requirements/recommendations for international students: Required—TOEFL (minimum score 580 paper-based; 92 iBT), TWE. *Application deadline:* For fall admission, 11/1 priority date for domestic students. Applications are processed on a rolling basis. Application fee: $80. Electronic applications accepted. *Financial support:* In 2017–18, 12 students received support. Research assistantships, career-related internships or

fieldwork, Federal Work-Study, institutionally sponsored loans, and scholarships/grants available. Support available to part-time students. Financial award application deadline: 4/1; financial award applicants required to submit FAFSA. *Faculty research:* Commercial real estate investment, commercial real estate capital markets, sustainable real estate, housing affordability, workplace trends. *Unit head:* Dr. Charles Tu, Academic Director, Real Estate Program, 619-260-5942, E-mail: tuc@sandiego.edu. *Application contact:* Monica Mahon, Associate Director of Graduate Admissions, 619-260-4524, Fax: 619-260-4158, E-mail: grads@sandiego.edu.
Website: http://www.sandiego.edu/business/graduate/ms-real-estate/

University of South Africa, College of Economic and Management Sciences, Pretoria, South Africa. Offers accounting (D Admin, D Com); accounting science (DA); auditing (D Admin, D Com); business administration (M Tech); business economics (D Admin); business leadership (DBL); business management (D Admin, D Com); economic management analysis (M Tech); economics (D Admin, D Com, PhD); human resource development (M Tech); industrial psychology (D Admin, D Com, PhD); logistics (D Com); marketing (M Tech); public administration (D Admin, D Com, DPA, PhD); public management (M Tech); quantitative management (D Admin, D Com); real estate (M Tech); statistics (D Admin, PhD); tourism management (D Admin, D Com); transport economics (D Admin, D Com).

University of Southern California, Graduate School, Sol Price School of Public Policy, Master of Real Estate Development Program, Los Angeles, CA 90089. Offers MRED, JD/MRED, M PI/MRED, MBA/MRED. *Program availability:* Part-time. *Degree requirements:* For master's, comprehensive exam. *Entrance requirements:* For master's, GRE, GMAT. Additional exam requirements/recommendations for international students: Required—TOEFL (minimum score 600 paper-based; 100 iBT). Electronic applications accepted. *Expenses:* Contact institution. *Faculty research:* Urban development, urban economics, real estate finance, housing markets.

University of South Florida, Muma College of Business, Department of Finance, Tampa, FL 33620-9951. Offers business administration (PhD), including finance; finance (MS); real estate (MSRE). *Program availability:* Part-time, evening/weekend. *Faculty:* 14 full-time (3 women). *Students:* 99 full-time (30 women), 26 part-time (13 women); includes 8 minority (4 Asian, non-Hispanic/Latino; 4 Hispanic/Latino), 94 international. Average age 25. 142 applicants, 58% accepted, 57 enrolled. In 2017, 57 master's, 1 doctorate awarded. Terminal master's awarded for partial completion of doctoral program. *Degree requirements:* For master's, comprehensive exam, thesis or alternative; for doctorate, comprehensive exam, thesis/dissertation. *Entrance requirements:* For master's, GMAT, minimum undergraduate GPA of 3.0 in upper-division coursework; for doctorate, GMAT or GRE, minimum undergraduate GPA of 3.0 in upper-division coursework, personal statement, recommendations, interview. Additional exam requirements/recommendations for international students: Required—TOEFL (minimum score 550 paper-based; 79 iBT) or IELTS (minimum score 6.5). *Application deadline:* For fall admission, 6/1 for domestic students, 1/2 for international students; for spring admission, 10/15 for domestic students, 7/1 for international students; for summer admission, 2/15 for domestic students, 1/1 for international students. Application fee: $30. Electronic applications accepted. *Financial support:* In 2017–18, 16 students received support, including 8 research assistantships (averaging $14,357 per year), 9 teaching assistantships with tuition reimbursements available (averaging $11,972 per year); scholarships/grants, health care benefits, and unspecified assistantships also available. Financial award application deadline: 6/30. *Faculty research:* International corporate finance, corporate finance, market efficiency, mergers and acquisitions, agency theory, corporate governance, investments, mutual fund industry, mergers and acquisitions, corporate creditworthiness, credit risk issues, empirical asset pricing, financial intermediation, corporate finance theory, public offerings, business strategy. *Unit head:* Dr. Scott Besley, Chairperson and Associate Professor, 813-974-6341, Fax: 813-974-3084, E-mail: sbesley@usf.edu. *Application contact:* Yuting DiGiovanni, 813-974-6358, Fax: 813-974-3084, E-mail: yuting2@usf.edu.
Website: http://business.usf.edu/departments/finance/

The University of Texas at Arlington, Graduate School, College of Business, Department of Finance and Real Estate, Arlington, TX 76019. Offers finance (PhD); quantitative finance (MS); real estate (MS). *Program availability:* Part-time, evening/weekend. *Degree requirements:* For master's, thesis optional; for doctorate, comprehensive exam, thesis/dissertation. *Entrance requirements:* For master's, GMAT/GRE, minimum GPA of 3.0; for doctorate, GMAT/GRE. Additional exam requirements/recommendations for international students: Required—TOEFL (minimum score 550 paper-based; 79 iBT).

The University of Texas at Dallas, Naveen Jindal School of Management, Program in Finance and Managerial Economics, Richardson, TX 75080. Offers finance (MS), including energy risk management, enterprise risk management, real estate, risk management insurance. *Program availability:* Part-time, evening/weekend. *Faculty:* 27 full-time (2 women), 10 part-time/adjunct (4 women). *Students:* 291 full-time (103 women), 80 part-time (33 women); includes 64 minority (7 Black or African American, non-Hispanic/Latino; 32 Asian, non-Hispanic/Latino; 17 Hispanic/Latino; 8 Two or more races, non-Hispanic/Latino), 227 international. Average age 26. 717 applicants, 48% accepted, 140 enrolled. In 2017, 190 master's awarded. *Entrance requirements:* For master's, GMAT or GRE. Additional exam requirements/recommendations for international students: Required—TOEFL (minimum score 550 paper-based). *Application deadline:* For fall admission, 7/15 for domestic students, 5/1 priority date for international students; for spring admission, 11/15 for domestic students, 9/1 priority date for international students. Applications are processed on a rolling basis. Application fee: $50 ($100 for international students). Electronic applications accepted. *Expenses:* Tuition, state resident: full-time $12,916; part-time $718 per credit hour. Tuition, nonresident: full-time $25,252; part-time $1403 per credit hour. *Financial support:* In 2017–18, 96 students received support, including 8 teaching assistantships with partial tuition reimbursements available (averaging $10,050 per year); research assistantships with partial tuition reimbursements available, career-related internships or fieldwork, Federal Work-Study, institutionally sponsored loans, scholarships/grants, and unspecified assistantships also available. Support available to part-time students. Financial award application deadline: 4/30; financial award applicants required to submit FAFSA. *Faculty research:* Econometrics, industrial organization, auction theory, file-sharing copyrights and bundling, international financial management, entrepreneurial finance. *Unit head:* Dr. Vikram Nanda, Area Coordinator, 972-883-5004, E-mail: vikram.nanda@utdallas.edu.
Website: http://jindal.utdallas.edu/finance

University of Utah, Graduate School, David Eccles School of Business, Master in Real Estate Development Program, Salt Lake City, UT 84112. Offers MRED, MRED/JD, MRED/M Arch, MRED/MCMP. MRED/M Arch, MRED/MCMP offered jointly with College of Architecture and Planning; MRED/JD with S.J. Quinney College of Law. *Program availability:* Part-time. *Faculty:* 2 full-time (1 woman), 15 part-time/adjunct (1 woman). *Students:* 27 full-time (5 women), 37 part-time (7 women); includes 7 minority (2 Black or African American, non-Hispanic/Latino; 3 Asian, non-Hispanic/Latino; 2 Native Hawaiian or other Pacific Islander, non-Hispanic/Latino), 3 international. Average age 26. 36 applicants, 86% accepted, 25 enrolled. In 2017, 31 master's awarded. *Degree*

requirements: For master's, professional project. *Entrance requirements:* For master's, GMAT or GRE, minimum undergraduate GPA of 3.0. Additional exam requirements/recommendations for international students: Required—TOEFL (minimum score 90 iBT), IELTS (minimum score 6.5). *Application deadline:* For fall admission, 7/28 for domestic students, 4/1 for international students; for winter admission, 12/7 for domestic students, 10/1 for international students. Applications are processed on a rolling basis. Application fee: $25. Electronic applications accepted. *Expenses:* Contact institution. *Financial support:* In 2017–18, 44 students received support, including 44 fellowships with partial tuition reimbursements available (averaging $7,400 per year); scholarships/grants and unspecified assistantships also available. Financial award application deadline: 4/15; financial award applicants required to submit FAFSA. *Unit head:* Danny Wall, Program Director, 801-581-8903, E-mail: danny.wall@eccles.utah.edu. *Application contact:* Regina Mavis, Admissions Coordinator, 801-585-0005, E-mail: regina.mavis@eccles.utah.edu.
Website: http://mred.eccles.utah.edu/

University of Wisconsin–Madison, Graduate School, Wisconsin School of Business, Doctoral Program in Real Estate and Urban Land Economics, Madison, WI 53706-1380. Offers PhD. *Degree requirements:* For doctorate, comprehensive exam, thesis/dissertation. *Entrance requirements:* For doctorate, GMAT or GRE. Additional exam requirements/recommendations for international students: Recommended—TOEFL (minimum score 623 paper-based; 106 iBT), IELTS (minimum score 7.5), TSE (minimum score 73). Electronic applications accepted. *Expenses:* Contact institution. *Faculty research:* Real estate finance, real estate equity investments, zoning restructurings, home ownership, international real estate and public policy, real estate economics.

University of Wisconsin–Madison, Graduate School, Wisconsin School of Business, Wisconsin Full-Time MBA Program, Madison, WI 53706. Offers applied security analysis (MBA); arts administration (MBA); brand and product management (MBA); corporate finance and investment banking (MBA); marketing research (MBA); operations and technology management (MBA); real estate (MBA); risk management and insurance (MBA); strategic human resource management (MBA); supply chain management (MBA). *Faculty:* 130 full-time (35 women), 42 part-time/adjunct (13 women). *Students:* 203 full-time (72 women); includes 34 minority (8 Black or African American, non-Hispanic/Latino; 10 Asian, non-Hispanic/Latino; 12 Hispanic/Latino; 4 Two or more races, non-Hispanic/Latino), 41 international. Average age 28. 556 applicants, 30% accepted, 104 enrolled. In 2017, 97 master's awarded. *Entrance requirements:* For master's, GMAT or GRE, bachelor's or equivalent degree, 2 years of work experience, essay, letter of recommendation, resume. Additional exam requirements/recommendations for international students: Required—TOEFL (minimum score 100 iBT), IELTS (minimum score 7.5). *Application deadline:* For fall admission, 11/2 for domestic and international students; for winter admission, 1/11 for domestic and international students; for spring admission, 3/1 for domestic and international students; for summer admission, 4/12 for domestic and international students. Applications are processed on a rolling basis. Application fee: $75 ($81 for international students). Electronic applications accepted. *Expenses:* $9,356 per semester resident, $18,288 non-resident. *Financial support:* In 2017–18, 183 students received support, including 14 fellowships with full tuition reimbursements available (averaging $25,420 per year), 7 research assistantships with full tuition reimbursements available (averaging $13,375 per year), 53 teaching assistantships with full tuition reimbursements available (averaging $13,375 per year); scholarships/grants, health care benefits, tuition waivers (full), and unspecified assistantships also available. Financial award application deadline: 4/11. *Faculty research:* Forms of competition and outcomes in dual distribution systems; explaining the accuracy of revised forecasts; supply chain planning for random demand surges; advanced demand information in a multi-product system; the effects of presentation salience and measurement subjectivity on nonprofessional investors' fair value judgments. *Unit head:* Dr. Don Hausch, Associate Dean, Full-time MBA Program, 608-262-9731, E-mail: don.hausch@wisc.edu. *Application contact:* Betsy Kacizak, Director of Admissions and Recruiting, Full-time MBA Program, 608-262-4000, E-mail: betsy.kacizak@wisc.edu.
Website: https://wsb.wisc.edu/

Villanova University, Villanova School of Business, MBA - The Flex Track Program, Villanova, PA 19085. Offers healthcare (MBA); international business (MBA); marketing (MBA); real estate (MBA); strategic management (MBA); JD/MBA. *Accreditation:* AACSB. *Program availability:* Part-time, evening/weekend, online learning. *Faculty:* 68 full-time (22 women), 65 part-time/adjunct (11 women). *Students:* 13 full-time (4 women), 410 part-time (137 women); includes 105 minority (28 Black or African American, non-Hispanic/Latino; 1 American Indian or Alaska Native, non-Hispanic/Latino; 41 Asian, non-Hispanic/Latino; 29 Hispanic/Latino; 6 Two or more races, non-Hispanic/Latino), 13 international. Average age 31. 94 applicants, 94% accepted, 79 enrolled. In 2017, 201 master's awarded. *Degree requirements:* For master's, minimum GPA of 3.0. *Entrance requirements:* For master's, GMAT or GRE, work experience, 2 letters of recommendation, 2 essays, resume, official transcript. Additional exam requirements/recommendations for international students: Required—TOEFL (minimum score 550 paper-based; 100 iBT). *Application deadline:* For fall admission, 6/30 for domestic and international students; for spring admission, 11/15 for domestic and international students; for summer admission, 3/31 for domestic and international students. Applications are processed on a rolling basis. Application fee: $65. Electronic applications accepted. *Expenses:* $50,016 per year tuition, $1,167 per credit; $50 semester fee. *Financial support:* In 2017–18, 19 research assistantships with full tuition reimbursements (averaging $16,245 per year) were awarded; scholarships/grants also available. Financial award application deadline: 6/30; financial award applicants required to submit FAFSA. *Faculty research:* Business analytics; creativity, innovation and entrepreneurship; global leadership; real estate; church management; business ethics. *Unit head:* Dr. Joyce Russell, Dean of Villanova School of Business, 610-519-5424, Fax: 610-519-6273, E-mail: joyce.russell@villanova.edu. *Application contact:* Claire Bruno, Director of Recruitment and Enrollment Management, 610-519-4336, Fax: 610-519-6273, E-mail: claire.bruno@villanova.edu.
Website: http://www1.villanova.edu/villanova/business/graduate/mba.html

Virginia Commonwealth University, Graduate School, School of Business, Program in Real Estate and Urban Land Development, Richmond, VA 23284-9005. Offers Postbaccalaureate Certificate. *Entrance requirements:* Additional exam requirements/recommendations for international students: Required—TOEFL (minimum score 600 paper-based; 100 iBT); Recommended—IELTS (minimum score 6.5). Electronic applications accepted.

Section 21
Transportation Management, Logistics, and Supply Chain Management

This section contains a directory of institutions offering graduate work in real estate, followed by an in-depth entry submitted by an institution that chose to prepare a detailed program description. Additional information about programs listed in the directory but not augmented by an in-depth entry may be obtained by writing directly to the dean of a graduate school or chair of a department at the address given in the directory.

For programs offering related work, see also in this book *Business Administration and Management*.

CONTENTS

Program Directories

Aviation Management

Arizona State University at the Tempe campus, Ira A. Fulton Schools of Engineering, The Polytechnic School, Programs in Technology Management, Mesa, AZ 85212. Offers aviation management and human factors (MS); environmental technology management (MS); global technology and development (MS); graphic information technology (MS); management of technology (MS). *Program availability:* Part-time, evening/weekend, online learning. *Degree requirements:* For master's, thesis or applied project and oral defense; interactive Program of Study (iPOS) submitted before completing 50 percent of required credit hours. *Entrance requirements:* For master's, GRE, minimum GPA of 3.0 or equivalent in last 2 years of work leading to bachelor's degree. Additional exam requirements/recommendations for international students: Required—TOEFL, IELTS, or PTE. Electronic applications accepted. *Faculty research:* Digital imaging, digital publishing, Internet development/e-commerce, information aviation human factors, pilot selection, databases, multimedia, commercial digital photography, digital workflow, computer graphics modeling and animation, information design, sociotechnology, visual and technical literacy, environmental management, quality management, project management, industrial ethics, hazardous materials, environmental chemistry.

Delta State University, Graduate Programs, College of Business, Department of Commercial Aviation, Cleveland, MS 38733-0001. Offers MCA. *Program availability:* Part-time, evening/weekend, online learning. *Degree requirements:* For master's, thesis or alternative. *Entrance requirements:* For master's, GMAT.

Embry-Riddle Aeronautical University–Worldwide, Department of Business Administration, Daytona Beach, FL 32114-3900. Offers aviation (MBAA); MS/MBA. *Program availability:* Part-time, evening/weekend, online only, EagleVision Classroom (between classrooms), EagleVision Home (faculty and students at home), and a blend of Classroom or Home. *Faculty:* 12 full-time (5 women), 60 part-time/adjunct (18 women). *Students:* 374 full-time (77 women), 292 part-time (65 women); includes 163 minority (54 Black or African American, non-Hispanic/Latino; 3 American Indian or Alaska Native, non-Hispanic/Latino; 27 Asian, non-Hispanic/Latino; 43 Hispanic/Latino; 4 Native Hawaiian or other Pacific Islander, non-Hispanic/Latino; 32 Two or more races, non-Hispanic/Latino), 55 international. Average age 35. 166 applicants, 74% accepted, 115 enrolled. In 2017, 214 master's awarded. *Degree requirements:* For master's, comprehensive exam. *Entrance requirements:* Additional exam requirements/recommendations for international students: Required—TOEFL (minimum score 550 paper-based; 79 iBT), IELTS (minimum score 6). *Application deadline:* Applications are processed on a rolling basis. Application fee: $50. Electronic applications accepted. *Expenses:* Contact institution. *Financial support:* Career-related internships or fieldwork and scholarships/grants available. Financial award applicants required to submit FAFSA. *Unit head:* Ronald Mau, PhD, Department Chair, E-mail: ronald.mau@erau.edu. *Application contact:* Worldwide Campus, 800-522-6787, E-mail: worldwide@erau.edu.
Website: http://worldwide.erau.edu/degrees-programs/colleges/business/department-of-business-admin/index.html

Florida Institute of Technology, College of Aeronautics, Program in Airport Development and Management, Melbourne, FL 32901-6975. Offers MSA. *Program availability:* Part-time. *Students:* 17 full-time (5 women), 3 part-time (0 women); includes 1 minority (Two or more races, non-Hispanic/Latino), 19 international. Average age 24. 29 applicants, 59% accepted, 9 enrolled. In 2017, 13 master's awarded. *Entrance requirements:* For master's, GRE General Test, 3 letters of recommendation, resume, statement of objectives. Additional exam requirements/recommendations for international students: Required—TOEFL (minimum score 550 paper-based; 79 iBT). *Application deadline:* Applications are processed on a rolling basis. Electronic applications accepted. *Expenses: Tuition:* Part-time $1241 per credit hour. Part-time tuition and fees vary according to campus/location. *Financial support:* Applicants required to submit FAFSA. *Unit head:* Dr. Stephen Rice, Chair of Graduate Programs, 321-674-8375, Fax: 321-674-8059, E-mail: srice@fit.edu. *Application contact:* Cheryl A. Brown, Associate Director of Graduate Admissions, 321-674-7581, Fax: 321-723-9468, E-mail: cbrown@fit.edu.
Website: http://coa.fit.edu

Lewis University, College of Arts and Sciences, Program in Aviation and Transportation, Romeoville, IL 60446. Offers administration (MS); safety and security (MS). *Program availability:* Part-time, evening/weekend, 100% online, blended/hybrid learning. *Students:* 29 full-time (7 women), 20 part-time (5 women); includes 11 minority (6 Black or African American, non-Hispanic/Latino; 3 Hispanic/Latino; 2 Two or more races, non-Hispanic/Latino), 7 international. Average age 30. *Degree requirements:* For master's, comprehensive exam (for some programs). *Entrance requirements:* For master's, bachelor's degree, minimum GPA of 3.0, personal statement, 2 letters of recommendation. Additional exam requirements/recommendations for international students: Required—TOEFL (minimum score 550 paper-based; 79 iBT), IELTS (minimum score 6). *Application deadline:* For fall admission, 5/1 priority date for international students; for spring admission, 11/15 priority date for international students. Applications are processed on a rolling basis. Application fee: $40. Electronic applications accepted. Tuition and fees vary according to program. *Financial support:* Federal Work-Study and unspecified assistantships available. Financial award application deadline: 5/1; financial award applicants required to submit FAFSA. *Total annual research expenditures:* $30. *Unit head:* Dr. Randal DeMik, Program Chair, 815-838-0500 Ext. 5559, E-mail: demikra@lewisu.edu. *Application contact:* Linda Campbell, Graduate Admissions Counselor, 815-836-5610, Fax: 815-836-5578, E-mail: grad@lewisu.edu.

Lynn University, College of Business and Management, Boca Raton, FL 33431-5598. Offers business administration (MBA), including aviation management, entrepreneurial management, financial valuation and investment management, hospitality management, human resource management, international business management, marketing, media management, social innovation management, sports management, Web development. *Program availability:* Part-time, evening/weekend, 100% online, blended/hybrid learning. *Faculty:* 29 full-time (11 women), 19 part-time/adjunct (7 women). *Students:* 287 full-time (124 women), 195 part-time (105 women); includes 110 minority (44 Black or African American, non-Hispanic/Latino; 2 American Indian or Alaska Native, non-Hispanic/Latino; 11 Asian, non-Hispanic/Latino; 47 Hispanic/Latino; 6 Two or more races, non-Hispanic/Latino), 135 international. Average age 28. 293 applicants, 94% accepted, 192 enrolled. In 2017, 236 master's awarded. *Degree requirements:* For master's, thesis, minimum GPA of 3.0, strategic management seminar, written presentation reflecting the integration and application of theory to practice. *Entrance requirements:* For master's, bachelor's degree from accredited institution, minimum undergraduate GPA of 2.5, official undergraduate transcripts, resume, personal statement, letter of recommendation from academic or professional sources, writing sample demonstrating capacity to perform at graduate level. Additional exam requirements/recommendations for international students: Required—TOEFL (minimum score 550 paper-based; 80 iBT), IELTS (minimum score 6.5). *Application deadline:* For fall admission, 8/18 for domestic students, 8/4 for international students; for spring admission, 12/15 for domestic students, 12/1 for international students; for summer admission, 4/17 for domestic students, 4/3 for international students. Applications are processed on a rolling basis. Application fee: $45. Electronic applications accepted. *Expenses:* $740 per credit. *Financial support:* Career-related internships or fieldwork, Federal Work-Study, scholarships/grants, tuition waivers (full and partial), and unspecified assistantships available. Support available to part-time students. Financial award application deadline: 3/1; financial award applicants required to submit FAFSA. *Faculty research:* Knowledge economy, urban economy, U.S. manufacturing industries, leadership personality, stock market reactions to terrorism, personality psychology, industrial/organizational psychology. *Unit head:* Dr. RT Good, Dean of the College of Business and Management, 561-237-7458, E-mail: rgood@lynn.edu. *Application contact:* Steven Pruitt, Director of Graduate and Undergraduate Evening Admission, 561-237-7834, Fax: 561-237-7100, E-mail: spruitt@lynn.edu.
Website: http://www.lynn.edu/academics/colleges/business-and-management

Middle Tennessee State University, College of Graduate Studies, College of Basic and Applied Sciences, Department of Aerospace, Program in Aviation Administration, Murfreesboro, TN 37132. Offers MS. *Program availability:* Part-time, evening/weekend, online learning. *Degree requirements:* For master's, comprehensive exam, thesis optional. *Entrance requirements:* For master's, GRE or MAT. Additional exam requirements/recommendations for international students: Required—TOEFL (minimum score 525 paper-based; 71 iBT) or IELTS (minimum score 6).

National American University, Roueche Graduate Center, Austin, TX 78731. Offers accounting (MBA); aviation management (MBA, MM); care coordination (MSN); community college leadership (Ed D); criminal justice (MM); e-marketing (MBA, MM); health care administration (MBA, MM); higher education (MM); human resources management (MBA, MM); information technology management (MBA, MM); international business (MBA); leadership (EMBA); management (MBA); nursing administration (MSN); nursing education (MSN); nursing informatics (MSN); operations and configuration management (MBA, MM); project and process management (MBA, MM). Master's programs offered online through the Harold D. Buckingham Graduate School. *Program availability:* Part-time, evening/weekend, online learning. *Entrance requirements:* For master's, minimum undergraduate GPA of 2.75. Additional exam requirements/recommendations for international students: Required—TOEFL, TWE. Electronic applications accepted. *Faculty research:* Tourism, finance, marketing.

Purdue University, Graduate School, College of Technology, Department of Aviation Technology, West Lafayette, IN 47907. Offers aviation and aerospace management (MS). *Faculty:* 22 full-time (2 women), 1 (woman) part-time/adjunct. *Students:* 44 full-time (15 women), 37 part-time (6 women); includes 18 minority (2 Black or African American, non-Hispanic/Latino; 7 Asian, non-Hispanic/Latino; 6 Hispanic/Latino; 1 Native Hawaiian or other Pacific Islander, non-Hispanic/Latino; 2 Two or more races, non-Hispanic/Latino), 20 international. Average age 28. 55 applicants, 85% accepted, 28 enrolled. In 2017, 34 master's awarded. *Entrance requirements:* For master's, GRE/GMAT, written and spoken communication skills; general knowledge of aviation industry operations and components; entry-level analytical tools and processes; group activity and interpersonal skills. Additional exam requirements/recommendations for international students: Required—TOEFL (minimum score 550 paper-based; 77 iBT); Recommended—TWE. *Application deadline:* For fall admission, 4/1 for domestic and international students; for spring admission, 10/1 for domestic students, 9/1 for international students; for summer admission, 4/1 for domestic students, 2/15 for international students. Applications are processed on a rolling basis. Application fee: $60 ($75 for international students). Electronic applications accepted. *Unit head:* Dr. Manoj S. Patankar, Head of the Graduate Program, 765-496-3136, E-mail: mspatankar@purdue.edu. *Application contact:* Emily Birge, Graduate Contact, 765-494-2884, E-mail: ebirge@purdue.edu.
Website: https://tech.purdue.edu/departments/aviation-technology

Southeastern Oklahoma State University, Department of Aviation Science, Durant, OK 74701-0609. Offers aerospace administration and logistics (MS). *Program availability:* Part-time, evening/weekend. *Entrance requirements:* For master's, minimum GPA of 3.0 in last 60 hours or 2.75 overall. Additional exam requirements/recommendations for international students: Required—TOEFL (minimum score 550 paper-based; 79 iBT). Electronic applications accepted.

Vaughn College of Aeronautics and Technology, Graduate Programs, Flushing, NY 11369. Offers airport management (MS). *Degree requirements:* For master's, project or thesis.

Logistics

Air Force Institute of Technology, Graduate School of Engineering and Management, Department of Operational Sciences, Dayton, OH 45433-7765. Offers logistics management (MS); operations research (MS, PhD); space operations (MS). *Program availability:* Part-time. *Degree requirements:* For master's, thesis; for doctorate, thesis/dissertation. *Entrance requirements:* For doctorate, GRE General Test, minimum GPA of 3.0, U.S. citizenship. *Faculty research:* Optimization, simulation, combat modeling and analysis, reliability and maintainability, resource scheduling.

Albany State University, College of Business, Albany, GA 31705-2717. Offers accounting (MBA); general business administration (MBA); healthcare (MBA); public administration (MBA); supply chain and logistics (MBA). *Accreditation:* ACBSP. *Program availability:* Part-time, evening/weekend. *Degree requirements:* For master's, comprehensive exam, internship, 3 hours of physical education. *Entrance requirements:* For master's, GMAT (minimum score of 450)/GRE (minimum score of 800) for those without earned master's degree or higher, minimum undergraduate GPA of 2.5, 2 letters of reference, official transcript, pre-entrance medical record and certificate of immunization. Electronic applications accepted. *Faculty research:* Diversity issues, ancestry, understanding finance through use of technology.

American Public University System, AMU/APU Graduate Programs, Charles Town, WV 25414. Offers accounting (MS); applied business analytics (MS); business administration (MBA); criminal justice (MA); cybersecurity studies (MS); educational leadership (M Ed); environmental policy and management (MS); global security (DGS); health information management (MS); history (MA), including American military history, American Revolution, civil war, war since 1945, World War II; information technology (MS); international relations and conflict resolution (MA), including American politics and government, comparative government and development, general, international relations, public policy; national security studies (MA); nursing (MSN); political science (MA); public policy (MPP); reverse logistics management (MA), including comparative and security issues, conflict resolution, international and transnational security issues, peacekeeping; space studies (MS); sports management (MS); strategic intelligence (DSI); teaching (M Ed), including secondary social studies; transportation and logistics management (MA). *Program availability:* Part-time, evening/weekend, online only, 100% online. *Students:* 455 full-time (227 women), 7,939 part-time (3,353 women); includes 2,793 minority (1,429 Black or African American, non-Hispanic/Latino; 48 American Indian or Alaska Native, non-Hispanic/Latino; 205 Asian, non-Hispanic/Latino; 766 Hispanic/Latino; 62 Native Hawaiian or other Pacific Islander, non-Hispanic/Latino; 283 Two or more races, non-Hispanic/Latino), 101 international. Average age 37. In 2017, 2,977 master's awarded. *Degree requirements:* For master's, comprehensive exam or practicum. *Entrance requirements:* For master's, official transcript showing earned bachelor's degree from institution accredited by recognized accrediting body. Additional exam requirements/recommendations for international students: Required—TOEFL (minimum score 550 paper-based), IELTS (minimum score 6.5). *Application deadline:* Applications are processed on a rolling basis. Application fee: $0. Electronic applications accepted. *Expenses: Tuition:* Full-time $6300; part-time $350 per credit. *Required fees:* $300; $50 per course. *Financial support:* Scholarships/grants available. Financial award applicants required to submit FAFSA. *Unit head:* Dr. Wallace Boston, President, 877-468-6268, Fax: 304-728-2348, E-mail: president@apus.edu. *Application contact:* Yoci Deal, Associate Vice President, Graduate and International Admissions, 877-468-6268, Fax: 304-724-3764, E-mail: info@apus.edu.
Website: http://www.apus.edu

Athens State University, Graduate Programs, Athens, AL 35611. Offers career and technical education (M Ed); global logistics and supply chain management (MS); religious studies (MA). *Students:* 28 full-time (19 women), 119 part-time (55 women). *Expenses:* Tuition, state resident: full-time $3900; part-time $325 per credit hour. Tuition, nonresident: full-time $3900; part-time $325 per credit hour.
Website: http://www.athens.edu/masters/

Benedictine University, Graduate Programs, Program in Business Administration, Lisle, IL 60532. Offers accounting (MBA); entrepreneurship and managing innovation (MBA); financial management (MBA); health administration (MBA); human resource management (MBA); information systems security (MBA); international business (MBA); management consulting (MBA); management information systems (MBA); marketing management (MBA); operations management and logistics (MBA); organizational leadership (MBA). *Program availability:* Part-time, evening/weekend, online learning. *Entrance requirements:* For master's, GMAT. Additional exam requirements/recommendations for international students: Required—TOEFL (minimum score 550 paper-based). Electronic applications accepted. *Faculty research:* Strategic leadership in professional organizations, sociology of professions, organizational change, social identity theory, applications to change management.

Case Western Reserve University, School of Graduate Studies, Case School of Engineering, Department of Electrical Engineering and Computer Science, Cleveland, OH 44106. Offers computer engineering (MS, PhD); computing and information sciences (MS, PhD); electrical engineering (MS, PhD); systems and control engineering (MS, PhD). *Program availability:* Part-time, evening/weekend, online only, 100% online. *Faculty:* 30 full-time (1 woman). *Students:* 219 full-time (46 women), 12 part-time (6 women); includes 11 minority (1 Black or African American, non-Hispanic/Latino; 7 Asian, non-Hispanic/Latino; 2 Hispanic/Latino; 1 Two or more races, non-Hispanic/Latino), 170 international. In 2017, 36 master's, 11 doctorates awarded. Terminal master's awarded for partial completion of doctoral program. *Degree requirements:* For master's, thesis; for doctorate, thesis/dissertation, qualifying exam, teaching experience. *Entrance requirements:* For master's and doctorate, GRE General Test. Additional exam requirements/recommendations for international students: Required—TOEFL. *Application deadline:* For fall admission, 2/1 for domestic students; for spring admission, 11/1 for domestic students. Applications are processed on a rolling basis. Application fee: $50. *Expenses: Tuition:* Full-time $43,854; part-time $1827 per credit hour. *Required fees:* $50; $50 per credit hour. Tuition and fees vary according to course load and program. *Financial support:* In 2017–18, 1 fellowship with tuition reimbursement, 76 research assistantships with tuition reimbursements, 10 teaching assistantships were awarded; career-related internships or fieldwork, Federal Work-Study, and institutionally sponsored loans also available. Support available to part-time students. Financial award application deadline: 3/1; financial award applicants required to submit FAFSA. *Faculty research:* Micro-/nano-systems; robotics and haptics; applied artificial intelligence; automation; computer-aided design and testing of digital systems. *Total annual research expenditures:* $5.1 million. *Unit head:* Alexis Abramson, Interim Department Chair, 216-368-4115, E-mail: alexis.abramson@case.edu. *Application contact:* Angela Beca, Student Affairs Specialist, 216-368-2800, Fax: 216-368-2801, E-mail: angela.beca@case.edu.
Website: http://eecs.cwru.edu/

Central Connecticut State University, School of Graduate Studies, School of Engineering, Science and Technology, Department of Manufacturing and Construction Management, New Britain, CT 06050-4010. Offers construction management (MS, Certificate); environmental and occupational safety (Certificate); lean manufacturing and Six Sigma (Certificate); supply chain and logistics (Certificate); technology management (MS). *Program availability:* Part-time, evening/weekend. *Faculty:* 8 full-time (1 woman), 3 part-time/adjunct (0 women). *Students:* 25 full-time (10 women), 92 part-time (16 women); includes 31 minority (17 Black or African American, non-Hispanic/Latino; 5 Asian, non-Hispanic/Latino; 8 Hispanic/Latino; 1 Two or more races, non-Hispanic/Latino), 11 international. Average age 32. 77 applicants, 71% accepted, 37 enrolled. In 2017, 40 master's, 6 other advanced degrees awarded. *Degree requirements:* For master's, comprehensive exam, special project; for Certificate, qualifying exam. *Entrance requirements:* For master's, minimum undergraduate GPA of 2.7. Additional exam requirements/recommendations for international students: Required—TOEFL

(minimum score 550 paper-based; 79 iBT); Recommended—IELTS (minimum score 6.5). *Application deadline:* For fall admission, 8/1 for domestic students, 5/1 for international students; for spring admission, 12/1 for domestic students, 11/1 for international students; for summer admission, 5/1 for domestic students. Applications are processed on a rolling basis. Application fee: $50. Electronic applications accepted. *Expenses: Tuition, area resident:* Full-time $6757. Tuition, state resident: full-time $9750; part-time $374 per credit. Tuition, nonresident: full-time $18,102; part-time $374 per credit. *Required fees:* $4635; $255 per credit. *Financial support:* In 2017–18, 17 students received support. Career-related internships or fieldwork, Federal Work-Study, scholarships/grants, and unspecified assistantships available. Support available to part-time students. Financial award application deadline: 3/1; financial award applicants required to submit FAFSA. *Faculty research:* All aspects of middle management, technical supervision in the workplace. *Unit head:* Dr. Ravindra Thamma, Chair, 860-832-1830, E-mail: thammarav@ccsu.edu. *Application contact:* Patricia Gardner, Associate Director of Graduate Studies, 860-832-2350, Fax: 860-832-2362.
Website: http://www.ccsu.edu/mcm/

Central Michigan University, Central Michigan University Global Campus, Program in Business Administration, Mount Pleasant, MI 48859. Offers enterprise resource planning (MBA, Certificate); human resource management (MBA); logistics management (MBA, Certificate); marketing (MBA); value-driven organization (MBA). *Program availability:* Part-time, evening/weekend. *Entrance requirements:* For master's, GMAT.

Central Michigan University, College of Graduate Studies, College of Business Administration, MBA Program, Mount Pleasant, MI 48859. Offers accounting (MBA); business economics (MBA); consulting (MBA); finance (MBA); general business (MBA); human resource management (MBA); information systems (MBA); international business (MBA); logistics management (MBA); marketing (MBA); value-driven organization (MBA). *Program availability:* Part-time, evening/weekend, online learning. Electronic applications accepted. *Faculty research:* Accounting, consulting, international business, marketing, information systems.

Colorado Technical University Colorado Springs, Graduate Studies, Program in Management, Colorado Springs, CO 80907. Offers accounting (MBA, MSA); business administration (MBA); finance (MBA); human resources management (MBA); logistics/supply chain management (MBA); management (DM); marketing (MBA); mediation and dispute resolution (MBA); operations management (MBA); project management (MBA); technology management (MBA). *Accreditation:* ACBSP. *Program availability:* Part-time, evening/weekend, online learning. *Degree requirements:* For master's, thesis or alternative; for doctorate, thesis/dissertation. *Entrance requirements:* For doctorate, minimum graduate GPA of 3.0, 5 years of related work experience. *Faculty research:* Sexual harassment, performance evaluation, critical thinking.

Copenhagen Business School, Graduate Programs, Copenhagen, Denmark. Offers business administration (Exec MBA, MBA, PhD); business administration and information systems (M Sc); business, language and culture (M Sc); economics and business administration (M Sc); health management (MHM); international business and politics (M Sc); public administration (MPA); shipping and logistics (Exec MBA); technology, market and organization (MBA).

East Carolina University, Graduate School, College of Engineering and Technology, Department of Technology Systems, Greenville, NC 27858-4353. Offers computer network professional (Certificate); cyber security professional (Certificate); information assurance (Certificate); Lean Six Sigma Black Belt (Certificate); network technology (MS), including computer networking management, digital communications technology, information security, Web technologies; occupational safety (MS); technology management (MS, PhD), including industrial distribution and logistics (MS); Website developer (Certificate). *Students:* 19 full-time (4 women), 158 part-time (35 women); includes 43 minority (28 Black or African American, non-Hispanic/Latino; 2 American Indian or Alaska Native, non-Hispanic/Latino; 3 Asian, non-Hispanic/Latino; 6 Hispanic/Latino; 4 Two or more races, non-Hispanic/Latino), 6 international. Average age 39. 44 applicants, 91% accepted, 37 enrolled. In 2017, 30 master's, 29 other advanced degrees awarded. *Entrance requirements:* For master's and Certificate, GRE General Test or MAT, minimum GPA of 2.5; for doctorate, GRE General Test, related work experience. Additional exam requirements/recommendations for international students: Recommended—TOEFL (minimum score 78 iBT), IELTS (minimum score 6.5). *Application deadline:* For fall admission, 6/1 priority date for domestic students. Applications are processed on a rolling basis. Application fee: $75. *Expenses:* Tuition, state resident: full-time $4749; part-time $297 per credit hour. Tuition, nonresident: full-time $17,898; part-time $1119 per credit hour. *Required fees:* $2691; $224 per credit hour. Part-time tuition and fees vary according to course load and program. *Financial support:* Application deadline: 6/1. *Unit head:* Dr. Tijjani Mohammed, Chair, 252-328-9668, E-mail: mohammedt@ecu.edu.
Website: http://www.ecu.edu/cs-cet/techsystems/index.cfm

Embry-Riddle Aeronautical University–Worldwide, Department of Decision Sciences, Daytona Beach, FL 32114-3900. Offers aviation and aerospace (MSPM); aviation/aerospace management (MSEM); financial management (MSEM, MSPM); general management (MSPM); global management (MSPM); human resources management (MSPM); information systems (MSPM); leadership (MSEM, MSPM); logistics and supply chain management (MSEM, MSLSCM, MSPM); management (MSEM, MSPM); project management (MSEM); systems engineering (MSEM, MSPM); technical management (MSPM). *Program availability:* Part-time, evening/weekend, EagleVision Classroom (between classrooms), EagleVision Home (faculty and students at home), and a blend of Classroom or Home. *Faculty:* 12 full-time (3 women), 53 part-time/adjunct (10 women). *Students:* 514 full-time (141 women), 476 part-time (111 women); includes 337 minority (136 Black or African American, non-Hispanic/Latino; 6 American Indian or Alaska Native, non-Hispanic/Latino; 39 Asian, non-Hispanic/Latino; 81 Hispanic/Latino; 4 Native Hawaiian or other Pacific Islander, non-Hispanic/Latino; 71 Two or more races, non-Hispanic/Latino), 21 international. Average age 36. 297 applicants, 72% accepted, 209 enrolled. In 2017, 292 master's awarded. *Degree requirements:* For master's, comprehensive exam (for some programs), thesis (for some programs). *Entrance requirements:* Additional exam requirements/recommendations for international students: Required—TOEFL (minimum score 550 paper-based; 79 iBT), IELTS (minimum score 6). *Application deadline:* Applications are processed on a rolling basis. Application fee: $50. Electronic applications accepted. *Expenses:* Contact institution. *Financial support:* Career-related internships or fieldwork and scholarships/grants available. Financial award applicants required to submit FAFSA. *Unit head:* Aman Gupta, PhD, Department Chair, E-mail: aman.gupta@erau.edu. *Application contact:* Worldwide Campus, 800-522-6787, E-mail: worldwide@erau.edu.

Florida Institute of Technology, Extended Studies Division, Melbourne, FL 32901-6975. Offers acquisition and contract management (MS); aerospace engineering (MS); business administration (MBA, DBA); computer information systems (MS); computer science (MS); electrical engineering (MS); engineering management (MS); human resources management (MS); logistics management (MS), including humanitarian and disaster relief logistics; management (MS), including acquisition and contract management, e-business, human resources management, information systems, logistics management, management, transportation management; material acquisition

Logistics

management (MS); mechanical engineering (MS); operations research (MS); project management (MS), including information systems, operations research; public administration (MPA); quality management (MS); software engineering (MS); space systems (MS); space systems management (MS); supply chain management (MS); systems management (MS), including information systems, operations research; technology management (MS). *Program availability:* Part-time, evening/weekend, online learning. *Students:* Average age 36. 962 applicants, 48% accepted, 323 enrolled. In 2017, 403 master's awarded. *Entrance requirements:* For master's, GMAT or resume showing 8 years of supervised experience, minimum GPA of 3.0, 2 letters of recommendation, resume. Additional exam requirements/recommendations for international students: Required—TOEFL (minimum score 550 paper-based; 79 iBT). *Application deadline:* For fall admission, 4/1 for international students; for spring admission, 9/30 for international students. Applications are processed on a rolling basis. Electronic applications accepted. *Expenses:* Contact institution. *Financial support:* Application deadline: 3/1; applicants required to submit FAFSA. *Unit head:* Dr. Theodore R. Richardson, III, Dean, 321-674-8123, Fax: 321-674-7597, E-mail: trichardson@fit.edu. *Application contact:* Carolyn Farrior, Director of Graduate Admissions, Online Learning and Off-Campus Programs, 321-674-7118, Fax: 321-674-8216, E-mail: cfarrior@fit.edu.
Website: http://es.fit.edu

Friends University, Graduate School, Wichita, KS 67213. Offers family therapy (MSFT); global business administration (MBA), including accounting, business law, change management, health care leadership, management information systems, supply chain management and logistics; health care leadership (MHCL); management information systems (MMIS); professional business administration (MBA), including accounting, business law, change management, health care leadership, management information systems, supply chain management and logistics. *Program availability:* Part-time, evening/weekend, online learning. *Degree requirements:* For master's, research project. *Entrance requirements:* For master's, bachelor's degree from accredited institution, official transcripts, interview with program director, letter(s) of recommendation. Additional exam requirements/recommendations for international students: Required—TOEFL (minimum score 560 paper-based). Electronic applications accepted.

George Mason University, Schar School of Policy and Government, Program in Transportation Policy, Operations and Logistics, Arlington, VA 22201. Offers MA. *Faculty:* 6 full-time (3 women), 2 part-time/adjunct (0 women). *Students:* 9 full-time (3 women), 20 part-time (7 women); includes 7 minority (2 Black or African American, non-Hispanic/Latino; 3 Hispanic/Latino; 2 Two or more races, non-Hispanic/Latino), 4 international. Average age 34. 15 applicants, 100% accepted, 8 enrolled. In 2017, 12 master's awarded. *Entrance requirements:* For master's, GRE (for students seeking merit-based scholarships), bachelor's degree with minimum GPA of 3.0, current resume, 2 letters of recommendation, expanded goals statement, 2 copies of official transcripts. Additional exam requirements/recommendations for international students: Required—TOEFL (minimum score 575 paper-based; 88 iBT), IELTS (minimum score 6.5), PTE (minimum score 59). *Application deadline:* For fall admission, 2/1 priority date for domestic and international students; for spring admission, 11/1 priority date for domestic and international students. Application fee: $75 ($80 for international students). Electronic applications accepted. *Expenses:* $795 per credit in-state tuition, $1,516 out-of-state. *Financial support:* Career-related internships or fieldwork, Federal Work-Study, and scholarships/grants available. Support available to part-time students. Financial award application deadline: 3/1; financial award applicants required to submit FAFSA. *Unit head:* Laurie Schintler, Director, 703-993-2256, Fax: 703-993-4557, E-mail: lschintl@gmu.edu. *Application contact:* Stephanie Ellis, Graduate Admissions Coordinator, 703-993-4478, E-mail: sellis11@gmu.edu.
Website: http://spgia.gmu.edu/programs/graduate-degrees/transportation-policy-operations-logistics-tpol/

Georgia College & State University, Graduate School, The J. Whitney Bunting School of Business, Logistics Education Center, Milledgeville, GA 31061. Offers MLSCM. *Program availability:* Part-time, evening/weekend. *Students:* 79 part-time (32 women); includes 26 minority (19 Black or African American, non-Hispanic/Latino; 4 Hispanic/Latino; 3 Two or more races, non-Hispanic/Latino), 2 international. Average age 34. 36 applicants, 83% accepted, 25 enrolled. In 2017, 21 master's awarded. *Degree requirements:* For master's, minimum overall GPA of 3.0 on all business courses taken at Georgia College, complete program within 7 years. *Entrance requirements:* For master's, GRE or GMAT (not required for students who earned business degree at AACSB-accredited business school and maintained minimum overall undergraduate GPA of 3.15), baccalaureate degree, transcript, certification of immunization, resume. *Application deadline:* For fall admission, 7/1 priority date for domestic students; for spring admission, 11/1 priority date for domestic students. Applications are processed on a rolling basis. Application fee: $40. Electronic applications accepted. *Expenses:* $6,770 per semester full-time tuition and fees. *Financial support:* Application deadline: 3/1; applicants required to submit FAFSA. *Unit head:* Dr. Dale Young, Dean, School of Business, 478-445-5497, Fax: 478-445-5249, E-mail: dale.young@gcsu.edu. *Application contact:* Lynn Hanson, Director of Graduate Programs in Business, 478-445-5115, E-mail: lynn.hanson@gcsu.edu.

Georgia Institute of Technology, Graduate Studies, College of Engineering, H. Milton Stewart School of Industrial and Systems Engineering, Program in International Logistics, Atlanta, GA 30332-0001. Offers MS. *Program availability:* Part-time. *Entrance requirements:* For master's, GRE General Test. Additional exam requirements/recommendations for international students: Required—TOEFL (minimum score 550 paper-based; 79 iBT). Electronic applications accepted. *Expenses:* Contact institution.

Georgia Southern University, Jack N. Averitt College of Graduate Studies, College of Business, Program in Logistics/Supply Chain Management, Statesboro, GA 30458. Offers PhD. *Faculty:* 15 full-time (2 women). *Students:* 8 full-time (3 women), 5 international. Average age 30. 20 applicants, 20% accepted, 3 enrolled. *Degree requirements:* For doctorate, comprehensive exam, thesis/dissertation. *Entrance requirements:* For doctorate, GMAT or GRE, minimum of three letters of reference; statement of purpose; resume. Additional exam requirements/recommendations for international students: Required—TOEFL (minimum score 550 paper-based; 80 iBT), IELTS (minimum score 6). *Application deadline:* For fall admission, 3/15 priority date for domestic and international students. Application fee: $50. Electronic applications accepted. *Expenses:* Tuition, state resident: full-time $4986; part-time $3324 per year. Tuition, nonresident: full-time $21,982; part-time $15,352 per year. *Required fees:* $2092; $1802 per credit hour. $901 per semester. Tuition and fees vary according to course load, campus/location and program. *Financial support:* In 2017–18, 5 students received support, including 6 research assistantships with full tuition reimbursements available (averaging $16,000 per year); teaching assistantships, career-related internships or fieldwork, Federal Work-Study, scholarships/grants, traineeships, and unspecified assistantships also available. Support available to part-time students. Financial award application deadline: 4/15; financial award applicants required to submit FAFSA. *Faculty research:* Buyer-supplier relationships, retail supply chain management, strategic sourcing/outsourcing, supply chain metrics, service scheduling, demand and supply planning, supply chain strategy, operations and supply management, decision

sciences. *Unit head:* Dr. Alan Mackelprang, PhD Program Director, 912-478-0379, E-mail: amackelprang@georgiasouthern.edu. *Application contact:* E-mail: coba@georgiasouthern.edu.
Website: http://cob.georgiasouthern.edu/lscm/phd/

HEC Montreal, School of Business Administration, Master of Science Programs in Administration, Program in International Logistics, Montréal, QC H3T 2A7, Canada. Offers M Sc. Program offered in French. *Students:* 23 full-time (13 women), 4 part-time (1 woman). 22 applicants, 59% accepted, 10 enrolled. In 2017, 15 master's awarded. *Entrance requirements:* For master's, BBA, undergraduate degree in another field, degree deemed equivalent by program director and minimum GPA of 3.0 on 4.3 scale. Additional exam requirements/recommendations for international students: Required—TAGE MAGE (minimum recommended score of 283), GMAT (minimum recommended score of 630), or GRE. *Application deadline:* For fall admission, 3/15 for domestic and international students; for winter admission, 9/15 for domestic and international students. Application fee: $88 Canadian dollars ($184 Canadian dollars for international students). Electronic applications accepted. *Expenses:* Tuition, state resident: full-time $2869 Canadian dollars; part-time $79.70 Canadian dollars per credit. Tuition, nonresident: full-time $8883 Canadian dollars; part-time $246.76 Canadian dollars per credit. *International tuition:* $19,648 Canadian dollars full-time. *Required fees:* $41.20 Canadian dollars per credit. $67.94 Canadian dollars per term. Tuition and fees vary according to degree level and program. *Financial support:* Research assistantships, teaching assistantships, and scholarships/grants available. Financial award application deadline: 9/2. *Unit head:* Dr. Marie-Helene Jobin, Director, 514-340-6283, E-mail: marie-helene.jobin@hec.ca. *Application contact:* Marianne de Moura, Administrative Director, 514-340-6151, Fax: 514-340-6411, E-mail: aide@hec.ca.
Website: http://www.hec.ca/programmes/maitrises/maitrise-logistique-internationale/index.html

Maryville University of Saint Louis, The John E. Simon School of Business, St. Louis, MO 63141-7299. Offers accounting (MBA, MS, Certificate); business studies (Certificate); cybersecurity (MBA, MS, Certificate); financial services (MBA, Certificate); healthcare practice management (MBA, Certificate); human resource management (MBA, Certificate); information technology (MBA, Certificate); management (MBA, Certificate); management and leadership (MA); marketing (MBA, Certificate); project management (MBA, Certificate); sport business management (MBA); supply chain management (Certificate); supply chain management/logistics (MBA). *Accreditation:* ACBSP. *Program availability:* Part-time, 100% online, blended/hybrid learning. *Faculty:* 5 full-time (3 women), 51 part-time/adjunct (16 women). *Students:* 222 full-time (96 women), 498 part-time (222 women); includes 185 minority (104 Black or African American, non-Hispanic/Latino; 5 American Indian or Alaska Native, non-Hispanic/Latino; 30 Asian, non-Hispanic/Latino; 37 Hispanic/Latino; 9 Two or more races, non-Hispanic/Latino), 26 international. Average age 33. In 2017, 106 master's awarded. *Degree requirements:* For master's, capstone course (for MBA). *Entrance requirements:* Additional exam requirements/recommendations for international students: Required—TOEFL (minimum score 563 paper-based; 85 iBT). *Application deadline:* Applications are processed on a rolling basis. Electronic applications accepted. *Expenses:* Contact institution. *Financial support:* Career-related internships or fieldwork, Federal Work-Study, tuition waivers (partial), and campus employment available. Financial award application deadline: 4/1; financial award applicants required to submit FAFSA. *Unit head:* Pam Horwitz, Interim Dean, 314-529-9680, Fax: 314-529-9975. *Application contact:* Dustin Loeffler, Director for Graduate Studies in Business, 314-529-9571, Fax: 314-529-9975, E-mail: dloeffler@maryville.edu.
Website: http://www.maryville.edu/bu/business-administration-masters/

Massachusetts Institute of Technology, School of Engineering, Supply Chain Management Program, Cambridge, MA 02139-4307. Offers logistics (M Eng). *Degree requirements:* For master's, thesis. *Entrance requirements:* Additional exam requirements/recommendations for international students: Required—TOEFL, IELTS. Electronic applications accepted. *Faculty research:* Logistics hubs and clusters; supply chain network risk management; urban logistics; carbon efficient supply chains; scenario planning; supply chain strategy alignment; supply chain innovation in emerging markets; supply chain resilience and security.

Michigan State University, The Graduate School, Eli Broad College of Business, Department of Supply Chain Management, East Lansing, MI 48224. Offers logistics (PhD); operations and sourcing management (PhD); supply chain management (MS), including logistics management, operations management, rail management, supply management. *Program availability:* Part-time. *Degree requirements:* For master's, field study/research project; for doctorate, comprehensive exam, thesis/dissertation. *Entrance requirements:* For master's, GMAT (taken within past 5 years), bachelor's degree, minimum GPA of 3.0 in junior/senior years, transcripts, at least 2 years of professional supply chain work experience, 3 letters of recommendation, essays, resume; for doctorate, GMAT or GRE, bachelor's or master's degree, transcripts, strong work experience, 3 letters of recommendation, statement of personal goals, interview. Additional exam requirements/recommendations for international students: Required—TOEFL (minimum score 600 paper-based). Electronic applications accepted. *Expenses:* Contact institution.

Naval Postgraduate School, Departments and Academic Groups, Graduate School of Business and Public Policy, Monterey, CA 93943. Offers acquisition and contract management (MBA); business administration (EMBA, MBA); contract management (MS); defense business management (MBA); defense systems analysis (MS), including management; defense systems management (international) (MBA); financial management (MBA); information management (MBA); manpower systems analysis (MS); material logistics support management (MBA); program management (MS); resource planning and management for international defense (MBA); supply chain management (MBA); systems acquisition management (MBA); transportation management (MBA). Program only open to commissioned officers of the United States and friendly nations and selected United States federal civilian employees. *Accreditation:* AACSB; NASPAA. *Program availability:* Part-time, online learning. *Degree requirements:* For master's, thesis (for some programs), terminal project/capstone (for some programs). *Faculty research:* U.S. and European public procurement policies for small and medium-sized enterprises, examining external validity criticisms in the choice of students as subjects in accounting experiment studies, assurance of learning in contract management education, contracting for cloud computing: opportunities and risks, NPS, Apple App Store as a business model supporting U.S. Navy requirements.

North Dakota State University, College of Graduate and Interdisciplinary Studies, Interdisciplinary Program in Transportation and Logistics, Fargo, ND 58102. Offers managerial logistics (MML); transportation and logistics (PhD); transportation and urban systems (MS). *Entrance requirements:* For doctorate, 1 year of calculus, statistics and probability, minimum GPA of 3.0. Additional exam requirements/recommendations for international students: Required—TOEFL (minimum score 550 paper-based; 79 iBT). *Faculty research:* Supply chain optimization, spatial analysis of transportation networks, advanced traffic analysis, transportation demand, railroad/intermodal freight.

Norwich University, College of Graduate and Continuing Studies, Master of Business Administration Program, Northfield, VT 05663. Offers construction management (MBA);

energy management (MBA); finance (MBA); logistics (MBA); organizational leadership (MBA); project management (MBA); supply chain management (MBA). *Accreditation:* ACBSP. *Program availability:* Evening/weekend, online only, mostly all online with a week-long residency requirement. *Degree requirements:* For master's, comprehensive exam. *Entrance requirements:* For master's, minimum undergraduate GPA of 2.75. Additional exam requirements/recommendations for international students: Required— TOEFL (minimum score 550 paper-based; 80 iBT), IELTS (minimum score 6.5). Electronic applications accepted. *Expenses:* Contact institution.

The Ohio State University, Graduate School, Max M. Fisher College of Business, Program in Business Logistics Engineering, Columbus, OH 43210. Offers MBLE. *Students:* 48 (25 women). Average age 23. In 2017, 38 master's awarded. *Entrance requirements:* For master's, GRE or GMAT. Additional exam requirements/ recommendations for international students: Required—TOEFL (minimum score 550 paper-based; 79 iBT), Michigan English Language Assessment Battery (minimum score 82); Recommended—IELTS (minimum score 7). *Application deadline:* For fall admission, 12/13 priority date for domestic students, 11/30 priority date for international students. Applications are processed on a rolling basis. Application fee: $60 ($70 for international students). Electronic applications accepted. *Financial support:* Scholarships/grants available. *Unit head:* Steve Denunzio, Program Director, 614-769-3155, E-mail: dununzio.4@osu.edu. *Application contact:* Graduate and Professional Admissions, 614-292-9444, Fax: 614-292-3895, E-mail: gpadmissions@osu.edu. Website: http://fisher.osu.edu/mble

Polytechnic University of Puerto Rico, Miami Campus, Graduate School, Miami, FL 33166. Offers accounting (MBA); business administration (MBA); construction management (MEM); environmental management (MEM); finance (MBA); human resources management (MBA); logistics and supply chain management (MBA); management of international enterprises (MBA); manufacturing management (MEM); marketing management (MBA); project management (MBA). *Program availability:* Part-time, evening/weekend, online learning. *Entrance requirements:* For master's, minimum GPA of 3.0. Electronic applications accepted.

Pontifical Catholic University of Puerto Rico, College of Business Administration, Program in Maritime Logistics and Transportation, Ponce, PR 00717-0777. Offers Professional Certificate.

Pontificia Universidad Catolica Madre y Maestra, Graduate School, Faculty of Engineering Sciences, Santiago, Dominican Republic. Offers earthquake engineering (ME); logistics management (ME).

Purdue University Global, School of Business, Davenport, IA 52807. Offers business administration (MBA); change leadership (MS); entrepreneurship (MBA); finance (MBA); health care management (MBA, MS); human resource (MBA); international business (MBA); management (MS); marketing (MBA); project management (MBA, MS); supply chain management and logistics (MBA, MS). *Accreditation:* ACBSP. *Program availability:* Part-time, evening/weekend, online learning. *Entrance requirements:* Additional exam requirements/recommendations for international students: Required— TOEFL (minimum score 550 paper-based; 80 iBT). Electronic applications accepted.

Rutgers University–Newark, Rutgers Business School–Newark and New Brunswick, Program in Real Estate and Logistics, Newark, NJ 07102. Offers MRE.

Shippensburg University of Pennsylvania, School of Graduate Studies, John L. Grove College of Business, Shippensburg, PA 17257-2299. Offers advanced studies in business (Certificate); advanced supply chain and logistics management (Certificate); business administration (MBA, DBA), including business administration (MBA), business analytics (MBA), finance (MBA), healthcare management (MBA), management information systems (MBA), supply chain management (MBA); finance (Certificate); health care management (Certificate); management information systems (Certificate). *Accreditation:* AACSB. *Program availability:* Part-time, evening/weekend, 100% online, blended/hybrid learning. *Faculty:* 23 full-time (5 women), 1 part-time/adjunct (0 women). *Students:* 46 full-time (14 women), 201 part-time (71 women); includes 35 minority (12 Black or African American, non-Hispanic/Latino; 10 Asian, non-Hispanic/Latino; 11 Hispanic/Latino; 2 Two or more races, non-Hispanic/Latino), 22 international. Average age 32. 169 applicants, 65% accepted, 77 enrolled. In 2017, 105 master's, 82 other advanced degrees awarded. *Degree requirements:* For master's, thesis optional, practicum; for doctorate, comprehensive exam, thesis/dissertation. *Entrance requirements:* For master's, GMAT (minimum score 450 if less than 5 years of mid-level experience, including management experience), current resume; relevant work/ classroom experience; 500-word statement of purpose; prerequisites of quantitative analysis, computer usage, and oral and written communications; laptop computer; for doctorate, GMAT (minimum score of 600 if less than 5 years of substantive professional or teaching experience), 2 letters of recommendation from professionals in academia or industry; 2-3 page personal and professional statement; interview; resume. Additional exam requirements/recommendations for international students: Required—TOEFL (minimum score 550 paper-based, 68 iBT) or IELTS (minimum score 6). *Application deadline:* For fall admission, 4/30 for international students; for spring admission, 9/30 for international students. Applications are processed on a rolling basis. Application fee: $45. Electronic applications accepted. *Expenses:* Tuition, state resident: part-time $500 per credit. Tuition, nonresident: part-time $750 per credit. *Required fees:* $145 per credit. *Financial support:* In 2017–18, 14 students received support. Career-related internships or fieldwork, scholarships/grants, unspecified assistantships, and resident hall director and student payroll positions available. Support available to part-time students. Financial award application deadline: 3/1; financial award applicants required to submit FAFSA. *Unit head:* Dr. John G. Kooti, Dean of the College of Business, 717-477-1435, Fax: 717-477-4003, E-mail: jgkooti@ship.edu. *Application contact:* Maya T. Mapp, Director of Admissions, 717-477-1231, Fax: 717-477-4016, E-mail: mtmapp@ ship.edu. Website: http://www.ship.edu/business

Stevens Institute of Technology, Graduate School, School of Systems and Enterprises, Program in Systems Design and Operational Effectiveness, Hoboken, NJ 07030. Offers Certificate. *Program availability:* Part-time, evening/weekend. *Students:* 5 part-time (0 women). Average age 38. 3 applicants, 100% accepted, 2 enrolled. In 2017, 10 Certificates awarded. *Degree requirements:* For Certificate, minimum B average. *Entrance requirements:* Additional exam requirements/recommendations for international students: Required—TOEFL (minimum score 74 iBT), IELTS (minimum score 6). *Application deadline:* For fall admission, 7/1 for domestic students, 4/15 for international students; for spring admission, 12/1 for domestic and international students. Applications are processed on a rolling basis. Application fee: $60. Electronic applications accepted. *Expenses:* Tuition: Full-time $34,494; part-time $1554 per credit. *Required fees:* $291 per semester. *Financial support:* Fellowships, research assistantships, teaching assistantships, career-related internships or fieldwork, Federal Work-Study, scholarships/grants, and unspecified assistantships available. Financial award application deadline: 2/15; financial award applicants required to submit FAFSA. *Unit head:* Dr. Dinesh Verma, Dean, 201-216-8645, Fax: 201-216-5541, E-mail: dinesh.verma@stevens.edu. *Application contact:* Graduate Admissions, 888-783-8367, Fax: 888-511-1306, E-mail: graduate@stevens.edu.

Trident University International, College of Business Administration, Program in Business Administration, Cypress, CA 90630. Offers business administration (PhD); conflict and negotiation management (MBA); criminal justice administration (MBA); entrepreneurship (MBA); finance (MBA); general management (MBA); government accounting (MBA); human resource management (MBA); information security and digital assurance management (MBA); information technology management (MBA); international business (MBA); logistics management (MBA); marketing (MBA); project management (MBA); public management (MBA); quality management (MBA); strategic leadership (MBA). *Program availability:* Part-time, evening/weekend, online learning. *Degree requirements:* For doctorate, comprehensive exam, thesis/dissertation, defense of dissertation. *Entrance requirements:* For master's, minimum GPA of 2.5 (students with GPA 3.0 or greater may transfer up to 30% of graduate level credits); for doctorate, minimum GPA of 3.4, curriculum vitae, course work in research methods or statistics. Additional exam requirements/recommendations for international students: Required— TOEFL. Electronic applications accepted.

Universidad del Turabo, Graduate Programs, School of Business and Entrepreneurship, Program in Logistics and Materials Management, Gurabo, PR 00778-3030. Offers MBA. *Program availability:* Part-time, evening/weekend. *Entrance requirements:* For master's, GRE, EXADEP or GMAT, interview, essay, official transcript, recommendation letters. Electronic applications accepted.

University at Buffalo, the State University of New York, Graduate School, School of Engineering and Applied Sciences, Program in Sustainable Transportation and Logistics, Buffalo, NY 14260. Offers MS.

University at Buffalo, the State University of New York, Graduate School, School of Management, Buffalo, NY 14260. Offers accounting (MS); analytics (MBA); business administration (PMBA); consulting (MBA); finance (MBA, MS), including financial risk management (MS); quantitative finance (MS); healthcare (MBA); information assurance (MBA); information systems (MBA); international management (MBA); management (EMBA, PhD); management information systems (MS); marketing (MBA); supply chain and operations (MBA); supply chains and operations management (MS); Au D/MBA; DDS/MBA; JD/MBA; M Arch/MBA; MD/MBA; MPH/MBA; MSW/MBA; Pharm D/MBA. *Accreditation:* AACSB. *Program availability:* Part-time, evening/weekend. *Faculty:* 80 full-time (26 women), 45 part-time/adjunct (12 women). *Students:* 597 full-time (251 women); includes 83 minority (19 Black or African American, non-Hispanic/Latino; 59 Asian, non-Hispanic/Latino; 5 Hispanic/Latino), 306 international. Average age 25. 2,109 applicants, 46% accepted, 376 enrolled. In 2017, 371 master's, 13 doctorates awarded. *Degree requirements:* For master's, capstone courses or projects; for doctorate, comprehensive exam, thesis/dissertation. *Entrance requirements:* For master's, GMAT (for MS in accounting, finance); GRE or GMAT (for MBA, MS in management information systems, supply chains and operations management), essays, letters of recommendation; for doctorate, GMAT or GRE, essays, writing sample, letters of recommendation. Additional exam requirements/recommendations for international students: Required—TOEFL (minimum score 95 iBT) or IELTS (minimum score 6.5); Recommended—TSE (minimum score 73). *Application deadline:* For fall admission, 10/ 15 priority date for domestic and international students; for winter admission, 2/1 priority date for domestic and international students; for spring admission, 4/15 for domestic students; for summer admission, 5/15 for domestic students. Application fee: $100. Electronic applications accepted. *Expenses:* Varies by program. *Financial support:* Fellowships with full and partial tuition reimbursements, research assistantships with full and partial tuition reimbursements, teaching assistantships with full and partial tuition reimbursements, career-related internships or fieldwork, Federal Work-Study, institutionally sponsored loans, scholarships/grants, health care benefits, and unspecified assistantships available. Financial award application deadline: 2/15. *Faculty research:* Data analytics, accounting and law, rate finance, consumer behavior, supply chain logistics, leadership and team effectiveness. *Total annual research expenditures:* $968,376. *Unit head:* Erin K. O'Brien, Assistant Dean and Director of Graduate Programs, 716-645-3204, Fax: 716-645-2341, E-mail: ekobrien@buffalo.edu. *Application contact:* Meghan Felser, Director of Admissions and Recruiting, 716-645-3204, Fax: 716-645-2341, E-mail: mpwood@buffalo.edu. Website: http://mgt.buffalo.edu/

The University of Alabama in Huntsville, School of Graduate Studies, College of Business Administration, Programs in Business and Management, Huntsville, AL 35899. Offers business analytics (MSMS); federal contracting and procurement management (Certificate); human resource management (MSM); management (MBA), including acquisition management, entrepreneurship, federal contract accounting, finance, human resource management, logistics and supply chain management, marketing, project management; supply chain management (Certificate); technology and innovation management (Certificate). *Accreditation:* AACSB. *Program availability:* Part-time, evening/weekend. *Degree requirements:* For master's, comprehensive exam, thesis or alternative. *Entrance requirements:* For master's, GMAT (minimum score 500), minimum AACSB index of 1080. Additional exam requirements/recommendations for international students: Required—TOEFL (minimum score 550 paper-based; 80 iBT), IELTS (minimum score 6.5). Electronic applications accepted. *Faculty research:* Supply chain management, management of research and development, international marketing and branding, organizational behavior and human resource management, social networks and computational economics.

University of Alaska Anchorage, College of Business and Public Policy, Program in Logistics, Anchorage, AK 99508. Offers global supply chain management (MS); supply chain management (Certificate). *Program availability:* Part-time, evening/weekend, online learning. *Degree requirements:* For master's, thesis or alternative, research project. *Entrance requirements:* Additional exam requirements/recommendations for international students: Required—TOEFL (minimum score 550 paper-based).

University of Dallas, Satish and Yasmin Gupta College of Business, Irving, TX 75062-4736. Offers accounting (MBA, MS); business administration (DBA); business analytics (MS); business management (MBA); corporate finance (MBA); cybersecurity (MS); finance (MS); financial services (MBA); global business (MBA, MS); health services management (MBA); human resource management (MBA); information and technology management (MS); information assurance (MBA); information technology (MBA); information technology service management (MBA); marketing management (MBA); organization development (MBA); project management (MBA); sports and entertainment management (MBA); strategic leadership (MBA); supply chain management (MBA). *Accreditation:* AACSB. *Program availability:* Part-time, evening/weekend, online learning. *Entrance requirements:* Additional exam requirements/recommendations for international students: Required—TOEFL. *Application deadline:* Applications are processed on a rolling basis. Application fee: $50. Electronic applications accepted. *Expenses:* Contact institution. *Financial support:* Application deadline: 2/15; applicants required to submit FAFSA. *Unit head:* Brett J.L. Landry, Dean, 972-721-5356, E-mail: blandry@udallas.edu. *Application contact:* Dr. David Sweet, Dean, Braniff Graduate School, 972-721-5288, Fax: 972-721-5280, E-mail: dsweet@udallas.edu. Website: http://www.udallas.edu/

University of Houston, College of Technology, Department of Information and Logistics Technology, Houston, TX 77204. Offers information security (MS); supply chain and logistics technology (MS); technology project management (MS). *Program*

Logistics

availability: Part-time. Degree requirements: For master's, project or thesis (most programs). Entrance requirements: For master's, GMAT. Additional exam requirements/recommendations for international students: Required—TOEFL (minimum score 550 paper-based; 79 iBT). Electronic applications accepted.

The University of Kansas, Graduate Studies, School of Business, Program in Business, Lawrence, KS 66045. Offers business and organizational leadership (MS); decision sciences and supply chain management (PhD); finance (PhD); human resources management (PhD); marketing (PhD); organizational behavior (PhD); strategic management (PhD); supply chain management and logistics (MS). Accreditation: AACSB. Program availability: Part-time. Students: 66 full-time (18 women), 227 part-time (76 women); includes 59 minority (21 Black or African American, non-Hispanic/Latino; 2 American Indian or Alaska Native, non-Hispanic/Latino; 13 Asian, non-Hispanic/Latino; 3 Hispanic/Latino; 20 Two or more races, non-Hispanic/Latino), 29 international. Average age 32. 329 applicants, 71% accepted, 185 enrolled. In 2017, 30 master's, 8 doctorates awarded. Entrance requirements: For master's, GMAT, official transcript, three letters of recommendation, resume, statement of purpose; for doctorate, GMAT or GRE, official transcript, three letters of recommendation, resume, statement of purpose. Additional exam requirements/recommendations for international students: Required—TOEFL (minimum score 600 paper-based; 100 iBT). Application deadline: For fall admission, 1/10 for domestic and international students. Application fee: $65 ($85 for international students). Electronic applications accepted. Financial support: Fellowships, research assistantships, teaching assistantships, scholarships/grants, health care benefits, tuition waivers (full), and unspecified assistantships available. Financial award application deadline: 1/10. Faculty research: Strategic human resource management, business ethics, organizational theory/behavior, corporate strategy, international business, supply chain management, Bayesian networks, game theory, decision analysis and time/series analysis, pricing, consumer effects, advertising and emotion. Unit head: Charly Edmonds, Director, 785-864-3841, E-mail: bschoolphd@ku.edu. Application contact: Graduate Admission Contact, 785-864-7500, E-mail: bschoolphd@ku.edu. Website: http://www.business.ku.edu/

University of Louisville, J. B. Speed School of Engineering, Department of Industrial Engineering, Louisville, KY 40292-0001. Offers engineering management (M Eng); industrial engineering (M Eng, MS, PhD); logistics and distribution (Certificate). Accreditation: ABET (one or more programs are accredited). Program availability: 100% online, blended/hybrid learning. Faculty: 9 full-time (4 women), 6 part-time/adjunct (2 women). Students: 84 full-time (28 women), 115 part-time (19 women); includes 33 minority (16 Black or African American, non-Hispanic/Latino; 1 American Indian or Alaska Native, non-Hispanic/Latino; 4 Asian, non-Hispanic/Latino; 6 Hispanic/Latino; 6 Two or more races, non-Hispanic/Latino), 81 international. Average age 31. 99 applicants, 70% accepted, 55 enrolled. In 2017, 29 master's, 2 doctorates awarded. Degree requirements: For master's and Certificate, thesis optional; for doctorate, comprehensive exam, thesis/dissertation. Entrance requirements: For master's and doctorate, GRE General Test, two letters of recommendation, official transcripts. Additional exam requirements/recommendations for international students: Required—TOEFL (minimum score 550 paper-based; 80 iBT), IELTS (minimum score 6.5). Application deadline: For fall admission, 5/1 priority date for domestic and international students; for spring admission, 11/1 priority date for domestic and international students; for summer admission, 3/1 priority date for domestic and international students. Applications are processed on a rolling basis. Application fee: $65. Electronic applications accepted. Expenses: Tuition, state resident: full-time $12,246; part-time $681 per credit hour. Tuition, nonresident: full-time $25,486; part-time $1417 per credit hour. Required fees: $196. Tuition and fees vary according to course load, program and reciprocity agreements. Financial support: In 2017–18, 2 fellowships with full tuition reimbursements (averaging $22,000 per year), 3 research assistantships with full tuition reimbursements (averaging $22,000 per year), 4 teaching assistantships with full tuition reimbursements (averaging $22,000 per year) were awarded; scholarships/grants, health care benefits, and tuition waivers (full) also available. Financial award application deadline: 1/1; financial award applicants required to submit FAFSA. Faculty research: Optimization, computer simulation, logistics and distribution, ergonomics and human factors, advanced manufacturing process. Total annual research expenditures: $620,986. Unit head: Dr. Suraj M. Alexander, Chair, 502-852-6342, Fax: 502-852-5633, E-mail: suraj.alexander@louisville.edu. Application contact: Lihui Bai, Director of Graduate Studies, 502-852-1416, E-mail: lihui.bai@louisville.edu. Website: http://www.louisville.edu/speed/industrial/

University of Missouri–St. Louis, College of Business Administration, St. Louis, MO 63121. Offers accounting (M Acc); business administration (MBA, DBA, PhD, Certificate), including logistics and supply chain management (PhD); business intelligence (Certificate); cybersecurity (Certificate); digital and social media marketing (Certificate); human resources management (Certificate); information systems (MS); logistics and supply chain management (Certificate); marketing management (Certificate). Program availability: Part-time, evening/weekend. Faculty: 51 full-time (21 women), 25 part-time/adjunct (5 women). Students: 146 full-time (77 women), 326 part-time (143 women); includes 82 minority (32 Black or African American, non-Hispanic/Latino; 1 American Indian or Alaska Native, non-Hispanic/Latino; 34 Asian, non-Hispanic/Latino; 11 Hispanic/Latino; 4 Two or more races, non-Hispanic/Latino), 89 international. 276 applicants, 83% accepted, 142 enrolled. Degree requirements: For doctorate, thesis/dissertation. Entrance requirements: For master's, GMAT, 2 letters of recommendation; for doctorate, GMAT or GRE, 3 letters of recommendation. Additional exam requirements/recommendations for international students: Recommended—TOEFL (minimum score 550 paper-based; 79 iBT), IELTS (minimum score 6.5). Application deadline: For fall admission, 7/1 priority date for domestic and international students; for spring admission, 12/1 priority date for domestic and international students. Applications are processed on a rolling basis. Application fee: $50 ($40 for international students). Electronic applications accepted. Expenses: Tuition, state resident: part-time $476.50 per credit hour. Tuition, nonresident: part-time $1169.70 per credit hour. Financial support: Research assistantships with tuition reimbursements, teaching assistantships with tuition reimbursements, career-related internships or fieldwork, Federal Work-Study, and institutionally sponsored loans available. Support available to part-time students. Financial award application deadline: 4/1; financial award applicants required to submit FAFSA. Faculty research: Statistical decision aids, commercial banking, corporate finance, operations management, information systems. Unit head: Charles E. Hoffman, Dean, 314-516-6109, Fax: 314-516-6420. Application contact: 314-516-5458, Fax: 314-516-6996, E-mail: gradadm@umsl.edu. Website: http://www.umsl.edu/divisions/business/

The University of North Carolina at Charlotte, William States Lee College of Engineering, Department of Systems Engineering and Engineering Management, Charlotte, NC 28223-0001. Offers energy analytics (Graduate Certificate); engineering management (MSEM); Lean Six Sigma (Graduate Certificate); logistics and supply chains (Graduate Certificate); systems analytics (Graduate Certificate). Program availability: Part-time, evening/weekend, 100% online, blended/hybrid learning. Faculty: 9 full-time (2 women), 1 part-time/adjunct (0 women). Students: 32 full-time (9 women), 54 part-time (11 women); includes 15 minority (8 Black or African American, non-Hispanic/Latino; 1 American Indian or Alaska Native, non-Hispanic/Latino; 2 Asian, non-

Hispanic/Latino; 2 Hispanic/Latino; 2 Two or more races, non-Hispanic/Latino), 33 international. Average age 29. 156 applicants, 62% accepted, 25 enrolled. In 2017, 20 master's, 5 other advanced degrees awarded. Degree requirements: For master's, project or thesis. Entrance requirements: For master's, GRE or GMAT, bachelor's degree in engineering or a closely-related technical or scientific field, or in business, provided relevant technical course requirements have been met; undergraduate coursework in engineering economics, calculus, or statistics; minimum GPA of 3.0; for Graduate Certificate, bachelor's degree in engineering or closely-related technical or scientific field, or in business, provided relevant technical course requirements have been met; minimum GPA of 3.0; undergraduate coursework in engineering economics, calculus, and statistics; written description of work experience. Additional exam requirements/recommendations for international students: Required—TOEFL (minimum score 523 paper-based; 70 iBT) or IELTS (6.5). Application deadline: For fall admission, 3/1 priority date for domestic and international students; for spring admission, 10/1 priority date for domestic and international students; for summer admission, 4/1 priority date for domestic and international students. Applications are processed on a rolling basis. Application fee: $75. Electronic applications accepted. Expenses: Contact institution. Financial support: Career-related internships or fieldwork, institutionally sponsored loans, scholarships/grants, and unspecified assistantships available. Support available to part-time students. Financial award application deadline: 3/1; financial award applicants required to submit FAFSA. Total annual research expenditures: $209,562. Unit head: Dr. Simon M. Hsiang, Chair, 704-687-1958, E-mail: shsiang1@uncc.edu. Application contact: Kathy B. Giddings, Director of Graduate Admissions, 704-687-5503, Fax: 704-687-1668, E-mail: gradadm@uncc.edu. Website: http://seem.uncc.edu/

University of North Florida, Coggin College of Business, MBA Program, Jacksonville, FL 32224. Offers accounting (MBA); construction management (MBA); e-commerce (MBA); economics (MBA); finance (MBA); human resource management (MBA); international business (MBA); logistics (MBA); management applications (MBA). Accreditation: AACSB. Program availability: Part-time, evening/weekend. Entrance requirements: For master's, GMAT or GRE, U.S. bachelor's degree from regionally-accredited university or equivalent foreign degree. Additional exam requirements/recommendations for international students: Required—TOEFL (minimum score 550 paper-based; 79 iBT). Faculty research: Performance measures, costing, and inventory issues in logistics and supply chain management; inter-organizational systems; international management and marketing practices; e-commerce; organizational learning and socialization processes.

University of North Texas, Robert B. Toulouse School of Graduate Studies, Denton, TX 76203-5459. Offers accounting (MS); applied anthropology (MA, MS); applied behavior analysis (Certificate); applied geography (MA); applied technology and performance improvement (M Ed, MS); art education (MA); art history (MA); art museum education (Certificate); arts leadership (Certificate); audiology (Au D); behavior analysis (MS); behavioral science (PhD); biochemistry and molecular biology (MS); biology (MA, MS); biomedical engineering (MS); business analysis (MS); chemistry (MS); clinical health psychology (PhD); communication studies (MA, MS); computer engineering (MS); computer science (MS); counseling (M Ed, MS), including clinical mental health counseling (MS), college and university counseling, elementary school counseling, secondary school counseling; creative writing (MA); criminal justice (MS); curriculum and instruction (M Ed); decision sciences (MBA); design (MA, MFA), including fashion design (MFA), innovation studies, interior design (MFA); early childhood studies (MS); economics (MS); educational leadership (M Ed, Ed D); educational psychology (MS, PhD), including family studies (MS), gifted and talented (MS), human development (MS), learning and cognition (MS), research, measurement and evaluation (MS); electrical engineering (MS); emergency management (MPA); engineering technology (MS); English (MA); English as a second language (MA); environmental science (MS); finance (MBA, MS); financial management (MPA); French (MA); health services management (MBA); higher education (M Ed, Ed D); history (MA, MS); hospitality management (MS); human resources management (MPA); information science (MS); information systems (PhD); information technologies (MBA); interdisciplinary studies (MA, MS); international studies (MA); international sustainable tourism (MS); jazz studies (MM); journalism (MA, MJ, Graduate Certificate), including interactive and virtual digital communication (Graduate Certificate), narrative journalism (Graduate Certificate), public relations (Graduate Certificate); kinesiology (MS); linguistics (MA); local government management (MPA); logistics (PhD); logistics and supply chain management (MBA); long-term care, senior housing, and aging services (MA); management (PhD); marketing (MBA); mathematics (MA, MS); mechanical and energy engineering (MS, PhD); music (MA), including ethnomusicology, music theory, musicology, performance; music composition (PhD); music education (MM Ed, PhD); nonprofit management (MPA); operations and supply chain management (MBA); performance (MM, DMA); philosophy (MA); political science (MA); professional and technical communication (MA); radio, television and film (MA, MFA); rehabilitation counseling (Certificate); sociology (MA); Spanish (MA); special education (M Ed); speech-language pathology (MA); strategic management (MBA); studio art (MFA); teaching (M Ed); MBA/MS. Program availability: Part-time, evening/weekend, online learning. Terminal master's awarded for partial completion of doctoral program. Degree requirements: For master's, variable foreign language requirement, comprehensive exam, thesis (for some programs); for doctorate, variable foreign language requirement, comprehensive exam (for some programs), thesis/dissertation; for other advanced degree, variable foreign language requirement, comprehensive exam (for some programs). Entrance requirements: For master's and doctorate, GRE, GMAT. Additional exam requirements/recommendations for international students: Required—TOEFL (minimum score 550 paper-based; 79 iBT). Electronic applications accepted.

University of South Africa, College of Economic and Management Sciences, Pretoria, South Africa. Offers accounting (D Admin, D Com); accounting science (DA); auditing (D Admin, D Com); business administration (M Tech); business economics (D Admin); business leadership (DBL); business management (D Admin, D Com); economic management analysis (M Tech); economics (D Admin, D Com, PhD); human resource development (M Tech); industrial psychology (D Admin, D Com, PhD); logistics (D Com); marketing (M Tech); public administration (D Admin, D Com, DPA, PhD); public management (M Tech); quantitative management (D Admin, D Com); real estate (M Tech); statistics (D Admin, PhD); tourism management (D Admin, D Com); transport economics (D Admin, D Com).

The University of Tennessee, Graduate School, College of Business Administration, Program in Business Administration, Knoxville, TN 37996. Offers accounting (PhD); finance (MBA, PhD); logistics and transportation (MBA, PhD); management (PhD); marketing (MBA, PhD); operations management (MBA); professional business administration (MBA); statistics (PhD); JD/MBA; MS/MBA; Pharm D/MBA. Pharm D/MBA offered jointly with The University of Tennessee Health Science Center. Accreditation: AACSB. Program availability: Online learning. Degree requirements: For master's, thesis or alternative; for doctorate, thesis/dissertation. Entrance requirements: For master's and doctorate, GMAT, minimum GPA of 2.7. Additional exam requirements/recommendations for international students: Required—TOEFL. Electronic applications accepted.

The University of Tennessee at Chattanooga, Engineering Management and Technology Program, Chattanooga, TN 37403. Offers construction management (Graduate Certificate); engineering management (MS); fundamentals of engineering management (Graduate Certificate); leadership and ethics (Graduate Certificate); logistics and supply chain management (Graduate Certificate); power systems management (Graduate Certificate); project and technology management (Graduate Certificate); quality management (Graduate Certificate). *Program availability:* 100% online, blended/hybrid learning. *Students:* 14 full-time (3 women), 50 part-time (11 women); includes 17 minority (10 Black or African American, non-Hispanic/Latino; 1 Asian, non-Hispanic/Latino; 6 Hispanic/Latino), 5 international. Average age 33. 34 applicants, 94% accepted, 20 enrolled. In 2017, 18 master's, 6 other advanced degrees awarded. *Degree requirements:* For master's, thesis. *Entrance requirements:* For master's, GRE General Test, letters of recommendation; minimum undergraduate GPA of 2.7 overall or 3.0 in final two years; for Graduate Certificate, baccalaureate degree and professional experience or have already been admitted to engineering/engineering management graduate program. Additional exam requirements/recommendations for international students: Required—TOEFL (minimum score 550 paper-based; 79 iBT), IELTS (minimum score 6). *Application deadline:* For fall admission, 6/15 priority date for domestic students, 7/1 for international students; for spring admission, 11/1 priority date for domestic students, 11/1 for international students. Applications are processed on a rolling basis. Application fee: $35 ($40 for international students). Electronic applications accepted. *Expenses:* Contact institution. *Financial support:* Research assistantships, teaching assistantships, career-related internships or fieldwork, scholarships/grants, and unspecified assistantships available. Support available to part-time students. Financial award application deadline: 7/1; financial award applicants required to submit FAFSA. *Faculty research:* Plant layout design, lean manufacturing, Six Sigma, value management, product development. *Total annual research expenditures:* $108,577. *Unit head:* Dr. Neslihan Alp, Department Head, 423-425-4032, Fax: 423-425-5818, E-mail: neslihan-alp@utc.edu. *Application contact:* Dr. Joanne Romagni, Dean of the Graduate School, 423-425-4478, Fax: 423-425-5223, E-mail: joanne-romagni@utc.edu. Website: https://www.utc.edu/college-engineering-computer-science/programs/engineering-management-and-technology/index.php

The University of Texas at Arlington, Graduate School, College of Engineering, Department of Industrial, Manufacturing, and Systems Engineering, Program in Logistics, Arlington, TX 76019. Offers MS. *Degree requirements:* For master's, comprehensive exam, thesis optional. *Entrance requirements:* For master's, GRE, GMAT, minimum GPA of 3.0. Additional exam requirements/recommendations for international students: Required—TOEFL (minimum score 550 paper-based).

University of Washington, Graduate School, Interdisciplinary Program in Global Trade, Transportation and Logistics Studies, Seattle, WA 98195. Offers Certificate.

Virginia International University, School of Business, Fairfax, VA 22030. Offers accounting (MBA, MS); entrepreneurship (MBA); executive management (Graduate Certificate); global logistics (MBA); health care management (MBA); hospitality and tourism management (MBA); human resources management (MBA); international business management (MBA); international finance (MBA); marketing management (MBA); mass media and public relations (MBA); project management (MBA, MS). *Program availability:* Part-time, online learning. *Entrance requirements:* For master's and Graduate Certificate, bachelor's degree. Additional exam requirements/recommendations for international students: Required—TOEFL (minimum score 550 paper-based; 80 iBT), IELTS (minimum score 6). Electronic applications accepted.

Wright State University, Graduate School, Raj Soin College of Business, Department of Information Systems and Operations Management, Logistics and Supply Chain Management Program, Dayton, OH 45435. Offers MS.

Supply Chain Management

Abilene Christian University, College of Graduate and Professional Studies, Program in Business Administration, Addison, TX 75001. Offers business analytics (MBA); corporate finance (MBA); general management (MBA); healthcare administration (MBA); human resource management (MBA); international business (MBA); management: business analytics (MS); management: healthcare administration (MS); management: international business (MS); management: marketing (MS); management: operations and supply chain management (MS); marketing (MBA); nonprofit leadership (MBA); operations and supply chain management (MBA). *Program availability:* Part-time, online only, 100% online. *Faculty:* 2 full-time (0 women), 6 part-time/adjunct (2 women). *Students:* 109 full-time (47 women), 51 part-time (22 women); includes 42 minority (33 Black or African American, non-Hispanic/Latino; 1 American Indian or Alaska Native, non-Hispanic/Latino; 2 Asian, non-Hispanic/Latino; 6 Hispanic/Latino). 125 applicants, 65% accepted, 58 enrolled. *Entrance requirements:* Additional exam requirements/recommendations for international students: Required—TOEFL (minimum score 80 iBT), IELTS (minimum score 6). *Application deadline:* For fall admission, 8/14 priority date for domestic students; for winter admission, 10/1 priority date for domestic students; for spring admission, 12/15 priority date for domestic students; for summer admission, 4/15 priority date for domestic students. Applications are processed on a rolling basis. Application fee: $50. Electronic applications accepted. *Expenses:* $700 per hour. *Financial support:* In 2017–18, 2 students received support. Application deadline: 4/1; applicants required to submit FAFSA. *Faculty research:* Organizational structure, financial management, cost accounting, unit analysis management. *Unit head:* Phil Vardiman, Program Director, 325-674-2153, E-mail: pxv02b@acu.edu. *Application contact:* Graduate Advisor, 817-219-7300, E-mail: gradonline@acu.edu. Website: http://www.acu.edu/online/academics/mba-business-administration.html

Adelphi University, Robert B. Willumstad School of Business, Program in Supply Chain Management, Garden City, NY 11530-0701. Offers MS. *Program availability:* Part-time, online learning. *Students:* 8 full-time (2 women), 2 part-time (0 women); includes 2 minority (1 Asian, non-Hispanic/Latino; 1 Hispanic/Latino), 3 international. Average age 33. 23 applicants, 35% accepted, 4 enrolled. In 2017, 2 master's awarded. *Entrance requirements:* For master's, GMAT, official transcripts, bachelor's degree, 500-word essay, letter of recommendation, resume. Additional exam requirements/recommendations for international students: Required—TOEFL (minimum score 550 paper-based; 80 iBT), IELTS (minimum score 6.5). Application fee: $50. *Expenses:* Contact institution. *Unit head:* Anthony Libertella, Dean, 516-877-4661, E-mail: libertel@adelphi.edu. *Application contact:* E-mail: graduateadmissions@adelphi.edu. Website: http://business.adelphi.edu/academics/graduate-degree-programs/ms-supply-chain-management/

Albany State University, College of Business, Albany, GA 31705-2717. Offers accounting (MBA); general business administration (MBA); healthcare (MBA); public administration (MBA); supply chain and logistics (MBA). *Accreditation:* ACBSP. *Program availability:* Part-time, evening/weekend. *Degree requirements:* For master's, comprehensive exam, internship, 3 hours of physical education. *Entrance requirements:* For master's, GMAT (minimum score of 450)/GRE (minimum score of 800) for those without earned master's degree or higher, minimum undergraduate GPA of 2.5, 2 letters of reference, official transcript, pre-entrance medical record and certificate of immunization. Electronic applications accepted. *Faculty research:* Diversity issues, ancestry, understanding finance through use of technology.

American Graduate University, Program in Business Administration, Covina, CA 91724. Offers acquisition and contracting (MBA); supply chain management (MBA). *Program availability:* Part-time, online learning. *Degree requirements:* For master's, thesis. *Entrance requirements:* For master's, undergraduate degree from institution accredited by accrediting agency recognized by the U.S. Department of Education. Additional exam requirements/recommendations for international students: Required—TOEFL. Electronic applications accepted.

American Graduate University, Program in Supply Chain Management, Covina, CA 91724. Offers MSCM, Certificate. *Program availability:* Part-time, online learning. *Degree requirements:* For master's, comprehensive exam or project. *Entrance requirements:* For master's, undergraduate degree from institution accredited by accrediting agency recognized by the U.S. Department of Education. Additional exam requirements/recommendations for international students: Required—TOEFL.

Anderson University, College of Business, Anderson, SC 29621-4035. Offers business administration (MBA); healthcare leadership (MBA); human resources (MBA); marketing (MBA); organizational leadership (MOL); supply chain management (MBA). *Accreditation:* ACBSP. *Expenses:* Contact institution. *Financial support:* Tuition waivers available. Financial award application deadline: 3/1; financial award applicants required to submit FAFSA. *Unit head:* Steve Nail, Dean, 864-MBA-6000. *Application contact:* Mallory Knight, Graduate Admission Counselor, 864-231-2182, Fax: 864-231-2115, E-mail: malloryknight@andersonuniversity.edu. Website: http://www.andersonuniversity.edu/business

Arizona State University at the Tempe campus, W. P. Carey School of Business, Program in Business Administration, Tempe, AZ 85287-4906. Offers entrepreneurship (MBA); finance (MBA); health sector management (MBA); international business (MBA); leadership (MBA); marketing (MBA); organizational behavior (PhD); strategic management (PhD); supply chain management (MBA, PhD); JD/MBA; MBA/M Acc; MBA/M Arch. *Accreditation:* AACSB. *Program availability:* Part-time, evening/weekend, online learning. Terminal master's awarded for partial completion of doctoral program. *Degree requirements:* For master's, thesis or alternative, internship, interactive Program of Study (iPOS) submitted before completing 50 percent of required credit hours; for doctorate, comprehensive exam, thesis/dissertation, interactive Program of Study (iPOS) submitted before completing 50 percent of required credit hours. *Entrance requirements:* For master's, GMAT, minimum GPA of 3.0 in last 2 years of work leading to bachelor's degree, 2 letters of recommendation, professional resume, official transcripts, 3 essays; for doctorate, GMAT or GRE, minimum GPA of 3.0 in last 2 years of work leading to bachelor's degree, 3 letters of recommendation, resume, personal statement/essay. Additional exam requirements/recommendations for international students: Required—TOEFL (minimum score 550 paper-based; 80 iBT), IELTS (minimum score 6.5). Electronic applications accepted. *Expenses:* Contact institution.

Ashland University, Dauch College of Business and Economics, Ashland, OH 44805-3702. Offers accounting (MBA); business analytics (MBA); entrepreneurship (MBA); financial management (MBA); global management (MBA); health care management and leadership (MBA); human resource management (MBA); human resources (MBA); management information systems (MBA); project management (MBA); sport management (MBA); supply chain management (MBA). *Accreditation:* ACBSP. *Program availability:* Part-time, evening/weekend, 100% online, blended/hybrid learning. *Faculty:* 20 full-time (8 women), 13 part-time/adjunct (2 women). *Students:* 458 full-time (210 women), 144 part-time (52 women); includes 88 minority (63 Black or African American, non-Hispanic/Latino; 1 American Indian or Alaska Native, non-Hispanic/Latino; 10 Asian, non-Hispanic/Latino; 14 Hispanic/Latino), 202 international. Average age 31. 216 applicants, 74% accepted, 115 enrolled. In 2017, 184 master's awarded. Terminal master's awarded for partial completion of doctoral program. *Degree requirements:* For master's, thesis optional, capstone course. *Entrance requirements:* For master's, 2 years of full-time work experience. Additional exam requirements/recommendations for international students: Required—TOEFL (minimum score 550 paper-based; 78 iBT). *Application deadline:* For fall admission, 8/1 priority date for domestic students; for spring admission, 12/1 priority date for domestic students. Applications are processed on a rolling basis. Application fee: $30. Electronic applications accepted. *Expenses:* $815 per credit hour, $15 technology fee for online sections. *Financial support:* Scholarships/grants, tuition waivers (partial), and unspecified assistantships available. Financial award application deadline: 4/15; financial award applicants required to submit FAFSA. *Faculty research:* Relationship marketing strategy, executive compensation and company performance, online marketplaces in electronic commerce, diversity training in campus recreation departments, entrepreneurship in developing and emerging economies. *Unit head:* Dr. Elad Granot, Dean, 419-289-5932, E-mail: egranot@ashland.edu. *Application contact:* Stephen W. Krispinsky, Executive Director of MBA Program, 419-289-5236, Fax: 419-289-5910, E-mail: skrispin@ashland.edu. Website: http://www.mba.ashland.edu

Athens State University, Graduate Programs, Athens, AL 35611. Offers career and technical education (M Ed); global logistics and supply chain management (MS); religious studies (MA). *Students:* 28 full-time (19 women), 119 part-time (55 women). *Expenses:* Tuition, state resident: full-time $3900; part-time $325 per credit hour. Tuition, nonresident: full-time $3900; part-time $325 per credit hour. Website: http://www.athens.edu/masters/

Binghamton University, State University of New York, Graduate School, School of Management, Program in Management, Binghamton, NY 13902-6000. Offers finance (PhD); management information systems (PhD); marketing (PhD); organizational studies (PhD); supply chain management (PhD). *Students:* 8 full-time (5 women), 12 part-time (5 women), 19 international. Average age 30. 57 applicants, 21% accepted, 7 enrolled. In 2017, 3 doctorates awarded. *Degree requirements:* For doctorate, thesis/dissertation. *Entrance requirements:* For doctorate, GMAT. *Application deadline:* For fall

Supply Chain Management

admission, 2/1 for domestic students. *Financial support:* In 2017–18, 18 students received support. *Unit head:* Dr. Upinder Dhillon, Dean, 607-777-2314, E-mail: dhillon@binghamton.edu. *Application contact:* Marianne Ferry, Administrative Assistant, Executive Education and PhD Programs, 607-777-2342, E-mail: mferry@binghamton.edu.

Boston University, Metropolitan College, Department of Administrative Sciences, Boston, MA 02215. Offers applied business analytics (MS); economic development and tourism management (MSAS); enterprise risk management (MS); financial management (MS); global marketing management (MS); innovation and technology (MSAS); insurance management (MS); project management (MS); supply chain management (MS). *Accreditation:* AACSB. *Program availability:* Part-time, evening/weekend, 100% online, blended/hybrid learning. *Faculty:* 21 full-time (5 women), 34 part-time/adjunct (5 women). *Students:* 297 full-time (156 women), 597 part-time (298 women); includes 183 minority (58 Black or African American, non-Hispanic/Latino; 2 American Indian or Alaska Native, non-Hispanic/Latino; 56 Asian, non-Hispanic/Latino; 51 Hispanic/Latino; 2 Native Hawaiian or other Pacific Islander, non-Hispanic/Latino; 14 Two or more races, non-Hispanic/Latino), 391 international. Average age 30. 963 applicants, 64% accepted, 209 enrolled. In 2017, 372 master's awarded. *Degree requirements:* For master's, thesis optional. *Entrance requirements:* For master's, 1 year of work experience, minimum GPA of 3.0. Additional exam requirements/recommendations for international students: Required—TOEFL (minimum score 84 iBT). *Application deadline:* Applications are processed on a rolling basis. Application fee: $85. Electronic applications accepted. *Expenses:* Contact institution. *Financial support:* In 2017–18, 15 students received support, including 16 research assistantships (averaging $8,400 per year), 12 teaching assistantships (averaging $2,700 per year); career-related internships or fieldwork, Federal Work-Study, and unspecified assistantships also available. Financial award applicants required to submit FAFSA. *Faculty research:* International business, innovative process. *Unit head:* Dr. John Sullivan, Chair, 617-353-3016, E-mail: adminsc@bu.edu. *Application contact:* Fiona Niven, Administrative Sciences Department, 617-353-3016, E-mail: adminsc@bu.edu.
Website: http://www.bu.edu/met/academic-community/departments/administrative-sciences/

Brigham Young University, Graduate Studies, BYU Marriott School of Business, MBA Program, Provo, UT 84602. Offers entrepreneurship (MBA); finance (MBA); global supply chain management (MBA); marketing (MBA); strategic human resources (MBA); JD/MBA; MBA/MS. *Accreditation:* AACSB. *Faculty:* 134 full-time (15 women), 65 part-time/adjunct (16 women). *Students:* 303 full-time (65 women); includes 26 minority (3 American Indian or Alaska Native, non-Hispanic/Latino; 8 Asian, non-Hispanic/Latino; 11 Hispanic/Latino; 4 Native Hawaiian or other Pacific Islander, non-Hispanic/Latino), 58 international. Average age 30. 339 applicants, 52% accepted, 136 enrolled. In 2017, 163 master's awarded. *Entrance requirements:* For master's, GMAT or GRE, commitment to BYU Honor Code, undergraduate degree. Additional exam requirements/recommendations for international students: Required—TOEFL (minimum score 590 paper-based; 100 iBT), IELTS (minimum score 7). *Application deadline:* For fall admission, 5/1 for domestic students, 3/1 for international students. Applications are processed on a rolling basis. Application fee: $50. Electronic applications accepted. *Expenses:* Contact institution. *Financial support:* Research assistantships, teaching assistantships, career-related internships or fieldwork, institutionally sponsored loans, and scholarships/grants available. Financial award application deadline: 3/1; financial award applicants required to submit FAFSA. *Faculty research:* Finance, marketing, supply chain management, entrepreneurship, strategic human resources. *Unit head:* Dr. Grant McQueen, Director, 801-422-3500, E-mail: mba@byu.edu. *Application contact:* Yvette Anderson, MBA Program Admissions Director, 801-422-3500, Fax: 801-422-0513, E-mail: mba@byu.edu.
Website: http://mba.byu.edu

Bryant University, Graduate School of Business, Smithfield, RI 02917. Offers accounting (MPAC); business administration (MBA), including business analytics, general management, global finance, global supply chain management, international business; taxation (MST). *Program availability:* Part-time, 100% online. *Faculty:* 30 full-time (5 women), 7 part-time/adjunct (2 women). *Students:* 84 full-time (31 women), 91 part-time (35 women); includes 24 minority (4 Black or African American, non-Hispanic/Latino; 1 American Indian or Alaska Native, non-Hispanic/Latino; 6 Asian, non-Hispanic/Latino; 8 Hispanic/Latino; 5 Two or more races, non-Hispanic/Latino), 6 international. Average age 26. 215 applicants, 66% accepted, 96 enrolled. In 2017, 118 master's awarded. *Degree requirements:* For master's, comprehensive exam (for some programs). *Entrance requirements:* For master's, GMAT, resume, recommendation, college transcripts. Additional exam requirements/recommendations for international students: Required—TOEFL (minimum score 580 paper-based; 95 iBT). *Application deadline:* For fall admission, 7/15 for domestic and international students; for spring admission, 11/15 for domestic and international students; for summer admission, 4/15 for domestic and international students. Applications are processed on a rolling basis. Application fee: $80. Electronic applications accepted. *Expenses:* $45,102 total, $1,118 per credit hour, $1,500 study abroad fee (for full-time MBA); $40,248 total, $1,118 per credit hour (for part-time MBA); $30,280 total, $1,176 per credit hour (for MP Ac and MST); $13,146, $1,118 per credit hour (for CGS). *Financial support:* In 2017–18, 95 fellowships with full and partial tuition reimbursements (averaging $9,825 per year), 9 research assistantships with full and partial tuition reimbursements (averaging $7,100 per year) were awarded; scholarships/grants and unspecified assistantships also available. Support available to part-time students. Financial award application deadline: 2/15; financial award applicants required to submit FAFSA. *Faculty research:* International business, public sector auditing, taxation of partnerships, information systems security, financial markets microstructure. *Unit head:* Bjorn Carlsson, Graduate Program Director, 401-232-6707, E-mail: bcarlsson@bryant.edu. *Application contact:* Terri Rogers, Admissions Assistant, 401-232-6230, Fax: 401-232-6494, E-mail: graduateprograms@bryant.edu.
Website: http://gradschool.bryant.edu/business/

California Polytechnic State University, San Luis Obispo, Orfalea College of Business, Program in Packaging Value Chain, San Luis Obispo, CA 93407. Offers MS. *Program availability:* Online learning. *Faculty:* 1 part-time/adjunct (0 women). *Expenses:* Tuition, state resident: full-time $7176; part-time $4164 per year. *Required fees:* $3690; $3219 per year. $1073 per trimester. *Unit head:* Dr. Sanjiv Jaggia, Associate Dean, 805-756-2705, E-mail: sjaggia@calpoly.edu. *Application contact:* Dr. Beena Khurana, Associate Dean, 805-756-7519, E-mail: bkhurana@calpoly.edu.
Website: https://gradbusiness.calpoly.edu/ms-packaging-value-chain/

California State University, East Bay, Office of Graduate Studies, College of Business and Economics, MBA Program, Option in Operations and Supply Chain Management, Hayward, CA 94542-3000. Offers MBA. *Degree requirements:* For master's, comprehensive exam or thesis. *Entrance requirements:* For master's, GMAT, minimum GPA of 2.75. Additional exam requirements/recommendations for international students: Required—TOEFL (minimum score 550 paper-based). *Application deadline:* For fall admission, 6/1 for domestic and international students. Application fee: $55. Electronic applications accepted. *Financial support:* Fellowships, career-related internships or fieldwork, Federal Work-Study, institutionally sponsored loans, and scholarships/grants

available. Support available to part-time students. Financial award application deadline: 3/1; financial award applicants required to submit FAFSA. *Unit head:* Dr. Zinovy Radovilsky, Program Advisor, 510-885-3307, E-mail: zinovy.radovilsky@csueastbay.edu. *Application contact:* Philip Cole-Regis, Administrative Support Coordinator, 510-885-3286, E-mail: philip.coleregis@csueastbay.edu.
Website: http://www.csueastbay.edu/cbe/mba-options/operations-and-supply-chain-management-option.html

California State University, San Bernardino, Graduate Studies, College of Business and Public Administration, Program in Business Administration, San Bernardino, CA 92407. Offers accounting (MBA); entrepreneurship (MBA); finance (MBA); global business (MBA); information management (MBA); information security (MBA); management (MBA); supply chain management (MBA). *Accreditation:* AACSB. *Program availability:* Part-time, evening/weekend, online learning. *Faculty:* 4 full-time (3 women), 6 part-time/adjunct (4 women). *Students:* 21 full-time (15 women), 122 part-time (30 women); includes 82 minority (15 Black or African American, non-Hispanic/Latino; 1 American Indian or Alaska Native, non-Hispanic/Latino; 19 Asian, non-Hispanic/Latino; 44 Hispanic/Latino; 3 Two or more races, non-Hispanic/Latino), 37 international. Average age 33. 258 applicants, 44% accepted, 50 enrolled. In 2017, 134 master's awarded. *Degree requirements:* For master's, comprehensive exam, thesis. *Entrance requirements:* Additional exam requirements/recommendations for international students: Required—TOEFL. *Application deadline:* For fall admission, 7/16 for domestic students, 7/20 for international students; for winter admission, 10/23 for domestic students, 10/20 for international students; for spring admission, 1/22 for domestic students, 1/20 for international students. Application fee: $55. *Expenses:* Contact institution. *Financial support:* Application deadline: 3/1. *Unit head:* Dr. Lawrence C. Rose, Dean, 909-537-3703, Fax: 909-537-7026, E-mail: lrose@csusb.edu. *Application contact:* Dr. Vipin Gupta, Associate Dean/MBA Director, 909-537-7380, Fax: 909-537-7026, E-mail: vgupta@csusb.edu.
Website: http://mba.csusb.edu/

Capella University, School of Business and Technology, Doctoral Programs in Technology, Minneapolis, MN 55402. Offers general information technology (PhD); global operations and supply chain management (DBA); information assurance and security (PhD); information technology education (PhD); information technology management (DBA, PhD).

Capella University, School of Business and Technology, Master's Programs in Technology, Minneapolis, MN 55402. Offers enterprise software architecture (MS); general information systems and technology management (MS); global operations and supply chain management (MS); information assurance and security (MS); information technology management (MBA); network management (MS).

Case Western Reserve University, Weatherhead School of Management, Department of Operations, Cleveland, OH 44106. Offers operations and supply chain management (MSM); operations research (PhD); MBA/MSM. *Program availability:* Part-time. *Degree requirements:* For doctorate, thesis/dissertation. *Entrance requirements:* For master's, GRE General Test; for doctorate, GMAT, GRE General Test. *Expenses:* Tuition: Full-time $43,854; part-time $1827 per credit hour. *Required fees:* $50; $50 per credit hour. Tuition and fees vary according to course load and program. *Faculty research:* Mathematical finance, mathematical programming, scheduling, stochastic optimization, environmental/energy models.

Central Connecticut State University, School of Graduate Studies, School of Engineering, Science and Technology, Department of Manufacturing and Construction Management, New Britain, CT 06050-4010. Offers construction management (MS, Certificate); environmental and occupational safety (Certificate); lean manufacturing and Six Sigma (Certificate); supply chain and logistics (Certificate); technology management (MS). *Program availability:* Part-time, evening/weekend. *Faculty:* 8 full-time (1 woman), 3 part-time/adjunct (0 women). *Students:* 25 full-time (10 women), 92 part-time (16 women); includes 31 minority (17 Black or African American, non-Hispanic/Latino; 5 Asian, non-Hispanic/Latino; 8 Hispanic/Latino; 1 Two or more races, non-Hispanic/Latino), 11 international. Average age 32. 77 applicants, 71% accepted, 37 enrolled. In 2017, 40 master's, 6 other advanced degrees awarded. *Degree requirements:* For master's, comprehensive exam, special project; for Certificate, qualifying exam. *Entrance requirements:* For master's, minimum undergraduate GPA of 2.7. Additional exam requirements/recommendations for international students: Required—TOEFL (minimum score 550 paper-based; 79 iBT); Recommended—IELTS (minimum score 6.5). *Application deadline:* For fall admission, 8/1 for domestic students, 5/1 for international students; for spring admission, 12/1 for domestic students, 11/1 for international students; for summer admission, 5/1 for domestic students. Applications are processed on a rolling basis. Application fee: $50. Electronic applications accepted. *Expenses:* Tuition, area resident: Full-time $6757. Tuition, state resident: full-time $9750; part-time $374 per credit. Tuition, nonresident: full-time $18,102; part-time $374 per credit. *Required fees:* $4635; $255 per credit. *Financial support:* In 2017–18, 17 students received support. Career-related internships or fieldwork, Federal Work-Study, scholarships/grants, and unspecified assistantships available. Support available to part-time students. Financial award application deadline: 3/1; financial award applicants required to submit FAFSA. *Faculty research:* All aspects of middle management, technical supervision in the workplace. *Unit head:* Dr. Ravindra Thamma, Chair, 860-832-1830, E-mail: thammarav@ccsu.edu. *Application contact:* Patricia Gardner, Associate Director of Graduate Studies, 860-832-2350, Fax: 860-832-2362.
Website: http://www.ccsu.edu/mcm/

Clarkson University, David D. Reh School of Business, Master's Program in Business Administration, Potsdam, NY 13699. Offers business fundamentals (Advanced Certificate); global supply chain management (Advanced Certificate); human resource management (Advanced Certificate); management and leadership (Advanced Certificate). *Accreditation:* AACSB. *Program availability:* Part-time, evening/weekend, 100% online, blended/hybrid learning. *Faculty:* 55 full-time (14 women), 38 part-time/adjunct (10 women). *Students:* 92 full-time (31 women), 50 part-time (24 women); includes 20 minority (5 Black or African American, non-Hispanic/Latino; 1 American Indian or Alaska Native, non-Hispanic/Latino; 8 Asian, non-Hispanic/Latino; 5 Hispanic/Latino; 1 Two or more races, non-Hispanic/Latino), 11 international. 174 applicants, 55% accepted, 67 enrolled. In 2017, 1 Advanced Certificate awarded. *Entrance requirements:* Additional exam requirements/recommendations for international students: Required—TOEFL (minimum score 550 paper-based, 80 iBT) or IELTS (6.5). *Application deadline:* Applications are processed on a rolling basis. Application fee: $50. Electronic applications accepted. *Expenses:* Tuition: Full-time $24,210; part-time $1345 per credit hour. Tuition and fees vary according to campus/location and program. *Financial support:* Scholarships/grants available. *Unit head:* Dr. Alan Bowman, Senior Associate Dean of Graduate Business Programs, 518-631-9887, E-mail: abowman@clarkson.edu. *Application contact:* Dan Capogna, Director of Graduate Admissions, 518-631-9910, E-mail: graduate@clarkson.edu.
Website: https://www.clarkson.edu/academics/graduate

Clayton State University, School of Graduate Studies, College of Business, Program in Business Administration, Morrow, GA 30260-0285. Offers accounting (MBA); human resource leadership (MBA); international business (MBA); sports and entertainment management (MBA); supply chain management (MBA). *Accreditation:* AACSB. *Program* availability: Part-time, evening/weekend. *Degree requirements:* For master's, thesis. *Entrance requirements:* For master's, GMAT, 3 letters of recommendation; statement of purpose; 2 official transcripts. Additional exam requirements/recommendations for international students: Required—TOEFL (minimum score 550 paper-based; 80 iBT). Electronic applications accepted. *Expenses:* Contact institution.

Clemson University, Graduate School, College of Business, Department of Management, Clemson, SC 29634. Offers business administration (PhD), including management information systems, strategy, entrepreneurship and organizational behavior, supply chain and operations management; management (MS). *Accreditation:* AACSB. *Faculty:* 34 full-time (12 women), 1 part-time/adjunct (0 women). *Students:* 14 full-time (3 women), 1 part-time (0 women), 9 international. Average age 33. 30 applicants, 13% accepted. In 2017, 4 master's, 4 doctorates awarded. Terminal master's awarded for partial completion of doctoral program. *Degree requirements:* For master's, comprehensive exam, thesis optional; for doctorate, comprehensive exam, thesis/dissertation. *Entrance requirements:* For master's and doctorate, GMAT or GRE General Test, unofficial transcripts, two letters of reference, curriculum vitae. Additional exam requirements/recommendations for international students: Required—TOEFL (minimum score 94 iBT), IELTS (minimum score 7), PTE (minimum score 64). *Application deadline:* For fall admission, 1/15 priority date for domestic and international students. Application fee: $80 ($90 for international students). Electronic applications accepted. *Expenses:* $6,564 per semester full-time resident, $12,538 per semester full-time non-resident, $743 per credit hour part-time resident, $1,486 per credit hour part-time non-resident, $1,203 per credit hour online, other fees may apply per session. *Financial support:* In 2017–18, 10 students received support, including 1 fellowship with partial tuition reimbursement available (averaging $1,000 per year), 1 research assistantship with partial tuition reimbursement available (averaging $12,000 per year), 2 teaching assistantships with partial tuition reimbursements available (averaging $18,770 per year); unspecified assistantships also available. Financial award application deadline: 1/15. *Faculty research:* Effective use of information technology in business, manufacturing and service operations strategy, lean operations and quality management, healthcare operations, behavioral market design. *Total annual research expenditures:* $89,179. *Unit head:* Dr. V. Sridharan, Department Chair, 864-656-2624, E-mail: suhas@clemson.edu. *Application contact:* Dr. Janis Miller, Graduate Program Coordinator, 864-656-3757, E-mail: janism@clemson.edu.
Website: https://www.clemson.edu/business/departments/management/

Concordia University, School of Graduate Studies, John Molson School of Business, Montreal, QC H3H 0A1, Canada. Offers administration (M Sc), including finance, management, marketing; business administration (MBA, PhD, Certificate, Diploma); executive business administration (EMBA); supply chain management (MSCM). PhD program offered jointly with HEC Montreal, McGill University, and Université du Québec à Montréal. *Program availability:* Part-time, evening/weekend. *Degree requirements:* For master's, one foreign language, thesis (for some programs), research project; for doctorate, one foreign language, thesis/dissertation; for other advanced degree, one foreign language. *Entrance requirements:* For master's, GMAT, minimum 2 years of work experience (for MBA); letters of recommendation, bachelor's degree from recognized university with minimum GPA of 3.0, curriculum vitae; for doctorate, GMAT (minimum score of 600), official transcripts, curriculum vitae, 3 letters of reference, statement of purpose; for other advanced degree, minimum GPA of 2.7, 2 letters of reference, statement of purpose, resume. Additional exam requirements/recommendations for international students: Required—TOEFL (minimum score 90 iBT), IELTS (minimum score 7). Electronic applications accepted. *Expenses:* Contact institution. *Faculty research:* General business, capital markets, international business.

Delaware Valley University, MBA Program, Doylestown, PA 18901-2697. Offers accounting (MBA); entrepreneurship (MBA); finance (MBA); food and agribusiness (MBA); general business (MBA); global executive leadership (MBA); human resource management (MBA); supply chain management (MBA). *Program availability:* Part-time, evening/weekend, online learning. *Entrance requirements:* For master's, minimum undergraduate GPA of 3.0. Electronic applications accepted. *Expenses:* Contact institution.

DePaul University, Kellstadt Graduate School of Business, Chicago, IL 60604. Offers accountancy (MBA, MSA); applied economics (MBA); audit and advisory services (MS); business administration (DBA); business analytics (MS); business strategy and decision-making (MBA); computational finance (MS); economics and policy analysis (MS); enterprise risk management (MS); entrepreneurship (MBA, MS); finance (MBA, MS); general business (MBA); hospitality leadership (MBA); hospitality leadership and operational performance (MS); human resources (MS); international business (MBA); management (MBA, MS); management information systems (MBA); marketing (MBA, MS); marketing analysis (MS); marketing strategy and planning (MBA); real estate (MS); real estate finance and investment (MBA); strategy, execution and valuation (MBA); supply chain management (MS); sustainable management (MS); taxation (MS); JD/MBA. *Accreditation:* AACSB. *Program availability:* Part-time, evening/weekend, online learning. *Entrance requirements:* For master's, GMAT/GRE, 2 letters of recommendation, resume, essay, official transcripts. Additional exam requirements/recommendations for international students: Required—TOEFL (minimum score 550 paper-based; 80 iBT). *Application deadline:* For fall admission, 7/1 for domestic students, 6/1 for international students; for winter admission, 10/1 for domestic students, 9/1 for international students; for spring admission, 2/1 for domestic students, 1/1 for international students. Applications are processed on a rolling basis. Application fee: $60. Electronic applications accepted. *Expenses:* Contact institution. *Financial support:* Application deadline: 4/1; applicants required to submit FAFSA. *Unit head:* Christa Hinton, Assistant Dean and Director, 312-362-8810, Fax: 312-362-6677, E-mail: chinton@depaul.edu. *Application contact:* Garry Cooke, Director of Recruitment and Admissions, 312-362-8810, Fax: 312-362-6677, E-mail: kgsb@depaul.edu.
Website: http://kellstadt.depaul.edu

DeSales University, Division of Business, Center Valley, PA 18034-9568. Offers accounting (MBA); computer information systems (MBA); finance (MBA); health care systems management (MBA); human resources management (MBA); management (MBA); marketing (MBA); project management (MBA); self-design (MBA); supply chain management (MBA); DNP/MBA; MSN/MBA. *Accreditation:* ACBSP. *Program availability:* Part-time, evening/weekend, 100% online, blended/hybrid learning. *Faculty:* 9 full-time (3 women), 32 part-time/adjunct (8 women). *Students:* 78 full-time (44 women), 323 part-time (164 women); includes 71 minority (22 Black or African American, non-Hispanic/Latino; 17 Asian, non-Hispanic/Latino; 24 Hispanic/Latino; 8 Two or more races, non-Hispanic/Latino), 1 international. Average age 34. 213 applicants, 40% accepted, 64 enrolled. In 2017, 123 master's awarded. *Entrance requirements:* For master's, GMAT (waived if undergraduate GPA is 3.0 or better), minimum GPA of 3.0 in undergraduate work, literacy in basic software, background or interest in the field of study, personal statement, 2 years of work experience. Additional exam requirements/recommendations for international students: Required—TOEFL. *Application deadline:* Applications are processed on a rolling basis. Application fee: $50. Electronic applications accepted. *Expenses:* Contact institution. *Financial support:* Applicants required to submit FAFSA. *Faculty research:* Quality improvement, executive development, productivity, cross-cultural managerial differences, leadership. *Unit head:*

Dr. David M. Gilfoil, Director, MBA Program, 610-282-1100 Ext. 1828, Fax: 610-282-2869, E-mail: david.gilfoil@desales.edu. *Application contact:* Julia Ferraro, Director of Graduate Admissions, 610-282-1100 Ext. 1768, E-mail: gradadmissions@desales.edu.

Duquesne University, Palumbo-Donahue School of Business, Pittsburgh, PA 15282-0001. Offers accounting (M Acc); finance (MBA); information systems management (MSISM); management (MBA, MS); marketing (MBA); sports business (MS); supply chain management (MS); sustainability (MBA); JD/MBA; MBA/M Acc; MBA/MA; MBA/MES; MBA/MHMS; MSISM/MBA; Pharm D/MBA. *Accreditation:* AACSB. *Program availability:* Part-time, evening/weekend, minimal on-campus study. *Faculty:* 59 full-time (23 women), 25 part-time/adjunct (6 women). *Students:* 232 full-time (83 women), 46 part-time (18 women); includes 28 minority (14 Black or African American, non-Hispanic/Latino; 8 Asian, non-Hispanic/Latino; 4 Hispanic/Latino; 2 Two or more races, non-Hispanic/Latino), 24 international. Average age 29. 220 applicants, 83% accepted, 121 enrolled. In 2017, 113 master's awarded. *Entrance requirements:* For master's, GMAT or GRE, undergraduate transcripts, 2 letters of recommendation, current resume, personal statement. Additional exam requirements/recommendations for international students: Required—TOEFL (minimum score 577 paper-based; 90 iBT), IELTS (minimum score 7). *Application deadline:* For fall admission, 7/1 priority date for domestic and international students; for spring admission, 12/1 for domestic and international students; for summer admission, 4/1 for domestic and international students. Applications are processed on a rolling basis. Application fee: $0. Electronic applications accepted. *Expenses:* $934 per credit (MS in management, sports business); $1,259 per credit (MBA, MS in accountancy, information systems management). *Financial support:* In 2017–18, 211 students received support, including 12 fellowships with partial tuition reimbursements available (averaging $14,200 per year), 20 research assistantships with partial tuition reimbursements available (averaging $22,662 per year); career-related internships or fieldwork, scholarships/grants, and unspecified assistantships also available. Support available to part-time students. Financial award application deadline: 7/1; financial award applicants required to submit FAFSA. *Faculty research:* Investment management, business ethics, technology management, supply chain management, entrepreneurship. *Unit head:* Dr. Karen Donovan, Associate Dean of Graduate Programs and Executive Education, 412-396-6276, Fax: 412-396-1726, E-mail: donovan6@duq.edu. *Application contact:* Jeff Jewett, Director of Admissions and Enrollment Management, 412-396-6244, Fax: 412-396-1726, E-mail: decrostam@duq.edu.
Website: http://www.duq.edu/business/grad

Eastern Michigan University, Graduate School, College of Business, Department of Marketing, Ypsilanti, MI 48197. Offers e-business (MBA); integrated marketing communications (MS, Postbaccalaureate Certificate); international business (MBA); marketing management (MBA); supply chain management (MBA). *Program availability:* Part-time, evening/weekend, online learning. *Faculty:* 21 full-time (8 women). *Students:* 24 full-time (20 women), 33 part-time (26 women); includes 15 minority (11 Black or African American, non-Hispanic/Latino; 3 Hispanic/Latino; 1 Two or more races, non-Hispanic/Latino). Average age 31. 41 applicants, 66% accepted, 23 enrolled. In 2017, 22 master's, 1 other advanced degree awarded. *Entrance requirements:* For master's, GMAT. Additional exam requirements/recommendations for international students: Required—TOEFL. *Application deadline:* For fall admission, 5/15 priority date for domestic students, 2/15 priority date for international students; for winter admission, 10/15 priority date for domestic students, 9/1 priority date for international students; for summer admission, 3/15 priority date for domestic students, 3/1 priority date for international students. Applications are processed on a rolling basis. Application fee: $45. *Financial support:* Fellowships, research assistantships with full tuition reimbursements, teaching assistantships with full tuition reimbursements, career-related internships or fieldwork, Federal Work-Study, institutionally sponsored loans, scholarships/grants, tuition waivers (partial), and unspecified assistantships available. Support available to part-time students. Financial award applicants required to submit FAFSA. *Unit head:* Dr. Lewis Hershey, Department Head, 734-487-3323, Fax: 734-487-7099, E-mail: lhershe1@emich.edu. *Application contact:* K. Michelle Henry, Director, Graduate Business Programs, 734-487-4444, Fax: 734-483-1316, E-mail: cob.graduate@emich.edu.
Website: http://www.mkt.emich.edu/index.html

Eastern Michigan University, Graduate School, College of Business, Programs in Business Administration, Ypsilanti, MI 48197. Offers business administration (MBA, Graduate Certificate); computer information systems (Graduate Certificate); e-business (MBA, Graduate Certificate); enterprise business intelligence (MBA); entrepreneurship (MBA, Graduate Certificate); finance (MBA, Graduate Certificate); human resources (MBA); human resources management (Graduate Certificate); information systems (MBA); internal auditing (MBA); international business (MBA, Graduate Certificate); marketing management (Graduate Certificate); nonprofit management (MBA); organizational development (Graduate Certificate); supply chain management (MBA, Graduate Certificate). *Accreditation:* AACSB. *Program availability:* Part-time, online learning. *Students:* 53 full-time (30 women), 297 part-time (170 women); includes 121 minority (72 Black or African American, non-Hispanic/Latino; 4 American Indian or Alaska Native, non-Hispanic/Latino; 15 Asian, non-Hispanic/Latino; 20 Hispanic/Latino; 10 Two or more races, non-Hispanic/Latino), 20 international. Average age 31. 247 applicants, 74% accepted, 94 enrolled. In 2017, 71 master's, 34 other advanced degrees awarded. *Entrance requirements:* For master's, GMAT (minimum score 450), minimum cumulative undergraduate GPA of 2.75. Additional exam requirements/recommendations for international students: Required—TOEFL. *Application deadline:* For fall admission, 5/15 priority date for domestic students, 2/15 priority date for international students; for winter admission, 10/15 priority date for domestic students, 9/1 priority date for international students; for summer admission, 3/15 priority date for domestic students, 3/1 priority date for international students. Applications are processed on a rolling basis. Application fee: $45. *Financial support:* Fellowships, research assistantships with full tuition reimbursements, teaching assistantships with full tuition reimbursements, career-related internships or fieldwork, Federal Work-Study, institutionally sponsored loans, scholarships/grants, tuition waivers (partial), and unspecified assistantships available. Support available to part-time students. Financial award applicants required to submit FAFSA. *Unit head:* K. Michelle Henry, Director, Graduate Business Programs, 734-487-4444, Fax: 734-483-1316, E-mail: cob.graduate@emich.edu.
Website: http://www.emich.edu/cob/mba/

Elmhurst College, Graduate Programs, Program in Supply Chain Management, Elmhurst, IL 60126-3296. Offers MS. *Program availability:* Part-time, evening/weekend. *Faculty:* 2 full-time (0 women), 4 part-time/adjunct (0 women). *Students:* 29 part-time (8 women); includes 9 minority (3 Black or African American, non-Hispanic/Latino; 4 Asian, non-Hispanic/Latino; 2 Hispanic/Latino), 3 international. Average age 31. 21 applicants, 62% accepted, 13 enrolled. In 2017, 15 master's awarded. *Entrance requirements:* For master's, 3 recommendations, resume, statement of purpose. Additional exam requirements/recommendations for international students: Required—TOEFL (minimum score 550 paper-based; 79 iBT). *Application deadline:* Applications are processed on a rolling basis. Application fee: $0. Electronic applications accepted. *Expenses:* Contact institution. *Financial support:* In 2017–18, 11 students received support. Scholarships/grants available. Support available to part-time students. Financial award application

deadline: 3/1; financial award applicants required to submit FAFSA. *Unit head:* Dr. Roby Thomas, Director, 630-617-3116, E-mail: rthomas@elmhurst.edu. *Application contact:* Timothy J. Panfil, Director of Enrollment Management, 630-617-3300 Ext. 3256, Fax: 630-617-6471, E-mail: panfilt@elmhurst.edu.
Website: http://www.elmhurst.edu/scm

Embry-Riddle Aeronautical University–Worldwide, Department of Decision Sciences, Daytona Beach, FL 32114-3900. Offers aviation and aerospace (MSPM); aviation/aerospace management (MSEM); financial management (MSEM, MSPM); general management (MSPM); global management (MSPM); human resources management (MSPM); information systems (MSPM); leadership (MSEM, MSPM); logistics and supply chain management (MSEM, MSLSCM, MSPM); management (MSEM, MSPM); project management (MSEM); systems engineering (MSEM, MSPM); technical management (MSPM). *Program availability:* Part-time, evening/weekend, EagleVision Classroom (between classrooms), EagleVision Home (faculty and students at home), and a blend of Classroom or Home. *Faculty:* 12 full-time (3 women), 53 part-time/adjunct (10 women). *Students:* 514 full-time (141 women), 476 part-time (111 women); includes 337 minority (136 Black or African American, non-Hispanic/Latino; 6 American Indian or Alaska Native, non-Hispanic/Latino; 39 Asian, non-Hispanic/Latino; 81 Hispanic/Latino; 4 Native Hawaiian or other Pacific Islander, non-Hispanic/Latino; 71 Two or more races, non-Hispanic/Latino), 21 international. Average age 36. 297 applicants, 72% accepted, 209 enrolled. In 2017, 292 master's awarded. *Degree requirements:* For master's, comprehensive exam (for some programs), thesis (for some programs). *Entrance requirements:* Additional exam requirements/recommendations for international students: Required—TOEFL (minimum score 550 paper-based; 79 iBT), IELTS (minimum score 6). *Application deadline:* Applications are processed on a rolling basis. Application fee: $50. Electronic applications accepted. *Expenses:* Contact institution. *Financial support:* Career-related internships or fieldwork and scholarships/grants available. Financial award applicants required to submit FAFSA. *Unit head:* Aman Gupta, PhD, Department Chair, E-mail: aman.gupta@erau.edu. *Application contact:* Worldwide Campus, 800-522-6787, E-mail: worldwide@erau.edu.

Fairleigh Dickinson University, Florham Campus, Silberman College of Business, Program in Supply Chain Management, Madison, NJ 07940-1099. Offers MS. *Entrance requirements:* For master's, GMAT.

Ferris State University, College of Business, Big Rapids, MI 49307. Offers business intelligence (MBA); design and innovation management (MBA); incident response (MBA); information security and intelligence (MS), including business intelligence, incident response, project management; lean systems and leadership (MBA); performance metrics (MBA); project management (MBA); supply chain management and lean logistics (MBA). *Accreditation:* ACBSP. *Program availability:* Part-time, evening/weekend, 100% online, blended/hybrid learning. *Faculty:* 18 full-time (7 women), 6 part-time/adjunct (3 women). *Students:* 19 full-time (10 women), 73 part-time (45 women); includes 8 minority (1 Black or African American, non-Hispanic/Latino; 2 Asian, non-Hispanic/Latino; 3 Hispanic/Latino; 2 Two or more races, non-Hispanic/Latino), 12 international. Average age 32. 52 applicants, 77% accepted, 16 enrolled. In 2017, 88 master's awarded. *Degree requirements:* For master's, comprehensive exam, thesis. *Entrance requirements:* For master's, GRE or GMAT, minimum GPA of 3.0 in junior-/senior-level classes and overall; statement of purpose; 3 letters of reference; resume; transcripts. Additional exam requirements/recommendations for international students: Required—TOEFL (minimum score 500 paper-based; 70 iBT), IELTS (minimum score 6.5). *Application deadline:* For fall admission, 7/1 priority date for domestic students, 6/15 for international students; for winter admission, 11/1 priority date for domestic students, 10/15 for international students; for spring admission, 3/1 priority date for domestic students, 2/15 for international students. Applications are processed on a rolling basis. Application fee: $0 ($30 for international students). Electronic applications accepted. *Expenses:* Contact institution. *Financial support:* Career-related internships or fieldwork, Federal Work-Study, scholarships/grants, and unspecified assistantships available. Support available to part-time students. Financial award application deadline: 3/15; financial award applicants required to submit FAFSA. *Faculty research:* Lifestyle medicine business models, lean systems value chain optimization, digital forensics/incident response, location-based services, passive data capture and analysis. *Unit head:* Dr. David Nicol, College of Business Dean, 231-591-2168, Fax: 231-591-3521, E-mail: davidnicol@ferris.edu. *Application contact:* Dr. Greg Gogolin, Professor, 231-591-3159, Fax: 231-591-3521, E-mail: greggogolin@ferris.edu.
Website: http://cbgp.ferris.edu/

Florida Institute of Technology, Extended Studies Division, Melbourne, FL 32901-6975. Offers acquisition and contract management (MS); aerospace engineering (MS); business administration (MBA, DBA); computer information systems (MS); computer science (MS); electrical engineering (MS); engineering management (MS); human resources management (MS); logistics management (MS), including humanitarian and disaster relief logistics; management (MS), including acquisition and contract management, e-business, human resources management, information systems, logistics management, management, transportation management; material acquisition management (MS); mechanical engineering (MS); operations research (MS); project management (MS), including information systems, operations research; public administration (MPA); quality management (MS); software engineering (MS); space systems (MS); space systems management (MS); supply chain management (MS); systems management (MS), including information systems, operations research; technology management (MS). *Program availability:* Part-time, evening/weekend, online learning. *Students:* Average age 36. 962 applicants, 48% accepted, 323 enrolled. In 2017, 403 master's awarded. *Entrance requirements:* For master's, GMAT or resume showing 8 years of supervised experience, minimum GPA of 3.0, 2 letters of recommendation, resume. Additional exam requirements/recommendations for international students: Required—TOEFL (minimum score 550 paper-based; 79 iBT). *Application deadline:* For fall admission, 4/1 for international students; for spring admission, 9/30 for international students. Applications are processed on a rolling basis. Electronic applications accepted. *Expenses:* Contact institution. *Financial support:* Application deadline: 3/1; applicants required to submit FAFSA. *Unit head:* Dr. Theodore R. Richardson, III, Dean, 321-674-8123, Fax: 321-674-7597, E-mail: trichardson@fit.edu. *Application contact:* Carolyn Farrior, Director of Graduate Admissions, Online Learning and Off-Campus Programs, 321-674-7118, Fax: 321-674-8216, E-mail: cfarrior@fit.edu.
Website: http://es.fit.edu

Fontbonne University, Graduate Programs, St. Louis, MO 63105-3098. Offers accounting (MBA, MS); art (MA); art (K-12) (MAT); business (MBA); computer science (MS); deaf education (MA); early intervention in deaf education (MA); education (MA), including autism spectrum disorders, curriculum and instruction, diverse learners, early childhood education, reading, special education; elementary education (MAT); family and consumer sciences (MA), including multidisciplinary health communication studies; fine arts (MFA); instructional design and technology (MS); management and leadership (MM); middle school education (MAT); secondary education (MAT); special education (MAT); speech-language pathology (MS); supply chain management (MS); theatre (MA). *Program availability:* Part-time, evening/weekend, online learning. *Degree requirements:* For master's, comprehensive exam (for some programs), thesis (for some

programs). *Entrance requirements:* Additional exam requirements/recommendations for international students: Required—TOEFL (minimum score 500 paper-based; 65 iBT). Electronic applications accepted.

Friends University, Graduate School, Wichita, KS 67213. Offers family therapy (MSFT); global business administration (MBA), including accounting, business law, change management, health care leadership, management information systems, supply chain management and logistics; health care leadership (MHCL); management information systems (MMIS); professional business administration (MBA), including accounting, business law, change management, health care leadership, management information systems, supply chain management and logistics. *Program availability:* Part-time, evening/weekend, online learning. *Degree requirements:* For master's, research project. *Entrance requirements:* For master's, bachelor's degree from accredited institution, official transcripts, interview with program director, letter(s) of recommendation. Additional exam requirements/recommendations for international students: Required—TOEFL (minimum score 560 paper-based). Electronic applications accepted.

Georgia Southern University, Jack N. Averitt College of Graduate Studies, College of Business, Program in Logistics/Supply Chain Management, Statesboro, GA 30458. Offers PhD. *Faculty:* 15 full-time (2 women). *Students:* 8 full-time (3 women), 5 international. Average age 30. 20 applicants, 20% accepted, 3 enrolled. *Degree requirements:* For doctorate, comprehensive exam, thesis/dissertation. *Entrance requirements:* For doctorate, GMAT or GRE, minimum of three letters of reference; statement of purpose; resume. Additional exam requirements/recommendations for international students: Required—TOEFL (minimum score 550 paper-based; 80 iBT), IELTS (minimum score 6). *Application deadline:* For fall admission, 3/15 priority date for domestic and international students. Application fee: $50. Electronic applications accepted. *Expenses:* Tuition, state resident: full-time $4986; part-time $3324 per year. Tuition, nonresident: full-time $21,982; part-time $15,352 per year. *Required fees:* $2092; $1802 per credit hour. $901 per semester. Tuition and fees vary according to course load, campus/location and program. *Financial support:* In 2017–18, 5 students received support, including 6 research assistantships with full tuition reimbursements available (averaging $16,000 per year); teaching assistantships, career-related internships or fieldwork, Federal Work-Study, scholarships/grants, traineeships, and unspecified assistantships also available. Support available to part-time students. Financial award application deadline: 4/15; financial award applicants required to submit FAFSA. *Faculty research:* Buyer-supplier relationships, retail supply chain management, strategic sourcing/outsourcing, supply chain metrics, service scheduling, demand and supply planning, supply chain strategy, operations and supply management, decision sciences. *Unit head:* Dr. Alan Mackelprang, PhD Program Director, 912-478-0379, E-mail: amackelprang@georgiasouthern.edu. *Application contact:* coba@georgiasouthern.edu.
Website: http://cob.georgiasouthern.edu/lscm/phd/

Golden Gate University, Ageno School of Business, San Francisco, CA 94105-2968. Offers accounting (MBA); adaptive leadership (MBA); advanced financial planning (MS); business administration (EMBA, MBA, DBA); business analytics (MBA, MS); entrepreneurship (MBA); finance (MBA, MS, Certificate); financial life planning (Certificate); financial planning (MS, Certificate); global supply chain management (MBA, Certificate); human resource management (MBA, MS, Certificate); information technology management (MBA, MS, Certificate); international business (MBA); marketing (MBA, MS, Certificate); project management (MBA, MS, Certificate); psychology (MA, Certificate); public administration (EMPA, MBA); public administration leadership (Certificate); JD/MBA. *Program availability:* Part-time, evening/weekend. *Faculty:* 17 full-time (7 women), 280 part-time/adjunct (95 women). *Students:* 309 full-time (147 women), 527 part-time (266 women); includes 286 minority (56 Black or African American, non-Hispanic/Latino; 1 American Indian or Alaska Native, non-Hispanic/Latino; 131 Asian, non-Hispanic/Latino; 83 Hispanic/Latino; 4 Native Hawaiian or other Pacific Islander, non-Hispanic/Latino; 11 Two or more races, non-Hispanic/Latino), 209 international. Average age 35. 549 applicants, 66% accepted, 185 enrolled. *Degree requirements:* For doctorate, thesis/dissertation, qualifying examination. *Entrance requirements:* For master's, GMAT (for MBA), minimum GPA of 2.5 (MS). Additional exam requirements/recommendations for international students: Required—TOEFL (minimum score 550 paper-based; 79 iBT). *Application deadline:* For fall admission, 5/15 for domestic and international students; for winter admission, 1/15 for domestic and international students; for spring admission, 9/15 for domestic and international students. Applications are processed on a rolling basis. Application fee: $65 ($105 for international students). Electronic applications accepted. *Expenses:* $3,150 per 3-unit course. *Financial support:* Career-related internships or fieldwork, Federal Work-Study, institutionally sponsored loans, and scholarships/grants available. Support available to part-time students. Financial award applicants required to submit FAFSA. *Unit head:* Marianne Koch, Associate Dean, 415-442-6542, Fax: 415-442-6579, E-mail: mkoch@ggu.edu. *Application contact:* Angela Melero, Enrollment Services, 415-442-7800, Fax: 415-442-7807, E-mail: info@ggu.edu.
Website: http://www.ggu.edu/programs/business-and-management

HEC Montreal, School of Business Administration, Graduate Diploma Programs in Administration, Program in Supply Chain Management, Montréal, QC H3T 2A7, Canada. Offers Graduate Diploma. All courses are given in French. *Program availability:* Part-time. *Students:* 10 full-time (5 women), 39 part-time (18 women). 56 applicants, 38% accepted, 16 enrolled. In 2017, 20 Graduate Diplomas awarded. *Entrance requirements:* For degree, bachelor's degree, working experience, letters of recommendation. *Application deadline:* For fall admission, 4/15 for domestic and international students; for winter admission, 9/15 for domestic and international students. Application fee: $88 Canadian dollars ($184 Canadian dollars for international students). Electronic applications accepted. *Expenses:* Tuition, state resident: full-time $2869 Canadian dollars; part-time $79.70 Canadian dollars per credit. Tuition, nonresident: full-time $8883 Canadian dollars; part-time $246.76 Canadian dollars per credit. *International tuition:* $19,648 Canadian dollars full-time. *Required fees:* $41.20 Canadian dollars per credit. $67.94 Canadian dollars per term. Tuition and fees vary according to degree level and program. *Financial support:* Research assistantships, teaching assistantships, and scholarships/grants available. Financial award application deadline: 9/2. *Unit head:* Renaud Lachance, Director, 514-340-7165, E-mail: renaud.lachance@hec.ca. *Application contact:* Anny Caron, Administrative Director, 514-340-6151, Fax: 514-340-6411, E-mail: aide@hec.ca.
Website: http://www.hec.ca/programmes/dess/dess-gestion-chaine-logistique/index.html

HEC Montreal, School of Business Administration, Master of Science Programs in Administration, Program in Global Supply Chain Management, Montréal, QC H3T 2A7, Canada. Offers M Sc. Program offered in English. *Students:* 60 full-time (23 women). 73 applicants, 62% accepted. In 2017, 17 master's awarded. *Entrance requirements:* For master's, BBA, undergraduate degree in another field, degree deemed equivalent by program director and minimum GPA of 3.0 on 4.3 scale. Additional exam requirements/recommendations for international students: Required—TAGE MAGE (minimum recommended score of 283), GMAT (minimum recommended score of 630), or GRE. *Application deadline:* For fall admission, 3/15 for domestic and international students; for winter admission, 9/15 for domestic and international students. Application fee: $88 ($184 for international students). Electronic applications accepted. *Expenses:* Tuition, state resident: full-time $2869 Canadian dollars; part-time $79.70 Canadian dollars per credit. Tuition, nonresident: full-time $8883 Canadian dollars; part-time $246.76 Canadian dollars per credit. *International tuition:* $19,648 Canadian dollars full-time. *Required fees:* $41.20 Canadian dollars per credit. $67.94 Canadian dollars per term. Tuition and fees vary according to degree level and program. *Financial support:* Research assistantships, teaching assistantships, and scholarships/grants available. Financial award application deadline: 9/2. *Unit head:* Dr. Marie-Helene Jobin, Director, 514-340-6283, E-mail: marie-helene.jobin@hec.ca. *Application contact:* Marianne de Moura, Administrative Director, 514-340-6151, Fax: 514-340-6411, E-mail: aide@hec.ca. Website: http://www.hec.ca/en/programs/masters/master-global-supply-chain-management/index.html

Howard University, School of Business, Graduate Programs in Business, Washington, DC 20059-0002. Offers accounting (MBA); entrepreneurship (MBA); finance (MBA); general management (MBA); human resources management (MBA); information systems (MBA); international business (MBA); marketing (MBA); supply chain management (MBA); JD/MBA. *Accreditation:* AACSB. *Program availability:* Part-time, evening/weekend, online learning. *Entrance requirements:* For master's, GMAT, minimum 1 year post undergraduate work experience, resume, 3 letters of recommendation, advanced college algebra. Additional exam requirements/recommendations for international students: Required—TOEFL. *Faculty research:* Marketing research in multi-ethnic populations, U.S. trade policies and international relations, risk management (finance).

Indiana University–Purdue University Indianapolis, Kelley School of Business, Evening MBA Program, Indianapolis, IN 46202-5151. Offers accounting (MBA); entrepreneurship (MBA); finance (MBA); general administration (MBA); marketing (MBA); supply chain management (MBA); MBA/JD; MBA/MD; MBA/MHA; MBA/MS; MBA/MSA; MBA/MSE. *Program availability:* Part-time-only, evening/weekend, online learning. *Entrance requirements:* For master's, GMAT or GRE, 2 years of professional work experience. Additional exam requirements/recommendations for international students: Required—TOEFL or IELTS. Electronic applications accepted. *Expenses:* Contact institution. *Faculty research:* Entrepreneurship; corporate finance; international business; consumer behavior; supply chain; business law.

Johnson & Wales University, Graduate Studies, MBA Program, Providence, RI 02903-3703. Offers accounting (MBA); business administration (MBA); finance (MBA); global fashion merchandising and management (MBA); hospitality (MBA); human resource management (MBA); information security/assurance (MBA); information technology (MBA); nonprofit management (MBA); operations and supply chain management (MBA); organizational leadership (MBA); organizational psychology (MBA); sport leadership (MBA). Program also offered on Denver campus. *Program availability:* Part-time, online learning. *Entrance requirements:* For master's, minimum GPA of 2.75. Additional exam requirements/recommendations for international students: Required—TOEFL (minimum score 550 paper-based); Recommended—IELTS, TWE. *Application deadline:* For fall admission, 8/15 priority date for domestic students, 6/28 priority date for international students; for winter admission, 11/10 priority date for domestic students, 9/20 priority date for international students; for spring admission, 2/5 priority date for domestic students, 12/20 priority date for international students. Applications are processed on a rolling basis. *Expenses: Tuition:* Full-time $12,636; part-time $702 per credit hour. *Financial support:* Tuition waivers (partial) and unspecified assistantships available. Support available to part-time students. Financial award application deadline: 5/1. *Faculty research:* International banking, global economy, international trade, cultural differences. *Unit head:* Dr. Karen Silva, Director, 401-598-2849, Fax: 401-598-1125. *Application contact:* Graduate School Admissions, 401-598-1015, Fax: 401-598-1286, E-mail: gradadm@jwu.edu.

Lindenwood University, Graduate Programs, Plaster School of Business and Entrepreneurship, St. Charles, MO 63301-1695. Offers accountancy (M Acc); accounting (MBA); business administration (MBA); entrepreneurial studies (MBA); finance (MBA, MS); human resource management (MBA); international business (MBA); leadership (MA); management (MBA); marketing (MBA, MS); nonprofit administration (MA); public administration (MBA); sport management (MA); supply chain management (MBA). *Accreditation:* ACBSP. *Program availability:* Part-time, evening/weekend, 100% online. *Faculty:* 15 full-time (8 women), 26 part-time/adjunct (9 women). *Students:* 201 full-time (116 women), 253 part-time (153 women); includes 102 minority (80 Black or African American, non-Hispanic/Latino; 2 American Indian or Alaska Native, non-Hispanic/Latino; 6 Asian, non-Hispanic/Latino; 7 Hispanic/Latino; 7 Two or more races, non-Hispanic/Latino), 61 international. Average age 32. 370 applicants, 42% accepted, 134 enrolled. In 2017, 178 master's awarded. *Degree requirements:* For master's, comprehensive exam (for some programs), thesis (for some programs), minimum GPA of 3.0. *Entrance requirements:* For master's, interview, minimum undergraduate cumulative GPA of 3.0, letter of recommendation. Additional exam requirements/recommendations for international students: Required—TOEFL (minimum score 550 paper-based; 80 iBT); Recommended—IELTS (minimum score 6.5). *Application deadline:* For fall admission, 8/27 priority date for domestic and international students; for winter admission, 1/14 priority date for domestic and international students; for spring admission, 3/18 for domestic students, 3/18 priority date for international students; for summer admission, 6/3 priority date for domestic and international students. Applications are processed on a rolling basis. Application fee: $30 ($100 for international students). Electronic applications accepted. *Expenses:* Contact institution. *Financial support:* In 2017–18, 439 students received support. Career-related internships or fieldwork, Federal Work-Study, institutionally sponsored loans, scholarships/grants, tuition waivers (partial), and unspecified assistantships available. Financial award application deadline: 6/30; financial award applicants required to submit FAFSA. *Unit head:* Roger Ellis, Dean, School of Business and Entrepreneurship, 636-949-4839, E-mail: rellis@lindenwood.edu. *Application contact:* Kara Schilli, Director, Evening and Graduate Admissions, 636-949-4349, Fax: 636-949-4109, E-mail: adultadmissions@lindenwood.edu. Website: http://www.lindenwood.edu/academics/academic-schools/robert-w-plaster-school-of-business-entrepreneurship/

Loyola University Chicago, Quinlan School of Business, Master of Science in Supply Chain Management Program, Chicago, IL 60611. Offers data warehousing (Certificate); information systems and supply chain management (MSSCM); supply chain management (MS, Certificate). *Program availability:* Part-time, evening/weekend. *Faculty:* 14 full-time (1 woman), 9 part-time/adjunct (1 woman). *Students:* 7 full-time (3 women), 8 part-time (3 women); includes 3 minority (1 Black or African American, non-Hispanic/Latino; 2 Hispanic/Latino), 6 international. Average age 30. 36 applicants, 53% accepted, 4 enrolled. In 2017, 14 master's, 3 other advanced degrees awarded. *Entrance requirements:* For master's, GMAT or GRE, official transcripts, two letters of recommendation, statement of purpose, resume. Additional exam requirements/recommendations for international students: Required—TOEFL (minimum score 90 iBT), IELTS (minimum score 6.5). *Application deadline:* For fall admission, 7/15 for domestic and international students; for winter admission, 10/1 for domestic and international students; for spring admission, 1/15 for domestic students, 1/14 for international students; for summer admission, 4/1 for domestic and international students. Applications are

processed on a rolling basis. Application fee: $50. Electronic applications accepted. Application fee is waived when completed online. *Expenses:* $4,488 per course. *Financial support:* In 2017–18, 2 students received support. Research assistantships, career-related internships or fieldwork, Federal Work-Study, scholarships/grants, and health care benefits available. *Faculty research:* Consistent vehicle routing policies, logistics, operations management. *Unit head:* Dr. Maciek Nowak, Chair, 312-915-7654, E-mail: mnowak4@luc.edu. Website: http://www.luc.edu/quinlan/mba/supply-chain-management-degrees/index.shtml

Loyola University Chicago, Quinlan School of Business, MBA Programs, Chicago, IL 60611. Offers accounting (MBA); business ethics (MBA); derivative markets (MBA); economics (MBA); entrepreneurship (MBA); finance (MBA); healthcare management (MBA); human resources management (MBA); information systems management (MBA); international business (MBA); management (MBA); marketing (MBA); risk management (MBA); supply chain management (MBA). *Program availability:* Part-time, evening/weekend. *Faculty:* 84 full-time (28 women), 12 part-time/adjunct (3 women). *Students:* 253 full-time (118 women), 76 part-time (35 women); includes 83 minority (21 Black or African American, non-Hispanic/Latino; 1 American Indian or Alaska Native, non-Hispanic/Latino; 33 Asian, non-Hispanic/Latino; 24 Hispanic/Latino; 4 Two or more races, non-Hispanic/Latino), 37 international. Average age 30. 334 applicants, 52% accepted, 80 enrolled. In 2017, 220 master's awarded. *Entrance requirements:* For master's, GMAT or GRE, official transcripts, two letters of recommendation, statement of purpose, resume. Additional exam requirements/recommendations for international students: Required—TOEFL (minimum score 90 iBT) or IELTS (minimum score 6.5). *Application deadline:* For fall admission, 7/15 for domestic and international students; for winter admission, 10/1 for domestic and international students; for spring admission, 1/15 for domestic and international students; for summer admission, 4/1 for domestic and international students. Applications are processed on a rolling basis. Application fee: $50. Electronic applications accepted. Application fee is waived when completed online. *Expenses:* $4,488 per course. *Financial support:* In 2017–18, 11 students received support. Research assistantships, career-related internships or fieldwork, Federal Work-Study, scholarships/grants, and health care benefits available. *Faculty research:* Social enterprise and responsibility, emerging markets, supply chain management, risk management. *Unit head:* Katherine Acles, Assistant Dean for Graduate Programs, 312-915-6124, Fax: 312-915-7207, E-mail: kacles@luc.edu.

Maine Maritime Academy, Loeb-Sullivan School of International Business and Logistics, Castine, ME 04420. Offers global logistics and maritime management (MS); international logistics management (MS). *Program availability:* Part-time, 100% online. *Faculty:* 6 full-time (1 woman), 5 part-time/adjunct (1 woman). *Students:* 8 full-time (2 women), 13 part-time (7 women). Average age 30. 26 applicants. In 2017, 17 master's awarded. *Degree requirements:* For master's, capstone course. *Entrance requirements:* For master's, GMAT or GRE, letter of recommendation. Additional exam requirements/recommendations for international students: Required—TOEFL, IELTS. *Application deadline:* For fall admission, 6/1 for domestic and international students; for spring admission, 3/15 for domestic and international students. Applications are processed on a rolling basis. Application fee: $40. Electronic applications accepted. Application fee is waived when completed online. *Financial support:* In 2017–18, 2 students received support, including teaching assistantships with full tuition reimbursements available (averaging $5,000 per year); career-related internships or fieldwork, Federal Work-Study, and institutionally sponsored loans also available. Support available to part-time students. Financial award application deadline: 4/15; financial award applicants required to submit FAFSA. *Faculty research:* Internet of things, trait intelligence, port operations, location theory. *Unit head:* Dr. Donald Maier, Dean, 207-326-2488, E-mail: donald.maier@mma.edu. *Application contact:* Debra Kingston, Program Coordinator, 207-326-2212, Fax: 207-326-2411, E-mail: debra.kingston@mma.edu. Website: http://ibl.mainemaritime.edu

Marquette University, Graduate School of Management, Executive MBA Program, Milwaukee, WI 53201-1881. Offers economics (MBA); finance (MBA); human resources (MBA); international business (MBA); management information systems (MBA); marketing (MBA); operations and supply chain management (MBA); sports business (MBA). *Accreditation:* AACSB. *Degree requirements:* For master's, international trip. *Entrance requirements:* For master's, GMAT or GRE, two letters of recommendation, official transcripts from current and previous colleges/universities. Additional exam requirements/recommendations for international students: Required—TOEFL (minimum score 550 paper-based; 88 iBT), IELTS (minimum score 6.5), PTE. Electronic applications accepted. *Expenses:* Contact institution. *Faculty research:* International trade and finance, customer relationship management, consumer satisfaction, customer service.

Marquette University, Graduate School of Management, Program in Business Administration, Milwaukee, WI 53201-1881. Offers business administration (MBA); economics (MBA); entrepreneurship (Certificate); finance (MBA); human resources (MBA); international business (MBA); management information systems (MBA); marketing (MBA); operations and supply chain management (MBA); sports business (MBA); JD/MBA; MBA/MA; MBA/MSN. *Accreditation:* AACSB. *Program availability:* Part-time, evening/weekend. *Degree requirements:* For Certificate, business plan. *Entrance requirements:* For master's, GMAT or GRE, letters of recommendation. Additional exam requirements/recommendations for international students: Required—TOEFL (minimum score 550 paper-based; 88 iBT), IELTS (minimum score 6.5), PTE. Electronic applications accepted. *Faculty research:* Ethics in the professions, services marketing, technology impact on decision-making, mentoring.

Maryville University of Saint Louis, The John E. Simon School of Business, St. Louis, MO 63141-7299. Offers accounting (MBA, MS, Certificate); business studies (Certificate); cybersecurity (MBA, MS, Certificate); financial services (MBA, Certificate); healthcare practice management (MBA, Certificate); human resource management (MBA, Certificate); information technology (MBA, Certificate); management (MBA, Certificate); management and leadership (MA); marketing (MBA, Certificate); project management (MBA, Certificate); sport business management (MBA); supply chain management (Certificate); supply chain management/logistics (MBA). *Accreditation:* ACBSP. *Program availability:* Part-time, 100% online, blended/hybrid learning. *Faculty:* 5 full-time (3 women), 51 part-time/adjunct (16 women). *Students:* 222 full-time (96 women), 498 part-time (222 women); includes 185 minority (104 Black or African American, non-Hispanic/Latino; 5 American Indian or Alaska Native, non-Hispanic/Latino; 30 Asian, non-Hispanic/Latino; 37 Hispanic/Latino; 9 Two or more races, non-Hispanic/Latino), 26 international. Average age 33. In 2017, 106 master's awarded. *Degree requirements:* For master's, capstone course (for MBA). *Entrance requirements:* Additional exam requirements/recommendations for international students: Required—TOEFL (minimum score 563 paper-based; 85 iBT). *Application deadline:* Applications are processed on a rolling basis. Electronic applications accepted. *Expenses:* Contact institution. *Financial support:* Career-related internships or fieldwork, Federal Work-Study, tuition waivers (partial), and campus employment available. Financial award application deadline: 4/1; financial award applicants required to submit FAFSA. *Unit head:* Pam Horwitz, Interim Dean, 314-529-9680, Fax: 314-529-9975. *Application contact:* Dustin Loeffler, Director for Graduate Studies in Business, 314-529-9571, Fax: 314-529-9975, E-mail: dloeffler@maryville.edu. Website: http://www.maryville.edu/bu/business-administration-masters/

Supply Chain Management

Metropolitan State University, College of Management, St. Paul, MN 55106-5000. Offers business administration (MBA, DBA); business analytics (Graduate Certificate); database administration (Graduate Certificate); global supply chain management (Graduate Certificate); information assurance security (Graduate Certificate); management information systems (MMIS); MIS generalist (Graduate Certificate); MIS systems analysis and design (Graduate Certificate); project management (Graduate Certificate). *Program availability:* Part-time, evening/weekend. *Degree requirements:* For master's, thesis optional, computer language (MMIS). *Entrance requirements:* For master's, GMAT (for MBA), resume. Additional exam requirements/recommendations for international students: Required—TOEFL (minimum score 550 paper-based). *Application deadline:* For fall admission, 7/15 for international students; for winter admission, 11/15 for international students; for spring admission, 3/15 for international students. Applications are processed on a rolling basis. Application fee: $20. Electronic applications accepted. *Expenses:* Tuition, state resident: part-time $388.55 per credit. Tuition, nonresident: part-time $777.11 per credit. *Required fees:* $35.11 per credit. Part-time tuition and fees vary according to campus/location and program. *Financial support:* Research assistantships with partial tuition reimbursements, career-related internships or fieldwork, and Federal Work-Study available. Support available to part-time students. Financial award applicants required to submit FAFSA. *Faculty research:* Yugoslav economic system, workers' cooperatives, participative management and job enrichment, global business systems. *Unit head:* Allen Bellas, Interim Dean, 612-659-7272, Fax: 612-659-7268, E-mail: allen.bellas@metrostate.edu. *Application contact:* Allen Bellas, Interim Dean, 612-659-7272, Fax: 612-659-7268, E-mail: allen.bellas@metrostate.edu.
Website: https://www.metrostate.edu/academics/management

Michigan State University, The Graduate School, Eli Broad College of Business, Department of Supply Chain Management, East Lansing, MI 48224. Offers logistics (PhD); operations and sourcing management (PhD); supply chain management (MS), including logistics management, operations management, rail management, supply management. *Program availability:* Part-time. *Degree requirements:* For master's, field study/research project; for doctorate, comprehensive exam, thesis/dissertation. *Entrance requirements:* For master's, GMAT (taken within past 5 years), bachelor's degree, minimum GPA of 3.0 in junior/senior years, transcripts, at least 2 years of professional supply chain work experience, 3 letters of recommendation, essays, resume; for doctorate, GMAT or GRE, bachelor's or master's degree, transcripts, strong work experience, 3 letters of recommendation, statement of personal goals, interview. Additional exam requirements/recommendations for international students: Required—TOEFL (minimum score 600 paper-based). Electronic applications accepted. *Expenses:* Contact institution.

Michigan State University, The Graduate School, Eli Broad College of Business, Program in Business Administration, East Lansing, MI 48224. Offers finance (MBA); human resource management (MBA); integrative management (MBA); marketing (MBA); supply chain management (MBA). MBA in integrative management is through Weekend MBA Program; other 4 concentrations are through Full-Time MBA Program. *Program availability:* Evening/weekend. *Degree requirements:* For master's, enrichment experience. *Entrance requirements:* For master's, GMAT or GRE, 4-year bachelor's degree; resume; work experience (minimum of 5 years for Weekend MBA); 2-3 personal essays; 2 letters of recommendation; personal interview. Additional exam requirements/recommendations for international students: Required—PTE (minimum score 70), TOEFL (minimum score 100 iBT) or IELTS (minimum score 7) for full-time MBA applicants. Electronic applications accepted. *Expenses:* Contact institution.

Moravian College, Graduate and Continuing Studies, Business and Management Programs, Bethlehem, PA 18018-6650. Offers accounting (MBA); business analytics (MBA); business management (MBA); health administration (MHA); healthcare management (MBA); HR leadership (MSHRM); human resource management (MBA); learning and performance management (MSHRM); supply chain management (MBA). *Program availability:* Part-time, evening/weekend. *Faculty:* 5 full-time (2 women), 9 part-time/adjunct (3 women). *Students:* 13 full-time (10 women), 80 part-time (45 women); includes 13 minority (6 Black or African American, non-Hispanic/Latino; 6 Hispanic/Latino; 1 Two or more races, non-Hispanic/Latino). Average age 31. 55 applicants, 91% accepted, 31 enrolled. In 2017, 29 master's awarded. *Entrance requirements:* For master's, current resume, official transcripts, 2 letters of recommendation. Additional exam requirements/recommendations for international students: Required—TOEFL (minimum score 550 paper-based), IELTS (minimum score 6.5). *Application deadline:* For fall admission, 8/1 priority date for domestic and international students; for spring admission, 1/1 priority date for domestic and international students; for summer admission, 5/1 priority date for domestic and international students. Applications are processed on a rolling basis. Electronic applications accepted. *Expenses: Tuition:* Full-time $15,714; part-time $2619 per course. *Required fees:* $45 per semester. Tuition and fees vary according to program. *Financial support:* In 2017–18, 3 students received support, including 2 research assistantships with full tuition reimbursements available. Financial award applicants required to submit FAFSA. *Faculty research:* Leadership, change management, human resources. *Unit head:* Dr. Liz Kleintop, Associate Chair of Graduate Business, 610-861-1400, Fax: 610-861-1466, E-mail: graduate@moravian.edu. *Application contact:* Sean Rossi, Student Experience Mentor, 610-861-1400, Fax: 610-861-1466, E-mail: graduate@moravian.edu.
Website: https://www.moravian.edu/graduate

Naval Postgraduate School, Departments and Academic Groups, Graduate School of Business and Public Policy, Monterey, CA 93943. Offers acquisition and contract management (MBA); business administration (EMBA, MBA); contract management (MS); defense business management (MBA); defense systems analysis (MS), including management; defense systems management (international) (MBA); financial management (MBA); information management (MBA); manpower systems analysis (MS); material logistics support management (MBA); program management (MS); resource planning and management for international defense (MBA); supply chain management (MBA); systems acquisition management (MBA); transportation management (MBA). Program only open to commissioned officers of the United States and friendly nations and selected United States federal civilian employees. *Accreditation:* AACSB; NASPAA. *Program availability:* Part-time, online learning. *Degree requirements:* For master's, thesis (for some programs), terminal project/capstone (for some programs). *Faculty research:* U.S. and European public procurement policies for small and medium-sized enterprises, examining external validity criticisms in the choice of students as subjects in accounting experiment studies, assurance of learning in contract management education, contracting for cloud computing: opportunities and risks, NPS, Apple App Store as a business model supporting U.S. Navy requirements.

New York Institute of Technology, School of Management, Department of Business Administration, Old Westbury, NY 11568-8000. Offers executive management (MBA), including finance, marketing, operations and supply chain management. *Accreditation:* AACSB. *Program availability:* Part-time. *Faculty:* 25 full-time (4 women), 20 part-time/adjunct (6 women). *Students:* 398 full-time (187 women), 138 part-time (63 women); includes 43 minority (9 Black or African American, non-Hispanic/Latino; 1 American Indian or Alaska Native, non-Hispanic/Latino; 22 Asian, non-Hispanic/Latino; 9 Hispanic/Latino; 2 Two or more races, non-Hispanic/Latino), 432 international. Average age 26. 635 applicants, 75% accepted, 196 enrolled. In 2017, 230 master's awarded. *Entrance requirements:* For master's, bachelor's degree; minimum undergraduate GPA of 3.0. Additional exam requirements/recommendations for international students: Required—TOEFL (minimum score 79 iBT), IELTS (minimum score 6). *Application deadline:* Applications are processed on a rolling basis. Application fee: $50. Electronic applications accepted. *Expenses:* $1,285 per credit plus fees. *Financial support:* Career-related internships or fieldwork, Federal Work-Study, scholarships/grants, tuition waivers (full and partial), and unspecified assistantships available. Support available to part-time students. Financial award application deadline: 2/15; financial award applicants required to submit FAFSA. *Faculty research:* Accounting, economics, finance, management, marketing. *Unit head:* Dr. Jess Boronico, Dean, 516-686-7838, E-mail: som@nyit.edu. *Application contact:* Alice Dolitsky, Director, Graduate Admissions, 516-686-7520, Fax: 516-686-1116, E-mail: nyitgrad@nyit.edu.
Website: http://www.nyit.edu/degrees/management_mba

Niagara University, Graduate Division of Business Administration, Niagara University, NY 14109. Offers accounting (MBA); business administration (MBA); finance (MBA, MS); financial planning (MBA); healthcare administration (MBA, MHA); human resources (MBA); international business (MBA); marketing (MBA); professional accountancy (MBA); strategic management (MBA); supply chain management (MBA). *Accreditation:* AACSB. *Program availability:* Part-time, evening/weekend. *Faculty:* 17 full-time, 11 part-time/adjunct (92 women), 77 part-time (39 women); includes 38 minority (8 Black or African American, non-Hispanic/Latino; 3 American Indian or Alaska Native, non-Hispanic/Latino; 8 Asian, non-Hispanic/Latino; 8 Hispanic/Latino; 11 Two or more races, non-Hispanic/Latino), 46 international. Average age 27. In 2017, 139 master's awarded. *Entrance requirements:* For master's, GMAT. Additional exam requirements/recommendations for international students: Required—TOEFL (minimum score 550 paper-based; 79 iBT), IELTS (minimum score 6). *Application deadline:* For fall admission, 8/1 for domestic students; for spring admission, 11/1 for domestic students. Applications are processed on a rolling basis. Electronic applications accepted. *Expenses:* Contact institution. *Financial support:* Fellowships, research assistantships, career-related internships or fieldwork, and Federal Work-Study available. Support available to part-time students. Financial award application deadline: 4/15; financial award applicants required to submit FAFSA. *Faculty research:* Capital flows, Federal Reserve policy, human resource management, public policy, issues in marketing, auctions, economics of information, risk and capital markets, management strategy, consumer behavior, Internet and social media marketing. *Unit head:* Dr. Paul Richardson, MBA Director/Chair of the Marketing Department, 716-286-8169, Fax: 716-286-8206, E-mail: psr@niagara.edu. *Application contact:* Evan Pierce, Associate Director for Graduate Recruitment, 716-286-8769, Fax: 716-286-8170, E-mail: epierce@niagara.edu.
Website: http://mba.niagara.edu

North Carolina Agricultural and Technical State University, School of Graduate Studies, School of Business and Economics, Greensboro, NC 27411. Offers accounting (MBA); business education (MAT); human resources management (MBA); supply chain systems (MBA).

North Carolina State University, Graduate School, Poole College of Management, Program in Business Administration, Raleigh, NC 27695. Offers biosciences management (MBA); entrepreneurship and technology commercialization (MBA); financial management (MBA); innovation management (MBA); marketing management (MBA); services management (MBA); supply chain management (MBA). *Accreditation:* AACSB. *Program availability:* Part-time. *Degree requirements:* For master's, thesis optional. *Entrance requirements:* For master's, GMAT, interview, 3 letters of recommendation. Additional exam requirements/recommendations for international students: Required—TOEFL (minimum score 600 paper-based; 100 iBT). Electronic applications accepted. *Faculty research:* Manufacturing strategy, information systems, technology commercialization, managing research and development, historical stock returns.

Norwich University, College of Graduate and Continuing Studies, Master of Business Administration Program, Northfield, VT 05663. Offers construction management (MBA); energy management (MBA); finance (MBA); logistics (MBA); organizational leadership (MBA); project management (MBA); supply chain management (MBA). *Accreditation:* ACBSP. *Program availability:* Evening/weekend, online only, mostly all online with a week-long residency requirement. *Degree requirements:* For master's, comprehensive exam. *Entrance requirements:* For master's, minimum undergraduate GPA of 2.75. Additional exam requirements/recommendations for international students: Required—TOEFL (minimum score 550 paper-based; 80 iBT), IELTS (minimum score 6.5). Electronic applications accepted. *Expenses:* Contact institution.

Nova Southeastern University, H. Wayne Huizenga College of Business and Entrepreneurship, Fort Lauderdale, FL 33314-7796. Offers accounting (M Acc); business (MBA); business intelligence/analytics (MBA); complex health systems (MBA); enterprise informatics (MBA); entrepreneurship (MBA); finance (MBA); human resource management (MBA); international business (MBA); management (MBA); marketing (MBA); process improvement (MBA); public administration (MPA); real estate development (MS); sport revenue generation (MBA); supply chain management (MBA). *Accreditation:* NASPAA. *Program availability:* Part-time, evening/weekend, 100% online, blended/hybrid learning. *Faculty:* 85 full-time (37 women), 59 part-time/adjunct (19 women). *Students:* 1,999 full-time (1,225 women), 335 part-time (210 women); includes 1,516 minority (597 Black or African American, non-Hispanic/Latino; 4 American Indian or Alaska Native, non-Hispanic/Latino; 92 Asian, non-Hispanic/Latino; 789 Hispanic/Latino; 3 Native Hawaiian or other Pacific Islander, non-Hispanic/Latino; 31 Two or more races, non-Hispanic/Latino), 291 international. Average age 34. 1,269 applicants, 59% accepted, 551 enrolled. In 2017, 1,055 master's awarded. *Entrance requirements:* For master's, GMAT or GRE (depending on undergraduate GPA), official transcripts from all schools attended while in pursuit of bachelor's degree; minimum GPA of 2.5 from regionally-accredited institution. Additional exam requirements/recommendations for international students: Required—TOEFL (minimum score 550 paper-based; 79 iBT), IELTS (minimum score 6), PTE (minimum score 54). *Application deadline:* For fall admission, 8/5 priority date for domestic students, 7/29 priority date for international students; for winter admission, 12/16 priority date for domestic students, 12/9 priority date for international students; for summer admission, 4/21 priority date for domestic and international students. Applications are processed on a rolling basis. Application fee: $50. Electronic applications accepted. *Expenses:* $37,785 (online), $35,640 (in-classroom). *Financial support:* In 2017–18, 325 students received support. Federal Work-Study and scholarships/grants available. Support available to part-time students. Financial award application deadline: 4/15; financial award applicants required to submit FAFSA. *Faculty research:* Entrepreneurship and venture capital, ethics and social responsibility, global commerce and cultures, business process management. *Unit head:* Dr. J. Preston Jones, Dean, 954-262-5127, E-mail: prestonj@nova.edu. *Application contact:* Zeida Rodriguez, Associate Director of Enrollment Services, 954-262-5163, Fax: 954-262-3822, E-mail: zeida@nova.edu.
Website: http://www.huizenga.nova.edu

Supply Chain Management

Old Dominion University, Strome College of Business, Program in Maritime Trade and Supply Chain Management, Norfolk, VA 23529. Offers MS. *Program availability:* Part-time, evening/weekend. *Students:* 5 full-time (3 women), 13 part-time (5 women); includes 4 minority (3 Asian, non-Hispanic/Latino; 1 Hispanic/Latino), 4 international. Average age 33. In 2017, 1 master's awarded. *Degree requirements:* For master's, capstone course. *Entrance requirements:* For master's, GRE or GMAT, bachelor's degree, official transcripts, two letters of recommendation, current resume, statement of professional goals. Additional exam requirements/recommendations for international students: Required—TOEFL (minimum score 550 paper-based; 79 iBT), IELTS (minimum score 6.5). *Application deadline:* For fall admission, 6/1 for domestic students, 4/15 for international students; for spring admission, 11/1 for domestic students, 10/1 for international students. Applications are processed on a rolling basis. Electronic applications accepted. *Expenses:* Tuition, state resident: full-time $8928; part-time $496 per credit. Tuition, nonresident: full-time $22,482; part-time $1249 per credit. *Required fees:* $66 per semester. *Financial support:* In 2017–18, 2 students received support. Unspecified assistantships available. *Total annual research expenditures:* $400,000. *Unit head:* Dr. Wayne Talley, Director, 757-683-3534.

Penn State Harrisburg, Graduate School, School of Business Administration, Middletown, PA 17057. Offers accounting (MPAC, Certificate); business administration (MBA); information systems (MS); operations and supply chain management (Certificate). *Program availability:* Part-time, evening/weekend. *Unit head:* Dr. Mukund S. Kulkarni, Chancellor, 717-948-6105, Fax: 717-948-6452. *Application contact:* Robert W. Coffman, Jr., Director of Enrollment Management, Recruitment and Admissions, 717-948-6250, Fax: 717-948-6325, E-mail: hbgadmit@psu.edu.
Website: https://harrisburg.psu.edu/business-administration/

Polytechnic University of Puerto Rico, Miami Campus, Graduate School, Miami, FL 33166. Offers accounting (MBA); business administration (MBA); construction management (MEM); environmental management (MEM); finance (MBA); human resources management (MBA); logistics and supply chain management (MBA); management of international enterprises (MEM); manufacturing management (MEM); marketing management (MBA); project management (MBA). *Program availability:* Part-time, evening/weekend, online learning. *Entrance requirements:* For master's, minimum GPA of 3.0. Electronic applications accepted.

Portland State University, Graduate Studies, The School of Business, MS in Global Supply Chain Management Program, Portland, OR 97207-0751. Offers MS. *Program availability:* Part-time, online learning. *Students:* 3 full-time (1 woman), 63 part-time (28 women); includes 20 minority (3 Black or African American, non-Hispanic/Latino; 9 Asian, non-Hispanic/Latino; 7 Hispanic/Latino; 1 Two or more races, non-Hispanic/Latino), 6 international. Average age 35. 41 applicants, 85% accepted, 25 enrolled. In 2017, 24 master's awarded. *Entrance requirements:* For master's, minimum undergraduate GPA of 3.0; two professional references; unofficial transcript from each college or university attended; statement of purpose; resume. Additional exam requirements/recommendations for international students: Required—TOEFL (minimum score 550 paper-based; 80 iBT). *Application deadline:* For fall admission, 5/1 priority date for domestic and international students; for winter admission, 12/1 for domestic and international students; for spring admission, 1/15 priority date for domestic and international students; for summer admission, 5/1 for domestic and international students. Application fee: $65. Electronic applications accepted. *Expenses:* Contact institution. *Financial support:* Career-related internships or fieldwork, Federal Work-Study, and scholarships/grants available. Support available to part-time students. Financial award applicants required to submit FAFSA. *Unit head:* Daniel Wong, Academic Director, 503-725-3710, E-mail: dwong@pdx.edu. *Application contact:* Abby Messenger, Recruiting and Admissions Specialist, 503-725-2291, Fax: 503-725-5850, E-mail: a.g.messenger@pdx.edu.
Website: https://www.pdx.edu/sba/ms-in-global-supply-chain-management

Purdue University Global, School of Business, Davenport, IA 52807. Offers business administration (MBA); change leadership (MS); entrepreneurship (MBA); finance (MBA); health care management (MBA, MS); human resource (MBA); international business (MBA); management (MS); marketing (MBA); project management (MBA, MS); supply chain management and logistics (MBA, MS). *Accreditation:* ACBSP. *Program availability:* Part-time, evening/weekend, online learning. *Entrance requirements:* Additional exam requirements/recommendations for international students: Required—TOEFL (minimum score 550 paper-based; 80 iBT). Electronic applications accepted.

Quinnipiac University, School of Business, Program in Business Administration, Hamden, CT 06518-1940. Offers finance (MBA); health care management (MBA); supply chain management (MBA); JD/MBA. *Accreditation:* AACSB. *Program availability:* Part-time, evening/weekend, 100% online, blended/hybrid learning. *Faculty:* 32 full-time (11 women), 8 part-time/adjunct (3 women). *Students:* 201 full-time (95 women), 215 part-time (95 women); includes 48 minority (9 Black or African American, non-Hispanic/Latino; 12 Asian, non-Hispanic/Latino; 20 Hispanic/Latino; 7 Two or more races, non-Hispanic/Latino), 19 international. 307 applicants, 79% accepted, 223 enrolled. In 2017, 264 master's awarded. *Entrance requirements:* For master's, GMAT or GRE, minimum GPA of 3.0. Additional exam requirements/recommendations for international students: Required—TOEFL (minimum score 575 paper-based; 90 iBT), IELTS (minimum score 6.5). *Application deadline:* For fall admission, 7/30 priority date for domestic students, 4/30 priority date for international students; for spring admission, 12/15 priority date for domestic students, 9/30 priority date for international students. Applications are processed on a rolling basis. Application fee: $45. Electronic applications accepted. *Expenses:* Contact institution. *Financial support:* Career-related internships or fieldwork, Federal Work-Study, scholarships/grants, and unspecified assistantships available. Financial award application deadline: 6/1; financial award applicants required to submit FAFSA. *Faculty research:* Financial markets and investments, international business, supply chain management, health care management, corporate governance. *Unit head:* Lisa Braiewa, Director of the MBA Program, 800-462-1944, Fax: 203-582-3443, E-mail: graduate@qu.edu. *Application contact:* Office of Graduate Admissions, 800-462-1944, Fax: 203-582-3443, E-mail: graduate@qu.edu.
Website: http://www.qu.edu/mba

Rensselaer Polytechnic Institute, Graduate School, Lally School of Management, Program in Supply Chain Management, Troy, NY 12180-3590. Offers MS, MS/MBA. *Program availability:* Part-time. *Faculty:* 36 full-time (9 women), 5 part-time/adjunct (1 women). *Students:* 11 full-time (3 women), 5 part-time (4 women); includes 6 minority (1 Asian, non-Hispanic/Latino; 2 Hispanic/Latino; 3 Two or more races, non-Hispanic/Latino), 7 international. Average age 24. 84 applicants, 44% accepted, 3 enrolled. In 2017, 3 master's awarded. *Entrance requirements:* For master's, GMAT or GRE, personal statement. Additional exam requirements/recommendations for international students: Required—TOEFL (minimum score 570 paper-based; 88 iBT), IELTS (minimum score 6.8), PTE (minimum score 60). *Application deadline:* For fall admission, 1/1 for domestic and international students. Applications are processed on a rolling basis. Application fee: $75. Electronic applications accepted. *Expenses: Tuition:* Full-time $52,550; part-time $2125 per credit hour. *Required fees:* $2890. *Financial support:* Scholarships/grants available. Financial award application deadline: 1/1. *Unit head:* Dr. T. Ravichandran, Graduate Program Director, 518-276-6842, E-mail: ravit@rpi.edu.
Website: https://lallyschool.rpi.edu/graduate-programs/ms-supplychainmanagement

Rutgers University–Newark, Rutgers Business School–Newark and New Brunswick, Doctoral Programs in Management, Newark, NJ 07102. Offers accounting (PhD); accounting information systems (PhD); economics (PhD); finance (PhD); individualized study (PhD); information technology (PhD); international business (PhD); management science (PhD); marketing science (PhD); organizational management (PhD); science, technology and management (PhD); supply chain management (PhD). *Degree requirements:* For doctorate, comprehensive exam, thesis/dissertation. *Entrance requirements:* For doctorate, GRE or GMAT. Additional exam requirements/recommendations for international students: Required—TOEFL (minimum score 550 paper-based; 79 iBT). Electronic applications accepted.

Saint Leo University, Graduate Studies in Business, Saint Leo, FL 33574-6665. Offers accounting (M Acc, MBA); cybersecurity (MS); cybersecurity management (MBA); data analytics (MBA); health care management (MBA); human resource management (MBA); international and experiential business administration (MBA); management (MBA, DBA); marketing (MBA); marketing research and social media analytics (MBA); project management (MBA); social media marketing (MBA); sport business (MBA); supply chain global integration management (MBA). *Accreditation:* ACBSP. *Program availability:* Part-time, evening/weekend, 100% online, blended/hybrid learning. *Faculty:* 54 full-time (18 women), 52 part-time/adjunct (18 women). *Students:* 9 full-time (3 women), 1,867 part-time (1,079 women); includes 861 minority (598 Black or African American, non-Hispanic/Latino; 3 American Indian or Alaska Native, non-Hispanic/Latino; 38 Asian, non-Hispanic/Latino; 186 Hispanic/Latino; 3 Native Hawaiian or other Pacific Islander, non-Hispanic/Latino; 33 Two or more races, non-Hispanic/Latino), 68 international. Average age 37. 868 applicants, 63% accepted, 537 enrolled. In 2017, 859 master's, 3 doctorates awarded. *Degree requirements:* For doctorate, comprehensive exam, thesis/ dissertation. *Entrance requirements:* For master's, GMAT with minimum score 500 (for M Acc), official transcripts, current resume, 2 professional recommendations, personal statement, bachelor's degree from regionally-accredited university; undergraduate degree in accounting and minimum undergraduate GPA of 3.0 (for M Acc); minimum undergraduate GPA of 3.0 in final 2 years of undergraduate study and 2 years' work experience (for MBA); for doctorate, GMAT (minimum score of 550) if master's GPA is under 3.25, official transcripts, current resume, 2 professional recommendations, personal statement, master's degree from regionally-accredited university with minimum GPA of 3.25, 3 years' work experience, interview. Additional exam requirements/ recommendations for international students: Required—TOEFL (minimum score 550 paper-based; 78 iBT). *Application deadline:* For fall admission, 7/1 priority date for domestic and international students; for spring admission, 11/12 priority date for domestic students, 11/1 for international students. Applications are processed on a rolling basis. Application fee: $80. Electronic applications accepted. *Expenses:* Contact institution. *Financial support:* In 2017–18, 106 students received support. Career-related internships or fieldwork, health care benefits, and tuition remission for Saint Leo employees and their dependents available. Financial award application deadline: 3/1; financial award applicants required to submit FAFSA. *Faculty research:* Servant leadership, work/life balance, emotional intelligence, pricing, marketing. *Unit head:* Dr. Charles Hale, Dean, School of Business, 352-588-8599, Fax: 352-588-8912, E-mail: mbaslu@saintleo.edu. *Application contact:* Mark Russum, Assistant Vice President, Enrollment, 800-707-8846, Fax: 352-588-7873, E-mail: grad.admissions@saintleo.edu.
Website: https://www.saintleo.edu/school-of-business

St. Norbert College, Master of Business Administration Program, De Pere, WI 54115-2099. Offers business (MBA); health care (MBA); supply chain and manufacturing (MBA). *Program availability:* Part-time-only, evening/weekend. *Faculty:* 10 full-time (3 women), 8 part-time/adjunct (2 women). *Students:* 68 part-time (40 women); includes 5 minority (1 American Indian or Alaska Native, non-Hispanic/Latino; 1 Asian, non-Hispanic/Latino; 2 Hispanic/Latino; 1 Two or more races, non-Hispanic/Latino), 1 international. Average age 33. 15 applicants, 100% accepted, 14 enrolled. In 2017, 12 master's awarded. *Entrance requirements:* For master's, official transcripts, letters of recommendation, professional resume, essay. *Application deadline:* For fall admission, 8/4 for domestic students; for winter admission, 12/15 for domestic students; for spring admission, 3/2 for domestic students; for summer admission, 4/20 for domestic students. Applications are processed on a rolling basis. Application fee: $50. Electronic applications accepted. *Expenses:* $675 per credit tuition, $37.50 per course technology fee. *Financial support:* Federal Work-Study available. Financial award application deadline: 1/1; financial award applicants required to submit FAFSA. *Faculty research:* Urban segregation, religious identity, crisis decision-making, normative ethics, psychological effects of change on individuals and organizations. *Unit head:* Lisa Gray, Coordinator of MBA Program, 920-403-3449, E-mail: lisa.gray@snc.edu. *Application contact:* Brenda Busch, Associate Director of Graduate Recruitment, 920-403-3942, Fax: 920-403-4072, E-mail: brenda.busch@snc.edu.
Website: http://www.snc.edu/mba/

Santa Clara University, Leavey School of Business, Santa Clara, CA 95053. Offers business administration (MBA); business analytics (MS); finance (MS); information systems (MS); supply chain management and analytics (MS); JD/MBA. *Accreditation:* AACSB. *Program availability:* Part-time, evening/weekend, online curriculum with 2 on-campus intensives. *Faculty:* 100 full-time (30 women), 42 part-time/adjunct (16 women). *Students:* 413 full-time (226 women), 308 part-time (131 women); includes 246 minority (10 Black or African American, non-Hispanic/Latino; 175 Asian, non-Hispanic/Latino; 40 Hispanic/Latino; 2 Native Hawaiian or other Pacific Islander, non-Hispanic/Latino; 19 Two or more races, non-Hispanic/Latino), 256 international. Average age 31. 761 applicants, 63% accepted, 271 enrolled. In 2017, 267 master's awarded. *Entrance requirements:* For master's, GMAT, resume, essays, 2 letters of recommendation, 2 official transcripts. Additional exam requirements/recommendations for international students: Required—TOEFL (minimum score 100 iBT) or IELTS (7.0). Application fee: $100 ($150 for international students). Electronic applications accepted. *Expenses:* Contact institution. *Financial support:* In 2017–18, 192 students received support. Career-related internships or fieldwork, scholarships/grants, and unspecified assistantships available. Financial award applicants required to submit FAFSA. *Faculty research:* Digital marketing, database mining and retail, product innovation, industry disruption, entrepreneurship and cluster dynamics, innovation and temporary advantage, platform strategy, ethics and leadership, bank regulation, monetary policy, poverty alleviation, costs of financial crises, information technology and business intelligence, supply chain management, corporate social responsibility and institutional ownership, audits and financial reporting. *Unit head:* Caryn Beck-Dudley, Dean, 408-554-4523, E-mail: cbeckdudley@scu.edu. *Application contact:* Lenore Grant, Director, Graduate Business Recruitment and Admissions, 408-551-1633, E-mail: lgrant@scu.edu.
Website: http://www.scu.edu/business/

Seton Hall University, Stillman School of Business, Programs in Business Administration, South Orange, NJ 07079-2697. Offers accounting (MBA); entrepreneurial studies (Certificate); finance (MBA); financial decision making (Certificate); information technology management (MBA); international business (MBA); management (MBA); marketing (MBA); sport management (MBA); supply chain management (MBA, Certificate). *Program availability:* Part-time, evening/weekend. *Faculty:* 29 full-time (4 women), 18 part-time/adjunct (0 women). *Students:* 140 full-time (58 women), 154 part-time (49 women); includes 66 minority (25 Black or African

Supply Chain Management

American, non-Hispanic/Latino; 14 Asian, non-Hispanic/Latino; 23 Hispanic/Latino; 4 Two or more races, non-Hispanic/Latino; 88 international. Average age 32. 406 applicants, 75% accepted, 100 enrolled. In 2017, 132 master's awarded. *Degree requirements:* For master's, 20 hours of community service (Social Responsibility Project). *Entrance requirements:* For master's, GMAT or CPA, GRE (waived based on work experience or advanced degree from AACSB institution), MS in business discipline, professional degree or designation (MD, JD, PhD, DVM, DDS, CPA, etc.), minimum undergraduate GPA of 3.0. Additional exam requirements/recommendations for international students: Required—TOEFL (minimum score 607 paper-based; 80 iBT), IELTS (minimum score 6), PTE. *Application deadline:* For fall admission, 5/31 priority date for domestic students, 4/30 priority date for international students; for spring admission, 10/31 priority date for domestic students, 9/30 priority date for international students; for summer admission, 3/31 priority date for domestic students. Applications are processed on a rolling basis. Application fee: $75. Electronic applications accepted. *Expenses:* $1,305 per credit; $126 fees (fall and spring semester), $51 (summer semester). *Financial support:* In 2017–18, 41 students received support, including 25 research assistantships with full tuition reimbursements available (averaging $3,644 per year); career-related internships or fieldwork, scholarships/grants, and unspecified assistantships also available. Financial award application deadline: 6/30; financial award applicants required to submit FAFSA. *Faculty research:* Sport, hedge funds, executive compensation, social media, legal studies. *Unit head:* Dr. Joyce Strawser, Dean, 973-761-9013, Fax: 973-761-9217, E-mail: joyce.strawser@shu.edu. *Application contact:* Alfred Ayoub, Director of Graduate Admissions, 973-761-9262, Fax: 973-761-9208, E-mail: alfred.ayoub@shu.edu.
Website: http://www.shu.edu/business/mba-programs.cfm

Shippensburg University of Pennsylvania, School of Graduate Studies, John L. Grove College of Business, Shippensburg, PA 17257-2299. Offers advanced studies in business (Certificate); advanced supply chain and logistics management (Certificate); business administration (MBA, DBA), including business administration (MBA), business analytics (MBA), finance (MBA), healthcare management (MBA), management information systems (MBA), supply chain management (MBA); finance (Certificate); health care management (Certificate); management information systems (Certificate). *Accreditation:* AACSB. *Program availability:* Part-time, evening/weekend, 100% online, blended/hybrid learning. *Faculty:* 23 full-time (5 women), 1 part-time/adjunct (0 women). *Students:* 46 full-time (14 women), 201 part-time (71 women); includes 35 minority (12 Black or African American, non-Hispanic/Latino; 10 Asian, non-Hispanic/Latino; 11 Hispanic/Latino; 2 Two or more races, non-Hispanic/Latino), 22 international. Average age 32. 169 applicants, 65% accepted, 77 enrolled. In 2017, 105 master's, 82 other advanced degrees awarded. *Degree requirements:* For master's, thesis optional, practicum; for doctorate, comprehensive exam, thesis/dissertation. *Entrance requirements:* For master's, GMAT (minimum score 450 if less than 5 years of mid-level experience, including management experience), current resume; relevant work/classroom experience; 500-word statement of purpose; prerequisites of quantitative analysis, computer usage, and oral and written communications; laptop computer; for doctorate, GMAT (minimum score of 600 if less than 5 years of substantive professional or teaching experience), 2 letters of recommendation from professionals in academia or industry; 2-3 page personal and professional statement; interview; resume. Additional exam requirements/recommendations for international students: Required—TOEFL (minimum score 550 paper-based, 68 iBT) or IELTS (minimum score 6). *Application deadline:* For fall admission, 4/30 for international students; for spring admission, 9/30 for international students. Applications are processed on a rolling basis. Application fee: $45. Electronic applications accepted. *Expenses:* Tuition, state resident: part-time $500 per credit. Tuition, nonresident: part-time $750 per credit. *Required fees:* $145 per credit. *Financial support:* In 2017–18, 14 students received support. Career-related internships or fieldwork, scholarships/grants, unspecified assistantships, and resident hall director and student payroll positions available. Support available to part-time students. Financial award application deadline: 3/1; financial award applicants required to submit FAFSA. *Unit head:* Dr. John G. Kooti, Dean of the College of Business, 717-477-1435, Fax: 717-477-4003, E-mail: jgkooti@ship.edu. *Application contact:* Maya T. Mapp, Director of Admissions, 717-477-1231, Fax: 717-477-4016, E-mail: mtmapp@ship.edu.
Website: http://www.ship.edu/business .

Southern Arkansas University–Magnolia, School of Graduate Studies, Magnolia, AR 71753. Offers agriculture (MS); business administration (MBA), including agribusiness, social entrepreneurship, supply chain management; clinical and mental health counseling (MS); computer and information sciences (MS), including cyber security and privacy, data science, information technology; gifted and talented (M Ed), including curriculum and instruction, educational administration and supervision, gifted and talented P-8/7-12, instructional specialist P-4; higher, adult and lifelong education (M Ed); kinesiology (M Ed), including coaching; library media and information specialist (M Ed); public administration (MPA); school counseling K-12 (M Ed); student affairs and college counseling (M Ed); teaching (MAT). *Accreditation:* NCATE. *Program availability:* Part-time, 100% online, blended/hybrid learning. *Faculty:* 36 full-time (20 women), 31 part-time/adjunct (12 women). *Students:* 242 full-time (89 women), 889 part-time (459 women); includes 167 minority (143 Black or African American, non-Hispanic/Latino; 7 American Indian or Alaska Native, non-Hispanic/Latino; 7 Asian, non-Hispanic/Latino; 3 Hispanic/Latino; 7 Two or more races, non-Hispanic/Latino), 562 international. Average age 28. 400 applicants, 100% accepted, 239 enrolled. In 2017, 875 master's awarded. *Degree requirements:* For master's, comprehensive exam (for some programs), thesis optional. *Entrance requirements:* For master's, GRE, MAT or GMAT, minimum GPA of 2.5. Additional exam requirements/recommendations for international students: Required—TOEFL (minimum score 550 paper-based), IELTS (minimum score 6). *Application deadline:* For fall admission, 7/20 for domestic students, 7/10 for international students; for spring admission, 12/1 for domestic students, 11/15 for international students; for summer admission, 4/1 for domestic students, 5/1 for international students. Applications are processed on a rolling basis. Application fee: $25 ($50 for international students). Electronic applications accepted. *Expenses:* Tuition, state resident: full-time $6038. Tuition, nonresident: full-time $8558. *Required fees:* $804. One-time fee: $110 full-time. Tuition and fees vary according to course load. *Financial support:* Career-related internships or fieldwork, Federal Work-Study, scholarships/grants, tuition waivers (full), and unspecified assistantships available. Financial award applicants required to submit FAFSA. *Faculty research:* Alternative certification for teachers, supervision of instruction, instructional leadership, counseling. *Unit head:* Dr. Kim Bloss, Dean, School of Graduate Studies, 870-235-4150, Fax: 870-235-5227, E-mail: kkbloss@saumag.edu. *Application contact:* Shrijana Malakar, Admissions Specialist, 870-235-4150, Fax: 870-235-5227, E-mail: smalakar@saumag.edu.
Website: http://www.saumag.edu/graduate

Southern New Hampshire University, School of Business, Manchester, NH 03106-1045. Offers accounting (MBA, Graduate Certificate); accounting finance (MS); accounting/auditing (MS); accounting/forensic accounting (MS); accounting/management accounting (MS); accounting/taxation (MS); applied economics (MS); athletic administration (MBA, Graduate Certificate); business administration (IMBA, Certificate), including business information systems (Certificate), human resource

management (Certificate); business analytics (MBA); business intelligence (MBA); communication (MA), including new media and marketing, public relations; community economic development (MBA); criminal justice (MBA); data analytics (MS); economics (MBA); engineering management (MBA); entrepreneurship (MBA); finance (MBA, MS, Graduate Certificate); finance/corporate finance (MS); finance/investments (MS); forensic accounting (MBA); forensic accounting and fraud examination (Graduate Certificate); healthcare informatics (MBA); healthcare management (MBA); human resource management (MS); human resources (MBA); information technology (MS); information technology management (MBA); international business (PhD); Internet marketing (MBA); leadership (MBA); leadership of nonprofit organizations (Graduate Certificate); management (MS); marketing (MBA, MS, Graduate Certificate); music business (MBA); operations and project management (MS); operations and supply chain management (MBA, Graduate Certificate); organizational leadership (MS); project management (MBA, Graduate Certificate); public administration (MBA, Graduate Certificate); quantitative analysis (MBA); Six Sigma (Graduate Certificate); Six Sigma quality (MBA); social media marketing (MBA, Graduate Certificate); sport management (MBA, MS, Graduate Certificate); sustainability and environmental compliance (MBA); MBA/Certificate. *Accreditation:* ACBSP. *Program availability:* Part-time, evening/weekend, online learning. Terminal master's awarded for partial completion of doctoral program. *Degree requirements:* For master's, one foreign language, comprehensive exam (for some programs), thesis or alternative; for doctorate, one foreign language, comprehensive exam, thesis/dissertation. *Entrance requirements:* For master's, minimum GPA of 2.5; for doctorate, GMAT. Additional exam requirements/recommendations for international students: Required—TOEFL (minimum score 500 paper-based). *Application deadline:* Applications are processed on a rolling basis. Application fee: $40. Electronic applications accepted. *Expenses: Tuition:* Part-time $627 per credit hour. Part-time tuition and fees vary according to campus/location and program. *Financial support:* Career-related internships or fieldwork, Federal Work-Study, institutionally sponsored loans, scholarships/grants, tuition waivers (partial), and unspecified assistantships available. Support available to part-time students. Financial award applicants required to submit FAFSA. *Unit head:* Dr. Bill Lightfoot, Dean, 603-644-3102, Fax: 603-644-3144. *Application contact:* Office of Graduate Admission, 888-327-SNHU, Fax: 603-644-3144, E-mail: enroll@snhu.edu.

Strayer University, Graduate Studies, Washington, DC 20005-2603. Offers accounting (MS); acquisition (MBA); business administration (MBA); communications technology (MS); educational management (M Ed); finance (MBA); health services administration (MHSA); hospitality and tourism management (MBA); human resource management (MBA); information systems (MS), including computer security management, decision support system management, enterprise resource management, network management, software engineering management, systems development management; management (MBA); management information systems (MS); marketing (MBA); professional accounting (MS), including accounting information systems, controllership, taxation; public administration (MPA); supply chain management (MBA); technology in education (M Ed). Programs also offered at campus locations in Birmingham, AL; Chamblee, GA; Cobb County, GA; Morrow, GA; White Marsh, MD; Charleston, SC; Columbia, SC; Greensboro, NC; Greenville, SC; Lexington, KY; Louisville, KY; Nashville, TN; North Raleigh, NC; Washington, DC. *Accreditation:* ACBSP. *Program availability:* Part-time, evening/weekend, online learning. *Degree requirements:* For master's, thesis. *Entrance requirements:* For master's, GMAT, GRE General Test, bachelor's degree from an accredited college or university, minimum undergraduate GPA of 2.75. Electronic applications accepted.

Suffolk University, Sawyer Business School, Master of Business Administration Program, Boston, MA 02108-2770. Offers accounting (MBA); entrepreneurship (MBA); executive business administration (EMBA); finance (MBA); global business administration (GMBA); health administration (MBA); international business (MBA); marketing (MBA); nonprofit management (MBA); organizational behavior (MBA); strategic management (MBA); supply chain management (MBA); taxation (MBA); JD/MBA; MBA/MHA; MBA/MSA; MBA/MSF; MBA/MST. *Accreditation:* AACSB. *Program availability:* Part-time, evening/weekend, 100% online. *Faculty:* 16 full-time (6 women), 9 part-time/adjunct (1 woman). *Students:* 106 full-time (57 women), 236 part-time (135 women); includes 80 minority (23 Black or African American, non-Hispanic/Latino; 23 Asian, non-Hispanic/Latino; 28 Hispanic/Latino; 6 Two or more races, non-Hispanic/Latino), 41 international. Average age 30. 354 applicants, 69% accepted, 115 enrolled. In 2017, 170 master's awarded. *Entrance requirements:* For master's, GMAT, minimum undergraduate GPA of 2.75 (MBA), 5 years of managerial experience (EMBA). Additional exam requirements/recommendations for international students: Required—TOEFL (minimum score 550 paper-based; 80 iBT). *Application deadline:* For fall admission, 3/15 priority date for domestic students, 10/15 priority date for international students; for spring admission, 10/15 priority date for domestic and international students. Applications are processed on a rolling basis. Application fee: $50. Electronic applications accepted. *Expenses:* $43,980 per year full-time, $1,466 per credit part-time (for MBA); $1,794 per credit part-time (for Executive MBA). *Financial support:* In 2017–18, 198 students received support, including 1 fellowship (averaging $2,325 per year); career-related internships or fieldwork, Federal Work-Study, institutionally sponsored loans, and scholarships/grants also available. Support available to part-time students. Financial award application deadline: 4/1; financial award applicants required to submit FAFSA. *Faculty research:* Foreign investments; career strategies and boundaryless careers; corporate ethics codes; interest rates, inflation, and growth options; innovation and product development performance. *Unit head:* Jodi Detjen, Director of MBA Programs, 617-573-8306, E-mail: jdetjen@suffolk.edu. *Application contact:* Mara Marzocchi, Associate Director of Graduate Admissions, 617-573-8302, Fax: 617-305-1733, E-mail: grad.admission@suffolk.edu.
Website: http://www.suffolk.edu/mba

Syracuse University, Martin J. Whitman School of Management, Master of Business Administration Program, Syracuse, NY 13244. Offers accounting (MBA); business analytics (MBA); entrepreneurship (MBA); marketing management (MBA); real estate (MBA); supply chain management (MBA); JD/MBA. *Program availability:* Part-time, 100% online. *Students:* 22 full-time (9 women), 495 part-time (147 women); includes 182 minority (81 Black or African American, non-Hispanic/Latino; 3 American Indian or Alaska Native, non-Hispanic/Latino; 42 Asian, non-Hispanic/Latino; 52 Hispanic/Latino; 4 Native Hawaiian or other Pacific Islander, non-Hispanic/Latino). Average age 32. 1,086 applicants, 73% accepted, 516 enrolled. In 2017, 84 master's awarded. *Entrance requirements:* For master's, GMAT or GRE, resume, essay, 5-minute video interview, two letters of recommendation, transcripts (unofficial). Additional exam requirements/recommendations for international students: Required—TOEFL (minimum score 100 iBT), IELTS (minimum score 7), PTE (minimum score 68). *Application deadline:* For fall admission, 11/30 for domestic students, 11/30 priority date for international students; for winter admission, 1/1 for domestic students, 1/1 priority date for international students; for spring admission, 2/15 for domestic and international students; for summer admission, 4/19 for domestic students. Application fee: $75. Electronic applications accepted. *Expenses:* Contact institution. *Financial support:* In 2017–18, 22 students received support. Merit scholarships available. Financial award application deadline: 2/15. *Faculty research:* Data analysis, economics of international business, financial markets and institutions, operations management, supply chain management. *Unit*

head: Dr. Alexander McKelvie, Associate Dean for Undergraduate and Full-time Master's Education, 315-443-7252, E-mail: mckelvie@syr.edu. *Application contact:* Shri Ramakrishnan, Assistant Director, Graduate Recruitment, 315-443-3497, Fax: 315-443-9517, E-mail: busgrad@syr.edu.
Website: http://whitman.syr.edu/ftmba/

Syracuse University, Martin J. Whitman School of Management, MS Program in Supply Chain Management, Syracuse, NY 13244. Offers MS. *Students:* Average age 22. 72 applicants, 36% accepted, 3 enrolled. In 2017, 5 master's awarded. *Entrance requirements:* For master's, GMAT or GRE, resume, essay, 5-minute video interview, two letters of recommendation, transcripts (unofficial). Additional exam requirements/recommendations for international students: Required—TOEFL (minimum score 100 iBT), IELTS (minimum score 7), PTE (minimum score 68), GMAT or GRE. *Application deadline:* For fall admission, 11/30 for domestic students, 11/30 priority date for international students; for winter admission, 1/1 for domestic students, 1/1 priority date for international students; for spring admission, 2/15 for domestic and international students; for summer admission, 4/19 for domestic students. Application fee: $75. Electronic applications accepted. *Expenses:* Contact institution. *Financial support:* In 2017–18, 3 students received support. Merit scholarships available. Financial award application deadline: 2/15. *Faculty research:* Supply chain management, logistics management, management information systems, risk sharing, buyer-seller alliances. *Unit head:* Fred Easton, Director, Operations Management/Professor of Supply Chain Management, 315-443-3463, E-mail: ffeaston@syr.edu. *Application contact:* Shri Ramakrishnan, Assistant Director, Graduate Recruitment, 315-443-3497, Fax: 315-443-9517, E-mail: sramak01@syr.edu.
Website: http://whitman.syr.edu/Academics/Marketing/SupplyChain/

Towson University, College of Business and Economics, Program in e-Business and Technology Management, Towson, MD 21252-0001. Offers project, program and portfolio management (Postbaccalaureate Certificate); supply chain management (MS). *Students:* 3 full-time (1 woman), 23 part-time (12 women); includes 5 minority (2 Black or African American, non-Hispanic/Latino; 1 Asian, non-Hispanic/Latino; 2 Two or more races, non-Hispanic/Latino), 3 international. *Entrance requirements:* For master's and Postbaccalaureate Certificate, GRE or GMAT, bachelor's degree in relevant field and/or three years of post-bachelor's experience working in supply chain related areas; minimum cumulative GPA of 3.0; resume; 2 reference letters. Additional exam requirements/recommendations for international students: Required—TOEFL (minimum score 550 paper-based). *Application deadline:* For fall admission, 1/17 for domestic students, 5/15 for international students; for spring admission, 10/15 for domestic students, 12/1 for international students. Applications are processed on a rolling basis. Application fee: $45. Electronic applications accepted. *Expenses:* Tuition, state resident: full-time $7960; part-time $398 per unit. Tuition, nonresident: full-time $16,480; part-time $824 per unit. *Required fees:* $2600; $130 per year. $390 per term. *Unit head:* Dr. Tobin Porterfield, Program Director, 410-704-3265, E-mail: tporterfield@towson.edu. *Application contact:* Coverley Beidleman, Assistant Director of Graduate Admissions, 410-704-5630, Fax: 410-704-3030, E-mail: cbeidleman@towson.edu.
Website: http://www.towson.edu/cbe/departments/ebusiness/grad/

University at Buffalo, the State University of New York, Graduate School, School of Management, Buffalo, NY 14260. Offers accounting (MS); analytics (MBA); business administration (PMBA); consulting (MBA); finance (MBA, MS), including financial risk management (MS); quantitative finance (MS); healthcare (MBA); information assurance (MBA); information systems (MBA); international management (MBA); management (EMBA, PhD); management information systems (MS); marketing (MBA); supply chain and operations (MBA); supply chains and operations management (MS); Au D/MBA; DDS/MBA; JD/MBA; M Arch/MBA; MD/MBA; MPH/MBA; MSW/MBA; Pharm D/MBA. *Accreditation:* AACSB. *Program availability:* Part-time, evening/weekend. *Faculty:* 80 full-time (26 women), 45 part-time/adjunct (12 women). *Students:* 597 full-time (251 women); includes 83 minority (19 Black or African American, non-Hispanic/Latino; 59 Asian, non-Hispanic/Latino; 5 Hispanic/Latino), 306 international. Average age 25. 2,109 applicants, 46% accepted, 376 enrolled. In 2017, 371 master's, 13 doctorates awarded. *Degree requirements:* For master's, capstone courses or projects; for doctorate, comprehensive exam, thesis/dissertation. *Entrance requirements:* For master's, GMAT (for MS in accounting, finance); GRE or GMAT (for MBA, MS in management information systems, supply chains and operations management), essays, letters of recommendation; for doctorate, GMAT or GRE, essays, writing sample, letters of recommendation. Additional exam requirements/recommendations for international students: Required—TOEFL (minimum score 95 iBT) or IELTS (minimum score 6.5); Recommended—TSE (minimum score 73). *Application deadline:* For fall admission, 10/15 priority date for domestic and international students; for winter admission, 2/1 priority date for domestic and international students; for spring admission, 4/15 for domestic students; for summer admission, 5/15 for domestic students. Application fee: $100. Electronic applications accepted. *Expenses:* Varies by program. *Financial support:* Fellowships with full and partial tuition reimbursements, research assistantships with full and partial tuition reimbursements, teaching assistantships with full and partial tuition reimbursements, career-related internships or fieldwork, Federal Work-Study, institutionally sponsored loans, scholarships/grants, health care benefits, and unspecified assistantships available. Financial award application deadline: 2/15. *Faculty research:* Data analytics, accounting and law, rate finance, consumer behavior, supply chain logistics, leadership and team effectiveness. *Total annual research expenditures:* $968,376. *Unit head:* Erin K. O'Brien, Assistant Dean and Director of Graduate Programs, 716-645-3204, Fax: 716-645-2341, E-mail: ekobrien@buffalo.edu. *Application contact:* Meghan Felser, Director of Admissions and Recruiting, 716-645-3204, Fax: 716-645-2341, E-mail: mpwood@buffalo.edu.
Website: http://mgt.buffalo.edu/

The University of Akron, Graduate School, College of Business Administration, Department of Management, Program in Supply Chain Management, Akron, OH 44325. Offers MBA. *Program availability:* Part-time. *Students:* 4 full-time (2 women), 8 part-time (1 woman); includes 1 minority (Asian, non-Hispanic/Latino), 7 international. Average age 30. 8 applicants, 75% accepted, 2 enrolled. In 2017, 12 master's awarded. *Entrance requirements:* For master's, GMAT, GRE, MCAT, LSAT, PCAT, or CAT, minimum GPA of 3.0 (preferred), two letters of recommendation, resume, statement of purpose. Additional exam requirements/recommendations for international students: Required—TOEFL (minimum score 79 iBT), IELTS (minimum score 6.5). *Application deadline:* For fall admission, 7/15 for domestic and international students; for spring admission, 11/15 for domestic and international students; for summer admission, 4/15 for domestic and international students. Application fee: $45 ($75 for international students). Electronic applications accepted. *Unit head:* Dr. Steve Ash, Chair, 330-972-6086, E-mail: ash@uakron.edu. *Application contact:* Dr. William Hauser, Director of Graduate Business Programs, 330-972-7043, Fax: 330-972-6588, E-mail: whauser@uakron.edu.
Website: http://www.uakron.edu/cba/graduate/programs/msm/

The University of Alabama in Huntsville, School of Graduate Studies, College of Business Administration, Programs in Business and Management, Huntsville, AL 35899. Offers business analytics (MSMS); federal contracting and procurement management (Certificate); human resource management (MSM); management (MBA), including acquisition management, entrepreneurship, federal contract accounting, finance, human resource management, logistics and supply chain management, marketing, project management; supply chain management (Certificate); technology and innovation management (Certificate). *Accreditation:* AACSB. *Program availability:* Part-time, evening/weekend. *Degree requirements:* For master's, comprehensive exam, thesis or alternative. *Entrance requirements:* For master's, GMAT (minimum score 500), minimum AACSB index of 1080. Additional exam requirements/recommendations for international students: Required—TOEFL (minimum score 550 paper-based; 80 iBT), IELTS (minimum score 6.5). Electronic applications accepted. *Faculty research:* Supply chain management, management of research and development, international marketing and branding, organizational behavior and human resource management, social networks and computational economics.

The University of Alabama in Huntsville, School of Graduate Studies, College of Business Administration, Programs in Information Systems, Huntsville, AL 35899. Offers cybersecurity (MS, Certificate); enterprise resource planning (Certificate); information systems (MSIS); supply chain and logistics management (MS); supply chain management (Certificate). *Program availability:* Part-time, evening/weekend. *Degree requirements:* For master's, comprehensive exam, thesis or alternative. *Entrance requirements:* For master's, GMAT (minimum score 500), minimum AACSB index of 1080. Additional exam requirements/recommendations for international students: Required—TOEFL (minimum score 550 paper-based; 80 iBT), IELTS (minimum score 6.5). Electronic applications accepted. *Faculty research:* Supply chain information systems, information assurance and security, databases and conceptual schema, workflow management, inter-organizational information sharing.

University of Dallas, Satish and Yasmin Gupta College of Business, Irving, TX 75062-4736. Offers accounting (MBA, MS); business administration (DBA); business analytics (MS); business management (MBA); corporate finance (MBA); cybersecurity (MS); finance (MS); financial services (MBA); global business (MBA, MS); health services management (MBA); human resource management (MBA); information and technology management (MS); information assurance (MBA); information technology (MBA); information technology service management (MBA); marketing management (MBA); organization development (MBA); project management (MBA); sports and entertainment management (MBA); strategic leadership (MBA); supply chain management (MBA). *Accreditation:* AACSB. *Program availability:* Part-time, evening/weekend, online learning. *Entrance requirements:* Additional exam requirements/recommendations for international students: Required—TOEFL. *Application deadline:* Applications are processed on a rolling basis. Application fee: $50. Electronic applications accepted. *Expenses:* Contact institution. *Financial support:* Application deadline: 2/15; applicants required to submit FAFSA. *Unit head:* Brett J.L. Landry, Dean, 972-721-5356, E-mail: blandry@udallas.edu. *Application contact:* Dr. David Sweet, Dean, Braniff Graduate School, 972-721-5288, Fax: 972-721-5280, E-mail: dsweet@udallas.edu.
Website: http://www.udallas.edu/cob/

University of Florida, Graduate School, Warrington College of Business Administration, Hough Graduate School of Business, Department of Information Systems and Operations Management, Gainesville, FL 32611. Offers information systems and operations management (PhD); supply chain management (Certificate). Terminal master's awarded for partial completion of doctoral program. *Degree requirements:* For doctorate, thesis/dissertation. *Entrance requirements:* For master's, GMAT or GRE General Test, minimum GPA of 3.0; for doctorate, GMAT (minimum score 650) or GRE General Test, minimum GPA of 3.0. Additional exam requirements/recommendations for international students: Required—TOEFL (minimum score 550 paper-based; 80 iBT), IELTS (minimum score 6). *Faculty research:* Expert systems, nonconvex optimization, manufacturing management, production and operation management, telecommunication.

University of Houston, College of Technology, Department of Information and Logistics Technology, Houston, TX 77204. Offers information security (MS); supply chain and logistics technology (MS); technology project management (MS). *Program availability:* Part-time. *Degree requirements:* For master's, project or thesis (most programs). *Entrance requirements:* For master's, GMAT. Additional exam requirements/recommendations for international students: Required—TOEFL (minimum score 550 paper-based; 79 iBT). Electronic applications accepted.

University of Houston–Downtown, Marilyn Davies College of Business, MBA Program, Houston, TX 77002. Offers accounting (MBA); finance (MBA); human resource management (MBA); international business (MBA); investment management (MBA); leadership (MBA); project management and process improvement (MBA); sales management and business development (MBA); supply chain management (MBA). *Accreditation:* AACSB. *Program availability:* Part-time, evening/weekend. *Faculty:* 36 full-time (13 women), 11 part-time/adjunct (6 women). *Students:* 4 full-time (2 women), 1,065 part-time (605 women); includes 821 minority (383 Black or African American, non-Hispanic/Latino; 3 American Indian or Alaska Native, non-Hispanic/Latino; 136 Asian, non-Hispanic/Latino; 299 Hispanic/Latino), 33 international. Average age 33. 418 applicants, 89% accepted, 308 enrolled. In 2017, 310 master's awarded. *Entrance requirements:* For master's, GMAT, two letters of recommendation from professional references, personal statement, resume. Additional exam requirements/recommendations for international students: Required—TOEFL (minimum score 81 iBT). *Application deadline:* For fall admission, 8/1 for domestic and international students. Application fee: $35 ($60 for international students). Electronic applications accepted. *Expenses:* $360 per credit resident; $725 per credit non-resident. *Financial support:* Federal Work-Study and scholarships/grants available. Financial award application deadline: 4/1; financial award applicants required to submit FAFSA. *Unit head:* Dr. Charles E. Gengler, Dean, 713-221-8179, Fax: 713-221-8675. *Application contact:* Ceshia Love, Director of Admissions, 713-221-8093, Fax: 713-223-7408, E-mail: gradadmissions@uhd.edu.
Website: http://mba.uhd.edu/

The University of Kansas, Graduate Studies, School of Business, Program in Business, Lawrence, KS 66045. Offers business and organizational leadership (MS); decision sciences and supply chain management (PhD); finance (PhD); human resources management (PhD); marketing (PhD); organizational behavior (PhD); strategic management (PhD); supply chain management and logistics (MS). *Accreditation:* AACSB. *Program availability:* Part-time. *Students:* 66 full-time (18 women), 227 part-time (76 women); includes 59 minority (21 Black or African American, non-Hispanic/Latino; 2 American Indian or Alaska Native, non-Hispanic/Latino; 13 Asian, non-Hispanic/Latino; 3 Hispanic/Latino; 20 Two or more races, non-Hispanic/Latino), 29 international. Average age 32. 329 applicants, 71% accepted, 185 enrolled. In 2017, 30 master's, 8 doctorates awarded. *Entrance requirements:* For master's, GMAT, official transcript, three letters of recommendation, resume, statement of purpose; for doctorate, GMAT or GRE, official transcript, three letters of recommendation, resume, statement of purpose. Additional exam requirements/recommendations for international students: Required—TOEFL (minimum score 600 paper-based; 100 iBT). *Application deadline:* For fall admission, 1/10 for domestic and international students. Application fee: $65 ($85 for international students). Electronic applications accepted. *Financial support:* Fellowships, research assistantships, teaching assistantships, scholarships/grants, health care benefits, tuition waivers (full), and unspecified assistantships available. Financial award application deadline: 1/10.

Supply Chain Management

Faculty research: Strategic human resource management, business ethics, organizational theory/behavior, corporate strategy, international business, supply chain management, Bayesian networks, game theory, decision analysis and time/series analysis, pricing, consumer effects, advertising and emotion. *Unit head:* Charly Edmonds, Director, 785-864-3841, E-mail: bschoolphd@ku.edu. *Application contact:* Graduate Admission Contact, 785-864-7500, E-mail: bschoolphd@ku.edu.
Website: http://www.business.ku.edu/

University of La Verne, College of Business and Public Management, Graduate Programs in Business Administration, La Verne, CA 91750-4443. Offers accounting (MBA, MBA-EP); finance (MBA, MBA-EP); health services management (MBA); information technology (MBA, MBA-EP); international business (MBA, MBA-EP); management and leadership (MBA, MBA-EP); marketing (MBA, MBA-EP); supply chain management (MBA, MBA-EP). *Program availability:* Part-time, evening/weekend. *Faculty:* 24 full-time (11 women), 25 part-time/adjunct (6 women). *Students:* 390 full-time (193 women), 93 part-time (48 women); includes 96 minority (7 Black or African American, non-Hispanic/Latino; 1 American Indian or Alaska Native, non-Hispanic/Latino; 17 Asian, non-Hispanic/Latino; 67 Hispanic/Latino; 1 Native Hawaiian or other Pacific Islander, non-Hispanic/Latino; 3 Two or more races, non-Hispanic/Latino), 336 international. Average age 28. *Entrance requirements:* For master's, GMAT, MAT, or GRE, minimum undergraduate GPA of 3.0, 2 letters of recommendation, resume, statement of purpose. Additional exam requirements/recommendations for international students: Required—TOEFL (minimum score 550 paper-based; 85 iBT). *Application deadline:* Applications are processed on a rolling basis. Application fee: $50. Tuition and fees vary according to program. *Financial support:* Institutionally sponsored loans and scholarships/grants available. Financial award application deadline: 3/2; financial award applicants required to submit FAFSA. *Unit head:* Dr. Abe Helou, Chairperson, 909-448-4455, Fax: 909-392-2704, E-mail: ihelou@laverne.edu. *Application contact:* Rina Lazarian-Chehab, Senior Associate Director of Graduate Admissions, 909-448-4317, Fax: 909-971-2295, E-mail: rlazarian@laverne.edu.
Website: https://business.laverne.edu/mba/

University of La Verne, Regional and Online Campuses, Graduate Programs, Inland Empire Campus, Ontario, CA 91730. Offers business administration (MBA, MBA-EP), including accounting (MBA), finance (MBA), health services management (MBA-EP), information technology (MBA-EP), international business (MBA), managed care (MBA), management and leadership (MBA-EP), marketing (MBA-EP), supply chain management (MBA); leadership and management (MS), including human resource management, nonprofit management, organizational development. *Program availability:* Part-time, evening/weekend. *Faculty:* 5 part-time/adjunct (1 woman). *Students:* 24 full-time (13 women), 72 part-time (44 women); includes 64 minority (12 Black or African American, non-Hispanic/Latino; 13 Asian, non-Hispanic/Latino; 36 Hispanic/Latino; 3 Two or more races, non-Hispanic/Latino). Average age 38. In 2017, 42 master's awarded. *Application deadline:* Applications are processed on a rolling basis. Application fee: $50. *Expenses:* Contact institution. *Financial support:* Application deadline: 3/2; applicants required to submit FAFSA. *Unit head:* Juli Roberts, Campus Director, Inland Empire Regional Campus in Ontario, 760-955-6448, E-mail: jroberts@laverne.edu. *Application contact:* Admissions, 877-468-6858, E-mail: gradadmission@laverne.edu.
Website: https://laverne.edu/locations/

University of Louisville, J. B. Speed School of Engineering, Department of Industrial Engineering, Louisville, KY 40292-0001. Offers engineering management (M Eng); industrial engineering (M Eng, MS, PhD); logistics and distribution (Certificate). *Accreditation:* ABET (one or more programs are accredited). *Program availability:* 100% online, blended/hybrid learning. *Faculty:* 9 full-time (4 women), 6 part-time/adjunct (2 women). *Students:* 84 full-time (28 women), 115 part-time (19 women); includes 33 minority (16 Black or African American, non-Hispanic/Latino; 1 American Indian or Alaska Native, non-Hispanic/Latino; 4 Asian, non-Hispanic/Latino; 6 Hispanic/Latino; 6 Two or more races, non-Hispanic/Latino), 81 international. Average age 31. 99 applicants, 70% accepted, 55 enrolled. In 2017, 29 master's, 2 doctorates awarded. *Degree requirements:* For master's and Certificate, thesis optional; for doctorate, comprehensive exam, thesis/dissertation. *Entrance requirements:* For master's and doctorate, GRE General Test, two letters of recommendation, official transcripts. Additional exam requirements/recommendations for international students: Required—TOEFL (minimum score 550 paper-based; 80 iBT), IELTS (minimum score 6.5). *Application deadline:* For fall admission, 5/1 priority date for domestic and international students; for spring admission, 11/1 priority date for domestic and international students; for summer admission, 3/1 priority date for domestic and international students. Applications are processed on a rolling basis. Application fee: $65. Electronic applications accepted. *Expenses:* Tuition, state resident: full-time $12,246; part-time $681 per credit hour. Tuition, nonresident: full-time $25,486; part-time $1417 per credit hour. *Required fees:* $196. Tuition and fees vary according to course load, program and reciprocity agreements. *Financial support:* In 2017–18, 2 fellowships with full tuition reimbursements (averaging $22,000 per year), 3 research assistantships with full tuition reimbursements (averaging $22,000 per year), 4 teaching assistantships with full tuition reimbursements (averaging $22,000 per year) were awarded; scholarships/grants, health care benefits, and tuition waivers (full) also available. Financial award application deadline: 1/1; financial award applicants required to submit FAFSA. *Faculty research:* Optimization, computer simulation, logistics and distribution, ergonomics and human factors, advanced manufacturing process. *Total annual research expenditures:* $620,986. *Unit head:* Dr. Suraj M. Alexander, Chair, 502-852-6342, Fax: 502-852-5633, E-mail: suraj.alexander@louisville.edu. *Application contact:* Lihui Bai, Director of Graduate Studies, 502-852-1416, E-mail: lihui.bai@louisville.edu.
Website: http://www.louisville.edu/speed/industrial/

The University of Manchester, Alliance Manchester Business School, M15 6PB, United Kingdom. Offers accounting and finance (M Sc); business (M Ent); business analysis and strategic management (M Sc); business analytics: operational research and risk analysis (M Sc); business psychology (M Sc); corporate communications and reputation management (M Sc); finance (M Sc); finance and business economics (M Sc); human resource management and industrial relations (M Sc); innovation management and entrepreneurship (M Sc); international business and management (M Sc); international human resource management and comparative industrial relations (M Sc); management (M Sc); marketing (M Sc); operations, project and supply chain management (M Sc); organizational psychology (M Sc); quantitative finance (M Sc). *Entrance requirements:* For master's, UK 2:1 honours degree or overseas equivalent. Additional exam requirements/recommendations for international students: Required—TOEFL (minimum score 100 iBT), IELTS (minimum score 7), PTE. Electronic applications accepted. *Faculty research:* Accounting and finance, management sciences and marketing, people management and organization, innovation management and policy, decision sciences.

University of Memphis, Graduate School, Fogelman College of Business and Economics, Program in Business Administration, Memphis, TN 38152. Offers accounting (MBA, PhD); business administration (IMBA); economics (PhD); executive business administration (MBA); finance (PhD); management (PhD); marketing (MS); marketing and supply chain management (PhD); real estate development (MS); JD/

MBA. *Accreditation:* AACSB. *Faculty:* 2 part-time/adjunct (0 women). *Students:* 166 full-time (76 women), 361 part-time (142 women); includes 161 minority (91 Black or African American, non-Hispanic/Latino; 51 Asian, non-Hispanic/Latino; 10 Hispanic/Latino; 9 Two or more races, non-Hispanic/Latino), 89 international. Average age 32. 263 applicants, 83% accepted, 157 enrolled. In 2017, 186 master's, 14 doctorates awarded. *Degree requirements:* For master's, comprehensive exam; for doctorate, comprehensive exam, thesis/dissertation. *Entrance requirements:* For master's, GMAT, resume; for doctorate, GMAT, interview, minimum GPA of 3.4, resume, letter of recommendation. Additional exam requirements/recommendations for international students: Required—TOEFL (minimum score 550 paper-based). *Application deadline:* For fall admission, 8/1 for domestic students; for spring admission, 12/1 for domestic students. Application fee: $35 ($60 for international students). *Financial support:* In 2017–18, 164 students received support, including 17 research assistantships with full tuition reimbursements available (averaging $53,750 per year), 13 teaching assistantships with full tuition reimbursements available (averaging $20,798 per year); career-related internships or fieldwork, Federal Work-Study, scholarships/grants, and unspecified assistantships also available. Financial award application deadline: 2/15; financial award applicants required to submit FAFSA. *Faculty research:* Competitive business strategy, finance microstructures, supply chain management innovations, health care economics, litigation risks and corporate audits. *Unit head:* Dr. Rajiv Grover, Dean, 901-678-3759, E-mail: rgrover@memphis.edu. *Application contact:* Dr. Carol V. Danehower, Associate Dean, 901-678-5402, Fax: 901-678-3579, E-mail: fcbegp@memphis.edu.
Website: https://web0.memphis.edu/gradcatalog/degreeprog/fcbe/fcbe.php

University of Michigan, Ross School of Business, Ann Arbor, MI 48109-1234. Offers accounting (M Acc); business (MBA); business administration (PhD); supply chain management (MSCM); JD/MBA; MBA/M Arch; MBA/M Eng; MBA/MA; MBA/MEM; MBA/MHSA; MBA/MM; MBA/MPP; MBA/MS; MBA/MSE; MBA/MSI; MBA/MSW; MBA/MUP; MD/MBA; MHSA/MBA. *Accreditation:* AACSB. *Program availability:* Part-time, evening/weekend. *Degree requirements:* For doctorate, comprehensive exam, thesis/dissertation, oral defense of dissertation, preliminary exam. *Entrance requirements:* For master's, GMAT or GRE, completion of equivalent of four-year U.S. bachelor's degree, two letters of recommendation, essays, resume; for doctorate, GMAT or GRE. Additional exam requirements/recommendations for international students: Required—TOEFL (minimum score 600 paper-based; 100 iBT). Electronic applications accepted. *Expenses:* Tuition, state resident: full-time $22,368; part-time $1201 per credit hour. Tuition, nonresident: full-time $45,156; part-time $2467 per credit hour. *Required fees:* $376 per term. Tuition and fees vary according to course load, degree level and program. *Faculty research:* Finance and accounting, marketing, technology and operations management, corporate strategy, management and organizations.

University of Michigan–Dearborn, College of Business, MS Program in Supply Chain Management, Dearborn, MI 48126. Offers MS. *Program availability:* Part-time, evening/weekend. *Faculty:* 45 full-time (19 women), 4 part-time/adjunct (2 women). *Students:* 5 full-time (2 women), 11 part-time (6 women); includes 4 minority (1 Black or African American, non-Hispanic/Latino; 2 Asian, non-Hispanic/Latino; 1 Two or more races, non-Hispanic/Latino), 7 international. Average age 27. 41 applicants, 39% accepted, 6 enrolled. In 2017, 9 master's awarded. *Entrance requirements:* For master's, GRE or GMAT, equivalent of four-year U.S. bachelor's degree from regionally-accredited institution, undergraduate course in finite math, pre-calculus, or calculus. Additional exam requirements/recommendations for international students: Required—TOEFL (minimum score 560 paper-based; 84 iBT), IELTS (minimum score 6.5). *Application deadline:* For fall admission, 8/1 for domestic students, 5/1 for international students; for winter admission, 12/1 for domestic students, 9/1 for international students; for spring admission, 4/1 for domestic students, 1/1 for international students. Applications are processed on a rolling basis. Application fee: $60. Electronic applications accepted. *Expenses:* $883 per credit hour in-state; $1,376 per credit hour out-state. *Financial support:* In 2017–18, 9 students received support. Scholarships/grants and non-resident tuition scholarships available. Financial award application deadline: 3/1; financial award applicants required to submit FAFSA. *Faculty research:* Business intelligence, behavioral finance, brand management and new media, management education, operations strategy. *Unit head:* Dr. Michael Kamen, Director, Graduate Programs, 313-593-5460, E-mail: mkamen@umich.edu. *Application contact:* Joan Doherty, Academic Advisor/Counselor, 313-593-5460, Fax: 313-271-9838, E-mail: umd-gradbusiness@umich.edu.
Website: http://umdearborn.edu/cob/ms-supply-chain/

University of Minnesota, Twin Cities Campus, Carlson School of Management, Carlson Full-Time MBA Program, Minneapolis, MN 55455. Offers finance (MBA); information technology (MBA); management (MBA); marketing (MBA); medical industry orientation (MBA); supply chain and operations (MBA); JD/MBA; MBA/MPP; MBA/MSBA; MD/MBA; MHA/MBA; Pharm D/MBA. *Accreditation:* AACSB. *Faculty:* 143 full-time (42 women), 24 part-time/adjunct (6 women). *Students:* 200 full-time (63 women); includes 25 minority (4 Black or African American, non-Hispanic/Latino; 13 Asian, non-Hispanic/Latino; 5 Hispanic/Latino; 3 Two or more races, non-Hispanic/Latino), 41 international. Average age 29. 606 applicants, 45% accepted, 104 enrolled. In 2017, 85 master's awarded. *Entrance requirements:* For master's, GMAT or GRE. Additional exam requirements/recommendations for international students: Required—TOEFL (minimum score 580 paper-based; 84 iBT), IELTS (minimum score 7), PTE. *Application deadline:* For fall admission, 4/1 for domestic students, 2/1 for international students. Application fee: $75. Electronic applications accepted. *Expenses:* $19,104 per semester resident tuition, $24,468 per semester non-resident tuition; $1,138 per semester fees; $1,050 per semester student health plan; $179 per semester (for international students). *Financial support:* In 2017–18, 147 students received support, including 147 fellowships with tuition reimbursements available (averaging $23,479 per year); research assistantships with partial tuition reimbursements available, teaching assistantships with partial tuition reimbursements available, career-related internships or fieldwork, Federal Work-Study, institutionally sponsored loans, scholarships/grants, health care benefits, and unspecified assistantships also available. Financial award application deadline: 4/1; financial award applicants required to submit FAFSA. *Faculty research:* Market regulation and asset pricing, social networks and data analytics, consumer behavior, innovation and entrepreneurship, workplace wellbeing and labor relationships. *Total annual research expenditures:* $577,440. *Unit head:* Philip J. Miller, Assistant Dean, MBA and MS Programs, 612-625-5555, Fax: 612-625-1012, E-mail: mba@umn.edu. *Application contact:* Linh Gilles, Director of Admissions and Recruiting, 612-625-5555, Fax: 612-625-1012, E-mail: ftmba@umn.edu.
Website: http://www.csom.umn.edu/MBA/full-time/

University of Minnesota, Twin Cities Campus, Carlson School of Management, Carlson Part-Time MBA Program, Minneapolis, MN 55455. Offers finance (MBA); information technology (MBA); management (MBA); marketing (MBA); medical industry orientation (MBA); supply chain and operations (MBA). *Program availability:* Part-time-only, evening/weekend, 100% online, blended/hybrid learning. *Faculty:* 143 full-time (42 women), 26 part-time/adjunct (6 women). *Students:* 919 part-time (291 women); includes 120 minority (14 Black or African American, non-Hispanic/Latino; 2 American Indian or Alaska Native, non-Hispanic/Latino; 55 Asian, non-Hispanic/Latino; 26 Hispanic/Latino; 1 Native Hawaiian or other Pacific Islander, non-Hispanic/Latino; 22

Two or more races, non-Hispanic/Latino), 57 international. Average age 28. 226 applicants, 85% accepted, 167 enrolled. In 2017, 289 master's awarded. *Entrance requirements:* For master's, GMAT or GRE. Additional exam requirements/recommendations for international students: Required—TOEFL (minimum score 580 paper-based; 84 iBT), IELTS (minimum score 7), PTE. *Application deadline:* For fall admission, 5/15 priority date for domestic and international students; for spring admission, 10/15 priority date for domestic and international students. Applications are processed on a rolling basis. Application fee: $75. Electronic applications accepted. *Expenses:* $1,375 per credit tuition, $314 per semester fees. *Financial support:* Applicants required to submit FAFSA. *Faculty research:* Market regulation and asset pricing, social networks and data analytics, consumer behavior, innovation and entrepreneurship, workplace wellbeing and labor relationships. *Total annual research expenditures:* $577,440. *Unit head:* Philip J. Miller, Assistant Dean, MBA and MS Programs, 612-625-2039, Fax: 612-625-1012, E-mail: mba@umn.edu. *Application contact:* Linh Gilles, Director of Admissions and Recruiting, 612-625-5555, Fax: 612-625-1012, E-mail: ptmba@umn.edu.
Website: http://www.carlsonschool.umn.edu/ptmba

University of Minnesota, Twin Cities Campus, Carlson School of Management, Doctoral Program in Business Administration, Minneapolis, MN 55455. Offers accounting (PhD); finance (PhD); information and decision sciences (PhD); marketing (PhD); strategic management and entrepreneurship (PhD); supply chain and operations (PhD); work and organizations (PhD). *Faculty:* 102 full-time (32 women). *Students:* 95 full-time (32 women); includes 10 minority (2 Black or African American, non-Hispanic/Latino; 7 Asian, non-Hispanic/Latino; 1 Hispanic/Latino), 68 international. Average age 30. 357 applicants, 6% accepted, 17 enrolled. In 2017, 14 doctorates awarded. *Degree requirements:* For doctorate, comprehensive exam, thesis/dissertation, written and oral preliminary exams, proposal defense, final defense. *Entrance requirements:* For doctorate, GMAT, GRE General Test, minimum undergraduate GPA of 3.0, graduate 3.5 (recommended). Additional exam requirements/recommendations for international students: Required—TOEFL (minimum score 600 paper-based, 100 iBT) or IELTS (minimum score 7.0). *Application deadline:* For fall admission, 12/15 for domestic students, 12/15 priority date for international students. Applications are processed on a rolling basis. Application fee: $75 ($95 for international students). Electronic applications accepted. *Expenses:* Contact institution. *Financial support:* In 2017–18, 80 students received support, including 80 fellowships with full tuition reimbursements available (averaging $13,000 per year), 73 research assistantships with full tuition reimbursements available (averaging $7,520 per year), 73 teaching assistantships with full tuition reimbursements available (averaging $7,520 per year); institutionally sponsored loans, scholarships/grants, health care benefits, unspecified assistantships, and full student service fee waivers also available. Financial award application deadline: 12/15. *Faculty research:* Finance, strategy and entrepreneurship, marketing, information and decision science, operations, accounting, supply chain, human resources and industrial relations, organizational behavior. *Unit head:* Dr. Shawn P. Curley, Director, 612-624-6546, Fax: 612-624-8221, E-mail: curley@umn.edu. *Application contact:* Sandy Herzan, Associate Director, 612-624-0875, Fax: 612-624-8221, E-mail: herza002@umn.edu.
Website: http://carlsonschool.umn.edu/degrees/phd

University of Missouri–St. Louis, College of Business Administration, St. Louis, MO 63121. Offers accounting (M Acc); business administration (MBA, DBA, PhD, Certificate), including logistics and supply chain management (PhD); business intelligence (Certificate); cybersecurity (Certificate); digital and social media marketing (Certificate); human resources management (Certificate); information systems (MS); logistics and supply chain management (Certificate); marketing management (Certificate). *Program availability:* Part-time, evening/weekend. *Faculty:* 51 full-time (21 women), 25 part-time/adjunct (5 women). *Students:* 146 full-time (77 women), 326 part-time (143 women); includes 82 minority (32 Black or African American, non-Hispanic/Latino; 1 American Indian or Alaska Native, non-Hispanic/Latino; 34 Asian, non-Hispanic/Latino; 11 Hispanic/Latino; 4 Two or more races, non-Hispanic/Latino), 89 international. 276 applicants, 83% accepted, 142 enrolled. *Degree requirements:* For doctorate, thesis/dissertation. *Entrance requirements:* For master's, GMAT, 2 letters of recommendation; for doctorate, GMAT or GRE, 3 letters of recommendation. Additional exam requirements/recommendations for international students: Recommended—TOEFL (minimum score 550 paper-based; 79 iBT), IELTS (minimum score 6.5). *Application deadline:* For fall admission, 7/1 priority date for domestic and international students; for spring admission, 12/1 priority date for domestic and international students. Applications are processed on a rolling basis. Application fee: $50 ($40 for international students). Electronic applications accepted. *Expenses:* Tuition, state resident: part-time $476.50 per credit hour. Tuition, nonresident: part-time $1169.70 per credit hour. *Financial support:* Research assistantships with tuition reimbursements, teaching assistantships with tuition reimbursements, career-related internships or fieldwork, Federal Work-Study, and institutionally sponsored loans available. Support available to part-time students. Financial award application deadline: 4/1; financial award applicants required to submit FAFSA. *Faculty research:* Statistical decision aids, commercial banking, corporate finance, operations management, information systems. *Unit head:* Charles E. Hoffman, Dean, 314-516-6109, Fax: 314-516-6420. *Application contact:* 314-516-5458, Fax: 314-516-6996, E-mail: gradadm@umsl.edu.
Website: http://www.umsl.edu/divisions/business/

The University of North Carolina at Charlotte, William States Lee College of Engineering, Department of Systems Engineering and Engineering Management, Charlotte, NC 28223-0001. Offers energy analytics (Graduate Certificate); engineering management (MSEM); Lean Six Sigma (Graduate Certificate); logistics and supply chains (Graduate Certificate); systems analytics (Graduate Certificate). *Program availability:* Part-time, evening/weekend, 100% online, blended/hybrid learning. *Faculty:* 9 full-time (2 women), 1 part-time/adjunct (0 women). *Students:* 32 full-time (9 women), 54 part-time (11 women); includes 15 minority (8 Black or African American, non-Hispanic/Latino; 1 American Indian or Alaska Native, non-Hispanic/Latino; 2 Asian, non-Hispanic/Latino; 2 Hispanic/Latino; 2 Two or more races, non-Hispanic/Latino), 33 international. Average age 29. 156 applicants, 62% accepted, 25 enrolled. In 2017, 20 master's, 5 other advanced degrees awarded. *Degree requirements:* For master's, project or thesis. *Entrance requirements:* For master's, GRE or GMAT, bachelor's degree in engineering or a closely-related technical or scientific field, or in business, provided relevant technical course requirements have been met; undergraduate coursework in engineering economics, calculus, or statistics; minimum GPA of 3.0; for Graduate Certificate, bachelor's degree in engineering or closely-related technical or scientific field, or in business, provided relevant technical course requirements have been met; minimum GPA of 3.0; undergraduate coursework in engineering economics, calculus, and statistics; written description of work experience. Additional exam requirements/recommendations for international students: Required—TOEFL (minimum score 523 paper-based, 70 iBT) or IELTS (6.5). *Application deadline:* For fall admission, 3/1 priority date for domestic and international students; for spring admission, 10/1 priority date for domestic and international students; for summer admission, 4/1 priority date for domestic and international students. Applications are processed on a rolling basis. Application fee: $75. Electronic applications accepted. *Expenses:* Contact institution. *Financial support:* Career-related internships or fieldwork, institutionally

sponsored loans, scholarships/grants, and unspecified assistantships available. Support available to part-time students. Financial award application deadline: 3/1; financial award applicants required to submit FAFSA. *Total annual research expenditures:* $209,562. *Unit head:* Dr. Simon M. Hsiang, Chair, 704-687-1958, E-mail: shsiang1@uncc.edu. *Application contact:* Kathy B. Giddings, Director of Graduate Admissions, 704-687-5503, Fax: 704-687-1668, E-mail: gradadm@uncc.edu.
Website: http://seem.uncc.edu/

The University of North Carolina at Greensboro, Graduate School, Bryan School of Business and Economics, Department of Information Systems and Supply Chain Management, Greensboro, NC 27412-5001. Offers information systems (PhD); information technology (Certificate); information technology and management (MS); supply chain management (Certificate). *Entrance requirements:* For master's, GMAT, GRE General Test. Additional exam requirements/recommendations for international students: Required—TOEFL. Electronic applications accepted.

University of North Texas, Robert B. Toulouse School of Graduate Studies, Denton, TX 76203-5459. Offers accounting (MS); applied anthropology (MA, MS); applied behavior analysis (Certificate); applied geography (MA); applied technology and performance improvement (M Ed, MS); art education (MA); art history (MA); art museum education (Certificate); arts leadership (Certificate); audiology (Au D); behavior analysis (MS); behavioral science (PhD); biochemistry and molecular biology (MS); biology (MA, MS); biomedical engineering (MS); business analysis (MS); chemistry (MS); clinical health psychology (PhD); communication studies (MA, MS); computer engineering (MS); computer science (MS); counseling (M Ed, MS), including clinical mental health counseling (MS), college and university counseling, elementary school counseling, secondary school counseling; creative writing (MA); criminal justice (MS); curriculum and instruction (M Ed); decision sciences (MBA); design (MA, MFA), including fashion design (MFA), innovation studies, interior design (MFA); early childhood studies (MS); economics (MS); educational leadership (M Ed, Ed D); educational psychology (MS, PhD), including family studies (MS), gifted and talented (MS), human development (MS), learning and cognition (MS), research, measurement and evaluation (MS); electrical engineering (MS); emergency management (MPA); engineering technology (MS); English (MA); English as a second language (MA); environmental science (MS); finance (MBA, MS); financial management (MPA); French (MA); health services management (MBA); higher education (M Ed, Ed D); history (MA, MS); hospitality management (MS); human resources management (MPA); information science (MS); information systems (PhD); information technologies (MBA); interdisciplinary studies (MA, MS); international studies (MA); international sustainable tourism (MS); jazz studies (MM); journalism (MA, MJ, Graduate Certificate), including interactive and virtual digital communication (Graduate Certificate), narrative journalism (Graduate Certificate), public relations (Graduate Certificate); kinesiology (MS); linguistics (MA); local government management (MPA); logistics (PhD); logistics and supply chain management (MBA); long-term care, senior housing, and aging services (MA); management (PhD); marketing (MBA); mathematics (MS); mechanical and energy engineering (MS, PhD); music (MA), including ethnomusicology, music theory, musicology, performance; music composition (PhD); music education (MM Ed, PhD); nonprofit management (MPA); operations and supply chain management (MBA); performance (MM, DMA); philosophy (MA); political science (MA); professional and technical communication (MA); radio, television and film (MA, MFA); rehabilitation counseling (Certificate); sociology (MA); Spanish (MA); special education (M Ed); speech-language pathology (MA); strategic management (MBA); studio art (MFA); teaching (M Ed); MBA/MS. *Program availability:* Part-time, evening/weekend, online learning. Terminal master's awarded for partial completion of doctoral program. *Degree requirements:* For master's, variable foreign language requirement, comprehensive exam (for some programs), thesis (for some programs); for doctorate, variable foreign language requirement, comprehensive exam (for some programs), thesis/dissertation; for other advanced degree, variable foreign language requirement, comprehensive exam (for some programs). *Entrance requirements:* For master's and doctorate, GRE, GMAT. Additional exam requirements/recommendations for international students: Required—TOEFL (minimum score 550 paper-based; 79 iBT). Electronic applications accepted.

University of Oklahoma, Price College of Business, Program in Business Administration, Oklahoma City, OK 73104. Offers business administration (MBA, PhD), including accounting (PhD), business administration, entrepreneurship and economic development (PhD), finance (PhD), management and international business (PhD), management of information systems (PhD), marketing/supply chain (PhD); JD/MBA; MBA/MS. *Accreditation:* AACSB. *Program availability:* Part-time, evening/weekend. *Students:* 100 full-time (27 women), 152 part-time (30 women); includes 36 minority (2 Black or African American, non-Hispanic/Latino; 4 American Indian or Alaska Native, non-Hispanic/Latino; 10 Asian, non-Hispanic/Latino; 13 Hispanic/Latino; 7 Two or more races, non-Hispanic/Latino), 32 international. Average age 31. 247 applicants, 29% accepted, 41 enrolled. In 2017, 118 master's, 9 doctorates awarded. *Degree requirements:* For doctorate, comprehensive exam, thesis/dissertation. *Entrance requirements:* For master's, GMAT or GRE, resume, 2 essays, interview; for doctorate, GMAT or GRE, resume, statement of goals, 3 letters of recommendation. Additional exam requirements/recommendations for international students: Required—TOEFL (minimum score 100 iBT) or IELTS (minimum score 7). *Application deadline:* For fall admission, 11/1 for domestic and international students; for summer admission, 11/1 for domestic and international students. Applications are processed on a rolling basis. Application fee: $50 ($100 for international students). Electronic applications accepted. *Expenses:* Contact institution. *Financial support:* In 2017–18, 107 students received support, including 6 fellowships with partial tuition reimbursements available (averaging $2,500 per year); research assistantships with full and partial tuition reimbursements available, teaching assistantships with full and partial tuition reimbursements available, career-related internships or fieldwork, scholarships/grants, health care benefits, and unspecified assistantships also available. Support available to part-time students. Financial award application deadline: 6/1; financial award applicants required to submit FAFSA. *Faculty research:* Energy finance; international accounting; organizational behavior and entrepreneurship; management information systems; supply chain. *Unit head:* Laku Chidambaram, Associate Dean for Academic Programs and Engagement, 405-325-8013. *Application contact:* Kate Hile, Associate Director of MBA Admissions, 405-325-4572, E-mail: khile@ou.edu.
Website: http://www.ou/price/divisions/graduate-programs/graduate.html

University of Pittsburgh, Katz Graduate School of Business, Master of Science in Supply Chain Management Program, Pittsburgh, PA 15260. Offers MS. *Faculty:* 91 full-time (30 women), 14 part-time/adjunct (4 women). *Students:* 9 full-time (4 women); includes 2 minority (both Hispanic/Latino), 7 international. Average age 24. 67 applicants, 64% accepted, 9 enrolled. In 2017, 8 master's awarded. *Degree requirements:* For master's, minimum GPA of 3.0. *Entrance requirements:* For master's, GMAT, GRE. Additional exam requirements/recommendations for international students: Required—TOEFL (minimum score 100 iBT), IELTS (minimum score 7). *Application deadline:* For fall admission, 7/1 priority date for domestic students, 5/1 priority date for international students. Applications are processed on a rolling basis. Application fee: $50. Electronic applications accepted. *Expenses:* Contact institution. *Financial support:* Scholarships/grants available. Financial award application deadline: 6/1; financial award applicants required to submit FAFSA. *Faculty research:* Accounting

Supply Chain Management

systems/financial reporting, corporate finance, shopper marketing/consumer behavior, management information systems, organizational behavior and entrepreneurship. *Total annual research expenditures:* $475,077. *Unit head:* Dr. Arjang A. Assad, Dean, 412-648-1556, Fax: 412-648-1552, E-mail: aassad@katz.pitt.edu. *Application contact:* Thomas Keller, Director of MBA Admissions, 412-648-1700, Fax: 412-648-1659, E-mail: mba@katz.pitt.edu.
Website: http://www.business.pitt.edu/katz/ms-programs/supply-chain

University of Rhode Island, Graduate School, College of Business, Program in Business Administration, Kingston, RI 02881. Offers finance (MBA); general business (MBA); management (MBA); marketing (MBA, PhD); operations and supply chain management (PhD); supply chain management (MBA); Pharm D/MBA. *Faculty:* 34 full-time (13 women). *Students:* 47 full-time (13 women), 146 part-time (72 women); includes 22 minority (3 Black or African American, non-Hispanic/Latino; 1 American Indian or Alaska Native, non-Hispanic/Latino; 11 Asian, non-Hispanic/Latino; 6 Hispanic/Latino; 1 Two or more races, non-Hispanic/Latino), 16 international. 131 applicants, 59% accepted, 58 enrolled. In 2017, 94 master's, 1 doctorate awarded. *Entrance requirements:* Additional exam requirements/recommendations for international students: Required—TOEFL. *Application deadline:* For fall admission, 6/30 for domestic students; for spring admission, 10/31 for domestic students; for summer admission, 3/31 for domestic students. Electronic applications accepted. *Expenses:* Tuition, state resident: full-time $12,706; part-time $786 per credit. Tuition, nonresident: full-time $25,216; part-time $1401 per credit. *Required fees:* $1598; $45 per credit. One-time fee: $30 part-time. *Financial support:* In 2017–18, 15 teaching assistantships (averaging $16,541 per year) were awarded. Financial award application deadline: 2/1. *Unit head:* Lisa Lancellotta, Coordinator, MBA Programs, 401-874-4241, E-mail: mba@uri.edu.

University of San Diego, School of Business, Program in Supply Chain Management, San Diego, CA 92110-2492. Offers MS, Certificate. *Program availability:* Part-time, online learning. *Students:* 2 full-time (both women), 66 part-time (27 women); includes 31 minority (6 Black or African American, non-Hispanic/Latino; 8 Asian, non-Hispanic/Latino; 14 Hispanic/Latino; 3 Two or more races, non-Hispanic/Latino). Average age 34. In 2017, 33 master's awarded. *Degree requirements:* For master's, capstone course. *Entrance requirements:* For master's, interview. Additional exam requirements/recommendations for international students: Required—TOEFL (minimum score 580 paper-based; 92 iBT), TWE. *Application deadline:* For fall admission, 11/1 priority date for domestic students. Applications are processed on a rolling basis. Application fee: $80. Electronic applications accepted. *Financial support:* In 2017–18, 4 students received support. Scholarships/grants and tuition waivers available. Financial award application deadline: 4/1; financial award applicants required to submit FAFSA. *Unit head:* Karen Kukta, Program Manager, Supply Chain Management, 619-260-7903, E-mail: kkukta@sandiego.edu. *Application contact:* Monica Mahon, Associate Director of Graduate Admissions, 619-260-4524, Fax: 619-260-4158, E-mail: grads@sandiego.edu.
Website: http://www.sandiego.edu/business/graduate/ms-supply-chain-management/

University of South Dakota, Graduate School, Beacom School of Business, Department of Business Administration, Vermillion, SD 57069. Offers business administration (MBA); business analytics (MBA, Graduate Certificate); health services administration (MBA); long term care management (Graduate Certificate); marketing (MBA, Graduate Certificate); operations and supply chain management (MBA, Graduate Certificate); JD/MBA. *Accreditation:* AACSB. *Program availability:* Part-time, blended/hybrid learning. *Degree requirements:* For master's, thesis or alternative. *Entrance requirements:* For master's, GMAT, minimum GPA of 2.7, resume. Additional exam requirements/recommendations for international students: Required—TOEFL (minimum score 550 paper-based; 79 iBT), IELTS (minimum score 6). *Application deadline:* For fall admission, 6/1 priority date for domestic students, 5/1 priority date for international students; for spring admission, 10/1 priority date for domestic students, 9/1 priority date for international students; for summer admission, 3/1 priority date for domestic students. Applications are processed on a rolling basis. Application fee: $35. Electronic applications accepted. *Expenses:* Contact institution. *Financial support:* Research assistantships with partial tuition reimbursements, teaching assistantships with partial tuition reimbursements, career-related internships or fieldwork, Federal Work-Study, and unspecified assistantships available. Financial award applicants required to submit FAFSA. *Application contact:* Graduate School, 605-658-6140, Fax: 605-677-6118, E-mail: grad@usd.edu.
Website: http://www.usd.edu/business/business-administration/graduate

University of Southern California, Graduate School, Viterbi School of Engineering, Daniel J. Epstein Department of Industrial and Systems Engineering, Los Angeles, CA 90089. Offers digital supply chain management (MS); engineering management (MS); engineering technology communication (Graduate Certificate); health systems operations (Graduate Certificate); industrial and systems engineering (MS, PhD, Engr); manufacturing engineering (MS); operations research engineering (MS); optimization and supply chain management (Graduate Certificate); product development engineering (MS); safety systems and security (MS); systems architecting and engineering (MS, Graduate Certificate); systems safety and security (Graduate Certificate); transportation systems (Graduate Certificate); MS/MBA. *Program availability:* Part-time, evening/weekend, online learning. Terminal master's awarded for partial completion of doctoral program. *Degree requirements:* For master's, thesis optional; for doctorate, thesis/dissertation. *Entrance requirements:* For master's and doctorate, GRE General Test. Additional exam requirements/recommendations for international students: Recommended—TOEFL. Electronic applications accepted. *Faculty research:* Health systems, music cognition and retrieval, transportation and logistics, manufacturing and automation, engineering systems design, risk and economic analysis.

The University of Tennessee at Chattanooga, Engineering Management and Technology Program, Chattanooga, TN 37403. Offers construction management (Graduate Certificate); engineering management (MS); fundamentals of engineering management (Graduate Certificate); leadership and ethics (Graduate Certificate); logistics and supply chain management (Graduate Certificate); power systems management (Graduate Certificate); project and technology management (Graduate Certificate); quality management (Graduate Certificate). *Program availability:* 100% online, blended/hybrid learning. *Students:* 14 full-time (3 women), 50 part-time (11 women); includes 17 minority (10 Black or African American, non-Hispanic/Latino; 1 Asian, non-Hispanic/Latino; 6 Hispanic/Latino), 5 international. Average age 33. 34 applicants, 94% accepted, 20 enrolled. In 2017, 18 master's, 6 other advanced degrees awarded. *Degree requirements:* For master's, thesis. *Entrance requirements:* For master's, GRE General Test, letters of recommendation; minimum undergraduate GPA of 2.7 overall or 3.0 in final two years; for Graduate Certificate, baccalaureate degree and professional experience or have already been admitted to engineering/engineering management graduate program. Additional exam requirements/recommendations for international students: Required—TOEFL (minimum score 550 paper-based; 79 iBT), IELTS (minimum score 6). *Application deadline:* For fall admission, 6/15 priority date for domestic students, 7/1 for international students; for spring admission, 11/1 priority date for domestic students, 11/1 for international students. Applications are processed on a rolling basis. Application fee: $35 ($40 for international students). Electronic applications accepted. *Expenses:* Contact institution. *Financial support:* Research assistantships,

teaching assistantships, career-related internships or fieldwork, scholarships/grants, and unspecified assistantships available. Support available to part-time students. Financial award application deadline: 7/1; financial award applicants required to submit FAFSA. *Faculty research:* Plant layout design, lean manufacturing, Six Sigma, value management, product development. *Total annual research expenditures:* $108,577. *Unit head:* Dr. Neslihan Alp, Department Head, 423-425-4032, Fax: 423-425-5818, E-mail: neslihan-alp@utc.edu. *Application contact:* Dr. Joanne Romagni, Dean of the Graduate School, 423-425-4478, Fax: 423-425-5223, E-mail: joanne-romagni@utc.edu.
Website: https://www.utc.edu/college-engineering-computer-science/programs/engineering-management-and-technology/index.php

The University of Texas at Austin, Graduate School, McCombs School of Business, Department of Information, Risk, and Operations Management, Austin, TX 78712-1111. Offers information management (MBA); information systems (PhD); information technology and management (MS); risk analysis and decision making (MS); risk management (MBA); supply chain and operations management (MBA, PhD). *Degree requirements:* For doctorate, thesis/dissertation. *Entrance requirements:* For doctorate, GMAT or GRE. Electronic applications accepted. *Faculty research:* Stochastic processing and queuing, discrete nonlinear and large-scale optimization simulation, quality assurance logistics, distributed artificial intelligence, organizational modeling.

The University of Texas at Dallas, Naveen Jindal School of Management, Program in Operations and Supply Chain Management, Richardson, TX 75080. Offers supply chain management (MS). *Faculty:* 15 full-time (3 women), 12 part-time/adjunct (4 women). *Students:* 262 full-time (105 women), 104 part-time (34 women); includes 24 minority (3 Black or African American, non-Hispanic/Latino; 16 Asian, non-Hispanic/Latino; 2 Hispanic/Latino; 3 Two or more races, non-Hispanic/Latino), 316 international. Average age 26. 393 applicants, 53% accepted, 118 enrolled. In 2017, 201 master's awarded. *Entrance requirements:* For master's, GMAT. Additional exam requirements/recommendations for international students: Required—TOEFL (minimum score 550 paper-based). *Application deadline:* For fall admission, 7/15 for domestic students, 5/1 priority date for international students; for spring admission, 11/15 for domestic students, 9/1 priority date for international students. Applications are processed on a rolling basis. Application fee: $50 ($100 for international students). Electronic applications accepted. *Expenses:* Tuition, state resident: full-time $12,916; part-time $718 per credit hour. Tuition, nonresident: full-time $25,252; part-time $1403 per credit hour. *Financial support:* In 2017–18, 93 students received support, including 13 teaching assistantships with partial tuition reimbursements available (averaging $10,050 per year); research assistantships, career-related internships or fieldwork, Federal Work-Study, institutionally sponsored loans, scholarships/grants, and unspecified assistantships also available. Support available to part-time students. Financial award application deadline: 4/30; financial award applicants required to submit FAFSA. *Faculty research:* Technology marketing, measuring information work productivity. *Unit head:* Dr. Milind Dawande, Professor, 972-883-2793, E-mail: milind@utdallas.edu. *Application contact:* 972-883-2750, Fax: 972-883-6425, E-mail: jindal@utdallas.edu.
Website: http://jindal.utdallas.edu/isom/operations-scm-programs/

University of Washington, Graduate School, Michael G. Foster School of Business, Seattle, WA 98195-3200. Offers auditing and assurance (MP Acc); business administration (MBA, PhD); entrepreneurship (MS); executive business administration (MBA); global executive business administration (MBA); information systems (MSIS); supply chain management (MSSCM); taxation (MP Acc); technology management (MBA); JD/MBA; MBA/MAIS; MBA/MHA. *Accreditation:* AACSB. *Program availability:* Part-time, evening/weekend, blended/hybrid learning. *Faculty:* 109 full-time (35 women), 54 part-time/adjunct (32 women). *Students:* 469 full-time (173 women), 638 part-time (216 women); includes 314 minority (15 Black or African American, non-Hispanic/Latino; 6 American Indian or Alaska Native, non-Hispanic/Latino; 246 Asian, non-Hispanic/Latino; 28 Hispanic/Latino; 5 Native Hawaiian or other Pacific Islander, non-Hispanic/Latino; 14 Two or more races, non-Hispanic/Latino), 125 international. Average age 32. 1,809 applicants, 84% accepted, 1107 enrolled. In 2017, 543 master's, 10 doctorates awarded. Terminal master's awarded for partial completion of doctoral program. *Degree requirements:* For doctorate, comprehensive exam, thesis/dissertation. *Entrance requirements:* For master's and doctorate, GMAT, GRE. Additional exam requirements/recommendations for international students: Required—TOEFL (minimum score 600 paper-based; 100 iBT). *Application deadline:* For fall admission, 3/15 for domestic students, 1/15 for international students. Application fee: $85. Electronic applications accepted. *Expenses:* Contact institution. *Financial support:* Fellowships with partial tuition reimbursements, research assistantships with partial tuition reimbursements, teaching assistantships with partial tuition reimbursements, Federal Work-Study, institutionally sponsored loans, and scholarships/grants available. Financial award application deadline: 2/28; financial award applicants required to submit FAFSA. *Faculty research:* Finance, consumer behavior, marketing analytics, technology management, supply chain. *Unit head:* Dr. James Jiambalvo, Dean, 206-543-4750, E-mail: jjiambal@uw.edu. *Application contact:* Erin Town, Director of Admissions, 206-543-4661, Fax: 206-616-7351, E-mail: mba@uw.edu.
Website: http://www.foster.washington.edu/

University of Wisconsin–Madison, Graduate School, Wisconsin School of Business, Wisconsin Full-Time MBA Program, Madison, WI 53706. Offers applied security analysis (MBA); arts administration (MBA); brand and product management (MBA); corporate finance and investment banking (MBA); marketing research (MBA); operations and technology management (MBA); real estate (MBA); risk management and insurance (MBA); strategic human resource management (MBA); supply chain management (MBA). *Faculty:* 130 full-time (35 women), 42 part-time/adjunct (13 women). *Students:* 203 full-time (72 women); includes 34 minority (8 Black or African American, non-Hispanic/Latino; 10 Asian, non-Hispanic/Latino; 12 Hispanic/Latino; 4 Two or more races, non-Hispanic/Latino), 41 international. Average age 28. 556 applicants, 30% accepted, 104 enrolled. In 2017, 97 master's awarded. *Entrance requirements:* For master's, GMAT or GRE, bachelor's or equivalent degree, 2 years of work experience, essay, letter of recommendation, resume. Additional exam requirements/recommendations for international students: Required—TOEFL (minimum score 100 iBT), IELTS (minimum score 7.5). *Application deadline:* For fall admission, 11/2 for domestic and international students; for winter admission, 1/11 for domestic and international students; for spring admission, 3/1 for domestic and international students; for summer admission, 4/12 for domestic and international students. Applications are processed on a rolling basis. Application fee: $75 ($81 for international students). Electronic applications accepted. *Expenses:* $9,356 per semester resident, $18,288 non-resident. *Financial support:* In 2017–18, 183 students received support, including 14 fellowships with full tuition reimbursements available (averaging $25,420 per year), 7 research assistantships with full tuition reimbursements available (averaging $13,375 per year), 53 teaching assistantships with full tuition reimbursements available (averaging $13,375 per year); scholarships/grants, health care benefits, tuition waivers (full), and unspecified assistantships also available. Financial award application deadline: 4/11. *Faculty research:* Forms of competition and outcomes in dual distribution systems; explaining the accuracy of revised forecasts; supply chain planning for random demand surges; advanced demand information in a multi-product system; the effects of presentation salience and measurement subjectivity on nonprofessional investors' fair value judgments. *Unit head:* Dr. Don Hausch, Associate Dean, Full-time MBA Program,

608-262-9731, E-mail: don.hausch@wisc.edu. *Application contact:* Betsy Kacizak, Director of Admissions and Recruiting, Full-time MBA Program, 608-262-4000, E-mail: betsy.kacizak@wisc.edu.
Website: https://wsb.wisc.edu/

University of Wisconsin–Platteville, School of Graduate Studies, Distance Learning Center, Online Master of Science in Integrated Supply Chain Management Program, Platteville, WI 53818-3099. Offers MS. *Program availability:* Part-time, online learning. *Students:* 2 full-time (0 women), 95 part-time (36 women); includes 26 minority (14 Black or African American, non-Hispanic/Latino; 1 American Indian or Alaska Native, non-Hispanic/Latino; 3 Asian, non-Hispanic/Latino; 8 Hispanic/Latino). 31 applicants, 77% accepted, 15 enrolled. In 2017, 28 master's awarded. *Entrance requirements:* Additional exam requirements/recommendations for international students: Required—TOEFL (minimum score 550 paper-based; 79 iBT), IELTS (minimum score 6.5). *Application deadline:* Applications are processed on a rolling basis. Application fee: $56. Electronic applications accepted. *Unit head:* Dawn Drake, Executive Director, 800-362-5460, Fax: 608-342-1071, E-mail: disted@uwplatt.edu.

University of Wisconsin–Stout, Graduate School, College of Management, Program in Operations and Supply Management, Menomonie, WI 54751. Offers operations management (MS); project management (MS); quality management (MS); supply chain management (MS).

Walden University, Graduate Programs, School of Management, Minneapolis, MN 55401. Offers accounting (MBA, MS, DBA), including accounting for the professional (MS), accounting with CPA emphasis (MS), self-designed (MS); advanced project management (Graduate Certificate); applied project management (Graduate Certificate); auditing (Graduate Certificate); bridge to business administration (Post-Doctoral Certificate); bridge to management (Post-Doctoral Certificate); business management (Graduate Certificate); communication (MBA); corporate finance (MBA); digital marketing (Graduate Certificate); entrepreneurship (DBA); entrepreneurship and small business (MBA); finance (MS, DBA), including finance for the professional (MS), finance with CFA/investment (MS), finance with CPA emphasis (MS); global supply chain management (DBA); healthcare management (MBA, DBA); human resource management (MBA, MS, Graduate Certificate), including functional human resource management (MS), general program (MS), integrating functional and strategic human resource management (MS), organizational strategy (MS); human resources management (DBA); information systems management (DBA); international business (MBA, DBA); leadership (MBA, MS, DBA, Graduate Certificate), including general program (MS), human resource leadership (MS), leader development (MS), self-designed (MS); management (MS, PhD), including communications (MS), finance (PhD), general program (MS), healthcare management (MS), human resource management (MS), human resources management (PhD), information systems management (PhD), international business (MS), leadership (MS), leadership and organizational change (PhD), marketing (MS), project management (MS), strategy and operations (MS); managerial accounting (Graduate Certificate); marketing (MBA, MS, DBA); project management (MBA, MS, DBA); self-designed (MBA, DBA); social impact management (DBA); technology entrepreneurship (DBA). *Accreditation:* ACBSP. *Program availability:* Part-time, evening/weekend, online only, 100% online. *Degree requirements:* For master's, thesis (for some programs), residency (for EMBA); for doctorate, thesis/dissertation, (for some programs), residency. *Entrance requirements:* For master's, bachelor's degree or higher; minimum GPA of 2.5; official transcripts; goal statement (for some programs); access to computer and Internet; for doctorate, master's degree or higher; three years of related professional or academic experience (preferred); minimum GPA of 3.0; goal statement and current resume (for select programs); official transcripts; access to computer and Internet; for other advanced degree, relevant work experience; access to computer and Internet. Additional exam requirements/recommendations for international students: Required—TOEFL (minimum score 550 paper-based, 79 iBT), IELTS (minimum score 6.5), Michigan English Language Assessment Battery (minimum score 82), or PTE (minimum score 53). Electronic applications accepted.

Washington University in St. Louis, Olin Business School, Program in Supply Chain Management, St. Louis, MO 63130-4899. Offers MS. *Program availability:* Part-time. *Faculty:* 98 full-time (25 women), 54 part-time/adjunct (12 women). *Students:* 54 full-time (31 women), 2 part-time (1 woman); includes 1 minority (American Indian or Alaska Native, non-Hispanic/Latino), 52 international. Average age 25. 140 applicants, 24% accepted, 20 enrolled. In 2017, 20 master's awarded. *Entrance requirements:* For master's, GMAT or GRE. Additional exam requirements/recommendations for international students: Required—TOEFL, IELTS. *Application deadline:* For fall admission, 10/3 for domestic students, 2/3 priority date for international students; for winter admission, 12/1 for domestic students; for spring admission, 4/3 for domestic students. Applications are processed on a rolling basis. Application fee: $100. Electronic applications accepted. *Financial support:* Institutionally sponsored loans and scholarships/grants available. Financial award applicants required to submit FAFSA. *Unit head:* Joe Fox, Associate Dean/Director of Specialized Master's Programs, 314-

935-6322, Fax: 314-935-4464, E-mail: fox@wustl.edu. *Application contact:* 314-935-7301, E-mail: olingradadmissions@wustl.edu.
Website: http://www.olin.wustl.edu/academicprograms/MSSCM/Pages/default.aspx

Western Illinois University, School of Graduate Studies, College of Business and Technology, Program in Business Administration, Macomb, IL 61455-1390. Offers business administration (MBA, Certificate); supply chain management (Certificate). *Accreditation:* AACSB. *Program availability:* Part-time. *Students:* 44 full-time (20 women), 63 part-time (23 women); includes 14 minority (2 Black or African American, non-Hispanic/Latino; 2 Asian, non-Hispanic/Latino; 9 Hispanic/Latino; 1 Two or more races, non-Hispanic/Latino), 9 international. Average age 32. 94 applicants, 65% accepted, 24 enrolled. In 2017, 42 master's awarded. *Degree requirements:* For master's, thesis or alternative. *Entrance requirements:* For master's, GMAT. Additional exam requirements/recommendations for international students: Required—TOEFL (minimum score 550 paper-based; 80 iBT). *Application deadline:* Applications are processed on a rolling basis. Application fee: $30. Electronic applications accepted. *Financial support:* Research assistantships with full tuition reimbursements and unspecified assistantships available. Financial award applicants required to submit FAFSA. *Unit head:* Dr. Bill Polley, Associate Dean, 309-298-2442. *Application contact:* Dr. Nancy Parsons, Associate Provost and Director of Graduate Studies, 309-298-1806, Fax: 309-298-2345, E-mail: grad-office@wiu.edu.
Website: http://wiu.edu/cbt

Wichita State University, Graduate School, W. Frank Barton School of Business, Program in Global Supply Chain Management, Wichita, KS 67260. Offers MS. *Unit head:* Dr. Mehmet Barut, Coordinator, 316-978-6930, E-mail: mehmet.barut@wichita.edu. *Application contact:* Jordan Oleson, Admissions Coordinator, 316-978-3095, Fax: 316-978-3253, E-mail: jordan.oleson@wichita.edu.

Wilfrid Laurier University, Faculty of Graduate and Postdoctoral Studies, School of Business and Economics, Department of Business, Waterloo, ON N2L 3C5, Canada. Offers accounting (PhD); finance (M Fin); financial economics (PhD); marketing (PhD); operations and supply chain management (PhD); organizational behavior and human resource management (M Sc); organizational behaviour and human resource management (PhD); supply chain management (M Sc); technology management (EMTM). *Accreditation:* AACSB. *Program availability:* Part-time, evening/weekend. *Degree requirements:* For master's, thesis optional; for doctorate, comprehensive exam, thesis/dissertation. *Entrance requirements:* For master's, GMAT, 4-year honors degree with minimum B+ average; for doctorate, GMAT, master's degree, minimum B+ average. Additional exam requirements/recommendations for international students: Required—TOEFL (minimum score 89 iBT). Electronic applications accepted. *Faculty research:* Financial economics, management and organizational behavior, operations and supply chain management.

Worcester Polytechnic Institute, Graduate Admissions, Foisie Business School, Worcester, MA 01609-2280. Offers business administration (PhD); information technology (MS), including information security management; management (Graduate Certificate); marketing and technological innovation (MS); operations design and leadership (MS); supply chain management (MS); technology (MS). *Accreditation:* AACSB. *Program availability:* Part-time, evening/weekend, 100% online, blended/hybrid learning. *Faculty:* 26 full-time (12 women), 9 part-time/adjunct (0 women). *Students:* 254 full-time (153 women), 150 part-time (52 women); includes 34 minority (3 Black or African American, non-Hispanic/Latino; 10 Asian, non-Hispanic/Latino; 14 Hispanic/Latino; 7 Two or more races, non-Hispanic/Latino), 230 international. Average age 29. 677 applicants, 71% accepted, 146 enrolled. In 2017, 188 master's, 14 doctorates awarded. *Degree requirements:* For master's, thesis optional. *Entrance requirements:* For master's and Graduate Certificate, GMAT or GRE General Test, 3 letters of recommendation, statement of purpose, resume. Additional exam requirements/recommendations for international students: Required—TOEFL (minimum score 563 paper-based; 84 iBT), IELTS (minimum score 7). *Application deadline:* For fall admission, 6/1 priority date for domestic and international students; for spring admission, 11/1 priority date for domestic students, 10/1 priority date for international students. Applications are processed on a rolling basis. Application fee: $70. Electronic applications accepted. *Expenses:* Tuition: Full-time $26,226; part-time $1457 per credit. *Required fees:* $60; $30 per credit. One-time fee: $15. Tuition and fees vary according to course load. *Financial support:* Career-related internships or fieldwork, institutionally sponsored loans, scholarships/grants, and unspecified assistantships available. Financial award application deadline: 6/1. *Unit head:* Melissa Terrio, Executive Director, 508-831-4665, Fax: 508-831-4665, E-mail: biz@wpi.edu. *Application contact:* Margaret Clancey, Recruiting Operations Coordinator, 508-831-4980, Fax: 508-831-5720, E-mail: maclancey@wpi.edu.
Website: https://www.wpi.edu/academics/business

Wright State University, Graduate School, Raj Soin College of Business, Department of Information Systems and Operations Management, Logistics and Supply Chain Management Program, Dayton, OH 45435. Offers MS.

Transportation Management

American Public University System, AMU/APU Graduate Programs, Charles Town, WV 25414. Offers accounting (MS); applied business analytics (MS); business administration (MBA); criminal justice (MA); cybersecurity studies (MS); educational leadership (M Ed); environmental policy and management (MS); global security (DGS); health information management (MS); history (MA), including American military history, American Revolution, civil war, war since 1945, World War II; information technology (MS); international relations and conflict resolution (MA), including American politics and government, comparative government and development, general, international relations, public policy; national security studies (MA); nursing (MSN); political science (MA); public policy (MPP); reverse logistics management (MA), including comparative and security issues, conflict resolution, international and transnational security issues, peacekeeping; space studies (MS); sports management (MS); strategic intelligence (DSI); teaching (M Ed), including secondary social studies; transportation and logistics management (MA). *Program availability:* Part-time, evening/weekend, online only, 100% online. *Students:* 455 full-time (227 women), 7,939 part-time (3,353 women); includes 2,793 minority (1,429 Black or African American, non-Hispanic/Latino; 48 American Indian or Alaska Native, non-Hispanic/Latino; 205 Asian, non-Hispanic/Latino; 766 Hispanic/Latino; 62 Native Hawaiian or other Pacific Islander, non-Hispanic/Latino; 283 Two or more races, non-Hispanic/Latino), 101 international. Average age 37. In 2017, 2,977 master's awarded. *Degree requirements:* For master's, comprehensive exam or practicum. *Entrance requirements:* For master's, official transcript showing earned

bachelor's degree from institution accredited by recognized accrediting body. Additional exam requirements/recommendations for international students: Required—TOEFL (minimum score 550 paper-based), IELTS (minimum score 6.5). *Application deadline:* Applications are processed on a rolling basis. Application fee: $0. Electronic applications accepted. *Expenses:* Tuition: Full-time $6300; part-time $350 per credit. *Required fees:* $300; $50 per course. *Financial support:* Scholarships/grants available. Financial award applicants required to submit FAFSA. *Unit head:* Dr. Wallace Boston, President, 877-468-6268, Fax: 304-728-2348, E-mail: president@apus.edu. *Application contact:* Yoci Deai, Associate Vice President, Graduate and International Admissions, 877-468-6268, Fax: 304-724-3764, E-mail: info@apus.edu.
Website: http://www.apus.edu

California State University Maritime Academy, Graduate Studies, Vallejo, CA 94590. Offers transportation and engineering management (MS), including engineering management, humanitarian disaster management, transportation. *Program availability:* Evening/weekend, online only, 100% online. *Faculty:* 16 part-time/adjunct (2 women). *Students:* 41 full-time (7 women); includes 10 minority (2 Black or African American, non-Hispanic/Latino; 5 Asian, non-Hispanic/Latino; 2 Hispanic/Latino; 1 Native Hawaiian or other Pacific Islander, non-Hispanic/Latino), 2 international. Average age 33. 32 applicants, 84% accepted, 22 enrolled. In 2017, 16 master's awarded. *Degree requirements:* For master's, comprehensive exam (for some programs), thesis, minimum GPA of 3.0 in 10 required courses including capstone course and project.

Transportation Management

Entrance requirements: For master's, GMAT/GRE (for applicants with fewer than five years of post-baccalaureate professional experience), equivalent of four-year U.S. bachelor's degree with minimum GPA of 2.5 during last two years (60 semester units or 90 quarter units) of coursework in degree program. Additional exam requirements/recommendations for international students: Required—TOEFL (minimum score 550 paper-based). *Application deadline:* Applications are processed on a rolling basis. Application fee: $55. Electronic applications accepted. *Expenses:* $900 per credit. *Financial support:* Applicants required to submit FAFSA. *Unit head:* Dr. Graham Benton, Associate Vice President, Academic Affairs, 707-654-1147. *Application contact:* Kathy Arnold, Program Coordinator, 707-654-1271, Fax: 707-654-1158, E-mail: karnold@csum.edu.
Website: http://www.csum.edu/web/industry/graduate-studies

Florida Institute of Technology, Extended Studies Division, Melbourne, FL 32901-6975. Offers acquisition and contract management (MS); aerospace engineering (MS); business administration (MBA, DBA); computer information systems (MS); computer science (MS); electrical engineering (MS); engineering management (MS); human resources management (MS); logistics management (MS), including humanitarian and disaster relief logistics; management (MS), including acquisition and contract management, e-business, human resources management, information systems, logistics management, management, transportation management; material acquisition management (MS); mechanical engineering (MS); operations research (MS); project management (MS), including information systems, operations research; public administration (MPA); quality management (MS); software engineering (MS); space systems (MS); space systems management (MS); supply chain management (MS); systems management (MS), including information systems, operations research; technology management (MS). *Program availability:* Part-time, evening/weekend, online learning. *Students:* Average age 36. 962 applicants, 48% accepted, 323 enrolled. In 2017, 403 master's awarded. *Entrance requirements:* For master's, GMAT or resume showing 8 years of supervised experience, minimum GPA of 3.0, 2 letters of recommendation, resume. Additional exam requirements/recommendations for international students: Required—TOEFL (minimum score 550 paper-based; 79 iBT). *Application deadline:* For fall admission, 4/1 for international students; for spring admission, 9/30 for international students. Applications are processed on a rolling basis. Electronic applications accepted. *Expenses:* Contact institution. *Financial support:* Application deadline: 3/1; applicants required to submit FAFSA. *Unit head:* Dr. Theodore R. Richardson, III, Dean, 321-674-8123, Fax: 321-674-7597, E-mail: trichardson@fit.edu. *Application contact:* Carolyn Farrior, Director of Graduate Admissions, Online Learning and Off-Campus Programs, 321-674-7118, Fax: 321-674-8216, E-mail: cfarrior@fit.edu.
Website: http://es.fit.edu

George Mason University, Schar School of Policy and Government, Program in Transportation Policy, Operations and Logistics, Arlington, VA 22201. Offers MA. *Faculty:* 6 full-time (3 women), 2 part-time/adjunct (0 women). *Students:* 9 full-time (3 women), 20 part-time (7 women); includes 7 minority (2 Black or African American, non-Hispanic/Latino; 3 Hispanic/Latino; 2 Two or more races, non-Hispanic/Latino), 4 international. Average age 34. 15 applicants, 100% accepted, 8 enrolled. In 2017, 12 master's awarded. *Entrance requirements:* For master's, GRE (for students seeking merit-based scholarships), bachelor's degree with minimum GPA of 3.0, current resume, 2 letters of recommendation, expanded goals statement, 2 copies of official transcripts. Additional exam requirements/recommendations for international students: Required—TOEFL (minimum score 575 paper-based; 88 iBT), IELTS (minimum score 6.5), PTE (minimum score 59). *Application deadline:* For fall admission, 2/1 priority date for domestic and international students; for spring admission, 11/1 priority date for domestic and international students. Application fee: $75 ($80 for international students). Electronic applications accepted. *Expenses:* $795 per credit in-state tuition, $1,516 out-of-state. *Financial support:* Career-related internships or fieldwork, Federal Work-Study, and scholarships/grants available. Support available to part-time students. Financial award application deadline: 3/1; financial award applicants required to submit FAFSA. *Unit head:* Laurie Schintler, Director, 703-993-2256, Fax: 703-993-4557, E-mail: lschintl@gmu.edu. *Application contact:* Stephanie Ellis, Graduate Admissions Coordinator, 703-993-4478, E-mail: sellis11@gmu.edu.
Website: http://spgia.gmu.edu/programs/graduate-degrees/transportation-policy-operations-logistics-tpol/

Instituto Tecnologico de Santo Domingo, Graduate School, Area of Engineering, Santo Domingo, Dominican Republic. Offers construction administration (MS, Certificate); data telecommunications (M Eng, MS, Certificate); industrial engineering (M Eng, Certificate); industrial management (M Mgmt); information technology (Certificate); maintenance engineering (M Eng); occupational hazard prevention (M Mgmt); production management (Certificate); quantitative methods (Certificate); sanitary and environmental engineering (M Eng); structural engineering (M Eng); systems engineering and electronic data processing (Certificate); transportation (Certificate).

Iowa State University of Science and Technology, Department of Community and Regional Planning, Ames, IA 50011. Offers community and regional planning (MCRP); transportation (MS); M Arch/MCRP; MBA/MCRP; MCRP/MLA; MCRP/MPA. *Accreditation:* ACSP (one or more programs are accredited). *Degree requirements:* For master's, thesis or alternative. *Entrance requirements:* For master's, GRE General Test. Additional exam requirements/recommendations for international students: Required—TOEFL (minimum score 550 paper-based; 79 iBT), IELTS (minimum score 6.5). Electronic applications accepted. *Faculty research:* Economic development, housing, land use, geographic information systems planning in developing nations, regional and community revitalization, transportation planning in developing countries.

Iowa State University of Science and Technology, Program in Transportation, Ames, IA 50011. Offers MS. *Entrance requirements:* For master's, GMAT or GRE General Test. Additional exam requirements/recommendations for international students: Required—TOEFL (minimum score 550 paper-based; 82 iBT), IELTS (minimum score 6.5). Electronic applications accepted.

Maine Maritime Academy, Loeb-Sullivan School of International Business and Logistics, Castine, ME 04420. Offers global logistics and maritime management (MS); international logistics management (MS). *Program availability:* Part-time, 100% online. *Faculty:* 6 full-time (1 woman), 5 part-time/adjunct (1 woman). *Students:* 8 full-time (2 women), 13 part-time (7 women). Average age 30. 26 applicants. In 2017, 17 master's awarded. *Degree requirements:* For master's, capstone course. *Entrance requirements:* For master's, GMAT or GRE, letter of recommendation. Additional exam requirements/recommendations for international students: Required—TOEFL, IELTS. *Application deadline:* For fall admission, 6/1 for domestic and international students; for spring admission, 3/15 for domestic and international students. Applications are processed on a rolling basis. Application fee: $40. Electronic applications accepted. Application fee is waived when completed online. *Financial support:* In 2017–18, 2 students received support, including teaching assistantships with full tuition reimbursements available (averaging $5,000 per year); career-related internships or fieldwork, Federal Work-Study, and institutionally sponsored loans also available. Support available to part-time students. Financial award application deadline: 4/15; financial award applicants required

to submit FAFSA. *Faculty research:* Internet of things, trait intelligence, port operations, location theory. *Unit head:* Dr. Donald Maier, Dean, 207-326-2488, E-mail: donald.maier@mma.edu. *Application contact:* Debra Kingston, Program Coordinator, 207-326-2212, Fax: 207-326-2411, E-mail: debra.kingston@mma.edu.
Website: http://ibl.mainemaritime.edu

McGill University, Faculty of Graduate and Postdoctoral Studies, Faculty of Engineering, School of Urban Planning, Montréal, QC H3A 2T5, Canada. Offers environmental planning (MUP); housing (MUP); transportation (MUP); urban design (MUP); urban planning, policy and design (PhD).

Naval Postgraduate School, Departments and Academic Groups, Graduate School of Business and Public Policy, Monterey, CA 93943. Offers acquisition and contract management (MBA); business administration (EMBA, MBA); contract management (MS); defense business management (MBA); defense systems analysis (MS), including management; defense systems management (international) (MBA); financial management (MBA); information management (MBA); manpower systems analysis (MS); material logistics support management (MBA); program management (MS); resource planning and management for international defense (MBA); supply chain management (MBA); systems acquisition management (MBA); transportation management (MBA). Program only open to commissioned officers of the United States and friendly nations and selected United States federal civilian employees. *Accreditation:* AACSB; NASPAA. *Program availability:* Part-time, online learning. *Degree requirements:* For master's, thesis (for some programs), terminal project/capstone (for some programs). *Faculty research:* U.S. and European public procurement policies for small and medium-sized enterprises, examining external validity criticisms in the choice of students as subjects in accounting experiment studies, assurance of learning in contract management education, contracting for cloud computing: opportunities and risks, NPS, Apple App Store as a business model supporting U.S. Navy requirements.

New Jersey Institute of Technology, Newark College of Engineering, Newark, NJ 07102. Offers biomedical engineering (MS, PhD); chemical engineering (MS, PhD); computer engineering (MS, PhD); electrical engineering (MS, PhD); engineering management (MS); environmental engineering (PhD); healthcare systems management (MS); industrial engineering (MS, PhD); Internet engineering (MS); manufacturing engineering (MS); mechanical engineering (MS, PhD); occupational safety and health engineering (MS); pharmaceutical bioprocessing (MS); pharmaceutical engineering (MS); pharmaceutical systems management (MS); power and energy systems (MS); telecommunications (MS); transportation (MS, PhD). *Program availability:* Part-time, evening/weekend. *Students:* Average age 27. 2,959 applicants, 51% accepted, 442 enrolled. In 2017, 595 master's, 29 doctorates awarded. Terminal master's awarded for partial completion of doctoral program. *Entrance requirements:* For master's, GRE General Test; for doctorate, GRE General Test, minimum graduate GPA of 3.5. Additional exam requirements/recommendations for international students: Required—TOEFL (minimum score 550 paper-based; 79 iBT). *Application deadline:* For fall admission, 6/1 priority date for domestic students, 5/1 priority date for international students; for spring admission, 11/15 priority date for domestic and international students. Applications are processed on a rolling basis. Application fee: $75. Electronic applications accepted. *Expenses:* Contact institution. *Financial support:* In 2017–18, 172 students received support, including 24 fellowships (averaging $7,124 per year), 112 research assistantships (averaging $19,407 per year), 101 teaching assistantships (averaging $24,173 per year); scholarships/grants also available. Financial award application deadline: 1/15. *Faculty research:* Nonlinear signal processing, intelligent medical image analysis, calibration issues in coherent localization, computer-aided design, neural network for tool wear measurement. *Total annual research expenditures:* $11.1 million. *Unit head:* Dr. Moshe Kam, Dean, 973-596-5534, E-mail: moshe.kam@njit.edu. *Application contact:* Stephen Eck, Director of Admissions, 973-596-3300, Fax: 973-596-3461, E-mail: admissions@njit.edu.
Website: http://engineering.njit.edu/

New York University, Tandon School of Engineering, Department of Civil and Urban Engineering, Major in Transportation Management, New York, NY 10012-1019. Offers MS. *Program availability:* Part-time, evening/weekend. *Faculty:* 17 full-time (5 women), 38 part-time/adjunct (4 women). *Students:* 2 full-time (1 woman), 5 part-time (1 woman); includes 2 minority (both Asian, non-Hispanic/Latino), 2 international. Average age 31. 10 applicants, 20% accepted, 1 enrolled. In 2017, 4 master's awarded. *Entrance requirements:* Additional exam requirements/recommendations for international students: Required—TOEFL (minimum score 550 paper-based; 90 iBT); Recommended—IELTS (minimum score 7). *Application deadline:* For fall admission, 2/15 priority date for domestic and international students; for spring admission, 11/1 priority date for domestic and international students. Applications are processed on a rolling basis. Application fee: $75. Electronic applications accepted. *Expenses:* Tuition: Full-time $41,352; part-time $19,968 per year. *Required fees:* $2496; $1628 per unit. $814 per term. Tuition and fees vary according to course load and program. *Financial support:* Fellowships, research assistantships, teaching assistantships, institutionally sponsored loans, scholarships/grants, and unspecified assistantships available. Support available to part-time students. Financial award applicants required to submit FAFSA. *Total annual research expenditures:* $2.5 million. *Unit head:* Dr. Elena S. Prassas, Program Manager, 646-997-3788, E-mail: eprassas@nyu.edu. *Application contact:* Elizabeth Ensweiler, Senior Director of Graduate Enrollment and Graduate Admissions, 646-997-3182, E-mail: elizabeth.ensweiler@nyu.edu.

North Dakota State University, College of Graduate and Interdisciplinary Studies, Interdisciplinary Program in Transportation and Logistics, Fargo, ND 58102. Offers managerial logistics (MML); transportation and logistics (PhD); transportation and urban systems (MS). *Entrance requirements:* For doctorate, 1 year of calculus, statistics and probability, minimum GPA of 3.0. Additional exam requirements/recommendations for international students: Required—TOEFL (minimum score 550 paper-based; 79 iBT). *Faculty research:* Supply chain optimization, spatial analysis of transportation networks, advanced traffic analysis, transportation demand, railroad/intermodal freight.

Pontifical Catholic University of Puerto Rico, College of Business Administration, Program in Maritime Logistics and Transportation, Ponce, PR 00717-0777. Offers Professional Certificate.

San Jose State University, Graduate Studies and Research, Lucas Graduate School of Business, San Jose, CA 95192-0065. Offers accountancy (MS); business administration (MBA); taxation (MS); transportation management (MS). *Program availability:* Part-time, evening/weekend, online learning. *Faculty:* 15 full-time (7 women), 6 part-time/adjunct (3 women). *Students:* 85 full-time (49 women), 51 part-time (28 women); includes 77 minority (2 Black or African American, non-Hispanic/Latino; 44 Asian, non-Hispanic/Latino; 16 Hispanic/Latino; 1 Native Hawaiian or other Pacific Islander, non-Hispanic/Latino; 14 Two or more races, non-Hispanic/Latino), 42 international. Average age 28. 328 applicants, 43% accepted, 89 enrolled. In 2017, 155 master's awarded. *Degree requirements:* For master's, graduate writing assessment, culminating project. *Entrance requirements:* Additional exam requirements/recommendations for international students: Required—TOEFL (minimum score 80 iBT), IELTS (minimum score 6.5), PTE (minimum score 53). *Application deadline:* For fall admission, 2/1 for domestic and international students. Applications are processed on a rolling basis. Application fee: $55. Electronic applications accepted. *Expenses:* Contact institution. *Financial support:* Fellowships, research assistantships, career-related internships or fieldwork, Federal Work-Study, institutionally sponsored loans, scholarships/grants, and unspecified assistantships available. Support available to part-time students. Financial award application deadline: 4/28; financial award applicants required to submit FAFSA. *Faculty research:* Financial effects of cyber-security breaches, health care analytics, innovation and teamwork, corporate bankruptcy prediction, multi-domain executive coaching. *Unit head:* Dr. Dan Moshavi, Dean, 408-924-3400, Fax: 408-924-3426, E-mail: dan.moshavi@sjsu.edu. Website: http://www.sjsu.edu/lucasschool/

State University of New York Maritime College, Program in International Transportation Management, Throggs Neck, NY 10465-4198. Offers MS. *Program availability:* Part-time, evening/weekend. *Degree requirements:* For master's, thesis. *Entrance requirements:* For master's, minimum GPA of 2.5. Additional exam requirements/recommendations for international students: Required—TOEFL. *Faculty research:* Ports, intermodal, shipping, logistics, port tax.

Temple University, Tyler School of Art, Department of Planning and Community Development, Ambler, PA 19335. Offers city and regional planning (MS); sustainable community planning (Graduate Certificate); transportation planning (Graduate Certificate). *Accreditation:* ACSP. *Program availability:* Part-time, evening/weekend. *Faculty:* 3 full-time (1 woman), 8 part-time/adjunct (5 women). *Students:* 1 (woman) part-time. 23 applicants, 70% accepted, 1 enrolled. In 2017, 2 master's awarded. *Entrance requirements:* For master's, GRE or GMAT, 2 letters of recommendation, minimum undergraduate GPA of 3.0, statement of goals. Additional exam requirements/recommendations for international students: Required—TOEFL (minimum score 550 paper-based; 79 iBT). *Application deadline:* For fall admission, 3/1 for domestic students, 12/15 for international students; for spring admission, 11/1 for domestic students, 8/1 for international students. Applications are processed on a rolling basis. Application fee: $60. *Expenses:* Tuition, state resident: full-time $16,164; part-time $898 per credit hour. Tuition, nonresident: full-time $22,158; part-time $1231 per credit hour. *Required fees:* $890; $445 per semester. Full-time tuition and fees vary according to course load, degree level, campus/location and program. *Financial support:* Fellowships with full tuition reimbursements, research assistantships with full tuition reimbursements, Federal Work-Study, scholarships/grants, health care benefits, and unspecified assistantships available. Financial award application deadline: 1/15; financial award applicants required to submit FAFSA. *Faculty research:* Regional environmental planning, collaboration, management community development through sustainable food systems, storm water management and floodplain mapping, land use policy innovations, community planning for aging. *Unit head:* Lynn Mandarano, Chair, 267-468-8300, Fax: 267-468-8315, E-mail: lynn.mandarano@temple.edu. Website: http://tyler.temple.edu/programs/planning-community-development

Texas A&M University, Galveston Campus, Department of Maritime Administration, College Station, TX 77843. Offers maritime administration and logistics (MMAL). *Program availability:* Part-time, evening/weekend. *Faculty:* 6. *Students:* 48 full-time (11 women), 15 part-time (3 women); includes 13 minority (1 Black or African American, non-Hispanic/Latino; 4 Asian, non-Hispanic/Latino; 6 Hispanic/Latino; 2 Two or more races, non-Hispanic/Latino). Average age 29. 10 applicants, 90% accepted, 9 enrolled. In 2017, 14 master's awarded. *Degree requirements:* For master's, comprehensive exam (for some programs), thesis (for some programs). *Entrance requirements:* For master's, GMAT, coursework in statistics, microeconomics, organizational behavior, financial and managerial accounting, management information systems. Additional exam requirements/recommendations for international students: Required—TOEFL (minimum score 550 paper-based; 80 iBT), IELTS (minimum score 6). *Application deadline:* For fall admission, 5/1 for domestic and international students; for spring admission, 10/15 for domestic students, 10/1 for international students. Application fee: $50 ($90 for international students). Electronic applications accepted. *Expenses:* Contact institution. *Financial support:* In 2017–18, 37 students received support, including 4 research assistantships (averaging $6,146 per year), 15 teaching assistantships (averaging $11,638 per year); scholarships/grants and unspecified assistantships also available. Financial award application deadline: 3/15; financial award applicants required to submit FAFSA. *Faculty research:* International trade, inland waterways management, brokerage and chartering, organizational behavior, transportation economics, port and terminal management. *Unit head:* Dr. Joan P. Mileski, Professor/Chair of Maritime Administration, 409-740-4978, E-mail: mileskij@tamug.edu. *Application contact:* Nicole Kinslow, Director of Graduate Studies, 409-740-4937, Fax: 409-740-4754, E-mail: kinslown@tamug.edu. Website: http://www.tamug.edu/mara/

Texas Southern University, School of Science and Technology, Program in Transportation, Planning and Management, Houston, TX 77004-4584. Offers MS.

Program availability: Part-time, evening/weekend. *Degree requirements:* For master's, comprehensive exam, thesis optional. *Entrance requirements:* For master's, GRE General Test, minimum GPA of 2.5. Additional exam requirements/recommendations for international students: Required—TOEFL. Electronic applications accepted. *Faculty research:* Highway traffic operations, transportation and policy planning, air quality in transportation, transportation modeling.

University at Buffalo, the State University of New York, Graduate School, School of Engineering and Applied Sciences, Program in Sustainable Transportation and Logistics, Buffalo, NY 14260. Offers MS.

The University of British Columbia, Sauder School of Business, Doctoral Program in Business Administration, Vancouver, BC V6T 1Z2, Canada. Offers accounting (PhD); finance (PhD); management information systems (PhD); management science (PhD); marketing (PhD); organizational behavior (PhD); strategy and business economics (PhD); transportation and logistics (PhD); urban land economics (PhD). *Degree requirements:* For doctorate, comprehensive exam, thesis/dissertation. *Entrance requirements:* For doctorate, GMAT or GRE. Additional exam requirements/recommendations for international students: Required—TOEFL (minimum score 600 paper-based; 100 iBT). Electronic applications accepted. *Expenses:* Contact institution.

University of California, Davis, College of Engineering, Graduate Group in Transportation Technology and Policy, Davis, CA 95616. Offers MS, PhD. Terminal master's awarded for partial completion of doctoral program. *Degree requirements:* For master's, comprehensive exam (for some programs), thesis (for some programs); for doctorate, thesis/dissertation. *Entrance requirements:* For master's, GRE General Test, minimum GPA of 3.0; for doctorate, GRE General Test, minimum GPA of 3.5. Additional exam requirements/recommendations for international students: Required—TOEFL (minimum score 550 paper-based). Electronic applications accepted.

University of California, Santa Barbara, Graduate Division, College of Letters and Sciences, Division of Mathematics, Life, and Physical Sciences, Department of Geography, Santa Barbara, CA 93106-4060. Offers cognitive science (PhD); geography (MA, PhD); global studies (PhD); quantitative methods in the social sciences (PhD); technology and society (PhD); transportation (PhD); MA/PhD. Terminal master's awarded for partial completion of doctoral program. *Degree requirements:* For master's, comprehensive exam (for some programs), thesis or alternative; for doctorate, comprehensive exam, thesis/dissertation, 1 quarter of teaching assistantship. *Entrance requirements:* For master's and doctorate, GRE (minimum combined verbal and quantitative scores above 1100 in old scoring system or 301 in new scoring system). Additional exam requirements/recommendations for international students: Required—TOEFL (minimum score 550 paper-based; 80 iBT), IELTS (minimum score 7). Electronic applications accepted. *Faculty research:* Earth system science; human environment relations; modeling, measurement, and computation.

University of Hawaii at Manoa, Office of Graduate Education, College of Social Sciences, Department of Urban and Regional Planning, Honolulu, HI 96822. Offers community planning (MURP); disaster management and humanitarian assistance (Graduate Certificate); environmental planning and sustainability (MURP); international development planning (MURP); land use, transportation and infrastructure planning (MURP); planning studies (Graduate Certificate); urban and regional planning (PhD, Graduate Certificate). *Accreditation:* ACSP. *Program availability:* Part-time. *Entrance requirements:* For master's, GRE General Test, minimum GPA of 3.0; for doctorate, GRE General Test. Additional exam requirements/recommendations for international students: Required—TOEFL (minimum score 500 paper-based; 61 iBT), IELTS (minimum score 5).

University of New Orleans, Graduate School, College of Liberal Arts, Department of Planning and Urban Studies, Program in Transportation, New Orleans, LA 70148. Offers MS. *Program availability:* Online learning.

The University of Tennessee, Graduate School, College of Business Administration, Program in Business Administration, Knoxville, TN 37996. Offers accounting (PhD); finance (MBA, PhD); logistics and transportation (MBA, PhD); management (PhD); marketing (MBA, PhD); operations management (MBA); professional business administration (MBA); statistics (PhD); JD/MBA; MS/MBA; Pharm D/MBA. Pharm D/MBA offered jointly with The University of Tennessee Health Science Center. *Accreditation:* AACSB. *Program availability:* Online learning. *Degree requirements:* For master's, thesis or alternative; for doctorate, thesis/dissertation. *Entrance requirements:* For master's and doctorate, GMAT, minimum GPA of 2.7. Additional exam requirements/recommendations for international students: Required—TOEFL. Electronic applications accepted.

University of Washington, Graduate School, Interdisciplinary Program in Global Trade, Transportation and Logistics Studies, Seattle, WA 98195. Offers Certificate.

ACADEMIC AND PROFESSIONAL PROGRAMS IN EDUCATION

Section 22
Education

This section contains a directory of institutions offering graduate work in education, followed by in-depth entries submitted by institutions that chose to prepare detailed program descriptions. Additional information about programs listed in the directory but not augmented by an in-depth entry may be obtained by writing directly to the dean of a graduate school or chair of a department at the address given in the directory.

For programs offering related work, see also in this book *Administration, Instruction, and Theory; Instructional Levels; Leisure Studies and Recreation; Physical Education and Kinesiology; Special Focus;* and *Subject Areas.* In other guides in this series:

Graduate Programs in the Humanities, Arts & Social Sciences
See *Psychology and Counseling (School Psychology)*
Graduate Programs in the Biological/Biomedical Sciences and Health-Related Medical Professions
See *Health-Related Professions*

CONTENTS

Program Directory

Featured Schools: Displays and Close-Ups

Education—General

Abilene Christian University, Graduate Programs, College of Education and Human Services, Abilene, TX 79699. Offers M Ed, MS, MSSW, Certificate. *Accreditation:* TEAC. *Faculty:* 4 full-time (3 women), 32 part-time/adjunct (23 women). *Students:* 177 full-time (165 women), 40 part-time (38 women); includes 36 minority (13 Black or African American, non-Hispanic/Latino; 1 American Indian or Alaska Native, non-Hispanic/Latino; 5 Asian, non-Hispanic/Latino; 17 Hispanic/Latino), 3 international. 600 applicants, 41% accepted, 141 enrolled. In 2017, 72 master's awarded. *Degree requirements:* For master's, comprehensive exam (for some programs), thesis (for some programs), practicum. *Entrance requirements:* For master's, GRE. Additional exam requirements/recommendations for international students: Required—TOEFL (minimum score 80 iBT), IELTS (minimum score 6), PTE. *Application deadline:* For fall admission, 8/15 priority date for domestic students; for winter admission, 10/1 priority date for domestic students; for spring admission, 12/15 priority date for domestic students; for summer admission, 4/15 for domestic students. Applications are processed on a rolling basis. Application fee: $50. Electronic applications accepted. *Expenses: Tuition:* Full-time $20,664; part-time $1148 per contact hour. *Financial support:* In 2017–18, 110 students received support. Career-related internships or fieldwork and scholarships/grants available. Financial award application deadline: 4/1; financial award applicants required to submit FAFSA. *Unit head:* Dr. Jennifer Shewmaker, Dean, 325-674-2700, Fax: 325-674-3707, E-mail: cehs@acu.edu. *Application contact:* Graduate Admission, 325-674-6911, Fax: 325-674-6717, E-mail: gradinfo@acu.edu.
Website: http://www.acu.edu/graduate/academics/education-and-human-services.html

Acacia University, American Graduate School of Education, Tempe, AZ 85284. Offers educational administration (M Ed); elementary education (MA); English as a second language (M Ed); secondary education (MA); special education (M Ed).

Acadia University, Faculty of Professional Studies, Inter-University Doctoral Program in Educational Studies, Wolfville, NS B4P 2R6, Canada. Offers PhD. Program offered jointly with Mount Saint Vincent University and St. Francis Xavier University. *Degree requirements:* For doctorate, thesis/dissertation, comprehensive research/scholarly portfolio. *Application deadline:* For spring admission, 11/15 priority date for domestic and international students. *Unit head:* Dr. Jennifer Mitton-Kukner, PhD Program Director/Coordinator, 902-867-3649, E-mail: jmitton@stfx.ca. *Application contact:* Rosie Hare, Administrative Assistant, 902-585-1597, Fax: 902-585-1086, E-mail: rosie.hare@acadiau.ca.
Website: http://www.educationphd.ns.ca/

Acadia University, Faculty of Professional Studies, School of Education, Wolfville, NS B4P 2R6, Canada. Offers counseling (M Ed); curriculum studies (M Ed), including curriculum studies, interprofessional health practice, music education; inclusive education (M Ed); leadership (M Ed). *Entrance requirements:* For master's, B Ed or the equivalent, 2 years of teaching or related experience. Additional exam requirements/recommendations for international students: Required—TOEFL (minimum score 580 paper-based; 93 iBT), IELTS (minimum score 6.5). *Application deadline:* Applications are processed on a rolling basis. Application fee: $50. *Financial support:* Application deadline: 2/1. *Unit head:* Dr. John J. Guinney Yallop, Director, 902-585-1229, Fax: 902-585-1071, E-mail: johnj.guiney.yallop@acadiau.ca. *Application contact:* Rosie Hare, Administrative Assistant, 902-585-1597, Fax: 902-585-1086, E-mail: rosie.hare@acadiau.ca.
Website: http://education.acadiau.ca

Adams State University, Office of Graduate Studies, Department of Teacher Education, Alamosa, CO 81101. Offers teacher education (MA), including adaptive leadership, curriculum and instruction, curriculum and instruction-STEM, educational leadership. *Program availability:* Part-time, online learning. *Degree requirements:* For master's, qualifying exam. *Entrance requirements:* For master's, GRE General Test or MAT, minimum undergraduate GPA of 3.0. *Application deadline:* For fall admission, 5/15 priority date for domestic students; for spring admission, 10/15 for domestic students. Applications are processed on a rolling basis. Application fee: $30. *Expenses: Tuition,* state resident: full-time $4800; part-time $2400 per credit. Tuition, nonresident: full-time $7100; part-time $3550 per credit. *Required fees:* $213; $106 per credit. One-time fee: $100. Tuition and fees vary according to campus/location and program. *Financial support:* In 2017–18, fellowships with partial tuition reimbursements (averaging $4,000 per year), teaching assistantships with partial tuition reimbursements (averaging $4,000 per year) were awarded; career-related internships or fieldwork, Federal Work-Study, institutionally sponsored loans, and unspecified assistantships also available. Support available to part-time students. Financial award application deadline: 4/15; financial award applicants required to submit FAFSA. *Unit head:* Dr. Cheri Meder, Interim Chair, 719-587-7934, Fax: 719-587-8145, E-mail: teachered@adams.edu. *Application contact:* Information Contact, 719-587-7776, Fax: 719-587-8145, E-mail: teachered@adams.edu.
Website: http://teachered.adams.edu

Adelphi University, Ruth S. Ammon School of Education, Garden City, NY 11530-0701. Offers MA, MS, DA, Certificate. *Accreditation:* NCATE. *Program availability:* Part-time, evening/weekend. *Faculty:* 66 full-time (43 women), 92 part-time/adjunct (66 women). *Students:* 457 full-time (362 women), 226 part-time (150 women); includes 215 minority (55 Black or African American, non-Hispanic/Latino; 1 American Indian or Alaska Native, non-Hispanic/Latino; 28 Asian, non-Hispanic/Latino; 123 Hispanic/Latino; 8 Two or more races, non-Hispanic/Latino), 18 international. Average age 27. 1,162 applicants, 50% accepted, 249 enrolled. In 2017, 320 master's, 7 doctorates, 90 other advanced degrees awarded. *Degree requirements:* For doctorate, one foreign language, comprehensive exam, thesis/dissertation. *Entrance requirements:* For master's, resume, letters of recommendation, minimum cumulative GPA of 2.75; for doctorate, GRE General Test, 3 letters of recommendation, interview. Additional exam requirements/recommendations for international students: Required—TOEFL (minimum score 550 paper-based; 80 iBT), IELTS (minimum score 6.5). *Application deadline:* For fall admission, 4/1 for international students; for spring admission, 11/1 for international students. Applications are processed on a rolling basis. Application fee: $50. Electronic applications accepted. *Expenses:* Contact institution. *Financial support:* In 2017–18, 97 teaching assistantships with full and partial tuition reimbursements (averaging $11,015 per year) were awarded; fellowships, research assistantships, career-related internships or fieldwork, Federal Work-Study, scholarships/grants, traineeships, tuition waivers (full and partial), unspecified assistantships, and tuition remission for employees also available. Support available to part-time students. Financial award application deadline: 2/15; financial award applicants required to submit FAFSA. *Faculty research:* Multicultural and gender issues, psychometric assessment, quantitative research methods. *Unit head:* Dr. Anne Mungai, Interim Dean, 516-877-4065, E-mail: mungai@adelphi.edu. *Application contact:* Kristen Capezza, Associate Vice President for Enrollment Management, 516-877-3021, Fax: 516-877-3039, E-mail: graduateadmissions@adelphi.edu.
Website: http://education.adelphi.edu

Alabama Agricultural and Mechanical University, School of Graduate Studies, College of Education, Humanities, and Behavioral Sciences, Huntsville, AL 35811.

Offers M Ed, MS, MS Ed, PhD, Ed S. *Accreditation:* NCATE. *Program availability:* Part-time, evening/weekend. *Degree requirements:* For master's, comprehensive exam. *Entrance requirements:* For master's, GRE General Test. Additional exam requirements/recommendations for international students: Required—TOEFL (minimum score 500 paper-based; 61 iBT). Electronic applications accepted. *Faculty research:* Speech defects, aging, blindness, multicultural education, learning styles.

Alabama State University, College of Education, Montgomery, AL 36101-0271. Offers M Ed, MS, Ed D, PhD, Ed S. *Accreditation:* NCATE. *Program availability:* Part-time. *Faculty:* 7 full-time (4 women), 7 part-time/adjunct (4 women). *Students:* 82 full-time (57 women), 190 part-time (146 women); includes 260 minority (259 Black or African American, non-Hispanic/Latino; 1 Two or more races, non-Hispanic/Latino), 2 international. Average age 22. 99 applicants, 68% accepted, 37 enrolled. In 2017, 76 master's, 4 doctorates, 17 other advanced degrees awarded. *Degree requirements:* For master's, comprehensive exam; for doctorate, thesis/dissertation; for Ed S, comprehensive exam, thesis. *Entrance requirements:* For master's, GRE General Test, MAT, writing competency test; for Ed S, writing competency test, GRE, MAT. Additional exam requirements/recommendations for international students: Required—TOEFL (minimum score 500 paper-based). *Application deadline:* For fall admission, 4/15 for domestic and international students; for spring admission, 11/15 for domestic and international students; for summer admission, 3/15 for domestic and international students. Applications are processed on a rolling basis. Application fee: $25. Electronic applications accepted. *Expenses:* Contact institution. *Financial support:* In 2017–18, 4 students received support. Research assistantships and unspecified assistantships available. Financial award application deadline: 6/30; financial award applicants required to submit FAFSA. *Faculty research:* Whole language instruction, African-American children's literature. *Unit head:* Dr. Alma Freeman, Interim Dean, 334-229-4250, E-mail: educan@alasu.edu. *Application contact:* Dr. William Person, Dean of Graduate Studies, 334-229-4274, Fax: 334-229-4928, E-mail: wperson@alasu.edu.
Website: http://www.alasu.edu/Education/

Alaska Pacific University, Graduate Programs, Education Department, Program in Teaching, Anchorage, AK 99508-4672. Offers teaching (K-8) (MAT). *Degree requirements:* For master's, research project. *Entrance requirements:* For master's, GRE or MAT, PRAXIS, minimum GPA of 3.0.

Albany State University, College of Education, Albany, GA 31705-2717. Offers early childhood education (M Ed); educational leadership (Ed S); health and physical education (M Ed); middle grades education (M Ed); school counseling (M Ed); special education (M Ed). *Accreditation:* NCATE. *Program availability:* Part-time, evening/weekend, online learning. *Degree requirements:* For master's, comprehensive exam, internship, GACE Content Exam. *Entrance requirements:* For master's, GRE or MAT. Electronic applications accepted. *Faculty research:* GACE preparation, STEM (science, technology, engineering, and mathematics), technology education, special education, professional teacher development, health implications liberation philosophy, NET-Q, learning community, disabled or at-risk students.

Albertus Magnus College, Master of Science in Education Program, New Haven, CT 06511-1189. Offers MS Ed. *Program availability:* Part-time, evening/weekend, blended/hybrid learning. *Degree requirements:* For master's, thesis, capstone. *Entrance requirements:* For master's, bachelor's degree, official transcripts of all undergraduate work, three letters of recommendation, resume, essay, valid Connecticut initial teacher certificate (preferred). Additional exam requirements/recommendations for international students: Recommended—TOEFL (minimum score 550 paper-based; 80 iBT). *Application deadline:* For fall admission, 8/15 for domestic students; for spring admission, 1/15 for domestic students. Application fee: $50. *Expenses:* Contact institution. *Financial support:* Federal Work-Study and unspecified assistantships available. Support available to part-time students. Financial award applicants required to submit FAFSA. *Faculty research:* Assessment, learning theory, educational leadership, differentiated instruction, multiculturalism. *Unit head:* Dr. Joan Venditto, Director, Education Programs, 203-773-8087, Fax: 203-773-4422, E-mail: jvenditto@albertus.edu. *Application contact:* Anthony Reich, Director of Admission, Division of Professional and Graduate Studies, 203-773-5032, E-mail: arreich@albertus.edu.
Website: http://www.albertus.edu/education/ms/

Albright College, Graduate Division, Reading, PA 19612-5234. Offers early childhood education (MS); elementary education (MS); English as a second language (MA); general education (MA); special education (MS). *Program availability:* Part-time, evening/weekend. *Degree requirements:* For master's, thesis. *Entrance requirements:* For master's, GRE General Test or MAT, minimum undergraduate GPA of 3.0, 2 letters of recommendation, interview. Additional exam requirements/recommendations for international students: Recommended—TOEFL (minimum score 525 paper-based). Electronic applications accepted.

Alcorn State University, School of Graduate Studies, School of Psychology and Education, Lorman, MS 39096-7500. Offers agricultural education (MS Ed); elementary education (MS Ed, Ed S); guidance and counseling (MS Ed); industrial education (MS Ed); secondary education (MS Ed), including health and physical education; special education (MS Ed). *Accreditation:* NCATE. *Degree requirements:* For master's, thesis optional.

Alfred University, Graduate School, Division of Education, Alfred, NY 14802-1205. Offers college student development (MS Ed); literacy (MS Ed). *Accreditation:* TEAC. *Program availability:* Part-time. *Entrance requirements:* For master's, Liberal Arts and Sciences Test (LAST), Assessment of Teaching Skills (written) (ATS-W), Content Specialty Test (CST). Additional exam requirements/recommendations for international students: Required—TOEFL (minimum score 590 paper-based; 90 iBT), IELTS (minimum score 6.5). Electronic applications accepted.

Alliant International University–Los Angeles, Shirley M. Hufstedler School of Education, TeachersCHOICE Preparation Programs, Alhambra, CA 91803. Offers MA, Credential. *Program availability:* Part-time. *Entrance requirements:* For master's, CBEST, CSET, interview; offer of employment as a teacher of record in a California school; minimum GPA of 2.5; 2 letters of recommendation. Additional exam requirements/recommendations for international students: Required—TOEFL (minimum score 550 paper-based). *Faculty research:* Multicultural and bilingual education pedagogy, teacher training pedagogy, curriculum development, instructional strategies.

Alliant International University–Sacramento, Shirley M. Hufstedler School of Education, TeachersCHOICE Preparation Programs, Sacramento, CA 95833. Offers MA, Credential. *Entrance requirements:* For master's, CBEST, CSET, interview; offer of employment as a teacher of record in a California school; minimum GPA of 3.0; 2 letters of recommendation. Electronic applications accepted. *Faculty research:* Innovative teacher education, educational leadership, cross-cultural education.

Alliant International University–San Diego, Shirley M. Hufstedler School of Education, Teacher Education Programs, San Diego, CA 92131. Offers preliminary single subject (Credential); professional clear multiple subject (Credential); professional clear single subject (Credential); teacher education (MA). *Program availability:* Part-time, evening/weekend. *Entrance requirements:* For degree, California Basic Educational Skills Test, minimum GPA of 2.5. Additional exam requirements/recommendations for international students: Required—TOEFL (minimum score 550 paper-based; 80 iBT), TWE (minimum score 5). Electronic applications accepted. *Faculty research:* Curriculum and instructional planning.

Alliant International University–San Francisco, Shirley M. Hufstedler School of Education, Teacher Education Programs, San Francisco, CA 94133. Offers auditory oral education (Certificate); CLAD (Certificate); education specialist: mild/moderate disabilities (Credential); preliminary multiple subject (Credential); preliminary single subject (Credential); professional clear multiple subject (Credential); professional clear single subject (Credential); special education (MA); teaching (MA); TESOL (Certificate). *Program availability:* Part-time, evening/weekend. *Degree requirements:* For master's, thesis. *Entrance requirements:* For degree, California Basic Educational Skills Test, minimum GPA of 2.5. Additional exam requirements/recommendations for international students: Required—TOEFL (minimum score 550 paper-based), TWE (minimum score 5). Electronic applications accepted. *Faculty research:* Curriculum development, first year teachers, cross-cultural issues in teaching, biliteracy.

Alvernia University, School of Graduate Studies, Program in Education, Reading, PA 19607-1799. Offers urban education (M Ed). *Program availability:* Part-time, evening/weekend. *Degree requirements:* For master's, thesis optional. *Entrance requirements:* For master's, GRE or MAT (alumni excluded). Electronic applications accepted.

Alverno College, School of Professional Studies - Education Division, Milwaukee, WI 53234-3922. Offers adaptive education (MA); administrative leadership (MA); adult education and organizational development (MA); adult educational and instructional design (MA); adult educational and instructional technology (MA); global connections in the humanities (MA); instructional leadership (MA); instructional technology for K-12 settings (MA); professional development (MA); reading education (MA); reading education with adaptive education (MA); science education (MA); special education (MA); teaching in alternative schools (MA). *Accreditation:* NCATE. *Program availability:* Part-time, evening/weekend. *Faculty:* 3 full-time (2 women), 23 part-time/adjunct (17 women). *Students:* 37 full-time (34 women), 68 part-time (65 women); includes 27 minority (16 Black or African American, non-Hispanic/Latino; 1 American Indian or Alaska Native, non-Hispanic/Latino; 1 Asian, non-Hispanic/Latino; 7 Hispanic/Latino; 2 Two or more races, non-Hispanic/Latino). Average age 35. 67 applicants, 100% accepted, 51 enrolled. In 2017, 68 master's awarded. *Degree requirements:* For master's, presentation/defense of proposal, conference presentation of inquiry projects. *Entrance requirements:* For master's, bachelor's degree in related field, communication samples from work setting, 3 letters of recommendation. Additional exam requirements/recommendations for international students: Required—TOEFL. *Application deadline:* For fall admission, 7/15 priority date for domestic and international students; for spring admission, 12/15 priority date for domestic and international students. Applications are processed on a rolling basis. Application fee: $0. Electronic applications accepted. *Expenses:* Contact institution. *Financial support:* Federal Work-Study and scholarships/grants available. Support available to part-time students. Financial award applicants required to submit FAFSA. *Faculty research:* Student self-assessment, self-reflection, integration of curriculum, identifying needs of students in strategic situations and designing appropriate classroom strategies. *Unit head:* Dr. Patricia Luebke, Dean, School of Professional Studies, 414-382-6368, Fax: 414-382-6354, E-mail: patricia.luebke@alverno.edu. *Application contact:* Katie Kipp, Graduate Admissions Counselor, 414-382-6045, Fax: 414-382-6354, E-mail: katie.kipp@alverno.edu.

American College of Education, Graduate Programs, Indianapolis, IN 46204. Offers curriculum and instruction (M Ed), including bilingual, ESL; educational leadership (M Ed); educational technology (M Ed).

American InterContinental University Online, Program in Education, Schaumburg, IL 60173. Offers curriculum and instruction (M Ed); educational assessment and evaluation (M Ed); instructional technology (M Ed); leadership of educational organizations (M Ed). *Accreditation:* TEAC. *Program availability:* Evening/weekend, online learning. *Entrance requirements:* Additional exam requirements/recommendations for international students: Required—TOEFL (minimum score 550 paper-based). Electronic applications accepted.

American International College, School of Education, Low Residency Programs, Springfield, MA 01109-3189. Offers counseling psychology (MA); educational leadership and supervision (Ed D); professional counseling and supervision (Ed D); teaching and learning (Ed D). *Program availability:* Evening/weekend. *Faculty:* 2 full-time (1 woman), 4 part-time/adjunct (all women). *Students:* 117 full-time (90 women); includes 32 minority (22 Black or African American, non-Hispanic/Latino; 1 Asian, non-Hispanic/Latino; 7 Hispanic/Latino; 2 Two or more races, non-Hispanic/Latino). Average age 40. 35 applicants, 86% accepted, 20 enrolled. In 2017, 8 master's, 12 doctorates awarded. *Degree requirements:* For doctorate, thesis/dissertation. *Entrance requirements:* For master's, minimum undergraduate GPA of 3.0, 2 letters of recommendation, personal goal statement, official transcript of all academic work (graduate and undergraduate); for doctorate, minimum master's GPA of 3.0, 3 letters of recommendation, personal goal statement/essay (6-8 pages), official transcript of all academic work (graduate and undergraduate). Additional exam requirements/recommendations for international students: Required—TOEFL. *Application deadline:* For fall admission, 8/15 for domestic and international students; for spring admission, 1/3 for domestic and international students; for summer admission, 5/15 for domestic and international students. Applications are processed on a rolling basis. Application fee: $50. *Expenses:* $6,515 per trimester (for EdD); $505 per credit (for MA); $30 per term registration fee; $100 one-time graduation fee. *Faculty research:* Educational leadership, curriculum, program evaluation, educational policy. *Unit head:* Dr. Nicholas Young, Dean, Low Residency Programs, 413-205-1726, E-mail: nicholas.young@aic.edu. *Application contact:* Kerry Barnes, Director of Graduate Admissions, 413-205-3703, Fax: 413-205-3051, E-mail: kerry.barnes@aic.edu.

American Jewish University, Graduate School of Education, Program in Education, Bel Air, CA 90077-1599. Offers MA Ed. *Degree requirements:* For master's, one foreign language. *Entrance requirements:* For master's, GRE General Test, interview, minimum GPA of 3.0. Additional exam requirements/recommendations for international students: Required—TOEFL. *Faculty research:* Philosophy of education, curriculum development, teacher training.

American Jewish University, Graduate School of Education, Program in Education for Working Professionals, Bel Air, CA 90077-1599. Offers MA Ed. *Degree requirements:* For master's, comprehensive exam, internships. *Entrance requirements:* For master's, GRE General Test, interview. Additional exam requirements/recommendations for international students: Required—TOEFL.

American University, School of Education, Washington, DC 20016-8030. Offers M Ed, MA, MAT, Certificate, M Ed/MPA, M Ed/MPP, MAT/MA. *Accreditation:* NCATE. *Program availability:* Part-time, evening/weekend. *Faculty:* 14 full-time (11 women), 56 part-time/

adjunct (37 women). *Students:* 58 full-time (48 women), 122 part-time (94 women); includes 78 minority (53 Black or African American, non-Hispanic/Latino; 8 Asian, non-Hispanic/Latino; 13 Hispanic/Latino; 4 Two or more races, non-Hispanic/Latino), 2 international. Average age 29. 213 applicants, 99% accepted, 180 enrolled. In 2017, 101 master's, 6 other advanced degrees awarded. *Degree requirements:* For master's, comprehensive exam, thesis or alternative. *Entrance requirements:* For master's, bachelor's degree, statement of purpose, transcripts, 2 letters of recommendation. Additional exam requirements/recommendations for international students: Required—TOEFL (minimum score 100 iBT). *Application deadline:* For fall admission, 2/1 priority date for domestic students. Applications are processed on a rolling basis. Application fee: $55. Electronic applications accepted. *Expenses:* Contact institution. *Financial support:* Research assistantships, teaching assistantships, institutionally sponsored loans, scholarships/grants, and unspecified assistantships available. Financial award application deadline: 2/1; financial award applicants required to submit FAFSA. *Unit head:* Cheryl Holcomb-McCoy, Dean, 202-885-3720, E-mail: educate@american.edu. *Application contact:* Graziella Covello, Graduate Program Coordinator, 202-885-3761, E-mail: gcovello@american.edu.
Website: https://www.american.edu/cas/education/

The American University in Cairo, Graduate School of Education, Cairo, Egypt. Offers educational leadership (MA); international and comparative education (MA). *Program availability:* Part-time, evening/weekend. *Faculty:* 9 full-time (6 women). *Students:* 6 full-time (4 women), 77 part-time (65 women). Average age 33. 40 applicants, 48% accepted, 11 enrolled. In 2017, 24 master's awarded. *Degree requirements:* For master's, thesis. *Entrance requirements:* Additional exam requirements/recommendations for international students: Required—TOEFL (minimum score 450 paper-based; 45 iBT), IELTS (minimum score 5). *Application deadline:* For fall admission, 2/1 priority date for domestic and international students; for spring admission, 10/15 priority date for domestic and international students. Applications are processed on a rolling basis. Application fee: $85. Electronic applications accepted. *Financial support:* Fellowships with partial tuition reimbursements, teaching assistantships, career-related internships or fieldwork, scholarships/grants, tuition waivers (partial), and unspecified assistantships available. Financial award application deadline: 3/10. *Faculty research:* Educational reform. *Unit head:* Dr. Ted Purinton, Dean, 20-2-2615-1490, E-mail: tedpurinton@aucegypt.edu. *Application contact:* Maha Hegazi, Director for Graduate Admissions, 20-2-2615-1462, E-mail: mahahegazi@aucegypt.edu.
Website: http://www.aucegypt.edu/GSE/Pages/default.aspx

The American University in Dubai, Graduate Programs, Dubai, United Arab Emirates. Offers construction management (MS); education (M Ed); finance (MBA); generalist (MBA); marketing (MBA). *Program availability:* Part-time, evening/weekend. *Degree requirements:* For master's, thesis optional. *Entrance requirements:* For master's, GMAT (for MBA); GRE (for M Ed and MS), minimum undergraduate GPA of 3.0, official transcripts, two reference forms, curriculum vitae/resume, statement of career objectives, work experience. Additional exam requirements/recommendations for international students: Required—TOEFL (minimum score 550 paper-based; 79 iBT). Electronic applications accepted.

American University of Beirut, Graduate Programs, Faculty of Arts and Sciences, 1107 2020, Lebanon. Offers anthropology (MA); Arab and Middle Eastern history (PhD); Arabic language and literature (MA, PhD); archaeology (MA); art history and curating (MA); biology (MS); cell and molecular biology (PhD); chemistry (MS); clinical psychology (MA); computational sciences (MS); computer science (MS); economics (MA); education (MA), including administration and policy studies, elementary education, mathematics education, psychology school guidance, psychology test and measurements, science education, teaching English as a foreign language; English language (MA); English literature (MA); environmental policy planning (MS); financial economics (MAFE); general psychology (MA); geology (MS); history (MA); Islamic studies (MA); mathematics (MS); media studies (MA); Middle East studies (MA); philosophy (MA); physics (MS); political studies (MA); public administration (MA); public policy and international affairs (MA); sociology (MA); theoretical physics (PhD). *Program availability:* Part-time. *Faculty:* 108 full-time (36 women), 5 part-time/adjunct (4 women). *Students:* 251 full-time (180 women), 233 part-time (172 women). Average age 26. 425 applicants, 65% accepted, 121 enrolled. In 2017, 47 master's, 2 doctorates awarded. *Degree requirements:* For master's, one foreign language, comprehensive exam, thesis (for some programs), project; for doctorate, one foreign language, comprehensive exam, thesis/dissertation. *Entrance requirements:* For master's, GRE General Test (for some programs); for doctorate, GRE General Test (GRE Subject Test for theoretical physics). Additional exam requirements/recommendations for international students: Required—TOEFL (minimum score 583 paper-based; 97 iBT), IELTS (minimum score 7). *Application deadline:* For fall admission, 2/8 for domestic students; for spring admission, 11/3 for domestic students. Application fee: $50. Electronic applications accepted. *Expenses:* Contact institution. *Financial support:* In 2017–18, 29 fellowships, 40 research assistantships were awarded; teaching assistantships, scholarships/grants, tuition waivers (full and partial), and unspecified assistantships also available. Financial award application deadline: 4/4. *Unit head:* Dr. Nadia Maria El Cheikh, Dean, Faculty of Arts and Sciences, 961-1-374374 Ext. 3800, Fax: 961-1-744461, E-mail: nmcheikh@aub.edu.lb. *Application contact:* Rima Rassi, Graduate Studies Officer, 961-1-350000 Ext. 3833, Fax: 961-1-744461, E-mail: rr46@aub.edu.lb.
Website: http://www.aub.edu.lb/fas/pages/default.aspx

American University of Puerto Rico, Program in Education, Bayamon, PR 00960-2037. Offers art education (M Ed); elementary education 4-6 (M Ed); elementary education K-3 (M Ed); general science education (M Ed); physical education (M Ed); special education (M Ed). *Program availability:* Part-time, evening/weekend. *Faculty:* 17 part-time/adjunct (7 women). *Students:* 22 full-time (18 women), 54 part-time (42 women); all minorities (all Hispanic/Latino). Average age 33. 22 applicants, 86% accepted, 19 enrolled. In 2017, 53 master's awarded. *Entrance requirements:* For master's, EXADEP, GRE, or MAT, 2 letters of recommendation, minimum GPA of 2.5. *Application deadline:* For fall admission, 8/1 for domestic students; for winter admission, 10/18 for domestic students; for spring admission, 3/15 for domestic students. Applications are processed on a rolling basis. Application fee: $25. Tuition and fees vary according to course load and degree level. *Financial support:* In 2017–18, 79 students received support, including 76 fellowships (averaging $400 per year), 55 teaching assistantships (averaging $1,741 per year). Financial award applicants required to submit FAFSA. *Unit head:* Prof. Bolivar Ramirez-Carlo, III, Dean of Faculty, 787-620-2040 Ext. 2010, Fax: 787-620-2958, E-mail: bramirez@aupr.edu. *Application contact:* Keren I. Llanos-Figueroa, Information Contact, 787-620-2040 Ext. 2021, Fax: 787-785-7377, E-mail: oficnaadmisiones@aupr.edu.

Anderson University, College of Education, Anderson, SC 29621-4035. Offers administration and supervision (M Ed); education (M Ed); elementary education (MAT). *Accreditation:* NCATE. *Program availability:* 100% online. *Expenses:* Contact institution. *Financial support:* Tuition waivers available. Financial award application deadline: 3/1; financial award applicants required to submit FAFSA. *Unit head:* Dr. Mark Butler, Dean, 864-231-2042. *Application contact:* Mallory Knight, Graduate Admission Counselor, 864-231-2182, Fax: 864-231-2115, E-mail: malloryknight@andersonuniversity.edu.
Website: https://www.andersonuniversity.edu/education

Education—General

Anderson University, School of Education, Anderson, IN 46012-3495. Offers M Ed. *Accreditation:* NCATE.

Andrews University, School of Graduate Studies, School of Education, Berrien Springs, MI 49104. Offers MA, MAT, MS, Ed D, PhD, Ed S. *Accreditation:* NCATE. *Program availability:* Part-time. *Faculty:* 21 full-time (9 women), 5 part-time/adjunct (2 women). *Students:* 131 full-time (84 women), 61 part-time (36 women); includes 64 minority (35 Black or African American, non-Hispanic/Latino; 4 Asian, non-Hispanic/Latino; 20 Hispanic/Latino; 5 Two or more races, non-Hispanic/Latino), 56 international. Average age 41. 166 applicants, 51% accepted, 42 enrolled. In 2017, 36 master's, 16 doctorates, 12 other advanced degrees awarded. Terminal master's awarded for partial completion of doctoral program. *Degree requirements:* For doctorate, thesis/dissertation. *Entrance requirements:* For master's, GRE Subject Test. Additional exam requirements/recommendations for international students: Required—TOEFL (minimum score 550 paper-based). *Application deadline:* Applications are processed on a rolling basis. Application fee: $40. *Financial support:* Fellowships, research assistantships, teaching assistantships, career-related internships or fieldwork, Federal Work-Study, institutionally sponsored loans, and tuition waivers (partial) available. Support available to part-time students. *Faculty research:* Church planting, bilingual education, leadership development, exercise education. *Unit head:* Dr. Robson Marinho, Dean, 269-471-3464. *Application contact:* Justina Clayburn, Supervisor of Graduate Admission, 800-253-2874, Fax: 269-471-6321, E-mail: graduate@andrews.edu.

Anna Maria College, Graduate Division, Program in Education, Paxton, MA 01612. Offers early childhood education (M Ed); education (CAGS); elementary education (M Ed); English language arts (M Ed); visual arts (M Ed). *Program availability:* Part-time, evening/weekend. *Entrance requirements:* For master's, bachelor's degree in liberal arts or sciences, minimum GPA of 3.0. Additional exam requirements/recommendations for international students: Required—TOEFL (minimum score 500 paper-based). Electronic applications accepted.

Antioch University Los Angeles, Program in Education, Culver City, CA 90230. Offers MA. *Program availability:* Evening/weekend. *Faculty:* 3. *Students:* 44 full-time (32 women), 1 (woman) part-time; includes 28 minority (8 Black or African American, non-Hispanic/Latino; 1 Asian, non-Hispanic/Latino; 14 Hispanic/Latino; 1 Native Hawaiian or other Pacific Islander, non-Hispanic/Latino; 4 Two or more races, non-Hispanic/Latino). Average age 34. 24 applicants, 79% accepted. *Entrance requirements:* Additional exam requirements/recommendations for international students: Required—TOEFL. *Application deadline:* For fall admission, 5/4 priority date for domestic students. Applications are processed on a rolling basis. Application fee: $60. *Financial support:* Career-related internships or fieldwork, Federal Work-Study, and scholarships/grants available. Support available to part-time students. Financial award application deadline: 3/24; financial award applicants required to submit CSS PROFILE or FAFSA. *Unit head:* Dr. Cheryl Armon, Head, 310-578-1080 Ext. 233, Fax: 310-822-4824, E-mail: cheryl_armon@antiochla.edu. *Application contact:* Information Contact, 310-578-1090, Fax: 310-822-4824, E-mail: admissions@antiochla.edu.

Antioch University New England, Graduate School, Department of Education, Keene, NH 03431-3552. Offers integrated learning (M Ed), including elementary and early childhood education, elementary education (M Ed, Certificate); teaching (M Ed, PMC), including foundations of education (M Ed), principal certification (PMC); Waldorf teacher training (M Ed, Certificate), including elementary education, foundations of education (M Ed). *Degree requirements:* For master's, thesis (for some programs), internship. *Entrance requirements:* Additional exam requirements/recommendations for international students: Required—TOEFL (minimum score 550 paper-based). Electronic applications accepted. *Expenses:* Contact institution. *Faculty research:* Classroom and school restructuring, problem-based learning, Waldorf collaborative leadership, ecological literacy.

Antioch University Santa Barbara, Program in Education/Teacher Credentialing, Santa Barbara, CA 93101-1581. Offers M Ed, MA. *Program availability:* Part-time. *Entrance requirements:* Additional exam requirements/recommendations for international students: Required—TOEFL (minimum score 550 paper-based). Electronic applications accepted.

Antioch University Seattle, Program in Education, Seattle, WA 98121. Offers adult education (MA); drama therapy (MA); individualized studies (MA); leadership in edible education (MA); teaching (MAT); urban environmental education (MA). *Program availability:* Part-time, evening/weekend. *Students:* 58 full-time (40 women), 15 part-time (12 women); includes 12 minority (2 Asian, non-Hispanic/Latino; 6 Hispanic/Latino; 4 Two or more races, non-Hispanic/Latino). Average age 36. *Degree requirements:* For master's, comprehensive exam (for some programs), thesis. *Entrance requirements:* For master's, WEST-B, WEST-E, current resume, transcripts of undergraduate degree and coursework (or for highest degree completed), two letters of recommendation, proof of fingerprinting and background check, moral character with fitness statement of understanding, documentation of 40 hours' experience in school classroom(s). *Application deadline:* Applications are processed on a rolling basis. *Expenses:* Contact institution. *Financial support:* Research assistantships, Federal Work-Study, scholarships/grants, and unspecified assistantships available. Financial award application deadline: 6/15. *Faculty research:* Visual thinking and science education, K-8 equity and engaged pedagogy in science education, K-12 inquiry-based mathematics education, education in prisons and other institutions of confinement. *Unit head:* Ed Mikel, Interim Dean, 206-268-4617, E-mail: emikel@antioch.edu. *Application contact:* Eileen Knight, Recruitment and Admissions Director, 206-268-4200, E-mail: eknight@antioch.edu.
Website: https://www.antioch.edu/seattle/degrees-programs/education-degrees/

Aquinas College, School of Education, Nashville, TN 37205-2005. Offers elementary education (MAT); secondary education (MAT); teaching and learning (M Ed).

Aquinas College, School of Education, Grand Rapids, MI 49506. Offers M Ed, MAT. *Accreditation:* TEAC. *Program availability:* Part-time, evening/weekend. *Students:* 4 full-time (1 woman), 104 part-time (92 women); includes 11 minority (2 Black or African American, non-Hispanic/Latino; 2 Asian, non-Hispanic/Latino; 6 Hispanic/Latino; 1 Two or more races, non-Hispanic/Latino). *Degree requirements:* For master's, teaching project; action research. *Entrance requirements:* For master's, Michigan Basic Skills Test, minimum undergraduate GPA of 3.0, teaching certificate. Additional exam requirements/recommendations for international students: Required—TOEFL (minimum score 550 paper-based). *Application deadline:* Applications are processed on a rolling basis. Application fee: $0. *Expenses:* Contact institution. *Financial support:* Scholarships/grants available. Support available to part-time students. Financial award application deadline: 3/15. *Unit head:* Dr. Susan English, Dean, 616-632-2800, Fax: 616-732-4465, E-mail: englisus@aquinas.edu. *Application contact:* Administrative Assistant, 616-632-2440.
Website: http://www.aquinas.edu/education/

Arcadia University, School of Education, Glenside, PA 19038-3295. Offers art education (M Ed); computer education (CAS); curriculum (CAS); curriculum studies (M Ed); early childhood education (M Ed), including individualized, master teacher, research in child development; educational leadership (M Ed, Ed D, CAS); elementary education (M Ed); English education (MA Ed); environmental education (MA Ed);

instructional technology (M Ed); language arts (M Ed); library science (M Ed); mathematics education (M Ed, MA Ed); music education (MA Ed); psychology (MA Ed); reading (M Ed, CAS); science education (M Ed, CAS); secondary education (M Ed, CAS); special education (M Ed, Ed D, CAS); theater arts (MA Ed); written communication (MA Ed). *Accreditation:* NASAD. *Program availability:* Part-time, evening/weekend, online learning. Electronic applications accepted. *Expenses:* Contact institution.

Argosy University, Atlanta, College of Education, Atlanta, GA 30328. Offers educational leadership (MAEd, Ed D, Ed S), including higher education administration (Ed D), K-12 education (Ed D); teaching and learning (MAEd, Ed D, Ed S), including education technology (Ed D), higher education (Ed D), K-12 education (Ed D).

Argosy University, Chicago, College of Education, Chicago, IL 60601. Offers adult education and training (MA Ed); community college executive leadership (Ed D); educational leadership (MA Ed, Ed D, Ed S), including district leadership (Ed D), higher education administration (Ed D), K-12 education (Ed D); instructional leadership (Ed D, Ed S), including higher education (Ed D), K-12 education (Ed D). *Program availability:* Online learning.

Argosy University, Hawai`i, College of Education, Honolulu, HI 96813. Offers adult education and training (MAEd); educational leadership (Ed D), including higher education administration, K-12 education; instructional leadership (Ed D), including higher education, K-12 education; school psychology (MA).

Argosy University, Los Angeles, College of Education, Los Angeles, CA 90045. Offers community college executive leadership (Ed D); educational leadership (MA Ed, Ed D), including higher education administration (Ed D), K-12 education (Ed D); instructional leadership (MA Ed, Ed D), including higher education (Ed D), K-12 education (Ed D), multiple subject teacher preparation (MA Ed), single subject teacher preparation (MA Ed).

Argosy University, Northern Virginia, College of Education, Arlington, VA 22209. Offers community college executive leadership (Ed D); educational leadership (MA Ed, Ed D, Ed S), including higher education administration (Ed D), K-12 education (Ed D); instructional leadership (MA Ed, Ed D, Ed S), including higher education (Ed D), K-12 education (Ed D).

Argosy University, Orange County, College of Education, Orange, CA 92868. Offers community college executive leadership (Ed D); educational leadership (MA Ed, Ed D), including higher education administration (Ed D), K-12 education (Ed D); instructional leadership (MA Ed, Ed D), including education technology (Ed D), higher education (Ed D), K-12 education (Ed D), multiple subject teacher preparation (MA Ed), single subject teacher preparation (MA Ed).

Argosy University, Phoenix, College of Education, Phoenix, AZ 85021. Offers adult education and training (MA Ed); advanced educational administration (Ed D, Ed S); community college executive leadership (Ed D); educational administration (MA Ed); educational leadership (MA Ed, Ed D, Ed S), including education technology (Ed D), higher education administration (Ed D), K-12 education (Ed D); higher and postsecondary education (MA Ed); initial educational administration (Ed D, Ed S); school psychology (MA); teaching and learning (MA Ed, Ed D, Ed S), including education technology (Ed D), higher education (Ed D), K-12 education (Ed D).

Argosy University, Seattle, College of Education, Seattle, WA 98121. Offers adult education and training (MA Ed); community college executive leadership (Ed D); educational leadership (MA Ed, Ed D), including higher education administration (Ed D), K-12 education (Ed D); higher and postsecondary education (MA Ed); instructional leadership (MA Ed, Ed D), including education technology (Ed D), higher education (Ed D), K-12 education (Ed D).

Argosy University, Tampa, College of Education, Tampa, FL 33607. Offers community college executive leadership (Ed D); educational leadership (MA Ed, Ed D, Ed S), including higher education administration (Ed D), K-12 education (Ed D); school counseling (MA); teaching and learning (MA Ed, Ed D, Ed S), including higher education (Ed D), K-12 education (Ed D).

Argosy University, Twin Cities, College of Education, Eagan, MN 55121. Offers advanced educational administration (Ed D, Ed S); educational leadership (MA Ed, Ed D, Ed S), including higher education administration (Ed D), K-12 education (Ed D); higher and postsecondary education (MA Ed); initial educational administration (Ed D, Ed S); instructional leadership (MA Ed, Ed D, Ed S), including education technology (Ed D), higher education (Ed D), K-12 education (Ed D).

Arizona State University at the Tempe campus, Mary Lou Fulton Teachers College, Phoenix, AZ 85069. Offers M Ed, MA, MC, MPE, Ed D, PhD, Graduate Certificate. *Program availability:* Part-time, evening/weekend, online learning. *Degree requirements:* For master's, comprehensive exam (for some programs), thesis (for some programs), interactive Program of Study (iPOS) submitted before completing 50 percent of required credit hours; for doctorate, comprehensive exam, thesis/dissertation, interactive Program of Study (iPOS) submitted before completing 50 percent of required credit hours. *Entrance requirements:* For master's and doctorate, GRE General Test or GMAT, minimum GPA of 3.0 or equivalent in last 2 years of work leading to bachelor's degree. Additional exam requirements/recommendations for international students: Required—TOEFL, IELTS, or PTE. Electronic applications accepted. *Expenses:* Contact institution.

Arkansas State University, Graduate School, College of Education and Behavioral Science, State University, AR 72467. Offers MAT, MRC, MS, MSE, Ed D, Ed S, Graduate Certificate, SCCT. *Accreditation:* NCATE. *Program availability:* Part-time, online learning. *Degree requirements:* For master's and other advanced degree, comprehensive exam, thesis or alternative; for doctorate, comprehensive exam, thesis/dissertation. *Entrance requirements:* For master's, GRE General Test or MAT, appropriate bachelor's degree, interview, letters of reference, official transcripts, immunization records; for doctorate, GRE General Test or MAT, interview, master's degree, letters of reference, official transcript, personal statement, immunization records, writing sample; for other advanced degree, GRE General Test, MAT, interview, master's degree, letters of reference, official transcript, 3 years of teaching experience, teaching license, immunization records. Additional exam requirements/recommendations for international students: Required—TOEFL (minimum score 550 paper-based; 79 iBT), IELTS (minimum score 6), PTE (minimum score 56). Electronic applications accepted.

Arkansas Tech University, College of Education, Russellville, AR 72801. Offers college student personnel (MS); educational leadership (M Ed, Ed S); instructional technology (M Ed); school counseling and leadership (M Ed); school leadership (Ed D); special education K-12 (M Ed); strength and conditioning studies (MS); teaching (MAT); teaching, learning, and leadership (M Ed). *Accreditation:* NCATE. *Program availability:* Part-time, evening/weekend, 100% online, blended/hybrid learning. *Students:* 80 full-time (45 women), 433 part-time (328 women); includes 114 minority (81 Black or African American, non-Hispanic/Latino; 4 American Indian or Alaska Native, non-Hispanic/Latino; 1 Asian, non-Hispanic/Latino; 13 Hispanic/Latino; 15 Two or more races, non-Hispanic/Latino), 2 international. Average age 34. In 2017, 132 master's, 8 doctorates, 3 other advanced degrees awarded. *Degree requirements:* For master's, comprehensive exam, thesis optional, action research project; for doctorate, thesis/dissertation. *Entrance requirements:*

Additional exam requirements/recommendations for international students: Required—TOEFL (minimum score 550 paper-based; 79 iBT), IELTS (minimum score 6.5), PTE (minimum score 58). *Application deadline:* For fall admission, 3/1 priority date for domestic students, 5/1 priority date for international students; for spring admission, 10/1 priority date for domestic and international students. Applications are processed on a rolling basis. Application fee: $40 ($90 for international students). Electronic applications accepted. *Expenses:* Tuition, state resident: full-time $6816; part-time $284 per credit hour. Tuition, nonresident: full-time $13,632; part-time $568 per credit hour. *Required fees:* $420 per semester. Tuition and fees vary according to course load. *Financial support:* In 2017–18, research assistantships with full and partial tuition reimbursements (averaging $4,800 per year), teaching assistantships with full and partial tuition reimbursements (averaging $4,800 per year) were awarded; career-related internships or fieldwork, Federal Work-Study, scholarships/grants, health care benefits, and unspecified assistantships also available. Support available to part-time students. Financial award application deadline: 4/15; financial award applicants required to submit FAFSA. *Unit head:* Dr. Mary Gunter, Dean, 479-964-3217, E-mail: mgunter@atu.edu. Website: http://www.atu.edu/education/

Arlington Baptist University, Program in Education, Arlington, TX 76012-3425. Offers curriculum and instruction (M Ed); educational leadership (M Ed). *Degree requirements:* For master's, professional portfolio; internship (for educational leadership). *Entrance requirements:* For master's, bachelor's degree from accredited college or university with minimum GPA of 3.0, minimum of 12 hours in Bible; minimum of three years' classroom teaching experience in an accredited K-12 public or private school (for educational leadership only).

Ashland University, Dwight Schar College of Education, Ashland, OH 44805-3702. Offers M Ed, Ed D. *Accreditation:* NCATE. *Program availability:* Part-time. *Degree requirements:* For master's, thesis optional, capstone project; for doctorate, comprehensive exam, thesis/dissertation. *Entrance requirements:* For master's, minimum GPA of 2.75; for doctorate, master's degree, minimum GPA of 3.3, writing sample, letters of recommendation. Additional exam requirements/recommendations for international students: Recommended—TOEFL, IELTS, TSE. *Application deadline:* Applications are processed on a rolling basis. Application fee: $30. Electronic applications accepted. *Expenses: Tuition:* Full-time $9621; part-time $4707 per credit hour. *Required fees:* $15 per semester. *Financial support:* Teaching assistantships with partial tuition reimbursements and scholarships/grants available. *Faculty research:* Teacher performance, administrative performance, collaborative learning groups, talent development, environmental education. *Unit head:* Dr. Donna Breault, Dean, 419-289-5377, E-mail: dbreault@ashland.edu. *Application contact:* Bernie Bannin, Director, Graduate, Online and Adult Admissions, 419-289-5291, E-mail: grad-admissions@ashland.edu.

Athabasca University, Centre for Distance Education, Athabasca, AB T9S 3A3, Canada. Offers distance education (MDE, Ed D); distance education technology (Advanced Diploma). *Program availability:* Part-time, online learning. *Degree requirements:* For master's, thesis optional. *Entrance requirements:* For master's, 3- or 4-year baccalaureate degree. Electronic applications accepted. *Expenses:* Contact institution. *Faculty research:* Role development, interaction, educational technology, and communities of practice in distance education; instructional design.

Athabasca University, Centre for Interdisciplinary Studies, Athabasca, AB T9S 3A3, Canada. Offers adult education (MA); community studies (MA); cultural studies (MA); educational studies (MA); global change (MA); heritage resource management (Postbaccalaureate Certificate); legislative drafting (Postbaccalaureate Certificate); work, organization, and leadership (MA). *Program availability:* Part-time, evening/weekend, online learning. *Degree requirements:* For master's, project. *Entrance requirements:* Additional exam requirements/recommendations for international students: Required—TOEFL (minimum score 560 paper-based). Electronic applications accepted. *Faculty research:* Women's history, literature and culture studies, sustainable development, labor and education.

Auburn University, Graduate School, College of Education, Auburn University, AL 36849. Offers M Ed, MS, Ed D, PhD, Ed S, Graduate Certificate. *Accreditation:* NCATE. *Program availability:* Part-time. *Faculty:* 99 full-time (63 women), 30 part-time/adjunct (20 women). *Students:* 501 full-time (357 women), 526 part-time (373 women); includes 258 minority (191 Black or African American, non-Hispanic/Latino; 3 American Indian or Alaska Native, non-Hispanic/Latino; 7 Asian, non-Hispanic/Latino; 36 Hispanic/Latino; 2 Native Hawaiian or other Pacific Islander, non-Hispanic/Latino; 19 Two or more races, non-Hispanic/Latino), 47 international. Average age 32. 800 applicants, 61% accepted, 327 enrolled. In 2017, 291 master's, 80 doctorates, 75 other advanced degrees awarded. *Degree requirements:* For master's, thesis (for some programs); for doctorate, thesis/dissertation. *Entrance requirements:* For master's, doctorate, and other advanced degree, GRE General Test. Application fee: $50 ($60 for international students). Electronic applications accepted. *Expenses:* Tuition, state resident: full-time $10,974; part-time $519 per credit hour. Tuition, nonresident: full-time $29,658; part-time $1557 per credit hour. *Required fees:* $816 per semester. Tuition and fees vary according to degree level and program. *Financial support:* Fellowships, research assistantships, teaching assistantships, career-related internships or fieldwork, and Federal Work-Study available. Support available to part-time students. Financial award application deadline: 3/15; financial award applicants required to submit FAFSA. *Faculty research:* Dropout phenomena, high school students and substance use and abuse. *Unit head:* Dr. Betty Lou Whitford, Dean, 334-844-4446. *Application contact:* Dr. George Flowers, Dean of the Graduate School, 334-844-2125. Website: http://www.education.auburn.edu/

Auburn University at Montgomery, College of Education, Montgomery, AL 36124-4023. Offers M Ed, Ed S. *Accreditation:* NCATE. *Program availability:* Part-time, evening/weekend. *Faculty:* 26 full-time (15 women), 11 part-time/adjunct (all women). *Students:* 82 full-time (66 women), 156 part-time (127 women); includes 91 minority (87 Black or African American, non-Hispanic/Latino; 4 Hispanic/Latino), 2 international. Average age 33. 198 applicants, 71% accepted, 73 enrolled. In 2017, 102 master's awarded. *Degree requirements:* For master's and Ed S, comprehensive exam. *Entrance requirements:* For master's, GRE General Test or MAT, BS in teaching, certification; for Ed S, GRE General Test or MAT, certification. Additional exam requirements/recommendations for international students: Recommended—TOEFL (minimum score 500 paper-based; 61 iBT), IELTS (minimum score 5.5), TSE (minimum score 44). *Application deadline:* For fall admission, 7/1 for international students; for spring admission, 11/1 for international students; for summer admission, 4/15 for international students. Applications are processed on a rolling basis. Application fee: $25. Electronic applications accepted. *Expenses:* Tuition, state resident: full-time $6930; part-time $385 per credit hour. Tuition, nonresident: full-time $15,588; part-time $866 per credit hour. *Required fees:* $640. *Financial support:* Teaching assistantships, career-related internships or fieldwork, and scholarships/grants available. Support available to part-time students. Financial award application deadline: 3/1; financial award applicants required to submit FAFSA. *Unit head:* Dr. Sheila Austin, Dean, 334-244-3425, Fax: 334-244-3102, E-mail: saustin1@aum.edu. *Application contact:* Dr. Rhonda Morton, Associate Dean/Graduate Coordinator, 334-224-3287, Fax: 334-244-3978, E-mail: rmorton@aum.edu. Website: http://www.education.aum.edu/

Augsburg University, Program in Education, Minneapolis, MN 55454-1351. Offers MAE. *Accreditation:* NCATE. *Program availability:* Part-time, evening/weekend. *Degree requirements:* For master's, comprehensive exam, final project. *Entrance requirements:* For master's, minimum GPA of 3.0. Additional exam requirements/recommendations for international students: Required—TOEFL (minimum score 600 paper-based). Electronic applications accepted.

Augustana University, MA in Education Program, Sioux Falls, SD 57197. Offers instructional strategies (MA); reading (MA); special populations (MA); STEM (MA); technology (MA). *Accreditation:* NCATE. *Program availability:* Part-time-only, evening/weekend, online only, 100% online. *Faculty:* 7 full-time (5 women), 6 part-time/adjunct (5 women). *Students:* 288 part-time (250 women); includes 20 minority (2 Black or African American, non-Hispanic/Latino; 2 American Indian or Alaska Native, non-Hispanic/Latino; 1 Asian, non-Hispanic/Latino; 11 Hispanic/Latino; 1 Native Hawaiian or other Pacific Islander, non-Hispanic/Latino; 3 Two or more races, non-Hispanic/Latino), 3 international. Average age 32. 47 applicants, 77% accepted, 35 enrolled. In 2017, 84 master's awarded. *Degree requirements:* For master's, thesis. *Entrance requirements:* For master's, appropriate bachelor's degree, minimum GPA of 3.0, teaching certificate. Additional exam requirements/recommendations for international students: Required—TOEFL (minimum score 550 paper-based). *Application deadline:* For fall admission, 8/1 for domestic and international students; for spring admission, 11/1 for domestic and international students; for summer admission, 4/1 for domestic and international students. Applications are processed on a rolling basis. Application fee: $60. Electronic applications accepted. *Expenses:* Contact institution. *Financial support:* Application deadline: 3/1; applicants required to submit FAFSA. *Faculty research:* Multicultural education, education of students with autism, well-being in school settings, factors that predict academic hopefulness. *Unit head:* Dr. Laurie Daily, Chair, 605-274-5211, E-mail: laurie.daily@augie.edu. *Application contact:* Julia Paulich, Graduate Coordinator, 605-274-4043, Fax: 605-274-4450, E-mail: graduate@augie.edu. Website: http://www.augie.edu/master-arts-education

Augusta University, College of Education, Augusta, GA 30912. Offers M Ed, MAT, Ed D, Ed S. *Accreditation:* NCATE. *Program availability:* Part-time, evening/weekend. *Entrance requirements:* For master's, GRE, MAT, minimum GPA of 2.5.

Aurora University, School of Education and Human Performance, Aurora, IL 60506-4892. Offers applied behavioral analysis (MS); bilingual-ESL education (MA); educational leadership with principal endorsement (MA); educational technology (MA); leadership in adult learning higher education (Ed D); leadership in curriculum and instruction (Ed D); leadership in educational administration (Ed D); reading instruction (MA); special education (MA). *Accreditation:* NCATE. *Program availability:* Part-time, evening/weekend. *Faculty:* 15 full-time (8 women), 39 part-time/adjunct (20 women). *Students:* 421 full-time (299 women), 142 part-time (89 women); includes 90 minority (25 Black or African American, non-Hispanic/Latino; 7 Asian, non-Hispanic/Latino; 50 Hispanic/Latino; 2 Native Hawaiian or other Pacific Islander, non-Hispanic/Latino; 6 Two or more races, non-Hispanic/Latino). Average age 37. 169 applicants, 95% accepted, 59 enrolled. In 2017, 175 master's, 36 doctorates awarded. *Degree requirements:* For master's, student teaching; for doctorate, comprehensive exam, thesis/dissertation. *Entrance requirements:* For master's, 2 years of teaching experience, valid teaching certificate, resume; for doctorate, appropriate master's degree, two references, curriculum vitae, personal statement, professional project, reflective essay. Additional exam requirements/recommendations for international students: Required—TOEFL (minimum score 550 paper-based; 79 iBT). *Application deadline:* For fall admission, 6/1 for international students; for spring admission, 10/1 for international students. Applications are processed on a rolling basis. Application fee: $0. Electronic applications accepted. *Expenses:* Contact institution. *Financial support:* In 2017–18, 34 students received support. Federal Work-Study, scholarships/grants, and unspecified assistantships available. Support available to part-time students. Financial award applicants required to submit FAFSA. *Unit head:* Dr. Jen Buckley, Dean, School of Education and Human Performance, 630-844-1542, Fax: 630-844-6155, E-mail: jbuckley@aurora.edu. *Application contact:* Elizabeth Botica, Graduate Education Recruiter, 630-947-8918, E-mail: ebotica@aurora.edu. Website: http://aurora.edu/education

Austin College, Austin Teacher Program, Sherman, TX 75090-4400. Offers MAT. *Program availability:* Part-time. *Faculty:* 3 full-time (all women), 3 part-time/adjunct (all women). *Students:* 14 full-time (5 women); includes 4 minority (1 Black or African American, non-Hispanic/Latino; 1 American Indian or Alaska Native, non-Hispanic/Latino; 1 Asian, non-Hispanic/Latino; 1 Hispanic/Latino). Average age 22. In 2017, 15 master's awarded. *Degree requirements:* For master's, one foreign language, thesis or alternative. *Entrance requirements:* For master's, Texas Academic Skills Program Test. *Application deadline:* For fall admission, 5/1 priority date for domestic students; for spring admission, 1/15 priority date for domestic students. Applications are processed on a rolling basis. Application fee: $35. Electronic applications accepted. *Financial support:* Career-related internships or fieldwork, Federal Work-Study, scholarships/grants, and unspecified assistantships available. Support available to part-time students. Financial award application deadline: 4/1; financial award applicants required to submit FAFSA. *Unit head:* Julia Shahid, Department Chair, 903-813-2457, E-mail: jshahid@austincollege.edu. *Application contact:* Nikki Christensen, Administrative Assistant, 903-813-2327, E-mail: nchristensen@austincollege.edu. Website: http://www.austincollege.edu/academics/atp/

Austin Peay State University, College of Graduate Studies, College of Education, Clarksville, TN 37044. Offers MA Ed, Ed S. *Accreditation:* NCATE. *Program availability:* Part-time, evening/weekend, online learning. *Faculty:* 16 full-time (10 women), 5 part-time/adjunct (4 women). *Students:* 73 full-time (54 women), 139 part-time (106 women); includes 49 minority (23 Black or African American, non-Hispanic/Latino; 4 Asian, non-Hispanic/Latino; 12 Hispanic/Latino; 10 Two or more races, non-Hispanic/Latino), 1 international. Average age 34. 72 applicants, 96% accepted, 42 enrolled. In 2017, 94 master's, 12 Ed Ss awarded. *Degree requirements:* For master's, comprehensive exam, thesis optional. *Entrance requirements:* For master's, GRE General Test, MAT, 3 letters of recommendation, minimum undergraduate GPA of 2.75; for Ed S, GRE General Test, master's degree, minimum graduate GPA of 3.0, 3 letters of recommendation. Additional exam requirements/recommendations for international students: Required—TOEFL (minimum score 500 paper-based). *Application deadline:* For fall admission, 8/8 priority date for domestic students. Applications are processed on a rolling basis. Application fee: $45 ($55 for international students). Electronic applications accepted. *Expenses:* Tuition, state resident: full-time $7686; part-time $427 per credit hour. Tuition, nonresident: full-time $20,268; part-time $1126 per credit hour. *Required fees:* $1529; $76.45 per credit hour. *Financial support:* Research assistantships with full tuition reimbursements, career-related internships or fieldwork, Federal Work-Study, institutionally sponsored loans, scholarships/grants, and unspecified assistantships available. Support available to part-time students. Financial award application deadline: 4/1; financial award applicants required to submit FAFSA. *Unit head:* Dr. Prentice Chandler, Dean, 931-221-7511, Fax: 931-221-1292, E-mail: chandlerp@apsu.edu. *Application contact:* Megan Mitchell, Coordinator of Graduate Admissions, 931-221-6189, Fax: 931-221-7641, E-mail: mitchellm@apsu.edu. Website: http://www.apsu.edu/education/index.php

Education—General

Averett University, Master in Education Program, Danville, VA 24541-3692. Offers administration and supervision (M Ed); curriculum and instruction (M Ed); special education with endorsement (M Ed); special education with licensure (M Ed). *Program availability:* Part-time, online only, 100% online. *Faculty:* 2 full-time (1 woman), 14 part-time/adjunct (11 women). *Students:* 38 full-time (32 women), 46 part-time (28 women); includes 33 minority (29 Black or African American, non-Hispanic/Latino; 1 Hispanic/Latino; 3 Two or more races, non-Hispanic/Latino). Average age 38. 155 applicants, 52% accepted, 59 enrolled. In 2017, 50 master's awarded. *Degree requirements:* For master's, 30-credit core curriculum, minimum GPA of 3.0 throughout program, completion of degree requirements within six years from start of program. *Entrance requirements:* For master's, PRAXIS I, GRE, or MAT; writing proficiency test, minimum cumulative GPA of 3.0 over the last 60 hours of undergraduate study toward a baccalaureate degree, three letters of recommendation, Virginia teaching license (or eligibility). Additional exam requirements/recommendations for international students: Required—TOEFL (minimum score 600 paper-based; 100 iBT). *Application deadline:* Applications are processed on a rolling basis. Electronic applications accepted. *Expenses:* Contact institution. *Financial support:* Application deadline: 3/1; applicants required to submit FAFSA. *Faculty research:* Digital story telling for instruction and assessment; online collaborative tools; digital field trips with Google Earth; teacher preparation in special education in Kenya, Malawi, Zambia, and Zimbabwe; self-efficacy of regular education teachers regarding inclusion of special education students in their classrooms. *Total annual research expenditures:* $5,000. *Unit head:* Dr. Sue Davis, Education Chair, 434-791-5741, Fax: 434-791-5020, E-mail: suedavis@averett.edu. Website: http://gps.averett.edu/online/education/

Avila University, School of Education, Kansas City, MO 64145-1698. Offers advanced classroom management (MA); art K-12 (Teaching Certificate); educational technology (MA, Certificate); elementary education (Teaching Certificate; English as a second language (MA); English language learners (Advanced Certificate); middle school (Teaching Certificate); physical education K-12 (Teaching Certificate); secondary education (Teaching Certificate); special education (Teaching Certificate); special reading (Advanced Certificate); teaching and learning (MA). *Program availability:* Part-time, evening/weekend, online learning. *Faculty:* 6 full-time (5 women), 9 part-time/adjunct (8 women). *Students:* 81 full-time (63 women), 20 part-time (11 women); includes 14 minority (8 Black or African American, non-Hispanic/Latino; 2 Asian, non-Hispanic/Latino; 3 Hispanic/Latino; 1 Two or more races, non-Hispanic/Latino), 4 international. Average age 35. 92 applicants, 62% accepted, 40 enrolled. In 2017, 24 master's awarded. *Entrance requirements:* For master's, minimum GPA of 3.0, writing sample, recommendation, interview; for other advanced degree, foreign language. Additional exam requirements/recommendations for international students: Required—TOEFL (minimum score 580 paper-based; 92 iBT). *Application deadline:* Applications are processed on a rolling basis. Electronic applications accepted. *Expenses:* Contact institution. *Financial support:* In 2017–18, 14 students received support. Unspecified assistantships available. Financial award applicants required to submit FAFSA. *Unit head:* Dr. Stacy Keith, Director of Graduate Education, 816-501-2446, Fax: 816-501-2915, E-mail: stacy.keith@avila.edu. *Application contact:* Cory Roup, Graduate Education Enrollment and Academic Advisor, 816-501-2464, E-mail: cory.roup@avila.edu.
Website: https://www.avila.edu/academics/graduate-studies/grad-education

Azusa Pacific University, School of Education, Azusa, CA 91702-7000. Offers M Ed, MA, MA Ed, Ed D. *Program availability:* Part-time, evening/weekend. *Degree requirements:* For doctorate, oral defense of dissertation, qualifying exam. *Entrance requirements:* For master's, minimum GPA of 3.0; for doctorate, GRE General Test or MAT, 5 years of experience, writing sample. Additional exam requirements/recommendations for international students: Required—TOEFL.

Baker University, School of Education, Baldwin City, KS 66006-0065. Offers MA Ed, MSSE, MSSL, Ed D. Master's-level programs also offered in Wichita, KS. *Accreditation:* NCATE; TEAC. *Program availability:* Part-time, evening/weekend, 100% online. *Students:* 11 full-time (9 women), 492 part-time (350 women); includes 79 minority (43 Black or African American, non-Hispanic/Latino; 5 American Indian or Alaska Native, non-Hispanic/Latino; 3 Asian, non-Hispanic/Latino; 18 Hispanic/Latino; 2 Native Hawaiian or other Pacific Islander, non-Hispanic/Latino; 8 Two or more races, non-Hispanic/Latino), 1 international. Average age 36. In 2017, 173 master's, 42 doctorates awarded. *Degree requirements:* For master's, portfolio of learning; for doctorate, thesis/dissertation, portfolio of learning. *Entrance requirements:* For master's, one year of full-time work experience, teaching certificate; for doctorate, interview. Additional exam requirements/recommendations for international students: Required—TOEFL (minimum score 600 paper-based; 100 iBT). *Application deadline:* Applications are processed on a rolling basis. Electronic applications accepted. *Expenses:* Contact institution. *Financial support:* Applicants required to submit FAFSA. *Unit head:* Dr. Marc Childress, Dean of the School of Education, 913-344-1235, E-mail: marcus.childress@bakeru.edu. *Application contact:* Linda Reynolds, Director of Graduate Education Enrollment, 913-344-6037, E-mail: linda.reynolds@bakeru.edu.
Website: https://www.bakeru.edu/SOE/

Baldwin Wallace University, Graduate Programs, School of Education, Berea, OH 44017-2088. Offers leadership in higher education (MA Ed); leadership in technology for teaching and learning (MA Ed); literacy (MA Ed); mild/moderate educational needs (MA Ed); school leadership (MA Ed). *Accreditation:* NCATE. *Program availability:* Part-time, evening/weekend, 100% online, blended/hybrid learning. *Faculty:* 10 full-time (4 women), 8 part-time/adjunct (1 woman). *Students:* 84 full-time (63 women), 81 part-time (64 women); includes 21 minority (14 Black or African American, non-Hispanic/Latino; 1 Hispanic/Latino; 6 Two or more races, non-Hispanic/Latino). Average age 31. 89 applicants, 62% accepted, 40 enrolled. In 2017, 69 master's awarded. *Degree requirements:* For master's, capstone, practica or portfolio. *Entrance requirements:* For master's, bachelor's degree in field, MAT or minimum GPA of 3.0, teaching license (for all but technology program). Additional exam requirements/recommendations for international students: Required—TOEFL (minimum score 550 paper-based; 79 iBT). *Application deadline:* For fall admission, 8/15 priority date for domestic students; for spring admission, 12/15 priority date for domestic students. Applications are processed on a rolling basis. Application fee: $25. Electronic applications accepted. Application fee is waived when completed online. *Expenses:* $721 per credit hour. *Financial support:* Career-related internships or fieldwork available. Financial award applicants required to submit FAFSA. *Faculty research:* Literacy, technology and literacy, diversity in education, assessment, special education, research methodology, leadership, and organization. *Unit head:* Dr. Karen Kaye, Dean, 440-826-2168, Fax: 440-826-3779, E-mail: kkaye@bw.edu. *Application contact:* Winnie W. Gerhardt, Director of Transfer, Adult and Graduate Admission, 440-826-2222, Fax: 440-826-3830, E-mail: admission@bw.edu.
Website: http://www.bw.edu/academics/master-of-arts-in-education

Ball State University, Graduate School, Teachers College, Muncie, IN 47306. Offers MA, MAE, MS, Ed D, PhD, Certificate, Ed S. *Accreditation:* NCATE. *Program availability:* Part-time, evening/weekend, 100% online, blended/hybrid learning. *Faculty:* 95 full-time (75 women), 68 part-time/adjunct (48 women). *Students:* 389 full-time (306 women), 2,873 part-time (2,450 women); includes 647 minority (259 Black or African

American, non-Hispanic/Latino; 86 Asian, non-Hispanic/Latino; 239 Hispanic/Latino; 3 Native Hawaiian or other Pacific Islander, non-Hispanic/Latino; 60 Two or more races, non-Hispanic/Latino), 39 international. Average age 31. 1,873 applicants, 65% accepted, 947 enrolled. In 2017, 1,002 master's, 29 doctorates, 286 other advanced degrees awarded. Terminal master's awarded for partial completion of doctoral program. *Degree requirements:* For doctorate, comprehensive exam, thesis/dissertation; for other advanced degree, comprehensive exam, thesis. *Entrance requirements:* For master's, minimum baccalaureate GPA of 2.75 or 3.0 in latter half of baccalaureate; for doctorate, GRE General Test, minimum graduate GPA of 3.2; for other advanced degree, GRE General Test. Additional exam requirements/recommendations for international students: Required—TOEFL (minimum score 550 paper-based; 79 iBT), IELTS (minimum score 6.5). *Application deadline:* For fall admission, 1/1 priority date for international students. Applications are processed on a rolling basis. Application fee: $60. Electronic applications accepted. *Financial support:* In 2017–18, 120 students received support, including 81 research assistantships with partial tuition reimbursements available (averaging $10,472 per year), 19 teaching assistantships with partial tuition reimbursements available (averaging $8,704 per year); unspecified assistantships also available. Financial award application deadline: 3/1; financial award applicants required to submit FAFSA. *Unit head:* Dr. Roy Weaver, Interim Dean, 765-285-5452, Fax: 765-285-5455, E-mail: rweaver@bsu.edu. *Application contact:* Stephanie D. Wilson, Graduate Recruiter, 765-285-6130, Fax: 765-285-1328, E-mail: shuffman@bsu.edu.
Website: http://www.bsu.edu/teachers/

Bank Street College of Education, Graduate School, New York, NY 10025. Offers Ed M, MS, MS Ed. *Degree requirements:* For master's, thesis. *Entrance requirements:* For master's, interview, essays. Additional exam requirements/recommendations for international students: Required—TOEFL (minimum score 600 paper-based; 100 iBT), IELTS (minimum score 7). Electronic applications accepted. *Faculty research:* Understanding developmental variations in inclusive classrooms, urban teacher education and technology, learner-centered education, improving teacher preparation.

Bard College, Master of Arts in Teaching Program, Annandale-on-Hudson, NY 12504. Offers secondary education (MAT), including biology, history, literature, mathematics, Spanish; MS/MAT. *Program availability:* Part-time. *Degree requirements:* For master's, year-long teaching residencies in area middle and high schools. *Entrance requirements:* For master's, GRE General Test, resume, 3 letters of recommendation, personal statement, official transcripts. Additional exam requirements/recommendations for international students: Required—TOEFL. Electronic applications accepted. Application fee is waived when completed online.

Barry University, School of Education, Miami Shores, FL 33161-6695. Offers MS, Ed D, PhD, Certificate, Ed S. *Program availability:* Part-time, evening/weekend, online learning. *Degree requirements:* For master's, comprehensive exam; for doctorate, thesis/dissertation. *Entrance requirements:* For master's, GRE General Test or MAT, minimum GPA of 3.0; for doctorate, GRE General Test, minimum GPA of 3.25; for other advanced degree, GRE General Test, minimum GPA of 3.0. Additional exam requirements/recommendations for international students: Required—TOEFL (minimum score 550 paper-based). Electronic applications accepted.

Bayamón Central University, Graduate Programs, Program in Education, Bayamón, PR 00960-1725. Offers administration and supervision (MA Ed); commercial education (MA Ed); elementary education (K–3) (MA Ed); family counseling (Graduate Certificate); guidance and counseling (MA Ed); pre-elementary teacher (MA Ed); rehabilitation counseling (MA Ed); special education (MA Ed), including attention deficit disorder, education of the autistic, learning disabilities. *Program availability:* Part-time, evening/weekend. *Degree requirements:* For master's, comprehensive exam. *Entrance requirements:* For master's, EXADEP, bachelor's degree in education or related field.

Baylor University, Graduate School, School of Education, Waco, TX 76798-7304. Offers MA, MS Ed, Ed D, PhD, Ed S. *Accreditation:* NCATE. *Program availability:* Part-time. *Faculty:* 42 full-time (26 women), 10 part-time/adjunct (6 women). *Students:* 140 full-time (94 women), 42 part-time (23 women); includes 47 minority (11 Black or African American, non-Hispanic/Latino; 5 Asian, non-Hispanic/Latino; 20 Hispanic/Latino; 1 Native Hawaiian or other Pacific Islander, non-Hispanic/Latino; 10 Two or more races, non-Hispanic/Latino), 7 international. 248 applicants, 35% accepted, 28 enrolled. In 2017, 66 master's, 4 doctorates, 7 other advanced degrees awarded. *Degree requirements:* For master's, variable foreign language requirement, comprehensive exam, thesis optional; for doctorate, variable foreign language requirement, comprehensive exam, thesis/dissertation. *Entrance requirements:* For master's and Ed S, GRE; for doctorate, GRE, 3 letters of recommendation, personal statement. Additional exam requirements/recommendations for international students: Required—TOEFL (minimum score 550 paper-based; 80 iBT), IELTS (minimum score 6.5). *Application deadline:* For fall admission, 2/1 priority date for domestic and international students. Applications are processed on a rolling basis. Application fee: $25. Electronic applications accepted. *Financial support:* In 2017–18, 181 students received support, including 38 research assistantships (averaging $12,050 per year), 68 teaching assistantships (averaging $12,050 per year); career-related internships or fieldwork, Federal Work-Study, institutionally sponsored loans, scholarships/grants, health care benefits, tuition waivers (partial), unspecified assistantships, and stipends also available. Support available to part-time students. Financial award application deadline: 2/1; financial award applicants required to submit FAFSA. *Faculty research:* Quantitative methods, gifted and talented, applied behavior analysis, sport management, marketing, civics/science education. *Total annual research expenditures:* $324,254. *Unit head:* Dr. Terrill F. Saxon, Dean, 254-710-3111, Fax: 254-710-3987, E-mail: terrill_saxon@baylor.edu.
Website: http://www.baylor.edu/soe/

Belhaven University, School of Education, Jackson, MS 39202-1789. Offers education (M Ed, MAT); educational leadership (Ed D, Ed S); reading literacy (M Ed). *Program availability:* Part-time, evening/weekend, 100% online, blended/hybrid learning. *Faculty:* 7 full-time (all women), 34 part-time/adjunct (23 women). *Students:* 4 full-time (all women), 505 part-time (413 women); includes 273 minority (257 Black or African American, non-Hispanic/Latino; 1 Asian, non-Hispanic/Latino; 5 Hispanic/Latino; 10 Two or more races, non-Hispanic/Latino). Average age 35. 203 applicants, 48% accepted, 92 enrolled. In 2017, 82 master's awarded. *Degree requirements:* For master's, comprehensive exam, portfolio; for doctorate, thesis/dissertation. *Entrance requirements:* For master's, PRAXIS I and II, minimum GPA of 2.8; for doctorate, MAT or GRE, master's degree in education or related field with minimum GPA of 3.0; essay; three professional letters of recommendation; minimum three years' experience in a PK-12 education context. *Application deadline:* Applications are processed on a rolling basis. Application fee: $25. Electronic applications accepted. *Expenses:* Contact institution. *Financial support:* Applicants required to submit FAFSA. *Unit head:* Dr. David Hand, Dean, 601-965-7020, E-mail: dhand@belhaven.edu. *Application contact:* Sean Kirnan, Assistant Vice President for Adult and Graduate Enrollment and Student Services, 601-968-8727, Fax: 601-968-5953, E-mail: gradadmission@belhaven.edu.

Bellarmine University, Annsley Frazier Thornton School of Education, Louisville, KY 40205. Offers education and district leadership (Ed D); education and social change (PhD); elementary education (MA Ed, MAT); leadership in higher education (PhD);

middle school education (MA Ed, MAT); principalship (Ed S); reading and writing (MA Ed); secondary education (MAT); teacher leadership (MA Ed). *Accreditation:* NCATE. *Program availability:* Part-time, evening/weekend. *Faculty:* 19 full-time (10 women), 36 part-time/adjunct (29 women). *Students:* 34 full-time (27 women), 204 part-time (158 women); includes 60 minority (43 Black or African American, non-Hispanic/Latino; 7 Asian, non-Hispanic/Latino; 7 Hispanic/Latino; 3 Two or more races, non-Hispanic/Latino). Average age 33. In 2017, 50 master's, 8 doctorates, 42 other advanced degrees awarded. *Degree requirements:* For master's, comprehensive exam (for some programs), thesis (for some programs); for doctorate, comprehensive exam (for some programs), thesis/dissertation; for Ed S, comprehensive exam (for some programs). *Entrance requirements:* For master's, GRE, baccalaureate degree from accredited institution; minimum cumulative GPA of 2.75; recommendations from employers, supervisors, or professors attesting to applicant's potential as graduate student; statement of intent to pursue graduate degree; for doctorate, GRE, minimum GPA of 3.5 in all graduate coursework; baccalaureate and master's degrees in education or fields directly relevant to education; three letters of recommendation; two essays (no more than 1,000 words each); resume or curriculum vitae; interview; for Ed S, master's degree in education; valid teaching certificate; three years of experience in teaching; three recommendations; minimum GPA of 3.0 in all graduate work; interview; essays; personal goal statement. Additional exam requirements/recommendations for international students: Required—TOEFL (minimum score 550 paper-based, 68 iBT), IELTS (minimum score 6), or Michigan English Language Assessment Battery. *Application deadline:* For fall admission, 8/1 priority date for domestic and international students; for spring admission, 12/1 priority date for domestic and international students; for summer admission, 4/10 priority date for domestic and international students. Applications are processed on a rolling basis. Application fee: $40. Electronic applications accepted. Tuition and fees vary according to program. *Financial support:* Scholarships/grants available. Financial award applicants required to submit FAFSA. *Faculty research:* Literacy, service-learning, dispositions, educational technology, special education. *Unit head:* Dr. Elizabeth Dinkins, Interim Dean, 502-272-7958, Fax: 502-272-8189, E-mail: edinkins@bellarmine.edu. *Application contact:* Sarah Schuble, Senior Graduate Admissions Recruiter, 502-272-8271, Fax: 502-272-8002, E-mail: sschuble@bellarmine.edu.
Website: http://www.bellarmine.edu/education/graduate

Bemidji State University, School of Graduate Studies, Bemidji, MN 56601. Offers biology (MS); education (MS); English (MA, MS); environmental studies (MS); mathematics (MS); mathematics (elementary and middle level education) (MS); special education (M Sp Ed). *Program availability:* Part-time, online learning. *Degree requirements:* For master's, comprehensive exam, thesis (for some programs). *Entrance requirements:* For master's, GRE; GMAT, letters of recommendation, letters of interest. Additional exam requirements/recommendations for international students: Required—TOEFL (minimum score 550 paper-based; 80 iBT). Electronic applications accepted. *Expenses:* Contact institution. *Faculty research:* Human performance, sport, and health: physical education teacher education, continuum models, spiritual health, intellectual health, resiliency, health priorities; psychology: health psychology, college student drinking behavior, micro-aggressions, infant cognition, false memories, leadership assessment; biology: structure and dynamics of forest communities, aquatic and riverine ecology, interaction between animal populations and aquatic environments, cellular motility.

Benedictine College, Master of Arts in Education Program, Atchison, KS 66002-1499. Offers MA. *Program availability:* Part-time, evening/weekend. *Students:* 1 (woman) part-time. Average age 24. *Entrance requirements:* For master's, minimum GPA of 3.0 in last two years (60 hours) of college course work from accredited institutions, official transcripts, bachelor's degree, teacher certification/licensure, resume, essay. Additional exam requirements/recommendations for international students: Recommended—TOEFL, IELTS. *Application deadline:* Applications are processed on a rolling basis. Application fee: $50. Electronic applications accepted. Application fee is waived when completed online. *Expenses:* Contact institution. *Financial support:* Unspecified assistantships available. Financial award applicants required to submit FAFSA. *Application contact:* Dr. Cheryl Reding, Director, Graduate Programs in Education, 913-360-7384, E-mail: creding@benedictine.edu.

Benedictine University, Graduate Programs, Program in Education, Lisle, IL 60532. Offers curriculum and instruction and collaborative teaching (M Ed); elementary education (MA Ed); leadership and administration (M Ed); reading and literacy (M Ed); secondary education (MA Ed); special education (MA Ed). *Program availability:* Part-time, evening/weekend. *Degree requirements:* For master's, comprehensive exam, thesis (for some programs). *Entrance requirements:* For master's, GRE or MAT. Additional exam requirements/recommendations for international students: Required—TOEFL (minimum score 550 paper-based). Electronic applications accepted. *Expenses:* Contact institution.

Berry College, Graduate Programs, Graduate Programs in Education, Mount Berry, GA 30149-0159. Offers curriculum and instruction (M Ed, MAT); early childhood education (M Ed, MAT); educational leadership (Ed S); middle-grades education and reading (M Ed, MAT), including middle grades education (MAT), middle-grades education (M Ed), reading (M Ed); secondary education (MA Ed). *Accreditation:* NCATE. *Program availability:* Part-time. *Faculty:* 1 full-time (0 women), 7 part-time/adjunct (5 women). *Students:* 16 full-time (10 women), 86 part-time (67 women); includes 20 minority (17 Black or African American, non-Hispanic/Latino; 3 Hispanic/Latino). Average age 41. In 2017, 12 master's, 46 other advanced degrees awarded. *Degree requirements:* For master's and Ed S, thesis, portfolio, oral exams. *Entrance requirements:* For master's, GRE General Test or MAT, minimum GPA of 2.5; for Ed S, M Ed from NCATE-accredited school, minimum GPA of 3.25. Additional exam requirements/recommendations for international students: Required—TOEFL (minimum score 550 paper-based). *Application deadline:* For fall admission, 7/20 for domestic students, 5/1 for international students; for spring admission, 12/1 for domestic students, 10/1 for international students. Applications are processed on a rolling basis. Application fee: $25 ($30 for international students). *Expenses:* $8,370 full-time tuition plus $176 fees per year; $465 per credit hour part-time tuition. *Financial support:* In 2017–18, 3 students received support. Research assistantships with full tuition reimbursements available, scholarships/grants, tuition waivers (partial), and unspecified assistantships available. Support available to part-time students. Financial award application deadline: 3/1; financial award applicants required to submit FAFSA. *Faculty research:* Focus on faculty research, school readiness, literacy, K-12 hiring, education policy, arts education. *Total annual research expenditures:* $11,064. *Unit head:* Dr. Jacqueline McDowell, Dean, Charter School of Education and Human Sciences, 706-236-1717, Fax: 706-238-5827, E-mail: jmcdowell@berry.edu. *Application contact:* Brett Kennedy, Assistant Vice President of Enrollment Management, 706-236-2215, Fax: 706-290-2178, E-mail: admissions@berry.edu.
Website: http://www.berry.edu/academics/education/graduate/

Bethany College, Master of Arts in Teaching Program, Bethany, WV 26032. Offers MAT. *Program availability:* Part-time. *Degree requirements:* For master's, thesis. *Entrance requirements:* For master's, baccalaureate degree from accredited U.S. college/university or international equivalent; minimum undergraduate GPA of 2.75.

Additional exam requirements/recommendations for international students: Required—TOEFL (minimum score 500 paper-based; 90 iBT); Recommended—IELTS (minimum score 7). Electronic applications accepted.

Bethel College, Adult and Graduate Programs, Program in Education, Mishawaka, IN 46545-5591. Offers M Ed, MAT. *Accreditation:* NCATE; TEAC. *Program availability:* Part-time. *Faculty:* 3 full-time (1 woman), 9 part-time/adjunct (5 women). *Students:* 11 full-time (10 women), 51 part-time (36 women); includes 11 minority (5 Black or African American, non-Hispanic/Latino; 2 Asian, non-Hispanic/Latino; 3 Hispanic/Latino; 1 Two or more races, non-Hispanic/Latino). Average age 35. 64 applicants, 39% accepted, 25 enrolled. In 2017, 23 master's awarded. *Entrance requirements:* Additional exam requirements/recommendations for international students: Required—TOEFL (minimum score 540 paper-based). *Application deadline:* For fall admission, 5/1 for international students; for spring admission, 10/1 for international students. Applications are processed on a rolling basis. Application fee: $0. Electronic applications accepted. Tuition and fees vary according to program. *Financial support:* Career-related internships or fieldwork available. Financial award applicants required to submit FAFSA. *Unit head:* James Bennett, Director, 574-807-7347, E-mail: jim.bennett@bethelcollege.edu.

Bethel University, Graduate School, St. Paul, MN 55112-6999. Offers business administration (MBA); classroom management (Certificate); counseling (MA); K-12 education (MA); leadership (Ed D); leadership foundations (Certificate); nurse educator (MS, Certificate); nurse-midwifery (MS); physician assistant (MS); special education (MA); strategic leadership (MA); teaching (MA); teaching and learning (Certificate). *Program availability:* Part-time, evening/weekend, 100% online, blended/hybrid learning. *Faculty:* 22 full-time (16 women), 70 part-time/adjunct (44 women). *Students:* 611 full-time (431 women), 393 part-time (249 women); includes 176 minority (82 Black or African American, non-Hispanic/Latino; 4 American Indian or Alaska Native, non-Hispanic/Latino; 31 Asian, non-Hispanic/Latino; 39 Hispanic/Latino; 2 Native Hawaiian or other Pacific Islander, non-Hispanic/Latino; 18 Two or more races, non-Hispanic/Latino), 9 international. Average age 36. 668 applicants, 42% accepted, 223 enrolled. In 2017, 287 master's, 30 doctorates, 172 other advanced degrees awarded. *Degree requirements:* For master's, comprehensive exam (for some programs), thesis (for some programs); for doctorate, comprehensive exam, thesis/dissertation. *Entrance requirements:* Additional exam requirements/recommendations for international students: Required—TOEFL (minimum score 550 paper-based, 80 iBT) or IELTS. *Application deadline:* Applications are processed on a rolling basis. Application fee: $0. Electronic applications accepted. *Expenses:* Contact institution. *Financial support:* Teaching assistantships, career-related internships or fieldwork, and scholarships/grants available. Support available to part-time students. Financial award applicants required to submit FAFSA. *Unit head:* Dr. Randy Bergen, Associate Provost, 651-635-8000, Fax: 651-635-8004, E-mail: r-bergen@bethel.edu. *Application contact:* Director of Admissions, 651-635-8000, Fax: 651-635-8004, E-mail: gs@bethel.edu.
Website: https://www.bethel.edu/graduate/

Binghamton University, State University of New York, Graduate School, College of Community and Public Affairs, Department of Teaching, Learning and Educational Leadership, Binghamton, NY 13902-6000. Offers adolescence education (MAT, MS Ed), including biology education, chemistry education, earth science education, English education, French education, mathematical sciences education, physics, social studies, Spanish education; childhood and early childhood education (MS Ed); educational leadership (Certificate); educational studies (MS); educational theory and practice (Ed D); literacy education (MS Ed); special education (MS Ed); TESOL education (MA, MS Ed). *Accreditation:* TEAC. *Program availability:* Part-time, evening/weekend. *Faculty:* 18 full-time (13 women). *Students:* 99 full-time (71 women), 136 part-time (107 women); includes 27 minority (5 Black or African American, non-Hispanic/Latino; 1 American Indian or Alaska Native, non-Hispanic/Latino; 2 Asian, non-Hispanic/Latino; 14 Hispanic/Latino; 5 Two or more races, non-Hispanic/Latino), 8 international. Average age 34. 158 applicants, 84% accepted, 86 enrolled. In 2017, 75 master's, 5 doctorates, 19 other advanced degrees awarded. *Degree requirements:* For doctorate, thesis/dissertation. *Entrance requirements:* For master's, GRE General Test, teaching certification; for doctorate, GRE General Test, writing sample. Additional exam requirements/recommendations for international students: Required—TOEFL (minimum score 550 paper-based; 80 iBT). Application fee: $75. Electronic applications accepted. *Financial support:* In 2017–18, 22 students received support, including 2 fellowships with full tuition reimbursements available (averaging $10,000 per year), 3 teaching assistantships with full tuition reimbursements available (averaging $15,500 per year); research assistantships, career-related internships or fieldwork, Federal Work-Study, institutionally sponsored loans, scholarships/grants, health care benefits, tuition waivers (full and partial), and unspecified assistantships also available. Financial award applicants required to submit FAFSA. *Unit head:* Dr. Susan Strehle, Dean, 607-777-7329, E-mail: sstrehle@binghamton.edu. *Application contact:* Ben Balkaya, Assistant Dean and Director, 607-777-2151, Fax: 607-777-2501, E-mail: balkaya@binghamton.edu.
Website: https://www.binghamton.edu/tlel/

Biola University, School of Education, La Mirada, CA 90639-0001. Offers curriculum and instruction (Certificate); early childhood (MA Ed, MAT); multiple subject (MAT); single subject (MAT); special education (MA Ed, MAT, Certificate). *Program availability:* Part-time, evening/weekend, online learning. *Faculty:* 16. *Students:* 67 full-time (52 women), 164 part-time (142 women); includes 97 minority (8 Black or African American, non-Hispanic/Latino; 1 American Indian or Alaska Native, non-Hispanic/Latino; 51 Asian, non-Hispanic/Latino; 30 Hispanic/Latino; 7 Two or more races, non-Hispanic/Latino), 4 international. 164 applicants, 87% accepted, 116 enrolled. In 2017, 25 master's awarded. *Entrance requirements:* For master's, CBEST, CSET, GRE (waived if cumulative GPA is 3.5 or above or if CBEST and all CSET subtests are passed). Additional exam requirements/recommendations for international students: Required—TOEFL (minimum score 100 iBT). *Application deadline:* For fall admission, 7/1 for domestic students, 6/1 for international students; for spring admission, 12/1 for domestic students; for summer admission, 5/1 for domestic students. Applications are processed on a rolling basis. Application fee: $65. Electronic applications accepted. *Financial support:* Scholarships/grants available. Support available to part-time students. Financial award applicants required to submit FAFSA. *Faculty research:* Early childhood education, elementary education, special education, curriculum development, teacher preparation. *Unit head:* Dr. June Hetzel, Dean, 562-903-4715. *Application contact:* Graduate Admissions Office, 562-903-4752, E-mail: graduate.admissions@biola.edu.
Website: http://education.biola.edu/

Bishop's University, School of Education, Sherbrooke, QC J1M 1Z7, Canada. Offers advanced studies in education (Diploma); education (M Ed, MA); teaching English as a second language (Certificate). *Program availability:* Part-time, online learning. *Degree requirements:* For master's, thesis (for some programs). *Entrance requirements:* For master's, teaching license, 2 years of teaching experience. *Faculty research:* Integration of special needs students, multigrade classes/small schools, leadership in organizational development, second language acquisition.

Bloomsburg University of Pennsylvania, School of Graduate Studies, College of Education, Bloomsburg, PA 17815-1301. Offers M Ed, MS, Certificate. *Accreditation:*

Education—General

NCATE. *Program availability:* Part-time. *Degree requirements:* For master's, thesis optional. *Entrance requirements:* For master's, minimum QPA of 3.0. Additional exam requirements/recommendations for international students: Required—TOEFL, IELTS. Electronic applications accepted. *Expenses:* Tuition, state resident: full-time $10,000; part-time $500 per credit hour. Tuition, nonresident: full-time $15,000; part-time $750 per credit hour. *Required fees:* $2484; $110.75 per credit hour. $75 per term. Tuition and fees vary according to program.

Bluefield College, School of Education, Bluefield, VA 24605-1799. Offers MA Ed. *Accreditation:* TEAC. *Program availability:* Part-time, online only, 100% online. *Degree requirements:* For master's, action research project. *Entrance requirements:* For master's, GRE, MAT or PRAXIS, bachelor's degree from regionally-accredited institution of higher education, minimum GPA of 2.75 in all college work, two letters of recommendation, Pre-Self-Assessment of Professional Temperament and Performance. Additional exam requirements/recommendations for international students: Required—TOEFL. Electronic applications accepted. *Expenses:* Contact institution.

Bluffton University, Programs in Education, Bluffton, OH 45817. Offers intervention specialist (MA Ed); leadership (MA Ed); reading (MA Ed). *Accreditation:* NCATE. *Program availability:* Part-time, 100% online, blended/hybrid learning, videoconference. *Faculty:* 2 full-time (1 woman), 1 part-time/adjunct (0 women). *Students:* 7 full-time (4 women), 11 part-time (10 women); includes 1 minority (Black or African American, non-Hispanic/Latino). Average age 29. 14 applicants, 64% accepted, 9 enrolled. In 2017, 7 master's awarded. *Degree requirements:* For master's, action research project, public presentation. *Entrance requirements:* For master's, PRAXIS I, bachelor's degree, minimum GPA of 3.0. Additional exam requirements/recommendations for international students: Required—TOEFL. *Application deadline:* For fall admission, 8/15 priority date for domestic students, 6/15 priority date for international students; for spring admission, 12/15 priority date for domestic students, 9/15 priority date for international students. Applications are processed on a rolling basis. Electronic applications accepted. *Expenses:* $456 per credit hour tuition, $50 per semester technology fee ($100 for more than 6 hours). *Financial support:* In 2017–18, 2 students received support. Unspecified assistantships available. Financial award application deadline: 9/15; financial award applicants required to submit FAFSA. *Unit head:* Dr. Amy K. Mullins, Director of Graduate Programs in Education, 419-358-3457, E-mail: mullinsa@bluffton.edu. *Application contact:* Nancey Schortgen, Program Representative, 419-358-3202, Fax: 419-358-3399, E-mail: schortgenn@bluffton.edu.
Website: http://www.bluffton.edu/grad/

Boise State University, College of Education, Boise, ID 83725-0399. Offers M Ed, MA, MET, MPE, MS, MS Ed, Ed D, Ed S, Graduate Certificate. *Accreditation:* NCATE. *Program availability:* Part-time, 100% online, blended/hybrid learning. *Faculty:* 106. *Students:* 131 full-time (106 women), 762 part-time (486 women); includes 88 minority (13 Black or African American, non-Hispanic/Latino; 4 American Indian or Alaska Native, non-Hispanic/Latino; 19 Asian, non-Hispanic/Latino; 46 Hispanic/Latino; 4 Native Hawaiian or other Pacific Islander, non-Hispanic/Latino; 2 Two or more races, non-Hispanic/Latino), 32 international. Average age 37. 399 applicants, 61% accepted, 146 enrolled. In 2017, 234 master's, 12 doctorates awarded. Terminal master's awarded for partial completion of doctoral program. *Degree requirements:* For master's, thesis (for some programs); for doctorate, thesis/dissertation. *Entrance requirements:* For master's, minimum GPA 3.0; for doctorate, GRE General Test, minimum GPA of 3.0. Additional exam requirements/recommendations for international students: Required—TOEFL (minimum score 550 paper-based; 80 iBT), IELTS (minimum score 6). Application fee: $65 ($95 for international students). Electronic applications accepted. *Expenses:* Tuition, state resident: full-time $6471; part-time $390 per credit. Tuition, nonresident: full-time $21,787; part-time $685 per credit. *Required fees:* $2283; $100 per term. Part-time tuition and fees vary according to course load and program. *Financial support:* Teaching assistantships, scholarships/grants, and unspecified assistantships available. Financial award applicants required to submit FAFSA. *Unit head:* Dr. Rich Osguthorpe, Dean, 208-426-1611, E-mail: richardosguthorpe@boisestate.edu.
Website: http://education.boisestate.edu/

Boston College, Lynch School of Education, Chestnut Hill, MA 02467. Offers M Ed, MA, MAT, MS, MST, Ed D, PhD, CAES, JD/MA, JD/MA, MA/MA, MBA/MA. *Accreditation:* TEAC. *Program availability:* Part-time. *Faculty:* 56 full-time (33 women). *Students:* 345 full-time (277 women), 422 part-time (318 women); includes 157 minority (50 Black or African American, non-Hispanic/Latino; 36 Asian, non-Hispanic/Latino; 50 Hispanic/Latino; 1 Native Hawaiian or other Pacific Islander, non-Hispanic/Latino; 20 Two or more races, non-Hispanic/Latino), 103 international. Average age 28. 1,385 applicants, 58% accepted, 322 enrolled. In 2017, 375 master's, 56 doctorates, 7 other advanced degrees awarded. Terminal master's awarded for partial completion of doctoral program. *Degree requirements:* For master's, comprehensive exam; for doctorate, comprehensive exam, thesis/dissertation. *Entrance requirements:* For master's, GRE, letters of recommendation, transcripts, personal statement, resume; for doctorate, GRE, letters of recommendation, transcripts, writing sample, personal statement, resume. Additional exam requirements/recommendations for international students: Required—TOEFL (minimum score 600 paper-based; 100 iBT); Recommended—IELTS (minimum score 7). *Application deadline:* For fall admission, 1/10 priority date for domestic and international students; for spring admission, 11/1 for domestic and international students; for summer admission, 5/15 for domestic and international students. Applications are processed on a rolling basis. Application fee: $65. Electronic applications accepted. *Financial support:* Fellowships with tuition reimbursements, research assistantships with tuition reimbursements, teaching assistantships with tuition reimbursements, career-related internships or fieldwork, Federal Work-Study, scholarships/grants, traineeships, health care benefits, tuition waivers (partial), and unspecified assistantships available. Support available to part-time students. Financial award applicants required to submit FAFSA. *Faculty research:* Curriculum, teaching and learning, whole person learning and development, educational change and leadership, assessment and evaluation, counseling and development. *Total annual research expenditures:* $19.1 million. *Unit head:* Dr. Stanton Wortham, Dean, 617-552-4200, Fax: 617-552-0812. *Application contact:* Jamie Grenon, Associate Dean for Graduate Admissions and Financial Aid, 617-552-4214, Fax: 617-552-0398, E-mail: grenonj@bc.edu.
Website: http://www.bc.edu/schools/lsoe

Boston University, Wheelock College of Education and Human Development, Boston, MA 02215. Offers Ed M, MAT, Ed D, PhD, CAGS. *Program availability:* Part-time, evening/weekend. *Students:* 234 full-time (183 women), 444 part-time (331 women); includes 168 minority (38 Black or African American, non-Hispanic/Latino; 46 Asian, non-Hispanic/Latino; 63 Hispanic/Latino; 1 Native Hawaiian or other Pacific Islander, non-Hispanic/Latino; 20 Two or more races, non-Hispanic/Latino), 53 international. Average age 27. 1,303 applicants, 65% accepted, 346 enrolled. In 2017, 286 master's, 26 doctorates, 6 other advanced degrees awarded. Terminal master's awarded for partial completion of doctoral program. *Degree requirements:* For master's, thesis (for some programs); for doctorate, comprehensive exam, thesis/dissertation; for CAGS, comprehensive exam. *Entrance requirements:* For master's, GRE or MAT (for Ed M in

counseling); for doctorate, GRE General Test; for CAGS, GRE General Test or MAT. Additional exam requirements/recommendations for international students: Required—TOEFL (minimum score 84 iBT), IELTS. *Application deadline:* For fall admission, 1/15 priority date for domestic and international students; for spring admission, 9/15 priority date for domestic and international students. Applications are processed on a rolling basis. Application fee: $95. Electronic applications accepted. *Financial support:* Fellowships with full tuition reimbursements, research assistantships, teaching assistantships with partial tuition reimbursements, career-related internships or fieldwork, Federal Work-Study, and scholarships/grants available. Support available to part-time students. Financial award applicants required to submit FAFSA. *Faculty research:* Deaf studies, social emotional learning, civic engagement and education, STEM education, pre-college educational pipelines. *Unit head:* Dr. David J. Chard, Interim Dean, 617-353-3213. *Application contact:* Katharine Nelson, Director of Graduate Student Services, 617-353-4237, E-mail: sedgrad@bu.edu.
Website: http://www.bu.edu/wheelock

Bowie State University, Graduate Programs, Program in Teaching, Bowie, MD 20715-9465. Offers MAT. *Accreditation:* NCATE. *Program availability:* Part-time, evening/weekend. *Entrance requirements:* For master's, PRAXIS I. Electronic applications accepted.

Bradley University, The Graduate School, College of Education and Health Sciences, Peoria, IL 61625-0002. Offers MA, MS, MSN, DNP, DPT, Certificate. *Accreditation:* NCATE. *Program availability:* Part-time, evening/weekend. *Degree requirements:* For master's, comprehensive exam, thesis optional. *Entrance requirements:* For master's, GRE General Test or MAT, letters of recommendation; for doctorate, GRE, letters of recommendation. Additional exam requirements/recommendations for international students: Required—TOEFL (minimum score 550 paper-based; 79 iBT), IELTS (minimum score 6.5). Electronic applications accepted. *Faculty research:* Health care, professional nurse traineeship, gifted education.

Brandman University, School of Education, Irvine, CA 92618. Offers curriculum and instruction (MAE); educational administration (MAE); educational leadership (MAE); educational leadership and administration (MA); elementary education (MAT); instructional technology: teaching the 21st century learner (MAE); leadership in early childhood education (MAE); organizational leadership (Ed D); school counseling (MAE); secondary education (MAT); special education (MA); teaching and learning (MAE). *Expenses:* Tuition: Part-time $640 per credit hour. Tuition and fees vary according to degree level and program. *Unit head:* Dr. Christine G. Zeppos, Dean, 949-341-9948, E-mail: zeppos@brandman.edu. *Application contact:* Dr. Christine G. Zeppos, Dean, 949-341-9948, E-mail: zeppos@brandman.edu.
Website: https://www.brandman.edu/academic-programs/education

Brandon University, Faculty of Education, Brandon, MB R7A 6A9, Canada. Offers curriculum and instruction (M Ed, Diploma); educational administration (M Ed, Diploma); guidance and counseling (M Ed, Diploma); special education (M Ed, Diploma). *Degree requirements:* For master's, thesis. *Entrance requirements:* For master's, minimum GPA of 3.0, teaching certificate or equivalent. Additional exam requirements/recommendations for international students: Required—TOEFL. *Faculty research:* Comparative education, environmental studies, parent/school council.

Brenau University, Sydney O. Smith Graduate School, College of Education, Gainesville, GA 30501. Offers early childhood (Ed S); early childhood education (M Ed, MAT); middle grades (Ed S); middle grades education (M Ed, MAT); secondary education (MAT); special education (M Ed, MAT). *Accreditation:* NCATE. *Program availability:* Part-time, evening/weekend, online learning. *Degree requirements:* For master's, thesis optional, comprehensive exam or applied research project, effective portfolio; for Ed S, thesis, applied research project. *Entrance requirements:* For master's, GRE, MAT, interview, minimum GPA of 3.0, 3 references, writing samples; for Ed S, GRE, MAT, master's degree, minimum GPA of 3.0, writing sample, letters of reference. Additional exam requirements/recommendations for international students: Required—TOEFL (minimum score 500 paper-based; 61 iBT); Recommended—IELTS (minimum score 5). Electronic applications accepted. *Expenses:* Contact institution.

Bridgewater State University, College of Graduate Studies, College of Education and Allied Studies, Bridgewater, MA 02325. Offers M Ed, MAT, MS, CAGS. *Accreditation:* NCATE. *Program availability:* Part-time, evening/weekend. *Degree requirements:* For CAGS, comprehensive exam. *Entrance requirements:* For master's, GRE General Test or Massachusetts Test for Educator Licensure; for CAGS, master's degree. Additional exam requirements/recommendations for international students: Required—TOEFL.

Brigham Young University, Graduate Studies, David O. McKay School of Education, Provo, UT 84602. Offers M Ed, MA, MS, Ed D, PhD, Ed S. *Accreditation:* TEAC. *Faculty:* 82 full-time (28 women), 11 part-time/adjunct (4 women). *Students:* 171 full-time (98 women), 136 part-time (84 women); includes 30 minority (1 Black or African American, non-Hispanic/Latino; 4 American Indian or Alaska Native, non-Hispanic/Latino; 6 Asian, non-Hispanic/Latino; 10 Hispanic/Latino; 9 Native Hawaiian or other Pacific Islander, non-Hispanic/Latino), 6 international. Average age 34. 312 applicants, 30% accepted, 86 enrolled. In 2017, 85 master's, 20 doctorates, 10 other advanced degrees awarded. Application fee: $50. Electronic applications accepted. *Expenses:* Tuition: Full-time $6880; part-time $405 per credit hour. Tuition and fees vary according to course load, program and student's religious affiliation. *Financial support:* In 2017–18, 168 students received support, including 64 fellowships (averaging $9,270 per year), 20 research assistantships with tuition reimbursements available (averaging $1,701 per year), 18 teaching assistantships with tuition reimbursements available (averaging $2,786 per year); career-related internships or fieldwork, Federal Work-Study, institutionally sponsored loans, scholarships/grants, traineeships, health care benefits, tuition waivers, and unspecified assistantships also available. Support available to part-time students. Financial award applicants required to submit FAFSA. *Unit head:* Dr. Mary Anne Prater, Dean, 801-422-1592, Fax: 801-422-0200, E-mail: prater@byu.edu. *Application contact:* Brandan Beerli, Director, Education Student Services, 801-422-9199, Fax: 801-422-0195.
Website: http://education.byu.edu/

Brock University, Faculty of Graduate Studies, Faculty of Education, St. Catharines, ON L2S 3A1, Canada. Offers M Ed, PhD. *Program availability:* Part-time, evening/weekend. *Degree requirements:* For master's, thesis optional; for doctorate, thesis/dissertation. *Entrance requirements:* For master's, 1 year of teaching experience, honors degree; for doctorate, master's degree. Additional exam requirements/recommendations for international students: Required—TOEFL (minimum score 550 paper-based; 80 iBT), IELTS (minimum score 6.5), TWE (minimum score 4). Electronic applications accepted. *Expenses:* Contact institution. *Faculty research:* International and comparative education, early childhood education, educational leadership, adult education.

Brooklyn College of the City University of New York, School of Education, Brooklyn, NY 11210-2889. Offers MA, MAT, MS Ed, AC. *Accreditation:* NCATE. *Program availability:* Part-time, evening/weekend. *Entrance requirements:* For master's, GRE, GMAT, MAT (depending on program). Additional exam requirements/recommendations for international students: Required—TOEFL or IELTS. Electronic applications accepted.

Brown University, Graduate School, Department of Education, Providence, RI 02912. Offers teaching (MAT), including elementary education, English, history/social studies, science, secondary education; urban education policy (AM). *Degree requirements:* For master's, student teaching, portfolio. *Entrance requirements:* For master's, GRE General Test, letters of recommendation, interview. Additional exam requirements/recommendations for international students: Recommended—TOEFL.

Bucknell University, Graduate Studies, College of Arts and Sciences, Department of Education, Lewisburg, PA 17837. Offers college student personnel (MS Ed). *Program availability:* Part-time. *Degree requirements:* For master's, comprehensive exam (for some programs), thesis or alternative. *Entrance requirements:* For master's, GRE General Test, minimum GPA of 3.0. Additional exam requirements/recommendations for international students: Required—TOEFL (minimum score 600 paper-based).

Buena Vista University, School of Education, Storm Lake, IA 50588. Offers curriculum and instruction (M Ed), including effective teaching, TESL; school guidance and counseling (MS Ed). Program offered in summer only. *Program availability:* Part-time, evening/weekend, online learning. *Degree requirements:* For master's, thesis, fieldwork/practicum, capstone portfolio. *Entrance requirements:* For master's, Analytical Writing Assessment (in-house), minimum undergraduate GPA of 2.75. Electronic applications accepted. *Faculty research:* Reading, curriculum, educational psychology, special education.

Butler University, College of Education, Indianapolis, IN 46208-3485. Offers applied educational neuroscience (Certificate); educational administration (MS); effective teaching and leadership (MS); licensed mental health counselor (Certificate); school counseling (MS); wellness and sport leadership (Certificate). *Accreditation:* ACA; NCATE. *Program availability:* Part-time. *Faculty:* 12 full-time (8 women), 10 part-time/adjunct (7 women). *Students:* 3 full-time (2 women), 131 part-time (102 women); includes 13 minority (7 Black or African American, non-Hispanic/Latino; 2 Asian, non-Hispanic/Latino; 2 Hispanic/Latino; 2 Two or more races, non-Hispanic/Latino). Average age 31. 65 applicants, 75% accepted, 41 enrolled. In 2017, 45 master's, 10 other advanced degrees awarded. *Degree requirements:* For master's, thesis. *Entrance requirements:* For master's, GRE (minimum score 291) or MAT (minimum score 396) unless undergraduate GPA is a 3.0 or higher, two letters of recommendation, transcripts, interview, professional resume. Additional exam requirements/recommendations for international students: Required—TOEFL (minimum score 550 paper-based; 79 iBT), IELTS (minimum score 6). *Application deadline:* For fall admission, 2/1 for domestic and international students; for spring admission, 11/1 for domestic and international students; for summer admission, 4/1 for domestic and international students. Applications are processed on a rolling basis. Application fee: $0. Electronic applications accepted. *Expenses:* $560 per credit. *Financial support:* In 2017–18, 64 students received support. Scholarships/grants, tuition waivers (full and partial), and unspecified assistantships available. Financial award application deadline: 7/15; financial award applicants required to submit FAFSA. *Faculty research:* Principals role in school improvement, leadership and school climate, retention of teachers in special education, the neuro-diversity brain, school counseling intervention. *Unit head:* Dr. Ena Shelley, Dean, 317-940-9752, Fax: 317-940-6481. *Application contact:* Diane Dubord, Graduate Student Services Specialist, 317-940-8100, Fax: 317-940-8250, E-mail: ddubord@butler.edu.
Website: https://www.butler.edu/coe/graduate-programs

Cairn University, School of Education, Langhorne, PA 19047-2990. Offers applied behavior analysis (MS Sp Ed, Certificate); educational leadership and administration (MS El); instruction (MS Sp Ed); teacher education (MS Ed). *Program availability:* Part-time, evening/weekend, 100% online, blended/hybrid learning. *Entrance requirements:* Additional exam requirements/recommendations for international students: Required—TOEFL (minimum score 550 paper-based). Electronic applications accepted. Application fee is waived when completed online. *Expenses:* Contact institution.

Caldwell University, School of Education, Caldwell, NJ 07006-6195. Offers curriculum and instruction (MA); education leadership (Ed D); educational administration (MA); elementary, secondary or preschool endorsement, special ed, ESL (Postbaccalaureate Certificate); learning disabilities teacher-consultant (Post-Master's Certificate); literacy instruction (MA); principal (Post-Master's Certificate); reading specialist (Post-Master's Certificate); special education (MA), including special education, teaching of students with disabilities, teaching of students with disabilities and learning disabilities teacher-consultant; superintendent (Post-Master's Certificate); supervisor (Post-Master's Certificate). *Program availability:* Part-time, evening/weekend. *Faculty:* 10 full-time (6 women), 21 part-time/adjunct (12 women). *Students:* 37 full-time (30 women), 225 part-time (177 women); includes 47 minority (19 Black or African American, non-Hispanic/Latino; 3 Asian, non-Hispanic/Latino; 23 Hispanic/Latino; 2 Two or more races, non-Hispanic/Latino). Average age 35. 189 applicants, 57% accepted, 85 enrolled. In 2017, 47 master's awarded. *Degree requirements:* For master's, comprehensive exam (for some programs), thesis (for some programs); for doctorate, thesis/dissertation. *Entrance requirements:* For master's, PRAXIS, 3 years of work experience, prior teaching certification; for doctorate, GRE or MAT; for other advanced degree, two letters of recommendation; interview (for some programs). Additional exam requirements/recommendations for international students: Required—TOEFL (minimum score 580 paper-based, 70 iBT), IELTS (6), or ELS Level 112 Certification of Completion. *Application deadline:* For fall admission, 6/1 for domestic students; for spring admission, 12/1 for domestic students; for summer admission, 4/1 for domestic students. Applications are processed on a rolling basis. Application fee: $50. Electronic applications accepted. *Expenses:* $950 per credit (for master's and certificate programs); $1,125 per credit (for doctoral programs). *Financial support:* Unspecified assistantships available. Financial award applicants required to submit FAFSA. *Faculty research:* Curriculum and instruction, secondary education, special education, education and technology, literacy instruction, higher education administration, education leadership. *Unit head:* Dr. Joan Moriarity, Associate Dean, 973-618-3626, E-mail: jmoriarity@caldwell.edu. *Application contact:* Tom Disch, Senior Admissions Counselor, 973-618-3544, E-mail: graduate@caldwell.edu.

California Baptist University, Program in Education, Riverside, CA 92504-3206. Offers educational leadership (MS); educational leadership for faith-based institutions (MS); educational leadership for public institutions (MS); educational technology (MS); instructional computer applications (MS); international education (MS); leadership and adult learning (MS); leadership and organizational studies (MS); online teaching and learning (MS); reading (MS); science education (MA); special education in mild/moderate disabilities (MS); special education in moderate/severe disabilities (MS); teacher leadership (MS); teaching (MS); teaching and learning (MS). *Program availability:* Part-time, evening/weekend, 100% online, blended/hybrid learning. *Faculty:* 19 full-time (11 women), 36 part-time/adjunct (22 women). *Students:* 232 full-time (182 women), 315 part-time (247 women); includes 264 minority (33 Black or African American, non-Hispanic/Latino; 4 American Indian or Alaska Native, non-Hispanic/Latino; 11 Asian, non-Hispanic/Latino; 186 Hispanic/Latino; 7 Native Hawaiian or other Pacific Islander, non-Hispanic/Latino; 23 Two or more races, non-Hispanic/Latino). Average age 31. 217 applicants, 64% accepted, 129 enrolled. In 2017, 196 master's awarded. *Degree requirements:* For master's, comprehensive exam, project, or thesis. *Entrance requirements:* For master's, minimum undergraduate GPA of 2.75; 500-word essay; three letters of recommendation; two prerequisite courses completed with

minimum C grade. Additional exam requirements/recommendations for international students: Required—TOEFL (minimum score 80 iBT). *Application deadline:* For fall admission, 8/1 priority date for domestic students, 7/1 for international students; for spring admission, 12/1 priority date for domestic students, 11/1 for international students. Applications are processed on a rolling basis. Application fee: $45. Electronic applications accepted. *Expenses:* Contact institution. *Financial support:* In 2017–18, 162 students received support. Federal Work-Study and scholarships/grants available. Financial award applicants required to submit CSS PROFILE or FAFSA. *Faculty research:* Leadership development, complexity theory, faith and learning, special education, social and philosophical contexts of education. *Unit head:* Dr. John Shoup, Dean, School of Education, 951-343-4516, E-mail: jshoup@calbaptist.edu. *Application contact:* Gavin Andrew, Graduate Admissions Counselor, 951-552-8437, E-mail: gandrew@calbaptist.edu.
Website: http://www.calbaptist.edu/mastersined/

California Coast University, School of Education, Santa Ana, CA 92701. Offers administration (M Ed); curriculum and instruction (M Ed); educational administration (Ed D); educational psychology (Ed D); organizational leadership (Ed D). *Program availability:* Online learning.

California Lutheran University, Graduate Studies, Graduate School of Education, Thousand Oaks, CA 91360-2787. Offers counseling and guidance (MS), including college student personnel, counseling and guidance; educational leadership (MA, Ed D), including educational leadership (K-12) (Ed D), higher education leadership (Ed D); special education (MS); teacher leadership (M Ed); teaching (M Ed). *Accreditation:* NCATE. *Program availability:* Part-time, evening/weekend. *Faculty:* 21 full-time (18 women), 40 part-time/adjunct (27 women). *Students:* 390 full-time (303 women), 61 part-time (51 women); includes 228 minority (6 Black or African American, non-Hispanic/Latino; 2 American Indian or Alaska Native, non-Hispanic/Latino; 13 Asian, non-Hispanic/Latino; 186 Hispanic/Latino; 1 Native Hawaiian or other Pacific Islander, non-Hispanic/Latino; 20 Two or more races, non-Hispanic/Latino). Average age 31. 201 applicants, 76% accepted, 121 enrolled. In 2017, 129 master's, 19 doctorates awarded. *Degree requirements:* For master's, comprehensive exam or thesis; for doctorate, thesis/dissertation. *Entrance requirements:* For master's, GRE General Test, interview, minimum GPA of 3.0. *Application deadline:* For fall admission, 7/1 priority date for domestic students; for spring admission, 11/1 priority date for domestic students; for summer admission, 4/1 priority date for domestic students. Applications are processed on a rolling basis. Application fee: $50. Electronic applications accepted. *Expenses:* Tuition: Full-time $15,000. Full-time tuition and fees vary according to degree level and program. *Unit head:* Dr. Michael Hillis, Dean, 805-493-3421. *Application contact:* 805-493-3325, Fax: 805-493-3861, E-mail: clugrad@callutheran.edu.

California Polytechnic State University, San Luis Obispo, College of Science and Mathematics, School of Education, San Luis Obispo, CA 93407. Offers MA. *Accreditation:* NCATE. *Program availability:* Part-time, evening/weekend. *Faculty:* 10 full-time (5 women), 8 part-time/adjunct (5 women). *Students:* 92 full-time (67 women), 4 part-time (1 woman); includes 32 minority (1 Black or African American, non-Hispanic/Latino; 5 Asian, non-Hispanic/Latino; 25 Hispanic/Latino; 1 Two or more races, non-Hispanic/Latino). Average age 30. 155 applicants, 42% accepted, 57 enrolled. In 2017, 42 master's awarded. *Degree requirements:* For master's, comprehensive exam (for some programs), thesis (for some programs). *Entrance requirements:* Additional exam requirements/recommendations for international students: Required—TOEFL (minimum score 80 iBT). *Application deadline:* For fall admission, 4/1 for domestic students, 3/1 for international students. Applications are processed on a rolling basis. Application fee: $55. Electronic applications accepted. *Expenses:* Tuition, state resident: full-time $7176; part-time $4164 per year. *Required fees:* $3690; $3219 per year. $1073 per trimester. *Financial support:* Fellowships, research assistantships, career-related internships or fieldwork, Federal Work-Study, and institutionally sponsored loans available. Support available to part-time students. Financial award application deadline: 3/2; financial award applicants required to submit FAFSA. *Faculty research:* Rural school counseling, partner school effectiveness, college student affairs, special education, educational leadership and administration. *Unit head:* Dr. Kevin Taylor, Director, 805-756-1503, E-mail: jktaylor@calpoly.edu. *Application contact:* E-mail: soe@calpoly.edu.
Website: http://soe.calpoly.edu/

California State University, Bakersfield, Division of Graduate Studies, School of Social Sciences and Education, Bakersfield, CA 93311. Offers MA, MS, MSW, Ed D. *Accreditation:* NCATE. *Students:* 239 full-time (206 women), 74 part-time (57 women); includes 222 minority (23 Black or African American, non-Hispanic/Latino; 4 American Indian or Alaska Native, non-Hispanic/Latino; 18 Asian, non-Hispanic/Latino; 161 Hispanic/Latino; 16 Two or more races, non-Hispanic/Latino), 8 international. Average age 33. 312 applicants, 64% accepted, 156 enrolled. *Degree requirements:* For master's, thesis or alternative, culminating projects. *Application deadline:* Applications are processed on a rolling basis. Application fee: $55. *Expenses:* Tuition, state resident: full-time $7176; part-time $4164 per year. *Unit head:* Dr. Steve Bacon, Dean, 661-664-2210, Fax: 661-664-2016, E-mail: sbacon@csub.edu. *Application contact:* Debbie Blowers, Assistant Director of Admissions, 661-664-3381, E-mail: dblowers@csub.edu.
Website: https://www.csub.edu/sse/index.html

California State University, Dominguez Hills, College of Education, Carson, CA 90747-0001. Offers MA, MS. *Accreditation:* NCATE. *Program availability:* Part-time, evening/weekend. *Degree requirements:* For master's, comprehensive exam, thesis or alternative. *Entrance requirements:* For master's, minimum GPA of 2.75. Additional exam requirements/recommendations for international students: Required—TOEFL. *Faculty research:* Science education, literacy, language acquisition, math, social adjustment.

California State University, East Bay, Office of Graduate Studies, College of Education and Allied Studies, Department of Teacher Education, Hayward, CA 94542-3000. Offers education (MS), including curriculum, early childhood education, educational technology and leadership, reading instruction. *Program availability:* Online learning. *Faculty:* 11 full-time (8 women), 56 part-time/adjunct (40 women). *Students:* 49 full-time (35 women), 15 part-time (13 women); includes 31 minority (5 Black or African American, non-Hispanic/Latino; 13 Asian, non-Hispanic/Latino; 11 Hispanic/Latino; 2 Two or more races, non-Hispanic/Latino), 7 international. Average age 31. 76 applicants, 82% accepted, 33 enrolled. In 2017, 83 master's awarded. *Degree requirements:* For master's, project or thesis. *Entrance requirements:* For master's, minimum GPA of 3.0 in field, 2.5 overall; teaching experience; baccalaureate degree; 3 letters of recommendation. Additional exam requirements/recommendations for international students: Required—TOEFL (minimum score 550 paper-based), IELTS. *Application deadline:* For fall admission, 6/1 for domestic and international students. Application fee: $55. Electronic applications accepted. *Financial support:* Career-related internships or fieldwork, Federal Work-Study, and institutionally sponsored loans available. Support available to part-time students. Financial award application deadline: 3/2; financial award applicants required to submit FAFSA. *Faculty research:* Online, pedagogy, writing, learning, teaching. *Unit head:* Dr. Eric Engdahl, Chair, 510-885-4599, E-mail: eric.engdahl@csueastbay.edu. *Application contact:* Prof. Valerie Helgren-Lempesis, Education Graduate Advisor, 510-885-3006, Fax: 510-885-4632, E-mail: valerie.helgren-lempesis@csueastbay.edu.
Website: http://www20.csueastbay.edu/ceas/departments/ted/index.html

Education—General

California State University, Fresno, Division of Research and Graduate Studies, Kremen School of Education and Human Development, Fresno, CA 93740-8027. Offers MA, MS, Ed D. *Accreditation:* NCATE. *Program availability:* Part-time, evening/weekend. *Degree requirements:* For master's, thesis or alternative; for doctorate, thesis/dissertation. *Entrance requirements:* For master's, GRE General Test, MAT; for doctorate, GRE or MAT, minimum GPA of 3.2, master's degree. Additional exam requirements/recommendations for international students: Required—TOEFL. Electronic applications accepted. *Faculty research:* Adult community education, parenting, gifted and talented curriculum and instruction, peer mediation and conflict resolution.

California State University, Long Beach, Graduate Studies, College of Education, Long Beach, CA 90840. Offers MA, MS, Ed D. *Accreditation:* NCATE. *Program availability:* Part-time, evening/weekend. *Entrance requirements:* For master's, GRE General Test, minimum GPA of 2.75. Electronic applications accepted. *Faculty research:* K-16 educational reform and partnership, gender issues related to teaching and learning, urban education (poverty, diversity, language), assessment and standards-based education.

California State University, Los Angeles, Graduate Studies, Charter College of Education, Los Angeles, CA 90032-8530. Offers MA, MS, Ed D, PhD, Graduate Certificate. *Accreditation:* NCATE. *Program availability:* Part-time, evening/weekend. *Degree requirements:* For doctorate, thesis/dissertation. *Entrance requirements:* For master's, minimum GPA of 2.75 in last 90 units of course work, teaching certificate; for doctorate, GRE General Test, master's degree; minimum undergraduate GPA of 3.0, graduate 3.5. Additional exam requirements/recommendations for international students: Required—TOEFL (minimum score 500 paper-based). Electronic applications accepted.

California State University, Monterey Bay, College of Education, Seaside, CA 93955-8001. Offers MAE. *Accreditation:* NCATE. *Program availability:* Part-time, evening/weekend. *Degree requirements:* For master's, one foreign language, thesis, 2 years of teaching experience. *Entrance requirements:* For master's, recommendations. Additional exam requirements/recommendations for international students: Required—TOEFL (minimum score 550 paper-based; 71 iBT). Electronic applications accepted. *Faculty research:* Multicultural education, linguistic diversity, behavior analysis.

California State University, Northridge, Graduate Studies, Michael D. Eisner College of Education, Northridge, CA 91330. Offers MA, MA Ed, MS, Ed D. *Accreditation:* NCATE. *Program availability:* Part-time, evening/weekend. *Students:* 351 full-time (296 women), 553 part-time (441 women); includes 477 minority (33 Black or African American, non-Hispanic/Latino; 2 American Indian or Alaska Native, non-Hispanic/Latino; 57 Asian, non-Hispanic/Latino; 355 Hispanic/Latino; 1 Native Hawaiian or other Pacific Islander, non-Hispanic/Latino; 29 Two or more races, non-Hispanic/Latino), 19 international. Average age 33. 703 applicants, 48% accepted, 300 enrolled. In 2017, 284 master's awarded. *Entrance requirements:* Additional exam requirements/recommendations for international students: Required—TOEFL. *Application deadline:* For fall admission, 11/30 for domestic students. Application fee: $55. *Financial support:* Fellowships, career-related internships or fieldwork, Federal Work-Study, institutionally sponsored loans, scholarships/grants, and tuition waivers (partial) available. Support available to part-time students. Financial award application deadline: 3/1. *Faculty research:* Federal teacher center support, bilingual teacher training. *Unit head:* Dr. Shari Tarver Behring, Dean, 818-677-2590, E-mail: coe.educ@csun.edu. Website: http://www.csun.edu/eisner-education

California State University, Sacramento, College of Education, Sacramento, CA 95819. Offers MA, MS, Ed D, Ed S. *Program availability:* Part-time, evening/weekend, blended/hybrid learning. *Students:* 381 full-time (294 women), 135 part-time (101 women); includes 296 minority (44 Black or African American, non-Hispanic/Latino; 1 American Indian or Alaska Native, non-Hispanic/Latino; 94 Asian, non-Hispanic/Latino; 153 Hispanic/Latino; 4 Native Hawaiian or other Pacific Islander, non-Hispanic/Latino). Average age 32. 550 applicants, 53% accepted, 292 enrolled. In 2017, 147 master's, 13 doctorates, 10 other advanced degrees awarded. *Degree requirements:* For master's, comprehensive exam, project, thesis, or writing proficiency exam; for doctorate, thesis/dissertation; for Ed S, project/thesis. *Entrance requirements:* For master's and doctorate, GRE. Additional exam requirements/recommendations for international students: Required—TOEFL (minimum score 550 paper-based; 80 iBT); Recommended—IELTS, TSE. *Application deadline:* For fall admission, 2/15 for domestic and international students; for spring admission, 9/15 for domestic and international students. Applications are processed on a rolling basis. Application fee: $55. Electronic applications accepted. *Financial support:* Teaching assistantships, career-related internships or fieldwork, and Federal Work-Study available. Support available to part-time students. Financial award application deadline: 3/1; financial award applicants required to submit FAFSA. *Unit head:* Dr. Alexander Sidorkin, Dean, 916-278-6639, E-mail: sidorkin@csus.edu. *Application contact:* Jose Martinez, Graduate Admissions Supervisor, 916-278-7871, E-mail: martinj@skymail.csus.edu. Website: http://www.edweb.csus.edu

California State University, San Bernardino, Graduate Studies, College of Education, Program in Education, San Bernardino, CA 92407. Offers MA. *Faculty:* 12 full-time (9 women), 10 part-time/adjunct (7 women). *Students:* 121 full-time (97 women), 200 part-time (156 women); includes 157 minority (20 Black or African American, non-Hispanic/Latino; 10 Asian, non-Hispanic/Latino; 117 Hispanic/Latino; 10 Two or more races, non-Hispanic/Latino), 47 international. Average age 35. 195 applicants, 78% accepted, 111 enrolled. In 2017, 121 master's awarded. *Degree requirements:* For master's, comprehensive exam (for some programs), thesis (for some programs). *Entrance requirements:* Additional exam requirements/recommendations for international students: Required—TOEFL. *Application deadline:* For fall admission, 7/16 for domestic students. Application fee: $55. *Unit head:* Dr. Jay Fiene, Dean, 909-537-5600, Fax: 909-537-7510, E-mail: jfiene@csusb.edu. *Application contact:* Dr. Dorota Huizinga, Dean of Graduate Studies, 909-537-3064, E-mail: dorota.huizinga@csusb.edu.

California State University, San Marcos, College of Education, Health and Human Services, School of Education, San Marcos, CA 92096-0001. Offers education (MA); educational administration (MA); educational leadership (Ed D); literacy education (MA); special education (MA). *Accreditation:* NCATE (one or more programs are accredited). *Program availability:* Part-time, evening/weekend. *Entrance requirements:* For master's, minimum GPA of 3.0, teaching credentials, 1 year of teaching experience. *Application deadline:* For fall admission, 2/1 priority date for domestic students. Applications are processed on a rolling basis. Application fee: $55. *Expenses:* Tuition, state resident: full-time $7176. Tuition, nonresident: full-time $9504. *Financial support:* Applicants required to submit FAFSA. *Faculty research:* Multicultural literature, art as knowledge, poetry and second language acquisition, restructuring K–12 education and improving the training of K–8 science teachers. *Unit head:* Pat Stall, Director, 760-750-4386, E-mail: pstall@csusm.edu. Website: http://www.csusm.edu/education/

California State University, Stanislaus, College of Education, Kinesiology and Social Work, Turlock, CA 95382. Offers MA, MSW, Ed D. *Accreditation:* NCATE. *Program availability:* Part-time, evening/weekend. *Degree requirements:* For master's, thesis.

Entrance requirements: For master's, MAT, minimum GPA of 3.0. Additional exam requirements/recommendations for international students: Required—TOEFL (minimum score 550 paper-based).

California University of Pennsylvania, School of Graduate Studies and Research, College of Education and Human Services, California, PA 15419-1394. Offers M Ed, MAT, MS, MSW, Ed D. *Accreditation:* NCATE. *Program availability:* Part-time, evening/weekend, online learning. *Degree requirements:* For master's, comprehensive exam, thesis optional. *Entrance requirements:* For master's, PRAXIS, MAT, minimum GPA of 3.0. Additional exam requirements/recommendations for international students: Required—TOEFL (minimum score 550 paper-based; 80 iBT). *Application deadline:* For fall admission, 8/1 priority date for domestic and international students; for winter admission, 12/1 priority date for domestic and international students; for spring admission, 5/1 priority date for domestic and international students. Applications are processed on a rolling basis. Application fee: $25. Electronic applications accepted. *Financial support:* Applicants required to submit FAFSA. *Faculty research:* Autism counseling, injury and education, early childhood education, National Board certification. *Unit head:* Geraldine Jones, Dean, 724-938-4125, E-mail: jones_gm@cup.edu. *Application contact:* Suzanne P. Powers, Director of Graduate Admissions and Recruitment, 724-938-4029, Fax: 724-938-5712, E-mail: powers_s@cup.edu. Website: http://www.calu.edu/academics/colleges/education/

Calvary University, Graduate School and Seminary, Kansas City, MO 64147. Offers Bible and theology (MS); Biblical counseling (MA); education (MS), including administration and leadership, Christian education, curriculum and instruction, elementary education; organizational development (MS); pastoral studies (M Div); worship arts (MS). *Program availability:* Part-time, evening/weekend. *Faculty:* 6 full-time (2 women), 2 part-time/adjunct (1 woman). *Students:* 11 full-time (3 women), 29 part-time (15 women); includes 12 minority (4 Black or African American, non-Hispanic/Latino; 1 American Indian or Alaska Native, non-Hispanic/Latino; 6 Asian, non-Hispanic/Latino; 1 Native Hawaiian or other Pacific Islander, non-Hispanic/Latino). Average age 39. *Degree requirements:* For master's, variable foreign language requirement, comprehensive exam, thesis or alternative. *Entrance requirements:* For master's, minimum GPA of 2.5, BA or BS, doctrine agreement. Additional exam requirements/recommendations for international students: Required—TOEFL (minimum score 550 paper-based). *Application deadline:* Applications are processed on a rolling basis. Application fee: $0. Electronic applications accepted. *Expenses:* Contact institution. *Financial support:* Scholarships/grants available. Financial award application deadline: 11/5; financial award applicants required to submit FAFSA. *Unit head:* Dr. Thomas Baurain, Director of Seminary, 816-322-0110 Ext. 1502, Fax: 816-331-4474, E-mail: thomas.baurain@calvary.edu. *Application contact:* Ann Rogers, Admissions Office Assistant, 800-326-3960 Ext. 1321, Fax: 816-331-4474, E-mail: admissions@calvary.edu. Website: http://www.calvary.edu

Calvin College, Graduate Programs in Education, Grand Rapids, MI 49546-4388. Offers curriculum and instruction (M Ed). *Accreditation:* TEAC. *Program availability:* Part-time. *Degree requirements:* For master's, thesis or seminar. *Entrance requirements:* For master's, teaching certificate. Additional exam requirements/recommendations for international students: Required—TOEFL (minimum score 550 paper-based; 80 iBT). Electronic applications accepted. *Expenses:* Contact institution. *Faculty research:* Literacy, racialized gender and gendered identity, teacher learning, learning disabilities identification, leadership.

Cambridge College, School of Education, Boston, MA 02129. Offers autism specialist (M Ed); autism/behavior analyst (M Ed); behavior analyst (Post-Master's Certificate); behavioral management (M Ed); early childhood teacher (M Ed); education specialist in curriculum and instruction (CAGS); educational leadership (Ed D); elementary teacher (M Ed); English as a second language (M Ed, Certificate); general science (M Ed); health education (Post-Master's Certificate); health/family and consumer sciences (M Ed); history (M Ed); individualized (M Ed); information technology literacy (M Ed); instructional technology (M Ed); interdisciplinary studies (M Ed); library teacher (M Ed); literacy education (M Ed); mathematics (M Ed); mathematics specialist (Certificate); middle school mathematics and science (M Ed); school administration (M Ed, CAGS); school guidance counselor (M Ed); school nurse education (M Ed); school social worker/school adjustment counselor (M Ed); special education administrator (CAGS); special education/moderate disabilities (M Ed); teaching skills and methodologies (M Ed). *Program availability:* Part-time, evening/weekend, online learning. *Degree requirements:* For master's, internship/practicum (licensure program only); for doctorate, thesis/dissertation; for other advanced degree, thesis. *Entrance requirements:* For master's, interview, resume, documentation of licensure, 2 professional references; for doctorate, official transcripts, interview, resume, documentation of licensure (if any), written personal statement/essay, portfolio of scholarly and professional work, qualifying assessment, 2 professional references, health insurance, immunizations form; for other advanced degree, official transcripts, interview, resume, documentation of licensure (if any), written personal statement/essay, 2 professional references, health insurance, immunizations form. Additional exam requirements/recommendations for international students: Required—TOEFL (minimum score 550 paper-based; 79 iBT), Michigan English Language Assessment Battery (minimum score 85); Recommended—IELTS (minimum score 6). Electronic applications accepted. *Expenses:* Contact institution. *Faculty research:* Adult education, accelerated learning, mathematics education, brain compatible learning, special education and law.

Cameron University, Office of Graduate Studies, Program in Education, Lawton, OK 73505-6377. Offers M Ed. *Accreditation:* NCATE. *Program availability:* Part-time, evening/weekend. *Degree requirements:* For master's, portfolio. *Entrance requirements:* Additional exam requirements/recommendations for international students: Required—TOEFL (minimum score 550 paper-based). Electronic applications accepted. *Faculty research:* Motivation, computer learning, special education mathematics, inquiry-based learning.

Cameron University, Office of Graduate Studies, Program in Teaching, Lawton, OK 73505-6377. Offers MAT. *Accreditation:* NCATE. *Degree requirements:* For master's, portfolio. *Entrance requirements:* Additional exam requirements/recommendations for international students: Required—TOEFL (minimum score 550 paper-based). Electronic applications accepted. *Faculty research:* Teacher retention/attrition, teacher education.

Campbellsville University, School of Education, Campbellsville, KY 42718-2799. Offers education (MA); school counseling (MA); school improvement (MA); special education (MASE); special education-teacher leader (MA); teacher leader (MA); teaching (MAT), including middle grades biology, middle grades chemistry, middle grades English. *Accreditation:* NCATE. *Program availability:* Part-time, evening/weekend, 100% online, blended/hybrid learning. *Faculty:* 15 full-time (10 women), 14 part-time/adjunct (9 women). *Students:* 26 full-time (20 women), 155 part-time (122 women); includes 14 minority (13 Black or African American, non-Hispanic/Latino; 1 Hispanic/Latino). Average age 35. 199 applicants, 34% accepted, 57 enrolled. In 2017, 96 master's awarded. *Degree requirements:* For master's, comprehensive exam (for some programs), thesis, research paper. *Entrance requirements:* For master's, GRE or PRAXIS, minimum undergraduate GPA of 2.75, teaching certificate, professional growth plan, letters of recommendation, interview. Additional exam requirements/

recommendations for international students: Recommended—TOEFL (minimum score 550 paper-based; 79 iBT), IELTS (minimum score 6). *Application deadline:* Applications are processed on a rolling basis. Application fee: $25. Electronic applications accepted. Application fee is waived when completed online. *Expenses:* $399 per credit hour. *Financial support:* Unspecified assistantships and employee tuition waivers available. Financial award applicants required to submit FAFSA. *Faculty research:* Professional development, curriculum development, school governance, assessment, special education. *Unit head:* Dr. Beverly Ennis, Dean, 270-789-5344, Fax: 270-789-5206, E-mail: bcennis@campbellsville.edu. *Application contact:* Monica Bamwine, Assistant Director of Graduate Admissions, 270-789-5221, Fax: 270-789-5071, E-mail: mkbamwine@campbellsville.edu.

Campbell University, Graduate and Professional Programs, School of Education, Buies Creek, NC 27506. Offers elementary education (M Ed); interdisciplinary studies (M Ed); middle grades education (M Ed); physical education (M Ed); school administration (MSA); school counseling (M Ed); secondary education (M Ed). *Accreditation:* NCATE. *Program availability:* Part-time, evening/weekend. *Degree requirements:* For master's, comprehensive exam. *Entrance requirements:* For master's, GRE General Test, minimum GPA of 2.7. *Faculty research:* Spiritual values and wellness issues in counseling, stress and professional burnout among counselors, thinking strategies, leadership, adaptive technology.

Canisius College, Graduate Division, School of Education and Human Services, Buffalo, NY 14208-1098. Offers MS, MS Ed, MSA, Certificate. *Program availability:* Part-time, evening/weekend, 100% online, blended/hybrid learning. *Faculty:* 26 full-time (15 women), 58 part-time/adjunct (39 women). *Students:* 328 full-time (219 women), 388 part-time (271 women); includes 102 minority (66 Black or African American, non-Hispanic/Latino; 3 American Indian or Alaska Native, non-Hispanic/Latino; 4 Asian, non-Hispanic/Latino; 19 Hispanic/Latino; 10 Two or more races, non-Hispanic/Latino), 13 international. Average age 31. 490 applicants, 86% accepted, 315 enrolled. In 2017, 449 master's awarded. *Degree requirements:* For master's, thesis (for some programs). *Entrance requirements:* For master's, GRE (if cumulative GPA less than 2.7), transcripts, BA from accredited institution. Additional exam requirements/recommendations for international students: Required—TOEFL (minimum score 550 paper-based, 79 iBT), IELTS (minimum score 6.5), or CAEL (minimum score 70). *Application deadline:* Applications are processed on a rolling basis. Application fee: $0. Electronic applications accepted. *Expenses: Tuition:* Full-time $22,860; part-time $820 per credit. *Required fees:* $720; $25 per credit. $65 per semester. One-time fee: $425. *Financial support:* Career-related internships or fieldwork, Federal Work-Study, scholarships/grants, tuition waivers (partial), and unspecified assistantships available. Support available to part-time students. Financial award application deadline: 4/30; financial award applicants required to submit FAFSA. *Faculty research:* Asperger's disease, autism, culturally congruent pedagogy in physical education, family as faculty, impact of trauma on adults, information processing and perceptual styles of athletes, integrating digital technologies in the classroom, long term psych-social impact on police officers, private higher education, qualities of effective coaches, reading strategies, student perceptions of online courses, teaching effectiveness, teaching methods, tutorial experiences in modern math. *Unit head:* Dr. Jeffrey R. Lindauer, Dean, 716-888-3294, Fax: 716-888-3164, E-mail: lindauej@canisius.edu.
Website: http://www.canisius.edu/graduate/

Capella University, School of Education, Doctoral Programs in Education, Minneapolis, MN 55402. Offers curriculum and instruction (PhD); educational leadership and management (Ed D); instructional design for online learning (PhD); K-12 studies in education (PhD); leadership for higher education (PhD); leadership in educational administration (PhD); postsecondary and adult education (PhD); professional studies in education (PhD); reading and literacy (Ed D); special education leadership (PhD); training and performance improvement (PhD).

Capella University, School of Education, Master's Programs in Education, Minneapolis, MN 55402. Offers adult education (MS); curriculum and instruction (MS); early childhood education (MS); enrollment management (MS); higher education leadership and management (MS); instructional design for online learning (MS); integrative studies (MS); K-12 studies in education (MS); leadership in educational administration (MS); reading and literacy (MS); special education teaching (MS).

Cardinal Stritch University, College of Education and Leadership, Milwaukee, WI 53217-3985. Offers MA, MS, Ed D, PHD. *Accreditation:* NCATE. *Program availability:* Part-time, evening/weekend, 100% online. *Students:* 226 part-time (146 women); includes 55 minority (32 Black or African American, non-Hispanic/Latino; 6 Asian, non-Hispanic/Latino; 14 Hispanic/Latino; 1 Native Hawaiian or other Pacific Islander, non-Hispanic/Latino; 2 Two or more races, non-Hispanic/Latino), 7 international. Average age 38. 356 applicants, 100% accepted, 189 enrolled. In 2017, 152 master's, 28 doctorates awarded. *Degree requirements:* For master's, comprehensive exam, thesis (for some programs); for doctorate, thesis/dissertation, practica/field experience. *Entrance requirements:* For doctorate, minimum GPA of 3.5 in master's coursework, portfolio, interview, 3 letters of recommendation. Additional exam requirements/recommendations for international students: Required—TOEFL (minimum score 79 iBT), IELTS (minimum score 6.5). *Application deadline:* For fall admission, 7/15 priority date for domestic students; for spring admission, 12/15 priority date for domestic students. Applications are processed on a rolling basis. Electronic applications accepted. *Expenses:* $680 per credit. *Financial support:* Fellowships, research assistantships with partial tuition reimbursements, career-related internships or fieldwork, Federal Work-Study, and scholarships/grants available. Financial award applicants required to submit FAFSA. *Unit head:* Dr. Freda Russell, Dean, 414-410-4735, E-mail: frrussell@stritch.edu. *Application contact:* Graduate Admissions, 800-347-8822 Ext. 4042, E-mail: admissions@stritch.edu.

Caribbean University, Graduate School, Bayamón, PR 00960-0493. Offers administration and supervision (MA Ed); criminal justice (MA); curriculum and instruction (MA Ed, PhD), including elementary education (MA Ed), English education (MA Ed), history education (MA Ed), mathematics education (MA Ed), primary education (MA Ed), science education (MA Ed), Spanish education (MA Ed); educational technology in instructional systems (MA Ed); gerontology (MSN); human resources (MBA); museology, archiving and art history (MA Ed); neonatal pediatrics (MSN); physical education (MA Ed); special education (MA Ed). *Entrance requirements:* For master's, interview, minimum GPA of 2.5.

Carlow University, College of Learning and Innovation, Pittsburgh, PA 15213-3165. Offers M Ed, MA, MFA, Certificate, Graduate Certificate. *Program availability:* Part-time, evening/weekend, 100% online, blended/hybrid learning, low-residency. *Students:* 51 full-time (47 women), 41 part-time (37 women); includes 16 minority (10 Black or African American, non-Hispanic/Latino; 1 American Indian or Alaska Native, non-Hispanic/Latino; 2 Asian, non-Hispanic/Latino; 3 Two or more races, non-Hispanic/Latino), 1 international. Average age 31. 23 applicants, 100% accepted, 19 enrolled. In 2017, 57 master's, 9 other advanced degrees awarded. *Entrance requirements:* For master's, personal essay (two for MFA); resume or curriculum vitae; two recommendations; official transcripts; interview; minimum undergraduate GPA of 3.0. Additional exam requirements/recommendations for international students: Required—TOEFL (minimum score 550 paper-based). *Application deadline:* Applications are processed on a rolling

basis. Application fee: $0. Electronic applications accepted. *Expenses:* Contact institution. *Financial support:* Application deadline: 4/1; applicants required to submit FAFSA. *Unit head:* Dr. Matthew Gordley, Dean, 412-578-6262, E-mail: megordley@carlow.edu. *Application contact:* 412-578-6059, E-mail: gradstudies@carlow.edu.
Website: http://www.carlow.edu/College_of_Learning_and_Innovation.aspx

Carroll University, Graduate Programs in Education, Waukesha, WI 53186-5593. Offers adult and continuing education (M Ed); educational leadership (MS); PK-12 (M Ed). *Program availability:* Part-time, evening/weekend. *Degree requirements:* For master's, thesis. *Entrance requirements:* For master's, minimum undergraduate GPA of 2.5 in related field. Additional exam requirements/recommendations for international students: Required—TOEFL. Electronic applications accepted. *Faculty research:* Qualitative research methods, whole language approaches to teaching, the writing process, multicultural education, gifted/talented learners.

Carson-Newman University, Graduate Program in Education, Jefferson City, TN 37760. Offers curriculum and instruction (M Ed); educational leadership (M Ed); elementary education (MAT); school counseling (MS); secondary education (MAT); teaching English as a second language (MATESL). *Accreditation:* NCATE. *Program availability:* Part-time, evening/weekend, 100% online, blended/hybrid learning. *Faculty:* 20 full-time (11 women), 16 part-time/adjunct (13 women). *Students:* 63 full-time (37 women), 488 part-time (362 women); includes 60 minority (46 Black or African American, non-Hispanic/Latino; 2 American Indian or Alaska Native, non-Hispanic/Latino; 1 Asian, non-Hispanic/Latino; 5 Hispanic/Latino; 1 Native Hawaiian or other Pacific Islander, non-Hispanic/Latino; 5 Two or more races, non-Hispanic/Latino), 29 international. Average age 35. 204 applicants, 100% accepted, 188 enrolled. In 2017, 211 master's awarded. *Degree requirements:* For master's, thesis or alternative. *Entrance requirements:* For master's, PRAXIS II or GRE with minimum score of 290 on the verbal and quantitative components (for MAT), minimum GPA of 3.0 in major, 2.5 overall. Additional exam requirements/recommendations for international students: Recommended—TOEFL (minimum score 79 iBT), IELTS (minimum score 6.5), TSE (minimum score 53). *Application deadline:* For fall admission, 7/15 priority date for domestic students. Applications are processed on a rolling basis. Application fee: $50. *Expenses: Tuition:* Full-time $10,516; part-time $478 per credit hour. *Required fees:* $240; $120 per semester. One-time fee: $150. *Financial support:* Federal Work-Study and unspecified assistantships available. Financial award applicants required to submit FAFSA. *Unit head:* Dr. Kim Hawkins, Chair, 865-471-3314, E-mail: khawkins@cn.edu. *Application contact:* Nilma Stewart, Graduate Admissions and Services Adviser, 865-471-3230, Fax: 865-471-3875, E-mail: adults@cn.edu.
Website: http://www.cn.edu/adult-graduate-studies

Carthage College, Division of Teacher Education, Kenosha, WI 53140. Offers classroom guidance and counseling (M Ed); creative arts (M Ed); gifted and talented children (M Ed); language arts (M Ed); modern language (M Ed); natural sciences (M Ed); reading (M Ed, Certificate); social sciences (M Ed); teacher leadership (M Ed). *Program availability:* Part-time, evening/weekend. *Degree requirements:* For master's, thesis optional. *Entrance requirements:* For master's, MAT, minimum B average, letters of reference.

Castleton University, Division of Graduate Studies, Department of Education, Castleton, VT 05735. Offers curriculum and instruction (MA Ed); educational leadership (MA Ed, CAGS); language arts and reading (MA Ed, CAGS); special education (MA Ed, CAGS). *Program availability:* Part-time, evening/weekend. *Degree requirements:* For master's, thesis or alternative; for CAGS, publishable paper. *Entrance requirements:* For master's, GRE General Test, MAT, interview, minimum undergraduate GPA of 3.0; for CAGS, educational research, master's degree, minimum undergraduate GPA of 3.0. *Faculty research:* Assessment, narrative.

The Catholic University of America, School of Arts and Sciences, Department of Education, Washington, DC 20064. Offers Catholic school leadership (MA); education (Certificate); secondary education (MA); special education (MA), including early childhood, non-categorical. *Accreditation:* NCATE. *Program availability:* Part-time. *Faculty:* 8 full-time (7 women), 3 part-time/adjunct (all women). *Students:* 9 full-time (all women), 25 part-time (14 women); includes 2 minority (both Hispanic/Latino), 4 international. Average age 39. 24 applicants, 63% accepted, 9 enrolled. In 2017, 9 master's awarded. *Degree requirements:* For master's, comprehensive exam, thesis or alternative; for Certificate, action research project. *Entrance requirements:* For master's, GRE General Test or MAT, statement of purpose, official copies of academic transcripts, three letters of recommendation, interview; for Certificate, PRAXIS I, statement of purpose, official copies of academic transcripts, three letters of recommendation, interview. Additional exam requirements/recommendations for international students: Required—TOEFL (minimum score 550 paper-based; 80 iBT). *Application deadline:* For fall admission, 7/15 priority date for domestic students, 7/1 for international students; for spring admission, 11/15 priority date for domestic students, 11/1 for international students. Applications are processed on a rolling basis. Application fee: $55. Electronic applications accepted. *Expenses:* Contact institution. *Financial support:* Fellowships, research assistantships, teaching assistantships, Federal Work-Study, scholarships/grants, tuition waivers (full and partial), and unspecified assistantships available. Financial award application deadline: 2/1; financial award applicants required to submit FAFSA. *Faculty research:* Special education, early childhood education, educational psychology, Catholic school administration, leadership and policy studies, counseling, curriculum and instruction. *Unit head:* Dr. Agnes Cave, Chair, 202-319-5805, Fax: 202-319-5815, E-mail: cave@cua.edu. *Application contact:* Dr. Steven Brown, Director of Graduate Admissions, 202-319-5057, Fax: 202-319-6533, E-mail: cua-admissions@cua.edu.
Website: http://education.cua.edu/

Cedar Crest College, Department of Education, Allentown, PA 18104-6196. Offers M Ed. *Program availability:* Part-time, evening/weekend, 100% online, blended/hybrid learning. *Faculty:* 3 full-time (all women), 8 part-time/adjunct (5 women). *Students:* 9 full-time (7 women), 57 part-time (50 women); includes 7 minority (3 Black or African American, non-Hispanic/Latino; 3 Hispanic/Latino; 1 Two or more races, non-Hispanic/Latino). Average age 34. In 2017, 38 master's awarded. *Entrance requirements:* Additional exam requirements/recommendations for international students: Required—TOEFL. *Application deadline:* For fall admission, 8/7 priority date for domestic and international students; for winter admission, 11/7 priority date for domestic and international students; for spring admission, 1/8 priority date for domestic and international students. Applications are processed on a rolling basis. Electronic applications accepted. *Expenses:* Contact institution. *Financial support:* In 2017–18, 60 students received support. Available to part-time students. Applicants required to submit FAFSA. *Faculty research:* Science education, reading, history of Pennsylvania, math education. *Unit head:* Dr. Jill Purdy, Graduate Program Director, 610-606-4666 Ext. 3419, E-mail: jepurdy@cedarcrest.edu. *Application contact:* Nancy Wunderly, Director of School of Adult and Graduate Education, 610-606-4666, E-mail: sage@cedarcrest.edu.

Centenary College of Louisiana, Graduate Programs, Department of Education, Shreveport, LA 71104. Offers elementary education (MAT); secondary education (MAT). *Program availability:* Part-time, evening/weekend. *Degree requirements:* For master's, comprehensive exam. *Entrance requirements:* For master's, PRAXIS I and II (for MAT), undergraduate degree, minimum GPA of 2.5. *Expenses:* Contact institution. *Faculty research:* Teachers as advocates for teachers, portfolio assessment, disabled readers.

Centenary University, Program in Education, Hackettstown, NJ 07840-2100. Offers education practice (M Ed); educational leadership (MA, Ed D); instructional leadership (MA); reading (M Ed); special education (MA). *Accreditation:* TEAC. *Program availability:* Part-time, evening/weekend, online learning. *Degree requirements:* For master's, thesis. *Entrance requirements:* For master's, interview, minimum undergraduate GPA of 2.8.

Central Connecticut State University, School of Graduate Studies, School of Education and Professional Studies, New Britain, CT 06050-4010. Offers MAT, MS, Ed D, AC, Certificate, Sixth Year Certificate. *Accreditation:* NCATE. *Program availability:* Part-time, evening/weekend. *Faculty:* 50 full-time (29 women), 61 part-time/adjunct (44 women). *Students:* 289 full-time (209 women), 824 part-time (622 women); includes 248 minority (98 Black or African American, non-Hispanic/Latino; 2 American Indian or Alaska Native, non-Hispanic/Latino; 9 Asian, non-Hispanic/Latino; 108 Hispanic/Latino; 1 Native Hawaiian or other Pacific Islander, non-Hispanic/Latino; 30 Two or more races, non-Hispanic/Latino), 3 international. Average age 33. 492 applicants, 74% accepted, 265 enrolled. In 2017, 257 master's, 13 doctorates, 126 other advanced degrees awarded. *Degree requirements:* For master's, comprehensive exam, thesis or alternative; for doctorate, thesis/dissertation; for other advanced degree, qualifying exam. *Entrance requirements:* For master's, minimum undergraduate GPA of 2.7; for doctorate, GRE. Additional exam requirements/recommendations for international students: Required—TOEFL (minimum score 550 paper-based; 79 iBT); Recommended—IELTS (minimum score 6.5). *Application deadline:* For fall admission, 8/1 for domestic students, 5/1 for international students; for spring admission, 11/1 for domestic and international students. Applications are processed on a rolling basis. Application fee: $50. Electronic applications accepted. *Expenses: Tuition, area resident:* Full-time $6757. Tuition, state resident: full-time $9750; part-time $374 per credit. Tuition, nonresident: full-time $18,102; part-time $374 per credit. *Required fees:* $4635; $255 per credit. *Financial support:* In 2017–18, 121 students received support. Career-related internships or fieldwork, Federal Work-Study, scholarships/grants, and unspecified assistantships available. Support available to part-time students. Financial award application deadline: 3/1; financial award applicants required to submit FAFSA. *Unit head:* Dr. Kimberly Kostelis, Interim Dean, 860-832-2101, E-mail: kimberly.kostelis@ccsu.edu. *Application contact:* Patricia Gardner, Associate Director of Graduate Studies, 860-832-2350, Fax: 860-832-2362.
Website: http://www.ccsu.edu/seps/

Central Methodist University, College of Graduate and Extended Studies, Fayette, MO 65248-1198. Offers clinical counseling (MS); clinical nurse leader (MSN); education (M Ed); music education (MME); nurse educator (MSN). *Program availability:* Part-time, evening/weekend, online learning. *Degree requirements:* For master's, thesis. *Entrance requirements:* For master's, GRE General Test, minimum GPA of 2.75. Electronic applications accepted.

Central Michigan University, Central Michigan University Global Campus, Program in Education, Mount Pleasant, MI 48859. Offers college teaching (Graduate Certificate); community college (MA); curriculum and instruction (MA); educational technology (MA, DET); reading and literacy K-12 (MA); school principalship (MA), including charter school leadership; training and development (MA). *Accreditation:* TEAC. *Program availability:* Part-time, evening/weekend. *Entrance requirements:* For master's, minimum GPA of 2.7 in major. Additional exam requirements/recommendations for international students: Required—TOEFL. Electronic applications accepted.

Central Michigan University, College of Graduate Studies, College of Education and Human Services, Mount Pleasant, MI 48859. Offers MA, MS, Ed D, Ed S, Graduate Certificate. *Accreditation:* TEAC. *Program availability:* Part-time, evening/weekend. *Degree requirements:* For master's and other advanced degree, thesis or alternative; for doctorate, thesis/dissertation. Electronic applications accepted.

Central Washington University, School of Graduate Studies and Research, College of Education and Professional Studies, Ellensburg, WA 98926. Offers M Ed, MS. *Program availability:* Part-time. *Entrance requirements:* For master's, minimum GPA of 3.0. Additional exam requirements/recommendations for international students: Required—TOEFL (minimum score 550 paper-based; 79 iBT). *Application deadline:* For fall admission, 2/1 priority date for domestic students; for winter admission, 10/1 for domestic students; for spring admission, 1/1 for domestic students. Applications are processed on a rolling basis. Application fee: $50. Electronic applications accepted. *Financial support:* Application deadline: 3/1; applicants required to submit FAFSA. *Unit head:* Dr. Paul Ballard, Dean, 509-963-1411, E-mail: paul.ballard@cwu.edu. *Application contact:* Justine Eason, Admissions Program Coordinator, 509-963-3103, Fax: 509-963-1799, E-mail: masters@cwu.edu.

Chadron State College, School of Professional and Graduate Studies, Department of Education, Chadron, NE 69337. Offers business (MA Ed); community counseling (MA Ed); educational administration (MS Ed, Sp Ed); elementary education (MS Ed); history (MA Ed); language and literature (MA Ed); secondary administration (MS Ed); secondary education (MS Ed). *Accreditation:* NCATE. *Program availability:* Part-time, evening/weekend, online learning. *Degree requirements:* For master's, thesis optional. *Entrance requirements:* For master's, GRE General Test, GRE Writing Test, minimum GPA of 2.75 or 12 graduate hours at CSC with minimum GPA of 3.25. Additional exam requirements/recommendations for international students: Required—TOEFL. Electronic applications accepted. *Faculty research:* Rural education, technology, mental health.

Chaminade University of Honolulu, Office of Professional and Continuing Education, Program in Education, Honolulu, HI 96816-1578. Offers child development (M Ed); early childhood education (Montessori) (MAT); early childhood education (PK-3) (MAT); educational leadership (M Ed); elementary education (MAT); instructional leadership (M Ed); Montessori (M Ed); secondary education (MAT); special education (MAT); teacher leader (M Ed). *Program availability:* Part-time, evening/weekend, 100% online, blended/hybrid learning. *Faculty:* 7 full-time (3 women), 8 part-time/adjunct (6 women). *Students:* 86 full-time (68 women), 88 part-time (64 women); includes 113 minority (7 Black or African American, non-Hispanic/Latino; 2 American Indian or Alaska Native, non-Hispanic/Latino; 46 Asian, non-Hispanic/Latino; 7 Hispanic/Latino; 51 Native Hawaiian or other Pacific Islander, non-Hispanic/Latino), 6 international. Average age 34. 61 applicants, 98% accepted, 49 enrolled. In 2017, 91 master's awarded. *Degree requirements:* For master's, thesis or alternative. *Entrance requirements:* For master's, PRAXIS (for MAT), minimum GPA of 2.75 (for M Ed), 3.0 (for MAT); 2 letters of recommendation, resume, writing sample (for MAT). Additional exam requirements/recommendations for international students: Required—TOEFL (minimum score 550 paper-based; 79 iBT). *Application deadline:* Applications are processed on a rolling basis. Application fee: $40. Electronic applications accepted. *Expenses:* $780 per credit hour plus $93 fee per online class. *Financial support:* Applicants required to submit FAFSA. *Unit head:* Dr. Dale Fryxell, Dean, 808-739-4652, Fax: 808-739-4607, E-mail: edu-office@chaminade.edu. *Application contact:* 808-735-4755, E-mail: gradserv@chaminade.edu.
Website: https://education.chaminade.edu/

Chapman University, Donna Ford Attallah College of Educational Studies, Orange, CA 92866. Offers counseling (MA), including school counseling (MA, Credential); curriculum and instruction (MA), including elementary education, secondary education; education (PhD), including cultural and curricular studies, disability studies, leadership studies, school psychology (PhD, Credential); educational psychology (MA); leadership development (MA); multiple subjects (Credential), including Spanish/English bilingual; pupil personnel services (Credential), including school counseling (MA, Credential); school psychology (PhD, Credential); school psychology (Ed S); single subject (Credential); special education (MA, Credential), including mild/moderate (Credential), moderate/severe (Credential); teaching (MA), including elementary education, secondary education, secondary music education. *Accreditation:* TEAC. *Program availability:* Part-time, evening/weekend. *Faculty:* 32 full-time (18 women), 37 part-time/adjunct (26 women). *Students:* 170 full-time (140 women), 180 part-time (129 women); includes 164 minority (6 Black or African American, non-Hispanic/Latino; 38 Asian, non-Hispanic/Latino; 101 Hispanic/Latino; 1 Native Hawaiian or other Pacific Islander, non-Hispanic/Latino; 18 Two or more races, non-Hispanic/Latino), 10 international. Average age 28. 143 applicants, 63% accepted, 64 enrolled. In 2017, 126 master's, 18 doctorates awarded. *Application deadline:* Applications are processed on a rolling basis. Application fee: $60. Electronic applications accepted. *Expenses:* Contact institution. *Financial support:* Fellowships and scholarships/grants available. Financial award application deadline: 3/2; financial award applicants required to submit FAFSA. *Unit head:* Dr. Margaret Grogan, Dean, 714-516-5968, E-mail: grogan@chapman.edu. *Application contact:* Shannon McCance, Graduate Admission Counselor, 714-516-5236, E-mail: smccance@chapman.edu.
Website: http://www.chapman.edu/CES/

Charleston Southern University, College of Education, Charleston, SC 29423-8087. Offers elementary administration and supervision (M Ed); elementary education (M Ed); secondary administration and supervision (M Ed). *Accreditation:* NCATE. *Program availability:* Part-time, evening/weekend. *Degree requirements:* For master's, thesis optional. *Entrance requirements:* For master's, GRE or MAT. Additional exam requirements/recommendations for international students: Required—TOEFL (minimum score 550 paper-based; 79 iBT). *Application deadline:* Applications are processed on a rolling basis. Application fee: $40. Electronic applications accepted. *Expenses:* Contact institution. *Financial support:* Research assistantships with full tuition reimbursements, career-related internships or fieldwork, and Federal Work-Study available. Financial award application deadline: 4/15; financial award applicants required to submit FAFSA. *Unit head:* Dr. George Metz, Dean, 843-863-7765, Fax: 843-863-7784, E-mail: gmetz@csuniv.edu.
Website: http://www.csuniv.edu/education/

Chatham University, Program in Education, Pittsburgh, PA 15232-2826. Offers early childhood education (MAT); elementary education (MAT); environmental education (K-12) (MAT); secondary art (MAT); secondary biology education (MAT); secondary chemistry education (MAT); secondary English education (MAT); secondary math education (MAT); secondary physics education (MAT); secondary social studies education (MAT); special education (MAT). *Faculty:* 1 (woman) full-time, 15 part-time/adjunct (13 women). *Students:* 31 full-time (23 women), 3 part-time (1 woman); includes 9 minority (8 Black or African American, non-Hispanic/Latino; 1 Hispanic/Latino). Average age 30. 25 applicants, 60% accepted, 9 enrolled. In 2017, 23 master's awarded. *Degree requirements:* For master's, thesis, teaching experience. *Entrance requirements:* For master's, minimum GPA of 3.0, sample of written work, recommendation letters. Additional exam requirements/recommendations for international students: Required—TOEFL (minimum score 600 paper-based; 100 iBT), IELTS (minimum score 7), TWE. *Application deadline:* For fall admission, 4/1 priority date for domestic and international students; for spring admission, 11/1 priority date for domestic students, 10/1 priority date for international students. Applications are processed on a rolling basis. Application fee: $45. Electronic applications accepted. Application fee is waived when completed online. *Expenses: Tuition:* Full-time $16,740; part-time $930 per credit. *Required fees:* $486; $27 per credit. $243 per semester. *Financial support:* Career-related internships or fieldwork available. Financial award applicants required to submit FAFSA. *Faculty research:* Gifted education, environmental education, technology in education, writing as learning, class size and achievement. *Application contact:* Katie Noel, Assistant Director of Graduate Admission, 412-365-2758, Fax: 412-365-1609, E-mail: gradadmissions@chatham.edu.
Website: http://www.chatham.edu/mat

Chestnut Hill College, School of Graduate Studies, Department of Education, Philadelphia, PA 19118-2693. Offers early education (M Ed), including early education; educational leadership (M Ed); elementary/middle education (M Ed); reading (M Ed), including reading specialist; secondary education (M Ed); special education (M Ed), including special education. *Program availability:* Part-time, evening/weekend. *Degree requirements:* For master's, thesis optional. *Entrance requirements:* For master's, PRAXIS I or proof of teaching certification, letters of recommendation, writing sample, 6 graduate credits with minimum B grade if undergraduate GPA less than 3.0. Additional exam requirements/recommendations for international students: Required—TOEFL (minimum score 500 paper-based), IELTS (minimum score 6.0), or TWE (minimum score 22). Electronic applications accepted. *Expenses:* Contact institution. *Faculty research:* Culturally responsive pedagogy, gender issues, autism, inclusive education, mentoring and induction programs.

Cheyney University of Pennsylvania, Graduate Programs, Cheyney, PA 19319. Offers M Ed, MPA, Certificate. *Program availability:* Part-time, evening/weekend. *Degree requirements:* For master's and Certificate, thesis or alternative. *Entrance requirements:* For master's and Certificate, GRE General Test, MAT, minimum GPA of 2.75. Electronic applications accepted. *Faculty research:* Teacher motivation, critical thinking.

Chicago State University, School of Graduate and Professional Studies, College of Education, Chicago, IL 60628. Offers M Ed, MA, MAT, MS Ed, Ed D. *Accreditation:* NCATE. *Program availability:* Part-time. *Entrance requirements:* For master's, minimum GPA of 2.75. *Application deadline:* For fall admission, 7/1 for domestic students; for spring admission, 11/10 for domestic students. Application fee: $25. *Unit head:* Dr. Sandra Westbrooks, Acting Dean, 773-995-2472, Fax: 773-995-2473. *Application contact:* Daphne G. Townsend, Admissions and Records Officer II, 773-995-2404, Fax: 773-995-3671, E-mail: g-studies1@csu.edu.

Chowan University, School of Graduate Studies, Murfreesboro, NC 27855. Offers education (M Ed). *Entrance requirements:* For master's, official transcripts, three letters of recommendation, personal statement, current teacher license. Additional exam requirements/recommendations for international students: Required—TOEFL. Application fee: $50. Electronic applications accepted. *Expenses: Tuition:* Part-time $400 per hour. *Unit head:* Dr. John Dilustro, Dean, 252-398-6528, E-mail: dilusj@chowan.edu. *Application contact:* Crystal Powell, Assistant Director of Graduate Admission, 252-398-6214, E-mail: powellcc@chowan.edu.
Website: https://www.chowan.edu/admissions/school-graduate-studies

Christian Brothers University, School of Arts, Memphis, TN 38104-5581. Offers Catholic studies (MACS); educational leadership (MSEL); teacher-leadership (M Ed); teaching (MAT). *Program availability:* Part-time, evening/weekend. *Entrance requirements:* For master's, GRE, GMAT, PRAXIS II. *Expenses:* Contact institution.

Christopher Newport University, Graduate Studies, Department of Teacher Preparation, Newport News, VA 23606-3072. Offers MAT. *Faculty:* 15 full-time (6 women), 16 part-time/adjunct (14 women). *Students:* 82 full-time (68 women); includes 3 minority (2 Asian, non-Hispanic/Latino; 1 Two or more races, non-Hispanic/Latino), 1 international. Average age 23. 96 applicants, 92% accepted, 78 enrolled. In 2017, 70 master's awarded. *Degree requirements:* For master's, comprehensive exam, thesis or alternative. *Entrance requirements:* For master's, PRAXIS II/Virginia Communication and Literacy Assessment (VCLA)/PRAXIS (core mathematics), minimum GPA of 3.0. Additional exam requirements/recommendations for international students: Required—TOEFL (minimum score 580 paper-based; 92 iBT), IELTS (minimum score 7). *Application deadline:* For spring admission, 10/15 for domestic students, 10/1 for international students; for summer admission, 12/1 for domestic and international students. Applications are processed on a rolling basis. Application fee: $65. Electronic applications accepted. *Expenses:* Tuition, state resident: full-time $6984; part-time $388 per credit hour. Tuition, nonresident: full-time $15,588; part-time $866 per credit hour. *Required fees:* $3906; $225 per credit hour. Tuition and fees vary according to course load. *Financial support:* In 2017–18, 3 students received support. Unspecified assistantships available. Financial award application deadline: 3/1; financial award applicants required to submit FAFSA. *Faculty research:* Early literacy development, instructional innovations, professional teaching standards, multicultural issues, aesthetic education. *Total annual research expenditures:* $27,000. *Unit head:* Dr. Jean Filetti, Director, 757-594-7388, Fax: 757-594-7803, E-mail: filetti@cnu.edu. *Application contact:* Lyn Sawyer, Associate Director, Graduate Admissions, 757-594-7544, Fax: 757-594-7649, E-mail: gradstdy@cnu.edu.
Website: http://cnu.edu/academics/departments/teacherprep/

The Citadel, The Military College of South Carolina, Citadel Graduate College, Zucker Family School of Education, Charleston, SC 29409. Offers elementary/secondary school administration and supervision (M Ed); elementary/secondary school counseling (M Ed); interdisciplinary STEM education (M Ed); literacy education (M Ed, Graduate Certificate); middle grades (MAT), including English, mathematics, science, social studies; physical education (grades K-12) (MAT); school superintendency (Ed S); secondary education (MAT), including biology, English, mathematics, social studies; student affairs (Graduate Certificate); student affairs and college counseling (M Ed). *Accreditation:* NCATE. *Program availability:* Part-time, evening/weekend, 100% online, blended/hybrid learning. *Degree requirements:* For master's, comprehensive exam (for some programs). *Entrance requirements:* For master's, GRE (minimum combined verbal and quantitative score of 290) or MAT (minimum score 396). Additional exam requirements/recommendations for international students: Required—TOEFL (minimum score 550 paper-based; 79 iBT). Electronic applications accepted. *Expenses:* Tuition, state resident: part-time $587 per credit hour. Tuition, nonresident: part-time $988 per credit hour. *Required fees:* $90 per term.

City College of the City University of New York, Graduate School, School of Education, New York, NY 10031-9198. Offers MA, MS, MS Ed, AC. *Accreditation:* NCATE. *Program availability:* Part-time, evening/weekend. *Entrance requirements:* For master's, Liberal Arts and Sciences Test (LAST), Content Specialty Test (CST). Additional exam requirements/recommendations for international students: Required—TOEFL.

City University of Seattle, Graduate Division, Albright School of Education, Seattle, WA 98121. Offers administrator certification (Certificate); curriculum and instruction (M Ed); elementary education (MIT); guidance and counseling (M Ed); leadership (M Ed); reading and literacy (M Ed); school counseling (M Ed); special education (MIT); superintendent certification (Certificate). *Program availability:* Part-time, evening/weekend, online learning. *Degree requirements:* For master's, comprehensive exam (for some programs), thesis (for some programs). *Entrance requirements:* For master's, baccalaureate degree or equivalent from an accredited or otherwise recognized institution. Additional exam requirements/recommendations for international students: Required—TOEFL (minimum score 567 paper-based; 87 iBT); Recommended—IELTS. Electronic applications accepted. *Expenses:* Contact institution.

Claremont Graduate University, Graduate Programs, School of Educational Studies, Claremont, CA 91711-6160. Offers Africana education (Certificate); education and policy (MA, PhD); higher education/student affairs (MA, PhD); human development (MA, PhD); public school administration (MA, PhD); quantitative evaluation (MA, PhD); special education (MA, PhD); teacher education (MA); teaching and learning (MA, PhD); urban leadership (PhD); MBA/PhD. PhD program offered jointly with San Diego State University. *Program availability:* Part-time. Terminal master's awarded for partial completion of doctoral program. *Entrance requirements:* For master's and doctorate, GRE General Test. Additional exam requirements/recommendations for international students: Required—TOEFL (minimum score 75 iBT). Electronic applications accepted. *Faculty research:* Education administration, K-12 and higher education, multicultural education, education policy, diversity in higher education, faculty issues.

Clarion University of Pennsylvania, College of Arts, Education and Sciences, Master of Education Program, Clarion, PA 16214. Offers curriculum and instruction (M Ed); early childhood (M Ed); math education (M Ed); reading (M Ed); science education (M Ed); special education (M Ed); technology (M Ed). *Accreditation:* NCATE. *Program availability:* Part-time, evening/weekend, online only, 100% online, blended/hybrid learning. *Faculty:* 6 full-time (3 women). *Students:* 11 full-time (all women), 101 part-time (82 women); includes 4 minority (2 Black or African American, non-Hispanic/Latino; 1 Hispanic/Latino; 1 Two or more races, non-Hispanic/Latino). Average age 30. 80 applicants, 98% accepted, 33 enrolled. In 2017, 52 master's awarded. *Degree requirements:* For master's, comprehensive exam, thesis, or portfolio. *Entrance requirements:* For master's, minimum QPA of 3.0. Additional exam requirements/recommendations for international students: Required—TOEFL (minimum score 550 paper-based, 80 iBT) or IELTS (7). *Application deadline:* For fall admission, 8/15 priority date for domestic students, 7/15 priority date for international students; for winter admission, 11/1 priority date for domestic students; for spring admission, 1/7 priority date for domestic students, 11/15 priority date for international students; for summer admission, 4/1 priority date for domestic students. Applications are processed on a rolling basis. Application fee: $40. Electronic applications accepted. *Expenses:* $655.05 per credit. *Financial support:* Career-related internships or fieldwork and scholarships/grants available. Support available to part-time students. Financial award application deadline: 3/1; financial award applicants required to submit FAFSA. *Unit head:* Dr. John McCullough, Chair, Department of Education, 814-393-2404, Fax: 814-393-2446, E-mail: gradstudies@clarion.edu. *Application contact:* Dana Bearer, Associate Director for Transfer, Adult, and Graduate Programs, 814-393-2337, Fax: 814-393-2722, E-mail: gradstudies@clarion.edu.

Clark Atlanta University, School of Education, Atlanta, GA 30314. Offers MA, MAT, Ed D, Ed S. *Accreditation:* NCATE. *Program availability:* Part-time, evening/weekend. *Faculty:* 13 full-time (7 women), 12 part-time/adjunct (5 women). *Students:* 84 full-time (57 women), 67 part-time (36 women); includes 112 minority (110 Black or African American, non-Hispanic/Latino; 1 Asian, non-Hispanic/Latino; 1 Hispanic/Latino), 31 international. Average age 32. 72 applicants, 96% accepted, 37 enrolled. In 2017, 33 master's, 21 doctorates, 1 other advanced degree awarded. *Degree requirements:* For master's, comprehensive exam; for doctorate, comprehensive exam, thesis/dissertation.

Entrance requirements: For master's, GRE General Test, minimum undergraduate GPA of 2.6; for doctorate, GRE General Test, minimum graduate GPA of 3.0. Additional exam requirements/recommendations for international students: Required—TOEFL (minimum score 500 paper-based; 61 iBT). *Application deadline:* For fall admission, 4/1 for domestic and international students; for spring admission, 11/1 for domestic and international students. Applications are processed on a rolling basis. Application fee: $40 ($55 for international students). Electronic applications accepted. *Financial support:* Career-related internships or fieldwork, Federal Work-Study, scholarships/grants, and unspecified assistantships available. Support available to part-time students. Financial award application deadline: 4/30; financial award applicants required to submit FAFSA. *Unit head:* Dr. Moses C. Norman, Dean, 404-880-8495, E-mail: mnorman@cau.edu.

Clarke University, Program in Education, Dubuque, IA 52001-3198. Offers instructional leadership (MAE). *Program availability:* Part-time, 100% online, blended/hybrid learning. *Faculty:* 3 full-time (all women), 2 part-time/adjunct (1 woman). *Students:* 3 full-time (all women), 27 part-time (19 women); includes 3 minority (1 Black or African American, non-Hispanic/Latino; 1 Hispanic/Latino; 1 Two or more races, non-Hispanic/Latino). Average age 29. 39 applicants, 87% accepted, 21 enrolled. In 2017, 15 master's awarded. *Degree requirements:* For master's, thesis optional. *Entrance requirements:* For master's, official transcripts documenting completion of undergraduate degree from accredited college or university, copy of teaching certificates and licenses, two recommendation forms, statement of goals and career plans, minimum GPA of 2.75. Additional exam requirements/recommendations for international students: Required—TOEFL (minimum score 550 paper-based; 80 iBT), IELTS (minimum score 6.5). *Application deadline:* Applications are processed on a rolling basis. Application fee: $35. Electronic applications accepted. *Expenses:* $515 per credit. *Financial support:* Applicants required to submit FAFSA. *Unit head:* Beth Putnam, Director of Graduate Education, 563-588-6573, E-mail: beth.putnam@clarke.edu. *Application contact:* Kimberly Roush, Director of Admission, Graduate and Adult Programs, 563-588-6539, Fax: 563-552-7994, E-mail: graduate@clarke.edu.

Clarkson University, Program in Education, Schenectady, NY 12308. Offers adolescence education 7-12 (MAT); teaching of English to speakers of other languages (MAT); technology education K-12 (MAT). *Accreditation:* TEAC. *Faculty:* 3 full-time (all women), 23 part-time/adjunct (14 women). *Students:* 22 full-time (13 women), 12 part-time (8 women); includes 4 minority (1 Black or African American, non-Hispanic/Latino; 3 Asian, non-Hispanic/Latino), 6 international. 39 applicants, 72% accepted, 21 enrolled. In 2017, 28 master's awarded. *Degree requirements:* For master's, thesis (for some programs), thesis or project. *Entrance requirements:* For master's, GRE, minimum undergraduate GPA of 3.0. Additional exam requirements/recommendations for international students: Required—TOEFL (minimum score 550 paper-based, 80 iBT) or IELTS (6.5). *Application deadline:* Applications are processed on a rolling basis. Application fee: $50. Electronic applications accepted. *Expenses:* Contact institution. *Financial support:* Scholarships/grants available. *Unit head:* Dr. Catherine Snyder, Chair of Education, 518-631-9870, E-mail: csnyder@clarkson.edu. *Application contact:* Dan Capogna, Director of Graduate Admissions, 518-631-9910, E-mail: graduate@clarkson.edu.
Website: https://www.clarkson.edu/academics/graduate

Clark University, Graduate School, Adam Institute for Urban Teaching and School Practice, Worcester, MA 01610-1477. Offers MAT, PhD. *Faculty:* 11 full-time (7 women), 8 part-time/adjunct (4 women). *Students:* 34 full-time (27 women); includes 7 minority (1 Black or African American, non-Hispanic/Latino; 3 Asian, non-Hispanic/Latino; 1 Hispanic/Latino; 2 Two or more races, non-Hispanic/Latino). Average age 24. 73 applicants, 52% accepted, 33 enrolled. In 2017, 28 master's awarded. *Degree requirements:* For master's, thesis or alternative, oral exam. *Entrance requirements:* For master's, GRE General Test, minimum GPA of 3.0, professional experience, 2 references, statement of purpose, resume. Additional exam requirements/recommendations for international students: Required—TOEFL (minimum score 575 paper-based; 90 iBT), IELTS (minimum score 6.5). *Application deadline:* For fall admission, 1/15 priority date for domestic students. Application fee: $75. Electronic applications accepted. *Expenses:* $2,265 tuition per 14-week course; $40 activity fee (full-time students only); $80 miscellaneous one-time fee. *Financial support:* Fellowships with tuition reimbursements, research assistantships with tuition reimbursements, teaching assistantships with tuition reimbursements, institutionally sponsored loans, and tuition waivers (partial) available. *Faculty research:* Developmental learning, instructional theory, educational program management, special education, urban education. *Unit head:* Dr. Thomas Del Prete, Co-Chair, 508-793-7197, E-mail: tdelprete@clarku.edu. *Application contact:* Andrea Allen, Program Administrator, 508-793-7685, E-mail: aallen@clarku.edu.
Website: http://www.clarku.edu/education/adam-institute/

Clayton State University, School of Graduate Studies, College of Arts and Sciences, Program in Education, Morrow, GA 30260-0285. Offers biology (MAT); English (MAT); history (MAT); mathematics (MAT). *Accreditation:* NCATE. *Entrance requirements:* For master's, GRE, GACE, 2 official copies of transcripts, 3 recommendation letters, statement of purpose. Additional exam requirements/recommendations for international students: Required—TOEFL (minimum score 550 paper-based). Electronic applications accepted.

Clemson University, Graduate School, College of Education, Clemson, SC 29634. Offers M Ed, MAT, MHRD, MS, Ed D, PhD, Certificate, Ed S. *Program availability:* Part-time, evening/weekend, 100% online. *Faculty:* 74 full-time (53 women), 1 part-time/adjunct (0 women). *Students:* 546 full-time (407 women), 616 part-time (467 women); includes 206 minority (118 Black or African American, non-Hispanic/Latino; 16 Asian, non-Hispanic/Latino; 44 Hispanic/Latino; 2 Native Hawaiian or other Pacific Islander, non-Hispanic/Latino; 26 Two or more races, non-Hispanic/Latino), 7 international. Average age 32. 797 applicants, 65% accepted, 343 enrolled. In 2017, 327 master's, 154 doctorates awarded. *Degree requirements:* For master's, comprehensive exam (for some programs), thesis (for some programs); for doctorate, comprehensive exam, thesis/dissertation. *Entrance requirements:* For master's, doctorate, and other advanced degree, GRE General Test, unofficial transcripts, letters of recommendation. Additional exam requirements/recommendations for international students: Required—TOEFL (minimum score 80 iBT), IELTS (minimum score 7), PTE (minimum score 54). *Application deadline:* Applications are processed on a rolling basis. Application fee: $80 ($90 for international students). Electronic applications accepted. *Expenses:* $5,174 per semester full-time resident, $9,714 per semester full-time non-resident, $511 per credit hour part-time resident, $1,017 per credit hour part-time non-resident; $741 per credit hour online; other fees may apply per session. *Financial support:* In 2017–18, 118 students received support, including 15 fellowships with partial tuition reimbursements available (averaging $7,689 per year), 2 research assistantships with partial tuition reimbursements available (averaging $13,689 per year), 24 teaching assistantships with partial tuition reimbursements available (averaging $14,822 per year); unspecified assistantships also available. *Faculty research:* Early literacy and motivation, STEAM education, legal/policy issues in education, leadership, special education interventions/assessment/policy. *Total annual research expenditures:* $2.8 million. *Unit head:* Dr. George Petersen, Founding Dean, 864-656-4444, E-mail: soedean@clemson.edu. *Application contact:* Julie Jones, Graduate Programs Coordinator, 864-656-5096, E-mail: jgambre@clemson.edu.
Website: http://www.clemson.edu/education/

Education—General

Cleveland State University, College of Graduate Studies, College of Education and Human Services, Cleveland, OH 44115. Offers M Ed, MPH, PhD, Certificate, Ed S. *Accreditation:* NCATE. *Program availability:* Part-time, evening/weekend, 100% online, blended/hybrid learning. *Faculty:* 86 full-time (60 women), 106 part-time/adjunct (81 women). *Students:* 266 full-time (199 women), 763 part-time (562 women); includes 324 minority (252 Black or African American, non-Hispanic/Latino; 1 American Indian or Alaska Native, non-Hispanic/Latino; 15 Asian, non-Hispanic/Latino; 34 Hispanic/Latino; 1 Native Hawaiian or other Pacific Islander, non-Hispanic/Latino; 21 Two or more races, non-Hispanic/Latino), 37 international. Average age 34. 487 applicants, 58% accepted, 178 enrolled. In 2017, 280 master's, 14 doctorates awarded. *Degree requirements:* For master's, comprehensive exam (for some programs), thesis optional; for doctorate, one foreign language, comprehensive exam, thesis/dissertation; for other advanced degree, comprehensive exam (for some programs), thesis optional, internship. *Entrance requirements:* For master's, GRE General Test or MAT, minimum undergraduate GPA of 2.75, 3.0 if undergraduate degree is 6 or more years old; for doctorate, GRE General Test, master's degree, minimum graduate GPA of 3.25; for other advanced degree, GRE General Test or MAT, master's degree, minimum graduate GPA of 3.0. Additional exam requirements/recommendations for international students: Required—TOEFL (minimum score 550 paper-based; 78 iBT). *Application deadline:* For fall admission, 7/1 priority date for domestic students, 5/15 for international students; for spring admission, 11/15 priority date for domestic students, 11/1 for international students; for summer admission, 4/1 for domestic students, 3/15 for international students. Applications are processed on a rolling basis. Application fee: $30. Electronic applications accepted. *Financial support:* In 2017–18, 64 students received support, including 38 research assistantships with full tuition reimbursements available (averaging $6,960 per year), 2 teaching assistantships with full tuition reimbursements available (averaging $7,800 per year); career-related internships or fieldwork, Federal Work-Study, scholarships/grants, tuition waivers (partial), and unspecified assistantships also available. Support available to part-time students. Financial award application deadline: 8/1; financial award applicants required to submit FAFSA. *Faculty research:* Adult learning and development, counseling theory and practice, equity issues in education (race, ethnicity, gender, socioeconomics), health care and health education, population nursing, urban educational leadership, curriculum and instruction. *Total annual research expenditures:* $7.5 million. *Unit head:* Dr. Sajit Zachariah, Dean, 216-523-7143, Fax: 216-687-5415, E-mail: sajit.zachariah@csuohio.edu. *Application contact:* Patricia Sokolowski, Office Coordinator/Assistant to the Dean, 216-523-7143, Fax: 216-687-5415, E-mail: p.sokolowski@csuohio.edu.
Website: http://www.csuohio.edu/cehs/

Coastal Carolina University, Spadoni College of Education, Conway, SC 29528-6054. Offers education (MAT); educational leadership (M Ed, Ed S); English for speakers of other languages (Certificate); instructional technology (M Ed, Ed S); language, literacy and culture (M Ed); learning and teaching (M Ed); online teaching and training (Certificate); special education (M Ed). *Accreditation:* NCATE. *Program availability:* Part-time, evening/weekend, 100% online, blended/hybrid learning. *Faculty:* 16 full-time (9 women), 22 part-time/adjunct (15 women). *Students:* 43 full-time (22 women), 345 part-time (290 women); includes 70 minority (51 Black or African American, non-Hispanic/Latino; 3 American Indian or Alaska Native, non-Hispanic/Latino; 3 Asian, non-Hispanic/Latino; 8 Hispanic/Latino; 1 Native Hawaiian or other Pacific Islander, non-Hispanic/Latino; 4 Two or more races, non-Hispanic/Latino). Average age 33. 288 applicants, 77% accepted, 157 enrolled. In 2017, 151 master's, 28 other advanced degrees awarded. *Degree requirements:* For master's and other advanced degree, comprehensive exam. *Entrance requirements:* For master's, GRE, GMAT, 2 letters of recommendation, evidence of teacher certification, official transcripts; for other advanced degree, official transcripts, 3 letters of reference, master's degree in related field with minimum overall cumulative GPA of 3.0. Additional exam requirements/recommendations for international students: Required—TOEFL (minimum score 550 paper-based; 79 iBT), IELTS (minimum score 6.5). *Application deadline:* For fall admission, 5/1 priority date for domestic and international students; for spring admission, 11/1 priority date for domestic and international students; for summer admission, 3/1 priority date for domestic and international students. Applications are processed on a rolling basis. Application fee: $45. Electronic applications accepted. *Expenses:* Tuition, state resident: full-time $5184; part-time $576 per credit hour. Tuition, nonresident: full-time $9369; part-time $1041 per credit hour. *Required fees:* $90; $5 per credit hour. *Financial support:* Fellowships, research assistantships, teaching assistantships, and tuition waivers available. Financial award application deadline: 3/1; financial award applicants required to submit FAFSA. *Unit head:* Dr. Edward Jadallah, Dean/Vice President for Online Education and Teaching Excellence, 843-349-2773, Fax: 843-349-2106, E-mail: ejadalla@coastal.edu. *Application contact:* Dr. James O. Luken, Associate Provost for Graduate Program/Vice-Dean of the Coastal Environment, 843-349-2235, Fax: 843-349-6444, E-mail: joluken@coastal.edu.
Website: https://www.coastal.edu/education/

The College at Brockport, State University of New York, School of Education, Health, and Human Services, Department of Education and Human Development, Brockport, NY 14420-2997. Offers adolescence education (MS Ed), including adolescence biology education, adolescence chemistry education, adolescence English, adolescence mathematics, adolescence physics, adolescence physics education, adolescence social studies education; bilingual education (MS Ed, AGC); childhood curriculum specialist (MS Ed); inclusive generalist education (MS Ed, AGC, Advanced Certificate), including biology (MS Ed, AGC), chemistry (MS Ed), English (MS Ed, Advanced Certificate), mathematics (MS Ed, Advanced Certificate), science (MS Ed, Advanced Certificate), social studies (MS Ed, Advanced Certificate); literacy education B-12 (MS Ed). *Accreditation:* NCATE. *Faculty:* 14 full-time (9 women), 12 part-time/adjunct (11 women). *Students:* 57 full-time (26 women), 168 part-time (130 women); includes 8 minority (3 Black or African American, non-Hispanic/Latino; 1 American Indian or Alaska Native, non-Hispanic/Latino; 1 Asian, non-Hispanic/Latino; 3 Hispanic/Latino). 107 applicants, 83% accepted, 63 enrolled. In 2017, 88 master's awarded. *Degree requirements:* For master's, thesis or alternative. *Entrance requirements:* For master's, minimum GPA of 3.0, letters of recommendation, interview (for some programs); statement of objectives, current resume. Additional exam requirements/recommendations for international students: Required—TOEFL (minimum score 550 paper-based; 79 iBT), IELTS (minimum score 6.5). *Application deadline:* For fall admission, 3/15 priority date for domestic and international students; for spring admission, 10/15 priority date for domestic and international students; for summer admission, 3/15 priority date for domestic and international students. Application fee: $80. Electronic applications accepted. *Expenses:* Tuition, state resident: full-time $10,870; part-time $453 per credit hour. Tuition, nonresident: full-time $22,210. *Required fees:* $988; $246 per semester. *Financial support:* In 2017–18, 1 fellowship with full tuition reimbursement (averaging $7,500 per year), 1 teaching assistantship with full tuition reimbursement (averaging $6,000 per year) were awarded; Federal Work-Study, scholarships/grants, and unspecified assistantships also available. Support available to part-time students. Financial award application deadline: 3/15; financial award applicants required to submit FAFSA. *Faculty research:* Educational assessment, literacy education, inclusive education, teacher preparation, qualitative methodology. *Unit head:* Dr. Sue Robb, Chairperson, 585-395-5550, Fax: 585-395-2172, E-mail: srobb@brockport.edu. *Application contact:* Anne Walton, Coordinator of Certification and Graduate Advisement, 585-395-2326, Fax: 585-395-2172, E-mail: awalton@brockport.edu.
Website: https://www.brockport.edu/academics/education_human_development/department.html

College of Charleston, Graduate School, School of Education, Health, and Human Performance, Charleston, SC 29424-0001. Offers M Ed, MAT, Certificate. *Accreditation:* NCATE. *Program availability:* Part-time, evening/weekend. *Degree requirements:* For master's, thesis or alternative, written qualifying exam, student teaching experience (MAT). *Entrance requirements:* For master's, teaching certificate (M Ed). Additional exam requirements/recommendations for international students: Required—TOEFL (minimum score 81 iBT). Electronic applications accepted. *Faculty research:* Computer-assisted instruction, higher education, faculty development, teaching study skills to college students.

The College of Idaho, Department of Education, Caldwell, ID 83605. Offers curriculum and instruction (M Ed); teaching (MAT). *Degree requirements:* For master's, thesis. *Entrance requirements:* For master's, GRE, portfolio, minimum undergraduate GPA of 3.0, interview. *Faculty research:* Discourse analysis, at-risk youth, children's literature, research design, program evaluation.

College of Mount Saint Vincent, School of Professional and Graduate Studies, Department of Teacher Education, Riverdale, NY 10471-1093. Offers instructional technology and global perspectives (Certificate); middle level education (Certificate); multicultural studies (Certificate); teaching English to speakers of other languages (MS Ed); urban and multicultural education (MS Ed). *Accreditation:* TEAC. *Program availability:* Part-time. *Degree requirements:* For master's, comprehensive exam. *Entrance requirements:* For master's, interview, New York teaching certificate. Additional exam requirements/recommendations for international students: Required—TOEFL.

The College of New Jersey, Office of Graduate and Advancing Education, School of Education, Ewing, NJ 08628. Offers M Ed, MA, MAT, Certificate, Ed S. *Accreditation:* NCATE. *Program availability:* Part-time, evening/weekend. *Degree requirements:* For master's, comprehensive exam. *Entrance requirements:* For master's, GRE, minimum GPA of 3.0 in field or 2.75 overall; for other advanced degree, previous master's degree or higher. Additional exam requirements/recommendations for international students: Required—TOEFL. Electronic applications accepted.

The College of New Rochelle, Graduate School, Division of Education, New Rochelle, NY 10805-2308. Offers art education (MS); childhood education/early childhood education (MS Ed), including childhood education, early childhood education; educational leadership (MS, Advanced Certificate, Advanced Diploma), including school building leader (MS, Advanced Certificate), school district leader (MS, Advanced Diploma); gifted education (Certificate); literacy education (MS Ed); multilingual/multicultural education (MS Ed, Certificate), including bilingual education (Certificate), multilingual/multicultural education (Certificate), teaching English to speakers of other languages; special education (MS Ed). *Program availability:* Part-time, evening/weekend. *Degree requirements:* For master's, comprehensive exam (for some programs), thesis (for some programs). *Entrance requirements:* For master's, interview, minimum GPA of 3.0 in field, 2.7 overall. Electronic applications accepted. *Expenses: Tuition:* Full-time $17,406. *Required fees:* $1120.

College of Saint Elizabeth, Program in Education, Morristown, NJ 07960-6989. Offers assistive technology (Certificate); education (MA); ESL (Certificate); Holocaust/genocide education (Certificate); middle school science (Certificate); online teaching in the 21st century (Certificate); teaching (Certificate), including K-12, K-6, teacher of students with disabilities. *Program availability:* Part-time. *Faculty:* 3 full-time (2 women), 8 part-time/adjunct (6 women). *Students:* 1 (woman) full-time, 34 part-time (29 women); includes 1 minority (Hispanic/Latino). Average age 32. 25 applicants, 100% accepted, 24 enrolled. In 2017, 23 master's awarded. *Degree requirements:* For master's and Certificate, thesis. *Entrance requirements:* For master's, certification. Additional exam requirements/recommendations for international students: Required—TOEFL (minimum score 550 paper-based; 79 iBT), IELTS (minimum score 6.5). *Application deadline:* For fall admission, 5/1 for international students. Applications are processed on a rolling basis. Application fee: $35. Electronic applications accepted. Application fee is waived when completed online. *Financial support:* Career-related internships or fieldwork, scholarships/grants, and unspecified assistantships available. Financial award applicants required to submit FAFSA. *Unit head:* Dr. Joseph Ciccone, 973-290-4383, Fax: 973-290-4389, E-mail: jciccone@cse.edu. *Application contact:* Lori J. Fragoso, Director of Graduate and Continuing Studies Admissions, 973-290-4413, Fax: 973-290-4710, E-mail: apply@cse.edu.
Website: http://www.cse.edu/academics/prof-studies/education/

College of St. Joseph, Graduate Programs, Division of Education, Rutland, VT 05701-3899. Offers elementary education (M Ed); general education (M Ed); reading (M Ed); secondary education (M Ed), including English, social studies; special education (M Ed). *Program availability:* Part-time, evening/weekend. *Degree requirements:* For master's, comprehensive exam. *Entrance requirements:* For master's, PRAXIS I, essay; two letters of reference from academic or professional sources; official transcripts of all graduate and undergraduate study. Additional exam requirements/recommendations for international students: Required—TOEFL (minimum score 550 paper-based). Electronic applications accepted. *Faculty research:* Co-teaching, Response to Intervention (RTI).

College of Saint Mary, Program in Teaching, Omaha, NE 68106. Offers MAT. *Program availability:* Evening/weekend. *Entrance requirements:* For master's, Pre-Professional Skills Tests (PPST), minimum cumulative GPA of 2.5, background check.

The College of Saint Rose, Graduate Studies, Thelma P. Lally School of Education, Albany, NY 12203-1419. Offers MS, MS Ed, Advanced Certificate, Certificate. *Accreditation:* NCATE. *Program availability:* Part-time, evening/weekend, 100% online. *Faculty:* 29 full-time (18 women), 78 part-time/adjunct (45 women). *Students:* 317 full-time (285 women), 907 part-time (694 women); includes 353 minority (154 Black or African American, non-Hispanic/Latino; 5 American Indian or Alaska Native, non-Hispanic/Latino; 25 Asian, non-Hispanic/Latino; 136 Hispanic/Latino; 1 Native Hawaiian or other Pacific Islander, non-Hispanic/Latino; 32 Two or more races, non-Hispanic/Latino), 14 international. Average age 33. 674 applicants, 65% accepted, 436 enrolled. In 2017, 312 master's, 695 other advanced degrees awarded. *Degree requirements:* For master's, comprehensive exam (for some programs), thesis (for some programs), capstone project. *Entrance requirements:* For master's, minimum undergraduate GPA of 3.0. Additional exam requirements/recommendations for international students: Required—TOEFL (minimum score 550 paper-based; 80 iBT), IELTS (minimum score 6), PTE (minimum score 56). *Application deadline:* For fall admission, 4/1 priority date for domestic and international students; for spring admission, 10/15 priority date for domestic and international students; for summer admission, 3/15 priority date for domestic and international students. Applications are processed on a rolling basis. Application fee: $40. Electronic applications accepted. *Expenses: Tuition:* Full-time $7191; part-time $799 per credit hour. *Required fees:* $924; $462 per credit hour. Tuition and fees vary according to course load. *Financial support:* Career-related internships or fieldwork, scholarships/grants, tuition waivers (partial), and unspecified assistantships available. Support available to part-time students. Financial award application deadline: 4/15. *Unit head:* Dr. Theresa Ward, Acting Associate Dean, 518-454-5125. *Application contact:* Cris Murray, Assistant Vice President for Graduate Recruitment and Enrollment, 518-454-5136, Fax: 518-458-5479, E-mail: grad@strose.edu. Website: https://www.strose.edu/academics/schools/school-of-education/

The College of St. Scholastica, Graduate Studies, Department of Education, Duluth, MN 55811-4199. Offers M Ed, MS, Certificate. *Accreditation:* TEAC. *Program availability:* Part-time, evening/weekend, online learning. *Entrance requirements:* Additional exam requirements/recommendations for international students: Required—TOEFL (minimum score 550 paper-based; 79 iBT). Electronic applications accepted.

College of Staten Island of the City University of New York, Graduate Programs, School of Education, Staten Island, NY 10314-6600. Offers MS Ed, Advanced Certificate, Post-Master's Certificate. *Accreditation:* NCATE. *Faculty:* 30 full-time, 28 part-time/adjunct. *Students:* 409. 212 applicants, 66% accepted, 113 enrolled. In 2017, 90 master's, 11 Advanced Certificates awarded. *Expenses:* Tuition, state resident: full-time $10,450; part-time $440 per credit. Tuition, nonresident: full-time $19,320; part-time $440 per credit. *Required fees:* $181.10 per semester. Tuition and fees vary according to program. *Unit head:* Dr. Kenneth Gold, Dean of School of Education, 718-982-3737, Fax: 718-982-3743, E-mail: kenneth.gold@csi.cuny.edu. *Application contact:* Sasha Spence, Associate Director for Graduate Admissions, 718-982-2019, Fax: 718-982-2500, E-mail: sasha.spence@csi.cuny.edu.
Website: https://www.csi.cuny.edu/academics-and-research/divisions-schools/school-education

★ **The College of William and Mary,** School of Education, Williamsburg, VA 23187-8795. Offers M Ed, MA Ed, Ed D, PhD, Ed S. *Accreditation:* NCATE. *Program availability:* Part-time, evening/weekend. *Faculty:* 54 full-time (31 women), 80 part-time/adjunct (40 women). *Students:* 220 full-time (163 women), 192 part-time (131 women); includes 103 minority (48 Black or African American, non-Hispanic/Latino; 7 Asian, non-Hispanic/Latino; 33 Hispanic/Latino; 15 Two or more races, non-Hispanic/Latino), 7 international. Average age 34. 538 applicants, 63% accepted, 242 enrolled. In 2017, 129 master's, 33 doctorates, 6 other advanced degrees awarded. *Degree requirements:* For master's, project; for doctorate, comprehensive exam, thesis/dissertation; for Ed S, internship. *Entrance requirements:* For master's, GRE, MAT, PRAXIS Core Academic Skills for Educators, minimum GPA of 2.5; for doctorate, GRE or MAT, minimum GPA of 3.5; for Ed S, GRE, minimum GPA of 3.0. Additional exam requirements/recommendations for international students: Required—TOEFL (minimum score 100 iBT), IELTS (minimum score 7). *Application deadline:* For fall admission, 1/15 for domestic and international students; for spring admission, 10/1 for domestic and international students. Application fee: $50. Electronic applications accepted. *Expenses:* $9,630 resident full-time, $535 resident part-time per credit hour; $25,920 nonresident full-time, $1,265 nonresident part-time per credit hour; $5,944 full-time fees. *Financial support:* In 2017–18, 143 students received support, including 1 fellowship with full tuition reimbursement available (averaging $20,000 per year), 93 research assistantships (averaging $17,316 per year); scholarships/grants and unspecified assistantships also available. Financial award application deadline: 1/15; financial award applicants required to submit FAFSA. *Faculty research:* Gifted education, curriculum and instruction, technology and education, leadership, classroom assessment. *Total annual research expenditures:* $6.8 million. *Unit head:* Dr. Spencer G. Niles, Dean, 757-221-2317, E-mail: sgniles@wm.edu. *Application contact:* Dorothy Smith Osborne, Assistant Dean for Academic Programs and Student Services, 757-221-2317, E-mail: dsosbo@wm.edu.
Website: http://education.wm.edu

See Display on this page and Close-Up on page 717.

Colorado Christian University, Program in Curriculum and Instruction, Lakewood, CO 80226. Offers corporate education (MACI); early childhood educator (MACI); elementary educator (MACI); instructional technology (MACI); master educator (MACI); online course developer (MACI); online teaching and learning (MACI); special education generalist (MACI). *Program availability:* Part-time, evening/weekend. *Degree requirements:* For master's, thesis optional, practicum. *Entrance requirements:* For master's, interviews, letters of recommendation. Additional exam requirements/recommendations for international students: Required—TOEFL. Electronic applications accepted. *Expenses:* Contact institution.

The Colorado College, Education Department, Colorado Springs, CO 80903-3294. Offers elementary education (MAT), including elementary school teaching; secondary education (MAT), including art teaching (K-12), English teaching, foreign language teaching, mathematics teaching, music teaching, science teaching, social studies teaching; teaching (MAT), including arts and humanities, integrated natural sciences, liberal arts, Southwest studies. *Degree requirements:* For master's, thesis, internship. Electronic applications accepted. *Faculty research:* Geology, environmental resources, urban education, educational psychology, arts integration in the classroom, literacy/early childhood.

Colorado Mesa University, Center for Teacher Education, Grand Junction, CO 81501-3122. Offers educational leadership (MAEd); English for speakers of other languages (MAEd); exceptional learner/special education (MAEd); teacher education (Graduate Certificate); teacher leader (MAEd). *Accreditation:* NCATE. *Program availability:* Part-time. *Degree requirements:* For master's, comprehensive exam (for some programs), capstone presentation. *Entrance requirements:* For master's, 3 professional letters of recommendation, Colorado teaching license, minimum baccalaureate GPA of 3.0; for Graduate Certificate, minimum baccalaureate GPA of 3.0. Additional exam requirements/recommendations for international students: Required—TOEFL (minimum score 550 paper-based). Electronic applications accepted. *Expenses:* Contact institution. *Faculty research:* K-8 STEM instruction, special education inclusion, elementary math literacy, secondary literacy, elementary/early childhood education literacy.

Colorado State University, College of Health and Human Sciences, School of Education, Fort Collins, CO 80523-1588. Offers adult education and training (M Ed); counseling and career development (MA); education and human resources (M Ed); education, equity, and transformation (PhD); higher education leadership (PhD); organizational learning, performance, and change (M Ed, PhD); student affairs in higher education (MS). *Accreditation:* ACA; TEAC. *Program availability:* Part-time, online only, 100% online, blended/hybrid learning. *Faculty:* 33 full-time (23 women), 19 part-time/adjunct (11 women). *Students:* 74 full-time (53 women), 548 part-time (357 women); includes 151 minority (37 Black or African American, non-Hispanic/Latino; 4 American Indian or Alaska Native, non-Hispanic/Latino; 14 Asian, non-Hispanic/Latino; 71 Hispanic/Latino; 25 Two or more races, non-Hispanic/Latino), 16 international. Average age 37. 456 applicants, 31% accepted, 123 enrolled. In 2017, 177 master's, 22 doctorates awarded. *Degree requirements:* For master's, thesis optional, professional portfolio or capstone project; for doctorate, comprehensive exam, thesis/dissertation. *Entrance requirements:* For master's, bachelor's degree; minimum GPA of 3.0 in last degree earned; for doctorate, GRE; GRE or GMAT (for organizational learning, performance and change only), master's degree; minimum GPA of 3.0 in last degree earned. Additional exam requirements/recommendations for international students:

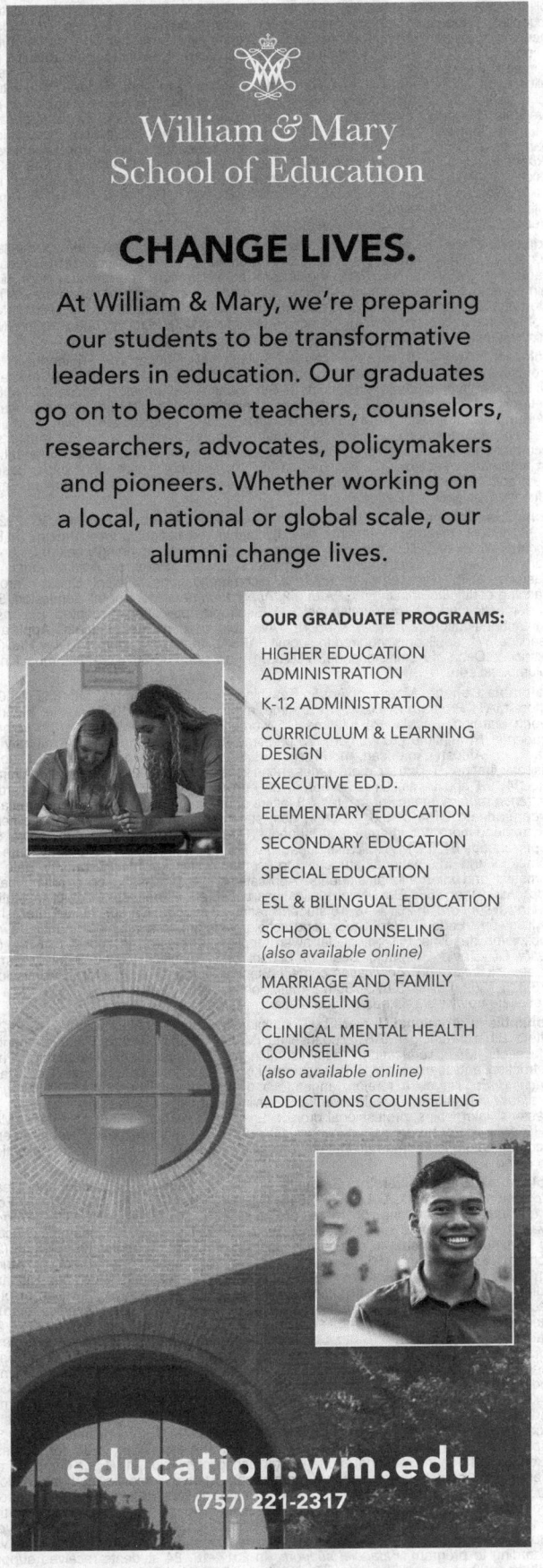

Education—General

Required—TOEFL (minimum score 550 paper-based; 80 iBT), IELTS (minimum score 6.5), PTE (minimum score 58). *Application deadline:* Applications are processed on a rolling basis. Application fee: $60 ($70 for international students). Electronic applications accepted. *Expenses:* Contact institution. *Financial support:* In 2017–18, 4 students received support, including 8 research assistantships with full and partial tuition reimbursements available (averaging $12,758 per year), 4 teaching assistantships with full and partial tuition reimbursements available (averaging $14,256 per year); fellowships with full and partial tuition reimbursements available, Federal Work-Study, scholarships/grants, tuition waivers (full and partial), and unspecified assistantships also available. Financial award applicants required to submit FAFSA. *Faculty research:* Diversity, equity, and inclusion; STEM education; higher education; occupational learning, performance, and change; teacher education. *Total annual research expenditures:* $312,562. *Unit head:* Dr. Louise Jennings, Co-Director, 970-491-6317, Fax: 970-491-1317, E-mail: louise.jennings@colostate.edu. *Application contact:* Kelli Clark, Graduate Programs Coordinator, 970-491-2093, Fax: 970-491-1317, E-mail: kelli.clark@colostate.edu.
Website: http://www.soe.chhs.colostate.edu/

Colorado State University–Global Campus, Graduate Programs, Greenwood Village, CO 80111. Offers criminal justice and law enforcement administration (MS); education leadership (MS); finance (MS); healthcare administration and management (MS); human resource management (MHRM); information technology management (MITM); international management (MS); management (MS); organizational leadership (MS); professional accounting (MPA); project management (MS); teaching and learning (MS). *Accreditation:* ACBSP. *Program availability:* Online learning.

Colorado State University–Pueblo, College of Education, Engineering and Professional Studies, Education Program, Pueblo, CO 81001-4901. Offers art education (M Ed); foreign language education (M Ed); health and physical education (M Ed); instructional technology (M Ed); linguistically diverse education (M Ed); music education (M Ed); special education (M Ed). *Accreditation:* TEAC. *Program availability:* Part-time. *Degree requirements:* For master's, portfolio. *Entrance requirements:* For master's, 3 recommendations, teaching license. Additional exam requirements/recommendations for international students: Required—TOEFL (minimum score 500 paper-based). Electronic applications accepted. *Faculty research:* Portfolio assessment, math education, science education.

Columbia College, Graduate Programs, Education Division, Columbia, SC 29203-5998. Offers divergent learning (M Ed); higher education administration (M Ed). *Accreditation:* NCATE. *Program availability:* Part-time, evening/weekend, online learning. *Degree requirements:* For master's, thesis. *Entrance requirements:* For master's, GRE General Test, MAT, 2 recommendations, current South Carolina teaching certificate, minimum GPA of 3.2. *Application deadline:* For fall admission, 8/22 for domestic students. Application fee: $50. Electronic applications accepted. *Expenses:* Contact institution. *Financial support:* Available to part-time students. Application deadline: 7/1; applicants required to submit FAFSA. *Application contact:* Myles Hacking, Associate Dean of Admissions, 803-786-3871, Fax: 803-786-3674, E-mail: mhacking@columbiasc.edu.

Columbia College, Master of Arts in Teaching Program, Columbia, MO 65216-0002. Offers MAT. *Program availability:* Part-time, evening/weekend, 100% online, blended/hybrid learning. *Faculty:* 24 full-time (15 women), 48 part-time/adjunct (31 women). *Students:* 14 full-time (10 women), 73 part-time (60 women); includes 22 minority (12 Black or African American, non-Hispanic/Latino; 1 Asian, non-Hispanic/Latino; 6 Hispanic/Latino; 3 Two or more races, non-Hispanic/Latino), 2 international. Average age 34. 99 applicants, 91% accepted, 56 enrolled. In 2017, 61 master's awarded. *Entrance requirements:* For master's, 3 letters of recommendation, minimum cumulative undergraduate GPA of 3.0, resume, goal statement. Additional exam requirements/recommendations for international students: Required—TOEFL (minimum score 500 paper-based; 61 iBT). *Application deadline:* For fall admission, 8/9 priority date for domestic and international students; for spring admission, 12/27 priority date for domestic and international students. Applications are processed on a rolling basis. Application fee: $55. Electronic applications accepted. *Expenses:* Contact institution. *Financial support:* In 2017–18, 16 students received support. Career-related internships or fieldwork, Federal Work-Study, and scholarships/grants available. Financial award application deadline: 3/15; financial award applicants required to submit FAFSA. *Unit head:* Dr. David Roebuck, Dean of School of Humanities, 573-875-7570, E-mail: cdroebuck@ccis.edu. *Application contact:* Stephanie Johnson, Director of Admissions, 573-875-7352, Fax: 573-875-7506, E-mail: sjohnson@ccis.edu.
Website: http://www.ccis.edu/graduate/academics/degrees.asp?MAT

Columbia International University, Columbia Graduate School, Columbia, SC 29203. Offers Bible teaching (MABT); counseling (MACN); early childhood and elementary education (MAT); educational administration (M Ed); educational leadership (PhD); instruction and learning (M Ed); teaching English as a foreign language (Certificate); teaching English as a foreign language and intercultural studies (MATF). *Program availability:* Part-time, evening/weekend, online learning. *Degree requirements:* For master's, internships, professional project. *Entrance requirements:* For master's, MAT, GRE (for some programs), minimum GPA of 2.7. Additional exam requirements/recommendations for international students: Required—TOEFL. Electronic applications accepted.

Columbus State University, Graduate Studies, College of Education and Health Professions, Columbus, GA 31907-5645. Offers M Ed, MAT, MS, MSN, Ed D, Ed S. *Accreditation:* ACA (one or more programs are accredited); NCATE. *Program availability:* Part-time, evening/weekend, 100% online, blended/hybrid learning. *Faculty:* 50 full-time (31 women), 46 part-time/adjunct (30 women). *Students:* 409 full-time (290 women), 632 part-time (503 women); includes 525 minority (445 Black or African American, non-Hispanic/Latino; 1 American Indian or Alaska Native, non-Hispanic/Latino; 20 Asian, non-Hispanic/Latino; 34 Hispanic/Latino; 1 Native Hawaiian or other Pacific Islander, non-Hispanic/Latino; 24 Two or more races, non-Hispanic/Latino), 2 international. Average age 37. 452 applicants, 50% accepted, 117 enrolled. In 2017, 202 master's, 18 doctorates, 118 other advanced degrees awarded. *Degree requirements:* For master's, thesis, exit exam; for doctorate, thesis/dissertation; for Ed S, thesis or alternative. *Entrance requirements:* For master's, GRE General Test, minimum undergraduate GPA of 2.75; for doctorate, GRE General Test, minimum graduate GPA of 3.5, four years of professional service; for Ed S, GRE General Test, minimum undergraduate GPA of 2.75, graduate 3.0. Additional exam requirements/recommendations for international students: Required—TOEFL (minimum score 550 paper-based; 79 iBT). *Application deadline:* For fall admission, 6/30 for domestic students, 5/1 for international students; for spring admission, 11/1 for domestic and international students; for summer admission, 3/1 for domestic and international students. Applications are processed on a rolling basis. Application fee: $50. Electronic applications accepted. *Expenses:* Tuition, state resident: full-time $3708; part-time $2472 per year. Tuition, nonresident: full-time $14,418; part-time $9612 per year. *International tuition:* $19,218 full-time. *Required fees:* $1605. Tuition and fees vary according to program. *Financial support:* In 2017–18, 84 students received support, including 29 research assistantships with partial tuition reimbursements available (averaging $3,000 per year); career-related internships or fieldwork, Federal Work-

Study, institutionally sponsored loans, scholarships/grants, tuition waivers (partial), and unspecified assistantships also available. Support available to part-time students. Financial award application deadline: 5/1; financial award applicants required to submit FAFSA. *Unit head:* Dr. Deirdre Greer, Dean, 706-507-8505, Fax: 706-569-3134, E-mail: greer_deirdre@columbusstate.edu. *Application contact:* Catrina Smith-edmond, Assistant Director for Graduate and Global Admission, 706-507-8824, Fax: 706-568-5091, E-mail: smithedmond_catrina@columbusstate.edu.
Website: http://coehp.columbusstate.edu/

Concordia College, Program in Education, Moorhead, MN 56562. Offers world language instruction (M Ed). *Degree requirements:* For master's, thesis/seminar. *Entrance requirements:* For master's, 2 professional references, 1 personal reference.

Concordia University, College of Education, Portland, OR 97211-6099. Offers career and technical education (M Ed); curriculum and instruction (M Ed), including adolescent literacy, career and technical education, e-learning/technology education, early childhood education, English for speakers of other languages, English language development, environmental education, mathematics, methods and curriculum, reading, science, teacher leadership, the inclusive classroom; early childhood (MAT); education leadership (Ed D); educational administration (M Ed); elementary education (MAT); secondary education (MAT); special education (M Ed); teacher leadership (Ed D). *Program availability:* Part-time, online learning. *Degree requirements:* For master's, comprehensive exam, work samples/portfolio. *Entrance requirements:* For master's, California Basic Educational Skills Test or PRAXIS I, minimum undergraduate GPA of 2.8, graduate 3.0; 2 letters of recommendation. Additional exam requirements/recommendations for international students: Required—TOEFL (minimum score 525 paper-based). Electronic applications accepted. *Faculty research:* Learner-centered classroom, brain-based learning, future of online learning.

Concordia University, School of Graduate Studies, Faculty of Arts and Science, Department of Education, Montréal, QC H3G 1M8, Canada. Offers adult education (Certificate, Diploma); applied linguistics (MA, Certificate), including applied linguistics (MA), teaching English as a second language (Certificate); child studies (MA); educational studies (MA); educational technology (MA); instructional technology (Diploma). *Degree requirements:* For master's, one foreign language, thesis optional.

Concordia University Chicago, College of Education, Program in Teaching, River Forest, IL 60305-1499. Offers early childhood education (MAT); elementary education (MAT); secondary education (MAT). *Degree requirements:* For master's, thesis or alternative. *Entrance requirements:* For master's, minimum GPA of 2.9. Additional exam requirements/recommendations for international students: Required—TOEFL (minimum score 550 paper-based). Electronic applications accepted.

Concordia University Irvine, School of Education, Irvine, CA 92612-3299. Offers curriculum and instruction (MA); education and preliminary teaching credential (M Ed); educational administration and preliminary administrative services credential (MA); educational technology (MA); school counseling with pupil personnel services credential (MA). *Program availability:* Part-time, evening/weekend, online learning. *Degree requirements:* For master's, action research project. *Entrance requirements:* For master's, California Basic Educational Skills Test, California Subject Examinations for Teachers (M Ed and MA in educational administration and preliminary administrative services credential), official college transcript(s), signed statement of intent, two references, copy of credential. Additional exam requirements/recommendations for international students: Required—TOEFL. Electronic applications accepted. *Expenses:* Contact institution.

Concordia University, Nebraska, Graduate Programs in Education, Seward, NE 68434. Offers M Ed, MPE, MS. *Accreditation:* NCATE. *Program availability:* Part-time, evening/weekend. *Degree requirements:* For master's, comprehensive exam, thesis or alternative. *Entrance requirements:* For master's, GRE, MAT, or NTE, minimum GPA of 3.0, BS in education or equivalent. Additional exam requirements/recommendations for international students: Required—TOEFL. Electronic applications accepted.

Concordia University, St. Paul, College of Education, St. Paul, MN 55104-5494. Offers classroom instruction (MA Ed), including K-12 reading; differentiated instruction (MA Ed); early childhood education (MA Ed); education (Ed D); educational leadership (MA Ed); educational technology (MA Ed, Certificate); K-12 principal licensure (Ed S); special education (MA Ed), including autism spectrum disorder, emotional and behavioral disorders, learning disabilities; superintendent (Ed S); teaching (MAT). *Accreditation:* NCATE. *Program availability:* Part-time, evening/weekend, 100% online, blended/hybrid learning. *Faculty:* 15 full-time (8 women), 86 part-time/adjunct (56 women). *Students:* 955 full-time (731 women), 42 part-time (28 women); includes 105 minority (35 Black or African American, non-Hispanic/Latino; 5 American Indian or Alaska Native, non-Hispanic/Latino; 31 Asian, non-Hispanic/Latino; 19 Hispanic/Latino; 15 Two or more races, non-Hispanic/Latino), 9 international. Average age 34. 409 applicants, 87% accepted, 347 enrolled. In 2017, 386 master's, 104 other advanced degrees awarded. *Degree requirements:* For master's, thesis (for some programs); for doctorate, thesis/dissertation, capstone projects; for other advanced degree, e-folio review of competencies. *Entrance requirements:* For master's, official transcripts from regionally-accredited institution stating the conferral of a bachelor's degree with minimum cumulative GPA of 3.0; personal statement; professional resume; practitioner in field through work or volunteerism; resume; for doctorate, minimum master's or specialist degree GPA of 3.25; transcript; writing sample; three letters of recommendation; current resume; on-campus interview; for other advanced degree, minimum master's or specialist degree GPA of 3.25; transcript; statement covering employment history and long-term academic and professional goals; two letters of recommendation; interview with program director. Additional exam requirements/recommendations for international students: Recommended—TOEFL (minimum score 547 paper-based; 78 iBT), IELTS (minimum score 6). *Application deadline:* For fall admission, 8/1 for domestic and international students; for spring admission, 12/1 for domestic and international students; for summer admission, 5/1 for domestic and international students. Applications are processed on a rolling basis. Application fee: $0. Electronic applications accepted. *Expenses:* $395 per credit (for MA in education); $440 per credit (for MAT); $615 per credit (for EdD). *Financial support:* In 2017–18, 105 students received support. Scholarships/grants and unspecified assistantships available. Financial award applicants required to submit FAFSA. *Faculty research:* Differentiated instruction in K-12 educational settings; educational leadership; effective online pedagogy in higher education; equine-assisted learning; faculty development in higher education. *Unit head:* Lonn Maly, Dean, 651-641-8203, E-mail: maly@csp.edu. *Application contact:* Amber Faletti, Director of Enrollment Management, 651-641-8838, Fax: 651-603-6320, E-mail: faletti@csp.edu.

Concordia University Texas, College of Education, Austin, TX 78726. Offers M Ed. *Program availability:* Part-time, evening/weekend. *Degree requirements:* For master's, thesis (for some programs), portfolio presentation.

Concordia University Wisconsin, Graduate Programs, Department of Education, Mequon, WI 53097-2402. Offers art education (MS Ed); early childhood (MS Ed); educational administration (MS Ed); environmental education (MS Ed); family studies (MS Ed); literacy (MS Ed); school counseling (MS Ed); special education (MS Ed). *Program availability:* Part-time, evening/weekend, online learning. *Degree requirements:*

For master's, comprehensive exam, thesis or alternative. *Entrance requirements:* For master's, minimum GPA of 3.0, teaching license. Additional exam requirements/recommendations for international students: Required—TOEFL. *Faculty research:* Motivation, developmental learning, learning styles.

Concord University, Graduate Studies, Athens, WV 24712-1000. Offers educational leadership and supervision (M Ed); health promotion (MA); reading specialist (M Ed); social work (MSW); special education (M Ed); teaching (MAT). *Program availability:* Part-time, evening/weekend, 100% online. *Faculty:* 16 full-time (10 women), 7 part-time/adjunct (4 women). *Students:* 146 full-time (117 women), 195 part-time (161 women); includes 26 minority (15 Black or African American, non-Hispanic/Latino; 1 American Indian or Alaska Native, non-Hispanic/Latino; 4 Asian, non-Hispanic/Latino; 1 Hispanic/Latino; 5 Two or more races, non-Hispanic/Latino). Average age 34. 591 applicants, 99% accepted, 144 enrolled. In 2017, 114 master's awarded. *Degree requirements:* For master's, thesis (for some programs). *Entrance requirements:* For master's, GRE or MAT, baccalaureate degree with minimum GPA of 2.5 from regionally-accredited institution; teaching license; 2 letters of recommendation; completed disposition assessment form. *Application deadline:* Applications are processed on a rolling basis. Application fee: $30. Electronic applications accepted. *Expenses:* Tuition, state resident: full-time $8132; part-time $453 per semester hour. Tuition, nonresident: full-time $14,180; part-time $788 per semester hour. *Financial support:* Tuition waivers and unspecified assistantships available. Financial award applicants required to submit FAFSA. *Unit head:* Dr. Cheryl Barnes, Director, 304-384-6306, E-mail: cbarnes@concord.edu. *Application contact:* Debra Moore, Special Events Assistant, 304-384-5113, E-mail: dlm@concord.edu.
Website: http://www.concord.edu/graduate

Coppin State University, Division of Graduate Studies, Division of Education, Department of Curriculum and Instruction, Program in Teaching, Baltimore, MD 21216-3698. Offers teacher education (MAT). *Program availability:* Part-time, evening/weekend, online learning. *Degree requirements:* For master's, thesis, exit portfolio. *Entrance requirements:* For master's, GRE, resume, references.

Corban University, Graduate School, Education Program, Salem, OR 97301-9392. Offers MS Ed.

Cornell University, Graduate School, Graduate Fields of Agriculture and Life Sciences, Field of Education, Ithaca, NY 14853. Offers adult and extension education (MPS, MS, PhD); learning, teaching, and social policy (MPS, MS, PhD); mathematics 7-12 (MS). Terminal master's awarded for partial completion of doctoral program. *Degree requirements:* For master's, thesis (MS); for doctorate, comprehensive exam, thesis/dissertation. *Entrance requirements:* For master's and doctorate, GRE General Test, sample of written work (recommended), 2 letters of recommendation. Additional exam requirements/recommendations for international students: Required—TOEFL (minimum score 550 paper-based; 77 iBT). Electronic applications accepted. *Faculty research:* Moral development and professional ethics, public issues education and community development, socio/political issues in public education, teacher education and curriculum in agricultural science and mathematics, extension research.

Cornerstone University, Graduate Programs, Grand Rapids, MI 49525-5897. Offers business administration (MBA); education (MA Ed); management (MSM); teaching English to speakers of other languages (MA, Graduate Certificate). Programs also offered at Holland, Kalamazoo, and Troy, MI campuses. *Program availability:* Part-time, online learning. *Degree requirements:* For master's, comprehensive exam (for some programs), thesis (for some programs). *Entrance requirements:* For master's, minimum GPA of 2.5, 2 letters of reference. Additional exam requirements/recommendations for international students: Required—TOEFL (minimum score 575 paper-based). Electronic applications accepted.

Covenant College, Program in Education, Lookout Mountain, GA 30750. Offers M Ed, MAT. *Program availability:* Part-time. *Degree requirements:* For master's, comprehensive exam, special project. *Entrance requirements:* For master's, GRE General Test, 2 professional recommendations, minimum GPA of 3.0, writing sample.

Crandall University, Graduate Programs, Moncton, NB E1C 9L7, Canada. Offers literacy education (M Ed); organizational management (MOM); resource education (M Ed).

Creighton University, Graduate School, College of Arts and Sciences, Department of Education, Omaha, NE 68178-0001. Offers educational leadership (MS), including elementary school administration, secondary school administration, teacher leadership; school counseling and preventive mental health (MS), including elementary school guidance, secondary school guidance; teaching (M Ed), including elementary teaching, secondary teaching. *Accreditation:* NCATE. *Program availability:* Part-time, 100% online, blended/hybrid learning. *Faculty:* 14 full-time (7 women). *Students:* 35 full-time (29 women), 170 part-time (123 women); includes 6 minority (2 Black or African American, non-Hispanic/Latino; 2 American Indian or Alaska Native, non-Hispanic/Latino; 1 Asian, non-Hispanic/Latino; 1 Native Hawaiian or other Pacific Islander, non-Hispanic/Latino), 3 international. Average age 33. 2 applicants, 100% accepted, 1 enrolled. In 2017, 85 master's awarded. *Degree requirements:* For master's, comprehensive exam (for some programs), portfolio. *Entrance requirements:* For master's, GRE General Test, PPST, 3 letters of recommendation, writing samples, resume. Additional exam requirements/recommendations for international students: Required—TOEFL (minimum score 90 iBT). *Application deadline:* For fall admission, 7/1 priority date for domestic students, 3/1 priority date for international students; for winter admission, 12/1 for domestic students, 7/1 for international students; for spring admission, 4/1 for domestic students, 10/1 for international students; for summer admission, 3/1 for domestic and international students. Application fee: $50. Electronic applications accepted. Part-time tuition and fees vary according to course load, degree level, campus/location and program. *Financial support:* Scholarships/grants and tuition waivers (partial) available. Support available to part-time students. Financial award applicants required to submit FAFSA. *Unit head:* Dr. Timothy J. Cook, Chair, 402-280-2561, E-mail: timothycook@creighton.edu. *Application contact:* Lindsay Johnson, Director of Graduate and Adult Recruitment, 402-280-2703, Fax: 402-280-2423, E-mail: gradschool@creighton.edu.

Cumberland University, Program in Education, Lebanon, TN 37087. Offers MAE. *Accreditation:* NCATE. *Program availability:* Part-time, evening/weekend, online learning. *Degree requirements:* For master's, comprehensive exam. *Entrance requirements:* For master's, GRE General Test, MAT, or NTE, 3 letters of recommendation. Additional exam requirements/recommendations for international students: Required—TOEFL (minimum score 500 paper-based).

Curry College, Graduate Studies, Program in Education, Milton, MA 02186-9984. Offers elementary education (M Ed); foundations (non-license) (M Ed); reading (M Ed, Certificate); special education (M Ed). *Program availability:* Part-time, evening/weekend. *Degree requirements:* For master's, project or thesis. *Entrance requirements:* For master's, interview, recommendations, resume, written statement. Additional exam requirements/recommendations for international students: Required—TOEFL (minimum score 550 paper-based; 80 iBT). *Expenses:* Contact institution. *Faculty research:* Classroom trauma, therapeutic writing, inclusionary practices.

Daemen College, Education Department, Amherst, NY 14226-3592. Offers adolescence education (MS); childhood education (MS); childhood special education (MS); childhood special-alternative certification (MS); early childhood special-alternative certification (MS). *Accreditation:* TEAC. *Program availability:* Part-time. *Degree requirements:* For master's, thesis optional, research thesis in lieu of comprehensive exam; completion of degree within 5 years. *Entrance requirements:* For master's, 2 letters of recommendation (professional and character), proof of initial certificate of license for professional programs, resume. Additional exam requirements/recommendations for international students: Required—TOEFL (minimum score 500 paper-based; 63 iBT), IELTS (minimum score 5.5). Electronic applications accepted. *Faculty research:* Transition for students with disabilities, early childhood special education, traumatic brain injury (TBI), reading assessment.

Dakota State University, College of Education, Madison, SD 57042-1799. Offers educational technology (MSET). *Accreditation:* NCATE. *Program availability:* Part-time-only, evening/weekend, online only, 100% online. *Faculty:* 4 full-time (0 women). *Students:* 8 part-time (5 women). Average age 32. 3 applicants, 100% accepted, 2 enrolled. In 2017, 5 master's awarded. *Degree requirements:* For master's, thesis optional, portfolio. *Entrance requirements:* For master's, GRE General Test, demonstration of technology skills, minimum GPA of 2.7. *Application deadline:* For fall admission, 6/15 for domestic students; for spring admission, 11/15 for domestic students; for summer admission, 4/15 for domestic students. Applications are processed on a rolling basis. Application fee: $35. Electronic applications accepted. *Expenses:* Tuition, state resident: full-time $5749. Tuition, nonresident: full-time $10,733. *Required fees:* $715. Tuition and fees vary according to campus/location and reciprocity agreements. *Financial support:* Unspecified assistantships and administrative assistantships available. Financial award applicants required to submit FAFSA. *Faculty research:* Educational technology evaluation, computer-supported collaborative learning, cognitive theory and visual representation of the effects of ubiquitous wireless computing on student learning and productivity, accessible learning, pedagogies for exceptional children. *Unit head:* Dr. Crystal Pauli, Dean of College of Education, 605-256-5799. *Application contact:* Dr. Kevin Smith, Program Coordinator, 605-256-5175, Fax: 605-256-7300, E-mail: kevin.smith@dsu.edu.
Website: http://dsu.edu/graduate-students/mset

Dakota Wesleyan University, Program in Education, Mitchell, SD 57301-4398. Offers curriculum and instruction (MA Ed); educational policy and administration (MA Ed); preK-12 principal certification (MA Ed); secondary certification (MA Ed). *Program availability:* Part-time, evening/weekend. *Degree requirements:* For master's, comprehensive exam, thesis optional, electronic portfolio. *Entrance requirements:* For master's, minimum GPA of 2.7, elementary statistics course, statement of purpose, official transcripts, resume, three letters of recommendation. Additional exam requirements/recommendations for international students: Required—TOEFL (minimum score 500 paper-based), IELTS (minimum score 6.5). Electronic applications accepted. *Faculty research:* Math, political policy, technology in the classroom.

Dallas Baptist University, Dorothy M. Bush College of Education, Teaching Program, Dallas, TX 75211-9299. Offers distance learning (MAT); early childhood through grade 6 certification (MAT); early childhood-12 (MAT); elementary (MAT); English as a second language (MAT); Montessori (MAT); multisensory (MAT); secondary (MAT). *Program availability:* Part-time, evening/weekend. *Application deadline:* Applications are processed on a rolling basis. Application fee: $25. Electronic applications accepted. Application fee is waived when completed online. *Expenses:* Tuition: Full-time $16,308; part-time $906 per credit hour. *Required fees:* $900; $450 per semester. Tuition and fees vary according to course load and degree level. *Unit head:* Dr. Neil Dugger, Dean, 214-333-5202, E-mail: neil@dbu.edu. *Application contact:* Dr. DeAnna Jenkins, Program Director, 214-333-5402, E-mail: deannaj@dbu.edu.
Website: http://www3.dbu.edu/graduate/mat.asp

Defiance College, Program in Education, Defiance, OH 43512-1610. Offers education (MAE); sport coaching (MAE). *Program availability:* Part-time-only. *Faculty:* 5 full-time (all women), 2 part-time/adjunct (both women). In 2017, 5 master's awarded. *Degree requirements:* For master's, thesis. *Entrance requirements:* For master's, teaching license. *Application deadline:* For fall admission, 8/1 for domestic students. Electronic applications accepted. *Unit head:* Dr. Carla Higgins, Assistant Professor of Education, 419-783-2571, E-mail: chiggins@defiance.edu. *Application contact:* Teresa Watkins, Administrative Assistant, 419-783-2323, Fax: 419-784-0426, E-mail: twatkins@defiance.edu.
Website: http://www.defiance.edu/graduate-programs/mae-home.html

Delaware State University, Graduate Programs, College of Education, Health and Public Policy, Dover, DE 19901-2277. Offers MA, MS, MSW, Ed D. *Accreditation:* NCATE. *Program availability:* Part-time, evening/weekend. *Degree requirements:* For master's, comprehensive exam, thesis optional. *Entrance requirements:* For master's, GRE General Test, minimum GPA of 3.0 in major, 2.75 overall. Additional exam requirements/recommendations for international students: Required—TOEFL (minimum score 500 paper-based). Electronic applications accepted.

Delta State University, Graduate Programs, College of Education, Cleveland, MS 38733-0001. Offers M Ed, MAT, MS, Ed D, Ed S. *Accreditation:* NCATE. *Program availability:* Part-time, evening/weekend. *Degree requirements:* For master's, thesis optional; for doctorate, thesis/dissertation. *Entrance requirements:* For doctorate, GRE General Test; for Ed S, master's degree, teaching certificate.

DePaul University, College of Education, Chicago, IL 60614. Offers bilingual-bicultural education (M Ed, MA); counseling (M Ed, MA), including clinical mental health counseling, college student development, school counseling; curriculum studies (M Ed, MA, Ed D); early childhood education (M Ed, MA, Ed D); educational leadership (M Ed, MA, Ed D), including Catholic leadership (M Ed, MA), general (M Ed, MA), higher education (M Ed, MA), physical education (M Ed, MA), principal preparation (M Ed); teacher preparation (M Ed); elementary education (M Ed, MA); middle grades education (M Ed); middle school mathematics education (MS); reading specialist (M Ed, MA); secondary education (M Ed, MA); social and cultural foundations in education (M Ed, MA); special education (M Ed); sport, fitness and recreation leadership (MS); value-creating education for global citizenship (M Ed); world languages education (M Ed, MA). *Program availability:* Part-time, evening/weekend, online learning. *Degree requirements:* For doctorate, thesis/dissertation. *Application deadline:* Applications are processed on a rolling basis. Application fee: $40. Electronic applications accepted. *Financial support:* Application deadline: 12/31; applicants required to submit FAFSA. *Unit head:* Dr. Paul Zionts, Dean, 773-325-7581, Fax: 773-325-7713, E-mail: pzionts@depaul.edu. *Application contact:* Dr. Paul Zionts, Dean, 773-325-7581, Fax: 773-325-7713, E-mail: pzionts@depaul.edu.
Website: http://education.depaul.edu

DePaul University, School for New Learning, Chicago, IL 60604. Offers applied professional studies (MA); applied technology (MS); educating adults (MA). *Program availability:* Part-time, evening/weekend. *Degree requirements:* For master's, thesis or alternative. *Entrance requirements:* For master's, resume, interview, official transcript. *Application deadline:* Applications are processed on a rolling basis. Application fee: $25. Electronic applications accepted. *Financial support:* Applicants required to submit

Education—General

FAFSA. *Unit head:* Dr. Don Opitz, Interim Dean, 312-362-8512, Fax: 312-362-8809. *Application contact:* Russ Rogers, Director, Graduate Programs, 312-362-8512, Fax: 312-362-8809, E-mail: rrogers@depaul.edu. Website: http://snl.depaul.edu.

DeSales University, Division of Liberal Arts and Social Sciences, Center Valley, PA 18034-9568. Offers criminal justice (MCJ); digital forensics (MCJ, Postbaccalaureate Certificate); education (M Ed), including instructional technology, secondary education, special education, teaching English to speakers of other languages; investigative forensics (MCJ, Postbaccalaureate Certificate). *Program availability:* Part-time, 100% online, blended/hybrid learning. *Faculty:* 5 full-time (3 women), 15 part-time/adjunct (9 women). *Students:* 54 full-time (36 women), 112 part-time (68 women); includes 23 minority (3 Black or African American, non-Hispanic/Latino; 1 Asian, non-Hispanic/Latino; 17 Hispanic/Latino; 2 Two or more races, non-Hispanic/Latino), 1 international. Average age 33. 114 applicants, 64% accepted, 41 enrolled. In 2017, 41 master's awarded. *Entrance requirements:* For master's, bachelor's degree from accredited institution, minimum undergraduate GPA of 3.0, personal statement showing potential of graduate study, three letters of recommendation, professional goal statement. Additional exam requirements/recommendations for international students: Required—TOEFL. *Application deadline:* Applications are processed on a rolling basis. Application fee: $50. Electronic applications accepted. *Expenses: Tuition:* Part-time $840 per credit. Full-time tuition and fees vary according to course load, degree level and program. *Financial support:* Applicants required to submit FAFSA. *Unit head:* Ronald Nordone, Dean of Graduate Education, 610-282-1100 Ext. 1289, E-mail: ronald.nordone@desales.edu. *Application contact:* Julia Ferraro, Director of Graduate Admissions, 610-282-1100 Ext. 1768, E-mail: gradadmissions@desales.edu.

Doane University, Program in Education, Crete, NE 68333-2430. Offers curriculum and instruction (M Ed); curriculum leadership (Ed S); education (Ed D); educational leadership (M Ed); school counseling (M Ed). *Accreditation:* NCATE. *Program availability:* Part-time, evening/weekend. *Faculty:* 10 full-time (7 women), 66 part-time/adjunct (50 women). *Students:* 228 full-time (172 women), 541 part-time (433 women); includes 51 minority (21 Black or African American, non-Hispanic/Latino; 4 American Indian or Alaska Native, non-Hispanic/Latino; 4 Asian, non-Hispanic/Latino; 12 Hispanic/Latino; 1 Native Hawaiian or other Pacific Islander, non-Hispanic/Latino; 9 Two or more races, non-Hispanic/Latino). Average age 33. In 2017, 284 master's, 1 other advanced degree awarded. *Degree requirements:* For master's, thesis; for doctorate, thesis/dissertation. *Entrance requirements:* For master's, minimum GPA of 2.5. Additional exam requirements/recommendations for international students: Required—TOEFL. *Application deadline:* Applications are processed on a rolling basis. Electronic applications accepted. *Expenses:* Contact institution. *Financial support:* Applicants required to submit FAFSA. *Unit head:* Dr. Lyn C. Forester, Dean, 402-826-8604, Fax: 402-826-8278. *Application contact:* Leah Schaber, Assistant Dean, 402-464-1223, Fax: 402-466-4228, E-mail: leah.schaber@doane.edu. Website: http://www.doane.edu/masters-degrees

Dominican College, Division of Teacher Education, Orangeburg, NY 10962-1210. Offers education/teaching of individuals with multiple disabilities (MS Ed). *Program availability:* Part-time, evening/weekend, online learning. *Faculty:* 2 full-time (1 woman), 7 part-time/adjunct (all women). *Students:* 3 full-time (all women), 48 part-time (30 women); includes 9 minority (1 Black or African American, non-Hispanic/Latino; 1 Asian, non-Hispanic/Latino; 7 Hispanic/Latino). In 2017, 18 master's awarded. *Degree requirements:* For master's, comprehensive exam (for some programs), thesis. *Entrance requirements:* For master's, 3 letters of recommendation (written by former or current work supervisors or instructors), interview. Additional exam requirements/recommendations for international students: Required—TOEFL (minimum score 90 iBT). *Application deadline:* Applications are processed on a rolling basis. *Expenses: Tuition:* Part-time $900 per credit. One-time fee: $200. Tuition and fees vary according to degree level and program. *Financial support:* Application deadline: 2/1; applicants required to submit FAFSA. *Unit head:* Dr. Mike Kelly, Director, 845-848-4090, Fax: 845-359-7802, E-mail: mike.kelly@dc.edu. *Application contact:* Christina Lifshey, Assistant Director of Graduate Admissions, 845-848-7908 Ext. 15, Fax: 845-365-3150, E-mail: admissions@dc.edu.

Dominican University, School of Education, River Forest, IL 60305-1099. Offers child life studies (MS); early childhood education (MS); education (MAT); elementary education (MA Ed); English as a second language (MA Ed); reading (MA Ed); secondary education (MAT); special education (MS). *Accreditation:* NCATE. *Program availability:* Part-time, evening/weekend, 100% online, blended/hybrid learning. *Faculty:* 8 full-time (6 women), 42 part-time/adjunct (38 women). *Students:* 5 full-time (all women), 261 part-time (206 women); includes 45 minority (16 Black or African American, non-Hispanic/Latino; 1 American Indian or Alaska Native, non-Hispanic/Latino; 5 Asian, non-Hispanic/Latino; 18 Hispanic/Latino; 5 Two or more races, non-Hispanic/Latino), 1 international. Average age 32. 95 applicants, 98% accepted, 72 enrolled. In 2017, 206 master's awarded. *Entrance requirements:* For master's, Illinois Test of Basic Skills. Additional exam requirements/recommendations for international students: Required—TOEFL (minimum score 550 paper-based; 79 iBT). *Application deadline:* Applications are processed on a rolling basis. Application fee: $25. *Expenses:* Contact institution. *Financial support:* Career-related internships or fieldwork, scholarships/grants, tuition waivers (partial), and unspecified assistantships available. Support available to part-time students. Financial award application deadline: 8/15; financial award applicants required to submit FAFSA. *Faculty research:* Governance of private education institutions, reading and language arts, inclusion, organizational planning, leadership and vision. *Unit head:* Dr. Colleen Reardon, Interim Executive Director, School of Education, 708-524-6643, Fax: 708-524-6665, E-mail: creardon@dom.edu. *Application contact:* Benjamin Mueller, Senior Graduate Marketing and Recruitment Coordinator, 708-524-6456, Fax: 708-524-6665, E-mail: bmueller@dom.edu. Website: http://educate.dom.edu/

Dominican University of California, School of Liberal Arts and Education, San Rafael, CA 94901-2298. Offers MA. *Program availability:* Part-time, evening/weekend. *Faculty:* 17 full-time (11 women), 11 part-time/adjunct (10 women). *Students:* 57 full-time (43 women), 99 part-time (75 women); includes 37 minority (4 Black or African American, non-Hispanic/Latino; 1 American Indian or Alaska Native, non-Hispanic/Latino; 4 Asian, non-Hispanic/Latino; 20 Hispanic/Latino; 2 Native Hawaiian or other Pacific Islander, non-Hispanic/Latino; 6 Two or more races, non-Hispanic/Latino), 2 international. Average age 37. 63 applicants, 98% accepted, 41 enrolled. In 2017, 51 master's awarded. *Degree requirements:* For master's, comprehensive exam (for some programs), thesis (for some programs). *Entrance requirements:* For master's, minimum GPA of 3.0. Additional exam requirements/recommendations for international students: Required—TOEFL (minimum score 550 paper-based; 80 iBT), IELTS (minimum score 6.5). *Application deadline:* For fall admission, 5/15 for domestic and international students; for spring admission, 11/15 for domestic and international students. Applications are processed on a rolling basis. Application fee: $0. Electronic applications accepted. *Expenses: Tuition:* Full-time $17,370; part-time $965 per credit. *Required fees:* $150 per semester. Tuition and fees vary according to course load and program. *Financial support:* In 2017–18, 69 students received support. Scholarships/grants available. Support available to part-time students. Financial award application deadline: 3/2; financial award applicants required to submit FAFSA. *Unit head:* Laura Stivers, Dean, 415-458-3734, E-mail: laura.stivers@dominican.edu. *Application contact:* Michael Lavigna, Assistant Director of Graduate Admissions, 415-485-3253, Fax: 415-485-3214, E-mail: gradmissions@dominican.edu. Website: https://www.dominican.edu/academics/lae/index_html

Dordt College, Program in Education, Sioux Center, IA 51250-1697. Offers M Ed. *Program availability:* Part-time, online learning. *Degree requirements:* For master's, comprehensive exam, thesis. *Entrance requirements:* For master's, GRE or MAT. Additional exam requirements/recommendations for international students: Required—TOEFL. Electronic applications accepted.

Drake University, School of Education, Des Moines, IA 50311-4516. Offers applied behavior analysis (MS); counseling (MS); education (PhD); education administration (Ed D); educational leadership (MSE, Ed D); effective teaching (MSE); leadership development (MS); literacy (Ed S); literacy education (MSE); rehabilitation administration (MS); rehabilitation placement (MS); special education (MSE); STEM education (MSE); teacher education (5-12) (MAT); teacher education (K-8) (MST); teacher effectiveness and professional development (MSE). *Program availability:* Part-time, evening/weekend. *Degree requirements:* For master's and Ed S, comprehensive exam, internships (for some programs); for doctorate, comprehensive exam, thesis/dissertation, internships (for some programs). *Entrance requirements:* For master's, GRE General Test, MAT, or Drake Writing Assessment, resume, 2 letters of recommendation; for doctorate, GRE General Test or MAT, master's degree, 3 letters of recommendation; for Ed S, GRE General Test or MAT. Additional exam requirements/recommendations for international students: Required—TOEFL (minimum score 550 paper-based). *Application deadline:* For fall admission, 7/1 priority date for domestic students, 6/1 priority date for international students; for spring admission, 11/1 priority date for domestic students, 10/1 priority date for international students. Applications are processed on a rolling basis. Application fee: $25. Electronic applications accepted. *Expenses:* Contact institution. *Financial support:* Research assistantships, career-related internships or fieldwork, and unspecified assistantships available. Support available to part-time students. *Faculty research:* Counseling and rehabilitation, behavioral supports, inquiry-based science methods, teacher quality enhancement. *Unit head:* Dr. Janet McMahill, Dean, 515-271-3829, E-mail: janet.mcmahill@drake.edu. Website: http://www.drake.edu/soe/

Drew University, Caspersen School of Graduate Studies, Madison, NJ 07940-1493. Offers conflict resolution and leadership (Certificate), including community leadership, moderation, peace building; education (M Ed); finance (MA); history and culture (MA, PhD), including American history, book history, British history, European history, Holocaust and genocide (M Litt, MA, D Litt, PhD), intellectual history, Irish history, print culture, public history; K-12 education (MAT), including art, biology, chemistry, elementary education, English, French, Italian, math, secondary education, special education, teacher of students with disabilities; liberal studies (M Litt, D Litt), including history, Holocaust and genocide (M Litt, MA, D Litt, PhD), Irish/Irish-American studies, literature (M Litt, MMH, D Litt, DMH, CMH); religion, spirituality, teaching in the two-year college, writing; medical humanities (MMH, DMH, CMH), including arts, health, healthcare, literature (M Litt, MMH, D Litt, DMH, CMH), scientific research; poetry (MFA). *Program availability:* Part-time, evening/weekend. *Faculty:* 4 full-time (2 women), 29 part-time/adjunct (15 women). *Students:* 77 full-time (42 women), 175 part-time (114 women); includes 39 minority (12 Black or African American, non-Hispanic/Latino; 6 Asian, non-Hispanic/Latino; 16 Hispanic/Latino; 5 Two or more races, non-Hispanic/Latino), 11 international. Average age 41. 126 applicants, 75% accepted, 52 enrolled. In 2017, 38 master's, 23 doctorates, 35 other advanced degrees awarded. Terminal master's awarded for partial completion of doctoral program. *Degree requirements:* For master's and other advanced degree, thesis (for some programs); for doctorate, one foreign language, comprehensive exam (for some programs), thesis/dissertation. *Entrance requirements:* For master's, PRAXIS Core and Subject Area tests (for MAT), GRE/GMAT (for M Fin), resume, transcripts, writing sample, personal statement, letters of recommendation; for doctorate, GRE (PhD in history and culture), resume, transcripts, writing sample, personal statement, letters of recommendation; for other advanced degree, resume, transcripts, personal statement. Additional exam requirements/recommendations for international students: Required—TOEFL (minimum score 587 paper-based; 80 iBT), IELTS (minimum score 6), TWE (minimum score 4). *Application deadline:* For fall admission, 8/1 for domestic students, 6/1 for international students; for spring admission, 12/1 for domestic students, 10/1 for international students. Applications are processed on a rolling basis. Application fee: $35. Electronic applications accepted. *Financial support:* Fellowships, research assistantships, teaching assistantships, career-related internships or fieldwork, Federal Work-Study, scholarships/grants, and unspecified assistantships available. Support available to part-time students. Financial award applicants required to submit FAFSA. *Faculty research:* Irish history and culture, conflict resolution and leadership. *Application contact:* Leanne Horinko, Director of Caspersen Admissions, 973-408-3280, E-mail: gradm@drew.edu. Website: http://www.drew.edu/caspersen

★ **Drexel University,** Goodwin College of Professional Studies, School of Education, Philadelphia, PA 19104-2875. Offers applied behavior analysis (MS); creativity and innovation (MS); education improvement and transformation (MS); educational administration (MS); educational leadership and management (Ed D); educational leadership development and learning technologies (PhD); global and international education (MS); higher education (MS); human resources development (MS); learning technologies (MS); mathematics, learning and teaching (MS); special education (MS); teaching, learning and curriculum (MS). *Program availability:* Part-time, evening/weekend, online learning. *Degree requirements:* For doctorate, thesis/dissertation. *Entrance requirements:* For doctorate, GRE or GMAT. Additional exam requirements/recommendations for international students: Required—TOEFL, IELTS. Electronic applications accepted. Application fee is waived when completed online. *Expenses:* Contact institution. *Faculty research:* Leadership development, mathematics education, literacy, autism, educational technology.
See Display on the next page and Close-Up on page 719.

Drury University, Master in Education Program, Springfield, MO 5802. Offers curriculum and instruction (M Ed), including elementary, middle school, secondary; gifted education (M Ed); instructional leadership (M Ed); instructional technology (M Ed); integrated learning (M Ed); online teaching (M Ed); special education (M Ed); special reading (M Ed). *Accreditation:* NCATE. *Program availability:* Part-time, evening/weekend, 100% online, blended/hybrid learning. *Entrance requirements:* For master's, GRE, bachelor's degree with minimum GPA of 2.75. Additional exam requirements/recommendations for international students: Recommended—TOEFL (minimum score 80 iBT), IELTS (minimum score 6.5). Electronic applications accepted. *Expenses:* Contact institution. *Faculty research:* Gifted students, instructional technology, autism, diversity and social justice.

Duke University, Graduate School, Program in Teaching, Durham, NC 27708. Offers MAT. *Accreditation:* NCATE. *Entrance requirements:* For master's, GRE General Test. Additional exam requirements/recommendations for international students: Required—TOEFL (minimum score 577 paper-based; 90 iBT) or IELTS (minimum score 7). Electronic applications accepted.

Duquesne University, School of Education, Pittsburgh, PA 15282-0001. Offers MS Ed, Ed D, PhD, Psy D, Post-Master's Certificate. *Accreditation:* NCATE. *Program availability:* Part-time, evening/weekend, 100% online, blended/hybrid learning. *Faculty:* 52 full-time (31 women), 83 part-time/adjunct (63 women). *Students:* 488 full-time (354 women), 52 part-time (35 women); includes 87 minority (51 Black or African American, non-Hispanic/Latino; 1 American Indian or Alaska Native, non-Hispanic/Latino; 12 Asian, non-Hispanic/Latino; 12 Hispanic/Latino; 11 Two or more races, non-Hispanic/Latino), 54 international. Average age 30. 439 applicants, 84% accepted, 180 enrolled. In 2017, 138 master's, 36 doctorates, 7 other advanced degrees awarded. *Degree requirements:* For master's, comprehensive exam (for some programs); for doctorate, comprehensive exam (for some programs), thesis/dissertation (for some programs); for Post-Master's Certificate, comprehensive exam (for some programs), thesis (for some programs). *Entrance requirements:* For master's, letters of recommendation, essay, personal statement, interview, bachelor's degree; for doctorate, GRE, letters of recommendation, essay, personal statement, interview, master's degree; for Post-Master's Certificate, GRE, letters of recommendation, essay, personal statement, interview, bachelor's/master's degree. Additional exam requirements/recommendations for international students: Required—TOEFL (minimum score 550 paper-based), IELTS (minimum score 7). *Application deadline:* For fall admission, 3/1 for domestic students; for spring admission, 9/1 for domestic students. Applications are processed on a rolling basis. Application fee: $0. Electronic applications accepted. *Expenses:* $1,259 per credit. *Financial support:* In 2017–18, 53 research assistantships with full and partial tuition reimbursements (averaging $3,603 per year) were awarded; teaching assistantships, career-related internships or fieldwork, Federal Work-Study, institutionally sponsored loans, and tuition waivers also available. Support available to part-time students. *Total annual research expenditures:* $249,745. *Unit head:* Dr. Cindy Walker, Dean, 412-396-6102, Fax: 412-396-5585. *Application contact:* Kelly McGinley, Graduate Admissions Assistant, 412-396-1559, Fax: 412-296-5585, E-mail: mcginleyk@duq.edu.
Website: http://www.duq.edu/academics/schools/education

D'Youville College, Department of Education, Buffalo, NY 14201-1084. Offers educational leadership (Ed D); elementary education (MS Ed); secondary education (MS Ed); special education (MS Ed). *Program availability:* Part-time, evening/weekend. *Degree requirements:* For master's, one foreign language, comprehensive exam, project or thesis. *Entrance requirements:* For master's, GRE (if GPA less than 2.75), minimum GPA of 3.0. Additional exam requirements/recommendations for international students: Required—TOEFL (minimum score 500 paper-based). Electronic applications accepted. *Faculty research:* Developmental disabilities, multiculturalism, early childhood education.

Earlham College, Graduate Programs, Richmond, IN 47374-4095. Offers M Ed, MAT. *Entrance requirements:* For master's, GRE, PRAXIS I, PRAXIS II.

East Carolina University, Graduate School, College of Education, Greenville, NC 27858-4353. Offers MA, MA Ed, MAT, MLS, MS, MSA, Ed D, Certificate, Ed S. *Accreditation:* NCATE. *Program availability:* Part-time, evening/weekend, online learning. *Students:* 186 full-time (145 women), 959 part-time (778 women); includes 266 minority (184 Black or African American, non-Hispanic/Latino; 13 American Indian or Alaska Native, non-Hispanic/Latino; 11 Asian, non-Hispanic/Latino; 33 Hispanic/Latino; 25 Two or more races, non-Hispanic/Latino), 6 international. Average age 37. 397 applicants, 96% accepted, 326 enrolled. In 2017, 317 master's, 23 doctorates, 71 other advanced degrees awarded. *Degree requirements:* For master's, comprehensive exam, thesis optional; for doctorate, thesis/dissertation. *Entrance requirements:* For master's, GRE or MAT, bachelor's degree in related field, minimum GPA of 2.5; for doctorate, GRE or MAT, interview, minimum GPA of 3.5. Additional exam requirements/recommendations for international students: Recommended—TOEFL (minimum score

78 iBT), IELTS (minimum score 6.5), TWE. *Application deadline:* For fall admission, 8/15 for domestic students, 2/1 for international students; for spring admission, 12/20 for domestic students, 10/1 for international students. Applications are processed on a rolling basis. Application fee: $75. Electronic applications accepted. *Expenses:* Tuition, state resident: full-time $4749; part-time $297 per credit hour. Tuition, nonresident: full-time $17,898; part-time $1119 per credit hour. *Required fees:* $2691; $224 per credit hour. Part-time tuition and fees vary according to course load and program. *Financial support:* Research assistantships with partial tuition reimbursements, teaching assistantships with partial tuition reimbursements, and Federal Work-Study available. Support available to part-time students. Financial award application deadline: 6/1. *Unit head:* Dr. Linda Ann Patriarca, Dean, 252-328-1000, Fax: 252-328-4219, E-mail: patriarcal@ecu.edu.
Website: http://www.ecu.edu/coe

East Central University, School of Graduate Studies, Department of Education, Ada, OK 74820. Offers M Ed. *Accreditation:* NCATE. *Program availability:* Part-time, evening/weekend. *Entrance requirements:* For master's, minimum GPA of 2.5. *Application deadline:* Applications are processed on a rolling basis. Application fee: $0 ($50 for international students). Electronic applications accepted. *Financial support:* Fellowships, career-related internships or fieldwork, and tuition waivers (partial) available. Support available to part-time students. *Unit head:* Phyllis Isaacs, Chair, 580-559-5240, E-mail: phylisa@ecok.edu. *Application contact:* Freda Low, Secretary, 580-559-5348, Fax: 580-282-8691, E-mail: freslow@ecok.edu.
Website: http://www.ecok.edu/academics/colleges-and-schools/college-education-and-psychology/department-education

Eastern Connecticut State University, School of Education and Professional Studies/Graduate Division, Willimantic, CT 06226-2295. Offers MS. *Accreditation:* NCATE. *Program availability:* Part-time, evening/weekend. *Faculty:* 27 full-time (12 women), 14 part-time/adjunct (8 women). *Students:* 90 full-time (57 women), 124 part-time (94 women); includes 46 minority (12 Black or African American, non-Hispanic/Latino; 4 American Indian or Alaska Native, non-Hispanic/Latino; 11 Asian, non-Hispanic/Latino; 15 Hispanic/Latino; 1 Native Hawaiian or other Pacific Islander, non-Hispanic/Latino; 3 Two or more races, non-Hispanic/Latino). Average age 34. 91 applicants, 74% accepted, 52 enrolled. In 2017, 61 master's awarded. *Degree requirements:* For master's, comprehensive exam, thesis optional. *Entrance requirements:* For master's, PRAXIS I, SAT, ACT, or GRE; PRAXIS II, minimum GPA of 2.7, 3.0 (for education). Additional exam requirements/recommendations for international students: Required—TOEFL (minimum score 550 paper-based; 79 iBT); Recommended—IELTS (minimum score 6). *Application deadline:* For fall admission, 7/6 priority date for domestic and international students; for spring admission, 11/3 priority date for domestic and international students; for summer admission, 4/5 priority date for domestic and international students. Applications are processed on a rolling basis. Application fee: $50. Electronic applications accepted. *Expenses: Tuition, area resident:* Full-time $12,252. Tuition, state resident: full-time $15,245; part-time $582 per credit hour. Tuition, nonresident: full-time $24,828; part-time $582 per credit hour. *Required fees:* $40 per semester. Full-time tuition and fees vary according to reciprocity agreements. *Financial support:* Research assistantships, teaching assistantships, career-related internships or fieldwork, scholarships/grants, and unspecified assistantships available. Financial award application deadline: 3/1; financial award applicants required to submit FAFSA. *Unit head:* Dr. Jacob Easley, II, Dean, 860-465-5293, Fax: 860-465-4538, E-mail: easleyj@easternct.edu. *Application contact:* Paula Goyette, Secretary II, 860-465-5292, Fax: 860-465-4538, E-mail: graduateadmissions@easternct.edu.
Website: http://www.easternct.edu/graduate/

Eastern Illinois University, Graduate School, College of Education and Professional Studies, Charleston, IL 61920. Offers MS, MS Ed, Ed S. *Accreditation:* NCATE. *Program*

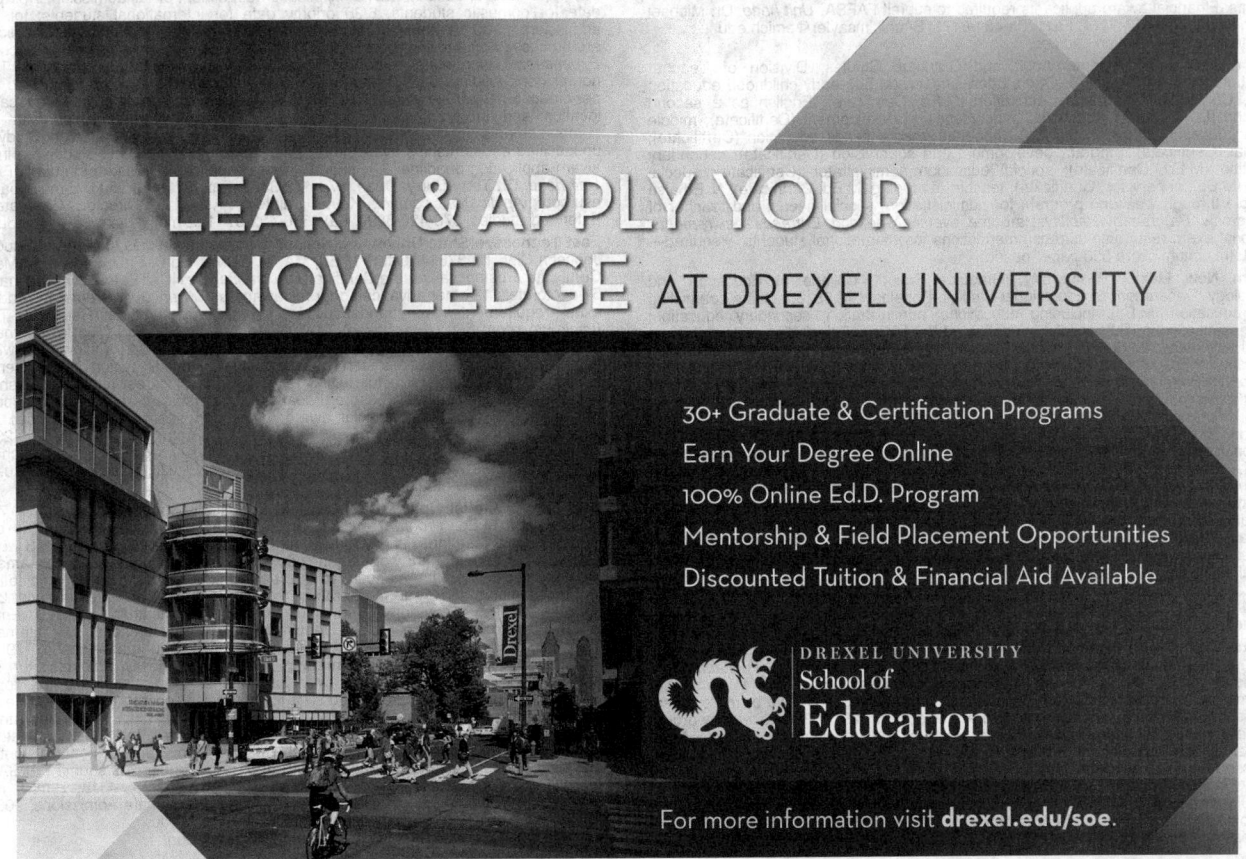

Education—General

availability: Part-time, evening/weekend. *Degree requirements:* For master's and Ed S, comprehensive exam (for some programs), thesis (for some programs). *Entrance requirements:* For master's and Ed S, GMAT or GRE. Additional exam requirements/recommendations for international students: Required—TOEFL (minimum score 500 paper-based; 61 iBT), IELTS (minimum score 6). *Application deadline:* For fall admission, 5/15 for domestic and international students; for spring admission, 10/15 for domestic and international students. Applications are processed on a rolling basis. Application fee: $30. Electronic applications accepted. *Financial support:* In 2017–18, 245 students received support. Research assistantships with full tuition reimbursements available, teaching assistantships with full tuition reimbursements available, career-related internships or fieldwork, Federal Work-Study, and unspecified assistantships available. Support available to part-time students. Financial award application deadline: 3/1; financial award applicants required to submit FAFSA. *Unit head:* Douglas J. Bower, Dean, 217-581-2200, Fax: 217-581-2518, E-mail: djbower@eiu.edu. *Application contact:* Douglas J. Bower, Dean, 217-581-2200, Fax: 217-581-2518, E-mail: djbower@eiu.edu.
Website: http://www.eiu.edu/ceps/programs.php

Eastern Kentucky University, The Graduate School, College of Education, Richmond, KY 40475-3102. Offers MA, MA Ed, MAT. *Accreditation:* NCATE. *Program availability:* Part-time, online learning. *Entrance requirements:* For master's, GRE General Test, minimum GPA of 2.5. *Faculty research:* Dispositions to teach, technology in education, distance learning.

Eastern Mennonite University, Program in Teacher Education, Harrisonburg, VA 22802-2462. Offers curriculum and instruction (MA Ed); diverse needs (MA Ed); literacy (MA Ed); restorative justice in education (MA Ed). *Accreditation:* NCATE. *Program availability:* Part-time. *Degree requirements:* For master's, portfolio, research projects. *Entrance requirements:* For master's, 1 year of teaching experience, interview, minimum undergraduate GPA of 2.75. Additional exam requirements/recommendations for international students: Required—TOEFL (minimum score 550 paper-based). *Application deadline:* Applications are processed on a rolling basis. Application fee: $50. Electronic applications accepted. *Expenses:* Contact institution. *Financial support:* Federal Work-Study and scholarships/grants available. Financial award application deadline: 6/30; financial award applicants required to submit FAFSA. *Faculty research:* Effective literacy instruction for middle school English language learners, beginning teacher's emotional experiences, constructivist learning environments, restorative discipline. *Unit head:* Cathy Smeltzer Erb, Chair, 540-432-4638. *Application contact:* Yvonne Martin, Office Assistant, 540-432-4350, Fax: 540-432-4071, E-mail: yvonne.martin@emu.edu.
Website: http://www.emu.edu/maed/

Eastern Michigan University, Graduate School, College of Education, Ypsilanti, MI 48197. Offers M Ed, MA, Ed D, PhD, Graduate Certificate, Post Master's Certificate, SPA. *Accreditation:* NCATE. *Program availability:* Part-time, evening/weekend, online learning. *Faculty:* 69 full-time (48 women). *Students:* 193 full-time (163 women), 681 part-time (523 women); includes 201 minority (136 Black or African American, non-Hispanic/Latino; 3 American Indian or Alaska Native, non-Hispanic/Latino; 11 Asian, non-Hispanic/Latino; 30 Hispanic/Latino; 21 Two or more races, non-Hispanic/Latino), 30 international. Average age 34. 693 applicants, 54% accepted, 196 enrolled. In 2017, 253 master's, 34 doctorates, 87 other advanced degrees awarded. *Degree requirements:* For doctorate, thesis/dissertation. *Entrance requirements:* For master's, GRE; for doctorate, GRE General Test. Additional exam requirements/recommendations for international students: Required—TOEFL. *Application deadline:* Applications are processed on a rolling basis. Application fee: $45. *Financial support:* Fellowships, research assistantships with full tuition reimbursements, teaching assistantships with full tuition reimbursements, career-related internships or fieldwork, Federal Work-Study, institutionally sponsored loans, scholarships/grants, tuition waivers (partial), and unspecified assistantships available. Support available to part-time students. Financial award applicants required to submit FAFSA. *Unit head:* Dr. Michael Sayler, Dean, 734-487-1414, Fax: 734-484-6471, E-mail: msayler@emich.edu.
Website: http://www.emich.edu/coe/

Eastern Nazarene College, Adult and Graduate Studies, Division of Teacher Education, Quincy, MA 02170. Offers administration (M Ed); early childhood education (M Ed, Certificate); elementary education (M Ed, Certificate); English as a second language (Certificate); instructional enrichment and development (Certificate); middle school education (M Ed, Certificate); moderate special needs education (Certificate); principal (Certificate); program development and supervision (Certificate); secondary education (M Ed, Certificate); special education administrator (Certificate); special needs (M Ed); supervisor (Certificate); teacher of reading (M Ed, Certificate). M Ed also available through weekend program for administration, special needs, and teacher of reading only. *Program availability:* Part-time, evening/weekend. *Entrance requirements:* Additional exam requirements/recommendations for international students: Required—TOEFL (minimum score 550 paper-based).

Eastern New Mexico University, Graduate School, College of Education and Technology, Department of Educational Studies, Portales, NM 88130. Offers counseling (MA); education (M Ed), including educational administration, secondary education; school counseling (M Ed); special education (M Ed, M Sp Ed), including early childhood special education (M Sp Ed), general special education (M Sp Ed), gifted education pedagogy (M Ed), special education pedagogy (M Ed). *Accreditation:* NCATE. *Program availability:* Part-time, evening/weekend, online learning. *Degree requirements:* For master's, comprehensive exam, thesis optional. *Entrance requirements:* For master's, writing assessment, minimum GPA of 3.0, letter of recommendation, photocopy of teaching license; Level II teaching license (for M Ed in educational administration). Additional exam requirements/recommendations for international students: Required—TOEFL (minimum score 550 paper-based; 79 iBT), IELTS (minimum score 6). *Application deadline:* For fall admission, 7/20 priority date for domestic students, 6/20 priority date for international students; for spring admission, 12/15 priority date for domestic students, 11/15 priority date for international students. Applications are processed on a rolling basis. Application fee: $10. Electronic applications accepted. *Financial support:* Applicants required to submit FAFSA. *Unit head:* Dr. Rebecca Davis, Educational Administration/Special Education Graduate Coordinator, 575-562-2526, Fax: 575-562-2559, E-mail: rebecca.davis@enmu.edu. *Application contact:* Cheryl Reeves, Senior Secretary, 575-562-2443, Fax: 575-562-2559, E-mail: cheryl.reeves@enmu.edu.
Website: http://education.enmu.edu

Eastern Oregon University, Master of Arts in Teaching Program, La Grande, OR 97850. Offers elementary education (MAT); secondary education (MAT). *Faculty:* 12 full-time (9 women), 4 part-time/adjunct (1 woman). *Students:* 53 full-time (41 women), 2 part-time (both women); includes 6 minority (5 Hispanic/Latino; 1 Two or more races, non-Hispanic/Latino), 1 international. Average age 29. In 2017, 32 master's awarded. *Degree requirements:* For master's, thesis. *Entrance requirements:* For master's, NTE. *Application deadline:* For fall admission, 3/1 for domestic students. Applications are processed on a rolling basis. Electronic applications accepted. *Expenses:* $404.50 per credit. *Financial support:* In 2017–18, 24 students received support. Federal Work-Study, scholarships/grants, and tuition waivers (full and partial) available. Support available to part-time students. *Unit head:* Dr. Danny Ray Mielke, Dean of College of Business and Education, 541-962-3399, Fax: 541-962-3701, E-mail: dmeilke@eou.edu.

Application contact: Janet Frye, Administrative Support, MAT/MS Graduate Admission, 541-962-3772, Fax: 541-962-3701, E-mail: jfrye@eou.edu.
Website: https://www.eou.edu/cobe/ed/mat/

Eastern Oregon University, Master of Science Program, La Grande, OR 97850-2899. Offers education (MS). *Program availability:* Part-time, online only, 100% online. *Faculty:* 10 full-time (6 women), 4 part-time/adjunct (2 women). *Students:* 9 full-time (all women), 52 part-time (44 women); includes 2 minority (both Hispanic/Latino). Average age 37. In 2017, 22 master's awarded. *Degree requirements:* For master's, thesis. *Entrance requirements:* For master's, minimum GPA of 3.0 on last 60 quarter hours completed of undergraduate upper-division coursework or 15 quarter hours of approved graduate-level coursework; two letters of professional reference attesting to applicant's ability to be successful; essay. *Application deadline:* Applications are processed on a rolling basis. Electronic applications accepted. *Expenses:* $232 per credit; $350 one-time matriculation fee. *Financial support:* In 2017–18, 8 students received support. Federal Work-Study, scholarships/grants, and tuition waivers (full and partial) available. Support available to part-time students. *Unit head:* Dr. Danny Ray Mielke, Coordinator, 541-962-3349, Fax: 541-962-3701, E-mail: danny.mielke@eou.edu.
Website: https://www.eou.edu/cobe/ed/ms/

Eastern Washington University, Graduate Studies, College of Arts, Letters and Education, Department of Education, Cheney, WA 99004-2431. Offers adult education (M Ed); curriculum development (M Ed); early childhood education (M Ed); educational foundations (M Ed); educational leadership (M Ed); literacy (M Ed); teaching K-8 (M Ed). *Program availability:* Part-time. *Faculty:* 13. *Students:* 32 full-time (25 women), 36 part-time (25 women); includes 5 minority (all Hispanic/Latino), 4 international. Average age 37. 38 applicants, 55% accepted, 18 enrolled. In 2017, 24 master's awarded. *Degree requirements:* For master's, comprehensive exam. *Entrance requirements:* For master's, minimum GPA of 3.0. Additional exam requirements/recommendations for international students: Required—TOEFL (minimum score 580 paper-based; 92 iBT), IELTS (minimum score 7), PTE (minimum score 63). *Application deadline:* For fall admission, 4/1 priority date for domestic students; for spring admission, 1/15 for domestic students. Applications are processed on a rolling basis. Application fee: $75. Electronic applications accepted. *Expenses:* Tuition, state resident: full-time $11,191; part-time $373.06 per credit. Tuition, nonresident: full-time $25,995; part-time $866.52 per credit. *Financial support:* Teaching assistantships with partial tuition reimbursements, career-related internships or fieldwork, Federal Work-Study, institutionally sponsored loans, scholarships/grants, health care benefits, tuition waivers (partial), and unspecified assistantships available. Support available to part-time students. Financial award application deadline: 2/1; financial award applicants required to submit FAFSA. *Unit head:* Dr. Tara Haskins, Education Department Chair/Associate Professor of Literacy, 509-359-2831, E-mail: thaskins@ewu.edu. *Application contact:* Dr. Robin Showalter, Graduate Program Coordinator, 509-359-6492, E-mail: rshowalter@ewu.edu.
Website: http://www.ewu.edu/CALE/Programs/Education.xml

East Stroudsburg University of Pennsylvania, Graduate and Extended Studies, College of Education, East Stroudsburg, PA 18301-2999. Offers M Ed, Ed D. *Program availability:* Part-time, evening/weekend, online learning. *Faculty:* 12 full-time (10 women), 9 part-time/adjunct (6 women). *Students:* 34 full-time (22 women), 244 part-time (196 women); includes 37 minority (13 Black or African American, non-Hispanic/Latino; 1 American Indian or Alaska Native, non-Hispanic/Latino; 2 Asian, non-Hispanic/Latino; 17 Hispanic/Latino; 4 Two or more races, non-Hispanic/Latino), 2 international. Average age 35. 146 applicants, 88% accepted, 90 enrolled. In 2017, 37 master's, 2 doctorates awarded. *Degree requirements:* For master's, comprehensive exam, thesis (for some programs). *Entrance requirements:* Additional exam requirements/recommendations for international students: Recommended—TOEFL (minimum score 560 paper-based; 83 iBT), IELTS. *Application deadline:* For fall admission, 7/31 priority date for domestic students, 6/30 priority date for international students; for spring admission, 11/30 for domestic students, 10/31 for international students. Applications are processed on a rolling basis. Application fee: $50. Electronic applications accepted. *Expenses:* Tuition, state resident: full-time $4500; part-time $3000 per credit. Tuition, nonresident: full-time $6750; part-time $4500 per credit. *Required fees:* $2642; $1756 per credit. $878 per semester. Tuition and fees vary according to course load, campus/location and program. *Financial support:* Research assistantships with tuition reimbursements, career-related internships or fieldwork, Federal Work-Study, and unspecified assistantships available. Support available to part-time students. Financial award application deadline: 3/1; financial award applicants required to submit FAFSA. *Unit head:* Dr. Terry Barry, Dean, 570-422-3377, Fax: 570-422-3506, E-mail: tbarry1@esu.edu. *Application contact:* Kevin Quintero, Associate Director, Graduate and Extended Studies, 570-422-3890, Fax: 570-422-3711, E-mail: kquintero@esu.edu.

East Tennessee State University, School of Graduate Studies, College of Education, Johnson City, TN 37614. Offers M Ed, MA, MAT, MS, Ed D, PhD, Ed S, Post-Master's Certificate, Postbaccalaureate Certificate. *Accreditation:* NCATE. In 2017, 198 master's, 51 doctorates, 12 other advanced degrees awarded. *Entrance requirements:* Additional exam requirements/recommendations for international students: Required—TOEFL (minimum score 550 paper-based; 79 iBT). Application fee: $55 ($65 for international students). Electronic applications accepted. *Financial support:* Fellowships with full tuition reimbursements, research assistantships with full tuition reimbursements, teaching assistantships with full tuition reimbursements, career-related internships or fieldwork, institutionally sponsored loans, scholarships/grants, and unspecified assistantships available. Financial award application deadline: 7/1; financial award applicants required to submit FAFSA. *Unit head:* Dr. Gregory F. Aloia, Dean, 423-439-7616, Fax: 423-439-7560, E-mail: aloiag@etsu.edu. *Application contact:* School of Graduate Studies, 423-439-4221, Fax: 423-439-5624, E-mail: gradsch@etsu.edu.
Website: http://www.etsu.edu/coe/

East Texas Baptist University, Master of Education Program, Marshall, TX 75670-1498. Offers M Ed. *Program availability:* Part-time, evening/weekend, 100% online, blended/hybrid learning. *Faculty:* 3 full-time (1 woman), 4 part-time/adjunct (3 women). *Students:* 32 part-time (18 women); includes 12 minority (8 Black or African American, non-Hispanic/Latino; 1 American Indian or Alaska Native, non-Hispanic/Latino; 1 Hispanic/Latino; 2 Two or more races, non-Hispanic/Latino). Average age 28. 70 applicants, 41% accepted, 21 enrolled. In 2017, 20 master's awarded. *Entrance requirements:* Additional exam requirements/recommendations for international students: Recommended—TOEFL (minimum score 550 paper-based; 79 iBT). *Application deadline:* For fall admission, 8/13 for domestic students; for spring admission, 1/7 for domestic students; for summer admission, 5/10 for domestic students. Applications are processed on a rolling basis. Application fee: $50. Electronic applications accepted. *Expenses:* $700 per credit hour tuition, $150 per semester fees ($75 per semester if less than 6 hours). *Financial support:* In 2017–18, 18 students received support. Federal Work-Study, scholarships/grants, unspecified assistantships, and staff grants available. Financial award applicants required to submit FAFSA. *Unit head:* Dr. PJ Winters, Director, 903-923-2276, Fax: 903-935-4318, E-mail: med@etbu.edu. *Application contact:* Den Murley, Director of Graduate Admissions, 903-923-2079, Fax: 903-934-8115, E-mail: gradadmissions@etbu.edu.
Website: https://www.etbu.edu/education/master-education/

Edgewood College, School of Education, Madison, WI 53711-1997. Offers adult learning (MA Ed); director of special education and pupil services (Certificate); education (MA Ed); teaching and learning (MA Ed). *Accreditation:* NCATE (one or more programs are accredited. *Program availability:* Part-time, evening/weekend. *Faculty:* 13 full-time (9 women), 15 part-time/adjunct (10 women). *Students:* 157 full-time (106 women), 188 part-time (133 women); includes 65 minority (26 Black or African American, non-Hispanic/Latino; 1 American Indian or Alaska Native, non-Hispanic/Latino; 8 Asian, non-Hispanic/Latino; 23 Hispanic/Latino; 7 Two or more races, non-Hispanic/Latino), 14 international. Average age 37. In 2017, 68 master's, 34 doctorates awarded. *Degree requirements:* For master's, practicum, research project; for doctorate, comprehensive exam, thesis/dissertation. *Entrance requirements:* For master's, minimum GPA of 2.75, 2 letters of recommendation, personal statement; for doctorate, resume, letter of intent, 2 letters of recommendation, interview, writing sample. Additional exam requirements/recommendations for international students: Required—TOEFL (minimum score 525 paper-based; 72 iBT). *Application deadline:* For fall admission, 8/15 for domestic students, 5/1 for international students; for spring admission, 1/8 for domestic students, 11/1 for international students. Applications are processed on a rolling basis. Application fee: $30. Electronic applications accepted. *Expenses: Tuition:* Part-time $930 per credit. *Financial support:* Applicants required to submit FAFSA. *Faculty research:* Urban high schools, transgender students, literacy pedagogy, funds of knowledge, English language learners. *Unit head:* Dr. Timothy D. Slekar, Dean, 608-663-2293, E-mail: tslekar@edgewood.edu. *Application contact:* Joann Eastman, Admissions Counselor, 608-663-3250, Fax: 608-663-2214, E-mail: gps@edgewood.edu.
Website: https://www.edgewood.edu/academics/schools/school-of-education

Elizabeth City State University, Department of Education, Psychology and Health, Elizabeth City, NC 27909-7806. Offers M Ed, MSA. *Program availability:* Part-time, evening/weekend. *Faculty:* 7 full-time (4 women), 1 (woman) part-time/adjunct. *Students:* 3 full-time (2 women), 42 part-time (33 women); includes 21 minority (20 Black or African American, non-Hispanic/Latino; 1 Two or more races, non-Hispanic/Latino). Average age 37. 3 applicants, 100% accepted, 2 enrolled. In 2017, 51 master's awarded. *Degree requirements:* For master's, comprehensive exam (for some programs), thesis. *Application deadline:* For fall admission, 11/1 priority date for domestic students; for spring admission, 3/15 priority date for domestic students. Applications are processed on a rolling basis. Application fee: $30. Electronic applications accepted. Tuition and fees vary according to course load and program. *Financial support:* In 2017–18, 25 students received support. Scholarships/grants and tuition waivers (partial) available. *Unit head:* Dr. Sharon D. Raynor, Director, Graduate Education Program, 252-335-3945, E-mail: sdraynor@ecsu.edu.
Website: http://www.ecsu.edu/academics/educationpsychology/index.cfm

Elms College, Division of Education, Chicopee, MA 01013-2839. Offers early childhood education (MAT); education (M Ed, CAGS); elementary education (MAT); English as a second language (MAT); reading (MAT); secondary education (MAT), including biology education, English education, Spanish education; special education (MAT). *Program availability:* Part-time, evening/weekend. *Faculty:* 4 full-time (all women), 8 part-time/adjunct (7 women). *Students:* 6 full-time (4 women), 127 part-time (107 women); includes 8 minority (2 Asian, non-Hispanic/Latino; 6 Hispanic/Latino). Average age 33. 42 applicants, 88% accepted, 36 enrolled. In 2017, 50 master's, 6 other advanced degrees awarded. *Degree requirements:* For master's, thesis (for some programs). *Entrance requirements:* For master's, Massachusetts Educators Certification Test, minimum GPA of 3.0; for CAGS, master's degree in education. Additional exam requirements/recommendations for international students: Required—TOEFL. *Application deadline:* For fall admission, 7/1 priority date for domestic students; for spring admission, 11/1 priority date for domestic students. Applications are processed on a rolling basis. Application fee: $30. *Expenses: Tuition:* Full-time $13,860; part-time $770 per credit hour. *Required fees:* $200. Tuition and fees vary according to degree level and program. *Financial support:* In 2017–18, 2 teaching assistantships with partial tuition reimbursements were awarded. Financial award applicants required to submit FAFSA. *Unit head:* Dr. Mary Janeczek, Chair, Division of Education, 413-594-2761, Fax: 413-592-4871, E-mail: janeczeke@elms.edu. *Application contact:* School of Graduate and Professional Studies, 413-265-2445, E-mail: graduateeducation@elms.edu.

Elon University, Program in Education, Elon, NC 27244-2010. Offers elementary education (M Ed); gifted education (M Ed); special education (M Ed). *Accreditation:* NCATE. *Program availability:* Part-time. *Faculty:* 8 full-time (6 women), 2 part-time/adjunct (both women). *Students:* 24 part-time (22 women); includes 13 minority (2 Black or African American, non-Hispanic/Latino; 2 Asian, non-Hispanic/Latino; 8 Hispanic/Latino; 1 Two or more races, non-Hispanic/Latino). Average age 23. 29 applicants, 69% accepted, 16 enrolled. In 2017, 10 master's awarded. *Entrance requirements:* For master's, GRE, MAT. Additional exam requirements/recommendations for international students: Required—TOEFL (minimum score 550 paper-based; 79 iBT). *Application deadline:* For fall admission, 5/1 for domestic students. Applications are processed on a rolling basis. Application fee: $50. Electronic applications accepted. *Financial support:* Federal Work-Study and scholarships/grants available. Support available to part-time students. Financial award application deadline: 6/1; financial award applicants required to submit FAFSA. *Faculty research:* Teaching reading to low-achieving second and third graders, pre- and post-student teaching attitudes, children's writing, whole language methodology, critical creative thinking. *Unit head:* Dr. Ann Bullock, Dean of the School of Education/Professor, 336-278-5900, E-mail: abullock9@elon.edu. *Application contact:* Art Fadde, Director of Graduate Admissions, 800-334-8448 Ext. 3, Fax: 336-278-7699, E-mail: afadde@elon.edu.
Website: http://www.elon.edu/med

Embry-Riddle Aeronautical University–Worldwide, Department of Aeronautics, Graduate Studies, Daytona Beach, FL 32114-3900. Offers aeronautics (MSA); aeronautics and design (MS); aviation maintenance (MAM); aviation/aerospace management (MS); aviation/aerospace research (MS); education (MS); human factors (MSHFS), including aerospace, systems engineering; occupational safety management (MS); operations (MS); safety/emergency response (MS); space systems (MS); unmanned systems (MS). *Program availability:* Part-time, evening/weekend. *Faculty:* 31 full-time (9 women), 145 part-time/adjunct (18 women). *Students:* 821 full-time (175 women), 972 part-time (146 women); includes 403 minority (136 Black or African American, non-Hispanic/Latino; 5 American Indian or Alaska Native, non-Hispanic/Latino; 65 Asian, non-Hispanic/Latino; 90 Hispanic/Latino; 8 Native Hawaiian or other Pacific Islander, non-Hispanic/Latino; 99 Two or more races, non-Hispanic/Latino), 128 international. Average age 37. 515 applicants, 75% accepted, 329 enrolled. In 2017, 514 master's awarded. *Degree requirements:* For master's, comprehensive exam, thesis or capstone project. *Entrance requirements:* For master's, GRE (for MSHFS). Additional exam requirements/recommendations for international students: Required—TOEFL (minimum score 550 paper-based, 79 iBT) or IELTS (6). *Application deadline:* Applications are processed on a rolling basis. Application fee: $50. Electronic applications accepted. *Expenses: Tuition:* Full-time $7680; part-time $640 per credit hour. Tuition and fees vary according to program. *Financial support:* Career-related internships or fieldwork and scholarships/grants available. Financial award applicants required to submit FAFSA. *Unit head:* Kenneth Witcher, PhD, Associate Professor and Dean, College of Aeronautics, E-mail: kenneth.witcher@erau.edu. *Application contact:*

Worldwide Campus, 800-522-6787, E-mail: worldwide@erau.edu.
Website: http://worldwide.erau.edu/colleges/aeronautics/department-aeronautics-graduate-studies/

Emmanuel College, Graduate and Professional Programs, Graduate Programs in Education, Boston, MA 02115. Offers moderate learning disabilities (Certificate); urban education (M Ed). *Program availability:* Part-time, evening/weekend. *Faculty:* 1 (woman) full-time, 7 part-time/adjunct (all women). *Students:* 5 full-time (all women), 11 part-time (7 women); includes 6 minority (1 Black or African American, non-Hispanic/Latino; 1 Asian, non-Hispanic/Latino; 4 Hispanic/Latino). Average age 28. 21 applicants, 38% accepted, 4 enrolled. In 2017, 13 master's awarded. *Degree requirements:* For master's, 36 credits, including 6-credit practicum. *Entrance requirements:* For master's, transcripts from all regionally-accredited institutions attended (showing proof of bachelor's degree completion), 2 letters of recommendation, essay, resume. Additional exam requirements/recommendations for international students: Required—TOEFL. *Application deadline:* Applications are processed on a rolling basis. Electronic applications accepted. *Expenses:* $24,112 (for M Ed); $6,576 (for Certificate in moderate disabilities). *Financial support:* Application deadline: 2/15; applicants required to submit FAFSA. *Unit head:* Cindy O'Callaghan, Dean of Academic Administration and Graduate and Professional Programs, 617-735-9700, E-mail: gpp@emmanuel.edu. *Application contact:* Helen Muterperl, Director of Graduate and Professional Programs, 617-735-9700, Fax: 617-507-0434, E-mail: gpp@emmanuel.edu.
Website: http://www.emmanuel.edu/graduate-professional-programs/academics/education.html

Emory & Henry College, Graduate Programs, Emory, VA 24327. Offers American history (MA Ed); education professional studies (M Ed); occupational therapy (MOT); organizational leadership (MCOL); physical therapy (DPT); physician assistant studies (MPAS); reading specialist (M Ed). *Program availability:* Part-time. *Faculty:* 7 full-time (3 women). *Students:* 194 full-time (128 women), 4 part-time (2 women); includes 6 minority (2 Black or African American, non-Hispanic/Latino; 1 American Indian or Alaska Native, non-Hispanic/Latino; 1 Asian, non-Hispanic/Latino; 2 Hispanic/Latino). Average age 25. 525 applicants, 21% accepted, 74 enrolled. In 2017, 24 master's awarded. *Degree requirements:* For master's, thesis optional; for doctorate, thesis/dissertation optional. *Entrance requirements:* For master's, GRE or PRAXIS I, official transcripts from all colleges previously attended, three professional recommendations, essay. Additional exam requirements/recommendations for international students: Recommended—TOEFL, IELTS (minimum score 6). *Application deadline:* Applications are processed on a rolling basis. Electronic applications accepted. *Expenses:* Contact institution. *Financial support:* Application deadline: 10/15; applicants required to submit FAFSA. *Unit head:* Dr. Michael Puglisi, Associate Dean for Academic Affairs, 276-944-6662, E-mail: mpuglisi@ehc.edu. *Application contact:* Mary Bolt, Director of Transfer and Graduate Admission, 276-944-6135, E-mail: mbolt@ehc.edu.

Emory University, Laney Graduate School, Division of Educational Studies, Atlanta, GA 30322-1100. Offers educational studies (MA, PhD); middle grades teaching (MAT); secondary teaching (MAT). *Accreditation:* NCATE. Terminal master's awarded for partial completion of doctoral program. *Degree requirements:* For master's, thesis; for doctorate, comprehensive exam, thesis/dissertation. *Entrance requirements:* For master's and doctorate, GRE General Test, minimum GPA of 3.0. Additional exam requirements/recommendations for international students: Required—TOEFL. Electronic applications accepted. *Faculty research:* Educational policy, educational measurement, urban and multicultural education, mathematics and science education, comparative education.

Emporia State University, Program in Teaching, Emporia, KS 66801-5415. Offers M Ed. *Program availability:* Part-time, online learning. *Faculty:* 10 full-time (3 women). *Students:* 6 full-time (4 women), 19 part-time (15 women); includes 1 minority (Black or African American, non-Hispanic/Latino). 14 applicants, 64% accepted, 6 enrolled. In 2017, 18 master's awarded. *Entrance requirements:* For master's, GRE or MAT, minimum GPA of 2.5 on last 60 undergraduate hours; two personal references. Application fee: $40. *Expenses:* Tuition, state resident: full-time $6084; part-time $253.50 per credit hour. Tuition, nonresident: full-time $18,924; part-time $788.50 per credit hour. *Required fees:* $1943; $80.95 per credit hour. Tuition and fees vary according to campus/location. *Unit head:* Dr. Daniel Stiffler, Chair, 620-341-5776, E-mail: dstiffle@emporia.edu. *Application contact:* Mary Sewell, Admissions Coordinator, 800-950-GRAD, Fax: 620-341-5909, E-mail: msewell@emporia.edu.

Evangel University, Department of Education, Springfield, MO 65802. Offers curriculum and instruction (M Ed); educational leadership (M Ed); literacy (M Ed); secondary teaching (M Ed). *Accreditation:* NCATE. *Program availability:* Part-time, evening/weekend, 100% online, blended/hybrid learning. *Faculty:* 8 full-time (5 women), 8 part-time/adjunct (5 women). *Students:* 1 (woman) full-time, 47 part-time (41 women); includes 2 minority (both Hispanic/Latino). Average age 37. 16 applicants, 100% accepted, 14 enrolled. In 2017, 14 master's awarded. *Entrance requirements:* For master's, PRAXIS II (preferred) or GRE, minimum undergraduate GPA of 3.0. Additional exam requirements/recommendations for international students: Required—TOEFL (minimum score 550 paper-based). *Application deadline:* For fall admission, 7/15 priority date for domestic students, 8/1 for international students; for spring admission, 11/15 priority date for domestic students, 12/1 for international students. Applications are processed on a rolling basis. Application fee: $25. Electronic applications accepted. Application fee is waived when completed online. *Expenses: Tuition:* Full-time $7200; part-time $4800 per credit hour. *Required fees:* $210; $155 per semester. *Financial support:* In 2017–18, 23 students received support. Scholarships/grants and unspecified assistantships available. Financial award application deadline: 4/1; financial award applicants required to submit FAFSA. *Unit head:* Dr. Susan Langston, Program Coordinator, 417-865-2815 Ext. 8552, E-mail: langstons@evangel.edu. *Application contact:* Michael Mann, Enrollment Coordinator, Graduate Studies, 417-865-2815 Ext. 8276, Fax: 417-575-5484, E-mail: mannm@evangel.edu.
Website: http://www.evangel.edu/academics/graduate-studies/graduate-programs

The Evergreen State College, Graduate Programs, Program in Teaching, Olympia, WA 98505. Offers MIT. *Faculty:* 6 full-time (5 women), 1 (woman) part-time/adjunct. *Students:* 57 full-time (40 women), 1 part-time (0 women); includes 16 minority (4 Black or African American, non-Hispanic/Latino; 1 American Indian or Alaska Native, non-Hispanic/Latino; 1 Asian, non-Hispanic/Latino; 4 Hispanic/Latino; 6 Two or more races, non-Hispanic/Latino). Average age 28. 46 applicants, 93% accepted, 40 enrolled. In 2017, 15 master's awarded. *Degree requirements:* For master's, project, 20-week teaching internship. *Entrance requirements:* For master's, Washington Educator Skills Test-Basic (WEST-B), Washington Educator Skills Test-Endorsements, minimum undergraduate GPA of 3.0 for last 90 quarter hours; official transcript; resume; 3 letters of recommendation; personal statement; thesis-based essay; Washington State Patrol and FBI background check; 4 quarter credits in college level math; 8 quarter credits in social sciences; 10 quarter credits of academic writing. Additional exam requirements/recommendations for international students: Required—TOEFL (minimum score 600 paper-based; 100 iBT). *Application deadline:* For fall admission, 4/2 priority date for domestic and international students. Applications are processed on a rolling basis. Application fee: $50. Electronic applications accepted. *Expenses:* Contact institution. *Financial support:* In 2017–18, 37 students received support, including 14 fellowships

with partial tuition reimbursements available (averaging $641 per year); career-related internships or fieldwork, institutionally sponsored loans, scholarships/grants, and tuition waivers (partial) also available. Financial award application deadline: 2/1; financial award applicants required to submit FAFSA. *Faculty research:* Literacy, children's and adolescent literature, language acquisition, learning theory, developmental psychology, multicultural education, qualitative research, critical pedagogy, feminist theory, teacher education, urban education, elementary education. *Unit head:* Dr. Patrick Naughton, Director, 360-867-6909, E-mail: naughtonp@evergreen.edu. *Application contact:* Maggie Foran, Associate Director, 360-867-6559, Fax: 360-867-6575, E-mail: foranm@evergreen.edu.
Website: http://www.evergreen.edu/mit/

Fairfield University, Graduate School of Education and Allied Professions, Fairfield, CT 06824. Offers applied behavior analysis (ATC); applied psychology (MA); clinical mental health counseling (MA, CAS); educational technology (MA); elementary education (MA, CAS); family studies (MA); integration of spirituality and religion in counseling (ATC); marriage and family therapy (MA); reading and language development (Sixth Year Certificate); school counseling (MA, CAS); school psychology (MA, CAS); school-based marriage and family therapy (ATC); secondary education (MA); special education (MA, CAS); substance abuse counseling (ATC); teaching (Certificate); teaching and foundations (MA, CAS); TESOL, world languages, and bilingual education (MA, CAS). *Accreditation:* NCATE. *Program availability:* Part-time, evening/weekend. *Faculty:* 23 full-time (17 women), 39 part-time/adjunct (28 women). *Students:* 199 full-time (168 women), 251 part-time (206 women); includes 85 minority (21 Black or African American, non-Hispanic/Latino; 9 Asian, non-Hispanic/Latino; 49 Hispanic/Latino; 6 Two or more races, non-Hispanic/Latino), 4 international. Average age 32. 370 applicants, 56% accepted, 125 enrolled. In 2017, 136 master's, 28 other advanced degrees awarded. *Degree requirements:* For master's, comprehensive exam. *Entrance requirements:* For master's, minimum GPA of 3.0, 2 recommendations, resume. Additional exam requirements/recommendations for international students: Required—TOEFL (minimum score 550 paper-based; 84 iBT) or IELTS (minimum score 7.5). *Application deadline:* For fall admission, 2/15 for international students; for spring admission, 10/1 for international students. Application fee: $60. Electronic applications accepted. *Expenses:* $750 per credit hour. *Financial support:* In 2017–18, 34 students received support. Career-related internships or fieldwork and unspecified assistantships available. Support available to part-time students. Financial award applicants required to submit FAFSA. *Faculty research:* Reading and literacy, writing, social justice and inequality in education, addictions and mental health issues, therapeutic relationships and clinical supervision. *Unit head:* Dr. Robert D. Hannafin, Dean, 203-254-4250, Fax: 203-254-4241, E-mail: rhannafin@fairfield.edu. *Application contact:* Marianne Gumpper, Director of Graduate Admission, 203-254-4184, Fax: 203-254-4073, E-mail: gradadmis@fairfield.edu.
Website: http://www.fairfield.edu/gseap

Fairleigh Dickinson University, Florham Campus, Maxwell Becton College of Arts and Sciences, Department of English, Communication and Philosophy, Program in Creative Writing and Literature for Educators, Madison, NJ 07940-1099. Offers MA.

Fairleigh Dickinson University, Florham Campus, University College: Arts, Sciences, and Professional Studies, Peter Sammartino School of Education, Madison, NJ 07940-1099. Offers education for certified teachers (MA, Certificate); educational leadership (MA); instructional technology (Certificate); literacy/reading (Certificate); teaching (MAT).

Fairleigh Dickinson University, Metropolitan Campus, University College: Arts, Sciences, and Professional Studies, Peter Sammartino School of Education, Teaneck, NJ 07666-1914. Offers dyslexia specialist (Certificate); education for certified teachers (MA); educational leadership (MA); instructional technology (Certificate); learning disabilities (MA); literacy/reading (Certificate); multilingual education (MA); teacher of the handicapped (Certificate); teaching (MAT). *Accreditation:* TEAC. *Program availability:* Part-time. *Degree requirements:* For master's, research project (MAT).

Fairmont State University, Programs in Education, Fairmont, WV 26554. Offers digital media, new literacies and learning (M Ed); education (MAT); exercise science, fitness and wellness (M Ed); professional studies (M Ed); reading (M Ed); special education (M Ed). *Accreditation:* NCATE. *Program availability:* Part-time, evening/weekend, 100% online. *Entrance requirements:* For master's, GRE. Additional exam requirements/recommendations for international students: Required—TOEFL (minimum score 80 iBT), IELTS (minimum score 6.5). Electronic applications accepted.

Faulkner University, College of Education, Montgomery, AL 36109-3398. Offers counseling (MS); curriculum and instruction (M Ed); elementary education (M Ed); school counseling (M Ed). *Program availability:* Part-time, evening/weekend, 100% online, blended/hybrid learning. *Faculty:* 13 full-time (8 women), 6 part-time/adjunct (1 woman). *Students:* 140 full-time (107 women), 16 part-time (13 women); includes 97 minority (92 Black or African American, non-Hispanic/Latino; 1 American Indian or Alaska Native, non-Hispanic/Latino; 1 Asian, non-Hispanic/Latino; 3 Hispanic/Latino). Average age 37. 92 applicants, 55% accepted, 48 enrolled. In 2017, 51 master's awarded. *Degree requirements:* For master's, 5+ hours in clinical training (for MS, M Ed in school counseling). *Entrance requirements:* For master's, MAT (minimum score of 370) or GRE (minimum score of 280) taken within last five years, bachelor's degree from regionally-accredited college or university; official transcripts from all colleges and universities attended; three letters of recommendation; goal statement (approximately 600 words); minimum cumulative GPA of 2.75 in undergraduate courses, 3.0 in graduate courses. Additional exam requirements/recommendations for international students: Required—TOEFL (minimum score 500 paper-based). *Application deadline:* For fall admission, 8/1 for domestic students; for spring admission, 12/1 for domestic students; for summer admission, 5/1 for domestic students. Application fee: $35. Electronic applications accepted. *Expenses:* Contact institution. *Financial support:* Applicants required to submit FAFSA. *Unit head:* Dr. Leslie S. Cowell, Dean, College of Education, 334-386-7224, Fax: 334-386-7194, E-mail: lcowell@faulkner.edu. *Application contact:* Rebecca L. Horn, Director, Graduate Education, 334-386-7264, Fax: 334-386-7194, E-mail: rhorn@faulkner.edu.
Website: https://www.faulkner.edu/graduate/graduate_academics/

Felician University, Program in Education, Lodi, NJ 07644-2117. Offers education (MA); educational leadership (principal/supervision) (MA); educational supervision (PMC); principal (PMC). *Accreditation:* TEAC. *Program availability:* Part-time, evening/weekend. *Faculty:* 2 full-time (1 woman), 7 part-time/adjunct (2 women). *Students:* 3 full-time (2 women), 51 part-time (48 women); includes 15 minority (4 Black or African American, non-Hispanic/Latino; 3 Asian, non-Hispanic/Latino; 8 Hispanic/Latino), 2 international. Average age 36. 29 applicants, 86% accepted, 12 enrolled. In 2017, 23 master's, 11 other advanced degrees awarded. *Degree requirements:* For master's and PMC, thesis, presentation. *Entrance requirements:* For master's, PRAXIS Core (Reading/Writing/Math), minimum GPA of 3.0, two professional letters of recommendation, personal statement, personal interview. Additional exam requirements/recommendations for international students: Required—TOEFL (minimum score 550 paper-based; 79 iBT), IELTS (minimum score 6.5), PTE (minimum score 56). *Application deadline:* Applications are processed on a rolling basis. Application fee: $40. Electronic applications accepted. Application fee is waived when completed online.

Expenses: Contact institution. *Financial support:* Federal Work-Study and scholarships/grants available. Financial award applicants required to submit FAFSA. *Faculty research:* Educational leadership, administration, supervision, curriculum. *Unit head:* Stephanie McGowan, Dean of Education, 201-559-3551, E-mail: mcgowans@felician.edu. *Application contact:* Michael Szarek, Assistant Vice-President, Graduate Admissions, 201-355-1450, E-mail: szarekm@felician.edu.

Ferris State University, College of Education and Human Services, School of Education, Big Rapids, MI 49307. Offers curriculum and instruction (M Ed), including special education, subject area; educational leadership (MS); instructor (MSCTE); post-secondary administration (MSCTE); training and development (MSCTE). *Program availability:* Part-time, evening/weekend, blended/hybrid learning. *Faculty:* 7 full-time (4 women), 9 part-time/adjunct (6 women). *Students:* 4 full-time (1 woman), 40 part-time (23 women); includes 7 minority (3 Black or African American, non-Hispanic/Latino; 2 Hispanic/Latino; 2 Two or more races, non-Hispanic/Latino), 4 international. Average age 37. 13 applicants, 92% accepted, 7 enrolled. In 2017, 36 master's awarded. *Degree requirements:* For master's, thesis, research paper or project. *Entrance requirements:* For master's, minimum undergraduate GPA of 3.0. Additional exam requirements/recommendations for international students: Required—TOEFL (minimum score 500 paper-based, 79 iBT) or IELTS. *Application deadline:* For fall admission, 7/1 priority date for domestic and international students; for spring admission, 11/1 priority date for domestic and international students; for summer admission, 3/1 priority date for domestic and international students. Applications are processed on a rolling basis. Application fee: $30. Electronic applications accepted. Application fee is waived when completed online. *Financial support:* Career-related internships or fieldwork and scholarships/grants available. Support available to part-time students. Financial award applicants required to submit FAFSA. *Faculty research:* Suicide prevention, reading, women in education, special needs, administration. *Unit head:* Arrick L. Jackson, Dean, 231-591-2702, Fax: 231-591-2043, E-mail: arrickjackson@ferris.edu. *Application contact:* Liza Ing, Graduate Program Coordinator, 231-591-5362, Fax: 231-591-2043, E-mail: lizaIng@ferris.edu.
Website: http://www.ferris.edu/education/education/

Fielding Graduate University, Graduate Programs, School of Leadership Studies, Programs in Education, Santa Barbara, CA 93105-3814. Offers digital teaching and learning (MA); leadership for change (Ed D). *Program availability:* Part-time, evening/weekend, 100% online, blended/hybrid learning. *Faculty:* 6 full-time (4 women), 16 part-time/adjunct (12 women). *Students:* 68 full-time (45 women), 8 part-time (6 women); includes 41 minority (20 Black or African American, non-Hispanic/Latino; 2 American Indian or Alaska Native, non-Hispanic/Latino; 1 Asian, non-Hispanic/Latino; 8 Hispanic/Latino; 10 Two or more races, non-Hispanic/Latino), 1 international. Average age 50. 15 applicants, 93% accepted, 5 enrolled. In 2017, 5 master's, 21 doctorates awarded. Terminal master's awarded for partial completion of doctoral program. *Degree requirements:* For master's, thesis or alternative, capstone; for doctorate, comprehensive exam, thesis/dissertation. *Entrance requirements:* For master's, bachelor's degree from regionally-accredited U.S. institution or equivalent, resume, statement of purpose, official transcript; for doctorate, bachelor's or master's degree from regionally-accredited U.S. institution or equivalent, resume, statement of purpose, reflexive essay, official transcript. *Application deadline:* For fall admission, 7/15 for domestic and international students; for spring admission, 11/1 for domestic and international students; for summer admission, 3/1 for domestic and international students. Application fee: $75. Electronic applications accepted. *Expenses:* Contact institution. *Financial support:* In 2017–18, 17 students received support. Research assistantships, teaching assistantships, and scholarships/grants available. Support available to part-time students. Financial award applicants required to submit FAFSA. *Unit head:* Dr. Barbara Mink, Program Director, E-mail: bmink@fielding.edu. *Application contact:* Enrollment Coordinator, 800-340-1099 Ext. 4098, Fax: 805-687-9793, E-mail: admissions@fielding.edu.
Website: http://www.fielding.edu/our-programs/school-of-leadership-studies/

Florida Agricultural and Mechanical University, Division of Graduate Studies, Research, and Continuing Education, College of Education, Tallahassee, FL 32307-3200. Offers M Ed, MBE, MS, MS Ed, PhD. *Accreditation:* NCATE. *Program availability:* Part-time, evening/weekend. *Degree requirements:* For master's, thesis (for some programs); for doctorate, thesis/dissertation. *Entrance requirements:* For master's, GRE General Test, minimum GPA of 3.0. Additional exam requirements/recommendations for international students: Required—TOEFL.

Florida Atlantic University, College of Education, Boca Raton, FL 33431-0991. Offers M Ed, MA, MS, Ed D, PhD, Ed S. *Accreditation:* NCATE. *Program availability:* Part-time, evening/weekend. *Faculty:* 76 full-time (44 women), 22 part-time/adjunct (13 women). *Students:* 324 full-time (242 women), 495 part-time (372 women); includes 344 minority (168 Black or African American, non-Hispanic/Latino; 13 Asian, non-Hispanic/Latino; 146 Hispanic/Latino; 17 Two or more races, non-Hispanic/Latino), 17 international. Average age 33. 986 applicants, 38% accepted, 259 enrolled. In 2017, 205 master's, 25 doctorates, 20 other advanced degrees awarded. *Degree requirements:* For doctorate, comprehensive exam, thesis/dissertation; for Ed S, departmental qualifying exam. *Entrance requirements:* For master's, doctorate, and Ed S, GRE General Test. Additional exam requirements/recommendations for international students: Required—TOEFL (minimum score 500 paper-based; 61 iBT), IELTS (minimum score 6). *Application deadline:* For fall admission, 5/1 for domestic students. Applications are processed on a rolling basis. Application fee: $30. Electronic applications accepted. *Expenses:* Tuition, state resident: full-time $7400; part-time $369.82 per credit. Tuition, nonresident: full-time $20,496; part-time $1042.81 per credit. *Financial support:* Fellowships with partial tuition reimbursements, research assistantships with partial tuition reimbursements, teaching assistantships with partial tuition reimbursements, career-related internships or fieldwork, Federal Work-Study, and unspecified assistantships available. *Faculty research:* Marriage and family counseling, multicultural education, self-directed learning, assessment, reading. *Unit head:* Dr. Valerie Bristor, Dean, 561-297-3357, E-mail: bristor@fau.edu.
Website: http://www.coe.fau.edu/

Florida Gulf Coast University, College of Education, Fort Myers, FL 33965-6565. Offers M Ed, MA. *Program availability:* Part-time, evening/weekend, online learning. *Faculty:* 27 full-time (19 women), 44 part-time/adjunct (30 women). *Students:* 13 full-time (11 women), 84 part-time (70 women); includes 44 minority (15 Black or African American, non-Hispanic/Latino; 4 Asian, non-Hispanic/Latino; 24 Hispanic/Latino; 1 Two or more races, non-Hispanic/Latino), 5 international. Average age 36. 62 applicants, 94% accepted, 46 enrolled. In 2017, 49 master's awarded. *Entrance requirements:* For master's, GRE General Test, MAT, minimum GPA of 3.0. Additional exam requirements/recommendations for international students: Required—TOEFL (minimum score 550 paper-based). *Application deadline:* For fall admission, 2/15 priority date for domestic students, 5/1 for international students; for spring admission, 12/1 for domestic students, 9/15 for international students. Applications are processed on a rolling basis. Application fee: $30. Electronic applications accepted. *Expenses:* Tuition, state resident: part-time $290 per credit hour. Tuition, nonresident: part-time $1173 per credit hour. *Required fees:* $127 per credit hour. Tuition and fees vary according to course load. *Financial support:* In 2017–18, 17 students received support. Application deadline: 6/30;

applicants required to submit FAFSA. *Faculty research:* Inclusion, emergent literacy, pre-service and in-service teacher education, education policy. *Total annual research expenditures:* $2.3 million. *Unit head:* Dr. Eunny Hyun, Dean, 239-590-7791, Fax: 239-590-7801, E-mail: ehyun@fgcu.edu. *Application contact:* Shannon Acosta, Graduate Studies Admissions, 239-590-7027, Fax: 239-590-7843, E-mail: sacosta@fgcu.edu. Website: http://www.fgcu.edu/

Florida Institute of Technology, College of Science, Program in Teaching, Melbourne, FL 32901-6975. Offers MAT. *Students:* Average age 29. 5 applicants, 20% accepted. In 2017, 1 master's awarded. *Degree requirements:* For master's, comprehensive exam, minimum GPA of 3.0, field experience. *Entrance requirements:* For master's, appropriate bachelor's degree, resume, statement of objectives. Additional exam requirements/recommendations for international students: Required—TOEFL (minimum score 550 paper-based; 79 iBT). *Application deadline:* Applications are processed on a rolling basis. Electronic applications accepted. *Expenses:* Tuition: Part-time $1241 per credit hour. Part-time tuition and fees vary according to campus/location. *Financial support:* Applicants required to submit FAFSA. *Unit head:* Dr. Kastro Hamed, Department Head, 321-674-7206, E-mail: khamed@fit.edu. *Application contact:* Cheryl A. Brown, Associate Director of Graduate Admissions, 321-674-7581, Fax: 321-723-9468, E-mail: cbrown@fit.edu. Website: http://cos.fit.edu/education/

Florida Memorial University, School of Education, Miami-Dade, FL 33054. Offers elementary education (MS); exceptional student education (MS); reading (MS). *Degree requirements:* For master's, comprehensive exam or thesis, field and clinical experiences, exit exam. *Entrance requirements:* For master's, GRE, CLAST, PRAXIS I, baccalaureate or graduate degree with minimum GPA of 3.0 in last 60 hours, 3 recommendations. Additional exam requirements/recommendations for international students: Recommended—TOEFL.

Florida Southern College, Programs in Teaching, Lakeland, FL 33801-5698. Offers collaborative teaching and learning (M Ed); educational leadership (M Ed, Ed D); teaching (MAT). *Program availability:* Part-time, evening/weekend, 100% online, blended/hybrid learning. *Faculty:* 11 full-time (4 women), 11 part-time/adjunct (7 women). *Students:* 41 full-time (36 women), 23 part-time (all women); includes 11 minority (6 Black or African American, non-Hispanic/Latino; 1 American Indian or Alaska Native, non-Hispanic/Latino; 2 Hispanic/Latino; 1 Native Hawaiian or other Pacific Islander, non-Hispanic/Latino; 1 Two or more races, non-Hispanic/Latino), 2 international. Average age 40. 130 applicants, 92% accepted, 95 enrolled. In 2017, 1 master's awarded. *Degree requirements:* For master's, comprehensive exam (for some programs), thesis (for some programs), FICE General Knowledge test and professional education exam (for MAT), eligibility for the Florida Professional Teacher Certificate (for M Ed); for doctorate, thesis/dissertation. *Entrance requirements:* For master's, Florida Teacher Certification exam (for MAT), letter of reference, resume, personal statement. Additional exam requirements/recommendations for international students: Required—TOEFL (minimum score 550 paper-based; 79 iBT), IELTS (minimum score 6.5). *Application deadline:* For fall admission, 8/1 for domestic and international students; for winter admission, 4/1 for domestic and international students; for spring admission, 12/1 for domestic and international students. Applications are processed on a rolling basis. Application fee: $30. Electronic applications accepted. *Expenses:* $410 per credit hour, $100 required fee. *Financial support:* In 2017–18, 3 students received support. Scholarships/grants available. Support available to part-time students. Financial award applicants required to submit FAFSA. *Unit head:* Dr. Tracey Tedder, Dean, 863-680-4177, Fax: 863-680-4102, E-mail: ttedder@flsouthern.edu. *Application contact:* Kathy Connelly, Evening Program Assistant Director, 863-680-4205, Fax: 863-680-3872, E-mail: kconnelly@flsouthern.edu.

Florida State University, The Graduate School, College of Education, Tallahassee, FL 32306. Offers MS, Ed D, PhD, Certificate, Ed S, MS/Ed S. *Accreditation:* NCATE. *Program availability:* Part-time, evening/weekend, blended/hybrid learning, asynchronous, minimal on-campus study. *Faculty:* 97 full-time (68 women), 46 part-time/adjunct (34 women). *Students:* 706 full-time (470 women), 438 part-time (311 women); includes 332 minority (135 Black or African American, non-Hispanic/Latino; 5 American Indian or Alaska Native, non-Hispanic/Latino; 13 Asian, non-Hispanic/Latino; 130 Hispanic/Latino; 49 Two or more races, non-Hispanic/Latino), 215 international. Average age 32. 937 applicants, 47% accepted, 238 enrolled. In 2017, 283 master's, 50 doctorates, 56 other advanced degrees awarded. Terminal master's awarded for partial completion of doctoral program. *Degree requirements:* For master's and other advanced degree, comprehensive exam, thesis optional; for doctorate, comprehensive exam, thesis/dissertation, diagnostic exam, preliminary exam, prospectus defense, dissertation defense. *Entrance requirements:* For master's, doctorate, and other advanced degree, GRE General Test, minimum upper-division GPA of 3.0. Additional exam requirements/recommendations for international students: Required—TOEFL (minimum score 550 paper-based, 80 iBT), IELTS (minimum score 6.5), Michigan English Language Assessment Battery (minimum score 77), or PTE (minimum score 55). Application fee: $30. Electronic applications accepted. *Financial support:* In 2017–18, 307 students received support, including 23 fellowships with tuition reimbursements available, 334 research assistantships with tuition reimbursements available, 248 teaching assistantships with tuition reimbursements available; scholarships/grants, tuition waivers (full and partial), and unspecified assistantships also available. Financial award application deadline: 1/15; financial award applicants required to submit FAFSA. *Faculty research:* Sport management and administration, educational psychology, instructional systems, teacher education, educational leadership and policy. *Total annual research expenditures:* $14.7 million. *Unit head:* Marcy P. Driscoll, Dean, 850-644-6885, Fax: 850-644-2725, E-mail: mdriscoll@fsu.edu. *Application contact:* Jennie H. Kroeger, Assistant Director, Office of Communication and Recruitment, 850-644-6885, Fax: 850-644-2725, E-mail: jennie.kroeger@fsu.edu. Website: http://education.fsu.edu

Fontbonne University, Graduate Programs, St. Louis, MO 63105-3098. Offers accounting (MBA, MS); art (MA); art (K-12) (MAT); business (MBA); computer science (MS); deaf education (MA); early intervention in deaf education (MA); education (MA), including autism spectrum disorders, curriculum and instruction, diverse learners, early childhood education, reading, special education; elementary education (MAT); family and consumer sciences (MA), including multidisciplinary health communication studies; fine arts (MFA); instructional design and technology (MS); management and leadership (MM); middle school education (MAT); secondary education (MAT); special education (MAT); speech-language pathology (MS); supply chain management (MS); theatre (MA). *Program availability:* Part-time, evening/weekend, online learning. *Degree requirements:* For master's, comprehensive exam (for some programs), thesis (for some programs). *Entrance requirements:* Additional exam requirements/recommendations for international students: Required—TOEFL (minimum score 500 paper-based; 65 iBT). Electronic applications accepted.

Fordham University, Graduate School of Education, New York, NY 10023. Offers MSE, MST, Ed D, PhD, Adv C. *Accreditation:* NCATE. *Program availability:* Part-time, evening/weekend. Terminal master's awarded for partial completion of doctoral program. *Degree requirements:* For master's and Adv C, comprehensive exam (for some programs); for doctorate, comprehensive exam (for some programs), thesis/

dissertation. *Entrance requirements:* For master's and Adv C, minimum GPA of 3.0; for doctorate, GRE or MAT. Additional exam requirements/recommendations for international students: Required—TOEFL (minimum score 577 paper-based, 90 iBT) or IELTS (minimum score 7.0). Electronic applications accepted. *Expenses:* Contact institution.

Fort Hays State University, Graduate School, College of Education, Hays, KS 67601-4099. Offers MS, MSE, Ed S. *Accreditation:* NCATE. *Program availability:* Part-time. *Degree requirements:* For master's, comprehensive exam, thesis or alternative. *Entrance requirements:* Additional exam requirements/recommendations for international students: Required—TOEFL (minimum score 550 paper-based). Electronic applications accepted.

Franciscan University of Steubenville, Graduate Programs, Department of Education, Steubenville, OH 43952-1763. Offers administration (MS Ed); teaching (MS Ed). *Accreditation:* NCATE. *Program availability:* Part-time, evening/weekend, online learning. *Degree requirements:* For master's, project. *Entrance requirements:* For master's, minimum undergraduate GPA of 2.5 or written exam. Additional exam requirements/recommendations for international students: Required—TOEFL. Electronic applications accepted. Application fee is waived when completed online. *Expenses:* Contact institution.

Francis Marion University, Graduate Programs, School of Education, Florence, SC 29502-0547. Offers learning disabilities (M Ed, MAT). *Accreditation:* NCATE. *Program availability:* Part-time. *Degree requirements:* For master's, comprehensive exam (for some programs), supervised internship (for MAT). *Entrance requirements:* For master's, GRE General Test, MAT, NTE, or PRAXIS II, official transcripts; two letters of recommendation. Additional exam requirements/recommendations for international students: Required—TOEFL (minimum score 550 paper-based; 79 iBT). *Faculty research:* Identification and alternate assessment of at-risk students.

Freed-Hardeman University, Program in Education, Henderson, TN 38340-2399. Offers curriculum and instruction (M Ed); school counseling (M Ed), including administration and supervision, special education; school leadership (Ed S). *Accreditation:* NCATE. *Program availability:* Part-time, evening/weekend. *Degree requirements:* For master's, comprehensive exam, thesis optional; for Ed S, thesis. *Entrance requirements:* For master's, GRE General Test or NTE; for Ed S, 3 years of teaching experience. Additional exam requirements/recommendations for international students: Required—TOEFL (minimum score 500 paper-based).

Fresno Pacific University, Graduate Programs, School of Education, Fresno, CA 93702-4709. Offers MA, MA Ed, Certificate. *Program availability:* Part-time, evening/weekend. *Degree requirements:* For master's, thesis (for some programs). *Entrance requirements:* For master's, interview; GMAT, GRE, MAT, or 6 units of course work with a faculty recommendation. Additional exam requirements/recommendations for international students: Required—TOEFL (minimum score 550 paper-based). Electronic applications accepted.

Frostburg State University, College of Education, Frostburg, MD 21532. Offers M Ed, MAT, MS, Ed D. *Accreditation:* NCATE. *Program availability:* Part-time, evening/weekend. *Faculty:* 24 full-time (17 women), 33 part-time/adjunct (26 women). *Students:* 89 full-time (63 women), 273 part-time (193 women); includes 31 minority (20 Black or African American, non-Hispanic/Latino; 1 Asian, non-Hispanic/Latino; 4 Hispanic/Latino; 6 Two or more races, non-Hispanic/Latino), 3 international. Average age 30. 210 applicants, 74% accepted, 103 enrolled. In 2017, 96 master's, 12 doctorates awarded. *Entrance requirements:* Additional exam requirements/recommendations for international students: Required—TOEFL. *Application deadline:* For fall admission, 7/15 priority date for domestic students. Applications are processed on a rolling basis. Application fee: $45. Electronic applications accepted. *Expenses:* Tuition, state resident: part-time $433 per credit hour. Tuition, nonresident: part-time $557 per credit hour. *Required fees:* $121 per credit hour. $27 per term. *Financial support:* In 2017–18, 29 research assistantships with full tuition reimbursements (averaging $5,000 per year) were awarded; career-related internships or fieldwork and Federal Work-Study also available. Financial award application deadline: 4/1; financial award applicants required to submit FAFSA. *Unit head:* Dr. Boyce Williams, Interim Dean, 301-687-4759, E-mail: bcwilliams@frostburg.edu. *Application contact:* Vickie Mazer, Director, Graduate Services, 301-687-7053, Fax: 301-687-4597, E-mail: vmmazer@frostburg.edu.

Furman University, Graduate Division, Department of Education, Greenville, SC 29613. Offers curriculum and instruction (MA); early childhood education (MA); educational leadership (Ed S); English as a second language (MA); literacy (MA); school leadership (MA); special education (MA). *Accreditation:* NCATE. *Program availability:* Part-time, online learning. *Degree requirements:* For master's, comprehensive exam (for some programs), thesis or alternative. *Entrance requirements:* For master's, PRAXIS II. *Faculty research:* Literacy, pedagogy and practice, social justice, advanced leadership, achievement in high poverty schools.

Gallaudet University, The Graduate School, Washington, DC 20002-3625. Offers American Sign Language/English bilingual early childhood deaf education: birth to 5 (Certificate); audiology (Au D); clinical psychology (PhD); deaf and hard of hearing infants, toddlers, and their families (Certificate); deaf education (MA, Ed S); deaf history (Certificate); deaf studies (Certificate); educating deaf students with disabilities (Certificate); education: teacher preparation (MA), including deaf education, early childhood education and deaf education, elementary education and deaf education, secondary education and deaf education; educational neuroscience (PhD); hearing, speech and language sciences (MS, PhD); international development (MA); interpretation (MA, PhD), including combined interpreting practice and research (MA), interpreting research (MA); linguistics (MA, PhD); mental health counseling (MA); peer mentoring (Certificate); public administration (MPA); school counseling (MA); school psychology (Psy S); sign language teaching (MA); social work (MSW); speech-language pathology (MS). *Program availability:* Part-time. Terminal master's awarded for partial completion of doctoral program. *Degree requirements:* For master's, comprehensive exam (for some programs), thesis optional; for doctorate, comprehensive exam, thesis/dissertation. *Entrance requirements:* For master's and doctorate, GRE General Test or MAT, letters of recommendation, interviews, goals statement, American Sign Language proficiency interview, written English competency. Additional exam requirements/recommendations for international students: Required—TOEFL. Electronic applications accepted. *Faculty research:* Signing math dictionaries, telecommunications access, cancer genetics, linguistics, visual language and visual learning, integrated quantum materials, deaf legal discourse, advance recruitment and retention in geosciences.

Gannon University, School of Graduate Studies, College of Humanities, Education, and Social Sciences, School of Education, Erie, PA 16541-0001. Offers curriculum and instruction (M Ed); curriculum supervisor (Certificate); English as a second language (Certificate); principal certification (Certificate); reading (M Ed); reading specialist (Certificate); superintendent letter of eligibility (Certificate). *Program availability:* Part-time, evening/weekend, 100% online. *Degree requirements:* For master's, thesis (for some programs), portfolio project. *Entrance requirements:* For master's, GRE, bachelor's degree from accredited institution, letters of recommendation, transcripts, teaching certificate (for some programs), minimum GPA of 3.0; for Certificate, GRE, master's degree (for some programs), teaching certificate, minimum GPA of 3.0, experience in field (for some programs). Additional exam requirements/recommendations for international students: Required—TOEFL (minimum score 79 iBT). Electronic applications accepted. Application fee is waived when completed online. *Expenses:* Contact institution.

Gardner-Webb University, Graduate School, School of Education, Boiling Springs, NC 28017. Offers curriculum and instruction (Ed D); educational leadership (Ed D); executive leadership studies (MA, Ed S); organizational leadership (Ed D); school administration (MA). *Accreditation:* NCATE. *Program availability:* Part-time, evening/weekend. *Faculty:* 15 full-time (7 women), 33 part-time/adjunct (20 women). *Students:* 13 full-time (10 women), 736 part-time (567 women); includes 332 minority (306 Black or African American, non-Hispanic/Latino; 6 American Indian or Alaska Native, non-Hispanic/Latino; 4 Asian, non-Hispanic/Latino; 9 Hispanic/Latino; 1 Native Hawaiian or other Pacific Islander, non-Hispanic/Latino; 6 Two or more races, non-Hispanic/Latino). Average age 33. *Degree requirements:* For master's, comprehensive exam. *Entrance requirements:* For master's, GRE General Test or NTE, PRAXIS, minimum GPA of 2.5. *Application deadline:* For fall admission, 8/1 priority date for domestic students. Applications are processed on a rolling basis. Electronic applications accepted. *Expenses:* Contact institution. *Financial support:* Unspecified assistantships available. *Application contact:* Office of Graduate Admissions, 877-498-4723, Fax: 704-406-3895, E-mail: gradinfo@gardner-webb.edu.

Geneva College, Master of Arts in Higher Education Program, Beaver Falls, PA 15010-3599. Offers campus ministry (MA); college teaching (MA); educational leadership (MA); student affairs administration (MA). *Program availability:* Part-time, evening/weekend, blended/hybrid learning. *Faculty:* 1 full-time (0 women), 6 part-time/adjunct (1 woman). *Students:* 44 full-time (27 women), 10 part-time (6 women); includes 8 minority (5 Black or African American, non-Hispanic/Latino; 2 Hispanic/Latino; 1 Two or more races, non-Hispanic/Latino), 1 international. Average age 27. 40 applicants, 75% accepted, 21 enrolled. In 2017, 18 master's awarded. *Degree requirements:* For master's, 36 hours (27 in core courses) including a capstone research project. *Entrance requirements:* For master's, minimum GPA of 3.0, writing sample, 3 letters of recommendation, essay on motivation for participation in the program. Additional exam requirements/recommendations for international students: Required—TOEFL. *Application deadline:* Applications are processed on a rolling basis. Application fee: $0. Electronic applications accepted. *Expenses:* $655 per credit. *Financial support:* Unspecified assistantships available. Financial award application deadline: 8/1; financial award applicants required to submit FAFSA. *Faculty research:* Learning theories, church-related higher education, organizational culture, sexual assault and transgender students at Christian colleges, emerging technology in higher education. *Unit head:* Dr. Keith Martel, Program Director, 724-847-6884, Fax: 724-847-6107, E-mail: hed@geneva.edu. *Application contact:* Allison Davis, Assistant Director, 724-847-6510, Fax: 724-847-6696, E-mail: hed@geneva.edu.
Website: http://www.geneva.edu/page/higher_ed

George Fox University, College of Education, Newberg, OR 97132-2697. Offers M Ed, MA, MAT, Ed D, Certificate, Ed S.

George Mason University, College of Education and Human Development, Fairfax, VA 22030. Offers M Ed, MS, PhD, Certificate. *Accreditation:* NCATE. *Program availability:* Part-time, evening/weekend, 100% online, blended/hybrid learning. *Faculty:* 122 full-time (86 women), 211 part-time/adjunct (144 women). *Students:* 476 full-time (377 women), 2,154 part-time (1,751 women); includes 773 minority (286 Black or African American, non-Hispanic/Latino; 9 American Indian or Alaska Native, non-Hispanic/Latino; 195 Asian, non-Hispanic/Latino; 221 Hispanic/Latino; 5 Native Hawaiian or other Pacific Islander, non-Hispanic/Latino; 57 Two or more races, non-Hispanic/Latino), 90 international. Average age 34. 1,321 applicants, 82% accepted, 788 enrolled. In 2017, 786 master's, 40 doctorates, 250 other advanced degrees awarded. *Degree requirements:* For doctorate, comprehensive exam, final project, internship. *Entrance requirements:* For master's, PRAXIS Core, GRE, or MAT (depending on program), minimum GPA of 3.0 in last 60 hours of course work, goals statement, interview or writing sample; for doctorate, GRE, appropriate master's degree, transcripts, resume, interview, 3 letters of recommendation, goals statement; 3 years of experience in educational, community, and human development settings (depending on program). Additional exam requirements/recommendations for international students: Required—TOEFL (minimum score 575 paper-based; 88 iBT), IELTS (minimum score 6.5), PTE (minimum score 59). *Application deadline:* For fall admission, 4/2 for domestic and international students; for spring admission, 11/1 for domestic and international students. Application fee: $75 ($80 for international students). Electronic applications accepted. *Expenses:* $795 per credit out-of-state tuition. *Financial support:* In 2017–18, 95 students received support, including 5 fellowships (averaging $6,080 per year), 75 research assistantships with tuition reimbursements available (averaging $13,826 per year), 32 teaching assistantships with tuition reimbursements available (averaging $5,037 per year); career-related internships or fieldwork, Federal Work-Study, scholarships/grants, unspecified assistantships, and health care benefits for full-time research or teaching assistantship recipients) also available. Support available to part-time students. Financial award application deadline: 3/1; financial award applicants required to submit FAFSA. *Faculty research:* Special education/human disabilities, mathematics/science/technology education, education leadership, school/community/agency/higher education, counseling and administration. *Total annual research expenditures:* $9.1 million. *Unit head:* Mark Ginsberg, Dean, 703-993-2004, Fax: 703-993-2001, E-mail: mginsber@gmu.edu. *Application contact:* Nicole Mariam, Graduate Admissions Coordinator, 703-993-3832, Fax: 703-993-2020, E-mail: nwhite5@gmu.edu.
Website: http://cehd.gmu.edu/

Georgetown College, Department of Education, Georgetown, KY 40324-1696. Offers reading and writing (MA Ed); special education (MA Ed); teaching (MA Ed). *Accreditation:* NCATE. *Program availability:* Part-time. *Degree requirements:* For master's, portfolio. *Entrance requirements:* For master's, teaching certificate, minimum GPA of 2.7 or GRE General Test.

The George Washington University, Graduate School of Education and Human Development, Washington, DC 20052. Offers M Ed, MA, MA Ed, MA Ed/HD, MAT, Ed D, PhD, Certificate, Ed S, Graduate Certificate, Teaching Certificate. *Accreditation:* NCATE. *Program availability:* Part-time, evening/weekend, online learning. *Faculty:* 87 full-time (55 women), 96 part-time/adjunct (61 women). *Students:* 411 full-time (327 women), 1,048 part-time (794 women); includes 526 minority (286 Black or African American, non-Hispanic/Latino; 7 American Indian or Alaska Native, non-Hispanic/Latino; 82 Asian, non-Hispanic/Latino; 111 Hispanic/Latino; 40 Two or more races, non-Hispanic/Latino), 115 international. Average age 36. 1,735 applicants, 65% accepted, 550 enrolled. In 2017, 388 master's, 68 doctorates, 108 other advanced degrees awarded. *Degree requirements:* For master's and other advanced degree, comprehensive exam; for doctorate, comprehensive exam, thesis/dissertation. *Entrance requirements:* For master's, GRE General Test or MAT, minimum GPA of 2.75; for doctorate, GRE General Test or MAT, interview, minimum GPA of 3.3; for other advanced degree, GRE General Test or MAT, minimum GPA of 3.3. *Application deadline:* For fall admission, 1/15 priority date for domestic students; for spring admission, 10/1 for domestic students. Applications are processed on a rolling basis.

Application fee: $75. Electronic applications accepted. *Expenses:* Tuition: Full-time $28,800; part-time $1655 per credit hour. *Required fees:* $45; $2.75 per credit hour. *Financial support:* In 2017–18, 279 students received support. Fellowships with tuition reimbursements available, research assistantships with tuition reimbursements available, teaching assistantships with tuition reimbursements available, career-related internships or fieldwork, Federal Work-Study, and tuition waivers (full and partial) available. Support available to part-time students. Financial award application deadline: 1/15. *Faculty research:* Policy, special education, bilingual education, counseling, human resource development. *Total annual research expenditures:* $4.6 million. *Unit head:* Michael Feuer, Dean, 202-994-6161, Fax: 202-994-7207, E-mail: mjfeuer@gwu.edu. *Application contact:* Sarah Lang, Director of Graduate Admissions, 202-994-1447, Fax: 202-994-7207, E-mail: slang@gwu.edu.
Website: http://gsehd.gwu.edu/

Georgia College & State University, Graduate School, The John H. Lounsbury College of Education, Milledgeville, GA 31061. Offers M Ed, MAT, Ed S. *Accreditation:* NCATE. *Program availability:* Evening/weekend, 100% online, blended/hybrid learning. *Faculty:* 29 full-time (25 women). *Students:* 68 full-time (47 women), 146 part-time (130 women); includes 73 minority (52 Black or African American, non-Hispanic/Latino; 5 Asian, non-Hispanic/Latino; 14 Hispanic/Latino; 2 Two or more races, non-Hispanic/Latino), 2 international. Average age 35. 72 applicants, 100% accepted, 58 enrolled. In 2017, 78 master's, 87 other advanced degrees awarded. *Degree requirements:* For master's, minimum GPA of 3.0, complete program within 6 years; for Ed S, minimum GPA of 3.0, complete program within 4 years. *Application deadline:* For fall admission, 7/1 priority date for domestic students; for spring admission, 11/1 priority date for domestic students; for summer admission, 4/1 priority date for domestic students. Applications are processed on a rolling basis. Application fee: $40. Electronic applications accepted. *Expenses:* Contact institution. *Financial support:* In 2017–18, 33 students received support. Unspecified assistantships available. Support available to part-time students. Financial award application deadline: 3/1; financial award applicants required to submit FAFSA. *Unit head:* Dr. Joseph Peters, Dean, College of Education, 478-445-2518, Fax: 478-445-6582, E-mail: joseph.peters@gcsu.edu. *Application contact:* Shanda Brand, Graduate Admissions Advisor, 478-445-1383, Fax: 478-445-6582, E-mail: shanda.brand@gcsu.edu.
Website: http://www.gcsu.edu/education/graduate/index.htm

Georgian Court University, School of Education, Lakewood, NJ 08701-2697. Offers administration and leadership (MA); autism spectrum disorders (Certificate); education (M Ed, MA, MAT); instructional technology (M Mat SE, Certificate). *Accreditation:* TEAC. *Program availability:* Part-time, evening/weekend. *Faculty:* 11 full-time (7 women), 40 part-time/adjunct (22 women). *Students:* 49 full-time (42 women), 472 part-time (388 women); includes 101 minority (42 Black or African American, non-Hispanic/Latino; 12 Asian, non-Hispanic/Latino; 44 Hispanic/Latino; 3 Two or more races, non-Hispanic/Latino). Average age 34. 412 applicants, 56% accepted, 153 enrolled. In 2017, 81 master's awarded. *Degree requirements:* For master's, comprehensive exam (for some programs), thesis (for some programs). *Entrance requirements:* For master's, GRE, GMAT or NTE/PRAXIS, 3 letters of recommendation. Additional exam requirements/recommendations for international students: Required—TOEFL (minimum score 550 paper-based). *Application deadline:* For fall admission, 8/15 priority date for domestic students, 5/1 for international students; for spring admission, 1/15 priority date for domestic students, 10/1 for international students. Applications are processed on a rolling basis. Application fee: $40. Electronic applications accepted. *Expenses: Tuition:* Part-time $839 per credit. *Required fees:* $248 per semester. Tuition and fees vary according to campus/location and program. *Financial support:* Scholarships/grants, health care benefits, and unspecified assistantships available. Financial award application deadline: 4/15; financial award applicants required to submit FAFSA. *Unit head:* Dr. Lynn DeCapua, Dean, 732-987-2729, E-mail: ldecapua@georgian.edu. *Application contact:* Patrick Givens, Director of Graduate and Professional Studies Admissions, 732-987-2736, Fax: 732-987-2000, E-mail: gps@georgian.edu.
Website: http://georgian.edu/academics/school-of-education/

Georgia Southern University, Jack N. Averitt College of Graduate Studies, College of Education, Statesboro, GA 30460. Offers M Ed, MAT, Ed D, Ed S. *Accreditation:* NCATE. *Program availability:* Part-time, evening/weekend, 100% online, blended/hybrid learning. *Faculty:* 77 full-time (52 women), 12 part-time/adjunct (5 women). *Students:* 351 full-time (279 women), 840 part-time (675 women); includes 357 minority (282 Black or African American, non-Hispanic/Latino; 2 American Indian or Alaska Native, non-Hispanic/Latino; 11 Asian, non-Hispanic/Latino; 39 Hispanic/Latino; 23 Two or more races, non-Hispanic/Latino), 3 international. Average age 33. 294 applicants, 89% accepted, 216 enrolled. In 2017, 378 master's, 44 doctorates, 65 other advanced degrees awarded. *Degree requirements:* For master's, comprehensive exam (for some programs), thesis optional, portfolio or assessments; for doctorate, comprehensive exam, thesis/dissertation, exams; for Ed S, thesis (for some programs), assessments, field-based research projects. *Entrance requirements:* For doctorate, GRE General Test or MAT, minimum GPA of 3.5, letters of reference, writing sample; for Ed S, GRE General Test or MAT, minimum graduate GPA of 3.25. Additional exam requirements/recommendations for international students: Required—TOEFL (minimum score 500 paper-based; 80 iBT), IELTS (minimum score 6). *Application deadline:* For fall admission, 3/1 priority date for domestic and international students; for spring admission, 10/1 priority date for domestic students, 10/1 for international students. Applications are processed on a rolling basis. Application fee: $50. Electronic applications accepted. *Expenses:* Tuition, state resident: full-time $4986; part-time $3324 per year. Tuition, nonresident: full-time $21,982; part-time $15,352 per year. *Required fees:* $2092; $1802 per credit hour. $901 per semester. Tuition and fees vary according to course load, campus/location and program. *Financial support:* In 2017–18, 146 students received support, including 1 teaching assistantship with full tuition reimbursement available (averaging $7,750 per year); research assistantships with partial tuition reimbursements available, career-related internships or fieldwork, scholarships/grants, and unspecified assistantships also available. Financial award application deadline: 4/15; financial award applicants required to submit FAFSA. *Faculty research:* Scholarship of teaching and learning, curriculum studies, STEM education, social justice/multicultural education, teacher education best practices. *Total annual research expenditures:* $497,630. *Unit head:* Dr. Thomas Koballa, Dean, 912-478-5648, Fax: 912-478-5093, E-mail: tkoballa@georgiasouthern.edu. *Application contact:* Dr. Lydia Cross, Director, Graduate Academic Services Center, 912-478-1447, E-mail: gasc@georgiasouthern.edu.
Website: http://coe.georgiasouthern.edu/

Georgia Southern University–Armstrong Campus, College of Graduate Studies, Department of Childhood and Exceptional Student Education, Savannah, GA 31419-1997. Offers early childhood education (M Ed, MAT); reading (Certificate); special education (M Ed, MAT); special education transition specialist (Certificate). *Accreditation:* NCATE. *Program availability:* Part-time, evening/weekend. *Faculty:* 14 full-time (11 women), 1 (woman) part-time/adjunct. *Students:* 11 full-time (6 women), 214 part-time (195 women); includes 79 minority (63 Black or African American, non-Hispanic/Latino; 3 Asian, non-Hispanic/Latino; 6 Hispanic/Latino; 7 Two or more races, non-Hispanic/Latino). Average age 34. 159 applicants, 50% accepted, 69 enrolled. In 2017, 72 master's, 3 other advanced degrees awarded. *Degree requirements:* For

master's, portfolio. *Entrance requirements:* For master's, MAT, Georgia Assessment for the Certification of Educators. Additional exam requirements/recommendations for international students: Required—TOEFL (minimum score 523 paper-based; 70 iBT). *Application deadline:* For fall admission, 7/1 priority date for domestic students, 5/1 priority date for international students; for spring admission, 11/15 priority date for domestic students, 9/15 priority date for international students; for summer admission, 4/15 priority date for domestic students, 9/15 for international students. Applications are processed on a rolling basis. Application fee: $30. Electronic applications accepted. *Expenses:* Tuition, state resident: part-time $211 per credit hour. Tuition, nonresident: part-time $782 per credit hour. *Required fees:* $737 per semester. Tuition and fees vary according to course load, degree level, campus/location and program. *Financial support:* In 2017–18, research assistantships with full tuition reimbursements (averaging $5,000 per year) were awarded; career-related internships or fieldwork, Federal Work-Study, and scholarships/grants also available. Support available to part-time students. Financial award application deadline: 3/15; financial award applicants required to submit FAFSA. *Faculty research:* Literacy, instructional design, poetry, working with local schools. *Unit head:* Dr. John Hobe, Department Head, 912-344-2619, Fax: 912-344-3443, E-mail: john.hobe@armstrong.edu. *Application contact:* McKenzie Peterman, Assistant Director of Graduate Admissions, 912-344-2503, Fax: 912-344-3417, E-mail: graduate@armstrong.edu.
Website: https://www.armstrong.edu/academic-departments/education-ceed

Georgia Southwestern State University, School of Education, Americus, GA 31709-4693. Offers early childhood education (M Ed, Ed S); middle grades education (Ed S); middle grades language arts (M Ed); middle grades mathematics (M Ed); special education (M Ed). *Accreditation:* NCATE. *Faculty:* 17 full-time (7 women), 7 part-time/adjunct (all women). *Students:* 221 full-time (206 women), 5 part-time (all women); includes 70 minority (all Black or African American, non-Hispanic/Latino). Average age 35. In 2017, 89 master's, 94 Ed Ss awarded. *Degree requirements:* For master's, minimum cumulative GPA of 3.0; maximum of 6 credit hours with C grade; no courses with D grade; degree completed within 7 calendar years; for Ed S, minimum GPA of 3.25 in all courses with no grade less than a B; degree must be completed within 7 calendar years from date of initial enrollment in graduate work. *Entrance requirements:* For master's, undergraduate degree from accredited institution; professional Georgia Teaching Certificate or eligibility; minimum undergraduate GPA of 2.75 as reported on official final transcripts from all accredited institutions attended; 2 confidential Administrative Recommendation Forms; for Ed S, master's degree from accredited college or university; professional Georgia Teaching Certificate or eligibility; minimum graduate GPA of 3.0 as reported on official final graduate transcripts from all accredited institutions attended; 2 confidential Administrative Recommendation Forms. *Application deadline:* For summer admission, 4/15 for domestic students. Application fee: $25. Electronic applications accepted. *Expenses:* $257 per credit hour for online courses plus fees which vary according to number of enrolled credit hours. *Financial support:* Application deadline: 6/1; applicants required to submit FAFSA. *Unit head:* Dr. Rachel Abbott, Dean, 229-931-2145. *Application contact:* Whitney Ford, Admissions Specialist, Office of Graduate Admissions, 800-338-0082, Fax: 229-931-2983.
Website: https://gsw.edu/Academics/Schools-and-Departments/School-of-Education/index

Georgia State University, College of Education and Human Development, Atlanta, GA 30302-3083. Offers M Ed, MAT, MS, Ed D, PhD, Ed S. *Accreditation:* NCATE. *Program availability:* Part-time, evening/weekend, online learning. *Faculty:* 103 full-time (64 women). *Students:* 874 full-time (662 women), 472 part-time (324 women); includes 656 minority (460 Black or African American, non-Hispanic/Latino; 1 American Indian or Alaska Native, non-Hispanic/Latino; 52 Asian, non-Hispanic/Latino; 92 Hispanic/Latino; 1 Native Hawaiian or other Pacific Islander, non-Hispanic/Latino; 50 Two or more races, non-Hispanic/Latino). 36 international. Average age 31. 1,084 applicants, 43% accepted, 333 enrolled. In 2017, 333 master's, 64 doctorates, 36 other advanced degrees awarded. Terminal master's awarded for partial completion of doctoral program. *Degree requirements:* For master's, comprehensive exam (for some programs), thesis (for some programs), minimum GPA of 3.0; for doctorate, comprehensive exam, thesis/dissertation, minimum GPA of 3.5; for Ed S, thesis or alternative, minimum GPA of 3.0. *Entrance requirements:* For master's, GRE, MAT (for some programs), minimum GPA of 2.5 on all undergraduate work attempted in which letter grades were awarded; for doctorate, GRE, MAT (for some programs), minimum GPA of 3.3 on all graduate coursework for which letter grades were awarded (for PhD); for Ed S, GRE, MAT (for some programs), graduate degree from regionally-accredited college or university unless specified otherwise by the program with minimum GPA of 3.25 on all graduate coursework for which letter grades were awarded. Application fee: $50. Electronic applications accepted. *Expenses:* Tuition, state resident: full-time $7020. Tuition, nonresident: full-time $22,518. *Required fees:* $2128. Tuition and fees vary according to degree level and program. *Financial support:* In 2017–18, fellowships with full tuition reimbursements (averaging $25,000 per year), research assistantships with tuition reimbursements (averaging $4,867 per year) teaching assistantships with tuition reimbursements (averaging $4,683 per year) were awarded; career-related internships or fieldwork, Federal Work-Study, scholarships/grants, tuition waivers (partial), and unspecified assistantships also available. Support available to part-time students. Financial award applicants required to submit FAFSA. *Faculty research:* Literacy, early, middle-secondary, adult and deaf/hard of hearing; teacher professional development, evaluation and urban education; STEM teacher education; health, physical activity and exercise science; school safety and counseling. *Unit head:* Dr. Paul A. Alberto, Interim Dean, 404-413-8100, Fax: 404-413-8103, E-mail: palberto@gsu.edu. *Application contact:* Nancy Keita, Director, Office of Academic Assistance and Graduate Admissions, 404-413-8001, E-mail: nkeita@gsu.edu.
Website: http://education.gsu.edu/main/

Goddard College, Graduate Division, Master of Arts in Education Program, Plainfield, VT 05667-9432. Offers community education (MA); teacher licensure (MA). *Program availability:* Part-time, online learning. *Degree requirements:* For master's, thesis. *Entrance requirements:* For master's, PRAXIS, 3 letters of recommendation, statement of purpose, interview. Electronic applications accepted. *Faculty research:* Democratic curriculum leadership, service-learning and academic achievement, middle grades curriculum, community education, dual language.

Gonzaga University, School of Education, Spokane, WA 99258. Offers clinical mental health counseling (MA); educational leadership (M Ed, Ed D); elementary education (MIT); marriage and family counseling (MA); school counseling (MA); secondary education (MIT); special education (M Ed, MIT); sport and athletic administration (MA). *Accreditation:* NCATE. *Program availability:* Part-time, evening/weekend, 100% online, blended/hybrid learning. *Faculty:* 16 full-time (11 women), 31 part-time/adjunct (19 women). *Students:* 108 full-time (90 women), 225 part-time (140 women); includes 34 minority (4 Black or African American, non-Hispanic/Latino; 2 American Indian or Alaska Native, non-Hispanic/Latino; 5 Asian, non-Hispanic/Latino; 18 Hispanic/Latino; 5 Two or more races, non-Hispanic/Latino), 114 international. Average age 31. 367 applicants, 74% accepted, 160 enrolled. In 2017, 175 master's awarded. *Degree requirements:* For master's, comprehensive exam. *Entrance requirements:* For master's, GRE, MAT, and/or Washington Educator Skills Test-Basic (WEST-B), Washington Educator Skills Test-Endorsements (WEST-E), official transcripts from all colleges or universities attended, interview, two letters of

recommendation, resume, essay, minimum GPA of 3.0. Additional exam requirements/recommendations for international students: Required—TOEFL (minimum score 580 paper-based, 88 iBT) or IELTS (minimum score 6.5). *Application deadline:* Applications are processed on a rolling basis. Application fee: $50. Electronic applications accepted. *Expenses:* $990 per credit. *Financial support:* In 2017–18, 51 students received support. Scholarships/grants and unspecified assistantships available. Support available to part-time students. Financial award applicants required to submit FAFSA. *Unit head:* Dr. Vincent Alfonso, Dean, 509-313-3594, Fax: 509-313-3821, E-mail: alfonso@gonzaga.edu. *Application contact:* Meg Martens, Graduate Admissions Program Specialist, 509-313-4314, E-mail: martens@gonzaga.edu.
Website: https://www.gonzaga.edu/school-of-education

Gordon College, Graduate Education Program, Wenham, MA 01984-1899. Offers early childhood (M Ed); educational leadership (M Ed, Ed S); elementary education (M Ed); English as a second language (M Ed, Ed S); math specialist (M Ed); mathematics specialist (Ed S); middle school education (M Ed); moderate disabilities (M Ed); Montessori education (M Ed); reading (M Ed, Ed S); secondary education (M Ed). *Program availability:* Part-time, evening/weekend. *Faculty:* 23 full-time (17 women), 32 part-time/adjunct (23 women). *Students:* 68 full-time (50 women), 114 part-time (99 women); includes 24 minority (2 Black or African American, non-Hispanic/Latino; 8 Asian, non-Hispanic/Latino; 13 Hispanic/Latino; 1 Two or more races, non-Hispanic/Latino), 10 international. Average age 34. 248 applicants, 100% accepted, 182 enrolled. In 2017, 99 master's, 16 Ed Ss awarded. *Degree requirements:* For master's, action research or clinical experience (for most programs); for Ed S, action research or clinical experience (for some programs). *Entrance requirements:* For master's, minimum undergraduate GPA of 3.0; 2 official undergraduate transcripts; professional resume; 3 recommendation letters (one professional reference, one academic reference, one personal reference); 500-700 word statement of purpose; for Ed S, minimum master's GPA of 3.3; 2 official transcripts from undergraduate and graduate schools; professional resume; 3 recommendation letters (one professional reference, one academic reference, one personal reference); 500-700 word statement of purpose. Additional exam requirements/recommendations for international students: Required—TOEFL (minimum score 550 paper-based, 80 iBT) or IELTS (minimum score 6.5). *Application deadline:* Applications are processed on a rolling basis. Application fee: $75. *Expenses:* $325 per credit tuition; $75 per semester administrative fee. *Financial support:* Applicants required to submit FAFSA. *Faculty research:* Reading, early childhood development, English language learners, universal design for learning. *Unit head:* Dr. Janet Arndt, Director of Graduate Studies, 978-867-4355, Fax: 978-867-4663. *Application contact:* Julie Lenocker, Program Administrator, 978-867-4322, Fax: 978-867-4663, E-mail: graduate-education@gordon.edu.
Website: http://www.gordon.edu/graduate

Goucher College, Graduate Programs in Education, Baltimore, MD 21204-2794. Offers at-risk and diverse learners (M Ed, Certificate); athletic program leadership and administration (M Ed, Certificate); elementary education (MAT); literacy strategies for content learning (M Ed); middle school (M Ed, Certificate); Montessori studies (M Ed); reading instruction (M Ed, Certificate); reducing student, classroom, and school disruption (M Ed); school improvement leadership (M Ed); secondary education (MAT); special education (MAT), including elementary education; special education for certified elementary and secondary teachers (M Ed); teacher as leader in technology (M Ed). *Program availability:* Part-time, evening/weekend. *Degree requirements:* For master's, thesis (M Ed), final presentation (MAT). *Entrance requirements:* For master's, minimum GPA of 3.0. Additional exam requirements/recommendations for international students: Required—TOEFL (minimum score 550 paper-based; 80 iBT), IELTS (minimum score 7). *Application deadline:* For fall admission, 9/1 for domestic students; for spring admission, 1/15 for domestic students. Applications are processed on a rolling basis. Application fee: $75. Electronic applications accepted. *Expenses:* Contact institution. *Financial support:* Career-related internships or fieldwork and unspecified assistantships available. Support available to part-time students. Financial award application deadline: 4/15; financial award applicants required to submit FAFSA. *Faculty research:* Urban education, middle school, school improvement, teacher education, at-risk student achievement. *Unit head:* Dr. Phyllis Sunshine, Assistant Provost, 410-337-6047, Fax: 410-337-6394, E-mail: psunshin@goucher.edu. *Application contact:* Carlton E. Surbeck, III, Director of Admissions, 410-337-6100, Fax: 410-337-6085, E-mail: admissions@goucher.edu.
Website: http://www.goucher.edu/graduate-programs/graduate-programs-in-education

Governors State University, College of Education, Program in Education, University Park, IL 60484. Offers MA. *Program availability:* Part-time. *Faculty:* 20 full-time (12 women), 40 part-time/adjunct (28 women). *Students:* 1 (woman) full-time, 23 part-time (20 women); includes 6 minority (2 Black or African American, non-Hispanic/Latino; 4 Hispanic/Latino). Average age 42. 2 applicants, 50% accepted. In 2017, 6 master's awarded. *Application deadline:* For fall admission, 4/1 for domestic students. Applications are processed on a rolling basis. Application fee: $50. Electronic applications accepted. *Expenses:* Tuition, state resident: full-time $8472; part-time $353 per credit hour. Tuition, nonresident: full-time $16,944; part-time $706 per credit hour. *Required fees:* $1824; $76 per credit hour. $38 per term. Tuition and fees vary according to course load, degree level and program. *Financial support:* Application deadline: 5/1; applicants required to submit FAFSA. *Unit head:* Timothy Harrington, Chair, Division of Education, 708-534-5000 Ext. 4361, E-mail: tharrington2@govst.edu.

Graceland University, Gleazer School of Education, Independence, MO 64050. Offers curriculum and instruction: collaborative learning and teaching (M Ed); differentiated instruction (M Ed); instructional leadership (M Ed); literacy instruction (M Ed); management in a quality classroom (M Ed); special education (M Ed); technology integration (M Ed). *Accreditation:* NCATE. *Program availability:* Part-time, 100% online. *Faculty:* 2 full-time (both women), 13 part-time/adjunct (10 women). *Students:* 117 full-time (102 women), 62 part-time (54 women); includes 8 minority (3 Black or African American, non-Hispanic/Latino; 1 Asian, non-Hispanic/Latino; 2 Hispanic/Latino; 1 Native Hawaiian or other Pacific Islander, non-Hispanic/Latino; 1 Two or more races, non-Hispanic/Latino), 1 international. Average age 35. 28 applicants, 100% accepted, 19 enrolled. In 2017, 64 master's awarded. *Degree requirements:* For master's, action research capstone. *Entrance requirements:* For master's, minimum GPA of 3.0, teaching certificate, current teaching contract and license, two letters of reference, statement of professional goals, verification of ongoing access to computer technology, including email and Internet. Additional exam requirements/recommendations for international students: Required—TOEFL (minimum score 550 paper-based; 79 iBT). *Application deadline:* For fall admission, 10/1 for domestic students; for winter admission, 11/15 for domestic students; for spring admission, 2/15 priority date for domestic students; for summer admission, 6/1 for domestic students. Application fee: $50. Electronic applications accepted. *Expenses:* Contact institution. *Financial support:* In 2017–18, 3 students received support. Tuition waivers available. Financial award applicants required to submit FAFSA. *Faculty research:* Literacy, technology, faculty mentoring, adult literacy, e-learning, online teaching. *Unit head:* Dr. Lee Bash, Interim Dean, 641-784-5072, E-mail: bash@graceland.edu. *Application contact:* Jeanette Calipetro, Admissions Representative, 816-423-4716, Fax: 816-833-2990, E-mail: jcali1@graceland.edu.
Website: http://www.graceland.edu/education

Education—General

Grambling State University, School of Graduate Studies and Research, College of Education, Grambling, LA 71245. Offers M Ed, MAT, MS, Ed D, PMC. *Accreditation:* NCATE. *Program availability:* Part-time, evening/weekend. *Degree requirements:* For master's, comprehensive exam, thesis (for some programs); for doctorate, comprehensive exam, thesis/dissertation. *Entrance requirements:* For master's, GRE; for doctorate, GRE (minimum score 1000, 500 on Verbal), master's degree, minimum GPA of 3.0 on last degree. Additional exam requirements/recommendations for international students: Required—TOEFL (minimum score 500 paper-based; 62 iBT). Electronic applications accepted.

Grand Canyon University, College of Education, Phoenix, AZ 85017-1097. Offers autism spectrum disorders (MA); curriculum and instruction (MA); early childhood education (M Ed); educational administration (M Ed); educational leadership (M Ed); elementary education (M Ed); gifted education (MA); instructional technology (MS); K-12 leadership (Ed S); reading (MA); secondary education (M Ed); secondary humanities education (M Ed); secondary STEM education (M Ed); special education (M Ed); teaching and learning (Ed D); teaching English to speakers of other languages (MA). *Program availability:* Part-time, evening/weekend, online learning. *Degree requirements:* For master's, publishable research paper (M Ed), e-portfolio. *Entrance requirements:* For master's, undergraduate degree from accredited, GCU-approved college, university, or program with minimum GPA 2.8. Additional exam requirements/recommendations for international students: Required—TOEFL (minimum score 550 paper-based; 79 iBT), IELTS (minimum score 6). Electronic applications accepted.

Grand Valley State University, College of Education, Programs in General Education, Allendale, MI 49401-9403. Offers adult and higher education (M Ed); early childhood education (M Ed); educational differentiation (M Ed); educational leadership (M Ed); educational technology integration (M Ed); elementary education (M Ed); middle level education (M Ed); school library media services (M Ed); secondary level education (M Ed); teaching English to speakers of other languages (M Ed). *Program availability:* Part-time, evening/weekend, 100% online, blended/hybrid learning. *Students:* 24 part-time (16 women). Average age 41. In 2017, 5 master's awarded. *Degree requirements:* For master's, project or thesis. *Entrance requirements:* For master's, GRE General Test or minimum GPA of 3.0, last 60 credits from regionally-accredited college/university, 3 letters of recommendation. Additional exam requirements/recommendations for international students: Required—TOEFL (minimum iBT score of 80), IELTS (6.5), or Michigan English Language Assessment Battery (77). *Application deadline:* Applications are processed on a rolling basis. Application fee: $30. Electronic applications accepted. *Expenses:* $652 per credit hour. *Financial support:* In 2017–18, 2 students received support, including 2 fellowships; career-related internships or fieldwork, Federal Work-Study, scholarships/grants, and unspecified assistantships also available. *Faculty research:* Effectiveness of technology in education, parental involvement, effective teaching, effective schools research. *Unit head:* Dr. David Bair, Department Director, 616-331-6489, Fax: 616-331-6489, E-mail: baird@gvsu.edu. *Application contact:* Thomas Owens, Director, Student Information and Services Center, 616-331-6282, Fax: 616-331-6217, E-mail: owenst@gvsu.edu.
Website: http://www.gvsu.edu/coe/

Gratz College, Graduate Programs, Program in Education, Melrose Park, PA 19027. Offers MA. *Program availability:* Part-time. *Degree requirements:* For master's, one foreign language, project. *Entrance requirements:* For master's, teaching certificate.

Greensboro College, Program in Education, Greensboro, NC 27401-1875. Offers elementary education (M Ed); special education (M Ed). *Program availability:* Part-time, evening/weekend. *Degree requirements:* For master's, thesis. *Entrance requirements:* For master's, GRE, teacher license, 2 years of teaching experience, 2 letters of recommendation. Additional exam requirements/recommendations for international students: Required—TOEFL (minimum score 550 paper-based). Electronic applications accepted.

Greenville University, Program in Education, Greenville, IL 62246-0159. Offers education (MAT); elementary education (MAE); secondary education (MAE). *Degree requirements:* For master's, thesis (for some programs). *Entrance requirements:* For master's, GRE, Illinois Basic Skills Test, teacher certification. Electronic applications accepted.

Gwynedd Mercy University, School of Education, Gwynedd Valley, PA 19437-0901. Offers education (Ed D); educational administration (MS); master teacher (MS); school counseling (MS); special education (MS). *Program availability:* Part-time, evening/weekend, 100% online. *Faculty:* 8 full-time (5 women), 38 part-time/adjunct (24 women). *Students:* 579 full-time (430 women); includes 130 minority (90 Black or African American, non-Hispanic/Latino; 11 Asian, non-Hispanic/Latino; 26 Hispanic/Latino; 3 Two or more races, non-Hispanic/Latino). Average age 36. 127 applicants, 18% accepted, 9 enrolled. In 2017, 106 master's awarded. *Degree requirements:* For master's, thesis, internship, practicum. *Entrance requirements:* For master's, GRE or MAT; PRAXIS I, minimum GPA of 3.0. *Application deadline:* Applications are processed on a rolling basis. *Expenses:* $550 per credit (master's degrees); $965 per credit (doctoral); $17 part-time fee, $165 graduation fee. *Financial support:* In 2017–18, 2 research assistantships were awarded; career-related internships or fieldwork, Federal Work-Study, institutionally sponsored loans, tuition waivers (full and partial), and unspecified assistantships also available. Financial award applicants required to submit FAFSA. *Faculty research:* Learning and the brain, reading literacy, ethics and moral judgment, leadership, teaching and multicultural education. *Unit head:* Dr. Heather Pfleger, Dean, 215-646-7300 Ext. 21581, E-mail: pfleger.h@gmercyu.edu. *Application contact:* Graduate Program Coordinator, 877-499-6333, E-mail: graduate@gmercyu.edu.
Website: https://www.gmercyu.edu/academics/graduate-education-programs

Hamline University, School of Education, St. Paul, MN 55104-1284. Offers education (MA Ed, Ed D); English as a second language (MA); literacy education (MA); natural science and environmental education (MA Ed); teaching (MAT); teaching English to speakers of other languages (MA). *Accreditation:* NCATE (one or more programs are accredited). *Program availability:* Part-time, evening/weekend, 100% online, blended/hybrid learning. *Faculty:* 23 full-time (15 women), 43 part-time/adjunct (30 women). *Students:* 79 full-time (60 women), 898 part-time (692 women); includes 139 minority (31 Black or African American, non-Hispanic/Latino; 1 American Indian or Alaska Native, non-Hispanic/Latino; 58 Asian, non-Hispanic/Latino; 33 Hispanic/Latino; 16 Two or more races, non-Hispanic/Latino), 8 international. Average age 35. 366 applicants, 78% accepted, 193 enrolled. In 2017, 236 master's, 7 doctorates awarded. *Degree requirements:* For master's, thesis (for some programs), thesis or capstone project; for doctorate, comprehensive exam, thesis/dissertation. *Entrance requirements:* For master's, official transcripts, essay, letters of recommendation, minimum GPA of 3.0 from bachelor's work; resume and/or writing samples (for some programs); for doctorate, personal statement, master's degree with minimum GPA of 3.0, letters of recommendation, writing sample. Additional exam requirements/recommendations for international students: Required—TOEFL (minimum score 550 paper-based; 80 iBT), IELTS (minimum score 6.5). *Application deadline:* For fall admission, 6/1 for domestic and international students; for spring admission, 11/1 for domestic and international students; for summer admission, 3/1 for domestic and international students. Applications are processed on a rolling basis. Application fee: $0 ($100 for international students). Electronic applications accepted. *Expenses:* $466 per credit (for MA Ed), $625 per credit (for MATESOL), $569 per credit (for MAT), $721 per credit plus fees (for EdD). *Financial support:* Career-related internships or fieldwork, Federal Work-Study, and scholarships/grants available. Support available to part-time students. Financial award application deadline: 4/20; financial award applicants required to submit FAFSA. *Faculty research:* Adult basic education, service-learning, teacher dispositions, diversity, technology. *Unit head:* Dr. Marcela Kostihova, Dean, 651-523-2206, Fax: 651-523-2489, E-mail: cladean@hamline.edu. *Application contact:* Shawn Skoog, Director of Graduate Recruitment and Admission, 651-523-2900, Fax: 651-523-3058, E-mail: gradprog@hamline.edu.
Website: http://www.hamline.edu/education

Hampton University, School of Liberal Arts and Education, Hampton, VA 23668. Offers MA, MS, MT, PhD, Ed S. *Accreditation:* NCATE. *Program availability:* Part-time, evening/weekend. *Students:* 85 full-time (52 women), 75 part-time (52 women); includes 144 minority (all Black or African American, non-Hispanic/Latino), 1 international. Average age 33. 79 applicants, 41% accepted, 4 enrolled. In 2017, 37 master's, 10 doctorates awarded. *Degree requirements:* For master's, comprehensive exam, thesis (for some programs); for doctorate, comprehensive exam, thesis/dissertation. *Entrance requirements:* For master's, GRE General Test, PRAXIS; for doctorate, GRE General Test, GMAT. *Application deadline:* For fall admission, 6/1 priority date for domestic students, 4/1 priority date for international students; for winter admission, 9/1 priority date for international students; for spring admission, 11/1 for domestic students; for summer admission, 4/15 for domestic students, 2/1 priority date for international students. Applications are processed on a rolling basis. Application fee: $35. Electronic applications accepted. *Expenses: Tuition:* Full-time $22,630; part-time $575 per semester hour. *Required fees:* $70. Tuition and fees vary according to program. *Financial support:* Fellowships, research assistantships, teaching assistantships, career-related internships or fieldwork, Federal Work-Study, institutionally sponsored loans, and scholarships/grants available. Support available to part-time students. Financial award application deadline: 5/1; financial award applicants required to submit FAFSA. *Unit head:* Dr. Linda Malone-Colon, Dean, 757-727-5400. *Application contact:* Dr. Michelle Penn-Marshall, Dean, Graduate College, 757-727-5454, E-mail: hugrad@hamptonu.edu.
Website: http://edhd.hamptonu.edu/

Hannibal-LaGrange University, Program in Education, Hannibal, MO 63401-1999. Offers literacy (MS Ed); teaching and learning (MS Ed). *Program availability:* Part-time, evening/weekend. *Degree requirements:* For master's, thesis, portfolio, documenting of program outcomes, public sharing of research. *Entrance requirements:* For master's, copy of current teaching certificate; minimum GPA of 2.75. *Faculty research:* Reading assessment, reading remediation, handwriting instruction, early childhood intervention.

Harding University, Cannon-Clary College of Education, Searcy, AR 72149-0001. Offers advanced studies in teaching and learning (M Ed); art (MSE); behavioral science (MSE); counseling (MS, Ed S); early childhood special education (M Ed, MSE); education (MSE); educational leadership (M Ed, Ed S); elementary education (M Ed); English (MSE); French (MSE); history/social science (MSE); kinesiology (MSE); math (MSE); reading (M Ed); secondary education (MSE); Spanish (MSE); teaching (MAT); teaching English as a second language (MSE). *Accreditation:* NCATE. *Program availability:* Part-time, evening/weekend. *Faculty:* 22 full-time (9 women), 51 part-time/adjunct (37 women). *Students:* 135 full-time (95 women), 316 part-time (231 women); includes 77 minority (46 Black or African American, non-Hispanic/Latino; 7 American Indian or Alaska Native, non-Hispanic/Latino; 4 Asian, non-Hispanic/Latino; 9 Hispanic/Latino; 11 Two or more races, non-Hispanic/Latino), 11 international. Average age 34. 128 applicants, 87% accepted, 111 enrolled. In 2017, 153 master's, 24 other advanced degrees awarded. *Degree requirements:* For master's, comprehensive exam (for some programs), thesis optional, portfolio(s); for Ed S, comprehensive exam, portfolio, project. *Entrance requirements:* For master's, GRE, MAT, PRAXIS; for Ed S, MAT or GRE. Additional exam requirements/recommendations for international students: Required—TOEFL (minimum score 550 paper-based; 79 iBT). *Application deadline:* For fall admission, 8/1 for domestic and international students; for spring admission, 1/1 for domestic and international students. Applications are processed on a rolling basis. Application fee: $35. Tuition and fees vary according to course load, degree level, campus/location and program. *Financial support:* In 2017–18, 33 students received support. Unspecified assistantships available. *Faculty research:* Reading, comprehension, school violence, educational technology, behavior, college choice, differentiated instruction, brain-based teaching. *Unit head:* Dr. Clara Carroll, Chair, 501-279-4501, Fax: 501-279-4083, E-mail: ccarroll@harding.edu. *Application contact:* Information Contact, 501-279-4315, E-mail: gradstudiesedu@harding.edu.
Website: http://www.harding.edu/education

Hardin-Simmons University, Graduate School, Irvin School of Education, Abilene, TX 79698-0001. Offers M Ed, Ed D. *Program availability:* Part-time. *Faculty:* 13 full-time (8 women), 5 part-time/adjunct (3 women). *Students:* 26 full-time (14 women), 99 part-time (69 women); includes 33 minority (16 Black or African American, non-Hispanic/Latino; 1 Asian, non-Hispanic/Latino; 13 Hispanic/Latino; 3 Two or more races, non-Hispanic/Latino), 4 international. Average age 33. 57 applicants, 98% accepted, 40 enrolled. In 2017, 34 master's, 1 doctorate awarded. *Degree requirements:* For master's, comprehensive exam; for doctorate, comprehensive exam, thesis/dissertation. *Entrance requirements:* For master's, minimum undergraduate GPA of 3.0 in major, 2.7 overall. Additional exam requirements/recommendations for international students: Required—TOEFL (minimum score 550 paper-based; 79 iBT). *Application deadline:* For fall admission, 8/15 priority date for domestic students, 4/1 for international students; for spring admission, 1/5 priority date for domestic students, 9/1 for international students. Applications are processed on a rolling basis. Application fee: $50. Electronic applications accepted. *Expenses: Tuition:* Full-time $13,500; part-time $750 per semester hour. *Required fees:* $220 per term. One-time fee: $50. Tuition and fees vary according to course load, campus/location and program. *Financial support:* In 2017–18, 50 students received support. Fellowships, career-related internships or fieldwork, scholarships/grants, and coaching assistantships available. Support available to part-time students. Financial award application deadline: 6/30; financial award applicants required to submit FAFSA. *Unit head:* Dr. Perry Kay Brown, Dean, 325-670-1021, Fax: 325-670-5859, E-mail: pkbrown@hsutx.edu. *Application contact:* Dr. Nancy Kucinski, Dean of Graduate Studies, 325-670-1298, Fax: 325-670-1564, E-mail: gradoff@hsutx.edu.
Website: http://www.hsutx.edu/academics/irvin

Harrison Middleton University, Graduate Program, Tempe, AZ 85282. Offers education (MA, Ed D); humanities (MA); imaginative literature (MA); interdisciplinary studies (DA); jurisprudence (MA); natural science (MA); philosophy and religion (MA); social science (MA). *Program availability:* Part-time, evening/weekend, online learning. *Degree requirements:* For master's and doctorate, capstone project. *Entrance requirements:* For master's, interview; for doctorate, 2 academic letters of reference, interview, essay. Additional exam requirements/recommendations for international students: Required—TOEFL (minimum score 550 paper-based; 80 iBT). Electronic applications accepted. *Faculty research:* Japanese animation, educational leadership, war art, John Muir's wilderness.

Harvard University, Harvard Graduate School of Education, Cambridge, MA 02138. Offers Ed M, Ed L D, PhD. *Program availability:* Part-time. *Degree requirements:* For doctorate, thesis/dissertation (for some programs), capstone project or thesis (for Ed.L.D.). *Entrance requirements:* For master's, GRE General Test, statement of purpose, 3 letters of recommendation, resume, official transcripts; for doctorate, GRE General Test or GMAT (for Ed.L.D. only), statement of purpose, 3 letters of recommendation, resume, official transcripts, 2 short essay questions (for Ed.L.D. only). Additional exam requirements/recommendations for international students: Required—TOEFL (minimum score 613 paper-based; 104 iBT), TWE (minimum score 5). Electronic applications accepted. *Expenses:* Contact institution. *Faculty research:* Learning and development, educational leadership and organizations, education policy analysis.

Hastings College, Department of Teacher Education, Hastings, NE 68901. Offers MAT. *Accreditation:* NCATE. *Program availability:* Part-time. *Degree requirements:* For master's, comprehensive exam, thesis, or oral teaching presentation; digital portfolio. *Entrance requirements:* For master's, minimum GPA of 2.5, 2 letters of reference, interview. Additional exam requirements/recommendations for international students: Required—TOEFL. Electronic applications accepted. *Faculty research:* Assessments, performance competencies.

Hebrew College, Shoolman Graduate School of Jewish Education, Newton Centre, MA 02459. Offers early childhood Jewish education (Certificate); Jewish day school education (Certificate); Jewish education (MJ Ed); Jewish family education (Certificate); Jewish special education (Certificate); Jewish youth education, informal education and camping (Certificate). *Program availability:* Part-time, evening/weekend, online learning. *Degree requirements:* For master's, one foreign language. *Entrance requirements:* For master's, GRE, interview. Additional exam requirements/recommendations for international students: Required—TOEFL.

Hebrew Union College–Jewish Institute of Religion, School of Education, New York, NY 10012-1186. Offers MARE. *Program availability:* Part-time. *Degree requirements:* For master's, one foreign language, thesis. *Entrance requirements:* For master's, GRE, minimum 2 years of college-level Hebrew.

Heidelberg University, Master of Arts in Education Program, Tiffin, OH 44883-2462. Offers MAE. *Accreditation:* NCATE. *Program availability:* Part-time, evening/weekend. *Students:* 14 part-time (4 women). In 2017, 15 master's awarded. *Degree requirements:* For master's, practicum. *Entrance requirements:* For master's, bachelor's degree with minimum cumulative GPA of 2.75; 3 letters of recommendation; goal statement. Additional exam requirements/recommendations for international students: Required—TOEFL (minimum score 550 paper-based, 79 iBT) or IELTS (minimum score 6.5). *Application deadline:* Applications are processed on a rolling basis. Application fee: $0. Electronic applications accepted. *Expenses:* $525 per semester hour. *Financial support:* Unspecified assistantships available. Financial award applicants required to submit FAFSA. *Unit head:* Dr. Karen Jones, Director of the School of Education, 419-448-2130, E-mail: kjones9@heidelberg.edu. *Application contact:* Katie Zeyen, Graduate Admissions Coordinator, 419-448-2602, Fax: 419-448-2565, E-mail: kzeyen@heidelberg.edu.
Website: https://www.heidelberg.edu/academics/programs/master-education

Henderson State University, Graduate Studies, Teachers College, Arkadelphia, AR 71999-0001. Offers MAT, MS, MSE, Ed S, Graduate Certificate. *Accreditation:* NCATE. *Program availability:* Part-time, 100% online. *Entrance requirements:* For master's, GRE General Test or MAT, minimum GPA of 2.7, teacher certification. Additional exam requirements/recommendations for international students: Required—TOEFL (minimum score 600 paper-based); Recommended—IELTS (minimum score 6.5).

Heritage University, Graduate Programs in Education, Toppenish, WA 98948-9599. Offers counseling (M Ed); educational administration (M Ed); professional studies (M Ed), including bilingual education/ESL, biology, English and literature, reading/literacy, special education; teaching (MIT). *Program availability:* Part-time, evening/weekend. *Degree requirements:* For master's, comprehensive exam, thesis (for some programs). *Entrance requirements:* For master's, interview, letters of recommendation, teaching certificate. Additional exam requirements/recommendations for international students: Recommended—TOEFL (minimum score 550 paper-based).

Hofstra University, School of Education, Hempstead, NY 11549. Offers MA, MS, MS Ed, Ed D, Advanced Certificate. *Accreditation:* TEAC. *Program availability:* Part-time, evening/weekend, blended/hybrid learning. *Faculty:* 26 full-time (16 women), 60 part-time/adjunct (41 women). *Students:* 267 full-time (193 women), 373 part-time (278 women); includes 159 minority (69 Black or African American, non-Hispanic/Latino; 1 American Indian or Alaska Native, non-Hispanic/Latino; 22 Asian, non-Hispanic/Latino; 64 Hispanic/Latino; 2 Native Hawaiian or other Pacific Islander, non-Hispanic/Latino; 1 Two or more races, non-Hispanic/Latino), 13 international. Average age 31. 433 applicants, 90% accepted, 225 enrolled. In 2017, 200 master's, 26 doctorates, 63 other advanced degrees awarded. *Degree requirements:* For master's, variable foreign language requirement, comprehensive exam, thesis (for some programs), capstone, minimum GPA of 3.0, electronic portfolio, student teaching, practicum, internship, seminars, field work, curriculum project, clinical hours; for doctorate, variable foreign language requirement, comprehensive exam (for some programs), thesis/dissertation, qualifying hearing; for Advanced Certificate, comprehensive exam (for some programs), thesis optional, electronic portfolio, fieldwork, internship, state exams, exit project. *Entrance requirements:* For master's, GRE, letters of recommendation, interview, portfolio, resume, essay, certification; for doctorate, GRE, 3 letters of recommendation, essay, interview, 2 years' full-time teaching. Additional exam requirements/recommendations for international students: Required—TOEFL (minimum score 550 paper-based; 80 iBT). *Application deadline:* Applications are processed on a rolling basis. Application fee: $75. Electronic applications accepted. *Expenses: Tuition:* Full-time $1292. *Required fees:* $970. Tuition and fees vary according to program. *Financial support:* In 2017–18, 315 students received support, including 164 fellowships with full and partial tuition reimbursements available (averaging $4,332 per year), 14 research assistantships with full and partial tuition reimbursements available (averaging $7,435 per year); career-related internships or fieldwork, Federal Work-Study, institutionally sponsored loans, scholarships/grants, traineeships, tuition waivers (full and partial), and unspecified assistantships also available. Support available to part-time students. Financial award applicants required to submit FAFSA. *Faculty research:* How children learn in contexts spanning from pre-school through high school and the learning needs of children with disabilities, the theory and practice of how teachers can effectively teach children in diverse contexts, educational leadership in K-12 and post secondary contexts. *Total annual research expenditures:* $163,678. *Unit head:* Dr. Benjamin Rifkin, Dean, 516-463-5411, Fax: 516-463-4861, E-mail: benjamin.rifkin@hofstra.edu. *Application contact:* Sunil Samuel, Assistant Vice President of Admissions, 516-463-4723, Fax: 516-463-4664, E-mail: graduateadmission@hofstra.edu.
Website: http://www.hofstra.edu/education/

Hollins University, Graduate Programs, Program in Teaching, Roanoke, VA 24020. Offers teaching (MAT); teaching and learning (MA). *Accreditation:* TEAC. *Program availability:* Part-time, evening/weekend. *Faculty:* 3 full-time (all women), 3 part-time/adjunct (1 woman). *Students:* 15 full-time (12 women), 14 part-time (13 women); includes 6 minority (2 Black or African American, non-Hispanic/Latino; 1 Asian, non-Hispanic/Latino; 2 Hispanic/Latino; 1 Two or more races, non-Hispanic/Latino). Average age 31. 13 applicants, 85% accepted, 9 enrolled. In 2017, 19 master's awarded. *Degree requirements:* For master's, thesis or alternative. *Entrance requirements:* For master's, PRAXIS I or ACT/SAT, three letters of recommendation, bachelor's degree, official transcripts with minimum GPA of 2.5, personal statement. Additional exam requirements/recommendations for international students: Required—TOEFL (minimum score 550 paper-based; 80 iBT), IELTS (minimum score 6.5). *Application deadline:* For fall admission, 8/1 priority date for domestic and international students; for spring admission, 12/1 priority date for domestic and international students; for summer admission, 5/1 priority date for domestic and international students. Applications are processed on a rolling basis. Application fee: $40. Electronic applications accepted. *Expenses:* Contact institution. *Financial support:* Scholarships/grants available. Financial award application deadline: 7/15; financial award applicants required to submit FAFSA. *Unit head:* Dr. Lorraine Lange, Director, 540-362-7460, Fax: 540-362-6288, E-mail: hugrad@hollins.edu. *Application contact:* Donna Martin, Administrative Assistant, 540-362-7460, Fax: 540-362-6288, E-mail: dmartin@hollins.edu.
Website: http://www.hollins.edu/academics/graduate-degrees/teaching

Holy Family University, Graduate and Professional Programs, School of Education, Philadelphia, PA 19114. Offers education (M Ed, Ed D), including early elementary education (PreK-Grade 4) (M Ed), education leadership (M Ed), educational leadership and professional studies (Ed D), general education (M Ed), reading specialist (M Ed), special education (M Ed), TESOL and literacy (M Ed). *Accreditation:* TEAC. *Program availability:* Part-time, evening/weekend. *Degree requirements:* For master's, comprehensive exam, thesis optional; for doctorate, comprehensive exam, thesis/dissertation. *Entrance requirements:* For master's, GRE or MAT (if GPA is below 3.0), interview, minimum GPA of 3.0, essay/personal statement, 2 letters of recommendation, official transcripts of all college or university work; for doctorate, GRE or MAT (taken within 5 years of application), minimum GPA of 3.5, 3 letters of recommendation, official transcripts of all college or university work, current resume, essay/personal statement, writing sample, interview. Additional exam requirements/recommendations for international students: Required—TOEFL (minimum score 550 paper-based; 79 iBT), IELTS (minimum score 6), or PTE (minimum score 54). Electronic applications accepted. *Expenses: Tuition:* Full-time $13,518; part-time $9012 per credit hour. Tuition and fees vary according to degree level and program.

Holy Names University, Graduate Division, Department of Education, Oakland, CA 94619-1699. Offers educational therapy (Certificate); mild/moderate disabilities (Ed S); multiple subject teaching (Credential); single subject teaching (Credential); urban education: educational therapy (M Ed); urban education: K-12 education (M Ed); urban education: special education (M Ed). *Program availability:* Part-time. *Degree requirements:* For master's, comprehensive exam, research paper, thesis or project. *Entrance requirements:* For master's, minimum undergraduate GPA of 2.6 overall, 3.0 in major; personal statement; two recommendations; interview. Additional exam requirements/recommendations for international students: Required—TOEFL (minimum score 550 paper-based; 79 iBT). Electronic applications accepted. Application fee is waived when completed online. *Faculty research:* Cognitive development, language development, learning handicaps.

Hood College, Graduate School, Department of Education, Frederick, MD 21701-8575. Offers curriculum and instruction (MS), including elementary education, elementary science and mathematics education, secondary education, special education; education, multidisciplinary studies (MS); educational leadership (MS, Certificate); reading specialization (MS); STEM education (Certificate). *Accreditation:* NCATE. *Program availability:* Part-time-only, evening/weekend. *Faculty:* 6 full-time (4 women), 35 part-time/adjunct (27 women). *Students:* 3 full-time (all women), 329 part-time (265 women); includes 62 minority (35 Black or African American, non-Hispanic/Latino; 4 Asian, non-Hispanic/Latino; 14 Hispanic/Latino; 9 Two or more races, non-Hispanic/Latino), 3 international. Average age 33. 76 applicants, 100% accepted, 63 enrolled. In 2017, 53 master's, 58 other advanced degrees awarded. *Degree requirements:* For master's, action research project, portfolio (for reading specialization); for Certificate, STEM capstone activity. *Entrance requirements:* For master's, minimum GPA of 2.75, teaching certification, writing sample during interview, letter of recommendation from principal (for educational leadership program only). Additional exam requirements/recommendations for international students: Required—TOEFL (minimum score 575 paper-based; 89 iBT), IELTS (minimum score 6.5). *Application deadline:* For fall admission, 8/15 priority date for domestic students, 8/5 for international students; for spring admission, 12/1 priority date for domestic students, 12/1 for international students; for summer admission, 5/1 priority date for domestic students, 4/15 for international students. Applications are processed on a rolling basis. Application fee: $35. Electronic applications accepted. *Expenses:* $465 per credit plus $110 comprehensive fee per semester. *Financial support:* Tuition waivers (partial) and unspecified assistantships available. Financial award applicants required to submit FAFSA. *Faculty research:* Leadership, action research, brain research, learning styles. *Unit head:* Dr. April M. Boulton, Dean of the Graduate School, 301-696-3612, E-mail: gofurther@hood.edu. *Application contact:* Jan Marcus, Assistant Director of Graduate Admissions, 301-696-3600, E-mail: gofurther@hood.edu.
Website: http://www.hood.edu/academics/education/index.html

Hope International University, School of Graduate and Professional Studies, Program in Education, Fullerton, CA 92831-3138. Offers education administration (MA); elementary education (ME); secondary education (ME). *Program availability:* Part-time, evening/weekend. *Degree requirements:* For master's, comprehensive exam (for some programs), thesis. *Entrance requirements:* For master's, minimum GPA of 3.0, 2 references. Additional exam requirements/recommendations for international students: Required—TOEFL (minimum score 550 paper-based; 86 iBT); Recommended—IELTS (minimum score 6.5). Electronic applications accepted. *Expenses:* Contact institution. *Faculty research:* Distance education.

Houston Baptist University, College of Education and Behavioral Sciences, Programs in Education, Houston, TX 77074-3298. Offers bilingual education (M Ed); counselor education (M Ed); curriculum and instruction (M Ed); curriculum and instruction (EC-6 bilingual) (M Ed); curriculum and instruction in all-level art, Spanish, music, or physical education (M Ed); curriculum and instruction in EC-6 and special education (EC-12) (M Ed); curriculum and instruction in instructional technology (M Ed); curriculum and instruction in mathematics, science, or social studies (4-8) (M Ed); curriculum and instruction with EC-6 generalist (M Ed); curriculum and instruction with English language arts and reading (4-8) (M Ed); educational administration (M Ed); educational diagnostician (M Ed); executive educational leadership (Ed D); higher education in business management (M Ed); higher education in Christian studies (M Ed); higher education in counseling (M Ed); higher education in educational technology (M Ed); reading (M Ed); special educational leadership (Ed D). *Program availability:* Part-time, evening/weekend, 100% online, blended/hybrid learning. *Students:* 83 full-time (65 women), 187 part-time (156 women); includes 189 minority (114 Black or African American, non-Hispanic/Latino; 2 American Indian or Alaska Native, non-Hispanic/Latino; 9 Asian, non-Hispanic/Latino; 58 Hispanic/Latino; 6 Two or more races, non-Hispanic/Latino), 7 international. Average age 36. 309 applicants, 31% accepted, 70

Education—General

enrolled. In 2017, 92 master's awarded. *Degree requirements:* For master's, comprehensive exam; for doctorate, thesis/dissertation. *Entrance requirements:* For master's, minimum GPA of 2.75, two recommendations, resume, bachelor's degree conferred transcript; interview (for non-certified teachers); for doctorate, GRE, 5 letters of recommendation. Additional exam requirements/recommendations for international students: Required—TOEFL (minimum score 80 iBT), IELTS (minimum score 6.5). *Application deadline:* For fall admission, 8/1 for domestic students, 6/1 for international students; for spring admission, 1/1 for domestic students, 11/1 for international students; for summer admission, 5/1 for domestic students, 3/1 for international students. Applications are processed on a rolling basis. Application fee: $0 ($100 for international students). Electronic applications accepted. Application fee is waived when completed online. *Expenses:* $22,000 tuition; $4,500 fees (general, technology and parking). *Financial support:* In 2017–18, 59 students received support. Research assistantships, teaching assistantships, Federal Work-Study, and scholarships/grants available. Support available to part-time students. Financial award application deadline: 4/1; financial award applicants required to submit FAFSA. *Faculty research:* Autism and inclusion, integrating technology into instruction, school change and leadership trust. *Unit head:* Dr. Charlotte Fontenot, Director, Graduate Programs, 281-649-3078, Fax: 281-649-3361, E-mail: cfontenot@hbu.edu. *Application contact:* Kristy Wright, Administrative Assistant for Graduate Programs, 281-649-3094, Fax: 281-649-3361, E-mail: kwright@hbu.edu.
Website: http://www.hbu.edu/MED

Houston Baptist University, School of Humanities, Program in Liberal Arts, Houston, TX 77074-3298. Offers education (EC-12 art, music, physical education, or Spanish) (MLA); education (EC-6 generalist) (MLA); general liberal arts (MLA); specialization in education (4-8 or 7-12) (MLA). *Program availability:* Part-time, evening/weekend. *Students:* 11 full-time (7 women), 13 part-time (9 women); includes 12 minority (5 Black or African American, non-Hispanic/Latino; 2 Asian, non-Hispanic/Latino; 5 Hispanic/Latino). Average age 31. 26 applicants, 73% accepted, 12 enrolled. In 2017, 15 master's awarded. *Entrance requirements:* For master's, minimum GPA of 2.5, essay/personal statement, resume, bachelor's degree transcript. Additional exam requirements/recommendations for international students: Required—TOEFL (minimum score 80 iBT), IELTS (minimum score 6.5). *Application deadline:* For fall admission, 8/1 for domestic students, 6/1 for international students; for spring admission, 1/1 for domestic students, 11/1 for international students; for summer admission, 5/1 for domestic students, 3/1 for international students. Applications are processed on a rolling basis. Application fee: $0 ($100 for international students). Electronic applications accepted. Application fee is waived when completed online. *Expenses:* $18,000 tuition; $4,500 fees (general, technology and parking). *Financial support:* In 2017–18, 12 students received support. Federal Work-Study and scholarships/grants available. Support available to part-time students. Financial award application deadline: 4/1; financial award applicants required to submit FAFSA. *Unit head:* Dr. Collin Garbarino, Graduate Programs Director, 281-649-3679, E-mail: cgarbarino@hbu.edu. *Application contact:* Kathy Holston, Administrative Assistant to the Dean, 281-649-3404, E-mail: kholston@hbu.edu.
Website: http://www.hbu.edu/mla

Howard University, School of Education, Washington, DC 20059. Offers M Ed, Ed D, PhD, CAGS. *Accreditation:* NCATE. *Faculty:* 39 full-time (27 women), 9 part-time/adjunct (4 women). *Students:* 115 full-time (85 women), 86 part-time (57 women); includes 163 minority (159 Black or African American, non-Hispanic/Latino; 3 Asian, non-Hispanic/Latino; 1 Hispanic/Latino), 28 international. Average age 32. 167 applicants, 63% accepted, 67 enrolled. In 2017, 8 master's, 35 doctorates awarded. *Degree requirements:* For master's, comprehensive exam, expository writing exam, practicum, PRAXIS II; for doctorate, one foreign language, comprehensive exam, thesis/dissertation, expository writing exam, internship. *Entrance requirements:* For master's, PRAXIS I or GRE General Test (for curriculum and instruction students only), minimum GPA of 3.0; for doctorate, GRE General Test, minimum GPA of 3.0. Additional exam requirements/recommendations for international students: Required—TOEFL (minimum score 550 paper-based; 79 iBT). *Application deadline:* For fall admission, 1/15 for domestic and international students. Applications are processed on a rolling basis. Application fee: $75. Electronic applications accepted. *Expenses:* $1,700 per credit. *Financial support:* In 2017–18, 69 students received support, including 5 fellowships (averaging $49,000 per year), 17 research assistantships (averaging $24,500 per year); career-related internships or fieldwork, Federal Work-Study, institutionally sponsored loans, scholarships/grants, tuition waivers (full and partial), and unspecified assistantships also available. Financial award application deadline: 2/15; financial award applicants required to submit FAFSA. *Faculty research:* Policy and practice issues affecting education for African-Americans; information technology use in underserved school populations; increasing literacy skills for public school students; violence intervention and prevention; successes, problems, and needs of disabled African-Americans. *Total annual research expenditures:* $1.3 million. *Unit head:* Dr. Dawn G. Williams, Dean, School of Education, 202-806-7340, Fax: 202-806-7018, E-mail: dgwilliams@howard.edu. *Application contact:* Dr. Kenneth A. Anderson, Interim Associate Dean for Academic Programs and Student Affairs, 202-806-7340, Fax: 202-806-7018, E-mail: kenneth.anderson@howard.edu.
Website: https://education.howard.edu/

Humboldt State University, Academic Programs, College of Professional Studies, School of Education, Arcata, CA 95521-8299. Offers MA. *Program availability:* Part-time, evening/weekend, online only, 100% online, blended/hybrid learning. *Degree requirements:* For master's, thesis or alternative. *Entrance requirements:* For master's, minimum GPA of 3.0, 3 letters of recommendation. Additional exam requirements/recommendations for international students: Required—TOEFL (minimum score 500 paper-based). Electronic applications accepted.

Hunter College of the City University of New York, Graduate School, School of Education, New York, NY 10065-5085. Offers MA, MS, MS Ed, Ed D, AC. *Accreditation:* NCATE. *Program availability:* Part-time, evening/weekend. *Degree requirements:* For master's, comprehensive exam (for some programs), thesis (for some programs), minimum overall GPA of 3.0; portfolio review; for doctorate, thesis/dissertation; for AC, comprehensive exam (for some programs), minimum overall GPA of 3.0; portfolio review; valid and appropriate NY state certification. *Entrance requirements:* For master's, GRE (for teacher preparation programs), transcript review requiring BA with minimum GPA of 3.0; personal statement, letters of recommendation and/or writing sample; for doctorate, GRE (for teacher preparation programs), official transcripts; letters of recommendation; essay; resume; minimum GPA of 3.5 in a master's program; interview; for AC, GRE (for teacher preparation programs), transcript review requiring minimum B average in graduate course work; teaching certificate; minimum 3 years of full-time teaching experience; personal statement, letters of recommendation and/or writing sample. Additional exam requirements/recommendations for international students: Required—TOEFL. Electronic applications accepted. *Faculty research:* Multicultural and multiracial urban education; mentoring new teachers; mathematics and science education; bilingual, bi-cultural, and special education.

Idaho State University, Office of Graduate Studies, College of Education, Pocatello, ID 83209-8059. Offers M Ed, MPE, Ed D, PhD, 5th Year Certificate, 6th Year Certificate,

Ed S. *Accreditation:* NCATE. *Program availability:* Part-time. *Degree requirements:* For master's, comprehensive exam, thesis optional, oral exam, written exam; for doctorate, comprehensive exam, thesis/dissertation, written exam; for other advanced degree, comprehensive exam, oral exam, written exam, practicum or field project. *Entrance requirements:* For master's, GRE General Test or MAT, minimum undergraduate GPA of 3.0, interview, bachelor's degree or equivalent; for doctorate, GRE General Test or MAT, minimum undergraduate GPA of 3.0, 3.5 graduate; departmental interview; current curriculum vitae, computer skill competency checklist; for other advanced degree, GRE General Test, minimum graduate GPA of 3.0, master's degree, letter from supervisor attesting to school administration potential. Additional exam requirements/recommendations for international students: Required—TOEFL (minimum score 550 paper-based; 80 iBT). Electronic applications accepted. *Faculty research:* School reform, inclusion, students at risk, teacher education standards, teaching cases, education leadership.

Illinois College, Program in Education, Jacksonville, IL 62650-2299. Offers MA Ed. *Program availability:* Part-time-only, evening/weekend. *Degree requirements:* For master's, action research capstone experience. Electronic applications accepted. *Expenses:* Contact institution.

Illinois State University, Graduate School, College of Education, Normal, IL 61790. Offers MS, MS Ed, Ed D, PhD, Certificate. *Accreditation:* NCATE. *Program availability:* Part-time. *Degree requirements:* For doctorate, thesis/dissertation, 2 terms of residency. *Entrance requirements:* For master's and doctorate, GRE General Test.

Indiana State University, College of Graduate and Professional Studies, Bayh College of Education, Terre Haute, IN 47809. Offers M Ed, MS, PhD, Ed S, MA/MS. *Accreditation:* NCATE. *Program availability:* Part-time, evening/weekend. *Degree requirements:* For doctorate, thesis/dissertation. *Entrance requirements:* For master's, minimum undergraduate GPA of 2.5; for doctorate, GRE General Test; for Ed S, GRE General Test, minimum graduate GPA of 3.25. Electronic applications accepted.

Indiana University Bloomington, School of Education, Bloomington, IN 47405-1006. Offers MS, Ed D, PhD, Ed S, Graduate Certificate. *Accreditation:* NCATE. *Program availability:* Part-time, 100% online, blended/hybrid learning. Terminal master's awarded for partial completion of doctoral program. *Degree requirements:* For master's, thesis optional; for doctorate, comprehensive exam, thesis/dissertation; for other advanced degree, comprehensive exam (for some programs), thesis (for some programs), comprehensive exam or project. *Entrance requirements:* For master's and other advanced degree, GRE General Test, minimum GPA of 3.0 (recommended), 3 letters of recommendation; for doctorate, GRE General Test, minimum GPA of 3.0, 3 letters of recommendation. Additional exam requirements/recommendations for international students: Required—TOEFL (minimum score 550 paper-based; 79 iBT). Electronic applications accepted.

Indiana University East, School of Education, Richmond, IN 47374-1289. Offers MS Ed. *Accreditation:* NCATE. *Entrance requirements:* For master's, 3 letters of recommendation, interview.

Indiana University Northwest, School of Education, Gary, IN 46408. Offers educational leadership (MS Ed); elementary education (MS Ed); K-12 online teaching (Graduate Certificate); secondary education (MS Ed). *Accreditation:* NCATE. *Program availability:* Part-time, evening/weekend. *Entrance requirements:* For master's, GRE General Test or MAT, minimum GPA of 3.0. Electronic applications accepted. *Expenses:* Contact institution.

Indiana University of Pennsylvania, School of Graduate Studies and Research, College of Education and Communications, Indiana, PA 15705. Offers M Ed, MA, MS, D Ed, PhD, Certificate. *Accreditation:* NCATE. *Program availability:* Part-time, evening/weekend. *Faculty:* 55 full-time (39 women), 12 part-time/adjunct (9 women). *Students:* 264 full-time (202 women), 411 part-time (272 women); includes 85 minority (52 Black or African American, non-Hispanic/Latino; 1 American Indian or Alaska Native, non-Hispanic/Latino; 3 Asian, non-Hispanic/Latino; 14 Hispanic/Latino; 15 Two or more races, non-Hispanic/Latino), 29 international. Average age 33. 622 applicants, 66% accepted, 182 enrolled. In 2017, 159 master's, 58 doctorates, 19 other advanced degrees awarded. Terminal master's awarded for partial completion of doctoral program. *Degree requirements:* For master's, thesis optional; for doctorate, comprehensive exam, thesis/dissertation. *Entrance requirements:* For master's and doctorate, 2 letters of recommendation. Additional exam requirements/recommendations for international students: Required—TOEFL (minimum score 540 paper-based; 76 iBT). *Application deadline:* Applications are processed on a rolling basis. Application fee: $50. Electronic applications accepted. *Expenses:* Tuition, state resident: full-time $12,000; part-time $500 per credit. Tuition, nonresident: full-time $18,000; part-time $750 per credit. Required fees: $4073; $165.55 per credit. $64 per term. *Financial support:* In 2017–18, 22 fellowships (averaging $919 per year), 135 research assistantships with tuition reimbursements (averaging $4,373 per year), 8 teaching assistantships with tuition reimbursements (averaging $18,450 per year) were awarded; career-related internships or fieldwork, Federal Work-Study, scholarships/grants, and unspecified assistantships also available. Support available to part-time students. Financial award application deadline: 4/15; financial award applicants required to submit FAFSA. *Unit head:* Dr. Lara Luetkehans, Dean, 724-357-2480, Fax: 724-357-5595. *Application contact:* Paula Stossel, Assistant Dean for Administration, 724-357-4511, Fax: 724-357-4862, E-mail: graduate-admissions@iup.edu.
Website: http://www.iup.edu/education

Indiana University–Purdue University Fort Wayne, College of Education and Public Policy, Fort Wayne, IN 46805-1499. Offers MPM, MS Ed, Certificate. *Accreditation:* NCATE. *Program availability:* Part-time. *Entrance requirements:* For master's, minimum GPA of 2.5, 3 professional letters of recommendation. Additional exam requirements/recommendations for international students: Required—TOEFL (minimum score 550 paper-based; 79 iBT). *Faculty research:* Alcoholism and sobriety, international faculty perceptions.

Indiana University–Purdue University Indianapolis, School of Education, Indianapolis, IN 46202-5155. Offers curriculum and instruction (MS); early childhood (MS); educational leadership (MS, Certificate); English as a second language (Certificate); kindergarten (Certificate); language education (MS); reading (Certificate); school counseling (MS); special education (MS, Certificate). *Program availability:* Part-time, evening/weekend. Terminal master's awarded for partial completion of doctoral program. *Degree requirements:* For master's, thesis optional. *Entrance requirements:* For master's, GRE General Test, minimum GPA of 2.5; for Certificate, official transcripts. Additional exam requirements/recommendations for international students: Required—TOEFL (minimum score 60 iBT), IELTS (minimum score 5.5). Electronic applications accepted. *Expenses:* Contact institution. *Faculty research:* Educational policies and school leaders' responses to these; issues of intersectionality in the experiences of African American lesbian, gay, and bisexual students attending historically black colleges and universities and those who belong to black Greek-letter organizations; students' experiential knowledge and their evolving disciplinary-specific literacy and understanding; innovative program development; urban ESL teacher preparation; target-based instructional coaching.

Indiana University South Bend, School of Education, South Bend, IN 46615. Offers addiction counseling (MS Ed); alcohol and drug counseling (Graduate Certificate); clinical mental health counseling (MS Ed); educational leadership (MS Ed); elementary education (MS Ed); marriage, couple, and family counseling (MS Ed); school counseling (MS Ed); secondary education (MS Ed); special education (MAT, MS Ed), including intense intervention (MS Ed), mild intervention (MS Ed). *Accreditation:* NCATE. *Program availability:* Part-time, evening/weekend. *Degree requirements:* For master's, thesis or alternative, exit project. *Entrance requirements:* For master's, letters of recommendation, GRE or minimum GPA of 3.0. Additional exam requirements/recommendations for international students: Required—TOEFL. Electronic applications accepted. *Expenses:* Contact institution. *Faculty research:* Professional dispositions, early childhood literacy, online learning, program assessments, problem-based learning.

Indiana University Southeast, School of Education, New Albany, IN 47150. Offers counselor education (MS Ed); elementary education (MS Ed); secondary education (MS Ed). *Accreditation:* NCATE. *Program availability:* Part-time, evening/weekend. *Entrance requirements:* For master's, minimum undergraduate GPA of 2.5, graduate 3.0. Electronic applications accepted. *Faculty research:* Learning styles, technology, constructivism, group process, innovative math strategies.

Institute for Christian Studies, Graduate Programs, Toronto, ON M5T 1R4, Canada. Offers education (M Phil F, PhD); history of philosophy (M Phil F, PhD); philosophical aesthetics (M Phil F, PhD); philosophy of religion (M Phil F, PhD); political theory (M Phil F, PhD); systematic philosophy (M Phil F, PhD); theology (M Phil F, PhD); worldview studies (MWS). *Program availability:* Part-time, online learning. *Degree requirements:* For master's, one foreign language, thesis; for doctorate, 2 foreign languages, thesis/dissertation. *Entrance requirements:* For master's and doctorate, philosophy background. Additional exam requirements/recommendations for international students: Required—TOEFL (minimum score 600 paper-based). *Faculty research:* Human rights, anthropology of self, medieval discourse, gender and body, post-modern thought; biblical hermeneutics, creational aesthetics, ecumenism, epistemology, political theory and public policy, relational psychotherapy.

Instituto Tecnologico de Santo Domingo, Graduate School, Area of Humanities and Social Sciences, Santo Domingo, Dominican Republic. Offers accounting (Certificate); adult education (Certificate); applied linguistics (MA); economics (MA); education (M Ed); educational psychology (MA, Certificate); gender and development (MA, Certificate); humanistic studies (MA); international marketing management (Certificate); international relations in the Caribbean basin (Certificate); intervention systems in family therapy (MA); linguistic and literary communication (Certificate); pedagogical support (MA); social science education (M Ed); sustainable human development (MA); terminal illness and death psychology (Certificate); youth and adult education (M Ed).

Instituto Tecnológico y de Estudios Superiores de Monterrey, Campus Central de Veracruz, Graduate Programs, Córdoba, Mexico. Offers administration (MA); administration of information technologies (MTI); computer sciences (MCC); education (MEE); educational institution administration (MAD); educational technology (MTE); electronic commerce (MCE); finance (MAF); humanistic studies (MEH); international business for Latin America (MNL); marketing (MMT); science (MCP). *Program availability:* Part-time, evening/weekend, online learning. *Degree requirements:* For master's, thesis (for some programs). *Entrance requirements:* For master's, PAEP College Board. Electronic applications accepted.

Instituto Tecnológico y de Estudios Superiores de Monterrey, Campus Ciudad de México, Virtual University Division, Ciudad de Mexico, Mexico. Offers administration of information technologies (MA); computer sciences (MA); education (MA, PhD); educational technology (MA); environmental engineering (MA); environmental systems (MA); humanistic studies (MA); industrial engineering (MA); international business for Latin America (MA); quality systems (MA); quality systems and productivity (MA). *Program availability:* Part-time, evening/weekend, online learning. *Entrance requirements:* For master's and doctorate, Instituto entrance exam. Additional exam requirements/recommendations for international students: Required—TOEFL.

Instituto Tecnológico y de Estudios Superiores de Monterrey, Campus Ciudad Juárez, Program in Education, Ciudad Juárez, Mexico. Offers M Ed.

Instituto Tecnológico y de Estudios Superiores de Monterrey, Campus Ciudad Obregón, Programs in Education, Ciudad Obregón, Mexico. Offers cognitive development (ME); communications (ME); mathematics (ME).

Instituto Tecnológico y de Estudios Superiores de Monterrey, Campus Estado de México, Professional and Graduate Division, Estado de Mexico, Mexico. Offers administration of information technologies (MITA); architecture (M Arch); business administration (GMBA, MBA); computer sciences (MCS, PhD); education (M Ed); educational institution administration (MAD); educational technology and innovation (PhD); electronic commerce (MEC); environmental systems (MS); finance (MAF); humanistic studies (MHS); information sciences and knowledge management (MISKM); information systems (MS); manufacturing systems (MS); marketing (MEM); quality systems and productivity (MS); science and materials engineering (PhD); telecommunications management (MTM). *Program availability:* Part-time, online learning. *Degree requirements:* For master's, one foreign language, thesis (for some programs); for doctorate, one foreign language, thesis/dissertation. *Entrance requirements:* For master's, E-PAEP 500, interview; for doctorate, E-PAEP 500, research proposal. Additional exam requirements/recommendations for international students: Required—TOEFL (minimum score 550 paper-based). *Faculty research:* Surface treatments by plasmas, mechanical properties, robotics, graphical computing, mechatronics security protocols.

Instituto Tecnológico y de Estudios Superiores de Monterrey, Campus Irapuato, Graduate Programs, Irapuato, Mexico. Offers administration (MBA); administration of information technology (MAIT); administration of telecommunications (MAT); architecture (M Arch); computer science (MCS); education (M Ed); educational administration (MEA); educational innovation and technology (DEIT); educational technology (MET); electronic commerce (MBA); environmental administration and planning (MEAP); environmental systems (MES); finances (MBA); humanistic studies (MHS); international management for Latin American executives (MIMLAE); library and information science (MLIS); manufacturing quality management (MMQM); marketing research (MBA).

Instituto Tecnológico y de Estudios Superiores de Monterrey, Campus Sonora Norte, Program in Education, Hermosillo, Mexico. Offers MA. *Entrance requirements:* For master's, MAT.

Inter American University of Puerto Rico, Arecibo Campus, Programs in Education, Arecibo, PR 00614-4050. Offers administration and educational supervision (MA Ed); counseling and guidance (MA Ed); curriculum and teaching (MA Ed), including biology education, English as a second language, history education, math education, Spanish; elementary education (MA Ed). *Accreditation:* TEAC. *Degree requirements:* For master's, comprehensive exam, thesis optional. *Entrance requirements:* For master's, GRE, EXADEP, bachelor's degree in education or teaching license (administration and supervision) or courses in education and psychology (counseling and guidance), minimum GPA of 2.5 in last 60 credits.

Inter American University of Puerto Rico, Barranquitas Campus, Program in Education, Barranquitas, PR 00794. Offers curriculum and teaching (M Ed), including biology, English as a second language, history, Spanish; educational leadership and management (MA); elementary education (M Ed); information and library service technology (M Ed); special education (MA). *Accreditation:* TEAC. *Program availability:* Part-time, evening/weekend. *Faculty:* 1 full-time (0 women), 3 part-time/adjunct (2 women). *Students:* 17 full-time (16 women), 2 part-time (both women); all minorities (all Hispanic/Latino). Average age 34. 9 applicants, 89% accepted, 8 enrolled. In 2017, 5 master's awarded. *Degree requirements:* For master's, 2 foreign languages, comprehensive exam, thesis (for some programs). *Entrance requirements:* For master's, GRE or EXADEP, bachelor's degree or its equivalent from accredited institution, official academic transcript from institution that conferred bachelor's degree, minimum GPA of 2.5, two recommendation letters, interview (for some programs), essay (for some programs). *Application deadline:* Applications are processed on a rolling basis. Application fee: $31. Electronic applications accepted. *Expenses:* $3,392 full-time tuition plus $652 fees. *Financial support:* Applicants required to submit FAFSA. *Unit head:* Juan A. Negron-Berrios, PhD, Chancellor, 787-857-3600 Ext. 2002, Fax: 787-857-2125, E-mail: janegron@br.inter.edu. *Application contact:* Aramilda Cartagena-Santiago, Dean of Students, 787-857-3600 Ext. 2009, Fax: 787-857-2125, E-mail: aramildacartagena@br.inter.edu.

Inter American University of Puerto Rico, Metropolitan Campus, Graduate Programs, Program in Education, San Juan, PR 00919-1293. Offers curriculum and instruction (Ed D); educational administration (Ed D); guidance and counseling (MA, Ed D); special education administration (Ed D). *Accreditation:* TEAC. *Degree requirements:* For doctorate, comprehensive exam, thesis/dissertation. *Entrance requirements:* For doctorate, GRE, MAT, or EXADEP. Electronic applications accepted.

International Baptist College and Seminary, Program in Education, Chandler, AZ 85286. Offers M Ed. *Degree requirements:* For master's, research paper/thesis. *Entrance requirements:* For master's, letter of recommendation.

Iona College, School of Arts and Science, Department of Education, New Rochelle, NY 10801-1890. Offers adolescence education: biology (MS Ed, MST); adolescence education: English (MS Ed); adolescence education: mathematics (MST); adolescence education: social studies (MS Ed, MST); adolescence education: Spanish (MS Ed); adolescence special education 5-12 (MST); childhood and special education (MST); early childhood and childhood (MST); educational leadership (MS Ed). *Accreditation:* NCATE. *Program availability:* Part-time, evening/weekend. *Faculty:* 7 full-time (5 women), 2 part-time/adjunct (1 woman). *Students:* 23 full-time (18 women), 26 part-time (19 women); includes 12 minority (4 Black or African American, non-Hispanic/Latino; 8 Hispanic/Latino). Average age 26. 33 applicants, 97% accepted, 20 enrolled. In 2017, 31 master's awarded. *Degree requirements:* For master's, thesis or alternative. *Entrance requirements:* For master's, minimum GPA of 3.0, NY State teaching certificate and bachelor's degree (for MS Ed). Additional exam requirements/recommendations for international students: Required—TOEFL (minimum score 550 paper-based; 80 iBT), IELTS (minimum score 6.5). *Application deadline:* For fall admission, 8/1 priority date for domestic students, 5/1 priority date for international students; for spring admission, 1/1 priority date for domestic students, 9/1 priority date for international students. Applications are processed on a rolling basis. Electronic applications accepted. Tuition and fees vary according to program. *Financial support:* In 2017–18, 16 students received support. Unspecified assistantships available. Support available to part-time students. Financial award application deadline: 4/15; financial award applicants required to submit FAFSA. *Faculty research:* Engaging teacher educators in scientific process, cross-national comparisons of mathematics teaching, questioning strategies in the classroom, research methods, literacy development. *Unit head:* Margaret Smith, PhD, Chair, 914-633-2710, Fax: 914-633-2608, E-mail: msmith@iona.edu. *Application contact:* Richard McMahon, Coordinator, Graduate School of Education, 914-633-2552, E-mail: rmcmahon@iona.edu. Website: http://www.iona.edu/Academics/School-of-Arts-Science/Departments/Education/Graduate-Programs.aspx

Iowa State University of Science and Technology, Department of Education, Ames, IA 50011. Offers curriculum and instructional technology (M Ed, MS, PhD); elementary education (M Ed, MS); historical, philosophical, and comparative studies in education (M Ed, MS); special education (M Ed, MS, PhD). *Degree requirements:* For master's, thesis or alternative; for doctorate, thesis/dissertation. *Entrance requirements:* For master's and doctorate, GRE General Test. Additional exam requirements/recommendations for international students: Required—TOEFL (minimum score 560 paper-based; 83 iBT), IELTS (minimum score 6.5). Electronic applications accepted.

Jackson State University, Graduate School, College of Education and Human Development, Jackson, MS 39217. Offers MS, MS Ed, Ed D, PhD, Ed S. *Accreditation:* NCATE. *Program availability:* Part-time, evening/weekend, 100% online, blended/hybrid learning. Terminal master's awarded for partial completion of doctoral program. *Degree requirements:* For master's, comprehensive exam; for doctorate, comprehensive exam, thesis/dissertation. *Entrance requirements:* For master's, GRE General Test; for doctorate, MAT, teaching experience. Additional exam requirements/recommendations for international students: Required—TOEFL (minimum score 520 paper-based; 67 iBT). Electronic applications accepted. *Expenses:* Contact institution.

Jacksonville State University, College of Graduate Studies and Continuing Education, College of Education and Professional Studies, Jacksonville, AL 36265-1602. Offers MS, MS Ed, Ed S. *Accreditation:* NCATE. *Program availability:* Part-time, evening/weekend, 100% online, blended/hybrid learning. *Degree requirements:* For master's, comprehensive exam, thesis (for some programs). *Entrance requirements:* For master's, GRE General Test or MAT. Additional exam requirements/recommendations for international students: Required—TOEFL (minimum score 500 paper-based; 61 iBT). Electronic applications accepted.

John Brown University, Graduate Education Programs, Siloam Springs, AR 72761-2121. Offers curriculum and instruction (M Ed); secondary education (MAT). *Program availability:* Part-time, evening/weekend. *Entrance requirements:* For master's, GRE (minimum score of 300). Additional exam requirements/recommendations for international students: Required—TOEFL (minimum score 550 paper-based; 79 iBT). Electronic applications accepted.

John Carroll University, Graduate Studies, Program in Professional Teacher Education, University Heights, OH 44118. Offers M Ed, MA. *Program availability:* Part-time, evening/weekend. *Faculty:* 9 full-time (5 women), 1 (woman) part-time/adjunct. *Students:* 27 full-time (20 women), 28 part-time (22 women); includes 7 minority (3 Black or African American, non-Hispanic/Latino; 1 Hispanic/Latino; 3 Two or more races, non-Hispanic/Latino), 1 international. Average age 30. In 2017, 57 master's awarded. *Degree requirements:* For master's, comprehensive exam, research essay or thesis (MA only). *Entrance requirements:* For master's, GRE General Test or MAT, minimum GPA of 2.75, interview. *Application deadline:* For fall admission, 8/15 priority date for domestic students; for spring admission, 1/3 for domestic students. Applications are processed on a rolling basis. Application fee: $25 ($35 for international students). Electronic applications accepted. *Expenses:* Tuition: Full-time $16,238; part-time $788 per credit hour. One-time fee: $200. Part-time tuition and fees vary according to course load and program. *Financial support:* Scholarships/grants, tuition waivers (partial), and unspecified assistantships available. Financial award application deadline: 3/1; financial award applicants required to submit FAFSA. *Unit head:* Dr. Barbara Garson, Coordinator, 216-397-4689, Fax: 216-397-3045, E-mail: bgarson@jcu.edu. *Application contact:* Jennifer L. Tucker, Records Management Assistant, 216-397-1925, Fax: 216-397-1835, E-mail: jtucker@jcu.edu.

John F. Kennedy University, School of Education and Liberal Arts, Department of Education, Pleasant Hill, CA 94523-4817. Offers MAT. *Program availability:* Part-time, evening/weekend. *Degree requirements:* For master's, thesis. *Entrance requirements:* For master's, California Basic Educational Skills Test, NTE, interview. Additional exam requirements/recommendations for international students: Required—TOEFL.

Johns Hopkins University, School of Education, Baltimore, MD 21218. Offers M Ed, MAT, MS, Ed D, PhD, Advanced Certificate, Graduate Certificate, Post-Master's Certificate. *Accreditation:* NCATE. *Program availability:* Part-time, evening/weekend, 100% online, blended/hybrid learning. *Degree requirements:* For master's, comprehensive exam (for some programs), portfolio, capstone project and/or internship; PRAXIS II (subject area assessments) for initial teacher preparation programs that lead to licensure; for doctorate, comprehensive exam, thesis/dissertation. *Entrance requirements:* For master's, GRE, (for full-time programs only); PRAXIS I/core or state-approved alternative (for initial teacher preparation programs that lead to licensure), minimum of bachelor's degree from regionally- or nationally-accredited institution; minimum GPA of 3.0 in all previous programs of study; official transcripts from all post-secondary institutions attended; essay; curriculum vitae/resume; letters of recommendation (3 for full-time programs, 2 for part-time programs); dispositions survey; for doctorate, GRE (for PhD only), master's degree from regionally- or nationally-accredited institution; minimum GPA of 3.0 in previous undergraduate and graduate studies (for Ed D only); official transcripts from all post-secondary institutions attended; three letters of recommendation; curriculum vitae/resume; personal statement; dispositions survey; for other advanced degree, minimum of bachelor's degree from regionally- or nationally-accredited institution (master's degree for some programs); minimum GPA of 3.0 in all previous programs of study; official transcripts from all post-secondary institutions attended; essay; curriculum vitae/resume; two letters of recommendation; dispositions survey. Additional exam requirements/recommendations for international students: Required—TOEFL (minimum score 600 paper-based; 100 iBT), IELTS (minimum score 7). Electronic applications accepted. *Expenses:* Contact institution. *Faculty research:* Comprehensive school reform, dropout prevention, evidence-based decision making in education, neuro-education, entrepreneurial leadership.

Johnson & Wales University, Graduate Studies, MAT Program in Teacher Education, Providence, RI 02903-3703. Offers business education and secondary special education (MAT); culinary arts education (MAT); elementary education and elementary special education (MAT). *Program availability:* Part-time, evening/weekend. *Entrance requirements:* For master's, MAT, minimum GPA of 2.75. Additional exam requirements/recommendations for international students: Required—TOEFL (minimum score 550 paper-based) or IELTS (recommended). *Application deadline:* For fall admission, 8/21 priority date for domestic students, 6/15 priority date for international students; for winter admission, 11/15 priority date for domestic students, 10/1 priority date for international students. Applications are processed on a rolling basis. Application fee: $0. *Expenses: Tuition:* Full-time $12,636; part-time $702 per credit hour. *Financial support:* Unspecified assistantships available. Financial award application deadline: 5/1. *Faculty research:* Secondary education, student teaching, educational reform, evaluation procedures. *Unit head:* Karen Swoboda, Director, 401-598-1922, Fax: 401-598-1125. *Application contact:* Graduate School Admissions, 401-598-1015, Fax: 401-598-1286, E-mail: gradadm@jwu.edu.

Johnson & Wales University, Graduate Studies, M Ed Program in Teaching and Learning, Providence, RI 02903-3703. Offers M Ed. *Program availability:* Evening/weekend. *Entrance requirements:* For master's, bachelor's degree with minimum GPA of 2.75 from accredited institution of higher education, valid teaching license. Additional exam requirements/recommendations for international students: Required—TOEFL (minimum score 550 paper-based, 80 iBT) or Michigan English Language Assessment Battery (minimum score 77). *Expenses: Tuition:* Full-time $12,636; part-time $702 per credit hour. *Unit head:* Karen Swoboda, Director of Teacher Education, 401-598-5139, Fax: 401-598-1125. *Application contact:* Graduate School Admissions, 401-598-1015, Fax: 401-598-1286, E-mail: gradadm@jwu.edu. Website: https://www.jwu.edu/academics/programs-by-campus/providence-programs/teaching-and-learning-med.html

Johnson University, Graduate and Professional Programs, Knoxville, TN 37998-1001. Offers biblical interpretation (Graduate Certificate); business administration (MBA); Christian ministries (Graduate Certificate); clinical mental health counseling (MA); educational technology (MA); intercultural studies (MA); leadership (MBA); leadership studies (PhD); New Testament (MA); nonprofit management (MBA); school counseling (MA); spiritual formation and leadership (Graduate Certificate); strategic ministry (MA); teacher education (MA). *Program availability:* Part-time, evening/weekend, 100% online, blended/hybrid learning. *Degree requirements:* For master's, variable foreign language requirement, comprehensive exam, thesis (for some programs), internships; for doctorate, variable foreign language requirement, comprehensive exam, thesis/dissertation, internships. *Entrance requirements:* For master's, PRAXIS (for MA in teacher education); MAT (for counseling); GRE or GMAT (for MBA), interview, 3 references, transcripts, essay, minimum GPA of 2.5 or 3.0 (depending on program); for doctorate, GRE or MAT (taken not less than 5 years prior), interview, 3 references, transcripts, essay, minimum GPA of 3.0; for Graduate Certificate, interview, 3 references, transcripts, essay, minimum GPA of 3.0. Additional exam requirements/recommendations for international students: Required—TOEFL (minimum score 527 paper-based; 71 iBT). Electronic applications accepted. *Expenses:* Contact institution.

Kansas State University, Graduate School, College of Education, Manhattan, KS 66506. Offers MS, Ed D, PhD, Certificate. *Accreditation:* NCATE. *Program availability:* Part-time, evening/weekend, online learning. Terminal master's awarded for partial completion of doctoral program. *Degree requirements:* For master's, thesis or alternative, oral or comprehensive exam; for doctorate, thesis/dissertation, residency. *Entrance requirements:* For master's and doctorate, GRE or MAT. Additional exam requirements/recommendations for international students: Required—GRE General Test or TOEFL. Electronic applications accepted. *Faculty research:* Teacher preparation, program evaluation, science education, ESL-bilingual education, rural issues in education.

Kean University, College of Education, Union, NJ 07083. Offers MA, MS. *Accreditation:* NCATE. *Program availability:* Part-time. *Faculty:* 43 full-time (26 women). *Students:* 27 full-time (13 women), 127 part-time (107 women); includes 60 minority (12 Black or African American, non-Hispanic/Latino; 14 Asian, non-Hispanic/Latino; 34 Hispanic/Latino), 2 international. Average age 33. 55 applicants, 98% accepted, 41 enrolled. In 2017, 66 master's awarded. *Degree requirements:* For master's, comprehensive exam, thesis, practicum, portfolio, field experience. *Entrance requirements:* Additional exam requirements/recommendations for international students: Required—TOEFL (minimum score 550 paper-based; 79 iBT), IELTS (minimum score 6.5). *Application deadline:* For

fall admission, 6/30 for domestic and international students; for spring admission, 12/1 for domestic and international students. Applications are processed on a rolling basis. Application fee: $75. Electronic applications accepted. *Expenses:* Tuition, state resident: full-time $13,419; part-time $653 per credit. Tuition, nonresident: full-time $18,188; part-time $801 per credit. *Required fees:* $3382; $154 per credit. Tuition and fees vary according to course level, course load, degree level and program. *Financial support:* Scholarships/grants and unspecified assistantships available. Financial award applicants required to submit FAFSA. *Unit head:* Dr. Anthony Pitmann, Acting Dean, 908-737-3750, Fax: 908-737-3760, E-mail: polirsts@kean.edu. *Application contact:* Brittany Gerstenhaber, Admissions Counselor, 908-737-7100, E-mail: gradadmissions@kean.edu.
Website: http://www.kean.edu/KU/College-of-Education

Keene State College, School of Professional and Graduate Studies, Keene, NH 03435. Offers curriculum and instruction (M Ed); education leadership (PMC); educational leadership (M Ed); school counselor (M Ed, PMC); special education (M Ed). *Accreditation:* NCATE. *Program availability:* Part-time, evening/weekend. *Faculty:* 6 full-time (3 women), 7 part-time/adjunct (2 women). *Students:* 20 full-time (14 women), 42 part-time (20 women); includes 2 minority (1 Black or African American, non-Hispanic/Latino; 1 Asian, non-Hispanic/Latino), 1 international. Average age 31. 33 applicants, 58% accepted, 17 enrolled. In 2017, 39 master's awarded. *Degree requirements:* For master's, thesis (for some programs). *Entrance requirements:* For master's, PRAXIS I, 3 references; official transcripts; minimum GPA of 2.5; interview; essay; teacher/educator certificate; work/internship experience. Additional exam requirements/recommendations for international students: Required—TOEFL (minimum score 550 paper-based; 61 iBT). *Application deadline:* For fall admission, 4/1 for domestic and international students; for spring admission, 11/1 for domestic and international students; for summer admission, 3/1 for domestic and international students. Applications are processed on a rolling basis. Application fee: $50. Electronic applications accepted. *Expenses:* Tuition, state resident: full-time $9360; part-time $520 per credit. Tuition, nonresident: full-time $10,260; part-time $570 per credit. *Required fees:* $1908; $106 per credit. Tuition and fees vary according to course load. *Financial support:* In 2017–18, 9 students received support. Career-related internships or fieldwork, Federal Work-Study, institutionally sponsored loans, scholarships/grants, and unspecified assistantships available. Support available to part-time students. Financial award application deadline: 3/1; financial award applicants required to submit FAFSA. *Unit head:* Dr. Karrie Kalich, Dean of Professional and Graduate Studies, 603-358-2885, E-mail: kkalich@keene.edu. *Application contact:* Carl Ditkoff, Graduate Program Assistant, 603-358-2497, E-mail: kscgraduatestudies@keene.edu.
Website: http://www.keene.edu/academics/graduate/

Keiser University, Master of Science in Education Program, Fort Lauderdale, FL 33309. Offers allied health teaching and leadership (MS Ed); career college administration (MS Ed); leadership (MS Ed); online teaching and learning (MS Ed); teaching and learning (MS Ed). *Program availability:* Part-time, online learning. *Unit head:* Brian Keintz, Chair of Graduate Programs.
Website: http://www.keiseruniversity.edu/graduateschool/

Kennesaw State University, Leland and Clarice C. Bagwell College of Education, Kennesaw, GA 30144. Offers M Ed, MAT, Ed D, Ed S. *Accreditation:* NCATE. *Program availability:* Part-time. *Degree requirements:* For master's, thesis or alternative. *Entrance requirements:* For master's, GRE General Test, minimum GPA of 2.75, renewable teaching certificate. Additional exam requirements/recommendations for international students: Required—TOEFL (minimum score 550 paper-based; 80 iBT), IELTS (minimum score 6.5). Electronic applications accepted.

Kent State University, College of Education, Health and Human Services, Kent, OH 44242-0001. Offers M Ed, MA, MAT, MS, Au D, PhD, Ed S. *Accreditation:* NCATE. *Program availability:* Part-time, evening/weekend, online learning. *Degree requirements:* For master's, thesis (for some programs); for doctorate, comprehensive exam, thesis/dissertation. *Entrance requirements:* For doctorate and Ed S, GRE General Test. Additional exam requirements/recommendations for international students: Required—TOEFL (minimum score 550 paper-based; 80 iBT). Electronic applications accepted. *Expenses:* Tuition, state resident: full-time $11,310; part-time $515 per credit hour. Tuition, nonresident: full-time $20,396; part-time $928 per credit hour. *International tuition:* $18,544 full-time.

Kent State University at Stark, Graduate School of Education, Health and Human Services, Canton, OH 44720-7599. Offers curriculum and instruction studies (M Ed, MA).

King's College, Program in Education, Wilkes-Barre, PA 18711-0801. Offers M Ed. *Accreditation:* NCATE. *Program availability:* Part-time, evening/weekend. *Degree requirements:* For master's, thesis. *Entrance requirements:* Additional exam requirements/recommendations for international students: Required—TOEFL (minimum score 600 paper-based).

Kutztown University of Pennsylvania, College of Education, Kutztown, PA 19530-0730. Offers M Ed, MA, MLS, MS, Ed D. *Accreditation:* NCATE. *Program availability:* Part-time, evening/weekend, 100% online, blended/hybrid learning. *Faculty:* 33 full-time (28 women), 3 part-time/adjunct (0 women). *Students:* 172 full-time (134 women), 366 part-time (293 women); includes 78 minority (30 Black or African American, non-Hispanic/Latino; 5 Asian, non-Hispanic/Latino; 35 Hispanic/Latino; 8 Two or more races, non-Hispanic/Latino), 2 international. Average age 30. 413 applicants, 85% accepted, 172 enrolled. In 2017, 147 master's awarded. *Degree requirements:* For master's, comprehensive exam; for doctorate, thesis/dissertation. *Entrance requirements:* For master's, GRE; for doctorate, master's (or specialist) degree in education or related field from regionally-accredited institution of higher education with minimum graduate GPA of 3.25, significant educational experience, full- or part-time employment in educational setting (preferred), candidate statement, 3-5 letters of recommendation. Additional exam requirements/recommendations for international students: Required—TOEFL (minimum score 550 paper-based, 79 iBT), IELTS (minimum score 6.5), or PTE (minimum score 53). *Application deadline:* For fall admission, 8/1 for domestic and international students; for spring admission, 12/1 for domestic and international students. Application fee: $35. Electronic applications accepted. *Expenses:* Tuition, state resident: part-time $500 per credit. Tuition, nonresident: part-time $750 per credit. *Required fees:* $115 per credit. One-time fee: $50 part-time. Tuition and fees vary according to degree level. *Financial support:* Career-related internships or fieldwork, Federal Work-Study, and unspecified assistantships available. Financial award application deadline: 3/1; financial award applicants required to submit FAFSA. *Unit head:* Dr. Kenneth Teitelbaum, Dean, 610-683-4253, Fax: 610-683-4255, E-mail: teitelba@kutztown.edu.
Website: http://www.kutztown.edu/Education

LaGrange College, Graduate Programs, Department of Education, LaGrange, GA 30240-2999. Offers curriculum and instruction (M Ed, Ed S); middle grades (MAT); secondary education (MAT). *Program availability:* Part-time, evening/weekend. *Degree requirements:* For master's, comprehensive exam. *Entrance requirements:* For master's, GRE, MAT, minimum GPA of 2.5. Additional exam requirements/recommendations for international students: Required—TOEFL (minimum score 550 paper-based).

Lake Erie College, School of Education and Professional Studies, Painesville, OH 44077-3389. Offers M Ed. *Accreditation:* TEAC. *Program availability:* Part-time, evening/weekend. *Degree requirements:* For master's, comprehensive exam (for some programs), thesis optional, applied research project. *Entrance requirements:* For master's, GRE General Test (minimum score of 440 verbal or 500 quantitative) or minimum GPA of 2.75, bachelor's degree from accredited 4-year institution; references; essay. Additional exam requirements/recommendations for international students: Required—TOEFL (minimum score 550 paper-based; 79 iBT), IELTS (minimum score 6), STEP Eiken 1st and pre-1st grade level (for Japanese students). Electronic applications accepted. Application fee is waived when completed online. *Expenses:* Contact institution.

Lake Forest College, Master of Arts in Teaching Program, Lake Forest, IL 60045. Offers elementary education (MAT); K-12 French (MAT); K-12 music (MAT); K-12 Spanish (MAT); K-12 visual art (MAT); secondary biology (MAT); secondary chemistry (MAT); secondary English (MAT); secondary history (MAT); secondary mathematics (MAT). *Degree requirements:* For master's, comprehensive exam, portfolio. *Entrance requirements:* For master's, GRE.

Lakehead University, Graduate Studies, Faculty of Education, Thunder Bay, ON P7B 5E1, Canada. Offers educational studies (PhD); gerontology (M Ed); women's studies (M Ed). *Program availability:* Part-time, evening/weekend. *Degree requirements:* For master's, project or thesis. *Entrance requirements:* For master's, minimum B average. Additional exam requirements/recommendations for international students: Required—TOEFL. *Faculty research:* Art education, AIDS education, language arts education, gerontology, women's studies.

Lakeland University, Graduate Studies Division, Program in Education, Plymouth, WI 53073. Offers M Ed. *Accreditation:* TEAC. *Degree requirements:* For master's, thesis. *Expenses:* Contact institution.

Lamar University, College of Graduate Studies, College of Education and Human Development, Beaumont, TX 77701. Offers M Ed, MS, Ed D, Certificate. *Accreditation:* NCATE. *Program availability:* Part-time, evening/weekend, online learning. *Faculty:* 76 full-time (54 women), 45 part-time/adjunct (33 women). *Students:* 74 full-time (46 women), 3,195 part-time (2,526 women); includes 1,404 minority (662 Black or African American, non-Hispanic/Latino; 16 American Indian or Alaska Native, non-Hispanic/Latino; 43 Asian, non-Hispanic/Latino; 653 Hispanic/Latino; 2 Native Hawaiian or other Pacific Islander, non-Hispanic/Latino; 28 Two or more races, non-Hispanic/Latino), 18 international. Average age 37. 3,498 applicants, 80% accepted, 564 enrolled. In 2017, 1,484 master's, 82 doctorates, 68 other advanced degrees awarded. *Degree requirements:* For master's, comprehensive exam, thesis optional; for doctorate, comprehensive exam, thesis/dissertation. *Entrance requirements:* For master's, GRE General Test, minimum GPA of 2.5; for doctorate, GRE, interview. Additional exam requirements/recommendations for international students: Required—TOEFL (minimum score 550 paper-based; 79 iBT), IELTS (minimum score 6.5). *Application deadline:* For fall admission, 8/10 for domestic students, 7/1 for international students; for spring admission, 1/5 for domestic students, 12/1 for international students. Applications are processed on a rolling basis. Application fee: $25 ($50 for international students). Electronic applications accepted. *Expenses:* Contact institution. *Financial support:* Fellowships, research assistantships, teaching assistantships, career-related internships or fieldwork, Federal Work-Study, institutionally sponsored loans, and scholarships/grants available. Support available to part-time students. Financial award application deadline: 4/1; financial award applicants required to submit FAFSA. *Faculty research:* School dropouts, suicide prevention in public school students, school climate and gifted performance, teacher evaluation. *Unit head:* Dr. Robert Spina, Dean, 409-880-8661. *Application contact:* Deidre Mayer, Interim Director, Admissions and Academic Services, 409-880-8888, Fax: 409-880-7419, E-mail: gradmissions@lamar.edu.
Website: http://education.lamar.edu

Lander University, Graduate Studies, Greenwood, SC 29649-2099. Offers clinical nurse leader (MSN); emergency management (MS); Montessori education (M Ed); teaching and learning (M Ed). *Accreditation:* NCATE. *Program availability:* Part-time, online learning. *Degree requirements:* For master's, comprehensive exam, thesis or alternative. *Entrance requirements:* For master's, GRE General Test. Additional exam requirements/recommendations for international students: Required—TOEFL (minimum score 550 paper-based). Electronic applications accepted.

Langston University, School of Education and Behavioral Sciences, Langston, OK 73050. Offers bilingual/multicultural (M Ed); elementary education (M Ed); English as a second language (M Ed); rehabilitation counseling (M Sc); urban education (M Ed). *Accreditation:* CORE; NCATE (one or more programs are accredited). *Program availability:* Part-time. *Degree requirements:* For master's, comprehensive exam, thesis optional. *Entrance requirements:* For master's, GRE, writing skills test, minimum GPA of 2.5, 3 letters of recommendation. Additional exam requirements/recommendations for international students: Required—TOEFL, TWE. *Faculty research:* Bilingual/multicultural education, financing post-secondary education.

La Salle University, School of Arts and Sciences, Program in Education, Philadelphia, PA 19141-1199. Offers autism spectrum disorders (MA, Certificate); bilingual/bicultural studies (MA); classroom management (MA); dual early childhood and special education (MA); dual middle-level science and math and special education (MA); education (MA); English (MA); English as a second language (Certificate); history (MA); instructional coach (Certificate); instructional leadership (MA); reading specialist (MA, Certificate); secondary education (MA); special education (MA, Certificate). *Program availability:* Part-time, evening/weekend. *Faculty:* 5 full-time (4 women), 8 part-time/adjunct (5 women). *Students:* 2 full-time (1 woman), 110 part-time (81 women); includes 23 minority (11 Black or African American, non-Hispanic/Latino; 1 Asian, non-Hispanic/Latino; 7 Hispanic/Latino; 4 Two or more races, non-Hispanic/Latino). Average age 33. 137 applicants, 70% accepted, 63 enrolled. In 2017, 148 master's awarded. *Degree requirements:* For master's, comprehensive exam. *Entrance requirements:* For master's, MAT or GRE, 2 letters of recommendation; for Certificate, GMAT or GRE, 2 letters of recommendation. Additional exam requirements/recommendations for international students: Required—TOEFL. *Application deadline:* For fall admission, 8/15 priority date for domestic students, 7/15 for international students; for spring admission, 12/15 priority date for domestic students, 11/15 for international students; for summer admission, 4/15 priority date for domestic students, 3/15 for international students. Applications are processed on a rolling basis. Application fee: $35. Electronic applications accepted. Application fee is waived when completed online. *Expenses:* Contact institution. *Financial support:* In 2017–18, 19 students received support. Scholarships/grants available. Support available to part-time students. Financial award application deadline: 8/31; financial award applicants required to submit FAFSA. *Unit head:* Dr. Greer Richardson, Director, 215-951-1806, Fax: 215-951-1843, E-mail: graded@lasalle.edu. *Application contact:* Elizabeth Heenan, Director, Graduate and Adult Enrollment, 215-951-1100, Fax: 215-951-1462, E-mail: heenan@lasalle.edu.
Website: http://www.lasalle.edu/grad-education-programs/

Lasell College, Graduate and Professional Studies in Education, Newton, MA 02466-2709. Offers curriculum, leadership, and inclusion (M Ed); elementary education (M Ed); special education (M Ed), including moderate disabilities; teaching bilingual/English learners with disabilities (Graduate Certificate). *Program availability:* Part-time-only, evening/weekend, blended/hybrid learning. *Faculty:* 3 full-time (all women), 5 part-time/adjunct (4 women). *Students:* 8 full-time (7 women), 43 part-time (38 women); includes 4 minority (2 Asian, non-Hispanic/Latino; 1 Hispanic/Latino; 1 Two or more races, non-Hispanic/Latino), 1 international. Average age 28. 23 applicants, 74% accepted, 10 enrolled. In 2017, 15 master's awarded. *Degree requirements:* For master's, minimum GPA of 3.0; practicum. *Entrance requirements:* For master's, Massachusetts Tests for Educator Licensure (MTEL) Curriculum and Literacy foundations of reading and writing subtest, one-page personal statement, 2 letters of recommendation, resume, bachelor's degree transcript. Additional exam requirements/recommendations for international students: Required—TOEFL (minimum score 550 paper-based, 79 iBT) or IELTS (minimum score 6). *Application deadline:* For fall admission, 8/31 priority date for domestic students, 6/30 priority date for international students; for spring admission, 12/31 priority date for domestic students, 10/31 priority date for international students. Applications are processed on a rolling basis. Electronic applications accepted. *Expenses:* $600 per credit. *Financial support:* Federal Work-Study, scholarships/grants, and tuition discounts available. Support available to part-time students. Financial award application deadline: 8/31; financial award applicants required to submit FAFSA. *Faculty research:* Inclusion, English language learners, literacy, and urban education; teacher inquiry; universal design for learning, deaf-blindness, and visual impairments; social and emotional learning; educational law, applied behavior analysis, and classroom management. *Unit head:* Eric Turner, Vice President of Graduate and Professional Studies, 617-243-2071, Fax: 617-243-2450, E-mail: gradinfo@lasell.edu. *Application contact:* Adrienne Franciosi, Director of Graduate Enrollment, 617-243-2214, Fax: 617-243-2450, E-mail: gradinfo@lasell.edu.
Website: http://www.lasell.edu/academics/graduate-and-professional-studies/programs-of-study/master-of-education.html

La Sierra University, School of Education, Riverside, CA 92505. Offers MA, MAT, Ed D, Ed S. *Program availability:* Part-time, evening/weekend. Terminal master's awarded for partial completion of doctoral program. *Degree requirements:* For doctorate, thesis/dissertation; for Ed S, thesis optional. *Entrance requirements:* For master's, minimum GPA of 3.0; for doctorate, GRE General Test, GRE Subject Test, minimum GPA of 3.3; for Ed S, minimum GPA of 3.3.

Lee University, Program in Education, Cleveland, TN 37320-3450. Offers art (MAT); curriculum and instruction (M Ed, Ed S); early childhood (MAT); educational leadership (M Ed, Ed S); elementary education (MAT); English and math (MAT); English and science (MAT); English and social studies (MAT); higher education administration (MS); history (MAT); history and economics (MAT); math and science (MAT); math and social studies (MAT); middle grades (MAT); science and social studies (MASW); secondary education (MAT); Spanish (MAT); special education (M Ed, MAT); TESOL (MAT). *Accreditation:* NCATE. *Program availability:* Part-time. *Faculty:* 15 full-time (7 women), 8 part-time/adjunct (3 women). *Students:* 28 full-time (21 women), 77 part-time (48 women); includes 12 minority (7 Black or African American, non-Hispanic/Latino; 2 Hispanic/Latino; 3 Two or more races, non-Hispanic/Latino), 1 international. Average age 31. 35 applicants, 83% accepted, 22 enrolled. In 2017, 54 master's, 4 other advanced degrees awarded. *Degree requirements:* For master's, variable foreign language requirement, thesis optional, internship. *Entrance requirements:* For master's, MAT or GRE General Test, minimum undergraduate GPA of 2.75, 3 letters of recommendation, interview, writing sample, official transcripts, background check; for Ed S, minimum undergraduate and master's GPA of 2.75, official transcripts for undergraduate and master's degrees. Additional exam requirements/recommendations for international students: Required—TOEFL (minimum score 61 iBT). *Application deadline:* For fall admission, 6/1 priority date for domestic and international students; for spring admission, 11/1 priority date for domestic and international students; for summer admission, 4/1 priority date for domestic and international students. Applications are processed on a rolling basis. Application fee: $25. Electronic applications accepted. *Expenses: Tuition:* Full-time $12,780; part-time $710 per credit hour. *Required fees:* $60; $60 per term. Tuition and fees vary according to program. *Financial support:* In 2017–18, 32 students received support. Career-related internships or fieldwork, Federal Work-Study, institutionally sponsored loans, scholarships/grants, and unspecified assistantships available. Financial award application deadline: 3/1; financial award applicants required to submit FAFSA. *Unit head:* Dr. William Kamm, Director, 423-614-8544, E-mail: wkamm@leeuniversity.edu. *Application contact:* Crystal Keeter, Graduate Education Secretary, 423-614-8544, E-mail: ckeeter@leeuniversity.edu.
Website: http://www.leeuniversity.edu/academics/graduate/education

Lehigh University, College of Education, Bethlehem, PA 18015. Offers M Ed, MA, MS, Ed D, PhD, Certificate, Ed S, Graduate Certificate, M Ed/MA. *Program availability:* Part-time, evening/weekend, online only, 100% online, blended/hybrid learning. *Faculty:* 34 full-time (24 women), 27 part-time/adjunct (17 women). *Students:* 181 full-time (155 women), 267 part-time (186 women); includes 54 minority (12 Black or African American, non-Hispanic/Latino; 13 Asian, non-Hispanic/Latino; 27 Hispanic/Latino; 1 Native Hawaiian or other Pacific Islander, non-Hispanic/Latino; 1 Two or more races, non-Hispanic/Latino), 48 international. Average age 31. 468 applicants, 52% accepted, 79 enrolled. In 2017, 148 master's, 15 doctorates, 9 other advanced degrees awarded. Terminal master's awarded for partial completion of doctoral program. *Degree requirements:* For master's, thesis (for some programs), internship; for doctorate, comprehensive exam, thesis/dissertation, internship. *Entrance requirements:* For master's, essay, transcripts, 2 recommendation letters; for doctorate, GRE and/or MAT, essay, transcripts, 2 recommendation letters. Additional exam requirements/recommendations for international students: Required—TOEFL (minimum score 600 paper-based, 93 iBT) or IELTS (6.5). *Application deadline:* For fall admission, 1/1 for domestic and international students; for spring admission, 11/1 for domestic and international students; for summer admission, 5/1 for domestic and international students. Applications are processed on a rolling basis. Application fee: $65. Electronic applications accepted. *Expenses:* $565 per credit. *Financial support:* In 2017–18, 133 students received support, including 4 fellowships with tuition reimbursements available (averaging $24,238 per year), 57 research assistantships with full and partial tuition reimbursements available (averaging $13,229 per year); unspecified assistantships also available. Financial award application deadline: 3/1. *Faculty research:* Urban educational leadership, special education, instructional technology, school and counseling psychology, international education. *Unit head:* Dr. Gary M. Sasso, Dean, 610-758-3221, Fax: 610-758-6223, E-mail: gary.sasso@lehigh.edu. *Application contact:* Donna M. Johnson, Manager of Admissions and Recruitment, 610-758-3231, Fax: 610-758-6223, E-mail: dmj4@lehigh.edu.
Website: https://ed.lehigh.edu

Lehman College of the City University of New York, School of Education, Bronx, NY 10468-1589. Offers MA, MS Ed. *Accreditation:* NCATE. *Program availability:* Part-time, evening/weekend.

Le Moyne College, Department of Education, Syracuse, NY 13214. Offers adolescent education (MS Ed, MST); adolescent education/special education (MS Ed, MST); adolescent English (MST), including grades 7-12; adolescent English/special education (MST), including grades 7-12; adolescent foreign language (MST), including grades 7-

Education—General

12; adolescent history (MST), including grades 7-12; childhood education (MS Ed); childhood education/special education (MS Ed); elementary education (MS Ed); general education (MS Ed); inclusive childhood education (MST); literacy education (MS Ed), including birth to grade 6, grades 5-12; school building leader (MS Ed); school building leadership (CAS); school district business leader (MS Ed, CAS); school district leader (MS Ed); school district leadership (CAS); secondary education (MS Ed); special education (MS Ed); teaching English to speakers of other languages (MS Ed); urban studies (MS Ed). *Accreditation:* TEAC. *Program availability:* Part-time, evening/weekend. *Faculty:* 7 full-time (5 women), 20 part-time/adjunct (12 women). *Students:* 30 full-time (19 women), 126 part-time (93 women); includes 15 minority (7 Black or African American, non-Hispanic/Latino; 1 American Indian or Alaska Native, non-Hispanic/Latino; 1 Asian, non-Hispanic/Latino; 6 Hispanic/Latino), 4 international. Average age 29. 139 applicants, 65% accepted, 76 enrolled. In 2017, 82 master's, 43 CASs awarded. *Degree requirements:* For master's, thesis. *Entrance requirements:* For master's, bachelor's degree with minimum undergraduate GPA of 3.0, 2 letters of recommendation, transcripts. Additional exam requirements/recommendations for international students: Required—TOEFL (minimum score 550 paper-based; 79 iBT); Recommended—IELTS (minimum score 6.5). *Application deadline:* For fall admission, 4/1 priority date for domestic and international students; for spring admission, 10/1 priority date for domestic and international students; for summer admission, 3/1 priority date for domestic and international students. Applications are processed on a rolling basis. Application fee: $50. Electronic applications accepted. *Expenses:* $700 per credit hour. *Financial support:* In 2017–18, 30 students received support. Career-related internships or fieldwork, scholarships/grants, and health care benefits available. Support available to part-time students. Financial award applicants required to submit FAFSA. *Faculty research:* Minority teachers, special education, multiculturalism, literacy, technology, media literacy learning, autism, school district organization, service-learning, higher level problem solving, teacher leadership. *Unit head:* Dr. Stephen C. Fleury, Chair, Department of Education, 315-445-4376, Fax: 315-445-4744, E-mail: fleurysc@lemoyne.edu. *Application contact:* Kristen P. Richards, Senior Director of Enrollment Management, 315-445-5444, Fax: 315-445-6092, E-mail: trapaskp@lemoyne.edu.
Website: http://www.lemoyne.edu/education

Lenoir-Rhyne University, Graduate Programs, School of Education, Hickory, NC 28601. Offers MA, MAT, MS. *Accreditation:* NCATE. *Program availability:* Part-time, evening/weekend, online learning. *Degree requirements:* For master's, comprehensive exam, thesis optional. *Entrance requirements:* Additional exam requirements/recommendations for international students: Required—TOEFL. Electronic applications accepted. *Expenses:* Contact institution.

Lesley University, Graduate School of Education, Cambridge, MA 02138-2790. Offers arts, community, and education (M Ed); autism studies (Certificate); curriculum and instruction (M Ed, CAGS); early childhood education (M Ed); ecological teaching and learning (MS); educational studies (PhD), including adult learning, educational leadership, individually designed; elementary education (M Ed); emergent technologies for educators (Certificate); ESLArts: language learning through the arts (M Ed); high school education (M Ed); individually designed (M Ed); integrated teaching through the arts (M Ed); literacy for K-8 classroom teachers (M Ed); mathematics education (M Ed); middle school education (M Ed); moderate disabilities (M Ed); online learning (Certificate); reading (CAGS); science in education (M Ed); severe disabilities (M Ed); special needs (CAGS); specialist teacher of reading (M Ed); teacher of visual art (M Ed); technology in education (M Ed, CAGS). *Accreditation:* TEAC. *Program availability:* Part-time, evening/weekend, online learning. *Degree requirements:* For master's, practicum; for doctorate, thesis/dissertation. *Entrance requirements:* For master's, Massachusetts Tests for Educator Licensure (MTEL), transcripts, statement of purpose, recommendations; interview (for special education); for doctorate, GRE General Test, transcripts, statement of purpose, recommendations, interview, master's degree, resume; for other advanced degree, interview, master's degree. Additional exam requirements/recommendations for international students: Required—TOEFL (minimum score 550 paper-based; 80 iBT). Electronic applications accepted. *Faculty research:* Assessment in literacy, mathematics and science; autism spectrum disorders; instructional technology and online learning; multicultural education and English language learners.

Lewis University, College of Education, Romeoville, IL 60446. Offers M Ed, MA, Ed D. *Accreditation:* NCATE. *Program availability:* Part-time, evening/weekend. *Students:* 59 full-time (41 women), 196 part-time (135 women); includes 70 minority (29 Black or African American, non-Hispanic/Latino; 4 Asian, non-Hispanic/Latino; 34 Hispanic/Latino; 3 Two or more races, non-Hispanic/Latino), 10 international. Average age 34. *Degree requirements:* For master's, thesis optional, departmental qualifying exam; for doctorate, thesis/dissertation. *Entrance requirements:* For master's, writing exam, minimum GPA of 2.75, 2 letters of recommendation, interview. Additional exam requirements/recommendations for international students: Required—TOEFL (minimum score 550 paper-based; 80 iBT), IELTS. *Application deadline:* For fall admission, 5/1 priority date for international students; for spring admission, 11/15 priority date for international students. Applications are processed on a rolling basis. Application fee: $40. Electronic applications accepted. Tuition and fees vary according to program. *Financial support:* Career-related internships or fieldwork, Federal Work-Study, scholarships/grants, and unspecified assistantships available. Financial award application deadline: 5/1; financial award applicants required to submit FAFSA. *Total annual research expenditures:* $34. *Unit head:* Dr. Pamela Jessee, Dean, 815-836-5316, E-mail: jesseepa@lewisu.edu. *Application contact:* Linda Campbell, Graduate Admission Counselor, 815-836-5704, Fax: 815-836-5578, E-mail: campbeli@lewisu.edu.

Liberty University, School of Education, Lynchburg, VA 24515. Offers curriculum and instruction (Ed D, Ed S), including elementary education, middle grades education, secondary education, special education; educational leadership (Ed D); gifted education (Certificate); math specialist (M Ed); middle grades (MAT, Certificate); reading specialist (M Ed); school leadership (Certificate); secondary education (MAT); sport management (MS), including coaching and athletic administration, outdoor adventure sport, sport administration, tourism. *Accreditation:* NCATE. *Program availability:* Part-time, online learning. *Students:* 1,966 full-time (1,428 women), 3,484 part-time (2,528 women); includes 1,323 minority (1,026 Black or African American, non-Hispanic/Latino; 29 American Indian or Alaska Native, non-Hispanic/Latino; 49 Asian, non-Hispanic/Latino; 100 Hispanic/Latino; 9 Native Hawaiian or other Pacific Islander, non-Hispanic/Latino; 110 Two or more races, non-Hispanic/Latino), 58 international. Average age 37. 3,748 applicants, 58% accepted, 1167 enrolled. In 2017, 656 master's, 110 doctorates, 316 other advanced degrees awarded. *Degree requirements:* For doctorate, comprehensive exam, thesis/dissertation. *Entrance requirements:* For master's, GRE General Test or MAT (if taken in or before 1999), 2 letters of recommendation, minimum undergraduate GPA of 3.0, curriculum vitae; for doctorate and other advanced degree, GRE General Test or MAT (if taken before 1999), minimum master's GPA of 3.0, 3 years of teaching experience. Additional exam requirements/recommendations for international students: Required—TOEFL (minimum score 600 paper-based; 100 iBT). *Application deadline:* For fall admission, 6/1 for domestic students; for spring admission, 11/1 for domestic students. Applications are processed on a rolling basis. Application fee: $50. Electronic

applications accepted. *Expenses:* Contact institution. *Financial support:* Federal Work-Study and tuition waivers (partial) available. *Faculty research:* Self-determination, character education, bibliotherapy, learning styles, distance education. *Unit head:* Dr. Heather Schoffstall, Dean, 434-582-2445, Fax: 434-582-2468, E-mail: awgunter@liberty.edu. *Application contact:* Jay Bridge, Director of Graduate Admissions, 800-424-9595, Fax: 800-628-7977, E-mail: gradadmissions@liberty.edu.
Website: http://www.liberty.edu/academics/education/graduate/

Lincoln Memorial University, Carter and Moyers School of Education, Harrogate, TN 37752-1901. Offers administration and supervision (M Ed); counseling and guidance (M Ed); curriculum and instruction (M Ed, Ed D, Ed S); English (M Ed); executive leadership (Ed D); higher education administration (Ed D); human resource development (Ed D); leadership and administration (Ed D). *Program availability:* Part-time, evening/weekend, online learning. *Degree requirements:* For master's, comprehensive exam, thesis optional; for Ed S, comprehensive exam. *Entrance requirements:* For master's, PRAXIS, NTE, GRE, MAT, letters of recommendation; for Ed S, graduate transcripts. Additional exam requirements/recommendations for international students: Recommended—TOEFL. *Faculty research:* Brain compatible teaching and learning; poverty in Appalachia; leadership for change; ethics, moral responsibility and social justice; human and organizational learning.

Lindenwood University, Graduate Programs, School of Education, St. Charles, MO 63301-1695. Offers behavioral analysis (MA); education (MA), including autism spectrum disorders, character education, early intervention in autism and sensory impairment, gifted, technology; educational administration (MA, Ed D, Ed S); English to speakers of other languages (MA); instructional leadership (Ed D, Ed S); library media (MA); professional counseling (MA); school administration (MA, Ed S); school counseling (MA); teaching (MA). *Program availability:* Part-time, evening/weekend, 100% online, blended/hybrid learning. *Faculty:* 47 full-time (31 women), 213 part-time/adjunct (135 women). *Students:* 434 full-time (319 women), 1,292 part-time (989 women); includes 387 minority (313 Black or African American, non-Hispanic/Latino; 9 American Indian or Alaska Native, non-Hispanic/Latino; 13 Asian, non-Hispanic/Latino; 37 Hispanic/Latino; 1 Native Hawaiian or other Pacific Islander, non-Hispanic/Latino; 14 Two or more races, non-Hispanic/Latino), 20 international. Average age 36. 828 applicants, 61% accepted, 378 enrolled. In 2017, 431 master's, 63 doctorates, 94 other advanced degrees awarded. *Degree requirements:* For master's, thesis (for some programs), minimum GPA of 3.0; for doctorate, thesis/dissertation, minimum GPA of 3.0; for Ed S, comprehensive exam, project, minimum GPA of 3.0. *Entrance requirements:* For master's, interview, minimum undergraduate cumulative GPA of 3.0, writing sample, letter of recommendation; for doctorate, GRE, minimum graduate GPA of 3.4, resume, interview, writing sample, 4 letters of recommendation; for Ed S, master's degree in education, relevant work experience. Additional exam requirements/recommendations for international students: Required—TOEFL (minimum score 550 paper-based; 80 iBT); Recommended—IELTS (minimum score 6.5). *Application deadline:* For fall admission, 8/27 priority date for domestic and international students; for spring admission, 1/14 priority date for domestic and international students; for summer admission, 6/4 priority date for domestic and international students. Applications are processed on a rolling basis. Application fee: $30 ($100 for international students). Electronic applications accepted. *Expenses:* Tuition: Full-time $16,300; part-time $460 per credit. *Required fees:* $660; $330 per credit. Tuition and fees vary according to degree level and program. *Financial support:* In 2017–18, 1,615 students received support. Career-related internships or fieldwork, Federal Work-Study, institutionally sponsored loans, scholarships/grants, tuition waivers (partial), and unspecified assistantships available. Financial award application deadline: 6/30; financial award applicants required to submit FAFSA. *Unit head:* Dr. Anthony Scheffler, Dean, School of Education, 636-949-4618, Fax: 636-949-4197, E-mail: ascheffler@lindenwood.edu. *Application contact:* Kara Schilli, Director, Evening and Graduate Admissions, 636-949-4349, Fax: 636-949-4109, E-mail: adultadmissions@lindenwood.edu.
Website: http://www.lindenwood.edu/academic-schools/school-of-education/

Lindenwood University–Belleville, Graduate Programs, Belleville, IL 62226. Offers business administration (MBA); communications (MA), including digital and multimedia, media management, promotions, training and development; counseling (MA); criminal justice administration (MS); education (MA); healthcare administration (MS); human resource management (MS); school administration (MA); teaching (MAT).

Lipscomb University, College of Education, Nashville, TN 37204-3951. Offers applied behavior analysis (MS, Certificate); coaching for learning (M Ed, Certificate, Ed S); educational leadership (M Ed, Ed S); English language learning (M Ed, Ed S); instructional coaching (M Ed, Certificate, Ed S); instructional practice (M Ed); learning organizations and strategic change (Ed D); literacy coaching (Certificate, Ed S); reading specialty (M Ed, Ed S); school counseling (M Ed, Ed S); special education (M Ed); teaching, learning, and leading (M Ed); technology integration (M Ed, Ed S); technology integration specialist (Certificate). *Accreditation:* NCATE. *Program availability:* Part-time, evening/weekend, 100% online. *Faculty:* 21 full-time (14 women), 42 part-time/adjunct (29 women). *Students:* 565 full-time (452 women), 59 part-time (45 women); includes 154 minority (102 Black or African American, non-Hispanic/Latino; 2 American Indian or Alaska Native, non-Hispanic/Latino; 8 Asian, non-Hispanic/Latino; 26 Hispanic/Latino; 16 Two or more races, non-Hispanic/Latino). Average age 32. 395 applicants, 54% accepted, 196 enrolled. In 2017, 162 master's, 30 doctorates, 54 other advanced degrees awarded. *Degree requirements:* For master's, comprehensive exam, portfolio, research project and presentation; for doctorate, practical capstone project in experiential setting. *Entrance requirements:* For master's, MAT (minimum score 31) or GRE General Test (minimum score 294), 2 reference letters, goals statement, writing sample, interview; for doctorate, MAT or GRE General Test, 3 reference letters, artifact of demonstrated academic excellence, written personal statements, interview. Additional exam requirements/recommendations for international students: Required—TOEFL (minimum score 570 paper-based; 80 iBT). *Application deadline:* For fall admission, 8/29 priority date for domestic students; for spring admission, 1/15 priority date for domestic students. Applications are processed on a rolling basis. Application fee: $50 ($75 for international students). Electronic applications accepted. *Expenses:* Contact institution. *Financial support:* Scholarships/grants, unspecified assistantships, and partnerships with local school districts available. Financial award applicants required to submit FAFSA. *Faculty research:* Facilitative learning styles, leadership, student assessment, interactive multimedia inclusion, learning organizations and strategic change. *Unit head:* Dr. Deborah Boyd, Director of Graduate Studies, 615-966-6263, E-mail: deborah.boyd@lipscomb.edu. *Application contact:* Amanda Logsdon, Director of Enrollment and Outreach, 615-966-7199, E-mail: amanda.logsdon@lipscomb.edu.
Website: http://www.lipscomb.edu/education/graduate-programs

Lock Haven University of Pennsylvania, College of Liberal Arts and Education, Lock Haven, PA 17745-2390. Offers alternative education (M Ed); educational leadership (M Ed); teaching and learning (M Ed). *Accreditation:* NCATE. *Program availability:* Part-time, evening/weekend, online learning. *Degree requirements:* For master's, thesis. *Entrance requirements:* For master's, minimum undergraduate GPA of 3.0. Additional exam requirements/recommendations for international students: Required—TOEFL. Electronic applications accepted.

London Metropolitan University, Graduate Programs, London, United Kingdom. Offers applied psychology (M Sc); architecture (MA); biomedical science (M Sc); blood science (M Sc); cancer pharmacology (M Sc); computer networking and cyber security (M Sc); computing and information systems (M Sc); conference interpreting (MA); counter-terrorism studies (M Sc); creative, digital and professional writing (MA); crime, violence and prevention (M Sc); criminology (M Sc); curating contemporary art (MA); data analytics (M Sc); digital media (MA); early childhood studies (MA); education (MA, Ed D); financial services law, regulation and compliance (LL M); food science (M Sc); forensic psychology (M Sc); health and social care management and policy (M Sc); human nutrition (M Sc); human resource management (MA); human rights and international conflict (MA); information technology (M Sc); intelligence and security studies (M Sc); international oil, gas and energy law (LL M); international relations (MA); interpreting (MA); learning and teaching in higher education (MA); legal practice (LL M); media and entertainment law (LL M); organizational and consumer psychology (M Sc); psychological therapy (M Sc); psychology of mental health (M Sc); public health (M Sc); public policy and management (MPA); security studies (M Sc); social work (M Sc); spatial planning and urban design (MA); sports therapy (M Sc); supporting older children and young people with dyslexia (MA); teaching languages (MA), including Arabic, English; translation (MA); woman and child abuse (MA).

Long Island University–LIU Brooklyn, School of Education, Brooklyn, NY 11201-8423. Offers adolescence urban education (MS Ed); applied behavior analysis (Advanced Certificate); bilingual education (Advanced Certificate); bilingual education in urban setting (MS Ed); bilingual school counselor (MS Ed, Advanced Certificate); childhood urban education (MS Ed); childhood/early childhood education (MS Ed); childhood/early childhood urban education (MS Ed); early childhood urban education (MS Ed, Advanced Certificate); educational leadership (Advanced Certificate); marriage and family therapy (MS, Advanced Certificate); mental health counseling (MS, Advanced Certificate); school building district leader (Advanced Certificate); school counselor (MS Ed, Advanced Certificate); school psychologist (MS Ed); teaching students with disabilities (MS Ed); teaching urban children with disabilities (MS Ed); TESOL (MS Ed, Advanced Certificate). *Accreditation:* TEAC. *Program availability:* Part-time, evening/weekend, 100% online. *Faculty:* 14 full-time (12 women), 42 part-time/adjunct (32 women). *Students:* 140 full-time (130 women), 563 part-time (414 women); includes 417 minority (183 Black or African American, non-Hispanic/Latino; 1 American Indian or Alaska Native, non-Hispanic/Latino; 32 Asian, non-Hispanic/Latino; 187 Hispanic/Latino; 14 Two or more races, non-Hispanic/Latino), 10 international. Average age 31. 449 applicants, 82% accepted, 264 enrolled. In 2017, 408 master's, 31 other advanced degrees awarded. *Entrance requirements:* For master's, GRE. Additional exam requirements/recommendations for international students: Required—TOEFL (minimum score 527 paper-based, 75 iBT), IELTS, or PTE. *Application deadline:* Applications are processed on a rolling basis. Application fee: $50. Electronic applications accepted. *Expenses: Tuition:* Full-time $21,618; part-time $1201 per credit. *Required fees:* $1840; $920 per term. Tuition and fees vary according to course load. *Financial support:* In 2017–18, 58 students received support. Career-related internships or fieldwork, Federal Work-Study, scholarships/grants, and unspecified assistantships available. Support available to part-time students. Financial award application deadline: 2/15; financial award applicants required to submit FAFSA. *Faculty research:* Diversity issues in education and mental health care, inclusion - disability studies, sustainability, teacher professional development. *Unit head:* Dean, 718-488-1055, E-mail: bkln-admissions@liu.edu. *Application contact:* Bayu Sutrisno, Graduate Admissions Counselor, 718-488-1011, Fax: 718-780-6110, E-mail: bkln-admissions@liu.edu. Website: http://www.liu.edu/Brooklyn/Academics/School-of-Education

Long Island University–LIU Post, College of Education, Information and Technology, Brookville, NY 11548-1300. Offers adolescence education (MS); adolescence education 7-12 (MS); archives and records management (AC); art education (MS); childhood education (MS); childhood education/literacy B-6 (MS); childhood education/special education (MS); clinical mental health counseling (MS, AC); early childhood education (MS); early childhood education/childhood education (MS); educational leadership (AC); educational technology (MS); information studies (PhD); interdisciplinary educational studies (Ed D); middle childhood education (MS); music education (MS); public library administration (AC); school counselor (MS); special education (MS Ed); speech-language pathology (MA); students with disabilities, 7-12 generalist (AC); TESOL (MA). *Accreditation:* TEAC. *Program availability:* Part-time, 100% online, blended/hybrid learning. *Faculty:* 40 full-time (26 women), 73 part-time/adjunct (38 women). *Students:* 472 full-time (400 women), 696 part-time (543 women); includes 254 minority (93 Black or African American, non-Hispanic/Latino; 46 Asian, non-Hispanic/Latino; 105 Hispanic/Latino; 10 Two or more races, non-Hispanic/Latino), 33 international. Average age 33. 917 applicants, 82% accepted, 357 enrolled. In 2017, 408 master's, 31 other advanced degrees awarded. Terminal master's awarded for partial completion of doctoral program. *Degree requirements:* For master's, variable foreign language requirement, comprehensive exam (for some programs), thesis optional; for doctorate, comprehensive exam, thesis/dissertation. *Entrance requirements:* For master's and AC, GRE (for some programs). Additional exam requirements/recommendations for international students: Required—TOEFL (minimum score 550 paper-based, 75 iBT), IELTS, or PTE. *Application deadline:* Applications are processed on a rolling basis. Application fee: $50. Electronic applications accepted. *Expenses: Tuition:* Full-time $21,618; part-time $1201 per credit. *Required fees:* $1840; $920 per term. Tuition and fees vary according to course load. *Financial support:* In 2017–18, 376 students received support. Career-related internships or fieldwork, Federal Work-Study, institutionally sponsored loans, scholarships/grants, tuition waivers (partial), and unspecified assistantships available. Support available to part-time students. Financial award application deadline: 2/15; financial award applicants required to submit FAFSA. *Faculty research:* Sleep; use of technology to develop executive function by students with disabilities; early childhood literacy development through play; social justice through education; using a structured protocol to discuss Bad News. *Unit head:* Dr. Albert Inserra, Dean, 516-299-2210, E-mail: albert.inserra@liu.edu. *Application contact:* Rita Langdon, Graduate Admissions, 516-299-2900, Fax: 516-299-2137, E-mail: post-enroll@liu.edu. Website: http://liu.edu/CWPost/Academics/College-of-Education-Information-and-Technology

Longwood University, College of Graduate and Professional Studies, College of Education and Human Services, Farmville, VA 23909. Offers education (MS), including algebra and middle school mathematics, counselor education, elementary and middle school mathematics, elementary education, elementary education initial licensure, health and physical education, special education general curriculum, special education initial licensure; reading, literacy and learning (M Ed); school librarianship (M Ed); social work and communication sciences and disorders (MS), including communication sciences and disorders. *Accreditation:* NCATE. *Program availability:* Part-time, evening/weekend. *Degree requirements:* For master's, comprehensive exam (for some programs), thesis optional, professional portfolio, internship, clinical experience, or practicum. *Entrance requirements:* For master's, PRAXIS I (for initial teaching licensure programs); GRE (for some programs), bachelor's degree from regionally-accredited institution, 2 recommendations (3 for some programs), minimum 500-word personal essay, official transcripts, minimum GPA of 2.75, valid teaching license (for some

programs). Additional exam requirements/recommendations for international students: Required—TOEFL (minimum score 570 paper-based), IELTS (minimum score 6.5). Electronic applications accepted. *Expenses:* Contact institution.

Louisiana College, Graduate Programs, Pineville, LA 71359-0001. Offers teaching (MAT).

Louisiana State University and Agricultural & Mechanical College, Graduate School, College of Human Sciences and Education, Baton Rouge, LA 70803. Offers M Ed, MA, MAT, MLIS, MS, MSW, PhD, Ed S. *Accreditation:* NCATE. *Faculty:* 69 full-time (33 women). *Students:* 767 full-time (589 women), 632 part-time (489 women); includes 488 minority (362 Black or African American, non-Hispanic/Latino; 7 American Indian or Alaska Native, non-Hispanic/Latino; 18 Asian, non-Hispanic/Latino; 76 Hispanic/Latino; 1 Native Hawaiian or other Pacific Islander, non-Hispanic/Latino; 24 Two or more races, non-Hispanic/Latino), 33 international. Average age 32. 958 applicants, 61% accepted, 401 enrolled. In 2017, 403 master's, 50 doctorates, 28 other advanced degrees awarded. *Financial support:* In 2017–18, 6 fellowships (averaging $15,183 per year), 14 research assistantships (averaging $19,155 per year), 158 teaching assistantships (averaging $16,233 per year) were awarded. *Total annual research expenditures:* $1.5 million.

Louisiana State University in Shreveport, College of Business, Education, and Human Development, Program in Education, Shreveport, LA 71115-2399. Offers curriculum and instruction (M Ed); leadership (M Ed); leadership studies (Ed D). *Accreditation:* NCATE. *Program availability:* Part-time. *Students:* 35 full-time (22 women), 215 part-time (181 women); includes 76 minority (62 Black or African American, non-Hispanic/Latino; 1 Asian, non-Hispanic/Latino; 10 Hispanic/Latino; 3 Two or more races, non-Hispanic/Latino), 5 international. Average age 36. 270 applicants, 96% accepted, 98 enrolled. In 2017, 59 master's, 3 doctorates awarded. *Degree requirements:* For master's, orally-presented project, 200-hour internship (educational leadership). *Entrance requirements:* For master's, GRE, minimum GPA of 2.5; teacher certification; recommendations and interview (for educational leadership). Additional exam requirements/recommendations for international students: Required—TOEFL (minimum score 550 paper-based; 61 iBT). *Application deadline:* For fall admission, 6/30 for domestic and international students; for spring admission, 11/30 for domestic and international students; for summer admission, 4/30 for domestic and international students. Applications are processed on a rolling basis. Application fee: $20 ($30 for international students). Electronic applications accepted. *Expenses: Tuition,* state resident: full-time $3098; part-time $344 per credit hour. Tuition, nonresident: full-time $9923; part-time $1103 per credit hour. *Required fees:* $384 per semester. Tuition and fees vary according to program. *Financial support:* In 2017–18, 5 research assistantships (averaging $2,150 per year) were awarded. *Unit head:* Dr. Pat Doerr, Coordinator, 318-797-5033, Fax: 318-798-4144, E-mail: pat.doerr@lsus.edu. *Application contact:* Mary Catherine Harvison, Director of Admissions, 318-797-2400, Fax: 318-797-5286, E-mail: mary.harvison@lsus.edu.

Louisiana Tech University, Graduate School, College of Education, Ruston, LA 71272. Offers counseling and guidance (MA), including clinical mental health counseling, human services, orientation and mobility; counseling psychology (PhD); curriculum and instruction (M Ed); cyber education (Graduate Certificate); dynamics of domestic and family violence (Graduate Certificate); early childhood education - PreK-3 (MAT); educational leadership (M Ed, Ed D); elementary education and special education mild/moderate grades 1-5 (MAT); higher education administration (Graduate Certificate); industrial/organizational psychology (MA, PhD); kinesiology (MS); middle school education (MAT), including mathematics; orientation and mobility (Graduate Certificate); rehabilitation teaching for the blind (Graduate Certificate); secondary education (MAT), including agriculture, biology, business, chemistry, English; special education: visually impaired (MAT); teacher leader education (Graduate Certificate); visual impairments - blind education (Graduate Certificate). *Accreditation:* NCATE. *Program availability:* Part-time. *Faculty:* 28 full-time (16 women), 23 part-time/adjunct (22 women). *Students:* 269 full-time (192 women), 194 part-time (150 women); includes 127 minority (94 Black or African American, non-Hispanic/Latino; 2 American Indian or Alaska Native, non-Hispanic/Latino; 6 Asian, non-Hispanic/Latino; 16 Hispanic/Latino; 1 Native Hawaiian or other Pacific Islander, non-Hispanic/Latino; 8 Two or more races, non-Hispanic/Latino), 8 international. Average age 34. 226 applicants, 74% accepted, 60 enrolled. In 2017, 5 master's, 2 doctorates, 1 other advanced degree awarded. *Degree requirements:* For master's, thesis; for doctorate, thesis/dissertation. *Entrance requirements:* For master's and doctorate, GRE General Test. Additional exam requirements/recommendations for international students: Required—TOEFL (minimum score 550 paper-based; 80 iBT), IELTS (minimum score 6.5). *Application deadline:* For fall admission, 9/1 priority date for domestic students, 6/1 for international students; for winter admission, 11/1 priority date for domestic students, 9/1 for international students; for spring admission, 2/1 priority date for domestic students, 12/1 for international students; for summer admission, 5/1 priority date for domestic students, 3/1 for international students. Application fee: $40. Electronic applications accepted. *Expenses: Tuition,* state resident: full-time $5146. Tuition, nonresident: full-time $10,147. *International tuition:* $10,267 full-time. *Required fees:* $2273. *Financial support:* In 2017–18, 40 students received support, including 23 research assistantships (averaging $10,346 per year), 15 teaching assistantships (averaging $6,887 per year); fellowships and career-related internships or fieldwork also available. Financial award application deadline: 2/1. *Faculty research:* Blindness and the best methods for increasing independence for individuals who are blind or visually impaired; educating and investigating factors contributing to improvements in human performance across the lifespan and a reduction in injury rates during training. *Total annual research expenditures:* $2.1 million. *Unit head:* Dr. Don Schillinger, Dean, 318-257-3712, E-mail: dschill@latech.edu. *Application contact:* Dr. Dawn Basinger, Associate Dean of Academic Affairs, 318-257-2977, Fax: 318-257-2379, E-mail: dbasing@latech.edu. Website: http://education.latech.edu/

Loyola Marymount University, School of Education, Los Angeles, CA 90045-2659. Offers MA, Ed D, JD/MA. *Accreditation:* NCATE. *Program availability:* Part-time, evening/weekend. *Faculty:* 35 full-time (24 women), 106 part-time/adjunct (71 women). *Students:* 773 full-time (601 women), 143 part-time (96 women); includes 551 minority (86 Black or African American, non-Hispanic/Latino; 79 Asian, non-Hispanic/Latino; 356 Hispanic/Latino; 2 Native Hawaiian or other Pacific Islander, non-Hispanic/Latino; 28 Two or more races, non-Hispanic/Latino), 64 international. Average age 29. 472 applicants, 73% accepted, 272 enrolled. In 2017, 376 master's, 14 doctorates awarded. *Degree requirements:* For doctorate, thesis/dissertation. *Entrance requirements:* For master's, official transcripts, letters of recommendation. Additional exam requirements/recommendations for international students: Required—TOEFL, IELTS. Application fee: $50. Electronic applications accepted. *Financial support:* Research assistantships, teaching assistantships, institutionally sponsored loans, scholarships/grants, and unspecified assistantships available. Support available to part-time students. Financial award application deadline: 4/15; financial award applicants required to submit FAFSA. *Unit head:* Dr. Shane P. Martin, Dean, School of Education, 310-338-7301, E-mail: smartin@lmu.edu. *Application contact:* Chake H. Kouyoumjian, Associate Dean of Graduate Studies, 310-338-2721, Fax: 310-338-6086, E-mail: graduateinfo@lmu.edu. Website: http://soe.lmu.edu

Education—General

Loyola University Chicago, School of Education, Chicago, IL 60660. Offers M Ed, MA, Ed D, PhD, Certificate, Ed S. *Accreditation:* NCATE. *Program availability:* Part-time, evening/weekend. *Faculty:* 49 full-time (32 women), 69 part-time/adjunct (50 women). *Students:* 386 full-time (297 women), 210 part-time (167 women); includes 221 minority (94 Black or African American, non-Hispanic/Latino; 1 American Indian or Alaska Native, non-Hispanic/Latino; 31 Asian, non-Hispanic/Latino; 78 Hispanic/Latino; 1 Native Hawaiian or other Pacific Islander, non-Hispanic/Latino; 16 Two or more races, non-Hispanic/Latino), 22 international. Average age 32. 842 applicants, 56% accepted, 198 enrolled. In 2017, 203 master's, 40 doctorates, 1 other advanced degree awarded. *Degree requirements:* For master's, comprehensive exam (for some programs), thesis (for some programs); for doctorate, comprehensive exam, thesis/dissertation; for other advanced degree, comprehensive exam. *Entrance requirements:* For master's, minimum GPA of 3.0, 3 letters of recommendation, resume, transcripts; for doctorate, GRE, interview, minimum GPA of 3.0, 3 letters of recommendation, resume; for other advanced degree, GRE, interview, minimum GPA of 3.0, letters of recommendation, resume, transcripts. Additional exam requirements/recommendations for international students: Required—TOEFL (minimum score 550 paper-based; 79 iBT). Application fee: $50. Electronic applications accepted. Application fee is waived when completed online. *Expenses:* $949 per semester hour, $2,847 per course, $8,541-$11,388 full-time semester tuition; $432 per semester fees, $225 additional fees (first semester only). *Financial support:* In 2017–18, 293 students received support, including 120 fellowships with partial tuition reimbursements available, 80 research assistantships with full tuition reimbursements available (averaging $14,000 per year), 93 teaching assistantships (averaging $4,000 per year); career-related internships or fieldwork, Federal Work-Study, institutionally sponsored loans, scholarships/grants, traineeships, health care benefits, and unspecified assistantships also available. Support available to part-time students. Financial award application deadline: 2/1; financial award applicants required to submit FAFSA. *Faculty research:* Policy studies, historical foundations, teacher education, research methodologies, comparative education. *Total annual research expenditures:* $2.2 million. *Unit head:* Dr. David Slavsky, Interim Dean, 312-915-6992, Fax: 312-915-6980, E-mail: dslavsk@luc.edu. *Application contact:* Mirtza Campbell, Information Contact, 312-915-8907, E-mail: mcampbell11@luc.edu.
Website: http://www.luc.edu/education

Loyola University Maryland, Graduate Programs, School of Education, Baltimore, MD 21210-2699. Offers M Ed, MA, MAT, CAS. *Accreditation:* NCATE. *Program availability:* Part-time, evening/weekend. *Faculty:* 36 full-time (27 women), 23 part-time/adjunct (15 women). *Students:* 104 full-time (89 women), 653 part-time (538 women); includes 269 minority (197 Black or African American, non-Hispanic/Latino; 15 Asian, non-Hispanic/Latino; 37 Hispanic/Latino; 2 Native Hawaiian or other Pacific Islander, non-Hispanic/Latino; 18 Two or more races, non-Hispanic/Latino), 6 international. Average age 32. In 2017, 333 master's, 3 other advanced degrees awarded. *Degree requirements:* For master's, thesis. *Entrance requirements:* Additional exam requirements/recommendations for international students: Required—TOEFL (minimum score 550 paper-based), IELTS (minimum score 7). *Application deadline:* For fall admission, 6/15 for domestic students. Applications are processed on a rolling basis. Application fee: $60. Electronic applications accepted. *Expenses:* Contact institution. *Financial support:* Research assistantships, scholarships/grants, and unspecified assistantships available. Financial award application deadline: 4/15; financial award applicants required to submit FAFSA. *Unit head:* Dr. Joshua Smith, Dean, School of Education, 410-617-5343, E-mail: jssmith2@loyola.edu. *Application contact:* Office of Graduate Admission, 410-617-5020, E-mail: graduate@loyola.edu.
Website: http://www.loyola.edu/education/

Loyola University New Orleans, College of Arts and Sciences, Master of Arts in Teaching Program, New Orleans, LA 70118-6195. Offers MAT. *Program availability:* Part-time. *Faculty:* 1 (woman) full-time, 1 (woman) part-time/adjunct. *Students:* 8 full-time (4 women), 12 part-time (8 women); includes 7 minority (3 Black or African American, non-Hispanic/Latino; 2 American Indian or Alaska Native, non-Hispanic/Latino; 1 Asian, non-Hispanic/Latino; 1 Hispanic/Latino). Average age 32. 10 applicants, 100% accepted, 10 enrolled. *Application deadline:* Applications are processed on a rolling basis. Electronic applications accepted. *Expenses:* $409 per credit hour. *Financial support:* Applicants required to submit FAFSA. *Unit head:* Dr. Glenda Hembree, Office of Teacher Education, 504-865-3081, E-mail: gghembre@loyno.edu. *Application contact:* 800-4LOYOLA, Fax: 504-865-3383, E-mail: admit@loyno.edu.
Website: http://cas.loyno.edu/teacher-education/mat

Lynn University, Donald E. and Helen L. Ross College of Education, Boca Raton, FL 33431-5598. Offers educational leadership (M Ed, Ed D), including K-12 (Ed D), school administration K-12 (M Ed); exceptional student education (M Ed), including school administration K-12. *Program availability:* Part-time, evening/weekend, online learning. *Faculty:* 6 full-time (4 women), 4 part-time/adjunct (3 women). *Students:* 31 full-time (23 women), 62 part-time (42 women); includes 32 minority (20 Black or African American, non-Hispanic/Latino; 1 American Indian or Alaska Native, non-Hispanic/Latino; 10 Hispanic/Latino; 1 Two or more races, non-Hispanic/Latino), 3 international. Average age 36. 46 applicants, 78% accepted, 30 enrolled. In 2017, 24 master's, 22 doctorates awarded. *Degree requirements:* For master's, comprehensive exam, thesis (for some programs), completion of degree in maximum of four calendar years; minimum cumulative GPA of 3.0 and B grade or higher in each course; orientation seminar (one credit); minimum of 40 credits; FTCE ESE K-12 Exam; for doctorate, thesis/dissertation, mid-program review; minimum cumulative GPA of 3.25 and B grade or higher in each course. *Entrance requirements:* For master's, bachelor's degree from accredited institution, minimum undergraduate GPA of 3.0, official undergraduate and graduate transcripts of all academic coursework attempted, current résumé, statement of professional goals, writing sample, two recent letters of recommendation; for doctorate, professional practice statement that identifies applicant's goals and explains how Lynn's program will help attain them, official transcript showing conferral of master's degree, two letters of recommendation from previous professors or employers, current resume, interview. Additional exam requirements/recommendations for international students: Required—TOEFL (minimum score 550 paper-based; 80 iBT), IELTS (minimum score 6.5). *Application deadline:* For fall admission, 8/18 for domestic students, 8/4 for international students; for spring admission, 12/15 for domestic students, 12/1 for international students; for summer admission, 4/17 for domestic students, 4/3 for international students. Applications are processed on a rolling basis. Application fee: $45. Electronic applications accepted. *Expenses:* $740 per credit (for master's degrees); $850 per credit (for EdD). *Financial support:* Career-related internships or fieldwork, Federal Work-Study, scholarships/grants, tuition waivers (partial), and unspecified assistantships available. Support available to part-time students. Financial award application deadline: 3/1; financial award applicants required to submit FAFSA. *Faculty research:* Student achievement, students with learning differences, teacher and student retention, student motivation and cognition, neuroscience leadership and learning. *Unit head:* Dr. Kathleen Weigel, Dean, College of Education, 561-237-7441, E-mail: kweigel@lynn.edu. *Application contact:* Steven Pruitt, Director of Graduate and Undergraduate Evening Admission, 561-237-7834, Fax: 561-237-7100, E-mail: spruitt@lynn.edu.
Website: http://www.lynn.edu/academics/colleges/education

Madonna University, Programs in Education, Livonia, MI 48150-1173. Offers Catholic school leadership (MSA); educational leadership (MSA); learning disabilities (MAT); literacy education (MAT); teaching and learning (MAT). *Accreditation:* NCATE. *Program availability:* Part-time, evening/weekend. *Degree requirements:* For master's, thesis or alternative. Electronic applications accepted.

Malone University, Graduate Program in Education, Canton, OH 44709. Offers curriculum and instruction (MA); curriculum, instruction, and professional development (MA); educational leadership (principal license) (MA); intervention specialist (MA). *Accreditation:* NCATE. *Program availability:* Part-time, evening/weekend. *Degree requirements:* For master's, research project. *Entrance requirements:* For master's, minimum GPA of 3.0, teaching license. Additional exam requirements/recommendations for international students: Required—TOEFL (minimum score 550 paper-based; 79 iBT). *Faculty research:* Educational leadership styles: Jesus as master teacher, assessment accommodations for English language learners, preparing culturally proficient teachers, using naturally occurring text in the classroom to meet the syntactic needs of students with learning disabilities, using tablet instructional technology to meet the needs of students with disabilities.

Manhattan College, Graduate Programs, School of Education and Health, Riverdale, NY 10471. Offers MA, MS, MS Ed, Advanced Certificate, Certificate, Professional Diploma. *Accreditation:* TEAC. *Program availability:* Part-time, evening/weekend, online learning. *Degree requirements:* For master's and other advanced degree, thesis, internship. *Entrance requirements:* For master's and other advanced degree, minimum GPA of 3.0. Additional exam requirements/recommendations for international students: Required—TOEFL. *Expenses:* Tuition: Part-time $1034 per credit. *Required fees:* $280 per term. One-time fee: $590 part-time. Tuition and fees vary according to program. *Faculty research:* Leadership, assessment, professional development, school improvement.

Manhattanville College, School of Education, Purchase, NY 10577-2132. Offers M Ed, MAT, MPS, Ed D, Advanced Certificate, Certificate, PD. *Accreditation:* NCATE. *Program availability:* Part-time, evening/weekend. *Faculty:* 24 full-time (15 women), 76 part-time/adjunct (49 women). *Students:* 239 full-time (167 women), 574 part-time (428 women); includes 123 minority (35 Black or African American, non-Hispanic/Latino; 8 Asian, non-Hispanic/Latino; 75 Hispanic/Latino; 2 Native Hawaiian or other Pacific Islander, non-Hispanic/Latino; 3 Two or more races, non-Hispanic/Latino), 4 international. Average age 34. 192 applicants, 77% accepted, 128 enrolled. In 2017, 228 master's, 17 doctorates, 30 other advanced degrees awarded. *Degree requirements:* For master's, comprehensive exam (for some programs), thesis (for some programs), student teaching, research seminars, portfolios, internships, writing assessment; for doctorate, comprehensive exam (for some programs), thesis/dissertation. *Entrance requirements:* For master's, GRE or MAT (for programs leading to certification), minimum GPA of 3.0, 2 letters of recommendation, interview, essay (2-3 page personal statement that describes reasons for choosing teaching or educational leadership as profession and philosophy of education), proof of immunization (for those born after 1957); for doctorate, GRE or MAT, minimum GPA of 3.0, 3 letters of recommendation, interview, writing sample (statement explaining interest in joining program, strengths applicant brings to role of education leader, leadership experience to date, and skills they hope to develop in program), proof of immunization (for those born after 1957). Additional exam requirements/recommendations for international students: Required—TOEFL (minimum score 600 paper-based; 110 iBT); Recommended—IELTS (minimum score 8). *Application deadline:* For summer admission, 1/1 for domestic students. Applications are processed on a rolling basis. Application fee: $75. Electronic applications accepted. *Expenses:* $915 per credit ($1,000 for those who completed all degree requirements from another institution and just need to complete dissertation). *Financial support:* Teaching assistantships, career-related internships or fieldwork, Federal Work-Study, institutionally sponsored loans, scholarships/grants, and unspecified assistantships available. Financial award application deadline: 3/15; financial award applicants required to submit FAFSA. *Faculty research:* Early childhood and technology, professional development schools and community schools, early childhood and technology, social capital, diversity in higher education, school leadership, social capital in relation to achievement gap, diversity in higher education, power of story for literacy development, English learners, education for sustainability, early childhood and physical education, students with emotional difficulties, literacy and adolescents, mindfulness, studying the effects of the en. *Total annual research expenditures:* $800. *Unit head:* Dr. Shelley Wepner, Dean, 914-323-3153, Fax: 914-323-5493, E-mail: shelly.wepner@mville.edu. *Application contact:* Alissa Wilson, Director, Graduate Admissions, 914-323-3150, E-mail: edschool@mville.edu.
Website: http://www.mville.edu/academics/school-education

Mansfield University of Pennsylvania, Graduate Studies, Department of Education and Special Education, Mansfield, PA 16933. Offers elementary education (M Ed); secondary education (MS); special education (M Ed). *Accreditation:* NCATE (one or more programs are accredited). *Program availability:* Part-time, evening/weekend, online learning. *Degree requirements:* For master's, comprehensive exam, thesis optional. *Entrance requirements:* For master's, minimum GPA of 3.0. Additional exam requirements/recommendations for international students: Required—TOEFL (minimum score 550 paper-based). Electronic applications accepted.

Maranatha Baptist University, Program in Teaching and Learning, Watertown, WI 53094. Offers M Ed. *Program availability:* Part-time, evening/weekend, 100% online. *Expenses:* Contact institution.

Marian University, Educators College, Indianapolis, IN 46222-1997. Offers MA, MAT. *Accreditation:* NCATE. *Program availability:* Part-time, evening/weekend, 100% online. *Faculty:* 10 full-time (6 women), 22 part-time/adjunct (18 women). *Students:* 36 full-time (29 women), 269 part-time (185 women); includes 92 minority (61 Black or African American, non-Hispanic/Latino; 8 Asian, non-Hispanic/Latino; 11 Hispanic/Latino; 12 Two or more races, non-Hispanic/Latino). Average age 30. 333 applicants, 59% accepted, 165 enrolled. In 2017, 105 master's awarded. *Degree requirements:* For master's, 2 classroom research courses, initial teacher licensure, final portfolio. *Entrance requirements:* For master's, Indiana CORE Academic Skills Assessment (or alternative). Additional exam requirements/recommendations for international students: Required—TOEFL (minimum score 69 iBT), IELTS. *Application deadline:* For fall admission, 3/1 priority date for domestic students. Applications are processed on a rolling basis. Application fee: $40. Electronic applications accepted. Application fee is waived when completed online. *Expenses:* $470 per credit hour. *Financial support:* Application deadline: 4/15; applicants required to submit FAFSA. *Unit head:* Dr. Kenith Britt, Senior Vice President of Teacher Learning Excellence/Dean, 317-955-6209, Fax: 317-955-6406, E-mail: kbritt@marian.edu.

Marian University, School of Education, Fond du Lac, WI 54935-4699. Offers curriculum and instruction leadership (PhD); educational administration (PhD); educational leadership (MAE); educational technology (MAE); leadership studies (PhD); special education (MAE); teacher education (MAE). *Accreditation:* NCATE. *Program availability:* Part-time, evening/weekend, online learning. *Degree requirements:* For master's, exam, field-based experience project, portfolio; for doctorate, comprehensive exam, thesis/dissertation, field-based experience. *Entrance requirements:* For master's, minimum GPA of 3.0, BA in education or related field, teaching license; for doctorate,

GRE, MAT, resume, 2 writing samples, interview. Additional exam requirements/recommendations for international students: Required—TOEFL (minimum score 525 paper-based; 70 iBT). *Faculty research:* At-risk youth, multicultural issues, values in education, teaching/learning strategies.

Marist College, Graduate Programs, School of Social and Behavioral Sciences, Poughkeepsie, NY 12601-1387. Offers education (M Ed, MA); mental health counseling (MA); school psychology (MA, Adv C). *Program availability:* Part-time, evening/weekend. *Degree requirements:* For master's, thesis optional. *Entrance requirements:* For master's, GRE General Test, letters of recommendation, minimum undergraduate GPA of 3.0, interview. Additional exam requirements/recommendations for international students: Required—TOEFL (minimum score 550 paper-based; 80 iBT); Recommended—IELTS (minimum score 6.5). Electronic applications accepted. *Faculty research:* AIDS prevention, educational intervention, humanistic counseling research, aging and development, neuroimaging.

Marquette University, Graduate School, College of Education, Milwaukee, WI 53201-1881. Offers M Ed, MA, MS, PhD, Certificate. *Accreditation:* NCATE. *Program availability:* Part-time. Terminal master's awarded for partial completion of doctoral program. *Degree requirements:* For master's, comprehensive exam, thesis (for some programs); for doctorate, thesis/dissertation, qualifying exam. *Entrance requirements:* For master's, GRE General Test or MAT, official transcripts from all current and previous colleges/universities except Marquette, three letters of recommendation, statement of purpose; for doctorate, GRE General Test, MAT, sample of written work, official transcripts from all current and previous colleges/universities except Marquette, three letters of recommendation, statement of purpose, resume/curriculum vitae; for Certificate, GRE General Test or MAT, master's degree. Additional exam requirements/recommendations for international students: Required—TOEFL (minimum score 530 paper-based). *Expenses:* Contact institution. *Faculty research:* Parenting, psychology of motivation, reading assessment, socialization of educational administrators, education philosophy of Cardinal Newman.

Marshall University, Academic Affairs Division, College of Education and Professional Development, Huntington, WV 25755. Offers MA, MAT, MS, Ed D, Certificate, Ed S. *Accreditation:* NCATE. *Program availability:* Part-time, evening/weekend. *Faculty:* 42 full-time (20 women), 10 part-time/adjunct (7 women). *Students:* 259 full-time (202 women), 735 part-time (519 women); includes 77 minority (33 Black or African American, non-Hispanic/Latino; 1 American Indian or Alaska Native, non-Hispanic/Latino; 6 Asian, non-Hispanic/Latino; 25 Hispanic/Latino; 2 Native Hawaiian or other Pacific Islander, non-Hispanic/Latino; 10 Two or more races, non-Hispanic/Latino). Average age 35. In 2017, 367 master's, 18 doctorates, 20 other advanced degrees awarded. *Degree requirements:* For master's, thesis optional, comprehensive or oral assessment. *Entrance requirements:* Additional exam requirements/recommendations for international students: Required—TOEFL. *Application deadline:* For fall admission, 5/1 for domestic students; for spring admission, 12/1 for domestic students. Applications are processed on a rolling basis. Application fee: $40. Electronic applications accepted. *Financial support:* Career-related internships or fieldwork, Federal Work-Study, tuition waivers (full and partial), and unspecified assistantships available. Support available to part-time students. Financial award applicants required to submit FAFSA. *Unit head:* Dr. Teresa Eagle, Dean, 304-746-8924, E-mail: thardman@marshall.edu. *Application contact:* Information Contact, 304-746-1900, Fax: 304-746-1902, E-mail: services@marshall.edu.
Website: http://www.marshall.edu/gsepd/

Martin Luther College, Graduate Studies, New Ulm, MN 56073. Offers early childhood director (MS Ed Admin); educational technology (MS Ed); instruction (MS Ed); leadership (MS Ed); principal (MS Ed Admin); special education (MS Ed). *Program availability:* Part-time, evening/weekend, online learning. *Faculty:* 8 full-time (1 woman), 21 part-time/adjunct (10 women). *Students:* 1 (woman) full-time, 81 part-time (28 women); includes 2 minority (1 Asian, non-Hispanic/Latino; 1 Two or more races, non-Hispanic/Latino), 2 international. Average age 37. 23 applicants, 100% accepted, 23 enrolled. In 2017, 25 master's awarded. *Degree requirements:* For master's, capstone project or comprehensive exam. *Entrance requirements:* For master's, undergraduate degree in education from an accredited college or university, minimum undergraduate GPA of 3.0. Additional exam requirements/recommendations for international students: Required—TOEFL (minimum score 550 paper-based; 80 iBT); Recommended—IELTS (minimum score 6.5). *Application deadline:* Applications are processed on a rolling basis. Application fee: $35. Electronic applications accepted. *Expenses:* $315 per credit. *Financial support:* In 2017–18, 4 students received support. Scholarships/grants available. Financial award application deadline: 9/1. *Faculty research:* Principal effectiveness, principal support, cognitive load in math instruction, reading strategies in multigrade classrooms, mentor provided professional development for new teachers. *Unit head:* John E. Meyer, Director of Graduate Studies, 507-354-8221 Ext. 398, E-mail: meyerjd@mlc-wels.edu.
Website: https://mlc-wels.edu/graduate-studies/

Mary Baldwin University, Graduate Studies, Program in Teaching, Staunton, VA 24401-3610. Offers elementary education (MAT); middle grades education (MAT). *Accreditation:* TEAC.

Marymount University, School of Education and Human Services, Program in Education, Arlington, VA 22207-4299. Offers curriculum and instruction (M Ed); elementary education (M Ed); professional studies (M Ed); secondary education (M Ed); special education: general curriculum (M Ed). *Accreditation:* NCATE. *Program availability:* Part-time, evening/weekend. *Faculty:* 7 full-time (all women), 10 part-time/adjunct (7 women). *Students:* 51 full-time (40 women), 92 part-time (61 women); includes 33 minority (9 Black or African American, non-Hispanic/Latino; 9 Asian, non-Hispanic/Latino; 10 Hispanic/Latino; 5 Two or more races, non-Hispanic/Latino), 11 international. Average age 34. 39 applicants, 97% accepted, 30 enrolled. In 2017, 72 master's awarded. *Degree requirements:* For master's, thesis or alternative, capstone/internship. *Entrance requirements:* For master's, GRE or MAT and PRAXIS I or SAT/ACT and Virginia Communication and Literacy Assessment (VCLA), 2 letters of recommendation, resume, interview, minimum undergraduate GPA of 2.75 or 3.25 in the last 60 hours. Additional exam requirements/recommendations for international students: Required—TOEFL (minimum score 600 paper-based; 96 iBT), IELTS (minimum score 6.5). *Application deadline:* Applications are processed on a rolling basis. Application fee: $40. Electronic applications accepted. *Expenses:* $715 per credit. *Financial support:* In 2017–18, 7 students received support, including 2 teaching assistantships with full and partial tuition reimbursements available (averaging $14,520 per year); career-related internships or fieldwork, Federal Work-Study, scholarships/grants, and unspecified assistantships also available. Support available to part-time students. Financial award application deadline: 3/1; financial award applicants required to submit FAFSA. *Unit head:* Dr. Lisa Turissini, Chair, Education, 703-526-1668, Fax: 703-284-1631, E-mail: lisa.turissini@marymount.edu. *Application contact:* Francesca Reed, Director, Graduate Admissions, 703-284-5901, Fax: 703-527-3815, E-mail: grad.admissions@marymount.edu.
Website: http://www.marymount.edu/Academics/School-of-Education-Human-Services/Graduate-Programs/Education-(M-Ed-)

Maryville University of Saint Louis, School of Education, St. Louis, MO 63141-7299. Offers early childhood education (MA Ed); educational leadership (Ed D); elementary education (MA Ed); higher education leadership (Ed D); literacy specialist (MA Ed); middle grades education (MA Ed); secondary teaching and inquiry (MA Ed); teacher as leader (MA Ed, Ed D). *Accreditation:* NCATE. *Program availability:* Part-time, 100% online, blended/hybrid learning. *Faculty:* 20 full-time (14 women), 19 part-time/adjunct (13 women). *Students:* 6 full-time (4 women), 337 part-time (250 women); includes 101 minority (85 Black or African American, non-Hispanic/Latino; 4 Asian, non-Hispanic/Latino; 8 Hispanic/Latino; 4 Two or more races, non-Hispanic/Latino), 3 international. Average age 38. In 2017, 34 master's, 67 doctorates awarded. *Degree requirements:* For master's, thesis, project. *Entrance requirements:* For master's, minimum cumulative GPA of 3.0, 3 professional recommendations, essays, interview with program faculty; for doctorate, minimum GPA of 3.0, 3 professional recommendations, essay, interview, on-site writing sample. Additional exam requirements/recommendations for international students: Required—TOEFL (minimum score 550 paper-based). *Application deadline:* Applications are processed on a rolling basis. Electronic applications accepted. *Expenses:* Contact institution. *Financial support:* Career-related internships or fieldwork, Federal Work-Study, tuition waivers (partial), and professional educator discounts available. Financial award application deadline: 4/1; financial award applicants required to submit FAFSA. *Faculty research:* Collaboration with public schools, pre-service program development, mathematics, diversity, literacy. *Unit head:* Dr. Cathy Bear, Dean, 314-529-9692, Fax: 314-529-9921, E-mail: cbear@maryville.edu. *Application contact:* Stacey Ruffin, Coordinator of Clinical Experiences and Graduate Programs, 314-529-9542, Fax: 314-529-9921, E-mail: teachered@maryville.edu.
Website: http://www.maryville.edu/ed/graduate-programs/

Marywood University, Academic Affairs, Reap College of Education and Human Development, Department of Education, Scranton, PA 18509-1598. Offers early childhood intervention (MS), including birth to age 9; higher education administration (MS); instructional leadership (MAT); PK-4 education (MAT); reading education (MS); school leadership (MS); secondary/K-12 education (MAT); special education (MS); special education administration and supervision (MS). *Accreditation:* NCATE. *Program availability:* Part-time. Electronic applications accepted.

Massachusetts College of Liberal Arts, Graduate Programs, North Adams, MA 01247-4100. Offers business (MBA); educational administration (M Ed); educational leadership (CAGS); instruction and curriculum (M Ed); instructional technology (M Ed); physical education and health (M Ed); reading (M Ed); special education (M Ed). *Program availability:* Part-time, evening/weekend. *Degree requirements:* For master's, thesis. *Entrance requirements:* For master's, writing sample.

McGill University, Faculty of Graduate and Postdoctoral Studies, Faculty of Education, Department of Integrated Studies in Education, Montréal, QC H3A 2T5, Canada. Offers culture and values in education (MA, PhD); curriculum studies (MA); educational studies (PhD); integrated studies in education (M Ed); second language education (MA, PhD).

McKendree University, Graduate Programs, Programs in Education, Lebanon, IL 62254-1299. Offers curriculum design and instruction (Ed D, Ed S); educational administration and leadership (MA Ed); educational studies (MA Ed); higher education administrative services (MA Ed); music education (MA Ed); reading (MA Ed); special education (MA Ed); teacher leadership (MA Ed); teaching certification (MA Ed). *Accreditation:* NCATE. *Program availability:* Part-time, evening/weekend, online learning. *Entrance requirements:* For master's, official transcripts from all institutions previously attended, minimum GPA of 3.0, resume, references; for doctorate, GRE (within the past 5 years), master's degree in education and Ed S, or the equivalent, from regionally-accredited institution; official transcripts from all institutions previously attended; curriculum vitae/resume; essay/personal statement; two years of teaching/professional experience; for Ed S, GRE (within the past 5 years), master's degree in education from regionally-accredited institution of higher education; official transcripts from all institutions previously attended; curriculum vitae/resume; essay/personal statement; two years of teaching/professional experience. Additional exam requirements/recommendations for international students: Required—TOEFL. Electronic applications accepted.

McNeese State University, Doré School of Graduate Studies, Burton College of Education, Department of Education Professions, Program in Multiple Levels Grades K-12, Lake Charles, LA 70609. Offers multiple levels grades K-12 (Postbaccalaureate Certificate), including art, health and physical education, music - instrumental, music - vocal. *Entrance requirements:* For degree, PRAXIS, 2 letters of recommendation, autobiography. *Application deadline:* For fall admission, 5/15 priority date for domestic and international students; for spring admission, 10/15 priority date for domestic and international students. Applications are processed on a rolling basis. Application fee: $20 ($30 for international students). *Financial support:* Application deadline: 5/1. *Unit head:* Dr. Veronica Faye White, Head, 337-475-5400, Fax: 337-475-5272, E-mail: vfwhite@mcneese.edu. *Application contact:* Dr. Dustin M. Hebert, Director of Dore' School of Graduate Studies, 337-475-5396, Fax: 337-475-5397, E-mail: admissions@mcneese.edu.

McPherson College, Program in Education, McPherson, KS 67460-1402. Offers M Ed. *Degree requirements:* For master's, project.

Medaille College, Program in Education, Buffalo, NY 14214-2695. Offers adolescent education (MS Ed); curriculum and instruction (MS Ed); education preparation (MS Ed); literacy (MS Ed); special education (MS). *Accreditation:* TEAC. *Program availability:* Part-time, evening/weekend. *Degree requirements:* For master's, comprehensive exam (for some programs), thesis or alternative. *Entrance requirements:* For master's, minimum undergraduate GPA of 2.7. Additional exam requirements/recommendations for international students: Required—TOEFL (minimum score 550 paper-based). Electronic applications accepted. *Faculty research:* Curriculum planning, truancy, tracking minority students, curriculum design, mentoring students.

Memorial University of Newfoundland, School of Graduate Studies, Faculty of Education, St. John's, NL A1C 5S7, Canada. Offers counseling psychology (M Ed); curriculum, teaching, and learning studies (M Ed); education (PhD); educational leadership studies (M Ed, Graduate Diploma); information technology (M Ed); post-secondary studies (M Ed, Diploma), including health professional education (Diploma). *Program availability:* Part-time. *Degree requirements:* For master's, thesis optional, internship, paper folio, project; for doctorate, comprehensive exam, thesis/dissertation, thesis seminar, oral defense of thesis. *Entrance requirements:* For master's, undergraduate degree with at least 2nd class standing, 1-2 years of work experience; for doctorate, minimum A average in graduate course work, MA in education, 2 years of professional experience; for other advanced degree, 2nd class degree, 2 years of work experience with adult learners, appropriate academic qualifications and work experience in a health-related field. Electronic applications accepted. *Faculty research:* Critical thinking, literacy, cognitive studies and counseling, educational change, technology in instruction.

Mercer University, Graduate Studies, Cecil B. Day Campus, Tift College of Education (Atlanta), Atlanta, GA 30341. Offers curriculum and instruction (PhD); early childhood education (M Ed, MAT, Ed S); educational leadership (PhD), including higher education

Education—General

leadership, P-12 school leadership; educational leadership P-12 (M Ed, Ed S); higher education leadership (M Ed); independent and charter school leadership (M Ed); middle grades education (M Ed, MAT); secondary education (M Ed, MAT); teacher leadership (Ed S). *Accreditation:* NCATE. *Program availability:* Part-time, evening/weekend. *Faculty:* 30 full-time (18 women), 34 part-time/adjunct (27 women). *Students:* 159 full-time (131 women), 284 part-time (229 women); includes 264 minority (232 Black or African American, non-Hispanic/Latino; 1 American Indian or Alaska Native, non-Hispanic/Latino; 9 Asian, non-Hispanic/Latino; 18 Hispanic/Latino; 4 Two or more races, non-Hispanic/Latino), 2 international. Average age 35. In 2017, 137 master's, 22 doctorates, 40 other advanced degrees awarded. *Degree requirements:* For master's and Ed S, research project; for doctorate, comprehensive exam, thesis/dissertation. *Entrance requirements:* For master's, GRE or MAT, minimum undergraduate GPA of 2.75; for doctorate, GRE; for Ed S, GRE or MAT, minimum GPA of 3.25; 3 years of certified teaching experience (for educational leadership and teacher leadership). Additional exam requirements/recommendations for international students: Required—TOEFL (minimum score 80 iBT). *Application deadline:* For fall admission, 8/1 for domestic and international students; for spring admission, 12/1 for domestic and international students; for summer admission, 5/1 for domestic and international students. Applications are processed on a rolling basis. Application fee: $25 ($50 for international students). Electronic applications accepted. *Expenses:* Contact institution. *Financial support:* Federal Work-Study and unspecified assistantships available. Support available to part-time students. Financial award application deadline: 5/1; financial award applicants required to submit FAFSA. *Faculty research:* Educational technology, multicultural and minority issues in education, educational leadership (P-12 and higher education), school discipline and school bullying, standards-based mathematics education. *Unit head:* Dr. Scott Davis, Dean, 478-301-2110, Fax: 478-301-5576.
Website: http://education.mercer.edu/

Mercer University, Graduate Studies, Macon Campus, Tift College of Education (Macon), Macon, GA 31207. Offers curriculum and instruction (PhD); early childhood education (M Ed, Ed S); educational leadership (M Ed, PhD, Ed S), including higher education (PhD), P-12; higher education leadership (M Ed); independent and charter school leadership (M Ed); secondary education (MAT), including STEM; teacher leadership (Ed S). *Accreditation:* NCATE. *Program availability:* Part-time, evening/weekend, 100% online, blended/hybrid learning. *Faculty:* 13 full-time (8 women), 1 part-time/adjunct (0 women). *Students:* 33 full-time (18 women), 51 part-time (37 women); includes 49 minority (44 Black or African American, non-Hispanic/Latino; 2 Asian, non-Hispanic/Latino; 2 Hispanic/Latino; 1 Two or more races, non-Hispanic/Latino), 1 international. Average age 32. In 2017, 22 master's, 17 doctorates awarded. *Degree requirements:* For master's, research project report; for doctorate, comprehensive exam, thesis/dissertation. *Entrance requirements:* For master's, GRE or MAT, minimum GPA of 2.75; for doctorate, GRE, minimum GPA of 3.5; interview; writing sample; 3 recommendations; for Ed S, GRE or MAT, minimum GPA of 3.5 (for teacher leadership), 3.0 (for educational leadership). Additional exam requirements/recommendations for international students: Required—TOEFL (minimum score 80 iBT). *Application deadline:* For fall admission, 8/1 for domestic and international students; for spring admission, 12/1 for domestic and international students. Applications are processed on a rolling basis. Application fee: $35. Electronic applications accepted. *Expenses:* Contact institution. *Financial support:* Federal Work-Study, institutionally sponsored loans, and unspecified assistantships available. Support available to part-time students. Financial award application deadline: 5/1; financial award applicants required to submit FAFSA. *Faculty research:* Teacher effectiveness, specific learning disabilities, inclusion. *Unit head:* Dr. Scott Davis, Dean, 478-301-2110, Fax: 478-301-5576, E-mail: davis_ds@mercer.edu.
Website: http://education.mercer.edu/

Mercy College, School of Education, Dobbs Ferry, NY 10522-1189. Offers MS, Advanced Certificate. *Program availability:* Part-time, evening/weekend, 100% online, blended/hybrid learning. *Students:* 187 full-time (163 women), 502 part-time (425 women); includes 345 minority (128 Black or African American, non-Hispanic/Latino; 2 American Indian or Alaska Native, non-Hispanic/Latino; 19 Asian, non-Hispanic/Latino; 189 Hispanic/Latino; 1 Native Hawaiian or other Pacific Islander, non-Hispanic/Latino; 6 Two or more races, non-Hispanic/Latino). Average age 32. 344 applicants, 40% accepted, 76 enrolled. In 2017, 410 master's, 38 other advanced degrees awarded. *Degree requirements:* For master's, comprehensive exam (for some programs), thesis (for some programs). *Entrance requirements:* For master's, GRE, resume, undergraduate transcript. Additional exam requirements/recommendations for international students: Required—TOEFL (minimum score 600 paper-based; 100 iBT), IELTS (minimum score 8). *Application deadline:* For fall admission, 8/1 for international students. Applications are processed on a rolling basis. Application fee: $40. Electronic applications accepted. *Expenses: Tuition:* Full-time $15,426; part-time $857 per credit hour. *Required fees:* $630; $158 per term. Tuition and fees vary according to course load, degree level and program. *Financial support:* Career-related internships or fieldwork, Federal Work-Study, scholarships/grants, and unspecified assistantships available. Support available to part-time students. Financial award applicants required to submit FAFSA. *Unit head:* Dean for the School of Education, 914-674-7350. *Application contact:* Allison Gurdineer, Senior Director of Admissions, 877-637-2946, Fax: 914-674-7382, E-mail: admissions@mercy.edu.
Website: https://www.mercy.edu/education/

Meredith College, School of Education, Health and Human Sciences, Raleigh, NC 27607-5298. Offers academically and intellectually gifted (M Ed); elementary education (M Ed, MAT); English as a second language (M Ed, MAT); health and physical education (MAT); nutrition, health and human performance (MS, Postbaccalaureate Certificate), including dietetic internship (Postbaccalaureate Certificate), nutrition (MS); psychology (MA), including industrial/organizational psychology; reading (M Ed); special education (MAT); special education (general curriculum) (M Ed). *Accreditation:* NCATE. *Program availability:* Part-time, evening/weekend. *Students:* 25 full-time (24 women), 22 part-time (all women); includes 13 minority (8 Black or African American, non-Hispanic/Latino; 1 American Indian or Alaska Native, non-Hispanic/Latino; 1 Asian, non-Hispanic/Latino; 3 Hispanic/Latino). Average age 31. 57 applicants, 54% accepted, 31 enrolled. In 2017, 14 master's awarded. *Degree requirements:* For master's, thesis optional. *Entrance requirements:* For master's, GRE General Test or MAT, minimum GPA of 2.5, teaching license, recommendations. Additional exam requirements/recommendations for international students: Required—TOEFL. *Application deadline:* For fall admission, 7/1 priority date for domestic students; for spring admission, 11/1 priority date for domestic students. Applications are processed on a rolling basis. Application fee: $50. Electronic applications accepted. *Expenses:* Contact institution. *Financial support:* Career-related internships or fieldwork, institutionally sponsored loans, and tuition waivers (partial) available. Support available to part-time students. Financial award application deadline: 2/15; financial award applicants required to submit FAFSA. *Unit head:* Dr. Monica McKinney, Graduate Program Manager, 919-760-8056, Fax: 919-760-2303, E-mail: mckinneym@meredith.edu.
Website: https://www.meredith.edu/school-of-education-health-and-human-sciences

Merrimack College, School of Education and Social Policy, North Andover, MA 01845-5800. Offers community engagement (M Ed), including community organizations, higher education, PreK-12 education; criminology and criminal justice (MS); curriculum and instruction (M Ed); early childhood education (M Ed); educational leadership (CAGS), including instructional leadership; elementary education (M Ed); English as a second language (PreK-6) (M Ed); high school education (M Ed); higher education (M Ed), including leadership and organizational development, student affairs; middle school education (M Ed); moderate disabilities (PreK-8) (M Ed); school counseling (M Ed). *Program availability:* Part-time, evening/weekend, 100% online courses with immersion events and in-classroom practicum close to home. *Faculty:* 15 full-time, 36 part-time/adjunct. *Students:* 212 full-time (175 women), 121 part-time (101 women); includes 42 minority (6 Black or African American, non-Hispanic/Latino; 6 Asian, non-Hispanic/Latino; 27 Hispanic/Latino; 3 Two or more races, non-Hispanic/Latino), 3 international. Average age 27. 420 applicants, 84% accepted, 250 enrolled. In 2017, 177 master's awarded. *Degree requirements:* For master's, practicum, portfolio, and state test (for licensure track); capstone (for higher education, curriculum and instruction, and community engagement tracks); for CAGS, capstone. *Entrance requirements:* For master's, Massachusetts Teacher Education Licensure (MTEL), official transcripts from other colleges, resume, personal statement, 2 letters of recommendation. Additional exam requirements/recommendations for international students: Required—TOEFL (minimum score 84 iBT), IELTS (minimum score 6.5), PTE (minimum score 56). *Application deadline:* For fall admission, 8/24 for domestic students, 7/30 for international students; for spring admission, 1/10 for domestic students, 12/10 for international students; for summer admission, 5/10 for domestic students, 4/10 for international students. Applications are processed on a rolling basis. Application fee: $0. Electronic applications accepted. *Expenses:* Contact institution. *Financial support:* Fellowships with full tuition reimbursements, career-related internships or fieldwork, scholarships/grants, and health care benefits available. Support available to part-time students. Financial award application deadline: 5/1; financial award applicants required to submit FAFSA. *Application contact:* Alyssa Orlando, Graduate Admissions Counselor, 978-837-3563, E-mail: orlandoaf@merrimack.edu.
Website: http://www.merrimack.edu/academics/graduate/education/

Metropolitan State University of Denver, School of Education, Denver, CO 80204. Offers elementary education (MAT); special education (MAT). *Expenses:* Contact institution.

Miami University, College of Education, Health and Society, Oxford, OH 45056. Offers M Ed, MA, MAT, MS, Ed D, PhD, Ed S. *Accreditation:* NCATE. *Expenses:* Tuition, state resident: full-time $13,812; part-time $575 per credit hour. Tuition, nonresident: full-time $30,860; part-time $1286 per credit hour. *Unit head:* Dr. Michael Dantley, Dean, 513-529-6317, E-mail: ehs@miamioh.edu. *Application contact:* Graduate Admission Coordinator, 513-529-3734, E-mail: applygrad@miamioh.edu.
Website: http://www.MiamiOH.edu/eap/

Michigan State University, The Graduate School, College of Education, East Lansing, MI 48824. Offers MA, MS, PhD, Ed S. *Accreditation:* TEAC. *Entrance requirements:* Additional exam requirements/recommendations for international students: Required—TOEFL. Electronic applications accepted.

MidAmerica Nazarene University, Professional and Graduate Studies in Education, Olathe, KS 66062-1899. Offers ESOL (M Ed); reading specialist (M Ed); technology enhanced teaching (M Ed). *Accreditation:* NCATE. *Program availability:* Part-time, evening/weekend, online only, 100% online. *Entrance requirements:* For master's, bachelor's degree from an accredited college or university, minimum undergraduate GPA of 3.0, valid teaching license. Additional exam requirements/recommendations for international students: Required—TOEFL (minimum score 81 iBT), IELTS (minimum score 6). Electronic applications accepted. *Expenses:* Contact institution.

Middle Tennessee State University, College of Graduate Studies, College of Education, Murfreesboro, TN 37132. Offers M Ed, PhD, Ed S. *Accreditation:* NCATE. *Program availability:* Part-time, evening/weekend, online learning. *Degree requirements:* For master's, comprehensive exam, thesis (for some programs); for doctorate, comprehensive exam, thesis/dissertation; for Ed S, comprehensive exam, thesis or alternative. *Entrance requirements:* For master's, doctorate, and Ed S, GRE, MAT, current teaching license or PRAXIS. Additional exam requirements/recommendations for international students: Required—TOEFL (minimum score 525 paper-based; 71 iBT) or IELTS (minimum score 6). Electronic applications accepted.

Midway University, Graduate Programs, Midway, KY 40347-1120. Offers education (MAT); leadership (MBA). *Degree requirements:* For master's, capstone course. *Entrance requirements:* For master's, GMAT (for MBA); GRE or PRAXIS I (for MAT); bachelor's degree; interview; minimum GPA of 3.0 (for MBA), 2.75 (for MAT); 3 years of professional work experience (for MBA). Additional exam requirements/recommendations for international students: Required—TOEFL (minimum score 550 paper-based; 80 iBT).

Midwestern State University, Billie Doris McAda Graduate School, West College of Education, Wichita Falls, TX 76308. Offers M Ed, MA. *Program availability:* Part-time, evening/weekend. *Degree requirements:* For master's, comprehensive exam, thesis (for some programs). *Entrance requirements:* For master's, GRE General Test or MAT. Additional exam requirements/recommendations for international students: Required—TOEFL (minimum score 550 paper-based). Electronic applications accepted. *Faculty research:* Assessment, reading education, vocabulary instruction, current role of the principal, educational research methodology.

Millersville University of Pennsylvania, College of Graduate Studies and Adult Learning, College of Education and Human Services, Millersville, PA 17551-0302. Offers M Ed, MS, MSW, DSW, Ed D, Post-Master's Certificate. *Accreditation:* NCATE. *Program availability:* Part-time, evening/weekend, coursework completed primarily online, with a weekend residency once a semester. *Faculty:* 48 full-time (33 women), 24 part-time/adjunct (17 women). *Students:* 150 full-time (120 women), 376 part-time (300 women); includes 74 minority (30 Black or African American, non-Hispanic/Latino; 3 American Indian or Alaska Native, non-Hispanic/Latino; 5 Asian, non-Hispanic/Latino; 32 Hispanic/Latino; 4 Two or more races, non-Hispanic/Latino), 3 international. Average age 30. 358 applicants, 87% accepted, 186 enrolled. In 2017, 176 master's awarded. *Degree requirements:* For master's, comprehensive exam (for some programs), thesis (for some programs). *Entrance requirements:* For master's, GRE; MAT, teaching certificate, resume (for some programs), academic references, transcripts; for doctorate, letters of recommendation, resume, writing sample. Additional exam requirements/recommendations for international students: Required—TOEFL (minimum score 80 iBT), IELTS (minimum score 6.5), PTE (minimum score 60). Application fee: $40. Electronic applications accepted. *Expenses:* $500 per credit resident tuition and fees; $750 per credit non-resident tuition and fees; $114.75 per credit general fee (maximum of 12 credits); technology fee $27 per credit (resident), $39 per credit (non-resident). *Financial support:* In 2017–18, 81 students received support. Unspecified assistantships available. Financial award application deadline: 3/15; financial award applicants required to submit FAFSA. *Unit head:* Dr. George Drake, Dean, 717-871-7333, E-mail: george.drake@millersville.edu. *Application contact:* Dr. Victor S. DeSantis, Dean of College of Graduate Studies and Adult Learning/Associate Provost for Civic and Community Engagement, 717-871-7619, Fax: 717-871-7954, E-mail: victor.desantis@millersville.edu.
Website: http://www.millersville.edu/education/

Milligan College, Area of Education, Milligan College, TN 37682. Offers combined preK-3/K-5 education (M Ed); educational leadership (Ed D, Ed S); K-5 education (M Ed); middle grades education (M Ed); preK-3 education (M Ed); preK-3 special education (M Ed); secondary education (M Ed). *Accreditation:* NCATE. *Program availability:* Part-time. *Faculty:* 6 full-time (4 women), 3 part-time/adjunct (2 women). *Students:* 27 full-time (20 women), 20 part-time (11 women); includes 2 minority (1 Hispanic/Latino; 1 Two or more races, non-Hispanic/Latino), 1 international. Average age 34. 17 applicants, 35% accepted, 6 enrolled. In 2017, 21 master's awarded. *Degree requirements:* For master's, thesis, portfolio, research project; for doctorate, thesis/dissertation, portfolio, research project. *Entrance requirements:* For master's, MAT, GRE General Test, ACT, SAT, or PRAXIS, undergraduate degree and supporting transcripts, professional recommendations, interview; for doctorate, MAT or GRE, master's degree and supporting transcripts, demonstrated scholastic ability, recognized leadership role within education, professional recommendations, essay/personal statement, portfolio (professional development plan, evidence of ability, knowledge and qualities), interview. Additional exam requirements/recommendations for international students: Required—TOEFL (minimum score 550 paper-based, 79 iBT) or IELTS (6.5). *Application deadline:* For fall admission, 8/1 priority date for domestic students, 6/1 for international students; for spring admission, 11/15 priority date for domestic students, 12/1 for international students; for summer admission, 4/1 for domestic students. Applications are processed on a rolling basis. Application fee: $30. Electronic applications accepted. *Expenses:* $360 per hour tuition (M Ed), $475 per hour (Ed D and Ed S); $325 per semester tech/activity fees. *Financial support:* Scholarships/grants available. Financial award application deadline: 12/1; financial award applicants required to submit FAFSA. *Faculty research:* Assessment; school mental health; literacy; technology; educator preparation. *Unit head:* Dr. Angela Hilton-Prillhart, Area Chair of Education, 423-461-8769, Fax: 423-461-3103, E-mail: anhilton-prillhart@milligan.edu. *Application contact:* Melissa Dillow, Graduate Admissions Recruiter, Education, 423-461-8306, Fax: 423-461-8982, E-mail: msdillow@milligan.edu. Website: http://www.Milligan.edu/GPS

Mills College, Graduate Studies, School of Education, Oakland, CA 94613-1000. Offers MA, Ed D, Certificate. *Program availability:* Part-time, evening/weekend. *Faculty:* 11 full-time (9 women), 16 part-time/adjunct (14 women). *Students:* 83 full-time (66 women), 115 part-time (100 women); includes 94 minority (26 Black or African American, non-Hispanic/Latino; 1 American Indian or Alaska Native, non-Hispanic/Latino; 19 Asian, non-Hispanic/Latino; 38 Hispanic/Latino; 1 Native Hawaiian or other Pacific Islander, non-Hispanic/Latino; 9 Two or more races, non-Hispanic/Latino), 7 international. Average age 32. 189 applicants, 72% accepted, 84 enrolled. In 2017, 60 master's, 17 doctorates, 49 other advanced degrees awarded. Terminal master's awarded for partial completion of doctoral program. *Degree requirements:* For master's, comprehensive exam, thesis (for some programs); for doctorate, thesis/dissertation. *Entrance requirements:* For master's, statement of purpose, official transcript, 3 recommendations. Additional exam requirements/recommendations for international students: Required—TOEFL (minimum score 550 paper-based; 80 iBT) or IELTS (minimum score 6). *Application deadline:* For fall admission, 12/31 priority date for domestic students, 12/15 for international students; for spring admission, 11/1 priority date for domestic students, 10/1 for international students. Applications are processed on a rolling basis. Application fee: $50. Electronic applications accepted. *Expenses:* Contact institution. *Financial support:* In 2017–18, 122 students received support, including 122 fellowships with tuition reimbursements available (averaging $5,462 per year), 15 teaching assistantships with tuition reimbursements available; career-related internships or fieldwork and scholarships/grants also available. Support available to part-time students. Financial award application deadline: 2/1; financial award applicants required to submit FAFSA. *Faculty research:* Early childhood education, teacher preparation, educational leadership. *Total annual research expenditures:* $1.2 million. *Unit head:* Dr. Diane Ketelle, School of Education Dean, 510-430-3190, Fax: 510-430-2159, E-mail: dketelle@mills.edu. *Application contact:* Robynne Lofton, Director of Admissions, 510-430-3295, Fax: 510-430-2159, E-mail: grad-admission@mills.edu. Website: http://www.mills.edu/education

Minnesota State University Mankato, College of Graduate Studies and Research, College of Education, Mankato, MN 56001. Offers MAT, MS, Ed D, Certificate. *Accreditation:* NCATE. *Program availability:* Part-time, evening/weekend. *Degree requirements:* For master's, comprehensive exam, thesis or alternative; for Certificate, thesis. *Entrance requirements:* For master's, GRE or MAT, minimum GPA of 3.0 during previous 2 years; for Certificate, minimum GPA of 3.0. Additional exam requirements/recommendations for international students: Required—TOEFL. Electronic applications accepted.

Minnesota State University Moorhead, Graduate Studies, College of Education and Human Services, Moorhead, MN 56563. Offers counseling and student affairs (MS); curriculum and instruction (MS); educational leadership (MS, Ed D, Ed S); special education (MS); speech-language pathology (MS). *Accreditation:* NCATE. *Program availability:* Part-time, 100% online, blended/hybrid learning. *Faculty:* 22. *Students:* 117 full-time (101 women), 337 part-time (253 women). Average age 32. 248 applicants, 49% accepted. In 2017, 149 master's, 16 other advanced degrees awarded. *Degree requirements:* For master's, comprehensive exam (for some programs), thesis, final oral defense; for doctorate, comprehensive exam (for some programs), thesis/dissertation, final oral defense. *Entrance requirements:* For master's, GRE, essay, letter of intent, letters of reference, teaching license, teaching verification, minimum cumulative GPA of 3.0; for doctorate, official transcripts; letter of intent; resume or curriculum vitae; master's degree; personal essay. Additional exam requirements/recommendations for international students: Required—TOEFL (minimum score 550 paper-based); Recommended—IELTS (minimum score 6.5). *Application deadline:* Applications are processed on a rolling basis. Application fee: $20. Electronic applications accepted. *Expenses:* Tuition, state resident: full-time $9000; part-time $374 per credit. Tuition, nonresident: full-time $18,000; part-time $748 per credit. *Required fees:* $1055; $43.96 per credit. Tuition and fees vary according to degree level, program and reciprocity agreements. *Financial support:* Federal Work-Study and unspecified assistantships available. Financial award application deadline: 10/1; financial award applicants required to submit FAFSA. *Unit head:* Dr. Ok-Hee Lee, Dean, 218-477-2095, E-mail: okheelee@mnstate.edu. *Application contact:* Karla Wenger, Office Manager, 218-477-2344, Fax: 218-477-2482, E-mail: wengerk@mnstate.edu. Website: http://www.mnstate.edu/cehs/

Misericordia University, College of Health Sciences and Education, Program in Education, Dallas, PA 18612-1098. Offers instructional technology (MS); reading specialist (MS); special education (MS). *Program availability:* Part-time, evening/weekend. *Entrance requirements:* For master's, minimum undergraduate GPA of 3.0. Additional exam requirements/recommendations for international students: Required—TOEFL. Electronic applications accepted.

Mississippi College, Graduate School, School of Education, Clinton, MS 39058. Offers M Ed, MS, Ed D, Ed S. *Accreditation:* NCATE. *Program availability:* Part-time, evening/weekend, online learning. *Degree requirements:* For master's, comprehensive exam, thesis optional. *Entrance requirements:* For master's, GRE or NTE, minimum GPA of 2.5, Class A Certificate (for some programs); for Ed S, NTE, minimum GPA of 3.0.

Additional exam requirements/recommendations for international students: Recommended—TOEFL, IELTS. Electronic applications accepted.

Mississippi State University, College of Education, Mississippi State, MS 39762. Offers MAT, MS, MSIT, MST, PhD, Ed S. *Accreditation:* NCATE. *Program availability:* Part-time, evening/weekend, blended/hybrid learning. *Faculty:* 97 full-time (51 women), 4 part-time/adjunct (3 women). *Students:* 158 full-time (169 women), 423 part-time (304 women); includes 243 minority (196 Black or African American, non-Hispanic/Latino; 10 American Indian or Alaska Native, non-Hispanic/Latino; 5 Asian, non-Hispanic/Latino; 15 Hispanic/Latino; 2 Native Hawaiian or other Pacific Islander, non-Hispanic/Latino; 15 Two or more races, non-Hispanic/Latino), 20 international. Average age 32. 413 applicants, 62% accepted, 202 enrolled. In 2017, 186 master's, 49 doctorates, 26 other advanced degrees awarded. Terminal master's awarded for partial completion of doctoral program. *Degree requirements:* For master's, thesis optional, comprehensive oral or written exam; for doctorate, thesis/dissertation; for Ed S, thesis or alternative, final written or oral exam. *Entrance requirements:* For master's, doctorate, and Ed S, GRE. Additional exam requirements/recommendations for international students: Required—TOEFL (minimum score 550 paper-based; 79 iBT); Recommended—IELTS (minimum score 6.5). *Application deadline:* For fall admission, 7/1 for domestic students, 5/1 for international students; for spring admission, 11/1 for domestic students, 9/1 for international students. Applications are processed on a rolling basis. Application fee: $60 ($80 for international students). Electronic applications accepted. *Expenses:* Tuition, state resident: full-time $8318; part-time $462.12 per credit hour. Tuition, nonresident: full-time $22,358; part-time $1242.12 per credit hour. *Required fees:* $110; $12.24 per credit hour. $6.12 per semester. *Financial support:* In 2017–18, 12 research assistantships (averaging $10,542 per year), 25 teaching assistantships (averaging $9,672 per year) were awarded; career-related internships or fieldwork, Federal Work-Study, institutionally sponsored loans, scholarships/grants, and unspecified assistantships also available. Financial award application deadline: 4/1; financial award applicants required to submit FAFSA. *Faculty research:* Leadership behavior, creativity measures, early childhood education, employability of the blind, quality indicators of professional educators. *Total annual research expenditures:* $2.1 million. *Unit head:* Dr. Richard Blackbourn, Dean, 662-325-3717, Fax: 662-325-8784, E-mail: rlb277@msstate.edu. *Application contact:* Marina Hunt, Admissions and Enrollment Assistant, 662-325-5188, E-mail: mhunt@grad.msstate.edu. Website: http://www.educ.msstate.edu/

Mississippi University for Women, Graduate School, College of Education and Human Sciences, Columbus, MS 39701-9998. Offers differentiated instruction (M Ed); educational leadership (M Ed); gifted studies (M Ed); reading/literacy (M Ed); teaching (MAT). *Accreditation:* ASHA; NCATE. *Program availability:* Part-time. *Degree requirements:* For master's, comprehensive exam, thesis optional. *Entrance requirements:* For master's, GRE General Test or NTE (M Ed in gifted education or MS in speech/language pathology), MAT (M Ed in instructional management), minimum QPA of 3.0.

Mississippi Valley State University, College of Education, Itta Bena, MS 38941-1400. Offers MAT, MS. *Accreditation:* NCATE. *Program availability:* Part-time, evening/weekend. *Degree requirements:* For master's, comprehensive exam, thesis (for some programs). *Entrance requirements:* Additional exam requirements/recommendations for international students: Required—TOEFL (minimum score 525 paper-based). *Expenses:* Contact institution.

Missouri Baptist University, Graduate Programs, St. Louis, MO 63141-8660. Offers business administration (MBA); Christian ministries (MACM); counseling (MAC); education (MSE); education administration (MEA); educational leadership (MSE, Ed S); teaching (MAT).

Missouri Southern State University, Program in Teaching, Joplin, MO 64801-1595. Offers MAT. Program offered jointly with Missouri State University. *Accreditation:* NCATE. *Degree requirements:* For master's, research seminar.

Molloy College, Graduate Education Program, Rockville Centre, NY 11571-5002. Offers adolescent education in biology (MS); adolescent special education (Advanced Certificate); bilingual extension (Advanced Certificate); childhood education (MS); childhood special education (Advanced Certificate); early childhood education (MS); educational technology (MS); English (MS); mathematics (MS); social studies (MS); Spanish (MS); special education on both childhood and adolescent levels (MS); teaching English to speakers of other languages (TESOL) in grades pre-K to 12 (MS); TESOL (Advanced Certificate). *Accreditation:* NCATE. *Program availability:* Part-time, evening/weekend. *Faculty:* 18 full-time (17 women), 11 part-time/adjunct (9 women). *Students:* 102 full-time (80 women), 217 part-time (167 women); includes 65 minority (16 Black or African American, non-Hispanic/Latino; 7 Asian, non-Hispanic/Latino; 38 Hispanic/Latino; 4 Two or more races, non-Hispanic/Latino), 1 international. Average age 41. 153 applicants, 68% accepted, 85 enrolled. In 2017, 95 master's, 3 other advanced degrees awarded. *Entrance requirements:* Additional exam requirements/recommendations for international students: Required—TOEFL (minimum score 550 paper-based; 79 iBT). *Application deadline:* Applications are processed on a rolling basis. Application fee: $60. Electronic applications accepted. *Expenses: Tuition:* Full-time $19,980; part-time $1110 per credit. *Required fees:* $1040. Tuition and fees vary according to course load and degree level. *Financial support:* Application deadline: 3/1; applicants required to submit FAFSA. *Faculty research:* English Language Learners; social emotional needs of students; gifted education; cultural diversity; collaborative teaching methods. *Unit head:* Joanne O'Brien, Associate Dean and Director of Graduate Education Programs, 516-323-3116, E-mail: jobrien@molloy.edu. *Application contact:* Jaclyn Machowicz, Assistant Director for Admissions, 516-323-4010, E-mail: jmachowicz@molloy.edu.

Monmouth University, Graduate Studies, School of Education, West Long Branch, NJ 07764-1898. Offers applied behavior analysis (Certificate); autism (Certificate); director of school counseling services (Post-Master's Certificate); early childhood (M Ed); educational leadership (Ed D); elementary education (MAT), including elementary level, secondary level; English as a second language (M Ed); learning disabilities teacher-consultant (Post-Master's Certificate); literacy (MS Ed); school counseling (MS Ed); special education (MS Ed), including autism, learning disabilities teacher-consultant, teacher of students with disabilities, teaching in inclusive settings; speech-language pathology (MS Ed); student affairs and college counseling (MS Ed); supervisor (Post-Master's Certificate); teaching English to speakers of other languages (Certificate). *Accreditation:* NCATE. *Program availability:* Part-time, evening/weekend, 100% online, blended/hybrid learning. *Faculty:* 23 full-time (19 women), 33 part-time/adjunct (25 women). *Students:* 175 full-time (163 women), 168 part-time (142 women); includes 54 minority (10 Black or African American, non-Hispanic/Latino; 4 Asian, non-Hispanic/Latino; 32 Hispanic/Latino; 8 Two or more races, non-Hispanic/Latino). Average age 27. In 2017, 160 master's, 3 other advanced degrees awarded. *Entrance requirements:* For master's, GRE taken within last 5 years (for MS Ed in speech-language pathology); SAT (minimum combined score of 1660 in 3 sections), ACT (23), GRE (minimum score of 4.0 on analytical writing section and minimum combined score of 310 on quantitative and verbal sections), or passing scores on 3 parts of Core Academic Skills Educators, minimum GPA of 3.0 in major; 2 letters of recommendation (for some programs); resume, personal statement or essay (depending on program). Additional exam

requirements/recommendations for international students: Required—TOEFL (minimum score 550 paper-based; 79 iBT), IELTS (minimum score 6), Michigan English Language Assessment Battery (minimum score 77) or Certificate of Advanced English (minimum score 160). *Application deadline:* For fall admission, 7/15 priority date for domestic students, 7/1 for international students; for spring admission, 12/1 priority date for domestic students, 11/1 for international students; for summer admission, 5/1 for domestic students. Applications are processed on a rolling basis. Application fee: $50. Electronic applications accepted. *Expenses: Tuition:* Full-time $21,366; part-time $7122 per credit. *Required fees:* $700; $175 per term. *Financial support:* In 2017–18, 125 students received support. Institutionally sponsored loans, scholarships/grants, and unspecified assistantships available. Support available to part-time students. Financial award applicants required to submit FAFSA. *Faculty research:* Multicultural literacy, science and mathematics teaching strategies, teacher as reflective practitioner, children with disabilities. *Unit head:* Dr. John E. Henning, Dean, 732-263-5513, Fax: 732-263-5277. *Application contact:* Laurie Kuhn, Associate Director of Graduate Admission, 732-571-3452, Fax: 732-263-5123, E-mail: gradadm@monmouth.edu.
Website: http://www.monmouth.edu/academics/schools/education/default.asp

Montana State University, The Graduate School, College of Education, Health, and Human Development, Department of Education, Bozeman, MT 59717. Offers adult and higher education (Ed D); curriculum and instruction (M Ed, Ed D), including professional educator (M Ed), technology education (M Ed); education (M Ed), including adult and higher education, educational leadership, school counseling; educational leadership (Ed D, Ed S). *Accreditation:* TEAC. *Program availability:* Part-time, online learning. *Degree requirements:* For master's, comprehensive exam; for doctorate, comprehensive exam, thesis/dissertation. *Entrance requirements:* For master's, GRE, 3 letters of reference, essays, BA transcripts; for doctorate, GRE, MAT, 3 letters of reference, essay, BA and M Ed transcripts; for Ed S, PRAXIS. Additional exam requirements/recommendations for international students: Required—TOEFL (minimum score 550 paper-based). Electronic applications accepted. *Faculty research:* Critical literacy; standards-based education; school Improvement, organizational change, leadership in rural education, leadership in Indian education; student Learning; multicultural/culturally responsive education for social justice Native American indigenous education, community-centered education teacher preparation.

Montana State University Billings, College of Education, Billings, MT 59101. Offers M Ed, MS Sp Ed, Certificate. *Accreditation:* NCATE. *Program availability:* Part-time, 100% online, blended/hybrid learning. *Degree requirements:* For master's, thesis optional. *Entrance requirements:* For master's, GRE General Test, minimum GPA of 3.0. Additional exam requirements/recommendations for international students: Required—TOEFL (minimum score 79 iBT), IELTS (minimum score 6.5). *Application deadline:* For fall admission, 7/15 for international students; for spring admission, 12/1 for international students. Applications are processed on a rolling basis. Application fee: $40. Electronic applications accepted. *Expenses:* Tuition, state resident: full-time $11,740; part-time $7880 per year. Tuition, nonresident: full-time $32,200; part-time $24,140 per year. *Financial support:* Research assistantships with partial tuition reimbursements, teaching assistantships with partial tuition reimbursements, career-related internships or fieldwork, Federal Work-Study, institutionally sponsored loans, scholarships/grants, tuition waivers (partial), and unspecified assistantships available. Support available to part-time students. Financial award application deadline: 5/1; financial award applicants required to submit FAFSA. *Faculty research:* Social studies education, science education. *Unit head:* Dr. Mary Susan Fishbaugh, Dean, 406-657-2286, Fax: 406-657-2299, E-mail: mfishbaugh@msubillings.edu. *Application contact:* Dr. Mary Susan Fishbaugh, Dean, 406-657-2286, Fax: 406-657-2299, E-mail: mfishbaugh@msubillings.edu.
Website: http://www.msubillings.edu/coe/

Montana State University–Northern, Graduate Programs, Option in Instruction and Learning, Havre, MT 59501-7751. Offers MS Ed. *Program availability:* Part-time, blended/hybrid learning. *Degree requirements:* For master's, comprehensive exam, thesis optional, oral exams. *Entrance requirements:* For master's, GRE General Test or MAT, minimum GPA of 3.0. Electronic applications accepted. *Expenses:* Contact institution.

Montclair State University, The Graduate School, College of Education and Human Services, Montclair, NJ 07043-1624. Offers M Ed, MA, MAT, MPH, MS, Ed D, PhD, Certificate, Post Master's Certificate, Postbaccalaureate Certificate. *Accreditation:* NCATE. *Program availability:* Part-time, evening/weekend. *Degree requirements:* For master's, comprehensive exam (for some programs), thesis (for some programs); for doctorate, comprehensive exam, thesis/dissertation. *Entrance requirements:* For master's, GRE, GMAT, MAT, 2 letters of recommendation; for doctorate, GRE General Test, 3 letters of recommendation. Additional exam requirements/recommendations for international students: Required—TOEFL (minimum score 83 iBT) or IELTS. Electronic applications accepted. *Faculty research:* Key factors in the preparation of teachers for urban schools, factors affecting upper extremity motion patterns and injuries, implementation fidelity of instructional interventions, data-based decision-making in educational contexts, nutrition and physical activity of the aging population in the U.S.

Moravian College, Graduate and Continuing Studies, Education Programs, Bethlehem, PA 18018-6650. Offers curriculum and instruction (M Ed); education (MAT). *Program availability:* Part-time, evening/weekend. *Faculty:* 4 full-time (2 women), 7 part-time/adjunct (3 women). *Students:* 8 full-time (4 women), 95 part-time (74 women); includes 4 minority (1 Asian, non-Hispanic/Latino; 2 Hispanic/Latino; 1 Two or more races, non-Hispanic/Latino), 1 international. Average age 32. 79 applicants, 56% accepted, 22 enrolled. In 2017, 7 master's awarded. *Degree requirements:* For master's, thesis. *Entrance requirements:* For master's, state teacher certification. Additional exam requirements/recommendations for international students: Required—TOEFL, IELTS. *Application deadline:* For fall admission, 8/1 priority date for domestic and international students; for spring admission, 1/1 priority date for domestic and international students; for summer admission, 5/1 priority date for domestic and international students. Applications are processed on a rolling basis. Electronic applications accepted. *Expenses:* Contact institution. *Financial support:* In 2017–18, 1 research assistantship with full tuition reimbursement was awarded. Financial award applicants required to submit FAFSA. *Faculty research:* Teacher action research, youth participatory research, practitioner inquiry, science education, deaf and hard of hearing education. *Unit head:* Scott Dams, Dean of Graduate and Adult Enrollment, 610-861-1400, Fax: 610-861-1466, E-mail: graduate@moravian.edu. *Application contact:* 610-861-1400, Fax: 610-861-1466, E-mail: graduate@moravian.edu.

Morehead State University, Graduate Programs, College of Education, Morehead, KY 40351. Offers MA, MA Ed, MAT, Ed S. *Accreditation:* NCATE. *Program availability:* Part-time, evening/weekend. *Degree requirements:* For master's, comprehensive exam, thesis or alternative; for Ed S, thesis. *Entrance requirements:* For master's, GRE General Test or PRAXIS, minimum overall undergraduate GPA of 2.5; for Ed S, GRE General Test, interview, master's degree, minimum GPA of 3.5, work experience. Additional exam requirements/recommendations for international students: Required—TOEFL (minimum score 500 paper-based). Electronic applications accepted. *Faculty research:* Regional economic development, computer applications for school administrators, effectiveness of teacher interns, perceptual processes, alcoholism.

Morgan State University, School of Graduate Studies, School of Education and Urban Studies, Baltimore, MD 21251. Offers MA, MAT, MS, Ed D, PhD. *Program availability:* Part-time. *Degree requirements:* For master's, comprehensive exam; for doctorate, comprehensive exam, thesis/dissertation. *Entrance requirements:* For doctorate, GRE General Test or MAT. Additional exam requirements/recommendations for international students: Required—TOEFL (minimum score 550 paper-based). *Application deadline:* For fall admission, 2/1 priority date for domestic students; for spring admission, 10/1 priority date for domestic students. Applications are processed on a rolling basis. Application fee: $0. *Expenses:* Tuition, state resident: part-time $433 per credit. Tuition, nonresident: part-time $851 per credit. *Required fees:* $81.50 per credit. *Financial support:* Application deadline: 2/1. *Faculty research:* Multicultural education, cooperative learning, psychology of cognition. *Unit head:* Dr. Patricia L. Welch, Dean, 443-885-3385, Fax: 443-885-8240, E-mail: patricia.welch@morgan.edu. *Application contact:* Dr. Dean Campbell, Graduate Recruitment Specialist, 443-885-3185, Fax: 443-885-8226, E-mail: dean.campbell@morgan.edu.

Morningside College, Graduate Programs, Sharon Walker School of Education, Sioux City, IA 51106. Offers professional educator (MAT); special education (MAT), including instructional strategist: mild/moderate (7-12), instructional strategist: mild/moderate (K-6), K-12 instructional strategist: behavior disorders/learning disabilities, K-12 instructional strategist: mental disabilities. *Program availability:* Part-time, online only, 100% online. *Faculty:* 4 full-time (1 woman), 83 part-time/adjunct (62 women). *Students:* 18 full-time (15 women), 864 part-time (721 women); includes 29 minority (4 Black or African American, non-Hispanic/Latino; 3 American Indian or Alaska Native, non-Hispanic/Latino; 1 Asian, non-Hispanic/Latino; 18 Hispanic/Latino; 1 Native Hawaiian or other Pacific Islander, non-Hispanic/Latino; 2 Two or more races, non-Hispanic/Latino), 1 international. Average age 33. 314 applicants, 73% accepted, 162 enrolled. In 2017, 375 master's awarded. *Entrance requirements:* For master's, writing sample. *Application deadline:* Applications are processed on a rolling basis. Electronic applications accepted. *Expenses:* Contact institution. *Financial support:* In 2017–18, 266 students received support. Institutionally sponsored loans and tuition waivers (partial) available. Support available to part-time students. Financial award applicants required to submit FAFSA. *Unit head:* Barbara Chambers, Director, 712-274-5465, Fax: 712-274-5488, E-mail: chambersb@morningside.edu. *Application contact:* Tracy Sursely, Student Records Enrollment Coordinator, 712-274-5576, Fax: 712-274-5101, E-mail: surselyt@morningside.edu.

Mount Mary University, Graduate Programs, Programs in Education, Milwaukee, WI 53222-4597. Offers professional development (MA). *Program availability:* Part-time, evening/weekend. *Degree requirements:* For master's, action research project. *Entrance requirements:* For master's, minimum GPA of 2.75, teaching license. Additional exam requirements/recommendations for international students: Required—TOEFL (minimum score 550 paper-based; 80 iBT). Recommended—IELTS (minimum score 6.5). Electronic applications accepted. *Expenses:* Contact institution. *Faculty research:* Staff development, writing across the curriculum, effective schools, critical thinking skills, mathematics education.

Mount Mercy University, Program in Education, Cedar Rapids, IA 52402-4797. Offers reading (MA Ed); special education (MA Ed); teacher leadership (MA Ed). *Entrance requirements:* For master's, minimum cumulative GPA of 3.0, 2 letters of recommendation, resume, valid teaching license. Additional exam requirements/recommendations for international students: Required—TOEFL (minimum score 570 paper-based; 88 iBT). Electronic applications accepted.

Mount St. Joseph University, Graduate Education Program, Cincinnati, OH 45233-1670. Offers adolescent to young adult education (MA); dyslexia (Certificate); inclusive early childhood education (MA); middle childhood education (MA); multicultural special education (MA); reading science (MA). *Accreditation:* TEAC. *Program availability:* Part-time, evening/weekend, 100% online, blended/hybrid learning. *Faculty:* 6 full-time (5 women), 11 part-time/adjunct (8 women). *Students:* 37 full-time (30 women), 91 part-time (83 women); includes 13 minority (11 Black or African American, non-Hispanic/Latino; 1 Hispanic/Latino; 1 Two or more races, non-Hispanic/Latino). Average age 34. In 2017, 79 master's awarded. *Degree requirements:* For master's, comprehensive exam, thesis, research project, student teaching, clinical and field-based experiences. *Entrance requirements:* For master's, GRE (if GPA is below 3.0), letter of intent, 2 referrals, background check, interview, resume, minimum undergraduate GPA of 3.0. Additional exam requirements/recommendations for international students: Required—TOEFL (minimum score 560 paper-based; 83 iBT). *Application deadline:* Applications are processed on a rolling basis. Application fee: $50. Electronic applications accepted. *Expenses:* $600 per credit hour. *Financial support:* Applicants required to submit FAFSA. *Faculty research:* Foreign and second language learning problems/reading disabilities, multicultural/bilingual special education, science education, pedagogical content knowledge, early childhood, response to intervention. *Unit head:* Dr. Laura Saylor, Dean, 513-244-3263, E-mail: laura.saylor@msj.edu. *Application contact:* Mary Brigham, Assistant Director of Graduate Recruitment, 513-244-4233, Fax: 513-244-4629, E-mail: mary.brigham@msj.edu.
Website: http://www.msj.edu/academics/graduate-programs/master-of-arts-initial-teacher-licensure-programs/

Mount Saint Mary College, Division of Education, Newburgh, NY 12550-3494. Offers adolescence and special education (MS Ed); childhood education (MS Ed); literacy education (MS Ed); middle school (7-9) (MS Ed). *Accreditation:* NCATE. *Program availability:* Part-time, evening/weekend. *Faculty:* 10 full-time (9 women), 3 part-time/adjunct (all women). *Students:* 11 full-time (9 women), 83 part-time (62 women); includes 9 minority (1 American Indian or Alaska Native, non-Hispanic/Latino; 6 Hispanic/Latino; 2 Two or more races, non-Hispanic/Latino). Average age 28. 20 applicants, 100% accepted, 16 enrolled. In 2017, 57 master's awarded. *Entrance requirements:* Additional exam requirements/recommendations for international students: Required—TOEFL (minimum score 80 iBT). *Application deadline:* Applications are processed on a rolling basis. Application fee: $45. Electronic applications accepted. Application fee is waived when completed online. *Expenses: Tuition:* Full-time $14,454; part-time $803 per credit. *Required fees:* $172; $86 per semester. *Financial support:* In 2017–18, 15 students received support. Unspecified assistantships available. Financial award application deadline: 4/15; financial award applicants required to submit FAFSA. *Faculty research:* Learning and teaching styles, computers in special education, language development. *Unit head:* Dr. Monica Merritt, Graduate Coordinator, 845-569-3430, Fax: 845-569-3535, E-mail: monica.merritt@msmc.edu. *Application contact:* Lisa Alvarez, Director of Admissions for Graduate Programs and Adult Degree Completion, 845-569-3166, Fax: 845-569-3450, E-mail: lisa.gallina@msmc.edu.
Website: http://www.msmc.edu/Academics/Graduate_Programs/Master_of_Science_in_Education

Mount Saint Mary's University, Graduate Division, Los Angeles, CA 90049. Offers business administration (MBA); counseling psychology (MS); creative writing (MFA); education (MS, Certificate); film and television (MFA); health policy and management (MS); humanities (MA); nursing (MSN, Certificate); physical therapy (DPT); religious studies (MA). *Program availability:* Part-time, evening/weekend. *Faculty:* 50 full-time (35 women), 116 part-time/adjunct (81 women). *Students:* 670 full-time (518 women), 147 part-time (116 women); includes 414 minority (73 Black or African American, non-

Hispanic/Latino; 4 American Indian or Alaska Native, non-Hispanic/Latino; 60 Asian, non-Hispanic/Latino; 259 Hispanic/Latino; 7 Native Hawaiian or other Pacific Islander, non-Hispanic/Latino; 11 Two or more races, non-Hispanic/Latino), 4 international. Average age 32. 1,398 applicants, 21% accepted, 242 enrolled. In 2017, 170 master's, 28 doctorates, 35 other advanced degrees awarded. *Entrance requirements:* Additional exam requirements/recommendations for international students: Required—TOEFL. *Application deadline:* For fall admission, 6/30 priority date for domestic and international students; for spring admission, 10/30 priority date for domestic and international students; for summer admission, 3/30 priority date for domestic and international students. Applications are processed on a rolling basis. Application fee: $50. Electronic applications accepted. *Expenses: Tuition:* Part-time $905 per unit. One-time fee: $155 part-time. Tuition and fees vary according to degree level and program. *Financial support:* Career-related internships or fieldwork, Federal Work-Study, institutionally sponsored loans, and tuition waivers (full and partial) available. Support available to part-time students. Financial award application deadline: 3/15; financial award applicants required to submit FAFSA. *Unit head:* Albert Ramos, Director of Graduate Admissions, 213-477-2800, E-mail: gradprograms@msmu.edu. *Application contact:* Shawn Peters, Graduate Admission Counselor, 213-477-2676, E-mail: gradprograms@msmu.edu.
Website: http://www.msmu.edu/graduate-programs/

Mount St. Mary's University, Program in Education, Emmitsburg, MD 21727-7799. Offers M Ed, MAT. *Accreditation:* NCATE. *Degree requirements:* For master's, thesis (for some programs), exit portfolio/presentation. *Entrance requirements:* For master's, PRAXIS I and II. Additional exam requirements/recommendations for international students: Required—TOEFL (minimum score 550 paper-based; 83 iBT). Electronic applications accepted. *Expenses:* Contact institution.

Mount Saint Vincent University, Graduate Programs, Faculty of Education, Halifax, NS B3M 2J6, Canada. Offers adult education (M Ed, MA Ed, MA-R); curriculum studies (M Ed, MA Ed, MA-R), including education of young adolescents, general studies, teaching English as a second language; educational foundations (M Ed, MA Ed, MA-R); educational psychology (M Ed, MA Ed, MA-R), including education of the blind or visually impaired (M Ed, MA Ed), education of the deaf or hard of hearing (M Ed, MA Ed), educational psychology (MA-R); human relations (M Ed, MA Ed); elementary education (M Ed, MA Ed, MA-R); literacy education (M Ed, MA Ed, MA-R); school psychology (MASP). *Program availability:* Part-time, evening/weekend, online learning. *Degree requirements:* For master's, thesis (for some programs), practicum. *Entrance requirements:* For master's, bachelor's degree in related field. Electronic applications accepted.

Mount Vernon Nazarene University, Department of Education, Mount Vernon, OH 43050-9500. Offers education (MA Ed); professional educator's license (MA Ed). *Accreditation:* NCATE. *Program availability:* Part-time, evening/weekend. *Degree requirements:* For master's, project.

Multnomah University, Graduate Programs, Portland, OR 97220-5898. Offers counseling (MA); global development and justice (MA); teaching (MA); TESOL (MA). *Program availability:* Part-time, evening/weekend. *Faculty:* 6 full-time (5 women), 12 part-time/adjunct (7 women). *Students:* 69 full-time (53 women), 18 part-time (13 women); includes 22 minority (5 Black or African American, non-Hispanic/Latino; 3 Asian, non-Hispanic/Latino; 9 Hispanic/Latino; 5 Two or more races, non-Hispanic/Latino). Average age 30. 71 applicants, 58% accepted, 30 enrolled. In 2017, 57 master's awarded. *Degree requirements:* For master's, variable foreign language requirement, comprehensive exam (for some programs), thesis (for some programs). *Entrance requirements:* For master's, interview; references; writing sample (for counseling). Additional exam requirements/recommendations for international students: Required—TOEFL (minimum score 550 paper-based). *Application deadline:* For fall admission, 8/1 for domestic students, 12/1 for international students; for spring admission, 12/1 for domestic and international students. Application fee: $40. Electronic applications accepted. *Expenses: Tuition:* Full-time $8720; part-time $5450 per credit hour. *Required fees:* $110; $55 per credit hour. Tuition and fees vary according to course load, degree level and program. *Financial support:* Career-related internships or fieldwork and scholarships/grants available. Support available to part-time students. Financial award application deadline: 7/1; financial award applicants required to submit FAFSA. *Unit head:* Dr. Daniel Scalberg, Academic Dean, 503-251-6441, E-mail: dscalberg@multnomah.edu. *Application contact:* Mindy Kate Hasenkamp, Director of Admissions, 503-251-6483, Fax: 503-254-1268, E-mail: admiss@multnomah.edu.

Murray State University, College of Education and Human Services, Murray, KY 42071. Offers MA Ed, MS, Ed D, Certificate, Ed S. PhD, EdD offered jointly with University of Kentucky. *Accreditation:* NCATE. *Program availability:* Part-time, evening/weekend, 100% online, blended/hybrid learning. *Faculty:* 75 full-time (47 women), 5 part-time/adjunct (2 women). *Students:* 128 full-time (101 women), 374 part-time (296 women); includes 50 minority (34 Black or African American, non-Hispanic/Latino; 1 American Indian or Alaska Native, non-Hispanic/Latino; 6 Asian, non-Hispanic/Latino; 5 Hispanic/Latino; 4 Two or more races, non-Hispanic/Latino), 9 international. Average age 33. 218 applicants, 66% accepted, 96 enrolled. In 2017, 92 master's, 16 doctorates, 12 other advanced degrees awarded. Terminal master's awarded for partial completion of doctoral program. *Entrance requirements:* For master's, doctorate, and other advanced degree, GRE or GMAT, minimum university GPA of 2.75. Additional exam requirements/recommendations for international students: Required—TOEFL (minimum score 527 paper-based; 71 iBT). *Application deadline:* Applications are processed on a rolling basis. Application fee: $40 ($50 for international students). Electronic applications accepted. *Expenses:* Tuition, state resident: full-time $9504. Tuition, nonresident: full-time $26,811. *International tuition:* $14,400 full-time. Tuition and fees vary according to course load, degree level and reciprocity agreements. *Financial support:* In 2017–18, 3 research assistantships were awarded; Federal Work-Study, scholarships/grants, and unspecified assistantships also available. Financial award applicants required to submit FAFSA. *Unit head:* Dr. David Whaley, Dean, College of Education and Human Services, 270-809-3817, Fax: 270-809-3889, E-mail: dwhaley2@murraystate.edu. *Application contact:* Kaitlyn Burzynski, Interim Assistant Director for Graduate Admission and Records, 270-809-5732, Fax: 270-809-3780, E-mail: msu.graduateadmissions@murraystate.edu.
Website: http://murraystate.edu/academics/CollegesDepartments/CollegeOfEducationandHumanServices/index.aspx

Muskingum University, Graduate Programs in Education, New Concord, OH 43762. Offers MAE, MAT. *Accreditation:* NCATE. *Program availability:* Part-time. *Entrance requirements:* For master's, minimum GPA of 2.7, teaching license. *Faculty research:* Brain behavior relationships, school partnerships, staff development, school law, proficiency testing, multi-age groupings.

National Louis University, National College of Education, Chicago, IL 60603. Offers administration and supervision (M Ed, Ed D, CAS, Ed S); curriculum and instruction (M Ed, MS Ed, CAS); early childhood administration (M Ed, CAS); early childhood education (M Ed, MAT, MS Ed, CAS); education (Ed D); educational psychology/human learning and development (M Ed, MS Ed, CAS, Ed S); elementary education (MAT); interdisciplinary curriculum and instruction (M Ed); mathematics education (M Ed, MS Ed, CAS); middle grades education (MAT); reading and language (M Ed, MS Ed,

CAS); school psychology (M Ed, Ed S); science education (M Ed, MS Ed, CAS); secondary education (MAT); special education (M Ed, MAT, CAS); technology in education (M Ed, CAS). *Accreditation:* NCATE. *Program availability:* Part-time, evening/weekend. *Degree requirements:* For doctorate, comprehensive exam, thesis/dissertation. *Entrance requirements:* For master's, MAT or GRE, minimum GPA of 3.0; for doctorate, GRE General Test, minimum GPA of 3.25, interview, resume, writing sample, 4 recommendations. Additional exam requirements/recommendations for international students: Required—TOEFL (minimum score 550 paper-based; 79 iBT).

National University, Academic Affairs, Sanford College of Education, La Jolla, CA 92037-1011. Offers advanced teaching practices (MS); applied behavior analysis (MS); applied school leadership (MS); e-teaching and learning (Certificate); education (MA); educational administration (MS); educational and instructional technology (MS); educational counseling (MS); higher education administration (MS); inspired teaching and learning (M Ed); school psychology (MS); special education (MA, MS). *Program availability:* Part-time, evening/weekend, 100% online, blended/hybrid learning. *Degree requirements:* For master's, thesis (for some programs). *Entrance requirements:* For master's, interview, minimum GPA of 2.5. Additional exam requirements/recommendations for international students: Required—TOEFL (minimum score 550 paper-based; 79 iBT), IELTS (minimum score 6). *Application deadline:* Applications are processed on a rolling basis. Application fee: $60 ($65 for international students). Electronic applications accepted. *Expenses: Tuition:* Part-time $430 per quarter hour. *Financial support:* Career-related internships or fieldwork, institutionally sponsored loans, scholarships/grants, and tuition waivers (partial) available. Support available to part-time students. Financial award application deadline: 6/30. *Faculty research:* Teacher education, special education, educational effectiveness, teaching abroad, school counseling. *Unit head:* Dr. Judy Mantle, Dean, 858-642-8320, E-mail: soe@nu.edu. *Application contact:* Brandon Jouganatos, Vice President for Enrollment Services, 800-628-8648, E-mail: advisor@nu.edu.
Website: http://www.nu.edu/OurPrograms/SchoolOfEducation.html

Nazareth College of Rochester, Graduate Studies, Department of Education, Rochester, NY 14618. Offers educational technology (MS Ed); inclusive adolescence education (MS Ed); inclusive childhood education (MS Ed); inclusive early childhood education (MS Ed); literacy education (MS Ed); teaching English to speakers of other languages (MS Ed). *Accreditation:* TEAC. *Program availability:* Part-time, evening/weekend. *Entrance requirements:* For master's, GRE or MAT (for education programs), minimum GPA of 3.0. Additional exam requirements/recommendations for international students: Required—TOEFL (minimum score 550 paper-based, 79 iBT) or IELTS (6.5). Electronic applications accepted.

Neumann University, Graduate Program in Education, Aston, PA 19014-1298. Offers education (MS), including administrative certification (school principal PK-12), autism, early elementary education, secondary education, special education. *Program availability:* Part-time, evening/weekend, 100% online, blended/hybrid learning. *Faculty:* 6 full-time (5 women), 16 part-time/adjunct (7 women). *Students:* 68 full-time (56 women), 108 part-time (93 women); includes 36 minority (28 Black or African American, non-Hispanic/Latino; 3 Hispanic/Latino; 5 Two or more races, non-Hispanic/Latino). Average age 33. 83 applicants, 69% accepted, 36 enrolled. In 2017, 114 master's awarded. *Entrance requirements:* For master's, official transcripts from all institutions attended, letter of intent, three professional references, copy of any teaching certifications. Additional exam requirements/recommendations for international students: Required—TOEFL (minimum score 70 iBT). *Application deadline:* Applications are processed on a rolling basis. Application fee: $0. Electronic applications accepted. *Expenses:* $700 per credit hour (for on-campus master's-level education courses); $480 per credit hour (for online or off-campus master's-level education courses). *Financial support:* Scholarships/grants and health care benefits available. Support available to part-time students. Financial award application deadline: 3/15; financial award applicants required to submit FAFSA. *Unit head:* Dr. Stephanie Smith-Budhai, Director of Graduate Education, 610-358-4249, E-mail: budhais@neumann.edu. *Application contact:* Dr. Erika K. Davis, Director of Adult and Graduate Admissions, 800-9-NEUMANN Ext. 5208, Fax: 610-361-2548, E-mail: gradadultadmiss@neumann.edu.
Website: http://www.neumann.edu/academics/grad/education/index.asp

New England College, Program in Education, Henniker, NH 03242-3293. Offers higher education administration (MS, Ed D); K-12 leadership (Ed D); literacy and language arts (M Ed); meeting the needs of all learners/special education (M Ed); teacher leadership/school reform (M Ed). *Program availability:* Part-time, evening/weekend.

New Jersey City University, Debra Cannon Partridge Wolfe College of Education, Jersey City, NJ 07305-1597. Offers MA, MAT, Ed D. *Program availability:* Part-time, evening/weekend. *Entrance requirements:* Additional exam requirements/recommendations for international students: Required—TOEFL (minimum score 79 iBT).

Newman University, Master of Science in Education Program, Wichita, KS 67213-2097. Offers building leadership (MS Ed); curriculum and instruction (MS Ed), including English as a second language, reading specialist; organizational leadership (MS Ed). *Accreditation:* NCATE. *Program availability:* Part-time, evening/weekend, online learning. *Degree requirements:* For master's, thesis optional. *Entrance requirements:* For master's, 3 years' full-time teaching experience, minimum GPA of 3.0, writing sample, 2 letters of recommendation, evidence of teaching certification. Additional exam requirements/recommendations for international students: Required—TOEFL (minimum score 600 paper-based; 100 iBT). Electronic applications accepted. *Expenses:* Contact institution. *Faculty research:* Online course design and deliver, staff engagement, classroom action.

New Mexico Highlands University, Graduate Studies, School of Education, Las Vegas, NM 87701. Offers curriculum and instruction (MA); educational leadership (MA); professional counseling (MA); special education (MA). *Accreditation:* NCATE. *Program availability:* Part-time. *Degree requirements:* For master's, comprehensive exam, thesis or alternative. *Entrance requirements:* For master's, minimum undergraduate GPA of 3.0. Additional exam requirements/recommendations for international students: Required—TOEFL (minimum score 540 paper-based). *Faculty research:* Middle school curriculum, integrated computer applications for pre-service classroom teachers, adolescent literacy, narrative cognitive modes in New Mexico multicultural setting, math and math education.

New Mexico State University, College of Education, Las Cruces, NM 88003. Offers MA, MAT, Ed D, PhD, Ed S, Graduate Certificate. *Accreditation:* NCATE. *Program availability:* Part-time-only, evening/weekend, blended/hybrid learning. *Faculty:* 62 full-time (43 women), 16 part-time/adjunct (9 women). *Students:* 254 full-time (188 women), 401 part-time (292 women); includes 397 minority (22 Black or African American, non-Hispanic/Latino; 16 American Indian or Alaska Native, non-Hispanic/Latino; 16 Asian, non-Hispanic/Latino; 1 Native Hawaiian or other Pacific Islander, non-Hispanic/Latino; 11 Two or more races, non-Hispanic/Latino), 47 international. Average age 36. 413 applicants, 53% accepted, 135 enrolled. In 2017, 167 master's, 32 doctorates, 24 other advanced degrees awarded. *Degree requirements:* For master's, comprehensive exam (for some programs), thesis (for some programs); for doctorate, comprehensive exam (for some programs), thesis/dissertation (for some programs); for

Education—General

other advanced degree, comprehensive exam, thesis (for some programs). *Entrance requirements:* Additional exam requirements/recommendations for international students: Required—TOEFL (minimum score 550 paper-based; 79 iBT), IELTS (minimum score 6.5). *Application deadline:* For fall admission, 3/15 for international students; for spring admission, 10/15 for international students. Applications are processed on a rolling basis. Application fee: $40 ($50 for international students). Electronic applications accepted. *Expenses:* Tuition, state resident: full-time $4390. Tuition, nonresident: full-time $15,309. *Required fees:* $853. *Financial support:* In 2017–18, 227 students received support, including 7 fellowships (averaging $4,390 per year), 11 research assistantships (averaging $16,015 per year), 56 teaching assistantships (averaging $13,836 per year); career-related internships or fieldwork, Federal Work-Study, scholarships/grants, traineeships, health care benefits, and unspecified assistantships also available. Support available to part-time students. Financial award application deadline: 3/1. *Faculty research:* Multicultural identity development, mindfulness, pediatric neuropsychology, multicultural training for teachers and school psychologists, counselor training and supervision, college student mental health, critical pedagogy, bilingual education, critical race feminisms, oral history, access to literacy, literacy comprehension strategies, early childhood education policy and reform, technology-based learning environments, family-school relations, immigrant parent involvement, language differences. *Total annual research expenditures:* $402,004. *Unit head:* Dr. Donald Pope Davis, Dean, 575-646-5858, Fax: 575-646-6032, E-mail: dpd@nmsu.edu. *Application contact:* Dr. David Rutledge, Graduate Education Advising, 575-646-5411, Fax: 575-646-6032, E-mail: rutledge@nmsu.edu. Website: http://education.nmsu.edu/

New York Institute of Technology, School of Interdisciplinary Studies and Education, Old Westbury, NY 11568-8000. Offers MA, MAT, MS, Advanced Certificate, Advanced Diploma. *Accreditation:* NCATE. *Program availability:* Part-time, evening/weekend, 100% online, blended/hybrid learning. *Faculty:* 12 full-time (7 women), 23 part-time/adjunct (14 women). *Students:* 80 full-time (67 women), 203 part-time (142 women); includes 72 minority (25 Black or African American, non-Hispanic/Latino; 13 Asian, non-Hispanic/Latino; 30 Hispanic/Latino; 4 Two or more races, non-Hispanic/Latino), 6 international. Average age 32. 151 applicants, 66% accepted, 65 enrolled. In 2017, 83 master's, 38 other advanced degrees awarded. *Entrance requirements:* Additional exam requirements/recommendations for international students: Required—TOEFL (minimum score 79 iBT), IELTS (minimum score 6). *Application deadline:* Applications are processed on a rolling basis. Application fee: $50. Electronic applications accepted. *Expenses:* $1,285 per credit plus fees. *Financial support:* Career-related internships or fieldwork, Federal Work-Study, scholarships/grants, tuition waivers (full and partial), and unspecified assistantships available. Support available to part-time students. Financial award application deadline: 2/15; financial award applicants required to submit FAFSA. *Unit head:* Dr. Christian Pomgratz, Interim Dean, 516-686-1474, E-mail: soeinfo@nyit.edu. *Application contact:* Alice Dolitsky, Director, Graduate Admissions, 516-686-7520, Fax: 516-686-1116, E-mail: nyitgrad@nyit.edu. Website: http://www.nyit.edu/interdisciplinary

New York University, Steinhardt School of Culture, Education, and Human Development, New York, NY 10003. Offers MA, MFA, MM, MPH, MS, DPS, DPT, Ed D, PhD, Advanced Certificate, Post Master's Certificate, Postbaccalaureate Certificate, Advanced Certificate/MPH, MA/Advanced Certificate, MA/MA, MA/MS, MLIS/MA. *Accreditation:* TEAC. *Program availability:* Part-time. *Students:* Average age 31. 6,757 applicants, 42% accepted, 1245 enrolled. In 2017, 1,316 master's, 109 doctorates, 36 other advanced degrees awarded. *Entrance requirements:* For doctorate, GRE General Test, interview. Additional exam requirements/recommendations for international students: Required—TOEFL (minimum score 100 iBT). *Application deadline:* Applications are processed on a rolling basis. Application fee: $75. Electronic applications accepted. *Expenses:* Contact institution. *Financial support:* Fellowships, research assistantships, teaching assistantships, career-related internships or fieldwork, Federal Work-Study, institutionally sponsored loans, scholarships/grants, traineeships, tuition waivers (partial), and unspecified assistantships available. Support available to part-time students. Financial award application deadline: 2/1; financial award applicants required to submit FAFSA. *Faculty research:* Equity, urban adolescents, arts in education, globalization, multivariate analysis, psychometrics. *Total annual research expenditures:* $30.4 million. *Unit head:* Dr. Dominic Brewer, Dean, 212-998-5000. *Application contact:* John Myers, Director of Enrollment Management, 212-998-5030, Fax: 212-995-4328, E-mail: steinhardt.gradadmissions@nyu.edu. Website: http://steinhardt.nyu.edu/

Niagara University, Graduate Division of Education, Niagara University, NY 14109. Offers applied behavior analysis (Certificate); educational leadership (MS Ed, PhD, Certificate), including leadership and policy (PhD), school building leader (MS Ed), school district business leader (Certificate), school district leader (MS Ed, Certificate); literacy instruction (MS Ed); mental health counseling (MS, Certificate); school counseling (MS Ed, Certificate); school psychology (MS); teacher education (MS, MS Ed, Certificate), including early childhood and childhood education (MS Ed, Certificate), early childhood special education (MS), middle and adolescence education (Certificate), special education (MS Ed), special education (grades 1-6) (Certificate), special education (grades 7-12) (Certificate), teaching English to speakers of other languages (TESOL) (Certificate). *Accreditation:* NCATE (one or more programs are accredited). *Program availability:* Part-time, evening/weekend. *Faculty:* 24 full-time, 49 part-time/adjunct. *Students:* 260 full-time (203 women), 311 part-time (239 women); includes 67 minority (35 Black or African American, non-Hispanic/Latino; 3 American Indian or Alaska Native, non-Hispanic/Latino; 3 Asian, non-Hispanic/Latino; 18 Hispanic/Latino; 8 Two or more races, non-Hispanic/Latino), 102 international. Average age 31. In 2017, 202 master's, 10 doctorates, 59 other advanced degrees awarded. *Entrance requirements:* For master's, GRE General Test or MAT. Additional exam requirements/recommendations for international students: Required—TOEFL (minimum score 550 paper-based; 79 iBT), IELTS (minimum score 6). *Application deadline:* For fall admission, 8/1 for domestic students. Applications are processed on a rolling basis. Application fee: $30. *Expenses:* Contact institution. *Financial support:* Research assistantships with tuition reimbursements, teaching assistantships with tuition reimbursements, career-related internships or fieldwork, Federal Work-Study, scholarships/grants, and unspecified assistantships available. Financial award application deadline: 4/15; financial award applicants required to submit FAFSA. *Faculty research:* Instructional supervision, appraisal and evaluation, career opportunities. *Unit head:* Dr. Chandra Foote, Dean, College of Education, 716-286-8549, Fax: 716-286-8561, E-mail: cjf@niagara.edu. *Application contact:* Evan Pierce, Associate Director for Graduate Recruitment, 716-286-8769, Fax: 716-286-8170, E-mail: epierce@niagara.edu. Website: http://www.niagara.edu/advance/

Nicholls State University, Graduate Studies, College of Education, Department of Teacher Education, Thibodaux, LA 70310. Offers curriculum and instruction (M Ed); educational leadership (M Ed); elementary education (MAT); human performance education (MAT); middle school education (MAT); secondary education (MAT). *Accreditation:* NCATE. *Program availability:* Part-time, evening/weekend, online learning. *Degree requirements:* For master's, comprehensive exam, portfolio. *Entrance requirements:* For master's, GRE General Test, teaching license. Electronic applications accepted.

Nipissing University, Faculty of Education, North Bay, ON P1B 8L7, Canada. Offers M Ed, Certificate. *Program availability:* Part-time, evening/weekend. *Degree requirements:* For master's, comprehensive exam (for some programs), thesis (for some programs). *Entrance requirements:* For master's, 1 year of experience, letters of recommendation, minimum undergraduate GPA of 3.0. Additional exam requirements/recommendations for international students: Required—TOEFL (minimum score 600 paper-based), IELTS (minimum score 7), TWE (minimum score 5).

Norfolk State University, School of Graduate Studies, School of Education, Norfolk, VA 23504. Offers MA, MAT. *Accreditation:* NCATE. *Program availability:* Part-time. *Degree requirements:* For master's, comprehensive exam. *Entrance requirements:* For master's, PRAXIS, GRE/GMAT, interview, teacher license. *Faculty research:* Urban, pre-elementary, and special education.

North Carolina Agricultural and Technical State University, School of Graduate Studies, School of Education, Greensboro, NC 27411. Offers MA Ed, MAT, MS. *Accreditation:* NCATE. *Program availability:* Part-time, evening/weekend. *Degree requirements:* For master's, comprehensive exam, qualifying exam. *Entrance requirements:* For master's, GRE General Test.

North Carolina Central University, School of Education, Durham, NC 27707-3129. Offers M Ed, MA, MAT, MS, MSA. *Accreditation:* NCATE. *Program availability:* Part-time, evening/weekend. *Degree requirements:* For master's, comprehensive exam, thesis or alternative. *Entrance requirements:* For master's, minimum GPA of 3.0 in major, 2.5 overall. Additional exam requirements/recommendations for international students: Required—TOEFL. *Application deadline:* For fall admission, 8/1 for domestic students. Application fee: $30. *Expenses:* Tuition, state resident: full-time $2770; part-time $692.50 per credit hour. Tuition, nonresident: full-time $9247; part-time $2311.75 per credit hour. *Financial support:* Application deadline: 5/1. *Unit head:* Audrey W. Beard, Dean, 919-530-6466, Fax: 919-530-7681, E-mail: awbeard@nccu.edu. *Application contact:* Audrey W. Beard, Dean, 919-530-6466, Fax: 919-530-7681, E-mail: awbeard@nccu.edu.

North Carolina State University, Graduate School, College of Education, Raleigh, NC 27695. Offers M Ed, MS, MS Ed, MSA, Ed D, PhD, Certificate. *Accreditation:* NCATE. *Program availability:* Part-time. *Degree requirements:* For doctorate, thesis/dissertation. *Entrance requirements:* For master's, doctorate, and Certificate, GRE General Test or MAT, minimum GPA of 3.0 in major. Electronic applications accepted. *Faculty research:* Moral/ethical development, financial policy analysis, middle years education, adult education.

North Central College, School of Graduate and Professional Studies, Department of Education, Naperville, IL 60566-7063. Offers MA Ed. *Program availability:* Part-time, evening/weekend. *Degree requirements:* For master's, thesis optional, clinical practicum, project. *Entrance requirements:* For master's, interview. Additional exam requirements/recommendations for international students: Required—TOEFL (minimum score 550 paper-based; 80 iBT), IELTS (minimum score 6.5). Electronic applications accepted. Application fee is waived when completed online. *Expenses:* Contact institution.

Northcentral University, Graduate Studies, San Diego, CA 92106. Offers business (MBA, DBA, PhD, Postbaccalaureate Certificate); education (M Ed, Ed D, PhD, Ed S, Post-Master's Certificate, Postbaccalaureate Certificate); marriage and family therapy (MA, DMFT, PhD, Post-Master's Certificate, Postbaccalaureate Certificate); psychology (MA, PhD, Post-Master's Certificate, Postbaccalaureate Certificate); technology (MS, PhD), including computer science, cybersecurity (MS), data science, technology and innovation management (PhD). *Program availability:* Part-time, evening/weekend, online only, 100% online. *Faculty:* 98 full-time (63 women), 385 part-time/adjunct (203 women). *Students:* 5,036 full-time (3,291 women), 5,747 part-time (3,977 women); includes 3,777 minority (2,550 Black or African American, non-Hispanic/Latino; 76 American Indian or Alaska Native, non-Hispanic/Latino; 192 Asian, non-Hispanic/Latino; 603 Hispanic/Latino; 39 Native Hawaiian or other Pacific Islander, non-Hispanic/Latino; 317 Two or more races, non-Hispanic/Latino). Average age 45. In 2017, 929 master's, 782 doctorates, 278 other advanced degrees awarded. *Degree requirements:* For doctorate, comprehensive exam, thesis/dissertation. *Entrance requirements:* For master's, bachelor's degree from regionally- or nationally-accredited institution, current resume or curriculum vitae, statement of intent, interview, and background check (for marriage and family therapy); for doctorate, post-baccalaureate master's degree and/or doctoral degree from nationally- or regionally-accredited academic institution; for other advanced degree, bachelor's-level or higher degree from accredited institution or university (for Post-Baccalaureate Certificate); master's and/or doctoral degree from regionally- or nationally-accredited academic institution (for Post-Master's Certificate). Additional exam requirements/recommendations for international students: Required—TOEFL (minimum score 550 paper-based; 79 iBT), IELTS (minimum score 6.5), PTE (minimum score 53). *Application deadline:* Applications are processed on a rolling basis. Application fee: $0. Electronic applications accepted. Tuition and fees vary according to program. *Financial support:* Scholarships/grants available. *Faculty research:* Business management, curriculum and instruction, educational leadership, health psychology, organizational behavior. *Unit head:* Dr. David Harpool, Acting Provost, 888-327-2877 Ext. 8181, E-mail: provost@ncu.edu. *Application contact:* Ken Boutelle, Vice President, Enrollment Services, 888-628-4979, E-mail: enrollmentservices@ncu.edu.

North Dakota State University, College of Graduate and Interdisciplinary Studies, College of Human Development and Education, School of Education, Fargo, ND 58102. Offers agricultural education (M Ed, MS), including agricultural education; counselor education (M Ed, MS, PhD), including clinical mental health counseling (M Ed, MS), counselor education and supervision (PhD), school counseling (M Ed, MS); curriculum and instruction (M Ed, MS); education (PhD); educational leadership (M Ed, MS, Ed S); family and consumer sciences education (M Ed, MS); history education (M Ed, MS); institutional analysis (Ed D); mathematics education (M Ed, MS); music education (M Ed, MS); occupational and adult education (Ed D); science education (M Ed, MS). *Accreditation:* NCATE. *Program availability:* Part-time, evening/weekend, online learning. *Degree requirements:* For master's, comprehensive exam; for doctorate, thesis/dissertation; for Ed S, thesis. *Entrance requirements:* For degree, GRE General Test, master's degree, minimum GPA of 3.25. Additional exam requirements/recommendations for international students: Required—TOEFL.

Northeastern Illinois University, College of Graduate Studies and Research, Daniel L. Goodwin College of Education, Chicago, IL 60625-4699. Offers MA, MAT, MS, MSI. *Program availability:* Part-time, evening/weekend. *Degree requirements:* For master's, comprehensive exam (for some programs), thesis (for some programs). *Entrance requirements:* For master's, minimum GPA of 2.75. Additional exam requirements/recommendations for international students: Required—TOEFL (minimum score 550 paper-based; 79 iBT). *Application deadline:* For fall admission, 4/1 priority date for domestic students; for spring admission, 8/15 for domestic students. Applications are processed on a rolling basis. Application fee: $30. Electronic applications accepted. *Expenses:* Tuition, state resident: full-time $7274; part-time $404.11 per credit hour. Tuition, nonresident: full-time $14,548; part-time $808.23 per credit hour. *Required fees:* $1284. *Financial support:* Applicants required to submit FAFSA. *Faculty research:* Leadership, problem-based learning strategies, school improvement, bilingual

education, use of technology. *Unit head:* Dr. Maureen D. Gillette, Dean, 773-442-5500. *Application contact:* Ada Umeh, Admission Director, Graduate College, 773-442-6008, Fax: 773-442-6040, E-mail: a-umeh@neiu.edu.
Website: https://www.neiu.edu/academics/college-of-education/

Northeastern State University, College of Education, Tahlequah, OK 74464-2399. Offers M Ed, MS. *Accreditation:* NCATE. *Program availability:* Part-time, evening/weekend. *Faculty:* 40 full-time (25 women), 9 part-time/adjunct (6 women). *Students:* 156 full-time (119 women), 362 part-time (300 women); includes 187 minority (20 Black or African American, non-Hispanic/Latino; 73 American Indian or Alaska Native, non-Hispanic/Latino; 6 Asian, non-Hispanic/Latino; 12 Hispanic/Latino; 76 Two or more races, non-Hispanic/Latino), 10 international. Average age 35. In 2017, 229 master's awarded. *Degree requirements:* For master's, thesis. *Entrance requirements:* For master's, GRE or MAT. Additional exam requirements/recommendations for international students: Required—TOEFL. *Application deadline:* For fall admission, 6/1 priority date for domestic students. Applications are processed on a rolling basis. Application fee: $25. Electronic applications accepted. *Expenses:* Tuition, state resident: part-time $222 per credit hour. Tuition, nonresident: part-time $501.75 per credit hour. *Required fees:* $37.40 per credit hour. Tuition and fees vary according to degree level. *Financial support:* Teaching assistantships, career-related internships or fieldwork, and Federal Work-Study available. Financial award application deadline: 3/1. *Unit head:* Dr. Vanessa Anton, Interim Dean of the College of Education, 918-444-3700, Fax: 918-458-2351, E-mail: anton@nsuok.edu. *Application contact:* Josh McCollum, Graduate Coordinator, 918-444-2093, E-mail: mccolluj@nsuok.edu.
Website: http://academics.nsuok.edu/education/EducationHome.aspx

Northern Arizona University, College of Education, Flagstaff, AZ 86011. Offers M Ed, MA, Ed D, PhD, Certificate, Ed S, Graduate Certificate. *Accreditation:* NCATE. *Program availability:* Part-time, 100% online, blended/hybrid learning. *Faculty:* 105 full-time (65 women), 10 part-time/adjunct (7 women). *Students:* 525 full-time (390 women), 1,207 part-time (870 women); includes 617 minority (107 Black or African American, non-Hispanic/Latino; 96 American Indian or Alaska Native, non-Hispanic/Latino; 24 Asian, non-Hispanic/Latino; 333 Hispanic/Latino; 6 Native Hawaiian or other Pacific Islander, non-Hispanic/Latino; 51 Two or more races, non-Hispanic/Latino), 24 international. Average age 36. 805 applicants, 80% accepted, 646 enrolled. In 2017, 597 master's, 21 doctorates, 74 other advanced degrees awarded. *Degree requirements:* For master's, variable foreign language requirement, comprehensive exam (for some programs), thesis (for some programs); for doctorate, variable foreign language requirement, comprehensive exam (for some programs), thesis/dissertation (for some programs); for other advanced degree, comprehensive exam (for some programs). *Entrance requirements:* Additional exam requirements/recommendations for international students: Required—TOEFL (minimum score 80 iBT), IELTS (minimum score 6.5). *Application deadline:* For fall admission, 3/1 for domestic and international students; for spring admission, 10/1 for domestic and international students. Application fee: $65. Electronic applications accepted. *Expenses:* Tuition, state resident: full-time $9240; part-time $458 per credit hour. Tuition, nonresident: full-time $21,588; part-time $1199 per credit hour. *Required fees:* $1021; $14 per credit hour. $646 per semester. Tuition and fees vary according to course load, campus/location and program. *Financial support:* In 2017–18, 79 students received support, including 2 fellowships with full and partial tuition reimbursements available (averaging $13,285 per year), 3 research assistantships with full and partial tuition reimbursements available (averaging $13,714 per year), 29 teaching assistantships with full and partial tuition reimbursements available (averaging $13,371 per year); institutionally sponsored loans, health care benefits, tuition waivers (full and partial), and unspecified assistantships also available. Financial award application deadline: 2/1; financial award applicants required to submit FAFSA. *Unit head:* Dr. Ramona Mellott, Dean, 928-523-7139, Fax: 928-523-1929, E-mail: ramona.mellott@nau.edu. *Application contact:* Tina Sutton, Coordinator, Graduate College, 928-523-4348, Fax: 928-523-8950, E-mail: graduate@nau.edu.
Website: https://nau.edu/coe

Northern Illinois University, Graduate School, College of Education, De Kalb, IL 60115-2854. Offers MS, MS Ed, Ed D, Ed S. *Accreditation:* NCATE. *Program availability:* Part-time, evening/weekend, online learning. *Faculty:* 110 full-time (66 women), 5 part-time/adjunct (3 women). *Students:* 328 full-time (199 women), 848 part-time (606 women); includes 284 minority (135 Black or African American, non-Hispanic/Latino; 2 American Indian or Alaska Native, non-Hispanic/Latino; 29 Asian, non-Hispanic/Latino; 84 Hispanic/Latino; 34 Two or more races, non-Hispanic/Latino), 59 international. Average age 35. 415 applicants, 77% accepted, 168 enrolled. In 2017, 359 master's, 62 doctorates, 20 other advanced degrees awarded. Terminal master's awarded for partial completion of doctoral program. *Degree requirements:* For master's and Ed S, comprehensive exam, thesis optional; for doctorate, thesis/dissertation, candidacy exam, dissertation defense. *Entrance requirements:* For master's, GRE General Test or MAT, minimum GPA of 2.75; for doctorate, GRE General Test or MAT, minimum GPA of 2.75 (undergraduate), 3.2 (graduate); for Ed S, GRE General Test, master's degree; minimum undergraduate GPA of 2.75, graduate 3.2. Additional exam requirements/recommendations for international students: Required—TOEFL (minimum score 550 paper-based). *Application deadline:* For fall admission, 6/1 for domestic students, 5/1 for international students; for spring admission, 11/1 for domestic students, 10/1 for international students. Applications are processed on a rolling basis. Application fee: $40. Electronic applications accepted. *Financial support:* In 2017–18, 1 research assistantship with full tuition reimbursement was awarded; fellowships with full tuition reimbursements, teaching assistantships with full tuition reimbursements, career-related internships or fieldwork, Federal Work-Study, scholarships/grants, tuition waivers (full), and staff assistantships also available. Support available to part-time students. Financial award applicants required to submit FAFSA. *Unit head:* Laurie Elish-Piper, Dean, 815-753-1949, Fax: 815-753-2100. *Application contact:* Graduate School Office, 815-753-0395, E-mail: gradsch@niu.edu.
Website: http://www.cedu.niu.edu/

Northern Kentucky University, Office of Graduate Programs, College of Education and Human Services, Highland Heights, KY 41099. Offers MA, MAT, MS, MSW, Ed D, Certificate, Ed S. *Accreditation:* NCATE. *Program availability:* Part-time, evening/weekend. *Degree requirements:* For master's, comprehensive exam (for some programs), thesis (for some programs). *Entrance requirements:* For master's, GRE. Additional exam requirements/recommendations for international students: Required—TOEFL (minimum score 550 paper-based; 79 iBT); Recommended—IELTS (minimum score 6.5). Electronic applications accepted.

Northern Michigan University, Office of Graduate Education and Research, College of Health Sciences and Professional Studies, School of Education, Leadership and Public Service, Marquette, MI 49855-5301. Offers administration and supervision (MAE); instruction (MAE); learning disabilities (MAE); postsecondary biology education (MS); reading education (MAE), including reading, reading specialist. *Accreditation:* TEAC. *Program availability:* Part-time, online learning. *Degree requirements:* For master's, thesis (for some programs). *Entrance requirements:* For master's, minimum GPA of 3.0. Additional exam requirements/recommendations for international students: Required—TOEFL (minimum score 550 paper-based; 79 iBT), IELTS (minimum score 6.5). *Application deadline:* For fall admission, 7/1 priority date for domestic students; for winter

admission, 11/15 for domestic students; for spring admission, 3/17 for domestic students. Applications are processed on a rolling basis. Application fee: $50. Electronic applications accepted. *Expenses:* Tuition, state resident: full-time $9417; part-time $542 per credit hour. Tuition, nonresident: full-time $12,873; part-time $758 per credit hour. Tuition and fees vary according to course load, degree level and program. *Financial support:* Research assistantships with full tuition reimbursements, career-related internships or fieldwork, Federal Work-Study, institutionally sponsored loans, and unspecified assistantships available. Support available to part-time students. Financial award application deadline: 3/1; financial award applicants required to submit FAFSA. *Unit head:* Dr. Joseph Lubig, Associate Dean for Teacher Education, 906-227-1880, Fax: 906-227-2764, E-mail: jlubig@nmu.edu. *Application contact:* Dr. Joseph Lubig, Associate Dean for Teacher Education, 906-227-1880, Fax: 906-227-2764, E-mail: jlubig@nmu.edu.
Website: http://www.nmu.edu/education/

Northern State University, MS Ed Program in Educational Studies, Aberdeen, SD 57401-7198. Offers MS Ed. *Program availability:* Part-time, online learning. *Degree requirements:* For master's, comprehensive exam, thesis optional. *Entrance requirements:* For master's, minimum GPA of 2.75. Additional exam requirements/recommendations for international students: Required—TOEFL (minimum score 550 paper-based; 78 iBT), IELTS (minimum score 6). Electronic applications accepted.

Northern Vermont University–Johnson, Program in Education, Johnson, VT 05656. Offers applied behavior analysis (MA Ed); curriculum and instruction (MA Ed); foundations of education (MA Ed); special education (MA Ed). *Program availability:* Part-time. *Faculty:* 5 full-time (3 women), 4 part-time/adjunct (3 women). *Students:* 3 full-time (all women), 36 part-time (30 women). In 2017, 23 master's awarded. *Degree requirements:* For master's, thesis or alternative, exit interview. *Entrance requirements:* For master's, interview. Additional exam requirements/recommendations for international students: Required—TOEFL. *Application deadline:* For fall admission, 5/1 for domestic students, 2/1 for international students. Applications are processed on a rolling basis. Electronic applications accepted. *Expenses:* Tuition, state resident: part-time $572 per credit hour. Tuition, nonresident: part-time $832 per credit hour. *Financial support:* Scholarships/grants and unspecified assistantships available. Financial award application deadline: 3/1; financial award applicants required to submit FAFSA. *Unit head:* Dr. Kathleen Brinegar, Chair, Department of Education, 802-635-1472, Fax: 802-635-1465, E-mail: kathleen.brinegar@jsc.edu. *Application contact:* Catherine H. Higley, Administrative Assistant, 800-635-2356 Ext. 1244, Fax: 802-635-1248, E-mail: catherine.higley@jsc.edu.
Website: http://www.jsc.edu/academics/education/majors-and-minors/master-of-arts-in-education/

Northern Vermont University–Lyndon, Graduate Programs in Education, Lyndonville, VT 05851. Offers education (M Ed), including curriculum and instruction, reading specialist, special education, teaching and counseling; natural sciences (MST), including science education. *Program availability:* Part-time, evening/weekend. *Degree requirements:* For master's, exam or major field project. *Entrance requirements:* Additional exam requirements/recommendations for international students: Recommended—TOEFL (minimum score 500 paper-based). *Faculty research:* Impaired reading, cognitive style, counseling relationship.

North Greenville University, T. Walter Brashier Graduate School, Greer, SC 29651. Offers Christian ministry (MCM, D Min); education (M Ed, MAT); financial planning (MBA); human resources (MBA). *Program availability:* Part-time, evening/weekend, online learning. *Degree requirements:* For master's, comprehensive exam (for some programs), thesis or alternative, capstone course. *Entrance requirements:* For master's, minimum GPA of 2.25 overall, 2.5 in major; for doctorate, MAT. Additional exam requirements/recommendations for international students: Required—TOEFL (minimum score 550 paper-based). Electronic applications accepted. *Faculty research:* Organizational behavior, church growth, homiletics, human resources, business strategy.

North Park University, School of Education, Chicago, IL 60625-4895. Offers MA. *Degree requirements:* For master's, thesis. *Entrance requirements:* For master's, GRE General Test. *Faculty research:* Teacher leadership, research design, teacher education.

Northwest Christian University, School of Education and Counseling, Eugene, OR 97401-3745. Offers clinical mental health counseling (MA); elementary teaching (MAT); English for speakers of other languages (MAT); physical education (MAT); school counseling (MA); secondary teaching (MAT); special education (MAT). *Program availability:* Part-time, evening/weekend, online learning. *Faculty:* 9 full-time (4 women), 14 part-time/adjunct (10 women). *Students:* 77 full-time (60 women), 44 part-time (30 women); includes 19 minority (4 Black or African American, non-Hispanic/Latino; 1 American Indian or Alaska Native, non-Hispanic/Latino; 3 Asian, non-Hispanic/Latino; 2 Hispanic/Latino; 1 Native Hawaiian or other Pacific Islander, non-Hispanic/Latino; 8 Two or more races, non-Hispanic/Latino). Average age 34. In 2017, 58 master's awarded. *Degree requirements:* For master's, thesis (for some programs). *Entrance requirements:* For master's, GRE or MAT, minimum undergraduate GPA of 3.0, interview, 2-3 page statement of purpose, two letters of recommendation, resume, background check. Additional exam requirements/recommendations for international students: Required—TOEFL (minimum score 550 paper-based; 80 iBT). *Application deadline:* Applications are processed on a rolling basis. Electronic applications accepted. *Expenses:* $640 to $660 per credit tuition, $90 per semester technology fee. *Financial support:* Applicants required to submit FAFSA. *Unit head:* Elizabeth Wosley-George, Director, 541-349-7465, Fax: 541-684-7310, E-mail: ewosleygeorge@nwcu.edu. *Application contact:* Billy Dorsch, Admission Counselor for Graduate Studies, 541-684-7279, Fax: 541-349-5281, E-mail: wdorsch@nwcu.edu.

Northwest College, Program in Education, Orange City, IA 51041-1996. Offers early childhood (M Ed); master teacher (M Ed); teacher leadership (M Ed, Graduate Certificate). *Program availability:* Online learning.

Northwestern Oklahoma State University, School of Professional Studies, Alva, OK 73717-2799. Offers adult education management and administration (M Ed); counseling psychology (MCP); curriculum and instruction (M Ed); educational leadership (M Ed); elementary education (M Ed); reading specialist (M Ed); school counseling (M Ed); secondary education (M Ed). *Accreditation:* NCATE (one or more programs are accredited). *Program availability:* Part-time. *Degree requirements:* For master's, comprehensive exam (for some programs), thesis optional, portfolio. *Entrance requirements:* For master's, GRE General Test or MAT, minimum GPA of 2.75.

Northwestern State University of Louisiana, Graduate Studies and Research, College of Education and Human Development, Natchitoches, LA 71497. Offers M Ed, MA, MAT, Ed S. *Accreditation:* NCATE. *Degree requirements:* For master's, comprehensive exam, thesis (for some programs); for Ed S, comprehensive exam, thesis. *Entrance requirements:* For master's, GRE General Test, GRE Subject Test, minimum undergraduate GPA of 2.5; for Ed S, GRE General Test. Additional exam requirements/recommendations for international students: Required—TOEFL. Electronic applications accepted. *Faculty research:* Teacher-parent-child-friendly physical activities for young children, Net generation and social media, positive emotion and multimedia learning, the effects of Web-based mathematics resources on the motivation and achievement of high school students with learning disabilities, educational leadership.

Education—General

Northwestern University, The Graduate School, School of Education and Social Policy, Evanston, IL 60208. Offers education (MS), including elementary teaching, secondary teaching, teacher leadership; human development and social policy (PhD); learning and organizational change (MS); learning sciences (MA, PhD). MA and PhD admissions and degrees offered through The Graduate School. *Program availability:* Part-time, evening/weekend. *Degree requirements:* For doctorate, comprehensive exam, thesis/dissertation. *Entrance requirements:* For master's and doctorate, GRE General Test. Electronic applications accepted. *Expenses:* Contact institution. *Faculty research:* Technology, curriculum design, welfare, education reform, learning.

Northwest Missouri State University, Graduate School, School of Education, Maryville, MO 64468-6001. Offers early childhood education (MS Ed); education leadership (MS Ed), including elementary, K-12, secondary; educational leadership (Ed S), including elementary school principalship, secondary school principalship, superintendency; educational leadership and policy analysis (Ed D); elementary education (MS Ed); elementary mathematics (MS Ed); higher education leadership (MS); middle school education (MS Ed); reading (MS Ed); special education (MS Ed); teacher leadership (MS Ed); teaching English language learners (MS Ed). *Accreditation:* NCATE. *Program availability:* Part-time. *Faculty:* 15 full-time (8 women). *Students:* 28 full-time (20 women), 170 part-time (114 women); includes 20 minority (7 Black or African American, non-Hispanic/Latino; 1 Asian, non-Hispanic/Latino; 8 Hispanic/Latino; 4 Two or more races, non-Hispanic/Latino). Average age 33. 168 applicants, 73% accepted, 114 enrolled. In 2017, 67 master's, 21 other advanced degrees awarded. *Degree requirements:* For master's, comprehensive exam; for Ed S, comprehensive exam, thesis. *Entrance requirements:* For master's, GRE General Test, writing sample; for Ed S, minimum graduate GPA of 3.25. Additional exam requirements/ recommendations for international students: Required—TOEFL (minimum score 550 paper-based). *Application deadline:* For fall admission, 7/1 for domestic and international students; for spring admission, 11/15 for domestic and international students. Applications are processed on a rolling basis. Application fee: $0 ($50 for international students). Electronic applications accepted. *Expenses:* $389.11 per credit hour in-state tuition and fees, $641.97 out-of-state; $9,750 total cost (for online-based education program). *Financial support:* Research assistantships with full tuition reimbursements, teaching assistantships with full tuition reimbursements, and unspecified assistantships available. Financial award application deadline: 4/1; financial award applicants required to submit FAFSA. *Unit head:* Dr. Tim Wall, Director, 660-562-1179, E-mail: timwall@nwmissouri.edu.
Website: https://www.nwmissouri.edu/education/index.htm

Northwest Nazarene University, Graduate Education Program, Nampa, ID 83686-5897. Offers curriculum and instruction (M Ed); educational leadership (M Ed, Ed D, PhD, Ed S), including building administrator (M Ed, Ed S), director of special education (Ed S), leadership and organizational development (Ed S), superintendent (Ed S). *Accreditation:* ACA (one or more programs are accredited); NCATE. *Program availability:* Part-time, online only, 100% online, 2-week face-to-face residency (for doctoral programs). *Students:* Average age 39. 96 applicants, 72% accepted, 67 enrolled. In 2017, 59 master's, 13 doctorates, 33 other advanced degrees awarded. *Degree requirements:* For master's, comprehensive exam (for some programs), action research project; for doctorate, thesis/dissertation; for Ed S, comprehensive exam, research project. *Entrance requirements:* For master's, minimum undergraduate GPA of 3.0 overall or during final 30 semester credits, undergraduate degree, valid teaching certificate; for doctorate, Ed S or equivalent, minimum GPA of 3.5; for Ed S, undergraduate degree, valid teaching certificate. Additional exam requirements/ recommendations for international students: Recommended—TOEFL. *Application deadline:* Applications are processed on a rolling basis. Application fee: $50. Electronic applications accepted. *Expenses:* Contact institution. *Financial support:* Research assistantships available. Financial award application deadline: 1/15; financial award applicants required to submit FAFSA. *Faculty research:* Action research, cooperative learning, accountability, institutional accreditation. *Unit head:* Dr. Heidi Curtis, Chair, 208-467-8250, E-mail: hlcurtis@nnu.edu. *Application contact:* Charlene Brown, Admissions Counselor, 208-467-8492, Fax: 208-467-8384, E-mail: gradeducationinfo@nnu.edu.
Website: http://www.nnu.edu/graded/

Northwest University, School of Education, Kirkland, WA 98033. Offers education (M Ed); teaching (MIT). *Program availability:* Part-time, evening/weekend. *Degree requirements:* For master's, action research project. *Entrance requirements:* For master's, Washington Educator Skills Test-Basic (WEST-B)/Washington Educator Skills Test-Endorsements (WEST-E), minimum GPA of 3.3. Additional exam requirements/ recommendations for international students: Recommended—TOEFL. Electronic applications accepted. *Expenses:* Contact institution.

Notre Dame de Namur University, Division of Academic Affairs, School of Education and Psychology, Program in Education, Belmont, CA 94002-1908. Offers curriculum and instruction (MA); disciplinary studies (MA). *Program availability:* Part-time, evening/weekend. *Students:* 5 full-time (2 women), 211 part-time (142 women). Average age 35. *Degree requirements:* For master's, thesis (for some programs). *Entrance requirements:* For master's, CBEST, CSET, valid teaching credential or substantial teaching experience. Additional exam requirements/recommendations for international students: Required—TOEFL (minimum score 550 paper-based; 79 iBT). *Application deadline:* For fall admission, 8/1 priority date for domestic students; for spring admission, 12/1 priority date for domestic students. Applications are processed on a rolling basis. Application fee: $60. Electronic applications accepted. *Expenses: Tuition:* Full-time $16,128; part-time $8064 per credit hour. *Required fees:* $80; $80 per credit hour. $40 per semester. *Financial support:* Career-related internships or fieldwork available. Support available to part-time students. Financial award applicants required to submit FAFSA. *Unit head:* Kim Tolley, Program Director, Master of Arts in Education, 650-508-3464, E-mail: ktolley@ndnu.edu.
Website: https://www.ndnu.edu/education-and-leadership/graduate/education/

Notre Dame of Maryland University, Graduate Studies, Program in Teaching, Baltimore, MD 21210-2476. Offers MA. *Accreditation:* NCATE. *Entrance requirements:* For master's, Watson-Glaser Critical Thinking Appraisal, writing test, grammar test, interview. Additional exam requirements/recommendations for international students: Required—TOEFL (minimum score 500 paper-based; 61 iBT). Electronic applications accepted.

Nova Southeastern University, Abraham S. Fischler College of Education, Fort Lauderdale, FL 33314. Offers education (MS, Ed D, PhD, Ed S); instructional technology and distance education (MS); teaching and learning (MA). *Accreditation:* NCATE. *Program availability:* Part-time, evening/weekend, 100% online, blended/hybrid learning. *Faculty:* 94 full-time (58 women), 204 part-time/adjunct (145 women). *Students:* 1,513 full-time (1,199 women), 1,583 part-time (1,259 women); includes 2,373 minority (1,224 Black or African American, non-Hispanic/Latino; 5 American Indian or Alaska Native, non-Hispanic/Latino; 34 Asian, non-Hispanic/Latino; 1,057 Hispanic/ Latino; 2 Native Hawaiian or other Pacific Islander, non-Hispanic/Latino; 51 Two or more races, non-Hispanic/Latino), 19 international. Average age 41. 1,753 applicants, 47% accepted, 581 enrolled. In 2017, 399 master's, 571 doctorates, 104 other advanced degrees awarded. *Degree requirements:* For master's, practicum, internship; for

doctorate, thesis/dissertation; for Ed S, thesis, practicum, internship. *Entrance requirements:* For master's, MAT or GRE (for some programs), CLAST, PRAXIS I, CBEST, General Knowledge Test, teaching certification, minimum GPA of 2.5, verification of teaching, BS; for doctorate, MAT or GRE, master's degree, minimum cumulative GPA of 3.0; for Ed S, MAT or GRE, master's degree, teaching certificate, minimum GPA of 3.0. Additional exam requirements/recommendations for international students: Recommended—TOEFL (minimum score 550 paper-based; 79 iBT), IELTS (minimum score 6). *Application deadline:* Applications are processed on a rolling basis. Application fee: $50. Electronic applications accepted. *Expenses:* Contact institution. *Financial support:* In 2017–18, 67 students received support. Career-related internships or fieldwork and Federal Work-Study available. Support available to part-time students. Financial award application deadline: 4/15; financial award applicants required to submit FAFSA. *Faculty research:* STEM education, educational technology, principal training, quality of life. *Total annual research expenditures:* $50,000. *Unit head:* Dr. Kimberly Durham, Interim Dean, 954-262-8731, Fax: 954-262-3894, E-mail: durham@nova.edu. *Application contact:* Adriana Garay, Executive Director for Marketing, Recruitment and Admissions, 800-986-3223 Ext. 8500, E-mail: fserecruit@nova.edu.
Website: http://www.fischlerschool.nova.edu/

Oakland City University, School of Education, Oakland City, IN 47660-1099. Offers educational leadership (Ed D); teaching (MA). *Accreditation:* NCATE. Terminal master's awarded for partial completion of doctoral program. *Degree requirements:* For master's, thesis; for doctorate, comprehensive exam, thesis/dissertation. *Entrance requirements:* For master's, MAT, minimum GPA of 3.0, interview, resume, letters of recommendation; for doctorate, MAT, GRE, minimum GPA of 3.2, interview, resume, letters of recommendation. *Expenses:* Contact institution. *Faculty research:* Assessment, cultural diversity, teacher education, education leadership.

Oakland University, Graduate Study and Lifelong Learning, School of Education and Human Services, Rochester, MI 48309-4401. Offers M Ed, MA, MAT, PhD, Certificate, Ed S, Graduate Certificate, PMC. *Accreditation:* TEAC. *Program availability:* Part-time, evening/weekend. *Degree requirements:* For doctorate, thesis/dissertation. *Entrance requirements:* For master's and doctorate, minimum GPA of 3.0. Additional exam requirements/recommendations for international students: Required—TOEFL (minimum score 550 paper-based). Electronic applications accepted. *Expenses: Tuition, state resident:* full-time $16,950; part-time $706.25 per credit. *Tuition, nonresident:* full-time $24,648; part-time $1027 per credit.

Ohio Dominican University, Division of Education, Columbus, OH 43219-2099. Offers curriculum and instruction (M Ed); educational leadership (M Ed); teaching English to speakers of other languages (MA). *Accreditation:* NCATE. *Program availability:* Part-time, evening/weekend, 100% online, blended/hybrid learning. *Faculty:* 15 full-time (10 women), 15 part-time/adjunct (11 women). *Students:* 7 full-time (all women), 103 part-time (83 women); includes 11 minority (5 Black or African American, non-Hispanic/ Latino; 1 Asian, non-Hispanic/Latino; 1 Hispanic/Latino; 4 Two or more races, non-Hispanic/Latino), 5 international. Average age 35. 59 applicants, 73% accepted, 41 enrolled. *Entrance requirements:* For master's, minimum undergraduate GPA of 3.0, teaching certificate/license, teaching experience, 2 letters of recommendation, currently teaching or access to academic classroom. Additional exam requirements/ recommendations for international students: Required—TOEFL (minimum score 550 paper-based), IELTS (minimum score 6.5). *Application deadline:* For fall admission, 8/15 for domestic students, 6/10 for international students; for spring admission, 1/4 for domestic students, 11/2 for international students. Applications are processed on a rolling basis. Application fee: $25. Electronic applications accepted. *Financial support:* Tuition waivers and tuition discounts (for diocesan teachers) available. Financial award applicants required to submit FAFSA. *Unit head:* Dr. JoAnn Hohenbrink, Chair, 614-251-4759, E-mail: hohenbrj@ohiodominican.edu. *Application contact:* John W. Naughton, Director for Graduate Admissions, 614-251-4721, Fax: 614-251-6654, E-mail: grad@ ohiodominican.edu.
Website: http://www.ohiodominican.edu/academics/graduate/master-of-education

The Ohio State University, Graduate School, College of Education and Human Ecology, Columbus, OH 43210. Offers M Ed, MA, MS, Ed D, PhD, and Ed S. *Accreditation:* NCATE. *Faculty:* 148. *Students:* 770 full-time (499 women), 269 part-time (196 women). Average age 31. In 2017, 284 master's, 91 doctorates, 2 other advanced degrees awarded. Terminal master's awarded for partial completion of doctoral program. *Degree requirements:* For master's, comprehensive exam (for some programs), thesis optional; for doctorate, comprehensive exam, thesis/dissertation. *Entrance requirements:* For master's and doctorate, GRE or GMAT. Additional exam requirements/ recommendations for international students: Required—TOEFL (minimum score 550 paper-based; 79 iBT), Michigan English Language Assessment Battery (minimum score 82); Recommended—IELTS (minimum score 7). *Application deadline:* Applications are processed on a rolling basis. Application fee: $60 ($70 for international students). Electronic applications accepted. *Financial support:* Fellowships with tuition reimbursements, research assistantships with tuition reimbursements, teaching assistantships with tuition reimbursements, career-related internships or fieldwork, Federal Work-Study, institutionally sponsored loans, scholarships/grants, traineeships, health care benefits, and unspecified assistantships available. Support available to part-time students. *Faculty research:* Math and science education; teaching professional development; issues related to urban education; health, well-being, and sports; literacy education. *Unit head:* Dr. Cheryl Achterberg, Dean, 614-292-2461, Fax: 614-292-8052, E-mail: achterberg.1@osu.edu. *Application contact:* Graduate and Professional Admissions, 614-292-9444, Fax: 614-292-3895, E-mail: gpadmissions@osu.edu.
Website: http://ehe.osu.edu/

The Ohio State University at Mansfield, Graduate Programs, Mansfield, OH 44906-1599. Offers education (MA); social work (MSW). *Program availability:* Part-time. *Faculty:* 39. *Students:* 1. *Degree requirements:* For master's, comprehensive exam (for some programs), thesis (for some programs). *Entrance requirements:* For master's, GRE, minimum GPA of 3.0. Additional exam requirements/recommendations for international students: Required—TOEFL (minimum 550 paper-based, 79 iBT), IELTS (minimum score 7) or Michigan English Language Assessment Battery (minimum score 82). *Application deadline:* For fall admission, 4/1 for domestic students, 3/1 for international students; for spring admission, 10/15 for domestic and international students. Applications are processed on a rolling basis. Application fee: $60 ($70 for international students). Electronic applications accepted. *Financial support:* Teaching assistantships with full tuition reimbursements, Federal Work-Study, and scholarships/ grants available. Support available to part-time students. Financial award application deadline: 2/15; financial award applicants required to submit FAFSA. *Unit head:* Dr. Norman W. Jones, Interim Dean and Director, E-mail: jones.2376@osu.edu. *Application contact:* Graduate and Professional Admissions, 614-292-9444, Fax: 614-292-3895, E-mail: gpadmissions@osu.edu.

The Ohio State University at Marion, Graduate Programs, Marion, OH 43302-5695. Offers education (MA), including teaching and learning. *Program availability:* Part-time. *Faculty:* 38. *Students:* 1. *Degree requirements:* For master's, comprehensive exam (for some programs), thesis (for some programs). *Entrance requirements:* For master's, GRE, minimum undergraduate GPA of 3.0. Additional exam requirements/ recommendations for international students: Required—TOEFL (minimum score 550 paper-based, 79 iBT), IELTS (minimum score 7) or Michigan English Language Assessment Battery (minimum score 82). *Application deadline:* Applications are processed on a rolling basis. Application fee: $60 ($70 for international students). Electronic applications accepted. *Financial support:* Application deadline: 2/15; applicants required to submit FAFSA. *Unit head:* Dr. Gregory S. Rose, Dean/Director, 740-725-6218, E-mail: rose.9@osu.edu. *Application contact:* Graduate and Professional Admissions, 614-292-9444, Fax: 614-292-3895, E-mail: gpadmissions@osu.edu.

The Ohio State University at Newark, Graduate Programs, Newark, OH 43055-1797. Offers education - teaching and learning (MA); social work (MSW). *Program availability:* Part-time. *Faculty:* 49. *Students:* 13 (12 women). Average age 33. Terminal master's awarded for partial completion of doctoral program. *Degree requirements:* For master's, comprehensive exam (for some programs), thesis (for some programs). *Entrance requirements:* For master's, GRE, minimum GPA of 3.0. Additional exam requirements/recommendations for international students: Required—TOEFL (minimum score 550 paper-based; 79 iBT, IELTS (minimum score 7), or Michigan English Language Assessment Battery (minimum score 82). *Application deadline:* For fall admission, 3/1 for domestic and international students. Applications are processed on a rolling basis. Application fee: $60 ($70 for international students). Electronic applications accepted. *Financial support:* Application deadline: 2/15. *Unit head:* Dr. William L. MacDonald, Dean and Director, 740-366-9333 Ext. 330, E-mail: macdonald.24@osu.edu. *Application contact:* Graduate and Professional Admissions, 614-292-9444, Fax: 614-292-3985, E-mail: gpadmissions@osu.edu.

Ohio University, Graduate College, Gladys W. and David H. Patton College of Education and Human Services, Athens, OH 45701-2979. Offers M Ed, MS, MSA, Ed D, PhD. *Accreditation:* NCATE. *Program availability:* Part-time, evening/weekend. *Degree requirements:* For master's, comprehensive exam (for some programs), thesis or alternative; for doctorate, comprehensive exam, thesis/dissertation. *Entrance requirements:* For master's, GRE General Test or MAT; for doctorate, GRE General Test, MAT, master's degree. Additional exam requirements/recommendations for international students: Required—TOEFL (minimum score 550 paper-based; 80 iBT) or IELTS (minimum score 6.5). Electronic applications accepted. *Faculty research:* School improvement, partnerships, literacy, rural education.

Ohio Valley University, School of Graduate Education, Vienna, WV 26105-8000. Offers curriculum and instruction (M Ed). *Program availability:* Online learning. *Entrance requirements:* For master's, 2 letters of recommendation, official transcripts from all previous institutions, essay, bachelor's degree.

Oklahoma State University, College of Education, Health and Aviation, Stillwater, OK 74078. Offers MS, Ed D, PhD, Ed S. *Accreditation:* NCATE. *Program availability:* Part-time, online learning. *Faculty:* 96 full-time (67 women), 69 part-time/adjunct (40 women). *Students:* 261 full-time (181 women), 542 part-time (345 women); includes 224 minority (58 Black or African American, non-Hispanic/Latino; 41 American Indian or Alaska Native, non-Hispanic/Latino; 10 Asian, non-Hispanic/Latino; 51 Hispanic/Latino; 2 Native Hawaiian or other Pacific Islander, non-Hispanic/Latino; 62 Two or more races, non-Hispanic/Latino), 34 international. Average age 35. 281 applicants, 67% accepted, 158 enrolled. In 2017, 174 master's, 58 doctorates awarded. *Degree requirements:* For master's, thesis or alternative; for doctorate, comprehensive exam, thesis/dissertation. *Entrance requirements:* For master's and doctorate, GRE or GMAT. Additional exam requirements/recommendations for international students: Required—TOEFL (minimum score 550 paper-based; 79 iBT). *Application deadline:* For fall admission, 3/1 priority date for domestic and international students; for spring admission, 8/1 priority date for domestic and international students. Applications are processed on a rolling basis. Application fee: $40 ($75 for international students). Electronic applications accepted. *Expenses:* Tuition, state resident: full-time $4019; part-time $2679.60 per year. Tuition, nonresident: full-time $15,286; part-time $10,190.40 per year. *Required fees:* $2129; $1419 per unit. Tuition and fees vary according to program. *Financial support:* In 2017-18, 75 research assistantships (averaging $9,598 per year), 105 teaching assistantships (averaging $11,392 per year) were awarded; career-related internships or fieldwork, Federal Work-Study, scholarships/grants, health care benefits, tuition waivers (partial), and unspecified assistantships also available. Support available to part-time students. Financial award application deadline: 3/1; financial award applicants required to submit FAFSA. *Unit head:* Dr. Robert Davis, Interim Dean, 405-744-6350, Fax: 405-744-6350, E-mail: robert.davis@okstate.edu.
Website: http://education.okstate.edu/

Old Dominion University, Darden College of Education, Norfolk, VA 23529. Offers MS, MS Ed, PhD, Ed S, Postbaccalaureate Certificate. *Program availability:* Part-time, evening/weekend, 100% online, blended/hybrid learning. *Faculty:* 94 full-time (55 women), 62 part-time/adjunct (40 women). *Students:* 541 full-time (448 women), 869 part-time (679 women); includes 448 minority (284 Black or African American, non-Hispanic/Latino; 6 American Indian or Alaska Native, non-Hispanic/Latino; 25 Asian, non-Hispanic/Latino; 71 Hispanic/Latino; 3 Native Hawaiian or other Pacific Islander, non-Hispanic/Latino; 59 Two or more races, non-Hispanic/Latino), 22 international. Average age 34. 755 applicants, 69% accepted, 382 enrolled. In 2017, 375 master's, 56 doctorates, 40 other advanced degrees awarded. *Degree requirements:* For master's, comprehensive exam (for some programs), thesis (for some programs); for doctorate, comprehensive exam, thesis/dissertation; for other advanced degree, comprehensive exam. *Entrance requirements:* For doctorate, GRE General Test, master's degree, minimum GPA of 3.25; for other advanced degree, GRE General Test or MAT. Additional exam requirements/recommendations for international students: Required—TOEFL (minimum score 550 paper-based). *Application deadline:* For fall admission, 6/1 priority date for domestic and international students; for spring admission, 11/1 priority date for domestic and international students. Applications are processed on a rolling basis. Application fee: $50. Electronic applications accepted. *Expenses:* Tuition, state resident: full-time $8928; part-time $496 per credit. Tuition, nonresident: full-time $22,482; part-time $1249 per credit. *Required fees:* $66 per semester. *Financial support:* In 2017–18, 141 students received support, including 4 fellowships with tuition reimbursements available (averaging $15,000 per year), 60 research assistantships with tuition reimbursements available (averaging $15,000 per year), 72 teaching assistantships with tuition reimbursements available (averaging $15,000 per year); career-related internships or fieldwork, Federal Work-Study, institutionally sponsored loans, scholarships/grants, tuition waivers (partial), and unspecified assistantships also available. Support available to part-time students. Financial award application deadline: 2/15; financial award applicants required to submit CSS PROFILE or FAFSA. *Faculty research:* Effective urban teaching practices, curriculum theory, clinical practices, special education, instructional technology. *Total annual research expenditures:* $11.9 million. *Unit head:* Dr. Jane S. Bray, Dean, 757-683-3938, Fax: 757-683-5083, E-mail: jsbray@odu.edu. *Application contact:* William Heffelfinger, Director of Graduate Admissions, 757-683-5554, Fax: 757-683-3255, E-mail: gradadmit@odu.edu.
Website: http://education.odu.edu/

Olivet Nazarene University, Graduate School, Division of Education, Bourbonnais, IL 60914. Offers curriculum and instruction (MAE); elementary education (MAT); library information specialist (MAE); reading specialist (MAE); school leadership (MAE); secondary education (MAT). *Accreditation:* NCATE. *Program availability:* Evening/weekend. *Degree requirements:* For master's, thesis or alternative.

Open University, Graduate Programs, Milton Keynes, United Kingdom. Offers business (MBA); education (M Ed); engineering (M Eng); history (MA); music (MA); philosophy (MA).

Oral Roberts University, School of Education, Tulsa, OK 74171. Offers Christian school administration (K-12) (MA Ed, Ed D); college and higher education administration (Ed D); curriculum and instruction (MA Ed); initial teaching with alternative licensure (MAT); initial teaching with licensure (MAT); public school administration (K-12) (MA Ed, Ed D). *Accreditation:* NCATE. *Program availability:* Part-time, online learning. *Faculty:* 7 full-time (2 women), 6 part-time/adjunct (2 women). *Students:* 344 full-time (223 women); includes 117 minority (93 Black or African American, non-Hispanic/Latino; 7 American Indian or Alaska Native, non-Hispanic/Latino; 11 Asian, non-Hispanic/Latino; 6 Hispanic/Latino). 80 applicants, 94% accepted, 65 enrolled. In 2017, 14 master's, 4 doctorates awarded. *Degree requirements:* For master's, comprehensive exam, thesis optional; for doctorate, comprehensive exam, thesis/dissertation. *Entrance requirements:* For master's, GRE General Test or MAT (minimum score in 80th percentile or higher); Oklahoma general education or subject area test (for MAT), minimum GPA of 3.0, bachelor's degree from regionally-accredited institution; for doctorate, minimum GPA of 3.0, master's degree from regionally-accredited institution. *Application deadline:* Applications are processed on a rolling basis. Application fee: $35. Electronic applications accepted. Application fee is waived when completed online. *Expenses:* Contact institution. *Financial support:* Fellowships and scholarships/grants available. Financial award application deadline: 3/15. *Faculty research:* Teacher effectiveness, college success in high achieving African-Americans, professional development practices. *Unit head:* Dr. Patrick Otto, Chair of Graduate School of Education, 918-495-7087, E-mail: jotto@oru.edu. *Application contact:* Audrey Ripley, Enrollment Counselor, 918-495-6375, E-mail: aripley@oru.edu.

Oregon State University, College of Education, Program in Education, Corvallis, OR 97331. Offers agricultural education (PhD); language equity and education policy (PhD); mathematics education (MS); science education (MS); science/mathematics education (PhD). *Program availability:* Part-time, 100% online, blended/hybrid learning. Terminal master's awarded for partial completion of doctoral program. *Degree requirements:* For master's, variable foreign language requirement, thesis (for some programs); for doctorate, variable foreign language requirement, thesis/dissertation. *Entrance requirements:* Additional exam requirements/recommendations for international students: Required—TOEFL (minimum score 575 paper-based). Application fee: $75 ($85 for international students). *Faculty research:* School administration, educational foundations, research methodology, education policy development, higher education administration. *Unit head:* Nick Cabot, Ecampus Counseling Lead, 541-737-8564, E-mail: cabotn@oregonstate.edu. *Application contact:* Nick Cabot, Ecampus Counseling Lead, 541-737-8564, E-mail: cabotn@oregonstate.edu.

Oregon State University, College of Education, Program in Teaching, Corvallis, OR 97331. Offers clinically based elementary education (MAT); elementary education (MAT); language arts (MAT); mathematics (MAT); music education (MAT); science (MAT); social studies (MAT). *Program availability:* Part-time, blended/hybrid learning. *Entrance requirements:* For master's, CBEST. Additional exam requirements/recommendations for international students: Required—TOEFL (minimum score 575 paper-based). *Application deadline:* For fall admission, 12/1 for domestic students. Application fee: $60. *Expenses:* Contact institution. *Unit head:* Jordon Zardinejad, 541-322-3118, E-mail: jordon.zardinejad@osucascades.edu. *Application contact:* Jordon Zardinejad, 541-322-3118, E-mail: jordon.zardinejad@osucascades.edu.
Website: http://education.oregonstate.edu/mat

Oregon State University–Cascades, Program in Education, Bend, OR 97701. Offers MAT.

Ottawa University, Graduate Studies-Arizona, Program in Education, Ottawa, KS 66067-3399. Offers community college counseling (MA); curriculum and instruction (MA); early childhood (MA); education intervention (MA); education leadership (MA); education technology (MA); Montessori early childhood education (MA); Montessori elementary education (MA); professional development (MA); school guidance counseling (MA); special education - cross categorical (MA). Programs offered in Mesa, Phoenix, Tempe and West Valley, AZ. *Accreditation:* NCATE. *Program availability:* Part-time. *Degree requirements:* For master's, thesis or alternative. *Entrance requirements:* For master's, minimum undergraduate GPA of 3.0, copy of current state certification or teaching license. Additional exam requirements/recommendations for international students: Required—TOEFL (minimum score 550 paper-based). Electronic applications accepted. *Expenses:* Contact institution.

Otterbein University, Department of Education, Westerville, OH 43081. Offers MAE, MAT. *Accreditation:* NCATE. *Degree requirements:* For master's, capstone project. *Entrance requirements:* For master's, 2 reference forms, essay, interview. Additional exam requirements/recommendations for international students: Required—TOEFL (minimum score 550 paper-based; 79 iBT). *Faculty research:* Computer technology middle level education, assessment, teacher leadership, multicultural education.

Pace University, School of Education, New York, NY 10038. Offers adolescent education (MST), including biology, chemistry, earth science, English, foreign languages, mathematics, physics, social studies; childhood education (MST); early childhood development, learning and intervention (MST); educational technology studies (MS); inclusive adolescent education (MST), including biology, chemistry, earth science, English, foreign languages, mathematics, physics, social studies; integrated instruction for educational technology (Certificate); integrated instruction for literacy and technology (Certificate); literacy (MS Ed); special education (MS Ed). *Accreditation:* NCATE. *Program availability:* Part-time, evening/weekend, 100% online, blended/hybrid learning. *Faculty:* 19 full-time (13 women), 86 part-time/adjunct (49 women). *Students:* 91 full-time (76 women), 548 part-time (401 women); includes 247 minority (112 Black or African American, non-Hispanic/Latino; 2 American Indian or Alaska Native, non-Hispanic/Latino; 31 Asian, non-Hispanic/Latino; 93 Hispanic/Latino; 1 Native Hawaiian or other Pacific Islander, non-Hispanic/Latino; 8 Two or more races, non-Hispanic/Latino), 6 international. Average age 30. 188 applicants, 86% accepted, 114 enrolled. In 2017, 213 master's, 8 other advanced degrees awarded. *Degree requirements:* For master's and Certificate, certification exams. *Entrance requirements:* For master's, GRE (for initial certification programs only), teaching certificate (for MS Ed in literacy and special education programs only). Additional exam requirements/recommendations for international students: Required—TOEFL (minimum score 88 iBT), IELTS or PTE. *Application deadline:* For fall admission, 8/1 priority date for domestic students, 6/1 for international students; for spring admission, 12/1 priority date for domestic students, 10/1 for international students. Applications are processed on a rolling basis. Application fee: $70. Electronic applications accepted. *Expenses:* Contact institution. *Financial support:* In 2017–18, 17 students received support, including 17 research assistantships with partial tuition reimbursements available (averaging $6,020 per year); career-related internships or fieldwork, Federal Work-Study, scholarships/grants, and unspecified assistantships also available. Financial award application deadline: 9/1; financial award applicants required to submit FAFSA. *Faculty research:* STEM education, TESOL, teacher education, special education, language and literary development. *Total annual research expenditures:* $29,706. *Unit head:* Dr. Xiao-Lei Wang, Dean, School of Education, 914-773-3876, E-mail: xwang@pace.edu.

Education—General

Application contact: Susan Ford-Goldschein, Director of Graduate Admissions, 212-346-1531, Fax: 212-346-1585, E-mail: graduateadmission@pace.edu. Website: http://www.pace.edu/school-of-education

Pacific Lutheran University, School of Education and Kinesiology, Tacoma, WA 98447. Offers MAE. *Accreditation:* NCATE. *Program availability:* Part-time, evening/weekend. *Degree requirements:* For master's, comprehensive exam, thesis optional. *Entrance requirements:* For master's, WEST-B or WEST-B Exemption, interview. Additional exam requirements/recommendations for international students: Required—TOEFL (minimum score 550 paper-based; 88 iBT). Electronic applications accepted. *Expenses:* Contact institution.

Pacific Oaks College, Graduate School, Program in Education, Pasadena, CA 91103. Offers preliminary education specialist (MA); preliminary multiple subject (MA). *Program availability:* Online learning. *Degree requirements:* For master's, practicum. *Entrance requirements:* For master's, bachelor's degree from accredited college or university.

Pacific Union College, Education Department, Angwin, CA 94508-9707. Offers education (M Ed); elementary teaching (MAT); secondary teaching (MAT). *Program availability:* Part-time. *Faculty:* 3 full-time (1 woman), 1 (woman) part-time/adjunct. *Students:* 3 full-time (2 women), 4 part-time (2 women); includes 1 minority (Black or African American, non-Hispanic/Latino). Average age 45. 4 applicants, 100% accepted, 4 enrolled. In 2017, 1 master's awarded. *Degree requirements:* For master's, thesis, action research project, field experiences. *Entrance requirements:* For master's, GRE General Test, two interviews, teaching credential, letters of recommendation, essay. *Application deadline:* For fall admission, 8/30 for domestic and international students; for summer admission, 6/1 for domestic and international students. Applications are processed on a rolling basis. Application fee: $0. *Expenses:* $29,469 per year, $9,823 per quarter. *Financial support:* Scholarships/grants available. Support available to part-time students. Financial award application deadline: 9/25. *Unit head:* Prof. Thomas Lee, Department Chair, 707-965-6646, Fax: 707-965-6645, E-mail: tdlee@puc.edu. *Application contact:* Cherith Mundy, Credential Analyst, 707-965-6643, Fax: 707-965-6645, E-mail: teachingcredentials@puc.edu. Website: http://www.puc.edu/academics/departments/education/

Pacific University, College of Education, Forest Grove, OR 97116-1797. Offers early childhood education (MAT); education (MAE); elementary education (MAT); ESOL (MAT); high school education (MAT); middle school education (MAT); special education (MAT); speech-language pathology (MS); STEM education (MAT); talented and gifted (M Ed); visual function in learning (M Ed). *Accreditation:* ASHA; NCATE. *Program availability:* Part-time, evening/weekend. *Degree requirements:* For master's, research project. *Entrance requirements:* For master's, California Basic Educational Skills Test, PRAXIS II, minimum undergraduate GPA of 2.75, 3.0 graduate. Additional exam requirements/recommendations for international students: Required—TOEFL. Electronic applications accepted. *Expenses:* Contact institution. *Faculty research:* Defining a culturally competent classroom, technology in the K-12 classroom, Socratic seminars, social studies education.

Palm Beach Atlantic University, School of Education and Behavioral Studies, West Palm Beach, FL 33416-4708. Offers counseling psychology (MS), including addictions/mental health, general counseling, marriage and family therapy, mental health counseling, school guidance counseling. *Program availability:* Part-time, evening/weekend. *Entrance requirements:* For master's, GRE or MAT, minimum GPA of 3.0, essay. Additional exam requirements/recommendations for international students: Required—TOEFL (minimum score 550 paper-based; 79 iBT). Electronic applications accepted. *Faculty research:* Group dynamics, phenomenology, spirituality, multicultural psychology.

Park University, School of Graduate and Professional Studies, Kansas City, MO 54105. Offers adult education (M Ed); business and government leadership (Graduate Certificate); business, government, and global society (MPA); communication and leadership (MA); creative and life writing (Graduate Certificate); disaster and emergency management (MPA, Graduate Certificate); educational leadership (M Ed); finance (MBA, Graduate Certificate); general business (MBA); global business (Graduate Certificate); healthcare administration (MHA); healthcare services management and leadership (Graduate Certificate); international business (MBA); language and literacy (M Ed), including English for speakers of other languages, special reading teacher/literacy coach; leadership of international healthcare organizations (Graduate Certificate); management information systems (MBA, Graduate Certificate); music performance (ADP, Graduate Certificate), including cello (MM, ADP), piano (MM, ADP), viola (MM, ADP), violin (MM, ADP); nonprofit and community services management (MPA); nonprofit leadership (Graduate Certificate); performance (MM), including cello (MM, ADP), piano (MM, ADP), viola (MM, ADP), violin (MM, ADP); public management (MPA); social work (MSW); teacher leadership (M Ed), including curriculum and assessment, instructional leader. *Program availability:* Part-time, evening/weekend, online learning. *Degree requirements:* For master's, comprehensive exam (for some programs), thesis (for some programs), internship (for some programs); exam (for some programs). *Entrance requirements:* For master's, GRE or GMAT (for some programs), teacher certification (for some M Ed programs), letters of recommendation, essay, resume (for some programs). Additional exam requirements/recommendations for international students: Required—TOEFL (minimum score 550 paper-based; 79 iBT), IELTS (minimum score 6). Electronic applications accepted.

Penn State Harrisburg, Graduate School, School of Behavioral Sciences and Education, Middletown, PA 17057. Offers adult education in the health and medical professions (Certificate); applied behavior analysis (MA); applied clinical psychology (MA); applied psychological research (MA); community psychology and social change (MA); English as a second language (ESL) program specialist and leadership (Certificate); health education (M Ed); lifelong learning and adult education (M Ed, D Ed); literacy education (M Ed); literacy leadership (Certificate); psychology: applications in clinical psychology (Certificate); psychology: health psychology (Certificate); teaching and curriculum (M Ed); training and development (M Ed, Certificate). *Program availability:* Part-time, evening/weekend. *Unit head:* Dr. Mukund S. Kulkarni, Chancellor, 717-948-6105, Fax: 717-948-6452. *Application contact:* Robert W. Coffman, Jr., Director of Enrollment Management, Recruitment and Admissions, 717-948-6250, Fax: 717-948-6325, E-mail: hbgadmit@psu.edu. Website: https://harrisburg.psu.edu/behavioral-sciences-and-education/

Penn State University Park, Graduate School, College of Education, University Park, PA 16802. Offers M Ed, MA, MS, D Ed, PhD, Certificate. *Accreditation:* NCATE. *Program availability:* Part-time, evening/weekend. *Students:* 478 full-time (342 women), 194 part-time (118 women). Average age 33. 531 applicants, 56% accepted, 168 enrolled. In 2017, 151 master's, 104 doctorates awarded. *Entrance requirements:* Additional exam requirements/recommendations for international students: Required—TOEFL (minimum score 550 paper-based; 80 iBT), IELTS. *Application deadline:* Applications are processed on a rolling basis. Application fee: $65. Electronic applications accepted. *Expenses:* Contact institution. *Financial support:* Fellowships, research assistantships, teaching assistantships, career-related internships or fieldwork, Federal Work-Study, scholarships/grants, traineeships, health care benefits, and unspecified assistantships available. Support available to part-time students. Financial

award application deadline: 2/15; financial award applicants required to submit FAFSA. *Unit head:* Dr. David H. Monk, Dean, 814-865-2523, Fax: 814-865-0555. *Application contact:* Lori Hawn, Director, Graduate Student Services, 814-865-1795, Fax: 814-863-4627, E-mail: l-gswww@lists.psu.edu. Website: http://ed.psu.edu/

Penn State York, Graduate School, York, PA 17403. Offers ESL specialist (Certificate); teaching and curriculum (M Ed). *Students:* 16 part-time (13 women); includes 2 minority (1 Black or African American, non-Hispanic/Latino; 1 Two or more races, non-Hispanic/Latino). Average age 35. 3 applicants, 67% accepted, 2 enrolled. In 2017, 2 master's awarded. Application fee: $65. *Expenses:* Contact institution. *Unit head:* Dr. Regina Vasilatos-Younken, Vice Provost for Graduate Education/Dean, Graduate School, 814-865-2516, Fax: 814-863-4627. *Application contact:* Lori Hawn, Director, Graduate Student Services, 814-865-1795, Fax: 814-863-4627, E-mail: l-gswww@lists.psu.edu. Website: http://www.gradschool.psu.edu/

Peru State College, Graduate Programs, Program in Education, Peru, NE 68421. Offers curriculum and instruction (MS Ed). *Accreditation:* NCATE. *Program availability:* Part-time. *Degree requirements:* For master's, comprehensive exam (for some programs), thesis optional.

Piedmont College, School of Education, Demorest, GA 30535. Offers art education (MA, MAT); curriculum and instruction (Ed D, Ed S); early childhood education (MA, MAT); instructional technology (MA); middle grades education (MA, MAT); music education (MA, MAT); secondary education (MA, MAT); special education (MA, MAT). *Program availability:* Part-time, evening/weekend. *Students:* 341 full-time (268 women), 682 part-time (571 women); includes 182 minority (136 Black or African American, non-Hispanic/Latino; 2 American Indian or Alaska Native, non-Hispanic/Latino; 11 Asian, non-Hispanic/Latino; 32 Hispanic/Latino; 1 Two or more races, non-Hispanic/Latino). Average age 37. 333 applicants, 77% accepted, 103 enrolled. In 2017, 292 master's, 9 doctorates, 318 other advanced degrees awarded. *Degree requirements:* For master's, thesis, field experience in the classroom teaching; for doctorate, thesis/dissertation. *Entrance requirements:* For master's, GRE General Test, MAT; for Ed S, minimum graduate GPA of 3.5, valid teaching certificate. Additional exam requirements/recommendations for international students: Required—TOEFL (minimum score 550 paper-based). *Application deadline:* For fall admission, 7/15 for domestic students; for spring admission, 12/1 for domestic students. Applications are processed on a rolling basis. Electronic applications accepted. *Expenses:* Tuition: Full-time $9360; part-time $520 per credit hour. *Required fees:* $200; $200 per year. $100 per term. *Financial support:* Career-related internships or fieldwork, Federal Work-Study, and unspecified assistantships available. Support available to part-time students. Financial award applicants required to submit FAFSA. *Unit head:* Dr. Don Gnecco, Dean, 706-778-3000 Ext. 1201, Fax: 706-776-9608, E-mail: dgnecco@piedmont.edu. *Application contact:* Kathleen Carter, Director of Graduate Enrollment Management, 706-778-8500 Ext. 1181, Fax: 706-778-0150, E-mail: kanderson@piedmont.edu.

Pittsburg State University, Graduate School, College of Education, Pittsburg, KS 66762. Offers MS, Ed S. *Accreditation:* NCATE. *Program availability:* Part-time, 100% online, blended/hybrid learning. *Students:* 595 (413 women); includes 80 minority (17 Black or African American, non-Hispanic/Latino; 12 American Indian or Alaska Native, non-Hispanic/Latino; 3 Asian, non-Hispanic/Latino; 24 Hispanic/Latino; 24 Two or more races, non-Hispanic/Latino), 1 international. In 2017, 266 master's, 13 other advanced degrees awarded. Terminal master's awarded for partial completion of doctoral program. *Degree requirements:* For master's, thesis or alternative. *Entrance requirements:* For master's, GRE. Additional exam requirements/recommendations for international students: Required—TOEFL (minimum score 520 paper-based; 68 iBT), IELTS (minimum score 6), PTE (minimum score 47). *Application deadline:* For fall admission, 6/1 for international students; for spring admission, 10/15 for international students; for summer admission, 4/1 for international students. Applications are processed on a rolling basis. Application fee: $35 ($60 for international students). Electronic applications accepted. *Expenses:* Contact institution. *Financial support:* In 2017–18, 25 teaching assistantships with full tuition reimbursements (averaging $5,500 per year) were awarded; career-related internships or fieldwork, Federal Work-Study, and unspecified assistantships also available. Financial award application deadline: 2/1; financial award applicants required to submit FAFSA. *Unit head:* Dr. Jim Truelove, Dean, 620-235-4518, Fax: 620-235-4520, E-mail: jtruelove@pittstate.edu. *Application contact:* Lisa Allen, Assistant Director of Graduate and Continuing Studies, 620-235-4223, Fax: 620-235-4219, E-mail: lallen@pittstate.edu. Website: http://www.pittstate.edu/edsc/

Plymouth State University, College of Graduate Studies, Graduate Studies in Education, Certificate of Advanced Graduate Studies Programs, Plymouth, NH 03264-1595. Offers clinical mental health counseling (CAGS); educational leadership (CAGS); higher education (CAGS); school psychology (CAGS). *Program availability:* Part-time, evening/weekend.

Point Loma Nazarene University, School of Education, Program in Teaching, San Diego, CA 92106-2899. Offers MAT. *Program availability:* Part-time, evening/weekend. *Students:* 229 full-time (162 women), 234 part-time (176 women); includes 208 minority (17 Black or African American, non-Hispanic/Latino; 2 American Indian or Alaska Native, non-Hispanic/Latino; 12 Asian, non-Hispanic/Latino; 148 Hispanic/Latino; 3 Native Hawaiian or other Pacific Islander, non-Hispanic/Latino; 26 Two or more races, non-Hispanic/Latino). Average age 30. 109 applicants, 97% accepted, 86 enrolled. In 2017, 47 master's awarded. *Entrance requirements:* For master's, letters of recommendation, essay, interview. *Application deadline:* For fall admission, 8/4 priority date for domestic students; for spring admission, 12/8 priority date for domestic students; for summer admission, 4/13 priority date for domestic students. Applications are processed on a rolling basis. Application fee: $50. Electronic applications accepted. *Expenses:* Contact institution. *Financial support:* Career-related internships or fieldwork, scholarships/grants, and unspecified assistantships available. Financial award applicants required to submit FAFSA. *Faculty research:* Teaching preparation, the lives of teachers, co-teaching, teacher dispositions. *Unit head:* Jill Hamilton Bunch, Associate Dean, Bakersfield Regional Center, 661-321-8187, E-mail: jillhamilton-bunch@pointloma.edu. *Application contact:* Joanie Joy, Senior Director of Enrollment Management, 619-329-6785, E-mail: gradinfo@pointloma.edu. Website: https://www.pointloma.edu/graduate-studies/programs/teaching-ma

Point Park University, School of Arts and Sciences, Department of Education, Pittsburgh, PA 15222-1984. Offers adult learning and training (MA); athletic coaching (M Ed); curriculum and instruction (MA); educational administration (MA); leadership and administration (Ed D); secondary education (M Ed); special education grades 7-12 (M Ed); special education PreK-grade 8 (M Ed). *Program availability:* Part-time, evening/weekend, 100% online, blended/hybrid learning. *Degree requirements:* For master's, comprehensive exam (for some programs), thesis or alternative. *Entrance requirements:* For master's, minimum GPA of 3.0, resume, 2 letters of recommendation. Additional exam requirements/recommendations for international students: Required—TOEFL. Electronic applications accepted.

Pontifical Catholic University of Puerto Rico, College of Education, Ponce, PR 00717-0777. Offers M Ed, MA Ed, MRE, PhD. *Accreditation:* TEAC. *Program*

availability: Part-time, evening/weekend. *Degree requirements:* For master's, comprehensive exam, thesis (for some programs). *Entrance requirements:* For master's, GRE General Test, 2 letters of recommendation, interview, minimum GPA of 2.75; for doctorate, EXADEP, GRE or MAT, 3 letters of recommendation. *Faculty research:* Teaching English as a second language, learning styles, leadership styles.

Portland State University, Graduate Studies, School of Education, Portland, OR 97207-0751. Offers M Ed, MA, MAT, MS, MST, Ed D. *Accreditation:* NCATE. *Program availability:* Part-time, evening/weekend. *Faculty:* 68 full-time (47 women), 108 part-time/adjunct (79 women). *Students:* 469 full-time (347 women), 841 part-time (661 women); includes 333 minority (38 Black or African American, non-Hispanic/Latino; 16 American Indian or Alaska Native, non-Hispanic/Latino; 55 Asian, non-Hispanic/Latino; 162 Hispanic/Latino; 4 Native Hawaiian or other Pacific Islander, non-Hispanic/Latino; 58 Two or more races, non-Hispanic/Latino), 28 international. Average age 36. 669 applicants, 45% accepted, 241 enrolled. In 2017, 456 master's, 17 doctorates awarded. *Degree requirements:* For master's, variable foreign language requirement, comprehensive exam (for some programs), thesis (for some programs); for doctorate, variable foreign language requirement, comprehensive exam, thesis/dissertation. *Entrance requirements:* Additional exam requirements/recommendations for international students: Required—TOEFL (minimum score 550 paper-based; 80 iBT). *Application deadline:* For fall admission, 4/1 for domestic and international students; for winter admission, 9/1 for domestic and international students; for spring admission, 11/1 for domestic and international students. Application fee: $65. Electronic applications accepted. *Expenses:* Tuition, state resident: full-time $14,436; part-time $401 per credit. Tuition, nonresident: full-time $21,780; part-time $605 per credit. *Required fees:* $1380; $22 per credit. $119 per quarter. One-time fee: $325. Tuition and fees vary according to program. *Financial support:* In 2017–18, 156 students received support, including 5 research assistantships with full and partial tuition reimbursements available (averaging $9,145 per year), 3 teaching assistantships with full and partial tuition reimbursements available (averaging $6,390 per year); career-related internships or fieldwork, Federal Work-Study, institutionally sponsored loans, scholarships/grants, and unspecified assistantships also available. Support available to part-time students. Financial award application deadline: 3/1; financial award applicants required to submit FAFSA. *Total annual research expenditures:* $3.2 million. *Unit head:* Dr. Marvin Lynn, Dean, 503-725-4697, Fax: 503-725-5399, E-mail: mlynn@pdx.edu. *Application contact:* Information Contact, 503-725-4619, Fax: 503-725-5599, E-mail: gseinfo@pdx.edu.
Website: http://www.pdx.edu/education/

Post University, Program in Education, Waterbury, CT 06723-2540. Offers curriculum and instruction (M Ed); education (M Ed); educational technology (M Ed); higher education administration (MS); learning design and technology (M Ed); online teaching (M Ed); teaching English to speakers of other languages (TESOL) (M Ed). *Program availability:* Online learning. *Entrance requirements:* For master's, resume. *Expenses:* Tuition: Part-time $730 per credit hour. Part-time tuition and fees vary according to degree level and program. *Application contact:* Veronica Montalvo, Vice President, Online Education Enrollment Management and Admissions, 203-596-6164, E-mail: vmontalvo@post.edu.

Prairie View A&M University, College of Education, Prairie View, TX 77446. Offers M Ed, MA, MA Ed, MS, MS Ed, PhD. *Accreditation:* NCATE. *Program availability:* Part-time, evening/weekend, blended/hybrid learning. *Faculty:* 23 full-time (13 women), 6 part-time/adjunct (5 women). *Students:* 111 full-time (81 women), 256 part-time (204 women); includes 347 minority (327 Black or African American, non-Hispanic/Latino; 1 Asian, non-Hispanic/Latino; 17 Hispanic/Latino; 1 Native Hawaiian or other Pacific Islander, non-Hispanic/Latino; 1 Two or more races, non-Hispanic/Latino), 6 international. Average age 35. 181 applicants, 88% accepted, 104 enrolled. In 2017, 150 master's, 11 doctorates awarded. *Degree requirements:* For master's, comprehensive exam, thesis optional, minimum GPA of 3.0; for doctorate, comprehensive exam, thesis/dissertation. *Entrance requirements:* For master's, GRE, 3 letters of reference, minimum undergraduate GPA of 2.75; for doctorate, GRE General Test, 3 letters of reference, minimum undergraduate GPA of 3.0, essay. Additional exam requirements/recommendations for international students: Required—TOEFL (minimum score 550 paper-based; 79 iBT). *Application deadline:* For fall admission, 5/1 priority date for domestic and international students; for spring admission, 10/1 priority date for domestic students, 9/1 priority date for international students; for summer admission, 3/1 priority date for domestic students, 2/1 priority date for international students. Applications are processed on a rolling basis. Application fee: $50. Electronic applications accepted. *Expenses:* Tuition, state resident: part-time $242 per credit. Tuition, nonresident: part-time $695 per credit. *Required fees:* $149 per credit. *Financial support:* Career-related internships or fieldwork, institutionally sponsored loans, scholarships/grants, and unspecified assistantships available. Support available to part-time students. Financial award application deadline: 4/1; financial award applicants required to submit FAFSA. *Faculty research:* Mentoring, assessment, humanistic education, diversity, literacy education, recruitment, student retention, school collaboration, leadership skills, structural equations. *Unit head:* Dr. Phyllis Metcalf-Turner, Dean, 936-261-3600, Fax: 936-261-3621, E-mail: pmmetcalf@pvamu.edu. *Application contact:* Pauline Walker, Administrative Assistant II, Research and Graduate Studies, 936-261-3521, Fax: 936-261-3529, E-mail: gradadmissions@pvamu.edu.

Prescott College, Graduate Programs, Program in Education, Prescott, AZ 86301. Offers early childhood education (MA); early childhood special education (MA); education (MA); elementary education (MA); environmental education leadership and administration (MA); equine-assisted learning (MA); school guidance counseling (MA); secondary education (MA); special education: learning disabilities (MA); special education: mental retardation (MA); special education: serious emotional disabilities (MA); student-directed independent study (MA); sustainability education (PhD). *Program availability:* Part-time, online learning. *Degree requirements:* For master's, thesis, fieldwork or internship, practicum; for doctorate, thesis/dissertation. *Entrance requirements:* For master's, 2 letters of recommendation, resume; for doctorate, 3 letters of recommendation, resume, official transcripts, personal statement, program proposal. Additional exam requirements/recommendations for international students: Required—TOEFL (minimum score 500 paper-based). Electronic applications accepted.

Purdue University, Graduate School, College of Education, West Lafayette, IN 47907. Offers MS, MS Ed, PhD, Ed S. *Accreditation:* NCATE. *Program availability:* Part-time, evening/weekend. *Faculty:* 70 full-time (51 women), 2 part-time/adjunct (1 woman). *Students:* 156 full-time (110 women), 530 part-time (370 women); includes 114 minority (41 Black or African American, non-Hispanic/Latino; 3 American Indian or Alaska Native, non-Hispanic/Latino; 18 Asian, non-Hispanic/Latino; 38 Hispanic/Latino; 1 Native Hawaiian or other Pacific Islander, non-Hispanic/Latino; 13 Two or more races, non-Hispanic/Latino), 97 international. Average age 34. 377 applicants, 64% accepted, 151 enrolled. In 2017, 40 master's, 145 doctorates, 6 other advanced degrees awarded. *Degree requirements:* For master's, thesis optional; for doctorate, thesis/dissertation, oral and written exams; for Ed S, oral presentation, project. *Entrance requirements:* For master's, GRE General Test (if undergraduate GPA is below 3.0), minimum undergraduate GPA of 3.0 or equivalent; for doctorate, GRE General Test (minimum combined verbal and quantitative score of 1000, 300 for new scoring), minimum undergraduate GPA of 3.0 or equivalent; master's degree with minimum GPA of 3.0 or

equivalent; for Ed S, GRE General Test (minimum combined verbal and quantitative score of 1000, 300 for new scoring), minimum undergraduate GPA of 3.0 or equivalent; master's degree. Additional exam requirements/recommendations for international students: Required—TOEFL (minimum score 550 paper-based; 77 iBT); Recommended—TWE. *Application deadline:* For fall admission, 12/15 for domestic students, 3/1 for international students; for spring admission, 9/15 for domestic students, 8/1 for international students. Application fee: $60 ($75 for international students). Electronic applications accepted. *Financial support:* Fellowships with full tuition reimbursements, research assistantships with full tuition reimbursements, teaching assistantships with full tuition reimbursements, career-related internships or fieldwork, and tuition waivers (full) available. Support available to part-time students. Financial award application deadline: 3/1; financial award applicants required to submit FAFSA. *Unit head:* Maryann Santos, Dean, College of Education, 765-494-2336, E-mail: msdb@purdue.edu. *Application contact:* Graduate School Admissions, 765-494-2600, Fax: 765-494-0136, E-mail: gradinfo@purdue.edu.
Website: http://www.education.purdue.edu/

Purdue University Global, School of Teacher Education, Davenport, IA 52807. Offers education (M Ed); secondary education (M Ed); teaching and learning (MA); teaching literacy and language: grades 6-12 (MA); teaching literacy and language: grades K-6 (MA); teaching mathematics: grades 6-8 (MA); teaching mathematics: grades 9-12 (MA); teaching mathematics: grades K-5 (MA); teaching science: grades 6-12 (MA); teaching science: grades K-6 (MA); teaching students with special needs (MA); teaching with technology (MA). *Program availability:* Part-time, evening/weekend, online learning. *Entrance requirements:* Additional exam requirements/recommendations for international students: Required—TOEFL (minimum score 550 paper-based; 80 iBT).

Purdue University Northwest, Graduate Studies Office, School of Education, Hammond, IN 46323-2094. Offers counseling (MS Ed), including human services, mental health counseling, school counseling; educational administration (MS Ed); instructional technology (MS Ed); special education (MS Ed). *Accreditation:* NCATE. *Entrance requirements:* Additional exam requirements/recommendations for international students: Required—TOEFL.

Queens College of the City University of New York, Division of Education, Queens, NY 11367-1597. Offers MA, MAT, MS Ed, AC. *Accreditation:* NCATE. *Program availability:* Part-time, evening/weekend. *Students:* 245 full-time (208 women), 1,114 part-time (864 women); includes 649 minority (97 Black or African American, non-Hispanic/Latino; 2 American Indian or Alaska Native, non-Hispanic/Latino; 193 Asian, non-Hispanic/Latino; 335 Hispanic/Latino; 1 Native Hawaiian or other Pacific Islander, non-Hispanic/Latino; 21 Two or more races, non-Hispanic/Latino), 31 international. Average age 29. *Degree requirements:* For master's, comprehensive exam (for some programs), thesis (for some programs), research project. *Entrance requirements:* For master's, minimum GPA of 3.0. Additional exam requirements/recommendations for international students: Required—TOEFL, IELTS. *Application deadline:* For fall admission, 4/1 for domestic students; for spring admission, 11/1 for domestic students. Applications are processed on a rolling basis. Application fee: $125. Electronic applications accepted. *Financial support:* Career-related internships or fieldwork available. Financial award application deadline: 4/1; financial award applicants required to submit FAFSA. *Unit head:* Dr. Craig Michaels, Dean, 718-997-5220, E-mail: craig.michaels@qc.cuny.edu. *Application contact:* Elizabeth D'Amico-Ramirez, Assistant Director of Graduate Admissions, 718-997-5203, E-mail: elizabeth.damicoramirez@qc.cuny.edu.

Queen's University at Kingston, School of Graduate Studies, Faculty of Education, Kingston, ON K7L 3N6, Canada. Offers M Ed, PhD. *Program availability:* Part-time. *Degree requirements:* For master's, thesis optional; for doctorate, comprehensive exam, thesis/dissertation. *Entrance requirements:* Additional exam requirements/recommendations for international students: Required—TOEFL (minimum score 580 paper-based); Recommended—TWE (minimum score 4). *Faculty research:* Literacy, assessment and evaluation, special needs, mathematics, science and technology education.

Queens University of Charlotte, Wayland H. Cato, Jr. School of Education, Charlotte, NC 28274-0002. Offers educational leadership (MA); K-6 (MAT); literacy K-12 (M Ed). *Accreditation:* NCATE. *Program availability:* Part-time, evening/weekend, online learning. *Degree requirements:* For master's, comprehensive exam. *Entrance requirements:* For master's, GRE General Test. *Expenses:* Contact institution.

Quincy University, Master of Science in Education Programs, Quincy, IL 62301-2699. Offers curriculum and instruction (MS Ed), including bilingual/English as a second language; education studies (MS Ed); leadership (MS Ed); reading education (MS Ed); teacher leader (MS Ed). *Program availability:* Part-time, evening/weekend, online learning. *Degree requirements:* For master's, comprehensive exam (for some programs), thesis optional. *Entrance requirements:* For master's, MAT or GRE, personal resume. Additional exam requirements/recommendations for international students: Required—TOEFL (minimum score 550 paper-based; 79 iBT). *Application deadline:* Applications are processed on a rolling basis. Application fee: $25. Electronic applications accepted. Application fee is waived when completed online. *Expenses:* Tuition: Part-time $450 per credit hour. *Financial support:* Applicants required to submit FAFSA. *Unit head:* Dr. Bruce Alan Spitzer, Director, 217-228-5432 Ext. 3106, E-mail: spitzbr@quincy.edu. *Application contact:* Office of Admissions, 217-228-5210, Fax: 217-228-5479, E-mail: admissions@quincy.edu.
Website: http://www.quincy.edu/academics/graduate-programs/education

Quinnipiac University, School of Education, Hamden, CT 06518-1940. Offers MAT, MS, Diploma. *Accreditation:* NCATE. *Faculty:* 15 full-time (12 women), 44 part-time/adjunct (30 women). *Students:* 107 full-time (97 women), 189 part-time (162 women); includes 41 minority (13 Black or African American, non-Hispanic/Latino; 3 Asian, non-Hispanic/Latino; 14 Hispanic/Latino; 11 Two or more races, non-Hispanic/Latino), 2 international. 149 applicants, 93% accepted, 123 enrolled. In 2017, 116 master's, 32 other advanced degrees awarded. *Application deadline:* Applications are processed on a rolling basis. Application fee: $45. Electronic applications accepted. *Financial support:* Career-related internships or fieldwork, Federal Work-Study, and unspecified assistantships available. Financial award application deadline: 6/1; financial award applicants required to submit FAFSA. *Faculty research:* Equity and excellence in education, school leadership.
Website: http://www.qu.edu/gradeducation

Randolph College, Programs in Education, Lynchburg, VA 24503. Offers curriculum and instruction (MAT); special education-learning disabilities (M Ed, MAT). *Accreditation:* TEAC. *Entrance requirements:* For master's, minimum GPA of 3.0 in prerequisite education coursework, 2.7 in major or field of interest (MAT); teaching license (M Ed); 2 recommendations; interview.

Regent University, Graduate School, School of Education, Virginia Beach, VA 23464-9800. Offers education (M Ed, Ed D, PhD), including adult education (Ed D, PhD, Ed S), advanced educational leadership (Ed D, PhD, Ed S), character education (Ed D, PhD, Ed S), Christian education leadership (Ed D, PhD, Ed S), Christian school administration (M Ed), curriculum and instruction (Ed D, PhD, Ed S), curriculum and instruction - adult education (M Ed), curriculum and instruction - Christian school (M Ed), curriculum and

Education—General

instruction - gifted and talented (M Ed), curriculum and instruction - STEM education (M Ed), curriculum and instruction - teacher leader (M Ed), discipleship for ministry (M Ed), educational leadership (M Ed), educational psychology (Ed D, PhD, Ed S), educational technology and online learning (Ed D, PhD, Ed S), elementary education (M Ed), exceptional education executive leadership (Ed D, PhD, Ed S), higher education (Ed D, PhD, Ed S), higher education leadership and management (Ed D, PhD, Ed S), instructional design and technology (M Ed), K-12 school leadership (Ed D, PhD, Ed S), K-12 special education (M Ed), leadership in mathematics education (M Ed), reading specialist (M Ed), special education (Ed D, PhD, Ed S), student affairs (M Ed), TESOL - adult education (M Ed), TESOL - K-12 (M Ed); educational specialist (Ed S), including adult education (Ed D, PhD, Ed S), advanced educational leadership (Ed D, PhD, Ed S), character education (Ed D, PhD, Ed S), Christian education leadership (Ed D, PhD, Ed S), curriculum and instruction (Ed D, PhD, Ed S), educational psychology (Ed D, PhD, Ed S), educational technology and online learning (Ed D, PhD, Ed S), exceptional education executive leadership (Ed D, PhD, Ed S), higher education (Ed D, PhD, Ed S), higher education leadership and management (Ed D, PhD, Ed S), K-12 school leadership (Ed D, PhD, Ed S), special education (Ed D, PhD, Ed S). *Accreditation:* TEAC. *Program availability:* Part-time, evening/weekend, 100% online, blended/hybrid learning. *Faculty:* 22 full-time (10 women), 44 part-time/adjunct (32 women). *Students:* 80 full-time (59 women), 945 part-time (750 women); includes 432 minority (352 Black or African American, non-Hispanic/Latino; 4 American Indian or Alaska Native, non-Hispanic/Latino; 14 Asian, non-Hispanic/Latino; 43 Hispanic/Latino; 19 Two or more races, non-Hispanic/Latino), 12 international. Average age 40. 1,125 applicants, 49% accepted, 436 enrolled. In 2017, 316 master's, 24 doctorates awarded. *Degree requirements:* For master's, thesis or alternative; for doctorate, comprehensive exam, thesis/dissertation. *Entrance requirements:* For master's, Virginia Communication and Literacy Assessment (VCLA), PRAXIS, college transcripts, writing sample, interview; for doctorate, GRE, writing sample, resume, transcripts, interview. Additional exam requirements/recommendations for international students: Required—TOEFL (minimum score 577 paper-based). *Application deadline:* For fall admission, 4/1 priority date for domestic students; for spring admission, 10/15 priority date for domestic students. Applications are processed on a rolling basis. Application fee: $50. Electronic applications accepted. *Expenses:* Contact institution. *Financial support:* In 2017–18, 669 students received support, including 1 fellowship (averaging $10,000 per year); career-related internships or fieldwork, scholarships/grants, and unspecified assistantships also available. Support available to part-time students. *Faculty research:* Christian school administration, curriculum and instruction, educational technology and online learning, higher education, special education. *Unit head:* Dr. Donald Finn, Dean, 757-352-4278, Fax: 757-352-4318, E-mail: dfinn@regent.edu. *Application contact:* Heidi Cece, Assistant Vice President of Enrollment Management, 800-373-5504, Fax: 757-352-4381, E-mail: admissions@regent.edu.
Website: https://www.regent.edu/school-of-education

Regis College, Department of Education, Weston, MA 02493. Offers elementary teacher (M Ed); higher education leadership (Ed D); special education (M Ed). *Program availability:* Part-time, evening/weekend. *Degree requirements:* For doctorate, thesis/dissertation, capstone project. *Entrance requirements:* For master's, GRE or MAT, personal statement, recommendations, resume/curriculum vitae, official transcripts, interview; for doctorate, personal statement, recommendations, resume/curriculum vitae, official transcripts, presentation/interview. Additional exam requirements/recommendations for international students: Required—TOEFL (minimum score 560 paper-based; 79 iBT); Recommended—IELTS (minimum score 6.5). *Application deadline:* Applications are processed on a rolling basis. Application fee: $65. Electronic applications accepted. *Financial support:* Federal Work-Study, scholarships/grants, and unspecified assistantships available. Financial award applicants required to submit FAFSA. *Unit head:* Dr. Priscilla Boerger, Department Chair/Graduate Program Director, 781-768-7422, E-mail: priscilla.boerger@regiscollege.edu.

Regis University, Regis College, Denver, CO 80221-1099. Offers biomedical sciences (MS); developmental practice (MDP); education (MA); environmental biology (MS). *Accreditation:* TEAC. *Program availability:* Part-time. *Degree requirements:* For master's, thesis (for some programs), capstone presentation. *Entrance requirements:* For master's, official transcript reflecting baccalaureate degree awarded from U.S.-based regionally-accredited college or university. Additional exam requirements/recommendations for international students: Required—TOEFL (minimum score 550 paper-based; 82 iBT). Electronic applications accepted. *Expenses:* Contact institution.

Reinhardt University, Price School of Education, Waleska, GA 30183-2981. Offers M Ed, MAT. *Program availability:* Part-time, evening/weekend, online learning. *Degree requirements:* For master's, comprehensive exam. *Entrance requirements:* For master's, GACE, background check. Additional exam requirements/recommendations for international students: Required—TOEFL. Electronic applications accepted.

Relay Graduate School of Education, Graduate Programs, New York, NY 10011. Offers MAT. Program also offered at Chicago, Delaware, Houston, Memphis, New Orleans, and Newark campuses. *Program availability:* Online learning.

Rhode Island College, School of Graduate Studies, Feinstein School of Education and Human Development, Program in Education, Providence, RI 02908-1991. Offers PhD. Program offered jointly with University of Rhode Island. *Accreditation:* NCATE. *Program availability:* Part-time, evening/weekend. *Faculty:* 8 part-time/adjunct (5 women). *Students:* 55 part-time (33 women); includes 13 minority (3 Black or African American, non-Hispanic/Latino; 1 American Indian or Alaska Native, non-Hispanic/Latino; 7 Asian, non-Hispanic/Latino; 2 Hispanic/Latino). Average age 42. In 2017, 9 doctorates awarded. *Degree requirements:* For doctorate, comprehensive exam, thesis/dissertation. *Entrance requirements:* For doctorate, GRE, two official transcripts from all colleges and universities attended, 3 letters of recommendation, personal statement, professional resume. Additional exam requirements/recommendations for international students: Recommended—TOEFL (minimum score 550 paper-based; 79 iBT). *Application deadline:* For fall admission, 1/29 for domestic students. Applications are processed on a rolling basis. Application fee: $65. Electronic applications accepted. *Expenses:* Tuition, state resident: full-time $9768; part-time $407 per credit. Tuition, nonresident: full-time $19,008; part-time $792 per credit. *Required fees:* $696; $29 per credit. One-time fee: $200 full-time; $100 part-time. Tuition and fees vary according to course load. *Financial support:* Health care benefits available. Support available to part-time students. Financial award application deadline: 5/15; financial award applicants required to submit FAFSA. *Unit head:* Dr. Janet Johnson, Co-Director, 401-456-8701. *Application contact:* Graduate Studies, 401-456-8700.
Website: http://www.ric.edu/feinsteinschooleducationhumandevelopment/jointPHD.php

Rice University, Graduate Programs, Programs in Education Certification, Houston, TX 77251-1892. Offers MAT. *Entrance requirements:* For master's, GRE General Test, minimum GPA of 3.0. Additional exam requirements/recommendations for international students: Required—TOEFL (minimum score 600 paper-based; 90 iBT). Electronic applications accepted. *Faculty research:* Assessment, integration of math and science.

Rider University, College of Education and Human Services, Lawrenceville, NJ 08648-3001. Offers MA, MAT, Certificate, Ed S. *Accreditation:* NCATE. *Program availability:* Part-time, evening/weekend. *Degree requirements:* For master's, comprehensive exam (for some programs), thesis or alternative, internship, portfolios; for other advanced

degree, internship, professional portfolio. *Entrance requirements:* For master's, GRE (counseling, school psychology), MAT, interview, resume, letters of recommendation; for other advanced degree, PRAXIS. Additional exam requirements/recommendations for international students: Required—TOEFL (minimum score 550 paper-based). Electronic applications accepted. *Faculty research:* Gifted students, self-esteem, hope and mental health, conflicts in group work, cultural diversity and counseling assessment of special needs in children.

Rivier University, School of Graduate Studies, Department of Education, Nashua, NH 03060. Offers curriculum and instruction (M Ed); early childhood education (M Ed); educational administration (M Ed); educational studies (M Ed); elementary education (M Ed); elementary education and general special education (M Ed); emotional and behavioral disorders (M Ed); general social education (M Ed); leadership and learning (Ed D, CAGS); learning disabilities (M Ed); learning disabilities and reading (M Ed); mental health counseling (MA); reading (M Ed); school counseling (M Ed). *Program availability:* Part-time, evening/weekend. *Degree requirements:* For master's, comprehensive exam (for some programs), internships. *Entrance requirements:* For master's, GRE General Test or MAT.

Robert Morris University, School of Education and Social Sciences, Moon Township, PA 15108-1189. Offers business education (MS); counseling psychology (MS); education (Postbaccalaureate Certificate); higher education (MS); instructional leadership (MS), including education; instructional management and leadership (PhD); literacy (MS); special education (MS). *Accreditation:* TEAC. *Program availability:* Part-time, evening/weekend, online learning. *Faculty:* 18 full-time (10 women), 5 part-time/adjunct (2 women). *Students:* 151 part-time (90 women); includes 23 minority (12 Black or African American, non-Hispanic/Latino; 2 Asian, non-Hispanic/Latino; 2 Hispanic/Latino; 7 Two or more races, non-Hispanic/Latino), 4 international. Average age 34. 51 applicants, 39% accepted, 10 enrolled. In 2017, 31 master's, 16 doctorates awarded. *Degree requirements:* For doctorate, thesis/dissertation. *Entrance requirements:* Additional exam requirements/recommendations for international students: Required—TOEFL (minimum score 550 paper-based; 79 iBT). *Application deadline:* For fall admission, 7/1 priority date for domestic and international students; for spring admission, 11/1 priority date for domestic and international students. Applications are processed on a rolling basis. Application fee: $35. Electronic applications accepted. *Expenses:* $890 per credit tuition, $80 per credit university fee. *Unit head:* Dr. George Semich, Acting Dean, 412-397-6032, Fax: 412-397-6044, E-mail: semich@rmu.edu. *Application contact:* E-mail: graduateadmissions@rmu.edu.
Website: http://www.rmu.edu/web/cms/schools/sess/

Roberts Wesleyan College, Graduate Teacher Education Programs, Rochester, NY 14624-1997. Offers adolescence and special education (M Ed); childhood and special education (M Ed); literacy education (M Ed); special education (M Ed). *Program availability:* Part-time, evening/weekend. *Degree requirements:* For master's, thesis. Electronic applications accepted.

Rockford University, Graduate Studies, Department of Education, Rockford, IL 61108-2393. Offers early childhood education (MAT); elementary education (MAT); instructional strategies (MAT); reading (MAT); secondary education (MAT); special education (MAT). *Program availability:* Part-time, evening/weekend. *Degree requirements:* For master's, thesis optional, professional portfolio (for instructional strategies program). *Entrance requirements:* For master's, GRE General Test, basic skills test (for students seeking certification), 3 letters of recommendation. Additional exam requirements/recommendations for international students: Required—TOEFL (minimum score 550 paper-based; 79 iBT). Electronic applications accepted.

Rockhurst University, College of Health and Human Services, Program in Education, Kansas City, MO 64110-2561. Offers M Ed. *Accreditation:* TEAC. *Program availability:* Part-time, evening/weekend. *Faculty:* 4 full-time (all women), 5 part-time/adjunct (all women). *Students:* 27 full-time (21 women), 43 part-time (30 women); includes 12 minority (6 Black or African American, non-Hispanic/Latino; 1 Asian, non-Hispanic/Latino; 3 Hispanic/Latino; 2 Two or more races, non-Hispanic/Latino), 1 international. Average age 29. 62 applicants, 69% accepted, 39 enrolled. In 2017, 22 master's awarded. *Entrance requirements:* For master's, minimum GPA of 2.5, 2 letters of recommendation. Additional exam requirements/recommendations for international students: Required—TOEFL (minimum score 550 paper-based; 79 iBT). *Application deadline:* Applications are processed on a rolling basis. Electronic applications accepted. *Expenses:* $495 per credit hour tuition; $790 per year in student fees, additional fees may apply. *Financial support:* Applicants required to submit FAFSA. *Faculty research:* English language learners, urban literacy, online discussions, character education, teaching K-12 students about math and literacy. *Unit head:* Dr. Hillary Logan, Chair, 816-501-3557, E-mail: hilary.logan@rockhurst.edu. *Application contact:* Kevin Roy, Graduate Admissions Coordinator and Recruiter, 816-501-4097, E-mail: kevin.roy@rockhurst.edu.
Website: https://www.rockhurst.edu/education

Roger Williams University, Feinstein School of Humanities, Arts and Education, Bristol, RI 02809. Offers literacy education (MA); middle school education (Certificate). *Program availability:* Part-time-only, evening/weekend. *Faculty:* 3 full-time (all women), 5 part-time/adjunct (4 women). *Students:* 14 part-time (all women); includes 1 minority (Hispanic/Latino). Average age 33. 10 applicants, 100% accepted, 7 enrolled. In 2017, 10 master's awarded. *Entrance requirements:* For master's, resume, 2 letters of recommendation, college transcript, letter of intent, verification of active teaching license. Additional exam requirements/recommendations for international students: Required—TOEFL (minimum score 85 iBT), IELTS (minimum score 6.5). *Application deadline:* Applications are processed on a rolling basis. Application fee: $50. Electronic applications accepted. *Expenses:* $573 per credit hour, $258 graduation fee. *Financial support:* Application deadline: 4/1; applicants required to submit FAFSA. *Unit head:* Jeffrey Meriwether, Interim Dean, 401-254-3780, E-mail: jmeriwether@rwu.edu. *Application contact:* Marcus Hanscom, Director of Graduate Admissions, 401-254-3345, Fax: 401-254-3557, E-mail: gradadm@rwu.edu.
Website: http://www.rwu.edu/academics/schools-and-colleges/fshae

Rollins College, Hamilton Holt School, Graduate Education Programs, Winter Park, FL 32789-4499. Offers elementary education (M Ed, MAT). *Program availability:* Part-time, evening/weekend. *Faculty:* 5 full-time (3 women), 1 part-time/adjunct (0 women). *Students:* 10 full-time (7 women), 4 part-time (3 women); includes 5 minority (2 Black or African American, non-Hispanic/Latino; 1 American Indian or Alaska Native, non-Hispanic/Latino; 2 Hispanic/Latino), 1 international. Average age 31. In 2017, 6 master's awarded. *Degree requirements:* For master's, comprehensive exam, Professional Education Test (PED) and Subject Area Examination (SAE) of the Florida Teacher Certification Examinations (FTCE), successful review of the Expanded Teacher Education Portfolio (ETEP). *Entrance requirements:* For master's, General Knowledge Test of the Florida Teacher Certification Examination (FTCE), official transcripts, letter(s) of recommendation, essay. Additional exam requirements/recommendations for international students: Required—TOEFL (minimum score 550 paper-based; 80 iBT). *Application deadline:* For fall admission, 8/11 for domestic students; for spring admission, 12/10 for domestic students. Applications are processed on a rolling basis. Application fee: $50. *Expenses:* $1,575 per course. *Financial support:* Scholarships/grants and unspecified assistantships available. Support available to part-time students.

Financial award applicants required to submit FAFSA. *Unit head:* Dr. H. James McLaughlin, Department Chair, 407-646-2242, E-mail: hmclaughlin@rollins.edu. *Application contact:* 407-646-1568, Fax: 407-975-6430.

Roosevelt University, Graduate Division, College of Education, Chicago, IL 60605. Offers MA. *Accreditation:* ACA; NCATE. *Program availability:* Part-time, evening/weekend. *Students:* 97 full-time (75 women), 218 part-time (159 women); includes 133 minority (68 Black or African American, non-Hispanic/Latino; 6 Asian, non-Hispanic/Latino; 51 Hispanic/Latino; 1 Native Hawaiian or other Pacific Islander, non-Hispanic/Latino; 7 Two or more races, non-Hispanic/Latino), 7 international. Average age 30. 175 applicants, 98% accepted, 103 enrolled. In 2017, 94 master's awarded. *Application deadline:* Applications are processed on a rolling basis. Application fee: $40. Electronic applications accepted. *Financial support:* Scholarships/grants and unspecified assistantships available. *Unit head:* Tom Philion, Dean, 312-853-4780. *Application contact:* Laura Lag, Associate Dean, 312-341-4753, E-mail: llag@roosevelt.edu. Website: https://www.roosevelt.edu/

Rosemont College, Schools of Graduate and Professional Studies, Graduate Education PreK-4 Program, Rosemont, PA 19010-1699. Offers elementary certification (MA); PreK-4 (MA). *Program availability:* Part-time, evening/weekend. *Degree requirements:* For master's, thesis optional. *Entrance requirements:* For master's, minimum college GPA of 3.0, 3 letters of recommendation. Additional exam requirements/recommendations for international students: Required—TOEFL. Electronic applications accepted. Application fee is waived when completed online.

Rowan University, Graduate School, College of Education, Glassboro, NJ 08028-1701. Offers M Ed, MA, MST, Ed D, CAGS, CGS, Ed S, Postbaccalaureate Certificate. *Accreditation:* NCATE. *Program availability:* Part-time, evening/weekend. *Degree requirements:* For master's, comprehensive exam, thesis; for doctorate, thesis/dissertation. *Entrance requirements:* For master's, GRE General Test, PRAXIS I, PRAXIS II; for doctorate, GRE, master's degree. Additional exam requirements/recommendations for international students: Required—TOEFL. Electronic applications accepted. *Expenses:* Tuition, state resident: full-time $15,020; part-time $751 per semester hour. Tuition, nonresident: full-time $15,020; part-time $751 per semester hour. *Required fees:* $3158; $157.90 per semester hour. Tuition and fees vary according to course load, campus/location and program.

Rutgers University–New Brunswick, Graduate School of Education, New Brunswick, NJ 08901. Offers Ed M, Ed D, PhD. *Accreditation:* TEAC. *Program availability:* Part-time, evening/weekend. Terminal master's awarded for partial completion of doctoral program. *Degree requirements:* For master's, comprehensive exam (for some programs); for doctorate, thesis/dissertation. *Entrance requirements:* For master's and doctorate, GRE General Test. Additional exam requirements/recommendations for international students: Required—TOEFL (minimum score 575 paper-based; 83 iBT). Electronic applications accepted.

Sacred Heart University, Graduate Programs, Isabelle Farrington College of Education, Fairfield, CT 06825. Offers M Ed, MAT, Professional Certificate. *Accreditation:* NCATE. *Program availability:* Part-time, evening/weekend. *Faculty:* 22 full-time (13 women), 29 part-time/adjunct (12 women). *Students:* 217 full-time (174 women), 503 part-time (383 women); includes 105 minority (33 Black or African American, non-Hispanic/Latino; 1 American Indian or Alaska Native, non-Hispanic/Latino; 8 Asian, non-Hispanic/Latino; 54 Hispanic/Latino; 9 Two or more races, non-Hispanic/Latino), 2 international. Average age 34. 261 applicants, 97% accepted, 222 enrolled. In 2017, 183 master's, 4 other advanced degrees awarded. *Degree requirements:* For master's, comprehensive exam (for some programs), thesis (for some programs). *Entrance requirements:* For master's, PRAXIS, minimum GPA of 2.67; for Professional Certificate, CT teacher certification. *Application deadline:* Applications are processed on a rolling basis. Application fee: $75. Electronic applications accepted. *Expenses:* Contact institution. *Financial support:* Teaching assistantships with partial tuition reimbursements and unspecified assistantships available. Financial award applicants required to submit FAFSA. *Faculty research:* Reading education, learning theory, teacher preparation, education of underachievers. *Unit head:* Dr. Michael Alfano, Dean, 203-365-7621, Fax: 203-365-7513, E-mail: alfanom3@sacredheart.edu. *Application contact:* Tara Chudy, Executive Director of Graduate Admissions, 203-365-4735, E-mail: chudyt@sacredheart.edu. Website: http://www.sacredheart.edu/academics/isabellefarringtoncollegeofeducation/

Sage Graduate School, Esteves School of Education, Troy, NY 12180-4115. Offers MS, MS Ed, Ed D, Post Master's Certificate. *Accreditation:* NCATE. *Program availability:* Part-time, evening/weekend. *Faculty:* 15 full-time (12 women), 22 part-time/adjunct (14 women). *Students:* 81 full-time (73 women), 323 part-time (252 women); includes 118 minority (51 Black or African American, non-Hispanic/Latino; 1 American Indian or Alaska Native, non-Hispanic/Latino; 19 Asian, non-Hispanic/Latino; 42 Hispanic/Latino; 1 Native Hawaiian or other Pacific Islander, non-Hispanic/Latino; 4 Two or more races, non-Hispanic/Latino). Average age 33. 432 applicants, 48% accepted, 139 enrolled. In 2017, 131 master's, 35 doctorates, 8 other advanced degrees awarded. *Entrance requirements:* Additional exam requirements/recommendations for international students: Required—TOEFL (minimum score 550 paper-based). *Application deadline:* Applications are processed on a rolling basis. Application fee: $30. Electronic applications accepted. Tuition and fees vary according to degree level and program. *Financial support:* Fellowships, research assistantships, scholarships/grants, and unspecified assistantships available. Financial award application deadline: 3/1; financial award applicants required to submit FAFSA. *Faculty research:* Literacy development in at-risk children, effective behavior strategies for class instruction. *Unit head:* Dr. John Pelizza, Interim Dean, Esteves School of Education, 518-244-2051, Fax: 518-244-2334, E-mail: pelizj@sage.edu. *Application contact:* Wendy D. Diefendorf, Director of Graduate and Adult Admission, 518-244-2443, Fax: 518-244-6880, E-mail: diefew@sage.edu.

Saginaw Valley State University, College of Education, University Center, MI 48710. Offers M Ed, MA, MAT, Ed S. *Accreditation:* NCATE. *Program availability:* Part-time, evening/weekend, online learning. *Faculty:* 13 full-time (11 women), 17 part-time/adjunct (2 women). *Students:* 20 full-time (16 women), 216 part-time (173 women); includes 17 minority (7 Black or African American, non-Hispanic/Latino; 1 American Indian or Alaska Native, non-Hispanic/Latino; 1 Asian, non-Hispanic/Latino; 4 Hispanic/Latino; 4 Two or more races, non-Hispanic/Latino), 11 international. Average age 34. 88 applicants, 95% accepted, 60 enrolled. In 2017, 114 master's, 7 other advanced degrees awarded. *Entrance requirements:* For master's, minimum GPA of 3.0, teaching certificate. Additional exam requirements/recommendations for international students: Required—TOEFL (minimum score 550 paper-based; 79 iBT). *Application deadline:* For fall admission, 7/15 for international students; for winter admission, 11/15 for international students; for spring admission, 4/15 for international students. Applications are processed on a rolling basis. Application fee: $30 ($90 for international students). Electronic applications accepted. *Expenses:* Tuition, state resident: full-time $10,156; part-time $564.20 per credit hour. Tuition, nonresident: full-time $19,336; part-time $1074.20 per credit hour. *Required fees:* $263; $14.60 per credit hour. Tuition and fees vary according to degree level and program. *Financial support:* Federal Work-Study and scholarships/grants available. Support available to part-time students. Financial award applicants required to submit FAFSA. *Unit head:* Dr. Craig Douglas, Dean, 989-964-

4057, Fax: 989-964-4563, E-mail: coeconnect@svsu.edu. *Application contact:* Jenna Briggs, Director, Graduate and International Admissions, 989-964-6096, Fax: 989-964-2788, E-mail: gradadm@svsu.edu. Website: http://www.svsu.edu/collegeofeducation

St. Ambrose University, School of Education, Davenport, IA 52803-2898. Offers early childhood education (M Ed); educational administration (M Ed). *Accreditation:* TEAC. *Program availability:* Part-time, evening/weekend, online learning. *Degree requirements:* For master's, comprehensive exam. *Entrance requirements:* For master's, GRE General Test or MAT, minimum GPA of 2.75. Additional exam requirements/recommendations for international students: Required—TOEFL. Electronic applications accepted. *Faculty research:* Disabilities and postsecondary career avenues, self-determination.

St. Bonaventure University, School of Graduate Studies, School of Education, St. Bonaventure, NY 14778-2284. Offers MS Ed, Adv C. *Accreditation:* NCATE. *Program availability:* Part-time, evening/weekend, 100% online, blended/hybrid learning. *Faculty:* 11 full-time (7 women), 11 part-time/adjunct (8 women). *Students:* 67 full-time (55 women), 101 part-time (72 women); includes 14 minority (7 Black or African American, non-Hispanic/Latino; 6 Hispanic/Latino; 1 Two or more races, non-Hispanic/Latino), 2 international. Average age 30. 85 applicants, 87% accepted, 60 enrolled. In 2017, 71 master's, 22 Adv Cs awarded. *Degree requirements:* For master's and Adv C, comprehensive exam, thesis optional, student teaching, electronic portfolio, internship, practicum. *Entrance requirements:* For master's, GRE or MAT, official transcripts, teacher certification, letters of recommendation, personal statement/writing sample. Additional exam requirements/recommendations for international students: Required—TOEFL (minimum score 550 paper-based; 79 iBT). *Application deadline:* For fall admission, 6/15 priority date for domestic students, 2/1 priority date for international students; for spring admission, 11/15 priority date for domestic students, 7/1 priority date for international students. Applications are processed on a rolling basis. Application fee: $0. Electronic applications accepted. *Expenses:* $733 per credit hour, $100 graduation fee. *Financial support:* Career-related internships or fieldwork, Federal Work-Study, scholarships/grants, health care benefits, and unspecified assistantships available. Support available to part-time students. Financial award application deadline: 4/15; financial award applicants required to submit FAFSA. *Faculty research:* Disproportionality in special education, gifted education, global competence, cyberbullying. *Unit head:* Dr. Lisa Buenaventura, Dean, 716-375-2394, Fax: 716-375-2360, E-mail: lbuenave@sbu.edu. *Application contact:* Bruce Campbell, Director of Graduate Admissions, 716-375-2429, Fax: 716-375-4015, E-mail: gradsch@sbu.edu.

St. Catherine University, Graduate Programs, Program in Education - Initial Licensure, St. Paul, MN 55105. Offers MA, Certificate. *Program availability:* Part-time, evening/weekend. *Students:* 10 full-time (all women), 13 part-time (11 women); includes 1 minority (Asian, non-Hispanic/Latino). Average age 31. In 2017, 27 master's, 37 other advanced degrees awarded. *Expenses:* $526 per credit. *Unit head:* David Stricker, Director, 651-690-6601, E-mail: drstricker@stkate.edu. *Application contact:* Sylvia Alexander-Sedey, Assistant Director of Admissions, 651-690-6243, Fax: 651-690-6064. Website: https://www.stkate.edu/academics/graduate-degrees/academic-programs/maed-licensed

St. Cloud State University, School of Graduate Studies, School of Education, St. Cloud, MN 56301-4498. Offers MS, Ed D. *Accreditation:* NCATE. *Program availability:* Part-time, evening/weekend, online learning. *Degree requirements:* For master's, comprehensive exam (for some programs), thesis or alternative; for doctorate, comprehensive exam, thesis/dissertation. *Entrance requirements:* For master's, GRE General Test (for some programs), minimum GPA of 2.75; for doctorate, GRE. Additional exam requirements/recommendations for international students: Required—Michigan English Language Assessment Battery; Recommended—TOEFL (minimum score 550 paper-based), IELTS (minimum score 6.5).

St. Edward's University, School of Education, Austin, TX 78704. Offers college student development (MA); counseling (MA); education (Certificate); liberal arts (MLA, Certificate), including humanities (MLA). *Program availability:* Part-time, evening/weekend. *Students:* 81 full-time (67 women), 172 part-time (139 women); includes 94 minority (16 Black or African American, non-Hispanic/Latino; 5 Asian, non-Hispanic/Latino; 65 Hispanic/Latino; 8 Two or more races, non-Hispanic/Latino), 2 international. Average age 35. 153 applicants, 55% accepted, 56 enrolled. In 2017, 99 master's awarded. *Entrance requirements:* Additional exam requirements/recommendations for international students: Required—TOEFL, IELTS. *Application deadline:* For fall admission, 6/1 priority date for domestic and international students; for spring admission, 10/1 priority date for domestic and international students. Applications are processed on a rolling basis. Application fee: $50. Electronic applications accepted. *Expenses:* Tuition: Full-time $26,406; part-time $1467 per hour. *Required fees:* $75 per trimester. Full-time tuition and fees vary according to course load and program. *Unit head:* Dr. Elizabeth Katz, MAC Program Director/Associate Professor of Counseling, 512-464-8833, E-mail: elizk@stedwards.edu. *Application contact:* Dave Bralower, Director of Graduate Admission, 512-233-1424, Fax: 512-464-8877, E-mail: davidcb@stedwards.edu.

Saint Francis University, Graduate Education Program, Loretto, PA 15940-0600. Offers education (M Ed); leadership (M Ed); reading (M Ed). *Program availability:* Part-time, 100% online, blended/hybrid learning. *Faculty:* 1 full-time (0 women), 15 part-time/adjunct (9 women). *Students:* 13 full-time (6 women), 96 part-time (65 women); includes 3 minority (2 Black or African American, non-Hispanic/Latino; 1 Hispanic/Latino). Average age 35. 22 applicants, 100% accepted, 16 enrolled. In 2017, 33 master's awarded. *Degree requirements:* For master's, comprehensive exam, thesis optional. *Entrance requirements:* For master's, GRE or MAT (if undergraduate GPA less than 3.0). Additional exam requirements/recommendations for international students: Required—TOEFL (minimum score 550 paper-based; 75 iBT), IELTS (minimum score 6.5), International Test of English proficiency (minimum score 4). *Application deadline:* Applications are processed on a rolling basis. Application fee: $30. Electronic applications accepted. *Expenses:* Contact institution. *Financial support:* Applicants required to submit FAFSA. *Unit head:* Dr. Janette D. Kelly, Director, 814-472-3068, Fax: 814-472-3864, E-mail: jkelly@francis.edu. *Application contact:* Sherri L. Toth, Coordinator, 814-472-3058, Fax: 814-472-3864, E-mail: stoth@francis.edu. Website: http://www.francis.edu/master-of-education/

St. Francis Xavier University, Graduate Studies, Graduate Studies in Education, Antigonish, NS B2G 2W5, Canada. Offers curriculum and instruction (M Ed); educational administration and leadership (M Ed). *Program availability:* Part-time, online learning. *Degree requirements:* For master's, thesis. *Entrance requirements:* For master's, minimum undergraduate B average, 2 years of teaching experience. *Faculty research:* Inclusive education, qualitative research.

St. John Fisher College, Ralph C. Wilson Jr. School of Education, Rochester, NY 14618-3597. Offers MS, MS Ed, Ed D, Certificate. *Accreditation:* NCATE. *Program availability:* Part-time, evening/weekend. *Faculty:* 22 full-time (18 women), 14 part-time/adjunct (13 women). *Students:* 150 full-time (99 women), 87 part-time (71 women); includes 88 minority (61 Black or African American, non-Hispanic/Latino; 2 American Indian or Alaska Native, non-Hispanic/Latino; 2 Asian, non-Hispanic/Latino; 18 Hispanic/Latino; 5 Two or more races, non-Hispanic/Latino). Average age 38. 171 applicants,

Education—General

76% accepted, 92 enrolled. In 2017, 66 master's, 47 doctorates, 1 other advanced degree awarded. *Degree requirements:* For doctorate, thesis/dissertation. *Entrance requirements:* For master's and doctorate, 2 letters of recommendation, current resume. Additional exam requirements/recommendations for international students: Required—TOEFL (minimum score 575 paper-based; 80 iBT). *Application deadline:* Applications are processed on a rolling basis. Application fee: $30. Electronic applications accepted. *Expenses:* Contact institution. *Financial support:* Scholarships/grants available. Financial award applicants required to submit FAFSA. *Unit head:* Dr. Michael Wischnowski, Dean, 585-385-7361, E-mail: mwischnowski@sjfc.edu. *Application contact:* Michelle Gosier, Director of Transfer and Graduate Admissions, 585-385-8064, E-mail: mgosier@sjfc.edu.
Website: https://www.sjfc.edu/schools/school-of-education/

St. John's University, The School of Education, Queens, NY 11439. Offers MS Ed, Ed D, PhD, Adv C. *Accreditation:* TEAC. *Faculty:* 53 full-time (34 women), 70 part-time/adjunct (29 women). *Students:* 218 full-time (169 women), 1,130 part-time (783 women); includes 565 minority (233 Black or African American, non-Hispanic/Latino; 2 American Indian or Alaska Native, non-Hispanic/Latino; 89 Asian, non-Hispanic/Latino; 211 Hispanic/Latino; 1 Native Hawaiian or other Pacific Islander, non-Hispanic/Latino; 29 Two or more races, non-Hispanic/Latino), 33 international. Average age 35. 559 applicants, 90% accepted, 479 enrolled. In 2017, 380 master's, 62 doctorates, 168 other advanced degrees awarded. *Entrance requirements:* For master's, GRE, MAT, or PRAXIS, statement of goals (personal essay), official undergraduate transcripts, initial teaching certification (unless career change); for doctorate, GRE, resume, letters of recommendation, master's transcripts; for Adv C, initial teaching certification, first master's transcripts. Additional exam requirements/recommendations for international students: Required—TOEFL, IELTS. *Application deadline:* For fall admission, 8/17 for domestic and international students; for summer admission, 5/15 for domestic and international students. Application fee: $70. Electronic applications accepted. *Expenses: Tuition:* Full-time $44,280; part-time $1230 per credit. *Required fees:* $340; $340 per credit. Tuition and fees vary according to course load, degree level and program. *Financial support:* In 2017–18, 10 students received support, including 5 fellowships with full tuition reimbursements available (averaging $16,000 per year), 5 research assistantships with full tuition reimbursements available (averaging $4,250 per year); scholarships/grants and unspecified assistantships also available. Support available to part-time students. Financial award application deadline: 2/1; financial award applicants required to submit FAFSA. *Total annual research expenditures:* $695,747. *Unit head:* Dr. Yvonne Pratt-Johnson, Interim Dean, 718-990-2645, E-mail: prattjoy@stjohns.edu. *Application contact:* Associate Director of Graduate Admissions, E-mail: graded@stjohns.edu.
Website: http://www.stjohns.edu/academics/schools-and-colleges/school-education

St. Joseph's College, New York, Programs in Education, Brooklyn, NY 11205-3688. Offers educational leadership (MA), including critical consciousness; literacy and cognition (MA); special education (MA), including severe and multiple disabilities. *Program availability:* Part-time, evening/weekend. *Faculty:* 5 full-time (all women), 4 part-time/adjunct (3 women). *Students:* 35 part-time (28 women); includes 7 minority (1 Black or African American, non-Hispanic/Latino; 6 Hispanic/Latino). Average age 23. 24 applicants, 96% accepted, 15 enrolled. In 2017, 18 master's awarded. *Entrance requirements:* For master's, GRE, PRAXIS or MAT, official transcripts, two letters of recommendation, resume, copy of teaching certification. Additional exam requirements/recommendations for international students: Required—TOEFL (minimum score 80 iBT). *Application deadline:* Applications are processed on a rolling basis. Application fee: $25. Electronic applications accepted. *Expenses: Tuition:* Full-time $17,550; part-time $975 per credit. *Required fees:* $362. *Financial support:* In 2017–18, 27 students received support. *Unit head:* Nancy Gilchriest, Professor/Department Chair, 631-687-1472, E-mail: ngilchriest@sjcny.edu.
Website: http://www.sjcny.edu

Saint Joseph's College of Maine, Master of Science in Education Program, Standish, ME 04084. Offers adult education and training (MS Ed); Catholic school leadership (MS Ed); health care educator (MS Ed); school educator (MS Ed). Program available by correspondence. *Program availability:* Part-time, online learning. Electronic applications accepted.

Saint Joseph's University, College of Arts and Sciences, Graduate Programs in Education, Philadelphia, PA 19131-1395. Offers curriculum supervisor (Certificate); educational leadership (MS, Ed D); elementary education (MS, Certificate); elementary/middle school education (Certificate); organizational development and leadership (MS); principal (Certificate); professional education (MS); reading specialist (MS, Certificate); reading supervisor (Certificate); secondary education (MS, Certificate); special education (MS); special education 7-12 (Certificate); special education PK-8 (Certificate); superintendent's letter of eligibility (Certificate); supervisor of special education (Certificate); teacher of the deaf and hard of hearing (Certificate). *Program availability:* Part-time, evening/weekend, blended/hybrid learning. *Faculty:* 18 full-time (16 women), 63 part-time/adjunct (44 women). *Students:* 79 full-time (60 women), 793 part-time (604 women); includes 179 minority (125 Black or African American, non-Hispanic/Latino; 5 American Indian or Alaska Native, non-Hispanic/Latino; 15 Asian, non-Hispanic/Latino; 27 Hispanic/Latino; 1 Native Hawaiian or other Pacific Islander, non-Hispanic/Latino; 6 Two or more races, non-Hispanic/Latino), 12 international. Average age 34. 375 applicants, 75% accepted, 189 enrolled. In 2017, 340 master's, 13 doctorates, 3 other advanced degrees awarded. *Degree requirements:* For master's, thesis or alternative; for doctorate, comprehensive exam, thesis/dissertation. *Entrance requirements:* For master's, 2 letters of recommendation, minimum GPA of 3.0, official transcripts, personal statement; for doctorate, GRE, master's degree from accredited institution, minimum graduate GPA of 3.5, computer competence, interview with program director. Additional exam requirements/recommendations for international students: Required—TOEFL (minimum score 550 paper-based; 80 iBT), IELTS (minimum score 6.5), PTE (minimum score 60). *Application deadline:* For fall admission, 7/15 for international students; for spring admission, 11/1 for international students. Applications are processed on a rolling basis. Application fee: $35. Electronic applications accepted. *Expenses:* Contact institution. *Financial support:* Scholarships/grants and unspecified assistantships available. Financial award application deadline: 5/1; financial award applicants required to submit FAFSA. *Faculty research:* Factors predicting early mathematics skills for low income children, early child care and development, preschool quality, parent communication and home-school collaboration issues, education of terminally ill children, preparing literacy teachers for urban schools. *Unit head:* Dr. John Vacca, Associate Dean, Education, 610-660-3131, E-mail: gradcas@sju.edu. *Application contact:* Graduate Admissions, College of Arts and Sciences, 610-660-3131, E-mail: gradcas@sju.edu.
Website: https://sites.sju.edu/education/graduate-programs/

St. Lawrence University, Department of Education, Canton, NY 13617. Offers counseling and human development (M Ed, MS, CAS), including mental health counseling (MS), school counseling (M Ed, CAS); educational leadership (M Ed, CAS), including combined school building leadership/school district leadership (M Ed), educational leadership (M Ed), school building leadership (M Ed), school district leadership (CAS); general studies in education (M Ed). *Accreditation:* TEAC. *Program availability:* Part-time, evening/weekend. *Degree requirements:* For master's, thesis

optional. *Entrance requirements:* For master's, GRE General Test. *Faculty research:* Defense mechanisms, conflict negotiations and mediation, teacher education policy.

Saint Leo University, Graduate Studies in Education, Saint Leo, FL 33574-6665. Offers educational leadership (M Ed), including Catholic school administration; exceptional student education (M Ed); instructional design (MS, Certificate); instructional leadership (M Ed); reading (M Ed, Certificate); school leadership (Ed S). *Program availability:* Part-time, evening/weekend, online only, 100% online. *Faculty:* 8 full-time (all women), 18 part-time/adjunct (11 women). *Students:* 1 (woman) full-time, 360 part-time (282 women); includes 95 minority (56 Black or African American, non-Hispanic/Latino; 1 American Indian or Alaska Native, non-Hispanic/Latino; 1 Asian, non-Hispanic/Latino; 31 Hispanic/Latino; 6 Two or more races, non-Hispanic/Latino), 1 international. Average age 37. 214 applicants, 69% accepted, 125 enrolled. In 2017, 158 master's, 5 other advanced degrees awarded. *Degree requirements:* For master's, appropriate State of Florida certification tests, internship. *Entrance requirements:* For master's, GRE (minimum score of 1000), MAT (minimum score of 410), or minimum undergraduate GPA of 3.0 in final 2 years, official transcripts, current resumé, 2 professional recommendations, personal statement, bachelor's degree from regionally-accredited university, valid professional teaching certificate; for other advanced degree, valid professional teaching certificate (for Ed S). Additional exam requirements/recommendations for international students: Required—TOEFL (minimum score 550 paper-based; 78 iBT). *Application deadline:* For fall admission, 7/1 priority date for domestic students, 7/1 for international students; for winter admission, 7/1 for international students; for spring admission, 11/1 priority date for domestic students. Applications are processed on a rolling basis. Application fee: $80. Electronic applications accepted. *Expenses:* $480 per credit (for M Ed), $670 per credit (for Ed S). *Financial support:* In 2017–18, 17 students received support. Career-related internships or fieldwork, scholarships/grants, health care benefits, and tuition remission for Saint Leo employees and their dependents available. Financial award application deadline: 3/1; financial award applicants required to submit FAFSA. *Faculty research:* Impact of partnerships with K-12 school and university programs. *Unit head:* Dr. Fern Aefsky, Director of Graduate Studies in Education, 352-588-8309, Fax: 352-588-8861, E-mail: kara.winkler@saintleo.edu. *Application contact:* Mark Russum, Assistant Vice President, Enrollment, 800-707-8846, Fax: 352-588-7873, E-mail: grad.admissions@saintleo.edu.
Website: https://www.saintleo.edu/education-master-degree

Saint Louis University, Graduate Programs, School of Education, Department of Educational Studies, St. Louis, MO 63103. Offers curriculum and instruction (MA, Ed D, PhD); educational foundations (MA, Ed D, PhD); special education (MA); teaching (MAT). *Accreditation:* NCATE. *Program availability:* Part-time. *Degree requirements:* For master's, comprehensive exam; for doctorate, comprehensive exam, thesis/dissertation, preliminary oral and written exams. *Entrance requirements:* For master's, GRE General Test or MAT, letters of recommendation, resume; for doctorate, GRE General Test, letters of recommendation, resumé, goal statement, transcripts. Additional exam requirements/recommendations for international students: Required—TOEFL (minimum score 525 paper-based). Electronic applications accepted. *Faculty research:* Teacher preparation, multicultural issues, children with special needs, qualitative research in education, inclusion.

Saint Martin's University, Office of Graduate Studies, College of Education, Lacey, WA 98503. Offers M Ed, MIT. *Accreditation:* TEAC. *Program availability:* Part-time, evening/weekend. *Faculty:* 8 full-time (6 women), 12 part-time/adjunct (6 women). *Students:* 26 full-time (15 women), 45 part-time (34 women); includes 7 minority (1 Black or African American, non-Hispanic/Latino; 2 Asian, non-Hispanic/Latino; 3 Hispanic/Latino; 1 Two or more races, non-Hispanic/Latino). Average age 35. 12 applicants, 92% accepted, 8 enrolled. In 2017, 28 master's awarded. *Degree requirements:* For master's, comprehensive exam (for some programs), thesis or alternative, project or comprehensives. *Entrance requirements:* For master's, GRE General Test or MAT, three letters of recommendation; curriculum vitae. Additional exam requirements/recommendations for international students: Required—TOEFL (minimum score 550 paper-based; 79 iBT); Recommended—IELTS (minimum score 6.5). *Application deadline:* For fall admission, 4/1 priority date for domestic and international students; for spring admission, 11/1 priority date for domestic and international students. Applications are processed on a rolling basis. Application fee: $50. Electronic applications accepted. *Expenses: Tuition:* Full-time $21,420; part-time $1190 per credit. *Financial support:* Career-related internships or fieldwork, Federal Work-Study, institutionally sponsored loans, and unspecified assistantships available. Support available to part-time students. Financial award application deadline: 3/1; financial award applicants required to submit FAFSA. *Faculty research:* Reader's theatre and reader/writer workshops, curriculum and assessment integration, gender and equity, classroom evaluations, organizational leadership. *Unit head:* Dr. Kathleen M. Boyle, College of Education and Counseling Psychology, 360-438-4333, Fax: 360-438-4486, E-mail: kboyle@stmartin.edu. *Application contact:* Casey Caronna, Administrative Assistant, 360-412-6128, E-mail: ccaronna@stmartin.edu.
Website: https://www.stmartin.edu/directory/office-graduate-studies

Saint Mary's College of California, Kalmanovitz School of Education, Moraga, CA 94575. Offers M Ed, MA, MA Ed, Ed D, Credential. *Program availability:* Part-time, evening/weekend. *Degree requirements:* For master's, thesis or alternative; for doctorate, thesis/dissertation. *Entrance requirements:* For master's, interview, minimum GPA of 3.0; for doctorate, GRE or MAT, interview, MA, minimum GPA of 3.0. *Expenses:* Contact institution. *Faculty research:* Teacher effectiveness, school-based management, multicultural teaching, language and literacy development.

St. Mary's College of Maryland, Department of Educational Studies, St. Mary's City, MD 20686-3001. Offers MAT. *Degree requirements:* For master's, internship, electronic portfolio, research projects, PRAXIS II. *Entrance requirements:* For master's, SAT, ACT, GRE or PRAXIS, 2 letters of recommendation, minimum GPA of 3.0. Additional exam requirements/recommendations for international students: Required—TOEFL. Electronic applications accepted. *Expenses:* Contact institution. *Faculty research:* Supporting English language learners across the curriculum, supporting women and minorities in math and science, instructional technology, multicultural young adult literature, educating teachers to be advocates for equity and social justice.

St. Mary's University, Graduate Studies, Program in Education, San Antonio, TX 78228. Offers MA. *Program availability:* Part-time, evening/weekend. *Students:* 1 full-time (0 women), all international. Average age 29. 10 applicants. *Entrance requirements:* For master's, GRE, minimum undergraduate GPA of 2.7. Additional exam requirements/recommendations for international students: Required—TOEFL (minimum score 550 paper-based; 80 iBT), IELTS (minimum score 6). *Application deadline:* For fall admission, 7/1 for domestic students; for spring admission, 11/15 for domestic students; for summer admission, 4/1 for domestic students. Applications are processed on a rolling basis. Electronic applications accepted. *Expenses: Tuition:* Full-time $16,200; part-time $900 per credit hour. *Required fees:* $810; $405 per semester. *Financial support:* Application deadline: 3/31; applicants required to submit FAFSA. *Faculty research:* Philosophy of education. *Unit head:* Dr. Dan Higgins, Program Director, 210-436-3121, E-mail: dhiggins@stmarytx.edu. *Application contact:* Kim Thornton, Director of Graduate Admission, 210-436-3101, E-mail: kthornton@stmarytx.edu.
Website: https://www.stmarytx.edu/academics/programs/master-of-education/

Saint Mary's University of Minnesota, Schools of Graduate and Professional Programs, Graduate School of Education, Education Program, Winona, MN 55987-1399. Offers culturally responsive teaching (Certificate); education (MA); gifted inclusive education (Certificate). *Unit head:* Lynn Albee, Director, 612-728-5128, Fax: 612-728-5121, E-mail: lalbee@smumn.edu. *Application contact:* James Callinan, Director of Admissions for Graduate and Professional Programs, 612-728-5158, Fax: 612-728-5121, E-mail: jcallina@smumn.edu.
Website: http://www.smumn.edu/graduate-home/areas-of-study/graduate-school-of-education/ma-in-education

Saint Mary's University of Minnesota, Schools of Graduate and Professional Programs, Graduate School of Education, Education-Wisconsin Program, Winona, MN 55987-1399. Offers MA. *Unit head:* Dr. Lynda Sullivan, Director, 877-442-4020, E-mail: lsulliva@smumn.edu. *Application contact:* James Callinan, Director of Admissions for Graduate and Professional Programs, 612-728-5158, Fax: 612-728-5121, E-mail: jcallina@smumn.edu.
Website: http://www.smumn.edu/graduate-home/areas-of-study/graduate-school-of-education/ma-in-education-wisconsin

Saint Mary's University of Minnesota, Schools of Graduate and Professional Programs, Graduate School of Education, Teaching and Learning Program, Winona, MN 55987-1399. Offers M Ed. *Unit head:* Tracy Lysne, Program Director, 612-238-4520, E-mail: tlysne@smumn.edu. *Application contact:* James Callinan, Director of Admissions for Graduate and Professional Programs, 612-728-5185, Fax: 612-728-5121, E-mail: jcallina@smumn.edu.
Website: http://www.smumn.edu/graduate-home/areas-of-study/graduate-school-of-education/med-in-teaching-learning

Saint Michael's College, Graduate Programs, Program in Education, Colchester, VT 05439. Offers arts in education (CAGS); literacy (M Ed); school leadership (CAGS); special education (M Ed). *Program availability:* Part-time, evening/weekend. *Students:* 7 full-time (3 women), 204 part-time (173 women); includes 8 minority (1 Black or African American, non-Hispanic/Latino; 1 American Indian or Alaska Native, non-Hispanic/Latino; 3 Hispanic/Latino; 3 Two or more races, non-Hispanic/Latino). Average age 38. 23 applicants, 65% accepted, 10 enrolled. In 2017, 32 master's awarded. *Degree requirements:* For master's, thesis. *Entrance requirements:* For master's, minimum GPA of 3.0, official transcripts, essay, interview. *Application deadline:* Applications are processed on a rolling basis. Application fee: $50. Electronic applications accepted. *Expenses: Tuition:* Part-time $590 per credit. *Financial support:* Fellowships with partial tuition reimbursements and scholarships/grants available. Support available to part-time students. Financial award applicants required to submit FAFSA. *Faculty research:* Integrative curriculum, moral and spiritual dimensions of education, learning styles, multiple intelligences, integrating technology into the curriculum. *Unit head:* Jonathan Silverman, Department Chair, 802-654-2306, Fax: 802-654-2664, E-mail: jsilverman@smcvt.edu. *Application contact:* Lindsay A. Damici, Marketing Communications Manager, 802-654-2556, Fax: 802-654-2732.
Website: http://www.smcvt.edu/graduate-programs/academic-programs/education.aspx

Saint Peter's University, Graduate Programs in Education, Jersey City, NJ 07306-5997. Offers director of school counseling services (Certificate); educational leadership (MA Ed, Ed D); higher education (Ed D); middle school mathematics (Certificate); professional/associate counselor (Certificate); reading (MA Ed); school business administrator (Certificate); school counseling (MA, Certificate); special education (MA Ed, Certificate), including applied behavioral analysis (MA Ed), literacy (MA Ed), teacher of students with disabilities (Certificate); teaching (MA Ed, Certificate), including 6-8 middle school education, K-12 secondary education, K-5 elementary education. *Accreditation:* TEAC. *Program availability:* Part-time, evening/weekend. *Degree requirements:* For master's, comprehensive exam; for doctorate, comprehensive exam, thesis/dissertation. *Entrance requirements:* For master's and doctorate, GRE or MAT. Additional exam requirements/recommendations for international students: Required—TOEFL. Electronic applications accepted.

St. Thomas Aquinas College, Division of Teacher Education, Sparkill, NY 10976. Offers adolescence education (MST); childhood and special education (MST); childhood education (MST); educational leadership (MS Ed); reading (MS Ed, PMC); special education (MS Ed, PMC); teaching (MS Ed), including elementary education, middle school education, secondary education. *Accreditation:* NCATE. *Program availability:* Part-time, evening/weekend. *Degree requirements:* For master's, comprehensive exam, comprehensive professional portfolio; for PMC, action research project. *Entrance requirements:* For master's, New York State Qualifying Exam, GRE General Test or minimum GPA of 3.0, teaching certificate; for PMC, GRE General Test or minimum GPA of 3.0. Electronic applications accepted. *Faculty research:* Computer applications in education, adolescent special education students, literacy development, inclusive practices for special education students.

St. Thomas University, School of Leadership Studies, Institute for Education, Miami Gardens, FL 33054-6459. Offers earth/space science (Certificate); educational administration (MS, Certificate); educational leadership (Ed D); elementary education (MS); ESOL (Certificate); gifted education (Certificate); instructional technology (MS, Certificate); professional/studies (Certificate); reading (MS, Certificate); special education (MS). *Program availability:* Part-time, evening/weekend. *Degree requirements:* For master's, comprehensive exam; for doctorate, comprehensive exam, thesis/dissertation. *Entrance requirements:* For master's, interview, minimum GPA of 3.0 or GRE; for doctorate, GRE or MAT. Additional exam requirements/recommendations for international students: Required—TOEFL (minimum score 550 paper-based; 79 iBT). Electronic applications accepted.

Saint Vincent College, Program in Education, Latrobe, PA 15650-2690. Offers curriculum and instruction (MS); instructional design and technology (MS); school administration and supervision (MS); special education (MS). *Program availability:* Part-time, evening/weekend. *Degree requirements:* For master's, comprehensive exam. *Entrance requirements:* For master's, GRE (if undergraduate GPA less than 3.0). Additional exam requirements/recommendations for international students: Required—TOEFL (minimum score 550 paper-based). *Faculty research:* Assessment and instructional technology.

Saint Xavier University, Graduate Studies, School of Education, Chicago, IL 60655-3105. Offers counseling (MA); curriculum and instruction (MA); early childhood education (MA); educational administration (MA); elementary education (MA); individualized studies (MA), including educational technology, English as a second language (ESL), ISTEM (integrative science, technology, engineering, and math), science education (MA); music education (MA); reading (MA); secondary education (MA); Spanish education (MA); special education (MA); teaching and leadership (MA). *Accreditation:* NCATE. *Program availability:* Part-time, evening/weekend. *Degree requirements:* For master's, thesis or project. *Entrance requirements:* For master's, minimum GPA of 3.0. *Expenses:* Contact institution.

Salem College, Graduate Studies, Winston-Salem, NC 27101. Offers art education (MAT); elementary education (M Ed, MAT); language and literacy (M Ed); middle school education (MAT); organ (MM); piano (MM); school counseling (M Ed); second language studies (MAT); secondary education (MAT); special education (M Ed, MAT).

Accreditation: NCATE. *Program availability:* Part-time, evening/weekend, online learning. *Faculty:* 8 full-time (all women), 11 part-time/adjunct (8 women). In 2017, 17 master's awarded. *Degree requirements:* For master's, practicum (MAT), action research project (M Ed). *Entrance requirements:* For master's, minimum GPA of 3.0, two academic/professional recommendations, acceptable criminal background check. Additional exam requirements/recommendations for international students: Recommended—TOEFL. *Application deadline:* For fall admission, 8/1 for domestic students, 7/15 for international students; for spring admission, 1/15 for domestic students; for summer admission, 5/1 for domestic students. Applications are processed on a rolling basis. Application fee: $30. Electronic applications accepted. *Expenses: Tuition:* Part-time $440 per semester hour. *Financial support:* Scholarships/grants available. Support available to part-time students. Financial award applicants required to submit FAFSA. *Faculty research:* Teacher professional development, adolescent literacy, instructional technology. *Application contact:* Sheryl Long, Director, 336-721-2658, Fax: 336-917-5384, E-mail: sheryl.long@salem.edu.
Website: http://www.salem.edu

Salem International University, School of Education, Salem, WV 26426-0500. Offers curriculum and instruction (M Ed); educational leadership (M Ed). *Program availability:* Part-time, evening/weekend, online learning. *Degree requirements:* For master's, comprehensive exam (for some programs), thesis (for some programs). *Entrance requirements:* For master's, GRE, MAT, NTE, 3 letters of recommendation. Additional exam requirements/recommendations for international students: Required—TOEFL (minimum score 550 paper-based). Electronic applications accepted. *Expenses:* Contact institution. *Faculty research:* Improved classroom effectiveness.

Samford University, Orlean Beeson School of Education, Birmingham, AL 35229. Offers educational leadership (MSE, Ed D); elementary education (MS Ed, MSE); gifted (MSE); instructional design and technology (MSE); instructional leadership (MSE, Ed S); secondary education (MSE); special education (MSE). *Accreditation:* NCATE. *Program availability:* Part-time, evening/weekend, 100% online, blended/hybrid learning. *Faculty:* 11 full-time (7 women), 22 part-time/adjunct (12 women). *Students:* 206 full-time (144 women), 102 part-time (75 women); includes 124 minority (113 Black or African American, non-Hispanic/Latino; 3 American Indian or Alaska Native, non-Hispanic/Latino; 3 Asian, non-Hispanic/Latino; 2 Hispanic/Latino; 3 Two or more races, non-Hispanic/Latino), 1 international. Average age 37. 134 applicants, 84% accepted, 76 enrolled. In 2017, 79 master's, 34 doctorates, 21 other advanced degrees awarded. *Degree requirements:* For master's and Ed S, comprehensive exam; for doctorate, comprehensive exam, thesis/dissertation. *Entrance requirements:* For master's, GRE, MAT, PRAXIS II, interview, transcripts, essay, recommendations, teaching certification; for doctorate, resume, transcripts, interview, essay; for Ed S, teaching certification, transcripts, essay, interview. Additional exam requirements/recommendations for international students: Required—TOEFL (minimum score 90 iBT), IELTS (minimum score 6.5). *Application deadline:* For fall admission, 7/15 for domestic and international students; for winter admission, 11/15 for domestic and international students; for spring admission, 11/15 for domestic and international students; for summer admission, 4/15 for domestic and international students. Application fee: $35. *Expenses:* $813 per credit hour, $100 School of Education fee, $175 technology fee. *Financial support:* In 2017–18, 220 students received support. Scholarships/grants and unspecified assistantships available. Financial award application deadline: 2/15; financial award applicants required to submit FAFSA. *Faculty research:* Principal leadership's and teacher organizational commitment mentoring, professional development, and middle grades leadership coaching and administrator effectiveness character development programs in schools teacher efficacy related STEM and professional growth. *Unit head:* Dr. Bonnie Rabe, Interim Dean, 205-726-2565, E-mail: brabe@samford.edu. *Application contact:* Brooke Karr, Graduate Admissions Office Coordinator, 205-729-2783, Fax: 205-726-4233, E-mail: kbgilrea@samford.edu.
Website: http://www.samford.edu/education/

Sam Houston State University, College of Education, Huntsville, TX 77341. Offers M Ed, MA, MLS, Ed D, PhD. *Accreditation:* NCATE. *Program availability:* Part-time, evening/weekend, online learning. *Degree requirements:* For master's, comprehensive exam (for some programs), thesis optional, portfolio, internship; for doctorate, comprehensive exam (for some programs), thesis/dissertation. *Entrance requirements:* For master's, GRE General Test, references, essay, face-to-face interview, personal statement, resume; for doctorate, GRE General Test, on-site interview, on-site professional presentation, on-site writing prompt, personal statement, five references, master's degree, resume. Additional exam requirements/recommendations for international students: Required—TOEFL (minimum score 550 paper-based; 79 iBT), IELTS (minimum score 6.5). Electronic applications accepted.

San Diego Christian College, Graduate Programs, Santee, CA 92071. Offers education (MAT); organization (MSL).

San Diego State University, Graduate and Research Affairs, College of Education, San Diego, CA 92182. Offers MA, MS, Ed D, PhD. *Accreditation:* NCATE. *Program availability:* Part-time, evening/weekend. *Degree requirements:* For master's, thesis optional; for doctorate, thesis/dissertation. *Entrance requirements:* For master's, GRE General Test, letters of reference; for doctorate, GRE General Test, 3 letters of reference, resumé. Additional exam requirements/recommendations for international students: Required—TOEFL. Electronic applications accepted. *Faculty research:* Special education, rehabilitation counseling, educational psychology.

San Francisco State University, Division of Graduate Studies, College of Education, San Francisco, CA 94132-1722. Offers MA, MS, Ed D, PhD, AC, Certificate, Credential. *Accreditation:* NCATE. *Unit head:* Dr. Nancy Robinson, Interim Dean, 415-338-2687, Fax: 415-338-7019, E-mail: nancyr@sfsu.edu. *Application contact:* Victoria Narkewicz, Executive Assistant, 415-338-2687, Fax: 415-338-7019, E-mail: toria@sfsu.edu.
Website: http://gcoe.sfsu.edu/

San Ignacio University, Graduate Programs, Doral, FL 33178. Offers business administration (MBA), including human resources management, international business, marketing management; education (M Ed), including early childhood education, educational leadership, special education; hospitality management (MA), including gastronomy and restaurant management, tourism management.

San Jose State University, Graduate Studies and Research, Connie L. Lurie College of Education, San Jose, CA 95192-0071. Offers child and adolescent development (MA); education (MA), including counseling and student personnel, curriculum and instruction, speech pathology; educational leadership (MA, Ed D), including administration and supervision (MA), educational leadership (MA); elementary education (MA), including curriculum and instruction. *Accreditation:* NCATE. *Program availability:* Part-time, evening/weekend. *Faculty:* 29 full-time (22 women), 47 part-time/adjunct (40 women). *Students:* 414 full-time (339 women), 115 part-time (93 women); includes 341 minority (14 Black or African American, non-Hispanic/Latino; 87 Asian, non-Hispanic/Latino; 176 Hispanic/Latino; 64 Two or more races, non-Hispanic/Latino), 9 international. Average age 30. 654 applicants, 34% accepted, 161 enrolled. In 2017, 286 master's, 7 doctorates awarded. Terminal master's awarded for partial completion of doctoral program. *Degree requirements:* For master's, project or theses, graduate

Education—General

writing assessment; for doctorate, thesis/dissertation. *Entrance requirements:* For master's, GRE General Test (for some programs). Additional exam requirements/recommendations for international students: Required—TOEFL (minimum score 550 paper-based; 80 iBT), IELTS (minimum score 6.5), PTE (minimum score 53). *Application deadline:* For fall admission, 2/1 for domestic and international students. Applications are processed on a rolling basis. Application fee: $55. Electronic applications accepted. *Expenses:* Tuition, state resident: full-time $7176. Tuition, nonresident: full-time $16,680. Tuition and fees vary according to course load and program. *Financial support:* In 2017–18, 4 research assistantships with partial tuition reimbursements (averaging $2,500 per year) were awarded; fellowships, career-related internships or fieldwork, Federal Work-Study, scholarships/grants, traineeships, and tuition waivers (full and partial) also available. Support available to part-time students. Financial award application deadline: 4/28; financial award applicants required to submit FAFSA. *Faculty research:* Equity and social justice in public education, interdisciplinary practices, teacher training, and effective pedagogy, clinical efficacy, typical and atypical development in children. *Unit head:* Dr. Paul Cascella, Interim Dean, 408-924-3600, Fax: 408-924-3713, E-mail: paul.cascella@sjsu.edu.
Website: http://www.sjsu.edu/education/

Santa Clara University, School of Education and Counseling Psychology, Santa Clara, CA 95053. Offers alternative and correctional education (Certificate); Catholic school teaching (MAT); counseling (MA); counseling psychology (MA); educational leadership (MA); interdisciplinary education (MA); teaching multiple subjects (MAT); teaching single subjects (MAT). *Program availability:* Part-time. *Faculty:* 31 full-time (21 women), 37 part-time/adjunct (25 women). *Students:* 253 full-time (195 women), 350 part-time (283 women); includes 296 minority (10 Black or African American, non-Hispanic/Latino; 1 American Indian or Alaska Native, non-Hispanic/Latino; 80 Asian, non-Hispanic/Latino; 179 Hispanic/Latino; 26 Two or more races, non-Hispanic/Latino), 41 international. Average age 31. 211 applicants, 75% accepted, 142 enrolled. In 2017, 266 master's awarded. *Entrance requirements:* For master's, official transcripts, 2-3 letters of recommendation, statement of purpose, resume or curriculum vitae. Additional exam requirements/recommendations for international students: Required—TOEFL (minimum score 90 iBT) or IELTS (6.5). *Application deadline:* For fall admission, 4/16 for international students; for summer admission, 3/12 for domestic students. Applications are processed on a rolling basis. Application fee: $50. Electronic applications accepted. *Expenses:* $607 per unit. *Financial support:* In 2017–18, 355 students received support. Fellowships, research assistantships, teaching assistantships, Federal Work-Study, scholarships/grants, and health care benefits available. Support available to part-time students. Financial award applicants required to submit FAFSA. *Unit head:* Dr. Sabrina Zirkel, Dean, 408-551-3074, Fax: 408-554-4367, E-mail: szirkel@scu.edu. *Application contact:* Victoria Rodriguez, Graduate Admissions Advisor, 408-554-4723, E-mail: v1rodriguez@scu.edu.
Website: http://www.scu.edu/ecp/

Sarah Lawrence College, Graduate Studies, Program in the Art of Teaching, Bronxville, NY 10708-5999. Offers MS Ed. *Program availability:* Part-time. *Degree requirements:* For master's, thesis, fieldwork, oral presentation. *Entrance requirements:* For master's, minimum B average in undergraduate coursework. Additional exam requirements/recommendations for international students: Required—TOEFL (minimum score 600 paper-based). Electronic applications accepted. *Expenses:* Contact institution.

Schreiner University, Department of Education, Kerrville, TX 78028-5697. Offers education (M Ed); principal (Certificate). *Program availability:* Part-time, evening/weekend, online learning. *Entrance requirements:* For master's, GRE (waived if undergraduate cumulative GPA is 3.0 or above), 3 references; transcripts; interview. Additional exam requirements/recommendations for international students: Required—TOEFL. Electronic applications accepted.

Seattle Pacific University, Doctoral Program in Education, Seattle, WA 98119-1997. Offers Ed D, PhD. *Accreditation:* NCATE. *Students:* 1 full-time (0 women), 33 part-time (23 women); includes 4 minority (3 Black or African American, non-Hispanic/Latino; 1 American Indian or Alaska Native, non-Hispanic/Latino), 2 international. Average age 44. 4 applicants, 75% accepted, 2 enrolled. In 2017, 8 doctorates awarded. *Degree requirements:* For doctorate, comprehensive exam, thesis/dissertation. *Entrance requirements:* For doctorate, GRE, MAT. *Application deadline:* For fall admission, 8/15 for domestic students; for winter admission, 11/15 for domestic students; for spring admission, 2/15 for domestic students; for summer admission, 5/15 for domestic students. Applications are processed on a rolling basis. Application fee: $50. *Expenses:* Contact institution. *Financial support:* Career-related internships or fieldwork available. Financial award applicants required to submit FAFSA. *Faculty research:* International education, curriculum and instruction, values and morals, school reform. *Unit head:* Nyaradzo Mvududu, Director of Doctoral Programs, 206-281-2551, E-mail: nyaradzo@spu.edu.
Website: http://spu.edu/academics/school-of-education/graduate-programs/doctoral-programs/doctor-of-philosophy-education-phd

Seattle University, College of Education, Seattle, WA 98122-1090. Offers M Ed, MA, MIT, Ed D, Certificate, Ed S, Post-Master's Certificate. *Accreditation:* NCATE. *Program availability:* Part-time, evening/weekend. *Faculty:* 27 full-time (15 women), 13 part-time/adjunct (9 women). *Students:* 250 full-time (196 women), 246 part-time (180 women); includes 180 minority (19 Black or African American, non-Hispanic/Latino; 7 American Indian or Alaska Native, non-Hispanic/Latino; 57 Asian, non-Hispanic/Latino; 67 Hispanic/Latino; 1 Native Hawaiian or other Pacific Islander, non-Hispanic/Latino; 29 Two or more races, non-Hispanic/Latino), 12 international. Average age 31. 460 applicants, 62% accepted, 146 enrolled. In 2017, 176 master's, 5 doctorates, 49 other advanced degrees awarded. *Degree requirements:* For master's and other advanced degree, comprehensive exam; for doctorate, comprehensive exam, thesis/dissertation. *Entrance requirements:* For doctorate, GRE General Test, MAT, interview, MA, minimum GPA of 3.5, 3 years of related experience. Additional exam requirements/recommendations for international students: Required—TOEFL. *Application deadline:* Applications are processed on a rolling basis. Application fee: $55. Electronic applications accepted. *Expenses:* Contact institution. *Financial support:* In 2017–18, 116 students received support. Career-related internships or fieldwork, Federal Work-Study, scholarships/grants, and unspecified assistantships available. Support available to part-time students. Financial award applicants required to submit FAFSA. *Faculty research:* Service-learning, learning and technology, assessment models of professional education, alternative delivery systems. *Unit head:* Dr. Deanna Sands, Dean, 206-296-5758, E-mail: sandsd@seattleu.edu. *Application contact:* Janet Shandley, Director of Graduate Admissions, 206-296-5900, Fax: 206-298-5656, E-mail: grad_admissions@seattleu.edu.
Website: https://www.seattleu.edu/education/

Seton Hall University, College of Education and Human Services, South Orange, NJ 07079-2697. Offers MA, MS, Ed D, Exec Ed D, PhD, Ed S. *Accreditation:* NCATE. *Program availability:* Part-time, evening/weekend, 100% online, blended/hybrid learning. *Degree requirements:* For master's, comprehensive exam (for some programs), internship; for doctorate, comprehensive exam, thesis/dissertation, internship. *Entrance requirements:* For master's, GRE or MAT, PRAXIS, letters of recommendation,

interview, personal statement, curriculum vitae, transcript; for doctorate, GRE, interview, letters of recommendation, personal statement, curriculum vitae, transcript; for Ed S, GRE or MAT, PRAXIS, interview, letters of recommendation, personal statement, curriculum vitae, transcript. Additional exam requirements/recommendations for international students: Required—TOEFL. Electronic applications accepted. *Expenses:* Contact institution. *Faculty research:* Integration of technology, education leadership, educational media, special education, school district management.

Shawnee State University, Program in Curriculum and Instruction, Portsmouth, OH 45662. Offers M Ed. *Accreditation:* NCATE.

Shenandoah University, School of Education and Leadership, Winchester, VA 22601. Offers administration and supervision (Certificate); administrative leadership (D Ed); early childhood literacy (MS); educational administration (MSE); elementary school teacher education (Certificate); emphasis in teaching (MSE); health and physical education (Certificate); individualized focus (MS, MSE); literacy education (MS); middle school teacher education (Certificate); organizational leadership (MS, D Prof); reading licensure (MS, Certificate); reading non-licensure (MS); secondary school teacher education (Certificate); special education (MSE); writing (MS). *Accreditation:* TEAC. *Program availability:* Part-time, evening/weekend. *Faculty:* 8 full-time (7 women), 22 part-time/adjunct (16 women). *Students:* 16 full-time (14 women), 221 part-time (167 women); includes 32 minority (17 Black or African American, non-Hispanic/Latino; 1 American Indian or Alaska Native, non-Hispanic/Latino; 6 Asian, non-Hispanic/Latino; 5 Hispanic/Latino; 1 Native Hawaiian or other Pacific Islander, non-Hispanic/Latino; 2 Two or more races, non-Hispanic/Latino), 3 international. Average age 38. 81 applicants, 99% accepted, 63 enrolled. In 2017, 53 master's, 11 doctorates, 49 other advanced degrees awarded. *Degree requirements:* For master's, comprehensive exam (for some programs), thesis (for some programs); for doctorate, comprehensive exam, thesis/dissertation. *Entrance requirements:* For degree, PRAXIS Academic Core, SAT/ACT, PRAXIS Academic Core Math, or VCLA, three letters of recommendation, writing sample, undergraduate degree. Additional exam requirements/recommendations for international students: Required—TOEFL (minimum score 550 paper-based, 79 iBT) or IELTS (6.5). *Application deadline:* For fall admission, 5/1 priority date for domestic students, 5/1 for international students; for spring admission, 10/15 priority date for domestic students, 10/15 for international students; for summer admission, 3/15 priority date for domestic students, 3/15 for international students. Application fee: $30. Electronic applications accepted. *Expenses:* $15,600 tuition plus $1,296 fees (technology and student services). *Financial support:* In 2017–18, 26 students received support. Scholarships/grants and unspecified assistantships available. Financial award applicants required to submit FAFSA. *Faculty research:* Mentoring, behavior support for students, teacher change agency, educational technology in pedagogy, literacy education. *Unit head:* Jill Lindsey, PhD, Director, 540-535-7324, Fax: 540-665-4726, E-mail: jlindsey@su.edu. *Application contact:* Andrew Woodall, Executive Director of Recruitment and Admissions, 540-665-4581, Fax: 540-665-4627, E-mail: admit@su.edu.
Website: http://www.su.edu/education/

Shippensburg University of Pennsylvania, School of Graduate Studies, College of Education and Human Services, Shippensburg, PA 17257-2299. Offers M Ed, MAT, MS, MSW, Ed D. *Accreditation:* NCATE. *Program availability:* Part-time, evening/weekend, blended/hybrid learning. *Faculty:* 49 full-time (26 women), 15 part-time/adjunct (9 women). *Students:* 145 full-time (112 women), 305 part-time (216 women); includes 60 minority (32 Black or African American, non-Hispanic/Latino; 5 Asian, non-Hispanic/Latino; 17 Hispanic/Latino; 6 Two or more races, non-Hispanic/Latino), 21 international. Average age 32. 331 applicants, 70% accepted, 168 enrolled. In 2017, 137 master's awarded. *Entrance requirements:* Additional exam requirements/recommendations for international students: Required—TOEFL (minimum score 550 paper-based, 68 iBT) or IELTS (minimum score 6). *Application deadline:* For fall admission, 4/30 for international students; for spring admission, 9/30 for international students. Applications are processed on a rolling basis. Application fee: $45. Electronic applications accepted. *Expenses:* Tuition, state resident: part-time $500 per credit. Tuition, nonresident: part-time $750 per credit. *Required fees:* $145 per credit. *Financial support:* In 2017–18, 72 students received support. Career-related internships or fieldwork, scholarships/grants, unspecified assistantships, and resident hall director and student payroll positions available. Support available to part-time students. Financial award application deadline: 3/1; financial award applicants required to submit FAFSA. *Unit head:* Dr. Nicole R. Hill, Dean of the College of Education and Human Services, 717-477-1373, Fax: 717-477-4012, E-mail: nrhill@ship.edu. *Application contact:* Maya T. Mapp, Director of Admissions, 717-477-1231, Fax: 717-477-4016, E-mail: mtmapp@ship.edu.
Website: http://www.ship.edu/COEHS/

Siena Heights University, Graduate College, Adrian, MI 49221-1796. Offers clinical mental health counseling (MA); educational leadership (Specialist); leadership (MA), including health care leadership, organizational leadership; teacher education (MA), including early childhood education, early childhood education: Montessori, education leadership: principal, elementary education: reading K-12, leadership: higher education, secondary education: reading K-12, special education: cognitive impairment, special education: learning disabilities. *Program availability:* Part-time, evening/weekend. *Degree requirements:* For master's, thesis, presentation. *Entrance requirements:* For master's, minimum GPA of 3.0, current resume, essay, all post-secondary transcripts, 3 letters of reference, conviction disclosure form; copy of teaching certificate (for some education programs); for Specialist, master's degree, minimum GPA of 3.0, current resume, essay, all post-secondary transcripts, 3 letters of reference, conviction disclosure form; copy of teaching certificate (for some education programs). Electronic applications accepted.

Sierra Nevada College, Teacher Education Program, Incline Village, NV 89451. Offers advanced teaching and leadership (M Ed); elementary education (MAT); secondary education (MAT). *Program availability:* Part-time, evening/weekend, online learning. *Degree requirements:* For master's, comprehensive exam, thesis, PRAXIS I and II. *Entrance requirements:* For master's, 2 letters of recommendation, minimum GPA of 3.0. Electronic applications accepted.

Silver Lake College of the Holy Family, Graduate School, Graduate Education Program, Manitowoc, WI 54220-9319. Offers administrative leadership (MA Ed); teacher leadership (MA Ed). *Program availability:* Part-time, evening/weekend, blended/hybrid learning. *Degree requirements:* For master's, comprehensive exam, thesis or alternative, capstone culminating project, comprehensive portfolio, or public presentation of project. *Entrance requirements:* For master's, ACT (preferred) or SAT, minimum undergraduate GPA of 3.0. Additional exam requirements/recommendations for international students: Required—TOEFL (minimum score 550 paper-based; 89 iBT). Electronic applications accepted. *Expenses:* Contact institution. *Faculty research:* Student development; school administration.

Simmons College, School of Social Work, Boston, MA 02115. Offers behavior analysis (MS, PhD, Ed S); education (MS Ed); social work (MSW, PhD); special education (MS Ed), including moderate and severe disabilities; teaching (MAT), including elementary education; MSW/MBA. *Accreditation:* CSWE (one or more programs are accredited). *Program availability:* Part-time, 100% online, blended/hybrid learning.

Faculty: 57 full-time (47 women), 48 part-time/adjunct (36 women). *Students:* 878 full-time (757 women), 979 part-time (869 women); includes 468 minority (213 Black or African American, non-Hispanic/Latino; 1 American Indian or Alaska Native, non-Hispanic/Latino; 45 Asian, non-Hispanic/Latino; 152 Hispanic/Latino; 3 Native Hawaiian or other Pacific Islander, non-Hispanic/Latino; 54 Two or more races, non-Hispanic/Latino), 12 international. Average age 30. 1,521 applicants, 74% accepted, 545 enrolled. In 2017, 611 master's, 7 doctorates, 1 other advanced degree awarded. Terminal master's awarded for partial completion of doctoral program. *Degree requirements:* For master's, thesis (for some programs); for doctorate, comprehensive exam (for some programs), thesis/dissertation (for some programs). *Entrance requirements:* For master's, GRE, MAT, Massachusetts Tests for Education Licensure (for different programs), minimum grade of B in introductory statistics course within five years prior to entering program, resume, transcripts, three letters of recommendation, personal statement; for doctorate, GRE, BCBA Analyst Exam. Additional exam requirements/recommendations for international students: Required—TOEFL (minimum score 600 paper-based; 100 iBT). *Application deadline:* For fall admission, 8/1 for domestic students; for spring admission, 12/15 for domestic students; for summer admission, 5/1 for domestic students. Applications are processed on a rolling basis. Application fee: $35. Electronic applications accepted. *Expenses:* $1,001 per credit hour, $3,003 per course, $55 activity fee per semester. *Financial support:* In 2017–18, 12 fellowships with partial tuition reimbursements were awarded; scholarships/grants and unspecified assistantships also available. Support available to part-time students. Financial award applicants required to submit FAFSA. *Unit head:* Dr. Cheryl Parks, Dean, 617-521-3293, E-mail: cheryl.parks@simmons.edu. *Application contact:* Carlos D. Frontado, Director of Admissions, 617-521-3920, Fax: 617-521-3980, E-mail: ssw@simmons.edu. Website: http://www.simmons.edu/ssw/

Simon Fraser University, Office of Graduate Studies and Postdoctoral Fellows, Faculty of Education, Burnaby, BC V5A 1S6, Canada. Offers M Ed, M Sc, MA, Ed D, PhD, Graduate Diploma. *Degree requirements:* For doctorate, thesis/dissertation. *Entrance requirements:* Additional exam requirements/recommendations for international students: Recommended—TOEFL (minimum score 580 paper-based; 93 iBT), IELTS (minimum score 7), TWE (minimum score 5). Electronic applications accepted.

Simpson College, Department of Education, Indianola, IA 50125-1297. Offers secondary education (MAT). *Degree requirements:* For master's, PRAXIS II, electronic portfolio. *Entrance requirements:* For master's, bachelor's degree; minimum cumulative GPA of 2.75, 3.0 in major; 3 letters of recommendation.

Simpson University, School of Education, Redding, CA 96003-8606. Offers education (MA), including curriculum, education leadership; education and preliminary administrative services credential (MA); education and preliminary teaching credential (MA); teaching (MA). *Program availability:* Part-time, evening/weekend. *Degree requirements:* For master's, thesis optional. *Entrance requirements:* For master's, statement of purpose, 2 professional references, professional essay, interview. Additional exam requirements/recommendations for international students: Required—TOEFL (minimum score 550 paper-based). Electronic applications accepted. *Expenses:* Contact institution.

Sinte Gleska University, Graduate Education Program, Mission, SD 57555. Offers elementary education (M Ed). *Program availability:* Part-time, evening/weekend. *Degree requirements:* For master's, thesis. *Entrance requirements:* For master's, 2 years of experience in elementary education, minimum GPA of 2.5, South Dakota elementary education certification. *Faculty research:* American Indian graduate education, teaching of Native American students.

Slippery Rock University of Pennsylvania, Graduate Studies (Recruitment), College of Education, Slippery Rock, PA 16057-1383. Offers M Ed, MA, MS, Ed D. *Accreditation:* NCATE. *Program availability:* Part-time, evening/weekend, 100% online. *Degree requirements:* For master's, comprehensive exam (for some programs), thesis (for some programs), internship (depending on program). *Entrance requirements:* For master's, GRE General Test or MAT (depending on program), official transcripts, minimum GPA of 2.75 (depending on program). Additional exam requirements/recommendations for international students: Required—TOEFL (minimum score 550 paper-based; 80 iBT). Electronic applications accepted. *Expenses:* Contact institution.

Smith College, Graduate and Special Programs, Department of Education and Child Study, Northampton, MA 01063. Offers elementary education (MAT), including elementary education, middle school education; secondary education (MAT), including secondary education. *Program availability:* Part-time. *Students:* 10 full-time (all women), 5 part-time (2 women); includes 3 minority (1 Asian, non-Hispanic/Latino; 2 Hispanic/Latino). Average age 26. 28 applicants, 93% accepted, 12 enrolled. In 2017, 14 master's awarded. *Entrance requirements:* Additional exam requirements/recommendations for international students: Required—TOEFL (minimum score 595 paper-based; 97 iBT), IELTS. *Application deadline:* For fall admission, 4/15 for domestic students, 1/15 for international students; for spring admission, 12/1 for domestic students. Applications are processed on a rolling basis. Application fee: $60. *Expenses:* Contact institution. *Financial support:* In 2017–18, 15 students received support, including 4 fellowships with full tuition reimbursements available; scholarships/grants and human resources employee benefit also available. Support available to part-time students. Financial award application deadline: 4/15; financial award applicants required to submit CSS PROFILE or FAFSA. *Unit head:* Alan Rudnitsky, Chair, 413-585-3261, Fax: 413-585-3268, E-mail: arudnits@smith.edu. *Application contact:* Ruth Morgan, Program Assistant, 413-585-3050, Fax: 413-585-3054, E-mail: gradstdy@smith.edu. Website: http://www.smith.edu/education

Sonoma State University, School of Education, Rohnert Park, CA 94928. Offers administrative services (Credential); curriculum, teaching, and learning (MA); early childhood education (MA); education specialist (Credential); educational leadership (MA); multiple subject (Credential); reading and literacy (MA, Credential); single subject (Credential); special education (MA). *Accreditation:* NCATE. *Program availability:* Part-time, evening/weekend. *Entrance requirements:* For master's, minimum GPA of 2.5. Additional exam requirements/recommendations for international students: Required—TOEFL (minimum score 500 paper-based). Application fee: $55. *Financial support:* Fellowships, research assistantships, career-related internships or fieldwork, and Federal Work-Study available. Support available to part-time students. Financial award application deadline: 3/2; financial award applicants required to submit FAFSA. *Unit head:* Dr. Carlos Ayala, Dean, 707-664-4412, E-mail: carlos.ayala@sonoma.edu. *Application contact:* Dr. Karen Grady, Coordinator of Graduate Studies, 707-664-3328, E-mail: karen.grady@sonoma.edu. Website: http://www.sonoma.edu/education/

South Carolina State University, College of Graduate and Professional Studies, Department of Education, Orangeburg, SC 29117-0001. Offers early childhood education (MAT); education (M Ed); elementary education (M Ed, MAT); English (MAT); general science/biology (MAT); mathematics (MAT); secondary education (M Ed), including biology education, business education, counselor education, English education, home economics education, industrial education, mathematics education, science education, social studies education; special education (M Ed), including emotionally handicapped, learning disabilities, mentally handicapped. *Accreditation:*

NCATE. *Program availability:* Part-time, evening/weekend. *Faculty:* 11 full-time (6 women), 4 part-time/adjunct (2 women). *Students:* 26 full-time (18 women), 22 part-time (17 women); includes 41 minority (all Black or African American, non-Hispanic/Latino), 1 international. Average age 33. 25 applicants, 100% accepted, 19 enrolled. In 2017, 6 master's awarded. *Degree requirements:* For master's, thesis optional, departmental qualifying exam. *Entrance requirements:* For master's, GRE General Test, NTE, interview, teaching certificate. *Application deadline:* For fall admission, 6/15 priority date for domestic students, 6/15 for international students; for spring admission, 11/1 for domestic and international students. Application fee: $25. Electronic applications accepted. *Expenses:* Tuition, state resident: full-time $9388; part-time $607 per credit hour. Tuition, nonresident: full-time $19,968; part-time $1194 per credit hour. *Required fees:* $766; $766 per credit hour. *Financial support:* Fellowships, career-related internships or fieldwork, Federal Work-Study, and scholarships/grants available. Financial award application deadline: 6/1. *Unit head:* Dr. Charlie Spell, Interim Chair, Department of Education, 803-536-8963, Fax: 803-516-4568, E-mail: cspell@scsu.edu. *Application contact:* Curtis Foskey, Coordinator of Graduate Studies, 803-536-8419, Fax: 803-536-8812, E-mail: cfoskey@scsu.edu.

South Dakota State University, Graduate School, College of Education and Human Sciences, Brookings, SD 57007. Offers M Ed, MFCS, MS, PhD. *Degree requirements:* For master's, thesis, oral exam. *Entrance requirements:* Additional exam requirements/recommendations for international students: Required—TOEFL.

Southeastern Louisiana University, College of Education, Hammond, LA 70402. Offers M Ed, MAT, Ed D. *Accreditation:* NCATE. *Program availability:* Part-time. *Faculty:* 24 full-time (18 women), 3 part-time/adjunct (2 women). *Students:* 24 full-time (20 women), 274 part-time (230 women); includes 85 minority (63 Black or African American, non-Hispanic/Latino; 11 Hispanic/Latino; 11 Two or more races, non-Hispanic/Latino), 2 international. Average age 38. 94 applicants, 55% accepted, 44 enrolled. In 2017, 73 master's, 2 doctorates awarded. *Degree requirements:* For master's, comprehensive exam (for some programs), thesis optional; for doctorate, thesis/dissertation. *Entrance requirements:* Additional exam requirements/recommendations for international students: Required—TOEFL (minimum score 500 paper-based; 61 iBT). *Application deadline:* For fall admission, 7/15 priority date for domestic students, 6/1 priority date for international students; for spring admission, 12/1 priority date for domestic students, 10/1 priority date for international students. Applications are processed on a rolling basis. Application fee: $20 ($30 for international students). Electronic applications accepted. *Expenses:* Tuition, state resident: full-time $6684. Tuition, nonresident: full-time $19,162. *Required fees:* $2088. *Financial support:* In 2017–18, 19 students received support, including 6 teaching assistantships (averaging $8,276 per year); research assistantships, career-related internships or fieldwork, Federal Work-Study, institutionally sponsored loans, scholarships/grants, and unspecified assistantships also available. Support available to part-time students. Financial award application deadline: 5/1; financial award applicants required to submit FAFSA. *Faculty research:* School effectiveness, using data to drive instruction, change leadership, dyslexia, struggling at risk readers. *Unit head:* Dr. Paula Calderon, Dean, 985-549-2217, Fax: 985-549-2070, E-mail: paula.calderon@southeastern.edu. *Application contact:* Amanda Harper, Graduate Admissions Analyst, 985-549-5620, Fax: 985-549-5632, E-mail: admissions@southeastern.edu. Website: http://www.southeastern.edu/acad_research/colleges/edu_hd/index.html

Southeastern Oklahoma State University, School of Education, Durant, OK 74701-0609. Offers math specialist (M Ed); reading specialist (M Ed); school administration (M Ed); school counseling (M Ed). *Accreditation:* NCATE. *Program availability:* Part-time, evening/weekend. *Degree requirements:* For master's, comprehensive exam, thesis optional, portfolio (M Ed). *Entrance requirements:* For master's, GRE General Test (for school counseling), minimum GPA of 3.0 in last 60 hours or 2.75 overall. Additional exam requirements/recommendations for international students: Required—TOEFL (minimum score 550 paper-based; 79 iBT). Electronic applications accepted.

Southeastern University, College of Education, Lakeland, FL 33801-6099. Offers curriculum and instruction (Ed D); educational leadership (M Ed); elementary education (M Ed); exceptional student education (M Ed); exceptional student education/educational therapy (M Ed); kinesiology (M Ed); organizational leadership (Ed D); reading education (M Ed); teaching English to speakers of other languages (M Ed). *Faculty:* 8 full-time (5 women), 12 part-time/adjunct (7 women). *Students:* 139 full-time (109 women), 225 part-time (172 women); includes 107 minority (57 Black or African American, non-Hispanic/Latino; 2 Asian, non-Hispanic/Latino; 48 Hispanic/Latino), 4 international. Average age 40. Application fee: $50. Electronic applications accepted. *Unit head:* James A. Anderson, Dean, 863-667-5366, E-mail: jaanderson2@seu.edu. Website: http://www.seu.edu/education/

Southern Adventist University, School of Education and Psychology, Collegedale, TN 37315-0370. Offers clinical mental health counseling (MS); instructional leadership (MS Ed); literacy education (MS Ed); outdoor education (MS Ed); professional school counseling (MS). *Accreditation:* NCATE. *Program availability:* Part-time, evening/weekend. *Degree requirements:* For master's, comprehensive exam (for some programs), thesis optional, position paper (MS), portfolio (MS Ed in outdoor education). *Entrance requirements:* For master's, interview (MS); 9 semester hours of upper-division course work in psychology or related field, including 1 course in psychology research or statistics; 9 semester hours of education (MS Ed). Additional exam requirements/recommendations for international students: Required—TOEFL (minimum score 600 paper-based; 100 iBT). *Application deadline:* For fall admission, 7/1 priority date for domestic students, 6/1 priority date for international students; for winter admission, 11/1 priority date for domestic students, 10/1 priority date for international students; for spring admission, 4/1 priority date for domestic students, 3/1 priority date for international students. Applications are processed on a rolling basis. Application fee: $40. Electronic applications accepted. *Expenses:* Tuition: Full-time $11,430; part-time $635 per credit hour. Tuition and fees vary according to degree level and program. *Financial support:* Research assistantships with full tuition reimbursements, teaching assistantships with full tuition reimbursements, career-related internships or fieldwork, scholarships/grants, tuition waivers (partial), and unspecified assistantships available. Support available to part-time students. Financial award application deadline: 4/1; financial award applicants required to submit FAFSA. *Unit head:* Bonnie Eder, Interim Dean, 423-236-2759, Fax: 423-236-1765, E-mail: beder@southern.edu. *Application contact:* Mikhaile Spence, Graduate Enrollment Counselor, 423-236-2496, Fax: 423-236-1765, E-mail: maspence@southern.edu. Website: https://www.southern.edu/academics/edpsych.html

Southern Arkansas University–Magnolia, School of Graduate Studies, Magnolia, AR 71753. Offers agriculture (MS); business administration (MBA), including agribusiness, social entrepreneurship, supply chain management; clinical and mental health counseling (MS); computer and information sciences (MS), including cyber security and privacy, data science, information technology; gifted and talented (M Ed), including curriculum and instruction, educational administration and supervision, gifted and talented P-8/7-12, instructional specialist P-4; higher, adult and lifelong education (M Ed); kinesiology (M Ed), including coaching; library media and information specialist (M Ed); public administration (MPA); school counseling K-12 (M Ed); student affairs and college counseling (M Ed); teaching (MAT). *Accreditation:* NCATE. *Program availability:* Part-time, 100% online,

Education—General

blended/hybrid learning. *Faculty:* 36 full-time (20 women), 31 part-time/adjunct (12 women). *Students:* 242 full-time (89 women), 889 part-time (459 women); includes 167 minority (143 Black or African American, non-Hispanic/Latino; 7 American Indian or Alaska Native, non-Hispanic/Latino; 7 Asian, non-Hispanic/Latino; 3 Hispanic/Latino; 7 Two or more races, non-Hispanic/Latino), 562 international. Average age 28. 400 applicants, 100% accepted, 239 enrolled. In 2017, 875 master's awarded. *Degree requirements:* For master's, comprehensive exam (for some programs), thesis optional. *Entrance requirements:* For master's, GRE, MAT or GMAT, minimum GPA of 2.5. Additional exam requirements/recommendations for international students: Required—TOEFL (minimum score 550 paper-based), IELTS (minimum score 6). *Application deadline:* For fall admission, 7/20 for domestic students, 7/10 for international students; for spring admission, 12/1 for domestic students, 11/15 for international students; for summer admission, 4/1 for domestic students, 5/1 for international students. Applications are processed on a rolling basis. Application fee: $25 ($50 for international students). Electronic applications accepted. *Expenses:* Tuition, state resident: full-time $6038. Tuition, nonresident: full-time $8558. *Required fees:* $804. One-time fee: $110 full-time. Tuition and fees vary according to course load. *Financial support:* Career-related internships or fieldwork, Federal Work-Study, scholarships/grants, tuition waivers (full), and unspecified assistantships available. Financial award applicants required to submit FAFSA. *Faculty research:* Alternative certification for teachers, supervision of instruction, instructional leadership, counseling. *Unit head:* Dr. Kim Bloss, Dean, School of Graduate Studies, 870-235-4150, Fax: 870-235-5227, E-mail: kkbloss@saumag.edu. *Application contact:* Shrijana Malakar, Admissions Specialist, 870-235-4150, Fax: 870-235-5227, E-mail: smalakar@saumag.edu.
Website: http://www.saumag.edu/graduate

Southern Connecticut State University, School of Graduate Studies, School of Education, New Haven, CT 06515-1355. Offers MLS, MS, MS Ed, Ed D, Diploma. *Accreditation:* NCATE. *Program availability:* Part-time. *Degree requirements:* For doctorate, comprehensive exam, thesis/dissertation. *Entrance requirements:* For degree, master's degree. Electronic applications accepted.

Southern Illinois University Carbondale, Graduate School, College of Education and Human Services, Carbondale, IL 62901-4701. Offers MPH, MS, MS Ed, MSW, PhD, JD/MSW. *Accreditation:* NCATE. *Program availability:* Part-time. Terminal master's awarded for partial completion of doctoral program. *Degree requirements:* For doctorate, thesis/dissertation. *Entrance requirements:* For master's, minimum GPA of 2.7. Additional exam requirements/recommendations for international students: Required—TOEFL (minimum score 550 paper-based; 80 iBT). Electronic applications accepted. *Faculty research:* Safety education, community health, curriculum development, gifted, effective schools.

Southern Illinois University Edwardsville, Graduate School, School of Education, Health, and Human Behavior, Edwardsville, IL 62062. Offers MA, MS, MS Ed, Ed D, Ed S, Post-Master's Certificate, Postbaccalaureate Certificate, SD. *Accreditation:* NCATE. *Program availability:* Part-time, evening/weekend. *Degree requirements:* For master's, comprehensive exam (for some programs), thesis (for some programs), final exam, portfolio. *Entrance requirements:* For master's, GRE. Additional exam requirements/recommendations for international students: Required—TOEFL (minimum score 550 paper-based; 79 iBT), IELTS (minimum score 6.5). Electronic applications accepted.

Southern Methodist University, Annette Caldwell Simmons School of Education and Human Development, Department of Teaching and Learning, Dallas, TX 75275. Offers bilingual/ESL education (MBE); education (M Ed, PhD); gifted education (MBE); reading and writing (M Ed); special education (M Ed). *Program availability:* Part-time, evening/weekend. Terminal master's awarded for partial completion of doctoral program. *Degree requirements:* For master's, comprehensive exam, minimum GPA of 3.0; for doctorate, thesis/dissertation, qualifying exams, major area paper, evidence of teaching competency, dissemination of research (e.g., conference presentation), professional portfolio. *Entrance requirements:* For master's, minimum GPA of 3.0 or GRE, 3 letters of recommendation; for doctorate, GRE, minimum GPA of 3.3, 3 years of full-time teaching, 3 letters of recommendation, interview. Additional exam requirements/recommendations for international students: Required—TOEFL. Electronic applications accepted. *Faculty research:* Reading intervention, mathematics intervention, bilingual education, new literacies.

Southern New Hampshire University, School of Education, Manchester, NH 03106-1045. Offers curriculum and instruction (M Ed), including dyslexia studies and language-based learning disabilities, educational leadership, reading, special education, technology integration; dyslexia studies and language-based learning disabilities (Certificate); early childhood and special education (M Ed); educational leadership (M Ed, Ed D); educational studies (M Ed); elementary and special education (M Ed); field based education (M Ed); higher education administration (MS); teaching English as a foreign language (MS). *Program availability:* Part-time, evening/weekend, online learning. *Degree requirements:* For master's, comprehensive exam (for some programs), thesis or alternative. *Entrance requirements:* For master's, PRAXIS I, minimum GPA of 2.75. Additional exam requirements/recommendations for international students: Required—TOEFL (minimum score 550 paper-based). *Application deadline:* Applications are processed on a rolling basis. Application fee: $40. Electronic applications accepted. *Expenses:* Contact institution. *Financial support:* Institutionally sponsored loans available. Financial award applicants required to submit FAFSA. *Unit head:* Raymond McNulty, Dean, 603-668-2211, Fax: 603-629-4673. *Application contact:* Office of Graduate Admission, 888-327-SNHU, Fax: 603-644-3144, E-mail: enroll@snhu.edu.

Southern Oregon University, Graduate Studies, School of Education, Ashland, OR 97520. Offers elementary education (MA Ed, MS Ed), including classroom teacher, early childhood, handicapped learner, reading, supervision; secondary education (MA Ed, MS Ed), including classroom teacher, handicapped learner, reading, supervision; teaching (MAT). *Program availability:* Online learning. *Degree requirements:* For master's, thesis optional. *Entrance requirements:* For master's, GRE General Test, minimum cumulative GPA of 3.0 in the last 90 quarter credits (60 semester credits) of undergraduate coursework. Additional exam requirements/recommendations for international students: Required—TOEFL (minimum score 540 paper-based; 76 iBT), IELTS (minimum score 6), ELPT (minimum score 964) or ELS (minimum score 112). Electronic applications accepted.

Southern University and Agricultural and Mechanical College, Graduate School, College of Education, Baton Rouge, LA 70813. Offers M Ed, MA, MS, PhD. *Accreditation:* NCATE. *Degree requirements:* For master's, comprehensive exam, thesis optional. *Entrance requirements:* For master's and doctorate, GRE General Test. Additional requirements/recommendations for international students: Required—TOEFL (minimum score 525 paper-based).

Southern Utah University, Program in Education, Cedar City, UT 84720-2498. Offers M Ed, MMus, Certificate. *Accreditation:* TEAC. *Program availability:* Part-time, 100% online. *Faculty:* 13 full-time (6 women), 16 part-time/adjunct (6 women). *Students:* 5 full-time (all women), 380 part-time (273 women); includes 22 minority (1 Black or African American, non-Hispanic/Latino; 8 Asian, non-Hispanic/Latino; 10 Hispanic/Latino; 3 Native Hawaiian or other Pacific Islander, non-Hispanic/Latino), 2 international. Average age 38. 72 applicants, 86% accepted, 45 enrolled. In 2017, 195 master's awarded. *Entrance requirements:* For master's, GRE (if GPA is less than 3.25). Additional exam requirements/recommendations for international students: Required—TOEFL (minimum score 550 paper-based, 79 iBT) or IELTS (minimum score 6). *Application deadline:* For fall admission, 7/15 for domestic and international students; for spring admission, 11/15 for domestic and international students; for summer admission, 4/15 for domestic and international students. Applications are processed on a rolling basis. Application fee: $60 ($65 for international students). Electronic applications accepted. *Expenses:* Contact institution. *Financial support:* Tuition waivers (partial) available. *Unit head:* Dr. Bart Reynolds, Department Chair, 435-865-8125, Fax: 435-865-8485, E-mail: reynolds@suu.edu. *Application contact:* Tamara Lovell, Program Specialist, 435-865-8759, Fax: 435-865-8485, E-mail: tamaralovell@suu.edu.
Website: https://www.suu.edu/ed/graduate/master.html

Southern Wesleyan University, Program in Education, Central, SC 29630-1020. Offers M Ed. Program also offered at Greenville, S. C. site. *Accreditation:* NCATE. *Program availability:* Evening/weekend. *Entrance requirements:* For master's, GRE General Test or MAT, 1 year teaching experience, minimum undergraduate GPA of 3.0, teacher certification. Additional exam requirements/recommendations for international students: Required—TOEFL (minimum score 500 paper-based).

Southwest Baptist University, Program in Education, Bolivar, MO 65613-2597. Offers education (MS); educational administration (MS, Ed S). *Program availability:* Part-time. *Degree requirements:* For master's, comprehensive exam, thesis optional, 6-hour residency; for Ed S, comprehensive exam, 5-hour residency. *Entrance requirements:* For master's, GRE or PRAXIS II, interviews, minimum GPA of 2.75; for Ed S, master's degree. Additional exam requirements/recommendations for international students: Required—TOEFL (minimum score 550 paper-based). *Faculty research:* At-risk programs, principal retention, mentoring beginning principals.

Southwestern Adventist University, Education Department, Keene, TX 76059. Offers curriculum and instruction with reading emphasis (M Ed); educational leadership (M Ed). *Program availability:* Part-time, evening/weekend. *Degree requirements:* For master's, thesis or alternative, professional paper. *Entrance requirements:* For master's, GRE General Test.

Southwestern Assemblies of God University, Thomas F. Harrison School of Graduate Studies, Program in Education, Waxahachie, TX 75165-5735. Offers Christian school administration (MS); curriculum development (MS); early education administration (M Ed); middle and secondary education (M Ed). *Degree requirements:* For master's, comprehensive written and oral exams. *Entrance requirements:* For master's, GRE General Test, minimum GPA of 2.5. Electronic applications accepted.

Southwestern College, Education Programs, Winfield, KS 67156-2499. Offers curriculum and instruction (M Ed); early childhood education (M Ed); educational leadership (Ed D), including higher education leadership, PK-12 education leadership; special education (M Ed), including high-incidence disabilities, low-incidence disabilities; teaching (MA). *Accreditation:* NCATE. *Program availability:* Part-time, evening/weekend, 100% online, blended/hybrid learning. *Faculty:* 6 full-time (5 women), 12 part-time/adjunct (10 women). *Students:* 12 full-time (10 women), 77 part-time (51 women); includes 12 minority (5 Black or African American, non-Hispanic/Latino; 2 American Indian or Alaska Native, non-Hispanic/Latino; 1 Asian, non-Hispanic/Latino; 3 Hispanic/Latino; 1 Native Hawaiian or other Pacific Islander, non-Hispanic/Latino), 10 international. Average age 39. 29 applicants, 86% accepted, 18 enrolled. In 2017, 52 master's, 11 doctorates awarded. *Degree requirements:* For master's, practicum, portfolio; for doctorate, thesis/dissertation, professional portfolio. *Entrance requirements:* For master's, baccalaureate degree, minimum GPA of 3.0, valid teaching certificate (for special education); for doctorate, GRE if no master's degree, baccalaureate degree with minimum GPA of 3.25 and current teaching experience, or master's degree with minimum GPA of 3.5. Additional exam requirements/recommendations for international students: Required—TOEFL (minimum score 550 paper-based; 80 iBT). *Application deadline:* Applications are processed on a rolling basis. Application fee: $40. Electronic applications accepted. *Expenses:* $577 per credit hour, $509 online (for master's programs); $609 per credit hour (for doctorate program). *Financial support:* In 2017–18, 9 students received support. Unspecified assistantships and employee tuition waivers available. Financial award applicants required to submit FAFSA. *Unit head:* Dana Pentz, Director of Education Operations, 620-229-6253, E-mail: dana.pentz@sckans.edu. *Application contact:* Dennis Russell, Director of Admissions and Student Services, 888-684-5335 Ext. 3372, Fax: 888-684-5218, E-mail: dennis.russell@sckans.edu.
Website: http://www.sckans.edu/graduate/education-med/

Southwestern Oklahoma State University, College of Professional and Graduate Studies, School of Behavioral Sciences and Education, Weatherford, OK 73096-3098. Offers community counseling (M Ed); early childhood education (M Ed); educational administration (M Ed); elementary education (M Ed); health sciences and microbiology (M Ed); kinesiology (M Ed); parks and recreation management (M Ed); school counseling (M Ed); school psychology (MS); school psychometry (M Ed); secondary education (M Ed); special education (M Ed). *Accreditation:* NCATE. *Program availability:* Part-time, evening/weekend, online learning. *Degree requirements:* For master's, exam. *Entrance requirements:* For master's, GRE General Test or minimum undergraduate GPA of 3.0. Additional exam requirements/recommendations for international students: Required—TOEFL.

Southwest Minnesota State University, Department of Education, Marshall, MN 56258. Offers ESL (MS); math (MS); reading (MS); special education (MS), including developmental disabilities, early childhood education, emotional behavioral disorders, learning disabilities; teaching, learning and leadership (MS). *Program availability:* Part-time, evening/weekend, online learning. *Entrance requirements:* Additional exam requirements/recommendations for international students: Required—TOEFL or IELTS; Recommended—TOEFL (minimum score 550 paper-based; 80 iBT), IELTS.

Spalding University, Graduate Studies, College of Education, Louisville, KY 40203-2188. Offers M Ed, MA, MAT, Ed D. *Accreditation:* NCATE. *Program availability:* Part-time, evening/weekend. *Degree requirements:* For doctorate, comprehensive exam, thesis/dissertation. *Entrance requirements:* For master's, GRE, GMAT, or MAT, transcripts, interview, letters of recommendation. Additional exam requirements/recommendations for international students: Required—TOEFL (minimum score 535 paper-based). Electronic applications accepted. Application fee is waived when completed online. *Expenses:* Contact institution. *Faculty research:* School leadership, assessment of student learning, classroom management.

Spring Arbor University, School of Education, Spring Arbor, MI 49283-9799. Offers education (MAE); reading (MAR); special education (MSE). *Accreditation:* TEAC. *Program availability:* Part-time, evening/weekend, online learning. *Degree requirements:* For master's, thesis. *Entrance requirements:* For master's, official transcripts from all institutions attended, including evidence of an earned bachelor's degree from regionally-accredited college or university with minimum cumulative GPA of 3.0 for the last two years of the bachelor's degree; two professional letters of recommendation. Additional exam requirements/recommendations for international students: Required—TOEFL (minimum score 600 paper-based). Electronic applications accepted.

Springfield College, Graduate Programs, Programs in Education, Springfield, MA 01109-3797. Offers early childhood education (M Ed); educational studies (M Ed); elementary education (M Ed); secondary education (M Ed); special education (M Ed, CAGS). *Program availability:* Part-time, evening/weekend. *Students:* 18 applicants, 72% accepted, 12 enrolled. In 2017, 22 master's awarded. *Entrance requirements:* For master's, Massachusetts Tests for Educator Licensure (MTEL). Additional exam requirements/recommendations for international students: Required—TOEFL (minimum score 550 paper-based); Recommended—IELTS (minimum score 7). *Application deadline:* For fall admission, 1/15 for domestic and international students; for winter admission, 11/1 for domestic and international students; for spring admission, 11/1 for domestic and international students. Applications are processed on a rolling basis. Application fee: $50. Electronic applications accepted. *Expenses:* Contact institution. *Financial support:* Fellowships with partial tuition reimbursements, teaching assistantships with partial tuition reimbursements, career-related internships or fieldwork, Federal Work-Study, institutionally sponsored loans, scholarships/grants, and unspecified assistantships available. Financial award application deadline: 3/1; financial award applicants required to submit FAFSA. *Unit head:* Linda Davis-Delano, Director of Education Preparation and Licensure, 413-748-3295, E-mail: ldelano@springfield.edu. *Application contact:* Anne Griffin, Director of Graduate Admissions, 413-748-3225, Fax: 413-748-3694, E-mail: agriffin2@springfield.edu.
Website: http://springfield.edu/wtp

Spring Hill College, Graduate Programs, Program in Education, Mobile, AL 36608-1791. Offers early childhood education (MAT, MS Ed); educational theory (MS Ed); elementary education (MAT, MS Ed); secondary education (MAT, MS Ed). *Program availability:* Part-time. *Faculty:* 2 full-time (both women). *Students:* 15 part-time (14 women); includes 6 minority (5 Black or African American, non-Hispanic/Latino; 1 Hispanic/Latino). Average age 30. In 2017, 5 master's awarded. *Degree requirements:* For master's, comprehensive exam, completion of program within 6 calendar years of entrance into graduate studies at Spring Hill; documentation of course field assignments (MS) or completion of internship (MAT). *Entrance requirements:* For master's, GRE, MAT, or PRAXIS (varies by program), bachelor's degree with minimum undergraduate GPA of 3.0; class B certificate (for MS); minimum number of hours in specific fields (for MAT). Additional exam requirements/recommendations for international students: Required—TOEFL (minimum score 550 paper-based; 80 iBT), IELTS (minimum score 6.5), CPE or CAE (minimum score C), Michigan English Language Assessment Battery (minimum score 90). *Application deadline:* For fall admission, 8/1 priority date for domestic and international students; for spring admission, 12/1 priority date for domestic and international students. Applications are processed on a rolling basis. Application fee: $25 ($35 for international students). Electronic applications accepted. *Expenses:* Contact institution. *Financial support:* Applicants required to submit FAFSA. *Unit head:* Dr. Lori P. Aultman, Chair of Education, Fax: 251-380-3473, Fax: 251-460-2184, E-mail: laultman@shc.edu. *Application contact:* Robert Stewart, Vice President of Enrollment, 251-380-3030, Fax: 251-460-2186, E-mail: rstewart@shc.edu.
Website: http://ug.shc.edu/graduate-degrees/master-science-education/

Stanford University, Graduate School of Education, Stanford, CA 94305-2004. Offers MA, MAE, PhD, MA/JD, MA/MBA, MPP/MA. *Accreditation:* NCATE. *Degree requirements:* For doctorate, thesis/dissertation. *Entrance requirements:* For master's and doctorate, GRE General Test. Electronic applications accepted. *Expenses: Tuition:* Full-time $48,987; part-time $10,620 per quarter. One-time fee: $400. Tuition and fees vary according to program.

State University of New York at Fredonia, College of Education, Fredonia, NY 14063-1136. Offers curriculum and instruction (MS Ed); literacy education (MS Ed), including birth-grade 12, grades 5-12; TESOL (MS Ed). *Accreditation:* NCATE. *Program availability:* Part-time. *Faculty:* 11 full-time (9 women), 1 part-time/adjunct (0 women). *Students:* Average age 29. 60 applicants, 97% accepted, 39 enrolled. In 2017, 33 master's awarded. *Degree requirements:* For master's, thesis. *Entrance requirements:* For master's, GRE, minimum undergraduate GPA of 3.0. Additional exam requirements/recommendations for international students: Required—TOEFL (minimum score 79 iBT), IELTS (minimum score 6.5). *Application deadline:* For fall admission, 4/1 priority date for domestic and international students; for spring admission, 11/1 priority date for domestic students, 11/1 for international students. Applications are processed on a rolling basis. Application fee: $75. Electronic applications accepted. *Expenses:* Tuition, state resident: full-time $8154. Tuition, nonresident: full-time $16,650. *Required fees:* $1209. *Financial support:* In 2017–18, 4 teaching assistantships with full and partial tuition reimbursements (averaging $7,075 per year) were awarded. Financial award application deadline: 3/15; financial award applicants required to submit FAFSA. *Faculty research:* Positive behavioral intervention and support (PBIS), place-based science education, peer support for education, primary source material for social studies education, policies and practices in learning English language. *Unit head:* Dr. Christine Givner, Dean, 716-673-3311, E-mail: christine.givner@fredonia.edu. *Application contact:* Wendy S. Dunst, Interim Graduate Recruitment and Admissions Associate, 716-673-3808, Fax: 716-673-3712, E-mail: wendy.dunst@fredonia.edu.
Website: http://www.fredonia.edu/coe/

State University of New York at New Paltz, Graduate and Extended Learning School, School of Education, New Paltz, NY 12561. Offers MAT, MPS, MS Ed, MST, AC, CAS. *Accreditation:* NCATE. *Program availability:* Part-time, evening/weekend. *Faculty:* 29 full-time (22 women), 20 part-time/adjunct (14 women). *Students:* 115 full-time (84 women), 236 part-time (184 women); includes 60 minority (11 Black or African American, non-Hispanic/Latino; 5 Asian, non-Hispanic/Latino; 39 Hispanic/Latino; 5 Two or more races, non-Hispanic/Latino). 180 applicants, 75% accepted, 113 enrolled. In 2017, 147 master's, 22 other advanced degrees awarded. *Degree requirements:* For master's, comprehensive exam (for some programs), portfolio. *Entrance requirements:* For master's, GRE, MAT, minimum GPA of 3.0, New York State Teaching Certificate; for other advanced degree, minimum GPA of 3.0. Additional exam requirements/recommendations for international students: Required—TOEFL (minimum score 550 paper-based; 80 iBT), IELTS (minimum score 6.5). *Application deadline:* For fall admission, 3/1 for domestic and international students; for spring admission, 10/1 for domestic and international students. Application fee: $50. Electronic applications accepted. *Financial support:* Scholarships/grants available. Financial award application deadline: 8/1. *Faculty research:* Kindergarten readiness, translation learning experiences, assessment in mathematics education, long and short term outcomes of delayed school entry, parental involvement in children's education. *Unit head:* Dr. Michael Rosenberg, Dean, 845-257-2800, E-mail: schoolofed@newpaltz.edu. *Application contact:* Vika Shock, Director of Graduate Admissions, 845-257-3285, Fax: 845-257-3284, E-mail: gradschool@newpaltz.edu.
Website: http://www.newpaltz.edu/schoolofed/

State University of New York at Oswego, Graduate Studies, School of Education, Oswego, NY 13126. Offers MAT, MS, MS Ed, MST, CAS, MS/CAS. *Accreditation:* NCATE. *Program availability:* Part-time. *Degree requirements:* For master's, comprehensive exam (for some programs), thesis optional. *Entrance requirements:* For degree, GRE General Test, interview, MA or MS, minimum GPA of 3.0. Additional exam requirements/recommendations for international students: Required—TOEFL (minimum score 560 paper-based).

State University of New York College at Cortland, Graduate Studies, School of Education, Cortland, NY 13045. Offers MS Ed, MST, CAS. *Accreditation:* NCATE. *Program availability:* Part-time, evening/weekend. *Entrance requirements:* Additional exam requirements/recommendations for international students: Required—TOEFL.

State University of New York College at Geneseo, Graduate Studies, School of Education, Geneseo, NY 14454-1401. Offers MS Ed. *Accreditation:* NCATE. *Program availability:* Part-time. *Faculty:* 11 full-time (9 women), 1 (woman) part-time/adjunct. *Students:* 27 full-time (24 women), 32 part-time (25 women); includes 3 minority (1 Asian, non-Hispanic/Latino; 2 Hispanic/Latino). Average age 25. 50 applicants, 78% accepted, 37 enrolled. In 2017, 56 master's awarded. *Degree requirements:* For master's, comprehensive exam (for some programs), thesis (for some programs). *Entrance requirements:* For master's, GRE, MAT, EAS, edTPA, PRAXIS, or another substantially equivalent test, proof of New York State initial certification or equivalent certification from another state. Additional exam requirements/recommendations for international students: Required—TOEFL (minimum score 525 paper-based; 71 iBT), IELTS (minimum score 6.5), PTE, iTEP. *Application deadline:* For fall admission, 4/1 priority date for domestic students; for spring admission, 11/1 priority date for domestic students; for summer admission, 4/1 priority date for domestic students. Applications are processed on a rolling basis. Application fee: $50. Electronic applications accepted. *Expenses:* Contact institution. *Financial support:* In 2017–18, 13 students received support, including 9 research assistantships with full tuition reimbursements available (averaging $8,823 per year); fellowships, career-related internships or fieldwork, scholarships/grants, tuition waivers (full and partial), and unspecified assistantships also available. Support available to part-time students. Financial award application deadline: 4/1; financial award applicants required to submit FAFSA. *Unit head:* Dr. Anjoo Sikka, Dean of School of Education, 585-245-5151, Fax: 585-245-5220, E-mail: sikka@geneseo.edu. *Application contact:* Michael R. George, Director of Graduate Admissions, 585-245-5148, Fax: 585-245-5550, E-mail: georgem@geneseo.edu.
Website: http://www.geneseo.edu/education/grad_programs

State University of New York College at Old Westbury, School of Education, Old Westbury, NY 11568-0210. Offers biology (MAT, MS); chemistry (MAT, MS); English language arts (MAT, MS); math (MAT, MS); social studies (MAT, MS); Spanish (MAT, MS). *Program availability:* Part-time, evening/weekend. *Students:* 164 full-time (80 women), 112 part-time (52 women); includes 87 minority (14 Black or African American, non-Hispanic/Latino; 38 Asian, non-Hispanic/Latino; 35 Hispanic/Latino), 2 international. Average age 30. 34 applicants, 82% accepted, 25 enrolled. In 2017, 25 master's awarded. *Entrance requirements:* For master's, Liberal Arts and Sciences Test, undergraduate degree with at least 30 semester hours of appropriate coursework as defined by the respective discipline; minimum cumulative undergraduate GPA of 3.0; two letters of recommendation (one from an academic source); essay. Additional exam requirements/recommendations for international students: Required—TOEFL (minimum score 550 paper-based); Recommended—IELTS. Application fee: $50. *Financial support:* Applicants required to submit FAFSA. *Unit head:* Dr. Nancy Brown, Dean, School of Education, 516-876-3275, E-mail: brownn@oldwestbury.edu. *Application contact:* Philip D'Angelo, Graduate Admissions Office, 516-876-3073, E-mail: enroll@oldwestbury.edu.

State University of New York College at Oneonta, Graduate Programs, Division of Education, Oneonta, NY 13820-4015. Offers educational psychology, counseling and special education (MS Ed, CAS), including school counselor K-12, special education (MS Ed); elementary education and reading (MS Ed), including childhood education, literacy education. *Accreditation:* NCATE. *Program availability:* Part-time, evening/weekend. *Entrance requirements:* For master's, GRE General Test.

State University of New York Empire State College, School for Graduate Studies, Programs in Education, Saratoga Springs, NY 12866-4391. Offers adult learning (MA); learning and emerging technologies (MA); teaching (MAT); teaching and learning (M Ed). *Program availability:* Online learning.

Stephen F. Austin State University, Graduate School, College of Education, Nacogdoches, TX 75962. Offers M Ed, MA, MS, Ed D. *Accreditation:* NCATE. *Program availability:* Part-time, evening/weekend. *Degree requirements:* For master's, comprehensive exam; for doctorate, thesis/dissertation. *Entrance requirements:* For master's, GRE General Test; for doctorate, GRE General Test, interview, writing sample. Additional exam requirements/recommendations for international students: Required—TOEFL.

Stetson University, College of Arts and Sciences, Division of Education, DeLand, FL 32723. Offers counselor education (MS), including marriage, couple and family counseling, mental health counseling, school counseling; teacher education (M Ed), including educational leadership. *Accreditation:* NCATE (one or more programs are accredited). *Program availability:* Part-time, evening/weekend. *Faculty:* 13 full-time (8 women), 6 part-time/adjunct (3 women). *Students:* 168 full-time (132 women), 14 part-time (12 women); includes 73 minority (19 Black or African American, non-Hispanic/Latino; 7 American Indian or Alaska Native, non-Hispanic/Latino; 1 Asian, non-Hispanic/Latino; 25 Hispanic/Latino; 1 Native Hawaiian or other Pacific Islander, non-Hispanic/Latino; 20 Two or more races, non-Hispanic/Latino), 5 international. Average age 32. 102 applicants, 85% accepted, 66 enrolled. In 2017, 81 master's awarded. *Entrance requirements:* For master's, GRE or MAT. *Application deadline:* For fall admission, 8/1 priority date for domestic students; for spring admission, 1/1 priority date for domestic students; for summer admission, 5/1 priority date for domestic students. Applications are processed on a rolling basis. Application fee: $50. Electronic applications accepted. *Expenses:* $911 per credit hour. *Financial support:* In 2017–18, 74 students received support. Career-related internships or fieldwork, Federal Work-Study, institutionally sponsored loans, scholarships/grants, unspecified assistantships, and tuition waivers (for staff and dependents) available. Support available to part-time students. Financial award applicants required to submit FAFSA. *Faculty research:* School leadership succession planning; teacher preparation, educational pedagogies; mission-driven leadership; restorative practices in schools. *Unit head:* Dr. Thomas Farrell, Interim Dean, 386-822-7515. *Application contact:* Jamie Vanderlip, Director of Admissions for Graduate, Transfer and Adult Programs, 386-822-7100, Fax: 386-822-7112, E-mail: jlvander@stetson.edu.

Stevenson University, Master of Arts in Teaching Program, Stevenson, MD 21153. Offers secondary biology (MAT); secondary chemistry (MAT); secondary mathematics (MAT). *Program availability:* Part-time, blended/hybrid learning. *Faculty:* 5 part-time/adjunct (all women). *Students:* 18 part-time (11 women); includes 6 minority (2 Black or African American, non-Hispanic/Latino; 2 Asian, non-Hispanic/Latino; 1 Hispanic/Latino; 1 Two or more races, non-Hispanic/Latino). Average age 31. 8 applicants, 100% accepted, 8 enrolled. *Degree requirements:* For master's, internship, portfolio, action research project. *Entrance requirements:* For master's, PRAXIS, GRE, SAT, or ACT, official transcripts from each college or university attended verifying completion of baccalaureate degree in a science or math discipline from regionally-accredited institution. *Application deadline:* Applications are processed on a rolling basis. Electronic applications accepted. *Expenses:* Contact institution. *Financial support:* Unspecified assistantships available. Financial award applicants required to submit FAFSA. *Unit head:* Anne P. Davis, Associate Dean of Teacher Education. *Application contact:* Amanda Courter, Senior Enrollment Counselor, 443-352-4243, Fax: 443-352-4440, E-mail: acourter@stevenson.edu.
Website: http://www.stevenson.edu/online/academics/online-graduate-programs/master-arts-teaching/

Education—General

Stockton University, Office of Graduate Studies, Program in Education, Galloway, NJ 08205-9441. Offers MA. *Accreditation:* TEAC. *Program availability:* Part-time, evening/weekend. *Faculty:* 8 full-time (7 women), 6 part-time/adjunct (3 women). *Students:* 9 full-time (7 women), 203 part-time (168 women); includes 25 minority (6 Black or African American, non-Hispanic/Latino; 1 Asian, non-Hispanic/Latino; 17 Hispanic/Latino; 1 Two or more races, non-Hispanic/Latino), 3 international. Average age 36. 145 applicants, 75% accepted, 91 enrolled. In 2017, 23 master's awarded. *Entrance requirements:* For master's, GRE, MAT, minimum GPA of 2.75, teaching certificate. *Application deadline:* For fall admission, 7/1 for domestic students; for spring admission, 12/1 for domestic students. Applications are processed on a rolling basis. Application fee: $50. Electronic applications accepted. *Expenses:* Contact institution. *Financial support:* Fellowships, research assistantships, career-related internships or fieldwork, Federal Work-Study, scholarships/grants, and unspecified assistantships available. Support available to part-time students. Financial award application deadline: 3/1; financial award applicants required to submit FAFSA. *Faculty research:* Curriculum instruction, math, science, special education, language arts, literacy. *Unit head:* Dr. Kim LeBak, Program Director, 609-626-3640, E-mail: gradschool@stockton.edu. *Application contact:* Tara Williams, Assistant Director of Graduate Enrollment Management, 609-626-3640, Fax: 609-626-6050, E-mail: gradschool@stockton.edu.

Strayer University, Graduate Studies, Washington, DC 20005-2603. Offers accounting (MS); acquisition (MBA); business administration (MBA); communications technology (MS); educational management (M Ed); finance (MBA); health services administration (MHSA); hospitality and tourism management (MBA); human resource management (MBA); information systems (MS), including computer security management, decision support system management, enterprise resource management, network management, software engineering management, systems development management; management (MBA); management information systems (MS); marketing (MBA); professional accounting (MS), including accounting information systems, controllership, taxation; public administration (MPA); supply chain management (MBA); technology in education (M Ed). Programs also offered at campus locations in Birmingham, AL; Chamblee, GA; Cobb County, GA; Morrow, GA; White Marsh, MD; Charleston, SC; Columbia, SC; Greensboro, NC; Greenville, SC; Lexington, KY; Louisville, KY; Nashville, TN; North Raleigh, NC; Washington, DC. *Accreditation:* ACBSP. *Program availability:* Part-time, evening/weekend, online learning. *Degree requirements:* For master's, thesis. *Entrance requirements:* For master's, GMAT, GRE General Test, bachelor's degree from an accredited college or university, minimum undergraduate GPA of 2.75. Electronic applications accepted.

Sul Ross State University, College of Professional Studies, Department of Education, Alpine, TX 79832. Offers counseling (M Ed); educational diagnostics (M Ed); reading specialist (M Ed, Certificate), including master reading teacher (Certificate), Texas reading specialist (M Ed); school administration (M Ed). *Program availability:* Part-time, evening/weekend. *Degree requirements:* For master's, thesis optional. *Entrance requirements:* For master's, GMAT or GRE General Test, minimum GPA of 2.5 in last 60 hours of undergraduate work. *Faculty research:* Critical thinking skills, adolescent eating disorders, reading-based study skills, cross-cultural adaptations, educational leadership.

Sul Ross State University, Rio Grande College of Sul Ross State University, Alpine, TX 79832. Offers business administration (MBA); teacher education (M Ed), including bilingual education, counseling, educational diagnostics, elementary education, general education, reading, school administration, secondary education. *Program availability:* Part-time, evening/weekend, online learning. *Degree requirements:* For master's, comprehensive exam, thesis optional, minimum GPA of 3.0. *Entrance requirements:* For master's, GMAT or GRE General Test, minimum GPA of 2.5 in last 60 hours of undergraduate work. Additional exam requirements/recommendations for international students: Required—TOEFL.

Sweet Briar College, Department of Education, Sweet Briar, VA 24595. Offers M Ed, MAT. *Program availability:* Part-time. *Degree requirements:* For master's, comprehensive exam (for some programs), thesis. *Entrance requirements:* For master's, PRAXIS I and II; Virginia Communication and Literacy Assessment, Virginia Reading Assessment (MAT); GRE (M Ed), current teaching license (M Ed). Additional exam requirements/recommendations for international students: Required—TOEFL (minimum score 550 paper-based; 79 iBT), IELTS (minimum score 6.5). Electronic applications accepted. *Faculty research:* Differentiation of K-12 student achievement, mentoring and teacher retention, teaching science by inquiry.

Syracuse University, School of Education, Syracuse, NY 13244. Offers M Mus, MM, MS, Ed D, PhD, CAS, Ed D/PhD. *Accreditation:* NCATE. *Program availability:* Part-time. *Faculty:* 50 full-time (29 women), 44 part-time/adjunct (29 women). *Students:* 298 full-time (205 women), 215 part-time (153 women); includes 122 minority (53 Black or African American, non-Hispanic/Latino; 5 American Indian or Alaska Native, non-Hispanic/Latino; 12 Asian, non-Hispanic/Latino; 36 Hispanic/Latino; 1 Native Hawaiian or other Pacific Islander, non-Hispanic/Latino; 15 Two or more races, non-Hispanic/Latino), 83 international. Average age 33. 470 applicants, 57% accepted, 144 enrolled. In 2017, 156 master's, 22 doctorates, 43 other advanced degrees awarded. *Degree requirements:* For master's, thesis or alternative; for doctorate, comprehensive exam, thesis/dissertation; for CAS, thesis. *Entrance requirements:* For master's, GRE (for some programs), baccalaureate degree from regionally-accredited college/university; for doctorate, GRE, master's degree. Additional exam requirements/recommendations for international students: Required—TOEFL (minimum score 100 iBT). *Application deadline:* Applications are processed on a rolling basis. Application fee: $75. Electronic applications accepted. *Financial support:* Fellowships with full tuition reimbursements, research assistantships, teaching assistantships, career-related internships or fieldwork, institutionally sponsored loans, scholarships/grants, health care benefits, tuition waivers (partial), and unspecified assistantships available. Financial award application deadline: 1/15; financial award applicants required to submit FAFSA. *Faculty research:* Literacy education, inclusive education, communication sciences and disorders, facilitated communication, school sustainability. *Unit head:* Dr. Joanna Masingila, Dean, 315-443-4751, E-mail: jomasing@syr.edu. *Application contact:* Speranza Migliore, Graduate Recruiter, School of Education, 315-443-2505, E-mail: gradrcrt@syr.edu.
Website: http://soeweb.syr.edu/

Taft University System, The Boyer Graduate School of Education, Denver, CO 80246. Offers M Ed.

Tarleton State University, College of Graduate Studies, College of Education, Stephenville, TX 76402. Offers M Ed, MS, Ed D, Certificate. *Program availability:* Part-time, evening/weekend, 100% online, blended/hybrid learning. *Faculty:* 29 full-time (14 women), 11 part-time/adjunct (6 women). *Students:* 71 full-time (45 women), 455 part-time (326 women); includes 122 minority (56 Black or African American, non-Hispanic/Latino; 2 American Indian or Alaska Native, non-Hispanic/Latino; 2 Asian, non-Hispanic/Latino; 53 Hispanic/Latino; 9 Two or more races, non-Hispanic/Latino), 4 international. Average age 39. 123 applicants, 92% accepted, 97 enrolled. In 2017, 162 master's, 14 doctorates awarded. *Degree requirements:* For master's, comprehensive exam, thesis (for some programs); for doctorate, thesis/dissertation. *Entrance requirements:* For master's, GRE General Test, minimum GPA of 3.0; for doctorate, GRE, 4 letters of reference, leadership portfolio. Additional exam requirements/recommendations for international students: Required—TOEFL (minimum score 550 paper-based; 80 iBT). *Application deadline:* For fall admission, 8/15 priority date for domestic students; for

spring admission, 1/7 for domestic students. Applications are processed on a rolling basis. Application fee: $45 ($130 for international students). Electronic applications accepted. *Expenses:* Tuition, state resident: full-time $3775. Tuition, nonresident: full-time $11,245. *Required fees:* $2920. *Financial support:* Research assistantships, teaching assistantships with partial tuition reimbursements, career-related internships or fieldwork, Federal Work-Study, institutionally sponsored loans, and tuition waivers (partial) available. Support available to part-time students. Financial award application deadline: 5/1; financial award applicants required to submit FAFSA. *Unit head:* Dr. Jordan Barkley, Dean, 254-968-9088, Fax: 254-968-9525, E-mail: jbarkley@tarleton.edu. *Application contact:* Wendy Weiss, Information Contact, 254-968-9104, Fax: 254-968-9670, E-mail: weiss@tarleton.edu.
Website: http://www.tarleton.edu/coe/index.html

Teachers College, Columbia University, Department of International and Transcultural Studies, New York, NY 10027-6696. Offers anthropology and education (MA, Ed D, PhD); applied anthropology (PhD); comparative and international education (MA, Ed D, PhD); international educational development (Ed M, MA, Ed D, PhD). *Program availability:* Part-time. *Students:* 150 full-time (120 women), 143 part-time (116 women); includes 95 minority (22 Black or African American, non-Hispanic/Latino; 33 Asian, non-Hispanic/Latino; 29 Hispanic/Latino; 11 Two or more races, non-Hispanic/Latino), 116 international. Average age 29. 433 applicants, 59% accepted, 120 enrolled. *Degree requirements:* For doctorate, thesis/dissertation. *Unit head:* Prof. Herve Varenne, Chair, 212-678-3190, E-mail: varenne@tc.columbia.edu. *Application contact:* David Estrella, Director of Admission, 212-678-3305, E-mail: estrella@tc.columbia.edu.

Teachers College, Columbia University, Department of Mathematics, Science and Technology, New York, NY 10027-6696. Offers biology 7-12 (MA); chemistry 7-12 (MA); communication and education (MA, Ed D); computing in education (MA, Ed D); earth science 7-12 (MA); instructional technology and media (Ed M, MA, Ed D); mathematics education (Ed M, MA, Ed D, Ed DCT, PhD); physics 7-12 (MA); science and dental education (MA); science education (Ed M, MS, Ed DCT, PhD); supervisor/teacher of science education (MA); technology specialist (MA). *Program availability:* Part-time, evening/weekend, online learning. *Students:* 187 full-time (129 women), 228 part-time (153 women); includes 143 minority (42 Black or African American, non-Hispanic/Latino; 64 Asian, non-Hispanic/Latino; 25 Hispanic/Latino; 12 Two or more races, non-Hispanic/Latino), 125 international. Average age 32. 484 applicants, 59% accepted, 141 enrolled. Terminal master's awarded for partial completion of doctoral program. *Degree requirements:* For doctorate, thesis/dissertation. *Unit head:* Prof. Erica Walker, Chair, E-mail: ewalker@tc.columbia.edu. *Application contact:* David Estrella, Director of Admission, 212-678-3305, E-mail: estrella@tc.columbia.edu.
Website: http://www.tc.columbia.edu/mathematics-science-and-technology/

Teachers College of San Joaquin, Master's Program in Education, Stockton, CA 95206. Offers early education (M Ed); educational inquiry (M Ed); educational leadership and school development (M Ed); science, technology, engineering, and mathematics (M Ed); special education (M Ed).

Temple University, College of Education, Philadelphia, PA 19122-6096. Offers Ed M, MS Ed, Ed D, PhD, Ed S. *Accreditation:* TEAC. *Program availability:* Part-time, evening/weekend. *Faculty:* 62 full-time (34 women), 97 part-time/adjunct (62 women). *Students:* 493 full-time (350 women), 554 part-time (361 women); includes 298 minority (184 Black or African American, non-Hispanic/Latino; 2 American Indian or Alaska Native, non-Hispanic/Latino; 41 Asian, non-Hispanic/Latino; 46 Hispanic/Latino; 1 Native Hawaiian or other Pacific Islander, non-Hispanic/Latino; 24 Two or more races, non-Hispanic/Latino), 43 international. 776 applicants, 53% accepted, 262 enrolled. In 2017, 262 master's, 50 doctorates, 63 other advanced degrees awarded. *Entrance requirements:* Additional exam requirements/recommendations for international students: Required—TOEFL. *Application deadline:* For fall admission, 4/1 for domestic students, 1/1 for international students; for spring admission, 10/1 for domestic students, 7/3 for international students. Applications are processed on a rolling basis. Application fee: $60. Electronic applications accepted. *Expenses:* Contact institution. *Financial support:* Research assistantships, teaching assistantships, career-related internships or fieldwork, Federal Work-Study, scholarships/grants, health care benefits, and unspecified assistantships available. Financial award application deadline: 1/15; financial award applicants required to submit FAFSA. *Faculty research:* Curriculum development, instruction, technology, learning, educational achievement. *Unit head:* Dr. Gregory Anderson, Dean, 215-204-8017, Fax: 215-204-5622, E-mail: coedean@temple.edu. *Application contact:* Elizabeth Jung, Enrollment Management, 215-204-5634, E-mail: educate@temple.edu.
Website: http://education.temple.edu/

Tennessee State University, The School of Graduate Studies and Research, College of Education, Nashville, TN 37209-1561. Offers M Ed, MA Ed, MS, Ed D, PhD, Ed S. *Accreditation:* NCATE. *Program availability:* Part-time, evening/weekend. *Degree requirements:* For doctorate, thesis/dissertation. *Entrance requirements:* For doctorate, minimum GPA of 3.25. *Faculty research:* Class size, biobehavioral research, equity, dropout rate, K-12 teachers: first 5 years of employment.

Tennessee Technological University, College of Graduate Studies, College of Education, Cookeville, TN 38505. Offers MA, PhD, and Ed S. *Accreditation:* NCATE. *Program availability:* Part-time, evening/weekend. *Faculty:* 58 full-time (16 women). *Students:* 115 full-time (88 women), 273 part-time (202 women); includes 34 minority (20 Black or African American, non-Hispanic/Latino; 1 Asian, non-Hispanic/Latino; 4 Hispanic/Latino; 9 Two or more races, non-Hispanic/Latino), 8 international. 222 applicants, 70% accepted, 117 enrolled. In 2017, 137 master's, 10 doctorates, 31 other advanced degrees awarded. *Degree requirements:* For master's and Ed S, comprehensive exam, thesis or alternative; for doctorate, comprehensive exam, thesis/dissertation. *Entrance requirements:* For master's, GRE or MAT; for doctorate, GRE; for Ed S, MAT or GRE. Additional exam requirements/recommendations for international students: Required—TOEFL (minimum score 527 paper-based; 71 iBT), IELTS (minimum score 5.5), PTE (minimum score 48), or TOEIC (Test of English as an International Communication). *Application deadline:* For fall admission, 8/1 for domestic students, 5/1 for international students; for spring admission, 12/1 for domestic students, 10/1 for international students; for summer admission, 5/1 for domestic students, 2/1 for international students. Applications are processed on a rolling basis. Application fee: $35 ($40 for international students). Electronic applications accepted. *Expenses:* Tuition, state resident: full-time $9925; part-time $565 per credit hour. Tuition, nonresident: full-time $22,993; part-time $1291 per credit hour. *Financial support:* Fellowships, research assistantships, teaching assistantships, and career-related internships or fieldwork available. Support available to part-time students. Financial award application deadline: 4/1. *Faculty research:* Teacher evaluation. *Unit head:* Dr. Lisa Zagumny, Dean, 931-372-3124, Fax: 931-372-6319, E-mail: lzagumny@tntech.edu. *Application contact:* Shelia K. Kendrick, Coordinator of Graduate Studies, 931-372-3808, Fax: 931-372-3497, E-mail: skendrick@tntech.edu.

Texas A&M International University, Office of Graduate Studies and Research, College of Education, Laredo, TX 78041. Offers MS, MS Ed. *Program availability:* Part-time, evening/weekend. *Degree requirements:* For master's, thesis (for some programs). *Entrance requirements:* For master's, GRE General Test. Additional exam requirements/recommendations for international students: Required—TOEFL (minimum score 550 paper-based; 79 iBT).

Texas A&M University, College of Education and Human Development, College Station, TX 77843. Offers M Ed, MS, Ed D, PhD. *Program availability:* Part-time, evening/weekend, blended/hybrid learning. *Faculty:* 170. *Students:* 671 full-time (470 women), 921 part-time (683 women); includes 532 minority (162 Black or African American, non-Hispanic/Latino; 5 American Indian or Alaska Native, non-Hispanic/Latino; 49 Asian, non-Hispanic/Latino; 282 Hispanic/Latino; 4 Native Hawaiian or other Pacific Islander, non-Hispanic/Latino; 30 Two or more races, non-Hispanic/Latino), 163 international. Average age 33. 580 applicants, 68% accepted, 282 enrolled. In 2017, 526 master's, 76 doctorates awarded. *Degree requirements:* For doctorate, thesis/dissertation. *Entrance requirements:* For master's and doctorate, GRE General Test. Additional exam requirements/recommendations for international students: Required—TOEFL (minimum score 550 paper-based; 80 iBT), IELTS (minimum score 6), PTE (minimum score 53). *Application deadline:* Applications are processed on a rolling basis. Application fee: $50 ($90 for international students). Electronic applications accepted. *Expenses:* Contact institution. *Financial support:* In 2017–18, 802 students received support, including 13 fellowships with tuition reimbursements available (averaging $22,861 per year), 221 research assistantships with tuition reimbursements available (averaging $10,462 per year), 132 teaching assistantships with tuition reimbursements available (averaging $9,872 per year); career-related internships or fieldwork, institutionally sponsored loans, scholarships/grants, traineeships, health care benefits, tuition waivers (full and partial), and unspecified assistantships also available. Support available to part-time students. Financial award application deadline: 3/15; financial award applicants required to submit FAFSA. *Unit head:* Dr. Joyce Alexander, Professor and Dean, 979-862-6649, E-mail: joycemalexander@tamu.edu. *Application contact:* Dr. Beverly Irby, Professor and Associate Dean for Academic Affairs, 979-845-5311, E-mail: beverly.irby@tamu.edu.
Website: http://education.tamu.edu/

Texas A&M University–Commerce, College of Education and Human Services, Commerce, TX 75429. Offers counseling (M Ed, MS, PhD); early childhood education (M Ed, MS); educational administration (M Ed, MS, Ed D); educational psychology (PhD); educational technology leadership (M Ed, MS); educational technology library science (M Ed, MS); elementary education (M Ed); health, kinesiology and sports studies (MS); higher education (MS, Ed D); psychology (MS); reading (M Ed, MS); secondary education (M Ed, MS); social work (MSW); special education (M Ed, MS); supervision, curriculum and instruction-elementary education (Ed D); training and development (MS). *Program availability:* Part-time, evening/weekend, 100% online, blended/hybrid learning. *Faculty:* 91 full-time (51 women), 38 part-time/adjunct (31 women). *Students:* 400 full-time (310 women), 1,400 part-time (1,117 women); includes 724 minority (412 Black or African American, non-Hispanic/Latino; 8 American Indian or Alaska Native, non-Hispanic/Latino; 24 Asian, non-Hispanic/Latino; 220 Hispanic/Latino; 60 Two or more races, non-Hispanic/Latino), 18 international. Average age 37. 951 applicants, 46% accepted, 331 enrolled. In 2017, 564 master's, 24 doctorates awarded. *Degree requirements:* For master's, comprehensive exam, thesis optional, departmental qualifying exams (for some programs); for doctorate, comprehensive exam, thesis/dissertation, departmental qualifying exams; for SSP, comprehensive exam, thesis optional. *Entrance requirements:* For master's and doctorate, GRE General Test. Additional exam requirements/recommendations for international students: Required—TOEFL (minimum score 550 paper-based; 79 iBT), IELTS (minimum score 6). *Application deadline:* For fall admission, 6/1 priority date for international students; for spring admission, 10/15 priority date for international students; for summer admission, 3/15 priority date for international students. Applications are processed on a rolling basis. Application fee: $50. Electronic applications accepted. *Expenses:* Tuition, state resident: full-time $3630. Tuition, nonresident: full-time $11,100. *Required fees:* $2564. Tuition and fees vary according to course load, degree level and program. *Financial support:* In 2017–18, 84 students received support, including 40 research assistantships with partial tuition reimbursements available (averaging $10,800 per year), 12 teaching assistantships with partial tuition reimbursements available (averaging $13,000 per year); career-related internships or fieldwork, Federal Work-Study, institutionally sponsored loans, scholarships/grants, health care benefits, and unspecified assistantships also available. Financial award application deadline: 6/15; financial award applicants required to submit FAFSA. *Faculty research:* Cognitive and bilingual education, positive behavioral intervention, literacy, math readiness. *Total annual research expenditures:* $1.1 million. *Unit head:* Dr. Timothy Letzring, Dean, 903-886-5181, Fax: 903-886-5905, E-mail: tim.letzring@tamuc.edu. *Application contact:* Vicky Turner, Doctoral Degree and Special Programs Coordinator, 903-886-5167, E-mail: vicky.turner@tamuc.edu.
Website: http://www.tamuc.edu/academics/graduateSchool/programs/education/default.aspx

Texas A&M University–Corpus Christi, College of Graduate Studies, College of Education and Human Development, Corpus Christi, TX 78412. Offers counseling (MS), including counseling; counselor education (PhD); curriculum and instruction (MS, PhD); early childhood education (MS); educational administration (MS); educational leadership (Ed D); elementary education (MS); instructional design and educational technology (MS); kinesiology (MS); reading (MS); secondary education (MS); special education (MS). *Program availability:* Part-time, evening/weekend, blended/hybrid learning. *Faculty:* 50 full-time (29 women), 29 part-time/adjunct (18 women). *Students:* 160 full-time (127 women), 366 part-time (293 women); includes 279 minority (40 Black or African American, non-Hispanic/Latino; 3 Asian, non-Hispanic/Latino; 228 Hispanic/Latino; 8 Two or more races, non-Hispanic/Latino), 18 international. Average age 35. 296 applicants, 65% accepted, 155 enrolled. In 2017, 103 master's, 27 doctorates awarded. *Degree requirements:* For master's, comprehensive exam, capstone; for doctorate, thesis/dissertation. *Entrance requirements:* For master's, GRE General Test, essay (300 words); for doctorate, GRE, essay, resume, 3-4 reference forms. *Application deadline:* For fall admission, 7/15 priority date for domestic students, 5/1 priority date for international students; for spring admission, 11/15 priority date for domestic students, 9/1 priority date for international students. Applications are processed on a rolling basis. Application fee: $50 ($70 for international students). Electronic applications accepted. *Expenses:* Tuition, state resident: full-time $3568; part-time $198.24 per credit hour. Tuition, nonresident: full-time $11,038; part-time $613.24 per credit hour. *Required fees:* $2129; $1422.58 per semester. Tuition and fees vary according to program. *Financial support:* Research assistantships, teaching assistantships, career-related internships or fieldwork, Federal Work-Study, institutionally sponsored loans, scholarships/grants, health care benefits, and unspecified assistantships available. Support available to part-time students. Financial award application deadline: 3/15; financial award applicants required to submit FAFSA. *Unit head:* Dr. David Scott, Dean, 361-825-2660, E-mail: david.scott@tamucc.edu. *Application contact:* Graduate Admissions Coordinator, 361-825-2177, Fax: 361-825-2755, E-mail: gradweb@tamucc.edu.
Website: http://education.tamucc.edu/

Texas A&M University–Kingsville, College of Graduate Studies, College of Education and Human Performance, Kingsville, TX 78363. Offers M Ed, MA, MS, Ed D, Certificate. *Program availability:* 100% online, blended/hybrid learning. *Entrance requirements:* Additional exam requirements/recommendations for international students: Required—TOEFL (minimum score 550 paper-based; 79 iBT); Recommended—IELTS. Electronic applications accepted.

Texas A&M University–San Antonio, Department of Educator and Leadership Preparation, San Antonio, TX 78224. Offers bilingual education (MS); early childhood education (M Ed); educational administration (MA); reading specialization (MS); special education (M Ed), including educational diagnostician. *Program availability:* Part-time, evening/weekend, online learning. *Faculty:* 19 full-time (14 women), 8 part-time/adjunct (2 women). *Students:* 24 full-time (21 women), 188 part-time (143 women); includes 163 minority (7 Black or African American, non-Hispanic/Latino; 1 Asian, non-Hispanic/Latino; 149 Hispanic/Latino; 6 Two or more races, non-Hispanic/Latino), 1 international. Average age 36. 191 applicants, 62% accepted, 67 enrolled. In 2017, 70 master's awarded. *Degree requirements:* For master's, comprehensive exam, thesis or alternative. *Entrance requirements:* For master's, GRE (Quantitative and Verbal) or MAT. Additional exam requirements/recommendations for international students: Required—TOEFL (minimum score 550 paper-based; 79 iBT), IELTS (minimum score 6). *Application deadline:* For fall admission, 3/15 priority date for domestic and international students; for spring admission, 11/1 priority date for domestic and international students; for summer admission, 4/1 priority date for domestic and international students. Applications are processed on a rolling basis. Application fee: $35 ($50 for international students). Electronic applications accepted. *Expenses:* Tuition, state resident: full-time $3475; part-time $1930 per semester. Tuition, nonresident: full-time $10,945; part-time $6080 per semester. *Required fees:* $2148; $1412 per year. $706 per semester. Tuition and fees vary according to course load. *Financial support:* In 2017–18, 16 students received support. Research assistantships, Federal Work-Study, scholarships/grants, and tuition waivers available. Financial award application deadline: 3/15; financial award applicants required to submit FAFSA. *Faculty research:* Equity in education, biliteracy practices among Latina and immigrants, academic achievement of low socio-economic students, equity practices in instruction and educational leadership in diverse settings, racial identity development and multicultural education. *Unit head:* Dr. Debbie Vera, Department Chair. *Application contact:* Caitie Garza, Graduate Admissions Coordinator, 210-784-1300, E-mail: beajaguar@tamusa.edu.
Website: http://www.tamusa.edu/collegeofeducationandhumandevelopment/educatorleadershippreparation/index.html

Texas A&M University–Texarkana, Graduate Studies and Research, College of Education and Liberal Arts, Texarkana, TX 75503. Offers adult education (MS); curriculum and instruction (M Ed); education (MS); educational administration (M Ed); English (MA); instructional technology (MS); interdisciplinary studies (MA, MS); special education (MS). *Program availability:* Part-time, evening/weekend. *Degree requirements:* For master's, comprehensive exam (for some programs), thesis optional. *Entrance requirements:* For master's, minimum GPA of 2.5 on last 60 hours of bachelor's degree. Additional exam requirements/recommendations for international students: Required—TOEFL. Electronic applications accepted.

Texas Christian University, College of Education, Fort Worth, TX 76129. Offers M Ed, MAT, Ed D, PhD, MBA/Ed D. *Program availability:* Part-time, evening/weekend. *Faculty:* 29 full-time (21 women), 3 part-time/adjunct (1 woman). *Students:* 204 full-time (151 women), 40 part-time (25 women); includes 39 minority (29 Black or African American, non-Hispanic/Latino; 2 American Indian or Alaska Native, non-Hispanic/Latino; 9 Asian, non-Hispanic/Latino; 45 Hispanic/Latino; 8 Two or more races, non-Hispanic/Latino), 7 international. Average age 33. 195 applicants, 72% accepted, 109 enrolled. In 2017, 62 master's, 12 doctorates awarded. *Degree requirements:* For master's, comprehensive exam (for some programs), thesis (for some programs); for doctorate, comprehensive exam, thesis/dissertation. *Entrance requirements:* For master's, GRE General Test; Pre-Admission Content Test or PRAXIS (for MAT); for doctorate, GRE General Test. Additional exam requirements/recommendations for international students: Required—TOEFL (minimum score 550 paper-based; 80 iBT), IELTS (minimum score 6.5). *Application deadline:* For fall admission, 2/1 for domestic and international students; for spring admission, 11/16 for domestic and international students; for summer admission, 2/1 for domestic and international students. Application fee: $60. Electronic applications accepted. *Financial support:* In 2017–18, 193 students received support, including 1 fellowship with full tuition reimbursement available (averaging $18,500 per year), 9 research assistantships with full tuition reimbursements available (averaging $18,500 per year), 36 teaching assistantships with full tuition reimbursements available (averaging $15,000 per year); career-related internships or fieldwork, scholarships/grants, health care benefits, and unspecified assistantships also available. Support available to part-time students. Financial award application deadline: 2/1. *Faculty research:* Science education, special education, literacy, educational leadership, higher education leadership, solution focused counseling. *Unit head:* Dr. Jan Lacina, Associate Dean, 817-257-6786, Fax: 817-257-7466, E-mail: j.lacina@tcu.edu. *Application contact:* Lori Kimball, Administrative Program Specialist, 817-257-7661, Fax: 817-257-7466, E-mail: l.kimball@tcu.edu.
Website: http://coe.tcu.edu/graduate-overview/

Texas Southern University, College of Education, Houston, TX 77004-4584. Offers M Ed, MS, Ed D. *Program availability:* Part-time, evening/weekend. *Degree requirements:* For master's, comprehensive exam; for doctorate, comprehensive exam, thesis/dissertation. *Entrance requirements:* For master's, GRE General Test, minimum GPA of 2.5; for doctorate, GRE General Test or MAT, master's degree, minimum B+ average. Additional exam requirements/recommendations for international students: Required—TOEFL. Electronic applications accepted.

Texas State University, The Graduate College, College of Education, San Marcos, TX 78666. Offers M Ed, MA, MS, MSRLS, Ed D, PhD, SSP. *Program availability:* Part-time, evening/weekend. *Faculty:* 136 full-time (86 women), 72 part-time/adjunct (50 women). *Students:* 543 full-time (411 women), 536 part-time (422 women); includes 474 minority (102 Black or African American, non-Hispanic/Latino; 35 Asian, non-Hispanic/Latino; 314 Hispanic/Latino; 23 Two or more races, non-Hispanic/Latino), 22 international. Average age 32. 921 applicants, 56% accepted, 247 enrolled. In 2017, 393 master's, 20 doctorates awarded. *Degree requirements:* For master's, comprehensive exam, thesis (for some programs); for doctorate, comprehensive exam, thesis/dissertation. *Entrance requirements:* For master's, GRE (for some programs), baccalaureate degree from regionally-accredited institution; letters of recommendation, statement of purpose, resume, and/or interview (for some programs); for doctorate, GRE, baccalaureate and master's degrees from regionally-accredited institution; letters of recommendation, statement of purpose, resume, and/or interview (for some programs). Additional exam requirements/recommendations for international students: Required—TOEFL (minimum score 550 paper-based; 78 iBT). *Application deadline:* For fall admission, 1/15 priority date for domestic and international students; for spring admission, 10/1 priority date for domestic and international students. Applications are processed on a rolling basis. Application fee: $40 ($90 for international students). Electronic applications accepted. *Expenses:* Tuition, state resident: full-time $7868; part-time $3934 per semester. Tuition, nonresident: full-time $17,828; part-time $8914 per semester. *Required fees:* $2092; $1435 per semester. Tuition and fees vary according to course load. *Financial support:* In 2017–18, 627 students received support, including 62 research assistantships (averaging $17,396 per year), 70 teaching assistantships (averaging $14,811 per year); fellowships, career-related internships or fieldwork, Federal Work-Study, institutionally sponsored loans, and scholarships/grants also available. Support available to part-time students. Financial award application deadline: 3/1; financial

Education—General

award applicants required to submit FAFSA. *Unit head:* Dr. Stan Carpenter, Dean, 512-245-2150, Fax: 512-245-3158, E-mail: sc33@txstate.edu. *Application contact:* Dr. Andrea Golato, Dean of Graduate School, 512-245-2581, Fax: 512-245-8365, E-mail: gradcollege@txstate.edu.
Website: http://www.education.txstate.edu/

Texas Tech University, Graduate School, College of Education, Lubbock, TX 79409. Offers M Ed, MS, Ed D, PhD. *Accreditation:* NCATE. *Program availability:* Part-time, evening/weekend. *Faculty:* 160 full-time (109 women), 12 part-time/adjunct (11 women). *Students:* 327 full-time (243 women), 884 part-time (695 women); includes 407 minority (110 Black or African American, non-Hispanic/Latino; 4 American Indian or Alaska Native, non-Hispanic/Latino; 15 Asian, non-Hispanic/Latino; 247 Hispanic/Latino; 31 Two or more races, non-Hispanic/Latino), 87 international. Average age 36. 667 applicants, 49% accepted, 256 enrolled. In 2017, 229 master's, 85 doctorates awarded. Terminal master's awarded for partial completion of doctoral program. *Degree requirements:* For master's, comprehensive exam (for some programs), thesis or alternative; for doctorate, thesis/dissertation. *Entrance requirements:* For master's and doctorate, GRE General Test. Additional exam requirements/recommendations for international students: Required—TOEFL (minimum score 550 paper-based; 79 iBT). *Application deadline:* For fall admission, 6/1 priority date for domestic students, 1/15 priority date for international students; for spring admission, 9/1 priority date for domestic students, 6/15 priority date for international students. Applications are processed on a rolling basis. Application fee: $60. Electronic applications accepted. *Expenses:* Contact institution. *Financial support:* In 2017–18, 462 students received support, including 452 fellowships (averaging $3,250 per year), 100 research assistantships (averaging $12,061 per year), 7 teaching assistantships (averaging $10,995 per year); career-related internships or fieldwork, Federal Work-Study, institutionally sponsored loans, scholarships/grants, traineeships, health care benefits, and unspecified assistantships also available. Support available to part-time students. Financial award application deadline: 2/1; financial award applicants required to submit FAFSA. *Faculty research:* Multicultural foundations of education, teacher education, psychological processes of teaching and learning, teaching populations with special needs, institutional technology, teacher preparation and educator quality, STEM education, blended and personalized learning using technology, autism and educational interventions around autism, partnerships for education and school reform. *Total annual research expenditures:* $10.1 million. *Unit head:* Dr. D. Scott Ridley, Dean, 806-834-1431, Fax: 806-742-2179, E-mail: scott.ridley@ttu.edu. *Application contact:* Brianna Sanchez, Coordinator, 806-834-2353, Fax: 806-742-2179, E-mail: brianna.sanchez@ttu.edu.
Website: http://www.educ.ttu.edu.

Texas Wesleyan University, Graduate Programs, Programs in Education, Fort Worth, TX 76105. Offers education (M Ed, Ed D). *Program availability:* Part-time, evening/weekend. *Faculty:* 12 full-time (8 women), 4 part-time/adjunct (3 women). *Students:* 38 full-time (25 women), 234 part-time (200 women); includes 127 minority (73 Black or African American, non-Hispanic/Latino; 3 American Indian or Alaska Native, non-Hispanic/Latino; 3 Asian, non-Hispanic/Latino; 48 Hispanic/Latino), 9 international. Average age 36. 48 applicants, 94% accepted, 39 enrolled. In 2017, 13 master's, 8 doctorates awarded. *Degree requirements:* For master's, comprehensive exam (for some programs); for doctorate, thesis/dissertation. *Entrance requirements:* For master's and doctorate, GRE General Test. Additional exam requirements/recommendations for international students: Required—TOEFL (minimum score 550 paper-based; 79 iBT), IELTS (minimum score 6.5). *Application deadline:* Applications are processed on a rolling basis. Electronic applications accepted. *Expenses:* Contact institution. *Financial support:* Career-related internships or fieldwork, Federal Work-Study, scholarships/grants, and tuition waivers (full and partial) available. Support available to part-time students. Financial award application deadline: 3/15; financial award applicants required to submit FAFSA. *Faculty research:* Teacher effectiveness, bilingual education, analytic teaching. *Unit head:* Dr. Carlos Martinez, Dean, School of Education, 817-531-4940, Fax: 817-531-4943. *Application contact:* Amy Orcutt, Interim Director of Graduate Admissions, 817-531-4288, Fax: 817-531-4261, E-mail: arorcutt@txwes.edu.
Website: https://txwes.edu/academics/school-of-education/

Texas Woman's University, Graduate School, College of Professional Education, Denton, TX 76204. Offers M Ed, MA, MAT, MLS, MS, PhD, Certificate. *Program availability:* Part-time, evening/weekend. *Faculty:* 69 full-time (56 women), 56 part-time/adjunct (42 women). *Students:* 318 full-time (301 women), 896 part-time (842 women); includes 448 minority (146 Black or African American, non-Hispanic/Latino; 2 American Indian or Alaska Native, non-Hispanic/Latino; 26 Asian, non-Hispanic/Latino; 246 Hispanic/Latino; 28 Two or more races, non-Hispanic/Latino), 13 international. Average age 35. 519 applicants, 65% accepted, 259 enrolled. In 2017, 301 master's, 25 doctorates awarded. Terminal master's awarded for partial completion of doctoral program. *Degree requirements:* For master's, comprehensive exam (for some programs), thesis (for some programs); for doctorate, comprehensive exam, thesis/dissertation; for Certificate, comprehensive exam. *Entrance requirements:* For master's, minimum GPA of 3.0 on the last 60 hours; for doctorate, minimum GPA of 3.0. Additional exam requirements/recommendations for international students: Required—TOEFL (minimum score 550 paper-based; 79 iBT); Recommended—IELTS (minimum score 6.5), TSE (minimum score 53). *Application deadline:* For fall admission, 3/1 priority date for domestic and international students; for spring admission, 11/1 priority date for domestic students, 7/1 priority date for international students. Applications are processed on a rolling basis. Application fee: $50 ($75 for international students). Electronic applications accepted. *Expenses:* $7,520 per year full-time in-state; $16,820 per year full-time out-of-state. *Financial support:* In 2017–18, 264 students received support, including 40 research assistantships (averaging $12,164 per year), 8 teaching assistantships (averaging $12,164 per year); career-related internships or fieldwork, Federal Work-Study, institutionally sponsored loans, scholarships/grants, traineeships, health care benefits, and unspecified assistantships also available. Support available to part-time students. Financial award application deadline: 3/1; financial award applicants required to submit FAFSA. *Total annual research expenditures:* $621,594. *Unit head:* Dr. Lisa Huffman, Dean, 940-898-2202, Fax: 940-898-2209, E-mail: cope@twu.edu. *Application contact:* Korie Hawkins, Associate Director of Admissions, Graduate Recruitment, 940-898-3188, Fax: 940-898-3081, E-mail: admissions@twu.edu.
Website: http://www.twu.edu/college-professional-education/

Thomas More College, Program in Teaching, Crestview Hills, KY 41017-3495. Offers MAT. *Program availability:* Part-time. *Degree requirements:* For master's, comprehensive exam. *Entrance requirements:* For master's, GRE (minimum scores: verbal 450, quantitative 490, and analytical 4.0) or PPST (minimum scores: math 174, reading 176, and writing 174), minimum undergraduate content GPA of 2.75, interview. Additional exam requirements/recommendations for international students: Required—TOEFL (minimum score 600 paper-based; 100 iBT). Electronic applications accepted. *Expenses:* Contact institution.

Thomas University, Department of Education, Thomasville, GA 31792-7499. Offers M Ed. *Program availability:* Part-time. *Entrance requirements:* For master's, resume, 2 academic/professional references. Additional exam requirements/recommendations for international students: Required—TOEFL (minimum score 600 paper-based). Electronic applications accepted.

Thompson Rivers University, Program in Education, Kamloops, BC V2C 0C8, Canada. Offers M Ed. *Program availability:* Part-time. *Entrance requirements:* For master's, 2 letters of reference, minimum GPA of 3.0 in final 2 years of undergraduate degree.

Tiffin University, Program in Education, Tiffin, OH 44883-2161. Offers educational technology management (M Ed); higher education administration (M Ed). *Program availability:* Part-time, evening/weekend, online only, 100% online, blended/hybrid learning. *Entrance requirements:* Additional exam requirements/recommendations for international students: Required—TOEFL. Electronic applications accepted. *Expenses:* Contact institution.

Touro College, Graduate School of Education, New York, NY 10010. Offers education and special education (MS); instructional technology (MS); mathematics education (MS); school leadership (MS); teaching English to speakers of other languages (MS); teaching literacy (MS). *Accreditation:* TEAC. *Program availability:* Part-time, evening/weekend, online learning. *Faculty:* 52 full-time (34 women), 199 part-time/adjunct (136 women). *Students:* 756 full-time (686 women), 3,833 part-time (3,492 women). Average age 33. 1,422 applicants, 50% accepted, 675 enrolled. In 2017, 6 master's awarded. *Entrance requirements:* Additional exam requirements/recommendations for international students: Required—TOEFL (minimum score 83 iBT), IELTS (minimum score 6.5). *Application deadline:* For fall admission, 8/26 for domestic students, 7/15 for international students; for spring admission, 12/31 for domestic students, 12/15 for international students. Applications are processed on a rolling basis. Application fee: $50. *Financial support:* Federal Work-Study available. Financial award applicants required to submit FAFSA. *Faculty research:* Equity assistance, language development, scholarly communications, Latin American studies and cultural sensitivity, behavior management techniques and strategies in special education. *Unit head:* Dr. Jacob Easley, III, Dean, 212-463-0400 Ext. 5561, Fax: 212-462-4889, E-mail: jeasley@touro.edu. *Application contact:* Sharmilee Hoopnarine, Admissions, 212-463-0400.

Touro University California, Graduate Programs, Vallejo, CA 94592. Offers education (MA); medical health sciences (MS); osteopathic medicine (DO); pharmacy (Pharm D); public health (MPH). *Accreditation:* AOsA; ARC-PA. *Program availability:* Part-time, evening/weekend. *Degree requirements:* For master's, comprehensive exam, thesis; for doctorate, comprehensive exam. *Entrance requirements:* For doctorate, BS/BA. Electronic applications accepted. *Faculty research:* Cancer, heart disease.

Towson University, College of Education, Program in Teaching, Towson, MD 21252-0001. Offers early childhood education (MAT); elementary education (MAT); secondary education (MAT); special education (MAT). *Students:* 64 full-time (44 women), 48 part-time (34 women); includes 16 minority (5 Black or African American, non-Hispanic/Latino; 5 Asian, non-Hispanic/Latino; 5 Hispanic/Latino; 1 Two or more races, non-Hispanic/Latino). *Entrance requirements:* For master's, ACT, GRE, PRAXIS I or SAT, 2 letters of reference, resume, minimum GPA of 3.0, essay. *Application deadline:* For fall admission, 1/17 for domestic students, 5/15 for international students; for spring admission, 10/15 for domestic students, 12/1 for international students. Applications are processed on a rolling basis. Application fee: $45. Electronic applications accepted. *Expenses:* Tuition, state resident: full-time $7960; part-time $398 per unit. Tuition, nonresident: full-time $16,480; part-time $824 per unit. *Required fees:* $2600; $130 per year. $390 per term. *Financial support:* Application deadline: 4/1. *Unit head:* Dr. Pamela Wruble, Graduate Program Director, 410-704-4935, E-mail: pwruble@towson.edu. *Application contact:* Coverley Beidleman, Assistant Director of Graduate Admissions, 410-704-5630, Fax: 410-704-3030, E-mail: grads@towson.edu.
Website: https://www.towson.edu/coe/departments/teaching/

Trevecca Nazarene University, Graduate Education Program, Nashville, TN 37210-2877. Offers accountability and instructional leadership (Ed S); curriculum and instruction for Christian school educators (M Ed); curriculum and instruction K-12 (M Ed); educational leadership (M Ed); English second language (M Ed); library and information science (MLI Sc); special education: visual impairments (M Ed); teaching (MAT), including teaching 6-12, teaching K-5. *Accreditation:* NCATE. *Program availability:* Part-time, evening/weekend, online learning. *Faculty:* 8 full-time (6 women), 22 part-time/adjunct (18 women). *Students:* 150 full-time (114 women), 3 part-time (1 woman); includes 54 minority (49 Black or African American, non-Hispanic/Latino; 4 Hispanic/Latino; 1 Two or more races, non-Hispanic/Latino). Average age 36. In 2017, 57 master's, 4 other advanced degrees awarded. *Degree requirements:* For master's, comprehensive exam, exit assessment/e-portfolio. *Entrance requirements:* For master's, GRE or MAT; PRAXIS (for MAT), minimum GPA of 3.0, official transcript from regionally-accredited institution, references, interview, writing sample, at least 3 years' successful teaching experience (for M Ed in educational leadership); for Ed S, GRE or MAT, master's degree with minimum GPA of 3.0, official transcript from regionally accredited institution, at least 3 years' successful teaching experience, interview, writing sample, background and fingerprinting check, recommendations. Additional exam requirements/recommendations for international students: Required—TOEFL (minimum score 550 paper-based). *Application deadline:* Applications are processed on a rolling basis. Electronic applications accepted. *Expenses:* Contact institution. *Financial support:* Applicants required to submit FAFSA. *Unit head:* Dr. Suzie Harris, Dean, School of Education, 615-248-1201, Fax: 615-248-1597, E-mail: admissions_ged@trevecca.edu. *Application contact:* 844-TNU-GRAD, E-mail: sgcsadmissions@trevecca.edu.
Website: http://www.trevecca.edu/soe

Trident University International, College of Education, Cypress, CA 90630. Offers MA Ed, PhD. *Program availability:* Part-time, evening/weekend, online learning. *Degree requirements:* For doctorate, comprehensive exam, thesis/dissertation, defense of dissertation. *Entrance requirements:* For master's, minimum GPA of 2.5 (students with GPA 3.0 or greater may transfer up to 30% of graduate level credits); for doctorate, minimum GPA of 3.4, curriculum vitae, course work in research methods or statistics. Additional exam requirements/recommendations for international students: Required—TOEFL (minimum score 525 paper-based). Electronic applications accepted.

Trinity International University, Trinity Graduate School, Deerfield, IL 60015-1284. Offers athletic training (MA); bioethics (MA); counseling psychology (MA); diverse learning (M Ed); leadership (MA); teaching (MA). *Program availability:* Part-time, evening/weekend, online learning. *Degree requirements:* For master's, comprehensive exam. *Entrance requirements:* For master's, GRE General Test or MAT, minimum undergraduate GPA of 3.0. Additional exam requirements/recommendations for international students: Required—TOEFL (minimum score 580 paper-based), TWE (minimum score 4). Electronic applications accepted.

Trinity University, Department of Education, San Antonio, TX 78212-7200. Offers school leadership (M Ed); school psychology (MA); teaching (MAT). *Accreditation:* NCATE. *Program availability:* Part-time, evening/weekend. *Faculty:* 9 full-time (all women), 14 part-time/adjunct (10 women). *Students:* 59 full-time (42 women), 11 part-time (8 women); includes 38 minority (7 Black or African American, non-Hispanic/Latino; 1 Asian, non-Hispanic/Latino; 27 Hispanic/Latino; 3 Two or more races, non-Hispanic/Latino), 3 international. Average age 29. *Financial support:* Application deadline: 5/1; applicants required to submit FAFSA. *Unit head:* Norvella Carter, Interim Chair, 210-999-7506, Fax: 210-999-7592, E-mail: ncarter1@trinity.edu. *Application contact:* Office of the Registrar, 210-999-7201, Fax: 210-999-7202, E-mail: roffice@trinity.edu.

Trinity Washington University, School of Education, Washington, DC 20017-1094. Offers clinical mental health counseling (MA); early childhood education (MAT); educating for change (M Ed); educational administration (MSA); elementary education (MAT); reading (M Ed); school counseling (MA); secondary education (MAT), including English, social studies; special education (MAT). *Accreditation:* NCATE. *Program availability:* Part-time, evening/weekend. *Degree requirements:* For master's, thesis (for some programs), capstone project(s). *Entrance requirements:* For master's, PRAXIS I, minimum GPA of 2.8. Additional exam requirements/recommendations for international students: Required—TOEFL (minimum score 550 paper-based). *Faculty research:* Technology, literacy, special education, organizations, inclusion models.

Troy University, Graduate School, College of Education, Troy, AL 36082. Offers MS, MS Ed, Ed S. *Accreditation:* NCATE. *Program availability:* Part-time, evening/weekend. *Faculty:* 75 full-time (45 women), 26 part-time/adjunct (19 women). *Students:* 424 full-time (349 women), 188 part-time (93 women); includes 305 minority (261 Black or African American, non-Hispanic/Latino; 5 American Indian or Alaska Native, non-Hispanic/Latino; 2 Asian, non-Hispanic/Latino; 23 Hispanic/Latino; 1 Native Hawaiian or other Pacific Islander, non-Hispanic/Latino; 13 Two or more races, non-Hispanic/Latino). Average age 35. 319 applicants, 93% accepted, 229 enrolled. In 2017, 109 master's, 22 other advanced degrees awarded. *Degree requirements:* For master's, comprehensive exam, thesis. *Entrance requirements:* For master's, GRE (minimum score of 850 on old exam or 290 on new exam), GMAT (minimum score of 380), or MAT (minimum score of 385), bachelor's degree; minimum undergraduate GPA of 2.5 or 3.0 on last 30 semester hours, letter of recommendation; for Ed S, GRE (minimum score of 850 on old exam or 290 on new exam), GMAT (minimum score of 380), or MAT (minimum score of 385), Alabama Class A certificate or equivalent, minimum graduate GPA of 3.0. Additional exam requirements/recommendations for international students: Required—TOEFL (minimum score 523 paper-based; 70 iBT), IELTS (minimum score 6). *Application deadline:* For fall admission, 1/1 for domestic students, 6/1 for international students; for spring admission, 10/15 for international students. Applications are processed on a rolling basis. Application fee: $50. Electronic applications accepted. *Expenses:* Tuition, state resident: part-time $417 per credit hour. Tuition, nonresident: part-time $834 per credit hour. *Required fees:* $42 per credit hour. $50 per semester. Tuition and fees vary according to campus/location. *Financial support:* Fellowships, career-related internships or fieldwork, and scholarships/grants available. Support available to part-time students. Financial award applicants required to submit FAFSA. *Unit head:* Dr. Royce Dasinger, Dean, 334-670-3365, Fax: 334-670-3474, E-mail: rdasinger@troy.edu. *Application contact:* Jessica A. Kimbro, Director of Graduate Admissions, 334-670-3178, E-mail: jacord@troy.edu.

Truman State University, Graduate School, School of Health Sciences and Education, Program in Education, Kirksville, MO 63501-4221. Offers MAE. *Accreditation:* NCATE. *Degree requirements:* For master's, comprehensive exam, thesis or alternative. *Entrance requirements:* For master's, GRE, minimum GPA of 2.75. Additional exam requirements/recommendations for international students: Required—TOEFL (minimum score 550 paper-based). Electronic applications accepted.

Tufts University, Graduate School of Arts and Sciences, Department of Education, Medford, MA 02155. Offers art education (MAT); education (MA, MAT, MS, PhD), including educational studies (MA), elementary education (MAT), middle and secondary education (MAT), museum education (MA), secondary education (MA), STEM education (MS, PhD); school psychology (MA, Ed S). *Program availability:* Part-time. *Students:* 95 full-time (78 women), 9 part-time (8 women); includes 17 minority (4 Black or African American, non-Hispanic/Latino; 6 Asian, non-Hispanic/Latino; 5 Hispanic/Latino; 2 Two or more races, non-Hispanic/Latino), 4 international. Average age 27. 197 applicants, 57% accepted, 65 enrolled. In 2017, 64 master's, 14 other advanced degrees awarded. *Degree requirements:* For master's, thesis optional; for doctorate, thesis/dissertation. *Entrance requirements:* For master's and doctorate, GRE General Test. Additional exam requirements/recommendations for international students: Required—TOEFL (minimum score 550 paper-based; 80 iBT), IELTS (minimum score 6.5). *Application deadline:* For fall admission, 1/2 for domestic and international students; for spring admission, 10/15 for domestic and international students. Applications are processed on a rolling basis. Application fee: $85. Electronic applications accepted. *Expenses:* Contact institution. *Financial support:* Teaching assistantships, Federal Work-Study, scholarships/grants, and tuition waivers (full and partial) available. Support available to part-time students. Financial award application deadline: 1/2. *Unit head:* Dr. David Hammer, Graduate Program Director, 617-627-2396. *Application contact:* Office of Graduate Admissions, 617-627-3395, E-mail: gradadmissions@tufts.edu.
Website: http://www.ase.tufts.edu/education/

Tusculum College, Program in Teaching, Greeneville, TN 37743-9997. Offers MAT. *Program availability:* Evening/weekend. *Entrance requirements:* For master's, PRAXIS I, GRE, MAT, minimum GPA of 3.0. *Unit head:* Dr. Tricia Hunsader, Dean, School of Education, 423-636-7300 Ext. 5693, E-mail: thunsader@tusculum.edu. *Application contact:* Lindsey Seal, Director of Enrollment, 423-636-7300 Ext. 5006, E-mail: lseal@tusculum.edu.
Website: http://home.tusculum.edu/gps/graduate-degrees/master-arts-teaching/

Union College, Graduate Programs, Department of Education, Barbourville, KY 40906-1499. Offers elementary education (MA); health and physical education (MA); middle grades (MA); music education (MA); principalship (MA); reading specialist (MA); secondary education (MA); special education (MA). *Degree requirements:* For master's, thesis optional. *Entrance requirements:* For master's, GRE General Test, NTE.

Union Institute & University, PhD Program in Interdisciplinary Studies, Cincinnati, OH 45206-1925. Offers educational studies (PhD), including Martin Luther King studies; ethical and creative leadership (PhD); humanities and culture (PhD); public policy and social change (PhD). Program requires participation in brief on-campus residencies twice each year (January and July). *Program availability:* Part-time, online only, blended/hybrid learning. *Degree requirements:* For doctorate, comprehensive exam, thesis/dissertation. *Entrance requirements:* For doctorate, master's degree, three letters of recommendation, statement of purpose. Additional exam requirements/recommendations for international students: Required—TOEFL. *Application deadline:* Applications are processed on a rolling basis. Application fee: $50. Electronic applications accepted. *Expenses:* Contact institution. *Financial support:* Federal Work-Study and scholarships/grants available. Financial award application deadline: 5/1; financial award applicants required to submit FAFSA. *Faculty research:* Social responsibility, ethical leadership, Martin Luther King studies. *Unit head:* Dr. Michael Raffanti, Dean of Graduate College, 800-641-6400 Ext. 1237, E-mail: michael.raffanti@myunion.edu. *Application contact:* Admissions Counselor, 800-486-3116.
Website: https://myunion.edu/academics/doctoral/

Union University, School of Education, Jackson, TN 38305-3697. Offers education (M Ed, MA Ed); education administration generalist (Ed S); educational leadership (Ed D); educational supervision (Ed S); higher education (Ed D). M Ed also available at Germantown campus. *Accreditation:* NCATE. *Program availability:* Part-time, evening/weekend, online learning. *Degree requirements:* For master's, thesis (for some programs), capstone research course (for MA Ed); performance exhibition (for M Ed); for doctorate, comprehensive exam, thesis/dissertation; for Ed S, thesis or alternative. *Entrance requirements:* For master's, MAT, PRAXIS II or GRE, minimum GPA of 3.0, teaching license (for M Ed only), writing sample; for doctorate, GRE, minimum graduate GPA of 3.2,

writing sample; for Ed S, PRAXIS II, minimum graduate GPA of 3.2, writing sample. Additional exam requirements/recommendations for international students: Required—TOEFL (minimum score 560 paper-based; 80 iBT). Electronic applications accepted. *Expenses:* Contact institution. *Faculty research:* Mathematics education, brain compatible learning, transformational teaching, cognitive strategy development, instructional technology.

Universidad Autonoma de Guadalajara, Graduate Programs, Guadalajara, Mexico. Offers administrative law and justice (LL M); advertising and corporate communications (MA); architecture (M Arch); business (MBA); computational science (MCC); education (Ed M, Ed D); English-Spanish translation (MA); entrepreneurship and management (MBA); integrated management of digital animation (MA); international business (MIB); international corporate law (LL M); internet technologies (MS); manufacturing systems (MMS); occupational health (MS); philosophy (MA, PhD); power electronics (MS); quality systems (MQS); renewable energy (MS); social evaluation of projects (MBA); strategic market research (MBA); tax law (MA); teaching mathematics (MA).

Universidad de las Americas, A.C., Program in Education, Mexico City, Mexico. Offers M Ed. *Entrance requirements:* For master's, 2 years of professional experience; undergraduate degree in early childhood education, human communication, psychology, science of education, special education or related fields.

Universidad de las Américas Puebla, Division of Graduate Studies, School of Social Sciences, Program in Education, Puebla, Mexico. Offers MA. *Program availability:* Part-time, evening/weekend. *Degree requirements:* For master's, one foreign language, thesis. *Faculty research:* Curriculum development, curriculum evaluation, instructional technology, critical thinking.

Universidad del Turabo, Graduate Programs, Programs in Education, Gurabo, PR 00778-3030. Offers M Ed, MPHE, D Ed. *Program availability:* Part-time, evening/weekend. *Degree requirements:* For master's, thesis (for some programs). *Entrance requirements:* For master's, GRE, EXADEP, GMAT, interview, official transcript, essay, recommendation letter; for doctorate, GRE, EXADEP, GMAT, official transcript, recommendation letters, essay, curriculum vitae, interview. Electronic applications accepted.

Universidad Metropolitana, School of Education, San Juan, PR 00928-1150. Offers administration and supervision (M Ed); curriculum and teaching (M Ed); educational administration and supervision (M Ed); managing recreation and sports services (M Ed); pre-school centers administration (M Ed); special education (M Ed); teaching of physical education (M Ed), including teaching of adult physical education, teaching of elementary physical education, teaching of secondary physical education. *Program availability:* Part-time, evening/weekend. *Degree requirements:* For master's, thesis or alternative. Electronic applications accepted.

Université de Moncton, Faculty of Education, Graduate Studies in Education, Moncton, NB E1A 3E9, Canada. Offers educational psychology (M Ed, MA Ed); guidance (M Ed, MA Ed); school administration (M Ed, MA Ed); teaching (M Ed, MA Ed). *Program availability:* Part-time. *Degree requirements:* For master's, proficiency in English and French. *Entrance requirements:* For master's, minimum GPA of 3.0. *Faculty research:* Guidance, ethnolinguistic vitality, children's rights, ecological education, entrepreneurship.

Université de Montréal, Faculty of Education, Montréal, QC H3C 3J7, Canada. Offers M Ed, MA, PhD, DESS. *Program availability:* Part-time, evening/weekend. *Degree requirements:* For doctorate, thesis/dissertation, general exam. Electronic applications accepted.

Université de Saint-Boniface, Department of Education, Saint-Boniface, MB R2H 0H7, Canada. Offers M Ed.

Université de Sherbrooke, Faculty of Education, Sherbrooke, QC J1K 2R1, Canada. Offers M Ed, MA, Diploma. *Program availability:* Part-time, evening/weekend. *Degree requirements:* For master's, thesis. *Faculty research:* Career education, teaching, professional instruction.

Université du Québec à Chicoutimi, Graduate Programs, Program in Education, Chicoutimi, QC G7H 2B1, Canada. Offers M Ed, MA, PhD. PhD offered jointly with Université du Québec à Rimouski, Université du Québec à Trois-Rivières, Université du Québec en Outaouais, Université du Québec en Abitibi-Témiscamingue, and Université du Québec à Montréal. *Program availability:* Part-time. *Degree requirements:* For doctorate, thesis/dissertation. *Entrance requirements:* For master's, appropriate bachelor's degree, proficiency in French; for doctorate, appropriate master's degree, proficiency in French.

Université du Québec à Montréal, Graduate Programs, Program in Education, Montréal, QC H3C 3P8, Canada. Offers education (M Ed, MA, PhD); education of the environmental sciences (Diploma). PhD offered jointly with Université du Québec à Chicoutimi, Université du Québec à Rimouski, Université du Québec à Trois-Rivières, Université du Québec en Outaouais, and Université du Québec en Abitibi-Témiscamingue. *Program availability:* Part-time. *Degree requirements:* For master's, thesis (for some programs); for doctorate, thesis/dissertation. *Entrance requirements:* For master's and Diploma, appropriate bachelor's degree or equivalent, proficiency in French; for doctorate, appropriate master's degree or equivalent, proficiency in French.

Université du Québec à Rimouski, Graduate Programs, Program in Education, Rimouski, QC G5L 3A1, Canada. Offers M Ed, MA, PhD, Diploma. M Ed and MA offered jointly with Université du Québec en Outaouais and Université du Québec en Abitibi-Témiscamingue; PhD with Université du Québec à Chicoutimi, Université du Québec à Trois-Rivières, Université du Québec en Outaouais, and Université du Québec en Abitibi-Témiscamingue. *Program availability:* Part-time. *Degree requirements:* For master's, thesis optional; for doctorate, thesis/dissertation. *Entrance requirements:* For master's, appropriate bachelor's degree, proficiency in French; for doctorate, appropriate master's degree, proficiency in French.

Université du Québec à Trois-Rivières, Graduate Programs, Program in Education, Trois-Rivières, QC G9A 5H7, Canada. Offers M Ed, PhD. *Program availability:* Part-time. *Degree requirements:* For master's, research report. *Entrance requirements:* For master's, appropriate bachelor's degree, proficiency in French.

Université du Québec en Abitibi-Témiscamingue, Graduate Programs, Program in Education, Rouyn-Noranda, QC J9X 5E4, Canada. Offers M Ed, MA, PhD, DESS. M Ed and MA offered jointly with Université du Québec à Rimouski and Université du Québec en Outaouais; PhD with Université du Québec à Chicoutimi, Université du Québec à Rimouski, Université du Québec à Trois-Rivières, Université du Québec en Outaouais, and Université du Québec à Montréal. *Program availability:* Part-time. *Degree requirements:* For master's, thesis optional; for doctorate, thesis/dissertation. *Entrance requirements:* For master's, appropriate bachelor's degree, proficiency in French; for doctorate, appropriate master's degree, proficiency in French.

Université du Québec en Outaouais, Graduate Programs, Program in Education, Gatineau, QC J8X 3X7, Canada. Offers M Ed, MA, PhD, DESS, Diploma. *Program availability:* Part-time. *Degree requirements:* For master's, thesis optional; for doctorate, thesis/dissertation. *Entrance requirements:* For master's, appropriate bachelor's degree, proficiency in French; for doctorate, appropriate master's degree, proficiency in French.

Education—General

Université Laval, Faculty of Education, Québec, QC G1K 7P4, Canada. Offers MA, PhD, Diploma. *Program availability:* Part-time. *Degree requirements:* For doctorate, comprehensive exam, thesis/dissertation. Electronic applications accepted.

Université Sainte-Anne, Program in Education, Church Point, NS B0W 1M0, Canada. Offers M Ed. *Program availability:* Part-time.

University at Albany, State University of New York, School of Education, Albany, NY 12222-0001. Offers MS, PhD, Psy D, CAS. *Accreditation:* TEAC. *Program availability:* Part-time, evening/weekend, 100% online, blended/hybrid learning. *Faculty:* 67 full-time (36 women), 75 part-time/adjunct (56 women). *Students:* 329 full-time (255 women), 505 part-time (383 women); includes 119 minority (37 Black or African American, non-Hispanic/Latino; 1 American Indian or Alaska Native, non-Hispanic/Latino; 25 Asian, non-Hispanic/Latino; 42 Hispanic/Latino; 14 Two or more races, non-Hispanic/Latino), 72 international. Average age 31. 588 applicants, 64% accepted, 310 enrolled. In 2017, 192 master's, 18 doctorates, 24 other advanced degrees awarded. *Degree requirements:* For doctorate, thesis/dissertation. *Entrance requirements:* For doctorate, GRE General Test. Additional exam requirements/recommendations for international students: Required—TOEFL (minimum score 550 paper-based). Application fee: $75. Electronic applications accepted. *Expenses:* Tuition, state resident: full-time $10,870; part-time $453 per credit hour. Tuition, nonresident: full-time $22,210; part-time $925 per credit hour. *Required fees:* $84.68 per credit hour. $508.06 per semester. Part-time tuition and fees vary according to course load and program. *Financial support:* Fellowships, career-related internships or fieldwork, and Federal Work-Study available. *Unit head:* Robert Bangert-Drowns, Dean, 518-442-4988, E-mail: rbangert-drowns@albany.edu.
Website: http://www.albany.edu/education/

University at Buffalo, the State University of New York, Graduate School, Graduate School of Education, Buffalo, NY 14260. Offers Ed M, MA, MS, Ed D, PhD, Advanced Certificate, Certificate, Certificate/Ed M. *Accreditation:* TEAC. *Program availability:* Part-time, 100% online. *Faculty:* 72 full-time (46 women), 144 part-time/adjunct (105 women). *Students:* 452 full-time (338 women), 748 part-time (554 women); includes 116 minority (78 Black or African American, non-Hispanic/Latino; 9 American Indian or Alaska Native, non-Hispanic/Latino; 22 Asian, non-Hispanic/Latino; 7 Hispanic/Latino), 94 international. Average age 33. 914 applicants, 72% accepted, 449 enrolled. In 2017, 290 master's, 50 doctorates, 78 other advanced degrees awarded. Terminal master's awarded for partial completion of doctoral program. *Degree requirements:* For master's, comprehensive exam; for doctorate, thesis/dissertation. *Entrance requirements:* For master's, GRE General Test; for doctorate, GRE, MAT. Additional exam requirements/recommendations for international students: Required—TOEFL (minimum score 79 iBT), PTE. *Application deadline:* Applications are processed on a rolling basis. Application fee: $50. Electronic applications accepted. *Financial support:* In 2017–18, 98 fellowships (averaging $5,401 per year), 125 research assistantships with tuition reimbursements (averaging $11,177 per year) were awarded; teaching assistantships, Federal Work-Study, institutionally sponsored loans, scholarships/grants, tuition waivers (full and partial), and unspecified assistantships also available. Support available to part-time students. Financial award applicants required to submit FAFSA. *Faculty research:* Early childhood mathematics education, finance and management of higher education, curricular policy, practice and reform, student behavior in small classes, psychological measurement and assessment. *Total annual research expenditures:* $3.8 million. *Unit head:* Dr. Suzanne Rosenblith, Dean, 716-645-1354, Fax: 716-645-2479, E-mail: gse-info@buffalo.edu. *Application contact:* Cory Meyers, Assistant Dean for Enrollment Management, 716-645-2110, Fax: 716-645-7937, E-mail: gse-info@buffalo.edu.
Website: http://www.gse.buffalo.edu/

The University of Akron, Graduate School, College of Education, Akron, OH 44325. Offers MA, MS. *Accreditation:* NCATE. *Program availability:* Part-time. *Faculty:* 26 full-time (18 women), 7 part-time/adjunct (6 women). *Students:* 67 full-time (40 women), 158 part-time (119 women); includes 38 minority (28 Black or African American, non-Hispanic/Latino; 3 Asian, non-Hispanic/Latino; 3 Hispanic/Latino; 4 Two or more races, non-Hispanic/Latino), 12 international. Average age 34. 79 applicants, 94% accepted, 74 enrolled. In 2017, 98 master's awarded. Terminal master's awarded for partial completion of doctoral program. *Degree requirements:* For master's, comprehensive exam, thesis optional. *Entrance requirements:* For master's, GRE, letters of recommendation, resume, statement of purpose. Additional exam requirements/recommendations for international students: Required—TOEFL (minimum score 550 paper-based; 79 iBT), IELTS (minimum score 6.5). *Application deadline:* Applications are processed on a rolling basis. Application fee: $45 ($70 for international students). Electronic applications accepted. *Financial support:* In 2017–18, 2 teaching assistantships with full tuition reimbursements were awarded; scholarships/grants and administrative assistantships also available. *Faculty research:* History, philosophy of education, ethnographic research in education, case study methodology in education, multiple linear regression. *Total annual research expenditures:* $288,213. *Unit head:* Dr. Jarrod Tudor, Acting Dean, 330-972-7750, E-mail: grt2@uakron.edu. *Application contact:* Kelly Chaff, College Program Specialist, 330-972-7028, E-mail: klchaff@uakron.edu.
Website: http://www.uakron.edu/education/

The University of Alabama at Birmingham, School of Education, Birmingham, AL 35294. Offers MA, MA Ed, Ed D, PhD, Ed S. *Accreditation:* NCATE. *Program availability:* Part-time, evening/weekend, online learning. *Degree requirements:* For master's, thesis optional; for doctorate, thesis/dissertation; for Ed S, comprehensive exam, thesis optional. *Entrance requirements:* For master's, GRE General Test, MAT, or NTE, minimum GPA of 3.0; for doctorate, GRE General Test, MAT, minimum GPA of 3.25; for Ed S, GRE General Test, MAT, minimum GPA of 3.0, master's degree. Electronic applications accepted.

The University of Alabama in Huntsville, School of Graduate Studies, College of Education, Huntsville, AL 35899. Offers autism spectrum disorders (M Ed, Graduate Certificate); biology (MAT); chemistry (MAT); differentiated instruction in elementary education (M Ed); English language arts (MAT); English speakers of other languages (M Ed, MAT); history (MAT); mathematics (MAT); physics (MAT); reading education (M Ed); secondary education (M Ed).

University of Alaska Anchorage, College of Education, Anchorage, AK 99508. Offers M Ed, Certificate. *Accreditation:* NCATE. *Program availability:* Part-time. *Degree requirements:* For master's, comprehensive exam, thesis or alternative, portfolio. *Entrance requirements:* For master's, interview, minimum GPA of 3.0. Additional exam requirements/recommendations for international students: Required—TOEFL (minimum score 550 paper-based).

University of Alaska Fairbanks, School of Education, Fairbanks, AK 99775-6480. Offers M Ed, Graduate Certificate. *Accreditation:* NCATE. *Program availability:* 100% online, blended/hybrid learning. *Degree requirements:* For master's, comprehensive exam, oral defense of project or thesis, student teaching. *Entrance requirements:* For master's and Graduate Certificate, bachelor's degree from accredited institution with minimum cumulative undergraduate and major GPA of 3.0. Additional exam requirements/recommendations for international students: Required—TOEFL (minimum score 550 paper-based; 79 iBT), IELTS (minimum score 6.5). Electronic applications

accepted. *Faculty research:* Native ways of knowing, classroom research in methods of literacy instruction, multiple intelligence theory, geometry concept development, mathematics and science curriculum development.

University of Alaska Southeast, Graduate Programs, Program in Education, Juneau, AK 99801. Offers educational leadership (M Ed); elementary education (MAT); learning design and technology (M Ed); mathematics education (M Ed); reading specialist (M Ed); secondary education (MAT); special education (M Ed, MAT). *Accreditation:* NCATE. *Program availability:* Part-time, evening/weekend, online learning. *Degree requirements:* For master's, comprehensive exam or project, portfolio. *Entrance requirements:* For master's, PRAXIS, minimum GPA of 3.0, writing sample, letters of recommendation. Electronic applications accepted. *Faculty research:* Applied classroom research, culturally responsive practices, action research, teaching effectiveness.

The University of Arizona, College of Education, Tucson, AZ 85721. Offers M Ed, MA, MS, Ed D, PhD, Certificate, Ed S. *Program availability:* Part-time, online learning. Terminal master's awarded for partial completion of doctoral program. *Degree requirements:* For master's, comprehensive exam, thesis (for some programs); for doctorate, comprehensive exam, thesis/dissertation. *Entrance requirements:* For doctorate, GRE. Additional exam requirements/recommendations for international students: Required—TOEFL (minimum score 550 paper-based; 79 iBT). Electronic applications accepted. *Faculty research:* Teacher effectiveness, pupil achievement, learning skills, program evaluation, instructional method effects.

University of Arkansas, Graduate School, College of Education and Health Professions, Fayetteville, AR 72701. Offers M Ed, MAT, MAT, MS, MSN, Ed D, PhD, Ed S. *Accreditation:* NCATE. In 2017, 399 master's, 43 doctorates awarded. *Degree requirements:* For doctorate, thesis/dissertation. *Application deadline:* For fall admission, 8/1 for domestic students, 4/1 for international students; for spring admission, 12/1 for domestic students, 10/1 for international students; for summer admission, 4/15 for domestic students, 3/1 for international students. Applications are processed on a rolling basis. Application fee: $60. Electronic applications accepted. *Expenses:* Tuition, state resident: full-time $3782. Tuition, nonresident: full-time $10,238. *Financial support:* In 2017–18, 110 research assistantships, 15 teaching assistantships were awarded; fellowships with tuition reimbursements, career-related internships or fieldwork, and Federal Work-Study also available. Support available to part-time students. Financial award application deadline: 4/1; financial award applicants required to submit FAFSA. *Unit head:* Dr. Michael T. Miller, Dean, 479-575-3582, Fax: 479-575-3119, E-mail: mtmille@uark.edu.
Website: http://coehp.uark.edu/

University of Arkansas at Little Rock, Graduate School, College of Education and Health Professions, Little Rock, AR 72204-1099. Offers M Ed, MA, MS, MSW, Ed D, Ed S, Graduate Certificate. *Accreditation:* CORE; NCATE (one or more programs are accredited). *Program availability:* Part-time, evening/weekend. *Degree requirements:* For doctorate, comprehensive exam, oral defense of dissertation, residency; for other advanced degree, comprehensive exam. *Entrance requirements:* For master's, minimum GPA of 2.75; for doctorate, GRE General Test or MAT, minimum graduate GPA of 3.0, teaching certificate, work experience; for other advanced degree, GRE General Test or MAT, teaching certificate.

University of Arkansas at Monticello, School of Education, Monticello, AR 71656. Offers education (M Ed, MAT); educational leadership (M Ed). *Accreditation:* NCATE. *Program availability:* Part-time, evening/weekend, online learning. *Degree requirements:* For master's, comprehensive exam. *Entrance requirements:* For master's, minimum GPA of 3.0. Additional exam requirements/recommendations for international students: Required—TOEFL (minimum score 550 paper-based). Electronic applications accepted.

University of Arkansas at Pine Bluff, School of Education, Pine Bluff, AR 71601-2799. Offers elementary education (M Ed); secondary education (M Ed), including English education, mathematics education, science education, social studies education; teaching (MAT). *Accreditation:* NCATE. *Program availability:* Part-time, evening/weekend. *Degree requirements:* For master's, comprehensive exam. *Entrance requirements:* For master's, GRE, minimum GPA of 2.75, NTE or Standard Arkansas Teaching Certificate. *Faculty research:* Teacher certification, accreditation, assessment, standards, portfolio development, rehabilitation, technology.

University of Bridgeport, School of Education, Department of Education, Bridgeport, CT 06604. Offers education (MS); educational management (Ed D, Diploma), including intermediate administrator or supervisor (Diploma), leadership (Ed D); elementary education (MS, Diploma), including early childhood education, elementary education; middle school education (MS); music education (MS); remedial reading and language arts (Diploma); secondary education (MS, Diploma), including computer specialist (Diploma), international education (Diploma), reading specialist, secondary education. *Program availability:* Part-time, evening/weekend. *Degree requirements:* For master's, final exam, final project, or thesis; for doctorate, comprehensive exam, thesis/dissertation; for Diploma, thesis or alternative, final project. *Entrance requirements:* For master's, minimum undergraduate QPA of 2.67; for doctorate, GRE, MAT; for Diploma, GRE General Test or MAT, minimum graduate QPA of 3.0. Additional exam requirements/recommendations for international students: Recommended—TOEFL (minimum score 550 paper-based; 80 iBT), IELTS (minimum score 6.5). Electronic applications accepted. *Expenses:* Contact institution.

The University of British Columbia, Faculty of Education, Vancouver, BC V6T1Z4, Canada. Offers M Ed, M Kin, M Sc, MA, MET, MHPCTL, Ed D, PhD, Diploma. *Program availability:* Part-time, evening/weekend, online learning. Terminal master's awarded for partial completion of doctoral program. *Degree requirements:* For master's, thesis (for some programs); for doctorate, comprehensive exam, thesis/dissertation. *Entrance requirements:* Additional exam requirements/recommendations for international students: Required—TOEFL. Electronic applications accepted. *Expenses:* Contact institution. *Faculty research:* Curriculum and pedagogy; school counseling psychology; educational administration; human kinetics; language and literacy education.

University of California, Berkeley, Graduate Division, School of Education, Berkeley, CA 94720-1500. Offers MA, PhD, MA/Credential, PhD/Credential, PhD/MA. Terminal master's awarded for partial completion of doctoral program. *Degree requirements:* For master's, exam or thesis; for doctorate, thesis/dissertation, oral qualifying exam (PhD). *Entrance requirements:* For master's and doctorate, GRE General Test, minimum undergraduate GPA of 3.0 during last 2 years, 3 letters of recommendation. Electronic applications accepted. *Faculty research:* Cognition and development; language, literacy and culture.

University of California, Berkeley, UC Berkeley Extension, Certificate Programs in Education, Berkeley, CA 94720-1500. Offers college admissions and career planning (Certificate); teaching English as a second language (Certificate).

University of California, Davis, Graduate Studies, Graduate Group in Education, Davis, CA 95616. Offers education (MA, Ed D); instructional studies (PhD); psychological studies (PhD); sociocultural studies (PhD). Ed D offered jointly with California State University, Fresno. Terminal master's awarded for partial completion of doctoral program. *Degree requirements:* For master's, comprehensive exam (for some programs), thesis (for some programs); for doctorate, thesis/dissertation. *Entrance* *requirements:* For master's and doctorate, GRE. Additional exam requirements/recommendations for international students: Required—TOEFL (minimum score 550 paper-based). Electronic applications accepted. *Faculty research:* Language and literacy, mathematics education, science education, teacher development, school psychology.

University of California, Irvine, School of Education, Irvine, CA 92697. Offers educational administration (Ed D); educational administration and leadership (Ed D); elementary and secondary education (MAT). *Program availability:* Part-time, evening/weekend. *Students:* 210 full-time (157 women), 1 (woman) part-time; includes 104 minority (1 Black or African American, non-Hispanic/Latino; 46 Asian, non-Hispanic/Latino; 39 Hispanic/Latino; 1 Native Hawaiian or other Pacific Islander, non-Hispanic/Latino; 17 Two or more races, non-Hispanic/Latino), 20 international. Average age 27. 451 applicants, 46% accepted, 147 enrolled. In 2017, 130 master's, 7 doctorates awarded. *Entrance requirements:* For master's, GRE, minimum GPA of 3.0; for doctorate, GRE General Test, minimum GPA of 3.0. Additional exam requirements/recommendations for international students: Required—TOEFL (minimum score 550 paper-based). *Application deadline:* For fall admission, 1/2 priority date for domestic students, 1/2 for international students. Application fee: $105 ($125 for international students). Electronic applications accepted. *Financial support:* Fellowships, research assistantships with full tuition reimbursements, institutionally sponsored loans, traineeships, health care benefits, and unspecified assistantships available. Financial award application deadline: 3/1; financial award applicants required to submit FAFSA. *Faculty research:* Education technology, learning theory, social theory, cultural diversity, postmodernism. *Unit head:* Richard Arum, Dean, 949-824-2534, E-mail: richard.arum@uci.edu. *Application contact:* Denise Earley, Assistant Director of Student Affairs, 949-824-4022, E-mail: denise.earley@uci.edu.
Website: http://education.uci.edu/

University of California, Los Angeles, Graduate Division, Graduate School of Education and Information Studies, Department of Education, Los Angeles, CA 90095. Offers M Ed, MA, Ed D, PhD. *Program availability:* Evening/weekend. *Degree requirements:* For master's, comprehensive exam; for doctorate, thesis/dissertation, oral and written qualifying exams. *Entrance requirements:* For master's, GRE General Test, minimum GPA of 3.0; for doctorate, GRE General Test, minimum undergraduate GPA of 3.0. Additional exam requirements/recommendations for international students: Required—TOEFL (minimum score 560 paper-based; 87 iBT). Electronic applications accepted.

University of California, Riverside, Graduate Division, Graduate School of Education, Riverside, CA 92521. Offers applied behavior analysis (M Ed); diversity and equity (M Ed); education policy analysis and leadership (PhD); education specialist (Credential); education, society, and culture (MA, PhD); educational psychology (MA, PhD); general education (M Ed); higher education administration and policy (M Ed, PhD); multiple subject (Credential); research, evaluation, measurement and statistics (MA); school psychology (PhD); single subject (Credential); special education (M Ed, PhD); special education and autism (MA); TESOL (M Ed). *Faculty:* 29 full-time (16 women), 2 part-time/adjunct (1 woman). *Students:* 241 full-time (188 women). 396 applicants, 42% accepted, 166 enrolled. In 2017, 130 master's, 15 doctorates, 14 other advanced degrees awarded. Terminal master's awarded for partial completion of doctoral program. *Degree requirements:* For master's, comprehensive exams or thesis (MA), case study or analytical report (M Ed); for doctorate, comprehensive exam, thesis/dissertation, written and oral qualifying exams, college teaching practicum. *Entrance requirements:* For master's, GRE General Test (for MA); CBEST and CSET (for M Ed in general education only), UCR Extension TESOL certificate (for M Ed with TESOL emphasis only); for doctorate, GRE General Test, writing sample; for Credential, CBEST, CSET. Additional exam requirements/recommendations for international students: Required—TOEFL (minimum score 550 paper-based; 80 iBT), IELTS (minimum score 7). *Application deadline:* For fall admission, 9/1 for domestic students, 6/1 for international students; for winter admission, 11/15 for domestic students, 9/1 for international students; for spring admission, 3/1 for domestic students, 12/1 for international students. Applications are processed on a rolling basis. Application fee: $80 ($100 for international students). Electronic applications accepted. *Expenses:* Tuition, state resident: full-time $5746. Tuition, nonresident: full-time $10,780. Tuition and fees vary according to campus/location and program. *Financial support:* In 2017–18, 105 students received support, including 16 fellowships with full tuition reimbursements available (averaging $31,000 per year), 25 research assistantships with full tuition reimbursements available (averaging $31,000 per year), 10 teaching assistantships with full tuition reimbursements available (averaging $31,000 per year); career-related internships or fieldwork, Federal Work-Study, institutionally sponsored loans, scholarships/grants, and unspecified assistantships also available. Financial award application deadline: 12/15. *Faculty research:* Responsiveness to intervention, faculty core, response to intervention of English language learners, advanced modeling techniques, study on social capital, trust, and motivation. *Total annual research expenditures:* $1.7 million. *Unit head:* Thomas Smith, Dean, 951-827-4633, E-mail: thomas.smith@ucr.edu. *Application contact:* Heather Killeen, Graduate Program Coordinator, 951-827-6362, E-mail: heather.killeen@ucr.edu.
Website: http://www.education.ucr.edu/

University of California, San Diego, Graduate Division, Program in Education Studies, La Jolla, CA 92093. Offers education (M Ed, PhD); educational leadership (Ed D); teaching and learning (MA, Ed D), including bilingual education (MA), curriculum design (MA). Ed D offered jointly with California State University, San Marcos. *Students:* 88 full-time (64 women), 54 part-time (36 women). 261 applicants, 57% accepted, 77 enrolled. In 2017, 68 master's, 13 doctorates awarded. *Degree requirements:* For master's, thesis (for some programs), student teaching; for doctorate, comprehensive exam, thesis/dissertation. *Entrance requirements:* For master's, GRE General Test; CBEST and appropriate CSET exam (for select tracks), current teaching or educational assignment (for select tracks); for doctorate, GRE General Test, current teaching or educational assignment (for select tracks). Additional exam requirements/recommendations for international students: Required—TOEFL (minimum score 550 paper-based; 80 iBT), IELTS (minimum score 7). *Application deadline:* For fall admission, 2/2 for domestic students. Application fee: $105 ($125 for international students). Electronic applications accepted. *Financial support:* Fellowships, career-related internships or fieldwork, and scholarships/grants available. Financial award applicants required to submit FAFSA. *Faculty research:* Language, culture and literacy development of deaf/hard of hearing children; equity issues in education; educational reform; evaluation, assessment, and research methodologies; distributed learning. *Unit head:* Carolyn Hofstetter, Chair, 858-822-6688, E-mail: ajdaly@ucsd.edu. *Application contact:* Giselle Van Luit, Graduate Coordinator, 858-534-2958, E-mail: edsinfo@ucsd.edu.

University of California, Santa Barbara, Graduate Division, Gevirtz Graduate School of Education, Santa Barbara, CA 93106-9490. Offers counseling, clinical and school psychology (MA, PhD, Credential), including clinical psychology (PhD), counseling psychology (MA, PhD), pupil personnel services (Credential), school psychology (PhD); education (MA, PhD, Credential); teacher education (M Ed, Credential), including multiple subject teaching (Credential), single subject teaching (Credential), special education (Credential), teaching (M Ed); MA/PhD. *Accreditation:* APA (one or more programs are

accredited). Terminal master's awarded for partial completion of doctoral program. *Degree requirements:* For master's, comprehensive exam (for some programs), thesis (for some programs); for doctorate, comprehensive exam (for some programs), thesis/dissertation. *Entrance requirements:* For master's and doctorate, GRE; for Credential, GRE or MAT, CSET, CBEST. Additional exam requirements/recommendations for international students: Required—TOEFL (minimum score 550 paper-based; 80 iBT), IELTS (minimum score 7). Electronic applications accepted. *Faculty research:* Needs of diverse students, school accountability and leadership, school violence, language learning and literacy, science/math education.

University of California, Santa Cruz, Division of Graduate Studies, Division of Social Sciences, Department of Education, Santa Cruz, CA 95064. Offers MA, PhD. Terminal master's awarded for partial completion of doctoral program. *Degree requirements:* For master's, thesis; for doctorate, thesis/dissertation. *Entrance requirements:* Additional exam requirements/recommendations for international students: Required—TOEFL (minimum score 550 paper-based; 83 iBT); Recommended—IELTS (minimum score 8). Electronic applications accepted. *Faculty research:* Bilingual/multicultural education, special education, curriculum and instruction, child development, gaps in the learning opportunities of underserved students, discovery of more effective practices.

University of Central Arkansas, Graduate School, College of Education, Conway, AR 72035-0001. Offers MA, MS, MSE, Ed S, Graduate Certificate, PMC. *Accreditation:* NCATE. *Program availability:* Part-time, evening/weekend, online learning. Terminal master's awarded for partial completion of doctoral program. *Degree requirements:* For master's, comprehensive exam, thesis optional, portfolio. *Entrance requirements:* For master's, GRE General Test, minimum GPA of 2.7. Additional exam requirements/recommendations for international students: Required—TOEFL (minimum score 550 paper-based; 80 iBT). Electronic applications accepted.

University of Central Arkansas, Graduate School, College of Education, Department of Teaching and Learning, Graduate Program in Teaching, Conway, AR 72035-0001. Offers MAT. *Program availability:* Part-time, online learning. *Degree requirements:* For master's, comprehensive exam, thesis optional. *Entrance requirements:* For master's, GRE General Test, minimum GPA of 2.7. Additional exam requirements/recommendations for international students: Required—TOEFL (minimum score 550 paper-based). Electronic applications accepted.

University of Central Arkansas, Graduate School, College of Education, Department of Teaching and Learning, Program in Advanced Studies of Teaching and Learning, Conway, AR 72035-0001. Offers MSE. *Program availability:* Evening/weekend, online learning. *Entrance requirements:* For master's, GRE General Test, minimum GPA of 2.7. Additional exam requirements/recommendations for international students: Required—TOEFL (minimum score 550 paper-based). Electronic applications accepted.

University of Central Missouri, The Graduate School, Warrensburg, MO 64093. Offers accountancy (MA); accounting (MBA); applied mathematics (MS); aviation safety (MA); biology (MS); business administration (MBA); career and technical education leadership (MS); college student personnel administration (MS); communication (MA); computer science (MS); counseling (MS); criminal justice (MS); educational leadership (Ed D); educational technology (MS); elementary and early childhood education (MSE); English (MA); environmental studies (MA); finance (MBA); history (MA); human services/educational technology (Ed S); human services/learning resources (Ed S); human services/professional counseling (Ed S); industrial hygiene (MS); industrial management (MS); information systems (MBA); information technology (MS); kinesiology (MS); library science and information services (MS); literacy education (MSE); marketing (MBA); mathematics (MS); music (MA); occupational safety management (MS); psychology (MS); rural family nursing (MS); school administration (MSE); social gerontology (MS); sociology (MA); special education (MSE); speech language pathology (MS); superintendency (Ed S); teaching (MAT); teaching English as a second language (MA); technology (MS); technology management (PhD); theatre (MA). *Program availability:* Part-time, 100% online, blended/hybrid learning. *Faculty:* 337 full-time (145 women), 41 part-time/adjunct (28 women). *Students:* 785 full-time (398 women), 1,633 part-time (1,063 women); includes 231 minority (102 Black or African American, non-Hispanic/Latino; 4 American Indian or Alaska Native, non-Hispanic/Latino; 16 Asian, non-Hispanic/Latino; 52 Hispanic/Latino; 57 Two or more races, non-Hispanic/Latino), 692 international. Average age 30. In 2017, 2,605 master's, 122 other advanced degrees awarded. *Degree requirements:* For master's and Ed S, comprehensive exam (for some programs), thesis (for some programs). *Entrance requirements:* Additional exam requirements/recommendations for international students: Required—TOEFL (minimum score 550 paper-based; 79 iBT). *Application deadline:* For fall admission, 6/1 priority date for domestic and international students; for spring admission, 10/1 priority date for domestic and international students; for summer admission, 4/1 priority date for domestic and international students. Applications are processed on a rolling basis. Application fee: $30 ($75 for international students). Electronic applications accepted. *Expenses:* Tuition, state resident: full-time $8771; part-time $292.35 per credit hour. Tuition, nonresident: full-time $17,541; part-time $584.70 per credit hour. *Required fees:* $372; $24.78 per credit hour. *Financial support:* In 2017–18, 99 students received support. Research assistantships, teaching assistantships, career-related internships or fieldwork, Federal Work-Study, scholarships/grants, and administrative and laboratory assistantships available. Support available to part-time students. Financial award application deadline: 3/1; financial award applicants required to submit FAFSA. *Unit head:* Shellie Hewitt, Director of Graduate and International Student Services, 660-543-4621, Fax: 660-543-4778, E-mail: hewitt@ucmo.edu. *Application contact:* 660-543-4621, E-mail: admit_intl@ucmo.edu.
Website: http://www.ucmo.edu/graduate/

University of Central Oklahoma, The Jackson College of Graduate Studies, College of Education and Professional Studies, Edmond, OK 73034-5209. Offers M Ed, MA, MS. *Accreditation:* NCATE. *Program availability:* Part-time. *Faculty:* 72 full-time (48 women), 30 part-time/adjunct (18 women). *Students:* 280 full-time (220 women), 615 part-time (501 women); includes 280 minority (115 Black or African American, non-Hispanic/Latino; 26 American Indian or Alaska Native, non-Hispanic/Latino; 15 Asian, non-Hispanic/Latino; 73 Hispanic/Latino; 51 Two or more races, non-Hispanic/Latino), 44 international. Average age 33. 486 applicants, 81% accepted, 255 enrolled. In 2017, 310 master's awarded. *Degree requirements:* For master's, comprehensive exam (for some programs), thesis (for some programs). *Entrance requirements:* For master's, GRE. Additional exam requirements/recommendations for international students: Required—TOEFL (minimum score 550 paper-based; 79 iBT), IELTS (minimum score 6.5). *Application deadline:* For fall admission, 7/15 for international students; for spring admission, 11/15 for international students. Applications are processed on a rolling basis. Application fee: $60. Electronic applications accepted. *Expenses:* Tuition, state resident: full-time $5375; part-time $268.75 per credit hour. Tuition, nonresident: full-time $13,295; part-time $664.75 per credit hour. *Required fees:* $626; $31.30 per credit hour. One-time fee: $50. Tuition and fees vary according to program. *Financial support:* In 2017–18, 179 students received support, including 19 research assistantships with partial tuition reimbursements available (averaging $4,047 per year), 2 teaching assistantships with partial tuition reimbursements available (averaging $4,436 per year); career-related internships or fieldwork, scholarships/grants, tuition waivers (partial), and unspecified assistantships also available. Financial award application deadline: 3/31;

Education—General

financial award applicants required to submit FAFSA. *Unit head:* Dr. James Machell, Dean, 405-974-5701, Fax: 405-974-3851. *Application contact:* Carlie Wellington, Assistant Director, CEPS Graduate Enrollment, 405-974-5105, Fax: 405-974-3851, E-mail: gradcoll@uco.edu.
Website: http://www.uco.edu/ceps/

University of Cincinnati, Graduate School, College of Education, Criminal Justice, and Human Services, Cincinnati, OH 45221. Offers M Ed, MA, MS, Ed D, PhD, CAGS, Certificate, Ed S, Graduate Certificate. *Accreditation:* NCATE. *Program availability:* Part-time, online learning. *Degree requirements:* For master's, comprehensive exam (for some programs), thesis (for some programs); for doctorate, comprehensive exam, thesis/dissertation. *Entrance requirements:* For master's and doctorate, GRE. Additional exam requirements/recommendations for international students: Required—TOEFL (minimum score 550 paper-based), OEPT 3. Electronic applications accepted. *Expenses: Tuition, area resident:* Full-time $14,468. Tuition, state resident: full-time $14,968; part-time $754 per credit hour. Tuition, nonresident: full-time $24,210; part-time $1311 per credit hour. *International tuition:* $26,460 full-time. *Required fees:* $3958; $84 per credit hour. One-time fee: $85 full-time. Tuition and fees vary according to course load, degree level and program. *Faculty research:* Alcohol and drug prevention, family-based prevention, criminal justice, literacy, urban education.

University of Colorado Boulder, Graduate School, School of Education, Boulder, CO 80309. Offers MA, PhD. *Accreditation:* NCATE. *Faculty:* 38 full-time (24 women). *Students:* 176 full-time (119 women), 153 part-time (126 women); includes 89 minority (11 Black or African American, non-Hispanic/Latino; 1 American Indian or Alaska Native, non-Hispanic/Latino; 3 Asian, non-Hispanic/Latino; 67 Hispanic/Latino; 1 Native Hawaiian or other Pacific Islander, non-Hispanic/Latino; 6 Two or more races, non-Hispanic/Latino), 5 international. Average age 33. 401 applicants, 52% accepted, 82 enrolled. In 2017, 133 master's, 11 doctorates awarded. Terminal master's awarded for partial completion of doctoral program. *Degree requirements:* For master's, comprehensive exam, thesis or alternative; for doctorate, one foreign language, comprehensive exam, thesis/dissertation. *Entrance requirements:* For master's, GRE General Test or MAT, minimum undergraduate GPA of 2.75; for doctorate, GRE General Test. *Application deadline:* For fall admission, 12/1 for domestic and international students; for spring admission, 9/1 for domestic and international students. Application fee: $60 ($80 for international students). Electronic applications accepted. Application fee is waived when completed online. *Financial support:* In 2017–18, 381 students received support, including 92 fellowships (averaging $4,091 per year), 46 research assistantships with full and partial tuition reimbursements available (averaging $32,538 per year), 35 teaching assistantships with full and partial tuition reimbursements available (averaging $10,002 per year); scholarships/grants, health care benefits, and unspecified assistantships also available. Financial award application deadline: 2/15; financial award applicants required to submit FAFSA. *Faculty research:* Teacher education; educational reform; literacy; equal educational opportunity; minority education. *Total annual research expenditures:* $9.1 million.
Website: http://www.colorado.edu/education/

University of Colorado Colorado Springs, College of Education, Colorado Springs, CO 80918. Offers counseling and human services (MA); curriculum and instruction (MA); educational leadership (MA); educational leadership, research and policy (PhD); special education (MA); teaching English to speakers of other languages (MA). *Accreditation:* ACA; NCATE. *Program availability:* Part-time, evening/weekend, 100% online, blended/hybrid learning. *Faculty:* 30 full-time (21 women), 61 part-time/adjunct (38 women). *Students:* 190 full-time (132 women), 286 part-time (202 women); includes 117 minority (20 Black or African American, non-Hispanic/Latino; 2 American Indian or Alaska Native, non-Hispanic/Latino; 12 Asian, non-Hispanic/Latino; 59 Hispanic/Latino; 24 Two or more races, non-Hispanic/Latino), 6 international. Average age 36. 169 applicants, 85% accepted, 113 enrolled. In 2017, 160 master's, 16 doctorates awarded. *Degree requirements:* For master's, comprehensive exam, thesis or alternative, microcomputer proficiency; for doctorate, comprehensive exam, thesis/dissertation, research lab. *Entrance requirements:* For master's and doctorate, GRE General Test. Additional exam requirements/recommendations for international students: Recommended—TOEFL (minimum score 550 paper-based; 80 iBT), IELTS (minimum score 6). *Application deadline:* For fall admission, 1/28 priority date for domestic and international students; for spring admission, 11/1 priority date for domestic and international students. Applications are processed on a rolling basis. Application fee: $60 ($100 for international students). Electronic applications accepted. *Expenses:* $10,350 per year resident tuition, $20,935 nonresident, $11,961 nonresidential online; annual costs vary depending on program, course-load, and residency status. *Financial support:* In 2017–18, 81 students received support. Career-related internships or fieldwork, Federal Work-Study, scholarships/grants, and unspecified assistantships available. Support available to part-time students. Financial award application deadline: 3/1; financial award applicants required to submit FAFSA. *Faculty research:* Linguistically diverse education (LDE), educational policy, evidence-based reading and writing instruction, relational and social aggression, positive behavior supports, inclusive schooling, K-12 education, policy. *Total annual research expenditures:* $607,967. *Unit head:* Dr. Valerie Martin Conley, Dean, 719-255-4133, E-mail: vmconley@uccs.edu. *Application contact:* The College of Education Student Resource Office, 719-255-4996, E-mail: education@uccs.edu.
Website: http://www.uccs.edu/coe

University of Colorado Denver, School of Education and Human Development, Denver, CO 80217. Offers MA, MS Ed, Ed D, PhD, Psy D, Ed S. *Accreditation:* NCATE. *Program availability:* Part-time, evening/weekend, online learning. *Degree requirements:* For master's and Ed S, comprehensive exam (for some programs); for doctorate, comprehensive exam, thesis/dissertation. *Entrance requirements:* Additional exam requirements/recommendations for international students: Required—TOEFL (minimum score 537 paper-based; 75 iBT); Recommended—IELTS (minimum score 6.5). Electronic applications accepted. *Expenses:* Contact institution. *Faculty research:* Educational equity: race, class, culture, power and privilege; analytic approaches to educational program effectiveness and measuring student learning; early childhood special education/early intervention policies; recruiting and retention of African-American teachers; secondary and postsecondary institutions; accountability systems to improve public education.

University of Connecticut, Graduate School, Neag School of Education, Storrs, CT 06269. Offers MA, PhD. *Accreditation:* NCATE. Terminal master's awarded for partial completion of doctoral program. *Degree requirements:* For master's, comprehensive exam, thesis or alternative; for doctorate, thesis/dissertation. *Entrance requirements:* For doctorate, GRE General Test. Additional exam requirements/recommendations for international students: Required—TOEFL (minimum score 550 paper-based). Electronic applications accepted.

University of Delaware, College of Education and Human Development, School of Education, Newark, DE 19716. Offers education (PhD); educational leadership (Ed D); higher education (M Ed); instruction (MI); reading (M Ed); school leadership (M Ed); school psychology (MA, Ed S); teaching English as a second language (TESL) (MA). *Accreditation:* NCATE. *Program availability:* Part-time, evening/weekend. Terminal master's awarded for partial completion of doctoral program. *Degree requirements:* For

master's, comprehensive exam (for some programs), thesis (for some programs); for doctorate, comprehensive exam (for some programs), thesis/dissertation. *Entrance requirements:* For master's and doctorate, GRE, 3 letters of recommendation. Additional exam requirements/recommendations for international students: Required—TOEFL (minimum score 600 paper-based). Electronic applications accepted. *Faculty research:* Teacher education; curriculum theory and development; community based education models, educational leadership.

University of Denver, Morgridge College of Education, Denver, CO 80208. Offers child, family and school psychology (MA, PhD, Ed S); counseling psychology (MA, PhD); curriculum and instruction (MA, Ed D, PhD); curriculum instruction and teaching (Certificate); early childhood special education (MA, Certificate); educational leadership and policy studies (MA, Ed D, PhD, Certificate); higher education (Ed D, PhD); library and information science (MLIS); research methods and statistics (MA, PhD). *Accreditation:* ALA; APA (one or more programs are accredited). *Program availability:* Part-time, evening/weekend, online learning. *Faculty:* 39 full-time (29 women), 60 part-time/adjunct (42 women). *Students:* 502 full-time (406 women), 361 part-time (267 women); includes 233 minority (54 Black or African American, non-Hispanic/Latino; 6 American Indian or Alaska Native, non-Hispanic/Latino; 25 Asian, non-Hispanic/Latino; 113 Hispanic/Latino; 35 Two or more races, non-Hispanic/Latino), 52 international. Average age 31. 1,167 applicants, 64% accepted, 415 enrolled. In 2017, 285 master's, 51 doctorates, 157 other advanced degrees awarded. Terminal master's awarded for partial completion of doctoral program. *Degree requirements:* For master's, comprehensive exam; for doctorate, 2 foreign languages, comprehensive exam, thesis/dissertation. *Entrance requirements:* For master's and doctorate, GRE General Test or GMAT. Additional exam requirements/recommendations for international students: Required—TOEFL (minimum score 550 paper-based; 80 iBT). *Application deadline:* Applications are processed on a rolling basis. Application fee: $65. Electronic applications accepted. *Expenses:* $31,935 per year full-time. *Financial support:* In 2017–18, 765 students received support, including 26 research assistantships with tuition reimbursements available (averaging $10,957 per year), 38 teaching assistantships with tuition reimbursements available (averaging $3,391 per year); career-related internships or fieldwork, Federal Work-Study, institutionally sponsored loans, scholarships/grants, and unspecified assistantships also available. Support available to part-time students. Financial award application deadline: 2/15; financial award applicants required to submit FAFSA. *Faculty research:* Early childhood education, educational leadership, access and opportunity to postsecondary education, marriage and family therapy, data management and archival research. *Unit head:* Dr. Karen Riley, Dean, 303-871-3665, Fax: 303-871-4456, E-mail: karen.riley@du.edu. *Application contact:* Jodi Dye, Director of Admissions, 303-871-2510, Fax: 303-871-4456, E-mail: jodi.dye@du.edu.
Website: http://morgridge.du.edu

The University of Findlay, Office of Graduate Admissions, Findlay, OH 45840. Offers applied security and analytics (MSAS); athletic training (MAT); business (MBA), including certified management accountant, certified public accountant, health care management, hospitality management; education (MA Ed, Ed D), including children's literature (MA Ed), curriculum and teaching (MA Ed), education (MA Ed), educational administration (MA Ed), human resource development (MA Ed), mathematics (MA Ed), reading (MA Ed), science education (MA Ed), superintendent (Ed D), teaching (Ed D), technology (MA Ed); environmental, safety, and health management (MSEM); health informatics (MS); occupational therapy (MOT); pharmacy (Pharm D); physical therapy (DPT); physician assistant (MPA); rhetoric and writing (MA); teaching English to speakers of other languages (TESOL) and applied linguistics (MA). *Program availability:* Part-time, evening/weekend, 100% online, blended/hybrid learning. *Students:* 688 full-time (430 women), 553 part-time (308 women), 170 international. Average age 28. In 2017, 366 master's, 137 doctorates awarded. *Degree requirements:* For master's, comprehensive exam (for some programs), thesis (for some programs), cumulative project, capstone project; for doctorate, thesis/dissertation (for some programs). *Entrance requirements:* For master's, GRE/GMAT, bachelor's degree from accredited institution, minimum undergraduate GPA of 2.5 in last 64 hours of course work; for doctorate, GRE, MAT, minimum cumulative GPA of 3.0. Additional exam requirements/recommendations for international students: Required—TOEFL (minimum score 79 iBT), IELTS (minimum score 7), PTE (minimum score 61). *Application deadline:* Applications are processed on a rolling basis. Electronic applications accepted. *Financial support:* In 2017–18, 10 research assistantships with partial tuition reimbursements (averaging $7,200 per year), 35 teaching assistantships with partial tuition reimbursements (averaging $7,200 per year) were awarded; Federal Work-Study, institutionally sponsored loans, and unspecified assistantships also available. Financial award applicants required to submit FAFSA. *Unit head:* Christopher M. Harris, Director of Admissions, 419-434-4347, E-mail: harrisc1@findlay.edu. *Application contact:* Madeline Fauser Brennan, Graduate Admissions Counselor, 419-434-4636, Fax: 419-434-4898, E-mail: fauserbrennan@findlay.edu.
Website: http://www.findlay.edu/admissions/graduate/Pages/default.aspx

University of Florida, Graduate School, College of Education, Gainesville, FL 32611. Offers M Ed, MAE, Ed D, PhD, Ed S, PhD/JD. *Accreditation:* NCATE. *Program availability:* Part-time, evening/weekend, online learning. Terminal master's awarded for partial completion of doctoral program. *Degree requirements:* For master's, comprehensive exam (for some programs), thesis (for some programs); for doctorate, comprehensive exam (for some programs), thesis/dissertation (for some programs), capstone project. *Entrance requirements:* For master's and doctorate, GRE General Test, minimum GPA of 3.0; for Ed S, GRE General Test. Additional exam requirements/recommendations for international students: Required—TOEFL (minimum score 550 paper-based; 80 iBT), IELTS (minimum score 6). Electronic applications accepted. *Faculty research:* Early childhood, teacher education, educator professional development, learning and intervention sciences, educational leadership and policy.

University of Georgia, College of Education, Athens, GA 30602. Offers M Ed, MA, MA Ed, MAT, MS, Ed D, PhD, Ed S. *Accreditation:* NCATE. *Degree requirements:* For doctorate, thesis/dissertation. *Entrance requirements:* For doctorate, GRE General Test. Electronic applications accepted.

University of Guam, Office of Graduate Studies, School of Education, Mangilao, GU 96923. Offers M Ed, MA. *Accreditation:* NCATE. *Program availability:* Part-time. *Degree requirements:* For master's, comprehensive oral and written exams. *Entrance requirements:* For master's, GRE General Test. Additional exam requirements/recommendations for international students: Required—TOEFL. *Faculty research:* Multicultural issues, computerized student advising.

University of Hartford, College of Education, Nursing, and Health Professions, West Hartford, CT 06117-1599. Offers M Ed, MS, MSN, MSPT, Ed D, CAGS, Sixth Year Certificate. *Accreditation:* NCATE. *Program availability:* Part-time, evening/weekend. *Degree requirements:* For doctorate, thesis/dissertation; for other advanced degree, comprehensive exam or research project. *Entrance requirements:* For doctorate, MAT. Additional exam requirements/recommendations for international students: Required—TOEFL (minimum score 550 paper-based). Electronic applications accepted. *Expenses:* Contact institution.

University of Hawaii at Hilo, Program in Education, Hilo, HI 96720-4091. Offers M Ed. *Program availability:* Part-time, evening/weekend. *Entrance requirements:* Additional exam requirements/recommendations for international students: Required—TOEFL, IELTS. Electronic applications accepted.

University of Hawaii at Hilo, Program in Teaching, Hilo, HI 96720-4091. Offers MA. *Entrance requirements:* Additional exam requirements/recommendations for international students: Required—TOEFL, IELTS. Electronic applications accepted.

University of Hawaii at Manoa, Office of Graduate Education, College of Education, Honolulu, HI 96822. Offers M Ed, M Ed T, MS, Ed D, PhD, Graduate Certificate. *Accreditation:* NCATE. *Program availability:* Part-time, evening/weekend. *Entrance requirements:* Additional exam requirements/recommendations for international students: Required—TOEFL or IELTS.

University of Holy Cross, Graduate Programs, New Orleans, LA 70131-7399. Offers biomedical sciences (MS); Catholic theology (MA); counseling (MA, PhD), including community counseling (MA), marriage and family counseling (MA), school counseling (MA); educational leadership (M Ed); executive leadership (Ed D); management (MS), including healthcare management, operations management; teaching and learning (M Ed). *Accreditation:* ACA; NCATE. *Program availability:* Part-time, evening/weekend, online learning. *Faculty:* 7 full-time (4 women), 8 part-time/adjunct (3 women). *Students:* 67 full-time (55 women), 69 part-time (55 women); includes 51 minority (46 Black or African American, non-Hispanic/Latino; 2 American Indian or Alaska Native, non-Hispanic/Latino; 1 Asian, non-Hispanic/Latino; 2 Hispanic/Latino). Average age 30. 20 applicants, 50% accepted. In 2017, 28 degrees awarded. *Degree requirements:* For master's, thesis. *Entrance requirements:* For master's, GRE General Test, minimum GPA of 2.7. *Application deadline:* For fall admission, 9/1 for domestic students. Application fee: $15. *Expenses: Tuition:* Full-time $10,890; part-time $605 per credit hour. *Required fees:* $1624; $812 per semester. One-time fee: $50. *Financial support:* Federal Work-Study and tuition waivers (partial) available. Support available to part-time students. Financial award application deadline: 6/1. *Unit head:* Dr. Myles Seghers, Dean of Humanities, Education, and Counseling, 504-394-7744 Ext. 214, Fax: 504-391-2421, E-mail: mseghers@olhcc.edu. *Application contact:* Anne-Katherine Lene, Director of Student Enrollment, 504-394-7744 Ext. 110, Fax: 504-391-2421, E-mail: aklene@olhcc.edu.

University of Houston, College of Education, Houston, TX 77204. Offers M Ed, Ed D, PhD. *Accreditation:* NCATE. *Program availability:* Part-time. *Degree requirements:* For master's, comprehensive exam or thesis; for doctorate, comprehensive exam, thesis/dissertation. *Entrance requirements:* For master's, GRE General Test, transcripts, 3 letters of recommendation, curriculum vita, goal statement; for doctorate, GRE General Test, transcripts, 3 letters of recommendation, curriculum vita, goal statement, writing sample, interview. Additional exam requirements/recommendations for international students: Required—TOEFL (minimum score 550 paper-based). Electronic applications accepted.

University of Houston–Clear Lake, School of Education, Houston, TX 77058-1002. Offers MS, Ed D. *Accreditation:* NCATE. *Program availability:* Part-time, evening/weekend. *Degree requirements:* For master's, thesis optional; for doctorate, comprehensive exam, thesis/dissertation. *Entrance requirements:* For master's, GRE or minimum GPA of 3.0 in last 60 hours; for doctorate, GRE, master's degree, letters of reference. Additional exam requirements/recommendations for international students: Required—TOEFL (minimum score 550 paper-based). Electronic applications accepted.

University of Houston–Victoria, School of Education, Health Professions and Human Development, Victoria, TX 77901-4450. Offers administration and supervision (M Ed); adult and higher education (M Ed); counselor education (M Ed); curriculum and instruction (M Ed); dyslexia education (Certificate); educational technology (M Ed); special education (M Ed). *Program availability:* Part-time, evening/weekend, online learning. *Degree requirements:* For master's, comprehensive exam, project or thesis. *Entrance requirements:* For master's, GRE General Test. Additional exam requirements/recommendations for international students: Required—TOEFL. Electronic applications accepted. *Faculty research:* Reading and language arts education, evaluation and diagnosis of special children's abilities.

University of Idaho, College of Graduate Studies, College of Education, Health and Human Sciences, Moscow, ID 83844. Offers M Ed, MS, MSAT, DAT, Ed D, PhD, Ed S. *Accreditation:* NCATE. *Faculty:* 61 full-time, 9 part-time/adjunct. *Students:* 164 full-time (94 women), 248 part-time (150 women). Average age 35. In 2017, 119 master's, 7 doctorates, 49 other advanced degrees awarded. *Degree requirements:* For doctorate, thesis/dissertation. *Entrance requirements:* For master's, minimum GPA of 3.0. Additional exam requirements/recommendations for international students: Required—TOEFL. *Application deadline:* For fall admission, 8/1 for domestic students; for spring admission, 12/15 for domestic students. Applications are processed on a rolling basis. Application fee: $60. Electronic applications accepted. *Expenses: Tuition,* state resident: full-time $6722; part-time $430 per credit hour. Tuition, nonresident: full-time $23,046; part-time $1337 per credit hour. *Required fees:* $2142; $63 per credit hour. *Financial support:* Teaching assistantships and Federal Work-Study available. Support available to part-time students. Financial award applicants required to submit FAFSA. *Faculty research:* Technology integration, curricular development for cooperative environments, increasing science literacy, best practices for online pedagogy. *Unit head:* Dr. Alison Carr-Chellman, Dean, 208-885-6772, E-mail: coe@uidaho.edu. *Application contact:* Sean Scoggin, Graduate Recruitment Coordinator, 208-885-4001, Fax: 208-885-4406, E-mail: graduateadmissions@uidaho.edu.
Website: http://www.uidaho.edu/ed/

University of Illinois at Chicago, College of Education, Chicago, IL 60607-7128. Offers M Ed, Ed D, PhD. *Program availability:* Part-time, evening/weekend. Terminal master's awarded for partial completion of doctoral program. *Degree requirements:* For doctorate, thesis/dissertation. *Entrance requirements:* For master's, minimum GPA of 2.75; for doctorate, GRE General Test, minimum GPA of 2.75. Additional exam requirements/recommendations for international students: Required—TOEFL. Electronic applications accepted. *Faculty research:* Teaching and learning, program design, school and classroom organization with emphasis on urban settings.

University of Illinois at Springfield, Graduate Programs, College of Education and Human Services, Springfield, IL 62703-5407. Offers MA, CAS, Certificate, Graduate Certificate. *Program availability:* Part-time, evening/weekend, 100% online, blended/hybrid learning. *Faculty:* 15 full-time (10 women), 16 part-time/adjunct (13 women). *Students:* 68 full-time (58 women), 222 part-time (167 women); includes 68 minority (44 Black or African American, non-Hispanic/Latino; 1 American Indian or Alaska Native, non-Hispanic/Latino; 1 Asian, non-Hispanic/Latino; 15 Hispanic/Latino; 7 Two or more races, non-Hispanic/Latino), 2 international. Average age 33. 145 applicants, 50% accepted, 65 enrolled. In 2017, 70 master's, 6 other advanced degrees awarded. *Entrance requirements:* Additional exam requirements/recommendations for international students: Required—TOEFL (minimum score 500 paper-based; 61 iBT). *Application deadline:* Applications are processed on a rolling basis. Application fee: $60 ($75 for international students). Electronic applications accepted. *Expenses: Tuition,* state resident: full-time $7896; part-time $329 per credit hour. Tuition, nonresident: full-time $16,200; part-time $675 per credit hour. Tuition and fees vary according to

program. *Financial support:* In 2017–18, research assistantships with full tuition reimbursements (averaging $10,249 per year), teaching assistantships with full tuition reimbursements (averaging $10,303 per year) were awarded; fellowships, career-related internships or fieldwork, Federal Work-Study, scholarships/grants, health care benefits, and unspecified assistantships also available. Support available to part-time students. Financial award application deadline: 11/15; financial award applicants required to submit FAFSA. *Unit head:* Dr. Hanfu Mi, Dean, 217-206-6784, Fax: 217-206-6775, E-mail: hmi2@uis.edu.

University of Illinois at Urbana–Champaign, Graduate College, College of Education, Champaign, IL 61820. Offers Ed M, MA, MS, Ed D, PhD, CAS. *Program availability:* Part-time, online learning.

University of Indianapolis, Graduate Programs, School of Education, Indianapolis, IN 46227-3697. Offers art education (MAT); biology (MAT); chemistry (MAT); curriculum and instruction (MA); earth sciences (MAT); education (MA, MAT); educational leadership (MA); elementary education (MA); English (MAT); French (MAT); math (MAT); physical education (MAT); physics (MAT); secondary education (MA), including art education, education, English education, social studies education; social studies (MAT); Spanish (MAT). *Accreditation:* NCATE. *Program availability:* Part-time, evening/weekend. *Entrance requirements:* For master's, GRE Subject Test, PRAXIS I, minimum GPA of 2.5, 3 letters of recommendation, interview. Additional exam requirements/recommendations for international students: Required—TOEFL (minimum score 550 paper-based). *Faculty research:* Assessment of teacher education, perceptions of prospective teachers by parents.

The University of Iowa, Graduate College, College of Education, Iowa City, IA 52242-1316. Offers MA, MAT, MM, PhD, Ed S. *Degree requirements:* For master's and Ed S, exam; for doctorate, comprehensive exam, thesis/dissertation. *Entrance requirements:* For master's, doctorate, and Ed S, GRE General Test, minimum GPA of 3.0. Additional exam requirements/recommendations for international students: Required—TOEFL (minimum score 550 paper-based; 81 iBT). Electronic applications accepted. *Faculty research:* Computer-assisted instrumentation, testing and measurement, instructional design.

University of Jamestown, Program in Education, Jamestown, ND 58405. Offers curriculum and instruction (M Ed). *Degree requirements:* For master's, thesis or project.

The University of Kansas, Graduate Studies, School of Education, Lawrence, KS 66045-3101. Offers MA, MS, MS Ed, MSE, Ed D, PhD, Certificate, Ed S. *Accreditation:* NCATE. *Program availability:* Part-time, online learning. *Students:* 503 full-time (326 women), 839 part-time (671 women); includes 212 minority (76 Black or African American, non-Hispanic/Latino; 11 American Indian or Alaska Native, non-Hispanic/Latino; 31 Asian, non-Hispanic/Latino; 43 Hispanic/Latino; 1 Native Hawaiian or other Pacific Islander, non-Hispanic/Latino; 50 Two or more races, non-Hispanic/Latino), 103 international. Average age 33. 907 applicants, 69% accepted, 450 enrolled. In 2017, 388 master's, 59 doctorates, 78 other advanced degrees awarded. *Entrance requirements:* For master's and other advanced degree, minimum GPA of 3.0; for doctorate, GRE General Test. Application fee: $65 ($85 for international students). Electronic applications accepted. *Financial support:* Fellowships, research assistantships, teaching assistantships, career-related internships or fieldwork, scholarships/grants, and unspecified assistantships available. Financial award application deadline: 2/1. *Unit head:* Dr. Rick J. Ginsberg, Dean, 785-864-3726, E-mail: ginsberg@ku.edu. *Application contact:* Kim Huggett, Graduate Student Services Manager, 785-864-4510, E-mail: khuggett@ku.edu.
Website: http://www.soe.ku.edu/

University of Kentucky, Graduate School, College of Education, Lexington, KY 40506-0032. Offers M Ed, MA Ed, MRC, MS Ed, Ed D, PhD, Ed S. *Accreditation:* NCATE. *Program availability:* Part-time, evening/weekend. Terminal master's awarded for partial completion of doctoral program. *Degree requirements:* For master's and Ed S, comprehensive exam; for doctorate, comprehensive exam, thesis/dissertation. *Entrance requirements:* For master's, GRE General Test, minimum undergraduate GPA of 2.75; for doctorate, GRE General Test, minimum graduate GPA of 3.0; for Ed S, GRE General Test. Additional exam requirements/recommendations for international students: Required—TOEFL (minimum score 550 paper-based). Electronic applications accepted.

University of La Verne, LaFetra College of Education, Credential Program in Teacher Education, La Verne, CA 91750-4443. Offers multiple subject (Credential); single subject (Credential); teaching (Credential). *Accreditation:* NCATE. *Program availability:* Part-time. *Faculty:* 13 full-time (9 women), 9 part-time/adjunct (8 women). *Students:* 18 full-time (13 women), 142 part-time (103 women); includes 91 minority (5 Black or African American, non-Hispanic/Latino; 1 American Indian or Alaska Native, non-Hispanic/Latino; 5 Asian, non-Hispanic/Latino; 73 Hispanic/Latino; 1 Native Hawaiian or other Pacific Islander, non-Hispanic/Latino; 6 Two or more races, non-Hispanic/Latino), 1 international. Average age 32. *Entrance requirements:* For degree, California Basic Educational Skills Test, minimum GPA of 3.0, interview, writing sample. Additional exam requirements/recommendations for international students: Required—TOEFL (minimum score 550 paper-based). *Application deadline:* Applications are processed on a rolling basis. Application fee: $50. *Expenses:* Contact institution. *Financial support:* Federal Work-Study, institutionally sponsored loans, and scholarships/grants available. Financial award application deadline: 3/2; financial award applicants required to submit FAFSA. *Unit head:* Dr. Jessica Decker, Assistant Professor, 909-448-4582, E-mail: jdecker@laverne.edu. *Application contact:* Christy Ranells, Associate Director of Graduate Admission, 909-448-4644, Fax: 909-971-2295, E-mail: cranells@laverne.edu.
Website: https://education.laverne.edu/certificates/

University of La Verne, LaFetra College of Education, Master of Arts in Teaching Program, La Verne, CA 91750-4443. Offers MA. *Faculty:* 13 full-time (9 women), 9 part-time/adjunct (8 women). *Students:* 21 part-time (18 women); includes 13 minority (1 Black or African American, non-Hispanic/Latino; 12 Hispanic/Latino). Average age 28. *Entrance requirements:* Additional exam requirements/recommendations for international students: Required—TOEFL (minimum score 550 paper-based; 80 iBT), IELTS (minimum score 6.5). *Application deadline:* Applications are processed on a rolling basis. Application fee: $50. Electronic applications accepted. Tuition and fees vary according to program. *Financial support:* Federal Work-Study, institutionally sponsored loans, and scholarships/grants available. Financial award application deadline: 3/2; financial award applicants required to submit FAFSA. *Unit head:* Dr. Kimberly White-Smith, Dean of LaFetra College of Education, 909-448-4583, E-mail: kwhite-smith@laverne.edu. *Application contact:* Christy Ranells, Associate Director of Graduate Admission, 909-448-4644, Fax: 909-971-2295, E-mail: cranells@laverne.edu.
Website: https://education.laverne.edu/teaching/

University of La Verne, LaFetra College of Education, Master's Program in Education, La Verne, CA 91750-4443. Offers advanced teaching skills (M Ed); education (M Ed); educational leadership (M Ed); special emphasis (M Ed). *Accreditation:* NCATE. *Program availability:* Part-time. *Students:* 35 full-time (23 women), 149 part-time (111 women); includes 92 minority (5 Black or African American, non-Hispanic/Latino; 2 American Indian or Alaska Native, non-Hispanic/Latino; 3 Asian, non-Hispanic/Latino; 78 Hispanic/Latino; 4 Two or more races, non-Hispanic/Latino). Average age 32. *Entrance requirements:* For master's, California Basic Educational Skills Test, interview,

Education—General

writing sample, minimum GPA of 3.0, 3 letters of recommendation. Additional exam requirements/recommendations for international students: Required—TOEFL (minimum score 550 paper-based). *Application deadline:* Applications are processed on a rolling basis. Application fee: $50. *Expenses:* Contact institution. *Financial support:* Institutionally sponsored loans and scholarships/grants available. Financial award application deadline: 3/2; financial award applicants required to submit FAFSA. *Unit head:* Dr. Jessica Decker, Chair, 909-448-4582, E-mail: jdecker@laverne.edu. *Application contact:* Christy Ranells, Associate Director of Graduate Admission, 909-448-4644, Fax: 909-392-2744, E-mail: cranells@laverne.edu. Website: https://education.laverne.edu/leadership/

University of La Verne, Regional and Online Campuses, Graduate Credential Program in Education, California Statewide Campus, La Verne, CA 91750-4443. Offers administration services (preliminary) (Credential); education specialist: mild/moderate (Credential); English (Certificate); multiple subject teaching (Credential); pupil personnel services: school counseling (Credential); single subject teaching (Credential); special education (MS); special emphasis (M Ed). *Accreditation:* NCATE. *Program availability:* Part-time. *Faculty:* 3 full-time (2 women), 25 part-time/adjunct (19 women). *Students:* 120 full-time (95 women), 62 part-time (47 women); includes 47 minority (3 Black or African American, non-Hispanic/Latino; 2 American Indian or Alaska Native, non-Hispanic/Latino; 2 Asian, non-Hispanic/Latino; 40 Hispanic/Latino). Average age 31. In 2017, 25 master's, 61 other advanced degrees awarded. *Entrance requirements:* For degree, California Basic Educational Skills Test, minimum undergraduate GPA of 2.75, 3 letters of recommendation, interview. *Application deadline:* Applications are processed on a rolling basis. Application fee: $50. *Expenses:* Contact institution. *Financial support:* Application deadline: 3/2; applicants required to submit FAFSA. *Unit head:* Pam Bergovoy, Assistant Dean, Regional and Online Campuses/Director, Center for Educators, 909-448-4953, E-mail: pbergovoy@laverne.edu. *Application contact:* 877-468-6858, E-mail: gradadmission@laverne.edu. Website: https://laverne.edu/locations/

University of La Verne, Regional and Online Campuses, Master's Programs in Education, California Statewide Campus, La Verne, CA 91750-4443. Offers administration services (preliminary) (Credential); education specialist: mild/moderate (Credential); educational counseling (MS); educational leadership (M Ed); multiple subject teaching (Credential); pupil personnel services: school counseling (Credential); single subject teaching (Credential); special education studies (MS); special emphasis (M Ed). *Accreditation:* NCATE. *Students:* 106 full-time (88 women), 75 part-time (55 women); includes 112 minority (4 Black or African American, non-Hispanic/Latino; 5 Asian, non-Hispanic/Latino; 102 Hispanic/Latino; 1 Two or more races, non-Hispanic/Latino). Average age 35. In 2017, 76 master's, 82 other advanced degrees awarded. *Entrance requirements:* For master's, California Basic Educational Skills Test, 3 letters of recommendation, teaching credential. *Application deadline:* Applications are processed on a rolling basis. Application fee: $50. *Expenses:* Contact institution. *Financial support:* Application deadline: 3/2; applicants required to submit FAFSA. *Unit head:* Pam Bergovoy, Assistant Dean, Regional and Online Campuses/Director, Center for Educators, 909-448-4953, E-mail: pbergovoy@laverne.edu. *Application contact:* 877-468-6858, E-mail: gradadmission@laverne.edu. Website: http://www.laverne.edu/locations

University of Lethbridge, School of Graduate Studies, Lethbridge, AB T1K 3M4, Canada. Offers addictions counseling (M Sc); agricultural biotechnology (M Sc); agricultural studies (M Sc, MA); anthropology (MA); archaeology (M Sc, MA); art (MA, MFA); biochemistry (M Sc); biological sciences (M Sc); biomolecular science (PhD); biosystems and biodiversity (PhD); Canadian studies (MA); chemistry (M Sc); computer science (M Sc); computer science and geographical information science (M Sc); counseling (MC); counseling psychology (M Ed); dramatic arts (MA); earth, space, and physical science (PhD); economics (MA); education (MA, PhD); educational leadership (M Ed); English (MA); environmental science (M Sc); evolution and behavior (PhD); exercise science (M Sc); French (MA); French/German (MA); French/Spanish (MA); general education (M Ed); geography (MA); German (MA); health sciences (M Sc); individualized multidisciplinary (M Sc, MA); kinesiology (M Sc, MA); management (M Sc), including accounting, finance, human resource management and labor relations, information systems, international management, marketing, policy and strategy; mathematics (M Sc); music (M Mus, MA); Native American studies (MA); neuroscience (M Sc, PhD); new media (MA, MFA); nursing (M Sc, MN); philosophy (MA); physics (M Sc); political science (MA); psychology (M Sc, MA); religious studies (MA); sociology (MA); theatre and dramatic arts (MFA); theoretical and computational science (PhD); urban and regional studies (MA); women and gender studies (MA). *Program availability:* Part-time, evening/weekend. *Degree requirements:* For master's, thesis (for some programs); for doctorate, comprehensive exam, thesis/dissertation. *Entrance requirements:* For master's, GMAT (for M Sc in management), bachelor's degree in related field, minimum GPA of 3.0 during previous 20 graded semester courses, 2 years' teaching or related experience (M Ed); for doctorate, master's degree, minimum graduate GPA of 3.5. Additional exam requirements/recommendations for international students: Required—TOEFL (minimum score 580 paper-based; 93 iBT). Electronic applications accepted. *Faculty research:* Movement and brain plasticity, gibberellin physiology, photosynthesis, carbon cycling, molecular properties of main-group ring components.

University of Louisiana at Lafayette, College of Education, Lafayette, LA 70504. Offers M Ed, Ed D. *Accreditation:* NCATE. *Program availability:* Part-time. *Degree requirements:* For master's, thesis or alternative. *Entrance requirements:* For master's, GRE General Test, teaching certificate. Additional exam requirements/recommendations for international students: Required—TOEFL (minimum score 550 paper-based). Electronic applications accepted.

University of Louisiana at Monroe, Graduate School, College of Arts, Education, and Sciences, School of Education, Monroe, LA 71209-0001. Offers curriculum and instruction (M Ed, Ed D), including curriculum and instruction; elementary education (MAT); secondary education (MAT); special education (MAT). *Accreditation:* NCATE. *Program availability:* Part-time, evening/weekend, online learning. *Faculty:* 11 full-time (7 women). *Students:* 35 full-time (25 women), 137 part-time (105 women); includes 50 minority (42 Black or African American, non-Hispanic/Latino; 1 Asian, non-Hispanic/Latino; 4 Hispanic/Latino; 3 Two or more races, non-Hispanic/Latino), 2 international. Average age 34. 133 applicants, 57% accepted, 55 enrolled. In 2017, 63 master's, 9 doctorates awarded. *Degree requirements:* For master's, thesis; for doctorate, comprehensive exam, thesis/dissertation. *Entrance requirements:* For master's, GRE General Test, PRAXIS, minimum GPA of 2.5; for doctorate, GRE General Test, minimum undergraduate GPA of 2.75, 3.25 graduate; 3 letters of recommendation; interview. Additional exam requirements/recommendations for international students: Required—TOEFL (minimum score 500 paper-based; 61 iBT). *Application deadline:* For fall admission, 8/24 priority date for domestic students, 7/1 for international students; for winter admission, 12/14 priority date for domestic students; for spring admission, 1/19 for domestic students, 11/1 for international students. Applications are processed on a rolling basis. Application fee: $20 ($30 for international students). Electronic applications accepted. *Expenses:* Tuition, state resident: full-time $6489; part-time $479 per hour.

Tuition, nonresident: full-time $12,100; part-time $479 per hour. *Required fees:* $8860; $802 per hour. $3273 per semester. *Financial support:* In 2017–18, 27 students received support. Research assistantships, career-related internships or fieldwork, Federal Work-Study, and unspecified assistantships available. Financial award application deadline: 4/1; financial award applicants required to submit FAFSA. Website: http://www.ulm.edu/education/index.html

University of Louisville, Graduate School, College of Education and Human Development, Louisville, KY 40292-0001. Offers M Ed, MA, MAT, MS, Ed D, PhD, Certificate, Ed S. *Accreditation:* NCATE. *Program availability:* Part-time, evening/weekend, 100% online, blended/hybrid learning. *Faculty:* 106 full-time (71 women), 71 part-time/adjunct (48 women). *Students:* 477 full-time (250 women), 717 part-time (431 women); includes 318 minority (184 Black or African American, non-Hispanic/Latino; 2 American Indian or Alaska Native, non-Hispanic/Latino; 23 Asian, non-Hispanic/Latino; 68 Hispanic/Latino; 2 Native Hawaiian or other Pacific Islander, non-Hispanic/Latino; 39 Two or more races, non-Hispanic/Latino), 14 international. Average age 32. 588 applicants, 70% accepted, 269 enrolled. In 2017, 194 master's, 7 doctorates, 19 other advanced degrees awarded. Terminal master's awarded for partial completion of doctoral program. *Degree requirements:* For master's, comprehensive exam (for some programs), thesis optional; for doctorate, comprehensive exam (for some programs), thesis/dissertation. *Entrance requirements:* For master's, GRE (for most programs); PRAXIS (for educator preparation programs), professional statement, recommendation letters, resume, transcripts; for doctorate and other advanced degree, GRE, professional statement, recommendation letters, resume, transcripts. Additional exam requirements/recommendations for international students: Required—TOEFL (minimum score 550 paper-based; 79 iBT); Recommended—IELTS (minimum score 6.5). *Application deadline:* For fall admission, 6/1 priority date for domestic students; for spring admission, 10/1 priority date for domestic students; for summer admission, 3/1 priority date for domestic students. Application fee: $65. *Expenses:* Tuition, state resident: full-time $12,246; part-time $681 per credit hour. Tuition, nonresident: full-time $25,486; part-time $1417 per credit hour. *Required fees:* $196. Tuition and fees vary according to course load, program and reciprocity agreements. *Financial support:* In 2017–18, 8 fellowships with full tuition reimbursements (averaging $20,694 per year), 34 research assistantships with full tuition reimbursements (averaging $20,694 per year), 13 teaching assistantships with full tuition reimbursements (averaging $20,694 per year) were awarded; Federal Work-Study, scholarships/grants, health care benefits, and unspecified assistantships also available. Financial award application deadline: 3/1; financial award applicants required to submit FAFSA. *Faculty research:* Teacher preparation and P-12 school partnerships, behavioral and psychological intervention and supports in P-20 settings, teacher capacities in effective STEM instruction and assessment, understanding workplace systems and cultures, health and sport sciences. *Total annual research expenditures:* $4.6 million. *Unit head:* Dr. Ann A. Larson, Dean, College of Education and Human Development, 502-852-6411, Fax: 502-852-1464, E-mail: cehdinfo@louisville.edu. *Application contact:* Betty Hampton, Director, Graduate Student Services, 502-852-0411, Fax: 502-852-1465, E-mail: edadvise@louisville.edu. Website: http://www.louisville.edu/education

University of Maine, Graduate School, College of Education and Human Development, Orono, ME 04469. Offers M Ed, MA, MAT, MS, Ed D, PhD, CAS, CGS. *Accreditation:* NCATE. *Program availability:* Part-time, evening/weekend. *Faculty:* 35 full-time (19 women), 47 part-time/adjunct (34 women). *Students:* 136 full-time (107 women), 258 part-time (214 women); includes 29 minority (3 Black or African American, non-Hispanic/Latino; 11 American Indian or Alaska Native, non-Hispanic/Latino; 3 Asian, non-Hispanic/Latino; 7 Hispanic/Latino; 5 Two or more races, non-Hispanic/Latino), 4 international. Average age 37. 230 applicants, 89% accepted, 125 enrolled. In 2017, 110 master's, 7 doctorates, 52 other advanced degrees awarded. Terminal master's awarded for partial completion of doctoral program. *Degree requirements:* For master's, thesis (for some programs); for doctorate, comprehensive exam, thesis/dissertation. *Entrance requirements:* For master's, GRE General Test, MAT; for doctorate, GRE General Test; for other advanced degree, MA, M Ed, or MS. Additional exam requirements/recommendations for international students: Required—TOEFL (minimum score 550 paper-based; 80 iBT), IELTS (minimum score 6.5). *Application deadline:* For fall admission, 1/15 priority date for domestic students. Applications are processed on a rolling basis. Application fee: $65. Electronic applications accepted. *Expenses:* Tuition, state resident: full-time $7722; part-time $429 per credit hour. Tuition, nonresident: full-time $25,146; part-time $1397 per credit hour. *Required fees:* $1162; $581 per credit hour. *Financial support:* In 2017–18, 51 students received support, including 22 teaching assistantships with full tuition reimbursements available (averaging $15,200 per year); career-related internships or fieldwork, Federal Work-Study, institutionally sponsored loans, scholarships/grants, and unspecified assistantships also available. Support available to part-time students. Financial award application deadline: 3/1. *Faculty research:* Student hazing and hazing prevention epidemiology and birth defects prevention theories of science thinking and learning using writing to improve performance in athletics rural poverty and education. *Total annual research expenditures:* $5 million. *Unit head:* Dr. Timothy Reagan, Dean, 207-581-2441, Fax: 207-581-2423. *Application contact:* Scott G. Delcourt, Senior Associate Dean of the Graduate School, 207-581-3291, Fax: 207-581-3232, E-mail: graduate@maine.edu. Website: http://umaine.edu/edhd/

University of Maine at Farmington, Graduate Programs in Education, Farmington, ME 04938. Offers early childhood education (MS Ed); educational leadership (MS Ed); instructional technology (M Ed). M Ed offered in collaboration with University of Maine and University of Southern Maine. *Accreditation:* NCATE. *Program availability:* Part-time-only, evening/weekend, 100% online, blended/hybrid learning. *Faculty:* 8 full-time (7 women), 2 part-time/adjunct (1 woman). *Students:* 106 part-time (92 women). Average age 36. 6 applicants, 100% accepted, 6 enrolled. In 2017, 29 master's awarded. *Degree requirements:* For master's, thesis, capstone research project. *Entrance requirements:* For master's, baccalaureate degree from accredited institution, valid teaching certificate or professional experience in education. Additional exam requirements/recommendations for international students: Required—TOEFL. *Application deadline:* For fall admission, 8/10 for domestic students; for spring admission, 1/5 for domestic students; for summer admission, 4/10 for domestic students. Applications are processed on a rolling basis. Application fee: $60. Electronic applications accepted. *Expenses:* Contact institution. *Financial support:* Applicants required to submit FAFSA. *Faculty research:* Teacher leadership, school improvement strategies, technology integration. *Unit head:* Dr. Johanna Prince, Director of Graduate Programs in Education, 207-778-7066, E-mail: gradstudies@maine.edu. *Application contact:* Valerie Soucie, Administrative Specialist, 207-778-7502, Fax: 207-778-8134, E-mail: gradstudies@maine.edu. Website: http://www2.umf.maine.edu/gradstudies/

The University of Manchester, School of Education, Manchester, United Kingdom. Offers counseling (D Couns); counseling psychology (D Couns); education (M Phil, Ed D, PhD); educational and child psychology (Ed D); educational psychology (Ed D).

University of Manitoba, Faculty of Graduate Studies, College Universitaire de Saint Boniface, Education Program, Winnipeg, MB R3T 2N2, Canada. Offers M Ed.

University of Manitoba, Faculty of Graduate Studies, Faculty of Education, Winnipeg, MB R3T 2N2, Canada. Offers M Ed, PhD. *Degree requirements:* For master's, thesis or alternative.

University of Mary, Liffrig Family School of Education and Behavioral Sciences, Department of Education, Bismarck, ND 58504-9652. Offers curriculum, instruction and assessment (M Ed); education (Ed D); elementary administration (M Ed); reading (M Ed); secondary administration (M Ed); special education strategist (M Ed). *Program availability:* Part-time. *Degree requirements:* For master's, portfolio or thesis. *Entrance requirements:* For master's, interview, letters of reference, minimum GPA of 2.5. Additional exam requirements/recommendations for international students: Required—TOEFL (minimum score 500 paper-based; 71 iBT). Electronic applications accepted.

University of Mary Hardin-Baylor, Graduate Studies in Education, Belton, TX 76513. Offers curriculum and instruction (M Ed); educational administration (M Ed, Ed D), including higher education (Ed D), leadership in nursing education (Ed D), P-12 (Ed D). *Program availability:* Part-time, evening/weekend. *Faculty:* 12 full-time (8 women), 5 part-time/adjunct (2 women). *Students:* 29 full-time (20 women), 79 part-time (55 women); includes 53 minority (35 Black or African American, non-Hispanic/Latino; 17 Hispanic/Latino; 1 Two or more races, non-Hispanic/Latino), 1 international. Average age 39. 15 applicants, 80% accepted, 10 enrolled. In 2017, 47 master's, 16 doctorates awarded. *Degree requirements:* For master's, comprehensive exam; for doctorate, thesis/dissertation. *Entrance requirements:* For master's, minimum GPA of 3.0, interview; for doctorate, minimum GPA of 3.5, interview, essay, resume, employment verification, 3 letters of recommendation. Additional exam requirements/recommendations for international students: Required—TOEFL (minimum score 60 iBT), IELTS (minimum score 4.5). *Application deadline:* For fall admission, 6/1 for domestic students, 4/30 priority date for international students; for spring admission, 11/1 for domestic students, 9/30 priority date for international students. Applications are processed on a rolling basis. Application fee: $35 ($135 for international students). Electronic applications accepted. *Expenses:* $920 per credit hour. *Financial support:* In 2017–18, 90 students received support. Federal Work-Study and scholarships for some active duty military personnel available. Support available to part-time students. Financial award application deadline: 6/1; financial award applicants required to submit FAFSA. *Faculty research:* Motivational orientation of preservice teachers. *Unit head:* Dr. Craig Hammonds, Director, Graduate Programs in Education, 254-295-4189, E-mail: rhammonds@umhb.edu. *Application contact:* Sharon Aguilera, Assistant Director, Graduate Admissions, 254-295-4835, E-mail: saguilera@umhb.edu. Website: https://go.umhb.edu/graduate/education/home

University of Maryland, Baltimore County, The Graduate School, College of Arts, Humanities and Social Sciences, Department of Education, Baltimore, MD 21250. Offers education (MAE, MAE), including K-8 mathematics instructional leadership (MAE), K-8 science education (MAE), K-8 STEM education (MAE), secondary science education (MAE), secondary STEM education (MAE); instructional systems development (MA, Graduate Certificate), including distance education (Graduate Certificate), instructional systems development, instructional technology (Graduate Certificate); teaching (MAT), including early childhood education, elementary education, teaching; teaching English to speakers of other languages (MA, Postbaccalaureate Certificate). *Accreditation:* NCATE. *Program availability:* Part-time, evening/weekend, online learning. *Faculty:* 21 full-time (15 women), 25 part-time/adjunct (19 women). *Students:* 71 full-time (52 women), 339 part-time (251 women); includes 99 minority (62 Black or African American, non-Hispanic/Latino; 1 American Indian or Alaska Native, non-Hispanic/Latino; 17 Asian, non-Hispanic/Latino; 15 Hispanic/Latino; 1 Native Hawaiian or other Pacific Islander, non-Hispanic/Latino; 3 Two or more races, non-Hispanic/Latino), 9 international. Average age 34. 90 applicants, 94% accepted, 80 enrolled. In 2017, 60 master's awarded. *Degree requirements:* For master's, comprehensive exam (for some programs), thesis (for some programs). *Entrance requirements:* For master's, GRE General Test, GRE Subject Test (for MA in TESOL); PRAXIS Core Examination or GRE with minimum score of 1000 (for MAT); PRAXIS II (for MAE), minimum GPA of 3.0. Additional exam requirements/recommendations for international students: Required—TOEFL. *Application deadline:* For fall admission, 6/1 for domestic and international students; for spring admission, 11/1 for domestic students, 6/1 for international students. Applications are processed on a rolling basis. Application fee: $50. Electronic applications accepted. *Expenses: Required fees:* $132. *Financial support:* In 2017–18, 12 students received support, including teaching assistantships with full tuition reimbursements available (averaging $12,000 per year); fellowships, career-related internships or fieldwork, Federal Work-Study, scholarships/grants, tuition waivers (partial), and unspecified assistantships also available. Financial award application deadline: 3/1. *Faculty research:* Teacher leadership; STEM education; ESOL/bilingual education; early childhood education; language, literacy and culture. *Total annual research expenditures:* $100,000. *Unit head:* Dr. Jon Singer, Department Chair, 410-455-2466, Fax: 410-455-3986, E-mail: jsinger@umbc.edu. *Application contact:* Dr. Susan M. Blunck, Graduate Program Director, 410-455-2869, Fax: 410-455-3986, E-mail: blunck@umbc.edu.
Website: http://www.umbc.edu/education/

University of Maryland, College Park, Academic Affairs, College of Education, College Park, MD 20742. Offers M Ed, MA, Ed D, PhD, AGSC, CAGS. *Accreditation:* NCATE. *Program availability:* Part-time, evening/weekend, online learning. *Degree requirements:* For doctorate, thesis/dissertation. *Entrance requirements:* For master's, GRE General Test or MAT, minimum GPA of 3.0. Electronic applications accepted.

University of Maryland Eastern Shore, Graduate Programs, Department of Education, Program in Teaching, Princess Anne, MD 21853. Offers MAT. Program offered jointly with Salisbury University. *Accreditation:* NCATE. *Degree requirements:* For master's, comprehensive exam, internship, seminar paper, PRAXIS II. *Entrance requirements:* For master's, PRAXIS I, interview, minimum GPA of 3.0, writing sample. Additional exam requirements/recommendations for international students: Required—TOEFL (minimum score 80 iBT). Electronic applications accepted.

University of Maryland University College, The Graduate School, Master of Arts in Teaching Program, Adelphi, MD 20783. Offers MAT. *Program availability:* Part-time, evening/weekend. *Students:* 8 full-time (5 women), 101 part-time (60 women); includes 29 minority (14 Black or African American, non-Hispanic/Latino; 7 Asian, non-Hispanic/Latino; 6 Hispanic/Latino; 2 Two or more races, non-Hispanic/Latino), 1 international. Average age 34. 64 applicants, 100% accepted, 26 enrolled. In 2017, 43 master's awarded. *Degree requirements:* For master's, comprehensive exam, thesis or alternative. *Application deadline:* Applications are processed on a rolling basis. Application fee: $50. Electronic applications accepted. *Financial support:* Federal Work-Study and scholarships/grants available. Support available to part-time students. Financial award application deadline: 6/1; financial award applicants required to submit FAFSA. *Unit head:* Dr. Warna Gillies, Program Chair, 240-684-2400, Fax: 240-684-2401, E-mail: warna.gillies@umuc.edu. *Application contact:* Coordinator, Graduate Admissions, 800-888-8682, Fax: 240-684-2151, E-mail: newgrad@umuc.edu. Website: http://www.umuc.edu/academic-programs/masters-degrees/teaching.cfm

University of Mary Washington, College of Education, Fredericksburg, VA 22401. Offers education (M Ed); elementary education (MS). *Program availability:* Part-time, evening/weekend. *Degree requirements:* For master's, one foreign language,

comprehensive exam (for some programs). *Entrance requirements:* For master's, PRAXIS Core Academic Skills for Educators (Reading; Writing; Math or Virginia Department of Education accepted equivalent). Additional exam requirements/recommendations for international students: Required—TOEFL (minimum score 570 paper-based; 88 iBT), IELTS (minimum score 6.5). Electronic applications accepted. Application fee is waived when completed online. *Expenses:* Contact institution.

University of Massachusetts Amherst, Graduate School, College of Education, Amherst, MA 01003. Offers M Ed, Ed D, PhD, Ed S. *Accreditation:* NCATE. *Program availability:* Part-time, online learning. Terminal master's awarded for partial completion of doctoral program. *Degree requirements:* For doctorate, comprehensive exam, thesis/dissertation. *Entrance requirements:* Additional exam requirements/recommendations for international students: Required—TOEFL (minimum score 550 paper-based; 80 iBT), IELTS (minimum score 6.5). Electronic applications accepted.

University of Massachusetts Boston, College of Education and Human Development, Boston, MA 02125-3393. Offers M Ed, MS, Ed D, PhD, CAGS. *Program availability:* Part-time, evening/weekend. *Faculty:* 56 full-time (40 women), 43 part-time/adjunct (26 women). *Students:* 350 full-time (269 women), 425 part-time (302 women); includes 21 minority (10 Black or African American, non-Hispanic/Latino; 6 Asian, non-Hispanic/Latino; 5 Hispanic/Latino), 1 international. Average age 33. 779 applicants, 56% accepted, 300 enrolled. In 2017, 306 master's, 17 doctorates, 139 other advanced degrees awarded. *Degree requirements:* For master's, comprehensive exam; for doctorate, comprehensive exam, thesis/dissertation. *Entrance requirements:* For master's, GRE General Test or MAT; for doctorate, GRE General Test or MAT, minimum GPA of 2.75; for CAGS, minimum GPA of 2.75. *Application deadline:* For fall admission, 3/1 for domestic students. *Expenses:* Tuition, state resident: full-time $17,375. Tuition, nonresident: full-time $33,915. *Required fees:* $355. *Financial support:* Research assistantships, teaching assistantships, career-related internships or fieldwork, Federal Work-Study, and unspecified assistantships available. Support available to part-time students. Financial award application deadline: 3/1; financial award applicants required to submit FAFSA. *Faculty research:* Effects of ethnicity on applied psychology and education, enhancing equity and excellence in public schools, diversity and change in higher education, improving the functioning of individuals with disabilities. *Unit head:* Dr. Joseph Berger, Dean, 617-287-7606. *Application contact:* Graduate Admissions Coordinator, 617-287-6400, Fax: 617-287-6236, E-mail: bos.gadm@dpc.umassp.edu.
Website: http://www.umb.edu/academics/cehd

University of Massachusetts Dartmouth, Graduate School, College of Arts and Sciences, School of Education, North Dartmouth, MA 02747-2300. Offers educational leadership (Ed D), including educational leadership and policy studies; STEM education and teacher development (MAT, PhD, Postbaccalaureate Certificate), including English as a second language (Postbaccalaureate Certificate), mathematics education (PhD), middle school education (MAT), secondary school education (MAT). *Program availability:* Part-time. *Faculty:* 13 full-time (6 women), 12 part-time/adjunct (8 women). *Students:* 37 full-time (24 women), 120 part-time (72 women); includes 27 minority (5 Black or African American, non-Hispanic/Latino; 1 American Indian or Alaska Native, non-Hispanic/Latino; 3 Asian, non-Hispanic/Latino; 10 Hispanic/Latino; 8 Two or more races, non-Hispanic/Latino), 3 international. Average age 34. 76 applicants, 91% accepted, 51 enrolled. In 2017, 45 master's, 11 doctorates awarded. Terminal master's awarded for partial completion of doctoral program. *Degree requirements:* For doctorate, comprehensive exam, thesis/dissertation. *Entrance requirements:* For master's, statement of purpose (minimum of 300 words), resume, 2 letters of recommendation, official transcripts; copy of Massachusetts Initial License (for professional licensure program); for doctorate, GRE, statement of purpose (minimum of 300 words), resume, 3 letters of recommendation, official transcripts; minimum 10-page scholarly writing sample (for educational leadership program); for Postbaccalaureate Certificate, statement of purpose (minimum of 300 words), resume, 2 letters of recommendation, official transcripts. Additional exam requirements/recommendations for international students: Required—TOEFL (minimum score 533 paper-based; 72 iBT), IELTS (minimum score 6). Application fee: $60. Electronic applications accepted. *Expenses:* Tuition, state resident: full-time $15,449; part-time $643.71 per credit. Tuition, nonresident: full-time $27,880; part-time $1161.67 per credit. *Required fees:* $405; $25.88 per credit. Tuition and fees vary according to course load and reciprocity agreements. *Financial support:* In 2017–18, 4 fellowships (averaging $18,500 per year), 4 research assistantships (averaging $20,656 per year), 2 teaching assistantships (averaging $16,000 per year) were awarded; tuition waivers (full), unspecified assistantships, and doctoral support also available. Support available to part-time students. Financial award application deadline: 3/1; financial award applicants required to submit FAFSA. *Faculty research:* Sociology of education, urban education, curriculum theory, mindfulness in education, literacies, assessment of teacher knowledge. *Total annual research expenditures:* $1.7 million. *Unit head:* Amy Shapiro, Interim Dean, College of Arts and Sciences, 508-910-9101, Fax: 508-999-9125, E-mail: ashapiro@umassd.edu. *Application contact:* Steven Briggs, Director of Marketing and Recruitment for Graduate Studies, 508-999-8604, Fax: 508-999-8183, E-mail: graduate@umassd.edu.
Website: http://www.umassd.edu/cas/schoolofeducation

University of Massachusetts Lowell, Graduate School of Education, Lowell, MA 01854. Offers curriculum and instruction (M Ed). *Accreditation:* NCATE. *Program availability:* Part-time, evening/weekend, online learning. Terminal master's awarded for partial completion of doctoral program. *Entrance requirements:* For master's, GRE General Test. Additional exam requirements/recommendations for international students: Required—TOEFL. Electronic applications accepted.

University of Memphis, Graduate School, College of Education, Memphis, TN 38152. Offers M Ed, MAT, MS, Ed D, PhD, Graduate Certificate. *Accreditation:* NCATE. *Program availability:* Part-time, evening/weekend, 100% online, blended/hybrid learning. *Faculty:* 58 full-time (36 women), 32 part-time/adjunct (21 women). *Students:* 2 full-time (1 woman), 22 part-time (15 women); includes 13 minority (11 Black or African American, non-Hispanic/Latino; 2 Two or more races, non-Hispanic/Latino). Average age 37. 13 applicants, 54% accepted, 6 enrolled. In 2017, 21 other advanced degrees awarded. Terminal master's awarded for partial completion of doctoral program. *Degree requirements:* For master's, comprehensive exam, thesis or alternative, practicum; for doctorate, comprehensive exam, thesis/dissertation, residency project, internship (for some). *Entrance requirements:* For master's, GRE General Test or MAT; for doctorate, GRE General Test, writing sample, interview, letters of reference; for Graduate Certificate, letters of reference. Additional exam requirements/recommendations for international students: Required—TOEFL (minimum score 550 paper-based; 79 iBT). *Application deadline:* Applications are processed on a rolling basis. Application fee: $35 ($60 for international students). Electronic applications accepted. *Expenses:* Contact institution. *Financial support:* In 2017–18, 921 students received support, including 18 research assistantships with full tuition reimbursements available, 14 teaching assistantships with full tuition reimbursements available; career-related internships or fieldwork, Federal Work-Study, scholarships/grants, tuition waivers (partial), and unspecified assistantships also available. Financial award application deadline: 2/1; financial award applicants required to submit FAFSA. *Faculty research:* Urban school effectiveness, literacy development, teacher effectiveness, exercise physiology, crisis counseling. *Total annual research expenditures:* $3.3 million. *Unit head:* Dr. Kandi Hill-Clarke, Dean, 901-678-5495, Fax: 901-678-4778, E-mail: k.hill-clarke@memphis.edu. *Application contact:* Dr. Suzanne Lease, Interim Assistant Dean of Education for Graduate Programs, 901-678-2352, Fax: 901-678-4476, E-mail: slease@memphis.edu. Website: http://www.memphis.edu/coe

University of Miami, Graduate School, School of Education and Human Development, Coral Gables, FL 33124. Offers MS Ed, Ed D, PhD, Certificate, Ed S. *Program availability:* 100% online. Terminal master's awarded for partial completion of doctoral program. *Degree requirements:* For master's, comprehensive exam (for some programs), thesis optional, electronic portfolio, special project, personal growth experience; for doctorate, thesis/dissertation, qualifying exam, portfolio. *Entrance requirements:* For master's and doctorate, GRE General Test. Additional exam requirements/recommendations for international students: Required—TOEFL (minimum score 550 paper-based; 80 iBT); Recommended—IELTS (minimum score 6.5). Electronic applications accepted. *Faculty research:* Social skills and learning disabilities, planning for mainstreamed pupils, alcohol and drug abuse, restructuring education for all learners.

University of Michigan, Rackham Graduate School, Combined Program in Education and Psychology, Ann Arbor, MI 48109. Offers PhD. *Accreditation:* TEAC. *Degree requirements:* For doctorate, thesis/dissertation, independent research project, preliminary exam, oral defense of dissertation. *Entrance requirements:* For doctorate, GRE General Test with Analytical Writing Test. Additional exam requirements/recommendations for international students: Required—TOEFL (minimum score 600 paper-based; 100 iBT). Electronic applications accepted. *Expenses:* Contact institution. *Faculty research:* Human development in context of schools, families, communities; cognitive and learning sciences; motivation and self-regulated learning; culture, ethnicity, social and class influences on learning and motivation.

University of Michigan, School of Education, Ann Arbor, MI 48109-1259. Offers MA, MS, PhD, MA/Certification, MBA/MA, MPP/MA, PhD/MA. *Accreditation:* TEAC. Terminal master's awarded for partial completion of doctoral program. *Degree requirements:* For master's, thesis optional; for doctorate, comprehensive exam, thesis/dissertation. *Entrance requirements:* For master's and doctorate, GRE General Test. Additional exam requirements/recommendations for international students: Required—TOEFL (minimum score 560 paper-based). Electronic applications accepted. *Expenses:* Tuition, state resident: full-time $22,368; part-time $1201 per credit hour. Tuition, nonresident: full-time $45,156; part-time $2467 per credit hour. *Required fees:* $376 per term. Tuition and fees vary according to course load, degree level and program. *Faculty research:* Teaching, learning, policy, leadership, technology.

University of Michigan–Dearborn, College of Education, Health, and Human Services, Master of Arts in Teaching Program, Dearborn, MI 48126-2638. Offers MAT. *Accreditation:* TEAC. *Program availability:* Part-time, evening/weekend. *Faculty:* 9 full-time (5 women), 8 part-time/adjunct (5 women). *Students:* 5 full-time (4 women), 5 part-time (all women); includes 1 minority (Black or African American, non-Hispanic/Latino). Average age 32. 6 applicants, 50% accepted, 3 enrolled. In 2017, 11 master's awarded. *Entrance requirements:* For master's, SAT, minimum cumulative GPA of 3.0, 3 letters of recommendation, statement of purpose. Additional exam requirements/recommendations for international students: Required—TOEFL (minimum score 560 paper-based; 84 iBT), IELTS (minimum score 6.5). *Application deadline:* For fall admission, 8/1 priority date for domestic students, 5/1 priority date for international students; for winter admission, 12/1 priority date for domestic students, 9/1 priority date for international students; for spring admission, 4/1 priority date for domestic students, 1/1 priority date for international students. Applications are processed on a rolling basis. Application fee: $60. Electronic applications accepted. *Expenses:* $683 per credit hour in-state; $1,176 per credit hour out-state. *Financial support:* In 2017–18, 3 students received support. Career-related internships or fieldwork and scholarships/grants available. Financial award application deadline: 3/1; financial award applicants required to submit FAFSA. *Faculty research:* Technology and teaching, learning disabilities, pedagogy and interventions, literacy, multiculturalism. *Unit head:* Dr. Stein Brunvand, Director, Master's Programs, 313-583-6415, E-mail: sbrunvan@umich.edu. *Application contact:* Office of Graduate Studies, 313-583-6321, E-mail: umd-graduatestudies@umich.edu.
Website: http://umdearborn.edu/cehhs/cehhs_mat/

University of Michigan–Dearborn, College of Education, Health, and Human Services, Master of Arts Program in Education, Dearborn, MI 48126-2638. Offers MA. *Accreditation:* TEAC. *Program availability:* Part-time, evening/weekend, 100% online. *Faculty:* 7 full-time (6 women), 8 part-time/adjunct (4 women). *Students:* 1 (woman) full-time, 68 part-time (58 women); includes 8 minority (1 Black or African American, non-Hispanic/Latino; 3 Asian, non-Hispanic/Latino; 3 Hispanic/Latino; 1 Two or more races, non-Hispanic/Latino), 1 international. Average age 33. 24 applicants, 83% accepted, 18 enrolled. In 2017, 21 master's awarded. *Entrance requirements:* For master's, minimum GPA of 3.0, 3 letters of recommendation, statement of purpose, valid state of Michigan teaching certificate (if seeking an additional endorsement). Additional exam requirements/recommendations for international students: Required—TOEFL (minimum score 560 paper-based; 84 iBT), IELTS (minimum score 6.5). *Application deadline:* For fall admission, 8/1 for domestic students, 5/1 for international students; for winter admission, 12/1 for domestic students, 9/1 for international students; for spring admission, 4/1 for domestic students, 1/1 for international students. Applications are processed on a rolling basis. Application fee: $60. Electronic applications accepted. *Expenses:* $683 per credit hour in-state; $1,176 per credit hour out-state. *Financial support:* In 2017–18, 12 students received support. Career-related internships or fieldwork and scholarships/grants available. Financial award application deadline: 3/1; financial award applicants required to submit FAFSA. *Faculty research:* Urban education, literacy, curriculum development, pedagogy and interventions, language acquisition. *Unit head:* Dr. Stein Brunvand, Director, Master's Programs, 313-583-6415, E-mail: sbrunvan@umich.edu. *Application contact:* Office of Graduate Studies, 313-583-6321, E-mail: umd-graduatestudies@umich.edu.
Website: http://umdearborn.edu/cehhs/cehhs_maed/

University of Michigan–Flint, School of Education and Human Services, Flint, MI 48502-1950. Offers MA, Ed D, Ed S. *Program availability:* Part-time, mixed mode format. *Faculty:* 18 full-time (11 women), 26 part-time/adjunct (13 women). *Students:* 34 full-time (23 women), 192 part-time (137 women); includes 61 minority (46 Black or African American, non-Hispanic/Latino; 2 Asian, non-Hispanic/Latino; 5 Hispanic/Latino; 2 Native Hawaiian or other Pacific Islander, non-Hispanic/Latino; 6 Two or more races, non-Hispanic/Latino), 2 international. Average age 39. 124 applicants, 87% accepted, 81 enrolled. In 2017, 89 master's, 3 doctorates awarded. *Degree requirements:* For master's, thesis optional; for doctorate, thesis/dissertation. *Entrance requirements:* For master's, bachelor's degree from regionally-accredited institution, minimum overall undergraduate GPA of 3.0; for doctorate, Ed S; minimum overall graduate GPA of 3.3 (6.0 on a 9.0 scale) or equivalent; at least 3 years of work experience in a P-16 educational institution or in an education-related position; for Ed S, MA or MS in an education-related field from accredited institution; minimum overall graduate GPA of 3.0 (6.0 on a 9.0 scale) or equivalent; at least 3 years of work experience in educational

setting. Additional exam requirements/recommendations for international students: Required—TOEFL (minimum score 84 iBT), IELTS (minimum score 6.5). *Application deadline:* For fall admission, 7/1 for domestic students, 4/1 for international students; for winter admission, 11/15 for domestic students, 9/1 for international students; for spring admission, 3/15 for domestic students, 1/1 for international students. Applications are processed on a rolling basis. Application fee: $55. Electronic applications accepted. *Expenses:* Contact institution. *Financial support:* Federal Work-Study and unspecified assistantships available. Support available to part-time students. Financial award application deadline: 3/1; financial award applicants required to submit FAFSA. *Unit head:* Dr. Bob Barnett, Dean, 810-766-6878, Fax: 810-766-6891, E-mail: rbarnett@umflint.edu. *Application contact:* Bradley T. Maki, Director of Graduate Admissions, 810-762-3171, Fax: 810-766-6789, E-mail: bmaki@umflint.edu.
Website: http://www.umflint.edu/sehs

University of Minnesota, Duluth, Graduate School, College of Education and Human Service Professions, Department of Education, Duluth, MN 55812-2496. Offers M Ed, Ed D. *Program availability:* Part-time, evening/weekend. *Degree requirements:* For doctorate, comprehensive exam. *Entrance requirements:* For doctorate, GRE, MA (preferred) minimum GPA of 3.0, 3 letters of recommendation, 3 work samples. Additional exam requirements/recommendations for international students: Required—TOEFL (minimum score 550 paper-based).

University of Minnesota, Twin Cities Campus, Graduate School, College of Education and Human Development, Minneapolis, MN 55455-0213. Offers M Ed, MA, MS, MSW, Ed D, PhD, Certificate, Ed S. *Accreditation:* NCATE. *Program availability:* Part-time. *Faculty:* 171 full-time (91 women). *Students:* 1,449 full-time (1,067 women), 727 part-time (498 women); includes 465 minority (129 Black or African American, non-Hispanic/Latino; 16 American Indian or Alaska Native, non-Hispanic/Latino; 112 Asian, non-Hispanic/Latino; 119 Hispanic/Latino; 3 Native Hawaiian or other Pacific Islander, non-Hispanic/Latino; 86 Two or more races, non-Hispanic/Latino), 188 international. Average age 32. 1,926 applicants, 53% accepted, 918 enrolled. In 2017, 767 master's, 112 doctorates, 79 other advanced degrees awarded. Application fee: $75 ($95 for international students). *Financial support:* In 2017–18, 101 fellowships, 291 research assistantships with full tuition reimbursements (averaging $12,285 per year), 218 teaching assistantships with full tuition reimbursements (averaging $11,848 per year) were awarded; scholarships/grants and tuition waivers (partial) also available. Financial award applicants required to submit FAFSA. *Faculty research:* Educational equity and achievement gap; living longer, living better - healthy aging across the lifespan; children's mental health, child welfare; autism spectrum disorders, neurodevelopment, developmental disability. *Total annual research expenditures:* $42.4 million. *Unit head:* Dr. Jean K. Quam, Dean, 612-626-9252, Fax: 612-626-7496, E-mail: jquam@umn.edu. *Application contact:* Dr. Brianne Keeney, Director of Graduate Education Initiatives, 612-626-9145, E-mail: keen0113@umn.edu.
Website: http://www.cehd.umn.edu

University of Mississippi, Graduate School, School of Education, University, MS 38677. Offers counselor education (M Ed, PhD); counselor education - play therapy (Ed S); early childhood (M Ed); educational leadership K-12 (M Ed, Ed D, PhD, Ed S); elementary education (M Ed, Ed D, Ed S); higher education/student personnel (Ed D, PhD); literacy education (M Ed); math education (Ed D); secondary education (M Ed, PhD, Ed S); special education (M Ed, PhD, Ed S); teacher corporations (MA); teacher education (MA). *Accreditation:* NCATE. *Faculty:* 65 full-time (40 women), 25 part-time/adjunct (5 women). *Students:* 185 full-time (148 women), 410 part-time (310 women); includes 193 minority (168 Black or African American, non-Hispanic/Latino; 7 Asian, non-Hispanic/Latino; 14 Hispanic/Latino; 4 Two or more races, non-Hispanic/Latino), 7 international. Average age 33. In 2017, 176 master's, 20 doctorates, 37 other advanced degrees awarded. *Entrance requirements:* For master's, GRE General Test, minimum GPA of 3.0; for doctorate, GRE General Test. Additional exam requirements/recommendations for international students: Required—TOEFL. *Application deadline:* For fall admission, 3/1 for domestic students; for spring admission, 10/1 for domestic students; for summer admission, 3/1 for domestic students. Applications are processed on a rolling basis. Application fee: $50. Electronic applications accepted. *Financial support:* Scholarships/grants available. Financial award application deadline: 3/1; financial award applicants required to submit FAFSA. *Unit head:* Dr. David Rock, Dean, 662-915-7063, Fax: 662-915-7249, E-mail: soe@olemiss.edu. *Application contact:* Dr. Joe Sumrall, Professor of Elementary Education, 662-915-7350, E-mail: soe@olemiss.edu.

University of Missouri, Office of Research and Graduate Studies, College of Education, Columbia, MO 65211. Offers M Ed, MA, Ed D, PhD, Certificate, Ed S. *Accreditation:* TEAC. *Program availability:* Part-time, evening/weekend. Terminal master's awarded for partial completion of doctoral program. *Degree requirements:* For master's, variable foreign language requirement, thesis (for some programs); for doctorate, variable foreign language requirement, comprehensive exam (for some programs), thesis/dissertation. *Entrance requirements:* For master's, minimum GPA of 3.0; for doctorate, GRE General Test. Additional exam requirements/recommendations for international students: Required—TOEFL (minimum score 550 paper-based; 80 iBT), IELTS (minimum score 6.5).

University of Missouri–Kansas City, School of Education, Kansas City, MO 64110-2499. Offers administration (Ed D); counseling and guidance (MA, Ed S), including mental health counseling (Ed S), school counseling (Ed S); counseling psychology (PhD); curriculum and instruction (MA, Ed S), including language and literacy (Ed S); education (PhD), including higher education administration, PK-12 education administration; educational administration (MA, Ed S), including advanced principal (Ed S), beginning principal (Ed S), district-level administration (Ed S); reading education (MA); special education (MA). PhD in education offered through the School of Graduate Studies. *Accreditation:* NCATE. *Program availability:* Part-time, evening/weekend. *Degree requirements:* For doctorate, thesis/dissertation, internship, practicum. *Entrance requirements:* For master's, GRE, minimum GPA of 2.75, 2 letters of reference, written statement of purpose; for doctorate, GRE, minimum GPA of 3.0; for Ed S, minimum GPA of 3.0. Additional exam requirements/recommendations for international students: Required—TOEFL (minimum score 550 paper-based; 80 iBT). *Faculty research:* Urban education, inquiry-based field study, theories of counseling and psychotherapy, school literacy, educational technology.

University of Missouri–St. Louis, College of Education, St. Louis, MO 63121. Offers M Ed, Ed D, PhD, Certificate, Ed S. *Accreditation:* NCATE. *Program availability:* Part-time, evening/weekend. *Faculty:* 69 full-time (41 women), 93 part-time/adjunct (76 women). *Students:* 226 full-time (179 women), 910 part-time (700 women); includes 309 minority (217 Black or African American, non-Hispanic/Latino; 5 American Indian or Alaska Native, non-Hispanic/Latino; 21 Asian, non-Hispanic/Latino; 53 Hispanic/Latino; 13 Two or more races, non-Hispanic/Latino), 12 international. 456 applicants, 88% accepted, 286 enrolled. *Degree requirements:* For master's, comprehensive exam, thesis optional; for doctorate, thesis/dissertation. *Entrance requirements:* For doctorate, GRE General Test, 3 letters of recommendation. Additional exam requirements/recommendations for international students: Recommended—TOEFL (minimum score 550 paper-based; 79 iBT), IELTS (minimum score 6.5). *Application deadline:* For fall admission, 7/1 priority date for domestic and international students; for spring

admission, 12/1 priority date for domestic and international students. Applications are processed on a rolling basis. Application fee: $50 ($40 for international students). Electronic applications accepted. *Expenses:* Tuition, state resident: part-time $476.50 per credit hour. Tuition, nonresident: part-time $1169.70 per credit hour. *Financial support:* Research assistantships with tuition reimbursements and teaching assistantships with tuition reimbursements available. Financial award application deadline: 4/1; financial award applicants required to submit FAFSA. *Faculty research:* Remedial reading, literacy, educational policy and research, science education. *Unit head:* Ann Taylor, Dean, 314-516-5109, Fax: 314-516-5227, E-mail: taylorann@ umsl.edu. *Application contact:* 314-516-5458, Fax: 314-516-6996, E-mail: gradadm@ umsl.edu.
Website: http://coe.umsl.edu/

University of Mobile, Graduate Studies, Program in Education, Mobile, AL 36613. Offers education (MA); higher education leadership and policy (M Ed). *Program availability:* Part-time, 100% online. *Degree requirements:* For master's, comprehensive exam, thesis optional. *Entrance requirements:* For master's, GRE, Alabama teaching certificate. Additional exam requirements/recommendations for international students: Required—TOEFL (minimum score 550 paper-based; 80 iBT). *Application deadline:* For fall admission, 8/3 priority date for domestic students, 8/3 for international students; for spring admission, 12/23 priority date for domestic students, 12/3 priority date for international students. Applications are processed on a rolling basis. Application fee: $40 ($50 for international students). Electronic applications accepted. *Financial support:* Application deadline: 8/1; applicants required to submit FAFSA. *Faculty research:* Retention, writing across the curriculum. *Unit head:* Dr. Carolyn D. Corliss, Dean, School of Education, 251-442-2276, Fax: 251-442-2523, E-mail: ccorliss@umobile.edu. *Application contact:* Brian Boyle, Director of Recruitment, 251-442-2727, Fax: 251-442-2523.
Website: http://umobile.edu/school-of-education/master-of-arts-in-education/

University of Montana, Graduate School, Phyllis J. Washington College of Education and Human Sciences, Missoula, MT 59812. Offers M Ed, MA, MS, Ed D, Ed S. *Accreditation:* NCATE. *Program availability:* Part-time. *Degree requirements:* For Ed S, thesis. *Entrance requirements:* For master's, GRE General Test, minimum GPA of 3.0; for Ed S, GRE General Test. Additional exam requirements/recommendations for international students: Required—TOEFL. *Faculty research:* Cooperative learning, administrative styles.

University of Montevallo, College of Education, Montevallo, AL 35115. Offers M Ed, Ed S. *Accreditation:* NCATE. *Program availability:* Part-time, evening/weekend. *Students:* 92 full-time (72 women), 164 part-time (121 women); includes 54 minority (41 Black or African American, non-Hispanic/Latino; 7 Hispanic/Latino; 6 Two or more races, non-Hispanic/Latino). *Degree requirements:* For master's, comprehensive exam. *Entrance requirements:* For master's, GRE General Test, MAT, minimum undergraduate GPA of 2.5. Additional exam requirements/recommendations for international students: Required—TOEFL (minimum score 550 paper-based). *Application deadline:* For fall admission, 7/15 for domestic students; for spring admission, 11/15 for domestic students. Application fee: $30. *Expenses:* Tuition, state resident: full-time $9888. Tuition, nonresident: full-time $21,144. *Required fees:* $1920. *Financial support:* Federal Work-Study, scholarships/grants, and unspecified assistantships available. *Unit head:* Dr. Charlotte Daughhetee, Interim Dean, 205-665-6360, E-mail: daughc@ montevallo.edu. *Application contact:* Colleen Kennedy, Graduate Program Assistant, 205-665-6350, E-mail: ckennedy@montevallo.edu.
Website: http://www.montevallo.edu/education/college-of-education/

University of Nebraska at Kearney, College of Education, Kearney, NE 68849-0001. Offers MA Ed, MS Ed, Ed S. *Accreditation:* NCATE. *Program availability:* Part-time, evening/weekend, 100% online. *Degree requirements:* For master's, comprehensive exam, thesis optional. *Entrance requirements:* Additional exam requirements/ recommendations for international students: Recommended—TOEFL (minimum score 550 paper-based; 79 iBT), IELTS (minimum score 6.5). Electronic applications accepted.

University of Nebraska at Omaha, Graduate Studies, College of Education, Omaha, NE 68182. Offers MA, MS, Ed D, PhD, Certificate, Ed S. *Accreditation:* NCATE. *Program availability:* Part-time, evening/weekend. *Degree requirements:* For master's, comprehensive exam (for some programs), thesis (for some programs); for doctorate, comprehensive exam, thesis/dissertation. *Entrance requirements:* Additional exam requirements/recommendations for international students: Required—TOEFL, IELTS, PTE. Electronic applications accepted.

University of Nevada, Las Vegas, Graduate College, College of Education, Las Vegas, NV 89154-3001. Offers M Ed, MS, Ed D, PhD, Advanced Certificate, Certificate, Ed S, PhD/JD. *Program availability:* Part-time. *Faculty:* 67 full-time (37 women), 50 part-time/ adjunct (38 women). *Students:* 691 full-time (525 women), 545 part-time (384 women); includes 509 minority (131 Black or African American, non-Hispanic/Latino; 4 American Indian or Alaska Native, non-Hispanic/Latino; 61 Asian, non-Hispanic/Latino; 231 Hispanic/Latino; 6 Native Hawaiian or other Pacific Islander, non-Hispanic/Latino; 76 Two or more races, non-Hispanic/Latino; 28 international. Average age 35. 582 applicants, 79% accepted, 379 enrolled. In 2017, 390 master's, 30 doctorates, 12 other advanced degrees awarded. *Degree requirements:* For master's, comprehensive exam (for some programs), thesis (for some programs); for doctorate, comprehensive exam, thesis/dissertation; for other advanced degree, comprehensive exam (for some programs). *Entrance requirements:* For master's and doctorate, GRE General Test. Additional exam requirements/recommendations for international students: Required— TOEFL (minimum score 550 paper-based; 80 iBT), IELTS (minimum score 7). Application fee: $60 ($95 for international students). Electronic applications accepted. *Expenses:* $275 per credit, $850 per course, $7,966 per year resident, $22,157 per year non-resident, $7,094 non-resident fee (7 credits or more), $1,307 annual health insurance fee. *Financial support:* In 2017–18, 120 students received support, including 54 research assistantships with partial tuition reimbursements available (averaging $15,952 per year), 66 teaching assistantships with partial tuition reimbursements available (averaging $18,625 per year); institutionally sponsored loans, scholarships/ grants, health care benefits, and unspecified assistantships also available. Financial award application deadline: 3/15; financial award applicants required to submit FAFSA. *Faculty research:* Technology integration in general and special education, assessment of behavioral and emotional disorders, teacher quality and student achievement, evidence-based practices in special education (autism and emotional and behavioral disorders), math and science education. *Total annual research expenditures:* $2.9 million. *Unit head:* Dr. Kim Metcalf, Dean, 702-895-3375, Fax: 702-895-4068, E-mail: kim.metcalf@unlv.edu.
Website: http://education.unlv.edu/

University of Nevada, Reno, Graduate School, College of Education, Reno, NV 89557. Offers M Ed, MA, MS, Ed D, PhD, Ed S. *Accreditation:* NCATE. Terminal master's awarded for partial completion of doctoral program. *Degree requirements:* For master's, thesis optional; for doctorate, thesis/dissertation. *Entrance requirements:* For master's, GRE, minimum GPA of 2.75; for doctorate, GRE, minimum GPA of 3.0. Additional exam requirements/recommendations for international students: Required—TOEFL (minimum

score 500 paper-based; 61 iBT), IELTS (minimum score 6). Electronic applications accepted.

University of New Brunswick Fredericton, School of Graduate Studies, Faculty of Education, Fredericton, NB E3B 5A3, Canada. Offers M Ed, PhD. *Program availability:* Part-time, online learning. *Degree requirements:* For master's, variable foreign language requirement, thesis optional; for doctorate, variable foreign language requirement, comprehensive exam, thesis/dissertation. *Entrance requirements:* For master's, minimum GPA of 3.0. Additional exam requirements/recommendations for international students: Required—TOEFL (minimum score 650 paper-based); Recommended—TWE (minimum score 5.5). Electronic applications accepted. *Faculty research:* Adult education, educational administration and leadership, counseling, exceptional learners, critical studies.

University of New England, College of Graduate and Professional Studies, Portland, ME 04005-9526. Offers advanced educational leadership (CAGS); applied nutrition (MS); career and technical education (MS Ed); curriculum and instruction (MS Ed); education (CAGS, Post-Master's Certificate); educational leadership (MS Ed, Ed D); generalist (MS Ed); health informatics (MS, Graduate Certificate); inclusion education (MS Ed); literacy K-12 (MS Ed); medical education leadership (MMEL); public health (MPH); public health (Graduate Certificate); reading specialist (MS Ed); social work (MSW). *Program availability:* Part-time, evening/weekend, online only, 100% online. *Faculty:* 125 part-time/adjunct (94 women). *Students:* 1,403 full-time (1,128 women), 594 part-time (475 women); includes 474 minority (332 Black or African American, non-Hispanic/Latino; 13 American Indian or Alaska Native, non-Hispanic/Latino; 83 Asian, non-Hispanic/Latino; 27 Hispanic/Latino; 11 Native Hawaiian or other Pacific Islander, non-Hispanic/Latino; 8 Two or more races, non-Hispanic/Latino). Average age 35. 3,153 applicants, 41% accepted, 990 enrolled. In 2017, 307 master's, 59 doctorates, 124 other advanced degrees awarded. *Application deadline:* Applications are processed on a rolling basis. Electronic applications accepted. Tuition and fees vary according to degree level, program and student level. *Financial support:* Application deadline: 5/1; applicants required to submit FAFSA. *Unit head:* Dr. Martha Wilson, Associate Provost for Online Worldwide Learning/Dean of the College of Graduate and Professional Studies, 207-221-4985, E-mail: mwilson13@une.edu.
Website: http://online.une.edu

University of New Hampshire, Graduate School, College of Liberal Arts, Department of Education, Durham, NH 03824. Offers assessment evaluation and policy (Postbaccalaureate Certificate); autism spectrum disorders (Postbaccalaureate Certificate); early childhood education (M Ed), including early childhood education, early childhood education: special needs; education (PhD, Postbaccalaureate Certificate), including children and youth in communities (PhD); curriculum and instruction leadership (Postbaccalaureate Certificate), education (PhD); educational administration and supervision (Ed S); educational studies (M Ed); elementary education (M Ed); mentoring teachers (Postbaccalaureate Certificate); secondary education (M Ed, MAT); special education (M Ed, Postbaccalaureate Certificate), including special education (M Ed), special education administration (Postbaccalaureate Certificate); technology integration (Postbaccalaureate Certificate). *Accreditation:* TEAC. *Program availability:* Part-time. *Students:* 81 full-time (59 women), 143 part-time (104 women); includes 11 minority (5 Asian, non-Hispanic/Latino; 5 Hispanic/Latino; 1 Two or more races, non-Hispanic/ Latino), 9 international. Average age 32. 113 applicants, 73% accepted, 62 enrolled. In 2017, 148 master's, 5 doctorates, 5 other advanced degrees awarded. *Entrance requirements:* For master's, doctorate, and other advanced degree, GRE General Test. Additional exam requirements/recommendations for international students: Required— TOEFL (minimum score 550 paper-based; 80 iBT). *Application deadline:* For fall admission, 4/1 priority date for domestic students, 4/1 for international students; for spring admission, 12/1 priority date for domestic students. Application fee: $65. Electronic applications accepted. *Financial support:* In 2017–18, 38 students received support, including 2 fellowships, 1 research assistantship, 17 teaching assistantships; career-related internships or fieldwork, Federal Work-Study, scholarships/grants, and tuition waivers (full and partial) also available. Support available to part-time students. Financial award application deadline: 2/15. *Unit head:* Paula Salvio, Chair, 603-862-0024, E-mail: education.department@unh.edu. *Application contact:* Cindy Glidden, Academic Department Coordinator, 603-862-2174, E-mail: education.department@ unh.edu.
Website: http://cola.unh.edu/education

University of New Hampshire, Graduate School Manchester Campus, Manchester, NH 03101. Offers business administration (MBA); cybersecurity policy and risk management (MS); educational administration and supervision (Ed S); educational studies (M Ed); elementary education (M Ed); information technology (MS); public administration (MPA); public health (MPH, Certificate); secondary education (M Ed, MAT); social work (MSW); substance use disorders (Certificate). *Program availability:* Part-time, evening/weekend. *Students:* 13 full-time (6 women), 17 part-time (0 women); includes 7 minority (1 Black or African American, non-Hispanic/Latino; 4 Asian, non-Hispanic/Latino; 1 Hispanic/Latino; 1 Two or more races, non-Hispanic/Latino), 10 international. Average age 33. 42 applicants, 71% accepted, 8 enrolled. In 2017, 4 master's awarded. *Entrance requirements:* Additional exam requirements/ recommendations for international students: Required—TOEFL (minimum score 550 paper-based; 80 iBT). *Application deadline:* For fall admission, 6/1 for domestic students, 4/1 for international students; for spring admission, 12/1 for domestic students. Application fee: $65. Electronic applications accepted. *Financial support:* Fellowships, research assistantships, teaching assistantships, Federal Work-Study, scholarships/ grants, health care benefits, and unspecified assistantships available. Support available to part-time students. Financial award application deadline: 2/15; financial award applicants required to submit FAFSA. *Unit head:* Candice Morey, Educational Programs Coordinator, 603-641-4313, E-mail: unhm.gradcenter@unh.edu.
Website: http://www.gradschool.unh.edu/manchester/

University of New Mexico, Graduate Studies, College of Education, Albuquerque, NM 87131-2039. Offers MA, MS, Ed D, PhD, Ed S, Graduate Certificate. *Accreditation:* NCATE. *Program availability:* Part-time, evening/weekend. *Faculty:* 110 full-time (70 women), 17 part-time/adjunct (12 women). *Students:* 353 full-time (244 women), 570 part-time (424 women); includes 436 minority (30 Black or African American, non-Hispanic/Latino; 68 American Indian or Alaska Native, non-Hispanic/Latino; 19 Asian, non-Hispanic/Latino; 298 Hispanic/Latino; 1 Native Hawaiian or other Pacific Islander, non-Hispanic/Latino; 20 Two or more races, non-Hispanic/Latino), 77 international. Average age 37. 398 applicants, 56% accepted, 212 enrolled. In 2017, 288 master's, 33 doctorates, 39 other advanced degrees awarded. *Degree requirements:* For master's, comprehensive exam (for some programs), thesis (for some programs); for doctorate, variable foreign language requirement, comprehensive exam, thesis/dissertation. *Entrance requirements:* Additional exam requirements/recommendations for international students: Required—TOEFL (minimum score 550 paper-based), IELTS (minimum score 7). *Application deadline:* For fall admission, 3/1 for international students; for spring admission, 8/1 for international students. Application fee: $50. Electronic applications accepted. *Financial support:* Career-related internships or fieldwork, Federal Work-Study, scholarships/grants, health care benefits, and unspecified assistantships available. Support available to part-time students. Financial

Education—General

award application deadline: 3/1; financial award applicants required to submit FAFSA. *Faculty research:* Best practices in pedagogy, quantitative analysis and assessment, socio-cultural issues, educational leadership, health and wellness across the lifespan. *Total annual research expenditures:* $578,105. *Unit head:* Dr. Richard Howell, Dean, 505-277-2231, Fax: 505-277-8427, E-mail: rhowell@unm.edu. *Application contact:* Academic Graduate Coordinator, 505-277-3190, E-mail: coeac@unm.edu. Website: http://coe.unm.edu/

University of New Orleans, Graduate School, College of Education and Human Development, New Orleans, LA 70148. Offers M Ed, MAT, PhD. *Accreditation:* NCATE. *Program availability:* Part-time, online learning. *Degree requirements:* For master's, comprehensive exam, thesis optional; for doctorate, comprehensive exam, thesis/dissertation. *Entrance requirements:* For master's and doctorate, GRE General Test. Additional exam requirements/recommendations for international students: Required—TOEFL (minimum score 550 paper-based; 79 iBT). Electronic applications accepted. *Faculty research:* Special education and habilitation, educational administration, exercise physiology, wellness, effective school instruction.

University of North Alabama, College of Education, Florence, AL 35632-0001. Offers MA, MA Ed, MS, Ed S. *Accreditation:* NCATE. *Program availability:* Part-time, 100% online, blended/hybrid learning. *Faculty:* 23 full-time (13 women), 8 part-time/adjunct (3 women). *Students:* 87 full-time (59 women), 203 part-time (155 women); includes 34 minority (23 Black or African American, non-Hispanic/Latino; 3 American Indian or Alaska Native, non-Hispanic/Latino; 2 Hispanic/Latino; 6 Two or more races, non-Hispanic/Latino), 3 international. Average age 32. 161 applicants, 61% accepted, 81 enrolled. In 2017, 106 master's, 32 other advanced degrees awarded. *Degree requirements:* For master's, comprehensive exam. *Entrance requirements:* For master's, GRE, MAT, PRAXIS II, or NTE, minimum GPA of 2.5, Alabama Class B Certificate or equivalent, teaching experience. Additional exam requirements/recommendations for international students: Required—TOEFL (minimum score 79 iBT), IELTS (minimum score 6), PTE (minimum score 54). *Application deadline:* Applications are processed on a rolling basis. Application fee: $50 ($100 for international students). Electronic applications accepted. *Expenses:* Tuition, state resident: full-time $7824; part-time $5943 per year. Tuition, nonresident: full-time $15,648; part-time $11,736 per year. *Required fees:* $3064; $2298 per unit. Tuition and fees vary according to course load and reciprocity agreements. *Financial support:* In 2017–18, 39 students received support. Federal Work-Study, scholarships/grants, and unspecified assistantships available. Financial award application deadline: 2/1; financial award applicants required to submit FAFSA. *Total annual research expenditures:* $2.6 million. *Unit head:* Dr. Donna Lefort, Dean, 256-765-4252, Fax: 256-765-4664, E-mail: dpjacobs@una.edu. *Application contact:* Hillary N. Coats, Graduate Admissions Coordinator, 256-765-4447, E-mail: graduate@una.edu. Website: http://www.una.edu/education/

The University of North Carolina at Chapel Hill, Graduate School, School of Education, Chapel Hill, NC 27514-3500. Offers M Ed, MA, MAT, MSA, Ed D, PhD. *Accreditation:* NCATE. *Program availability:* Part-time. *Degree requirements:* For master's, comprehensive exam, thesis (for some programs); for doctorate, comprehensive exam, thesis/dissertation. *Entrance requirements:* For master's and doctorate, GRE General Test, minimum GPA of 3.0 during last 2 years of undergraduate course work. Additional exam requirements/recommendations for international students: Required—TOEFL (minimum score 550 paper-based). Electronic applications accepted. *Faculty research:* Curriculum development; school success and intervention; professional development, recruitment and retention; service-learning; evaluation.

The University of North Carolina at Charlotte, Cato College of Education, Charlotte, NC 28223-0001. Offers M Ed, MA, MAT, MSA, Ed D, PhD, Graduate Certificate, Post-Master's Certificate, Postbaccalaureate Certificate. *Accreditation:* ACA (one or more programs are accredited); NCATE. *Program availability:* Part-time, evening/weekend, 100% online, blended/hybrid learning. *Faculty:* 108 full-time (64 women), 40 part-time/adjunct (27 women). *Students:* 294 full-time (232 women), 1,126 part-time (897 women); includes 436 minority (315 Black or African American, non-Hispanic/Latino; 3 American Indian or Alaska Native, non-Hispanic/Latino; 20 Asian, non-Hispanic/Latino; 76 Hispanic/Latino; 22 Two or more races, non-Hispanic/Latino), 27 international. Average age 34. 966 applicants, 79% accepted, 570 enrolled. In 2017, 265 master's, 31 doctorates, 272 other advanced degrees awarded. *Entrance requirements:* For master's, bachelor's degree, or its U.S. equivalent, from regionally-accredited college or university; minimum overall GPA of 3.0 on all previous work beyond high school; statement of purpose (essay); at least three recommendation forms; for doctorate, bachelor's degree (or its U.S. equivalent) from regionally-accredited college or university; minimum overall GPA of 3.5 in master's degree program; for other advanced degree, bachelor's degree from regionally-accredited university; minimum GPA of 2.75 on all post-secondary work attempted; transcripts; personal statement outlining why the applicant seeks admission to the program. Additional exam requirements/recommendations for international students: Required—TOEFL (minimum score 523 paper-based, 70 iBT) or IELTS (6.5). *Application deadline:* Applications are processed on a rolling basis. Application fee: $75. Electronic applications accepted. *Expenses:* Tuition, state resident: full-time $4337. Tuition, nonresident: full-time $17,771. *Required fees:* $3211. Tuition and fees vary according to course load and program. *Financial support:* In 2017–18, 44 students received support, including 38 research assistantships (averaging $12,881 per year), 4 teaching assistantships (averaging $3,500 per year); career-related internships or fieldwork, institutionally sponsored loans, scholarships/grants, unspecified assistantships, and administrative assistantships also available. Support available to part-time students. Financial award application deadline: 3/1; financial award applicants required to submit FAFSA. *Faculty research:* Quality classroom instruction, culturally responsive instruction, teacher education policy and practice, early intervention, counseling practices. *Total annual research expenditures:* $6.4 million. *Unit head:* Dr. Ellen McIntyre, Dean, 704-687-8722, E-mail: ellen.mcintyre@uncc.edu. *Application contact:* Kathy B. Giddings, Director of Graduate Admissions, 704-687-5503, Fax: 704-687-1668, E-mail: gradadm@uncc.edu. Website: https://education.uncc.edu/

The University of North Carolina at Greensboro, Graduate School, School of Education, Greensboro, NC 27412-5001. Offers M Ed, MLIS, MS, MSA, Ed D, PhD, Certificate, Ed S, PMC, MS/Ed S, MS/PhD. *Accreditation:* NCATE. *Program availability:* Part-time, evening/weekend. *Degree requirements:* For doctorate, thesis/dissertation. *Entrance requirements:* For master's, doctorate, and other advanced degree, GRE General Test. Additional exam requirements/recommendations for international students: Required—TOEFL. Electronic applications accepted. *Faculty research:* Effects of homogeneous grouping, women in higher education, assessment of student achievement.

The University of North Carolina at Pembroke, The Graduate School, School of Education, Pembroke, NC 28372-1510. Offers MA, MA Ed, MAT, MSA. *Accreditation:* NCATE. *Program availability:* Part-time, evening/weekend. *Degree requirements:* For master's, comprehensive exam (for some programs), thesis optional. *Entrance requirements:* For master's, GRE General Test or MAT, minimum GPA of 3.0 in major, 2.5 overall. Additional exam requirements/recommendations for international students: Required—TOEFL. *Application deadline:* For fall admission, 7/15 priority date for domestic and international students; for spring admission, 12/1 priority date for domestic

and international students. Applications are processed on a rolling basis. Application fee: $45 ($60 for international students). *Financial support:* Application deadline: 4/15. *Unit head:* Dr. Alfred Bryant, Jr., Dean, 910-775-4009, Fax: 910-521-6165, E-mail: alfred.bryant@uncp.edu. Website: http://www.uncp.edu/soe/

The University of North Carolina Wilmington, Watson College of Education, Wilmington, NC 28403-3297. Offers M Ed, MAT, MS, MSA, Ed D. *Accreditation:* NCATE. *Program availability:* Part-time. *Faculty:* 51 full-time (35 women), 8 part-time/adjunct (6 women). *Students:* 159 full-time (118 women), 331 part-time (256 women); includes 136 minority (86 Black or African American, non-Hispanic/Latino; 10 American Indian or Alaska Native, non-Hispanic/Latino; 5 Asian, non-Hispanic/Latino; 22 Hispanic/Latino; 2 Native Hawaiian or other Pacific Islander, non-Hispanic/Latino; 11 Two or more races, non-Hispanic/Latino), 1 international. Average age 34. 199 applicants, 79% accepted, 125 enrolled. In 2017, 180 master's, 20 doctorates awarded. *Degree requirements:* For doctorate, comprehensive exam, thesis/dissertation. *Entrance requirements:* For doctorate, education statement of interest essay, master's degree in education field, 3 years of leadership experience. Additional exam requirements/recommendations for international students: Required—TOEFL (minimum score 550 paper-based; 79 iBT), IELTS (minimum score 6.5). *Application deadline:* Applications are processed on a rolling basis. Application fee: $75. Electronic applications accepted. *Expenses:* Tuition, state resident: full-time $4626; part-time $226.76 per credit hour. Tuition, nonresident: full-time $17,834; part-time $874.22 per credit hour. *Required fees:* $2124. Tuition and fees vary according to program. *Financial support:* Scholarships/grants and unspecified assistantships available. Financial award application deadline: 1/1; financial award applicants required to submit FAFSA. *Unit head:* Dr. Van Dempsey, Dean, 910-962-3354, Fax: 910-962-4081, E-mail: dempseyv@uncw.edu. *Application contact:* Kimberly Harris, Administrative Specialist, Graduate School, 910-962-7449, Fax: 910-962-3787, E-mail: harrisk@uncw.edu. Website: http://www.uncw.edu/ed/degree_grad.html

University of North Dakota, Graduate School, College of Education and Human Development, Grand Forks, ND 58202. Offers M Ed, MA, MS, MSW, Ed D, PhD, Ed S. *Accreditation:* NCATE. *Program availability:* Part-time, evening/weekend, online learning. *Degree requirements:* For master's, comprehensive exam, thesis or alternative; for doctorate, comprehensive exam, thesis/dissertation; for Ed S, comprehensive exam (for some programs), thesis (for some programs). *Entrance requirements:* For master's, GRE General Test, MAT, GRE Subject Test, minimum GPA of 3.0; for doctorate, GRE Subject Test, minimum GPA of 3.5. Additional exam requirements/recommendations for international students: Required—TOEFL (minimum score 550 paper-based; 79 iBT), IELTS (minimum score 6.5). Electronic applications accepted.

University of Northern British Columbia, Office of Graduate Studies, Prince George, BC V2N 4Z9, Canada. Offers business administration (Diploma); community health science (M Sc); disability management (MA); education (M Ed); first nations studies (MA); gender studies (MA); history (MA); interdisciplinary studies (MA); international studies (MA); mathematical, computer and physical sciences (M Sc); natural resources and environmental studies (M Sc, MA, MNRES, PhD); political science (MA); psychology (M Sc, PhD); social work (MSW). *Program availability:* Part-time, evening/weekend, online learning. *Degree requirements:* For master's, thesis; for doctorate, thesis/dissertation. *Entrance requirements:* For master's, GRE, minimum B average in undergraduate course work; for doctorate, candidacy exam, minimum A average in graduate course work.

University of Northern Colorado, Graduate School, College of Education and Behavioral Sciences, Greeley, CO 80639. Offers MA, MAT, MS, Ed D, PhD, Ed S. *Accreditation:* NCATE. *Program availability:* Part-time, online learning. *Degree requirements:* For master's, comprehensive exam, thesis optional; for doctorate, comprehensive exam, thesis/dissertation; for Ed S, comprehensive exam, thesis. *Entrance requirements:* For doctorate, GRE General Test.

University of Northern Iowa, Graduate College, College of Education, Cedar Falls, IA 50614. Offers MA, MAE, MS, Ed D, Ed S. *Program availability:* Part-time, evening/weekend. *Degree requirements:* For Ed S, thesis or alternative. *Entrance requirements:* For master's, minimum GPA of 3.0; for doctorate, GRE, master's degree, minimum GPA of 3.5; for Ed S, GRE General Test, GRE Subject Test. Additional exam requirements/recommendations for international students: Required—TOEFL (minimum score 500 paper-based; 61 iBT). Electronic applications accepted.

University of North Florida, College of Education and Human Services, Jacksonville, FL 32224. Offers M Ed, MS, Ed D. *Accreditation:* NCATE. *Program availability:* Part-time, evening/weekend. Terminal master's awarded for partial completion of doctoral program. *Degree requirements:* For doctorate, thesis/dissertation. *Entrance requirements:* For master's, GRE General Test, minimum GPA of 3.0 in last 60 hours, interview, 3 letters of recommendation; for doctorate, GRE General Test, master's degree, interview, writing sample, 3 letters of recommendation. Additional exam requirements/recommendations for international students: Required—TOEFL (minimum score 500 paper-based). Electronic applications accepted. *Faculty research:* Effective instruction, technology education, exceptional student education, multiculturalism.

University of North Georgia, Master of Arts in Teaching Program, Dahlonega, GA 30597. Offers physical education (MAT); secondary education - English (MAT); secondary education - history (MAT); secondary education - mathematics (MAT); secondary education - middle grades (MAT). *Students:* 27 part-time (20 women). Average age 29. 12 applicants, 75% accepted, 7 enrolled. In 2017, 15 master's awarded. *Degree requirements:* For master's, internship, capstone. *Entrance requirements:* For master's, GRE or MAT, GACE I and II, GA pre-service application, lawful presence verification, official transcripts, GA Educator Ethics Program entry assessment. Additional exam requirements/recommendations for international students: Required—TOEFL (minimum score 550 paper-based; 79 iBT), IELTS (minimum score 6.5). *Application deadline:* For summer admission, 2/1 for domestic students. Application fee: $40. Electronic applications accepted. *Expenses:* Contact institution. *Financial support:* Application deadline: 3/17; applicants required to submit FAFSA. *Unit head:* Dr. Susan Brandenburg-Ayres, Dean, 706-864-1998, E-mail: susan.ayres@ung.edu. *Application contact:* Melinda Maxwell, Director of Graduate Admissions, 706-867-2077, E-mail: melinda.maxwell@ung.edu. Website: https://ung.edu/teacher-education/graduate/master-of-arts-teaching.php

University of North Texas, Robert B. Toulouse School of Graduate Studies, Denton, TX 76203-5459. Offers accounting (MS); applied anthropology (MA, MS); applied behavior analysis (Certificate); applied geography (MA); applied technology and performance improvement (M Ed, MS); art education (MA); art history (MA); art museum education (Certificate); arts leadership (Certificate); audiology (Au D); behavior analysis (MS); behavioral science (PhD); biochemistry and molecular biology (MS); biology (MA, MS); biomedical engineering (MS); business analysis (MS); chemistry (MS); clinical health psychology (PhD); communication studies (MA, MS); computer engineering (MS); computer science (MS); counseling (M Ed, MS), including clinical mental health counseling (MS), college and university counseling, elementary school counseling, secondary school counseling; creative writing (MA); criminal justice (MS); curriculum and instruction (M Ed); decision sciences (MBA); design (MA, MFA), including fashion design (MFA), innovation studies, interior design (MFA); early childhood studies (MS); economics (MS); educational leadership (M Ed, Ed D); educational psychology (MS, PhD), including family studies (MS), gifted and talented (MS), human development (MS), learning and cognition (MS), research, measurement and evaluation (MS); electrical engineering (MS); emergency management (MPA); engineering technology (MS); English (MA); English as a second language (MA); environmental science (MS); finance (MBA, MS); financial management (MPA); French (MA); health services management (MBA); higher education (M Ed, Ed D); history (MA, MS); hospitality management (MS); human resources management (MPA); information science (MS); information systems (PhD); information technologies (MBA); interdisciplinary studies (MA, MS); international studies (MA); international sustainable tourism (MS); jazz studies (MM); journalism (MA, MJ, Graduate Certificate), including interactive and virtual digital communication (Graduate Certificate), narrative journalism (Graduate Certificate), public relations (Graduate Certificate); kinesiology (MS); linguistics (MA); local government management (MPA); logistics (PhD); logistics and supply chain management (MBA); long-term care, senior housing, and aging services (MA); management (PhD); marketing (MBA); mathematics (MA, MS); mechanical and energy engineering (MS, PhD); music (MA), including ethnomusicology, music theory, musicology, performance; music composition (PhD); music education (MM Ed, PhD); nonprofit management (MPA); operations and supply chain management (MBA); performance (MM, DMA); philosophy (MA); political science (MA); professional and technical communication (MA); radio, television and film (MA, MFA); rehabilitation counseling (Certificate); sociology (MA); Spanish (MA); special education (M Ed); speech-language pathology (MA); strategic management (MBA); studio art (MFA); teaching (M Ed); MBA/MS. *Program availability:* Part-time, evening/weekend, online learning. Terminal master's awarded for partial completion of doctoral program. *Degree requirements:* For master's, variable foreign language requirement, comprehensive exam (for some programs), thesis (for some programs); for doctorate, variable foreign language requirement, comprehensive exam (for some programs), thesis/dissertation; for other advanced degree, variable foreign language requirement, comprehensive exam (for some programs). *Entrance requirements:* For master's and doctorate, GRE, GMAT. Additional exam requirements/recommendations for international students: Required—TOEFL (minimum score 550 paper-based; 79 iBT). Electronic applications accepted.

University of Northwestern–St. Paul, Master of Arts in Education Program, St. Paul, MN 55113-1598. Offers MA Ed. *Program availability:* Part-time, evening/weekend, online learning. *Application deadline:* Applications are processed on a rolling basis. Electronic applications accepted. *Expenses:* Contact institution. *Application contact:* Graduate Studies Admissions, 651-631-5200, E-mail: gradstudies@unwsp.edu. Website: https://www.unwsp.edu/web/graduate-studies/master-of-arts-in-education

University of Notre Dame, Graduate School, College of Arts and Letters, Division of Social Science, Institute for Educational Initiatives, Notre Dame, IN 46556. Offers M Ed, MA. Enrollment restricted to participants in the Alliance for Catholic Education (ACE) program. *Entrance requirements:* For master's, GRE General Test, acceptance into the Alliance for Catholic Education program. Electronic applications accepted. *Faculty research:* Effective teaching, motivation, social and ethical development, literacy.

University of Oklahoma, Jeannine Rainbolt College of Education, Norman, OK 73019. Offers M Ed, Ed D, PhD, Graduate Certificate. *Accreditation:* NCATE. *Program availability:* Part-time, evening/weekend. *Faculty:* 73 full-time (44 women), 5 part-time/adjunct (2 women). *Students:* 253 full-time (178 women), 503 part-time (383 women); includes 224 minority (75 Black or African American, non-Hispanic/Latino; 36 American Indian or Alaska Native, non-Hispanic/Latino; 12 Asian, non-Hispanic/Latino; 50 Hispanic/Latino; 1 Native Hawaiian or other Pacific Islander, non-Hispanic/Latino; 50 Two or more races, non-Hispanic/Latino), 35 international. Average age 34. 359 applicants, 64% accepted, 189 enrolled. In 2017, 199 master's, 43 doctorates, 6 other advanced degrees awarded. Terminal master's awarded for partial completion of doctoral program. *Degree requirements:* For master's, comprehensive exam (for some programs), thesis (for some programs); for doctorate, comprehensive exam (for some programs), thesis/dissertation (for some programs). *Entrance requirements:* Additional exam requirements/recommendations for international students: Required—TOEFL (minimum score 79 iBT) or IELTS (minimum score 6.5). Application fee: $50 ($100 for international students). Electronic applications accepted. *Expenses:* Tuition, state resident: full-time $5119; part-time $213.30 per credit hour. Tuition, nonresident: full-time $19,778; part-time $824.10 per credit hour. *Required fees:* $3458; $133.55 per credit hour. $126.50 per semester. *Financial support:* In 2017–18, 468 students received support, including 45 research assistantships with full and partial tuition reimbursements available (averaging $12,416 per year), 12 teaching assistantships with full and partial tuition reimbursements available (averaging $12,723 per year); fellowships with full and partial tuition reimbursements available, career-related internships or fieldwork, Federal Work-Study, institutionally sponsored loans, scholarships/grants, traineeships, health care benefits, and unspecified assistantships also available. Support available to part-time students. Financial award application deadline: 6/1; financial award applicants required to submit FAFSA. *Total annual research expenditures:* $5.2 million. *Unit head:* Dr. Gregg Garn, Dean, 405-325-1082, Fax: 405-325-7390, E-mail: garn@ou.edu. *Application contact:* Anna Steele, Graduate Programs Officer, 405-325-4525, E-mail: jrcoe_gps@ou.edu.
Website: http://www.ou.edu/

University of Oregon, Graduate School, College of Education, Eugene, OR 97403. Offers communication disorders and sciences (MA, MS, PhD); counseling psychology (PhD); couples and family therapy (MS); critical and sociocultural studies in education (PhD); curriculum and teacher education (MA, MS); educational leadership (MS, D Ed, PhD); prevention science (M Ed, MS, PhD); school psychology (MS, PhD); special education (M Ed, MA, MS, PhD). *Program availability:* Part-time. Terminal master's awarded for partial completion of doctoral program. *Degree requirements:* For master's, exam, paper, or project; for doctorate, comprehensive exam, thesis/dissertation. *Entrance requirements:* Additional exam requirements/recommendations for international students: Required—TOEFL. *Faculty research:* Basic and applied research in teaching, learning and habilitation in all settings, schooling effectiveness.

University of Ottawa, Faculty of Graduate and Postdoctoral Studies, Faculty of Education, Ottawa, ON K1N 6N5, Canada. Offers M Ed, MA Ed, PhD, Certificate. *Program availability:* Online learning. *Degree requirements:* For master's, thesis or alternative; for doctorate, comprehensive exam, thesis/dissertation, seminar. *Entrance requirements:* For master's, honors degree or equivalent, minimum B average; for doctorate, master's degree, minimum B+ average. Electronic applications accepted. *Faculty research:* Teaching, learning and evaluation; second language education; organizational studies in education; society, culture and literacies; educational counseling.

★ **University of Pennsylvania,** Graduate School of Education, Philadelphia, PA 19104. Offers M Phil, MS, MS Ed, Ed D, PhD, Certificate. *Program availability:* Part-time, evening/weekend, online learning. *Faculty:* 73 full-time (30 women), 45 part-time/adjunct (21 women). *Students:* 1,057 full-time (751 women), 299 part-time (203 women); includes 432 minority (208 Black or African American, non-Hispanic/Latino; 99 Asian, non-Hispanic/Latino; 81 Hispanic/Latino; 1 Native Hawaiian or other Pacific Islander, non-Hispanic/Latino; 43 Two or more races,

non-Hispanic/Latino), 355 international. Average age 31. 3,105 applicants, 51% accepted, 888 enrolled. In 2017, 559 master's, 77 doctorates awarded. Terminal master's awarded for partial completion of doctoral program. Application fee: $80. Electronic applications accepted. *Unit head:* Dr. Pam Grossman, Dean, 215-898-7014, Fax: 215-746-6884, E-mail: admissions@gse.upenn.edu.
Website: http://www.gse.upenn.edu/
See Display on page 705 and Close-Up on page 721.

University of Pennsylvania, Graduate School of Education, Division of Teaching, Learning, and Leadership, Program in Teaching, Learning, and Teacher Education, Philadelphia, PA 19104. Offers Ed D, PhD.

University of Phoenix–Bay Area Campus, College of Education, San Jose, CA 95134-1805. Offers administration and supervision (MA Ed); adult education and training (MA Ed); early childhood education (MA Ed); education (Ed S); educational leadership (Ed D); elementary teacher education (MA Ed); higher education administration (PhD); secondary teacher education (MA Ed); special education (MA Ed); teacher leadership (MA Ed). *Program availability:* Evening/weekend, online learning. *Degree requirements:* For master's, thesis (for some programs). *Entrance requirements:* For master's, minimum undergraduate GPA of 2.5, 3 years of work experience. Additional exam requirements/recommendations for international students: Required—TOEFL (minimum score 550 paper-based; 79 iBT). Electronic applications accepted.

University of Phoenix–Central Valley Campus, College of Education, Fresno, CA 93720-1552. Offers curriculum and instruction (MA Ed); curriculum and instruction-computer education (MA Ed); elementary teacher education (MA Ed); secondary teacher education (MA Ed).

University of Phoenix–Dallas Campus, College of Education, Dallas, TX 75251. Offers curriculum and instruction (MA Ed).

University of Phoenix–Hawaii Campus, College of Education, Honolulu, HI 96813-3800. Offers administration and supervision (MA Ed); curriculum and instruction (MA Ed); elementary education (MA Ed); secondary education (MA Ed); special education (MA Ed); teacher education for elementary licensure (MA Ed). *Program availability:* Evening/weekend. *Degree requirements:* For master's, thesis (for some programs). *Entrance requirements:* For master's, minimum undergraduate GPA of 2.5, 3 years of work experience. Additional exam requirements/recommendations for international students: Required—TOEFL (minimum score 550 paper-based; 79 iBT). Electronic applications accepted.

University of Phoenix–Houston Campus, College of Education, Houston, TX 77079-2004. Offers curriculum and instruction (MA Ed).

University of Phoenix–Las Vegas Campus, College of Education, Las Vegas, NV 89135. Offers administration and supervision (MA Ed); curriculum and instruction (MA Ed); school counseling (MSC); teacher education-elementary licensure (MA Ed). *Program availability:* Evening/weekend. *Degree requirements:* For master's, thesis (for some programs). *Entrance requirements:* For master's, minimum undergraduate GPA of 2.5, 3 years of work experience. Additional exam requirements/recommendations for international students: Required—TOEFL (minimum score 550 paper-based; 79 iBT). Electronic applications accepted.

University of Phoenix–Online Campus, College of Education, Phoenix, AZ 85034-7209. Offers administration and supervision (MAEd, Certificate); adult education and training (MAEd); curriculum and instruction (MAEd), including computer education, curriculum and instruction, English as a second language, language arts, mathematics, reading; early childhood education (MAEd); educational studies (MAEd); elementary teacher education (MAEd), including early childhood, elementary teacher education, high school middle level, middle level; principal licensure (Certificate); secondary teacher education (MAEd); special education (MAEd, Certificate); teacher education (MAEd), including middle level generalist; teacher education middle level mathematics (MAEd), including middle level mathematics; teacher education middle level science (MAEd), including middle level science; teacher education secondary mathematics (MAEd); teacher education secondary science (MAEd); teacher leadership (MAEd); teachers of English learners (Certificate); transition to teaching (Certificate), including elementary education, secondary education. *Program availability:* Evening/weekend, online learning. *Entrance requirements:* Additional exam requirements/recommendations for international students: Required—TOEFL, TOEIC (Test of English as an International Communication), Berlitz Online English Proficiency Exam, PTE, or IELTS. Electronic applications accepted. *Expenses:* Contact institution.

University of Phoenix–Phoenix Campus, College of Education, Tempe, AZ 85282-2371. Offers administration and supervision (MA Ed); adult education and training (MA Ed); curriculum and instruction reading (MA Ed); early childhood education (MA Ed); education studies (MA Ed); elementary teacher education (MA Ed); secondary teacher education (MA Ed); special education (MA Ed); teacher leadership (MA Ed). *Program availability:* Evening/weekend, online learning. *Entrance requirements:* Additional exam requirements/recommendations for international students: Required—TOEFL, TOEIC (Test of English as an International Communication), Berlitz Online English Proficiency Exam, PTE, or IELTS. Electronic applications accepted. *Expenses:* Contact institution.

University of Phoenix–Sacramento Valley Campus, College of Education, Sacramento, CA 95833-4334. Offers adult education (MA Ed); curriculum instruction (MA Ed); elementary teacher education (MA Ed); secondary teacher education (MA Ed); teacher education (Certificate). *Program availability:* Evening/weekend. *Degree requirements:* For master's, thesis (for some programs). *Entrance requirements:* For master's, 3 years of work experience, minimum undergraduate GPA of 2.5. Additional exam requirements/recommendations for international students: Required—TOEFL (minimum score 550 paper-based; 79 iBT). Electronic applications accepted.

University of Phoenix–San Diego Campus, College of Education, San Diego, CA 92123. Offers curriculum and instruction (MA Ed), including computer education, curriculum and instruction, English as a second language; elementary teacher education (MA Ed); secondary teacher education (MA Ed). *Program availability:* Evening/weekend. *Degree requirements:* For master's, thesis (for some programs). *Entrance requirements:* For master's, 3 years of work experience, minimum undergraduate GPA of 3.0. Additional exam requirements/recommendations for international students: Required—TOEFL (minimum score 550 paper-based; 79 iBT). Electronic applications accepted.

University of Pikeville, Patton College of Education, Pikeville, KY 41501. Offers teacher leader (MA). *Program availability:* Part-time, evening/weekend. *Faculty:* 10 part-time/adjunct (6 women). *Students:* 66 full-time (56 women), 15 part-time (11 women). Average age 35. In 2017, 25 master's awarded. *Degree requirements:* For master's, comprehensive exam. *Application deadline:* For fall admission, 8/15 for domestic students. Applications are processed on a rolling basis. Application fee: $50. *Expenses:* Contact institution. *Financial support:* Application deadline: 2/1; applicants required to submit FAFSA. *Unit head:* Dr. Coletta Parsley, Division Chair, 606-218-5318, E-mail: colettaparsley@upike.edu. *Application contact:* Fairy Coleman, Administrative Assistant, 606-218-5314, E-mail: fairycoleman@upike.edu.
Website: http://www.upike.edu/COE/

University of Pittsburgh, School of Education, Pittsburgh, PA 15260. Offers M Ed, MA, MAT, MS, Ed D, PhD. *Program availability:* Part-time, evening/weekend, online learning. Terminal master's awarded for partial completion of doctoral program. *Degree requirements:* For master's, comprehensive exam, thesis (for some programs); for doctorate, comprehensive exam, thesis/dissertation. *Entrance requirements:* For doctorate, GRE. Additional exam requirements/recommendations for international students: Required—TOEFL (minimum score 550 paper-based; 80 iBT). Electronic applications accepted.

See Display below and Close-Up on page 723.

University of Portland, School of Education, Portland, OR 97203-5798. Offers education (MA, MAT); educational leadership (M Ed); English for speakers of other languages (M Ed); initial administrator licensure (M Ed); neuroeducation (M Ed, Ed D); organizational leadership and development (Ed D); reading (M Ed); school leadership and development (Ed D); special education (M Ed). M Ed also available through the Graduate Outreach Program for teachers residing in the Oregon and Washington state areas. *Accreditation:* NCATE. *Program availability:* Part-time, evening/weekend. *Entrance requirements:* For master's, minimum GPA of 3.0, teaching certificate, letters of recommendation, resume, statement of goals, official transcripts. Additional exam requirements/recommendations for international students: Required—TOEFL (minimum score 550 paper-based; 80 iBT), IELTS (minimum score 7). *Faculty research:* Multicultural education, supervision/leadership.

University of Prince Edward Island, Faculty of Education, Charlottetown, PE C1A 4P3, Canada. Offers educational studies (PhD); leadership in learning (M Ed). *Program availability:* Part-time. *Degree requirements:* For master's, thesis. *Entrance requirements:* For master's, 2 years of professional experience, bachelor of education, professional certificate. Additional exam requirements/recommendations for international students: Required—TOEFL (minimum score 550 paper-based; 80 iBT), Canadian Academic English Language Assessment, Michigan English Language Assessment Battery, Canadian Test of English for Scholars and Trainees. *Faculty research:* Distance learning, aboriginal communities and education leadership development, international development, immersion language learning.

University of Puerto Rico–Río Piedras, College of Education, San Juan, PR 00931-3300. Offers M Ed, MS, Ed D. *Accreditation:* NCATE. *Program availability:* Part-time. *Degree requirements:* For master's, thesis; for doctorate, thesis/dissertation, internship. *Entrance requirements:* For master's, GRE or PAEG, minimum GPA of 3.0, letter of recommendation; for doctorate, GRE or PAEG, master's degree, minimum GPA of 3.0, letter of recommendation (2), interview. *Faculty research:* Curriculum, math teaching.

University of Puget Sound, School of Education, Tacoma, WA 98416. Offers M Ed, MAT. *Program availability:* Part-time. *Degree requirements:* For master's, capstone course (for M Ed); project (for MAT). *Entrance requirements:* For master's, GRE General Test, WEST-E or NES, WEST-B or ACT/SAT, two education foundation prerequisite courses (for MAT); interview (for M Ed). Additional exam requirements/recommendations for international students: Required—TOEFL (minimum score 550 paper-based; 90 iBT). Electronic applications accepted. *Expenses:* Contact institution. *Faculty research:* Pre-service teacher learning and public school partnerships, creating equitable classrooms, literacy development, teaching social studies, suicide prevention.

University of Redlands, School of Education, Redlands, CA 92373-0999. Offers MA, Ed D, Certificate. *Program availability:* Part-time, evening/weekend. *Entrance requirements:* For master's, minimum undergraduate GPA of 3.0, 2 letters of recommendation. Additional exam requirements/recommendations for international students: Required—TOEFL (minimum score 550 paper-based). *Expenses:* Contact institution.

University of Regina, Faculty of Graduate Studies and Research, Faculty of Education, Regina, SK S4S 0A2, Canada. Offers M Ed, MA Ed, MHRD, PhD, Master's Certificate. *Program availability:* Part-time. *Faculty:* 48 full-time (33 women), 13 part-time/adjunct (6 women). *Students:* 99 full-time (76 women), 285 part-time (223 women). 297 applicants, 41% accepted. In 2017, 119 master's, 8 doctorates, 2 other advanced degrees awarded. *Degree requirements:* For master's, thesis (for some programs), practicum, project, or thesis; for doctorate, thesis/dissertation. *Entrance requirements:* For master's, 4-year B Ed or equivalent, two years of teaching or other relevant professional experience. Additional exam requirements/recommendations for international students: Required—TOEFL (minimum score 580 paper-based; 80 iBT), IELTS (minimum score 6.5), PTE (minimum score 59). *Application deadline:* For fall admission, 2/15 for domestic and international students; for winter admission, 10/15 for domestic and international students; for spring admission, 2/15 for domestic and international students. Application fee: $100. Electronic applications accepted. *Expenses:* $10,681. *Financial support:* In 2017–18, 15 fellowships (averaging $5,042 per year), 25 teaching assistantships (averaging $2,562 per year) were awarded; research assistantships, career-related internships or fieldwork, and scholarships/grants also available. Financial award application deadline: 6/15. *Faculty research:* Curriculum and instruction, educational administration, educational psychology, human resource development, adult education. *Unit head:* Dr. Paul Clarke, Associate Dean, Research and Graduate Programs in Education, 306-585-5353, Fax: 306-585-5387, E-mail: paul.clarke@uregina.ca. *Application contact:* Linda Jiang, Graduate Program Coordinator, 306-585-4506, Fax: 306-585-5387, E-mail: edgrad@uregina.ca. Website: http://www.uregina.ca/education

University of Rhode Island, Graduate School, Alan Shawn Feinstein College of Education and Professional Studies, School of Education, Kingston, RI 02881. Offers education (PhD); reading (MA); special education (MA). *Accreditation:* NCATE. *Program availability:* Part-time, evening/weekend. *Faculty:* 18 full-time (12 women). *Students:* 59 full-time (44 women), 145 part-time (114 women); includes 24 minority (6 Black or African American, non-Hispanic/Latino; 6 American Indian or Alaska Native, non-Hispanic/Latino; 7 Asian, non-Hispanic/Latino; 3 Hispanic/Latino; 2 Two or more races, non-Hispanic/Latino), 6 international. 91 applicants, 65% accepted, 53 enrolled. In 2017, 50 master's, 9 doctorates awarded. *Entrance requirements:* For master's, 2 letters of recommendation; personal statement; two official transcripts; interview and minimum undergraduate GPA of 3.0 (for special education applicants); for doctorate, GRE, 3 letters of recommendation, resume, personal statement, two copies of official transcripts. Additional exam requirements/recommendations for international students: Required—TOEFL. Application fee: $65. Electronic applications accepted. *Expenses:* Tuition, state resident: full-time $12,706; part-time $786 per credit. Tuition, nonresident: full-time $25,216; part-time $1401 per credit. *Required fees:* $1598; $45 per credit. One-time fee: $30 part-time. *Financial support:* In 2017–18, 1 research assistantship with tuition reimbursement (averaging $8,862 per year), 5 teaching assistantships with tuition reimbursements (averaging $17,795 per year) were awarded. Financial award applicants required to submit FAFSA. *Unit head:* Dr. David Byrd, Director, School of Education, 401-874-5484, Fax: 401-874-5471, E-mail: dbyrd@uri.edu. *Application contact:* Graduate Admissions, 401-874-2262, E-mail: gradadm@etal.uri.edu. Website: http://www.uri.edu/hss/education/

University of Rio Grande, Graduate School, Rio Grande, OH 45674. Offers athletic coaching leadership (M Ed); educational leadership (M Ed); integrated arts (M Ed); intervention specialist in early childhood (M Ed); intervention specialist in mild/moderate (M Ed). *Accreditation:* NCATE. *Program availability:* Part-time. *Degree requirements:* For master's, final research project, portfolio. *Entrance requirements:* For master's, minimum GPA of 2.7 in major, 2.5 overall. Additional exam requirements/recommendations for international students: Required—TOEFL. *Faculty research:* Interagency collaboration, reading and mathematics, learning styles, college access, literacy.

Pitt Education
University of Pittsburgh School of Education

$3.5 MILLION
in scholarship support awarded through endowed funds, scholarships, and student assistantships

5 DEPARTMENTS
Administrative & Policy Studies I Health & Physical Activity I Instruction & Learning I Learning Sciences & Policy I Psychology in Education

6 CENTERS & INSTITUTES
in areas such as urban education, motivation, child development, and physical activity/weight management

$22 MILLION
in funded research for more than 50 research projects in 2017-18

More Than **60** PROGRAMS OFFERED
undergraduate I online I master's I certification I EdD I PhD

More Than **150** FACULTY MEMBERS

Nearly **1,000** GRADUATE STUDENTS

#1 PUBLIC GRADUATE EDUCATION PROGRAM IN PA
U.S. News & World Report

#14 ONLINE M.Ed. PROGRAM IN THE NATION
BestColleges.com

#34 GRADUATE EDUCATION PROGRAM IN THE NATION
U.S. News & World Report

education.pitt.edu

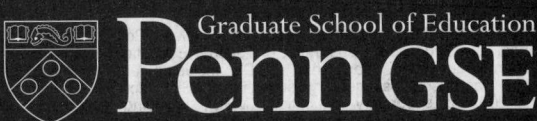
University of Rochester, Margaret Warner Graduate School of Education and Human Development, Rochester, NY 14627. Offers MS, Ed D, PhD. *Accreditation:* ACA (one or more programs are accredited); NCATE. *Program availability:* Part-time, evening/weekend. Terminal master's awarded for partial completion of doctoral program. *Degree requirements:* For master's, thesis (for some programs); for doctorate, thesis/dissertation, qualifying exam.

University of St. Francis, College of Education, Joliet, IL 60435-6169. Offers educational leadership (MS, Ed D); elementary education (M Ed); reading (MS); secondary education (M Ed), including English education, math education, science education, social studies education, visual arts education; special education (M Ed); teaching and learning (MS); TESOL (Certificate). *Accreditation:* NCATE. *Program availability:* Part-time, evening/weekend, 100% online, blended/hybrid learning. *Faculty:* 11 full-time (8 women), 52 part-time/adjunct (36 women). *Students:* 39 full-time (32 women), 411 part-time (318 women); includes 106 minority (57 Black or African American, non-Hispanic/Latino; 8 Asian, non-Hispanic/Latino; 37 Hispanic/Latino; 4 Two or more races, non-Hispanic/Latino), 4 international. Average age 37. 277 applicants, 55% accepted, 137 enrolled. In 2017, 199 master's, 28 doctorates awarded. *Degree requirements:* For master's, comprehensive exam; for doctorate, thesis/dissertation. *Entrance requirements:* Additional exam requirements/recommendations for international students: Required—TOEFL (minimum score 550 paper-based; 79 iBT), IELTS (minimum score 6). *Application deadline:* Applications are processed on a rolling basis. Application fee: $30. Electronic applications accepted. Application fee is waived when completed online. *Expenses:* $365 to $748 per credit hour. *Financial support:* In 2017–18, 40 students received support. Scholarships/grants and unspecified assistantships available. Support available to part-time students. Financial award applicants required to submit FAFSA. *Unit head:* Dr. John Gambro, Dean, 815-740-3829, Fax: 815-740-2264, E-mail: jgambro@stfrancis.edu. *Application contact:* Sandra Sloka, Director of Admissions for Graduate and Degree Completion Programs, 800-735-7500, Fax: 815-740-3431, E-mail: ssloka@stfrancis.edu.
Website: http://www.stfrancis.edu/academics/college-of-education/

University of Saint Francis, Graduate School, Department of Education, Fort Wayne, IN 46808-3994. Offers secondary education (MAT); special education (MS Ed), including intense intervention, mild intervention. *Accreditation:* NCATE. *Program availability:* Part-time, evening/weekend, online only, 100% online. *Faculty:* 4 full-time (3 women), 3 part-time/adjunct (all women). *Students:* 6 full-time (5 women), 19 part-time (15 women); includes 1 minority (Hispanic/Latino). Average age 33. 17 applicants, 100% accepted, 14 enrolled. In 2017, 8 master's awarded. *Entrance requirements:* For master's, GRE (minimum composite score of 280 verbal and quantitative subtests) or MAT (minimum score of 389) if undergraduate GPA is below a 2.8 or prior graduate level GPA is below 3.0; GRE, ACT, SAT, or CASA exam if no license, minimum undergraduate GPA of 2.8; resume (if GPA is below 3.0); standard teaching license and/or bachelor's degree from regionally-accredited institution; background check; two professional recommendations. Additional exam requirements/recommendations for international students: Required—TOEFL (minimum score 550 paper-based) or IELTS (minimum score 6.5). *Application deadline:* For fall admission, 7/1 for international students; for spring admission, 11/1 for international students; for summer admission, 3/1 for international students. Applications are processed on a rolling basis. Application fee: $0. Electronic applications accepted. *Expenses:* $475 per hour (for MAT); $905 per hour (for MS Ed). *Financial support:* Federal Work-Study, scholarships/grants, and unspecified assistantships available. Financial award application deadline: 4/15; financial award applicants required to submit FAFSA. *Unit head:* Mary Riepenhoff, Assistant Professor/Department Chair, 260-399-7700 Ext. 8409, Fax: 260-399-8170, E-mail: mriepenhoff@sf.edu. *Application contact:* Kyle Richardson, Associate Director of Enrollment Services for Adult Learning, 260-399-7700 Ext. 6310, Fax: 260-399-8152, E-mail: krichardson@sf.edu.
Website: https://education.sf.edu/

University of Saint Joseph, Department of Education, West Hartford, CT 06117-2700. Offers curriculum and instruction (MA); elementary education (MAT); instructional technology (MA); literacy (MA); secondary education (MAT); TESOL (MA). *Program availability:* Part-time, evening/weekend. *Degree requirements:* For master's, comprehensive exam, thesis or alternative. *Entrance requirements:* For master's, 2 letters of recommendation. *Application deadline:* Applications are processed on a rolling basis. Application fee: $50. Electronic applications accepted. Application fee is waived when completed online. *Financial support:* Career-related internships or fieldwork and unspecified assistantships available. Support available to part-time students. Financial award applicants required to submit FAFSA.
Website: https://www.usj.edu/academics/schools/sasbe/education/

University of Saint Mary, Graduate Programs, Program in Education, Leavenworth, KS 66048-5082. Offers MA. *Accreditation:* NCATE. *Program availability:* Part-time, evening/weekend, online learning. *Degree requirements:* For master's, thesis, oral presentation. *Entrance requirements:* For master's, minimum undergraduate GPA of 2.75, bachelor's degree from accredited college, interview, official transcripts, two letters of recommendation, essay. Electronic applications accepted. *Expenses:* Contact institution. *Faculty research:* Curriculum and instruction.

University of Saint Mary, Graduate Programs, Program in Teaching, Leavenworth, KS 66048-5082. Offers MAT. *Program availability:* Part-time, online only, 100% online. *Degree requirements:* For master's, thesis. *Entrance requirements:* For master's, minimum undergraduate GPA of 2.75. Electronic applications accepted. *Expenses:* Contact institution.

University of St. Thomas, College of Education, Leadership and Counseling, St. Paul, MN 55105-1096. Offers MA, Ed D, Psy D, Certificate, Ed S. *Program availability:* Part-time, evening/weekend, 100% online, blended/hybrid learning. *Degree requirements:* For doctorate, thesis/dissertation. *Entrance requirements:* For master's, minimum GPA of 3.0 or MAT. Additional exam requirements/recommendations for international students: Required—TOEFL (minimum score 550 paper-based; 80 iBT). *Application deadline:* For fall admission, 7/15 priority date for domestic students, 7/15 for international students; for spring admission, 12/9 priority date for domestic students, 12/9 for international students; for summer admission, 4/3 for domestic and international students. Applications are processed on a rolling basis. Electronic applications accepted. *Expenses:* Contact institution. *Financial support:* Research assistantships, career-related internships or fieldwork, institutionally sponsored loans, scholarships/grants, and unspecified assistantships available. Support available to part-time students. Financial award application deadline: 8/1; financial award applicants required to submit FAFSA. *Unit head:* Dr. Joseph L. Kreitzer, Dean, 651-962-6032, Fax: 651-962-4169, E-mail: jlkreitzer@stthomas.edu.
Website: https://www.stthomas.edu/celc/

University of St. Thomas, School of Education and Human Services, Houston, TX 77006-4696. Offers all level education (M Ed); bilingual/dual language (M Ed); Catholic school teaching (M Ed); Catholic/private school leadership (M Ed); counselor education (M Ed); curriculum and instruction (M Ed); education (Ed D); educational leadership (M Ed); elementary teaching (M Ed); English as a second language (M Ed); exceptionality/educational diagnostician (M Ed); exceptionality/special education (M Ed); generalist (M Ed); reading (M Ed); secondary teaching (M Ed); teaching (MAT).

Education—General

Accreditation: TEAC. *Program availability:* Part-time, evening/weekend, online learning. *Faculty:* 33 full-time (22 women), 43 part-time/adjunct (26 women). *Students:* 119 full-time (97 women), 597 part-time (529 women); includes 478 minority (166 Black or African American, non-Hispanic/Latino; 29 Asian, non-Hispanic/Latino; 277 Hispanic/Latino; 2 Native Hawaiian or other Pacific Islander, non-Hispanic/Latino; 4 Two or more races, non-Hispanic/Latino), 19 international. Average age 36. 306 applicants, 91% accepted, 181 enrolled. In 2017, 328 master's awarded. *Degree requirements:* For master's, thesis, field experience. *Entrance requirements:* For master's, GRE or MAT if GPA is below 3.0, bachelor's degree; minimum GPA of 2.75 in bachelor's degree or last 60 credit hours; official transcripts from all institutions; goal statement of 250-300 words; 1 reference. Additional exam requirements/recommendations for international students: Required—TOEFL (minimum score 94 iBT), IELTS (minimum score 7), PTE (minimum score 53). *Application deadline:* Applications are processed on a rolling basis. Application fee: $35. Electronic applications accepted. *Expenses:* Contact institution. *Financial support:* In 2017–18, 27 students received support. Federal Work-Study, scholarships/grants, and state work-study, institutional employment available. Support available to part-time students. Financial award application deadline: 4/15; financial award applicants required to submit FAFSA. *Faculty research:* Leadership, diversity, personality traits, second language acquisition. *Unit head:* Dr. Paul C. Paese, Dean, 713-942-5999, Fax: 713-525-3871, E-mail: paesep@stthom.edu. *Application contact:* 713-525-3540, E-mail: education@stthom.edu.
Website: http://www.stthom.edu/Academics/ School_of_Education_and_Human_Services/Index.aqf

University of San Diego, School of Leadership and Education Sciences, San Diego, CA 92110-2492. Offers M Ed, MA, PhD, Certificate. *Accreditation:* NCATE. *Program availability:* Part-time, evening/weekend. *Faculty:* 32 full-time (18 women), 74 part-time/adjunct (49 women). *Students:* 385 full-time (317 women), 473 part-time (358 women); includes 355 minority (47 Black or African American, non-Hispanic/Latino; 1 American Indian or Alaska Native, non-Hispanic/Latino; 60 Asian, non-Hispanic/Latino; 209 Hispanic/Latino; 2 Native Hawaiian or other Pacific Islander, non-Hispanic/Latino; 36 Two or more races, non-Hispanic/Latino), 48 international. Average age 31. In 2017, 273 master's, 15 doctorates awarded. *Degree requirements:* For master's, international experience; for doctorate, comprehensive exam (for some programs), thesis/dissertation (for some programs), international experience. *Entrance requirements:* For doctorate, GRE General Test, master's degree. Additional exam requirements/recommendations for international students: Required—TOEFL (minimum score 580 paper-based; 83 iBT), TWE. Application fee: $45. *Financial support:* In 2017–18, 424 students received support. Career-related internships or fieldwork, Federal Work-Study, institutionally sponsored loans, unspecified assistantships, and stipends available. Support available to part-time students. Financial award application deadline: 4/1; financial award applicants required to submit FAFSA. *Unit head:* Dr. Nicholas Ladany, Dean, 619-260-4540, Fax: 619-260-6835, E-mail: nladany@sandiego.edu. *Application contact:* Monica Mahon, Associate Director of Graduate Admissions, 619-260-4524, Fax: 619-260-4158, E-mail: grads@sandiego.edu.
Website: http://www.sandiego.edu/soles/

University of San Francisco, School of Education, San Francisco, CA 94117-1080. Offers MA, Ed D. *Program availability:* Part-time, evening/weekend. *Degree requirements:* For doctorate, thesis/dissertation. *Entrance requirements:* For master's, CBEST, CSET, and/or CSET Writing Skills (depending on program); for doctorate, GRE or MAT. Additional exam requirements/recommendations for international students: Required—TOEFL (minimum score 580 paper-based; 92 iBT), IELTS (minimum score 7), PTE (minimum score 62). Electronic applications accepted.

University of Saskatchewan, College of Graduate Studies and Research, College of Education, Saskatoon, SK S7N 5A2, Canada. Offers M Ed, MC Ed, PhD, Diploma. *Program availability:* Part-time. *Degree requirements:* For master's, thesis (for some programs); for doctorate, comprehensive exam (for some programs), thesis/dissertation. *Entrance requirements:* Additional exam requirements/recommendations for international students: Required—TOEFL (minimum score 80 iBT); Recommended—IELTS (minimum score 6.5). Electronic applications accepted.

The University of Scranton, Panuska College of Professional Studies, Department of Education, Scranton, PA 18510. Offers curriculum and instruction (MS); educational administration (MS); reading education (MS); secondary education (MS). *Accreditation:* NCATE; TEAC. *Program availability:* Part-time, evening/weekend, online learning. *Faculty research:* Meta-analysis as a research tool, family involvement in school activities, effect of curriculum integration on student learning and attitude, the effects of inclusion on students, development of emotional intelligence of young children.

University of Sioux Falls, Fredrikson School of Education, Sioux Falls, SD 57105-1699. Offers educational administration (Ed S), including principal leadership, superintendent and district leadership; leadership in reading (M Ed); leadership in schools (M Ed); leadership in technology (M Ed); teaching (M Ed). Admission in summer only. *Accreditation:* NCATE. *Program availability:* Part-time, evening/weekend. *Degree requirements:* For master's, comprehensive exam (for some programs), research application project; for Ed S, comprehensive exam, portfolio. *Entrance requirements:* For master's, minimum GPA of 3.0, 1 year of teaching experience; for Ed S, minimum 3 years of teaching experience, minimum cumulative GPA of 3.5, 1 year of administrative experience. Additional exam requirements/recommendations for international students: Required—TOEFL. *Faculty research:* Reading, literacy, leadership.

University of South Africa, College of Human Sciences, Pretoria, South Africa. Offers adult education (M Ed); African languages (MA, PhD); African politics (MA, PhD); Afrikaans (MA, PhD); ancient history (MA, PhD); ancient Near Eastern studies (MA, PhD); anthropology (MA, PhD); applied linguistics (MA); Arabic (MA, PhD); archaeology (MA); art history (MA); Biblical archaeology (MA); Biblical studies (M Th, D Th, PhD); Christian spirituality (M Th, D Th); church history (M Th, D Th); classical studies (MA, PhD); clinical psychology (MA); communication (MA, PhD); comparative education (M Ed, Ed D); consulting psychology (D Admin, D Com, PhD); curriculum studies (M Ed, Ed D); development studies (M Admin, MA, D Admin, PhD); didactics (M Ed, Ed D); education (M Tech); education management (M Ed, Ed D); educational psychology (M Ed); English (MA); environmental education (M Ed); French (MA, PhD); German (MA, PhD); Greek (MA); guidance and counseling (M Ed); health studies (MA, PhD), including health sciences education (MA), health services management (MA), medical and surgical nursing science (critical care general) (MA), midwifery and neonatal nursing science (MA), trauma and emergency care (MA); history (MA, PhD); history of education (Ed D); inclusive education (M Ed, Ed D); information and communications technology policy and regulation (MA); information science (MA, MIS, PhD); international politics (MA, PhD); Islamic studies (MA, PhD); Italian (MA, PhD); Judaica (MA, PhD); linguistics (MA, PhD); mathematical education (M Ed); mathematics education (MA); missiology (M Th, D Th); modern Hebrew (MA, PhD); musicology (MA, MMus, D Mus, PhD); natural science education (M Tech); New Testament (M Th, D Th); Old Testament (D Th); pastoral therapy (M Th, D Th); philosophy (MA); philosophy of education (M Ed, Ed D); politics (MA, PhD); Portuguese (MA, PhD); practical theology (M Th, D Th); psychology (MA, MS, PhD); psychology of education (M Ed, Ed D); public health (MA); religious studies (MA, D Th, PhD); Romance languages (MA); Russian (MA, PhD); Semitic languages (MA, PhD); social behavior studies in HIV/AIDS (MA); social science (mental health) (MA); social science in development studies (MA); social science in psychology (MA); social science in social work (MA); social science in sociology (MA); social work (MSW, DSW, PhD); socio-education (M Ed, Ed D); sociolinguistics (MA); sociology (MA, PhD); Spanish (MA, PhD); systematic theology (M Th, D Th); TESOL (teaching English to speakers of other languages) (MA); theological ethics (M Th, D Th); theory of literature (MA, PhD); urban ministries (D Th); urban ministry (M Th).

University of South Alabama, College of Education and Professional Studies, Mobile, AL 36688. Offers M Ed, MS, Ed D, PhD, Ed S. *Accreditation:* NCATE. *Program availability:* Part-time, evening/weekend. *Faculty:* 34 full-time (20 women), 20 part-time/adjunct (15 women). *Students:* 361 full-time (254 women), 142 part-time (109 women); includes 140 minority (106 Black or African American, non-Hispanic/Latino; 4 American Indian or Alaska Native, non-Hispanic/Latino; 10 Asian, non-Hispanic/Latino; 17 Hispanic/Latino; 3 Two or more races, non-Hispanic/Latino), 9 international. Average age 33. 258 applicants, 55% accepted, 112 enrolled. In 2017, 128 master's, 17 doctorates, 10 other advanced degrees awarded. *Degree requirements:* For master's, comprehensive exam; for doctorate, comprehensive exam, thesis/dissertation. *Entrance requirements:* For master's, GRE General Test or MAT; for doctorate, GRE, minimum graduate GPA of 3.25, 3 years of experience in field, 3 letters of recommendation, interview, official transcripts, statement of purpose; for Ed S, GRE, Class A certification, master's degree, two years of teaching experience, three letters of recommendation. Additional exam requirements/recommendations for international students: Required—TOEFL (minimum score 525 paper-based; 71 iBT). *Application deadline:* For fall admission, 7/15 priority date for domestic students, 6/15 priority date for international students; for spring admission, 11/15 priority date for domestic students, 11/1 priority date for international students; for summer admission, 4/15 priority date for domestic students, 4/1 for international students. Applications are processed on a rolling basis. Application fee: $35. Electronic applications accepted. *Expenses:* Tuition, state resident: full-time $10,104; part-time $421 per semester hour. Tuition, nonresident: full-time $20,208; part-time $842 per semester hour. *Financial support:* Fellowships, research assistantships, teaching assistantships, career-related internships or fieldwork, Federal Work-Study, institutionally sponsored loans, scholarships/grants, and unspecified assistantships available. Support available to part-time students. Financial award application deadline: 3/31; financial award applicants required to submit FAFSA. *Faculty research:* Mixed methods research and program evaluation. *Unit head:* Dr. Andrea M. Kent, Dean, College of Education, 251-380-2738, Fax: 251-380-2748, E-mail: akent@southalabama.edu. *Application contact:* Dr. Susan Santoli, Director of Graduate Studies, 251-380-2738, Fax: 251-380-2758, E-mail: ssantoli@ southalabama.edu.
Website: http://www.southalabama.edu/colleges/ceps/

University of South Carolina, The Graduate School, College of Education, Columbia, SC 29208. Offers IMA, M Ed, MAT, MS, MT, Ed D, PhD, Certificate, Ed S. *Accreditation:* NCATE. *Program availability:* Part-time, evening/weekend, online learning. *Degree requirements:* For master's, comprehensive exam, thesis (for some programs), foreign language (MA); for doctorate, one foreign language, comprehensive exam, thesis/dissertation. *Entrance requirements:* For master's, GRE General Test or MAT, official transcripts, letters of recommendation, letter of intent; for doctorate, GRE General Test or MAT/qualifying exams, letters of recommendation, letters of intent, interview. Electronic applications accepted. *Faculty research:* Inquiry learning, assessment of student learning, equity issues in education, multicultural education, cultural diversity.

University of South Carolina Upstate, Graduate Programs, Spartanburg, SC 29303-4999. Offers early childhood education (M Ed); elementary education (M Ed); informatics (MS); special education: visual impairment (M Ed). *Accreditation:* NCATE. *Program availability:* Part-time, evening/weekend. *Degree requirements:* For master's, professional portfolio. *Entrance requirements:* For master's, GRE General Test or MAT, interview, minimum undergraduate GPA of 2.5, teaching certificate, 2 letters of recommendation. *Faculty research:* Promoting university diversity awareness, rough and tumble play, social justice education, American Indian literatures and cultures, diversity and multicultural education, science teaching strategy.

University of South Dakota, Graduate School, School of Education, Vermillion, SD 57069. Offers MA, MS, Ed D, PhD, Certificate, Ed S. *Accreditation:* NCATE. *Program availability:* Part-time, evening/weekend, 100% online, blended/hybrid learning. *Degree requirements:* For master's and other advanced degree, comprehensive exam, thesis or alternative; for doctorate, comprehensive exam, thesis/dissertation. *Entrance requirements:* For master's and doctorate, GRE General Test or MAT, minimum GPA of 2.7. Additional exam requirements/recommendations for international students: Required—TOEFL (minimum score 550 paper-based; 79 iBT). *Application deadline:* For summer admission, 3/1 for domestic students. Applications are processed on a rolling basis. Application fee: $35. Electronic applications accepted. *Financial support:* Research assistantships with partial tuition reimbursements, teaching assistantships with partial tuition reimbursements, career-related internships or fieldwork, Federal Work-Study, and unspecified assistantships available. Support available to part-time students. Financial award applicants required to submit FAFSA. *Application contact:* Graduate School, 605-658-6140, Fax: 605-677-6118.
Website: http://www.usd.edu/education

University of Southern California, Graduate School, Rossier School of Education, Los Angeles, CA 90089. Offers MAT, ME, MMFT, Ed D, PhD. *Degree requirements:* For master's, thesis optional; for doctorate, thesis/dissertation. *Entrance requirements:* For master's and doctorate, GRE. Additional exam requirements/recommendations for international students: Required—TOEFL (minimum score 100 iBT). Electronic applications accepted. *Faculty research:* Data-driven decision-making in K-12 schools and districts; examination of college and university leadership and management in U. S. and Asia; studies in facilitating student learning; organizational change and the role of leaders; leadership, diversity, learning and accountability.

University of Southern Indiana, Graduate Studies, Pott College of Science, Engineering, and Education, Department of Teacher Education, Evansville, IN 47712-3590. Offers educational leadership (Ed D), including administrative leadership, pedagogical leadership; elementary education (MSE); school administration and leadership (MSE); secondary education (MSE), including secondary education. *Accreditation:* NCATE. *Program availability:* Part-time, evening/weekend. *Faculty:* 4 full-time (3 women), 2 part-time/adjunct (1 woman). *Students:* 14 full-time (9 women), 7 part-time (all women); includes 1 minority (Black or African American, non-Hispanic/Latino). Average age 34. In 2017, 12 master's awarded. *Entrance requirements:* For master's, PRAXIS II, bachelor's degree with minimum cumulative GPA of 2.75 from college or university accredited by NCATE or comparable association; minimum GPA of 3.0 in all courses taken at graduate level at all schools attended; teaching license; for doctorate, GRE, master's degree transcript; essay; two letters of recommendation; resume/curriculum vitae. Additional exam requirements/recommendations for international students: Required—TOEFL (minimum score 550 paper-based; 79 iBT), IELTS (minimum score 6). *Application deadline:* For fall admission, 7/1 priority date for domestic students, 1/1 priority date for international students. Applications are processed on a rolling basis. Application fee: $40. Electronic applications accepted. *Expenses:* Tuition, state resident: full-time $9394. Tuition, nonresident: full-time $17,917. Required fees: $510. *Financial support:* In 2017–18, 6 students received

support. Federal Work-Study, scholarships/grants, tuition waivers (full and partial), and unspecified assistantships available. Financial award application deadline: 3/1; financial award applicants required to submit FAFSA. *Unit head:* Dr. Bonnie Beach, Associate Dean, 812-465-1620, E-mail: blbeach@usi.edu. *Application contact:* Dr. Mayola Rowser, Director, Graduate Studies, 812-465-7015, Fax: 812-464-1956, E-mail: mrowser@usi.edu.
Website: http://www.usi.edu/science/teacher-education

University of Southern Maine, College of Management and Human Service, School of Education and Human Development, Gorham, ME 04038. Offers MS, MS Ed, Psy D, CAS, CGS. *Accreditation:* TEAC. *Program availability:* Part-time, evening/weekend, online learning. Terminal master's awarded for partial completion of doctoral program. *Degree requirements:* For master's, comprehensive exam (for some programs), thesis or alternative; for doctorate, thesis/dissertation; for other advanced degree, thesis or alternative. *Entrance requirements:* For master's, GRE General Test or MAT, proof of teacher certification; for doctorate, GRE General Test; for other advanced degree, master's degree. Additional exam requirements/recommendations for international students: Required—TOEFL (minimum score 550 paper-based; 79 iBT). Electronic applications accepted. *Faculty research:* Teacher development, library technology outreach, literacy through literature, college-bound, multicultural education, school psychology, education policy and evaluation.

University of Southern Mississippi, College of Education and Psychology, Hattiesburg, MS 39406-0001. Offers M Ed, MA, MAT, MLIS, MS, Ed D, PhD, Ed S, Graduate Certificate. *Accreditation:* NCATE. *Program availability:* Part-time. *Students:* 136 full-time (104 women), 16 part-time (14 women). 387 applicants, 48% accepted, 136 enrolled. In 2017, 16 master's, 10 doctorates awarded. Terminal master's awarded for partial completion of doctoral program. *Degree requirements:* For master's, comprehensive exam, thesis (for some programs); for doctorate, comprehensive exam, thesis/dissertation; for other advanced degree, comprehensive exam, thesis. *Entrance requirements:* For master's, GRE General Test, MAT, minimum GPA of 2.75 on last 60 hours; for doctorate, GRE General Test, minimum GPA of 3.5; for other advanced degree, GRE General Test. Additional exam requirements/recommendations for international students: Required—TOEFL, IELTS. *Application deadline:* For fall admission, 3/1 priority date for domestic students, 3/1 for international students; for spring admission, 11/1 priority date for domestic students, 11/1 for international students. Applications are processed on a rolling basis. Application fee: $60. Electronic applications accepted. *Expenses:* Tuition, state resident: full-time $3830. *Financial support:* Research assistantships with full tuition reimbursements, teaching assistantships with full tuition reimbursements, career-related internships or fieldwork, Federal Work-Study, institutionally sponsored loans, scholarships/grants, health care benefits, and unspecified assistantships available. Financial award application deadline: 3/15; financial award applicants required to submit FAFSA. *Faculty research:* Reading, sleep, animal cognition. *Unit head:* Dr. Trent Gould, Dean, 601-266-4224, Fax: 601-266-4175, E-mail: trent.gould@usm.edu.
Website: https://www.usm.edu/education-psychology

University of South Florida, College of Education, Tampa, FL 33620-9951. Offers M Ed, MA, MAT, Ed D, PhD, Ed S. *Accreditation:* NCATE. *Program availability:* Part-time, evening/weekend, online learning. *Faculty:* 89 full-time (54 women). *Students:* 466 full-time (344 women), 687 part-time (487 women); includes 341 minority (165 Black or African American, non-Hispanic/Latino; 5 American Indian or Alaska Native, non-Hispanic/Latino; 27 Asian, non-Hispanic/Latino; 126 Hispanic/Latino; 1 Native Hawaiian or other Pacific Islander, non-Hispanic/Latino; 17 Two or more races, non-Hispanic/Latino), 104 international. Average age 35. 843 applicants, 55% accepted, 308 enrolled. In 2017, 280 master's, 68 doctorates, 17 other advanced degrees awarded. *Degree requirements:* For master's, comprehensive exam, thesis (for some programs), project (for some programs); for doctorate, comprehensive exam, thesis/dissertation, philosophies of inquiry; multiple research methods. *Entrance requirements:* For master's, GRE General Test, minimum GPA of 3.5 in last 60 hours of course work; for doctorate, GRE General Test, minimum GPA of 3.5; for Ed S, GRE General Test. Additional exam requirements/recommendations for international students: Required—TOEFL (minimum score 550 paper-based). *Application deadline:* For fall admission, 2/15 for domestic students, 1/2 for international students; for spring admission, 10/15 for domestic students, 6/1 for international students. Application fee: $30. Electronic applications accepted. *Financial support:* In 2017–18, 206 students received support, including 9 fellowships with full tuition reimbursements available (averaging $15,000 per year), 2 research assistantships with full tuition reimbursements available (averaging $15,000 per year); career-related internships or fieldwork, Federal Work-Study, institutionally sponsored loans, scholarships/grants, health care benefits, and unspecified assistantships also available. Support available to part-time students. Financial award applicants required to submit FAFSA. *Faculty research:* Scholarship of teaching and learning, educator preparation, diversity issues as they relate to PK-20 education, urban education. *Total annual research expenditures:* $13.9 million. *Unit head:* Dr. Colleen S. Kennedy, Dean, 813-974-3400, Fax: 813-974-3826. *Application contact:* Dr. Diane Briscoe, Coordinator of Graduate Studies, 813-974-1804, Fax: 813-974-3391, E-mail: briscoe@usf.edu.
Website: http://www.coedu.usf.edu/

University of South Florida, St. Petersburg, College of Education, St. Petersburg, FL 33701. Offers educational leadership development (M Ed); elementary education (MA), including math/science; English education (MA); middle grades STEM education (MS); reading education (MA). *Program availability:* Part-time. *Degree requirements:* For master's, comprehensive exam, practicum, internship, comprehensive portfolio. *Entrance requirements:* For master's, State of Florida General Knowledge Test (GKT), Florida Teaching Certificate (for non-initial certification programs), letters of recommendation. Additional exam requirements/recommendations for international students: Required—TOEFL (minimum score 550 paper-based; 79 iBT); Recommended—IELTS. Electronic applications accepted.

The University of Tampa, Programs in Education, Tampa, FL 33606-1490. Offers curriculum and instruction (M Ed); educational leadership (M Ed); instructional design and technology (MS). *Program availability:* Part-time, evening/weekend. *Faculty:* 5 full-time (4 women), 7 part-time/adjunct (5 women). *Students:* 41 full-time (27 women), 69 part-time (52 women); includes 20 minority (18 Black or African American, non-Hispanic/Latino; 2 Two or more races, non-Hispanic/Latino), 14 international. Average age 32. 126 applicants, 40% accepted, 29 enrolled. In 2017, 47 master's awarded. *Degree requirements:* For master's, capstone. *Entrance requirements:* For master's, GMAT or GRE, current Florida Professional Teaching Certificate, statement of eligibility for Florida Professional Teaching Certificate, or professional teaching certificate from another state; bachelor's degree in an area of education. Additional exam requirements/recommendations for international students: Required—TOEFL (minimum score 577 paper-based; 90 iBT), IELTS (minimum score 7.5). *Application deadline:* Applications are processed on a rolling basis. Application fee: $40. Electronic applications accepted. *Expenses:* Contact institution. *Financial support:* In 2017–18, 20 students received support. Career-related internships or fieldwork, scholarships/grants, and unspecified assistantships available. Financial award applicants required to submit FAFSA. *Faculty research:* Diversity in the classroom, technology integration, assessment

methodologies, complex and ill-structured problem solving, communities of practice. *Unit head:* Dr. Antony Erben, Chair, 813-257-3414, E-mail: terben@ut.edu. *Application contact:* Chanelle Cox, Staff Assistant, Admissions for Graduate and Continuing Studies, 813-253-6249, E-mail: ccox@ut.edu.
Website: http://www.ut.edu/graduate/education/

The University of Tennessee, Graduate School, College of Education, Health and Human Sciences, Knoxville, TN 37996. Offers MPH, MS, Ed D, PhD, Ed S, MS/MPH. *Accreditation:* NCATE. *Program availability:* Part-time, evening/weekend, online learning. Terminal master's awarded for partial completion of doctoral program. *Degree requirements:* For master's and Ed S, thesis optional; for doctorate, thesis/dissertation. *Entrance requirements:* For master's, minimum GPA of 2.7; for doctorate and Ed S, GRE General Test, minimum GPA of 2.7. Additional exam requirements/recommendations for international students: Required—TOEFL. Electronic applications accepted.

The University of Tennessee at Chattanooga, School of Education, Chattanooga, TN 37403. Offers counseling (M Ed), including community counseling, school counseling; education (M Ed, Post-Master's Certificate), including elementary education (M Ed); school leadership (Post-Master's Certificate); elementary education (M Ed); learning and leadership (Ed D), including educational leadership; school leadership (Post-Master's Certificate); school leadership: principal licensure (Ed S); secondary education (M Ed); special education (M Ed). *Accreditation:* ACA; NCATE. *Program availability:* Part-time. *Students:* 43 full-time (30 women), 58 part-time (47 women); includes 18 minority (9 Black or African American, non-Hispanic/Latino; 1 Asian, non-Hispanic/Latino; 1 Hispanic/Latino; 7 Two or more races, non-Hispanic/Latino). Average age 31. 118 applicants, 75% accepted, 33 enrolled. In 2017, 59 master's, 7 other advanced degrees awarded. *Degree requirements:* For master's, comprehensive exam, thesis optional, culminating experience; for other advanced degree, internship. *Entrance requirements:* For master's, GRE General Test, PPST 1, teaching certificate; for other advanced degree, two letters of recommendation, graduate degree in education, teaching certificate with three years of experience. Additional exam requirements/recommendations for international students: Required—TOEFL (minimum score 550 paper-based; 79 iBT), IELTS (minimum score 6). *Application deadline:* For fall admission, 6/15 for domestic students, 7/1 for international students; for spring admission, 11/1 for domestic and international students. Applications are processed on a rolling basis. Application fee: $35 ($40 for international students). Electronic applications accepted. *Expenses:* Contact institution. *Financial support:* Research assistantships, teaching assistantships, career-related internships or fieldwork, institutionally sponsored loans, scholarships/grants, and unspecified assistantships available. Support available to part-time students. Financial award application deadline: 7/1; financial award applicants required to submit FAFSA. *Faculty research:* School counseling, community counseling, elementary and secondary education, school leadership and administration. *Total annual research expenditures:* $576,495. *Unit head:* Dr. Renee Murley, Director, 423-425-4684, Fax: 423-425-5380, E-mail: renee-murley@utc.edu. *Application contact:* Dr. Joanne Romagni, Dean of the Graduate School, 423-425-4478, Fax: 423-425-5223, E-mail: joanne-romagni@utc.edu.
Website: https://www.utc.edu/school-education

The University of Tennessee at Martin, Graduate Programs, College of Education, Health and Behavioral Sciences, Martin, TN 38238. Offers MS Ed. *Accreditation:* NCATE. *Program availability:* Part-time, online only, 100% online. *Faculty:* 47. *Students:* 37 full-time (32 women), 164 part-time (127 women); includes 31 minority (21 Black or African American, non-Hispanic/Latino; 3 Hispanic/Latino; 5 Native Hawaiian or other Pacific Islander, non-Hispanic/Latino; 2 Two or more races, non-Hispanic/Latino). Average age 33. 125 applicants, 61% accepted, 52 enrolled. In 2017, 33 master's awarded. *Degree requirements:* For master's, comprehensive exam. *Entrance requirements:* For master's, GRE General Test, minimum GPA of 2.5. Additional exam requirements/recommendations for international students: Required—TOEFL (minimum score 525 paper-based; 71 iBT). *Application deadline:* For fall admission, 7/27 priority date for domestic and international students; for spring admission, 12/17 priority date for domestic and international students; for summer admission, 5/10 priority date for domestic and international students. Applications are processed on a rolling basis. Application fee: $30 ($130 for international students). Electronic applications accepted. *Expenses:* Tuition, state resident: full-time $8658; part-time $481 per credit hour. Tuition, nonresident: full-time $14,418; part-time $801 per credit hour. *International tuition:* $22,602 full-time. *Required fees:* $1404; $79 per credit hour. Part-time tuition and fees vary according to course load. *Financial support:* In 2017–18, 42 students received support, including 2 research assistantships with full tuition reimbursements available (averaging $6,912 per year), 7 teaching assistantships with full tuition reimbursements available (averaging $6,796 per year); scholarships/grants and tuition waivers (full and partial) also available. Financial award application deadline: 2/1; financial award applicants required to submit FAFSA. *Faculty research:* Environmental education, self-concept, science education, attention deficit disorder, special education. *Unit head:* Cynthia West, Dean, 731-881-7127, Fax: 731-881-7975, E-mail: cwest@utm.edu. *Application contact:* Jolene L. Cunningham, Student Services Specialist, 731-881-7012, Fax: 731-881-7499, E-mail: jcunningham@utm.edu.
Website: http://www.utm.edu/departments/cehbs/

The University of Texas at Arlington, Graduate School, College of Education, Arlington, TX 76019. Offers M Ed, M Ed T, PhD.

The University of Texas at Austin, Graduate School, College of Education, Austin, TX 78712-1111. Offers M Ed, MA, MS, Ed D, PhD. *Program availability:* Part-time. *Entrance requirements:* For master's and doctorate, GRE General Test. Electronic applications accepted.

The University of Texas at El Paso, Graduate School, College of Education, El Paso, TX 79968-0001. Offers M Ed, MA, Ed D, PhD. *Program availability:* Part-time, evening/weekend, online learning. *Degree requirements:* For master's, thesis optional; for doctorate, thesis/dissertation. *Entrance requirements:* For master's, minimum GPA of 3.0, letter of intent, resume, letters of recommendation, copy of teaching certificate, district service record; for doctorate, GRE, resume, letters of recommendation, scholarly paper. Additional exam requirements/recommendations for international students: Required—TOEFL; Recommended—IELTS. Electronic applications accepted.

The University of Texas of the Permian Basin, Office of Graduate Studies, School of Education, Odessa, TX 79762-0001. Offers MA. *Accreditation:* NCATE. *Entrance requirements:* For master's, GRE General Test. Additional exam requirements/recommendations for international students: Required—TOEFL (minimum score 550 paper-based).

The University of Texas Rio Grande Valley, College of Education and P-16 Integration, Edinburg, TX 78539. Offers M Ed, MA, Ed D. *Program availability:* Part-time, evening/weekend. *Students:* 968. In 2017, 343 master's, 10 doctorates awarded. *Degree requirements:* For master's, comprehensive exam (for some programs), thesis optional; for doctorate, comprehensive exam, thesis/dissertation. *Entrance requirements:* Additional exam requirements/recommendations for international students: Required—TOEFL (minimum score 550 paper-based; 79 iBT), IELTS (minimum score 6.5). *Application deadline:* For fall admission, 4/15 for domestic

Education—General

students; for spring admission, 11/15 for domestic students; for summer admission, 3/1 for domestic students. Application fee: $50 ($75 for international students). Electronic applications accepted. *Expenses:* Tuition, state resident: full-time $5550; part-time $417 per credit hour. Tuition, nonresident: full-time $13,020; part-time $832 per credit hour. *Required fees:* $1169. *Financial support:* Research assistantships, teaching assistantships, career-related internships or fieldwork, Federal Work-Study, institutionally sponsored loans, and scholarships/grants available. Support available to part-time students. Financial award application deadline: 4/15; financial award applicants required to submit FAFSA. *Faculty research:* Literacy development, bilingual education, special education, counseling, school leadership. *Unit head:* Dr. Alma Rodriguez, Interim Dean, 956-665-3627, E-mail: cep@utrgv.edu. *Application contact:* Stephanie Ozuna, Graduate Student Recruiter, 956-665-3558, E-mail: stephanie.ozuna@utrgv.edu.

University of the Cumberlands, Graduate Programs in Education, Williamsburg, KY 40769-1372. Offers all grades (P-12) (M Ed); business and marketing (MA Ed, MAT); counselor education and supervision (Ed D); director of pupil personnel (Certificate); director of special education (Certificate); educational administration and supervision (Ed S); educational leadership (Ed D); elementary education (MA Ed, MAT); instructional leadership - principalship (MA Ed); instructional leadership - school principal (Certificate); middle school education (MA Ed, MAT); reading and writing (MA Ed); school counseling (MA Ed); school superintendent (Certificate); secondary education (MA Ed, MAT); special education (MAT); supervisor of instruction (Certificate); teacher leader (MA Ed). *Program availability:* Part-time, evening/weekend, online learning. *Degree requirements:* For master's, comprehensive exam. Electronic applications accepted.

University of the Incarnate Word, Dreeben School of Education, San Antonio, TX 78209-6397. Offers M Ed, MA, MAT, PhD. *Program availability:* Part-time, evening/weekend, online learning. *Faculty:* 10 full-time (6 women), 5 part-time/adjunct (4 women). *Students:* 90 full-time (54 women), 105 part-time (64 women); includes 116 minority (23 Black or African American, non-Hispanic/Latino; 2 Asian, non-Hispanic/Latino; 87 Hispanic/Latino; 4 Two or more races, non-Hispanic/Latino), 22 international. In 2017, 33 master's, 17 doctorates awarded. *Degree requirements:* For master's, capstone course; for doctorate, thesis/dissertation, qualifying exam. *Entrance requirements:* For master's, baccalaureate degree, interview; for doctorate, master's degree, interview, supervised writing sample. Additional exam requirements/recommendations for international students: Required—TOEFL (minimum score 560 paper-based; 83 iBT). *Application deadline:* Applications are processed on a rolling basis. Application fee: $20. Electronic applications accepted. *Expenses: Tuition:* Full-time $16,470; part-time $915 per credit hour. Tuition and fees vary according to degree level, program and student level. *Financial support:* In 2017–18, 4 research assistantships were awarded; Federal Work-Study, scholarships/grants, tuition waivers (partial), and unspecified assistantships also available. Financial award applicants required to submit FAFSA. *Faculty research:* Political and social contexts of education, teaching children mathematics and science, thoughtfully adaptive teachers, college student success for underrepresented populations, technology integration in education. *Unit head:* Dr. Denise Staudt, Dean, 210-829-2761, Fax: 210-829-2765, E-mail: staudt@uiwtx.edu. *Application contact:* Johnny Garcia, Graduate Admissions Counselor, 210-805-3554, Fax: 210-829-3921, E-mail: admis@uiwtx.edu. Website: http://www.uiw.edu/education/index.htm

University of the Pacific, Gladys L. Benerd School of Education, Stockton, CA 95211-0197. Offers curriculum and instruction (MA, Ed D); education (M Ed); educational administration and leadership (MA, Ed D); educational and school psychology (MA, Ed D); school psychology (Ed S); special education (MA); teacher education (MA). *Accreditation:* NCATE. *Faculty:* 19 full-time (12 women), 48 part-time/adjunct (39 women). *Students:* 141 full-time (115 women), 305 part-time (236 women); includes 219 minority (41 Black or African American, non-Hispanic/Latino; 44 Asian, non-Hispanic/Latino; 105 Hispanic/Latino; 2 Native Hawaiian or other Pacific Islander, non-Hispanic/Latino; 27 Two or more races, non-Hispanic/Latino), 7 international. Average age 33. 144 applicants, 83% accepted, 94 enrolled. In 2017, 231 master's, 8 doctorates awarded. *Degree requirements:* For doctorate, thesis/dissertation. *Entrance requirements:* For master's, GRE General Test; for doctorate, GRE General Test, GRE Subject Test. Additional exam requirements/recommendations for international students: Required—TOEFL. *Application deadline:* For fall admission, 3/1 priority date for domestic students; for spring admission, 10/15 for domestic students. Applications are processed on a rolling basis. Application fee: $75. *Financial support:* Teaching assistantships and institutionally sponsored loans available. Support available to part-time students. Financial award application deadline: 3/1; financial award applicants required to submit FAFSA. *Unit head:* Dr. Vanessa Sheared, Dean, 209-946-2683, E-mail: lwebster@pacific.edu. *Application contact:* Office of Graduate Admissions, 209-946-2344.

University of the Sacred Heart, Graduate Programs, Department of Education, San Juan, PR 00914-0383. Offers early childhood education (M Ed); information technology and multimedia (Certificate); instruction systems and education technology (M Ed), including English, information technology and multimedia, instructional design, mathematics, Spanish. *Program availability:* Part-time, evening/weekend. *Degree requirements:* For master's, thesis. *Entrance requirements:* For master's, EXADEP, minimum undergraduate GPA of 2.75, interview.

University of the Southwest, Graduate Programs, Hobbs, NM 88240-9129. Offers business administration (MBA); curriculum and instruction (MSE); curriculum and instruction: bilingual (MSE); curriculum and instruction: TESOL (MSE); early childhood education (MSE); educational administration (MSE); mental health counseling (MSE); school counseling (MSE); special education (MSE); sports management (MBA). *Program availability:* Part-time, evening/weekend, online learning. *Degree requirements:* For master's, comprehensive exam, thesis (for some programs). *Entrance requirements:* Additional exam requirements/recommendations for international students: Recommended—TOEFL. Electronic applications accepted.

University of the Virgin Islands, School of Education, St. Thomas, VI 00802. Offers creative leadership for innovation and change (PhD); educational leadership (MA); school counseling (MA); school psychology (Ed S). *Program availability:* Part-time, evening/weekend. *Degree requirements:* For master's, comprehensive exam, thesis or alternative; for doctorate, comprehensive exam, thesis/dissertation, qualifying examination; for Ed S, comprehensive exam. *Entrance requirements:* For master's, GRE, minimum GPA of 2.5, BA degree from accredited institution. Additional exam requirements/recommendations for international students: Required—TOEFL (minimum score 550 paper-based). Electronic applications accepted. *Expenses:* Contact institution.

The University of Toledo, College of Graduate Studies, Judith Herb College of Education, Toledo, OH 43606-3390. Offers MAE, ME, MES, MME, DE, PhD, Certificate, Ed S. *Accreditation:* NCATE. *Program availability:* Part-time, evening/weekend. Terminal master's awarded for partial completion of doctoral program. *Degree requirements:* For master's, thesis; for doctorate, comprehensive exam (for some programs), thesis/dissertation (for some programs); for other advanced degree, thesis optional. *Entrance requirements:* For master's and other advanced degree, minimum

cumulative GPA of 2.7 for all previous academic work, letters of recommendation, statement of purpose, transcripts from all prior institutions attended; for doctorate, GRE, minimum cumulative GPA of 2.7 for all previous academic work, 3.0 for occupational therapy and physical therapy; letters of recommendation; statement of purpose; transcripts from all prior institutions attended. Additional exam requirements/recommendations for international students: Required—TOEFL (minimum score 550 paper-based; 80 iBT). Electronic applications accepted.

University of Toronto, School of Graduate Studies, Ontario Institute for Studies in Education, Toronto, ON M5S 1A1, Canada. Offers M Ed, MA, MT, Ed D, PhD. *Program availability:* Part-time, evening/weekend. *Degree requirements:* For master's, thesis (for some programs); for doctorate, thesis/dissertation. *Entrance requirements:* For master's, minimum B average in final year, 1 year of professional experience in field (MA, M Ed); for doctorate, minimum B+ average, professional experience in education or a relevant field (Ed D). Additional exam requirements/recommendations for international students: Required—TOEFL (minimum score 580 paper-based; 93 iBT), TWE (minimum score 5). *Expenses:* Contact institution.

The University of Tulsa, Graduate School, Kendall College of Arts and Sciences, School of Education, Tulsa, OK 74104-3189. Offers mathematics and science education (MSMSE); teaching arts (MTA), including art, biology, English, history, mathematics; urban education (MA). *Accreditation:* TEAC. *Program availability:* Part-time. *Faculty:* 9 full-time (5 women), 2 part-time/adjunct (both women). *Students:* 8 full-time (4 women), 6 part-time (5 women); includes 4 minority (1 Black or African American, non-Hispanic/Latino; 1 American Indian or Alaska Native, non-Hispanic/Latino; 1 Asian, non-Hispanic/Latino; 1 Two or more races, non-Hispanic/Latino). Average age 31. 22 applicants, 9% accepted. In 2017, 10 master's awarded. *Degree requirements:* For master's, thesis optional. *Entrance requirements:* For master's, GRE General Test. Additional exam requirements/recommendations for international students: Required—TOEFL (minimum score 577 paper-based; 91 iBT), IELTS (minimum score 6.5). *Application deadline:* For fall admission, 2/1 priority date for domestic students. Applications are processed on a rolling basis. Application fee: $55. Electronic applications accepted. *Expenses: Tuition:* Full-time $22,230. *Required fees:* $2000. Tuition and fees vary according to course load and program. *Financial support:* In 2017–18, 3 students received support, including 3 teaching assistantships with full tuition reimbursements available (averaging $13,410 per year); fellowships with tuition reimbursements available, research assistantships with tuition reimbursements available, career-related internships or fieldwork, Federal Work-Study, scholarships/grants, health care benefits, tuition waivers (full and partial), and unspecified assistantships also available. Support available to part-time students. Financial award application deadline: 2/1; financial award applicants required to submit FAFSA. *Faculty research:* Elementary/secondary certification, math/science education, teaching arts. *Unit head:* Dr. Elizabeth Smith, Chair, 918-631-2238, Fax: 918-631-3721, E-mail: elizabeth-smith-43@utulsa.edu. *Application contact:* Dr. David Brown, Advisor, 918-631-2719, Fax: 918-631-2133, E-mail: david-brown@utulsa.edu.
Website: http://artsandsciences.utulsa.edu/academics/departments-schools/urban-education/

University of Utah, Graduate School, College of Education, Salt Lake City, UT 84112. Offers M Ed, M Stat, MA, MS, Ed D, PhD, Ed S, MPA/PhD. *Accreditation:* TEAC. *Faculty:* 48 full-time (30 women), 23 part-time/adjunct (17 women). *Students:* 286 full-time (208 women), 328 part-time (227 women); includes 144 minority (16 Black or African American, non-Hispanic/Latino; 2 American Indian or Alaska Native, non-Hispanic/Latino; 15 Asian, non-Hispanic/Latino; 96 Hispanic/Latino; 15 Two or more races, non-Hispanic/Latino), 10 international. Average age 30. 548 applicants, 47% accepted, 211 enrolled. In 2017, 167 master's, 35 doctorates awarded. *Degree requirements:* For master's, variable foreign language requirement, comprehensive exam (for some programs), thesis (for some programs); for doctorate, variable foreign language requirement, comprehensive exam (for some programs), thesis/dissertation. *Entrance requirements:* For master's and doctorate, minimum GPA of 3.0. Additional exam requirements/recommendations for international students: Required—TOEFL. *Application deadline:* For fall admission, 2/15 for domestic and international students; for spring admission, 11/1 for domestic and international students. Application fee: $55 ($65 for international students). Electronic applications accepted. *Expenses:* Contact institution. *Financial support:* Fellowships with tuition reimbursements, research assistantships with tuition reimbursements, teaching assistantships with tuition reimbursements, career-related internships or fieldwork, Federal Work-Study, institutionally sponsored loans, scholarships/grants, health care benefits, tuition waivers (full), and unspecified assistantships available. Support available to part-time students. Financial award application deadline: 2/1; financial award applicants required to submit FAFSA. *Faculty research:* Leadership, autism, reading instruction, mental retardation, diagnosis. *Unit head:* Elaine Clark, Dean, 801-581-8221.
Website: http://education.utah.edu/

University of Vermont, Graduate College, College of Education and Social Services, Burlington, VT 05405. Offers M Ed, MAT, MS, MSW, Ed D, PhD. *Accreditation:* NCATE. *Program availability:* Part-time, evening/weekend. *Students:* 337 (251 women). 506 applicants, 61% accepted, 169 enrolled. In 2017, 119 master's, 19 doctorates awarded. *Degree requirements:* For doctorate, thesis/dissertation. *Entrance requirements:* Additional exam requirements/recommendations for international students: Required—TOEFL (minimum score 550 paper-based, 90 iBT) or IELTS (6.5). Application fee: $65. Electronic applications accepted. *Expenses:* Tuition, state resident: full-time $11,628; part-time $646 per credit. Tuition, nonresident: full-time $29,340; part-time $1630 per credit. *Required fees:* $1994; $10 per credit. Tuition and fees vary according to course load and program. *Financial support:* Fellowships, research assistantships, teaching assistantships, career-related internships or fieldwork, Federal Work-Study, scholarships/grants, and health care benefits available. *Unit head:* Dr. Scott L. Thomas, Dean, 802-656-3424, E-mail: cessstsv@uvm.edu. *Application contact:* Roman Vogel, Administrative Coordinator of Graduate Programs, 802-656-2936, E-mail: roman.vogel@uvm.edu.
Website: https://www.uvm.edu/cess

University of Victoria, Faculty of Graduate Studies, Faculty of Education, Victoria, BC V8W 2Y2, Canada. Offers M Ed, M Sc, MA, PhD.

University of Virginia, Curry School of Education, Charlottesville, VA 22903. Offers M Ed, MS, MT, Ed D, PhD, Ed S, MBA/M Ed, MPP/PhD. *Accreditation:* TEAC. *Faculty:* 136 full-time (81 women), 6 part-time/adjunct (4 women). *Students:* 746 full-time (608 women), 79 part-time (53 women); includes 175 minority (60 Black or African American, non-Hispanic/Latino; 43 Asian, non-Hispanic/Latino; 40 Hispanic/Latino; 32 Two or more races, non-Hispanic/Latino), 30 international. Average age 26. 470 applicants, 92% accepted, 281 enrolled. In 2017, 205 master's, 19 doctorates, 17 other advanced degrees awarded. *Degree requirements:* For master's, comprehensive exam (for some programs), thesis (for some programs); for doctorate, comprehensive exam (for some programs), thesis/dissertation. *Entrance requirements:* For master's, doctorate, and Ed S, GRE General Test, letters of recommendation. Additional exam requirements/recommendations for international students: Required—TOEFL (minimum score 600 paper-based; 90 iBT), IELTS (minimum score 7). *Application deadline:* Applications are processed on a rolling basis. Application fee: $60. Electronic applications accepted. *Expenses:* Contact institution. *Financial support:* Fellowships, research assistantships,

teaching assistantships, and Federal Work-Study available. Financial award application deadline: 1/5; financial award applicants required to submit FAFSA. *Unit head:* Robert C. Pianta, Dean, 434-924-3334, E-mail: pianta@virginia.edu. *Application contact:* E-mail: curry-admissions@virginia.edu.
Website: http://curry.edschool.virginia.edu/

University of Washington, Graduate School, College of Education, Seattle, WA 98195. Offers curriculum and instruction (M Ed, Ed D, PhD), including educational technology, general curriculum (Ed D, PhD), language, literacy, and culture, mathematics education, multicultural education, reading and language arts education (Ed D), science education, social studies education, teaching and curriculum (M Ed); educational leadership and policy studies (M Ed, Ed D, PhD), including administration (Ed D), educational policy, organization, and leadership (M Ed, PhD), higher education, leadership for learning (Ed D), social and cultural foundations of education (M Ed, PhD); educational psychology (M Ed, PhD), including educational psychology (PhD), human development and cognition (M Ed), learning sciences, measurement, statistics and research design (M Ed), school psychology (M Ed); instructional leadership (M Ed); intercollegiate athletic leadership (M Ed); special education (M Ed, Ed D, PhD), including early childhood special education (M Ed), emotional and behavioral disabilities (M Ed), learning disabilities (M Ed), low-incidence disabilities (M Ed), severe disabilities (M Ed), special education (Ed D, PhD); teacher education (MIT). *Accreditation:* APA. *Program availability:* Part-time, evening/weekend. *Degree requirements:* For master's, thesis optional; for doctorate, thesis/dissertation. *Entrance requirements:* For master's and doctorate, GRE General Test, minimum GPA of 3.0. Additional exam requirements/recommendations for international students: Required—TOEFL. Electronic applications accepted. *Faculty research:* School restructuring/effective schools, special education interventions, literacy and writing, technology, school partnerships, teacher preparation.

University of Washington, Bothell, Program in Education, Bothell, WA 98011. Offers education (M Ed); leadership development for educators (M Ed); secondary/middle level endorsement (M Ed). *Program availability:* Part-time, evening/weekend. *Degree requirements:* For master's, thesis. *Entrance requirements:* Additional exam requirements/recommendations for international students: Required—TOEFL. Electronic applications accepted. *Faculty research:* Multicultural education in citizenship education, intercultural education, knowledge and practice in the principalship, educational public policy, national board certification for teachers, teacher learning in literacy, technology and its impact on teaching and learning of mathematics, reading assessments, professional development in literacy education and mobility, digital media, education and class.

University of Washington, Tacoma, Graduate Programs, Program in Education, Tacoma, WA 98402-3100. Offers education (M Ed); educational administration (principal or program administrator certification) (M Ed); elementary education teacher certification (M Ed); elementary education/special education teacher certification (M Ed); secondary science or math teacher certification (M Ed). *Program availability:* Part-time, evening/weekend. *Degree requirements:* For master's, culminating project. *Entrance requirements:* For master's, WEST-B, WEST-E (teacher certification programs only), official sealed transcript from every college/university attended, personal goal statement, letters of recommendation, copy of valid teaching certificate. Additional exam requirements/recommendations for international students: Required—TOEFL (minimum score 580 paper-based; 92 iBT). Electronic applications accepted. *Faculty research:* Global learning communities for English/Chinese languages, evaluation of mathematics and reading intervention programs, response to intervention, school-wide behavioral and emotional support, mathematics education and culturally responsive mathematics education.

The University of West Alabama, School of Graduate Studies, College of Education, Livingston, AL 35470. Offers M Ed, MAT, MS, MSCE, Ed S. *Accreditation:* NCATE. *Program availability:* Part-time, evening/weekend, 100% online. *Faculty:* 46 full-time (29 women), 71 part-time/adjunct (46 women). *Students:* 2,298 (1,937 women); includes 815 minority (744 Black or African American, non-Hispanic/Latino; 17 American Indian or Alaska Native, non-Hispanic/Latino; 7 Asian, non-Hispanic/Latino; 18 Hispanic/Latino; 1 Native Hawaiian or other Pacific Islander, non-Hispanic/Latino; 28 Two or more races, non-Hispanic/Latino). Average age 35. 724 applicants, 96% accepted, 507 enrolled. In 2017, 532 master's, 152 other advanced degrees awarded. *Degree requirements:* For master's, comprehensive exam, thesis optional; for Ed S, comprehensive exam. *Entrance requirements:* For master's, GRE, minimum GPA of 2.75. Additional exam requirements/recommendations for international students: Required—TOEFL (minimum score 500 paper-based; 61 iBT). *Application deadline:* Applications are processed on a rolling basis. Application fee: $40. Electronic applications accepted. *Expenses:* Tuition, state resident: part-time $371 per credit hour. Tuition, nonresident: part-time $742 per credit hour. *Required fees:* $130 per semester. *Financial support:* In 2017–18, 1 teaching assistantship (averaging $7,344 per year) was awarded; Federal Work-Study, scholarships/grants, and unspecified assistantships also available. Support available to part-time students. Financial award application deadline: 3/1; financial award applicants required to submit FAFSA. *Unit head:* Dr. B. J. Kimbrough, Dean of Graduate Studies, 205-652-3647, Fax: 205-652-3670, E-mail: bkimbrough@uwa.edu.
Website: http://www.uwa.edu/academics/collegeofeducation

The University of Western Ontario, Faculty of Graduate Studies, Social Sciences Division, Faculty of Education, London, ON N6A 5B8, Canada. Offers M Ed. *Program availability:* Part-time. *Entrance requirements:* For master's, minimum B average.

University of West Georgia, College of Education, Carrollton, GA 30118. Offers business education (M Ed); early childhood education (M Ed, Ed S); educational leadership (M Ed, Ed S); media (M Ed, Ed S); professional counseling (M Ed, Ed S); professional counseling and supervision (Ed D); reading instruction (M Ed); school improvement (Ed D); secondary education (M Ed); special education (M Ed, Ed S), including teaching (M Ed); speech language pathology (M Ed); teaching (MAT). *Accreditation:* NCATE. *Program availability:* Part-time, evening/weekend, 100% online, blended/hybrid learning. *Faculty:* 45 full-time (28 women). *Students:* 344 full-time (286 women), 1,243 part-time (1,039 women); includes 538 minority (456 Black or African American, non-Hispanic/Latino; 19 Asian, non-Hispanic/Latino; 46 Hispanic/Latino; 1 Native Hawaiian or other Pacific Islander, non-Hispanic/Latino; 16 Two or more races, non-Hispanic/Latino), 7 international. Average age 36. 685 applicants, 78% accepted, 429 enrolled. In 2017, 299 master's, 30 doctorates, 218 other advanced degrees awarded. *Entrance requirements:* Additional exam requirements/recommendations for international students: Required—TOEFL (minimum score 523 paper-based; 69 iBT); Recommended—IELTS (minimum score 6.5). *Application deadline:* For fall admission, 7/21 for domestic students, 6/1 for international students; for spring admission, 11/30 for domestic students, 10/15 for international students; for summer admission, 4/15 for domestic students, 3/30 for international students. Applications are processed on a rolling basis. Application fee: $40. Electronic applications accepted. Tuition and fees vary according to degree level and program. *Financial support:* Fellowships, research assistantships, teaching assistantships, career-related internships or fieldwork, Federal Work-Study, institutionally sponsored loans, scholarships/grants, and unspecified assistantships available. Support available to part-time students. Financial award application deadline: 4/1; financial award applicants required to submit FAFSA. *Unit head:* Dr. Diane Hoff, Dean, College of Education, 678-839-6570, Fax: 678-839-6098,

E-mail: dhoff@westga.edu. *Application contact:* Dr. Toby Ziglar, Assistant Dean of the Graduate School, 678-839-1394, Fax: 678-839-1395, E-mail: graduate@westga.edu.
Website: http://www.westga.edu/education/

University of Windsor, Faculty of Graduate Studies, Faculty of Education, Windsor, ON N9B 3P4, Canada. Offers education (M Ed); educational studies (PhD). *Program availability:* Part-time, evening/weekend. *Degree requirements:* For master's, thesis or alternative; for doctorate, comprehensive exam, thesis/dissertation. *Entrance requirements:* For master's, minimum B average, teaching certificate; for doctorate, M Ed or MA in education, minimum A average, evidence of research competencies. Additional exam requirements/recommendations for international students: Required—TOEFL (minimum score 600 paper-based). Electronic applications accepted. *Faculty research:* School structures, teacher morale, cognitive deficits, new technologies in art education, internal and external factors that affect learning and teaching.

University of Wisconsin–Eau Claire, College of Education and Human Sciences, Eau Claire, WI 54702-4004. Offers ME-PD, MS, MSE, MST. *Degree requirements:* For master's, comprehensive exam. *Entrance requirements:* For master's, GRE (MAT, MST, MSE, MS); pre-professional skills test (MAT), minimum undergraduate GPA of 2.75 or 3.0 in the last half of undergraduate work. Additional exam requirements/recommendations for international students: Required—TOEFL (minimum score 79 iBT). Electronic applications accepted.

University of Wisconsin–Green Bay, Graduate Studies, Program in Applied Leadership for Teaching and Learning, Green Bay, WI 54311-7001. Offers MS Ed. *Program availability:* Part-time, evening/weekend. *Degree requirements:* For master's, thesis or alternative. *Entrance requirements:* For master's, minimum GPA of 3.0. Electronic applications accepted. *Faculty research:* Curriculum design, assessment.

University of Wisconsin–La Crosse, School of Education, La Crosse, WI 54601-3742. Offers English language arts elementary (Graduate Certificate); professional development in education (ME-PD); reading (MS Ed); special education (MS Ed). *Program availability:* Part-time, evening/weekend. *Faculty:* 6 full-time (4 women), 8 part-time/adjunct (6 women). *Students:* 70 part-time (51 women); includes 2 minority (1 Asian, non-Hispanic/Latino; 1 Two or more races, non-Hispanic/Latino). Average age 30. 59 applicants, 100% accepted, 34 enrolled. In 2017, 69 master's, 1 other advanced degree awarded. *Entrance requirements:* For master's, GRE. Additional exam requirements/recommendations for international students: Required—TOEFL (minimum score 550 paper-based; 79 iBT). *Application deadline:* Applications are processed on a rolling basis. Electronic applications accepted. *Financial support:* Research assistantships, Federal Work-Study, scholarships/grants, health care benefits, and tuition waivers (partial) available. Support available to part-time students. Financial award application deadline: 3/15; financial award applicants required to submit FAFSA. *Unit head:* Marcie Wycoff-Horn, Dean, School of Education, 608-785-6786, E-mail: mwycoff-horn@uwlax.edu. *Application contact:* Brandon Schaller, Senior Graduate Student Status Examiner, 608-785-8941, E-mail: admissions@uwlax.edu.
Website: https://www.uwlax.edu/soe/

University of Wisconsin–Madison, Graduate School, School of Education, Madison, WI 53706-1380. Offers MA, MFA, MS, PhD, Certificate. *Degree requirements:* For doctorate, thesis/dissertation. *Entrance requirements:* Additional exam requirements/recommendations for international students: Required—TOEFL (minimum score 580 paper-based; 92 iBT), IELTS (minimum score 7).

University of Wisconsin–Milwaukee, Graduate School, School of Education, Milwaukee, WI 53201. Offers MS, PhD, CAS, Ed S, Graduate Certificate. *Program availability:* Part-time. *Students:* 261 full-time (200 women), 370 part-time (278 women); includes 181 minority (74 Black or African American, non-Hispanic/Latino; 6 American Indian or Alaska Native, non-Hispanic/Latino; 23 Asian, non-Hispanic/Latino; 12 Hispanic/Latino; 1 Native Hawaiian or other Pacific Islander, non-Hispanic/Latino; 65 Two or more races, non-Hispanic/Latino), 9 international. Average age 34. 518 applicants, 51% accepted, 181 enrolled. In 2017, 169 master's, 24 doctorates, 32 other advanced degrees awarded. *Entrance requirements:* For doctorate, GRE General Test. *Application deadline:* For fall admission, 1/1 priority date for domestic students; for spring admission, 9/1 for domestic students. Application fee: $56 ($96 for international students). Electronic applications accepted. *Financial support:* Fellowships, teaching assistantships, career-related internships or fieldwork, Federal Work-Study, health care benefits, unspecified assistantships, and project assistantships available. Support available to part-time students. Financial award application deadline: 4/15; financial award applicants required to submit FAFSA. *Total annual research expenditures:* $1.8 million. *Unit head:* Alan Shoho, Dean, 414-229-4181, E-mail: shoho@uwm.edu. *Application contact:* Education Office of Student Services, 414-229-4721, E-mail: soeoss@uwm.edu.
Website: http://uwm.edu/education

University of Wisconsin–Oshkosh, Graduate Studies, College of Education and Human Services, Oshkosh, WI 54901. Offers MS, MSE. *Program availability:* Part-time, evening/weekend. *Degree requirements:* For master's, comprehensive exam (for some programs), thesis or alternative, field report, PPST, PRAXIS II. *Entrance requirements:* For master's, PPST, PRAXIS II, teaching license, letters of recommendation, interview. Additional exam requirements/recommendations for international students: Required—TOEFL (minimum score 550 paper-based; 79 iBT). Electronic applications accepted.

University of Wisconsin–Platteville, School of Graduate Studies, College of Liberal Arts and Education, School of Education, Platteville, WI 53818-3099. Offers adult education (MSE). *Accreditation:* NCATE. *Program availability:* Part-time, evening/weekend. *Students:* 41 full-time (32 women), 109 part-time (82 women); includes 14 minority (12 Black or African American, non-Hispanic/Latino; 1 Asian, non-Hispanic/Latino; 1 Hispanic/Latino). 37 applicants, 86% accepted, 25 enrolled. In 2017, 62 master's awarded. *Degree requirements:* For master's, thesis or alternative. *Entrance requirements:* Additional exam requirements/recommendations for international students: Required—TOEFL (minimum score 550 paper-based; 79 iBT), IELTS (minimum score 6.5). *Application deadline:* For fall admission, 9/1 for domestic students, 7/1 for international students; for spring admission, 1/1 for domestic students, 11/15 for international students. Applications are processed on a rolling basis. Application fee: $56. Electronic applications accepted. *Financial support:* Research assistantships with partial tuition reimbursements, career-related internships or fieldwork, Federal Work-Study, institutionally sponsored loans, scholarships/grants, and unspecified assistantships available. Support available to part-time students. Financial award applicants required to submit FAFSA. *Unit head:* Dr. Dominic Barraclough, Interim Director, 608-342-1131, Fax: 608-342-1133, E-mail: education@uwplatt.edu. *Application contact:* Dee Dunbar, School of Graduate Studies, 608-342-1322, Fax: 608-342-1454, E-mail: gradstudies@uwplatt.edu.
Website: http://www.uwplatt.edu

University of Wisconsin–River Falls, Outreach and Graduate Studies, College of Education and Professional Studies, Department of Teacher Education, River Falls, WI 54022. Offers elementary education (MSE); professional development shared inquiry communities (MSE); reading (MSE). *Program availability:* Part-time. *Degree requirements:* For master's, comprehensive exam, thesis or alternative. *Entrance requirements:* For master's, minimum GPA of 2.75. Additional exam requirements/recommendations for international students: Required—TOEFL (minimum score 500 paper-based; 65 iBT), IELTS (minimum score 5.5). Electronic applications accepted.

University of Wisconsin–Stevens Point, College of Professional Studies, School of Education, Stevens Point, WI 54481-3897. Offers education—general/reading (MSE); education—general/special (MSE); educational administration (MSE); educational sustainability (Ed D); elementary education (MSE); guidance and counseling (MSE). *Program availability:* Part-time. *Degree requirements:* For master's, comprehensive exam, thesis or alternative. *Entrance requirements:* For master's, teacher certification, minimum undergraduate GPA of 3.0, 2 years of teaching experience, letters of recommendation. Additional exam requirements/recommendations for international students: Required—TOEFL (minimum score 523 paper-based). *Faculty research:* Gifted education, early childhood special education, curriculum and instruction, standards-based education.

University of Wisconsin–Stout, Graduate School, College of Education, Health and Human Sciences, School of Education, Menomonie, WI 54751. Offers MS, MS Ed, Ed D, Ed S. *Accreditation:* NCATE. *Program availability:* Part-time, online learning. *Degree requirements:* For master's and Ed S, thesis. *Entrance requirements:* For degree, minimum GPA of 3.25. Additional exam requirements/recommendations for international students: Required—TOEFL (minimum score 500 paper-based; 61 iBT). Electronic applications accepted.

University of Wisconsin–Superior, Graduate Division, Department of Teacher Education, Superior, WI 54880-4500. Offers instruction (MSE); special education (MSE), including emotional/behavior disabilities, learning disabilities; teaching reading (MSE). *Program availability:* Part-time, evening/weekend, online learning. *Degree requirements:* For master's, research project. *Entrance requirements:* For master's, minimum GPA of 2.75, teaching certificate. Electronic applications accepted. *Faculty research:* Science teaching.

University of Wisconsin–Whitewater, School of Graduate Studies, College of Education and Professional Studies, Whitewater, WI 53190-1790. Offers MS, MSE, Postbaccalaureate Certificate. *Accreditation:* NCATE. *Program availability:* Part-time, evening/weekend, online learning. *Entrance requirements:* Additional exam requirements/recommendations for international students: Required—TOEFL (minimum score 550 paper-based). Electronic applications accepted.

Upper Iowa University, Master of Education Program, Fayette, IA 52142-1857. Offers early childhood (M Ed); English as a second language (M Ed); higher education (M Ed); instructional strategist (M Ed); reading (M Ed); teacher leadership (M Ed).

Urbana University–A Branch Campus of Franklin University, College of Education and Sports Studies, Urbana, OH 43078-2091. Offers classroom education (M Ed). *Program availability:* Part-time, evening/weekend. *Degree requirements:* For master's, comprehensive oral exam, capstone research project. *Entrance requirements:* For master's, minimum GPA of 2.7, teaching license. Additional exam requirements/recommendations for international students: Required—TOEFL (minimum score 550 paper-based). *Faculty research:* Best professional practices, reading/special education, classroom management, teaching models, school finance.

Utah State University, School of Graduate Studies, Emma Eccles Jones College of Education and Human Services, Logan, UT 84322. Offers M Ed, MA, MFHD, MRC, MS, Au D, Ed D, PhD, Ed S. *Accreditation:* TEAC. *Program availability:* Part-time, evening/weekend, online learning. *Degree requirements:* For doctorate, comprehensive exam, thesis/dissertation. *Entrance requirements:* For master's, GRE General Test, minimum GPA of 3.0; for doctorate, GRE General Test, master's degree; for Ed S, GRE General Test, GRE Subject Test. Additional exam requirements/recommendations for international students: Required—TOEFL (minimum score 550 paper-based). *Faculty research:* Literacy instruction, design and delivery of instruction, children at-risk and their families, hearing assessment and management, language and literacy development.

Utah Valley University, Program in Education, Orem, UT 84058-5999. Offers educational technology (M Ed); elementary mathematics (M Ed); elementary STEM (M Ed); English as a second language (M Ed); reading (M Ed); teachers as leaders (M Ed). *Accreditation:* TEAC. *Program availability:* Part-time. *Degree requirements:* For master's, project. *Entrance requirements:* For master's, GRE, 3 letters of recommendation, interview, essay. Additional exam requirements/recommendations for international students: Required—TOEFL (minimum score 83 iBT). Electronic applications accepted. *Expenses:* Contact institution.

Utica College, Teacher Education Programs, Utica, NY 13502-4892. Offers MS, MS Ed, CAS. *Accreditation:* TEAC. *Faculty:* 10 full-time (7 women). *Students:* 24 full-time (18 women), 27 part-time (17 women); includes 2 minority (1 Black or African American, non-Hispanic/Latino; 1 Hispanic/Latino). Average age 27. 21 applicants, 76% accepted, 14 enrolled. In 2017, 17 master's awarded. *Degree requirements:* For master's, comprehensive exam or thesis. *Entrance requirements:* For master's, CST, LAST, minimum GPA of 3.0. Additional exam requirements/recommendations for international students: Required—TOEFL (minimum score 525 paper-based). *Application deadline:* Applications are processed on a rolling basis. Application fee: $50. Electronic applications accepted. *Expenses:* Contact institution. *Financial support:* Career-related internships or fieldwork, scholarships/grants, tuition waivers (partial), and unspecified assistantships available. Support available to part-time students. Financial award application deadline: 3/15; financial award applicants required to submit FAFSA. *Unit head:* Dr. Patrice Hallock, Dean of Health Professions and Education, 315-792-3162, E-mail: phallock@utica.edu. *Application contact:* John D. Rowe, Director of Graduate Admissions, 315-792-3824, Fax: 315-792-3003, E-mail: jrowe@utica.edu.

Valley City State University, Online Graduate Programs, Valley City, ND 58072. Offers elementary education (M Ed); English education (M Ed); library and information technologies (M Ed); teaching (MAT); teaching and technology (M Ed); teaching English language learners (M Ed); technology education (M Ed). *Accreditation:* NCATE. *Program availability:* Part-time, evening/weekend, online only, 100% online. *Faculty:* 21 full-time (12 women), 15 part-time/adjunct (11 women). *Students:* 12 full-time (9 women), 138 part-time (99 women); includes 5 minority (3 Hispanic/Latino; 2 Two or more races, non-Hispanic/Latino). Average age 36. 13 applicants, 92% accepted, 12 enrolled. In 2017, 45 master's awarded. *Degree requirements:* For master's, action research report, comprehensive portfolio. *Entrance requirements:* For master's, GRE, MAT, PRAXIS II or National Teaching Board for Professional Standards (if GPA is less than 3.0). Additional exam requirements/recommendations for international students: Required—TOEFL (minimum score 525 paper-based; 71 iBT); Recommended—IELTS (minimum score 5.5). *Application deadline:* For fall admission, 7/21 for domestic and international students; for spring admission, 12/8 for domestic and international students; for summer admission, 5/5 for domestic and international students. Applications are processed on a rolling basis. Application fee: $35. Electronic applications accepted. *Expenses:* $384.21 per credit. *Financial support:* In 2017–18, 16 students received support. Scholarships/grants, tuition waivers (full and partial), and unspecified assistantships available. Financial award applicants required to submit FAFSA. *Faculty research:* Universal accessibility, instructional design and technology, gender communication, STEM education in K-12, English language learners. *Unit head:* Dr. Sheri Okland, Dean, 701-845-7184, E-mail: sheri.l.okland@vcsu.edu. *Application contact:* Misty Lindgren, Graduate Studies, 701-845-7303, Fax: 701-845-7190, E-mail: misty.lindgren@vcsu.edu.
Website: http://www.vcsu.edu/graduate

Valparaiso University, Graduate School and Continuing Education, Programs in Education, Valparaiso, IN 46383. Offers initial licensure (M Ed), including Chinese teaching, elementary education, secondary education; instructional leadership (M Ed); school psychology (Ed S); secondary education (M Ed); M Ed/Ed S. *Accreditation:* NCATE. *Program availability:* Part-time, evening/weekend, online learning. *Entrance requirements:* For master's, GRE General Test, minimum GPA of 3.0. Additional exam requirements/recommendations for international students: Required—TOEFL (minimum score 550 paper-based; 80 iBT), IELTS (minimum score 6). Electronic applications accepted. *Expenses:* Tuition: Full-time $11,340; part-time $630 per credit hour. *Required fees:* $520; $250 per year. $125 per semester. Tuition and fees vary according to program and reciprocity agreements.

Vanderbilt University, Peabody College, Nashville, TN 37240-1001. Offers M Ed, MPP, Ed D. *Accreditation:* APA (one or more programs are accredited); NCATE. *Program availability:* Part-time, online courses with semester immersions on campus. *Faculty:* 166 full-time (107 women), 85 part-time/adjunct (53 women). *Students:* 518 full-time (424 women), 217 part-time (149 women); includes 142 minority (63 Black or African American, non-Hispanic/Latino; 1 American Indian or Alaska Native, non-Hispanic/Latino; 27 Asian, non-Hispanic/Latino; 30 Hispanic/Latino; 1 Native Hawaiian or other Pacific Islander, non-Hispanic/Latino; 20 Two or more races, non-Hispanic/Latino), 80 international. Average age 27. 1,488 applicants, 63% accepted, 377 enrolled. In 2017, 315 master's, 22 doctorates awarded. *Degree requirements:* For master's, comprehensive exam (for some programs), thesis optional; for doctorate, thesis/dissertation, qualifying examinations, residency. *Entrance requirements:* For master's and doctorate, GRE General Test. Additional exam requirements/recommendations for international students: Required—TOEFL (minimum score 550 paper-based; 80 iBT). *Application deadline:* For fall admission, 12/31 priority date for domestic and international students; for spring admission, 11/1 priority date for domestic and international students. Applications are processed on a rolling basis. Electronic applications accepted. *Expenses:* $1,708 per credit; $3,253 health insurance per year; $289 recreation fee per year; $168 activity fee per year; $100 one-time transcript fee. *Financial support:* In 2017–18, 520 students received support. Fellowships with partial tuition reimbursements available, research assistantships with partial tuition reimbursements available, teaching assistantships with partial tuition reimbursements available, career-related internships or fieldwork, Federal Work-Study, institutionally sponsored loans, scholarships/grants, traineeships, tuition waivers (partial), and unspecified assistantships available. Support available to part-time students. Financial award application deadline: 1/15; financial award applicants required to submit FAFSA. *Total annual research expenditures:* $38.2 million. *Unit head:* Dr. Camilla P. Benbow, Dean, 615-322-8407, Fax: 615-322-8501, E-mail: camilla.benbow@vanderbilt.edu. *Application contact:* Kimberly Brazil, Director of Graduate and Professional Admissions, 615-332-8410, Fax: 615-343-3474, E-mail: kim.brazil@vanderbilt.edu.
Website: http://peabody.vanderbilt.edu/

See Display on the next page and Close-Up on page 725.

Vanderbilt University, Program in Learning, Teaching and Diversity, Nashville, TN 37240-1001. Offers PhD. *Faculty:* 18 full-time (10 women), 1 (woman) part-time/adjunct. *Students:* 36 full-time (29 women); includes 11 minority (2 Black or African American, non-Hispanic/Latino; 5 Asian, non-Hispanic/Latino; 4 Two or more races, non-Hispanic/Latino), 2 international. Average age 32. 126 applicants, 7% accepted, 7 enrolled. In 2017, 9 doctorates awarded. *Degree requirements:* For doctorate, comprehensive exam, thesis/dissertation, qualifying examinations. *Entrance requirements:* For doctorate, GRE General Test. Additional exam requirements/recommendations for international students: Required—TOEFL (minimum score 570 paper-based; 88 iBT). *Application deadline:* For fall admission, 12/1 for domestic and international students. Application fee: $0. Electronic applications accepted. *Expenses:* Contact institution. *Financial support:* Fellowships with partial tuition reimbursements, research assistantships with full tuition reimbursements, teaching assistantships with full tuition reimbursements, Federal Work-Study, institutionally sponsored loans, scholarships/grants, traineeships, and health care benefits available. Financial award application deadline: 1/15; financial award applicants required to submit CSS PROFILE or FAFSA. *Faculty research:* New pedagogies for math, science, and language; the support of English language learners; the uses of new technology and media in the classroom; middle school mathematics and the institutional setting of teaching. *Unit head:* Dr. Melissa Gresalfi, Director of Graduate Studies, 615-322-8227, Fax: 615-322-8014, E-mail: melissa.gresalfi@vanderbilt.edu. *Application contact:* Angela Saylor, Educational Coordinator, 615-322-8092, Fax: 615-322-8014, E-mail: angela.saylor@vanderbilt.edu.
Website: http://peabody.vanderbilt.edu/departments/tl/index.php

Vanguard University of Southern California, Graduate Programs in Education, Costa Mesa, CA 92626. Offers MA. *Program availability:* Evening/weekend. *Degree requirements:* For master's, thesis or alternative. *Entrance requirements:* For master's, California Basic Educational Skills Test, California Subject Examinations for Teachers, minimum GPA of 3.0. Additional exam requirements/recommendations for international students: Required—TOEFL (minimum score 550 paper-based; 79 iBT). Electronic applications accepted. *Expenses:* Contact institution. *Faculty research:* Reading, educational administration.

Villanova University, Graduate School of Liberal Arts and Sciences, Department of Education and Counseling, Villanova, PA 19085-1699. Offers elementary school counseling (MS), including counseling and human relations; teacher leadership (MA). *Program availability:* Part-time, evening/weekend. *Faculty:* 24. *Students:* 80 full-time (58 women), 37 part-time (28 women); includes 15 minority (7 Black or African American, non-Hispanic/Latino; 2 Asian, non-Hispanic/Latino; 5 Hispanic/Latino; 1 Two or more races, non-Hispanic/Latino), 2 international. Average age 30. 62 applicants, 74% accepted, 32 enrolled. In 2017, 49 master's awarded. *Degree requirements:* For master's, comprehensive exam. *Entrance requirements:* For master's, GRE or MAT, minimum GPA of 3.0, statement of goals. *Application deadline:* For fall admission, 3/1 priority date for domestic students, 5/1 for international students; for spring admission, 11/15 priority date for domestic students, 10/15 for international students; for summer admission, 5/1 for domestic students. Applications are processed on a rolling basis. Application fee: $50. Electronic applications accepted. *Financial support:* Research assistantships, teaching assistantships, scholarships/grants, and unspecified assistantships available. Financial award applicants required to submit FAFSA. *Unit head:* Dr. Christopher Schmidt, Chairperson, 610-519-4618. *Application contact:* Dean, Graduate School of Liberal Arts and Sciences.
Website: http://www.education.villanova.edu/

Virginia Commonwealth University, Graduate School, School of Education, Richmond, VA 23284-9005. Offers M Ed, MT, Ed D, PhD, Certificate. *Accreditation:* NCATE. *Program availability:* Part-time. *Degree requirements:* For doctorate, thesis/dissertation. *Entrance requirements:* For master's, GRE General Test or MAT; for doctorate, GRE (PhD only), MAT (Ed D only), interview, master's degree. Additional exam requirements/recommendations for international students: Required—TOEFL (minimum score 600 paper-based; 100 iBT); Recommended—IELTS (minimum score 6.5). Electronic applications accepted.

Virginia International University, School of Education, Fairfax, VA 22030. Offers applied linguistics (MS); education (M Ed); teaching English to speakers of other languages (MA). *Program availability:* Part-time, online learning. *Entrance requirements:* For master's, bachelor's degree. Additional exam requirements/recommendations for international students: Required—TOEFL (minimum score 550 paper-based; 80 iBT), IELTS (minimum score 6). Electronic applications accepted.

Virginia Polytechnic Institute and State University, VT Online, Blacksburg, VA 24061. Offers advanced transportation systems (Certificate); aerospace engineering (MS); agricultural and life sciences (MSLFS); business information systems (Graduate Certificate); career and technical education (MS); civil engineering (MS); computer engineering (M Eng, MS); decision support systems (Graduate Certificate); eLearning leadership (MA); electrical engineering (M Eng, MS); engineering administration (MEA); environmental engineering (Certificate); environmental politics and policy (Graduate Certificate); environmental sciences and engineering (MS); foundations of political analysis (Graduate Certificate); health product risk management (Graduate Certificate); industrial and systems engineering (MS); information policy and society (Graduate Certificate); information security (Graduate Certificate); information technology (MIT); instructional technology (MA); integrative STEM education (MA Ed); liberal arts (Graduate Certificate); life sciences: health product risk management (MS); natural resources (MNR, Graduate Certificate); networking (Graduate Certificate); nonprofit and nongovernmental organization management (Graduate Certificate); ocean engineering (MS); political science (MA); security studies (Graduate Certificate); software development (Graduate Certificate). *Expenses:* Tuition, state resident: full-time $15,072; part-time $718.50 per credit hour. Tuition, nonresident: full-time $28,810; part-time $1448.25 per credit hour. *Required fees:* $2741; $502 per semester. Tuition and fees vary according to course load, campus/location and program.

Virginia State University, College of Graduate Studies, College of Education, Petersburg, VA 23806-0001. Offers M Ed, MS, Ed D.

Virginia State University, College of Graduate Studies, College of Humanities and Social Sciences, Petersburg, VA 23806-0001. Offers M Ed, MA, MS. *Accreditation:* NCATE. *Program availability:* Part-time, evening/weekend.

Virginia Union University, Evelyn R. Syphax School of Education, Psychology and Interdisciplinary Studies, Richmond, VA 23220-1170. Offers curriculum and instruction (MA).

Virginia Wesleyan University, Graduate Studies, Virginia Beach, VA 23455. Offers business administration (MBA); secondary and PreK-12 education (MA Ed). *Program availability:* Online learning.

Viterbo University, Graduate Programs in Education, La Crosse, WI 54601-4797. Offers cross-categorical special education (Certificate); director of instruction (Certificate); director of special education and pupil services (Certificate); early childhood (Certificate); education (MAE); literacy coaching (Certificate); PreK-12 principal/supervisor of special education (Certificate); principal (Certificate); reading specialist endorsement (Certificate); reading teacher (Certificate); reading teacher 5-12 endorsement (Certificate); reading teacher K-8 endorsement (Certificate); superintendent (Certificate); talented and gifted endorsement (Certificate); Wisconsin school business administrator (Certificate). Weekend courses available in summer. *Accreditation:* NCATE. *Program availability:* Part-time, evening/weekend. *Degree requirements:* For master's, comprehensive exam, thesis, 30 credits of course work. *Entrance requirements:* For master's, BS, transcripts, teaching license, written narrative. Electronic applications accepted. *Expenses:* Contact institution.

Wagner College, Division of Graduate Studies, Education Department, Staten Island, NY 10301-4495. Offers childhood education/students with disabilities (MS Ed), including childhood education; early childhood education/students with disabilities (birth-grade 2) (MS Ed); higher education and learning organizations leadership (MA); secondary education/students with disabilities (MS Ed), including secondary education 7-12. *Accreditation:* NCATE. *Program availability:* Part-time, evening/weekend. *Faculty:* 5 full-time (4 women). *Students:* 41 full-time (29 women), 18 part-time (12 women); includes 14 minority (7 Black or African American, non-Hispanic/Latino; 3 Asian, non-Hispanic/Latino; 2 Hispanic/Latino; 2 Two or more races, non-Hispanic/Latino), 1 international. Average age 25. 47 applicants, 68% accepted, 25 enrolled. In 2017, 27 master's awarded. *Degree requirements:* For master's, thesis (for some programs). *Entrance requirements:* For master's, GRE, minimum GPA of 3.0. Additional exam requirements/recommendations for international students: Required—TOEFL (minimum score 550 paper-based; 79 iBT), IELTS (minimum score 6.5). *Application deadline:* For fall admission, 12/1 priority date for domestic and international students. Applications are processed on a rolling basis. Application fee: $60. Electronic applications accepted. *Financial support:* Unspecified assistantships and alumni fellowship available. Financial award application deadline: 4/15; financial award applicants required to submit FAFSA. *Faculty research:* School-community partnerships, civic engagement, educational accountability, micro-aggression and bullying, cross-cultural pedagogy with students and families. *Unit head:* Dr. Jason Fitzgerald, Department Chair, 718-420-4129, Fax: 718-390-3456, E-mail: jason.fitzgerald@wagner.edu. *Application contact:* Patricia Clancy, Assistant Director of Enrollment, 718-420-4464, Fax: 718-390-3105, E-mail: patricia.clancy@wagner.edu.
Website: http://www.wagner.edu/education/

Wake Forest University, Graduate School of Arts and Sciences, Department of Education, Winston-Salem, NC 27109. Offers secondary education (MA Ed). *Accreditation:* ACA; NCATE. *Faculty:* 6 full-time (3 women). *Students:* 12 full-time (8 women); includes 2 minority (1 Black or African American, non-Hispanic/Latino; 1 Hispanic/Latino). Average age 24. 20 applicants, 75% accepted, 12 enrolled. In 2017, 10 master's awarded. *Degree requirements:* For master's, thesis optional. *Entrance requirements:* For master's, GRE General Test. Additional exam requirements/recommendations for international students: Required—TOEFL (minimum score 550 paper-based). *Application deadline:* For fall admission, 1/15 for domestic students, 1/15 priority date for international students. Application fee: $75. Electronic applications accepted. *Expenses:* Contact institution. *Financial support:* In 2017–18, 13 students received support, including 10 fellowships with full tuition reimbursements available (averaging $49,000 per year), 3 teaching assistantships with full tuition reimbursements available (averaging $49,000 per year); scholarships/grants and tuition waivers (full and partial) also available. Financial award application deadline: 2/15. *Faculty research:* Teaching and learning. *Unit head:* Dr. Adam Friedman, Chair, 336-758-5507, Fax: 336-758-4591, E-mail: amfriedman@wfu.edu. *Application contact:* Dr. Leah McCoy, Program Director, 336-758-5498, Fax: 336-758-4591, E-mail: mccoy@wfu.edu.
Website: http://college.wfu.edu/education/graduate-program/overview-of-graduate-programs/

Walden University, Graduate Programs, Richard W. Riley College of Education and Leadership, Minneapolis, MN 55401. Offers adult education (Post-Master's Certificate); adult learning (Graduate Certificate); college teaching and learning (Graduate Certificate); community college leadership (Ed D); curriculum, instruction and assessment (Ed D, Ed S, Graduate Certificate); developmental education (Graduate Certificate); early childhood administration, management, and leadership (Graduate Certificate); early childhood education (Ed D, Ed S); early childhood public policy and advocacy (Graduate Certificate); early childhood studies (MS), including administration, management and leadership, early childhood public policy and advocacy, teaching adults in the early childhood field, teaching and diversity in early childhood education; education (MS, PhD), including adolescent literacy and learning (MS), curriculum,

VANDERBILT PEABODY COLLEGE

Great Change begins with great ideas.

For more information on Peabody's graduate programs, visit **peabody.vanderbilt.edu.**

instruction, and assessment (grades K-12) (MS), curriculum, instruction, assessment, and evaluation (PhD), early childhood leadership and advocacy (PhD), early childhood special education (PhD), educational leadership (MS), educational leadership and administration (principal preparation) (MS), educational technology and design (PhD), elementary reading and literacy (PreK-6) (MS), elementary reading and mathematics (grades K-6) (MS), global and comparative education (PhD), higher education leadership management and policy (PhD), integrating technology in the classroom (grades K-12) (MS), learning, instruction and innovation (PhD), mathematics (grades 5-8) (MS), mathematics (grades K-6) (MS), mathematics and science (grades K-8) (MS), organizational research, assessment, and evaluation (PhD), reading and literacy with a reading K-12 endorsement (MS), reading literacy assessment and evaluation (PhD), science (grades K-8) (MS), special education (non-licensure) (grades K-12) (MS), teacher leadership (grades K-12) (MS), teaching English language learners (grades K-12) (MS); educational administration and leadership (Ed D); educational leadership and administration (principal preparation) (Ed S); educational technology (Ed D, Ed S, Post Master's Certificate); elementary reading and literacy (Graduate Certificate); engaging culturally diverse learners (Graduate Certificate); enrollment management and institutional marketing (Graduate Certificate); higher education (MS), including adult learning, college teaching and learning, enrollment management and institutional marketing, global higher education, leadership for student success, online and distance learning; higher education and adult learning (Ed D); higher education leadership and management (Ed D); higher education leadership for student success (Graduate Certificate); instructional design and technology (MS, Postbaccalaureate Certificate), including general program (MS), online learning (MS), training and performance improvement (MS); integrating technology in the classroom (Graduate Certificate); mathematics 5-8 (Graduate Certificate); mathematics K-6 (Graduate Certificate); online teaching for adult educators (Graduate Certificate); reading, literacy, and assessment (Ed D, Ed S); science K-8 (Graduate Certificate); special education Ed D, Ed S, Graduate Certificate); special education (K-age 21) (MAT); teacher leadership (Graduate Certificate); teaching adults English as a second language (Graduate Certificate); teaching adults in the early childhood field (Graduate Certificate); teaching and diversity in early childhood education (Graduate Certificate); teaching English language learners (grades K-12) (Graduate Certificate); teaching K-12 students online (Graduate Certificate). *Accreditation:* NCATE. *Program availability:* Part-time, evening/weekend, online only, 100% online. *Degree requirements:* For doctorate, thesis/dissertation (for some programs), residency; for other advanced degree, residency (for some programs). *Entrance requirements:* For master's, bachelor's degree or higher; minimum GPA of 2.5; official transcripts; goal statement (for some programs); access to computer and Internet; for doctorate, master's degree or higher; three years of related professional or academic experience (preferred); minimum GPA of 3.0; goal statement and current resume (for select programs); official transcripts; access to computer and Internet; for other advanced degree, relevant work experience; access to computer and Internet. Additional exam requirements/recommendations for international students: Required—TOEFL (minimum score 550 paper-based, 79 iBT), IELTS (minimum score 6.5), Michigan English Language Assessment Battery (minimum score 82), or PTE (minimum score 53). Electronic applications accepted.

Walla Walla University, Graduate Studies, School of Education and Psychology, College Place, WA 99324. Offers curriculum and instruction (M Ed, MAT); educational leadership (M Ed, MAT); literacy instruction (M Ed, MAT); special education (M Ed, MAT). *Program availability:* Part-time. *Entrance requirements:* For master's, GRE General Test, minimum GPA of 2.75. Additional exam requirements/recommendations for international students: Required—TOEFL (minimum score 550 paper-based; 79 iBT). *Application deadline:* For fall admission, 4/1 priority date for domestic students. Applications are processed on a rolling basis. Application fee: $50. Electronic applications accepted. *Financial support:* Research assistantships, teaching assistantships, Federal Work-Study, and tuition waivers (partial) available. Support available to part-time students. Financial award application deadline: 4/30; financial award applicants required to submit FAFSA. *Faculty research:* Admissions/retention, instructional psychology, moral development, teaching of reading. *Unit head:* Dr. Debbie Muthersbaugh, Dean, 509-527-2212, Fax: 509-527-2248, E-mail: debbie.muthersbaugh@wallawalla.edu. *Application contact:* Dr. Joe G. Galusha, Dean of Graduate Studies, 509-527-2421, Fax: 509-527-2237, E-mail: joe.galusha@wallawalla.edu.
Website: https://wallawalla.edu/academics/areas-of-study/undergraduate-programs/education-and-psychology/

Walsh University, Graduate Programs, Program in Education, North Canton, OH 44720-3396. Offers leadership with principal license (MA Ed); reading literacy (MA Ed). *Accreditation:* NCATE. *Program availability:* Part-time, evening/weekend. *Degree requirements:* For master's, comprehensive exam (for some programs), thesis optional, action research project or comprehensive exam. *Entrance requirements:* For master's, MAT (minimum score 396), GRE (minimum scores: verbal 145, quantitative 146, combined 291, writing 3.0), or minimum GPA of 3.0 on the baccalaureate transcript, interview, minimum GPA of 3.0, writing sample, 3 recommendation forms, notarized affidavit of good moral character. Additional exam requirements/recommendations for international students: Required—TOEFL (minimum score 500 paper-based; 61 iBT). Electronic applications accepted. Application fee is waived when completed online. *Expenses:* Contact institution. *Faculty research:* Learning and the brain, primary STEM, effective assessment practices, literacy.

Warner Pacific University, Graduate Programs, Portland, OR 97215-4099. Offers human services (MA); not-for-profit leadership (MS); organizational leadership (MS); teaching (MAT). *Program availability:* Part-time, evening/weekend. *Degree requirements:* For master's, thesis or alternative, presentation of defense. *Entrance requirements:* For master's, interview, minimum GPA of 2.5, letters of recommendation. *Faculty research:* New Testament studies, nineteenth-century Wesleyan theology, preaching and church growth, Christian ethics.

Warner University, School of Education, Lake Wales, FL 33859. Offers curriculum and instruction (MAEd); elementary education (MAEd); science, technology, engineering, and mathematics (STEM) (MAEd). *Program availability:* Part-time, evening/weekend, online learning. *Degree requirements:* For master's, thesis, accomplished practices portfolio. *Entrance requirements:* For master's, minimum GPA of 3.0 in last 60 hours of undergraduate coursework; 2 letters of recommendation. Additional exam requirements/recommendations for international students: Required—TOEFL (minimum score 550 paper-based). Electronic applications accepted.

Washburn University, College of Arts and Sciences, Department of Education, Topeka, KS 66621. Offers curriculum and instruction (M Ed); educational leadership (M Ed); reading (M Ed); special education (M Ed). *Accreditation:* NCATE. *Program availability:* Part-time. *Degree requirements:* For master's, comprehensive exam, thesis or alternative, portfolio, comprehensive paper, or action research project. *Entrance requirements:* For master's, department exam, GRE General Test, or MAT, minimum GPA of 3.0 in graduate coursework or last 60 hours of undergraduate coursework. Additional exam requirements/recommendations for international students: Required—TOEFL (minimum score 80 iBT). *Faculty research:* Reading/literature/literacy, foundations, special education, diversity, teaching and technology.

Washington State University, College of Education, Pullman, WA 99164-2114. Offers Ed M, MA, MIT, Ed D, PhD. *Degree requirements:* For master's, comprehensive exam (for some programs), thesis (for some programs), oral and written exams; for doctorate, comprehensive exam, thesis/dissertation, oral and written exams, internship. *Entrance requirements:* For master's, GRE General Test, minimum GPA of 3.0, 3 letters of recommendation, transcripts showing all college or university course work, statement of professional objectives, current curriculum vitae/resume; for doctorate, GRE General Test or MAT, minimum GPA of 3.0, 3 letters of recommendation, transcripts showing all college or university course work, statement of professional objectives, current curriculum vitae/resume. Additional exam requirements/recommendations for international students: Required—TOEFL (minimum score 550 paper-based; 80 iBT). Electronic applications accepted.

Washington University in St. Louis, The Graduate School, Department of Education, St. Louis, MO 63130-4899. Offers educational research (PhD); elementary education (MA Ed); secondary education (MAT). *Degree requirements:* For master's, thesis or alternative; for doctorate, thesis/dissertation. *Entrance requirements:* For master's and doctorate, GRE General Test. Additional exam requirements/recommendations for international students: Required—TOEFL. Electronic applications accepted. *Faculty research:* Teacher education, educational studies, urban education, policy studies, science and math education, second language research.

Wayland Baptist University, Graduate Programs, Program in Education, Plainview, TX 79072-6998. Offers education administration (M Ed); education diagnostics (M Ed); education literacy (M Ed); elementary certification (M Ed); English (M Ed); English as a second language (M Ed); higher education administration (M Ed); human resources (M Ed); instructional leadership (M Ed); instructional technology (M Ed); leadership training and development (M Ed); science education (M Ed); secondary certification (M Ed); social studies (M Ed); special education (M Ed); sports administration and management (M Ed). *Program availability:* Part-time, evening/weekend, 100% online. *Faculty:* 33 full-time (17 women), 28 part-time/adjunct (17 women). *Students:* 16 full-time (13 women), 221 part-time (143 women); includes 97 minority (26 Black or African American, non-Hispanic/Latino; 1 American Indian or Alaska Native, non-Hispanic/Latino; 5 Asian, non-Hispanic/Latino; 54 Hispanic/Latino; 11 Two or more races, non-Hispanic/Latino), 1 international. Average age 39. 32 applicants, 97% accepted, 23 enrolled. In 2017, 78 master's awarded. *Degree requirements:* For master's, comprehensive exam, capstone course. *Entrance requirements:* For master's, GRE, GMAT or MAT. Additional exam requirements/recommendations for international students: Required—TOEFL (minimum score 500 paper-based; 61 iBT). *Application deadline:* Applications are processed on a rolling basis. Application fee: $50. Electronic applications accepted. *Expenses: Tuition:* Full-time $11,250; part-time $625 per credit hour. *Required fees:* $1200. *Financial support:* Federal Work-Study, institutionally sponsored loans, and scholarships/grants available. Support available to part-time students. Financial award application deadline: 5/1; financial award applicants required to submit FAFSA. *Unit head:* Dr. Gene Whitfill, Dean, 806-291-1047, Fax: 806-291-1951, E-mail: whitfillg@wbu.edu. *Application contact:* Amanda Stanton, Coordinator of Graduate Studies, 806-291-3423, Fax: 806-291-1950, E-mail: stanton@wbu.edu.

Wayne State College, School of Education and Counseling, Wayne, NE 68787. Offers MSE, Ed S. *Accreditation:* NCATE. *Program availability:* Part-time, evening/weekend. *Degree requirements:* For master's, comprehensive exam, thesis (for some programs). *Entrance requirements:* For master's, GRE General Test, minimum cumulative GPA of 3.0; for Ed S, GRE General Test, minimum GPA of 3.2 in all program coursework. Additional exam requirements/recommendations for international students: Required—TOEFL (minimum score 550 paper-based).

Wayne State University, College of Education, Detroit, MI 48202. Offers M Ed, MA, MAT, MSAT, Ed D, PhD, Certificate, Ed S, M Ed/MA. *Accreditation:* TEAC. *Program availability:* Part-time, evening/weekend, 100% online, blended/hybrid learning. *Faculty:* 46. *Students:* 426 full-time (307 women), 926 part-time (692 women); includes 511 minority (382 Black or African American, non-Hispanic/Latino; 3 American Indian or Alaska Native, non-Hispanic/Latino; 22 Asian, non-Hispanic/Latino; 44 Hispanic/Latino; 2 Native Hawaiian or other Pacific Islander, non-Hispanic/Latino; 58 Two or more races, non-Hispanic/Latino), 52 international. Average age 35. 919 applicants, 36% accepted, 228 enrolled. In 2017, 322 master's, 53 doctorates, 64 other advanced degrees awarded. *Degree requirements:* For master's, thesis (for some programs); for doctorate, thesis/dissertation, written exam. *Entrance requirements:* For master's, baccalaureate degree with minimum upper-division GPA of 2.75; teaching certificate (for some M Ed programs); for doctorate, written exam of writing ability, minimum undergraduate GPA of 3.0, 3 years of teaching experience (for some programs); master's degree (for most programs); for other advanced degree, minimum upper-division GPA of 2.75 or 3.4 in master's program (for Ed S); master's degree; 3 years of teaching experience (for some areas). Additional exam requirements/recommendations for international students: Required—TOEFL (minimum score 550 paper-based; 79 iBT), TWE (minimum score 5.5); Recommended—IELTS (minimum score 6.5). *Application deadline:* For fall admission, 6/1 priority date for domestic students, 5/1 for international students; for winter admission, 10/1 priority date for domestic students, 9/1 priority date for international students; for spring admission, 2/1 priority date for domestic students, 1/1 priority date for international students. Application fee: $50. Electronic applications accepted. *Expenses: Tuition,* state resident: full-time $10,224; part-time $638.98 per credit hour. Tuition, nonresident: full-time $22,145; part-time $1384.04 per credit hour. Tuition and fees vary according to course load and program. *Financial support:* In 2017–18, 303 students received support, including 4 fellowships with tuition reimbursements available (averaging $13,500 per year), 13 research assistantships with tuition reimbursements available (averaging $18,339 per year), 5 teaching assistantships with tuition reimbursements available (averaging $18,534 per year); Federal Work-Study, scholarships/grants, traineeships, health care benefits, and unspecified assistantships also available. Support available to part-time students. Financial award applicants required to submit FAFSA. *Unit head:* Dr. R. Douglas Whitman, Dean, 313-577-1620, E-mail: dwhitman@wayne.edu. *Application contact:* Paul W. Johnson, Assistant Dean of Academic Services, 313-577-1606, E-mail: askcoe@wayne.edu.
Website: http://coe.wayne.edu/

Weber State University, Jerry and Vickie Moyes College of Education, Ogden, UT 84408-1001. Offers M Ed, MSAT. *Accreditation:* NCATE; TEAC. *Program availability:* Part-time, evening/weekend. *Faculty:* 27 full-time (14 women), 2 part-time/adjunct (1 woman). *Students:* 45 full-time (22 women), 106 part-time (83 women); includes 3 minority (2 Asian, non-Hispanic/Latino; 1 Hispanic/Latino), 6 international. Average age 35. In 2017, 44 master's awarded. *Degree requirements:* For master's, project presentation, exam. *Entrance requirements:* For master's, GRE. Additional exam requirements/recommendations for international students: Required—TOEFL (minimum score 525 paper-based). *Application deadline:* For fall admission, 5/15 for domestic students; for spring admission, 9/15 for domestic students; for summer admission, 1/15 for domestic students. Application fee: $60 ($90 for international students). *Expenses:* Contact institution. *Financial support:* In 2017–18, 30 students received support. Institutionally sponsored loans, scholarships/grants, tuition waivers (full and partial), and unspecified assistantships available. Support available to part-time students. Financial award application deadline: 4/1; financial award applicants required to submit FAFSA. *Unit head:* Dr. Jack Rasmussen, Dean, 801-626-6273, Fax: 801-626-7427, E-mail: jrasmussen@weber.edu. *Application contact:* Nathan Alexander, College of Education Recruiter, 801-626-8124, Fax: 801-626-7427, E-mail: nathanalexander@weber.edu. Website: http://www.weber.edu/education/

Webster University, School of Education, St. Louis, MO 63119-3194. Offers MA, MAT, MET, Ed S. *Accreditation:* NCATE. *Program availability:* Part-time, online learning. *Degree requirements:* For master's, thesis (for some programs). *Entrance requirements:* For master's, minimum GPA of 2.5. Additional exam requirements/recommendations for international students: Required—TOEFL.

Wesleyan College, Department of Education, Macon, GA 31210-4462. Offers early childhood education (MA). *Program availability:* Part-time. *Degree requirements:* For master's, thesis or alternative, practicum, professional portfolio. *Entrance requirements:* For master's, GRE or MAT, interview, teaching certificate, 3 letters of recommendation. Additional exam requirements/recommendations for international students: Required—TOEFL. *Faculty research:* Neuroscience, gender bias in science and mathematics.

Wesley College, Education Program, Dover, DE 19901-3875. Offers M Ed, MA Ed, MAT. *Accreditation:* NCATE. *Program availability:* Part-time, evening/weekend. *Degree requirements:* For master's, thesis optional. *Entrance requirements:* For master's, GRE. *Faculty research:* Learning styles, community-higher education partnerships, curriculum models, science learning and teaching, literacy development in early elementary.

West Chester University of Pennsylvania, College of Education and Social Work, West Chester, PA 19383. Offers M Ed, MS, MSW, Ed D, Certificate, Post Master's Certificate, Teaching Certificate. *Accreditation:* NCATE. *Program availability:* Part-time, evening/weekend, 100% online, blended/hybrid learning. *Faculty:* 62 full-time (45 women), 22 part-time/adjunct (15 women). *Students:* 394 full-time (325 women), 615 part-time (531 women); includes 233 minority (157 Black or African American, non-Hispanic/Latino; 11 Asian, non-Hispanic/Latino; 38 Hispanic/Latino; 27 Two or more races, non-Hispanic/Latino), 4 international. Average age 30. 759 applicants, 76% accepted, 379 enrolled. In 2017, 299 master's, 57 other advanced degrees awarded. *Degree requirements:* For master's, comprehensive exam (for some programs), thesis (for some programs). *Entrance requirements:* Additional exam requirements/recommendations for international students: Required—TOEFL or IELTS. *Application deadline:* For fall admission, 5/15 for international students; for spring admission, 10/15 for international students. Applications are processed on a rolling basis. Application fee: $50. Electronic applications accepted. *Expenses:* Tuition: state resident: full-time $9000; part-time $500 per credit. Tuition, nonresident: full-time $13,500; part-time $750 per credit. *Required fees:* $2959; $149.79 per credit. *Financial support:* Scholarships/grants and unspecified assistantships available. Financial award application deadline: 2/15; financial award applicants required to submit FAFSA. *Unit head:* Dr. Kenneth D. Witmer, Jr., Dean, 610-436-2321, Fax: 610-436-3102, E-mail: kwitmer@wcupa.edu. *Application contact:* Office of Graduate Studies and Extended Education, 610-436-2943, Fax: 610-436-2763, E-mail: gradstudy@wcupa.edu. Website: http://www.wcupa.edu/education-socialWork/staff.aspx

Western Carolina University, Graduate School, College of Education and Allied Professions, Cullowhee, NC 28723. Offers MA. *Accreditation:* NCATE. *Program availability:* Part-time, evening/weekend, online learning. *Degree requirements:* For master's, comprehensive exam, thesis. *Entrance requirements:* For master's, GRE, appropriate undergraduate degree with minimum GPA of 3.0, 3 recommendations, writing sample, resume, interview. Additional exam requirements/recommendations for international students: Required—TOEFL (minimum score 550 paper-based; 79 iBT). *Expenses:* Tuition, state resident: full-time $4436. Tuition, nonresident: full-time $14,842. *Required fees:* $2926. *Faculty research:* Evolutionary psychology, marital and family development, program evaluation, rural education, special education, educational leadership, employee recruitment/retention.

Western Connecticut State University, Division of Graduate Studies, School of Professional Studies, Department of Education and Educational Psychology, Danbury, CT 06810-6885. Offers clinical mental health counseling (MS); curriculum (MS); instructional leadership (Ed D); instructional technology (MS); reading (MS); school counseling (MS); special education (MS). *Accreditation:* NCATE. *Program availability:* Part-time. *Degree requirements:* For master's, thesis or alternative, completion of program in 6 years. *Entrance requirements:* For master's, MAT (if GPA is below 2.8), valid teaching certificate, letters of reference; for doctorate, GRE or MAT, resume, three recommendations (one in a supervisory capacity in an educational setting), satisfactory interview with WCSU representatives from the Ed D Admissions Committee. Additional exam requirements/recommendations for international students: Recommended—TOEFL (minimum score 550 paper-based; 79 iBT), IELTS (minimum score 6). *Expenses:* Contact institution. *Faculty research:* Cultural diversity in teacher and counselor education programs, African-American educational leaders, urban education and equity.

Western Governors University, Teachers College, Salt Lake City, UT 84107. Offers curriculum and instruction (MS); educational leadership (MS); educational studies (MA); educational studies (5-12) (MA), including mathematics; elementary education (K-8) (MAT, Postbaccalaureate Certificate); elementary education (PreK-8) (MAT); English language learning (K-12) (MA); instructional design (MAT); learning and technology (M Ed, MA); management and innovation (M Ed); mathematics (5-12) (MAT, Postbaccalaureate Certificate); mathematics (5-9) (MAT, Postbaccalaureate Certificate); mathematics education (5-12) (MA); mathematics education (5-9) (MA); mathematics education (K-6) (MA); measurement and evaluation (M Ed); science (5-12) (Postbaccalaureate Certificate); science (5-9) (MAT, Postbaccalaureate Certificate); science education (5-12) (MA), including biology, chemistry, geology, physics; science education (5-9) (MA); social science (5-12) (MAT, Postbaccalaureate Certificate); special education (MAT, MS). *Accreditation:* NCATE. *Program availability:* Evening/weekend, online learning. *Degree requirements:* For master's, capstone project. *Entrance requirements:* For master's and Postbaccalaureate Certificate, Readiness Assessment, transcripts. Additional exam requirements/recommendations for international students: Required—TOEFL (minimum score 450 paper-based; 80 iBT). Electronic applications accepted. *Expenses:* Contact institution.

Western Illinois University, School of Graduate Studies, College of Education and Human Services, Macomb, IL 61455-1390. Offers MA, MS, MS Ed, Ed D, Certificate, Ed S. *Accreditation:* NCATE. *Program availability:* Part-time, evening/weekend, online learning. *Students:* 319 full-time (171 women), 407 part-time (284 women); includes 130 minority (67 Black or African American, non-Hispanic/Latino; 6 Asian, non-Hispanic/Latino; 44 Hispanic/Latino; 13 Two or more races, non-Hispanic/Latino), 33 international. Average age 31. 397 applicants, 84% accepted, 201 enrolled. In 2017, 212 master's, 12 doctorates, 7 other advanced degrees awarded. *Degree requirements:* For master's, comprehensive exam (for some programs), thesis or alternative; for doctorate, comprehensive exam, thesis/dissertation, electronic portfolio. *Entrance requirements:* For master's, GRE and MAT (for selected programs); for doctorate, GRE. Additional exam requirements/recommendations for international students: Required—TOEFL. *Application deadline:* Applications are processed on a rolling basis. Application fee: $30. Electronic applications accepted. *Financial support:* Research assistantships with full

tuition reimbursements, teaching assistantships with full tuition reimbursements, and unspecified assistantships available. Financial award applicants required to submit FAFSA. *Unit head:* Dr. Erskine Smith, Dean, 309-298-1690. *Application contact:* Dr. Nancy Parsons, Associate Provost and Director of Graduate Studies, 309-298-1806, Fax: 309-298-2345, E-mail: grad-office@wiu.edu. Website: http://wiu.edu/coehs

Western Michigan University, Graduate College, College of Education and Human Development, Kalamazoo, MI 49008. Offers MA, MS, Ed D, PhD, Ed S, Graduate Certificate. *Accreditation:* NCATE. *Program availability:* Part-time. *Degree requirements:* For doctorate, thesis/dissertation; for other advanced degree, thesis.

Western New Mexico University, Graduate Division, School of Education, Silver City, NM 88062-0680. Offers bilingual education (MAT); educational leadership (MA); elementary education (MAT); reading (MAT); secondary education (MAT); special education (MAT); TESOL (teaching English to speakers of other languages) (MAT). *Accreditation:* NCATE. *Program availability:* Part-time, online learning. *Degree requirements:* For master's, comprehensive exam. *Entrance requirements:* For master's, minimum GPA of 3.0 in last 64 hours of undergraduate study. Additional exam requirements/recommendations for international students: Required—TOEFL (minimum score 550 paper-based; 79 iBT). Electronic applications accepted. *Faculty research:* International education, electronic reading assessment, developing STEM teachers.

Western Oregon University, Graduate Programs, College of Education, Monmouth, OR 97361. Offers MAT, MS, MS Ed. *Accreditation:* NCATE. *Program availability:* Part-time, evening/weekend, online learning. *Degree requirements:* For master's, comprehensive exam (for some programs), thesis optional, written exam. *Entrance requirements:* For master's, minimum GPA of 3.0. Additional exam requirements/recommendations for international students: Required—TOEFL (minimum score 550 paper-based; 79 iBT), IELTS (minimum score 6.5). *Faculty research:* Effectiveness of work, sample methodology, documentation of learning gains, appropriateness of advanced proficiency.

Western State Colorado University, Graduate Programs in Education, Gunnison, CO 81231. Offers education administrator leadership (MA); reading leadership (MA); teacher leadership (MA). *Program availability:* Online learning. *Degree requirements:* For master's, capstone.

Western Washington University, Graduate School, Woodring College of Education, Bellingham, WA 98225-5996. Offers M Ed, MA, MIT. *Accreditation:* NCATE. *Program availability:* Part-time, online learning. *Degree requirements:* For master's, comprehensive exam, thesis optional. *Entrance requirements:* For master's, GRE General Test or MAT, minimum GPA of 3.0 in last 60 semester hours or last 90 quarter hours. Additional exam requirements/recommendations for international students: Required—TOEFL (minimum score 567 paper-based). Electronic applications accepted.

Westfield State University, College of Graduate and Continuing Education, Department of Education, Westfield, MA 01086. Offers early childhood education (M Ed); elementary education (M Ed); reading specialist (M Ed); secondary education (M Ed), including biology teacher education, chemistry teacher education, general science teacher education, history teacher education, mathematics teacher education, physical education teacher education; special education (M Ed), including moderate disabilities, 5-12, moderate disabilities, preK-8; vocational technical education (M Ed). *Accreditation:* NCATE. *Program availability:* Part-time, evening/weekend. *Faculty:* 6 full-time (all women), 17 part-time/adjunct (13 women). *Students:* 12 full-time (8 women), 137 part-time (110 women); includes 5 minority (1 Black or African American, non-Hispanic/Latino; 1 Asian, non-Hispanic/Latino; 1 Hispanic/Latino; 2 Two or more races, non-Hispanic/Latino). Average age 31. 65 applicants, 98% accepted, 50 enrolled. In 2017, 60 master's awarded. *Degree requirements:* For master's, comprehensive exam, practicum. *Entrance requirements:* For master's, GRE General Test or MAT, minimum undergraduate GPA of 2.8. Additional exam requirements/recommendations for international students: Recommended—TOEFL (minimum score 550 paper-based; 79 iBT). *Application deadline:* For fall admission, 7/1 for domestic students; for spring admission, 11/1 for domestic students; for summer admission, 4/1 for domestic students. Applications are processed on a rolling basis. Application fee: $50. *Expenses:* Tuition, state resident: part-time $332 per credit. Tuition, nonresident: part-time $332 per credit. *Required fees:* $75 per semester. Tuition and fees vary according to program. *Financial support:* Unspecified assistantships and SOS scholarships (for education majors only) available. Financial award application deadline: 3/1; financial award applicants required to submit FAFSA. *Faculty research:* Collaborative teacher education, developmental early childhood education. *Unit head:* Dr. Laura Baker, Department Chair, 413-572-5324, E-mail: lbaker@westfield.ma.edu. *Application contact:* Shelly Henrichon, Coordinator of College of Graduate and Continuing Education Admissions, 413-572-8022, Fax: 413-572-5227, E-mail: mhenrichon@westfield.ma.edu. Website: http://www.westfield.ma.edu/academics/degrees/education-graduate-programs

West Liberty University, College of Education and Human Performance, West Liberty, WV 26074. Offers community education research and leadership (MA Ed); innovative instruction (MA Ed); leadership in disability services (MA Ed); leadership studies (MA Ed); multi-categorical special education (MA Ed); reading specialist (MA Ed); sports leadership and coaching (MA Ed). *Accreditation:* NCATE. *Program availability:* Part-time, evening/weekend. *Students:* 18 full-time (12 women), 74 part-time (60 women); includes 2 minority (1 Black or African American, non-Hispanic/Latino; 1 Native Hawaiian or other Pacific Islander, non-Hispanic/Latino). Average age 32. *Degree requirements:* For master's, capstone experience. *Entrance requirements:* For master's, minimum GPA of 2.5 or 3.0 (depending on track). Additional exam requirements/recommendations for international students: Required—TOEFL. *Application deadline:* Applications are processed on a rolling basis. Application fee: $0. Electronic applications accepted. Tuition and fees vary according to course load and program. *Financial support:* Teaching assistantships and unspecified assistantships available. *Unit head:* Dr. Catherine Monteroso, Interim Dean, 304-336-8247, E-mail: cmonteroso@westliberty.edu. *Application contact:* Sara Sweeney, Director, Office of Graduate Studies, 304-336-8545, E-mail: sara.sweeney@westliberty.edu. Website: http://westliberty.edu/education/

Westminster College, School of Education, Salt Lake City, UT 84105-3697. Offers community leadership (MACL); education (M Ed); teaching (MAT). *Accreditation:* TEAC. *Program availability:* Part-time, evening/weekend. *Faculty:* 14 full-time (9 women), 23 part-time/adjunct (19 women). *Students:* 57 full-time (44 women), 64 part-time (51 women); includes 30 minority (3 Black or African American, non-Hispanic/Latino; 1 American Indian or Alaska Native, non-Hispanic/Latino; 5 Asian, non-Hispanic/Latino; 18 Hispanic/Latino; 1 Native Hawaiian or other Pacific Islander, non-Hispanic/Latino; 2 Two or more races, non-Hispanic/Latino), 6 international. Average age 34. 56 applicants, 88% accepted, 34 enrolled. In 2017, 61 master's awarded. *Degree requirements:* For master's, thesis (for some programs), project or thesis. *Entrance requirements:* For master's, GRE, PRAXIS II, personal statement (2-pages), 2 letters of recommendation, personal resume, official transcript, minimum GPA of 3.0. Additional exam requirements/recommendations for international students: Required—TOEFL

Education—General

(minimum score 84 iBT), IELTS (minimum score 7). *Application deadline:* For fall admission, 6/1 priority date for domestic and international students; for spring admission, 10/1 priority date for domestic and international students; for summer admission, 1/1 priority date for domestic and international students. Applications are processed on a rolling basis. Application fee: $50. Electronic applications accepted. *Expenses:* $695 per credit hour plus $13 student fee per credit hour (for M Ed fall and spring only); $29,190 for entire program (for MAT); $715 per credit hour plus $13 student fee per credit hour (for MACL fall and spring only). *Financial support:* In 2017–18, 49 students received support. Career-related internships or fieldwork, scholarships/grants, unspecified assistantships, and tuition remission available. Financial award applicants required to submit FAFSA. *Faculty research:* Identity development, space among marginalized populations, adult education, Latin American studies and economic developments, educational travel, learning in social movements. *Unit head:* Melanie Agnew, Dean, School of Education, 801-832-2470, Fax: 801-832-3105. *Application contact:* Andrea Pischnotte, Admissions Counselor, 801-832-2220, Fax: 801-832-3101, E-mail: apischnotte@westminstercollege.edu.
Website: https://www.westminstercollege.edu/graduate/programs

West Texas A&M University, College of Education and Social Sciences, Department of Education, Canyon, TX 79015. Offers counseling (MA); curriculum and instruction (M Ed); educational diagnostician (M Ed); educational leadership (M Ed); instructional design and technology (M Ed); reading education (M Ed); school counseling (M Ed); teaching (MAT). *Program availability:* Part-time, evening/weekend, online learning. *Degree requirements:* For master's, comprehensive exam, thesis optional. *Entrance requirements:* For master's, GRE General Test. Additional exam requirements/recommendations for international students: Required—TOEFL. Electronic applications accepted.

West Virginia University, College of Education and Human Services, Morgantown, WV 26506. Offers audiology (Au D); autism spectrum disorder (MA); clinical rehabilitation and mental health counseling (MS); communication science and disorders (PhD); counseling (MA); counseling psychology (PhD); curriculum and instruction (Ed D); early childhood education (MA); early intervention (MA); education (PhD); educational leadership (MA, Ed D); educational leadership/public school administration (MA); educational psychology (MA, Ed D); elementary education (MA); gifted education (MA); higher education administration (MA, Ed D); higher education curriculum and teaching (MA); institutional design and technology (MA); instructional design and technology (Ed D); literacy education (MA); secondary education (MA); secondary education/English (MA); special education (Ed D); speech pathology (MS). *Accreditation:* NCATE. *Program availability:* Part-time, evening/weekend, online learning. *Students:* 423 full-time (347 women), 367 part-time (316 women); includes 57 minority (14 Black or African American, non-Hispanic/Latino; 7 Asian, non-Hispanic/Latino; 20 Hispanic/Latino; 16 Two or more races, non-Hispanic/Latino), 13 international. *Degree requirements:* For master's, content exams; for doctorate, comprehensive exam, thesis/dissertation. *Entrance requirements:* Additional exam requirements/recommendations for international students: Required—TOEFL (minimum score 500 paper-based; 61 iBT). *Application deadline:* For fall admission, 8/1 for domestic students; for spring admission, 1/1 for domestic students; for summer admission, 5/1 for domestic students. Application fee: $60. Electronic applications accepted. *Expenses:* Tuition, state resident: full-time $9450. Tuition, nonresident: full-time $24,390. *Financial support:* Fellowships, research assistantships, teaching assistantships, career-related internships or fieldwork, Federal Work-Study, institutionally sponsored loans, health care benefits, tuition waivers (full and partial), and administrative assistantships available. Financial award applicants required to submit FAFSA. *Faculty research:* Internet training and integration for teachers, rural education, teacher preparation, organization of schools, evaluation of personnel. *Unit head:* Dr. Gypsy Denzine, Dean, 304-293-5703, Fax: 304-293-7565, E-mail: gypsy.denzine@mail.wvu.edu. *Application contact:* Dr. M. Cecil Smith, Associate Dean for Research and Graduate Education, 304-293-2174, Fax: 304-293-3802, E-mail: mcecil.smith@mail.wvu.edu.
Website: http://cehs.wvu.edu/

West Virginia Wesleyan College, Department of Education, Buckhannon, WV 26201. Offers M Ed. *Accreditation:* NCATE.

Wheaton College, Graduate School, Department of Education, Wheaton, IL 60187-5593. Offers elementary education (MAT); secondary education (MAT). *Accreditation:* NCATE. *Faculty:* 1 full-time (0 women), 1 part-time/adjunct (0 women). *Students:* 24 full-time (13 women); includes 4 minority (3 Asian, non-Hispanic/Latino; 1 Hispanic/Latino), 1 international. Average age 24. 18 applicants, 100% accepted, 17 enrolled. In 2017, 11 master's awarded. *Degree requirements:* For master's, thesis or alternative. *Entrance requirements:* For master's, GRE General Test or MAT. Additional exam requirements/recommendations for international students: Required—TOEFL (minimum score 550 paper-based; 80 iBT), IELTS (minimum score 6.5). *Application deadline:* For fall admission, 5/1 for domestic students, 1/1 for international students; for spring admission, 11/1 for domestic students. Applications are processed on a rolling basis. Application fee: $30. Electronic applications accepted. *Expenses:* Tuition: Full-time $19,800; part-time $825 per credit hour. Tuition and fees vary according to degree level and program. *Financial support:* Career-related internships or fieldwork and Federal Work-Study available. Financial award application deadline: 3/1; financial award applicants required to submit FAFSA. *Unit head:* Dr. Paul Egeland, Chair, 630-752-5041, E-mail: education.dept@wheaton.edu. *Application contact:* Director of Graduate Admissions, 630-752-5195, Fax: 630-752-7047, E-mail: graduate.admissions@wheaton.edu.
Website: https://www.wheaton.edu/academics/programs/education/master-of-arts-in-teaching/

Whittier College, Graduate Programs, Department of Education and Child Development, Whittier, CA 90608-0634. Offers educational administration (MA Ed); elementary education (MA Ed); secondary education (MA Ed). *Program availability:* Part-time, evening/weekend. *Degree requirements:* For master's, thesis. *Entrance requirements:* For master's, GRE General Test, MAT, minimum GPA of 3.5, academic writing sample.

Whitworth University, School of Education, Graduate Studies in Education, Spokane, WA 99251-0001. Offers administration (M Ed); counseling (M Ed), including school counselors, social agency/church setting; elementary education (M Ed); gifted and talented (MAT); secondary education (M Ed); special education (MAT); teaching (MIT). *Accreditation:* NCATE. *Program availability:* Part-time, evening/weekend. *Degree requirements:* For master's, comprehensive exam, thesis (for some programs). *Entrance requirements:* For master's, GRE General Test, MAT. Additional exam requirements/recommendations for international students: Required—TOEFL. *Faculty research:* Rural program development, mainstreaming, special needs learners.

Wichita State University, Graduate School, College of Education, Wichita, KS 67260. Offers M Ed, MAT, Ed D, Ed S. *Accreditation:* NCATE. *Program availability:* Part-time, evening/weekend, 100% online, blended/hybrid learning. *Unit head:* Dr. Shirley Lefever, Dean, 316-978-3301, Fax: 316-978-3302, E-mail: shirley.lefever@wichita.edu. *Application contact:* Jordan Oleson, Admissions Coordinator, 316-978-3095, Fax: 316-978-3253, E-mail: jordan.oleson@wichita.edu.
Website: http://www.wichita.edu/education

Widener University, School of Human Service Professions, Center for Education, Chester, PA 19013-5792. Offers adult education (M Ed); counseling in higher education (M Ed); counselor education (M Ed); early childhood education (M Ed); educational foundations (M Ed); educational leadership (M Ed); educational psychology (M Ed); elementary education (M Ed); English and language arts (M Ed); health education (M Ed); higher education leadership (Ed D); home and school visitor (M Ed); human sexuality (M Ed, PhD); mathematics education (M Ed); middle school education (M Ed); principalship (M Ed); reading and language arts (Ed D); reading education (M Ed); school administration (Ed D); science education (M Ed); social studies education (M Ed); special education (M Ed); technology education (M Ed). *Accreditation:* NCATE. *Program availability:* Part-time, evening/weekend. *Faculty:* 34 full-time (22 women), 37 part-time/adjunct (14 women). *Students:* 131 full-time (112 women), 244 part-time (179 women); includes 94 minority (58 Black or African American, non-Hispanic/Latino; 1 American Indian or Alaska Native, non-Hispanic/Latino; 1 Asian, non-Hispanic/Latino; 22 Hispanic/Latino; 12 Two or more races, non-Hispanic/Latino), 12 international. Average age 37. 140 applicants, 38% accepted, 26 enrolled. In 2017, 45 master's, 21 doctorates awarded. Terminal master's awarded for partial completion of doctoral program. *Degree requirements:* For doctorate, thesis/dissertation. *Entrance requirements:* For master's, minimum GPA of 2.5; for doctorate, GRE or MAT, minimum GPA of 2.0 (undergraduate), 3.5 (graduate). *Application deadline:* Applications are processed on a rolling basis. Application fee: $25 ($300 for international students). Electronic applications accepted. *Expenses:* Contact institution. *Financial support:* Career-related internships or fieldwork, tuition waivers (full and partial), and unspecified assistantships available. Support available to part-time students. Financial award application deadline: 5/1. *Faculty research:* Reading and cognition, adult education, technology education, educational leadership, special education. *Unit head:* Dr. Shawn Fitzgerald, Dean, 610-499-4294, Fax: 610-499-4623, E-mail: smfitzgerald@widener.edu. *Application contact:* Megan Kuft, Director of Graduate Admissions, 610-499-4124, E-mail: gradprograms@widener.edu.
Website: http://www.widener.edu/academics/schools/eics

Wilkes University, College of Graduate and Professional Studies, School of Education, Wilkes-Barre, PA 18766-0002. Offers educational development and strategies (MS Ed); educational leadership (MS Ed, Ed D); effective teaching (MS Ed); instructional media (MS Ed); instructional technology (MS Ed); international school leadership (MS Ed); international teaching and learning (MS Ed); literacy specialist (MS Ed); middle level education (MS Ed); online teaching (MS Ed); school business leadership (MS Ed); special education (MS Ed); teaching English to speakers of other languages (MS Ed). *Program availability:* Part-time, evening/weekend, 100% online, blended/hybrid learning. *Students:* 76 full-time (57 women), 1,586 part-time (1,204 women); includes 82 minority (10 Black or African American, non-Hispanic/Latino; 12 Asian, non-Hispanic/Latino; 41 Hispanic/Latino; 1 Native Hawaiian or other Pacific Islander, non-Hispanic/Latino; 18 Two or more races, non-Hispanic/Latino). Average age 34. In 2017, 619 master's, 23 doctorates awarded. *Entrance requirements:* Additional exam requirements/recommendations for international students: Required—TOEFL (minimum score 550 paper-based; 79 iBT). *Application deadline:* Applications are processed on a rolling basis. Application fee: $45 ($65 for international students). Electronic applications accepted. *Expenses:* Contact institution. *Financial support:* Unspecified assistantships available. Financial award application deadline: 3/1; financial award applicants required to submit FAFSA. *Unit head:* Dr. Rhonda Rabbitt, Dean, 570-408-4680, Fax: 570-408-7872, E-mail: rhonda.rabbitt@wilkes.edu. *Application contact:* Stephanie Wasmanski, Associate Director of Graduate Admissions, 570-408-5535, Fax: 570-408-7846, E-mail: stephanie.wasmanski@wilkes.edu.
Website: http://www.wilkes.edu/academics/graduate-programs/masters-programs/graduate-education/index.aspx

William Carey University, School of Education, Hattiesburg, MS 39401. Offers art education (M Ed); art of teaching (M Ed); elementary education (M Ed, Ed S); English education (M Ed); gifted education (M Ed); history and social science (M Ed); mild/moderate disabilities (M Ed); secondary education (M Ed). *Accreditation:* NCATE. *Program availability:* Part-time. *Degree requirements:* For master's, comprehensive exam. *Entrance requirements:* For master's, GRE, MAT, minimum GPA of 2.5, Class A teacher's license. Additional exam requirements/recommendations for international students: Required—TOEFL (minimum score 550 paper-based).

William Jessup University, Program in Teaching, Rocklin, CA 95765. Offers single subject English (MAT); single subject math (MAT). *Program availability:* Evening/weekend.

William Jewell College, Department of Education, Liberty, MO 64068-1843. Offers differentiated instruction (MS Ed).

William Paterson University of New Jersey, College of Education, Wayne, NJ 07470-8420. Offers curriculum and learning (M Ed); early childhood education (Certificate); educational leadership (M Ed); educational media specialist (Certificate); elementary education (MAT, Certificate); elementary education subject area (Certificate); higher education administration (MA); learning disabilities consultant (Certificate); literacy (M Ed); middle level education (M Ed); middle school education subject area (Certificate); professional counseling (M Ed); reading specialist (Certificate); school library media specialist (Certificate); school principal (Certificate); school supervisor (Certificate); secondary education (MAT); special education (M Ed); teacher of students with disabilities (Certificate). *Accreditation:* NCATE. *Program availability:* Part-time, evening/weekend. *Faculty:* 37 full-time (25 women), 21 part-time/adjunct (16 women). *Students:* 73 full-time (54 women), 480 part-time (409 women); includes 153 minority (48 Black or African American, non-Hispanic/Latino; 13 Asian, non-Hispanic/Latino; 81 Hispanic/Latino; 11 Two or more races, non-Hispanic/Latino), 1 international. Average age 35. 347 applicants, 87% accepted, 226 enrolled. In 2017, 136 master's awarded. *Degree requirements:* For master's, comprehensive exam, thesis (for some programs), exit interview (for some programs); practicum/internship; minimum GPA of 3.0 (for some programs); exit portfolio (for some programs). *Entrance requirements:* For master's, GRE/MAT, minimum GPA of 2.75; teaching certificate; essay; interview; 2 letters of recommendation; personal statement. Additional exam requirements/recommendations for international students: Required—TOEFL (minimum score 550 paper-based; 79 iBT), IELTS (minimum score 6). *Application deadline:* For fall admission, 6/1 for domestic students, 3/1 for international students; for spring admission, 11/1 for domestic students, 10/1 for international students. Applications are processed on a rolling basis. Application fee: $50. Electronic applications accepted. *Expenses:* Tuition, state resident: full-time $13,920; part-time $6264 per year. Tuition, nonresident: full-time $21,700; part-time $9765 per year. *Required fees:* $80; $36 per year. Tuition and fees vary according to course load, degree level and program. *Financial support:* In 2017–18, 8,416 students received support. Career-related internships or fieldwork, Federal Work-Study, scholarships/grants, and unspecified assistantships available. Support available to part-time students. Financial award application deadline: 3/15; financial award applicants required to submit FAFSA. *Faculty research:* Code switching and creative writing, language instruction, teacher evaluation, preschools, history of educational theories. *Total annual research expenditures:* $311,226. *Unit head:* Dr. Dorothy Feola, Dean, 973-720-2138, Fax: 973-720-3647, E-mail: feolad@wpunj.edu. *Application contact:* Liana Fornarotto, Director of Education Enrollment and Certification, 973-720-2206, Fax: 973-720-2989, E-mail: fornarottol@wpunj.edu.
Website: http://www.wpunj.edu/coe

Williams Baptist College, Graduate Programs, Walnut Ridge, AR 72476. Offers teaching (MAT).

Wilmington College, Department of Education, Wilmington, OH 45177. Offers reading (M Ed); special education (M Ed). *Accreditation:* TEAC. *Program availability:* Part-time. *Degree requirements:* For master's, comprehensive exam. *Entrance requirements:* For master's, GRE or MAT, minimum GPA of 3.0, 2 letters of recommendation. Additional exam requirements/recommendations for international students: Required—TOEFL. *Faculty research:* Reading instruction, special education practices, conflict resolution in the schools, models of higher education for teachers.

Wilmington University, College of Education, New Castle, DE 19720-6491. Offers applied technology in education (M Ed); career and technical education (M Ed); educational leadership (Ed D); elementary and secondary school counseling (M Ed); elementary studies (M Ed); ESOL literacy (M Ed); higher education leadership (Ed D); instruction: gifted and talented (M Ed); instruction: teacher of reading (M Ed); instruction: teaching and learning (M Ed); organizational leadership (Ed D); school leadership (M Ed); secondary education (MAT); special education (M Ed). *Accreditation:* NCATE. *Program availability:* Part-time, evening/weekend. *Faculty:* 23 full-time (13 women), 162 part-time/adjunct (99 women). *Students:* 546 full-time (394 women), 960 part-time (732 women); includes 320 minority (241 Black or African American, non-Hispanic/Latino; 12 American Indian or Alaska Native, non-Hispanic/Latino; 11 Asian, non-Hispanic/Latino; 28 Hispanic/Latino; 3 Native Hawaiian or other Pacific Islander, non-Hispanic/Latino; 25 Two or more races, non-Hispanic/Latino), 7 international. Average age 34. 1,068 applicants, 64% accepted, 582 enrolled. In 2017, 430 master's, 59 doctorates awarded. *Entrance requirements:* For master's, 2 letters of recommendation, interview. Additional exam requirements/recommendations for international students: Required—TOEFL (minimum score 500 paper-based). *Application deadline:* For fall admission, 4/30 for domestic students. Applications are processed on a rolling basis. Application fee: $35. Electronic applications accepted. *Expenses: Tuition:* Part-time $466 per credit. *Required fees:* $25 per semester. Tuition and fees vary according to degree level and campus/location. *Financial support:* Applicants required to submit FAFSA. *Unit head:* Dr. John C. Gray, Dean, 302-295-1139. *Application contact:* Laura Morris, Director of Admissions, 877-967-5464, E-mail: infocenter@wilmu.edu.
Website: http://www.wilmu.edu/education/

Wilson College, Graduate Programs, Chambersburg, PA 17201-1285. Offers accounting (M Acc); choreography and visual art (MFA); education (M Ed); educational technology (MET); healthcare administration (MHA); humanities (MA), including art and culture, critical/cultural theory, English language and literature, women's studies; management (MSM); nursing (MSN), including nursing education, nursing leadership and management; special education (MSE). *Program availability:* Evening/weekend. *Degree requirements:* For master's, project. *Entrance requirements:* For master's, PRAXIS, minimum undergraduate cumulative GPA of 3.0, 2 letters of recommendation, current certification for eligibility to teach in grades K-12, resume, personal interview. Electronic applications accepted.

Wingate University, Thayer School of Education, Wingate, NC 28174. Offers community college executive leadership (Ed D); educational leadership (MA Ed, Ed S); elementary education (MA Ed, MAT). *Accreditation:* NCATE. *Program availability:* Part-time, evening/weekend. *Degree requirements:* For master's, portfolio. *Entrance requirements:* For master's, GRE General Test or MAT, teaching certificate (MA Ed).

Winona State University, College of Education, Department of Education Studies, Winona, MN 55987. Offers multicultural education (Certificate). *Accreditation:* NCATE. *Program availability:* Part-time, evening/weekend.

Winston-Salem State University, MAT Program, Winston-Salem, NC 27110-0003. Offers middle grades education (MAT); special education (MAT). *Accreditation:* NCATE. *Program availability:* Part-time, evening/weekend, online learning. *Entrance requirements:* For master's, GRE, MAT, NC teacher licensure. Electronic applications accepted. *Faculty research:* Action research on issues in elementary classroom.

Winthrop University, College of Education, Rock Hill, SC 29733. Offers M Ed, MAT. *Accreditation:* NCATE. *Program availability:* Part-time. *Students:* 167 full-time (132 women), 89 part-time (80 women); includes 74 minority (61 Black or African American, non-Hispanic/Latino; 1 American Indian or Alaska Native, non-Hispanic/Latino; 2 Asian, non-Hispanic/Latino; 6 Hispanic/Latino; 1 Native Hawaiian or other Pacific Islander, non-Hispanic/Latino; 3 Two or more races, non-Hispanic/Latino), 2 international. Average age 38. In 2017, 137 master's awarded. *Degree requirements:* For master's, comprehensive exam (for some programs). *Entrance requirements:* Additional exam requirements/recommendations for international students: Required—TOEFL (minimum paper-based score of 520, iBT 68) or IELTS (minimum score of 6). *Application deadline:* For fall admission, 7/15 priority date for domestic students; for spring admission, 12/1 for domestic students. Applications are processed on a rolling basis. Application fee: $50. Electronic applications accepted. *Financial support:* Research assistantships with full tuition reimbursements, career-related internships or fieldwork, Federal Work-Study, scholarships/grants, and unspecified assistantships available. Support available to part-time students. Financial award application deadline: 2/1; financial award applicants required to submit FAFSA. *Unit head:* Dr. Jeannie Rakestraw, Dean, 803-323-2151, Fax: 803-323-4369, E-mail: rakestrawj@winthrop.edu. *Application contact:* 800-411-7041, Fax: 803-323-2292, E-mail: gradschool@winthrop.edu.
Website: http://www.winthrop.edu/coe

Wittenberg University, Graduate Program, Springfield, OH 45501-0720. Offers education (MA). *Accreditation:* NCATE.

Worcester State University, Graduate School, Department of Education, Worcester, MA 01602-2597. Offers curriculum and instruction (Ed S); early childhood education (M Ed, Postbaccalaureate Certificate); education (M Ed); elementary education (M Ed, Postbaccalaureate Certificate); English as a second language (M Ed, Postbaccalaureate Certificate); health education (M Ed); leadership and administration (M Ed); middle school education (M Ed, Postbaccalaureate Certificate); moderate disabilities (M Ed, Postbaccalaureate Certificate); reading (M Ed, Postbaccalaureate Certificate); school psychology (M Ed, Ed S); secondary education (M Ed, Ed S, Postbaccalaureate Certificate). *Program availability:* Part-time, evening/weekend. *Faculty:* 6 full-time, 21 part-time/adjunct. *Students:* 41 full-time (36 women), 289 part-time (209 women); includes 29 minority (5 Black or African American, non-Hispanic/Latino; 3 American Indian or Alaska Native, non-Hispanic/Latino; 1 Asian, non-Hispanic/Latino; 13 Hispanic/Latino; 7 Two or more races, non-Hispanic/Latino), 1 international. Average age 34. 237 applicants, 70% accepted, 101 enrolled. In 2017, 74 master's, 141 Ed Ss awarded. *Degree requirements:* For master's, comprehensive exam (for some programs), thesis (for some programs). *Entrance requirements:* For master's, GRE General Test, MAT or GMAT, teaching certificate. Additional exam requirements/recommendations for international students: Required—TOEFL (minimum score 550 paper-based; 79 iBT). *Application deadline:* For fall admission, 6/15 for domestic and international students; for spring admission, 11/1 for domestic and international students; for summer admission, 4/1 for domestic and international students. Applications are processed on a rolling basis. Application fee: $50. Electronic applications accepted. *Expenses: Tuition,* state resident: full-time $3042; part-time $169 per credit hour. Tuition, nonresident: full-time $3042; part-time $169 per credit hour. *Required fees:* $2754; $153 per credit hour. *Financial support:* Career-related internships or fieldwork, scholarships/grants, and unspecified assistantships available. Financial award application deadline: 3/1; financial award applicants required to submit FAFSA. *Unit head:* Dr. Sue Foo, Department Chair, 508-929-8071, E-mail: sfoo@worcester.edu. *Application contact:* Sara Grady, Associate Dean of Graduate and Continuing Education, 508-929-8130, Fax: 508-929-8100, E-mail: sara.grady@worcester.edu.

Wright State University, Graduate School, College of Education and Human Services, Dayton, OH 45435. Offers M Ed, MA, MRC, MS, Ed S. *Accreditation:* NCATE. *Program availability:* Part-time, evening/weekend. *Degree requirements:* For Ed S, thesis. *Entrance requirements:* For master's, GRE General Test, MAT, PRAXIS II; for Ed S, GRE General Test, MAT. Additional exam requirements/recommendations for international students: Required—TOEFL.

Xavier University, College of Social Sciences, Health and Education, School of Education, Cincinnati, OH 45207. Offers M Ed, MA, MS, Ed D. *Accreditation:* TEAC. *Entrance requirements:* Additional exam requirements/recommendations for international students: Required—TOEFL (minimum score 550 paper-based; 79 iBT). Electronic applications accepted. Application fee is waived when completed online. *Expenses:* Contact institution. *Faculty research:* Early childhood literacy, service-learning, family resiliency/special needs families, technology integration, leadership theory, Montessori methodology.

Xavier University of Louisiana, Graduate School, Programs in Education, New Orleans, LA 70125. Offers counseling (MA); curriculum and instruction (MA); educational leadership (MA). *Accreditation:* NCATE. *Program availability:* Part-time, evening/weekend. *Degree requirements:* For master's, comprehensive exam, thesis or alternative. *Entrance requirements:* For master's, GRE General Test, MAT, minimum GPA of 2.5. Additional exam requirements/recommendations for international students: Required—TOEFL.

York College of Pennsylvania, Master of Education Program, York, PA 17403-3651. Offers educational leadership (M Ed); educational technology (M Ed); reading specialist (M Ed). *Program availability:* Part-time-only, evening/weekend. *Faculty:* 2 full-time (1 woman), 7 part-time/adjunct (3 women). *Students:* 87 part-time (62 women); includes 2 minority (1 Hispanic/Latino; 1 Two or more races, non-Hispanic/Latino), 1 international. Average age 33. 57 applicants, 79% accepted, 39 enrolled. In 2017, 7 master's awarded. *Degree requirements:* For master's, comprehensive exam (for some programs), thesis (for some programs). *Entrance requirements:* For master's, PRAXIS, statement of applicant's professional and academic goals, 2 letters of recommendation, letter from current supervisor, official undergraduate and graduate transcript(s), copy of teaching certificate(s), current professional resume, interview. *Application deadline:* For fall admission, 7/15 priority date for domestic students; for spring admission, 11/15 priority date for domestic students; for summer admission, 4/15 priority date for domestic students. Applications are processed on a rolling basis. Application fee: $0. Electronic applications accepted. *Expenses:* $620 per credit. *Financial support:* Scholarships/grants available. Financial award applicants required to submit FAFSA. *Faculty research:* Classroom technology, assessment, educational leadership, professional development, literacy. *Unit head:* Dr. Joshua D. DeSantis, Director, Master of Education Program, 717-815-1936, E-mail: jdesant1@ycp.edu.
Website: https://www.ycp.edu/med

York University, Faculty of Graduate Studies, Faculty of Education, Toronto, ON M3J 1P3, Canada. Offers M Ed, PhD. *Program availability:* Part-time. *Degree requirements:* For master's, thesis or alternative; for doctorate, comprehensive exam, thesis/dissertation. Electronic applications accepted.

Youngstown State University, Graduate School, Beeghly College of Education, Youngstown, OH 44555-0001. Offers MS Ed, Ed D. *Accreditation:* NCATE. *Program availability:* Part-time, evening/weekend. *Degree requirements:* For master's, comprehensive exam; for doctorate, comprehensive exam, thesis/dissertation. *Entrance requirements:* For master's, minimum GPA of 2.7; for doctorate, GRE General Test, GRE Subject Test, interview, minimum GPA of 3.5. Additional exam requirements/recommendations for international students: Required—TOEFL. *Faculty research:* Euthanasia, psychometrics, ethical issues, community relations, educational law.

THE COLLEGE OF WILLIAM AND MARY

School of Education

 For more information, visit http://petersons.to/williammaryeducation

Programs of Study

Curriculum and Instruction—Teacher Education: The School of Education prepares tomorrow's educational leaders, because it attracts highly qualified students to its teacher education programs and then provides them with exemplary professional educational experiences. The School of Education offers one-year master's programs in elementary education, secondary education, special education, and ESL/bilingual education. (http://education.wm.edu/academics/ci/index.php)

Counseling and School Psychology: The school psychology and counseling programs at William and Mary prepare highly qualified professionals to practice in the public schools or in related educational and mental health settings. The School offers two-year master's programs in clinical mental health, couples, marriage and family, addictions, and school counseling. For students who want to study beyond the master's level, the School offers a Ph.D. in counselor education, which can be completed in three to four years of full-time enrollment. For students interested in school psychology, the School offers a three-year Ed.S. program that culminates in a year-long internship experience. For students who want to study online, William and Mary offers online counseling programs with concentrations in clinical mental health and school counseling. (http://education.wm.edu/academics/space/index.php)

Educational Policy, Planning and Leadership: The Educational Policy, Planning and Leadership department prepares students with the knowledge and skills necessary to guide, influence, and shape institutions at all levels of education, and to enhance the effectiveness of complex educational organizations through leadership, scholarship, and service. The School of Education offers master's degrees in K–12 administration and higher education administration. In addition, the School offers doctoral programs in general K–12 administration, gifted administration, curriculum learning and design, and higher education administration. Full-time students can expect to finish the doctorate in three to four years. (http://education.wm.edu/academics/eppl/index.php)

Research Facilities

The School of Education building was completed in May 2010. The facility houses W&M's nationally-ranked School of Education and brings all of its academic programs, outreach centers and research projects together in a highly professional setting designed to stimulate collaboration and innovation.

One such project, the Center for Gifted Education, provides services to educators, policy makers, graduate students, researchers, parents, and students in support of the needs of gifted and talented individuals. The center has established an international reputation for excellence in research, curriculum development, and service.

Another outreach center, the New Horizons Family Counseling Center, provides free services to families of children attending public schools in the local area. Families may be referred to the clinic by teachers, principals, counselors, school psychologists, or school social workers. Students in counseling programs complete clinical internships in the center. Under licensed faculty supervision, students serve as administrators, supervisors, and family counselors for the center.

Financial Aid

Financial assistance is available in the form of assistantships, fellowships, scholarships, and awards earmarked for School of Education students. Both full-time and part-time assistantships are available to full-time students. Awards and scholarships are merit based. Other forms of aid are available through the university's financial aid office. For more information about assistantships, prospective students should visit http://education.wm.edu/admissions/financialaid/assistantships/index.php. For more information about scholarships and awards, visit http://education.wm.edu/admissions/financialaid/soeawards/index.php.

Cost of Study

In 2018–19, the tuition and general fee for students is approximately $15,760 per year for residents of Virginia and $33,354 per year for nonresidents. Details about tuition can be found at http://education.wm.edu/admissions/graduate/tuition/index.php.

Living and Housing Costs

The College offers a limited number of graduate student housing spaces on campus, with costs averaging approximately $4,000 per semester. Application is made by submission of the housing request form after a student is admitted. In addition, the College maintains a website for off-campus student housing available in the Williamsburg community.

Student Group

The School of Education enrolls approximately 500 students each semester. Of those, 77 percent are degree-seeking students; 34 percent are pursuing doctorate degrees; 41 percent are enrolled full time; 18 percent are students of color; 19 percent are male; and 4 percent are international students. The average age is 28.

Admission is competitive. The average undergraduate GPA of admitted students is 3.4; the average GRE verbal score is the 69th percentile; the average GRE quantitative score is the 46th percentile.

Student Outcomes

Graduates of the School of Education find work in public and private K–12 schools, nonprofit organizations, clinical practices, and institutions of higher education, just to name a few.

Location

Williamsburg is on a Chesapeake Bay peninsula between the York and James rivers, 50 miles from Richmond and 150 miles from Washington, D.C. The College is located in a beautiful and historic city, constituting an integral part of Colonial Williamsburg. Williamsburg is serviced by Newport News, Norfolk, and Richmond airports; bus and railway services are also available.

The College

Although it retains the historic name under which it was chartered in 1693, the College of William and Mary in Virginia is a residential, full-time, coeducational, state-supported university. It is the second oldest college in the nation, but also a cutting-edge research university. It is selective, but also public, offering a world-class education without the sticker shock. It is a "Public Ivy"—one of only eight in the nation, which means it offers a superior education that's accessible to everyone.

Applying

Applications are available online at http://education.wm.edu/admissions/graduate/applying/index.php. The deadline for all application materials to be received, including transcripts, test scores, and letters of recommendation, is January 15 each year. The counseling and school psychology programs require the GRE (general test only); the educational leadership and administrative programs require either the GRE or the MAT. The initial teacher preparation programs require the Praxis Core Academic Skills for Educators exam. The school psychology program and doctorate in counselor education require admission interviews. Students are notified of admission decisions no later than mid-March.

Correspondence and Information

Dorothy Smith Osborne, Assistant Dean
School of Education—Office of Academic Programs
The College of William and Mary
P.O. Box 8795
Williamsburg, Virginia 23187-8795
United States
Phone: 757-221-2317
E-mail: graded@wm.edu
Website: https://education.wm.edu/
Request Information: http://education.wm.edu/admissions/graduate/requestinfo/index.php

THE FACULTY AND THEIR RESEARCH

The School of Education has 42 tenure-line faculty members, of which 8 hold endowed professorships, combined with other personnel for a total of 90 faculty and staff members.

Spencer Niles, Dean and Professor—Ph.D., The Pennsylvania State University.

Virginia Ambler, Executive Assistant Professor, Ph.D., The College of William and Mary.

James Barber, Associate Professor, Ph.D., University of Michigan.

Katherine Barko-Alva, Instructor, Ph.D., University of Florida.

Stephanie Blackmon, Assistant Professor, Ph.D., University of Alabama, Tuscaloosa.

Brian Blouet, Professor, Ph.D., University of Hull.

Bruce Bracken, Professor, Ph.D., University of Georgia.

Johnston Brendel, Clinical Associate Professor, Ed.D., The College of William and Mary.

Jason Chen, Assistant Professor, Ph.D., Emory University.

Eddie Cole, Assistant Professor, Ph.D., Indiana University.

Kristen Conradi, Assistant Professor, Ph.D., University of Virginia.

Margaret A. Constatino, Ph.D., University of Southern Mississippi.

Kristen Conradi, Assistant Professor, Ph.D., University of Virginia.

Tracy Cross, Professor, Ph.D., University of Tennessee, Knoxville.

Michael DiPaola, Professor, Ed.D., Rutgers, The State University of New Jersey.

Jamel Donnor, Associate Professor, Ph.D., University of Wisconsin–Madison.

Pamela Eddy, Associate Professor, Ph.D., Michigan State University.

Victoria Foster, Professor, Ed.D., North Carolina State University.

Christopher Gareis, Professor, Ed.D., The College of William and Mary.

W. Fanchon Glover, Executive Assistant Professor, Ed.D., The College of William and Mary.

Leslie Grant, Associate Professor, Ph.D., The College of William and Mary.

Charles Gressard, Professor, Ph.D., University of Iowa.

Daniel Gutierrez, Assistant Professor, Ph.D., University of Central Florida.

Judith Harris, Professor, Ph.D., University of Virginia.

Natoya Haskins, Assistant Professor, Ph.D., The College of William and Mary.

Judith Harris, Professor, Ph.D., University of Virginia.

Mark Hofer, Professor, Ph.D., University of Virginia.

Heartley Huber, Ph.D., Vanderbilt University.

C. Denise Johnson, Professor, Ph.D., University of Memphis.

Meredith Kier, Assistant Professor, Ph.D., North Carolina State University.

Kyung Kim, Associate Professor, Ph.D., Korea University; Ph.D., University of Georgia.

Lori Korinek, Professor, Ph.D., University of Florida.

Gladys Krause, Assistant Professor, Ph.D., University of Texas at Austin.

Marguerite Mason, Professor, Ph.D., University of Iowa.

Charles McAdams, Professor, Ed.D., North Carolina State University.

Gail McEachron, Professor, Ph.D., University of Texas at Austin.

Ryan J. McGill, Assistant Professor, Ph.D., Chapman University.

Virginia McLaughlin, Professor, Ed.D., Memphis State University.

Patrick R. Mullin, Assistant Professor, Ph.D., University of Central Florida.

Janise Parker, Assistant Professor, Ph.D., University of Florida.

Patricia Popp, Clinical Associate Professor, Ph.D., The College of William and Mary.

Deborah Ramer, Instructor, Ed.S., University of Virginia.

Jacqueline Rodriguez, Assistant Professor, Ph.D., University of Central Florida.

Drew Stelljis, Executive Assistant Professor, Ph.D., The College of William and Mary.

Jeremy Stoddard, Associate Professor, Ph.D., University of Wisconsin–Madison.

James Stronge, Professor, Ph.D., University of Alabama at Tuscaloosa.

Carol Tieso, Professor, Ph.D., University of Connecticut.

Megan Tschannen-Moran, Professor, Ph.D., The Ohio State University.

Thomas Ward, Professor, The Pennsylvania State University.

DREXEL UNIVERSITY
School of Education

 For more information, visit http://petersons.to/drexelu_education

Programs of Study

Drexel University's School of Education strives to meet the professional needs and career objectives of those who are currently working in the education field, or who wish to pursue careers as teachers, faculty members, education administrators, and staff members at all levels of education. Through challenging course work taught by experienced faculty, students are exposed to current research and trends on teaching and administration including the latest developments in pedagogy and instructional technology. The School of Education goes well beyond teacher training: it produces education leaders.

The School of Education offers undergraduate, graduate, and doctoral degree programs and a wide variety of certificate, certification, and professional development programs to meet the needs of educators and educational administrators. Drexel University is a premier technology university, and the School of Education provides cutting-edge technology-based curricula with an orientation in science, technology, and math.

Graduates of the School of Education are known for their creativity, technological savvy, preparedness, and leadership skills. The School of Education's faculty members are carefully chosen for their expertise in developing these traits and skills in students. The School of Education continues to explore new opportunities for graduate programs and for collaboration and partnership with the education community. These initiatives provide additional opportunities to students who wish to make a difference in the rapidly expanding and diverse field of education.

M.S. in Applied Behavioral Analysis: Drexel's Master of Science in Applied Behavioral Analysis enables students to effectively analyze, understand, and guide change in human behavior from a systematic, data-driven approach. The M.S. in Applied Behavioral Analysis degree program with the Autism Spectrum concentration is approved by the Behavior Analyst Certification Board and is ideal for students who plan to work with children and adults who are affected by this disorder. The program offers a practicum at the A. J. Drexel Autism Institute or with EI programs, residential and community behavior health providers, or educational agencies.

M.S. in Creativity and Innovation: Drexel's online Master of Science in Creativity and Innovation degree program enables students to develop and apply their own creativity to find innovative solutions in the full gamut of work environments, from education to marketing and public relations to engineering to healthcare. Students have access to the prestigious Drexel-Torrance Center for Creativity and Innovation, a valuable resource that helps students develop leadership and problem-solving skills.

M.S. in Educational Administration (principal certification available): Drexel's online Master of Science in Educational Administration degree program offers innovative training based on a framework of state and national leadership standards for elementary and secondary instructors and counselors to become school administrators. The M.S. in Educational Administration degree program is ideal for those with an initial teaching certification who are interested in furthering their career by obtaining principal certification with a master's degree. For those interested in a singular leadership credential without principal certification, it offers leadership training that can be applied in any educational setting in the United States and around the world.

M.S. in Educational Improvement and Transformation: Drexel's flexible online Master of Science in Educational Improvement and Transformation degree program allows students to approach a master's degree in several unique ways. Students select from 10 Professional Development Concentration Sets to customize their degree, including: Collaborative Special Education Law and Process, Creativity and Innovation, Educational Policy, e-Learning Leadership, Evaluation and Assessment, Instructional Design, Leadership in Educational Settings, Learning Technologies, Special Education Leadership, and Urban Education.

Knowledge gained in this program prepares the student for leadership positions in several educational settings, including public and private schools, colleges and universities, national associations, government organizations, nonprofit organizations, learning science organizations, and more.

M.S. in Global and International Education: Drexel's online Master of Science in Global and International Education degree program prepares students to work within the complex economic, political, cultural, and social structures that shape learning in different parts of the world. Graduates of the Global and International Education program will acquire the leadership skills necessary to develop, analyze, implement, and evaluate educational policies at a variety of institutions and organizations, through interpersonal advocacy skills and cross-cultural communication, using emerging information technologies. It is ideal for those who have already completed a study-abroad program, for those who want to transition back to the international realm, for those working abroad, and individuals interested in a second career opportunity.

M.S. in Higher Education: Drexel's online Master of Science in Higher Education degree program prepares students to lead complex administrative and management positions at universities and colleges, national and international associations and organizations, government agencies, foundations, and corporations in the United States and around the world. The Higher Education program offers an interdisciplinary, experiential curriculum of coursework drawn from Drexel's School of Education. Foundation study provides a thorough overview of education from the colonial era to present-day virtual models, and examines the organizational and administrative structure of institutional hierarchy.

Students take a primary concentration in administration and organizational management and can select a secondary concentration from one of the following areas: Community College Administration and Leadership, Enrollment Management, Global and International Education, Educational Policy, Institutional Research and Planning, e-Learning Technologies and Instructional Design, Neuroscience, Learning and Online Instruction, and Student Development and Affairs.

M.S. in Learning Technologies: Drexel's online Master of Science in Learning Technologies degree program is a unique online program that prepares students as leaders who can create learning solutions for an increasingly fluid, interconnected, and complex world. The curriculum is framed by national technology standards in twenty-first century learning, digital media literacy, design thinking, learning sciences, and diverse field experiences. The Learning Technologies course work builds on Drexel's leadership in the latest educational research and technologies and provides students with a complete framework for understanding the learning sciences and media literacy—from initial concepts and development of instructional design to how individuals use learning software—from the obstacles they encounter to the solutions that help them succeed.

M.S. in Mathematics Learning and Teaching: Drexel's online Master of Science in Mathematics Learning and Teaching program trains graduates to improve mathematics in middle and high schools through shared, solution-oriented teaching methods. The Mathematics Learning and Teaching curriculum builds on leading-edge aspects of education and math in areas such as evaluation and diagnostic teaching, and offers electives that explore higher education and learning technologies. Students work independently on rigorous math assignments and collaborate on the outcome within a community of fellow students and faculty members to produce student-centered, technology-enhanced strategies for middle and high school math learners of all abilities.

M.S. in Special Education: Drexel's online Master of Science in Special Education degree program is designed to produce highly qualified professionals to expand educational horizons for all children in need. The Special Education program is a flexible online program with course work that builds on the essentials of special education. Students can hone their skills by pursuing on of four concentration areas: Autism Spectrum Disorders, Technologies for Special Education, Multisensory Reading Instruction Level 1 (includes Wilson® Language Level 1 certification), Collaborative Special Education Law and Process, and Customized Study (for individuals who already possess special education certification).

M.S. in Sport Coaching Leadership: Drexel's online Master of Science in Sport Coaching Leadership engages students in the areas of coaching theory, developing a sports program, coaching philosophy, goal-setting, understanding the needs of athletes, recruiting, developing training programs, budgeting, program planning, forecasting, NCAA compliance, and fundraising. Students will also select a concentration to specialize in a particular sport or create a custom-designed specialization to meet their career goals. Coaches at the youth, scholastic, club, collegiate, Olympic, and professional levels can customize their course to their level and sport(s) of interest. Offered fully

Drexel University

online, this program is well-suited to coaches with a busy schedule, at any level of their career.

M.S. in Teaching, Learning, and Curriculum: Drexel's online Master of Science in Teaching, Learning, and Curriculum program is customized to each student's goals and is rooted in Drexel's philosophy of experiential learning through field experiences and a focus on integrated technology in research. Students have two degree options to pursue:

- Master of Science in Teaching, Learning, and Curriculum: Teaching Certification
- Master of Science in Teaching, Learning, and Curriculum: Advanced Studies

The degree program trains students using current learning trends, from advanced techniques of instruction and assessment to the impact of multimedia and new learning technologies. Students focus on diversities in the classroom, such as students with special needs and intercultural learners, and develop solution-oriented strategies for instructional leadership.

Ed.D. in Education Leadership and Management: Drexel's Ed.D. in Educational Leadership and Management degree program stands alone as a rigorous, accelerated doctoral program that produces leaders with the skills and knowledge to create educational reform. The Ed.D. program offers an elite professional practitioner's degree as a completely online program or in a blended delivery format that combines on-campus classes and online education.

For achievement-oriented students interested in educational management, the Ed.D. program provides a path to the Superintendent Letter of Eligibility in Pennsylvania. The program also provides a competitive creative career track into leadership roles within public school districts and private institutions, universities and colleges, national and global foundations, organizations, corporations, and government agencies.

The Ed.D. program is an expansive, leading-edge program that prepares students for a full range of educational opportunities connected to human and societal development, with a real understanding of the operations and responsibilities faced by rapidly changing, global learning environments.

Ph.D. in Education: Drexel's Ph.D. in Education program is a rigorous, highly competitive program designed for those who aspire to be leaders in the field of education as researchers, scholars, and instructors in higher education and in other educational settings. Small by design, the Ph.D. degree program admits 6–10 students per cohort and provides students with benefits such as research and teaching assistantships that offer generous stipends, tuition remission, and health insurance subsidies. The major emphasis of the program is on engaging individual students in collaborative inquiry and research with faculty experts. Specific areas of concentration for doctoral students include Science, Technology, Engineering, and Mathematics (STEM) Education and Educational Leadership.

Faculty

Drexel University's School of Education has diverse faculty expertise in many areas, including teacher education, higher education, global and international education, educational administration and leadership, learning technologies, and adult education and organization development. Collaborative research associated with these areas and more is expansive, interdisciplinary, and focused, with a particular emphasis on technology-enhanced education and the learning sciences.

Research productivity, measured both by peer-reviewed publications and funded research expenditures continues to be high priority, encouraging scholarly inquiry to improve education practices locally and globally.

The School of Education's faculty directory is available online at drexel.edu/soe/faculty-and-staff/faculty.

Financial Aid

Prospective students should visit http://drexel.edu/drexelcentral/finaid/prospective-students/grad/ for details on the financial aid application. Information for international students is also available at this site.

Costs

The most up-to-date information on tuition and fees can be found at http://drexel.edu/drexelcentral/costs/grad.

Admissions

For details on requirements for Drexel's School of Education's graduate programs, prospective students should visit http://drexel.edu/soe/admissions/graduate.

Applying

Specific information for applying to the School of Education's on-campus or blended graduate programs, as well as the online graduate programs, is available at drexel.edu/soe/admissions/overview.

Correspondence and Information

School of Education
Drexel University
3141 Chestnut Street
Philadelphia, Pennsylvania 19104
United States
Phone: 215-895-6770
E-mail: education@drexel.edu
Website: Drexel.edu/soe

Drexel University was founded as the Drexel Institute in 1891 (pictured above). It has since grown to include 3 Philadelphia campuses, regional sites, international partnerships in China and Israel, and Drexel Online.

Drexel offers robust educational offerings, both online and in-person, at its modern campus located in Philadelphia, Pennsylvania, including the Papadakis Integrated Sciences Building (left) and the James Marks Intercultural Center (right).

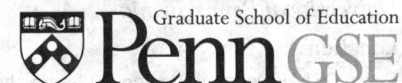

UNIVERSITY OF PENNSYLVANIA
Graduate School of Education

 For more information, visit http://petersons.to/penneducation

Programs of Study

The University of Pennsylvania Graduate School of Education (Penn GSE) is currently ranked in the top 10 in the nation, is home to a world-class faculty and a diverse population of students from across the globe and at various levels of their careers. The school prepares national leaders in education research, as well as dedicated, innovative teachers and administrators. The school is notably entrepreneurial, launching innovative degree programs for practicing professionals, unique partnerships with local educators, and the first-ever business plan competition devoted exclusively to educational products and programs.

The Ph.D. in Education: GSE offers an intensive, theory-based Doctor of Philosophy (Ph.D.) degree for students pursuing careers in scholarship at the university level. Courses offer hands-on experience and practical skills through mentoring, research assistantships, and service-based placements. Ph.D. students can specialize in one of eight subfields: education, culture, and society; education policy; educational linguistics; higher education; interdisciplinary studies in human development; quantitative methods; reading/writing/literacy; and teaching, learning, and teacher education.

The Ed.D. for Leaders in Education: The Doctor of Education (Ed.D.) is designed for students pursuing senior leadership positions in education. Courses and research opportunities engage students in a variety of educational fields including policy, consulting, K–12 leadership, and postsecondary education. The Ed.D. is offered in educational leadership; educational linguists; higher education; reading/writing/literacy; and teaching, learning, and teacher education. Students already working at senior levels in their organizations may choose to pursue the Penn CLO Executive Doctoral Program, the Mid-Career Doctoral Program in Educational Leadership, or the Executive Doctoral Program in Higher Education Management.

Master's Degrees in Education: GSE offers more than 20 master's-level programs to educators interested in developing extensive foundational knowledge and professional preparation in a broad range of positions. The Master of Science in Education (M.S.Ed.) degree is offered in the following fields: counseling and mental health services; education, culture, and society; education entrepreneurship; education policy; higher education; interdisciplinary studies in human development; intercultural communication; international educational development; learning sciences and technologies; Penn residency master's in teaching program; reading/writing/literacy (reading specialist certification); school leadership; urban teacher education programs; teaching English to speakers of other languages (TESOL); and teaching, learning, and leadership.

GSE also offers a medical educator's program, a reading specialist certification, and an executive master's program in professional school counseling.

The Master of Philosophy in Education (M.Phil.Ed.), which is designed for students who already hold master's degrees but want to expand their skills, is offered in two concentrations: professional counseling and mental health services, and quantitative methods. A Master of Science (M.S.) in statistics, measurement, assessment, and research technology (SMART) degree program is also available.

Research Accomplishments and Opportunities

In addition to offering nearly 30 degree programs and 5 degree options, Penn GSE offers students the opportunity to work with more than 30 in-house centers and initiatives that produce cutting-edge research and translate that research to practice. Faculty members and students focus on the challenges of urban education, the opportunities of international education, issues of race and equity, and qualitative and quantitative research that informs policy and practice.

Penn GSE is one of the nation's premiere research education schools. The school has long been recognized for its strengths in research on teaching and learning, the cultural contexts of education, language education, qualitative research methods, and practitioner inquiry. In recent years, those strengths have deepened to include national leadership in policy research, urban education, developmental psychology, and quantitative and multi-method inquiry. Stand-out examples include: the Alliance for Higher Education and Democracy (AHEAD) which is dedicated to promoting the public purposes of higher education in fostering open, equitable, and democratic societies; the Center on Minority Serving Institutions (MSIs) at Penn which serves as a repository for research, data, best practices, emerging innovations and ideas on and within MSIs; and the Penn Child Research Center which develops social and scientific policy to promote the educational and psychological well-being of children.

Urban Education is a central interest of research and practice at Penn GSE. Located in the heart of West Philadelphia, the school engages deeply in local, urban communities through projects like the Penn Alexander School and the Penn Partnership Schools that put research into practice to improve educational outcomes for urban students.

Financial Aid

The Graduate School of Education is committed to making education affordable through generous scholarships, assistantships, and fellowships. All traditional, full-time Ph.D. and Ed.D. students receive fellowships, and 75 percent of incoming students receive merit aid. Penn GSE Ph.D. students are fully funded. More information on financial aid and additional scholarships is available at http://www.ges.upenn.edu/admssions_financial/finaid.

Cost of Study

The most current tuition rates can be found online at: http://www.gse.upenn.edu/admissions_financial/tuition.

Student Group

The Penn GSE student body is one of the most diverse schools at the University of Pennsylvania. One-third of the student body originates from more than 30 international countries. Penn GSE students range from recent college graduates to career changers and experienced practitioners. Nearly 35 percent of our students are enrolled in executive-format programs designed for working professionals (http://www.gse.upenn.edu/admissions_financial/classprofile).

University of Pennsylvania

Location

Penn GSE is located on the 302-acre, Ivy League campus of the University of Pennsylvania, in West Philadelphia, Pennsylvania. Its location provides students with unique opportunities to practice and conduct research within the fifth-largest city in America. The city's cultural and recreational life includes a world-class orchestra and opera, dozens of museums, professional sports teams, art galleries, jazz clubs, an Italian market, and a renowned international film festival. The city is conveniently located in the mid-Atlantic region of the United States, offering easy access to New York City, Baltimore, Maryland, and Washington, D.C.

The School

Penn GSE was founded in 1914, is ranked in the top 10 in the country, and is noted for excellence in educational research in the areas of policy, evaluation, sociocultural foundations, and urban education. Penn GSE strives to foster an inclusive community of scholars, administrators, and students who possess diverse knowledge, experiences, and research interests, and who service and learn from diverse communities.

Penn GSE is deeply committed to the city of Philadelphia through both research and practice. Students, faculty, and staff are involved in hundreds of initiatives throughout the Greater Philadelphia area, including high-quality after school programs, research that sparks national conversations, and the development of an acclaimed public school partnership with the School District of Philadelphia.

Graduates of Penn GSE are part of a rich heritage of educators and thought leaders. The more than 16,000 graduates who comprise the diverse alumni network live and work across the globe and pursue careers in a variety of fields, including schools, government agencies, universities, think tanks, foundations, and corporations. In these fields, they work in positions that include superintendents, principals, teachers, counselors, university professors, policy analysts, researchers, foundation officers, psychologists, and higher education administrators.

Faculty

Penn GSE's world-class professors are leading the conversation about critical issues in education. As a relatively small school of education with a standing faculty of 40 members, the school has an outsize impact on education policy and practice on a global scale.

A full list of all Penn GSE faculty members, including associated faculty members, can be found online at http://www.ges.upenn.edu/directory/fac_div.

Applying

Penn GSE seeks students who are interested in promoting a deeper understanding of educational issues and contributing to societal change on the local, national, and global level. The curriculum places a strong emphasis on the interactive relationship of theory, research, and practice, often focusing on urban education. Students engage in extensive fieldwork throughout their studies and are both learners and agents of change within the University and the surrounding Philadelphia neighborhoods.

The University of Pennsylvania Graduate School of Education's admissions web page can be found at: http://www.gse.upenn.edu/admissions_financial. Information regarding application deadlines is available at https://www.gse.upenn.edu/admissions_financial/deadlines.

Correspondence and Information

Dr. Pam Grossman, Dean
Graduate School of Education
University of Pennsylvania
3700 Walnut Street
Philadelphia, Pennsylvania 19104
United States
Phone: 215-898-7014
215-898-6415
Fax: 215-746-6884
E-mail: admissions@gse.upenn.edu
Website: https://www.gse.upenn.edu

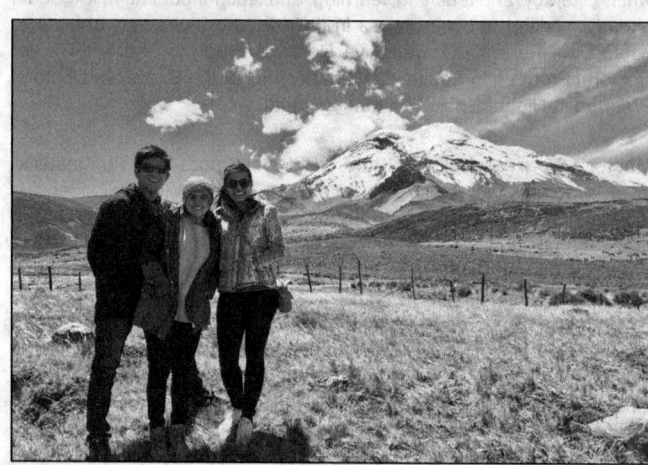

UNIVERSITY OF PITTSBURGH

Graduate Programs in Education

 For more information, visit http://petersons.to/upitt_education

Programs of Study

The University of Pittsburgh School of Education (SOE) offers numerous opportunities to pursue graduate studies in education, including over 50 graduate degree programs. As the school begins its second century, it is focused on advancing education through the following:

- Improving the educational experience for students in urban schools
- Exploring the synergy between public policy and classroom practice
- Understanding the factors and strategies that lead to success in the classroom
- Developing obesity prevention and intervention programs

The School of Education's **Department of Administrative and Policy Studies (ADMPS)** helps to develop school leaders and policymakers who can effectively advocate advancements while managing K–12 and higher education systems. Master's, Ph.D., and Ed.D. degrees are offered in higher education management, school leadership, and social and comparative analysis in education. Administrative and supervisory certificates are also offered in school leadership. More information is available online at http://www.education.pitt.edu/AcademicDepartments/AdministrativePolicyStudies.aspx.

The **Department of Health and Physical Activity (HPA)** promotes the importance of physically active lifestyles and other health-related behaviors that lead to better quality of life. Master's degrees are offered in the areas of health and fitness, as well as health, physical activity, and chronic disease. HPA also offers a Ph.D. program in exercise physiology, and an Ed.D. in health and physical activity. Additional details can be found at http://www.education.pitt.edu/AcademicDepartments/HealthPhysicalActivity.aspx.

The **Department of Instruction and Learning (DIL)** program prepares expert and leader teachers in specific subject areas by shaping an understanding of educating and learning from various perspectives. The department awards a variety of master's degrees, initial and add-on teaching certificate options, supervisory certificates, as well as Ph.D. and Ed.D. options. Areas of focus include but are not limited to: early childhood and elementary education; secondary education: English and communications, foreign language, mathematics, science, and social studies; teaching English to speakers of other languages (TESOL); language, literacy, and culture; special education; reading education; early intervention; applied behavioral analysis; and vision studies. More information is available online at http://www.education.pitt.edu/AcademicDepartments/InstructionLearning.aspx.

The **Psychology in Education (PIE) Department** prepares graduates for professional careers in and out of the classroom (applied developmental psychology) and in the lab (research methodology). Master's and Ph.D. degrees, as well as teaching certificates, are awarded in applied developmental psychology. The school also offers master's and Ph.D. degrees in research methodology. Additional details can be found at http://www.education.pitt.edu/AcademicDepartments/PsychologyinEducation.aspx.

The **Learning Sciences and Policy (LSAP) Department** at the School of Education offers a Ph.D. in LSAP, which incorporates the inclusion of learning sciences into education and teaching, and emphasizes organizational and policy change with the goal of improving instruction. The department also offers an E.D. program in Out-of-School Learning, which is intended for experienced informal learning professionals seeking advanced training for leadership positions in museums, after-school learning, media, digital design, university outreach/extension, and other areas where learning environments exist outside of schools. More information is available online at http://www.education.pitt.edu AcademicDepartments/LearningSciencesPolicy.aspx.

Research and Outreach

The SOE has many partnerships with centers, institutes, and initiatives both on campus and regionally, and has developed some of its own centers, such as the Center for Urban Education (CUE), Healthy Lifestyle Institute (HLI), and the Motivation Center (MC), to enhance the education of its students and students in the local communities. These include outreach programs such as the Western PA Writing Project and the Educational Leadership Initiative.

The tuition-based Falk Laboratory School, affiliated with the SOE, is a K–8 laboratory school that provides faculty members, student interns, practicum students, and researchers with opportunities to develop and support new and innovative practices in education.

Financial Aid

The School of Education offers some departmental aid options to students pursuing advanced degrees. Financial assistance is available to a limited number of graduate students through graduate student assistantships (GSA), teaching assistantships (TA), teaching fellowships (TF), graduate student researchers (GSR), and tuition remission. In addition to departmental aid, the SOE has numerous endowed scholarships and fellowships available that were established through gifts or grants.

Many of the students in the School of Education fund their schooling through the use of Federal Stafford Loans and Graduate PLUS loans, as well as private alternative educational loans. University policy holds that international students must provide evidence of their ability to fully fund their studies in the United States prior to acceptance. International students are not eligible for Federal Stafford Loan funds or private alternative loan funds.

Cost of Study

For the 2018–19 academic year, tuition for Pennsylvania students in graduate programs in the School of Education is $11,423 per term plus $425 in fees for full-time students and $920 per credit and $270 in fees for part-time students. For out-of-state residents, full-time tuition is $19,368 per term with $425 in fees and for part-time students, $1,583 per credit with $270 in fees.

Living and Housing

The University owns several hundred apartments that are available to graduate students. University-owned apartments are unfurnished and range from efficiencies to three-bedroom units. These units are not considered on-campus housing and are administered via a lease, security deposit, and monthly payments.

Applications for University-owned apartments are accepted by Off-Campus Living (http://www.ocl.pitt.edu) beginning the second Monday in January on a first-come, first-served basis. Students also may apply online.

Student Group

In the fall of 2017, there were 842 graduate students in the SOE's programs; 13.9 percent of those were international students. There were 86 graduate student appointments, 9 fellowships, 56 teaching assistants, and 21 research assistants. For the 2016-17 academic year, the SOE conferred 614 master's degrees and 174 doctoral degrees.

The Council of Graduate Students in Education (CGSE) is run by graduate students in the School of Education; students within the school are automatically members of the organization. CGSE is supported primarily through the student activity fee fund with additional support from the Dean's office.

With more than 33,000 SOE alumni across the globe, graduates are connected to a strong and involved fellowship that is changing the field of education through life-changing work.

Location

The main campus of the University of Pittsburgh is situated on 132 urban acres in Pittsburgh's historic Oakland section. Much of the campus, including its centerpiece 42-story Cathedral of Learning, falls within the Oakland Civic Center and Schenley Farms National Historic District, a park populated with buildings that replicate the city's architectural history.

The main campus borders or is within a short walking distance of many recreational, cultural, and educational institutions that also populate the Oakland neighborhood. The campus is directly adjacent to Schenley Plaza, the main branch of the Carnegie Public Library, the Carnegie Museums of Natural History and Art, and the Carnegie Music Hall.

The campus is widely recognized for its commitment to environmental sustainability and has won multiple Green Star Awards from the Professional Grounds Management Society.

The University and The School

The University of Pittsburgh (Pitt), in western Pennsylvania, was founded in 1787 and is one of the oldest public institutions of higher education in the nation. *U.S. News & World Report* ranks the University of Pittsburgh School of Education graduate program among its top 30 graduate education programs in the nation.

For more than 100 years, the University of Pittsburgh's School of Education has been dedicated to preparing students for life-changing careers, whether they desire to be teachers, researchers, public policy experts, administrators or health educators. The SOE consists of five academic departments: Administrative and Policy Studies; Health and Physical Activity; Instruction and Learning; Learning Sciences and Policy; and Psychology in Education. Through these departments, the school awards over 50 graduate degrees and offers 12 certificate programs.

Faculty

The School of Education at University of Pittsburgh has 80 full-time faculty members on staff with a 4:1 ratio of doctoral students to full-time faculty members. Faculty members and graduate students are involved in a variety of collaborative research experiences ranging from more basic research to research that is applied to school settings. Additional information and a complete listing about SOE faculty members is available at http://www.education.pitt.edu/AboutUs/Faculty.aspx.

Applying

Deadlines vary by program. Specific information regarding dates can be found on the School of Education website, specifically, on the admission requirements page for the program for which the applicant is applying. Supplemental materials that must be submitted with the online application also vary by program, and details can also be found on the admission requirement page for the program. Applicants are also welcome to direct questions to soeinfo@pitt.edu or call 412-648-2230. To begin the online application process, applicants should visit http://www.education.pitt.edu/FutureStudents/AdmissionsProcedures.aspx.

For the fall of 2016, nearly 600 students applied for admission to the various master's degree programs in the SOE; 86 percent were accepted. Approximately 230 students sought admission to the Ph.D. and Ed.D. programs; 50 percent were accepted.

Correspondence and Information

Dr. Valerie Kinloch, Dean
School of Education
University of Pittsburgh
Wesley W. Posvar Hall
230 S. Bouquet St.
Pittsburgh, Pennsylvania 15260
United States
Phone: 412-648-6944
Fax: 412-648-1825

Kaitlin Yacob
Director of Admissions
School of Education
Phone: 412-648-7362
Fax: 412-648-1899
E-mail: soeinfo@pitt.edu

The Cathedral of Learning, a Pittsburgh landmark listed in the National Register of Historic Places, is the centerpiece of the University of Pittsburgh's main campus in the Oakland neighborhood of Pittsburgh. The 42-story Late Gothic Revival Cathedral is the second-tallest university building in the world. The Cathedral of Learning contains more than 2,000 rooms and windows, and functions as one of the primary classroom and administrative centers of the university.

A point of convergence for Pitt students, faculty, and staff since it was erected in fall 2001, this panther statue greets those who enter the south side of the University's William Pitt Union. The bronze statue was cast in Parma, Italy, and serves as both a tribute to Pitt and a reminder of the University's fierce Panther Pride. A time capsule, to be opened in 2051, lies buried beneath the statue.

VANDERBILT UNIVERSITY
Peabody College

Programs of Study

Vanderbilt University's Peabody College of Education and Human Development offers programs leading to the Master of Education (M.Ed.), Master of Public Policy (M.P.P.), and Doctor of Education (Ed.D.) degrees. The Vanderbilt Graduate School, through Peabody departments, offers the Doctor of Philosophy (Ph.D.) degree. Peabody is committed to preparing students to become research scholars or innovative practitioners in the field of education and human development. Students may attend full- or part-time. Weekend courses are offered in several programs for working professionals who want to earn an advanced degree.

Students may pursue the Master of Education (M.Ed.) in child studies; community development and action; elementary education; English language learners; higher education administration (including specializations in administration, student life, and service learning); human development counseling (with specializations in school and community counseling); independent school leadership; international education policy and management; leadership and organizational performance; learning, diversity, and urban studies; learning and design (including specializations in teaching and learning; digital literacies; language, culture, and international studies; science and mathematics; or an individualized program); quantitative methods; reading education; secondary education; and special education (including specializations in applied behavior analysis, early childhood, high-incidence disabilities, and low-incidence disabilities). A Master of Public Policy is available in education policy. Peabody also offers a joint M.P.P./J.D. program and a dual degree with the Vanderbilt Divinity School.

Students interested in doctoral study may enroll in educational leadership and policy (Ed.D.); educational neuroscience (Ph.D); higher education leadership and policy (Ed.D.); community research and action (Ph.D.); leadership and learning in organizations (online Ed.D.); leadership and policy studies (Ph.D., with specializations in educational leadership and policy, higher education leadership and policy, and international education policy and management); learning, teaching, and diversity (Ph.D., with specializations in development, learning, and diversity; language, literacy, and culture; mathematics and science; and science and learning environment design); psychological sciences (Ph.D., with specializations in clinical science, cognitive science, developmental science, and quantitative methods and evaluation); and special education (Ph.D., with specializations in early childhood, high-incidence disabilities, and severe disabilities).

Peabody's teacher education and advanced certification programs are approved by the National Council for Accreditation of Teacher Education (NCATE). Programs in psychology and counseling are accredited by the American Psychological Association and the Council on Accreditation of Counseling and Related Educational Programs (CACREP), respectively.

Research Opportunities

In addition to the Vanderbilt University Library System, which has more than 2.6 million volumes, excellent research facilities and opportunities to conduct research are available through the Vanderbilt Kennedy Center for Research on Human Development, the Peabody Research Institute, the Susan Gray School, the National Center on School Choice, the National Center on Performance Initiatives, and the Center for Community Studies. The many local field sites available for research include hospitals, Metropolitan Nashville Public Schools, private schools, rehabilitation centers, schools for people with disabilities, government agencies, corporations, and nonprofit organizations.

Financial Aid

More than 70 percent of new students at Peabody receive financial aid. The College sponsors several substantial scholarship programs with offerings that range from partial to full tuition. In addition, assistantships, traineeships, loans, and part-time employment are available. Awards are made annually, and every attempt is made to meet a student's financial need. Application for financial aid does not affect the admission decision.

Cost of Study

Tuition for study at Peabody College for the 2018–19 academic year is $1,828 per semester credit hour for the M.Ed., M.P.P., and Ed.D. programs, and $1,967 per semester credit hour for programs offered through the Graduate School.

Living and Housing Costs

Vanderbilt's location in Nashville offers students the advantage of a wide range of living choices. Costs for housing, food, and other living expenses are moderate when compared with other metropolitan areas nationwide.

Student Group

Vanderbilt has a diverse student body of about 12,000. Peabody has an enrollment of approximately 1,800 students, of whom about 700 are graduate students. Women make up about 65 percent of Peabody's graduate students, while students from underrepresented groups make up about 20 percent. Students have a broad range of academic backgrounds and include recent graduates of baccalaureate programs as well as men and women who have many years of professional experience. The median age of current students is 27.

Student Outcomes

Graduates who earn a master's or doctoral degree from Peabody are prepared to work for educational, corporate, government, and service organizations in a variety of roles. More than 10,000 alumni are practicing teachers, more than 175 are school superintendents, and more than 50 are current or former college or university presidents.

Location

Nashville, the capital of Tennessee, is a cosmopolitan city with a metropolitan area population of 1.7 million. Vanderbilt University is one of more than a dozen institutions of higher learning located in Nashville and the surrounding area, leading Nashville to be called the "Athens of the South."

Nashville offers residents and visitors much in the way of music, art, and recreation. More than 100 local venues provide a wide variety of music, while classical and contemporary music is performed by the Nashville Symphony Orchestra and the Nashville Chamber Orchestra. The Tennessee Performing Arts Center (TPAC) is home to two theater companies, a ballet company, and an opera company. Vanderbilt's own Great Performances series frequently brings the best in chamber music, new music, theater, and all forms of dance to the Vanderbilt campus. Outstanding exhibitions of fine art can be seen at the Frist Center for the Visual Arts and at Cheekwood Botanical Garden and Museum of Art. There are more than 6,000 acres of public parks in the city, and the surrounding region of rolling hills and lakes is dotted with state parks and recreation areas.

Nashville has been named one of the 15 best U.S. cities for work and family by *Fortune* magazine, was ranked as the most popular U.S. city for corporate relocations by *Expansion Management* magazine, and was named by *Forbes* magazine as one of the 25 cities most likely to have the country's highest job growth over the coming five years. More information on Nashville can be found online at http://www.vanderbilt.edu/nashville.

The University and The College

Vanderbilt University, founded in 1873, is a private nondenominational institution with a strong tradition of graduate and professional education. Peabody, recognized for more than a century as one of the nation's foremost independent colleges of education, merged with Vanderbilt University in 1979. Peabody seeks to create knowledge through research, to prepare leaders, to support practitioners, and to strengthen communities at all levels.

Applying

Admission to professional degree programs is based on an evaluation of the applicant's potential for academic success and professional service, with consideration given to transcripts of previous course work, GRE General Test or MAT scores, letters of reference, and a letter outlining personal goals. Additional supporting credentials, such as a sample of the applicant's scholarly writing or a personal interview, may also be required.

Applicants who apply after the deadline should know that admission and financial assistance depend upon the availability of space and funds in the department in which they seek to study. Deadlines are December 1 for the Ph.D. and Ed.D. programs and December 31 for the M.Ed. and M.P.P. programs.

Correspondence and Information

Graduate Admissions
Peabody College of Vanderbilt University
Peabody Station, Box 227
Nashville, Tennessee 37203
United States
Phone: 615-322-8410
Fax: 615-322-4029
E-mail: peabody.admissions@vanderbilt.edu
Website: http://peabody.vanderbilt.edu

THE FACULTY

Department of Human and Organizational Development
Sandra Barnes, Professor; Ph.D., Georgia State.
Kimberly D. Bess, Assistant Professor; Ph.D., Vanderbilt.
Mark D. Cannon, Associate Professor; Ph.D., Harvard.
Ashley Carse, Assistant Professor; Ph.D., North Carolina at Chapel Hill.
Brian Christens, Associate Professor; Ph.D., Vanderbilt.
Nicole Cobb, Senior Lecturer; Ed.D., Tennessee.
David K. Diehl, Assistant Professor; Ph.D., Stanford.
Bradley Erford, Professor; Ph.D., Virginia.
Andrew J. Finch, Associate Professor of the Practice; Ph.D., Vanderbilt.
Anjali Forber-Pratt, Assistant Professor; Ph.D., Illinois at Urbana-Champaign.
James C. Fraser, Associate Professor; Ph.D., Georgia State.
Gina Frieden, Assistant Professor of the Practice; Ph.D., Memphis State.
Susan K. Friedman, Lecturer; M.B.A., Arizona State.
Leigh Gilchrist, Assistant Professor of the Practice; Ed.D., Vanderbilt.
Leslie Kirby, Principal Senior Lecturer; Ph.D., Vanderbilt.
Heather Lefkowitz, Lecturer; M.Div., Vanderbilt.
Mark Lipsey, Research Professor; Ph.D., Johns Hopkins.
Velma McBride Murry, Professor; Ph.D., Missouri–Columbia.
Yolanda McDonald, Assistant Professor.
Maury Nation, Associate Professor; Ph.D., South Carolina.
Carol Nixon, Research Assistant Professor; Ph.D., Vanderbilt.

Vanderbilt University

Nancy Nolan, Lecturer; M.Ed., Vanderbilt.
Douglas Perkins, Professor; Ph.D., NYU.
Jessica Perkins, Assistant Professor; Ph.D., Harvard.
Sara Safransky, Assistant Professor; Ph.D., North Carolina at Chapel Hill.
Sharon Shields, Professor of the Practice; Ph.D., George Peabody.
Marybeth Shinn, Professor; Ph.D., Michigan.
Heather Smith, Assistant Professor of the Practice; Ph.D., Central Florida.
Paul Speer, Professor; Ph.D., Missouri–Kansas City.
Sarah V. Suiter, Assistant Professor of the Practice; Ph.D., Vanderbilt.
Kristen C. Tompkins, Lecturer; M.Ed., Vanderbilt.
Andrew Van Schaack, Principal Senior Lecturer; Ph.D., Utah State.

Department of Leadership, Policy, and Organizations

Robert Dale Ballou, Associate Professor; Ph.D., Yale.
Angela Boatman, Assistant Professor; Ed.D., Harvard.
Christopher Candelaria; Assistant Professor; Ph.D., Stanford.
Marisa A. Cannata, Research Assistant Professor; Ph.D., Michigan.
Sean Corcoran, Associate Professor.
Jose Cossa, Senior Lecturer; Ph.D., Chicago.
Xiu Cravens, Associate Professor of the Practice; Ph.D., Vanderbilt.
Shaun Dougherty, Associate Professor.
Susan Douglas, Assistant Professor of the Practice; Ph.D., Vanderbilt.
Corbette Doyle, Senior Lecturer; M.B.A., Vanderbilt.
William R. Doyle, Associate Professor; Ph.D., Stanford.
Brent Evans, Assistant Professor; Ph.D., Stanford.
Joanne Golann, Assistant Professor; Ph.D., Princeton.
Ellen Goldring, Professor; Ph.D., Chicago.
Jason Grissom, Associate Professor; Ph.D., Stanford.
Carolyn J. Heinrich, Professor; Ph.D., Chicago.
Gary T. Henry, Professor; Ph.D., Wisconsin.
Brian L. Heuser, Assistant Professor; Ed.D., Vanderbilt.
David Laird, Assistant Professor of the Practice; Ed.D., Vanderbilt.
Daniel LeBreton; Lecturer.
Catherine Gavin Loss, Assistant Professor of the Practice; Ph.D., Virginia.
Christopher P. Loss, Associate Professor; Ph.D., Virginia.
Brenda McKenzie, Senior Lecturer; Ph.D., Kent.
Joseph Murphy, Professor; Ph.D., Ohio State.
Christine Quinn Trank, Associate Professor of the Practice; Ph.D., Iowa.
Mollie Rubin, Research Assistant Professor.
Patrick J. Schuermann, Assistant Professor; Ed.D., Vanderbilt.
Matthew Shaw, Assistant Professor; Ed.D., Harvard.
Claire Smrekar, Associate Professor; Ph.D., Stanford.
Adela Soliz, Assistant Professor; Ed.D., Harvard.
Matthew Springer, Associate Professor; Ph.D., Vanderbilt.
Deborah Tobey, Senior Lecturer; Ed.D., Vanderbilt.

Department of Psychology and Human Development

Camilla P. Benbow, Professor; Ed.D., Johns Hopkins.
Amy Booth, Professor; Ph.D., Pittsburgh.
James Booth, Professor; Ph.D., Maryland.
Sarah Brown-Schmidt, Associate Professor; Ph.D., Rochester.
Sun-Joo Cho, Associate Professor; Ph.D., Georgia.
David A. Cole, Professor; Ph.D., Houston.
Bruce E. Compas, Professor; Ph.D., UCLA.
Elizabeth May Dykens, Professor; Ph.D., Kansas.
Lisa K. Fazio, Assistant Professor; Ph.D., Duke.
Judy Garber, Professor; Ph.D., Minnesota, Twin Cities.
Vicki S. Harris, Assistant Clinical Professor; Ph.D., Pennsylvania.
Kathryn Humphreys, Assistant Professor; Ph.D., California.
Shane Hutton, Lecturer; Ph.D., North Carolina–Chapel Hill.
Autumn Kujawa, Assistant Professor; Ph.D., SUNY.
Jonathan Lane, Assistant Professor; Ph.D., Michigan.
Daniel T. Levin, Professor; Ph.D., Cornell.
David Lubinski, Professor; Ph.D., Minnesota.
Nina Martin, Associate Clinical Professor; Ed.D., Harvard.
Amy Needham, Professor; Ph.D., Illinois.
Julia Noland, Senior Lecturer; Ph.D., Cornell.
Laura R. Novick, Associate Professor; Ph.D., Stanford.
Georgine Pion, Research Associate Professor; Ph.D., Claremont.
Kristopher J. Preacher, Professor; Ph.D., Ohio.
Gavin Price, Assistant Professor; Ph.D., Jyväskylä (Finland).
John R. Rieser, Professor; Ph.D., Minnesota, Twin Cities.
Bethany Rittle-Johnson, Professor; Ph.D., Carnegie Mellon.
Joseph Lee Rodgers III, Professor; Ph.D., North Carolina.
Megan M. Saylor, Associate Professor; Ph.D., Oregon.
Craig A. Smith, Associate Professor; Ph.D., Stanford.
Sonya Sterba, Associate Professor; Ph.D., North Carolina–Chapel Hill.
Georgene Troseth, Associate Professor; Ph.D., Illinois at Urbana-Champaign.
Leigh Wadsworth, Senior Lecturer; Ph.D., Arizona State.
Tedra Ann Walden, Professor; Ph.D., Florida.
Duane Watson, Associate Professor; Ph.D., Rochester.
Bahr Weiss, Associate Professor; Ph.D., North Carolina–Chapel Hill.

Department of Special Education

Marcia Barnes, Professor; Ph.D., McMaster.
Erin Barton, Associate Professor; Ph.D., Vanderbilt.
Andrea Capizzi, Assistant Professor of the Practice; Ph.D., Vanderbilt.
Erik W. Carter, Professor; Ph.D., Vanderbilt.
Laurie Cutting, Professor; Ph.D., Northwestern.
Alex da Fonte, Assistant Professor of the Practice; M.S., Purdue.
Donna Y. Ford, Professor; Ph.D., Cleveland State.

Douglas Fuchs, Professor; Ph.D., Minnesota.
Lynn Fuchs, Professor; Ph.D., Minnesota.
Ted S. Hasselbring, Research Professor; Ed.D., Indiana.
Deborah D. Hatton, Associate Professor; Ph.D., North Carolina.
Mary Louise Hemmeter, Professor; Ph.D., Vanderbilt.
Robert Hodapp, Professor; Ph.D., Boston University.
Nealetta J. Houchins-Juarez, Instructor of the Practice; M.A., Nevada.
Ann Kaiser, Professor; Ph.D., Kansas.
Joseph Lambert, Assistant Professor of the Practice; Ph.D., Utah State.
Jennifer Ledford, Assistant Professor; Ph.D., Vanderbilt.
Christopher Lemons, Associate Professor; Ph.D., Vanderbilt.
Blair Lloyd, Assistant Professor; Ph.D., Vanderbilt. Kim Paulsen, Professor of the Practice; Ed.D., Nevada, Las Vegas.
Naomi Tyler, Associate Professor of the Practice; Ph.D., New Mexico State.
Jeanne Wanzek, Associate Professor; Ph.D., University of Texas.
Joseph H. Wehby, Associate Professor; Ph.D., Vanderbilt.
Sandra Wilson, Research Assistant Professor; Ph.D., Vanderbilt.
Paul J. Yoder, Professor; Ph.D., North Carolina.

Department of Teaching and Learning

Corey Brady, Assistant Professor; Ph.D., Dartmouth.
Caroline Christopher, Research Assistant Professor.
Douglas Clark, Professor; Ph.D., Berkeley.
Paul A. Cobb, Research Professor; Ph.D., Georgia.
Molly F. Collins, Lecturer; Ed.D., Boston University. Shannon M. Daniel, Lecturer; Ph.D., Maryland.
Ana Christine DaSilva, Professor of the Practice; Ph.D., Nevada.
David Dickinson, Professor; Ed.D., Harvard.
Teresa Dunleavy, Assistant Professor of the Practice; Ph.D., Washington (Seattle).
Kelley Durkin, Research Assistant Professor.
Noel Enyedy, Professor.
Dale C. Farran, Research Professor; Ph.D., Bryn Mawr.
Emily Galloway, Assistant Professor; D.Ed., Harvard.
Kathy A. Ganske, Professor of the Practice; Ph.D., Virginia.
Amanda P. Goodwin, Associate Professor; Ph.D., Miami.
Melissa Sommerfield Gresalfi, Associate Professor; Ph.D., Stanford.
Rogers Hall, Professor; Ph.D., California, Irvine.
Andrea W. Henrie, Lecturer; Ph.D., Tennessee.
Ilana Horn, Associate Professor; Ph.D., Berkeley.
Andrew L. Hostetler, Assistant Professor of the Practice; Ph.D., Kent State.
Melanie K. Hundley, Associate Professor of the Practice; Ph.D., Georgia.
Robert T. Jimenez, Professor; Ph.D., Illinois at Urbana-Champaign.
Heather J. Johnson, Assistant Professor of the Practice; Ph.D., Northwestern.
Nicole Joseph, Assistant Professor; Ph.D., Washington.
Ocheze Joseph, Lecturer; Ed.D., Maryland.
Kara Krinks, Lecturer; Ph.D., Vanderbilt.
Kevin Leander, Associate Professor; Ph.D., Illinois.
Deborah L. Lehrer, Lecturer; M.Ed., Edinboro.
Richard Lehrer, Professor; Ph.D., Chicago.
Luis Leyva, Assistant Professor; Ed.M., Rutgers.
Jeannette Mancilla-Martinez, Associate Professor; Ed.D., Harvard.
Ebony O. McGee, Assistant Professor; Ph.D., Illinois.
Catherine McTamaney, Senior Lecturer; Ed.D., Vanderbilt.
Kristen W. Neal, Lecturer; Ph.D., Vanderbilt.
Ann M. Neely, Associate Professor of the Practice; Ed.D., Georgia.
Amy Palmeri, Assistant Professor of the Practice; Ph.D., Indiana Bloomington.
Emily Pendergrass, Senior Lecturer; Ph.D., Georgia.
Jeanne H. Peter, Lecturer; Ed.D., Vanderbilt.
Rebecca Peterson, Lecturer; M.Ed., Vanderbilt.
Lisa Pray, Professor of the Practice; Ph.D., Arizona State.
Deborah W. Rowe, Professor; Ph.D., Indiana.
Leona Schauble, Professor; Ph.D., Columbia.
Elizabeth Self, Lecturer; Ph.D., Vanderbilt.
Virginia L. Shepherd, Research Professor; Ph.D., Iowa.
Marcy Singer-Gabella, Professor; Ph.D., Stanford.
Barbara Stengel, Professor of the Practice; Ph.D., Pittsburgh.
Anita Wager, Professor of the Practice; Ph.D., Wisconsin.

The Faye and Joe Wyatt Center for Education.

Section 23
Administration, Instruction, and Theory

This section contains a directory of institutions offering graduate work in administration, instruction, and theory. Additional information about programs listed in the directory but not augmented by an in-depth entry may be obtained by writing directly to the dean of a graduate school or chair of a department at the address given in the directory.

For programs offering related work, see also in this book *Education, Instructional Levels, Leisure Studies and Recreation, Physical Education and Kinesiology, Special Focus,* and *Subject Areas.* In other guides in this series:

Graduate Programs in the Humanities, Arts & Social Sciences
See *Psychology and Counseling (School Psychology)*
Graduate Programs in the Biological/Biomedical Sciences and Health-Related Medical Professions
See *Health-Related Professions*

CONTENTS

Program Directories

Featured Schools: Displays and Close-Ups

See also:

Curriculum and Instruction

Acadia University, Faculty of Professional Studies, School of Education, Program in Curriculum Studies, Wolfville, NS B4P 2R6, Canada. Offers curriculum studies (M Ed); interprofessional health practice (M Ed); music education (M Ed). *Program availability:* Part-time. *Entrance requirements:* For master's, B Ed or the equivalent, minimum B average in undergraduate course work, 2 years of teaching experience. Additional exam requirements/recommendations for international students: Required—TOEFL (minimum score 580 paper-based; 93 iBT), IELTS (minimum score 6.5). *Application deadline:* For fall admission, 3/15 priority date for domestic and international students. Applications are processed on a rolling basis. Application fee: $50. *Financial support:* Application deadline: 3/15. *Faculty research:* Literacy development, postmodern philosophy and curriculum theory, historiography, philosophy of education, learning and technology. *Unit head:* Dr. Ann Vibert, Director, 902-585-1229, E-mail: ann.vibert@acadiau.ca. *Application contact:* Rosie Hare, Administrative Assistant, 902-585-1597, Fax: 902-585-1086, E-mail: rosie.hare@acadiau.ca.
Website: http://education.acadiau.ca/

Adams State University, Office of Graduate Studies, Department of Teacher Education, Alamosa, CO 81101. Offers teacher education (MA), including adaptive leadership, curriculum and instruction, curriculum and instruction-STEM, educational leadership. *Program availability:* Part-time, online learning. *Degree requirements:* For master's, qualifying exam. *Entrance requirements:* For master's, GRE General Test or MAT, minimum undergraduate GPA of 3.0. *Application deadline:* For fall admission, 5/15 priority date for domestic students; for spring admission, 10/15 for domestic students. Applications are processed on a rolling basis. Application fee: $30. *Expenses:* Tuition, state resident: full-time $4800; part-time $2400 per credit. Tuition, nonresident: full-time $7100; part-time $3550 per credit. *Required fees:* $213; $106 per credit. One-time fee: $100. Tuition and fees vary according to campus/location and program. *Financial support:* In 2017–18, fellowships with partial tuition reimbursements (averaging $4,000 per year), teaching assistantships with partial tuition reimbursements (averaging $4,000 per year) were awarded; career-related internships or fieldwork, Federal Work-Study, institutionally sponsored loans, and unspecified assistantships also available. Support available to part-time students. Financial award application deadline: 4/15; financial award applicants required to submit FAFSA. *Unit head:* Dr. Cheri Meder, Interim Chair, 719-587-7934, Fax: 719-587-8145, E-mail: teachered@adams.edu. *Application contact:* Information Contact, 719-587-7776, Fax: 719-587-8145, E-mail: teachered@adams.edu.
Website: http://teachered.adams.edu

American College of Education, Graduate Programs, Indianapolis, IN 46204. Offers curriculum and instruction (M Ed), including bilingual, ESL; educational leadership (M Ed); educational technology (M Ed).

American InterContinental University Online, Program in Education, Schaumburg, IL 60173. Offers curriculum and instruction (M Ed); educational assessment and evaluation (M Ed); instructional technology (M Ed); leadership of educational organizations (M Ed). *Accreditation:* TEAC. *Program availability:* Evening/weekend, online learning. *Entrance requirements:* Additional exam requirements/recommendations for international students: Required—TOEFL (minimum score 550 paper-based). Electronic applications accepted.

Andrews University, School of Graduate Studies, School of Education, Department of Teaching, Learning, and Curriculum, Program in Curriculum and Instruction, Berrien Springs, MI 49104. Offers MA, Ed D, PhD, Ed S. *Students:* 11 full-time (7 women), 6 part-time (5 women); includes 4 minority (all Black or African American, non-Hispanic/Latino), 8 international. Average age 41. 19 applicants, 26% accepted, 2 enrolled. In 2017, 3 doctorates awarded. *Degree requirements:* For master's, thesis optional; for doctorate, thesis/dissertation. *Entrance requirements:* For master's, GRE Subject Test. Additional exam requirements/recommendations for international students: Required—TOEFL (minimum score 550 paper-based). *Application deadline:* Applications are processed on a rolling basis. Application fee: $40. *Financial support:* Fellowships, research assistantships, teaching assistantships, career-related internships or fieldwork, Federal Work-Study, institutionally sponsored loans, and tuition waivers (partial) available. Support available to part-time students. *Unit head:* Dr. Larry D. Burton, Coordinator, 269-971-6674. *Application contact:* Justina Clayburn, Supervisor of Graduate Admission, 800-253-2874, Fax: 269-471-6321, E-mail: graduate@andrews.edu.

Angelo State University, College of Graduate Studies and Research, College of Education, Department of Curriculum and Instruction, San Angelo, TX 76909. Offers curriculum and instruction (MA); educational administration (M Ed); guidance and counseling (M Ed); student development and leadership in higher education (M Ed). *Program availability:* Part-time, evening/weekend, online learning. *Students:* 405 full-time (332 women), 449 part-time (380 women); includes 291 minority (98 Black or African American, non-Hispanic/Latino; 3 American Indian or Alaska Native, non-Hispanic/Latino; 3 Asian, non-Hispanic/Latino; 178 Hispanic/Latino; 9 Two or more races, non-Hispanic/Latino), 1 international. Average age 35. *Application deadline:* For fall admission, 7/15 priority date for domestic students, 6/10 for international students; for spring admission, 12/1 priority date for domestic students, 11/1 for international students. Application fee: $40 ($50 for international students). *Expenses:* Tuition, state resident: full-time $3856. Tuition, nonresident: full-time $11,324. *Required fees:* $2650. *Unit head:* Dr. Jim Summerlin, Chair, 325-942-2647, Fax: 325-942-2039, E-mail: james.summerlin@angelo.edu. *Application contact:* Lesley Casarez, Graduate Advisor, 325-486-6775, E-mail: lesley.casarez@angelo.edu.
Website: http://www.angelo.edu/dept/ci/

Appalachian State University, Cratis D. Williams Graduate School, Department of Curriculum and Instruction, Boone, NC 28608. Offers curriculum specialist (MA); educational media (MA); elementary education (MA); middle grades education (MA), including language arts, mathematics, science, social studies. *Accreditation:* NCATE. *Program availability:* Part-time, evening/weekend, online learning. *Degree requirements:* For master's, comprehensive exam, thesis or alternative. *Entrance requirements:* For master's, GRE General Test or MAT, 3 letters of recommendation. Additional exam requirements/recommendations for international students: Required—TOEFL (minimum score 570 paper-based; 79 iBT), IELTS (minimum score 6.5). Electronic applications accepted. *Faculty research:* Media literacy, elementary teaching, curriculum development, online learning environments.

Arcadia University, School of Education, Glenside, PA 19038-3295. Offers art education (M Ed); computer education (CAS); curriculum (CAS); curriculum studies (M Ed); early childhood education (M Ed), including individualized, master teacher, research in child development; educational leadership (M Ed, Ed D, CAS); elementary education (M Ed); English education (MA Ed); environmental education (MA Ed); instructional technology (M Ed); language arts (M Ed); library science (M Ed);

mathematics education (M Ed, MA Ed); music education (MA Ed); psychology (MA Ed); reading (M Ed, CAS); science education (M Ed, CAS); secondary education (M Ed, CAS); special education (M Ed, Ed D, CAS); theater arts (MA Ed); written communication (MA Ed). *Accreditation:* NASAD. *Program availability:* Part-time, evening/weekend, online learning. Electronic applications accepted. *Expenses:* Contact institution.

Arizona State University at the Tempe campus, Mary Lou Fulton Teachers College, Program in Curriculum and Instruction, Phoenix, AZ 85069. Offers curriculum and instruction (M Ed, MA); elementary education (M Ed); physical education (MPE); secondary education (M Ed). *Program availability:* Part-time, evening/weekend, online learning. Terminal master's awarded for partial completion of doctoral program. *Degree requirements:* For master's, thesis or alternative, applied project, interactive Program of Study (iPOS) submitted before completing 50 percent of required credit hours. *Entrance requirements:* For master's, GRE or GMAT (for some programs), minimum GPA of 3.0 or equivalent in last 2 years of work leading to bachelor's degree, 3 letters of recommendation, personal statement describing research and career goals, curriculum vitae or resume, IVP fingerprint clearance card (for those seeking Arizona certification). Additional exam requirements/recommendations for international students: Required—TOEFL, IELTS, or PTE. Electronic applications accepted. *Expenses:* Contact institution. *Faculty research:* Early childhood, media and computers, elementary education, secondary education, English education, bilingual education, language and literacy, science education, engineering education, exercise and wellness education.

Arlington Baptist University, Program in Education, Arlington, TX 76012-3425. Offers curriculum and instruction (M Ed); educational leadership (M Ed). *Degree requirements:* For master's, professional portfolio; internship (for educational leadership). *Entrance requirements:* For master's, bachelor's degree from accredited college or university with minimum GPA of 3.0, minimum of 12 hours in Bible; minimum of three years' classroom teaching experience in an accredited K-12 public or private school (for educational leadership only).

Auburn University, Graduate School, College of Education, Department of Educational Foundations, Leadership, and Technology, Auburn University, AL 36849. Offers adult education (PhD, Ed S); curriculum supervision (M Ed, PhD); higher education administration (PhD); library media (Ed S); school administration (M Ed, PhD). *Accreditation:* NCATE. *Program availability:* Part-time. *Faculty:* 30 full-time (17 women), 8 part-time/adjunct (5 women). *Students:* 139 full-time (94 women), 254 part-time (171 women); includes 109 minority (95 Black or African American, non-Hispanic/Latino; 1 American Indian or Alaska Native, non-Hispanic/Latino; 2 Asian, non-Hispanic/Latino; 1 Native Hawaiian or other Pacific Islander, non-Hispanic/Latino; 6 Two or more races, non-Hispanic/Latino), 12 international. Average age 37. 216 applicants, 72% accepted, 94 enrolled. In 2017, 92 master's, 46 doctorates, 58 other advanced degrees awarded. *Degree requirements:* For master's, thesis (for some programs); for doctorate, thesis/dissertation; for Ed S, field project. *Entrance requirements:* For master's, doctorate, and Ed S, GRE General Test. *Application deadline:* Applications are processed on a rolling basis. Application fee: $50 ($60 for international students). Electronic applications accepted. *Expenses:* Tuition, state resident: full-time $10,974; part-time $519 per credit hour. Tuition, nonresident: full-time $29,658; part-time $1557 per credit hour. *Required fees:* $816 per semester. Tuition and fees vary according to degree level and program. *Financial support:* Teaching assistantships and Federal Work-Study available. Support available to part-time students. Financial award application deadline: 3/15; financial award applicants required to submit FAFSA. *Unit head:* Dr. Sherida Downer, Head, 334-844-3060. *Application contact:* Dr. George Flowers, Dean of the Graduate School, 334-844-4700.
Website: http://www.education.auburn.edu/academic_departments/eflt/

Augusta University, College of Education, Program in Curriculum and Instruction, Augusta, GA 30912. Offers curriculum and instruction (Ed S); elementary education (MAT); foreign language education (MAT); instruction (M Ed); middle grades education (MAT); music education (MAT); secondary education (MAT); special education (MAT). *Degree requirements:* For master's, thesis, portfolio. *Entrance requirements:* For master's, GRE, MAT, minimum GPA of 2.5.

Aurora University, School of Education and Human Performance, Aurora, IL 60506-4892. Offers applied behavioral analysis (MS); bilingual-ESL education (MA); educational leadership with principal endorsement (MA); educational technology (MA); leadership in adult learning higher education (Ed D); leadership in curriculum and instruction (Ed D); leadership in educational administration (Ed D); reading instruction (MA); special education (MA). *Accreditation:* NCATE. *Program availability:* Part-time, evening/weekend. *Faculty:* 15 full-time (8 women), 39 part-time/adjunct (20 women). *Students:* 421 full-time (299 women), 142 part-time (89 women); includes 90 minority (25 Black or African American, non-Hispanic/Latino; 7 Asian, non-Hispanic/Latino; 50 Hispanic/Latino; 2 Native Hawaiian or other Pacific Islander, non-Hispanic/Latino; 6 Two or more races, non-Hispanic/Latino). Average age 37. 169 applicants, 95% accepted, 59 enrolled. In 2017, 175 master's, 36 doctorates awarded. *Degree requirements:* For master's, student teaching; for doctorate, comprehensive exam, thesis/dissertation. *Entrance requirements:* For master's, 2 years of teaching experience, valid teaching certificate, resume; for doctorate, appropriate master's degree, two references, curriculum vitae, personal statement, professional project, reflective essay. Additional exam requirements/recommendations for international students: Required—TOEFL (minimum score 550 paper-based; 79 iBT). *Application deadline:* For fall admission, 6/1 for international students; for spring admission, 10/1 for international students. Applications are processed on a rolling basis. Application fee: $0. Electronic applications accepted. *Expenses:* Contact institution. *Financial support:* In 2017–18, 34 students received support. Federal Work-Study, scholarships/grants, and unspecified assistantships available. Support available to part-time students. Financial award applicants required to submit FAFSA. *Unit head:* Dr. Jen Buckley, Dean, School of Education and Human Performance, 630-844-1542, Fax: 630-844-6155, E-mail: jbuckley@aurora.edu. *Application contact:* Elizabeth Botica, Graduate Education Recruiter, 630-947-8918, E-mail: ebotica@aurora.edu.
Website: http://aurora.edu/education

Austin Peay State University, College of Graduate Studies, College of Education, Department of Educational Specialties, Clarksville, TN 37044. Offers administration and supervision (Ed S); counseling and guidance (Ed S); curriculum and instruction (MA Ed); education leadership (MA Ed); elementary education (Ed S); reading (MA Ed); secondary education (Ed S). *Program availability:* Part-time, evening/weekend, online learning. *Faculty:* 15 full-time (9 women), 5 part-time/adjunct (4 women). *Students:* 73 full-time (54 women), 139 part-time (106 women); includes 49 minority (23 Black or African American, non-Hispanic/Latino; 4 Asian, non-Hispanic/Latino; 12 Hispanic/Latino; 10 Two or more races, non-Hispanic/Latino), 1 international. Average age 35. 72

applicants, 96% accepted, 42 enrolled. In 2017, 94 master's, 12 Ed Ss awarded. *Degree requirements:* For master's, comprehensive exam, thesis optional. *Entrance requirements:* For master's, GRE General Test, MAT, minimum undergraduate GPA of 2.75. Additional exam requirements/recommendations for international students: Required—TOEFL (minimum score 500 paper-based). *Application deadline:* For fall admission, 8/8 priority date for domestic students. Applications are processed on a rolling basis. Application fee: $45 ($50 for international students). Electronic applications accepted. *Expenses:* Tuition, state resident: full-time $7686; part-time $427 per credit hour. Tuition, nonresident: full-time $20,268; part-time $1126 per credit hour. *Required fees:* $1529; $76.45 per credit hour. *Financial support:* Research assistantships with full tuition reimbursements, career-related internships or fieldwork, Federal Work-Study, institutionally sponsored loans, scholarships/grants, and unspecified assistantships available. Support available to part-time students. Financial award application deadline: 4/1; financial award applicants required to submit FAFSA. *Unit head:* Dr. Moniqueka Gold, Chair, 931-221-7696, Fax: 931-221-1292, E-mail: goldm@apsu.edu. *Application contact:* Megan Mitchell, Coordinator of Graduate Admissions, 800-859-4723, Fax: 931-221-7641, E-mail: gradadmissions@apsu.edu.

Averett University, Master in Education Program, Danville, VA 24541-3692. Offers administration and supervision (M Ed); curriculum and instruction (M Ed); special education with endorsement (M Ed); special education with licensure (M Ed). *Program availability:* Part-time, online only, 100% online. *Faculty:* 2 full-time (1 woman), 14 part-time/adjunct (11 women). *Students:* 38 full-time (32 women), 46 part-time (28 women); includes 33 minority (29 Black or African American, non-Hispanic/Latino; 1 Hispanic/Latino; 3 Two or more races, non-Hispanic/Latino). Average age 38. 155 applicants, 52% accepted, 59 enrolled. In 2017, 50 master's awarded. *Degree requirements:* For master's, 30-credit core curriculum, minimum GPA of 3.0 throughout program, completion of degree requirements within six years from start of program. *Entrance requirements:* For master's, PRAXIS I, GRE, or MAT; writing proficiency test, minimum cumulative GPA of 3.0 over the last 60 hours of undergraduate study toward a baccalaureate degree, three letters of recommendation, Virginia teaching license (or eligibility). Additional exam requirements/recommendations for international students: Required—TOEFL (minimum score 600 paper-based; 100 iBT). *Application deadline:* Applications are processed on a rolling basis. Electronic applications accepted. *Expenses:* Contact institution. *Financial support:* Application deadline: 3/1; applicants required to submit FAFSA. *Faculty research:* Digital story telling for instruction and assessment; online collaborative tools; digital field trips with Google Earth; teacher preparation in special education in Kenya, Malawi, Zambia, and Zimbabwe; self-efficacy of regular education teachers regarding inclusion of special education students in their classrooms. *Total annual research expenditures:* $5,000. *Unit head:* Dr. Sue Davis, Education Chair, 434-791-5741, Fax: 434-791-5020; E-mail: suedavis@averett.edu. Website: http://gps.averett.edu/online/education/

Azusa Pacific University, School of Education, Department of Teacher Education, Program in Teaching, Azusa, CA 91702-7000. Offers MA Ed.

Ball State University, Graduate School, Teachers College, Department of Educational Studies, Program in Curriculum and Educational Technology, Muncie, IN 47306. Offers MA. *Accreditation:* NCATE. *Program availability:* Part-time, online only, 100% online. *Students:* 3 full-time (all women), 42 part-time (32 women); includes 5 minority (3 Black or African American, non-Hispanic/Latino; 1 Hispanic/Latino; 1 Two or more races, non-Hispanic/Latino). Average age 33. 9 applicants, 78% accepted, 6 enrolled. In 2017, 24 master's awarded. *Entrance requirements:* For master's, minimum baccalaureate GPA of 2.75 or 3.0 in latter half of baccalaureate. Additional exam requirements/recommendations for international students: Required—TOEFL (minimum score 550 paper-based; 79 iBT), IELTS (minimum score 6.5). *Application deadline:* Applications are processed on a rolling basis. Application fee: $60. Electronic applications accepted. *Financial support:* Research assistantships with partial tuition reimbursements, teaching assistantships with partial tuition reimbursements, and unspecified assistantships available. Financial award application deadline: 3/1; financial award applicants required to submit FAFSA. *Unit head:* Dr. Ayesha Sadaf, Program Director, 785-285-4246, Fax: 785-285-5489, E-mail: sadaf@bsu.edu. Website: http://www.bsu.edu/edstudies

Ball State University, Graduate School, Teachers College, Department of Educational Studies, Program in Educational Studies, Muncie, IN 47306. Offers educational studies (PhD), including cultural and educational policy studies, curriculum, educational technology. *Program availability:* Part-time, blended/hybrid learning. *Students:* 8 full-time (4 women), 16 part-time (11 women); includes 4 minority (2 Black or African American, non-Hispanic/Latino; 1 Asian, non-Hispanic/Latino; 1 Two or more races, non-Hispanic/Latino), 3 international. Average age 43. 14 applicants, 57% accepted, 4 enrolled. In 2017, 3 doctorates awarded. *Degree requirements:* For doctorate, thesis/dissertation. *Entrance requirements:* For doctorate, GRE General Test, minimum graduate GPA of 3.2, curriculum vitae, writing sample, three letters of reference. Additional exam requirements/recommendations for international students: Required—TOEFL (minimum score 550 paper-based; 79 iBT), IELTS (minimum score 6.5). *Application deadline:* Applications are processed on a rolling basis. Application fee: $60. Electronic applications accepted. *Financial support:* Research assistantships with partial tuition reimbursements and teaching assistantships with partial tuition reimbursements available. Financial award application deadline: 3/1; financial award applicants required to submit FAFSA. *Faculty research:* Emerging curriculum trends, secondary teacher preparation, issues of equity and social justice in education, teacher technology integration, teaching for transformative understanding, teacher leadership, history of educational policy and practices, ethics and education. *Unit head:* Dr. Theresa Kruczek, Interim Chair, 765-285-8049, E-mail: tkruczek@bsu.edu. Website: http://www.bsu.edu/edstudies

Barry University, School of Education, Program in Curriculum and Instruction, Miami Shores, FL 33161-6695. Offers accomplished teacher (Ed S); culture, language and literacy (TESOL) (PhD); curriculum evaluation and research (PhD); early childhood (Ed S); early childhood education (PhD); elementary (Ed S); elementary education (PhD); ESOL (Ed S); gifted (Ed S); Montessori (Ed S); PKP/elementary (Ed S); reading (Ed S); reading, language and cognition (PhD). *Entrance requirements:* For doctorate, GRE, minimum GPA of 3.25.

Baylor University, Graduate School, School of Education, Department of Curriculum and Instruction, Waco, TX 76798. Offers MA, MS Ed, Ed D, PhD. *Accreditation:* NCATE. *Program availability:* Part-time. *Faculty:* 13 full-time (9 women). *Students:* 24 full-time (15 women), 8 part-time (5 women); includes 5 minority (2 Black or African American, non-Hispanic/Latino; 2 Hispanic/Latino; 1 Two or more races, non-Hispanic/Latino), 2 international. Average age 30. 26 applicants, 65% accepted, 14 enrolled. In 2017, 12 master's, 3 doctorates awarded. *Degree requirements:* For master's, comprehensive exam, thesis optional; for doctorate, comprehensive exam, thesis/dissertation. *Entrance requirements:* For master's, GRE General Test (including Analytic Writing), 3 letters of recommendation, personal statement, interview; for doctorate, GRE General Test (including Analytic Writing), 3 letters of recommendation, personal statement, interview, writing sample. Additional exam requirements/recommendations for international students: Required—TOEFL (minimum score 550 paper-based; 80 iBT). *Application deadline:* For fall admission, 3/15 priority date for domestic and international students;

for spring admission, 10/15 priority date for domestic and international students. Applications are processed on a rolling basis. Application fee: $25. Electronic applications accepted. *Expenses:* $1,650 per hour. *Financial support:* In 2017–18, 35 students received support, including 15 research assistantships with partial tuition reimbursements available (averaging $10,000 per year), 1 teaching assistantship with full tuition reimbursement available (averaging $19,000 per year); Federal Work-Study, institutionally sponsored loans, scholarships/grants, health care benefits, and unspecified assistantships also available. Support available to part-time students. Financial award application deadline: 3/15. *Faculty research:* Curriculum and pedagogy, elementary education, English language arts education, literacy and reading education, mathematics education, qualitative research, science education, social foundations and cultural studies, social studies education, secondary education, teacher education, technology education, media literacy, civics education, historically black colleges. *Total annual research expenditures:* $75,000. *Unit head:* Dr. Trena Wilkerson, Graduate Program Director, 254-710-6162, Fax: 254-710-3160, E-mail: trena_wilkerson@baylor.edu. *Application contact:* Carol Stukenbroeker, Administrative Assistant, 254-710-2410, Fax: 254-710-3160, E-mail: carol_stukenbroeker@baylor.edu. Website: http://www.baylor.edu/soe/ci/

Bay Path University, Program in Curriculum and Instruction, Longmeadow, MA 01106-2292. Offers MS Ed. *Program availability:* Part-time, 100% online. *Students:* 17 full-time (all women), 37 part-time (35 women); includes 4 minority (3 Black or African American, non-Hispanic/Latino; 1 Hispanic/Latino). Average age 31. In 2017, 4 master's awarded. *Application deadline:* Applications are processed on a rolling basis. Application fee: $45. Electronic applications accepted. Application fee is waived when completed online. *Expenses:* $505 per credit. *Financial support:* Unspecified assistantships available. Financial award applicants required to submit FAFSA. *Unit head:* Andrea Hickson, Program Director, E-mail: ahickson@baypath.edu. *Application contact:* Diane Ranaldi, Dean of Graduate Admissions, 413-565-1332, Fax: 413-565-1250, E-mail: dranaldi@baypath.edu.

Benedictine University, Graduate Programs, Program in Education, Lisle, IL 60532. Offers curriculum and instruction and collaborative teaching (M Ed); elementary education (MA Ed); leadership and administration (M Ed); reading and literacy (M Ed); secondary education (MA Ed); special education (MA Ed). *Program availability:* Part-time, evening/weekend. *Degree requirements:* For master's, comprehensive exam, thesis (for some programs). *Entrance requirements:* For master's, GRE or MAT. Additional exam requirements/recommendations for international students: Required—TOEFL (minimum score 550 paper-based). Electronic applications accepted. *Expenses:* Contact institution.

Berry College, Graduate Programs, Graduate Programs in Education, Program in Curriculum and Instruction, Mount Berry, GA 30149-0159. Offers M Ed, Ed S. *Accreditation:* NCATE. In 2017, 7 master's awarded. *Degree requirements:* For master's and Ed S, thesis, portfolio, oral exams. *Entrance requirements:* For master's, GRE or MAT, minimum GPA of 2.5; for Ed S, M Ed from NCATE-accredited school, minimum GPA of 3.25. Additional exam requirements/recommendations for international students: Required—TOEFL (minimum score 550 paper-based). *Application deadline:* For fall admission, 7/20 for domestic students, 5/1 for international students; for spring admission, 12/1 for domestic students, 10/1 for international students. Applications are processed on a rolling basis. Application fee: $25 ($30 for international students). Electronic applications accepted. *Expenses:* $8,370 full-time tuition plus $176 fees per year; $465 per credit hour part-time tuition. *Financial support:* Research assistantships, scholarships/grants, tuition waivers, and unspecified assistantships available. Support available to part-time students. Financial award application deadline: 3/1; financial award applicants required to submit FAFSA. *Unit head:* Dr. Jacqueline McDowell, Dean, 706-236-1717, Fax: 706-238-5827, E-mail: jmcdowell@berry.edu. *Application contact:* Brett Kennedy, Assistant Vice President of Enrollment Management, 706-236-2215, Fax: 706-290-2178, E-mail: admissions@berry.edu. Website: http://www.berry.edu/academics/education/graduate/

Biola University, School of Education, La Mirada, CA 90639-0001. Offers curriculum and instruction (Certificate); early childhood (MA Ed, MAT); multiple subject (MAT); single subject (MAT); special education (MA Ed, MAT, Certificate). *Program availability:* Part-time, evening/weekend, online learning. *Faculty:* 16. *Students:* 67 full-time (52 women), 164 part-time (142 women); includes 97 minority (8 Black or African American, non-Hispanic/Latino; 1 American Indian or Alaska Native, non-Hispanic/Latino; 51 Asian, non-Hispanic/Latino; 30 Hispanic/Latino; 7 Two or more races, non-Hispanic/Latino), 4 international. 164 applicants, 87% accepted, 116 enrolled. In 2017, 25 master's awarded. *Entrance requirements:* For master's, CBEST, CSET, GRE (waived if cumulative GPA is 3.5 or above or if CBEST and all CSET subtests are passed). Additional exam requirements/recommendations for international students: Required—TOEFL (minimum score 100 iBT). *Application deadline:* For fall admission, 7/1 for domestic students, 6/1 for international students; for spring admission, 12/1 for domestic students; for summer admission, 5/1 for domestic students. Applications are processed on a rolling basis. Application fee: $65. Electronic applications accepted. *Financial support:* Scholarships/grants available. Support available to part-time students. Financial award applicants required to submit FAFSA. *Faculty research:* Early childhood education, elementary education, special education, curriculum development, teacher preparation. *Unit head:* Dr. June Hetzel, Dean, 562-903-4715. *Application contact:* Graduate Admissions Office, 562-903-4752, E-mail: graduate.admissions@biola.edu. Website: http://education.biola.edu/

Black Hills State University, Graduate Studies, Program in Curriculum and Instruction, Spearfish, SD 57799. Offers MS. *Program availability:* Part-time. *Entrance requirements:* Additional exam requirements/recommendations for international students: Required—TOEFL (minimum score 500 paper-based; 60 iBT).

Bloomsburg University of Pennsylvania, School of Graduate Studies, College of Education, Department of Teaching and Learning, Program in Curriculum and Instruction, Bloomsburg, PA 17815-1301. Offers M Ed, Certificate. *Accreditation:* NCATE. *Degree requirements:* For master's, thesis. *Entrance requirements:* For master's, MAT, GRE, or PRAXIS, minimum QPA of 3.0, interview. Additional exam requirements/recommendations for international students: Required—TOEFL (minimum score 550 paper-based; 79 iBT), IELTS. Electronic applications accepted. *Expenses:* Tuition, state resident: full-time $10,000; part-time $500 per credit hour. Tuition, nonresident: full-time $15,000; part-time $750 per credit hour. *Required fees:* $2484; $110.75 per credit hour. $75 per term. Tuition and fees vary according to program.

Bloomsburg University of Pennsylvania, School of Graduate Studies, College of Education, Department of Teaching and Learning, Program in Educational Leadership, Bloomsburg, PA 17815-1301. Offers college student affairs (M Ed); PreK-12 curriculum and instruction (M Ed); PreK-12 school counseling (M Ed); PreK-12 school principal (M Ed). *Degree requirements:* For master's, practicum. *Entrance requirements:* For master's, 3 letters of recommendation, resume, minimum QPA of 3.0, personal statement, interview. Additional exam requirements/recommendations for international students: Required—TOEFL, IELTS. Electronic applications accepted. *Expenses:* Tuition, state resident: full-time $10,000; part-time $500 per credit hour. Tuition, nonresident: full-time $15,000; part-time $750 per credit hour. *Required fees:* $2484; $110.75 per credit hour. $75 per term. Tuition and fees vary according to program.

Curriculum and Instruction

Bluffton University, Programs in Education, Bluffton, OH 45817. Offers intervention specialist (MA Ed); leadership (MA Ed); reading (MA Ed). *Accreditation:* NCATE. *Program availability:* Part-time, 100% online, blended/hybrid learning, videoconference. *Faculty:* 2 full-time (1 woman), 1 part-time/adjunct (0 women). *Students:* 7 full-time (4 women), 11 part-time (10 women); includes 1 minority (Black or African American, non-Hispanic/Latino). Average age 29. 14 applicants, 64% accepted, 9 enrolled. In 2017, 7 master's awarded. *Degree requirements:* For master's, action research project, public presentation. *Entrance requirements:* For master's, PRAXIS I, bachelor's degree, minimum GPA of 3.0. Additional exam requirements/recommendations for international students: Required—TOEFL. *Application deadline:* For fall admission, 8/15 priority date for domestic students, 6/15 priority date for international students; for spring admission, 12/15 priority date for domestic students, 9/15 priority date for international students. Applications are processed on a rolling basis. Electronic applications accepted. *Expenses:* $456 per credit hour tuition, $50 per semester technology fee ($100 for more than 6 hours). *Financial support:* In 2017–18, 2 students received support. Unspecified assistantships available. Financial award application deadline: 9/15; financial award applicants required to submit FAFSA. *Unit head:* Dr. Amy K. Mullins, Director of Graduate Programs in Education, 419-358-3457, E-mail: mullinsa@bluffton.edu. *Application contact:* Nancey Schortgen, Program Representative, 419-358-3202, Fax: 419-358-3399, E-mail: schortgenn@bluffton.edu.
Website: http://www.bluffton.edu/grad/

Bob Jones University, Graduate Programs, Greenville, SC 29614. Offers accountancy (MS); Bible (MA); Bible translation (MA); Biblical studies (Certificate); broadcast management (MS); business administration (MBA); church history (MA, PhD); church ministries (MA); church music (MM); cinema and video production (MA); counseling (MS); curriculum and instruction (Ed D); divinity (M Div); dramatic production (MA); educational leadership (MS, Ed D, Ed S); elementary education (M Ed, MAT); English (M Ed, MA, MAT); fine arts (MA); graphic design (MA); history (M Ed, MA); illustration (MA); interpretative speech (MA); mathematics (M Ed, MAT); medical missions (Certificate); ministry (MM, D Min); multi-categorical special education (M Ed, MAT); music (M Ed); New Testament interpretation (PhD); Old Testament interpretation (PhD); orchestral instrument performance (MM); organ performance (MM); pastoral studies (MA); personnel services (MS, Ed S); piano pedagogy (MM); piano performance (MM); platform arts (MA); radio and television broadcasting (MS); rhetoric and public address (MA); secondary education (M Ed); studio art (MA); teaching Bible (MA); theology (MA, PhD); voice performance (MM); youth ministries (MA); M Div/MA.

Boise State University, College of Education, Department of Curriculum, Instruction and Foundational Studies, Boise, ID 83725-0399. Offers curriculum and instruction (MA Ed, Ed D); educational leadership (M Ed); executive educational leadership (Ed S). *Accreditation:* NCATE. *Program availability:* Part-time. *Faculty:* 36. *Students:* 24 full-time (18 women), 180 part-time (113 women); includes 19 minority (1 Black or African American, non-Hispanic/Latino; 3 American Indian or Alaska Native, non-Hispanic/Latino; 3 Asian, non-Hispanic/Latino; 12 Hispanic/Latino), 6 international. Average age 36. 79 applicants, 67% accepted, 35 enrolled. In 2017, 36 master's, 6 other advanced degrees awarded. *Degree requirements:* For master's, thesis optional. *Entrance requirements:* For master's, minimum GPA of 3.0. Additional exam requirements/recommendations for international students: Required—TOEFL (minimum score 550 paper-based; 80 iBT), IELTS (minimum score 6). *Application deadline:* For fall admission, 3/1 for domestic and international students; for spring admission, 10/15 for domestic students, 10/1 for international students. Application fee: $65 ($95 for international students). Electronic applications accepted. *Expenses:* Tuition, state resident: full-time $6471; part-time $390 per credit. Tuition, nonresident: full-time $21,787; part-time $685 per credit. *Required fees:* $2283; $100 per term. Part-time tuition and fees vary according to course load and program. *Financial support:* Scholarships/grants and unspecified assistantships available. Financial award application deadline: 3/1; financial award applicants required to submit FAFSA. *Unit head:* Dr. Kathleen Budge, Department Chair, 208-426-3758. *Application contact:* Dr. Esther Enright, Program Coordinator, 208-426-1693, E-mail: estherenright@boisestate.edu.
Website: http://education.boisestate.edu/cifs/

Boston College, Lynch School of Education, Program in Curriculum and Instruction, Chestnut Hill, MA 02467-3800. Offers M Ed, PhD, CAES, JD/M Ed. *Program availability:* Part-time, evening/weekend. *Students:* 77 full-time (64 women), 70 part-time (53 women); includes 23 minority (6 Black or African American, non-Hispanic/Latino; 3 Asian, non-Hispanic/Latino; 13 Hispanic/Latino; 1 Two or more races, non-Hispanic/Latino), 27 international. Average age 28. 165 applicants, 68% accepted, 58 enrolled. In 2017, 47 master's, 12 doctorates awarded. Terminal master's awarded for partial completion of doctoral program. *Degree requirements:* For master's and CAES, comprehensive exam; for doctorate, comprehensive exam, thesis/dissertation. *Entrance requirements:* For master's and CAES, GRE General Test or MAT; for doctorate, GRE General Test. Additional exam requirements/recommendations for international students: Required—TOEFL (minimum score 550 paper-based; 100 iBT). *Application deadline:* For fall admission, 12/1 priority date for domestic and international students; for spring admission, 11/1 priority date for domestic and international students. Application fee: $65. Electronic applications accepted. *Financial support:* Federal Work-Study, scholarships/grants, and tuition waivers (partial) available. Support available to part-time students. Financial award applicants required to submit FAFSA. *Unit head:* Dr. Susan Bruce, Chairperson, 617-552-4214, Fax: 617-552-0398. *Application contact:* Kimberly Rose, Graduate Admission Assistant, 617-552-4214, Fax: 617-552-0398, E-mail: roseki@bc.edu.

Bowling Green State University, Graduate College, College of Education and Human Development, School of Teaching and Learning, Program in Curriculum and Teaching, Bowling Green, OH 43403. Offers M Ed. *Program availability:* Part-time, evening/weekend. *Degree requirements:* For master's, thesis or alternative. *Entrance requirements:* For master's, GRE General Test or PRAXIS. Additional exam requirements/recommendations for international students: Required—TOEFL. Electronic applications accepted. *Faculty research:* Cognitive development in cultural context, sociocultural and activity theory, philosophy in education, performance assessment.

Bradley University, The Graduate School, College of Education and Health Sciences, Department of Teacher Education, Peoria, IL 61625-0002. Offers curriculum and instruction (MA). *Accreditation:* NCATE. *Program availability:* Part-time, evening/weekend. *Degree requirements:* For master's, comprehensive exam, thesis optional. *Entrance requirements:* For master's, GRE General Test or MAT, 2 letters of recommendation. Additional exam requirements/recommendations for international students: Required—TOEFL (minimum score 550 paper-based; 79 iBT), IELTS (minimum score 6.5). Electronic applications accepted.

Brandman University, School of Education, Irvine, CA 92618. Offers curriculum and instruction (MAE); educational administration (MAE); educational leadership (MAE); educational leadership and administration (MA); elementary education (MAT); instructional technology: teaching the 21st century learner (MAE); leadership in early childhood education (MAE); organizational leadership (Ed D); school counseling (MA); secondary education (MAT); special education (MA); teaching and learning (MAE).

Expenses: Tuition: Part-time $640 per credit hour. Tuition and fees vary according to degree level and program. *Unit head:* Dr. Christine G. Zeppos, Dean, 949-341-9948, E-mail: zeppos@brandman.edu. *Application contact:* Dr. Christine G. Zeppos, Dean, 949-341-9948, E-mail: zeppos@brandman.edu.
Website: https://www.brandman.edu/academic-programs/education

Brandon University, Faculty of Education, Brandon, MB R7A 6A9, Canada. Offers curriculum and instruction (M Ed, Diploma); educational administration (M Ed, Diploma); guidance and counseling (M Ed, Diploma); special education (M Ed, Diploma). *Degree requirements:* For master's, thesis. *Entrance requirements:* For master's, minimum GPA of 3.0, teaching certificate or equivalent. Additional exam requirements/recommendations for international students: Required—TOEFL. *Faculty research:* Comparative education, environmental studies, parent/school council.

Brescia University, Program in Teacher Leadership, Owensboro, KY 42301-3023. Offers MSTL. *Program availability:* Part-time, evening/weekend. *Degree requirements:* For master's, action research project. *Entrance requirements:* For master's, PRAXIS II, NTE, or GRE, interview, minimum GPA of 2.75, BA or BS, two letters of reference, professional resume. Electronic applications accepted.

Buena Vista University, School of Education, Storm Lake, IA 50588. Offers curriculum and instruction (M Ed), including effective teaching, TESL; school guidance and counseling (MS Ed). Program offered in summer only. *Program availability:* Part-time, evening/weekend, online learning. *Degree requirements:* For master's, thesis, fieldwork/practicum, capstone portfolio. *Entrance requirements:* For master's, Analytical Writing Assessment (in-house), minimum undergraduate GPA of 2.75. Electronic applications accepted. *Faculty research:* Reading, curriculum, educational psychology, special education.

Cabrini University, Academic Affairs, Radnor, PA 19087. Offers accounting (M Acc); autism spectrum disorder (M Ed); biological sciences (MS), including civic leadership; criminology and criminal justice (MA); curriculum, instruction, and assessment (M Ed); educational leadership (M Ed, Ed D), including curriculum and instructional leadership (Ed D), preK-12 leadership (Ed D); English as a second language (M Ed); organizational leadership (DBA, PhD); preK to 4 (M Ed); reading specialist (M Ed); secondary education (M Ed), including biology, chemistry, English, English/communication, mathematics, social studies; special education grades 7-12 (M Ed); special education preK-8 (M Ed); teaching and learning (M Ed). *Program availability:* Part-time, evening/weekend. *Faculty:* 23 full-time (17 women), 46 part-time/adjunct (38 women). *Students:* 60 full-time (35 women), 559 part-time (435 women); includes 93 minority (66 Black or African American, non-Hispanic/Latino; 1 American Indian or Alaska Native, non-Hispanic/Latino; 8 Asian, non-Hispanic/Latino; 15 Hispanic/Latino; 3 Two or more races, non-Hispanic/Latino), 4 international. Average age 33. 290 applicants, 82% accepted, 154 enrolled. In 2017, 283 master's awarded. *Degree requirements:* For master's, comprehensive exam (for some programs), thesis (for some programs); for doctorate, comprehensive exam (for some programs), thesis/dissertation. *Entrance requirements:* For master's, professional resume, personal statement, two recommendations, official transcripts; for doctorate, official transcripts, minimum master's GPA of 3.0, two recommendations, interview with admissions committee. Additional exam requirements/recommendations for international students: Required—TOEFL (minimum score 80 iBT). *Application deadline:* For fall admission, 8/26 for domestic students, 8/1 for international students; for winter admission, 1/13 for domestic students, 12/20 for international students; for spring admission, 1/13 for domestic students, 12/20 for international students; for summer admission, 5/20 for domestic students, 4/30 for international students. Applications are processed on a rolling basis. Application fee: $50. Electronic applications accepted. Application fee is waived when completed online. *Expenses:* Contact institution. *Financial support:* In 2017–18, 1,459 students received support. Tuition waivers and unspecified assistantships available. Financial award application deadline: 5/1; financial award applicants required to submit FAFSA. *Unit head:* Dr. Maliha Zaman, 610-902-8502, Fax: 610-902-8797, E-mail: msz37@cabrini.edu. *Application contact:* Diane Greenwood, Director of Graduate Admissions, 610-902-8291, E-mail: diane.l.greenwood@cabrini.edu.
Website: http://cabrini.edu/graduate

Caldwell University, School of Education, Caldwell, NJ 07006-6195. Offers curriculum and instruction (MA); education leadership (Ed D); educational administration (MA); elementary, secondary or preschool endorsement, special ed, ESL (Postbaccalaureate Certificate); learning disabilities teacher-consultant (Post-Master's Certificate); literacy instruction (MA); principal (Post-Master's Certificate); reading specialist (Post-Master's Certificate); special education (MA), including special education, teaching of students with disabilities, teaching of students with disabilities and learning disabilities teacher-consultant; superintendent (Post-Master's Certificate); supervisor (Post-Master's Certificate). *Program availability:* Part-time, evening/weekend. *Faculty:* 10 full-time (6 women), 21 part-time/adjunct (12 women). *Students:* 37 full-time (30 women), 225 part-time (177 women); includes 47 minority (19 Black or African American, non-Hispanic/Latino; 3 Asian, non-Hispanic/Latino; 23 Hispanic/Latino; 2 Two or more races, non-Hispanic/Latino). Average age 35. 189 applicants, 57% accepted, 85 enrolled. In 2017, 47 master's awarded. *Degree requirements:* For master's, comprehensive exam (for some programs), thesis (for some programs); for doctorate, thesis/dissertation. *Entrance requirements:* For master's, PRAXIS, 3 years of work experience, prior teaching certification; for doctorate, GRE or MAT; for other advanced degree, two letters of recommendation; interview (for some programs). Additional exam requirements/recommendations for international students: Required—TOEFL (minimum score 580 paper-based, 70 iBT), IELTS (6), or ELS Level 112 Certification of Completion. *Application deadline:* For fall admission, 6/1 for domestic students; for spring admission, 12/1 for domestic students; for summer admission, 4/1 for domestic students. Applications are processed on a rolling basis. Application fee: $50. Electronic applications accepted. *Expenses:* $950 per credit (for master's and certificate programs); $1,125 per credit (for doctoral programs). *Financial support:* Unspecified assistantships available. Financial award applicants required to submit FAFSA. *Faculty research:* Curriculum and instruction, secondary education, special education, education and technology, literacy instruction, higher education administration, education leadership. *Unit head:* Dr. Joan Moriarity, Associate Dean, 973-618-3626, E-mail: jmoriarity@caldwell.edu. *Application contact:* Tom Disch, Senior Admissions Counselor, 973-618-3544, E-mail: graduate@caldwell.edu.

California Baptist University, Program in Education, Riverside, CA 92504-3206. Offers educational leadership (MS); educational leadership for faith-based institutions (MS); educational leadership for public institutions (MS); educational technology (MS); instructional computer applications (MS); international education (MS); leadership and adult learning (MS); leadership and organizational studies (MS); online teaching and learning (MS); reading (MS); science education (MA); special education in mild/moderate disabilities (MS); special education in moderate/severe disabilities (MS); teacher leadership (MS); teaching (MS); teaching and learning (MS). *Program availability:* Part-time, evening/weekend, 100% online, blended/hybrid learning. *Faculty:* 19 full-time (11 women), 36 part-time/adjunct (22 women). *Students:* 232 full-time (182 women), 315 part-time (247 women); includes 264 minority (33 Black or African American, non-Hispanic/Latino; 4 American Indian or Alaska Native, non-Hispanic/Latino; 11 Asian, non-Hispanic/Latino; 186 Hispanic/Latino; 7 Native Hawaiian or other

Pacific Islander, non-Hispanic/Latino; 23 Two or more races, non-Hispanic/Latino). Average age 31. 217 applicants, 64% accepted, 129 enrolled. In 2017, 196 master's awarded. *Degree requirements:* For master's, comprehensive exam, project, or thesis. *Entrance requirements:* For master's, minimum undergraduate GPA of 2.75; 500-word essay; three letters of recommendation; two prerequisite courses completed with minimum C grade. Additional exam requirements/recommendations for international students: Required—TOEFL (minimum score 80 iBT). *Application deadline:* For fall admission, 8/1 priority date for domestic students, 7/1 for international students; for spring admission, 12/1 priority date for domestic students, 11/1 for international students. Applications are processed on a rolling basis. Application fee: $45. Electronic applications accepted. *Expenses:* Contact institution. *Financial support:* In 2017–18, 162 students received support. Federal Work-Study and scholarships/grants available. Financial award applicants required to submit CSS PROFILE or FAFSA. *Faculty research:* Leadership development, complexity theory, faith and learning, special education, social and philosophical contexts of education. *Unit head:* Dr. John Shoup, Dean, School of Education, 951-343-4516, E-mail: jshoup@calbaptist.edu. *Application contact:* Gavin Andrew, Graduate Admissions Counselor, 951-552-8437, E-mail: gandrew@calbaptist.edu.
Website: http://www.calbaptist.edu/mastersined/

California Coast University, School of Education, Santa Ana, CA 92701. Offers administration (M Ed); curriculum and instruction (M Ed); educational administration (Ed D); educational psychology (Ed D); organizational leadership (Ed D). *Program availability:* Online learning.

California State Polytechnic University, Pomona, Master's Programs in Education, Pomona, CA 91768-2557. Offers curriculum and instruction (MA), including literacy studies. *Program availability:* Part-time, evening/weekend. *Students:* 19 full-time (14 women), 71 part-time (43 women); includes 58 minority (6 Black or African American, non-Hispanic/Latino; 10 Asian, non-Hispanic/Latino; 39 Hispanic/Latino; 3 Two or more races, non-Hispanic/Latino), 5 international. Average age 35. 45 applicants, 56% accepted, 13 enrolled. In 2017, 43 master's awarded. *Entrance requirements:* Additional exam requirements/recommendations for international students: Required—TOEFL (minimum score 550 paper-based). *Application deadline:* Applications are processed on a rolling basis. Application fee: $55. Electronic applications accepted. *Expenses:* Contact institution. *Financial support:* Application deadline: 3/2; applicants required to submit FAFSA. *Unit head:* Dr. Richard A. Navarro, Professor/Graduate Coordinator, 909-869-2081, Fax: 909-869-4822, E-mail: ranavarro@cpp.edu. *Application contact:* Deborah L. Brandon, Executive Director of Admissions and Enrollment Planning, 909-869-3427, Fax: 909-869-5315, E-mail: dlbrandon@cpp.edu. Website: http://www.cpp.edu/~ceis/education/masters-programs/index.shtml

California State University, Chico, Office of Graduate Studies, College of Communication and Education, School of Education, Chico, CA 95929-0722. Offers curriculum and instruction (MA); teaching English learners and special education advising patterns (MA), including special education, teaching English learners. *Program availability:* Part-time. *Degree requirements:* For master's, thesis or project and comprehensive exam. *Entrance requirements:* For master's, writing assessment, two letters of recommendation, statement of purpose. Additional exam requirements/recommendations for international students: Required—TOEFL (minimum score 550 paper-based; 80 iBT), IELTS (minimum score 6.5), PTE (minimum score 59). Electronic applications accepted.

California State University, Fresno, Division of Research and Graduate Studies, Kremen School of Education and Human Development, Department of Curriculum and Instruction, Fresno, CA 93740-8027. Offers education (MA), including curriculum and instruction. *Accreditation:* NCATE. *Program availability:* Part-time, evening/weekend. *Degree requirements:* For master's, thesis or alternative. *Entrance requirements:* For master's, GRE General Test, MAT, minimum GPA of 2.75. Additional exam requirements/recommendations for international students: Required—TOEFL. Electronic applications accepted. *Faculty research:* Teacher excellence, teacher quality improvement, online assessment.

California State University, Los Angeles, Graduate Studies, Charter College of Education, Division of Curriculum and Instruction, Los Angeles, CA 90032-8530. Offers elementary teaching (MA). *Program availability:* Part-time, evening/weekend. *Entrance requirements:* For master's, minimum GPA of 2.75 in last 90 units of course work, teaching certificate. Additional exam requirements/recommendations for international students: Required—TOEFL (minimum score 500 paper-based). Electronic applications accepted. *Faculty research:* Media, language arts, mathematics, computers, drug-free schools.

California State University, Northridge, Graduate Studies, Michael D. Eisner College of Education, Department of Elementary Education, Northridge, CA 91330. Offers curriculum and instruction (MA); language and literacy (MA); multilingual/multicultural education (MA). *Accreditation:* NCATE. *Program availability:* Part-time, evening/weekend. *Students:* 3 full-time (all women), 62 part-time (56 women); includes 37 minority (7 Asian, non-Hispanic/Latino; 26 Hispanic/Latino; 4 Two or more races, non-Hispanic/Latino). Average age 30. 42 applicants, 50% accepted, 19 enrolled. In 2017, 103 master's awarded. *Degree requirements:* For master's, comprehensive exam. *Entrance requirements:* For master's, GRE General Test or minimum GPA of 3.0. Additional exam requirements/recommendations for international students: Required—TOEFL. *Application deadline:* For fall admission, 11/30 for domestic students. Application fee: $55. *Financial support:* Federal Work-Study available. Financial award application deadline: 3/1. *Unit head:* Dr. Joyce Burstein, Chair, 818-677-2621. Website: http://www.csun.edu/eisner-education/elementary-education

California State University, Sacramento, College of Education, Graduate and Professional Studies in Education, Sacramento, CA 95819. Offers behavioral science and gender equity (MA); child development (MA); counseling (MS); curriculum and instruction (MA); education (Ed D), including K-12 and community college; education leadership and policy studies (MA), including higher education, PreK-12; education specialist (Ed S), including school psychology; educational technology (MA); language and literacy (MA); multicultural education (MA); school psychology (MA); special education (MA); workforce development advocacy (MA). *Program availability:* Part-time, evening/weekend, blended/hybrid learning. *Students:* 381 full-time (294 women), 135 part-time (101 women); includes 296 minority (44 Black or African American, non-Hispanic/Latino; 1 American Indian or Alaska Native, non-Hispanic/Latino; 94 Asian, non-Hispanic/Latino; 153 Hispanic/Latino; 4 Native Hawaiian or other Pacific Islander, non-Hispanic/Latino), 3 international. Average age 32. 553 applicants, 53% accepted, 292 enrolled. In 2017, 147 master's, 13 doctorates, 10 other advanced degrees awarded. *Degree requirements:* For master's, thesis or project; writing proficiency exam; for doctorate, thesis/dissertation. *Entrance requirements:* For master's and doctorate, GRE. Additional exam requirements/recommendations for international students: Required—TOEFL (minimum score 550 paper-based; 80 iBT); Recommended—IELTS (minimum score 7), TSE. *Application deadline:* For fall admission, 2/15 for domestic students, 1/15 for international students. Applications are processed on a rolling basis. Application fee: $55. Electronic applications accepted. *Expenses:* Contact institution. *Financial support:* Career-related internships or fieldwork, Federal Work-Study, and scholarships/grants available. Support available to part-time students. Financial award

application deadline: 3/1; financial award applicants required to submit FAFSA. *Unit head:* Dr. Elizabeth Liles, Chair, 916-278-5942, E-mail: coe@csus.edu. *Application contact:* Jose Martinez, Graduate Admissions Supervisor, 916-278-7871, E-mail: martinj@skymail.csus.edu.
Website: http://www.csus.edu/coe/academics/graduate/index.html

California State University, Stanislaus, College of Education, Kinesiology and Social Work, MA Program in Education, Turlock, CA 95382. Offers curriculum and instruction (MA), including education technology, elementary education, multilingual education, physical education, reading, secondary education, special education; school administration (MA); school counseling (MA). *Program availability:* Part-time, evening/weekend. *Degree requirements:* For master's, comprehensive exam (for some programs), thesis (for some programs). *Entrance requirements:* For master's, MAT, GRE, or CBEST (varies by concentration), 3 letters of recommendation, personal statement. Additional exam requirements/recommendations for international students: Required—TOEFL (minimum score 550 paper-based). Electronic applications accepted. *Faculty research:* Children's perspectives on historical events, method elementary schools dual language education, K-12 reading programs.

Calvary University, Graduate School and Seminary, Kansas City, MO 64147. Offers Bible and theology (MS); Biblical counseling (MA); education (MS), including administration and leadership, Christian education, curriculum and instruction, elementary education; organizational development (MS); pastoral studies (M Div); worship arts (MS). *Program availability:* Part-time, evening/weekend. *Faculty:* 6 full-time (2 women), 2 part-time/adjunct (1 woman). *Students:* 11 full-time (3 women), 29 part-time (15 women); includes 12 minority (4 Black or African American, non-Hispanic/Latino; 1 American Indian or Alaska Native, non-Hispanic/Latino; 6 Asian, non-Hispanic/Latino; 1 Native Hawaiian or other Pacific Islander, non-Hispanic/Latino). Average age 39. *Degree requirements:* For master's, variable foreign language requirement, comprehensive exam, thesis or alternative. *Entrance requirements:* For master's, minimum GPA of 2.5, BA or BS, doctrine agreement. Additional exam requirements/recommendations for international students: Required—TOEFL (minimum score 550 paper-based). *Application deadline:* Applications are processed on a rolling basis. Application fee: $0. Electronic applications accepted. *Expenses:* Contact institution. *Financial support:* Scholarships/grants available. Financial award application deadline: 11/5; financial award applicants required to submit FAFSA. *Unit head:* Dr. Thomas Baurain, Director of Seminary, 816-322-0110 Ext. 1502, Fax: 816-331-4474, E-mail: thomas.baurain@calvary.edu. *Application contact:* Ann Rogers, Admissions Office Assistant, 800-326-3960 Ext. 1321, Fax: 816-331-4474, E-mail: admissions@calvary.edu.
Website: http://www.calvary.edu

Calvin College, Graduate Programs in Education, Grand Rapids, MI 49546-4388. Offers curriculum and instruction (M Ed). *Accreditation:* TEAC. *Program availability:* Part-time. *Degree requirements:* For master's, thesis or seminar. *Entrance requirements:* For master's, teaching certificate. Additional exam requirements/recommendations for international students: Required—TOEFL (minimum score 550 paper-based; 80 iBT). Electronic applications accepted. *Expenses:* Contact institution. *Faculty research:* Literacy, racialized gender and gendered identity, teacher learning, learning disabilities identification, leadership.

Cambridge College, School of Education, Boston, MA 02129. Offers autism specialist (M Ed); autism/behavior analyst (M Ed); behavior analyst (Post-Master's Certificate); behavioral management (M Ed); early childhood teacher (M Ed); education specialist in curriculum and instruction (CAGS); educational leadership (Ed D); elementary teacher (M Ed); English as a second language (M Ed, Certificate); general science (M Ed); health education (Post-Master's Certificate); health/family and consumer sciences (M Ed); history (M Ed); individualized (M Ed); information technology literacy (M Ed); instructional technology (M Ed); interdisciplinary studies (M Ed); library teacher (M Ed); literacy education (M Ed); mathematics (M Ed); mathematics specialist (Certificate); middle school mathematics and science (M Ed); school administration (M Ed, CAGS); school guidance counselor (M Ed); school nurse education (M Ed); school social worker/school adjustment counselor (M Ed); special education administrator (CAGS); special education/moderate disabilities (M Ed); teaching skills and methodologies (M Ed). *Program availability:* Part-time, evening/weekend, online learning. *Degree requirements:* For master's, thesis, internship/practicum (licensure program only); for doctorate, thesis/dissertation; for other advanced degree, thesis. *Entrance requirements:* For master's, interview, resume, documentation of licensure, 2 professional references; for doctorate, official transcripts, interview, resume, documentation of licensure (if any), written personal statement/essay, portfolio of scholarly and professional work, qualifying assessment, 2 professional references, health insurance, immunizations form; for other advanced degree, official transcripts, interview, resume, documentation of licensure (if any), written personal statement/essay, 2 professional references, health insurance, immunizations form. Additional exam requirements/recommendations for international students: Required—TOEFL (minimum score 550 paper-based; 79 iBT), Michigan English Language Assessment Battery (minimum score 85); Recommended—IELTS (minimum score 6). Electronic applications accepted. *Expenses:* Contact institution. *Faculty research:* Adult education, accelerated learning, mathematics education, brain compatible learning, special education and law.

Capella University, School of Education, Doctoral Programs in Education, Minneapolis, MN 55402. Offers curriculum and instruction (PhD); educational leadership and management (Ed D); instructional design for online learning (PhD); K-12 studies in education (PhD); leadership for higher education (PhD); leadership in educational administration (PhD); postsecondary and adult education (PhD); professional studies in education (PhD); reading and literacy (Ed D); special education leadership (PhD); training and performance improvement (PhD).

Capella University, School of Education, Master's Programs in Education, Minneapolis, MN 55402. Offers adult education (MS); curriculum and instruction (MS); early childhood education (MS); enrollment management (MS); higher education leadership and management (MS); instructional design for online learning (MS); integrative studies (MS); K-12 studies in education (MS); leadership in educational administration (MS); reading and literacy (MS); special education teaching (MS).

Caribbean University, Graduate School, Bayamón, PR 00960-0493. Offers administration and supervision (MA Ed); criminal justice (MA); curriculum and instruction (MA Ed, PhD), including elementary education (MA Ed), English education (MA Ed), history education (MA Ed), mathematics education (MA Ed), primary education (MA Ed), science education (MA Ed), Spanish education (MA Ed); educational technology in instructional systems (MA Ed); gerontology (MSN); human resources (MBA); museology, archiving and art history (MA Ed); neonatal pediatrics (MSN); physical education (MA Ed); special education (MA Ed). *Entrance requirements:* For master's, interview, minimum GPA of 2.5.

Carlow University, College of Learning and Innovation, Program in Curriculum and Instruction, Pittsburgh, PA 15213-3165. Offers autism (M Ed); early childhood leadership (M Ed); online learning instructional design (M Ed); STEM (M Ed). *Program availability:* Part-time, evening/weekend. *Entrance requirements:* For master's, personal essay; resume or curriculum vitae; two recommendations; official transcripts; interview;

Curriculum and Instruction

minimum undergraduate GPA of 3.0. Additional exam requirements/recommendations for international students: Required—TOEFL (minimum score 550 paper-based). *Application deadline:* Applications are processed on a rolling basis. Electronic applications accepted. *Expenses: Tuition:* Full-time $12,103; part-time $825 per credit hour. Tuition and fees vary according to program. *Financial support:* Application deadline: 4/1; applicants required to submit FAFSA. *Unit head:* Dr. Keeley Baronak, Chair, 412-578-6135, Fax: 412-578-6326, E-mail: kobaronak@carlow.edu. *Application contact:* 412-578-6059, Fax: 412-578-6321, E-mail: gradstudies@carlow.edu. Website: http://www.carlow.edu/Curriculum_and_Instruction_MEd.aspx

Carson-Newman University, Graduate Program in Education, Jefferson City, TN 37760. Offers curriculum and instruction (M Ed); educational leadership (M Ed); elementary education (MAT); school counseling (MS); secondary education (MAT); teaching English as a second language (MATESL). *Accreditation:* NCATE. *Program availability:* Part-time, evening/weekend, 100% online, blended/hybrid learning. *Faculty:* 20 full-time (11 women), 16 part-time/adjunct (13 women). *Students:* 63 full-time (37 women), 488 part-time (362 women); includes 60 minority (46 Black or African American, non-Hispanic/Latino; 2 American Indian or Alaska Native, non-Hispanic/Latino; 1 Asian, non-Hispanic/Latino; 5 Hispanic/Latino; 1 Native Hawaiian or other Pacific Islander, non-Hispanic/Latino; 5 Two or more races, non-Hispanic/Latino), 29 international. Average age 35. 204 applicants, 100% accepted, 188 enrolled. In 2017, 211 master's awarded. *Degree requirements:* For master's, thesis or alternative. *Entrance requirements:* For master's, PRAXIS II or GRE with minimum score of 290 on the verbal and quantitative components (for MAT), minimum GPA of 3.0 in major, 2.5 overall. Additional exam requirements/recommendations for international students: Recommended—TOEFL (minimum score 79 iBT), IELTS (minimum score 6.5), TSE (minimum score 53). *Application deadline:* For fall admission, 7/15 priority date for domestic students. Applications are processed on a rolling basis. Application fee: $50. *Expenses: Tuition:* Full-time $10,516; part-time $478 per credit hour. *Required fees:* $240; $120 per semester. One-time fee: $150. *Financial support:* Federal Work-Study and unspecified assistantships available. Financial award applicants required to submit FAFSA. *Unit head:* Dr. Kim Hawkins, Chair, 865-471-3314, E-mail: khawkins@cn.edu. *Application contact:* Nilma Stewart, Graduate Admissions and Services Adviser, 865-471-3230, Fax: 865-471-3875, E-mail: adults@cn.edu. Website: http://www.cn.edu/adult-graduate-studies

Castleton University, Division of Graduate Studies, Department of Education, Program in Curriculum and Instruction, Castleton, VT 05735. Offers MA Ed. *Program availability:* Part-time, evening/weekend. *Degree requirements:* For master's, thesis or alternative. *Entrance requirements:* For master's, GRE General Test, MAT, interview, minimum undergraduate GPA of 3.0.

Central Michigan University, Central Michigan University Global Campus, Program in Education, Mount Pleasant, MI 48859. Offers college teaching (Graduate Certificate); community college (MA); curriculum and instruction (MA); educational technology (MA, DET); reading and literacy K-12 (MA); school principalship (MA), including charter school leadership; training and development (MA). *Accreditation:* TEAC. *Program availability:* Part-time, evening/weekend. *Entrance requirements:* For master's, minimum GPA of 2.7 in major. Additional exam requirements/recommendations for international students: Required—TOEFL. Electronic applications accepted.

Central Michigan University, College of Graduate Studies, College of Education and Human Services, Department of Educational Leadership, Mount Pleasant, MI 48859. Offers educational leadership (Ed D), including educational technology (Ed D, Ed S), higher education leadership, K-12 curriculum, K-12 leadership; general educational administration (Ed S), including administrative leadership K-12, educational technology (Ed D, Ed S), higher education administration, instructional leadership K-12; school principalship (MA), including charter school leadership, site-based leadership; student affairs administration (MA); teacher leadership (MA). *Program availability:* Part-time, evening/weekend. *Degree requirements:* For master's and Ed S, thesis or alternative; for doctorate, thesis/dissertation. *Entrance requirements:* For doctorate, GRE or MAT, master's degree, minimum GPA of 3.5, 3 years of professional education experience. Electronic applications accepted. *Faculty research:* Elementary administration, secondary administration, student achievement, in-service training, internships in administration.

Central Washington University, School of Graduate Studies and Research, College of Education and Professional Studies, Department of Curriculum, Supervision, and Educational Leadership, Program in Master Teacher, Ellensburg, WA 98926. Offers M Ed. *Program availability:* Part-time. *Degree requirements:* For master's, comprehensive exam (for some programs), thesis or alternative. *Entrance requirements:* For master's, minimum GPA of 3.0, 1 year of contracted teaching experience. Additional exam requirements/recommendations for international students: Required—TOEFL (minimum score 550 paper-based; 79 iBT), IELTS (minimum score 6.5). *Application deadline:* For fall admission, 2/1 priority date for domestic students; for winter admission, 10/1 for domestic students; for spring admission, 1/1 for domestic students. Applications are processed on a rolling basis. Application fee: $50. Electronic applications accepted. *Financial support:* Application deadline: 3/1; applicants required to submit FAFSA. *Unit head:* Dr. Denise Shaw, Graduate Coordinator, 509-963-2259, E-mail: denise.shaw@cwu.edu. *Application contact:* Justine Eason, Admissions Program Coordinator, 509-963-3103, Fax: 509-963-1799, E-mail: masters@cwu.edu. Website: http://www.cwu.edu/~education/master.html

Chapman University, Donna Ford Attallah College of Educational Studies, Orange, CA 92866. Offers counseling (MA), including school counseling (MA, Credential); curriculum and instruction (MA), including elementary education, secondary education; education (PhD), including cultural and curricular studies, disability studies, leadership studies, school psychology (PhD, Credential); educational psychology (MA); leadership development (MA); multiple subjects (Credential), including Spanish/English bilingual; pupil personnel services (Credential), including school counseling (MA, Credential), school psychology (PhD, Credential); school psychology (Ed S); single subject (Credential); special education (MA, Credential), including mild/moderate (Credential), moderate/severe (Credential); teaching (MA), including elementary education, secondary education, secondary music education. *Accreditation:* TEAC. *Program availability:* Part-time, evening/weekend. *Faculty:* 32 full-time (18 women), 37 part-time/adjunct (26 women). *Students:* 170 full-time (140 women), 180 part-time (129 women); includes 164 minority (6 Black or African American, non-Hispanic/Latino; 38 Asian, non-Hispanic/Latino; 101 Hispanic/Latino; 1 Native Hawaiian or other Pacific Islander, non-Hispanic/Latino; 18 Two or more races, non-Hispanic/Latino), 10 international. Average age 28. 143 applicants, 63% accepted, 64 enrolled. In 2017, 126 master's, 18 doctorates awarded. *Application deadline:* Applications are processed on a rolling basis. Application fee: $60. Electronic applications accepted. *Expenses:* Contact institution. *Financial support:* Fellowships and scholarships/grants available. Financial award application deadline: 3/2; financial award applicants required to submit FAFSA. *Unit head:* Dr. Margaret Grogan, Dean, 714-516-5968, E-mail: grogan@chapman.edu. *Application contact:* Shannon McCance, Graduate Admission Counselor, 714-516-5236, E-mail: smccance@chapman.edu. Website: http://www.chapman.edu/CES/

City University of Seattle, Graduate Division, Albright School of Education, Seattle, WA 98121. Offers administrator certification (Certificate); curriculum and instruction (M Ed); elementary education (MIT); guidance and counseling (M Ed); leadership (M Ed); reading and literacy (M Ed); school counseling (M Ed); special education (MIT); superintendent certification (Certificate). *Program availability:* Part-time, evening/weekend, online learning. *Degree requirements:* For master's, comprehensive exam (for some programs), thesis (for some programs). *Entrance requirements:* For master's, baccalaureate degree or equivalent from an accredited or otherwise recognized institution. Additional exam requirements/recommendations for international students: Required—TOEFL (minimum score 567 paper-based; 87 iBT); Recommended—IELTS. Electronic applications accepted. *Expenses:* Contact institution.

Clarion University of Pennsylvania, College of Arts, Education and Sciences, Master of Education Program, Clarion, PA 16214. Offers curriculum and instruction (M Ed); early childhood (M Ed); math education (M Ed); reading (M Ed); science education (M Ed); special education (M Ed); technology (M Ed). *Accreditation:* NCATE. *Program availability:* Part-time, evening/weekend, online only, 100% online, blended/hybrid learning. *Faculty:* 6 full-time (3 women). *Students:* 11 full-time (all women), 101 part-time (82 women); includes 4 minority (2 Black or African American, non-Hispanic/Latino; 1 Hispanic/Latino; 1 Two or more races, non-Hispanic/Latino). Average age 30. 80 applicants, 98% accepted, 33 enrolled. In 2017, 52 master's awarded. *Degree requirements:* For master's, comprehensive exam, thesis, or portfolio. *Entrance requirements:* For master's, minimum QPA of 3.0. Additional exam requirements/recommendations for international students: Required—TOEFL (minimum score 550 paper-based, 80 iBT) or IELTS (7). *Application deadline:* For fall admission, 8/15 priority date for domestic students, 7/15 priority date for international students; for winter admission, 11/1 priority date for domestic students; for spring admission, 1/7 priority date for domestic students, 11/15 priority date for international students; for summer admission, 4/1 priority date for domestic students. Applications are processed on a rolling basis. Application fee: $40. Electronic applications accepted. *Expenses:* $655.05 per credit. *Financial support:* Career-related internships or fieldwork and scholarships/grants available. Support available to part-time students. Financial award application deadline: 3/1; financial award applicants required to submit FAFSA. *Unit head:* Dr. John McCullough, Chair, Department of Education, 814-393-2404, Fax: 814-393-2446, E-mail: gradstudies@clarion.edu. *Application contact:* Dana Bearer, Associate Director for Transfer, Adult, and Graduate Programs, 814-393-2337, Fax: 814-393-2722, E-mail: gradstudies@clarion.edu.

Clark Atlanta University, School of Education, Department of Curriculum and Instruction, Atlanta, GA 30314. Offers special education general curriculum (MA); teaching math and science (MAT). *Program availability:* Part-time. *Faculty:* 5 full-time (4 women), 6 part-time/adjunct (2 women). *Students:* 8 full-time (2 women), 4 part-time (1 woman); includes 6 minority (all Black or African American, non-Hispanic/Latino), 5 international. Average age 34. 10 applicants, 90% accepted, 3 enrolled. In 2017, 1 master's awarded. *Degree requirements:* For master's, one foreign language, comprehensive exam. *Entrance requirements:* For master's, GRE General Test, minimum undergraduate GPA of 2.6. Additional exam requirements/recommendations for international students: Required—TOEFL (minimum score 500 paper-based; 61 iBT). *Application deadline:* For fall admission, 4/1 for domestic and international students; for spring admission, 11/1 for domestic and international students. Applications are processed on a rolling basis. Application fee: $40 ($55 for international students). *Financial support:* Career-related internships or fieldwork, Federal Work-Study, scholarships/grants, and unspecified assistantships available. Support available to part-time students. Financial award application deadline: 4/30; financial award applicants required to submit FAFSA. *Unit head:* Dr. James Young, Chairperson, 404-880-6079, E-mail: jyoung@cau.edu. Website: http://www.cau.edu/school-of-education/Dept-of-Curriculum-and-Instruction/index.html

Clarks Summit University, Online Master's Programs, South Abington Township, PA 18411. Offers Bible (MA); counseling (MA, MS); curriculum and instruction (M Ed); educational administration (M Ed); literature (MA); organizational leadership (MA). *Program availability:* Part-time, evening/weekend, online learning. *Entrance requirements:* Additional exam requirements/recommendations for international students: Required—TOEFL (minimum score 500 paper-based). *Application deadline:* Applications are processed on a rolling basis. Application fee: $30. *Financial support:* Institutionally sponsored loans and scholarships/grants available. Financial award application deadline: 8/20; financial award applicants required to submit FAFSA. *Unit head:* Dr. James Lytle, President, 570-586-2400 Ext. 9222, Fax: 570-586-1753. *Application contact:* Drew Whipple, Vice President for Enrollment Management, 570-585-9370, Fax: 570-585-9299, E-mail: awhipple@clarkssummitu.edu. Website: https://www.clarkssummitu.edu/online-masters-degrees/

Clemson University, Graduate School, College of Education, Department of Teaching and Learning, Clemson, SC 29634. Offers curriculum and instruction (PhD); middle level education (MAT); secondary math and science (MAT); STEAM education (Certificate); teaching and learning (M Ed). *Program availability:* Part-time, evening/weekend, 100% online. *Faculty:* 21 full-time (17 women). *Students:* 41 full-time (27 women), 94 part-time (78 women); includes 16 minority (8 Black or African American, non-Hispanic/Latino; 6 Hispanic/Latino; 1 Native Hawaiian or other Pacific Islander, non-Hispanic/Latino; 1 Two or more races, non-Hispanic/Latino), 3 international. Average age 29. 65 applicants, 62% accepted, 33 enrolled. In 2017, 74 master's awarded. *Degree requirements:* For master's, comprehensive exam; for doctorate, comprehensive exam, thesis/dissertation. *Entrance requirements:* For master's, doctorate, and Certificate, GRE General Test, unofficial transcripts, letters of recommendation. Additional exam requirements/recommendations for international students: Required—TOEFL (minimum score 540 paper-based; 80 iBT), IELTS (minimum score 7), PTE (minimum score 45). *Application deadline:* For fall admission, 4/15 for domestic and international students. Applications are processed on a rolling basis. Application fee: $80 ($90 for international students). Electronic applications accepted. *Expenses:* $5,767 per semester full-time resident, $10,918 per semester full-time non-resident, $656 per credit hour part-time resident, $1,310 per credit hour part-time non-resident, $915 per credit hour online; other fees may apply per session. *Financial support:* In 2017–18, 8 students received support, including 2 fellowships with partial tuition reimbursements available (averaging $3,500 per year), 1 research assistantship with partial tuition reimbursement available (averaging $18,000 per year), 5 teaching assistantships with partial tuition reimbursements available (averaging $18,000 per year); career-related internships or fieldwork also available. Financial award application deadline: 4/1. *Faculty research:* STEAM education, inquiry-based instruction, cultural hegemony and mathematics, equity and ethics, teacher effectiveness. *Total annual research expenditures:* $1.6 million. *Unit head:* Dr. Jeff Marshall, Department Chair, 864-656-2059, E-mail: marsha9@clemson.edu. *Application contact:* Alison Search, Student Services Coordinator, 864-250-8880, E-mail: alisonp@clemson.edu. Website: http://www.clemson.edu/education/departments/teaching-learning/index.html

Coker College, Graduate Programs, Hartsville, SC 29550. Offers college athletic administration (MS); criminal and social justice policy (MS); curriculum and instructional technology (M Ed); literacy studies (M Ed); management and leadership (MS). *Program*

availability: Part-time, 100% online. *Faculty:* 9 full-time (4 women), 3 part-time/adjunct (2 women). *Students:* 77 full-time (47 women), 9 part-time (4 women); includes 21 minority (15 Black or African American, non-Hispanic/Latino; 1 American Indian or Alaska Native, non-Hispanic/Latino; 1 Hispanic/Latino; 4 Two or more races, non-Hispanic/Latino), 1 international. Average age 30. *Degree requirements:* For master's, comprehensive exam, portfolio. *Entrance requirements:* For master's, GRE or GMAT, minimum overall GPA of 2.85 in bachelor's program, official transcripts, resume, three letters of recommendation, teacher licensure. *Application deadline:* Applications are processed on a rolling basis. Application fee: $25. Electronic applications accepted. *Expenses: Tuition:* Full-time $14,424; part-time $601 per credit hour. *Required fees:* $176; $176 per credit hour. Tuition and fees vary according to course load and program. *Financial support:* Unspecified assistantships available. Financial award application deadline: 6/30; financial award applicants required to submit FAFSA. *Application contact:* Lacey Rice-Serafin, Director of Graduate Programs, 843-857-4128, E-mail: lriceserafin@coker.edu.

The College at Brockport, State University of New York, School of Education, Health, and Human Services, Department of Education and Human Development, Program in Childhood Curriculum Specialist, Brockport, NY 14420-2997. Offers MS Ed. *Accreditation:* NCATE. *Program availability:* Part-time. In 2017, 2 master's awarded. *Degree requirements:* For master's, thesis or alternative. *Entrance requirements:* For master's, minimum GPA of 3.0, letters of recommendation, statement of objectives, current resume. Additional exam requirements/recommendations for international students: Required—TOEFL (minimum score 550 paper-based; 79 iBT), IELTS (minimum score 6.5). *Application deadline:* For fall admission, 3/15 priority date for domestic and international students; for spring admission, 10/15 priority date for domestic and international students. Application fee: $80. Electronic applications accepted. *Expenses:* Tuition, state resident: full-time $10,870; part-time $453 per credit hour. Tuition, nonresident: full-time $22,210. *Required fees:* $988; $246 per semester. *Financial support:* Federal Work-Study, scholarships/grants, and unspecified assistantships available. Support available to part-time students. Financial award application deadline: 3/15; financial award applicants required to submit FAFSA. *Unit head:* Dr. Sue Robb, Chairperson, 585-395-5935, Fax: 585-395-2172, E-mail: srobb@brockport.edu. *Application contact:* Anne Walton, Coordinator of Certification and Graduate Advisement, 585-395-2326, Fax: 585-395-2172, E-mail: awalton@brockport.edu.
Website: https://www.brockport.edu/academics/education_human_development/department.html

The College of Idaho, Department of Education, Caldwell, ID 83605. Offers curriculum and instruction (M Ed); teaching (MAT). *Degree requirements:* For master's, thesis. *Entrance requirements:* For master's, GRE, portfolio, minimum undergraduate GPA of 3.0, interview. *Faculty research:* Discourse analysis, at-risk youth, children's literature, research design, program evaluation.

The College of Saint Rose, Graduate Studies, Thelma P. Lally School of Education, Teacher Education Programs, Albany, NY 12203-1419. Offers adolescence education (MS Ed, Advanced Certificate); adolescence education/special education (Advanced Certificate); childhood education (MS Ed); curriculum and instruction (MS Ed); early childhood education (MS Ed). *Students:* 69 full-time (60 women), 21 part-time (16 women); includes 7 minority (4 Black or African American, non-Hispanic/Latino; 2 Hispanic/Latino; 1 Two or more races, non-Hispanic/Latino), 1 international. Average age 27. 46 applicants, 52% accepted, 23 enrolled. In 2017, 43 master's awarded. *Entrance requirements:* For master's, minimum undergraduate GPA of 3.0. Additional exam requirements/recommendations for international students: Required—TOEFL (minimum score 550 paper-based; 80 iBT), IELTS (minimum score 6), PTE (minimum score 56). *Application deadline:* For fall admission, 4/1 priority date for domestic and international students; for spring admission, 10/15 priority date for domestic and international students; for summer admission, 3/15 priority date for domestic and international students. Applications are processed on a rolling basis. Application fee: $40. Electronic applications accepted. *Expenses: Tuition:* Full-time $7191; part-time $799 per credit hour. *Required fees:* $924; $462 per credit hour. Tuition and fees vary according to course load. *Financial support:* Career-related internships or fieldwork, scholarships/grants, tuition waivers (partial), and unspecified assistantships available. Support available to part-time students. Financial award application deadline: 4/15. *Unit head:* Dr. Drey Martone, Chair, 518-454-5262, E-mail: martoned@strose.edu. *Application contact:* Cris Murray, Assistant Vice President for Graduate Recruitment and Enrollment, 518-485-3390, Fax: 518-458-5479, E-mail: grad@strose.edu.
Website: https://www.strose.edu/academics/schools/school-of-education/

The College of William and Mary, School of Education, Program in Curriculum and Instruction, Williamsburg, VA 23187-8795. Offers elementary education (MA Ed); English as a second language/bilingual education (MA Ed); gifted education (MA Ed); literacy leadership (MA Ed); math specialist (MA Ed); secondary education (MA Ed), including English, foreign language, math, science, social studies; special education (MA Ed). *Accreditation:* NCATE. *Program availability:* Part-time. *Faculty:* 23 full-time (16 women), 40 part-time/adjunct (32 women). *Students:* 85 full-time (63 women), 16 part-time (15 women); includes 18 minority (5 Black or African American, non-Hispanic/Latino; 4 Asian, non-Hispanic/Latino; 7 Hispanic/Latino; 2 Two or more races, non-Hispanic/Latino), 1 international. Average age 27. 152 applicants, 83% accepted, 90 enrolled. In 2017, 67 master's awarded. *Degree requirements:* For master's, project. *Entrance requirements:* For master's, GRE, MAT, PRAXIS Core Academic Skills for Educators, minimum GPA of 2.5. Additional exam requirements/recommendations for international students: Required—TOEFL (minimum score 100 iBT), IELTS (minimum score 7). *Application deadline:* For fall admission, 1/15 for domestic and international students; for spring admission, 10/1 for domestic and international students. Application fee: $50. Electronic applications accepted. *Expenses:* $9,630 resident full-time, $535 resident part-time per credit hour; $25,920 nonresident full-time, $1,265 nonresident part-time per credit hour; $5,944 full-time fees. *Financial support:* In 2017–18, 35 students received support, including 7 research assistantships (averaging $6,678 per year); scholarships/grants and unspecified assistantships also available. Financial award application deadline: 1/15; financial award applicants required to submit FAFSA. *Faculty research:* Educational technology, professional development and evaluation, inclusive education, rural education, education policy. *Unit head:* Dr. Jeremy D. Stoddard, Department Chair, 757-221-2348, E-mail: jdstod@wm.edu. *Application contact:* Dorothy Smith Osborne, Assistant Dean for Academic Programs and Student Services, 757-221-2317, E-mail: dsosbo@wm.edu.
Website: http://education.wm.edu

The College of William and Mary, School of Education, Program in Education Policy, Planning, and Leadership, Williamsburg, VA 23187-8795. Offers curriculum and educational technology (PhD); curriculum leadership (Ed D, PhD); educational leadership (M Ed), including higher education administration (M Ed, Ed D, PhD), K-12 administration and supervision; educational policy, planning, and leadership (Ed D, PhD), including general education administration, gifted education administration, higher education administration (M Ed, Ed D, PhD). *Accreditation:* NCATE. *Program availability:* Part-time, evening/weekend. *Faculty:* 20 full-time (10 women), 21 part-time/adjunct (13 women). *Students:* 54 full-time (35 women), 172 part-time (113 women);

includes 70 minority (42 Black or African American, non-Hispanic/Latino; 1 Asian, non-Hispanic/Latino; 19 Hispanic/Latino; 8 Two or more races, non-Hispanic/Latino), 3 international. Average age 39. 163 applicants, 71% accepted, 89 enrolled. In 2017, 23 master's, 37 doctorates awarded. *Degree requirements:* For doctorate, comprehensive exam, thesis/dissertation. *Entrance requirements:* For master's, GRE or MAT, minimum GPA of 2.5; for doctorate, GRE or MAT, minimum GPA of 3.0. Additional exam requirements/recommendations for international students: Required—TOEFL (minimum score 100 iBT), IELTS (minimum score 7). *Application deadline:* For fall admission, 1/15 for domestic and international students. Application fee: $50. Electronic applications accepted. *Expenses:* $9,630 resident full-time, $535 resident part-time per credit hour; $25,920 nonresident full-time, $1,265 nonresident part-time per credit hour; $5,944 full-time fees. *Financial support:* In 2017–18, 59 students received support, including 1 fellowship (averaging $20,000 per year), 43 research assistantships (averaging $20,535 per year); scholarships/grants and unspecified assistantships also available. Support available to part-time students. Financial award application deadline: 1/15; financial award applicants required to submit FAFSA. *Faculty research:* Higher education policy, evaluation of teachers, program evaluation, civil rights and higher education, program evaluation. *Unit head:* Dr. Michael F. Dipaola, Department Chair, 757-221-2344, E-mail: mfdipa@wm.edu. *Application contact:* Dorothy Smith Osborne, Assistant Dean for Academic Programs and Student Services, 757-221-2317, E-mail: dsosbo@wm.edu.
Website: http://education.wm.edu

Colorado Christian University, Program in Curriculum and Instruction, Lakewood, CO 80226. Offers corporate education (MACI); early childhood educator (MACI); elementary educator (MACI); instructional technology (MACI); master educator (MACI); online course developer (MACI); online teaching and learning (MACI); special education generalist (MACI). *Program availability:* Part-time, evening/weekend. *Degree requirements:* For master's, thesis optional, practicum. *Entrance requirements:* For master's, interviews, letters of recommendation. Additional exam requirements/recommendations for international students: Required—TOEFL. Electronic applications accepted. *Expenses:* Contact institution.

Columbia International University, Columbia Graduate School, Columbia, SC 29203. Offers Bible teaching (MABT); counseling (MACN); early childhood and elementary education (MAT); educational administration (M Ed); educational leadership (PhD); instruction and learning (M Ed); teaching English as a foreign language (Certificate); teaching English as a foreign language and intercultural studies (MATF). *Program availability:* Part-time, evening/weekend, online learning. *Degree requirements:* For master's, internships, professional project. *Entrance requirements:* For master's, MAT, GRE (for some programs), minimum GPA of 2.7. Additional exam requirements/recommendations for international students: Required—TOEFL. Electronic applications accepted.

Columbus State University, Graduate Studies, College of Education and Health Professions, Department of Counseling, Foundations, and Leadership, Columbus, GA 31907-5645. Offers clinical mental health counseling (MS); curriculum and leadership (Ed D), including curriculum, educational leadership, higher education (M Ed, Ed D); educational leadership (M Ed, Ed S), including higher education (M Ed, Ed D); school counseling (M Ed, Ed S). *Accreditation:* ACA; NCATE. *Program availability:* Part-time, evening/weekend, 100% online, blended/hybrid learning. *Faculty:* 18 full-time (8 women), 20 part-time/adjunct (10 women). *Students:* 248 full-time (166 women), 308 part-time (236 women); includes 315 minority (278 Black or African American, non-Hispanic/Latino; 11 Asian, non-Hispanic/Latino; 15 Hispanic/Latino; 1 Native Hawaiian or other Pacific Islander, non-Hispanic/Latino; 10 Two or more races, non-Hispanic/Latino), 2 international. Average age 39. 155 applicants, 38% accepted, 40 enrolled. In 2017, 41 master's, 18 doctorates, 110 other advanced degrees awarded. *Degree requirements:* For master's, thesis, exit exam; for doctorate, comprehensive exam, thesis/dissertation; for Ed S, thesis or alternative. *Entrance requirements:* For master's, GRE General Test, minimum undergraduate GPA of 2.75; for doctorate, GRE General Test, minimum graduate GPA of 3.5, four years of professional service; for Ed S, GRE General Test, minimum undergraduate GPA of 2.75, graduate 3.0. Additional exam requirements/recommendations for international students: Required—TOEFL (minimum score 550 paper-based; 79 iBT). *Application deadline:* For fall admission, 6/30 for domestic and international students; for spring admission, 11/1 for domestic and international students; for summer admission, 3/1 for domestic and international students. Applications are processed on a rolling basis. Application fee: $50. Electronic applications accepted. *Expenses:* Tuition, state resident: full-time $3708; part-time $2472 per year. Tuition, nonresident: full-time $14,418; part-time $9612 per year. *International tuition:* $19,218 full-time. *Required fees:* $1605. Tuition and fees vary according to program. *Financial support:* In 2017–18, 34 students received support, including 14 research assistantships with partial tuition reimbursements available (averaging $3,000 per year); career-related internships or fieldwork, Federal Work-Study, institutionally sponsored loans, scholarships/grants, tuition waivers (partial), and unspecified assistantships also available. Support available to part-time students. Financial award application deadline: 5/1; financial award applicants required to submit FAFSA. *Unit head:* Dr. Tom Hackett, Department Chair, 706-507-8968, Fax: 706-569-3134, E-mail: hackett_paul@columbusstate.edu. *Application contact:* Catrina Smith-Edmond, Assistant Director for Graduate and Global Admission, 706-507-8824, Fax: 706-568-5091, E-mail: smithedmond_catrina@columbusstate.edu.
Website: http://cfl.columbusstate.edu/

Columbus State University, Graduate Studies, College of Education and Health Professions, Department of Teacher Education, Columbus, GA 31907-5645. Offers curriculum and instruction in accomplished teaching (M Ed); early childhood education (M Ed, MAT, Ed S); middle grades education (M Ed, MAT, Ed S); secondary education (M Ed, MAT, Ed S), including biology (MAT), chemistry (MAT), earth and space science (MAT), English/language arts, general science (M Ed), history (MAT), mathematics, science (Ed S), social science (M Ed, Ed S); special education (M Ed, MAT, Ed S), including general curriculum (M Ed, MAT); teacher leadership (M Ed). *Accreditation:* NCATE. *Program availability:* Part-time, evening/weekend, 100% online, blended/hybrid learning. *Faculty:* 19 full-time (12 women), 24 part-time/adjunct (18 women). *Students:* 99 full-time (76 women), 181 part-time (143 women); includes 109 minority (94 Black or African American, non-Hispanic/Latino; 1 American Indian or Alaska Native, non-Hispanic/Latino; 1 Asian, non-Hispanic/Latino; 6 Hispanic/Latino; 7 Two or more races, non-Hispanic/Latino). Average age 34. 136 applicants, 63% accepted, 56 enrolled. In 2017, 119 master's, 8 other advanced degrees awarded. *Degree requirements:* For Ed S, thesis or alternative. *Entrance requirements:* For master's, GRE General Test, minimum undergraduate GPA of 2.75; for Ed S, GRE General Test, minimum undergraduate GPA of 2.75, graduate 3.0. Additional exam requirements/recommendations for international students: Required—TOEFL (minimum score 550 paper-based; 79 iBT). *Application deadline:* For fall admission, 6/30 for domestic students, 5/1 for international students; for spring admission, 11/1 for domestic and international students; for summer admission, 3/1 for domestic and international students. Applications are processed on a rolling basis. Application fee: $50. Electronic applications accepted. *Expenses:* Tuition, state resident: full-time $3708; part-time $2472 per year. Tuition, nonresident: full-time $14,418; part-time $9612 per year. *International tuition:* $19,218 full-time. *Required fees:* $1605. Tuition and fees vary according to program. *Financial support:* In 2017–18, 45 students received support, including 9 research assistantships with partial tuition reimbursements available (averaging $3,000 per year); career-related internships or fieldwork, Federal Work-Study, institutionally sponsored loans, scholarships/grants, tuition waivers (partial), and unspecified assistantships also available. Support available to part-time students. Financial award application deadline: 5/1; financial award applicants required to submit FAFSA. *Unit head:* Dr. Jan Burcham, Department Chair, 706-507-8519, Fax: 706-568-3134, E-mail: burcham_jan@columbusstate.edu. *Application contact:* Catrina Smith-Edmond, Assistant Director for Graduate and Global Admission, 706-507-8824, Fax: 706-568-5091, E-mail: smithedmond_catrina@columbusstate.edu. Website: http://te.columbusstate.edu/

Concordia University, College of Education, Portland, OR 97211-6099. Offers career and technical education (M Ed); curriculum and instruction (M Ed), including adolescent literacy, career and technical education, e-learning/technology education, early childhood education, English for speakers of other languages, English language development, environmental education, mathematics, methods and curriculum, reading, science, teacher leadership, the inclusive classroom; early childhood (MAT); education leadership (Ed D); educational administration (M Ed); elementary education (MAT); secondary education (MAT); special education (M Ed); teacher leadership (Ed D). *Program availability:* Part-time, online learning. *Degree requirements:* For master's, comprehensive exam, work samples/portfolio. *Entrance requirements:* For master's, California Basic Educational Skills Test or PRAXIS I, minimum undergraduate GPA of 2.8, graduate 3.0; 2 letters of recommendation. Additional exam requirements/recommendations for international students: Required—TOEFL (minimum score 525 paper-based). Electronic applications accepted. *Faculty research:* Learner-centered classroom, brain-based learning, future of online learning.

Concordia University Ann Arbor, Graduate Programs, Ann Arbor, MI 48105-2797. Offers curriculum and instruction (MS); educational leadership (MS); organizational leadership and administration (MS). *Program availability:* Part-time, evening/weekend. *Degree requirements:* For master's, thesis. *Entrance requirements:* Additional exam requirements/recommendations for international students: Required—TOEFL (minimum score 80 iBT); Recommended—IELTS (minimum score 6.5). Electronic applications accepted.

Concordia University Chicago, College of Education, Program in Curriculum and Instruction, River Forest, IL 60305-1499. Offers MA. MA offered jointly with the Chicago Consortium of Colleges and Universities. *Accreditation:* NCATE. *Program availability:* Part-time, evening/weekend. *Degree requirements:* For master's, comprehensive exam, thesis. *Entrance requirements:* For master's, minimum GPA of 2.9. Additional exam requirements/recommendations for international students: Required—TOEFL (minimum score 550 paper-based). Electronic applications accepted. *Faculty research:* School discipline, school improvement, leadership.

Concordia University Irvine, School of Education, Irvine, CA 92612-3299. Offers curriculum and instruction (MA); education and preliminary teaching credential (M Ed); educational administration and preliminary administrative services credential (MA); educational technology (MA); school counseling with pupil personnel services credential (MA). *Program availability:* Part-time, evening/weekend, online learning. *Degree requirements:* For master's, action research project. *Entrance requirements:* For master's, California Basic Educational Skills Test, California Subject Examinations for Teachers (M Ed and MA in educational administration and preliminary administrative services credential), official college transcript(s), signed statement of intent, two references, copy of credential. Additional exam requirements/recommendations for international students: Required—TOEFL. Electronic applications accepted. *Expenses:* Contact institution.

Concordia University, St. Paul, College of Education, St. Paul, MN 55104-5494. Offers classroom instruction (MA Ed), including K-12 reading; differentiated instruction (MA Ed); early childhood education (MA Ed); education (Ed D); educational leadership (MA Ed); educational technology (MA Ed, Certificate); K-12 principal licensure (Ed S); special education (MA Ed), including autism spectrum disorder, emotional and behavioral disorders, learning disabilities; superintendent (Ed S); teaching (MAT). *Accreditation:* NCATE. *Program availability:* Part-time, evening/weekend, 100% online, blended/hybrid learning. *Faculty:* 15 full-time (8 women), 86 part-time/adjunct (56 women). *Students:* 955 full-time (731 women), 42 part-time (28 women); includes 105 minority (35 Black or African American, non-Hispanic/Latino; 5 American Indian or Alaska Native, non-Hispanic/Latino; 31 Asian, non-Hispanic/Latino; 19 Hispanic/Latino; 15 Two or more races, non-Hispanic/Latino), 9 international. Average age 34. 409 applicants, 87% accepted, 347 enrolled. In 2017, 386 master's, 104 other advanced degrees awarded. *Degree requirements:* For master's, thesis (for some programs); for doctorate, thesis/dissertation, capstone projects; for other advanced degree, e-folio review of competencies. *Entrance requirements:* For master's, official transcripts from regionally-accredited institution stating the conferral of a bachelor's degree with minimum cumulative GPA of 3.0; personal statement; professional resume; practitioner in field through work or volunteerism; resume; for doctorate, minimum master's or specialist degree GPA of 3.25; transcript; writing sample; three letters of recommendation; current resume; on-campus interview; for other advanced degree, minimum master's or specialist degree GPA of 3.25; transcript; statement covering employment history and long-term academic and professional goals; two letters of recommendation; interview with program director. Additional exam requirements/recommendations for international students: Recommended—TOEFL (minimum score 547 paper-based; 78 iBT), IELTS (minimum score 6). *Application deadline:* For fall admission, 8/1 for domestic and international students; for spring admission, 12/1 for domestic and international students; for summer admission, 5/1 for domestic and international students. Applications are processed on a rolling basis. Application fee: $0. Electronic applications accepted. *Expenses:* $395 per credit (for MA in education); $440 per credit (for MAT); $615 per credit (for EdD). *Financial support:* In 2017–18, 105 students received support. Scholarships/grants and unspecified assistantships available. Financial award applicants required to submit FAFSA. *Faculty research:* Differentiated instruction in K-12 educational settings; educational leadership; effective online pedagogy in higher education; equine-assisted learning; faculty development in higher education. *Unit head:* Lonn Maly, Dean, 651-641-8203, E-mail: maly@csp.edu. *Application contact:* Amber Faletti, Director of Enrollment Management, 651-641-8838, Fax: 651-603-6320, E-mail: faletti@csp.edu.

Coppin State University, Division of Graduate Studies, Division of Education, Department of Curriculum and Instruction, Program in Curriculum and Instruction, Baltimore, MD 21216-3698. Offers M Ed. *Program availability:* Part-time, evening/weekend, online learning. *Degree requirements:* For master's, thesis. *Entrance requirements:* For master's, GRE or MAT, minimum GPA of 3.0, teacher certification.

Cornell University, Graduate School, Graduate Fields of Agriculture and Life Sciences, Field of Education, Ithaca, NY 14853. Offers adult and extension education (MPS, MS, PhD); learning, teaching, and social policy (MPS, MS, PhD); mathematics 7-12 (MS). Terminal master's awarded for partial completion of doctoral program. *Degree requirements:* For master's, thesis (MS); for doctorate, comprehensive exam, thesis/dissertation. *Entrance requirements:* For master's and doctorate, GRE General Test, sample of written work (recommended), 2 letters of recommendation. Additional exam requirements/recommendations for international students: Required—TOEFL (minimum

score 550 paper-based; 77 iBT). Electronic applications accepted. *Faculty research:* Moral development and professional ethics, public issues education and community development, socio/political issues in public education, teacher education and curriculum in agricultural science and mathematics, extension research.

Dakota Wesleyan University, Program in Education, Mitchell, SD 57301-4398. Offers curriculum and instruction (MA Ed); educational policy and administration (MA Ed); preK-12 principal certification (MA Ed); secondary certification (MA Ed). *Program availability:* Part-time, evening/weekend. *Degree requirements:* For master's, comprehensive exam, thesis optional, electronic portfolio. *Entrance requirements:* For master's, minimum GPA of 2.7, elementary statistics course, statement of purpose, official transcripts, resume, three letters of recommendation. Additional exam requirements/recommendations for international students: Required—TOEFL (minimum score 500 paper-based), IELTS (minimum score 6.5). Electronic applications accepted. *Faculty research:* Math, political policy, technology in the classroom.

Dallas Baptist University, Dorothy M. Bush College of Education, Program in Curriculum and Instruction, Dallas, TX 75211-9299. Offers Christian school administration (M Ed); distance learning (M Ed); English as a second language (M Ed); instructional technology (M Ed); professional life coaching (M Ed); special education (M Ed); supervision (M Ed). *Program availability:* Part-time, evening/weekend, online learning. *Application deadline:* Applications are processed on a rolling basis. Application fee: $25. Electronic applications accepted. Application fee is waived when completed online. *Expenses: Tuition:* Full-time $16,308; part-time $906 per credit hour. *Required fees:* $900; $450 per semester. Tuition and fees vary according to course load and degree level. *Unit head:* Dr. Neil Dugger, Dean, 214-333-5202, E-mail: neil@dbu.edu. *Application contact:* Dr. Deborah Tribble, Program Director, 214-333-5831, E-mail: debbiet@dbu.edu. Website: http://www3.dbu.edu/graduate/curriculum_instruction.asp

Delaware State University, Graduate Programs, College of Education, Health and Public Policy, Program in Curriculum and Instruction, Dover, DE 19901-2277. Offers MA. *Program availability:* Part-time, evening/weekend. *Degree requirements:* For master's, comprehensive exam, thesis optional. *Entrance requirements:* For master's, GRE General Test, minimum GPA of 3.0 in major, 2.75 overall. Additional exam requirements/recommendations for international students: Required—TOEFL (minimum score 550 paper-based). Electronic applications accepted.

Delaware Valley University, Program in Educational Leadership, Doylestown, PA 18901-2697. Offers instruction, curriculum and technology (MS); school administration and leadership (MS). *Program availability:* Part-time, evening/weekend. *Entrance requirements:* For master's, minimum undergraduate GPA of 3.0.

DePaul University, College of Education, Chicago, IL 60614. Offers bilingual-bicultural education (M Ed, MA); counseling (M Ed, MA), including clinical mental health counseling, college student development, school counseling; curriculum studies (M Ed, MA, Ed D); early childhood education (M Ed, MA, Ed D); educational leadership (M Ed, MA, Ed D), including Catholic leadership (M Ed, MA), general (M Ed, MA), higher education (M Ed, MA), physical education (M Ed, MA), principal preparation (M Ed); teacher preparation (M Ed); elementary education (M Ed, MA); middle grades education (M Ed); middle school mathematics education (MS); reading specialist (M Ed, MA); secondary education (M Ed, MA); social and cultural foundations in education (M Ed, MA); special education (M Ed); sport, fitness and recreation leadership (MS); value-creating education for global citizenship (M Ed); world languages education (M Ed, MA). *Program availability:* Part-time, evening/weekend, online learning. *Degree requirements:* For doctorate, thesis/dissertation. *Application deadline:* Applications are processed on a rolling basis. Application fee: $40. Electronic applications accepted. *Financial support:* Application deadline: 12/31; applicants required to submit FAFSA. *Unit head:* Dr. Paul Zionts, Dean, 773-325-7581, Fax: 773-325-7713, E-mail: pzionts@depaul.edu. *Application contact:* Dr. Paul Zionts, Dean, 773-325-7581, Fax: 773-325-7713, E-mail: pzionts@depaul.edu. Website: http://education.depaul.edu

DeVry University–Folsom Campus, Graduate Programs, Folsom, CA 95630. Offers accounting (M Acc); accounting and financial management (MAFM); business administration (MBA); curriculum leadership (M Ed); educational leadership (M Ed); educational technology (M Ed); higher education leadership (M Ed); human resource management (MHRM); information systems management (MISM); network and communications management (MNCM); project management (MPM); public administration (MPA).

Doane University, Program in Education, Crete, NE 68333-2430. Offers curriculum and instruction (M Ed); curriculum leadership (Ed S); education (Ed D); educational leadership (M Ed); school counseling (M Ed). *Accreditation:* NCATE. *Program availability:* Part-time, evening/weekend. *Faculty:* 10 full-time (7 women), 66 part-time/adjunct (50 women). *Students:* 228 full-time (172 women), 541 part-time (433 women); includes 51 minority (21 Black or African American, non-Hispanic/Latino; 4 American Indian or Alaska Native, non-Hispanic/Latino; 4 Asian, non-Hispanic/Latino; 12 Hispanic/Latino; 1 Native Hawaiian or other Pacific Islander, non-Hispanic/Latino; 9 Two or more races, non-Hispanic/Latino). Average age 33. In 2017, 284 master's, 1 other advanced degree awarded. *Degree requirements:* For master's, thesis; for doctorate, thesis/dissertation. *Entrance requirements:* For master's, minimum GPA of 2.5. Additional exam requirements/recommendations for international students: Required—TOEFL. *Application deadline:* Applications are processed on a rolling basis. Electronic applications accepted. *Expenses:* Contact institution. *Financial support:* Applicants required to submit FAFSA. *Unit head:* Dr. Lyn C. Forester, Dean, 402-826-8604, Fax: 402-826-8278. *Application contact:* Leah Schaber, Assistant Dean, 402-464-1223, Fax: 402-466-4228, E-mail: leah.schaber@doane.edu. Website: http://www.doane.edu/masters-degrees

Drexel University, Goodwin College of Professional Studies, School of Education, Philadelphia, PA 19104-2875. Offers applied behavior analysis (MS); creativity and innovation (MS); education improvement and transformation (MS); educational administration (MS); educational leadership and management (Ed D); educational leadership development and learning technologies (PhD); global and international education (MS); higher education (MS); human resources development (MS); learning technologies (MS); mathematics, learning and teaching (MS); special education (MS); teaching, learning and curriculum (MS). *Program availability:* Part-time, evening/weekend, online learning. *Degree requirements:* For doctorate, thesis/dissertation. *Entrance requirements:* For doctorate, GRE or GMAT. Additional exam requirements/recommendations for international students: Required—TOEFL, IELTS. Electronic applications accepted. Application fee is waived when completed online. *Expenses:* Contact institution. *Faculty research:* Leadership development, mathematics education, literacy, autism, educational technology.

See Display on page 654 and Close-Up on page 719.

Drury University, Master in Education Program, Springfield, MO 5802. Offers curriculum and instruction (M Ed), including elementary, middle school, secondary; gifted education (M Ed); instructional leadership (M Ed); instructional technology (M Ed); integrated learning (M Ed); online teaching (M Ed); special education (M Ed); special reading (M Ed). *Accreditation:* NCATE. *Program availability:* Part-time, evening/weekend, 100% online, blended/hybrid learning. *Entrance requirements:* For master's, GRE, bachelor's degree with minimum GPA of 2.75. Additional exam requirements/recommendations for international students: Recommended—TOEFL (minimum score 80 iBT), IELTS (minimum score 6.5). Electronic applications accepted. *Expenses:* Contact institution. *Faculty research:* Gifted students, instructional technology, autism, diversity and social justice.

Duquesne University, School of Education, Department of Educational Foundations and Leadership, Program in School Administration and Supervision, Pittsburgh, PA 15282-0001. Offers curriculum and instruction (Post-Master's Certificate); school administration K-12 (MS Ed, Post-Master's Certificate); school supervision (MS Ed). *Program availability:* Part-time, evening/weekend. *Faculty:* 1 (woman) full-time. *Students:* 19 full-time (13 women), 5 part-time (3 women); includes 4 minority (all Black or African American, non-Hispanic/Latino), 1 international. Average age 36. 17 applicants, 100% accepted, 10 enrolled. In 2017, 21 master's, 1 other advanced degree awarded. *Entrance requirements:* For master's, bachelor's degree; minimum GPA of 3.0 overall or on most recent 48 credits, or minimum overall GPA of 2.8 and MAT (minimum score 396); resume that documents competence and effectiveness in professional work; 3 letters of professional reference; for Post-Master's Certificate, bachelor's degree. Additional exam requirements/recommendations for international students: Required—TOEFL (minimum score 550 paper-based), IELTS (minimum score 7). *Application deadline:* For fall admission, 9/1 for domestic students; for spring admission, 1/2 for domestic students. Applications are processed on a rolling basis. Application fee: $0. Electronic applications accepted. *Expenses:* $1,259 per credit. *Financial support:* Research assistantships available. Support available to part-time students. *Faculty research:* Building culturally relevant systems of training for educational and helping professionals; preservice/in service teacher beliefs (self, content, equity); principal beliefs about teacher evaluation; beliefs about classroom assessment; school achievement and school effectiveness. *Unit head:* Dr. Fran Serenka, Associate Professor and Director, 412-396-5274, Fax: 412-396-1274, E-mail: serenkaf@duq.edu. *Application contact:* Kelly McGinley, Graduate Admissions Assistant, 412-396-1559, Fax: 412-396-5585, E-mail: mcginleyk@duq.edu.
Website: http://www.duq.edu/academics/schools/education/graduate-programs-education/school-admin-and-supervision

East Carolina University, Graduate School, College of Education, Department of Literacy Studies, English and History Education, Greenville, NC 27858-4353. Offers curriculum and instruction (MA Ed); English education (MAT); history education (MAT); reading education (MA Ed). *Accreditation:* NCATE. *Program availability:* Part-time, evening/weekend, online learning. *Students:* 4 full-time (3 women), 50 part-time (47 women); includes 4 minority (2 Black or African American, non-Hispanic/Latino; 1 Hispanic/Latino; 1 Two or more races, non-Hispanic/Latino). Average age 33. 18 applicants, 94% accepted, 17 enrolled. In 2017, 17 master's awarded. *Degree requirements:* For master's, comprehensive exam, thesis optional. *Entrance requirements:* For master's, GRE General Test or MAT, interview, minimum GPA of 2.5, bachelor's degree in related field, teaching license (MA Ed). Additional exam requirements/recommendations for international students: Required—TOEFL. *Application deadline:* For fall admission, 6/1 priority date for domestic students. Applications are processed on a rolling basis. Application fee: $75. *Expenses:* Tuition, state resident: full-time $4749; part-time $297 per credit hour. Tuition, nonresident: full-time $17,898; part-time $1119 per credit hour. *Required fees:* $2691; $224 per credit hour. Part-time tuition and fees vary according to course load and program. *Financial support:* Research assistantships, teaching assistantships, and Federal Work-Study available. Support available to part-time students. Financial award application deadline: 6/1. *Unit head:* Katherine Misulis, Chair, 252-328-6128, E-mail: misulisk@ecu.edu.
Website: http://www.ecu.edu/cs-educ/libs/index.cfm

East Carolina University, Graduate School, College of Education, Department of Special Education, Foundations, and Research, Greenville, NC 27858-4353. Offers assistive technology (Certificate); autism (Certificate); special education (MA Ed, MAT), including behavioral-emotional disabilities (MA Ed), intellectual disabilities (MA Ed), learning disabilities (MA Ed), low-incidence disabilities (MA Ed). *Program availability:* Part-time, evening/weekend, online learning. *Students:* 1 (woman) full-time, 61 part-time (56 women); includes 15 minority (8 Black or African American, non-Hispanic/Latino; 2 American Indian or Alaska Native, non-Hispanic/Latino; 1 Asian, non-Hispanic/Latino; 2 Hispanic/Latino; 2 Two or more races, non-Hispanic/Latino). Average age 31. 26 applicants, 92% accepted, 22 enrolled. In 2017, 10 master's, 6 other advanced degrees awarded. *Degree requirements:* For master's, comprehensive exam, thesis optional. *Entrance requirements:* For master's, GRE General Test or MAT, interview, bachelor's degree in related field, minimum GPA of 2.5, teaching license. Additional exam requirements/recommendations for international students: Required—TOEFL. *Application deadline:* For fall admission, 6/1 priority date for domestic students. Applications are processed on a rolling basis. Application fee: $75. *Expenses:* Tuition, state resident: full-time $4749; part-time $297 per credit hour. Tuition, nonresident: full-time $17,898; part-time $1119 per credit hour. *Required fees:* $2691; $224 per credit hour. Part-time tuition and fees vary according to course load and program. *Financial support:* Research assistantships, teaching assistantships, and Federal Work-Study available. Support available to part-time students. Financial award application deadline: 6/1; financial award applicants required to submit FAFSA. *Unit head:* Dr. Guili Zhang, Interim Chair, 252-328-4989, E-mail: zhangg@ecu.edu.
Website: http://www.ecu.edu/cs-educ/sefr/index.cfm

Eastern Illinois University, Graduate School, College of Education and Professional Studies, Department of Early Childhood, Elementary and Middle Level Education, Charleston, IL 61920. Offers curriculum and instruction (MS Ed). *Accreditation:* NCATE. *Program availability:* Part-time, evening/weekend. *Degree requirements:* For master's, comprehensive exam (for some programs), thesis (for some programs). *Entrance requirements:* For master's, GMAT or GRE. Additional exam requirements/recommendations for international students: Required—TOEFL (minimum score 500 paper-based; 61 iBT), IELTS (minimum score 6). *Application deadline:* For fall admission, 5/15 for domestic and international students; for spring admission, 10/15 for domestic and international students. Applications are processed on a rolling basis. Application fee: $30. Electronic applications accepted. *Financial support:* Research assistantships with full tuition reimbursements, teaching assistantships with full tuition reimbursements, career-related internships or fieldwork, Federal Work-Study, and unspecified assistantships available. Support available to part-time students. Financial award application deadline: 3/1; financial award applicants required to submit FAFSA. *Unit head:* Jeanne E. Okrasinski, Chair, 217-581-5728, Fax: 217-581-6300, E-mail: jeokrasinski@eiu.edu. *Application contact:* Jeanne E. Okrasinski, Chair, 217-581-5728, Fax: 217-581-6300, E-mail: jeokrasinski@eiu.edu.
Website: http://www.eiu.edu/elegrad/

Eastern Kentucky University, The Graduate School, College of Education, Department of Curriculum and Instruction, Richmond, KY 40475-3102. Offers elementary education (MA Ed), including early elementary education, reading; library science (MA Ed); music education (MA Ed); secondary and higher education (MA Ed), including secondary education; teaching (MAT). *Accreditation:* NCATE. *Program*

availability: Part-time. *Degree requirements:* For master's, portfolio is part of exam. *Entrance requirements:* For master's, GRE General Test, PRAXIS II (KY), minimum GPA of 2.5. *Faculty research:* Technology in education, reading instruction, e-portfolios, induction to teacher education, dispositions of teachers.

Eastern Mennonite University, Program in Teacher Education, Harrisonburg, VA 22802-2462. Offers curriculum and instruction (MA Ed); diverse needs (MA Ed); literacy (MA Ed); restorative justice in education (MA Ed). *Accreditation:* NCATE. *Program availability:* Part-time. *Degree requirements:* For master's, portfolio, research projects. *Entrance requirements:* For master's, 1 year of teaching experience, interview, minimum undergraduate GPA of 2.75. Additional exam requirements/recommendations for international students: Required—TOEFL (minimum score 550 paper-based). *Application deadline:* Applications are processed on a rolling basis. Application fee: $50. Electronic applications accepted. *Expenses:* Contact institution. *Financial support:* Federal Work-Study and scholarships/grants available. Financial award application deadline: 6/30; financial award applicants required to submit FAFSA. *Faculty research:* Effective literacy instruction for middle school English language learners, beginning teacher's emotional experiences, constructivist learning environments, restorative discipline. *Unit head:* Cathy Smeltzer Erb, Chair, 540-432-4638. *Application contact:* Yvonne Martin, Office Assistant, 540-432-4350, Fax: 540-432-4071, E-mail: yvonne.martin@emu.edu.
Website: http://www.emu.edu/maed/

Eastern Michigan University, Graduate School, College of Education, Department of Teacher Education, Programs in Curriculum and Instruction, Ypsilanti, MI 48197. Offers advanced teaching and learning (MA); early literacy instruction (Graduate Certificate); instructional leadership (MA); learning, motivation and creativity (Graduate Certificate); literacy coaching (Graduate Certificate); online teaching (Certificate); secondary literacy instruction (Graduate Certificate); urban and diversity education (MA). *Students:* 1 full-time (0 women), 22 part-time (19 women); includes 6 minority (2 Black or African American, non-Hispanic/Latino; 1 Hispanic/Latino; 3 Two or more races, non-Hispanic/Latino). Average age 31. 15 applicants, 67% accepted, 7 enrolled. In 2017, 15 master's, 1 other advanced degree awarded. Application fee: $45. *Application contact:* Dr. Virginia Harder, Graduate Coordinator/Advisor, 734-487-2729, Fax: 734-487-2101, E-mail: vharder1@emich.edu.

Eastern New Mexico University, Graduate School, College of Education and Technology, Department of Curriculum and Instruction, Portales, NM 88130. Offers alternative licensure in elementary education (M Ed); bilingual education (M Ed); career and technical education (M Ed); educational technology (M Ed); elementary education (M Ed); English as a second language (M Ed); pedagogy and learning (M Ed); reading/literacy (M Ed). *Program availability:* Part-time, online learning. *Degree requirements:* For master's, comprehensive exam, thesis optional. *Entrance requirements:* For master's, writing assessment, minimum GPA of 3.0, photocopy of teaching license, letter of recommendation. Additional exam requirements/recommendations for international students: Required—TOEFL (minimum score 550 paper-based; 79 iBT), IELTS (minimum score 6). *Application deadline:* For fall admission, 7/20 priority date for domestic students, 6/20 priority date for international students; for spring admission, 12/15 priority date for domestic students, 11/15 priority date for international students. Applications are processed on a rolling basis. Application fee: $10. Electronic applications accepted. *Financial support:* Applicants required to submit FAFSA. *Unit head:* Dr. Mary Daughrity, Graduate Coordinator, 575-562-2481, Fax: 575-562-2559, E-mail: mary.daughrity@enmu.edu. *Application contact:* Cheryl Reeves, Senior Secretary, 575-562-2443, E-mail: cheryl.reeves@enmu.edu.
Website: http://education.enmu.edu

Eastern Washington University, Graduate Studies, College of Arts, Letters and Education, Department of Education, Program in Curriculum Development, Cheney, WA 99004-2431. Offers M Ed. *Students:* 2 full-time (both women), 6 part-time (5 women); includes 1 minority (Asian, non-Hispanic/Latino), 2 international. Average age 33. 7 applicants, 57% accepted, 3 enrolled. *Degree requirements:* For master's, comprehensive exam. *Entrance requirements:* For master's, minimum GPA of 3.0. Additional exam requirements/recommendations for international students: Required—TOEFL (minimum score 580 paper-based; 92 iBT), IELTS (minimum score 7), PTE (minimum score 63). *Application deadline:* For fall admission, 4/1 priority date for domestic students; for spring admission, 1/15 for domestic students. Applications are processed on a rolling basis. Application fee: $75. Electronic applications accepted. *Expenses:* Tuition, state resident: full-time $11,191; part-time $373.06 per credit. Tuition, nonresident: full-time $25,995; part-time $866.52 per credit. *Financial support:* In 2017–18, teaching assistantships with partial tuition reimbursements (averaging $10,000 per year) were awarded; career-related internships or fieldwork, Federal Work-Study, institutionally sponsored loans, scholarships/grants, health care benefits, tuition waivers (partial), and unspecified assistantships also available. Support available to part-time students. Financial award application deadline: 2/1. *Unit head:* Dr. Vince Aleccia, Program Coordinator, 509-359-7024, E-mail: valeccia@ewu.edu.

East Tennessee State University, School of Graduate Studies, College of Education, Department of Curriculum and Instruction, Johnson City, TN 37614. Offers advanced studies in teaching and learning (M Ed), including childhood literacy; educational technology (M Ed), including educational communications and technology, school library media; elementary education (M Ed); reading (M Ed, MA), including reading education (MA), storytelling (MA); response to intervention (Post-Master's Certificate); school library professional (Post-Master's Certificate); secondary education (M Ed); STEAM K-12 education (Postbaccalaureate Certificate); storytelling (Postbaccalaureate Certificate); teacher education (MAT), including elementary education K-5, middle grades education 4-8, middle grades education 6-8, secondary education 6-12 and preK-12, secondary education K-12. *Accreditation:* NCATE. *Program availability:* Part-time, evening/weekend, online learning. *Degree requirements:* For master's, comprehensive exam, thesis optional, student teaching, practicum; for other advanced degree, field work (school library); culminating experience (storytelling). *Entrance requirements:* For master's, GRE, SAT, ACT, PRAXIS, minimum GPA of 3.0, interview, 3 letters of recommendation, background check; for other advanced degree, master's degree, TN teaching license. Additional exam requirements/recommendations for international students: Required—TOEFL (minimum score 550 paper-based; 79 iBT). *Application deadline:* For fall admission, 6/1 for domestic students, 4/29 for international students; for spring admission, 11/1 for domestic students, 4/29 for international students. Application fee: $55 ($65 for international students). Electronic applications accepted. *Financial support:* Research assistantships with full tuition reimbursements, teaching assistantships with tuition reimbursements, career-related internships or fieldwork, institutionally sponsored loans, scholarships/grants, and unspecified assistantships available. Financial award application deadline: 7/1; financial award applicants required to submit FAFSA. *Faculty research:* Critical thinking; curriculum development in reading, math, and science education; cultural diversity; cognitive processes; effective teaching strategies. *Unit head:* Dr. Karin Keith, Chair, 423-439-7598, Fax: 423-439-8362, E-mail: keithkj@etsu.edu. *Application contact:* Dr. Aimee Govett, Graduate Coordinator, 423-439-7804, Fax: 423-439-5624, E-mail: govett@etsu.edu.
Website: http://www.etsu.edu/coe/cuai/

Curriculum and Instruction

Emporia State University, Program in Curriculum and Instruction, Emporia, KS 66801-5415. Offers curriculum leadership (MS); effective practitioner (MS); national board certification (MS). *Accreditation:* NCATE. *Program availability:* Part-time, online only, 100% online. *Faculty:* 10 full-time (3 women). *Students:* 6 full-time (all women), 105 part-time (91 women); includes 7 minority (2 Black or African American, non-Hispanic/Latino; 2 Hispanic/Latino; 3 Two or more races, non-Hispanic/Latino). 19 applicants, 95% accepted, 15 enrolled. In 2017, 60 master's awarded. *Degree requirements:* For master's, comprehensive exam or thesis, practicum. *Entrance requirements:* For master's, GRE or MAT, appropriate bachelor's degree, teacher certification, 1 year of teaching experience, letters of recommendation. *Application deadline:* For fall admission, 8/15 priority date for domestic students. Applications are processed on a rolling basis. Application fee: $30 ($75 for international students). Electronic applications accepted. *Expenses:* Tuition, state resident: full-time $6084; part-time $253.50 per credit hour. Tuition, nonresident: full-time $18,924; part-time $788.50 per credit hour. *Required fees:* $1943; $80.95 per credit hour. Tuition and fees vary according to campus/location. *Financial support:* Career-related internships or fieldwork, Federal Work-Study, institutionally sponsored loans, health care benefits, and unspecified assistantships available. Financial award application deadline: 3/15; financial award applicants required to submit FAFSA. *Unit head:* Dr. Daniel Stiffler, Chair, 620-341-5776, E-mail: dstiffle@emporia.edu. *Application contact:* Mary Sewell, Admissions Coordinator, 800-950-GRAD, Fax: 620-341-5909, E-mail: msewell@emporia.edu.

Emporia State University, Program in Instructional Specialist, Emporia, KS 66801-5415. Offers elementary subject matter (MS); reading (MS). *Accreditation:* NCATE. *Program availability:* Part-time. *Faculty:* 30 full-time (24 women), 1 part-time/adjunct (0 women). *Students:* 2 full-time (1 woman), 88 part-time (80 women); includes 3 minority (1 Black or African American, non-Hispanic/Latino; 1 Asian, non-Hispanic/Latino; 1 Two or more races, non-Hispanic/Latino). 14 applicants, 93% accepted, 11 enrolled. In 2017, 15 master's awarded. *Degree requirements:* For master's, comprehensive exam or thesis, practicum. *Entrance requirements:* For master's, GRE General Test or MAT, essay exam, appropriate bachelor's degree, letters of recommendation. Additional exam requirements/recommendations for international students: Required—TOEFL (minimum score 520 paper-based; 68 iBT). *Application deadline:* For fall admission, 8/15 priority date for domestic students. Applications are processed on a rolling basis. Application fee: $30 ($75 for international students). Electronic applications accepted. *Expenses:* Tuition, state resident: full-time $6084; part-time $253.50 per credit hour. Tuition, nonresident: full-time $18,924; part-time $788.50 per credit hour. *Required fees:* $1943; $80.95 per credit hour. Tuition and fees vary according to campus/location. *Financial support:* Federal Work-Study, institutionally sponsored loans, health care benefits, and unspecified assistantships available. Financial award application deadline: 3/15; financial award applicants required to submit FAFSA. *Unit head:* Dr. Matt Siemears, Chair, 620-341-6057, E-mail: msiemear@emporia.edu. *Application contact:* Mary Sewell, Admissions Coordinator, 800-950-GRAD, Fax: 620-341-5909, E-mail: msewell@emporia.edu.

Evangel University, Department of Education, Springfield, MO 65802. Offers curriculum and instruction (M Ed); educational leadership (M Ed); literacy (M Ed); secondary teaching (M Ed). *Accreditation:* NCATE. *Program availability:* Part-time, evening/weekend, 100% online, blended/hybrid learning. *Faculty:* 8 full-time (5 women), 8 part-time/adjunct (5 women). *Students:* 1 (woman) full-time, 47 part-time (41 women); includes 2 minority (both Hispanic/Latino). Average age 37. 16 applicants, 100% accepted, 14 enrolled. In 2017, 14 master's awarded. *Entrance requirements:* For master's, PRAXIS II (preferred) or GRE, minimum undergraduate GPA of 3.0. Additional exam requirements/recommendations for international students: Required—TOEFL (minimum score 550 paper-based). *Application deadline:* For fall admission, 7/15 priority date for domestic students, 8/1 for international students; for spring admission, 11/15 priority date for domestic students, 12/1 for international students. Applications are processed on a rolling basis. Application fee: $25. Electronic applications accepted. Application fee is waived when completed online. *Expenses: Tuition:* Full-time $7200; part-time $4800 per credit hour. *Required fees:* $210; $155 per semester. *Financial support:* In 2017–18, 23 students received support. Scholarships/grants and unspecified assistantships available. Financial award application deadline: 4/1; financial award applicants required to submit FAFSA. *Unit head:* Dr. Susan Langston, Program Coordinator, 417-865-2815 Ext. 8552, E-mail: langstons@evangel.edu. *Application contact:* Michael Mann, Enrollment Coordinator, Graduate Studies, 417-865-2815 Ext. 8276, Fax: 417-575-5484, E-mail: mannm@evangel.edu.
Website: http://www.evangel.edu/academics/graduate-studies/graduate-programs

Evangel University, Doctor of Education in Educational Leadership, Curriculum, and Instruction Program, Springfield, MO 65802. Offers Ed D. *Program availability:* Part-time, evening/weekend. *Faculty:* 5 full-time (3 women), 6 part-time/adjunct (3 women). *Students:* 14 full-time (12 women), 25 part-time (17 women); includes 3 minority (1 Black or African American, non-Hispanic/Latino; 1 American Indian or Alaska Native, non-Hispanic/Latino; 1 Two or more races, non-Hispanic/Latino). Average age 40. 13 applicants, 85% accepted, 8 enrolled. *Degree requirements:* For doctorate, thesis/dissertation. *Entrance requirements:* For doctorate, MA in education (preferred). Additional exam requirements/recommendations for international students: Required—TOEFL (minimum score 550 paper-based). *Application deadline:* For fall admission, 7/15 priority date for domestic students, 8/1 for international students; for spring admission, 11/15 priority date for domestic students, 12/1 for international students. Applications are processed on a rolling basis. Application fee: $25. Electronic applications accepted. *Expenses: Tuition:* Full-time $7200; part-time $4800 per credit hour. *Required fees:* $210; $155 per semester. *Financial support:* In 2017–18, 15 students received support. Scholarships/grants available. Support available to part-time students. Financial award application deadline: 4/1; financial award applicants required to submit FAFSA. *Unit head:* Dr. Susan Langston, Program Coordinator, 417-865-2815 Ext. 8552, E-mail: langstons@evangel.edu. *Application contact:* Michael Mann, Enrollment Coordinator, Graduate Studies, 417-865-2811 Ext. 8276, Fax: 417-575-5484, E-mail: mannm@evangel.edu.
Website: https://www.evangel.edu/programs/doctor-education-educational-leadership-curriculum-instruction/

Fairleigh Dickinson University, Metropolitan Campus, University College: Arts, Sciences, and Professional Studies, Peter Sammartino School of Education, Teaneck, NJ 07666-1914. Offers dyslexia specialist (Certificate); education for certified teachers (MA); educational leadership (MA); instructional technology (Certificate); learning disabilities (MA); literacy/reading (Certificate); multilingual education (MA); teacher of the handicapped (Certificate); teaching (MAT). *Accreditation:* TEAC. *Program availability:* Part-time. *Degree requirements:* For master's, research project (MAT).

Faulkner University, College of Education, Montgomery, AL 36109-3398. Offers counseling (MS); curriculum and instruction (M Ed); elementary education (M Ed); school counseling (M Ed). *Program availability:* Part-time, evening/weekend, 100% online, blended/hybrid learning. *Faculty:* 13 full-time (8 women), 6 part-time/adjunct (1 woman). *Students:* 140 full-time (107 women), 16 part-time (13 women); includes 97 minority (92 Black or African American, non-Hispanic/Latino; 1 American Indian or Alaska Native, non-Hispanic/Latino; 1 Asian, non-Hispanic/Latino; 3 Hispanic/Latino). Average age 37. 92 applicants, 55% accepted, 48 enrolled. In 2017, 51 master's

awarded. *Degree requirements:* For master's, 5+ hours in clinical training (for MS, M Ed in school counseling). *Entrance requirements:* For master's, MAT (minimum score of 370) or GRE (minimum score of 280) taken within last five years, bachelor's degree from regionally-accredited college or university; official transcripts from all colleges and universities attended; three letters of recommendation; goal statement (approximately 600 words); minimum cumulative GPA of 2.75 in undergraduate courses, 3.0 in graduate courses. Additional exam requirements/recommendations for international students: Required—TOEFL (minimum score 500 paper-based). *Application deadline:* For fall admission, 8/1 for domestic students; for spring admission, 12/1 for domestic students; for summer admission, 5/1 for domestic students. Application fee: $35. Electronic applications accepted. *Expenses:* Contact institution. *Financial support:* Applicants required to submit FAFSA. *Unit head:* Dr. Leslie S. Cowell, Dean, College of Education, 334-386-7224, Fax: 334-386-7194, E-mail: lcowell@faulkner.edu. *Application contact:* Rebecca L. Horn, Director, Graduate Education, 334-386-7264, Fax: 334-386-7194, E-mail: rhorn@faulkner.edu.
Website: https://www.faulkner.edu/graduate/graduate_academics/

Ferris State University, College of Education and Human Services, School of Education, Big Rapids, MI 49307. Offers curriculum and instruction (M Ed), including special education, subject area; educational leadership (MS); instructor (MSCTE); post-secondary administration (MSCTE); training and development (MSCTE). *Program availability:* Part-time, evening/weekend, blended/hybrid learning. *Faculty:* 7 full-time (4 women), 9 part-time/adjunct (6 women). *Students:* 4 full-time (1 woman), 40 part-time (23 women); includes 7 minority (3 Black or African American, non-Hispanic/Latino; 2 Hispanic/Latino; 2 Two or more races, non-Hispanic/Latino), 4 international. Average age 37. 13 applicants, 92% accepted, 7 enrolled. In 2017, 36 master's awarded. *Degree requirements:* For master's, thesis, research paper or project. *Entrance requirements:* For master's, minimum undergraduate GPA of 3.0. Additional exam requirements/recommendations for international students: Required—TOEFL (minimum score 500 paper-based, 79 iBT) or IELTS. *Application deadline:* For fall admission, 7/1 priority date for domestic and international students; for spring admission, 11/1 priority date for domestic and international students; for summer admission, 3/1 priority date for domestic and international students. Applications are processed on a rolling basis. Application fee: $30. Electronic applications accepted. Application fee is waived when completed online. *Financial support:* Career-related internships or fieldwork and scholarships/grants available. Support available to part-time students. Financial award applicants required to submit FAFSA. *Faculty research:* Suicide prevention, reading, women in education, special needs, administration. *Unit head:* Arrick L. Jackson, Dean, 231-591-2702, Fax: 231-591-2043, E-mail: arrickjackson@ferris.edu. *Application contact:* Liza Ing, Graduate Program Coordinator, 231-591-5362, Fax: 231-591-2043, E-mail: lizaing@ferris.edu.
Website: http://www.ferris.edu/education/education/

Fitchburg State University, Division of Graduate and Continuing Education, Program in Curriculum and Teaching, Fitchburg, MA 01420-2697. Offers M Ed. *Program availability:* Part-time, evening/weekend. *Students:* 137 full-time (92 women), 114 part-time (89 women); includes 16 minority (3 Black or African American, non-Hispanic/Latino; 2 Asian, non-Hispanic/Latino; 6 Hispanic/Latino; 5 Two or more races, non-Hispanic/Latino). Average age 36. 83 applicants, 100% accepted, 80 enrolled. In 2017, 132 master's awarded. *Entrance requirements:* Additional exam requirements/recommendations for international students: Required—TOEFL (minimum score 550 paper-based; 79 iBT). *Application deadline:* For fall admission, 7/15 for international students; for spring admission, 12/1 for international students. Applications are processed on a rolling basis. Application fee: $50. Electronic applications accepted. *Expenses:* Contact institution. *Financial support:* In 2017–18, research assistantships with partial tuition reimbursements (averaging $5,500 per year) were awarded; Federal Work-Study, scholarships/grants, and unspecified assistantships also available. Support available to part-time students. Financial award application deadline: 3/1; financial award applicants required to submit FAFSA. *Unit head:* Dr. Janna Heiligenstein, Chair, 978-665-3477, Fax: 978-665-3658, E-mail: gce@fitchburgstate.edu. *Application contact:* Jinawa McNeil, Director of Admissions, 978-665-3140, Fax: 978-665-4540, E-mail: admissions@fitchburgstate.edu.
Website: http://www.fitchburgstate.edu

Florida Atlantic University, College of Education, Department of Curriculum, Culture, and Educational Inquiry, Boca Raton, FL 33431-0991. Offers curriculum and instruction (M Ed, PhD, Ed S); early childhood education (M Ed); multicultural education (M Ed); TESOL and bilingual education (MA). *Program availability:* Part-time, evening/weekend. *Faculty:* 10 full-time (8 women), 2 part-time/adjunct (both women). *Students:* 15 full-time (13 women), 81 part-time (65 women); includes 28 minority (11 Black or African American, non-Hispanic/Latino; 3 Asian, non-Hispanic/Latino; 12 Hispanic/Latino; 2 Two or more races, non-Hispanic/Latino), 3 international. Average age 36. 54 applicants, 37% accepted, 14 enrolled. In 2017, 23 master's, 5 doctorates, 4 other advanced degrees awarded. *Entrance requirements:* Additional exam requirements/recommendations for international students: Required—TOEFL (minimum score 500 paper-based; 61 iBT), IELTS (minimum score 6). *Application deadline:* For fall admission, 7/1 for domestic students, 2/15 for international students; for spring admission, 11/1 for domestic students, 7/15 for international students. Application fee: $30. *Expenses:* Tuition, state resident: full-time $7400; part-time $369.82 per credit. Tuition, nonresident: full-time $20,496; part-time $1042.81 per credit. *Faculty research:* Multicultural education, early intervention strategies, family literacy, religious diversity in schools, early childhood curriculum. *Unit head:* Dr. Dilys Schoorman, Chair, 561-297-3965, E-mail: dschoorm@fau.edu. *Application contact:* Dr. Eliah Watlington, Associate Dean, 561-296-8520, Fax: 261-297-2991, E-mail: ewatling@fau.edu.
Website: http://www.coe.fau.edu/academicdepartments/ccei/

Florida Atlantic University, College of Education, Department of Teaching and Learning, Boca Raton, FL 33431-0991. Offers curriculum and instruction (M Ed), including art, biology, chemistry, English, French, German, mathematics, music, physics, Pre-K and primary education, reading, social sciences, Spanish; elementary education (M Ed); environmental education (M Ed); reading education (M Ed); social foundations of education (M Ed), including educational psychology, educational technology, multilingual education. *Accreditation:* NCATE. *Program availability:* Part-time, evening/weekend. *Faculty:* 13 full-time (10 women), 1 part-time/adjunct (0 women). *Students:* 26 full-time (22 women), 43 part-time (39 women); includes 19 minority (9 Black or African American, non-Hispanic/Latino; 1 Asian, non-Hispanic/Latino; 8 Hispanic/Latino; 1 Two or more races, non-Hispanic/Latino), 3 international. Average age 30. 91 applicants, 57% accepted, 33 enrolled. In 2017, 25 master's awarded. *Entrance requirements:* For master's, GRE General Test, minimum GPA of 3.0 in last 2 years of undergraduate course work. Additional exam requirements/recommendations for international students: Required—TOEFL (minimum score 500 paper-based; 61 iBT), IELTS (minimum score 6). *Application deadline:* For fall admission, 7/1 for domestic students, 2/15 for international students; for spring admission, 11/1 for domestic students, 7/15 for international students. Applications are processed on a rolling basis. Application fee: $30. *Expenses:* Tuition, state resident: full-time $7400; part-time $369.82 per credit. Tuition, nonresident: full-time $20,496; part-time $1042.81 per credit. *Financial support:* Fellowships with partial tuition reimbursements, research assistantships with partial tuition reimbursements, teaching

assistantships with partial tuition reimbursements, career-related internships or fieldwork, scholarships/grants, and unspecified assistantships available. *Faculty research:* Technology, teaching English to speakers of other languages, math teaching, electronic portfolio assessment, global perspectives through social studies. *Unit head:* Dr. Barbara Ridener, Chairperson, 561-297-3588, E-mail: bridener@fau.edu. *Application contact:* Dr. Eliah Watlington, Associate Dean, 561-296-8520, Fax: 261-297-2991, E-mail: ewatling@fau.edu.
Website: http://www.coe.fau.edu/academicdepartments/tl/

Florida Gulf Coast University, College of Education, Program in Curriculum and Instruction, Fort Myers, FL 33965-6565. Offers elementary education (M Ed); English education (M Ed); English speakers of other languages endorsement (M Ed); gifted education (M Ed); mathematics education (M Ed); middle school education (M Ed); reading education (M Ed); science education (M Ed); social science education (M Ed); special education (M Ed). *Program availability:* Part-time, evening/weekend, online learning. *Faculty:* 27 full-time (19 women), 44 part-time/adjunct (30 women). *Students:* 3 full-time (all women), 16 part-time (14 women); includes 4 minority (2 Black or African American, non-Hispanic/Latino; 2 Hispanic/Latino). Average age 30. 6 applicants, 100% accepted, 5 enrolled. In 2017, 4 master's awarded. *Degree requirements:* For master's, final project or portfolio. *Entrance requirements:* For master's, GRE General Test, MAT, minimum undergraduate GPA of 3.0 in last 2 years. Additional exam requirements/recommendations for international students: Required—TOEFL (minimum score 550 paper-based). *Application deadline:* For fall admission, 2/15 priority date for domestic students, 5/1 for international students; for spring admission, 12/1 for domestic students, 9/15 for international students. Applications are processed on a rolling basis. Application fee: $30. Electronic applications accepted. *Expenses:* Tuition, state resident: part-time $290 per credit hour. Tuition, nonresident: part-time $1173 per credit hour. *Required fees:* $127 per credit hour. Tuition and fees vary according to course load. *Financial support:* In 2017–18, 2 students received support. Application deadline: 6/30; applicants required to submit FAFSA. *Faculty research:* Internet in schools, technology in pre-service and in-service teacher training. *Unit head:* Dr. Vickie Johnston, Instructor, 239-590-7754, Fax: 239-590-7801, E-mail: vjohnston@fgcu.edu. *Application contact:* Keiana Desmore, Adviser/Counselor, 239-590-7759, Fax: 239-590-7801, E-mail: kdesmore@fgcu.edu.
Website: http://coe.fgcu.edu/c-imed/

Florida International University, College of Arts, Sciences, and Education, Department of Teaching and Learning, Miami, FL 33199. Offers art education (MA, MS); curriculum and instruction (MS, Ed D, PhD, Ed S), including curriculum development (MS), elementary education (MS), English education (MS), learning technologies (MS), mathematics education (MS), modern language education (MS), physical education (MS), science education (MS), social studies education (MS), special education (MS); early childhood education (MS); exceptional student education (Ed D); foreign language education (MS), including foreign language education, teaching English to speakers of other languages (TESOL); language, literacy and culture (PhD); mathematics, science, and learning technologies (PhD); physical education (MS), including sport and fitness; reading education (MS). *Program availability:* Part-time, evening/weekend. *Faculty:* 60 full-time (41 women), 112 part-time/adjunct (77 women). *Students:* 165 full-time (139 women), 191 part-time (148 women); includes 270 minority (56 Black or African American, non-Hispanic/Latino; 12 Asian, non-Hispanic/Latino; 191 Hispanic/Latino; 11 Two or more races, non-Hispanic/Latino), 13 international. Average age 34. 238 applicants, 68% accepted, 107 enrolled. In 2017, 184 master's, 15 doctorates awarded. *Degree requirements:* For doctorate, comprehensive exam, thesis/dissertation. *Entrance requirements:* For master's, GRE General Test, Florida General Knowledge Test or Florida College Level Academic Skills Test; for doctorate and Ed S, GRE General Test. Additional exam requirements/recommendations for international students: Required—TOEFL (minimum score 550 paper-based; 80 iBT), IELTS (minimum score 6.3). *Application deadline:* For fall admission, 6/1 priority date for domestic students, 4/1 for international students; for winter admission, 10/1 priority date for domestic students, 9/1 for international students; for spring admission, 3/1 priority date for domestic students, 2/1 for international students. Applications are processed on a rolling basis. Application fee: $30. Electronic applications accepted. *Expenses:* Tuition, state resident: full-time $8912; part-time $446 per credit hour. Tuition, nonresident: full-time $21,393; part-time $992 per credit hour. *Required fees:* $390; $195 per semester. *Financial support:* Research assistantships with tuition reimbursements and teaching assistantships with tuition reimbursements available. *Unit head:* Dr. Lynn Miller, Chair, 305-348-2005, Fax: 305-348-2086, E-mail: lynne.miller@fiu.edu. *Application contact:* Nanett Rojas, Assistant Director, Graduate Admissions, 305-348-7464, Fax: 305-348-7441, E-mail: gradadm@fiu.edu.
Website: https://tl.fiu.edu/

Florida State University, The Graduate School, College of Education, School of Teacher Education, Tallahassee, FL 32306-4450. Offers curriculum and instruction (MS, PhD, Ed S), including early childhood education, elementary education, English education, foreign and second language education, mathematics education, reading and language arts, science education, social science education, special education, visual disabilities education (MS); teaching English to speakers of other languages (Certificate). *Program availability:* Part-time, evening/weekend, 100% online, blended/hybrid learning, asynchronous, minimal on-campus study. *Faculty:* 41 full-time (33 women), 21 part-time/adjunct (18 women). *Students:* 133 full-time (93 women), 84 part-time (69 women); includes 48 minority (20 Black or African American, non-Hispanic/Latino; 2 Asian, non-Hispanic/Latino; 19 Hispanic/Latino; 7 Two or more races, non-Hispanic/Latino), 52 international. Average age 31. 146 applicants, 56% accepted, 52 enrolled. In 2017, 91 master's, 7 doctorates, 1 other advanced degree awarded. Terminal master's awarded for partial completion of doctoral program. *Degree requirements:* For master's and other advanced degree, comprehensive exam, thesis optional; for doctorate, comprehensive exam, thesis/dissertation, diagnostic exam, preliminary exam, prospectus defense, dissertation defense. *Entrance requirements:* For master's, doctorate, and other advanced degree, GRE General Test, minimum upper-division GPA of 3.0. Additional exam requirements/recommendations for international students: Required—TOEFL (minimum score 550 paper-based, 80 iBT), Michigan English Language Assessment Battery (minimum score 77), IELTS (minimum score 6.5) or PTE (minimum score 55). Application fee: $30. Electronic applications accepted. *Financial support:* Fellowships, research assistantships, teaching assistantships, scholarships/grants, tuition waivers (full and partial), and unspecified assistantships available. Financial award application deadline: 1/15; financial award applicants required to submit FAFSA. *Faculty research:* Identifying effective intervention strategies to improve reading skills; improving literacy teaching and learning through technology; understanding of student sense making, problem solving, the history and structure of STEM disciplines, and teacher education to support the development of ambitious instruction that supports the STEM learning of all students; examining practices of international education; identifying ways to support the professional development of teachers. *Unit head:* Dr. Sherry Southerland, Professor/Department Chair, 850-644-6885, Fax: 850-644-2725, E-mail: ssoutherland@admin.fsu.edu. *Application contact:* Britni DeZerga, Academic Program Specialist, 850-644-2122, Fax: 850-644-7736, E-mail: bpurvis@fsu.edu.
Website: http://education.fsu.edu

Fontbonne University, Graduate Programs, St. Louis, MO 63105-3098. Offers accounting (MBA, MS); art (MA); art (K-12) (MAT); business (MBA); computer science (MS); deaf education (MA); early intervention in deaf education (MA); education (MA), including autism spectrum disorders, curriculum and instruction, diverse learners, early childhood education, reading, special education; elementary education (MAT); family and consumer sciences (MA), including multidisciplinary health communication studies; fine arts (MFA); instructional design and technology (MS); management and leadership (MM); middle school education (MAT); secondary education (MAT); special education (MAT); speech-language pathology (MS); supply chain management (MS); theatre (MA). *Program availability:* Part-time, evening/weekend, online learning. *Degree requirements:* For master's, comprehensive exam (for some programs), thesis (for some programs). *Entrance requirements:* Additional exam requirements/recommendations for international students: Required—TOEFL (minimum score 500 paper-based; 65 iBT). Electronic applications accepted.

Fordham University, Graduate School of Education, Division of Curriculum and Teaching, New York, NY 10023. Offers curriculum and teaching (MSE); childhood education (MSE); elementary education (MST); special education (MSE, Adv C); teaching English as a second language (MSE). *Accreditation:* NCATE. *Program availability:* Part-time, evening/weekend. *Degree requirements:* For Adv C, thesis. *Entrance requirements:* Additional exam requirements/recommendations for international students: Required—TOEFL (minimum score 577 paper-based; 90 iBT), IELTS (minimum score 7). Electronic applications accepted.

Framingham State University, Graduate Studies, Program in Curriculum and Instructional Technology, Framingham, MA 01701-9101. Offers M Ed. *Program availability:* Online learning. *Unit head:* Kim Cochrane, Visiting Associate Professor, E-mail: kcochrane1@framingham.edu. *Application contact:* 508-626-4550, Fax: 508-626-4030, E-mail: dgce@frc.mass.edu.

Franciscan University of Steubenville, Graduate Programs, Department of Education, Steubenville, OH 43952-1763. Offers administration (MS Ed); teaching (MS Ed). *Accreditation:* NCATE. *Program availability:* Part-time, evening/weekend, online learning. *Degree requirements:* For master's, project. *Entrance requirements:* For master's, minimum undergraduate GPA of 2.5 or written exam. Additional exam requirements/recommendations for international students: Required—TOEFL. Electronic applications accepted. Application fee is waived when completed online. *Expenses:* Contact institution.

Franklin Pierce University, Graduate and Professional Studies, Rindge, NH 03461-0060. Offers curriculum and instruction (M Ed); elementary education (MS Ed); emerging network technologies (Graduate Certificate); energy and sustainability studies (MBA, Graduate Certificate); health administration (MBA, Graduate Certificate); human resource management (MBA, Graduate Certificate); information technology (MBA); leadership (MBA); nursing education (MS); nursing leadership (MS); physical therapy (DPT); physician assistant studies (MPAS); special education (M Ed); sports management (MBA). *Accreditation:* APTA. *Program availability:* Part-time, 100% online, blended/hybrid learning. *Degree requirements:* For master's, concentrated original research projects; student teaching; fieldwork and/or internship; leadership project; PRAXIS I and II (for M Ed); for doctorate, concentrated original research projects, clinical fieldwork and/or internship, leadership project. *Entrance requirements:* For master's, minimum GPA of 2.5, 3 letters of recommendation; competencies in accounting, economics, statistics, and computer skills through life experience or undergraduate coursework (for MBA); certification/e-portfolio, minimum C grade in all education courses (for M Ed); license to practice as RN (for MS); for doctorate, GRE, 80 hours of observation/work in PT settings; completion of anatomy, chemistry, physics, and statistics; minimum GPA of 3.0. Additional exam requirements/recommendations for international students: Required—TOEFL (minimum score 550 paper-based; 61 iBT). Electronic applications accepted. *Faculty research:* Evidence-based practice in sports physical therapy, human resource management in economic crisis, leadership in nursing, innovation in sports facility management, differentiated learning and understanding by design.

Freed-Hardeman University, Program in Education, Henderson, TN 38340-2399. Offers curriculum and instruction (M Ed); school counseling (M Ed), including administration and supervision, special education; school leadership (Ed S). *Accreditation:* NCATE. *Program availability:* Part-time, evening/weekend. *Degree requirements:* For master's, comprehensive exam, thesis optional; for Ed S, thesis. *Entrance requirements:* For master's, GRE General Test or NTE; for Ed S, 3 years of teaching experience. Additional exam requirements/recommendations for international students: Required—TOEFL (minimum score 500 paper-based).

Fresno Pacific University, Graduate Programs, School of Education, Program in Curriculum and Teaching, Fresno, CA 93702-4709. Offers MA. *Program availability:* Part-time, evening/weekend, online learning. *Degree requirements:* For master's, thesis or alternative. *Entrance requirements:* For master's, interview, statement of intent, three letters of recommendation, official transcript, BA/BS, minimum GPA of 2.75. Additional exam requirements/recommendations for international students: Required—TOEFL (minimum score 550 paper-based). Electronic applications accepted. *Expenses:* Contact institution.

Frostburg State University, College of Education, Department of Educational Professions, Program in Curriculum and Instruction, Frostburg, MD 21532. Offers curriculum and instruction (Ed D); educational technology (M Ed); elementary education (M Ed); secondary education (M Ed). *Program availability:* Part-time, evening/weekend. *Faculty:* 2. *Students:* 45 part-time (33 women); includes 1 minority (Two or more races, non-Hispanic/Latino). Average age 34. 15 applicants, 93% accepted, 11 enrolled. In 2017, 5 master's, 1 doctorate awarded. *Degree requirements:* For master's, thesis or alternative. *Entrance requirements:* For master's, teaching certificate. Additional exam requirements/recommendations for international students: Required—TOEFL. *Application deadline:* For fall admission, 7/15 priority date for domestic students. Applications are processed on a rolling basis. Application fee: $45. Electronic applications accepted. *Expenses:* Tuition, state resident: part-time $433 per credit hour. Tuition, nonresident: part-time $557 per credit hour. *Required fees:* $121 per credit hour. $27 per term. *Financial support:* In 2017–18, 2 research assistantships with full tuition reimbursements (averaging $5,000 per year) were awarded. Financial award application deadline: 4/1; financial award applicants required to submit FAFSA. *Unit head:* Dr. Jennifer Rankin, Coordinator, 301-687-7010, E-mail: jerankin@frostburg.edu. *Application contact:* Vickie Mazer, Director, Graduate Services, 301-687-7053, Fax: 301-687-4597, E-mail: vmmazer@frostburg.edu.

Furman University, Graduate Division, Department of Education, Greenville, SC 29613. Offers curriculum and instruction (MA); early childhood education (MA); educational leadership (Ed S); English as a second language (MA); literacy (MA); school leadership (MA); special education (MA). *Accreditation:* NCATE. *Program availability:* Part-time, online learning. *Degree requirements:* For master's, comprehensive exam (for some programs), thesis or alternative. *Entrance requirements:* For master's, PRAXIS II. *Faculty research:* Literacy, pedagogy and practice, social justice, advanced leadership, achievement in high poverty schools.

Curriculum and Instruction

Gannon University, School of Graduate Studies, College of Humanities, Education, and Social Sciences, School of Education, Program in Curriculum and Instruction, Erie, PA 16541-0001. Offers M Ed. *Program availability:* Part-time, evening/weekend, 100% online. *Degree requirements:* For master's, thesis or alternative, portfolio project. *Entrance requirements:* For master's, bachelor's degree from regionally-accredited college or university with minimum GPA of 3.0, official transcripts, 3 letters of recommendation. Additional exam requirements/recommendations for international students: Required—TOEFL (minimum score 79 iBT). Electronic applications accepted. Application fee is waived when completed online. *Expenses:* Contact institution.

Gannon University, School of Graduate Studies, College of Humanities, Education, and Social Sciences, School of Education, Program in Curriculum Supervisor, Erie, PA 16541-0001. Offers Certificate. *Program availability:* Part-time, evening/weekend, online learning. *Degree requirements:* For Certificate, internship. *Entrance requirements:* Additional exam requirements/recommendations for international students: Required—TOEFL (minimum score 79 iBT). Electronic applications accepted. Application fee is waived when completed online. *Expenses:* Contact institution.

Gardner-Webb University, Graduate School, School of Education, Boiling Springs, NC 28017. Offers curriculum and instruction (Ed D); educational leadership (Ed D); executive leadership studies (MA, Ed S); organizational leadership (Ed D); school administration (MA). *Accreditation:* NCATE. *Program availability:* Part-time, evening/weekend. *Faculty:* 15 full-time (7 women), 33 part-time/adjunct (20 women). *Students:* 13 full-time (10 women), 736 part-time (567 women); includes 332 minority (306 Black or African American, non-Hispanic/Latino; 6 American Indian or Alaska Native, non-Hispanic/Latino; 4 Asian, non-Hispanic/Latino; 9 Hispanic/Latino; 1 Native Hawaiian or other Pacific Islander, non-Hispanic/Latino; 6 Two or more races, non-Hispanic/Latino). Average age 33. *Degree requirements:* For master's, comprehensive exam. *Entrance requirements:* For master's, GRE General Test or NTE, PRAXIS, minimum GPA of 2.5. *Application deadline:* For fall admission, 8/1 priority date for domestic students. Applications are processed on a rolling basis. Electronic applications accepted. *Expenses:* Contact institution. *Financial support:* Unspecified assistantships available. *Application contact:* Office of Graduate Admissions, 877-498-4723, Fax: 704-406-3895, E-mail: gradinfo@gardner-webb.edu.

George Mason University, College of Education and Human Development, Programs in Curriculum and Instruction, Fairfax, VA 22030. Offers advanced international baccalaureate (M Ed); assistive technology (M Ed); designing digital learning in schools (M Ed); early childhood education (M Ed); early childhood education for diverse learners (M Ed); elementary education (M Ed); English as a second language (M Ed); gifted child education (M Ed); history (M Ed); literacy (M Ed), including PK-12 classroom teachers, reading specialist; literacy leadership for diverse schools (M Ed), including K-12 reading; physical education (M Ed); science K-12 (M Ed); secondary education (M Ed), including biology, chemistry, earth science, English, history/social science, math, physics; special education (M Ed); teacher leadership (M Ed); teaching culturally, linguistically diverse and exceptional learners (M Ed); transformative teaching (M Ed). *Program availability:* Part-time, evening/weekend, 100% online, blended/hybrid learning. *Faculty:* 41 full-time (36 women), 45 part-time/adjunct (37 women). *Students:* 173 full-time (151 women), 729 part-time (611 women); includes 271 minority (65 Black or African American, non-Hispanic/Latino; 5 American Indian or Alaska Native, non-Hispanic/Latino; 88 Asian, non-Hispanic/Latino; 94 Hispanic/Latino; 1 Native Hawaiian or other Pacific Islander, non-Hispanic/Latino; 18 Two or more races, non-Hispanic/Latino), 28 international. Average age 32. 426 applicants, 91% accepted, 289 enrolled. In 2017, 349 master's awarded. *Degree requirements:* For master's, thesis. *Entrance requirements:* For master's, PRAXIS Core (for some programs), 2 letters of recommendation, interview, program goals statement; 9 hours of complete licensure endorsement requirements (for elementary education); minimum GPA of 3.0 in applicant's last 60 hours of undergraduate coursework (for secondary education); at least 1 year of teaching experience (for literacy). Additional exam requirements/recommendations for international students: Required—TOEFL (minimum score 575 paper-based; 88 iBT), IELTS (minimum score 6.5), PTE (minimum score 59). *Application deadline:* For fall admission, 4/2 priority date for domestic and international students; for spring admission, 11/1 for domestic and international students. Application fee: $75 ($80 for international students). Electronic applications accepted. *Expenses:* Tuition, state resident: full-time $11,228; part-time $459.50 per credit. Tuition, nonresident: full-time $30,932; part-time $1280.50 per credit. *Required fees:* $3252; $135.50 per credit. Part-time tuition and fees vary according to course load and program. *Financial support:* In 2017–18, 2 students received support, including 2 teaching assistantships; career-related internships or fieldwork, Federal Work-Study, scholarships/grants, unspecified assistantships, and health care benefits (for full-time research or teaching assistantship recipients) also available. Support available to part-time students. Financial award application deadline: 3/1; financial award applicants required to submit FAFSA. *Faculty research:* Teacher preparation and professional development; adaptive teaching; wonder in science teacher preparation; literacy (digital, adolescent); site based course instruction. *Unit head:* Rebecca Fox, Professor and Academic Program Coordinator, 703-993-4123, E-mail: rfox@gmu.edu. *Website:* http://gse.gmu.edu/programs/gsemasters

The George Washington University, Graduate School of Education and Human Development, Department of Curriculum and Pedagogy, Program in Curriculum and Instruction, Washington, DC 20052. Offers MA Ed, Ed D, Ed S, Graduate Certificate. *Accreditation:* NCATE. *Program availability:* Evening/weekend. *Students:* 23 full-time (20 women), 44 part-time (36 women); includes 15 minority (9 Black or African American, non-Hispanic/Latino; 4 Asian, non-Hispanic/Latino; 2 Hispanic/Latino), 16 international. Average age 34. 81 applicants, 58% accepted, 13 enrolled. In 2017, 12 master's, 9 doctorates awarded. *Degree requirements:* For master's and other advanced degree, comprehensive exam; for doctorate, comprehensive exam, thesis/dissertation. *Entrance requirements:* For master's, GRE General Test or MAT, minimum GPA of 2.75, resume; for doctorate and other advanced degree, GRE General Test or MAT, interview, minimum GPA of 3.3. *Application deadline:* For fall admission, 1/15 priority date for domestic students; for spring admission, 10/1 for domestic students. Applications are processed on a rolling basis. Application fee: $75. *Expenses: Tuition:* Full-time $28,800; part-time $1655 per credit hour. *Required fees:* $45; $2.75 per credit hour. *Financial support:* In 2017–18, 25 students received support. Fellowships, research assistantships, career-related internships or fieldwork, Federal Work-Study, and tuition waivers (partial) available. Financial award application deadline: 1/15; financial award applicants required to submit FAFSA. *Faculty research:* Cognitive skills-teaching, metacognitive strategies, adult basic literacy. *Unit head:* Dr. Sharon Lynch, Faculty Coordinator, 202-994-6174, E-mail: slynch@gwu.edu. *Application contact:* Sarah Lang, Director of Graduate Admissions, 202-994-1447, Fax: 202-994-7207, E-mail: slang@gwu.edu.

Georgia College & State University, Graduate School, The John H. Lounsbury College of Education, Program in Curriculum and Instruction, Milledgeville, GA 31061. Offers M Ed. *Program availability:* Part-time, evening/weekend, online only, 100% online. *Students:* 17 part-time (13 women); includes 8 minority (6 Black or African American, non-Hispanic/Latino; 1 Hispanic/Latino; 1 Two or more races, non-Hispanic/Latino). Average age 30. *Degree requirements:* For master's, minimum GPA of 3.0, complete program within 6 years. *Entrance requirements:* For master's, minimum GPA

of 2.75; clear renewable level 4 Georgia Teacher Certificate or eligibility, two professional recommendations, official transcripts, verification of immunization. Additional exam requirements/recommendations for international students: Recommended—TOEFL. *Application deadline:* For fall admission, 7/1 priority date for domestic students; for spring admission, 11/1 priority date for domestic students; for summer admission, 4/1 priority date for domestic students. Application fee: $40. Electronic applications accepted. *Expenses:* $288 per semester hour full-time, $2,592 per semester; $343 per semester fees. *Financial support:* Applicants required to submit FAFSA. *Unit head:* Dr. Marcie Peck, Coordinator, 478-445-2513, E-mail: marcia.peck@gcsu.edu. *Application contact:* Shanda Brand, Graduate Admissions Advisor, 478-445-1383, Fax: 478-445-6582, E-mail: shanda.brand@gcsu.edu. *Website:* http://www.gcsu.edu/education/proflearning/curriculum-instruction-med

Georgia Southern University, Jack N. Averitt College of Graduate Studies, College of Education, Department of Curriculum, Foundations, and Reading, Program in Curriculum Studies, Statesboro, GA 30460. Offers curriculum studies (Ed D), including cultural curriculum, instructional improvement, multicultural studies, teaching and learning. *Program availability:* Part-time. *Students:* 24 full-time (19 women), 119 part-time (93 women); includes 39 minority (28 Black or African American, non-Hispanic/Latino; 2 Asian, non-Hispanic/Latino; 5 Hispanic/Latino; 4 Two or more races, non-Hispanic/Latino), 2 international. Average age 41. In 2017, 26 doctorates awarded. *Degree requirements:* For doctorate, comprehensive exam, thesis/dissertation, exams; assessments. *Entrance requirements:* For doctorate, GRE or MAT, letters of reference, minimum GPA of 3.5, writing sample. Additional exam requirements/recommendations for international students: Required—TOEFL (minimum score 550 paper-based; 80 iBT), IELTS (minimum score 6). *Application deadline:* For summer admission, 1/30 for domestic students. Application fee: $50. Electronic applications accepted. *Expenses:* Tuition, state resident: full-time $4986; part-time $3324 per year. Tuition, nonresident: full-time $21,982; part-time $15,352 per year. *Required fees:* $2092; $1802 per credit hour. $901 per semester. Tuition and fees vary according to course load, campus/location and program. *Financial support:* In 2017–18, 7 students received support, including 1 research assistantship with full tuition reimbursement available (averaging $7,750 per year); teaching assistantships, career-related internships or fieldwork, Federal Work-Study, scholarships/grants, and unspecified assistantships also available. Financial award application deadline: 4/15; financial award applicants required to submit FAFSA. *Faculty research:* Curriculum theory, cultural studies, narrative research, postmodern theory, critical race theory, international education, feminism, media literacy, documentary studies, post human condition, social and cultural foundations of education, democracy and education. *Unit head:* Dr. Daniel Chapman, Program Coordinator, 912-478-5715, E-mail: dechapman@georgiasouthern.edu. *Application contact:* Dr. Lydia Cross, Coordinator for Graduate Student Recruitment, 912-478-8664, E-mail: lcross@georgiasouthern.edu. *Website:* http://coe.georgiasouthern.edu/cs/

Georgia Southern University, Jack N. Averitt College of Graduate Studies, College of Education, Department of Teaching and Learning, Program in Curriculum and Instruction - Accomplished Teaching, Statesboro, GA 30458. Offers M Ed. *Program availability:* Part-time, evening/weekend, 100% online. *Students:* 39 full-time (29 women), 182 part-time (157 women); includes 69 minority (57 Black or African American, non-Hispanic/Latino; 2 Asian, non-Hispanic/Latino; 5 Hispanic/Latino; 5 Two or more races, non-Hispanic/Latino). Average age 30. 66 applicants, 97% accepted, 48 enrolled. In 2017, 101 master's awarded. *Degree requirements:* For master's, key assessments. *Entrance requirements:* For master's, current Georgia teaching certificate. Additional exam requirements/recommendations for international students: Required—TOEFL (minimum score 550 paper-based; 80 iBT), IELTS (minimum score 6). *Application deadline:* For fall admission, 8/16 for domestic students; for spring admission, 1/11 for domestic students; for summer admission, 5/14 for domestic students. Applications are processed on a rolling basis. Application fee: $50. Electronic applications accepted. *Expenses:* Tuition, state resident: full-time $4986; part-time $3324 per year. Tuition, nonresident: full-time $21,982; part-time $15,352 per year. *Required fees:* $2092; $1802 per credit hour. $901 per semester. Tuition and fees vary according to course load, campus/location and program. *Financial support:* In 2017–18, 1 student received support. Scholarships/grants available. Support available to part-time students. Financial award application deadline: 4/20; financial award applicants required to submit FAFSA. *Faculty research:* Teacher preparation, curriculum design, assessment for improved student outcomes, reflective practices of infield teachers, diversity responsive methods in instruction. *Unit head:* Dr. Kymberly Harris, Program Director, 912-478-5041, E-mail: kharris@georgiasouthern.edu. *Application contact:* Dr. Lydia Cross, Coordinator for Graduate Student Recruitment, 912-478-8664, E-mail: lcross@georgiasouthern.edu.

Georgia Southern University–Armstrong Campus, College of Graduate Studies, Department of Secondary, Adult, and Physical Education, Savannah, GA 31419-1997. Offers adolescent and adult education (Certificate); adult education and community leadership (M Ed); curriculum and instruction (M Ed); secondary education (MAT). *Program availability:* Part-time, evening/weekend, online learning. *Faculty:* 8 full-time (all women), 4 part-time/adjunct (3 women). *Students:* 19 full-time (16 women), 106 part-time (60 women); includes 41 minority (31 Black or African American, non-Hispanic/Latino; 1 Asian, non-Hispanic/Latino; 3 Hispanic/Latino; 6 Two or more races, non-Hispanic/Latino), 1 international. Average age 33. 83 applicants, 48% accepted, 40 enrolled. In 2017, 43 master's, 1 other advanced degree awarded. *Degree requirements:* For master's, comprehensive exam (for some programs), thesis (for some programs), capstone project (for M Ed). *Entrance requirements:* For master's, edTPA (for MAT). Additional exam requirements/recommendations for international students: Required—TOEFL (minimum score 523 paper-based). *Application deadline:* For fall admission, 6/30 priority date for domestic students, 5/1 priority date for international students; for spring admission, 11/15 priority date for domestic students, 9/15 priority date for international students; for summer admission, 4/15 priority date for domestic students, 9/15 for international students. Applications are processed on a rolling basis. Application fee: $30. Electronic applications accepted. *Expenses:* Tuition, state resident: part-time $211 per credit hour. Tuition, nonresident: part-time $782 per credit hour. *Required fees:* $737 per semester. Tuition and fees vary according to course load, degree level, campus/location and program. *Financial support:* In 2017–18, research assistantships with full tuition reimbursements (averaging $5,000 per year) were awarded; career-related internships or fieldwork, Federal Work-Study, scholarships/grants, and unspecified assistantships also available. Support available to part-time students. Financial award application deadline: 3/15; financial award applicants required to submit FAFSA. *Faculty research:* Quality of teacher leadership, classroom management and first year teachers; edTPA preparation and success of candidates; social justice issues related to educational preparation; recruitment of STEM teachers. *Unit head:* Dr. Amelia Adkins, Department Head, 912-344-2562, E-mail: amee.adkins@armstrong.edu. *Application contact:* McKenzie Peterman, Graduate Admissions Specialist, 912-478-5678, Fax: 912-478-0740, E-mail: mpeterman@georgiasouthern.edu. *Website:* http://www.armstrong.edu/Education/adolescent_adult_education2/aaed_welcome

Georgia State University, College of Education and Human Development, Department of Middle and Secondary Education, Atlanta, GA 30302-3083. Offers curriculum and instruction (Ed D); English education (MAT); mathematics education (M Ed, MAT);

middle level education (MAT); reading, language and literacy education (M Ed, MAT), including reading instruction (M Ed); science education (M Ed, MAT), including biology (MAT), broad field science (MAT), chemistry (MAT), earth science (MAT), physics (MAT); social studies education (M Ed, MAT), including economics (MAT), geography (MAT), history (MAT), political science (MAT); teaching and learning (PhD), including language and literacy, mathematics education, music education, science education, social studies education, teaching and teacher education. *Accreditation:* NCATE. *Program availability:* Part-time, evening/weekend, online learning. *Faculty:* 24 full-time (18 women). *Students:* 179 full-time (110 women), 192 part-time (133 women); includes 193 minority (130 Black or African American, non-Hispanic/Latino; 1 American Indian or Alaska Native, non-Hispanic/Latino; 23 Asian, non-Hispanic/Latino; 25 Hispanic/Latino; 14 Two or more races, non-Hispanic/Latino), 6 international. Average age 33. 175 applicants, 58% accepted, 83 enrolled. In 2017, 81 master's, 17 doctorates awarded. *Entrance requirements:* For master's, GRE; GACE I (for initial teacher preparation programs), baccalaureate degree or equivalent, resume, goals statement, two letters of recommendation, minimum undergraduate GPA of 2.5; proof of initial teacher certification in the content area (for M Ed); for doctorate, GRE, resume, goals statement, writing sample, two letters of recommendation, minimum graduate GPA of 3.3, interview. *Application deadline:* For fall admission, 1/15 priority date for domestic and international students; for spring admission, 10/1 for domestic and international students. Application fee: $50. Electronic applications accepted. *Expenses:* Tuition, state resident: full-time $7020. Tuition, nonresident: full-time $22,518. *Required fees:* $2128. Tuition and fees vary according to degree level and program. *Financial support:* In 2017–18, fellowships with full tuition reimbursements (averaging $19,667 per year), research assistantships with full tuition reimbursements (averaging $5,436 per year), teaching assistantships with full tuition reimbursements (averaging $2,779 per year) were awarded; career-related internships or fieldwork, Federal Work-Study, scholarships/grants, health care benefits, tuition waivers (full and partial), and unspecified assistantships also available. Financial award application deadline: 3/15. *Faculty research:* Teacher education in language and literacy, mathematics, science, and social studies in urban middle and secondary school settings; learning technologies in school, community, and corporate settings; multicultural education and education for social justice; urban education; international education. *Unit head:* Dr. Dana L. Fox, Chair, 404-413-8060, Fax: 404-413-8063, E-mail: dfox@gsu.edu. *Application contact:* Bobbie Turner, Administrative Coordinator, 404-413-8405, Fax: 404-413-8063, E-mail: bnturner@gsu.edu.
Website: http://mse.education.gsu.edu/

Graceland University, Gleazer School of Education, Independence, MO 64050. Offers curriculum and instruction: collaborative learning and teaching (M Ed); differentiated instruction (M Ed); instructional leadership (M Ed); literacy instruction (M Ed); management in a quality classroom (M Ed); special education (M Ed); technology integration (M Ed). *Accreditation:* NCATE. *Program availability:* Part-time, 100% online. *Faculty:* 2 full-time (both women), 13 part-time/adjunct (10 women). *Students:* 117 full-time (102 women), 62 part-time (54 women); includes 8 minority (3 Black or African American, non-Hispanic/Latino; 1 Asian, non-Hispanic/Latino; 2 Hispanic/Latino; 1 Native Hawaiian or other Pacific Islander, non-Hispanic/Latino; 1 Two or more races, non-Hispanic/Latino), 1 international. Average age 35. 28 applicants, 100% accepted, 19 enrolled. In 2017, 64 master's awarded. *Degree requirements:* For master's, action research capstone. *Entrance requirements:* For master's, minimum GPA of 3.0, teaching certificate, current teaching contract and license, two letters of reference, statement of professional goals, verification of ongoing access to computer technology, including email and Internet. Additional exam requirements/recommendations for international students: Required—TOEFL (minimum score 550 paper-based; 79 iBT). *Application deadline:* For fall admission, 10/1 for domestic students; for winter admission, 11/15 for domestic students; for spring admission, 2/15 priority date for domestic students; for summer admission, 6/1 for domestic students. Application fee: $50. Electronic applications accepted. *Expenses:* Contact institution. *Financial support:* In 2017–18, 3 students received support. Tuition waivers available. Financial award applicants required to submit FAFSA. *Faculty research:* Literacy, technology, faculty mentoring, adult literacy, e-learning, online teaching. *Unit head:* Dr. Lee Bash, Interim Dean, 641-784-5072, E-mail: bash@graceland.edu. *Application contact:* Jeanette Calipetro, Admissions Representative, 816-423-4716, Fax: 816-833-2990, E-mail: jcali1@graceland.edu.
Website: http://www.graceland.edu/education

Grambling State University, School of Graduate Studies and Research, College of Education, Department of Curriculum and Instruction, Grambling, LA 71245. Offers curriculum and instruction (MS); special education (M Ed). *Program availability:* Part-time. *Degree requirements:* For master's, comprehensive exam, thesis (for some programs). *Entrance requirements:* Additional exam requirements/recommendations for international students: Required—TOEFL (minimum score 500 paper-based; 62 iBT).

Grambling State University, School of Graduate Studies and Research, College of Education, Department of Educational Leadership, Grambling, LA 71245. Offers developmental education (MS, Ed D, PMC), including curriculum and instructional design (Ed D), English (MS), guidance and counseling (MS), higher education administration and management (Ed D), mathematics (MS), reading (MS), science (MS), student development and personnel services (Ed D); educational leadership (M Ed). *Program availability:* Part-time, evening/weekend. *Degree requirements:* For master's, comprehensive exam, thesis (for some programs); for doctorate, comprehensive exam, thesis/dissertation. *Entrance requirements:* For master's, GRE, minimum GPA of 2.5 on last degree; for doctorate, GRE (minimum score 1000, 500 on Verbal), master's degree, minimum GPA of 3.0 on last degree. Additional exam requirements/recommendations for international students: Required—TOEFL (minimum score 500 paper-based; 62 iBT). Electronic applications accepted.

Grand Canyon University, College of Education, Phoenix, AZ 85017-1097. Offers autism spectrum disorders (MA); curriculum and instruction (MA); early childhood education (M Ed); educational administration (M Ed); educational leadership (M Ed); elementary education (M Ed); gifted education (MA); instructional technology (MS); K-12 leadership (Ed S); reading (MA); secondary education (M Ed); secondary humanities education (M Ed); secondary STEM education (M Ed); special education (M Ed); teaching and learning (Ed D); teaching English to speakers of other languages (MA). *Program availability:* Part-time, evening/weekend, online learning. *Degree requirements:* For master's, publishable research paper (M Ed), e-portfolio. *Entrance requirements:* For master's, undergraduate degree from accredited, GCU-approved college, university, or program with minimum GPA 2.8. Additional exam requirements/recommendations for international students: Required—TOEFL (minimum score 550 paper-based; 79 iBT), IELTS (minimum score 6). Electronic applications accepted.

Grand Valley State University, College of Education, Program in Instruction and Curriculum, Allendale, MI 49401-9403. Offers M Ed. *Program availability:* Part-time, evening/weekend. *Students:* 36 full-time (28 women), 136 part-time (119 women); includes 16 minority (5 Black or African American, non-Hispanic/Latino; 2 American Indian or Alaska Native, non-Hispanic/Latino; 1 Asian, non-Hispanic/Latino; 5 Hispanic/Latino; 3 Two or more races, non-Hispanic/Latino), 4 international. Average age 32. 43 applicants, 98% accepted, 16 enrolled. In 2017, 74 master's awarded. *Degree requirements:* For master's, project or thesis. *Entrance requirements:* For master's, minimum GPA of 3.0 or GRE General Test, last 60 credits from a regionally-accredited

college/university, 3 letters of recommendation. Additional exam requirements/recommendations for international students: Required—TOEFL (minimum iBT score of 80), IELTS (6.5), or Michigan English Language Assessment Battery (77). *Application deadline:* Applications are processed on a rolling basis. Application fee: $30. Electronic applications accepted. *Expenses:* $652 per credit hour. *Financial support:* In 2017–18, 23 students received support, including 22 fellowships; research assistantships and unspecified assistantships also available. *Unit head:* Paula Lancaster, Department Director, 616-331-6593, Fax: 616-331-6291, E-mail: lanscastp@gvsu.edu. *Application contact:* Thomas Owens, Director, Student Information and Services Center, 616-331-6282, Fax: 616-331-6217, E-mail: owenst@gvsu.edu.
Website: http://www.gvsu.edu/grad/instruction/

Harvard University, Harvard Graduate School of Education, Master's Programs in Education, Cambridge, MA 02138. Offers arts in education (Ed M); education policy and management (Ed M); higher education (Ed M); human development and psychology (Ed M); international education policy (Ed M); language and literacy (Ed M); learning and teaching (Ed M); mind, brain, and education (Ed M); prevention science and practice (Ed M); school leadership (Ed M); special studies (Ed M); teacher education (Ed M); technology, innovation, and education (Ed M). *Program availability:* Part-time. *Entrance requirements:* For master's, GRE General Test, statement of purpose, 3 letters of recommendation, resume, official transcripts. Additional exam requirements/recommendations for international students: Required—TOEFL (minimum score 613 paper-based; 104 iBT), TWE (minimum score 5). Electronic applications accepted. *Faculty research:* Learning and development, educational leadership and organizations, education policy analysis.

Henderson State University, Graduate Studies, Teachers College, Department of Advanced Instructional Studies, Arkadelphia, AR 71999-0001. Offers developmental therapy (MSE); dyslexia therapy (Graduate Certificate); education (MAT); educational technology leadership (Graduate Certificate); English as a second language (MSE, Graduate Certificate); instructional facilitator (MSE, Graduate Certificate); middle level education (MAT); special education (K-12) (MAT, MSE); special education/early childhood (MAT). *Accreditation:* NCATE. *Program availability:* Part-time. *Entrance requirements:* For master's, GRE General Test or MAT, minimum GPA of 2.7, teacher certification. Additional exam requirements/recommendations for international students: Required—TOEFL (minimum score 600 paper-based); Recommended—IELTS (minimum score 6.5).

Hood College, Graduate School, Department of Education, Frederick, MD 21701-8575. Offers curriculum and instruction (MS), including elementary education, elementary science and mathematics education, secondary education, special education; education, multidisciplinary studies (MS); educational leadership (MS, Certificate); reading specialization (MS); STEM education (Certificate). *Accreditation:* NCATE. *Program availability:* Part-time-only, evening/weekend. *Faculty:* 6 full-time (4 women), 35 part-time/adjunct (27 women). *Students:* 3 full-time (all women), 329 part-time (265 women); includes 62 minority (35 Black or African American, non-Hispanic/Latino; 4 Asian, non-Hispanic/Latino; 14 Hispanic/Latino; 9 Two or more races, non-Hispanic/Latino), 3 international. Average age 33. 76 applicants, 100% accepted, 63 enrolled. In 2017, 53 master's, 58 other advanced degrees awarded. *Degree requirements:* For master's, action research project, portfolio (for reading specialization); for Certificate, STEM capstone activity. *Entrance requirements:* For master's, minimum GPA of 2.75, teaching certification, writing sample during interview; letter of recommendation from principal (for educational leadership program only). Additional exam requirements/recommendations for international students: Required—TOEFL (minimum score 575 paper-based; 89 iBT), IELTS (minimum score 6.5). *Application deadline:* For fall admission, 8/15 priority date for domestic students, 8/5 for international students; for spring admission, 12/1 priority date for domestic students, 12/1 for international students; for summer admission, 5/1 priority date for domestic students, 4/15 for international students. Applications are processed on a rolling basis. Application fee: $35. Electronic applications accepted. *Expenses:* $465 per credit plus $110 comprehensive fee per semester. *Financial support:* Tuition waivers (partial) and unspecified assistantships available. Financial award applicants required to submit FAFSA. *Faculty research:* Leadership, action research, brain research, learning styles. *Unit head:* Dr. April M. Boulton, Dean of the Graduate School, 301-696-3612, E-mail: gofurther@hood.edu. *Application contact:* Jan Marcus, Assistant Director of Graduate Admissions, 301-696-3600, E-mail: gofurther@hood.edu.
Website: http://www.hood.edu/academics/education/index.html

Houston Baptist University, College of Education and Behavioral Sciences, Programs in Education, Houston, TX 77074-3298. Offers bilingual education (M Ed); counselor education (M Ed); curriculum and instruction (M Ed); curriculum and instruction (EC-6 bilingual) (M Ed); curriculum and instruction in all-level art, Spanish, music, or physical education (M Ed); curriculum and instruction in EC-6 and special education (EC-12) (M Ed); curriculum and instruction in instructional technology (M Ed); curriculum and instruction in mathematics, science, or social studies (4-8) (M Ed); curriculum and instruction with EC-6 generalist (M Ed); curriculum and instruction with English language arts and reading (4-8) (M Ed); educational administration (M Ed); educational diagnostician (M Ed); executive educational leadership (Ed D); higher education in business management (M Ed); higher education in Christian studies (M Ed); higher education in counseling (M Ed); higher education in educational technology (M Ed); reading (M Ed); special educational leadership (Ed D). *Program availability:* Part-time, evening/weekend, 100% online, blended/hybrid learning. *Students:* 83 full-time (65 women), 187 part-time (156 women); includes 189 minority (114 Black or African American, non-Hispanic/Latino; 2 American Indian or Alaska Native, non-Hispanic/Latino; 9 Asian, non-Hispanic/Latino; 58 Hispanic/Latino; 6 Two or more races, non-Hispanic/Latino), 7 international. Average age 36. 309 applicants, 31% accepted, 70 enrolled. In 2017, 92 master's awarded. *Degree requirements:* For master's, comprehensive exam; for doctorate, thesis/dissertation. *Entrance requirements:* For master's, minimum GPA of 2.75, two recommendations, resume, bachelor's degree conferred transcript; interview (for non-certified teachers); for doctorate, GRE, 5 letters of recommendation. Additional exam requirements/recommendations for international students: Required—TOEFL (minimum score 80 iBT), IELTS (minimum score 6.5). *Application deadline:* For fall admission, 8/1 for domestic students, 6/1 for international students; for spring admission, 1/1 for domestic students, 11/1 for international students; for summer admission, 5/1 for domestic students, 3/1 for international students. Applications are processed on a rolling basis. Application fee: $0 ($100 for international students). Electronic applications accepted. Application fee is waived when completed online. *Expenses:* $22,000 tuition; $4,500 fees (general, technology and parking). *Financial support:* In 2017–18, 59 students received support. Research assistantships, teaching assistantships, Federal Work-Study, and scholarships/grants available. Support available to part-time students. Financial award application deadline: 4/1; financial award applicants required to submit FAFSA. *Faculty research:* Autism and inclusion, integrating technology into instruction, school change and leadership trust. *Unit head:* Dr. Charlotte Fontenot, Director, Graduate Programs, 281-649-3078, Fax: 281-649-3361, E-mail: cfontenot@hbu.edu. *Application contact:* Kristy Wright, Administrative Assistant for Graduate Programs, 281-649-3094, Fax: 281-649-3361, E-mail: kwright@hbu.edu.
Website: http://www.hbu.edu/MED

Curriculum and Instruction

Illinois State University, Graduate School, College of Education, Department of Curriculum and Instruction, Normal, IL 61790. Offers curriculum and instruction (MS, MS Ed, Ed D); educational policies (Ed D); postsecondary education (Ed D); reading (MS Ed); supervision (Ed D). *Accreditation:* NCATE. *Degree requirements:* For master's, variable foreign language requirement, thesis or alternative; for doctorate, variable foreign language requirement, thesis/dissertation, 2 terms of residency, internship. *Entrance requirements:* For master's, GRE General Test, minimum GPA of 3.0 in last 60 hours of course work; for doctorate, GRE General Test. *Faculty research:* In-service and pre-service teacher education for teachers of English language learners; teachers for all children: developing a model for alternative, bilingual elementary certification for paraprofessionals in Illinois; Illinois Geographic Alliance, Connections Project.

Indiana State University, College of Graduate and Professional Studies, Bayh College of Education, Department of Teaching and Learning, Terre Haute, IN 47809. Offers curriculum and instruction (M Ed, PhD); educational technology (MS). *Accreditation:* NCATE. *Degree requirements:* For doctorate, thesis/dissertation. *Entrance requirements:* For doctorate, GRE General Test. Electronic applications accepted. *Faculty research:* Discipline FERPA reading, teacher strengths and needs.

Indiana University Bloomington, School of Education, Department of Curriculum and Instruction, Bloomington, IN 47405-7000. Offers art education (MS, Ed D, PhD); curriculum studies (Ed D, PhD); elementary education (MS, Ed D, PhD, Ed S); mathematics education (MS, Ed D, PhD); science education (MS, Ed D, PhD); secondary education (MS, Ed D, PhD); social studies education (MS, Ed D, PhD); special education (PhD, Ed S). *Accreditation:* NCATE. *Program availability:* Part-time, evening/weekend. Terminal master's awarded for partial completion of doctoral program. *Degree requirements:* For doctorate, thesis/dissertation; for Ed S, comprehensive exam or project. *Entrance requirements:* For master's, doctorate, and Ed S, GRE General Test. Electronic applications accepted.

Indiana University of Pennsylvania, School of Graduate Studies and Research, College of Education and Communications, Department of Professional Studies in Education, Program in Curriculum and Instruction, Indiana, PA 15705. Offers D Ed. *Accreditation:* NCATE. *Program availability:* Part-time, evening/weekend. *Faculty:* 13 full-time (11 women), 3 part-time/adjunct (2 women). *Students:* 8 full-time (3 women), 85 part-time (62 women); includes 7 minority (3 Black or African American, non-Hispanic/ Latino; 2 Hispanic/Latino; 2 Two or more races, non-Hispanic/Latino), 12 international. Average age 41. 42 applicants, 79% accepted, 12 enrolled. In 2017, 20 doctorates awarded. *Degree requirements:* For doctorate, one foreign language, comprehensive exam, thesis/dissertation. *Entrance requirements:* For doctorate, 2 letters of recommendation; recorded five-minute, research-based presentation; 1.5 hour online writing task. Additional exam requirements/recommendations for international students: Required—TOEFL (minimum score 540 paper-based). *Application deadline:* Applications are processed on a rolling basis. Application fee: $50. Electronic applications accepted. *Expenses:* Contact institution. *Financial support:* In 2017–18, 3 fellowships with full tuition reimbursements (averaging $2,137 per year), 14 research assistantships with tuition reimbursements (averaging $4,690 per year), 2 teaching assistantships with partial tuition reimbursements (averaging $21,363 per year) were awarded; career-related internships or fieldwork, Federal Work-Study, scholarships/ grants, and unspecified assistantships also available. Support available to part-time students. Financial award application deadline: 4/15; financial award applicants required to submit FAFSA. *Unit head:* Dr. Kelli Jo Kerry-Moran, Graduate Coordinator, 724-357-7931, E-mail: kjkmoran@iup.edu.
Website: http://www.iup.edu/grad/CandI/default.aspx

Indiana University–Purdue University Indianapolis, School of Education, Indianapolis, IN 46202-5155. Offers curriculum and instruction (MS); early childhood (MS); educational leadership (MS, Certificate); English as a second language (Certificate); kindergarten (Certificate); language education (MS); reading (Certificate); school counseling (MS); special education (MS, Certificate). *Program availability:* Part-time, evening/weekend. Terminal master's awarded for partial completion of doctoral program. *Degree requirements:* For master's, thesis optional. *Entrance requirements:* For master's, GRE General Test, minimum GPA of 2.5; for Certificate, official transcripts. Additional exam requirements/recommendations for international students: Required—TOEFL (minimum score 60 iBT), IELTS (minimum score 5.5). Electronic applications accepted. *Expenses:* Contact institution. *Faculty research:* Educational policies and school leaders' responses to these; issues of intersectionality in the experiences of African American lesbian, gay, and bisexual students attending historically black colleges and universities and those who belong to black Greek-letter organizations; students' experiential knowledge and their evolving disciplinary-specific literacy and understanding; innovative program development; urban ESL teacher preparation; target-based instructional coaching.

Inter American University of Puerto Rico, Arecibo Campus, Programs in Education, Arecibo, PR 00614-4050. Offers administration and educational supervision (MA Ed); counseling and guidance (MA Ed); curriculum and teaching (MA Ed), including biology education, English as a second language, history education, math education, Spanish; elementary education (MA Ed). *Accreditation:* TEAC. *Degree requirements:* For master's, comprehensive exam, thesis optional. *Entrance requirements:* For master's, GRE, EXADEP, bachelor's degree in education or teaching license (administration and supervision) or courses in education and psychology (counseling and guidance), minimum GPA of 2.5 in last 60 credits.

Inter American University of Puerto Rico, Barranquitas Campus, Program in Education, Barranquitas, PR 00794. Offers curriculum and teaching (M Ed), including biology, English as a second language, history, Spanish; educational leadership and management (MA); elementary education (M Ed); information and library service technology (M Ed); special education (MA). *Accreditation:* TEAC. *Program availability:* Part-time, evening/weekend. *Faculty:* 1 full-time (0 women), 3 part-time/adjunct (2 women). *Students:* 17 full-time (16 women), 2 part-time (both women); all minorities (all Hispanic/Latino). Average age 34. 9 applicants, 89% accepted, 8 enrolled. In 2017, 5 master's awarded. *Degree requirements:* For master's, 2 foreign languages, comprehensive exam, thesis (for some programs). *Entrance requirements:* For master's, GRE or EXADEP, bachelor's degree or its equivalent from accredited institution, official academic transcript from institution that conferred bachelor's degree, minimum GPA of 2.5, two recommendation letters, interview (for some programs), essay (for some programs). *Application deadline:* Applications are processed on a rolling basis. Application fee: $31. Electronic applications accepted. *Expenses:* $3,392 full-time tuition plus $652 fees. *Financial support:* Applicants required to submit FAFSA. *Unit head:* Juan A. Negron-Berrios, PhD, Chancellor, 787-857-3600 Ext. 2002, Fax: 787-857-2125, E-mail: janegron@br.inter.edu. *Application contact:* Aramilda Cartagena-Santiago, Dean of Students, 787-857-3600 Ext. 2009, Fax: 787-857-2125, E-mail: aramildacartagena@br.inter.edu.

Inter American University of Puerto Rico, Metropolitan Campus, Graduate Programs, Program in Education, San Juan, PR 00919-1293. Offers curriculum and instruction (Ed D); educational administration (Ed D); guidance and counseling (MA, Ed D); special education administration (Ed D). *Accreditation:* TEAC. *Degree*

requirements: For doctorate, comprehensive exam, thesis/dissertation. *Entrance requirements:* For doctorate, GRE, MAT, or EXADEP. Electronic applications accepted.

Inter American University of Puerto Rico, San Germán Campus, Graduate Studies Center, Program in Curriculum and Instruction, San Germán, PR 00683-5008. Offers Ed D. *Program availability:* Part-time, evening/weekend.

Iowa State University of Science and Technology, Department of Education, Ames, IA 50011. Offers curriculum and instructional technology (M Ed, MS, PhD); elementary education (M Ed, MS); historical, philosophical, and comparative studies in education (M Ed, MS); special education (M Ed, MS, PhD). *Degree requirements:* For master's, thesis or alternative; for doctorate, thesis/dissertation. *Entrance requirements:* For master's and doctorate, GRE General Test. Additional exam requirements/ recommendations for international students: Required—TOEFL (minimum score 560 paper-based; 83 iBT), IELTS (minimum score 6.5). Electronic applications accepted.

John Brown University, Graduate Education Programs, Siloam Springs, AR 72761-2121. Offers curriculum and instruction (M Ed); secondary education (MAT). *Program availability:* Part-time, evening/weekend. *Entrance requirements:* For master's, GRE (minimum score of 300). Additional exam requirements/recommendations for international students: Required—TOEFL (minimum score 550 paper-based; 79 iBT). Electronic applications accepted.

Kansas State University, Graduate School, College of Education, Department of Curriculum and Instruction, Manhattan, KS 66506. Offers curriculum and instruction (Ed D, PhD); digital teaching and learning (MS); educational computing, design and online learning (MS); elementary/middle level curriculum and instruction (MS); online learning (Certificate); reading specialist endorsement (MS); reading/language arts (MS); teacher leader/school improvement (MS); teaching and learning (Certificate). *Accreditation:* NCATE. *Program availability:* Part-time, online learning. *Degree requirements:* For master's, comprehensive exam, portfolio, project, report or thesis; for doctorate, comprehensive exam, thesis/dissertation, preliminary exam; for Certificate, comprehensive exam, portfolio. *Entrance requirements:* For master's, minimum GPA of 3.0, 3 letters of recommendation; for doctorate, GRE, minimum GPA of 3.0, 3 letters of recommendation, evidence of scholarly writing; for Certificate, minimum GPA of 3.0, letters of recommendation. Additional exam requirements/recommendations for international students: Required—TOEFL (minimum score 550 paper-based; 80 iBT) or IELTS. Electronic applications accepted. *Faculty research:* Literacy and technology, critical race theory and diversity, achievement gaps, school improvement, teacher education.

Kean University, College of Education, Program in Instruction and Curriculum, Union, NJ 07083. Offers bilingual/bicultural education (MA); teaching English as a second language (MA). *Accreditation:* NCATE. *Program availability:* Part-time. *Faculty:* 13 full-time (7 women). *Students:* 3 full-time (2 women), 26 part-time (23 women); includes 19 minority (1 Black or African American, non-Hispanic/Latino; 18 Hispanic/Latino), 2 international. Average age 35. 10 applicants, 100% accepted, 8 enrolled. In 2017, 10 master's awarded. *Degree requirements:* For master's, comprehensive exam (for some programs), thesis optional, two-semester advanced seminar. *Entrance requirements:* For master's, GRE General Test or MAT; PRAXIS (for some programs), minimum GPA of 3.0, personal statement, professional resume/curriculum vitae, commitment to working with children, certification (for some programs), two letters of recommendation. Additional exam requirements/recommendations for international students: Required— TOEFL (minimum score 550 paper-based; 79 iBT), IELTS (minimum score 6.5). *Application deadline:* For fall admission, 6/30 for domestic and international students; for spring admission, 12/1 for domestic and international students. Applications are processed on a rolling basis. Application fee: $75. Electronic applications accepted. *Expenses:* Tuition, state resident: full-time $13,419; part-time $653 per credit. Tuition, nonresident: full-time $18,188; part-time $801 per credit. *Required fees:* $3382; $154 per credit. Tuition and fees vary according to course level, course load, degree level and program. *Financial support:* Scholarships/grants and unspecified assistantships available. Financial award applicants required to submit FAFSA. *Unit head:* Dr. Gail Verdi, Program Coordinator, 908-737-3908, E-mail: gverdi@kean.edu. *Application contact:* Brittany Gerstenhaber, Admissions Counselor, 908-737-7100, E-mail: grad-adm@kean.edu.
Website: http://grad.kean.edu/masters-programs/bilingualbicultural-education-instruction-and-curriculum

Keene State College, School of Professional and Graduate Studies, Keene, NH 03435. Offers curriculum and instruction (M Ed); education leadership (PMC); educational leadership (M Ed); school counselor (M Ed, PMC); special education (M Ed). *Accreditation:* NCATE. *Program availability:* Part-time, evening/weekend. *Faculty:* 6 full-time (3 women), 7 part-time/adjunct (2 women). *Students:* 20 full-time (14 women), 42 part-time (20 women); includes 2 minority (1 Black or African American, non-Hispanic/ Latino; 1 Asian, non-Hispanic/Latino), 1 international. Average age 31. 33 applicants, 58% accepted, 17 enrolled. In 2017, 39 master's awarded. *Degree requirements:* For master's, thesis (for some programs). *Entrance requirements:* For master's, PRAXIS I, 3 references; official transcripts; minimum GPA of 2.5; interview; essay; teacher/educator certificate; work/internship experience. Additional exam requirements/recommendations for international students: Required—TOEFL (minimum score 550 paper-based; 61 iBT). *Application deadline:* For fall admission, 4/1 for domestic and international students; for spring admission, 11/1 for domestic and international students; for summer admission, 3/1 for domestic and international students. Applications are processed on a rolling basis. Application fee: $50. Electronic applications accepted. *Expenses:* Tuition, state resident: full-time $9960; part-time $520 per credit. Tuition, nonresident: full-time $10,260; part-time $570 per credit. *Required fees:* $1908; $106 per credit. Tuition and fees vary according to course load. *Financial support:* In 2017–18, 19 students received support. Career-related internships or fieldwork, Federal Work-Study, institutionally sponsored loans, scholarships/grants, and unspecified assistantships available. Support available to part-time students. Financial award application deadline: 3/1; financial award applicants required to submit FAFSA. *Unit head:* Dr. Karrie Kalich, Dean of Professional and Graduate Studies, 603-358-2885, E-mail: kkalich@keene.edu. *Application contact:* Carl Ditkoff, Graduate Program Assistant, 603-358-2497, E-mail: kscgraduatestudies@keene.edu.
Website: http://www.keene.edu/academics/graduate/

Kent State University, College of Education, Health and Human Services, School of Teaching, Learning and Curriculum Studies, Program in Curriculum and Instruction, Kent, OH 44242-0001. Offers M Ed, PhD, Ed S. *Accreditation:* NCATE. *Program availability:* Part-time, evening/weekend. *Degree requirements:* For doctorate, comprehensive exam, thesis/dissertation. *Entrance requirements:* For master's, 2 letters of reference, goals statement; for doctorate, GRE General Test, 2 letters of reference, goals statement, writing sample, resume; for Ed S, GRE General Test, 2 letters of reference, goals statement. Additional exam requirements/recommendations for international students: Required—TOEFL (minimum score 550 paper-based; 80 iBT). Electronic applications accepted. *Expenses:* Tuition, state resident: full-time $11,310; part-time $515 per credit hour. Tuition, nonresident: full-time $20,396; part-time $928 per credit hour. *International tuition:* $18,544 full-time. *Faculty research:* Gender equity issues in teaching, learning math and science, teaching as inquiry artistry, curriculum studies for democratic humanism.

Kent State University at Stark, Graduate School of Education, Health and Human Services, Canton, OH 44720-7599. Offers curriculum and instruction studies (M Ed, MA).

Kutztown University of Pennsylvania, College of Education, Program in Secondary Education, Kutztown, PA 19530-0730. Offers biology (M Ed); curriculum and instruction (M Ed); English (M Ed); mathematics (M Ed); middle level (M Ed); social studies (M Ed); teaching (M Ed); transformational teaching and learning (Ed D). *Accreditation:* NCATE. *Program availability:* Part-time, evening/weekend, 100% online, blended/hybrid learning. *Faculty:* 4 full-time (3 women), 1 part-time/adjunct (0 women). *Students:* 33 full-time (21 women), 76 part-time (49 women); includes 6 minority (3 Black or African American, non-Hispanic/Latino; 3 Hispanic/Latino). Average age 32. 76 applicants, 91% accepted, 43 enrolled. In 2017, 31 master's awarded. *Degree requirements:* For master's, comprehensive exam, thesis optional; for doctorate, thesis/dissertation. *Entrance requirements:* For master's, GRE General Test, minimum undergraduate major GPA of 3.0, 3 letters of recommendation, copy of PRAXIS II or valid instructional I or II teaching certificate; for doctorate, master's or specialist degree in education or related field from regionally-accredited institution of higher learning with minimum graduate GPA of 3.25, significant educational experience, employment in an education setting (preferred). Additional exam requirements/recommendations for international students: Required—TOEFL (minimum score 550 paper-based, 79 iBT), IELTS (minimum score 6.5), or PTE (minimum score 53). *Application deadline:* For fall admission, 8/1 for domestic and international students; for spring admission, 12/1 for domestic and international students. Application fee: $35. Electronic applications accepted. *Expenses:* Tuition, state resident: part-time $500 per credit. Tuition, nonresident: part-time $750 per credit. *Required fees:* $115 per credit. One-time fee: $50 part-time. Tuition and fees vary according to degree level. *Financial support:* Career-related internships or fieldwork, Federal Work-Study, scholarships/grants, and unspecified assistantships available. Financial award application deadline: 3/1; financial award applicants required to submit FAFSA. *Unit head:* Dr. Theresa Stahler, Department Chair, 610-683-4259, Fax: 610-683-1338, E-mail: stahler@kutztown.edu. *Application contact:* Dr. Patricia Walsh Coates, Graduate Coordinator, 610-638-4289, Fax: 610-683-1338, E-mail: coates@kutztown.edu.
Website: https://www.kutztown.edu/academcs/graduate-programs/secondary-education.htm

LaGrange College, Graduate Programs, Department of Education, LaGrange, GA 30240-2999. Offers curriculum and instruction (M Ed, Ed S); middle grades (MAT); secondary education (MAT). *Program availability:* Part-time, evening/weekend. *Degree requirements:* For master's, comprehensive exam. *Entrance requirements:* For master's, GRE, MAT, minimum GPA of 2.5. Additional exam requirements/recommendations for international students: Required—TOEFL (minimum score 550 paper-based).

Lasell College, Graduate and Professional Studies in Education, Newton, MA 02466-2709. Offers curriculum, leadership, and inclusion (M Ed); elementary education (M Ed); special education (M Ed), including moderate disabilities; teaching bilingual/English learners with disabilities (Graduate Certificate). *Program availability:* Part-time-only, evening/weekend, blended/hybrid learning. *Faculty:* 3 full-time (all women), 5 part-time/adjunct (4 women). *Students:* 8 full-time (7 women), 43 part-time (38 women); includes 4 minority (2 Asian, non-Hispanic/Latino; 1 Hispanic/Latino; 1 Two or more races, non-Hispanic/Latino), 1 international. Average age 28. 23 applicants, 74% accepted, 10 enrolled. In 2017, 15 master's awarded. *Degree requirements:* For master's, minimum GPA of 3.0; practicum. *Entrance requirements:* For master's, Massachusetts Tests for Educator Licensure (MTEL) Curriculum and Literacy foundations of reading and writing subtest, one-page personal statement, 2 letters of recommendation, resume, bachelor's degree transcript. Additional exam requirements/recommendations for international students: Required—TOEFL (minimum score 550 paper-based, 79 iBT) or IELTS (minimum score 6). *Application deadline:* For fall admission, 8/31 priority date for domestic students, 6/30 priority date for international students; for spring admission, 12/31 priority date for domestic students, 10/31 priority date for international students. Applications are processed on a rolling basis. Electronic applications accepted. *Expenses:* $600 per credit. *Financial support:* Federal Work-Study, scholarships/grants, and tuition discounts available. Support available to part-time students. Financial award application deadline: 8/31; financial award applicants required to submit FAFSA. *Faculty research:* Inclusion, English language learners, literacy, and urban education; teacher inquiry; universal design for learning, deaf-blindness, and visual impairments; social and emotional learning; educational law, applied behavior analysis, and classroom management. *Unit head:* Eric Turner, Vice President of Graduate and Professional Studies, 617-243-2071, Fax: 617-243-2450, E-mail: gradinfo@lasell.edu. *Application contact:* Adrienne Franciosi, Director of Graduate Enrollment, 617-243-2214, Fax: 617-243-2450, E-mail: gradinfo@lasell.edu.
Website: http://www.lasell.edu/academics/graduate-and-professional-studies/programs-of-study/master-of-education.html

La Sierra University, School of Education, Department of Curriculum and Instruction, Riverside, CA 92505. Offers curriculum and instruction (MA, Ed D, Ed S); teaching (MAT). *Program availability:* Part-time, evening/weekend. *Degree requirements:* For doctorate, thesis/dissertation; for Ed S, thesis optional. *Entrance requirements:* For master's, minimum GPA of 3.0; for doctorate, GRE General Test, GRE Subject Test, minimum GPA of 3.3; for Ed S, minimum GPA of 3.3. *Faculty research:* New teacher success, politics of knowledge, computer-assisted instruction, diversity issues.

Lee University, Program in Education, Cleveland, TN 37320-3450. Offers art (MAT); curriculum and instruction (M Ed, Ed S); early childhood (MAT); educational leadership (M Ed, Ed S); elementary education (MAT); English and math (MAT); English and science (MAT); English and social studies (MAT); higher education administration (MS); history (MAT); history and economics (MAT); math and science (MAT); math and social studies (MAT); middle grades (MAT); science and social studies (MASW); secondary education (MAT); Spanish (MAT); special education (M Ed, MAT); TESOL (MAT). *Accreditation:* NCATE. *Program availability:* Part-time. *Faculty:* 15 full-time (7 women), 8 part-time/adjunct (3 women). *Students:* 28 full-time (21 women), 77 part-time (48 women); includes 12 minority (7 Black or African American, non-Hispanic/Latino; 2 Hispanic/Latino; 3 Two or more races, non-Hispanic/Latino), 1 international. Average age 31. 35 applicants, 83% accepted, 22 enrolled. In 2017, 54 master's, 4 other advanced degrees awarded. *Degree requirements:* For master's, variable foreign language requirement, thesis optional, internship. *Entrance requirements:* For master's, MAT or GRE General Test, minimum undergraduate GPA of 2.75, 3 letters of recommendation, interview, writing sample, official transcripts, background check; for Ed S, minimum undergraduate and master's GPA of 2.75, official transcripts for undergraduate and master's degrees. Additional exam requirements/recommendations for international students: Required—TOEFL (minimum score 61 iBT). *Application deadline:* For fall admission, 6/1 priority date for domestic and international students; for spring admission, 11/1 priority date for domestic and international students; for summer admission, 4/1 priority date for domestic and international students. Applications are processed on a rolling basis. Application fee: $25. Electronic applications accepted. *Expenses:* Tuition: Full-time $12,780; part-time $710 per credit hour. *Required fees:* $60; $60 per term. Tuition and fees vary according to program. *Financial support:* In 2017–18, 32 students received support. Career-related internships or fieldwork, Federal

Work-Study, institutionally sponsored loans, scholarships/grants, and unspecified assistantships available. Financial award application deadline: 3/1; financial award applicants required to submit FAFSA. *Unit head:* Dr. William Kamm, Director, 423-614-8544, E-mail: wkamm@leeuniversity.edu. *Application contact:* Crystal Keeter, Graduate Education Secretary, 423-614-8544, E-mail: ckeeter@leeuniversity.edu.
Website: http://www.leeuniversity.edu/academics/graduate/education

Lehigh University, College of Education, Program in Educational Leadership, Bethlehem, PA 18015. Offers curriculum and instruction (Certificate); educational leadership (M Ed, Ed D); K-12 principal (Certificate); superintendent letter (Certificate). *Program availability:* Part-time, evening/weekend, online learning. *Faculty:* 5 full-time (2 women), 7 part-time/adjunct (3 women). *Students:* 6 full-time (5 women), 111 part-time (70 women); includes 14 minority (1 Black or African American, non-Hispanic/Latino; 1 Asian, non-Hispanic/Latino; 12 Hispanic/Latino), 6 international. Average age 34. 82 applicants, 67% accepted, 9 enrolled. In 2017, 52 master's, 9 Certificates awarded. Terminal master's awarded for partial completion of doctoral program. *Degree requirements:* For master's, thesis (for some programs); for doctorate, comprehensive exam, thesis/dissertation. *Entrance requirements:* For master's, minimum undergraduate GPA of 3.0, essay, transcripts, 2 letters of recommendation; for doctorate, GRE General Test or MAT, minimum graduate GPA of 3.6, 2 letters of recommendation, essay, transcript; for Certificate, minimum undergraduate GPA of 3.0. Additional exam requirements/recommendations for international students: Required—TOEFL (minimum score 600 paper-based, 93 iBT) or IELTS. *Application deadline:* For fall admission, 1/15 for domestic and international students; for spring admission, 12/1 for domestic and international students; for summer admission, 5/1 for domestic and international students. Applications are processed on a rolling basis. Application fee: $65. Electronic applications accepted. *Expenses:* $565 per credit; $225 internship fee. *Financial support:* In 2017–18, 18 students received support, including 3 research assistantships (averaging $8,092 per year); fellowships and unspecified assistantships also available. Financial award application deadline: 1/31; financial award applicants required to submit FAFSA. *Faculty research:* Supervision of instruction, middle-level education, organizational change, leadership preparation and development, international school leadership, urban school leadership, comparative education, social justice, education and human services, social network, principal leadership, policy implementation, teacher evaluation, teaching quality. *Unit head:* Dr. Floyd D. Beachum, Director, 610-758-5955, Fax: 610-758-3227, E-mail: fdb209@lehigh.edu. *Application contact:* Kristi Ball, Coordinator, 610-758-3250, Fax: 610-758-6223, E-mail: kmb618@lehigh.edu.
Website: https://ed.lehigh.edu/academics/programs/educational-leadership

Lesley University, Graduate School of Education, Cambridge, MA 02138-2790. Offers arts, community, and education (M Ed); autism studies (Certificate); curriculum and instruction (M Ed, CAGS); early childhood education (M Ed); ecological teaching and learning (MS); educational studies (PhD), including adult learning, educational leadership, individually designed; elementary education (M Ed); emergent technologies for educators (Certificate); ESLArts: language learning through the arts (M Ed); high school education (M Ed); individually designed (M Ed); integrated teaching through the arts (M Ed); literacy for K-8 classroom teachers (M Ed); mathematics education (M Ed); middle school education (M Ed); moderate disabilities (M Ed); online learning (Certificate); reading (CAGS); science in education (M Ed); severe disabilities (M Ed); special needs (CAGS); specialist teacher of reading (M Ed); teacher of visual art (M Ed); technology in education (M Ed, CAGS). *Accreditation:* TEAC. *Program availability:* Part-time, evening/weekend, online learning. *Degree requirements:* For master's, practicum; for doctorate, thesis/dissertation. *Entrance requirements:* For master's, Massachusetts Tests for Educator Licensure (MTEL), transcripts, statement of purpose, recommendations; interview (for special education); for doctorate, GRE General Test, transcripts, statement of purpose, recommendations, interview, master's degree, resume; for other advanced degree, interview, master's degree. Additional exam requirements/recommendations for international students: Required—TOEFL (minimum score 550 paper-based; 80 iBT). Electronic applications accepted. *Faculty research:* Assessment in literacy, mathematics and science; autism spectrum disorders; instructional technology and online learning; multicultural education and English language learners.

LeTourneau University, Graduate Programs, Longview, TX 75607-7001. Offers business (MBA); counseling (MA), including licensed professional counselor, marriage and family therapy, school counseling; curriculum and instruction (M Ed); educational administration (M Ed); engineering (ME, MS); engineering management (MEM); health care administration (MS); marriage and family therapy (MA); psychology (MA); strategic leadership (MSL); teacher leadership (M Ed); teaching and learning (M Ed). *Program availability:* Part-time, 100% online, blended/hybrid learning. *Students:* 55 full-time (35 women), 337 part-time (266 women); includes 218 minority (140 Black or African American, non-Hispanic/Latino; 2 American Indian or Alaska Native, non-Hispanic/Latino; 5 Asian, non-Hispanic/Latino; 32 Hispanic/Latino; 39 Two or more races, non-Hispanic/Latino), 3 international. Average age 37. *Entrance requirements:* Additional exam requirements/recommendations for international students: Required—TOEFL. *Application deadline:* For fall admission, 8/22 for domestic students, 8/29 for international students; for winter admission, 10/10 for domestic students; for spring admission, 1/2 for domestic students, 1/10 for international students; for summer admission, 5/1 for domestic and international students. Applications are processed on a rolling basis. Electronic applications accepted. *Expenses:* Contact institution. *Financial support:* Research assistantships, institutionally sponsored loans, and unspecified assistantships available. Financial award applicants required to submit FAFSA.
Website: http://www.letu.edu

Lewis & Clark College, Graduate School of Education and Counseling, Department of Teacher Education, Program in Curriculum and Instruction, Portland, OR 97219-7899. Offers M Ed. *Program availability:* Part-time, evening/weekend. *Entrance requirements:* For master's, minimum GPA of 2.75. Additional exam requirements/recommendations for international students: Required—TOEFL (minimum score 575 paper-based). Electronic applications accepted.

Lewis University, College of Education, Program in Curriculum and Instruction: Technology Learning and Design, Romeoville, IL 60446. Offers M Ed. *Program availability:* Part-time, evening/weekend. *Students:* 1 (woman) full-time, 2 part-time (1 woman), 1 international. Average age 35. *Degree requirements:* For master's, departmental qualifying exam. *Entrance requirements:* For master's, writing exam, bachelor's degree, minimum GPA of 2.75, two letters of recommendation, interview. Additional exam requirements/recommendations for international students: Required—TOEFL (minimum score 550 paper-based; 79 iBT), IELTS (minimum score 6). *Application deadline:* For fall admission, 5/1 priority date for international students; for spring admission, 11/15 priority date for international students. Applications are processed on a rolling basis. Application fee: $40. Electronic applications accepted. Tuition and fees vary according to program. *Financial support:* Career-related internships or fieldwork, Federal Work-Study, institutionally sponsored loans, and unspecified assistantships available. Financial award application deadline: 5/1; financial award applicants required to submit FAFSA. *Unit head:* Dr. Seung Kim, Program Director, 815-838-0500, E-mail: kimse@lewisu.edu. *Application contact:* Kathy Lisak, Graduate Admission Counselor, 815-836-5610, E-mail: grad@lewisu.edu.

Curriculum and Instruction

Liberty University, School of Education, Lynchburg, VA 24515. Offers curriculum and instruction (Ed D, Ed S), including elementary education, middle grades education, secondary education, special education; educational leadership (Ed D); gifted education (Certificate); math specialist (M Ed); middle grades (MAT, Certificate); reading specialist (M Ed); school leadership (Certificate); secondary education (MAT); sport management (MS); including coaching and athletic administration, outdoor adventure sport, sport administration, tourism. *Accreditation:* NCATE. *Program availability:* Part-time, online learning. *Students:* 1,966 full-time (1,428 women), 3,484 part-time (2,528 women); includes 1,323 minority (1,026 Black or African American, non-Hispanic/Latino; 29 American Indian or Alaska Native, non-Hispanic/Latino; 49 Asian, non-Hispanic/Latino; 100 Hispanic/Latino; 9 Native Hawaiian or other Pacific Islander, non-Hispanic/Latino; 110 Two or more races, non-Hispanic/Latino), 58 international. Average age 37. 3,748 applicants, 58% accepted, 1167 enrolled. In 2017, 656 master's, 110 doctorates, 316 other advanced degrees awarded. *Degree requirements:* For doctorate, comprehensive exam, thesis/dissertation. *Entrance requirements:* For master's, GRE General Test or MAT (if taken in or before 1999), 2 letters of recommendation, minimum undergraduate GPA of 3.0, curriculum vitae; for doctorate and other advanced degree, GRE General Test or MAT (if taken before 1999), minimum master's GPA of 3.0, 3 years of teaching experience. Additional exam requirements/recommendations for international students: Required—TOEFL (minimum score 600 paper-based; 100 iBT). *Application deadline:* For fall admission, 6/1 for domestic students; for spring admission, 11/1 for domestic students. Applications are processed on a rolling basis. Application fee: $50. Electronic applications accepted. *Expenses:* Contact institution. *Financial support:* Federal Work-Study and tuition waivers (partial) available. *Faculty research:* Self-determination, character education, bibliotherapy, learning styles, distance education. *Unit head:* Dr. Heather Schoffstall, Dean, 434-582-2445, Fax: 434-582-2468, E-mail: awgunter@liberty.edu. *Application contact:* Jay Bridge, Director of Graduate Admissions, 800-424-9595, Fax: 800-628-7977, E-mail: gradadmissions@liberty.edu.
Website: http://www.liberty.edu/academics/education/graduate/

Lincoln Memorial University, Carter and Moyers School of Education, Harrogate, TN 37752-1901. Offers administration and supervision (M Ed, Ed S); counseling and guidance (M Ed); curriculum and instruction (M Ed, Ed D, Ed S); educational leadership (M Ed); executive leadership (Ed D); higher education administration (Ed D); human resource development (Ed D); leadership and administration (Ed D). *Program availability:* Part-time, evening/weekend, online learning. *Degree requirements:* For master's, comprehensive exam, thesis optional; for Ed S, comprehensive exam. *Entrance requirements:* For master's, PRAXIS, NTE, GRE, MAT, letters of recommendation; for Ed S, graduate transcripts. Additional exam requirements/recommendations for international students: Recommended—TOEFL. *Faculty research:* Brain compatible teaching and learning; poverty in Appalachia; leadership for change; ethics, moral responsibility and social justice; human and organizational learning.

Louisiana State University in Shreveport, College of Business, Education, and Human Development, Program in Education, Shreveport, LA 71115-2399. Offers curriculum and instruction (M Ed); leadership (M Ed); leadership studies (Ed D). *Accreditation:* NCATE. *Program availability:* Part-time. *Students:* 35 full-time (22 women), 215 part-time (181 women); includes 76 minority (62 Black or African American, non-Hispanic/Latino; 1 Asian, non-Hispanic/Latino; 10 Hispanic/Latino; 3 Two or more races, non-Hispanic/Latino), 5 international. Average age 36. 270 applicants, 96% accepted, 98 enrolled. In 2017, 59 master's, 3 doctorates awarded. *Degree requirements:* For master's, orally-presented project, 200-hour internship (educational leadership). *Entrance requirements:* For master's, GRE, minimum GPA of 2.5; teacher certification; recommendations and interview (for educational leadership). Additional exam requirements/recommendations for international students: Required—TOEFL (minimum score 550 paper-based; 61 iBT). *Application deadline:* For fall admission, 6/30 for domestic and international students; for spring admission, 11/30 for domestic and international students; for summer admission, 4/30 for domestic and international students. Applications are processed on a rolling basis. Application fee: $20 ($30 for international students). Electronic applications accepted. *Expenses:* Tuition, state resident: full-time $3098; part-time $344 per credit hour. Tuition, nonresident: full-time $9923; part-time $1103 per credit hour. *Required fees:* $384 per semester. Tuition and fees vary according to program. *Financial support:* In 2017–18, 5 research assistantships (averaging $2,150 per year) were awarded. *Unit head:* Dr. Pat Doerr, Coordinator, 318-797-5033, Fax: 318-798-4144, E-mail: pat.doerr@lsus.edu. *Application contact:* Mary Catherine Harvison, Director of Admissions, 318-797-2400, Fax: 318-797-5286, E-mail: mary.harvison@lsus.edu.

Louisiana Tech University, Graduate School, College of Education, Ruston, LA 71272. Offers counseling and guidance (MA), including clinical mental health counseling, human services, orientation and mobility; counseling psychology (PhD); curriculum and instruction (M Ed); cyber education (Graduate Certificate); dynamics of domestic and family violence (Graduate Certificate); early childhood education - PreK-3 (MAT); educational leadership (M Ed, Ed D); elementary education and special education mild/moderate grades 1-5 (MAT); higher education administration (Graduate Certificate); industrial/organizational psychology (MA, PhD); kinesiology (MS); middle school education (MAT), including mathematics; orientation and mobility (Graduate Certificate); rehabilitation teaching for the blind (Graduate Certificate); secondary education (MAT), including agriculture, biology, business, chemistry, English; special education: visually impaired (MAT); teacher leader education (Graduate Certificate); visual impairments - blind education (Graduate Certificate). *Accreditation:* NCATE. *Program availability:* Part-time. *Faculty:* 28 full-time (16 women), 23 part-time/adjunct (22 women). *Students:* 269 full-time (192 women), 194 part-time (150 women); includes 127 minority (94 Black or African American, non-Hispanic/Latino; 2 American Indian or Alaska Native, non-Hispanic/Latino; 6 Asian, non-Hispanic/Latino; 16 Hispanic/Latino; 1 Native Hawaiian or other Pacific Islander, non-Hispanic/Latino; 8 Two or more races, non-Hispanic/Latino), 8 international. Average age 34. 226 applicants, 74% accepted, 60 enrolled. In 2017, 5 master's, 2 doctorates, 1 other advanced degree awarded. *Degree requirements:* For master's, thesis; for doctorate, thesis/dissertation. *Entrance requirements:* For master's and doctorate, GRE General Test. Additional exam requirements/recommendations for international students: Required—TOEFL (minimum score 550 paper-based; 80 iBT), IELTS (minimum score 6.5). *Application deadline:* For fall admission, 9/1 priority date for domestic students, 6/1 for international students; for winter admission, 11/1 priority date for domestic students, 9/1 for international students; for spring admission, 2/1 priority date for domestic students, 12/1 for international students; for summer admission, 5/1 priority date for domestic students, 3/1 for international students. Application fee: $40. Electronic applications accepted. *Expenses:* Tuition, state resident: full-time $5146. Tuition, nonresident: full-time $10,147. *International tuition:* $10,267 full-time. *Required fees:* $2273. *Financial support:* In 2017–18, 40 students received support, including 23 research assistantships (averaging $10,346 per year), 15 teaching assistantships (averaging $6,887 per year); fellowships and career-related internships or fieldwork also available. Financial award application deadline: 2/1. *Faculty research:* Blindness and the best methods for increasing independence for individuals who are blind or visually impaired; educating and investigating factors contributing to improvements in human performance across the lifespan and a reduction in injury rates during training. *Total annual research expenditures:* $2.1 million. *Unit head:* Dr. Don Schillinger, Dean, 318-257-3712, E-mail: dschill@latech.edu. *Application contact:* Dr. Dawn Basinger,

Associate Dean of Academic Affairs, 318-257-2977, Fax: 318-257-2379, E-mail: dbasing@latech.edu.
Website: http://education.latech.edu/

Lourdes University, Graduate School, Sylvania, OH 43560-2898. Offers business (MBA); leadership (M Ed); nurse anesthesia (MSN); nurse educator (MSN); nurse leader (MSN); organizational leadership (MOL); reading (M Ed); teaching and curriculum (M Ed); theology (MA). *Program availability:* Evening/weekend. *Entrance requirements:* Additional exam requirements/recommendations for international students: Required—TOEFL.

Loyola University Chicago, School of Education, Program in Curriculum and Instruction, Chicago, IL 60660. Offers M Ed, Ed D. *Program availability:* Part-time, evening/weekend. *Faculty:* 18 full-time (12 women), 33 part-time/adjunct (29 women). *Students:* 26 full-time (17 women), 22 part-time (19 women); includes 16 minority (7 Black or African American, non-Hispanic/Latino; 3 Asian, non-Hispanic/Latino; 5 Hispanic/Latino; 1 Two or more races, non-Hispanic/Latino), 5 international. Average age 37. 35 applicants, 43% accepted, 11 enrolled. In 2017, 4 master's, 6 doctorates awarded. *Degree requirements:* For master's, comprehensive exam; for doctorate, comprehensive exam, thesis/dissertation. *Entrance requirements:* For master's, 3 references, minimum GPA of 3.0, resume; for doctorate, GRE, 3 references, interview, minimum GPA of 3.0, resume. Additional exam requirements/recommendations for international students: Required—TOEFL (minimum score 550 paper-based; 79 iBT). *Application deadline:* For fall admission, 1/1 for domestic and international students. Applications are processed on a rolling basis. Application fee: $50. Electronic applications accepted. Application fee is waived when completed online. *Expenses:* $949 per semester hour, $2,847 per course, $8,541-$11,388 full-time semester tuition; $432 per semester fees, $225 additional fees (first semester only). *Financial support:* In 2017–18, 9 research assistantships with full tuition reimbursements (averaging $14,000 per year) were awarded; fellowships with partial tuition reimbursements, institutionally sponsored loans, scholarships/grants, and unspecified assistantships also available. Support available to part-time students. Financial award application deadline: 2/1; financial award applicants required to submit FAFSA. *Faculty research:* School improvement, technology, change, reading. *Unit head:* Dr. Hank Bohanon, Director, 312-915-7099, E-mail: hbohano@luc.edu. *Application contact:* Mirtza Campbell, Information Contact, 312-915-8907, E-mail: mcampbell11@luc.edu.

Loyola University Maryland, Graduate Programs, School of Education, Program in Curriculum and Instruction, Baltimore, MD 21210-2699. Offers MA. *Program availability:* Part-time. *Faculty:* 36 full-time (27 women), 23 part-time/adjunct (15 women). *Students:* 1 full-time (0 women), 43 part-time (39 women); includes 17 minority (11 Black or African American, non-Hispanic/Latino; 2 Asian, non-Hispanic/Latino; 3 Hispanic/Latino; 1 Two or more races, non-Hispanic/Latino). Average age 31. *Degree requirements:* For master's, thesis. *Entrance requirements:* For master's, essay, transcripts, resume. Additional exam requirements/recommendations for international students: Required—TOEFL (minimum score 550 paper-based), IELTS (minimum score 7). *Application deadline:* For fall admission, 6/15 for domestic students; for winter admission, 11/1 for domestic students. Applications are processed on a rolling basis. Application fee: $60. Electronic applications accepted. *Expenses:* Contact institution. *Financial support:* Scholarships/grants available. Financial award application deadline: 4/15; financial award applicants required to submit FAFSA. *Unit head:* Stephanie Flores-Koulish, Director, 410-617-5456, E-mail: sfloreskoulish@loyola.edu. *Application contact:* Office of Graduate Admission, 410-617-5020, E-mail: graduate@loyola.edu.

Malone University, Graduate Program in Education, Canton, OH 44709. Offers curriculum and instruction (MA); curriculum, instruction, and professional development (MA); educational leadership (principal license) (MA); intervention specialist (MA). *Accreditation:* NCATE. *Program availability:* Part-time, evening/weekend. *Degree requirements:* For master's, research project. *Entrance requirements:* For master's, minimum GPA of 3.0, teaching license. Additional exam requirements/recommendations for international students: Required—TOEFL (minimum score 550 paper-based; 79 iBT). *Faculty research:* Educational leadership styles; Jesus as master teacher, assessment accommodations for English language learners, preparing culturally proficient teachers, using naturally occurring text in the classroom to meet the syntactic needs of students with learning disabilities, using tablet instructional technology to meet the needs of students with disabilities.

Marian University, School of Education, Fond du Lac, WI 54935-4699. Offers curriculum and instruction leadership (PhD); educational administration (PhD); educational leadership (MAE); educational technology (MAE); leadership studies (PhD); special education (MAE); teacher education (MAE). *Accreditation:* NCATE. *Program availability:* Part-time, evening/weekend, online learning. *Degree requirements:* For master's, exam, field-based experience project, portfolio; for doctorate, comprehensive exam, thesis/dissertation, field-based experience. *Entrance requirements:* For master's, minimum GPA of 3.0, BA in education or related field, teaching license; for doctorate, GRE, MAT, resume, 2 writing samples, interview. Additional exam requirements/recommendations for international students: Required—TOEFL (minimum score 525 paper-based; 70 iBT). *Faculty research:* At-risk youth, multicultural issues, values in education, teaching/learning strategies.

Marquette University, Graduate School, College of Education, Department of Educational Policy and Leadership, Milwaukee, WI 53201-1881. Offers college student personnel administration (M Ed); curriculum and instruction (MA); education (MA); educational administration (M Ed); educational policy and foundations (MA); elementary education (Certificate); literacy (MA); principal (Certificate); reading specialist (Certificate); reading teacher (Certificate); secondary education (Certificate); superintendent (Certificate). *Program availability:* Part-time, evening/weekend. Terminal master's awarded for partial completion of doctoral program. *Degree requirements:* For master's, comprehensive exam, thesis (for some programs); for doctorate, thesis/dissertation, qualifying exam. *Entrance requirements:* For master's, GRE General Test or MAT, official transcripts from all current and previous colleges/universities except Marquette, three letters of recommendation, statement of purpose; for doctorate, GRE General Test, MAT, sample of written work, official transcripts from all current and previous colleges/universities except Marquette, three letters of recommendation, statement of purpose, resume/curriculum vitae; for Certificate, GRE General Test or MAT, master's degree. Additional exam requirements/recommendations for international students: Required—TOEFL (minimum score 530 paper-based). *Expenses:* Contact institution. *Faculty research:* Leadership; social justice in education; development of lifelong learners; race, class, and schooling in historical perspective; urban teacher education.

Martin Luther College, Graduate Studies, New Ulm, MN 56073. Offers early childhood director (MS Ed Admin); educational technology (MS Ed); instruction (MS Ed); leadership (MS Ed); principal (MS Ed Admin); special education (MS Ed). *Program availability:* Part-time, evening/weekend, online learning. *Faculty:* 8 full-time (1 woman), 21 part-time/adjunct (10 women). *Students:* 1 (woman) full-time, 81 part-time (28 women); includes 2 minority (1 Asian, non-Hispanic/Latino; 1 Two or more races, non-Hispanic/Latino), 2 international. Average age 37. 23 applicants, 100% accepted, 23 enrolled. In 2017, 25 master's awarded. *Degree requirements:* For master's, capstone project or comprehensive exam. *Entrance requirements:* For master's, undergraduate

degree in education from an accredited college or university, minimum undergraduate GPA of 3.0. Additional exam requirements/recommendations for international students: Required—TOEFL (minimum score 550 paper-based; 80 iBT); Recommended—IELTS (minimum score 6.5). *Application deadline:* Applications are processed on a rolling basis. Application fee: $35. Electronic applications accepted. *Expenses:* $315 per credit. *Financial support:* In 2017–18, 4 students received support. Scholarships/grants available. Financial award application deadline: 9/1. *Faculty research:* Principal effectiveness, principal support, cognitive load in math instruction, reading strategies in multigrade classrooms, mentor provided professional development for new teachers. *Unit head:* John E. Meyer, Director of Graduate Studies, 507-354-8221 Ext. 398, E-mail: meyerjd@mlc-wels.edu.
Website: https://mlc-wels.edu/graduate-studies/

Marygrove College, Graduate Studies, Detroit, MI 48221-2599. Offers autism spectrum disorders (M Ed, Certificate); curriculum instruction and assessment (MAT); educational leadership (MA); educational technology (M Ed); effective teaching in the 21st century-classroom focus (MAT); effective teaching in the 21st century-technology focus (MAT); human resource management (MA, Certificate); mathematics 6-8 (MAT); mathematics K-5 (MAT); reading and literacy K-6 (MAT); reading specialist (M Ed); school administrator (Certificate); social justice (MA); special education (MAT); special education - learning disabilities (M Ed); teaching - pre-elementary education (M Ed); teaching - pre-secondary education (M Ed). *Program availability:* Part-time, evening/weekend, 100% online, blended/hybrid learning. *Students:* 163 full-time (123 women), 264 part-time (186 women). Average age 34. *Entrance requirements:* For master's, all official bachelor's transcripts. Additional exam requirements/recommendations for international students: Required—TOEFL (minimum score 550 paper-based; 80 iBT). *Application deadline:* Applications are processed on a rolling basis. Electronic applications accepted. *Expenses: Tuition:* Part-time $590 per credit hour. *Required fees:* $120 per semester. One-time fee: $25 part-time. *Financial support:* Applicants required to submit FAFSA. *Unit head:* Marygrove College Admissions, 313-927-1240, E-mail: info@marygrove.edu. *Application contact:* Marygrove College Admissions, 313-927-1240, E-mail: info@marygrove.edu.

Marymount University, School of Education and Human Services, Program in Education, Arlington, VA 22207-4299. Offers curriculum and instruction (M Ed); elementary education (M Ed); professional studies (M Ed); secondary education (M Ed); special education: general curriculum (M Ed). *Accreditation:* NCATE. *Program availability:* Part-time, evening/weekend. *Faculty:* 7 full-time (all women), 10 part-time/adjunct (7 women). *Students:* 51 full-time (40 women), 92 part-time (61 women); includes 33 minority (9 Black or African American, non-Hispanic/Latino; 9 Asian, non-Hispanic/Latino; 10 Hispanic/Latino; 5 Two or more races, non-Hispanic/Latino), 11 international. Average age 34. 39 applicants, 97% accepted, 30 enrolled. In 2017, 72 master's awarded. *Degree requirements:* For master's, thesis or alternative, capstone/internship. *Entrance requirements:* For master's, GRE or MAT and PRAXIS I or SAT/ACT and Virginia Communication and Literacy Assessment (VCLA), 2 letters of recommendation, resume, interview, minimum undergraduate GPA of 2.75 or 3.25 in the last 60 hours. Additional exam requirements/recommendations for international students: Required—TOEFL (minimum score 600 paper-based; 96 iBT), IELTS (minimum score 6.5). *Application deadline:* Applications are processed on a rolling basis. Application fee: $40. Electronic applications accepted. *Expenses:* $715 per credit. *Financial support:* In 2017–18, 7 students received support, including 2 teaching assistantships with full and partial tuition reimbursements available (averaging $14,520 per year); career-related internships or fieldwork, Federal Work-Study, scholarships/grants, and unspecified assistantships also available. Support available to part-time students. Financial award application deadline: 3/1; financial award applicants required to submit FAFSA. *Unit head:* Dr. Lisa Turissini, Chair, Education, 703-526-1668, Fax: 703-284-1631, E-mail: lisa.turissini@marymount.edu. *Application contact:* Francesca Reed, Director, Graduate Admissions, 703-284-5901, Fax: 703-527-3815, E-mail: grad.admissions@marymount.edu.
Website: http://www.marymount.edu/Academics/School-of-Education-Human-Services/Graduate-Programs/Education-(M-Ed-)

Massachusetts College of Liberal Arts, Graduate Programs, North Adams, MA 01247-4100. Offers business (MBA); educational administration (M Ed); educational leadership (CAGS); instruction and curriculum (M Ed); instructional technology (M Ed); physical education and health (M Ed); reading (M Ed); special education (M Ed). *Program availability:* Part-time, evening/weekend. *Degree requirements:* For master's, thesis. *Entrance requirements:* For master's, writing sample.

McDaniel College, Graduate and Professional Studies, Program in Curriculum and Instruction, Westminster, MD 21157-4390. Offers MS. *Program availability:* Part-time, evening/weekend, 100% online, blended/hybrid learning. *Faculty:* 4 full-time (all women), 18 part-time/adjunct (13 women). *Students:* 3 full-time (all women), 254 part-time (201 women); includes 34 minority (18 Black or African American, non-Hispanic/Latino; 2 Asian, non-Hispanic/Latino; 11 Hispanic/Latino; 1 Native Hawaiian or other Pacific Islander, non-Hispanic/Latino; 2 Two or more races, non-Hispanic/Latino), 1 international. Average age 30. 36 applicants, 100% accepted, 25 enrolled. In 2017, 106 master's awarded. *Degree requirements:* For master's, comprehensive exam (for some programs), thesis optional. *Entrance requirements:* For master's, one reference. Additional exam requirements/recommendations for international students: Required—TOEFL (minimum score 79 iBT), IELTS (minimum score 6). *Application deadline:* For fall admission, 6/1 priority date for domestic students; for spring admission, 11/1 priority date for domestic students; for summer admission, 3/1 priority date for domestic students. Applications are processed on a rolling basis. Application fee: $75. Electronic applications accepted. *Expenses: Tuition:* Full-time $11,760; part-time $490 per credit hour. Tuition and fees vary according to course load and program. *Financial support:* Application deadline: 3/1; applicants required to submit FAFSA. *Unit head:* Fax: 410-857-2515, E-mail: gradadms@mcdaniel.edu. *Application contact:* Penny Pfeiffer, Senior Graduate Enrollment Management Specialist, 410-857-2513, Fax: 410-857-2515, E-mail: ppfeiffer@mcdaniel.edu.

McGill University, Faculty of Graduate and Postdoctoral Studies, Faculty of Education, Department of Integrated Studies in Education, Montréal, QC H3A 2T5, Canada. Offers culture and values in education (MA, PhD); curriculum studies (MA); educational leadership (MA, Certificate); educational studies (PhD); integrated studies in education (M Ed); second language education (MA, PhD).

McKendree University, Graduate Programs, Programs in Education, Lebanon, IL 62254-1299. Offers curriculum design and instruction (Ed D, Ed S); educational administration and leadership (MA Ed); educational studies (MA Ed); higher education administrative services (MA Ed); music education (MA Ed); reading (MA Ed); special education (MA Ed); teacher leadership (MA Ed); teaching certification (MA Ed). *Accreditation:* NCATE. *Program availability:* Part-time, evening/weekend, online learning. *Entrance requirements:* For master's, official transcripts from all institutions previously attended, minimum GPA of 3.0, resume, references; for doctorate, GRE (within the past 5 years), master's degree in education and Ed S, or the equivalent, from regionally-accredited institution; official transcripts from all institutions previously attended; curriculum vitae/resume; essay/personal statement; two years of teaching/professional experience; for Ed S, GRE (within the past 5 years), master's degree in

education from regionally-accredited institution of higher education; official transcripts from all institutions previously attended; curriculum vitae/resume; essay/personal statement; two years of teaching/professional experience. Additional exam requirements/recommendations for international students: Required—TOEFL. Electronic applications accepted.

McNeese State University, Doré School of Graduate Studies, Burton College of Education, Department of Education Professions, Program in Curriculum and Instruction, Lake Charles, LA 70609. Offers academically gifted education (M Ed); elementary education (M Ed); reading (M Ed); secondary education (M Ed); special education (M Ed). *Program availability:* Evening/weekend. *Entrance requirements:* For master's, GRE, teaching certificate. *Application deadline:* For fall admission, 5/15 priority date for domestic and international students; for spring admission, 10/15 priority date for domestic and international students. Applications are processed on a rolling basis. Application fee: $20 ($30 for international students). *Financial support:* Application deadline: 5/1. *Unit head:* Dr. Brett C. Welch, Director, 337-475-5405, Fax: 337-475-5272, E-mail: bwelch@mcneese.edu. *Application contact:* Dr. Dustin M. Hebert, Director of Doré School of Graduate Studies, 337-475-5396, Fax: 337-475-5397, E-mail: admissions@mcneese.edu.

Medaille College, Program in Education, Buffalo, NY 14214-2695. Offers adolescent education (MS Ed); curriculum and instruction (MS Ed); education preparation (MS Ed); literacy (MS Ed); special education (MS). *Accreditation:* TEAC. *Program availability:* Part-time, evening/weekend. *Degree requirements:* For master's, comprehensive exam (for some programs), thesis or alternative. *Entrance requirements:* For master's, minimum undergraduate GPA of 2.7. Additional exam requirements/recommendations for international students: Required—TOEFL (minimum score 550 paper-based). Electronic applications accepted. *Faculty research:* Curriculum planning, truancy, tracking minority students, curriculum design, mentoring students.

Memorial University of Newfoundland, School of Graduate Studies, Faculty of Education, St. John's, NL A1C 5S7, Canada. Offers counseling psychology (M Ed); curriculum, teaching, and learning studies (M Ed); education (PhD); educational leadership studies (M Ed, Graduate Diploma); information technology (M Ed); post-secondary studies (M Ed, Diploma), including health professional education (Diploma). *Program availability:* Part-time. *Degree requirements:* For master's, thesis optional, internship, paper folio, project; for doctorate, comprehensive exam, thesis/dissertation, thesis seminar, oral defense of thesis. *Entrance requirements:* For master's, undergraduate degree with at least 2nd class standing, 1-2 years of work experience; for doctorate, minimum A average in graduate course work, MA in education, 2 years of professional experience; for other advanced degree, 2nd class degree, 2 years of work experience with adult learners, appropriate academic qualifications and work experience in a health-related field. Electronic applications accepted. *Faculty research:* Critical thinking, literacy, cognitive studies and counseling, educational change, technology in instruction.

Mercer University, Graduate Studies, Cecil B. Day Campus, Tift College of Education (Atlanta), Atlanta, GA 30341. Offers curriculum and instruction (PhD); early childhood education (M Ed, MAT, Ed S); educational leadership (PhD), including higher education leadership, P-12 school leadership; educational leadership P-12 (M Ed, Ed S); higher education leadership (M Ed); independent and charter school leadership (M Ed); middle grades education (M Ed, MAT); secondary education (M Ed, MAT); teacher leadership (Ed S). *Accreditation:* NCATE. *Program availability:* Part-time, evening/weekend. *Faculty:* 30 full-time (16 women), 34 part-time/adjunct (27 women). *Students:* 159 full-time (131 women), 284 part-time (229 women); includes 264 minority (232 Black or African American, non-Hispanic/Latino; 1 American Indian or Alaska Native, non-Hispanic/Latino; 9 Asian, non-Hispanic/Latino; 18 Hispanic/Latino; 4 Two or more races, non-Hispanic/Latino), 2 international. Average age 35. In 2017, 137 master's, 22 doctorates, 40 other advanced degrees awarded. *Degree requirements:* For master's and Ed S, research project; for doctorate, comprehensive exam, thesis/dissertation. *Entrance requirements:* For master's, GRE or MAT, minimum undergraduate GPA of 2.75; for doctorate, GRE; for Ed S, GRE or MAT, minimum GPA of 3.25; 3 years of certified teaching experience (for educational leadership and teacher leadership). Additional exam requirements/recommendations for international students: Required—TOEFL (minimum score 80 iBT). *Application deadline:* For fall admission, 8/1 for domestic and international students; for spring admission, 12/1 for domestic and international students; for summer admission, 5/1 for domestic and international students. Applications are processed on a rolling basis. Application fee: $25 ($50 for international students). Electronic applications accepted. *Expenses:* Contact institution. *Financial support:* Federal Work-Study and unspecified assistantships available. Support available to part-time students. Financial award application deadline: 5/1; financial award applicants required to submit FAFSA. *Faculty research:* Educational technology, multicultural and minority issues in education, educational leadership (P-12 and higher education), school discipline and school bullying, standards-based mathematics education. *Unit head:* Dr. Scott Davis, Dean, 478-301-2110, Fax: 478-301-5576.
Website: http://education.mercer.edu/

Mercer University, Graduate Studies, Macon Campus, Tift College of Education (Macon), Macon, GA 31207. Offers curriculum and instruction (PhD); early childhood education (M Ed, Ed S); educational leadership (M Ed, PhD, Ed S), including higher education (PhD), P-12; higher education leadership (M Ed); independent and charter school leadership (M Ed); secondary education (MAT), including STEM; teacher leadership (Ed S). *Accreditation:* NCATE. *Program availability:* Part-time, evening/weekend, 100% online, blended/hybrid learning. *Faculty:* 13 full-time (8 women), 1 part-time/adjunct (0 women). *Students:* 33 full-time (18 women), 51 part-time (37 women); includes 49 minority (44 Black or African American, non-Hispanic/Latino; 2 Asian, non-Hispanic/Latino; 2 Hispanic/Latino; 1 Two or more races, non-Hispanic/Latino), 1 international. Average age 32. In 2017, 22 master's, 17 doctorates awarded. *Degree requirements:* For master's, research project report; for doctorate, comprehensive exam, thesis/dissertation. *Entrance requirements:* For master's, GRE or MAT, minimum GPA of 2.75; for doctorate, GRE, minimum GPA of 3.5; interview; writing sample; 3 recommendations; for Ed S, GRE or MAT, minimum GPA of 3.5 (for teacher leadership), 3.0 (for educational leadership). Additional exam requirements/recommendations for international students: Required—TOEFL (minimum score 80 iBT). *Application deadline:* For fall admission, 8/1 for domestic and international students; for spring admission, 12/1 for domestic and international students. Applications are processed on a rolling basis. Application fee: $35. Electronic applications accepted. *Expenses:* Contact institution. *Financial support:* Federal Work-Study, institutionally sponsored loans, and unspecified assistantships available. Support available to part-time students. Financial award application deadline: 5/1; financial award applicants required to submit FAFSA. *Faculty research:* Teacher effectiveness, specific learning disabilities, inclusion. *Unit head:* Dr. Scott Davis, Dean, 478-301-2110, Fax: 478-301-5576, E-mail: davis_ds@mercer.edu.
Website: http://education.mercer.edu/

Merrimack College, School of Education and Social Policy, North Andover, MA 01845-5800. Offers community engagement (M Ed), including community organizations, higher education, PreK-12 education; criminology and criminal justice (MS); curriculum and instruction (M Ed); early childhood education (M Ed); educational leadership (CAGS), including instructional leadership; elementary education (M Ed); English as a second language (PreK-6) (M Ed); high school education (M Ed); higher education (M Ed),

Curriculum and Instruction

including leadership and organizational development, student affairs; middle school education (M Ed); moderate disabilities (PreK-8) (M Ed); school counseling (M Ed). *Program availability:* Part-time, evening/weekend, 100% online courses with immersion events and in-classroom practicum close to home. *Faculty:* 15 full-time, 36 part-time/adjunct. *Students:* 212 full-time (175 women), 121 part-time (101 women); includes 42 minority (6 Black or African American, non-Hispanic/Latino; 6 Asian, non-Hispanic/Latino; 27 Hispanic/Latino; 3 Two or more races, non-Hispanic/Latino), 3 international. Average age 27. 420 applicants, 84% accepted, 250 enrolled. In 2017, 177 master's awarded. *Degree requirements:* For master's, practicum, portfolio, and state test (for licensure track); capstone (for higher education, curriculum and instruction, and community engagement tracks); for CAGS, capstone. *Entrance requirements:* For master's, Massachusetts Teacher Education Licensure (MTEL), official transcripts from other colleges, resume, personal statement, 2 letters of recommendation. Additional exam requirements/recommendations for international students: Required—TOEFL (minimum score 84 iBT), IELTS (minimum score 6.5), PTE (minimum score 56). *Application deadline:* For fall admission, 8/24 for domestic students, 7/30 for international students; for spring admission, 1/10 for domestic students, 12/10 for international students; for summer admission, 5/10 for domestic students, 4/10 for international students. Applications are processed on a rolling basis. Application fee: $0. Electronic applications accepted. *Expenses:* Contact institution. *Financial support:* Fellowships with full tuition reimbursements, career-related internships or fieldwork, scholarships/grants, and health care benefits available. Support available to part-time students. Financial award application deadline: 5/1; financial award applicants required to submit FAFSA. *Application contact:* Alyssa Orlando, Graduate Admissions Counselor, 978-837-3563, E-mail: orlandoaf@merrimack.edu.
Website: http://www.merrimack.edu/academics/graduate/education/

Messiah College, Program in Education, Mechanicsburg, PA 17055. Offers curriculum and instruction (M Ed); special education (M Ed); teaching English to speakers of other languages (M Ed). *Program availability:* Part-time, online learning. Electronic applications accepted. *Faculty research:* Socio-cultural perspectives on education, TESOL, autism, special education.

Michigan State University, The Graduate School, College of Education, Department of Teacher Education, East Lansing, MI 48824. Offers curriculum, instruction and teacher education (PhD, Ed S); teaching and curriculum (MA). *Entrance requirements:* Additional exam requirements/recommendations for international students: Required—TOEFL. Electronic applications accepted.

Middle Tennessee State University, College of Graduate Studies, College of Education, Department of Educational Leadership, Program in Curriculum and Instruction, Murfreesboro, TN 37132. Offers curriculum and instruction (M Ed, Ed S); English as a second language (M Ed, Ed S); secondary education (M Ed); technology and curriculum design (Ed S). *Accreditation:* NCATE. *Program availability:* Part-time, evening/weekend, online learning. *Degree requirements:* For master's, comprehensive exam; for Ed S, comprehensive exam, thesis or alternative. *Entrance requirements:* For master's and Ed S, GRE, MAT or PRAXIS. Additional exam requirements/recommendations for international students: Required—TOEFL (minimum score 525 paper-based; 71 iBT) or IELTS (minimum score 6). Electronic applications accepted.

Midwestern State University, Billie Doris McAda Graduate School, West College of Education, Program in Curriculum and Instruction, Wichita Falls, TX 76308. Offers M Ed. *Program availability:* Part-time, evening/weekend. *Degree requirements:* For master's, comprehensive exam. *Entrance requirements:* For master's, GRE General Test, MAT, or GMAT. Additional exam requirements/recommendations for international students: Required—TOEFL (minimum score 550 paper-based). Electronic applications accepted. *Faculty research:* Role of the twenty-first century principal, instructional effectiveness, motivation, curriculum theory, educational research methodology.

Minnesota State University Moorhead, Graduate Studies, College of Education and Human Services, Moorhead, MN 56563. Offers counseling and student affairs (MS); curriculum and instruction (MS); educational leadership (MS, Ed D, Ed S); special education (MS); speech-language pathology (MS). *Accreditation:* NCATE. *Program availability:* Part-time, 100% online, blended/hybrid learning. *Faculty:* 22. *Students:* 117 full-time (101 women), 337 part-time (253 women). Average age 32. 248 applicants, 49% accepted. In 2017, 149 master's, 16 other advanced degrees awarded. *Degree requirements:* For master's, comprehensive exam (for some programs), thesis, final oral defense; for doctorate, comprehensive exam (for some programs), thesis/dissertation, final oral defense. *Entrance requirements:* For master's, GRE, essay, letter of intent, letters of reference, teaching license, teaching verification, minimum cumulative GPA of 3.0; for doctorate, official transcripts; letter of intent; resume or curriculum vitae; master's degree; personal essay. Additional exam requirements/recommendations for international students: Required—TOEFL (minimum score 550 paper-based); Recommended—IELTS (minimum score 6.5). *Application deadline:* Applications are processed on a rolling basis. Application fee: $20. Electronic applications accepted. *Expenses:* Tuition, state resident: full-time $9000; part-time $374 per credit. Tuition, nonresident: full-time $18,000; part-time $748 per credit. *Required fees:* $1055; $43.96 per credit. Tuition and fees vary according to degree level, program and reciprocity agreements. *Financial support:* Federal Work-Study and unspecified assistantships available. Financial award application deadline: 10/1; financial award applicants required to submit FAFSA. *Unit head:* Dr. Ok-Hee Lee, Dean, 218-477-2095, E-mail: okheelee@mnstate.edu. *Application contact:* Karla Wenger, Office Manager, 218-477-2344, Fax: 218-477-2482, E-mail: wengerk@mnstate.edu.
Website: http://www.mnstate.edu/cehs/

Misericordia University, College of Health Sciences and Education, Program in Education, Dallas, PA 18612-1098. Offers instructional technology (MS); reading specialist (MS); special education (MS). *Program availability:* Part-time, evening/weekend. *Entrance requirements:* For master's, minimum undergraduate GPA of 3.0. Additional exam requirements/recommendations for international students: Required—TOEFL. Electronic applications accepted.

Mississippi College, Graduate School, School of Education, Department of Teacher Education and Leadership, Clinton, MS 39058. Offers art (M Ed); biological science (M Ed); business education (M Ed); computer science (M Ed); dyslexia therapy (M Ed); educational leadership (M Ed, Ed D, Ed S); elementary education (M Ed, Ed S); English (M Ed); higher education administration (MS); mathematics (M Ed); secondary education (M Ed); social studies (history) (M Ed); teaching arts (M Ed). *Program availability:* Part-time, online learning. *Degree requirements:* For master's, comprehensive exam, thesis optional. *Entrance requirements:* For master's, NTE. Additional exam requirements/recommendations for international students: Recommended—TOEFL, IELTS. Electronic applications accepted.

Mississippi State University, College of Education, Department of Curriculum, Instruction and Special Education, Mississippi State, MS 39762. Offers early childhood education (PhD); elementary education (MS, PhD, Ed S), including early childhood education (MS), general elementary education (MS), middle level education (MS); general curriculum and instruction (PhD); reading education (PhD); secondary education (MAT, MS, PhD, Ed S); special education (MAT, MS, PhD, Ed S). *Accreditation:* NCATE. *Program availability:* Part-time, evening/weekend. *Faculty:* 22 full-time (16

women), 1 (woman) part-time/adjunct. *Students:* 38 full-time (26 women), 170 part-time (131 women); includes 46 minority (37 Black or African American, non-Hispanic/Latino; 4 American Indian or Alaska Native, non-Hispanic/Latino; 2 Hispanic/Latino; 1 Native Hawaiian or other Pacific Islander, non-Hispanic/Latino; 2 Two or more races, non-Hispanic/Latino), 4 international. Average age 32. 88 applicants, 53% accepted, 39 enrolled. In 2017, 68 master's, 4 doctorates, 5 other advanced degrees awarded. *Degree requirements:* For master's, comprehensive exam; for doctorate, thesis/dissertation; for Ed S, comprehensive exam, thesis or alternative. *Entrance requirements:* For master's, GRE, minimum GPA of 2.75 in junior and senior year, eligibility for initial teacher certification; for doctorate, GRE, minimum GPA of 3.4 on previous graduate work; for Ed S, GRE, minimum GPA of 3.2 on master's degree. Additional exam requirements/recommendations for international students: Required—TOEFL (minimum score 550 paper-based; 79 iBT); Recommended—IELTS (minimum score 6.5). *Application deadline:* For fall admission, 3/1 priority date for domestic students, 5/1 for international students; for spring admission, 9/1 priority date for domestic students, 9/1 for international students. Applications are processed on a rolling basis. Application fee: $60 ($80 for international students). Electronic applications accepted. *Expenses:* Tuition, state resident: full-time $8318; part-time $462.12 per credit hour. Tuition, nonresident: full-time $22,358; part-time $1242.12 per credit hour. *Required fees:* $110; $12.24 per credit hour. $6.12 per semester. *Financial support:* In 2017–18, 6 research assistantships with partial tuition reimbursements (averaging $11,307 per year) were awarded; Federal Work-Study, institutionally sponsored loans, scholarships/grants, and unspecified assistantships also available. Financial award application deadline: 4/1; financial award applicants required to submit FAFSA. *Faculty research:* Early childhood education, reading, rural schools, multicultural education, use of technology in instruction. *Unit head:* Dr. Linda Cornelious, Professor and Interim Head, 662-325-3747, Fax: 662-325-7857, E-mail: lcornelious@colled.msstate.edu. *Application contact:* Laken Drinker, Admissions and Enrollment Assistant, 662-325-8951, E-mail: ldrinker@grad.msstate.edu.
Website: http://www.cise.msstate.edu/

Mississippi University for Women, Graduate School, College of Education and Human Sciences, Columbus, MS 39701-9998. Offers differentiated instruction (M Ed); educational leadership (M Ed); gifted studies (M Ed); reading/literacy (M Ed); teaching (MAT). *Accreditation:* ASHA; NCATE. *Program availability:* Part-time. *Degree requirements:* For master's, comprehensive exam, thesis optional. *Entrance requirements:* For master's, GRE General Test or NTE (M Ed in gifted education or MS in speech/language pathology), MAT (M Ed in instructional management), minimum QPA of 3.0.

Montana State University, The Graduate School, College of Education, Health, and Human Development, Department of Education, Bozeman, MT 59717. Offers adult and higher education (Ed D); curriculum and instruction (M Ed, Ed D), including professional educator (M Ed), technology education (M Ed); education (M Ed), including adult and higher education, educational leadership, school counseling; educational leadership (Ed D, Ed S). *Accreditation:* TEAC. *Program availability:* Part-time, online learning. *Degree requirements:* For master's, comprehensive exam; for doctorate, comprehensive exam, thesis/dissertation. *Entrance requirements:* For master's, GRE, 3 letters of reference, essays, BA transcripts; for doctorate, GRE, MAT, 3 letters of reference, essay, BA and M Ed transcripts; for Ed S, PRAXIS. Additional exam requirements/recommendations for international students: Required—TOEFL (minimum score 550 paper-based). Electronic applications accepted. *Faculty research:* Critical literacy; standards-based education; school Improvement, organizational change, leadership in rural education, leadership in Indian education; student Learning; multicultural/culturally responsive education for social justice Native American indigenous education, community-centered education teacher preparation.

Montana State University Billings, College of Education, Department of Educational Theory and Practice, Option in Curriculum and Instruction, Billings, MT 59101. Offers K-8 elementary education (M Ed); secondary education (M Ed). *Accreditation:* NCATE. *Program availability:* Part-time. *Degree requirements:* For master's, thesis or professional paper and/or field experience. *Entrance requirements:* For master's, GRE General Test or MAT, minimum GPA of 3.0. Additional exam requirements/recommendations for international students: Required—TOEFL (minimum score 79 iBT), IELTS (minimum score 6.5). *Application deadline:* Applications are processed on a rolling basis. Application fee: $40. Electronic applications accepted. *Expenses:* Tuition, state resident: full-time $11,740; part-time $7880 per year. Tuition, nonresident: full-time $32,200; part-time $24,140 per year. *Financial support:* Teaching assistantships with partial tuition reimbursements, career-related internships or fieldwork, Federal Work-Study, institutionally sponsored loans, scholarships/grants, tuition waivers (partial), and unspecified assistantships available. Support available to part-time students. Financial award application deadline: 5/1; financial award applicants required to submit FAFSA. *Faculty research:* Social studies education, science education. *Unit head:* Dr. Cindy Dell, Chair, Educational Theory and Practice, 406-657-1614, Fax: 406-657-2807, E-mail: cdell@msubillings.edu. *Application contact:* Dr. Cindy Dell, Chair, Educational Theory and Practice, 406-657-1614, Fax: 406-657-2807, E-mail: cdell@msubillings.edu.
Website: http://www.msubillings.edu/grad/program-med_curric_and_instruct.htm

Montclair State University, The Graduate School, College of Education and Human Services, MAT Program in Teaching, Montclair, NJ 07043-1624. Offers art (MAT); biology (MAT); chemistry (MAT); earth science (MAT); English (MAT); French (MAT); health and physical education (MAT); health education (MAT); mathematics (MAT); music (MAT); physical education (MAT); physical science (MAT); social studies (MAT); Spanish (MAT); teacher of English as a second language (MAT). *Degree requirements:* For master's, comprehensive exam, thesis or alternative. *Entrance requirements:* For master's, interview, 2 letters of recommendation. Additional exam requirements/recommendations for international students: Required—TOEFL (minimum score 83 iBT), IELTS (minimum score 6.5). Electronic applications accepted.

Moravian College, Graduate and Continuing Studies, Education Programs, Bethlehem, PA 18018-6650. Offers curriculum and instruction (M Ed); education (MAT). *Program availability:* Part-time, evening/weekend. *Faculty:* 4 full-time (2 women), 7 part-time/adjunct (3 women). *Students:* 8 full-time (7 women), 95 part-time (74 women); includes 4 minority (1 Asian, non-Hispanic/Latino; 2 Hispanic/Latino; 1 Two or more races, non-Hispanic/Latino), 1 international. Average age 32. 79 applicants, 56% accepted, 22 enrolled. In 2017, 7 master's awarded. *Degree requirements:* For master's, thesis. *Entrance requirements:* For master's, state teacher certification. Additional exam requirements/recommendations for international students: Required—TOEFL, IELTS. *Application deadline:* For fall admission, 8/1 priority date for domestic and international students; for spring admission, 1/1 priority date for domestic and international students; for summer admission, 5/1 priority date for domestic and international students. Applications are processed on a rolling basis. Electronic applications accepted. *Expenses:* Contact institution. *Financial support:* In 2017–18, 1 research assistantship with full tuition reimbursement was awarded. Financial award applicants required to submit FAFSA. *Faculty research:* Teacher action research, youth participatory research, practitioner inquiry, science education, deaf and hard of hearing education. *Unit head:* Scott Dams, Dean of Graduate and Adult Enrollment, 610-861-1400, Fax: 610-861-1466, E-mail: graduate@moravian.edu. *Application contact:* 610-861-1400, Fax: 610-861-1466, E-mail: graduate@moravian.edu.

Morehead State University, Graduate Programs, College of Education, Department of Curriculum and Instruction, Morehead, KY 40351. Offers curriculum and instruction (Ed S); elementary education (MA Ed), including elementary education, international education, middle school education, reading; secondary education (MA Ed); special education (MA Ed); teaching (MAT). *Program availability:* Part-time, evening/weekend. *Degree requirements:* For master's, comprehensive exam, thesis optional; for Ed S, thesis, oral exam. *Entrance requirements:* For master's, GRE General Test, minimum GPA of 2.75, teaching certificate; for Ed S, GRE General Test, interview, master's degree, minimum GPA of 3.5, work experience. Additional exam requirements/ recommendations for international students: Required—TOEFL (minimum score 500 paper-based). Electronic applications accepted. *Faculty research:* Communicative competence of learning-disabled students, teaching social studies in elementary schools, ungraded primary school organization, study skills.

Morehead State University, Graduate Programs, College of Education, Department of Foundational and Graduate Studies in Education, Morehead, KY 40351. Offers adult and higher education (MA, Ed S); certified professional counselor (MA); counseling P-12 (MA); curriculum and instruction (Ed S); educational technology (MA Ed); instructional leadership (Ed S); school administration (MA); school counseling (Ed S); teacher leader business and marketing content (MA Ed); teacher leader business and marketing technology (MA Ed); teacher leader educational technology (MA Ed); teacher leader English (MA Ed); teacher leader gifted education (MA Ed); teacher leader IECE certification (MA Ed); teacher leader interdisciplinary education P-5 (MA Ed); teacher leader middle grades (MA Ed); teacher leader non IECE certification (MA Ed); teacher leader reading/writing - non-certification (MA Ed); teacher leader reading/writing certification (MA Ed); teacher leader school communication - certification (MA Ed); teacher leader school communication - non-certification (MA Ed); teacher leader social studies (MA Ed); teacher leader special education (MA Ed). *Accreditation:* NCATE. *Program availability:* Part-time, evening/weekend. *Degree requirements:* For master's, thesis optional, oral and/or written comprehensive exams; for Ed S, thesis, oral exam. *Entrance requirements:* For master's, GRE General Test, minimum overall undergraduate GPA of 2.5; for Ed S, GRE General Test, interview, master's degree, minimum GPA of 3.5, work experience. Additional exam requirements/ recommendations for international students: Required—TOEFL (minimum score 500 paper-based). Electronic applications accepted. *Faculty research:* Character education, school accountability, computer applications for school administrators.

Mount Saint Vincent University, Graduate Programs, Faculty of Education, Program in Curriculum Studies, Halifax, NS B3M 2J6, Canada. Offers education of young adolescents (M Ed, MA Ed, MA-R); general studies (M Ed, MA Ed, MA-R); teaching English as a second language (M Ed, MA Ed, MA-R). *Program availability:* Part-time, evening/weekend, online learning. *Degree requirements:* For master's, thesis (for some programs). *Entrance requirements:* For master's, bachelor's degree in related field, minimum B average, 1 year of teaching experience. Electronic applications accepted. *Faculty research:* Science education, cultural studies, international education, curriculum development.

National Louis University, National College of Education, Chicago, IL 60603. Offers administration and supervision (M Ed, Ed D, CAS, Ed S); curriculum and instruction (M Ed, MS Ed, CAS); early childhood administration (M Ed, CAS); early childhood education (M Ed, MAT, MS Ed, CAS); education (Ed D); educational psychology/human learning and development (M Ed, MS Ed, CAS, Ed S); elementary education (MAT); interdisciplinary curriculum and instruction (M Ed); mathematics education (M Ed, MS Ed, CAS); middle grades education (MAT); reading and language (M Ed, MS Ed, CAS); school psychology (M Ed, Ed S); science education (M Ed, MS Ed, CAS); secondary education (MAT); special education (M Ed, MAT, CAS); technology in education (M Ed, CAS). *Accreditation:* NCATE. *Program availability:* Part-time, evening/weekend. *Degree requirements:* For doctorate, comprehensive exam, thesis/ dissertation. *Entrance requirements:* For master's, MAT or GRE, minimum GPA of 3.0; for doctorate, GRE General Test, minimum GPA of 3.25, interview, resume, writing sample, 4 recommendations. Additional exam requirements/recommendations for international students: Required—TOEFL (minimum score 550 paper-based; 79 iBT).

Newman University, Master of Science in Education Program, Wichita, KS 67213-2097. Offers building leadership (MS Ed); curriculum and instruction (MS Ed), including English as a second language, reading specialist; organizational leadership (MS Ed). *Accreditation:* NCATE. *Program availability:* Part-time, evening/weekend, online learning. *Degree requirements:* For master's, thesis optional. *Entrance requirements:* For master's, 3 years' full-time teaching experience, minimum GPA of 3.0, writing sample, 2 letters of recommendation, evidence of teaching certification. Additional exam requirements/recommendations for international students: Required—TOEFL (minimum score 600 paper-based; 100 iBT). Electronic applications accepted. *Expenses:* Contact institution. *Faculty research:* Online course design and deliver, staff engagement, classroom action.

New Mexico Highlands University, Graduate Studies, School of Education, Las Vegas, NM 87701. Offers curriculum and instruction (MA); educational leadership (MA); professional counseling (MA); special education (MA). *Accreditation:* NCATE. *Program availability:* Part-time. *Degree requirements:* For master's, comprehensive exam, thesis or alternative. *Entrance requirements:* For master's, minimum undergraduate GPA of 3.0. Additional exam requirements/recommendations for international students: Required—TOEFL (minimum score 540 paper-based). *Faculty research:* Middle school curriculum, integrated computer applications for pre-service classroom teachers, adolescent literacy, narrative cognitive modes in New Mexico multicultural setting, math and math education.

New Mexico State University, College of Education, Department of Curriculum and Instruction, Las Cruces, NM 88003. Offers bilingual education (MA); curriculum and instruction (MA, Ed D, PhD); early childhood education (MA); educational diagnostics (Ed S); language, literacy and culture (MA); learning design and technologies (MA); teaching (MAT), including dance, Spanish; teaching English to speakers of other languages (MA). *Accreditation:* NCATE. *Program availability:* Part-time, evening/ weekend, 100% online. *Faculty:* 22 full-time (17 women), 7 part-time/adjunct (2 women). *Students:* 113 full-time (79 women), 194 part-time (138 women); includes 171 minority (15 Black or African American, non-Hispanic/Latino; 3 American Indian or Alaska Native, non-Hispanic/Latino; 4 Asian, non-Hispanic/Latino; 142 Hispanic/Latino; 7 Two or more races, non-Hispanic/Latino), 37 international. Average age 36. 106 applicants, 80% accepted, 56 enrolled. In 2017, 82 master's, 15 doctorates, 1 other advanced degree awarded. *Entrance requirements:* For master's, minimum cumulative GPA of 3.0; for doctorate, portfolio, minimum cumulative GPA of 3.0. Additional exam requirements/ recommendations for international students: Required—TOEFL (minimum score 550 paper-based; 79 iBT), IELTS (minimum score 6.5). *Application deadline:* For fall admission, 12/15 priority date for domestic and international students; for spring admission, 11/1 for domestic students. Applications are processed on a rolling basis. Application fee: $40 ($50 for international students). Electronic applications accepted. *Expenses:* Tuition, state resident: full-time $4390. Tuition, nonresident: full-time $15,309. *Required fees:* $853. *Financial support:* In 2017–18, 97 students received support, including 2 fellowships (averaging $4,390 per year), 1 research assistantship (averaging $17,368 per year), 10 teaching assistantships (averaging $17,489 per year);

career-related internships or fieldwork, Federal Work-Study, scholarships/grants, traineeships, health care benefits, and unspecified assistantships also available. Support available to part-time students. Financial award application deadline: 3/1. *Faculty research:* STEM education, bilingual and English as a second language education, critical pedagogy/multicultural education, learning design and technology, early childhood education. *Total annual research expenditures:* $13,518. *Unit head:* Dr. David Rutledge, Department Head, 575-646-5411, Fax: 575-646-5436, E-mail: rutledge@nmsu.edu. *Application contact:* Dr. David Rutledge, Associate Department Head for Graduate Programs, 575-646-5411, Fax: 575-646-5436, E-mail: rutledge@ nmsu.edu.
Website: http://tpal.nmsu.edu/

Nicholls State University, Graduate Studies, College of Education, Department of Teacher Education, Thibodaux, LA 70310. Offers curriculum and instruction (M Ed); educational leadership (M Ed); elementary education (MAT); human performance education (MAT); middle school education (MAT); secondary education (MAT). *Accreditation:* NCATE. *Program availability:* Part-time, evening/weekend, online learning. *Degree requirements:* For master's, comprehensive exam, portfolio. *Entrance requirements:* For master's, GRE General Test, teaching license. Electronic applications accepted.

North Carolina State University, Graduate School, College of Education, Department of Curriculum and Instruction, Program in Curriculum and Instruction, Raleigh, NC 27695. Offers M Ed, MS, PhD. *Accreditation:* NCATE. *Degree requirements:* For master's, thesis (for some programs); for doctorate, thesis/dissertation. *Entrance requirements:* For master's, GRE General Test or MAT, minimum GPA of 3.0 in major; for doctorate, GRE General Test, minimum GPA of 3.0 in major. Electronic applications accepted. *Faculty research:* Curriculum development, teacher development, intervention for exceptional children, literacy development.

North Dakota State University, College of Graduate and Interdisciplinary Studies, College of Human Development and Education, School of Education, Program in Curriculum and Instruction, Fargo, ND 58102. Offers M Ed, MS. *Degree requirements:* For master's, comprehensive exam, thesis (for some programs). *Entrance requirements:* For master's, Cooperative English Test, GRE General Test, MAT. Additional exam requirements/recommendations for international students: Required—TOEFL.

Northern Arizona University, College of Education, Department of Teaching and Learning, Flagstaff, AZ 86011. Offers curriculum and instruction (Ed D); early childhood education (M Ed); elementary education (M Ed); secondary education (M Ed). *Program availability:* Part-time, 100% online, blended/hybrid learning. *Faculty:* 28 full-time (24 women), 1 (woman) part-time/adjunct. *Students:* 82 full-time (71 women), 181 part-time (167 women); includes 87 minority (19 Black or African American, non-Hispanic/Latino; 11 American Indian or Alaska Native, non-Hispanic/Latino; 4 Asian, non-Hispanic/ Latino; 47 Hispanic/Latino; 1 Native Hawaiian or other Pacific Islander, non-Hispanic/ Latino; 5 Two or more races, non-Hispanic/Latino), 7 international. Average age 36. 106 applicants, 95% accepted, 99 enrolled. In 2017, 79 master's, 5 doctorates awarded. *Degree requirements:* For master's, variable foreign language requirement, comprehensive exam (for some programs), thesis (for some programs); for doctorate, variable foreign language requirement, comprehensive exam (for some programs), thesis/dissertation (for some programs). *Entrance requirements:* Additional exam requirements/recommendations for international students: Required—TOEFL (minimum score 80 iBT), IELTS (minimum score 6.5). *Application deadline:* For fall admission, 2/15 for domestic and international students; for spring admission, 9/15 for domestic and international students. Applications are processed on a rolling basis. Application fee: $65. Electronic applications accepted. *Expenses:* Tuition, state resident: full-time $9240; part-time $458 per credit hour. Tuition, nonresident: full-time $21,588; part-time $1199 per credit hour. *Required fees:* $1021; $14 per credit hour. $646 per semester. Tuition and fees vary according to course load, campus/location and program. *Financial support:* In 2017–18, 5 students received support, including 1 research assistantship with full and partial tuition reimbursement available (averaging $13,500 per year), 4 teaching assistantships with full and partial tuition reimbursements available (averaging $13,500 per year); institutionally sponsored loans, health care benefits, tuition waivers (full and partial), and unspecified assistantships also available. Financial award application deadline: 2/1; financial award applicants required to submit FAFSA. *Unit head:* Dr. Pamela Powell, Chair, 928-523-5644, Fax: 928-523-1929, E-mail: pamela.powell@nau.edu. *Application contact:* Tina Sutton, Coordinator, Graduate College, 928-523-4348, Fax: 928-523-8950, E-mail: graduate@nau.edu.
Website: https://nau.edu/coe/Teaching-and-Learning/

Northern Illinois University, Graduate School, College of Education, Department of Curriculum and Instruction, De Kalb, IL 60115-2854. Offers curriculum and instruction (Ed D), including reading; literacy education (MS Ed). *Program availability:* Part-time, evening/weekend. *Faculty:* 12 full-time (10 women), 1 part-time/adjunct (0 women). *Students:* 8 full-time (all women), 183 part-time (162 women); includes 31 minority (6 Black or African American, non-Hispanic/Latino; 5 Asian, non-Hispanic/Latino; 19 Hispanic/Latino; 1 Two or more races, non-Hispanic/Latino), 2 international. Average age 35. 40 applicants, 65% accepted, 10 enrolled. In 2017, 78 master's, 6 doctorates awarded. *Degree requirements:* For master's, comprehensive exam, thesis optional; for doctorate, thesis/dissertation, candidacy exam, dissertation defense. *Entrance requirements:* For master's, GRE General Test or MAT, minimum undergraduate GPA of 2.75; for doctorate, GRE General Test, minimum GPA of 2.75 (undergraduate), 3.2 (graduate). Additional exam requirements/recommendations for international students: Required—TOEFL (minimum score 550 paper-based). *Application deadline:* For fall admission, 3/1 priority date for domestic students, 5/1 for international students; for spring admission, 11/1 for domestic students, 10/1 for international students. Applications are processed on a rolling basis. Application fee: $40. Electronic applications accepted. *Financial support:* In 2017–18, 3 research assistantships with full tuition reimbursements, 13 teaching assistantships with full tuition reimbursements were awarded; fellowships with full tuition reimbursements, career-related internships or fieldwork, Federal Work-Study, scholarships/grants, tuition waivers (full), and staff assistantships also available. Support available to part-time students. Financial award applicants required to submit FAFSA. *Faculty research:* Early reading development, literacy for bilingual students, family literacy, expository writing, fluency. *Unit head:* Dr. Anne E. Gregory, Chair, 815-753-8556, E-mail: ltcy@niu.edu. *Application contact:* Graduate School Office, 815-753-0395, E-mail: gradsch@niu.edu.
Website: http://cedu.niu.edu/leed/programs/masters1.shtml

Northern Illinois University, Graduate School, College of Education, Department of Special and Early Education, De Kalb, IL 60115-2854. Offers curriculum and instruction (MS Ed); early childhood education (MS Ed); elementary education (MS Ed); special education (MS Ed). *Program availability:* Part-time, evening/weekend. *Faculty:* 22 full-time (14 women), 2 part-time/adjunct (both women). *Students:* 40 full-time (33 women), 79 part-time (65 women); includes 16 minority (5 Black or African American, non-Hispanic/Latino; 3 Asian, non-Hispanic/Latino; 6 Hispanic/Latino; 2 Two or more races, non-Hispanic/Latino). Average age 32. 48 applicants, 83% accepted, 25 enrolled. In 2017, 58 master's awarded. *Degree requirements:* For master's, comprehensive exam, thesis optional. *Entrance requirements:* For master's, GRE General Test or MAT, minimum undergraduate GPA of 2.75. Additional exam requirements/recommendations

for international students: Required—TOEFL (minimum score 550 paper-based). *Application deadline:* For fall admission, 6/1 for domestic students, 5/1 for international students; for spring admission, 11/1 for domestic students, 10/1 for international students. Applications are processed on a rolling basis. Application fee: $40. Electronic applications accepted. *Financial support:* In 2017–18, 17 research assistantships with full tuition reimbursements were awarded; fellowships with full tuition reimbursements, teaching assistantships with full tuition reimbursements, career-related internships or fieldwork, Federal Work-Study, scholarships/grants, tuition waivers (full), and unspecified assistantships also available. Support available to part-time students. Financial award applicants required to submit FAFSA. *Faculty research:* Teacher certification, stress reduction during student teaching, teaching history, portfolios in student teaching. *Unit head:* Gregory Conderman, Chair, 815-753-1619, E-mail: seed@niu.edu. *Application contact:* Gail Myers, Clerk, Graduate Advising, 815-753-0381, E-mail: gmyers@niu.edu.
Website: http://www.cedu.niu.edu/seed/

Northern Michigan University, Office of Graduate Education and Research, College of Health Sciences and Professional Studies, School of Education, Leadership and Public Service, Marquette, MI 49855-5301. Offers administration and supervision (MAE); instruction (MAE); learning disabilities (MAE); postsecondary biology education (MS); reading education (MAE), including reading, reading specialist. *Accreditation:* TEAC. *Program availability:* Part-time, online learning. *Degree requirements:* For master's, thesis (for some programs). *Entrance requirements:* For master's, minimum GPA of 3.0. Additional exam requirements/recommendations for international students: Required—TOEFL (minimum score 550 paper-based; 79 iBT), IELTS (minimum score 6.5). *Application deadline:* For fall admission, 7/1 priority date for domestic students; for winter admission, 11/15 for domestic students; for spring admission, 3/17 for domestic students. Applications are processed on a rolling basis. Application fee: $50. Electronic applications accepted. *Expenses:* Tuition, state resident: full-time $9417; part-time $542 per credit hour. Tuition, nonresident: full-time $12,873; part-time $758 per credit hour. Tuition and fees vary according to course load, degree level and program. *Financial support:* Research assistantships with full tuition reimbursements, career-related internships or fieldwork, Federal Work-Study, institutionally sponsored loans, and unspecified assistantships available. Support available to part-time students. Financial award application deadline: 3/1; financial award applicants required to submit FAFSA. *Unit head:* Dr. Joseph Lubig, Associate Dean for Teacher Education, 906-227-1880, Fax: 906-227-2764, E-mail: jlubig@nmu.edu. *Application contact:* Dr. Joseph Lubig, Associate Dean for Teacher Education, 906-227-1880, Fax: 906-227-2764, E-mail: jlubig@nmu.edu.
Website: http://www.nmu.edu/education/

Northern State University, MS Ed Program in Teaching and Learning, Aberdeen, SD 57401-7198. Offers MS Ed. *Accreditation:* NCATE. *Program availability:* Part-time, evening/weekend, online learning. *Degree requirements:* For master's, comprehensive exam, thesis optional. *Entrance requirements:* For master's, minimum GPA of 2.75. Additional exam requirements/recommendations for international students: Required—TOEFL (minimum score 550 paper-based; 78 iBT), IELTS (minimum score 6). Electronic applications accepted.

Northern Vermont University–Johnson, Program in Education, Johnson, VT 05656. Offers applied behavior analysis (MA Ed); curriculum and instruction (MA Ed); foundations of education (MA Ed); special education (MA Ed). *Program availability:* Part-time. *Faculty:* 5 full-time (3 women), 4 part-time/adjunct (3 women). *Students:* 3 full-time (all women), 36 part-time (30 women). In 2017, 23 master's awarded. *Degree requirements:* For master's, thesis or alternative, exit interview. *Entrance requirements:* For master's, interview. Additional exam requirements/recommendations for international students: Required—TOEFL. *Application deadline:* For fall admission, 5/1 for domestic students, 2/1 for international students. Applications are processed on a rolling basis. Electronic applications accepted. *Expenses:* Tuition, state resident: part-time $572 per credit hour. Tuition, nonresident: part-time $832 per credit hour. *Financial support:* Scholarships/grants and unspecified assistantships available. Financial award application deadline: 3/1; financial award applicants required to submit FAFSA. *Unit head:* Dr. Kathleen Brinegar, Chair, Department of Education, 802-635-1472, Fax: 802-635-1465, E-mail: kathleen.brinegar@jsc.edu. *Application contact:* Catherine H. Higley, Administrative Assistant, 800-635-2356 Ext. 1244, Fax: 802-635-1248, E-mail: catherine.higley@jsc.edu.
Website: http://www.jsc.edu/academics/education/majors-and-minors/master-of-arts-in-education/

Northern Vermont University–Lyndon, Graduate Programs in Education, Department of Education, Lyndonville, VT 05851. Offers curriculum and instruction (M Ed); reading specialist (M Ed); special education (M Ed); teaching and counseling (M Ed). *Program availability:* Part-time, evening/weekend. *Degree requirements:* For master's, exam or major field project. *Entrance requirements:* Additional exam requirements/recommendations for international students: Recommended—TOEFL (minimum score 500 paper-based).

Northwestern Oklahoma State University, School of Professional Studies, Program in Curriculum and Instruction, Alva, OK 73717-2799. Offers M Ed. *Program availability:* Part-time. *Degree requirements:* For master's, thesis optional, portfolio. *Entrance requirements:* For master's, GRE General Test or MAT, minimum GPA of 2.75.

Northwestern State University of Louisiana, Graduate Studies and Research, College of Education and Human Development, Program in Curriculum and Instruction, Natchitoches, LA 71497. Offers M Ed. *Entrance requirements:* Additional exam requirements/recommendations for international students: Required—TOEFL. Electronic applications accepted.

Northwest Nazarene University, Graduate Education Program, Nampa, ID 83686-5897. Offers curriculum and instruction (M Ed); educational leadership (M Ed, Ed D, PhD, Ed S), including building administrator (M Ed, Ed S), director of special education (Ed S), leadership and organizational development (Ed S), superintendent (Ed S). *Accreditation:* ACA (one or more programs are accredited); NCATE. *Program availability:* Part-time, online only, 100% online, 2-week face-to-face residency (for doctoral programs). *Students:* Average age 39. 96 applicants, 72% accepted, 67 enrolled. In 2017, 59 master's, 13 doctorates, 33 other advanced degrees awarded. *Degree requirements:* For master's, comprehensive exam (for some programs), action research project; for doctorate, thesis/dissertation; for Ed S, comprehensive exam, research project. *Entrance requirements:* For master's, minimum undergraduate GPA of 3.0 overall or during final 30 semester credits, undergraduate degree, valid teaching certificate; for doctorate, Ed S or equivalent, minimum GPA of 3.5; for Ed S, undergraduate degree, valid teaching certificate. Additional exam requirements/recommendations for international students: Recommended—TOEFL. *Application deadline:* Applications are processed on a rolling basis. Application fee: $50. Electronic applications accepted. *Expenses:* Contact institution. *Financial support:* Research assistantships available. Financial award application deadline: 1/15; financial award applicants required to submit FAFSA. *Faculty research:* Action research, cooperative learning, accountability, institutional accreditation. *Unit head:* Dr. Heidi Curtis, Chair, 208-467-8250, E-mail: hlcurtis@nnu.edu. *Application contact:* Charlene Brown, Admissions Counselor, 208-467-8492, Fax: 208-467-8384, E-mail: gradeducationinfo@nnu.edu.
Website: http://www.nnu.edu/graded/

Notre Dame de Namur University, Division of Academic Affairs, School of Education and Psychology, Program in Education, Belmont, CA 94002-1908. Offers curriculum and instruction (MA); disciplinary studies (MA). *Program availability:* Part-time, evening/weekend. *Students:* 5 full-time (2 women), 211 part-time (142 women). Average age 35. *Degree requirements:* For master's, thesis (for some programs). *Entrance requirements:* For master's, CBEST, CSET, valid teaching credential or substantial teaching experience. Additional exam requirements/recommendations for international students: Required—TOEFL (minimum score 550 paper-based; 79 iBT). *Application deadline:* For fall admission, 8/1 priority date for domestic students; for spring admission, 12/1 priority date for domestic students. Applications are processed on a rolling basis. Application fee: $60. Electronic applications accepted. *Expenses:* Tuition: Full-time $16,128; part-time $8064 per credit hour. *Required fees:* $80; $80 per credit hour. $40 per semester. *Financial support:* Career-related internships or fieldwork available. Support available to part-time students. Financial award applicants required to submit FAFSA. *Unit head:* Kim Tolley, Program Director, Master of Arts in Education, 650-508-3464, E-mail: ktolley@ndnu.edu.
Website: https://www.ndnu.edu/education-and-leadership/graduate/education/

Ohio Dominican University, Division of Education, Program in Curriculum and Instruction, Columbus, OH 43219-2099. Offers M Ed. *Program availability:* Part-time, evening/weekend, 100% online, blended/hybrid learning. *Faculty:* 7 full-time (5 women), 7 part-time/adjunct (5 women). *Students:* 3 full-time (all women), 33 part-time (28 women); includes 3 minority (all Two or more races, non-Hispanic/Latino). Average age 34. 14 applicants, 79% accepted, 10 enrolled. In 2017, 12 master's awarded. *Entrance requirements:* For master's, bachelor's degree from regionally-accredited institution; teaching certificate/license; currently teaching or have access to an academic classroom; minimum undergraduate GPA of 3.0. Additional exam requirements/recommendations for international students: Required—TOEFL (minimum score 550 paper-based), IELTS (minimum score 6.5). *Application deadline:* For fall admission, 8/15 for domestic students, 6/10 for international students; for spring admission, 1/4 for domestic students, 11/2 for international students; for summer admission, 5/30 for domestic students. Applications are processed on a rolling basis. Application fee: $25. Electronic applications accepted. *Expenses:* $538 per credit hour, $175 per semester technology fee, $50 per semester activity fee. *Financial support:* Applicants required to submit FAFSA. *Unit head:* Dr. JoAnn Hohenbrink, Associate Professor/Chair of Education Division, 614-251-4759, E-mail: hohenbrj@ohiodominican.edu. *Application contact:* John W. Naughton, Associate Vice President for Enrollment Management, 614-251-4721, Fax: 614-251-6654, E-mail: grad@ohiodominican.edu.
Website: http://www.ohiodominican.edu/academics/graduate/master-of-education/curriculum-instruction

Ohio University, Graduate College, Gladys W. and David H. Patton College of Education and Human Services, Department of Teacher Education, Athens, OH 45701-2979. Offers adolescent to young adult education (M Ed); curriculum and instruction (M Ed, PhD); early childhood/special education (M Ed); intervention specialist/mild-moderate needs (M Ed); intervention specialist/moderate-intensive needs (M Ed); middle childhood education (M Ed); reading education (M Ed). *Program availability:* Part-time, evening/weekend. *Degree requirements:* For master's, thesis or alternative; for doctorate, comprehensive exam, thesis/dissertation. *Entrance requirements:* For master's, GRE General Test or MAT (if GPA is below 2.9); for doctorate, GRE General Test, minimum GPA of 3.4, work experience. Additional exam requirements/recommendations for international students: Required—TOEFL (minimum score 550 paper-based; 80 iBT) or IELTS (minimum score 6.5). Electronic applications accepted. *Faculty research:* Cognition literacy, character education, teacher's education reform, disabilities.

Ohio Valley University, School of Graduate Education, Vienna, WV 26105-8000. Offers curriculum and instruction (M Ed). *Program availability:* Online learning. *Entrance requirements:* For master's, 2 letters of recommendation, official transcripts from all previous institutions, essay, bachelor's degree.

Oklahoma State University, College of Education, Health and Aviation, School of Teaching and Curriculum Leadership, Stillwater, OK 74078. Offers MS, PhD. *Program availability:* Part-time. *Faculty:* 37 full-time (32 women), 29 part-time/adjunct (25 women). *Students:* 26 full-time (24 women), 152 part-time (123 women); includes 41 minority (9 Black or African American, non-Hispanic/Latino; 4 American Indian or Alaska Native, non-Hispanic/Latino; 2 Asian, non-Hispanic/Latino; 6 Hispanic/Latino; 16 Two or more races, non-Hispanic/Latino), 7 international. Average age 38. 45 applicants, 91% accepted, 35 enrolled. In 2017, 61 master's, 8 doctorates awarded. *Entrance requirements:* For master's and doctorate, GRE or GMAT. Additional exam requirements/recommendations for international students: Required—TOEFL (minimum score 550 paper-based; 79 iBT). *Application deadline:* For fall admission, 3/1 priority date for international students; for spring admission, 8/1 priority date for international students. Applications are processed on a rolling basis. Application fee: $40 ($75 for international students). Electronic applications accepted. *Expenses:* Tuition, state resident: full-time $4019; part-time $2679.60 per year. Tuition, nonresident: full-time $15,286; part-time $10,190.40 per year. *Required fees:* $2129; $1419 per unit. Tuition and fees vary according to program. *Financial support:* Research assistantships, teaching assistantships, career-related internships or fieldwork, Federal Work-Study, scholarships/grants, health care benefits, tuition waivers (partial), and unspecified assistantships available. Support available to part-time students. Financial award application deadline: 3/1; financial award applicants required to submit FAFSA. *Unit head:* Dr. Jennifer Sanders, Interim Department Head, 405-744-9214, Fax: 405-744-6290, E-mail: jenn.sanders10@okstate.edu.
Website: http://education.okstate.edu/

Old Dominion University, Darden College of Education, Doctoral Program in Curriculum and Instruction, Norfolk, VA 23529. Offers PhD. *Program availability:* Part-time, evening/weekend. *Faculty:* 8 full-time (6 women). *Students:* 9 full-time (7 women), 8 part-time (all women); includes 2 minority (both Black or African American, non-Hispanic/Latino). Average age 44. 19 applicants, 53% accepted, 8 enrolled. In 2017, 5 doctorates awarded. *Degree requirements:* For doctorate, comprehensive exam, thesis/dissertation. *Entrance requirements:* For doctorate, GRE, letters of recommendation; minimum undergraduate GPA of 2.8, graduate 3.2. Additional exam requirements/recommendations for international students: Required—TOEFL (minimum score 600 paper-based). *Application deadline:* For fall admission, 3/15 priority date for domestic and international students; for spring admission, 11/15 for domestic and international students. Applications are processed on a rolling basis. Application fee: $50. Electronic applications accepted. *Expenses:* Tuition, state resident: full-time $8928; part-time $496 per credit. Tuition, nonresident: full-time $22,482; part-time $1249 per credit. *Required fees:* $66 per semester. *Financial support:* In 2017–18, 7 students received support, including fellowships with full tuition reimbursements available (averaging $20,000 per year), 4 teaching assistantships with full tuition reimbursements available (averaging $20,000 per year); research assistantships also available. Financial award application deadline: 4/15. *Faculty research:* Curriculum change, language arts, library science, multicultural education, foundations in education. *Unit head:* Dr. Richard Overbaugh, Graduate Program Director, 757-683-3284, Fax: 757-683-5862, E-mail: roverbau@odu.edu. *Application contact:* William Heffelfinger, Director of Graduate Admissions, 757-683-5554, Fax: 757-683-3255, E-mail: gradadmit@odu.edu.
Website: http://education.odu.edu/eci/ciphd/

Old Dominion University, Darden College of Education, Program in Physical Education, Curriculum and Instruction Emphasis, Norfolk, VA 23529. Offers human movement sciences (PhD), including health and sport pedagogy; physical education (MS Ed), including adapted physical education, coaching education, curriculum and instruction. *Program availability:* Part-time, evening/weekend. *Faculty:* 3 full-time (1 woman). *Students:* 2 full-time (1 woman), 5 part-time (1 woman); includes 1 minority (1 Black or African American, non-Hispanic/Latino; 1 Two or more races, non-Hispanic/Latino). Average age 29. 2 applicants, 50% accepted. In 2017, 2 master's awarded. *Degree requirements:* For master's, comprehensive exam (for some programs), thesis or alternative, internship, research project. *Entrance requirements:* For master's, GRE, PRAXIS tests (for licensure only), minimum GPA of 2.8 overall, 3.0 in major. Additional exam requirements/recommendations for international students: Required—TOEFL (minimum score 500 paper-based; 97 iBT). *Application deadline:* For fall admission, 3/1 priority date for domestic students; for spring admission, 11/1 for domestic students. Applications are processed on a rolling basis. Application fee: $50. Electronic applications accepted. *Expenses:* Tuition, state resident: full-time $8928; part-time $496 per credit. Tuition, nonresident: full-time $22,482; part-time $1249 per credit. *Required fees:* $66 per semester. *Financial support:* Unspecified assistantships available. Financial award application deadline: 4/15. *Faculty research:* Motor development, physical activity and fitness, motivation and learning in physical education, curriculum and instruction, adapted physical education. *Total annual research expenditures:* $104,000. *Unit head:* Dr. Lynn Ridinger, Chair, 757-683-4995, E-mail: lridinge@odu.edu. *Application contact:* William Heffelfinger, Director of Graduate Admissions, 757-683-5554, Fax: 757-683-3255, E-mail: gradadmit@odu.edu. Website: https://www.odu.edu/hms/academics/hpe/graduate

Olivet Nazarene University, Graduate School, Division of Education, Program in Curriculum and Instruction, Bourbonnais, IL 60914. Offers MAE. *Program availability:* Evening/weekend. *Degree requirements:* For master's, thesis or alternative.

Oral Roberts University, School of Education, Tulsa, OK 74171. Offers Christian school administration (K-12) (MA Ed, Ed D); college and higher education administration (Ed D); curriculum and instruction (MA Ed); initial teaching with alternative licensure (MAT); initial teaching with licensure (MAT); public school administration (K-12) (MA Ed, Ed D). *Accreditation:* NCATE. *Program availability:* Part-time, online learning. *Faculty:* 7 full-time (2 women), 6 part-time/adjunct (2 women). *Students:* 344 full-time (223 women); includes 117 minority (93 Black or African American, non-Hispanic/Latino; 7 American Indian or Alaska Native, non-Hispanic/Latino; 11 Asian, non-Hispanic/Latino; 6 Hispanic/Latino). 80 applicants, 94% accepted, 65 enrolled. In 2017, 14 master's, 4 doctorates awarded. *Degree requirements:* For master's, comprehensive exam, thesis optional; for doctorate, comprehensive exam, thesis/dissertation. *Entrance requirements:* For master's, GRE General Test or MAT (minimum score in 80th percentile or higher); Oklahoma general education or subject area test (for MAT), minimum GPA of 3.0, bachelor's degree from regionally-accredited institution; for doctorate, minimum GPA of 3.0, master's degree from regionally-accredited institution. *Application deadline:* Applications are processed on a rolling basis. Application fee: $35. Electronic applications accepted. Application fee is waived when completed online. *Expenses:* Contact institution. *Financial support:* Fellowships and scholarships/grants available. Financial award application deadline: 3/15. *Faculty research:* Teacher effectiveness, college success in high achieving African-Americans, professional development practices. *Unit head:* Dr. Patrick Otto, Chair of Graduate School of Education, 918-495-7087, E-mail: jotto@oru.edu. *Application contact:* Audrey Ripley, Enrollment Counselor, 918-495-6375, E-mail: aripley@oru.edu.

Ottawa University, Graduate Studies-Arizona, Program in Education, Ottawa, KS 66067-3399. Offers community college counseling (MA); curriculum and instruction (MA); early childhood (MA); education intervention (MA); education leadership (MA); education technology (MA); Montessori early childhood education (MA); Montessori elementary education (MA); professional development (MA); school guidance counseling (MA); special education - cross categorical (MA). Programs offered in Mesa, Phoenix, Tempe and West Valley, AZ. *Accreditation:* NCATE. *Program availability:* Part-time. *Degree requirements:* For master's, thesis or alternative. *Entrance requirements:* For master's, minimum undergraduate GPA of 3.0, copy of current state certification or teaching license. Additional exam requirements/recommendations for international students: Required—TOEFL (minimum score 550 paper-based). Electronic applications accepted. *Expenses:* Contact institution.

Our Lady of the Lake University, College of Professional Studies, Program in Curriculum and Instruction, San Antonio, TX 78207-4689. Offers integrated science teaching (M Ed). *Program availability:* Part-time, evening/weekend. *Faculty:* 4 full-time (all women), 3 part-time/adjunct (2 women). *Students:* 20 part-time (17 women); includes 14 minority (all Hispanic/Latino). Average age 39. In 2017, 1 master's awarded. *Degree requirements:* For master's, comprehensive exam. *Entrance requirements:* For master's, GRE General Test or MAT, official transcripts demonstrating bachelor's degree with minimum cumulative GPA of 2.75, personal statement, 2 references, completed FERPA Consent to Release Education Records and Information form, interview. Additional exam requirements/recommendations for international students: Required—TOEFL. *Application deadline:* For fall admission, 6/15 for domestic and international students; for spring admission, 11/15 for domestic and international students; for summer admission, 4/15 for domestic and international students. Applications are processed on a rolling basis. Application fee: $40 ($50 for international students). Electronic applications accepted. Application fee is waived when completed online. *Expenses: Tuition:* Full-time $10,668; part-time $5334 per year. *Required fees:* $816; $816 per year. $408 per semester. *Financial support:* Federal Work-Study, scholarships/grants, unspecified assistantships, and tuition discounts available. Support available to part-time students. Financial award application deadline: 5/1; financial award applicants required to submit FAFSA. *Faculty research:* Multicultural Issues, technology integration, mentoring teachers, teacher retention. *Unit head:* Dr. Alycia Maurer, Chair, Education Department, 210-434-6711 Ext. 7152, E-mail: admaurer@ollusa.edu. *Application contact:* Office of Graduate Admissions, 210-431-3995, Fax: 210-431-3945, E-mail: gradadm@lake.ollusa.edu. Website: http://www.ollusa.edu/s/1190/hybrid/default-hybrid-ollu.aspx?sid-1190&gid-1&pgid-7883

Pacific Lutheran University, School of Education and Kinesiology, Program in Initial Teaching Certification, Tacoma, WA 98447. Offers MAE. *Accreditation:* NCATE. *Program availability:* Part-time, evening/weekend. *Degree requirements:* For master's, comprehensive exam, thesis optional. *Entrance requirements:* For master's, WEST-B or WEST-B Exemption (or CBEST and/or PRAXIS for out-of-state applicants), interview. Additional exam requirements/recommendations for international students: Required—TOEFL (minimum score 550 paper-based; 88 iBT), ACTFL (American Council on the Teaching of Foreign Languages) oral proficiency exam. Electronic applications accepted. *Expenses:* Contact institution.

Park University, School of Graduate and Professional Studies, Kansas City, MO 54105. Offers adult education (M Ed); business and government leadership (Graduate Certificate); business, government, and global society (MPA); communication and leadership (MA); creative and life writing (Graduate Certificate); disaster and emergency management (MPA, Graduate Certificate); educational leadership (M Ed); finance (MBA, Graduate Certificate); general business (MBA); global business (Graduate Certificate); healthcare administration (MHA); healthcare services management and leadership (Graduate Certificate); international business (MBA); language and literacy (M Ed), including English for speakers of other languages, special reading teacher/literacy coach; leadership of international healthcare organizations (Graduate Certificate); management information systems (MBA, Graduate Certificate); music performance (ADP, Graduate Certificate), including cello (MM, ADP), piano (MM, ADP), viola (MM, ADP), violin (MM, ADP); nonprofit and community services management (MPA); nonprofit leadership (Graduate Certificate); performance (MM), including cello (MM, ADP), piano (MM, ADP), viola (MM, ADP), violin (MM, ADP); public management (MPA); social work (MSW); teacher leadership (M Ed), including curriculum and assessment, instructional leader. *Program availability:* Part-time, evening/weekend, online learning. *Degree requirements:* For master's, comprehensive exam (for some programs), thesis (for some programs), internship (for some programs); exam (for some programs). *Entrance requirements:* For master's, GRE or GMAT (for some programs), teacher certification (for some M Ed programs), letters of recommendation, essay, resume (for some programs). Additional exam requirements/recommendations for international students: Required—TOEFL (minimum score 550 paper-based; 79 iBT), IELTS (minimum score 6). Electronic applications accepted.

Penn State Harrisburg, Graduate School, School of Behavioral Sciences and Education, Middletown, PA 17057. Offers adult education in the health and medical professions (Certificate); applied behavior analysis (MA); applied clinical psychology (MA); applied psychological research (MA); community psychology and social change (MA); English as a second language (ESL) program specialist and leadership (Certificate); health education (M Ed); lifelong learning and adult education (M Ed, D Ed); literacy education (M Ed); literacy leadership (Certificate); psychology: applications in clinical psychology (Certificate); psychology: health psychology (Certificate); teaching and curriculum (M Ed); training and development (M Ed, Certificate). *Program availability:* Part-time, evening/weekend. *Unit head:* Dr. Mukund S. Kulkarni, Chancellor, 717-948-6105, Fax: 717-948-6452. *Application contact:* Robert W. Coffman, Jr., Director of Enrollment Management, Recruitment and Admissions, 717-948-6250, Fax: 717-948-6325, E-mail: hbgadmit@psu.edu. Website: https://harrisburg.psu.edu/behavioral-sciences-and-education/

Penn State University Park, Graduate School, College of Education, Department of Curriculum and Instruction, University Park, PA 16802. Offers M Ed, MS, PhD, Certificate. *Accreditation:* NCATE. *Unit head:* Dr. David H. Monk, Dean, 814-865-2523, Fax: 814-865-0555. *Application contact:* Lori Hawn, Director, Graduate Student Services, 814-865-1795, Fax: 814-863-4627, E-mail: l-gswww@lists.psu.edu. Website: http://ed.psu.edu/c-and-i

Penn State York, Graduate School, York, PA 17403. Offers ESL specialist (Certificate); teaching and curriculum (M Ed). *Students:* 16 part-time (13 women); includes 2 minority (1 Black or African American, non-Hispanic/Latino; 1 Two or more races, non-Hispanic/Latino). Average age 35. 3 applicants, 67% accepted, 2 enrolled. In 2017, 2 master's awarded. Application fee: $65. *Expenses:* Contact institution. *Unit head:* Dr. Regina Vasilatos-Younken, Vice Provost for Graduate Education/Dean, Graduate School, 814-865-2516, Fax: 814-863-4627. *Application contact:* Lori Hawn, Director, Graduate Student Services, 814-865-1795, Fax: 814-863-4627, E-mail: l-gswww@lists.psu.edu. Website: http://www.gradschool.psu.edu/

Pensacola Christian College, Graduate Studies, Pensacola, FL 32503-2267. Offers business administration (MBA); curriculum and instruction (MS, Ed D, Ed S); dramatics (MFA); educational leadership (MS, Ed D, Ed S); graphic design (MA, MFA); music (MA); nursing (MSN); performance studies (MA); studio art (MA, MFA).

Peru State College, Graduate Programs, Program in Education, Peru, NE 68421. Offers curriculum and instruction (MS Ed). *Accreditation:* NCATE. *Program availability:* Part-time. *Degree requirements:* For master's, comprehensive exam (for some programs), thesis optional.

Piedmont College, School of Education, Demorest, GA 30535. Offers art education (MA, MAT); curriculum and instruction (Ed D, Ed S); early childhood education (MA, MAT); instructional technology (MA); middle grades education (MA, MAT); music education (MA, MAT); secondary education (MA, MAT); special education (MA, MAT). *Program availability:* Part-time, evening/weekend. *Students:* 341 full-time (268 women), 682 part-time (571 women); includes 182 minority (136 Black or African American, non-Hispanic/Latino; 2 American Indian or Alaska Native, non-Hispanic/Latino; 11 Asian, non-Hispanic/Latino; 32 Hispanic/Latino; 1 Two or more races, non-Hispanic/Latino). Average age 37. 333 applicants, 77% accepted, 103 enrolled. In 2017, 292 master's, 9 doctorates, 318 other advanced degrees awarded. *Degree requirements:* For master's, thesis, field experience in the classroom teaching; for doctorate, thesis/dissertation. *Entrance requirements:* For master's, GRE General Test, MAT; for Ed S, minimum graduate GPA of 3.5, valid teaching certificate. Additional exam requirements/recommendations for international students: Required—TOEFL (minimum score 550 paper-based). *Application deadline:* For fall admission, 7/15 for domestic students; for spring admission, 12/1 for domestic students. Applications are processed on a rolling basis. Electronic applications accepted. *Expenses: Tuition:* Full-time $9360; part-time $520 per credit hour. *Required fees:* $200; $200 per year. $100 per term. *Financial support:* Career-related internships or fieldwork, Federal Work-Study, and unspecified assistantships available. Support available to part-time students. Financial award applicants required to submit FAFSA. *Unit head:* Dr. Don Gnecco, Dean, 706-778-3000 Ext. 1201, Fax: 706-776-9608, E-mail: dgnecco@piedmont.edu. *Application contact:* Kathleen Carter, Director of Graduate Enrollment Management, 706-778-8500 Ext. 1181, Fax: 706-778-0150, E-mail: kanderson@piedmont.edu.

Piedmont International University, Graduate School, Winston-Salem, NC 27101-5197. Offers Biblical studies (PhD); curriculum and instruction (M Ed); divinity (M Div); educational leadership (M Ed); leadership (MA, PhD); ministry (MA Min, D Min); non-language track (MABS); PhD preparation track (MABS). *Program availability:* Part-time, online learning. Terminal master's awarded for partial completion of doctoral program. *Degree requirements:* For master's, 2 foreign languages, comprehensive exam, thesis or alternative; for doctorate, 2 foreign languages, comprehensive exam. *Entrance requirements:* For master's, GRE General Test; for doctorate, Hebrew and Greek proficiency, MA. Additional exam requirements/recommendations for international students: Required—TOEFL (minimum score 500 paper-based; 60 iBT). Electronic applications accepted. *Faculty research:* Theological and biblical studies.

Plymouth State University, College of Graduate Studies, Graduate Studies in Education, Program in Secondary Education, Plymouth, NH 03264-1595. Offers curriculum and instruction (M Ed); language education (M Ed); library media (M Ed); physical education (M Ed); social studies education (M Ed); special education (M Ed). *Program availability:* Part-time, evening/weekend. *Entrance requirements:* For master's, MAT.

Point Park University, School of Arts and Sciences, Department of Education, Pittsburgh, PA 15222-1984. Offers adult learning and training (MA); athletic coaching (M Ed); curriculum and instruction (MA); educational administration (MA); leadership and administration (Ed D); secondary education (M Ed); special education grades 7-12 (M Ed); special education PreK-grade 8 (M Ed). *Program availability:* Part-time, evening/

weekend, 100% online, blended/hybrid learning. *Degree requirements:* For master's, comprehensive exam (for some programs), thesis or alternative. *Entrance requirements:* For master's, minimum GPA of 3.0, resume, 2 letters of recommendation. Additional exam requirements/recommendations for international students: Required—TOEFL. Electronic applications accepted.

Pontifical Catholic University of Puerto Rico, College of Education, Doctoral Program in Curriculum and Instruction, Ponce, PR 00717-0777. Offers PhD. *Degree requirements:* For doctorate, thesis/dissertation. *Entrance requirements:* For doctorate, EXADEP, GRE General Test or MAT, 3 letters of recommendation.

Pontifical Catholic University of Puerto Rico, College of Education, Master's Program in Curriculum and Instruction, Ponce, PR 00717-0777. Offers M Ed. *Degree requirements:* For master's, comprehensive exam, thesis (for some programs). *Entrance requirements:* For master's, GRE, 2 letters of recommendation, interview, minimum GPA of 2.75.

Post University, Program in Education, Waterbury, CT 06723-2540. Offers curriculum and instruction (M Ed); education (M Ed); educational technology (M Ed); higher education administration (MS); learning design and technology (M Ed); online teaching (M Ed); teaching English to speakers of other languages (TESOL) (M Ed). *Program availability:* Online learning. *Entrance requirements:* For master's, resume. *Expenses: Tuition:* Part-time $730 per credit hour. Part-time tuition and fees vary according to degree level and program. *Application contact:* Veronica Montalvo, Vice President, Online Education Enrollment Management and Admissions, 203-596-6164, E-mail: vmontalvo@post.edu.

Prairie View A&M University, College of Education, Department of Curriculum and Instruction, Prairie View, TX 77446. Offers M Ed, MA Ed, MS Ed. *Accreditation:* NCATE. *Program availability:* Part-time, evening/weekend. *Faculty:* 5 full-time (4 women), 1 (woman) part-time/adjunct. *Students:* 12 full-time (all women), 30 part-time (all women); includes 40 minority (39 Black or African American, non-Hispanic/Latino; 1 Hispanic/Latino), 1 international. Average age 33. 27 applicants, 93% accepted, 15 enrolled. In 2017, 12 master's awarded. *Degree requirements:* For master's, comprehensive exam, thesis optional. *Entrance requirements:* For master's, GRE, minimum GPA of 2.5, 3 references. Additional exam requirements/recommendations for international students: Required—TOEFL (minimum score 550 paper-based; 79 iBT). *Application deadline:* For fall admission, 5/1 priority date for domestic and international students; for spring admission, 10/1 priority date for domestic students, 9/1 priority date for international students; for summer admission, 3/1 priority date for domestic students, 2/1 priority date for international students. Applications are processed on a rolling basis. Application fee: $50. Electronic applications accepted. *Expenses:* Tuition, state resident: part-time $242 per credit. Tuition, nonresident: part-time $695 per credit. *Required fees:* $149 per credit. *Financial support:* Career-related internships or fieldwork, institutionally sponsored loans, scholarships/grants, health care benefits, tuition waivers (full and partial), and unspecified assistantships available. Support available to part-time students. Financial award application deadline: 4/1; financial award applicants required to submit FAFSA. *Faculty research:* Metacognitive strategies, emotionally disturbed, language arts, teachers recruit, diversity, recruitment, retention, school collaboration. *Unit head:* Dr. Douglas Butler, Interim Department Head, 936-261-3410, Fax: 936-261-3419, E-mail: dmbutler@pvamu.edu. *Application contact:* Pauline Walker, Administrative Assistant II, Research and Graduate Studies, 936-261-3521, Fax: 936-261-3529, E-mail: gradadmissions@pvamu.edu.

Purdue University, Graduate School, College of Education, Department of Curriculum and Instruction, West Lafayette, IN 47907. Offers agricultural and extension education (MS, MS Ed, PhD, Ed S); art education (PhD); career and technical education (MS Ed, PhD, Ed S); curriculum studies (MS Ed, PhD, Ed S); educational technology (MS Ed, PhD, Ed S); elementary education (MS Ed); family and consumer sciences education (MS Ed, PhD, Ed S); foreign language education (MS Ed, PhD, Ed S); industrial technology (PhD, Ed S); language arts (MS Ed, PhD, Ed S); literacy (MS Ed, PhD, Ed S); mathematics education (MS, MS Ed, PhD, Ed S); science education (MS, MS Ed, PhD, Ed S); social studies education (MS Ed, PhD, Ed S). *Accreditation:* NCATE. *Program availability:* Part-time, evening/weekend. *Faculty:* 37 full-time (27 women), 1 (woman) part-time/adjunct. *Students:* 78 full-time (50 women), 286 part-time (195 women); includes 68 minority (25 Black or African American, non-Hispanic/Latino; 3 American Indian or Alaska Native, non-Hispanic/Latino; 10 Asian, non-Hispanic/Latino; 22 Hispanic/Latino; 1 Native Hawaiian or other Pacific Islander, non-Hispanic/Latino; 7 Two or more races, non-Hispanic/Latino), 44 international. Average age 36. 150 applicants, 79% accepted, 73 enrolled. In 2017, 107 master's, 20 doctorates, 2 other advanced degrees awarded. *Degree requirements:* For master's, thesis optional; for doctorate, thesis/dissertation, oral and written exams; for Ed S, oral presentation, project. *Entrance requirements:* For master's, GRE General Test (if undergraduate GPA is below 3.0), minimum undergraduate GPA of 3.0 or equivalent; for doctorate, GRE General Test (minimum combined verbal and quantitative score of 1000, 300 for new scoring), minimum undergraduate GPA of 3.0 or equivalent; master's degree with minimum GPA of 3.0 or equivalent; for Ed S, GRE General Test (minimum combined verbal and quantitative score of 1000, 300 for new scoring), minimum undergraduate GPA of 3.0 or equivalent; master's degree. Additional exam requirements/recommendations for international students: Required—TOEFL (minimum score 550 paper-based; 77 iBT). *Application deadline:* For fall admission, 12/15 for domestic students, 3/1 for international students; for spring admission, 9/15 for domestic students, 8/1 for international students. Application fee: $60 ($75 for international students). Electronic applications accepted. *Financial support:* Fellowships with full tuition reimbursements, research assistantships with full tuition reimbursements, teaching assistantships with full tuition reimbursements, career-related internships or fieldwork, and tuition waivers (full) available. Support available to part-time students. Financial award application deadline: 3/1; financial award applicants required to submit FAFSA. *Faculty research:* Literacy acquisition and development, teacher beliefs and knowledge, recruitment and retention of underrepresented students, economic education, literacy discourse. *Unit head:* Janet M. Alsup, Head, 765-494-9667, E-mail: alsupj@purdue.edu. *Application contact:* Heather Brinkman, Graduate Contact, 765-494-2345, E-mail: hbrinkma@purdue.edu.
Website: http://www.edci.purdue.edu/

Quincy University, Master of Science in Education Programs, Quincy, IL 62301-2699. Offers curriculum and instruction (MS Ed), including bilingual/English as a second language; education studies (MS Ed); leadership (MS Ed); reading education (MS Ed); teacher leader (MS Ed). *Program availability:* Part-time, evening/weekend, online learning. *Degree requirements:* For master's, comprehensive exam (for some programs), thesis optional. *Entrance requirements:* For master's, MAT or GRE, personal resume. Additional exam requirements/recommendations for international students: Required—TOEFL (minimum score 550 paper-based; 79 iBT). *Application deadline:* Applications are processed on a rolling basis. Application fee: $25. Electronic applications accepted. Application fee is waived when completed online. *Expenses: Tuition:* Part-time $450 per credit hour. *Financial support:* Applicants required to submit FAFSA. *Unit head:* Dr. Bruce Alan Spitzer, Director, 217-228-5432 Ext. 3106, E-mail: spitzbr@quincy.edu. *Application contact:* Office of Admissions, 217-228-5210, Fax: 217-228-5479, E-mail: admissions@quincy.edu.
Website: http://www.quincy.edu/academics/graduate-programs/education

Randolph College, Programs in Education, Lynchburg, VA 24503. Offers curriculum and instruction (MAT); special education-learning disabilities (M Ed, MAT). *Accreditation:* TEAC. *Entrance requirements:* For master's, minimum GPA of 3.0 in prerequisite education coursework, 2.7 in major or field of interest (MAT); teaching license (M Ed); 2 recommendations; interview.

Regent University, Graduate School, School of Education, Virginia Beach, VA 23464-9800. Offers education (M Ed, Ed D, PhD), including adult education (Ed D, PhD, Ed S), advanced educational leadership (Ed D, PhD, Ed S), character education (Ed D, PhD, Ed S), Christian education leadership (Ed D, PhD, Ed S), Christian school administration (M Ed), curriculum and instruction (Ed D, PhD, Ed S), curriculum and instruction - adult education (M Ed), curriculum and instruction - Christian school (M Ed), curriculum and instruction - gifted and talented (M Ed), curriculum and instruction - STEM education (M Ed), curriculum and instruction - teacher leader (M Ed), discipleship for ministry (M Ed), educational leadership (M Ed), educational psychology (Ed D, PhD, Ed S), educational technology and online learning (Ed D, PhD, Ed S), elementary education (M Ed), exceptional education executive leadership (Ed D, PhD, Ed S), higher education (Ed D, PhD, Ed S), higher education leadership and management (Ed D, PhD, Ed S), instructional design and technology (M Ed), K-12 school leadership (Ed D, PhD, Ed S), K-12 special education (M Ed), leadership in mathematics education (M Ed), reading specialist (M Ed), special education (Ed D, PhD, Ed S), student affairs (M Ed), TESOL - adult education (M Ed), TESOL - K-12 (M Ed); educational specialist (Ed S), including adult education (Ed D, PhD, Ed S), advanced educational leadership (Ed D, PhD, Ed S), character education (Ed D, PhD, Ed S), Christian education leadership (Ed D, PhD, Ed S), curriculum and instruction (Ed D, PhD, Ed S), educational psychology (Ed D, PhD, Ed S), educational technology and online learning (Ed D, PhD, Ed S), exceptional education executive leadership (Ed D, PhD, Ed S), higher education (Ed D, PhD, Ed S), higher education leadership and management (Ed D, PhD, Ed S), K-12 school leadership (Ed D, PhD, Ed S), special education (Ed D, PhD, Ed S). *Accreditation:* TEAC. *Program availability:* Part-time, evening/weekend, 100% online, blended/hybrid learning. *Faculty:* 22 full-time (10 women), 44 part-time/adjunct (32 women). *Students:* 80 full-time (59 women), 945 part-time (750 women); includes 432 minority (352 Black or African American, non-Hispanic/Latino; 4 American Indian or Alaska Native, non-Hispanic/Latino; 14 Asian, non-Hispanic/Latino; 43 Hispanic/Latino; 19 Two or more races, non-Hispanic/Latino), 12 international. Average age 40. 1,125 applicants, 49% accepted, 436 enrolled. In 2017, 316 master's, 24 doctorates awarded. *Degree requirements:* For master's, thesis or alternative; for doctorate, comprehensive exam, thesis/dissertation. *Entrance requirements:* For master's, Virginia Communication and Literacy Assessment (VCLA), PRAXIS, college transcripts, writing sample, interview; for doctorate, GRE, writing sample, resume, transcripts, interview. Additional exam requirements/recommendations for international students: Required—TOEFL (minimum score 577 paper-based). *Application deadline:* For fall admission, 4/1 priority date for domestic students; for spring admission, 10/15 priority date for domestic students. Applications are processed on a rolling basis. Application fee: $50. Electronic applications accepted. *Expenses:* Contact institution. *Financial support:* In 2017–18, 669 students received support, including 1 fellowship (averaging $10,000 per year); career-related internships or fieldwork, scholarships/grants, and unspecified assistantships also available. Support available to part-time students. *Faculty research:* Christian school administration, curriculum and instruction, educational technology and online learning, higher education, special education. *Unit head:* Dr. Donald Finn, Dean, 757-352-4278, Fax: 757-352-4318, E-mail: dfinn@regent.edu. *Application contact:* Heidi Cece, Assistant Vice President of Enrollment Management, 800-373-5504, Fax: 757-352-4381, E-mail: admissions@regent.edu.
Website: https://www.regent.edu/school-of-education/

Regis University, College of Contemporary Liberal Studies, Denver, CO 80221-1099. Offers creative writing (MFA); criminology (M Sc); curriculum, instruction and assessment (M Ed); education - teacher leadership (M Ed); educational leadership (M Ed); elementary education (M Ed); literacy (Certificate); reading (M Ed); secondary education (M Ed); special education (M Ed); teacher academic leadership (Certificate); teacher leadership (MA); teacher/educational leadership (M Ed); teaching the linguistically diverse (M Ed). *Program availability:* Part-time, evening/weekend, 100% online, blended/hybrid learning. *Degree requirements:* For master's, thesis (for some programs). *Entrance requirements:* For master's, official transcript reflecting baccalaureate degree awarded from regionally-accredited college or university, work experience, resume, letters of recommendation. Additional exam requirements/recommendations for international students: Required—TOEFL (minimum score 550 paper-based; 82 iBT). Electronic applications accepted. *Expenses:* Contact institution.

Rivier University, School of Graduate Studies, Department of Education, Nashua, NH 03060. Offers curriculum and instruction (M Ed); early childhood education (M Ed); educational administration (M Ed); educational studies (M Ed); elementary education (M Ed); elementary education and general special education (M Ed); emotional and behavioral disorders (M Ed); general social education (M Ed); leadership and learning (Ed D, CAGS); learning disabilities (M Ed); learning disabilities and reading (M Ed); mental health counseling (MA); reading (M Ed); school counseling (M Ed). *Program availability:* Part-time, evening/weekend. *Degree requirements:* For master's, comprehensive exam (for some programs), internships. *Entrance requirements:* For master's, GRE General Test or MAT.

St. Catherine University, Graduate Programs, Program in Education—Curriculum and Instruction, St. Paul, MN 55105. Offers MA. *Program availability:* Part-time, evening/weekend, online learning. *Faculty:* 14 full-time (11 women). *Students:* 71 part-time (57 women); includes 2 minority (1 Asian, non-Hispanic/Latino; 1 Two or more races, non-Hispanic/Latino). Average age 32. 18 applicants, 100% accepted, 15 enrolled. In 2017, 25 master's awarded. *Degree requirements:* For master's, thesis. *Entrance requirements:* For master's, current teaching license, classroom experience, minimum GPA of 3.0. Additional exam requirements/recommendations for international students: Required—Michigan English Language Assessment Battery or TOEFL (minimum score 600 paper-based; 100 iBT). *Application deadline:* For fall admission, 6/1 priority date for domestic students; for winter admission, 1/1 priority date for domestic students; for spring admission, 5/1 priority date for domestic students. Applications are processed on a rolling basis. Application fee: $35. *Expenses:* Contact institution. *Financial support:* In 2017–18, 39 students received support. Application deadline: 4/1; applicants required to submit FAFSA. *Unit head:* Siri Anderson, Associate Professor/Director of Online Learning, 651-690-6121, E-mail: ssanderson2@stkate.edu. *Application contact:* Sylvia Alexander-Sedey, Assistant Director of Admissions, 651-690-6243, Fax: 651-690-6064.

St. Cloud State University, School of Graduate Studies, School of Education, Department of Teacher Development, St. Cloud, MN 56301-4498. Offers curriculum and instruction (MS). *Degree requirements:* For master's, thesis or alternative. *Entrance requirements:* For master's, GRE General Test, minimum GPA of 2.75. Additional exam requirements/recommendations for international students: Required—Michigan English Language Assessment Battery; Recommended—TOEFL (minimum score 550 paper-based), IELTS (minimum score 6.5). Electronic applications accepted.

St. Francis Xavier University, Graduate Studies, Graduate Studies in Education, Antigonish, NS B2G 2W5, Canada. Offers curriculum and instruction (M Ed); educational administration and leadership (M Ed). *Program availability:* Part-time, online learning. *Degree requirements:* For master's, thesis. *Entrance requirements:* For master's, minimum undergraduate B average, 2 years of teaching experience. *Faculty research:* Inclusive education, qualitative research.

St. John's University, The School of Education, Department of Curriculum and Instruction, PhD in Curriculum and Instruction Program, Queens, NY 11439. Offers early childhood (PhD); global education (PhD); STEM education (PhD); teaching, learning, and knowing (PhD). *Program availability:* Part-time-only. *Degree requirements:* For doctorate, comprehensive exam, thesis/dissertation. *Entrance requirements:* For doctorate, teacher certification (or equivalent), at least three years' teaching experience or the equivalent in informal learning environments, master's degree. Additional exam requirements/recommendations for international students: Required—TOEFL. *Application deadline:* Applications are processed on a rolling basis. Application fee: $70. Electronic applications accepted. *Expenses: Tuition:* Full-time $44,280; part-time $1230 per credit. *Required fees:* $340; $340 per credit. Tuition and fees vary according to course load, degree level and program. *Financial support:* Fellowships, research assistantships, and scholarships/grants available. Support available to part-time students. Financial award application deadline: 2/1; financial award applicants required to submit FAFSA. *Faculty research:* Literacies, early childhood, STEM, school culture, global education. *Unit head:* Dr. Sandra Schamroth Abrams, PhD Program Director, 718-990-8313, E-mail: abramss@stjohns.edu. *Application contact:* Dr. Sandra Schamroth Abrams, PhD Program Director, 718-990-8313, E-mail: abramss@stjohns.edu.
Website: https://www.stjohns.edu/academics/schools-and-colleges/school-education/programs-and-majors/phd-curriculum-and-instruction

Saint Joseph's University, College of Arts and Sciences, Graduate Programs in Education, Philadelphia, PA 19131-1395. Offers curriculum supervisor (Certificate); educational leadership (MS, Ed D); elementary education (MS, Certificate); elementary/middle school education (Certificate); organizational development and leadership (MS); principal (Certificate); professional education (MS); reading specialist (MS, Certificate); reading supervisor (Certificate); secondary education (MS, Certificate); special education (MS); special education 7-12 (Certificate); special education PK-8 (Certificate); superintendent's letter of eligibility (Certificate); supervisor of special education (Certificate); teacher of the deaf and hard of hearing (Certificate). *Program availability:* Part-time, evening/weekend, blended/hybrid learning. *Faculty:* 18 full-time (16 women), 63 part-time/adjunct (44 women). *Students:* 79 full-time (60 women), 793 part-time (604 women); includes 179 minority (125 Black or African American, non-Hispanic/Latino; 5 American Indian or Alaska Native, non-Hispanic/Latino; 15 Asian, non-Hispanic/Latino; 27 Hispanic/Latino; 1 Native Hawaiian or other Pacific Islander, non-Hispanic/Latino; 6 Two or more races, non-Hispanic/Latino), 12 international. Average age 34. 375 applicants, 75% accepted, 189 enrolled. In 2017, 340 master's, 13 doctorates, 3 other advanced degrees awarded. *Degree requirements:* For master's, thesis or alternative; for doctorate, comprehensive exam, thesis/dissertation. *Entrance requirements:* For master's, 2 letters of recommendation, minimum GPA of 3.0, official transcripts, personal statement; for doctorate, GRE, master's degree from accredited institution, minimum graduate GPA of 3.5, computer competence, interview with program director. Additional exam requirements/recommendations for international students: Required—TOEFL (minimum score 550 paper-based; 80 iBT), IELTS (minimum score 6.5), PTE (minimum score 60). *Application deadline:* For fall admission, 7/15 for international students; for spring admission, 11/1 for international students. Applications are processed on a rolling basis. Application fee: $35. Electronic applications accepted. *Expenses:* Contact institution. *Financial support:* Scholarships/grants and unspecified assistantships available. Financial award application deadline: 5/1; financial award applicants required to submit FAFSA. *Faculty research:* Factors predicting early mathematics skills for low income children, early child care and development, preschool quality, parent communication and home-school collaboration issues, education of terminally ill children, preparing literacy teachers for urban schools. *Unit head:* Dr. John Vacca, Associate Dean, Education, 610-660-3131, E-mail: gradcas@sju.edu. *Application contact:* Graduate Admissions, College of Arts and Sciences, 610-660-3131, E-mail: gradcas@sju.edu.
Website: https://sites.sju.edu/education/graduate-programs/

Saint Louis University, Graduate Programs, School of Education, Department of Educational Studies, St. Louis, MO 63103. Offers curriculum and instruction (MA, Ed D, PhD); educational foundations (MA, Ed D, PhD); special education (MA); teaching (MAT). *Accreditation:* NCATE. *Program availability:* Part-time. *Degree requirements:* For master's, comprehensive exam; for doctorate, comprehensive exam, thesis/dissertation, preliminary oral and written exams. *Entrance requirements:* For master's, GRE General Test or MAT, letters of recommendation, resume; for doctorate, GRE General Test, letters of recommendation, resumé, goal statement, transcripts. Additional exam requirements/recommendations for international students: Required—TOEFL (minimum score 525 paper-based). Electronic applications accepted. *Faculty research:* Teacher preparation, multicultural issues, children with special needs, qualitative research in education, inclusion.

Saint Vincent College, Program in Education, Latrobe, PA 15650-2690. Offers curriculum and instruction (MS); instructional design and technology (MS); school administration and supervision (MS); special education (MS). *Program availability:* Part-time, evening/weekend. *Degree requirements:* For master's, comprehensive exam. *Entrance requirements:* For master's, GRE (if undergraduate GPA less than 3.0). Additional exam requirements/recommendations for international students: Required—TOEFL (minimum score 550 paper-based). *Faculty research:* Assessment and instructional technology.

Saint Xavier University, Graduate Studies, School of Education, Chicago, IL 60655-3105. Offers counseling (MA); curriculum and instruction (MA); early childhood education (MA); educational administration (MA); elementary education (MA); individualized studies (MA), including educational technology, English as a second language (ESL), ISTEM (integrative science, technology, engineering, and math); science education; music education (MA); reading (MA); secondary education (MA); Spanish education (MA); special education (MA); teaching and leadership (MA). *Accreditation:* NCATE. *Program availability:* Part-time, evening/weekend. *Degree requirements:* For master's, thesis or project. *Entrance requirements:* For master's, minimum GPA of 3.0. *Expenses:* Contact institution.

Salem International University, School of Education, Salem, WV 26426-0500. Offers curriculum and instruction (M Ed); educational leadership (M Ed). *Program availability:* Part-time, evening/weekend, online learning. *Degree requirements:* For master's, comprehensive exam (for some programs), thesis (for some programs). *Entrance requirements:* For master's, GRE, MAT, NTE, 3 letters of recommendation. Additional exam requirements/recommendations for international students: Required—TOEFL (minimum score 550 paper-based). Electronic applications accepted. *Expenses:* Contact institution. *Faculty research:* Improved classroom effectiveness.

Salisbury University, Program in Curriculum and Instruction, Salisbury, MD 21801-6837. Offers M Ed. *Program availability:* Part-time, evening/weekend. *Faculty:* 5 full-time (4 women), 3 part-time/adjunct (2 women). *Students:* 18 full-time (10 women), 83 part-time (71 women); includes 10 minority (4 Black or African American, non-Hispanic/Latino; 1 Asian, non-Hispanic/Latino; 1 Hispanic/Latino; 1 Native Hawaiian or other Pacific Islander, non-Hispanic/Latino; 3 Two or more races, non-Hispanic/Latino), 1 international. Average age 29. 37 applicants, 59% accepted, 20 enrolled. In 2017, 27 master's awarded. *Entrance requirements:* For master's, three letters of recommendation; transcripts from all colleges and universities attended; personal statement; minimum GPA of 3.0; resume. Additional exam requirements/recommendations for international students: Required—TOEFL (minimum score 550 paper-based; 79 iBT), IELTS (minimum score 6.5). *Application deadline:* For fall admission, 3/1 priority date for domestic and international students; for spring admission, 10/1 priority date for domestic and international students; for summer admission, 3/1 priority date for domestic and international students. Applications are processed on a rolling basis. Application fee: $65. Electronic applications accepted. *Expenses:* $392 per credit hour resident; $703 per credit hour non-resident; $92 per credit hour fees. *Financial support:* In 2017–18, 4 students received support, including 13 teaching assistantships with full tuition reimbursements available (averaging $8,191 per year); career-related internships or fieldwork and scholarships/grants also available. Support available to part-time students. Financial award application deadline: 3/1; financial award applicants required to submit FAFSA. *Faculty research:* Technology; literacy; social justice; STEM; mathematics. *Unit head:* Dr. Diana Wagner, Graduate Program Director, Curriculum and Instruction, 410-677-5490, E-mail: dmwagner@salisbury.edu.
Website: http://www.salisbury.edu/gsr/gradstudies/MEDpage

Sam Houston State University, College of Education, Department of Curriculum and Instruction, Huntsville, TX 77341. Offers curriculum and instruction (M Ed). *Accreditation:* NCATE. *Program availability:* Part-time, evening/weekend. *Degree requirements:* For master's, comprehensive exam, thesis optional; for doctorate, comprehensive exam, thesis/dissertation. *Entrance requirements:* For master's, GRE General Test; for doctorate, GRE General Test, three letters of recommendation, sample of professional work, three years of working experience. Additional exam requirements/recommendations for international students: Required—TOEFL (minimum score 550 paper-based; 79 iBT), IELTS (minimum score 6.5). Electronic applications accepted.

San Diego State University, Graduate and Research Affairs, College of Education, School of Teacher Education, Program in Elementary Curriculum and Instruction, San Diego, CA 92182. Offers MA. *Accreditation:* NCATE. *Program availability:* Evening/weekend. *Entrance requirements:* For master's, GRE General Test, letters of reference. Additional exam requirements/recommendations for international students: Required—TOEFL. Electronic applications accepted.

San Diego State University, Graduate and Research Affairs, College of Education, School of Teacher Education, Program in Secondary Curriculum and Instruction, San Diego, CA 92182. Offers MA. *Accreditation:* NCATE. *Entrance requirements:* For master's, GRE General Test, letters of reference. Additional exam requirements/recommendations for international students: Required—TOEFL. Electronic applications accepted.

San Jose State University, Graduate Studies and Research, Connie L. Lurie College of Education, San Jose, CA 95192-0071. Offers child and adolescent development (MA); education (MA), including counseling and student personnel, curriculum and instruction, speech pathology; educational leadership (MA, Ed D), including administration and supervision (MA), educational leadership (MA); elementary education (MA), including curriculum and instruction. *Accreditation:* NCATE. *Program availability:* Part-time, evening/weekend. *Faculty:* 29 full-time (22 women), 47 part-time/adjunct (40 women). *Students:* 414 full-time (339 women), 115 part-time (93 women); includes 341 minority (14 Black or African American, non-Hispanic/Latino; 87 Asian, non-Hispanic/Latino; 176 Hispanic/Latino; 64 Two or more races, non-Hispanic/Latino), 9 international. Average age 30. 654 applicants, 34% accepted, 161 enrolled. In 2017, 286 master's, 7 doctorates awarded. Terminal master's awarded for partial completion of doctoral program. *Degree requirements:* For master's, project or theses, graduate writing assessment; for doctorate, thesis/dissertation. *Entrance requirements:* For master's, GRE General Test (for some programs). Additional exam requirements/recommendations for international students: Required—TOEFL (minimum score 550 paper-based; 80 iBT), IELTS (minimum score 6.5), PTE (minimum score 53). *Application deadline:* For fall admission, 2/1 for domestic and international students. Applications are processed on a rolling basis. Application fee: $55. Electronic applications accepted. *Expenses:* Tuition, state resident: full-time $7176. Tuition, nonresident: full-time $16,680. Tuition and fees vary according to course load and program. *Financial support:* In 2017–18, 4 research assistantships with partial tuition reimbursements (averaging $2,500 per year) were awarded; fellowships, career-related internships or fieldwork, Federal Work-Study, scholarships/grants, traineeships, and tuition waivers (full and partial) also available. Support available to part-time students. Financial award application deadline: 4/28; financial award applicants required to submit FAFSA. *Faculty research:* Equity and social justice in public education, interdisciplinary practices, teacher training, and effective pedagogy, clinical efficacy, typical and atypical development in children. *Unit head:* Dr. Paul Cascella, Interim Dean, 408-924-3600, Fax: 408-924-3713, E-mail: paul.cascella@sjsu.edu.
Website: http://www.sjsu.edu/education/

Shawnee State University, Program in Curriculum and Instruction, Portsmouth, OH 45662. Offers M Ed. *Accreditation:* NCATE.

Shaw University, Department of Education, Raleigh, NC 27601-2399. Offers curriculum and instruction (MS), including early childhood education. *Program availability:* Part-time, evening/weekend. *Degree requirements:* For master's, comprehensive exam, thesis, practicum/internship, PRAXIS II. *Entrance requirements:* For master's, GRE General Test, letters of recommendation. Additional exam requirements/recommendations for international students: Required—TOEFL (minimum score 500 paper-based). Electronic applications accepted. *Faculty research:* Multicultural education, instructional technology.

Shepherd University, Program in Curriculum and Instruction, Shepherdstown, WV 25443. Offers MA. *Accreditation:* NCATE.

Shippensburg University of Pennsylvania, School of Graduate Studies, College of Education and Human Services, Department of Teacher Education, Shippensburg, PA 17257-2299. Offers curriculum and instruction (M Ed), including biology, early childhood education, elementary education, geography/earth science, history, mathematics, middle school education, modern languages; reading (M Ed). *Accreditation:* NCATE. *Program availability:* Part-time, evening/weekend, 100% online, blended/hybrid learning. *Faculty:* 13 full-time (8 women), 1 (woman) part-time/adjunct. *Students:* 10 full-time (7 women), 94 part-time (81 women); includes 10 minority (3 Black or African American, non-Hispanic/Latino; 2 Asian, non-Hispanic/Latino; 5 Hispanic/Latino), 1 international. Average age 34. 71 applicants, 86% accepted, 35 enrolled. In 2017, 23 master's awarded. *Degree requirements:* For master's, comprehensive exam (for some programs), thesis optional, practicum or internship; capstone seminar (for some programs). *Entrance requirements:* For master's, MAT or GRE (if GPA less than 2.75),

Curriculum and Instruction

interview, 3 letters of reference, questionnaire of teaching background and future goals, resume. Additional exam requirements/recommendations for international students: Required—TOEFL (minimum score 550 paper-based, 68 iBT) or IELTS (minimum score 6). *Application deadline:* For fall admission, 4/1 priority date for domestic students, 4/30 for international students; for spring admission, 9/1 priority date for domestic students, 9/30 for international students; for summer admission, 2/1 priority date for domestic students. Applications are processed on a rolling basis. Application fee: $45. Electronic applications accepted. *Expenses:* Tuition, state resident: part-time $500 per credit. Tuition, nonresident: part-time $750 per credit. *Required fees:* $145 per credit. *Financial support:* In 2017–18, 1 student received support. Career-related internships or fieldwork, scholarships/grants, unspecified assistantships, and resident hall director and student payroll positions available. Support available to part-time students. Financial award application deadline: 3/1; financial award applicants required to submit FAFSA. *Unit head:* Dr. Christine A. Royce, Chairperson, 717-477-1688, Fax: 717-477-4046, E-mail: caroyc@ship.edu. *Application contact:* Maya T. Mapp, Director of Admissions, 717-477-1231, Fax: 717-477-4016, E-mail: mtmapp@ship.edu.
Website: http://www.ship.edu/teacher/

Simon Fraser University, Office of Graduate Studies and Postdoctoral Fellows, Faculty of Education, Programs in Curriculum and Instruction, Burnaby, BC V5A 1S6, Canada. Offers curriculum and instruction (M Ed); curriculum and instruction foundations (M Ed, MA); curriculum theory and implementation (PhD); educational practice (M Ed); philosophy of education (PhD). *Degree requirements:* For master's, comprehensive exam (for some programs), thesis (for some programs); for doctorate, comprehensive exam, thesis/dissertation. *Entrance requirements:* For master's, minimum GPA of 3.0 (on scale of 4.33) or 3.33 based on last 60 credits of undergraduate courses; for doctorate, minimum GPA of 3.5 (on scale of 4.33). Additional exam requirements/recommendations for international students: Recommended—TOEFL (minimum score 580 paper-based; 93 iBT), IELTS (minimum score 7), TWE (minimum score 5). Electronic applications accepted. *Faculty research:* Philosophy of education, applied and comparative epistemology, ethics and moral education, critical multicultural practices.

Simpson University, School of Education, Redding, CA 96003-8606. Offers education (MA), including curriculum, education leadership; education and preliminary administrative services credential (MA); education and preliminary teaching credential (MA); teaching (MA). *Program availability:* Part-time, evening/weekend. *Degree requirements:* For master's, thesis optional. *Entrance requirements:* For master's, statement of purpose, 2 professional references, professional essay, interview. Additional exam requirements/recommendations for international students: Required—TOEFL (minimum score 550 paper-based). Electronic applications accepted. *Expenses:* Contact institution.

Sitting Bull College, Graduate Programs, Fort Yates, ND 58538-9701. Offers curriculum and instruction (M Ed); environmental science (MS). *Faculty:* 2 full-time (0 women). *Students:* 14 full-time (13 women). 16 applicants, 100% accepted, 14 enrolled. *Entrance requirements:* For master's, GRE, official transcripts from all previous colleges and universities, three letters of recommendation, curriculum vitae, letter of intent. *Application deadline:* For fall admission, 4/30 priority date for domestic students. Application fee: $0. *Expenses:* Tuition, area resident: Full-time $6300; part-time $350 per credit hour. *Required fees:* $310; $310 per year. $155 per semester. Tuition and fees vary according to course load. *Financial support:* Fellowships and scholarships/grants available. *Unit head:* Chris Fried, Division of Education Director, 701-854-8000, Fax: 701-854-8197, E-mail: travis.frank@sittingbull.edu. *Application contact:* Chris Fried, Division of Education Director, 701-854-8000, Fax: 701-854-8197, E-mail: travis.frank@sittingbull.edu.

Sonoma State University, School of Education, Rohnert Park, CA 94928. Offers administrative services (Credential); curriculum, teaching, and learning (MA); early childhood education (MA); education specialist (Credential); educational leadership (MA); multiple subject (Credential); reading and literacy (MA, Credential); single subject (Credential); special education (MA). *Accreditation:* NCATE. *Program availability:* Part-time, evening/weekend. *Entrance requirements:* For master's, minimum GPA of 2.5. Additional exam requirements/recommendations for international students: Required—TOEFL (minimum score 500 paper-based). Application fee: $55. *Financial support:* Fellowships, research assistantships, career-related internships or fieldwork, and Federal Work-Study available. Support available to part-time students. Financial award application deadline: 3/2; financial award applicants required to submit FAFSA. *Unit head:* Dr. Carlos Ayala, Dean, 707-664-4412, E-mail: carlos.ayala@sonoma.edu. *Application contact:* Dr. Karen Grady, Coordinator of Graduate Studies, 707-664-3328, E-mail: karen.grady@sonoma.edu.
Website: http://www.sonoma.edu/education/

South Dakota State University, Graduate School, College of Education and Human Sciences, Department of Teaching, Learning and Leadership, Brookings, SD 57007. Offers agricultural education (MS); curriculum and instruction (M Ed); educational administration (M Ed). *Program availability:* Part-time, evening/weekend, online learning. *Degree requirements:* For master's, portfolio, oral exam. *Entrance requirements:* For master's, minimum GPA of 2.75. Additional exam requirements/recommendations for international students: Required—TOEFL (minimum score 550 paper-based; 80 iBT). *Faculty research:* Inclusion school climate, K-12 reform and restructuring, rural development, ESL, leadership.

Southeastern Louisiana University, College of Education, Department of Teaching and Learning, Hammond, LA 70402. Offers curriculum and instruction (M Ed); elementary education (MAT); special education (M Ed); special education: early interventionist (MAT). *Accreditation:* NCATE. *Program availability:* Part-time, evening/weekend. *Faculty:* 14 full-time (all women), 2 part-time/adjunct (1 woman). *Students:* 19 full-time (16 women), 115 part-time (104 women); includes 13 minority (3 Black or African American, non-Hispanic/Latino; 5 Hispanic/Latino; 5 Two or more races, non-Hispanic/Latino), 1 international. Average age 37. 55 applicants, 45% accepted, 18 enrolled. In 2017, 29 master's awarded. *Degree requirements:* For master's, comprehensive exam (for some programs), thesis (for some programs), action research project, oral defense of research project, portfolio, teaching certificate, minimum cumulative GPA of 3.0. *Entrance requirements:* For master's, GRE (verbal and quantitative), PRAXIS (for MAT), Prospective Education Candidate (PEC) self-assessment survey; competency on a technology performance assessment in education or three-hour graduate-level technology course; orientation seminar. Additional exam requirements/recommendations for international students: Required—TOEFL (minimum score 500 paper-based; 61 iBT). *Application deadline:* For fall admission, 7/15 priority date for domestic students, 6/1 priority date for international students; for spring admission, 12/1 priority date for domestic students, 10/1 priority date for international students. Applications are processed on a rolling basis. Application fee: $20 ($30 for international students). Electronic applications accepted. *Expenses:* Tuition, state resident: full-time $6684. Tuition, nonresident: full-time $19,162. *Required fees:* $2088. *Financial support:* In 2017–18, 5 students received support. Research assistantships, teaching assistantships, career-related internships or fieldwork, Federal Work-Study, institutionally sponsored loans, scholarships/grants, and unspecified assistantships available. Support available to part-time students. Financial award application deadline:

5/1; financial award applicants required to submit FAFSA. *Faculty research:* Teacher in services, STEM, educational technology, pre-service teacher education. *Unit head:* Dr. Colleen Klein-Ezell, Department Head, 985-549-2221, Fax: 985-549-5009, E-mail: colleen.klein-ezell@southeastern.edu. *Application contact:* Amanda Harper, Graduate Admissions Analyst, 985-549-5620, Fax: 985-549-5632, E-mail: admissions@southeastern.edu.
Website: http://www.southeastern.edu/acad_research/depts/teach_lrn/index.html

Southeastern University, College of Education, Lakeland, FL 33801-6099. Offers curriculum and instruction (Ed D); educational leadership (M Ed); elementary education (M Ed); exceptional student education (M Ed); exceptional student education/educational therapy (M Ed); kinesiology (M Ed); organizational leadership (Ed D); reading education (M Ed); teaching English to speakers of other languages (M Ed). *Faculty:* 8 full-time (5 women), 12 part-time/adjunct (7 women). *Students:* 139 full-time (109 women), 225 part-time (172 women); includes 107 minority (57 Black or African American, non-Hispanic/Latino; 2 Asian, non-Hispanic/Latino; 48 Hispanic/Latino), 4 international. Average age 40. Application fee: $50. Electronic applications accepted. *Unit head:* James A. Anderson, Dean, 863-667-5366, E-mail: jaanderson2@seu.edu.
Website: http://www.seu.edu/education/

Southern Arkansas University–Magnolia, School of Graduate Studies, Magnolia, AR 71753. Offers agriculture (MS); business administration (MBA), including agribusiness, social entrepreneurship, supply chain management; clinical and mental health counseling (MS); computer and information sciences (MS), including cyber security and privacy, data science, information technology; gifted and talented (M Ed); curriculum and instruction, educational administration and supervision, gifted and talented P-8/7-12, instructional specialist P-4; higher, adult and lifelong education (M Ed); kinesiology (M Ed), including coaching; library media and information specialist (M Ed); public administration (MPA); school counseling K-12 (M Ed); student affairs and college counseling (M Ed); teaching (MAT). *Accreditation:* NCATE. *Program availability:* Part-time, 100% online, blended/hybrid learning. *Faculty:* 36 full-time (20 women), 31 part-time/adjunct (12 women). *Students:* 242 full-time (89 women), 889 part-time (459 women); includes 167 minority (143 Black or African American, non-Hispanic/Latino; 7 American Indian or Alaska Native, non-Hispanic/Latino; 7 Asian, non-Hispanic/Latino; 3 Hispanic/Latino; 7 Two or more races, non-Hispanic/Latino), 562 international. Average age 28. 400 applicants, 100% accepted, 239 enrolled. In 2017, 875 master's awarded. *Degree requirements:* For master's, comprehensive exam (for some programs), thesis optional. *Entrance requirements:* For master's, GRE, MAT or GMAT, minimum GPA of 2.5. Additional exam requirements/recommendations for international students: Required—TOEFL (minimum score 550 paper-based), IELTS (minimum score 6). *Application deadline:* For fall admission, 7/20 for domestic students, 7/10 for international students; for spring admission, 12/1 for domestic students, 11/15 for international students; for summer admission, 4/1 for domestic students, 5/1 for international students. Applications are processed on a rolling basis. Application fee: $25 ($50 for international students). Electronic applications accepted. *Expenses:* Tuition, state resident: full-time $6038. Tuition, nonresident: full-time $8558. *Required fees:* $804. One-time fee: $110 full-time. Tuition and fees vary according to course load. *Financial support:* Career-related internships or fieldwork, Federal Work-Study, scholarships/grants, tuition waivers (full), and unspecified assistantships available. Financial award applicants required to submit FAFSA. *Faculty research:* Alternative certification for teachers, supervision of instruction, instructional leadership, counseling. *Unit head:* Dr. Kim Bloss, Dean, School of Graduate Studies, 870-235-4150, Fax: 870-235-5227, E-mail: kkbloss@saumag.edu. *Application contact:* Shrijana Malakar, Admissions Specialist, 870-235-4150, Fax: 870-235-5227, E-mail: smalakar@saumag.edu.
Website: http://www.saumag.edu/graduate

Southern Illinois University Carbondale, Graduate School, College of Education and Human Services, Department of Curriculum and Instruction, Carbondale, IL 62901-4701. Offers MS Ed, PhD. *Accreditation:* NCATE. *Program availability:* Part-time. *Degree requirements:* For doctorate, variable foreign language requirement, thesis/dissertation. *Entrance requirements:* For master's, minimum GPA of 2.7; for doctorate, GRE, minimum GPA of 3.25. Additional exam requirements/recommendations for international students: Required—TOEFL. *Faculty research:* Early childhood, science/environmental education, teacher education, instructional development/technology, reading.

Southern Illinois University Edwardsville, Graduate School, School of Education, Health, and Human Behavior, Department of Curriculum and Instruction, Program in Curriculum and Instruction, Edwardsville, IL 62026. Offers MS Ed. *Accreditation:* NCATE. *Program availability:* Part-time, evening/weekend. *Degree requirements:* For master's, thesis (for some programs), final exam/paper. *Entrance requirements:* For master's, teaching certificate. Additional exam requirements/recommendations for international students: Required—TOEFL (minimum score 550 paper-based; 79 iBT), IELTS (minimum score 6.5). Electronic applications accepted.

Southern New Hampshire University, School of Education, Manchester, NH 03106-1045. Offers curriculum and instruction (M Ed), including dyslexia studies and language-based learning disabilities, educational leadership, reading, special education, technology integration; dyslexia studies and language-based learning disabilities (Certificate); early childhood and special education (M Ed); educational leadership (M Ed, Ed D); educational studies (M Ed); elementary and special education (M Ed); field based education (M Ed); higher education administration (MS); teaching English as a foreign language (MS). *Program availability:* Part-time, evening/weekend, online learning. *Degree requirements:* For master's, comprehensive exam (for some programs), thesis or alternative. *Entrance requirements:* For master's, PRAXIS I, minimum GPA of 2.75. Additional exam requirements/recommendations for international students: Required—TOEFL (minimum score 550 paper-based). *Application deadline:* Applications are processed on a rolling basis. Application fee: $40. Electronic applications accepted. *Expenses:* Contact institution. *Financial support:* Institutionally sponsored loans available. Financial award applicants required to submit FAFSA. *Unit head:* Raymond McNulty, Dean, 603-668-2211, Fax: 603-629-4673. *Application contact:* Office of Graduate Admission, 888-327-SNHU, Fax: 603-644-3144, E-mail: enroll@snhu.edu.

Southwestern Adventist University, Education Department, Keene, TX 76059. Offers curriculum and instruction with reading emphasis (M Ed); educational leadership (M Ed). *Program availability:* Part-time, evening/weekend. *Degree requirements:* For master's, thesis or alternative, professional paper. *Entrance requirements:* For master's, GRE General Test.

Southwestern Assemblies of God University, Thomas F. Harrison School of Graduate Studies, Program in Education, Waxahachie, TX 75165-5735. Offers Christian school administration (MS); curriculum development (MS); early education administration (M Ed); middle and secondary education (M Ed). *Degree requirements:* For master's, comprehensive written and oral exams. *Entrance requirements:* For master's, GRE General Test, minimum GPA of 2.5. Electronic applications accepted.

Southwestern College, Education Programs, Winfield, KS 67156-2499. Offers curriculum and instruction (M Ed); early childhood education (M Ed); educational leadership (Ed D), including higher education leadership, PK-12 education leadership; special education (M Ed), including high-incidence disabilities, low-incidence disabilities; teaching (MA). *Accreditation:* NCATE. *Program availability:* Part-time, evening/weekend, 100% online, blended/hybrid learning. *Faculty:* 6 full-time (5 women), 12 part-time/adjunct (10 women). *Students:* 12 full-time (10 women), 77 part-time (51 women); includes 12 minority (5 Black or African American, non-Hispanic/Latino; 2 American Indian or Alaska Native, non-Hispanic/Latino; 1 Asian, non-Hispanic/Latino; 3 Hispanic/Latino; 1 Native Hawaiian or other Pacific Islander, non-Hispanic/Latino), 10 international. Average age 39. 29 applicants, 86% accepted, 18 enrolled. In 2017, 52 master's, 11 doctorates awarded. *Degree requirements:* For master's, practicum, portfolio; for doctorate, thesis/dissertation, professional portfolio. *Entrance requirements:* For master's, baccalaureate degree, minimum GPA of 3.0, valid teaching certificate (for special education); for doctorate, GRE if no master's degree, baccalaureate degree with minimum GPA of 3.25 and current teaching experience, or master's degree with minimum GPA of 3.5. Additional exam requirements/recommendations for international students: Required—TOEFL (minimum score 550 paper-based; 80 iBT). *Application deadline:* Applications are processed on a rolling basis. Application fee: $40. Electronic applications accepted. *Expenses:* Tuition: $577 per credit hour, $509 online (for master's programs); $609 per credit hour (for doctorate program). *Financial support:* In 2017–18, 9 students received support. Unspecified assistantships and employee tuition waivers available. Financial award applicants required to submit FAFSA. *Unit head:* Dana Pentz, Director of Education Operations, 620-229-6253, E-mail: dana.pentz@sckans.edu. *Application contact:* Dennis Russell, Director of Admissions and Student Services, 888-684-5335 Ext. 3372, Fax: 888-684-5218, E-mail: dennis.russell@sckans.edu. Website: http://www.sckans.edu/graduate/education-med/

Stanford University, Graduate School of Education, Program in Curriculum and Teacher Education, Stanford, CA 94305-2004. Offers MA. *Degree requirements:* For master's, thesis (for some programs). *Entrance requirements:* For master's, GRE General Test. Electronic applications accepted. *Expenses:* Tuition: Full-time $48,987; part-time $10,620 per quarter. One-time fee: $400. Tuition and fees vary according to program.

State University of New York at Fredonia, College of Education, Fredonia, NY 14063-1136. Offers curriculum and instruction (MS Ed); literacy education (MS Ed), including birth-grade 12, grades 5-12; TESOL (MS Ed). *Accreditation:* NCATE. *Program availability:* Part-time. *Faculty:* 11 full-time (9 women), 1 part-time/adjunct (0 women). *Students:* Average age 29. 60 applicants, 97% accepted, 39 enrolled. In 2017, 33 master's awarded. *Degree requirements:* For master's, thesis. *Entrance requirements:* For master's, GRE, minimum undergraduate GPA of 3.0. Additional exam requirements/recommendations for international students: Required—TOEFL (minimum score 79 iBT), IELTS (minimum score 6.5). *Application deadline:* For fall admission, 4/1 priority date for domestic and international students; for spring admission, 11/1 priority date for domestic students, 11/1 for international students. Applications are processed on a rolling basis. Application fee: $75. Electronic applications accepted. *Expenses:* Tuition, state resident: full-time $8154. Tuition, nonresident: full-time $16,650. *Required fees:* $1209. *Financial support:* In 2017–18, 4 teaching assistantships with full and partial tuition reimbursements (averaging $7,075 per year) were awarded. Financial award application deadline: 3/15; financial award applicants required to submit FAFSA. *Faculty research:* Positive behavioral intervention and support (PBIS), place-based science education, peer support for education, primary source material for social studies education, policies and practices in learning English language. *Unit head:* Dr. Christine Givner, Dean, 716-673-3311, E-mail: christine.givner@fredonia.edu. *Application contact:* Wendy S. Dunst, Interim Graduate Recruitment and Admissions Associate, 716-673-3808, Fax: 716-673-3712, E-mail: wendy.dunst@fredonia.edu. Website: http://www.fredonia.edu/coe/

State University of New York at Oswego, Graduate Studies, School of Education, Department of Curriculum and Instruction, Oswego, NY 13126. Offers adolescence education (MST); art education (MAT); childhood education (MST); curriculum and instruction (MS Ed); literacy education (MS Ed); special education (MS Ed). *Program availability:* Part-time, evening/weekend. *Degree requirements:* For master's, comprehensive exam (for some programs), thesis optional. *Entrance requirements:* For master's, GRE General Test, minimum GPA of 2.7, provisional teaching certificate. Additional exam requirements/recommendations for international students: Required—TOEFL (minimum score 560 paper-based). *Faculty research:* Classroom applications for microcomputers; classroom questioning, wait-time, and achievement; values clarification and academic achievement.

State University of New York at Plattsburgh, School of Education, Health, and Human Services, Program in Teacher Education: Teaching and Learning, Plattsburgh, NY 12901-2681. Offers MS Ed. *Program availability:* Part-time, evening/weekend. *Entrance requirements:* For master's, minimum GPA of 2.5. Additional exam requirements/recommendations for international students: Required—TOEFL.

State University of New York College at Potsdam, School of Education and Professional Studies, Program in Curriculum and Instruction, Potsdam, NY 13676. Offers childhood education (MST); curriculum and instruction (MS Ed). *Accreditation:* NCATE. *Program availability:* Online learning. *Degree requirements:* For master's, thesis (for some programs). *Entrance requirements:* For master's, minimum GPA of 2.75 in last 60 credit hours of undergraduate study. Additional exam requirements/recommendations for international students: Required—TOEFL (minimum score 550 paper-based; 80 iBT), IELTS (minimum score 6). Electronic applications accepted.

Syracuse University, School of Education, Programs in Instructional Design, Development, and Evaluation, Syracuse, NY 13244. Offers MS, PhD, CAS. *Program availability:* Part-time. *Students:* Average age 34. *Degree requirements:* For master's, thesis or alternative; for doctorate, comprehensive exam, thesis/dissertation. *Entrance requirements:* For master's, GRE or MAT, baccalaureate degree from regionally-accredited college/university, statement of goals, three letters of recommendation, transcripts; for doctorate, GRE, master's degree in instructional design or equivalent, statement of goals, three letters of recommendation, transcripts; for CAS, GRE (recommended), master's degree in instructional design or equivalent, statement of goals, three letters of recommendation, transcripts. Additional exam requirements/recommendations for international students: Required—TOEFL (minimum score 100 iBT). *Application deadline:* For fall admission, 1/15 priority date for domestic and international students; for spring admission, 10/15 priority date for domestic and international students. Applications are processed on a rolling basis. Application fee: $75. Electronic applications accepted. *Financial support:* Fellowships with full tuition reimbursements, research assistantships, teaching assistantships, career-related internships or fieldwork, and scholarships/grants available. Financial award application deadline: 1/15. *Faculty research:* Digital media production, technologies for instructional settings, strategies in educational project management, educational technology in international settings. *Unit head:* Dr. Jing Lei, Chair, 315-443-3703, E-mail: jlei@syr.edu. *Application contact:* Speranza Migliore, Graduate Admissions Recruiter, 315-443-2505, E-mail: gradrcrt@syr.edu. Website: http://soe.syr.edu/academic/Instructional_Design_Development_and_Evaluation/

Syracuse University, School of Education, Programs in Teaching and Curriculum, Syracuse, NY 13244. Offers MS, PhD. *Program availability:* Part-time. *Students:* Average age 37. *Degree requirements:* For master's, thesis or alternative; for doctorate, comprehensive exam, thesis/dissertation. *Entrance requirements:* For master's, baccalaureate degree from regionally-accredited college/university, relevant work experience, three letters of recommendation, personal statement, transcripts; for doctorate, GRE, master's degree, writing sample, three years of professional experience, resume, interview. Additional exam requirements/recommendations for international students: Required—TOEFL (minimum score 100 iBT). *Application deadline:* For fall admission, 1/15 priority date for domestic students, 5/15 priority date for international students; for spring admission, 10/15 priority date for domestic and international students; for summer admission, 1/15 priority date for domestic and international students. Applications are processed on a rolling basis. Application fee: $75. Electronic applications accepted. *Financial support:* Fellowships with full tuition reimbursements, research assistantships, teaching assistantships, scholarships/grants, and tuition waivers available. Financial award application deadline: 1/15. *Faculty research:* Theory and practice of curriculum, the lives and careers of teachers, policies and practices of teacher education, research design, implementation and analysis, forms of scholarly expression. *Unit head:* Dr. Benjamin Dotger, Chair of Teaching and Leadership/Professor, 315-443-2685, E-mail: bdotger@syr.edu. *Application contact:* Speranza Migliore, Graduate Admissions Recruiter, 315-443-2505, E-mail: gradrcrt@syr.edu. Website: http://soe.syr.edu/academic/teaching_and_leadership/graduate/masters/teaching_and_curriculum/

Tarleton State University, College of Graduate Studies, College of Education, Department of Curriculum and Instruction, Stephenville, TX 76402. Offers curriculum and instruction (M Ed); educational diagnostician (M Ed); elementary education (M Ed); instructional design and technology (M Ed); instructional leadership (M Ed); secondary education (M Ed); special education (M Ed); technology applications (M Ed); technology director (M Ed). *Program availability:* Part-time, evening/weekend. *Faculty:* 7 full-time (5 women), 4 part-time/adjunct (2 women). *Students:* 7 full-time (6 women), 156 part-time (137 women); includes 40 minority (11 Black or African American, non-Hispanic/Latino; 25 Hispanic/Latino; 4 Two or more races, non-Hispanic/Latino). Average age 38. 55 applicants, 96% accepted, 46 enrolled. In 2017, 33 master's awarded. *Degree requirements:* For master's, comprehensive exam, thesis (for some programs). *Entrance requirements:* For master's, GRE General Test, minimum GPA of 3.0. Additional exam requirements/recommendations for international students: Required—TOEFL (minimum score 550 paper-based; 80 iBT), IELTS (minimum score 6). *Application deadline:* For fall admission, 8/15 priority date for domestic students; for spring admission, 1/7 for domestic students. Applications are processed on a rolling basis. Application fee: $45 ($145 for international students). Electronic applications accepted. *Expenses:* Contact institution. *Financial support:* Research assistantships, teaching assistantships, career-related internships or fieldwork, Federal Work-Study, and institutionally sponsored loans available. Support available to part-time students. Financial award application deadline: 5/1; financial award applicants required to submit FAFSA. *Unit head:* Dr. Jordan Barkley, Dean, 254-968-9089, E-mail: jbarkley@tarleton.edu. *Application contact:* Information Contact, 254-968-9104, Fax: 254-968-9670, E-mail: gradoffice@tarleton.edu. Website: http://www.tarleton.edu/cimasters/

Teachers College, Columbia University, Department of Curriculum and Teaching, New York, NY 10027-6696. Offers curriculum and teaching (Ed M, MA, Ed D); curriculum and teaching: elementary education (MA); curriculum and teaching: secondary education (MA); early childhood education (MA, Ed D); early childhood education: special education (MA); elementary education-gifted extension (MA); elementary inclusive education (MA); gifted education (MA); literacy specialist (MA); secondary inclusive education (MA); special inclusive elementary education (MA). *Program availability:* Part-time, evening/weekend. *Students:* 196 full-time (181 women), 181 part-time (161 women); includes 141 minority (45 Black or African American, non-Hispanic/Latino; 2 American Indian or Alaska Native, non-Hispanic/Latino; 45 Asian, non-Hispanic/Latino; 35 Hispanic/Latino; 14 Two or more races, non-Hispanic/Latino), 37 international. Average age 30. 509 applicants, 72% accepted, 155 enrolled. Terminal master's awarded for partial completion of doctoral program. *Degree requirements:* For doctorate, thesis/dissertation. *Unit head:* Prof. Daniel Friedrich, Chair, E-mail: friedrich@exchange.tc.columbia.edu. *Application contact:* David Estrella, Director of Admission, 212-678-3305, Fax: 212-678-4171, E-mail: estrella@tc.columbia.edu.

Tennessee State University, The School of Graduate Studies and Research, College of Education, Department of Teaching and Learning, Program in Curriculum and Instruction, Nashville, TN 37209-1561. Offers M Ed, Ed D. *Accreditation:* NCATE. *Degree requirements:* For master's, thesis optional; for doctorate, thesis/dissertation. *Entrance requirements:* For master's, GRE General Test or MAT, minimum GPA of 2.5; for doctorate, GRE General Test or MAT, minimum GPA of 3.25. Additional exam requirements/recommendations for international students: Required—TOEFL.

Tennessee Technological University, College of Graduate Studies, College of Education, Department of Curriculum and Instruction, Program in Curriculum, Cookeville, TN 38505. Offers MA, Ed S. *Accreditation:* NCATE. *Program availability:* Part-time, evening/weekend. *Faculty:* 2 full-time (1 woman). *Students:* 7 full-time (all women), 28 part-time (26 women); includes 1 minority (Two or more races, non-Hispanic/Latino), 1 international. 23 applicants, 52% accepted, 8 enrolled. In 2017, 27 master's, 5 other advanced degrees awarded. *Degree requirements:* For master's and Ed S, comprehensive exam, thesis or alternative. *Entrance requirements:* For master's and Ed S, MAT or GRE. Additional exam requirements/recommendations for international students: Required—TOEFL (minimum score 527 paper-based; 71 iBT), IELTS (minimum score 5.5), PTE (minimum score 48), or TOEIC (Test of English as an International Communication). *Application deadline:* For fall admission, 8/1 for domestic students, 5/1 for international students; for spring admission, 12/1 for domestic students, 10/1 for international students; for summer admission, 5/1 for domestic students, 2/1 for international students. Applications are processed on a rolling basis. Application fee: $35 ($40 for international students). Electronic applications accepted. *Expenses:* Tuition, state resident: full-time $9925; part-time $565 per credit hour. Tuition, nonresident: full-time $22,993; part-time $1291 per credit hour. *Financial support:* Fellowships, research assistantships, and teaching assistantships available. Financial award application deadline: 4/1. *Unit head:* Dr. Jeremy Wendt, Interim Chairperson, 931-372-3181, Fax: 931-372-6270, E-mail: jwendt@tntech.edu. *Application contact:* Shelia K. Kendrick, Coordinator of Graduate Studies, 931-372-3808, Fax: 931-372-3497, E-mail: skendrick@tntech.edu.

Texas A&M International University, Office of Graduate Studies and Research, College of Education, Department of Curriculum and Pedagogy, Laredo, TX 78041. Offers MS. *Degree requirements:* For master's, comprehensive exam. *Entrance requirements:* Additional exam requirements/recommendations for international students: Required—TOEFL (minimum score 550 paper-based; 79 iBT).

Texas A&M University, College of Education and Human Development, Department of Teaching, Learning, and Culture, College Station, TX 77843. Offers curriculum and instruction (M Ed, MS, Ed D, PhD). *Program availability:* Part-time. *Faculty:* 43. *Students:* 183 full-time (149 women), 304 part-time (251 women); includes 141 minority

Curriculum and Instruction

(51 Black or African American, non-Hispanic/Latino; 13 Asian, non-Hispanic/Latino; 70 Hispanic/Latino; 7 Two or more races, non-Hispanic/Latino), 64 international. Average age 34. 104 applicants, 87% accepted, 69 enrolled. In 2017, 161 master's, 21 doctorates awarded. *Degree requirements:* For master's, comprehensive exam, thesis (for some programs); for doctorate, comprehensive exam, thesis/dissertation. *Entrance requirements:* For master's, GRE General Test, minimum GPA of 3.0; for doctorate, GRE General Test, 3 years of teaching experience. Additional exam requirements/recommendations for international students: Required—TOEFL (minimum score 550 paper-based; 80 iBT), IELTS (minimum score 6), PTE (minimum score 53). *Application deadline:* For fall admission, 3/1 for domestic students, 1/1 for international students; for spring admission, 10/1 for domestic students, 8/1 for international students. Application fee: $50 ($90 for international students). Electronic applications accepted. *Expenses:* Contact institution. *Financial support:* In 2017–18, 206 students received support, including 3 fellowships with tuition reimbursements available (averaging $21,229 per year), 48 research assistantships with tuition reimbursements available (averaging $10,869 per year), 33 teaching assistantships with tuition reimbursements available (averaging $10,567 per year); career-related internships or fieldwork, institutionally sponsored loans, scholarships/grants, traineeships, health care benefits, tuition waivers (full and partial), and unspecified assistantships also available. Support available to part-time students. Financial award application deadline: 3/15; financial award applicants required to submit FAFSA. *Unit head:* Dr. Lynn Burlbaw, Professor and Interim Department Co-Head, 979-845-8384, Fax: 979-845-9663, E-mail: burlbaw@neo.tamu.edu. *Application contact:* Sarah Oakley, Academic Advisor II, 979-845-5063, Fax: 979-845-9663, E-mail: sarahoakley@tamu.edu.
Website: http://tlac.tamu.edu

Texas A&M University–Central Texas, Graduate Studies and Research, Killeen, TX 76549. Offers accounting (MS); business administration (MBA); clinical mental health counseling (MS); criminal justice (MCJ); curriculum and instruction (M Ed); educational administration (M Ed); educational psychology - experimental psychology (MS); history (MA); human resource management (MS); information systems (MS); liberal studies (MS); management and leadership (MS); marriage and family therapy (MS); mathematics (MS); political science (MA); school counseling (M Ed); school psychology (Ed S).

Texas A&M University–Commerce, College of Education and Human Services, Commerce, TX 75429. Offers counseling (M Ed, MS, PhD); early childhood education (M Ed, MS); educational administration (M Ed, MS, Ed D); educational psychology (PhD); educational technology leadership (M Ed, MS); educational technology library science (M Ed, MS); elementary education (M Ed); health, kinesiology and sports studies (MS); higher education (MS, Ed D); psychology (MS); reading (M Ed, MS); secondary education (M Ed, MS); social work (MSW); special education (M Ed, MS); supervision, curriculum and instruction-elementary education (Ed D); training and development (MS). *Program availability:* Part-time, evening/weekend, 100% online, blended/hybrid learning. *Faculty:* 91 full-time (51 women), 38 part-time/adjunct (31 women). *Students:* 400 full-time (310 women), 1,400 part-time (1,117 women); includes 724 minority (412 Black or African American, non-Hispanic/Latino; 8 American Indian or Alaska Native, non-Hispanic/Latino; 24 Asian, non-Hispanic/Latino; 220 Hispanic/Latino; 60 Two or more races, non-Hispanic/Latino), 18 international. Average age 37. 951 applicants, 46% accepted, 331 enrolled. In 2017, 564 master's, 24 doctorates awarded. *Degree requirements:* For master's, comprehensive exam, thesis optional, departmental qualifying exams (for some programs); for doctorate, comprehensive exam, thesis/dissertation, departmental qualifying exam; for SSP, comprehensive exam, thesis optional. *Entrance requirements:* For master's and doctorate, GRE General Test. Additional exam requirements/recommendations for international students: Required—TOEFL (minimum score 550 paper-based; 79 iBT), IELTS (minimum score 6). *Application deadline:* For fall admission, 6/1 priority date for international students; for spring admission, 10/15 priority date for international students; for summer admission, 3/15 priority date for international students. Applications are processed on a rolling basis. Application fee: $50. Electronic applications accepted. *Expenses:* Tuition, state resident: full-time $3630. Tuition, nonresident: full-time $11,100. *Required fees:* $2564. Tuition and fees vary according to course load, degree level and program. *Financial support:* In 2017–18, 84 students received support, including 40 research assistantships with partial tuition reimbursements available (averaging $10,800 per year), 12 teaching assistantships with partial tuition reimbursements available (averaging $13,000 per year); career-related internships or fieldwork, Federal Work-Study, institutionally sponsored loans, scholarships/grants, health care benefits, and unspecified assistantships also available. Financial award application deadline: 6/15; financial award applicants required to submit FAFSA. *Faculty research:* Cognitive and bilingual education, positive behavioral intervention, literacy, math readiness. *Total annual research expenditures:* $1.1 million. *Unit head:* Dr. Timothy Letzring, Dean, 903-886-5181, Fax: 903-886-5905, E-mail: tim.letzring@tamuc.edu. *Application contact:* Vicky Turner, Doctoral Degree and Special Programs Coordinator, 903-886-5167, E-mail: vicky.turner@tamuc.edu.
Website: http://www.tamuc.edu/academics/graduateSchool/programs/education/default.aspx

Texas A&M University–Corpus Christi, College of Graduate Studies, College of Education and Human Development, Program in Curriculum and Instruction, Corpus Christi, TX 78412. Offers MS, PhD. *Program availability:* Part-time, evening/weekend. *Students:* 8 full-time (6 women), 49 part-time (44 women); includes 37 minority (2 Black or African American, non-Hispanic/Latino; 35 Hispanic/Latino). Average age 38. 11 applicants, 73% accepted, 7 enrolled. In 2017, 13 master's, 8 doctorates awarded. *Degree requirements:* For master's, comprehensive exam; for doctorate, thesis/dissertation. *Entrance requirements:* For master's, minimum GPA of 3.0 in last 60 hours; essay (approximately 300-400 words in length); for doctorate, GMAT/GRE (taken within 5 years), master's degree, minimum GPA of 3.0 in last 60 hours, 4 reference forms, 3 years' teaching experience, interview. Additional exam requirements/recommendations for international students: Required—TOEFL (minimum score 550 paper-based; 79 iBT), IELTS (minimum score 6.5). *Application deadline:* For fall admission, 8/10 for domestic students, 5/1 for international students; for spring admission, 1/10 for domestic students, 9/1 for international students; for summer admission, 6/15 for domestic students, 2/1 for international students. Applications are processed on a rolling basis. Application fee: $50 ($70 for international students). Electronic applications accepted. *Expenses:* Tuition, state resident: full-time $3568; part-time $198.24 per credit hour. Tuition, nonresident: full-time $11,038; part-time $613.24 per credit hour. *Required fees:* $2129; $1422.58 per semester. Tuition and fees vary according to program. *Financial support:* Research assistantships, teaching assistantships, career-related internships or fieldwork, Federal Work-Study, institutionally sponsored loans, scholarships/grants, health care benefits, and unspecified assistantships available. Support available to part-time students. Financial award application deadline: 3/15; financial award applicants required to submit FAFSA. *Unit head:* Dr. Faye Bruun, Chair, 361-825-2417, E-mail: faye.bruun@tamucc.edu. *Application contact:* Graduate Admissions Coordinator, 361-825-2177, Fax: 361-825-2755, E-mail: gradweb@tamucc.edu.
Website: http://education.tamucc.edu

Texas A&M University–Texarkana, Graduate Studies and Research, College of Education and Liberal Arts, Texarkana, TX 75503. Offers adult education (MS);

curriculum and instruction (M Ed); education (MS); educational administration (M Ed); English (MA); instructional technology (MS); interdisciplinary studies (MA, MS); special education (MS). *Program availability:* Part-time, evening/weekend. *Degree requirements:* For master's, comprehensive exam (for some programs), thesis optional. *Entrance requirements:* For master's, minimum GPA of 2.5 on last 60 hours of bachelor's degree. Additional exam requirements/recommendations for international students: Required—TOEFL. Electronic applications accepted.

Texas Christian University, College of Education, Doctoral Programs in Education, Fort Worth, TX 76129. Offers counseling and counselor education (PhD); curriculum studies (PhD); educational leadership (Ed D); higher educational leadership (Ed D); science education (PhD); MBA/Ed D. *Program availability:* Part-time, evening/weekend. *Faculty:* 29 full-time (21 women), 3 part-time/adjunct (1 woman). *Students:* 80 full-time (57 women), 26 part-time (13 women); includes 41 minority (15 Black or African American, non-Hispanic/Latino; 6 Asian, non-Hispanic/Latino; 17 Hispanic/Latino; 3 Two or more races, non-Hispanic/Latino), 6 international. Average age 39. 109 applicants, 50% accepted, 23 enrolled. In 2017, 12 doctorates awarded. *Degree requirements:* For doctorate, comprehensive exam, thesis/dissertation. *Entrance requirements:* For doctorate, GRE General Test. Additional exam requirements/recommendations for international students: Required—TOEFL (minimum score 550 paper-based; 80 iBT). *Application deadline:* For fall admission, 2/1 for domestic and international students; for winter admission, 2/1 for domestic and international students; for spring admission, 11/16 for domestic and international students. Application fee: $60. Electronic applications accepted. *Financial support:* In 2017–18, 69 students received support, including 1 fellowship with full tuition reimbursement available (averaging $18,500 per year), 8 research assistantships with full tuition reimbursements available (averaging $18,500 per year), 7 teaching assistantships with full tuition reimbursements available (averaging $18,500 per year); career-related internships or fieldwork, scholarships/grants, health care benefits, and unspecified assistantships also available. Support available to part-time students. Financial award application deadline: 2/1. *Unit head:* Dr. Jan Lacina, Associate Dean, 817-257-6786, Fax: 817-257-7466, E-mail: j.lacina@tcu.edu. *Application contact:* Lori Kimball, Administrative Program Specialist, 817-257-7661, Fax: 817-257-7466, E-mail: l.kimball@tcu.edu.
Website: http://coe.tcu.edu/graduate-overview/

Texas Christian University, College of Education, Master's Programs in Education, Fort Worth, TX 76129. Offers counseling (M Ed); curriculum and instruction (M Ed), including curriculum studies, language and literacy, math education, science education; education (MAT); educational leadership (M Ed); special education (M Ed). *Program availability:* Part-time, evening/weekend. *Faculty:* 29 full-time (21 women), 3 part-time/adjunct (1 woman). *Students:* 124 full-time (94 women), 14 part-time (12 women); includes 52 minority (14 Black or African American, non-Hispanic/Latino; 2 American Indian or Alaska Native, non-Hispanic/Latino; 3 Asian, non-Hispanic/Latino; 28 Hispanic/Latino; 5 Two or more races, non-Hispanic/Latino), 1 international. Average age 28. 172 applicants, 69% accepted, 86 enrolled. In 2017, 62 master's awarded. *Degree requirements:* For master's, comprehensive exam (for some programs), thesis (for some programs). *Entrance requirements:* For master's, GRE General Test; Pre-Admission Content Test (for MAT). Additional exam requirements/recommendations for international students: Required—TOEFL (minimum score 550 paper-based; 80 iBT). *Application deadline:* For fall admission, 3/1 for domestic and international students; for spring admission, 11/16 for domestic and international students; for summer admission, 3/1 for domestic and international students. Application fee: $60. Electronic applications accepted. *Financial support:* In 2017–18, 124 students received support, including 1 research assistantship with full tuition reimbursement available (averaging $15,000 per year), 29 teaching assistantships with full tuition reimbursements available (averaging $15,000 per year); career-related internships or fieldwork, scholarships/grants, and unspecified assistantships also available. Support available to part-time students. Financial award application deadline: 3/1. *Unit head:* Dr. Jan Lacina, Associate Dean, 817-257-6786, Fax: 817-257-7466, E-mail: j.lacina@tcu.edu. *Application contact:* Lori Kimball, Administrative Program Specialist, 817-257-7661, Fax: 817-257-7466, E-mail: l.kimball@tcu.edu.
Website: http://coe.tcu.edu/graduate-overview/

Texas Southern University, College of Education, Area of Curriculum and Instruction, Houston, TX 77004-4584. Offers bilingual education (M Ed); curriculum and instruction (Ed D); secondary education (M Ed). *Program availability:* Part-time, evening/weekend. *Degree requirements:* For master's, comprehensive exam; for doctorate, comprehensive exam, thesis/dissertation. *Entrance requirements:* For master's, GRE General Test, minimum GPA of 2.5; for doctorate, GRE General Test or MAT, master's degree, minimum B+ average. Additional exam requirements/recommendations for international students: Required—TOEFL. Electronic applications accepted.

Texas Tech University, Graduate School, College of Education, Department of Curriculum and Instruction, Lubbock, TX 79409. Offers bilingual education (M Ed); curriculum and instruction (M Ed); elementary education (M Ed); language/literacy education (M Ed); multidisciplinary science (MS); secondary education (M Ed). *Accreditation:* NCATE. *Program availability:* Part-time, evening/weekend, online learning. *Faculty:* 22 full-time (14 women), 2 part-time/adjunct (1 woman). *Students:* 64 full-time (50 women), 247 part-time (205 women); includes 100 minority (26 Black or African American, non-Hispanic/Latino; 1 American Indian or Alaska Native, non-Hispanic/Latino; 11 Asian, non-Hispanic/Latino; 54 Hispanic/Latino; 8 Two or more races, non-Hispanic/Latino), 39 international. Average age 39. 157 applicants, 56% accepted, 71 enrolled. In 2017, 20 master's, 21 doctorates awarded. Terminal master's awarded for partial completion of doctoral program. *Degree requirements:* For master's, comprehensive exam (for some programs), thesis optional; for doctorate, comprehensive exam, thesis/dissertation. *Entrance requirements:* For master's, bachelor's degree; resume; letter of intent; academic writing sample; 2 letters of recommendation; for doctorate, GRE, master's degree; resume; letter of intent; academic writing sample; 3 letters of recommendation. Additional exam requirements/recommendations for international students: Required—TOEFL (minimum score 550 paper-based; 79 iBT). *Application deadline:* For fall admission, 6/1 priority date for domestic students, 1/15 priority date for international students; for spring admission, 9/1 priority date for domestic students, 6/15 priority date for international students. Applications are processed on a rolling basis. Application fee: $60. Electronic applications accepted. *Expenses:* Contact institution. *Financial support:* In 2017–18, 96 students received support, including 92 fellowships (averaging $3,321 per year), 37 research assistantships (averaging $12,336 per year); teaching assistantships, Federal Work-Study, institutionally sponsored loans, scholarships/grants, health care benefits, and unspecified assistantships also available. Support available to part-time students. Financial award application deadline: 2/1; financial award applicants required to submit FAFSA. *Faculty research:* Teacher education, curriculum studies, bilingual education, science and math education, language and literacy education. *Total annual research expenditures:* $107,999. *Unit head:* Dr. Fanni Liu Coward, Interim Chairperson, 806-834-4475, Fax: 806-742-2179, E-mail: fanni.coward@ttu.edu. *Application contact:* Brianna Sanchez, Coordinator, 806-834-2353, Fax: 806-742-2179, E-mail: brianna.sanchez@ttu.edu.
Website: http://www.educ.ttu.edu

Texas Woman's University, Graduate School, College of Professional Education, Department of Teacher Education, Denton, TX 76204. Offers educational administration (M Ed, MA); special education (M Ed, PhD), including educational diagnostician (M Ed); intervention specialist (M Ed); teaching, learning, and curriculum (M Ed, MA). *Program availability:* Part-time. *Faculty:* 9 full-time (7 women), 1 (woman) part-time/adjunct. *Students:* 20 full-time (17 women), 92 part-time (79 women); includes 41 minority (11 Black or African American, non-Hispanic/Latino; 1 American Indian or Alaska Native, non-Hispanic/Latino; 3 Asian, non-Hispanic/Latino; 24 Hispanic/Latino; 2 Two or more races, non-Hispanic/Latino), 1 international. Average age 38. 48 applicants, 71% accepted, 29 enrolled. In 2017, 36 master's, 4 doctorates awarded. Terminal master's awarded for partial completion of doctoral program. *Degree requirements:* For master's, comprehensive exam, thesis, professional paper (M Ed); for doctorate, comprehensive exam, thesis/dissertation, residency. *Entrance requirements:* For master's, minimum GPA of 3.0 on last 60 undergraduate hours, 2 letters of reference, resume, copy of certifications, teacher service record, statement of intent, interview (for MAT); for doctorate, GRE General Test, minimum GPA of 3.0, 3 letters of reference, resume, copy of certifications, teacher service record, statement of intent. Additional exam requirements/recommendations for international students: Required—TOEFL (minimum score 550 paper-based; 79 iBT); Recommended—IELTS (minimum score 6.5), TSE (minimum score 53). *Application deadline:* For fall admission, 7/1 priority date for domestic students, 3/1 priority date for international students; for spring admission, 11/1 priority date for domestic students, 7/1 priority date for international students. Applications are processed on a rolling basis. Application fee: $50 ($75 for international students). Electronic applications accepted. *Expenses:* $7,520 per year full-time in-state; $16,820 per year full-time out-of-state. *Financial support:* In 2017–18, 21 students received support, including 5 research assistantships (averaging $32,980 per year); career-related internships or fieldwork, Federal Work-Study, institutionally sponsored loans, scholarships/grants, traineeships, health care benefits, and unspecified assistantships also available. Support available to part-time students. Financial award application deadline: 3/1; financial award applicants required to submit FAFSA. *Faculty research:* Experiential learning, classroom management, learning disabilities, staff and professional development, technology in the classroom. *Total annual research expenditures:* $272,198. *Unit head:* Dr. Diane Myers, Chair, 940-898-2271, Fax: 940-898-2270, E-mail: teachereducation@twu.edu. *Application contact:* Korie Hawkins, Associate Director of Admissions, Graduate Recruitment, 940-898-3188, Fax: 940-898-3081, E-mail: admissions@twu.edu.
Website: http://www.twu.edu/teacher-education/

Trevecca Nazarene University, Graduate Education Program, Nashville, TN 37210-2877. Offers accountability and instructional leadership (Ed S); curriculum and instruction for Christian school educators (M Ed); curriculum and instruction K-12 (M Ed); educational leadership (M Ed); English second language (M Ed); library and information science (MLI Sc); special education: visual impairments (M Ed); teaching (MAT), including teaching 6-12, teaching K-5. *Accreditation:* NCATE. *Program availability:* Part-time, evening/weekend, online learning. *Faculty:* 8 full-time (6 women), 22 part-time/adjunct (18 women). *Students:* 150 full-time (114 women), 3 part-time (1 woman); includes 54 minority (49 Black or African American, non-Hispanic/Latino; 4 Hispanic/Latino; 1 Two or more races, non-Hispanic/Latino). Average age 36. In 2017, 57 master's, 4 other advanced degrees awarded. *Degree requirements:* For master's, comprehensive exam, exit assessment/e-portfolio. *Entrance requirements:* For master's, GRE or MAT; PRAXIS (for MAT), minimum GPA of 3.0, official transcript from regionally-accredited institution, references, interview, writing sample, at least 3 years' successful teaching experience (for M Ed in educational leadership); for Ed S, GRE or MAT, master's degree with minimum GPA of 3.0, official transcript from regionally accredited institution, at least 3 years' successful teaching experience, interview, writing sample, background and fingerprinting check, recommendations. Additional exam requirements/recommendations for international students: Required—TOEFL (minimum score 550 paper-based). *Application deadline:* Applications are processed on a rolling basis. Electronic applications accepted. *Expenses:* Contact institution. *Financial support:* Applicants required to submit FAFSA. *Unit head:* Dr. Suzie Harris, Dean, School of Education, 615-248-1201, Fax: 615-248-1597, E-mail: admissions_ged@trevecca.edu. *Application contact:* 844-TNU-GRAD, E-mail: sgcsadmissions@trevecca.edu.
Website: http://www.trevecca.edu/soe

Trinity Baptist College, Graduate Programs, Jacksonville, FL 32221. Offers Bible (MA); curriculum and instruction (M Ed); educational leadership (M Ed); special education (M Ed). *Program availability:* Online learning. *Faculty:* 6 full-time (1 woman), 5 part-time/adjunct (1 woman). *Students:* 13 part-time (5 women). *Entrance requirements:* For master's, GRE (for M Ed), 2 letters of recommendation; minimum GPA of 2.5 (for M Min), 3.0 (for M Ed); goals essay; official transcripts. Application fee: $45. *Expenses:* Tuition: Part-time $295 per hour. *Required fees:* $50 per term. One-time fee: $45 part-time. *Unit head:* Dr. Matthew Beemer, Senior Vice President, 904-596-2400, Fax: 904-596-2531, E-mail: mbeemer@tbc.edu.

Trinity Washington University, School of Education, Washington, DC 20017-1094. Offers clinical mental health counseling (MA); early childhood education (MAT); educating for change (M Ed); educational administration (MSA); elementary education (MAT); reading (M Ed); school counseling (MA); secondary education (MAT), including English, social studies; special education (MAT). *Accreditation:* NCATE. *Program availability:* Part-time, evening/weekend. *Degree requirements:* For master's, thesis (for some programs), capstone project(s). *Entrance requirements:* For master's, PRAXIS I, minimum GPA of 2.8. Additional exam requirements/recommendations for international students: Required—TOEFL (minimum score 550 paper-based). *Faculty research:* Technology, literacy, special education, organizations, inclusion models.

Tusculum College, Program in Curriculum and Instruction, Greeneville, TN 37743-9997. Offers special education (MA Ed). *Program availability:* Evening/weekend. *Degree requirements:* For master's, thesis or alternative. *Entrance requirements:* For master's, NTE, PRAXIS II, GRE, MAT, 3 years of work experience, minimum GPA of 3.0, bachelor's degree. Additional exam requirements/recommendations for international students: Required—TOEFL (minimum score 540 paper-based; 73 iBT). *Application deadline:* Applications are processed on a rolling basis. Application fee: $0. *Unit head:* Dr. Tricia Hunsader, Dean, School of Education, 423-636-7300 Ext. 5693, E-mail: thunsader@tusculum.edu. *Application contact:* Lindsey Seal, Director of Enrollment, 423-636-7300 Ext. 5006, E-mail: lseal@tusculum.edu.
Website: http://home.tusculum.edu/gps/graduate-degrees/master-arts-education-curriculum-instruction/

Universidad Adventista de las Antillas, EGECED Department, Mayagüez, PR 00681-0118. Offers curriculum and instruction (M Ed); medical surgical nursing (MN); school administration and supervision (M Ed). *Degree requirements:* For master's, comprehensive exam (for some programs), thesis (for some programs). *Entrance requirements:* For master's, EXADEP or GRE General Test, recommendations. Electronic applications accepted.

Universidad del Turabo, Graduate Programs, Programs in Education, Program in Curriculum and Instruction and Appropriate Environment, Gurabo, PR 00778-3030. Offers D Ed. *Program availability:* Part-time, evening/weekend. *Entrance requirements:* For doctorate, EXADEP, GRE or GMAT, official transcript, recommendation letters, essay, curriculum vitae, interview. Electronic applications accepted.

Universidad del Turabo, Graduate Programs, Programs in Education, Program in Curriculum and Teaching, Gurabo, PR 00778-3030. Offers M Ed. *Program availability:* Part-time, evening/weekend. *Entrance requirements:* For master's, EXADEP, GRE or GMAT, interview, official transcript, essay, recommendation letter. Electronic applications accepted.

Universidad Metropolitana, School of Education, Program in Curriculum and Teaching, San Juan, PR 00928-1150. Offers M Ed. *Program availability:* Part-time, evening/weekend. *Degree requirements:* For master's, thesis or alternative. *Entrance requirements:* For master's, EXADEP, interview.

Université de Montréal, Faculty of Education, Department of Didactics, Montréal, QC H3C 3J7, Canada. Offers M Ed, MA, PhD, DESS. Terminal master's awarded for partial completion of doctoral program. *Degree requirements:* For master's, thesis (for some programs); for doctorate, thesis/dissertation, general exam. Electronic applications accepted. *Faculty research:* Teaching of French as a first or second language, teaching of science and technology, teaching of mathematics, teaching of arts.

Université Laval, Faculty of Education, Department of Teaching and Learning Studies, Programs in Didactics, Québec, QC G1K 7P4, Canada. Offers MA, PhD. Terminal master's awarded for partial completion of doctoral program. *Degree requirements:* For master's, thesis (for some programs); for doctorate, comprehensive exam, thesis/dissertation. *Entrance requirements:* For master's and doctorate, English exam (comprehension of written English), knowledge of French. Electronic applications accepted.

University at Albany, State University of New York, School of Education, Department of Educational Theory and Practice, Albany, NY 12222-0001. Offers curriculum and instruction (PhD, CAS); curriculum development and instructional technology (MS); general education studies (MS). *Program availability:* Part-time, evening/weekend, 100% online, blended/hybrid learning. *Faculty:* 13 full-time (6 women), 26 part-time/adjunct (18 women). *Students:* 80 full-time (58 women), 215 part-time (157 women); includes 29 minority (6 Black or African American, non-Hispanic/Latino; 8 Asian, non-Hispanic/Latino; 12 Hispanic/Latino; 3 Two or more races, non-Hispanic/Latino), 27 international. Average age 31. 197 applicants, 68% accepted, 120 enrolled. In 2017, 83 master's, 4 doctorates, 8 other advanced degrees awarded. *Degree requirements:* For doctorate, one foreign language, thesis/dissertation. *Entrance requirements:* For doctorate, GRE General Test. Additional exam requirements/recommendations for international students: Required—TOEFL (minimum score 550 paper-based). *Application deadline:* For fall admission, 2/1 for domestic students, 1/31 for international students. Application fee: $75. Electronic applications accepted. *Expenses:* Tuition, state resident: full-time $10,870; part-time $453 per credit hour. Tuition, nonresident: full-time $22,210; part-time $925 per credit hour. *Required fees:* $84.68 per credit hour. $508.06 per semester. Part-time tuition and fees vary according to course load and program. *Financial support:* Fellowships available. *Unit head:* Jianwei Zhang, Chair, 518-442-5006, E-mail: jzhang@albany.edu.

University at Buffalo, the State University of New York, Graduate School, Graduate School of Education, Department of Learning and Instruction, Buffalo, NY 14260. Offers biology education (Ed M, Certificate); chemistry education (Ed M, Certificate); childhood education (Ed M); childhood education with bilingual extension (Ed M); college teaching (Advanced Certificate); curriculum, instruction and the science of learning (PhD); early childhood education (Ed M); early childhood education with bilingual extension (Ed M); earth science education (Ed M, Certificate); education and technology (Ed M); education studies (Ed M); educational technology and new literacies (Certificate); educational technology and new literacies (Advanced Certificate); elementary education (Ed D); English education (Ed M, Certificate); English education studies (Ed M); English for speakers of other languages (Ed M); foreign and second language education (PhD); French education (Ed M, Certificate); German education (Ed M, Certificate); gifted education (Certificate); Latin education (Ed M, Certificate); literacy education studies (Ed M); literacy specialist (Ed M); literacy teaching and learning (Certificate); mathematics education (Ed M, Certificate); music education (Ed M, Certificate); music education studies (Ed M); music learning theory (Advanced Certificate); online education (Advanced Certificate); physics education (Ed M, Certificate); science and the public (Ed M); social studies education (Ed M, Certificate); Spanish education (Ed M, Certificate); special education (PhD); teaching English to speakers of other languages (Ed M). *Program availability:* Part-time, evening/weekend, 100% online. *Faculty:* 26 full-time (19 women), 74 part-time/adjunct (52 women). *Students:* 172 full-time (122 women), 325 part-time (226 women); includes 44 minority (25 Black or African American, non-Hispanic/Latino; 5 American Indian or Alaska Native, non-Hispanic/Latino; 14 Asian, non-Hispanic/Latino), 57 international. Average age 33. 316 applicants, 78% accepted, 174 enrolled. In 2017, 109 master's, 34 doctorates, 15 other advanced degrees awarded. *Degree requirements:* For master's, comprehensive exam; for doctorate, thesis/dissertation, research analysis exam, research experience. *Entrance requirements:* For master's, letters of reference; for doctorate, GRE General Test or MAT, interview, writing sample, letters of recommendation. Additional exam requirements/recommendations for international students: Required—TOEFL (minimum score 600 paper-based; 96 iBT). *Application deadline:* For fall admission, 2/1 priority date for domestic and international students; for spring admission, 11/15 priority date for domestic students, 10/1 for international students. Applications are processed on a rolling basis. Application fee: $50. Electronic applications accepted. *Financial support:* In 2017–18, 42 fellowships (averaging $5,181 per year), 44 research assistantships with tuition reimbursements (averaging $10,908 per year) were awarded; teaching assistantships, career-related internships or fieldwork, Federal Work-Study, institutionally sponsored loans, scholarships/grants, tuition waivers (full and partial), and unspecified assistantships also available. Financial award application deadline: 2/28; financial award applicants required to submit FAFSA. *Faculty research:* Science assessment, foreign language teaching and learning, early learning, new literacies, gender and education. *Total annual research expenditures:* $413,233. *Unit head:* Dr. David Bruce, Chair, 716-645-4069, Fax: 716-645-3161, E-mail: gse-info@buffalo.edu. *Application contact:* Luann Zak, Admissions Assistant, 716-645-2110, Fax: 716-645-7937, E-mail: luannzak@buffalo.edu.
Website: http://gse.buffalo.edu/lai

The University of Akron, Graduate School, College of Education, Department of Curricular and Instructional Studies, Program in Curriculum and Instruction with Licensure Options, Akron, OH 44325. Offers MS. *Entrance requirements:* For master's, minimum GPA of 3.0. Additional exam requirements/recommendations for international students: Required—TOEFL (minimum score 79 iBT), IELTS (minimum score 6.5). *Application deadline:* Applications are processed on a rolling basis. Application fee: $45 ($70 for international students). *Unit head:* Dr. Evonn Welton, Interim Department Chair, 330-972-6742, E-mail: ewelton@uakron.edu. *Application contact:* Kelly Chaff, College Program Specialist, 330-972-7028, E-mail: klchaff@uakron.edu.
Website: http://www.uakron.edu/education/academic-programs/graduate-programs.dot

The University of Alabama at Birmingham, School of Education, Program in Curriculum Education, Birmingham, AL 35294. Offers Ed S. *Program availability:* Part-time, online learning. *Degree requirements:* For Ed S, comprehensive exam, thesis optional. *Entrance requirements:* For degree, GRE General Test, MAT, minimum GPA of 3.0, master's degree. Electronic applications accepted.

Curriculum and Instruction

University of Arkansas, Graduate School, College of Education and Health Professions, Department of Curriculum and Instruction, Program in Curriculum and Instruction, Fayetteville, AR 72701. Offers M Ed, PhD, Ed S. *Program availability:* Part-time. In 2017, 5 master's, 10 doctorates awarded. *Degree requirements:* For doctorate, thesis/dissertation. *Entrance requirements:* For doctorate, GRE General Test. *Application deadline:* For fall admission, 8/1 for domestic students, 4/1 for international students; for spring admission, 12/1 for domestic students, 10/1 for international students; for summer admission, 4/15 for domestic students, 3/1 for international students. Applications are processed on a rolling basis. Application fee: $60. Electronic applications accepted. *Expenses:* Tuition, state resident: full-time $3782. Tuition, nonresident: full-time $10,238. *Financial support:* In 2017–18, 12 research assistantships, 2 teaching assistantships were awarded; fellowships with tuition reimbursements also available. Financial award application deadline: 4/1. *Unit head:* Dr. Cheryl A. Murphy, Interim Department Head, 479-575-5111, E-mail: cmurphy@uark.edu. *Application contact:* Dr. Derrick Mears, Graduate Coordinator, 479-575-6195, Fax: 479-575-6676, E-mail: dmears@uark.edu.
Website: http://cied.uark.edu/

University of Arkansas at Little Rock, Graduate School, College of Education and Health Professions, Department of Teacher Education, Program in Curriculum and Instruction, Little Rock, AR 72204-1099. Offers M Ed. *Entrance requirements:* For master's, teaching license.

The University of British Columbia, Faculty of Education, Department of Curriculum and Pedagogy, Vancouver, BC V6T 1Z4, Canada. Offers art education (M Ed, MA); curriculum studies (M Ed, MA, PhD); home economics education (M Ed, MA); mathematics education (M Ed, MA); media and technology studies education (M Ed, MA); music education (M Ed, MA); physical education (M Ed, MA); science education (M Ed, MA); social studies education (M Ed, MA). *Program availability:* Part-time, online learning. *Degree requirements:* For master's, thesis (MA); for doctorate, comprehensive exam, thesis/dissertation. *Entrance requirements:* Additional exam requirements/recommendations for international students: Required—TOEFL, IELTS. Electronic applications accepted. *Expenses:* Contact institution. *Faculty research:* School subjects, teaching and learning.

University of Calgary, Faculty of Graduate Studies, Werklund School of Education, Graduate Division of Educational Research, Calgary, AB T2N 1N4, Canada. Offers adult learning (M Ed, MA, Ed D, PhD); curriculum and learning (M Ed, MA, Ed D, PhD); educational leadership (M Ed, MA, Ed D, PhD); languages and diversity (M Ed, MA, Ed D, PhD); learning sciences (M Ed, MA, Ed D, PhD). Ed D in educational leadership offered via distance delivery. *Program availability:* Part-time, evening/weekend, online learning. *Degree requirements:* For master's, thesis (for some programs); for doctorate, thesis/dissertation, candidacy exam. *Entrance requirements:* For master's, minimum GPA of 3.0, 3 letters of reference; for doctorate, minimum GPA of 3.5, 3 letters of reference. Additional exam requirements/recommendations for international students: Required—TOEFL, IELTS. Electronic applications accepted. *Faculty research:* Curriculum, leadership, technology, contexts, gifted, second language teaching, work place and adult learning.

University of California, Davis, Graduate Studies, Graduate Group in Education, Davis, CA 95616. Offers education (MA, Ed D); instructional studies (PhD); psychological studies (PhD); sociocultural studies (PhD). Ed D offered jointly with California State University, Fresno. Terminal master's awarded for partial completion of doctoral program. *Degree requirements:* For master's, comprehensive exam (for some programs), thesis (for some programs); for doctorate, thesis/dissertation. *Entrance requirements:* For master's and doctorate, GRE. Additional exam requirements/recommendations for international students: Required—TOEFL (minimum score 550 paper-based). Electronic applications accepted. *Faculty research:* Language and literacy, mathematics education, science education, teacher development, school psychology.

University of California, San Diego, Graduate Division, Program in Education Studies, La Jolla, CA 92093. Offers education (M Ed, PhD); educational leadership (Ed D); teaching and learning (MA, Ed D), including bilingual education (MA), curriculum design (MA). Ed D offered jointly with California State University, San Marcos. *Students:* 88 full-time (64 women), 54 part-time (36 women). 261 applicants, 57% accepted, 77 enrolled. In 2017, 68 master's, 13 doctorates awarded. *Degree requirements:* For master's, thesis (for some programs), student teaching; for doctorate, comprehensive exam, thesis/dissertation. *Entrance requirements:* For master's, GRE General Test; CBEST and appropriate CSET exam (for select tracks), current teaching or educational assignment (for select tracks); for doctorate, GRE General Test, current teaching or educational assignment (for select tracks). Additional exam requirements/recommendations for international students: Required—TOEFL (minimum score 550 paper-based; 80 iBT), IELTS (minimum score 7). *Application deadline:* For fall admission, 2/2 for domestic students. Application fee: $105 ($125 for international students). Electronic applications accepted. *Financial support:* Fellowships, career-related internships or fieldwork, and scholarships/grants available. Financial award applicants required to submit FAFSA. *Faculty research:* Language, culture and literacy development of deaf/hard of hearing children; equity issues in education; educational reform; evaluation, assessment, and research methodologies; distributed learning. *Unit head:* Carolyn Hofstetter, Chair, 858-822-6688, E-mail: ajdaly@ucsd.edu. *Application contact:* Giselle Van Luit, Graduate Coordinator, 858-534-2958, E-mail: edsinfo@ucsd.edu.

University of Central Arkansas, Graduate School, College of Education, Department of Leadership Studies, Conway, AR 72035-0001. Offers college student personnel (MS); district-level administration (PMC); educational leadership - district level (Ed S); instructional technology (MS); library media and information technology (MS); school counseling (MS); school leadership (MS); school-based leadership adult education program administration (PMC); school-based leadership building administration (PMC); school-based leadership curriculum administration (PMC); school-based leadership gifted and talented program administration (PMC); school-based leadership special education program administration (PMC). *Accreditation:* NCATE. *Program availability:* Part-time, evening/weekend, online learning. *Degree requirements:* For master's and other advanced degree, comprehensive exam. *Entrance requirements:* For master's, GRE. Additional exam requirements/recommendations for international students: Required—TOEFL (minimum score 80 iBT). Electronic applications accepted. *Expenses:* Contact institution.

University of Central Florida, College of Community Innovation and Education, Department of Learning Sciences and Educational Research, Applied Learning and Instruction Program, Orlando, FL 32816. Offers MA. *Accreditation:* NCATE. *Program availability:* Part-time, evening/weekend. *Students:* 32 full-time (31 women), 126 part-time (105 women); includes 57 minority (19 Black or African American, non-Hispanic/Latino; 1 American Indian or Alaska Native, non-Hispanic/Latino; 8 Asian, non-Hispanic/Latino; 27 Hispanic/Latino; 2 Two or more races, non-Hispanic/Latino), 3 international. Average age 33. 154 applicants, 79% accepted, 80 enrolled. In 2017, 47 master's awarded. *Degree requirements:* For master's, thesis or alternative. *Entrance requirements:* For master's, goal statement, writing sample. Additional exam requirements/recommendations for international students: Required—TOEFL. *Application deadline:* For fall admission, 7/15 for domestic students. Application fee:

$30. Electronic applications accepted. *Expenses:* Tuition, state resident: part-time $288.16 per credit hour. Tuition, nonresident: part-time $1073.31 per credit hour. Tuition and fees vary according to program. *Financial support:* In 2017–18, 2 students received support, including 1 fellowship with partial tuition reimbursement available (averaging $1,000 per year), 1 research assistantship with partial tuition reimbursement available (averaging $1,526 per year); career-related internships or fieldwork, Federal Work-Study, institutionally sponsored loans, health care benefits, and unspecified assistantships also available. Financial award application deadline: 3/1; financial award applicants required to submit FAFSA. *Unit head:* Dr. Bobby Hoffman, Program Coordinator, 407-823-1770, E-mail: bobby.hoffman@ucf.edu. *Application contact:* Associate Director, Graduate Admissions, 407-823-2766, Fax: 407-823-6442, E-mail: gradadmissions@ucf.edu.
Website: https://edcollege.ucf.edu/academic-programs/graduate/applied-learning-instruction/

University of Central Florida, College of Community Innovation and Education, Education Doctoral Programs, Orlando, FL 32816. Offers curriculum and instruction (Ed D); education (PhD), including communication sciences and disorders, counselor education, early childhood education, elementary education, exceptional education, exercise physiology, higher education, instructional design and technology, mathematics education, methodology, measurement and analysis, reading education, science education, social science education, TESOL; educational leadership (Ed D). *Students:* 122 full-time (86 women), 129 part-time (88 women); includes 64 minority (24 Black or African American, non-Hispanic/Latino; 1 American Indian or Alaska Native, non-Hispanic/Latino; 9 Asian, non-Hispanic/Latino; 24 Hispanic/Latino; 6 Two or more races, non-Hispanic/Latino), 26 international. Average age 38. 195 applicants, 47% accepted, 72 enrolled. In 2017, 89 doctorates awarded. *Entrance requirements:* For doctorate, GRE, letters of recommendation, goal statement, resume, writing sample. Application fee: $30. Electronic applications accepted. *Expenses:* Tuition, state resident: part-time $288.16 per credit hour. Tuition, nonresident: part-time $1073.31 per credit hour. Tuition and fees vary according to program. *Financial support:* In 2017–18, 77 students received support, including 28 fellowships with partial tuition reimbursements available (averaging $5,733 per year), 29 research assistantships with partial tuition reimbursements available (averaging $10,230 per year), 54 teaching assistantships with partial tuition reimbursements available (averaging $11,614 per year); health care benefits also available. Financial award application deadline: 3/1; financial award applicants required to submit FAFSA. *Unit head:* Dr. Edward Robinson, Director of Doctoral Programs, 407-823-6106, E-mail: edward.robinson@ucf.edu. *Application contact:* Associate Director, Graduate Admissions, 407-823-2766, Fax: 407-823-6442, E-mail: gradadmissions@ucf.edu.
Website: https://edcollege.ucf.edu/academic-programs/graduate/

University of Central Florida, College of Community Innovation and Education, School of Teacher Education, Orlando, FL 32816. Offers applied learning and instruction (MA); curriculum and instruction (M Ed); elementary education (M Ed, MA); exceptional student education (M Ed, MA, Certificate), including autism spectrum disorders (Certificate), exceptional student education (M Ed), exceptional student education K-12 (MA), intervention specialist (Certificate), pre-kindergarten disabilities (Certificate), severe or profound disabilities (Certificate), special education (Certificate); K-8 mathematics and science education (M Ed, Certificate); reading education (M Ed, Certificate); teacher education (MAT), including art education, English language, mathematics education, middle school mathematics, middle school science, science education, social science education; world languages education - English for speakers of other languages (ESOL) (Certificate); world languages education - languages other than English (LOTE) (Certificate). *Program availability:* Part-time, evening/weekend. *Students:* 63 full-time (59 women), 218 part-time (190 women); includes 104 minority (34 Black or African American, non-Hispanic/Latino; 1 American Indian or Alaska Native, non-Hispanic/Latino; 13 Asian, non-Hispanic/Latino; 52 Hispanic/Latino; 4 Two or more races, non-Hispanic/Latino), 5 international. Average age 31. 189 applicants, 78% accepted, 98 enrolled. In 2017, 124 master's, 16 other advanced degrees awarded. *Degree requirements:* For Certificate, thesis or alternative. *Entrance requirements:* For degree, GRE General Test, minimum GPA of 3.0. Additional exam requirements/recommendations for international students: Required—TOEFL. *Application deadline:* For fall admission, 7/15 for domestic students; for spring admission, 12/15 for domestic students. Application fee: $30. Electronic applications accepted. *Expenses:* Tuition, state resident: part-time $288.16 per credit hour. Tuition, nonresident: part-time $1073.31 per credit hour. Tuition and fees vary according to program. *Financial support:* In 2017–18, 5 students received support, including 1 fellowship with partial tuition reimbursement available (averaging $1,000 per year), 4 research assistantships with partial tuition reimbursements available (averaging $5,617 per year), 1 teaching assistantship with partial tuition reimbursement available (averaging $9,086 per year); career-related internships or fieldwork, Federal Work-Study, institutionally sponsored loans, health care benefits, tuition waivers (partial), and unspecified assistantships also available. Financial award application deadline: 3/1; financial award applicants required to submit FAFSA. *Unit head:* Dr. Michael Hynes, Director, 407-823-1768, E-mail: michael.hynes@ucf.edu. *Application contact:* Associate Director, Graduate Admissions, 407-823-2766, Fax: 407-823-6442, E-mail: gradadmissions@ucf.edu.
Website: https://ccie.ucf.edu/teachered/

University of Cincinnati, Graduate School, College of Education, Criminal Justice, and Human Services, School of Education, Program in Curriculum and Instruction, Cincinnati, OH 45221. Offers M Ed, Ed D. *Accreditation:* NCATE. *Program availability:* Part-time. *Degree requirements:* For master's, thesis; for doctorate, thesis/dissertation. *Entrance requirements:* For master's, GRE General Test; for doctorate, GRE General Test, GRE Subject Test. Additional exam requirements/recommendations for international students: Required—TOEFL (minimum score 550 paper-based), TWE (minimum score 4.5), OEPT. Electronic applications accepted. *Expenses:* Tuition, area resident: Full-time $14,468. Tuition, state resident: full-time $14,968; part-time $754 per credit hour. Tuition, nonresident: full-time $24,210; part-time $1311 per credit hour. International tuition: $26,460 full-time. Required fees: $3958; $84 per credit hour. One-time fee: $85 full-time. Tuition and fees vary according to course load, degree level and program.

University of Colorado Boulder, Graduate School, School of Education, Division of Curriculum and Instruction, Boulder, CO 80309. Offers MA, PhD. *Accreditation:* NCATE. *Students:* 69 full-time (38 women), 39 part-time (31 women); includes 14 minority (1 Black or African American, non-Hispanic/Latino; 1 Asian, non-Hispanic/Latino; 11 Hispanic/Latino; 1 Two or more races, non-Hispanic/Latino), 1 international. Average age 29. 125 applicants, 64% accepted, 28 enrolled. In 2017, 31 master's, 3 doctorates awarded. Terminal master's awarded for partial completion of doctoral program. *Degree requirements:* For master's, comprehensive exam, thesis or alternative; for doctorate, one foreign language, comprehensive exam, thesis/dissertation. *Entrance requirements:* For master's, GRE General Test or MAT, minimum undergraduate GPA of 2.75; for doctorate, GRE General Test. *Application deadline:* For fall admission, 12/1 for domestic and international students; for spring admission, 9/1 for domestic and international students. Application fee: $60 ($80 for international students). Electronic applications accepted. Application fee is waived when completed online. *Financial support:* In 2017–18, 104 students received support, including 32 fellowships (averaging $2,338 per year),

17 research assistantships with full and partial tuition reimbursements available (averaging $33,041 per year), 9 teaching assistantships with full and partial tuition reimbursements available (averaging $13,907 per year); institutionally sponsored loans, scholarships/grants, health care benefits, and unspecified assistantships also available. Financial award application deadline: 2/15; financial award applicants required to submit FAFSA. *Application contact:* E-mail: edadvise@colorado.edu. Website: http://www.colorado.edu/education/.

University of Colorado Colorado Springs, College of Education, Colorado Springs, CO 80918. Offers counseling and human services (MA); curriculum and instruction (MA); educational leadership (MA); educational leadership, research and policy (PhD); special education (MA); teaching English to speakers of other languages (MA). *Accreditation:* ACA; NCATE. *Program availability:* Part-time, evening/weekend, 100% online, blended/hybrid learning. *Faculty:* 30 full-time (21 women), 61 part-time/adjunct (38 women). *Students:* 190 full-time (132 women), 286 part-time (202 women); includes 117 minority (20 Black or African American, non-Hispanic/Latino; 2 American Indian or Alaska Native, non-Hispanic/Latino; 12 Asian, non-Hispanic/Latino; 59 Hispanic/Latino; 24 Two or more races, non-Hispanic/Latino), 6 international. Average age 36. 169 applicants, 85% accepted, 113 enrolled. In 2017, 160 master's, 16 doctorates awarded. *Degree requirements:* For master's, comprehensive exam, thesis or alternative, microcomputer proficiency; for doctorate, comprehensive exam, thesis/dissertation, research lab. *Entrance requirements:* For master's and doctorate, GRE General Test. Additional exam requirements/recommendations for international students: Recommended—TOEFL (minimum score 550 paper-based; 80 iBT), IELTS (minimum score 6). *Application deadline:* For fall admission, 1/28 priority date for domestic and international students; for spring admission, 11/1 priority date for domestic and international students. Applications are processed on a rolling basis. Application fee: $60 ($100 for international students). Electronic applications accepted. *Expenses:* $10,350 per year resident tuition, $20,935 nonresident, $11,961 nonresidential online; annual costs vary depending on program, course-load, and residency status. *Financial support:* In 2017–18, 81 students received support. Career-related internships or fieldwork, Federal Work-Study, scholarships/grants, and unspecified assistantships available. Support available to part-time students. Financial award application deadline: 3/1; financial award applicants required to submit FAFSA. *Faculty research:* Linguistically diverse education (LDE), educational policy, evidence-based reading and writing instruction, relational and social aggression, positive behavior supports, inclusive schooling, K-12 education policy. *Total annual research expenditures:* $607,967. *Unit head:* Dr. Valerie Martin Conley, Dean, 719-255-4133, E-mail: vmconley@uccs.edu. *Application contact:* The College of Education Student Resource Office, 719-255-4996, E-mail: education@uccs.edu.
Website: http://www.uccs.edu/coe

University of Connecticut, Graduate School, Neag School of Education, Department of Educational Psychology, Cognition, Instruction, and Learning Technology Program, Storrs, CT 06269. Offers MA, PhD. *Degree requirements:* For master's, comprehensive exam; for doctorate, thesis/dissertation. *Entrance requirements:* For doctorate, GRE General Test. Additional exam requirements/recommendations for international students: Required—TOEFL (minimum score 550 paper-based). Electronic applications accepted.

University of Delaware, College of Education and Human Development, School of Education, Newark, DE 19716. Offers education (PhD); educational leadership (Ed D); higher education (M Ed); instruction (MI); reading (M Ed); school leadership (M Ed); school psychology (MA, Ed S); teaching English as a second language (TESL) (MA). *Accreditation:* NCATE. *Program availability:* Part-time, evening/weekend. Terminal master's awarded for partial completion of doctoral program. *Degree requirements:* For master's, comprehensive exam (for some programs), thesis (for some programs); for doctorate, comprehensive exam (for some programs), thesis/dissertation. *Entrance requirements:* For master's and doctorate, GRE, 3 letters of recommendation. Additional exam requirements/recommendations for international students: Required—TOEFL (minimum score 600 paper-based). Electronic applications accepted. *Faculty research:* Teacher education; curriculum theory and development; community based education models, educational leadership.

University of Denver, Morgridge College of Education, Denver, CO 80208. Offers child, family and school psychology (MA, PhD, Ed S); counseling psychology (MA, PhD); curriculum and instruction (MA, Ed D, PhD); curriculum instruction and teaching (Certificate); early childhood special education (MA, Certificate); educational leadership and policy studies (MA, Ed D, PhD, Certificate); higher education (Ed D, PhD); library and information science (MLIS); research methods and statistics (MA, PhD). *Accreditation:* ALA; APA (one or more programs are accredited). *Program availability:* Part-time, evening/weekend, online learning. *Faculty:* 39 full-time (29 women), 60 part-time/adjunct (42 women). *Students:* 502 full-time (406 women), 361 part-time (267 women); includes 233 minority (54 Black or African American, non-Hispanic/Latino; 6 American Indian or Alaska Native, non-Hispanic/Latino; 25 Asian, non-Hispanic/Latino; 113 Hispanic/Latino; 35 Two or more races, non-Hispanic/Latino), 52 international. Average age 31. 1,167 applicants, 64% accepted, 415 enrolled. In 2017, 285 master's, 51 doctorates, 157 other advanced degrees awarded. Terminal master's awarded for partial completion of doctoral program. *Degree requirements:* For master's, comprehensive exam; for doctorate, 2 foreign languages, comprehensive exam, thesis/dissertation. *Entrance requirements:* For master's and doctorate, GRE General Test or GMAT. Additional exam requirements/recommendations for international students: Required—TOEFL (minimum score 550 paper-based; 80 iBT). *Application deadline:* Applications are processed on a rolling basis. Application fee: $65. Electronic applications accepted. *Expenses:* $31,935 per year full-time. *Financial support:* In 2017–18, 765 students received support, including 26 research assistantships with tuition reimbursements available (averaging $10,957 per year), 38 teaching assistantships with tuition reimbursements available (averaging $3,391 per year); career-related internships or fieldwork, Federal Work-Study, institutionally sponsored loans, scholarships/grants, and unspecified assistantships also available. Support available to part-time students. Financial award application deadline: 2/15; financial award applicants required to submit FAFSA. *Faculty research:* Early childhood education, educational leadership, access and opportunity to postsecondary education, marriage and family therapy, data management and archival research. *Unit head:* Dr. Karen Riley, Dean, 303-871-3665, Fax: 303-871-4456, E-mail: karen.riley@du.edu. *Application contact:* Jodi Dye, Director of Admissions, 303-871-2510, Fax: 303-871-4456, E-mail: jodi.dye@du.edu.
Website: http://morgridge.du.edu

University of Detroit Mercy, College of Liberal Arts and Education, Detroit, MI 48221. Offers addiction counseling (MA); addiction studies (Certificate); clinical mental health counseling (MA); clinical psychology (MA, PhD); computer and information systems (MS); criminal justice (MA); curriculum and instruction (MA); economics (MA); educational administration (MA); financial economics (MA); industrial/organizational psychology (MA); information assurance (MS); intelligence analysis (MA); liberal studies (MALS); religious studies (MA); school counseling (MA, Certificate); school psychology (Spec); security administration (MS); special education: emotionally impaired/behaviorally disordered (MA); special education: learning disabilities (MA). *Program availability:* Part-time, evening/weekend. *Degree requirements:* For doctorate,

departmental qualifying exam. *Faculty research:* Psychology of aging, history of technology, Renaissance humanism, U.S. and Japanese economic relations.

University of Florida, Graduate School, College of Education, School of Teaching and Learning, Gainesville, FL 32611. Offers curriculum and instruction (M Ed, MAE, Ed D, PhD, Ed S); elementary education (M Ed, MAE); English education (M Ed, MAE); mathematics education (M Ed, MAE); reading education (M Ed, MAE); science education (M Ed, MAE); social studies education (M Ed, MAE). *Accreditation:* NCATE. *Program availability:* Part-time, evening/weekend, online learning. Terminal master's awarded for partial completion of doctoral program. *Degree requirements:* For master's, comprehensive exam (for some programs), thesis (for some programs); for doctorate, comprehensive exam (for some programs), thesis/dissertation (for some programs). *Entrance requirements:* For master's and doctorate, GRE General Test, minimum GPA of 3.0; for Ed S, GRE General Test. Additional exam requirements/recommendations for international students: Required—TOEFL (minimum score 550 paper-based; 80 iBT), IELTS (minimum score 6). Electronic applications accepted. *Faculty research:* STEM education; curriculum; teaching and teacher education; languages and literacy; schools, culture, and society; theories and processes of learning.

University of Hawaii at Manoa, Office of Graduate Education, College of Education, Department of Curriculum Studies, Honolulu, HI 96822. Offers curriculum studies (M Ed); early childhood education (M Ed). *Program availability:* Part-time. *Degree requirements:* For master's, thesis optional. *Entrance requirements:* Additional exam requirements/recommendations for international students: Required—TOEFL (minimum score 500 paper-based; 61 iBT), IELTS (minimum score 5).

University of Hawaii at Manoa, Office of Graduate Education, College of Education, PhD in Education Program, Honolulu, HI 96822. Offers curriculum and instruction (PhD); educational administration (PhD); educational foundations (PhD); educational policy studies (PhD); educational psychology (PhD); exceptionalities (PhD); kinesiology (PhD); learning design and technology (PhD). *Program availability:* Part-time, evening/weekend. *Degree requirements:* For doctorate, thesis/dissertation. *Entrance requirements:* For doctorate, GRE General Test, sample of written work. Additional exam requirements/recommendations for international students: Required—TOEFL (minimum score 600 paper-based; 100 iBT), IELTS (minimum score 7).

University of Houston, College of Education, Department of Curriculum and Instruction, Houston, TX 77204. Offers administration and supervision (M Ed); curriculum and instruction (M Ed, Ed D); professional leadership (Ed D). *Accreditation:* NCATE. *Program availability:* Part-time, evening/weekend. *Degree requirements:* For master's, comprehensive exam, thesis optional; for doctorate, comprehensive exam, thesis/dissertation. *Entrance requirements:* For master's and doctorate, GRE, minimum cumulative undergraduate GPA of 2.6, 3 letters of recommendation, resume/vita, goal statement. Additional exam requirements/recommendations for international students: Required—TOEFL (minimum score 550 paper-based; 79 iBT). Electronic applications accepted. *Faculty research:* Teaching-learning process, instructional technology in schools, teacher education, classroom management, at-risk students.

University of Houston–Clear Lake, School of Education, Program in Curriculum and Instruction, Houston, TX 77058-1002. Offers curriculum and instruction (MS); early childhood education (MS); reading (MS); school library and information science (MS). *Program availability:* Part-time, evening/weekend. *Degree requirements:* For master's, thesis (for some programs). *Entrance requirements:* For master's, GRE or minimum GPA of 3.0 in last 60 hours. Additional exam requirements/recommendations for international students: Required—TOEFL (minimum score 550 paper-based). Electronic applications accepted.

University of Houston–Downtown, College of Public Service, Department of Urban Education, Houston, TX 77002. Offers curriculum and instruction (MAT). *Program availability:* Part-time, evening/weekend. *Faculty:* 12 full-time (6 women), 2 part-time/adjunct (0 women). *Students:* 10 full-time (7 women), 45 part-time (44 women); includes 44 minority (19 Black or African American, non-Hispanic/Latino; 1 American Indian or Alaska Native, non-Hispanic/Latino; 1 Asian, non-Hispanic/Latino; 23 Hispanic/Latino). Average age 36. 29 applicants, 93% accepted, 14 enrolled. In 2017, 7 master's awarded. *Degree requirements:* For master's, capstone course with completed project, position paper, grant proposal, empirical study, curriculum development/revision, or advanced technology project presented at annual Graduate Project Exhibition. *Entrance requirements:* For master's, GRE, personal statement, 3 recommendation forms. Additional exam requirements/recommendations for international students: Required—TOEFL (minimum score 550 paper-based; 80 iBT). *Application deadline:* For fall admission, 7/15 for domestic and international students; for spring admission, 11/15 for domestic and international students. Application fee: $35 ($60 for international students). Electronic applications accepted. *Expenses:* $335 per credit resident; $700 per credit non-resident. *Financial support:* Federal Work-Study and scholarships/grants available. Financial award application deadline: 4/1; financial award applicants required to submit FAFSA. *Unit head:* Dr. Christal Burnett, Department Chair, 713-226-5521, Fax: 713-226-5294, E-mail: burnettc@uhd.edu. *Application contact:* Ceshia Love, Director of Admissions, 713-221-8093, Fax: 713-223-7408, E-mail: gradadmissions@uhd.edu.
Website: https://www.uhd.edu/academics/public-service/urban-education/Pages/default.aspx

University of Houston–Victoria, School of Education, Health Professions and Human Development, Victoria, TX 77901-4450. Offers administration and supervision (M Ed); adult and higher education (M Ed); counselor education (M Ed); curriculum and instruction (M Ed); dyslexia education (Certificate); educational technology (M Ed); special education (M Ed). *Program availability:* Part-time, evening/weekend, online learning. *Degree requirements:* For master's, comprehensive exam, project or thesis. *Entrance requirements:* For master's, GRE General Test. Additional exam requirements/recommendations for international students: Required—TOEFL. Electronic applications accepted. *Faculty research:* Reading and language arts education, evaluation and diagnosis of special children's abilities.

University of Idaho, College of Graduate Studies, College of Education, Health and Human Sciences, Department of Curriculum and Instruction, Moscow, ID 83844. Offers career and technology education (M Ed); curriculum and instruction (M Ed, Ed S); special education (M Ed). *Faculty:* 29. *Students:* 25 full-time (19 women), 39 part-time (34 women). Average age 37. In 2017, 33 master's, 2 Ed Ss awarded. *Entrance requirements:* For master's, minimum GPA of 3.0. Additional exam requirements/recommendations for international students: Required—TOEFL (minimum score 79 iBT). *Application deadline:* For fall admission, 8/1 for domestic students; for spring admission, 12/15 for domestic students. Applications are processed on a rolling basis. Application fee: $60. Electronic applications accepted. *Expenses:* Tuition, state resident: full-time $6722; part-time $430 per credit hour. Tuition, nonresident: full-time $23,046; part-time $1337 per credit hour. *Required fees:* $2142; $63 per credit hour. *Financial support:* Research assistantships and teaching assistantships available. Financial award applicants required to submit FAFSA. *Unit head:* Dr. Allen Kitchel, Interim Chair, 208-885-6587, E-mail: teached@uidaho.edu. *Application contact:* Sean Scoggin, Graduate Recruitment Coordinator, 208-885-4001, Fax: 208-885-4406, E-mail: graduateadmissions@uidaho.edu.
Website: http://www.uidaho.edu/ed/ci

Curriculum and Instruction

University of Illinois at Chicago, College of Education, Department of Curriculum and Instruction, Chicago, IL 60607-7128. Offers curriculum studies (PhD); elementary education (M Ed); secondary education (M Ed). *Program availability:* Part-time, evening/weekend. *Degree requirements:* For doctorate, thesis/dissertation. *Entrance requirements:* For master's, minimum GPA of 2.75; for doctorate, GRE General Test, minimum GPA of 2.75. Additional exam requirements/recommendations for international students: Required—TOEFL. Electronic applications accepted. *Faculty research:* Curriculum theory, curriculum development, research on teaching, curriculum and context, reading/literacy.

University of Illinois at Urbana–Champaign, Graduate College, College of Education, Department of Curriculum and Instruction, Champaign, IL 61820. Offers curriculum and instruction (Ed M, MA, MS, Ed D, PhD, CAS); early childhood education (Ed M); elementary education (Ed M); secondary education (Ed M). *Program availability:* Part-time, online learning.

University of Indianapolis, Graduate Programs, School of Education, Indianapolis, IN 46227-3697. Offers art education (MAT); biology (MAT); chemistry (MAT); curriculum and instruction (MA); earth sciences (MAT); education (MA, MAT); educational leadership (MA); elementary education (MA); English (MAT); French (MAT); math (MAT); physical education (MAT); physics (MAT); secondary education (MA), including art education, education, English education, social studies education; social studies (MAT); Spanish (MAT). *Accreditation:* NCATE. *Program availability:* Part-time, evening/weekend. *Entrance requirements:* For master's, GRE Subject Test, PRAXIS I, minimum GPA of 2.5, 3 letters of recommendation, interview. Additional exam requirements/recommendations for international students: Required—TOEFL (minimum score 550 paper-based). *Faculty research:* Assessment of teacher education, perceptions of prospective teachers by parents.

University of Jamestown, Program in Education, Jamestown, ND 58405. Offers curriculum and instruction (M Ed). *Degree requirements:* For master's, thesis or project.

The University of Kansas, Graduate Studies, School of Education, Department of Curriculum and Teaching, Lawrence, KS 66045-3101. Offers MA, MS Ed, PhD. *Program availability:* Part-time, evening/weekend, online learning. *Students:* 71 full-time (45 women), 306 part-time (255 women); includes 47 minority (16 Black or African American, non-Hispanic/Latino; 3 American Indian or Alaska Native, non-Hispanic/Latino; 7 Asian, non-Hispanic/Latino; 9 Hispanic/Latino; 12 Two or more races, non-Hispanic/Latino), 16 international. Average age 34. 206 applicants, 74% accepted, 128 enrolled. In 2017, 145 master's, 12 doctorates awarded. *Entrance requirements:* For master's, minimum GPA of 3.0, official transcript(s), resume, statement of goals/purpose, three letters of recommendation; for doctorate, GRE General Test, minimum graduate GPA of 3.5, official transcript(s), resume, statement of goals/purpose, three letters of recommendation, writing sample. Additional exam requirements/recommendations for international students: Required—TOEFL, IELTS. *Application deadline:* For fall admission, 3/15 priority date for domestic and international students; for spring admission, 10/15 priority date for domestic and international students. Application fee: $65 ($85 for international students). Electronic applications accepted. *Financial support:* Fellowships, research assistantships, teaching assistantships, Federal Work-Study, scholarships/grants, and unspecified assistantships available. Financial award application deadline: 3/15; financial award applicants required to submit FAFSA. *Faculty research:* Community-based field experiences in teacher education, vocabulary and narrative development of primary students, narrative inquiry, engaging students in critical thinking by using technology in the classroom, argumentation and evaluation intervention in science education. *Unit head:* Dr. Steven Hugh White, Chair of Curriculum and Teaching, 785-864-9662, E-mail: s-white@ku.edu. *Application contact:* Susan M. McGee, Graduate Admissions Coordinator, 785-864-4437, E-mail: ctdepartment@ku.edu.
Website: http://ct.soe.ku.edu/

University of Kentucky, Graduate School, College of Education, Program in Curriculum and Instruction, Lexington, KY 40506-0032. Offers curriculum and instruction (Ed D, PhD); elementary education (MA Ed); instructional system design (MS Ed); literacy (MA Ed); middle school education (MA Ed, MS Ed); secondary education (MA Ed, MS Ed). *Accreditation:* NCATE. *Degree requirements:* For master's, comprehensive exam, thesis optional; for doctorate, comprehensive exam, thesis/dissertation. *Entrance requirements:* For master's, GRE General Test, minimum undergraduate GPA of 2.75; for doctorate, GRE General Test, minimum graduate GPA of 3.0. Additional exam requirements/recommendations for international students: Required—TOEFL (minimum score 550 paper-based). Electronic applications accepted. *Faculty research:* Educational reform, multicultural education, classroom instructional practices, performance based assessment, primary school programs.

University of Louisiana at Lafayette, College of Education, Graduate Studies and Research in Education, Program in Curriculum and Instruction, Lafayette, LA 70504. Offers M Ed. *Accreditation:* NCATE. *Degree requirements:* For master's, thesis or alternative. *Entrance requirements:* For master's, GRE General Test, teaching certificate. Additional exam requirements/recommendations for international students: Required—TOEFL (minimum score 550 paper-based). Electronic applications accepted.

University of Louisiana at Monroe, Graduate School, College of Arts, Education, and Sciences, School of Education, Program in Curriculum and Instruction, Monroe, LA 71209-0001. Offers curriculum and instruction (M Ed, Ed D). *Accreditation:* NCATE. *Faculty:* 11 full-time (7 women). *Students:* 13 full-time (10 women), 75 part-time (60 women); includes 24 minority (19 Black or African American, non-Hispanic/Latino; 1 Asian, non-Hispanic/Latino; 3 Hispanic/Latino; 1 Two or more races, non-Hispanic/Latino), 1 international. Average age 35. 36 applicants, 58% accepted, 17 enrolled. In 2017, 10 master's, 9 doctorates awarded. *Degree requirements:* For master's, comprehensive exam (for some programs), thesis; for doctorate, thesis/dissertation, internships. *Entrance requirements:* For master's, GRE General Test; for doctorate, GRE General Test, minimum undergraduate GPA of 2.75, graduate 3.25. Additional exam requirements/recommendations for international students: Required—TOEFL (minimum score 500 paper-based; 61 iBT). *Application deadline:* For fall admission, 8/24 priority date for domestic students, 7/1 for international students; for winter admission, 12/14 priority date for domestic students; for spring admission, 1/19 for domestic students, 11/1 for international students. Applications are processed on a rolling basis. Application fee: $20 ($30 for international students). Electronic applications accepted. *Expenses:* Tuition, state resident: full-time $6489; part-time $479 per hour. Tuition, nonresident: full-time $12,100; part-time $479 per hour. *Required fees:* $8860; $802 per hour. $3273 per semester. *Financial support:* Research assistantships, career-related internships or fieldwork, Federal Work-Study, and unspecified assistantships available. Financial award application deadline: 4/1; financial award applicants required to submit FAFSA.

University of Louisville, Graduate School, College of Education and Human Development, Departments of Early Childhood and Elementary Education, Middle and Secondary Education, and Special Education, Louisville, KY 40292-0001. Offers art education (MAT); autism and applied behavior analysis (Certificate); curriculum and instruction (PhD); early elementary education (MAT); exercise physiology (MS); health and physical education (MAT); health professions education (Certificate); higher education (MA); human resources and organization development (MS); instructional technology (M Ed); interdisciplinary early childhood education (MAT); middle school education (MAT); music education (MAT); secondary education (MAT); special education (MAT); sport administration (MS); teacher leadership (M Ed). *Program availability:* Part-time, evening/weekend. *Students:* 114 full-time (73 women), 173 part-time (114 women); includes 49 minority (19 Black or African American, non-Hispanic/Latino; 5 Asian, non-Hispanic/Latino; 13 Hispanic/Latino; 12 Two or more races, non-Hispanic/Latino), 7 international. Average age 29. 132 applicants, 73% accepted, 57 enrolled. In 2017, 70 master's, 2 doctorates, 2 other advanced degrees awarded. *Application deadline:* For spring admission, 1/1 priority date for international students. Application fee: $65. *Expenses:* Tuition, state resident: full-time $12,246; part-time $681 per credit hour. Tuition, nonresident: full-time $25,486; part-time $1417 per credit hour. *Required fees:* $196. Tuition and fees vary according to course load, program and reciprocity agreements. *Financial support:* Application deadline: 6/1; applicants required to submit FAFSA. *Faculty research:* STEM teaching and learning; content literacy for English language learners; social justice in teacher education; adolescent literacy; mathematics teacher development. *Total annual research expenditures:* $1.7 million. *Unit head:* Dr. Ann E. Larson, Dean, College of Education and Human Development, 502-852-6411, Fax: 502-852-1464, E-mail: ann@louisville.edu. *Application contact:* Betty Hampton, Director of Graduate Student Services, 502-852-5597, Fax: 502-852-1465, E-mail: edadvise@louisville.edu.
Website: http://louisville.edu/delphi

University of Lynchburg, Graduate Studies, M Ed Program in Curriculum and Instruction, Lynchburg, VA 24501-3199. Offers instructional leadership (M Ed); teacher licensure (M Ed). *Program availability:* Part-time, evening/weekend. *Faculty:* 17 full-time (10 women). *Students:* 2 full-time (both women), 13 part-time (11 women); includes 3 minority (all Black or African American, non-Hispanic/Latino). Average age 32. 5 applicants, 100% accepted, 2 enrolled. In 2017, 2 master's awarded. *Degree requirements:* For master's, comprehensive exam, internship, state license exam. *Entrance requirements:* For master's, GRE, minimum GPA of 3.0 (preferred), official transcripts (bachelor's, others as relevant), three letters of recommendation, career goals statement. Additional exam requirements/recommendations for international students: Required—TOEFL (minimum score 550 paper-based; 80 iBT), IELTS (minimum score 6). *Application deadline:* For fall admission, 7/31 for domestic students, 6/1 for international students; for spring admission, 11/30 for domestic students, 10/15 for international students. Applications are processed on a rolling basis. Application fee: $30. Electronic applications accepted. Application fee is waived when completed online. *Expenses:* $510 per credit tuition, $100 fees. *Financial support:* Federal Work-Study, scholarships/grants, health care benefits, and unspecified assistantships available. Support available to part-time students. Financial award application deadline: 7/31; financial award applicants required to submit FAFSA. *Unit head:* Dr. Mary Ann Mayhew, Assistant Professor/Program Director, Curriculum and Instruction, 434-544-8515, E-mail: mayhew.m@lynchburg.edu. *Application contact:* Ellen Thompson, Graduate Admissions Counselor, 434-544-8841, E-mail: thompson_e@lynchburg.edu.
Website: http://www.lynchburg.edu/graduate/master-of-education-in-curriculum-and-instruction/

University of Manitoba, Faculty of Graduate Studies, Faculty of Education, Department of Curriculum, Teaching and Learning, Winnipeg, MB R3T 2N2, Canada. Offers language and literacy (M Ed); second language education (M Ed); studies in curriculum, teaching and learning (M Ed). *Degree requirements:* For master's, thesis or alternative.

University of Mary, Liffrig Family School of Education and Behavioral Sciences, Department of Education, Bismarck, ND 58504-9652. Offers curriculum, instruction and assessment (M Ed); education (Ed D); elementary administration (M Ed); reading (M Ed); secondary administration (M Ed); special education strategist (M Ed). *Program availability:* Part-time. *Degree requirements:* For master's, portfolio or thesis. *Entrance requirements:* For master's, interview, letters of reference, minimum GPA of 2.5. Additional exam requirements/recommendations for international students: Required—TOEFL (minimum score 500 paper-based; 71 iBT). Electronic applications accepted.

University of Mary Hardin-Baylor, Graduate Studies in Education, Belton, TX 76513. Offers curriculum and instruction (M Ed); educational administration (M Ed, Ed D), including higher education (Ed D), leadership in nursing education (Ed D), P-12 (Ed D). *Program availability:* Part-time, evening/weekend. *Faculty:* 12 full-time (8 women), 5 part-time/adjunct (2 women). *Students:* 29 full-time (20 women), 79 part-time (55 women); includes 53 minority (35 Black or African American, non-Hispanic/Latino; 17 Hispanic/Latino; 1 Two or more races, non-Hispanic/Latino), 1 international. Average age 39. 15 applicants, 80% accepted, 10 enrolled. In 2017, 47 master's, 16 doctorates awarded. *Degree requirements:* For master's, comprehensive exam; for doctorate, thesis/dissertation. *Entrance requirements:* For master's, minimum GPA of 3.0, interview; for doctorate, minimum GPA of 3.5, interview, essay, resume, employment verification, 3 letters of recommendation. Additional exam requirements/recommendations for international students: Required—TOEFL (minimum score 60 iBT), IELTS (minimum score 4.5). *Application deadline:* For fall admission, 6/1 for domestic students, 4/30 priority date for international students; for spring admission, 11/1 for domestic students, 9/30 priority date for international students. Applications are processed on a rolling basis. Application fee: $35 ($135 for international students). Electronic applications accepted. *Expenses:* $920 per credit hour. *Financial support:* In 2017–18, 90 students received support. Federal Work-Study and scholarships for some active duty military personnel available. Support available to part-time students. Financial award application deadline: 6/1; financial award applicants required to submit FAFSA. *Faculty research:* Motivational orientation of preservice teachers. *Unit head:* Dr. Craig Hammonds, Director, Graduate Programs in Education, 254-295-4189, E-mail: rhammonds@umhb.edu. *Application contact:* Sharon Aguilera, Assistant Director, Graduate Admissions, 254-295-4835, E-mail: saguilera@umhb.edu.
Website: https://go.umhb.edu/graduate/education/home

University of Maryland, College Park, Academic Affairs, College of Education, Department of Teaching, Learning, Policy and Leadership, College Park, MD 20742. Offers reading (M Ed, MA, PhD, CAGS); secondary education (M Ed, MA, Ed D, PhD, CAGS); teaching English to speakers of other languages (M Ed). *Accreditation:* NCATE. *Program availability:* Part-time, evening/weekend, online learning. *Degree requirements:* For master's, comprehensive exam, seminar paper; for doctorate, comprehensive exam, thesis/dissertation, published paper, oral exam. *Entrance requirements:* For master's, GRE General Test or MAT, minimum GPA of 3.0, 3 letters of recommendation; for doctorate, GRE General Test or MAT, minimum undergraduate GPA of 3.0, graduate 3.5; 3 letters of recommendation. Electronic applications accepted. *Faculty research:* Teacher preparation, curriculum study, in-service education.

University of Massachusetts Lowell, Graduate School of Education, Lowell, MA 01854. Offers curriculum and instruction (M Ed). *Accreditation:* NCATE. *Program availability:* Part-time, evening/weekend, online learning. Terminal master's awarded for partial completion of doctoral program. *Entrance requirements:* For master's, GRE General Test. Additional exam requirements/recommendations for international students: Required—TOEFL. Electronic applications accepted.

University of Memphis, Graduate School, College of Education, Department of Instruction and Curriculum Leadership, Memphis, TN 38152. Offers advanced studies in

teaching and learning (M Ed); applied behavior analysis (Graduate Certificate); autism studies (Graduate Certificate); early childhood education (MAT, MS, Ed D); elementary education (MAT); instruction and curriculum (MS, Ed D); instruction design and technology (MS, Ed D); instructional design and technology (Graduate Certificate); literacy, leadership, and coaching (Graduate Certificate); reading (MS, Ed D); school library information specialist (Graduate Certificate); secondary education (MAT); special education (MAT, MS, Ed D); STEM teacher leadership (Graduate Certificate); urban education (Graduate Certificate). *Accreditation:* NCATE (one or more programs are accredited). *Program availability:* Part-time. *Faculty:* 22 full-time (14 women), 14 part-time/adjunct (10 women). *Students:* 36 full-time (27 women), 351 part-time (271 women); includes 159 minority (132 Black or African American, non-Hispanic/Latino; 1 American Indian or Alaska Native, non-Hispanic/Latino; 7 Asian, non-Hispanic/Latino; 10 Hispanic/Latino; 9 Two or more races, non-Hispanic/Latino), 4 international. Average age 35. 170 applicants, 85% accepted, 111 enrolled. In 2017, 84 master's, 14 doctorates, 32 other advanced degrees awarded. Terminal master's awarded for partial completion of doctoral program. *Degree requirements:* For master's, comprehensive exam, thesis or alternative; for doctorate, comprehensive exam, thesis/dissertation. *Entrance requirements:* For master's, GRE General Test, PRAXIS, minimum GPA of 2.5, letters of reference; for doctorate, GRE General Test, GRE Subject Test, 2 years of teaching experience, letters of reference, statement of purpose, interview. Additional exam requirements/recommendations for international students: Required—TOEFL (minimum score 550 paper-based; 79 iBT). *Application deadline:* For fall admission, 4/1 priority date for domestic students; for spring admission, 10/1 priority date for domestic students; for summer admission, 2/1 priority date for domestic students. Applications are processed on a rolling basis. Application fee: $35 ($60 for international students). Electronic applications accepted. *Expenses:* Contact institution. *Financial support:* In 2017–18, 2 research assistantships with full tuition reimbursements (averaging $10,000 per year), 3 teaching assistantships with full tuition reimbursements (averaging $10,666 per year) were awarded; career-related internships or fieldwork, Federal Work-Study, institutionally sponsored loans, scholarships/grants, traineeships, and unspecified assistantships also available. Support available to part-time students. Financial award application deadline: 2/1; financial award applicants required to submit FAFSA. *Faculty research:* Effective urban teachers, preparation and retention of urban teachers, technology utilization in schools, field-based teacher preparation programs, effective use of online instruction. *Unit head:* Dr. Angiline Powell, Interim Chair, 901-678-3310, E-mail: apowell3@memphis.edu. *Application contact:* Dr. James Meindl, Coordinator of Graduate Studies, 901-678-3310, E-mail: jnmeindl@memphis.edu.
Website: http://www.memphis.edu/icl/

University of Michigan–Dearborn, College of Education, Health, and Human Services, Doctoral Program in Education, Dearborn, MI 48126. Offers curriculum and practice (Ed D); educational leadership (Ed D); metropolitan education (Ed D). *Program availability:* Part-time, evening/weekend. *Faculty:* 5 full-time (3 women), 1 part-time/adjunct (0 women). *Students:* 2 full-time (1 woman), 13 part-time (9 women); includes 8 minority (7 Black or African American, non-Hispanic/Latino; 1 Hispanic/Latino). Average age 45. 15 applicants, 27% accepted, 3 enrolled. In 2017, 9 doctorates awarded. *Degree requirements:* For doctorate, comprehensive exam, thesis/dissertation. *Entrance requirements:* For doctorate, GRE (taken within the last 5 years), master's degree with minimum GPA of 3.3, 3 letters of recommendation (1 from faculty), 3 years' professional and/or teaching experience. Additional exam requirements/recommendations for international students: Required—TOEFL (minimum score 560 paper-based; 84 iBT), IELTS (minimum score 6.5). *Application deadline:* For fall admission, 3/1 for domestic and international students. Application fee: $60. Electronic applications accepted. *Expenses:* $683 per credit hour in-state; $1,176 per credit hour out-state. *Financial support:* In 2017–18, 2 students received support. Scholarships/grants available. Financial award application deadline: 3/1; financial award applicants required to submit FAFSA. *Faculty research:* Urban education, educational leadership, assessment and evaluation, research methods, science education. *Unit head:* Dr. Chris Burke, Director, 313-593-5319, E-mail: cjfburke@umich.edu. *Application contact:* Office of Graduate Studies, 313-583-6321, E-mail: umd-graduatestudies@umich.edu.
Website: http://umdearborn.edu/cehhs/cehhs_edd/

University of Michigan–Dearborn, College of Education, Health, and Human Services, Education Specialist Program, Dearborn, MI 48126. Offers curriculum and practice (Ed S); educational leadership (Ed S); metropolitan education (Ed S). *Program availability:* Part-time, evening/weekend. *Faculty:* 1 (woman) full-time, 1 part-time/adjunct (0 women). *Students:* 6 part-time (3 women). Average age 40. 5 applicants, 60% accepted, 1 enrolled. *Entrance requirements:* For degree, master's degree with minimum GPA of 3.3; at least 3 years' teaching experience or the equivalent experience working in a professional setting. Additional exam requirements/recommendations for international students: Required—TOEFL (minimum score 560 paper-based; 84 iBT), IELTS (minimum score 6.5). *Application deadline:* For fall admission, 8/1 for domestic students, 5/1 for international students; for winter admission, 12/1 for domestic students, 9/1 for international students; for spring admission, 4/1 for domestic students, 1/1 for international students. Applications are processed on a rolling basis. Application fee: $60. Electronic applications accepted. *Expenses:* $683 per credit hour in-state; $1,176 per credit hour out-state. *Financial support:* In 2017–18, 1 student received support. Scholarships/grants available. Financial award application deadline: 3/1; financial award applicants required to submit FAFSA. *Faculty research:* Educational leadership, curriculum development, education policy, organizational development, K-12administration. *Unit head:* Dr. Bonnie Beyer, Director, 313-593-5583, E-mail: beyer@umich.edu. *Application contact:* Office of Graduate Studies, 313-583-6321, E-mail: umd-graduatestudies@umich.edu.
Website: http://umdearborn.edu/cehhs/cehhs_eds/

University of Michigan–Flint, School of Education and Human Services, Department of Education, Flint, MI 48502-1950. Offers curriculum and instruction (Ed S); early childhood education (MA); education (Ed D); educational leadership (Ed S); educational technology (MA), including curriculum and instruction, developer; literacy education (MA); secondary education with certification (MA). *Program availability:* Part-time, evening/weekend, 100% online, mixed mode format (for some programs). *Faculty:* 18 full-time (11 women), 26 part-time/adjunct (13 women). *Students:* 34 full-time (23 women), 192 part-time (137 women); includes 61 minority (46 Black or African American, non-Hispanic/Latino; 2 Asian, non-Hispanic/Latino; 5 Hispanic/Latino; 1 Native Hawaiian or other Pacific Islander, non-Hispanic/Latino; 6 Two or more races, non-Hispanic/Latino), 2 international. Average age 39. 124 applicants, 87% accepted, 81 enrolled. In 2017, 89 master's, 3 doctorates awarded. *Degree requirements:* For master's, thesis optional; for doctorate, thesis/dissertation. *Entrance requirements:* For master's, bachelor's degree from regionally-accredited institution, minimum overall undergraduate GPA of 3.0; for doctorate, Ed S; minimum overall graduate GPA of 3.3 (6.0 on a 9.0 scale) or equivalent; at least 3 years of work experience in a P-16 educational institution or in an education-related position; for Ed S, MA or MS in education-related field from accredited institution; minimum overall graduate GPA of 3.0 (6.0 on a 9.0 scale) or equivalent; at least 3 years of work experience in an educational setting. Additional exam requirements/recommendations for international students: Required—TOEFL (minimum score 84 iBT), IELTS (minimum score 6.5). *Application deadline:* For fall admission, 8/1 for domestic students, 5/1 for international students; for winter admission, 11/15 for domestic students, 9/15 for international students; for spring admission, 3/15 for domestic students, 1/15 for international students; for summer admission, 5/15 for domestic students. Applications are processed on a rolling basis. Application fee: $55. Electronic applications accepted. *Expenses:* Contact institution. *Financial support:* Federal Work-Study, scholarships/grants, and unspecified assistantships available. Financial award application deadline: 3/1; financial award applicants required to submit FAFSA. *Unit head:* Dr. Mary Jo Finney, Department Chair/Associate Professor, 810-766-6617, E-mail: mjfinney@umflint.edu. *Application contact:* Bradley T. Maki, Director of Graduate Admissions, 810-762-3171, Fax: 810-766-6789, E-mail: bmaki@umflint.edu.
Website: https://www.umflint.edu/education/graduate-programs

University of Minnesota, Twin Cities Campus, Graduate School, College of Education and Human Development, Department of Curriculum and Instruction, Program in Curriculum and Instruction, Minneapolis, MN 55455-0213. Offers M Ed, MA, PhD. *Students:* 150 full-time (102 women), 167 part-time (130 women); includes 75 minority (10 Black or African American, non-Hispanic/Latino; 4 American Indian or Alaska Native, non-Hispanic/Latino; 19 Asian, non-Hispanic/Latino; 28 Hispanic/Latino; 1 Native Hawaiian or other Pacific Islander, non-Hispanic/Latino; 9 Two or more races, non-Hispanic/Latino), 34 international. Average age 37. 255 applicants, 47% accepted, 101 enrolled. In 2017, 53 master's, 30 doctorates awarded. Application fee: $75 ($95 for international students). *Unit head:* Dr. Cynthia Lewis, Chair, 612-625-6313, Fax: 612-624-8277, E-mail: lewis@umn.edu. *Application contact:* Dr. Gillian Roehrig, Director of Graduate Studies, 612-625-3692, E-mail: roehr013@umn.edu.
Website: http://www.cehd.umn.edu/ci

University of Missouri, Office of Research and Graduate Studies, College of Education, Department of Educational, School, and Counseling Psychology, Columbia, MO 65211. Offers counseling psychology (M Ed, MA, PhD, Ed S); educational psychology (M Ed, MA, PhD, Ed S); learning and instruction (M Ed); school psychology (M Ed, MA, PhD, Ed S). *Accreditation:* APA (one or more programs are accredited). *Program availability:* Part-time. *Degree requirements:* For doctorate, thesis/dissertation. *Entrance requirements:* For master's, doctorate, and Ed S, GRE General Test, minimum GPA of 3.0. Additional exam requirements/recommendations for international students: Required—TOEFL (minimum score 580 paper-based; 92 iBT). Electronic applications accepted.

University of Missouri, Office of Research and Graduate Studies, College of Education, Department of Learning, Teaching and Curriculum, Columbia, MO 65211. Offers agricultural education (M Ed, PhD, Ed S); art education (M Ed, PhD, Ed S); business and office education (M Ed, PhD, Ed S); early childhood education (M Ed, PhD, Ed S); elementary education (M Ed, PhD, Ed S); English education (M Ed, PhD, Ed S); foreign language education (M Ed, PhD, Ed S); health education and promotion (M Ed, PhD); learning and instruction (M Ed); marketing education (M Ed, PhD, Ed S); mathematics education (M Ed, PhD, Ed S); music education (M Ed, PhD, Ed S); reading education (M Ed, PhD, Ed S); science education (M Ed, PhD, Ed S); social studies education (M Ed, PhD, Ed S); vocational education (M Ed, PhD, Ed S). *Program availability:* Part-time. Terminal master's awarded for partial completion of doctoral program. *Degree requirements:* For doctorate, thesis/dissertation. *Entrance requirements:* For master's and Ed S, GRE General Test or MAT, minimum GPA of 3.0; for doctorate, GRE General Test, minimum GPA of 3.0. Additional exam requirements/recommendations for international students: Required—TOEFL (minimum score 600 paper-based; 100 iBT). Electronic applications accepted.

University of Missouri, Office of Research and Graduate Studies, College of Education, Department of Special Education, Columbia, MO 65211. Offers administration and supervision of special education (PhD); behavior disorders (M Ed, PhD); curriculum development of exceptional students (M Ed, PhD); early childhood special education (M Ed, PhD); general special education (M Ed, MA, PhD); learning and instruction (M Ed); learning disabilities (M Ed, PhD); mental retardation (M Ed, PhD). *Accreditation:* TEAC. *Program availability:* Part-time, evening/weekend, online learning. *Degree requirements:* For master's, comprehensive exam, thesis or alternative; for doctorate, comprehensive exam, thesis/dissertation. *Entrance requirements:* For master's and doctorate, GRE General Test, letters of recommendation. Additional exam requirements/recommendations for international students: Required—TOEFL (minimum score 500 paper-based; 61 iBT). Electronic applications accepted.

University of Missouri–Kansas City, School of Education, Kansas City, MO 64110-2499. Offers administration (Ed D); counseling and guidance (MA, Ed S), including mental health counseling (Ed S), school counseling (Ed S); counseling psychology (PhD); curriculum and instruction (MA, Ed S), including language and literacy (Ed S); education (PhD), including higher education administration, PK-12 education administration; educational administration (MA, Ed S), including advanced principal (Ed S), beginning principal (Ed S), district-level administration (Ed S); reading education (MA); special education (MA). PhD in education offered through the School of Graduate Studies. *Accreditation:* NCATE. *Program availability:* Part-time, evening/weekend. *Degree requirements:* For doctorate, thesis/dissertation, internship, practicum. *Entrance requirements:* For master's, GRE, minimum GPA of 2.75, 2 letters of reference, written statement of purpose; for doctorate, GRE, minimum GPA of 3.0; for Ed S, minimum GPA of 3.0. Additional exam requirements/recommendations for international students: Required—TOEFL (minimum score 550 paper-based; 80 iBT). *Faculty research:* Urban education, inquiry-based field study, theories of counseling and psychotherapy, school literacy, educational technology.

University of Missouri–St. Louis, College of Education, Department of Educator Preparation, Innovation and Research, St. Louis, MO 63121. Offers elementary education (M Ed), including early childhood, general, reading; secondary education (M Ed), including curriculum and instruction, general, middle level education, reading, teaching English to speakers of other languages (TESOL); special education (M Ed), including autism and developmental disabilities, early childhood special education. *Program availability:* Part-time, evening/weekend. *Students:* 75 full-time (63 women), 462 part-time (363 women); includes 127 minority (85 Black or African American, non-Hispanic/Latino; 2 American Indian or Alaska Native, non-Hispanic/Latino; 8 Asian, non-Hispanic/Latino; 24 Hispanic/Latino; 8 Two or more races, non-Hispanic/Latino), 1 international. 247 applicants, 92% accepted, 153 enrolled. *Degree requirements:* For master's, comprehensive exam. *Entrance requirements:* Additional exam requirements/recommendations for international students: Recommended—TOEFL (minimum score 550 paper-based; 79 iBT), IELTS (minimum score 6.5). *Application deadline:* For fall admission, 7/1 priority date for domestic and international students; for spring admission, 12/1 priority date for domestic and international students. Application fee: $50 ($40 for international students). Electronic applications accepted. *Expenses:* Tuition, state resident: part-time $476.50 per credit hour. Tuition, nonresident: part-time $1169.70 per credit hour. *Financial support:* Application deadline: 4/1; applicants required to submit FAFSA. *Unit head:* Dr. Gayle Wilkinson, Chair, 314-516-5791. *Application contact:* 314-516-5458, Fax: 314-516-6996, E-mail: gadadm@umsl.edu.
Website: https://coe.umsl.edu/dept/epir.html

University of Montana, Graduate School, Phyllis J. Washington College of Education and Human Sciences, Department of Teaching and Learning, Missoula, MT 59812. Offers curriculum and instruction (M Ed, Ed D); early childhood education (M Ed);

education (MA); teaching and learning (PhD). *Program availability:* Part-time. *Degree requirements:* For doctorate, thesis/dissertation. *Entrance requirements:* For master's, GRE General Test. Additional exam requirements/recommendations for international students: Required—TOEFL.

University of Nebraska at Kearney, College of Education, Department of Teacher Education, Kearney, NE 68849-0001. Offers curriculum and instruction (MA Ed), including early childhood education, elementary education, English as a second language, instructional effectiveness, reading/special education, secondary education; instructional technology (MS Ed), including information technology, instructional technology, school librarian; reading PK-12 (MA Ed); special education (MA Ed), including advanced practitioner: assistive technology specialist, advanced practitioner: behavioral interventionist, advanced practitioner: inclusive collaboration specialist, gifted, teacher education. *Program availability:* Part-time, evening/weekend, online only, 100% online. *Degree requirements:* For master's, comprehensive exam, thesis optional. *Entrance requirements:* For master's, portfolio or GRE. Additional exam requirements/recommendations for international students: Recommended—TOEFL (minimum score 550 paper-based; 79 iBT), IELTS (minimum score 6.5). Electronic applications accepted. *Expenses:* Contact institution.

University of Nebraska–Lincoln, Graduate College, College of Education and Human Sciences, Department of Teaching, Learning and Teacher Education, Lincoln, NE 68588. Offers adult and continuing education (MA); educational studies (Ed D, PhD), including special education (Ed D); teaching, learning and teacher education (M Ed, MA, MST, Ed D, PhD); vocational and adult education (M Ed, MA). *Accreditation:* NCATE. *Degree requirements:* For master's, thesis optional. *Entrance requirements:* Additional exam requirements/recommendations for international students: Required—TOEFL (minimum score 550 paper-based). Electronic applications accepted. *Faculty research:* Teacher education, instructional leadership, literacy education, technology, improvement of school curriculum.

University of Nebraska–Lincoln, Graduate College, College of Education and Human Sciences, Interdepartmental Area of Administration, Curriculum and Instruction, Lincoln, NE 68588. Offers Ed D, PhD, JD/PhD. *Accreditation:* NCATE. *Program availability:* Online learning. *Degree requirements:* For doctorate, comprehensive exam, thesis/dissertation. *Entrance requirements:* For doctorate, GRE, curriculum vitae. Additional exam requirements/recommendations for international students: Required—TOEFL (minimum score 550 paper-based). Electronic applications accepted.

University of Nevada, Las Vegas, Graduate College, College of Education, Department of Teaching and Learning, Las Vegas, NV 89154-3005. Offers curriculum and instruction (M Ed, MS, Ed D, PhD, Ed S), including teacher education (PhD); elementary teaching (Certificate); online teaching and training (Certificate); secondary teaching (Certificate); social justice studies (Certificate); teaching and learning (PhD). *Program availability:* Part-time, evening/weekend. *Faculty:* 27 full-time (13 women), 10 part-time/adjunct (8 women). *Students:* 315 full-time (222 women), 244 part-time (161 women); includes 226 minority (58 Black or African American, non-Hispanic/Latino; 2 American Indian or Alaska Native, non-Hispanic/Latino; 24 Asian, non-Hispanic/Latino; 104 Hispanic/Latino; 2 Native Hawaiian or other Pacific Islander, non-Hispanic/Latino; 36 Two or more races, non-Hispanic/Latino), 10 international. Average age 35. 234 applicants, 89% accepted, 174 enrolled. In 2017, 153 master's, 16 doctorates, 3 other advanced degrees awarded. *Degree requirements:* For master's, comprehensive exam (for some programs), thesis (for some programs); for doctorate, comprehensive exam, thesis/dissertation, defense of dissertation; for other advanced degree, comprehensive exam (for some programs), oral presentation of special project or professional paper. *Entrance requirements:* For master's, bachelor's degree with minimum GPA 2.75; for doctorate, GRE General Test, master's degree with minimum GPA of 3.0; statement of purpose; demonstration of oral communication skills; 3 letters of recommendation; for other advanced degree, PRAXIS Core (for some programs); PRAXIS II (for some programs), bachelor's degree (for some programs). Additional exam requirements/recommendations for international students: Required—TOEFL (minimum score 550 paper-based; 80 iBT), IELTS (minimum score 7). *Application deadline:* For fall admission, 6/1 for domestic students, 5/1 for international students; for spring admission, 11/1 for domestic students, 10/1 for international students; for summer admission, 3/15 for domestic students. Application fee: $60 ($95 for international students). Electronic applications accepted. *Expenses:* $275 per credit, $850 per course, $7,969 per year resident, $22,157 per year non-resident, $7,094 non-resident fee (7 credits or more), $1,307 annual health insurance fee. *Financial support:* In 2017–18, 36 students received support, including 13 research assistantships with full tuition reimbursements available (averaging $18,065 per year), 23 teaching assistantships with full tuition reimbursements available (averaging $19,564 per year); institutionally sponsored loans, scholarships/grants, health care benefits, and unspecified assistantships also available. Financial award application deadline: 3/15; financial award applicants required to submit FAFSA. *Faculty research:* Content area and critical literacy, education in content areas, teacher education, STEM education, immersive environments/simulations/games. *Total annual research expenditures:* $1.1 million. *Unit head:* Dr. Emily Lin, Chair/Professor, 702-895-6407, Fax: 702-895-4898, E-mail: emily.lin@unlv.edu. *Application contact:* Dr. Travis Olson, Graduate Coordinator, 702-895-0471, Fax: 702-895-4898, E-mail: travis.olson@unlv.edu.
Website: http://tl.unlv.edu/

University of Nevada, Reno, Graduate School, College of Education, Department of Curriculum, Teaching and Learning, Program in Curriculum and Instruction, Reno, NV 89557. Offers PhD. *Degree requirements:* For doctorate, thesis/dissertation. *Entrance requirements:* For doctorate, GRE General Test, minimum GPA of 3.0. Additional exam requirements/recommendations for international students: Required—TOEFL (minimum score 500 paper-based; 61 iBT), IELTS (minimum score 6). Electronic applications accepted. *Faculty research:* Education, development, pedagogy.

University of Nevada, Reno, Graduate School, College of Education, Department of Curriculum, Teaching and Learning, Program in Curriculum, Teaching and Learning, Reno, NV 89557. Offers Ed D, PhD. *Degree requirements:* For doctorate, comprehensive exam, thesis/dissertation. *Entrance requirements:* For doctorate, GRE General Test, minimum GPA of 3.0. Additional exam requirements/recommendations for international students: Required—TOEFL (minimum score 500 paper-based; 61 iBT), IELTS (minimum score 6). Electronic applications accepted. *Faculty research:* Education, trends, pedagogy.

University of New England, College of Graduate and Professional Studies, Portland, ME 04005-9526. Offers advanced educational leadership (CAGS); applied nutrition (MS); career and technical education (MS Ed); curriculum and instruction (MS Ed); education (CAGS, Post-Master's Certificate); educational leadership (MS Ed, Ed D); generalist (MS Ed); health informatics (MS, Graduate Certificate); inclusion education (MS Ed); literacy K-12 (MS Ed); medical education leadership (MMEL); public health (MPH); public health (Graduate Certificate); reading specialist (MS Ed); social work (MSW). *Program availability:* Part-time, evening/weekend, online only, 100% online. *Faculty:* 125 part-time/adjunct (94 women). *Students:* 1,403 full-time (1,128 women), 594 part-time (475 women); includes 474 minority (332 Black or African American, non-Hispanic/Latino; 13 American Indian or Alaska Native, non-Hispanic/Latino; 83 Asian, non-Hispanic/Latino; 27 Hispanic/Latino; 11 Native Hawaiian or other Pacific Islander,

non-Hispanic/Latino; 8 Two or more races, non-Hispanic/Latino). Average age 35. 3,153 applicants, 41% accepted, 990 enrolled. In 2017, 307 master's, 59 doctorates, 124 other advanced degrees awarded. *Application deadline:* Applications are processed on a rolling basis. Electronic applications accepted. Tuition and fees vary according to degree level, program and student level. *Financial support:* Application deadline: 5/1; applicants required to submit FAFSA. *Unit head:* Dr. Martha Wilson, Associate Provost for Online Worldwide Learning/Dean of the College of Graduate and Professional Studies, 207-221-4985, E-mail: mwilson13@une.edu.
Website: http://online.une.edu

University of New Hampshire, Graduate School, College of Liberal Arts, Department of Education, Program in Education, Durham, NH 03824. Offers children and youth in communities (PhD); curriculum and instruction leadership (Postbaccalaureate Certificate); education (PhD). *Students:* 33 full-time (23 women), 22 part-time (13 women); includes 3 minority (2 Asian, non-Hispanic/Latino; 1 Hispanic/Latino), 8 international. Average age 38. 24 applicants, 46% accepted, 4 enrolled. In 2017, 5 doctorates awarded. *Entrance requirements:* For doctorate, GRE General Test. Additional exam requirements/recommendations for international students: Required—TOEFL (minimum score 550 paper-based; 80 iBT). *Application deadline:* For fall admission, 12/15 priority date for domestic students, 12/15 for international students. Application fee: $65. Electronic applications accepted. *Financial support:* In 2017–18, 21 students received support, including 2 fellowships, 1 research assistantship, 15 teaching assistantships; Federal Work-Study, scholarships/grants, and tuition waivers (full and partial) also available. Support available to part-time students. Financial award application deadline: 2/15. *Unit head:* Paula Salvio, Chair, 603-862-0024. *Application contact:* Cindy Glidden, Department Coordinator, 603-862-2311, E-mail: education.department@unh.edu.
Website: http://cola.unh.edu/education

University of New Orleans, Graduate School, College of Education and Human Development, Department of Curriculum and Instruction, New Orleans, LA 70148. Offers M Ed, PhD. *Accreditation:* NCATE. *Program availability:* Evening/weekend. *Degree requirements:* For doctorate, variable foreign language requirement, thesis/dissertation. *Entrance requirements:* For master's, GRE General Test; for doctorate, GRE General Test, GRE Subject Test. Additional exam requirements/recommendations for international students: Required—TOEFL (minimum score 550 paper-based; 79 iBT). Electronic applications accepted.

The University of North Carolina at Chapel Hill, Graduate School, School of Education, Program in Education, Chapel Hill, NC 27599. Offers culture, curriculum and change (MA, PhD); early childhood, intervention and literacy (MA, PhD); educational psychology, measurement and evaluation (MA, PhD). *Accreditation:* NCATE. *Degree requirements:* For master's, thesis; for doctorate, comprehensive exam, thesis/dissertation. *Entrance requirements:* For master's, GRE General Test, minimum GPA of 3.0 during last 2 years of undergraduates course work; for doctorate, GRE General Test, minimum GPA of 3.0 during last 2 years of undergraduate course work. Additional exam requirements/recommendations for international students: Required—TOEFL (minimum score 550 paper-based). Electronic applications accepted.

The University of North Carolina at Charlotte, Cato College of Education, Interdisciplinary Education Programs, Charlotte, NC 28223-0001. Offers art education (Graduate Certificate); child and family development: early childhood education (MAT); curriculum and instruction (PhD); elementary education (MAT); foreign language education (MAT); middle grades education (MAT); secondary education (MAT); special education (MAT); teaching (Graduate Certificate); teaching English as a second language (MAT); theatre education (Graduate Certificate). *Program availability:* Part-time, 100% online, blended/hybrid learning. *Students:* 86 full-time (63 women), 533 part-time (423 women); includes 229 minority (169 Black or African American, non-Hispanic/Latino; 1 American Indian or Alaska Native, non-Hispanic/Latino; 7 Asian, non-Hispanic/Latino; 39 Hispanic/Latino; 13 Two or more races, non-Hispanic/Latino), 13 international. Average age 32. 382 applicants, 91% accepted, 253 enrolled. In 2017, 182 master's, 10 doctorates, 172 other advanced degrees awarded. *Degree requirements:* For master's, thesis or alternative, research project/portfolio. *Entrance requirements:* For master's, GRE or MAT, bachelor's degree, or its U.S. equivalent, from regionally-accredited college or university; minimum overall GPA of 3.0 on all previous work beyond high school; statement of purpose (essay); at least three recommendation forms; for doctorate, GRE or MAT, bachelor's degree (or its U.S. equivalent) from regionally-accredited college or university; minimum overall GPA of 3.5 in master's degree program; for Graduate Certificate, bachelor's degree from regionally-accredited university; minimum GPA of 2.75 on all post-secondary work attempted; transcripts; personal statement outlining why the applicant seeks admission to the program. Additional exam requirements/recommendations for international students: Required—TOEFL (minimum score 523 paper-based, 70 iBT) or IELTS (6.5). *Application deadline:* For fall admission, 3/1 priority date for domestic and international students; for spring admission, 10/1 priority date for domestic and international students; for summer admission, 4/1 priority date for domestic and international students. Applications are processed on a rolling basis. Application fee: $75. Electronic applications accepted. *Expenses:* Tuition, state resident: full-time $4337. Tuition, nonresident: full-time $17,771. *Required fees:* $3211. Tuition and fees vary according to course load and program. *Financial support:* Career-related internships or fieldwork, institutionally sponsored loans, scholarships/grants, and unspecified assistantships available. Support available to part-time students. Financial award application deadline: 3/1; financial award applicants required to submit FAFSA. *Unit head:* Dr. Ellen McIntyre, Dean, 704-687-8722, E-mail: ellen.mcintyre@uncc.edu. *Application contact:* Kathy B. Giddings, Director of Graduate Admissions, 704-687-5503, Fax: 704-687-1668, E-mail: gradadm@uncc.edu.
Website: http://education.uncc.edu/academic-programs

The University of North Carolina at Greensboro, Graduate School, School of Education, Department of Educational Leadership and Cultural Foundations, Greensboro, NC 27412-5001. Offers curriculum and teaching (PhD), including cultural studies; educational leadership (Ed D, Ed S); school administration (MSA). *Accreditation:* NCATE. *Degree requirements:* For doctorate, thesis/dissertation. *Entrance requirements:* For master's, doctorate, and Ed S, GRE General Test. Additional exam requirements/recommendations for international students: Required—TOEFL. Electronic applications accepted.

The University of North Carolina at Greensboro, Graduate School, School of Education, Department of Teacher Education and Higher Education, Greensboro, NC 27412-5001. Offers college teaching and adult learning (Certificate); curriculum and instruction (M Ed), including chemistry education, elementary education, English as a second language, French education, instructional technology, mathematics education, middle grades education, reading education, science education, social studies education, Spanish education; curriculum and teaching (PhD), including higher education, teacher education and development; English as a second language (Certificate); higher education (M Ed); supervision (M Ed). *Accreditation:* NCATE. *Program availability:* Part-time. *Degree requirements:* For doctorate, thesis/dissertation. *Entrance requirements:* For master's and doctorate, GRE General Test. Additional exam requirements/recommendations for international students: Required—TOEFL. Electronic applications accepted. *Faculty research:* Community college literacy program, middle school mathematics/computer mathematics.

The University of North Carolina Wilmington, Watson College of Education, Department of Educational Leadership, Wilmington, NC 28403-3297. Offers curriculum, instruction and supervision (M Ed); educational leadership and administration (Ed D), including curriculum and instruction; higher education (M Ed); school administration (MSA), including school administration. *Program availability:* Part-time, 100% online. *Faculty:* 14 full-time (11 women), 6 part-time/adjunct (4 women). *Students:* 39 full-time (24 women), 150 part-time (109 women); includes 56 minority (41 Black or African American, non-Hispanic/Latino; 7 American Indian or Alaska Native, non-Hispanic/Latino; 2 Asian, non-Hispanic/Latino; 4 Hispanic/Latino; 2 Native Hawaiian or other Pacific Islander, non-Hispanic/Latino), 1 international. Average age 36. 80 applicants, 74% accepted, 50 enrolled. In 2017, 53 master's, 20 doctorates awarded. *Degree requirements:* For master's, thesis or culminating project, e-Portfolio (for school administration); for doctorate, comprehensive exam, thesis/dissertation. *Entrance requirements:* For master's, GRE General Test, MAT, minimum B average in undergraduate work, 3 letters of recommendation, education statement of interest essay, autobiographical statement, NC Class A teacher licensure in related field, minimum of 3 years' teaching experience; for doctorate, education statement of interest essay, master's degree in education field, 3 years of leadership experience. Additional exam requirements/recommendations for international students: Required—TOEFL (minimum score 550 paper-based; 79 iBT), IELTS (minimum score 6.5). *Application deadline:* For fall admission, 5/15 for domestic students; for spring admission, 10/15 for domestic students; for summer admission, 3/15 for domestic students. Applications are processed on a rolling basis. Application fee: $75. Electronic applications accepted. *Expenses:* Tuition, state resident: full-time $4626; part-time $226.76 per credit hour. Tuition, nonresident: full-time $17,834; part-time $874.22 per credit hour. *Required fees:* $2124. Tuition and fees vary according to program. *Financial support:* Scholarships/grants and unspecified assistantships available. Financial award application deadline: 1/1; financial award applicants required to submit FAFSA. *Unit head:* Dr. Marsha Carr, Interim Chair, 910-962-2913, Fax: 910-962-3609, E-mail: carrm@uncw.edu. *Application contact:* Dr. William Sterrett, Graduate Program Coordinator, 910-962-7995, E-mail: stewettw@uncw.edu.
Website: http://uncw.edu/ed/el/

University of Northern Colorado, Graduate School, College of Education and Behavioral Sciences, School of Teacher Education, Greeley, CO 80639. Offers curriculum studies (MAT); educational studies (Ed D); elementary education (MAT); English education (MAT); literacy (MA); multilingual education (MA), including TESOL, world languages; teaching diverse learners (MA). *Accreditation:* NCATE. *Program availability:* Part-time, evening/weekend. *Degree requirements:* For master's, comprehensive exam, thesis or alternative; for doctorate, comprehensive exam, thesis/dissertation. *Entrance requirements:* For master's and doctorate, GRE General Test, 3 letters of recommendation. Electronic applications accepted.

University of Northern Iowa, Graduate College, College of Education, Ed D Program in Education, Cedar Falls, IA 50614. Offers allied health, recreation, and community services (Ed D); curriculum and instruction (Ed D); educational leadership (Ed D). *Program availability:* Part-time, evening/weekend. *Degree requirements:* For doctorate, thesis/dissertation. *Entrance requirements:* For doctorate, GRE, minimum GPA of 3.0, master's degree. Additional exam requirements/recommendations for international students: Required—TOEFL (minimum score 500 paper-based; 61 iBT).

University of North Georgia, Program in Curriculum and Instruction, Dahlonega, GA 30597. Offers M Ed. *Program availability:* Part-time. *Students:* 4 full-time (3 women), 27 part-time (23 women); includes 4 minority (2 Hispanic/Latino; 2 Two or more races, non-Hispanic/Latino). Average age 33. In 2017, 1 master's awarded. *Entrance requirements:* For master's, GRE (minimum score 301 verbal and quantitative combined) or MAT (minimum score 391), baccalaureate degree with minimum GPA of 2.75, clear renewable teaching certificate. Additional exam requirements/recommendations for international students: Required—TOEFL (minimum score 550 paper-based; 79 iBT), IELTS (minimum score 6.5). *Application deadline:* For fall admission, 8/10 for domestic students; for spring admission, 12/10 for domestic students; for summer admission, 5/15 for domestic students. Application fee: $40. Electronic applications accepted. *Expenses:* Tuition, state resident: full-time $2025. Tuition, nonresident: full-time $8082. Tuition and fees vary according to course load, degree level and program. *Financial support:* Application deadline: 3/17; applicants required to submit FAFSA. *Unit head:* Dr. Susan Brandenburg-Ayres, Dean, 706-864-1998, E-mail: susan.ayres@ung.edu. *Application contact:* Melinda Maxwell, Director of Graduate Admissions, 706-867-2077, E-mail: melinda.maxwell@ung.edu.
Website: https://ung.edu/teacher-education/graduate/master-education-curriculum-instruction.php

University of North Texas, Robert B. Toulouse School of Graduate Studies, Denton, TX 76203-5459. Offers accounting (MS); applied anthropology (MA, MS); applied behavior analysis (Certificate); applied geography (MA); applied technology and performance improvement (M Ed, MS); art education (MA); art history (MA); art museum education (Certificate); arts leadership (Certificate); audiology (Au D); behavior analysis (MS); behavioral science (PhD); biochemistry and molecular biology (MS); biology (MA, MS); biomedical engineering (MS); business analysis (MS); chemistry (MS); clinical health psychology (PhD); communication studies (MA, MS); computer engineering (MS); computer science (MS); counseling (M Ed, MS), including clinical mental health counseling (MS), college and university counseling, elementary school counseling, secondary school counseling; creative writing (MA); criminal justice (MS); curriculum and instruction (M Ed); decision sciences (MBA); design (MA, MFA), including fashion design (MFA), innovation studies, interior design (MFA); early childhood studies (MS); economics (MS); educational leadership (M Ed, Ed D); educational psychology (MS, PhD), including family studies (MS), gifted and talented (MS), human development (MS), learning and cognition (MS), research, measurement and evaluation (MS); electrical engineering (MS); emergency management (MPA); engineering technology (MS); English (MA); English as a second language (MA); environmental science (MS); finance (MBA, MS); financial management (MPA); French (MA); health services management (MBA); higher education (M Ed, Ed D); history (MA, MS); hospitality management (MS); human resources management (MPA); information science (MS); information systems (PhD); information technologies (MBA); interdisciplinary studies (MA, MS); international studies (MA); international sustainable tourism (MS); jazz studies (MM); journalism (MA, MJ, Graduate Certificate), including interactive and virtual digital communication (Graduate Certificate), narrative journalism (Graduate Certificate), public relations (Graduate Certificate); kinesiology (MS); linguistics (MA); local government management (MPA); logistics (PhD); logistics and supply chain management (MBA); long-term care, senior housing, and aging services (MA); management (PhD); marketing (MBA); mathematics (MA, MS); mechanical and energy engineering (MS, PhD); music (MA), including ethnomusicology, music theory, musicology, performance; music composition (PhD); music education (MM Ed, PhD); nonprofit management (MPA); operations and supply chain management (MBA); performance (MM, DMA); philosophy (MA); political science (MA); professional and technical communication (MA); radio, television and film (MA, MFA); rehabilitation counseling (Certificate); sociology (MA); Spanish (MA); special education (M Ed); speech-language pathology (MA); strategic management (MBA); studio art (MFA); teaching (M Ed); MBA/MS. *Program availability:* Part-time, evening/weekend, online learning. Terminal master's awarded for partial

completion of doctoral program. *Degree requirements:* For master's, variable foreign language requirement, comprehensive exam (for some programs), thesis (for some programs); for doctorate, variable foreign language requirement, comprehensive exam (for some programs), thesis/dissertation; for other advanced degree, variable foreign language requirement, comprehensive exam (for some programs). *Entrance requirements:* For master's and doctorate, GRE, GMAT. Additional exam requirements/recommendations for international students: Required—TOEFL (minimum score 550 paper-based; 79 iBT). Electronic applications accepted.

University of North Texas at Dallas, Graduate School, Dallas, TX 75241. Offers accounting (MBA); counseling (M Ed, MS); criminal justice (MS); curriculum and instruction (M Ed); educational administration (M Ed); human resources and organizational behavior (MBA); public leadership (MS); strategic management (MBA).

University of Oklahoma, Jeannine Rainbolt College of Education, Department of Educational Leadership and Policy Studies, Program in Educational Administration, Curriculum and Supervision, Norman, OK 73019. Offers M Ed, Ed D, PhD. *Accreditation:* NCATE. *Program availability:* Part-time, evening/weekend, blended/hybrid learning. *Students:* 28 full-time (23 women), 177 part-time (127 women); includes 66 minority (27 Black or African American, non-Hispanic/Latino; 14 American Indian or Alaska Native, non-Hispanic/Latino; 13 Hispanic/Latino; 12 Two or more races, non-Hispanic/Latino), 2 international. Average age 36. 91 applicants, 80% accepted, 61 enrolled. In 2017, 46 master's, 14 doctorates awarded. *Degree requirements:* For master's, comprehensive exam, thesis (for some programs); for doctorate, comprehensive exam, thesis/dissertation. *Entrance requirements:* For doctorate, GRE. Additional exam requirements/recommendations for international students: Required—TOEFL (minimum score 79 iBT) or IELTS (minimum score 6.5). *Application deadline:* Applications are processed on a rolling basis. Application fee: $50 ($100 for international students). Electronic applications accepted. *Expenses:* Tuition, state resident: full-time $5119; part-time $213.30 per credit hour. Tuition, nonresident: full-time $19,778; part-time $824.10 per credit hour. *Required fees:* $3458; $133.55 per credit hour. $126.50 per semester. *Financial support:* In 2017–18, 111 students received support. Fellowships, research assistantships, teaching assistantships, career-related internships or fieldwork, Federal Work-Study, institutionally sponsored loans, scholarships/grants, health care benefits, tuition waivers, and unspecified assistantships available. Support available to part-time students. Financial award application deadline: 6/1; financial award applicants required to submit FAFSA. *Faculty research:* Improvement science; leadership and ethics; education and social policy; gender and equity; organizational reform and change. *Unit head:* John Jones, Associate Professor, 405-325-4165, E-mail: jjones@ou.edu.
Website: http://www.ou.edu/education/elps

University of Oklahoma, Jeannine Rainbolt College of Education, Department of Instructional Leadership and Academic Curriculum, Norman, OK 73019. Offers instructional leadership and academic curriculum (M Ed, PhD), including biomedical education (PhD), early childhood education, elementary education, English education, instructional leadership, mathematics education, reading education, science education, social studies education, world languages education (M Ed); reading specialist (M Ed). *Accreditation:* NCATE. *Program availability:* Part-time. *Faculty:* 19 full-time (15 women), 1 (woman) part-time/adjunct. *Students:* 37 full-time (28 women), 121 part-time (98 women); includes 32 minority (7 Black or African American, non-Hispanic/Latino; 4 American Indian or Alaska Native, non-Hispanic/Latino; 5 Asian, non-Hispanic/Latino; 6 Hispanic/Latino; 1 Native Hawaiian or other Pacific Islander, non-Hispanic/Latino; 9 Two or more races, non-Hispanic/Latino), 12 international. Average age 35. 39 applicants, 77% accepted, 22 enrolled. In 2017, 49 master's, 12 doctorates awarded. Terminal master's awarded for partial completion of doctoral program. *Degree requirements:* For master's, comprehensive exam (for some programs), thesis (for some programs); for doctorate, comprehensive exam (for some programs), thesis/dissertation. *Entrance requirements:* For doctorate, GRE. Additional exam requirements/recommendations for international students: Required—TOEFL (minimum score 79 iBT) or IELTS (minimum score 6.5). Application fee: $50 ($100 for international students). Electronic applications accepted. *Expenses:* Tuition, state resident: full-time $5119; part-time $213.30 per credit hour. Tuition, nonresident: full-time $19,778; part-time $824.10 per credit hour. *Required fees:* $3458; $133.55 per credit hour. $126.50 per semester. *Financial support:* In 2017–18, 90 students received support, including 8 research assistantships (averaging $11,248 per year), 6 teaching assistantships (averaging $12,188 per year); fellowships, scholarships/grants, and unspecified assistantships also available. Financial award application deadline: 6/1; financial award applicants required to submit FAFSA. *Faculty research:* Teacher preparation; instruction; curriculum; learning; constructivist theory. *Total annual research expenditures:* $707,690. *Unit head:* Dr. Stacy Reeder, Chair, 405-325-1498, Fax: 405-325-4061, E-mail: reeder@ou.edu. *Application contact:* Anna Steele, Graduate Programs Officer, 405-325-4525, E-mail: anna.steele@ou.edu.
Website: http://www.ou.edu/education/ilac

University of Oregon, Graduate School, College of Education, Eugene, OR 97403. Offers communication disorders and sciences (MA, MS, PhD); counseling psychology (PhD); couples and family therapy (MS); critical and sociocultural studies in education (PhD); curriculum and teacher education (MA, MS); educational leadership (MS, D Ed, PhD); prevention science (M Ed, MS, PhD); school psychology (MS, PhD); special education (M Ed, MA, MS, PhD). *Program availability:* Part-time. Terminal master's awarded for partial completion of doctoral program. *Degree requirements:* For master's, exam, paper, or project; for doctorate, comprehensive exam, thesis/dissertation. *Entrance requirements:* Additional exam requirements/recommendations for international students: Required—TOEFL. *Faculty research:* Basic and applied research in teaching, learning and habilitation in all settings, schooling effectiveness.

University of Phoenix–Central Valley Campus, College of Education, Fresno, CA 93720-1552. Offers curriculum and instruction (MA Ed); curriculum and instruction-computer education (MA Ed); elementary teacher education (MA Ed); secondary teacher education (MA Ed).

University of Phoenix–Dallas Campus, College of Education, Dallas, TX 75251. Offers curriculum and instruction (MA Ed).

University of Phoenix–Hawaii Campus, College of Education, Honolulu, HI 96813-3800. Offers administration and supervision (MA Ed); curriculum and instruction (MA Ed); elementary education (MA Ed); secondary education (MA Ed); special education (MA Ed); teacher education for elementary licensure (MA Ed). *Program availability:* Evening/weekend. *Degree requirements:* For master's, thesis (for some programs). *Entrance requirements:* For master's, minimum undergraduate GPA of 2.5, 3 years of work experience. Additional exam requirements/recommendations for international students: Required—TOEFL (minimum score 550 paper-based; 79 iBT). Electronic applications accepted.

University of Phoenix–Houston Campus, College of Education, Houston, TX 77079-2004. Offers curriculum and instruction (MA Ed).

University of Phoenix–Las Vegas Campus, College of Education, Las Vegas, NV 89135. Offers administration and supervision (MA Ed); curriculum and instruction (MA Ed); school counseling (MSC); teacher education-elementary licensure (MA Ed).

Curriculum and Instruction

Program availability: Evening/weekend. *Degree requirements:* For master's, thesis (for some programs). *Entrance requirements:* For master's, minimum undergraduate GPA of 2.5, 3 years of work experience. Additional exam requirements/recommendations for international students: Required—TOEFL (minimum score 550 paper-based; 79 iBT). Electronic applications accepted.

University of Phoenix–Online Campus, College of Education, Phoenix, AZ 85034-7209. Offers administration and supervision (MAEd, Certificate); adult education and training (MAEd); curriculum and instruction (MAEd), including computer education, curriculum and instruction, English as a second language, language arts, mathematics, reading; early childhood education (MAEd); educational studies (MAEd); elementary teacher education (MAEd), including early childhood, elementary teacher education, high school middle level, middle level; principal licensure (Certificate); secondary teacher education (MAEd); special education (MAEd, Certificate); teacher education (MAEd), including middle level generalist; teacher education middle level mathematics (MAEd), including middle level mathematics; teacher education middle level science (MAEd), including middle level science; teacher education secondary mathematics (MAEd); teacher education secondary science (MAEd); teacher leadership (MAEd); teachers of English learners (Certificate); transition to teaching (Certificate), including elementary education, secondary education. *Program availability:* Evening/weekend, online learning. *Entrance requirements:* Additional exam requirements/recommendations for international students: Required—TOEFL, TOEIC (Test of English as an International Communication), Berlitz Online English Proficiency Exam, PTE, or IELTS. Electronic applications accepted. *Expenses:* Contact institution.

University of Phoenix–Online Campus, School of Advanced Studies, Phoenix, AZ 85034-7209. Offers business administration (DBA); education (Ed S); educational leadership (Ed D), including curriculum and instruction, education technology, educational leadership; health administration (DHA); higher education administration (PhD); industrial/organizational psychology (PhD); nursing (PhD); organizational leadership (DM), including information systems and technology, organizational leadership. *Program availability:* Evening/weekend, online learning. *Degree requirements:* For doctorate, thesis/dissertation. *Entrance requirements:* Additional exam requirements/recommendations for international students: Required—TOEFL, TOEIC (Test of English as an International Communication), Berlitz Online English Proficiency Exam, PTE, or IELTS. Electronic applications accepted. *Expenses:* Contact institution.

University of Phoenix–Phoenix Campus, College of Education, Tempe, AZ 85282-2371. Offers administration and supervision (MA Ed); adult education and training (MA Ed); curriculum and instruction reading (MA Ed); early childhood education (MA Ed); education studies (MA Ed); elementary teacher education (MA Ed); secondary teacher education (MA Ed); special education (MA Ed); teacher leadership (MA Ed). *Program availability:* Evening/weekend, online learning. *Entrance requirements:* Additional exam requirements/recommendations for international students: Required—TOEFL, TOEIC (Test of English as an International Communication), Berlitz Online English Proficiency Exam, PTE, or IELTS. Electronic applications accepted. *Expenses:* Contact institution.

University of Phoenix–Sacramento Valley Campus, College of Education, Sacramento, CA 95833-4334. Offers adult education (MA Ed); curriculum instruction (MA Ed); elementary teacher education (MA Ed); secondary teacher education (MA Ed); teacher education (Certificate). *Program availability:* Evening/weekend. *Degree requirements:* For master's, thesis (for some programs). *Entrance requirements:* For master's, 3 years of work experience, minimum undergraduate GPA of 2.5. Additional exam requirements/recommendations for international students: Required—TOEFL (minimum score 550 paper-based; 79 iBT). Electronic applications accepted.

University of Phoenix–San Antonio Campus, College of Education, San Antonio, TX 78230. Offers curriculum and instruction (MA Ed).

University of Phoenix–San Diego Campus, College of Education, San Diego, CA 92123. Offers curriculum and instruction (MA Ed), including computer education, curriculum and instruction, English as a second language; elementary teacher education (MA Ed); secondary teacher education (MA Ed). *Program availability:* Evening/weekend. *Degree requirements:* For master's, thesis (for some programs). *Entrance requirements:* For master's, 3 years of work experience, minimum undergraduate GPA of 3.0. Additional exam requirements/recommendations for international students: Required—TOEFL (minimum score 550 paper-based; 79 iBT). Electronic applications accepted.

University of Puerto Rico–Río Piedras, College of Education, Program in Curriculum and Teaching, San Juan, PR 00931-3300. Offers biology education (M Ed); chemistry education (M Ed); curriculum and teaching (Ed D); history education (M Ed); mathematics education (M Ed); physics education (M Ed); Spanish education (M Ed). *Program availability:* Part-time. *Degree requirements:* For master's, thesis; for doctorate, thesis/dissertation, internship. *Entrance requirements:* For master's, PAEG or GRE, minimum GPA of 3.0, letter of recommendation; for doctorate, GRE or PAEG, master's degree, minimum GPA of 3.0, letter of recommendation (2), interview. *Faculty research:* Curriculum, math teaching.

University of Regina, Faculty of Graduate Studies and Research, Faculty of Education, Department of Curriculum and Instruction, Regina, SK S4S 0A2, Canada. Offers M Ed. *Program availability:* Part-time. *Faculty:* 38 full-time (26 women), 2 part-time/adjunct (both women). *Students:* 15 full-time (11 women), 128 part-time (108 women). 111 applicants, 63% accepted. In 2017, 65 master's awarded. *Degree requirements:* For master's, thesis (for some programs), practicum, project, or thesis. *Entrance requirements:* For master's, bachelor's degree in education, 2 years of teaching or other relevant professional experience. Additional exam requirements/recommendations for international students: Required—TOEFL (minimum score 580 paper-based; 80 iBT), IELTS (minimum score 6.5), PTE (minimum score 59). *Application deadline:* For fall admission, 2/15 for domestic and international students; for winter admission, 10/15 for domestic and international students; for spring admission, 2/15 for domestic students. Application fee: $100. Electronic applications accepted. *Expenses:* $10,681. *Financial support:* In 2017–18, 3 fellowships (averaging $6,000 per year), 5 teaching assistantships (averaging $2,562 per year) were awarded; research assistantships and scholarships/grants also available. Financial award application deadline: 6/15. *Faculty research:* Writing process and pedagogy; the Saskatchewan Writing Project; second language reading, writing, and spoken acquisition; assessing experiential learning; multicultural and anti-racist relations issues in curriculum; social media and open education. *Unit head:* Dr. Paul Clarke, Associate Dean, Faculty Development and Human Resources, 306-585-5353, Fax: 306-585-5387, E-mail: paul.clarke@uregina.ca. *Application contact:* Linda Jiang, Graduate Program Coordinator, 306-585-5387, Fax: 306-585-5387, E-mail: edgrad@uregina.ca.
Website: http://www.uregina.ca/education/

University of Rochester, Eastman School of Music, Program in Music Theory Pedagogy, Rochester, NY 14627. Offers MA.

University of Rochester, Margaret Warner Graduate School of Education and Human Development, Doctoral Programs in Education, Rochester, NY 14627. Offers counseling (Ed D); educational administration (Ed D); educational policy and theory (PhD); higher education (PhD); human development in educational context (PhD); teaching, curriculum, and change (PhD).

University of Rochester, Margaret Warner Graduate School of Education and Human Development, Master's Program in Teaching and Curriculum, Rochester, NY 14627. Offers MS.

University of St. Francis, College of Education, Joliet, IL 60435-6169. Offers educational leadership (MS, Ed D); elementary education (M Ed); reading (MS); secondary education (M Ed), including English education, math education, science education, social studies education, visual arts education; special education (M Ed); teaching and learning (MS); TESOL (Certificate). *Accreditation:* NCATE. *Program availability:* Part-time, evening/weekend, 100% online, blended/hybrid learning. *Faculty:* 11 full-time (8 women), 52 part-time/adjunct (36 women). *Students:* 39 full-time (32 women), 411 part-time (318 women); includes 106 minority (57 Black or African American, non-Hispanic/Latino; 8 Asian, non-Hispanic/Latino; 37 Hispanic/Latino; 4 Two or more races, non-Hispanic/Latino), 4 international. Average age 37. 277 applicants, 55% accepted, 137 enrolled. In 2017, 199 master's, 28 doctorates awarded. *Degree requirements:* For master's, comprehensive exam; for doctorate, thesis/dissertation. *Entrance requirements:* Additional exam requirements/recommendations for international students: Required—TOEFL (minimum score 550 paper-based; 79 iBT), IELTS (minimum score 6). *Application deadline:* Applications are processed on a rolling basis. Application fee: $30. Electronic applications accepted. Application fee is waived when completed online. *Expenses:* $365 to $748 per credit hour. *Financial support:* In 2017–18, 40 students received support. Scholarships/grants and unspecified assistantships available. Support available to part-time students. Financial award applicants required to submit FAFSA. *Unit head:* Dr. John Gambro, Dean, 815-740-3829, Fax: 815-740-2264, E-mail: jgambro@stfrancis.edu. *Application contact:* Sandra Sloka, Director of Admissions for Graduate and Degree Completion Programs, 800-735-7500, Fax: 815-740-3431, E-mail: ssloka@stfrancis.edu.
Website: http://www.stfrancis.edu/academics/college-of-education/

University of Saint Joseph, Department of Education, West Hartford, CT 06117-2700. Offers curriculum and instruction (MA); elementary education (MAT); instructional technology (MA); literacy (MA); secondary education (MAT); TESOL (MA). *Program availability:* Part-time, evening/weekend. *Degree requirements:* For master's, comprehensive exam, thesis or alternative. *Entrance requirements:* For master's, 2 letters of recommendation. *Application deadline:* Applications are processed on a rolling basis. Application fee: $50. Electronic applications accepted. Application fee is waived when completed online. *Financial support:* Career-related internships or fieldwork and unspecified assistantships available. Support available to part-time students. Financial award applicants required to submit FAFSA.
Website: https://www.usj.edu/academics/schools/sasbe/education/

University of St. Thomas, School of Education and Human Services, Houston, TX 77006-4696. Offers all level education (M Ed); bilingual/dual language (M Ed); Catholic school teaching (M Ed); Catholic/private school leadership (M Ed); counselor education (M Ed); curriculum and instruction (M Ed); education (Ed D); educational leadership (M Ed); elementary teaching (M Ed); English as a second language (M Ed); exceptionality/educational diagnostician (M Ed); exceptionality/special education (M Ed); generalist (M Ed); reading (M Ed); secondary teaching (M Ed); teaching (MAT). *Accreditation:* TEAC. *Program availability:* Part-time, evening/weekend, online learning. *Faculty:* 33 full-time (22 women), 43 part-time/adjunct (26 women). *Students:* 119 full-time (97 women), 597 part-time (529 women); includes 478 minority (166 Black or African American, non-Hispanic/Latino; 29 Asian, non-Hispanic/Latino; 277 Hispanic/Latino; 2 Native Hawaiian or other Pacific Islander, non-Hispanic/Latino; 4 Two or more races, non-Hispanic/Latino), 19 international. Average age 36. 306 applicants, 91% accepted, 181 enrolled. In 2017, 328 master's awarded. *Degree requirements:* For master's, thesis, field experience. *Entrance requirements:* For master's, GRE or MAT if GPA is below 3.0, bachelor's degree; minimum GPA of 2.75 in bachelor's degree or last 60 credit hours; official transcripts from all institutions; goal statement of 250-300 words; 1 reference. Additional exam requirements/recommendations for international students: Required—TOEFL (minimum score 94 iBT), IELTS (minimum score 7), PTE (minimum score 53). *Application deadline:* Applications are processed on a rolling basis. Application fee: $35. Electronic applications accepted. *Expenses:* Contact institution. *Financial support:* In 2017–18, 27 students received support. Federal Work-Study, scholarships/grants, and state work-study, institutional employment available. Support available to part-time students. Financial award application deadline: 4/15; financial award applicants required to submit FAFSA. *Faculty research:* Leadership, diversity, personality traits, second language acquisition. *Unit head:* Dr. Paul C. Paese, Dean, 713-942-5999, Fax: 713-525-3871, E-mail: paesep@stthom.edu. *Application contact:* 713-525-3540, E-mail: education@stthom.edu.
Website: http://www.stthom.edu/Academics/School_of_Education_and_Human_Services/Index.aqf

University of San Diego, School of Leadership and Education Sciences, Department of Learning and Teaching, San Diego, CA 92110-2492. Offers curriculum and instruction (M Ed); inclusive learning (M Ed); literacy and digital learning (M Ed); school leadership (M Ed); special education (M Ed); STEAM (science, technology, engineering, arts, and mathematics) (M Ed); TESOL, literacy and culture (M Ed). *Program availability:* Part-time, evening/weekend. *Faculty:* 9 full-time (7 women), 30 part-time/adjunct (24 women). *Students:* 160 full-time (128 women), 221 part-time (176 women); includes 131 minority (10 Black or African American, non-Hispanic/Latino; 24 Asian, non-Hispanic/Latino; 83 Hispanic/Latino; 1 Native Hawaiian or other Pacific Islander, non-Hispanic/Latino; 13 Two or more races, non-Hispanic/Latino), 20 international. Average age 33. 398 applicants, 84% accepted, 196 enrolled. In 2017, 151 master's awarded. *Degree requirements:* For master's, thesis (for some programs), international experience. *Entrance requirements:* For master's, California Basic Educational Skills Test, California Subject Examination for Teachers. Additional exam requirements/recommendations for international students: Required—TOEFL (minimum score 580 paper-based; 83 iBT), TWE. *Application deadline:* Applications are processed on a rolling basis. Application fee: $45. Electronic applications accepted. *Financial support:* In 2017–18, 65 students received support. Career-related internships or fieldwork, Federal Work-Study, institutionally sponsored loans, and stipends available. Financial award application deadline: 4/1; financial award applicants required to submit FAFSA. *Faculty research:* Action research methodology, cultural studies, instructional theories and practices, second language acquisition, school reform. *Unit head:* Dr. Maya Kalyanpur, Chair, 619-260-7655, E-mail: mkalyanpur@sandiego.edu. *Application contact:* Monica Mahon, Associate Director of Graduate Admissions, 619-260-4524, Fax: 619-260-4158, E-mail: grads@sandiego.edu.
Website: http://www.sandiego.edu/soles/learning-and-teaching/

University of San Francisco, School of Education, Department of Learning and Instruction, San Francisco, CA 94117-1080. Offers digital technologies for teaching and learning (MA); learning and instruction (MA, Ed D); special education (MA, Ed D); teaching reading (MA). *Program availability:* Part-time, evening/weekend. *Degree requirements:* For doctorate, thesis/dissertation. *Entrance requirements:* Additional exam requirements/recommendations for international students: Required—TOEFL, IELTS, PTE. Electronic applications accepted.

University of Saskatchewan, College of Graduate Studies and Research, College of Education, Department of Curriculum Studies, Saskatoon, SK S7N 5A2, Canada. Offers M Ed, PhD, Diploma. *Program availability:* Part-time. *Degree requirements:* For master's, thesis (for some programs); for doctorate, comprehensive exam (for some programs), thesis/dissertation. *Entrance requirements:* For master's, MAT. Additional exam requirements/recommendations for international students: Required—TOEFL (minimum score 80 iBT); Recommended—IELTS (minimum score 6.5). Electronic applications accepted.

The University of Scranton, Panuska College of Professional Studies, Department of Education, Program in Curriculum and Instruction, Scranton, PA 18510. Offers MS. *Program availability:* Part-time, evening/weekend, online only, 100% online.

University of South Africa, College of Human Sciences, Pretoria, South Africa. Offers adult education (M Ed); African languages (MA, PhD); African politics (MA, PhD); Afrikaans (MA, PhD); ancient history (MA, PhD); ancient Near Eastern studies (MA, PhD); anthropology (MA, PhD); applied linguistics (MA); Arabic (MA, PhD); archaeology (MA); art history (MA); Biblical archaeology (MA); Biblical studies (M Th, D Th, PhD); Christian spirituality (M Th, D Th); church history (M Th, D Th); classical studies (MA, PhD); clinical psychology (MA); communication (MA, PhD); comparative education (M Ed, Ed D); consulting psychology (D Admin, D Com, PhD); curriculum studies (M Ed, Ed D); development studies (M Admin, MA, D Admin, PhD); didactics (M Ed, Ed D); education (M Tech); education management (M Ed, Ed D); educational psychology (M Ed); English (MA); environmental education (M Ed); French (MA, PhD); German (MA, PhD); Greek (MA); guidance and counseling (M Ed); health studies (MA, PhD), including health sciences education (MA), health services management (MA), medical and surgical nursing science (critical care general) (MA), midwifery and neonatal nursing science (MA), trauma and emergency care (MA); history (MA, PhD); history of education (Ed D); inclusive education (M Ed, Ed D); information and communications technology policy and regulation (MA); information science (MA, MIS, PhD); international politics (MA, PhD); Islamic studies (MA, PhD); Italian (MA, PhD); Judaica (MA, PhD); linguistics (MA, PhD); mathematical education (M Ed); mathematics education (MA); missiology (M Th, D Th); modern Hebrew (MA, PhD); musicology (MA, MMus, D Mus, PhD); natural science education (M Ed); New Testament (M Th, D Th); Old Testament (D Th); pastoral therapy (M Th, D Th); philosophy (MA); philosophy of education (M Ed, Ed D); politics (MA, PhD); Portuguese (MA, PhD); practical theology (M Th, D Th); psychology (MA, MS, PhD); psychology of education (M Ed, Ed D); public health (MA); religious studies (MA, D Th, PhD); Romance languages (MA); Russian (MA, PhD); Semitic languages (MA, PhD); social behavior studies in HIV/AIDS (MA); social science (mental health) (MA); social science in development studies (MA); social science in psychology (MA); social science in social work (MA); social science in sociology (MA); social work (MSW, DSW, PhD); socio-education (M Ed, Ed D); sociolinguistics (MA); sociology (MA, PhD); Spanish (MA, PhD); systematic theology (M Th, D Th); TESOL (teaching English to speakers of other languages) (MA); theological ethics (M Th, D Th); theory of literature (MA, PhD); urban ministries (D Th); urban ministry (M Th).

University of South Carolina, The Graduate School, College of Education, Department of Instruction and Teacher Education, Program in Curriculum and Instruction, Columbia, SC 29208. Offers Ed D. This degree cuts across two departments and represents 6 different concentrations. *Accreditation:* NCATE. *Program availability:* Part-time, evening/weekend. *Degree requirements:* For doctorate, comprehensive exam, thesis/dissertation. *Entrance requirements:* For doctorate, GRE General Test or MAT, interview, resume, letter of intent, letters of reference. Electronic applications accepted. *Faculty research:* Teacher education, historian recording project, curriculum development in international areas, human sexuality.

University of South Dakota, Graduate School, School of Education, Division of Curriculum and Instruction, Vermillion, SD 57069. Offers American Indian education (Certificate); curriculum and instruction (Ed D, Ed S); elementary education (MA), including elementary education; English language learners (Certificate); literacy leadership and coaching (Certificate); reading interventionist (Certificate); science, technology and math pedagogy (Certificate); secondary education (MA), including secondary education; special education (MA), including special education; technology for education and training (MS), including technology for education and training. *Accreditation:* NCATE. *Program availability:* Part-time, online learning. *Degree requirements:* For master's and other advanced degree, comprehensive exam, thesis or alternative; for doctorate, comprehensive exam, thesis/dissertation. *Entrance requirements:* For master's, doctorate, and other advanced degree, GRE General Test, MAT, minimum GPA of 2.7. Additional exam requirements/recommendations for international students: Required—TOEFL (minimum score 550 paper-based; 79 iBT). *Application deadline:* Applications are processed on a rolling basis. Application fee: $35. Electronic applications accepted. *Financial support:* Research assistantships with partial tuition reimbursements, teaching assistantships with partial tuition reimbursements, career-related internships or fieldwork, Federal Work-Study, and unspecified assistantships available. Financial award applicants required to submit FAFSA. *Application contact:* Graduate School, 605-658-6140, Fax: 605-677-6118, E-mail: grad@usd.edu. Website: http://www.usd.edu/ci

University of Southern Mississippi, College of Education and Psychology, Department of Curriculum, Instruction and Special Education, Hattiesburg, MS 39406-0001. Offers elementary education (M Ed, PhD); instructional technology (MS); instructional technology and design (PhD); secondary education (MAT); special education (M Ed, PhD). *Program availability:* Part-time, online learning. *Students:* 25 full-time (18 women), 5 part-time (3 women). 41 applicants, 59% accepted, 22 enrolled. *Degree requirements:* For master's, comprehensive exam, thesis (for some programs); for doctorate, comprehensive exam, thesis/dissertation. *Entrance requirements:* For master's, GRE General Test, MAT, minimum GPA of 3.0; for doctorate, GRE General Test, minimum GPA of 3.5. Additional exam requirements/recommendations for international students: Required—TOEFL, IELTS. *Application deadline:* For fall admission, 3/1 priority date for domestic students, 3/1 for international students; for spring admission, 1/10 priority date for domestic and international students. Applications are processed on a rolling basis. Application fee: $60. *Expenses:* Tuition, state resident: full-time $3830. *Financial support:* Research assistantships with tuition reimbursements, teaching assistantships with full tuition reimbursements, Federal Work-Study, institutionally sponsored loans, scholarships/grants, health care benefits, tuition waivers (partial), and unspecified assistantships available. Financial award application deadline: 3/15; financial award applicants required to submit FAFSA. *Faculty research:* Mathematical problem solving, integrative curriculum, writing process, teacher education models. *Unit head:* Dr. Jeff Hinton, Chair. Website: https://www.usm.edu/elementary-special-technology-education

University of South Florida Sarasota-Manatee, College of Liberal Arts and Social Sciences, Sarasota, FL 34243. Offers criminal justice (MA); education (MA); educational leadership (M Ed), including curriculum leadership, K-12 public school leadership, non-public/charter school leadership; elementary education (MAT); English education (MA); social work (MSW). *Program availability:* Part-time, 100% online, blended/hybrid learning. *Faculty:* 15 full-time (12 women), 8 part-time/adjunct (6 women). *Students:* 11 full-time (10 women), 43 part-time (37 women); includes 17 minority (7 Black or African

American, non-Hispanic/Latino; 2 Asian, non-Hispanic/Latino; 8 Hispanic/Latino), 1 international. Average age 35. 62 applicants, 27% accepted, 14 enrolled. In 2017, 32 master's awarded. *Degree requirements:* For master's, comprehensive exam (for some programs). *Entrance requirements:* For master's, GRE. Additional exam requirements/recommendations for international students: Required—TOEFL (minimum score 550 paper-based; 79 iBT), IELTS (minimum score 6.5). *Application deadline:* For fall admission, 3/1 priority date for domestic students, 3/1 for international students; for spring admission, 10/1 priority date for domestic students, 10/1 for international students. Applications are processed on a rolling basis. Application fee: $30. Electronic applications accepted. *Expenses:* Tuition, state resident: full-time $8350; part-time $418 per credit hour. Tuition, nonresident: full-time $19,047; part-time $863 per credit hour. *Required fees:* $1689. Tuition and fees vary according to degree level and program. *Financial support:* In 2017–18, 1 student received support. Career-related internships or fieldwork, institutionally sponsored loans, scholarships/grants, health care benefits, and unspecified assistantships available. Support available to part-time students. Financial award application deadline: 3/1; financial award applicants required to submit FAFSA. *Faculty research:* Educational leadership, secondary education, elementary education, criminal justice, social work. *Total annual research expenditures:* $72,000. *Unit head:* Dr. Jane Rose, Dean, 941-359-4469, Fax: 941-359-4778, E-mail: jane.rose@sar.usf.edu. *Application contact:* Brandon Avery, Assistant Director, Admissions, 941-359-4331, E-mail: bavery@sar.usf.edu.

The University of Tampa, Programs in Education, Tampa, FL 33606-1490. Offers curriculum and instruction (M Ed); educational leadership (M Ed); instructional design and technology (MS). *Program availability:* Part-time, evening/weekend. *Faculty:* 5 full-time (4 women), 7 part-time/adjunct (5 women). *Students:* 41 full-time (27 women), 69 part-time (52 women); includes 20 minority (18 Black or African American, non-Hispanic/Latino; 2 Two or more races, non-Hispanic/Latino), 14 international. Average age 32. 126 applicants, 40% accepted, 29 enrolled. In 2017, 47 master's awarded. *Degree requirements:* For master's, capstone. *Entrance requirements:* For master's, GMAT or GRE, current Florida Professional Teaching Certificate, statement of eligibility for Florida Professional Teaching Certificate, or professional teaching certificate from another state; bachelor's degree in an area of education. Additional exam requirements/recommendations for international students: Required—TOEFL (minimum score 577 paper-based; 90 iBT), IELTS (minimum score 7.5). *Application deadline:* Applications are processed on a rolling basis. Application fee: $40. Electronic applications accepted. *Expenses:* Contact institution. *Financial support:* In 2017–18, 20 students received support. Career-related internships or fieldwork, scholarships/grants, and unspecified assistantships available. Financial award applicants required to submit FAFSA. *Faculty research:* Diversity in the classroom, technology integration, assessment methodologies, complex and ill-structured problem solving, communities of practice. *Unit head:* Dr. Antony Erben, Chair, 813-257-3414, E-mail: terben@ut.edu. *Application contact:* Chanelle Cox, Staff Assistant, Admissions for Graduate and Continuing Studies, 813-253-6249, E-mail: ccox@ut.edu. Website: http://www.ut.edu/graduate/education/

The University of Tennessee, Graduate School, College of Education, Health and Human Sciences, Program in Education, Knoxville, TN 37996. Offers art education (MS); counseling education (PhD); cultural studies in education (PhD); curriculum (MS, Ed S); curriculum, educational research and evaluation (Ed D, PhD); early childhood education (PhD); early childhood special education (MS); education of deaf and hard of hearing (MS); educational administration and policy studies (Ed D, PhD); educational administration and supervision (Ed S); educational psychology (Ed D, PhD); elementary education (MS, Ed S); elementary teaching (MS); English education (MS, Ed S); exercise science (PhD); foreign language/ESL education (MS, Ed S); instructional technology (MS, Ed D, PhD, Ed S); literacy, language and ESL education (PhD); literacy, language education, and ESL education (Ed D); mathematics education (MS, Ed S); modified and comprehensive special education (MS); reading education (MS, Ed S); school counseling (Ed S); school psychology (PhD, Ed S); science education (MS, Ed S); secondary teaching (MS); social foundations (MS); social science education (MS, Ed S); socio-cultural foundations of sports and education (PhD); special education (Ed S); teacher education (Ed D, PhD). *Accreditation:* NCATE. *Program availability:* Part-time, evening/weekend. *Degree requirements:* For master's and Ed S, thesis optional; for doctorate, variable foreign language requirement, thesis/dissertation. *Entrance requirements:* For master's, minimum GPA of 2.7; for doctorate and Ed S, GRE General Test, minimum GPA of 2.7. Additional exam requirements/recommendations for international students: Required—TOEFL. Electronic applications accepted.

The University of Tennessee at Martin, Graduate Programs, College of Education, Health and Behavioral Sciences, Program in Teaching, Martin, TN 38238. Offers curriculum and instruction (MS Ed), including 7-12, K-6; initial licensure (MS Ed), including elementary education, secondary education; initial licensure K-12 (MS Ed), including physical education, special education; interdisciplinary (MS Ed). *Program availability:* Part-time, online only, 100% online. *Students:* 20 full-time (17 women), 92 part-time (66 women); includes 20 minority (14 Black or African American, non-Hispanic/Latino; 2 Hispanic/Latino; 4 Two or more races, non-Hispanic/Latino). Average age 32. 79 applicants, 70% accepted, 38 enrolled. In 2017, 14 master's awarded. *Entrance requirements:* Additional exam requirements/recommendations for international students: Required—TOEFL (minimum score 525 paper-based; 71 iBT). *Application deadline:* For fall admission, 7/27 for domestic and international students; for spring admission, 12/17 for domestic and international students; for summer admission, 5/10 for domestic and international students. Applications are processed on a rolling basis. Electronic applications accepted. *Expenses:* Tuition, state resident: full-time $8658; part-time $481 per credit hour. Tuition, nonresident: full-time $14,418; part-time $801 per credit hour. *International tuition:* $22,602 full-time. *Required fees:* $1404; $79 per credit hour. Part-time tuition and fees vary according to course load. *Financial support:* In 2017–18, 26 students received support, including 1 research assistantship with full tuition reimbursement available (averaging $6,283 per year), 5 teaching assistantships with full tuition reimbursements available (averaging $7,001 per year); scholarships/grants and tuition waivers also available. Financial award applicants required to submit FAFSA. *Faculty research:* Special education, science/math/technology, school reform, reading. *Unit head:* Cynthia West, Dean, 731-881-7125, Fax: 731-881-7975, E-mail: cwest@utm.edu. *Application contact:* Jolene L. Cunningham, Student Services Specialist, 731-881-7012, Fax: 731-881-7499, E-mail: jcunningham@utm.edu.

The University of Texas at Arlington, Graduate School, College of Education, Department of Curriculum and Instruction, Arlington, TX 76019. Offers curriculum and instruction (M Ed), including literacy studies, mathematics education, mind, brain, and education, science education; teaching (with certification) (M Ed T). *Accreditation:* NCATE. *Program availability:* Part-time, evening/weekend, online learning. *Degree requirements:* For master's, comprehensive exam (for some programs), comprehensive activity, research project. *Entrance requirements:* For master's, GRE General Test, minimum undergraduate GPA of 3.0 in last 60 hours of course work, writing sample, 3 letters of recommendation. Additional exam requirements/recommendations for international students: Required—TOEFL (minimum score 550 paper-based). Electronic applications accepted.

Curriculum and Instruction

The University of Texas at Austin, Graduate School, College of Education, Department of Curriculum and Instruction, Austin, TX 78712-1111. Offers bilingual/bicultural education (M Ed, MA, PhD); cultural studies in education (M Ed, MA, PhD); early childhood education (M Ed, MA, PhD); language and literacy studies (M Ed, PhD); learning technologies (M Ed, MA, PhD); physical education (M Ed, MA, PhD). Terminal master's awarded for partial completion of doctoral program. *Degree requirements:* For doctorate, thesis/dissertation. *Entrance requirements:* For master's and doctorate, GRE General Test. Electronic applications accepted.

The University of Texas at El Paso, Graduate School, College of Education, Department of Teacher Education, El Paso, TX 79968-0001. Offers education (MA); instruction (M Ed); reading education (M Ed); teaching, learning, and culture (PhD). *Program availability:* Part-time, evening/weekend. *Degree requirements:* For master's, thesis optional. *Entrance requirements:* For master's, GRE General Test, minimum GPA of 3.0. Additional exam requirements/recommendations for international students: Required—TOEFL. Electronic applications accepted.

The University of Texas at San Antonio, College of Education and Human Development, Department of Interdisciplinary Learning and Teaching, San Antonio, TX 78249-0617. Offers education (MA), including curriculum and instruction, early childhood and elementary education, instructional technology, reading and literacy, special education; interdisciplinary learning and teaching (PhD). *Program availability:* Part-time, evening/weekend. *Faculty:* 24 full-time (16 women), 5 part-time/adjunct (3 women). *Students:* 73 full-time (57 women), 227 part-time (206 women); includes 179 minority (25 Black or African American, non-Hispanic/Latino; 10 Asian, non-Hispanic/Latino; 140 Hispanic/Latino; 1 Native Hawaiian or other Pacific Islander, non-Hispanic/Latino; 3 Two or more races, non-Hispanic/Latino), 7 international. Average age 34. 107 applicants, 88% accepted, 70 enrolled. In 2017, 103 master's, 5 doctorates awarded. *Degree requirements:* For master's, comprehensive exam, thesis optional, 36 hours of course work without thesis (33 with thesis); for doctorate, comprehensive exam, thesis/dissertation, minimum of 60 semester credit hours. *Entrance requirements:* For master's, bachelor's degree with minimum GPA of 3.0 in last 60 hours of coursework; 18 hours of undergraduate coursework in education or related field; for doctorate, GRE, transcripts from all colleges and universities attended, professional vitae demonstrating experience in work environment where education was primary professional emphasis, 3 letters of recommendation, statement of purpose, minimum GPA of 3.5. Additional exam requirements/recommendations for international students: Required—TOEFL (minimum score 550 paper-based; 79 iBT), IELTS (minimum score 6.5). *Application deadline:* For fall admission, 6/15 for domestic students, 3/1 for international students; for spring admission, 10/15 for domestic students, 9/15 for international students. Applications are processed on a rolling basis. Application fee: $50 ($90 for international students). Electronic applications accepted. *Expenses:* Tuition, state resident: full-time $5495. Tuition, nonresident: full-time $21,938. *Required fees:* $1915. Tuition and fees vary according to program. *Financial support:* Career-related internships or fieldwork, Federal Work-Study, and scholarships/grants available. Support available to part-time students. *Faculty research:* Explorations of science, learning and teaching, family involvement in early childhood, culturally-responsive literacy instruction in diverse settings, STEM education, autism spectrum disorder. *Total annual research expenditures:* $511,331. *Unit head:* Dr. Mari R. Cortez, Department Chair, 210-458-4414, Fax: 210-458-7281, E-mail: mari.cortez@utsa.edu. *Application contact:* Elizabeth Narvaez, Student Development Specialist, 210-458-7443, E-mail: elizabeth.narvaez@utsa.edu.
Website: http://education.utsa.edu/interdisciplinary_learning_and_teaching/

The University of Texas Rio Grande Valley, College of Education and P-16 Integration, Department of Teaching and Learning, Edinburg, TX 78539. Offers curriculum and instruction (M Ed, Ed D); educational technology (M Ed). *Program availability:* Part-time, evening/weekend. *Faculty:* 24. *Students:* 199. In 2017, 54 master's, 2 doctorates awarded. *Degree requirements:* For master's, comprehensive exam, thesis optional; for doctorate, comprehensive exam, thesis/dissertation. *Entrance requirements:* For master's, minimum GPA of 3.0. Additional exam requirements/recommendations for international students: Required—TOEFL (minimum score 550 paper-based; 79 iBT), IELTS (minimum score 6.5). *Application deadline:* For fall admission, 4/15 for domestic students; for spring admission, 11/1 for domestic students; for summer admission, 3/1 for domestic students. Applications are processed on a rolling basis. Application fee: $50 ($75 for international students). Electronic applications accepted. *Expenses:* Tuition, state resident: full-time $5550; part-time $417 per credit hour. Tuition, nonresident: full-time $13,020; part-time $832 per credit hour. *Required fees:* $1169. *Financial support:* Research assistantships, institutionally sponsored loans, scholarships/grants, and unspecified assistantships available. Financial award application deadline: 4/15; financial award applicants required to submit FAFSA. *Faculty research:* Teacher education, mathematics education, science education, educational technology, pedagogy. *Unit head:* Dr. James Jupp, Chair, 956-665-3401, E-mail: james.jupp@utrgv.edu. *Application contact:* Stephanie Ozuna, Graduate Student Recruiter, 956-665-3558, E-mail: stephanie.ozuna@utrgv.edu.

University of the Pacific, Gladys L. Benerd School of Education, Stockton, CA 95211-0197. Offers curriculum and instruction (MA, Ed D); education (M Ed); educational administration and leadership (MA, Ed D); educational and school psychology (MA, Ed D); school psychology (Ed S); special education (MA); teacher education (MA). *Accreditation:* NCATE. *Faculty:* 19 full-time (12 women), 48 part-time/adjunct (39 women). *Students:* 141 full-time (115 women), 305 part-time (236 women); includes 219 minority (41 Black or African American, non-Hispanic/Latino; 44 Asian, non-Hispanic/Latino; 105 Hispanic/Latino; 2 Native Hawaiian or other Pacific Islander, non-Hispanic/Latino; 27 Two or more races, non-Hispanic/Latino), 7 international. Average age 33. 144 applicants, 83% accepted, 94 enrolled. In 2017, 231 master's, 8 doctorates awarded. *Degree requirements:* For doctorate, thesis/dissertation. *Entrance requirements:* For master's, GRE General Test; for doctorate, GRE General Test, GRE Subject Test. Additional exam requirements/recommendations for international students: Required—TOEFL. *Application deadline:* For fall admission, 3/1 priority date for domestic students; for spring admission, 10/15 for domestic students. Applications are processed on a rolling basis. Application fee: $75. *Financial support:* Teaching assistantships and institutionally sponsored loans available. Support available to part-time students. Financial award application deadline: 3/1; financial award applicants required to submit FAFSA. *Unit head:* Dr. Vanessa Sheared, Dean, 209-946-2683, E-mail: lwebster@pacific.edu. *Application contact:* Office of Graduate Admissions, 209-946-2344.

University of the Southwest, Graduate Programs, Hobbs, NM 88240-9129. Offers business administration (MBA); curriculum and instruction (MSE); curriculum and instruction: bilingual (MSE); curriculum and instruction: TESOL (MSE); early childhood education (MSE); educational administration (MSE); mental health counseling (MSE); school counseling (MSE); special education (MSE); sports management (MBA). *Program availability:* Part-time, evening/weekend, online learning. *Degree requirements:* For master's, comprehensive exam, thesis (for some programs). *Entrance requirements:* Additional exam requirements/recommendations for international students: Recommended—TOEFL. Electronic applications accepted.

The University of Toledo, College of Graduate Studies, Judith Herb College of Education, Department of Curriculum and Instruction, Toledo, OH 43606-3390. Offers art education (ME); career and technical education (ME, Ed S); curriculum and instruction (ME, PhD, Ed S); early childhood education (Ed S); education and anthropology (MAE); education and biology (MES); education and chemistry (MES); education and classics (MAE); education and economics (MAE); education and English (MAE); education and French (MAE); education and geology (MES); education and German (MAE); education and history (MAE); education and mathematics (MAE, MES); education and physics (MES); education and political science (MAE); education and sociology (MAE); education and Spanish (MAE); educational media (PhD); educational technology (ME); educational technology: virtual educator (Certificate); elementary education (PhD); English as a second language (MAE); gifted and talented education (PhD); middle childhood education (ME); secondary education (ME, PhD); special education (PhD). *Accreditation:* NCATE. *Program availability:* Part-time, evening/weekend. *Degree requirements:* For master's, comprehensive exam, thesis or alternative; for doctorate, comprehensive exam, thesis/dissertation; for other advanced degree, thesis optional. *Entrance requirements:* For master's, doctorate, and other advanced degree, minimum cumulative GPA of 2.7 for all previous academic work, letters of recommendation. Additional exam requirements/recommendations for international students: Required—TOEFL (minimum score 550 paper-based; 80 iBT). Electronic applications accepted.

University of Vermont, Graduate College, College of Education and Social Services, Program in Curriculum and Instruction, Burlington, VT 05405. Offers M Ed. *Accreditation:* NCATE. *Program availability:* Blended/hybrid learning. *Students:* 8 (4 women). 16 applicants, 88% accepted, 8 enrolled. In 2017, 2 master's awarded. *Entrance requirements:* For master's, GRE General Test, VT PRAXIS II, or equivalent teacher examination scores from another state (e.g. Massachusetts Tests for Educator Licensure, MTEL), resume. Additional exam requirements/recommendations for international students: Required—TOEFL (minimum score 550 paper-based; 90 iBT), IELTS (minimum score 6.5). *Application deadline:* For fall admission, 3/1 for domestic and international students; for spring admission, 10/1 for domestic and international students; for summer admission, 3/1 for domestic and international students. Application fee: $65. Electronic applications accepted. *Expenses:* Tuition, state resident: full-time $11,628; part-time $646 per credit. Tuition, nonresident: full-time $29,340; part-time $1630 per credit. *Required fees:* $1994; $10 per credit. Tuition and fees vary according to course load and program. *Financial support:* Fellowships, teaching assistantships, career-related internships or fieldwork, and scholarships/grants available. Financial award application deadline: 3/1. *Unit head:* Dr. George Salembier, Chair, 802-656-1410, E-mail: george.salembier@uvm.edu. *Application contact:* Karen Orr, Curriculum and Instruction Program Support, 802-656-1410, E-mail: crclmins@uvm.edu.
Website: https://www.uvm.edu/cess/doe/curriculum

University of Vermont, Graduate College, College of Education and Social Services, Program in Middle Level Education, Burlington, VT 05405. Offers curriculum and instruction (MAT), including middle level education. *Program availability:* Part-time. *Entrance requirements:* For master's, resume, writing sample. Additional exam requirements/recommendations for international students: Required—TOEFL (minimum iBT score of 90) or IELTS (6.5). *Application deadline:* Applications are processed on a rolling basis. Application fee: $65. Electronic applications accepted. *Expenses:* Tuition, state resident: full-time $11,628; part-time $646 per credit. Tuition, nonresident: full-time $29,340; part-time $1630 per credit. *Required fees:* $1994; $10 per credit. Tuition and fees vary according to course load and program. *Financial support:* Career-related internships or fieldwork and scholarships/grants available. *Unit head:* Ken Reissig, Coordinator, 802-656-1411, E-mail: kenneth.reissig@uvm.edu.
Website: https://www.uvm.edu/cess/doe/mat_middlelevel

University of Vermont, Graduate College, College of Education and Social Services, Program in Secondary Education, Burlington, VT 05405. Offers curriculum and instruction (MAT), including secondary education. *Entrance requirements:* For master's, major or its equivalent in a state-approved licensing area. Additional exam requirements/recommendations for international students: Required—TOEFL (minimum iBT score of 90) or IELTS (6.5). *Application deadline:* For fall admission, 2/1 for domestic and international students. Application fee: $65. Electronic applications accepted. *Expenses:* Tuition, state resident: full-time $11,628; part-time $646 per credit. Tuition, nonresident: full-time $29,340; part-time $1630 per credit. *Required fees:* $1994; $10 per credit. Tuition and fees vary according to course load and program. *Financial support:* In 2017–18, 2 students received support. Career-related internships or fieldwork and scholarships/grants available. Financial award application deadline: 3/1. *Unit head:* Regina Toolin, Coordinator, 802-656-1411, E-mail: regina.toolin@uvm.edu.
Website: https://www.uvm.edu/cess/doe/mat_secondary

University of Victoria, Faculty of Graduate Studies, Faculty of Education, Department of Curriculum and Instruction, Victoria, BC V8W 2Y2, Canada. Offers art education (M Ed, PhD); curriculum studies (M Ed, MA, PhD); early childhood education (M Ed, PhD); educational studies (PhD); language and literacy (M Ed, MA, PhD); mathematics (M Ed, MA, PhD); music education (M Ed, MA, PhD); science (M Ed, MA, PhD); social studies (M Ed, MA); social, cultural and foundational studies (MA, PhD); technology and environmental education (PhD). *Program availability:* Part-time. *Degree requirements:* For master's, thesis, project (M Ed); for doctorate, comprehensive exam, thesis/dissertation. *Entrance requirements:* For master's, minimum B average. Additional exam requirements/recommendations for international students: Required—TOEFL (minimum score 575 paper-based), IELTS (minimum score 7). Electronic applications accepted. *Faculty research:* Elementary and secondary English, language arts, curriculum theory and practice, educational media and technology, educational administration and leadership, history and philosophy of education.

University of Virginia, Curry School of Education, Department of Curriculum, Instruction, and Special Education, Program in Curriculum and Instruction, Charlottesville, VA 22903. Offers curriculum and instruction (M Ed, Ed S); elementary education (M Ed, Ed D); English education (M Ed, Ed D); foreign language education (M Ed); mathematics education (M Ed, Ed D); science education (Ed D); social studies education (M Ed); MBA/M Ed. *Program availability:* 100% online. *Students:* 38 full-time (31 women), 15 part-time (12 women); includes 6 minority (2 Asian, non-Hispanic/Latino; 2 Hispanic/Latino; 2 Two or more races, non-Hispanic/Latino), 2 international. Average age 32. 92 applicants, 64% accepted, 47 enrolled. In 2017, 47 master's, 9 doctorates, 8 other advanced degrees awarded. *Degree requirements:* For master's, comprehensive exam (for some programs); for doctorate, comprehensive exam, thesis/dissertation; for Ed S, comprehensive exam. *Entrance requirements:* For master's, doctorate, and Ed S, GRE General Test, 2 letters of recommendation. Additional exam requirements/recommendations for international students: Required—TOEFL (minimum score 600 paper-based; 90 iBT), IELTS (minimum score 7). *Application deadline:* Applications are processed on a rolling basis. Application fee: $60. Electronic applications accepted. *Financial support:* Fellowships with tuition reimbursements, research assistantships with tuition reimbursements, and teaching assistantships with tuition reimbursements available. Financial award application deadline: 1/5; financial award applicants required to submit FAFSA. *Unit head:* Susan Mintz, Program Area Director, 434-924-3128, E-mail: slm4r@virginia.edu. *Application contact:* E-mail: curry-admissions@virginia.edu.
Website: http://curry.virginia.edu/academics/areas-of-study/curriculum-teaching-learning

University of Virginia, Curry School of Education, Program in Education, Charlottesville, VA 22903. Offers administration and supervision (PhD); applied developmental science (PhD); counselor education (PhD); curriculum and instruction (PhD); early childhood special education (MT); education evaluation (PhD); educational psychology (PhD); educational research (PhD); elementary education (MT); English education (MT, PhD); foreign language education (MT); higher education (PhD); instructional technology (PhD); kinesiology (MT, PhD); math education (PhD); reading education (PhD); research, statistics and evaluation (PhD); school psychology (PhD); science education (PhD); social studies education (MT, PhD); special education (PhD); world languages education (MT). *Students:* 431 full-time (353 women), 15 part-time (14 women); includes 100 minority (32 Black or African American, non-Hispanic/Latino; 33 Asian, non-Hispanic/Latino; 16 Hispanic/Latino; 19 Two or more races, non-Hispanic/Latino), 14 international. Average age 25. 264 applicants, 49% accepted, 83 enrolled. In 2017, 142 master's, 33 doctorates awarded. *Degree requirements:* For master's, comprehensive exam (for some programs), field project; for doctorate, comprehensive exam, thesis/dissertation. *Entrance requirements:* For doctorate, GRE General Test. Additional exam requirements/recommendations for international students: Required—TOEFL (minimum score 600 paper-based; 90 iBT), IELTS (minimum score 7). *Application deadline:* Applications are processed on a rolling basis. Application fee: $60. Electronic applications accepted. *Financial support:* Fellowships, research assistantships, and teaching assistantships available. Financial award application deadline: 1/5; financial award applicants required to submit FAFSA. *Unit head:* Robert C. Pianta, Dean, 434-924-3334, E-mail: pianta@virginia.edu. *Application contact:* E-mail: curry-admissions@virginia.edu.
Website: http://curry.virginia.edu/teacher-education

University of Washington, Graduate School, College of Education, Seattle, WA 98195. Offers curriculum and instruction (M Ed, Ed D, PhD), including educational technology, general curriculum (Ed D, PhD), language, literacy, and culture, mathematics education, multicultural education, reading and language arts education (Ed D), science education, social studies education, teaching and curriculum (M Ed); educational leadership and policy studies (M Ed, Ed D, PhD), including administration (Ed D), educational policy, organization, and leadership (M Ed, PhD), higher education, leadership for learning (Ed D), social and cultural foundations of education (M Ed, PhD); educational psychology (M Ed, PhD), including educational psychology (PhD), human development and cognition (M Ed), learning sciences, measurement, statistics and research design (M Ed), school psychology (M Ed); instructional leadership (M Ed); intercollegiate athletic leadership (M Ed); special education (M Ed, Ed D, PhD), including early childhood special education (M Ed), emotional and behavioral disabilities (M Ed), learning disabilities (M Ed), low-incidence disabilities (M Ed), severe disabilities (M Ed), special education (Ed D, PhD); teacher education (MIT). *Accreditation:* APA. *Program availability:* Part-time, evening/weekend. *Degree requirements:* For master's, thesis optional; for doctorate, thesis/dissertation. *Entrance requirements:* For master's and doctorate, GRE General Test, minimum GPA of 3.0. Additional exam requirements/recommendations for international students: Required—TOEFL. Electronic applications accepted. *Faculty research:* School restructuring/effective schools, special education interventions, literacy and writing, technology, school partnerships, teacher preparation.

The University of Western Ontario, Faculty of Graduate Studies, Social Sciences Division, Faculty of Education, Program in Educational Studies, London, ON N6A 5B8, Canada. Offers curriculum studies (M Ed); educational policy studies (M Ed); educational psychology/special education (M Ed). *Program availability:* Part-time. *Faculty research:* Reflective practice, gender and schooling, feminist pedagogy, narrative inquiry, second language, multiculturalism in Canada, education and law.

University of West Florida, College of Education and Professional Studies, Department of Research and Advanced Studies, Ed S Program in Curriculum and Instruction, Pensacola, FL 32514-5750. Offers Ed S. *Accreditation:* NCATE. *Program availability:* Evening/weekend. *Entrance requirements:* Additional exam requirements/recommendations for international students: Required—TOEFL (minimum score 550 paper-based).

University of West Florida, College of Education and Professional Studies, Department of Teacher Education and Educational Leadership, Program in Curriculum and Instruction, Pensacola, FL 32514-5750. Offers elementary education (M Ed); middle level education (M Ed); secondary education (M Ed). *Program availability:* Part-time, evening/weekend. *Entrance requirements:* For master's, GRE (minimum score 450 verbal) or MAT (minimum score 396) if bachelor's GPA less than 3.0, state teaching certification; letter of intent; two professional references. Additional exam requirements/recommendations for international students: Required—TOEFL (minimum score 550 paper-based).

University of Wisconsin–Madison, Graduate School, School of Education, Department of Curriculum and Instruction, Madison, WI 53706-1380. Offers curriculum and instruction (MS, PhD); English as a second language (MS). *Accreditation:* NASM (one or more programs are accredited). *Degree requirements:* For doctorate, thesis/dissertation.

University of Wisconsin–Milwaukee, Graduate School, School of Education, Department of Curriculum and Instruction, Milwaukee, WI 53201-0413. Offers curriculum and instruction (MS), including cross-curricular focus, early childhood education, English education, mathematics education, middle childhood/early adolescence education, reading education, science education, urban social studies education. *Program availability:* Part-time. *Students:* 17 full-time (13 women), 45 part-time (39 women); includes 13 minority (2 Black or African American, non-Hispanic/Latino; 3 Asian, non-Hispanic/Latino; 1 Hispanic/Latino; 7 Two or more races, non-Hispanic/Latino). Average age 33. 32 applicants, 66% accepted, 16 enrolled. In 2017, 26 master's awarded. *Entrance requirements:* Additional exam requirements/recommendations for international students: Required—TOEFL (minimum score 550 paper-based; 79 iBT), IELTS (minimum score 6.5). *Application deadline:* For fall admission, 1/1 priority date for domestic students; for spring admission, 9/1 for domestic students. Application fee: $56 ($96 for international students). Electronic applications accepted. *Financial support:* Fellowships, research assistantships, teaching assistantships, career-related internships or fieldwork, health care benefits, unspecified assistantships, and project assistantships available. Support available to part-time students. Financial award application deadline: 4/15; financial award applicants required to submit FAFSA. *Application contact:* General Information Contact, 414-229-4721, E-mail: soeinfo@uwm.edu.
Website: http://uwm.edu/education/academics/curriculum-instruction-department/

University of Wisconsin–Milwaukee, Graduate School, School of Education, Department of Exceptional Education, Milwaukee, WI 53201-0413. Offers autism spectrum disorders (Graduate Certificate); exceptional education (MS); transition for students with disabilities (Graduate Certificate); urban education (MS), including adult, continuing and higher education leadership, art education, curriculum and instruction, exceptional education, mathematics education, multicultural studies, social foundations of education. *Program availability:* Part-time. *Students:* 45 full-time (34 women), 68 part-time (54 women); includes 46 minority (27 Black or African American, non-Hispanic/Latino; 7 Asian, non-Hispanic/Latino; 1 Hispanic/Latino; 11 Two or more races, non-Hispanic/Latino), 4 international. Average age 39. 43 applicants, 53% accepted, 19

enrolled. In 2017, 12 master's, 13 doctorates, 8 other advanced degrees awarded. *Entrance requirements:* Additional exam requirements/recommendations for international students: Required—TOEFL (minimum score 550 paper-based; 79 iBT), IELTS (minimum score 6.5). *Application deadline:* For fall admission, 1/1 priority date for domestic students; for spring admission, 9/1 for domestic students. Application fee: $56 ($96 for international students). Electronic applications accepted. *Financial support:* Fellowships, research assistantships, teaching assistantships, career-related internships or fieldwork, health care benefits, and unspecified assistantships available. Support available to part-time students. Financial award application deadline: 4/15; financial award applicants required to submit FAFSA. *Faculty research:* Emotional disturbance, hearing impairment, learning disabilities, mental retardation. *Application contact:* General Information Contact, 414-229-4721, E-mail: soeinfo@uwm.edu.
Website: http://uwm.edu/education/academics/exceptional-edu-department

University of Wisconsin–Oshkosh, Graduate Studies, College of Education and Human Services, Department of Curriculum and Instruction, Oshkosh, WI 54901. Offers MSE. *Program availability:* Part-time, evening/weekend. *Degree requirements:* For master's, thesis or alternative, seminar paper. *Entrance requirements:* For master's, teaching license, letters of recommendation. Additional exam requirements/recommendations for international students: Required—TOEFL (minimum score 550 paper-based; 79 iBT). Electronic applications accepted. *Faculty research:* Early childhood, middle school teaching, literacy, elementary teaching, bilingual education.

University of Wisconsin–Superior, Graduate Division, Department of Teacher Education, Program in Instruction, Superior, WI 54880-4500. Offers MSE. *Program availability:* Part-time, evening/weekend. *Degree requirements:* For master's, comprehensive exam, thesis or alternative, research project. *Entrance requirements:* For master's, minimum GPA of 2.75, teaching certificate. Electronic applications accepted.

University of Wyoming, College of Education, Programs in Curriculum and Instruction, Laramie, WY 82071. Offers MA, Ed D, PhD. *Program availability:* Part-time, online learning. Terminal master's awarded for partial completion of doctoral program. *Degree requirements:* For master's, comprehensive exam, thesis; for doctorate, comprehensive exam, thesis/dissertation. *Entrance requirements:* For master's, minimum GPA of 3.0, 3 letters of reference, writing samples; for doctorate, accredited master's degree, 3 letters of reference, 3 years of teaching experience, writing sample. Additional exam requirements/recommendations for international students: Required—TOEFL (minimum score 525 paper-based). *Faculty research:* Teaching and learning teacher education, multi-cultural education, early childhood, discipline-specific pedagogy.

Utah State University, School of Graduate Studies, Emma Eccles Jones College of Education and Human Services, Doctoral Program in Education, Logan, UT 84322. Offers business information systems (Ed D, PhD); curriculum and instruction (Ed D, PhD); research and evaluation (PhD). *Degree requirements:* For doctorate, comprehensive exam, thesis/dissertation. *Entrance requirements:* For doctorate, GRE General Test, minimum GPA of 3.0, master's degree. Additional exam requirements/recommendations for international students: Required—TOEFL. Electronic applications accepted. *Faculty research:* Language and literacy development, math and science education, instructional technology, hearing problems/deafness, domestic violence and animal abuse.

Virginia Commonwealth University, Graduate School, School of Education, Doctoral Program in Education, Richmond, VA 23284-9005. Offers art education (PhD); counselor education and supervision (PhD); curriculum, culture and change (PhD); educational leadership (PhD); educational psychology (PhD); leadership (Ed D); research and evaluation (PhD); special education and disability leadership (PhD); sport leadership (PhD); urban services leadership (PhD). *Accreditation:* NCATE. *Program availability:* Part-time. *Degree requirements:* For doctorate, thesis/dissertation. *Entrance requirements:* For doctorate, GRE (for PhD), MAT (for Ed D), interview, master's degree, writing sample. Additional exam requirements/recommendations for international students: Required—TOEFL (minimum score 600 paper-based; 100 iBT). Electronic applications accepted.

Virginia Polytechnic Institute and State University, Graduate School, College of Liberal Arts and Human Sciences, Blacksburg, VA 24061. Offers career and technical education (MS Ed, Ed S); communication (MA); counselor education (MA); creative writing (MFA); curriculum and instruction (MA Ed, Ed S); educational leadership and policy studies (Ed S); educational research and evaluation (PhD); English (MA); social, political, ethical, and cultural thought (PhD); Ed D/PhD. *Faculty:* 411 full-time (213 women), 3 part-time/adjunct (all women). *Students:* 623 full-time (427 women), 431 part-time (278 women); includes 203 minority (115 Black or African American, non-Hispanic/Latino; 4 American Indian or Alaska Native, non-Hispanic/Latino; 29 Asian, non-Hispanic/Latino; 33 Hispanic/Latino; 2 Native Hawaiian or other Pacific Islander, non-Hispanic/Latino; 20 Two or more races, non-Hispanic/Latino), 87 international. Average age 34. 898 applicants, 50% accepted, 329 enrolled. In 2017, 314 master's, 102 doctorates awarded. *Degree requirements:* For master's, comprehensive exam (for some programs), thesis (for some programs); for doctorate, comprehensive exam (for some programs), thesis/dissertation (for some programs). *Entrance requirements:* For master's and doctorate, GRE/GMAT. Additional exam requirements/recommendations for international students: Required—TOEFL (minimum score 80 iBT). *Application deadline:* For fall admission, 8/1 for domestic students, 4/1 for international students; for spring admission, 1/1 for domestic students, 9/1 for international students. Applications are processed on a rolling basis. Application fee: $75. Electronic applications accepted. *Expenses:* Tuition, state resident: full-time $15,072; part-time $718.50 per credit hour. Tuition, nonresident: full-time $28,810; part-time $1448.25 per credit hour. *Required fees:* $2741; $502 per semester. Tuition and fees vary according to course load, campus/location and program. *Financial support:* In 2017–18, 19 research assistantships with full tuition reimbursements (averaging $19,611 per year), 226 teaching assistantships with full tuition reimbursements (averaging $16,220 per year) were awarded. Financial award application deadline: 3/1; financial award applicants required to submit FAFSA. *Total annual research expenditures:* $7.9 million. *Unit head:* Dr. Rosemary Blieszner, Dean, 540-231-6779, Fax: 540-231-7157, E-mail: rmb@vt.edu. *Application contact:* Chelsea Blanchet, Executive Assistant, 540-231-6779, Fax: 540-231-7157, E-mail: bchels1@vt.edu.
Website: http://www.liberalarts.vt.edu/

Virginia Union University, Evelyn R. Syphax School of Education, Psychology and Interdisciplinary Studies, Richmond, VA 23220-1170. Offers curriculum and instruction (MA).

Walden University, Graduate Programs, Richard W. Riley College of Education and Leadership, Minneapolis, MN 55401. Offers adult education (Post-Master's Certificate); adult learning (Graduate Certificate); college teaching and learning (Graduate Certificate); community college leadership (Ed D); curriculum, instruction and assessment (Ed D, Ed S, Graduate Certificate); developmental education (Graduate Certificate); early childhood administration, management, and leadership (Graduate Certificate); early childhood education (Ed D, Ed S); early childhood public policy and advocacy (Graduate Certificate); early childhood studies (MS), including administration, management and leadership, early childhood public policy and advocacy, teaching adults in the early childhood field, teaching and diversity in early childhood education; education (MS, PhD), including adolescent literacy and learning (MS), curriculum, instruction, and assessment (grades K-12) (MS), curriculum, instruction, assessment and evaluation (PhD), early childhood leadership and advocacy (PhD), early childhood special education (PhD), educational leadership (MS), educational leadership and administration (principal preparation) (MS), educational technology and design (PhD), elementary reading and literacy (PreK-6) (MS), elementary reading and mathematics (grades K-6) (MS), global and comparative education (PhD), higher education leadership management and policy (PhD), integrating technology in the classroom (grades K-12) (MS), learning, instruction and innovation (PhD), mathematics (grades 5-8) (MS), mathematics (grades K-6) (MS), mathematics and science (grades K-8) (MS), organizational research, assessment, and evaluation (PhD), reading and literacy with a reading K-12 endorsement (MS), reading literacy assessment and evaluation (PhD), science (grades K-8) (MS), special education (non-licensure) (grades K-12) (MS), teacher leadership (grades K-12) (MS), teaching English language learners (grades K-12) (MS); educational administration and leadership (Ed D); educational leadership and administration (principal preparation) (Ed S); educational technology (Ed D, Ed S, Post Master's Certificate); elementary reading and literacy (Graduate Certificate); engaging culturally diverse learners (Graduate Certificate); enrollment management and institutional marketing (Graduate Certificate); higher education (MS), including adult learning, college teaching and learning, enrollment management and institutional marketing, global higher education, leadership for student success, online and distance learning; higher education and adult learning (Ed D); higher education leadership and management (Ed D); higher education leadership for student success (Graduate Certificate); instructional design and technology (MS, Postbaccalaureate Certificate), including general program (MS), online learning (MS), training and performance improvement (MS); integrating technology in the classroom (Graduate Certificate); mathematics 5-8 (Graduate Certificate); mathematics K-6 (Graduate Certificate); online teaching for adult educators (Graduate Certificate); reading, literacy, and assessment (Ed D, Ed S); science K-8 (Graduate Certificate); special education (Ed D, Ed S, Graduate Certificate); special education (K-age 21) (MAT); teacher leadership (Graduate Certificate); teaching adults English as a second language (Graduate Certificate); teaching adults in the early childhood field (Graduate Certificate); teaching and diversity in early childhood education (Graduate Certificate); teaching English language learners (grades K-12) (Graduate Certificate); teaching K-12 students online (Graduate Certificate). *Accreditation:* NCATE. *Program availability:* Part-time, evening/weekend, online only, 100% online. *Degree requirements:* For doctorate, thesis/dissertation (for some programs), residency; for other advanced degree, residency (for some programs). *Entrance requirements:* For master's, bachelor's degree or higher; minimum GPA of 2.5; official transcripts; goal statement (for some programs); access to computer and Internet; for doctorate, master's degree or higher; three years of related professional or academic experience (preferred); minimum GPA of 3.0; goal statement and current resume (for select programs); official transcripts; access to computer and Internet; for other advanced degree, relevant work experience; access to computer and Internet. Additional exam requirements/recommendations for international students: Required—TOEFL (minimum score 550 paper-based, 79 iBT), IELTS (minimum score 6.5), Michigan English Language Assessment Battery (minimum score 82), or PTE (minimum score 53). Electronic applications accepted.

Walla Walla University, Graduate Studies, School of Education and Psychology, College Place, WA 99324. Offers curriculum and instruction (M Ed, MAT); educational leadership (M Ed, MAT); literacy instruction (M Ed, MAT); special education (M Ed, MAT). *Program availability:* Part-time. *Entrance requirements:* For master's, GRE General Test, minimum GPA of 2.75. Additional exam requirements/recommendations for international students: Required—TOEFL (minimum score 550 paper-based; 79 iBT). *Application deadline:* For fall admission, 4/1 priority date for domestic students. Applications are processed on a rolling basis. Application fee: $50. Electronic applications accepted. *Financial support:* Research assistantships, teaching assistantships, Federal Work-Study, and tuition waivers (partial) available. Support available to part-time students. Financial award application deadline: 4/30; financial award applicants required to submit FAFSA. *Faculty research:* Admissions/retention, instructional psychology, moral development, teaching of reading. *Unit head:* Dr. Debbie Muthersbaugh, Dean, 509-527-2212, Fax: 509-527-2248, E-mail: debbie.muthersbaugh@wallawalla.edu. *Application contact:* Dr. Joe G. Galusha, Dean of Graduate Studies, 509-527-2421, Fax: 509-527-2237, E-mail: joe.galusha@wallawalla.edu.
Website: https://wallawalla.edu/academics/areas-of-study/undergraduate-programs/education-and-psychology/

Warner University, School of Education, Lake Wales, FL 33859. Offers curriculum and instruction (MAEd); elementary education (MAEd); science, technology, engineering, and mathematics (STEM) (MAEd). *Program availability:* Part-time, evening/weekend, online learning. *Degree requirements:* For master's, thesis, accomplished practices portfolio. *Entrance requirements:* For master's, minimum GPA of 3.0 in last 60 hours of undergraduate coursework; 2 letters of recommendation. Additional exam requirements/recommendations for international students: Required—TOEFL (minimum score 550 paper-based). Electronic applications accepted.

Washburn University, College of Arts and Sciences, Department of Education, Topeka, KS 66621. Offers curriculum and instruction (M Ed); educational leadership (M Ed); reading (M Ed); special education (M Ed). *Accreditation:* NCATE. *Program availability:* Part-time. *Degree requirements:* For master's, comprehensive exam, thesis or alternative, portfolio, comprehensive paper, or action research project. *Entrance requirements:* For master's, department exam, GRE General Test, or MAT, minimum GPA of 3.0 in graduate coursework or last 60 hours of undergraduate coursework. Additional exam requirements/recommendations for international students: Required—TOEFL (minimum score 80 iBT). *Faculty research:* Reading/literature/literacy, foundations, special education, diversity, teaching and technology.

Washington State University, College of Education, Department of Teaching and Learning, Pullman, WA 99164-2132. Offers cultural studies and social thought in education (PhD); curriculum and instruction (Ed M, MA); English language learners (Ed M, MA); language, literacy and technology (PhD); literacy education (Ed M, MA); mathematics education (PhD); special education (Ed M, MA, PhD); teacher leadership (Ed D); teaching (MIT), including elementary education, secondary education. Programs offered at the Pullman, Spokane, Tri-cities, Vancouver and Global (online) campuses. *Program availability:* Part-time, online learning. *Degree requirements:* For master's, comprehensive exam, thesis, oral or written exam; for doctorate, comprehensive exam, thesis/dissertation, oral and written exam. *Entrance requirements:* For master's, GRE General Test, minimum GPA of 3.0, 3 letters of recommendation, letter of intent, transcripts, resume/curriculum vitae; for doctorate, GRE General Test, minimum GPA of 3.0, 3 letters of recommendation, letter of intent, transcripts, writing sample, resume/curriculum vitae. Additional exam requirements/recommendations for international students: Required—TOEFL (minimum score 550 paper-based; 80 iBT). Electronic applications accepted. *Faculty research:* Intersection of gender, youth cultures and schooling; examination of ideology of power in children's literature; early childhood special education; analyzing pre-service and in-service teacher development; second language acquisition.

Waynesburg University, Graduate and Professional Studies, Canonsburg, PA 15370. Offers business (MBA), including energy management, finance, health systems, human resources, leadership, market development; counseling (MA), including addictions counseling, clinical mental health; counselor education and supervision (PhD); criminal investigation (MA); education (M Ed), including autism, curriculum and instruction, educational leadership, online teaching; nursing (MSN), including administration, education, informatics; nursing practice (DNP); special education (M Ed); technology (M Ed); MSN/MBA. *Accreditation:* AACN. *Program availability:* Part-time, evening/weekend. *Degree requirements:* For doctorate, thesis/dissertation. *Entrance requirements:* Additional exam requirements/recommendations for international students: Required—TOEFL. Electronic applications accepted.

Wayne State College, School of Education and Counseling, Department of Educational Foundations and Leadership, Program in Curriculum and Instruction, Wayne, NE 68787. Offers alternative education (MSE); business and information technology education (MSE); communication arts education (MSE); early childhood education (MSE); elementary education (MSE); English as a second language (MSE); English education (MSE); family and consumer sciences education (MSE); industrial technology and vocational education (MSE); learning communities (MSE); mathematics education (MSE); music education (MSE); science education (MSE); social science education (MSE). *Accreditation:* NCATE. *Program availability:* Part-time, evening/weekend. *Degree requirements:* For master's, comprehensive exam, thesis optional. *Entrance requirements:* For master's, GRE General Test. Additional exam requirements/recommendations for international students: Required—TOEFL (minimum score 550 paper-based).

Wayne State University, College of Education, Division of Teacher Education, Detroit, MI 48202. Offers art education (M Ed); bilingual/bicultural education (Certificate); curriculum and instruction (Ed D, PhD, Ed S), including English as a second language (MAT, Ed D, Ed S), K-12 curriculum (PhD); elementary education (MAT), including bilingual/bicultural education (M Ed, MAT), early childhood education (M Ed, MAT), English as a second language (MAT, Ed D, Ed S), foreign language education, science education (M Ed, MAT), special education (M Ed, MAT); elementary mathematics specialist (Certificate); English as a second language (Certificate); reading (M Ed, Ed S); reading, language and literature (Ed D); secondary education (MAT), including bilingual/bicultural education (M Ed, MAT), early childhood education (M Ed, MAT), English as a second language (MAT, Ed D, Ed S), English education, foreign language education, mathematics education (M Ed, MAT), science education (M Ed, MAT), social studies education (M Ed, MAT); special education (MAT), including career and technical education; teaching and learning (M Ed), including bilingual/bicultural education (M Ed, MAT), early childhood education (M Ed, MAT), elementary education, foreign language, mathematics education (M Ed, MAT), science education (M Ed, MAT), social studies education (M Ed, MAT), special education (M Ed, MAT). *Program availability:* Part-time, blended/hybrid learning. *Faculty:* 22. *Students:* 126 full-time (96 women), 317 part-time (258 women); includes 134 minority (95 Black or African American, non-Hispanic/Latino; 1 American Indian or Alaska Native, non-Hispanic/Latino; 8 Asian, non-Hispanic/Latino; 17 Hispanic/Latino; 1 Native Hawaiian or other Pacific Islander, non-Hispanic/Latino; 12 Two or more races, non-Hispanic/Latino), 13 international. Average age 37. 260 applicants, 33% accepted, 57 enrolled. In 2017, 111 master's, 13 doctorates, 7 other advanced degrees awarded. *Degree requirements:* For master's, essay or project (for some M Ed programs), professional field experience (for MAT programs); for doctorate, thesis/dissertation. *Entrance requirements:* For master's, Michigan Test for Teacher Certification (for most programs), verification of participation in group work with children (for MAT programs), Michigan State Police criminal background check; for doctorate, minimum undergraduate GPA of 3.0, graduate 3.5; interview; curriculum vitae; references; master's degree (for most programs). Additional exam requirements/recommendations for international students: Required—TOEFL (minimum score 550 paper-based; 79 iBT), TWE (minimum score 5.5); Recommended—IELTS (minimum score 6.5). *Application deadline:* For fall admission, 6/1 priority date for domestic students, 5/1 priority date for international students; for winter admission, 10/1 priority date for domestic students, 9/1 priority date for international students; for spring admission, 2/1 priority date for domestic students, 1/1 priority date for international students. Applications are processed on a rolling basis. Application fee: $50. Electronic applications accepted. *Expenses:* Tuition, state resident: full-time $10,224; part-time $638.98 per credit hour. Tuition, nonresident: full-time $22,145; part-time $1384.04 per credit hour. Tuition and fees vary according to course load and program. *Financial support:* In 2017–18, 78 students received support, including 4 fellowships (averaging $13,500 per year), 1 research assistantship with tuition reimbursement available (averaging $16,000 per year); Federal Work-Study, scholarships/grants, and unspecified assistantships also available. Support available to part-time students. Financial award applicants required to submit FAFSA. *Faculty research:* Improving students' skill achievement in mathematics, improving elementary children's understanding of informational text, teachers' use of their pedagogical and mathematical knowledge in the interactive work of teaching, the intersection of identity construction in teaching and learning, identifying effective methods of literacy instruction and assessments for bilingual students in elementary language arts classrooms. *Unit head:* Dr. Thomas Edwards, Interim Associate Dean for Teacher Education, 313-577-3886, E-mail: t.g.edwards@wayne.edu. *Application contact:* 313-577-0902, E-mail: askcoe@wayne.edu.
Website: http://coe.wayne.edu/ted/index.php

Weber State University, Jerry and Vickie Moyes College of Education, Program in Curriculum and Instruction, Ogden, UT 84408-1001. Offers M Ed. *Accreditation:* NCATE. *Program availability:* Part-time, evening/weekend. *Faculty:* 20 full-time (13 women), 1 (woman) part-time/adjunct. *Students:* 8 full-time (7 women), 128 part-time (105 women); includes 2 minority (1 Asian, non-Hispanic/Latino; 1 Hispanic/Latino), 1 international. Average age 37. In 2017, 42 master's awarded. *Degree requirements:* For master's, thesis or alternative, project presentation, exam. *Entrance requirements:* For master's, MAT or GRE, minimum GPA of 3.0. Additional exam requirements/recommendations for international students: Required—TOEFL (minimum score 85 iBT). *Application deadline:* For fall admission, 5/15 for domestic students; for spring admission, 9/15 for domestic students; for summer admission, 1/15 for domestic students. Application fee: $60 ($90 for international students). Electronic applications accepted. *Expenses:* Contact institution. *Financial support:* In 2017–18, 6 students received support. Scholarships/grants available. Financial award application deadline: 4/1; financial award applicants required to submit FAFSA. *Unit head:* Dr. Peggy Saunders, Director, 801-626-7673, Fax: 801-626-7427, E-mail: psaunders@weber.edu. *Application contact:* Nathan Alexander, College of Education Recruiter, 801-626-8124, Fax: 801-626-7427, E-mail: nathanalexander@weber.edu.
Website: http://www.weber.edu/COE/med.html

Western Connecticut State University, Division of Graduate Studies, School of Professional Studies, Department of Education and Educational Psychology, Curriculum Option, Danbury, CT 06810-6885. Offers MS. *Program availability:* Part-time. *Degree requirements:* For master's, thesis or alternative, thesis research project or 3 extra classes and comprehensive exam, completion of program in 6 years. *Entrance requirements:* For master's, minimum GPA of 2.8 or MAT, teaching certificate in elementary or secondary education. Additional exam requirements/recommendations for international students: Recommended—TOEFL (minimum score 550 paper-based; 79 iBT), IELTS (minimum score 6). *Expenses:* Tuition, state resident: full-time $6757; part-time $374 per credit hour. Tuition, nonresident: full-time $18,102; part-time $374 per credit hour. *Required fees:* $4994; $190 per credit hour. $60 per term. Tuition and fees vary according to degree level and program. *Faculty research:* Teaching various methods of instruction that include class discussions, lectures, independent projects, cooperative learning, experiential learning and field studies, recitals, demonstrations, shows, group projects, and technology-enhanced instruction.

Western Illinois University, School of Graduate Studies, College of Education and Human Services, Department of Curriculum and Instruction, Program in Curriculum and Instruction, Macomb, IL 61455-1390. Offers MS Ed. *Accreditation:* NCATE. *Program availability:* Part-time. *Students:* 82 part-time (76 women); includes 4 minority (1 Black or African American, non-Hispanic/Latino; 1 Asian, non-Hispanic/Latino; 2 Hispanic/Latino). Average age 34. 14 applicants, 93% accepted, 10 enrolled. In 2017, 33 master's awarded. *Degree requirements:* For master's, thesis or alternative. *Entrance requirements:* Additional exam requirements/recommendations for international students: Required—TOEFL (minimum score 550 paper-based; 80 iBT). *Application deadline:* Applications are processed on a rolling basis. Application fee: $30. Electronic applications accepted. *Financial support:* Applicants required to submit FAFSA. *Unit head:* Dr. Barry Witten, Interim Chairperson, 309-298-1961. *Application contact:* Dr. Nancy Parsons, Assistant Director of Graduate Studies, 309-298-1806, Fax: 309-298-2345, E-mail: grad-office@wiu.edu.
Website: http://wiu.edu/curriculum

Western New England University, College of Arts and Sciences, Program in Curriculum and Instruction, Springfield, MA 01119. Offers M Ed. *Program availability:* Part-time, evening/weekend, online learning. *Faculty:* 3 full-time (2 women). *Students:* 8 part-time (all women). Average age 28. 11 applicants, 100% accepted, 10 enrolled. In 2017, 8 master's awarded. *Entrance requirements:* For master's, initial license for elementary teaching, two letters of recommendation, official transcript, resume, personal statement. Additional exam requirements/recommendations for international students: Required—TOEFL (minimum score 79 iBT). *Application deadline:* Applications are processed on a rolling basis. Application fee: $30. Electronic applications accepted. *Expenses:* Contact institution. *Financial support:* Application deadline: 4/15; applicants required to submit FAFSA. *Unit head:* Dr. Saeed Ghahramani, Dean, 413-782-1218, Fax: 413-796-2118, E-mail: sghahram@wne.edu. *Application contact:* Matthew Fox, Director of Admissions for Graduate Students and Adult Learners, 413-782-1410, Fax: 413-782-1777, E-mail: study@wne.edu.
Website: http://www1.wne.edu/academics/graduate/education-curriculum-and-instruction.cfm

West Texas A&M University, College of Education and Social Sciences, Department of Education, Program in Curriculum and Instruction, Canyon, TX 79015. Offers M Ed. *Program availability:* Part-time, evening/weekend, online learning. *Degree requirements:* For master's, comprehensive exam, thesis optional. *Entrance requirements:* For master's, GRE General Test, 18 semester hours of education course work. Additional exam requirements/recommendations for international students: Required—TOEFL (minimum score 550 paper-based). Electronic applications accepted.

West Virginia University, College of Education and Human Services, Morgantown, WV 26506. Offers audiology (Au D); autism spectrum disorder (MA); clinical rehabilitation and mental health counseling (MS); communication science and disorders (PhD); counseling (MA); counseling psychology (PhD); curriculum and instruction (Ed D); early childhood education (MA); early intervention (MA); education (PhD); educational leadership (MA, Ed D); educational leadership/public school administration (MA); educational psychology (MA, Ed D); elementary education (MA); gifted education (MA); higher education administration (MA, Ed D); higher education curriculum and teaching (MA); institutional design and technology (MA); instructional design and technology (Ed D); literacy education (MA); secondary education (MA); secondary education/English (MA); special education (Ed D); speech pathology (MS). *Accreditation:* NCATE. *Program availability:* Part-time, evening/weekend, online learning. *Students:* 423 full-time (347 women), 367 part-time (316 women); includes 57 minority (14 Black or African American, non-Hispanic/Latino; 7 Asian, non-Hispanic/Latino; 20 Hispanic/Latino; 16 Two or more races, non-Hispanic/Latino), 13 international. *Degree requirements:* For master's, content exams; for doctorate, comprehensive exam, thesis/dissertation. *Entrance requirements:* Additional exam requirements/recommendations for international students: Required—TOEFL (minimum score 500 paper-based; 61 iBT). *Application deadline:* For fall admission, 8/1 for domestic students; for spring admission, 1/1 for domestic students; for summer admission, 5/1 for domestic students. Application fee: $60. Electronic applications accepted. *Expenses:* Tuition, state resident: full-time $9450. Tuition, nonresident: full-time $24,390. *Financial support:* Fellowships, research assistantships, teaching assistantships, career-related internships or fieldwork, Federal Work-Study, institutionally sponsored loans, health care benefits, tuition waivers (full and partial), and administrative assistantships available. Financial award applicants required to submit FAFSA. *Faculty research:* Internet training and integration for teachers, rural education, teacher preparation, organization of schools, evaluation of personnel. *Unit head:* Dr. Gypsy Denzine, Dean, 304-293-5703, Fax: 304-293-7565, E-mail: gypsy.denzine@mail.wvu.edu. *Application contact:* Dr. M. Cecil Smith, Associate Dean for Research and Graduate Education, 304-293-2174, Fax: 304-293-3802, E-mail: mcecil.smith@mail.wvu.edu.
Website: http://cehs.wvu.edu/

Wichita State University, Graduate School, College of Education, Department of Curriculum and Instruction, Wichita, KS 67260. Offers learning and instructional design (M Ed); special education (M Ed), including early childhood (M Ed, MAT), gifted, high incidence, low incidence; teaching (MAT), including early childhood (M Ed, MAT), middle level/secondary, transition to teaching. *Accreditation:* NCATE. *Program availability:* Part-time, evening/weekend, 100% online, blended/hybrid learning. *Entrance requirements:* For master's, MAT, minimum GPA of 2.75. *Unit head:* Dr. Kimberly McDowell, Department Head, 316-978-3322, E-mail: kim.mcdowell@wichita.edu. *Application contact:* Jordan Oleson, Admission Coordinator, 316-978-3095, Fax: 316-978-3253, E-mail: jordan.oleson@wichita.edu.

William Woods University, Graduate and Adult Studies, Fulton, MO 65251-1098. Offers administration (M Ed); athletic/activities administration (M Ed); curriculum and instruction (M Ed, Ed S); educational leadership (Ed D); equestrian education (M Ed); health management (MBA); human resources (MBA); leadership (MBA); marketing, advertising, and public relations (MBA); teaching and technology (M Ed). *Program availability:* Part-time, evening/weekend. *Degree requirements:* For master's, capstone course (MBA), action research (M Ed); for Ed S, field experience. *Entrance requirements:* Additional exam requirements/recommendations for international students: Required—TOEFL (minimum score 550 paper-based). Electronic applications accepted. *Expenses:* Contact institution.

Wisconsin Lutheran College, College of Adult and Graduate Studies, Milwaukee, WI 53226-9942. Offers high performance instruction (MA Ed); instructional technology (MA Ed); leadership and innovation (MA Ed); science instruction (MA Ed).

Worcester State University, Graduate School, Department of Education, Worcester, MA 01602-2597. Offers curriculum and instruction (Ed S); early childhood education (M Ed, Postbaccalaureate Certificate); education (M Ed); elementary education (M Ed, Postbaccalaureate Certificate); English as a second language (M Ed, Postbaccalaureate Certificate); health education (M Ed); leadership and administration (M Ed); middle school education (M Ed, Postbaccalaureate Certificate); moderate disabilities (M Ed, Postbaccalaureate Certificate); reading (M Ed, Postbaccalaureate Certificate); school psychology (M Ed, Ed S); secondary education (M Ed, Ed S, Postbaccalaureate Certificate). *Program availability:* Part-time, evening/weekend. *Faculty:* 6 full-time, 21 part-time/adjunct. *Students:* 41 full-time (36 women), 289 part-time (209 women); includes 29 minority (5 Black or African American, non-Hispanic/Latino; 3 American Indian or Alaska Native, non-Hispanic/Latino; 1 Asian, non-Hispanic/Latino; 13 Hispanic/Latino; 7 Two or more races, non-Hispanic/Latino), 1 international. Average age 34. 237 applicants, 70% accepted, 101 enrolled. In 2017, 74 master's, 141 Ed Ss awarded. *Degree requirements:* For master's, comprehensive exam (for some programs), thesis (for some programs). *Entrance requirements:* For master's, GRE General Test, MAT or GMAT, teaching certificate. Additional exam requirements/recommendations for international students: Required—TOEFL (minimum score 550 paper-based; 79 iBT). *Application deadline:* For fall admission, 6/15 for domestic and international students; for spring admission, 11/1 for domestic and international students; for summer admission, 4/1 for domestic and international students. Applications are processed on a rolling basis. Application fee: $50. Electronic applications accepted. *Expenses:* Tuition, state resident: full-time $3042; part-time $169 per credit hour. Tuition, nonresident: full-time $3042; part-time $169 per credit hour. *Required fees:* $2754; $153 per credit hour. *Financial support:* Career-related internships or fieldwork, scholarships/grants, and unspecified assistantships available. Financial award application deadline: 3/1; financial award applicants required to submit FAFSA. *Unit head:* Dr. Sue Foo, Department Chair, 508-929-8071, E-mail: sfoo@worcester.edu. *Application contact:* Sara Grady, Associate Dean of Graduate and Continuing Education, 508-929-8130, Fax: 508-929-8100, E-mail: sara.grady@worcester.edu.

Wright State University, Graduate School, College of Education and Human Services, Department of Educational Leadership, Program in Advanced Educational Leadership, Dayton, OH 45435. Offers advanced curriculum and instruction (Ed S). *Accreditation:* NCATE. *Degree requirements:* For Ed S, thesis. *Entrance requirements:* For degree, GRE General Test, MAT. Additional exam requirements/recommendations for international students: Required—TOEFL.

Xavier University of Louisiana, Graduate School, Programs in Education, New Orleans, LA 70125. Offers counseling (MA); curriculum and instruction (MA); educational leadership (MA). *Accreditation:* NCATE. *Program availability:* Part-time, evening/weekend. *Degree requirements:* For master's, comprehensive exam, thesis or alternative. *Entrance requirements:* For master's, GRE General Test, MAT, minimum GPA of 2.5. Additional exam requirements/recommendations for international students: Required—TOEFL.

Youngstown State University, Graduate School, Beeghly College of Education, Department of Teacher Education, Youngstown, OH 44555-0001. Offers adolescent/young adult education (MS Ed); content area concentration (MS Ed); early childhood education (MS Ed); educational technology (MS Ed); literacy (MS Ed); middle childhood education (MS Ed); special education (MS Ed), including gifted and talented education, special education. *Accreditation:* NCATE. *Program availability:* Part-time, evening/weekend. *Degree requirements:* For master's, comprehensive exam. *Entrance requirements:* For master's, GRE, MAT, or teaching certificate; minimum GPA of 2.7. Additional exam requirements/recommendations for international students: Required—TOEFL. *Faculty research:* Multicultural literacy, hands-on mathematics teaching, integrated instruction, reading comprehension, emergent curriculum.

Distance Education Development

Athabasca University, Centre for Distance Education, Athabasca, AB T9S 3A3, Canada. Offers distance education (MDE, Ed D); distance education technology (Advanced Diploma). *Program availability:* Part-time, online learning. *Degree requirements:* For master's, thesis optional. *Entrance requirements:* For master's, 3- or 4-year baccalaureate degree. Electronic applications accepted. *Expenses:* Contact institution. *Faculty research:* Role development, interaction, educational technology, and communities of practice in distance education; instructional design.

Barry University, School of Education, Graduate Certificate Programs, Miami Shores, FL 33161-6695. Offers advanced teaching and learning with technology (Certificate); distance education (Certificate); higher education technology integration (Certificate); human resources: not for profit and religious organizations (Certificate); K-12 technology integration (Certificate).

Boise State University, College of Education, Department of Educational Technology, Boise, ID 83725-0399. Offers educational technology (MET, MS, Ed D); online teaching (Graduate Certificate); school technology coordination (Graduate Certificate);

technology integration (Graduate Certificate). *Accreditation:* NCATE. *Program availability:* Part-time, 100% online, blended/hybrid learning. *Faculty:* 27. *Students:* 13 full-time (7 women), 422 part-time (242 women); includes 41 minority (11 Black or African American, non-Hispanic/Latino; 1 American Indian or Alaska Native, non-Hispanic/Latino; 9 Asian, non-Hispanic/Latino; 17 Hispanic/Latino; 1 Native Hawaiian or other Pacific Islander, non-Hispanic/Latino; 2 Two or more races, non-Hispanic/Latino), 17 international. Average age 38. 192 applicants, 68% accepted, 72 enrolled. In 2017, 151 master's awarded. Terminal master's awarded for partial completion of doctoral program. *Degree requirements:* For master's, thesis optional; for doctorate, thesis/dissertation. *Entrance requirements:* For master's, minimum GPA of 3.0; for doctorate, GRE General Test. Additional exam requirements/recommendations for international students: Required—TOEFL (minimum score 550 paper-based; 80 iBT), IELTS (minimum score 6). *Application deadline:* For fall admission, 2/15 for domestic and international students; for spring admission, 9/15 for domestic and international students. Applications are processed on a rolling basis. Application fee: $65 ($95 for international students). Electronic applications accepted. *Expenses:* Tuition, state resident: full-time $6471; part-time $390 per credit. Tuition, nonresident: full-time $21,787; part-time $685 per credit. *Required fees:* $2283; $100 per term. Part-time tuition and fees vary according to course load and program. *Financial support:* Teaching assistantships, scholarships/grants, and unspecified assistantships available. Financial award application deadline: 3/1; financial award applicants required to submit FAFSA. *Unit head:* Dr. Brett Shelton, Department Chair, 208-426-3391, E-mail: brettshelton@boisestate.edu. *Application contact:* Dr. Ross Perkins, Admissions Coordinator, 208-426-4875, E-mail: edtechdoc@boisestate.edu. Website: http://edtech.boisestate.edu/

Brandeis University, Rabb School of Continuing Studies, Division of Graduate Professional Studies, Master of Science in Instructional Design and Technology Program, Waltham, MA 02454-9110. Offers MS. *Program availability:* Part-time-only. *Faculty:* 55 part-time/adjunct (18 women). *Students:* 11 part-time (7 women). Average age 35. 1 applicant, 100% accepted, 1 enrolled. In 2017, 4 master's awarded. *Entrance requirements:* For master's, four-year bachelor's degree from regionally-accredited U.S. institution or equivalent; official transcript(s) from every college or university attended; resume or curriculum vitae; statement of goals; letter of recommendation. Additional exam requirements/recommendations for international students: Required—TWE (minimum score 4.5), TOEFL (minimum score: 600 paper-based, 100 iBT), IELTS (7), or PTE (68). *Application deadline:* For fall admission, 6/20 priority date for domestic and international students; for winter admission, 9/12 priority date for domestic and international students; for spring admission, 12/19 priority date for domestic and international students; for summer admission, 3/13 priority date for domestic and international students. Applications are processed on a rolling basis. Application fee: $75. Electronic applications accepted. *Expenses:* $825 per credit. *Financial support:* Applicants required to submit FAFSA. *Unit head:* Brian Salerno, Chair, 781-736-3443, E-mail: bsalerno@brandeis.edu. *Application contact:* Frances Stearns, Director of Student and Faculty Operations, 781-736-8785, E-mail: fstearns@brandeis.edu. Website: http://www.brandeis.edu/gps/future-students/learn-about-our-programs/instructional-design.html

California Baptist University, Program in Education, Riverside, CA 92504-3206. Offers educational leadership (MS); educational leadership for faith-based institutions (MS); educational leadership for public institutions (MS); educational technology (MS); instructional computer applications (MS); international education (MS); leadership and adult learning (MS); leadership and organizational studies (MS); online teaching and learning (MS); reading (MS); science education (MA); special education in mild/moderate disabilities (MS); special education in moderate/severe disabilities (MS); teacher leadership (MS); teaching (MS); teaching and learning (MS). *Program availability:* Part-time, evening/weekend, 100% online, blended/hybrid learning. *Faculty:* 19 full-time (11 women), 36 part-time/adjunct (22 women). *Students:* 232 full-time (182 women), 315 part-time (247 women); includes 264 minority (33 Black or African American, non-Hispanic/Latino; 4 American Indian or Alaska Native, non-Hispanic/Latino; 11 Asian, non-Hispanic/Latino; 186 Hispanic/Latino; 7 Native Hawaiian or other Pacific Islander, non-Hispanic/Latino; 23 Two or more races, non-Hispanic/Latino). Average age 31. 217 applicants, 64% accepted, 129 enrolled. In 2017, 196 master's awarded. *Degree requirements:* For master's, comprehensive exam, project, or thesis. *Entrance requirements:* For master's, minimum undergraduate GPA of 2.75; 500-word essay; three letters of recommendation; two prerequisite courses completed with minimum C grade. Additional exam requirements/recommendations for international students: Required—TOEFL (minimum score 80 iBT). *Application deadline:* For fall admission, 8/1 priority date for domestic students, 7/1 for international students; for spring admission, 12/1 priority date for domestic students, 11/1 for international students. Applications are processed on a rolling basis. Application fee: $45. Electronic applications accepted. *Expenses:* Contact institution. *Financial support:* In 2017–18, 162 students received support. Federal Work-Study and scholarships/grants available. Financial award applicants required to submit CSS PROFILE or FAFSA. *Faculty research:* Leadership development, complexity theory, faith and learning, special education, social and philosophical contexts of education. *Unit head:* Dr. John Shoup, Dean, School of Education, 951-343-4516, E-mail: jshoup@calbaptist.edu. *Application contact:* Gavin Andrew, Graduate Admissions Counselor, 951-552-8437, E-mail: gandrew@calbaptist.edu. Website: http://www.calbaptist.edu/mastersined/

Capella University, School of Education, Doctoral Programs in Education, Minneapolis, MN 55402. Offers curriculum and instruction (PhD); educational leadership and management (Ed D); instructional design for online learning (PhD); K-12 studies in education (PhD); leadership for higher education (PhD); leadership in educational administration (PhD); postsecondary and adult education (PhD); professional studies in education (PhD); reading and literacy (Ed D); special education leadership (PhD); training and performance improvement (PhD).

Capella University, School of Education, Master's Programs in Education, Minneapolis, MN 55402. Offers adult education (MS); curriculum and instruction (MS); early childhood education (MS); enrollment management (MS); higher education leadership and management (MS); instructional design for online learning (MS); integrative studies (MS); K-12 studies in education (MS); leadership in educational administration (MS); reading and literacy (MS); special education teaching (MS).

Carlow University, College of Learning and Innovation, Program in Education, Pittsburgh, PA 15213-3165. Offers early childhood education (M Ed); education (M Ed); online instructional design and technology (Certificate); special education (M Ed), including early childhood. *Program availability:* Part-time, evening/weekend, 100% online, blended/hybrid learning. *Students:* 44 full-time (41 women), 14 part-time (13 women); includes 12 minority (8 Black or African American, non-Hispanic/Latino; 1 Asian, non-Hispanic/Latino; 3 Two or more races, non-Hispanic/Latino). Average age 31. 16 applicants, 100% accepted, 12 enrolled. In 2017, 22 master's, 1 Certificate awarded. *Entrance requirements:* For master's, personal essay; resume or curriculum vitae; two recommendations; official transcripts; interview; minimum undergraduate GPA of 3.0. Additional exam requirements/recommendations for international students: Required—TOEFL (minimum score 550 paper-based). *Application deadline:* Applications are processed on a rolling basis. Electronic applications accepted. *Expenses: Tuition:* Full-time $12,103; part-time $825 per credit hour. Tuition and fees vary according to program. *Financial support:* Application deadline: 4/1; applicants required to submit FAFSA. *Unit head:* Dr. Keeley Baronak, Chair, Department of Education, 412-578-6135, Fax: 412-578-8816, E-mail: kobaronak@carlow.edu. *Application contact:* 412-578-6059, E-mail: gradstudies@carlow.edu. Website: http://www.carlow.edu/education.aspx

Clemson University, Graduate School, College of Behavioral, Social and Health Sciences, Department of Parks, Recreation, and Tourism Management, Clemson, SC 29634. Offers international parks and tourism (Certificate); parks, recreation and tourism management (MS, PhD), including recreational therapy (PhD); public administration (MPA, Certificate); recreational therapy (MS); youth development leadership (MS, Certificate). *Program availability:* Part-time, evening/weekend, 100% online. *Faculty:* 31 full-time (10 women), 3 part-time/adjunct (0 women). *Students:* 90 full-time (62 women), 193 part-time (114 women); includes 57 minority (44 Black or African American, non-Hispanic/Latino; 1 American Indian or Alaska Native, non-Hispanic/Latino; 1 Asian, non-

Hispanic/Latino; 8 Hispanic/Latino; 3 Two or more races, non-Hispanic/Latino), 14 international. Average age 32. 245 applicants, 80% accepted, 129 enrolled. In 2017, 37 master's, 5 doctorates, 38 other advanced degrees awarded. *Degree requirements:* For master's, comprehensive exam (for some programs), thesis (for some programs); for doctorate, comprehensive exam, thesis/dissertation; for Certificate, portfolio. *Entrance requirements:* For master's and doctorate, GRE General Test, unofficial transcripts, letter of intent, letters of reference; for Certificate, letter of recommendation, unofficial transcripts, personal statement, resume. Additional exam requirements/recommendations for international students: Required—TOEFL (minimum score 610 paper-based; 80 iBT), IELTS (minimum score 6.5), PTE (minimum score 54). *Application deadline:* For fall admission, 1/15 priority date for domestic and international students; for spring admission, 11/15 priority date for domestic and international students. Applications are processed on a rolling basis. Application fee: $80 ($90 for international students). Electronic applications accepted. *Expenses:* $5,767 per semester full-time resident, $10,918 per semester full-time non-resident, $656 per credit hour part-time resident, $1,310 per credit hour part-time non-resident, $915 per credit hour online; $5,174 per semester full-time resident, $9,714 per semester full-time non-resident, $511 per credit hour part-time resident, $1,017 per credit hour part-time non-resident, $741 per credit hour online (for online non-thesis ms and doctoral programs); $613 per credit hour (for online youth development leadership); other fees may apply per session. *Financial support:* In 2017–18, 68 students received support, including 4 fellowships with partial tuition reimbursements available (averaging $5,250 per year), 7 research assistantships with partial tuition reimbursements available (averaging $11,653 per year), 52 teaching assistantships with partial tuition reimbursements available (averaging $8,517 per year); career-related internships or fieldwork and unspecified assistantships also available. Financial award application deadline: 1/15. *Faculty research:* Human behavior, land use, recreational therapy, sustainability, tourism. *Total annual research expenditures:* $400,772. *Unit head:* Dr. Fran McGuire, Interim Chair, 864-656-3036, E-mail: lefty@clemson.edu. *Application contact:* Dr. Jeff Hallo, Graduate Coordinator, 864-656-3237, E-mail: jhallo@clemson.edu. Website: http://www.clemson.edu/hehd/departments/prtm/

Coastal Carolina University, Spadoni College of Education, Conway, SC 29528-6054. Offers education (MAT); educational leadership (M Ed, Ed S); English for speakers of other languages (Certificate); instructional technology (M Ed, Ed S); language, literacy and culture (M Ed); learning and teaching (M Ed); online teaching and training (Certificate); special education (M Ed). *Accreditation:* NCATE. *Program availability:* Part-time, evening/weekend, 100% online, blended/hybrid learning. *Faculty:* 16 full-time (9 women), 22 part-time/adjunct (15 women). *Students:* 43 full-time (22 women), 345 part-time (290 women); includes 70 minority (51 Black or African American, non-Hispanic/Latino; 3 American Indian or Alaska Native, non-Hispanic/Latino; 3 Asian, non-Hispanic/Latino; 8 Hispanic/Latino; 1 Native Hawaiian or other Pacific Islander, non-Hispanic/Latino; 4 Two or more races, non-Hispanic/Latino). Average age 33. 288 applicants, 77% accepted, 157 enrolled. In 2017, 151 master's, 28 other advanced degrees awarded. *Degree requirements:* For master's and other advanced degree, comprehensive exam. *Entrance requirements:* For master's, GRE, GMAT, 2 letters of recommendation, evidence of teacher certification, official transcripts; for other advanced degree, official transcripts, 3 letters of reference, master's degree in related field with minimum overall cumulative GPA of 3.0. Additional exam requirements/recommendations for international students: Required—TOEFL (minimum score 550 paper-based; 79 iBT), IELTS (minimum score 6.5). *Application deadline:* For fall admission, 5/1 priority date for domestic and international students; for spring admission, 11/1 priority date for domestic and international students; for summer admission, 3/1 priority date for domestic and international students. Applications are processed on a rolling basis. Application fee: $45. Electronic applications accepted. *Expenses:* Tuition, state resident: full-time $5184; part-time $576 per credit hour. Tuition, nonresident: full-time $9369; part-time $1041 per credit hour. *Required fees:* $90; $5 per credit hour. *Financial support:* Fellowships, research assistantships, teaching assistantships, and tuition waivers available. Financial award application deadline: 3/1; financial award applicants required to submit FAFSA. *Unit head:* Dr. Edward Jadallah, Dean/Vice President for Online Education and Teaching Excellence, 843-349-2773, Fax: 843-349-2106, E-mail: ejadalla@coastal.edu. *Application contact:* Dr. James O. Luken, Associate Provost for Graduate Program/Vice-Dean of the Coastal Environment, 843-349-2235, Fax: 843-349-6444, E-mail: joluken@coastal.edu. Website: https://www.coastal.edu/education/

College of Saint Elizabeth, Program in Education, Morristown, NJ 07960-6989. Offers assistive technology (Certificate); education (MA); ESL (Certificate); Holocaust/genocide education (Certificate); middle school science (Certificate); online teaching in the 21st century (Certificate); teaching (Certificate), including K-12, K-6, teacher of students with disabilities. *Program availability:* Part-time. *Faculty:* 3 full-time (2 women), 8 part-time/adjunct (6 women). *Students:* 1 (woman) full-time, 34 part-time (29 women); includes 1 minority (Hispanic/Latino). Average age 32. 25 applicants, 100% accepted, 24 enrolled. In 2017, 23 master's awarded. *Degree requirements:* For master's and Certificate, thesis. *Entrance requirements:* For master's, certification. Additional exam requirements/recommendations for international students: Required—TOEFL (minimum score 550 paper-based; 79 iBT), IELTS (minimum score 6.5). *Application deadline:* For fall admission, 5/1 for international students. Applications are processed on a rolling basis. Application fee: $35. Electronic applications accepted. Application fee is waived when completed online. *Financial support:* Career-related internships or fieldwork, scholarships/grants, and unspecified assistantships available. Financial award applicants required to submit FAFSA. *Unit head:* Dr. Joseph Ciccone, 973-290-4383, Fax: 973-290-4389, E-mail: jciccone@cse.edu. *Application contact:* Lori J. Fragoso, Director of Graduate and Continuing Studies Admissions, 973-290-4413, Fax: 973-290-4710, E-mail: apply@cse.edu. Website: http://www.cse.edu/academics/prof-studies/education/

Colorado Christian University, Program in Curriculum and Instruction, Lakewood, CO 80226. Offers corporate education (MACI); early childhood educator (MACI); elementary educator (MACI); instructional technology (MACI); master educator (MACI); online course developer (MACI); online teaching and learning (MACI); special education generalist (MACI). *Program availability:* Part-time, evening/weekend. *Degree requirements:* For master's, thesis optional, practicum. *Entrance requirements:* For master's, interviews, letters of recommendation. Additional exam requirements/recommendations for international students: Required—TOEFL. Electronic applications accepted. *Expenses:* Contact institution.

Dallas Baptist University, Dorothy M. Bush College of Education, Program in Curriculum and Instruction, Dallas, TX 75211-9299. Offers Christian school administration (M Ed); distance learning (M Ed); English as a second language (M Ed); instructional technology (M Ed); professional life coaching (M Ed); special education (M Ed); supervision (M Ed). *Program availability:* Part-time, evening/weekend, online learning. *Application deadline:* Applications are processed on a rolling basis. Application fee: $25. Electronic applications accepted. Application fee is waived when completed online. *Expenses: Tuition:* Full-time $16,308; part-time $906 per credit hour. *Required fees:* $900; $450 per semester. Tuition and fees vary according to course load and degree level. *Unit head:* Dr. Neil Dugger, Dean, 214-333-5202, E-mail: neil@dbu.edu. *Application contact:* Dr. Deborah Tribble, Program Director, 214-333-5831, E-mail: debbiet@dbu.edu. Website: http://www3.dbu.edu/graduate/curriculum_instruction.asp

Dallas Baptist University, Dorothy M. Bush College of Education, Teaching Program, Dallas, TX 75211-9299. Offers distance learning (MAT); early childhood through grade 6 certification (MAT); early childhood-12 (MAT); elementary (MAT); English as a second language (MAT); Montessori (MAT); multisensory (MAT); secondary (MAT). *Program availability:* Part-time, evening/weekend. *Application deadline:* Applications are processed on a rolling basis. Application fee: $25. Electronic applications accepted. Application fee is waived when completed online. *Expenses: Tuition:* Full-time $16,308; part-time $906 per credit hour. *Required fees:* $900; $450 per semester. Tuition and fees vary according to course load and degree level. *Unit head:* Dr. Neil Dugger, Dean, 214-333-5202, E-mail: neil@dbu.edu. *Application contact:* Dr. DeAnna Jenkins, Program Director, 214-333-5402, E-mail: deannaj@dbu.edu. Website: http://www3.dbu.edu/graduate/mat.asp

Dallas Baptist University, Gary Cook School of Leadership, Program in Higher Education, Dallas, TX 75211-9299. Offers leadership studies (M Ed); student affairs leadership (M Ed), including community college leadership, distance learning, interdisciplinary studies, student affairs leadership. *Program availability:* Part-time, evening/weekend. *Application deadline:* Applications are processed on a rolling basis. Application fee: $25. Electronic applications accepted. Application fee is waived when completed online. *Expenses: Tuition:* Full-time $16,308; part-time $906 per credit hour. *Required fees:* $900; $450 per semester. Tuition and fees vary according to course load and degree level. *Unit head:* Dr. Jack Goodyear, Dean, 214-333-5595, Fax: 214-333-6809, E-mail: jackg@dbu.edu. *Application contact:* Dr. Sena Baker, Program Director, 214-333-6850, E-mail: sena@dbu.edu. Website: http://www4.dbu.edu/leadership/hied/

Drury University, Master in Education Program, Springfield, MO 5802. Offers curriculum and instruction (M Ed), including elementary, middle school, secondary; gifted education (M Ed); instructional leadership (M Ed); instructional technology (M Ed); integrated learning (M Ed); online teaching (M Ed); special education (M Ed); special reading (M Ed). *Accreditation:* NCATE. *Program availability:* Part-time, evening/weekend, 100% online, blended/hybrid learning. *Entrance requirements:* For master's, GRE, bachelor's degree with minimum GPA of 2.75. Additional exam requirements/recommendations for international students: Recommended—TOEFL (minimum score 80 iBT), IELTS (minimum score 6.5). Electronic applications accepted. *Expenses:* Contact institution. *Faculty research:* Gifted students, instructional technology, autism, diversity and social justice.

East Carolina University, Graduate School, College of Education, Department of Mathematics, Science, and Instructional Technology Education, Greenville, NC 27858-4353. Offers distance learning and administration (Certificate); elementary mathematics education (Certificate); instructional technology (MA Ed, MS); mathematics education (MA Ed); science education (MA Ed, MAT); special endorsement in computer education (Certificate). *Program availability:* Part-time, evening/weekend. *Students:* 12 full-time (10 women), 202 part-time (153 women); includes 49 minority (31 Black or African American, non-Hispanic/Latino; 2 American Indian or Alaska Native, non-Hispanic/Latino; 2 Asian, non-Hispanic/Latino; 9 Hispanic/Latino; 5 Two or more races, non-Hispanic/Latino). Average age 38. 56 applicants, 100% accepted, 50 enrolled. In 2017, 76 master's, 30 other advanced degrees awarded. *Degree requirements:* For master's, comprehensive exam, thesis optional. *Entrance requirements:* For master's, GRE General Test or MAT, interview, minimum GPA of 2.5, bachelor's degree in related field, teaching license (MA Ed). Additional exam requirements/recommendations for international students: Required—TOEFL. *Application deadline:* For fall admission, 6/1 priority date for domestic students. Applications are processed on a rolling basis. Application fee: $75. *Expenses: Tuition,* state resident: full-time $4749; part-time $297 per credit hour. Tuition, nonresident: full-time $17,898; part-time $1119 per credit hour. *Required fees:* $2691; $224 per credit hour. Part-time tuition and fees vary according to course load and program. *Financial support:* Research assistantships, teaching assistantships, and Federal Work-Study available. Support available to part-time students. Financial award application deadline: 6/1. *Unit head:* Susan Ganter, Chair, 252-737-3001, E-mail: ganters@ecu.edu. Website: http://www.ecu.edu/cs-educ/msite/

Eastern Michigan University, Graduate School, College of Education, Department of Teacher Education, Programs in Curriculum and Instruction, Ypsilanti, MI 48197. Offers advanced teaching and learning (MA); early literacy instruction (Graduate Certificate); instructional leadership (MA); learning, motivation and creativity (Graduate Certificate); literacy coaching (Graduate Certificate); online teaching (Certificate); secondary literacy instruction (Graduate Certificate); urban and diversity education (MA). *Students:* 1 full-time (0 women), 22 part-time (19 women); includes 6 minority (2 Black or African American, non-Hispanic/Latino; 1 Hispanic/Latino; 3 Two or more races, non-Hispanic/Latino). Average age 31. 15 applicants, 67% accepted, 7 enrolled. In 2017, 15 master's, 1 other advanced degree awarded. Application fee: $45. *Application contact:* Dr. Virginia Harder, Graduate Coordinator/Advisor, 734-487-2729, Fax: 734-487-2101, E-mail: vharder1@emich.edu.

Emporia State University, Department of Instructional Design and Technology, Emporia, KS 66801-5415. Offers elearning/online teaching (Certificate); teaching with technology (Certificate). *Accreditation:* NCATE. *Program availability:* Part-time, online only, 100% online. *Faculty:* 7 full-time (4 women). *Students:* 25 full-time (20 women), 40 part-time (30 women); includes 6 minority (2 Black or African American, non-Hispanic/Latino; 2 Asian, non-Hispanic/Latino; 1 Hispanic/Latino; 1 Two or more races, non-Hispanic/Latino), 24 international. 26 applicants, 77% accepted, 11 enrolled. In 2017, 43 master's, 31 other advanced degrees awarded. *Degree requirements:* For master's, comprehensive exam (for some programs), thesis (for some programs), project. *Entrance requirements:* For master's, appropriate bachelor's degree, letters of recommendation. Additional exam requirements/recommendations for international students: Required—TOEFL (minimum score 520 paper-based; 68 iBT). *Application deadline:* For fall admission, 8/15 priority date for domestic students. Applications are processed on a rolling basis. Application fee: $30 ($75 for international students). Electronic applications accepted. *Expenses:* Tuition, state resident: full-time $6084; part-time $253.50 per credit hour. Tuition, nonresident: full-time $18,924; part-time $788.50 per credit hour. *Required fees:* $1943; $80.95 per credit hour. Tuition and fees vary according to campus/location. *Financial support:* In 2017–18, 7 teaching assistantships with full tuition reimbursements (averaging $6,295 per year) were awarded; Federal Work-Study, institutionally sponsored loans, health care benefits, and unspecified assistantships also available. Financial award application deadline: 3/15; financial award applicants required to submit FAFSA. *Unit head:* Dr. Zeni Colorado Resa, Chair, 620-341-5477, E-mail: jcolorad@emporia.edu. *Application contact:* Mary Sewell, Admissions Coordinator, 800-950-GRAD, Fax: 620-341-5909, E-mail: msewell@emporia.edu. Website: http://www.emporia.edu/idt/

Endicott College, Van Loan School of Graduate and Professional Studies, Program in Integrative Education, Beverly, MA 01915-2096. Offers M Ed. Program offered in conjunction with The Institute for Educational Studies (TIES). *Program availability:* Part-time, online only, 100% online. *Faculty:* 1 full-time (0 women). *Students:* 33 full-time (31 women); includes 1 minority (Hispanic/Latino). Average age 35. 15 applicants, 100% accepted, 13 enrolled. In 2017, 16 master's awarded. *Degree requirements:* For

master's, thesis. *Entrance requirements:* For master's, undergraduate transcript. Additional exam requirements/recommendations for international students: Required—TOEFL. *Application deadline:* Applications are processed on a rolling basis. Application fee: $50. Electronic applications accepted. *Expenses:* Contact institution. *Financial support:* Tuition waivers (partial) available. Financial award applicants required to submit FAFSA. *Faculty research:* Neurophenomenology, autopoiesis, systems view. *Unit head:* Dr. Phil Snow Gang, Academic Dean, 888-722-4547, Fax: 978-232-3000, E-mail: ties@endicott.edu. *Application contact:* Ian Menchini, Director, Graduate Enrollment and Advising, 978-232-5292, E-mail: imenchin@endicott.edu. Website: https://vanloan.endicott.edu/programs-of-study/masters-programs/montessori-integrative-education-program-med

The George Washington University, Graduate School of Education and Human Development, Department of Educational Leadership, Program in E-Learning, Washington, DC 20052. Offers Graduate Certificate. *Students:* 1 (woman) part-time. Average age 33. 1 applicant, 100% accepted, 1 enrolled. In 2017, 1 Graduate Certificate awarded. *Expenses: Tuition:* Full-time $28,800; part-time $1655 per credit hour. *Required fees:* $45; $2.75 per credit hour. *Unit head:* Dr. Virginia Roach, Chair, 202-994-3094, E-mail: vroach@gwu.edu. *Application contact:* Sarah Lang, Director of Graduate Admissions, 202-994-1447, Fax: 202-994-7207, E-mail: slang@gwu.edu. Website: http://gsehd.gwu.edu/e-learning-certificate

Kansas State University, Graduate School, College of Education, Department of Curriculum and Instruction, Manhattan, KS 66506. Offers curriculum and instruction (Ed D, PhD); digital teaching and learning (MS); educational computing, design and online learning (MS); elementary/middle level curriculum and instruction (MS); online learning (Certificate); reading specialist endorsement (MS); reading/language arts (MS); teacher leader/school improvement (MS); teaching and learning (Certificate). *Accreditation:* NCATE. *Program availability:* Part-time, online learning. *Degree requirements:* For master's, comprehensive exam, portfolio, project, report or thesis; for doctorate, comprehensive exam, thesis/dissertation, preliminary exam; for Certificate, comprehensive exam, portfolio. *Entrance requirements:* For master's, minimum GPA of 3.0, 3 letters of recommendation; for doctorate, GRE, minimum GPA of 3.0, 3 letters of recommendation, evidence of scholarly writing; for Certificate, minimum GPA of 3.0, letters of recommendation. Additional exam requirements/recommendations for international students: Required—TOEFL (minimum score 550 paper-based; 80 iBT) or IELTS. Electronic applications accepted. *Faculty research:* Literacy and technology, critical race theory and diversity, achievement gaps, school improvement, teacher education.

Keiser University, Master of Science in Education Program, Fort Lauderdale, FL 33309. Offers allied health teaching and leadership (MS Ed); career college administration (MS Ed); leadership (MS Ed); online teaching and learning (MS Ed); teaching and learning (MS Ed). *Program availability:* Part-time, online learning. *Unit head:* Brian Keintz, Chair of Graduate Programs. Website: http://www.keiseruniversity.edu/graduateschool/

Lenoir-Rhyne University, Graduate Programs, School of Education, Program in Online Teaching and Instructional Design, Hickory, NC 28601. Offers MS. *Program availability:* Online learning. *Entrance requirements:* For master's, GRE or MAT, essay; minimum GPA of 2.7 undergraduate, 3.0 graduate. Additional exam requirements/recommendations for international students: Required—TOEFL (minimum score 600 paper-based). Electronic applications accepted. *Expenses:* Contact institution.

Lesley University, Graduate School of Education, Cambridge, MA 02138-2790. Offers arts, community, and education (M Ed); autism studies (Certificate); curriculum and instruction (M Ed, CAGS); early childhood education (M Ed); ecological teaching and learning (MS); educational studies (PhD), including adult learning, educational leadership, individually designed; elementary education (M Ed); emergent technologies for educators (Certificate); ESLArts: language learning through the arts (M Ed); high school education (M Ed); individually designed (M Ed); integrated teaching through the arts (M Ed); literacy for K-8 classroom teachers (M Ed); mathematics education (M Ed); middle school education (M Ed); moderate disabilities (M Ed); online learning (Certificate); reading (CAGS); science in education (M Ed); severe disabilities (M Ed); special needs (CAGS); specialist teacher of reading (M Ed); teacher of visual art (M Ed); technology in education (M Ed, CAGS). *Accreditation:* TEAC. *Program availability:* Part-time, evening/weekend, online learning. *Degree requirements:* For master's, practicum; for doctorate, thesis/dissertation. *Entrance requirements:* For master's, Massachusetts Tests for Educator Licensure (MTEL), transcripts, statement of purpose, recommendations; interview (for special education); for doctorate, GRE General Test, transcripts, statement of purpose, recommendations, interview, master's degree; for other advanced degree, interview, master's degree. Additional exam requirements/recommendations for international students: Required—TOEFL (minimum score 550 paper-based; 80 iBT). Electronic applications accepted. *Faculty research:* Assessment in literacy, mathematics and science; autism spectrum disorders; instructional technology and online learning; multicultural education and English language learners.

Millersville University of Pennsylvania, College of Graduate Studies and Adult Learning, College of Education and Human Services, Department of Educational Foundations, Program in Assessment, Curriculum and Teaching - Online Teaching Option, Millersville, PA 17551-0302. Offers M Ed. *Program availability:* Part-time, evening/weekend, online only, 100% online. *Faculty:* 9 full-time (8 women), 8 part-time/adjunct (5 women). *Students:* 12 part-time (7 women). Average age 33. 7 applicants, 100% accepted, 6 enrolled. *Degree requirements:* For master's, thesis/capstone experience. *Entrance requirements:* For master's, GRE or MAT (if undergraduate cumulative GPA is lower than 2.8), teaching certificate. Additional exam requirements/recommendations for international students: Required—TOEFL (minimum score 80 iBT), IELTS (minimum score 6.5), PTE (minimum score 60). *Application deadline:* Applications are processed on a rolling basis. Application fee: $40. Electronic applications accepted. *Expenses:* $500 per credit resident tuition, $581.75 per credit non-resident tuition, $59.25 academic support fee. *Financial support:* Unspecified assistantships available. Financial award application deadline: 3/15; financial award applicants required to submit FAFSA. *Faculty research:* Online teacher efficacy, factors that impact on-line instructional quality, pedagogical content knowledge in instructional technology. *Unit head:* Dr. Tim E. Mahoney, Chair, 717-871-7202, E-mail: tim.mahoney@millersville.edu. *Application contact:* Dr. Victor S. DeSantis, Dean of College of Graduate Studies and Adult Learning/Associate Provost for Civic and Community Engagement, 717-871-7619, Fax: 717-871-7954, E-mail: victor.desantis@millersville.edu. Website: http://millersville.edu/academics/educ/edfoundations/master-online-teaching.php

National University, Academic Affairs, Sanford College of Education, La Jolla, CA 92037-1011. Offers advanced teaching practices (MS); applied behavior analysis (MS); applied school leadership (MS); e-teaching and learning (Certificate); education (MA); educational administration (MS); educational and instructional technology (MS); educational counseling (MS); higher education administration (MS); inspired teaching and learning (M Ed); school psychology (MS); special education (MA, MS). *Program availability:* Part-time, evening/weekend, 100% online, blended/hybrid learning. *Degree*

requirements: For master's, thesis (for some programs). *Entrance requirements:* For master's, interview, minimum GPA of 2.5. Additional exam requirements/recommendations for international students: Required—TOEFL (minimum score 550 paper-based; 79 iBT), IELTS (minimum score 6). *Application deadline:* Applications are processed on a rolling basis. Application fee: $60 ($65 for international students). Electronic applications accepted. *Expenses: Tuition:* Part-time $430 per quarter hour. *Financial support:* Career-related internships or fieldwork, institutionally sponsored loans, scholarships/grants, and tuition waivers (partial) available. Support available to part-time students. Financial award application deadline: 6/30. *Faculty research:* Teacher education, special education, educational effectiveness, teaching abroad, school counseling. *Unit head:* Dr. Judy Mantle, Dean, 858-642-8320, E-mail: soe@nu.edu. *Application contact:* Brandon Jouganatos, Vice President for Enrollment Services, 800-628-8648, E-mail: advisor@nu.edu.
Website: http://www.nu.edu/OurPrograms/SchoolOfEducation.html

New Mexico State University, College of Education, Online Teaching and Learning Program, Las Cruces, NM 88003. Offers Graduate Certificate. *Program availability:* Part-time, 100% online. *Students:* 4 full-time (2 women), 7 part-time (5 women); includes 1 minority (Black or African American, non-Hispanic/Latino), 3 international. Average age 42. 8 applicants, 75% accepted, 4 enrolled. In 2017, 10 Graduate Certificates awarded. *Degree requirements:* For Graduate Certificate, minimum grade of B in all 5 courses; practicum. *Entrance requirements:* Additional exam requirements/recommendations for international students: Required—TOEFL (minimum score 550 paper-based; 79 iBT), IELTS (minimum score 6.5). *Application deadline:* Applications are processed on a rolling basis. Application fee: $40 ($50 for international students). Electronic applications accepted. *Expenses:* Tuition, state resident: full-time $4390. Tuition, nonresident: full-time $15,309. *Required fees:* $853. *Financial support:* Career-related internships or fieldwork, Federal Work-Study, scholarships/grants, traineeships, health care benefits, and unspecified assistantships available. Support available to part-time students. Financial award application deadline: 3/1. *Faculty research:* Learning design, technology, and innovation including intersections of technology, pedagogy and content knowledge (TPACK); online/blended/hyflex teaching and learning; emerging technologies; and critical and culturally responsive teaching with technology. *Unit head:* Dr. David Rutledge, Interim Department Head, 575-646-5411, Fax: 575-646-5436, E-mail: rutledge@nmsu.edu. *Application contact:* Dr. Julia Parra, Director of Online Teaching and Learning Program, 575-646-1767, Fax: 575-646-5436, E-mail: juparra@nmsu.edu.
Website: http://otl.nmsu.edu/

Nova Southeastern University, Abraham S. Fischler College of Education, Fort Lauderdale, FL 33314. Offers education (MS, Ed D, PhD, Ed S); instructional technology and distance education (MS); teaching and learning (MA). *Accreditation:* NCATE. *Program availability:* Part-time, evening/weekend, 100% online, blended/hybrid learning. *Faculty:* 94 full-time (58 women), 204 part-time/adjunct (145 women). *Students:* 1,513 full-time (1,199 women), 1,583 part-time (1,259 women); includes 2,373 minority (1,224 Black or African American, non-Hispanic/Latino; 5 American Indian or Alaska Native, non-Hispanic/Latino; 34 Asian, non-Hispanic/Latino; 1,057 Hispanic/Latino; 2 Native Hawaiian or other Pacific Islander, non-Hispanic/Latino; 51 Two or more races, non-Hispanic/Latino), 19 international. Average age 41. 1,753 applicants, 47% accepted, 581 enrolled. In 2017, 399 master's, 571 doctorates, 104 other advanced degrees awarded. *Degree requirements:* For master's, practicum, internship; for doctorate, thesis/dissertation; for Ed S, thesis, practicum, internship. *Entrance requirements:* For master's, MAT or GRE (for some programs), CLAST, PRAXIS I, CBEST, General Knowledge Test, teaching certification, minimum GPA of 2.5, verification of teaching, BS; for doctorate, MAT or GRE, master's degree, minimum cumulative GPA of 3.0; for Ed S, MAT or GRE, master's degree, teaching certificate, minimum GPA of 3.0. Additional exam requirements/recommendations for international students: Recommended—TOEFL (minimum score 550 paper-based; 79 iBT), IELTS (minimum score 6). *Application deadline:* Applications are processed on a rolling basis. Application fee: $50. Electronic applications accepted. *Expenses:* Contact institution. *Financial support:* In 2017–18, 67 students received support. Career-related internships or fieldwork and Federal Work-Study available. Support available to part-time students. Financial award application deadline: 4/15; financial award applicants required to submit FAFSA. *Faculty research:* STEM education, educational technology, principal training, quality of life. *Total annual research expenditures:* $50,000. *Unit head:* Dr. Kimberly Durham, Interim Dean, 954-262-8731, Fax: 954-262-3894, E-mail: durham@nova.edu. *Application contact:* Adriana Garay, Executive Director for Marketing, Recruitment and Admissions, 800-986-3223 Ext. 8500, E-mail: fserecruit@nova.edu.
Website: http://www.fischlerschool.nova.edu/

Post University, Program in Education, Waterbury, CT 06723-2540. Offers curriculum and instruction (M Ed); education (M Ed); educational technology (M Ed); higher education administration (MS); learning design and technology (M Ed); online learning (M Ed); teaching English to speakers of other languages (TESOL) (M Ed). *Program availability:* Online learning. *Entrance requirements:* For master's, resume. *Expenses: Tuition:* Part-time $730 per credit hour. Part-time tuition and fees vary according to degree level and program. *Application contact:* Veronica Montalvo, Vice President, Online Education Enrollment Management and Admissions, 203-596-6164, E-mail: vmontalvo@post.edu.

Regent University, Graduate School, School of Education, Virginia Beach, VA 23464-9800. Offers education (M Ed, Ed D, PhD), including adult education (Ed D, PhD, Ed S), advanced educational leadership (Ed D, PhD, Ed S), character education (Ed D, PhD, Ed S), Christian education leadership (Ed D, PhD, Ed S), Christian school administration (M Ed), curriculum and instruction (Ed D, PhD, Ed S), curriculum and instruction - adult education (M Ed), curriculum and instruction - Christian school (M Ed), curriculum and instruction - gifted and talented (M Ed), curriculum and instruction - STEM education (M Ed), curriculum and instruction - teacher leader (M Ed), discipleship for ministry (M Ed), educational leadership (M Ed), educational psychology (Ed D, PhD, Ed S), educational technology and online learning (Ed D, PhD, Ed S), elementary education (M Ed), exceptional education executive leadership (Ed D, PhD, Ed S), higher education (Ed D, PhD, Ed S), higher education leadership and management (Ed D, PhD, Ed S), instructional design and technology (M Ed), K-12 school leadership (Ed D, PhD, Ed S), K-12 special education (M Ed), leadership in mathematics education (M Ed), reading specialist (M Ed), special education (Ed D, PhD, Ed S), student affairs (M Ed), TESOL - adult education (M Ed), TESOL - K-12 (M Ed); educational specialist (Ed S), including adult education (Ed D, PhD, Ed S), advanced educational leadership (Ed D, PhD, Ed S), character education (Ed D, PhD, Ed S), Christian education leadership (Ed D, PhD, Ed S), curriculum and instruction (Ed D, PhD, Ed S), educational psychology (Ed D, PhD, Ed S), educational technology and online learning (Ed D, PhD, Ed S), exceptional education executive leadership (Ed D, PhD, Ed S), higher education (Ed D, PhD, Ed S), higher education leadership and management (Ed D, PhD, Ed S), K-12 school leadership (Ed D, PhD, Ed S), special education (Ed D, PhD, Ed S). *Accreditation:* TEAC. *Program availability:* Part-time, evening/weekend, 100% online, blended/hybrid learning. *Faculty:* 22 full-time (10 women), 44 part-time/adjunct (32 women). *Students:* 80 full-time (59 women), 945 part-time (750 women); includes 432 minority (352 Black or African American, non-Hispanic/Latino; 4 American Indian or Alaska Native, non-Hispanic/Latino; 14 Asian, non-Hispanic/Latino; 43 Hispanic/Latino; 19 Two or more races, non-Hispanic/Latino), 12 international. Average age 40. 1,125 applicants, 49% accepted, 436 enrolled. In 2017, 316 master's, 24 doctorates awarded. *Degree requirements:* For master's, thesis or alternative; for doctorate, comprehensive exam, thesis/dissertation. *Entrance requirements:* For master's, Virginia Communication and Literacy Assessment (VCLA), PRAXIS, college transcripts, writing sample, interview; for doctorate, GRE, writing sample, resume, transcripts, interview. Additional exam requirements/recommendations for international students: Required—TOEFL (minimum score 577 paper-based). *Application deadline:* For fall admission, 4/1 priority date for domestic students; for spring admission, 10/15 priority date for domestic students. Applications are processed on a rolling basis. Application fee: $50. Electronic applications accepted. *Expenses:* Contact institution. *Financial support:* In 2017–18, 669 students received support, including 1 fellowship (averaging $10,000 per year); career-related internships or fieldwork, scholarships/grants, and unspecified assistantships also available. Support available to part-time students. *Faculty research:* Christian school administration, curriculum and instruction, educational technology and online learning, higher education, special education. *Unit head:* Dr. Donald Finn, Dean, 757-352-4278, Fax: 757-352-4318, E-mail: dfinn@regent.edu. *Application contact:* Heidi Cece, Assistant Vice President of Enrollment Management, 800-373-5504, Fax: 757-352-4381, E-mail: admissions@regent.edu.
Website: https://www.regent.edu/school-of-education/

Télé-université, Graduate Programs, Québec, QC G1K 9H5, Canada. Offers computer science (PhD); corporate finance (MS); distance learning (MS). *Program availability:* Part-time.

Thomas Edison State University, Heavin School of Arts and Sciences, Program in Educational Technology and Online Learning, Trenton, NJ 08608. Offers educational technology and online learning (MA); online learning and teaching (Graduate Certificate). *Program availability:* Part-time, online learning. *Degree requirements:* For master's, practicum. *Entrance requirements:* Additional exam requirements/recommendations for international students: Required—TOEFL (minimum score 550 paper-based; 79 iBT). Electronic applications accepted.

University at Buffalo, the State University of New York, Graduate School, Graduate School of Education, Department of Learning and Instruction, Buffalo, NY 14260. Offers biology education (Ed M, Certificate); chemistry education (Ed M, Certificate); childhood education (Ed M); childhood education with bilingual extension (Ed M); college teaching (Advanced Certificate); curriculum, instruction and the science of learning (PhD); early childhood education (Ed M); early childhood education with bilingual extension (Ed M); earth science education (Ed M, Certificate); education and technology (Ed M); education studies (Ed M); educational technology and new literacies (Certificate); educational technology and new literacies (Advanced Certificate); elementary education (Ed D); English education (Ed M, Certificate); English education studies (Ed M); English for speakers of other languages (Ed M); foreign and second language education (PhD); French education (Ed M, Certificate); German education (Ed M, Certificate); gifted education (Certificate); Latin education (Ed M, Certificate); literacy education studies (Ed M); literacy specialist (Ed M); literacy teaching and learning (Certificate); mathematics education (Ed M, Certificate); music education (Ed M, Certificate); music education studies (Ed M); music learning theory (Advanced Certificate); online education (Advanced Certificate); physics education (Ed M, Certificate); science and the public (Ed M); social studies education (Ed M, Certificate); Spanish education (Ed M, Certificate); special education (PhD); teaching English to speakers of other languages (Ed M). *Program availability:* Part-time, evening/weekend, 100% online. *Faculty:* 26 full-time (19 women), 74 part-time/adjunct (52 women). *Students:* 172 full-time (122 women), 325 part-time (226 women); includes 44 minority (25 Black or African American, non-Hispanic/Latino; 5 American Indian or Alaska Native, non-Hispanic/Latino; 14 Asian, non-Hispanic/Latino), 57 international. Average age 33. 316 applicants, 78% accepted, 174 enrolled. In 2017, 109 master's, 34 doctorates, 15 other advanced degrees awarded. *Degree requirements:* For master's, comprehensive exam; for doctorate, thesis/dissertation, research analysis exam, research experience. *Entrance requirements:* For master's, letters of reference; for doctorate, GRE General Test or MAT, interview, writing sample, letters of recommendation. Additional exam requirements/recommendations for international students: Required—TOEFL (minimum score 600 paper-based; 96 iBT). *Application deadline:* For fall admission, 2/1 priority date for domestic and international students; for spring admission, 11/15 priority date for domestic students, 10/1 for international students. Applications are processed on a rolling basis. Application fee: $50. Electronic applications accepted. *Financial support:* In 2017–18, 42 fellowships (averaging $5,181 per year), 44 research assistantships with tuition reimbursements (averaging $10,908 per year) were awarded; teaching assistantships, career-related internships or fieldwork, Federal Work-Study, institutionally sponsored loans, scholarships/grants, tuition waivers (full and partial), and unspecified assistantships also available. Financial award application deadline: 2/28; financial award applicants required to submit FAFSA. *Faculty research:* Science assessment, foreign language teaching and learning, early learning, new literacies, gender and education. *Total annual research expenditures:* $413,233. *Unit head:* Dr. David Bruce, Chair, 716-645-4069, Fax: 716-645-3161, E-mail: gse-info@buffalo.edu. *Application contact:* Luann Zak, Admissions Assistant, 716-645-2110, Fax: 716-645-7937, E-mail: luannzak@buffalo.edu.
Website: http://gse.buffalo.edu/lai

University of Colorado Denver, School of Education and Human Development, Information and Learning Technologies Program, Denver, CO 80217. Offers e-learning design and implementation (MA); instructional design and adult learning (MA); K-12 teaching (MA). *Program availability:* Part-time, evening/weekend, online learning. *Degree requirements:* For master's, comprehensive exam (for some programs), comprehensive exam or online portfolio; 30 credit hours. *Entrance requirements:* For master's, GRE or MAT (if GPA is below 2.75), resume, statement of intent, three letters of recommendation, transcripts from all colleges/universities previously attended. Additional exam requirements/recommendations for international students: Required—TOEFL (minimum score 537 paper-based; 75 iBT); Recommended—IELTS (minimum score 6.5). Electronic applications accepted. *Expenses:* Contact institution. *Faculty research:* Technology for educational management, instructional design foundations, e-learning, educational design.

University of Illinois at Springfield, Graduate Programs, College of Education and Human Services, Department of Educational Leadership, Springfield, IL 62703-5407. Offers chief school business official (CAS); educational leadership (MA, CAS); educational technology (Graduate Certificate); English as a second language (Graduate Certificate); higher education online pedagogy (Graduate Certificate); leadership and learning (Graduate Certificate); legal aspects of education (Graduate Certificate). *Program availability:* Part-time, evening/weekend, 100% online, blended/hybrid learning. *Faculty:* 4 full-time (1 woman), 14 part-time/adjunct (11 women). *Students:* 2 full-time (1 woman), 109 part-time (70 women); includes 15 minority (10 Black or African American, non-Hispanic/Latino; 1 American Indian or Alaska Native, non-Hispanic/Latino; 1 Asian, non-Hispanic/Latino; 3 Hispanic/Latino). Average age 35. 46 applicants, 57% accepted, 23 enrolled. In 2017, 30 master's, 5 other advanced degrees awarded. *Degree requirements:* For master's, capstone course. *Entrance requirements:* For master's, minimum undergraduate GPA of 3.0, valid Illinois Teaching License, minimum of two

years of successful teaching experience, portfolio that includes letters of recommendation, interview. Additional exam requirements/recommendations for international students: Required—TOEFL (minimum score 500 paper-based; 61 iBT). *Application deadline:* Applications are processed on a rolling basis. Application fee: $60 ($75 for international students). Electronic applications accepted. *Expenses:* Tuition, state resident: full-time $7896; part-time $329 per credit hour. Tuition, nonresident: full-time $16,200; part-time $675 per credit hour. Tuition and fees vary according to program. *Financial support:* In 2017–18, research assistantships with full tuition reimbursements (averaging $10,249 per year), teaching assistantships with full tuition reimbursements (averaging $10,303 per year) were awarded; fellowships, career-related internships or fieldwork, Federal Work-Study, scholarships/grants, health care benefits, and unspecified assistantships also available. Support available to part-time students. Financial award application deadline: 11/15; financial award applicants required to submit FAFSA. *Unit head:* Dr. Scott Day, Program Administrator, 217-206-7520, Fax: 217-206-6775, E-mail: day.scott@uis.edu.
Website: http://www.uis.edu/edl/

University of Maryland, Baltimore County, The Graduate School, College of Arts, Humanities and Social Sciences, Department of Education, Program in Instructional Systems Development, Halethorpe, MD 21227. Offers distance education (Graduate Certificate); instructional systems development (MA, Graduate Certificate), including distance education (Graduate Certificate); instructional technology (Graduate Certificate). *Program availability:* Part-time, evening/weekend, 100% online, blended/hybrid learning. *Faculty:* 2 full-time (0 women), 9 part-time/adjunct (3 women). *Students:* 4 full-time (2 women), 81 part-time (65 women); includes 29 minority (19 Black or African American, non-Hispanic/Latino; 4 Asian, non-Hispanic/Latino; 4 Hispanic/Latino; 2 Two or more races, non-Hispanic/Latino). Average age 41. 53 applicants, 96% accepted, 24 enrolled. In 2017, 27 master's, 60 other advanced degrees awarded. *Degree requirements:* For master's, comprehensive exam (for some programs), portfolio (for some programs). *Entrance requirements:* Additional exam requirements/recommendations for international students: Required—TOEFL (minimum score 99 iBT), GRE. *Application deadline:* For fall admission, 8/1 priority date for domestic students, 1/1 priority date for international students; for spring admission, 12/1 priority date for domestic students; for summer admission, 4/1 priority date for domestic students. Applications are processed on a rolling basis. Application fee: $50. Electronic applications accepted. *Expenses: Required fees:* $132. *Financial support:* Application deadline: 2/14; applicants required to submit FAFSA. *Faculty research:* E-learning, distance education, instructional design. *Unit head:* Dr. Greg Williams, Graduate Program Director, 443-543-5447, Fax: 443-543-5096, E-mail: gregw@umbc.edu. *Application contact:* Renee Eisenhuth, Graduate Program Coordinator, 443-543-5446, Fax: 443-543-5096, E-mail: reisen@umbc.edu.
Website: http://isd.umbc.edu

University of Maryland University College, The Graduate School, Program in Distance Education and E-learning, Adelphi, MD 20783. Offers MDE. *Program availability:* Part-time, evening/weekend, online learning. *Students:* 94 part-time (69 women); includes 40 minority (33 Black or African American, non-Hispanic/Latino; 1 Asian, non-Hispanic/Latino; 4 Hispanic/Latino; 2 Two or more races, non-Hispanic/Latino), 6 international. Average age 44. 5 applicants, 100% accepted, 2 enrolled. In 2017, 25 master's awarded. *Degree requirements:* For master's, thesis or alternative. *Application deadline:* Applications are processed on a rolling basis. Application fee: $50. Electronic applications accepted. *Financial support:* Federal Work-Study and scholarships/grants available. Support available to part-time students. Financial award application deadline: 6/1; financial award applicants required to submit FAFSA. *Unit head:* Dr. Randall Hansen, Director, 240-684-2400, Fax: 240-684-2401, E-mail: randall.hansen@umuc.edu. *Application contact:* Coordinator, Graduate Admissions, 800-888-8682, Fax: 240-684-2151, E-mail: newgrad@umuc.edu.
Website: http://www.umuc.edu/academic-programs/masters-degrees/distance-education.cfm

University of Nevada, Las Vegas, Graduate College, College of Education, Department of Teaching and Learning, Las Vegas, NV 89154-3005. Offers curriculum and instruction (M Ed, MS, Ed D, PhD, Ed S), including teacher education (PhD); elementary teaching (Certificate); online teaching and training (Certificate); secondary teaching (Certificate); social justice studies (Certificate); teaching and learning (PhD). *Program availability:* Part-time, evening/weekend. *Faculty:* 27 full-time (13 women), 10 part-time/adjunct (8 women). *Students:* 315 full-time (222 women), 244 part-time (161 women); includes 226 minority (58 Black or African American, non-Hispanic/Latino; 2 American Indian or Alaska Native, non-Hispanic/Latino; 24 Asian, non-Hispanic/Latino; 104 Hispanic/Latino; 2 Native Hawaiian or other Pacific Islander, non-Hispanic/Latino; 36 Two or more races, non-Hispanic/Latino), 10 international. Average age 35. 234 applicants, 89% accepted, 174 enrolled. In 2017, 153 master's, 16 doctorates, 3 other advanced degrees awarded. *Degree requirements:* For master's, comprehensive exam (for some programs), thesis (for some programs); for doctorate, comprehensive exam, thesis/dissertation, defense of dissertation; for other advanced degree, comprehensive exam (for some programs), oral presentation of special project or professional paper. *Entrance requirements:* For master's, bachelor's degree with minimum GPA 2.75; for doctorate, GRE General Test, master's degree with minimum GPA of 3.0; statement of purpose; demonstration of oral communication skills; 3 letters of recommendation; for other advanced degree, PRAXIS Core (for some programs); PRAXIS II (for some programs), bachelor's degree (for some programs). Additional exam requirements/recommendations for international students: Required—TOEFL (minimum score 550 paper-based; 80 iBT), IELTS (minimum score 7). *Application deadline:* For fall admission, 6/1 for domestic students, 5/1 for international students; for spring admission, 11/1 for domestic students, 10/1 for international students; for summer admission, 3/15 for domestic students, 2/15 for international students. Application fee: $60 ($95 for international students). Electronic applications accepted. *Expenses:* $275 per credit, $850 per course, $7,969 per year resident, $22,157 per year non-resident, $7,094 non-resident fee (7 credits or more), $1,307 annual health insurance fee. *Financial support:* In 2017–18, 36 students received support, including 13 research assistantships with full tuition reimbursements available (averaging $18,065 per year), 23 teaching assistantships with full tuition reimbursements available (averaging $19,564 per year); institutionally sponsored loans, scholarships/grants, health care benefits, and unspecified assistantships also available. Financial award application deadline: 3/15; financial award applicants required to submit FAFSA. *Faculty research:* Content area and critical literacy, education in content areas, teacher education, STEM education, immersive environments/simulations/games. *Total annual research expenditures:* $1.1 million. *Unit head:* Dr. Emily Lin, Chair/Professor, 702-895-6407, Fax: 702-895-4898, E-mail: emily.lin@unlv.edu. *Application contact:* Dr. Travis Olson, Graduate Coordinator, 702-895-0471, Fax: 702-895-4898, E-mail: travis.olson@unlv.edu.
Website: http://tl.unlv.edu/

University of South Florida, Innovative Education, Tampa, FL 33620-9951. Offers adult, career and higher education (Graduate Certificate), including college teaching, leadership in developing human resources, leadership in higher education; Africana studies (Graduate Certificate), including diasporas and health disparities, genocide and human rights; aging studies (Graduate Certificate), including gerontology; art research (Graduate Certificate), including museum studies; business foundations (Graduate

Certificate); chemical and biomedical engineering (Graduate Certificate), including materials science and engineering, water, health and sustainability; child and family studies (Graduate Certificate), including positive behavior support; civil and industrial engineering (Graduate Certificate), including transportation systems analysis; community and family health (Graduate Certificate), including maternal and child health, social marketing and public health, violence and injury: prevention and intervention, women's health; criminology (Graduate Certificate), including criminal justice administration; data science for public administration (Graduate Certificate); digital humanities (Graduate Certificate); educational measurement and research (Graduate Certificate), including evaluation; English (Graduate Certificate), including comparative literary studies, creative writing, professional and technical communication; entrepreneurship (Graduate Certificate); environmental health (Graduate Certificate), including safety management; epidemiology and biostatistics (Graduate Certificate), including applied biostatistics, biostatistics, concepts and tools of epidemiology, epidemiology, epidemiology of infectious diseases; geography, environment and planning (Graduate Certificate), including community development, environmental policy and management, geographical information systems; geology (Graduate Certificate), including hydrogeology; global health (Graduate Certificate), including disaster management, global health and Latin American and Caribbean studies, global health practice, humanitarian assistance, infection control; government and international affairs (Graduate Certificate), including Cuban studies, globalization studies; health policy and management (Graduate Certificate), including health management and leadership, public health policy and programs; hearing specialist: early intervention (Graduate Certificate); industrial and management systems engineering (Graduate Certificate), including systems engineering, technology management; information studies (Graduate Certificate), including school library media specialist; information systems/decision sciences (Graduate Certificate), including analytics and business intelligence; instructional technology (Graduate Certificate), including distance education, Florida digital/virtual educator, instructional design, multimedia design, Web design; internal medicine, bioethics and medical humanities (Graduate Certificate), including biomedical ethics; Latin American and Caribbean studies (Graduate Certificate); leadership for coastal resiliency planning (Graduate Certificate); mass communications (Graduate Certificate), including multimedia journalism; mathematics and statistics (Graduate Certificate), including mathematics; medicine (Graduate Certificate), including aging and neuroscience, bioinformatics, biotechnology, brain fitness and memory management, clinical investigation, hand and upper limb rehabilitation, health informatics, health sciences, integrative weight management, intellectual property, medicine and gender, metabolic and nutritional medicine, metabolic cardiology, pharmacy sciences; national and competitive intelligence (Graduate Certificate); nursing (Graduate Certificate), including simulation based academic fellowship in advanced pain management; psychological and social foundations (Graduate Certificate), including career counseling, college teaching, diversity in education, mental health counseling, school counseling; public affairs (Graduate Certificate), including nonprofit management, public management, research administration; public health (Graduate Certificate), including assessing chemical toxicity and public health risks, health equity, pharmacoepidemiology, public health generalist, toxicology, translational research in adolescent behavioral health; public health practices (Graduate Certificate), including planning for healthy communities; rehabilitation and mental health counseling (Graduate Certificate), including integrative mental health care, marriage and family therapy, rehabilitation technology; secondary education (Graduate Certificate), including ESOL, foreign language education: culture and content, foreign language education: professional; social work (Graduate Certificate), including geriatric social work/clinical gerontology; special education (Graduate Certificate), including autism spectrum disorder, disabilities education: severe/profound; world languages (Graduate Certificate), including teaching English as a second language (TESL) or foreign language. *Unit head:* Dr. Cynthia DeLuca, Associate Vice President and Assistant Vice Provost, 813-974-3077, Fax: 813-974-7061, E-mail: deluca@usf.edu. *Application contact:* Owen Hooper, Director, Summer and Alternative Calendar Programs, 813-974-6917, E-mail: hooper@usf.edu.
Website: http://www.usf.edu/innovative-education/

Virginia Polytechnic Institute and State University, VT Online, Blacksburg, VA 24061. Offers advanced transportation systems (Certificate); aerospace engineering (MS); agricultural and life sciences (MSLFS); business information systems (Graduate Certificate); career and technical education (MS); civil engineering (MS); computer engineering (M Eng, MS); decision support systems (Graduate Certificate); eLearning leadership (MA); electrical engineering (M Eng, MS); engineering administration (MEA); environmental engineering (Certificate); environmental politics and policy (Graduate Certificate); environmental sciences and engineering (MS); foundations of political analysis (Graduate Certificate); health product risk management (Graduate Certificate); industrial and systems engineering (MS); information policy and society (Graduate Certificate); information security (Graduate Certificate); information technology (MIT); instructional technology (MA); integrative STEM education (MA Ed); liberal arts (Graduate Certificate); life sciences: health product risk management (MS); natural resources (MNR, Graduate Certificate); networking (Graduate Certificate); nonprofit and nongovernmental organization management (Graduate Certificate); ocean engineering (MS); political science (MA); security studies (Graduate Certificate); software development (Graduate Certificate). *Expenses:* Tuition, state resident: full-time $15,072; part-time $718.50 per credit hour. Tuition, nonresident: full-time $28,810; part-time $1448.25 per credit hour. *Required fees:* $2741; $502 per semester. Tuition and fees vary according to course load, campus/location and program.

Walden University, Graduate Programs, Richard W. Riley College of Education and Leadership, Minneapolis, MN 55401. Offers adult education (Post-Master's Certificate); adult learning (Graduate Certificate); college teaching and learning (Graduate Certificate); community college leadership (Ed D); curriculum, instruction and assessment (Ed D, Ed S, Graduate Certificate); developmental education (Graduate Certificate); early childhood administration, management, and leadership (Graduate Certificate); early childhood education (Ed D, Ed S); early childhood public policy and advocacy (Graduate Certificate); early childhood studies (MS), including administration, management and leadership, early childhood public policy and advocacy, teaching adults in the early childhood field, teaching and diversity in early childhood education; education (MS, PhD), including adolescent literacy and learning (MS), curriculum, instruction, and assessment (grades K-12) (MS), curriculum, instruction, assessment, and evaluation (PhD), early childhood leadership and advocacy (PhD), early childhood special education (PhD), educational leadership (MS), educational leadership and administration (principal preparation) (MS), educational technology and design (PhD), elementary reading and literacy (PreK-6) (MS), elementary reading and mathematics (grades K-6) (MS), global and comparative education (PhD), higher education leadership management and policy (PhD), integrating technology in the classroom (grades K-12) (MS), learning, instruction and innovation (PhD), mathematics (grades 5-8) (MS), mathematics (grades K-6) (MS), mathematics and science (grades K-8) (MS), organizational research, assessment, and evaluation (PhD), reading and literacy with a reading K-12 endorsement (MS), reading literacy assessment and evaluation (PhD), science (grades K-8) (MS), special education (non-licensure) (grades K-12) (MS), teacher leadership (grades K-12) (MS), teaching English language learners (grades K-

12) (MS); educational administration and leadership (Ed D); educational leadership and administration (principal preparation) (Ed S); educational technology (Ed D, Ed S, Post Master's Certificate); elementary reading and literacy (Graduate Certificate); engaging culturally diverse learners (Graduate Certificate); enrollment management and institutional marketing (Graduate Certificate); higher education (MS), including adult learning, college teaching and learning, enrollment management and institutional marketing, global higher education, leadership for student success, online and distance learning; higher education and adult learning (Ed D); higher education leadership and management (Ed D); higher education leadership for student success (Graduate Certificate); instructional design and technology (MS, Postbaccalaureate Certificate), including general program (MS), online learning (MS), training and performance improvement (MS); integrating technology in the classroom (Graduate Certificate); mathematics 5-8 (Graduate Certificate); mathematics K-6 (Graduate Certificate); online teaching for adult educators (Graduate Certificate); reading, literacy, and assessment (Ed D, Ed S); science K-8 (Graduate Certificate); special education (Ed D, Ed S, Graduate Certificate); special education (K-age 21) (MAT); teacher leadership (Graduate Certificate); teaching adults English as a second language (Graduate Certificate); teaching adults in the early childhood field (Graduate Certificate); teaching and diversity in early childhood education (Graduate Certificate); teaching English language learners (grades K-12) (Graduate Certificate); teaching K-12 students online (Graduate Certificate). *Accreditation:* NCATE. *Program availability:* Part-time, evening/ weekend, online only, 100% online. *Degree requirements:* For doctorate, thesis/ dissertation (for some programs), residency; for other advanced degree, residency (for some programs). *Entrance requirements:* For master's, bachelor's degree or higher; minimum GPA of 2.5; official transcripts; goal statement (for some programs); access to computer and Internet; for doctorate, master's degree or higher; three years of related professional or academic experience (preferred); minimum GPA of 3.0; goal statement and current resume (for select programs); official transcripts; access to computer and Internet; for other advanced degree, relevant work experience; access to computer and Internet. Additional exam requirements/recommendations for international students: Required—TOEFL (minimum score 550 paper-based; 79 iBT), IELTS (minimum score 6.5), Michigan English Language Assessment Battery (minimum score 82), or PTE (minimum score 53). Electronic applications accepted.

Waynesburg University, Graduate and Professional Studies, Canonsburg, PA 15370. Offers business (MBA), including energy management, finance, health systems, human resources, leadership, market development; counseling (MA), including addictions counseling, clinical mental health; counselor education and supervision (PhD); criminal investigation (MA); education (M Ed), including autism, curriculum and instruction, educational leadership, online teaching; nursing (MSN), including administration, education, informatics; nursing practice (DNP); special education (M Ed); technology (M Ed); MSN/MBA. *Accreditation:* AACN. *Program availability:* Part-time, evening/ weekend. *Degree requirements:* For doctorate, thesis/dissertation. *Entrance requirements:* Additional exam requirements/recommendations for international students: Required—TOEFL. Electronic applications accepted.

Wayne State University, College of Education, Division of Administrative and Organizational Studies, Detroit, MI 48202. Offers educational administration and supervision (Ed S); educational leadership (M Ed); educational leadership and policy studies (Ed D, PhD); educational technology (Certificate); learning design and technology (M Ed, Ed D, PhD, Ed S); online teaching (Certificate). *Program availability:* Part-time, 100% online, blended/hybrid learning. *Faculty:* 7. *Students:* 50 full-time (30 women), 266 part-time (184 women); includes 158 minority (130 Black or African American, non-Hispanic/Latino; 1 American Indian or Alaska Native, non-Hispanic/ Latino; 5 Asian, non-Hispanic/Latino; 9 Hispanic/Latino; 1 Native Hawaiian or other Pacific Islander, non-Hispanic/Latino; 12 Two or more races, non-Hispanic/Latino), 9 international. Average age 39. 187 applicants, 31% accepted, 42 enrolled. In 2017, 48 master's, 17 doctorates, 47 other advanced degrees awarded. *Degree requirements:* For master's, thesis (for some programs); for doctorate, thesis/dissertation. *Entrance requirements:* For master's, baccalaureate degree from accredited U.S. institution or equivalent from college or university of government-recognized standing; minimum undergraduate GPA of 2.75 in upper-division coursework; personal statement; for doctorate, GRE (instructional design and technology), interview; curriculum vitae; three to four recommendations; master's degree (for educational leadership and policy studies); minimum graduate GPA of 3.5; autobiographical statement; research

experience (for PhD program). Additional exam requirements/recommendations for international students: Required—TOEFL (minimum score 550 paper-based; 79 iBT); Recommended—IELTS (minimum score 6.5), TWE (minimum score 5.5). *Application deadline:* For fall admission, 6/1 priority date for domestic students, 5/1 priority date for international students; for winter admission, 10/1 priority date for domestic students, 9/1 priority date for international students; for spring admission, 2/1 priority date for domestic students, 1/1 priority date for international students. Applications are processed on a rolling basis. Application fee: $50. Electronic applications accepted. *Expenses:* Tuition, state resident: full-time $10,224; part-time $638.98 per credit hour. Tuition, nonresident: full-time $22,145; part-time $1384.04 per credit hour. Tuition and fees vary according to course load and program. *Financial support:* In 2017–18, 85 students received support, including 4 research assistantships with tuition reimbursements available (averaging $18,534 per year); fellowships with tuition reimbursements available, scholarships/ grants, and unspecified assistantships also available. Support available to part-time students. Financial award applicants required to submit FAFSA. *Faculty research:* Total quality management, participatory management, administering educational technology, school improvement, principalship. *Unit head:* Dr. William Hill, Assistant Dean, 313-577-9316, E-mail: ad2107@wayne.edu. *Application contact:* Graduate Advisor, 313-577-1605, E-mail: askcoe@wayne.edu.
Website: http://coe.wayne.edu/aos/index.php

Western Illinois University, School of Graduate Studies, College of Business and Technology, Program in Instructional Design and Technology, Macomb, IL 61455-1390. Offers educational technology specialist (Certificate); instructional design and technology (MS); instructional media development (Certificate); online and distance learning development (Certificate); technology integration in education (Certificate); workplace learning and performance (Certificate). *Program availability:* Part-time, online learning. *Students:* 8 full-time (4 women), 48 part-time (29 women); includes 4 minority (2 Black or African American, non-Hispanic/Latino; 1 Asian, non-Hispanic/Latino; 1 Hispanic/Latino), 2 international. Average age 35. 12 applicants, 83% accepted, 6 enrolled. In 2017, 18 master's awarded. *Degree requirements:* For master's, thesis or alternative. *Entrance requirements:* Additional exam requirements/recommendations for international students: Required—TOEFL (minimum score 550 paper-based; 80 iBT). *Application deadline:* Applications are processed on a rolling basis. Application fee: $30. Electronic applications accepted. *Financial support:* Teaching assistantships and unspecified assistantships available. Financial award applicants required to submit FAFSA. *Unit head:* Dr. Hoyet Hemphill, Chairperson, 309-298-1952. *Application contact:* Dr. Nancy Parsons, Associate Provost and Director of Graduate Studies, 309-298-1806, Fax: 309-298-2345, E-mail: grad-office@wiu.edu.
Website: http://wiu.edu/idt

Wilkes University, College of Graduate and Professional Studies, School of Education, Wilkes-Barre, PA 18766-0002. Offers educational development and strategies (MS Ed); educational leadership (MS Ed, Ed D); effective teaching (MS Ed); instructional media (MS Ed); instructional technology (MS Ed); international school leadership (MS Ed); international teaching and learning (MS Ed); literacy specialist (MS Ed); middle level education (MS Ed); online teaching (MS Ed); school business leadership (MS Ed); special education (MS Ed); teaching English to speakers of other languages (MS Ed). *Program availability:* Part-time, evening/weekend, 100% online, blended/hybrid learning. *Students:* 76 full-time (57 women), 1,586 part-time (1,204 women); includes 82 minority (10 Black or African American, non-Hispanic/Latino; 12 Asian, non-Hispanic/Latino; 41 Hispanic/Latino; 1 Native Hawaiian or other Pacific Islander, non-Hispanic/Latino; 18 Two or more races, non-Hispanic/Latino). Average age 34. In 2017, 619 master's, 23 doctorates awarded. *Entrance requirements:* Additional exam requirements/ recommendations for international students: Required—TOEFL (minimum score 550 paper-based; 79 iBT). *Application deadline:* Applications are processed on a rolling basis. Application fee: $45 ($65 for international students). Electronic applications accepted. *Expenses:* Contact institution. *Financial support:* Unspecified assistantships available. Financial award application deadline: 3/1; financial award applicants required to submit FAFSA. *Unit head:* Dr. Rhonda Rabbitt, Dean, 570-408-4680, Fax: 570-408-7872, E-mail: rhonda.rabbitt@wilkes.edu. *Application contact:* Stephanie Wasmanski, Associate Director of Graduate Admissions, 570-408-5535, Fax: 570-408-7846, E-mail: stephanie.wasmanski@wilkes.edu.
Website: http://www.wilkes.edu/academics/graduate-programs/masters-programs/graduate-education/index.aspx

Educational Leadership and Administration

Abilene Christian University, College of Graduate and Professional Studies, Instruction and Learning Program, Abilene, TX 79699. Offers conflict management (M Ed); learning with emerging technologies (M Ed, Certificate). *Program availability:* Part-time, online only. *Faculty:* 2 full-time (1 woman), 1 part-time/adjunct (0 women). *Students:* 14 full-time (11 women); includes 3 minority (all Black or African American, non-Hispanic/Latino). 25 applicants, 44% accepted, 5 enrolled. *Degree requirements:* For master's, comprehensive exam, practicum. *Entrance requirements:* Additional exam requirements/recommendations for international students: Required—TOEFL (minimum score 80 iBT), IELTS (minimum score 6), PTE. *Application deadline:* For fall admission, 8/15 priority date for domestic students; for winter admission, 10/1 priority date for domestic students; for spring admission, 12/15 priority date for domestic students; for summer admission, 4/15 priority date for domestic students. Applications are processed on a rolling basis. Application fee: $50. Electronic applications accepted. *Expenses:* $600 per hour. *Financial support:* Application deadline: 4/1; applicants required to submit FAFSA. *Unit head:* Dr. Peter Williams, Program Director, 214-721-0685, E-mail: peter.williams@acu.edu. *Application contact:* Graduate Admissions, 855-219-7300, E-mail: gradonline@acu.edu.
Website: http://www.acu.edu/online/academics/master-of-education-in-instructional-leadership.html

Abilene Christian University, College of Graduate and Professional Studies, Program in Organizational Leadership, Addison, TX 75001. Offers Ed D. *Program availability:* Part-time, online only, 100% online. *Faculty:* 9 full-time (6 women), 18 part-time/adjunct (10 women). *Students:* 251 full-time (167 women), 106 part-time (64 women); includes 147 minority (131 Black or African American, non-Hispanic/Latino; 3 American Indian or Alaska Native, non-Hispanic/Latino; 4 Asian, non-Hispanic/Latino; 9 Hispanic/Latino), 1 international. 266 applicants, 46% accepted, 116 enrolled. *Degree requirements:* For doctorate, thesis/dissertation. *Entrance requirements:* Additional exam requirements/ recommendations for international students: Required—TOEFL (minimum score 80 iBT), IELTS (minimum score 6). *Application deadline:* For fall admission, 8/15 priority date for domestic students; for winter admission, 10/1 priority date for domestic students; for spring admission, 12/15 priority date for domestic students; for summer

admission, 4/15 priority date for domestic students. Applications are processed on a rolling basis. Application fee: $50. Electronic applications accepted. *Expenses:* $700 per hour. *Financial support:* Scholarships/grants available. Financial award application deadline: 4/1; financial award applicants required to submit FAFSA. *Unit head:* Dr. Sarah Lee, Interim Program Director, 214-308-9500, E-mail: skm00c@acu.edu. *Application contact:* Graduate Advisor, 855-219-7300, E-mail: gradonline@acu.edu.
Website: http://www.acu.edu/online/academics/organizational-leadership.html

Acacia University, American Graduate School of Education, Tempe, AZ 85284. Offers educational administration (M Ed); elementary education (MA); English as a second language (M Ed); secondary education (MA); special education (M Ed).

Acadia University, Faculty of Professional Studies, School of Education, Program in Leadership, Wolfville, NS B4P 2R6, Canada. Offers M Ed. *Program availability:* Part-time. *Degree requirements:* For master's, thesis optional. *Entrance requirements:* For master's, B Ed or the equivalent, 2 years of teaching or related experience. Additional exam requirements/recommendations for international students: Required—TOEFL (minimum score 580 paper-based; 93 iBT), IELTS (minimum score 6.5). *Application deadline:* For fall admission, 3/15 priority date for domestic and international students. Applications are processed on a rolling basis. Application fee: $50. *Financial support:* Application deadline: 3/15. *Faculty research:* Organizational theory and structural change, professionalism, sexuality education. *Unit head:* Dr. Ann Vibert, Director, 902-585-1229, E-mail: ann.vibert@acadiau.ca. *Application contact:* Shauna Sweeney, Secretary, 902-585-1759, Fax: 902-585-1071, E-mail: shauna.sweeney@acadiau.ca.
Website: http://education.acadiau.ca/

Adams State University, Office of Graduate Studies, Department of Teacher Education, Alamosa, CO 81101. Offers teacher education (MA), including adaptive leadership, curriculum and instruction, curriculum and instruction-STEM, educational leadership. *Program availability:* Part-time, online learning. *Degree requirements:* For master's, qualifying exam. *Entrance requirements:* For master's, GRE General Test or MAT, minimum undergraduate GPA of 3.0. *Application deadline:* For fall admission, 5/15 priority date for domestic students; for spring admission, 10/15 for domestic students.

Applications are processed on a rolling basis. Application fee: $30. *Expenses:* Tuition, state resident: full-time $4800; part-time $2400 per credit. Tuition, nonresident: full-time $7100; part-time $3550 per credit. *Required fees:* $213; $106 per credit. One-time fee: $100. Tuition and fees vary according to campus/location and program. *Financial support:* In 2017–18, fellowships with partial tuition reimbursements (averaging $4,000 per year), teaching assistantships with partial tuition reimbursements (averaging $4,000 per year) were awarded; career-related internships or fieldwork, Federal Work-Study, institutionally sponsored loans, and unspecified assistantships also available. Support available to part-time students. Financial award application deadline: 4/15; financial award applicants required to submit FAFSA. *Unit head:* Dr. Cheri Meder, Interim Chair, 719-587-7934, Fax: 719-587-8145, E-mail: teachered@adams.edu. *Application contact:* Information Contact, 719-587-7776, Fax: 719-587-8145, E-mail: teachered@adams.edu.
Website: http://teachered.adams.edu

Alabama State University, College of Education, Department of Instructional Support Programs, Montgomery, AL 36101-0271. Offers applied technology (MS); counselor education (M Ed, MS, Ed S), including general counseling (MS, Ed S), school counseling (M Ed, Ed S); educational administration (M Ed, Ed D, PhD, Ed S), including educational administration (Ed S), educational leadership, policy and law (Ed D, PhD), instructional leadership (M Ed), teacher leadership (Ed S); library education media (M Ed, Ed S). *Program availability:* Part-time. *Faculty:* 11 full-time (6 women), 7 part-time/adjunct (5 women). *Students:* 35 full-time (20 women), 112 part-time (81 women); includes 139 minority (all Black or African American, non-Hispanic/Latino), 1 international. Average age 37. 48 applicants, 75% accepted, 16 enrolled. In 2017, 31 master's, 4 doctorates awarded. Terminal master's awarded for partial completion of doctoral program. *Degree requirements:* For master's, comprehensive exam; for Ed S, comprehensive exam, thesis. *Entrance requirements:* For master's, GRE General Test, MAT, writing competency test, bachelor's degree or its equivalent from accredited college or university with minimum GPA of 2.5; for Ed S, GRE General Test, MAT, writing competency test, minimum GPA of 3.25. Additional exam requirements/recommendations for international students: Required—TOEFL (minimum score 500 paper-based). *Application deadline:* For fall admission, 4/15 for domestic and international students; for spring admission, 11/15 for domestic and international students; for summer admission, 3/15 for domestic and international students. Applications are processed on a rolling basis. Application fee: $25. Electronic applications accepted. *Expenses:* Contact institution. *Financial support:* In 2017–18, 3 students received support. Research assistantships and unspecified assistantships available. Financial award application deadline: 6/30; financial award applicants required to submit FAFSA. *Unit head:* Dr. Sonja Harrington, Chair, 334-229-8828, Fax: 334-229-6831, E-mail: sharrington@alasu.edu. *Application contact:* Dr. William Person, Dean of Graduate Studies, 334-229-4275, Fax: 334-229-4928, E-mail: wperson@alasu.edu.
Website: http://www.alasu.edu/academics/colleges—departments/college-of-education/instructional-support-programs/index.aspx

Albany State University, College of Education, Albany, GA 31705-2717. Offers early childhood education (M Ed); educational leadership (Ed S); health and physical education (M Ed); middle grades education (M Ed); school counseling (M Ed); special education (M Ed). *Accreditation:* NCATE. *Program availability:* Part-time, evening/weekend, online learning. *Degree requirements:* For master's, comprehensive exam, internship, GACE Content Exam. *Entrance requirements:* For master's, GRE or MAT. Electronic applications accepted. *Faculty research:* GACE preparation, STEM (science, technology, engineering, and mathematics), technology education, special education, professional teacher development, health implications liberation philosophy, NET-Q, learning community, disabled or at-risk students.

Alliant International University–San Diego, Shirley M. Hufstedler School of Education, Educational Leadership Programs, San Diego, CA 92131. Offers educational administration (MA); educational leadership and management (K-12) (Ed D); higher education (Ed D, Certificate); preliminary administrative services (Credential). *Program availability:* Part-time. *Degree requirements:* For doctorate, comprehensive exam, thesis/dissertation. *Entrance requirements:* For master's, minimum GPA of 2.5, letters of recommendation; for doctorate, minimum GPA of 3.0, letters of recommendation. Additional exam requirements/recommendations for international students: Required—TOEFL (minimum score 550 paper-based; 80 iBT), TWE (minimum score 5). Electronic applications accepted. *Faculty research:* Global education, women and international educational opportunities.

Alliant International University–San Francisco, Shirley M. Hufstedler School of Education, Educational Leadership Programs, San Francisco, CA 94133. Offers community college administration (Ed D); educational administration (MA); educational leadership and management (K-12) (Ed D); higher education (Ed D); preliminary administrative services (Credential). *Program availability:* Part-time. *Degree requirements:* For doctorate, comprehensive exam, thesis/dissertation. *Entrance requirements:* For master's and doctorate, minimum GPA of 3.0, letters of recommendation. Additional exam requirements/recommendations for international students: Required—TOEFL (minimum score 550 paper-based; 80 iBT), TWE (minimum score 5). Electronic applications accepted. *Faculty research:* Leadership in higher education, community colleges.

Alverno College, School of Professional Studies - Education Division, Milwaukee, WI 53234-3922. Offers adaptive education (MA); administrative leadership (MA); adult education and organizational development (MA); adult educational and instructional design (MA); adult educational and instructional technology (MA); global connections in the humanities (MA); instructional leadership (MA); instructional technology for K-12 settings (MA); professional development (MA); reading education (MA); reading education with adaptive education (MA); science education (MA); special education (MA); teaching in alternative schools (MA). *Accreditation:* NCATE. *Program availability:* Part-time, evening/weekend. *Faculty:* 3 full-time (2 women), 23 part-time/adjunct (17 women). *Students:* 37 full-time (34 women), 68 part-time (65 women); includes 27 minority (16 Black or African American, non-Hispanic/Latino; 1 American Indian or Alaska Native, non-Hispanic/Latino; 1 Asian, non-Hispanic/Latino; 7 Hispanic/Latino; 2 Two or more races, non-Hispanic/Latino). Average age 35. 67 applicants, 100% accepted, 51 enrolled. In 2017, 68 master's awarded. *Degree requirements:* For master's, presentation/defense of proposal, conference presentation of inquiry projects. *Entrance requirements:* For master's, bachelor's degree in related field, communication samples from work setting, 3 letters of recommendation. Additional exam requirements/recommendations for international students: Required—TOEFL. *Application deadline:* For fall admission, 7/15 priority date for domestic and international students; for spring admission, 12/15 priority date for domestic and international students. Applications are processed on a rolling basis. Application fee: $0. Electronic applications accepted. *Expenses:* Contact institution. *Financial support:* Federal Work-Study and scholarships/grants available. Support available to part-time students. Financial award applicants required to submit FAFSA. *Faculty research:* Student self-assessment, self-reflection, integration of curriculum, identifying needs of students in strategic situations and designing appropriate classroom strategies. *Unit head:* Dr. Patricia Luebke, Dean, School of Professional Studies, 414-382-6368, Fax: 414-382-6354, E-mail: patricia.luebke@alverno.edu. *Application contact:* Katie Kipp, Graduate Admissions Counselor, 414-382-6045, Fax: 414-382-6354, E-mail: katie.kipp@alverno.edu.

American College of Education, Graduate Programs, Indianapolis, IN 46204. Offers curriculum and instruction (M Ed), including bilingual, ESL; educational leadership (M Ed); educational technology (M Ed).

American InterContinental University Online, Program in Education, Schaumburg, IL 60173. Offers curriculum and instruction (M Ed); educational assessment and evaluation (M Ed); instructional technology (M Ed); leadership of educational organizations (M Ed). *Accreditation:* TEAC. *Program availability:* Evening/weekend, online learning. *Entrance requirements:* Additional exam requirements/recommendations for international students: Required—TOEFL (minimum score 550 paper-based). Electronic applications accepted.

American International College, School of Education, Low Residency Programs, Springfield, MA 01109-3189. Offers counseling psychology (MA); educational leadership and supervision (Ed D); professional counseling and supervision (Ed D); teaching and learning (Ed D). *Program availability:* Evening/weekend. *Faculty:* 2 full-time (1 woman), 4 part-time/adjunct (all women). *Students:* 117 full-time (90 women); includes 32 minority (22 Black or African American, non-Hispanic/Latino; 1 Asian, non-Hispanic/Latino; 7 Hispanic/Latino; 2 Two or more races, non-Hispanic/Latino). Average age 40. 35 applicants, 86% accepted, 20 enrolled. In 2017, 8 master's, 12 doctorates awarded. *Degree requirements:* For doctorate, thesis/dissertation. *Entrance requirements:* For master's, minimum undergraduate GPA of 3.0, 2 letters of recommendation, personal goal statement, official transcript of all academic work (graduate and undergraduate); for doctorate, minimum master's GPA of 3.0, 3 letters of recommendation, personal goal statement/essay (6-8 pages), official transcript of all academic work (graduate and undergraduate). Additional exam requirements/recommendations for international students: Required—TOEFL. *Application deadline:* For fall admission, 8/15 for domestic and international students; for spring admission, 1/3 for domestic and international students; for summer admission, 5/15 for domestic and international students. Applications are processed on a rolling basis. Application fee: $50. *Expenses:* $6,515 per trimester (for EdD); $505 per credit (for MA); $30 per term registration fee; $100 one-time graduation fee. *Faculty research:* Educational leadership, curriculum, program evaluation, educational policy. *Unit head:* Dr. Nicholas Young, Dean, Low Residency Programs, 413-205-1726, E-mail: nicholas.young@aic.edu. *Application contact:* Kerry Barnes, Director of Graduate Admissions, 413-205-3703, Fax: 413-205-3051, E-mail: kerry.barnes@aic.edu.

American Public University System, AMU/APU Graduate Programs, Charles Town, WV 25414. Offers accounting (MS); applied business analytics (MS); business administration (MBA); criminal justice (MA); cybersecurity studies (MS); educational leadership (M Ed); environmental policy and management (MS); global security (DGS); health information management (MS); history (MA), including American military history, American Revolution, civil war, war since 1945, World War II; information technology (MS); international relations and conflict resolution (MA), including American politics and government, comparative government and development, general, international relations, public policy; national security studies (MA); nursing (MSN); political science (MA); public policy (MPP); reverse logistics management (MA), including comparative and security issues, conflict resolution, international and transnational security issues, peacekeeping; space studies (MS); sports management (MS); strategic intelligence (DSI); teaching (M Ed), including secondary social studies; transportation and logistics management (MA). *Program availability:* Part-time, evening/weekend, online only, 100% online. *Students:* 455 full-time (227 women), 7,939 part-time (3,353 women); includes 2,793 minority (1,429 Black or African American, non-Hispanic/Latino; 48 American Indian or Alaska Native, non-Hispanic/Latino; 205 Asian, non-Hispanic/Latino; 766 Hispanic/Latino; 62 Native Hawaiian or other Pacific Islander, non-Hispanic/Latino; 283 Two or more races, non-Hispanic/Latino), 101 international. Average age 37. In 2017, 2,977 master's awarded. *Degree requirements:* For master's, comprehensive exam or practicum. *Entrance requirements:* For master's, official transcript showing earned bachelor's degree from institution accredited by recognized accrediting body. Additional exam requirements/recommendations for international students: Required—TOEFL (minimum score 550 paper-based), IELTS (minimum score 6.5). *Application deadline:* Applications are processed on a rolling basis. Application fee: $0. Electronic applications accepted. *Expenses: Tuition:* Full-time $6300; part-time $350 per credit. *Required fees:* $300; $50 per course. *Financial support:* Scholarships/grants available. Financial award applicants required to submit FAFSA. *Unit head:* Dr. Wallace Boston, President, 877-468-6268, Fax: 304-728-2348, E-mail: president@apus.edu. *Application contact:* Yoci Deal, Associate Vice President, Graduate and International Admissions, 877-468-6268, Fax: 304-724-3764, E-mail: info@apus.edu.
Website: http://www.apus.edu

The American University in Cairo, Graduate School of Education, Cairo, Egypt. Offers educational leadership (MA); international and comparative education (MA). *Program availability:* Part-time, evening/weekend. *Faculty:* 9 full-time (6 women). *Students:* 6 full-time (4 women), 77 part-time (65 women). Average age 33. 40 applicants, 48% accepted, 11 enrolled. In 2017, 24 master's awarded. *Degree requirements:* For master's, thesis. *Entrance requirements:* Additional exam requirements/recommendations for international students: Required—TOEFL (minimum score 450 paper-based; 45 iBT), IELTS (minimum score 5). *Application deadline:* For fall admission, 2/1 priority date for domestic and international students; for spring admission, 10/15 priority date for domestic and international students. Applications are processed on a rolling basis. Application fee: $85. Electronic applications accepted. *Financial support:* Fellowships with partial tuition reimbursements, teaching assistantships, career-related internships or fieldwork, scholarships/grants, tuition waivers (partial), and unspecified assistantships available. Financial award application deadline: 3/10. *Faculty research:* Educational reform. *Unit head:* Dr. Ted Purinton, Dean, 20-2-2615-1490, E-mail: tedpurinton@aucegypt.edu. *Application contact:* Maha Hegazi, Director for Graduate Admissions, 20-2-2615-1462, E-mail: mahahegazi@aucegypt.edu.
Website: http://www.aucegypt.edu/GSE/Pages/default.aspx

American University of Beirut, Graduate Programs, Faculty of Arts and Sciences, 1107 2020, Lebanon. Offers anthropology (MA); Arab and Middle Eastern history (PhD); Arabic language and literature (MA, PhD); archaeology (MA); art history and curating (MA); biology (MS); cell and molecular biology (PhD); chemistry (MS); clinical psychology (MA); computational sciences (MS); computer science (MS); economics (MA); education (MA), including administration and policy studies, elementary education, mathematics education, psychology school guidance, psychology test and measurements, science education, teaching English as a foreign language; English language (MA); English literature (MA); environmental policy planning (MS); financial economics (MAFE); general psychology (MA); geology (MS); history (MA); Islamic studies (MA); mathematics (MS); media studies (MA); Middle East studies (MA); philosophy (MA); physics (MS); political studies (MA); public administration (MA); public policy and international affairs (MA); sociology (MA); theoretical physics (PhD). *Program availability:* Part-time. *Faculty:* 108 full-time (36 women), 5 part-time/adjunct (4 women). *Students:* 251 full-time (180 women), 233 part-time (172 women). Average age 26. 425 applicants, 65% accepted, 121 enrolled. In 2017, 47 master's, 2 doctorates awarded.

Educational Leadership and Administration

Degree requirements: For master's, one foreign language, comprehensive exam, thesis (for some programs), project; for doctorate, one foreign language, comprehensive exam, thesis/dissertation. *Entrance requirements:* For master's, GRE General Test (for some programs); for doctorate, GRE General Test (GRE Subject Test for theoretical physics). Additional exam requirements/recommendations for international students: Required—TOEFL (minimum score 583 paper-based; 97 iBT), IELTS (minimum score 7). *Application deadline:* For fall admission, 2/8 for domestic students; for spring admission, 11/3 for domestic students. Application fee: $50. Electronic applications accepted. *Expenses:* Contact institution. *Financial support:* In 2017–18, 29 fellowships, 40 research assistantships were awarded; teaching assistantships, scholarships/grants, tuition waivers (full and partial), and unspecified assistantships also available. Financial award application deadline: 4/4. *Unit head:* Dr. Nadia Maria El Cheikh, Dean, Faculty of Arts and Sciences, 961-1-374374 Ext. 3800, Fax: 961-1-744461, E-mail: nmcheikh@aub.edu.lb. *Application contact:* Rima Rassi, Graduate Studies Officer, 961-1-350000 Ext. 3833, Fax: 961-1-744461, E-mail: rr46@aub.edu.lb. Website: http://www.aub.edu.lb/fas/pages/default.aspx

Anderson University, College of Education, Anderson, SC 29621-4035. Offers administration and supervision (M Ed); education (M Ed); elementary education (MAT). *Accreditation:* NCATE. *Program availability:* 100% online. *Expenses:* Contact institution. *Financial support:* Tuition waivers available. Financial award application deadline: 3/1; financial award applicants required to submit FAFSA. *Unit head:* Dr. Mark Butler, Dean, 864-231-2042. *Application contact:* Mallory Knight, Graduate Admission Counselor, 864-231-2182, Fax: 864-231-2115, E-mail: malloryknight@andersonuniversity.edu. Website: https://www.andersonuniversity.edu/education

Andrews University, School of Graduate Studies, School of Education, Department of Leadership and Educational Administration, Program in Educational Administration and Leadership, Berrien Springs, MI 49104. Offers MA, Ed D, PhD, Ed S. *Students:* 17 full-time (10 women), 20 part-time (11 women); includes 18 minority (10 Black or African American, non-Hispanic/Latino; 3 Asian, non-Hispanic/Latino; 3 Hispanic/Latino; 2 Two or more races, non-Hispanic/Latino), 8 international. Average age 46. 26 applicants, 69% accepted, 10 enrolled. In 2017, 6 master's, 3 doctorates, 4 other advanced degrees awarded. *Degree requirements:* For master's, thesis or alternative; for doctorate, thesis/dissertation. *Entrance requirements:* For master's and doctorate, GRE Subject Test. Additional exam requirements/recommendations for international students: Required—TOEFL (minimum score 550 paper-based). *Application deadline:* Applications are processed on a rolling basis. Application fee: $40. *Financial support:* Research assistantships available. *Unit head:* Dr. Robson Marinho, Coordinator, 269-471-3487. *Application contact:* Justina Clayburn, Supervisor of Graduate Admission, 800-253-2874, Fax: 269-471-6321, E-mail: graduate@andrews.edu.

Andrews University, School of Graduate Studies, School of Education, Department of Leadership and Educational Administration, Program in Leadership, Berrien Springs, MI 49104. Offers MA, Ed D, PhD, Ed S. *Students:* 24 full-time (11 women), 26 part-time (12 women); includes 14 minority (3 Black or African American, non-Hispanic/Latino; 1 Asian, non-Hispanic/Latino; 9 Hispanic/Latino; 1 Two or more races, non-Hispanic/Latino), 14 international. Average age 49. 32 applicants, 50% accepted, 5 enrolled. In 2017, 4 master's awarded. *Entrance requirements:* For master's, GRE. Additional exam requirements/recommendations for international students: Required—TOEFL (minimum score 550 paper-based). Application fee: $40. *Unit head:* Dr. Robson Marinho, Chair, 269-471-6580. *Application contact:* Justina Clayburn, Supervisor of Graduate Admission, 800-253-2874, Fax: 269-471-6321, E-mail: graduate@andrews.edu.

Angelo State University, College of Graduate Studies and Research, College of Education, Department of Curriculum and Instruction, San Angelo, TX 76909. Offers curriculum and instruction (MA); educational administration (M Ed); guidance and counseling (M Ed); student development and leadership in higher education (M Ed). *Program availability:* Part-time, evening/weekend, online learning. *Students:* 405 full-time (332 women), 449 part-time (380 women); includes 291 minority (98 Black or African American, non-Hispanic/Latino; 3 American Indian or Alaska Native, non-Hispanic/Latino; 3 Asian, non-Hispanic/Latino; 178 Hispanic/Latino; 9 Two or more races, non-Hispanic/Latino), 1 international. Average age 35. *Application deadline:* For fall admission, 7/15 priority date for domestic students, 6/10 for international students; for spring admission, 12/1 priority date for domestic students, 11/1 for international students. Application fee: $40 ($50 for international students). *Expenses:* Tuition, state resident: full-time $3856. Tuition, nonresident: full-time $11,324. *Required fees:* $2650. *Unit head:* Dr. Jim Summerlin, Chair, 325-942-2647, Fax: 325-942-2039, E-mail: james.summerlin@angelo.edu. *Application contact:* Lesley Casarez, Graduate Advisor, 325-486-6775, E-mail: lesley.casarez@angelo.edu. Website: http://www.angelo.edu/dept/ci/

Antioch University New England, Graduate School, Department of Education, Experienced Educators Program, Keene, NH 03431-3552. Offers foundations of education (M Ed), including applied behavioral analysis, autism spectrum disorders, educating for sustainability, next-generation learning using technology, problem-based learning using critical skills, teacher leadership; principal certification (PMC). *Degree requirements:* For master's, thesis, practicum. *Entrance requirements:* For master's, previous course work and work experience in education. Additional exam requirements/recommendations for international students: Required—TOEFL (minimum score 550 paper-based). Electronic applications accepted. *Expenses:* Contact institution. *Faculty research:* Classroom action research, school restructuring, problem-based learning, brain-based learning.

Appalachian State University, Cratis D. Williams Graduate School, Department of Leadership and Educational Studies, Boone, NC 28608. Offers educational administration (Ed S); educational media (MA); higher education (MA, Ed S); library science (MLS); school administration (MSA). *Program availability:* Part-time, evening/weekend, online learning. *Degree requirements:* For master's and Ed S, comprehensive exam, thesis optional. *Entrance requirements:* For master's and Ed S, GRE or MAT, 3 letters of recommendation. Additional exam requirements/recommendations for international students: Required—TOEFL (minimum score 570 paper-based; 79 iBT), IELTS (minimum score 6.5). Electronic applications accepted. *Faculty research:* Brain, learning and meditation; leadership of teaching and learning.

Arcadia University, School of Education, Glenside, PA 19038-3295. Offers art education (M Ed); computer education (CAS); curriculum (CAS); curriculum studies (M Ed); early childhood education (M Ed), including individualized, master teacher, research in child development; educational leadership (M Ed, Ed D, CAS); elementary education (M Ed); English education (MA Ed); environmental education (MA Ed); instructional technology (M Ed); language arts (M Ed); library science (M Ed); mathematics education (M Ed, MA Ed); music education (MA Ed); psychology (MA Ed); reading (M Ed, CAS); science education (M Ed, CAS); secondary education (M Ed, CAS); special education (M Ed, Ed D, CAS); theater arts (MA Ed); written communication (MA Ed). *Accreditation:* NASAD. *Program availability:* Part-time, evening/weekend, online learning. Electronic applications accepted. *Expenses:* Contact institution.

Argosy University, Atlanta, College of Education, Atlanta, GA 30328. Offers educational leadership (MAEd, Ed D, Ed S), including higher education administration (Ed D), K-12 education (Ed D); teaching and learning (MAEd, Ed D, Ed S), including education technology (Ed D), higher education (Ed D), K-12 education (Ed D).

Argosy University, Chicago, College of Education, Chicago, IL 60601. Offers adult education and training (MA Ed); community college executive leadership (Ed D); educational leadership (MA Ed, Ed D, Ed S), including district leadership (Ed D), higher education administration (Ed D), K-12 education (Ed D); instructional leadership (Ed D, Ed S), including higher education (Ed D), K-12 education (Ed D). *Program availability:* Online learning.

Argosy University, Hawai`i, College of Education, Honolulu, HI 96813. Offers adult education and training (MAEd); educational leadership (Ed D), including higher education administration, K-12 education; instructional leadership (Ed D), including higher education, K-12 education; school psychology (MA).

Argosy University, Los Angeles, College of Education, Los Angeles, CA 90045. Offers community college executive leadership (Ed D); educational leadership (MA Ed, Ed D), including higher education administration (Ed D), K-12 education (Ed D); instructional leadership (MA Ed, Ed D), including higher education (Ed D), K-12 education (Ed D), multiple subject teacher preparation (MA Ed), single subject teacher preparation (MA Ed).

Argosy University, Northern Virginia, College of Education, Arlington, VA 22209. Offers community college executive leadership (Ed D); educational leadership (MA Ed, Ed D, Ed S), including higher education administration (Ed D), K-12 education (Ed D); instructional leadership (MA Ed, Ed D, Ed S), including higher education (Ed D), K-12 education (Ed D).

Argosy University, Orange County, College of Education, Orange, CA 92868. Offers community college executive leadership (Ed D); educational leadership (MA Ed, Ed D), including higher education administration (Ed D), K-12 education (Ed D); instructional leadership (MA Ed, Ed D), including education technology (Ed D), higher education (Ed D), K-12 education (Ed D), multiple subject teacher preparation (MA Ed), single subject teacher preparation (MA Ed).

Argosy University, Phoenix, College of Education, Phoenix, AZ 85021. Offers adult education and training (MA Ed); advanced educational administration (Ed D, Ed S); community college executive leadership (Ed D); educational administration (MA Ed); educational leadership (MA Ed, Ed D, Ed S), including education technology (Ed D), higher education administration (Ed D), K-12 education (Ed D); higher and postsecondary education (MA Ed); initial educational administration (Ed D, Ed S); school psychology (MA); teaching and learning (MA Ed, Ed D, Ed S), including education technology (Ed D), higher education (Ed D), K-12 education (Ed D).

Argosy University, Seattle, College of Education, Seattle, WA 98121. Offers adult education and training (MA Ed); community college executive leadership (Ed D); educational leadership (MA Ed, Ed D), including higher education administration (Ed D), K-12 education (Ed D); higher and postsecondary education (MA Ed); instructional leadership (MA Ed, Ed D), including education technology (Ed D), higher education (Ed D), K-12 education (Ed D).

Argosy University, Tampa, College of Education, Tampa, FL 33607. Offers community college executive leadership (Ed D); educational leadership (MA Ed, Ed D, Ed S), including higher education administration (Ed D), K-12 education (Ed D); school counseling (MA); teaching and learning (MA Ed, Ed D, Ed S), including higher education (Ed D), K-12 education (Ed D).

Argosy University, Twin Cities, College of Education, Eagan, MN 55121. Offers advanced educational administration (Ed D, Ed S); educational leadership (MA Ed, Ed D, Ed S), including higher education administration (Ed D), K-12 education (Ed D); higher and postsecondary education (MA Ed); initial educational administration (Ed D, Ed S); instructional leadership (MA Ed, Ed D, Ed S), including education technology (Ed D), higher education (Ed D), K-12 education (Ed D).

Arizona State University at the Tempe campus, Mary Lou Fulton Teachers College, Program in Educational Leadership, Phoenix, AZ 85069. Offers educational leadership (M Ed); leadership and innovation (Ed D). *Program availability:* Part-time, evening/weekend, online learning. Terminal master's awarded for partial completion of doctoral program. *Degree requirements:* For master's, thesis or alternative, written portfolio, internship, interactive Program of Study (iPOS) submitted before completing 50 percent of required credit hours; for doctorate, thesis/dissertation, interactive Program of Study (iPOS) submitted before completing 50 percent of required credit hours. *Entrance requirements:* For master's, minimum GPA of 3.0 or equivalent in last 2 years of work leading to bachelor's degree, 1 year of teaching experience, 3 letters of recommendation, personal statement, writing sample, curriculum vitae or resume; for doctorate, master's degree in education or related field, resume, personal statement, writing samples based on short writing prompts, 3 letters of recommendation. Additional exam requirements/recommendations for international students: Required—TOEFL, IELTS, or PTE. Electronic applications accepted.

Arkansas State University, Graduate School, College of Education and Behavioral Science, School of Teacher Education and Leadership, State University, AR 72467. Offers community college administration (SCCT); curriculum and instruction (MSE); early childhood education (MSE); early childhood services (MS); educational leadership (MSE, Ed D, Ed S); educational theory and practice (MSE); middle level education (MAT, MSE); reading (MSE, Ed S); special education - gifted, talented, and creative (MSE); special education - instructional specialist grades 4-12 (MSE); special education - instructional specialist grades P-4 (MSE); special education, K-12 (MSE). *Accreditation:* NCATE. *Program availability:* Part-time, online learning. *Degree requirements:* For master's, comprehensive exam, thesis or alternative; for doctorate, comprehensive exam, thesis/dissertation; for other advanced degree, comprehensive exam. *Entrance requirements:* For master's, GRE General Test or MAT, appropriate bachelor's degree, official transcripts, immunization records, letters of reference, interview; for doctorate, GRE General Test or MAT, interview, master's degree, letters of reference, official transcript, personal statement, writing sample, immunization records; for other advanced degree, GRE General Test or MAT, interview, master's degree, official transcript, immunization records, letters of reference, 3 years of teaching experience, teaching license. Additional exam requirements/recommendations for international students: Required—TOEFL (minimum score 550 paper-based; 79 iBT), IELTS (minimum score 6), PTE (minimum score 56). Electronic applications accepted.

Arkansas Tech University, College of Education, Russellville, AR 72801. Offers college student personnel (MS); educational leadership (M Ed, Ed S); instructional technology (M Ed); school counseling and leadership (M Ed); school leadership (Ed D); special education K-12 (M Ed); strength and conditioning studies (MS); teaching (MAT); teaching, learning, and leadership (M Ed). *Accreditation:* NCATE. *Program availability:* Part-time, evening/weekend, 100% online, blended/hybrid learning. *Students:* 80 full-time (45 women), 433 part-time (328 women); includes 114 minority (81 Black or African American, non-Hispanic/Latino; 4 American Indian or Alaska Native, non-Hispanic/Latino; 1 Asian, non-Hispanic/Latino; 13 Hispanic/Latino; 15 Two or more races, non-Hispanic/Latino), 2 international. Average age 34. In 2017, 132 master's, 8 doctorates, 3 other advanced degrees awarded. *Degree requirements:* For master's, comprehensive exam, thesis optional, action research project; for doctorate, thesis/dissertation.

Entrance requirements: Additional exam requirements/recommendations for international students: Required—TOEFL (minimum score 550 paper-based; 79 iBT), IELTS (minimum score 6.5), PTE (minimum score 58). *Application deadline:* For fall admission, 3/1 priority date for domestic students, 5/1 priority date for international students; for spring admission, 10/1 priority date for domestic and international students. Applications are processed on a rolling basis. Application fee: $40 ($90 for international students). Electronic applications accepted. *Expenses:* Tuition, state resident: full-time $6816; part-time $284 per credit hour. Tuition, nonresident: full-time $13,632; part-time $568 per credit hour. *Required fees:* $420 per semester. Tuition and fees vary according to course load. *Financial support:* In 2017–18, research assistantships with full and partial tuition reimbursements (averaging $4,800 per year), teaching assistantships with full and partial tuition reimbursements (averaging $4,800 per year) were awarded; career-related internships or fieldwork, Federal Work-Study, scholarships/grants, health care benefits, and unspecified assistantships also available. Support available to part-time students. Financial award application deadline: 4/15; financial award applicants required to submit FAFSA. *Unit head:* Dr. Mary Gunter, Dean, 479-964-3217, E-mail: mgunter@atu.edu.
Website: http://www.atu.edu/education/

Arlington Baptist University, Program in Education, Arlington, TX 76012-3425. Offers curriculum and instruction (M Ed); educational leadership (M Ed). *Degree requirements:* For master's, professional portfolio; internship (for educational leadership). *Entrance requirements:* For master's, bachelor's degree from accredited college or university with minimum GPA of 3.0, minimum of 12 hours in Bible; minimum of three years' classroom teaching experience in an accredited K-12 public or private school (for educational leadership only).

Asbury University, School of Graduate and Professional Studies, Wilmore, KY 40390-1198. Offers biology: alternative certificate (MA Ed); chemistry: alternative certificate (MA Ed); English (MA Ed); English as a second language (MA Ed); ESL (MA Ed); French (MA Ed); Latin: alternative certificate (MA Ed); mathematics: alternative certificate (MA Ed); reading/writing endorsement (MA Ed); social studies (MA Ed); social work (MSW), including child and family services; Spanish (MA Ed); special education (MA Ed); special education: alternative certificate (MA Ed); teacher as leader endorsement (MA Ed). *Accreditation:* NCATE. *Program availability:* Part-time. *Degree requirements:* For master's, action research project, portfolio. *Entrance requirements:* For master's, PRAXIS/NTE, minimum GPA of 2.75, letters of recommendation. Additional exam requirements/recommendations for international students: Required—TOEFL (minimum score 550 paper-based). Electronic applications accepted.

Ashland University, Dwight Schar College of Education, Doctoral Program in Educational Leadership Studies, Ashland, OH 44805-3702. Offers executive leadership studies (Ed D); leadership studies (Ed D). *Degree requirements:* For doctorate, comprehensive exam, thesis/dissertation. *Entrance requirements:* For doctorate, master's degree, minimum GPA of 3.3, writing sample, letters of recommendation, leadership statement, resume. Additional exam requirements/recommendations for international students: Recommended—TOEFL, IELTS, TSE. *Application deadline:* For spring admission, 3/1 for domestic students. Applications are processed on a rolling basis. Application fee: $30. Electronic applications accepted. *Expenses:* Contact institution. *Financial support:* Teaching assistantships and scholarships/grants available. Financial award applicants required to submit FAFSA. *Faculty research:* School funding, charter schools, administrative jobs, continuous improvement, marginalized groups, school finance, minority superintendent trends, teacher salaries, minority recruiting, women's issues. *Unit head:* Dr. James Olive, Director, 419-207-6643, E-mail: jolive@ashland.edu. *Application contact:* Bernie Bannin, Director, Graduate, Online, and Adult Admissions, 419-289-5291, E-mail: grad-admissions@ashland.edu.
Website: http://www.ashland.edu/edd/

Ashland University, Dwight Schar College of Education, Program in Educational Leadership and Administration, Ashland, OH 44805-3702. Offers educational leadership and administration (M Ed). *Program availability:* Part-time. *Degree requirements:* For master's, thesis or alternative, internship. *Entrance requirements:* For master's, teaching certificate or license, bachelor's degree, minimum cumulative GPA of 2.75. Additional exam requirements/recommendations for international students: Recommended—TOEFL, IELTS, TSE. *Application deadline:* Applications are processed on a rolling basis. Application fee: $30. Electronic applications accepted. *Expenses: Tuition:* Full-time $9621; part-time $4707 per credit hour. *Required fees:* $15 per semester. *Financial support:* Institutionally sponsored loans and scholarships/grants available. Financial award application deadline: 4/15. *Faculty research:* Gender and religious considerations in employment, Interstate School Leaders Licensure Consortium (ISLLC) standards, adjunct faculty training, politics of school finance, ethnicity and employment. *Unit head:* Dr. Amy Klinger, Chair, 419-289-5314, E-mail: aklinger@ashland.edu. *Application contact:* Bernie Bannin, Director, Graduate, Online, and Adult Admissions, 419-289-5291, E-mail: grad-admissions@ashland.edu.

Auburn University, Graduate School, College of Education, Department of Educational Foundations, Leadership, and Technology, Auburn University, AL 36849. Offers adult education (PhD, Ed S); curriculum supervision (M Ed, PhD); higher education administration (PhD); library media (Ed S); school administration (M Ed, PhD). *Accreditation:* NCATE. *Program availability:* Part-time. *Faculty:* 30 full-time (17 women), 8 part-time/adjunct (5 women). *Students:* 139 full-time (94 women), 254 part-time (171 women); includes 109 minority (95 Black or African American, non-Hispanic/Latino; 1 American Indian or Alaska Native, non-Hispanic/Latino; 2 Asian, non-Hispanic/Latino; 4 Hispanic/Latino; 1 Native Hawaiian or other Pacific Islander, non-Hispanic/Latino; 6 Two or more races, non-Hispanic/Latino), 12 international. Average age 37. 216 applicants, 72% accepted, 94 enrolled. In 2017, 92 master's, 46 doctorates, 58 other advanced degrees awarded. *Degree requirements:* For master's, thesis (for some programs); for doctorate, thesis/dissertation; for Ed S, field project. *Entrance requirements:* For master's, doctorate, and Ed S, GRE General Test. *Application deadline:* Applications are processed on a rolling basis. Application fee: $50 ($60 for international students). Electronic applications accepted. *Expenses:* Tuition, state resident: full-time $10,974; part-time $519 per credit hour. Tuition, nonresident: full-time $29,658; part-time $1557 per credit hour. *Required fees:* $816 per semester. Tuition and fees vary according to degree level and program. *Financial support:* Teaching assistantships and Federal Work-Study available. Support available to part-time students. Financial award application deadline: 3/15; financial award applicants required to submit FAFSA. *Unit head:* Dr. Sherida Downer, Head, 334-844-3060. *Application contact:* Dr. George Flowers, Dean of the Graduate School, 334-844-4700.
Website: http://www.education.auburn.edu/academic_departments/eflt/

Auburn University at Montgomery, College of Education, Department of Counselor, Leadership, and Special Education, Montgomery, AL 36124-4023. Offers counselor education (M Ed, Ed S), including clinical mental health counseling, school counseling; early childhood special education (M Ed); instructional leadership (M Ed, Ed S); special education/collaborative teacher (M Ed, Ed S). *Accreditation:* ACA; NCATE. *Program availability:* Part-time, evening/weekend. *Faculty:* 7 full-time (4 women), 2 part-time/adjunct (both women). *Students:* 27 full-time (23 women), 57 part-time (51 women); includes 40 minority (38 Black or African American, non-Hispanic/Latino; 2 Hispanic/

Latino). Average age 34. 76 applicants, 72% accepted, 26 enrolled. In 2017, 37 master's awarded. *Degree requirements:* For master's and Ed S, comprehensive exam. *Entrance requirements:* For master's, GRE General Test or MAT, certification, BS in teaching; for Ed S, GRE General Test or MAT, certification. Additional exam requirements/recommendations for international students: Recommended—TOEFL (minimum score 500 paper-based; 61 iBT), IELTS (minimum score 5.5), TSE (minimum score 44). *Application deadline:* For fall admission, 7/15 for international students; for spring admission, 11/15 for international students; for summer admission, 4/15 for international students. Applications are processed on a rolling basis. Electronic applications accepted. *Expenses:* Tuition, state resident: full-time $6930; part-time $385 per credit hour. Tuition, nonresident: full-time $15,588; part-time $866 per credit hour. *Required fees:* $640. *Financial support:* Career-related internships or fieldwork and scholarships/grants available. Support available to part-time students. Financial award application deadline: 3/1; financial award applicants required to submit FAFSA. *Unit head:* Dr. Samuel Flynt, Head, 334-244-3835, Fax: 334-244-3101, E-mail: sflynt@aum.edu. *Application contact:* Dr. Rhonda Morton, Associate Dean/Graduate Coordinator, 334-244-3287, Fax: 334-244-3978, E-mail: rmorton@aum.edu.
Website: http://education.aum.edu/academic-departments/counselor-leadership-and-special-education

Augusta University, College of Education, Department of Counselor Education, Leadership, and Research, Augusta, GA 30912. Offers counselor education (M Ed, Ed S), including clinical mental health counseling (M Ed), school counselor (M Ed). *Accreditation:* ACA; NCATE. *Program availability:* Part-time, evening/weekend. *Degree requirements:* For master's, comprehensive exam; for Ed S, comprehensive exam, thesis. *Entrance requirements:* For master's, GRE, MAT, minimum GPA of 2.5; for Ed S, GRE, MAT. *Faculty research:* Restructuring schools, financing education, student transition.

Augusta University, College of Education, Program in Leadership, Augusta, GA 30912. Offers leadership (Ed S); school administration (M Ed); teacher leadership (M Ed). *Entrance requirements:* For master's, GRE or MAT, minimum baccalaureate GPA of 2.5.

Aurora University, School of Education and Human Performance, Aurora, IL 60506-4892. Offers applied behavioral analysis (MS); bilingual-ESL education (MA); educational leadership with principal endorsement (MA); educational technology (MA); leadership in adult learning higher education (Ed D); leadership in curriculum and instruction (Ed D); leadership in educational administration (Ed D); reading instruction (MA); special education (MA). *Accreditation:* NCATE. *Program availability:* Part-time, evening/weekend. *Faculty:* 15 full-time (8 women), 39 part-time/adjunct (20 women). *Students:* 421 full-time (299 women), 142 part-time (89 women); includes 90 minority (25 Black or African American, non-Hispanic/Latino; 7 Asian, non-Hispanic/Latino; 50 Hispanic/Latino; 2 Native Hawaiian or other Pacific Islander, non-Hispanic/Latino; 6 Two or more races, non-Hispanic/Latino). Average age 37. 169 applicants, 95% accepted, 59 enrolled. In 2017, 175 master's, 36 doctorates awarded. *Degree requirements:* For master's, student teaching; for doctorate, comprehensive exam, thesis/dissertation. *Entrance requirements:* For master's, 2 years of teaching experience, valid teaching certificate, resume; for doctorate, appropriate master's degree, two references, curriculum vitae, personal statement, professional project, reflective essay. Additional exam requirements/recommendations for international students: Required—TOEFL (minimum score 550 paper-based; 79 iBT). *Application deadline:* For fall admission, 6/1 for international students; for spring admission, 10/1 for international students. Applications are processed on a rolling basis. Application fee: $0. Electronic applications accepted. *Expenses:* Contact institution. *Financial support:* In 2017–18, 34 students received support. Federal Work-Study, scholarships/grants, and unspecified assistantships available. Support available to part-time students. Financial award applicants required to submit FAFSA. *Unit head:* Dr. Jen Buckley, Dean, School of Education and Human Performance, 630-844-1542, Fax: 630-844-6155, E-mail: jbuckley@aurora.edu. *Application contact:* Elizabeth Botica, Graduate Education Recruiter, 630-947-8918, E-mail: ebotica@aurora.edu.
Website: http://aurora.edu/education

Austin Peay State University, College of Graduate Studies, College of Education, Department of Educational Specialties, Clarksville, TN 37044. Offers administration and supervision (Ed S); counseling and guidance (Ed S); curriculum and instruction (MA Ed); education leadership (MA Ed); elementary education (Ed S); reading (MA Ed); secondary education (Ed S). *Program availability:* Part-time, evening/weekend, online learning. *Faculty:* 15 full-time (9 women), 5 part-time/adjunct (4 women). *Students:* 73 full-time (54 women), 139 part-time (106 women); includes 49 minority (23 Black or African American, non-Hispanic/Latino; 4 Asian, non-Hispanic/Latino; 12 Hispanic/Latino; 10 Two or more races, non-Hispanic/Latino), 1 international. Average age 35. 72 applicants, 96% accepted, 42 enrolled. In 2017, 94 master's, 12 Ed Ss awarded. *Degree requirements:* For master's, comprehensive exam, thesis optional. *Entrance requirements:* For master's, GRE General Test, MAT, minimum undergraduate GPA of 2.75. Additional exam requirements/recommendations for international students: Required—TOEFL (minimum score 500 paper-based). *Application deadline:* For fall admission, 8/8 priority date for domestic students. Applications are processed on a rolling basis. Application fee: $45 ($50 for international students). Electronic applications accepted. *Expenses:* Tuition, state resident: full-time $7686; part-time $427 per credit hour. Tuition, nonresident: full-time $20,268; part-time $1126 per credit hour. *Required fees:* $1529; $76.45 per credit hour. *Financial support:* Research assistantships with full tuition reimbursements, career-related internships or fieldwork, Federal Work-Study, institutionally sponsored loans, scholarships/grants, and unspecified assistantships available. Support available to part-time students. Financial award application deadline: 4/1; financial award applicants required to submit FAFSA. *Unit head:* Dr. Moniqueka Gold, Chair, 931-221-7696, Fax: 931-221-1292, E-mail: goldm@apsu.edu. *Application contact:* Megan Mitchell, Coordinator of Graduate Admissions, 800-859-4723, Fax: 931-221-7641, E-mail: gradadmissions@apsu.edu.

Averett University, Master in Education Program, Danville, VA 24541-3692. Offers administration and supervision (M Ed); curriculum and instruction (M Ed); special education with endorsement (M Ed); special education with licensure (M Ed). *Program availability:* Part-time, online only, 100% online. *Faculty:* 2 full-time (1 woman), 14 part-time/adjunct (11 women). *Students:* 38 full-time (32 women), 46 part-time (28 women); includes 33 minority (29 Black or African American, non-Hispanic/Latino; 1 Hispanic/Latino; 3 Two or more races, non-Hispanic/Latino). Average age 38. 155 applicants, 52% accepted, 59 enrolled. In 2017, 50 master's awarded. *Degree requirements:* For master's, 30-credit core curriculum, minimum GPA of 3.0 throughout program, completion of degree requirements within six years from start of program. *Entrance requirements:* For master's, PRAXIS I, GRE, or MAT; writing proficiency test, minimum cumulative GPA of 3.0 over the last 60 hours of undergraduate study toward a baccalaureate degree, three letters of recommendation, Virginia teaching license (or eligibility). Additional exam requirements/recommendations for international students: Required—TOEFL (minimum score 600 paper-based; 100 iBT). *Application deadline:* Applications are processed on a rolling basis. Electronic applications accepted. *Expenses:* Contact institution. *Financial support:* Application deadline: 3/1; applicants required to submit FAFSA. *Faculty research:* Digital story telling for instruction and

Educational Leadership and Administration

assessment; online collaborative tools; digital field trips with Google Earth; teacher preparation in special education in Kenya, Malawi, Zambia, and Zimbabwe; self-efficacy of regular education teachers regarding inclusion of special education students in their classrooms. *Total annual research expenditures:* $5,000. *Unit head:* Dr. Sue Davis, Education Chair, 434-791-5741, Fax: 434-791-5020, E-mail: suedavis@averett.edu. Website: http://gps.averett.edu/online/education/

Azusa Pacific University, School of Behavioral and Applied Sciences, Department of Higher Education, Azusa, CA 91702-7000. Offers college counseling and student development (MS); higher education (PhD); higher education leadership (Ed D)

Azusa Pacific University, School of Education, Department of Educational Leadership, Azusa, CA 91702-7000. Offers MA, Ed D. *Program availability:* Part-time, evening/weekend. *Degree requirements:* For doctorate, oral defense of dissertation, qualifying exam. *Entrance requirements:* For doctorate, GRE General Test or MAT, 5 years of experience, writing sample. Additional exam requirements/recommendations for international students: Required—TOEFL. *Expenses:* Contact institution. *Faculty research:* Ethics in educational administration.

Baldwin Wallace University, Graduate Programs, School of Education, Leadership in Higher Education Program, Berea, OH 44017-2088. Offers MA Ed. *Program availability:* Part-time, evening/weekend. *Students:* 28 full-time (20 women), 1 (woman) part-time; includes 5 minority (all Black or African American, non-Hispanic/Latino). Average age 27. 32 applicants, 38% accepted, 9 enrolled. In 2017, 12 master's awarded. *Degree requirements:* For master's, comprehensive exam (for some programs), capstone project, portfolio. *Entrance requirements:* For master's, bachelor's degree, MAT or minimum GPA of 3.0. Additional exam requirements/recommendations for international students: Required—TOEFL (minimum score 550 paper-based; 79 iBT). *Application deadline:* For fall admission, 8/15 for domestic students; for spring admission, 12/15 for domestic students. Applications are processed on a rolling basis. Application fee: $25. Electronic applications accepted. Application fee is waived when completed online. *Expenses:* $721 per credit hour. *Financial support:* Paid internships (for full-time students) available. Financial award applicants required to submit FAFSA. *Faculty research:* Program development in higher education, leadership styles, the psychology of leadership and learning in higher education. *Unit head:* Dr. Ken Schneck, Director, 440-826-8062, Fax: 440-826-3779, E-mail: kschneck@bw.edu. *Application contact:* Lydia Avery, Associate Director of Transfer, Adult and Graduate Admission, 440-826-2222, Fax: 440-826-3830, E-mail: admission@bw.edu.
Website: https://www.bw.edu/academics/master-of-arts-in-education/maed-school-leadership/

Baldwin Wallace University, Graduate Programs, School of Education, Specialization in School Leadership, Berea, OH 44017-2088. Offers MA Ed. *Program availability:* Part-time, evening/weekend, 100% online. *Students:* 21 full-time (12 women), 25 part-time (18 women); includes 4 minority (1 Black or African American, non-Hispanic/Latino; 3 Two or more races, non-Hispanic/Latino). Average age 33. 19 applicants, 95% accepted, 13 enrolled. In 2017, 16 master's awarded. *Degree requirements:* For master's, 2-semester internship. *Entrance requirements:* For master's, bachelor's degree in field, MAT or minimum GPA of 3.0. Additional exam requirements/recommendations for international students: Required—TOEFL (minimum score 550 paper-based; 79 iBT). *Application deadline:* For fall admission, 8/15 priority date for domestic students; for spring admission, 12/15 priority date for domestic students. Applications are processed on a rolling basis. Application fee: $25. Electronic applications accepted. Application fee is waived when completed online. *Expenses:* $721 per credit hour. *Financial support:* Career-related internships or fieldwork available. Financial award applicants required to submit FAFSA. *Faculty research:* Leadership styles, instructional strategies, formative assessment. *Unit head:* Dr. Joseph Hruby, Coordinator, 440-826-8539, Fax: 440-826-3779, E-mail: jhruby@bw.edu. *Application contact:* Winnie W. Gerhardt, Director of Transfer, Adult and Graduate Admission, 440-826-2222, Fax: 440-826-3830, E-mail: admission@bw.edu.
Website: http://www.bw.edu/academics/master-of-arts-in-education/maed-school-leadership/

Ball State University, Graduate School, Teachers College, Department of Educational Leadership, Program in Educational Administration and Supervision, Muncie, IN 47306. Offers MA, Ed D. *Accreditation:* NCATE. *Program availability:* Part-time, 100% online, blended/hybrid learning. *Students:* 25 full-time (17 women), 334 part-time (187 women); includes 32 minority (21 Black or African American, non-Hispanic/Latino; 8 Hispanic/Latino; 3 Two or more races, non-Hispanic/Latino). Average age 34. 83 applicants, 84% accepted, 59 enrolled. In 2017, 86 master's, 11 doctorates awarded. *Degree requirements:* For master's, thesis/dissertation. *Entrance requirements:* For master's, minimum baccalaureate GPA of 2.75 or 3.0 in latter half of baccalaureate; for doctorate, GRE General Test, interview, minimum graduate GPA of 3.2. Additional exam requirements/recommendations for international students: Required—TOEFL (minimum score 550 paper-based; 79 iBT), IELTS (minimum score 6.5). *Application deadline:* Applications are processed on a rolling basis. Application fee: $60. Electronic applications accepted. *Financial support:* Research assistantships with partial tuition reimbursements available. Financial award application deadline: 3/1; financial award applicants required to submit FAFSA. *Unit head:* Dr. Lori Boyland, Chairperson, 765-285-8491, Fax: 765-285-5455, E-mail: lgboyland@bsu.edu. *Application contact:* Dr. Marilynn Quick, Specialist and Doctoral Graduate Advisor, 765-285-3287, Fax: 765-285-5455, E-mail: mquick@bsu.edu.
Website: http://www.bsu.edu/edleadership

Ball State University, Graduate School, Teachers College, Department of Educational Leadership, Program in School Superintendency, Muncie, IN 47306. Offers Ed S. *Accreditation:* NCATE. *Program availability:* Part-time, online only, 100% online. *Students:* 2 full-time (both women), 39 part-time (13 women); includes 5 minority (all Black or African American, non-Hispanic/Latino). Average age 40. 11 applicants, 55% accepted, 6 enrolled. In 2017, 15 Ed Ss awarded. *Degree requirements:* For Ed S, thesis. *Entrance requirements:* For degree, GRE General Test, minimum graduate GPA of 3.2, professional portfolio including platform statement, writing sample, curriculum vitae, five references. Additional exam requirements/recommendations for international students: Required—TOEFL (minimum score 550 paper-based; 79 iBT), IELTS (minimum score 6.5). *Application deadline:* Applications are processed on a rolling basis. Application fee: $60. Electronic applications accepted. *Financial support:* Application deadline: 3/1; applicants required to submit FAFSA. *Unit head:* Dr. Lori Boyland, Chairperson, 765-285-8491, Fax: 765-285-5455, E-mail: lgboyland@bsu.edu. *Application contact:* Dr. Marilynn Quick, Doctoral and Specialist Graduate Advisor, 765-285-8488, Fax: 765-285-2166, E-mail: mquick@bsu.edu.
Website: http://www.bsu.edu/edleadership

Ball State University, Graduate School, Teachers College, Department of Educational Studies, Program in Executive Development for Public Service, Muncie, IN 47306. Offers MA. *Program availability:* Part-time, online only, 100% online, blended/hybrid learning. *Students:* 9 full-time (7 women), 38 part-time (33 women); includes 10 minority (all Black or African American, non-Hispanic/Latino). Average age 38. 9 applicants, 89% accepted, 8 enrolled. In 2017, 19 master's awarded. *Entrance requirements:* For master's, minimum baccalaureate GPA of 2.75 or 3.0 in latter half of baccalaureate. Additional exam requirements/recommendations for international students: Required—

TOEFL (minimum score 550 paper-based; 79 iBT), IELTS (minimum score 6.5). *Application deadline:* For fall admission, 7/1 priority date for domestic students; for spring admission, 12/1 priority date for domestic students; for summer admission, 4/1 priority date for domestic students. Applications are processed on a rolling basis. Application fee: $60. Electronic applications accepted. *Financial support:* Research assistantships with partial tuition reimbursements and unspecified assistantships available. Financial award application deadline: 3/1; financial award applicants required to submit FAFSA. *Unit head:* Dr. Theresa Kruczek, Interim Chair, 765-285-8049, E-mail: tkruczek@bsu.edu.

Ball State University, Graduate School, Teachers College, Department of Educational Studies, Program in Student Affairs Administration in Higher Education, Muncie, IN 47306. Offers MA. *Accreditation:* NCATE. *Students:* 42 full-time (24 women), 1 (woman) part-time; includes 14 minority (8 Black or African American, non-Hispanic/Latino; 1 Asian, non-Hispanic/Latino; 4 Hispanic/Latino; 1 Two or more races, non-Hispanic/Latino). Average age 23. 156 applicants, 20% accepted, 31 enrolled. In 2017, 30 master's awarded. *Entrance requirements:* For master's, GRE General Test, minimum baccalaureate GPA of 2.75 or 3.0 in latter half of baccalaureate, resume, three professional references. Additional exam requirements/recommendations for international students: Required—TOEFL (minimum score 550 paper-based; 79 iBT), IELTS (minimum score 6.5). *Application deadline:* For fall admission, 1/1 priority date for domestic students. Applications are processed on a rolling basis. Application fee: $60. Electronic applications accepted. *Financial support:* Teaching assistantships with partial tuition reimbursements and unspecified assistantships available. Financial award application deadline: 3/1; financial award applicants required to submit FAFSA. *Unit head:* Dr. Theresa Kruczek, Interim Chair, 765-285-8049, E-mail: tkruczek@bsu.edu.
Website: http://www.bsu.edu/edstudies

Bank Street College of Education, Graduate School, Programs in Educational Leadership, New York, NY 10025. Offers early childhood leadership (MS Ed); educational leadership (MS Ed); leadership for educational change (Ed M, MS Ed); leadership in community-based learning (MS Ed); leadership in mathematics education (MS Ed); leadership in museum education (MS Ed); leadership in the arts: creative writing (MS Ed); leadership in the arts: visual arts (MS Ed). *Degree requirements:* For master's, thesis. *Entrance requirements:* For master's, interview, essays, minimum of 2 years experience as a classroom teacher. Additional exam requirements/recommendations for international students: Required—TOEFL (minimum score 600 paper-based; 100 iBT), IELTS (minimum score 7). Electronic applications accepted. *Faculty research:* Leadership in urban schools, leadership in small schools, mathematics in elementary schools, professional development in early childhood, leadership in arts education, leadership in special education, museum leadership, community-based leadership.

Barry University, School of Education, Program in Educational Leadership, Miami Shores, FL 33161-6695. Offers MS, Ed D, Certificate, Ed S. *Program availability:* Part-time, evening/weekend. *Degree requirements:* For master's and other advanced degree, comprehensive exam. *Entrance requirements:* For master's, GRE General Test or MAT, minimum GPA of 3.0; for other advanced degree, GRE General Test, minimum GPA of 3.0. Electronic applications accepted.

Barry University, School of Education, Program in Higher Education Administration, Miami Shores, FL 33161-6695. Offers MS. *Program availability:* Part-time, evening/weekend. *Degree requirements:* For master's, comprehensive exam. *Entrance requirements:* For master's, GRE General Test or MAT, minimum GPA of 3.0. Electronic applications accepted.

Barry University, School of Education, Program in Leadership and Education, Miami Shores, FL 33161-6695. Offers educational technology (PhD); exceptional student education (PhD); higher education administration (PhD); human resource development (PhD); leadership (PhD). *Program availability:* Part-time, evening/weekend. *Degree requirements:* For doctorate, thesis/dissertation. *Entrance requirements:* For doctorate, GRE General Test, minimum GPA of 3.25. Electronic applications accepted.

Baruch College of the City University of New York, Austin W. Marxe School of Public and International Affairs, Program in Educational Leadership, New York, NY 10010-5585. Offers educational leadership (MS Ed); school building leadership (Advanced Certificate); school district leadership (Advanced Certificate). *Program availability:* Part-time, evening/weekend. *Degree requirements:* For master's, internship. *Entrance requirements:* For master's, GRE or master's degree. Additional exam requirements/recommendations for international students: Required—TOEFL. Electronic applications accepted. *Faculty research:* School administration, program development, school leadership, violence in schools, school leadership development, school reform, school discipline policy, program development.

Baruch College of the City University of New York, Austin W. Marxe School of Public and International Affairs, Program in Higher Education Administration, New York, NY 10010-5585. Offers MS Ed. *Program availability:* Part-time, evening/weekend. *Entrance requirements:* For master's, GRE General Test. Additional exam requirements/recommendations for international students: Required—TOEFL. Electronic applications accepted. *Expenses:* Contact institution.

Bayamón Central University, Graduate Programs, Program in Education, Bayamón, PR 00960-1725. Offers administration and supervision (MA Ed); commercial education (MA Ed); elementary education (K–3) (MA Ed); family counseling (Graduate Certificate); guidance and counseling (MA Ed); pre-elementary teacher (MA Ed); rehabilitation counseling (MA Ed); special education (MA Ed), including attention deficit disorder, education of the autistic, learning disabilities. *Program availability:* Part-time, evening/weekend. *Degree requirements:* For master's, comprehensive exam. *Entrance requirements:* For master's, EXADEP, bachelor's degree in education or related field.

Baylor University, Graduate School, School of Education, Department of Educational Leadership, Waco, TX 76798. Offers MS Ed, Ed S. *Accreditation:* NCATE. *Faculty:* 9 full-time (2 women), 6 part-time/adjunct (3 women). *Students:* 71 full-time (38 women), 23 part-time (8 women); includes 26 minority (8 Black or African American, non-Hispanic/Latino; 2 Asian, non-Hispanic/Latino; 8 Hispanic/Latino; 1 Native Hawaiian or other Pacific Islander, non-Hispanic/Latino; 7 Two or more races, non-Hispanic/Latino), 1 international. 90 applicants, 44% accepted, 14 enrolled. In 2017, 30 master's awarded. *Entrance requirements:* For master's, GRE General Test. *Application deadline:* Applications are processed on a rolling basis. Application fee: $25. *Financial support:* In 2017–18, 20 students received support, including 2 research assistantships; teaching assistantships, Federal Work-Study, institutionally sponsored loans, and scholarships/grants also available. *Faculty research:* Christian higher education sport management marketing and impact. *Total annual research expenditures:* $69,060. *Unit head:* Dr. Robert Cloud, Graduate Program Director, 254-710-6110, Fax: 254-710-3265, E-mail: robert_cloud@baylor.edu. *Application contact:* Julie Baker, Administrative Assistant, 254-710-3050, Fax: 254-710-3870, E-mail: julie_l_baker@baylor.edu.
Website: http://www.baylor.edu/soe/edl/

Bay Path University, Program in Higher Education Administration, Longmeadow, MA 01106-2292. Offers enrollment management (MS); general administration (MS); institutional advancement (MS); online teaching and program administration (MS). *Program availability:* Part-time, online only, 100% online. *Students:* 3 full-time (all

women), 47 part-time (33 women); includes 19 minority (9 Black or African American, non-Hispanic/Latino; 8 Hispanic/Latino; 2 Two or more races, non-Hispanic/Latino). Average age 34. In 2017, 15 master's awarded. *Degree requirements:* For master's, 8 core courses (24 credits) and 4 elective courses (12 credits) for a total of 36 credits. *Application deadline:* Applications are processed on a rolling basis. Application fee: $45. Electronic applications accepted. Application fee is waived when completed online. *Expenses:* $760 per credit. *Financial support:* Unspecified assistantships available. Financial award applicants required to submit FAFSA. *Unit head:* Dr. Lauren Way, Program Director, 413-565-1193, E-mail: lway@baypath.edu. *Application contact:* Diane Ranaldi, Dean of Graduate Admissions, 413-565-1332, Fax: 413-565-1250, E-mail: dranaldi@baypath.edu.
Website: http://graduate.baypath.edu/Graduate-Programs/Programs-Online/MS-Programs/Higher-Education-Administration

Belhaven University, School of Education, Jackson, MS 39202-1789. Offers education (M Ed, MAT); educational leadership (Ed D, Ed S); reading literacy (M Ed). *Program availability:* Part-time, evening/weekend, 100% online, blended/hybrid learning. *Faculty:* 7 full-time (all women), 34 part-time/adjunct (23 women). *Students:* 4 full-time (all women), 505 part-time (413 women); includes 273 minority (257 Black or African American, non-Hispanic/Latino; 1 Asian, non-Hispanic/Latino; 5 Hispanic/Latino; 10 Two or more races, non-Hispanic/Latino). Average age 35. 203 applicants, 48% accepted, 92 enrolled. In 2017, 82 master's awarded. *Degree requirements:* For master's, comprehensive exam, portfolio; for doctorate, thesis/dissertation. *Entrance requirements:* For master's, PRAXIS I and II, minimum GPA of 2.8; for doctorate, MAT or GRE, master's degree in education or related field with minimum GPA of 3.0; essay; three professional letters of recommendation; minimum three years' experience in a PK-12 education context. *Application deadline:* Applications are processed on a rolling basis. Application fee: $25. Electronic applications accepted. *Expenses:* Contact institution. *Financial support:* Applicants required to submit FAFSA. *Unit head:* Dr. David Hand, Dean, 601-965-7020, E-mail: dhand@belhaven.edu. *Application contact:* Sean Kirnan, Assistant Vice President for Adult and Graduate Enrollment and Student Services, 601-968-8727, Fax: 601-968-5953, E-mail: gradadmission@belhaven.edu.

Bellarmine University, Annsley Frazier Thornton School of Education, Louisville, KY 40205. Offers education and district leadership (Ed D); education and social change (PhD); elementary education (MA Ed, MAT); leadership in higher education (PhD); middle school education (MA Ed, MAT); principalship (Ed S); reading and writing (MA Ed); secondary education (MAT); teacher leadership (MA Ed). *Accreditation:* NCATE. *Program availability:* Part-time, evening/weekend. *Faculty:* 19 full-time (10 women), 36 part-time/adjunct (29 women). *Students:* 34 full-time (27 women), 204 part-time (158 women); includes 60 minority (43 Black or African American, non-Hispanic/Latino; 7 Asian, non-Hispanic/Latino; 7 Hispanic/Latino; 3 Two or more races, non-Hispanic/Latino). Average age 33. In 2017, 50 master's, 8 doctorates, 42 other advanced degrees awarded. *Degree requirements:* For master's, comprehensive exam (for some programs), thesis (for some programs); for doctorate, comprehensive exam (for some programs), thesis/dissertation; for Ed S, comprehensive exam (for some programs). *Entrance requirements:* For master's, GRE, baccalaureate degree from accredited institution; minimum cumulative GPA of 2.75; recommendations from employers, supervisors, or professors attesting to applicant's potential as graduate student; statement of intent to pursue graduate degree; for doctorate, GRE, minimum GPA of 3.5 in all graduate coursework; baccalaureate and master's degrees in education or fields directly relevant to education; three letters of recommendation; two essays (no more than 1,000 words each); resume or curriculum vitae; interview; for Ed S, master's degree in education; valid teaching certificate; three years of experience in teaching; three recommendations; minimum GPA of 3.0 in all graduate work; interview; essays; personal goal statement. Additional exam requirements/recommendations for international students: Required—TOEFL (minimum score 550 paper-based, 68 iBT), IELTS (minimum score 6), or Michigan English Language Assessment Battery. *Application deadline:* For fall admission, 8/1 priority date for domestic and international students; for spring admission, 12/1 priority date for domestic and international students; for summer admission, 4/10 priority date for domestic and international students. Applications are processed on a rolling basis. Application fee: $40. Electronic applications accepted. Tuition and fees according to program. *Financial support:* Scholarships/grants available. Financial award applicants required to submit FAFSA. *Faculty research:* Literacy, service-learning, dispositions, educational technology, special education. *Unit head:* Dr. Elizabeth Dinkins, Interim Dean, 502-272-7958, Fax: 502-272-8189, E-mail: edinkins@bellarmine.edu. *Application contact:* Sarah Schuble, Senior Graduate Admissions Recruiter, 502-272-8271, Fax: 502-272-8002, E-mail: sschuble@bellarmine.edu.
Website: http://www.bellarmine.edu/education/graduate

Benedictine College, Master of Arts in School Leadership Program, Atchison, KS 66002-1499. Offers MA. *Accreditation:* NCATE. *Program availability:* Part-time, evening/weekend. *Faculty:* 3 part-time/adjunct (1 woman). *Students:* 11 full-time (4 women), 14 part-time (9 women). Average age 33. In 2017, 8 master's awarded. *Degree requirements:* For master's, comprehensive exam, practicum. *Entrance requirements:* For master's, minimum GPA of 3.0. Additional exam requirements/recommendations for international students: Recommended—TOEFL, IELTS. *Application deadline:* Applications are processed on a rolling basis. Application fee: $50. Electronic applications accepted. Application fee is waived when completed online. *Expenses:* Contact institution. *Financial support:* Scholarships/grants and unspecified assistantships available. Financial award applicants required to submit FAFSA. *Faculty research:* Teacher leadership, special education issues, diversity in schools, Catholic school leadership, professional development. *Application contact:* Dr. Cheryl Reding, Director, Graduate Programs in Education, 913-360-7384, E-mail: creding@benedictine.edu.
Website: http://www.benedictine.edu/academics/graduate-programs/masl

Benedictine University, Graduate Programs, Program in Education, Lisle, IL 60532. Offers curriculum and instruction and collaborative teaching (M Ed); elementary education (MA Ed); leadership and administration (M Ed); reading and literacy (M Ed); secondary education (MA Ed); special education (MA Ed). *Program availability:* Part-time, evening/weekend. *Degree requirements:* For master's, comprehensive exam, thesis (for some programs). *Entrance requirements:* For master's, GRE or MAT. Additional exam requirements/recommendations for international students: Required—TOEFL (minimum score 550 paper-based). Electronic applications accepted. *Expenses:* Contact institution.

Benedictine University, Graduate Programs, Program in Higher Education and Organizational Change, Lisle, IL 60532. Offers Ed D.

Berry College, Graduate Programs, Graduate Programs in Education, Program in Educational Leadership, Mount Berry, GA 30149-0159. Offers Ed S. *Faculty:* 1 full-time (0 women), 7 part-time/adjunct (5 women). *Students:* 16 full-time (10 women), 86 part-time (67 women); includes 20 minority (17 Black or African American, non-Hispanic/Latino; 3 Hispanic/Latino). Average age 41. In 2017, 46 Ed Ss awarded. *Degree requirements:* For Ed S, thesis, portfolio, oral exams. *Entrance requirements:* For degree, M Ed from NCATE-accredited school, minimum GPA of 3.25. Additional exam requirements/recommendations for international students: Required—TOEFL (minimum score 550 paper-based). *Application deadline:* For fall admission, 7/20 for domestic

students, 5/1 for international students; for spring admission, 12/1 for domestic students, 10/1 for international students. Applications are processed on a rolling basis. Application fee: $25 ($30 for international students). Electronic applications accepted. *Expenses:* $8,370 full-time tuition plus $176 fees per year; $465 per credit hour part-time tuition. *Financial support:* Research assistantships, scholarships/grants, and unspecified assistantships available. Support available to part-time students. Financial award application deadline: 3/1; financial award applicants required to submit FAFSA. *Unit head:* Dr. Jacqueline McDowell, Dean, Charter School of Education and Human Sciences, 706-236-1717, Fax: 706-238-5827, E-mail: jmcdowell@berry.edu. *Application contact:* Brett Kennedy, Assistant Vice President of Enrollment Management, 706-236-2215, Fax: 706-290-2178, E-mail: admissions@berry.edu.
Website: http://www.berry.edu/academics/education/graduate/

Bethel University, Graduate Programs, McKenzie, TN 38201. Offers administration and supervision (MA Ed); business administration (MBA); conflict resolution (MA); physician assistant studies (MS). *Program availability:* Part-time, evening/weekend. *Degree requirements:* For master's, thesis (for some programs). *Entrance requirements:* For master's, GRE General Test or MAT, minimum undergraduate GPA of 2.5.

Bethel University, Graduate School, St. Paul, MN 55112-6999. Offers business administration (MBA); classroom management (Certificate); counseling (MA); K-12 education (MA); leadership (Ed D); leadership foundations (Certificate); nurse educator (MS, Certificate); nurse-midwifery (MS); physician assistant (MS); special education (MA); strategic leadership (MA); teaching (MA); teaching and learning (Certificate). *Program availability:* Part-time, evening/weekend, 100% online, blended/hybrid learning. *Faculty:* 22 full-time (16 women), 70 part-time/adjunct (44 women). *Students:* 611 full-time (431 women), 393 part-time (249 women); includes 176 minority (82 Black or African American, non-Hispanic/Latino; 4 American Indian or Alaska Native, non-Hispanic/Latino; 31 Asian, non-Hispanic/Latino; 39 Hispanic/Latino; 2 Native Hawaiian or other Pacific Islander, non-Hispanic/Latino; 18 Two or more races, non-Hispanic/Latino), 9 international. Average age 36. 668 applicants, 42% accepted, 223 enrolled. In 2017, 287 master's, 30 doctorates, 172 other advanced degrees awarded. *Degree requirements:* For master's, comprehensive exam (for some programs), thesis (for some programs); for doctorate, comprehensive exam, thesis/dissertation. *Entrance requirements:* Additional exam requirements/recommendations for international students: Required—TOEFL (minimum score 550 paper-based, 80 iBT) or IELTS. *Application deadline:* Applications are processed on a rolling basis. Application fee: $0. Electronic applications accepted. *Expenses:* Contact institution. *Financial support:* Teaching assistantships, career-related internships or fieldwork, and scholarships/grants available. Support available to part-time students. Financial award applicants required to submit FAFSA. *Unit head:* Dr. Randy Bergen, Associate Provost, 651-635-8000, Fax: 651-635-8004, E-mail: r-bergen@bethel.edu. *Application contact:* Director of Admissions, 651-635-8000, Fax: 651-635-8004, E-mail: gs@bethel.edu.
Website: https://www.bethel.edu/graduate/

Binghamton University, State University of New York, Graduate School, College of Community and Public Affairs, Department of Student Affairs Administration, Binghamton, NY 13902-6000. Offers MS. *Program availability:* Part-time. *Faculty:* 4 full-time (3 women). *Students:* 50 full-time (30 women), 14 part-time (10 women); includes 19 minority (7 Black or African American, non-Hispanic/Latino; 3 Asian, non-Hispanic/Latino; 4 Hispanic/Latino; 5 Two or more races, non-Hispanic/Latino), 2 international. Average age 27. 75 applicants, 89% accepted, 31 enrolled. In 2017, 16 master's awarded. *Degree requirements:* For master's, comprehensive exam. *Entrance requirements:* For master's, GRE General Test. Additional exam requirements/recommendations for international students: Required—TOEFL (minimum score 80 iBT). *Application deadline:* For fall admission, 4/15 priority date for domestic and international students; for spring admission, 11/15 priority date for domestic and international students. Application fee: $75. Electronic applications accepted. *Financial support:* In 2017–18, 34 students received support. Fellowships, career-related internships or fieldwork, Federal Work-Study, institutionally sponsored loans, scholarships/grants, health care benefits, and unspecified assistantships available. Financial award applicants required to submit FAFSA. *Unit head:* Brianna King, Director of Student Admissions, 607-777-2719, E-mail: bking@binghamton.edu. *Application contact:* Ben Balkaya, Assistant Dean and Director, 607-777-2151, Fax: 607-777-2501, E-mail: balkaya@binghamton.edu.
Website: http://www2.binghamton.edu/ccpa/student-affairs-administration/

Binghamton University, State University of New York, Graduate School, College of Community and Public Affairs, Department of Teaching, Learning and Educational Leadership, Binghamton, NY 13902-6000. Offers adolescence education (MAT, MS Ed), including biology education, chemistry education, earth science education, English education, French education, mathematical sciences education, physics, social studies, Spanish education; childhood and early childhood education (MS Ed); educational leadership (Certificate); educational studies (MS); educational theory and practice (Ed D); literacy education (MS Ed); special education (MS Ed); TESOL education (MA, MS Ed). *Accreditation:* TEAC. *Program availability:* Part-time, evening/weekend. *Faculty:* 18 full-time (13 women). *Students:* 99 full-time (71 women), 136 part-time (107 women); includes 27 minority (5 Black or African American, non-Hispanic/Latino; 1 American Indian or Alaska Native, non-Hispanic/Latino; 2 Asian, non-Hispanic/Latino; 14 Hispanic/Latino; 5 Two or more races, non-Hispanic/Latino), 8 international. Average age 34. 158 applicants, 84% accepted, 86 enrolled. In 2017, 75 master's, 5 doctorates, 19 other advanced degrees awarded. *Degree requirements:* For doctorate, thesis/dissertation. *Entrance requirements:* For master's, GRE General Test, teaching certification; for doctorate, GRE General Test, writing sample. Additional exam requirements/recommendations for international students: Required—TOEFL (minimum score 550 paper-based; 80 iBT). Application fee: $75. Electronic applications accepted. *Financial support:* In 2017–18, 22 students received support, including 2 fellowships with full tuition reimbursements available (averaging $10,000 per year), 3 teaching assistantships with full tuition reimbursements available (averaging $15,500 per year); research assistantships, career-related internships or fieldwork, Federal Work-Study, institutionally sponsored loans, scholarships/grants, health care benefits, tuition waivers (full and partial), and unspecified assistantships available. Financial award applicants required to submit FAFSA. *Unit head:* Dr. Susan Strehle, Dean, 607-777-7329, E-mail: sstrehle@binghamton.edu. *Application contact:* Ben Balkaya, Assistant Dean and Director, 607-777-2151, Fax: 607-777-2501, E-mail: balkaya@binghamton.edu.
Website: https://www.binghamton.edu/tlel/

Bloomsburg University of Pennsylvania, School of Graduate Studies, College of Education, Department of Teaching and Learning, Program in Educational Leadership, Bloomsburg, PA 17815-1301. Offers college student affairs (M Ed); PreK-12 curriculum and instruction (M Ed); PreK-12 school counseling (M Ed); PreK-12 school principal (M Ed). *Degree requirements:* For master's, practicum. *Entrance requirements:* For master's, 3 letters of recommendation, resume, minimum QPA of 3.0, personal statement, interview. Additional exam requirements/recommendations for international students: Required—TOEFL, IELTS. Electronic applications accepted. *Expenses:* Tuition, state resident: full-time $10,000; part-time $500 per credit hour. Tuition, nonresident: full-time $15,000; part-time $750 per credit hour. *Required fees:* $2484; $110.75 per credit hour. $75 per term. Tuition and fees vary according to program.

Educational Leadership and Administration

Bluffton University, Programs in Education, Bluffton, OH 45817. Offers intervention specialist (MA Ed); leadership (MA Ed); reading (MA Ed). *Accreditation:* NCATE. *Program availability:* Part-time, 100% online, blended/hybrid learning, videoconference. *Faculty:* 2 full-time (1 woman), 1 part-time/adjunct (0 women). *Students:* 7 full-time (4 women), 11 part-time (10 women); includes 1 minority (Black or African American, non-Hispanic/Latino). Average age 29. 14 applicants, 64% accepted, 9 enrolled. In 2017, 7 master's awarded. *Degree requirements:* For master's, action research project, public presentation. *Entrance requirements:* For master's, PRAXIS I, bachelor's degree, minimum GPA of 3.0. Additional exam requirements/recommendations for international students: Required—TOEFL. *Application deadline:* For fall admission, 8/15 priority date for domestic students, 6/15 priority date for international students; for spring admission, 12/15 priority date for domestic students, 9/15 priority date for international students. Applications are processed on a rolling basis. Electronic applications accepted. *Expenses:* $456 per credit hour tuition, $50 per semester technology fee ($100 for more than 6 hours). *Financial support:* In 2017–18, 2 students received support. Unspecified assistantships available. Financial award application deadline: 9/15; financial award applicants required to submit FAFSA. *Unit head:* Dr. Amy K. Mullins, Director of Graduate Programs in Education, 419-358-3457, E-mail: mullinsa@bluffton.edu. *Application contact:* Nancey Schortgen, Program Representative, 419-358-3202, Fax: 419-358-3399, E-mail: schortgenn@bluffton.edu.
Website: http://www.bluffton.edu/grad/

Bob Jones University, Graduate Programs, Greenville, SC 29614. Offers accountancy (MS); Bible (MA); Bible translation (MA); Biblical studies (Certificate); broadcast management (MS); business administration (MBA); church history (MA, PhD); church ministries (MA); church music (MM); cinema and video production (MA); counseling (MS); curriculum and instruction (Ed D); divinity (M Div); dramatic production (MA); educational leadership (MS, Ed D, Ed S); elementary education (M Ed, MAT); English (M Ed, MA, MAT); fine arts (MA); graphic design (MA); history (M Ed, MA); illustration (MA); interpretative speech (MA); mathematics (M Ed, MAT); medical missions (Certificate); ministry (MM, D Min); multi-categorical special education (M Ed, MAT); music (M Ed); New Testament interpretation (PhD); Old Testament interpretation (PhD); orchestral instrument performance (MM); organ performance (MM); pastoral studies (MA); personnel services (MS, Ed S); piano pedagogy (MM); piano performance (MM); platform arts (MA); radio and television broadcasting (MS); rhetoric and public address (MA); secondary education (M Ed); studio art (MA); teaching Bible (MA); theology (MA, PhD); voice performance (MM); youth ministries (MA); M Div/MM.

Boise State University, College of Education, Department of Curriculum, Instruction and Foundational Studies, Boise, ID 83725-0399. Offers curriculum and instruction (MA Ed, Ed D); educational leadership (M Ed); executive educational leadership (Ed S). *Accreditation:* NCATE. *Program availability:* Part-time. *Faculty:* 36. *Students:* 24 full-time (18 women), 180 part-time (113 women); includes 19 minority (1 Black or African American, non-Hispanic/Latino; 3 American Indian or Alaska Native, non-Hispanic/Latino; 3 Asian, non-Hispanic/Latino; 12 Hispanic/Latino), 6 international. Average age 36. 79 applicants, 67% accepted, 35 enrolled. In 2017, 36 master's, 6 other advanced degrees awarded. *Degree requirements:* For master's, thesis optional. *Entrance requirements:* For master's, minimum GPA of 3.0. Additional exam requirements/recommendations for international students: Required—TOEFL (minimum score 550 paper-based; 80 iBT), IELTS (minimum score 6). *Application deadline:* For fall admission, 3/1 for domestic and international students; for spring admission, 10/15 for domestic students, 10/1 for international students. Application fee: $65 ($95 for international students). Electronic applications accepted. *Expenses:* Tuition, state resident: full-time $6471; part-time $390 per credit. Tuition, nonresident: full-time $21,787; part-time $685 per credit. *Required fees:* $2283; $100 per term. Part-time tuition and fees vary according to course load and program. *Financial support:* Scholarships/grants and unspecified assistantships available. Financial award application deadline: 3/1; financial award applicants required to submit FAFSA. *Unit head:* Dr. Kathleen Budge, Department Chair, 208-426-3758. *Application contact:* Dr. Esther Enright, Program Coordinator, 208-426-1693, E-mail: estherenright@boisestate.edu.
Website: http://education.boisestate.edu/cifs/

Boston College, Lynch School of Education, Program in Educational Leadership, Chestnut Hill, MA 02467-3800. Offers M Ed, Ed D, CAES, JD/M Ed. *Program availability:* Part-time, evening/weekend. *Students:* 11 full-time (5 women), 51 part-time (29 women); includes 11 minority (5 Black or African American, non-Hispanic/Latino; 1 Asian, non-Hispanic/Latino; 4 Hispanic/Latino; 1 Two or more races, non-Hispanic/Latino), 3 international. Average age 38. 92 applicants, 48% accepted, 33 enrolled. In 2017, 18 master's awarded. Terminal master's awarded for partial completion of doctoral program. *Degree requirements:* For master's and CAES, comprehensive exam. *Entrance requirements:* For master's and CAES, GRE General Test or MAT; for doctorate, GRE General Test. Additional exam requirements/recommendations for international students: Required—TOEFL (minimum score 100 iBT). *Application deadline:* For fall admission, 12/1 priority date for domestic and international students; for spring admission, 11/1 priority date for domestic and international students. Application fee: $65. Electronic applications accepted. *Financial support:* Research assistantships with tuition reimbursements, Federal Work-Study, scholarships/grants, and tuition waivers (partial) available. Support available to part-time students. Financial award applicants required to submit FAFSA. *Unit head:* Lauri Johnson, Department Chair, 617-552-1039, E-mail: lauri.johnson.1@bc.edu. *Application contact:* Kimberly Rose, Graduate Admission Assistant, 617-552-4214, Fax: 617-552-0398, E-mail: roseki@bc.edu.

Bowie State University, Graduate Programs, Program in Educational Leadership/Executive Fellows, Bowie, MD 20715-9465. Offers Ed D. *Program availability:* Part-time, evening/weekend. *Degree requirements:* For doctorate, comprehensive exam, thesis/dissertation. Electronic applications accepted.

Bowie State University, Graduate Programs, Program in Elementary and Secondary School Administration, Bowie, MD 20715-9465. Offers M Ed. *Program availability:* Part-time, evening/weekend. *Degree requirements:* For master's, comprehensive exam. *Entrance requirements:* For master's, copy of teaching certificate, 3 years of teaching experience, letter of recommendation from current supervisor. Electronic applications accepted.

Bowie State University, Graduate Programs, Program in School Administration and Supervision, Bowie, MD 20715-9465. Offers M Ed. *Program availability:* Part-time, evening/weekend. *Degree requirements:* For master's, comprehensive exam, thesis optional, research paper. *Entrance requirements:* For master's, minimum undergraduate GPA of 3.0, 3 years of teaching experience, teaching certificate.

Bowling Green State University, Graduate College, College of Education and Human Development, Department of Higher Education and Student Affairs, Program in Higher Education Administration, Bowling Green, OH 43403. Offers PhD. *Accreditation:* NCATE. *Program availability:* Part-time. *Degree requirements:* For doctorate, comprehensive exam, thesis/dissertation. *Entrance requirements:* For doctorate, GRE General Test. Additional exam requirements/recommendations for international students: Required—TOEFL. Electronic applications accepted. *Faculty research:* Adult learners, legal issues, intellectual development.

Bowling Green State University, Graduate College, College of Education and Human Development, School of Educational Foundations, Leadership and Policy, Program in Educational Administration and Supervision, Bowling Green, OH 43403. Offers educational leadership (M Ed, Ed S); leadership studies (Ed D). *Accreditation:* NCATE. *Program availability:* Part-time, evening/weekend. *Degree requirements:* For master's, thesis or alternative; for doctorate, comprehensive exam, thesis/dissertation; for Ed S, thesis or alternative, field experience or internship. *Entrance requirements:* For master's, doctorate, and Ed S, GRE General Test. Additional exam requirements/recommendations for international students: Required—TOEFL. Electronic applications accepted. *Faculty research:* Professional development for school leaders, organizational development, school finance, legal challenges to school decision making, administering urban schools.

Bradley University, The Graduate School, College of Education and Health Sciences, Department of Leadership in Education, Nonprofits and Counseling, Peoria, IL 61625-0002. Offers counseling (MA), including clinical mental health counseling, professional school counseling; leadership in educational administration (MA); nonprofit leadership (MA). *Accreditation:* ACA; NCATE. *Program availability:* Part-time, evening/weekend. *Degree requirements:* For master's, comprehensive exam, thesis optional. *Entrance requirements:* For master's, GRE General Test or MAT, interview, 3 letters of recommendation. Additional exam requirements/recommendations for international students: Required—TOEFL (minimum score 550 paper-based; 79 iBT), IELTS (minimum score 6.5). Electronic applications accepted.

Brandeis University, Graduate School of Arts and Sciences, Program in Education, Waltham, MA 02454-9110. Offers Jewish day schools (MAT); public elementary education (MAT); secondary education (MAT), including Bible, biology, chemistry, Chinese, English, history, Jewish day schools, math, physics; teacher leadership (Ed M, AGC). *Faculty:* 4 full-time (2 women), 11 part-time/adjunct (10 women). *Students:* 21 full-time (19 women), 38 part-time (33 women); includes 5 minority (1 Black or African American, non-Hispanic/Latino; 3 Asian, non-Hispanic/Latino; 1 Hispanic/Latino), 8 international. Average age 34. 93 applicants, 78% accepted, 55 enrolled. In 2017, 43 master's, 10 other advanced degrees awarded. *Degree requirements:* For master's, thesis or alternative, internship; research project. *Entrance requirements:* For master's, GRE General Test or MAT, transcripts, letters of recommendation, resume, statement of purpose. Additional exam requirements/recommendations for international students: Required—PTE (minimum score 68), TOEFL (minimum score 600 paper-based, 100 iBT) or IELTS (7). *Application deadline:* For fall admission, 12/1 priority date for domestic students. Applications are processed on a rolling basis. Application fee: $75. Electronic applications accepted. *Expenses:* $32,440 (MAT), $17,520 (M Ed), $23,360 (AGS); $88 fees. *Financial support:* In 2017–18, 61 students received support. Scholarships/grants available. Financial award application deadline: 4/15; financial award applicants required to submit FAFSA. *Faculty research:* Teacher education, education, teaching, elementary education, secondary education, Jewish education, English, history, biology, chemistry, physics, math, Chinese, Bible/Tanakh. *Unit head:* Marya Levenson, Director, 781-736-2002, E-mail: mlevenso@brandeis.edu. *Application contact:* Manuel Tuan, Department Coordinator, 781-736-2002, E-mail: tuan@brandeis.edu.
Website: http://www.brandeis.edu/gsas/programs/education.html

Brandman University, School of Education, Irvine, CA 92618. Offers curriculum and instruction (MAE); educational administration (MAE); educational leadership (MAE); educational leadership and administration (MA); elementary education (MAT); instructional technology: teaching the 21st century learner (MAE); leadership in early childhood education (MAE); organizational leadership (Ed D); school counseling (MA); secondary education (MAT); special education (MA); teaching and learning (MAE). *Expenses:* Tuition: Part-time $640 per credit hour. Tuition and fees vary according to degree level and program. *Unit head:* Dr. Christine G. Zeppos, Dean, 949-341-9948, E-mail: zeppos@brandman.edu. *Application contact:* Dr. Christine G. Zeppos, Dean, 949-341-9948, E-mail: zeppos@brandman.edu.
Website: https://www.brandman.edu/academic-programs/education

Brandon University, Faculty of Education, Brandon, MB R7A 6A9, Canada. Offers curriculum and instruction (M Ed, Diploma); educational administration (M Ed, Diploma); guidance and counseling (M Ed, Diploma); special education (M Ed, Diploma). *Degree requirements:* For master's, thesis. *Entrance requirements:* For master's, minimum GPA of 3.0, teaching certificate or equivalent. Additional exam requirements/recommendations for international students: Required—TOEFL. *Faculty research:* Comparative education, environmental studies, parent/school council.

Bridgewater State University, College of Graduate Studies, College of Education and Allied Studies, Department of Secondary Education and Professional Programs, Program in Educational Leadership, Bridgewater, MA 02325. Offers M Ed, CAGS. *Accreditation:* NCATE. *Program availability:* Part-time, evening/weekend. *Degree requirements:* For master's and CAGS, comprehensive exam. *Entrance requirements:* For master's, GRE General Test or Massachusetts Test for Educator Licensure, work experience; for CAGS, master's degree.

Brigham Young University, Graduate Studies, David O. McKay School of Education, Department of Educational Leadership and Foundations, Provo, UT 84602. Offers educational leadership and foundations (Ed D); educational leadership: education policy studies (M Ed); educational leadership: school leadership (M Ed). *Program availability:* Part-time, evening/weekend. *Faculty:* 12 full-time (2 women), 1 part-time/adjunct (0 women). *Students:* 31 full-time (25 women), 62 part-time (31 women); includes 8 minority (2 American Indian or Alaska Native, non-Hispanic/Latino; 1 Asian, non-Hispanic/Latino; 4 Hispanic/Latino; 1 Native Hawaiian or other Pacific Islander, non-Hispanic/Latino). Average age 42. 78 applicants, 49% accepted, 39 enrolled. In 2017, 29 master's, 10 doctorates awarded. Terminal master's awarded for partial completion of doctoral program. *Degree requirements:* For master's, comprehensive exam; for doctorate, comprehensive exam, thesis/dissertation, prospectus. *Entrance requirements:* For master's, GRE, LSAT, GMAT, or MAT, level 2 teaching license; for doctorate, GRE, LSAT, or GMAT, master's degree. Additional exam requirements/recommendations for international students: Required—TOEFL (minimum score 580 paper-based; 85 iBT). *Application deadline:* For fall admission, 5/1 for domestic and international students; for winter admission, 9/15 for domestic and international students; for spring admission, 1/15 for domestic and international students. Application fee: $50. Electronic applications accepted. *Expenses:* Contact institution. *Financial support:* In 2017–18, 38 students received support, including 19 research assistantships (averaging $2,100 per year); scholarships/grants also available. Financial award application deadline: 8/15. *Faculty research:* Inequality of educational opportunity, value of principals academies, role of trust in educational leadership, social networks in education, factors and indicators leading to the improvement of educational settings. *Unit head:* Pamela Hallam, Chair, 801-422-3600, Fax: 801-422-0196, E-mail: pam_hallam@byu.edu. *Application contact:* Michele Price, Department Secretary, 801-422-3813, Fax: 801-422-0196, E-mail: michele_price@byu.edu.
Website: http://education.byu.edu/edlf/

Brooklyn College of the City University of New York, School of Education, Program in Educational Leadership, Brooklyn, NY 11210-2889. Offers school building leader (MS Ed); school district leader (MS Ed). *Program availability:* Part-time, evening/weekend. *Entrance requirements:* For master's, 2 supervisory letters of recommendation, essay, resume, teaching certificate, interview. Additional exam requirements/recommendations for international students: Required—TOEFL (minimum score 500 paper-based; 61 iBT). Electronic applications accepted.

Buffalo State College, State University of New York, The Graduate School, Faculty of Applied Science and Education, Department of Elementary Education and Reading, Program in Educational Leadership, Buffalo, NY 14222-1095. Offers CAS. *Accreditation:* NCATE. *Program availability:* Part-time, evening/weekend. *Degree requirements:* For CAS, internship. *Entrance requirements:* For degree, master's degree, New York teaching certificate, 3 years of teaching experience. Additional exam requirements/recommendations for international students: Required—TOEFL (minimum score 550 paper-based).

Butler University, College of Education, Indianapolis, IN 46208-3485. Offers applied educational neuroscience (Certificate); educational administration (MS); effective teaching and leadership (MS); licensed mental health counselor (Certificate); school counseling (MS); wellness and sport leadership (Certificate). *Accreditation:* ACA; NCATE. *Program availability:* Part-time. *Faculty:* 12 full-time (8 women), 10 part-time/adjunct (7 women). *Students:* 3 full-time (2 women), 131 part-time (102 women); includes 13 minority (7 Black or African American, non-Hispanic/Latino; 2 Asian, non-Hispanic/Latino; 2 Hispanic/Latino; 2 Two or more races, non-Hispanic/Latino). Average age 31. 65 applicants, 75% accepted, 41 enrolled. In 2017, 45 master's, 10 other advanced degrees awarded. *Degree requirements:* For master's, thesis. *Entrance requirements:* For master's, GRE (minimum score 291) or MAT (minimum score 396) unless undergraduate GPA is a 3.0 or higher, two letters of recommendation, transcripts, interview, professional resume. Additional exam requirements/recommendations for international students: Required—TOEFL (minimum score 550 paper-based; 79 iBT), IELTS (minimum score 6). *Application deadline:* For fall admission, 2/1 for domestic and international students; for spring admission, 11/1 for domestic and international students; for summer admission, 4/1 for domestic and international students. Applications are processed on a rolling basis. Application fee: $0. Electronic applications accepted. *Expenses:* $560 per credit. *Financial support:* In 2017–18, 64 students received support. Scholarships/grants, tuition waivers (full and partial), and unspecified assistantships available. Financial award application deadline: 7/15; financial award applicants required to submit FAFSA. *Faculty research:* Principals role in school improvement, leadership and school climate, retention of teachers in special education, the neuro-diversity brain, school counseling intervention. *Unit head:* Dr. Ena Shelley, Dean, 317-940-9752, Fax: 317-940-6481. *Application contact:* Diane Dubord, Graduate Student Services Specialist, 317-940-8100, Fax: 317-940-8250, E-mail: ddubord@butler.edu.
Website: https://www.butler.edu/coe/graduate-programs

Cabrini University, Academic Affairs, Radnor, PA 19087. Offers accounting (M Acc); autism spectrum disorder (M Ed); biological sciences (MS), including civic leadership; criminology and criminal justice (MA); curriculum, instruction, and assessment (M Ed); educational leadership (M Ed, Ed D), including curriculum and instructional leadership (Ed D), preK-12 leadership (Ed D); English as a second language (M Ed); organizational leadership (DBA, PhD); preK to 4 (M Ed); reading specialist (M Ed); secondary education (M Ed), including biology, chemistry, English, English/communication, mathematics, social studies; special education grades 7-12 (M Ed); special education preK-8 (M Ed); teaching and learning (M Ed). *Program availability:* Part-time, evening/weekend. *Faculty:* 23 full-time (17 women), 46 part-time/adjunct (38 women). *Students:* 60 full-time (35 women), 559 part-time (435 women); includes 93 minority (66 Black or African American, non-Hispanic/Latino; 1 American Indian or Alaska Native, non-Hispanic/Latino; 8 Asian, non-Hispanic/Latino; 3 Two or more races, non-Hispanic/Latino), 4 international. Average age 33. 290 applicants, 82% accepted, 154 enrolled. In 2017, 283 master's awarded. *Degree requirements:* For master's, comprehensive exam (for some programs), thesis (for some programs); for doctorate, comprehensive exam (for some programs), thesis/dissertation. *Entrance requirements:* For master's, professional resume, personal statement, two recommendations, official transcripts; for doctorate, official transcripts, minimum master's GPA of 3.0, two recommendations, interview with admissions committee. Additional exam requirements/recommendations for international students: Required—TOEFL (minimum score 80 iBT). *Application deadline:* For fall admission, 8/26 for domestic students, 8/1 for international students; for winter admission, 1/13 for domestic students, 12/20 for international students; for spring admission, 1/13 for domestic students, 12/20 for international students; for summer admission, 5/20 for domestic students, 4/30 for international students. Applications are processed on a rolling basis. Application fee: $50. Electronic applications accepted. Application fee is waived when completed online. *Expenses:* Contact institution. *Financial support:* In 2017–18, 1,459 students received support. Tuition waivers and unspecified assistantships available. Financial award application deadline: 5/1; financial award applicants required to submit FAFSA. *Unit head:* Dr. Maliha Zaman, 610-902-8502, Fax: 610-902-8797, E-mail: msz37@cabrini.edu. *Application contact:* Diane Greenwood, Director of Graduate Admissions, 610-902-8291, E-mail: diane.l.greenwood@cabrini.edu.
Website: http://cabrini.edu/graduate

Cairn University, School of Education, Langhorne, PA 19047-2990. Offers applied behavior analysis (MS Sp Ed, Certificate); educational leadership and administration (MS El); instruction (MS Sp Ed); teacher education (MS Ed). *Program availability:* Part-time, evening/weekend, 100% online, blended/hybrid learning. *Entrance requirements:* Additional exam requirements/recommendations for international students: Required—TOEFL (minimum score 550 paper-based). Electronic applications accepted. Application fee is waived when completed online. *Expenses:* Contact institution.

Caldwell University, School of Education, Caldwell, NJ 07006-6195. Offers curriculum and instruction (MA); education leadership (Ed D); educational administration (MA); elementary, secondary or preschool endorsement, special ed, ESL (Postbaccalaureate Certificate); learning disabilities teacher-consultant (Post-Master's Certificate); literacy instruction (MA); principal (Post-Master's Certificate); reading specialist (Post-Master's Certificate); special education (MA), including special education, teaching of students with disabilities, teaching of students with disabilities and learning disabilities teacher-consultant; superintendent (Post-Master's Certificate); supervisor (Post-Master's Certificate). *Program availability:* Part-time, evening/weekend. *Faculty:* 10 full-time (6 women), 21 part-time/adjunct (12 women). *Students:* 37 full-time (30 women), 225 part-time (177 women); includes 47 minority (19 Black or African American, non-Hispanic/Latino; 3 Asian, non-Hispanic/Latino; 23 Hispanic/Latino; 2 Two or more races, non-Hispanic/Latino). Average age 35. 189 applicants, 57% accepted, 85 enrolled. In 2017, 47 master's awarded. *Degree requirements:* For master's, comprehensive exam (for some programs), thesis (for some programs); for doctorate, thesis/dissertation. *Entrance requirements:* For master's, PRAXIS, 3 years of work experience, prior teaching certification; for doctorate, GRE or MAT; for other advanced degree, two letters of recommendation; interview (for some programs). Additional exam requirements/recommendations for international students: Required—TOEFL (minimum score 580 paper-based, 70 iBT), IELTS (6), or ELS Level 112 Certification of Completion. *Application deadline:* For fall admission, 6/1 for domestic students; for spring admission, 12/1 for domestic students; for summer admission, 4/1 for domestic students. Applications are processed on a rolling basis. Application fee: $50. Electronic applications accepted. *Expenses:* $950 per credit (for master's and certificate programs); $1,125 per credit (for doctoral programs). *Financial support:* Unspecified assistantships available. Financial award applicants required to submit FAFSA. *Faculty research:* Curriculum and instruction, secondary education, special education, education

and technology, literacy instruction, higher education administration, education leadership. *Unit head:* Dr. Joan Moriarity, Associate Dean, 973-618-3626, E-mail: jmoriarity@caldwell.edu. *Application contact:* Tom Disch, Senior Admissions Counselor, 973-618-3544, E-mail: graduate@caldwell.edu.

California Baptist University, Program in Education, Riverside, CA 92504-3206. Offers educational leadership (MS); educational leadership for faith-based institutions (MS); educational leadership for public institutions (MS); educational technology (MS); instructional computer applications (MS); international education (MS); leadership and adult learning (MS); leadership and organizational studies (MS); online teaching and learning (MS); reading (MS); science education (MA); special education in mild/moderate disabilities (MS); special education in moderate/severe disabilities (MS); teacher leadership (MS); teaching (MS); teaching and learning (MS). *Program availability:* Part-time, evening/weekend, 100% online, blended/hybrid learning. *Faculty:* 19 full-time (11 women), 36 part-time/adjunct (22 women). *Students:* 232 full-time (182 women), 315 part-time (247 women); includes 264 minority (33 Black or African American, non-Hispanic/Latino; 4 American Indian or Alaska Native, non-Hispanic/Latino; 11 Asian, non-Hispanic/Latino; 186 Hispanic/Latino; 7 Native Hawaiian or other Pacific Islander, non-Hispanic/Latino; 23 Two or more races, non-Hispanic/Latino). Average age 31. 217 applicants, 64% accepted, 129 enrolled. In 2017, 196 master's awarded. *Degree requirements:* For master's, comprehensive exam, project, or thesis. *Entrance requirements:* For master's, minimum undergraduate GPA of 2.75; 500-word essay; three letters of recommendation; two prerequisite courses completed with minimum C grade. Additional exam requirements/recommendations for international students: Required—TOEFL (minimum score 80 iBT). *Application deadline:* For fall admission, 8/1 priority date for domestic students, 7/1 for international students; for spring admission, 12/1 priority date for domestic students, 11/1 for international students. Applications are processed on a rolling basis. Application fee: $45. Electronic applications accepted. *Expenses:* Contact institution. *Financial support:* In 2017–18, 162 students received support. Federal Work-Study and scholarships/grants available. Financial award applicants required to submit CSS PROFILE or FAFSA. *Faculty research:* Leadership development, complexity theory, faith and learning, special education, social and philosophical contexts of education. *Unit head:* Dr. John Shoup, Dean, School of Education, 951-343-4516, E-mail: jshoup@calbaptist.edu. *Application contact:* Gavin Andrew, Graduate Admissions Counselor, 951-552-8437, E-mail: gandrew@calbaptist.edu.
Website: http://www.calbaptist.edu/mastersined/

California Baptist University, Program in Leadership and Adult Learning, Riverside, CA 92504-3206. Offers MA. *Program availability:* Part-time, evening/weekend. *Faculty:* 1 full-time (0 women). *Degree requirements:* For master's, CCCAOE professional training or leadership tactics. *Entrance requirements:* For master's, minimum undergraduate GPA of 2.75, bachelor's degree transcripts, three letters of recommendation, essay, resume. Additional exam requirements/recommendations for international students: Required—TOEFL (minimum score 80 iBT). *Application deadline:* For fall admission, 8/1 priority date for domestic students, 7/1 priority date for international students; for spring admission, 12/1 priority date for domestic students, 11/1 priority date for international students. Applications are processed on a rolling basis. Application fee: $45. Electronic applications accepted. *Expenses:* Contact institution. *Financial support:* Applicants required to submit CSS PROFILE or FAFSA. *Unit head:* Dr. John Shoup, Dean, School of Education, 951-343-4205, E-mail: jshoup@calbaptist.edu.

California Coast University, School of Education, Santa Ana, CA 92701. Offers administration (M Ed); curriculum and instruction (M Ed); educational administration (Ed D); educational psychology (Ed D); organizational leadership (Ed D). *Program availability:* Online learning.

California Lutheran University, Graduate Studies, Graduate School of Education, Thousand Oaks, CA 91360-2787. Offers counseling and guidance (MS), including college student personnel, counseling and guidance; educational leadership (MA, Ed D), including educational leadership (K-12) (Ed D), higher education leadership (Ed D); special education (MS); teacher leadership (M Ed); teaching (M Ed). *Accreditation:* NCATE. *Program availability:* Part-time, evening/weekend. *Faculty:* 21 full-time (18 women), 40 part-time/adjunct (27 women). *Students:* 390 full-time (303 women), 61 part-time (51 women); includes 228 minority (6 Black or African American, non-Hispanic/Latino; 2 American Indian or Alaska Native, non-Hispanic/Latino; 13 Asian, non-Hispanic/Latino; 186 Hispanic/Latino; 1 Native Hawaiian or other Pacific Islander, non-Hispanic/Latino; 20 Two or more races, non-Hispanic/Latino). Average age 31. 201 applicants, 76% accepted, 121 enrolled. In 2017, 129 master's, 19 doctorates awarded. *Degree requirements:* For master's, comprehensive exam or thesis; for doctorate, thesis/dissertation. *Entrance requirements:* For master's, GRE General Test, interview, minimum GPA of 3.0. *Application deadline:* For fall admission, 7/1 priority date for domestic students; for spring admission, 11/1 priority date for domestic students; for summer admission, 4/1 priority date for domestic students. Applications are processed on a rolling basis. Application fee: $50. Electronic applications accepted. *Expenses:* Tuition: Full-time $15,000. Full-time tuition and fees vary according to degree level and program. *Unit head:* Dr. Michael Hillis, Dean, 805-493-3421. *Application contact:* 805-493-3325, Fax: 805-493-3861, E-mail: clugrad@callutheran.edu.

California State Polytechnic University, Pomona, Ed D Program in Educational Leadership, Pomona, CA 91768-2557. Offers Ed D. *Program availability:* Part-time, evening/weekend. *Students:* 1 (woman) full-time, 45 part-time (34 women); includes 33 minority (8 Black or African American, non-Hispanic/Latino; 5 Asian, non-Hispanic/Latino; 18 Hispanic/Latino; 2 Two or more races, non-Hispanic/Latino), 1 international. Average age 43. 23 applicants, 87% accepted, 13 enrolled. In 2017, 14 doctorates awarded. *Entrance requirements:* Additional exam requirements/recommendations for international students: Required—TOEFL (minimum score 550 paper-based). *Application deadline:* Applications are processed on a rolling basis. Application fee: $55. Electronic applications accepted. *Expenses:* Contact institution. *Financial support:* Applicants required to submit FAFSA. *Unit head:* Dr. Betty T Alford, Professor/Doctoral Program Co-Director, 909-869-5369, Fax: 909-869-4822, E-mail: btalford@cpp.edu. *Application contact:* Dr. Nancy M. Sanders, Professor/Doctoral Program Co-Director, 909-869-2579, Fax: 909-869-5416, E-mail: nmsanders@cpp.edu.
Website: http://www.cpp.edu/~doctoralstudies/

California State University, Bakersfield, Division of Graduate Studies, School of Social Sciences and Education, Program in Educational Administration, Bakersfield, CA 93311. Offers MA. *Faculty:* 6 part-time/adjunct (4 women). *Students:* 26 full-time (18 women); includes 11 minority (3 Black or African American, non-Hispanic/Latino; 1 American Indian or Alaska Native, non-Hispanic/Latino; 1 Asian, non-Hispanic/Latino; 6 Hispanic/Latino). Average age 40. *Degree requirements:* For master's, thesis or alternative, project or culminating exam. *Application deadline:* Applications are processed on a rolling basis. Application fee: $55. *Expenses:* Tuition, state resident: full-time $7176; part-time $4164 per year. *Unit head:* Dr. Michael Cosimano, Director, 661-664-2482, Fax: 661-664-2479, E-mail: mcosimano@csub.edu. *Application contact:* Julia Bavier, Admissions and Graduation Advisor, 661-664-3193, Fax: 661-654-2479, E-mail: jbavier@csub.edu.
Website: https://www.csub.edu/sse/departments/advancededucationalstudies/educational_administration/index.html

Educational Leadership and Administration

California State University, Bakersfield, Division of Graduate Studies, School of Social Sciences and Education, Program in Educational Leadership, Bakersfield, CA 93311. Offers Ed D. *Faculty:* 3 full-time (1 woman). *Students:* 25 full-time (16 women), 1 (woman) part-time; includes 17 minority (4 Black or African American, non-Hispanic/Latino; 2 American Indian or Alaska Native, non-Hispanic/Latino; 3 Asian, non-Hispanic/Latino; 6 Hispanic/Latino; 2 Two or more races, non-Hispanic/Latino). Average age 39. 23 applicants, 96% accepted, 18 enrolled. *Degree requirements:* For doctorate, thesis/dissertation. *Expenses:* Tuition, state resident: full-time $7176; part-time $4164 per year. *Financial support:* In 2017–18, fellowships (averaging $1,850 per year) were awarded; Federal Work-Study, scholarships/grants, and tuition waivers (full and partial) also available. Financial award application deadline: 3/2; financial award applicants required to submit FAFSA. *Unit head:* Amanda Taggart, Director, 661-654-3140, E-mail: edd@csub.edu. *Application contact:* Timothy Lafond, Doctoral Program Coordinator, 661-654-3140, Fax: 661-654-2479, E-mail: tlafond@csub.edu.

California State University, East Bay, Office of Graduate Studies, College of Education and Allied Studies, Department of Educational Leadership, Hayward, CA 94542-3000. Offers MS, Ed D. *Accreditation:* NCATE. *Program availability:* Part-time, evening/weekend, online learning. *Students:* Average age 42. 66 applicants, 83% accepted, 42 enrolled. In 2017, 60 master's, 16 doctorates awarded. *Degree requirements:* For master's, comprehensive exam, project or thesis; for doctorate, thesis/dissertation. *Entrance requirements:* For master's, CBEST, teaching or services credential and experience; minimum GPA of 3.0; for doctorate, GRE, MA with minimum GPA of 3.0; PK-12 leadership position; portfolio of work samples; employer/district support agreement. Additional exam requirements/recommendations for international students: Required—TOEFL (minimum score 550 paper-based). *Application deadline:* For fall admission, 6/30 for domestic and international students. Application fee: $55. Electronic applications accepted. *Financial support:* Career-related internships or fieldwork, Federal Work-Study, and institutionally sponsored loans available. Support available to part-time students. Financial award application deadline: 3/2; financial award applicants required to submit FAFSA. *Unit head:* Prof. Peg Winkelman, Chair, 510-885-4145, E-mail: peg.winkelman@csueastbay.edu. *Application contact:* Prof. Gilberto Arriaza, Graduate Advisor, 510-885-2905, E-mail: gilberto.arriaza@csueastbay.edu.
Website: http://www20.csueastbay.edu/ceas/departments/el/

California State University, East Bay, Office of Graduate Studies, College of Education and Allied Studies, Department of Teacher Education, Hayward, CA 94542-3000. Offers education (MS), including curriculum, early childhood education, educational technology and leadership, reading instruction. *Program availability:* Online learning. *Faculty:* 11 full-time (8 women), 56 part-time/adjunct (40 women). *Students:* 49 full-time (35 women), 15 part-time (13 women); includes 31 minority (5 Black or African American, non-Hispanic/Latino; 13 Asian, non-Hispanic/Latino; 11 Hispanic/Latino; 2 Two or more races, non-Hispanic/Latino), 7 international. Average age 31. 76 applicants, 82% accepted, 33 enrolled. In 2017, 83 master's awarded. *Degree requirements:* For master's, project or thesis. *Entrance requirements:* For master's, minimum GPA of 3.0 in field, 2.5 overall; teaching experience; baccalaureate degree; 3 letters of recommendation. Additional exam requirements/recommendations for international students: Required—TOEFL (minimum score 550 paper-based), IELTS. *Application deadline:* For fall admission, 6/1 for domestic and international students. Application fee: $55. Electronic applications accepted. *Financial support:* Career-related internships or fieldwork, Federal Work-Study, and institutionally sponsored loans available. Support available to part-time students. Financial award application deadline: 3/2; financial award applicants required to submit FAFSA. *Faculty research:* Online pedagogy, writing, learning, teaching. *Unit head:* Dr. Eric Engdahl, Chair, 510-885-4599, E-mail: eric.engdahl@csueastbay.edu. *Application contact:* Prof. Valerie Helgren-Lempesis, Education Graduate Advisor, 510-885-3006, Fax: 510-885-4632, E-mail: valerie.helgren-lempesis@csueastbay.edu.
Website: http://www20.csueastbay.edu/ceas/departments/ted/index.html

California State University, Fresno, Division of Research and Graduate Studies, Kremen School of Education and Human Development, Department of Educational Leadership, Fresno, CA 93740-8027. Offers education (MA), including educational leadership and administration. *Accreditation:* NCATE. *Program availability:* Part-time, evening/weekend. *Degree requirements:* For master's, thesis or alternative. *Entrance requirements:* For master's, GRE General Test, MAT, minimum GPA of 2.75. Additional exam requirements/recommendations for international students: Required—TOEFL. Electronic applications accepted. *Faculty research:* Substance abuse on youth education.

California State University, Fresno, Division of Research and Graduate Studies, Kremen School of Education and Human Development, Doctoral Program in Educational Leadership, Fresno, CA 93740-8027. Offers Ed D. *Program availability:* Part-time. *Degree requirements:* For doctorate, thesis/dissertation. *Entrance requirements:* For doctorate, GRE, minimum GPA of 3.0, master's degree, personal interview, written statement of purpose. Additional exam requirements/recommendations for international students: Required—TOEFL. Electronic applications accepted. *Expenses:* Contact institution. *Faculty research:* Minority special education leadership, literacy, ethics of leadership, organizational planning, language development.

California State University, Fullerton, Graduate Studies, College of Education, Department of Educational Leadership, Fullerton, CA 92831-3599. Offers educational administration (MS); educational leadership (Ed D). *Accreditation:* NCATE. *Program availability:* Part-time. *Faculty:* 7 full-time (4 women), 4 part-time/adjunct (1 woman). *Students:* 2 full-time (both women), 239 part-time (172 women); includes 163 minority (31 Black or African American, non-Hispanic/Latino; 39 Asian, non-Hispanic/Latino; 82 Hispanic/Latino; 1 Native Hawaiian or other Pacific Islander, non-Hispanic/Latino; 10 Two or more races, non-Hispanic/Latino), 5 international. Average age 36. 311 applicants, 36% accepted, 98 enrolled. *Degree requirements:* For master's, thesis or alternative, project. *Entrance requirements:* For master's, minimum GPA of 2.5. Application fee: $55. *Financial support:* Career-related internships or fieldwork, Federal Work-Study, institutionally sponsored loans, and scholarships/grants available. Support available to part-time students. Financial award application deadline: 3/1; financial award applicants required to submit FAFSA. *Faculty research:* Creation of a substance abuse prevention training and demonstration program. *Unit head:* Jennifer Goldstein, Head, 657-278-3963. *Application contact:* Admissions/Applications, 657-278-2371.

California State University, Long Beach, Graduate Studies, College of Education, Department of Advanced Studies in Education and Counseling, Long Beach, CA 90840. Offers counseling (MS), including marriage and family therapy, school counseling, student development in higher education; education (MA, Ed D); educational administration (MA, Ed D); educational psychology (MA); special education (MS). *Program availability:* Part-time, evening/weekend. *Entrance requirements:* For master's, GRE General Test, minimum GPA of 2.75. Electronic applications accepted.

California State University, Northridge, Graduate Studies, Michael D. Eisner College of Education, Department of Educational Leadership and Policy Studies, Northridge, CA 91330. Offers education (MA); educational administration (MA); educational leadership (Ed D). *Accreditation:* NCATE. *Program availability:* Part-time, evening/weekend.

Students: 18 full-time (13 women), 239 part-time (180 women); includes 160 minority (13 Black or African American, non-Hispanic/Latino; 2 American Indian or Alaska Native, non-Hispanic/Latino; 9 Asian, non-Hispanic/Latino; 130 Hispanic/Latino; 6 Two or more races, non-Hispanic/Latino). Average age 38. 98 applicants, 84% accepted, 70 enrolled. In 2017, 78 master's awarded. *Entrance requirements:* For master's, 2 letters of recommendation. Additional exam requirements/recommendations for international students: Required—TOEFL. *Application deadline:* For fall admission, 11/30 for domestic students. Application fee: $55. *Financial support:* Fellowships available. Financial award application deadline: 3/1. *Faculty research:* Bilingual educational training. *Unit head:* Jody Dunlap, Chair, 818-677-2591, E-mail: jody.dunlap@csun.edu. Website: http://www.csun.edu/eisner-education/educational-leadership-policy-studies

California State University, Sacramento, College of Education, Graduate and Professional Studies in Education, Sacramento, CA 95819. Offers behavioral science and gender equity (MA); child development (MA); counseling (MS); curriculum and instruction (MA); education (Ed D), including K-12 and community college; education leadership and policy studies (MA), including higher education, PreK-12; education specialist (Ed S), including school psychology; educational technology (MA); language and literacy (MA); multicultural education (MA); school psychology (MA); special education (MA); workforce development advocacy (MA). *Program availability:* Part-time, evening/weekend, blended/hybrid learning. *Students:* 381 full-time (294 women), 135 part-time (101 women); includes 296 minority (44 Black or African American, non-Hispanic/Latino; 1 American Indian or Alaska Native, non-Hispanic/Latino; 94 Asian, non-Hispanic/Latino; 153 Hispanic/Latino; 4 Native Hawaiian or other Pacific Islander, non-Hispanic/Latino), 3 international. Average age 32. 553 applicants, 53% accepted, 292 enrolled. In 2017, 147 master's, 13 doctorates, 10 other advanced degrees awarded. *Degree requirements:* For master's, thesis or project; writing proficiency exam; for doctorate, thesis/dissertation. *Entrance requirements:* For master's and doctorate, GRE. Additional exam requirements/recommendations for international students: Required—TOEFL (minimum score 550 paper-based; 80 iBT); Recommended—IELTS (minimum score 7), TSE. *Application deadline:* For fall admission, 2/15 for domestic students, 1/15 for international students. Applications are processed on a rolling basis. Application fee: $55. Electronic applications accepted. *Expenses:* Contact institution. *Financial support:* Career-related internships or fieldwork, Federal Work-Study, and scholarships/grants available. Support available to part-time students. Financial award application deadline: 3/1; financial award applicants required to submit FAFSA. *Unit head:* Dr. Elizabeth Liles, Chair, 916-278-5942, E-mail: coe@csus.edu. *Application contact:* Jose Martinez, Graduate Admissions Supervisor, 916-278-7871, E-mail: martinj@skymail.csus.edu.
Website: http://www.csus.edu/coe/academics/graduate/index.html

California State University, San Bernardino, Graduate Studies, College of Education, Program in Educational Administration, San Bernardino, CA 92407. Offers MA. *Program availability:* Part-time, evening/weekend. *Faculty:* 21 full-time (11 women), 35 part-time/adjunct (26 women). *Students:* 35 full-time (24 women), 33 part-time (21 women); includes 40 minority (8 Black or African American, non-Hispanic/Latino; 1 American Indian or Alaska Native, non-Hispanic/Latino; 28 Hispanic/Latino; 3 Two or more races, non-Hispanic/Latino), 1 international. Average age 39. 44 applicants, 77% accepted, 30 enrolled. In 2017, 55 master's awarded. *Degree requirements:* For master's, thesis or alternative. *Entrance requirements:* Additional exam requirements/recommendations for international students: Required—TOEFL. *Application deadline:* For fall admission, 7/16 for domestic students; for winter admission, 10/16 for domestic students; for spring admission, 2/5 for domestic students. Application fee: $55. *Unit head:* Dr. Jay Fiene, Dean, 909-537-5600, E-mail: jfiene@csusb.edu. *Application contact:* Dr. Dorota Huizinga, Dean of Graduate Studies, 909-537-3064, E-mail: dorota.huizinga@csusb.edu.

California State University, San Bernardino, Graduate Studies, College of Education, Program in Educational Leadership: Community College Specialization, San Bernardino, CA 92407. Offers MA. *Program availability:* Part-time, evening/weekend. *Students:* 14 full-time (8 women), 10 part-time (6 women); includes 10 minority (1 Asian, non-Hispanic/Latino; 8 Hispanic/Latino; 1 Two or more races, non-Hispanic/Latino), 1 international. Average age 39. 15 applicants, 67% accepted, 8 enrolled. *Degree requirements:* For master's, thesis optional. *Entrance requirements:* Additional exam requirements/recommendations for international students: Required—TOEFL. *Application deadline:* For fall admission, 7/17 for domestic students. Application fee: $55. *Unit head:* Dr. Jay Fiene, Dean, 909-537-7621, E-mail: jfiene@csusb.edu. *Application contact:* Dr. Dorota Huizinga, Dean of Graduate Studies, 909-537-3064, E-mail: dorota.huizinga@csusb.edu.

California State University, San Bernardino, Graduate Studies, College of Education, Program in Educational Leadership: P-12 Specialization, San Bernardino, CA 92407. Offers Ed D. *Students:* 4 full-time (3 women), 45 part-time (32 women); includes 39 minority (14 Black or African American, non-Hispanic/Latino; 2 Asian, non-Hispanic/Latino; 22 Hispanic/Latino; 1 Two or more races, non-Hispanic/Latino). Average age 43. 11 applicants, 91% accepted, 10 enrolled. In 2017, 7 doctorates awarded. *Entrance requirements:* Additional exam requirements/recommendations for international students: Required—TOEFL. *Application deadline:* For fall admission, 7/16 for domestic students. Application fee: $55. *Unit head:* Dr. Jay Fiene, Dean, 909-537-7621, E-mail: jfiene@csusb.edu. *Application contact:* Dr. Dorota Huizinga, Dean of Graduate Studies, 909-537-3064, E-mail: dorota.huizinga@csusb.edu.

California State University, San Marcos, College of Education, Health and Human Services, School of Education, San Marcos, CA 92096-0001. Offers education (MA); educational administration (MA); educational leadership (Ed D); literacy education (MA); special education (MA). *Accreditation:* NCATE (one or more programs are accredited). *Program availability:* Part-time, evening/weekend. *Entrance requirements:* For master's, minimum GPA of 3.0, teaching credentials, 1 year of teaching experience. *Application deadline:* For fall admission, 2/1 priority date for domestic students. Applications are processed on a rolling basis. Application fee: $55. *Expenses:* Tuition, state resident: full-time $7176. Tuition, nonresident: full-time $9504. *Financial support:* Applicants required to submit FAFSA. *Faculty research:* Multicultural literature, art as knowledge, poetry and second language acquisition, restructuring K-12 education and improving the training of K-8 science teachers. *Unit head:* Pat Stall, Director, 760-750-4386, E-mail: pstall@csusm.edu.
Website: http://www.csusm.edu/education/

California State University, Stanislaus, College of Education, Kinesiology and Social Work, Doctor of Education in Educational Leadership Programs, Turlock, CA 95382. Offers community college leadership (Ed D); P-12 leadership (Ed D). *Program availability:* Part-time, evening/weekend. *Degree requirements:* For doctorate, thesis/dissertation. *Entrance requirements:* For doctorate, GRE, minimum GPA of 3.0, 3 letters of reference, interview, personal statement. Additional exam requirements/recommendations for international students: Required—TOEFL (minimum score 550 paper-based). Electronic applications accepted.

California State University, Stanislaus, College of Education, Kinesiology and Social Work, MA Program in Education, Turlock, CA 95382. Offers curriculum and instruction (MA), including education technology, elementary education, multilingual education, physical education, reading, secondary education, special education; school administration (MA); school counseling (MA). *Program availability:* Part-time, evening/weekend. *Degree requirements:* For master's, comprehensive exam (for some programs), thesis (for some programs). *Entrance requirements:* For master's, MAT, GRE, or CBEST (varies by concentration), 3 letters of recommendation, personal statement. Additional exam requirements/recommendations for international students: Required—TOEFL (minimum score 550 paper-based). Electronic applications accepted. *Faculty research:* Children's perspectives on historical events, method elementary schools dual language education, K-12 reading programs.

California University of Pennsylvania, School of Graduate Studies and Research, College of Education and Human Services, Program in School Administration, California, PA 15419-1394. Offers education administration and leadership (Ed D); educational leadership (M Ed), including educational studies, weather and climatology. *Accreditation:* NCATE. *Program availability:* Part-time, evening/weekend, online learning. *Degree requirements:* For master's, comprehensive exam, thesis optional. *Entrance requirements:* For master's, MAT, interview, minimum GPA of 3.0, teaching certificate, 2 years of teaching experience. Additional exam requirements/recommendations for international students: Required—TOEFL (minimum score 550 paper-based; 80 iBT). *Application deadline:* For spring admission, 5/1 priority date for domestic and international students. Applications are processed on a rolling basis. Application fee: $25. Electronic applications accepted. *Financial support:* Career-related internships or fieldwork, scholarships/grants, traineeships, and unspecified assistantships available. Financial award applicants required to submit FAFSA. *Faculty research:* Educational leadership, peer coaching, online education-effective teaching strategies, instruction strategies, school law. *Unit head:* Dr. Silvia Braidic, Program Coordinator, 724-938-4757, E-mail: braidic@calu.edu. *Application contact:* Suzanne C. Powers, Director of Graduate Admissions and Recruitment, 724-938-4029, Fax: 724-938-5712, E-mail: powers_s@cup.edu.

Calumet College of Saint Joseph, Program in Leadership in Teaching, Whiting, IN 46394-2195. Offers MS Ed.

Calvary University, Graduate School and Seminary, Kansas City, MO 64147. Offers Bible and theology (MS); Biblical counseling (MA); education (MS), including administration and leadership, Christian education, curriculum and instruction, elementary education; organizational development (MS); pastoral studies (M Div); worship arts (MS). *Program availability:* Part-time, evening/weekend. *Faculty:* 6 full-time (2 women), 2 part-time/adjunct (1 woman). *Students:* 11 full-time (3 women), 29 part-time (15 women); includes 12 minority (4 Black or African American, non-Hispanic/Latino; 1 American Indian or Alaska Native, non-Hispanic/Latino; 6 Asian, non-Hispanic/Latino; 1 Native Hawaiian or other Pacific Islander, non-Hispanic/Latino). Average age 39. *Degree requirements:* For master's, variable foreign language requirement, comprehensive exam, thesis or alternative. *Entrance requirements:* For master's, minimum GPA of 2.5, BA or BS, doctrine agreement. Additional exam requirements/recommendations for international students: Required—TOEFL (minimum score 550 paper-based). *Application deadline:* Applications are processed on a rolling basis. Application fee: $0. Electronic applications accepted. *Expenses:* Contact institution. *Financial support:* Scholarships/grants available. Financial award application deadline: 11/5; financial award applicants required to submit FAFSA. *Unit head:* Dr. Thomas Baurain, Director of Seminary, 816-322-0110 Ext. 1502, Fax: 816-331-4474, E-mail: thomas.baurain@calvary.edu. *Application contact:* Ann Rogers, Admissions Office Assistant, 800-326-3960 Ext. 1321, Fax: 816-331-4474, E-mail: admissions@calvary.edu.
Website: http://www.calvary.edu

Cambridge College, School of Education, Boston, MA 02129. Offers autism specialist (M Ed); autism/behavior analyst (M Ed); behavior analyst (Post-Master's Certificate); behavioral management (M Ed); early childhood teacher (M Ed); education specialist in curriculum and instruction (CAGS); educational leadership (Ed D); elementary teacher (M Ed); English as a second language (M Ed, Certificate); general science (M Ed); health education (Post-Master's Certificate); health/family and consumer sciences (M Ed); history (M Ed); individualized (M Ed); information technology literacy (M Ed); instructional technology (M Ed); interdisciplinary studies (M Ed); library teacher (M Ed); literacy education (M Ed); mathematics (M Ed); mathematics specialist (Certificate); middle school mathematics and science (M Ed); school administration (M Ed, CAGS); school guidance counselor (M Ed); school nurse education (M Ed); school social worker/school adjustment counselor (M Ed); special education administrator (CAGS); special education/moderate disabilities (M Ed); teaching skills and methodologies (M Ed). *Program availability:* Part-time, evening/weekend, online learning. *Degree requirements:* For master's, thesis, internship/practicum (licensure program only); for doctorate, thesis/dissertation; for other advanced degree, thesis. *Entrance requirements:* For master's, interview, resume, documentation of licensure, 2 professional references; for doctorate, official transcripts, interview, resume, documentation of licensure (if any), written personal statement/essay, portfolio of scholarly and professional work, qualifying assessment, 2 professional references, health insurance, immunizations form; for other advanced degree, official transcripts, interview, resume, documentation of licensure (if any), written personal statement/essay, 2 professional references, health insurance, immunizations form. Additional exam requirements/recommendations for international students: Required—TOEFL (minimum score 550 paper-based; 79 iBT), Michigan English Language Assessment Battery (minimum score 85); Recommended—IELTS (minimum score 6). Electronic applications accepted. *Expenses:* Contact institution. *Faculty research:* Adult education, accelerated learning, mathematics education, brain compatible learning, special education and law.

Cameron University, Office of Graduate Studies, Program in Educational Leadership, Lawton, OK 73505-6377. Offers MS. *Program availability:* Part-time, evening/weekend. *Degree requirements:* For master's, portfolio.

Campbellsville University, School of Education, Campbellsville, KY 42718-2799. Offers education (MA); school counseling (MA); school improvement (MA); special education (MASE); special education-teacher leader (MA); teacher leader (MA); teaching (MAT), including middle grades biology, middle grades chemistry, middle grades English. *Accreditation:* NCATE. *Program availability:* Part-time, evening/weekend, 100% online, blended/hybrid learning. *Faculty:* 15 full-time (10 women), 14 part-time/adjunct (9 women). *Students:* 26 full-time (20 women), 155 part-time (122 women); includes 14 minority (13 Black or African American, non-Hispanic/Latino; 1 Hispanic/Latino). Average age 35. 199 applicants, 34% accepted, 57 enrolled. In 2017, 96 master's awarded. *Degree requirements:* For master's, comprehensive exam (for some programs), thesis, research paper. *Entrance requirements:* For master's, GRE or PRAXIS, minimum undergraduate GPA of 2.75, teaching certificate, professional growth plan, letters of recommendation, interview. Additional exam requirements/recommendations for international students: Recommended—TOEFL (minimum score 550 paper-based; 79 iBT), IELTS (minimum score 6). *Application deadline:* Applications are processed on a rolling basis. Application fee: $25. Electronic applications accepted. Application fee is waived when completed online. *Expenses:* $399 per credit hour. *Financial support:* Unspecified assistantships and employee tuition waivers available. Financial award applicants required to submit FAFSA. *Faculty research:* Professional development, curriculum development, school governance, assessment, special education. *Unit head:* Dr. Beverly Ennis, Dean, 270-789-5344, Fax: 270-789-5206,

E-mail: bcennis@campbellsville.edu. *Application contact:* Monica Bamwine, Assistant Director of Graduate Admissions, 270-789-5221, Fax: 270-789-5071, E-mail: mkbamwine@campbellsville.edu.

Campbell University, Graduate and Professional Programs, School of Education, Buies Creek, NC 27506. Offers elementary education (M Ed); interdisciplinary studies (M Ed); middle grades education (M Ed); physical education (M Ed); school administration (MSA); school counseling (M Ed); secondary education (M Ed). *Accreditation:* NCATE. *Program availability:* Part-time, evening/weekend. *Degree requirements:* For master's, comprehensive exam. *Entrance requirements:* For master's, GRE General Test, minimum GPA of 2.7. *Faculty research:* Spiritual values and wellness issues in counseling, stress and professional burnout among counselors, thinking strategies, leadership, adaptive technology.

Canisius College, Graduate Division, School of Education and Human Services, Department of Graduate Education and Leadership, Buffalo, NY 14208-1098. Offers business and marketing education (MS Ed); college student personnel (MS Ed); deaf education (MS Ed); deaf/adolescent education, grades 7-12 (MS Ed); deaf/childhood education, grades 1-6 (MS Ed); differentiated instruction (MS Ed); education administration (MS); educational administration (MS Ed); educational technologies (Certificate); gifted education extension (Certificate); literacy (MS Ed); reading (Certificate); school building leadership (MS Ed, Certificate); school district leadership (Certificate); teacher leader (Certificate); TESOL (MS Ed). *Accreditation:* NCATE. *Program availability:* Part-time, evening/weekend, 100% online, blended/hybrid learning. *Faculty:* 5 full-time (all women), 21 part-time/adjunct (16 women). *Students:* 85 full-time (67 women), 189 part-time (151 women); includes 31 minority (18 Black or African American, non-Hispanic/Latino; 3 American Indian or Alaska Native, non-Hispanic/Latino; 3 Asian, non-Hispanic/Latino; 4 Hispanic/Latino; 3 Two or more races, non-Hispanic/Latino), 1 international. Average age 31. 83 applicants, 96% accepted, 74 enrolled. In 2017, 94 master's, 47 other advanced degrees awarded. *Entrance requirements:* For master's, GRE (if cumulative GPA less than 2.7), transcripts, two letters of recommendation. Additional exam requirements/recommendations for international students: Required—TOEFL (minimum score 550 paper-based, 79 iBT), IELTS (minimum score 6.5), or CAEL (minimum score 70). *Application deadline:* Applications are processed on a rolling basis. Application fee: $0. Electronic applications accepted. *Expenses: Tuition:* Full-time $22,860; part-time $820 per credit. *Required fees:* $720; $25 per credit. $65 per semester. One-time fee: $425. *Financial support:* Career-related internships or fieldwork, Federal Work-Study, scholarships/grants, tuition waivers (partial), and unspecified assistantships available. Support available to part-time students. Financial award application deadline: 4/30; financial award applicants required to submit FAFSA. *Faculty research:* Asperger's disease, autism, private higher education, reading strategies. *Unit head:* Dr. Anne Marie Tryjankowski, Chair/Associate Professor of Graduate Education and Leadership, 716-888-3715, Fax: 716-888-3142, E-mail: tryjanka@canisius.edu.

Capella University, School of Education, Doctoral Programs in Education, Minneapolis, MN 55402. Offers curriculum and instruction (PhD); educational leadership and management (Ed D); instructional design for online learning (PhD); K-12 studies in education (PhD); leadership for higher education (PhD); leadership in educational administration (PhD); postsecondary and adult education (PhD); professional studies in education (PhD); reading and literacy (Ed D); special education leadership (PhD); training and performance improvement (PhD).

Capella University, School of Education, Master's Programs in Education, Minneapolis, MN 55402. Offers adult education (MS); curriculum and instruction (MS); early childhood education (MS); enrollment management (MS); higher education leadership and management (MS); instructional design for online learning (MS); integrative studies (MS); K-12 studies in education (MS); leadership in educational administration (MS); reading and literacy (MS); special education teaching (MS).

Cardinal Stritch University, College of Education and Leadership, Department of Education, Milwaukee, WI 53217-3985. Offers educational leadership (MS); higher education student affairs leadership (MS); leadership for the advancement of learning and service (Ed D, PhD); leadership for the advancement of learning and service in higher education (Ed D, PhD); teaching (MAT); urban education (MA). *Accreditation:* NCATE. *Program availability:* Part-time, evening/weekend, 100% online, blended/hybrid learning. *Students:* 73 full-time (57 women), 332 part-time (220 women); includes 113 minority (59 Black or African American, non-Hispanic/Latino; 2 American Indian or Alaska Native, non-Hispanic/Latino; 10 Asian, non-Hispanic/Latino; 38 Hispanic/Latino; 1 Native Hawaiian or other Pacific Islander, non-Hispanic/Latino; 3 Two or more races, non-Hispanic/Latino), 7 international. Average age 35. 137 applicants, 97% accepted, 104 enrolled. In 2017, 135 master's, 28 doctorates awarded. *Degree requirements:* For master's, comprehensive exam, thesis (for some programs), research project, faculty recommendation; for doctorate, thesis/dissertation, practica, field experience. *Entrance requirements:* For master's, 2 letters of recommendation, minimum GPA of 3.0; for doctorate, minimum GPA of 3.5 in master's coursework, 3 letters of recommendation. Additional exam requirements/recommendations for international students: Required—TOEFL (minimum score 550 paper-based; 79 iBT), IELTS (minimum score 6.5). *Application deadline:* For fall admission, 7/15 priority date for domestic students; for spring admission, 12/15 priority date for domestic students. Applications are processed on a rolling basis. Application fee: $0. Electronic applications accepted. *Expenses:* Tuition varies by program. *Financial support:* Fellowships, research assistantships with partial tuition reimbursements, career-related internships or fieldwork, Federal Work-Study, and scholarships/grants available. Financial award applicants required to submit FAFSA. *Application contact:* 800-347-8822 Ext. 4042, E-mail: admissions@stritch.edu.

Caribbean University, Graduate School, Bayamón, PR 00960-0493. Offers administration and supervision (MA Ed); criminal justice (MA); curriculum and instruction (MA Ed, PhD), including elementary education (MA Ed), English education (MA Ed), history education (MA Ed), mathematics education (MA Ed), primary education (MA Ed), science education (MA Ed), Spanish education (MA Ed); educational technology in instructional systems (MA Ed); gerontology (MSN); human resources (MBA); museology, archiving and art history (MA Ed); neonatal pediatrics (MSN); physical education (MA Ed); special education (MA Ed). *Entrance requirements:* For master's, interview, minimum GPA of 2.5.

Carroll University, Graduate Programs in Education, Waukesha, WI 53186-5593. Offers adult and continuing education (M Ed); educational leadership (MS); PK-12 (M Ed). *Program availability:* Part-time, evening/weekend. *Degree requirements:* For master's, thesis. *Entrance requirements:* For master's, minimum undergraduate GPA of 2.5 in related field. Additional exam requirements/recommendations for international students: Required—TOEFL. Electronic applications accepted. *Faculty research:* Qualitative research methods, whole language approaches to teaching, the writing process, multicultural education, gifted/talented learners.

Carson-Newman University, Graduate Program in Education, Jefferson City, TN 37760. Offers curriculum and instruction (M Ed); educational leadership (M Ed); elementary education (MAT); school counseling (MS); secondary education (MAT); teaching English as a second language (MATESL). *Accreditation:* NCATE. *Program availability:* Part-time, evening/weekend, 100% online, blended/hybrid learning. *Faculty:*

Educational Leadership and Administration

20 full-time (11 women), 16 part-time/adjunct (13 women). *Students:* 63 full-time (37 women), 488 part-time (362 women); includes 60 minority (46 Black or African American, non-Hispanic/Latino; 2 American Indian or Alaska Native, non-Hispanic/Latino; 1 Asian, non-Hispanic/Latino; 5 Hispanic/Latino; 1 Native Hawaiian or other Pacific Islander, non-Hispanic/Latino; 5 Two or more races, non-Hispanic/Latino), 29 international. Average age 35. 204 applicants, 100% accepted, 188 enrolled. In 2017, 211 master's awarded. *Degree requirements:* For master's, thesis or alternative. *Entrance requirements:* For master's, PRAXIS II or GRE with minimum score of 290 on the verbal and quantitative components (for MAT), minimum GPA of 3.0 in major, 2.5 overall. Additional exam requirements/recommendations for international students: Recommended—TOEFL (minimum score 79 iBT), IELTS (minimum score 6.5), TSE (minimum score 53). *Application deadline:* For fall admission, 7/15 priority date for domestic students. Applications are processed on a rolling basis. Application fee: $50. *Expenses: Tuition:* Full-time $10,516; part-time $478 per credit hour. *Required fees:* $240; $120 per semester. One-time fee: $150. *Financial support:* Federal Work-Study and unspecified assistantships available. Financial award application required to submit FAFSA. *Unit head:* Dr. Kim Hawkins, Chair, 865-471-3314, E-mail: khawkins@cn.edu. *Application contact:* Nilma Stewart, Graduate Admissions and Services Adviser, 865-471-3230, Fax: 865-471-3875, E-mail: adults@cn.edu.
Website: http://www.cn.edu/adult-graduate-studies

Carthage College, Division of Teacher Education, Kenosha, WI 53140. Offers classroom guidance and counseling (M Ed); creative arts (M Ed); gifted and talented children (M Ed); language arts (M Ed); modern language (M Ed); natural sciences (M Ed); reading (M Ed, Certificate); social sciences (M Ed); teacher leadership (M Ed). *Program availability:* Part-time, evening/weekend. *Degree requirements:* For master's, thesis optional. *Entrance requirements:* For master's, MAT, minimum B average, letters of reference.

Castleton University, Division of Graduate Studies, Department of Education, Program in Educational Leadership, Castleton, VT 05735. Offers MA Ed, CAGS. *Program availability:* Part-time, evening/weekend. *Degree requirements:* For master's, thesis or alternative; for CAGS, publishable paper. *Entrance requirements:* For master's, GRE General Test, MAT, interview, minimum undergraduate GPA of 3.0; for CAGS, educational research, master's degree, minimum undergraduate GPA of 3.0.

The Catholic University of America, School of Arts and Sciences, Department of Education, Washington, DC 20064. Offers Catholic school leadership (MA); education (Certificate); secondary education (MA); special education (MA), including early childhood, non-categorical. *Accreditation:* NCATE. *Program availability:* Part-time. *Faculty:* 8 full-time (7 women), 3 part-time/adjunct (all women). *Students:* 9 full-time (all women), 25 part-time (14 women); includes 2 minority (both Hispanic/Latino), 4 international. Average age 39. 24 applicants, 63% accepted, 9 enrolled. In 2017, 9 master's awarded. *Degree requirements:* For master's, comprehensive exam, thesis or alternative; for Certificate, action research project. *Entrance requirements:* For master's, GRE General Test or MAT, statement of purpose, official copies of academic transcripts, three letters of recommendation, interview; for Certificate, PRAXIS I, statement of purpose, official copies of academic transcripts, three letters of recommendation, interview. Additional exam requirements/recommendations for international students: Required—TOEFL (minimum score 550 paper-based; 80 iBT). *Application deadline:* For fall admission, 7/15 priority date for domestic students, 7/1 for international students; for spring admission, 11/15 priority date for domestic students, 11/1 for international students. Applications are processed on a rolling basis. Application fee: $55. Electronic applications accepted. *Expenses:* Contact institution. *Financial support:* Fellowships, research assistantships, teaching assistantships, Federal Work-Study, scholarships/grants, tuition waivers (full and partial), and unspecified assistantships available. Financial award application deadline: 2/1; financial award applicants required to submit FAFSA. *Faculty research:* Special education, early childhood education, educational psychology, Catholic school administration, leadership and policy studies, counseling, curriculum and instruction. *Unit head:* Dr. Agnes Cave, Chair, 202-319-5805, Fax: 202-319-5815, E-mail: cave@cua.edu. *Application contact:* Dr. Steven Brown, Director of Graduate Admissions, 202-319-5057, Fax: 202-319-6533, E-mail: cua-admissions@cua.edu.
Website: http://education.cua.edu/

Centenary University, Program in Education, Hackettstown, NJ 07840-2100. Offers education practice (M Ed); educational leadership (MA, Ed D); instructional leadership (MA); reading (M Ed); special education (MA). *Accreditation:* TEAC. *Program availability:* Part-time, evening/weekend, online learning. *Degree requirements:* For master's, thesis. *Entrance requirements:* For master's, interview, minimum undergraduate GPA of 2.8.

Central Connecticut State University, School of Graduate Studies, School of Education and Professional Studies, Department of Educational Leadership, Policy and Instructional Technology, New Britain, CT 06050-4010. Offers MS, Ed D, AC, Sixth Year Certificate. *Program availability:* Part-time, evening/weekend. *Faculty:* 16 full-time (7 women), 22 part-time/adjunct (11 women). *Students:* 5 full-time (3 women), 376 part-time (268 women); includes 70 minority (34 Black or African American, non-Hispanic/Latino; 1 American Indian or Alaska Native, non-Hispanic/Latino; 5 Asian, non-Hispanic/Latino; 20 Hispanic/Latino; 1 Native Hawaiian or other Pacific Islander, non-Hispanic/Latino; 9 Two or more races, non-Hispanic/Latino), 1 international. Average age 35. 92 applicants, 82% accepted, 39 enrolled. In 2017, 40 master's, 13 doctorates, 92 other advanced degrees awarded. *Degree requirements:* For master's, thesis or alternative; for doctorate, thesis/dissertation or alternative; for other advanced degree, thesis or alternative, qualifying exam. *Entrance requirements:* For master's, minimum undergraduate GPA of 2.7; for doctorate, GRE, master's degree, minimum GPA of 3.0 on all graduate coursework, essay, interview, resume, letters of recommendation; for other advanced degree, master's degree with minimum GPA of 3.0, essay, portfolio, letters of recommendation. Additional exam requirements/recommendations for international students: Required—TOEFL (minimum score 550 paper-based; 79 iBT); Recommended—IELTS (minimum score 6.5). *Application deadline:* For summer admission, 11/1 for domestic and international students. Applications are processed on a rolling basis. Application fee: $50. Electronic applications accepted. *Expenses: Tuition, area resident:* Full-time $6757. Tuition, state resident: full-time $9750; part-time $374 per credit. Tuition, nonresident: full-time $18,102; part-time $374 per credit. *Required fees:* $4635; $255 per credit. *Financial support:* In 2017–18, 10 students received support. Career-related internships or fieldwork, Federal Work-Study, scholarships/grants, and unspecified assistantships available. Support available to part-time students. Financial award application deadline: 3/1; financial award applicants required to submit FAFSA. *Faculty research:* Curriculum development, organizational leadership in educational settings, educational planning and development. *Unit head:* Dr. Ethan Heinen, Chair, 860-832-2130, E-mail: heineneth@ccsu.edu. *Application contact:* Patricia Gardner, Associate Director of Graduate Studies, 860-832-2350, Fax: 860-832-2362.
Website: http://www.ccsu.edu/elpit/

Central Connecticut State University, School of Graduate Studies, School of Engineering, Science and Technology, Department of Mathematical Sciences, New Britain, CT 06050-4010. Offers data mining (MS, Certificate); mathematics (MA, MS), including actuarial science (MA), computer science (MA), statistics (MA); mathematics

education leadership (Sixth Year Certificate); mathematics for secondary education (Certificate). *Program availability:* Part-time, evening/weekend, 100% online. *Faculty:* 15 full-time (4 women). *Students:* 17 full-time (10 women), 65 part-time (36 women); includes 17 minority (8 Black or African American, non-Hispanic/Latino; 5 Asian, non-Hispanic/Latino; 3 Hispanic/Latino; 1 Two or more races, non-Hispanic/Latino), 2 international. Average age 35. 68 applicants, 81% accepted, 31 enrolled. In 2017, 21 master's, 5 other advanced degrees awarded. *Degree requirements:* For master's, comprehensive exam, thesis or alternative, special project; for other advanced degree, qualifying exam. *Entrance requirements:* For master's, minimum undergraduate GPA of 2.7; for other advanced degree, minimum undergraduate GPA of 3.0, essay, letters of recommendation. Additional exam requirements/recommendations for international students: Required—TOEFL (minimum score 550 paper-based; 79 iBT); Recommended—IELTS (minimum score 6.5). *Application deadline:* For fall admission, 8/1 for domestic students, 5/1 for international students; for spring admission, 11/1 for domestic and international students. Applications are processed on a rolling basis. Application fee: $50. Electronic applications accepted. *Expenses: Tuition, area resident:* Full-time $6757. Tuition, state resident: full-time $9750; part-time $374 per credit. Tuition, nonresident: full-time $18,102; part-time $374 per credit. *Required fees:* $4635; $255 per credit. *Financial support:* In 2017–18, 25 students received support. Career-related internships or fieldwork, Federal Work-Study, scholarships/grants, and unspecified assistantships available. Support available to part-time students. Financial award application deadline: 3/1; financial award applicants required to submit FAFSA. *Faculty research:* Statistics, actuarial mathematics, computer systems and engineering, computer programming techniques, operations research. *Unit head:* Dr. Philip Halloran, Chair, 860-832-2835, E-mail: halloranp@ccsu.edu. *Application contact:* Patricia Gardner, Associate Director of Graduate Studies, 860-832-2350, Fax: 860-832-2362.
Website: http://www.ccsu.edu/mathematics/

Central Michigan University, Central Michigan University Global Campus, Program in Education, Mount Pleasant, MI 48859. Offers college teaching (Graduate Certificate); community college (MA); curriculum and instruction (MA); educational technology (MA, DET); reading and literacy K-12 (MA); school principalship (MA), including charter school leadership; training and development (MA). *Accreditation:* TEAC. *Program availability:* Part-time, evening/weekend. *Entrance requirements:* For master's, minimum GPA of 2.7 in major. Additional exam requirements/recommendations for international students: Required—TOEFL. Electronic applications accepted.

Central Michigan University, Central Michigan University Global Campus, Program in Educational Leadership, Mount Pleasant, MI 48859. Offers K-12 leadership (Ed D). *Program availability:* Part-time, evening/weekend. *Entrance requirements:* Additional exam requirements/recommendations for international students: Required—TOEFL. Electronic applications accepted.

Central Michigan University, College of Graduate Studies, College of Education and Human Services, Department of Educational Leadership, Mount Pleasant, MI 48859. Offers educational leadership (Ed D), including educational technology (Ed D, Ed S), higher education leadership, K-12 curriculum, K-12 leadership; general educational administration (Ed S), including administrative leadership K-12, educational technology (Ed D, Ed S), higher education administration, instructional leadership K-12; school principalship (MA), including charter school leadership, site-based leadership; student affairs administration (MA); teacher leadership (MA). *Program availability:* Part-time, evening/weekend. *Degree requirements:* For master's and Ed S, thesis or alternative; for doctorate, thesis/dissertation. *Entrance requirements:* For doctorate, GRE or MAT, master's degree, minimum GPA of 3.5, 3 years of professional education experience. Electronic applications accepted. *Faculty research:* Elementary administration, secondary administration, student achievement, in-service training, internships in administration.

Central Washington University, School of Graduate Studies and Research, College of Education and Professional Studies, Department of Curriculum, Supervision, and Educational Leadership, Ellensburg, WA 98926. Offers higher education (M Ed); master teacher (M Ed). *Program availability:* Part-time. *Degree requirements:* For master's, comprehensive exam (for some programs), thesis or alternative. *Entrance requirements:* For master's, 1 year of contracted teaching experience. Additional exam requirements/recommendations for international students: Required—TOEFL (minimum score 550 paper-based; 79 iBT), IELTS (minimum score 6.5). *Application deadline:* For fall admission, 2/1 for domestic students; for winter admission, 10/1 for domestic students; for spring admission, 1/1 for domestic students. Applications are processed on a rolling basis. Application fee: $50. Electronic applications accepted. *Financial support:* Application deadline: 3/1; applicants required to submit FAFSA. *Unit head:* Traci Pantano, Chair, 509-963-2661, E-mail: traci.seely@cwu.edu. *Application contact:* Justine Eason, Admissions Program Coordinator, 509-963-3103, Fax: 509-963-1799, E-mail: masters@cwu.edu.
Website: http://www.cwu.edu/~edfoundations/

Chadron State College, School of Professional and Graduate Studies, Department of Education, Chadron, NE 69337. Offers business (MA Ed); community counseling (MA Ed); educational administration (MS Ed, Sp Ed); elementary education (MS Ed); history (MA Ed); language and literature (MA Ed); secondary administration (MS Ed); secondary education (MS Ed). *Accreditation:* NCATE. *Program availability:* Part-time, evening/weekend, online learning. *Degree requirements:* For master's, thesis optional. *Entrance requirements:* For master's, GRE General Test, GRE Writing Test, minimum GPA of 2.75 or 12 graduate hours at CSC with minimum GPA of 3.25. Additional exam requirements/recommendations for international students: Required—TOEFL. Electronic applications accepted. *Faculty research:* Rural education, technology, mental health.

Chaminade University of Honolulu, Office of Professional and Continuing Education, Program in Education, Honolulu, HI 96816-1578. Offers child development (M Ed); early childhood education (Montessori) (MAT); early childhood education (PK-3) (MAT); educational leadership (M Ed); elementary education (MAT); instructional leadership (M Ed); Montessori (M Ed); secondary education (MAT); special education (MAT); teacher leader (M Ed). *Program availability:* Part-time, evening/weekend, 100% online, blended/hybrid learning. *Faculty:* 7 full-time (3 women), 8 part-time/adjunct (6 women). *Students:* 86 full-time (68 women), 88 part-time (64 women); includes 113 minority (7 Black or African American, non-Hispanic/Latino; 2 American Indian or Alaska Native, non-Hispanic/Latino; 46 Asian, non-Hispanic/Latino; 7 Hispanic/Latino; 51 Native Hawaiian or other Pacific Islander, non-Hispanic/Latino), 6 international. Average age 34. 61 applicants, 98% accepted, 49 enrolled. In 2017, 91 master's awarded. *Degree requirements:* For master's, thesis or alternative. *Entrance requirements:* For master's, PRAXIS (for MAT), minimum GPA of 2.75 (for M Ed), 3.0 (for MAT); 2 letters of recommendation, resume, writing sample (for MAT). Additional exam requirements/recommendations for international students: Required—TOEFL (minimum score 550 paper-based; 79 iBT). *Application deadline:* Applications are processed on a rolling basis. Application fee: $40. Electronic applications accepted. *Expenses:* $780 per credit hour plus $93 fee per online class. *Financial support:* Applicants required to submit FAFSA. *Unit head:* Dr. Dale Fryxell, Dean, 808-739-4652, Fax: 808-739-4607, E-mail: edu-office@chaminade.edu. *Application contact:* 808-735-4755, E-mail: gradserv@chaminade.edu.
Website: https://education.chaminade.edu/

Chapman University, Donna Ford Attallah College of Educational Studies, Orange, CA 92866. Offers counseling (MA), including school counseling (MA, Credential); curriculum and instruction (MA), including elementary education, secondary education; education (PhD), including cultural and curricular studies, disability studies, leadership studies, school psychology (PhD, Credential); educational psychology (MA); leadership development (MA); multiple subjects (Credential), including Spanish/English bilingual; pupil personnel services (Credential), including school counseling (MA, Credential), school psychology (PhD, Credential); school psychology (Ed S); single subject (Credential); special education (MA, Credential), including mild/moderate (Credential), moderate/severe (Credential); teaching (MA), including elementary education, secondary education, secondary music education. *Accreditation:* TEAC. *Program availability:* Part-time, evening/weekend. *Faculty:* 32 full-time (18 women), 37 part-time/adjunct (26 women). *Students:* 170 full-time (140 women), 180 part-time (129 women); includes 164 minority (6 Black or African American, non-Hispanic/Latino; 38 Asian, non-Hispanic/Latino; 101 Hispanic/Latino; 1 Native Hawaiian or other Pacific Islander, non-Hispanic/Latino; 18 Two or more races, non-Hispanic/Latino), 10 international. Average age 28. 143 applicants, 63% accepted, 64 enrolled. In 2017, 126 master's, 18 doctorates awarded. *Application deadline:* Applications are processed on a rolling basis. Application fee: $60. Electronic applications accepted. *Expenses:* Contact institution. *Financial support:* Fellowships and scholarships/grants available. Financial award application deadline: 3/2; financial award applicants required to submit FAFSA. *Unit head:* Dr. Margaret Grogan, Dean, 714-516-5968, E-mail: grogan@chapman.edu. *Application contact:* Shannon McCance, Graduate Admission Counselor, 714-516-5236, E-mail: smccance@chapman.edu.
Website: http://www.chapman.edu/CES/

Charleston Southern University, College of Education, Charleston, SC 29423-8087. Offers elementary administration and supervision (M Ed); elementary education (M Ed); secondary administration and supervision (M Ed). *Accreditation:* NCATE. *Program availability:* Part-time, evening/weekend. *Degree requirements:* For master's, thesis optional. *Entrance requirements:* For master's, GRE or MAT. Additional exam requirements/recommendations for international students: Required—TOEFL (minimum score 550 paper-based; 79 iBT). *Application deadline:* Applications are processed on a rolling basis. Application fee: $40. Electronic applications accepted. *Expenses:* Contact institution. *Financial support:* Research assistantships with full tuition reimbursements, career-related internships or fieldwork, and Federal Work-Study available. Financial award application deadline: 4/15; financial award applicants required to submit FAFSA. *Unit head:* Dr. George Metz, Dean, 843-863-7765, Fax: 843-863-7784, E-mail: gmetz@csuniv.edu.
Website: http://www.csuniv.edu/education/

Chestnut Hill College, School of Graduate Studies, Department of Education, Program in Educational Leadership, Philadelphia, PA 19118-2693. Offers M Ed. *Program availability:* Part-time, evening/weekend. *Degree requirements:* For master's, thesis optional. *Entrance requirements:* For master's, PRAXIS I or proof of teaching certification, letters of recommendation, writing sample, 6 graduate credits with minimum B grade if undergraduate GPA less than 3.0. Additional exam requirements/recommendations for international students: Required—TOEFL (minimum score 500 paper-based), IELTS (minimum score 6.0), or TWE (minimum score 22). Electronic applications accepted. *Expenses:* Contact institution. *Faculty research:* Mentoring and induction program.

Cheyney University of Pennsylvania, Graduate Programs, Principal Certification Program (K-12), Cheyney, PA 19319. Offers Certificate. Program also offered on campus of West Chester University of Pennsylvania. *Entrance requirements:* For degree, five years of professional school experience.

Cheyney University of Pennsylvania, Graduate Programs, Program in Educational Leadership, Cheyney, PA 19319. Offers M Ed, Certificate. *Program availability:* Part-time, evening/weekend. *Degree requirements:* For master's, thesis or alternative; for Certificate, internship. *Entrance requirements:* For master's, minimum GPA of 3.0, writing sample. Electronic applications accepted. *Faculty research:* Teacher motivation, critical thinking.

Chicago State University, School of Graduate and Professional Studies, College of Education, Department of Educational Leadership, Curriculum and Foundations, Program in Educational Leadership, Chicago, IL 60628. Offers educational leadership (Ed D); higher education administration (MA); principal preparation (MA). *Accreditation:* NCATE. *Degree requirements:* For master's, comprehensive exam, thesis optional. *Entrance requirements:* For master's, minimum GPA of 2.75. *Application deadline:* For fall admission, 7/1 for domestic students; for spring admission, 11/10 for domestic students. Application fee: $25. *Unit head:* Dr. Athanase Gahungu, Program Facilitator, 773-995-2086, E-mail: agahungu@csu.edu. *Application contact:* Anika Miller, Graduate Studies Office, 773-995-2404, E-mail: g-studies1@csu.edu.

Christian Brothers University, School of Arts, Memphis, TN 38104-5581. Offers Catholic studies (MACS); educational leadership (MSEL); teacher-leadership (M Ed); teaching (MAT). *Program availability:* Part-time, evening/weekend. *Entrance requirements:* For master's, GRE, GMAT, PRAXIS II. *Expenses:* Contact institution.

The Citadel, The Military College of South Carolina, Citadel Graduate College, Zucker Family School of Education, Charleston, SC 29409. Offers elementary/secondary school administration and supervision (M Ed); elementary/secondary school counseling (M Ed); interdisciplinary STEM education (M Ed); literacy education (M Ed, Graduate Certificate); middle grades (MAT), including English, mathematics, science, social studies; physical education (grades K-12) (MAT); school superintendency (Ed S); secondary education (MAT), including biology, English, mathematics, social studies; student affairs (Graduate Certificate); student affairs and college counseling (M Ed). *Accreditation:* NCATE. *Program availability:* Part-time, evening/weekend, 100% online, blended/hybrid learning. *Degree requirements:* For master's, comprehensive exam (for some programs). *Entrance requirements:* For master's, GRE (minimum combined verbal and quantitative score of 290) or MAT (minimum score 396). Additional exam requirements/recommendations for international students: Required—TOEFL (minimum score 500 paper-based; 79 iBT). Electronic applications accepted. *Expenses:* Tuition, state resident: part-time $587 per credit hour. Tuition, nonresident: part-time $988 per credit hour. *Required fees:* $90 per term.

City College of the City University of New York, Graduate School, School of Education, Department of Leadership and Special Education, New York, NY 10031-9198. Offers educational leadership (MS, AC); teacher of students with disabilities in adolescent education (MS Ed); teacher of students with disabilities in childhood education (MS Ed). *Degree requirements:* For master's, thesis, research paper. *Entrance requirements:* For master's, Liberal Arts and Sciences Test (LAST), Content Specialty Test (CST), interview; minimum GPA of 3.0 in major, 2.5 overall. Additional exam requirements/recommendations for international students: Required—TOEFL. *Faculty research:* Dynamics of organizational change, impact of laws on educational policy, leadership development in schools.

City University of Seattle, Graduate Division, Albright School of Education, Seattle, WA 98121. Offers administrator certification (Certificate); curriculum and instruction (M Ed); elementary education (MIT); guidance and counseling (M Ed); leadership (M Ed); reading and literacy (M Ed); school counseling (M Ed); special education (MIT); superintendent certification (Certificate). *Program availability:* Part-time, evening/weekend, online learning. *Degree requirements:* For master's, comprehensive exam (for some programs), thesis (for some programs). *Entrance requirements:* For master's, baccalaureate degree or equivalent from an accredited or otherwise recognized institution. Additional exam requirements/recommendations for international students: Required—TOEFL (minimum score 567 paper-based; 87 iBT); Recommended—IELTS. Electronic applications accepted. *Expenses:* Contact institution.

City University of Seattle, Graduate Division, Division of Doctoral Studies, Seattle, WA 98121. Offers leadership (Ed D). *Program availability:* Online learning. *Entrance requirements:* For doctorate, master's degree from an accredited or otherwise recognized institution; resume/curriculum vitae that demonstrates two or more years in a leadership capacity; interview with a member of the program faculty.

Claremont Graduate University, Graduate Programs, School of Educational Studies, Claremont, CA 91711-6160. Offers Africana education (Certificate); education and policy (MA, PhD); higher education/student affairs (MA, PhD); human development (MA, PhD); public school administration (MA, PhD); quantitative evaluation (MA, PhD); special education (MA, PhD); teacher education (MA); teaching and learning (MA, PhD); urban leadership (PhD); MBA/PhD. PhD program offered jointly with San Diego State University. *Program availability:* Part-time. Terminal master's awarded for partial completion of doctoral program. *Entrance requirements:* For master's and doctorate, GRE General Test. Additional exam requirements/recommendations for international students: Required—TOEFL (minimum score 75 iBT). Electronic applications accepted. *Faculty research:* Education administration, K-12 and higher education, multicultural education, education policy, diversity in higher education, faculty issues.

Clark Atlanta University, School of Education, Department of Educational Leadership, Atlanta, GA 30314. Offers MA, Ed D, Ed S. *Program availability:* Part-time, evening/weekend. *Faculty:* 4 full-time (1 woman), 3 part-time/adjunct (1 woman). *Students:* 41 full-time (29 women), 44 part-time (21 women); includes 61 minority (59 Black or African American, non-Hispanic/Latino; 1 Asian, non-Hispanic/Latino; 1 Hispanic/Latino), 20 international. Average age 34. 27 applicants, 93% accepted, 14 enrolled. In 2017, 16 master's, 21 doctorates, 1 other advanced degree awarded. *Degree requirements:* For master's and Ed S, comprehensive exam; for doctorate, comprehensive exam, thesis/dissertation. *Entrance requirements:* For master's, GRE General Test, minimum undergraduate GPA of 2.6; for doctorate and Ed S, GRE General Test, minimum graduate GPA of 3.0. Additional exam requirements/recommendations for international students: Required—TOEFL (minimum score 500 paper-based; 61 iBT). *Application deadline:* For fall admission, 4/1 for domestic and international students; for spring admission, 11/1 for domestic and international students. Applications are processed on a rolling basis. Application fee: $40 ($55 for international students). Electronic applications accepted. *Financial support:* Career-related internships or fieldwork, Federal Work-Study, scholarships/grants, and unspecified assistantships available. Support available to part-time students. Financial award application deadline: 4/30; financial award applicants required to submit FAFSA. *Unit head:* Dr. Barbara Hill, Chairperson, 404-880-6126, E-mail: bhill@cau.edu.

Clarke University, Program in Education, Dubuque, IA 52001-3198. Offers instructional leadership (MAE). *Program availability:* Part-time, 100% online, blended/hybrid learning. *Faculty:* 3 full-time (all women), 2 part-time/adjunct (1 woman). *Students:* 3 full-time (all women), 27 part-time (19 women); includes 3 minority (1 Black or African American, non-Hispanic/Latino; 1 Hispanic/Latino; 1 Two or more races, non-Hispanic/Latino). Average age 29. 39 applicants, 87% accepted, 21 enrolled. In 2017, 15 master's awarded. *Degree requirements:* For master's, thesis optional. *Entrance requirements:* For master's, official transcripts documenting completion of undergraduate degree from accredited college or university, copy of teaching certificates and licenses, two recommendation forms, statement of goals and career plans, minimum GPA of 2.75. Additional exam requirements/recommendations for international students: Required—TOEFL (minimum score 550 paper-based; 80 iBT), IELTS (minimum score 6.5). *Application deadline:* Applications are processed on a rolling basis. Application fee: $35. Electronic applications accepted. *Expenses:* $515 per credit. *Financial support:* Applicants required to submit FAFSA. *Unit head:* Beth Putnam, Director of Graduate Education, 563-588-6573, E-mail: beth.putnam@clarke.edu. *Application contact:* Kimberly Roush, Director of Admission, Graduate and Adult Programs, 563-588-6539, Fax: 563-552-7994, E-mail: graduate@clarke.edu.

Clarks Summit University, Online Master's Programs, South Abington Township, PA 18411. Offers Bible (MA); counseling (MA, MS); curriculum and instruction (M Ed); educational administration (M Ed); literature (MA); organizational leadership (MA). *Program availability:* Part-time, evening/weekend, online learning. *Entrance requirements:* Additional exam requirements/recommendations for international students: Required—TOEFL (minimum score 500 paper-based). *Application deadline:* Applications are processed on a rolling basis. Application fee: $30. *Financial support:* Institutionally sponsored loans and scholarships/grants available. Financial award application deadline: 8/20; financial award applicants required to submit FAFSA. *Unit head:* Dr. James Lytle, President, 570-586-2400 Ext. 9222, Fax: 570-586-1753. *Application contact:* Drew Whipple, Vice President for Enrollment Management, 570-585-9370, Fax: 570-585-9299, E-mail: awhipple@clarkssummitu.edu.
Website: https://www.clarkssummitu.edu/online-masters-degrees/

Clemson University, Graduate School, College of Education, Department of Educational and Organizational Leadership Development, Clemson, SC 29634. Offers administration and supervision (M Ed, Ed S); athletic leadership (MS, Certificate); education systems improvement science (Ed D); educational leadership (PhD), including higher education, P-12; human resource development (MHRD), including human resource development; leadership (Certificate); student affairs (M Ed). *Program availability:* Part-time, evening/weekend, 100% online. *Faculty:* 21 full-time (14 women), 1 part-time/adjunct (0 women). *Students:* 55 full-time (32 women), 285 part-time (169 women); includes 89 minority (71 Black or African American, non-Hispanic/Latino; 1 American Indian or Alaska Native, non-Hispanic/Latino; 1 Asian, non-Hispanic/Latino; 13 Hispanic/Latino; 3 Two or more races, non-Hispanic/Latino), 2 international. Average age 35. 216 applicants, 69% accepted, 100 enrolled. In 2017, 58 master's, 16 doctorates, 20 other advanced degrees awarded. *Degree requirements:* For master's, thesis (for some programs); for doctorate, comprehensive exam, thesis/dissertation. *Entrance requirements:* For master's, doctorate, and other advanced degree, GRE General Test, unofficial transcripts, letters of recommendation. Additional exam requirements/recommendations for international students: Required—TOEFL (minimum score 80 iBT), IELTS (minimum score 7), PTE (minimum score 54). *Application deadline:* For fall admission, 3/1 priority date for domestic and international students; for spring admission, 10/1 priority date for domestic and international students. Applications are processed on a rolling basis. Application fee: $80 ($90 for international students). Electronic applications accepted. *Expenses:* $5,174 per semester full-time resident, $9,714 per semester full-time non-resident, $511 per credit hour part-time resident, $1,017 per credit hour part-time non-resident; $741 per credit hour online; other fees may apply per session. *Financial support:* In 2017–18, 20 students received support, including 4 fellowships with partial tuition reimbursements available (averaging $8,750 per year), 1 research assistantship with partial tuition reimbursement available

Educational Leadership and Administration

(averaging $9,378 per year); career-related internships or fieldwork and unspecified assistantships also available. Financial award application deadline: 3/1. *Total annual research expenditures:* $31,201. *Unit head:* Dr. Roy Jones, Interim Department Chair, 864-656-7915, E-mail: royj@clemson.edu. *Application contact:* Alison Search, Student Services Program Coordinator, 864-250-8880, E-mail: alisonp@clemson.edu.
Website: http://www.clemson.edu/education/departments/educational-organizational-leadership-development/index.html

Cleveland State University, College of Graduate Studies, College of Education and Human Services, Department of Counseling, Administration, Supervision and Adult Learning (CASAL), Cleveland, OH 44115. Offers adult learning and development (M Ed); counselor education (PhD); early childhood mental health counseling (Certificate); educational administration and supervision (M Ed). *Accreditation:* ACA (one or more programs are accredited). *Program availability:* Part-time, evening/weekend. *Faculty:* 15 full-time (8 women), 19 part-time/adjunct (10 women). *Students:* 121 full-time (98 women), 272 part-time (198 women); includes 127 minority (106 Black or African American, non-Hispanic/Latino; 1 American Indian or Alaska Native, non-Hispanic/Latino; 4 Asian, non-Hispanic/Latino; 11 Hispanic/Latino; 5 Two or more races, non-Hispanic/Latino), 8 international. Average age 33. 57 applicants, 93% accepted, 51 enrolled. In 2017, 99 master's awarded. *Degree requirements:* For master's, comprehensive exam (for some programs), thesis optional, internship. *Entrance requirements:* For master's, GRE General Test or MAT, letter of recommendation and minimum GPA of 2.75 (for counseling); 2 letters of recommendation and interviews (for organizational leadership). Additional exam requirements/recommendations for international students: Required—TOEFL (minimum score 550 paper-based; 78 iBT), IELTS (minimum score 6). *Application deadline:* For fall admission, 6/21 for domestic students, 5/15 for international students; for spring admission, 8/31 for domestic students, 11/1 for international students. Application fee: $40. Electronic applications accepted. *Financial support:* In 2017–18, 19 students received support, including 10 research assistantships with tuition reimbursements available (averaging $11,882 per year), 5 teaching assistantships with tuition reimbursements available (averaging $11,882 per year); scholarships/grants and unspecified assistantships also available. Support available to part-time students. *Faculty research:* Education law, career development, bullying, psychopharmacology, counseling and spirituality. *Total annual research expenditures:* $225,821. *Unit head:* Dr. R. Elliott Ingersoll, Chair/Professor, 216-687-4582, Fax: 216-687-5378, E-mail: r.ingersoll@csuohio.edu. *Application contact:* Deborah L. Brown, Interim Assistant Director, Graduate Admissions, 216-523-7572, Fax: 216-687-5400, E-mail: d.l.brown@csuohio.edu.
Website: http://www.csuohio.edu/cehs/departments/CASAL/casal_dept.html

Cleveland State University, College of Graduate Studies, College of Education and Human Services, Program in Urban Education, Specialization in School Administration, Cleveland, OH 44115. Offers PhD. *Program availability:* Part-time. *Faculty:* 4 full-time (0 women). *Students:* 3 full-time (1 woman), 6 part-time (3 women); includes 5 minority (4 Black or African American, non-Hispanic/Latino; 1 Hispanic/Latino). Average age 40. 10 applicants, 40% accepted. In 2017, 1 doctorate awarded. *Entrance requirements:* For doctorate, GRE General Test (minimum score of 297 for combined Verbal and Quantitative exams, 4.0 preferred for Analytical Writing), minimum graduate GPA of 3.25, curriculum vitae or resume, personal statement, 2 letters of recommendation. Additional exam requirements/recommendations for international students: Required—TOEFL (minimum score 550 paper-based; 78 iBT), IELTS (minimum score 6). Application fee: $40. Electronic applications accepted. *Financial support:* In 2017–18, 1 student received support. Teaching assistantships and tuition waivers available. Support available to part-time students. Financial award application deadline: 4/1; financial award applicants required to submit FAFSA. *Faculty research:* Theory and practice of management and leadership in educational, government, human resource development, and social service settings. *Unit head:* Dr. Graham Stead, Director, Doctoral Studies, 216-687-3828, E-mail: g.b.stead@csuohio.edu. *Application contact:* Rita M. Grabowski, Administrative Coordinator, 216-687-4697, Fax: 216-875-9697, E-mail: r.grabowski@csuohio.edu.
Website: http://www.csuohio.edu/cehs/casal/programs-1

Coastal Carolina University, Spadoni College of Education, Conway, SC 29528-6054. Offers education (MAT); educational leadership (M Ed, Ed S); English for speakers of other languages (Certificate); instructional technology (M Ed, Ed S); language, literacy and culture (M Ed); learning and teaching (M Ed); online teaching and training (Certificate); special education (M Ed). *Accreditation:* NCATE. *Program availability:* Part-time, evening/weekend, 100% online, blended/hybrid learning. *Faculty:* 16 full-time (9 women), 22 part-time/adjunct (15 women). *Students:* 43 full-time (22 women), 345 part-time (290 women); includes 70 minority (51 Black or African American, non-Hispanic/Latino; 3 American Indian or Alaska Native, non-Hispanic/Latino; 3 Asian, non-Hispanic/Latino; 8 Hispanic/Latino; 1 Native Hawaiian or other Pacific Islander, non-Hispanic/Latino; 4 Two or more races, non-Hispanic/Latino). Average age 33. 288 applicants, 77% accepted, 157 enrolled. In 2017, 151 master's, 28 other advanced degrees awarded. *Degree requirements:* For master's and other advanced degree, comprehensive exam. *Entrance requirements:* For master's, GRE, GMAT, 2 letters of recommendation, evidence of teacher certification, official transcripts; for other advanced degree, official transcripts, 3 letters of reference, master's degree in related field with minimum overall cumulative GPA of 3.0. Additional exam requirements/recommendations for international students: Required—TOEFL (minimum score 550 paper-based; 79 iBT), IELTS (minimum score 6.5). *Application deadline:* For fall admission, 5/1 priority date for domestic and international students; for spring admission, 11/1 priority date for domestic and international students; for summer admission, 3/1 priority date for domestic and international students. Applications are processed on a rolling basis. Application fee: $45. Electronic applications accepted. *Expenses:* Tuition, state resident: full-time $5184; part-time $576 per credit hour. Tuition, nonresident: full-time $9369; part-time $1041 per credit hour. *Required fees:* $90; $5 per credit hour. *Financial support:* Fellowships, research assistantships, teaching assistantships, and tuition waivers available. Financial award application deadline: 3/1; financial award applicants required to submit FAFSA. *Unit head:* Dr. Edward Jadallah, Dean/Vice President for Online Education and Teaching Excellence, 843-349-2773, Fax: 843-349-2106, E-mail: ejadalla@coastal.edu. *Application contact:* Dr. James O. Luken, Associate Provost for Graduate Program/Vice-Dean of the Coastal Environment, 843-349-2235, Fax: 843-349-6444, E-mail: joluken@coastal.edu.
Website: https://www.coastal.edu/education/

The College at Brockport, State University of New York, School of Education, Health, and Human Services, Department of Counselor Education, Brockport, NY 14420-2997. Offers college counseling (MS Ed, CAS); mental health counseling (MS, CAS); school counseling (MS Ed, CAS); school counselor supervision (CAS). *Accreditation:* ACA (one or more programs are accredited). *Program availability:* Part-time. *Faculty:* 5 full-time (3 women), 6 part-time/adjunct (4 women). *Students:* 32 full-time (23 women), 74 part-time (63 women); includes 24 minority (13 Black or African American, non-Hispanic/Latino; 1 Asian, non-Hispanic/Latino; 4 Hispanic/Latino; 6 Two or more races, non-Hispanic/Latino). 94 applicants, 60% accepted, 24 enrolled. In 2017, 31 master's, 6 other advanced degrees awarded. *Degree requirements:* For master's, thesis, internship. *Entrance requirements:* For master's, group interview, letters of recommendation, written objectives, audio response; for CAS, master's degree, New

York state school counselor certificate. Additional exam requirements/recommendations for international students: Required—TOEFL (minimum score 550 paper-based; 79 iBT), IELTS (minimum score 6.5). *Application deadline:* For fall admission, 2/1 priority date for domestic and international students; for spring admission, 9/1 priority date for domestic and international students; for summer admission, 2/1 priority date for domestic and international students. Application fee: $80. Electronic applications accepted. *Expenses:* Tuition, state resident: full-time $10,870; part-time $453 per credit hour. Tuition, nonresident: full-time $22,210. *Required fees:* $988; $246 per semester. *Financial support:* In 2017–18, 1 fellowship with full tuition reimbursement (averaging $7,500 per year), 1 teaching assistantship with full tuition reimbursement (averaging $6,000 per year) were awarded; Federal Work-Study, scholarships/grants, and unspecified assistantships also available. Support available to part-time students. Financial award application deadline: 3/15; financial award applicants required to submit FAFSA. *Faculty research:* Gender and diversity issues; counseling outcomes; spirituality; school, college and mental health counseling; obesity. *Unit head:* Dr. Susan Seem, Chair, 585-395-5492, Fax: 585-395-2366, E-mail: sseem@brockport.edu. *Application contact:* Danielle A. Welch, Graduate Admissions Counselor, 585-395-5465, Fax: 585-395-2515.
Website: https://www.brockport.edu/academics/counselor_education

The College at Brockport, State University of New York, School of Education, Health, and Human Services, Department of Educational Administration, Brockport, NY 14420-2997. Offers school building leader (CAS); school building leader/school district leader (CAS); school district business leader (CAS); school district leader (CAS); teacher leadership (CAS). *Program availability:* Part-time. *Faculty:* 3 full-time (1 woman), 6 part-time/adjunct (3 women). *Students:* 1 (woman) full-time, 99 part-time (64 women); includes 10 minority (6 Black or African American, non-Hispanic/Latino; 1 Asian, non-Hispanic/Latino; 3 Hispanic/Latino). 60 applicants, 90% accepted, 44 enrolled. In 2017, 29 CASs awarded. *Degree requirements:* For other advanced degree, thesis or alternative, internship. *Entrance requirements:* For degree, minimum GPA of 3.0, letter of recommendation. Additional exam requirements/recommendations for international students: Required—TOEFL (minimum score 550 paper-based; 79 iBT), IELTS (minimum score 6.5). *Application deadline:* For fall admission, 7/15 priority date for domestic and international students; for spring admission, 11/15 priority date for domestic and international students. Application fee: $80. Electronic applications accepted. *Expenses:* Tuition, state resident: full-time $10,870; part-time $453 per credit hour. Tuition, nonresident: full-time $22,210. *Required fees:* $988; $246 per semester. *Financial support:* Federal Work-Study, scholarships/grants, and unspecified assistantships available. Support available to part-time students. Financial award application deadline: 3/15; financial award applicants required to submit FAFSA. *Faculty research:* Superintendency, budgeting, school business administration, leadership, special education administration. *Unit head:* Jeffrey Linn, Graduate Director, 585-395-2661, Fax: 585-395-2172, E-mail: jlinn@brockport.edu. *Application contact:* Danielle A. Welch, Graduate Admissions Counselor, 585-395-2525, Fax: 585-395-2515.
Website: https://www.brockport.edu/academics/educational_administration/

The College of New Jersey, Office of Graduate and Advancing Education, School of Education, Department of Educational Administration and Secondary Education, Program in Educational Leadership, Ewing, NJ 08628. Offers M Ed, Certificate. *Program availability:* Part-time, evening/weekend. *Degree requirements:* For master's, comprehensive exam. *Entrance requirements:* For master's, GRE, minimum GPA of 3.0 in field or 2.75 overall; for Certificate, previous master's degree or higher. Additional exam requirements/recommendations for international students: Required—TOEFL. Electronic applications accepted.

The College of New Rochelle, Graduate School, Division of Education, Program in Educational Leadership, New Rochelle, NY 10805-2308. Offers school building leader (MS, Advanced Certificate); school district leader (MS, Advanced Diploma). *Degree requirements:* For master's, internship. *Entrance requirements:* For master's, interview, minimum GPA of 3.0 in field, 2.7 overall, minimum 3 years teaching or education administration experience. *Expenses:* Tuition: Full-time $17,406. *Required fees:* $1120.

College of Saint Elizabeth, Department of Educational Leadership, Morristown, NJ 07960-6989. Offers educational leadership (MA, Ed D), including higher education (Ed D), Pre-K to 12th grade (Ed D); supervisor (Certificate). *Program availability:* Part-time. *Faculty:* 3 full-time (0 women), 8 part-time/adjunct (3 women). *Students:* 4 full-time (3 women), 74 part-time (51 women); includes 34 minority (20 Black or African American, non-Hispanic/Latino; 2 Asian, non-Hispanic/Latino; 11 Hispanic/Latino; 1 Two or more races, non-Hispanic/Latino). Average age 44. 33 applicants, 97% accepted, 28 enrolled. In 2017, 15 master's, 6 doctorates awarded. *Degree requirements:* For master's, thesis or alternative; for doctorate, thesis/dissertation. *Entrance requirements:* For master's, baccalaureate degree with minimum GPA of 2.75, standard teaching certificate, three years of exemplary certified teaching experience, writing sample, two letters of recommendation from school(s) of employment, personal interview (for educational leadership); for doctorate, MA in educational leadership or related field; leadership experience including certification as principal and/or supervisor; letter of recommendation from college/university professor attesting to candidate's ability to perform a high level of academic work in the program; for Certificate, MA in education; certification; baccalaureate degree with minimum GPA of 2.75; personal written statement; two letters of recommendation; official transcripts from all colleges attended. Additional exam requirements/recommendations for international students: Required—TOEFL (minimum score 550 paper-based; 79 iBT), IELTS (minimum score 6.5). *Application deadline:* For fall admission, 5/1 for international students. Applications are processed on a rolling basis. Application fee: $35. Electronic applications accepted. Application fee is waived when completed online. *Expenses:* Contact institution. *Financial support:* Career-related internships or fieldwork, scholarships/grants, and unspecified assistantships available. Financial award applicants required to submit FAFSA. *Unit head:* Dr. Joseph Ciccone, Program Chair, 973-290-4383, Fax: 973-290-4389, E-mail: jciccone@cse.edu. *Application contact:* Lori J. Fragoso, Director of Graduate and Continuing Studies Admissions, 973-290-4413, Fax: 973-290-4710, E-mail: apply@cse.edu.
Website: http://www.cse.edu/academics/prof-studies/education/

College of Saint Mary, Program in Education, Omaha, NE 68106. Offers assessment leadership (MSE); English as a second language (MSE). *Program availability:* Part-time. *Entrance requirements:* For master's, technology competency test or equivalent, minimum cumulative GPA of 3.0, teaching certificate, 2 letters of reference, resume.

The College of Saint Rose, Graduate Studies, Thelma P. Lally School of Education, Programs in Educational Leadership and Administration, Albany, NY 12203-1419. Offers educational leadership (MS Ed); school building leader (Certificate); school district business leader (Certificate); school district leader (Certificate). *Program availability:* Part-time, evening/weekend. *Students:* 3 full-time (2 women), 785 part-time (596 women); includes 305 minority (138 Black or African American, non-Hispanic/Latino; 4 American Indian or Alaska Native, non-Hispanic/Latino; 20 Asian, non-Hispanic/Latino; 115 Hispanic/Latino; 1 Native Hawaiian or other Pacific Islander, non-Hispanic/Latino; 27 Two or more races, non-Hispanic/Latino), 1 international. Average age 37. 373 applicants, 82% accepted, 295 enrolled. In 2017, 9 master's, 671 Certificates awarded. *Degree requirements:* For master's, comprehensive exam or thesis. *Entrance requirements:* For master's, minimum undergraduate GPA of 3.0, timed

writing sample, interview, permanent certification or 3 years of teaching experience. Additional exam requirements/recommendations for international students: Required—TOEFL (minimum score 550 paper-based; 80 iBT), IELTS (minimum score 6), PTE (minimum score 56). *Application deadline:* For fall admission, 4/1 priority date for domestic and international students; for spring admission, 10/15 priority date for domestic and international students; for summer admission, 3/15 priority date for domestic students, 3/14 priority date for international students. Applications are processed on a rolling basis. Application fee: $40. Electronic applications accepted. *Expenses: Tuition:* Full-time $7191; part-time $799 per credit hour. *Required fees: $924;* $462 per credit hour. Tuition and fees vary according to course load. *Financial support:* Career-related internships or fieldwork, scholarships/grants, tuition waivers (partial), and unspecified assistantships available. Support available to part-time students. Financial award application deadline: 4/15. *Unit head:* Dr. Kevin S. Baughman, Program Director, 518-454-5259, E-mail: baughmak@strose.edu. *Application contact:* Cris Murray, Assistant Vice President for Graduate Recruitment and Enrollment, 518-485-3390, Fax: 518-458-5479, E-mail: grad@strose.edu.
Website: https://www.strose.edu/educational-leadership-and-administration/

The College of Saint Rose, Graduate Studies, Thelma P. Lally School of Education, Programs in Higher Education Leadership and Administration, Albany, NY 12203-1419. Offers MS Ed, Advanced Certificate. *Program availability:* Part-time, evening/weekend. *Students:* 2 full-time (1 woman), 10 part-time (3 women); includes 1 minority (Hispanic/Latino), 1 international. Average age 29. 8 applicants, 63% accepted, 3 enrolled. In 2017, 9 master's, 2 Advanced Certificates awarded. *Degree requirements:* For master's, capstone seminar. *Entrance requirements:* For master's, resume, letter of recommendation. Additional exam requirements/recommendations for international students: Required—TOEFL (minimum score 550 paper-based; 80 iBT), IELTS (minimum score 6), PTE (minimum score 56). *Application deadline:* For fall admission, 4/1 priority date for domestic and international students; for spring admission, 10/15 priority date for domestic and international students; for summer admission, 3/15 priority date for domestic and international students. Applications are processed on a rolling basis. Application fee: $40. Electronic applications accepted. *Expenses: Tuition:* Full-time $7191; part-time $799 per credit hour. *Required fees: $924;* $462 per credit hour. Tuition and fees vary according to course load. *Financial support:* Scholarships/grants, tuition waivers (partial), and unspecified assistantships available. Support available to part-time students. Financial award application deadline: 4/15. *Unit head:* Dr. Margaret McLane, Interim Provost and Vice President for Academic Affairs, 518-454-5160, E-mail: mclanem@strose.edu. *Application contact:* Cris Murray, Assistant Vice President for Graduate Recruitment and Enrollment, 518-454-5136, Fax: 518-458-5479, E-mail: grad@strose.edu.
Website: https://www.strose.edu/higher-education-leadership-and-administration/

College of Staten Island of the City University of New York, Graduate Programs, School of Education, Program in Leadership in Education, Staten Island, NY 10314-6600. Offers leadership in education (Post-Master's Certificate), including school building leader/school district leader, school district leader. *Program availability:* Part-time, evening/weekend. *Faculty:* 2 full-time, 3 part-time/adjunct. *Students:* 36. 25 applicants, 80% accepted, 18 enrolled. In 2017, 11 Post-Master's Certificates awarded. *Degree requirements:* For Post-Master's Certificate, 30 credits: 24 credits in supervision, administration, curriculum, policy analysis, human relations; theory, research, and practice in educational leadership. *Entrance requirements:* For degree, master's degree with minimum GPA of 3.0, 3 professional recommendations, letter of intent, interview with faculty; evidence of 4 years' teaching experience (school building leader and school district leader track); 3 years' full-time teaching or pupil personnel services experiences (school district leader track). Additional exam requirements/recommendations for international students: Required—TOEFL (minimum score 550 paper-based; 79 iBT), IELTS (minimum score 6.5). *Application deadline:* For fall admission, 6/20 priority date for domestic and international students; for spring admission, 12/2 priority date for domestic and international students. Applications are processed on a rolling basis. Application fee: $125. Electronic applications accepted. *Expenses:* Tuition, state resident: full-time $10,450; part-time $440 per credit. Tuition, nonresident: full-time $19,320; part-time $440 per credit. *Required fees:* $181.10 per semester. Tuition and fees vary according to program. *Faculty research:* Supervision of instruction, school-community partnerships, education reform, history of education, organizational theory. *Unit head:* Dr. Susan Sullivan, 718-982-3744, E-mail: susan.sullivan@csi.cuny.edu. *Application contact:* Sasha Spence, Associate Director for Graduate Admissions, 718-982-2019, Fax: 718-982-2500, E-mail: sasha.spence@csi.cuny.edu.
Website: https://www.csi.cuny.edu/sites/default/files/pdf/admissions/grad/pdf/PostMasters%20in%20Leadership%20Fact%20Sheet.pdf

The College of William and Mary, School of Education, Program in Education Policy, Planning, and Leadership, Williamsburg, VA 23187-8795. Offers curriculum and educational technology (PhD); curriculum leadership (Ed D, PhD); educational leadership (M Ed), including higher education administration (M Ed, Ed D, PhD), K-12 administration and supervision; educational policy, planning, and leadership (Ed D, PhD), including general education administration, gifted education administration, higher education administration (M Ed, Ed D, PhD). *Accreditation:* NCATE. *Program availability:* Part-time, evening/weekend. *Faculty:* 20 full-time (10 women), 21 part-time/adjunct (13 women). *Students:* 54 full-time (35 women), 172 part-time (113 women); includes 70 minority (42 Black or African American, non-Hispanic/Latino; 1 Asian, non-Hispanic/Latino; 19 Hispanic/Latino; 8 Two or more races, non-Hispanic/Latino), 3 international. Average age 39. 163 applicants, 71% accepted, 89 enrolled. In 2017, 23 master's, 37 doctorates awarded. *Degree requirements:* For doctorate, comprehensive exam, thesis/dissertation. *Entrance requirements:* For master's, GRE or MAT, minimum GPA of 2.5; for doctorate, GRE or MAT, minimum GPA of 3.0. Additional exam requirements/recommendations for international students: Required—TOEFL (minimum score 100 iBT), IELTS (minimum score 7). *Application deadline:* For fall admission, 1/15 for domestic and international students. Application fee: $50. Electronic applications accepted. *Expenses:* $9,630 resident full-time, $535 resident part-time per credit hour; $25,920 nonresident full-time, $1,265 nonresident part-time per credit hour; $5,944 full-time fees. *Financial support:* In 2017–18, 59 students received support, including 1 fellowship (averaging $20,000 per year), 43 research assistantships (averaging $20,535 per year); scholarships/grants and unspecified assistantships also available. Support available to part-time students. Financial award application deadline: 1/15; financial award applicants required to submit FAFSA. *Faculty research:* Higher education policy, evaluation of teachers, program evaluation, civil rights and higher education, program evaluation. *Unit head:* Dr. Michael F. Dipaola, Department Chair, 757-221-2344, E-mail: mfdipa@wm.edu. *Application contact:* Dorothy Smith Osborne, Assistant Dean for Academic Programs and Student Services, 757-221-2317, E-mail: dsosbo@wm.edu.
Website: http://education.wm.edu

Colorado Mesa University, Center for Teacher Education, Grand Junction, CO 81501-3122. Offers educational leadership (MAEd); English for speakers of other languages (MAEd); exceptional learner/special education (MAEd); teacher education (Graduate Certificate); teacher leader (MAEd). *Accreditation:* NCATE. *Program availability:* Part-time. *Degree requirements:* For master's, comprehensive exam (for some programs), capstone presentation. *Entrance requirements:* For master's, 3 professional letters of recommendation, Colorado teaching license, minimum baccalaureate GPA of 3.0; for

Graduate Certificate, minimum baccalaureate GPA of 3.0. Additional exam requirements/recommendations for international students: Required—TOEFL (minimum score 550 paper-based). Electronic applications accepted. *Expenses:* Contact institution. *Faculty research:* K-8 STEM instruction, special education inclusion, elementary math literacy, secondary literacy, elementary/early childhood education literacy.

Colorado State University, College of Health and Human Sciences, School of Education, Fort Collins, CO 80523-1588. Offers adult education and training (M Ed); counseling and career development (MA); education and human resources (M Ed); education, equity, and transformation (PhD); higher education leadership (PhD); organizational learning, performance, and change (M Ed, PhD); student affairs in higher education (MS). *Accreditation:* ACA; TEAC. *Program availability:* Part-time, online only, 100% online, blended/hybrid learning. *Faculty:* 33 full-time (23 women), 19 part-time/adjunct (11 women). *Students:* 74 full-time (53 women), 548 part-time (357 women); includes 151 minority (37 Black or African American, non-Hispanic/Latino; 4 American Indian or Alaska Native, non-Hispanic/Latino; 14 Asian, non-Hispanic/Latino; 71 Hispanic/Latino; 25 Two or more races, non-Hispanic/Latino), 16 international. Average age 37. 456 applicants, 31% accepted, 123 enrolled. In 2017, 177 master's, 22 doctorates awarded. *Degree requirements:* For master's, thesis optional, professional portfolio or capstone project; for doctorate, comprehensive exam, thesis/dissertation. *Entrance requirements:* For master's, bachelor's degree; minimum GPA of 3.0 in last degree earned; for doctorate, GRE; GRE or GMAT (for organizational learning, performance and change only), master's degree; minimum GPA of 3.0 in last degree earned. Additional exam requirements/recommendations for international students: Required—TOEFL (minimum score 550 paper-based; 80 iBT), IELTS (minimum score 6.5), PTE (minimum score 58). *Application deadline:* Applications are processed on a rolling basis. Application fee: $60 ($70 for international students). Electronic applications accepted. *Expenses:* Contact institution. *Financial support:* In 2017–18, 4 students received support, including 8 research assistantships with full and partial tuition reimbursements available (averaging $12,758 per year), 4 teaching assistantships with full and partial tuition reimbursements available (averaging $14,256 per year); fellowships with full and partial tuition reimbursements available, Federal Work-Study, scholarships/grants, tuition waivers (full and partial), and unspecified assistantships also available. Financial award applicants required to submit FAFSA. *Faculty research:* Diversity, equity, and inclusion; STEM education; higher education; occupational learning, performance, and change; teacher education. *Total annual research expenditures:* $312,562. *Unit head:* Dr. Louise Jennings, Co-Director, 970-491-6317, Fax: 970-491-1317, E-mail: louise.jennings@colostate.edu. *Application contact:* Kelli Clark, Graduate Programs Coordinator, 970-491-2093, Fax: 970-491-1317, E-mail: kelli.clark@colostate.edu.
Website: http://www.soe.chhs.colostate.edu/

Colorado State University–Global Campus, Graduate Programs, Greenwood Village, CO 80111. Offers criminal justice and law enforcement administration (MS); education leadership (MS); finance (MS); healthcare administration and management (MS); human resource management (MHRM); information technology management (MITM); international management (MS); management (MS); organizational leadership (MS); professional accounting (MPA); project management (MS); teaching and learning (MS). *Accreditation:* ACBSP. *Program availability:* Online learning.

Columbia College, Graduate Programs, Education Division, Columbia, SC 29203-5998. Offers divergent learning (M Ed); higher education administration (M Ed). *Accreditation:* NCATE. *Program availability:* Part-time, evening/weekend, online learning. *Degree requirements:* For master's, thesis. *Entrance requirements:* For master's, GRE General Test, MAT, 2 recommendations, current South Carolina teaching certificate, minimum GPA of 3.2. *Application deadline:* For fall admission, 8/22 for domestic students. Application fee: $50. Electronic applications accepted. *Expenses:* Contact institution. *Financial support:* Available to part-time students. Application deadline: 7/1; applicants required to submit FAFSA. *Application contact:* Myles Hacking, Associate Dean of Admissions, 803-786-3871, Fax: 803-786-3674, E-mail: mhacking@columbiasc.edu.

Columbia College, Master of Education in Educational Leadership Program, Columbia, MO 65216-0002. Offers M Ed. *Program availability:* Part-time, evening/weekend, 100% online, blended/hybrid learning. *Faculty:* 24 full-time (15 women), 7 part-time/adjunct (all women). *Students:* 7 full-time (all women), 49 part-time (33 women); includes 4 minority (3 Black or African American, non-Hispanic/Latino; 1 Hispanic/Latino). Average age 35. 30 applicants, 100% accepted, 21 enrolled. In 2017, 9 master's awarded. *Entrance requirements:* Additional exam requirements/recommendations for international students: Required—TOEFL (minimum score 550 paper-based; 61 iBT). *Application deadline:* For fall admission, 8/9 priority date for domestic and international students; for spring admission, 12/27 priority date for domestic and international students. Applications are processed on a rolling basis. Application fee: $55. Electronic applications accepted. *Expenses:* Contact institution. *Financial support:* In 2017–18, 20 students received support. Federal Work-Study and scholarships/grants available. Financial award application deadline: 3/1; financial award applicants required to submit FAFSA. *Unit head:* Dr. David Roebuck, Dean of the School of Humanities, 573-875-7570, E-mail: cdroebuck@ccis.edu. *Application contact:* Stephanie Johnson, Director of Admissions, 573-875-7352, Fax: 573-875-7506, E-mail: sjohnson@ccis.edu.

Columbia International University, Columbia Graduate School, Columbia, SC 29203. Offers Bible teaching (MABT); counseling (MACN); early childhood and elementary education (MAT); educational administration (M Ed); educational leadership (PhD); instruction and learning (M Ed); teaching English as a foreign language (Certificate); teaching English as a foreign language and intercultural studies (MATF). *Program availability:* Part-time, evening/weekend, online learning. *Degree requirements:* For master's, internships, professional project. *Entrance requirements:* For master's, MAT, GRE (for some programs), minimum GPA of 2.7. Additional exam requirements/recommendations for international students: Required—TOEFL. Electronic applications accepted.

Columbus State University, Graduate Studies, College of Education and Health Professions, Department of Counseling, Foundations, and Leadership, Columbus, GA 31907-5645. Offers clinical mental health counseling (MS); curriculum and leadership (Ed D), including curriculum, educational leadership, higher education (M Ed, Ed D); educational leadership (M Ed, Ed S), including higher education (M Ed, Ed D); school counseling (M Ed, Ed S). *Accreditation:* ACA; NCATE. *Program availability:* Part-time, evening/weekend, 100% online, blended/hybrid learning. *Faculty:* 18 full-time (8 women), 20 part-time/adjunct (10 women). *Students:* 248 full-time (166 women), 308 part-time (236 women); includes 315 minority (278 Black or African American, non-Hispanic/Latino; 11 Asian, non-Hispanic/Latino; 15 Hispanic/Latino; 1 Native Hawaiian or other Pacific Islander, non-Hispanic/Latino; 10 Two or more races, non-Hispanic/Latino), 2 international. Average age 39. 155 applicants, 38% accepted, 40 enrolled. In 2017, 41 master's, 18 doctorates, 110 other advanced degrees awarded. *Degree requirements:* For master's, thesis, exit exam; for doctorate, comprehensive exam, thesis/dissertation; for Ed S, thesis or alternative. *Entrance requirements:* For master's, GRE General Test, minimum undergraduate GPA of 2.75; for doctorate, GRE General Test, minimum graduate GPA of 3.5, four years of professional service; for Ed S, GRE

Educational Leadership and Administration

General Test, minimum undergraduate GPA of 2.75, graduate 3.0. Additional exam requirements/recommendations for international students: Required—TOEFL (minimum score 550 paper-based; 79 iBT). *Application deadline:* For fall admission, 6/30 for domestic and international students; for spring admission, 11/1 for domestic and international students; for summer admission, 3/1 for domestic and international students. Applications are processed on a rolling basis. Application fee: $50. Electronic applications accepted. *Expenses:* Tuition, state resident: full-time $3708; part-time $2472 per year. Tuition, nonresident: full-time $14,418; part-time $9612 per year. *International tuition:* $19,218 full-time. *Required fees:* $1605. Tuition and fees vary according to program. *Financial support:* In 2017–18, 34 students received support, including 14 research assistantships with partial tuition reimbursements available (averaging $3,000 per year); career-related internships or fieldwork, Federal Work-Study, institutionally sponsored loans, scholarships/grants, tuition waivers (partial), and unspecified assistantships also available. Support available to part-time students. Financial award application deadline: 5/1; financial award applicants required to submit FAFSA. *Unit head:* Dr. Tom Hackett, Department Chair, 706-507-8968, Fax: 706-569-3134, E-mail: hackett_paul@columbusstate.edu. *Application contact:* Catrina Smith-Edmond, Assistant Director for Graduate and Global Admission, 706-507-8824, Fax: 706-568-5091, E-mail: smithedmond_catrina@columbusstate.edu. Website: http://cfl.columbusstate.edu/

Columbus State University, Graduate Studies, College of Education and Health Professions, Department of Teacher Education, Columbus, GA 31907-5645. Offers curriculum and instruction in accomplished teaching (M Ed); early childhood education (M Ed, MAT, Ed S); middle grades education (M Ed, MAT, Ed S); secondary education (M Ed, MAT, Ed S), including biology (MAT), chemistry (MAT), earth and space science (MAT), English/language arts, general science (M Ed), history (MAT), mathematics, science (Ed S), social science (M Ed, Ed S); special education (M Ed, MAT, Ed S), including general curriculum (M Ed, MAT); teacher leadership (M Ed). *Accreditation:* NCATE. *Program availability:* Part-time, evening/weekend, 100% online, blended/hybrid learning. *Faculty:* 19 full-time (12 women), 24 part-time/adjunct (18 women). *Students:* 99 full-time (76 women), 181 part-time (143 women); includes 109 minority (94 Black or African American, non-Hispanic/Latino; 1 American Indian or Alaska Native, non-Hispanic/Latino; 1 Asian, non-Hispanic/Latino; 6 Hispanic/Latino; 7 Two or more races, non-Hispanic/Latino). Average age 34. 136 applicants, 63% accepted, 56 enrolled. In 2017, 119 master's, 8 other advanced degrees awarded. *Degree requirements:* For Ed S, thesis or alternative. *Entrance requirements:* For master's, GRE General Test, minimum undergraduate GPA of 2.75; for Ed S, GRE General Test, minimum undergraduate GPA of 2.75, graduate 3.0. Additional exam requirements/recommendations for international students: Required—TOEFL (minimum score 550 paper-based; 79 iBT). *Application deadline:* For fall admission, 6/30 for domestic students, 5/1 for international students; for spring admission, 11/1 for domestic and international students; for summer admission, 3/1 for domestic and international students. Applications are processed on a rolling basis. Application fee: $50. Electronic applications accepted. *Expenses:* Tuition, state resident: full-time $3708; part-time $2472 per year. Tuition, nonresident: full-time $14,418; part-time $9612 per year. *International tuition:* $19,218 full-time. *Required fees:* $1605. Tuition and fees vary according to program. *Financial support:* In 2017–18, 45 students received support, including 9 research assistantships with partial tuition reimbursements available (averaging $3,000 per year); career-related internships or fieldwork, Federal Work-Study, institutionally sponsored loans, scholarships/grants, tuition waivers (partial), and unspecified assistantships also available. Support available to part-time students. Financial award application deadline: 5/1; financial award applicants required to submit FAFSA. *Unit head:* Dr. Jan Burcham, Department Chair, 706-507-8519, Fax: 706-569-3134, E-mail: burcham_jan@columbusstate.edu. *Application contact:* Catrina Smith-Edmond, Assistant Director for Graduate and Global Admission, 706-507-8824, Fax: 706-568-5091, E-mail: smithedmond_catrina@columbusstate.edu. Website: http://te.columbusstate.edu/

Concordia University, College of Education, Portland, OR 97211-6099. Offers career and technical education (M Ed); curriculum and instruction (M Ed), including adolescent literacy, career and technical education, e-learning/technology education, early childhood education, English for speakers of other languages, English language development, environmental education, mathematics, methods and curriculum, reading, science, teacher leadership, the inclusive classroom; early childhood (MAT); education leadership (Ed D); educational administration (M Ed); elementary education (MAT); secondary education (MAT); special education (M Ed); teacher leadership (Ed D). *Program availability:* Part-time, online learning. *Degree requirements:* For master's, comprehensive exam, work samples/portfolio. *Entrance requirements:* For master's, California Basic Educational Skills Test or PRAXIS I, minimum undergraduate GPA of 2.8, graduate 3.0; 2 letters of recommendation. Additional exam requirements/recommendations for international students: Required—TOEFL (minimum score 525 paper-based). Electronic applications accepted. *Faculty research:* Learner-centered classroom, brain-based learning, future of online learning.

Concordia University Ann Arbor, Graduate Programs, Ann Arbor, MI 48105-2797. Offers curriculum and instruction (MS); educational leadership (MS); organizational leadership and administration (MS). *Program availability:* Part-time, evening/weekend. *Degree requirements:* For master's, thesis. *Entrance requirements:* Additional exam requirements/recommendations for international students: Required—TOEFL (minimum score 80 iBT); Recommended—IELTS (minimum score 6.5). Electronic applications accepted.

Concordia University Chicago, College of Education, Program in School Leadership, River Forest, IL 60305-1499. Offers MA, Ed D, CAS. MA offered jointly with the Chicago Consortium of Colleges and Universities. *Accreditation:* NCATE. *Program availability:* Part-time, evening/weekend. *Degree requirements:* For master's, comprehensive exam, thesis optional; for CAS, thesis, final project. *Entrance requirements:* For master's, minimum GPA of 2.9; for CAS, master's degree. Additional exam requirements/recommendations for international students: Required—TOEFL (minimum score 550 paper-based). Electronic applications accepted. *Faculty research:* Effectiveness of urban Lutheran schools in impacting children's faith development, effectiveness of centers for urban ministries in supporting urban ministry and teaching science.

Concordia University Irvine, School of Education, Irvine, CA 92612-3299. Offers curriculum and instruction (MA); education and preliminary teaching credential (M Ed); educational administration and preliminary administrative services credential (MA); educational technology (MA); school counseling with pupil personnel services credential (MA). *Program availability:* Part-time, evening/weekend, online learning. *Degree requirements:* For master's, action research project. *Entrance requirements:* For master's, California Basic Educational Skills Test, California Subject Examinations for Teachers (M Ed and MA in educational administration and preliminary administrative services credential), official college transcript(s), signed statement of intent, two references, copy of credential. Additional exam requirements/recommendations for international students: Required—TOEFL. Electronic applications accepted. *Expenses:* Contact institution.

Concordia University, Nebraska, Graduate Programs in Education, Program in Educational Administration, Seward, NE 68434. Offers elementary and secondary education (M Ed); elementary education (M Ed); secondary education (M Ed). *Accreditation:* NCATE. *Program availability:* Part-time. *Degree requirements:* For master's, thesis or alternative. *Entrance requirements:* For master's, GRE, MAT, or NTE, BS in education or equivalent, minimum GPA of 3.0.

Concordia University, St. Paul, College of Education, St. Paul, MN 55104-5494. Offers classroom instruction (MA Ed), including K-12 reading; differentiated instruction (MA Ed); early childhood education (MA Ed); education (Ed D); educational leadership (MA Ed); educational technology (MA Ed, Certificate); K-12 principal licensure (Ed S); special education (MA Ed), including autism spectrum disorder, emotional and behavioral disorders, learning disabilities; superintendent (Ed S); teaching (MAT). *Accreditation:* NCATE. *Program availability:* Part-time, evening/weekend, 100% online, blended/hybrid learning. *Faculty:* 15 full-time (8 women), 86 part-time/adjunct (56 women). *Students:* 955 full-time (731 women), 42 part-time (28 women); includes 105 minority (35 Black or African American, non-Hispanic/Latino; 5 American Indian or Alaska Native, non-Hispanic/Latino; 31 Asian, non-Hispanic/Latino; 19 Hispanic/Latino; 15 Two or more races, non-Hispanic/Latino), 9 international. Average age 34. 409 applicants, 87% accepted, 347 enrolled. In 2017, 386 master's, 104 other advanced degrees awarded. *Degree requirements:* For master's, thesis (for some programs); for doctorate, thesis/dissertation, capstone projects; for other advanced degree, e-folio review of competencies. *Entrance requirements:* For master's, official transcripts from regionally-accredited institution stating the conferral of a bachelor's degree with minimum cumulative GPA of 3.0; personal statement; professional resume; practitioner in field through work or volunteerism; resume; for doctorate, minimum master's or specialist degree GPA of 3.25; transcript; writing sample; three letters of recommendation; current resume; on-campus interview; for other advanced degree, minimum master's or specialist degree GPA of 3.25; transcript; statement covering employment history and long-term academic and professional goals; two letters of recommendation; interview with program director. Additional exam requirements/recommendations for international students: Recommended—TOEFL (minimum score 547 paper-based; 78 iBT), IELTS (minimum score 6). *Application deadline:* For fall admission, 8/1 for domestic and international students; for spring admission, 12/1 for domestic and international students; for summer admission, 5/1 for domestic and international students. Applications are processed on a rolling basis. Application fee: $0. Electronic applications accepted. *Expenses:* $395 per credit (for MA in education); $440 per credit (for MAT); $615 per credit (for EdD). *Financial support:* In 2017–18, 105 students received support. Scholarships/grants and unspecified assistantships available. Financial award applicants required to submit FAFSA. *Faculty research:* Differentiated instruction in K-12 educational settings; educational leadership; effective online pedagogy in higher education; equine-assisted learning; faculty development in higher education. *Unit head:* Lonn Maly, Dean, 651-641-8203, E-mail: maly@csp.edu. *Application contact:* Amber Faletti, Director of Enrollment Management, 651-641-8838, Fax: 651-603-6320, E-mail: faletti@csp.edu.

Concordia University Wisconsin, Graduate Programs, Department of Education, Program in Educational Administration, Mequon, WI 53097-2402. Offers MS Ed. *Program availability:* Part-time, evening/weekend, online learning. *Degree requirements:* For master's, comprehensive exam, thesis or alternative. *Entrance requirements:* For master's, minimum GPA of 3.0. Additional exam requirements/recommendations for international students: Required—TOEFL.

Concord University, Graduate Studies, Athens, WV 24712-1000. Offers educational leadership and supervision (M Ed); health promotion (MA); reading specialist (M Ed); social work (MSW); special education (M Ed); teaching (MAT). *Program availability:* Part-time, evening/weekend, 100% online. *Faculty:* 16 full-time (10 women), 7 part-time/adjunct (4 women). *Students:* 146 full-time (117 women), 195 part-time (161 women); includes 26 minority (15 Black or African American, non-Hispanic/Latino; 1 American Indian or Alaska Native, non-Hispanic/Latino; 4 Asian, non-Hispanic/Latino; 1 Hispanic/Latino; 5 Two or more races, non-Hispanic/Latino). Average age 34. 591 applicants, 99% accepted, 144 enrolled. In 2017, 114 master's awarded. *Degree requirements:* For master's, thesis (for some programs). *Entrance requirements:* For master's, GRE or MAT, baccalaureate degree with minimum GPA of 2.5 from regionally-accredited institution; teaching license; 2 letters of recommendation; completed disposition assessment form. *Application deadline:* Applications are processed on a rolling basis. Application fee: $30. Electronic applications accepted. *Expenses:* Tuition, state resident: full-time $8132; part-time $453 per semester hour. Tuition, nonresident: full-time $14,180; part-time $788 per semester hour. *Financial support:* Tuition waivers and unspecified assistantships available. Financial award applicants required to submit FAFSA. *Unit head:* Dr. Cheryl Barnes, Director, 304-384-6306, E-mail: cbarnes@concord.edu. *Application contact:* Debra Moore, Special Events Assistant, 304-384-5113, E-mail: dlm@concord.edu. Website: http://www.concord.edu/graduate

Converse College, Education Specialist Program, Spartanburg, SC 29302. Offers administration and leadership (Ed S); administration and supervision (Ed S); literacy (Ed S). *Accreditation:* AAMFT/COAMFTE. *Program availability:* Part-time. *Entrance requirements:* For degree, GRE or MAT (marriage and family therapy), minimum GPA of 3.0. *Application deadline:* For fall admission, 8/1 for domestic and international students; for winter admission, 11/15 for domestic and international students; for spring admission, 1/15 for domestic and international students. Applications are processed on a rolling basis. Application fee: $40. Electronic applications accepted. *Unit head:* Lienne Medford, Dean of Graduate Studies and Distance Education, 864-596-9082, E-mail: lienne.medford@converse.edu. *Application contact:* Kimberly Newton-Burgess, Director of Post-Traditional and Online Admissions, 864-596-9746, E-mail: kimberly.newton-burgess@converse.edu.

Converse College, Program in Educational Administration and Supervision, Spartanburg, SC 29302. Offers administration and supervision (M Ed). *Degree requirements:* For master's, capstone paper. *Entrance requirements:* For master's, NTE, minimum GPA of 2.75, nomination by school district, 3 recommendations. *Application deadline:* For fall admission, 8/1 for domestic and international students; for winter admission, 11/15 for domestic and international students; for spring admission, 1/15 for domestic and international students. Application fee: $40. Electronic applications accepted. *Unit head:* Lienne Medford, Dean of Graduate Studies and Distance Education, 864-596-9082, Fax: lienne.medford@converse.edu. *Application contact:* 864-596-9404, E-mail: graduate@converse.edu.

Creighton University, Graduate School, College of Arts and Sciences, Department of Education, Program in Educational Leadership, Omaha, NE 68178-0001. Offers MS. *Program availability:* Part-time, online only, 100% online, blended/hybrid learning. *Faculty:* 10 full-time (5 women). *Students:* 106 part-time (72 women); includes 1 minority (Black or African American, non-Hispanic/Latino), 2 international. Average age 36. 2 applicants, 100% accepted, 1 enrolled. In 2017, 44 master's awarded. *Degree requirements:* For master's, portfolio. *Entrance requirements:* For master's, 2 writing samples, 3 letters of recommendation. Additional exam requirements/recommendations for international students: Required—TOEFL (minimum score 90 iBT). *Application deadline:* For fall admission, 7/1 for domestic students, 3/1 for international students; for winter admission, 10/1 for domestic students, 5/1 for international students; for spring admission, 3/1 for domestic students, 10/1 for international students. Applications are processed on a rolling basis. Application fee: $50. Electronic applications accepted. Part-time tuition and fees vary according to course load, degree level, campus/location and program. *Financial support:* Scholarships/grants and tuition waivers (partial) available. Support available to part-time students. Financial award application deadline: 5/1; financial award applicants required to submit FAFSA. *Faculty research:* Catholic school leadership, early childhood education. *Unit head:* Dr. Timothy J. Cook, Professor of Education, 402-280-2561, E-mail: timcook@creighton.edu. *Application contact:* Lindsay Johnson, Director of Graduate and Adult Recruitment, 402-280-2703, Fax: 402-280-2423, E-mail: gradschool@creighton.edu.

Creighton University, Graduate School, Department of Interdisciplinary Studies, Interdisciplinary Ed D Program in Leadership, Omaha, NE 68178-0001. Offers Ed D. *Program availability:* Part-time, online only, blended/hybrid learning. *Faculty:* 7 full-time (5 women), 23 part-time/adjunct (12 women). *Students:* 45 full-time (29 women), 271 part-time (127 women); includes 57 minority (39 Black or African American, non-Hispanic/Latino; 1 American Indian or Alaska Native, non-Hispanic/Latino; 5 Asian, non-Hispanic/Latino; 9 Hispanic/Latino; 2 Native Hawaiian or other Pacific Islander, non-Hispanic/Latino; 1 Two or more races, non-Hispanic/Latino), 4 international. Average age 42. 67 applicants, 78% accepted, 37 enrolled. In 2017, 44 doctorates awarded. *Degree requirements:* For doctorate, thesis/dissertation. *Entrance requirements:* For doctorate, master's or equivalent professional degree, current resume, official transcripts, three recommendations. Additional exam requirements/recommendations for international students: Required—TOEFL (minimum score 90 iBT). *Application deadline:* For fall admission, 6/15 priority date for domestic students, 6/15 for international students; for winter admission, 10/15 for domestic and international students; for spring admission, 3/15 priority date for domestic students, 3/15 for international students; for summer admission, 3/1 for domestic and international students. Applications are processed on a rolling basis. Application fee: $50. Electronic applications accepted. *Expenses:* $1,205 per credit hour. *Financial support:* In 2017–18, 6 students received support. Scholarships/grants available. Financial award application deadline: 5/1; financial award applicants required to submit FAFSA. *Unit head:* Dr. Jennifer Moss Breen, Director, 402-280-3952, E-mail: jennifermossbreen@creighton.edu. *Application contact:* Tara Waln-Lewellyn, Program Manager, 402-280-2392, Fax: 402-280-2423, E-mail: tarawaln-lewellyn@creighton.edu. Website: https://www.creighton.edu/gradschool/edd/home/

Dakota Wesleyan University, Program in Education, Mitchell, SD 57301-4398. Offers curriculum and instruction (MA Ed); educational policy and administration (MA Ed); preK-12 principal certification (MA Ed); secondary certification (MA Ed). *Program availability:* Part-time, evening/weekend. *Degree requirements:* For master's, comprehensive exam, thesis optional, electronic portfolio. *Entrance requirements:* For master's, minimum GPA of 2.7, elementary statistics course, statement of purpose, official transcripts, resume, three letters of recommendation. Additional exam requirements/recommendations for international students: Required—TOEFL (minimum score 500 paper-based), IELTS (minimum score 6.5). Electronic applications accepted. *Faculty research:* Math, political policy, technology in the classroom.

Dallas Baptist University, Dorothy M. Bush College of Education, Program in Curriculum and Instruction, Dallas, TX 75211-9299. Offers Christian school administration (M Ed); distance learning (M Ed); English as a second language (M Ed); instructional technology (M Ed); professional life coaching (M Ed); special education (M Ed); supervision (M Ed). *Program availability:* Part-time, evening/weekend, online learning. *Application deadline:* Applications are processed on a rolling basis. Application fee: $25. Electronic applications accepted. Application fee is waived when completed online. *Expenses: Tuition:* Full-time $16,308; part-time $906 per credit hour. *Required fees:* $900; $450 per semester. Tuition and fees vary according to course load and degree level. *Unit head:* Dr. Neil Dugger, Dean, 214-333-5202, E-mail: neil@dbu.edu. *Application contact:* Dr. Deborah Tribble, Program Director, 214-333-5831, E-mail: debbiet@dbu.edu.
Website: http://www3.dbu.edu/graduate/curriculum_instruction.asp

Dallas Baptist University, Dorothy M. Bush College of Education, Program in Educational Leadership, Dallas, TX 75211-9299. Offers charter school administration (M Ed); educational leadership (M Ed); educational leadership K-12 (Ed D). *Program availability:* Part-time, evening/weekend, online learning. *Application deadline:* Applications are processed on a rolling basis. Application fee: $25. Electronic applications accepted. Application fee is waived when completed online. *Expenses: Tuition:* Full-time $16,308; part-time $906 per credit hour. *Required fees:* $900; $450 per semester. Tuition and fees vary according to course load and degree level. *Unit head:* Dr. Neil Dugger, Dean, 214-333-5202, E-mail: neil@dbu.edu. *Application contact:* Dr. Carolyn Spain, Program Director, 214-333-5217, E-mail: carolyns@dbu.edu.
Website: http://www3.dbu.edu/graduate/education.asp

Dallas Baptist University, Gary Cook School of Leadership, Program in Educational Leadership, Dallas, TX 75211-9299. Offers higher education leadership (Ed D), including educational ministry leadership, general leadership, higher education leadership. *Program availability:* Part-time. *Degree requirements:* For doctorate, thesis/dissertation. *Application deadline:* Applications are processed on a rolling basis. Application fee: $25. Electronic applications accepted. Application fee is waived when completed online. *Expenses: Tuition:* Full-time $16,308; part-time $906 per credit hour. *Required fees:* $900; $450 per semester. Tuition and fees vary according to course load and degree level. *Unit head:* Dr. Jack Goodyear, Dean, 214-333-5595, E-mail: jackg@dbu.edu. *Application contact:* Dr. Ozzie Ingram, Program Director, 214-333-6875, E-mail: ozzie@dbu.edu.
Website: http://www4.dbu.edu/leadership/education-leadership-ed-d

Dallas Theological Seminary, Graduate Programs, Dallas, TX 75204-6499. Offers adult education (Th M); apologetics (Th M); Bible backgrounds (Th M); Bible translation (Th M); Biblical and theological studies (Certificate); biblical counseling (MA); biblical exegesis and linguistics (MA); biblical exposition (PhD); biblical studies (MA); Biblical theology (Th M); children's education (Th M); Christian education (MA, D Min); Christian leadership (MA); cross-cultural ministries (MA); educational administration (Th M); educational leadership (Th M); evangelism and discipleship (Th M); exposition of Biblical books (Th M); family life education (Th M); general studies (Th M); Hebrew and cognate studies (Th M); hermeneutics (Th M); historical theology (Th M); homiletics (Th M); intercultural ministries (Th M); Jesus studies (Th M); leadership studies (Th M); media and communication (MA); media arts (Th M); ministry (D Min); ministry with women (Th M); New Testament studies (Th M, PhD); Old Testament studies (Th M, PhD); parachurch ministries (Th M); pastoral care and counseling (Th M); pastoral theology and practice (Th M); philosophy (Th M); sacred theology (STM); spiritual formation (Th M); systematic theology (Th M); teaching in Christian institutions (Th M); theological studies (PhD); urban ministries (Th M); worship studies (Th M); youth education (Th M). *Program availability:* Part-time, online learning. *Degree requirements:* For master's, variable foreign language requirement, thesis (for some programs); for doctorate, 2 foreign languages, thesis/dissertation. *Entrance requirements:* For master's, GRE or MAT (if minimum undergraduate cumulative GPA is below 2.5 or undergraduate degree is unaccredited). Additional exam requirements/recommendations for international students: Required—TOEFL (minimum score 575 paper-based; 85 iBT), TWE. Electronic applications accepted.

Delaware State University, Graduate Programs, College of Education, Health and Public Policy, Program in Educational Leadership, Dover, DE 19901-2277. Offers MA, Ed D. *Entrance requirements:* Additional exam requirements/recommendations for international students: Required—TOEFL (minimum score 550 paper-based).

Delaware Valley University, Program in Educational Leadership, Doylestown, PA 18901-2697. Offers instruction, curriculum and technology (MS); school administration and leadership (MS). *Program availability:* Part-time, evening/weekend. *Entrance requirements:* For master's, minimum undergraduate GPA of 3.0.

Delta State University, Graduate Programs, College of Education, Division of Teacher Education, Leadership, and Research, Program in Professional Studies, Cleveland, MS 38733-0001. Offers counselor education (Ed D); elementary education (Ed D); higher education (Ed D). *Program availability:* Part-time, evening/weekend. *Degree requirements:* For doctorate, thesis/dissertation. *Entrance requirements:* For doctorate, GRE General Test.

Delta State University, Graduate Programs, College of Education, Division of Teacher Education, Leadership, and Research, Programs in Educational Administration and Supervision, Cleveland, MS 38733-0001. Offers M Ed, Ed S. *Accreditation:* NCATE. *Program availability:* Part-time, evening/weekend. *Degree requirements:* For master's, thesis optional. *Entrance requirements:* For master's, GRE General Test or MAT; for Ed S, master's degree, teaching certificate.

DePaul University, College of Education, Chicago, IL 60614. Offers bilingual-bicultural education (M Ed, MA); counseling (M Ed, MA), including clinical mental health counseling, college student development, school counseling; curriculum studies (M Ed, MA, Ed D); early childhood education (M Ed, MA, Ed D); educational leadership (M Ed, MA, Ed D), including Catholic leadership (M Ed, MA), general (M Ed, MA), higher education (M Ed, MA), physical education (M Ed, MA), principal preparation (M Ed), teacher preparation (M Ed); elementary education (M Ed, MA); middle grades education (M Ed); middle school mathematics education (MS); reading specialist (M Ed, MA); secondary education (M Ed, MA); social and cultural foundations in education (M Ed, MA); special education (M Ed); sport, fitness and recreation leadership (MS); value-creating education for global citizenship (M Ed); world languages education (M Ed, MA). *Program availability:* Part-time, evening/weekend, online learning. *Degree requirements:* For doctorate, thesis/dissertation. *Application deadline:* Applications are processed on a rolling basis. Application fee: $40. Electronic applications accepted. *Financial support:* Application deadline: 12/31; applicants required to submit FAFSA. *Unit head:* Dr. Paul Zionts, Dean, 773-325-7581, Fax: 773-325-7713, E-mail: pzionts@depaul.edu. *Application contact:* Dr. Paul Zionts, Dean, 773-325-7581, Fax: 773-325-7713, E-mail: pzionts@depaul.edu.
Website: http://education.depaul.edu

DeVry University–Folsom Campus, Graduate Programs, Folsom, CA 95630. Offers accounting (M Acc); accounting and financial management (MAFM); business administration (MBA); curriculum leadership (M Ed); educational leadership (M Ed); educational technology (M Ed); higher education leadership (M Ed); human resource management (MHRM); information systems management (MISM); network and communications management (MNCM); project management (MPM); public administration (MPA).

Doane University, Program in Education, Crete, NE 68333-2430. Offers curriculum and instruction (M Ed); curriculum leadership (Ed S); education (Ed D); educational leadership (M Ed); school counseling (M Ed). *Accreditation:* NCATE. *Program availability:* Part-time, evening/weekend. *Faculty:* 10 full-time (7 women), 66 part-time/adjunct (50 women). *Students:* 228 full-time (172 women), 541 part-time (433 women); includes 51 minority (21 Black or African American, non-Hispanic/Latino; 4 American Indian or Alaska Native, non-Hispanic/Latino; 4 Asian, non-Hispanic/Latino; 12 Hispanic/Latino; 1 Native Hawaiian or other Pacific Islander, non-Hispanic/Latino; 9 Two or more races, non-Hispanic/Latino). Average age 33. In 2017, 284 master's, 1 other advanced degree awarded. *Degree requirements:* For master's, thesis; for doctorate, thesis/dissertation. *Entrance requirements:* For master's, minimum GPA of 2.5. Additional exam requirements/recommendations for international students: Required—TOEFL. *Application deadline:* Applications are processed on a rolling basis. Electronic applications accepted. *Expenses:* Contact institution. *Financial support:* Applicants required to submit FAFSA. *Unit head:* Dr. Lyn C. Forester, Dean, 402-826-8604, Fax: 402-826-8278. *Application contact:* Leah Schaber, Assistant Dean, 402-464-1223, Fax: 402-466-4228, E-mail: leah.schaber@doane.edu.
Website: http://www.doane.edu/masters-degrees

Drake University, School of Education, Des Moines, IA 50311-4516. Offers applied behavior analysis (MS); counseling (MS); education (PhD); education administration (Ed D); educational leadership (MSE, Ed D); effective teaching (MSE); leadership development (MS); literacy (Ed S); literacy education (MSE); rehabilitation administration (MS); rehabilitation placement (MS); special education (MSE); STEM education (MSE); teacher education (5-12) (MAT); teacher education (K-8) (MST); teacher effectiveness and professional development (MSE). *Program availability:* Part-time, evening/weekend. *Degree requirements:* For master's and Ed S, comprehensive exam, internships (for some programs); for doctorate, comprehensive exam, thesis/dissertation, internships (for some programs). *Entrance requirements:* For master's, GRE General Test, MAT, or Drake Writing Assessment, resume, 2 letters of recommendation; for doctorate, GRE General Test or MAT, master's degree, 3 letters of recommendation; for Ed S, GRE General Test or MAT. Additional exam requirements/recommendations for international students: Required—TOEFL (minimum score 550 paper-based). *Application deadline:* For fall admission, 7/1 priority date for domestic students, 6/1 priority date for international students; for spring admission, 11/1 priority date for domestic students, 10/1 priority date for international students. Applications are processed on a rolling basis. Application fee: $25. Electronic applications accepted. *Expenses:* Contact institution. *Financial support:* Research assistantships, career-related internships or fieldwork, and unspecified assistantships available. Support available to part-time students. *Faculty research:* Counseling and rehabilitation, behavioral supports, inquiry-based science methods, teacher quality enhancement. *Unit head:* Dr. Janet McMahill, Dean, 515-271-3829, E-mail: janet.mcmahill@drake.edu.
Website: http://www.drake.edu/soe/

Drexel University, Goodwin College of Professional Studies, School of Education, Philadelphia, PA 19104-2875. Offers applied behavior analysis (MS); creativity and innovation (MS); education improvement and transformation (MS); educational administration (MS); educational leadership and management (Ed D); educational leadership development and learning technologies (PhD); global and international education (MS); higher education (MS); human resources development (MS); learning technologies (MS); mathematics, learning and teaching (MS); special education (MS); teaching, learning and curriculum (MS). *Program availability:* Part-time, evening/weekend, online learning. *Degree requirements:* For doctorate, thesis/dissertation. *Entrance requirements:* For doctorate, GRE or GMAT. Additional exam requirements/recommendations for international students: Required—TOEFL, IELTS. Electronic applications accepted. Application fee is waived when completed online. *Expenses:* Contact institution. *Faculty research:* Leadership development, mathematics education, literacy, autism, educational technology.

See Display on page 654 and Close-Up on page 719.

Educational Leadership and Administration

Drury University, Master in Education Program, Springfield, MO 5802. Offers curriculum and instruction (M Ed), including elementary, middle school, secondary; gifted education (M Ed); instructional leadership (M Ed); instructional technology (M Ed); integrated learning (M Ed); online teaching (M Ed); special education (M Ed); special reading (M Ed). *Accreditation:* NCATE. *Program availability:* Part-time, evening/weekend, 100% online, blended/hybrid learning. *Entrance requirements:* For master's, GRE, bachelor's degree with minimum GPA of 2.75. Additional exam requirements/recommendations for international students: Recommended—TOEFL (minimum score 80 iBT), IELTS (minimum score 6.5). Electronic applications accepted. *Expenses:* Contact institution. *Faculty research:* Gifted students, instructional technology, autism, diversity and social justice.

Duquesne University, School of Education, Department of Educational Foundations and Leadership, Ed D in Educational Leadership Program, Pittsburgh, PA 15282-0001. Offers Ed D. *Program availability:* Part-time, evening/weekend. *Faculty:* 7 full-time (3 women). *Students:* 37 full-time (26 women); includes 13 minority (12 Black or African American, non-Hispanic/Latino; 1 Asian, non-Hispanic/Latino), 2 international. Average age 40. 18 applicants, 89% accepted, 15 enrolled. In 2017, 10 doctorates awarded. *Degree requirements:* For doctorate, thesis/dissertation. *Entrance requirements:* For doctorate, GRE, current curriculum vitae or resume; minimum GPA of 3.0 on last 30 hours of graduate work; master's degree in education or related field from accredited institution; 2 written essays; 3 letters of recommendation. Additional exam requirements/recommendations for international students: Required—TOEFL (minimum score 550 paper-based), IELTS (minimum score 7). *Application deadline:* For fall admission, 1/23 for domestic students. Application fee: $0. Electronic applications accepted. *Expenses:* $1,259 per credit. *Faculty research:* Effective school leadership; classroom assessment and social justice; evidence-based decision making; c-engaged educational improvement; scholarship of teaching. *Unit head:* Dr. Connie Moss, Associate Professor, 412-396-4433, Fax: 412-396-6017, E-mail: moss@duq.edu. *Application contact:* Kelly McGinley, Graduate Admissions Assistant, 412-396-1559, Fax: 412-396-5585, E-mail: mcginleyk@duq.edu.
Website: http://wwwtest.duq.edu/academics/schools/education/graduate-programs-education/educational-leadership

Duquesne University, School of Education, Department of Educational Foundations and Leadership, Program in School Administration and Supervision, Pittsburgh, PA 15282-0001. Offers curriculum and instruction (Post-Master's Certificate); school administration K-12 (MS Ed, Post-Master's Certificate); school supervision (MS Ed). *Program availability:* Part-time, evening/weekend. *Faculty:* 1 (woman) full-time. *Students:* 19 full-time (13 women), 5 part-time (3 women); includes 4 minority (all Black or African American, non-Hispanic/Latino), 1 international. Average age 36. 17 applicants, 100% accepted, 10 enrolled. In 2017, 21 master's, 1 other advanced degree awarded. *Entrance requirements:* For master's, bachelor's degree; minimum GPA of 3.0 overall or on most recent 48 credits, or minimum overall GPA of 2.8 and MAT (minimum score 396); resume that documents competence and effectiveness in professional work; 3 letters of professional reference; for Post-Master's Certificate, bachelor's degree. Additional exam requirements/recommendations for international students: Required—TOEFL (minimum score 550 paper-based), IELTS (minimum score 7). *Application deadline:* For fall admission, 9/1 for domestic students; for spring admission, 1/2 for domestic students. Applications are processed on a rolling basis. Application fee: $0. Electronic applications accepted. *Expenses:* $1,259 per credit. *Financial support:* Research assistantships available. Support available to part-time students. *Faculty research:* Building culturally relevant systems of training for educational and helping professionals; preservice/in service teacher beliefs (self, content, equity); principal beliefs about teacher evaluation; beliefs about classroom assessment; school achievement and school effectiveness. *Unit head:* Dr. Fran Serenka, Associate Professor and Director, 412-396-5274, Fax: 412-396-1274, E-mail: serenkaf@duq.edu. *Application contact:* Kelly McGinley, Graduate Admissions Assistant, 412-396-1559, Fax: 412-396-5585, E-mail: mcginleyk@duq.edu.
Website: http://www.duq.edu/academics/schools/education/graduate-programs-education/school-admin-and-supervision

D'Youville College, Department of Education, Buffalo, NY 14201-1084. Offers educational leadership (Ed D); elementary education (MS Ed); secondary education (MS Ed); special education (MS Ed). *Program availability:* Part-time, evening/weekend. *Degree requirements:* For master's, one foreign language, comprehensive exam, project or thesis. *Entrance requirements:* For master's, GRE (if GPA less than 2.75), minimum GPA of 3.0. Additional exam requirements/recommendations for international students: Required—TOEFL (minimum score 500 paper-based). Electronic applications accepted. *Faculty research:* Developmental disabilities, multiculturalism, early childhood education.

East Carolina University, Graduate School, College of Education, Department of Educational Leadership, Greenville, NC 27858-4353. Offers educational administration and supervision (Ed S); educational leadership (Ed D); school administration (MSA). *Accreditation:* NCATE. *Program availability:* Part-time, evening/weekend, online learning. *Students:* 29 full-time (19 women), 226 part-time (151 women); includes 76 minority (60 Black or African American, non-Hispanic/Latino; 2 American Indian or Alaska Native, non-Hispanic/Latino; 2 Asian, non-Hispanic/Latino; 8 Hispanic/Latino; 4 Two or more races, non-Hispanic/Latino), 6 international. Average age 41. 73 applicants, 99% accepted, 60 enrolled. In 2017, 41 master's, 23 doctorates, 12 other advanced degrees awarded. *Degree requirements:* For master's, comprehensive exam, thesis optional; for doctorate, thesis/dissertation. *Entrance requirements:* For master's, GRE General Test or MAT, interview, minimum GPA of 2.5, bachelor's degree in related field, teaching license (MA Ed); for doctorate, GRE or MAT, interview, minimum GPA of 3.5. Additional exam requirements/recommendations for international students: Required—TOEFL. *Application deadline:* For fall admission, 6/1 priority date for domestic students. Applications are processed on a rolling basis. Application fee: $75. *Expenses:* Tuition, state resident: full-time $4749; part-time $297 per credit hour. Tuition, nonresident: full-time $17,898; part-time $1119 per credit hour. *Required fees:* $2691; $224 per credit hour. Part-time tuition and fees vary according to course load and program. *Financial support:* Research assistantships with partial tuition reimbursements, teaching assistantships with partial tuition reimbursements, and Federal Work-Study available. Support available to part-time students. Financial award application deadline: 6/1. *Unit head:* Wiliam A. Rouse, Interim Chair, 252-328-6135, E-mail: rousew@ecu.edu.
Website: http://www.ecu.edu/cs-educ/leed/index.cfm

Eastern Illinois University, Graduate School, College of Education and Professional Studies, Department of Educational Leadership, Charleston, IL 61920. Offers educational administration (Ed S); educational leadership (MS Ed). *Accreditation:* NCATE. *Program availability:* Part-time, evening/weekend. *Degree requirements:* For master's, comprehensive exam; for Ed S, comprehensive exam, thesis. *Entrance requirements:* For master's and Ed S, GMAT or GRE. Additional exam requirements/recommendations for international students: Required—TOEFL (minimum score 500 paper-based; 61 iBT), IELTS (minimum score 6). *Application deadline:* For fall admission, 5/15 for domestic and international students; for spring admission, 10/15 for domestic and international students. Applications are processed on a rolling basis. Application fee: $30. Electronic applications accepted. *Financial support:* Research

assistantships with tuition reimbursements, teaching assistantships with tuition reimbursements, career-related internships or fieldwork, Federal Work-Study, and unspecified assistantships available. Support available to part-time students. Financial award application deadline: 3/1; financial award applicants required to submit FAFSA. *Unit head:* Chair, 217-581-2400, Fax: 217-581-6673. *Application contact:* Chair, 217-581-2400, Fax: 217-581-6673.
Website: http://www.eiu.edu/~edadmin/

Eastern Kentucky University, The Graduate School, College of Education, Department of Counseling and Educational Leadership, Richmond, KY 40475-3102. Offers human services (MA); instructional leadership (MA Ed); mental health counseling (MA); school counseling (MA Ed). *Accreditation:* ACA (one or more programs are accredited); NCATE. *Program availability:* Part-time, online learning. *Entrance requirements:* For master's, GRE General Test, minimum GPA of 2.5.

Eastern Michigan University, Graduate School, College of Education, Department of Leadership and Counseling, Programs in Educational Leadership, Ypsilanti, MI 48197. Offers community college leadership (Graduate Certificate); educational leadership (MA, Ed D, SPA); higher education/general administration (MA); higher education/student affairs (MA); K-12 administration (MA); K-12 basic administration (Post Master's Certificate). *Program availability:* Part-time, evening/weekend, online learning. *Students:* 50 full-time (34 women), 286 part-time (186 women); includes 108 minority (85 Black or African American, non-Hispanic/Latino; 3 American Indian or Alaska Native, non-Hispanic/Latino; 1 Asian, non-Hispanic/Latino; 12 Hispanic/Latino; 7 Two or more races, non-Hispanic/Latino), 2 international. Average age 40. 200 applicants, 72% accepted, 76 enrolled. In 2017, 88 master's, 22 doctorates, 28 other advanced degrees awarded. *Degree requirements:* For master's, portfolio. *Entrance requirements:* For doctorate, GRE. Additional exam requirements/recommendations for international students: Required—TOEFL. *Application deadline:* For winter admission, 2/1 for domestic and international students. Applications are processed on a rolling basis. Application fee: $45. *Financial support:* Fellowships, research assistantships with full tuition reimbursements, teaching assistantships with full tuition reimbursements, career-related internships or fieldwork, Federal Work-Study, institutionally sponsored loans, scholarships/grants, tuition waivers (partial), and unspecified assistantships available. Support available to part-time students. *Application contact:* Dr. Jaclynn Tracy, Coordinator of Advising, Programs in Educational Leadership, 734-487-0255, Fax: 734-487-4608, E-mail: jtracy@emich.edu.

Eastern Michigan University, Graduate School, College of Education, Department of Special Education, Ypsilanti, MI 48197. Offers autism spectrum disorders (MA); cognitive impairment (M Ed); emotional impairment (M Ed); learning disabilities (MA); physical/other health impairment (M Ed); special education (MA, SPA), including administration and supervision (SPA), special education (MA); speech-language pathology (MA); visual impairment (M Ed). *Accreditation:* NCATE. *Program availability:* Part-time, evening/weekend, online learning. *Faculty:* 20 full-time (15 women). *Students:* 96 full-time (89 women), 140 part-time (115 women); includes 27 minority (13 Black or African American, non-Hispanic/Latino; 5 Asian, non-Hispanic/Latino; 5 Hispanic/Latino; 4 Two or more races, non-Hispanic/Latino), 7 international. Average age 32. 267 applicants, 30% accepted, 40 enrolled. In 2017, 75 master's, 3 other advanced degrees awarded. *Entrance requirements:* For master's, GRE General Test. Additional exam requirements/recommendations for international students: Required—TOEFL. *Application deadline:* Applications are processed on a rolling basis. Application fee: $45. *Financial support:* Fellowships, research assistantships with full tuition reimbursements, teaching assistantships with full tuition reimbursements, career-related internships or fieldwork, Federal Work-Study, institutionally sponsored loans, scholarships/grants, tuition waivers (partial), and unspecified assistantships available. Support available to part-time students. Financial award applicants required to submit FAFSA. *Unit head:* Dr. David Winters, Department Head, 734-487-3300, Fax: 734-487-2473, E-mail: david.winters@emich.edu. *Application contact:* Dr. Derrick Fries, Graduate Coordinator, 734-487-2720, Fax: 734-487-2473, E-mail: dfries@emich.edu.
Website: http://www.emich.edu/coe/sped/

Eastern Michigan University, Graduate School, College of Education, Department of Teacher Education, Programs in Curriculum and Instruction, Ypsilanti, MI 48197. Offers advanced teaching and learning (MA); early literacy instruction (Graduate Certificate); instructional leadership (MA); learning, motivation and creativity (Graduate Certificate); literacy coaching (Graduate Certificate); online teaching (Certificate); secondary literacy instruction (Graduate Certificate); urban and diversity education (MA). *Students:* 1 full-time (0 women), 22 part-time (19 women); includes 6 minority (2 Black or African American, non-Hispanic/Latino; 1 Hispanic/Latino; 3 Two or more races, non-Hispanic/Latino). Average age 31. 15 applicants, 67% accepted, 7 enrolled. In 2017, 15 master's, 1 other advanced degree awarded. Application fee: $45. *Application contact:* Dr. Virginia Harder, Graduate Coordinator/Advisor, 734-487-2729, Fax: 734-487-2101, E-mail: vharder1@emich.edu.

Eastern Nazarene College, Adult and Graduate Studies, Division of Teacher Education, Quincy, MA 02170. Offers administration (M Ed); early childhood education (M Ed, Certificate); elementary education (M Ed, Certificate); English as a second language (Certificate); instructional enrichment and development (Certificate); middle school education (M Ed, Certificate); moderate special needs education (Certificate); principal (Certificate); program development and supervision (Certificate); secondary education (M Ed, Certificate); special education administrator (Certificate); special needs (M Ed); supervisor (Certificate); teacher of reading (M Ed, Certificate). M Ed also available through weekend program for administration, special needs, and teacher of reading only. *Program availability:* Part-time, evening/weekend. *Entrance requirements:* Additional exam requirements/recommendations for international students: Required—TOEFL (minimum score 550 paper-based).

Eastern New Mexico University, Graduate School, College of Education and Technology, Department of Educational Studies, Portales, NM 88130. Offers counseling (MA); education (M Ed), including educational administration, secondary education; school counseling (M Ed); special education (M Ed, M Sp Ed), including early childhood special education (M Sp Ed), general special education (M Sp Ed), gifted education pedagogy (M Ed), special education pedagogy (M Ed). *Accreditation:* NCATE. *Program availability:* Part-time, evening/weekend, online learning. *Degree requirements:* For master's, comprehensive exam, thesis optional. *Entrance requirements:* For master's, writing assessment, minimum GPA of 3.0, letter of recommendation, photocopy of teaching license; Level II teaching license (for M Ed in educational administration). Additional exam requirements/recommendations for international students: Required—TOEFL (minimum score 550 paper-based; 79 iBT), IELTS (minimum score 6). *Application deadline:* For fall admission, 7/20 priority date for domestic students, 6/20 priority date for international students; for spring admission, 12/15 priority date for domestic students, 11/15 priority date for international students. Applications are processed on a rolling basis. Application fee: $10. Electronic applications accepted. *Financial support:* Applicants required to submit FAFSA. *Unit head:* Dr. Rebecca Davis, Educational Administration/Special Education Graduate Coordinator, 575-562-2526, Fax: 575-562-2559, E-mail: rebecca.davis@enmu.edu. *Application contact:* Cheryl Reeves, Senior Secretary, 575-562-2443, Fax: 575-562-2559, E-mail: cheryl.reeves@enmu.edu.
Website: http://education.enmu.edu

Eastern University, Graduate Education Programs, St. Davids, PA 19087-3696. Offers ESL program specialist (K-12) (Certificate); general supervisor (PreK-12) (Certificate); health and physical education (K-12) (Certificate); middle level (4-8) (Certificate); multicultural education (M Ed); music (K-12) (Certificate); Pre K-4 (Certificate); Pre K-4 with special education (Certificate); reading (M Ed); reading specialist (K-12) (Certificate); reading supervisor (K-12) (Certificate); school counseling (MA, CAGS); school principalship (preK-12) (Certificate); school psychology (MS, CAGS); secondary biology education (7-12) (Certificate); secondary chemistry education (7-12) (Certificate); secondary communication education (7-12) (Certificate); secondary English education (7-12) (Certificate); secondary math education (7-12) (Certificate); secondary social studies education (7-12) (Certificate); special education (M Ed); special education (7-12) (Certificate); special education (Pre K-8) (Certificate); special education supervisor (K-12) (Certificate); TESOL (M Ed); world language (Certificate), including Spanish. *Program availability:* Part-time, evening/weekend, online learning. *Students:* 46 full-time (40 women), 115 part-time (93 women); includes 65 minority (42 Black or African American, non-Hispanic/Latino; 3 Asian, non-Hispanic/Latino; 14 Hispanic/Latino; 6 Two or more races, non-Hispanic/Latino), 1 international. Average age 32. In 2017, 72 master's awarded. *Entrance requirements:* Additional exam requirements/recommendations for international students: Required—TOEFL. *Application deadline:* Applications are processed on a rolling basis. Application fee: $35. Electronic applications accepted. Application fee is waived when completed online. *Expenses:* Contact institution. *Unit head:* Michael Dziedziak, Executive Director of Enrollment, 800-452-0996, E-mail: gpsadmissions@eastern.edu.
Website: https://www.eastern.edu/academics/programs/education-department-graduate-programs/graduate-programs

Eastern University, Program in Organizational Leadership, St. Davids, PA 19087-3696. Offers leadership studies (CAGS); organizational leadership (PhD), including business management, educational administration, public and nonprofit administration. *Students:* 98 full-time (60 women); includes 31 minority (26 Black or African American, non-Hispanic/Latino; 2 Asian, non-Hispanic/Latino; 2 Hispanic/Latino; 1 Two or more races, non-Hispanic/Latino), 4 international. Average age 47. In 2017, 8 doctorates, 10 other advanced degrees awarded. *Application deadline:* Applications are processed on a rolling basis. Application fee: $75. Electronic applications accepted. *Expenses:* Contact institution. *Unit head:* Michael Dziedziak, Executive Director of Enrollment, 800-452-0996, E-mail: gpsadmissions@eastern.edu.
Website: https://www.eastern.edu/academics/programs/phd-organizational-leadership/phd-organizational-leadership-0

Eastern Washington University, Graduate Studies, College of Arts, Letters and Education, Department of Education, Cheney, WA 99004-2431. Offers adult education (M Ed); curriculum development (M Ed); early childhood education (M Ed); educational foundations (M Ed); educational leadership (M Ed); literacy (M Ed); teaching K-8 (M Ed). *Program availability:* Part-time. *Faculty:* 13. *Students:* 32 full-time (25 women), 36 part-time (25 women); includes 5 minority (all Hispanic/Latino), 4 international. Average age 37. 38 applicants, 55% accepted, 18 enrolled. In 2017, 24 master's awarded. *Degree requirements:* For master's, comprehensive exam. *Entrance requirements:* For master's, minimum GPA of 3.0. Additional exam requirements/recommendations for international students: Required—TOEFL (minimum score 580 paper-based; 92 iBT), IELTS (minimum score 7), PTE (minimum score 63). *Application deadline:* For fall admission, 4/1 priority date for domestic students; for spring admission, 1/15 for domestic students. Applications are processed on a rolling basis. Application fee: $75. Electronic applications accepted. *Expenses:* Tuition, state resident: full-time $11,191; part-time $373.06 per credit. Tuition, nonresident: full-time $25,995; part-time $866.52 per credit. *Financial support:* Teaching assistantships with partial tuition reimbursements, career-related internships or fieldwork, Federal Work-Study, institutionally sponsored loans, scholarships/grants, health care benefits, tuition waivers (partial), and unspecified assistantships available. Support available to part-time students. Financial award application deadline: 2/1; financial award applicants required to submit FAFSA. *Unit head:* Dr. Tara Haskins, Education Department Chair/Associate Professor of Literacy, 509-359-2831, E-mail: thaskins@ewu.edu. *Application contact:* Dr. Robin Showalter, Graduate Program Coordinator, 509-359-6492, E-mail: rshowalter@ewu.edu.
Website: http://www.ewu.edu/CALE/Programs/Education.xml

East Tennessee State University, School of Graduate Studies, College of Education, Department of Educational Leadership and Policy Analysis, Johnson City, TN 37614. Offers administrative endorsement (Ed D, Ed S); classroom leadership (Ed D); community college leadership (Postbaccalaureate Certificate); counselor leadership (Ed S); postsecondary and private sector leadership (Ed D); school and administrator leadership (M Ed); school system leadership (Ed D, Ed S); student personnel leadership (M Ed); teacher leadership (M Ed, Ed S). *Accreditation:* NCATE. *Program availability:* Part-time, online learning. *Degree requirements:* For master's, comprehensive exam, portfolio development and presentation, performance assessment; for doctorate, comprehensive exam, thesis/dissertation, residency, internship; for other advanced degree, comprehensive exam, field experience; internship (for some programs). *Entrance requirements:* For master's, writing assessment, minimum GPA of 2.75, professional resume, teaching certificate, 3 years of teaching experience, interview, four letters of recommendation; for doctorate, GRE General Test, writing assessment, professional resume, teaching certificate (for some programs), interview, four letters of recommendation; for other advanced degree, writing assessment, professional resume, teaching certificate (for some programs), four letters of recommendation. Additional exam requirements/recommendations for international students: Required—TOEFL (minimum score 550 paper-based; 79 iBT). *Application deadline:* For fall admission, 5/1 for domestic and international students; for spring admission, 10/1 for domestic and international students; for summer admission, 2/1 for domestic and international students. Application fee: $55 ($65 for international students). Electronic applications accepted. *Financial support:* Fellowships with full tuition reimbursements, research assistantships with full tuition reimbursements, career-related internships or fieldwork, institutionally sponsored loans, scholarships/grants, and unspecified assistantships available. Financial award application deadline: 7/1; financial award applicants required to submit FAFSA. *Faculty research:* Assessment and evaluation; examining school leadership, management, and accountability systems that limit learning; college and university enrollment and retention issues. *Unit head:* Dr. Bill Flora, Chair, 423-439-7617, Fax: 423-439-7636, E-mail: elpa@etsu.edu. *Application contact:* Dr. Bill Flora, Chair, 423-439-7617, Fax: 423-439-7636, E-mail: elpa@etsu.edu.
Website: http://www.etsu.edu/coe/elpa/

Edgewood College, School of Education, Madison, WI 53711-1997. Offers adult learning (MA Ed); director of special education and pupil services (Certificate); education (MA Ed); teaching and learning (MA Ed). *Accreditation:* NCATE (one or more programs are accredited). *Program availability:* Part-time, evening/weekend. *Faculty:* 13 full-time (9 women), 15 part-time/adjunct (10 women). *Students:* 157 full-time (106 women), 188 part-time (133 women); includes 65 minority (26 Black or African American, non-Hispanic/Latino; 1 American Indian or Alaska Native, non-Hispanic/Latino; 8 Asian, non-Hispanic/Latino; 23 Hispanic/Latino; 7 Two or more races, non-Hispanic/Latino), 14 international. Average age 37. In 2017, 68 master's, 34 doctorates awarded. *Degree requirements:* For master's, practicum, research project; for doctorate,

comprehensive exam, thesis/dissertation. *Entrance requirements:* For master's, minimum GPA of 2.75, 2 letters of recommendation, personal statement; for doctorate, resume, letter of intent, 2 letters of recommendation, interview, writing sample. Additional exam requirements/recommendations for international students: Required—TOEFL (minimum score 525 paper-based; 72 iBT). *Application deadline:* For fall admission, 8/15 for domestic students, 5/1 for international students; for spring admission, 1/8 for domestic students, 11/1 for international students. Applications are processed on a rolling basis. Application fee: $30. Electronic applications accepted. *Expenses: Tuition:* Part-time $930 per credit. *Financial support:* Applicants required to submit FAFSA. *Faculty research:* Urban high schools, transgender students, literacy pedagogy, funds of knowledge, English language learners. *Unit head:* Dr. Timothy D. Slekar, Dean, 608-663-2293, E-mail: tslekar@edgewood.edu. *Application contact:* Joann Eastman, Admissions Counselor, 608-663-3250, Fax: 608-663-2214, E-mail: gps@edgewood.edu.
Website: https://www.edgewood.edu/academics/schools/school-of-education

Edinboro University of Pennsylvania, Department of Middle and Secondary Education and Educational Leadership, Edinboro, PA 16444. Offers educational leadership (M Ed); middle and secondary instruction (M Ed). *Program availability:* Part-time, evening/weekend. *Degree requirements:* For master's, comprehensive exam, thesis or alternative, project. *Entrance requirements:* For master's, GRE or MAT, minimum QPA of 2.5. Electronic applications accepted.

Elizabeth City State University, Department of Education, Psychology and Health, Master of School Administration Program, Elizabeth City, NC 27909-7806. Offers MSA. *Program availability:* Part-time, evening/weekend. *Faculty:* 3 full-time (1 woman). *Students:* 1 full-time (0 women), 30 part-time (23 women); includes 15 minority (all Black or African American, non-Hispanic/Latino). Average age 38. 2 applicants, 100% accepted, 2 enrolled. In 2017, 44 master's awarded. *Degree requirements:* For master's, thesis or alternative, electronic portfolio. *Entrance requirements:* For master's, MAT, GRE, minimum GPA of 3.0, 3 years of teaching experience, 3 letters of recommendation, two official transcripts from all undergraduate/graduate schools attended, teacher license, 3-4 page statement of purpose. Additional exam requirements/recommendations for international students: Required—TOEFL (minimum score 550 paper-based, 80 iBT) or IELTS (minimum score 6.5). *Application deadline:* For fall admission, 7/15 priority date for domestic students, 7/15 for international students; for spring admission, 11/15 priority date for domestic students, 11/15 for international students; for summer admission, 3/15 priority date for domestic and international students. Applications are processed on a rolling basis. Application fee: $30. Electronic applications accepted. Tuition and fees vary according to course load and program. *Financial support:* In 2017–18, 25 students received support. Scholarships/grants and health care benefits available. Financial award application deadline: 6/30; financial award applicants required to submit FAFSA. *Faculty research:* Mentoring, assessment, professional learning communities, common core standards, Interstate School Leaders Licensure Consortium (ISLLC), differentiating instruction. *Unit head:* Dr. Saundra S. Copeland, Coordinator, 252-335-3337, Fax: 252-335-3554, E-mail: sscopeland@mail.ecsu.edu. *Application contact:* Dr. Sharon D. Raynor, Director, Graduate Education Program, 252-335-3945, E-mail: sdraynor@escu.edu.
Website: http://www.ecsu.edu/academics/graduate/schooladmin/index.cfm

Elmhurst College, Graduate Programs, Program in Teacher Leadership, Elmhurst, IL 60126-3296. Offers M Ed. *Program availability:* Part-time, evening/weekend. *Faculty:* 3 full-time (all women). *Students:* 40 part-time (30 women); includes 4 minority (2 American Indian or Alaska Native, non-Hispanic/Latino; 2 Hispanic/Latino). Average age 30. 21 applicants, 81% accepted, 17 enrolled. In 2017, 3 master's awarded. *Entrance requirements:* For master's, 3 recommendations, resume, statement of purpose. Additional exam requirements/recommendations for international students: Required—TOEFL (minimum score 550 paper-based; 79 iBT). *Application deadline:* Applications are processed on a rolling basis. Application fee: $0. Electronic applications accepted. *Expenses:* Contact institution. *Financial support:* In 2017–18, 7 students received support. Scholarships/grants available. Support available to part-time students. Financial award application deadline: 3/1; financial award applicants required to submit FAFSA. *Unit head:* Diana Brannon, Director, 630-617-3458, E-mail: brannond@elmhurst.edu. *Application contact:* Timothy J. Panfil, Director of Enrollment Management, 630-617-3300 Ext. 3256, Fax: 630-617-6471, E-mail: panfilt@elmhurst.edu.
Website: http://www.elmhurst.edu/tl

Emporia State University, Program in Curriculum and Instruction, Emporia, KS 66801-5415. Offers curriculum leadership (MS); effective practitioner (MS); national board certification (MS). *Accreditation:* NCATE. *Program availability:* Part-time, online only, 100% online. *Faculty:* 10 full-time (3 women). *Students:* 6 full-time (all women), 105 part-time (91 women); includes 7 minority (2 Black or African American, non-Hispanic/Latino; 2 Hispanic/Latino; 3 Two or more races, non-Hispanic/Latino). 19 applicants, 95% accepted, 15 enrolled. In 2017, 60 master's awarded. *Degree requirements:* For master's, comprehensive exam or thesis, practicum. *Entrance requirements:* For master's, GRE or MAT, appropriate bachelor's degree, teacher certification, 1 year of teaching experience, letters of recommendation. *Application deadline:* For fall admission, 8/15 priority date for domestic students. Applications are processed on a rolling basis. Application fee: $30 ($75 for international students). Electronic applications accepted. *Expenses:* Tuition, state resident: full-time $6084; part-time $253.50 per credit hour. Tuition, nonresident: full-time $18,924; part-time $788.50 per credit hour. *Required fees:* $1943; $80.95 per credit hour. Tuition and fees vary according to campus/location. *Financial support:* Career-related internships or fieldwork, Federal Work-Study, institutionally sponsored loans, health care benefits, and unspecified assistantships available. Financial award application deadline: 3/15; financial award applicants required to submit FAFSA. *Unit head:* Dr. Daniel Stiffler, Chair, 620-341-5776, E-mail: dstiffle@emporia.edu. *Application contact:* Mary Sewell, Admissions Coordinator, 800-950-GRAD, Fax: 620-341-5909, E-mail: msewell@emporia.edu.

Emporia State University, Program in Educational Administration, Emporia, KS 66801-5415. Offers elementary administration (MS); elementary/secondary administration (MS); secondary administration (MS). *Accreditation:* NCATE. *Program availability:* Part-time. *Faculty:* 10 full-time (3 women). *Students:* 3 full-time (0 women), 100 part-time (53 women); includes 6 minority (3 Black or African American, non-Hispanic/Latino; 1 Hispanic/Latino; 2 Two or more races, non-Hispanic/Latino). 19 applicants, 79% accepted, 12 enrolled. In 2017, 45 master's awarded. *Degree requirements:* For master's, comprehensive exam or thesis, practicum. *Entrance requirements:* For master's, GRE or MAT, appropriate bachelor's degree, letters of recommendation, teacher certification, 1 year of teaching experience. *Application deadline:* For fall admission, 8/15 priority date for domestic students. Applications are processed on a rolling basis. Application fee: $30 ($75 for international students). Electronic applications accepted. *Expenses:* Tuition, state resident: full-time $6084; part-time $253.50 per credit hour. Tuition, nonresident: full-time $18,924; part-time $788.50 per credit hour. *Required fees:* $1943; $80.95 per credit hour. Tuition and fees vary according to campus/location. *Financial support:* In 2017–18, 1 research assistantship with partial tuition reimbursement (averaging $7,344 per year) was awarded; career-related internships or fieldwork, Federal Work-Study, institutionally sponsored loans, health care benefits, and unspecified assistantships also available. Financial award application deadline: 3/15; financial award applicants required to submit FAFSA. *Unit head:* Dr. Daniel Stiffler, Chair, 620-341-5776, E-mail: dstiffle@emporia.edu. *Application contact:* Mary Sewell, Admissions Coordinator, 800-950-GRAD, Fax: 620-341-5909, E-mail: msewell@emporia.edu.

Endicott College, Van Loan School of Graduate and Professional Studies, Program in Administrative Leadership, Beverly, MA 01915. Offers M Ed. *Program availability:* Part-time, evening/weekend. *Faculty:* 21 part-time/adjunct (10 women). *Students:* 34 full-time (22 women), 11 part-time (6 women). Average age 36. 10 applicants, 100% accepted, 10 enrolled. In 2017, 38 master's awarded. *Entrance requirements:* For master's, Massachusetts Tests for Educator Licensure (MTEL) Communication and Literacy Test; MAT or GRE, baccalaureate degree, at least three years of school-based employment. Additional exam requirements/recommendations for international students: Required—TOEFL. *Application deadline:* Applications are processed on a rolling basis. Application fee: $50. Electronic applications accepted. *Expenses:* Contact institution. *Financial support:* Scholarships/grants available. Financial award applicants required to submit FAFSA. *Unit head:* Dr. Aubry Threlkeld, Director of Graduate Licensure Programs, 978-232-2408, E-mail: athrelke@endicott.edu. *Application contact:* Ian Menchini, Director, Graduate Enrollment and Advising, 978-232-5292.
Website: https://vanloan.endicott.edu/programs-of-study/masters-programs/educator-preparation-program/administrative-leadership-program

Endicott College, Van Loan School of Graduate and Professional Studies, Program in Educational Leadership, Beverly, MA 01915-2096. Offers Ed D. *Program availability:* Part-time, evening/weekend. *Faculty:* 1 (woman) full-time, 4 part-time/adjunct (2 women). *Students:* 6 full-time (all women), 11 part-time (8 women); includes 3 minority (1 Black or African American, non-Hispanic/Latino; 1 Asian, non-Hispanic/Latino; 1 Two or more races, non-Hispanic/Latino). Average age 40. 8 applicants, 100% accepted, 7 enrolled. In 2017, 8 doctorates awarded. *Degree requirements:* For doctorate, comprehensive exam, thesis/dissertation, apprenticeship. *Entrance requirements:* For doctorate, GRE or MAT, official undergraduate and graduate transcripts, three letters of recommendation, personal statement, resume or curriculum vitae, writing sample, interview. Additional exam requirements/recommendations for international students: Required—TOEFL. *Application deadline:* For fall admission, 6/1 for domestic students. Application fee: $50. *Expenses:* Contact institution. *Faculty research:* Learning styles in post-secondary education, leadership in the professoriate, collapsing boundaries PreK-PhD. *Unit head:* Dr. Lynne Celli, Associate Dean of Graduate Education, 978-816-7651, Fax: 978-232-3000, E-mail: lcelli@endicott.edu. *Application contact:* Ian Menchini, Director, Graduate Enrollment and Advising, 978-232-5292, Fax: 978-232-3000, E-mail: imenchin@endicott.edu.
Website: https://vanloan.endicott.edu/programs-of-study/doctoral-programs/doctor-of-education—-educational-leadership-in-higher-education-program

Evangel University, Department of Education, Springfield, MO 65802. Offers curriculum and instruction (M Ed); educational leadership (M Ed); literacy (M Ed); secondary teaching (M Ed). *Accreditation:* NCATE. *Program availability:* Part-time, evening/weekend, 100% online, blended/hybrid learning. *Faculty:* 8 full-time (5 women), 8 part-time/adjunct (5 women). *Students:* 1 (woman) full-time, 47 part-time (41 women); includes 2 minority (both Hispanic/Latino). Average age 37. 16 applicants, 100% accepted, 14 enrolled. In 2017, 14 master's awarded. *Entrance requirements:* For master's, PRAXIS II (preferred) or GRE, minimum undergraduate GPA of 3.0. Additional exam requirements/recommendations for international students: Required—TOEFL (minimum score 550 paper-based). *Application deadline:* For fall admission, 7/15 priority date for domestic students, 8/1 for international students; for spring admission, 11/15 priority date for domestic students, 12/1 for international students. Applications are processed on a rolling basis. Application fee: $25. Electronic applications accepted. Application fee is waived when completed online. *Expenses: Tuition:* Full-time $7200; part-time $4800 per credit hour. *Required fees:* $210; $155 per semester. *Financial support:* In 2017–18, 23 students received support. Scholarships/grants and unspecified assistantships available. Financial award application deadline: 4/1; financial award applicants required to submit FAFSA. *Unit head:* Dr. Susan Langston, Program Coordinator, 417-865-2815 Ext. 8552, E-mail: langstons@evangel.edu. *Application contact:* Michael Mann, Enrollment Coordinator, Graduate Studies, 417-865-2815 Ext. 8276, Fax: 417-575-5484, E-mail: mannm@evangel.edu.
Website: http://www.evangel.edu/academics/graduate-studies/graduate-programs

Evangel University, Doctor of Education in Educational Leadership, Curriculum, and Instruction Program, Springfield, MO 65802. Offers Ed D. *Program availability:* Part-time, evening/weekend. *Faculty:* 5 full-time (3 women), 6 part-time/adjunct (3 women). *Students:* 14 full-time (12 women), 25 part-time (17 women); includes 3 minority (1 Black or African American, non-Hispanic/Latino; 1 American Indian or Alaska Native, non-Hispanic/Latino; 1 Two or more races, non-Hispanic/Latino). Average age 40. 13 applicants, 85% accepted, 8 enrolled. *Degree requirements:* For doctorate, thesis/dissertation. *Entrance requirements:* For doctorate, MA in education (preferred). Additional exam requirements/recommendations for international students: Required—TOEFL (minimum score 550 paper-based). *Application deadline:* For fall admission, 7/15 priority date for domestic students, 8/1 for international students; for spring admission, 11/15 priority date for domestic students, 12/1 for international students. Applications are processed on a rolling basis. Application fee: $25. Electronic applications accepted. *Expenses: Tuition:* Full-time $7200; part-time $4800 per credit hour. *Required fees:* $210; $155 per semester. *Financial support:* In 2017–18, 15 students received support. Scholarships/grants available. Support available to part-time students. Financial award application deadline: 4/1; financial award applicants required to submit FAFSA. *Unit head:* Dr. Susan Langston, Program Coordinator, 417-865-2815 Ext. 8552, E-mail: langstons@evangel.edu. *Application contact:* Michael Mann, Enrollment Coordinator, Graduate Studies, 417-865-2811 Ext. 8276, Fax: 417-575-5484, E-mail: mannm@evangel.edu.
Website: https://www.evangel.edu/programs/doctor-education-educational-leadership-curriculum-instruction/

Fairleigh Dickinson University, Florham Campus, University College: Arts, Sciences, and Professional Studies, Peter Sammartino School of Education, Program in Educational Leadership, Madison, NJ 07940-1099. Offers MA.

Fairleigh Dickinson University, Metropolitan Campus, University College: Arts, Sciences, and Professional Studies, Peter Sammartino School of Education, Program in Educational Leadership, Teaneck, NJ 07666-1914. Offers MA.

Fayetteville State University, Graduate School, Programs in Educational Leadership and School Administration, Fayetteville, NC 28301-4298. Offers school administration (MSA). *Accreditation:* NCATE (one or more programs are accredited). *Program availability:* Part-time, evening/weekend. *Faculty:* 9 full-time (4 women), 1 part-time/adjunct (0 women). *Students:* 73 full-time (53 women), 33 part-time (24 women); includes 78 minority (67 Black or African American, non-Hispanic/Latino; 3 American Indian or Alaska Native, non-Hispanic/Latino; 1 Asian, non-Hispanic/Latino; 5 Hispanic/Latino; 2 Two or more races, non-Hispanic/Latino). Average age 42. 44 applicants, 98% accepted, 32 enrolled. In 2017, 10 master's, 17 doctorates awarded. *Degree requirements:* For master's, internship, written and oral exams; for doctorate, thesis/dissertation. *Entrance requirements:* For master's, GRE or MAT, minimum GPA of 2.5.

Additional exam requirements/recommendations for international students: Required—TOEFL. *Application deadline:* For fall admission, 4/1 for domestic students. Applications are processed on a rolling basis. Application fee: $40. Electronic applications accepted. *Expenses:* Tuition, state resident: full-time $8604. Tuition, nonresident: full-time $19,669. *Financial support:* Application deadline: 3/1; applicants required to submit FAFSA. *Faculty research:* First-generation college students and academic successes, educational law and higher education, educational policy and K-12/higher education. *Unit head:* Dr. Abul Pitre, Chair and Professor, Department of Educational Leadership, 910-672-1731, Fax: 910-672-2075, E-mail: lwilson-jones@uncfsu.edu. *Application contact:* Mable Hawkins, Administrative Support Associate, 910-672-1731, Fax: 910-672-2075, E-mail: mhawkins@uncfsu.edu.

Felician University, Program in Education, Lodi, NJ 07644-2117. Offers education (MA); educational leadership (principal/supervision) (MA); educational supervision (PMC); principal (PMC). *Accreditation:* TEAC. *Program availability:* Part-time, evening/weekend. *Faculty:* 2 full-time (1 woman), 7 part-time/adjunct (2 women). *Students:* 3 full-time (2 women), 51 part-time (48 women); includes 15 minority (4 Black or African American, non-Hispanic/Latino; 3 Asian, non-Hispanic/Latino; 8 Hispanic/Latino), 2 international. Average age 36. 29 applicants, 86% accepted, 12 enrolled. In 2017, 23 master's, 11 other advanced degrees awarded. *Degree requirements:* For master's and PMC, thesis, presentation. *Entrance requirements:* For master's, PRAXIS Core (Reading/Writing/Math), minimum GPA of 3.0, two professional letters of recommendation, personal statement, personal interview. Additional exam requirements/recommendations for international students: Required—TOEFL (minimum score 550 paper-based; 79 iBT), IELTS (minimum score 6.5), PTE (minimum score 56). *Application deadline:* Applications are processed on a rolling basis. Application fee: $40. Electronic applications accepted. Application fee is waived when completed online. *Expenses:* Contact institution. *Financial support:* Federal Work-Study and scholarships/grants available. Financial award applicants required to submit FAFSA. *Faculty research:* Educational leadership, administration, supervision, curriculum. *Unit head:* Stephanie McGowan, Dean of Education, 201-559-3551, E-mail: mcgowans@felician.edu. *Application contact:* Michael Szarek, Assistant Vice-President, Graduate Admissions, 201-355-1450, E-mail: szarekm@felician.edu.

Ferris State University, College of Education and Human Services, School of Education, Big Rapids, MI 49307. Offers curriculum and instruction (M Ed), including special education, subject area; educational leadership (MS); instructor (MSCTE); post-secondary administration (MSCTE); training and development (MSCTE). *Program availability:* Part-time, evening/weekend, blended/hybrid learning. *Faculty:* 7 full-time (4 women), 9 part-time/adjunct (6 women). *Students:* 4 full-time (1 woman), 40 part-time (23 women); includes 7 minority (3 Black or African American, non-Hispanic/Latino; 2 Hispanic/Latino; 2 Two or more races, non-Hispanic/Latino), 4 international. Average age 37. 13 applicants, 92% accepted, 7 enrolled. In 2017, 36 master's awarded. *Degree requirements:* For master's, thesis, research paper or project. *Entrance requirements:* For master's, minimum undergraduate GPA of 3.0. Additional exam requirements/recommendations for international students: Required—TOEFL (minimum score 500 paper-based, 79 iBT) or IELTS. *Application deadline:* For fall admission, 7/1 priority date for domestic and international students; for spring admission, 11/1 priority date for domestic and international students; for summer admission, 3/1 priority date for domestic and international students. Applications are processed on a rolling basis. Application fee: $30. Electronic applications accepted. Application fee is waived when completed online. *Financial support:* Career-related internships or fieldwork and scholarships/grants available. Support available to part-time students. Financial award applicants required to submit FAFSA. *Faculty research:* Suicide prevention, reading, women in education, special needs, administration. *Unit head:* Arrick L. Jackson, Dean, 231-591-2702, Fax: 231-591-2043, E-mail: arrickjackson@ferris.edu. *Application contact:* Liza Ing, Graduate Program Coordinator, 231-591-5362, Fax: 231-591-2043, E-mail: lizaIng@ferris.edu.
Website: http://www.ferris.edu/education/education/

Ferris State University, Extended and International Operations, Big Rapids, MI 49307. Offers community college leadership (Ed D). *Program availability:* Evening/weekend, blended/hybrid learning. *Faculty:* 25 part-time/adjunct (15 women). *Students:* 103 full-time (72 women), 2 part-time (0 women); includes 29 minority (19 Black or African American, non-Hispanic/Latino; 1 Asian, non-Hispanic/Latino; 9 Hispanic/Latino). Average age 46. 41 applicants, 73% accepted, 27 enrolled. In 2017, 11 doctorates awarded. *Degree requirements:* For doctorate, thesis/dissertation, e-portfolio demonstrating completion of program outcomes. *Entrance requirements:* For doctorate, master's degree with minimum GPA of 3.25, fierce commitment to the mission of community colleges, essay, writing samples. *Application deadline:* For fall admission, 12/15 for domestic and international students; for winter admission, 1/27 for domestic and international students; for spring admission, 4/15 for domestic students, 4/18 for international students. Applications are processed on a rolling basis. Application fee: $0. Electronic applications accepted. *Expenses:* Contact institution. *Financial support:* In 2017–18, 4 teaching assistantships (averaging $1,000 per year) were awarded. Financial award application deadline: 5/1; financial award applicants required to submit FAFSA. *Faculty research:* Community college leadership. *Unit head:* Dr. Roberta Teahen, Director, 231-591-3805, E-mail: robertateahen@ferris.edu. *Application contact:* Megan Biller, Coordinator, 231-591-2710, E-mail: meganbiller@ferris.edu.

Fitchburg State University, Division of Graduate and Continuing Education, Program in Educational Leadership and Management, Fitchburg, MA 01420-2697. Offers education technology (Certificate); educational leadership and management (M Ed, CAGS); higher education administration (CAGS); school principal (M Ed, CAGS); supervisor/director (M Ed, CAGS). *Accreditation:* NCATE. *Program availability:* Part-time, evening/weekend. *Students:* 15 full-time (12 women), 23 part-time (17 women). Average age 39. 9 applicants, 100% accepted, 8 enrolled. In 2017, 4 master's, 6 CAGSs awarded. *Entrance requirements:* Additional exam requirements/recommendations for international students: Required—TOEFL (minimum score 550 paper-based; 79 iBT). *Application deadline:* For fall admission, 7/15 for international students; for spring admission, 12/1 for international students. Applications are processed on a rolling basis. Application fee: $50. Electronic applications accepted. *Expenses:* Contact institution. *Financial support:* In 2017–18, research assistantships with partial tuition reimbursements (averaging $5,500 per year) were awarded; Federal Work-Study, scholarships/grants, and unspecified assistantships also available. Support available to part-time students. Financial award application deadline: 3/1; financial award applicants required to submit FAFSA. *Unit head:* Dr. Janna Heiligenstein, Chair, 978-665-3477, Fax: 978-665-3658, E-mail: gce@fitchburgstate.edu. *Application contact:* Jinawa McNeil, Director of Admissions, 978-665-3140, Fax: 978-665-4540, E-mail: admissions@fitchburgstate.edu.
Website: http://www.fitchburgstate.edu

Florida Agricultural and Mechanical University, Division of Graduate Studies, Research, and Continuing Education, College of Education, Department of Educational Leadership and Human Services, Tallahassee, FL 32307-3200. Offers administration and supervision (M Ed, MS, PhD); adult education (M Ed, MS); educational leadership (PhD); guidance and counseling (M Ed, MS). *Accreditation:* NCATE. *Degree* *requirements:* For master's, thesis (for some programs); for doctorate, thesis/dissertation. *Entrance requirements:* For master's, GRE General Test, minimum GPA of 3.0. Additional exam requirements/recommendations for international students: Required—TOEFL.

Florida Atlantic University, College of Education, Department of Educational Leadership and Research Methodology, Boca Raton, FL 33431-0991. Offers adult and community education (M Ed, PhD, Ed S); educational leadership (M Ed, PhD, Ed S); higher education (M Ed, PhD); K-12 school leadership (M Ed, PhD, Ed S). *Accreditation:* NCATE. *Program availability:* Part-time, evening/weekend, online learning. *Faculty:* 22 full-time (12 women), 13 part-time/adjunct (8 women). *Students:* 98 full-time (55 women), 240 part-time (162 women); includes 165 minority (94 Black or African American, non-Hispanic/Latino; 4 Asian, non-Hispanic/Latino; 60 Hispanic/Latino; 7 Two or more races, non-Hispanic/Latino), 6 international. Average age 36. 205 applicants, 61% accepted, 105 enrolled. In 2017, 67 master's, 15 doctorates, 8 other advanced degrees awarded. *Degree requirements:* For doctorate, comprehensive exam, thesis/dissertation, departmental qualifying exam; for Ed S, departmental qualifying exam. *Entrance requirements:* For master's, GRE General Test, minimum GPA of 3.0 during previous 2 years; for doctorate, GRE General Test, minimum GPA of 3.5; for Ed S, GRE General Test. Additional exam requirements/recommendations for international students: Required—TOEFL (minimum score 500 paper-based; 61 iBT), IELTS (minimum score 6). *Application deadline:* For fall admission, 7/1 for domestic students, 2/15 for international students; for spring admission, 9/15 for domestic students, 7/15 for international students. Applications are processed on a rolling basis. Application fee: $30. Electronic applications accepted. *Expenses:* Tuition, state resident: full-time $7400; part-time $369.82 per credit. Tuition, nonresident: full-time $20,496; part-time $1042.81 per credit. *Financial support:* Fellowships, research assistantships, teaching assistantships, career-related internships or fieldwork, and tuition waivers (partial) available. *Faculty research:* Self-directed learning, school reform issues, legal issues, mentoring, school leadership. *Unit head:* Dr. Robert E. Shockley, Chair, 561-297-3550, Fax: 561-297-3618, E-mail: shockley@fau.edu. *Application contact:* Kathy DuBois, Senior Secretary, 561-297-3550, Fax: 561-297-3618, E-mail: edleadership@fau.edu. Website: http://www.coe.fau.edu/academicdepartments/el/

Florida Gulf Coast University, College of Education, Program in Educational Leadership, Fort Myers, FL 33965-6565. Offers M Ed, MA. *Program availability:* Part-time, evening/weekend. *Faculty:* 27 full-time (19 women), 44 part-time/adjunct (30 women). *Students:* 4 full-time (3 women), 40 part-time (34 women); includes 13 minority (5 Black or African American, non-Hispanic/Latino; 1 Asian, non-Hispanic/Latino; 7 Hispanic/Latino), 2 international. Average age 34. 21 applicants, 90% accepted, 16 enrolled. In 2017, 26 master's awarded. *Degree requirements:* For master's, thesis or alternative, learning and professional portfolios. *Entrance requirements:* For master's, GRE General Test, MAT, minimum GPA of 3.0. Additional exam requirements/recommendations for international students: Required—TOEFL (minimum score 550 paper-based). *Application deadline:* For fall admission, 2/15 priority date for domestic students, 5/1 for international students; for spring admission, 12/1 for domestic students, 9/15 for international students. Applications are processed on a rolling basis. Application fee: $30. Electronic applications accepted. *Expenses:* Tuition, state resident: part-time $290 per credit hour. Tuition, nonresident: part-time $1173 per credit hour. *Required fees:* $127 per credit hour. Tuition and fees vary according to course load. *Financial support:* In 2017–18, 3 students received support. Application deadline: 6/30; applicants required to submit FAFSA. *Faculty research:* Inclusion, technology in teaching, curriculum development in educational leadership, education policy and law. *Unit head:* Dr. Thomas Roberts, Associate Professor, 239-590-7806, Fax: 239-590-7801, E-mail: troberts@fgcu.edu. *Application contact:* Keiana Desmore, Adviser/Counselor, 239-590-7759, Fax: 239-590-7801, E-mail: kdesmore@fgcu.edu.

Florida International University, College of Arts, Sciences, and Education, Department of Leadership and Professional Studies, Miami, FL 33199. Offers adult education and human resource development (MS, Ed D); counseling (MS), including rehabilitation counseling, school counseling; counselor education (MS), including clinical mental health counseling; educational administration and supervision (Ed D); educational leadership (MS, Certificate, Ed S); higher education (Ed D); higher education administration (MS); international and comparative education (MS); recreation and sport management (MS), including recreation and sport management, recreational therapy; school psychology (Ed S); urban education (MS), including instruction in urban settings, learning technologies, multicultural/bilingual, multicultural/TESOL, urban education. *Program availability:* Part-time, evening/weekend. *Faculty:* 60 full-time (41 women), 112 part-time/adjunct (77 women). *Students:* 221 full-time (162 women), 301 part-time (239 women); includes 418 minority (127 Black or African American, non-Hispanic/Latino; 9 Asian, non-Hispanic/Latino; 271 Hispanic/Latino; 11 Two or more races, non-Hispanic/Latino), 10 international. Average age 31. 330 applicants, 55% accepted, 100 enrolled. In 2017, 181 master's, 6 doctorates awarded. *Degree requirements:* For doctorate, thesis/dissertation. *Entrance requirements:* For master's, minimum GPA of 3.0; for doctorate and other advanced degree, GRE General Test. Additional exam requirements/recommendations for international students: Required—TOEFL (minimum score 550 paper-based; 80 iBT), IELTS (minimum score 6.3). *Application deadline:* For fall admission, 6/1 priority date for domestic students, 4/1 for international students; for winter admission, 10/1 priority date for domestic students, 9/1 for international students; for spring admission, 3/1 priority date for domestic students, 2/1 for international students. Applications are processed on a rolling basis. Application fee: $30. Electronic applications accepted. *Expenses:* Tuition, state resident: full-time $8912; part-time $446 per credit hour. Tuition, nonresident: full-time $21,393; part-time $992 per credit hour. *Required fees:* $390; $195 per semester. *Financial support:* Fellowships, research assistantships with tuition reimbursements, teaching assistantships with tuition reimbursements, Federal Work-Study, and tuition waivers (full and partial) available. Support available to part-time students. Financial award applicants required to submit FAFSA. *Unit head:* Dr. Benjamin Baez, Chair, 305-348-3214, Fax: 305-348-1515, E-mail: benjamin.baez@fiu.edu. *Application contact:* Nanett Rojas, Assistant Director, Graduate Admissions, 305-348-7464, Fax: 305-348-7441, E-mail: gradadm@fiu.edu. Website: http://education.fiu.edu

Florida Southern College, Programs in Teaching, Lakeland, FL 33801-5698. Offers collaborative teaching and learning (M Ed); educational leadership (M Ed, Ed D); teaching (MAT). *Program availability:* Part-time, evening/weekend, 100% online, blended/hybrid learning. *Faculty:* 11 full-time (4 women), 11 part-time/adjunct (7 women). *Students:* 41 full-time (36 women), 23 part-time (all women); includes 16 minority (6 Black or African American, non-Hispanic/Latino; 1 American Indian or Alaska Native, non-Hispanic/Latino; 2 Hispanic/Latino; 1 Native Hawaiian or other Pacific Islander, non-Hispanic/Latino; 1 Two or more races, non-Hispanic/Latino), 2 international. Average age 40. 130 applicants, 92% accepted, 95 enrolled. In 2017, 1 master's awarded. *Degree requirements:* For master's, comprehensive exam (for some programs), thesis (for some programs), FICE General Knowledge test and professional education exam (for MAT), eligibility for the Florida Professional Teacher Certificate (for M Ed); for doctorate, thesis/dissertation. *Entrance requirements:* For master's, Florida Teacher Certification exam (for MAT), letter of reference, resume, personal statement. Additional exam requirements/recommendations for international students: Required—

TOEFL (minimum score 550 paper-based; 79 iBT), IELTS (minimum score 6.5). *Application deadline:* For fall admission, 8/1 for domestic and international students; for winter admission, 4/1 for domestic and international students; for spring admission, 12/1 for domestic and international students. Applications are processed on a rolling basis. Application fee: $30. Electronic applications accepted. *Expenses:* $410 per credit hour, $100 required fee. *Financial support:* In 2017–18, 3 students received support. Scholarships/grants available. Support available to part-time students. Financial award applicants required to submit FAFSA. *Unit head:* Dr. Tracey Tedder, Dean, 863-680-4177, Fax: 863-680-4102, E-mail: ttedder@flsouthern.edu. *Application contact:* Kathy Connelly, Evening Program Assistant Director, 863-680-4205, Fax: 863-680-3872, E-mail: kconnelly@flsouthern.edu.

Florida State University, The Graduate School, College of Education, Department of Educational Leadership and Policy Studies, Tallahassee, FL 32306. Offers educational leadership and administration (Certificate); educational leadership and policy (MS, Ed D, PhD, Ed S), including education policy and evaluation (MS, Ed D, PhD), educational leadership and administration; foundations of education (MS, PhD), including history and philosophy of education, international and multicultural education; higher education (MS, PhD); institutional research (Certificate); program evaluation (Certificate). *Program availability:* Part-time, evening/weekend, 100% online, blended/hybrid learning, asynchronous, minimal on-campus study. *Faculty:* 19 full-time (15 women), 10 part-time/adjunct (7 women). *Students:* 151 full-time (105 women), 196 part-time (138 women); includes 127 minority (55 Black or African American, non-Hispanic/Latino; 4 Asian, non-Hispanic/Latino; 49 Hispanic/Latino; 19 Two or more races, non-Hispanic/Latino), 33 international. Average age 35. 229 applicants, 54% accepted, 66 enrolled. In 2017, 49 master's, 10 doctorates, 17 other advanced degrees awarded. *Degree requirements:* For master's, comprehensive exam, thesis optional; for doctorate, comprehensive exam, thesis/dissertation, diagnostic exam, preliminary exam, prospectus defense, dissertation defense. *Entrance requirements:* For master's, doctorate, and other advanced degree, GRE General Test, minimum GPA of 3.0. Additional exam requirements/recommendations for international students: Required—TOEFL (minimum score 550 paper-based, 80 iBT), IELTS (minimum score 6.5), Michigan English Language Assessment Battery (minimum score 77), or PTE (minimum score 55). Application fee: $30. Electronic applications accepted. *Financial support:* Fellowships, research assistantships, teaching assistantships, scholarships/grants, tuition waivers (full and partial), and unspecified assistantships available. Financial award application deadline: 1/15; financial award applicants required to submit FAFSA. *Faculty research:* Post-secondary success; leadership education; education policy; international education; multicultural education. *Unit head:* Dr. Robert A. Schwartz, Chair, 850-644-6885, Fax: 850-644-2725, E-mail: raschwartz@fsu.edu. *Application contact:* Linda Lyons, Academic Support Assistant, 850-644-7077, Fax: 850-644-1258, E-mail: ljlyons@fsu.edu.

Fordham University, Graduate School of Education, Division of Educational Leadership, Administration and Policy, New York, NY 10023. Offers administration and supervision (MSE, Adv C); administration and supervision for church leaders (PhD); educational administration and supervision (Ed D, PhD). *Accreditation:* NCATE. *Program availability:* Part-time, evening/weekend. *Degree requirements:* For master's, comprehensive exam (for some programs); for doctorate, comprehensive exam (for some programs), thesis/dissertation. *Entrance requirements:* For doctorate, MAT, GRE General Test. Electronic applications accepted.

Fort Hays State University, Graduate School, College of Education, Department of Educational Administration and Counseling, Program in Educational Administration, Hays, KS 67601-4099. Offers MS, Ed S. *Accreditation:* NCATE. *Degree requirements:* For master's and Ed S, comprehensive exam, thesis or alternative. *Entrance requirements:* For master's, GRE General Test or MAT. Additional exam requirements/recommendations for international students: Required—TOEFL (minimum score 550 paper-based). Electronic applications accepted. *Faculty research:* Guide to negotiations, nutrition program for disadvantaged, accountability, student insurance practices, student liability.

Fort Lewis College, Program in Teacher Leadership, Durango, CO 81301-3999. Offers MA, Certificate. *Degree requirements:* For master's, culminating research project. *Entrance requirements:* For master's and Certificate, baccalaureate degree from regionally-accredited college or university; minimum cumulative undergraduate and graduate GPA of 3.0; one year of full-time teaching experience in P-12 schools.

Framingham State University, Graduate Studies, Program in Educational Leadership, Framingham, MA 01701-9101. Offers MA. *Program availability:* Part-time, evening/weekend. *Entrance requirements:* For master's, MAT. *Unit head:* Joyce M. Fahey, Associate Director, 508-626-4964, Fax: 508-626-4030, E-mail: jfahey@framingham.edu. *Application contact:* 508-626-4550, Fax: 508-626-4030, E-mail: dgce@frc.mass.edu.

Franciscan University of Steubenville, Graduate Programs, Department of Education, Steubenville, OH 43952-1763. Offers administration (MS Ed); teaching (MS Ed). *Accreditation:* NCATE. *Program availability:* Part-time, evening/weekend, online learning. *Degree requirements:* For master's, project. *Entrance requirements:* For master's, minimum undergraduate GPA of 2.5 or written exam. Additional exam requirements/recommendations for international students: Required—TOEFL. Electronic applications accepted. Application fee is waived when completed online. *Expenses:* Contact institution.

Freed-Hardeman University, Program in Education, Henderson, TN 38340-2399. Offers curriculum and instruction (M Ed); school counseling (M Ed), including administration and supervision, special education; school leadership (Ed S). *Accreditation:* NCATE. *Program availability:* Part-time, evening/weekend. *Degree requirements:* For master's, comprehensive exam, thesis optional; for Ed S, thesis. *Entrance requirements:* For master's, GRE General Test or NTE; for Ed S, 3 years of teaching experience. Additional exam requirements/recommendations for international students: Required—TOEFL (minimum score 500 paper-based).

Fresno Pacific University, Graduate Programs, School of Education, Division of Administrative Services, Fresno, CA 93702-4709. Offers MA. *Program availability:* Part-time, evening/weekend. *Degree requirements:* For master's, thesis or alternative, 4 practica. *Entrance requirements:* Additional exam requirements/recommendations for international students: Required—TOEFL (minimum score 550 paper-based). Electronic applications accepted. *Expenses:* Contact institution.

Frostburg State University, College of Education, Department of Educational Professions, Program in Educational Administration and Supervision, Frostburg, MD 21532. Offers educational administration and supervision (Ed D); elementary (M Ed); secondary (M Ed). *Program availability:* Part-time, evening/weekend. *Faculty:* 4. *Students:* 6 full-time (3 women), 102 part-time (66 women); includes 2 minority (both Black or African American, non-Hispanic/Latino). Average age 37. 12 applicants, 67% accepted, 5 enrolled. In 2017, 25 master's, 5 doctorates awarded. *Degree requirements:* For master's, thesis or alternative. *Entrance requirements:* For master's, teaching certificate. Additional exam requirements/recommendations for international students: Required—TOEFL. *Application deadline:* For fall admission, 7/15 priority date for domestic students. Applications are processed on a rolling basis. Application fee: $45.

Educational Leadership and Administration

Electronic applications accepted. *Expenses:* Tuition, state resident: part-time $433 per credit hour. Tuition, nonresident: part-time $557 per credit hour. $27 per term. *Financial support:* In 2017–18, 1 research assistantship with full tuition reimbursement (averaging $5,000 per year) was awarded; career-related internships or fieldwork also available. Financial award application deadline: 4/1; financial award applicants required to submit FAFSA. *Faculty research:* Practicum experience in schools. *Unit head:* Dr. John Stoothoff, Coordinator, 301-527-2736, E-mail: jlstoothoff@frostburg.edu. *Application contact:* Vickie Mazer, Director, Graduate Services, 301-687-7053, Fax: 301-687-4597, E-mail: vmmazer@frostburg.edu.

Furman University, Graduate Division, Department of Education, Greenville, SC 29613. Offers curriculum and instruction (MA); early childhood education (MA); educational leadership (Ed S); English as a second language (MA); literacy (MA); school leadership (MA); special education (MA). *Accreditation:* NCATE. *Program availability:* Part-time, online learning. *Degree requirements:* For master's, comprehensive exam (for some programs), thesis or alternative. *Entrance requirements:* For master's, PRAXIS II. *Faculty research:* Literacy, pedagogy and practice, social justice, advanced leadership, achievement in high poverty schools.

Gannon University, School of Graduate Studies, College of Humanities, Education, and Social Sciences, School of Education, Program in Principal Certification, Erie, PA 16541-0001. Offers Certificate. *Program availability:* Part-time, evening/weekend. *Degree requirements:* For Certificate, internship, portfolio. *Entrance requirements:* For degree, transcripts, master's degree in education or related field from regionally-accredited college or university with minimum GPA of 3.0, 3 letters of recommendation, documentation of 3 years of educational experience working under a certificate. Additional exam requirements/recommendations for international students: Required—TOEFL (minimum score 79 iBT). Electronic applications accepted. Application fee is waived when completed online. *Expenses:* Contact institution.

Gannon University, School of Graduate Studies, College of Humanities, Education, and Social Sciences, School of Education, Program in Superintendent Letter of Eligibility Certification, Erie, PA 16541-0001. Offers Certificate. *Program availability:* Part-time, evening/weekend. *Degree requirements:* For Certificate, thesis or alternative, superintendent internship, portfolio. *Entrance requirements:* For degree, transcripts, master's degree in education or related field from regionally-accredited college or university with minimum GPA of 3.0, 3 letters of recommendation, documentation of 6 years of educational experience working under a certificate. Additional exam requirements/recommendations for international students: Required—TOEFL (minimum score 79 iBT). Electronic applications accepted. Application fee is waived when completed online. *Expenses:* Contact institution.

Gannon University, School of Graduate Studies, College of Humanities, Education, and Social Sciences, School of Humanities, Program in Organizational Learning and Leadership, Erie, PA 16541-0001. Offers PhD. *Program availability:* Part-time, evening/weekend. *Degree requirements:* For doctorate, thesis/dissertation. *Entrance requirements:* For doctorate, GRE, master's or other post-baccalaureate professional graduate-level degree from regionally-accredited institution of higher education with minimum GPA of 3.5; 2 years of post-baccalaureate work experience; 3 letters of recommendation; transcripts; resume; statement of purpose. Additional exam requirements/recommendations for international students: Required—TOEFL (minimum score 79 iBT). Electronic applications accepted. Application fee is waived when completed online.

Gardner-Webb University, Graduate School, School of Education, Boiling Springs, NC 28017. Offers curriculum and instruction (Ed D); educational leadership (Ed D); executive leadership studies (MA, Ed S); organizational leadership (Ed D); school administration (MA). *Accreditation:* NCATE. *Program availability:* Part-time, evening/weekend. *Faculty:* 15 full-time (7 women), 33 part-time/adjunct (20 women). *Students:* 13 full-time (10 women), 736 part-time (567 women); includes 332 minority (306 Black or African American, non-Hispanic/Latino; 6 American Indian or Alaska Native, non-Hispanic/Latino; 4 Asian, non-Hispanic/Latino; 9 Hispanic/Latino; 1 Native Hawaiian or other Pacific Islander, non-Hispanic/Latino; 6 Two or more races, non-Hispanic/Latino). Average age 33. *Degree requirements:* For master's, comprehensive exam. *Entrance requirements:* For master's, GRE General Test or NTE, PRAXIS, minimum GPA of 2.5. *Application deadline:* For fall admission, 8/1 priority date for domestic students. Applications are processed on a rolling basis. Electronic applications accepted. *Expenses:* Contact institution. *Financial support:* Unspecified assistantships available. *Application contact:* Office of Graduate Admissions, 877-498-4723, Fax: 704-406-3895, E-mail: gradinfo@gardner-webb.edu.

Gateway Seminary, Graduate and Professional Programs, Ontario, CA 91761-8642. Offers divinity (M Div); early childhood education (Certificate); education leadership (MAEL, Diploma); ministry (D Min); theological studies (MTS); theology (Th M); youth ministry (Certificate). *Accreditation:* ACIPE; ATS. *Program availability:* Part-time, evening/weekend. *Degree requirements:* For master's, thesis (for some programs); for doctorate, 2 foreign languages, thesis/dissertation. *Entrance requirements:* For doctorate, MAT. Additional exam requirements/recommendations for international students: Required—TOEFL (minimum score 550 paper-based). Electronic applications accepted.

Geneva College, Master of Arts in Higher Education Program, Beaver Falls, PA 15010-3599. Offers campus ministry (MA); college teaching (MA); educational leadership (MA); student affairs administration (MA). *Program availability:* Part-time, evening/weekend, blended/hybrid learning. *Faculty:* 1 full-time (0 women), 6 part-time/adjunct (1 woman). *Students:* 44 full-time (27 women), 10 part-time (6 women); includes 8 minority (5 Black or African American, non-Hispanic/Latino; 2 Hispanic/Latino; 1 Two or more races, non-Hispanic/Latino), 1 international. Average age 27. 40 applicants, 75% accepted, 21 enrolled. In 2017, 18 master's awarded. *Degree requirements:* For master's, 36 hours (27 in core courses) including a capstone research project. *Entrance requirements:* For master's, minimum GPA of 3.0, writing sample, 3 letters of recommendation, essay on motivation for participation in the program. Additional exam requirements/recommendations for international students: Required—TOEFL. *Application deadline:* Applications are processed on a rolling basis. Application fee: $0. Electronic applications accepted. *Expenses:* $655 per credit. *Financial support:* Unspecified assistantships available. Financial award application deadline: 8/1; financial award applicants required to submit FAFSA. *Faculty research:* Learning theories, church-related higher education, organizational culture, sexual assault and transgender students at Christian colleges, emerging technology in higher education. *Unit head:* Dr. Keith Martel, Program Director, 724-847-6884, Fax: 724-847-6107, E-mail: hed@geneva.edu. *Application contact:* Allison Davis, Assistant Director, 724-847-6510, Fax: 724-847-6696, E-mail: hed@geneva.edu. Website: http://www.geneva.edu/page/higher_ed

George Fox University, College of Education, Doctor of Education in Educational Leadership Program, Newberg, OR 97132-2697. Offers Ed D. *Program availability:* Online learning.

George Fox University, College of Education, Graduate Teaching and Leading Program, Newberg, OR 97132-2697. Offers administrative leadership (Ed S); continuing administrator license (Certificate); educational leadership (M Ed); educational technology (M Ed); English for speakers of other languages (M Ed); ESOL (Certificate); initial administrator license (Certificate); reading (M Ed, Certificate); special education

(M Ed); teaching (MAT). *Accreditation:* NCATE. *Program availability:* Part-time, evening/weekend, online learning. *Degree requirements:* For master's, thesis (for some programs). *Entrance requirements:* For master's, minimum undergraduate GPA of 3.0 during previous 2 years of course work, resume, 3 professional recommendations on university forms, official transcripts. Additional exam requirements/recommendations for international students: Required—TOEFL (minimum score 577 paper-based; 90 iBT). Electronic applications accepted. *Expenses:* Contact institution.

George Mason University, College of Education and Human Development, Program in Education Leadership, Fairfax, VA 22030. Offers M Ed, Certificate. *Accreditation:* NCATE. *Program availability:* Part-time, evening/weekend, 100% online, blended/hybrid learning. *Faculty:* 5 full-time (2 women), 8 part-time/adjunct (3 women). *Students:* 3 full-time (2 women), 333 part-time (259 women); includes 67 minority (37 Black or African American, non-Hispanic/Latino; 7 Asian, non-Hispanic/Latino; 17 Hispanic/Latino; 6 Two or more races, non-Hispanic/Latino). Average age 35. 201 applicants, 90% accepted, 141 enrolled. In 2017, 123 master's, 18 Certificates awarded. *Entrance requirements:* For master's, bachelor's degree from regionally-accredited institution with minimum GPA of 3.0 overall or in last 60 credit hours; 2 official transcripts; expanded goals statement; 3 letters of recommendation; 3 years of documented teaching experience. Additional exam requirements/recommendations for international students: Required—TOEFL (minimum score 575 paper-based; 88 iBT), IELTS (minimum score 6.5), PTE (minimum score 59). *Application deadline:* For fall admission, 3/1 priority date for domestic and international students; for spring admission, 10/1 for domestic and international students. Application fee: $75 ($80 for international students). Electronic applications accepted. *Expenses:* Tuition, state resident: full-time $11,228; part-time $459.50 per credit. Tuition, nonresident: full-time $30,932; part-time $1280.50 per credit. *Required fees:* $3252; $135.50 per credit. Part-time tuition and fees vary according to course load and program. *Financial support:* Federal Work-Study, scholarships/grants, unspecified assistantships, and health care benefits (for full-time research or teaching assistantship recipients) available. Financial award application deadline: 3/1; financial award applicants required to submit FAFSA. *Faculty research:* Understanding of the complexities of change in schools, communities, and organizations; education law; foundations of education leadership, history and leadership. *Unit head:* Farnoosh Shahrokhi, Academic Program Coordinator, 703-993-2009, E-mail: fshahrok@gmu.edu. Website: http://gse.gmu.edu/programs/edleadership/

George Mason University, College of Education and Human Development, Programs in Curriculum and Instruction, Fairfax, VA 22030. Offers advanced international baccalaureate (M Ed); assistive technology (M Ed); designing digital learning in schools (M Ed); early childhood education (M Ed); early childhood education for diverse learners (M Ed); elementary education (M Ed); English as a second language (M Ed); gifted child education (M Ed); history (M Ed); literacy (M Ed), including PK-12 classroom teachers, reading specialist; literacy leadership for diverse schools (M Ed), including K-12 reading; physical education (M Ed); science K-12 (M Ed); secondary education (M Ed), including biology, chemistry, earth science, English, history/social science, math, physics; special education (M Ed); teacher leadership (M Ed); teaching culturally, linguistically diverse and exceptional learners (M Ed); transformative teaching (M Ed). *Program availability:* Part-time, evening/weekend, 100% online, blended/hybrid learning. *Faculty:* 41 full-time (36 women), 45 part-time/adjunct (37 women). *Students:* 173 full-time (151 women), 729 part-time (611 women); includes 271 minority (65 Black or African American, non-Hispanic/Latino; 5 American Indian or Alaska Native, non-Hispanic/Latino; 88 Asian, non-Hispanic/Latino; 94 Hispanic/Latino; 1 Native Hawaiian or other Pacific Islander, non-Hispanic/Latino; 18 Two or more races, non-Hispanic/Latino), 28 international. Average age 32. 426 applicants, 91% accepted, 289 enrolled. In 2017, 349 master's awarded. *Degree requirements:* For master's, thesis. *Entrance requirements:* For master's, PRAXIS Core (for some programs), 2 letters of recommendation, interview, program goals statement; 9 hours of complete licensure endorsement requirements (for elementary education); minimum GPA of 3.0 in applicant's last 60 hours of undergraduate coursework (for secondary education); at least 1 year of teaching experience (for literacy). Additional exam requirements/recommendations for international students: Required—TOEFL (minimum score 575 paper-based; 88 iBT), IELTS (minimum score 6.5), PTE (minimum score 59). *Application deadline:* For fall admission, 4/2 priority date for domestic and international students; for spring admission, 11/1 for domestic and international students. Application fee: $75 ($80 for international students). Electronic applications accepted. *Expenses:* Tuition, state resident: full-time $11,228; part-time $459.50 per credit. Tuition, nonresident: full-time $30,932; part-time $1280.50 per credit. *Required fees:* $3252; $135.50 per credit. Part-time tuition and fees vary according to course load and program. *Financial support:* In 2017–18, 2 students received support, including 2 teaching assistantships; career-related internships or fieldwork, Federal Work-Study, scholarships/grants, unspecified assistantships, and health care benefits (for full-time research or teaching assistantship recipients) also available. Support available to part-time students. Financial award application deadline: 3/1; financial award applicants required to submit FAFSA. *Faculty research:* Teacher preparation and professional development; adaptive teaching; wonder in science teacher preparation; literacy (digital, adolescent); site based course instruction. *Unit head:* Rebecca Fox, Professor and Academic Program Coordinator, 703-993-4123, E-mail: rfox@gmu.edu. Website: http://gse.gmu.edu/programs/gsemasters

George Mason University, College of Humanities and Social Sciences, Higher Education Program, Fairfax, VA 22030. Offers higher education administration (Certificate); higher education and student development (MA). *Faculty:* 4 full-time (all women), 1 part-time/adjunct (0 women). *Students:* 1 full-time (0 women), 13 part-time (7 women); includes 4 minority (2 Black or African American, non-Hispanic/Latino; 1 Asian, non-Hispanic/Latino; 1 Hispanic/Latino). Average age 43. 6 applicants, 50% accepted, 3 enrolled. In 2017, 3 other advanced degrees awarded. *Degree requirements:* For master's, thesis optional, practicum; for Certificate, practicum. *Entrance requirements:* For master's and Certificate, transcript, resume, writing sample, goals statement, 3 letters of recommendation. Additional exam requirements/recommendations for international students: Required—TOEFL (minimum score 575 paper-based; 88 iBT), IELTS (minimum score 6.5), PTE (minimum score 59). *Application deadline:* For fall admission, 3/1 for domestic and international students; for spring admission, 10/15 for domestic and international students. Application fee: $75 ($80 for international students). Electronic applications accepted. *Expenses:* Tuition, state resident: full-time $11,228; part-time $459.50 per credit. Tuition, nonresident: full-time $30,932; part-time $1280.50 per credit. *Required fees:* $3252; $135.50 per credit. Part-time tuition and fees vary according to course load and program. *Financial support:* Career-related internships or fieldwork, Federal Work-Study, and scholarships/grants available. Support available to part-time students. Financial award application deadline: 3/1; financial award applicants required to submit FAFSA. *Faculty research:* Multicultural issues, leadership, assessment, scholarship of teaching and learning, learning analytics. *Total annual research expenditures:* $24,019. *Unit head:* Jan Arminio, Director, 703-993-2064, Fax: 703-993-2307, E-mail: jarminio@gmu.edu. *Application contact:* Katie Richards, Administrative Coordinator, 703-993-2310, Fax: 703-993-2307, E-mail: kricha22@gmu.edu. Website: http://highered.gmu.edu/

The George Washington University, Graduate School of Education and Human Development, Department of Educational Leadership, Program in Educational Administration and Policy Studies, Washington, DC 20052. Offers education policy (Ed D); educational administration (Ed D). Ed D in educational administration offered at Newport News and Alexandria, VA. *Accreditation:* NCATE. *Students:* 3 full-time (1 woman), 104 part-time (75 women); includes 47 minority (36 Black or African American, non-Hispanic/Latino; 5 Asian, non-Hispanic/Latino; 4 Hispanic/Latino; 1 Native Hawaiian or other Pacific Islander, non-Hispanic/Latino; 1 Two or more races, non-Hispanic/Latino), 1 international. Average age 41. 45 applicants, 44% accepted. In 2017, 17 doctorates awarded. *Degree requirements:* For doctorate, comprehensive exam, thesis/dissertation. *Entrance requirements:* For doctorate, GRE General Test or MAT, interview, minimum GPA of 3.3. *Application deadline:* For fall admission, 1/15 priority date for domestic students; for spring admission, 10/1 for domestic students. Applications are processed on a rolling basis. Application fee: $75. *Expenses: Tuition:* Full-time $28,800; part-time $1655 per credit hour. *Required fees:* $45; $2.75 per credit hour. *Financial support:* In 2017–18, 9 students received support. Fellowships, research assistantships, teaching assistantships, career-related internships or fieldwork, Federal Work-Study, and tuition waivers (partial) available. Financial award application deadline: 1/15; financial award applicants required to submit FAFSA. *Unit head:* Michael Feuer, Dean, 202-994-6161, E-mail: mjfeuer@gwu.edu. *Application contact:* Sarah Lang, Director, Admissions and Marketing, 202-994-1447, Fax: 202-994-7207, E-mail: slang@gwu.edu.

The George Washington University, Graduate School of Education and Human Development, Department of Educational Leadership, Program in Educational Leadership and Administration, Washington, DC 20052. Offers MA Ed, Certificate, Ed S. Programs offered at Newport News and Alexandria, VA. *Accreditation:* NCATE. *Program availability:* Evening/weekend. *Students:* 17 full-time (13 women), 188 part-time (153 women); includes 97 minority (65 Black or African American, non-Hispanic/Latino; 1 American Indian or Alaska Native, non-Hispanic/Latino; 6 Asian, non-Hispanic/Latino; 22 Hispanic/Latino; 3 Two or more races, non-Hispanic/Latino), 11 international. Average age 37. 243 applicants, 78% accepted, 146 enrolled. In 2017, 30 master's, 24 Certificates awarded. *Entrance requirements:* For master's, GRE General Test or MAT, interview, minimum GPA of 2.75. *Application deadline:* For fall admission, 1/15 priority date for domestic students; for spring admission, 10/1 for domestic students. Applications are processed on a rolling basis. Application fee: $75. *Expenses: Tuition:* Full-time $28,800; part-time $1655 per credit hour. *Required fees:* $45; $2.75 per credit hour. *Financial support:* Fellowships, teaching assistantships, career-related internships or fieldwork, and Federal Work-Study available. Financial award application deadline: 1/15; financial award applicants required to submit FAFSA. *Faculty research:* Organizational learning. *Unit head:* Michael Feuer, Dean, 202-994-6161, E-mail: mjfeuer@gwu.edu. *Application contact:* Sarah Lang, Director of Graduate Admissions, 202-994-1447, Fax: 202-994-7207, E-mail: slang@gwu.edu.

The George Washington University, Graduate School of Education and Human Development, Department of Educational Leadership, Program in Higher Education Administration, Washington, DC 20052. Offers college teaching and academic leadership (MA Ed/HD, Ed S); general administration (MA Ed/HD, Ed S); higher education administration (Ed D); higher education finance (MA Ed/HD, Ed S); international education (MA Ed/HD, Ed S); policy (MA Ed/HD, Ed S); student affairs administration (MA Ed/HD, Ed S). *Accreditation:* NCATE. *Students:* 18 full-time (15 women), 65 part-time (44 women); includes 30 minority (17 Black or African American, non-Hispanic/Latino; 7 Asian, non-Hispanic/Latino; 5 Hispanic/Latino; 1 Two or more races, non-Hispanic/Latino), 2 international. Average age 32. 139 applicants, 76% accepted, 27 enrolled. In 2017, 34 master's, 9 doctorates, 1 other advanced degree awarded. *Degree requirements:* For master's and Ed S, comprehensive exam; for doctorate, comprehensive exam, thesis/dissertation. *Entrance requirements:* For master's, GRE General Test or MAT, minimum GPA of 2.75; for doctorate, GRE General Test or MAT, interview, minimum GPA of 3.3; for Ed S, GRE General Test or MAT, minimum GPA of 3.3. *Application deadline:* For fall admission, 1/15 priority date for domestic students; for spring admission, 10/1 for domestic students. Applications are processed on a rolling basis. Application fee: $75. *Expenses: Tuition:* Full-time $28,800; part-time $1655 per credit hour. *Required fees:* $45; $2.75 per credit hour. *Financial support:* In 2017–18, 17 students received support. Fellowships, research assistantships, career-related internships or fieldwork, Federal Work-Study, and tuition waivers (partial) available. Financial award application deadline: 1/15; financial award applicants required to submit FAFSA. *Faculty research:* Technology in higher education administration. *Unit head:* Michael Feuer, Dean, 202-994-6161, E-mail: mjfeuer@gwu.edu. *Application contact:* Sarah Lang, Director of Graduate Admissions, 202-994-1447, Fax: 202-994-7207, E-mail: slang@gwu.edu.

The George Washington University, Graduate School of Education and Human Development, Department of Educational Leadership, Program in Leadership in Educational Technology, Washington, DC 20052. Offers Graduate Certificate. *Students:* 1 (woman) part-time. Average age 44. 1 applicant, 100% accepted. In 2017, 1 Graduate Certificate awarded. *Expenses: Tuition:* Full-time $28,800; part-time $1655 per credit hour. *Required fees:* $45; $2.75 per credit hour. *Unit head:* Dr. Natalie Milman, Coordinator, 202-994-1884, E-mail: nmilman@gwu.edu. *Application contact:* Sarah Lang, Director of Graduate Admissions, 202-994-1447, Fax: 202-994-7207, E-mail: slang@gwu.edu.
Website: http://gsehd.gwu.edu/

Georgia College & State University, Graduate School, The John H. Lounsbury College of Education, Program in Educational Leadership, Milledgeville, GA 31061. Offers M Ed, Ed S. *Accreditation:* NCATE. *Program availability:* Part-time, evening/weekend, online only, 100% online. *Students:* 65 full-time (43 women), 10 part-time (9 women); includes 35 minority (34 Black or African American, non-Hispanic/Latino; 1 Native Hawaiian or other Pacific Islander, non-Hispanic/Latino). Average age 39. 17 applicants, 100% accepted, 12 enrolled. In 2017, 1 master's, 63 Ed Ss awarded. *Degree requirements:* For master's, comprehensive exam, electronic portfolio presentation; for Ed S, comprehensive exam, minimum GPA of 3.0, electronic portfolio presentation. *Entrance requirements:* For master's, GACE, 2 professional recommendations, transcript, documentation of completing coursework for the identification and education of children with special needs, verification of immunization, minimum GPA of 2.5; for Ed S, GACE, certification in educational leadership, leadership position at P-12 school or local unit of administration, 2 professional recommendations, transcripts, minimum GPA of 3.25, verification of immunization. *Application deadline:* For fall admission, 7/1 priority date for domestic students; for spring admission, 11/1 priority date for domestic students; for summer admission, 4/1 priority date for domestic students. Applications are processed on a rolling basis. Application fee: $40. Electronic applications accepted. *Expenses:* $288 per credit hour full-time, $2,592 per semester; $343 per semester fees. *Financial support:* Application deadline: 3/1; applicants required to submit FAFSA. *Unit head:* Dr. Joseph Peters, Dean, College of Education, 478-445-2518, Fax: 478-445-6582, E-mail: joseph.peters@gcsu.edu. *Application contact:* Shanda Brand, Graduate Admission Advisor, 478-445-1383.

Georgian Court University, School of Education, Lakewood, NJ 08701-2697. Offers administration and leadership (MA); autism spectrum disorders (Certificate); education (M Ed, MA, MAT); instructional technology (M Mat SE, Certificate). *Accreditation:* TEAC. *Program availability:* Part-time, evening/weekend. *Faculty:* 11 full-time (7 women), 40 part-time/adjunct (22 women). *Students:* 49 full-time (42 women), 472 part-time (388 women); includes 101 minority (42 Black or African American, non-Hispanic/Latino; 12 Asian, non-Hispanic/Latino; 44 Hispanic/Latino; 3 Two or more races, non-Hispanic/Latino). Average age 34. 412 applicants, 56% accepted, 153 enrolled. In 2017, 81 master's awarded. *Degree requirements:* For master's, comprehensive exam (for some programs), thesis (for some programs). *Entrance requirements:* For master's, GRE, GMAT or NTE/PRAXIS, 3 letters of recommendation. Additional exam requirements/recommendations for international students: Required—TOEFL (minimum score 550 paper-based). *Application deadline:* For fall admission, 8/15 priority date for domestic students, 5/1 for international students; for spring admission, 1/15 priority date for domestic students, 10/1 for international students. Applications are processed on a rolling basis. Application fee: $40. Electronic applications accepted. *Expenses: Tuition:* Part-time $839 per credit. *Required fees:* $248 per semester. Tuition and fees vary according to campus/location and program. *Financial support:* Scholarships/grants, health care benefits, and unspecified assistantships available. Financial award application deadline: 4/15; financial award applicants required to submit FAFSA. *Unit head:* Dr. Lynn DeCapua, Dean, 732-987-2729, E-mail: ldecapua@georgian.edu. *Application contact:* Patrick Givens, Director of Graduate and Professional Studies Admissions, 732-987-2736, Fax: 732-987-2000, E-mail: gps@georgian.edu.
Website: http://georgian.edu/academics/school-of-education/

Georgia Southern University, Jack N. Averitt College of Graduate Studies, College of Education, Department of Leadership, Technology, and Human Development, Ed D Program in Educational Leadership, Statesboro, GA 30460. Offers educational leadership (Ed S); higher education leadership (Ed D); P-12 leadership (Ed D). *Program availability:* Part-time, evening/weekend, 100% online, blended/hybrid learning. *Students:* 13 full-time (6 women), 86 part-time (53 women); includes 38 minority (31 Black or African American, non-Hispanic/Latino; 6 Hispanic/Latino; 1 Two or more races, non-Hispanic/Latino). Average age 37. 39 applicants, 74% accepted, 22 enrolled. In 2017, 8 doctorates, 10 other advanced degrees awarded. *Degree requirements:* For doctorate, comprehensive exam, thesis/dissertation, exams. *Entrance requirements:* For doctorate, GRE General Test or MAT, minimum GPA of 3.5, letters of reference, resume. Additional exam requirements/recommendations for international students: Required—TOEFL (minimum score 550 paper-based; 80 iBT), IELTS (minimum score 6). *Application deadline:* For fall admission, 4/1 for domestic students, 3/1 for international students; for spring admission, 11/1 for domestic students, 10/1 for international students. Application fee: $50. Electronic applications accepted. *Expenses:* Tuition, state resident: full-time $4986; part-time $3324 per year. Tuition, nonresident: full-time $21,982; part-time $15,352 per year. *Required fees:* $2092; $1802 per credit hour. $901 per semester. Tuition and fees vary according to course load, campus/location and program. *Financial support:* In 2017–18, 5 students received support. Research assistantships with partial tuition reimbursements available, teaching assistantships with partial tuition reimbursements available, Federal Work-Study, scholarships/grants, and unspecified assistantships available. Support available to part-time students. Financial award application deadline: 4/15; financial award applicants required to submit FAFSA. *Faculty research:* National and local policies regarding school renewal, student achievement, and university leadership; development of an instrument to measure student dispositions; the impact of cultural context on leadership practices and behaviors; technology leadership preparation. *Unit head:* Dr. Teri Melton, Program Director, 912-478-7267, Fax: 912-478-7140, E-mail: tamelton@georgiasouthern.edu. *Application contact:* Dr. Lydia Cross, Graduate Academic Service Center, 912-478-8664, E-mail: lcross@georgiasouthern.edu.
Website: http://coe.georgiasouthern.edu/edld/

Georgia Southern University, Jack N. Averitt College of Graduate Studies, College of Education, Department of Leadership, Technology, and Human Development, M Ed Program in Educational Leadership, Statesboro, GA 30460. Offers M Ed, Ed S. *Accreditation:* NCATE. *Program availability:* Part-time, evening/weekend. *Students:* 13 full-time (6 women), 86 part-time (53 women); includes 38 minority (31 Black or African American, non-Hispanic/Latino; 6 Hispanic/Latino; 1 Two or more races, non-Hispanic/Latino). Average age 37. 39 applicants, 74% accepted, 22 enrolled. In 2017, 3 master's, 10 Ed Ss awarded. *Degree requirements:* For master's, comprehensive exam, transition point assessments; for Ed S, transition point assessments. *Entrance requirements:* For master's, GRE General Test or MAT, minimum GPA of 2.5, 3 years of teaching experience; for Ed S, GRE General Test or MAT, minimum graduate GPA of 3.25. Additional exam requirements/recommendations for international students: Required—TOEFL (minimum score 550 paper-based; 80 iBT), IELTS (minimum score 6). *Application deadline:* For fall admission, 4/1 for domestic students, 3/1 for international students; for spring admission, 10/1 for domestic and international students. Application fee: $50. Electronic applications accepted. *Expenses:* Tuition, state resident: full-time $4986; part-time $3324 per year. Tuition, nonresident: full-time $21,982; part-time $15,352 per year. *Required fees:* $2092; $1802 per credit hour. $901 per semester. Tuition and fees vary according to course load, campus/location and program. *Financial support:* In 2017–18, 5 students received support, including 1 fellowship with full tuition reimbursement available (averaging $7,750 per year); research assistantships with partial tuition reimbursements available, teaching assistantships with partial tuition reimbursements available, career-related internships or fieldwork, Federal Work-Study, scholarships/grants, tuition waivers (full), and unspecified assistantships also available. Support available to part-time students. Financial award application deadline: 4/15; financial award applicants required to submit FAFSA. *Faculty research:* Principalship, performance-based leadership preparation, instructional technology for school leaders, dispositions of educational leaders, school/system-wide support services, student-oriented support services, universal vs. cultural contextuality of international educational leadership characteristics and behaviors. *Unit head:* Dr. Teri Melton, Program Coordinator, 912-478-0510, Fax: 912-478-7104, E-mail: tamelton@georgiasouthern.edu. *Application contact:* Dr. Lydia Cross, Coordinator for Graduate Academic Services Center, 912-478-8664, E-mail: lcross@georgiasouthern.edu.
Website: http://cogs.georgiasouthern.edu/admission/GraduatePrograms/coe_mededleader.php

Georgia Southern University, Jack N. Averitt College of Graduate Studies, College of Education, Department of Leadership, Technology, and Human Development, Program in Higher Education, Statesboro, GA 30460. Offers educational leadership (Ed D); higher education administration (M Ed). *Accreditation:* NCATE. *Program availability:* Part-time, evening/weekend. *Students:* 1 part-time (0 women). Average age 38. In 2017, 7 master's awarded. *Degree requirements:* For master's, portfolio, practicum, transition point assessments; for doctorate, comprehensive exam, thesis/dissertation. *Entrance requirements:* For master's, minimum GPA of 2.5. Additional exam requirements/recommendations for international students: Required—TOEFL (minimum score 550 paper-based; 80 iBT), IELTS (minimum score 6). *Application deadline:* For fall admission, 4/1 priority date for domestic students, 3/1 for international students; for spring admission, 10/1 for domestic and international students. Applications are processed on a rolling basis. Application fee: $50. Electronic applications accepted. *Expenses:* Tuition, state resident: full-time $4986; part-time $3324 per year. Tuition, nonresident: full-time $21,982; part-time $15,352 per year. *Required fees:* $2092; $1802

Educational Leadership and Administration

per credit hour. $901 per semester. Tuition and fees vary according to course load, campus/location and program. *Financial support:* In 2017–18, 1 student received support. Research assistantships with partial tuition reimbursements available, teaching assistantships with partial tuition reimbursements available, career-related internships or fieldwork, Federal Work-Study, scholarships/grants, and unspecified assistantships available. Support available to part-time students. Financial award application deadline: 4/15; financial award applicants required to submit FAFSA. *Faculty research:* Global issues in higher education, leadership and identity development in higher education, student affairs. *Unit head:* Dr. Daniel Calhoun, Program Coordinator, 912-478-1428, Fax: 912-478-7140, E-mail: dwcalhoun@georgiasouthern.edu. *Application contact:* Dr. Lydia Cross, Coordinator for Graduate Academic Services Center, 912-478-8664, E-mail: lcross@georgiasouthern.edu.
Website: http://coe.georgiasouthern.edu/edld/

Georgia Southern University, Jack N. Averitt College of Graduate Studies, College of Education, Department of Leadership, Technology, and Human Development, Program in Higher Education Administration, Statesboro, GA 30458. Offers M Ed. *Program availability:* Part-time, evening/weekend. *Students:* 29 full-time (22 women), 150 part-time (123 women); includes 47 minority (35 Black or African American, non-Hispanic/Latino; 2 Asian, non-Hispanic/Latino; 5 Hispanic/Latino; 5 Two or more races, non-Hispanic/Latino), 2 international. Average age 40. In 2017, 56 master's awarded. *Entrance requirements:* For master's, GRE, minimum GPA of 2.5. Additional exam requirements/recommendations for international students: Required—TOEFL (minimum score 550 paper-based; 80 iBT), IELTS (minimum score 6). *Application deadline:* For fall admission, 4/1 for domestic students; for spring admission, 11/1 for domestic students. Application fee: $50. Electronic applications accepted. *Expenses:* Tuition, state resident: full-time $4986; part-time $3324 per year. Tuition, nonresident: full-time $21,982; part-time $15,352 per year. *Required fees:* $2092; $1802 per credit hour. $901 per semester. Tuition and fees vary according to course load, campus/location and program. *Financial support:* In 2017–18, 16 students received support, including 3 fellowships with full tuition reimbursements available (averaging $7,750 per year). Financial award application deadline: 4/20; financial award applicants required to submit FAFSA. *Faculty research:* Higher education administration, student affairs. *Unit head:* Dr. Daniel Calhoun, Program Director, 912-478-1428, Fax: 912-478-7104, E-mail: dwcalhoun@georgiasouthern.edu.

Georgia State University, College of Education and Human Development, Department of Educational Policy Studies, Program in Educational Leadership, Atlanta, GA 30302-3083. Offers educational leadership (M Ed, Ed D, Ed S); urban teacher leadership (M Ed). *Accreditation:* NCATE. *Program availability:* Part-time. *Entrance requirements:* For master's, GRE; for doctorate and Ed S, GRE, MAT. *Application deadline:* Applications are processed on a rolling basis. Application fee: $50. Electronic applications accepted. *Expenses:* Tuition, state resident: full-time $7020. Tuition, nonresident: full-time $22,518. *Required fees:* $2128. Tuition and fees vary according to degree level and program. *Financial support:* Fellowships, research assistantships, teaching assistantships, career-related internships or fieldwork, scholarships/grants, health care benefits, tuition waivers, and unspecified assistantships available. Support available to part-time students. Financial award application deadline: 3/15. *Faculty research:* Practices with diverse populations, leadership and success, the cohort model of instruction, technology in the schools, instructional supervision and academic coaching. *Unit head:* Dr. Jami Berry, Clinical Assistant Professor, 404-413-8030, Fax: 404-413-8003, E-mail: jberry2@gsu.edu. *Application contact:* Aishah Cowan, Administrative Academic Specialist, 404-413-8273, Fax: 404-413-8033, E-mail: acowan@gsu.edu.
Website: http://eps.education.gsu.edu/programs-courses/educational-leadership/

Gonzaga University, School of Education, Spokane, WA 99258. Offers clinical mental health counseling (MA); educational leadership (M Ed, Ed D); elementary education (MIT); marriage and family counseling (MA); school counseling (MA); secondary education (MIT); special education (M Ed, MIT); sport and athletic administration (MA). *Accreditation:* NCATE. *Program availability:* Part-time, evening/weekend, 100% online, blended/hybrid learning. *Faculty:* 16 full-time (11 women), 31 part-time/adjunct (19 women). *Students:* 108 full-time (90 women), 225 part-time (140 women); includes 34 minority (4 Black or African American, non-Hispanic/Latino; 2 American Indian or Alaska Native, non-Hispanic/Latino; 5 Asian, non-Hispanic/Latino; 18 Hispanic/Latino; 5 Two or more races, non-Hispanic/Latino), 114 international. Average age 31. 367 applicants, 74% accepted, 160 enrolled. In 2017, 175 master's awarded. *Degree requirements:* For master's, comprehensive exam. *Entrance requirements:* For master's, GRE, MAT, and/or Washington Educator Skills Test-Basic (WEST-B), Washington Educator Skills Test-Endorsements (WEST-E), official transcripts from all colleges or universities attended, interview, two letters of recommendation, resume, essay, minimum GPA of 3.0. Additional exam requirements/recommendations for international students: Required—TOEFL (minimum score 580 paper-based, 88 iBT) or IELTS (minimum score 6.5). *Application deadline:* Applications are processed on a rolling basis. Application fee: $50. Electronic applications accepted. *Expenses:* $990 per credit. *Financial support:* In 2017–18, 51 students received support. Scholarships/grants and unspecified assistantships available. Support available to part-time students. Financial award applicants required to submit FAFSA. *Unit head:* Dr. Vincent Alfonso, Dean, 509-313-3594, Fax: 509-313-5821, E-mail: alfonso@gonzaga.edu. *Application contact:* Meg Martens, Graduate Admissions Program Specialist, 509-313-4314, E-mail: martens@gonzaga.edu.
Website: https://www.gonzaga.edu/school-of-education

Gordon College, Graduate Education Program, Wenham, MA 01984-1899. Offers early childhood (M Ed); educational leadership (M Ed, Ed S); elementary education (M Ed); English as a second language (M Ed, Ed S); math specialist (M Ed); mathematics specialist (Ed S); middle school education (M Ed); moderate disabilities (M Ed); Montessori education (M Ed); reading (M Ed, Ed S); secondary education (M Ed). *Program availability:* Part-time, evening/weekend. *Faculty:* 23 full-time (17 women), 32 part-time/adjunct (23 women). *Students:* 68 full-time (50 women), 114 part-time (99 women); includes 24 minority (2 Black or African American, non-Hispanic/Latino; 8 Asian, non-Hispanic/Latino; 13 Hispanic/Latino; 1 Two or more races, non-Hispanic/Latino), 10 international. Average age 34. 248 applicants, 100% accepted, 182 enrolled. In 2017, 99 master's, 16 Ed Ss awarded. *Degree requirements:* For master's, action research or clinical experience (for most programs); for Ed S, action research or clinical experience (for some programs). *Entrance requirements:* For master's, minimum undergraduate GPA of 3.0; 2 official undergraduate transcripts; professional resume; 3 recommendation letters (one professional reference, one academic reference, one personal reference); 500-700 word statement of purpose; for Ed S, minimum master's GPA of 3.3; 2 official transcripts from undergraduate and graduate schools; professional resume; 3 recommendation letters (one professional reference, one academic reference, one personal reference); 500-700 word statement of purpose. Additional exam requirements/recommendations for international students: Required—TOEFL (minimum score 550 paper-based, 80 iBT) or IELTS (minimum score 6.5). *Application deadline:* Applications are processed on a rolling basis. Application fee: $75. *Expenses:* $325 per credit tuition; $75 per semester administrative fee. *Financial support:* Applicants required to submit FAFSA. *Faculty research:* Reading, early childhood development, English language learners, universal design for learning. *Unit head:* Dr.

Janet Arndt, Director of Graduate Studies, 978-867-4355, Fax: 978-867-4663. *Application contact:* Julie Lenocker, Program Administrator, 978-867-4322, Fax: 978-867-4663, E-mail: graduate-education@gordon.edu.
Website: http://www.gordon.edu/graduate

Gordon College, Graduate Leadership Program, Wenham, MA 01984-1899. Offers leadership (MA, Ed S). *Faculty:* 8 part-time/adjunct (2 women). *Students:* 34 full-time (23 women), 14 part-time (11 women); includes 1 minority (Black or African American, non-Hispanic/Latino), 2 international. Average age 40. 9 applicants, 100% accepted, 8 enrolled. *Degree requirements:* For master's, capstone research. *Entrance requirements:* For master's, official transcripts of all degrees from undergraduate schools; professional resume; 3 references (one academic, one personal, one professional); 500-700 word statement of purpose; minimum undergraduate GPA of 3.0; for Ed S, official transcript of master's degree from accredited school; minimum GPA of 3.3 in master's program; statement of purpose essay, generally 500-700 words; professional resume; professional reference. *Application deadline:* For summer admission, 4/7 for domestic students. Application fee: $75. *Expenses:* $700 per credit tuition; $75 per semester administrative fee. *Unit head:* Dr. Janet Arndt, Director of Graduate Studies, 978-867-4663. *Application contact:* Julie Lenocker, Program Administrator, 978-867-4322, Fax: 978-867-4663, E-mail: graduate-education@gordon.edu.
Website: http://www.gordon.edu/graduate/leadership

Goucher College, Graduate Programs in Education, Baltimore, MD 21204-2794. Offers at-risk and diverse learners (M Ed, Certificate); athletic program leadership and administration (M Ed, Certificate); elementary education (MAT); literacy strategies for content learning (M Ed); middle school (M Ed, Certificate); Montessori studies (M Ed); reading instruction (M Ed, Certificate); reducing student, classroom, and school disruption (M Ed); school improvement leadership (M Ed); secondary education (MAT); special education (MAT), including elementary education; special education for certified elementary and secondary teachers (M Ed); teacher as leader in technology (M Ed). *Program availability:* Part-time, evening/weekend. *Degree requirements:* For master's, thesis (M Ed), final presentation (MAT). *Entrance requirements:* For master's, minimum GPA of 3.0. Additional exam requirements/recommendations for international students: Required—TOEFL (minimum score 550 paper-based; 80 iBT), IELTS (minimum score 7). *Application deadline:* For fall admission, 9/1 for domestic students; for spring admission, 1/15 for domestic students. Applications are processed on a rolling basis. Application fee: $75. Electronic applications accepted. *Expenses:* Contact institution. *Financial support:* Career-related internships or fieldwork and unspecified assistantships available. Support available to part-time students. Financial award application deadline: 4/15; financial award applicants required to submit FAFSA. *Faculty research:* Urban education, middle school, school improvement, teacher education, at-risk student achievement. *Unit head:* Dr. Phyllis Sunshine, Assistant Provost, 410-337-6047, Fax: 410-337-6394, E-mail: psunshin@goucher.edu. *Application contact:* Carlton E. Surbeck, III, Director of Admissions, 410-337-6100, Fax: 410-337-6085, E-mail: admissions@goucher.edu.
Website: http://www.goucher.edu/graduate-programs/graduate-programs-in-education

Governors State University, College of Education, Program in Educational Administration and Supervision, University Park, IL 60484. Offers MA. *Program availability:* Part-time. *Faculty:* 20 full-time (12 women), 40 part-time/adjunct (28 women). *Students:* 1 (woman) full-time, 57 part-time (39 women); includes 21 minority (19 Black or African American, non-Hispanic/Latino; 1 Hispanic/Latino; 1 Two or more races, non-Hispanic/Latino). Average age 36. 29 applicants, 79% accepted, 22 enrolled. In 2017, 35 master's awarded. *Application deadline:* For fall admission, 4/1 for domestic students. Applications are processed on a rolling basis. Application fee: $50. Electronic applications accepted. *Expenses:* Tuition, state resident: full-time $8472; part-time $353 per credit hour. Tuition, nonresident: full-time $16,944; part-time $706 per credit hour. *Required fees:* $1824; $76 per credit hour. $38 per term. Tuition and fees vary according to course load, degree level and program. *Financial support:* Application deadline: 5/1; applicants required to submit FAFSA. *Unit head:* Timothy Harrington, Chair, Division of Education, 708-534-5000 Ext. 4361, E-mail: tharrington2@govst.edu.

Governors State University, College of Education, Program in Interdisciplinary Leadership, University Park, IL 60484. Offers higher education administration (Ed D). *Program availability:* Part-time. *Faculty:* 20 full-time (12 women), 40 part-time/adjunct (28 women). *Students:* 23 full-time (16 women), 17 part-time (10 women); includes 24 minority (19 Black or African American, non-Hispanic/Latino; 5 Hispanic/Latino). Average age 41. 41 applicants, 37% accepted, 14 enrolled. In 2017, 7 doctorates awarded. *Application deadline:* For fall admission, 4/1 for domestic students. Applications are processed on a rolling basis. Application fee: $75. Electronic applications accepted. *Expenses:* Contact institution. *Financial support:* Application deadline: 5/1; applicants required to submit FAFSA. *Unit head:* Timothy Harrington, Chair, Division of Education, 708-534-5000 Ext. 4361, E-mail: tharrington2@govst.edu.

Graceland University, Gleazer School of Education, Independence, MO 64050. Offers curriculum and instruction: collaborative learning and teaching (M Ed); differentiated instruction (M Ed); instructional leadership (M Ed); literacy instruction (M Ed); management in a quality classroom (M Ed); special education (M Ed); technology integration (M Ed). *Accreditation:* NCATE. *Program availability:* Part-time, 100% online. *Faculty:* 2 full-time (both women), 13 part-time/adjunct (10 women). *Students:* 117 full-time (102 women), 62 part-time (54 women); includes 8 minority (3 Black or African American, non-Hispanic/Latino; 1 Asian, non-Hispanic/Latino; 2 Hispanic/Latino; 1 Native Hawaiian or other Pacific Islander, non-Hispanic/Latino; 1 Two or more races, non-Hispanic/Latino), 1 international. Average age 35. 28 applicants, 100% accepted, 19 enrolled. In 2017, 64 master's awarded. *Degree requirements:* For master's, action research capstone. *Entrance requirements:* For master's, minimum GPA of 3.0, teaching certificate, current teaching contract and license, two letters of reference, statement of professional goals, verification of ongoing access to computer technology, including email and Internet. Additional exam requirements/recommendations for international students: Required—TOEFL (minimum score 550 paper-based; 79 iBT). *Application deadline:* For fall admission, 10/1 for domestic students; for winter admission, 11/15 for domestic students; for spring admission, 2/15 priority date for domestic students; for summer admission, 6/1 for domestic students. Application fee: $50. Electronic applications accepted. *Expenses:* Contact institution. *Financial support:* In 2017–18, 3 students received support. Tuition waivers available. Financial award applicants required to submit FAFSA. *Faculty research:* Literacy, technology, faculty mentoring, adult literacy, e-learning, online teaching. *Unit head:* Dr. Lee Bash, Interim Dean, 641-784-5072, E-mail: bash@graceland.edu. *Application contact:* Jeanette Calipetro, Admissions Representative, 816-423-4716, Fax: 816-833-2990, E-mail: jcali1@graceland.edu.
Website: http://www.graceland.edu/education

Grambling State University, School of Graduate Studies and Research, College of Education, Department of Educational Leadership, Grambling, LA 71245. Offers developmental education (MS, Ed D, PMC), including curriculum and instructional design (Ed D), English (MS), guidance and counseling (MS), higher education administration and management (Ed D), mathematics (MS), reading (MS), science (MS), student development and personnel services (Ed D); educational leadership

(M Ed). *Program availability:* Part-time, evening/weekend. *Degree requirements:* For master's, comprehensive exam, thesis (for some programs); for doctorate, comprehensive exam, thesis/dissertation. *Entrance requirements:* For master's, GRE, minimum GPA of 2.5 on last degree; for doctorate, GRE (minimum score 1000, 500 on Verbal), master's degree, minimum GPA of 3.0 on last degree. Additional exam requirements/recommendations for international students: Required—TOEFL (minimum score 500 paper-based; 62 iBT). Electronic applications accepted.

Grand Canyon University, College of Education, Phoenix, AZ 85017-1097. Offers autism spectrum disorders (MA); curriculum and instruction (MA); early childhood education (M Ed); educational administration (M Ed); educational leadership (M Ed); elementary education (M Ed); gifted education (MA); instructional technology (MS); K-12 leadership (Ed S); reading (MA); secondary education (M Ed); secondary humanities education (M Ed); secondary STEM education (M Ed); special education (M Ed); teaching and learning (Ed D); teaching English to speakers of other languages (MA). *Program availability:* Part-time, evening/weekend, online learning. *Degree requirements:* For master's, publishable research paper (M Ed), e-portfolio. *Entrance requirements:* For master's, undergraduate degree from accredited, GCU-approved college, university, or program with minimum GPA 2.8. Additional exam requirements/recommendations for international students: Required—TOEFL (minimum score 550 paper-based; 79 iBT), IELTS (minimum score 6). Electronic applications accepted.

Grand Valley State University, College of Education, Program in Educational Leadership, Allendale, MI 49401-9403. Offers M Ed. *Program availability:* Part-time. *Students:* 13 full-time (7 women), 258 part-time (188 women); includes 40 minority (25 Black or African American, non-Hispanic/Latino; 2 Asian, non-Hispanic/Latino; 10 Hispanic/Latino; 3 Two or more races, non-Hispanic/Latino), 2 international. Average age 35. 88 applicants, 100% accepted, 49 enrolled. In 2017, 70 master's awarded. *Degree requirements:* For master's, thesis or project. *Entrance requirements:* For master's, minimum undergraduate GPA of 3.0 or GRE General Test, last 60 credits from regionally-accredited college/university, 3 letters of recommendation. Additional exam requirements/recommendations for international students: Required—TOEFL (minimum iBT score of 80), IELTS (6.5), or Michigan English Language Assessment Battery (77). *Application deadline:* Applications are processed on a rolling basis. *Expenses:* $652 per credit hour. *Financial support:* In 2017–18, 75 students received support, including 74 fellowships; research assistantships and unspecified assistantships also available. *Unit head:* Dr. Jay Cooper, Director, 616-331-0336, Fax: 616-331-6241, E-mail: cooperj@gvsu.edu. *Application contact:* Dr. Cathy Meyer-Looze, Graduate Program Director, 616-331-6280, Fax: 616-331-6422, E-mail: meyerlca@gvsu.edu.
Website: http://www.gvsu.edu/grad/eduleadership/

Grand Valley State University, College of Education, Program in Leadership, Allendale, MI 49401-9403. Offers Ed S. *Program availability:* Part-time, evening/weekend. *Students:* 1 (woman) full-time, 25 part-time (15 women); includes 10 minority (9 Black or African American, non-Hispanic/Latino; 1 Hispanic/Latino). Average age 40. 3 applicants, 100% accepted, 1 enrolled. In 2017, 15 Ed Ss awarded. *Entrance requirements:* For degree, GRE, master's degree with minimum GPA of 3.0, resume, 3 recommendations. Additional exam requirements/recommendations for international students: Required—TOEFL (minimum iBT score of 80), IELTS (6.5), or Michigan English Language Assessment Battery (77). *Application deadline:* Applications are processed on a rolling basis. Application fee: $30. Electronic applications accepted. *Expenses:* $652 per credit hour. *Financial support:* In 2017–18, 3 students received support, including 2 fellowships; research assistantships and unspecified assistantships also available. *Unit head:* Cathy Meyer-Looze, Graduate Program Coordinator, 616-331-6280, Fax: 616-331-6422, E-mail: meyerlca@gvsu.edu. *Application contact:* Thomas Owens, Director, Student Information and Services Center, 616-331-6282, Fax: 616-331-6217, E-mail: owenst@gvsu.edu.

Grand Valley State University, College of Education, Programs in General Education, Allendale, MI 49401-9403. Offers adult and higher education (M Ed); early childhood education (M Ed); educational differentiation (M Ed); educational leadership (M Ed); educational technology integration (M Ed); elementary education (M Ed); middle level education (M Ed); school library media services (M Ed); secondary level education (M Ed); teaching English to speakers of other languages (M Ed). *Program availability:* Part-time, evening/weekend, 100% online, blended/hybrid learning. *Students:* 24 part-time (16 women). Average age 41. In 2017, 5 master's awarded. *Degree requirements:* For master's, project or thesis. *Entrance requirements:* For master's, GRE General Test or minimum GPA of 3.0, last 60 credits from regionally-accredited college/university, 3 letters of recommendation. Additional exam requirements/recommendations for international students: Required—TOEFL (minimum iBT score of 80), IELTS (6.5), or Michigan English Language Assessment Battery (77). *Application deadline:* Applications are processed on a rolling basis. Application fee: $30. Electronic applications accepted. *Expenses:* $652 per credit hour. *Financial support:* In 2017–18, 2 students received support, including 2 fellowships; career-related internships or fieldwork, Federal Work-Study, scholarships/grants, and unspecified assistantships also available. *Faculty research:* Effectiveness of technology in education, parental involvement, effective teaching, effective schools research. *Unit head:* Dr. David Bair, Department Director, 616-331-6489, Fax: 616-331-6489, E-mail: baird@gvsu.edu. *Application contact:* Thomas Owens, Director, Student Information and Services Center, 616-331-6282, Fax: 616-331-6217, E-mail: owenst@gvsu.edu.
Website: http://www.gvsu.edu/coe/

Grand View University, Graduate Studies, Des Moines, IA 50316-1599. Offers athletic training (MS); clinical nurse leader (MSN, Post Master's Certificate); nursing education (MSN, Post Master's Certificate); organizational leadership (MS); sport management (MS); teacher leadership (M Ed); urban education (M Ed). *Program availability:* Part-time, evening/weekend. *Degree requirements:* For master's, completion of all required coursework in common core and selected track with minimum cumulative GPA of 3.0 and no more than two grades of C. *Entrance requirements:* For master's, GRE, GMAT, or essay, minimum undergraduate GPA of 3.0, professional resume, 3 letters of recommendation, interview. Additional exam requirements/recommendations for international students: Required—TOEFL (minimum score 550 paper-based). Electronic applications accepted.

Gratz College, Graduate Programs, Program in Jewish Education, Melrose Park, PA 19027. Offers education leadership (Ed D); Jewish instructional education (MA); MA/MA. *Program availability:* Part-time, evening/weekend, online learning. *Degree requirements:* For master's, one foreign language, internship. *Entrance requirements:* For master's, interview.

Gwynedd Mercy University, School of Education, Gwynedd Valley, PA 19437-0901. Offers education (Ed D); educational administration (MS); master teacher (MS); school counseling (MS); special education (MS). *Program availability:* Part-time, evening/weekend, 100% online. *Faculty:* 8 full-time (5 women), 38 part-time/adjunct (24 women). *Students:* 579 full-time (430 women); includes 130 minority (90 Black or African American, non-Hispanic/Latino; 11 Asian, non-Hispanic/Latino; 26 Hispanic/Latino; 3 Two or more races, non-Hispanic/Latino). Average age 36. 127 applicants, 18% accepted, 9 enrolled. In 2017, 106 master's awarded. *Degree requirements:* For master's, thesis, internship, practicum. *Entrance requirements:* For master's, GRE or

MAT; PRAXIS I, minimum GPA of 3.0. *Application deadline:* Applications are processed on a rolling basis. *Expenses:* $550 per credit (master's degrees), $965 per credit (doctoral); $17 part-time fee, $165 graduation fee. *Financial support:* In 2017–18, 2 research assistantships were awarded; career-related internships or fieldwork, Federal Work-Study, institutionally sponsored loans, tuition waivers (full and partial), and unspecified assistantships also available. Financial award applicants required to submit FAFSA. *Faculty research:* Learning and the brain, reading literacy, ethics and moral judgment, leadership, teaching and multicultural education. *Unit head:* Dr. Heather Pfleger, Dean, 215-646-7300 Ext. 21581, E-mail: pfleger.h@gmercyu.edu. *Application contact:* Graduate Program Coordinator, 877-499-6333, E-mail: graduate@gmercyu.edu.
Website: https://www.gmercyu.edu/academics/graduate-education-programs

Hampton University, School of Liberal Arts and Education, Program in Educational Leadership, Virginia Beach, VA 23462. Offers MA. *Entrance requirements:* For master's, GRE. Additional exam requirements/recommendations for international students: Required—TOEFL (minimum score 525 paper-based) or IELTS (6.5). *Application deadline:* For fall admission, 6/1 priority date for domestic students, 4/1 priority date for international students; for spring admission, 11/1 priority date for domestic students, 9/1 priority date for international students; for summer admission, 4/1 priority date for domestic students, 2/1 priority date for international students. Applications are processed on a rolling basis. Application fee: $35. Electronic applications accepted. *Expenses:* Tuition: Full-time $22,630; part-time $575 per semester hour. *Required fees:* $70. Tuition and fees vary according to program. *Unit head:* Dr. Martha Jallim-Hall, Graduate Program Coordinator, 757-727-5793, E-mail: martha-jallim-hall@hamptonu.edu.

Hampton University, School of Liberal Arts and Education, Program in Educational Management, Hampton, VA 23668. Offers PhD. *Faculty:* 2. *Students:* 11 full-time (9 women), 40 part-time (27 women); includes 47 minority (all Black or African American, non-Hispanic/Latino). Average age 42. 3 applicants, 100% accepted, 3 enrolled. In 2017, 12 doctorates awarded. *Degree requirements:* For doctorate, comprehensive exam, thesis/dissertation. *Entrance requirements:* Additional exam requirements/recommendations for international students: Required—TOEFL (minimum score 525 paper-based), IELTS (minimum score 6.5). *Application deadline:* For summer admission, 1/15 for domestic students. Applications are processed on a rolling basis. Application fee: $50. Electronic applications accepted. *Expenses:* Tuition: Full-time $22,630; part-time $575 per semester hour. *Required fees:* $70. Tuition and fees vary according to program. *Financial support:* Application deadline: 6/30; applicants required to submit FAFSA. *Unit head:* Dr. Martha Jallim-Hall, Graduate Program Coordinator, 757-727-5793.

Harding University, Cannon-Clary College of Education, Searcy, AR 72149-0001. Offers advanced studies in teaching and learning (M Ed); art (MSE); behavioral science (MSE); counseling (MS, Ed S); early childhood special education (M Ed, MSE); education (MSE); educational leadership (M Ed, Ed S); elementary education (M Ed); English (MSE); French (MSE); history/social science (MSE); kinesiology (MSE); math (MSE); reading (M Ed); secondary education (M Ed); Spanish (MSE); teaching (MAT); teaching English as a second language (MSE). *Accreditation:* NCATE. *Program availability:* Part-time, evening/weekend. *Faculty:* 22 full-time (9 women), 51 part-time/adjunct (37 women). *Students:* 135 full-time (95 women), 316 part-time (231 women); includes 77 minority (46 Black or African American, non-Hispanic/Latino; 7 American Indian or Alaska Native, non-Hispanic/Latino; 4 Asian, non-Hispanic/Latino; 9 Hispanic/Latino; 11 Two or more races, non-Hispanic/Latino), 11 international. Average age 34. 128 applicants, 87% accepted, 111 enrolled. In 2017, 153 master's, 24 other advanced degrees awarded. *Degree requirements:* For master's, comprehensive exam (for some programs), thesis optional, portfolio(s); for Ed S, comprehensive exam, portfolio, project. *Entrance requirements:* For master's, GRE, MAT, PRAXIS; for Ed S, MAT or GRE. Additional exam requirements/recommendations for international students: Required—TOEFL (minimum score 550 paper-based; 79 iBT). *Application deadline:* For fall admission, 8/1 for domestic and international students; for spring admission, 1/1 for domestic and international students. Applications are processed on a rolling basis. Application fee: $35. Tuition and fees vary according to course load, degree level, campus/location and program. *Financial support:* In 2017–18, 33 students received support. Unspecified assistantships available. *Faculty research:* Reading, comprehension, school violence, educational technology, behavior, college choice, differentiated instruction, brain-based teaching. *Unit head:* Dr. Clara Carroll, Chair, 501-279-4501, Fax: 501-279-4083, E-mail: ccarroll@harding.edu. *Application contact:* Information Contact, 501-279-4315, E-mail: gradstudiesedu@harding.edu.
Website: http://www.harding.edu/education

Hardin-Simmons University, Graduate School, Irvin School of Education, Program in Education Leadership, Abilene, TX 79698-0001. Offers educational leadership in superintendency (Ed D); higher education leadership (Ed D). *Program availability:* Part-time. *Faculty:* 3 full-time (all women), 3 part-time/adjunct (1 woman). *Students:* 32 part-time (27 women); includes 3 minority (all Hispanic/Latino), 1 international. Average age 39. 12 applicants, 100% accepted, 6 enrolled. In 2017, 1 doctorate awarded. *Entrance requirements:* For doctorate, minimum master's GPA of 3.5; resume or curriculum vitae; three recommendations from doctoral degree holder, employer/supervisor, and professional colleague. Additional exam requirements/recommendations for international students: Required—TOEFL (minimum score 550 paper-based; 79 iBT), TWE (minimum score 5). *Application deadline:* For fall admission, 7/15 priority date for domestic students, 4/1 for international students; for spring admission, 1/5 priority date for domestic students, 8/1 for international students. Applications are processed on a rolling basis. Application fee: $50 ($150 for international students). Electronic applications accepted. *Expenses:* Tuition: Full-time $13,500; part-time $750 per semester hour. *Required fees:* $220 per term. One-time fee: $50. Tuition and fees vary according to course load, campus/location and program. *Financial support:* In 2017–18, 22 students received support. Fellowships and scholarships/grants available. Support available to part-time students. Financial award application deadline: 6/30; financial award applicants required to submit FAFSA. *Unit head:* Dr. Mary Christopher, Program Director, 325-670-1510, Fax: 325-670-5859, E-mail: leadership@hsutx.edu. *Application contact:* Dr. Nancy Kucinski, Dean of Graduate Studies, 325-670-1298, Fax: 325-670-1564, E-mail: gradoff@hsutx.edu.
Website: http://www.hsutx.edu/doctorateinleadership

Harvard University, Harvard Graduate School of Education, Doctor of Education Leadership (Ed.L.D.) Program, Cambridge, MA 02138. Offers E L D. *Degree requirements:* For doctorate, thesis/dissertation, capstone project. *Entrance requirements:* For doctorate, GRE or GMAT, statement of purpose, 3 letters of recommendation, resume, official transcripts, 2 short essay questions. Additional exam requirements/recommendations for international students: Required—TOEFL (minimum score 613 paper-based; 104 iBT), TWE (minimum score 5). Electronic applications accepted. *Expenses:* Contact institution. *Faculty research:* System level leadership in education.

Harvard University, Harvard Graduate School of Education, Master's Programs in Education, Cambridge, MA 02138. Offers arts in education (Ed M); education policy and management (Ed M); higher education (Ed M); human development and psychology

Educational Leadership and Administration

(Ed M); international education policy (Ed M); language and literacy (Ed M); learning and teaching (Ed M); mind, brain, and education (Ed M); prevention science and practice (Ed M); school leadership (Ed M); special studies (Ed M); teacher education (Ed M); technology, innovation, and education (Ed M). *Program availability:* Part-time. *Entrance requirements:* For master's, GRE General Test, statement of purpose, 3 letters of recommendation, resume, official transcripts. Additional exam requirements/recommendations for international students: Required—TOEFL (minimum score 613 paper-based; 104 iBT), TWE (minimum score 5). Electronic applications accepted. *Faculty research:* Learning and development, educational leadership and organizations, education policy analysis.

Hawai`i Pacific University, College of Professional Studies, Program in Educational Leadership, Honolulu, HI 96813. Offers M Ed. *Program availability:* Evening/weekend, online only, 100% online, blended/hybrid learning. *Faculty:* 4 full-time (3 women), 6 part-time/adjunct (3 women). *Students:* 6 full-time (all women); includes 4 minority (1 American Indian or Alaska Native, non-Hispanic/Latino; 1 Hispanic/Latino; 2 Two or more races, non-Hispanic/Latino). Average age 25. 7 applicants, 100% accepted, 6 enrolled. *Entrance requirements:* For master's, transcripts, personal statement, interview, two letters of recommendation. Additional exam requirements/recommendations for international students: Recommended—TOEFL (minimum score 550 paper-based; 80 iBT), IELTS (minimum score 6), TWE (minimum score 5). *Application deadline:* For fall admission, 1/15 priority date for domestic students. Applications are processed on a rolling basis. Application fee: $50. Electronic applications accepted. *Expenses: Tuition:* Full-time $18,000; part-time $1000 per credit. *Required fees:* $200; $26 per credit. Tuition and fees vary according to course load and program. *Financial support:* In 2017–18, 1 student received support. Career-related internships or fieldwork, Federal Work-Study, scholarships/grants, tuition waivers (partial), and unspecified assistantships available. Financial award application deadline: 3/1; financial award applicants required to submit FAFSA. *Unit head:* Dr. Roger Kiyomura, Director, 808-544-1477, E-mail: rkiyomura@hpu.edu. *Application contact:* Danny Lam, Assistant Director of Graduate Admissions, 808-544-1135, E-mail: graduate@hpu.edu.
Website: https://www.hpu.edu/cps/education/ma-educational-leader.html

Henderson State University, Graduate Studies, Teachers College, Department of Advanced Instructional Studies, Arkadelphia, AR 71999-0001. Offers developmental therapy (MSE); dyslexia therapy (Graduate Certificate); education (MAT); educational technology leadership (Graduate Certificate); English as a second language (MSE, Graduate Certificate); instructional facilitator (MSE, Graduate Certificate); middle level education (MAT); special education (K-12) (MAT, MSE); special education/early childhood (MAT). *Accreditation:* NCATE. *Program availability:* Part-time. *Entrance requirements:* For master's, GRE General Test or MAT, minimum GPA of 2.7, teacher certification. Additional exam requirements/recommendations for international students: Required—TOEFL (minimum score 600 paper-based); Recommended—IELTS (minimum score 6.5).

Henderson State University, Graduate Studies, Teachers College, Department of Educational Leadership, Arkadelphia, AR 71999-0001. Offers curriculum leadership (Ed S); educational leadership (MSE, Ed S, Graduate Certificate). *Program availability:* Part-time, 100% online. *Entrance requirements:* For master's, GRE or MAT, minimum GPA of 2.7, teacher licensure. Additional exam requirements/recommendations for international students: Required—TOEFL (minimum score 600 paper-based); Recommended—IELTS (minimum score 6.5).

Heritage University, Graduate Programs in Education, Program in . Educational Administration, Toppenish, WA 98948-9599. Offers M Ed. *Program availability:* Part-time, evening/weekend. *Degree requirements:* For master's, comprehensive exam, thesis optional, special project. *Entrance requirements:* For master's, valid teaching certificate, 3 years of teaching experience, interview, letters of recommendation.

High Point University, Norcross Graduate School, High Point, NC 27268. Offers athletic training (MSAT); business administration (MBA); educational leadership (M Ed, Ed D); elementary education (M Ed, MAT); pharmacy (Pharm D); physical therapy (DPT); physician assistant studies (MPAS); secondary mathematics (M Ed, MAT); special education (M Ed); strategic communication (MA). *Accreditation:* NCATE. *Program availability:* Part-time, evening/weekend. *Degree requirements:* For master's, comprehensive exam (for some programs), thesis (for some programs). *Entrance requirements:* For master's, GMAT (MBA), GRE, MAT, minimum GPA of 3.0. Additional exam requirements/recommendations for international students: Required—TOEFL (minimum score 550 paper-based). Electronic applications accepted.

High Tech High Graduate School of Education, Program in Educational Leadership, San Diego, CA 92106. Offers M Ed. *Program availability:* Part-time. *Degree requirements:* For master's, project, leadership fieldwork.

Hofstra University, School of Education, Specialized Programs in Education, Hempstead, NY 11549. Offers applied behavior analysis (Advanced Certificate); childhood special education (MS Ed); early childhood special education (MS Ed, Advanced Certificate); educational and policy leadership (Ed D); educational leadership (Advanced Certificate), including school building leader/school district business leader; educational leadership and policy studies (MS Ed), including K-12; elementary special education (MS Ed); gifted education (Advanced Certificate), including school building leader/school district business leader; health education (MS); health professions pedagogy and leadership (MS); higher education leadership and policy studies (MS Ed); inclusive early childhood special education (MS Ed); inclusive elementary special education (MS Ed); inclusive secondary special education (MS Ed); literacy studies (MA, MS Ed, Ed D, Advanced Certificate), including birth-grade 6 (MS Ed, Advanced Certificate), grades 5-12 (MS Ed, Advanced Certificate), literacy studies (Ed D); pedagogy for health professions (Advanced Certificate); physical education (MS); school district business leader (Advanced Certificate); secondary education generalist - students with disabilities 7-12 (MS Ed), including students with disabilities 7-12; secondary special education generalist (MS Ed), including extension in secondary education; special education (MS Ed, Advanced Certificate); special education assessment and diagnosis (Advanced Certificate); special education early childhood intervention (MS Ed); special education: international perspectives (MS Ed); teaching students with severe or multiple disabilities (Advanced Certificate). *Program availability:* Part-time, evening/weekend, blended/hybrid learning. *Students:* 148 full-time (110 women), 249 part-time (188 women); includes 105 minority (54 Black or African American, non-Hispanic/Latino; 1 American Indian or Alaska Native, non-Hispanic/Latino; 13 Asian, non-Hispanic/Latino; 35 Hispanic/Latino; 1 Native Hawaiian or other Pacific Islander, non-Hispanic/Latino; 1 Two or more races, non-Hispanic/Latino), 1 international. Average age 32. 228 applicants, 93% accepted, 132 enrolled. In 2017, 97 master's, 22 doctorates, 31 other advanced degrees awarded. *Degree requirements:* For master's, one foreign language, comprehensive exam (for some programs), thesis (for some programs), electronic portfolio, capstone course, internship, practicum, student teaching, seminars, minimum GPA of 3.0; for doctorate, one foreign language, comprehensive exam, thesis/dissertation, qualifying hearing. *Entrance requirements:* For master's, GRE, interview, letters of recommendation, portfolio, essay, certification; for doctorate, GRE or MAT, interview, resume, essay, master's degree, 3 letters of recommendation, writing sample; for Advanced Certificate, GRE, interview, letters of

recommendation, essay, professional experience, resume, master's degree. Additional exam requirements/recommendations for international students: Required—TOEFL (minimum score 550 paper-based; 80 iBT). *Application deadline:* Applications are processed on a rolling basis. Application fee: $75. Electronic applications accepted. *Expenses: Tuition:* Full-time $1292. *Required fees:* $970. Tuition and fees vary according to program. *Financial support:* In 2017–18, 225 students received support, including 118 fellowships with full and partial tuition reimbursements available (averaging $3,887 per year), 12 research assistantships with full and partial tuition reimbursements available (averaging $7,215 per year); career-related internships or fieldwork, Federal Work-Study, institutionally sponsored loans, scholarships/grants, traineeships, tuition waivers (full and partial), and unspecified assistantships also available. Support available to part-time students. Financial award applicants required to submit FAFSA. *Faculty research:* Collaborative teaching and learning; language and culture; new media literacies; applied behavior analysis; K-12 leadership development. *Unit head:* Dr. Elfreda Blue, Chairperson, 516-463-5762, Fax: 516-463-6184, E-mail: elfreda.blue@hofstra.edu. *Application contact:* Sunil Samuel, Assistant Vice President of Admissions, 516-463-4723, Fax: 516-463-4664, E-mail: graduateadmission@hofstra.edu.
Website: http://www.hofstra.edu/education/

Holy Family University, Graduate and Professional Programs, School of Education, Doctor of Education Programs, Philadelphia, PA 19114. Offers educational leadership and professional studies (Ed D). *Degree requirements:* For doctorate, thesis/dissertation. Electronic applications accepted. *Expenses: Tuition:* Full-time $13,518; part-time $9012 per credit hour. Tuition and fees vary according to degree level and program.

Holy Family University, Graduate and Professional Programs, School of Education, Master of Education Programs, Philadelphia, PA 19114. Offers early elementary education (PreK-Grade 4) (M Ed); education leadership (M Ed); general education (M Ed); reading specialist (M Ed); special education (M Ed); TESOL and literacy (M Ed). *Program availability:* Part-time. *Degree requirements:* For master's, thesis optional. Electronic applications accepted. *Expenses: Tuition:* Full-time $13,518; part-time $9012 per credit hour. Tuition and fees vary according to degree level and program.

Hood College, Graduate School, Department of Education, Frederick, MD 21701-8575. Offers curriculum and instruction (MS), including elementary education, elementary science and mathematics education, secondary education, special education; education, multidisciplinary studies (MS); educational leadership (MS, Certificate); reading specialization (MS); STEM education (Certificate). *Accreditation:* NCATE. *Program availability:* Part-time-only, evening/weekend. *Faculty:* 6 full-time (4 women), 35 part-time/adjunct (27 women). *Students:* 3 full-time (all women), 329 part-time (265 women); includes 62 minority (35 Black or African American, non-Hispanic/Latino; 4 Asian, non-Hispanic/Latino; 14 Hispanic/Latino; 9 Two or more races, non-Hispanic/Latino), 3 international. Average age 33. 76 applicants, 100% accepted, 63 enrolled. In 2017, 53 master's, 58 other advanced degrees awarded. *Degree requirements:* For master's, action research project, portfolio (for reading specialization); for Certificate, STEM capstone activity. *Entrance requirements:* For master's, minimum GPA of 2.75, teaching certification, writing sample during interview, letter of recommendation from principal (for educational leadership program only). Additional exam requirements/recommendations for international students: Required—TOEFL (minimum score 575 paper-based; 89 iBT), IELTS (minimum score 6.5). *Application deadline:* For fall admission, 8/15 priority date for domestic students, 8/5 for international students; for spring admission, 12/1 priority date for domestic students, 12/1 for international students; for summer admission, 5/1 priority date for domestic students, 4/15 for international students. Applications are processed on a rolling basis. Application fee: $35. Electronic applications accepted. *Expenses:* $465 per credit plus $110 comprehensive fee per semester. *Financial support:* Tuition waivers (partial) and unspecified assistantships available. Financial award applicants required to submit FAFSA. *Faculty research:* Leadership, action research, brain research, learning styles. *Unit head:* Dr. April M. Boulton, Dean of the Graduate School, 301-696-3612, E-mail: gofurther@hood.edu. *Application contact:* Jan Marcus, Assistant Director of Graduate Admissions, 301-696-3600, E-mail: gofurther@hood.edu.
Website: http://www.hood.edu/academics/education/index.html

Hope International University, School of Graduate and Professional Studies, Program in Education, Fullerton, CA 92831-3138. Offers education administration (MA); elementary education (ME); secondary education (ME). *Program availability:* Part-time, evening/weekend. *Degree requirements:* For master's, comprehensive exam (for some programs), thesis. *Entrance requirements:* For master's, minimum GPA of 3.0, 2 references. Additional exam requirements/recommendations for international students: Required—TOEFL (minimum score 550 paper-based; 86 iBT); Recommended—IELTS (minimum score 6.5). Electronic applications accepted. *Expenses:* Contact institution. *Faculty research:* Distance education.

Houston Baptist University, College of Education and Behavioral Sciences, Programs in Education, Houston, TX 77074-3298. Offers bilingual education (M Ed); counselor education (M Ed); curriculum and instruction (M Ed); curriculum and instruction (EC-6 bilingual) (M Ed); curriculum and instruction in all-level art, Spanish, music, or physical education (M Ed); curriculum and instruction in EC-6 and special education (EC-12) (M Ed); curriculum and instruction in instructional technology (M Ed); curriculum and instruction in mathematics, science, or social studies (4-8) (M Ed); curriculum and instruction with EC-6 generalist (M Ed); curriculum and instruction with English language arts and reading (4-8) (M Ed); educational administration (M Ed); educational diagnostician (M Ed); executive educational leadership (Ed D); higher education in business management (M Ed); higher education in Christian studies (M Ed); higher education in counseling (M Ed); higher education in educational technology (M Ed); reading (M Ed); special educational leadership (Ed D). *Program availability:* Part-time, evening/weekend, 100% online, blended/hybrid learning. *Students:* 83 full-time (65 women), 187 part-time (156 women); includes 189 minority (114 Black or African American, non-Hispanic/Latino; 2 American Indian or Alaska Native, non-Hispanic/Latino; 9 Asian, non-Hispanic/Latino; 58 Hispanic/Latino; 6 Two or more races, non-Hispanic/Latino), 7 international. Average age 36. 309 applicants, 31% accepted, 70 enrolled. In 2017, 92 master's awarded. *Degree requirements:* For master's, comprehensive exam; for doctorate, thesis/dissertation. *Entrance requirements:* For master's, minimum GPA of 2.75, two recommendations, resume, bachelor's degree conferred transcript; interview (for non-certified teachers); for doctorate, GRE, 5 letters of recommendation. Additional exam requirements/recommendations for international students: Required—TOEFL (minimum score 80 iBT), IELTS (minimum score 6.5). *Application deadline:* For fall admission, 8/1 for domestic students, 6/1 for international students; for spring admission, 1/1 for domestic students, 11/1 for international students; for summer admission, 5/1 for domestic students, 3/1 for international students. Applications are processed on a rolling basis. Application fee: $0 ($100 for international students). Electronic applications accepted. Application fee is waived when completed online. *Expenses:* $22,000 tuition; $4,500 fees (general, technology and parking). *Financial support:* In 2017–18, 59 students received support. Research assistantships, teaching assistantships, Federal Work-Study, and scholarships/grants available. Support available to part-time students. Financial award application deadline: 4/1;

financial award applicants required to submit FAFSA. *Faculty research:* Autism and inclusion, integrating technology into instruction, school change and leadership trust. *Unit head:* Dr. Charlotte Fontenot, Director, Graduate Programs, 281-649-3078, Fax: 281-649-3361, E-mail: cfontenot@hbu.edu. *Application contact:* Kristy Wright, Administrative Assistant for Graduate Programs, 281-649-3094, Fax: 281-649-3361, E-mail: kwright@hbu.edu.
Website: http://www.hbu.edu/MED

Howard Payne University, Program in Instructional Leadership, Brownwood, TX 76801-2715. Offers M Ed. *Program availability:* Part-time, evening/weekend, online only. *Degree requirements:* For master's, comprehensive exam (for some programs), thesis or alternative. *Entrance requirements:* For master's, undergraduate degree, valid teaching certificate. Additional exam requirements/recommendations for international students: Required—TOEFL (minimum score 79 iBT). Electronic applications accepted. *Expenses:* Contact institution.

Howard University, School of Education, Department of Educational Leadership and Policy Studies, Washington, DC 20059. Offers educational administration (Ed D); educational administration and supervision (M Ed, CAGS). *Program availability:* Part-time. *Degree requirements:* For master's, comprehensive exam, School Leaders Licensure Assessment, practicum; for doctorate, comprehensive exam, thesis/dissertation, internship; for CAGS, thesis. *Entrance requirements:* For master's, minimum GPA of 2.7; for doctorate, minimum GPA of 3.0. Additional exam requirements/recommendations for international students: Required—TOEFL (minimum score 550 paper-based; 79 iBT). Electronic applications accepted.

Hunter College of the City University of New York, Graduate School, School of Education, Department of Curriculum and Teaching, Program in Educational Supervision and Administration, New York, NY 10065-5085. Offers administration and supervision (AC); instructional leadership (Ed D). *Degree requirements:* For AC, portfolio review. *Entrance requirements:* For degree, minimum B average in graduate course work, teaching certificate, minimum 3 years of full-time teaching experience, interview, 2 letters of support. Additional exam requirements/recommendations for international students: Required—TOEFL. *Faculty research:* Supervision of instruction, theory in action, human relations and leadership.

Husson University, Graduate Nursing Program, Bangor, ME 04401-2999. Offers educational leadership (MSN); family and community nurse practitioner (MSN, PMC); psychiatric mental health nurse practitioner (MSN, PMC). *Accreditation:* AACN. *Program availability:* Part-time, evening/weekend. *Faculty:* 4 full-time (all women), 4 part-time/adjunct (all women). *Students:* 1 full-time (0 women), 62 part-time (54 women); includes 3 minority (2 Black or African American, non-Hispanic/Latino; 1 Hispanic/Latino), 1 international. Average age 36. 62 applicants, 55% accepted, 26 enrolled. In 2017, 9 master's awarded. *Degree requirements:* For master's, comprehensive exam (for some programs), research project. *Entrance requirements:* For master's, proof of RN licensure. Additional exam requirements/recommendations for international students: Required—TOEFL (minimum score 550 paper-based; 80 iBT), IELTS (minimum score 6.5). *Application deadline:* For fall admission, 7/15 for domestic students; for spring admission, 10/30 for domestic students. Application fee: $50. Electronic applications accepted. *Expenses:* $577 per credit; $110 to $480 yearly fee depending on credit load. *Financial support:* In 2017–18, 1 student received support. Federal Work-Study, institutionally sponsored loans, traineeships, and unspecified assistantships available. Financial award application deadline: 3/31; financial award applicants required to submit FAFSA. *Faculty research:* Health disparities and methods to better identify and provide healthcare services to those most in need. *Unit head:* Prof. Mary Jude, Director, Graduate Nursing, 207-941-7769, Fax: 207-941-7198, E-mail: judem@husson.edu. *Application contact:* Kristen Card, Director of Graduate Admissions, 207-404-5660, Fax: 207-941-7935, E-mail: cardk@husson.edu.
Website: http://www.husson.edu/college-of-health-and-education/school-of-nursing/graduate-nursing/

Huston-Tillotson University, Graduate Programs, Austin, TX 78702. Offers educational leadership (M Ed). *Students:* 6 full-time (2 women), 44 part-time (31 women); includes 45 minority (34 Black or African American, non-Hispanic/Latino; 11 Hispanic/Latino). In 2017, 4 master's awarded. Application fee: $100. *Unit head:* Dr. Jan Seiter, Interim Chair, Educator Preparation Program, 512-505-3091, E-mail: jpseiter@htu.edu.

Idaho State University, Office of Graduate Studies, College of Education, Department of School Psychology and Educational Leadership, Pocatello, ID 83209-8059. Offers educational administration (M Ed, 6th Year Certificate, Ed S); educational leadership (Ed D), including higher education administration, K-12 school administration; school psychology (M Ed, Ed S). *Program availability:* Part-time. *Degree requirements:* For master's, comprehensive exam, thesis optional, internship, oral exam or deferred thesis; for doctorate, comprehensive exam, thesis/dissertation, written exam; for other advanced degree, comprehensive exam, thesis (for some programs), written and oral exam. *Entrance requirements:* For master's, MAT, bachelor's degree, minimum GPA of 3.0, 1 year of training experience; for doctorate, GRE General Test or MAT, minimum GPA of 3.0 (undergraduate), 3.5 (graduate); departmental interview; for other advanced degree, GRE General Test, minimum GPA of 3.0, master's degree. Additional exam requirements/recommendations for international students: Required—TOEFL (minimum score 550 paper-based; 80 iBT). Electronic applications accepted. *Faculty research:* Educational leadership, gender issues in education and sport, staff development.

Illinois State University, Graduate School, College of Education, Department of Educational Administration and Foundations, Normal, IL 61790. Offers college student personnel administration (MS); educational administration (MS, MS Ed, Ed D, PhD). *Accreditation:* NCATE. *Degree requirements:* For doctorate, variable foreign language requirement, thesis/dissertation, 2 terms of residency. *Entrance requirements:* For master's, GRE General Test, minimum GPA of 2.6 in last 60 hours of course work; for doctorate, GRE General Test, master's degree or equivalent, minimum GPA of 3.5. *Faculty research:* Illinois Principals Association, special populations professional development and technical assistance project, Illinois state action for education leadership project.

Immaculata University, College of Graduate Studies, Program in Educational Leadership, Immaculata, PA 19345. Offers educational leadership (MA, Ed D); principal (Certificate); secondary education (Certificate); supervisor of special education (Certificate). *Program availability:* Part-time, evening/weekend. *Degree requirements:* For master's, comprehensive exam, thesis optional; for doctorate, comprehensive exam, thesis/dissertation. *Entrance requirements:* For master's, GRE or MAT, minimum GPA of 3.0; for doctorate, GRE General Test or MAT, minimum GPA of 3.5. Additional exam requirements/recommendations for international students: Required—TOEFL. Electronic applications accepted. *Faculty research:* Cooperative learning, school-based management, whole language, performance assessment.

Indiana State University, College of Graduate and Professional Studies, Bayh College of Education, Department of Educational Leadership, Terre Haute, IN 47809. Offers educational administration (PhD); higher education leadership (PhD); K-12 district leadership (PhD); school administration (Ed S); school administration and supervision (M Ed); student affairs and higher education (MS). *Accreditation:* NCATE. *Program*

availability: Part-time, evening/weekend. Terminal master's awarded for partial completion of doctoral program. *Degree requirements:* For master's, thesis; for doctorate, thesis/dissertation. *Entrance requirements:* For master's, GRE General Test, minimum undergraduate GPA of 2.5; for doctorate, GRE General Test, minimum undergraduate GPA of 3.5; for Ed S, GRE General Test, minimum graduate GPA of 3.25. Electronic applications accepted.

Indiana University Bloomington, School of Education, Department of Educational Leadership and Policy Studies, Bloomington, IN 47405. Offers educational leadership (MS, Ed D, Ed S); higher education (Ed D, PhD); higher education and student affairs (MS); history and philosophy of education (MS); history, philosophy, and policy in education (PhD), including education policy studies, history of education, philosophy of education; international and comparative education (MS). *Accreditation:* NCATE. *Degree requirements:* For master's, thesis optional; for doctorate, comprehensive exam, thesis/dissertation; for Ed S, comprehensive exam or project. *Entrance requirements:* For master's, doctorate, and Ed S, GRE General Test. Additional exam requirements/recommendations for international students: Required—TOEFL (minimum score 79 iBT). Electronic applications accepted. *Faculty research:* Culturally engaging campus environments, school choice policy analysis, democracy and education in the national and international context, and principal leadership.

Indiana University Northwest, School of Education, Gary, IN 46408. Offers educational leadership (MS Ed); elementary education (MS Ed); K-12 online teaching (Graduate Certificate); secondary education (MS Ed). *Accreditation:* NCATE. *Program availability:* Part-time, evening/weekend. *Entrance requirements:* For master's, GRE General Test or MAT, minimum GPA of 3.0. Electronic applications accepted. *Expenses:* Contact institution.

Indiana University of Pennsylvania, School of Graduate Studies and Research, College of Education and Communications, Department of Professional Studies in Education, Doctoral Program in Administration and Leadership Studies, Indiana, PA 15705. Offers D Ed. Program also offered jointly with East Stroudsburg University of Pennsylvania. *Program availability:* Part-time, evening/weekend. *Faculty:* 13 full-time (11 women), 3 part-time/adjunct (2 women). *Students:* 2 full-time (both women), 107 part-time (61 women); includes 14 minority (9 Black or African American, non-Hispanic/Latino; 1 American Indian or Alaska Native, non-Hispanic/Latino; 3 Asian, non-Hispanic/Latino; 1 Hispanic/Latino), 4 international. Average age 39. 1 applicant, 100% accepted. In 2017, 23 doctorates awarded. *Degree requirements:* For doctorate, one foreign language, comprehensive exam, thesis/dissertation, written exam. *Entrance requirements:* For doctorate, 2 letters of recommendation, interview. *Application deadline:* Applications are processed on a rolling basis. Application fee: $50. Electronic applications accepted. *Expenses:* Tuition, state resident: full-time $12,000; part-time $500 per credit. Tuition, nonresident: full-time $18,000; part-time $750 per credit. *Required fees:* $4073; $165.55 per credit. $64 per term. *Financial support:* In 2017–18, 10 fellowships with full tuition reimbursements (averaging $496 per year), 7 research assistantships with tuition reimbursements (averaging $4,719 per year) were awarded; teaching assistantships, career-related internships or fieldwork, Federal Work-Study, scholarships/grants, and unspecified assistantships also available. Support available to part-time students. Financial award application deadline: 4/15; financial award applicants required to submit FAFSA. *Unit head:* Dr. Robert Millward, Graduate Coordinator, 724-357-5593, E-mail: robert.millward@iup.edu.
Website: http://www.iup.edu/pse/grad/administration-leadership-studies-ded/default.aspx

Indiana University of Pennsylvania, School of Graduate Studies and Research, College of Education and Communications, Department of Professional Studies in Education, Principal Certification Program, Indiana, PA 15705. Offers Certificate. *Program availability:* Part-time, evening/weekend. *Faculty:* 13 full-time (11 women), 3 part-time/adjunct (2 women). *Students:* 25 part-time (17 women); includes 1 minority (Hispanic/Latino). Average age 39. 29 applicants, 97% accepted, 14 enrolled. *Entrance requirements:* For degree, 2 letters of recommendation. Additional exam requirements/recommendations for international students: Required—TOEFL (minimum score 540 paper-based). *Application deadline:* For fall admission, 7/1 priority date for domestic students; for spring admission, 11/1 for domestic students. Applications are processed on a rolling basis. Application fee: $50. Electronic applications accepted. *Expenses:* Tuition, state resident: full-time $12,000; part-time $500 per credit. Tuition, nonresident: full-time $18,000; part-time $750 per credit. *Required fees:* $4073; $165.55 per credit. $64 per term. *Financial support:* Career-related internships or fieldwork, Federal Work-Study, and scholarships/grants available. Support available to part-time students. Financial award application deadline: 4/15; financial award applicants required to submit FAFSA. *Unit head:* Dr. Susan Sibert, Graduate Coordinator, 724-357-3023, E-mail: susan.sibert@iup.edu.
Website: http://www.iup.edu/pse/programs/principalcert/default.aspx

Indiana University–Purdue University Fort Wayne, College of Education and Public Policy, Department of Professional Studies, Fort Wayne, IN 46805-1499. Offers couple and family counseling (MS Ed); educational leadership (MS Ed); school counseling (MS Ed); special education (MS Ed, Certificate). *Program availability:* Part-time. *Degree requirements:* For master's, comprehensive exam, practicum, internship, portfolio. *Entrance requirements:* For master's, minimum GPA of 2.5, three professional letters of recommendation. Additional exam requirements/recommendations for international students: Required—TOEFL (minimum score 550 paper-based; 79 iBT). *Faculty research:* Learning opportunities with deafness and the hearing impaired, adolescent emotion, student evaluation of teaching.

Indiana University–Purdue University Indianapolis, School of Education, Indianapolis, IN 46202-5155. Offers curriculum and instruction (MS); early childhood (MS); educational leadership (MS, Certificate); English as a second language (Certificate); kindergarten (Certificate); language education (MS); reading (Certificate); school counseling (MS); special education (MS, Certificate). *Program availability:* Part-time, evening/weekend. Terminal master's awarded for partial completion of doctoral program. *Degree requirements:* For master's, thesis optional. *Entrance requirements:* For master's, GRE General Test, minimum GPA of 2.5; for Certificate, official transcripts. Additional exam requirements/recommendations for international students: Required—TOEFL (minimum score 60 iBT), IELTS (minimum score 5.5). Electronic applications accepted. *Expenses:* Contact institution. *Faculty research:* Educational policies and school leaders' responses to these; issues of intersectionality in the experiences of African American lesbian, gay, and bisexual students attending historically black colleges and universities and those who belong to black Greek-letter organizations; students' experiential knowledge and their evolving disciplinary-specific literacy and understanding; innovative program development; urban ESL teacher preparation; target-based instructional coaching.

Indiana University South Bend, School of Education, South Bend, IN 46615. Offers addiction counseling (MS Ed); alcohol and drug counseling (Graduate Certificate); clinical mental health counseling (MS Ed); educational leadership (MS Ed); elementary education (MS Ed); marriage, couple, and family counseling (MS Ed); school counseling (MS Ed); secondary education (MS Ed); special education (MAT, MS Ed), including intense intervention (MS Ed), mild intervention (MS Ed). *Accreditation:* NCATE. *Program availability:* Part-time, evening/weekend. *Degree requirements:* For master's,

Educational Leadership and Administration

thesis or alternative, exit project. *Entrance requirements:* For master's, letters of recommendation, GRE or minimum GPA of 3.0. Additional exam requirements/recommendations for international students: Required—TOEFL. Electronic applications accepted. *Expenses:* Contact institution. *Faculty research:* Professional dispositions, early childhood literacy, online learning, program assessments, problem-based learning.

Indiana Wesleyan University, College of Adult and Professional Studies, School of Educational Leadership, Marion, IN 46953. Offers M Ed, Ed S. *Accreditation:* NCATE. *Program availability:* Part-time, evening/weekend, online learning. *Degree requirements:* For master's, portfolio. *Entrance requirements:* For master's, minimum GPA of 2.75, teaching experience, teaching license. Additional exam requirements/recommendations for international students: Required—TOEFL (minimum score 550 paper-based). Electronic applications accepted. *Faculty research:* Mentoring, performance-based assessments, faith integration, integration of technology, program assessment.

Instituto Tecnologico de Santo Domingo, Graduate School, Area of Humanities and Social Sciences, Santo Domingo, Dominican Republic. Offers accounting (Certificate); adult education (Certificate); applied linguistics (MA); economics (MA); education (M Ed); educational psychology (MA, Certificate); gender and development (MA, Certificate); humanistic studies (MA); international marketing management (Certificate); international relations in the Caribbean basin (Certificate); intervention systems in family therapy (MA); linguistic and literary communication (Certificate); pedagogical support (MA); social science education (M Ed); sustainable human development (MA); terminal illness and death psychology (Certificate); youth and adult education (M Ed).

Instituto Tecnológico y de Estudios Superiores de Monterrey, Campus Central de Veracruz, Graduate Programs, Córdoba, Mexico. Offers administration (MA); administration of information technologies (MTI); computer sciences (MCC); education (MEE); educational institution administration (MAD); educational technology (MTE); electronic commerce (MCE); finance (MAF); humanistic studies (MEH); international business for Latin America (MNL); marketing (MMT); science (MCP). *Program availability:* Part-time, evening/weekend, online learning. *Degree requirements:* For master's, thesis (for some programs). *Entrance requirements:* For master's, PAEP College Board. Electronic applications accepted.

Instituto Tecnológico y de Estudios Superiores de Monterrey, Campus Ciudad Juárez, Program in Educational Administration, Ciudad Juárez, Mexico. Offers MEA.

Instituto Tecnológico y de Estudios Superiores de Monterrey, Campus Estado de México, Professional and Graduate Division, Estado de Mexico, Mexico. Offers administration of information technologies (MITA); architecture (M Arch); business administration (GMBA, MBA); computer sciences (MCS, PhD); education (M Ed); educational institution administration (MAD); educational technology and innovation (PhD); electronic commerce (MEC); environmental systems (MS); finance (MAF); humanistic studies (MHS); information sciences and knowledge management (MISKM); information systems (MS); manufacturing systems (MS); marketing (MEM); quality systems and productivity (MS); science and materials engineering (PhD); telecommunications management (MTM). *Program availability:* Part-time, online learning. *Degree requirements:* For master's, one foreign language, thesis (for some programs); for doctorate, one foreign language, thesis/dissertation. *Entrance requirements:* For master's, E-PAEP 500, interview; for doctorate, E-PAEP 500, research proposal. Additional exam requirements/recommendations for international students: Required—TOEFL (minimum score 550 paper-based). *Faculty research:* Surface treatments by plasmas, mechanical properties, robotics, graphical computing, mechatronics security protocols.

Instituto Tecnológico y de Estudios Superiores de Monterrey, Campus Irapuato, Graduate Programs, Irapuato, Mexico. Offers administration (MBA); administration of information technology (MAIT); administration of telecommunications (MAT); architecture (M Arch); computer science (MCS); education (M Ed); educational administration (MEA); educational innovation and technology (DEIT); educational technology (MET); electronic commerce (MBA); environmental administration and planning (MEAP); environmental systems (MES); finances (MBA); humanistic studies (MHS); international management for Latin American executives (MIMLAE); library and information science (MLIS); manufacturing quality management (MMQM); marketing research (MBA).

Inter American University of Puerto Rico, Aguadilla Campus, Graduate School, Aguadilla, PR 00605. Offers accounting (MBA); counseling psychology specializing in family (MS); criminal justice (MA); educative management and leadership (MA); elementary education (M Ed); finance (MBA); human resources (MBA); industrial management (MBA); management information systems (MBA); marketing (MBA). *Program availability:* Part-time, evening/weekend. *Degree requirements:* For master's, comprehensive exam. *Entrance requirements:* For master's, EXADEP, 2 letters of recommendation, minimum GPA of 2.5. Electronic applications accepted.

Inter American University of Puerto Rico, Arecibo Campus, Programs in Education, Arecibo, PR 00614-4050. Offers administration and educational supervision (MA Ed); counseling and guidance (MA Ed); curriculum and teaching (MA Ed), including biology education, English as a second language, history education, math education, Spanish; elementary education (MA Ed). *Accreditation:* TEAC. *Degree requirements:* For master's, comprehensive exam, thesis optional. *Entrance requirements:* For master's, GRE, EXADEP, bachelor's degree in education or teaching license (administration and supervision) or courses in education and psychology (counseling and guidance), minimum GPA of 2.5 in last 60 credits.

Inter American University of Puerto Rico, Barranquitas Campus, Program in Education, Barranquitas, PR 00794. Offers curriculum and teaching (M Ed), including biology, English as a second language, history, Spanish; educational leadership and management (MA); elementary education (M Ed); information and library service technology (M Ed); special education (MA). *Accreditation:* TEAC. *Program availability:* Part-time, evening/weekend. *Faculty:* 1 full-time (0 women), 3 part-time/adjunct (2 women). *Students:* 17 full-time (16 women), 2 part-time (both women); all minorities (all Hispanic/Latino). Average age 34. 9 applicants, 89% accepted, 8 enrolled. In 2017, 5 master's awarded. *Degree requirements:* For master's, 2 foreign languages, comprehensive exam, thesis (for some programs). *Entrance requirements:* For master's, GRE or EXADEP, bachelor's degree or its equivalent from accredited institution, official academic transcript from institution that conferred bachelor's degree, minimum GPA of 2.5, two recommendation letters, interview (for some programs), essay (for some programs). *Application deadline:* Applications are processed on a rolling basis. Application fee: $31. Electronic applications accepted. *Expenses:* $3,392 full-time tuition plus $652 fees. *Financial support:* Applicants required to submit FAFSA. *Unit head:* Juan A. Negron-Berrios, PhD, Chancellor, 787-857-3600 Ext. 2002, Fax: 787-857-2125, E-mail: janegron@br.inter.edu. *Application contact:* Aramilda Cartagena-Santiago, Dean of Students, 787-857-3600 Ext. 2009, Fax: 787-857-2125, E-mail: aramildacartagena@br.inter.edu.

Inter American University of Puerto Rico, Fajardo Campus, Graduate Programs, Fajardo, PR 00738-7003. Offers computer science (MS); educational management and leadership (MA Ed); general business (MBA); human resources (MBA); management information systems (MBA); marketing (MBA); special education (MA Ed). *Program*

availability: Online learning. *Faculty:* 1 full-time (0 women), 25 part-time/adjunct (13 women). *Students:* 1 (woman) full-time, 126 part-time (81 women).

Inter American University of Puerto Rico, Metropolitan Campus, Graduate Programs, Program in Education, San Juan, PR 00919-1293. Offers curriculum and instruction (Ed D); educational administration (Ed D); guidance and counseling (MA, Ed D); special education administration (Ed D). *Accreditation:* TEAC. *Degree requirements:* For doctorate, comprehensive exam, thesis/dissertation. *Entrance requirements:* For doctorate, GRE, MAT, or EXADEP. Electronic applications accepted.

Iona College, School of Arts and Science, Department of Education, New Rochelle, NY 10801-1890. Offers adolescence education: biology (MS Ed, MST); adolescence education: English (MS Ed); adolescence education: mathematics (MST); adolescence education: social studies (MS Ed, MST); adolescence education: Spanish (MS Ed); adolescence special education 5-12 (MST); childhood and special education (MST); early childhood and childhood (MST); educational leadership (MS Ed). *Accreditation:* NCATE. *Program availability:* Part-time, evening/weekend. *Faculty:* 7 full-time (5 women), 2 part-time/adjunct (1 woman). *Students:* 23 full-time (18 women), 26 part-time (19 women); includes 12 minority (4 Black or African American, non-Hispanic/Latino; 8 Hispanic/Latino). Average age 26. 33 applicants, 97% accepted, 20 enrolled. In 2017, 31 master's awarded. *Degree requirements:* For master's, thesis or alternative. *Entrance requirements:* For master's, minimum GPA of 3.0, NY State teaching certificate and bachelor's degree (for MS Ed). Additional exam requirements/recommendations for international students: Required—TOEFL (minimum score 550 paper-based; 80 iBT), IELTS (minimum score 6.5). *Application deadline:* For fall admission, 8/1 priority date for domestic students, 5/1 priority date for international students; for spring admission, 1/1 priority date for domestic students, 9/1 priority date for international students. Applications are processed on a rolling basis. Electronic applications accepted. Tuition and fees vary according to program. *Financial support:* In 2017–18, 16 students received support. Unspecified assistantships available. Support available to part-time students. Financial award application deadline: 4/15; financial award applicants required to submit FAFSA. *Faculty research:* Engaging teacher educators in scientific process, cross-national comparisons of mathematics teaching, questioning strategies in the classroom, research methods, literacy development. *Unit head:* Margaret Smith, PhD, Chair, 914-633-2210, Fax: 914-633-2608, E-mail: msmith@iona.edu. *Application contact:* Richard McMahon, Coordinator, Graduate School of Education, 914-633-2552, E-mail: rmcmahon@iona.edu.
Website: http://www.iona.edu/Academics/School-of-Arts-Science/Departments/Education/Graduate-Programs.aspx

Iowa State University of Science and Technology, Department of Educational Leadership and Policy Studies, Ames, IA 50011. Offers counselor education (M Ed, MS); educational administration (M Ed, MS); educational leadership (PhD); higher education (M Ed, MS); organizational learning and human resource development (M Ed, MS); research and evaluation (MS); student affairs (MS). *Degree requirements:* For master's, thesis or alternative; for doctorate, thesis/dissertation. *Entrance requirements:* For master's and doctorate, GRE General Test. Additional exam requirements/recommendations for international students: Required—TOEFL (minimum score 560 paper-based; 83 iBT), IELTS (minimum score 6.5). Electronic applications accepted.

Jackson State University, Graduate School, College of Education and Human Development, Department of Educational Leadership, Jackson, MS 39217. Offers education administration and supervision (Ed S); educational administration and supervision (MS Ed, PhD); higher education (Ed S). *Accreditation:* NCATE. *Program availability:* Part-time, evening/weekend, online only, 100% online, blended/hybrid learning. *Degree requirements:* For master's and Ed S, comprehensive exam, thesis; for doctorate, comprehensive exam, thesis/dissertation. *Entrance requirements:* For master's, GRE General Test; for doctorate, MAT, GRE, teaching experience. Additional exam requirements/recommendations for international students: Required—TOEFL (minimum score 520 paper-based; 67 iBT). Electronic applications accepted. *Expenses:* Contact institution.

Jacksonville State University, College of Graduate Studies and Continuing Education, College of Education and Professional Studies, Program in Instructional Leadership, Jacksonville, AL 36265-1602. Offers MS Ed, Ed S. *Accreditation:* NCATE. *Program availability:* Part-time, evening/weekend. *Degree requirements:* For master's, comprehensive exam, thesis (for some programs). *Entrance requirements:* For master's, GRE General Test or MAT. Additional exam requirements/recommendations for international students: Required—TOEFL (minimum score 500 paper-based; 61 iBT). Electronic applications accepted.

Jacksonville University, College of Arts and Sciences, MS in Education Leadership Program, Jacksonville, FL 32211. Offers leadership and learning (MS). *Program availability:* Part-time, evening/weekend. *Faculty:* 22 full-time (11 women), 77 part-time/adjunct (44 women). *Students:* 25 part-time (20 women); includes 8 minority (all Black or African American, non-Hispanic/Latino), 1 international. Average age 36. 1,010 applicants, 100% accepted, 55 enrolled. In 2017, 1,111 master's awarded. *Degree requirements:* For master's, comprehensive exam, practicum. *Entrance requirements:* For master's, GRE or minimum cumulative GPA of 3.3 and 3 years' relative work experience, baccalaureate degree from regionally-accredited institution with minimum GPA of 3.3; official transcripts; 2 letters of recommendation (1 from school principal); statement of professional goals (250-word minimum); resume. Additional exam requirements/recommendations for international students: Required—TOEFL. *Application deadline:* For fall admission, 2/15 priority date for domestic students. Applications are processed on a rolling basis. Application fee: $50. Electronic applications accepted. *Expenses:* $615 per credit hour. *Financial support:* Career-related internships or fieldwork, Federal Work-Study, and institutionally sponsored loans available. Support available to part-time students. Financial award application deadline: 3/15. *Unit head:* Dr. Sandra Coyle, Interim Dean for the College of Arts and Sciences/Professor of English, 904-256-7100, E-mail: scoyle@ju.eduscoyle@ju.edu. *Application contact:* Rakia Naze, Assistant Director of Graduate Admissions, 904-256-7004, E-mail: rnaze@ju.edu.

James Madison University, The Graduate School, College of Education, Program in Education, Harrisonburg, VA 22807. Offers early childhood education (preK-3) (MAT); educational leadership (M Ed); educational technology (M Ed); elementary education (MAT); equity and cultural diversity (M Ed); inclusive early childhood education (MAT); K-8 mathematics specialist (M Ed); middle education (MAT); reading education (M Ed); secondary education (MAT); Spanish language and culture for educators (M Ed); TESOL (MAT). *Accreditation:* NCATE. *Program availability:* Part-time, evening/weekend. *Students:* 260 full-time (233 women), 158 part-time (100 women); includes 48 minority (10 Black or African American, non-Hispanic/Latino; 4 Asian, non-Hispanic/Latino; 26 Hispanic/Latino; 1 Native Hawaiian or other Pacific Islander, non-Hispanic/Latino; 7 Two or more races, non-Hispanic/Latino), 2 international. Average age 30. In 2017, 262 master's awarded. Application fee: $55. Electronic applications accepted. *Expenses:* Tuition, state resident: full-time $10,512; part-time $438 per credit hour. Tuition, nonresident: full-time $28,358; part-time $1162 per credit hour. *Required fees:* $1128. *Financial support:* In 2017–18, 23 students received support, including 1 teaching assistantship; career-related internships or fieldwork, Federal Work-Study, and 22 assistantships (averaging $7911) also available. Financial award application deadline: 3/1; financial award applicants required to submit FAFSA. *Unit head:* Dr.

Phillip M. Wishon, Dean, 540-568-6572, E-mail: wishonpm@jmu.edu. *Application contact:* Lynette D. Michael, Director of Graduate Admissions, 540-568-6131 Ext. 6395, Fax: 540-568-7860, E-mail: michaeld@jmu.edu.
Website: http://www.jmu.edu/coe/index.shtml

Johns Hopkins University, School of Education, Certificate Programs in Education, Baltimore, MD 21218. Offers advanced methods for differentiated instruction and inclusive education (Graduate Certificate); applied behavior analysis (Post-Master's Certificate); clinical mental health counseling (Post-Master's Certificate); counseling (Advanced Certificate); data-based decision making and organizational improvement (Graduate Certificate); early intervention/preschool special education specialist (Graduate Certificate); education of students with autism and other pervasive developmental disorders (Graduate Certificate); educational leadership for independent schools (Graduate Certificate); evidence-based teaching in the health professions (Post-Master's Certificate); gifted education (Graduate Certificate); leadership in technology integration (Graduate Certificate); mind, brain and teaching (Graduate Certificate); school administration and supervision (Graduate Certificate); urban education (Graduate Certificate). *Program availability:* Part-time-only, evening/weekend, 100% online, blended/hybrid learning. *Entrance requirements:* For degree, minimum of bachelor's degree from regionally- or nationally-accredited institution (master's degree for some programs); minimum GPA of 3.0 in all previous programs of study; official transcripts from all post-secondary institutions attended; essay; curriculum vitae/resume; two letters of recommendation; dispositions survey. Electronic applications accepted. *Expenses:* Contact institution.

Johns Hopkins University, School of Education, Doctoral Programs in Education, Baltimore, MD 21218. Offers Ed D, PhD. *Program availability:* Part-time, evening/weekend, 100% online. *Degree requirements:* For doctorate, comprehensive exam, thesis/dissertation. *Entrance requirements:* For doctorate, GRE (for PhD only), master's degree from regionally- or nationally-accredited institution; minimum GPA of 3.0 in previous undergraduate and graduate studies (for Ed D only); official transcripts from all post-secondary institutions attended; three letters of recommendation; curriculum vitae/resume; personal statement; dispositions survey. Additional exam requirements/recommendations for international students: Required—TOEFL (minimum score 600 paper-based; 100 iBT), IELTS (minimum score 7). Electronic applications accepted. *Expenses:* Contact institution.

Johns Hopkins University, School of Education, Master's Programs in Education, Baltimore, MD 21218. Offers counseling (MS), including clinical mental health counseling, school counseling; education (MS), including educational studies, gifted education, reading, school administration and supervision, technology for educators; elementary education (MAT); health professions (M Ed); intelligence analysis (MS); organizational leadership (MS); secondary education (MAT), including biology, chemistry, earth/space science, English, physics, social studies; special education (MS), including early childhood special education, general special education studies, mild to moderate disabilities, severe disabilities. *Program availability:* Part-time, evening/weekend, 100% online, blended/hybrid learning. *Degree requirements:* For master's, comprehensive exam (for some programs), portfolio, capstone project and/or internship; PRAXIS II (subject area assessments) for initial teacher preparation programs that lead to licensure. *Entrance requirements:* For master's (for full-time programs only); PRAXIS I/core or state-approved alternative (for initial teacher preparation programs that lead to licensure), minimum of bachelor's degree from regionally- or nationally-accredited institution; minimum GPA of 3.0 in all previous programs of study; official transcripts from all post-secondary institutions attended; essay; curriculum vitae/resume; letters of recommendation (3 for full-time programs, 2 for part-time programs); dispositions survey. Additional exam requirements/recommendations for international students: Required—TOEFL (minimum score 600 paper-based; 100 iBT), IELTS (minimum score 7). Electronic applications accepted. *Expenses:* Contact institution.

Johnson & Wales University, Graduate Studies, Ed D Program in Educational Leadership, Providence, RI 02903-3703. Offers Ed D. *Program availability:* Part-time. *Degree requirements:* For doctorate, thesis/dissertation. *Entrance requirements:* For doctorate, MAT, minimum GPA of 3.25; master's degree in appropriate field from accredited institution. Additional exam requirements/recommendations for international students: Required—TOEFL (minimum score 550 paper-based); Recommended—IELTS, TWE. *Application deadline:* Applications are processed on a rolling basis. Application fee: $0. *Expenses: Tuition:* Full-time $12,636; part-time $702 per credit hour. *Financial support:* Application deadline: 5/1. *Faculty research:* Site-based management, collaborative learning, technology and education, K-16 education. *Unit head:* Karen Swoboda, Director, 401-598-5139, Fax: 401-598-1162. *Application contact:* Graduate School Admission, 401-598-1015, Fax: 401-598-1286, E-mail: gradadm@jwu.edu.
Website: https://www.jwu.edu/academics/programs-by-campus/providence-programs/educational-leadership-edd.html

Kansas State University, Graduate School, College of Education, Department of Curriculum and Instruction, Manhattan, KS 66506. Offers curriculum and instruction (Ed D, PhD); digital teaching and learning (MS); educational computing, design and online learning (MS); elementary/middle level curriculum and instruction (MS); online learning (Certificate); reading specialist endorsement (MS); reading/language arts (MS); teacher leader/school improvement (MS); teaching and learning (Certificate). *Accreditation:* NCATE. *Program availability:* Part-time, online learning. *Degree requirements:* For master's, comprehensive exam, portfolio, project, report or thesis; for doctorate, comprehensive exam, thesis/dissertation, preliminary exam; for Certificate, comprehensive exam, portfolio. *Entrance requirements:* For master's, minimum GPA of 3.0, 3 letters of recommendation; for doctorate, GRE, minimum GPA of 3.0, 3 letters of recommendation, evidence of scholarly writing; for Certificate, minimum GPA of 3.0, letters of recommendation. Additional exam requirements/recommendations for international students: Required—TOEFL (minimum score 550 paper-based; 80 iBT) or IELTS. Electronic applications accepted. *Faculty research:* Literacy and technology, critical race theory and diversity, achievement gaps, school improvement, teacher education.

Kansas State University, Graduate School, College of Education, Department of Educational Leadership, Manhattan, KS 66506. Offers adult learning (Certificate); educational leadership (MS, Ed D, PhD); leadership dynamics for adult learners (Certificate); qualitative research (Certificate); social justice education (Certificate); teaching English as a second language for adult learners (Certificate). *Accreditation:* NCATE. *Program availability:* Online learning. *Degree requirements:* For master's, comprehensive exam; for doctorate, comprehensive exam, thesis/dissertation. *Entrance requirements:* For master's, minimum undergraduate GPA of 3.0; for doctorate, MAT (for educational administration); GRE General Test (for adult education), minimum GPA of 3.0 in last 60 hours. Additional exam requirements/recommendations for international students: Required—TOEFL. Electronic applications accepted. *Faculty research:* Educational law, school finance, school facilities, organizational leadership, adult learning, distance learning/education.

Kean University, College of Natural, Applied and Health Sciences, Doctorate Program in Nursing Educational Leadership, Union, NJ 07083. Offers educational leadership (PhD). *Accreditation:* ACEN. *Faculty:* 12 full-time (all women). *Students:* 1 (woman) full-time, 19 part-time (17 women); includes 6 minority (5 Black or African American, non-Hispanic/Latino; 1 Asian, non-Hispanic/Latino). Average age 53. *Degree requirements:*

For doctorate, comprehensive exam, thesis/dissertation. *Entrance requirements:* For doctorate, GRE, MSN, minimum cumulative GPA of 3.2 in last degree obtained, official transcripts from all institutions attended, valid RN license, three letters of recommendation, professional resume/curriculum vitae, personal statement. Additional exam requirements/recommendations for international students: Required—TOEFL (minimum score 550 paper-based; 79 iBT), IELTS (minimum score 6.5). *Application deadline:* For fall admission, 5/1 for domestic students; for spring admission, 12/1 for domestic and international students. Application fee: $75. Electronic applications accepted. *Expenses:* Contact institution. *Financial support:* Scholarships/grants and unspecified assistantships available. *Unit head:* Dr. Joan Valas, Program Coordinator, 908-737-6210, E-mail: nursing@kean.edu. *Application contact:* Pedro Lopes, Admissions Counselor, 908-737-7100, E-mail: gradadmissions@kean.edu.
Website: http://grad.kean.edu/doctoral-programs/doctor-nursing-educational-leadership

Kean University, Nathan Weiss Graduate College, Doctorate Program in Educational Leadership, Union, NJ 07083. Offers Ed D. *Program availability:* Part-time. *Faculty:* 3 full-time (2 women). *Students:* 2 full-time (1 woman), 43 part-time (32 women); includes 30 minority (21 Black or African American, non-Hispanic/Latino; 1 American Indian or Alaska Native, non-Hispanic/Latino; 1 Asian, non-Hispanic/Latino; 7 Hispanic/Latino). Average age 44. 15 applicants, 93% accepted, 8 enrolled. In 2017, 8 doctorates awarded. *Degree requirements:* For doctorate, comprehensive exam, thesis/dissertation. *Entrance requirements:* For doctorate, GRE or MAT, master's degree from accredited college or university, minimum GPA of 3.0 in last degree attained, substantial experience working in education or family support agencies, 2 letters of recommendation, personal interview, transcripts, leadership portfolio, resume, letter of endorsement from superintendent or agency director. Additional exam requirements/recommendations for international students: Required—TOEFL (minimum score 550 paper-based; 79 iBT), IELTS (minimum score 6.5). *Application deadline:* For fall admission, 6/30 for domestic and international students. Applications are processed on a rolling basis. Application fee: $75. Electronic applications accepted. *Expenses:* Contact institution. *Financial support:* Scholarships/grants and unspecified assistantships available. Financial award applicants required to submit FAFSA. *Unit head:* Dr. Soundaram Ramaswami, Program Coordinator, 908-737-5979, E-mail: sramaswa@kean.edu. *Application contact:* Brittany Gerstenhaber, Admissions Counselor, 908-737-7100, E-mail: grad-adm@kean.edu.
Website: http://grad.kean.edu/edleadership/edd

Kean University, Nathan Weiss Graduate College, Program in Educational Administration, Union, NJ 07083. Offers school business administrator (MA); supervisor and principal (MA); supervisors, principals, and school business administrators (MA). *Accreditation:* NCATE. *Program availability:* Part-time, 100% online. *Faculty:* 3 full-time (2 women). *Students:* 16 full-time (10 women), 82 part-time (50 women); includes 36 minority (21 Black or African American, non-Hispanic/Latino; 1 Asian, non-Hispanic/Latino; 13 Hispanic/Latino; 1 Two or more races, non-Hispanic/Latino). Average age 35. 33 applicants, 85% accepted, 23 enrolled. In 2017, 23 master's awarded. *Degree requirements:* For master's, comprehensive exam (for some programs), portfolio, field experience, research component, internship, teaching experience. *Entrance requirements:* For master's, GRE General Test or MAT, minimum GPA of 3.0; New Jersey or out-of-state Standard Instructional or Educational Services Certificate; one year of experience under the appropriate certificate; official transcripts from all institutions attended; two letters of recommendation; personal statement; professional resume/curriculum vitae. Additional exam requirements/recommendations for international students: Required—TOEFL (minimum score 550 paper-based; 79 iBT), IELTS (minimum score 6.5). *Application deadline:* For fall admission, 6/30 for domestic and international students; for spring admission, 12/1 for domestic and international students; for summer admission, 5/15 for domestic and international students. Applications are processed on a rolling basis. Application fee: $75. Electronic applications accepted. *Expenses:* Tuition, state resident: full-time $13,419; part-time $653 per credit. Tuition, nonresident: full-time $18,188; part-time $801 per credit. *Required fees:* $3382; $154 per credit. Tuition and fees vary according to course level, course load, degree level and program. *Financial support:* Scholarships/grants and unspecified assistantships available. Financial award applicants required to submit FAFSA. *Unit head:* Dr. Steven Locasio, Program Coordinator, 908-737-5977, E-mail: locascst@kean.edu. *Application contact:* Brittany Gerstenhaber, Admissions Counselor, 908-737-7100, E-mail: gradadmissions@kean.edu.
Website: http://grad.kean.edu/edleadership/ma-combined

Keene State College, School of Professional and Graduate Studies, Keene, NH 03435. Offers curriculum and instruction (M Ed); education leadership (PMC); educational leadership (M Ed); school counselor (M Ed, PMC); special education (M Ed). *Accreditation:* NCATE. *Program availability:* Part-time, evening/weekend. *Faculty:* 6 full-time (3 women), 7 part-time/adjunct (2 women). *Students:* 20 full-time (14 women), 42 part-time (20 women); includes 2 minority (1 Black or African American, non-Hispanic/Latino; 1 Asian, non-Hispanic/Latino), 1 international. Average age 31. 33 applicants, 58% accepted, 17 enrolled. In 2017, 39 master's awarded. *Degree requirements:* For master's, thesis (for some programs). *Entrance requirements:* For master's, PRAXIS I, 3 references; official transcripts; minimum GPA of 2.5; interview; essay; teacher/educator certificate; work/internship experience. Additional exam requirements/recommendations for international students: Required—TOEFL (minimum score 550 paper-based; 61 iBT). *Application deadline:* For fall admission, 4/1 for domestic and international students; for spring admission, 11/1 for domestic and international students; for summer admission, 3/1 for domestic and international students. Applications are processed on a rolling basis. Application fee: $50. Electronic applications accepted. *Expenses:* Tuition, state resident: full-time $9360; part-time $520 per credit. Tuition, nonresident: full-time $10,260; part-time $570 per credit. *Required fees:* $1908; $106 per credit. Tuition and fees vary according to course load. *Financial support:* In 2017–18, 19 students received support. Career-related internships or fieldwork, Federal Work-Study, institutionally sponsored loans, scholarships/grants, and unspecified assistantships available. Support available to part-time students. Financial award application deadline: 3/1; financial award applicants required to submit FAFSA. *Unit head:* Dr. Karrie Kalich, Dean of Professional and Graduate Studies, 603-358-2885, E-mail: kkalich@keene.edu. *Application contact:* Carl Ditkoff, Graduate Program Assistant, 603-358-2497, E-mail: kscgraduatestudies@keene.edu.
Website: http://www.keene.edu/academics/graduate/

Keiser University, Ed S in Educational Leadership Program, Fort Lauderdale, FL 33309. Offers Ed S.
Website: https://www.keiseruniversity.edu/education-specialist-in-educational-leadership-eds/

Keiser University, Joint MS Ed/MBA Program, Fort Lauderdale, FL 33309. Offers MS Ed/MBA.
Website: http://www.keiseruniversity.edu/graduateschool/msed-mba.php

Keiser University, Master of Science in Education Program, Fort Lauderdale, FL 33309. Offers allied health teaching and leadership (MS Ed); career college administration (MS Ed); leadership (MS Ed); online teaching and learning (MS Ed); teaching and learning (MS Ed). *Program availability:* Part-time, online learning. *Unit head:* Brian Keintz, Chair of Graduate Programs.
Website: http://www.keiseruniversity.edu/graduateschool/

Educational Leadership and Administration

Keiser University, PhD in Educational Leadership Program, Fort Lauderdale, FL 33309. Offers PhD.
Website: https://www.keiseruniversity.edu/doctor-of-philosophy-in-educational-leadership-phd/

Kennesaw State University, Leland and Clarice C. Bagwell College of Education, Program in Graduate Education, Kennesaw, GA 30144. Offers educational leadership (M Ed); educational leadership technology (M Ed); elementary and early childhood education (M Ed); instructional technology (M Ed); middle grades education (M Ed); reading (M Ed); secondary education (M Ed); special education (M Ed); teaching English to speakers of other languages (M Ed). *Accreditation:* NCATE. *Program availability:* Part-time. *Degree requirements:* For master's, thesis or alternative. *Entrance requirements:* For master's, GRE General Test, T-4 state certification, minimum GPA of 2.75. Additional exam requirements/recommendations for international students: Required—TOEFL (minimum score 550 paper-based; 80 iBT), IELTS (minimum score 6.5). Electronic applications accepted.

Kennesaw State University, Leland and Clarice C. Bagwell College of Education, Program in Leadership for Learning, Kennesaw, GA 30144. Offers Ed D, Ed S. *Program availability:* Part-time, evening/weekend. *Degree requirements:* For doctorate, thesis/dissertation. *Entrance requirements:* For doctorate, GRE General Test, minimum graduate GPA of 3.0, resume. Additional exam requirements/recommendations for international students: Required—TOEFL (minimum score 550 paper-based; 80 iBT), IELTS (minimum score 6.5). Electronic applications accepted.

Kent State University, College of Education, Health and Human Services, School of Foundations, Leadership and Administration, Program in K-12 Leadership, Kent, OH 44242-0001. Offers M Ed, PhD, Ed S. *Degree requirements:* For master's, thesis optional; for doctorate, comprehensive exam, thesis/dissertation. *Entrance requirements:* For master's, GRE if GPA is below 3.0, 2 letters of reference, goals statement; for doctorate, GRE, minimum master's-level GPA of 3.5, interview, resume, 2 letters of reference, goals statement; for Ed S, GRE. Additional exam requirements/recommendations for international students: Required—TOEFL (minimum score 550 paper-based; 80 iBT). Electronic applications accepted. *Expenses:* Tuition, state resident: full-time $11,310; part-time $515 per credit hour. Tuition, nonresident: full-time $20,396; part-time $928 per credit hour. *International tuition:* $18,544 full-time.

Keystone College, Program in Early Childhood Education Leadership, La Plume, PA 18440. Offers M Ed. *Program availability:* Part-time, blended/hybrid learning. *Faculty:* 1 (woman) full-time, 4 part-time/adjunct (all women). *Students:* 49 part-time (all women); includes 24 minority (6 Black or African American, non-Hispanic/Latino; 1 American Indian or Alaska Native, non-Hispanic/Latino; 17 Hispanic/Latino). 23 applicants, 83% accepted, 18 enrolled. In 2017, 19 master's awarded. *Degree requirements:* For master's, thesis or alternative. *Entrance requirements:* For master's, GRE, college transcripts, resume or curriculum vitae, current clearances. Additional exam requirements/recommendations for international students: Required—TOEFL (minimum score 80 iBT) or IELTS (minimum score 6.5). *Application deadline:* For fall admission, 8/1 for domestic students; for spring admission, 12/1 for domestic students; for summer admission, 5/1 for domestic students. Applications are processed on a rolling basis. Application fee: $0. Electronic applications accepted. *Expenses:* $650 per credit. *Financial support:* Unspecified assistantships available. Financial award application deadline: 5/1; financial award applicants required to submit FAFSA. *Unit head:* Fran Langan, PhD, Dean, School of Professional Studies, 570-945-8472, E-mail: fran.langan@keystone.edu. *Application contact:* Jennifer Sekol, Director of Admissions, 570-945-8117, Fax: 570-945-7916, E-mail: jennifer.sekol@keystone.edu.

Kutztown University of Pennsylvania, College of Education, Program in Student Affairs in Higher Education, Kutztown, PA 19530-0730. Offers M Ed. *Accreditation:* NCATE. *Program availability:* Part-time, evening/weekend. *Faculty:* 1 (woman) full-time, 1 (woman) part-time/adjunct. *Students:* 31 full-time (18 women), 16 part-time (12 women); includes 14 minority (6 Black or African American, non-Hispanic/Latino; 1 Asian, non-Hispanic/Latino; 6 Hispanic/Latino; 1 Two or more races, non-Hispanic/Latino). Average age 26. 37 applicants, 81% accepted, 14 enrolled. In 2017, 15 master's awarded. *Degree requirements:* For master's, comprehensive exam. *Entrance requirements:* For master's, GRE General Test, 3 letters of recommendation, minimum undergraduate GPA of 3.0, department interview, statement of knowledge and experience in student affairs. Additional exam requirements/recommendations for international students: Required—TOEFL (minimum score 550 paper-based, 79 iBT), IELTS (minimum score 6.5), or PTE (minimum score 53). *Application deadline:* For fall admission, 3/1 for domestic and international students; for spring admission, 10/1 for domestic and international students. Application fee: $35. Electronic applications accepted. *Expenses:* Tuition, state resident: part-time $500 per credit. Tuition, nonresident: part-time $750 per credit. *Required fees:* $115 per credit. One-time fee: $50 part-time. Tuition and fees vary according to degree level. *Financial support:* Career-related internships or fieldwork, Federal Work-Study, and unspecified assistantships available. Financial award application deadline: 3/1; financial award applicants required to submit FAFSA. *Unit head:* Dr. Kelley Kenney, Professor, 610-683-4223, E-mail: kenney@kutztown.edu.
Website: https://www.kutztown.edu/academics/graduate-programs/counseling.htm

Lamar University, College of Graduate Studies, College of Education and Human Development, Department of Educational Leadership, Beaumont, TX 77701. Offers digital learning and leading (M Ed); education administration (M Ed); educational leadership (Ed D); educational technology (M Ed). *Program availability:* Part-time, evening/weekend. *Faculty:* 21 full-time (13 women), 10 part-time/adjunct (5 women). *Students:* 9 full-time (6 women), 1,576 part-time (1,093 women); includes 589 minority (242 Black or African American, non-Hispanic/Latino; 9 American Indian or Alaska Native, non-Hispanic/Latino; 17 Asian, non-Hispanic/Latino; 305 Hispanic/Latino; 16 Two or more races, non-Hispanic/Latino), 8 international. Average age 37. 1,961 applicants, 87% accepted, 264 enrolled. In 2017, 709 master's, 68 doctorates awarded. Terminal master's awarded for partial completion of doctoral program. *Degree requirements:* For master's, comprehensive exam, thesis optional; for doctorate, thesis/dissertation. *Entrance requirements:* For master's, GRE General Test, minimum GPA of 2.5; for doctorate, GRE. Additional exam requirements/recommendations for international students: Required—TOEFL (minimum score 550 paper-based; 79 iBT), IELTS (minimum score 6.5). *Application deadline:* For fall admission, 8/10 priority date for domestic students, 7/1 for international students; for spring admission, 1/5 priority date for domestic students, 12/1 for international students. Applications are processed on a rolling basis. Application fee: $25 ($50 for international students). Electronic applications accepted. *Expenses:* Contact institution. *Financial support:* In 2017–18, 3 fellowships (averaging $20,000 per year), 1 research assistantship with tuition reimbursement (averaging $6,500 per year) were awarded; teaching assistantships with tuition reimbursements, career-related internships or fieldwork, and scholarships/grants also available. Support available to part-time students. Financial award application deadline: 4/1; financial award applicants required to submit FAFSA. *Faculty research:* School dropouts, suicide prevention in public school students, school climate and gifted performance, teacher evaluation. *Unit head:* Dr. Kaye Shelton, Director, 409-880-8689, Fax: 409-880-8685. *Application contact:* Deidre Mayer, Interim Director, Admissions and Academic Services, 409-880-8888, Fax: 409-880-7419, E-mail: gradmissions@lamar.edu.
Website: http://education.lamar.edu/educational-leadership

Lamar University, College of Graduate Studies, College of Education and Human Development, Department of Teacher Education, Beaumont, TX 77701. Offers teacher leadership (M Ed). *Faculty:* 14 full-time (13 women), 4 part-time/adjunct (all women). *Students:* 199 part-time (183 women); includes 58 minority (25 Black or African American, non-Hispanic/Latino; 1 American Indian or Alaska Native, non-Hispanic/Latino; 5 Asian, non-Hispanic/Latino; 38 Hispanic/Latino). Average age 37. 148 applicants, 95% accepted, 37 enrolled. In 2017, 99 master's awarded. *Entrance requirements:* Additional exam requirements/recommendations for international students: Required—TOEFL (minimum score 550 paper-based; 79 iBT), IELTS (minimum score 6.5). *Application deadline:* For fall admission, 8/10 for domestic students, 7/1 for international students; for spring admission, 1/5 for domestic and international students. *Expenses:* Contact institution. *Financial support:* Application deadline: 4/1; applicants required to submit FAFSA. *Unit head:* Dr. Lulu Henry, 409-880-8217, Fax: 409-880-7788. *Application contact:* Deidre Mayer, Interim Director, Admissions and Academic Services, 409-880-8888, Fax: 409-880-7419, E-mail: gradmissions@lamar.edu.
Website: http://education.lamar.edu/teacher-education

La Salle University, School of Arts and Sciences, Program in Education, Philadelphia, PA 19141-1199. Offers autism spectrum disorders (MA, Certificate); bilingual/bicultural studies (MA); classroom management (MA); dual early childhood and special education (MA); dual middle-level science and math and special education (MA); education (MA); English (MA); English as a second language (Certificate); history (MA); instructional coach (Certificate); instructional leadership (MA); reading specialist (MA, Certificate); secondary education (MA); special education (MA, Certificate). *Program availability:* Part-time, evening/weekend. *Faculty:* 5 full-time (4 women), 8 part-time/adjunct (5 women). *Students:* 2 full-time (1 woman), 110 part-time (81 women); includes 23 minority (11 Black or African American, non-Hispanic/Latino; 1 Asian, non-Hispanic/Latino; 7 Hispanic/Latino; 4 Two or more races, non-Hispanic/Latino). Average age 33. 137 applicants, 70% accepted, 63 enrolled. In 2017, 148 master's awarded. *Degree requirements:* For master's, comprehensive exam. *Entrance requirements:* For master's, MAT or GRE, 2 letters of recommendation; for Certificate, GMAT or GRE, 2 letters of recommendation. Additional exam requirements/recommendations for international students: Required—TOEFL. *Application deadline:* For fall admission, 8/15 priority date for domestic students, 7/15 for international students; for spring admission, 12/15 priority date for domestic students, 11/15 for international students; for summer admission, 4/15 priority date for domestic students, 3/15 for international students. Applications are processed on a rolling basis. Application fee: $35. Electronic applications accepted. Application fee is waived when completed online. *Expenses:* Contact institution. *Financial support:* In 2017–18, 19 students received support. Scholarships/grants available. Support available to part-time students. Financial award application deadline: 8/31; financial award applicants required to submit FAFSA. *Unit head:* Dr. Greer Richardson, Director, 215-951-1806, Fax: 215-951-1843, E-mail: graded@lasalle.edu. *Application contact:* Elizabeth Heenan, Director, Graduate and Adult Enrollment, 215-951-1100, Fax: 215-951-1462, E-mail: heenan@lasalle.edu.
Website: http://www.lasalle.edu/grad-education-programs/

Lasell College, Graduate and Professional Studies in Education, Newton, MA 02466-2709. Offers curriculum, leadership, and inclusion (M Ed); elementary education (M Ed); special education (M Ed), including moderate disabilities; teaching bilingual/English learners with disabilities (Graduate Certificate). *Program availability:* Part-time-only, evening/weekend, blended/hybrid learning. *Faculty:* 3 full-time (all women), 5 part-time/adjunct (4 women). *Students:* 8 full-time (7 women), 43 part-time (38 women); includes 4 minority (2 Asian, non-Hispanic/Latino; 1 Hispanic/Latino; 1 Two or more races, non-Hispanic/Latino), 1 international. Average age 28. 23 applicants, 74% accepted, 10 enrolled. In 2017, 15 master's awarded. *Degree requirements:* For master's, minimum GPA of 3.0; practicum. *Entrance requirements:* For master's, Massachusetts Tests for Educator Licensure (MTEL) Curriculum and Literacy foundations of reading and writing subtest, one-page personal statement, 2 letters of recommendation, resume, bachelor's degree transcript. Additional exam requirements/recommendations for international students: Required—TOEFL (minimum score 550 paper-based, 79 iBT) or IELTS (minimum score 6). *Application deadline:* For fall admission, 8/31 priority date for domestic students, 6/30 priority date for international students; for spring admission, 12/31 priority date for domestic students, 10/31 priority date for international students. Applications are processed on a rolling basis. Electronic applications accepted. *Expenses:* $600 per credit. *Financial support:* Federal Work-Study, scholarships/grants, and tuition discounts available. Support available to part-time students. Financial award application deadline: 8/31; financial award applicants required to submit FAFSA. *Faculty research:* Inclusion, English language learners, literacy, and urban education; teacher inquiry; universal design for learning, deaf-blindness, and visual impairments; social and emotional learning; educational law, applied behavior analysis, and classroom management. *Unit head:* Eric Turner, Vice President of Graduate and Professional Studies, 617-243-2071, Fax: 617-243-2450, E-mail: gradinfo@lasell.edu. *Application contact:* Adrienne Franciosi, Director of Graduate Enrollment, 617-243-2214, Fax: 617-243-2450, E-mail: gradinfo@lasell.edu.
Website: http://www.lasell.edu/academics/graduate-and-professional-studies/programs-of-study/master-of-education.html

La Sierra University, School of Education, Department of Administration and Leadership, Riverside, CA 92505. Offers MA, Ed D, Ed S. *Program availability:* Part-time, evening/weekend. Terminal master's awarded for partial completion of doctoral program. *Degree requirements:* For master's, thesis optional; for doctorate, thesis/dissertation, fieldwork, qualifying exam; for Ed S, thesis optional, fieldwork. *Entrance requirements:* For master's, minimum GPA of 3.0; for doctorate, GRE General Test, GRE Subject Test, minimum GPA of 3.3, Ed S; for Ed S, master's degree, minimum GPA of 3.3.

Lee University, Program in Education, Cleveland, TN 37320-3450. Offers art (MAT); curriculum and instruction (M Ed, Ed S); early childhood (MAT); educational leadership (M Ed, Ed S); elementary education (MAT); English and math (MAT); English and science (MAT); English and social studies (MAT); higher education administration (MS); history (MAT); history and economics (MAT); math and science (MAT); math and social studies (MAT); middle grades (MAT); science and social studies (MASW); secondary education (MAT); Spanish (MAT); special education (M Ed, MAT); TESOL (MAT). *Accreditation:* NCATE. *Program availability:* Part-time. *Faculty:* 15 full-time (7 women), 8 part-time/adjunct (3 women). *Students:* 28 full-time (21 women), 77 part-time (48 women); includes 12 minority (7 Black or African American, non-Hispanic/Latino; 2 Hispanic/Latino; 3 Two or more races, non-Hispanic/Latino), 1 international. Average age 31. 35 applicants, 83% accepted, 22 enrolled. In 2017, 54 master's, 4 other advanced degrees awarded. *Degree requirements:* For master's, variable foreign language requirement, thesis optional, internship. *Entrance requirements:* For master's, MAT or GRE General Test, minimum undergraduate GPA of 2.75, 3 letters of recommendation, interview, writing sample, official transcripts, background check; for Ed S, minimum undergraduate and master's GPA of 2.75, official transcripts for undergraduate and master's degrees. Additional exam requirements/recommendations for international students: Required—TOEFL (minimum score 61 iBT). *Application deadline:* For fall admission, 6/1 priority date for domestic and international students; for spring admission, 11/1 priority date for domestic and international students; for summer

admission, 4/1 priority date for domestic and international students. Applications are processed on a rolling basis. Application fee: $25. Electronic applications accepted. *Expenses: Tuition:* Full-time $12,780; part-time $710 per credit hour. *Required fees:* $60; $60 per term. Tuition and fees vary according to program. *Financial support:* In 2017–18, 32 students received support. Career-related internships or fieldwork, Federal Work-Study, institutionally sponsored loans, scholarships/grants, and unspecified assistantships available. Financial award application deadline: 3/1; financial award applicants required to submit FAFSA. *Unit head:* Dr. William Kamm, Director, 423-614-8544, E-mail: wkamm@leeuniversity.edu. *Application contact:* Crystal Keeter, Graduate Education Secretary, 423-614-8544, E-mail: ckeeter@leeuniversity.edu.
Website: http://www.leeuniversity.edu/academics/graduate/education

Lehigh University, College of Education, Program in Educational Leadership, Bethlehem, PA 18015. Offers curriculum and instruction (Certificate); educational leadership (M Ed, Ed D); K-12 principal (Certificate); superintendent letter (Certificate). *Program availability:* Part-time, evening/weekend, online learning. *Faculty:* 5 full-time (2 women), 7 part-time/adjunct (3 women). *Students:* 6 full-time (5 women), 111 part-time (70 women); includes 14 minority (1 Black or African American, non-Hispanic/Latino; 1 Asian, non-Hispanic/Latino; 12 Hispanic/Latino), 6 international. Average age 34. 82 applicants, 67% accepted, 9 enrolled. In 2017, 52 master's, 9 Certificates awarded. Terminal master's awarded for partial completion of doctoral program. *Degree requirements:* For master's, thesis (for some programs); for doctorate, comprehensive exam, thesis/dissertation. *Entrance requirements:* For master's, minimum undergraduate GPA of 3.0, essay, transcripts, 2 letters of recommendation; for doctorate, GRE General Test or MAT, minimum graduate GPA of 3.6, 2 letters of recommendation, essay, transcript; for Certificate, minimum undergraduate GPA of 3.0. Additional exam requirements/recommendations for international students: Required—TOEFL (minimum score 600 paper-based, 93 iBT) or IELTS. *Application deadline:* For fall admission, 1/15 for domestic and international students; for spring admission, 12/1 for domestic and international students; for summer admission, 5/1 for domestic and international students. Applications are processed on a rolling basis. Application fee: $65. Electronic applications accepted. *Expenses:* $565 per credit; $225 internship fee. *Financial support:* In 2017–18, 18 students received support, including 3 research assistantships (averaging $8,092 per year); fellowships and unspecified assistantships also available. Financial award application deadline: 1/31; financial award applicants required to submit FAFSA. *Faculty research:* Supervision of instruction, middle-level education, organizational change, leadership preparation and development, international school leadership, urban school leadership, comparative education, social justice, education and human services, social network, principal leadership, policy implementation, teacher evaluation, teaching quality. *Unit head:* Dr. Floyd D. Beachum, Director, 610-758-5955, Fax: 610-758-3227, E-mail: fdb209@lehigh.edu. *Application contact:* Kristi Ball, Coordinator, 610-758-3250, Fax: 610-758-6223, E-mail: kmb618@lehigh.edu.
Website: https://ed.lehigh.edu/academics/programs/educational-leadership

Le Moyne College, Department of Education, Syracuse, NY 13214. Offers adolescent education (MS Ed, MST); adolescent education/special education (MS Ed, MST); adolescent English (MST), including grades 7-12; adolescent English/special education (MST), including grades 7-12; adolescent foreign language (MST), including grades 7-12; adolescent history (MST), including grades 7-12; childhood education (MS Ed); childhood education/special education (MS Ed); elementary education (MS Ed); general education (MS Ed); inclusive childhood education (MST); literacy education (MS Ed), including birth to grade 6, grades 5-12; school building leader (MS Ed); school building leadership (CAS); school district business leader (MS Ed, CAS); school district leader (MS Ed); school district leadership (CAS); secondary education (MS Ed); special education (MS Ed); teaching English to speakers of other languages (MS Ed); urban studies (MS Ed). *Accreditation:* TEAC. *Program availability:* Part-time, evening/weekend. *Faculty:* 7 full-time (5 women), 20 part-time/adjunct (12 women). *Students:* 30 full-time (19 women), 126 part-time (93 women); includes 15 minority (7 Black or African American, non-Hispanic/Latino; 1 American Indian or Alaska Native, non-Hispanic/Latino; 1 Asian, non-Hispanic/Latino; 6 Hispanic/Latino), 4 international. Average age 29. 139 applicants, 65% accepted, 76 enrolled. In 2017, 82 master's, 43 CASs awarded. *Degree requirements:* For master's, thesis. *Entrance requirements:* For master's, bachelor's degree with minimum undergraduate GPA of 3.0, 2 letters of recommendation, transcripts. Additional exam requirements/recommendations for international students: Required—TOEFL (minimum score 550 paper-based; 79 iBT); Recommended—IELTS (minimum score 6.5). *Application deadline:* For fall admission, 4/1 priority date for domestic and international students; for spring admission, 10/1 priority date for domestic and international students; for summer admission, 3/1 priority date for domestic and international students. Applications are processed on a rolling basis. Application fee: $50. Electronic applications accepted. *Expenses:* $700 per credit hour. *Financial support:* In 2017–18, 30 students received support. Career-related internships or fieldwork, scholarships/grants, and health care benefits available. Support available to part-time students. Financial award applicants required to submit FAFSA. *Faculty research:* Minority teachers, special education, multiculturalism, literacy, technology, media literacy learning, autism, school district organization, service-learning, higher level problem solving, teacher leadership. *Unit head:* Dr. Stephen C. Fleury, Chair, Department of Education, 315-445-4376, Fax: 315-445-4744, E-mail: fleurysc@lemoyne.edu. *Application contact:* Kristen P. Richards, Senior Director of Enrollment Management, 315-445-5444, Fax: 315-445-6092, E-mail: trapaskp@lemoyne.edu.
Website: http://www.lemoyne.edu/education

Lenoir-Rhyne University, Graduate Programs, School of Education, Program in Leadership, Hickory, NC 28601. Offers community and nonprofit leadership (MA); general management (MA); higher education leadership (MA); second language community services (MA). *Program availability:* Online learning. *Entrance requirements:* Additional exam requirements/recommendations for international students: Required—TOEFL (minimum score 600 paper-based). Electronic applications accepted. *Expenses:* Contact institution.

Lesley University, Graduate School of Education, Cambridge, MA 02138-2790. Offers arts, community, and education (M Ed); autism studies (Certificate); curriculum and instruction (M Ed, CAGS); early childhood education (M Ed); ecological teaching and learning (MS); educational studies (PhD), including adult learning, educational leadership, individually designed; elementary education (M Ed); emergent technologies for educators (Certificate); ESLArts: language learning through the arts (M Ed); high school education (M Ed); individually designed (M Ed); integrated teaching through the arts (M Ed); literacy for K-8 classroom teachers (M Ed); mathematics education (M Ed); middle school education (M Ed); moderate disabilities (M Ed); online learning (Certificate); reading (CAGS); science in education (M Ed); severe disabilities (M Ed); special needs (CAGS); specialist teacher of reading (M Ed); teacher of visual art (M Ed); technology in education (M Ed, CAGS). *Accreditation:* TEAC. *Program availability:* Part-time, evening/weekend, online learning. *Degree requirements:* For master's, practicum; for doctorate, thesis/dissertation. *Entrance requirements:* For master's, Massachusetts Tests for Educator Licensure (MTEL), transcripts, statement of purpose, recommendations; interview (for special education); for doctorate, GRE General Test, transcripts, statement of purpose, recommendations, interview, master's degree,

resume; for other advanced degree, interview, master's degree. Additional exam requirements/recommendations for international students: Required—TOEFL (minimum score 550 paper-based; 80 iBT). Electronic applications accepted. *Faculty research:* Assessment in literacy, mathematics and science; autism spectrum disorders; instructional technology and online learning; multicultural education and English language learners.

LeTourneau University, Graduate Programs, Longview, TX 75607-7001. Offers business (MBA); counseling (MA), including licensed professional counselor, marriage and family therapy, school counseling; curriculum and instruction (M Ed); educational administration (M Ed); engineering (ME, MS); engineering management (MEM); health care administration (MS); marriage and family therapy (MA); psychology (MA); strategic leadership (MSL); teacher leadership (M Ed); teaching and learning (M Ed). *Program availability:* Part-time, 100% online, blended/hybrid learning. *Students:* 55 full-time (35 women), 337 part-time (266 women); includes 218 minority (140 Black or African American, non-Hispanic/Latino; 2 American Indian or Alaska Native, non-Hispanic/Latino; 5 Asian, non-Hispanic/Latino; 32 Hispanic/Latino; 39 Two or more races, non-Hispanic/Latino), 3 international. Average age 37. *Entrance requirements:* Additional exam requirements/recommendations for international students: Required—TOEFL. *Application deadline:* For fall admission, 8/22 for domestic students, 8/29 for international students; for winter admission, 10/10 for domestic students; for spring admission, 1/2 for domestic students, 1/10 for international students; for summer admission, 5/1 for domestic and international students. Applications are processed on a rolling basis. Electronic applications accepted. *Expenses:* Contact institution. *Financial support:* Research assistantships, institutionally sponsored loans, and unspecified assistantships available. Financial award applicants required to submit FAFSA.
Website: http://www.letu.edu

Lewis & Clark College, Graduate School of Education and Counseling, Department of Educational Leadership, Program in Educational Leadership, Portland, OR 97219-7899. Offers educational administration (M Ed, Ed S); educational leadership (Ed D); student affairs administration (MA). *Program availability:* Part-time, evening/weekend. *Degree requirements:* For doctorate, thesis/dissertation. *Entrance requirements:* For master's, minimum undergraduate GPA of 2.75, Oregon teaching or personnel service license, three years of successful teaching and/or personnel service experience in the public schools or regionally-accredited private schools; for doctorate, master's degree plus minimum of 14 degree-applicable, post-master's semester credits; minimum undergraduate GPA of 2.75. Additional exam requirements/recommendations for international students: Required—TOEFL (minimum score 575 paper-based). Electronic applications accepted.

Lewis University, College of Education, Program in Educational Leadership for Teaching and Learning, Romeoville, IL 60446. Offers Ed D. *Program availability:* Part-time-only, evening/weekend. *Students:* 57 part-time (33 women); includes 28 minority (19 Black or African American, non-Hispanic/Latino; 1 Asian, non-Hispanic/Latino; 8 Hispanic/Latino), 1 international. Average age 43. *Degree requirements:* For doctorate, thesis/dissertation. *Entrance requirements:* For doctorate, master's degree, letters of recommendation, personal statement, academic and scholarly work, interview. Additional exam requirements/recommendations for international students: Required—TOEFL (minimum score 550 paper-based; 79 iBT), IELTS (minimum score 6). *Application deadline:* For fall admission, 5/1 priority date for international students; for spring admission, 11/1 priority date for international students. Application fee: $40. Electronic applications accepted. Tuition and fees vary according to program. *Financial support:* Federal Work-Study, institutionally sponsored loans, scholarships/grants, and unspecified assistantships available. Financial award application deadline: 5/1; financial award applicants required to submit FAFSA. *Unit head:* Dr. Lauren Hoffman, Director, 815-838-0500 Ext. 5501, E-mail: hoffmala@lewisu.edu. *Application contact:* Nina Nowaczyk, Assistant Director, Graduate Admission, 815-836-5610, E-mail: grad@lewisu.edu.

Lewis University, College of Education, Program in Educational Leadership with Principal Preparation Endorsement, Romeoville, IL 60446. Offers M Ed, MA. *Program availability:* Part-time, evening/weekend. *Students:* 10 part-time (3 women); includes 2 minority (both Black or African American, non-Hispanic/Latino). Average age 34. *Degree requirements:* For master's, departmental qualifying exams. *Entrance requirements:* For master's, bachelor's degree, minimum GPA of 2.75, two letters of recommendation, resume, interview, four years' teaching experience, portfolio. Additional exam requirements/recommendations for international students: Required—TOEFL (minimum score 550 paper-based; 79 iBT), IELTS (minimum score 6). *Application deadline:* For fall admission, 5/1 priority date for international students; for spring admission, 11/15 priority date for international students. Applications are processed on a rolling basis. Application fee: $40. Electronic applications accepted. Tuition and fees vary according to program. *Financial support:* Career-related internships or fieldwork, Federal Work-Study, scholarships/grants, and unspecified assistantships available. Financial award application deadline: 5/1; financial award applicants required to submit FAFSA. *Unit head:* Dr. Lauren Hoffman, Director, 815-838-0500 Ext. 5501, Fax: 815-836-5879, E-mail: hoffmala@lewisu.edu. *Application contact:* Nina Nowaczyk, Assistant Director, Graduate Admission, 815-836-5610, E-mail: grad@lewisu.edu.

Lewis University, College of Education, Program in Educational Leadership with Teacher Leader Endorsement, Romeoville, IL 60446. Offers M Ed. *Program availability:* Part-time, evening/weekend. *Students:* 1 full-time (0 women), 4 part-time (3 women), 1 international. Average age 34. *Degree requirements:* For master's, comprehensive exam. *Entrance requirements:* For master's, bachelor's degree, minimum GPA of 2.75, two letters of recommendation, resume, interview, three years' teaching experience, portfolio. Additional exam requirements/recommendations for international students: Required—TOEFL (minimum score 550 paper-based; 79 iBT), IELTS (minimum score 6). *Application deadline:* For fall admission, 5/1 priority date for international students; for spring admission, 11/1 priority date for international students. Application fee: $40. Electronic applications accepted. Tuition and fees vary according to program. *Financial support:* Federal Work-Study and unspecified assistantships available. Financial award application deadline: 5/1; financial award applicants required to submit FAFSA. *Unit head:* Dr. Pamela Jessee, Dean, 815-836-5316, E-mail: jesseepa@lewisu.edu. *Application contact:* Nina Nowaczyk, Assistant Director, Graduate Admissions, 815-836-5610, E-mail: grad@lewisu.edu.
Website: http://www.lewisu.edu/academics/grad-education/teacherleadership/index.htm

Liberty University, School of Education, Lynchburg, VA 24515. Offers curriculum and instruction (Ed D, Ed S), including elementary education, middle grades education, secondary education, special education; educational leadership (Ed D); gifted education (Certificate); math specialist (M Ed); middle grades (MAT, Certificate); reading specialist (M Ed); school leadership (Certificate); secondary education (MAT); sport management (MS), including coaching and athletic administration, outdoor adventure sport, sport administration, tourism. *Accreditation:* NCATE. *Program availability:* Part-time, online learning. *Students:* 1,966 full-time (1,428 women), 3,484 part-time (2,528 women); includes 1,323 minority (1,026 Black or African American, non-Hispanic/Latino; 29 American Indian or Alaska Native, non-Hispanic/Latino; 49 Asian, non-Hispanic/Latino; 100 Hispanic/Latino; 9 Native Hawaiian or other Pacific Islander, non-Hispanic/Latino; 110 Two or more races, non-Hispanic/Latino), 58 international. Average age 37. 3,748

Educational Leadership and Administration

applicants, 58% accepted, 1167 enrolled. In 2017, 656 master's, 110 doctorates, 316 other advanced degrees awarded. *Degree requirements:* For doctorate, comprehensive exam, thesis/dissertation. *Entrance requirements:* For master's, GRE General Test or MAT (if taken in or before 1999), 2 letters of recommendation, minimum undergraduate GPA of 3.0, curriculum vitae; for doctorate and other advanced degree, GRE General Test or MAT (if taken before 1999), minimum master's GPA of 3.0, 3 years of teaching experience. Additional exam requirements/recommendations for international students: Required—TOEFL (minimum score 600 paper-based; 100 iBT). *Application deadline:* For fall admission, 6/1 for domestic students; for spring admission, 11/1 for domestic students. Applications are processed on a rolling basis. Application fee: $50. Electronic applications accepted. *Expenses:* Contact institution. *Financial support:* Federal Work-Study and tuition waivers (partial) available. *Faculty research:* Self-determination, character education, bibliotherapy, learning styles, distance education. *Unit head:* Dr. Heather Schoffstall, Dean, 434-582-2445, Fax: 434-582-2468, E-mail: awgunter@liberty.edu. *Application contact:* Jay Bridge, Director of Graduate Admissions, 800-424-9595, Fax: 800-628-7977, E-mail: gradadmissions@liberty.edu.
Website: http://www.liberty.edu/academics/education/graduate/

Lincoln Memorial University, Carter and Moyers School of Education, Harrogate, TN 37752-1901. Offers administration and supervision (M Ed, Ed S); counseling and guidance (M Ed); curriculum and instruction (M Ed, Ed D, Ed S); English (M Ed); executive leadership (Ed D); higher education administration (Ed D); human resource development (Ed D); leadership and administration (Ed D). *Program availability:* Part-time, evening/weekend, online learning. *Degree requirements:* For master's, comprehensive exam, thesis optional; for Ed S, comprehensive exam. *Entrance requirements:* For master's, PRAXIS, NTE, GRE, MAT, letters of recommendation; for Ed S, graduate transcripts. Additional exam requirements/recommendations for international students: Recommended—TOEFL. *Faculty research:* Brain compatible teaching and learning; poverty in Appalachia; leadership for change; ethics, moral responsibility and social justice; human and organizational learning.

Lincoln University, Graduate Programs, Philadelphia, PA 19104. Offers counseling (MSC); early childhood education (M Ed), including PreK-4; early childhood education and special education (M Ed); educational leadership (M Ed), including principal certification; finance (MBA); human resources management (MBA); human services delivery (MAHS). *Program availability:* Part-time, evening/weekend. *Faculty:* 9 full-time (3 women), 25 part-time/adjunct (15 women). *Students:* 196 full-time (138 women), 68 part-time (46 women); includes 236 minority (227 Black or African American, non-Hispanic/Latino; 1 American Indian or Alaska Native, non-Hispanic/Latino; 7 Hispanic/Latino; 1 Two or more races, non-Hispanic/Latino), 3 international. Average age 34. 120 applicants, 100% accepted, 95 enrolled. In 2017, 126 master's awarded. *Degree requirements:* For master's, comprehensive exam, thesis al alternative, capstone, grant proposal. *Entrance requirements:* For master's, official academic transcript(s), letters of recommendation, personal statement, resume, supervisor's evaluation form. Additional exam requirements/recommendations for international students: Recommended—TOEFL (minimum score 500 paper-based; 71 iBT), IELTS. *Application deadline:* For fall admission, 8/1 priority date for domestic students, 7/1 priority date for international students; for spring admission, 12/1 priority date for domestic students, 10/1 for international students. Applications are processed on a rolling basis. Application fee: $50. Electronic applications accepted. *Expenses:* Contact institution. *Financial support:* Scholarships/grants available. Financial award application deadline: 6/30; financial award applicants required to submit FAFSA. *Unit head:* Dr. Patricia Pierce Ramsey, Provost, 484-365-7437, Fax: 484-365-8108, E-mail: provost@lincoln.edu. *Application contact:* Jernice Lea, Director, University City Student Services and Admissions, 215-590-8231, Fax: 215-387-3859, E-mail: jlea@lincoln.edu.
Website: http://www.lincoln.edu/admissions/graduate-admissions

Lindenwood University, Graduate Programs, School of Education, St. Charles, MO 63301-1695. Offers behavioral analysis (MA); education (MA), including autism spectrum disorders, character education, early intervention in autism and sensory impairment, gifted, technology; educational administration (MA, Ed D, Ed S); English to speakers of other languages (MA); instructional leadership (Ed D, Ed S); library media (MA); professional counseling (MA); school administration (MA, Ed S); school counseling (MA); teaching (MA). *Program availability:* Part-time, evening/weekend, 100% online, blended/hybrid learning. *Faculty:* 47 full-time (31 women), 213 part-time/adjunct (135 women). *Students:* 434 full-time (319 women), 1,292 part-time (989 women); includes 387 minority (313 Black or African American, non-Hispanic/Latino; 9 American Indian or Alaska Native, non-Hispanic/Latino; 13 Asian, non-Hispanic/Latino; 37 Hispanic/Latino; 1 Native Hawaiian or other Pacific Islander, non-Hispanic/Latino; 14 Two or more races, non-Hispanic/Latino), 20 international. Average age 36. 828 applicants, 61% accepted, 378 enrolled. In 2017, 431 master's, 63 doctorates, 94 other advanced degrees awarded. *Degree requirements:* For master's, thesis (for some programs), minimum GPA of 3.0; for doctorate, thesis/dissertation, minimum GPA of 3.0; for Ed S, comprehensive exam, project, minimum GPA of 3.0. *Entrance requirements:* For master's, interview, minimum undergraduate cumulative GPA of 3.0, writing sample, letter of recommendation; for doctorate, GRE, minimum graduate GPA of 3.4, resume, interview, writing sample, 4 letters of recommendation; for Ed S, master's degree in education, relevant work experience. Additional exam requirements/recommendations for international students: Required—TOEFL (minimum score 550 paper-based; 80 iBT); Recommended—IELTS (minimum score 6.5). *Application deadline:* For fall admission, 8/27 priority date for domestic and international students; for spring admission, 1/14 priority date for domestic and international students; for summer admission, 6/4 priority date for domestic and international students. Applications are processed on a rolling basis. Application fee: $30 ($100 for international students). Electronic applications accepted. *Expenses: Tuition:* Full-time $16,300; part-time $460 per credit. *Required fees:* $660; $330 per credit. Tuition and fees vary according to degree level and program. *Financial support:* In 2017–18, 1,615 students received support. Career-related internships or fieldwork, Federal Work-Study, institutionally sponsored loans, scholarships/grants, tuition waivers (partial), and unspecified assistantships available. Financial award application deadline: 6/30; financial award applicants required to submit FAFSA. *Unit head:* Dr. Anthony Scheffler, Dean, School of Education, 636-949-4618, Fax: 636-949-4197, E-mail: ascheffler@lindenwood.edu. *Application contact:* Kara Schilli, Director, Evening and Graduate Admissions, 636-949-4349, Fax: 636-949-4109, E-mail: adultadmissions@lindenwood.edu.
Website: http://www.lindenwood.edu/academics/academic-schools/school-of-education/

Lindenwood University–Belleville, Graduate Programs, Belleville, IL 62226. Offers business administration (MBA); communications (MA), including digital and multimedia, media management, promotions, training and development; counseling (MA); criminal justice administration (MS); education (MA); healthcare administration (MS); human resource management (MS); school administration (MA); teaching (MAT).

Lindsey Wilson College, Division of Education, Columbia, KY 42728. Offers teacher as leader (M Ed). *Program availability:* Online learning. *Entrance requirements:* For master's, bachelor's degree from accredited institution, minimum undergraduate GPA of 3.0, letters of recommendation.

Lipscomb University, College of Education, Nashville, TN 37204-3951. Offers applied behavior analysis (MS, Certificate); coaching for learning (M Ed, Certificate, Ed S);

educational leadership (M Ed, Ed S); English language learning (M Ed, Ed S); instructional coaching (M Ed, Certificate, Ed S); instructional practice (M Ed); learning organizations and strategic change (Ed D); literacy coaching (Certificate, Ed S); reading specialty (M Ed, Ed S); school counseling (M Ed, Ed S); special education (M Ed); teaching, learning, and leading (M Ed); technology integration (M Ed, Ed S); technology integration specialist (Certificate). *Accreditation:* NCATE. *Program availability:* Part-time, evening/weekend, 100% online. *Faculty:* 21 full-time (14 women), 42 part-time/adjunct (29 women). *Students:* 565 full-time (452 women), 59 part-time (45 women); includes 154 minority (102 Black or African American, non-Hispanic/Latino; 2 American Indian or Alaska Native, non-Hispanic/Latino; 8 Asian, non-Hispanic/Latino; 26 Hispanic/Latino; 16 Two or more races, non-Hispanic/Latino). Average age 32. 395 applicants, 54% accepted, 196 enrolled. In 2017, 162 master's, 30 doctorates, 54 other advanced degrees awarded. *Degree requirements:* For master's, comprehensive exam, portfolio, research project and presentation; for doctorate, practical capstone project in experiential setting. *Entrance requirements:* For master's, MAT (minimum score 31) or GRE General Test (minimum score 294), 2 reference letters, goals statement, writing sample, interview; for doctorate, MAT or GRE General Test, 3 reference letters, artifact of demonstrated academic excellence, written personal statements, interview. Additional exam requirements/recommendations for international students: Required—TOEFL (minimum score 570 paper-based; 80 iBT). *Application deadline:* For fall admission, 8/29 priority date for domestic students; for spring admission, 1/15 priority date for domestic students. Applications are processed on a rolling basis. Application fee: $50 ($75 for international students). Electronic applications accepted. *Expenses:* Contact institution. *Financial support:* Scholarships/grants, unspecified assistantships, and partnerships with local school districts available. Financial award applicants required to submit FAFSA. *Faculty research:* Facilitative learning styles, leadership, student assessment, interactive multimedia inclusion, learning organizations and strategic change. *Unit head:* Dr. Deborah Boyd, Director of Graduate Studies, 615-966-6263, E-mail: deborah.boyd@lipscomb.edu. *Application contact:* Amanda Logsdon, Director of Enrollment and Outreach, 615-966-7199, E-mail: amanda.logsdon@lipscomb.edu.
Website: http://www.lipscomb.edu/education/graduate-programs

Lock Haven University of Pennsylvania, College of Liberal Arts and Education, Lock Haven, PA 17745-2390. Offers alternative education (M Ed); educational leadership (M Ed); teaching and learning (M Ed). *Accreditation:* NCATE. *Program availability:* Part-time, evening/weekend, online learning. *Degree requirements:* For master's, thesis. *Entrance requirements:* For master's, minimum undergraduate GPA of 3.0. Additional exam requirements/recommendations for international students: Required—TOEFL. Electronic applications accepted.

Long Island University–Brentwood Campus, Graduate Programs, Brentwood, NY 11717. Offers childhood education (MS), including grades 1-6; childhood education/literacy B-6 (MS); childhood education/special education (grades 1-6) (MS); clinical mental health counseling (MS, Advanced Certificate); criminal justice (MS); early childhood education (MS); educational leadership (MS Ed); family nurse practitioner (MS, Advanced Certificate); health administration (MPA); library and information science (MS); literacy (B-6) (MS Ed); school counselor (MS, Advanced Certificate); social work (MSW); special education (MS Ed); students with disabilities generalist (grades 7-12) (Advanced Certificate). *Program availability:* Part-time. *Faculty:* 14 full-time (9 women), 22 part-time/adjunct (11 women). *Students:* 111 full-time (89 women), 47 part-time (34 women); includes 35 minority (8 Black or African American, non-Hispanic/Latino; 1 American Indian or Alaska Native, non-Hispanic/Latino; 3 Asian, non-Hispanic/Latino; 22 Hispanic/Latino; 1 Two or more races, non-Hispanic/Latino), 1 international. Average age 30. 110 applicants, 82% accepted, 63 enrolled. In 2017, 58 master's, 5 other advanced degrees awarded. *Entrance requirements:* For master's and Advanced Certificate, GRE. Additional exam requirements/recommendations for international students: Required—TOEFL or IELTS. *Application deadline:* Applications are processed on a rolling basis. Application fee: $50. Electronic applications accepted. *Expenses: Tuition:* Full-time $21,168; part-time $1201 per credit. *Required fees:* $1840; $920 per term. Tuition and fees vary according to course load. *Financial support:* In 2017–18, 121 students received support. Scholarships/grants available. Support available to part-time students. Financial award application deadline: 2/15; financial award applicants required to submit FAFSA. *Unit head:* Dr. Abby Van Vlerah, Dean and Chief Operating Officer, 631-299-3831, E-mail: abagail.vanvlerah@liu.edu. *Application contact:* Scott Aug, Associate Director of Enrollment Management, 631-287-8506, E-mail: scott.aug@liu.edu.
Website: http://liu.edu/brentwood

Long Island University–Hudson, Graduate School, Purchase, NY 10577. Offers autism (Advanced Certificate); bilingual education (Advanced Certificate); childhood education (MS Ed); crisis management (Advanced Certificate); early childhood education (MS Ed); educational leadership (MS Ed); health administration (MPA); literacy (MS Ed); marriage and family therapy (MS); mental health counseling (MS, Advanced Certificate), including credentialed alcoholism and substance abuse counselor (MS); middle childhood and adolescence education (MS Ed); pharmaceutics (MS), including cosmetic science, industrial pharmacy; public administration (MPA); school counseling (MS Ed, Advanced Certificate); school psychology (MS Ed); special education (MS Ed); TESOL (MS Ed); TESOL (all grades) (Advanced Certificate). *Program availability:* Part-time, evening/weekend. *Faculty:* 8 full-time (6 women), 41 part-time/adjunct (24 women). *Students:* 69 full-time (54 women), 249 part-time (200 women); includes 102 minority (29 Black or African American, non-Hispanic/Latino; 1 American Indian or Alaska Native, non-Hispanic/Latino; 9 Asian, non-Hispanic/Latino; 62 Hispanic/Latino; 1 Native Hawaiian or other Pacific Islander, non-Hispanic/Latino). Average age 33. 153 applicants, 96% accepted, 103 enrolled. In 2017, 138 master's, 36 other advanced degrees awarded. *Entrance requirements:* Additional exam requirements/recommendations for international students: Required—TOEFL. *Application deadline:* Applications are processed on a rolling basis. Application fee: $50. Electronic applications accepted. *Expenses:* Contact institution. *Financial support:* In 2017–18, 32 students received support. Scholarships/grants available. Support available to part-time students. Financial award application deadline: 2/15; financial award applicants required to submit FAFSA. *Unit head:* Dr. Sylvia Blake, Dean and Chief Operating Officer, 914-831-2700, E-mail: westchester@liu.edu. *Application contact:* Dr. Sylvia Blake, Dean and Chief Operating Officer, 914-831-2700, E-mail: westchester@liu.edu.

Long Island University–LIU Brooklyn, School of Education, Brooklyn, NY 11201-8423. Offers adolescence urban education (MS Ed); applied behavior analysis (Advanced Certificate); bilingual education (Advanced Certificate); bilingual education in urban setting (MS Ed); bilingual school counselor (MS Ed, Advanced Certificate); childhood urban education (MS Ed); childhood/early childhood education (MS Ed); childhood/early childhood urban education (MS Ed); early childhood urban education (MS Ed, Advanced Certificate); educational leadership (Advanced Certificate); marriage and family therapy (MS, Advanced Certificate); mental health counseling (MS, Advanced Certificate); school building district leader (Advanced Certificate); school counselor (MS Ed, Advanced Certificate); school psychologist (MS Ed); teaching students with disabilities (MS Ed); teaching urban children with disabilities (MS Ed); TESOL (MS Ed, Advanced Certificate). *Accreditation:* TEAC. *Program availability:* Part-time, evening/weekend, 100% online. *Faculty:* 14 full-time (12 women), 42 part-time/

adjunct (32 women). *Students:* 140 full-time (130 women), 563 part-time (414 women); includes 417 minority (183 Black or African American, non-Hispanic/Latino; 1 American Indian or Alaska Native, non-Hispanic/Latino; 32 Asian, non-Hispanic/Latino; 187 Hispanic/Latino; 14 Two or more races, non-Hispanic/Latino), 10 international. Average age 31. 449 applicants, 82% accepted, 264 enrolled. In 2017, 408 master's, 31 other advanced degrees awarded. *Entrance requirements:* For master's, GRE. Additional exam requirements/recommendations for international students: Required—TOEFL (minimum score 527 paper-based, 75 iBT), IELTS, or PTE. *Application deadline:* Applications are processed on a rolling basis. Application fee: $50. Electronic applications accepted. *Expenses: Tuition:* Full-time $21,618; part-time $1201 per credit. *Required fees:* $1840; $920 per term. Tuition and fees vary according to course load. *Financial support:* In 2017–18, 58 students received support. Career-related internships or fieldwork, Federal Work-Study, scholarships/grants, and unspecified assistantships available. Support available to part-time students. Financial award application deadline: 2/15; financial award applicants required to submit FAFSA. *Faculty research:* Diversity issues in education and mental health care, inclusion - disability studies, sustainability, teacher professional development. *Unit head:* Dean, 718-488-1055, E-mail: bkln-admissions@liu.edu. *Application contact:* Bayu Sutrisno, Graduate Admissions Counselor, 718-488-1011, Fax: 718-780-6110, E-mail: bkln-admissions@liu.edu. Website: http://www.liu.edu/Brooklyn/Academics/School-of-Education

Long Island University–LIU Post, College of Education, Information and Technology, Brookville, NY 11548-1300. Offers adolescence education (MS); adolescence education 7-12 (MS); archives and records management (AC); art education (MS); childhood education (MS); childhood education/literacy B-6 (MS); childhood education/special education (MS); clinical mental health counseling (MS, AC); early childhood education (MS); early childhood education/childhood education (MS); educational leadership (AC); educational technology (MS); information studies (PhD); interdisciplinary educational studies (Ed D); middle childhood education (MS); music education (MS); public library administration (AC); school counselor (MS); special education (MS Ed); speech-language pathology (MA); students with disabilities, 7-12 generalist (AC); TESOL (MA). *Accreditation:* TEAC. *Program availability:* Part-time, 100% online, blended/hybrid learning. *Faculty:* 40 full-time (26 women), 73 part-time/adjunct (38 women). *Students:* 472 full-time (400 women), 696 part-time (543 women); includes 254 minority (93 Black or African American, non-Hispanic/Latino; 46 Asian, non-Hispanic/Latino; 105 Hispanic/Latino; 10 Two or more races, non-Hispanic/Latino), 33 international. Average age 33. 917 applicants, 82% accepted, 357 enrolled. In 2017, 408 master's, 31 other advanced degrees awarded. Terminal master's awarded for partial completion of doctoral program. *Degree requirements:* For master's, variable foreign language requirement, comprehensive exam (for some programs), thesis optional; for doctorate, comprehensive exam, thesis/dissertation. *Entrance requirements:* For master's and AC, GRE (for some programs). Additional exam requirements/recommendations for international students: Required—TOEFL (minimum score 550 paper-based, 75 iBT), IELTS, or PTE. *Application deadline:* Applications are processed on a rolling basis. Application fee: $50. Electronic applications accepted. *Expenses: Tuition:* Full-time $21,618; part-time $1201 per credit. *Required fees:* $1840; $920 per term. Tuition and fees vary according to course load. *Financial support:* In 2017–18, 376 students received support. Career-related internships or fieldwork, Federal Work-Study, institutionally sponsored loans, scholarships/grants, tuition waivers (partial), and unspecified assistantships available. Support available to part-time students. Financial award application deadline: 2/15; financial award applicants required to submit FAFSA. *Faculty research:* Sleep; use of technology to develop executive function by students with disabilities; early childhood literacy development through play; social justice through education; using a structured protocol to discuss Bad News. *Unit head:* Dr. Albert Inserra, Dean, 516-299-2210, E-mail: albert.inserra@liu.edu. *Application contact:* Rita Langdon, Graduate Admissions, 516-299-2900, Fax: 516-299-2137, E-mail: post-enroll@liu.edu. Website: http://liu.edu/CWPost/Academics/College-of-Education-Information-and-Technology

Loras College, Graduate Division, Program in Educational Leadership, Dubuque, IA 52004-0178. Offers MA. *Program availability:* Part-time, evening/weekend. *Degree requirements:* For master's, comprehensive exam, thesis optional. *Entrance requirements:* For master's, minimum cumulative undergraduate GPA of 3.0.

Louisiana State University and Agricultural & Mechanical College, Graduate School, College of Human Sciences and Education, Department of Educational Theory, Policy and Practice, Baton Rouge, LA 70803. Offers counseling (M Ed, MA, Ed S); educational administration (M Ed, MA, PhD, Ed S); educational technology (MA); elementary education (M Ed, MAT); higher education (PhD); research methodology (PhD); secondary education (M Ed, MAT). *Accreditation:* ACA (one or more programs are accredited); NCATE. *Faculty:* 34 full-time (22 women). *Students:* 213 full-time (159 women), 228 part-time (178 women); includes 164 minority (123 Black or African American, non-Hispanic/Latino; 7 Asian, non-Hispanic/Latino; 27 Hispanic/Latino; 1 Native Hawaiian or other Pacific Islander, non-Hispanic/Latino; 6 Two or more races, non-Hispanic/Latino), 13 international. Average age 32. 231 applicants, 61% accepted, 82 enrolled. In 2017, 125 master's, 26 doctorates, 28 other advanced degrees awarded. *Financial support:* In 2017–18, 3 fellowships (averaging $12,129 per year), 2 research assistantships (averaging $16,019 per year), 96 teaching assistantships (averaging $16,061 per year) were awarded. *Total annual research expenditures:* $356,867.

Louisiana State University in Shreveport, College of Business, Education, and Human Development, Program in Education, Shreveport, LA 71115-2399. Offers curriculum and instruction (M Ed); leadership (M Ed); leadership studies (Ed D). *Accreditation:* NCATE. *Program availability:* Part-time. *Students:* 35 full-time (22 women), 215 part-time (181 women); includes 76 minority (62 Black or African American, non-Hispanic/Latino; 1 Asian, non-Hispanic/Latino; 10 Hispanic/Latino; 3 Two or more races, non-Hispanic/Latino), 5 international. Average age 36. 270 applicants, 96% accepted, 98 enrolled. In 2017, 59 master's, 3 doctorates awarded. *Degree requirements:* For master's, orally-presented project, 200-hour internship (educational leadership). *Entrance requirements:* For master's, GRE, minimum GPA of 2.5; teacher certification; recommendations and interview (for educational leadership). Additional exam requirements/recommendations for international students: Required—TOEFL (minimum score 550 paper-based; 61 iBT). *Application deadline:* For fall admission, 6/30 for domestic and international students; for spring admission, 11/30 for domestic and international students; for summer admission, 4/30 for domestic and international students. Applications are processed on a rolling basis. Application fee: $20 ($30 for international students). Electronic applications accepted. *Expenses: Tuition:* state resident: full-time $3098; part-time $344 per credit hour. Tuition, nonresident: full-time $9923; part-time $1103 per credit hour. *Required fees:* $384 per semester. Tuition and fees vary according to program. *Financial support:* In 2017–18, 5 research assistantships (averaging $2,150 per year) were awarded. *Unit head:* Dr. Pat Doerr, Coordinator, 318-797-5033, Fax: 318-798-4144, E-mail: pat.doerr@lsus.edu. *Application contact:* Mary Catherine Harvison, Director of Admissions, 318-797-2400, Fax: 318-797-5286, E-mail: mary.harvison@lsus.edu.

Louisiana Tech University, Graduate School, College of Education, Ruston, LA 71272. Offers counseling and guidance (MA), including clinical mental health counseling,

human services, orientation and mobility; counseling psychology (PhD); curriculum and instruction (M Ed); cyber education (Graduate Certificate); dynamics of domestic and family violence (Graduate Certificate); early childhood education - PreK-3 (MAT); educational leadership (M Ed, Ed D); elementary education and special education mild/moderate grades 1-5 (MAT); higher education administration (Graduate Certificate); industrial/organizational psychology (MA, PhD); kinesiology (MS); middle school education (MAT), including mathematics; orientation and mobility (Graduate Certificate); rehabilitation teaching for the blind (Graduate Certificate); secondary education (MAT), including agriculture, biology, business, chemistry, English; special education: visually impaired (MAT); teacher leader education (Graduate Certificate); visual impairments - blind education (Graduate Certificate). *Accreditation:* NCATE. *Program availability:* Part-time. *Faculty:* 28 full-time (16 women), 23 part-time/adjunct (22 women). *Students:* 269 full-time (192 women), 194 part-time (150 women); includes 127 minority (94 Black or African American, non-Hispanic/Latino; 2 American Indian or Alaska Native, non-Hispanic/Latino; 6 Asian, non-Hispanic/Latino; 16 Hispanic/Latino; 1 Native Hawaiian or other Pacific Islander, non-Hispanic/Latino; 8 Two or more races, non-Hispanic/Latino), 8 international. Average age 34. 226 applicants, 74% accepted, 60 enrolled. In 2017, 5 master's, 2 doctorates, 1 other advanced degree awarded. *Degree requirements:* For master's, thesis; for doctorate, thesis/dissertation. *Entrance requirements:* For master's and doctorate, GRE General Test. Additional exam requirements/recommendations for international students: Required—TOEFL (minimum score 550 paper-based; 80 iBT), IELTS (minimum score 6.5). *Application deadline:* For fall admission, 9/1 priority date for domestic students, 6/1 for international students; for winter admission, 11/1 priority date for domestic students, 9/1 for international students; for spring admission, 2/1 priority date for domestic students, 12/1 for international students; for summer admission, 5/1 priority date for domestic students, 3/1 for international students. Application fee: $40. Electronic applications accepted. *Expenses:* Tuition, state resident: full-time $5146. Tuition, nonresident: full-time $10,147. *International tuition:* $10,267 full-time. *Required fees:* $2273. *Financial support:* In 2017–18, 40 students received support, including 23 research assistantships (averaging $10,346 per year), 15 teaching assistantships (averaging $6,887 per year); fellowships and career-related internships or fieldwork also available. Financial award application deadline: 2/1. *Faculty research:* Blindness and the best methods for increasing independence for individuals who are blind or visually impaired; educating and investigating factors contributing to improvements in human performance across the lifespan and a reduction in injury rates during training. *Total annual research expenditures:* $2.1 million. *Unit head:* Dr. Don Schillinger, Dean, 318-257-3712, E-mail: dschill@latech.edu. *Application contact:* Dr. Dawn Basinger, Associate Dean of Academic Affairs, 318-257-2977, Fax: 318-257-2379, E-mail: dbasing@latech.edu. Website: http://education.latech.edu/

Lourdes University, Graduate School, Sylvania, OH 43560-2898. Offers business (MBA); leadership (M Ed); nurse anesthesia (MSN); nurse educator (MSN); nurse leader (MSN); organizational leadership (MOL); reading (M Ed); teaching and curriculum (M Ed); theology (MA). *Program availability:* Evening/weekend. *Entrance requirements:* Additional exam requirements/recommendations for international students: Required—TOEFL.

Loyola Marymount University, School of Education, Doctorate in Educational Leadership for Social Justice Program, Los Angeles, CA 90045-2659. Offers Ed D. *Unit head:* Dr. Jill Bickett, Director, Doctorate in Educational Leadership for Social Justice, 310-338-3777, E-mail: jbickett@lmu.edu. *Application contact:* Chake H. Kouyoumjian, Associate Dean of Graduate Studies, 310-338-2721, Fax: 310-338-6086, E-mail: graduateinfo@lmu.edu. Website: http://soe.lmu.edu/academics/doctoral

Loyola Marymount University, School of Education, Program in Catholic School Administration, Los Angeles, CA 90045-2659. Offers MA. *Unit head:* Dr. Mary McCullough, Director, Catholic School Leadership Programs, 310-338-7312, E-mail: mmccullo@lmu.edu. *Application contact:* Chake H. Kouyoumjian, Associate Dean of Graduate Studies, 310-338-2721, Fax: 310-338-6086, E-mail: graduateinfo@lmu.edu. Website: http://soe.lmu.edu/academics/catholicschooladministrationma

Loyola Marymount University, School of Education, Program in School Administration, Los Angeles, CA 90045-2659. Offers MA. *Unit head:* Dr. Manuel Ponce, Jr., Director, Institute of School Leadership and Administration, 310-568-7165, E-mail: mponce8@lmu.edu. *Application contact:* Chake H. Kouyoumjian, Associate Dean of Graduate Studies, 310-338-2721, Fax: 310-338-6086, E-mail: graduateinfo@lmu.edu. Website: http://soe.lmu.edu/academics/isla

Loyola University Chicago, School of Education, Program in Administration and Supervision, Chicago, IL 60660. Offers M Ed, Ed D, Certificate. *Program availability:* Part-time, evening/weekend. *Faculty:* 5 full-time (4 women), 8 part-time/adjunct (3 women). *Students:* 52 full-time (39 women), 17 part-time (12 women); includes 27 minority (15 Black or African American, non-Hispanic/Latino; 3 Asian, non-Hispanic/Latino; 8 Hispanic/Latino; 1 Two or more races, non-Hispanic/Latino), 1 international. Average age 42. 12 applicants, 83% accepted, 9 enrolled. In 2017, 10 master's, 6 doctorates awarded. *Degree requirements:* For master's, comprehensive exam; for doctorate, comprehensive exam, thesis/dissertation. *Entrance requirements:* For master's, minimum GPA of 3.0, letters of recommendation, resume, transcripts; for doctorate, GRE General Test, interview, minimum GPA of 3.0, letters of recommendation, resume. Additional exam requirements/recommendations for international students: Required—TOEFL (minimum score 550 paper-based; 79 iBT). *Application deadline:* For fall admission, 2/15 for domestic and international students. Applications are processed on a rolling basis. Application fee: $50. Electronic applications accepted. Application fee is waived when completed online. *Expenses:* $949 per semester hour, $2,847 per course, $8,541-$11,388 full-time semester tuition; $432 per semester fees, $225 additional fees (first semester only). *Financial support:* In 2017–18, 40 fellowships, 1 research assistantship (averaging $14,000 per year) were awarded; career-related internships or fieldwork, institutionally sponsored loans, scholarships/grants, and unspecified assistantships also available. Support available to part-time students. Financial award application deadline: 2/1; financial award applicants required to submit FAFSA. *Faculty research:* Leadership, school law, school administration, supervision, ethics. *Unit head:* Dr. Siobhan Cafferty, Director, 312-915-7002, Fax: 312-915-6980, E-mail: scaffer@luc.edu. *Application contact:* Mirtza Campbell, Information Contact, 312-915-8907, E-mail: mcampbell11@luc.edu.

Loyola University Maryland, Graduate Programs, School of Education, Program in Educational Leadership, Baltimore, MD 21210-2699. Offers M Ed, CAS. *Program availability:* Part-time. *Faculty:* 36 full-time (27 women), 23 part-time/adjunct (15 women). *Students:* 2 full-time (0 women), 182 part-time (136 women); includes 84 minority (67 Black or African American, non-Hispanic/Latino; 11 Hispanic/Latino; 1 Native Hawaiian or other Pacific Islander, non-Hispanic/Latino; 5 Two or more races, non-Hispanic/Latino), 1 international. Average age 33. *Entrance requirements:* For master's, transcripts, essay, resume. Additional exam requirements/recommendations for international students: Required—TOEFL (minimum score 550 paper-based), IELTS (minimum score 7). *Application deadline:* For fall admission, 6/15 priority date for domestic students; for winter admission, 11/1 for domestic students; for spring admission, 3/15 priority date for domestic students. Applications are processed on a rolling basis. Application fee: $60. Electronic applications accepted. *Expenses:* Contact institution. *Financial support:* Application deadline: 4/15; applicants required to submit FAFSA. *Unit head:* Dr. Peter Litchka, Director, 410-617-1656, E-mail: prlitchka@loyola.edu. *Application contact:* Office of Graduate Admission, 410-617-5020, E-mail: graduate@loyola.edu.

Lynn University, Donald E. and Helen L. Ross College of Education, Boca Raton, FL 33431-5598. Offers educational leadership (M Ed, Ed D), including K-12 (Ed D), school administration K-12 (M Ed); exceptional student education (M Ed), including school administration K-12. *Program availability:* Part-time, evening/weekend, online learning. *Faculty:* 6 full-time (4 women), 4 part-time/adjunct (3 women). *Students:* 31 full-time (23 women), 62 part-time (42 women); includes 32 minority (20 Black or African American, non-Hispanic/Latino; 1 American Indian or Alaska Native, non-Hispanic/Latino; 10 Hispanic/Latino; 1 Two or more races, non-Hispanic/Latino), 3 international. Average age 36. 46 applicants, 78% accepted, 30 enrolled. In 2017, 24 master's, 22 doctorates awarded. *Degree requirements:* For master's, comprehensive exam, thesis (for some programs), completion of degree in maximum of four calendar years; minimum cumulative GPA of 3.0 and B grade or higher in each course; orientation seminar (one credit); minimum of 40 credits; FTCE ESE K-12 Exam; for doctorate, thesis/dissertation, mid-program review; minimum cumulative GPA of 3.25 and B grade or higher in each course. *Entrance requirements:* For master's, bachelor's degree from accredited institution, minimum undergraduate GPA of 3.0, official undergraduate and graduate transcripts of all academic coursework attempted, current résumé, statement of professional goals, writing sample, two recent letters of recommendation; for doctorate, professional practice statement that identifies applicant's goals and explains how Lynn's program will help attain them, official transcript showing conferral of master's degree, two letters of recommendation from previous professors or employers, current resume, interview. Additional exam requirements/recommendations for international students: Required—TOEFL (minimum score 550 paper-based; 80 iBT), IELTS (minimum score 6.5). *Application deadline:* For fall admission, 8/18 for domestic students, 8/4 for international students; for spring admission, 12/15 for domestic students, 12/1 for international students; for summer admission, 4/17 for domestic students, 4/3 for international students. Applications are processed on a rolling basis. Application fee: $45. Electronic applications accepted. *Expenses:* $740 per credit (for master's degrees); $850 per credit (for EdD). *Financial support:* Career-related internships or fieldwork, Federal Work-Study, scholarships/grants, tuition waivers (partial), and unspecified assistantships available. Support available to part-time students. Financial award application deadline: 3/1; financial award applicants required to submit FAFSA. *Faculty research:* Student achievement, students with learning differences, teacher and student retention, student motivation and cognition, neuroscience leadership and learning. *Unit head:* Dr. Kathleen Weigel, Dean, College of Education, 561-237-7441, E-mail: kweigel@lynn.edu. *Application contact:* Steven Pruitt, Director of Graduate and Undergraduate Evening Admission, 561-237-7834, Fax: 561-237-7100, E-mail: spruitt@lynn.edu.
Website: http://www.lynn.edu/academics/colleges/education

Madonna University, Programs in Education, Livonia, MI 48150-1173. Offers Catholic school leadership (MSA); educational leadership (MSA); learning disabilities (MAT); literacy education (MAT); teaching and learning (MAT). *Accreditation:* NCATE. *Program availability:* Part-time, evening/weekend. *Degree requirements:* For master's, thesis or alternative. Electronic applications accepted.

Malone University, Graduate Program in Education, Canton, OH 44709. Offers curriculum and instruction (MA); curriculum, instruction, and professional development (MA); educational leadership (principal license) (MA); intervention specialist (MA). *Accreditation:* NCATE. *Program availability:* Part-time, evening/weekend. *Degree requirements:* For master's, research project. *Entrance requirements:* For master's, minimum GPA of 3.0, teaching license. Additional exam requirements/recommendations for international students: Required—TOEFL (minimum score 550 paper-based; 79 iBT). *Faculty research:* Educational leadership styles: Jesus as master teacher, assessment accommodations for English language learners, preparing culturally proficient teachers, using naturally occurring text in the classroom to meet the syntactic needs of students with learning disabilities, using tablet instructional technology to meet the needs of students with disabilities.

Manhattan College, Graduate Programs, School of Education and Health, Program in Educational Leadership, Riverdale, NY 10471. Offers advanced leadership studies (MS Ed, Advanced Certificate), including school district leadership; school building leadership (MS Ed, Advanced Certificate). *Program availability:* Part-time, evening/weekend, blended/hybrid learning. *Faculty:* 3 full-time (all women), 6 part-time/adjunct (3 women). *Students:* 41 full-time (34 women), 14 part-time (10 women); includes 27 minority (12 Black or African American, non-Hispanic/Latino; 2 Asian, non-Hispanic/Latino; 13 Hispanic/Latino). Average age 37. 48 applicants, 81% accepted, 29 enrolled. In 2017, 2 master's, 15 Advanced Certificates awarded. *Degree requirements:* For master's, thesis, internship; for Advanced Certificate, internship. *Entrance requirements:* For master's, GRE (for the first graduate course), baccalaureate degree, minimum GPA of 3.0, 3 years of pupil personnel service, professional recommendation; for Advanced Certificate, New York State certification examination, master's degree; 3 years of personnel service; minimum GPA of 3.0; professional recommendations. Additional exam requirements/recommendations for international students: Required—TOEFL (minimum score 550 paper-based). *Application deadline:* For fall admission, 8/1 priority date for domestic students, 4/1 priority date for international students; for spring admission, 1/1 priority date for domestic students, 9/1 priority date for international students. Applications are processed on a rolling basis. Application fee: $110. Electronic applications accepted. *Expenses:* $925 per credit tuition; $110 registration fee. *Financial support:* In 2017–18, 5 students received support. Scholarships/grants and unspecified assistantships available. Financial award application deadline: 4/1; financial award applicants required to submit FAFSA. *Faculty research:* Distance learning and teacher efficacy, leadership and student achievement, professional development and student achievement, leadership development, professional development for teachers, authentic assessment strategies, curriculum development and adaptation. *Unit head:* Dr. Remigia Kushner, Program Director, 718-862-7473, Fax: 718-862-7816, E-mail: sr.remigia.kushner@manhattan.edu.
Website: http://manhattan.edu/academics/education/school-building-leadership

Manhattanville College, School of Education, Program in Educational Leadership, Purchase, NY 10577-2132. Offers education leadership (Ed D); educational leadership (MPS); educational leadership - school building leader (PD); educational leadership - school district leader (PD); higher education leadership (Ed D); school district leader (Advanced Certificate). *Program availability:* Part-time, evening/weekend. *Faculty:* 7 full-time (2 women), 6 part-time/adjunct (3 women). *Students:* 81 full-time (54 women), 53 part-time (32 women); includes 28 minority (14 Black or African American, non-Hispanic/Latino; 4 Asian, non-Hispanic/Latino; 10 Hispanic/Latino), 1 international. Average age 43. 36 applicants, 75% accepted, 25 enrolled. In 2017, 1 master's, 17 doctorates, 17 Advanced Certificates awarded. *Degree requirements:* For master's, comprehensive exam (for some programs), thesis (for some programs), student teaching, research seminars, portfolios, internships, writing assessment; for doctorate, thesis/dissertation, professional portfolio; for other advanced degree, comprehensive exam (for some

programs). *Entrance requirements:* For master's, GRE or MAT (for programs leading to certification), minimum GPA of 3.0, 2 letters of recommendation, interview, essay (2-3 page personal statement that describes reasons for choosing teaching or educational leadership as profession and philosophy of education), proof of immunization (for those born after 1957); for doctorate, GRE or MAT, minimum GPA of 3.0, 3 letters of recommendation, interview, writing sample (statement explaining interest in joining program, strengths applicant brings to role of education leader, leadership experience to date, and skills they hope to develop in program), proof of immunization (for those born after 1957). Additional exam requirements/recommendations for international students: Required—TOEFL (minimum score 600 paper-based; 110 iBT); Recommended—IELTS (minimum score 8). *Application deadline:* Applications are processed on a rolling basis. Application fee: $75. Electronic applications accepted. *Expenses:* $1,000 per credit (for doctoral program); $915 per credit (for MS). *Financial support:* Teaching assistantships, career-related internships or fieldwork, Federal Work-Study, institutionally sponsored loans, scholarships/grants, and unspecified assistantships available. Financial award application deadline: 3/15; financial award applicants required to submit FAFSA. *Faculty research:* Social capital, diversity in higher education, school leadership. *Unit head:* Dr. Shelly Wepner, Dean, 914-323-3153, Fax: 914-323-5493, E-mail: shelly.wepner@mville.edu. *Application contact:* Alissa Wilson, Director, Graduate Admissions, 914-323-3150, Fax: 914-694-1732, E-mail: edschool@mville.edu.
Website: http://www.mville.edu/programs/educational-leadership

Marconi International University, Graduate Programs, Pembroke Pines, FL 33028. Offers business administration (DBA); education leadership (Ed D); education leadership, management and emerging technologies (M Ed); international business administration (IMBA).

Marian University, School of Education, Fond du Lac, WI 54935-4699. Offers curriculum and instruction leadership (PhD); educational administration (PhD); educational leadership (MAE); educational technology (MAE); leadership studies (PhD); special education (MAE); teacher education (MAE). *Accreditation:* NCATE. *Program availability:* Part-time, evening/weekend, online learning. *Degree requirements:* For master's, exam, field-based experience project, portfolio; for doctorate, comprehensive exam, thesis/dissertation, field-based experience. *Entrance requirements:* For master's, minimum GPA of 3.0, BA in education or related field, teaching license; for doctorate, GRE, MAT, resume, 2 writing samples, interview. Additional exam requirements/recommendations for international students: Required—TOEFL (minimum score 525 paper-based; 70 iBT). *Faculty research:* At-risk youth, multicultural issues, values in education, teaching/learning strategies.

Marquette University, Graduate School, College of Education, Department of Educational Policy and Leadership, Milwaukee, WI 53201-1881. Offers college student personnel administration (M Ed); curriculum and instruction (MA); education (MA); educational administration (M Ed); educational policy and foundations (MA); elementary education (Certificate); literacy (MA); principal (Certificate); reading specialist (Certificate); reading teacher (Certificate); secondary education (Certificate); superintendent (Certificate). *Program availability:* Part-time, evening/weekend. Terminal master's awarded for partial completion of doctoral program. *Degree requirements:* For master's, comprehensive exam, thesis (for some programs); for doctorate, thesis/dissertation, qualifying exam. *Entrance requirements:* For master's, GRE General Test or MAT, official transcripts from all current and previous colleges/universities except Marquette, three letters of recommendation, statement of purpose; for doctorate, GRE General Test, MAT, sample of written work, official transcripts from all current and previous colleges/universities except Marquette, three letters of recommendation, statement of purpose, resume/curriculum vitae; for Certificate, GRE General Test or MAT, master's degree. Additional exam requirements/recommendations for international students: Required—TOEFL (minimum score 530 paper-based). *Expenses:* Contact institution. *Faculty research:* Leadership; social justice in education; development of lifelong learners; race, class, and schooling in historical perspective; urban teacher education.

Marshall University, Academic Affairs Division, College of Education and Professional Development, Program in Leadership Studies, Huntington, WV 25755. Offers MA. *Program availability:* Part-time, evening/weekend. *Students:* 27 full-time (16 women), 291 part-time (143 women); includes 38 minority (15 Black or African American, non-Hispanic/Latino; 1 Asian, non-Hispanic/Latino; 18 Hispanic/Latino; 2 Native Hawaiian or other Pacific Islander, non-Hispanic/Latino; 2 Two or more races, non-Hispanic/Latino). Average age 39. In 2017, 112 master's awarded. *Degree requirements:* For master's, thesis optional, comprehensive or oral assessment. *Entrance requirements:* For master's, GRE General Test or MAT. Application fee: $40. *Financial support:* Career-related internships or fieldwork, Federal Work-Study, tuition waivers (full), and unspecified assistantships available. Support available to part-time students. Financial award applicants required to submit FAFSA. *Unit head:* Dr. Michael Cunningham, Program Director, 800-642-9842 Ext. 61912, E-mail: mcunningham@marshall.edu. *Application contact:* Information Contact, 304-746-1900, Fax: 304-746-1902, E-mail: services@marshall.edu.

Martin Luther College, Graduate Studies, New Ulm, MN 56073. Offers early childhood director (MS Ed Admin); educational technology (MS Ed); instruction (MS Ed); leadership (MS Ed); principal (MS Ed Admin); special education (MS Ed). *Program availability:* Part-time, evening/weekend, online learning. *Faculty:* 8 full-time (1 woman), 21 part-time/adjunct (10 women). *Students:* 1 (woman) full-time, 81 part-time (81 women); includes 2 minority (1 Asian, non-Hispanic/Latino; 1 Two or more races, non-Hispanic/Latino), 2 international. Average age 37. 23 applicants, 100% accepted, 23 enrolled. In 2017, 25 master's awarded. *Degree requirements:* For master's, capstone project or comprehensive exam. *Entrance requirements:* For master's, undergraduate degree in education from an accredited college or university, minimum undergraduate GPA of 3.0. Additional exam requirements/recommendations for international students: Required—TOEFL (minimum score 550 paper-based; 80 iBT); Recommended—IELTS (minimum score 6.5). *Application deadline:* Applications are processed on a rolling basis. Application fee: $35. Electronic applications accepted. *Expenses:* $315 per credit. *Financial support:* In 2017–18, 4 students received support. Scholarships/grants available. Financial award application deadline: 9/1. *Faculty research:* Principal effectiveness, principal support, cognitive load in math instruction, reading strategies in multigrade classrooms, mentor provided professional development for new teachers. *Unit head:* John E. Meyer, Director of Graduate Studies, 507-354-8221 Ext. 398, E-mail: meyerjd@mlc-wels.edu.
Website: https://mlc-wels.edu/graduate-studies/

Marygrove College, Graduate Studies, Detroit, MI 48221-2599. Offers autism spectrum disorders (M Ed, Certificate); curriculum instruction and assessment (MAT); educational leadership (MA); educational technology (M Ed); effective teaching in the 21st century-classroom focus (MAT); effective teaching in the 21st century-technology focus (MAT); human resource management (MA, Certificate); mathematics 6-8 (MAT); mathematics K-5 (MAT); reading and literacy K-6 (MAT); reading specialist (M Ed); school administrator (Certificate); social justice (MA); special education (MAT); special education - learning disabilities (M Ed); teaching - pre-elementary education (M Ed); teaching - pre-secondary education (M Ed). *Program availability:* Part-time, evening/

weekend, 100% online, blended/hybrid learning. *Students:* 163 full-time (123 women), 264 part-time (186 women). Average age 34. *Entrance requirements:* For master's, all official bachelor's transcripts. Additional exam requirements/recommendations for international students: Required—TOEFL (minimum score 550 paper-based; 80 iBT). *Application deadline:* Applications are processed on a rolling basis. Electronic applications accepted. *Expenses: Tuition:* Part-time $590 per credit hour. *Required fees:* $120 per semester. One-time fee: $25 part-time. *Financial support:* Applicants required to submit FAFSA. *Unit head:* Marygrove College Admissions, 313-927-1240, E-mail: info@marygrove.edu. *Application contact:* Marygrove College Admissions, 313-927-1240, E-mail: info@marygrove.edu.

Maryville University of Saint Louis, School of Education, St. Louis, MO 63141-7299. Offers early childhood education (MA Ed); educational leadership (Ed D); elementary education (MA Ed); higher education leadership (Ed D); literacy specialist (MA Ed); middle grades education (MA Ed); secondary teaching and inquiry (MA Ed); teacher as leader (MA Ed, Ed D). *Accreditation:* NCATE. *Program availability:* Part-time, 100% online, blended/hybrid learning. *Faculty:* 20 full-time (14 women), 19 part-time/adjunct (13 women). *Students:* 6 full-time (4 women), 337 part-time (250 women); includes 101 minority (85 Black or African American, non-Hispanic/Latino; 4 Asian, non-Hispanic/Latino; 8 Hispanic/Latino; 4 Two or more races, non-Hispanic/Latino), 3 international. Average age 38. In 2017, 34 master's, 67 doctorates awarded. *Degree requirements:* For master's, thesis, project. *Entrance requirements:* For master's, minimum cumulative GPA of 3.0, 3 professional recommendations, essays, interview with program faculty; for doctorate, minimum GPA of 3.0, 3 professional recommendations, essay, interview, on-site writing sample. Additional exam requirements/recommendations for international students: Required—TOEFL (minimum score 550 paper-based). *Application deadline:* Applications are processed on a rolling basis. Electronic applications accepted. *Expenses:* Contact institution. *Financial support:* Career-related internships or fieldwork, Federal Work-Study, tuition waivers (partial), and professional educator discounts available. Financial award application deadline: 4/1; financial award applicants required to submit FAFSA. *Faculty research:* Collaboration with public schools, pre-service program development, mathematics, diversity, literacy. *Unit head:* Dr. Cathy Bear, Dean, 314-529-9692, Fax: 314-529-9921, E-mail: cbear@maryville.edu. *Application contact:* Stacey Ruffin, Coordinator of Clinical Experiences and Graduate Programs, 314-529-9542, Fax: 314-529-9921, E-mail: teachered@maryville.edu. Website: http://www.maryville.edu/ed/graduate-programs/

Marywood University, Academic Affairs, Center for Interdisciplinary Studies, Scranton, PA 18509-1598. Offers human development (PhD), including educational administration, health promotion, higher education administration, instructional leadership, social work. *Program availability:* Part-time. Electronic applications accepted. *Expenses:* Contact institution.

Marywood University, Academic Affairs, Reap College of Education and Human Development, Department of Education, Program in Higher Education Administration, Scranton, PA 18509-1598. Offers MS. *Program availability:* Part-time, evening/weekend. Electronic applications accepted. *Faculty research:* Integrated thematic instruction.

Marywood University, Academic Affairs, Reap College of Education and Human Development, Department of Education, Program in Instructional Leadership, Scranton, PA 18509-1598. Offers M Ed. *Program availability:* Part-time. Electronic applications accepted.

Marywood University, Academic Affairs, Reap College of Education and Human Development, Department of Education, Program in School Leadership, Scranton, PA 18509-1598. Offers MS. *Accreditation:* NCATE. *Program availability:* Part-time. Electronic applications accepted.

Marywood University, Academic Affairs, Reap College of Education and Human Development, Department of Education, Program in Special Education Administration and Supervision, Scranton, PA 18509-1598. Offers MS. *Accreditation:* NCATE. *Program availability:* Part-time. Electronic applications accepted.

Massachusetts College of Liberal Arts, Graduate Programs, North Adams, MA 01247-4100. Offers business (MBA); educational administration (M Ed); educational leadership (CAGS); instruction and curriculum (M Ed); instructional technology (M Ed); physical education and health (M Ed); reading (M Ed); special education (M Ed). *Program availability:* Part-time, evening/weekend. *Degree requirements:* For master's, thesis. *Entrance requirements:* For master's, writing sample.

McDaniel College, Graduate and Professional Studies, Program in Educational Leadership, Westminster, MD 21157-4390. Offers MS. *Program availability:* Part-time-only, evening/weekend. *Faculty:* 2 full-time (1 woman), 16 part-time/adjunct (6 women). *Students:* 262 part-time (210 women); includes 36 minority (28 Black or African American, non-Hispanic/Latino; 1 American Indian or Alaska Native, non-Hispanic/Latino; 3 Asian, non-Hispanic/Latino; 3 Hispanic/Latino; 1 Two or more races, non-Hispanic/Latino), 1 international. Average age 38. 203 applicants, 99% accepted, 156 enrolled. In 2017, 11 master's awarded. *Degree requirements:* For master's, comprehensive exam (for some programs), thesis optional, portfolio. *Entrance requirements:* For master's, 3 recommendations, Principal Mentor Form. Additional exam requirements/recommendations for international students: Required—TOEFL (minimum score 79 iBT), IELTS (minimum score 6). *Application deadline:* For fall admission, 6/1 priority date for domestic students; for spring admission, 11/1 priority date for domestic students; for summer admission, 3/1 priority date for domestic students. Applications are processed on a rolling basis. Application fee: $75. Electronic applications accepted. *Expenses: Tuition:* Full-time $11,760; part-time $490 per credit hour. Tuition and fees vary according to course load and program. *Financial support:* Career-related internships or fieldwork available. Financial award application deadline: 3/1; financial award applicants required to submit FAFSA. *Unit head:* Fax: 410-857-2515, E-mail: gradadms@mcdaniel.edu. *Application contact:* Penny Pfeiffer, Senior Graduate Enrollment Management Specialist, 410-857-2513, Fax: 410-857-2515, E-mail: ppfeiffer@mcdaniel.edu.

McGill University, Faculty of Graduate and Postdoctoral Studies, Faculty of Education, Department of Integrated Studies in Education, Montréal, QC H3A 2T5, Canada. Offers culture and values in education (MA, PhD); curriculum studies (MA); educational leadership (MA, Certificate); educational studies (PhD); integrated studies in education (M Ed); second language education (MA, PhD).

McKendree University, Graduate Programs, Programs in Education, Lebanon, IL 62254-1299. Offers curriculum design and instruction (Ed D, Ed S); educational administration and leadership (MA Ed); educational studies (MA Ed); higher education administrative services (MA Ed); music education (MA Ed); reading (MA Ed); special education (MA Ed); teacher leadership (MA Ed); teaching certification (MA Ed). *Accreditation:* NCATE. *Program availability:* Part-time, evening/weekend, online learning. *Entrance requirements:* For master's, official transcripts from all institutions previously attended, minimum GPA of 3.0, resume, references; for doctorate, GRE (within the past 5 years), master's degree in education and Ed S, or the equivalent, from regionally-accredited institution; official transcripts from all institutions previously attended; curriculum vitae/resume; essay/personal statement; two years of teaching/professional experience; for Ed S, GRE (within the past 5 years), master's degree in

education from regionally-accredited institution of higher education; official transcripts from all institutions previously attended; curriculum vitae/resume; essay/personal statement; two years of teaching/professional experience. Additional exam requirements/recommendations for international students: Required—TOEFL. Electronic applications accepted.

McNeese State University, Doré School of Graduate Studies, Burton College of Education, Department of Education Professions, Program in Educational Leadership, Lake Charles, LA 70609. Offers educational leadership (M Ed, Ed S); educational technology (Ed S). *Program availability:* Evening/weekend. *Entrance requirements:* For master's, GRE, teaching certificate, 3 years of full-time teaching experience; for Ed S, teaching certificate, 3 years of teaching experience, 1 year of administration or supervision experience, master's degree with 12 semester hours in education. *Application deadline:* For fall admission, 5/15 priority date for domestic and international students; for spring admission, 10/15 priority date for domestic and international students. Applications are processed on a rolling basis. Application fee: $20 ($30 for international students). *Financial support:* Application deadline: 5/1. *Unit head:* Dr. Brett C. Welch, Director, 337-475-5405, Fax: 337-475-5272, E-mail: bwelch@mcneese.edu. *Application contact:* Dr. Dustin M. Hebert, Director of Doré' School of Graduate Studies, 337-475-5396, Fax: 337-475-5397, E-mail: admissions@mcneese.edu.

Memorial University of Newfoundland, School of Graduate Studies, Faculty of Education, St. John's, NL A1C 5S7, Canada. Offers counseling psychology (M Ed); curriculum, teaching, and learning studies (M Ed); education (PhD); educational leadership studies (M Ed, Graduate Diploma); information technology (M Ed); post-secondary studies (M Ed, Diploma), including health professional education (Diploma). *Program availability:* Part-time. *Degree requirements:* For master's, thesis optional, internship, paper folio, project; for doctorate, comprehensive exam, thesis/dissertation, thesis seminar, oral defense of thesis. *Entrance requirements:* For master's, undergraduate degree with at least 2nd class standing, 1-2 years of work experience; for doctorate, minimum A average in graduate course work, MA in education, 2 years of professional experience; for other advanced degree, 2nd class degree, 2 years of work experience with adult learners, appropriate academic qualifications and work experience in a health-related field. Electronic applications accepted. *Faculty research:* Critical thinking, literacy, cognitive studies and counseling, educational change, technology in instruction.

Mercer University, Graduate Studies, Cecil B. Day Campus, Tift College of Education (Atlanta), Atlanta, GA 30341. Offers curriculum and instruction (PhD); early childhood education (M Ed, MAT, Ed S); educational leadership (PhD), including higher education leadership, P-12 school leadership; educational leadership P-12 (M Ed, Ed S); higher education leadership (M Ed); independent and charter school leadership (M Ed); middle grades education (M Ed, MAT); secondary education (M Ed, MAT); teacher leadership (Ed S). *Accreditation:* NCATE. *Program availability:* Part-time, evening/weekend. *Faculty:* 30 full-time (18 women), 34 part-time/adjunct (27 women). *Students:* 159 full-time (131 women), 284 part-time (229 women); includes 264 minority (232 Black or African American, non-Hispanic/Latino; 1 American Indian or Alaska Native, non-Hispanic/Latino; 9 Asian, non-Hispanic/Latino; 18 Hispanic/Latino; 4 Two or more races, non-Hispanic/Latino), 2 international. Average age 35. In 2017, 137 master's, 22 doctorates, 40 other advanced degrees awarded. *Degree requirements:* For master's and Ed S, research project; for doctorate, comprehensive exam, thesis/dissertation. *Entrance requirements:* For master's, GRE or MAT, minimum undergraduate GPA of 2.75; for doctorate, GRE; for Ed S, GRE or MAT, minimum GPA of 3.25; 3 years of certified teaching experience (for educational leadership and teacher leadership). Additional exam requirements/recommendations for international students: Required—TOEFL (minimum score 80 iBT). *Application deadline:* For fall admission, 8/1 for domestic and international students; for spring admission, 12/1 for domestic and international students; for summer admission, 5/1 for domestic and international students. Applications are processed on a rolling basis. Application fee: $25 ($50 for international students). Electronic applications accepted. *Expenses:* Contact institution. *Financial support:* Federal Work-Study and unspecified assistantships available. Support available to part-time students. Financial award application deadline: 5/1; financial award applicants required to submit FAFSA. *Faculty research:* Educational technology, multicultural and minority issues in education, educational leadership (P-12 and higher education), school discipline and school bullying, standards-based mathematics education. *Unit head:* Dr. Scott Davis, Dean, 478-301-2110, Fax: 478-301-5576.
Website: http://education.mercer.edu/

Mercer University, Graduate Studies, Macon Campus, Tift College of Education (Macon), Macon, GA 31207. Offers curriculum and instruction (PhD); early childhood education (M Ed, Ed S); educational leadership (M Ed, PhD, Ed S), including higher education (PhD), P-12; higher education leadership (M Ed); independent and charter school leadership (M Ed); secondary education (MAT), including STEM; teacher leadership (Ed S). *Accreditation:* NCATE. *Program availability:* Part-time, evening/weekend, 100% online, blended/hybrid learning. *Faculty:* 13 full-time (8 women), 1 part-time/adjunct (0 women). *Students:* 33 full-time (18 women), 51 part-time (37 women); includes 49 minority (44 Black or African American, non-Hispanic/Latino; 2 Asian, non-Hispanic/Latino; 2 Hispanic/Latino; 1 Two or more races, non-Hispanic/Latino), 1 international. Average age 32. In 2017, 22 master's, 17 doctorates awarded. *Degree requirements:* For master's, research project report; for doctorate, comprehensive exam, thesis/dissertation. *Entrance requirements:* For master's, GRE or MAT, minimum GPA of 2.75; for doctorate, GRE, minimum GPA of 3.5; interview; writing sample; 3 recommendations; for Ed S, GRE or MAT, minimum GPA of 3.5 (for teacher leadership), 3.0 (for educational leadership). Additional exam requirements/recommendations for international students: Required—TOEFL (minimum score 80 iBT). *Application deadline:* For fall admission, 8/1 for domestic and international students; for spring admission, 12/1 for domestic and international students. Applications are processed on a rolling basis. Application fee: $35. Electronic applications accepted. *Expenses:* Contact institution. *Financial support:* Federal Work-Study, institutionally sponsored loans, and unspecified assistantships available. Support available to part-time students. Financial award application deadline: 5/1; financial award applicants required to submit FAFSA. *Faculty research:* Teacher effectiveness, specific learning disabilities, inclusion. *Unit head:* Dr. Scott Davis, Dean, 478-301-2110, Fax: 478-301-5576, E-mail: davis_ds@mercer.edu.
Website: http://education.mercer.edu/

Mercy College, School of Education, Advanced Certificate Program in Educational Leadership, Dobbs Ferry, NY 10522-1189. Offers educational leadership (Advanced Certificate). *Program availability:* Part-time, evening/weekend. *Students:* 9 part-time (4 women); includes 4 minority (3 Black or African American, non-Hispanic/Latino; 1 Hispanic/Latino). Average age 37. 1 applicant, 100% accepted, 1 enrolled. *Degree requirements:* For Advanced Certificate, thesis or alternative, capstone. *Entrance requirements:* For degree, initial or professional teaching certification; interview with program director or faculty advisor; two years of teaching or specialty area experience; resume; master's degree from accredited institution. Additional exam requirements/recommendations for international students: Required—TOEFL (minimum score 600 paper-based; 100 iBT), IELTS (minimum score 8). *Application deadline:* For fall admission, 8/1 for international students. Applications are processed on a rolling basis.

Educational Leadership and Administration

Application fee: $40. Electronic applications accepted. *Expenses: Tuition:* Full-time $15,426; part-time $857 per credit hour. *Required fees:* $630; $158 per term. Tuition and fees vary according to course load, degree level and program. *Financial support:* Career-related internships or fieldwork, Federal Work-Study, scholarships/grants, and unspecified assistantships available. Support available to part-time students. Financial award applicants required to submit FAFSA. *Faculty research:* School law, leadership, supervision. *Unit head:* Dr. Rose Rudnitski, Dean, School of Education, 914-674-7447, Fax: 914-674-7352, E-mail: rrudnitski@mercy.edu. *Application contact:* Mary Ellen Hoffman, Director, Graduate Education Programs, 914-674-7334, E-mail: mhoffman@mercy.edu.
Website: https://www.mercy.edu/education/educational-leadership

Mercy College, School of Education, Program in Educational Leadership, Dobbs Ferry, NY 10522-1189. Offers MS. *Program availability:* Part-time, evening/weekend, blended/hybrid learning. *Students:* 3 full-time (all women), 105 part-time (79 women); includes 49 minority (20 Black or African American, non-Hispanic/Latino; 1 Asian, non-Hispanic/Latino; 28 Hispanic/Latino). Average age 32. 25 applicants, 60% accepted, 10 enrolled. In 2017, 80 master's awarded. *Degree requirements:* For master's, comprehensive exam (for some programs), thesis (for some programs). *Entrance requirements:* For master's, GRE, resume, interview, undergraduate transcript. Additional exam requirements/recommendations for international students: Required—TOEFL (minimum score 600 paper-based; 100 iBT), IELTS (minimum score 8). *Application deadline:* For fall admission, 8/1 for international students. Applications are processed on a rolling basis. Application fee: $40. Electronic applications accepted. *Expenses: Tuition:* Full-time $15,426; part-time $857 per credit hour. *Required fees:* $630; $158 per term. Tuition and fees vary according to course load, degree level and program. *Financial support:* Career-related internships or fieldwork, Federal Work-Study, scholarships/grants, and unspecified assistantships available. Support available to part-time students. Financial award applicants required to submit FAFSA. *Unit head:* Dr. Rose Rudnitski, Dean for the School of Education, 914-674-7447, Fax: 914-674-7352, E-mail: rrudnitski@mercy.edu. *Application contact:* Allison Gurdineer, Senior Director of Admissions, 877-637-2946, Fax: 914-674-7382, E-mail: admissions@mercy.edu.
Website: https://www.mercy.edu/education/educational-leadership

Mercyhurst University, Graduate Studies, Program in Organizational Leadership, Erie, PA 16546. Offers accounting (MS); higher education administration (MS); human resources (MS); organizational leadership (MS, Certificate); sports leadership (MS); strategy and innovation (MS). *Program availability:* Part-time, evening/weekend. *Degree requirements:* For master's, thesis. *Entrance requirements:* For master's, GRE General Test or MAT, interview, resume, essay, three professional references, transcripts. Additional exam requirements/recommendations for international students: Required—TOEFL (minimum score 80 iBT), IELTS (minimum score 6.5). Electronic applications accepted. *Faculty research:* Leadership training, organizational communication, leadership pedagogy.

Merrimack College, School of Education and Social Policy, North Andover, MA 01845-5800. Offers community engagement (M Ed), including community organizations, higher education, PreK-12 education; criminology and criminal justice (MS); curriculum and instruction (M Ed); early childhood education (M Ed); educational leadership (CAGS), including instructional leadership; elementary education (M Ed); English as a second language (PreK-6) (M Ed); high school education (M Ed); higher education (M Ed), including leadership and organizational development, student affairs; middle school education (M Ed); moderate disabilities (PreK-8) (M Ed); school counseling (M Ed). *Program availability:* Part-time, evening/weekend, 100% online courses with immersion events and in-classroom practicum close to home. *Faculty:* 15 full-time, 36 part-time/adjunct. *Students:* 212 full-time (175 women), 121 part-time (101 women); includes 42 minority (6 Black or African American, non-Hispanic/Latino; 6 Asian, non-Hispanic/Latino; 27 Hispanic/Latino; 3 Two or more races, non-Hispanic/Latino), 3 international. Average age 27. 420 applicants, 84% accepted, 250 enrolled. In 2017, 177 master's awarded. *Degree requirements:* For master's, practicum, portfolio, and state test (for licensure track); capstone (for higher education, curriculum and instruction, and community engagement tracks); for CAGS, capstone. *Entrance requirements:* For master's, Massachusetts Teacher Education Licensure (MTEL), official transcripts from other colleges, resume, personal statement, 2 letters of recommendation. Additional exam requirements/recommendations for international students: Required—TOEFL (minimum score 84 iBT), IELTS (minimum score 6.5), PTE (minimum score 56). *Application deadline:* For fall admission, 8/24 for domestic students, 7/30 for international students; for spring admission, 1/10 for domestic students, 12/10 for international students; for summer admission, 5/10 for domestic students, 4/10 for international students. Applications are processed on a rolling basis. Application fee: $0. Electronic applications accepted. *Expenses:* Contact institution. *Financial support:* Fellowships with full tuition reimbursements, career-related internships or fieldwork, scholarships/grants, and health care benefits available. Support available to part-time students. Financial award application deadline: 5/1; financial award applicants required to submit FAFSA. *Application contact:* Alyssa Orlando, Graduate Admissions Counselor, 978-837-3563, E-mail: orlandoaf@merrimack.edu.
Website: http://www.merrimack.edu/academics/graduate/education/

Miami University, College of Education, Health and Society, Department of Educational Leadership, Oxford, OH 45056. Offers educational leadership (Ed D, PhD); school leadership (M Ed); student affairs in higher education (MS, PhD); transformative education (M Ed). *Accreditation:* NCATE. *Students:* 83 full-time (57 women), 138 part-time (91 women); includes 50 minority (22 Black or African American, non-Hispanic/Latino; 1 American Indian or Alaska Native, non-Hispanic/Latino; 10 Asian, non-Hispanic/Latino; 10 Hispanic/Latino; 7 Two or more races, non-Hispanic/Latino), 11 international. Average age 35. In 2017, 50 master's, 12 doctorates awarded. *Expenses:* Tuition, state resident: full-time $13,812; part-time $575 per credit hour. Tuition, nonresident: full-time $30,860; part-time $1286 per credit hour. *Unit head:* Dr. Kathleen Knight Abowitz, Chair and Professor, 513-529-6848, E-mail: knightk2@miamioh.edu. *Application contact:* Dr. Thomas Poetter, Professor and Director of Graduate Studies, 513-529-6825, E-mail: poettets@miamioh.edu.
Website: http://www.MiamiOH.edu/EDL

Michigan State University, The Graduate School, College of Education, Department of Educational Administration, East Lansing, MI 48824. Offers higher, adult and lifelong education (MA, PhD); K–12 educational administration (MA, PhD, Ed S); student affairs administration (MA). *Program availability:* Part-time. *Entrance requirements:* Additional exam requirements/recommendations for international students: Required—TOEFL. Electronic applications accepted.

Middle Tennessee State University, College of Graduate Studies, College of Education, Department of Educational Leadership, Program in Administration and Supervision, Murfreesboro, TN 37132. Offers M Ed, Ed S. *Program availability:* Part-time, evening/weekend, online learning. *Degree requirements:* For master's, comprehensive exam; for Ed S, comprehensive exam, thesis or alternative. *Entrance requirements:* For master's and Ed S, GRE, MAT or current teaching license. Additional exam requirements/recommendations for international students: Required—TOEFL (minimum score 525 paper-based; 71 iBT) or IELTS (minimum score 6). Electronic applications accepted.

Midwestern State University, Billie Doris McAda Graduate School, West College of Education, Programs in Educational Leadership and Technology, Wichita Falls, TX 76308. Offers educational leadership (M Ed); educational technology (M Ed). *Program availability:* Part-time, evening/weekend. *Degree requirements:* For master's, comprehensive exam. *Entrance requirements:* For master's, GRE General Test or MAT. Additional exam requirements/recommendations for international students: Required—TOEFL (minimum score 550 paper-based). Electronic applications accepted. *Faculty research:* Role of the principal in the twenty-first century, culturally proficient leadership, human diversity, immigration, teacher collaboration.

Millersville University of Pennsylvania, College of Graduate Studies and Adult Learning, College of Education and Human Services, Department of Educational Foundations, Program in Educational Leadership, Millersville, PA 17551-0302. Offers Ed D. *Program availability:* Part-time, evening/weekend, blended/hybrid learning. *Faculty:* 9 full-time (8 women), 8 part-time/adjunct (5 women). *Students:* 16 part-time (11 women); includes 1 minority (Black or African American, non-Hispanic/Latino). Average age 41. 11 applicants, 82% accepted, 4 enrolled. *Degree requirements:* For doctorate, comprehensive exam, thesis/dissertation, candidacy exam. *Entrance requirements:* For doctorate, teaching certificate; interview; 3-5 years of professional experience as specified by PDE; three letters of recommendation; 500- to 1000-word goal statement addressing goals and objectives for doctoral study in educational leadership and how program will assist in achieving those outcomes. Additional exam requirements/recommendations for international students: Required—TOEFL (minimum score 80 iBT), IELTS (minimum score 6.5), PTE (minimum score 60). *Application deadline:* Applications are processed on a rolling basis. Application fee: $40. Electronic applications accepted. *Expenses:* $650 per credit resident tuition, $975 per credit non-resident tuition. *Financial support:* Unspecified assistantships available. Financial award application deadline: 3/15; financial award applicants required to submit FAFSA. *Faculty research:* Follett management methods, teacher supervision and evaluation, poverty and educational outcomes. *Unit head:* Dr. Tim E. Mahoney, Chair, 717-871-7202, E-mail: tim.mahoney@millersville.edu. *Application contact:* Dr. Victor S. DeSantis, Dean of College of Graduate Studies and Adult Learning/Associate Provost for Civic and Community Engagement, 717-871-7619, Fax: 717-871-7954, E-mail: victor.desantis@millersville.edu.
Website: http://www.millersville.edu/graduate/programs/doctorate/doctorate-of-education-in-educational-leadership.php

Millersville University of Pennsylvania, College of Graduate Studies and Adult Learning, College of Education and Human Services, Department of Educational Foundations, Program in Leadership for Teaching and Learning, Millersville, PA 17551-0302. Offers M Ed. *Program availability:* Part-time, evening/weekend. *Faculty:* 9 full-time (8 women), 8 part-time/adjunct (5 women). *Students:* 16 part-time (8 women); includes 1 minority (Black or African American, non-Hispanic/Latino). Average age 34. 2 applicants, 100% accepted, 2 enrolled. In 2017, 11 master's awarded. *Degree requirements:* For master's, comprehensive exam, applied practicum experience, portfolio review. *Entrance requirements:* For master's, GRE or MAT, teaching certificate; interview. Additional exam requirements/recommendations for international students: Required—TOEFL (minimum score 80 iBT), IELTS (minimum score 6.5), PTE (minimum score 60). *Application deadline:* Applications are processed on a rolling basis. Application fee: $40. Electronic applications accepted. *Expenses:* $500 per credit resident tuition and fees; $750 per credit non-resident tuition and fees; $114.75 per credit general fee (maximum of 12 credits); technology fee $27 per credit (resident), $39 per credit (non-resident). *Financial support:* Unspecified assistantships available. Financial award application deadline: 3/15; financial award applicants required to submit FAFSA. *Faculty research:* Support for LGBT teachers, teacher supervision and instructional assessment, effective school leadership. *Unit head:* Dr. Tim E. Mahoney, Chair, 717-871-7202, E-mail: tim.mahoney@millersville.edu. *Application contact:* Dr. Victor S. DeSantis, Dean of College of Graduate Studies and Adult Learning/Associate Provost for Civic and Community Engagement, 717-871-7619, Fax: 717-871-7954, E-mail: victor.desantis@millersville.edu.
Website: https://www.millersville.edu/edfoundations/m_ed_leadership.php

Milligan College, Area of Education, Milligan College, TN 37682. Offers combined preK-3/K-5 education (M Ed); educational leadership (Ed D, Ed S); K-5 education (M Ed); middle grades education (M Ed); preK-3 education (M Ed); preK-3 special education (M Ed); secondary education (M Ed). *Accreditation:* NCATE. *Program availability:* Part-time. *Faculty:* 6 full-time (4 women), 3 part-time/adjunct (2 women). *Students:* 27 full-time (20 women), 20 part-time (11 women); includes 2 minority (1 Hispanic/Latino; 1 Two or more races, non-Hispanic/Latino), 1 international. Average age 34. 17 applicants, 35% accepted, 6 enrolled. In 2017, 21 master's awarded. *Degree requirements:* For master's, thesis, portfolio, research project; for doctorate, thesis/dissertation, portfolio, research project. *Entrance requirements:* For master's, MAT, GRE General Test, ACT, SAT, or PRAXIS, undergraduate degree and supporting transcripts, professional recommendations, interview; for doctorate, MAT or GRE, master's degree and supporting transcripts, demonstrated scholastic ability, recognized leadership role within education, professional recommendations, essay/personal statement, portfolio (professional development plan, evidence of ability, knowledge and qualities), interview. Additional exam requirements/recommendations for international students: Required—TOEFL (minimum score 550 paper-based, 79 iBT) or IELTS (6.5). *Application deadline:* For fall admission, 8/1 priority date for domestic students, 6/1 for international students; for spring admission, 11/15 priority date for domestic students, 12/1 for international students; for summer admission, 4/1 for domestic students. Applications are processed on a rolling basis. Application fee: $30. Electronic applications accepted. *Expenses:* $360 per hour tuition (M Ed), $475 per hour (Ed D and Ed S); $325 per semester tech/activity fees. *Financial support:* Scholarships/grants available. Financial award application deadline: 12/1; financial award applicants required to submit FAFSA. *Faculty research:* Assessment; school mental health; literacy; technology; educator preparation. *Unit head:* Dr. Angela Hilton-Prillhart, Area Chair of Education, 423-461-8769, Fax: 423-461-3103, E-mail: anhilton-prillhart@milligan.edu. *Application contact:* Melissa Dillow, Graduate Admissions Recruiter, Education, 423-461-8306, Fax: 423-461-8982, E-mail: msdillow@milligan.edu.
Website: http://www.Milligan.edu/GPS

Mills College, Graduate Studies, MBA/MA Program in Educational Leadership, Oakland, CA 94613-1000. Offers MBA/MA. Program offered jointly between School of Education and Lorry I. Lokey Graduate School of Business. *Faculty:* 1 (woman) full-time. *Students:* 2 full-time (both women), 1 (woman) part-time; all minorities (1 Black or African American, non-Hispanic/Latino; 1 Asian, non-Hispanic/Latino; 1 Hispanic/Latino). Average age 29. 1 applicant, 100% accepted. *Entrance requirements:* Additional exam requirements/recommendations for international students: Required—TOEFL (minimum score 550 paper-based; 80 iBT) or IELTS (minimum score 6). *Application deadline:* For fall admission, 2/1 priority date for domestic students, 12/15 priority date for international students. Applications are processed on a rolling basis. Application fee: $50. Electronic applications accepted. *Expenses: Tuition:* Full-time $33,480; part-time $1000 per credit. *Required fees:* $1479. Tuition and fees vary according to program. *Financial support:* In 2017–18, 2 students received support, including 2 fellowships with tuition reimbursements available (averaging $7,500 per year), 1 teaching assistantship with tuition reimbursement available (averaging $1,986 per year). Financial award application deadline: 2/1; financial award applicants required to submit FAFSA. *Unit head:* Alice McDonald, Program Head, E-mail: amcdonald@mills.edu. *Application contact:* Robynne Lofton, Director of Admissions, 510-430-3295, Fax: 510-430-2159, E-mail: grad-admission@mills.edu. *Website:* http://www.mills.edu/MBAMAEdLdrshp

Minnesota State University Mankato, College of Graduate Studies and Research, College of Education, Department of Educational Leadership, Program in Experiential Education, Mankato, MN 56001. Offers MS. *Accreditation:* NCATE. *Program availability:* Part-time, evening/weekend. *Degree requirements:* For master's, thesis or alternative. *Entrance requirements:* For master's, minimum GPA of 3.0 during previous 2 years. Additional exam requirements/recommendations for international students: Required—TOEFL. Electronic applications accepted.

Minnesota State University Moorhead, Graduate Studies, College of Education and Human Services, Moorhead, MN 56563. Offers counseling and student affairs (MS); curriculum and instruction (MS); educational leadership (MS, Ed D, Ed S); special education (MS); speech-language pathology (MS). *Accreditation:* NCATE. *Program availability:* Part-time, 100% online, blended/hybrid learning. *Faculty:* 22. *Students:* 117 full-time (101 women), 337 part-time (253 women). Average age 32. 248 applicants, 49% accepted. In 2017, 149 master's, 16 other advanced degrees awarded. *Degree requirements:* For master's, comprehensive exam (for some programs), thesis, final oral defense; for doctorate, comprehensive exam (for some programs), thesis/dissertation, final oral defense. *Entrance requirements:* For master's, GRE, essay, letter of intent, letters of reference, teaching license, teaching verification, minimum cumulative GPA of 3.0; for doctorate, official transcripts; letter of intent; resume or curriculum vitae; master's degree; personal essay. Additional exam requirements/recommendations for international students: Required—TOEFL (minimum score 550 paper-based); Recommended—IELTS (minimum score 6.5). *Application deadline:* Applications are processed on a rolling basis. Application fee: $20. Electronic applications accepted. *Expenses:* Tuition, state resident: full-time $9000; part-time $374 per credit. Tuition, nonresident: full-time $18,000; part-time $748 per credit. *Required fees:* $1055; $43.96 per credit. Tuition and fees vary according to degree level, program and reciprocity agreements. *Financial support:* Federal Work-Study and unspecified assistantships available. Financial award application deadline: 10/1; financial award applicants required to submit FAFSA. *Unit head:* Dr. Ok-Hee Lee, Dean, 218-477-2095, E-mail: okheelee@mnstate.edu. *Application contact:* Karla Wenger, Office Manager, 218-477-2344, Fax: 218-477-2482, E-mail: wengerk@mnstate.edu. *Website:* http://www.mnstate.edu/cehs/

Mississippi College, Graduate School, School of Education, Department of Teacher Education and Leadership, Clinton, MS 39058. Offers art (M Ed); biological science (M Ed); business education (M Ed); computer science (M Ed); dyslexia therapy (M Ed); educational leadership (M Ed, Ed D, Ed S); elementary education (M Ed, Ed S); English (M Ed); higher education administration (MS); mathematics (M Ed); secondary education (M Ed); social studies (history) (M Ed); teaching arts (M Ed). *Program availability:* Part-time, online learning. *Degree requirements:* For master's, comprehensive exam, thesis optional. *Entrance requirements:* For master's, NTE. Additional exam requirements/recommendations for international students: Recommended—TOEFL, IELTS. Electronic applications accepted.

Mississippi College, Graduate School, School of Education, Program in Higher Education Administration, Clinton, MS 39058. Offers MS. *Program availability:* Part-time, online learning. *Degree requirements:* For master's, comprehensive exam, thesis optional. *Entrance requirements:* For master's, GRE or GMAT, minimum GPA of 3.0. Additional exam requirements/recommendations for international students: Recommended—TOEFL, IELTS.

Mississippi State University, College of Agriculture and Life Sciences, School of Human Sciences, Mississippi State, MS 39762. Offers agriculture and extension education (MS), including communication, leadership; agriculture science (PhD), including agriculture and extension education; fashion design and merchandising (MS), including design and product development, merchandising; human development and family studies (MS, PhD). *Accreditation:* NCATE (one or more programs are accredited). *Program availability:* Part-time. *Faculty:* 20 full-time (11 women). *Students:* 31 full-time (23 women), 54 part-time (38 women); includes 19 minority (15 Black or African American, non-Hispanic/Latino; 1 Hispanic/Latino; 3 Two or more races, non-Hispanic/Latino), 5 international. Average age 36. 26 applicants, 65% accepted, 15 enrolled. In 2017, 19 master's, 2 doctorates awarded. *Degree requirements:* For master's, thesis optional, comprehensive oral or written exam. *Entrance requirements:* For master's, GRE, minimum GPA of 2.75 in last 4 semesters of course work; for doctorate, minimum GPA of 3.0 on prior graduate work. Additional exam requirements/recommendations for international students: Required—TOEFL (minimum score 477 paper-based; 53 iBT); Recommended—IELTS (minimum score 4.5). *Application deadline:* For fall admission, 7/1 for domestic students, 5/1 for international students; for spring admission, 11/1 for domestic students, 9/1 for international students. Applications are processed on a rolling basis. Application fee: $60 ($80 for international students). Electronic applications accepted. *Expenses:* Tuition, state resident: full-time $8318; part-time $462.12 per credit hour. Tuition, nonresident: full-time $22,358; part-time $1242.12 per credit hour. *Required fees:* $110; $12.24 per credit hour. $6.12 per semester. *Financial support:* In 2017–18, 13 research assistantships (averaging $13,718 per year) were awarded; Federal Work-Study, institutionally sponsored loans, and unspecified assistantships also available. Financial award application deadline: 4/1; financial award applicants required to submit FAFSA. *Faculty research:* Animal welfare, agroscience, information technology, learning styles, problem solving. *Unit head:* Dr. Michael Newman, Professor and Director, 662-325-2950, E-mail: mnewman@humansci.msstate.edu. *Application contact:* Marina Hunt, Admissions and Enrollment Assistant, 662-325-5188, E-mail: mhunt@grad.msstate.edu. *Website:* http://www.humansci.msstate.edu

Mississippi State University, College of Education, Educational Leadership Program, Mississippi State, MS 39762. Offers community college education (MAT); community college leadership (PhD); higher education leadership (PhD); P-12 school leadership (PhD); school administration (MS, Ed S); student affairs and higher education (MS); workforce education leadership (MS). MS in workforce education leadership held jointly with Alcorn State University. *Faculty:* 12 full-time (9 women). *Students:* 62 full-time (33 women), 149 part-time (93 women); includes 94 minority (79 Black or African American, non-Hispanic/Latino; 5 American Indian or Alaska Native, non-Hispanic/Latino; 4 Hispanic/Latino; 1 Native Hawaiian or other Pacific Islander, non-Hispanic/Latino; 5 Two or more races, non-Hispanic/Latino). Average age 36. 95 applicants, 79% accepted, 64 enrolled. In 2017, 41 master's, 32 doctorates, 7 other advanced degrees awarded. *Degree requirements:* For master's and Ed S, comprehensive exam, thesis; for doctorate, comprehensive exam, thesis/dissertation. *Entrance requirements:* For master's, GRE, minimum GPA of 2.75 in junior and senior courses; for doctorate, GRE, minimum GPA of 3.4 on previous graduate work; for Ed S, GRE, minimum GPA of 3.2, master's degree. Additional exam requirements/recommendations for international students: Required—TOEFL (minimum score 550 paper-based; 79 iBT); Recommended—IELTS (minimum score 6.5). *Application deadline:* For fall admission, 7/1 for domestic students, 5/1 for international students; for spring admission, 11/1 for

domestic students, 9/1 for international students. Application fee: $60 ($80 for international students). Electronic applications accepted. *Expenses:* Tuition, state resident: full-time $8318; part-time $462.12 per credit hour. Tuition, nonresident: full-time $22,358; part-time $1242.12 per credit hour. *Required fees:* $110; $12.24 per credit hour. $6.12 per semester. *Financial support:* In 2017–18, 1 research assistantship with full tuition reimbursement (averaging $10,879 per year) was awarded; Federal Work-Study, institutionally sponsored loans, and unspecified assistantships also available. Financial award application deadline: 4/1; financial award applicants required to submit FAFSA. *Unit head:* Dr. Eric Moyen, Associate Professor and Head, 662-325-0969, Fax: 662-325-0975, E-mail: em1621@msstate.edu. *Application contact:* Nathan Drake, Admissions and Enrollment Assistant, 662-325-3804, E-mail: ndrake@grad.msstate.edu. *Website:* http://www.educationalleadership.msstate.edu/

Mississippi University for Women, Graduate School, College of Education and Human Sciences, Columbus, MS 39701-9998. Offers differentiated instruction (M Ed); educational leadership (M Ed); gifted studies (M Ed); reading/literacy (M Ed); teaching (MAT). *Accreditation:* ASHA; NCATE. *Program availability:* Part-time. *Degree requirements:* For master's, comprehensive exam, thesis optional. *Entrance requirements:* For master's, GRE General Test or NTE (M Ed in gifted education or MS in speech/language pathology), MAT (M Ed in instructional management), minimum QPA of 3.0.

Missouri Baptist University, Graduate Programs, St. Louis, MO 63141-8660. Offers business administration (MBA); Christian ministries (MACM); counseling (MAC); education (MSE); education administration (MEA); educational leadership (MSE, Ed S); teaching (MAT).

Missouri State University, Graduate College, College of Education, Department of Counseling, Leadership, and Special Education, Program in Educational Administration, Springfield, MO 65897. Offers elementary principal (MS Ed, Ed S); secondary principal (MS Ed, Ed S); superintendent (Ed S). *Program availability:* Part-time, evening/weekend. *Faculty:* 5 full-time (2 women), 1 part-time/adjunct (0 women). *Students:* 8 full-time (4 women), 60 part-time (42 women); includes 7 minority (1 American Indian or Alaska Native, non-Hispanic/Latino; 4 Hispanic/Latino; 2 Two or more races, non-Hispanic/Latino). Average age 26. 46 applicants, 98% accepted, 31 enrolled. In 2017, 18 master's, 8 Ed Ss awarded. *Degree requirements:* For master's and Ed S, comprehensive exam, thesis or alternative. *Entrance requirements:* For master's, minimum GPA of 2.75; for Ed S, GRE General Test, MAT, minimum GPA of 2.75. Additional exam requirements/recommendations for international students: Required—TOEFL (minimum score 550 paper-based; 79 iBT), IELTS (minimum score 6). *Application deadline:* For fall admission, 7/20 priority date for domestic students, 5/1 for international students; for spring admission, 12/20 priority date for domestic students, 9/1 for international students; for summer admission, 5/20 priority date for domestic students. Applications are processed on a rolling basis. Application fee: $35 ($50 for international students). Electronic applications accepted. *Expenses:* Tuition, state resident: full-time $2915; part-time $2021 per credit hour. Tuition, nonresident: full-time $5354; part-time $3647 per credit hour. *International tuition:* $11,992 full-time. *Required fees:* $173; $173 per credit hour. Tuition and fees vary according to class time, course level, course load, degree level, campus/location and program. *Financial support:* Career-related internships or fieldwork, Federal Work-Study, institutionally sponsored loans, scholarships/grants, and unspecified assistantships available. Financial award application deadline: 3/31; financial award applicants required to submit FAFSA. *Unit head:* Dr. James Satterfield, Department Head, 417-836-5392, Fax: 417-836-4918, E-mail: clse@missouristate.edu. *Application contact:* Stephanie Praschan, Director, Graduate Enrollment Management, 417-836-5330, Fax: 417-836-6200, E-mail: stephaniepraschan@missouristate.edu. *Website:* http://education.missouristate.edu/edadmin/

Missouri State University, Graduate College, College of Education, Department of Reading, Foundations, and Technology, Springfield, MO 65897. Offers educational technology (MS Ed); literacy (MS Ed, Certificate, Graduate Certificate); teacher leadership (Certificate, Ed S); teaching (MAT); teaching and learning (MA, Certificate). *Program availability:* Part-time, evening/weekend, 100% online, blended/hybrid learning. *Faculty:* 13 full-time (6 women), 8 part-time/adjunct (7 women). *Students:* 25 full-time (22 women), 180 part-time (153 women); includes 10 minority (9 Hispanic/Latino; 1 Two or more races, non-Hispanic/Latino), 6 international. Average age 26. 67 applicants, 79% accepted, 33 enrolled. In 2017, 69 master's, 3 other advanced degrees awarded. *Degree requirements:* For master's, comprehensive exam, thesis or alternative. *Entrance requirements:* Additional exam requirements/recommendations for international students: Required—TOEFL (minimum score 550 paper-based; 79 iBT), IELTS (minimum score 6). *Application deadline:* For fall admission, 7/20 priority date for domestic students, 5/1 for international students; for spring admission, 12/20 priority date for domestic students, 9/1 for international students; for summer admission, 5/20 priority date for domestic students. Applications are processed on a rolling basis. Application fee: $35 ($50 for international students). Electronic applications accepted. *Expenses:* Tuition, state resident: full-time $2915; part-time $2021 per credit hour. Tuition, nonresident: full-time $5354; part-time $3647 per credit hour. *International tuition:* $11,992 full-time. *Required fees:* $173; $173 per credit hour. Tuition and fees vary according to class time, course level, course load, degree level, campus/location and program. *Financial support:* Federal Work-Study, institutionally sponsored loans, scholarships/grants, and unspecified assistantships available. Financial award application deadline: 3/31; financial award applicants required to submit FAFSA. *Faculty research:* Literacy and technology, struggling readers, community service learning. *Unit head:* Dr. Emmett Sawyer, Interim Department Head, 417-836-6769, Fax: 417-836-6252, E-mail: rft@missouristate.edu. *Application contact:* Stephanie Praschan, Director, Graduate Enrollment Management, 417-836-5330, Fax: 417-836-6200, E-mail: stephaniepraschan@missouristate.edu. *Website:* http://education.missouristate.edu/rft/

Monmouth University, Graduate Studies, School of Education, West Long Branch, NJ 07764-1898. Offers applied behavior analysis (Certificate); autism (Certificate); director of school counseling services (Post-Master's Certificate); early childhood (M Ed); educational leadership (Ed D), including elementary level, secondary level; English as a second language (M Ed); learning disabilities teacher-consultant (Post-Master's Certificate); literacy (MS Ed); school counseling (MS Ed); special education (MS Ed), including autism, learning disabilities teacher-consultant, teacher of students with disabilities, teaching in inclusive settings; speech-language pathology (MS Ed); student affairs and college counseling (MS Ed); supervisor (Post-Master's Certificate); teaching English to speakers of other languages (Certificate). *Accreditation:* NCATE. *Program availability:* Part-time, evening/weekend, 100% online, blended/hybrid learning. *Faculty:* 23 full-time (19 women), 33 part-time/adjunct (25 women). *Students:* 175 full-time (163 women), 168 part-time (142 women); includes 54 minority (10 Black or African American, non-Hispanic/Latino; 4 Asian, non-Hispanic/Latino; 32 Hispanic/Latino; 8 Two or more races, non-Hispanic/Latino). Average age 27. In 2017, 160 master's, 3 other advanced degrees awarded. *Entrance requirements:* For master's, GRE taken within last 5 years (for MS Ed in speech-language pathology); SAT (minimum combined score of 1660 in 3 sections), ACT (23), GRE (minimum score of 4.0

Educational Leadership and Administration

on analytical writing section and minimum combined score of 310 on quantitative and verbal sections), or passing scores on 3 parts of Core Academic Skills Educators, minimum GPA of 3.0 in major; 2 letters of recommendation (for some programs); resume, personal statement or essay (depending on program). Additional exam requirements/recommendations for international students: Required—TOEFL (minimum score 550 paper-based; 79 iBT), IELTS (minimum score 6), Michigan English Language Assessment Battery (minimum score 77) or Certificate of Advanced English (minimum score 160). *Application deadline:* For fall admission, 7/15 priority date for domestic students, 7/1 for international students; for spring admission, 12/1 priority date for domestic students, 11/1 for international students; for summer admission, 5/1 for domestic students. Applications are processed on a rolling basis. Application fee: $50. Electronic applications accepted. *Expenses: Tuition:* Full-time $21,366; part-time $7122 per credit. *Required fees:* $700; $175 per term. *Financial support:* In 2017–18, 125 students received support. Institutionally sponsored loans, scholarships/grants, and unspecified assistantships available. Support available to part-time students. Financial award applicants required to submit FAFSA. *Faculty research:* Multicultural literacy, science and mathematics teaching strategies, teacher as reflective practitioner, children with disabilities. *Unit head:* Dr. John E. Henning, Dean, 732-263-5513, Fax: 732-263-5277. *Application contact:* Laurie Kuhn, Associate Director of Graduate Admission, 732-571-3452, Fax: 732-263-5123, E-mail: gradadm@monmouth.edu.
Website: http://www.monmouth.edu/academics/schools/education/default.asp

Montana State University, The Graduate School, College of Education, Health, and Human Development, Department of Education, Bozeman, MT 59717. Offers adult and higher education (Ed D); curriculum and instruction (M Ed, Ed D), including professional educator (M Ed); technology education (M Ed); education (M Ed), including adult and higher education, educational leadership, school counseling; educational leadership (Ed D, Ed S). *Accreditation:* TEAC. *Program availability:* Part-time, online learning. *Degree requirements:* For master's, comprehensive exam; for doctorate, comprehensive exam, thesis/dissertation. *Entrance requirements:* For master's, GRE, 3 letters of reference, essays, BA transcripts; for doctorate, GRE, MAT, 3 letters of reference, essay, BA and M Ed transcripts; for Ed S, PRAXIS. Additional exam requirements/recommendations for international students: Required—TOEFL (minimum score 550 paper-based). Electronic applications accepted. *Faculty research:* Critical literacy; standards-based education; school Improvement, organizational change, leadership in rural education, leadership in Indian education; student Learning; multicultural/culturally responsive education for social justice Native American indigenous education, community-centered education teacher preparation.

Montclair State University, The Graduate School, College of Education and Human Services, Doctoral Program in Teacher Education and Teacher Development, Montclair, NJ 07043-1624. Offers PhD. *Program availability:* Part-time, evening/weekend. *Degree requirements:* For doctorate, comprehensive exam (for some programs), thesis/dissertation. *Entrance requirements:* For doctorate, GRE General Test, interview, 3 letters of recommendation, essay. Additional exam requirements/recommendations for international students: Required—TOEFL (minimum score 83 iBT), IELTS (minimum score 6.5). Electronic applications accepted.

Montclair State University, The Graduate School, College of Education and Human Services, Program in Educational Leadership, Montclair, NJ 07043-1624. Offers MA. *Program availability:* Part-time, evening/weekend. *Degree requirements:* For master's, comprehensive exam, thesis or alternative. *Entrance requirements:* For master's, GRE General Test, interview, 2 letters of recommendation. Additional exam requirements/recommendations for international students: Required—TOEFL (minimum score 83 iBT), IELTS (minimum score 6.5). Electronic applications accepted.

Morehead State University, Graduate Programs, College of Education, Department of Foundational and Graduate Studies in Education, Morehead, KY 40351. Offers adult and higher education (MA, Ed S); certified professional counselor (Ed S); counseling P-12 (MA); curriculum and instruction (Ed S); educational technology (MA Ed); instructional leadership (Ed S); school administration (MA); school counseling (Ed S); teacher leader business and marketing content (MA Ed); teacher leader business and marketing technology (MA Ed); teacher leader educational technology (MA Ed); teacher leader English (MA Ed); teacher leader gifted education (MA Ed); teacher leader IECE certification (MA Ed); teacher leader interdisciplinary education P-5 (MA Ed); teacher leader middle grades (MA Ed); teacher leader non IECE certification (MA Ed); teacher leader reading/writing - non-certification (MA Ed); teacher leader reading/writing certification (MA Ed); teacher leader school communication - certification (MA Ed); teacher leader school communication - non-certification (MA Ed); teacher leader social studies (MA Ed); teacher leader special education (MA Ed). *Accreditation:* NCATE. *Program availability:* Part-time, evening/weekend. *Degree requirements:* For master's, thesis optional, oral and/or written comprehensive exams; for Ed S, thesis, oral exam. *Entrance requirements:* For master's, GRE General Test, minimum overall undergraduate GPA of 2.5; for Ed S, GRE General Test, interview, master's degree, minimum GPA of 3.5, work experience. Additional exam requirements/recommendations for international students: Required—TOEFL (minimum score 500 paper-based). Electronic applications accepted. *Faculty research:* Character education, school accountability, computer applications for school administrators.

Morgan State University, School of Graduate Studies, School of Education and Urban Studies, Department of Advanced Studies, Leadership and Policy, Program in Community College Leadership, Baltimore, MD 21251. Offers Ed D. *Accreditation:* NCATE. *Program availability:* Part-time, evening/weekend. *Degree requirements:* For doctorate, comprehensive exam, thesis/dissertation. *Entrance requirements:* For doctorate, GRE General Test or MAT. Additional exam requirements/recommendations for international students: Required—TOEFL (minimum score 550 paper-based). *Application deadline:* For fall admission, 2/1 priority date for domestic students; for spring admission, 10/1 priority date for domestic students. Applications are processed on a rolling basis. Application fee: $0. *Expenses:* Tuition, state resident: part-time $433 per credit. Tuition, nonresident: part-time $851 per credit. *Required fees:* $81.50 per credit. *Financial support:* Application deadline: 2/1. *Faculty research:* Multicultural education, cooperative learning, psychology of cognition. *Unit head:* Carolyn Anderson, Interim Director, 443-885-4497, Fax: 443-885-8231, E-mail: carolyn.anderson@morgan.edu. *Application contact:* Dr. Dean Campbell, Graduate Recruitment Specialist, 443-885-3185, Fax: 443-885-8226, E-mail: dean.campbell@morgan.edu.

Morgan State University, School of Graduate Studies, School of Education and Urban Studies, Department of Advanced Studies, Leadership and Policy, Program in Higher Education Administration, Baltimore, MD 21251. Offers higher education (PhD); higher education and student affairs administration (MA). *Degree requirements:* For doctorate, comprehensive exam, thesis/dissertation. *Entrance requirements:* For doctorate, GRE General Test or MAT, minimum GPA of 3.0. *Application deadline:* For fall admission, 2/1 priority date for domestic students; for spring admission, 10/1 priority date for domestic students. Applications are processed on a rolling basis. Application fee: $0. *Expenses:* Tuition, state resident: part-time $433 per credit. Tuition, nonresident: part-time $851 per credit. *Required fees:* $81.50 per credit. *Financial support:* Application deadline: 2/1. *Unit head:* Dr. Sean Robinson, Admissions Coordinator, E-mail: sean.robinson@morgan.edu. *Application contact:* Dr. Dean Campbell, Graduate Recruitment Specialist, 443-885-3185, Fax: 443-885-8226, E-mail: dean.campbell@morgan.edu.

Mount Holyoke College, Professional and Graduate Education (PaGE), South Hadley, MA 01075. Offers mathematics teaching (MAMT); teacher leadership (MATL); teaching (MAT). *Program availability:* Part-time, 100% online, blended/hybrid learning. *Faculty:* 39 part-time/adjunct. *Students:* 20 full-time (18 women), 104 part-time (88 women); includes 18 minority (6 Black or African American, non-Hispanic/Latino; 2 Asian, non-Hispanic/Latino; 8 Hispanic/Latino; 2 Two or more races, non-Hispanic/Latino), 8 international. Average age 34. 100 applicants, 94% accepted, 68 enrolled. In 2017, 32 master's awarded. *Degree requirements:* For master's, practicum (for MAT); capstone project (for MATL); capstone portfolio (for MAMT). *Entrance requirements:* For master's, MTEL (for MAT initial licensure), bachelor's degree; subject area knowledge in desired teaching discipline; personal statement; essay; official transcripts; two letters of recommendation; history of effective classroom teaching (for MATL). Additional exam requirements/recommendations for international students: Required—TOEFL, IELTS. *Application deadline:* For fall admission, 8/15 for domestic students, 8/16 for international students; for winter admission, 12/15 for domestic and international students; for spring admission, 1/8 for domestic and international students; for summer admission, 5/15 for domestic and international students. Applications are processed on a rolling basis. Application fee: $50. Electronic applications accepted. *Expenses: Tuition:* Full-time $24,500; part-time $766 per credit hour. *Required fees:* $100. Tuition and fees vary according to course load and program. *Financial support:* Fellowships, research assistantships, scholarships/grants, and unspecified assistantships available. Support available to part-time students. *Faculty research:* Social justice; special education/moderate disabilities; English language learners and literacy; research and assessment; professional development and facilitating professional learning. *Unit head:* Dr. Tiffany Espinosa, Executive Director of Professional and Graduate Education, 413-538-3478, Fax: 413-538-3098, E-mail: tespinos@mtholyoke.edu.
Website: https://www.mtholyoke.edu/professional-graduate

Mount Mercy University, Program in Education, Cedar Rapids, IA 52402-4797. Offers reading (MA Ed); special education (MA Ed); teacher leadership (MA Ed). *Entrance requirements:* For master's, minimum cumulative GPA of 3.0, 2 letters of recommendation, resume, valid teaching license. Additional exam requirements/recommendations for international students: Required—TOEFL (minimum score 570 paper-based; 88 iBT). Electronic applications accepted.

Murray State University, College of Education and Human Services, Department of Adolescent, Career, and Special Education, Murray, KY 42071. Offers career and technical education (MS); middle school teacher leader (MA Ed); secondary teacher leader (MA Ed); special education (MA Ed), including mild learning and behavior disorders, moderate to severe disabilities (P-12), teacher leader in special education learning and behavior disorders; teacher education and professional development (Ed S). *Accreditation:* NCATE. *Program availability:* Part-time. *Faculty:* 10 full-time (9 women). *Students:* 4 full-time (2 women), 78 part-time (56 women); includes 4 minority (2 Black or African American, non-Hispanic/Latino; 1 Asian, non-Hispanic/Latino; 1 Hispanic/Latino), 2 international. Average age 33. 13 applicants, 100% accepted, 8 enrolled. In 2017, 19 master's awarded. *Entrance requirements:* For master's and Ed S, GRE or GMAT, minimum university GPA of 2.75. Additional exam requirements/recommendations for international students: Required—TOEFL (minimum score 527 paper-based; 71 iBT). *Application deadline:* Applications are processed on a rolling basis. Application fee: $40 ($50 for international students). Electronic applications accepted. *Expenses:* Tuition, state resident: full-time $9504. Tuition, nonresident: full-time $26,811. *International tuition:* $14,400 full-time. Tuition and fees vary according to course load, degree level and reciprocity agreements. *Financial support:* Federal Work-Study and unspecified assistantships available. Financial award applicants required to submit FAFSA. *Unit head:* Dr. Barbara Washington, Chair, Department of Adolescent, Career and Special Education, 270-809-2262, Fax: 270-809-2540, E-mail: bwashington@murraystate.edu. *Application contact:* Kaitlyn Burzynski, Interim Assistant Director of Graduate Admission and Records, 270-809-5732, Fax: 270-809-3780, E-mail: msu.graduateadmissions@murraystate.edu.
Website: http://www.murraystate.edu/academics/CollegesDepartments/CollegeOfEducationandHumanServices/coehsacademicunits/AdolescentCareerSpecialEd/index.aspx

Murray State University, College of Education and Human Services, Department of Early Childhood and Elementary Education, Murray, KY 42071. Offers elementary teacher leader (MA Ed); interdisciplinary early childhood education (MA Ed), including elementary education (MA Ed, Ed S), reading and writing; teacher education and professional development (Ed S), including elementary education (MA Ed, Ed S). *Accreditation:* NCATE. *Program availability:* Part-time. *Faculty:* 17 full-time (16 women), 1 (woman) part-time/adjunct. *Students:* 10 full-time (all women), 91 part-time (87 women); includes 7 minority (4 Black or African American, non-Hispanic/Latino; 1 Hispanic/Latino; 2 Two or more races, non-Hispanic/Latino). Average age 33. 27 applicants, 89% accepted, 19 enrolled. In 2017, 35 master's awarded. *Entrance requirements:* For master's and Ed S, GRE or GMAT, minimum university GPA of 2.75. Additional exam requirements/recommendations for international students: Required—TOEFL (minimum score 527 paper-based; 71 iBT). *Application deadline:* Applications are processed on a rolling basis. Application fee: $40 ($50 for international students). Electronic applications accepted. *Expenses:* Tuition, state resident: full-time $9504. Tuition, nonresident: full-time $26,811. *International tuition:* $14,400 full-time. Tuition and fees vary according to course load, degree level and reciprocity agreements. *Financial support:* Federal Work-Study and unspecified assistantships available. Financial award applicants required to submit FAFSA. *Unit head:* Dr. Jacqueline Hansen, Chair, Department of Early Childhood and Elementary Education, 270-809-2500, Fax: 270-809-3799, E-mail: jhansen@murraystate.edu. *Application contact:* Kaitlyn Burzynski, Interim Assistant Director for Graduate Admission and Records, 270-809-5732, Fax: 270-809-3780, E-mail: msu.graduateadmissions@murraystate.edu.
Website: http://www.murraystate.edu/academics/CollegesDepartments/CollegeOfEducationandHumanServices/coehsacademicunits/EarlyChildhoodandElementaryEducation/in

Murray State University, College of Education and Human Services, Department of Educational Studies, Leadership and Counseling, Murray, KY 42071. Offers college advising (Certificate); education administration (MA Ed); human development and leadership (MS, Certificate); library media (MA Ed); middle school teacher leader (MA Ed); P-20 and community leadership (Ed D); postsecondary education administration (MA Ed); school counseling (MA Ed); school guidance and counseling (Ed S); secondary teacher leader (MA Ed). *Program availability:* Part-time, evening/weekend, 100% online, blended/hybrid learning. *Faculty:* 38 full-time (16 women), 3 part-time/adjunct (1 woman). *Students:* 45 full-time (22 women), 190 part-time (140 women); includes 33 minority (25 Black or African American, non-Hispanic/Latino; 4 Asian, non-Hispanic/Latino; 3 Hispanic/Latino; 1 Two or more races, non-Hispanic/Latino), 6 international. Average age 35. 87 applicants, 77% accepted, 51 enrolled. In 2017, 21 master's, 16 doctorates, 12 other advanced degrees awarded. *Entrance requirements:* For master's and other advanced degree, GRE or GMAT, minimum university GPA of 2.75. Additional exam requirements/recommendations for international students: Required—TOEFL (minimum score 527 paper-based; 71 iBT). *Application deadline:* Applications are processed on a rolling basis. Application fee: $40 ($50 for international students). Electronic applications accepted. *Expenses:* Tuition,

state resident: full-time $9504. Tuition, nonresident: full-time $26,811. *International tuition:* $14,400 full-time. Tuition and fees vary according to course load, degree level and reciprocity agreements. *Financial support:* Federal Work-Study and unspecified assistantships available. Financial award applicants required to submit FAFSA. *Unit head:* Dr. Susana Bloomdahl, Chair, Department of Educational Studies, Leadership, and Counseling, 270-809-6471, Fax: 270-809-3799, E-mail: sbloomdahl@murraystate.edu. *Application contact:* Kaitlyn Burzynski, Interim Assistant Director for Graduate Admission and Records, 270-809-5732, Fax: 270-809-3780, E-mail: msu.graduateadmissions@murraystate.edu.
Website: http://www.murraystate.edu/academics/CollegesDepartments/CollegeOfEducationandHumanServices/coehsacademicunits/EducationalStudiesLeadershipandCounseli

National American University, Roueche Graduate Center, Austin, TX 78731. Offers accounting (MBA); aviation management (MBA, MM); care coordination (MSN); community college leadership (Ed D); criminal justice (MM); e-marketing (MBA, MM); health care administration (MBA, MM); higher education (MM); human resources management (MBA, MM); information technology management (MBA, MM); international business (MBA); leadership (EMBA); management (MBA); nursing administration (MSN); nursing education (MSN); nursing informatics (MSN); operations and configuration management (MBA, MM); project and process management (MBA, MM). Master's programs offered online through the Harold D. Buckingham Graduate School. *Program availability:* Part-time, evening/weekend, online learning. *Entrance requirements:* For master's, minimum undergraduate GPA of 2.75. Additional exam requirements/recommendations for international students: Required—TOEFL, TWE. Electronic applications accepted. *Faculty research:* Tourism, finance, marketing.

National Louis University, National College of Education, Chicago, IL 60603. Offers administration and supervision (M Ed, Ed D, CAS, Ed S); curriculum and instruction (M Ed, MS Ed, CAS); early childhood administration (M Ed, CAS); early childhood education (M Ed, MAT, MS Ed, CAS); education (Ed D); educational psychology/human learning and development (M Ed, MS Ed, CAS, Ed S); elementary education (MAT); interdisciplinary curriculum and instruction (M Ed); mathematics education (M Ed, MS Ed, CAS); middle grades education (MAT); reading and language (M Ed, MS Ed, CAS); school psychology (M Ed, Ed S); science education (M Ed, MS Ed, CAS); secondary education (MAT); special education (M Ed, MAT, CAS); technology in education (M Ed, CAS). *Accreditation:* NCATE. *Program availability:* Part-time, evening/weekend. *Degree requirements:* For doctorate, comprehensive exam, thesis/dissertation. *Entrance requirements:* For master's, MAT or GRE, minimum GPA of 3.0; for doctorate, GRE General Test, minimum GPA of 3.25, interview, resume, writing sample, 4 recommendations. Additional exam requirements/recommendations for international students: Required—TOEFL (minimum score 550 paper-based; 79 iBT).

National University, Academic Affairs, Sanford College of Education, La Jolla, CA 92037-1011. Offers advanced teaching practices (MS); applied behavior analysis (MS); applied school leadership (MS); e-teaching and learning (Certificate); education (MA); educational administration (MS); educational and instructional technology (MS); educational counseling (MS); higher education administration (MS); inspired teaching and learning (M Ed); school psychology (MS); special education (MA, MS). *Program availability:* Part-time, evening/weekend, 100% online, blended/hybrid learning. *Degree requirements:* For master's, thesis (for some programs). *Entrance requirements:* For master's, interview, minimum GPA of 2.5. Additional exam requirements/recommendations for international students: Required—TOEFL (minimum score 550 paper-based; 79 iBT), IELTS (minimum score 6). *Application deadline:* Applications are processed on a rolling basis. Application fee: $60 ($65 for international students). Electronic applications accepted. *Expenses:* Tuition: Part-time $430 per quarter hour. *Financial support:* Career-related internships or fieldwork, institutionally sponsored loans, scholarships/grants, and tuition waivers (partial) available. Support available to part-time students. Financial award application deadline: 6/30. *Faculty research:* Teacher education, special education, educational effectiveness, teaching abroad, school counseling. *Unit head:* Dr. Judy Mantle, Dean, 858-642-8320, E-mail: soe@nu.edu. *Application contact:* Brandon Jouganatos, Vice President for Enrollment Services, 800-628-8648, E-mail: advisor@nu.edu.
Website: http://www.nu.edu/OurPrograms/SchoolOfEducation.html

Neumann University, Graduate Program in Education, Aston, PA 19014-1298. Offers education (MS), including administrative certification (school principal PK-12), autism, early elementary education, secondary education, special education. *Program availability:* Part-time, evening/weekend, 100% online, blended/hybrid learning. *Faculty:* 6 full-time (5 women), 16 part-time/adjunct (7 women). *Students:* 68 full-time (56 women), 108 part-time (93 women); includes 36 minority (28 Black or African American, non-Hispanic/Latino; 3 Hispanic/Latino; 5 Two or more races, non-Hispanic/Latino). Average age 33. 83 applicants, 69% accepted, 36 enrolled. In 2017, 114 master's awarded. *Entrance requirements:* For master's, official transcripts from all institutions attended, letter of intent, three professional references, copy of any teaching certifications. Additional exam requirements/recommendations for international students: Required—TOEFL (minimum score 70 iBT). *Application deadline:* Applications are processed on a rolling basis. Application fee: $0. Electronic applications accepted. *Expenses:* $700 per credit hour (for on-campus master's-level education courses); $480 per credit hour (for online or off-campus master's-level education courses). *Financial support:* Scholarships/grants and health care benefits available. Support available to part-time students. Financial award application deadline: 3/15; financial award applicants required to submit FAFSA. *Unit head:* Dr. Stephanie Smith-Budhai, Director of Graduate Education, 610-358-4249, E-mail: budhais@neumann.edu. *Application contact:* Dr. Erika K. Davis, Director of Adult and Graduate Admissions, 800-9-NEUMANN Ext. 5208, Fax: 610-361-2548, E-mail: gradadultadmiss@neumann.edu.
Website: https://www.neumann.edu/academics/grad/education/index.asp

Neumann University, Program in Educational Leadership, Aston, PA 19014-1298. Offers educational leadership (Ed D), including PreK-12, superintendent's letter of eligibility. *Program availability:* Part-time, evening/weekend. *Faculty:* 3 full-time (1 woman), 4 part-time/adjunct (1 woman). *Students:* 2 full-time (1 woman), 37 part-time (19 women); includes 6 minority (5 Black or African American, non-Hispanic/Latino; 1 Two or more races, non-Hispanic/Latino). Average age 41. 25 applicants, 56% accepted, 9 enrolled. In 2017, 11 doctorates awarded. *Degree requirements:* For doctorate, comprehensive exam, thesis/dissertation. *Entrance requirements:* For doctorate, master's degree, official transcripts from all institutions attended, resume or curriculum vitae, three official letters of recommendation, two essays. Additional exam requirements/recommendations for international students: Required—TOEFL (minimum score 70 iBT). *Application deadline:* For fall admission, 7/1 for domestic and international students. Application fee: $0. Electronic applications accepted. *Expenses:* $830 per credit hour. *Financial support:* Scholarships/grants and health care benefits available. Support available to part-time students. Financial award application deadline: 3/15; financial award applicants required to submit FAFSA. *Unit head:* Dr. Cynthia Speace, Director of Ed D Program, 610-358-4243, E-mail: speacec@neumann.edu. *Application contact:* Dr. Erika K. Davis, Director of Adult and Graduate Admissions, 800-9-NEUMANN Ext. 5208, Fax: 610-361-2548, E-mail: gradadultadmiss@neumann.edu.

New England College, Program in Education, Henniker, NH 03242-3293. Offers higher education administration (MS, Ed D); K-12 leadership (Ed D); literacy and language arts (M Ed); meeting the needs of all learners/special education (M Ed); teacher leadership/school reform (M Ed). *Program availability:* Part-time, evening/weekend.

New Jersey City University, Debra Cannon Partridge Wolfe College of Education, Department of Educational Leadership and Counseling, Jersey City, NJ 07305-1597. Offers counselor education (MA); educational administration and supervision (MA); urban education (MA). *Accreditation:* TEAC. *Program availability:* Part-time, evening/weekend. *Entrance requirements:* Additional exam requirements/recommendations for international students: Required—TOEFL (minimum score 79 iBT).

Newman University, Master of Science in Education Program, Wichita, KS 67213-2097. Offers building leadership (MS Ed); curriculum and instruction (MS Ed), including English as a second language, reading specialist; organizational leadership (MS Ed). *Accreditation:* NCATE. *Program availability:* Part-time, evening/weekend, online learning. *Degree requirements:* For master's, thesis optional. *Entrance requirements:* For master's, 3 years' full-time teaching experience, minimum GPA of 3.0, writing sample, 2 letters of recommendation, evidence of teaching certification. Additional exam requirements/recommendations for international students: Required—TOEFL (minimum score 600 paper-based; 100 iBT). Electronic applications accepted. *Expenses:* Contact institution. *Faculty research:* Online course design and deliver, staff engagement, classroom action.

New Mexico Highlands University, Graduate Studies, School of Education, Las Vegas, NM 87701. Offers curriculum and instruction (MA); educational leadership (MA); professional counseling (MA); special education (MA). *Accreditation:* NCATE. *Program availability:* Part-time. *Degree requirements:* For master's, comprehensive exam, thesis or alternative. *Entrance requirements:* For master's, minimum undergraduate GPA of 3.0. Additional exam requirements/recommendations for international students: Required—TOEFL (minimum score 540 paper-based). *Faculty research:* Middle school curriculum, integrated computer applications for pre-service classroom teachers, adolescent literacy, narrative cognitive modes in New Mexico multicultural setting, math and math education.

New Mexico State University, College of Education, Department of Educational Leadership and Administration, Las Cruces, NM 88003. Offers educational administration (MA), including community college and university administration, PK-12 public school administration; educational leadership (Ed D, PhD). *Accreditation:* NCATE. *Program availability:* Part-time only, evening/weekend, blended/hybrid learning. *Faculty:* 6 full-time (5 women), 2 part-time/adjunct (1 woman). *Students:* 11 full-time (10 women), 124 part-time (88 women); includes 93 minority (2 Black or African American, non-Hispanic/Latino; 8 American Indian or Alaska Native, non-Hispanic/Latino; 3 Asian, non-Hispanic/Latino; 78 Hispanic/Latino; 1 Native Hawaiian or other Pacific Islander, non-Hispanic/Latino; 1 Two or more races, non-Hispanic/Latino), 1 international. Average age 41. 29 applicants, 28% accepted, 8 enrolled. In 2017, 26 master's, 9 doctorates awarded. *Degree requirements:* For master's, comprehensive exam, internship; for doctorate, comprehensive exam, thesis/dissertation, internship. *Entrance requirements:* For doctorate, minimum GPA of 3.0, master's degree. Additional exam requirements/recommendations for international students: Required—TOEFL (minimum score 550 paper-based; 79 iBT), IELTS (minimum score 6.5). *Application deadline:* For spring admission, 11/15 for domestic and international students. Application fee: $40 ($50 for international students). Electronic applications accepted. *Expenses:* Tuition, state resident: full-time $4390. Tuition, nonresident: full-time $15,309. *Required fees:* $853. *Financial support:* In 2017–18, 21 students received support, including 4 research assistantships (averaging $17,489 per year), 1 teaching assistantship (averaging $8,684 per year); career-related internships or fieldwork, Federal Work-Study, scholarships/grants, traineeships, health care benefits, and unspecified assistantships also available. Support available to part-time students. Financial award application deadline: 3/1. *Faculty research:* Leadership in pk-12 and postsecondary education, community college administration, distance education administration, leadership for social justice, educational change. *Total annual research expenditures:* $2,456. *Unit head:* Dr. Azadeh Osanloo, Department Head, 575-646-5976, Fax: 575-646-4767, E-mail: azadeh@nmsu.edu. *Application contact:* Denise Rodriguez-Strawn, Program Coordinator, 575-646-3825, Fax: 575-646-4767, E-mail: edmandev@nmsu.edu.
Website: http://ela.nmsu.edu/

New York Institute of Technology, School of Interdisciplinary Studies and Education, Department of School Leadership and Technology, Old Westbury, NY 11568-8000. Offers Advanced Diploma. *Program availability:* Part-time, evening/weekend, online only, 100% online. *Faculty:* 1 full-time (0 women), 6 part-time/adjunct (4 women). *Students:* 44 part-time (26 women); includes 8 minority (3 Black or African American, non-Hispanic/Latino; 4 Hispanic/Latino; 1 Two or more races, non-Hispanic/Latino). Average age 36. 13 applicants, 85% accepted, 7 enrolled. In 2017, 13 Advanced Diplomas awarded. *Degree requirements:* For Advanced Diploma, internship. *Entrance requirements:* For degree, master's degree with minimum cumulative GPA of 3.0; personal statement; at least 3 years of full-time teaching experience; professional NY state teacher certification; demonstration of computer competency; two letters of reference from school building or district administrator. Additional exam requirements/recommendations for international students: Required—TOEFL (minimum score 79 iBT), IELTS (minimum score 6). *Application deadline:* Applications are processed on a rolling basis. Application fee: $50. Electronic applications accepted. *Expenses:* $1,285 per credit plus fees. *Financial support:* Career-related internships or fieldwork, scholarships/grants, and unspecified assistantships available. Support available to part-time students. Financial award application deadline: 2/15; financial award applicants required to submit FAFSA. *Faculty research:* College readiness; school-community partnerships; administrator-school counselor relationships. *Unit head:* Dr. Robert Feirsen, Chair, 516-686-1169, E-mail: rfeirsen@nyit.edu. *Application contact:* Alice Dolitsky, Director, Graduate Admissions, 516-686-7520, Fax: 516-686-1116, E-mail: nyitgrad@nyit.edu.
Website: https://www.nyit.edu/programs/school_leadership_technology

New York University, Steinhardt School of Culture, Education, and Human Development, Department of Administration, Leadership, and Technology, Program in Educational Leadership, New York, NY 10012. Offers educational leadership (Ed D, PhD); educational leadership, politics and advocacy (MA); school building leader (MA); school district leader (Advanced Certificate). *Program availability:* Part-time, evening/weekend. *Students:* Average age 34. 127 applicants, 54% accepted, 30 enrolled. In 2017, 35 master's, 4 doctorates, 1 other advanced degree awarded. *Entrance requirements:* For doctorate, GRE General Test, interview; for Advanced Certificate, master's degree. Additional exam requirements/recommendations for international students: Required—TOEFL (minimum score 100 iBT). *Application deadline:* For fall admission, 12/1 priority date for domestic and international students; for spring admission, 10/1 for domestic and international students. Applications are processed on a rolling basis. Application fee: $75. Electronic applications accepted. *Expenses:* Tuition: Full-time $41,352; part-time $19,968 per year. *Required fees:* $2496; $1628 per unit. $814 per term. Tuition and fees vary according to course load and program. *Financial support:* Fellowships with full and partial tuition reimbursements, teaching

Educational Leadership and Administration

assistantships with partial tuition reimbursements, career-related internships or fieldwork, Federal Work-Study, institutionally sponsored loans, scholarships/grants, tuition waivers (partial), and unspecified assistantships available. Support available to part-time students. Financial award application deadline: 2/1; financial award applicants required to submit FAFSA. *Faculty research:* Schools and communities; critical theories of race, class and gender; school restructuring; educational reform; social organization of schools, educational advocacy. *Unit head:* Prof. Terry A. Astuto, Director, 212-998-5520, Fax: 212-995-4041, E-mail: terry.astuto@nyu.edu. *Application contact:* 212-998-5030, Fax: 212-995-4328, E-mail: steinhardt.gradadmissions@nyu.edu. Website: http://steinhardt.nyu.edu/alt/edleadership

New York University, Steinhardt School of Culture, Education, and Human Development, Department of Administration, Leadership, and Technology, Program in Higher Education, New York, NY 10012. Offers higher and postsecondary education (PhD); higher education administration (Ed D); higher education and student affairs (MA). *Accreditation:* TEAC. *Program availability:* Part-time. *Students:* Average age 36. 222 applicants, 18% accepted, 34 enrolled. In 2017, 52 master's, 10 doctorates awarded. *Entrance requirements:* For master's, interview, 2 letters of recommendation; for doctorate, GRE General Test, interview. Additional exam requirements/recommendations for international students: Required—TOEFL (minimum score 100 iBT). *Application deadline:* For fall admission, 12/1 priority date for domestic and international students; for spring admission, 10/1 for domestic and international students. Applications are processed on a rolling basis. Application fee: $75. Electronic applications accepted. *Expenses: Tuition:* Full-time $41,352; part-time $19,968 per year. *Required fees:* $2496; $1628 per unit. $814 per term. Tuition and fees vary according to course load and program. *Financial support:* Fellowships with full and partial tuition reimbursements, career-related internships or fieldwork, Federal Work-Study, institutionally sponsored loans, scholarships/grants, tuition waivers (partial), and unspecified assistantships available. Support available to part-time students. Financial award application deadline: 2/1; financial award applicants required to submit FAFSA. *Faculty research:* Organizational theory and culture, systemic change, leadership development, access, equity and diversity. *Unit head:* Prof. Ann Marcus, Director, 212-998-5276, Fax: 212-995-4041, E-mail: alm1@nyu.edu. *Application contact:* 212-998-5030, Fax: 212-995-4328, E-mail: steinhardt.gradadmissions@nyu.edu. Website: http://steinhardt.nyu.edu/alt/highered

Niagara University, Graduate Division of Education, Concentration in Educational Leadership, Niagara University, NY 14109. Offers leadership and policy (PhD); school building leader (MS Ed); school district business leader (Certificate); school district leader (MS Ed, Certificate). *Program availability:* Part-time, evening/weekend, 100% online. *Students:* 52 full-time (32 women), 149 part-time (105 women); includes 30 minority (16 Black or African American, non-Hispanic/Latino; 2 Asian, non-Hispanic/Latino; 7 Hispanic/Latino; 5 Two or more races, non-Hispanic/Latino), 45 international. Average age 38. In 2017, 21 master's, 10 doctorates, 18 other advanced degrees awarded. *Entrance requirements:* For master's, GRE General Test or MAT; for Certificate, GRE General Test and GRE Subject Test or MAT. Additional exam requirements/recommendations for international students: Required—TOEFL (minimum score 550 paper-based; 79 iBT), IELTS (minimum score 6). *Application deadline:* For fall admission, 8/1 for domestic students. Applications are processed on a rolling basis. Application fee: $30. *Expenses:* Contact institution. *Financial support:* In 2017–18, 1 research assistantship with tuition reimbursement was awarded; teaching assistantships with tuition reimbursements, career-related internships or fieldwork, Federal Work-Study, scholarships/grants, and unspecified assistantships also available. Support available to part-time students. Financial award application deadline: 4/15; financial award applicants required to submit FAFSA. *Unit head:* Dr. James Mills, Coordinator of Educational Leadership, 716-286-8553, E-mail: jmills@niagara.edu. *Application contact:* Evan Pierce, Associate Director, Graduate Studies, 716-286-8327, E-mail: epierce@niagara.edu.
Website: http://www.niagara.edu/educational-leadership-online

Nicholls State University, Graduate Studies, College of Education, Department of Teacher Education, Thibodaux, LA 70310. Offers curriculum and instruction (M Ed); educational leadership (M Ed); elementary education (MAT); human performance education (MAT); middle school education (MAT); secondary education (MAT). *Accreditation:* NCATE. *Program availability:* Part-time, evening/weekend, online learning. *Degree requirements:* For master's, comprehensive exam, portfolio. *Entrance requirements:* For master's, GRE General Test, teaching license. Electronic applications accepted.

Norfolk State University, School of Graduate Studies, School of Education, Department of Secondary Education and School Leadership, Norfolk, VA 23504. Offers principal preparation (MA); secondary education (MAT); urban education/administration (MA), including teaching. *Accreditation:* NCATE. *Program availability:* Part-time. *Entrance requirements:* For master's, GRE General Test, PRAXIS I, minimum GPA of 3.0 in major, 2.5 overall. Additional exam requirements/recommendations for international students: Required—TOEFL (minimum score 500 paper-based).

North American University, Program in Educational Leadership, Stafford, TX 77477. Offers M Ed.

North Carolina Agricultural and Technical State University, School of Graduate Studies, School of Education, Department of Human Development and Services, Greensboro, NC 27411. Offers adult education (MS); counseling (MS); school administration (MS). *Accreditation:* ACA. *Program availability:* Part-time, evening/weekend. *Degree requirements:* For master's, comprehensive exam, thesis, qualifying exam. *Entrance requirements:* For master's, GRE General Test, minimum GPA of 3.0.

North Carolina Central University, School of Education, Program in School Administration, Durham, NC 27707-3129. Offers MSA. *Expenses:* Tuition, state resident: full-time $2770; part-time $692.50 per credit hour. Tuition, nonresident: full-time $9247; part-time $2311.75 per credit hour. *Unit head:* Agnes L. DeWitt, Program Coordinator, 919-530-7696, E-mail: adewitt@nccu.edu. *Application contact:* Agnes L. DeWitt, Program Coordinator, 919-530-7696, E-mail: adewitt@nccu.edu.

North Carolina State University, Graduate School, College of Education, Department of Adult and Higher Education, Program in Higher Education Administration, Raleigh, NC 27695. Offers M Ed, MS, Ed D. *Degree requirements:* For master's, thesis (for some programs); for doctorate, thesis/dissertation. *Entrance requirements:* For master's and doctorate, GRE General Test or MAT, minimum GPA of 3.0 in major. Electronic applications accepted.

North Carolina State University, Graduate School, College of Education, Department of Educational Leadership and Policy Studies, Program in Educational Administration and Supervision, Raleigh, NC 27695. Offers Ed D. *Degree requirements:* For doctorate, thesis/dissertation. *Entrance requirements:* For doctorate, GRE General Test or MAT, minimum GPA of 3.0, interview, sample of work. Electronic applications accepted.

North Carolina State University, Graduate School, College of Education, Department of Educational Leadership and Policy Studies, Program in School Administration, Raleigh, NC 27695. Offers MSA. *Degree requirements:* For master's, comprehensive exam, thesis optional. *Entrance requirements:* For master's, GRE General Test or MAT, minimum GPA of 3.0 in major, 3 years of teaching experience. Electronic applications

accepted. *Faculty research:* State and national policy, educational evaluation, cohort preparation programs.

North Central College, School of Graduate and Professional Studies, Program in Leadership Studies, Naperville, IL 60566-7063. Offers MLD. *Program availability:* Part-time, evening/weekend. *Degree requirements:* For master's, thesis optional, project. *Entrance requirements:* For master's, interview. Additional exam requirements/recommendations for international students: Required—TOEFL (minimum score 550 paper-based; 80 iBT), IELTS (minimum score 6.5). Electronic applications accepted. Application fee is waived when completed online. *Expenses:* Contact institution.

North Dakota State University, College of Graduate and Interdisciplinary Studies, College of Human Development and Education, School of Education, Program in Educational Leadership, Fargo, ND 58102. Offers M Ed, MS, Ed S. MS and Ed S offered jointly with Minnesota State University Moorhead. *Accreditation:* NCATE. *Program availability:* Part-time, evening/weekend, online learning. *Entrance requirements:* For degree, GRE General Test, master's degree, minimum GPA of 3.25. Additional exam requirements/recommendations for international students: Required—TOEFL. *Faculty research:* Organizational change and development, goal setting and systematic planning, beginning teacher assistance.

Northeastern Illinois University, College of Graduate Studies and Research, Daniel L. Goodwin College of Education, Program in School Leadership, Chicago, IL 60625. Offers educational administration and supervision (MA), including chief school business official. *Program availability:* Part-time, evening/weekend. *Degree requirements:* For master's, comprehensive exam, practicum. *Entrance requirements:* For master's, 2 years of teaching experience, minimum GPA of 2.75. Additional exam requirements/recommendations for international students: Required—TOEFL (minimum score 550 paper-based; 79 iBT). *Application deadline:* For fall admission, 4/1 priority date for domestic students; for spring admission, 8/15 for domestic students. Applications are processed on a rolling basis. Application fee: $30. Electronic applications accepted. *Expenses:* Tuition, state resident: full-time $7274; part-time $404.11 per credit hour. Tuition, nonresident: full-time $14,548; part-time $808.23 per credit hour. *Required fees:* $1284. *Faculty research:* Student motivation, leadership, teacher expectation, educational partnerships, community/school relations. *Unit head:* Dr. Howard Bultinck, Department Chair, 773-442-5809, E-mail: h-bultinck@neiu.edu. *Application contact:* Martha Narvaez, Graduate Admission Representative, 773-442-6006, E-mail: m-narvaez@neiu.edu.

Northeastern State University, College of Education, Department of Educational Leadership, Program in Higher Education Leadership, Tahlequah, OK 74464-2399. Offers MS. *Faculty:* 12 full-time (9 women), 2 part-time/adjunct (1 woman). *Students:* 10 full-time (8 women), 18 part-time (16 women); includes 12 minority (7 American Indian or Alaska Native, non-Hispanic/Latino; 1 Asian, non-Hispanic/Latino; 4 Two or more races, non-Hispanic/Latino), 4 international. Average age 37. In 2017, 18 master's awarded. *Degree requirements:* For master's, thesis. *Entrance requirements:* For master's, MAT or GRE. Additional exam requirements/recommendations for international students: Required—TOEFL. *Application deadline:* For fall admission, 6/1 priority date for domestic students. Applications are processed on a rolling basis. Application fee: $25. Electronic applications accepted. *Expenses:* Tuition, state resident: part-time $222 per credit hour. Tuition, nonresident: part-time $501.75 per credit hour. *Required fees:* $37.40 per credit hour. Tuition and fees vary according to degree level. *Financial support:* Application deadline: 3/1. *Unit head:* Dr. Renee Cambiano, Program Chair, 918-444-3741, E-mail: cambiare@nsuok.edu. *Application contact:* Josh McCollum, Graduate Coordinator, 918-444-2093, E-mail: mccolluj@nsuok.edu.
Website: http://academics.nsuok.edu/education/DegreePrograms/GraduatePrograms/HigherEducationLeadership.aspx

Northeastern State University, College of Education, Department of Educational Leadership, Program in Instructional Leadership, Tahlequah, OK 74464-2399. Offers M Ed. *Program availability:* Part-time, evening/weekend. *Faculty:* 12 full-time (9 women), 2 part-time/adjunct (1 woman). *Students:* 12 full-time (10 women), 11 part-time (9 women); includes 12 minority (1 Black or African American, non-Hispanic/Latino; 5 American Indian or Alaska Native, non-Hispanic/Latino; 6 Two or more races, non-Hispanic/Latino). Average age 34. In 2017, 8 master's awarded. *Degree requirements:* For master's, thesis. *Entrance requirements:* For master's, MAT or GRE. Additional exam requirements/recommendations for international students: Required—TOEFL. *Application deadline:* For fall admission, 7/1 priority date for domestic and international students; for spring admission, 10/1 priority date for domestic and international students. Applications are processed on a rolling basis. Application fee: $25. Electronic applications accepted. *Expenses:* Tuition, state resident: part-time $222 per credit hour. Tuition, nonresident: part-time $501.75 per credit hour. *Required fees:* $37.40 per credit hour. Tuition and fees vary according to degree level. *Financial support:* Federal Work-Study available. Financial award application deadline: 3/1. *Unit head:* Dr. Renee Cambiano, Program Chair, 918-444-3741, E-mail: cambiare@nsuok.edu. *Application contact:* Josh McCollum, Graduate Coordinator, 918-444-2093, E-mail: mccolluj@nsuok.edu.

Northeastern State University, College of Education, Department of Educational Leadership, Program in School Administration, Tahlequah, OK 74464-2399. Offers M Ed. *Program availability:* Part-time, evening/weekend. *Faculty:* 12 full-time (9 women), 2 part-time/adjunct (1 woman). *Students:* 19 full-time (11 women), 61 part-time (39 women); includes 28 minority (3 Black or African American, non-Hispanic/Latino; 9 American Indian or Alaska Native, non-Hispanic/Latino; 2 Hispanic/Latino; 14 Two or more races, non-Hispanic/Latino). Average age 38. In 2017, 36 master's awarded. *Degree requirements:* For master's, thesis. *Entrance requirements:* For master's, MAT or GRE, minimum GPA of 3.0. Additional exam requirements/recommendations for international students: Required—TOEFL. *Application deadline:* For fall admission, 6/1 priority date for domestic students. Applications are processed on a rolling basis. Application fee: $25. Electronic applications accepted. *Expenses:* Tuition, state resident: part-time $222 per credit hour. Tuition, nonresident: part-time $501.75 per credit hour. *Required fees:* $37.40 per credit hour. Tuition and fees vary according to degree level. *Financial support:* Teaching assistantships and Federal Work-Study available. Financial award application deadline: 3/1. *Unit head:* Dr. Jim Ferrell, Department Chair, 918-444-3722, E-mail: ferrellj@nsuok.edu. *Application contact:* Josh McCollum, Graduate Coordinator, 918-444-2093, E-mail: mccolluj@nsuok.edu.
Website: http://academics.nsuok.edu/education/DegreePrograms/GraduatePrograms/SchoolAdministration.aspx

Northeastern University, College of Professional Studies, Boston, MA 02115-5096. Offers applied nutrition (MS); college athletics administration (MSL); commerce and economic development (MS); corporate and organizational communication (MS); criminal justice (MS); digital media (MPS); elearning and instructional design (M Ed); elementary education (MAT); geographic information technology (MPS); global studies and international relations (MS); higher education administration (M Ed); homeland security (MA); human services (M Ed); informatics (MPS); leadership (MS); learning analytics (M Ed); learning and instruction (M Ed); nonprofit management (MS); professional sports administration (MSL); project management (MS); regulatory affairs for drugs, biologics, and medical devices (MS); respiratory care leadership (MS); special education (M Ed); technical communication (MS). *Program availability:* Part-time,

evening/weekend, 100% online, blended/hybrid learning. *Faculty:* 82 full-time (51 women), 853 part-time/adjunct (366 women). *Students:* 5,278 part-time (3,230 women). In 2017, 1,586 master's awarded. *Application deadline:* Applications are processed on a rolling basis. Application fee: $0. Electronic applications accepted. *Expenses:* Contact institution. *Financial support:* Applicants required to submit FAFSA. *Unit head:* Dr. Mary Loeffelholz, Dean of the College of Professional Studies. *Application contact:* E-mail: cpsadmissions@northeastern.edu.
Website: https://cps.northeastern.edu/

Northern Arizona University, College of Education, Department of Educational Leadership, Flagstaff, AZ 86011. Offers community college teaching and learning (Graduate Certificate); educational leadership (M Ed, Ed D), including community college/higher education (M Ed), educational foundations (M Ed), instructional leadership K-12 school leadership (M Ed), principal certification K-12 (M Ed); principal (Graduate Certificate); superintendent (Graduate Certificate). *Program availability:* Part-time. *Faculty:* 24 full-time (10 women), 1 (woman) part-time/adjunct. *Students:* 193 full-time (128 women), 648 part-time (425 women); includes 329 minority (54 Black or African American, non-Hispanic/Latino; 63 American Indian or Alaska Native, non-Hispanic/Latino; 10 Asian, non-Hispanic/Latino; 169 Hispanic/Latino; 1 Native Hawaiian or other Pacific Islander, non-Hispanic/Latino; 32 Two or more races, non-Hispanic/Latino), 2 international. Average age 38. 298 applicants, 98% accepted, 291 enrolled. In 2017, 252 master's, 12 doctorates, 48 other advanced degrees awarded. *Degree requirements:* For master's, comprehensive exam, thesis (for some programs); for doctorate, comprehensive exam, thesis/dissertation; for Graduate Certificate, comprehensive exam (for some programs). *Entrance requirements:* Additional exam requirements/recommendations for international students: Required—TOEFL (minimum score 80 iBT), IELTS (minimum score 6.5). *Application deadline:* For fall admission, 3/1 for domestic and international students; for spring admission, 10/1 for domestic and international students. Applications are processed on a rolling basis. Application fee: $65. Electronic applications accepted. *Expenses:* Tuition, state resident: full-time $9240; part-time $458 per credit hour. Tuition, nonresident: full-time $21,588; part-time $1199 per credit hour. *Required fees:* $1021; $14 per credit hour. $646 per semester. Tuition and fees vary according to course load, campus/location and program. *Financial support:* In 2017–18, 1 student received support. Institutionally sponsored loans, health care benefits, tuition waivers (partial), and unspecified assistantships available. Financial award application deadline: 2/1; financial award applicants required to submit FAFSA. *Unit head:* Dr. Michael Schwanenberger, Chair, 928-523-3202, Fax: 928-523-1929, E-mail: michael.schwanenberger@nau.edu. *Application contact:* Jennifer Offutt, Administrative Assistant, 928-523-3202, Fax: 928-523-1929, E-mail: jennifer.offutt@nau.edu.
Website: https://nau.edu/coe/Ed-Leadership/

Northern Illinois University, Graduate School, College of Education, Department of Leadership, Educational Psychology and Foundations, De Kalb, IL 60115-2854. Offers educational administration (MS Ed, Ed D, Ed S); educational psychology (MS Ed, Ed D); foundations of education (MS Ed); school business management (MS Ed). *Program availability:* Part-time, evening/weekend, online learning. *Faculty:* 23 full-time (12 women). *Students:* 11 full-time (7 women), 241 part-time (151 women); includes 42 minority (19 Black or African American, non-Hispanic/Latino; 3 Asian, non-Hispanic/Latino; 11 Hispanic/Latino; 9 Two or more races, non-Hispanic/Latino), 7 international. Average age 39. 76 applicants, 80% accepted, 26 enrolled. In 2017, 47 master's, 28 doctorates, 20 other advanced degrees awarded. *Degree requirements:* For master's, comprehensive exam, thesis optional; for doctorate, thesis/dissertation, candidacy exam, dissertation defense. *Entrance requirements:* For master's, minimum undergraduate GPA of 2.75; for doctorate, GRE General Test, minimum undergraduate GPA of 2.75, 3.2 graduate; for Ed S, GRE General Test, minimum GPA of 2.75 (undergraduate), 3.2 (graduate). Additional exam requirements/recommendations for international students: Required—TOEFL (minimum score 550 paper-based). *Application deadline:* For fall admission, 6/1 for domestic students, 5/1 for international students; for spring admission, 11/1 for domestic students, 10/1 for international students. Applications are processed on a rolling basis. Application fee: $40. Electronic applications accepted. *Financial support:* In 2017–18, 1 research assistantship with full tuition reimbursement, 2 teaching assistantships with full tuition reimbursements were awarded; fellowships with full tuition reimbursements, career-related internships or fieldwork, Federal Work-Study, scholarships/grants, tuition waivers (full), and staff assistantships also available. Support available to part-time students. Financial award applicants required to submit FAFSA. *Faculty research:* Interpersonal forgiveness, learner-centered education, psychedelic studies, senior theory, professional growth. *Unit head:* Carolyn V. Schee, Chair, 815-753-4404, E-mail: lepf@niu.edu. *Application contact:* Graduate School Office, 815-753-0395, E-mail: gradsch@niu.edu.
Website: http://cedu.niu.edu/LEPF/

Northern Kentucky University, Office of Graduate Programs, College of Education and Human Services, Doctor of Education in Educational Leadership Program, Highland Heights, KY 41099. Offers Ed D. *Program availability:* Part-time, evening/weekend. *Entrance requirements:* For doctorate, master's (or specialist) degree in education or a related field; minimum GPA of 3.25; five or more years of educational leadership experience; letter describing educational and leadership background, goals, style, and philosophy; professional vitae; leadership situation account; 3 letters of recommendation; interview. Additional exam requirements/recommendations for international students: Required—TOEFL (minimum score 79 iBT); Recommended—IELTS (minimum score 6.5). Electronic applications accepted. *Faculty research:* Educator dispositions, civic engagement and service-learning in education, school leadership, technology in education, professional development.

Northern Kentucky University, Office of Graduate Programs, College of Education and Human Services, Education Program: Teacher as a Leader, Highland Heights, KY 41099. Offers MA, Certificate. *Program availability:* Part-time, evening/weekend, online learning. *Degree requirements:* For master's, thesis optional, portfolio. *Entrance requirements:* For master's, GRE, teacher certification, bachelor's degree in appropriate subject area, minimum GPA of 2.5, 3 letters of recommendation, 1 year of teaching experience, statement of personal goals. Additional exam requirements/recommendations for international students: Required—TOEFL (minimum score 79 iBT); Recommended—IELTS (minimum score 6.5). Electronic applications accepted. *Faculty research:* Teaching with technology, middle school education, children with disabilities, teaching in the content areas, diversifying faculty.

Northern Kentucky University, Office of Graduate Programs, College of Education and Human Services, Education Specialist in Educational Leadership Program, Highland Heights, KY 41099. Offers Ed S. *Degree requirements:* For Ed S, capstone and two presentations. *Entrance requirements:* For degree, copy of valid teaching certificate showing successful completion of 3 years' full-time documented classroom teaching experience, official transcripts, 3 letters of recommendation, minimum GPA of 3.5, 3 essays, professional folio, interview. Additional exam requirements/recommendations for international students: Required—TOEFL (minimum score 79 iBT); Recommended—IELTS (minimum score 6.5). Electronic applications accepted.

Northern Michigan University, Office of Graduate Education and Research, College of Health Sciences and Professional Studies, School of Education, Leadership and Public Service, Marquette, MI 49855-5301. Offers administration and supervision (MAE); instruction (MAE); learning disabilities (MAE); postsecondary biology education (MS); reading education (MAE), including reading, reading specialist. *Accreditation:* TEAC. *Program availability:* Part-time, online learning. *Degree requirements:* For master's, thesis (for some programs). *Entrance requirements:* For master's, minimum GPA of 3.0. Additional exam requirements/recommendations for international students: Required—TOEFL (minimum score 550 paper-based; 79 iBT), IELTS (minimum score 6.5). *Application deadline:* For fall admission, 7/1 priority date for domestic students; for winter admission, 11/15 for domestic students; for spring admission, 3/17 for domestic students. Applications are processed on a rolling basis. Application fee: $50. Electronic applications accepted. *Expenses:* Tuition, state resident: full-time $9417; part-time $542 per credit hour. Tuition, nonresident: full-time $12,873; part-time $758 per credit hour. Tuition and fees vary according to course load, degree level and program. *Financial support:* Research assistantships with full tuition reimbursements, career-related internships or fieldwork, Federal Work-Study, institutionally sponsored loans, and unspecified assistantships available. Support available to part-time students. Financial award application deadline: 3/1; financial award applicants required to submit FAFSA. *Unit head:* Dr. Joseph Lubig, Associate Dean for Teacher Education, 906-227-1880, Fax: 906-227-2764, E-mail: jlubig@nmu.edu. *Application contact:* Dr. Joseph Lubig, Associate Dean for Teacher Education, 906-227-1880, Fax: 906-227-2764, E-mail: jlubig@nmu.edu.
Website: http://www.nmu.edu/education/

Northern State University, MS Ed Program in Leadership and Administration, Aberdeen, SD 57401-7198. Offers MS Ed. *Accreditation:* NCATE. *Program availability:* Part-time, evening/weekend, online learning. *Degree requirements:* For master's, comprehensive exam, thesis optional. *Entrance requirements:* For master's, minimum GPA of 2.75. Additional exam requirements/recommendations for international students: Required—TOEFL (minimum score 550 paper-based; 78 iBT), IELTS (minimum score 6). Electronic applications accepted.

Northwestern College, Program in Education, Orange City, IA 51041-1996. Offers early childhood (M Ed); master teacher (M Ed); teacher leadership (M Ed, Graduate Certificate). *Program availability:* Online learning.

Northwestern Oklahoma State University, School of Professional Studies, Program in Educational Leadership, Alva, OK 73717-2799. Offers M Ed. *Program availability:* Part-time. *Degree requirements:* For master's, thesis optional, portfolio. *Entrance requirements:* For master's, GRE General Test or MAT, minimum GPA of 2.75.

Northwestern State University of Louisiana, Graduate Studies and Research, College of Education and Human Development, Programs in Educational Leadership and Instruction, Natchitoches, LA 71497. Offers counseling (Ed S); educational leadership (M Ed, Ed S); educational technology (Ed S); elementary teaching (Ed S); reading (Ed S); secondary teaching (Ed S); special education (Ed S). *Accreditation:* NASAD. *Degree requirements:* For master's, comprehensive exam, thesis (for some programs). *Entrance requirements:* For master's and Ed S, GRE General Test. Additional exam requirements/recommendations for international students: Required—TOEFL. Electronic applications accepted.

Northwestern University, The Graduate School, School of Education and Social Policy, Education and Social Policy Program, Evanston, IL 60035. Offers elementary teaching (MS); secondary teaching (MS); teacher leadership (MS). *Program availability:* Part-time, evening/weekend. *Degree requirements:* For master's, research project. *Entrance requirements:* For master's, GRE General Test, Illinois State Board of Education Basic Skills Exam (secondary and elementary), bachelor's degree. Additional exam requirements/recommendations for international students: Recommended—TOEFL. Electronic applications accepted. *Faculty research:* Cultural context and literacy, philosophy of education and interpretive discussion, productivity, enhancing research and teaching, motivation, new and junior faculty issues, professional development for K-12 teachers to improve math and science teaching, female/underrepresented students/faculty in STEM disciplines.

Northwest Missouri State University, Graduate School, School of Education, Maryville, MO 64468-6001. Offers early childhood education (MS Ed); education leadership (MS Ed), including elementary, K-12, secondary; educational leadership (Ed S), including elementary school principalship, secondary school principalship, superintendency; educational leadership and policy analysis (Ed D); elementary education (MS Ed); elementary mathematics (MS Ed); higher education leadership (MS); middle school education (MS Ed); reading (MS Ed); special education (MS Ed); teacher leadership (MS Ed); teaching English language learners (MS Ed). *Accreditation:* NCATE. *Program availability:* Part-time. *Faculty:* 15 full-time (8 women). *Students:* 28 full-time (20 women), 170 part-time (114 women); includes 20 minority (7 Black or African American, non-Hispanic/Latino; 1 Asian, non-Hispanic/Latino; 8 Hispanic/Latino; 4 Two or more races, non-Hispanic/Latino). Average age 33. 168 applicants, 73% accepted, 114 enrolled. In 2017, 67 master's, 21 other advanced degrees awarded. *Degree requirements:* For master's, comprehensive exam; for Ed S, comprehensive exam, thesis. *Entrance requirements:* For master's, GRE General Test, writing sample; for Ed S, minimum graduate GPA of 3.25. Additional exam requirements/recommendations for international students: Required—TOEFL (minimum score 550 paper-based). *Application deadline:* For fall admission, 7/1 for domestic and international students; for spring admission, 11/15 for domestic and international students. Applications are processed on a rolling basis. Application fee: $0 ($50 for international students). Electronic applications accepted. *Expenses:* $389.11 per credit hour in-state tuition and fees, $641.97 out-of-state; $9,750 total cost (for online-based education program). *Financial support:* Research assistantships with full tuition reimbursements, teaching assistantships with full tuition reimbursements, and unspecified assistantships available. Financial award application deadline: 4/1; financial award applicants required to submit FAFSA. *Unit head:* Dr. Tim Wall, Director, 660-562-1179, E-mail: timwall@nwmissouri.edu.
Website: https://www.nwmissouri.edu/education/index.htm

Northwest Nazarene University, Graduate Education Program, Nampa, ID 83686-5897. Offers curriculum and instruction (M Ed); educational leadership (M Ed, Ed D, PhD, Ed S), including building administrator (M Ed, Ed S), director of special education (Ed S), leadership and organizational development (Ed S), superintendent (Ed S). *Accreditation:* ACA (one or more programs are accredited); NCATE. *Program availability:* Part-time, online only, 100% online, 2-week face-to-face residency (for doctoral programs). *Students:* Average age 39. 96 applicants, 72% accepted, 67 enrolled. In 2017, 59 master's, 13 doctorates, 33 other advanced degrees awarded. *Degree requirements:* For master's, comprehensive exam (for some programs), action research project; for doctorate, thesis/dissertation; for Ed S, comprehensive exam, research project. *Entrance requirements:* For master's, minimum undergraduate GPA of 3.0 overall or during final 30 semester credits, undergraduate degree, valid teaching certificate; for doctorate, Ed S or equivalent, minimum GPA of 3.5; for Ed S, undergraduate degree, valid teaching certificate. Additional exam requirements/recommendations for international students: Recommended—TOEFL. *Application deadline:* Applications are processed on a rolling basis. Application fee: $50. Electronic applications accepted. *Expenses:* Contact institution. *Financial support:* Research assistantships available. Financial award application deadline: 1/15; financial award

Educational Leadership and Administration

applicants required to submit FAFSA. *Faculty research:* Action research, cooperative learning, accountability, institutional accreditation. *Unit head:* Dr. Heidi Curtis, Chair, 208-467-8250, E-mail: hlcurtis@nnu.edu. *Application contact:* Charlene Brown, Admissions Counselor, 208-467-8492, Fax: 208-467-8384, E-mail: gradeducationinfo@nnu.edu.
Website: http://www.nnu.edu/graded/

Notre Dame de Namur University, Division of Academic Affairs, School of Education and Psychology, Program in School Administration, Belmont, CA 94002-1908. Offers MA. *Program availability:* Part-time, evening/weekend. *Students:* 1 (woman) full-time, 17 part-time (7 women). Average age 37. *Degree requirements:* For master's, thesis optional, capstone course. *Entrance requirements:* For master's, interview, valid teaching credential, minimum 1 year of classroom teaching experience. Additional exam requirements/recommendations for international students: Required—TOEFL (minimum score 550 paper-based; 79 iBT). *Application deadline:* For fall admission, 8/1 priority date for domestic students; for spring admission, 12/1 priority date for domestic students. Applications are processed on a rolling basis. Application fee: $60. Electronic applications accepted. *Expenses: Tuition:* Full-time $16,128; part-time $8064 per credit hour. *Required fees:* $80; $80 per credit hour. $40 per semester. *Financial support:* Career-related internships or fieldwork available. Support available to part-time students. Financial award applicants required to submit FAFSA. *Application contact:* Susan Charles, Program Director, Master's in School Administration, 650-508-3473, E-mail: scharles@ndnu.edu.

Notre Dame of Maryland University, Graduate Studies, Leadership in Teaching Program, Baltimore, MD 21210-2476. Offers MA. *Entrance requirements:* For master's, interview, 1 year of teaching experience, minimum GPA of 3.0. Additional exam requirements/recommendations for international students: Required—TOEFL (minimum score 500 paper-based; 61 iBT). Electronic applications accepted.

Notre Dame of Maryland University, Graduate Studies, Program in Instructional Leadership for Changing Populations, Baltimore, MD 21210-2476. Offers PhD. *Entrance requirements:* Additional exam requirements/recommendations for international students: Required—TOEFL (minimum score 500 paper-based; 61 iBT).

Oakland City University, School of Education, Oakland City, IN 47660-1099. Offers educational leadership (Ed D); teaching (MA). *Accreditation:* NCATE. Terminal master's awarded for partial completion of doctoral program. *Degree requirements:* For master's, thesis; for doctorate, comprehensive exam, thesis/dissertation. *Entrance requirements:* For master's, MAT, minimum GPA of 3.0, interview, resume, letters of recommendation; for doctorate, MAT, GRE, minimum GPA of 3.2, interview, resume, letters of recommendation. *Expenses:* Contact institution. *Faculty research:* Assessment, cultural diversity, teacher education, education leadership.

Oakland University, Graduate Study and Lifelong Learning, School of Education and Human Services, Department of Organizational Leadership, Rochester, MI 48309-4401. Offers educational leadership (M Ed, PhD); higher education (Certificate); school administration (Ed S). *Entrance requirements:* Additional exam requirements/recommendations for international students: Required—TOEFL (minimum score 550 paper-based). *Expenses:* Tuition, state resident: full-time $16,950; part-time $706.25 per credit. Tuition, nonresident: full-time $24,648; part-time $1027 per credit.

Oakland University, Graduate Study and Lifelong Learning, School of Education and Human Services, Department of Teacher Development and Educational Studies, Rochester, MI 48309-4401. Offers educational studies (M Ed); elementary education (MAT); secondary education (MAT); teaching and learning (Graduate Certificate). *Entrance requirements:* For master's, minimum GPA of 3.0. Electronic applications accepted. *Expenses:* Tuition, state resident: full-time $16,950; part-time $706.25 per credit. Tuition, nonresident: full-time $24,648; part-time $1027 per credit.

Oglala Lakota College, Graduate Studies, Program in Educational Administration, Kyle, SD 57752-0490. Offers MA. *Program availability:* Part-time, evening/weekend. *Entrance requirements:* For master's, minimum GPA of 2.5.

Ohio Dominican University, Division of Education, Program in Educational Leadership, Columbus, OH 43219-2099. Offers M Ed. *Program availability:* Part-time, evening/weekend, 100% online, blended/hybrid learning. *Faculty:* 7 full-time (5 women), 7 part-time/adjunct (5 women). *Students:* 2 full-time (both women), 57 part-time (44 women); includes 7 minority (5 Black or African American, non-Hispanic/Latino; 1 Hispanic/Latino; 1 Two or more races, non-Hispanic/Latino), 2 international. Average age 38. 35 applicants, 77% accepted, 27 enrolled. In 2017, 26 master's awarded. *Entrance requirements:* For master's, bachelor's degree from regionally-accredited institution; teaching certificate/license; currently teaching or have access to an academic classroom. Additional exam requirements/recommendations for international students: Required—TOEFL (minimum score 550 paper-based), IELTS (minimum score 6.5). *Application deadline:* For fall admission, 8/15 for domestic students, 6/10 for international students; for spring admission, 1/4 for domestic students, 11/2 for international students; for summer admission, 5/30 for domestic students. Applications are processed on a rolling basis. Application fee: $25. Electronic applications accepted. *Expenses:* $538 per credit hour, $175 per semester technology fee, $50 per semester activity fee. *Financial support:* Applicants required to submit FAFSA. *Unit head:* Dr. JoAnn Hohenbrink, Associate Professor/Chair of Education Division, 614-251-4759, E-mail: hohenbrj@ohiodominican.edu. *Application contact:* John W. Naughton, Associate Vice President for Enrollment Management, 614-251-4721, Fax: 614-251-6654, E-mail: grad@ohiodominican.edu.
Website: http://www.ohiodominican.edu/academics/graduate/master-of-education/educational-leadership

The Ohio State University, Graduate School, College of Education and Human Ecology, Department of Educational Studies, Columbus, OH 43210. Offers M Ed, MA, PhD, Ed S. *Accreditation:* NCATE. *Program availability:* Part-time. *Faculty:* 55. *Students:* 307 full-time (201 women), 157 part-time (114 women); includes 106 minority (61 Black or African American, non-Hispanic/Latino; 15 Asian, non-Hispanic/Latino; 17 Hispanic/Latino; 13 Two or more races, non-Hispanic/Latino), 48 international. Average age 32. In 2017, 115 master's, 36 doctorates, 1 other advanced degree awarded. *Degree requirements:* For master's, thesis optional; for doctorate, thesis/dissertation. *Entrance requirements:* For master's and doctorate, GRE General Test. Additional exam requirements/recommendations for international students: Required—TOEFL (minimum score 550 paper-based; 79 iBT), Michigan English Language Assessment Battery (minimum score 82); Recommended—IELTS (minimum score 7). *Application deadline:* For fall admission, 12/1 priority date for domestic and international students; for spring admission, 11/1 for domestic and international students; for summer admission, 3/1 for domestic and international students. Applications are processed on a rolling basis. Application fee: $60 ($70 for international students). Electronic applications accepted. *Financial support:* Fellowships with tuition reimbursements, research assistantships with tuition reimbursements, teaching assistantships with tuition reimbursements, Federal Work-Study, institutionally sponsored loans, and unspecified assistantships available. Support available to part-time students. *Unit head:* Dr. Eric Anderman, Chair and Professor, 614-688-5721, E-mail: anderman.1@osu.edu. *Application contact:* Graduate and Professional Admissions, 614-292-9444, E-mail: gpadmissions@osu.edu.
Website: http://ehe.osu.edu/educational-studies/

Ohio University, Graduate College, Gladys W. and David H. Patton College of Education and Human Services, Department of Educational Studies, Athens, OH 45701-2979. Offers computer education and technology (M Ed); educational administration (M Ed, Ed D); educational research and evaluation (M Ed, PhD); instructional technology (PhD). *Program availability:* Part-time, evening/weekend, online learning. *Degree requirements:* For master's, thesis or alternative; for doctorate, comprehensive exam, thesis/dissertation. *Entrance requirements:* For master's, GRE General Test (if GPA less than 2.9); for doctorate, GRE General Test, GRE Subject Test, minimum GPA of 2.9, work experience, 3 letters of reference, autobiography. Additional exam requirements/recommendations for international students: Required—TOEFL (minimum score 550 paper-based; 80 iBT) or IELTS (minimum score 6.5). Electronic applications accepted. *Faculty research:* Race, class and gender; computer programs; development and organization theory; evaluation/development of instruments, leadership.

Oklahoma State University, College of Education, Health and Aviation, School of Teaching and Curriculum Leadership, Stillwater, OK 74078. Offers MS, PhD. *Program availability:* Part-time. *Faculty:* 37 full-time (32 women), 29 part-time/adjunct (25 women). *Students:* 26 full-time (24 women), 152 part-time (123 women); includes 41 minority (9 Black or African American, non-Hispanic/Latino; 8 American Indian or Alaska Native, non-Hispanic/Latino; 2 Asian, non-Hispanic/Latino; 6 Hispanic/Latino; 16 Two or more races, non-Hispanic/Latino), 7 international. Average age 38. 45 applicants, 91% accepted, 35 enrolled. In 2017, 61 master's, 8 doctorates awarded. *Entrance requirements:* For master's and doctorate, GRE or GMAT. Additional exam requirements/recommendations for international students: Required—TOEFL (minimum score 550 paper-based; 79 iBT). *Application deadline:* For fall admission, 3/1 priority date for international students; for spring admission, 8/1 priority date for international students. Applications are processed on a rolling basis. Application fee: $40 ($75 for international students). Electronic applications accepted. *Expenses:* Tuition, state resident: full-time $4019; part-time $2679.60 per year. Tuition, nonresident: full-time $15,286; part-time $10,190.40 per year. *Required fees:* $2129; $1419 per unit. Tuition and fees vary according to program. *Financial support:* Research assistantships, teaching assistantships, career-related internships or fieldwork, Federal Work-Study, scholarships/grants, health care benefits, tuition waivers (partial), and unspecified assistantships available. Support available to part-time students. Financial award application deadline: 3/1; financial award applicants required to submit FAFSA. *Unit head:* Dr. Jennifer Sanders, Interim Department Head, 405-744-9214, Fax: 405-744-6290, E-mail: jenn.sanders10@okstate.edu.
Website: http://education.okstate.edu/

Old Dominion University, Darden College of Education, Educational Leadership Services Programs, Norfolk, VA 23529. Offers educational leadership (MS Ed, PhD, Ed S). *Accreditation:* NCATE. *Program availability:* Part-time, evening/weekend, 100% online, blended/hybrid learning. *Faculty:* 4 full-time (1 woman), 26 part-time/adjunct (6 women). *Students:* 8 full-time (5 women), 249 part-time (187 women); includes 107 minority (83 Black or African American, non-Hispanic/Latino; 3 Asian, non-Hispanic/Latino; 8 Hispanic/Latino; 13 Two or more races, non-Hispanic/Latino). Average age 36. 42 applicants, 98% accepted, 34 enrolled. In 2017, 51 master's, 5 doctorates, 35 other advanced degrees awarded. *Degree requirements:* For master's and Ed S, comprehensive exam, thesis optional, internship, portfolio, school leadership licensure assessment; for doctorate, comprehensive exam, thesis/dissertation. *Entrance requirements:* For master's, minimum GPA of 3.0 in major, letters of recommendation, resume, 2 essays; for doctorate, GRE, minimum graduate GPA of 3.5, 3 letters of recommendation, essays, resume; for Ed S, minimum GPA of 3.0 in major, 2 letters of recommendation, essays, resume. Additional exam requirements/recommendations for international students: Required—TOEFL (minimum score 550 paper-based). *Application deadline:* For fall admission, 8/15 priority date for domestic students, 2/15 priority date for international students; for winter admission, 10/1 priority date for international students; for spring admission, 1/1 priority date for domestic students, 2/1 priority date for international students; for summer admission, 5/1 for domestic students. Applications are processed on a rolling basis. Application fee: $50. Electronic applications accepted. *Expenses:* Tuition, state resident: full-time $8928; part-time $496 per credit. Tuition, nonresident: full-time $22,482; part-time $1249 per credit. *Required fees:* $66 per semester. *Financial support:* In 2017–18, 2 students received support, including 2 fellowships (averaging $7,500 per year); teaching assistantships, career-related internships or fieldwork, scholarships/grants, and tuition waivers also available. Support available to part-time students. Financial award application deadline: 2/15; financial award applicants required to submit FAFSA. *Faculty research:* Leadership preparation, supervision, policy studies, finance, learning sciences. *Total annual research expenditures:* $500,000. *Unit head:* Dr. Karen L. Sanzo, Graduate Program Director, 757-683-6698, Fax: 757-683-4413, E-mail: ksanzo@odu.edu. *Application contact:* William Heffelfinger, Director of Graduate Admissions, 757-683-5554, Fax: 757-683-3255, E-mail: gradadmit@odu.edu.
Website: https://www.odu.edu/efl/academics/els#.WO1RPbznsow

Olivet Nazarene University, Graduate School, Division of Education, Program in School Leadership, Bourbonnais, IL 60914. Offers MAE.

Oral Roberts University, School of Education, Tulsa, OK 74171. Offers Christian school administration (K-12) (MA Ed, Ed D); college and higher education administration (Ed D); curriculum and instruction (MA Ed); initial teaching with alternative licensure (MAT); initial teaching with licensure (MAT); public school administration (K-12) (MA Ed, Ed D). *Accreditation:* NCATE. *Program availability:* Part-time, online learning. *Faculty:* 7 full-time (2 women), 6 part-time/adjunct (2 women). *Students:* 344 full-time (223 women); includes 117 minority (93 Black or African American, non-Hispanic/Latino; 7 American Indian or Alaska Native, non-Hispanic/Latino; 11 Asian, non-Hispanic/Latino; 6 Hispanic/Latino). 80 applicants, 94% accepted, 65 enrolled. In 2017, 14 master's, 4 doctorates awarded. *Degree requirements:* For master's, comprehensive exam, thesis optional; for doctorate, comprehensive exam, thesis/dissertation. *Entrance requirements:* For master's, GRE General Test or MAT (minimum score in 80th percentile or higher); Oklahoma general education or subject area test (for MAT), minimum GPA of 3.0, bachelor's degree from regionally-accredited institution; for doctorate, minimum GPA of 3.0, master's degree from regionally-accredited institution. *Application deadline:* Applications are processed on a rolling basis. Application fee: $35. Electronic applications accepted. Application fee is waived when completed online. *Expenses:* Contact institution. *Financial support:* Fellowships and scholarships/grants available. Financial award application deadline: 3/15. *Faculty research:* Teacher effectiveness, college success in high achieving African-Americans, professional development practices. *Unit head:* Dr. Patrick Otto, Chair of Graduate School of Education, 918-495-7087, E-mail: jotto@oru.edu. *Application contact:* Audrey Ripley, Enrollment Counselor, 918-495-6375, E-mail: aripley@oru.edu.

Oregon State University, College of Education, Program in Adult and Higher Education, Corvallis, OR 97331. Offers Ed M, Ed D, PhD. *Accreditation:* NCATE. *Program availability:* Part-time, blended/hybrid learning. *Entrance requirements:* For master's, minimum GPA of 3.0 in last 90 hours. Additional exam requirements/recommendations for international students: Required—TOEFL (minimum score 575 paper-based). *Application deadline:* For fall admission, 3/15 for domestic students.

Applications are processed on a rolling basis. Application fee: $75 ($85 for international students). *Unit head:* Dr. Erich N. Pitcher, Program Lead, 541-737-3574. *Application contact:* Dr. Erich N. Pitcher, Program Lead, 541-737-3574.
Website: http://education.oregonstate.edu/adult-education-masters-degree-program

Ottawa University, Graduate Studies-Arizona, Program in Education, Ottawa, KS 66067-3399. Offers community college counseling (MA); curriculum and instruction (MA); early childhood (MA); education intervention (MA); education leadership (MA); education technology (MA); Montessori early childhood education (MA); Montessori elementary education (MA); professional development (MA); school guidance counseling (MA); special education - cross categorical (MA). Programs offered in Mesa, Phoenix, Tempe and West Valley, AZ. *Accreditation:* NCATE. *Program availability:* Part-time. *Degree requirements:* For master's, thesis or alternative. *Entrance requirements:* For master's, minimum undergraduate GPA of 3.0, copy of current state certification or teaching license. Additional exam requirements/recommendations for international students: Required—TOEFL (minimum score 550 paper-based). Electronic applications accepted. *Expenses:* Contact institution.

Park University, School of Graduate and Professional Studies, Kansas City, MO 54105. Offers adult education (M Ed); business and government leadership (Graduate Certificate); business, government, and global society (MPA); communication and leadership (MA); creative and life writing (Graduate Certificate); disaster and emergency management (MPA, Graduate Certificate); educational leadership (M Ed); finance (MBA, Graduate Certificate); general business (MBA); global business (Graduate Certificate); healthcare administration (MHA); healthcare services management and leadership (Graduate Certificate); international business (MBA); language and literacy (M Ed), including English for speakers of other languages, special reading teacher/literacy coach; leadership of international healthcare organizations (Graduate Certificate); management information systems (MBA, Graduate Certificate); music performance (ADP, Graduate Certificate), including cello (MM, ADP), piano (MM, ADP), viola (MM, ADP), violin (MM, ADP); nonprofit and community services management (MPA); nonprofit leadership (Graduate Certificate); performance (MM), including cello (MM, ADP), piano (MM, ADP), viola (MM, ADP), violin (MM, ADP); public management (MPA); social work (MSW); teacher leadership (M Ed), including curriculum and assessment, instructional leader. *Program availability:* Part-time, evening/weekend, online learning. *Degree requirements:* For master's, comprehensive exam (for some programs), thesis (for some programs), internship (for some programs); exam (for some programs). *Entrance requirements:* For master's, GRE or GMAT (for some programs), teacher certification (for some M Ed programs), letters of recommendation, essay, resume (for some programs). Additional exam requirements/recommendations for international students: Required—TOEFL (minimum score 550 paper-based; 79 iBT), IELTS (minimum score 6). Electronic applications accepted.

Penn State University Park, Graduate School, College of Education, Department of Education Policy Studies, University Park, PA 16802. Offers educational leadership (M Ed, D Ed, PhD, Certificate); educational theory and policy (MA, PhD); higher education (M Ed, D Ed, PhD). *Accreditation:* NCATE. *Program availability:* Online learning. *Unit head:* Dr. David N. Monk, Dean, 814-865-2523, Fax: 814-865-0555. *Application contact:* Lori Hawn, Director, Graduate Student Services, 814-865-1795, Fax: 814-863-4627, E-mail: l-gswww@lists.psu.edu.
Website: http://ed.psu.edu/eps

Pensacola Christian College, Graduate Studies, Pensacola, FL 32503-2267. Offers business administration (MBA); curriculum and instruction (MS, Ed D, Ed S); dramatics (MFA); educational leadership (MS, Ed D, Ed S); graphic design (MA, MFA); music (MA); nursing (MSN); performance studies (MA); studio art (MA, MFA).

Pepperdine University, Graduate School of Education and Psychology, Division of Education, Los Angeles, CA 90263. Offers administration and preliminary administrative services (MS); education (MA); educational leadership, administration, and policy (Ed D); global leadership and change (PhD); learning technologies (MA, Ed D); organizational leadership (Ed D); social entrepreneurship and change (MA); teaching (MA); teaching: TESOL (MA). *Program availability:* Part-time, evening/weekend, blended/hybrid learning. *Students:* 214 full-time (139 women), 327 part-time (216 women); includes 248 minority (113 Black or African American, non-Hispanic/Latino; 2 American Indian or Alaska Native, non-Hispanic/Latino; 48 Asian, non-Hispanic/Latino; 61 Hispanic/Latino; 6 Native Hawaiian or other Pacific Islander, non-Hispanic/Latino; 18 Two or more races, non-Hispanic/Latino), 49 international. Average age 39. 410 applicants, 91% accepted, 160 enrolled. In 2017, 151 master's, 88 doctorates awarded. *Degree requirements:* For doctorate, thesis/dissertation. *Entrance requirements:* For master's, GRE General Test; for doctorate, GRE General Test, MAT. Additional exam requirements/recommendations for international students: Required—TOEFL. *Application deadline:* Applications are processed on a rolling basis. Application fee: $55. Electronic applications accepted. *Expenses:* Contact institution. *Financial support:* Research assistantships, teaching assistantships, career-related internships or fieldwork, institutionally sponsored loans, and scholarships/grants available. Support available to part-time students. Financial award application deadline: 7/1; financial award applicants required to submit FAFSA. *Unit head:* Dr. Martine Jago, Associate Dean, Education Division, 310-568-2828, E-mail: martine.jago@pepperdine.edu. *Application contact:* Chris Costa, Director of Enrollment, 310-568-2850, E-mail: chris.costa@pepperdine.edu.
Website: http://gsep.pepperdine.edu/masters-education/

Piedmont International University, Graduate School, Winston-Salem, NC 27101-5197. Offers Biblical studies (PhD); curriculum and instruction (M Ed); divinity (M Div); educational leadership (M Ed); leadership (MA, PhD); ministry (MA Min, D Min); non-language track (MABS); PhD preparation track (MABS). *Program availability:* Part-time, online learning. Terminal master's awarded for partial completion of doctoral program. *Degree requirements:* For master's, 2 foreign languages, comprehensive exam, thesis or alternative; for doctorate, 2 foreign languages, comprehensive exam. *Entrance requirements:* For master's, GRE General Test; for doctorate, Hebrew and Greek proficiency, MA. Additional exam requirements/recommendations for international students: Required—TOEFL (minimum score 500 paper-based; 60 iBT). Electronic applications accepted. *Faculty research:* Theological and biblical studies.

Pittsburg State University, Graduate School, College of Education, Department of Teaching and Leadership, Advanced Studies in Leadership Program, Pittsburg, KS 66762. Offers advanced studies in leadership (Ed S), including general school administration, special education. *Program availability:* Part-time, online only, 100% online. *Students:* 87. In 2017, 11 Ed Ss awarded. *Degree requirements:* For Ed S, thesis optional. *Entrance requirements:* Additional exam requirements/recommendations for international students: Required—TOEFL (minimum score 520 paper-based; 68 iBT), IELTS (minimum score 6), PTE (minimum score 47). *Application deadline:* For fall admission, 6/1 for international students; for spring admission, 10/15 for international students; for summer admission, 4/1 for international students. Applications are processed on a rolling basis. Application fee: $35 ($65 for international students). Electronic applications accepted. *Expenses:* Contact institution. *Financial support:* Application deadline: 2/1; applicants required to submit FAFSA. *Unit head:* Dr. Brenda Roberts, Program Coordinator, 620-235-4498, Fax: 620-235-4520, E-mail: broberts@

pittstate.edu. *Application contact:* Lisa Allen, Assistant Director of Graduate and Continuing Studies, 620-235-4218, Fax: 620-235-4219, E-mail: lallen@pittstate.edu.

Pittsburg State University, Graduate School, College of Education, Department of Teaching and Leadership, Program in Educational Leadership, Pittsburg, KS 66762. Offers MS. *Program availability:* Part-time-only, online only, 100% online. *Students:* 87. In 2017, 42 master's awarded. Terminal master's awarded for partial completion of doctoral program. *Degree requirements:* For master's, thesis optional. *Entrance requirements:* Additional exam requirements/recommendations for international students: Required—TOEFL (minimum score 520 paper-based; 68 iBT), IELTS (minimum score 6), PTE (minimum score 47). *Application deadline:* For fall admission, 7/15 for domestic students, 6/1 for international students; for spring admission, 12/15 for domestic students, 10/15 for international students; for summer admission, 5/15 for domestic students, 4/1 for international students. Applications are processed on a rolling basis. Electronic applications accepted. *Expenses:* Contact institution. *Financial support:* Application deadline: 2/1; applicants required to submit FAFSA. *Unit head:* Dr. Brenda Roberts, Program Coordinator, 620-235-4498, Fax: 620-235-4520, E-mail: broberts@pittstate.edu. *Application contact:* Lisa Allen, Assistant Director of Graduate and Continuing Studies, 620-235-4223, Fax: 620-235-4219, E-mail: lallen@pittstate.edu.

Plymouth State University, College of Graduate Studies, Graduate Studies in Education, Certificate of Advanced Graduate Studies Programs, Plymouth, NH 03264-1595. Offers clinical mental health counseling (CAGS); educational leadership (CAGS); higher education (CAGS); school psychology (CAGS). *Program availability:* Part-time, evening/weekend.

Plymouth State University, College of Graduate Studies, Graduate Studies in Education, Program in Educational Leadership, Plymouth, NH 03264-1595. Offers M Ed. *Accreditation:* NCATE. *Program availability:* Part-time, evening/weekend. *Degree requirements:* For master's, thesis optional, PRAXIS. *Entrance requirements:* For master's, MAT, minimum GPA of 3.0.

Point Loma Nazarene University, School of Education, Program in Education, San Diego, CA 92106-2899. Offers counseling and guidance (MA); educational administration (MA); leadership in learning (MA). *Program availability:* Part-time, evening/weekend. *Students:* 67 full-time (54 women), 161 part-time (128 women); includes 137 minority (7 Black or African American, non-Hispanic/Latino; 14 Asian, non-Hispanic/Latino; 104 Hispanic/Latino; 3 Native Hawaiian or other Pacific Islander, non-Hispanic/Latino; 9 Two or more races, non-Hispanic/Latino), 2 international. Average age 34. 60 applicants, 98% accepted, 53 enrolled. In 2017, 59 master's awarded. *Entrance requirements:* For master's, interview, letters of recommendation, essay. Additional exam requirements/recommendations for international students: Required—TOEFL. *Application deadline:* For fall admission, 8/4 priority date for domestic students; for spring admission, 12/8 priority date for domestic students; for summer admission, 4/12 priority date for domestic students. Applications are processed on a rolling basis. Application fee: $50. Electronic applications accepted. *Expenses:* Contact institution. *Financial support:* Federal Work-Study and scholarships/grants available. Support available to part-time students. Financial award applicants required to submit FAFSA. *Unit head:* Conni Campbell, Associate Dean of the School of Education, 619-849-2532, Fax: 619-849-2532, E-mail: connicampbell@pointloma.edu. *Application contact:* Joanie Joy, Senior Director of Enrollment Management, 619-329-6785, E-mail: gradinfo@pointloma.edu.
Website: https://www.pointloma.edu/schools-departments-colleges/school-education

Point Park University, Center for Innovative Learning, Pittsburgh, PA 15222-1984. Offers community engagement (PhD). *Expenses:* Contact institution.

Point Park University, School of Arts and Sciences, Department of Education, Pittsburgh, PA 15222-1984. Offers adult learning and training (MA); athletic coaching (M Ed); curriculum and instruction (MA); educational administration (MA); leadership and administration (Ed D); secondary education (M Ed); special education grades 7-12 (M Ed); special education PreK-grade 8 (M Ed). *Program availability:* Part-time, evening/weekend, 100% online, blended/hybrid learning. *Degree requirements:* For master's, comprehensive exam (for some programs), thesis or alternative. *Entrance requirements:* For master's, minimum GPA of 3.0, resume, 2 letters of recommendation. Additional exam requirements/recommendations for international students: Required—TOEFL. Electronic applications accepted.

Pontifical Catholic University of Puerto Rico, College of Education, Program in Educational Leadership and Administration, Ponce, PR 00717-0777. Offers PhD.

Post University, Program in Education, Waterbury, CT 06723-2540. Offers curriculum and instruction (M Ed); education (M Ed); educational technology (M Ed); higher education administration (MS); learning design and technology (M Ed); online teaching (M Ed); teaching English to speakers of other languages (TESOL) (M Ed). *Program availability:* Online learning. *Entrance requirements:* For master's, resume. *Expenses:* Tuition: Part-time $730 per credit hour. Part-time tuition and fees vary according to degree level and program. *Application contact:* Veronica Montalvo, Vice President, Online Education Enrollment Management and Admissions, 203-596-6164, E-mail: vmontalvo@post.edu.

Prairie View A&M University, College of Education, Department of Educational Leadership and Counseling, Prairie View, TX 77446. Offers M Ed, MA, MS Ed, PhD. *Accreditation:* NCATE. *Program availability:* Part-time, evening/weekend. *Faculty:* 14 full-time (5 women), 5 part-time/adjunct (4 women). *Students:* 73 full-time (55 women), 222 part-time (178 women); includes 277 minority (261 Black or African American, non-Hispanic/Latino; 1 Asian, non-Hispanic/Latino; 15 Hispanic/Latino), 5 international. Average age 37. 136 applicants, 85% accepted, 75 enrolled. In 2017, 125 master's, 11 doctorates awarded. *Degree requirements:* For master's, thesis optional; for doctorate, comprehensive exam, thesis/dissertation. *Entrance requirements:* For master's, GRE General Test, 3 letters of reference, minimum undergraduate GPA of 2.5; for doctorate, GRE General Test, 3 letters of reference. Additional exam requirements/recommendations for international students: Required—TOEFL (minimum score 550 paper-based; 79 iBT). *Application deadline:* For fall admission, 5/1 priority date for domestic students, 5/1 for international students; for spring admission, 10/1 priority date for domestic students, 9/1 for international students; for summer admission, 3/1 for domestic students, 2/1 for international students. Applications are processed on a rolling basis. Application fee: $50. Electronic applications accepted. *Expenses:* Tuition, state resident: part-time $242 per credit. Tuition, nonresident: part-time $695 per credit. *Required fees:* $149 per credit. *Financial support:* Career-related internships or fieldwork available. Support available to part-time students. Financial award application deadline: 4/1; financial award applicants required to submit FAFSA. *Faculty research:* Mentoring, personality assessment, holistic/humanistic education. *Unit head:* Dr. Maduakolam Ireh, Department Head, 936-261-3565, Fax: 936-261-3617, E-mail: maireh@pvamu.edu. *Application contact:* Pauline Walker, Administrative Assistant II, Research and Graduate Studies, 936-261-3521, Fax: 936-261-3529, E-mail: gradadmissions@pvamu.edu.

Prescott College, Graduate Programs, Program in Education, Prescott, AZ 86301. Offers early childhood education (MA); early childhood special education (MA); education (MA); elementary education (MA); environmental education leadership and

Educational Leadership and Administration

administration (MA); equine-assisted learning (MA); school guidance counseling (MA); secondary education (MA); special education: learning disabilities (MA); special education: mental retardation (MA); special education: serious emotional disabilities (MA); student-directed independent study (MA); sustainability education (PhD). *Program availability:* Part-time, online learning. *Degree requirements:* For master's, thesis, fieldwork or internship, practicum; for doctorate, thesis/dissertation. *Entrance requirements:* For master's, 2 letters of recommendation, resume; for doctorate, 3 letters of recommendation, resume, official transcripts, personal statement, program proposal. Additional exam requirements/recommendations for international students: Required—TOEFL (minimum score 500 paper-based). Electronic applications accepted.

Providence College, Programs in Administration, Providence, RI 02918. Offers elementary administration (M Ed); secondary administration (M Ed). *Program availability:* Part-time, evening/weekend. *Degree requirements:* For master's, comprehensive exam, portfolio. *Entrance requirements:* Additional exam requirements/recommendations for international students: Required—TOEFL (minimum score 577 paper-based; 90 iBT).

Purdue University, Graduate School, College of Education, Department of Educational Studies, West Lafayette, IN 47907. Offers administration (MS Ed, PhD, Ed S); counseling and development (MS Ed, PhD); education of the gifted (MS Ed); educational psychology (MS Ed, PhD); foundations of education (MS Ed, PhD); higher education administration (MS Ed, PhD); special education (MS Ed, PhD). *Accreditation:* ACA (one or more programs are accredited); NCATE (one or more programs are accredited). *Program availability:* Part-time, evening/weekend. *Faculty:* 29 full-time (22 women), 1 part-time/adjunct (0 women). *Students:* 78 full-time (60 women), 226 part-time (162 women); includes 45 minority (16 Black or African American, non-Hispanic/Latino; 8 Asian, non-Hispanic/Latino; 15 Hispanic/Latino; 6 Two or more races, non-Hispanic/Latino), 45 international. Average age 32. 214 applicants, 53% accepted, 70 enrolled. In 2017, 38 master's, 20 doctorates, 4 other advanced degrees awarded. *Degree requirements:* For master's, thesis optional; for doctorate, thesis/dissertation, oral and written exams; for Ed S, oral presentation, project. *Entrance requirements:* For master's, GRE General Test (except for special education if undergraduate GPA is higher than a 3.0), minimum undergraduate GPA of 3.0; for doctorate and Ed S, GRE General Test (minimum combined score of 1000, 300 for new scoring), minimum undergraduate GPA of 3.0. Additional exam requirements/recommendations for international students: Required—TOEFL (minimum score 550 paper-based; 77 iBT), TWE (minimum score 5). *Application deadline:* Applications are processed on a rolling basis. Application fee: $60 ($75 for international students). Electronic applications accepted. *Financial support:* Fellowships with full tuition reimbursements, research assistantships with full tuition reimbursements, teaching assistantships with full tuition reimbursements, career-related internships or fieldwork, and tuition waivers (full) available. Support available to part-time students. Financial award application deadline: 3/1; financial award applicants required to submit FAFSA. *Faculty research:* Motivation, learning disabilities, school learning, group processes, cognitive development. *Unit head:* F. Richard Olenchak, Head, 765-494-9170, E-mail: olenchak@purdue.edu. *Application contact:* Heather Brinkman, Graduate Contact, 765-494-2345, Fax: 765-494-5832, E-mail: hbrinkma@purdue.edu. Website: http://www.edst.purdue.edu/

Purdue University Global, School of Higher Education Studies, Davenport, IA 52807. Offers college administration and leadership (MS); college teaching and learning (MS); student services (MS). *Program availability:* Part-time, evening/weekend, online learning. *Entrance requirements:* Additional exam requirements/recommendations for international students: Required—TOEFL (minimum score 550 paper-based; 80 iBT).

Purdue University Northwest, Graduate Studies Office, School of Education, Program in Educational Administration, Hammond, IN 46323-2094. Offers MS Ed. *Entrance requirements:* Additional exam requirements/recommendations for international students: Required—TOEFL.

Queens College of the City University of New York, Division of Education, Department of Educational and Community Programs, Queens, NY 11367-1597. Offers bilingual pupil personnel (AC); counselor education (MS Ed); mental health counseling (MS); school building leader (AC); school district leader (AC); school psychologist (MS Ed); special education-childhood education (AC); special education-early childhood (MS Ed); teacher of special education 1-6 (MS Ed); teacher of special education birth-2 (MS Ed); teaching students with disabilities, grades 7-12 (MS Ed, AC). *Program availability:* Part-time. *Faculty:* 20 full-time (14 women), 63 part-time/adjunct (37 women). *Students:* 105 full-time (94 women), 423 part-time (350 women); includes 241 minority (40 Black or African American, non-Hispanic/Latino; 2 American Indian or Alaska Native, non-Hispanic/Latino; 50 Asian, non-Hispanic/Latino; 142 Hispanic/Latino; 1 Native Hawaiian or other Pacific Islander, non-Hispanic/Latino; 6 Two or more races, non-Hispanic/Latino), 5 international. Average age 28. 515 applicants, 57% accepted, 230 enrolled. In 2017, 163 master's, 74 other advanced degrees awarded. *Degree requirements:* For master's, research project; for AC, internship. *Entrance requirements:* For master's, minimum GPA of 3.0. Additional exam requirements/recommendations for international students: Required—TOEFL, IELTS. *Application deadline:* For fall admission, 3/1 for domestic students. Applications are processed on a rolling basis. Application fee: $125. Electronic applications accepted. *Financial support:* Career-related internships or fieldwork available. Financial award application deadline: 4/1; financial award applicants required to submit FAFSA. *Unit head:* Dr. Emilia Lopez, Chair, 718-997-5250, E-mail: emilia.lopez@qc.cuny.edu. *Application contact:* Elizabeth D'Amico-Ramirez, Assistant Director of Graduate Admissions, 718-997-5203, E-mail: elizabeth.damicoramirez@qc.cuny.edu.

Queens University of Charlotte, Wayland H. Cato, Jr. School of Education, Charlotte, NC 28274-0002. Offers educational leadership (MA); K-6 (MAT); literacy K-12 (M Ed). *Accreditation:* NCATE. *Program availability:* Part-time, evening/weekend, online learning. *Degree requirements:* For master's, comprehensive exam. *Entrance requirements:* For master's, GRE General Test. *Expenses:* Contact institution.

Quincy University, Master of Science in Education Programs, Quincy, IL 62301-2699. Offers curriculum and instruction (MS Ed), including bilingual/English as a second language; education studies (MS Ed); leadership (MS Ed); reading education (MS Ed); teacher leader (MS Ed). *Program availability:* Part-time, evening/weekend, online learning. *Degree requirements:* For master's, comprehensive exam (for some programs), thesis optional. *Entrance requirements:* For master's, MAT or GRE, personal resume. Additional exam requirements/recommendations for international students: Required—TOEFL (minimum score 550 paper-based; 79 iBT). *Application deadline:* Applications are processed on a rolling basis. Application fee: $25. Electronic applications accepted. Application fee is waived when completed online. *Expenses:* Tuition: Part-time $450 per credit hour. *Financial support:* Applicants required to submit FAFSA. *Unit head:* Dr. Bruce Alan Spitzer, Director, 217-228-5432 Ext. 3106, E-mail: spitzbr@quincy.edu. *Application contact:* Office of Admissions, 217-228-5210, Fax: 217-228-5479, E-mail: admissions@quincy.edu.
Website: http://www.quincy.edu/academics/graduate-programs/education

Quinnipiac University, School of Education, Program in Educational Leadership, Hamden, CT 06518-1940. Offers Diploma. *Program availability:* Part-time-only, evening/

weekend. *Faculty:* 1 (woman) full-time, 5 part-time/adjunct (2 women). *Students:* 1 (woman) full-time, 60 part-time (49 women); includes 5 minority (2 Black or African American, non-Hispanic/Latino; 1 Hispanic/Latino; 2 Two or more races, non-Hispanic/Latino). 26 applicants, 96% accepted, 24 enrolled. In 2017, 26 Diplomas awarded. *Entrance requirements:* For degree, 3 years of experience in pre K-12 setting, interview, 3 credits in special education course. *Application deadline:* For fall admission, 7/30 priority date for domestic students; for spring admission, 12/15 priority date for domestic students; for summer admission, 5/30 priority date for domestic students. Applications are processed on a rolling basis. Application fee: $45. Electronic applications accepted. *Expenses:* Contact institution. *Financial support:* Federal Work-Study and unspecified assistantships available. Financial award application deadline: 6/1; financial award applicants required to submit FAFSA. *Faculty research:* Leadership and teacher quality, leadership and student achievement. *Unit head:* Gail Gilmore, Program Director, 203-582-3289, E-mail: gail.gilmore@qu.edu. *Application contact:* Office of Graduate Admissions, 800-462-1944, Fax: 203-582-3443, E-mail: graduate@qu.edu.
Website: http://www.qu.edu/edleadership

Quinnipiac University, School of Education, Program in Teacher Leadership, Hamden, CT 06518-1940. Offers MS. *Program availability:* Part-time-only, evening/weekend, online only, 100% online. *Faculty:* 2 full-time (both women), 4 part-time/adjunct (3 women). *Students:* 40 part-time (33 women). 17 applicants, 82% accepted, 14 enrolled. In 2017, 14 master's awarded. *Degree requirements:* For master's, capstone experience. *Application deadline:* For fall admission, 8/15 for domestic students; for spring admission, 1/15 for domestic students. Applications are processed on a rolling basis. Application fee: $45. Electronic applications accepted. *Expenses:* Contact institution. *Financial support:* Federal Work-Study and unspecified assistantships available. Financial award application deadline: 6/1; financial award applicants required to submit FAFSA. *Faculty research:* Leadership and school climate, distributed leadership, teacher retention. *Unit head:* Gail Gilmore, Program Director, 203-582-3289, E-mail: gail.gilmore@qu.edu. *Application contact:* Quinnipiac University Online Admissions Office, 800-462-1944, E-mail: quonlineadmissions@qu.edu.
Website: https://quonline.quinnipiac.edu/online-programs/online-graduate-programs/ms-in-teacher-leadership/

Radford University, College of Graduate Studies and Research, Program in Educational Leadership, Radford, VA 24142. Offers MS. *Accreditation:* NCATE. *Program availability:* Part-time, evening/weekend, 100% online, blended/hybrid learning. *Faculty:* 1 full-time (0 women), 4 part-time/adjunct (1 woman). *Students:* 39 part-time (26 women); includes 3 minority (2 Black or African American, non-Hispanic/Latino; 1 Hispanic/Latino). Average age 37. 21 applicants, 100% accepted, 19 enrolled. In 2017, 27 master's awarded. *Degree requirements:* For master's, comprehensive exam. *Entrance requirements:* For master's, GRE or MAT (waived for any applicant with advanced degree), minimum GPA of 2.75, 3 years of K-12 classroom experience, writing sample, 3 letters of reference, resume, official transcripts. Additional exam requirements/recommendations for international students: Required—TOEFL (minimum score 550 paper-based; 79 iBT), IELTS (minimum score 6.5). *Application deadline:* For fall admission, 2/15 priority date for domestic students, 12/1 for international students; for spring admission, 7/1 for international students. Applications are processed on a rolling basis. Application fee: $50. Electronic applications accepted. *Expenses:* Tuition, state resident: full-time $8336; part-time $347 per credit hour. Tuition, nonresident: full-time $16,862; part-time $702 per credit hour. *Required fees:* $3220; $135 per credit hour. Tuition and fees vary according to course load and program. *Financial support:* In 2017–18, 2 students received support. Career-related internships or fieldwork, scholarships/grants, and unspecified assistantships available. Support available to part-time students. Financial award application deadline: 3/1; financial award applicants required to submit FAFSA. *Unit head:* Dr. Brad Bizzell, Coordinator, 540-831-5140, E-mail: bbizzell@radford.edu.
Website: http://www.radford.edu/content/cehd/home/teacher-ed/programs/education-leadership.html

Ramapo College of New Jersey, Master of Arts in Educational Leadership Program, Mahwah, NJ 07430-1680. Offers MA. *Program availability:* Part-time. *Faculty:* 1 full-time (0 women), 9 part-time/adjunct (1 woman). *Students:* 28 full-time (21 women), 30 part-time (20 women); includes 7 minority (1 Black or African American, non-Hispanic/Latino; 1 American Indian or Alaska Native, non-Hispanic/Latino; 1 Asian, non-Hispanic/Latino; 3 Hispanic/Latino; 1 Two or more races, non-Hispanic/Latino). Average age 35. 51 applicants, 86% accepted, 31 enrolled. In 2017, 44 master's awarded. *Degree requirements:* For master's, capstone project. *Entrance requirements:* For master's, PRAXIS, official transcripts of baccalaureate degree from accredited institution with minimum GPA of 3.0; minimum two years' employment under respective certification (preferred). Additional exam requirements/recommendations for international students: Required—TOEFL (minimum score 550 paper-based; 79 iBT); Recommended—IELTS (minimum score 6). *Application deadline:* For fall admission, 5/1 for domestic and international students; for spring admission, 12/1 for domestic and international students; for summer admission, 5/1 for domestic and international students. Applications are processed on a rolling basis. Application fee: $65. Electronic applications accepted. *Expenses:* $690.60 per credit tuition, $56.95 per credit fees. *Financial support:* Career-related internships or fieldwork available. Financial award application deadline: 3/1; financial award applicants required to submit FAFSA. *Faculty research:* Elements and indicators of effective modern learning organizations and application of systems thinking to guide contemporary educational leaders. *Unit head:* Dr. Brian P. Chinni, Associate Professor, Educational Leadership, 201-684-7613, E-mail: bchinni@ramapo.edu. *Application contact:* M. Joyce Wilson, Secretarial Assistant, 201-684-7721, Fax: 201-684-6699, E-mail: jwilson@ramapo.edu.
Website: http://www.ramapo.edu/mael/

Regent University, Graduate School, School of Education, Virginia Beach, VA 23464-9800. Offers education (M Ed, Ed D, PhD), including adult education (Ed D, PhD, Ed S), advanced educational leadership (Ed D, PhD, Ed S), character education (Ed D, PhD, Ed S), Christian education leadership (Ed D, PhD, Ed S), Christian school administration (M Ed), curriculum and instruction (Ed D, PhD, Ed S), curriculum and instruction - adult education (M Ed), curriculum and instruction - Christian school (M Ed), curriculum and instruction - gifted and talented (M Ed), curriculum and instruction - STEM education (M Ed), curriculum and instruction - teacher leader (M Ed), discipleship for ministry (M Ed), educational leadership (M Ed), educational psychology (Ed D, PhD, Ed S), educational technology and online learning (Ed D, PhD, Ed S), elementary education (M Ed), exceptional education executive leadership (Ed D, PhD, Ed S), higher education (Ed D, PhD, Ed S), higher education leadership and management (Ed D, PhD, Ed S), instructional design and technology (M Ed), K-12 school leadership (Ed D, PhD, Ed S), K-12 special education (M Ed), leadership in mathematics education (M Ed), reading specialist (M Ed), special education (Ed D, PhD, Ed S), student affairs (M Ed), TESOL - adult education (M Ed), TESOL - K-12 (M Ed); educational specialist (Ed S), including adult education (Ed D, PhD, Ed S), advanced educational leadership (Ed D, PhD, Ed S), character education (Ed D, PhD, Ed S), Christian education leadership (Ed D, PhD, Ed S), curriculum and instruction (Ed D, PhD, Ed S), educational psychology (Ed D, PhD, Ed S), educational technology and online learning (Ed D, PhD, Ed S), exceptional education executive leadership (Ed D, PhD, Ed S), higher education (Ed D, PhD, Ed S), higher education leadership and management (Ed D, PhD, Ed S), K-12 school

leadership (Ed D, PhD, Ed S), special education (Ed D, PhD, Ed S). *Accreditation:* TEAC. *Program availability:* Part-time, evening/weekend, 100% online, blended/hybrid learning. *Faculty:* 22 full-time (10 women), 44 part-time/adjunct (32 women). *Students:* 80 full-time (59 women), 945 part-time (750 women); includes 432 minority (352 Black or African American, non-Hispanic/Latino; 4 American Indian or Alaska Native, non-Hispanic/Latino; 14 Asian, non-Hispanic/Latino; 43 Hispanic/Latino; 19 Two or more races, non-Hispanic/Latino; 12 international. Average age 40. 1,125 applicants, 49% accepted, 436 enrolled. In 2017, 316 master's, 24 doctorates awarded. *Degree requirements:* For master's, thesis or alternative; for doctorate, comprehensive exam, thesis/dissertation. *Entrance requirements:* For master's, Virginia Communication and Literacy Assessment (VCLA), PRAXIS, college transcripts, writing sample, interview; for doctorate, GRE, writing sample, resume, transcripts, interview. Additional exam requirements/recommendations for international students: Required—TOEFL (minimum score 577 paper-based). *Application deadline:* For fall admission, 4/1 priority date for domestic students; for spring admission, 10/15 priority date for domestic students. Applications are processed on a rolling basis. Application fee: $50. Electronic applications accepted. *Expenses:* Contact institution. *Financial support:* In 2017–18, 669 students received support, including 1 fellowship (averaging $10,000 per year); career-related internships or fieldwork, scholarships/grants, and unspecified assistantships also available. Support available to part-time students. *Faculty research:* Christian school administration, curriculum and instruction, educational technology and online learning, higher education, special education. *Unit head:* Dr. Donald Finn, Dean, 757-352-4278, Fax: 757-352-4318, E-mail: dfinn@regent.edu. *Application contact:* Heidi Cece, Assistant Vice President of Enrollment Management, 800-373-5504, Fax: 757-352-4381, E-mail: admissions@regent.edu.
Website: https://www.regent.edu/school-of-education/

Regis College, Department of Education, Weston, MA 02493. Offers elementary teacher (M Ed); higher education leadership (Ed D); special education (M Ed). *Program availability:* Part-time, evening/weekend. *Degree requirements:* For doctorate, thesis/dissertation, capstone project. *Entrance requirements:* For master's, GRE or MAT, personal statement, recommendations, resume/curriculum vitae, official transcripts, interview; for doctorate, personal statement, recommendations, resume/curriculum vitae, official transcripts, presentation/interview. Additional exam requirements/recommendations for international students: Required—TOEFL (minimum score 560 paper-based; 79 iBT); Recommended—IELTS (minimum score 6.5). *Application deadline:* Applications are processed on a rolling basis. Application fee: $65. Electronic applications accepted. *Financial support:* Federal Work-Study, scholarships/grants, and unspecified assistantships available. Financial award applicants required to submit FAFSA. *Unit head:* Dr. Priscilla Boerger, Department Chair/Graduate Program Director, 781-768-7422, E-mail: priscilla.boerger@regiscollege.edu.

Regis University, College of Contemporary Liberal Studies, Denver, CO 80221-1099. Offers creative writing (MFA); criminology (M Sc); curriculum, instruction and assessment (M Ed); education - teacher leadership (M Ed); educational leadership (M Ed); elementary education (M Ed); literacy (Certificate); reading (M Ed); secondary education (M Ed); special education (M Ed); teacher academic leadership (Certificate); teacher leadership (MA); teacher/educational leadership (M Ed); teaching the linguistically diverse (M Ed). *Program availability:* Part-time, evening/weekend, 100% online, blended/hybrid learning. *Degree requirements:* For master's, thesis (for some programs). *Entrance requirements:* For master's, official transcript reflecting baccalaureate degree awarded from regionally-accredited college or university, work experience, resume, letters of recommendation. Additional exam requirements/recommendations for international students: Required—TOEFL (minimum score 550 paper-based; 82 iBT). Electronic applications accepted. *Expenses:* Contact institution.

Rhode Island College, School of Graduate Studies, Feinstein School of Education and Human Development, Department of Counseling, Educational Leadership, and School Psychology, Providence, RI 02908-1991. Offers advanced counseling (CGS); agency counseling (MA); clinical mental health counseling (MS); co-occurring disorders (MA, CGS); educational leadership (M Ed); mental health counseling (CAGS); school counseling (MA); school psychology (CAGS); teacher leadership (CGS). *Accreditation:* ACA; NCATE. *Program availability:* Part-time, evening/weekend. *Faculty:* 10. *Students:* 31 full-time (25 women), 75 part-time (65 women); includes 16 minority (4 Black or African American, non-Hispanic/Latino; 11 Hispanic/Latino; 1 Two or more races, non-Hispanic/Latino). Average age 32. In 2017, 40 master's, 15 other advanced degrees awarded. *Degree requirements:* For master's and other advanced degree, comprehensive exam (for some programs), thesis (for some programs). *Entrance requirements:* For master's, GRE General Test or MAT, undergraduate transcripts; minimum undergraduate GPA of 3.0; for other advanced degree, GRE or MAT (for most programs), undergraduate transcripts; minimum undergraduate GPA of 3.0; 3 letters of recommendation; current resume. Additional exam requirements/recommendations for international students: Recommended—TOEFL (minimum score 550 paper-based; 79 iBT). *Application deadline:* For fall admission, 3/1 for domestic students; for spring admission, 11/1 for domestic students. Applications are processed on a rolling basis. Application fee: $50. Electronic applications accepted. *Expenses:* Tuition, state resident: full-time $9768; part-time $407 per credit. Tuition, nonresident: full-time $19,008; part-time $792 per credit. *Required fees:* $696; $29 per credit. One-time fee: $200 full-time; $100 part-time. Tuition and fees vary according to course load. *Financial support:* In 2017–18, 4 teaching assistantships with full tuition reimbursements (averaging $2,063 per year) were awarded; career-related internships or fieldwork, Federal Work-Study, scholarships/grants, health care benefits, and unspecified assistantships also available. Support available to part-time students. Financial award application deadline: 5/15; financial award applicants required to submit FAFSA. *Unit head:* Dr. John Eagle, Chair, 401-456-8023. *Application contact:* Graduate Studies, 401-456-8700.
Website: http://www.ric.edu/counselingEducationalLeadershipSchoolPsychology/index.php

Rider University, College of Education and Human Services, Program in Educational Administration, Lawrenceville, NJ 08648-3001. Offers educational administration (MA); educational leadership (MA); principal (Certificate); school business administrator (Certificate); supervisor of instruction (Certificate); teacher leadership (MA). *Accreditation:* NCATE. *Program availability:* Part-time, evening/weekend. *Degree requirements:* For master's, comprehensive exam, research project. *Entrance requirements:* For master's, interview, resume, 2 letters of recommendation. Additional exam requirements/recommendations for international students: Required—TOEFL (minimum score 550 paper-based). Electronic applications accepted. *Faculty research:* National/state standards, urban education, administrative leadership, financing public education, community school linkages.

Rivier University, School of Graduate Studies, Department of Education, Nashua, NH 03060. Offers curriculum and instruction (M Ed); early childhood education (M Ed); educational administration (M Ed); educational studies (M Ed); elementary education (M Ed); elementary education and general special education (M Ed); emotional and behavioral disorders (M Ed); general social education (M Ed); leadership and learning (Ed D, CAGS); learning disabilities (M Ed); learning disabilities and reading (M Ed); mental health counseling (MA); reading (M Ed); school counseling (M Ed). *Program*

availability: Part-time, evening/weekend. *Degree requirements:* For master's, comprehensive exam (for some programs), internships. *Entrance requirements:* For master's, GRE General Test or MAT.

Robert Morris University, School of Education and Social Sciences, Moon Township, PA 15108-1189. Offers business education (MS); counseling psychology (MS); education (Postbaccalaureate Certificate); higher education (MS); instructional leadership (MS), including education; instructional management and leadership (PhD); literacy (MS); special education (MS). *Accreditation:* TEAC. *Program availability:* Part-time, evening/weekend, online learning. *Faculty:* 18 full-time (10 women), 5 part-time/adjunct (2 women). *Students:* 151 part-time (90 women); includes 23 minority (12 Black or African American, non-Hispanic/Latino; 2 Asian, non-Hispanic/Latino; 2 Hispanic/Latino; 7 Two or more races, non-Hispanic/Latino), 4 international. Average age 34. 51 applicants, 39% accepted, 10 enrolled. In 2017, 31 master's, 16 doctorates awarded. *Degree requirements:* For doctorate, thesis/dissertation. *Entrance requirements:* Additional exam requirements/recommendations for international students: Required—TOEFL (minimum score 550 paper-based; 79 iBT). *Application deadline:* For fall admission, 7/1 priority date for domestic and international students; for spring admission, 11/1 priority date for domestic and international students. Applications are processed on a rolling basis. Application fee: $35. Electronic applications accepted. *Expenses:* $890 per credit tuition, $80 per credit university fee. *Unit head:* Dr. George Semich, Acting Dean, 412-397-6032, Fax: 412-397-6044, E-mail: semich@rmu.edu. *Application contact:* E-mail: graduateadmissions@rmu.edu.
Website: http://www.rmu.edu/web/cms/schools/sess/

Robert Morris University Illinois, Morris Graduate School of Management, Chicago, IL 60605. Offers accounting (MBA); accounting/finance (MBA); business analytics (MIS); health care administration (MM); higher education administration (MM); human performance (MS); human resource management (MBA); information security (MIS); information systems management (MIS); law enforcement administration (MM); management (MBA); management/finance (MBA); management/human resource management (MBA); sports administration (MM). *Program availability:* Part-time, evening/weekend. *Faculty:* 2 full-time (0 women), 26 part-time/adjunct (8 women). *Students:* 186 full-time (108 women), 114 part-time (57 women); includes 167 minority (88 Black or African American, non-Hispanic/Latino; 15 Asian, non-Hispanic/Latino; 62 Hispanic/Latino; 1 Native Hawaiian or other Pacific Islander, non-Hispanic/Latino; 1 Two or more races, non-Hispanic/Latino), 18 international. Average age 32. 157 applicants, 78% accepted, 72 enrolled. In 2017, 191 master's awarded. *Entrance requirements:* For master's, official transcripts and letters of recommendation (for some programs); written personal statement. Additional exam requirements/recommendations for international students: Required—TOEFL (minimum score 550 paper-based). *Application deadline:* Applications are processed on a rolling basis. Application fee: $20 ($100 for international students). Electronic applications accepted. *Expenses:* Tuition: Full-time $17,100; part-time $2850 per course. *Financial support:* In 2017–18, 381 students received support. Federal Work-Study, scholarships/grants, and unspecified assistantships available. Support available to part-time students. Financial award applicants required to submit FAFSA. *Unit head:* Kayed Akkawi, Dean, 312-935-6050, Fax: 312-935-6020, E-mail: kakkawi@robertmorris.edu. *Application contact:* Mark Daugherty, Director of Admissions, 312-935-4814, Fax: 312-935-6020, E-mail: mdaugherty@robertmorris.edu.

Rocky Mountain College, Program in Educational Leadership, Billings, MT 59102-1796. Offers M Ed. *Faculty:* 2 full-time (both women). *Students:* 19 full-time (7 women). Average age 37. In 2017, 20 master's awarded. *Entrance requirements:* For master's, valid (current) teaching certificate. Additional exam requirements/recommendations for international students: Required—TOEFL (minimum score 570 paper-based; 88 iBT), IELTS (minimum score 6.5). *Application deadline:* Applications are processed on a rolling basis. Application fee: $35 ($40 for international students). Electronic applications accepted. Application fee is waived when completed online. *Expenses:* Contact institution. *Financial support:* In 2017–18, 19 students received support. Scholarships/grants available. Financial award applicants required to submit FAFSA. *Unit head:* Dr. Stevie Schmitz, Director of Educational Leadership and Distance Education, 406-657-1134, E-mail: schmitzs@rocky.edu.
Website: http://rocky.edu/academics/academic-programs/graduate-programs/mel/index.php

Roosevelt University, Graduate Division, College of Education, Program in Instructional Leadership, Chicago, IL 60605. Offers MA. *Students:* 1 full-time (0 women), 46 part-time (28 women); includes 13 minority (3 Black or African American, non-Hispanic/Latino; 3 Asian, non-Hispanic/Latino; 6 Hispanic/Latino; 1 Two or more races, non-Hispanic/Latino). Average age 36. 32 applicants, 100% accepted, 27 enrolled. In 2017, 1 master's awarded. *Application deadline:* Applications are processed on a rolling basis. Application fee: $40. Electronic applications accepted. *Financial support:* Scholarships/grants and unspecified assistantships available. *Application contact:* Laura Lag, Associate Dean for Graduate Admission, 312-853-4753, E-mail: llag@roosevelt.edu.
Website: https://www.roosevelt.edu/academics/programs/masters-in-instructional-leadership-iled

Rowan University, Graduate School, College of Education, Department of Educational Services and Leadership, Program in Educational Leadership, Glassboro, NJ 08028-1701. Offers Ed D, CAGS. *Accreditation:* NCATE. *Program availability:* Part-time, evening/weekend. *Degree requirements:* For doctorate, thesis/dissertation. *Entrance requirements:* For doctorate, GMAT or GRE General Test, master's degree. Additional exam requirements/recommendations for international students: Required—TOEFL. *Expenses:* Tuition, state resident: full-time $15,020; part-time $751 per semester hour. Tuition, nonresident: full-time $15,020; part-time $751 per semester hour. *Required fees:* $3158; $157.90 per semester hour. Tuition and fees vary according to course load, campus/location and program.

Rowan University, Graduate School, College of Education, Department of Educational Services and Leadership, Program in Higher Education Administration, Glassboro, NJ 08028-1701. Offers MA. *Accreditation:* NCATE. *Program availability:* Part-time, evening/weekend. *Degree requirements:* For master's, comprehensive exam, thesis. *Entrance requirements:* For master's, GRE General Test, minimum GPA of 2.8, 2 years of teaching experience. Additional exam requirements/recommendations for international students: Required—TOEFL. Electronic applications accepted. *Expenses:* Tuition, state resident: full-time $15,020; part-time $751 per semester hour. Tuition, nonresident: full-time $15,020; part-time $751 per semester hour. *Required fees:* $3158; $157.90 per semester hour. Tuition and fees vary according to course load, campus/location and program.

Rowan University, Graduate School, College of Education, Department of Educational Services and Leadership, Program in Principal Preparation, Glassboro, NJ 08028-1701. Offers CAGS. *Program availability:* Part-time, evening/weekend. *Degree requirements:* For CAGS, comprehensive exam, thesis, internship. *Entrance requirements:* For degree, GRE General Test, minimum GPA of 2.81, 1 year of teaching experience. Additional exam requirements/recommendations for international students: Required—TOEFL. Electronic applications accepted. *Expenses:* Tuition, state resident: full-time $15,020; part-time $751 per semester hour. Tuition, nonresident: full-time $15,020; part-time $751 per semester hour. *Required fees:* $3158; $157.90 per semester hour. Tuition and fees vary according to course load, campus/location and program.

Educational Leadership and Administration

Rowan University, Graduate School, College of Education, Department of Educational Services and Leadership, Program in School Administration, Glassboro, NJ 08028-1701. Offers MA. Electronic applications accepted. *Expenses:* Tuition, state resident: full-time $15,020; part-time $751 per semester hour. Tuition, nonresident: full-time $15,020; part-time $751 per semester hour. *Required fees:* $3158; $157.90 per semester hour. Tuition and fees vary according to course load, campus/location and program.

Rowan University, Graduate School, College of Education, Department of Educational Services and Leadership, Program in Supervisor Certification, Glassboro, NJ 08028-1701. Offers CAGS. Electronic applications accepted. *Expenses:* Tuition, state resident: full-time $15,020; part-time $751 per semester hour. Tuition, nonresident: full-time $15,020; part-time $751 per semester hour. *Required fees:* $3158; $157.90 per semester hour. Tuition and fees vary according to course load, campus/location and program.

Rowan University, Graduate School, College of Education, Department of Interdisciplinary and Inclusive Education, Program in Teacher Leadership, Glassboro, NJ 08028-1701. Offers M Ed. *Program availability:* Part-time, evening/weekend. *Degree requirements:* For master's, thesis. *Entrance requirements:* For master's, GRE General Test, minimum GPA of 2.8, 1 year of teaching experience. Additional exam requirements/recommendations for international students: Required—TOEFL. Electronic applications accepted. *Expenses:* Tuition, state resident: full-time $15,020; part-time $751 per semester hour. Tuition, nonresident: full-time $15,020; part-time $751 per semester hour. *Required fees:* $3158; $157.90 per semester hour. Tuition and fees vary according to course load, campus/location and program.

Rutgers University–Camden, Graduate School of Arts and Sciences, Department of Public Policy and Administration, Camden, NJ 08102. Offers education policy and leadership (MPA); international public service and development (MPA); public management (MPA); JD/MPA; MPA/MA. *Accreditation:* NASPAA. *Program availability:* Part-time, evening/weekend. *Degree requirements:* For master's, directed study, research workshop, 42 credits. *Entrance requirements:* For master's, GRE General Test, GMAT or LSAT, 3 letters of recommendation; resume. Additional exam requirements/recommendations for international students: Required—TOEFL (minimum score 550 paper-based), IELTS. Electronic applications accepted. *Faculty research:* Nonprofit management, county and municipal administration, health and human services, government communication, administrative law, educational finance.

Rutgers University–New Brunswick, Graduate School of Education, Department of Educational Theory, Policy and Administration, Programs in Educational Administration and Supervision, Piscataway, NJ 08854-8097. Offers Ed M, Ed D. *Program availability:* Part-time, evening/weekend. *Degree requirements:* For doctorate, thesis/dissertation, qualifying exam. *Entrance requirements:* For master's, GRE General Test, minimum GPA of 3.0; for doctorate, GRE General Test, minimum GPA of 3.0, master's degree in educational administration. Additional exam requirements/recommendations for international students: Required—TOEFL. Electronic applications accepted. *Faculty research:* Leadership of education, finance, law, schools as organizations.

Sacred Heart University, Graduate Programs, Isabelle Farrington College of Education, Department of Leadership/Literacy, Fairfield, CT 06825. Offers advanced studies in administration (Professional Certificate); advanced studies in literacy (Professional Certificate). *Program availability:* Part-time, evening/weekend. *Faculty:* 7 full-time (3 women), 17 part-time/adjunct (8 women). *Students:* 70 part-time (67 women); includes 5 minority (2 Black or African American, non-Hispanic/Latino; 1 American Indian or Alaska Native, non-Hispanic/Latino; 1 Asian, non-Hispanic/Latino; 1 Hispanic/Latino). Average age 37. 162 applicants, 98% accepted, 143 enrolled. In 2017, 59 Professional Certificates awarded. *Degree requirements:* For Professional Certificate, thesis or alternative. *Entrance requirements:* For degree, CT teacher certification. *Application deadline:* Applications are processed on a rolling basis. Application fee: $75. Electronic applications accepted. *Expenses:* Contact institution. *Financial support:* Unspecified assistantships available. Financial award applicants required to submit FAFSA. *Unit head:* Randall Glading, Chair/Assistant Professor, 203-396-8312, E-mail: gladingr@sacredheart.edu. *Application contact:* Tara Chudy, Executive Director of Graduate Admissions, 203-365-4735, E-mail: chudyt@sacredheart.edu.

Sage Graduate School, Esteves School of Education, Program in Educational Leadership, Troy, NY 12180-4115. Offers Ed D. *Program availability:* Part-time. *Faculty:* 7 full-time (5 women), 6 part-time/adjunct (2 women). *Students:* 107 part-time (77 women); includes 63 minority (34 Black or African American, non-Hispanic/Latino; 4 Asian, non-Hispanic/Latino; 23 Hispanic/Latino; 1 Native Hawaiian or other Pacific Islander, non-Hispanic/Latino; 1 Two or more races, non-Hispanic/Latino). Average age 45. 124 applicants, 44% accepted, 44 enrolled. In 2017, 35 doctorates awarded. *Degree requirements:* For doctorate, comprehensive exam. *Entrance requirements:* For doctorate, three letters of professional reference that address candidate's potential in relationship to New York State Education Department's nine essential characteristics of effective school leader; on-demand writing sample to determine readiness and capability for scholarly writing; current resume; statement of career goals. Additional exam requirements/recommendations for international students: Required—TOEFL (minimum score 550 paper-based). *Application deadline:* Applications are processed on a rolling basis. Application fee: $30. Electronic applications accepted. *Expenses:* Contact institution. *Financial support:* Fellowships, research assistantships, scholarships/grants, and unspecified assistantships available. Financial award applicants required to submit FAFSA. *Unit head:* Dr. John Pelizza, Interim Dean, Esteves School of Education, 518-244-2051, Fax: 518-244-2334, E-mail: pelizj@sage.edu. *Application contact:* Janice White, Chair, Doctor of Education Program in Educational Leadership, 518-244-4588, Fax: 518-266-1391, E-mail: whitej5@sage.edu.

Saginaw Valley State University, College of Education, Program in Educational Leadership, University Center, MI 48710. Offers M Ed, Ed S. *Accreditation:* NCATE. *Program availability:* Part-time, evening/weekend, online learning. *Students:* 1 (woman) full-time, 68 part-time (42 women); includes 8 minority (3 Black or African American, non-Hispanic/Latino; 1 American Indian or Alaska Native, non-Hispanic/Latino; 1 Asian, non-Hispanic/Latino; 2 Hispanic/Latino; 1 Two or more races, non-Hispanic/Latino). Average age 35. 34 applicants, 100% accepted, 24 enrolled. In 2017, 34 master's, 7 Ed Ss awarded. *Degree requirements:* For master's, capstone course. *Entrance requirements:* For master's, minimum GPA of 3.0, teaching certificate; for Ed S, master's degree with minimum GPA of 3.3. Additional exam requirements/recommendations for international students: Required—TOEFL (minimum score 550 paper-based; 79 iBT). *Application deadline:* For fall admission, 7/15 for international students; for winter admission, 11/15 for international students; for spring admission, 4/15 for international students. Applications are processed on a rolling basis. Application fee: $30 ($90 for international students). Electronic applications accepted. *Expenses:* Tuition, state resident: full-time $10,156; part-time $564.20 per credit hour. Tuition, nonresident: full-time $19,336; part-time $1074.20 per credit hour. *Required fees:* $263; $14.60 per credit hour. Tuition and fees vary according to degree level and program. *Financial support:* Federal Work-Study and scholarships/grants available. Support available to part-time students. Financial award applicants required to submit FAFSA. *Unit head:* Dr. Jonathan Gould, Associate Professor of Teacher Education, 989-964-4978, Fax: 989-964-4981, E-mail: jagould@svsu.edu. *Application contact:* Jenna Briggs, Director, Graduate and International Admissions, 989-964-6096, Fax: 989-964-2788, E-mail: gradadm@svsu.edu.

St. Ambrose University, School of Education, Davenport, IA 52803-2898. Offers early childhood education (M Ed); educational administration (M Ed). *Accreditation:* TEAC. *Program availability:* Part-time, evening/weekend, online learning. *Degree requirements:* For master's, comprehensive exam. *Entrance requirements:* For master's, GRE General Test or MAT, minimum GPA of 2.75. Additional exam requirements/recommendations for international students: Required—TOEFL. Electronic applications accepted. *Faculty research:* Disabilities and postsecondary career avenues, self-determination.

St. Bonaventure University, School of Graduate Studies, School of Education, Program in Educational Leadership, St. Bonaventure, NY 14778-2284. Offers educational leadership (MS Ed); school building leader (Adv C); school district leader (Adv C). *Program availability:* Part-time, evening/weekend, online learning. *Faculty:* 1 (woman) full-time, 3 part-time/adjunct (2 women). *Students:* 1 (woman) full-time, 50 part-time (35 women); includes 4 minority (3 Black or African American, non-Hispanic/Latino; 1 Hispanic/Latino). Average age 37. 20 applicants, 100% accepted, 13 enrolled. In 2017, 7 master's, 17 Adv Cs awarded. *Degree requirements:* For master's, comprehensive exam, thesis optional, minimum cumulative GPA of 3.0, practicum, internship, electronic portfolio; for Adv C, comprehensive exam, minimum cumulative GPA of 3.0, practicum, internship, electronic portfolio. *Entrance requirements:* For master's, teaching, counseling or other school certification; three years of K-12 school experience; transcripts from all colleges previously attended; two references (one from supervising principal or superintendent); interview; writing sample (academic or professional); for Adv C, master's degree in education or certification-related area; three years of K-12 school experience; teaching or counseling certification; transcripts from all colleges previously attended; two references (one from supervising principal or superintendent); interview; writing sample. Additional exam requirements/recommendations for international students: Required—TOEFL (minimum score 550 paper-based; 79 iBT). *Application deadline:* For fall admission, 6/15 priority date for domestic students, 2/1 priority date for international students; for spring admission, 11/1 for domestic students. Applications are processed on a rolling basis. Application fee: $0. Electronic applications accepted. *Expenses:* $733 per credit hour, $100 graduation fee. *Financial support:* Federal Work-Study, scholarships/grants, health care benefits, and unspecified assistantships available. Support available to part-time students. Financial award application deadline: 4/15; financial award applicants required to submit FAFSA. *Faculty research:* Global competence, teacher leadership. *Unit head:* Dr. Margaret Jones-Carey, Director, 716-375-4026, Fax: 716-375-2360, E-mail: mjonesca@sbu.edu. *Application contact:* Bruce Campbell, Director of Graduate Admissions, 716-375-2429, Fax: 716-375-4015, E-mail: gradsch@sbu.edu.
Website: http://www.sbu.edu/academics/schools/education/graduate-degrees-certificates/msed-in-educational-leadership

St. Cloud State University, School of Graduate Studies, School of Education, Department of Educational Leadership and Higher Education, Program in Higher Education Administration, St. Cloud, MN 56301-4498. Offers MS, Ed D.

St. Cloud State University, School of Graduate Studies, School of Health and Human Services, Department of Counseling and Community Psychology, Program in Educational Administration and Leadership, St. Cloud, MN 56301-4498. Offers MS. *Program availability:* Part-time. *Degree requirements:* For master's, comprehensive exam (for some programs), thesis or alternative. *Entrance requirements:* For master's, GRE General Test, minimum GPA of 2.75. Additional exam requirements/recommendations for international students: Required—Michigan English Language Assessment Battery; Recommended—TOEFL (minimum score 550 paper-based), IELTS (minimum score 6.5). Electronic applications accepted.

Saint Francis University, Graduate Education Program, Loretto, PA 15940-0600. Offers education (M Ed); leadership (M Ed); reading (M Ed). *Program availability:* Part-time, 100% online, blended/hybrid learning. *Faculty:* 1 full-time (0 women), 15 part-time/adjunct (9 women). *Students:* 13 full-time (6 women), 96 part-time (65 women); includes 3 minority (2 Black or African American, non-Hispanic/Latino; 1 Hispanic/Latino). Average age 35. 22 applicants, 100% accepted, 16 enrolled. In 2017, 33 master's awarded. *Degree requirements:* For master's, comprehensive exam, thesis optional. *Entrance requirements:* For master's, GRE or MAT (if undergraduate GPA less than 3.0). Additional exam requirements/recommendations for international students: Required—TOEFL (minimum score 550 paper-based; 75 iBT), IELTS (minimum score 6.5), International Test of English proficiency (minimum score 4). *Application deadline:* Applications are processed on a rolling basis. Application fee: $30. Electronic applications accepted. *Expenses:* Contact institution. *Financial support:* Applicants required to submit FAFSA. *Unit head:* Dr. Janette D. Kelly, Director, 814-472-3068, Fax: 814-472-3864, E-mail: jkelly@francis.edu. *Application contact:* Sherri L. Toth, Coordinator, 814-472-3058, Fax: 814-472-3864, E-mail: stoth@francis.edu.
Website: http://www.francis.edu/master-of-education/

St. Francis Xavier University, Graduate Studies, Graduate Studies in Education, Antigonish, NS B2G 2W5, Canada. Offers curriculum and instruction (M Ed); educational administration and leadership (M Ed). *Program availability:* Part-time, online learning. *Degree requirements:* For master's, thesis. *Entrance requirements:* For master's, minimum undergraduate B average, 2 years of teaching experience. *Faculty research:* Inclusive education, qualitative research.

St. John Fisher College, Ralph C. Wilson Jr. School of Education, Educational Leadership Program, Rochester, NY 14618-3597. Offers MS Ed. *Program availability:* Part-time, evening/weekend. *Faculty:* 1 (woman) full-time, 2 part-time/adjunct (both women). *Students:* 22 part-time (18 women); includes 4 minority (1 Black or African American, non-Hispanic/Latino; 1 Asian, non-Hispanic/Latino; 1 Hispanic/Latino; 1 Two or more races, non-Hispanic/Latino). Average age 39. 16 applicants, 75% accepted, 11 enrolled. In 2017, 8 master's awarded. *Degree requirements:* For master's, capstone project, internship. *Entrance requirements:* For master's, teacher certification, minimum 2 years of teaching experience, 2 letters of recommendation, current resume. Additional exam requirements/recommendations for international students: Required—TOEFL (minimum score 575 paper-based; 80 iBT). *Application deadline:* Applications are processed on a rolling basis. Application fee: $30. Electronic applications accepted. *Expenses:* Contact institution. *Financial support:* Scholarships/grants available. Financial award applicants required to submit FAFSA. *Faculty research:* Urban school leadership, assessment, effective school leadership. *Unit head:* Dr. Diane Reed, Director, 585-385-7257, E-mail: dreed@sjfc.edu. *Application contact:* Michelle Gosier, Director of Transfer and Graduate Admissions, 585-385-8064, E-mail: mgosier@sjfc.edu.
Website: https://www.sjfc.edu/graduate-programs/ms-in-educational-leadership

St. John Fisher College, Ralph C. Wilson Jr. School of Education, Executive Leadership Program, Rochester, NY 14618-3597. Offers Ed D. *Program availability:* Evening/weekend. *Faculty:* 11 full-time (9 women), 2 part-time/adjunct (both women). *Students:* 102 full-time (74 women), 68 part-time (42 women); includes 91 minority (70 Black or African American, non-Hispanic/Latino; 3 American Indian or Alaska Native, non-Hispanic/Latino; 1 Asian, non-Hispanic/Latino; 15 Hispanic/Latino; 2 Two or more races, non-Hispanic/Latino). Average age 45. 84 applicants, 79% accepted, 57 enrolled.

In 2017, 47 doctorates awarded. *Degree requirements:* For doctorate, comprehensive exam, thesis/dissertation, field experiences. *Entrance requirements:* For doctorate, 3 professional writing samples, 2 letters of reference, interview, minimum of 3 years' management experience, master's degree. Additional exam requirements/recommendations for international students: Required—TOEFL (minimum score 575 paper-based; 80 iBT). *Application deadline:* For fall admission, 3/1 for domestic and international students. Applications are processed on a rolling basis. Electronic applications accepted. *Expenses:* Contact institution. *Financial support:* Scholarships/grants available. Financial award applicants required to submit FAFSA. *Faculty research:* Leadership, organizational development. *Unit head:* Dr. Jeannine Dingus-Eason, Program Director, 585-385-8002, E-mail: jdingus@sjfc.edu. *Application contact:* Michelle Gosier, Director of Transfer and Graduate Admissions, 585-385-8064, E-mail: mgosier@sjfc.edu.
Website: https://www.sjfc.edu/graduate-programs/executive-leadership-edd/

St. John's University, The School of Education, Department of Administrative and Instructional Leadership, Program in Administration and Supervision, Queens, NY 11439. Offers Ed D. *Program availability:* Part-time, blended/hybrid learning. *Students:* 4 full-time (3 women), 253 part-time (164 women); includes 84 minority (42 Black or African American, non-Hispanic/Latino; 7 Asian, non-Hispanic/Latino; 30 Hispanic/Latino; 5 Two or more races, non-Hispanic/Latino), 4 international. Average age 43. 152 applicants, 98% accepted, 119 enrolled. In 2017, 36 doctorates awarded. *Degree requirements:* For doctorate, comprehensive exam, thesis/dissertation. *Entrance requirements:* For doctorate, GRE, official master's transcript, statement of purpose. Additional exam requirements/recommendations for international students: Required—TOEFL, IELTS. *Application deadline:* For fall admission, 8/17 for domestic and international students; for summer admission, 5/15 for domestic and international students. Application fee: $70. Electronic applications accepted. *Expenses: Tuition:* Full-time $44,280; part-time $1230 per credit. *Required fees:* $340; $340 per credit. Tuition and fees vary according to course load, degree level and program. *Financial support:* Fellowships, research assistantships, scholarships/grants, and unspecified assistantships available. Support available to part-time students. Financial award application deadline: 2/1; financial award applicants required to submit FAFSA. *Faculty research:* School administrators' accountability in response to New York state and federal regulations and reforms; budgetary and expenditure decision-making among school district administrators; compliance, and changing demographics; twenty-first century technological tools in today's schools; teacher decision-making models based on decision theory. *Unit head:* Dr. Rene Parmar, Chair, 718-990-2503, E-mail: parmarr@stjohns.edu. *Application contact:* Associate Director of Graduate Admissions.
Website: http://www.stjohns.edu/academics/schools-and-colleges/school-education/programs-and-majors/administration-and-supervision-doctor-education

St. John's University, The School of Education, Department of Administrative and Instructional Leadership, Program in Instructional Leadership, Queens, NY 11439. Offers gifted education (Adv C); instructional leadership (Ed D, Adv C). *Program availability:* Part-time, blended/hybrid learning. *Students:* 9 full-time (7 women), 128 part-time (83 women); includes 48 minority (27 Black or African American, non-Hispanic/Latino; 1 American Indian or Alaska Native, non-Hispanic/Latino; 8 Asian, non-Hispanic/Latino; 11 Hispanic/Latino; 1 Two or more races, non-Hispanic/Latino), 3 international. Average age 41. 51 applicants, 96% accepted, 30 enrolled. In 2017, 24 doctorates, 3 Adv Cs awarded. *Degree requirements:* For doctorate, comprehensive exam, thesis/dissertation. *Entrance requirements:* For doctorate, GRE, official master's transcript, statement of purpose; for Adv C, statement of purpose, official master's transcripts, teaching certification. Additional exam requirements/recommendations for international students: Required—TOEFL, IELTS. *Application deadline:* For fall admission, 8/17 for domestic and international students; for summer admission, 5/15 for domestic and international students. Application fee: $70. Electronic applications accepted. *Expenses: Tuition:* Full-time $44,280; part-time $1230 per credit. *Required fees:* $340; $340 per credit. Tuition and fees vary according to course load, degree level and program. *Financial support:* Fellowships, research assistantships, scholarships/grants, and unspecified assistantships available. Support available to part-time students. Financial award application deadline: 2/1; financial award applicants required to submit FAFSA. *Faculty research:* Mathematics learning disabilities and difficulties with students identified as learning disabled or students who are English language learners, identification of mathematical giftedness in students who are English language learners, effects of parental participation and parenting behaviors on the science and mathematics academic achievement of school-age students, analysis of major theoretical perspectives in curriculum design and implementation. *Unit head:* Dr. Rene Parmar, Chair, 718-990-2503, E-mail: parmarr@stjohns.edu. *Application contact:* Dr. Rene Parmar, Chair, 718-990-2503, E-mail: parmarr@stjohns.edu.
Website: https://www.stjohns.edu/academics/schools-and-colleges/school-education/programs-and-majors/instructional-leadership-doctor-education

St. John's University, The School of Education, Department of Administrative and Instructional Leadership, Program in School Building Leadership, Queens, NY 11439. Offers MS Ed, Adv C. *Program availability:* Part-time, evening/weekend. *Students:* 8 full-time (5 women), 83 part-time (63 women); includes 20 minority (12 Black or African American, non-Hispanic/Latino; 2 Asian, non-Hispanic/Latino; 6 Hispanic/Latino), 5 international. Average age 37. 30 applicants, 100% accepted, 28 enrolled. In 2017, 25 master's, 81 Adv Cs awarded. *Degree requirements:* For master's, internship. *Entrance requirements:* For master's, GRE, MAT, or PRAXIS, statement of goals (personal essay), official undergraduate transcripts, initial teaching certification; for Adv C, initial teaching certification, first master's transcripts, statement of purpose. Additional exam requirements/recommendations for international students: Required—TOEFL, IELTS. *Application deadline:* For fall admission, 8/17 for domestic and international students; for summer admission, 5/15 for domestic and international students. Application fee: $70. Electronic applications accepted. *Expenses: Tuition:* Full-time $44,280; part-time $1230 per credit. *Required fees:* $340; $340 per credit. Tuition and fees vary according to course load, degree level and program. *Financial support:* Fellowships, research assistantships, scholarships/grants, and unspecified assistantships available. Support available to part-time students. Financial award application deadline: 2/1; financial award applicants required to submit FAFSA. *Faculty research:* Analysis of non-public school graduate student outcomes in programs and certification, Catholic school parents' perceptions of school and after school programs, issues in school business leadership from a financial management perspective. *Unit head:* Dr. Rene Parmar, Chair, 718-990-2503, E-mail: parmarr@stjohns.edu. *Application contact:* Dr. Rene Parmar, Chair, 718-990-2503, E-mail: parmarr@stjohns.edu.
Website: https://stjohns.edu/academics/schools-and-colleges/school-education/programs-and-majors/school-building-leadership-master-science-education

St. John's University, The School of Education, Department of Administrative and Instructional Leadership, Program in School District Leadership, Queens, NY 11439. Offers Adv C. *Program availability:* Part-time, evening/weekend, blended/hybrid learning. *Students:* 2 part-time (1 woman). Average age 35. 2 applicants, 100% accepted, 1 enrolled. In 2017, 1 Adv C awarded. *Degree requirements:* For Adv C, internship. *Entrance requirements:* For degree, initial teaching certification, first master's transcripts, statement of purpose. Additional exam requirements/recommendations for international students: Required—TOEFL, IELTS. *Application deadline:* For fall

admission, 8/17 for domestic and international students; for summer admission, 5/15 for domestic and international students. Application fee: $70. Electronic applications accepted. *Expenses: Tuition:* Full-time $44,280; part-time $1230 per credit. *Required fees:* $340; $340 per credit. Tuition and fees vary according to course load, degree level and program. *Financial support:* Fellowships, research assistantships, scholarships/grants, and unspecified assistantships available. Support available to part-time students. Financial award application deadline: 2/1; financial award applicants required to submit FAFSA. *Faculty research:* Analysis of school district finances related to resource allocation and decision-making, responsiveness of districts to New York State Proposition 13 (property tax caps), implementation of technology planning for the twenty-first century at the school district level. *Unit head:* Dr. Rene Parmar, Chair, 718-990-2503, E-mail: parmarr@stjohns.edu. *Application contact:* Dr. Rene Parmar, Chair, 718-990-2503, E-mail: parmarr@stjohns.edu.
Website: http://www.stjohns.edu/academics/schools-and-colleges/school-education/programs-and-majors/school-district-leadership-advanced-certificate

St. Joseph's College, Long Island Campus, Programs in Education, Field in Educational Leadership, Patchogue, NY 11772-2399. Offers MA. *Program availability:* Part-time, evening/weekend. *Faculty:* 4 part-time/adjunct (1 woman). *Students:* 1 (woman) full-time, 9 part-time (7 women); includes 4 minority (1 Black or African American, non-Hispanic/Latino; 3 Hispanic/Latino). Average age 28. 7 applicants, 100% accepted, 4 enrolled. *Entrance requirements:* Additional exam requirements/recommendations for international students: Recommended—TOEFL (minimum score 550 paper-based). *Application deadline:* Applications are processed on a rolling basis. Application fee: $25. Electronic applications accepted. *Expenses: Tuition:* Full-time $17,550; part-time $975 per credit. *Required fees:* $362. *Financial support:* In 2017–18, 3 students received support. *Unit head:* Nancy Gilchriest, Associate Professor/Department Chair, 631-687-1472, E-mail: ngilchriest@sjcny.edu.
Website: http://www.sjcny.edu/long-island

St. Joseph's College, New York, Programs in Education, Field in Educational Leadership, Brooklyn, NY 11205-3688. Offers MA. *Program availability:* Part-time, evening/weekend. *Faculty:* 1 part-time/adjunct (0 women). *Students:* 3 part-time (2 women). Average age 25. 2 applicants, 100% accepted. *Entrance requirements:* For master's, GRE, PRAXIS, or MAT, official transcripts, teaching certificate, 2 letters of recommendation, personal statement, resume. Additional exam requirements/recommendations for international students: Required—TOEFL (minimum score 80 iBT). *Application deadline:* Applications are processed on a rolling basis. Application fee: $25. Electronic applications accepted. *Expenses: Tuition:* Full-time $17,550; part-time $975 per credit. *Required fees:* $362. *Financial support:* In 2017–18, 2 students received support. Alumni grants and/or alumni excellence awards available. Financial award applicants required to submit FAFSA. *Unit head:* Nancy Gilchriest, Associate Professor/Department Chair, 631-687-1472, E-mail: ngilchriest@sjcny.edu.
Website: https://www.sjcny.edu

Saint Joseph's College of Maine, Master of Science in Education Program, Standish, ME 04084. Offers adult education and training (MS Ed); Catholic school leadership (MS Ed); health care educator (MS Ed); school educator (MS Ed). Program available by correspondence. *Program availability:* Part-time, online learning. Electronic applications accepted.

Saint Joseph's University, College of Arts and Sciences, Graduate Programs in Education, Philadelphia, PA 19131-1395. Offers curriculum supervisor (Certificate); educational leadership (MS, Ed D); elementary education (MS, Certificate); elementary/middle school education (Certificate); organizational development and leadership (MS); principal (Certificate); professional education (MS); reading specialist (MS, Certificate); reading supervisor (Certificate); secondary education (MS, Certificate); special education (MS); special education 7-12 (Certificate); special education PK-8 (Certificate); superintendent's letter of eligibility (Certificate); supervisor of special education (Certificate); teacher of the deaf and hard of hearing (Certificate). *Program availability:* Part-time, evening/weekend, blended/hybrid learning. *Faculty:* 18 full-time (16 women), 63 part-time/adjunct (44 women). *Students:* 79 full-time (60 women), 793 part-time (604 women); includes 179 minority (125 Black or African American, non-Hispanic/Latino; 5 American Indian or Alaska Native, non-Hispanic/Latino; 15 Asian, non-Hispanic/Latino; 27 Hispanic/Latino; 1 Native Hawaiian or other Pacific Islander, non-Hispanic/Latino; 6 Two or more races, non-Hispanic/Latino), 12 international. Average age 34. 375 applicants, 75% accepted, 189 enrolled. In 2017, 340 master's, 13 doctorates, 3 other advanced degrees awarded. *Degree requirements:* For master's, thesis or alternative; for doctorate, comprehensive exam, thesis/dissertation. *Entrance requirements:* For master's, 2 letters of recommendation, minimum GPA of 3.0, official transcripts, personal statement; for doctorate, GRE, master's degree from accredited institution, minimum graduate GPA of 3.5, computer competence, interview with program director. Additional exam requirements/recommendations for international students: Required—TOEFL (minimum score 550 paper-based; 80 iBT), IELTS (minimum score 6.5), PTE (minimum score 60). *Application deadline:* For fall admission, 7/15 for international students; for spring admission, 11/1 for international students. Applications are processed on a rolling basis. Application fee: $35. Electronic applications accepted. *Expenses:* Contact institution. *Financial support:* Scholarships/grants and unspecified assistantships available. Financial award application deadline: 5/1; financial award applicants required to submit FAFSA. *Faculty research:* Factors predicting early mathematics skills for low income children, early child care and development, preschool quality, parent communication and home-school collaboration issues, education of terminally ill children, preparing literacy teachers for urban schools. *Unit head:* Dr. John Vacca, Associate Dean, Education, 610-660-3131, E-mail: gradcas@sju.edu. *Application contact:* Graduate Admissions, College of Arts and Sciences, 610-660-3131, E-mail: gradcas@sju.edu.
Website: https://sites.sju.edu/education/graduate-programs/

St. Lawrence University, Department of Education, Program in Educational Leadership, Canton, NY 13617. Offers combined school building leadership/school district leadership (CAS); educational leadership (M Ed); school building leadership (M Ed); school district leadership (CAS). *Program availability:* Part-time, evening/weekend. *Entrance requirements:* For master's, GRE General Test. *Faculty research:* Leadership.

Saint Leo University, Graduate Studies in Education, Saint Leo, FL 33574-6665. Offers educational leadership (M Ed), including Catholic school administration; exceptional student education (M Ed); instructional design (MS, Certificate); instructional leadership (M Ed); reading (M Ed, Certificate); school leadership (Ed S). *Program availability:* Part-time, evening/weekend, online only, 100% online. *Faculty:* 8 full-time (all women), 18 part-time/adjunct (11 women). *Students:* 1 (woman) full-time, 360 part-time (282 women); includes 95 minority (56 Black or African American, non-Hispanic/Latino; 1 American Indian or Alaska Native, non-Hispanic/Latino; 1 Asian, non-Hispanic/Latino; 31 Hispanic/Latino; 6 Two or more races, non-Hispanic/Latino), 1 international. Average age 37. 214 applicants, 69% accepted, 125 enrolled. In 2017, 158 master's, 5 other advanced degrees awarded. *Degree requirements:* For master's, appropriate State of Florida certification tests, internship. *Entrance requirements:* For master's, GRE (minimum score of 1000), MAT (minimum score of 410), or minimum undergraduate GPA of 3.0 in final 2 years, official transcripts, current resumé, 2 professional recommendations, personal statement, bachelor's degree from regionally-accredited university, valid professional teaching certificate; for other advanced degree, valid professional teaching certificate (for Ed S). Additional exam requirements/recommendations for international students: Required—TOEFL (minimum score 550 paper-based; 78 iBT). *Application deadline:* For fall admission, 7/1 priority date for domestic students, 7/1 for international students; for winter admission, 7/1 for international students; for spring admission, 11/1 priority date for domestic students. Applications are processed on a rolling basis. Application fee: $80. Electronic applications accepted. *Expenses:* $480 per credit (for M Ed), $670 per credit (for Ed S). *Financial support:* In 2017–18, 17 students received support. Career-related internships or fieldwork, scholarships/grants, health care benefits, and tuition remission for Saint Leo employees and their dependents available. Financial award application deadline: 3/1; financial award applicants required to submit FAFSA. *Faculty research:* Impact of partnerships with K-12 school and university programs. *Unit head:* Dr. Fern Aefsky, Director of Graduate Studies in Education, 352-588-8309, Fax: 352-588-8861, E-mail: kara.winkler@saintleo.edu. *Application contact:* Mark Russum, Assistant Vice President, Enrollment, 800-707-8846, Fax: 352-588-7873, E-mail: grad.admissions@saintleo.edu. Website: https://www.saintleo.edu/education-master-degree

Saint Louis University, Graduate Programs, School of Education and Graduate Programs, Department of Educational Leadership and Higher Education, St. Louis, MO 63103. Offers Catholic school leadership (MA); educational administration (MA, Ed D, PhD, Ed S); higher education (MA, Ed D, PhD); student personnel administration (MA). *Accreditation:* NCATE. *Program availability:* Part-time. *Degree requirements:* For master's, comprehensive written and oral exam; for doctorate, comprehensive exam, thesis/dissertation, preliminary oral and written exams. *Entrance requirements:* For master's, GRE General Test, MAT, LSAT, GMAT or MCAT, letters of recommendation, resume; for doctorate and Ed S, GRE General Test, LSAT, GMAT or MCAT, letters of recommendation, resumé, goal statement, transcripts. Additional exam requirements/recommendations for international students: Required—TOEFL (minimum score 525 paper-based). Electronic applications accepted. *Faculty research:* Superintendent of schools, school finance, school facilities, student personal administration, building leadership.

Saint Mary's College of California, Kalmanovitz School of Education, Program in Early Childhood Education, Moraga, CA 94575. Offers supervision and leadership (MA). *Program availability:* Part-time, evening/weekend. *Degree requirements:* For master's, thesis or alternative. *Entrance requirements:* For master's, interview, minimum GPA of 3.0.

Saint Mary's College of California, Kalmanovitz School of Education, Program in Educational Administration, Moraga, CA 94575. Offers educational administration (MA); educational leadership (Ed D); preliminary administrative services (Credential). *Program availability:* Part-time, evening/weekend. *Degree requirements:* For master's, thesis or alternative; for doctorate, thesis/dissertation. *Entrance requirements:* For master's, interview, minimum GPA of 3.0, teaching credential; for doctorate, GRE or MAT, interview, MA, minimum GPA of 3.0. *Faculty research:* Building communities, programs in educational leadership, alignment of curriculum to standards.

Saint Mary's College of California, Kalmanovitz School of Education, Teaching Leadership Program, Moraga, CA 94575. Offers MA.

St. Mary's University, Graduate Studies, Program in Catholic School Leadership, San Antonio, TX 78228. Offers MA. *Program availability:* Part-time, evening/weekend, online learning. *Students:* 10 part-time (9 women); includes 6 minority (all Hispanic/Latino). Average age 43. 9 applicants, 56% accepted, 2 enrolled. *Degree requirements:* For master's, comprehensive exam. *Entrance requirements:* For master's, GRE, minimum undergraduate GPA of 2.7. Additional exam requirements/recommendations for international students: Required—TOEFL (minimum score 550 paper-based; 80 iBT), IELTS (minimum score 6). *Application deadline:* For fall admission, 7/1 for domestic students; for spring admission, 11/15 for domestic students; for summer admission, 4/1 for domestic students. Applications are processed on a rolling basis. Application fee: $0. Electronic applications accepted. *Expenses: Tuition:* Full-time $16,200; part-time $900 per credit hour. *Required fees:* $810; $405 per semester. *Financial support:* Career-related internships or fieldwork, Federal Work-Study, institutionally sponsored loans, scholarships/grants, health care benefits, and unspecified assistantships available. Financial award application deadline: 3/31; financial award applicants required to submit FAFSA. *Faculty research:* Classical American philosophy, philosophy of education. *Unit head:* Dr. Dan Higgins, Program Director, 210-436-3121, E-mail: dhiggins@stmarytx.edu. *Application contact:* Kim Thornton, Director of Graduate Admission, 210-436-3101, E-mail: kthornton@stmarytx.edu. Website: https://www.stmarytx.edu/academics/programs/master-catholic-school-leadership/

St. Mary's University, Graduate Studies, Program in Educational Leadership, San Antonio, TX 78228. Offers MA. *Program availability:* Part-time, evening/weekend. *Students:* 7 full-time (5 women), 9 part-time (8 women); includes 8 minority (all Hispanic/Latino), 3 international. Average age 29. 7 applicants, 57% accepted, 3 enrolled. In 2017, 7 master's awarded. *Entrance requirements:* For master's, GRE, minimum undergraduate GPA of 2.7. Additional exam requirements/recommendations for international students: Required—TOEFL (minimum score 550 paper-based; 80 iBT), IELTS (minimum score 6). *Application deadline:* For fall admission, 7/1 for domestic students; for spring admission, 11/15 for domestic students; for summer admission, 4/1 for domestic students. Applications are processed on a rolling basis. Application fee: $0. Electronic applications accepted. *Expenses: Tuition:* Full-time $16,200; part-time $900 per credit hour. *Required fees:* $810; $405 per semester. *Financial support:* Fellowships, career-related internships or fieldwork, Federal Work-Study, institutionally sponsored loans, scholarships/grants, health care benefits, and unspecified assistantships available. Financial award application deadline: 3/31; financial award applicants required to submit FAFSA. *Faculty research:* Philosophy of education. *Unit head:* Dr. Dan Higgins, Program Director, 210-436-3121, E-mail: dhiggins@stmarytx.edu. *Application contact:* Kim Thornton, Director of Graduate Admission, 210-436-3101, E-mail: kthornton@stmarytx.edu. Website: https://www.stmarytx.edu/academics/programs/master-educational-leadership/

Saint Mary's University of Minnesota, Schools of Graduate and Professional Programs, Graduate School of Education, Educational Administration Program, Winona, MN 55987-1399. Offers educational administration (Certificate, Ed S), including director of special education, K-12 principal, superintendent. *Unit head:* Dr. William Bjorum, Director, 612-728-5126, Fax: 612-728-5121, E-mail: wbjorum@smumn.edu. *Application contact:* James Callinan, Director of Admissions for Graduate and Professional Programs, 612-728-5158, Fax: 612-728-5121, E-mail: jcallina@smumn.edu. Website: https://www.smumn.edu/academics/graduate/education/programs/ed.s.-in-educational-administration

Saint Mary's University of Minnesota, Schools of Graduate and Professional Programs, Graduate School of Education, Educational Leadership Program, Winona, MN 55987-1399. Offers MA, Ed D. *Program availability:* Online learning. *Unit head:* Dr. John McClure, Director, 612-728-5216, Fax: 612-728-5121, E-mail: jmcclure@

smumn.edu. *Application contact:* James Callinan, Director of Admissions for Graduate and Professional Programs, 612-728-5158, Fax: 612-728-5121, E-mail: jcallina@smumn.edu. Website: http://www.smumn.edu/graduate-home/areas-of-study/graduate-school-of-education/edd-in-leadership

Saint Mary's University of Minnesota, Schools of Graduate and Professional Programs, Graduate School of Education, Institute for LaSallian Studies, Winona, MN 55987-1399. Offers LaSallian leadership (MA); LaSallian studies (MA). *Unit head:* Dr. Roxanne Eubank, Director, 612-728-5217, E-mail: reubank@smumn.edu. *Application contact:* James Callinan, Director of Admissions for Graduate and Professional Programs, 612-728-5158, Fax: 612-728-5121, E-mail: jcallina@smumn.edu. Website: http://www.smumn.edu/graduate-home/areas-of-study/graduate-school-of-education/ma-in-lasallian-studies

Saint Michael's College, Graduate Programs, Program in Education, Colchester, VT 05439. Offers arts in education (CAGS); literacy (M Ed); school leadership (CAGS); special education (M Ed). *Program availability:* Part-time, evening/weekend. *Students:* 7 full-time (3 women), 204 part-time (173 women); includes 8 minority (1 Black or African American, non-Hispanic/Latino; 1 American Indian or Alaska Native, non-Hispanic/Latino; 3 Hispanic/Latino; 3 Two or more races, non-Hispanic/Latino). Average age 38. 23 applicants, 65% accepted, 10 enrolled. In 2017, 32 master's awarded. *Degree requirements:* For master's, thesis. *Entrance requirements:* For master's, minimum GPA of 3.0, official transcripts, essay, interview. *Application deadline:* Applications are processed on a rolling basis. Application fee: $50. Electronic applications accepted. *Expenses: Tuition:* Part-time $590 per credit. *Financial support:* Fellowships with partial tuition reimbursements and scholarships/grants available. Support available to part-time students. Financial award applicants required to submit FAFSA. *Faculty research:* Integrative curriculum, moral and spiritual dimensions of education, learning styles, multiple intelligences, integrating technology into the curriculum. *Unit head:* Jonathan Silverman, Department Chair, 802-654-2306, Fax: 802-654-2664, E-mail: jsilverman@smcvt.edu. *Application contact:* Lindsay A. Damici, Marketing Communications Manager, 802-654-2556, Fax: 802-654-2732. Website: http://www.smcvt.edu/graduate-programs/academic-programs/education.aspx

Saint Peter's University, Graduate Programs in Education, Program in Educational Leadership, Jersey City, NJ 07306-5997. Offers MA Ed, Ed D. *Program availability:* Part-time, evening/weekend. *Degree requirements:* For master's, comprehensive exam; for doctorate, comprehensive exam, thesis/dissertation. *Entrance requirements:* For master's and doctorate, GRE or MAT. Additional exam requirements/recommendations for international students: Required—TOEFL. Electronic applications accepted.

St. Thomas Aquinas College, Division of Teacher Education, Sparkill, NY 10976. Offers adolescence education (MST); childhood and special education (MST); childhood education (MST); educational leadership (MS Ed); reading (MS Ed, PMC); special education (MS Ed, PMC); teaching (MS Ed), including elementary education, middle school education, secondary education. *Accreditation:* NCATE. *Program availability:* Part-time, evening/weekend. *Degree requirements:* For master's, comprehensive exam, comprehensive professional portfolio; for PMC, action research project. *Entrance requirements:* For master's, New York State Qualifying Exam, GRE General Test or minimum GPA of 3.0, teaching certificate; for PMC, GRE General Test or minimum GPA of 3.0. Electronic applications accepted. *Faculty research:* Computer applications in education, adolescent special education students, literacy development, inclusive practices for special education students.

St. Thomas University, School of Leadership Studies, Institute for Education, Miami Gardens, FL 33054-6459. Offers earth/space science (Certificate); educational administration (MS, Certificate); educational leadership (Ed D); elementary education (MS); ESOL (Certificate); gifted education (Certificate); instructional technology (MS, Certificate); professional/studies (Certificate); reading (MS, Certificate); special education (MS). *Program availability:* Part-time, evening/weekend. *Degree requirements:* For master's, comprehensive exam; for doctorate, comprehensive exam, thesis/dissertation. *Entrance requirements:* For master's, interview, minimum GPA of 3.0 or GRE; for doctorate, GRE or MAT. Additional exam requirements/recommendations for international students: Required—TOEFL (minimum score 550 paper-based; 79 iBT). Electronic applications accepted.

Saint Vincent College, Program in Education, Latrobe, PA 15650-2690. Offers curriculum and instruction (MS); instructional design and technology (MS); school administration and supervision (MS); special education (MS). *Program availability:* Part-time, evening/weekend. *Degree requirements:* For master's, comprehensive exam. *Entrance requirements:* For master's, GRE (if undergraduate GPA less than 3.0). Additional exam requirements/recommendations for international students: Required—TOEFL (minimum score 550 paper-based). *Faculty research:* Assessment and instructional technology.

Saint Xavier University, Graduate Studies, School of Education, Chicago, IL 60655-3105. Offers counseling (MA); curriculum and instruction (MA); early childhood education (MA); educational administration (MA); elementary education (MA); individualized studies (MA), including educational technology, English as a second language (ESL), ISTEM (integrative science, technology, engineering, and math), science education; music education (MA); reading (MA); secondary education (MA); Spanish education (MA); special education (MA); teaching and leadership (MA). *Accreditation:* NCATE. *Program availability:* Part-time, evening/weekend. *Degree requirements:* For master's, thesis or project. *Entrance requirements:* For master's, minimum GPA of 3.0. *Expenses:* Contact institution.

Salem International University, School of Education, Salem, WV 26426-0500. Offers curriculum and instruction (M Ed); educational leadership (M Ed). *Program availability:* Part-time, evening/weekend, online learning. *Degree requirements:* For master's, comprehensive exam (for some programs), thesis (for some programs). *Entrance requirements:* For master's, GRE, MAT, NTE, 3 letters of recommendation. Additional exam requirements/recommendations for international students: Required—TOEFL (minimum score 550 paper-based). Electronic applications accepted. *Expenses:* Contact institution. *Faculty research:* Improved classroom effectiveness.

Salem State University, School of Graduate Studies, Program in Higher Education in Student Affairs, Salem, MA 01970-5353. Offers M Ed. *Program availability:* Part-time, evening/weekend. *Entrance requirements:* For master's, GRE or MAT. Additional exam requirements/recommendations for international students: Required—TOEFL (minimum score 550 paper-based; 80 iBT) or IELTS (minimum score 5.5).

Salisbury University, Program in Educational Leadership, Salisbury, MD 21801-6837. Offers M Ed. *Program availability:* Part-time, evening/weekend. *Faculty:* 1 full-time (0 women), 3 part-time/adjunct (1 woman). *Students:* 38 part-time (24 women); includes 8 minority (6 Black or African American, non-Hispanic/Latino; 2 Two or more races, non-Hispanic/Latino). Average age 32. 18 applicants, 78% accepted, 14 enrolled. In 2017, 13 master's awarded. *Degree requirements:* For master's, comprehensive exam. *Entrance requirements:* For master's, three letters of recommendation; transcripts from all colleges and universities attended; personal statement; minimum GPA of 3.0; resume; minimum two years' satisfactory teaching. Additional exam requirements/recommendations for international students: Required—TOEFL (minimum score 550

paper-based; 79 iBT), IELTS (minimum score 6.5). *Application deadline:* For fall admission, 3/1 priority date for domestic and international students; for spring admission, 10/1 priority date for domestic and international students; for summer admission, 3/1 priority date for domestic and international students. Applications are processed on a rolling basis. Application fee: $65. Electronic applications accepted. *Expenses:* $392 per credit hour resident; $703 per credit hour non-resident; $92 per credit hour fees. *Financial support:* Career-related internships or fieldwork and scholarships/grants available. Support available to part-time students. Financial award application deadline: 3/1; financial award applicants required to submit FAFSA. *Faculty research:* Leadership; organizational change; school administration; teacher shortage; principal mentoring. *Unit head:* Dr. Douglas DeWitt, Graduate Program Director, Educational Leadership, 410-543-6286, E-mail: dmdewitt@salisbury.edu. *Application contact:* Claire Williams, Program Management Specialist, 410-677-0001, E-mail: clwilliams@salisbury.edu.
Website: http://www.salisbury.edu/gsr/gradstudies/MEDpage.html

Salve Regina University, Program in Catholic School Leadership, Newport, RI 02840-4192. Offers CGS. *Entrance requirements:* For degree, minimum undergraduate cumulative GPA of 3.0; minimum of five years' teaching experience.

Samford University, Orlean Beeson School of Education, Birmingham, AL 35229. Offers educational leadership (MSE, Ed D); elementary education (MS Ed, MSE); gifted (MSE); instructional design and technology (MSE); instructional leadership (MSE, Ed S); secondary education (MSE); special education (MSE). *Accreditation:* NCATE. *Program availability:* Part-time, evening/weekend, 100% online, blended/hybrid learning. *Faculty:* 11 full-time (7 women), 22 part-time/adjunct (12 women). *Students:* 206 full-time (144 women), 102 part-time (75 women); includes 124 minority (113 Black or African American, non-Hispanic/Latino; 3 American Indian or Alaska Native, non-Hispanic/Latino; 3 Asian, non-Hispanic/Latino; 2 Hispanic/Latino; 3 Two or more races, non-Hispanic/Latino), 1 international. Average age 37. 134 applicants, 84% accepted, 76 enrolled. In 2017, 79 master's, 34 doctorates, 21 other advanced degrees awarded. *Degree requirements:* For master's and Ed S, comprehensive exam; for doctorate, comprehensive exam, thesis/dissertation. *Entrance requirements:* For master's, GRE, MAT, PRAXIS II, interview, transcripts, essay, recommendations, teaching certification; for doctorate, resume, transcripts, interview, essay; for Ed S, teaching certification, transcripts, essay, interview. Additional exam requirements/recommendations for international students: Required—TOEFL (minimum score 90 iBT), IELTS (minimum score 6.5). *Application deadline:* For fall admission, 7/15 for domestic and international students; for winter admission, 11/15 for domestic and international students; for spring admission, 11/15 for domestic and international students; for summer admission, 4/15 for domestic and international students. Application fee: $35. Electronic applications accepted. *Expenses:* $813 per credit hour, $100 School of Education fee, $175 technology fee. *Financial support:* In 2017–18, 220 students received support. Scholarships/grants and unspecified assistantships available. Financial award application deadline: 2/15; financial award applicants required to submit FAFSA. *Faculty research:* Principal leadership's and teacher organizational commitment mentoring, professional development, and middle grades leadership coaching and administrator effectiveness character development programs in schools teacher efficacy related STEM and professional growth. *Unit head:* Dr. Bonnie Rabe, Interim Dean, 205-726-2565, E-mail: brabe@samford.edu. *Application contact:* Brooke Karr, Graduate Admissions Office Coordinator, 205-729-2783, Fax: 205-726-4233, E-mail: kbgilrea@samford.edu.
Website: http://www.samford.edu/education/

Sam Houston State University, College of Education, Department of Educational Leadership, Huntsville, TX 77341. Offers administration (M Ed); developmental education administration (Ed D); educational leadership (Ed D); higher education administration (MA); higher education leadership (Ed D); instructional leadership (M Ed, MA). *Program availability:* Part-time, evening/weekend, online learning. *Degree requirements:* For master's, comprehensive exam (for some programs), thesis (for some programs); for doctorate, comprehensive exam, thesis/dissertation. *Entrance requirements:* For master's, GRE General Test, references, personal essay, resume, professional statement; for doctorate, GRE General Test, master's degree, references, personal essay, resume. Additional exam requirements/recommendations for international students: Required—TOEFL (minimum score 550 paper-based; 79 iBT), IELTS (minimum score 6.5). Electronic applications accepted.

San Diego State University, Graduate and Research Affairs, College of Education, Department of Administration, Rehabilitation and Post-Secondary Education, San Diego, CA 92182. Offers educational leadership in post-secondary education (MA); rehabilitation counseling (MS), including deafness. *Program availability:* Evening/weekend, online learning. *Degree requirements:* For master's, comprehensive exam (for some programs), thesis (for some programs). *Entrance requirements:* For master's, GRE General Test, letters of reference. Additional exam requirements/recommendations for international students: Required—TOEFL. Electronic applications accepted. *Faculty research:* Rehabilitation in cultural diversity, distance learning technology.

San Diego State University, Graduate and Research Affairs, College of Education, Department of Educational Leadership, San Diego, CA 92182. Offers MA. *Accreditation:* NCATE. *Program availability:* Evening/weekend. *Entrance requirements:* For master's, GRE General Test, letters of reference. Additional exam requirements/recommendations for international students: Required—TOEFL. Electronic applications accepted.

San Francisco State University, Division of Graduate Studies, College of Education, Department of Equity, Leadership Studies, and Instructional Technologies, Program in Educational Administration, San Francisco, CA 94132-1722. Offers MA, Credential. *Accreditation:* NCATE. *Application deadline:* Applications are processed on a rolling basis. *Unit head:* Dr. Doris Flowers, Chair, 415-338-2614, Fax: 415-338-0568, E-mail: dflowers@sfsu.edu. *Application contact:* Dr. Davide Celoria, Graduate Coordinator, 415-405-3659, Fax: 415-338-0568, E-mail: deceloria@sfsu.edu.
Website: http://elsit.sfsu.edu/

San Francisco State University, Division of Graduate Studies, College of Education, Program in Educational Leadership, San Francisco, CA 94132-1722. Offers Ed D. *Unit head:* Dr. Barbara Henderson, Interim Director, 415-405-4103, Fax: 415-338-7019, E-mail: barbarah@sfsu.edu. *Application contact:* Dr. Andrea Goldfien, Graduate Coordinator, 415-338-7873, Fax: 415-338-7019, E-mail: goldfien@sfsu.edu.
Website: http://edd.sfsu.edu/

San Ignacio University, Graduate Programs, Doral, FL 33178. Offers business administration (MBA), including human resources management, international business, marketing management; education (M Ed), including early childhood education, educational leadership, special education; hospitality management (MA), including gastronomy and restaurant management, tourism management.

San Jose State University, Graduate Studies and Research, Connie L. Lurie College of Education, San Jose, CA 95192-0071. Offers child and adolescent development (MA); education (MA), including counseling and student personnel, curriculum and instruction, speech pathology; educational leadership (MA, Ed D), including administration and supervision (MA), educational leadership (MA); elementary education (MA), including curriculum and instruction. *Accreditation:* NCATE. *Program availability:* Part-time, evening/weekend. *Faculty:* 29 full-time (22 women), 47 part-time/adjunct (40 women). *Students:* 414 full-time (339 women), 115 part-time (93 women); includes 341 minority (14 Black or African American, non-Hispanic/Latino; 87 Asian, non-Hispanic/Latino; 176 Hispanic/Latino; 64 Two or more races, non-Hispanic/Latino), 9 international. Average age 30. 654 applicants, 34% accepted, 161 enrolled. In 2017, 286 master's, 7 doctorates awarded. Terminal master's awarded for partial completion of doctoral program. *Degree requirements:* For master's, project or theses, graduate writing assessment; for doctorate, thesis/dissertation. *Entrance requirements:* For master's, GRE General Test (for some programs). Additional exam requirements/recommendations for international students: Required—TOEFL (minimum score 550 paper-based; 80 iBT), IELTS (minimum score 6.5), PTE (minimum score 53). *Application deadline:* For fall admission, 2/1 for domestic and international students. Applications are processed on a rolling basis. Application fee: $55. Electronic applications accepted. *Expenses:* Tuition, state resident: full-time $7176. Tuition, nonresident: full-time $16,680. Tuition and fees vary according to course load and program. *Financial support:* In 2017–18, 4 research assistantships with partial tuition reimbursements (averaging $2,500 per year) were awarded; fellowships, career-related internships or fieldwork, Federal Work-Study, scholarships/grants, traineeships, and tuition waivers (full and partial) also available. Support available to part-time students. Financial award application deadline: 4/28; financial award applicants required to submit FAFSA. *Faculty research:* Equity and social justice in public education, interdisciplinary practices, teacher training, and effective pedagogy, clinical efficacy, typical and atypical development in children. *Unit head:* Dr. Paul Cascella, Interim Dean, 408-924-3600, Fax: 408-924-3713, E-mail: paul.cascella@sjsu.edu.
Website: http://www.sjsu.edu/education/

Santa Clara University, School of Education and Counseling Psychology, Santa Clara, CA 95053. Offers alternative and correctional education (Certificate); Catholic school teaching (MA); counseling (MA); counseling psychology (MA); educational leadership (MA); interdisciplinary education (MA); teaching multiple subjects (MAT); teaching single subjects (MAT). *Program availability:* Part-time. *Faculty:* 31 full-time (21 women), 37 part-time/adjunct (25 women). *Students:* 253 full-time (195 women), 350 part-time (283 women); includes 296 minority (10 Black or African American, non-Hispanic/Latino; 1 American Indian or Alaska Native, non-Hispanic/Latino; 80 Asian, non-Hispanic/Latino; 179 Hispanic/Latino; 26 Two or more races, non-Hispanic/Latino), 41 international. Average age 31. 211 applicants, 75% accepted, 142 enrolled. In 2017, 266 master's awarded. *Entrance requirements:* For master's, official transcripts, 2-3 letters of recommendation, statement of purpose, resume or curriculum vitae. Additional exam requirements/recommendations for international students: Required—TOEFL (minimum score 90 iBT) or IELTS (6.5). *Application deadline:* For fall admission, 4/16 for international students; for summer admission, 3/12 for domestic students. Applications are processed on a rolling basis. Application fee: $50. Electronic applications accepted. *Expenses:* $607 per unit. *Financial support:* In 2017–18, 355 students received support. Fellowships, research assistantships, teaching assistantships, Federal Work-Study, scholarships/grants, and health care benefits available. Support available to part-time students. Financial award applicants required to submit FAFSA. *Unit head:* Dr. Sabrina Zirkel, Dean, 408-551-3074, Fax: 408-554-4367, E-mail: szirkel@scu.edu. *Application contact:* Victoria Rodriguez, Graduate Admissions Advisor, 408-554-4723, E-mail: v1rodriguez@scu.edu.
Website: http://www.scu.edu/ecp/

Schreiner University, Department of Education, Kerrville, TX 78028-5697. Offers education (M Ed); principal (Certificate). *Program availability:* Part-time, evening/weekend, online learning. *Entrance requirements:* For master's, GRE (waived if undergraduate cumulative GPA is 3.0 or above), 3 references; transcripts; interview. Additional exam requirements/recommendations for international students: Required—TOEFL. Electronic applications accepted.

Seattle Pacific University, Educational Leadership Programs, Seattle, WA 98119-1997. Offers educational leadership (M Ed, Ed D); principal (Certificate); program administrator (Certificate); superintendent (Certificate). *Accreditation:* NCATE. *Program availability:* Part-time, evening/weekend. *Students:* 5 full-time (all women), 57 part-time (43 women); includes 6 minority (1 Black or African American, non-Hispanic/Latino; 3 Asian, non-Hispanic/Latino; 1 Hispanic/Latino; 1 Two or more races, non-Hispanic/Latino). Average age 42. 21 applicants, 57% accepted, 11 enrolled. In 2017, 14 master's awarded. *Degree requirements:* For master's, comprehensive exam; for doctorate, comprehensive exam, thesis/dissertation. *Entrance requirements:* For master's, GRE (preferred minimum scores of Verbal: 148 and Quantitative: 147), MAT (preferred minimum scaled score of 400), or minimum GPA of 3.0, copy of Residency Teacher certificate or Educational Staff Associate (ESA) certificate; Career Tech Educator (CTE) certificate (for principal certificate candidates only); official transcript; resume; personal statement; minimum GPA of 3.0 in last 45 quarter credits of coursework completed; two letters of recommendation; for doctorate, GRE General Test or MAT, minimum GPA of 3.0, formal interview. *Application deadline:* For fall admission, 8/15 priority date for domestic students; for winter admission, 11/15 for domestic students; for spring admission, 2/15 priority date for domestic students; for summer admission, 5/15 for domestic students. Applications are processed on a rolling basis. Application fee: $50. Electronic applications accepted. *Financial support:* Career-related internships or fieldwork available. Financial award applicants required to submit FAFSA. *Unit head:* Dr. William Prenevost, Chair, 206-281-2370, Fax: 206-281-2756, E-mail: prenew@spu.edu. *Application contact:* The Graduate Center, 206-281-2091.
Website: http://spu.edu/academics/school-of-education/graduate-programs/masters-programs/educational-leadership-med

Seattle Pacific University, Master of Education in Teacher Leadership Program, Seattle, WA 98119-1997. Offers M Ed. *Accreditation:* NCATE. *Program availability:* Part-time, evening/weekend. *Students:* 35 part-time (22 women); includes 3 minority (2 Asian, non-Hispanic/Latino; 1 Two or more races, non-Hispanic/Latino), 1 international. Average age 32. 22 applicants, 77% accepted, 13 enrolled. In 2017, 7 master's awarded. *Degree requirements:* For master's, comprehensive exam. *Entrance requirements:* For master's, GRE General Test or MAT, copy of teaching certificate, official transcript(s), resume, personal statement, two letters of recommendation. Additional exam requirements/recommendations for international students: Required—TOEFL (minimum score 550 paper-based). *Application deadline:* For fall admission, 8/15 priority date for domestic students, 7/1 for international students; for winter admission, 11/15 for domestic students; for spring admission, 2/15 for domestic students, 3/1 for international students; for summer admission, 5/15 for domestic students. Applications are processed on a rolling basis. Application fee: $50. Electronic applications accepted. *Expenses:* Contact institution. *Financial support:* Applicants required to submit FAFSA. *Faculty research:* Educational technology, classroom environments, character education. *Unit head:* Robin Henrikson, Chair, 360-461-4422, E-mail: henrir@spu.edu. *Application contact:* The Graduate Center, 206-281-2091.
Website: http://spu.edu/academics/school-of-education/graduate-programs/masters-programs/teacher-leadership

Educational Leadership and Administration

Seattle University, College of Education, Program in Educational Administration, Seattle, WA 98122-1090. Offers M Ed, MA, Certificate, Ed S. *Accreditation:* NCATE. *Program availability:* Part-time, evening/weekend. *Faculty:* 3 full-time (1 woman), 3 part-time/adjunct (all women). *Students:* 4 full-time (all women), 10 part-time (8 women); includes 3 minority (2 Hispanic/Latino; 1 Native Hawaiian or other Pacific Islander, non-Hispanic/Latino). Average age 37. In 2017, 4 master's, 2 other advanced degrees awarded. *Degree requirements:* For master's and other advanced degree, comprehensive exam. *Entrance requirements:* For master's, GRE, MAT, or minimum GPA of 3.0; interview; 1 year of related experience. Additional exam requirements/recommendations for international students: Required—TOEFL. *Application deadline:* For fall admission, 8/20 priority date for domestic students; for winter admission, 11/20 for domestic students; for spring admission, 2/20 for domestic students. Applications are processed on a rolling basis. Application fee: $55. *Expenses: Tuition:* Full-time $12,960. *Required fees:* $570. Tuition and fees vary according to program. *Financial support:* In 2017–18, 7 students received support. Career-related internships or fieldwork and Federal Work-Study available. Support available to part-time students. Financial award applicants required to submit FAFSA. *Unit head:* Dr. Michael Silver, Director, 206-296-5798, E-mail: silverm@seattleu.edu. *Application contact:* Janet Shandley, Associate Dean of Graduate Admissions, 206-296-5900, Fax: 206-298-5656, E-mail: grad_admissions@seattleu.edu.
Website: https://www.seattleu.edu/education/edadmin/

Seattle University, College of Education, Program in Educational Leadership, Seattle, WA 98122-1090. Offers Ed D. *Accreditation:* NCATE. *Program availability:* Part-time, evening/weekend. *Faculty:* 5 full-time (3 women), 2 part-time/adjunct (0 women). *Students:* 11 full-time (7 women), 45 part-time (28 women); includes 21 minority (6 Black or African American, non-Hispanic/Latino; 2 American Indian or Alaska Native, non-Hispanic/Latino; 6 Asian, non-Hispanic/Latino; 4 Hispanic/Latino; 3 Two or more races, non-Hispanic/Latino), 6 international. Average age 42. In 2017, 5 doctorates awarded. *Degree requirements:* For doctorate, comprehensive exam, thesis/dissertation. *Entrance requirements:* For doctorate, GRE General Test, MAT, interview, MA, minimum GPA of 3.5, 3 years of related experience. Additional exam requirements/recommendations for international students: Required—TOEFL. *Application deadline:* For fall admission, 4/1 for domestic students. Application fee: $55. *Expenses:* Contact institution. *Financial support:* In 2017–18, 11 students received support. Career-related internships or fieldwork and Federal Work-Study available. Support available to part-time students. Financial award applicants required to submit FAFSA. *Unit head:* Dr. Laurie Stevahn, Chair, 206-296-5750, E-mail: stevahnl@seattleu.edu. *Application contact:* Janet Shandley, Associate Dean of Graduate Admissions, 206-296-5900, Fax: 206-298-5656, E-mail: grad_admissions@seattleu.edu.
Website: https://www.seattleu.edu/education/edlr/

Seattle University, College of Education, Program in Student Development Administration, Seattle, WA 98122-1090. Offers M Ed, MA. *Program availability:* Part-time, evening/weekend. *Faculty:* 4 full-time (3 women). *Students:* 23 full-time (16 women), 40 part-time (29 women); includes 45 minority (3 Black or African American, non-Hispanic/Latino; 1 American Indian or Alaska Native, non-Hispanic/Latino; 15 Asian, non-Hispanic/Latino; 21 Hispanic/Latino; 5 Two or more races, non-Hispanic/Latino). Average age 26. 82 applicants, 80% accepted, 26 enrolled. In 2017, 24 master's awarded. *Degree requirements:* For master's, comprehensive exam. *Entrance requirements:* For master's, GRE, MAT, or minimum GPA of 3.0; two recommendations; resume; self-assessment form; autobiography. Additional exam requirements/recommendations for international students: Required—TOEFL. *Application deadline:* For fall admission, 1/15 priority date for domestic students; for winter admission, 11/20 for domestic students; for spring admission, 2/20 for domestic students. Applications are processed on a rolling basis. Application fee: $55. *Expenses: Tuition:* Full-time $12,960. *Required fees:* $570. Tuition and fees vary according to program. *Financial support:* In 2017–18, 19 students received support. Career-related internships or fieldwork, Federal Work-Study, and unspecified assistantships available. Support available to part-time students. Financial award applicants required to submit FAFSA. *Unit head:* Dr. Jeremy Stringer, Coordinator, 206-296-6170, E-mail: stringer@seattleu.edu. *Application contact:* Janet Shandley, Associate Dean of Graduate Admissions, 206-296-5900, Fax: 206-298-5656, E-mail: grad_admissions@seattleu.edu.
Website: https://www.seattleu.edu/education/sda/

Seton Hall University, College of Education and Human Services, Department of Education Leadership, Management and Policy, Program in Higher Education Administration, South Orange, NJ 07079-2697. Offers Ed D, PhD. *Accreditation:* NCATE. *Program availability:* Part-time, evening/weekend. *Degree requirements:* For doctorate, comprehensive exam, thesis/dissertation, internship. *Entrance requirements:* For doctorate, GRE or MAT, interview, minimum GPA of 3.5. Additional exam requirements/recommendations for international students: Required—TOEFL.

Seton Hall University, College of Education and Human Services, Department of Education Leadership, Management and Policy, Program in K–12 Leadership, Management and Policy, South Orange, NJ 07079-2697. Offers Ed D, Exec Ed D, Ed S. *Program availability:* Part-time, evening/weekend. *Degree requirements:* For doctorate, comprehensive exam, thesis/dissertation. *Entrance requirements:* For doctorate, MAT or GRE, interview. Additional exam requirements/recommendations for international students: Required—TOEFL.

Shasta Bible College, Program in School and Church Administration, Redding, CA 96002. Offers MS. *Program availability:* Part-time, evening/weekend. *Degree requirements:* For master's, comprehensive exam (for some programs), thesis or alternative. *Entrance requirements:* For master's, cumulative GPA of 3.0, 9 semester hours of education or psychology courses. Additional exam requirements/recommendations for international students: Required—TOEFL (minimum score 550 paper-based).

Shenandoah University, School of Education and Leadership, Winchester, VA 22601. Offers administration and supervision (Certificate); administrative leadership (D Ed); early childhood literacy (MS); educational administration (MSE); elementary school teacher education (Certificate); emphasis in teaching (MSE); health and physical education (Certificate); individualized focus (MS, MSE); literacy education (MS); middle school teacher education (Certificate); organizational leadership (MS, D Prof); reading licensure (MS, Certificate); reading non-licensure (MS); secondary school teacher education (Certificate); special education (MSE); writing (MS). *Accreditation:* TEAC. *Program availability:* Part-time, evening/weekend. *Faculty:* 8 full-time (7 women), 22 part-time/adjunct (16 women). *Students:* 16 full-time (14 women), 221 part-time (167 women); includes 32 minority (17 Black or African American, non-Hispanic/Latino; 1 American Indian or Alaska Native, non-Hispanic/Latino; 6 Asian, non-Hispanic/Latino; 5 Hispanic/Latino; 1 Native Hawaiian or other Pacific Islander, non-Hispanic/Latino; 2 Two or more races, non-Hispanic/Latino), 3 international. Average age 38. 81 applicants, 99% accepted, 63 enrolled. In 2017, 53 master's, 11 doctorates, 49 other advanced degrees awarded. *Degree requirements:* For master's, comprehensive exam (for some programs), thesis (for some programs); for doctorate, comprehensive exam, thesis/dissertation. *Entrance requirements:* For degree, PRAXIS Academic Core, SAT/ACT, PRAXIS Academic Core Math, or VCLA, three letters of recommendation, writing sample, undergraduate degree. Additional exam requirements/recommendations for international students: Required—TOEFL (minimum score 550 paper-based, 79 iBT) or IELTS (6.5). *Application deadline:* For fall admission, 5/1 priority date for domestic students, 5/1 for international students; for spring admission, 10/15 priority date for domestic students, 10/15 for international students; for summer admission, 3/15 priority date for domestic students, 3/15 for international students. Application fee: $30. Electronic applications accepted. *Expenses:* $15,600 tuition plus $1,296 fees (technology and student services). *Financial support:* In 2017–18, 26 students received support. Scholarships/grants and unspecified assistantships available. Financial award applicants required to submit FAFSA. *Faculty research:* Mentoring, behavior support for students, teacher change agency, educational technology in pedagogy, literacy education. *Unit head:* Jill Lindsey, PhD, Director, 540-535-7324, Fax: 540-665-4726, E-mail: jlindsey@su.edu. *Application contact:* Andrew Woodall, Executive Director of Recruitment and Admissions, 540-665-4581, Fax: 540-665-4627, E-mail: admit@su.edu.
Website: http://www.su.edu/education/

Shippensburg University of Pennsylvania, School of Graduate Studies, College of Education and Human Services, Department of Educational Leadership and Special Education, Shippensburg, PA 17257-2299. Offers educational leadership (M Ed, Ed D); special education (M Ed), including behavior disorders, intellectual disabilities, learning disabilities. *Accreditation:* NCATE. *Program availability:* Part-time, evening/weekend, blended/hybrid learning. *Faculty:* 6 full-time (2 women), 8 part-time/adjunct (5 women). *Students:* 13 full-time (7 women), 106 part-time (60 women); includes 5 minority (3 Black or African American, non-Hispanic/Latino; 1 Asian, non-Hispanic/Latino; 1 Two or more races, non-Hispanic/Latino), 16 international. Average age 34. 80 applicants, 69% accepted, 44 enrolled. In 2017, 22 master's awarded. *Degree requirements:* For master's, candidacy, thesis, or practicum; for doctorate, comprehensive exam, thesis/dissertation, candidacy exam; 24 credits (six 4-credit residencies) of field-based courses leading to the superintendent's letter of eligibility. *Entrance requirements:* For master's, GRE or MAT (if GPA is less than 2.75), 2 years of successful teaching experience; 3 letters of reference; 2 years of successful teaching experience; interview; statement of purpose; writing sample; personal goals statement; resume; for doctorate, resume; three letters of recommendation; 500-1000 word goals statement; teaching certifications and endorsements currently held; experience as public school administrator or supervisor that requires an administrative/supervisory certificate. Additional exam requirements/recommendations for international students: Required—TOEFL (minimum score 550 paper-based, 68 iBT) or IELTS (minimum score 6). *Application deadline:* For fall admission, 2/1 for domestic students, 4/30 for international students; for spring admission, 7/1 for domestic students, 9/30 for international students. Applications are processed on a rolling basis. Application fee: $45. Electronic applications accepted. *Expenses:* Tuition, state resident: part-time $500 per credit. Tuition, nonresident: part-time $750 per credit. *Required fees:* $145 per credit. *Financial support:* In 2017–18, 2 students received support. Career-related internships or fieldwork, scholarships/grants, unspecified assistantships, and resident hall director and student payroll positions available. Support available to part-time students. Financial award application deadline: 3/1; financial award applicants required to submit FAFSA. *Unit head:* Dr. Thomas C. Gibbon, Departmental Chair, 717-477-1498, Fax: 717-477-4036, E-mail: tcgibb@ship.edu. *Application contact:* Maya T. Mapp, Director of Admissions, 717-477-1231, Fax: 717-477-4016, E-mail: mtmap@ship.edu.
Website: http://www.ship.edu/else/

Siena Heights University, Graduate College, Adrian, MI 49221-1796. Offers clinical mental health counseling (MA); educational leadership (Specialist); leadership (MA), including health care leadership, organizational leadership; teacher education (MA), including early childhood education, early childhood education: Montessori, education leadership: principal, elementary education: reading K-12, leadership: higher education, secondary education: reading K-12, special education: cognitive impairment, special education: learning disabilities. *Program availability:* Part-time, evening/weekend. *Degree requirements:* For master's, thesis, presentation. *Entrance requirements:* For master's, minimum GPA of 3.0, current resume, essay, all post-secondary transcripts, 3 letters of reference, conviction disclosure form; copy of teaching certificate (for some education programs); for Specialist, master's degree, minimum GPA of 3.0, current resume, essay, all post-secondary transcripts, 3 letters of reference, conviction disclosure form; copy of teaching certificate (for some education programs). Electronic applications accepted.

Sierra Nevada College, Teacher Education Program, Incline Village, NV 89451. Offers advanced teaching and leadership (M Ed); elementary education (MAT); secondary education (MAT). *Program availability:* Part-time, evening/weekend, online learning. *Degree requirements:* For master's, comprehensive exam, thesis, PRAXIS I and II. *Entrance requirements:* For master's, 2 letters of recommendation, minimum GPA of 3.0. Electronic applications accepted.

Silver Lake College of the Holy Family, Graduate School, Graduate Education Program, Manitowoc, WI 54220-9319. Offers administrative leadership (MA Ed); teacher leadership (MA Ed). *Program availability:* Part-time, evening/weekend, blended/hybrid learning. *Degree requirements:* For master's, comprehensive exam, thesis or alternative, capstone culminating project, comprehensive portfolio, or public presentation of project. *Entrance requirements:* For master's, ACT (preferred) or SAT, minimum undergraduate GPA of 3.0. Additional exam requirements/recommendations for international students: Required—TOEFL (minimum score 550 paper-based; 89 iBT). Electronic applications accepted. *Expenses:* Contact institution. *Faculty research:* Student development; school administration.

Simon Fraser University, Office of Graduate Studies and Postdoctoral Fellows, Faculty of Education, Program in Educational Leadership, Burnaby, BC V5A 1S6, Canada. Offers M Ed, MA, Ed D. *Program availability:* Part-time, evening/weekend. *Degree requirements:* For master's, comprehensive exam (for some programs), thesis (for some programs); for doctorate, comprehensive exam, thesis/dissertation. *Entrance requirements:* For master's, minimum GPA of 3.0 (on scale of 4.33) or 3.33 based on last 60 credits of undergraduate courses; for doctorate, minimum GPA of 3.5 (on scale of 4.33). Additional exam requirements/recommendations for international students: Recommended—TOEFL (minimum score 580 paper-based; 93 iBT), IELTS (minimum score 7), TWE (minimum score 5). Electronic applications accepted. *Faculty research:* Language learning, assessment and accountability policy, intersections between student affairs and services, recruitment and retention, indigenous peoples, student success in post-secondary education.

Simpson University, School of Education, Redding, CA 96003-8606. Offers education (MA), including curriculum, education leadership; education and preliminary administrative services credential (MA); education and preliminary teaching credential (MA); teaching (MA). *Program availability:* Part-time, evening/weekend. *Degree requirements:* For master's, thesis optional. *Entrance requirements:* For master's, statement of purpose, 2 professional references, professional essay, interview. Additional exam requirements/recommendations for international students: Required—TOEFL (minimum score 550 paper-based). Electronic applications accepted. *Expenses:* Contact institution.

SIT Graduate Institute, Graduate Programs, Master of Education Program in Global Youth Development and Leadership, Brattleboro, VT 05302-0676. Offers M Ed.

Slippery Rock University of Pennsylvania, Graduate Studies (Recruitment), College of Education, Department of Special Education, Slippery Rock, PA 16057-1383. Offers autism (M Ed); master teacher (M Ed), including birth to grade 8, grades 7 to 12; special education (Ed D); supervision (M Ed); technology for online instruction (M Ed). *Accreditation:* NCATE. *Program availability:* Part-time, evening/weekend, 100% online. *Degree requirements:* For master's, thesis optional. *Entrance requirements:* For master's, minimum GPA of 3.0, official transcripts, teaching certification. Additional exam requirements/recommendations for international students: Required—TOEFL (minimum score 550 paper-based; 80 iBT). Electronic applications accepted. *Expenses:* Contact institution.

Soka University of America, Graduate School, Aliso Viejo, CA 92656. Offers educational leadership and societal change (MA). *Program availability:* Evening/weekend. *Entrance requirements:* For master's, GRE. Additional exam requirements/recommendations for international students: Required—TOEFL (minimum score 600 paper-based; 100 iBT).
See Display below and Close-Up on page 933.

Sonoma State University, School of Education, Rohnert Park, CA 94928. Offers administrative services (Credential); curriculum, teaching, and learning (MA); early childhood education (MA); education specialist (Credential); educational leadership (MA); multiple subject (Credential); reading and literacy (MA, Credential); single subject (Credential); special education (MA). *Accreditation:* NCATE. *Program availability:* Part-time, evening/weekend. *Entrance requirements:* For master's, minimum GPA of 2.5. Additional exam requirements/recommendations for international students: Required—TOEFL (minimum score 500 paper-based). Application fee: $55. *Financial support:* Fellowships, research assistantships, career-related internships or fieldwork, and Federal Work-Study available. Support available to part-time students. Financial award application deadline: 3/2; financial award applicants required to submit FAFSA. *Unit head:* Dr. Carlos Ayala, Dean, 707-664-4412, E-mail: carlos.ayala@sonoma.edu. *Application contact:* Dr. Karen Grady, Coordinator of Graduate Studies, 707-664-3328, E-mail: karen.grady@sonoma.edu.
Website: http://www.sonoma.edu/education/

South Carolina State University, College of Graduate and Professional Studies, Department of Educational Leadership, Orangeburg, SC 29117-0001. Offers educational leadership and administration (Ed D, Ed S). *Accreditation:* ACA; NCATE. *Program availability:* Part-time, evening/weekend. *Faculty:* 5 full-time (1 woman), 2 part-time/adjunct (0 women). *Students:* 19 full-time (15 women), 82 part-time (50 women); includes 93 minority (92 Black or African American, non-Hispanic/Latino; 1 American Indian or Alaska Native, non-Hispanic/Latino), 1 international. Average age 41. 36 applicants, 100% accepted, 33 enrolled. In 2017, 7 doctorates, 10 other advanced degrees awarded. *Degree requirements:* For doctorate, comprehensive exam, thesis/dissertation, preliminary exams, internship, practicum; for Ed S, thesis. *Entrance requirements:* For doctorate, GRE General Test or MAT, teaching certificate, teaching experience; for Ed S, GRE General Test or MAT, interview, teaching certificate, teaching experience. *Application deadline:* For fall admission, 6/15 priority date for domestic students, 6/15 for international students; for spring admission, 11/1 for domestic and international students. Application fee: $25. Electronic applications accepted. *Expenses:* Tuition, state resident: full-time $9388; part-time $607 per credit hour. Tuition, nonresident: full-time $19,968; part-time $1194 per credit hour. *Required fees:* $766; $766 per credit hour. *Financial support:* Career-related internships or fieldwork available. Financial award application deadline: 6/1. *Unit head:* Dr. Frederick Evans, Interim Chair, Department of Educational Leadership, 803-536-4734, Fax: 803-536-8812, E-mail: fevans6@scsu.edu. *Application contact:* Curtis Foskey, Coordinator of

Graduate Enrollment, 803-536-8809, Fax: 803-536-8812, E-mail: cfoskey@scsu.edu. Website: http://www.scsu.edu/schoolofgraduatestudies/doctorofeducation.aspx

South Dakota State University, Graduate School, College of Education and Human Sciences, Department of Teaching, Learning and Leadership, Brookings, SD 57007. Offers agricultural education (MS); curriculum and instruction (M Ed); educational administration (M Ed). *Program availability:* Part-time, evening/weekend, online learning. *Degree requirements:* For master's, portfolio, oral exam. *Entrance requirements:* For master's, minimum GPA of 2.75. Additional exam requirements/recommendations for international students: Required—TOEFL (minimum score 550 paper-based; 80 iBT). *Faculty research:* Inclusion school climate, K-12 reform and restructuring, rural development, ESL, leadership.

Southeastern Louisiana University, College of Education, Department of Educational Leadership and Technology, Hammond, LA 70402. Offers educational leadership (M Ed, Ed D). *Program availability:* Part-time. *Faculty:* 11 full-time (6 women), 1 (woman) part-time/adjunct. *Students:* 5 full-time (4 women), 159 part-time (126 women); includes 72 minority (60 Black or African American, non-Hispanic/Latino; 6 Hispanic/Latino; 6 Two or more races, non-Hispanic/Latino), 1 international. Average age 39. 39 applicants, 69% accepted, 26 enrolled. In 2017, 44 master's, 2 doctorates awarded. *Degree requirements:* For master's, comprehensive exam; for doctorate, comprehensive exam, thesis/dissertation. *Entrance requirements:* For master's, GRE (minimum score of 500), copy of valid teaching certificate, verification of minimum of one successful year of teaching experience in either public or private schools, completed recommendation form from school official who can attest to applicant's leadership potential and likelihood of success in program; for doctorate, GRE (minimum scores: Verbal 145; Quantitative 145 taken August 2011 or after), three recommendation letters, verification of at least three years of appropriate professional experience, minimum GPA of 3.0 on all graduate-level course work. Additional exam requirements/recommendations for international students: Required—TOEFL (minimum score 500 paper-based; 61 iBT). *Application deadline:* For fall admission, 7/15 priority date for domestic students, 6/1 priority date for international students; for spring admission, 12/1 priority date for domestic students, 10/1 priority date for international students. Applications are processed on a rolling basis. Application fee: $20 ($30 for international students). Electronic applications accepted. *Expenses:* Tuition, state resident: full-time $6684. Tuition, nonresident: full-time $19,162. *Required fees:* $2088. *Financial support:* In 2017–18, 14 students received support, including 3 teaching assistantships (averaging $10,224 per year); research assistantships, career-related internships or fieldwork, Federal Work-Study, institutionally sponsored loans, scholarships/grants, and unspecified assistantships also available. Support available to part-time students. Financial award application deadline: 5/1; financial award applicants required to submit FAFSA. *Faculty research:* School effectiveness, online instruction, federal constitutional rights of students and teachers, using data to drive instruction, change leadership. *Unit head:* Dr. Thomas Devaney, Department Head, 985-549-5713, Fax: 985-549-5712, E-mail: tdevaney@southeastern.edu. *Application contact:* Amanda Harper, Graduate Admissions Analyst, 985-549-2066, Fax: 985-549-5632, E-mail: admissions@southeastern.edu.
Website: http://www.southeastern.edu/acad_research/depts/edlt

Southeastern Oklahoma State University, School of Education, Durant, OK 74701-0609. Offers math specialist (M Ed); reading specialist (M Ed); school administration (M Ed); school counseling (M Ed). *Accreditation:* NCATE. *Program availability:* Part-time, evening/weekend. *Degree requirements:* For master's, comprehensive exam, thesis optional, portfolio (M Ed). *Entrance requirements:* For master's, GRE General Test (for school counseling), minimum GPA of 3.0 in last 60 hours or 2.75 overall. Additional exam requirements/recommendations for international students: Required—TOEFL (minimum score 550 paper-based; 79 iBT). Electronic applications accepted.

Educational Leadership and Administration

Southeastern University, College of Education, Lakeland, FL 33801-6099. Offers curriculum and instruction (Ed D); educational leadership (M Ed); elementary education (M Ed); exceptional student education (M Ed); exceptional student education/educational therapy (M Ed); kinesiology (M Ed); organizational leadership (Ed D); reading education (M Ed); teaching English to speakers of other languages (M Ed). *Faculty:* 8 full-time (5 women), 12 part-time/adjunct (7 women). *Students:* 139 full-time (109 women), 225 part-time (172 women); includes 107 minority (57 Black or African American, non-Hispanic/Latino; 2 Asian, non-Hispanic/Latino; 48 Hispanic/Latino), 4 international. Average age 40. Application fee: $50. Electronic applications accepted. *Unit head:* James A. Anderson, Dean, 863-667-5366, E-mail: jaanderson2@seu.edu. Website: http://www.seu.edu/education/

Southeast Missouri State University, School of Graduate Studies, Department of Educational Leadership and Counseling, Program in Educational Administration, Cape Girardeau, MO 63701-4799. Offers educational leadership (Ed D); higher education administration (MA); secondary administration (MA); teacher leadership (MA, Ed S). *Accreditation:* NCATE. *Program availability:* Part-time, evening/weekend, online only, 100% online. *Faculty:* 7 full-time (4 women), 4 part-time/adjunct (1 woman). *Students:* 45 full-time (31 women), 203 part-time (133 women); includes 24 minority (18 Black or African American, non-Hispanic/Latino; 1 American Indian or Alaska Native, non-Hispanic/Latino; 4 Asian, non-Hispanic/Latino; 1 Two or more races, non-Hispanic/Latino), 13 international. Average age 32. 105 applicants, 100% accepted, 105 enrolled. In 2017, 29 master's, 31 other advanced degrees awarded. *Degree requirements:* For master's and Ed S, comprehensive exam, thesis or alternative, paper; for doctorate, comprehensive exam, thesis/dissertation. *Entrance requirements:* For master's, minimum GPA of 3.5; for doctorate, GRE, interview; for Ed S, minimum GPA of 3.7. Additional exam requirements/recommendations for international students: Required—TOEFL (minimum score 550 paper-based; 79 iBT), IELTS (minimum score 6), PTE (minimum score 53). *Application deadline:* For fall admission, 8/1 for domestic students, 6/1 for international students; for spring admission, 11/21 for domestic students, 10/1 for international students; for summer admission, 5/15 for domestic students. Applications are processed on a rolling basis. Application fee: $30 ($40 for international students). Electronic applications accepted. *Expenses:* $270.35 per credit hour in-state tuition, $33.40 per credit hour fees. *Financial support:* In 2017–18, 22 students received support. Career-related internships or fieldwork, Federal Work-Study, scholarships/grants, traineeships, tuition waivers (full), and unspecified assistantships available. Financial award application deadline: 6/30; financial award applicants required to submit FAFSA. *Faculty research:* Learning and technology; leadership, equity and social justice in P-12 schools and higher education; school culture; leadership and academic achievement; school leadership and student success. *Unit head:* Dr. C. P. Gause, Professor/Chair, 573-651-2137, Fax: 573-986-6512, E-mail: cgause@semo.edu. *Application contact:* Dr. Lisa Bertrand, Professor/Coordinator, 573-651-5080, Fax: 573-986-6512, E-mail: lbertrand@semo.edu. Website: http://www.semo.edu/eduleadcounsel/

Southern Adventist University, School of Education and Psychology, Collegedale, TN 37315-0370. Offers clinical mental health counseling (MS); instructional leadership (MS Ed); literacy education (MS Ed); outdoor education (MS Ed); professional school counseling (MS). *Accreditation:* NCATE. *Program availability:* Part-time, evening/weekend. *Degree requirements:* For master's, comprehensive exam (for some programs), thesis optional, position paper (MS), portfolio (MS Ed in outdoor education). *Entrance requirements:* For master's, interview (MS); 9 semester hours of upper-division course work in psychology or related field, including 1 course in psychology research or statistics; 9 semester hours of education (MS Ed). Additional exam requirements/recommendations for international students: Required—TOEFL (minimum score 600 paper-based; 100 iBT). *Application deadline:* For fall admission, 7/1 priority date for domestic students, 6/1 priority date for international students; for winter admission, 11/1 priority date for domestic students, 10/1 priority date for international students; for spring admission, 4/1 priority date for domestic students, 3/1 priority date for international students. Applications are processed on a rolling basis. Application fee: $40. Electronic applications accepted. *Expenses: Tuition:* Full-time $11,430; part-time $635 per credit hour. Tuition and fees vary according to degree level and program. *Financial support:* Research assistantships with full tuition reimbursements, teaching assistantships with full tuition reimbursements, career-related internships or fieldwork, scholarships/grants, tuition waivers (partial), and unspecified assistantships available. Support available to part-time students. Financial award application deadline: 4/1; financial award applicants required to submit FAFSA. *Unit head:* Bonnie Eder, Interim Dean, 423-236-2759, Fax: 423-236-1765, E-mail: beder@southern.edu. *Application contact:* Mikhaile Spence, Graduate Enrollment Counselor, 423-236-2496, Fax: 423-236-1765, E-mail: maspence@southern.edu. Website: https://www.southern.edu/academics/edpsych.html

Southern Arkansas University–Magnolia, School of Graduate Studies, Magnolia, AR 71753. Offers agriculture (MS); business administration (MBA), including agribusiness, social entrepreneurship, supply chain management; clinical and mental health counseling (MS); computer and information sciences (MS), including cyber security and privacy, data science, information technology; gifted and talented (M Ed), including curriculum and instruction, educational administration and supervision, gifted and talented P-8/7-12, instructional specialist P-4; higher, adult and lifelong education (M Ed); kinesiology (M Ed), including coaching; library media and information specialist (M Ed); public administration (MPA); school counseling K-12 (M Ed); student affairs and college counseling (M Ed); teaching (MAT). *Accreditation:* NCATE. *Program availability:* Part-time, 100% online, blended/hybrid learning. *Faculty:* 36 full-time (20 women), 31 part-time/adjunct (12 women). *Students:* 242 full-time (89 women), 889 part-time (459 women); includes 167 minority (143 Black or African American, non-Hispanic/Latino; 7 American Indian or Alaska Native, non-Hispanic/Latino; 7 Asian, non-Hispanic/Latino; 3 Hispanic/Latino; 7 Two or more races, non-Hispanic/Latino), 562 international. Average age 28. 400 applicants, 100% accepted, 239 enrolled. In 2017, 875 master's awarded. *Degree requirements:* For master's, comprehensive exam (for some programs), thesis optional. *Entrance requirements:* For master's, GRE, MAT or GMAT, minimum GPA of 2.5. Additional exam requirements/recommendations for international students: Required—TOEFL (minimum score 550 paper-based), IELTS (minimum score 6). *Application deadline:* For fall admission, 7/20 for domestic students, 7/10 for international students; for spring admission, 12/1 for domestic students, 11/15 for international students; for summer admission, 4/1 for domestic students, 5/1 for international students. Applications are processed on a rolling basis. Application fee: $25 ($50 for international students). Electronic applications accepted. *Expenses:* Tuition, state resident: full-time $6038. Tuition, nonresident: full-time $8558. *Required fees:* $804. One-time fee: $110 full-time. Tuition and fees vary according to course load. *Financial support:* Career-related internships or fieldwork, Federal Work-Study, scholarships/grants, tuition waivers (full), and unspecified assistantships available. Financial award applicants required to submit FAFSA. *Faculty research:* Alternative certification for teachers, supervision of instruction, instructional leadership, counseling. *Unit head:* Dr. Kim Bloss, Dean, School of Graduate Studies, 870-235-4150, Fax: 870-235-5227, E-mail: kkbloss@saumag.edu. *Application contact:* Shrijana Malakar, Admissions Specialist, 870-235-4150, Fax: 870-235-5227, E-mail: smalakar@saumag.edu. Website: http://www.saumag.edu/graduate

Southern Connecticut State University, School of Graduate Studies, School of Education, Department of Educational Leadership, New Haven, CT 06515-1355. Offers educational leadership (Ed D, Diploma); research, statistics, and measurement (MS). *Program availability:* Part-time, evening/weekend. *Entrance requirements:* For degree, master's degree, minimum GPA of 3.0, writing sample. Electronic applications accepted.

Southern Illinois University Carbondale, Graduate School, College of Education and Human Services, Department of Educational Administration and Higher Education, Program in Educational Administration, Carbondale, IL 62901-4701. Offers MS Ed, PhD. PhD offered jointly with Southeast Missouri State University. *Accreditation:* NCATE. *Program availability:* Part-time. *Degree requirements:* For master's, thesis or alternative; for doctorate, thesis/dissertation. *Entrance requirements:* For master's, minimum GPA of 2.7; for doctorate, GRE General Test, MAT, minimum GPA of 3.5. Additional exam requirements/recommendations for international students: Required—TOEFL. *Faculty research:* School principalship, history and philosophy of education, supervision.

Southern Illinois University Edwardsville, Graduate School, School of Education, Health, and Human Behavior, Department of Educational Leadership, Program in Educational Administration, Edwardsville, IL 62026. Offers MS Ed, Ed S. *Accreditation:* NCATE. *Program availability:* Part-time, evening/weekend. *Degree requirements:* For master's, thesis or alternative, portfolio. *Entrance requirements:* Additional exam requirements/recommendations for international students: Required—TOEFL (minimum score 550 paper-based; 79 iBT), IELTS (minimum score 6.5). Electronic applications accepted.

Southern Illinois University Edwardsville, Graduate School, School of Education, Health, and Human Behavior, Department of Educational Leadership, Program in Educational Leadership, Edwardsville, IL 62026. Offers Ed D. *Program availability:* Part-time, evening/weekend. *Degree requirements:* For doctorate, thesis/dissertation or alternative, project. *Entrance requirements:* For doctorate, GRE. Additional exam requirements/recommendations for international students: Required—TOEFL (minimum score 550 paper-based; 79 iBT), IELTS (minimum score 6.5). Electronic applications accepted.

Southern New Hampshire University, School of Education, Manchester, NH 03106-1045. Offers curriculum and instruction (M Ed), including dyslexia studies and language-based learning disabilities, educational leadership, reading, special education, technology integration; dyslexia studies and language-based learning disabilities (Certificate); early childhood and special education (M Ed); educational leadership (M Ed, Ed D); educational studies (M Ed); elementary and special education (M Ed); field based education (M Ed); higher education administration (MS); teaching English as a foreign language (MS). *Program availability:* Part-time, evening/weekend, online learning. *Degree requirements:* For master's, comprehensive exam (for some programs), thesis or alternative. *Entrance requirements:* For master's, PRAXIS I, minimum GPA of 2.75. Additional exam requirements/recommendations for international students: Required—TOEFL (minimum score 550 paper-based). *Application deadline:* Applications are processed on a rolling basis. Application fee: $40. Electronic applications accepted. *Expenses:* Contact institution. *Financial support:* Institutionally sponsored loans available. Financial award applicants required to submit FAFSA. *Unit head:* Raymond McNulty, Dean, 603-668-2211, Fax: 603-629-4673. *Application contact:* Office of Graduate Admission, 888-327-SNHU, Fax: 603-644-3144, E-mail: enroll@snhu.edu.

Southern Oregon University, Graduate Studies, School of Education, Ashland, OR 97520. Offers elementary education (MA Ed, MS Ed), including classroom teacher, early childhood, handicapped learner, reading, supervision; secondary education (MA Ed, MS Ed), including classroom teacher, handicapped learner, reading, supervision; teaching (MAT). *Program availability:* Online learning. *Degree requirements:* For master's, thesis optional. *Entrance requirements:* For master's, GRE General Test, minimum cumulative GPA of 3.0 in the last 90 quarter credits (60 semester credits) of undergraduate coursework. Additional exam requirements/recommendations for international students: Required—TOEFL (minimum score 540 paper-based; 76 iBT), IELTS (minimum score 6), ELPT (minimum score 964) or ELS (minimum score 112). Electronic applications accepted.

Southern University and Agricultural and Mechanical College, Graduate School, College of Education, Department of Behavioral Studies and Educational Leadership, Program in Administration and Supervision, Baton Rouge, LA 70813. Offers M Ed.

Southern University and Agricultural and Mechanical College, Graduate School, College of Education, Department of Behavioral Studies and Educational Leadership, Program in Educational Leadership, Baton Rouge, LA 70813. Offers M Ed. *Entrance requirements:* For master's, GRE General Test.

Southwest Baptist University, Program in Education, Bolivar, MO 65613-2597. Offers education (MS); educational administration (MS, Ed S). *Program availability:* Part-time. *Degree requirements:* For master's, comprehensive exam, thesis optional, 6-hour residency; for Ed S, comprehensive exam, 5-hour residency. *Entrance requirements:* For master's, GRE or PRAXIS II, interviews, minimum GPA of 2.75; for Ed S, master's degree. Additional exam requirements/recommendations for international students: Required—TOEFL (minimum score 550 paper-based). *Faculty research:* At-risk programs, principal retention, mentoring beginning principals.

Southwestern Adventist University, Education Department, Keene, TX 76059. Offers curriculum and instruction with reading emphasis (M Ed); educational leadership (M Ed). *Program availability:* Part-time, evening/weekend. *Degree requirements:* For master's, thesis or alternative, professional paper. *Entrance requirements:* For master's, GRE General Test.

Southwestern Assemblies of God University, Thomas F. Harrison School of Graduate Studies, Program in Education, Waxahachie, TX 75165-5735. Offers Christian school administration (MS); curriculum development (MS); early education administration (M Ed); middle and secondary education (M Ed). *Degree requirements:* For master's, comprehensive written and oral exams. *Entrance requirements:* For master's, GRE General Test, minimum GPA of 2.5. Electronic applications accepted.

Southwestern College, Education Programs, Winfield, KS 67156-2499. Offers curriculum and instruction (M Ed); early childhood education (M Ed); educational leadership (Ed D), including higher education leadership, PK-12 education leadership; special education (M Ed), including high-incidence disabilities, low-incidence disabilities; teaching (MA). *Accreditation:* NCATE. *Program availability:* Part-time, evening/weekend, 100% online, blended/hybrid learning. *Faculty:* 6 full-time (5 women), 12 part-time/adjunct (10 women). *Students:* 12 full-time (10 women), 77 part-time (51 women); includes 12 minority (5 Black or African American, non-Hispanic/Latino; 2 American Indian or Alaska Native, non-Hispanic/Latino; 1 Asian, non-Hispanic/Latino; 3 Hispanic/Latino; 1 Native Hawaiian or other Pacific Islander, non-Hispanic/Latino), 10 international. Average age 39. 29 applicants, 86% accepted, 18 enrolled. In 2017, 52 master's, 11 doctorates awarded. *Degree requirements:* For master's, practicum, portfolio; for doctorate, thesis/dissertation, professional portfolio. *Entrance requirements:* For master's, baccalaureate degree, minimum GPA of 3.0, valid teaching certificate (for special education); for doctorate, GRE if no master's degree, baccalaureate degree with minimum GPA of 3.25 and current teaching experience, or master's degree with minimum GPA of 3.5. Additional exam requirements/recommendations for international students: Required—TOEFL (minimum score 550 paper-based; 80 iBT). *Application deadline:* Applications are processed on a rolling basis. Application fee: $40. Electronic applications accepted. *Expenses:* $577 per credit hour, $509 online (for master's programs); $609 per credit hour (for doctorate program). *Financial support:* In 2017–18, 9 students received support. Unspecified assistantships and employee tuition waivers available. Financial award applicants required to submit FAFSA. *Unit head:* Dana Pentz, Director of Education Operations, 620-229-6253, E-mail: dana.pentz@sckans.edu. *Application contact:* Dennis Russell, Director of Admissions and Student Services, 888-684-5335 Ext. 3372, Fax: 888-684-5218, E-mail: dennis.russell@sckans.edu. Website: http://www.sckans.edu/graduate/education-med/

Southwestern Oklahoma State University, College of Professional and Graduate Studies, School of Behavioral Sciences and Education, Specialization in Educational Administration, Weatherford, OK 73096-3098. Offers M Ed. M Ed distance learning degree program offered to Oklahoma residents only. *Accreditation:* NCATE. *Program availability:* Part-time, evening/weekend, online learning. *Degree requirements:* For master's, exam. *Entrance requirements:* For master's, GRE General Test or minimum undergraduate GPA of 3.0, portfolio. Additional exam requirements/recommendations for international students: Required—TOEFL.

Southwest Minnesota State University, Department of Education, Marshall, MN 56258. Offers ESL (MS); math (MS); reading (MS); special education (MS), including developmental disabilities, early childhood education, emotional behavioral disorders, learning disabilities; teaching, learning and leadership (MS). *Program availability:* Part-time, evening/weekend, online learning. *Entrance requirements:* Additional exam requirements/recommendations for international students: Required—TOEFL or IELTS; Recommended—TOEFL (minimum score 550 paper-based; 80 iBT), IELTS.

Spalding University, Graduate Studies, College of Education, Program in Leadership Education, Louisville, KY 40203-2188. Offers executive (Ed D); scholar-practitioner (Ed D). *Accreditation:* NCATE. *Program availability:* Part-time, evening/weekend. *Degree requirements:* For doctorate, comprehensive exam, thesis/dissertation. *Entrance requirements:* For doctorate, GRE General Test or MAT, interview, letters of recommendation, resume, transcripts. Additional exam requirements/recommendations for international students: Required—TOEFL (minimum score 535 paper-based). Electronic applications accepted. *Faculty research:* Leadership of schools, achievement gap, women in leadership.

Spalding University, Graduate Studies, College of Education, Programs in Education, Louisville, KY 40203-2188. Offers art teacher education (MAT); business teacher education (MAT); elementary school education (MAT); foreign language (MAT); high school education (MAT); middle school education (MAT); secondary education (MAT); special education (learning and behavioral disorders) (MAT); student guidance counselor (MA); teacher leader (M Ed). *Accreditation:* NCATE. *Program availability:* Part-time, evening/weekend. *Entrance requirements:* For master's, GRE General Test or MAT, interview, letters of recommendation, resume. Additional exam requirements/recommendations for international students: Required—TOEFL (minimum score 535 paper-based). Electronic applications accepted. *Faculty research:* Instructional technology, achievement gap, classroom management, assessment.

Springfield College, Graduate Programs, Programs in Physical Education, Springfield, MA 01109-3797. Offers adapted physical education (MS); advanced-level coaching (M Ed); athletic administration (MS); exercise physiology (PhD); health promotion and disease prevention (MS); physical education initial licensure (CAGS); sport and exercise psychology (PhD); teaching and administration (PhD). *Program availability:* Part-time. *Students:* 82 applicants, 73% accepted, 37 enrolled. *Degree requirements:* For master's, comprehensive exam, thesis (for some programs). *Entrance requirements:* For master's and doctorate, GRE General Test. Additional exam requirements/recommendations for international students: Required—TOEFL (minimum score 550 paper-based); Recommended—IELTS (minimum score 7). *Application deadline:* For fall admission, 1/15 priority date for domestic students, 1/15 for international students; for winter admission, 11/1 for domestic and international students; for spring admission, 11/1 for domestic and international students. Applications are processed on a rolling basis. Application fee: $50. Electronic applications accepted. *Financial support:* Fellowships with partial tuition reimbursements, teaching assistantships with partial tuition reimbursements, career-related internships or fieldwork, Federal Work-Study, institutionally sponsored loans, scholarships/grants, and unspecified assistantships available. Financial award application deadline: 3/1; financial award applicants required to submit FAFSA. *Unit head:* Dr. Michelle Moosbrugger, Graduate Coordinator, 413-748-3486, E-mail: mmoosbrugger@springfield.edu. *Application contact:* Anne Griffin, Director of Graduate Admissions, 413-748-3225, Fax: 413-748-3694, E-mail: agriffin2@springfield.edu. Website: http://springfield.edu/gradpe

Stanford University, Graduate School of Education, Program in Policy, Organization, and Leadership Studies, Stanford, CA 94305-2004. Offers MA, MA/MBA. *Degree requirements:* For master's, thesis (for some programs). *Entrance requirements:* For master's, GRE General Test. Electronic applications accepted. *Expenses:* Tuition: Full-time $48,987; part-time $10,620 per quarter. One-time fee: $400. Tuition and fees vary according to program.

State University of New York at New Paltz, Graduate and Extended Learning School, School of Education, Department of Educational Foundations and Leadership, New Paltz, NY 12561. Offers educational leadership (MS Ed); school building leader (CAS); school district business leader (CAS); school district leader (CAS). *Program availability:* Part-time, evening/weekend. *Faculty:* 1 full-time (0 women), 5 part-time/adjunct (4 women). *Students:* 4 full-time (3 women), 45 part-time (28 women); includes 6 minority (2 Black or African American, non-Hispanic/Latino; 4 Hispanic/Latino). 17 applicants, 88% accepted, 13 enrolled. In 2017, 22 CASs awarded. *Entrance requirements:* For master's, GRE General Test or MAT, minimum GPA of 3.0, New York state teaching certificate; for CAS, minimum GPA of 3.0, proof of 3 years' teaching experience, New York state teaching certificate. Additional exam requirements/recommendations for international students: Required—TOEFL (minimum score 550 paper-based; 80 iBT), IELTS (minimum score 6.5). *Application deadline:* Applications are processed on a rolling basis. Application fee: $50. Electronic applications accepted. *Financial support:* Application deadline: 8/1. *Faculty research:* Time management of administrators, social justice, women in educational leadership, diversity in educational leadership, superintendency. *Unit head:* Prof. Devon Duhaney, Program Director, 845-257-2853, E-mail: duhaneyd@newpaltz.edu. *Application contact:* Vika Shock, Director of Graduate Admissions, 845-257-3286, Fax: 845-257-3284, E-mail: gradschool@newpaltz.edu. Website: http://www.newpaltz.edu/edadmin/

State University of New York at New Paltz, Graduate and Extended Learning School, School of Education, Department of Educational Studies and Leadership, New Paltz, NY 12561. Offers humanistic/multicultural education (MPS, AC), including humanistic/multicultural education (MPS), multicultural education (AC); special education (MS Ed), including adolescence special education (7-12), adolescence special education and literacy, childhood special education (1-6), childhood special education and literacy, early childhood special education (B-2). *Program availability:* Part-time, evening/

weekend. *Faculty:* 7 full-time (6 women). *Students:* 18 full-time (13 women), 63 part-time (49 women); includes 13 minority (3 Black or African American, non-Hispanic/Latino; 1 Asian, non-Hispanic/Latino; 9 Hispanic/Latino), 1 international. 37 applicants, 78% accepted, 29 enrolled. In 2017, 42 master's awarded. *Entrance requirements:* For master's, minimum GPA of 3.0, New York state teaching certificate (MS Ed). Additional exam requirements/recommendations for international students: Required—TOEFL (minimum score 550 paper-based; 80 iBT), IELTS (minimum score 6.5). *Application deadline:* For fall admission, 3/15 priority date for domestic students, 3/15 for international students; for spring admission, 10/15 for domestic and international students. Application fee: $50. Electronic applications accepted. *Financial support:* Scholarships/grants available. Financial award application deadline: 8/1. *Unit head:* Dr. Kate Mccoy, Chair, 845-257-2834, E-mail: mccoyk@newpaltz.edu. *Application contact:* Vika Shock, Director of Graduate Admissions, 845-257-3286, E-mail: gradschool@newpaltz.edu. Website: http://www.newpaltz.edu/edstudies/

State University of New York at Oswego, Graduate Studies, School of Education, Department of Educational Administration, Oswego, NY 13126. Offers educational administration (CAS); school building leadership (CAS). *Program availability:* Part-time. *Degree requirements:* For CAS, comprehensive exam, internship. *Entrance requirements:* For degree, interview, MA or MS, minimum GPA of 3.0, teaching certificate. Additional exam requirements/recommendations for international students: Required—TOEFL (minimum score 560 paper-based). *Faculty research:* Professional growth and development, leadership, governance, strategic planning, shared decision-making.

State University of New York at Plattsburgh, School of Education, Health, and Human Services, Program in Educational Leadership, Plattsburgh, NY 12901-2681. Offers CAS. *Program availability:* Part-time, evening/weekend. *Entrance requirements:* Additional exam requirements/recommendations for international students: Required—TOEFL.

State University of New York College at Cortland, Graduate Studies, School of Education, Program in Educational Leadership, Cortland, NY 13045. Offers school building leader (CAS); school building leader and school district leader (CAS); school district business leader (CAS); school district leader (CAS). *Program availability:* Part-time, evening/weekend. *Degree requirements:* For CAS, one foreign language. *Entrance requirements:* For degree, MS in education, permanent New York teaching certificate. Additional exam requirements/recommendations for international students: Required—TOEFL.

Stephen F. Austin State University, Graduate School, College of Education, Department of Secondary Education and Educational Leadership, Nacogdoches, TX 75962. Offers educational leadership (Ed D); secondary education (M Ed). *Accreditation:* NCATE. *Degree requirements:* For master's, comprehensive exam; for doctorate, thesis/dissertation. *Entrance requirements:* For master's, GRE General Test; for doctorate, GRE General Test, interview, writing sample. Additional exam requirements/recommendations for international students: Required—TOEFL. Electronic applications accepted.

Stetson University, College of Arts and Sciences, Division of Education, DeLand, FL 32723. Offers counselor education (MS), including marriage, couple and family counseling, mental health counseling, school counseling; teacher education (M Ed), including educational leadership. *Accreditation:* NCATE (one or more programs are accredited). *Program availability:* Part-time, evening/weekend. *Faculty:* 13 full-time (8 women), 6 part-time/adjunct (3 women). *Students:* 168 full-time (132 women), 14 part-time (12 women); includes 73 minority (19 Black or African American, non-Hispanic/Latino; 7 American Indian or Alaska Native, non-Hispanic/Latino; 1 Asian, non-Hispanic/Latino; 25 Hispanic/Latino; 1 Native Hawaiian or other Pacific Islander, non-Hispanic/Latino; 20 Two or more races, non-Hispanic/Latino), 5 international. Average age 32. 102 applicants, 85% accepted, 66 enrolled. In 2017, 81 master's awarded. *Entrance requirements:* For master's, GRE or MAT. *Application deadline:* For fall admission, 8/1 priority date for domestic students; for spring admission, 1/1 priority date for domestic students; for summer admission, 5/1 priority date for domestic students. Applications are processed on a rolling basis. Application fee: $50. Electronic applications accepted. *Expenses:* $911 per credit hour. *Financial support:* In 2017–18, 74 students received support. Career-related internships or fieldwork, Federal Work-Study, institutionally sponsored loans, scholarships/grants, unspecified assistantships, and tuition waivers (for staff and dependents) available. Support available to part-time students. Financial award applicants required to submit FAFSA. *Faculty research:* School leadership succession planning; teacher preparation, educational pedagogies; mission-driven leadership; restorative practices in schools. *Unit head:* Dr. Thomas Farrell, Interim Dean, 386-822-7515. *Application contact:* Jamie Vanderlip, Director of Admissions for Graduate, Transfer and Adult Programs, 386-822-7100, Fax: 386-822-7112, E-mail: jlvander@stetson.edu.

Stetson University, College of Arts and Sciences, Division of Education, Department of Teacher Education, Program in Educational Leadership, DeLand, FL 32723. Offers M Ed. *Accreditation:* NCATE. *Program availability:* Evening/weekend. *Faculty:* 5 full-time (3 women), 1 (woman) part-time/adjunct. *Students:* 68 full-time (50 women), 5 part-time (3 women); includes 36 minority (10 Black or African American, non-Hispanic/Latino; 3 American Indian or Alaska Native, non-Hispanic/Latino; 1 Asian, non-Hispanic/Latino; 10 Hispanic/Latino; 1 Native Hawaiian or other Pacific Islander, non-Hispanic/Latino; 11 Two or more races, non-Hispanic/Latino). Average age 36. 60 applicants, 90% accepted, 44 enrolled. In 2017, 57 master's awarded. *Degree requirements:* For master's, comprehensive exam. *Entrance requirements:* For master's, GRE or MAT, transcripts, three letters of recommendation, copy of professional teaching certificate. Additional exam requirements/recommendations for international students: Required—TOEFL (minimum score 90 iBT), IELTS (minimum score 7). *Application deadline:* For fall admission, 8/1 priority date for domestic students; for spring admission, 1/1 priority date for domestic students; for summer admission, 5/1 priority date for domestic students. Applications are processed on a rolling basis. Application fee: $50. Electronic applications accepted. *Expenses:* $911 per credit hour. *Financial support:* In 2017–18, 45 students received support. Career-related internships or fieldwork, Federal Work-Study, scholarships/grants, unspecified assistantships, and tuition waivers (for staff and dependents) available. Support available to part-time students. Financial award applicants required to submit FAFSA. *Faculty research:* School leadership succession planning; teacher preparation, educational pedagogies; mission-driven leadership; restorative practices in schools. *Unit head:* Dr. Debra Touchton, Director, 386-822-7075. *Application contact:* Jamie Vanderlip, Director of Admissions for Graduate, Transfer and Adult Programs, 386-822-7100, Fax: 386-822-7112, E-mail: jlvander@stetson.edu.

Stevenson University, Program in Community-Based Education and Leadership, Stevenson, MD 21153. Offers MS. *Program availability:* Part-time, evening/weekend. *Faculty:* 6 part-time/adjunct (5 women). *Students:* 18 part-time (12 women); includes 8 minority (6 Black or African American, non-Hispanic/Latino; 1 Asian, non-Hispanic/Latino; 1 Two or more races, non-Hispanic/Latino). Average age 31. 27 applicants, 78% accepted, 18 enrolled. *Degree requirements:* For master's, capstone. *Entrance requirements:* For master's, bachelor's degree from regionally-accredited institution, official college transcript from degree-granting institution, minimum cumulative GPA of

3.0 in past acadmeic work, two letters of recommendation, resume of professional experience, personal statement. *Application deadline:* Applications are processed on a rolling basis. Electronic applications accepted. *Expenses: Tuition:* Full-time $12,060; part-time $670 per credit. *Required fees:* $250; $125 per semester. Tuition and fees vary according to program. *Financial support:* Unspecified assistantships available. Financial award applicants required to submit FAFSA. *Unit head:* Anne Davis, Associate Dean. *Application contact:* Tonia Cristino, Assistant Director, SUO Admissions, 443-352-4058, Fax: 443-352-4440, E-mail: tcristino@stevenson.edu.
Website: http://www.stevenson.edu/online/academics/online-graduate-programs/community-based-education-leadership/

Stony Brook University, State University of New York, School of Professional Development, Stony Brook, NY 11794. Offers biology (MAT); chemistry (MAT); coaching (Graduate Certificate); earth science (MAT); educational computing (Graduate Certificate); educational leadership (Advanced Certificate); English (MAT); environmental management (MPS, Graduate Certificate); French (MAT); German (MAT); higher education administration (MA, Certificate); human resource management (MS, Graduate Certificate); industrial management (Graduate Certificate); information systems management (Graduate Certificate); Italian (MAT); liberal studies (MA); mathematics (MAT); operations research (Graduate Certificate); physics (MAT); school district business leadership (Advanced Certificate); social studies (MAT); Spanish (MAT). *Program availability:* Part-time, evening/weekend, online learning. *Faculty:* 3 full-time (2 women), 101 part-time/adjunct (45 women). *Students:* 190 full-time (126 women), 974 part-time (708 women); includes 255 minority (88 Black or African American, non-Hispanic/Latino; 2 American Indian or Alaska Native, non-Hispanic/Latino; 31 Asian, non-Hispanic/Latino; 113 Hispanic/Latino; 1 Native Hawaiian or other Pacific Islander, non-Hispanic/Latino; 20 Two or more races, non-Hispanic/Latino), 6 international. Average age 33. 411 applicants, 91% accepted, 288 enrolled. In 2017, 333 master's, 180 other advanced degrees awarded. *Entrance requirements:* Additional exam requirements/recommendations for international students: Required—TOEFL (minimum score 85 iBT). *Application deadline:* For fall admission, 1/15 for domestic students, 6/1 for international students; for spring admission, 10/1 for domestic and international students. Applications are processed on a rolling basis. Application fee: $100. *Expenses:* Contact institution. *Financial support:* Fellowships, research assistantships, teaching assistantships, and career-related internships or fieldwork available. Support available to part-time students. *Unit head:* Dr. Ken Lindblom, Dean, 631-632-7049, Fax: 631-632-9046, E-mail: kenneth.lindblom@stonybrook.edu. *Application contact:* Melissa Jordan, Assistant Dean, 631-632-7751, E-mail: melissa.jordan@stonybrook.edu.
Website: http://www.stonybrook.edu/spd/

Suffolk University, College of Arts and Sciences, Department of Philosophy, Boston, MA 02108-2770. Offers administration of higher education (M Ed, CAGS); disability services (Certificate); ethics and public policy (MS). *Program availability:* Part-time, evening/weekend. *Faculty:* 4 full-time (0 women), 2 part-time/adjunct (0 women). *Students:* 23 full-time (11 women), 37 part-time (27 women); includes 17 minority (6 Black or African American, non-Hispanic/Latino; 2 Asian, non-Hispanic/Latino; 7 Hispanic/Latino; 2 Two or more races, non-Hispanic/Latino), 2 international. Average age 31. 24 applicants, 75% accepted, 3 enrolled. In 2017, 21 master's awarded. *Degree requirements:* For master's, internship or thesis; practicum (for M Ed). *Entrance requirements:* For master's, GRE General Test, MAT, GMAT, statement of professional goals, official transcripts, 2 letters of recommendation, resume. Additional exam requirements/recommendations for international students: Required—TOEFL (minimum score 550 paper-based; 80 iBT). *Application deadline:* For fall admission, 3/15 priority date for domestic and international students; for spring admission, 10/15 priority date for domestic and international students. Applications are processed on a rolling basis. Application fee: $50. Electronic applications accepted. *Expenses:* $29,520 per year full-time tuition; $1,230 per credit part-time. *Financial support:* In 2017–18, 50 students received support, including 13 fellowships (averaging $5,915 per year); career-related internships or fieldwork, Federal Work-Study, institutionally sponsored loans, and unspecified assistantships also available. Support available to part-time students. Financial award application deadline: 4/1; financial award applicants required to submit FAFSA. *Faculty research:* Predicting competent Head Start preschoolers, cultural differences, school counseling technology, sibling attachment in divorce cases, consequences of ethical breaches by human resource professionals. *Unit head:* Dr. Greg Fried, Chair of Philosophy Department, 617-573-8109, E-mail: gfried@suffolk.edu. *Application contact:* Mara Marzocchi, Associate Director of Graduate Admissions, 617-573-8302, Fax: 617-305-1733, E-mail: grad.admission@suffolk.edu.
Website: http://www.suffolk.edu/college/graduate/69296.php

Sul Ross State University, College of Professional Studies, Department of Education, Program in School Administration, Alpine, TX 79832. Offers M Ed. *Program availability:* Part-time, evening/weekend. *Degree requirements:* For master's, thesis optional. *Entrance requirements:* For master's, GMAT or GRE General Test, minimum GPA of 2.5 in last 60 hours of undergraduate work.

Sul Ross State University, Rio Grande College of Sul Ross State University, Alpine, TX 79832. Offers business administration (MBA); teacher education (M Ed), including bilingual education, counseling, educational diagnostics, elementary education, general education, reading, school administration, secondary education. *Program availability:* Part-time, evening/weekend, online learning. *Degree requirements:* For master's, comprehensive exam, thesis optional, minimum GPA of 3.0. *Entrance requirements:* For master's, GMAT or GRE General Test, minimum GPA of 2.5 in last 60 hours of undergraduate work. Additional exam requirements/recommendations for international students: Required—TOEFL.

Syracuse University, School of Education, CAS Program in School District Business Leadership, Syracuse, NY 13244. Offers CAS. *Program availability:* Part-time. *Degree requirements:* For CAS, thesis or alternative, internship. *Entrance requirements:* For degree, master's degree, transcripts, resume. Additional exam requirements/recommendations for international students: Required—TOEFL (minimum score 100 iBT). *Application deadline:* For fall admission, 1/15 priority date for domestic and international students; for spring admission, 10/15 priority date for domestic and international students; for summer admission, 4/15 priority date for domestic and international students. Applications are processed on a rolling basis. Electronic applications accepted. *Financial support:* Fellowships, research assistantships, teaching assistantships, career-related internships or fieldwork, and scholarships/grants available. Financial award application deadline: 1/15. *Faculty research:* Education management, procurement, human resource management, educational leadership and administration, long-term strategic planning. *Unit head:* Dr. Benjamin Dotger, Chair of Teaching and Leadership/Professor, 315-443-2685, E-mail: bdotger@syr.edu. *Application contact:* Speranza Migliore, Graduate Admissions Recruiter, 315-443-2505, E-mail: gradrcrt@syr.edu.
Website: http://soeweb.syr.edu/academic/teaching_and_leadership/graduate/CAS/school_district_business_leadership/default.aspx

Syracuse University, School of Education, Programs in Educational Leadership, Syracuse, NY 13244. Offers MS, Ed D, CAS. *Program availability:* Part-time. In 2017, 1 master's, 1 doctorate, 22 other advanced degrees awarded. *Degree requirements:* For master's, thesis or alternative; for doctorate, comprehensive exam, thesis/dissertation; for CAS, thesis. *Entrance requirements:* For master's, personal statement, transcripts, three letters of recommendation, resume; for doctorate, GRE, master's degree, writing sample, resume, three letters of recommendation, transcripts; for CAS, master's degree, minimum three years of teaching experience, resume, personal statement, three letters of reference. Additional exam requirements/recommendations for international students: Required—TOEFL (minimum score 100 iBT). *Application deadline:* For fall admission, 6/15 for domestic and international students; for spring admission, 12/1 for domestic students, 10/15 for international students; for summer admission, 3/1 for domestic and international students. Applications are processed on a rolling basis. Application fee: $75. Electronic applications accepted. *Financial support:* Fellowships with full tuition reimbursements, research assistantships, teaching assistantships, career-related internships or fieldwork, and scholarships/grants available. Financial award application deadline: 1/15; financial award applicants required to submit FAFSA. *Faculty research:* Curriculum and instruction leadership for equity and excellence, information management in school, supervision of instruction, leadership for literacy development, assessment of teaching. *Unit head:* Dr. Benjamin Dotger, Chair of Teaching and Leadership/Professor, 315-443-2685, E-mail: bdotger@syr.edu. *Application contact:* Speranza Migliore, Graduate Admissions Recruiter, 315-443-2505, E-mail: gradrcrt@syr.edu.
Website: http://soe.syr.edu/academic/teaching_and_leadership/graduate/CAS/educational_leadership/default.aspx

Tarleton State University, College of Graduate Studies, College of Education, Department of Curriculum and Instruction, Stephenville, TX 76402. Offers curriculum and instruction (M Ed); educational diagnostician (M Ed); elementary education (M Ed); instructional design and technology (M Ed); instructional leadership (M Ed); secondary education (M Ed); special education (M Ed); technology applications (M Ed); technology director (M Ed). *Program availability:* Part-time, evening/weekend. *Faculty:* 7 full-time (5 women), 4 part-time/adjunct (2 women). *Students:* 7 full-time (6 women), 156 part-time (137 women); includes 40 minority (11 Black or African American, non-Hispanic/Latino; 25 Hispanic/Latino; 4 Two or more races, non-Hispanic/Latino). Average age 38. 55 applicants, 96% accepted, 46 enrolled. In 2017, 33 master's awarded. *Degree requirements:* For master's, comprehensive exam, thesis (for some programs). *Entrance requirements:* For master's, GRE General Test, minimum GPA of 3.0. Additional exam requirements/recommendations for international students: Required—TOEFL (minimum score 550 paper-based; 80 iBT), IELTS (minimum score 6). *Application deadline:* For fall admission, 8/15 priority date for domestic students; for spring admission, 1/7 for domestic students. Applications are processed on a rolling basis. Application fee: $45 ($145 for international students). Electronic applications accepted. *Expenses:* Contact institution. *Financial support:* Research assistantships, teaching assistantships, career-related internships or fieldwork, Federal Work-Study, and institutionally sponsored loans available. Support available to part-time students. Financial award application deadline: 5/1; financial award applicants required to submit FAFSA. *Unit head:* Dr. Jordan Barkley, Dean, 254-968-9089, E-mail: jbarkley@tarleton.edu. *Application contact:* Information Contact, 254-968-9104, Fax: 254-968-9670, E-mail: gradoffice@tarleton.edu.
Website: http://www.tarleton.edu/cimasters/

Tarleton State University, College of Graduate Studies, College of Education, Department of Educational Leadership and Technology, Stephenville, TX 76402. Offers educational administration (M Ed); educational leadership (Ed D, Certificate). *Program availability:* Part-time, evening/weekend, 100% online, blended/hybrid learning. *Faculty:* 7 full-time (3 women), 4 part-time/adjunct (3 women). *Students:* 7 full-time (5 women), 116 part-time (75 women); includes 36 minority (23 Black or African American, non-Hispanic/Latino; 2 American Indian or Alaska Native, non-Hispanic/Latino; 1 Asian, non-Hispanic/Latino; 9 Hispanic/Latino; 1 Two or more races, non-Hispanic/Latino), 1 international. Average age 42. 44 applicants, 48% accepted, 18 enrolled. In 2017, 36 master's, 13 doctorates awarded. *Degree requirements:* For master's, comprehensive exam, thesis optional; for doctorate, thesis/dissertation. *Entrance requirements:* For master's, GRE General Test, minimum GPA of 3.0; for doctorate, GRE, 4 letters of reference, leadership portfolio. Additional exam requirements/recommendations for international students: Required—TOEFL (minimum score 550 paper-based; 80 iBT), IELTS (minimum score 6). *Application deadline:* For fall admission, 8/15 priority date for domestic students; for spring admission, 1/7 for domestic students. Applications are processed on a rolling basis. Application fee: $45 ($145 for international students). Electronic applications accepted. *Expenses:* Contact institution. *Financial support:* Teaching assistantships, career-related internships or fieldwork, Federal Work-Study, and institutionally sponsored loans available. Support available to part-time students. Financial award application deadline: 5/1; financial award applicants required to submit FAFSA. *Unit head:* Dr. Don Beach, Interim Doctoral Program Coordinator, 254-968-9092, E-mail: beach@tarleton.edu. *Application contact:* Information Contact, 254-968-9104, Fax: 254-968-9670, E-mail: gradoffice@tarleton.edu.
Website: http://www.tarleton.edu/edlps/

Teachers College, Columbia University, Department of Organization and Leadership, New York, NY 10027-6696. Offers adult education guided intensive study (Ed D); adult learning and leadership (Ed M, MA, Ed D); educational leadership (Ed D); higher and postsecondary education (MA, Ed D); leadership, policy and politics (Ed D); nurse executive (MA, Ed D), including administration studies (MA), professorial studies (MA); private school leadership (Ed M, MA); public school building leadership (Ed M, MA); social and organizational psychology (MA); urban education leaders (Ed D); MA/MBA. *Program availability:* Part-time, evening/weekend. *Students:* 342 full-time (244 women), 378 part-time (256 women); includes 288 minority (106 Black or African American, non-Hispanic/Latino; 69 Asian, non-Hispanic/Latino; 92 Hispanic/Latino; 21 Two or more races, non-Hispanic/Latino), 86 international. Average age 33. 1,063 applicants, 59% accepted, 405 enrolled. *Degree requirements:* For doctorate, thesis/dissertation. *Unit head:* Prof. Bill Baldwin, Chair, E-mail: wjb12@tc.columbia.edu. *Application contact:* David Estrella, Director of Admission, 212-678-3305, E-mail: estrella@tc.columbia.edu.

Teachers College of San Joaquin, Master's Program in Education, Stockton, CA 95206. Offers early education (M Ed); educational inquiry (M Ed); educational leadership and school development (M Ed); science, technology, engineering, and mathematics (M Ed); special education (M Ed).

Temple University, College of Education, Department of Educational Leadership and Policy Studies, Philadelphia, PA 19122-6096. Offers Ed M, Ed D. *Program availability:* Part-time, evening/weekend. *Faculty:* 7 full-time (3 women). *Students:* 19 full-time (15 women), 70 part-time (41 women); includes 32 minority (19 Black or African American, non-Hispanic/Latino; 1 American Indian or Alaska Native, non-Hispanic/Latino; 5 Asian, non-Hispanic/Latino; 7 Hispanic/Latino), 2 international. 136 applicants, 63% accepted, 51 enrolled. In 2017, 4 master's awarded. Terminal master's awarded for partial completion of doctoral program. *Degree requirements:* For master's, comprehensive exam, thesis or alternative, internship; for doctorate, thesis/dissertation, preliminary exam. *Entrance requirements:* For master's, GRE General Test or MAT, minimum undergraduate GPA of 3.0, 2 letters of recommendation, goal statement, resume; for doctorate, GRE General Test or MAT, minimum undergraduate GPA of 3.0, 3 letters of recommendation, goal statement, resume. Additional exam requirements/recommendations for international students: Required—TOEFL (minimum score 550

paper-based; 79 iBT). *Application deadline:* For fall admission, 1/5 for domestic students, 10/7 for international students; for spring admission, 11/1 for domestic students, 11/3 for international students. Application fee: $60. Electronic applications accepted. *Expenses:* Tuition, state resident: full-time $16,164; part-time $898 per credit hour. Tuition, nonresident: full-time $22,158; part-time $1231 per credit hour. *Required fees:* $890; $445 per semester. Full-time tuition and fees vary according to course load, degree level, campus/location and program. *Financial support:* In 2017–18, 2 students received support, including 1 research assistantship with full tuition reimbursement available (averaging $20,333 per year), 1 teaching assistantship with full tuition reimbursement available (averaging $17,046 per year); career-related internships or fieldwork, Federal Work-Study, scholarships/grants, health care benefits, and unspecified assistantships also available. Financial award application deadline: 1/15; financial award applicants required to submit FAFSA. *Faculty research:* School leadership, educational policy, educational accountability, democratic leadership, equity and access. *Unit head:* Dr. Joan Shapiro, Professor, 215-204-6645, E-mail: joan.shapiro@temple.edu. *Application contact:* Felicia Neuber, Enrollment Management, 215-204-8011, E-mail: educate@temple.edu.
Website: http://education.temple.edu/leadership

Tennessee Technological University, College of Graduate Studies, College of Education, Department of Curriculum and Instruction, Program in Instructional Leadership, Cookeville, TN 38505. Offers MA, Ed S. *Accreditation:* NCATE. *Program availability:* Part-time, evening/weekend. *Faculty:* 9 full-time (3 women). *Students:* 7 full-time (5 women), 41 part-time (27 women); includes 8 minority (7 Black or African American, non-Hispanic/Latino; 1 Two or more races, non-Hispanic/Latino). 24 applicants, 63% accepted, 13 enrolled. In 2017, 4 master's, 16 other advanced degrees awarded. *Degree requirements:* For master's and Ed S, comprehensive exam, thesis or alternative. *Entrance requirements:* For master's and Ed S, MAT or GRE. Additional exam requirements/recommendations for international students: Required—TOEFL (minimum score 527 paper-based; 71 iBT), IELTS (minimum score 5.5), PTE (minimum score 48), or TOEIC (Test of English as an International Communication). *Application deadline:* For fall admission, 8/1 for domestic students, 5/1 for international students; for spring admission, 12/1 for domestic students, 10/1 for international students; for summer admission, 5/1 for domestic students, 2/1 for international students. Applications are processed on a rolling basis. Application fee: $35 ($40 for international students). Electronic applications accepted. *Expenses:* Tuition, state resident: full-time $9925; part-time $565 per credit hour. Tuition, nonresident: full-time $22,993; part-time $1291 per credit hour. *Financial support:* Fellowships, research assistantships, teaching assistantships, and career-related internships or fieldwork available. Financial award application deadline: 4/1. *Faculty research:* School board member training, community school education. *Unit head:* Dr. Jeremy Wendt, Interim Chairperson, 931-372-3181, Fax: 931-372-6270, E-mail: jwendt@tntech.edu. *Application contact:* Shelia K. Kendrick, Coordinator of Graduate Studies, 931-372-3808, Fax: 931-372-3497, E-mail: skendrick@tntech.edu.

Texas A&M International University, Office of Graduate Studies and Research, College of Education, Department of Professional Programs, Laredo, TX 78041. Offers educational administration (MS Ed); generic special education (MS Ed); school counseling (MS). *Entrance requirements:* Additional exam requirements/recommendations for international students: Required—TOEFL (minimum score 550 paper-based; 79 iBT).

Texas A&M University, College of Education and Human Development, Department of Educational Administration and Human Resource Development, College Station, TX 77843. Offers educational administration (M Ed, MS, Ed D, PhD); educational human resource development (MS, PhD). *Program availability:* Part-time. *Faculty:* 29. *Students:* 100 full-time (70 women), 275 part-time (169 women); includes 141 minority (45 Black or African American, non-Hispanic/Latino; 10 Asian, non-Hispanic/Latino; 78 Hispanic/Latino; 2 Native Hawaiian or other Pacific Islander, non-Hispanic/Latino; 6 Two or more races, non-Hispanic/Latino), 27 international. Average age 36. 144 applicants, 69% accepted, 81 enrolled. In 2017, 98 master's, 14 doctorates awarded. *Degree requirements:* For master's, thesis optional; for doctorate, thesis/dissertation. *Entrance requirements:* For master's, GRE General Test, writing exam, interview, professional experience; for doctorate, GRE General Test, writing exam, interview/presentation, professional experience. Additional exam requirements/recommendations for international students: Required—TOEFL (minimum score 550 paper-based; 80 iBT), IELTS (minimum score 6), PTE (minimum score 53). *Application deadline:* For fall admission, 12/1 for domestic and international students; for spring admission, 8/15 for domestic and international students. Application fee: $50 ($90 for international students). Electronic applications accepted. *Expenses:* Contact institution. *Financial support:* In 2017–18, 182 students received support, including 4 fellowships with tuition reimbursements available (averaging $1,170 per year), 38 research assistantships with tuition reimbursements available (averaging $9,628 per year), 21 teaching assistantships with tuition reimbursements available (averaging $11,667 per year); career-related internships or fieldwork, institutionally sponsored loans, scholarships/grants, traineeships, health care benefits, tuition waivers (full and partial), and unspecified assistantships also available. Support available to part-time students. Financial award application deadline: 3/15; financial award applicants required to submit FAFSA. *Faculty research:* Higher education administration, public school administration, student affairs. *Unit head:* Dr. Fred M. Nafukho, Head, 979-862-3395, Fax: 979-862-4347, E-mail: fnafukho@tamu.edu. *Application contact:* Joyce Nelson, Director of Academic Advising, 979-845-3017, Fax: 979-862-4347, E-mail: eahradvisor@tamu.edu.
Website: http://eahr.tamu.edu

Texas A&M University–Central Texas, Graduate Studies and Research, Killeen, TX 76549. Offers accounting (MS); business administration (MBA); clinical mental health counseling (MS); criminal justice (MCJ); curriculum and instruction (M Ed); educational administration (M Ed); educational psychology - experimental psychology (MS); history (MA); human resource management (MS); information systems (MS); liberal studies (MS); management and leadership (MS); marriage and family therapy (MS); mathematics (MS); political science (MA); school counseling (M Ed); school psychology (Ed S).

Texas A&M University–Commerce, College of Education and Human Services, Commerce, TX 75429. Offers counseling (M Ed, MS, PhD); early childhood education (M Ed, MS); educational administration (M Ed, MS, Ed D); educational psychology (PhD); educational technology leadership (M Ed, MS); educational technology library science (M Ed, MS); elementary education (M Ed); health, kinesiology and sports studies (MS); higher education (MS, Ed D); psychology (MS); reading (M Ed, MS); secondary education (M Ed, MS); social work (MSW); special education (M Ed, MS); supervision, curriculum and instruction-elementary education (Ed D); training and development (MS). *Program availability:* Part-time, evening/weekend, 100% online, blended/hybrid learning. *Faculty:* 91 full-time (51 women), 38 part-time/adjunct (31 women). *Students:* 400 full-time (310 women), 1,400 part-time (1,117 women); includes 724 minority (412 Black or African American, non-Hispanic/Latino; 8 American Indian or Alaska Native, non-Hispanic/Latino; 24 Asian, non-Hispanic/Latino; 220 Hispanic/Latino; 60 Two or more races, non-Hispanic/Latino), 18 international. Average age 37. 951 applicants, 46% accepted, 331 enrolled. In 2017, 564 master's, 24 doctorates awarded.

Degree requirements: For master's, comprehensive exam, thesis optional, departmental qualifying exams (for some programs); for doctorate, comprehensive exam, thesis/dissertation, departmental qualifying exam; for SSP, comprehensive exam, thesis optional. *Entrance requirements:* For master's and doctorate, GRE General Test. Additional exam requirements/recommendations for international students: Required—TOEFL (minimum score 550 paper-based; 79 iBT), IELTS (minimum score 6). *Application deadline:* For fall admission, 6/1 priority date for international students; for spring admission, 10/15 priority date for international students; for summer admission, 3/15 priority date for international students. Applications are processed on a rolling basis. Application fee: $50. Electronic applications accepted. *Expenses:* Tuition, state resident: full-time $3630. Tuition, nonresident: full-time $11,100. *Required fees:* $2564. Tuition and fees vary according to course load, degree level and program. *Financial support:* In 2017–18, 84 students received support, including 40 research assistantships with partial tuition reimbursements available (averaging $10,800 per year), 12 teaching assistantships with partial tuition reimbursements available (averaging $13,000 per year); career-related internships or fieldwork, Federal Work-Study, institutionally sponsored loans, scholarships/grants, health care benefits, and unspecified assistantships also available. Financial award application deadline: 6/15; financial award applicants required to submit FAFSA. *Faculty research:* Cognitive and bilingual education, positive behavioral intervention, literacy, math readiness. *Total annual research expenditures:* $1.1 million. *Unit head:* Dr. Timothy Letzring, Dean, 903-886-5181, Fax: 903-886-5905, E-mail: tim.letzring@tamuc.edu. *Application contact:* Vicky Turner, Doctoral Degree and Special Programs Coordinator, 903-886-5167, E-mail: vicky.turner@tamuc.edu.
Website: http://www.tamuc.edu/academics/graduateSchool/programs/education/default.aspx

Texas A&M University–Corpus Christi, College of Graduate Studies, College of Education and Human Development, Program in Educational Administration, Corpus Christi, TX 78412. Offers MS. *Program availability:* Part-time, evening/weekend. *Students:* 2 full-time (1 woman), 40 part-time (28 women); includes 31 minority (all Hispanic/Latino). Average age 34. 16 applicants, 81% accepted, 11 enrolled. In 2017, 17 master's awarded. *Degree requirements:* For master's, comprehensive exam. *Entrance requirements:* For master's, minimum GPA of 3.0 in last 60 hours; essay (approximately 300-400 words in length). Additional exam requirements/recommendations for international students: Required—TOEFL (minimum score 550 paper-based; 79 iBT), IELTS (minimum score 6.5). *Application deadline:* For fall admission, 8/10 for domestic students, 5/1 for international students; for spring admission, 1/10 for domestic students, 9/1 for international students; for summer admission, 5/15 for domestic students, 2/1 for international students. Applications are processed on a rolling basis. Application fee: $50 ($70 for international students). Electronic applications accepted. *Expenses:* Tuition, state resident: full-time $3568; part-time $198.24 per credit hour. Tuition, nonresident: full-time $11,038; part-time $613.24 per credit hour. *Required fees:* $2129; $1422.58 per semester. Tuition and fees vary according to program. *Financial support:* In 2017–18, 8 students received support. Research assistantships, teaching assistantships, career-related internships or fieldwork, Federal Work-Study, institutionally sponsored loans, scholarships/grants, health care benefits, and unspecified assistantships available. Support available to part-time students. Financial award application deadline: 3/15; financial award applicants required to submit FAFSA. *Unit head:* Dr. Lynn Hemmer, Chair, 361-825-3702, E-mail: lynn.hemmer@tamucc.edu. *Application contact:* Graduate Admissions Coordinator, 361-825-2177, Fax: 361-825-2755, E-mail: gradweb@tamucc.edu.
Website: http://education.tamucc.edu/

Texas A&M University–Corpus Christi, College of Graduate Studies, College of Education and Human Development, Program in Educational Leadership, Corpus Christi, TX 78412. Offers Ed D. *Program availability:* Part-time, evening/weekend. *Students:* 9 full-time (7 women), 46 part-time (38 women); includes 31 minority (all Hispanic/Latino). Average age 45. 17 applicants, 76% accepted, 13 enrolled. In 2017, 13 doctorates awarded. *Degree requirements:* For doctorate, thesis/dissertation. *Entrance requirements:* For doctorate, GMAT/GRE (taken within 5 years), master's degree, minimum graduate GPA of 3.0 in last 60 hours, essay (300-400 words in length), 4 reference forms, resume or curriculum vitae. Additional exam requirements/recommendations for international students: Required—TOEFL (minimum score 550 paper-based; 79 iBT), IELTS (minimum score 6.5). *Application deadline:* For fall admission, 6/5 for domestic students, 6/15 for international students; for spring admission, 10/15 for domestic and international students; for summer admission, 2/15 for domestic and international students. Applications are processed on a rolling basis. Application fee: $50 ($70 for international students). Electronic applications accepted. *Expenses:* Tuition, state resident: full-time $3568; part-time $198.24 per credit hour. Tuition, nonresident: full-time $11,038; part-time $613.24 per credit hour. *Required fees:* $2129; $1422.58 per semester. Tuition and fees vary according to program. *Financial support:* Research assistantships, career-related internships or fieldwork, Federal Work-Study, institutionally sponsored loans, scholarships/grants, health care benefits, and unspecified assistantships available. Support available to part-time students. Financial award application deadline: 3/15; financial award applicants required to submit FAFSA. *Unit head:* Dr. Randall Bowden, Associate Professor, 361-825-6034, E-mail: randall.bowden@tamucc.edu. *Application contact:* Graduate Admissions Coordinator, 361-825-2177, Fax: 361-825-2755, E-mail: gradweb@tamucc.edu.
Website: http://elci.tamucc.edu/

Texas A&M University–Kingsville, College of Graduate Studies, College of Education and Human Performance, Department of Educational Leadership and Counseling, Program in Educational Administration, Kingsville, TX 78363. Offers MA, MS. *Program availability:* Part-time, evening/weekend, online only, 100% online, blended/hybrid learning. *Entrance requirements:* Additional exam requirements/recommendations for international students: Required—TOEFL (minimum score 550 paper-based; 79 iBT); Recommended—IELTS. Electronic applications accepted.

Texas A&M University–Kingsville, College of Graduate Studies, College of Education and Human Performance, Department of Educational Leadership and Counseling, Program in Educational Leadership, Kingsville, TX 78363. Offers PhD. Program offered jointly with Texas A&M University. *Program availability:* Part-time, evening/weekend. *Degree requirements:* For doctorate, variable foreign language requirement, comprehensive exam, thesis/dissertation (for some programs). *Entrance requirements:* For doctorate, GRE, MAT, GMAT, two-page statement of desire to pursue doctoral degree in educational leadership; 3 letters of recommendation; curriculum vitae listing accomplishments or any other evidence of scholarship, leadership, and/or professionalism. Additional exam requirements/recommendations for international students: Required—TOEFL (minimum score 550 paper-based; 79 iBT). Electronic applications accepted.

Texas A&M University–San Antonio, Department of Educator and Leadership Preparation, San Antonio, TX 78224. Offers bilingual education (MS); early childhood education (M Ed); educational administration (MA); reading specialization (MS); special education (M Ed), including educational diagnostician. *Program availability:* Part-time, evening/weekend, online learning. *Faculty:* 19 full-time (14 women), 8 part-time/adjunct (2 women). *Students:* 24 full-time (21 women), 188 part-time (143 women); includes 163

Educational Leadership and Administration

minority (7 Black or African American, non-Hispanic/Latino; 1 Asian, non-Hispanic/Latino; 149 Hispanic/Latino; 6 Two or more races, non-Hispanic/Latino), 1 international. Average age 36. 191 applicants, 62% accepted, 67 enrolled. In 2017, 70 master's awarded. *Degree requirements:* For master's, comprehensive exam, thesis or alternative. *Entrance requirements:* For master's, GRE (Quantitative and Verbal) or MAT. Additional exam requirements/recommendations for international students: Required—TOEFL (minimum score 550 paper-based; 79 iBT), IELTS (minimum score 6). *Application deadline:* For fall admission, 3/15 priority date for domestic and international students; for spring admission, 11/1 priority date for domestic and international students; for summer admission, 4/1 priority date for domestic and international students. Applications are processed on a rolling basis. Application fee: $35 ($50 for international students). Electronic applications accepted. *Expenses:* Tuition, state resident: full-time $3475; part-time $1930 per semester. Tuition, nonresident: full-time $10,945; part-time $6080 per semester. *Required fees:* $2148; $1412 per year. $706 per semester. Tuition and fees vary according to course load. *Financial support:* In 2017–18, 16 students received support. Research assistantships, Federal Work-Study, scholarships/grants, and tuition waivers available. Financial award application deadline: 3/15; financial award applicants required to submit FAFSA. *Faculty research:* Equity in education, biliteracy practices among Latina and immigrants, academic achievement of low socio-economic students, equity practices in instruction and educational leadership in diverse settings, racial identity development and multicultural education. *Unit head:* Dr. Debbie Vera, Department Chair. *Application contact:* Caitie Garza, Graduate Admissions Coordinator, 210-784-1300, E-mail: beajaguar@tamusa.edu.
Website: http://www.tamusa.edu/collegeofeducationandhumandevelopment/educatorleadershippreparation/index.html

Texas A&M University–Texarkana, Graduate Studies and Research, College of Education and Liberal Arts, Texarkana, TX 75503. Offers adult education (MS); curriculum and instruction (M Ed); education (MS); educational administration (M Ed); English (MA); instructional technology (MS); interdisciplinary studies (MA, MS); special education (MS). *Program availability:* Part-time, evening/weekend. *Degree requirements:* For master's, comprehensive exam (for some programs), thesis optional. *Entrance requirements:* For master's, minimum GPA of 2.5 on last 60 hours of bachelor's degree. Additional exam requirements/recommendations for international students: Required—TOEFL. Electronic applications accepted.

Texas Christian University, College of Education, Doctoral Programs in Education, Fort Worth, TX 76129. Offers counseling and counselor education (PhD); curriculum studies (PhD); educational leadership (Ed D); higher educational leadership (Ed D); science education (PhD); MBA/Ed D. *Program availability:* Part-time, evening/weekend. *Faculty:* 29 full-time (21 women), 3 part-time/adjunct (1 woman). *Students:* 80 full-time (57 women), 26 part-time (13 women); includes 41 minority (15 Black or African American, non-Hispanic/Latino; 6 Asian, non-Hispanic/Latino; 17 Hispanic/Latino; 3 Two or more races, non-Hispanic/Latino), 6 international. Average age 39. 109 applicants, 50% accepted, 23 enrolled. In 2017, 12 doctorates awarded. *Degree requirements:* For doctorate, comprehensive exam, thesis/dissertation. *Entrance requirements:* For doctorate, GRE General Test. Additional exam requirements/recommendations for international students: Required—TOEFL (minimum score 550 paper-based; 80 iBT). *Application deadline:* For fall admission, 2/1 for domestic and international students; for winter admission, 2/1 for domestic and international students; for spring admission, 11/16 for domestic and international students. Application fee: $60. Electronic applications accepted. *Financial support:* In 2017–18, 69 students received support, including 1 fellowship with full tuition reimbursement available (averaging $18,500 per year), 8 research assistantships with full tuition reimbursements available (averaging $18,500 per year), 7 teaching assistantships with full tuition reimbursements available (averaging $18,500 per year); career-related internships or fieldwork, scholarships/grants, health care benefits, and unspecified assistantships also available. Support available to part-time students. Financial award application deadline: 2/1. *Unit head:* Dr. Jan Lacina, Associate Dean, 817-257-6786, Fax: 817-257-7466, E-mail: j.lacina@tcu.edu. *Application contact:* Lori Kimball, Administrative Program Specialist, 817-257-7661, Fax: 817-257-7466, E-mail: l.kimball@tcu.edu.
Website: http://coe.tcu.edu/graduate-overview/

Texas Christian University, College of Education, Master's Programs in Education, Fort Worth, TX 76129. Offers counseling (M Ed); curriculum and instruction (M Ed), including curriculum studies, language and literacy, math education, science education; education (MAT); educational leadership (M Ed); special education (M Ed). *Program availability:* Part-time, evening/weekend. *Faculty:* 29 full-time (21 women), 3 part-time/adjunct (1 woman). *Students:* 124 full-time (94 women), 14 part-time (12 women); includes 52 minority (14 Black or African American, non-Hispanic/Latino; 2 American Indian or Alaska Native, non-Hispanic/Latino; 3 Asian, non-Hispanic/Latino; 28 Hispanic/Latino; 5 Two or more races, non-Hispanic/Latino), 1 international. Average age 28. 172 applicants, 69% accepted, 86 enrolled. In 2017, 62 master's awarded. *Degree requirements:* For master's, comprehensive exam (for some programs), thesis (for some programs). *Entrance requirements:* For master's, GRE General Test; Pre-Admission Content Test (for MAT). Additional exam requirements/recommendations for international students: Required—TOEFL (minimum score 550 paper-based; 80 iBT). *Application deadline:* For fall admission, 3/1 for domestic and international students; for spring admission, 11/16 for domestic and international students; for summer admission, 3/1 for domestic and international students. Application fee: $60. Electronic applications accepted. *Financial support:* In 2017–18, 124 students received support, including 1 research assistantship with full tuition reimbursement available (averaging $15,000 per year), 29 teaching assistantships with full tuition reimbursements available (averaging $15,000 per year); career-related internships or fieldwork, scholarships/grants, and unspecified assistantships also available. Support available to part-time students. Financial award application deadline: 3/1. *Unit head:* Dr. Jan Lacina, Associate Dean, 817-257-6786, Fax: 817-257-7466, E-mail: j.lacina@tcu.edu. *Application contact:* Lori Kimball, Administrative Program Specialist, 817-257-7661, Fax: 817-257-7466, E-mail: l.kimball@tcu.edu.
Website: http://coe.tcu.edu/graduate-overview/

Texas Southern University, College of Education, Department of Educational Administration and Foundation, Houston, TX 77004-4584. Offers educational administration (M Ed, Ed D). *Program availability:* Part-time, evening/weekend. *Degree requirements:* For master's, comprehensive exam; for doctorate, comprehensive exam, thesis/dissertation. *Entrance requirements:* For master's, GRE General Test, minimum GPA of 2.5; for doctorate, GRE General Test or MAT, master's degree, minimum B+ average. Additional exam requirements/recommendations for international students: Required—TOEFL. Electronic applications accepted.

Texas State University, The Graduate College, College of Education, Program in Educational Leadership, San Marcos, TX 78666. Offers educational leadership (M Ed); instructional leadership (MA). *Program availability:* Part-time, evening/weekend. *Faculty:* 1 (woman) full-time, 15 part-time/adjunct (10 women). *Students:* 2 full-time (both women), 98 part-time (76 women); includes 39 minority (8 Black or African American, non-Hispanic/Latino; 1 Asian, non-Hispanic/Latino; 29 Hispanic/Latino; 1 Two or more races, non-Hispanic/Latino). Average age 35. 48 applicants, 67% accepted, 21 enrolled.

In 2017, 51 master's awarded. *Degree requirements:* For master's, comprehensive exam, thesis (for some programs). *Entrance requirements:* For master's, GRE General Test (preferred), baccalaureate degree from regionally-accredited institution with minimum GPA of 2.75 in last 60 hours of undergraduate course work. Additional exam requirements/recommendations for international students: Required—TOEFL (minimum score 550 paper-based; 78 iBT), IELTS (minimum score 6.5). *Application deadline:* For fall admission, 3/1 priority date for domestic and international students; for summer admission, 5/1 for domestic students, 3/15 for international students. Applications are processed on a rolling basis. Application fee: $40 ($90 for international students). Electronic applications accepted. *Expenses:* Tuition, state resident: full-time $7868; part-time $3934 per semester. Tuition, nonresident: full-time $17,828; part-time $8914 per semester. *Required fees:* $2092; $1435 per semester. Tuition and fees vary according to course load. *Financial support:* In 2017–18, 33 students received support. Research assistantships, teaching assistantships, career-related internships or fieldwork, Federal Work-Study, institutionally sponsored loans, and scholarships/grants available. Support available to part-time students. Financial award application deadline: 3/1; financial award applicants required to submit FAFSA. *Unit head:* Dr. Bergeron Harris, Graduate Advisor, 512-245-9909, E-mail: bh26@txstate.edu. *Application contact:* Dr. Andrea Golato, Dean of Graduate School, 512-245-2581, Fax: 512-245-8365, E-mail: gradcollege@txstate.edu.
Website: http://www.txstate.edu/clas/Educational-Leadership.html

Texas State University, The Graduate College, College of Education, Program in School Improvement, San Marcos, TX 78666. Offers PhD. *Program availability:* Part-time. *Faculty:* 11 full-time (3 women), 1 part-time/adjunct (0 women). *Students:* 21 full-time (13 women), 55 part-time (32 women); includes 36 minority (6 Black or African American, non-Hispanic/Latino; 30 Hispanic/Latino), 1 international. Average age 42. 44 applicants, 36% accepted, 4 enrolled. In 2017, 8 doctorates awarded. *Degree requirements:* For doctorate, comprehensive exam, thesis/dissertation. *Entrance requirements:* For doctorate, baccalaureate and master's degrees from regionally-accredited university (master's degree in an area related to proposed studies with minimum graduate GPA of 3.5); statement of purpose (500 words); 3 letters of reference addressing professional and academic background; resume. Additional exam requirements/recommendations for international students: Required—TOEFL (minimum score 78 iBT), IELTS (minimum score 6.5). *Application deadline:* For fall admission, 2/1 for domestic and international students. Applications are processed on a rolling basis. Application fee: $40 ($90 for international students). Electronic applications accepted. *Expenses:* Tuition, state resident: full-time $7868; part-time $3934 per semester. Tuition, nonresident: full-time $17,828; part-time $8914 per semester. *Required fees:* $2092; $1435 per semester. Tuition and fees vary according to course load. *Financial support:* In 2017–18, 45 students received support, including 7 research assistantships (averaging $26,111 per year), 1 teaching assistantship (averaging $12,152 per year); scholarships/grants and unspecified assistantships also available. Financial award application deadline: 3/1; financial award applicants required to submit FAFSA. *Faculty research:* Increasing college readiness and creating a college-going culture. *Total annual research expenditures:* $15,920. *Unit head:* Dr. Melissa Martinez, PhD Program Director, 512-245-4587, E-mail: mm224@txstate.edu. *Application contact:* Dr. Andrea Golato, Dean of Graduate School, 512-245-2581, Fax: 512-245-8365, E-mail: gradcollege@txstate.edu.
Website: http://si.education.txstate.edu

Texas Tech University, Graduate School, College of Education, Department of Educational Psychology and Leadership, Lubbock, TX 79409. Offers counselor education (M Ed, PhD); educational leadership (M Ed, Ed D, PhD); educational psychology (M Ed, PhD); higher education (M Ed); higher education administration (Ed D); higher education research (PhD); instructional technology (M Ed, Ed D); special education (M Ed, Ed D, PhD). *Accreditation:* ACA; NCATE. *Program availability:* Part-time, evening/weekend. *Faculty:* 64 full-time (30 women), 6 part-time/adjunct (all women). *Students:* 263 full-time (193 women), 637 part-time (490 women); includes 307 minority (84 Black or African American, non-Hispanic/Latino; 3 American Indian or Alaska Native, non-Hispanic/Latino; 4 Asian, non-Hispanic/Latino; 193 Hispanic/Latino; 23 Two or more races, non-Hispanic/Latino), 48 international. Average age 36. 510 applicants, 47% accepted, 185 enrolled. In 2017, 209 master's, 64 doctorates awarded. Terminal master's awarded for partial completion of doctoral program. *Degree requirements:* For master's, comprehensive exam, thesis optional; for doctorate, comprehensive exam, thesis/dissertation. *Entrance requirements:* For master's, GRE (for some programs); for doctorate, GRE. Additional exam requirements/recommendations for international students: Required—TOEFL (minimum score 550 paper-based; 79 iBT). *Application deadline:* For fall admission, 6/1 priority date for domestic students, 1/15 priority date for international students; for spring admission, 9/1 priority date for domestic students, 6/15 priority date for international students. Applications are processed on a rolling basis. Application fee: $60. Electronic applications accepted. *Expenses:* Contact institution. *Financial support:* In 2017–18, 366 students received support, including 360 fellowships (averaging $3,231 per year), 63 research assistantships (averaging $11,899 per year); teaching assistantships, scholarships/grants, and unspecified assistantships also available. Support available to part-time students. Financial award application deadline: 1/3; financial award applicants required to submit FAFSA. *Faculty research:* Cognitive, motivational, and developmental processes in learning; counseling education; instructional technology; generic special education and sensory impairment; community college administration; K-12 school administration. *Total annual research expenditures:* $127,956. *Unit head:* Dr. Hansel Burley, Chair, 806-834-5135, Fax: 806-742-2179, E-mail: hansel.burley@ttu.edu. *Application contact:* Pam Smith, Admissions Advisor, 806-834-2969, Fax: 806-742-2179, E-mail: pam.smith@ttu.edu.
Website: http://www.educ.ttu.edu/

Texas Woman's University, Graduate School, College of Professional Education, Department of Teacher Education, Denton, TX 76204. Offers educational administration (M Ed, MA); special education (M Ed, PhD), including educational diagnostician (M Ed); intervention specialist (M Ed); teaching, learning, and curriculum (M Ed, MA). *Program availability:* Part-time. *Faculty:* 9 full-time (7 women), 1 (woman) part-time/adjunct. *Students:* 20 full-time (17 women), 92 part-time (79 women); includes 41 minority (11 Black or African American, non-Hispanic/Latino; 1 American Indian or Alaska Native, non-Hispanic/Latino; 3 Asian, non-Hispanic/Latino; 24 Hispanic/Latino; 2 Two or more races, non-Hispanic/Latino), 1 international. Average age 38. 48 applicants, 71% accepted, 29 enrolled. In 2017, 36 master's, 4 doctorates awarded. Terminal master's awarded for partial completion of doctoral program. *Degree requirements:* For master's, comprehensive exam, thesis, professional paper (M Ed); for doctorate, comprehensive exam, thesis/dissertation, residency. *Entrance requirements:* For master's, minimum GPA of 3.0 on last 60 undergraduate hours, 2 letters of reference, resume, copy of certifications, teacher service record, statement of intent, interview (for MAT); for doctorate, GRE General Test, minimum GPA of 3.0, 3 letters of reference, resume, copy of certifications, teacher service record, statement of intent. Additional exam requirements/recommendations for international students: Required—TOEFL (minimum score 550 paper-based; Recommended—IELTS (minimum score 6.5), TSE (minimum score 53). *Application deadline:* For fall admission, 7/1 priority date for domestic students, 3/1 priority date for international students; for spring admission, 11/1

priority date for domestic students, 7/1 priority date for international students. Applications are processed on a rolling basis. Application fee: $50 ($75 for international students). Electronic applications accepted. *Expenses:* $7,520 per year full-time in-state; $16,820 per year full-time out-of-state. *Financial support:* In 2017–18, 21 students received support, including 5 research assistantships (averaging $32,980 per year); career-related internships or fieldwork, Federal Work-Study, institutionally sponsored loans, scholarships/grants, traineeships, health care benefits, and unspecified assistantships also available. Support available to part-time students. Financial award application deadline: 3/1; financial award applicants required to submit FAFSA. *Faculty research:* Experiential learning, classroom management, learning disabilities, staff and professional development, technology in the classroom. *Total annual research expenditures:* $272,198. *Unit head:* Dr. Diane Myers, Chair, 940-898-2271, Fax: 940-898-2270, E-mail: teachereducation@twu.edu. *Application contact:* Korie Hawkins, Associate Director of Admissions, Graduate Recruitment, 940-898-3188, Fax: 940-898-3081, E-mail: admissions@twu.edu.
Website: http://www.twu.edu/teacher-education/

Thomas Edison State University, Heavin School of Arts and Sciences, Program in Educational Leadership, Trenton, NJ 08608. Offers MAEL, Graduate Certificate. *Program availability:* Part-time, online learning. *Degree requirements:* For master's, field-based practicum, professional portfolio development. *Entrance requirements:* For master's, at least 3 years of teaching experience; valid teacher's certification; letter of recommendation from a building-level administrator; school setting and on-site mentor available to conduct site-based fieldwork and inquiry projects successfully for each course; statement of goals and objectives. Additional exam requirements/recommendations for international students: Required—TOEFL (minimum score 550 paper-based; 79 iBT). Electronic applications accepted.

Thomas More College, Program in Teacher Leader, Crestview Hills, KY 41017-3495. Offers M Ed. *Program availability:* Part-time, evening/weekend. *Degree requirements:* For master's, comprehensive exam. *Entrance requirements:* For master's, GRE, minimum undergraduate cumulative GPA of 2.7. Additional exam requirements/recommendations for international students: Required—TOEFL (minimum score 100 iBT). Electronic applications accepted.

Tiffin University, Program in Education, Tiffin, OH 44883-2161. Offers educational technology management (M Ed); higher education administration (M Ed). *Program availability:* Part-time, evening/weekend, online only, 100% online, blended/hybrid learning. *Entrance requirements:* Additional exam requirements/recommendations for international students: Required—TOEFL. Electronic applications accepted. *Expenses:* Contact institution.

Touro College, Graduate School of Education, New York, NY 10010. Offers education and special education (MS); instructional technology (MS); mathematics education (MS); school leadership (MS); teaching English to speakers of other languages (MS); teaching literacy (MS). *Accreditation:* TEAC. *Program availability:* Part-time, evening/weekend, online learning. *Faculty:* 52 full-time (34 women), 199 part-time/adjunct (136 women). *Students:* 756 full-time (686 women), 3,833 part-time (3,492 women). Average age 33. 1,422 applicants, 50% accepted, 675 enrolled. In 2017, 6 master's awarded. *Entrance requirements:* Additional exam requirements/recommendations for international students: Required—TOEFL (minimum score 83 iBT), IELTS (minimum score 6.5). *Application deadline:* For fall admission, 8/26 for domestic students, 7/15 for international students; for spring admission, 12/31 for domestic students, 12/15 for international students. Applications are processed on a rolling basis. Application fee: $50. *Financial support:* Federal Work-Study available. Financial award applicants required to submit FAFSA. *Faculty research:* Equity assistance, language development, scholarly communications, Latin American studies and cultural sensitivity, behavior management techniques and strategies in special education. *Unit head:* Dr. Jacob Easley, III, Dean, 212-463-0400 Ext. 5561, Fax: 212-462-4889, E-mail: jeasley@touro.edu. *Application contact:* Sharmilee Hoopnarine, Admissions, 212-463-0400.

Towson University, College of Education, Program in Instructional Leadership and Professional Development, Towson, MD 21252-0001. Offers CAS, Postbaccalaureate Certificate. *Students:* 3 full-time (2 women), 82 part-time (68 women); includes 25 minority (20 Black or African American, non-Hispanic/Latino; 2 Asian, non-Hispanic/Latino; 1 Hispanic/Latino; 2 Two or more races, non-Hispanic/Latino). *Application deadline:* For fall admission, 1/17 for domestic students, 5/15 for international students; for spring admission, 10/15 for domestic students, 12/1 for international students. Applications are processed on a rolling basis. Application fee: $45. Electronic applications accepted. *Expenses:* Tuition, state resident: full-time $7960; part-time $398 per unit. Tuition, nonresident: full-time $16,480; part-time $824 per unit. *Required fees:* $2600; $130 per year. $390 per term. *Unit head:* Carla Finkelstein, Graduate Director, 410-704-2974, E-mail: cfinkelstein@towson.edu. *Application contact:* Coverley Beidleman, Assistant Director of Graduate Admissions, 410-704-5630, Fax: 410-704-3030, E-mail: cbeidleman@towson.edu.
Website: http://www.towson.edu/coe/departments/leadership/grad/

Towson University, College of Education, Program in Special Education, Towson, MD 21252-0001. Offers special education (M Ed); teacher as leader in autism spectrum disorder (M Ed). *Accreditation:* NCATE. *Program availability:* Part-time, evening/weekend. *Students:* 3 full-time (all women), 156 part-time (145 women); includes 19 minority (6 Black or African American, non-Hispanic/Latino; 2 Asian, non-Hispanic/Latino; 10 Hispanic/Latino; 1 Two or more races, non-Hispanic/Latino). *Degree requirements:* For master's, thesis optional. *Entrance requirements:* For master's, letter of recommendation, bachelor's degree, professional teacher certification, minimum GPA of 3.0. *Application deadline:* For fall admission, 1/17 for domestic students, 5/15 for international students; for spring admission, 10/15 for domestic students, 12/1 for international students. Applications are processed on a rolling basis. Application fee: $45. Electronic applications accepted. *Expenses:* Tuition, state resident: full-time $7960; part-time $398 per unit. Tuition, nonresident: full-time $16,480; part-time $824 per unit. *Required fees:* $2600; $130 per year. $390 per term. *Unit head:* Dr. Andrea Parrish, Graduate Program Director, 410-704-3835, E-mail: aparrish@towson.edu. *Application contact:* Coverley Beidleman, Assistant Director of Graduate Admissions, 410-704-5630, Fax: 410-704-3030, E-mail: cbeidleman@towson.edu.
Website: http://www.towson.edu/coe/departments/specialed/gradspecialed/

Towson University, College of Liberal Arts, Program in Human Resource Development, Towson, MD 21252-0001. Offers education leadership (MS); general human resource management (MS). *Program availability:* Part-time, evening/weekend. *Students:* 23 full-time (19 women), 252 part-time (195 women); includes 63 minority (39 Black or African American, non-Hispanic/Latino; 11 Asian, non-Hispanic/Latino; 7 Hispanic/Latino; 6 Two or more races, non-Hispanic/Latino), 2 international. *Degree requirements:* For master's, comprehensive exam. *Entrance requirements:* For master's, bachelor's degree, 2 letters of recommendation, minimum GPA of 3.0, essay, resume. Additional exam requirements/recommendations for international students: Required—TOEFL. *Application deadline:* For fall admission, 1/17 for domestic students, 5/15 for international students; for spring admission, 10/15 for domestic students, 12/1 for international students. Applications are processed on a rolling basis. Application fee: $45. Electronic applications accepted. *Expenses:* Tuition, state resident: full-time $7960; part-time $398 per unit. Tuition, nonresident: full-time $16,480; part-time $824

per unit. *Required fees:* $2600; $130 per year. $390 per term. *Financial support:* Application deadline: 4/1. *Unit head:* Dr. Abby Mello, Graduate Program Director, 410-704-3364, E-mail: amello@towson.edu. *Application contact:* Coverley Beidleman, Assistant Director of Graduate Admissions, 410-704-5630, Fax: 410-704-3030, E-mail: cbeidleman@towson.edu.
Website: http://www.towson.edu/cla/departments/interdisciplinary/grad/hr/

Towson University, Jess and Mildred Fisher College of Science and Mathematics, Program in Integrated STEM Instructional Leadership, Towson, MD 21252-0001. Offers Postbaccalaureate Certificate. *Students:* 10 part-time (8 women); includes 1 minority (Two or more races, non-Hispanic/Latino). *Entrance requirements:* For degree, bachelor's degree, two years of teaching experience, minimum GPA of 3.0, two letters of recommendation, one-page personal statement, resume. *Application deadline:* For fall admission, 1/17 for domestic students, 5/15 for international students; for spring admission, 10/15 for domestic students, 12/1 for international students. Applications are processed on a rolling basis. Electronic applications accepted. *Expenses:* Tuition, state resident: full-time $7960; part-time $398 per unit. Tuition, nonresident: full-time $16,480; part-time $824 per unit. *Required fees:* $2600; $130 per year. $390 per term. *Unit head:* Dr. Pam Lottero-Perdue, Program Director, 410-704-4598, E-mail: plotteroperdue@towson.edu. *Application contact:* Coverley Beidleman, Assistant Director of Graduate Admissions, 410-704-5630, Fax: 410-704-3030, E-mail: cbeidleman@towson.edu.
Website: http://www.towson.edu/fcsm/departments/physics/grad/stempbc/

Trevecca Nazarene University, Graduate Education Program, Nashville, TN 37210-2877. Offers accountability and instructional leadership (Ed S); curriculum and instruction for Christian school educators (M Ed); curriculum and instruction K-12 (M Ed); educational leadership (M Ed); English second language (M Ed); library and information science (MLI Sc); special education: visual impairments (M Ed); teaching (MAT), including teaching 6-12, teaching K-5. *Accreditation:* NCATE. *Program availability:* Part-time, evening/weekend, online learning. *Faculty:* 8 full-time (6 women), 22 part-time/adjunct (18 women). *Students:* 150 full-time (114 women), 3 part-time (1 woman); includes 54 minority (49 Black or African American, non-Hispanic/Latino; 4 Hispanic/Latino; 1 Two or more races, non-Hispanic/Latino). Average age 36. In 2017, 57 master's, 4 other advanced degrees awarded. *Degree requirements:* For master's, comprehensive exam, exit assessment/e-portfolio. *Entrance requirements:* For master's, GRE or MAT; PRAXIS (for MAT), minimum GPA of 3.0, official transcript from regionally-accredited institution, references, interview, writing sample, at least 3 years' successful teaching experience (for M Ed in educational leadership); for Ed S, GRE or MAT, master's degree with minimum GPA of 3.0, official transcript from regionally accredited institution, at least 3 years' successful teaching experience, interview, writing sample, background and fingerprinting check, recommendations. Additional exam requirements/recommendations for international students: Required—TOEFL (minimum score 550 paper-based). *Application deadline:* Applications are processed on a rolling basis. Electronic applications accepted. *Expenses:* Contact institution. *Financial support:* Applicants required to submit FAFSA. *Unit head:* Dr. Suzie Harris, Dean, School of Education, 615-248-1201, Fax: 615-248-1597, E-mail: admissions_ged@trevecca.edu. *Application contact:* 844-TNU-GRAD, E-mail: sgcsadmissions@trevecca.edu.
Website: http://www.trevecca.edu/soe

Trevecca Nazarene University, Graduate Leadership Programs, Nashville, TN 37210-2877. Offers leadership and professional practice (Ed D); organizational leadership (MOL). *Program availability:* Online learning. *Faculty:* 9 full-time (5 women), 27 part-time/adjunct (12 women). *Students:* 282 full-time (205 women), 214 part-time (141 women); includes 302 minority (254 Black or African American, non-Hispanic/Latino; 4 American Indian or Alaska Native, non-Hispanic/Latino; 1 Asian, non-Hispanic/Latino; 25 Hispanic/Latino; 1 Native Hawaiian or other Pacific Islander, non-Hispanic/Latino; 17 Two or more races, non-Hispanic/Latino), 1 international. Average age 40. In 2017, 68 master's, 75 doctorates awarded. *Degree requirements:* For master's, capstone course; for doctorate, thesis/dissertation, proposal study, symposium presentation. *Entrance requirements:* For master's, minimum GPA of 2.5, official transcript from regionally accredited institution; for doctorate, minimum GPA of 3.4, official transcript from regionally accredited institution, resume, writing sample, references. Additional exam requirements/recommendations for international students: Required—TOEFL (minimum score 550 paper-based; 80 iBT). *Application deadline:* Applications are processed on a rolling basis. Application fee: $0. Electronic applications accepted. *Expenses:* $420 per credit hour (MOL); $699 per credit hour (EdD). *Financial support:* Applicants required to submit FAFSA. *Unit head:* Dr. Ricky Christman, Associate Vice President and Dean, Graduate and Continuing Studies/Director of Master of Organizational Leadership, 615-248-1529, E-mail: sgcsadmissions@trevecca.edu. *Application contact:* 844-TNU-GRAD, E-mail: sgcsadmissions@trevecca.edu.

Trident University International, College of Education, Program in Educational Leadership, Cypress, CA 90630. Offers e-learning leadership (MA Ed, PhD); educational leadership (MA Ed); higher education leadership (PhD); K-12 leadership (PhD). *Program availability:* Part-time, evening/weekend, online learning. *Degree requirements:* For doctorate, comprehensive exam, thesis/dissertation, defense of dissertation. *Entrance requirements:* For master's, minimum GPA of 2.5 (students with GPA 3.0 or greater may transfer up to 30% of graduate level credits); for doctorate, minimum GPA of 3.4, course work in research methods or statistics. Additional exam requirements/recommendations for international students: Required—TOEFL. Electronic applications accepted.

Trinity Baptist College, Graduate Programs, Jacksonville, FL 32221. Offers Bible (MA); curriculum and instruction (M Ed); educational leadership (M Ed); special education (M Ed). *Program availability:* Online learning. *Faculty:* 6 full-time (1 woman), 5 part-time/adjunct (1 woman). *Students:* 13 part-time (5 women). *Entrance requirements:* For master's, GRE (for M Ed), 2 letters of recommendation; minimum GPA of 2.5 (for M Min), 3.0 (for M Ed); goals essay; official transcripts. Application fee: $45. *Expenses:* Tuition: Part-time $295 per hour. *Required fees:* $50 per term. One-time fee: $45 part-time. *Unit head:* Dr. Matthew Beemer, Senior Vice President, 904-596-2400, Fax: 904-596-2531, E-mail: mbeemer@tbc.edu.

Trinity University, Department of Education, Master of Education in School Leadership Program, San Antonio, TX 78212-7200. Offers M Ed. *Accreditation:* NCATE. *Program availability:* Part-time, evening/weekend. *Entrance requirements:* For master's, GRE or MAT, nomination from home school district, phone interview, interactive daylong leadership simulation process. Application fee: $50. *Financial support:* Fellowships, institutionally sponsored loans, and scholarships/grants available. Support available to part-time students. Financial award application deadline: 5/1; financial award applicants required to submit FAFSA. *Unit head:* Norvella Carter, Interim Chair, 210-999-7506, E-mail: ncarter1@trinity.edu. *Application contact:* Norvella Carter, Interim Chair, 210-999-7506, E-mail: ncarter1@trinity.edu.
Website: https://new.trinity.edu/academics/departments/education/master-education-school-leadership

Trinity Washington University, School of Education, Washington, DC 20017-1094. Offers clinical mental health counseling (MA); early childhood education (MAT); educating for change (M Ed); educational administration (MSA); elementary education (MAT); reading (M Ed); school counseling (MA); secondary education (MAT), including English, social studies; special education (MAT). *Accreditation:* NCATE. *Program*

Educational Leadership and Administration

availability: Part-time, evening/weekend. *Degree requirements:* For master's, thesis (for some programs), capstone project(s). *Entrance requirements:* For master's, PRAXIS I, minimum GPA of 2.8. Additional exam requirements/recommendations for international students: Required—TOEFL (minimum score 550 paper-based). *Faculty research:* Technology, literacy, special education, organizations, inclusion models.

Trinity Western University, School of Graduate Studies, Program in Leadership, Langley, BC V2Y 1Y1, Canada. Offers business (MA, Certificate); Christian ministry (MA); education (MA, Certificate); healthcare (MA, Certificate); non-profit (MA, Certificate). *Program availability:* Online learning. *Degree requirements:* For master's, major project. *Entrance requirements:* For master's, minimum GPA of 2.7. Additional exam requirements/recommendations for international students: Required—TOEFL (minimum score 620 paper-based; 105 iBT). Electronic applications accepted. *Expenses:* Contact institution. *Faculty research:* Servant leadership.

Troy University, Graduate School, College of Education, Program in Educational Administration/Leadership, Troy, AL 36082. Offers MS, Ed S. *Accreditation:* NCATE. *Program availability:* Part-time, evening/weekend. *Faculty:* 7 full-time (4 women), 1 (woman) part-time/adjunct. *Students:* 9 full-time (7 women), 23 part-time (19 women); includes 9 minority (all Black or African American, non-Hispanic/Latino). Average age 35. 11 applicants, 91% accepted, 5 enrolled. In 2017, 9 master's, 9 other advanced degrees awarded. *Degree requirements:* For master's, comprehensive exam, thesis, internship. *Entrance requirements:* For master's, GRE (minimum score of 850 on old exam or 290 on new exam), GMAT (minimum score of 380), or MAT (minimum score of 385), bachelor's degree; minimum undergraduate GPA of 2.5 or 3.0 on last 30 semester hours, letter of recommendation; 3 years of teaching experience; for Ed S, GRE (minimum score of 850 on old exam or 290 on new exam), GMAT (minimum score of 380), or MAT (minimum score of 380), master's degree. Additional exam requirements/recommendations for international students: Required—TOEFL (minimum score 523 paper-based; 70 iBT), IELTS (minimum score 6). *Application deadline:* Applications are processed on a rolling basis. Application fee: $50. Electronic applications accepted. *Expenses:* Tuition, state resident: part-time $417 per credit hour. Tuition, nonresident: part-time $834 per credit hour. *Required fees:* $42 per credit hour. $50 per semester. Tuition and fees vary according to campus/location. *Financial support:* Available to part-time students. Applicants required to submit FAFSA. *Unit head:* Dr. Jan Oliver, Associate Professor, 334-670-3444, Fax: 334-670-3474, E-mail: oliverj@troy.edu. *Application contact:* Jessica A. Kimbro, Graduate Admissions, 334-670-3178, E-mail: jacord@troy.edu.

Union College, Graduate Programs, Department of Education, Barbourville, KY 40906-1499. Offers elementary education (MA); health and physical education (MA); middle grades (MA); music education (MA); principalship (MA); reading specialist (MA); secondary education (MA); special education (MA). *Degree requirements:* For master's, thesis optional. *Entrance requirements:* For master's, GRE General Test, NTE.

Union College, Graduate Programs, Educational Leadership Program, Barbourville, KY 40906-1499. Offers principalship (MA).

Union University, School of Education, Jackson, TN 38305-3697. Offers education (M Ed, MA Ed); education administration generalist (Ed S); educational leadership (Ed D); educational supervision (Ed S); higher education (Ed D). M Ed also available at Germantown campus. *Accreditation:* NCATE. *Program availability:* Part-time, evening/weekend, online learning. *Degree requirements:* For master's, thesis (for some programs), capstone research course (for MA Ed); performance exhibition (for M Ed); for doctorate, comprehensive exam, thesis/dissertation; for Ed S, thesis or alternative. *Entrance requirements:* For master's, MAT, PRAXIS II or GRE, minimum GPA of 3.0, teaching license (for M Ed only), writing sample; for doctorate, GRE, minimum graduate GPA of 3.2, writing sample; for Ed S, PRAXIS II, minimum graduate GPA of 3.2, writing sample. Additional exam requirements/recommendations for international students: Required—TOEFL (minimum score 560 paper-based; 80 iBT). Electronic applications accepted. *Expenses:* Contact institution. *Faculty research:* Mathematics education, brain compatible learning, transformational teaching, cognitive strategy development, instructional technology.

Universidad Adventista de las Antillas, EGECED Department, Mayagüez, PR 00681-0118. Offers curriculum and instruction (M Ed); medical surgical nursing (MN); school administration and supervision (M Ed). *Degree requirements:* For master's, comprehensive exam (for some programs), thesis (for some programs). *Entrance requirements:* For master's, EXADEP or GRE General Test, recommendations. Electronic applications accepted.

Universidad del Turabo, Graduate Programs, Programs in Education, Program in Educational Administration, Gurabo, PR 00778-3030. Offers M Ed. *Program availability:* Part-time, evening/weekend. *Entrance requirements:* For master's, GRE, EXADEP, GMAT, interview, official transcript, essay, recommendation letters. Electronic applications accepted.

Universidad del Turabo, Graduate Programs, Programs in Education, Program in Educational Leadership, Gurabo, PR 00778-3030. Offers D Ed. *Program availability:* Part-time, evening/weekend. *Entrance requirements:* For doctorate, GRE, EXADEP, GMAT, official transcript, recommendation letters, essay, curriculum vitae, interview. Electronic applications accepted.

Universidad Iberoamericana, Graduate School, Santo Domingo D.N., Dominican Republic. Offers business administration (MBA, PMBA); constitutional law (LL M); dentistry (DMD); educational management (MA); integrated marketing communication (MA); psychopedagogical intervention (M Ed); real estate law (LL M); strategic management of human talent (MM).

Universidad Metropolitana, School of Education, Program in Educational Administration and Supervision, San Juan, PR 00928-1150. Offers M Ed. *Program availability:* Part-time. *Degree requirements:* For master's, thesis or alternative. *Entrance requirements:* For master's, EXADEP, interview. Electronic applications accepted.

Universidad Metropolitana, School of Education, Program in Pre-School Centers Administration, San Juan, PR 00928-1150. Offers M Ed. *Program availability:* Part-time. *Degree requirements:* For master's, thesis or alternative. *Entrance requirements:* For master's, EXADEP, interview. Electronic applications accepted.

Université de Moncton, Faculty of Education, Graduate Studies in Education, Moncton, NB E1A 3E9, Canada. Offers educational psychology (M Ed, MA Ed); guidance (M Ed, MA Ed); school administration (M Ed, MA Ed); teaching (M Ed, MA Ed). *Program availability:* Part-time. *Degree requirements:* For master's, proficiency in English and French. *Entrance requirements:* For master's, minimum GPA of 3.0. *Faculty research:* Guidance, ethnolinguistic vitality, children's rights, ecological education, entrepreneurship.

Université de Montréal, Faculty of Education, Department of Administration and Foundations of Education, Montréal, QC H3C 3J7, Canada. Offers M Ed, MA, PhD, DESS. *Program availability:* Part-time. *Degree requirements:* For master's, thesis; for doctorate, thesis/dissertation, general exam. *Entrance requirements:* For master's and DESS, bachelor's degree in related field with minimum B average; for doctorate, master's degree in related field with minimum B average. Electronic applications

accepted. *Faculty research:* Pluriethnicity, formative education, comparative education, diagnostic evaluation.

Université de Sherbrooke, Faculty of Education, Program in School Administration, Sherbrooke, QC J1K 2R1, Canada. Offers M Ed. *Program availability:* Part-time, evening/weekend. *Degree requirements:* For master's, thesis.

Université du Québec à Trois-Rivières, Graduate Programs, Program in Educational Administration, Trois-Rivières, QC G9A 5H7, Canada. Offers DESS.

Université Laval, Faculty of Education, Department of Foundations and Interventions in Education, Programs in Educational Administration and Evaluation, Québec, QC G1K 7P4, Canada. Offers MA, PhD. Terminal master's awarded for partial completion of doctoral program. *Degree requirements:* For master's, thesis (for some programs); for doctorate, comprehensive exam, thesis/dissertation. *Entrance requirements:* For master's and doctorate, English exam (comprehension of written English), knowledge of French and English. Electronic applications accepted.

Université Laval, Faculty of Education, Department of Foundations and Interventions in Education, Programs in Educational Practice, Québec, QC G1K 7P4, Canada. Offers educational pedagogy (Diploma); pedagogy management and development (Diploma); school adaptation (Diploma). *Program availability:* Part-time. *Entrance requirements:* For degree, English exam (comprehension of written English), knowledge of French and English. Electronic applications accepted.

University at Albany, State University of New York, School of Education, Department of Educational Policy and Leadership, Albany, NY 12222-0001. Offers educational policy and leadership (MS, PhD); higher education (MS); international education management (CAS). *Program availability:* Evening/weekend. *Faculty:* 11 full-time (3 women), 13 part-time/adjunct (10 women). *Students:* 37 full-time (21 women), 93 part-time (51 women); includes 28 minority (14 Black or African American, non-Hispanic/Latino; 1 Asian, non-Hispanic/Latino; 11 Hispanic/Latino; 2 Two or more races, non-Hispanic/Latino), 21 international. Average age 32. 72 applicants, 71% accepted, 48 enrolled. In 2017, 11 master's, 7 doctorates, 12 other advanced degrees awarded. *Degree requirements:* For doctorate, one foreign language, thesis/dissertation. *Entrance requirements:* For doctorate, GRE General Test, GRE Subject Test. Additional exam requirements/recommendations for international students: Required—TOEFL (minimum score 550 paper-based). *Application deadline:* For fall admission, 2/1 for domestic students, 5/1 for international students; for spring admission, 9/1 for domestic students, 11/1 for international students. Applications are processed on a rolling basis. Application fee: $75. Electronic applications accepted. *Expenses:* Tuition, state resident: full-time $10,870; part-time $453 per credit hour. Tuition, nonresident: full-time $22,210; part-time $925 per credit hour. *Required fees:* $84.68 per credit hour. $508.06 per semester. Part-time tuition and fees vary according to course load and program. *Financial support:* Fellowships and career-related internships or fieldwork available. Financial award application deadline: 3/15. *Unit head:* Jason Lane, Chair, 518-442-5092, E-mail: jlane@albany.edu.
Website: http://www.albany.edu/epl/

University at Buffalo, the State University of New York, Graduate School, Graduate School of Education, Department of Educational Leadership and Policy, Buffalo, NY 14260. Offers economics and education policy analysis (MA); education studies (Ed M); educational administration (Ed M, Ed D, PhD); educational culture, policy and society (PhD); higher education administration (Ed M, PhD); school building leadership (Certificate); school business and human resource administration (Certificate); school district business leadership (Certificate); school district leadership (Certificate). *Program availability:* Part-time, evening/weekend. *Faculty:* 16 full-time (10 women), 9 part-time/adjunct (6 women). *Students:* 65 full-time (44 women), 125 part-time (82 women); includes 29 minority (23 Black or African American, non-Hispanic/Latino; 3 Asian, non-Hispanic/Latino; 3 Hispanic/Latino), 19 international. Average age 35. 153 applicants, 75% accepted, 59 enrolled. In 2017, 45 master's, 4 doctorates, 23 other advanced degrees awarded. *Degree requirements:* For master's, comprehensive exam (for some programs), thesis optional; for doctorate, comprehensive exam, thesis/dissertation. *Entrance requirements:* For master's, interview, letters of reference; for doctorate, GRE General Test or MAT, writing sample, letters of reference. Additional exam requirements/recommendations for international students: Required—TOEFL (minimum score 550 paper-based; 79 iBT). *Application deadline:* For fall admission, 2/1 priority date for domestic students, 2/1 for international students; for spring admission, 11/15 priority date for domestic students, 10/1 for international students. Applications are processed on a rolling basis. Application fee: $50. Electronic applications accepted. *Financial support:* In 2017–18, 18 fellowships (averaging $5,673 per year), 34 research assistantships with tuition reimbursements (averaging $12,055 per year) were awarded; career-related internships or fieldwork, Federal Work-Study, institutionally sponsored loans, scholarships/grants, health care benefits, tuition waivers (full and partial), and unspecified assistantships also available. Financial award application deadline: 3/15; financial award applicants required to submit FAFSA. *Faculty research:* College access and choice, school leadership preparation and practice, public policy, curriculum and pedagogy, comparative and international education. *Total annual research expenditures:* $637,951. *Unit head:* Dr. Janina C. Brutt-Griffler, Chair, 716-645-2471, Fax: 716-645-2481, E-mail: bruttg@buffalo.edu. *Application contact:* Veronica Kase, Admission Assistant, 716-645-2110, Fax: 716-645-7937, E-mail: vakase@buffalo.edu. Website: http://gse.buffalo.edu/elp

The University of Akron, Graduate School, College of Education, Department of Educational Foundations and Leadership, Program in Higher Education Administration, Akron, OH 44325. Offers MA, MS. *Accreditation:* NCATE. *Students:* 8 full-time (4 women), 10 part-time (8 women); includes 2 minority (1 Black or African American, non-Hispanic/Latino; 1 Hispanic/Latino). Average age 34. 8 applicants, 63% accepted, 3 enrolled. In 2017, 20 master's awarded. *Degree requirements:* For master's, comprehensive exam. *Entrance requirements:* For master's, GRE (if an applicant's GPA is between 2.75 and 2.99), minimum GPA of 2.75, declaration of intent that includes statement of professional goals and reasons for choosing the field of higher education administration and The University of Akron. Additional exam requirements/recommendations for international students: Required—TOEFL (minimum score 79 iBT), IELTS (minimum score 6.5). *Application deadline:* Applications are processed on a rolling basis. Application fee: $45 ($70 for international students). Electronic applications accepted. *Financial support:* Research assistantships and teaching assistantships available. *Unit head:* Dr. Evonn Welton, Interim Department Chair, 330-972-6742, E-mail: ewelton@uakron.edu. *Application contact:* Kelly Chaff, College Program Specialist, 330-972-7028, E-mail: klchaff@uakron.edu.
Website: http://www.uakron.edu/education/academic-programs/graduate-programs.dot

The University of Akron, Graduate School, College of Education, Department of Educational Foundations and Leadership, Program in Principalship, Akron, OH 44325. Offers MA, MS. *Students:* 1 (woman) full-time, 13 part-time (5 women); includes 3 minority (2 Black or African American, non-Hispanic/Latino; 1 Hispanic/Latino). Average age 32. 13 applicants, 100% accepted, 5 enrolled. In 2017, 3 master's awarded. *Degree requirements:* For master's, internship. *Entrance requirements:* For master's, minimum GPA of 2.75, valid Ohio teacher license. Additional exam requirements/recommendations for international students: Required—TOEFL (minimum score 79

iBT), IELTS (minimum score 6.5). *Application deadline:* Applications are processed on a rolling basis. Application fee: $45 ($70 for international students). Electronic applications accepted. *Unit head:* Dr. Evonn Welton, Interim Department Chair, 330-972-6742, E-mail: ewelton@uakron.edu. *Application contact:* Kelly Chaff, College Program Specialist, 330-972-7028, E-mail: klchaff@uakron.edu.
Website: http://www.uakron.edu/education/academic-programs/graduate-programs.dot

The University of Alabama, Graduate School, College of Education, Department of Educational Leadership, Policy, and Technology Studies, Educational Administration Program, Tuscaloosa, AL 35487. Offers Ed D, PhD. *Program availability:* Part-time, evening/weekend. *Students:* 1 (woman) full-time, 26 part-time (14 women); includes 8 minority (6 Black or African American, non-Hispanic/Latino; 1 American Indian or Alaska Native, non-Hispanic/Latino; 1 Hispanic/Latino), 1 international. Average age 41. 2 applicants. In 2017, 8 doctorates awarded. *Degree requirements:* For doctorate, comprehensive exam, thesis/dissertation. *Entrance requirements:* For doctorate, GRE or MAT, master's degree in field, minimum GPA of 3.0. Additional exam requirements/recommendations for international students: Recommended—TOEFL. *Application deadline:* For fall admission, 4/30 priority date for domestic and international students; for winter admission, 11/1 priority date for domestic students, 11/1 for international students; for spring admission, 11/1 priority date for domestic and international students. Applications are processed on a rolling basis. Application fee: $50 ($60 for international students). Electronic applications accepted. *Financial support:* In 2017–18, research assistantships with tuition reimbursements (averaging $11,900 per year) were awarded; health care benefits and unspecified assistantships also available. Financial award application deadline: 4/1. *Faculty research:* Organizational theory, instructional supervision, data-based decision-making. *Unit head:* Dr. David R. Dagley, Professor of Educational Leadership, 205-348-5159, Fax: 205-348-2161, E-mail: ddagley@bamaed.ua.edu. *Application contact:* Dr. Kathy S. Wetzel, Assistant Dean for Student Services, 205-348-1154, Fax: 205-348-0080, E-mail: kwetzel@bamaed.ua.edu.
Website: http://www.elpts.ua.edu

The University of Alabama, Graduate School, College of Education, Department of Educational Leadership, Policy, and Technology Studies, Educational Leadership Program, Tuscaloosa, AL 35487. Offers MA, Ed S. *Program availability:* Part-time, evening/weekend. *Students:* 1 (woman) full-time, 16 part-time (6 women); includes 7 minority (6 Black or African American, non-Hispanic/Latino; 1 Hispanic/Latino), 1 international. Average age 41. 5 applicants. *Degree requirements:* For master's, comprehensive exam, internship. *Entrance requirements:* For master's, MAT or GRE, 3 years of teaching experience, teaching certification, interview, portfolio, minimum GPA of 3.0; for Ed S, MAT or GRE, master's degree, minimum GPA of 3.0. Additional exam requirements/recommendations for international students: Required—TOEFL. *Application deadline:* For fall admission, 4/30 priority date for domestic and international students; for winter admission, 11/1 priority date for domestic and international students; for spring admission, 11/1 priority date for domestic and international students. Application fee: $50 ($60 for international students). Electronic applications accepted. *Financial support:* In 2017–18, research assistantships with full tuition reimbursements (averaging $11,900 per year) were awarded; health care benefits also available. *Faculty research:* Instructional supervision, school effectiveness, organizational theory, politics of education, educational law. *Unit head:* Dr. Philip Todd Westbrook, Professor of Educational Leadership, 205-348-3469, Fax: 205-348-2161, E-mail: ptwestbrook@ua.edu. *Application contact:* Dr. Kathy S. Wetzel, Assistant Dean for Student Services, 205-348-1154, Fax: 205-348-0080, E-mail: kwetzel@bamaed.ua.edu.
Website: http://education.ua.edu/academics/elpts/edle/

The University of Alabama, Graduate School, College of Education, Department of Educational Leadership, Policy, and Technology Studies, Higher Education Administration Program, Tuscaloosa, AL 35487. Offers MA, Ed D, PhD. *Program availability:* Evening/weekend, 100% online. *Students:* 8 full-time (2 women), 22 part-time (13 women); includes 5 minority (3 Black or African American, non-Hispanic/Latino; 1 American Indian or Alaska Native, non-Hispanic/Latino; 1 Two or more races, non-Hispanic/Latino). Average age 36. 31 applicants, 58% accepted, 16 enrolled. In 2017, 9 master's awarded. Terminal master's awarded for partial completion of doctoral program. *Degree requirements:* For master's, capstone seminar; for doctorate, comprehensive exam, thesis/dissertation. *Entrance requirements:* For master's, GRE or MAT, minimum GPA of 3.0; for doctorate, GRE (for PhD), GRE or MAT (for Ed D), master's degree, minimum GPA of 3.0. Additional exam requirements/recommendations for international students: Required—TOEFL. *Application deadline:* For fall admission, 1/15 priority date for domestic and international students. Application fee: $60 ($75 for international students). Electronic applications accepted. *Financial support:* In 2017–18, research assistantships with full tuition reimbursements (averaging $11,900 per year) were awarded; career-related internships or fieldwork, scholarships/grants, health care benefits, and unspecified assistantships also available. *Faculty research:* College teaching and learning, faculty-administration relations, community colleges, organizational change, student affairs. *Unit head:* Dr. Karri Holley, Coordinator and Associate Professor, 205-348-7825, Fax: 205-348-2161, E-mail: kaholley@ua.edu. *Application contact:* Donna Smith, Administrative Assistant, 205-348-6871, Fax: 205-348-2161, E-mail: dbsmith@ua.edu.
Website: http://education.ua.edu/academics/elpts/hea/

The University of Alabama, Graduate School, College of Education, Department of Educational Leadership, Policy, and Technology Studies, Instructional Leadership Program, Tuscaloosa, AL 35487. Offers Ed D, PhD. *Program availability:* Part-time, evening/weekend. *Students:* 48 full-time (43 women), 114 part-time (89 women); includes 47 minority (34 Black or African American, non-Hispanic/Latino; 2 American Indian or Alaska Native, non-Hispanic/Latino; 2 Asian, non-Hispanic/Latino; 3 Hispanic/Latino; 2 Native Hawaiian or other Pacific Islander, non-Hispanic/Latino; 4 Two or more races, non-Hispanic/Latino), 3 international. Average age 43. 25 applicants, 76% accepted, 16 enrolled. In 2017, 28 doctorates awarded. *Degree requirements:* For doctorate, comprehensive exam, thesis/dissertation. *Entrance requirements:* Additional exam requirements/recommendations for international students: Recommended—TOEFL. *Application deadline:* Applications are processed on a rolling basis. Application fee: $50 ($60 for international students). Electronic applications accepted. *Financial support:* In 2017–18, research assistantships with tuition reimbursements (averaging $11,900 per year), teaching assistantships with tuition reimbursements (averaging $11,900 per year) were awarded; health care benefits and unspecified assistantships also available. Financial award application deadline: 5/15. *Unit head:* Dr. John Petrovic, Professor of Social and Cultural Studies in Education, 205-348-0465, Fax: 205-348-2161, E-mail: petrovic@ua.edu. *Application contact:* John Petrovic, Professor of Social and Cultural Studies in Education, 205-348-0465, Fax: 205-348-2161, E-mail: petrovic@bamaed.ua.edu.
Website: http://www.elpts.ua.edu

The University of Alabama at Birmingham, School of Education, Program in Educational Leadership, Birmingham, AL 35294. Offers MA Ed, Ed D, Ed S. Ed D, PhD offered jointly with The University of Alabama (Tuscaloosa). *Accreditation:* NCATE. *Program availability:* Part-time. *Degree requirements:* For master's, thesis optional; for doctorate, thesis/dissertation; for Ed S, comprehensive exam, thesis optional. *Entrance requirements:* For master's, MAT, minimum GPA of 3.0, 3 years' teaching, interview; for

doctorate, MAT (at or above 50th percentile), minimum GPA of 3.0, Ed S in educational leadership, school leadership experience, references, writing sample; for Ed S, MAT (minimum score of 388), minimum GPA of 3.0, master's degree or Class A certification, references. Electronic applications accepted. *Faculty research:* Roles of assistant principals; mission, vision, and values of K-12; bullying.

University of Alaska Anchorage, College of Education, Program in Educational Leadership, Anchorage, AK 99508. Offers educational leadership (M Ed); principal licensure (Certificate); superintendent (Certificate). *Program availability:* Part-time. *Entrance requirements:* For master's, GRE or MAT, interview, minimum GPA of 3.0. Additional exam requirements/recommendations for international students: Required—TOEFL (minimum score 550 paper-based).

University of Alaska Southeast, Graduate Programs, Program in Education, Juneau, AK 99801. Offers educational leadership (M Ed); elementary education (MAT); learning design and technology (M Ed); mathematics education (M Ed); reading specialist (M Ed); secondary education (MAT); special education (M Ed, MAT). *Accreditation:* NCATE. *Program availability:* Part-time, evening/weekend, online learning. *Degree requirements:* For master's, comprehensive exam or project, portfolio. *Entrance requirements:* For master's, PRAXIS, minimum GPA of 3.0, writing sample, letters of recommendation. Electronic applications accepted. *Faculty research:* Applied classroom research, culturally responsive practices, action research, teaching effectiveness.

University of Alberta, Faculty of Graduate Studies and Research, Department of Educational Policy Studies, Edmonton, AB T6G 2E1, Canada. Offers adult education (M Ed, Ed D, PhD); educational administration and leadership (M Ed, Ed D, PhD, Postgraduate Diploma); First Nations education (M Ed, Ed D, PhD); theoretical, cultural and international studies in education (M Ed, Ed D, PhD). *Degree requirements:* For master's, thesis (for some programs); for doctorate, thesis/dissertation. *Entrance requirements:* For master's, minimum GPA of 6.5 on a 9.0 scale; for doctorate, minimum GPA of 7.5 on a 9.0 scale. Additional exam requirements/recommendations for international students: Required—TOEFL (minimum score 580 paper-based). Electronic applications accepted.

The University of Arizona, College of Education, Department of Educational Policy Studies and Practice, Program of Educational Leadership, Tucson, AZ 85721. Offers M Ed, Ed D, Ed S. *Program availability:* Part-time. *Degree requirements:* For master's and Ed S, capstone experience; for doctorate, comprehensive exam, thesis/dissertation. *Entrance requirements:* For master's, leadership experience; for doctorate, GRE General Test, minimum GPA of 3.5, 3 letters of recommendation, curriculum vitae, writing sample. Additional exam requirements/recommendations for international students: Required—TOEFL (minimum score 550 paper-based; 79 iBT). Electronic applications accepted. *Faculty research:* School governance, higher order thinking, restructuring schools, bilingual education policy, authority in education.

University of Arkansas, Graduate School, College of Education and Health Professions, Department of Curriculum and Instruction, Program in Educational Leadership, Fayetteville, AR 72701. Offers M Ed, Ed D, Ed S. *Accreditation:* NCATE. *Program availability:* Part-time, evening/weekend. In 2017, 8 master's, 2 doctorates awarded. *Degree requirements:* For doctorate, thesis/dissertation. *Entrance requirements:* For master's, GRE General Test, MAT or minimum GPA of 3.0; for doctorate, GRE General Test or MAT. *Application deadline:* For fall admission, 8/1 for domestic students, 4/1 for international students; for spring admission, 12/1 for domestic students, 10/1 for international students; for summer admission, 4/15 for domestic students, 3/1 for international students. Applications are processed on a rolling basis. Application fee: $60. Electronic applications accepted. *Expenses:* Tuition, state resident: full-time $3782. Tuition, nonresident: full-time $10,238. *Financial support:* Fellowships with tuition reimbursements, research assistantships, teaching assistantships, career-related internships or fieldwork, and Federal Work-Study available. Support available to part-time students. Financial award application deadline: 4/1; financial award applicants required to submit FAFSA. *Unit head:* Dr. Ed Bengtson, Program Coordinator, 479-575-5092, Fax: 479-575-5119, E-mail: egbengts@uark.edu. *Application contact:* Dr. Ed Bengtson, Graduate Coordinator, 479-575-5092, Fax: 479-575-6676, E-mail: egbents@uark.edu.
Website: https://edle.uark.edu

University of Arkansas at Little Rock, Graduate School, College of Education and Health Professions, Department of Educational Leadership, Program in Educational Administration and Supervision, Little Rock, AR 72204-1099. Offers M Ed, Ed D, Ed S. *Program availability:* Part-time, evening/weekend. *Degree requirements:* For master's, comprehensive exam; for doctorate, comprehensive exam, oral defense of dissertation, residency; for Ed S, comprehensive exam, professional project. *Entrance requirements:* For master's, GRE General Test or MAT, 4 years of work experience (minimum 3 in teaching), interview, minimum GPA of 2.75, teaching certificate; for doctorate, GRE General Test or MAT, 4 years of work experience, minimum graduate GPA of 3.0, teaching certificate; for Ed S, GRE General Test or MAT, 4 years of work experience, minimum GPA of 2.75, teaching certificate.

University of Arkansas at Little Rock, Graduate School, College of Education and Health Professions, Department of Educational Leadership, Program in Higher Education, Little Rock, AR 72204-1099. Offers administration (MA); college student affairs (MA); health professions teaching and learning (MA); higher education (Ed D); two-year college teaching (MA). *Degree requirements:* For doctorate, comprehensive exam, oral defense of dissertation, residency. *Entrance requirements:* For master's, GRE General Test or MAT, interview, minimum graduate GPA of 3.0; for doctorate, GRE General Test, interview, minimum graduate GPA of 3.5, teaching certificate, three years of work experience.

University of Arkansas at Monticello, School of Education, Monticello, AR 71656. Offers education (M Ed, MAT); educational leadership (M Ed). *Accreditation:* NCATE. *Program availability:* Part-time, evening/weekend, online learning. *Degree requirements:* For master's, comprehensive exam. *Entrance requirements:* For master's, minimum GPA of 3.0. Additional exam requirements/recommendations for international students: Required—TOEFL (minimum score 550 paper-based). Electronic applications accepted.

University of Bridgeport, School of Education, Department of Education, Bridgeport, CT 06604. Offers education (MS); educational management (Ed D, Diploma), including intermediate administrator or supervisor (Diploma); leadership (Ed D); elementary education (MS, Diploma), including early childhood education, elementary education; middle school education (MS); music education (MS); remedial reading and language arts (Diploma); secondary education (MS, Diploma), including computer specialist (Diploma), international education (Diploma), reading specialist, secondary education. *Program availability:* Part-time, evening/weekend. *Degree requirements:* For master's, final exam, final project, or thesis; for doctorate, comprehensive exam, thesis/dissertation; for Diploma, thesis or alternative, final project. *Entrance requirements:* For master's, minimum undergraduate QPA of 2.67; for doctorate, GRE, MAT; for Diploma, GRE General Test or MAT, minimum graduate QPA of 3.0. Additional exam requirements/recommendations for international students: Recommended—TOEFL (minimum score 550 paper-based; 80 iBT), IELTS (minimum score 6.5). Electronic applications accepted. *Expenses:* Contact institution.

Educational Leadership and Administration

University of Bridgeport, School of Education, Department of Educational Leadership, Bridgeport, CT 06604. Offers intermediate administrator or supervisor (Diploma); leadership (Ed D). *Degree requirements:* For doctorate, comprehensive exam, thesis/dissertation; for Diploma, thesis or alternative, final project. *Entrance requirements:* For doctorate, GRE, MAT; for Diploma, GRE General Test or MAT, minimum graduate QPA of 3.0. Additional exam requirements/recommendations for international students: Recommended—TOEFL (minimum score 550 paper-based; 80 iBT), IELTS (minimum score 6.5). Electronic applications accepted. *Expenses:* Contact institution.

The University of British Columbia, Faculty of Education, Department of Educational Studies, Vancouver, BC V6T 1Z1, Canada. Offers adult learning and education (M Ed); adult learning and global change (M Ed); curriculum and leadership (M Ed); educational administration and leadership (M Ed); educational leadership and policy (Ed D); educational studies (M Ed, MA, PhD); higher education (M Ed); society, culture and politics in education (M Ed). *Program availability:* Part-time, evening/weekend. Terminal master's awarded for partial completion of doctoral program. *Degree requirements:* For master's, thesis; for doctorate, comprehensive exam, thesis/dissertation. *Entrance requirements:* For master's, minimum B+ average, 4-year undergraduate degree, field-related experience; for doctorate, minimum B+ average, 4-year undergraduate degree, master's degree, field-related experience. Additional exam requirements/recommendations for international students: Required—TOEFL (minimum score 600 paper-based; 100 iBT) or IELTS (minimum score 6.5). Electronic applications accepted. *Expenses:* Contact institution. *Faculty research:* Educational leadership educational administration adult education politics in education, global change and adult learning.

University of Calgary, Faculty of Graduate Studies, Werklund School of Education, Graduate Division of Educational Research, Calgary, AB T2N 1N4, Canada. Offers adult learning (M Ed, MA, Ed D, PhD); curriculum and learning (M Ed, MA, Ed D, PhD); educational leadership (M Ed, MA, Ed D, PhD); languages and diversity (M Ed, MA, Ed D, PhD); learning sciences (M Ed, MA, Ed D, PhD). Ed D in educational leadership offered via distance delivery. *Program availability:* Part-time, evening/weekend, online learning. *Degree requirements:* For master's, thesis (for some programs); for doctorate, thesis/dissertation, candidacy exam. *Entrance requirements:* For master's, minimum GPA of 3.0, 3 letters of reference; for doctorate, minimum GPA of 3.5, 3 letters of reference. Additional exam requirements/recommendations for international students: Required—TOEFL, IELTS. Electronic applications accepted. *Faculty research:* Curriculum, leadership, technology, contexts, gifted, second language teaching, work place and adult learning.

University of California, Berkeley, Graduate Division, School of Education, Programs in Education, Berkeley, CA 94720-1500. Offers development in mathematics and science (MA); education in mathematics, science, and technology (MA, PhD); human development and education (MA, PhD); leadership education (MA); special education (PhD); teacher education (MA); MA/Credential; PhD/Credential; PhD/MA. Terminal master's awarded for partial completion of doctoral program. *Degree requirements:* For master's, exam or thesis; for doctorate, thesis/dissertation, oral qualifying exam. *Entrance requirements:* For master's and doctorate, GRE General Test, minimum GPA of 3.0 during last 2 years of undergraduate course work. Electronic applications accepted. *Faculty research:* Human development, social and moral educational psychology, developmental teacher preparation.

University of California, Irvine, School of Education, Irvine, CA 92697. Offers educational administration (Ed D); educational administration and leadership (Ed D); elementary and secondary education (MAT). *Program availability:* Part-time, evening/weekend. *Students:* 210 full-time (157 women), 1 (woman) part-time; includes 104 minority (1 Black or African American, non-Hispanic/Latino; 46 Asian, non-Hispanic/Latino; 39 Hispanic/Latino; 1 Native Hawaiian or other Pacific Islander, non-Hispanic/Latino; 17 Two or more races, non-Hispanic/Latino), 20 international. Average age 27. 451 applicants, 46% accepted, 147 enrolled. In 2017, 130 master's, 7 doctorates awarded. *Entrance requirements:* For master's, GRE, minimum GPA of 3.0; for doctorate, GRE General Test, minimum GPA of 3.0. Additional exam requirements/recommendations for international students: Required—TOEFL (minimum score 550 paper-based). *Application deadline:* For fall admission, 1/2 priority date for domestic students, 1/2 for international students. Application fee: $105 ($125 for international students). Electronic applications accepted. *Financial support:* Fellowships, research assistantships with full tuition reimbursements, institutionally sponsored loans, traineeships, health care benefits, and unspecified assistantships available. Financial award application deadline: 3/1; financial award applicants required to submit FAFSA. *Faculty research:* Education technology, learning theory, social theory, cultural diversity, postmodernism. *Unit head:* Richard Arum, Dean, 949-824-2534, E-mail: richard.arum@uci.edu. *Application contact:* Denise Earley, Assistant Director of Student Affairs, 949-824-4022, E-mail: denise.earley@uci.edu.
Website: http://education.uci.edu/

University of California, Los Angeles, Graduate Division, Graduate School of Education and Information Studies, Program in Educational Leadership, Los Angeles, CA 90095. Offers Ed D. *Program availability:* Evening/weekend. *Degree requirements:* For doctorate, thesis/dissertation, oral and written qualifying exams. *Entrance requirements:* For doctorate, GRE General Test, minimum undergraduate GPA of 3.0, resume. Electronic applications accepted.

University of California, Riverside, Graduate Division, Graduate School of Education, Riverside, CA 92521. Offers applied behavior analysis (M Ed); diversity and equity (M Ed); education policy analysis and leadership (PhD); education specialist (Credential); education, society, and culture (MA, PhD); educational psychology (MA, PhD); general education (M Ed); higher education administration and policy (M Ed, PhD); multiple subject (Credential); research, evaluation, measurement and statistics (MA); school psychology (PhD); single subject (Credential); special education (M Ed, PhD); special education and autism (MA); TESOL (M Ed). *Faculty:* 29 full-time (16 women), 2 part-time/adjunct (1 woman). *Students:* 241 full-time (188 women). 396 applicants, 42% accepted, 166 enrolled. In 2017, 130 master's, 15 doctorates, 14 other advanced degrees awarded. Terminal master's awarded for partial completion of doctoral program. *Degree requirements:* For master's, comprehensive exams or thesis (MA), case study or analytical report (M Ed); for doctorate, comprehensive exam, thesis/dissertation, written and oral qualifying exams, college teaching practicum. *Entrance requirements:* For master's, GRE General Test (for MA); CBEST and CSET (for M Ed in general education only), UCR Extension TESOL certificate (for M Ed with TESOL emphasis only); for doctorate, GRE General Test, writing sample; for Credential, CBEST, CSET. Additional exam requirements/recommendations for international students: Required—TOEFL (minimum score 550 paper-based; 80 iBT), IELTS (minimum score 7). *Application deadline:* For fall admission, 9/1 for domestic students, 6/1 for international students; for winter admission, 11/15 for domestic students, 9/1 for international students; for spring admission, 3/1 for domestic students, 12/1 for international students. Applications are processed on a rolling basis. Application fee: $80 ($100 for international students). Electronic applications accepted. *Expenses:* Tuition, state resident: full-time $5746. Tuition, nonresident: full-time $10,780. Tuition and fees vary according to campus/location and program. *Financial support:* In 2017–18, 105 students received support, including 16 fellowships with full tuition reimbursements available (averaging $31,000 per year), 25 research assistantships with full tuition reimbursements available (averaging $31,000 per year), 10 teaching assistantships with full tuition reimbursements available (averaging $31,000 per year); career-related internships or fieldwork, Federal Work-Study, institutionally sponsored loans, scholarships/grants, and unspecified assistantships also available. Financial award application deadline: 12/15. *Faculty research:* Responsiveness to intervention, faculty core, response to intervention of English language learners, advanced modeling techniques, study on social capital, trust, and motivation. *Total annual research expenditures:* $1.7 million. *Unit head:* Thomas Smith, Dean, 951-827-4633, E-mail: thomas.smith@ucr.edu. *Application contact:* Heather Killeen, Graduate Program Coordinator, 951-827-6362, E-mail: heather.killeen@ucr.edu.
Website: http://www.education.ucr.edu/

University of California, San Diego, Graduate Division, Program in Education Studies, La Jolla, CA 92093. Offers education (M Ed, PhD); educational leadership (Ed D); teaching and learning (MA, Ed D), including bilingual education (MA), curriculum design (MA). Ed D offered jointly with California State University, San Marcos. *Students:* 88 full-time (64 women), 54 part-time (36 women). 261 applicants, 57% accepted, 77 enrolled. In 2017, 68 master's, 13 doctorates awarded. *Degree requirements:* For master's, thesis (for some programs), student teaching; for doctorate, comprehensive exam, thesis/dissertation. *Entrance requirements:* For master's, GRE General Test; CBEST and appropriate CSET exam (for select tracks), current teaching or educational assignment (for select tracks); for doctorate, GRE General Test, current teaching or educational assignment (for select tracks). Additional exam requirements/recommendations for international students: Required—TOEFL (minimum score 550 paper-based; 80 iBT), IELTS (minimum score 7). *Application deadline:* For fall admission, 2/2 for domestic students. Application fee: $105 ($125 for international students). Electronic applications accepted. *Financial support:* Fellowships, career-related internships or fieldwork, and scholarships/grants available. Financial award applicants required to submit FAFSA. *Faculty research:* Language, culture and literacy development of deaf/hard of hearing children; equity issues in education; educational reform; evaluation, assessment, and research methodologies; distributed learning. *Unit head:* Carolyn Hofstetter, Chair, 858-822-6688, E-mail: ajdaly@ucsd.edu. *Application contact:* Giselle Van Luit, Graduate Coordinator, 858-534-2958, E-mail: edsinfo@ucsd.edu.

University of Central Arkansas, Graduate School, College of Education, Department of Leadership Studies, Conway, AR 72035-0001. Offers college student personnel (MS); district-level administration (PMC); educational leadership - district level (Ed S); instructional technology (MS); library media and information technology (MS); school counseling (MS); school leadership (MS); school-based leadership adult education program administration (PMC); school-based leadership building administration (PMC); school-based leadership curriculum administration (PMC); school-based leadership gifted and talented program administration (PMC); school-based leadership special education program administration (PMC). *Accreditation:* NCATE. *Program availability:* Part-time, evening/weekend, online learning. *Degree requirements:* For master's and other advanced degree, comprehensive exam. *Entrance requirements:* For master's, GRE. Additional exam requirements/recommendations for international students: Required—TOEFL (minimum score 80 iBT). Electronic applications accepted. *Expenses:* Contact institution.

University of Central Florida, College of Community Innovation and Education, Department of Educational Leadership and Higher Education, Orlando, FL 32816. Offers career and technical education (MA); educational leadership (M Ed, MA, Ed S); higher education/college teaching and leadership (MA); higher education/student personnel (MA). *Program availability:* Part-time, evening/weekend. *Students:* 86 full-time (65 women), 233 part-time (184 women); includes 136 minority (66 Black or African American, non-Hispanic/Latino; 1 American Indian or Alaska Native, non-Hispanic/Latino; 4 Asian, non-Hispanic/Latino; 59 Hispanic/Latino; 6 Two or more races, non-Hispanic/Latino). Average age 31. 235 applicants, 82% accepted, 113 enrolled. In 2017, 114 master's, 16 other advanced degrees awarded. *Degree requirements:* For master's, thesis or alternative; for Ed S, thesis or alternative, final exam. *Entrance requirements:* For master's, GRE General Test; for Ed S, GRE General Test, minimum GPA of 3.0, resume, letters of recommendation. Additional exam requirements/recommendations for international students: Required—TOEFL. *Application deadline:* For fall admission, 6/20 for domestic students; for spring admission, 9/20 for domestic students. Application fee: $30. Electronic applications accepted. *Expenses:* Tuition, state resident: part-time $288.16 per credit hour. Tuition, nonresident: part-time $1073.31 per credit hour. Tuition and fees vary according to program. *Financial support:* In 2017–18, 12 students received support, including 2 fellowships with partial tuition reimbursements available (averaging $3,000 per year), 10 research assistantships with partial tuition reimbursements available (averaging $8,387 per year), 2 teaching assistantships with partial tuition reimbursements available (averaging $12,166 per year); career-related internships or fieldwork, Federal Work-Study, institutionally sponsored loans, health care benefits, tuition waivers (partial), and unspecified assistantships also available. Financial award application deadline: 3/1; financial award applicants required to submit FAFSA. *Unit head:* Dr. Kenneth Murray, Program Coordinator, 407-832-1468, E-mail: kenneth.murray@ucf.edu. *Application contact:* Associate Director, Graduate Admissions, 407-823-2766, Fax: 407-823-6442, E-mail: gradadmissions@ucf.edu.
Website: https://ccie.ucf.edu/elhe/

University of Central Florida, College of Community Innovation and Education, Education Doctoral Programs, Orlando, FL 32816. Offers curriculum and instruction (Ed D); education (PhD), including communication sciences and disorders, counselor education, early childhood education, elementary education, exceptional education, exercise physiology, higher education, instructional design and technology, mathematics education, methodology, measurement and analysis, reading education, science education, social science education, TESOL; educational leadership (Ed D). *Students:* 122 full-time (86 women), 129 part-time (88 women); includes 64 minority (24 Black or African American, non-Hispanic/Latino; 1 American Indian or Alaska Native, non-Hispanic/Latino; 9 Asian, non-Hispanic/Latino; 24 Hispanic/Latino; 6 Two or more races, non-Hispanic/Latino), 26 international. Average age 38. 195 applicants, 47% accepted, 72 enrolled. In 2017, 89 doctorates awarded. *Entrance requirements:* For doctorate, GRE, letters of recommendation, goal statement, resume, writing sample. Application fee: $30. Electronic applications accepted. *Expenses:* Tuition, state resident: part-time $288.16 per credit hour. Tuition, nonresident: part-time $1073.31 per credit hour. Tuition and fees vary according to program. *Financial support:* In 2017–18, 77 students received support, including 28 fellowships with partial tuition reimbursements available (averaging $5,733 per year), 29 research assistantships with partial tuition reimbursements available (averaging $10,230 per year), 54 teaching assistantships with partial tuition reimbursements available (averaging $11,614 per year); health care benefits also available. Financial award application deadline: 3/1; financial award applicants required to submit FAFSA. *Unit head:* Dr. Edward Robinson, Director of Doctoral Programs, 407-823-6106, E-mail: edward.robinson@ucf.edu. *Application contact:* Associate Director, Graduate Admissions, 407-823-2766, Fax: 407-823-6442, E-mail: gradadmissions@ucf.edu.
Website: https://edcollege.ucf.edu/academic-programs/graduate/

University of Central Missouri, The Graduate School, Warrensburg, MO 64093. Offers accountancy (MA); accounting (MBA); applied mathematics (MS); aviation safety (MA);

biology (MS); business administration (MBA); career and technical education leadership (MS); college student personnel administration (MS); communication (MA); computer science (MS); counseling (MS); criminal justice (MS); educational leadership (Ed D); educational technology (MS); elementary and early childhood education (MSE); English (MA); environmental studies (MA); finance (MBA); history (MA); human services/educational technology (Ed S); human services/learning resources (Ed S); human services/professional counseling (Ed S); industrial hygiene (MS); industrial management (MS); information systems (MBA); information technology (MS); kinesiology (MS); library science and information services (MS); literacy education (MSE); marketing (MBA); mathematics (MS); music (MA); occupational safety management (MS); psychology (MS); rural family nursing (MS); school administration (MSE); social gerontology (MS); sociology (MA); special education (MSE); speech language pathology (MS); superintendency (Ed S); teaching (MAT); teaching English as a second language (MA); technology (MS); technology management (PhD); theatre (MA). *Program availability:* Part-time, 100% online, blended/hybrid learning. *Faculty:* 337 full-time (145 women), 41 part-time/adjunct (28 women). *Students:* 785 full-time (398 women), 1,633 part-time (1,063 women); includes 231 minority (102 Black or African American, non-Hispanic/Latino; 4 American Indian or Alaska Native, non-Hispanic/Latino; 16 Asian, non-Hispanic/Latino; 52 Hispanic/Latino; 57 Two or more races, non-Hispanic/Latino), 692 international. Average age 30. In 2017, 2,605 master's, 122 other advanced degrees awarded. *Degree requirements:* For master's and Ed S, comprehensive exam (for some programs), thesis (for some programs). *Entrance requirements:* Additional exam requirements/recommendations for international students: Required—TOEFL (minimum score 550 paper-based; 79 iBT). *Application deadline:* For fall admission, 6/1 priority date for domestic and international students; for spring admission, 10/1 priority date for domestic and international students; for summer admission, 4/1 priority date for domestic and international students. Applications are processed on a rolling basis. Application fee: $30 ($75 for international students). Electronic applications accepted. *Expenses:* Tuition, state resident: full-time $8771; part-time $292.35 per credit hour. Tuition, nonresident: full-time $17,541; part-time $584.70 per credit hour. *Required fees:* $372; $24.78 per credit hour. *Financial support:* In 2017–18, 99 students received support. Research assistantships, teaching assistantships, career-related internships or fieldwork, Federal Work-Study, scholarships/grants, and administrative and laboratory assistantships available. Support available to part-time students. Financial award application deadline: 3/1; financial award applicants required to submit FAFSA. *Unit head:* Shellie Hewitt, Director of Graduate and International Student Services, 660-543-4621, Fax: 660-543-4778, E-mail: hewitt@ucmo.edu. *Application contact:* 660-543-4621, E-mail: admit_intl@ucmo.edu.
Website: http://www.ucmo.edu/graduate/

University of Central Oklahoma, The Jackson College of Graduate Studies, College of Education and Professional Studies, Donna Nigh Department of Advanced Professional and Special Services, Edmond, OK 73034-5209. Offers educational leadership (M Ed); library media education (M Ed); reading (M Ed); school counseling (M Ed); special education (M Ed), including mild/moderate disabilities, severe-profound/multiple disabilities; speech-language pathology (MS). *Accreditation:* ASHA. *Program availability:* Part-time. *Faculty:* 17 full-time (12 women), 8 part-time/adjunct (4 women). *Students:* 73 full-time (65 women), 286 part-time (239 women); includes 91 minority (41 Black or African American, non-Hispanic/Latino; 8 American Indian or Alaska Native, non-Hispanic/Latino; 5 Asian, non-Hispanic/Latino; 20 Hispanic/Latino; 17 Two or more races, non-Hispanic/Latino), 3 international. Average age 35. 146 applicants, 83% accepted, 91 enrolled. In 2017, 128 master's awarded. *Degree requirements:* For master's, comprehensive exam (for some programs), thesis (for some programs). *Entrance requirements:* Additional exam requirements/recommendations for international students: Required—TOEFL (minimum score 550 paper-based; 79 iBT), IELTS (minimum score 6.5). *Application deadline:* For fall admission, 7/15 for international students; for spring admission, 11/15 for international students; for summer admission, 1/31 for domestic students. Applications are processed on a rolling basis. Application fee: $60. Electronic applications accepted. *Expenses:* Tuition, state resident: full-time $5375; part-time $268.75 per credit hour. Tuition, nonresident: full-time $13,295; part-time $664.75 per credit hour. *Required fees:* $626; $31.30 per credit hour. One-time fee: $50. Tuition and fees vary according to program. *Financial support:* In 2017–18, 74 students received support, including 1 research assistantship with partial tuition reimbursement available (averaging $2,958 per year), 1 teaching assistantship with partial tuition reimbursement available (averaging $5,915 per year); career-related internships or fieldwork, scholarships/grants, tuition waivers (partial), and unspecified assistantships also available. Financial award application deadline: 3/31; financial award applicants required to submit FAFSA. *Unit head:* Dr. Cheryl Evans, Chair, 405-974-5437, Fax: 405-974-3857. *Application contact:* Carlie Wellington, Assistant Director, CEPS Graduate Enrollment, 405-974-5105, Fax: 405-974-3851, E-mail: gradcoll@uco.edu.
Website: http://sites.uco.edu/ceps/dept/Education-Programs/apss/index.asp

University of Cincinnati, Graduate School, College of Education, Criminal Justice, and Human Services, School of Education, Program in Educational Leadership, Cincinnati, OH 45221. Offers M Ed, Ed S. *Accreditation:* NCATE. *Program availability:* Part-time, online learning. *Degree requirements:* For master's, thesis or alternative. *Entrance requirements:* For master's, GRE General Test, 3 letters of reference, resume, minimum GPA of 2.8; for Ed S, references, interview. Additional exam requirements/recommendations for international students: Required—TOEFL (minimum score 550 paper-based). Electronic applications accepted. *Expenses:* Tuition, area resident: Full-time $14,468. Tuition, state resident: full-time $14,968; part-time $754 per credit hour. Tuition, nonresident: full-time $24,210; part-time $1311 per credit hour. *International tuition:* $26,460 full-time. *Required fees:* $3958; $84 per credit hour. One-time fee: $85 full-time. Tuition and fees vary according to course load, degree level and program.

University of Cincinnati, Graduate School, College of Education, Criminal Justice, and Human Services, School of Education, Program in Urban Educational Leadership, Cincinnati, OH 45221. Offers Ed D. *Degree requirements:* For doctorate, thesis/dissertation. *Entrance requirements:* For doctorate, GRE General Test, GRE Subject Test. Additional exam requirements/recommendations for international students: Required—TOEFL (minimum score 550 paper-based), OEPT. *Expenses:* Tuition, area resident: Full-time $14,468. Tuition, state resident: full-time $14,968; part-time $754 per credit hour. Tuition, nonresident: full-time $24,210; part-time $1311 per credit hour. *International tuition:* $26,460 full-time. *Required fees:* $3958; $84 per credit hour. One-time fee: $85 full-time. Tuition and fees vary according to course load, degree level and program.

University of Colorado Colorado Springs, College of Education, Colorado Springs, CO 80918. Offers counseling and human services (MA); curriculum and instruction (MA); educational leadership (MA); educational leadership, research and policy (PhD); special education (MA); teaching English to speakers of other languages (MA). *Accreditation:* ACA; NCATE. *Program availability:* Part-time, evening/weekend, 100% online, blended/hybrid learning. *Faculty:* 30 full-time (21 women), 8 part-time/adjunct (38 women). *Students:* 190 full-time (132 women), 286 part-time (202 women); includes 117 minority (20 Black or African American, non-Hispanic/Latino; 2 American Indian or Alaska Native, non-Hispanic/Latino; 12 Asian, non-Hispanic/Latino; 59 Hispanic/Latino; 24 Two or more races, non-Hispanic/Latino), 6 international. Average age 36. 169

applicants, 85% accepted, 113 enrolled. In 2017, 160 master's, 16 doctorates awarded. *Degree requirements:* For master's, comprehensive exam, thesis or alternative, microcomputer proficiency; for doctorate, comprehensive exam, thesis/dissertation, research lab. *Entrance requirements:* For master's and doctorate, GRE General Test. Additional exam requirements/recommendations for international students: Recommended—TOEFL (minimum score 550 paper-based; 80 iBT), IELTS (minimum score 6). *Application deadline:* For fall admission, 1/28 priority date for domestic and international students; for spring admission, 11/1 priority date for domestic and international students. Applications are processed on a rolling basis. Application fee: $60 ($100 for international students). Electronic applications accepted. *Expenses:* $10,350 per year resident tuition, $20,935 nonresident, $11,961 nonresidential online; annual costs vary depending on program, course-load, and residency status. *Financial support:* In 2017–18, 81 students received support. Career-related internships or fieldwork, Federal Work-Study, scholarships/grants, and unspecified assistantships available. Support available to part-time students. Financial award application deadline: 3/1; financial award applicants required to submit FAFSA. *Faculty research:* Linguistically diverse education (LDE), educational policy, evidence-based reading and writing instruction, relational and social aggression, positive behavior supports, inclusive schooling, K-12 education policy. *Total annual research expenditures:* $607,967. *Unit head:* Dr. Valerie Martin Conley, Dean, 719-255-4133, E-mail: vmconley@uccs.edu. *Application contact:* The College of Education Student Resource Office, 719-255-4996, E-mail: education@uccs.edu.
Website: http://www.uccs.edu/coe

University of Colorado Denver, School of Education and Human Development, Administrative Leadership and Policy Studies Program, Denver, CO 80217. Offers MA, Ed S. *Accreditation:* NCATE. *Program availability:* Part-time, evening/weekend. *Degree requirements:* For master's, comprehensive exam, 9 credit hours beyond the 32 required for principal-administrator licensure; for Ed S, comprehensive exam, 9 credit hours beyond the 32 required for principal-administrator licensure (for those already holding MA). *Entrance requirements:* For master's and Ed S, GRE or MAT (if GPA is below 2.75), minimum GPA of 2.75, interview, 3 letters of recommendation, resume. Additional exam requirements/recommendations for international students: Required—TOEFL (minimum score 525 paper-based; 71 iBT); Recommended—IELTS (minimum score 6.3). Electronic applications accepted. *Expenses:* Contact institution. *Faculty research:* Learning cultures, teaching and learning in educational administration.

University of Colorado Denver, School of Education and Human Development, Program in Educational Leadership and Innovation, Denver, CO 80217. Offers educational studies and research (PhD), including administrative leadership and policy, early childhood special education, math education, research, assessment and evaluation, science education, urban ecologies. *Program availability:* Part-time, evening/weekend. *Degree requirements:* For doctorate, comprehensive exam, thesis/dissertation, 75 credit hours (for PhD). *Entrance requirements:* For doctorate, GRE or equivalent, resume or curriculum vitae, letters of recommendation, master's degree or equivalent, completion of basic or advanced statistics course with minimum B grade. Additional exam requirements/recommendations for international students: Required—TOEFL (minimum score 537 paper-based; 75 iBT); Recommended—IELTS (minimum score 6.5). Electronic applications accepted. *Expenses:* Contact institution. *Faculty research:* Administrative leadership and policy studies, early childhood education, research in diversity, paraprofessionals in education, urban schools lab.

University of Colorado Denver, School of Education and Human Development, Program in Leadership for Educational Equity, Denver, CO 80217. Offers executive leadership (Ed D); instructional leadership (Ed D). *Degree requirements:* For doctorate, thesis/dissertation, 69 credit hours, including 24 in dissertation and independent study. *Entrance requirements:* For doctorate, GRE General Test, resume with minimum of 5 years experience in an educational background, 2-3 professional artifacts illuminating leadership experiences, three professional letters of recommendation, master's degree with recommended minimum GPA of 3.2. Additional exam requirements/recommendations for international students: Required—TOEFL (minimum score 550 paper-based; 80 iBT); Recommended—IELTS (minimum score 6.8). Electronic applications accepted.

University of Connecticut, Graduate School, Neag School of Education, Department of Educational Leadership, Field of Educational Administration, Storrs, CT 06269. Offers MA. *Accreditation:* NCATE. *Entrance requirements:* Additional exam requirements/recommendations for international students: Required—TOEFL (minimum score 550 paper-based). Electronic applications accepted.

University of Dayton, Department of Counselor Education and Human Services, Dayton, OH 45469. Offers clinical mental health counseling (MS Ed); college student personnel (MS Ed); higher education administration (MS Ed); human services (MS Ed); school counseling (MS Ed); school psychology (MS Ed, Ed S). *Accreditation:* ACA; NCATE. *Program availability:* Part-time. *Faculty:* 11 full-time (6 women), 34 part-time/adjunct (24 women). *Students:* 194 full-time (153 women), 83 part-time (58 women); includes 58 minority (37 Black or African American, non-Hispanic/Latino; 2 Asian, non-Hispanic/Latino; 9 Hispanic/Latino; 10 Two or more races, non-Hispanic/Latino), 3 international. Average age 30. 426 applicants, 28% accepted. In 2017, 107 master's, 6 Ed Ss awarded. *Degree requirements:* For master's, thesis (for some programs); for Ed S, thesis (for some programs), professional portfolio. *Entrance requirements:* For master's, MAT or GRE (if GPA less than 2.75), essays (for some programs). Additional exam requirements/recommendations for international students: Required—TOEFL (minimum score 550 paper-based; 80 iBT). *Application deadline:* For fall admission, 1/10 priority date for domestic and international students; for spring admission, 9/10 priority date for domestic and international students; for summer admission, 11/10 priority date for domestic and international students. Application fee: $0 ($50 for international students). Electronic applications accepted. *Expenses:* Contact institution. *Financial support:* In 2017–18, 5 research assistantships with partial tuition reimbursements (averaging $9,950 per year) were awarded; career-related internships or fieldwork, institutionally sponsored loans, and unspecified assistantships also available. Financial award application deadline: 3/1; financial award applicants required to submit FAFSA. *Faculty research:* Student school bonding, traumatic brain injuries, wellness and counseling, creativity in education. *Unit head:* Dr. Alan Demmitt, Chair, 937-229-3644, Fax: 937-229-1055, E-mail: ademmitt1@udayton.edu. *Application contact:* Kathleen Brown, Administrative Assistant, 937-229-3644, Fax: 937-229-1055, E-mail: kbrown1@udayton.edu.
Website: https://www.udayton.edu/education/departments_and_programs/edc/

University of Dayton, Department of Educational Administration, Dayton, OH 45469. Offers Catholic school leadership (MS Ed); educational leadership (MS Ed, Ed S); leadership for educational systems (MS Ed). Ed S program in educational leadership offered jointly by the Graduate Schools of the University of Dayton and Wright State University. *Program availability:* Part-time, blended/hybrid learning. *Faculty:* 6 full-time (3 women), 17 part-time/adjunct (3 women). *Students:* 58 full-time (37 women), 65 part-time (46 women); includes 12 minority (7 Black or African American, non-Hispanic/Latino; 2 Hispanic/Latino; 3 Two or more races, non-Hispanic/Latino), 3 international. Average age 34. 74 applicants, 31% accepted. In 2017, 69 master's awarded. *Degree requirements:* For master's, thesis optional; for Ed S, thesis. *Entrance requirements:* For

SECTION 23: ADMINISTRATION, INSTRUCTION, AND THEORY

Educational Leadership and Administration

master's, MAT or GRE if undergraduate GPA is below 2.75. Additional exam requirements/recommendations for international students: Required—TOEFL (minimum score 550 paper-based; 80 iBT). *Application deadline:* For fall admission, 8/20 for domestic students; for spring admission, 1/10 for domestic students; for summer admission, 5/10 for domestic students. Applications are processed on a rolling basis. Application fee: $0 ($50 for international students). Electronic applications accepted. *Expenses:* Contact institution. *Financial support:* In 2017–18, 5 research assistantships with partial tuition reimbursements (averaging $9,640 per year) were awarded; career-related internships or fieldwork and institutionally sponsored loans also available. Financial award application deadline: 3/1; financial award applicants required to submit FAFSA. *Faculty research:* Data use for equity, school law, religion in education. *Unit head:* Dr. David D. Dolph, Chair, 937-229-3105, Fax: 937-229-1055, E-mail: ddolph1@udayton.edu. *Application contact:* Janice Keivel, Administrative Associate, 937-229-3738, Fax: 937-229-1055, E-mail: jkeivel1@udayton.edu.
Website: https://www.udayton.edu/education/departments_and_programs/eda/index.php

University of Dayton, Department of Teacher Education, Dayton, OH 45469. Offers adolescence to young adult education (MS Ed); early childhood leadership and advocacy (MS Ed); interdisciplinary education (MS Ed), including visual arts; interdisciplinary education studies (MS Ed); leadership in educational systems (MS Ed); literacy (MS Ed); mathematics education (MS Ed); middle childhood education (MS Ed); multi-age education (MS Ed), including world languages; music education (MS Ed); teacher as leader (MS Ed); teacher education (MS Ed); technology-enhanced learning (MS Ed); trans-disciplinary early childhood education (MS Ed). *Program availability:* Part-time, 100% online. *Faculty:* 23 full-time (20 women), 41 part-time/adjunct (36 women). *Students:* 45 full-time (38 women), 68 part-time (57 women); includes 7 minority (3 Black or African American, non-Hispanic/Latino; 1 Hispanic/Latino; 3 Two or more races, non-Hispanic/Latino), 6 international. Average age 31. 106 applicants, 28% accepted. In 2017, 70 master's awarded. *Degree requirements:* For master's, variable foreign language requirement, thesis or alternative, internship (for teaching licensure or endorsement). *Entrance requirements:* For master's, GRE (minimum score of 149 verbal, 4 on writing) or MAT (minimum score of 396) if undergraduate GPA was under 2.75, minimum GPA of 2.75, 3 letters of recommendation, personal statement or resume, official transcripts. Additional exam requirements/recommendations for international students: Required—TOEFL (minimum score 550 paper-based; 80 iBT); Recommended—IELTS (minimum score 6.5). *Application deadline:* Applications are processed on a rolling basis. Application fee: $0 ($50 for international students). Electronic applications accepted. *Expenses:* Contact institution. *Financial support:* In 2017–18, 5 research assistantships with partial tuition reimbursements (averaging $9,640 per year) were awarded; teaching assistantships, career-related internships or fieldwork, institutionally sponsored loans, and unspecified assistantships also available. Financial award application deadline: 3/1; financial award applicants required to submit FAFSA. *Faculty research:* Social emotional learning, culturally responsive teaching, urban teaching, literacy, instructional strategies, pre-service teacher education preparation. *Unit head:* Dr. Connie L. Bowman, Chair, 937-229-3348, E-mail: cbowman1@udayton.edu. *Application contact:* Gina Seiter, Coordinator of Graduate Programs and Licensing, 937-229-3103, E-mail: gseiter1@udayton.edu.
Website: https://www.udayton.edu/education/departments_and_programs/edt

University of Dayton, PhD Program in Educational Leadership, Dayton, OH 45469. Offers educational leadership (PhD). *Program availability:* Part-time. *Faculty:* 1 full-time (0 women), 5 part-time/adjunct (2 women). *Students:* 50 full-time (31 women); includes 7 minority (5 Black or African American, non-Hispanic/Latino; 1 Hispanic/Latino; 1 Two or more races, non-Hispanic/Latino), 3 international. Average age 42. 36 applicants, 19% accepted. In 2017, 7 doctorates awarded. *Degree requirements:* For doctorate, comprehensive exam, thesis/dissertation. *Entrance requirements:* For doctorate, GRE (minimum score of 149 verbal, 4.0 writing), official transcripts, 3 letters of recommendation, 500-700 word essay, current resume, interview. Additional exam requirements/recommendations for international students: Required—TOEFL (minimum score 550 paper-based; 80 iBT), GRE. *Application deadline:* For fall admission, 8/21 for domestic students. Applications are processed on a rolling basis. Application fee: $0 ($50 for international students). Electronic applications accepted. *Expenses:* Contact institution. *Financial support:* In 2017–18, 1 research assistantship with full and partial tuition reimbursement (averaging $13,920 per year) was awarded; fellowships, teaching assistantships, career-related internships or fieldwork, Federal Work-Study, and institutionally sponsored loans also available. Financial award application deadline: 3/1; financial award applicants required to submit FAFSA. *Faculty research:* School law; school finance; leadership, diversity, research methodology. *Unit head:* Dr. Charles Russo, Director, 937-229-3722, E-mail: crusso1@udayton.edu. *Application contact:* Elizabeth Pearn, Publication and Doctoral Program Specialist, 937-229-4003, E-mail: epearn1@udayton.edu.
Website: https://www.udayton.edu/education/departments_and_programs/phd/index.php

University of Delaware, College of Education and Human Development, School of Education, Newark, DE 19716. Offers education (PhD); educational leadership (Ed D); higher education (M Ed); instruction (MI); reading (M Ed); school leadership (M Ed); school psychology (MA, Ed S); teaching English as a second language (TESL) (MA). *Accreditation:* NCATE. *Program availability:* Part-time, evening/weekend. Terminal master's awarded for partial completion of doctoral program. *Degree requirements:* For master's, comprehensive exam (for some programs), thesis (for some programs); for doctorate, comprehensive exam (for some programs), thesis/dissertation. *Entrance requirements:* For master's and doctorate, GRE, 3 letters of recommendation. Additional exam requirements/recommendations for international students: Required—TOEFL (minimum score 600 paper-based). Electronic applications accepted. *Faculty research:* Teacher education; curriculum theory and development; community based education models, educational leadership.

University of Denver, Morgridge College of Education, Denver, CO 80208. Offers child, family and school psychology (MA, PhD, Ed S); counseling psychology (MA, PhD); curriculum and instruction (MA, Ed D, PhD); curriculum instruction and teaching (Certificate); early childhood special education (MA, Certificate); educational leadership and policy studies (MA, Ed D, PhD, Certificate); higher education (Ed D, PhD); library and information science (MLIS); research methods and statistics (MA, PhD). *Accreditation:* ALA; APA (one or more programs are accredited). *Program availability:* Part-time, evening/weekend, online learning. *Faculty:* 39 full-time (29 women), 60 part-time/adjunct (42 women). *Students:* 502 full-time (406 women), 361 part-time (267 women); includes 233 minority (54 Black or African American, non-Hispanic/Latino; 6 American Indian or Alaska Native, non-Hispanic/Latino; 25 Asian, non-Hispanic/Latino; 113 Hispanic/Latino; 35 Two or more races, non-Hispanic/Latino), 52 international. Average age 31. 1,167 applicants, 64% accepted, 415 enrolled. In 2017, 285 master's, 51 doctorates, 157 other advanced degrees awarded. Terminal master's awarded for partial completion of doctoral program. *Degree requirements:* For master's, comprehensive exam; for doctorate, 2 foreign languages, comprehensive exam, thesis/dissertation. *Entrance requirements:* For master's and doctorate, GRE General Test or GMAT. Additional exam requirements/recommendations for international students: Required—TOEFL (minimum score 550 paper-based; 80 iBT). *Application deadline:*

Applications are processed on a rolling basis. Application fee: $65. Electronic applications accepted. *Expenses:* $31,935 per year full-time. *Financial support:* In 2017–18, 765 students received support, including 26 research assistantships with tuition reimbursements available (averaging $10,957 per year), 38 teaching assistantships with tuition reimbursements available (averaging $3,391 per year); career-related internships or fieldwork, Federal Work-Study, institutionally sponsored loans, scholarships/grants, and unspecified assistantships also available. Support available to part-time students. Financial award application deadline: 2/15; financial award applicants required to submit FAFSA. *Faculty research:* Early childhood education, educational leadership, access and opportunity to postsecondary education, marriage and family therapy, data management and archival research. *Unit head:* Dr. Karen Riley, Dean, 303-871-3665, Fax: 303-871-4456, E-mail: karen.riley@du.edu. *Application contact:* Jodi Dye, Director of Admissions, 303-871-2510, Fax: 303-871-4456, E-mail: jodi.dye@du.edu.
Website: http://morgridge.du.edu

University of Detroit Mercy, College of Liberal Arts and Education, Detroit, MI 48221. Offers addiction counseling (MA); addiction studies (Certificate); clinical mental health counseling (MA); clinical psychology (MA, PhD); computer and information systems (MS); criminal justice (MA); curriculum and instruction (MA); economics (MA); educational administration (MA); financial economics (MA); industrial/organizational psychology (MA); information assurance (MS); intelligence analysis (MA); liberal studies (MALS); religious studies (MA); school counseling (MA, Certificate); school psychology (Spec); security administration (MS); special education: emotionally impaired/behaviorally disordered (MA); special education: learning disabilities (MA). *Program availability:* Part-time, evening/weekend. *Degree requirements:* For doctorate, departmental qualifying exam. *Faculty research:* Psychology of aging, history of technology, Renaissance humanism, U.S. and Japanese economic relations.

The University of Findlay, Office of Graduate Admissions, Findlay, OH 45840. Offers applied security and analytics (MSAS); athletic training (MAT); business (MBA), including certified management accountant, certified public accountant, health care management, hospitality management; education (MA Ed, Ed D), including children's literature (MA Ed), curriculum and teaching (MA Ed), education (MA Ed), educational administration (MA Ed), human resource development (MA Ed), mathematics (MA Ed), reading (MA Ed), science education (MA Ed), superintendent (Ed D), teaching (Ed D), technology (MA Ed); environmental, safety, and health management (MSEM); health informatics (MS); occupational therapy (MOT); pharmacy (Pharm D); physical therapy (DPT); physician assistant (MPA); rhetoric and writing (MA); teaching English to speakers of other languages (TESOL) and applied linguistics (MA). *Program availability:* Part-time, evening/weekend, 100% online, blended/hybrid learning. *Students:* 688 full-time (430 women), 553 part-time (308 women), 170 international. Average age 28. In 2017, 366 master's, 137 doctorates awarded. *Degree requirements:* For master's, comprehensive exam (for some programs), thesis (for some programs), cumulative project, capstone project; for doctorate, thesis/dissertation (for some programs). *Entrance requirements:* For master's, GRE/GMAT, bachelor's degree from accredited institution, minimum undergraduate GPA of 2.5 in last 64 hours of course work; for doctorate, GRE, MAT, minimum cumulative GPA of 3.0. Additional exam requirements/recommendations for international students: Required—TOEFL (minimum score 79 iBT), IELTS (minimum score 7), PTE (minimum score 61). *Application deadline:* Applications are processed on a rolling basis. Electronic applications accepted. *Financial support:* In 2017–18, 10 research assistantships with partial tuition reimbursements (averaging $7,200 per year), 35 teaching assistantships with partial tuition reimbursements (averaging $7,200 per year) were awarded; Federal Work-Study, institutionally sponsored loans, and unspecified assistantships also available. Financial award applicants required to submit FAFSA. *Unit head:* Christopher M. Harris, Director of Admissions, 419-434-4347, E-mail: harrisc1@findlay.edu. *Application contact:* Madeline Fauser Brennan, Graduate Admissions Counselor, 419-434-4636, Fax: 419-434-4898, E-mail: fauserbrennan@findlay.edu.
Website: http://www.findlay.edu/admissions/graduate/Pages/default.aspx

University of Florida, Graduate School, College of Education, School of Human Development and Organizational Studies in Education, Gainesville, FL 32611. Offers counseling and counselor education (Ed D, PhD), including counseling and counselor education, marriage and family counseling, mental health counseling, school counseling and guidance; educational leadership (M Ed, MAE, Ed D, PhD, Ed S), including educational leadership (Ed D, PhD), educational policy (Ed D, PhD); higher education administration (Ed D, PhD), including education policy (Ed D), educational policy, higher education administration; marriage and family counseling (M Ed, MAE, Ed D, PhD, Ed S); mental health counseling (M Ed, MAE, Ed D, PhD, Ed S); research and evaluation methodology (M Ed, MAE, Ed D, PhD); school counseling and guidance (M Ed, MAE, Ed D, PhD, Ed S); student personnel in higher education (M Ed, MAE). *Accreditation:* ACA (one or more programs are accredited); NCATE. *Program availability:* Part-time, online learning. Terminal master's awarded for partial completion of doctoral program. *Degree requirements:* For master's, thesis optional; for doctorate, comprehensive exam, thesis/dissertation. *Entrance requirements:* For master's and doctorate, GRE General Test, minimum GPA of 3.0 (undergraduate), 3.5 (graduate); for Ed S, GRE General Test. Additional exam requirements/recommendations for international students: Required—TOEFL (minimum score 550 paper-based; 80 iBT), IELTS (minimum score 6). Electronic applications accepted.

University of Georgia, College of Education, Department of Lifelong Education, Administration and Policy, Athens, GA 30602. Offers adult education (Ed D, Ed S); lifelong education, administration and policy (PhD). *Accreditation:* NCATE. *Entrance requirements:* For doctorate, GRE General Test; for Ed S, GRE General Test or MAT. Electronic applications accepted.

University of Guam, Office of Graduate Studies, School of Education, Program in Administration and Supervision, Mangilao, GU 96923. Offers M Ed. *Degree requirements:* For master's, comprehensive oral and written exams, special project or thesis. *Entrance requirements:* For master's, GRE General Test. Additional exam requirements/recommendations for international students: Required—TOEFL.

University of Hartford, College of Education, Nursing, and Health Professions, Doctoral Program in Educational Leadership, West Hartford, CT 06117-1599. Offers Ed D. *Accreditation:* NCATE. *Program availability:* Part-time, evening/weekend. *Degree requirements:* For doctorate, thesis/dissertation. *Entrance requirements:* For doctorate, MAT, 3 letters of recommendation, writing samples, interview, resume, letter of support from employer. *Expenses:* Contact institution.

University of Hartford, College of Education, Nursing, and Health Professions, Program in Educational Leadership, West Hartford, CT 06117-1599. Offers administration and supervision (CAGS). *Accreditation:* NCATE. *Program availability:* Part-time, evening/weekend. *Degree requirements:* For CAGS, comprehensive exam or research project. *Entrance requirements:* For degree, GRE General Test or MAT, interview. Additional exam requirements/recommendations for international students: Required—TOEFL (minimum score 550 paper-based). Electronic applications accepted.

University of Hawaii at Manoa, Office of Graduate Education, College of Education, Department of Educational Administration, Honolulu, HI 96822. Offers M Ed. *Program* *availability:* Part-time. *Degree requirements:* For master's, thesis optional. *Entrance requirements:* Additional exam requirements/recommendations for international students: Required—TOEFL (minimum score 600 paper-based; 100 iBT), IELTS (minimum score 7). *Faculty research:* Leadership, educational policy, organizational processes, finance.

University of Hawaii at Manoa, Office of Graduate Education, College of Education, Ed D in Professional Practice Program, Honolulu, HI 96822. Offers Ed D. *Entrance requirements:* Additional exam requirements/recommendations for international students: Required—TOEFL (minimum score 600 paper-based; 100 iBT).

University of Hawaii at Manoa, Office of Graduate Education, College of Education, PhD in Education Program, Honolulu, HI 96822. Offers curriculum and instruction (PhD); educational administration (PhD); educational foundations (PhD); educational policy studies (PhD); educational psychology (PhD); exceptionalities (PhD); kinesiology (PhD); learning design and technology (PhD). *Program availability:* Part-time, evening/weekend. *Degree requirements:* For doctorate, thesis/dissertation. *Entrance requirements:* For doctorate, GRE General Test, sample of written work. Additional exam requirements/recommendations for international students: Required—TOEFL (minimum score 600 paper-based; 100 iBT), IELTS (minimum score 7).

University of Holy Cross, Graduate Programs, New Orleans, LA 70131-7399. Offers biomedical sciences (MS); Catholic theology (MA); counseling (MA, PhD), including community counseling (MA), marriage and family counseling (MA), school counseling (MA); educational leadership (M Ed); executive leadership (Ed D); management (MS), including healthcare management, operations management; teaching and learning (M Ed). *Accreditation:* ACA; NCATE. *Program availability:* Part-time, evening/weekend, online learning. *Faculty:* 7 full-time (4 women), 8 part-time/adjunct (3 women). *Students:* 67 full-time (55 women), 69 part-time (55 women); includes 51 minority (46 Black or African American, non-Hispanic/Latino; 2 American Indian or Alaska Native, non-Hispanic/Latino; 1 Asian, non-Hispanic/Latino; 2 Hispanic/Latino). Average age 30. 20 applicants, 50% accepted. In 2017, 28 degrees awarded. *Degree requirements:* For master's, thesis. *Entrance requirements:* For master's, GRE General Test, minimum GPA of 2.7. *Application deadline:* For fall admission, 9/1 for domestic students. Application fee: $15. *Expenses: Tuition:* Full-time $10,890; part-time $605 per credit hour. *Required fees:* $1624; $812 per semester. One-time fee: $50. *Financial support:* Federal Work-Study and tuition waivers (partial) available. Support available to part-time students. Financial award application deadline: 6/1. *Unit head:* Dr. Myles Seghers, Dean of Humanities, Education, and Counseling, 504-394-7744 Ext. 214, Fax: 504-391-2421, E-mail: mseghers@olhcc.edu. *Application contact:* Anne-Katherine Lene, Director of Student Enrollment, 504-394-7744 Ext. 110, Fax: 504-391-2421, E-mail: aklene@olhcc.edu.

University of Houston, College of Education, Department of Curriculum and Instruction, Houston, TX 77204. Offers administration and supervision (M Ed); curriculum and instruction (M Ed, Ed D); professional leadership (Ed D). *Accreditation:* NCATE. *Program availability:* Part-time, evening/weekend. *Degree requirements:* For master's, comprehensive exam, thesis optional; for doctorate, comprehensive exam, thesis/dissertation. *Entrance requirements:* For master's and doctorate, GRE, minimum cumulative undergraduate GPA of 2.6, 3 letters of recommendation, resume/vita, goal statement. Additional exam requirements/recommendations for international students: Required—TOEFL (minimum score 550 paper-based; 79 iBT). Electronic applications accepted. *Faculty research:* Teaching-learning process, instructional technology in schools, teacher education, classroom management, at-risk students.

University of Houston, College of Education, Department of Educational Leadership and Cultural Studies, Houston, TX 77204. Offers administration and supervision (M Ed, Ed D); higher education (M Ed); historical, social, and cultural foundations of education (M Ed). *Accreditation:* NCATE. *Program availability:* Part-time, evening/weekend. *Degree requirements:* For master's, comprehensive exam or thesis; for doctorate, comprehensive exam, thesis/dissertation. *Entrance requirements:* For master's, GRE General Test, minimum cumulative GPA of 2.6, 3 letters of recommendation, resume/vitae, goal statement; for doctorate, GRE General Test, minimum cumulative GPA of 2.6, 3 letters of recommendation, resume/vitae, goal statement, writing sample, interview. Additional exam requirements/recommendations for international students: Required—TOEFL (minimum score 550 paper-based; 79 iBT). Electronic applications accepted. *Faculty research:* Change, supervision, multiculturalism, evaluation, policy.

University of Houston, College of Education, Department of Educational Psychology, Houston, TX 77204. Offers administration and supervision - higher education (M Ed); counseling (M Ed); counseling psychology (PhD); educational psychology (M Ed); school psychology (PhD); school psychology and individual differences (PhD); special education (M Ed). *Accreditation:* NCATE. *Program availability:* Part-time, evening/weekend, online learning. *Degree requirements:* For master's, comprehensive exam or thesis; for doctorate, comprehensive exam, thesis/dissertation. *Entrance requirements:* For master's, GRE, transcripts, 3 letters of recommendation, curriculum vita, goal statement; for doctorate, GRE, transcripts, 3 letters of recommendation, curriculum vita, goal statement, writing sample, interview. Additional exam requirements/recommendations for international students: Required—TOEFL (minimum score 550 paper-based; 79 iBT), IELTS (minimum score 6.5). Electronic applications accepted. *Faculty research:* Evidence-based assessment and intervention, multicultural issues in psychology, social and cultural context of learning, systemic barriers to college, motivational aspects of self-regulated learning.

University of Houston–Clear Lake, School of Education, Program in Educational Leadership, Houston, TX 77058-1002. Offers educational leadership (Ed D); educational management (MS). *Degree requirements:* For master's, thesis optional; for doctorate, comprehensive exam, thesis/dissertation.

University of Houston–Victoria, School of Education, Health Professions and Human Development, Victoria, TX 77901-4450. Offers administration and supervision (M Ed); adult and higher education (M Ed); counselor education (M Ed); curriculum and instruction (M Ed); dyslexia education (Certificate); educational technology (M Ed); special education (M Ed). *Program availability:* Part-time, evening/weekend, online learning. *Degree requirements:* For master's, comprehensive exam, project or thesis. *Entrance requirements:* For master's, GRE General Test. Additional exam requirements/recommendations for international students: Required—TOEFL. Electronic applications accepted. *Faculty research:* Reading and language arts education, evaluation and diagnosis of special children's abilities.

University of Idaho, College of Graduate Studies, College of Education, Health and Human Sciences, Department of Leadership and Counseling, Boise, ID 83844-2282. Offers adult/organizational learning and leadership (Ed S); educational leadership (Ed S); rehabilitation counseling and human services (M Ed); school counseling (M Ed, MS). *Faculty:* 14 full-time, 6 part-time/adjunct. *Students:* 29 full-time (20 women), 147 part-time (78 women). Average age 38. In 2017, 62 master's, 32 other advanced degrees awarded. *Entrance requirements:* For master's, minimum GPA of 3.0, writing sample. Additional exam requirements/recommendations for international students: Required—TOEFL (minimum score 79 iBT). *Application deadline:* Applications are processed on a rolling basis. Application fee: $60. Electronic applications accepted. *Expenses:* Tuition, state resident: full-time $6722; part-time $430 per credit hour.

Tuition, nonresident: full-time $23,046; part-time $1337 per credit hour. *Required fees:* $2142; $63 per credit hour. *Financial support:* Applicants required to submit FAFSA. *Unit head:* Dr. Kathy Canfield-Davis, Chair, 208-364-4047, E-mail: lead@uidaho.edu. *Application contact:* Sean Scoggin, Graduate Recruitment Coordinator, 208-885-4723, Fax: 208-885-4406, E-mail: graduateadmissions@uidaho.edu.
Website: https://www.uidaho.edu/ed/lc

University of Illinois at Chicago, College of Education, Department of Educational Policy Studies, Chicago, IL 60607-7128. Offers policy studies (M Ed); policy studies in urban education (PhD); urban education leadership (Ed D). *Faculty research:* Social foundations of education, educational organizations and leadership, education policy analysis, understanding and addressing educational problems in urban contexts.

University of Illinois at Springfield, Graduate Programs, College of Education and Human Services, Department of Educational Leadership, Springfield, IL 62703-5407. Offers chief school business official (CAS); educational leadership (MA, CAS); educational technology (Graduate Certificate); English as a second language (Graduate Certificate); higher education online pedagogy (Graduate Certificate); leadership and learning (Graduate Certificate); legal aspects of education (Graduate Certificate). *Program availability:* Part-time, evening/weekend, 100% online, blended/hybrid learning. *Faculty:* 4 full-time (1 woman), 14 part-time/adjunct (11 women). *Students:* 2 full-time (1 woman), 109 part-time (70 women); includes 15 minority (10 Black or African American, non-Hispanic/Latino; 1 American Indian or Alaska Native, non-Hispanic/Latino; 1 Asian, non-Hispanic/Latino; 3 Hispanic/Latino). Average age 35. 46 applicants, 57% accepted, 23 enrolled. In 2017, 30 master's, 5 other advanced degrees awarded. *Degree requirements:* For master's, capstone course. *Entrance requirements:* For master's, minimum undergraduate GPA of 3.0, valid Illinois Teaching License, minimum of two years of successful teaching experience, portfolio that includes letters of recommendation, interview. Additional exam requirements/recommendations for international students: Required—TOEFL (minimum score 500 paper-based; 61 iBT). *Application deadline:* Applications are processed on a rolling basis. Application fee: $60 ($75 for international students). Electronic applications accepted. *Expenses:* Tuition, state resident: full-time $7896; part-time $329 per credit hour. Tuition, nonresident: full-time $16,200; part-time $675 per credit hour. Tuition and fees vary according to program. *Financial support:* In 2017–18, research assistantships with full tuition reimbursements (averaging $10,249 per year), teaching assistantships with full tuition reimbursements (averaging $10,303 per year) were awarded; fellowships, career-related internships or fieldwork, Federal Work-Study, scholarships/grants, health care benefits, and unspecified assistantships also available. Support available to part-time students. Financial award application deadline: 11/15; financial award applicants required to submit FAFSA. *Unit head:* Dr. Scott Day, Program Administrator, 217-206-7520, Fax: 217-206-6775, E-mail: day.scott@uis.edu.
Website: http://www.uis.edu/edl

University of Illinois at Urbana–Champaign, Graduate College, College of Education, Department of Education Policy, Organization, and Leadership, Champaign, IL 61820. Offers educational organization and leadership (Ed M, MS, Ed D, PhD, CAS); educational policy studies (Ed M, MA, PhD); human resource education (Ed M, MS, Ed D, PhD, CAS). *Program availability:* Part-time, online learning.

University of Indianapolis, Graduate Programs, School of Education, Indianapolis, IN 46227-3697. Offers art education (MAT); biology (MAT); chemistry (MAT); curriculum and instruction (MA); earth sciences (MAT); education (MA, MAT); educational leadership (MA); elementary education (MA); English (MAT); French (MAT); math (MAT); physical education (MAT); physics (MAT); secondary education (MA), including art education, education, English education, social studies education; social studies (MAT); Spanish (MAT). *Accreditation:* NCATE. *Program availability:* Part-time, evening/weekend. *Entrance requirements:* For master's, GRE Subject Test, PRAXIS I, minimum GPA of 2.5, 3 letters of recommendation, interview. Additional exam requirements/recommendations for international students: Required—TOEFL (minimum score 550 paper-based). *Faculty research:* Assessment of teacher education, perceptions of prospective teachers by parents.

The University of Iowa, Graduate College, College of Education, Department of Educational Policy and Leadership Studies, Program in Educational Leadership, Iowa City, IA 52242-1316. Offers MA, PhD, Ed S. *Degree requirements:* For master's and Ed S, exam; for doctorate, comprehensive exam, thesis/dissertation. *Entrance requirements:* For master's, doctorate, and Ed S, GRE General Test, minimum GPA of 3.0. Additional exam requirements/recommendations for international students: Required—TOEFL (minimum score 550 paper-based; 81 iBT). Electronic applications accepted.

The University of Kansas, Graduate Studies, School of Education, Department of Educational Leadership and Policy Studies, Education Leadership and Policy Program, Lawrence, KS 66045-3101. Offers policy studies (PhD); social and cultural studies in education (MSE, PhD). *Program availability:* Part-time, evening/weekend. *Students:* 128 full-time (70 women), 45 part-time (24 women); includes 37 minority (14 Black or African American, non-Hispanic/Latino; 2 American Indian or Alaska Native, non-Hispanic/Latino; 4 Asian, non-Hispanic/Latino; 8 Hispanic/Latino; 9 Two or more races, non-Hispanic/Latino), 30 international. Average age 38. 66 applicants, 68% accepted, 36 enrolled. In 2017, 23 doctorates awarded. *Entrance requirements:* For master's, minimum GPA of 3.0, resume or curriculum vitae, statement of purpose, official academic transcripts, three letters of recommendation; for doctorate, GRE General Test, minimum graduate GPA of 3.5, resume or curriculum vitae, statement of purpose, official academic transcripts, three letters of recommendation, writing sample. *Application deadline:* For fall admission, 7/1 for domestic and international students; for spring admission, 11/1 for domestic and international students; for summer admission, 4/1 for domestic and international students. Application fee: $65 ($85 for international students). Electronic applications accepted. *Financial support:* Fellowships, research assistantships, teaching assistantships, scholarships/grants, and unspecified assistantships available. Financial award application deadline: 3/15. *Faculty research:* Historical and philosophical issues in education, education policy and leadership, higher education faculty, research on college students, education technology. *Unit head:* Dr. Susan B. Twombly, Chair, 785-864-9721, E-mail: stwombly@ku.edu. *Application contact:* Denise Brubaker, Admissions Coordinator, 785-864-7973, E-mail: brubaker@ku.edu.
Website: http://elps.soe.ku.edu/

The University of Kansas, Graduate Studies, School of Education, Department of Educational Leadership and Policy Studies, Program in Educational Administration, Lawrence, KS 66045-3101. Offers MSE, Ed D, PhD. Program begins in summer semester only. *Program availability:* Part-time, evening/weekend, online learning. *Students:* 3 full-time (1 woman), 115 part-time (67 women); includes 22 minority (13 Black or African American, non-Hispanic/Latino; 1 American Indian or Alaska Native, non-Hispanic/Latino; 1 Asian, non-Hispanic/Latino; 3 Hispanic/Latino; 4 Two or more races, non-Hispanic/Latino), 2 international. Average age 32. 54 applicants, 85% accepted, 38 enrolled. In 2017, 20 master's awarded. *Entrance requirements:* For master's, minimum GPA of 3.0, resume, statement of purpose, official transcript, three letters of recommendation; for doctorate, GRE General Test, minimum graduate GPA of 3.5, resume, statement of purpose, academic transcripts, three letters of

recommendation, writing sample. *Application deadline:* For summer admission, 4/1 for domestic and international students. Application fee: $65 ($85 for international students). Electronic applications accepted. *Financial support:* Research assistantships, teaching assistantships, Federal Work-Study, scholarships/grants, and unspecified assistantships available. Financial award application deadline: 3/1. *Unit head:* Dr. Susan B. Twombly, Chair, 785-864-9721, Fax: 785-864-4697, E-mail: stwombly@ku.edu. *Application contact:* Denise Brubaker, Admissions Coordinator, 785-864-7973, Fax: 785-864-4697, E-mail: brubaker@ku.edu.
Website: http://elps.soe.ku.edu/academics/edadmin/mse

University of Kentucky, Graduate School, College of Education, Program in Educational Leadership Studies, Lexington, KY 40506-0032. Offers educational leadership (M Ed, Ed D, PhD, Ed S); educational sciences (PhD); family resource and youth services (M Ed, Ed S); principalship (Ed D, Ed S); school technology leadership (M Ed, PhD, Ed S); teacher leadership (M Ed, Ed S). *Degree requirements:* For master's and Ed S, comprehensive exam; for doctorate, comprehensive exam, thesis/dissertation. *Entrance requirements:* For master's, GRE General Test, minimum undergraduate GPA of 2.75; for doctorate, GRE General Test, minimum graduate GPA of 3.0. Additional exam requirements/recommendations for international students: Required—TOEFL (minimum score 550 paper-based). Electronic applications accepted. *Faculty research:* School governance, teacher empowerment, planned change, systemic reform, issues of equity and fairness.

University of La Verne, LaFetra College of Education, Doctoral Program in Organizational Leadership, La Verne, CA 91750-4443. Offers Ed D. *Program availability:* Part-time. *Faculty:* 8 full-time (5 women). *Students:* 103 full-time (75 women), 40 part-time (23 women); includes 77 minority (19 Black or African American, non-Hispanic/Latino; 6 Asian, non-Hispanic/Latino; 48 Hispanic/Latino; 4 Two or more races, non-Hispanic/Latino), 1 international. Average age 45. *Entrance requirements:* For doctorate, GRE or MAT, minimum graduate GPA of 3.0, resume or curriculum vitae, 2 endorsement forms. Additional exam requirements/recommendations for international students: Required—TOEFL (minimum score 550 paper-based). *Application deadline:* Applications are processed on a rolling basis. Application fee: $75. *Expenses:* Contact institution. *Financial support:* Institutionally sponsored loans and scholarships/grants available. Financial award application deadline: 3/2; financial award applicants required to submit FAFSA. *Unit head:* Dr. Rich Whitney, Assistant Professor, Organizational Leadership, 909-448-4790, E-mail: rwhitney@laverne.edu. *Application contact:* Christy Ranells, Associate Director of Graduate Admission, 909-448-4644, Fax: 909-971-2295, E-mail: cranells@laverne.edu.
Website: https://laverne.edu/edd/

University of La Verne, LaFetra College of Education, Master's Program in Education, La Verne, CA 91750-4443. Offers advanced teaching skills (M Ed); education (M Ed); educational leadership (M Ed); special emphasis (M Ed). *Accreditation:* NCATE. *Program availability:* Part-time. *Students:* 35 full-time (23 women), 149 part-time (111 women); includes 92 minority (5 Black or African American, non-Hispanic/Latino; 2 American Indian or Alaska Native, non-Hispanic/Latino; 3 Asian, non-Hispanic/Latino; 78 Hispanic/Latino; 4 Two or more races, non-Hispanic/Latino). Average age 32. *Entrance requirements:* For master's, California Basic Educational Skills Test, interview, writing sample, minimum GPA of 3.0, 3 letters of recommendation. Additional exam requirements/recommendations for international students: Required—TOEFL (minimum score 550 paper-based). *Application deadline:* Applications are processed on a rolling basis. Application fee: $50. *Expenses:* Contact institution. *Financial support:* Institutionally sponsored loans and scholarships/grants available. Financial award application deadline: 3/2; financial award applicants required to submit FAFSA. *Unit head:* Dr. Jessica Decker, Chair, 909-448-4582, E-mail: jdecker@laverne.edu. *Application contact:* Christy Ranells, Associate Director of Graduate Admission, 909-448-4644, Fax: 909-392-2744, E-mail: cranells@laverne.edu.
Website: https://education.laverne.edu/leadership/

University of La Verne, Regional and Online Campuses, Graduate Credential Program in Education, California Statewide Campus, La Verne, CA 91750-4443. Offers administration services (preliminary) (Credential); education specialist: mild/moderate (Credential); English (Certificate); multiple subject teaching (Credential); pupil personnel services: school counseling (Credential); single subject teaching (Credential); special education (MS); special emphasis (M Ed). *Accreditation:* NCATE. *Program availability:* Part-time. *Faculty:* 3 full-time (2 women), 25 part-time/adjunct (19 women). *Students:* 120 full-time (95 women), 62 part-time (47 women); includes 47 minority (3 Black or African American, non-Hispanic/Latino; 2 American Indian or Alaska Native, non-Hispanic/Latino; 2 Asian, non-Hispanic/Latino; 40 Hispanic/Latino). Average age 31. In 2017, 25 master's, 61 other advanced degrees awarded. *Entrance requirements:* For degree, California Basic Educational Skills Test, minimum undergraduate GPA of 2.75, 3 letters of recommendation, interview. *Application deadline:* Applications are processed on a rolling basis. Application fee: $50. *Expenses:* Contact institution. *Financial support:* Application deadline: 3/2; applicants required to submit FAFSA. *Unit head:* Pam Bergovoy, Assistant Dean, Regional and Online Campuses/Director, Center for Educators, 909-448-4953, E-mail: pbergovoy@laverne.edu. *Application contact:* 877-468-6858, E-mail: gradadmission@laverne.edu.
Website: https://laverne.edu/locations/

University of La Verne, Regional and Online Campuses, Graduate Programs, High Desert Campus, Victorville, CA 92392. Offers business administration for experienced professionals (MBA); educational (special emphasis) (M Ed); educational counseling (MS); leadership and management (MS); multiple subject (elementary) (Credential); preliminary administrative services (Credential); pupil personnel services (Credential); single subject (secondary) (Credential). *Students:* 7 full-time (3 women), 16 part-time (12 women); includes 14 minority (3 Black or African American, non-Hispanic/Latino; 1 American Indian or Alaska Native, non-Hispanic/Latino; 1 Asian, non-Hispanic/Latino; 9 Hispanic/Latino). Average age 41. In 2017, 9 master's awarded. *Application deadline:* Applications are processed on a rolling basis. Application fee: $50. *Expenses:* Contact institution. *Financial support:* Application deadline: 3/2; applicants required to submit FAFSA. *Unit head:* Juli Roberts, Regional Campus Director, 760-955-6448, Fax: 760-843-9505, E-mail: jroberts@laverne.edu. *Application contact:* Admissions, 760-955-6440, Fax: 760-955-6443, E-mail: hdcv@laverne.edu.
Website: https://laverne.edu/locations/

University of La Verne, Regional and Online Campuses, Graduate Programs, Kern County Campus, Bakersfield, CA 93301. Offers business administration for experienced professionals (MBA-EP); education (special emphasis) (M Ed); educational counseling (MS); educational leadership (M Ed); health administration (MHA); leadership and management (MS); mild/moderate education specialist (Credential); multiple subject (elementary) (Credential); organizational leadership (Ed D); preliminary administrative services (Credential); single subject (secondary) (Credential); special education studies (MS). *Program availability:* Part-time, evening/weekend. *Students:* Average age 36. In 2017, 3 master's awarded. *Application deadline:* Applications are processed on a rolling basis. Application fee: $50. *Expenses:* Contact institution. *Financial support:* Institutionally sponsored loans available. Financial award application deadline: 3/2; financial award applicants required to submit FAFSA. *Unit head:* Nora Dominguez, Regional Campus Director, 661-861-6802, E-mail: ndominguez@laverne.edu.

Application contact: Rebecca Murillo, Associate Director of Admissions, 661-861-6807, E-mail: rmurillo@laverne.edu.
Website: https://laverne.edu/locations/

University of La Verne, Regional and Online Campuses, Graduate Programs, Orange County Campus, Irvine, CA 92840. Offers business administration for experienced professionals (MBA); educational counseling (MS); educational leadership (M Ed); health administration (MHA); leadership and management (MS); preliminary administrative services (Credential); pupil personnel services (Credential). *Program availability:* Part-time. *Students:* 19 full-time (11 women), 51 part-time (30 women); includes 47 minority (12 Black or African American, non-Hispanic/Latino; 2 American Indian or Alaska Native, non-Hispanic/Latino; 12 Asian, non-Hispanic/Latino; 21 Hispanic/Latino). Average age 39. In 2017, 43 master's awarded. *Application deadline:* Applications are processed on a rolling basis. Application fee: $50. *Expenses:* Contact institution. *Financial support:* Application deadline: 3/2; applicants required to submit FAFSA. *Unit head:* Alison Rodriguez-Balles, Interim Campus Director, 714-505-6943, Fax: 909-505-6937, E-mail: arodriguez2@laverne.edu. *Application contact:* 877-468-6858, E-mail: gradadmission@laverne.edu.
Website: https://laverne.edu/locations/

University of La Verne, Regional and Online Campuses, Graduate Programs, San Fernando Valley Campus, Burbank, CA 91505. Offers business administration for experienced professionals (MBA-EP); educational counseling (MS); educational leadership (M Ed); leadership and management (MS); preliminary administrative services (Credential); pupil personnel services (Credential). *Program availability:* Part-time, evening/weekend. *Students:* 43 full-time (26 women), 97 part-time (49 women); includes 88 minority (21 Black or African American, non-Hispanic/Latino; 1 American Indian or Alaska Native, non-Hispanic/Latino; 15 Asian, non-Hispanic/Latino; 49 Hispanic/Latino; 1 Native Hawaiian or other Pacific Islander, non-Hispanic/Latino; 1 Two or more races, non-Hispanic/Latino). Average age 38. In 2017, 65 master's awarded. *Application deadline:* Applications are processed on a rolling basis. Application fee: $50. *Expenses:* Contact institution. *Financial support:* Application deadline: 3/2; applicants required to submit FAFSA. *Unit head:* Dr. Nelly Kazman, Senior Executive Director, 818-295-6502, E-mail: nkazman@laverne.edu. *Application contact:* Debi Hrboka, Associate Director of Admissions, 818-295-6508, E-mail: dhrboka@laverne.edu.
Website: https://laverne.edu/locations/

University of La Verne, Regional and Online Campuses, Graduate Programs, Ventura County/Point Mugu Naval Air Station Campuses, Oxnard, CA 93036. Offers business administration for experienced professionals (MS); educational counseling (MS); educational leadership (M Ed); leadership and management (MS); multiple subject (elementary) (Credential); pupil personnel services (Credential); single subject (secondary) (Credential). *Program availability:* Part-time, evening/weekend. *Students:* Average age 38. In 2017, 19 master's awarded. Application fee: $50. *Expenses:* Contact institution. *Financial support:* Institutionally sponsored loans available. Financial award application deadline: 3/2; financial award applicants required to submit FAFSA. *Unit head:* Kitt Vincent, Senior Executive Director, 805-788-6202, E-mail: kvincent@laverne.edu. *Application contact:* Mike Stadler, Assistant Director/Academic Advisor, 805-986-6909, E-mail: mstadler3@laverne.edu.
Website: https://laverne.edu/locations/

University of La Verne, Regional and Online Campuses, Master's Programs in Education, California Statewide Campus, La Verne, CA 91750-4443. Offers administration services (preliminary) (Credential); education specialist: mild/moderate (Credential); educational counseling (MS); educational leadership (M Ed); multiple subject teaching (Credential); pupil personnel services: school counseling (Credential); single subject teaching (Credential); special education studies (MS); special emphasis (M Ed). *Accreditation:* NCATE. *Students:* 106 full-time (88 women), 75 part-time (55 women); includes 112 minority (4 Black or African American, non-Hispanic/Latino; 5 Asian, non-Hispanic/Latino; 102 Hispanic/Latino; 1 Two or more races, non-Hispanic/Latino). Average age 35. In 2017, 76 master's, 82 other advanced degrees awarded. *Entrance requirements:* For master's, California Basic Educational Skills Test, 3 letters of recommendation, teaching credential. *Application deadline:* Applications are processed on a rolling basis. Application fee: $50. *Expenses:* Contact institution. *Financial support:* Application deadline: 3/2; applicants required to submit FAFSA. *Unit head:* Pam Bergovoy, Assistant Dean, Regional and Online Campuses/Director, Center for Educators, 909-448-4953, E-mail: pbergovoy@laverne.edu. *Application contact:* 877-468-6858, E-mail: gradadmission@laverne.edu.
Website: http://www.laverne.edu/locations

University of Lethbridge, School of Graduate Studies, Lethbridge, AB T1K 3M4, Canada. Offers addictions counseling (M Sc); agricultural biotechnology (M Sc); agricultural studies (M Sc, MA); anthropology (MA); archaeology (M Sc, MA); art (MA, MFA); biochemistry (M Sc); biological sciences (M Sc); biomolecular science (PhD); biosystems and biodiversity (PhD); Canadian studies (MA); chemistry (M Sc); computer science (M Sc); computer science and geographical information science (M Sc); counseling (MC); counseling psychology (M Ed); dramatic arts (MA); earth, space, and physical science (PhD); economics (MA); education (MA, PhD); educational leadership (M Ed); English (MA); environmental science (M Sc); evolution and behavior (PhD); exercise science (M Sc); French (MA); French/German (MA); French/Spanish (MA); general education (M Ed); geography (M Sc, MA); German (MA); health sciences (M Sc); individualized multidisciplinary (M Sc, MA); kinesiology (M Sc, MA); management (M Sc), including accounting, finance, human resource management and labor relations, information systems, international management, marketing, policy and strategy; mathematics (M Sc); music (M Mus, MA); Native American studies (MA); neuroscience (M Sc, PhD); new media (MA, MFA); nursing (M Sc, MN); philosophy (MA); physics (M Sc); political science (M Sc, MA); psychology (M Sc, MA); religious studies (MA); sociology (MA); theatre and dramatic arts (MFA); theoretical and computational science (PhD); urban and regional studies (MA); women and gender studies (MA). *Program availability:* Part-time, evening/weekend. *Degree requirements:* For master's, thesis (for some programs); for doctorate, comprehensive exam, thesis/dissertation. *Entrance requirements:* For master's, GMAT (for M Sc in management), bachelor's degree in related field, minimum GPA of 3.0 during previous 20 graded semester courses, 2 years' teaching or related experience (M Ed); for doctorate, master's degree, minimum graduate GPA of 3.5. Additional exam requirements/recommendations for international students: Required—TOEFL (minimum score 580 paper-based; 93 iBT). Electronic applications accepted. *Faculty research:* Movement and brain plasticity, gibberellin physiology, photosynthesis, carbon cycling, molecular properties of main-group ring components.

University of Louisiana at Lafayette, College of Education, Graduate Studies and Research in Education, Program in Administration and Supervision, Lafayette, LA 70504. Offers M Ed. *Degree requirements:* For master's, thesis or alternative. *Entrance requirements:* For master's, GRE General Test, teaching certificate. Additional exam requirements/recommendations for international students: Required—TOEFL (minimum score 550 paper-based). Electronic applications accepted.

University of Louisiana at Lafayette, College of Education, Graduate Studies and Research in Education, Program in Educational Leadership, Lafayette, LA 70504. Offers M Ed, Ed D. *Entrance requirements:* Additional exam requirements/recommendations for international students: Required—TOEFL (minimum score 550 paper-based).

University of Louisville, Graduate School, College of Education and Human Development, Department of Educational Leadership, Evaluation and Organizational Development, Louisville, KY 40292-0001. Offers educational leadership and organizational development (Ed D, PhD), including evaluation (PhD), human resource development (PhD), P-12 administration (PhD), post-secondary administration (PhD), sport administration (PhD); health professions education (Certificate); higher education administration (MA); human resources and organization development (MS), including health professions education, human resource leadership, workplace learning and performance; P-12 educational administration (Ed S), including principalship, supervisor of instruction. *Accreditation:* NCATE. *Program availability:* Part-time, evening/weekend, online learning. *Students:* 190 full-time (64 women), 516 part-time (298 women); includes 218 minority (131 Black or African American, non-Hispanic/Latino; 1 American Indian or Alaska Native, non-Hispanic/Latino; 16 Asian, non-Hispanic/Latino; 47 Hispanic/Latino; 2 Native Hawaiian or other Pacific Islander, non-Hispanic/Latino; 21 Two or more races, non-Hispanic/Latino), 3 international. Average age 36. 232 applicants, 84% accepted, 141 enrolled. In 2017, 68 master's, 2 doctorates, 17 other advanced degrees awarded. Application fee: $65. *Expenses:* Tuition, state resident: full-time $12,246; part-time $681 per credit hour. Tuition, nonresident: full-time $25,486; part-time $1417 per credit hour. *Required fees:* $196. Tuition and fees vary according to course load, program and reciprocity agreements. *Financial support:* Application deadline: 6/1; applicants required to submit FAFSA. *Faculty research:* Urban educational leadership and policy, human resource and organizational development, program evaluation, community and military partnerships, higher education, and economic education. *Total annual research expenditures:* $256,111. *Unit head:* Dr. Jeffrey Sun, Chair and Professor, 502-852-0618, E-mail: jeffrey.sun@louisville.edu. *Application contact:* Betty Hampton, Director of Graduate Student Services, 502-852-5597, Fax: 502-852-1465, E-mail: edadvise@louisville.edu.
Website: http://louisville.edu/education/departments/eleod

University of Louisville, Graduate School, College of Education and Human Development, Departments of Early Childhood and Elementary Education, Middle and Secondary Education, and Special Education, Louisville, KY 40292-0001. Offers art education (MAT); autism and applied behavior analysis (Certificate); curriculum and instruction (PhD); early elementary education (MAT); exercise physiology (MS); health and physical education (MAT); health professions education (Certificate); higher education (MA); human resources and organization development (MS); instructional technology (M Ed); interdisciplinary early childhood education (MAT); middle school education (MAT); music education (MAT); secondary education (MAT); special education (MAT); sport administration (MS); teacher leadership (M Ed). *Program availability:* Part-time, evening/weekend. *Students:* 114 full-time (73 women), 173 part-time (114 women); includes 49 minority (19 Black or African American, non-Hispanic/Latino; 5 Asian, non-Hispanic/Latino; 13 Hispanic/Latino; 12 Two or more races, non-Hispanic/Latino), 7 international. Average age 29. 132 applicants, 73% accepted, 57 enrolled. In 2017, 70 master's, 2 doctorates, 2 other advanced degrees awarded. *Application deadline:* For spring admission, 1/1 priority date for international students. Application fee: $65. *Expenses:* Tuition, state resident: full-time $12,246; part-time $681 per credit hour. Tuition, nonresident: full-time $25,486; part-time $1417 per credit hour. *Required fees:* $196. Tuition and fees vary according to course load, program and reciprocity agreements. *Financial support:* Application deadline: 6/1; applicants required to submit FAFSA. *Faculty research:* STEM teaching and learning; content literacy for English language learners; social justice in teacher education; adolescent literacy; mathematics teacher development. *Total annual research expenditures:* $1.7 million. *Unit head:* Dr. Ann E. Larson, Dean, College of Education and Human Development, 502-852-6411, Fax: 502-852-1464, E-mail: ann@louisville.edu. *Application contact:* Betty Hampton, Director of Graduate Student Services, 502-852-5597, Fax: 502-852-1465, E-mail: edadvise@louisville.edu.
Website: http://louisville.edu/delphi

University of Lynchburg, Graduate Studies, Ed D in Leadership Studies Program, Lynchburg, VA 24501-3199. Offers educational leadership (Ed D). *Program availability:* Part-time, evening/weekend. *Faculty:* 14 full-time (6 women). *Students:* 6 full-time (5 women), 33 part-time (19 women); includes 10 minority (6 Black or African American, non-Hispanic/Latino; 2 Hispanic/Latino; 2 Two or more races, non-Hispanic/Latino), 2 international. Average age 45. 27 applicants, 100% accepted, 10 enrolled. In 2017, 5 doctorates awarded. *Degree requirements:* For doctorate, comprehensive exam, thesis/dissertation. *Entrance requirements:* For doctorate, GRE or GMAT, current resume or curriculum vitae, career goals statement, master's degree, official transcripts (bachelor's, master's, others of relevance), master's-level research course, three letters of recommendation, evidence of strong writing skills. Additional exam requirements/recommendations for international students: Required—TOEFL (minimum score 550 paper-based; 80 iBT), IELTS (minimum score 6). *Application deadline:* For fall admission, 7/31 for domestic students, 6/1 for international students; for spring admission, 11/30 for domestic students, 10/15 for international students. Applications are processed on a rolling basis. Application fee: $30. Electronic applications accepted. Application fee is waived when completed online. *Expenses:* $645 per credit hour; $100 fees. *Financial support:* Unspecified assistantships available. Financial award application deadline: 7/31; financial award applicants required to submit FAFSA. *Unit head:* Dr. John Walker, Program Director, 434-544-8032, E-mail: walker.jc@lynchburg.edu. *Application contact:* Ellen Thompson, Graduate Admissions Counselor, 434-544-8841, E-mail: thompson_e@lynchburg.edu.
Website: http://www.lynchburg.edu/graduate/doctor-of-education-edd-in-leadership-studies/

University of Lynchburg, Graduate Studies, M Ed Program in Educational Leadership, Lynchburg, VA 24501-3199. Offers higher education (M Ed); PK-12 administrative and supervisory (M Ed). *Program availability:* Part-time, evening/weekend. *Faculty:* 17 full-time (10 women). *Students:* 10 full-time (4 women), 41 part-time (32 women); includes 6 minority (all Black or African American, non-Hispanic/Latino). Average age 34. 14 applicants, 100% accepted, 7 enrolled. In 2017, 43 master's awarded. *Degree requirements:* For master's, comprehensive exam (for some programs), internship; SLLC exam or comprehensive exam. *Entrance requirements:* For master's, GRE, minimum GPA of 3.0 (preferred), official transcripts (bachelor's, others as relevant), three letters of recommendation, career goals statement. Additional exam requirements/recommendations for international students: Required—TOEFL (minimum score 550 paper-based; 80 iBT), IELTS (minimum score 6). *Application deadline:* For fall admission, 7/31 for domestic students, 6/1 for international students; for spring admission, 11/30 for domestic students, 10/5 for international students. Applications are processed on a rolling basis. Application fee: $30. Electronic applications accepted. Application fee is waived when completed online. *Expenses:* $510 per credit tuition, $100 fees. *Financial support:* Career-related internships or fieldwork, Federal Work-Study, scholarships/grants, health care benefits, and unspecified assistantships available. Support available to part-time students. Financial award application deadline: 7/31; financial award applicants required to submit FAFSA. *Unit head:* Dr. John Walker, Professor/Director, Leadership Studies, 434-544-8032, E-mail: walker.jc@lynchburg.edu. *Application contact:* Ellen Thompson, Graduate Admissions Counselor, 434-544-8841, E-mail: thompson_e@lynchburg.edu.

Website: http://www.lynchburg.edu/graduate/master-of-education-in-educational-leadership/

University of Maine, Graduate School, College of Education and Human Development, School of Educational Leadership, Higher Education, and Human Development, Orono, ME 04469. Offers educational leadership (M Ed, CAS); higher education (CAS); human development (MS). *Program availability:* Part-time. *Faculty:* 11 full-time (7 women), 10 part-time/adjunct (5 women). *Students:* 42 full-time (31 women), 67 part-time (49 women); includes 8 minority (1 Black or African American, non-Hispanic/Latino; 2 American Indian or Alaska Native, non-Hispanic/Latino; 3 Hispanic/Latino; 2 Two or more races, non-Hispanic/Latino). Average age 36. 73 applicants, 82% accepted, 25 enrolled. In 2017, 30 master's, 4 doctorates, 16 other advanced degrees awarded. *Degree requirements:* For master's, thesis (for some programs); for doctorate, comprehensive exam, thesis/dissertation. *Entrance requirements:* For master's, GRE General Test, MAT; for doctorate, GRE. Additional exam requirements/recommendations for international students: Required—TOEFL (minimum score 550 paper-based; 80 iBT), IELTS (minimum score 6.5). *Application deadline:* For fall admission, 2/1 priority date for domestic students. Applications are processed on a rolling basis. Application fee: $65. Electronic applications accepted. *Expenses:* Tuition, state resident: full-time $7722; part-time $429 per credit hour. Tuition, nonresident: full-time $25,146; part-time $1397 per credit hour. *Required fees:* $1162; $581 per credit hour. *Financial support:* In 2017–18, 30 students received support, including 5 teaching assistantships with full tuition reimbursements available (averaging $14,600 per year); career-related internships or fieldwork, Federal Work-Study, institutionally sponsored loans, tuition waivers (full and partial), and unspecified assistantships also available. Financial award application deadline: 3/1. *Faculty research:* Student hazing and hazing prevention, sexuality education, cross cultural perspectives on family, early childhood development, fatherhood/parenting, campus climate, social justice, rural higher education, gender in higher education, discourse, rural sociology, school-community relationships, instructional supervision, rural educational leadership. *Total annual research expenditures:* $130,000. *Unit head:* Dr. Jim Artesani, Associate Dean of Accreditation and Graduate Affairs, 207-581-4061, Fax: 207-581-3120. *Application contact:* Scott G. Delcourt, Senior Associate Dean of the Graduate School, 207-581-3291, Fax: 207-581-3232, E-mail: graduate@maine.edu.
Website: http://www.umaine.edu/edhd/

University of Maine at Farmington, Graduate Programs in Education, Farmington, ME 04938. Offers early childhood education (MS Ed); educational leadership (MS Ed); instructional technology (M Ed). M Ed offered in collaboration with University of Maine and University of Southern Maine. *Accreditation:* NCATE. *Program availability:* Part-time-only, evening/weekend, 100% online, blended/hybrid learning. *Faculty:* 8 full-time (7 women), 2 part-time/adjunct (1 woman). *Students:* 106 part-time (92 women). Average age 36. 6 applicants, 100% accepted, 6 enrolled. In 2017, 29 master's awarded. *Degree requirements:* For master's, thesis, capstone research project. *Entrance requirements:* For master's, baccalaureate degree from accredited institution, valid teaching certificate or professional experience in education. Additional exam requirements/recommendations for international students: Required—TOEFL. *Application deadline:* For fall admission, 8/10 for domestic students; for spring admission, 1/5 for domestic students; for summer admission, 4/10 for domestic students. Applications are processed on a rolling basis. Application fee: $60. Electronic applications accepted. *Expenses:* Contact institution. *Financial support:* Applicants required to submit FAFSA. *Faculty research:* Teacher leadership, school improvement strategies, technology integration. *Unit head:* Dr. Johanna Prince, Director of Graduate Programs in Education, 207-778-7066, E-mail: gradstudies@maine.edu. *Application contact:* Valerie Soucie, Administrative Specialist, 207-778-7502, Fax: 207-778-8134, E-mail: gradstudies@maine.edu.
Website: http://www2.umf.maine.edu/gradstudies/

University of Manitoba, Faculty of Graduate Studies, Faculty of Education, Department of Educational Administration, Foundations and Psychology, Winnipeg, MB R3T 2N2, Canada. Offers adult and post-secondary education (M Ed); educational administration (M Ed); guidance and counseling (M Ed); inclusive special education (M Ed); social foundations of education (M Ed). *Degree requirements:* For master's, thesis or alternative.

University of Mary, Liffrig Family School of Education and Behavioral Sciences, Department of Education, Bismarck, ND 58504-9652. Offers curriculum, instruction and assessment (M Ed); education (Ed D); elementary administration (M Ed); reading (M Ed); secondary administration (M Ed); special education strategist (M Ed). *Program availability:* Part-time. *Degree requirements:* For master's, portfolio or thesis. *Entrance requirements:* For master's, interview, letters of reference, minimum GPA of 2.5. Additional exam requirements/recommendations for international students: Required—TOEFL (minimum score 500 paper-based; 71 iBT). Electronic applications accepted.

University of Mary Hardin-Baylor, Graduate Studies in Education, Belton, TX 76513. Offers curriculum and instruction (M Ed); educational administration (M Ed), including higher education (Ed D), leadership in nursing education (Ed D), P-12 (Ed D). *Program availability:* Part-time, evening/weekend. *Faculty:* 12 full-time (8 women), 5 part-time/adjunct (2 women). *Students:* 29 full-time (20 women), 79 part-time (55 women); includes 53 minority (35 Black or African American, non-Hispanic/Latino; 17 Hispanic/Latino; 1 Two or more races, non-Hispanic/Latino), 1 international. Average age 36. 15 applicants, 80% accepted, 10 enrolled. In 2017, 47 master's, 16 doctorates awarded. *Degree requirements:* For master's, comprehensive exam; for doctorate, thesis/dissertation. *Entrance requirements:* For master's, minimum GPA of 3.0, interview; for doctorate, minimum GPA of 3.5, interview, essay, resume, employment verification, 3 letters of recommendation. Additional exam requirements/recommendations for international students: Required—TOEFL (minimum score 60 iBT), IELTS (minimum score 4.5). *Application deadline:* For fall admission, 6/1 for domestic students, 4/30 priority date for international students; for spring admission, 11/1 for domestic students, 9/30 priority date for international students. Applications are processed on a rolling basis. Application fee: $35 ($135 for international students). Electronic applications accepted. *Expenses:* $920 per credit hour. *Financial support:* In 2017–18, 90 students received support. Federal Work-Study and scholarships for some active duty military personnel available. Support available to part-time students. Financial award application deadline: 6/1; financial award applicants required to submit FAFSA. *Faculty research:* Motivational orientation of preservice teachers. *Unit head:* Dr. Craig Hammonds, Director, Graduate Programs in Education, 254-295-4189, E-mail: rhammonds@umhb.edu. *Application contact:* Sharon Aguilera, Assistant Director, Graduate Admissions, 254-295-4835, E-mail: saguilera@umhb.edu.
Website: https://go.umhb.edu/graduate/education/home

University of Maryland, College Park, Academic Affairs, College of Education, Department of Counseling, Higher Education and Special Education, College Park, MD 20742. Offers college student personnel (M Ed, MA); college student personnel administration (PhD); community counseling (CAGS); community/career counseling (M Ed, MA); counseling and personnel services (M Ed, MA, PhD), including art therapy (M Ed), college student personnel (M Ed), counseling and personnel services (PhD), counseling psychology (M Ed), mental health counseling (M Ed), school counseling (M Ed); counseling psychology (PhD); counselor education (PhD); rehabilitation counseling (M Ed, MA, AGSC); school counseling (M Ed, MA); school psychology (M Ed, MA, PhD). *Accreditation:* APA (one or more programs are accredited); NCATE. *Program availability:* Part-time, evening/weekend, online learning. *Degree requirements:* For master's, thesis (for some programs); for doctorate, thesis/dissertation. *Entrance requirements:* For master's, GRE General Test or MAT, minimum GPA of 3.0, 3 letters of recommendation; for doctorate, GRE General Test or MAT, minimum GPA of 3.5, 3 letters of recommendation. Additional exam requirements/recommendations for international students: Required—TOEFL. Electronic applications accepted. *Faculty research:* Educational psychology, counseling, health.

University of Maryland, College Park, Academic Affairs, College of Education, Department of Education Policy and Leadership, College Park, MD 20742. Offers curriculum and educational communications (M Ed, MA, Ed D, PhD); social foundations of education (M Ed, MA, Ed D, PhD, CAGS). *Accreditation:* NCATE. *Program availability:* Part-time, evening/weekend, online learning. *Degree requirements:* For master's, thesis or alternative, internship and/or field experience; for doctorate, comprehensive exam, thesis/dissertation, practicum or internship. *Entrance requirements:* For master's, GRE General Test or MAT, minimum GPA of 3.0, scholarly writing sample, 3 letters of recommendation; for doctorate, GRE General Test or MAT, scholarly writing sample; minimum undergraduate GPA of 3.0, graduate 3.5. *Faculty research:* Educational technology, adult and higher education.

University of Maryland Eastern Shore, Graduate Programs, Department of Education, Program in Education Leadership, Princess Anne, MD 21853. Offers Ed D. *Program availability:* Evening/weekend. *Degree requirements:* For doctorate, comprehensive exam, thesis/dissertation, internship. *Entrance requirements:* For doctorate, interview, writing sample, state certification in a standard area, 3 years of recent teaching or successful professional experience in K-12 school setting. Additional exam requirements/recommendations for international students: Required—TOEFL (minimum score 80 iBT). Electronic applications accepted.

University of Massachusetts Amherst, Graduate School, College of Education, Program in Education, Amherst, MA 01003. Offers bilingual, English as a second language, and multicultural education (M Ed, Ed S); child study and early education (M Ed); children, families and schools (Ed D, Ed S); early childhood and elementary teacher education (M Ed); educational leadership (M Ed); educational policy and leadership (Ed D); higher education (M Ed); international education (M Ed); language, literacy and culture (Ed D); learning, media and technology (M Ed, Ed S); mathematics, science, and learning technologies (Ed D); reading and writing (M Ed); research, educational measurement and psychometrics (Ed D); school counselor education (M Ed, Ed S); school psychology (Ed S); science education (Ed S); secondary teacher education (M Ed); social justice education (M Ed, Ed D, Ed S); special education (M Ed, Ed D, Ed S); teacher education and school improvement (Ed D, Ed S). *Accreditation:* NCATE. *Program availability:* Part-time, online learning. Terminal master's awarded for partial completion of doctoral program. *Degree requirements:* For doctorate, comprehensive exam, thesis/dissertation. *Entrance requirements:* Additional exam requirements/recommendations for international students: Required—TOEFL (minimum score 550 paper-based; 80 iBT), IELTS (minimum score 6.5). Electronic applications accepted.

University of Massachusetts Boston, College of Education and Human Development, Program in Educational Administration, Boston, MA 02125-3393. Offers M Ed, CAGS. *Program availability:* Part-time, evening/weekend. *Students:* 21 part-time (11 women); includes 12 minority (3 Black or African American, non-Hispanic/Latino; 1 Asian, non-Hispanic/Latino; 7 Hispanic/Latino; 1 Two or more races, non-Hispanic/Latino), 2 international. Average age 35. 59 applicants, 68% accepted, 21 enrolled. In 2017, 20 master's, 17 CAGSs awarded. *Application deadline:* For fall admission, 3/1 priority date for domestic students; for spring admission, 11/1 for domestic students. Application fee: $25 ($40 for international students). *Expenses:* Tuition, state resident: full-time $17,375. Tuition, nonresident: full-time $33,915. *Required fees:* $355. *Financial support:* Research assistantships, teaching assistantships, career-related internships or fieldwork, Federal Work-Study, and unspecified assistantships available. Support available to part-time students. Financial award application deadline: 3/1; financial award applicants required to submit FAFSA. *Faculty research:* Power in the classroom, teacher leadership, professional development schools. *Unit head:* Dr. Joseph Berger, Professor of Education, 617-287-5000. *Application contact:* Graduate Admissions Coordinator, 617-287-6400, Fax: 617-287-6236, E-mail: bos.gadm@dpc.umassp.edu.

University of Massachusetts Boston, College of Education and Human Development, Program in Urban Education, Leadership, and Policy Studies, Boston, MA 02125-3393. Offers Ed D, PhD. *Program availability:* Part-time, evening/weekend. *Faculty:* 13 full-time (8 women), 21 part-time/adjunct (12 women). *Students:* 7 full-time (all women), 32 part-time (22 women); includes 17 minority (6 Black or African American, non-Hispanic/Latino; 1 American Indian or Alaska Native, non-Hispanic/Latino; 8 Hispanic/Latino; 2 Two or more races, non-Hispanic/Latino), 3 international. Average age 36. 31 applicants, 45% accepted, 9 enrolled. In 2017, 3 doctorates awarded. *Entrance requirements:* For doctorate, GRE General Test or MAT, minimum GPA of 2.75. *Application deadline:* For fall admission, 3/15 for domestic students. Application fee: $25 ($40 for international students). *Expenses:* Tuition, state resident: full-time $17,375. Tuition, nonresident: full-time $33,915. *Required fees:* $355. *Financial support:* Research assistantships, teaching assistantships, career-related internships or fieldwork, Federal Work-Study, and unspecified assistantships available. Support available to part-time students. Financial award application deadline: 3/1; financial award applicants required to submit FAFSA. *Faculty research:* School reform, race and culture in schools, race and higher education, language, literacy and writing. *Unit head:* Dr. Tricia Kress, Director, 617-287-7646, E-mail: tricia.kress@umb.edu. *Application contact:* Graduate Admissions Coordinator, 617-287-6400, Fax: 617-287-6236, E-mail: bos.gadm@dpc.umassp.edu.

University of Massachusetts Dartmouth, Graduate School, College of Arts and Sciences, School of Education, Department of Educational Leadership, North Dartmouth, MA 02747-2300. Offers educational leadership and policy studies (Ed D, PhD). *Program availability:* Part-time. *Faculty:* 4 full-time (0 women), 1 (woman) part-time/adjunct. *Students:* 11 full-time (9 women), 18 part-time (12 women); includes 11 minority (3 Black or African American, non-Hispanic/Latino; 1 American Indian or Alaska Native, non-Hispanic/Latino; 1 Asian, non-Hispanic/Latino; 4 Hispanic/Latino; 2 Two or more races, non-Hispanic/Latino), 1 international. Average age 42. 16 applicants, 88% accepted. In 2017, 9 doctorates awarded. *Degree requirements:* For doctorate, comprehensive exam, thesis/dissertation. *Entrance requirements:* For doctorate, GRE or GMAT, statement of purpose (minimum of 300 words), resume, 3 letters of recommendation, official transcripts, scholarly writing sample (minimum of 10 pages of writing). Additional exam requirements/recommendations for international students: Required—TOEFL (minimum score 600 paper-based; 100 iBT), IELTS (minimum score 6.5). *Application deadline:* For fall admission, 4/30 priority date for domestic students, 3/30 priority date for international students. Application fee: $60. Electronic applications accepted. *Expenses:* Tuition, state resident: full-time $15,449; part-time $643.71 per credit. Tuition, nonresident: full-time $27,880; part-time $1161.67 per credit. *Required fees:* $405; $25.88 per credit. Tuition and fees vary according to course load and reciprocity agreements. *Financial support:* In 2017–18, 2 fellowships (averaging

$21,000 per year) were awarded; tuition waivers (full), unspecified assistantships, and doctoral support also available. Support available to part-time students. Financial award application deadline: 3/1; financial award applicants required to submit FAFSA. *Faculty research:* Sociology of education, critical theory, curriculum theory, globalization and education, urban education, teacher education. *Total annual research expenditures:* $99,000. *Unit head:* Amy Shapiro, Interim Dean, College of Arts and Sciences, 508-999-8352, E-mail: ashapiro@umassd.edu. *Application contact:* Steven Briggs, Director of Marketing and Recruitment for Graduate Studies, 508-999-8604, Fax: 508-999-8183, E-mail: graduate@umassd.edu.
Website: http://www.umassd.edu/educationalleadership

University of Memphis, Graduate School, College of Education, Department of Instruction and Curriculum Leadership, Memphis, TN 38152. Offers advanced studies in teaching and learning (M Ed); applied behavior analysis (Graduate Certificate); autism studies (Graduate Certificate); early childhood education (MAT, MS, Ed D); elementary education (MAT); instruction and curriculum (MS, Ed D); instruction design and technology (MS, Ed D); instructional design and technology (Graduate Certificate); literacy, leadership, and coaching (Graduate Certificate); reading (MS, Ed D); school library information specialist (Graduate Certificate); secondary education (MAT); special education (MAT, MS, Ed D); STEM teacher leadership (Graduate Certificate); urban education (Graduate Certificate). *Accreditation:* NCATE (one or more programs are accredited). *Program availability:* Part-time. *Faculty:* 22 full-time (14 women), 14 part-time/adjunct (10 women). *Students:* 36 full-time (27 women), 351 part-time (271 women); includes 159 minority (132 Black or African American, non-Hispanic/Latino; 1 American Indian or Alaska Native, non-Hispanic/Latino; 7 Asian, non-Hispanic/Latino; 10 Hispanic/Latino; 9 Two or more races, non-Hispanic/Latino), 4 international. Average age 35. 170 applicants, 85% accepted, 111 enrolled. In 2017, 84 master's, 14 doctorates, 32 other advanced degrees awarded. Terminal master's awarded for partial completion of doctoral program. *Degree requirements:* For master's, comprehensive exam, thesis or alternative; for doctorate, comprehensive exam, thesis/dissertation. *Entrance requirements:* For master's, GRE General Test, PRAXIS, minimum GPA of 2.5, letters of reference; for doctorate, GRE General Test, GRE Subject Test, 2 years of teaching experience, letters of reference, statement of purpose, interview. Additional exam requirements/recommendations for international students: Required—TOEFL (minimum score 550 paper-based; 79 iBT). *Application deadline:* For fall admission, 4/1 priority date for domestic students; for spring admission, 10/1 priority date for domestic students; for summer admission, 2/1 priority date for domestic students. Applications are processed on a rolling basis. Application fee: $35 ($60 for international students). Electronic applications accepted. *Expenses:* Contact institution. *Financial support:* In 2017–18, 2 research assistantships with full tuition reimbursements (averaging $10,000 per year), 3 teaching assistantships with full tuition reimbursements (averaging $10,666 per year) were awarded; career-related internships or fieldwork, Federal Work-Study, institutionally sponsored loans, scholarships/grants, traineeships, and unspecified assistantships also available. Support available to part-time students. Financial award application deadline: 2/1; financial award applicants required to submit FAFSA. *Faculty research:* Effective urban teachers, preparation and retention of urban teachers, technology utilization in schools, field-based teacher preparation programs, effective use of online instruction. *Unit head:* Dr. Angiline Powell, Interim Chair, 901-678-3310, E-mail: apowell3@memphis.edu. *Application contact:* Dr. James Meindl, Coordinator of Graduate Studies, 901-678-3310, E-mail: jnmeindl@memphis.edu.
Website: http://www.memphis.edu/icl/

University of Memphis, Graduate School, College of Education, Department of Leadership, Memphis, TN 38152. Offers adult education (Ed D); community college teaching and leadership (Graduate Certificate); community education (Ed D); educational leadership (Ed D); higher education (Ed D); leadership (MS); policy studies (Ed D); school administration and supervision (MS); student personnel (MS). *Accreditation:* NCATE. *Program availability:* Part-time, evening/weekend, online learning. *Faculty:* 9 full-time (5 women), 6 part-time/adjunct (2 women). *Students:* 13 full-time (9 women), 154 part-time (96 women). Average age 35. 54 applicants, 93% accepted, 44 enrolled. In 2017, 19 master's, 26 doctorates, 4 other advanced degrees awarded. *Degree requirements:* For master's, comprehensive exam, thesis optional; for doctorate, comprehensive exam, thesis/dissertation. *Entrance requirements:* For master's, GRE, resume, letters of reference, statement of professional goals, current teacher certification, sample work, interview; for doctorate, GRE, resume, letters of reference, statement of professional goals, interview. Additional exam requirements/recommendations for international students: Required—TOEFL (minimum score 550 paper-based; 79 iBT). *Application deadline:* For fall admission, 6/15 for domestic students; for spring admission, 9/15 for domestic students; for summer admission, 2/15 for domestic students. Application fee: $35 ($60 for international students). Electronic applications accepted. *Expenses:* Contact institution. *Financial support:* In 2017–18, 70 students received support, including 4 research assistantships with full tuition reimbursements available (averaging $14,700 per year); teaching assistantships, Federal Work-Study, scholarships/grants, and unspecified assistantships also available. Financial award application deadline: 2/1; financial award applicants required to submit FAFSA. *Faculty research:* School improvement, social justice, online learning, adult learning, diversity. *Unit head:* Dr. Reginald Green, Interim Chair, 901-678-3445, E-mail: rlgreen1@memphis.edu.
Website: http://www.memphis.edu/lead

University of Michigan–Dearborn, College of Education, Health, and Human Services, Doctoral Program in Education, Dearborn, MI 48126. Offers curriculum and practice (Ed D); educational leadership (Ed D); metropolitan education (Ed D). *Program availability:* Part-time, evening/weekend. *Faculty:* 5 full-time (3 women), 1 part-time/adjunct (0 women). *Students:* 2 full-time (1 woman), 13 part-time (9 women); includes 8 minority (7 Black or African American, non-Hispanic/Latino; 1 Hispanic/Latino). Average age 45. 15 applicants, 27% accepted, 3 enrolled. In 2017, 9 doctorates awarded. *Degree requirements:* For doctorate, comprehensive exam, thesis/dissertation. *Entrance requirements:* For doctorate, GRE (taken within the last 5 years), master's degree with minimum GPA of 3.3, 3 letters of recommendation (1 from faculty), 3 years' professional and/or teaching experience. Additional exam requirements/recommendations for international students: Required—TOEFL (minimum score 560 paper-based; 84 iBT), IELTS (minimum score 6.5). *Application deadline:* For fall admission, 3/1 for domestic and international students. Application fee: $60. Electronic applications accepted. *Expenses:* $683 per credit hour in-state; $1,176 per credit hour out-state. *Financial support:* In 2017–18, 2 students received support. Scholarships/grants available. Financial award application deadline: 3/1; financial award applicants required to submit FAFSA. *Faculty research:* Urban education, educational leadership, assessment and evaluation, research methods, science education. *Unit head:* Dr. Chris Burke, Director, 313-593-5319, E-mail: cjfburke@umich.edu. *Application contact:* Office of Graduate Studies, 313-583-6321, E-mail: umd-graduatestudies@umich.edu.
Website: http://umdearborn.edu/cehhs/cehhs_edd

University of Michigan–Dearborn, College of Education, Health, and Human Services, Education Specialist Program, Dearborn, MI 48126. Offers curriculum and practice (Ed S); educational leadership (Ed S); metropolitan education (Ed S). *Program availability:* Part-time, evening/weekend. *Faculty:* 1 (woman) full-time, 1 part-time/adjunct (0 women). *Students:* 6 part-time (3 women). Average age 40. 5 applicants, 60%

accepted, 1 enrolled. *Entrance requirements:* For degree, master's degree with minimum GPA of 3.3; at least 3 years' teaching experience or the equivalent experience working in a professional setting. Additional exam requirements/recommendations for international students: Required—TOEFL (minimum score 560 paper-based; 84 iBT), IELTS (minimum score 6.5). *Application deadline:* For fall admission, 8/1 for domestic students, 5/1 for international students; for winter admission, 12/1 for domestic students, 9/1 for international students; for spring admission, 4/1 for domestic students, 1/1 for international students. Applications are processed on a rolling basis. Application fee: $60. Electronic applications accepted. *Expenses:* $683 per credit hour in-state; $1,176 per credit hour out-state. *Financial support:* In 2017–18, 1 student received support. Scholarships/grants available. Financial award application deadline: 3/1; financial award applicants required to submit FAFSA. *Faculty research:* Educational leadership, curriculum development, education policy, organizational development, K-12administration. *Unit head:* Dr. Bonnie Beyer, Director, 313-593-5583, E-mail: beyer@umich.edu. *Application contact:* Office of Graduate Studies, 313-583-6321, E-mail: umd-graduatestudies@umich.edu.
Website: http://umdearborn.edu/cehhs/cehhs_eds/

University of Michigan–Dearborn, College of Education, Health, and Human Services, Master of Arts Program in Educational Leadership, Dearborn, MI 48126. Offers MA. *Program availability:* Part-time, evening/weekend. *Faculty:* 1 (woman) full-time, 2 part-time/adjunct (0 women). *Students:* 4 full-time (3 women), 19 part-time (16 women); includes 1 minority (Black or African American, non-Hispanic/Latino). Average age 32. 10 applicants, 90% accepted, 4 enrolled. In 2017, 14 master's awarded. *Entrance requirements:* Additional exam requirements/recommendations for international students: Required—TOEFL (minimum score 560 paper-based; 84 iBT), IELTS (minimum score 6.5). *Application deadline:* For fall admission, 8/1 priority date for domestic students, 5/1 for international students; for winter admission, 12/1 priority date for domestic students, 9/1 for international students; for spring admission, 4/1 priority date for domestic students, 1/1 for international students. Applications are processed on a rolling basis. Application fee: $60. Electronic applications accepted. *Expenses:* $683 per credit hour in-state; $1,176 per credit hour out-state. *Financial support:* In 2017–18, 4 students received support. Scholarships/grants available. Financial award application deadline: 3/1; financial award applicants required to submit FAFSA. *Faculty research:* Educational leadership, curriculum development, education policy, organizational development, K-12 administration. *Unit head:* Dr. Stein Brunvand, Director, Master's Programs, 313-583-6415, E-mail: sbrunvan@umich.edu. *Application contact:* Office of Graduate Studies, 313-583-6321, E-mail: umd-graduatestudies@umich.edu.
Website: http://umdearborn.edu/cehhs/cehhs_mael/

University of Michigan–Flint, Graduate Programs, Program in Public Administration, Flint, MI 48502-1950. Offers administration of non-profit agencies (MPA); criminal justice administration (MPA); educational administration (MPA); general public administration (MPA); healthcare administration (MPA). *Program availability:* Part-time. *Faculty:* 1 full-time (0 women), 2 part-time/adjunct (both women). *Students:* 13 full-time (6 women), 88 part-time (59 women); includes 38 minority (29 Black or African American, non-Hispanic/Latino; 3 American Indian or Alaska Native, non-Hispanic/Latino; 2 Asian, non-Hispanic/Latino; 4 Two or more races, non-Hispanic/Latino), 3 international. Average age 37. 63 applicants, 81% accepted, 37 enrolled. In 2017, 55 master's awarded. *Degree requirements:* For master's, thesis or alternative, internship. *Entrance requirements:* For master's, bachelor's degree from regionally-accredited institution, minimum overall undergraduate GPA of 3.0. Additional exam requirements/recommendations for international students: Required—TOEFL (minimum score 84 iBT), IELTS (minimum score 6.5). *Application deadline:* For fall admission, 8/1 for domestic students, 5/1 for international students; for winter admission, 11/15 for domestic students, 9/1 for international students; for spring admission, 3/15 for domestic students, 1/1 for international students; for summer admission, 5/15 for domestic students. Applications are processed on a rolling basis. Application fee: $55. Electronic applications accepted. *Expenses:* Contact institution. *Financial support:* Career-related internships or fieldwork, Federal Work-Study, and scholarships/grants available. Support available to part-time students. Financial award application deadline: 3/1; financial award applicants required to submit FAFSA. *Unit head:* Dr. Kathryn Schellenberg, Director, 810-762-3340, E-mail: kathsch@umflint.edu. *Application contact:* Bradley T. Maki, Director of Graduate Admissions, 810-762-3171, Fax: 810-766-6789, E-mail: bmaki@umflint.edu.
Website: http://www.umflint.edu/graduateprograms/public-administration-mpa

University of Michigan–Flint, School of Education and Human Services, Department of Education, Flint, MI 48502-1950. Offers curriculum and instruction (Ed S); early childhood education (MA); education (Ed D); educational leadership (Ed S); educational technology (MA), including curriculum and instruction, developer; literacy education (MA); secondary education with certification (MA). *Program availability:* Part-time, evening/weekend, 100% online, mixed mode format (for some programs). *Faculty:* 18 full-time (11 women), 26 part-time/adjunct (13 women). *Students:* 34 full-time (23 women), 192 part-time (137 women); includes 61 minority (46 Black or African American, non-Hispanic/Latino; 2 Asian, non-Hispanic/Latino; 5 Hispanic/Latino; 2 Native Hawaiian or other Pacific Islander, non-Hispanic/Latino; 6 Two or more races, non-Hispanic/Latino), 2 international. Average age 39. 124 applicants, 87% accepted, 81 enrolled. In 2017, 89 master's, 3 doctorates awarded. *Degree requirements:* For master's, thesis optional; for doctorate, thesis/dissertation. *Entrance requirements:* For master's, bachelor's degree from regionally-accredited institution, minimum overall undergraduate GPA of 3.0; for doctorate, Ed S; minimum overall graduate GPA of 3.3 (6.0 on a 9.0 scale) or equivalent; at least 3 years of work experience in a P-16 educational institution or in an education-related position; for Ed S, MA or MS in education-related field from accredited institution; minimum overall graduate GPA of 3.0 (6.0 on a 9.0 scale) or equivalent; at least 3 years of work experience in an educational setting. Additional exam requirements/recommendations for international students: Required—TOEFL (minimum score 84 iBT), IELTS (minimum score 6.5). *Application deadline:* For fall admission, 8/1 for domestic students, 5/1 for international students; for winter admission, 11/15 for domestic students, 9/15 for international students; for spring admission, 3/15 for domestic students, 1/15 for international students; for summer admission, 5/15 for domestic students. Applications are processed on a rolling basis. Application fee: $55. Electronic applications accepted. *Expenses:* Contact institution. *Financial support:* Federal Work-Study, scholarships/grants, and unspecified assistantships available. Financial award application deadline: 3/1; financial award applicants required to submit FAFSA. *Unit head:* Dr. Mary Jo Finney, Department Chair/Associate Professor, 810-766-6617, E-mail: mjfinney@umflint.edu. *Application contact:* Bradley T. Maki, Director of Graduate Admissions, 810-762-3171, Fax: 810-766-6789, E-mail: bmaki@umflint.edu.
Website: https://www.umflint.edu/education/graduate-programs

University of Minnesota, Twin Cities Campus, Graduate School, College of Education and Human Development, Department of Organizational Leadership, Policy and Development, Program in Education Policy and Leadership, Minneapolis, MN 55455-0213. Offers educational policy and leadership (MA, Ed D, PhD); leadership in education (M Ed). *Students:* 85 full-time (59 women), 87 part-time (55 women); includes 35 minority (11 Black or African American, non-Hispanic/Latino; 1 American Indian or Alaska Native, non-Hispanic/Latino; 7 Asian, non-Hispanic/Latino; 8 Hispanic/Latino; 8 Two or more races, non-Hispanic/Latino), 4 international. Average age 36. 141

applicants, 77% accepted, 84 enrolled. In 2017, 16 master's, 6 doctorates awarded. Application fee: $75 ($95 for international students). *Unit head:* Dr. Heidi Barajas, Chair, 612-625-4823, E-mail: hbarajas@umn.edu. *Application contact:* Dr. Jeremy J. Hernandez, Director of Graduate Studies, 612-626-9377, E-mail: herna220@umn.edu.
Website: http://www.cehd.umn.edu/OLPD/grad-programs/EPL/

University of Mississippi, Graduate School, School of Education, University, MS 38677. Offers counselor education (M Ed, PhD); counselor education - play therapy (Ed S); early childhood (M Ed); educational leadership K-12 (M Ed, Ed D, PhD, Ed S); elementary education (M Ed, Ed D, Ed S); higher education/student personnel (Ed D, PhD); literacy education (M Ed); math education (Ed D); secondary education (M Ed, PhD, Ed S); special education (M Ed, PhD, Ed S); teacher corporations (MA); teacher education (MA). *Accreditation:* NCATE. *Faculty:* 65 full-time (40 women), 25 part-time/adjunct (5 women). *Students:* 185 full-time (148 women), 410 part-time (310 women); includes 193 minority (168 Black or African American, non-Hispanic/Latino; 7 Asian, non-Hispanic/Latino; 14 Hispanic/Latino; 4 Two or more races, non-Hispanic/Latino), 7 international. Average age 33. In 2017, 176 master's, 20 doctorates, 37 other advanced degrees awarded. *Entrance requirements:* For master's, GRE General Test, minimum GPA of 3.0; for doctorate, GRE General Test. Additional exam requirements/recommendations for international students: Required—TOEFL. *Application deadline:* For fall admission, 3/1 for domestic students; for spring admission, 10/1 for domestic students; for summer admission, 3/1 for domestic students. Applications are processed on a rolling basis. Application fee: $50. Electronic applications accepted. *Financial support:* Scholarships/grants available. Financial award application deadline: 3/1; financial award applicants required to submit FAFSA. *Unit head:* Dr. David Rock, Dean, 662-915-7063, Fax: 662-915-7249, E-mail: soe@olemiss.edu. *Application contact:* Dr. Joe Sumrall, Professor of Elementary Education, 662-915-7350, E-mail: soe@olemiss.edu.

University of Missouri, Office of Research and Graduate Studies, College of Education, Department of Educational Leadership and Policy Analysis, Columbia, MO 65211. Offers education administration (M Ed, MA, Ed D, PhD, Ed S); higher and adult education (M Ed, MA, Ed D, PhD, Ed S). *Program availability:* Part-time. *Degree requirements:* For doctorate, variable foreign language requirement, comprehensive exam (for some programs), thesis/dissertation. *Entrance requirements:* For master's, doctorate, and Ed S, minimum GPA of 3.0. Additional exam requirements/recommendations for international students: Required—TOEFL (minimum score 500 paper-based; 61 iBT), IELTS (minimum score 5.5). Electronic applications accepted.

University of Missouri–Kansas City, School of Education, Kansas City, MO 64110-2499. Offers administration (Ed D); counseling and guidance (MA, Ed S), including mental health counseling (Ed S), school counseling (Ed S); counseling psychology (PhD); curriculum and instruction (MA, Ed S), including language and literacy (Ed S); education (PhD), including higher education administration, PK-12 education administration; educational administration (MA, Ed S), including advanced principal (Ed S), beginning principal (Ed S), district-level administration (Ed S); reading education (MA); special education (MA). PhD in education offered through the School of Graduate Studies. *Accreditation:* NCATE. *Program availability:* Part-time, evening/weekend. *Degree requirements:* For doctorate, thesis/dissertation, internship, practicum. *Entrance requirements:* For master's, GRE, minimum GPA of 2.75, 2 letters of reference, written statement of purpose; for doctorate, GRE, minimum GPA of 3.0; for Ed S, minimum GPA of 3.0. Additional exam requirements/recommendations for international students: Required—TOEFL (minimum score 550 paper-based; 80 iBT). *Faculty research:* Urban education, inquiry-based field study, theories of counseling and psychotherapy, school literacy, educational technology.

University of Missouri–St. Louis, College of Education, Interdisciplinary Doctoral Programs, St. Louis, MO 63121. Offers counseling (PhD); educational leadership and policy studies (PhD); educational psychology (PhD); leadership in educational practice (Ed D); teaching-learning processes (PhD). *Faculty:* 50 full-time (29 women), 82 part-time/adjunct (66 women). *Students:* 131 full-time (98 women), 428 part-time (319 women); includes 174 minority (126 Black or African American, non-Hispanic/Latino; 3 American Indian or Alaska Native, non-Hispanic/Latino; 13 Asian, non-Hispanic/Latino; 27 Hispanic/Latino; 5 Two or more races, non-Hispanic/Latino), 11 international. 187 applicants, 84% accepted, 121 enrolled. *Degree requirements:* For doctorate, thesis/dissertation. *Entrance requirements:* For doctorate, GRE General Test, 3 letters of recommendation; personal interview. Additional exam requirements/recommendations for international students: Recommended—TOEFL (minimum score 550 paper-based; 79 iBT), IELTS (minimum score 6.5). *Application deadline:* For fall admission, 3/1 for domestic and international students; for spring admission, 10/1 for domestic and international students. Application fee: $50 ($40 for international students). Electronic applications accepted. *Expenses:* Tuition, state resident: part-time $476.50 per credit hour. Tuition, nonresident: part-time $1169.70 per credit hour. *Financial support:* Research assistantships and teaching assistantships available. Financial award application deadline: 4/1; financial award applicants required to submit FAFSA. *Faculty research:* Higher education law and policy, gender and higher education, student retention, lifelong learning orientation, school counselor's role in violence prevention. *Unit head:* Dr. Kathleen Haywood, Director of Graduate Studies, 314-516-5483, Fax: 314-516-5227, E-mail: kathleen_haywood@umsl.edu. *Application contact:* 314-516-5458, Fax: 314-516-6996, E-mail: gradadm@umsl.edu.

University of Mobile, Graduate Studies, Program in Education, Mobile, AL 36613. Offers education (MA); higher education leadership and policy (M Ed). *Program availability:* Part-time, 100% online. *Degree requirements:* For master's, comprehensive exam, thesis optional. *Entrance requirements:* For master's, GRE, Alabama teaching certificate. Additional exam requirements/recommendations for international students: Required—TOEFL (minimum score 550 paper-based; 80 iBT). *Application deadline:* For fall admission, 8/3 priority date for domestic students, 8/3 for international students; for spring admission, 12/23 priority date for domestic students, 12/3 priority date for international students. Applications are processed on a rolling basis. Application fee: $40 ($50 for international students). Electronic applications accepted. *Financial support:* Application deadline: 8/1; applicants required to submit FAFSA. *Faculty research:* Retention, writing across the curriculum. *Unit head:* Dr. Carolyn D. Corliss, Dean, School of Education, 251-442-2276, Fax: 251-442-2523, E-mail: ccorliss@umobile.edu. *Application contact:* Brian Boyle, Director of Recruitment, 251-442-2727, Fax: 251-442-2523.
Website: http://umobile.edu/school-of-education/master-of-arts-in-education/

University of Montana, Graduate School, Phyllis J. Washington College of Education and Human Sciences, Department of Educational Leadership, Missoula, MT 59812. Offers M Ed, Ed D, Ed S. *Degree requirements:* For doctorate, thesis/dissertation; for Ed S, thesis. *Entrance requirements:* For master's and Ed S, GRE General Test. Additional exam requirements/recommendations for international students: Required—TOEFL.

University of Montevallo, College of Education, Program in Educational Administration, Montevallo, AL 35115. Offers M Ed, Ed S. *Accreditation:* NCATE. *Program availability:* Part-time, evening/weekend. *Students:* 50 part-time (40 women); includes 7 minority (all Black or African American, non-Hispanic/Latino). *Entrance requirements:* For master's, GRE General Test or MAT. Additional exam requirements/

Educational Leadership and Administration

recommendations for international students: Required—TOEFL (minimum score 550 paper-based). *Application deadline:* For fall admission, 7/15 for domestic students; for spring admission, 11/15 for domestic students. Application fee: $30. *Expenses:* Tuition, state resident: full-time $9888. Tuition, nonresident: full-time $21,144. *Required fees:* $1920. *Financial support:* Federal Work-Study, scholarships/grants, and unspecified assistantships available. *Unit head:* Dr. Charlotte Daughhetee, Interim Dean, 205-665-6360, E-mail: daughc@montevallo.edu. *Application contact:* Colleen Kennedy, Graduate Program Assistant, 205-665-6350, E-mail: ckennedy@montevallo.edu. Website: http://www.montevallo.edu/education/college-of-education/traditional-masters-degrees/leadership/

University of Mount Union, Program in Educational Leadership, Alliance, OH 44601-3993. Offers MA. *Program availability:* Part-time, online only, 100% online. *Faculty:* 1 (woman) full-time, 2 part-time/adjunct (both women). *Students:* 27 full-time (18 women), 1 (woman) part-time; includes 2 minority (both Hispanic/Latino). Average age 29. In 2017, 11 master's awarded. *Entrance requirements:* For master's, two recommendations, official transcript from each college or university previously attended, curriculum vitae or resume, personal statement. Additional exam requirements/recommendations for international students: Required—TOEFL (minimum score 100 iBT). *Application deadline:* For fall admission, 7/31 for domestic and international students; for summer admission, 4/30 for domestic and international students. Applications are processed on a rolling basis. Application fee: $30. Electronic applications accepted. *Expenses:* $10,635. *Financial support:* Applicants required to submit FAFSA. *Unit head:* Dr. Mandy Capel, Director, 330-829-8159, E-mail: capelml@mountunion.edu. *Application contact:* Eric Young, Director of Admission, 330-829-8238, E-mail: younger@mountunion.edu.
Website: http://www.mountunion.edu/mael

University of Nebraska at Kearney, College of Education, Department of Educational Administration, Kearney, NE 68849-0001. Offers curriculum supervisor of academic area (MA Ed); school principalship 7-12 (MA Ed); school principalship PK-8 (MA Ed); school superintendent (Ed S); supervisor of special education (MA Ed). *Accreditation:* NCATE. *Program availability:* Part-time, evening/weekend, online only, 100% online. *Degree requirements:* For master's and Ed S, comprehensive exam, thesis optional. *Entrance requirements:* For master's, letters of recommendation, resume, letter of interest; for Ed S, letters of recommendation, resume, essay. Additional exam requirements/recommendations for international students: Recommended—TOEFL (minimum score 550 paper-based; 79 iBT), IELTS (minimum score 6.5). Electronic applications accepted. *Faculty research:* Leadership and organizational behavior.

University of Nebraska at Omaha, Graduate Studies, College of Education, Department of Educational Administration, Omaha, NE 68182. Offers educational administration and supervision (Ed D); educational leadership (MS, Ed S). *Accreditation:* NCATE. *Program availability:* Part-time, evening/weekend. *Degree requirements:* For master's, comprehensive exam, thesis (for some programs); for doctorate, comprehensive exam, thesis/dissertation; for Ed S, comprehensive exam, thesis. *Entrance requirements:* For master's, minimum GPA of 3.0, transcripts, resume, copy of teaching certificate, 3 letters of recommendation, statement of purpose; for doctorate, GRE General Test, resume, 3 samples of research/written work, 3 letters of recommendation, statement of purpose, transcripts. Additional exam requirements/recommendations for international students: Required—TOEFL, IELTS, PTE. Electronic applications accepted.

University of Nebraska–Lincoln, Graduate College, College of Education and Human Sciences, Department of Educational Administration, Lincoln, NE 68588. Offers M Ed, MA, Ed D, Certificate. Ed D offered jointly with University of Nebraska at Omaha. *Accreditation:* NCATE. *Degree requirements:* For master's, thesis optional; for doctorate, comprehensive exam, thesis/dissertation. *Entrance requirements:* For master's, GRE or MAT; for doctorate, GRE General Test, administrative certification. Additional exam requirements/recommendations for international students: Required—TOEFL (minimum score 550 paper-based). Electronic applications accepted. *Faculty research:* Educational policy, school finance, school law, school restructuring, leadership behavior.

University of Nebraska–Lincoln, Graduate College, College of Education and Human Sciences, Interdepartmental Area of Administration, Curriculum and Instruction, Lincoln, NE 68588. Offers Ed D, PhD, JD/PhD. *Accreditation:* NCATE. *Program availability:* Online learning. *Degree requirements:* For doctorate, comprehensive exam, thesis/dissertation. *Entrance requirements:* For doctorate, GRE, curriculum vitae. Additional exam requirements/recommendations for international students: Required—TOEFL (minimum score 550 paper-based). Electronic applications accepted.

University of Nevada, Las Vegas, Graduate College, College of Education, Department of Educational Psychology and Higher Education, Las Vegas, NV 89154-3002. Offers chief diversity officer in higher education (Certificate); college sport leadership (Certificate); educational psychology (M Ed, MS, PhD, Ed S); higher education (M Ed, PhD, Certificate); psychology/learning and technology (PhD), including learning and technology; workforce development/educational leadership (PhD); PhD/JD. *Program availability:* Part-time, evening/weekend, 100% online, blended/hybrid learning. *Faculty:* 22 full-time (15 women), 12 part-time/adjunct (8 women). *Students:* 95 full-time (73 women), 108 part-time (75 women); includes 72 minority (19 Black or African American, non-Hispanic/Latino; 9 Asian, non-Hispanic/Latino; 32 Hispanic/Latino; 12 Two or more races, non-Hispanic/Latino), 5 international. Average age 36. 86 applicants, 65% accepted, 44 enrolled. In 2017, 33 master's, 6 doctorates, 8 other advanced degrees awarded. *Degree requirements:* For master's, comprehensive exam (for some programs), thesis (for some programs); for doctorate, comprehensive exam, thesis/dissertation. *Entrance requirements:* For master's, GRE General Test or GMAT (for some programs), letters of recommendation; writing sample; bachelor's degree; for doctorate, GMAT or GRE General Test, writing exam; for other advanced degree, GRE General Test (for some programs). Additional exam requirements/recommendations for international students: Required—TOEFL (minimum score 550 paper-based; 80 iBT), IELTS (minimum score 7). Application fee: $60 ($95 for international students). Electronic applications accepted. *Expenses:* $275 per credit, $850 per course, $7,969 per year resident, $22,157 per year non-resident, $7,094 non-resident fee (7 credits or more), $1,307 annual health insurance fee. *Financial support:* In 2017–18, 49 students received support, including 31 research assistantships with partial tuition reimbursements available (averaging $15,769 per year), 18 teaching assistantships with partial tuition reimbursements available (averaging $19,486 per year); institutionally sponsored loans, scholarships/grants, health care benefits, and unspecified assistantships also available. Financial award application deadline: 3/15; financial award applicants required to submit FAFSA. *Faculty research:* Innovation and change in educational settings; educational policy, finance, and marketing; psycho-educational assessment; student retention, persistence, development, language, and culture; statistical modeling, program evaluation, qualitative and quantitative research methods. *Total annual research expenditures:* $470,161. *Unit head:* Dr. Alice Corkill, Chair/Professor, 702-895-4164, E-mail: alice.corkill@unlv.edu. *Application contact:* Dr. Steve McCafferty, Graduate Coordinator, 702-895-3245, Fax: 702-895-1658, E-mail: mccaffes@unlv.nevada.edu.
Website: http://education.unlv.edu/ephe/

University of Nevada, Reno, Graduate School, College of Education, Department of Educational Leadership, Reno, NV 89557. Offers M Ed, MA, MS, Ed D, PhD, Ed S. *Accreditation:* NCATE. Terminal master's awarded for partial completion of doctoral program. *Degree requirements:* For master's, comprehensive exam, thesis optional; for doctorate, comprehensive exam, thesis/dissertation. *Entrance requirements:* For master's, minimum GPA of 2.75; for doctorate, GRE General Test, minimum GPA of 3.0. Additional exam requirements/recommendations for international students: Required—TOEFL (minimum score 500 paper-based; 61 iBT), IELTS (minimum score 6). Electronic applications accepted. *Faculty research:* Law, finance, supervision, organizational theory, principalship.

University of New England, College of Graduate and Professional Studies, Portland, ME 04005-9526. Offers advanced educational leadership (CAGS); applied nutrition (MS); career and technical education (MS Ed); curriculum and instruction (MS Ed); education (CAGS, Post-Master's Certificate); educational leadership (MS Ed, Ed D); generalist (MS Ed); health informatics (MS, Graduate Certificate); inclusion education (MS Ed); literacy K-12 (MS Ed); medical education leadership (MMEL); public health (MPH); public health (Graduate Certificate); reading specialist (MS Ed); social work (MSW). *Program availability:* Part-time, evening/weekend, online only, 100% online. *Faculty:* 125 part-time/adjunct (94 women). *Students:* 1,403 full-time (1,128 women), 594 part-time (475 women); includes 474 minority (332 Black or African American, non-Hispanic/Latino; 13 American Indian or Alaska Native, non-Hispanic/Latino; 83 Asian, non-Hispanic/Latino; 27 Hispanic/Latino; 11 Native Hawaiian or other Pacific Islander, non-Hispanic/Latino; 8 Two or more races, non-Hispanic/Latino). Average age 35. 3,153 applicants, 41% accepted, 990 enrolled. In 2017, 307 master's, 59 doctorates, 124 other advanced degrees awarded. *Application deadline:* Applications are processed on a rolling basis. Electronic applications accepted. Tuition and fees vary according to degree level, program and student level. *Financial support:* Application deadline: 5/1; applicants required to submit FAFSA. *Unit head:* Dr. Martha Wilson, Associate Provost for Online Worldwide Learning/Dean of the College of Graduate and Professional Studies, 207-221-4985, E-mail: mwilson13@une.edu.
Website: http://online.une.edu

University of New Hampshire, Graduate School, College of Liberal Arts, Department of Education, Program in Educational Administration and Supervision, Durham, NH 03824. Offers Ed S. *Program availability:* Part-time. *Students:* 14 part-time (7 women); includes 1 minority (Asian, non-Hispanic/Latino). Average age 41. 6 applicants, 83% accepted, 4 enrolled. In 2017, 2 Ed Ss awarded. *Entrance requirements:* For degree, master's degree in educational administration or equivalent. Additional exam requirements/recommendations for international students: Required—TOEFL (minimum score 550 paper-based; 80 iBT). *Application deadline:* For fall admission, 8/15 for domestic students; for spring admission, 1/15 for domestic students; for summer admission, 5/15 for domestic students. Application fee: $65. Electronic applications accepted. *Financial support:* Fellowships, research assistantships, teaching assistantships, career-related internships or fieldwork, Federal Work-Study, scholarships/grants, and tuition waivers (full and partial) available. Support available to part-time students. Financial award application deadline: 2/15. *Unit head:* Paula Salvio, Chair, 603-862-0024, E-mail: education.department@unh.edu. *Application contact:* Cindy Glidden, Department Coordinator, 603-862-2311, E-mail: education.department@unh.edu.
Website: http://cola.unh.edu/education

University of New Hampshire, Graduate School, College of Liberal Arts, Department of Education, Program in Special Education, Durham, NH 03824. Offers special education (M Ed); special education administration (Postbaccalaureate Certificate). *Program availability:* Part-time. *Students:* 6 full-time (all women), 1 part-time (0 women). Average age 24. 8 applicants, 88% accepted, 5 enrolled. In 2017, 9 master's awarded. *Entrance requirements:* For master's, PRAXIS, Department of Education background check. Additional exam requirements/recommendations for international students: Required—TOEFL (minimum score 550 paper-based; 80 iBT). *Application deadline:* For fall admission, 4/15 for domestic and international students; for spring admission, 11/1 for domestic students; for summer admission, 4/1 for domestic students. Application fee: $65. Electronic applications accepted. *Financial support:* In 2017–18, 1 student received support. Fellowships, research assistantships, teaching assistantships, career-related internships or fieldwork, Federal Work-Study, scholarships/grants, and tuition waivers (full and partial) available. Support available to part-time students. Financial award application deadline: 2/15. *Unit head:* Paula Salvio, Chair, 603-862-0024, E-mail: education.department@unh.edu. *Application contact:* Cindy Glidden, Department Coordinator, 603-862-2311, E-mail: education.department@unh.edu.
Website: http://cola.unh.edu/education

University of New Hampshire, Graduate School Manchester Campus, Manchester, NH 03101. Offers business administration (MBA); cybersecurity policy and risk management (MS); educational administration and supervision (Ed S); educational studies (M Ed); elementary education (M Ed); information technology (MS); public administration (MPA); public health (MPH, Certificate); secondary education (M Ed, MAT); social work (MSW); substance use disorders (Certificate). *Program availability:* Part-time, evening/weekend. *Students:* 13 full-time (6 women), 17 part-time (0 women); includes 7 minority (1 Black or African American, non-Hispanic/Latino; 4 Asian, non-Hispanic/Latino; 1 Hispanic/Latino; 1 Two or more races, non-Hispanic/Latino), 10 international. Average age 33. 42 applicants, 71% accepted, 8 enrolled. In 2017, 4 master's awarded. *Entrance requirements:* Additional exam requirements/recommendations for international students: Required—TOEFL (minimum score 550 paper-based; 80 iBT). *Application deadline:* For fall admission, 6/1 for domestic students, 4/1 for international students; for spring admission, 12/1 for domestic students. Application fee: $65. Electronic applications accepted. *Financial support:* Fellowships, research assistantships, teaching assistantships, Federal Work-Study, scholarships/grants, health care benefits, and unspecified assistantships available. Support available to part-time students. Financial award application deadline: 2/15; financial award applicants required to submit FAFSA. *Unit head:* Candice Morey, Educational Programs Coordinator, 603-641-4313, E-mail: unhm.gradcenter@unh.edu.
Website: http://www.gradschool.unh.edu/manchester/

University of New Mexico, Graduate Studies, College of Education, Program in Educational Leadership, Albuquerque, NM 87131-2039. Offers MA, Ed D, Ed S. *Accreditation:* NCATE. *Program availability:* Part-time, evening/weekend, online learning. *Faculty:* 11 full-time (7 women). *Students:* 29 full-time (21 women), 119 part-time (86 women); includes 84 minority (4 Black or African American, non-Hispanic/Latino; 24 American Indian or Alaska Native, non-Hispanic/Latino; 52 Hispanic/Latino; 1 Native Hawaiian or other Pacific Islander, non-Hispanic/Latino; 3 Two or more races, non-Hispanic/Latino), 3 international. Average age 41. 57 applicants, 72% accepted, 41 enrolled. In 2017, 13 master's, 5 doctorates, 17 other advanced degrees awarded. *Degree requirements:* For master's, comprehensive exam; for doctorate, comprehensive exam, thesis/dissertation. *Entrance requirements:* For master's, bachelor's degree; for doctorate, GRE, master's degree. *Application deadline:* For fall admission, 6/1 for domestic students; for spring admission, 10/1 for domestic students. Applications are processed on a rolling basis. Application fee: $50. Electronic applications accepted. *Financial support:* Research assistantships, career-related internships or fieldwork, and scholarships/grants available. Financial award application deadline: 3/1; financial award applicants required to submit FAFSA. *Faculty research:* K-20 educational and organizational leadership, individual and organizational learning, policy, legal and political contexts. *Unit head:* Dr. Patricia Boverie, Head, 505-277-2408, Fax: 505-277-5553, E-mail: pboverie@unm.edu. *Application contact:* Linda Wood, Information Contact, 505-277-0441, Fax: 505-277-5553, E-mail: woodl@unm.edu. Website: http://coe.unm.edu/departments-programs/teelp/education-leadership-program/index.html

University of New Orleans, Graduate School, College of Education and Human Development, Department of Educational Leadership, Counseling, and Foundations, Program in Educational Leadership, New Orleans, LA 70148. Offers M Ed, PhD. *Accreditation:* NCATE. *Program availability:* Evening/weekend. Terminal master's awarded for partial completion of doctoral program. *Degree requirements:* For doctorate, variable foreign language requirement, thesis/dissertation. *Entrance requirements:* For master's and doctorate, GRE General Test. Additional exam requirements/recommendations for international students: Required—TOEFL (minimum score 550 paper-based; 79 iBT). Electronic applications accepted.

University of North Alabama, College of Education, Department of Secondary Education, Program in Instructional Leadership, Florence, AL 35632-0001. Offers instructional leadership (MA Ed, Ed S); teacher leader (Ed S). *Accreditation:* NCATE. *Program availability:* Part-time, 100% online, blended/hybrid learning. *Faculty:* 7 full-time (3 women), 2 part-time/adjunct (1 woman). *Students:* 5 full-time (1 woman), 43 part-time (25 women); includes 3 minority (all Black or African American, non-Hispanic/Latino). Average age 40. 23 applicants, 96% accepted, 15 enrolled. In 2017, 14 master's, 27 Ed Ss awarded. *Entrance requirements:* Additional exam requirements/recommendations for international students: Required—TOEFL (minimum score 79 iBT), IELTS (minimum score 6), PTE (minimum score 54). *Application deadline:* Applications are processed on a rolling basis. Application fee: $50 ($100 for international students). Electronic applications accepted. *Expenses:* Tuition, state resident: full-time $7824; part-time $5943 per year. Tuition, nonresident: full-time $15,648; part-time $11,736 per year. *Required fees:* $3064; $2298 per unit. Tuition and fees vary according to course load and reciprocity agreements. *Financial support:* In 2017–18, 10 students received support. Federal Work-Study, scholarships/grants, and unspecified assistantships available. Financial award application deadline: 2/1; financial award applicants required to submit FAFSA. *Unit head:* Dr. Jessica Mitchell, Interim Chair, 256-765-4575, E-mail: jmitchell12@una.edu. *Application contact:* Hillary N. Coats, Graduate Admissions Counselor, 256-765-4447, E-mail: graduate@una.edu. Website: https://www.una.edu/education/departments/secondary-education.html

The University of North Carolina at Chapel Hill, Graduate School, School of Education, Programs in Educational Leadership and School Administration, Chapel Hill, NC 27599. Offers educational leadership (Ed D); school administration (MSA). *Accreditation:* NCATE. *Program availability:* Part-time. *Degree requirements:* For master's, comprehensive exam; for doctorate, comprehensive exam, thesis/dissertation. *Entrance requirements:* For master's, GRE General Test or MAT, minimum GPA of 3.2 during last 2 years of undergraduate course work, 3 years of school-based professional experience; for doctorate, GRE General Test, minimum GPA of 3.2 during last 2 years of undergraduate course work, 3 years of school-based professional experience. Additional exam requirements/recommendations for international students: Required—TOEFL (minimum score 550 paper-based). *Faculty research:* Gender, race, and class issues; school leadership; school finance and reform.

The University of North Carolina at Charlotte, Cato College of Education, Department of Educational Leadership, Charlotte, NC 28223-0001. Offers education research, measurement, and evaluation (PhD); educational leadership (Ed D); instructional systems technology (M Ed, Graduate Certificate); quantitative analysis (Graduate Certificate); school administration (MSA, Post-Master's Certificate); university and college teaching (Graduate Certificate). *Program availability:* Part-time, evening/weekend, 100% online, blended/hybrid learning. *Faculty:* 20 full-time (11 women), 16 part-time/adjunct (9 women). *Students:* 38 full-time (26 women), 257 part-time (163 women); includes 87 minority (64 Black or African American, non-Hispanic/Latino; 1 American Indian or Alaska Native, non-Hispanic/Latino; 7 Asian, non-Hispanic/Latino; 14 Hispanic/Latino; 1 Two or more races, non-Hispanic/Latino), 5 international. Average age 35. 155 applicants, 78% accepted, 103 enrolled. In 2017, 27 master's, 13 doctorates, 32 other advanced degrees awarded. *Degree requirements:* For master's, thesis or alternative, internship, capstone project; for doctorate, comprehensive exam (for some programs), thesis/dissertation, portfolio. *Entrance requirements:* For master's, GRE or MAT, bachelor's degree, or its U.S. equivalent, from regionally-accredited college or university; minimum overall GPA of 3.5 on all previous work beyond high school; statement of purpose (essay); at least three recommendation forms; for doctorate, GRE or MAT, bachelor's degree (or its U.S. equivalent) from regionally-accredited college or university; minimum overall GPA of 3.5 in master's degree program; for other advanced degree, bachelor's degree from regionally-accredited university; minimum GPA of 2.75 on all post-secondary work attempted; transcripts; personal statement outlining why the applicant seeks admission to the program. Additional exam requirements/recommendations for international students: Required—TOEFL (minimum score 523 paper-based, 70 iBT) or IELTS (6.5). *Application deadline:* For fall admission, 3/1 priority date for domestic and international students; for spring admission, 10/1 priority date for domestic and international students; for summer admission, 4/1 priority date for domestic and international students. Applications are processed on a rolling basis. Application fee: $75. Electronic applications accepted. *Expenses:* Tuition, state resident: full-time $4337. Tuition, nonresident: full-time $17,771. *Required fees:* $3211. Tuition and fees vary according to course load and program. *Financial support:* In 2017–18, 8 students received support, including 8 research assistantships (averaging $11,961 per year); career-related internships or fieldwork, institutionally sponsored loans, scholarships/grants, and unspecified assistantships also available. Support available to part-time students. Financial award application deadline: 3/1; financial award applicants required to submit FAFSA. *Total annual research expenditures:* $1.9 million. *Unit head:* Dr. Claudia Flowers, Chair, 704-687-8862, E-mail: cpflower@uncc.edu. *Application contact:* Kathy B. Giddings, Director of Graduate Admissions, 704-687-5503, Fax: 704-687-1668, E-mail: gradadm@uncc.edu. Website: http://edld.uncc.edu/

The University of North Carolina at Charlotte, Cato College of Education, Interdisciplinary Education Programs, Charlotte, NC 28223-0001. Offers art education (Graduate Certificate); child and family development: early childhood education (MAT); curriculum and instruction (PhD); elementary education (MAT); foreign language education (MAT); middle grades education (MAT); secondary education (MAT); special education (MAT); teaching (Graduate Certificate); teaching English as a second language (MAT); theatre education (Graduate Certificate). *Program availability:* Part-time, 100% online, blended/hybrid learning. *Students:* 86 full-time (63 women), 533 part-time (423 women); includes 229 minority (169 Black or African American, non-Hispanic/Latino; 1 American Indian or Alaska Native, non-Hispanic/Latino; 7 Asian, non-Hispanic/Latino; 39 Hispanic/Latino; 13 Two or more races, non-Hispanic/Latino), 13 international. Average age 32. 382 applicants, 91% accepted, 253 enrolled. In 2017, 182

master's, 10 doctorates, 172 other advanced degrees awarded. *Degree requirements:* For master's, thesis or alternative, research project/portfolio. *Entrance requirements:* For master's, GRE or MAT, bachelor's degree, or its U.S. equivalent, from regionally-accredited college or university; minimum overall GPA of 3.0 on all previous work beyond high school; statement of purpose (essay); at least three recommendation forms; for doctorate, GRE or MAT, bachelor's degree (or its U.S. equivalent) from regionally-accredited college or university; minimum overall GPA of 3.5 in master's degree program; for Graduate Certificate, bachelor's degree from regionally-accredited university; minimum GPA of 2.75 on all post-secondary work attempted; transcripts; personal statement outlining why the applicant seeks admission to the program. Additional exam requirements/recommendations for international students: Required—TOEFL (minimum score 523 paper-based, 70 iBT) or IELTS (6.5). *Application deadline:* For fall admission, 3/1 priority date for domestic and international students; for spring admission, 10/1 priority date for domestic and international students; for summer admission, 4/1 priority date for domestic and international students. Applications are processed on a rolling basis. Application fee: $75. Electronic applications accepted. *Expenses:* Tuition, state resident: full-time $4337. Tuition, nonresident: full-time $17,771. *Required fees:* $3211. Tuition and fees vary according to course load and program. *Financial support:* Career-related internships or fieldwork, institutionally sponsored loans, scholarships/grants, and unspecified assistantships available. Support available to part-time students. Financial award application deadline: 3/1; financial award applicants required to submit FAFSA. *Unit head:* Dr. Ellen McIntyre, Dean, 704-687-8722, E-mail: ellen.mcintyre@uncc.edu. *Application contact:* Kathy B. Giddings, Director of Graduate Admissions, 704-687-5503, Fax: 704-687-1668, E-mail: gradadm@uncc.edu. Website: http://education.uncc.edu/academic-programs

The University of North Carolina at Greensboro, Graduate School, School of Education, Department of Educational Leadership and Cultural Foundations, Greensboro, NC 27412-5001. Offers curriculum and teaching (PhD), including cultural studies; educational leadership (Ed D, Ed S); school administration (MSA). *Accreditation:* NCATE. *Degree requirements:* For doctorate, thesis/dissertation. *Entrance requirements:* For master's, doctorate, and Ed S, GRE General Test. Additional exam requirements/recommendations for international students: Required—TOEFL. Electronic applications accepted.

The University of North Carolina at Greensboro, Graduate School, School of Education, Department of Teacher Education and Higher Education, Greensboro, NC 27412-5001. Offers college teaching and adult learning (Certificate); curriculum and instruction (M Ed), including chemistry education, elementary education, English as a second language, French education, instructional technology, mathematics education, middle grades education, reading education, science education, social studies education, Spanish education; curriculum and teaching (PhD), including higher education, teacher education and development; English as a second language (Certificate); higher education (M Ed); supervision (M Ed). *Accreditation:* NCATE. *Program availability:* Part-time. *Degree requirements:* For doctorate, thesis/dissertation. *Entrance requirements:* For master's and doctorate, GRE General Test. Additional exam requirements/recommendations for international students: Required—TOEFL. Electronic applications accepted. *Faculty research:* Community college literacy program, middle school mathematics/computer mathematics.

The University of North Carolina at Pembroke, The Graduate School, School of Education, Program in School Administration, Pembroke, NC 28372-1510. Offers MSA. *Program availability:* Part-time, evening/weekend. *Entrance requirements:* For master's, GRE General Test or MAT, minimum GPA of 3.0 in major, 2.5 overall; 3 years of teaching experience; two recommendations. Additional exam requirements/recommendations for international students: Required—TOEFL. *Application deadline:* For fall admission, 7/1 for domestic and international students; for spring admission, 11/1 for domestic and international students. Applications are processed on a rolling basis. Application fee: $45 ($60 for international students). *Financial support:* Application deadline: 4/15; applicants required to submit FAFSA. *Unit head:* Dr. Jeffrey M. Warren, Department Chair, 910-775-4414, E-mail: jeffrey.warren@uncp.edu.

The University of North Carolina Wilmington, Watson College of Education, Department of Early Childhood, Elementary, Middle, Literacy and Special Education, Wilmington, NC 28403-3297. Offers educational leadership, policy, and advocacy (M Ed); elementary education (M Ed, MAT); language and literacy (M Ed); middle grades education (MAT). *Accreditation:* NCATE. *Program availability:* Part-time, blended/hybrid learning. *Faculty:* 22 full-time (15 women), 2 part-time/adjunct (both women). *Students:* 82 full-time (70 women), 91 part-time (84 women); includes 51 minority (33 Black or African American, non-Hispanic/Latino; 3 American Indian or Alaska Native, non-Hispanic/Latino; 1 Asian, non-Hispanic/Latino; 8 Hispanic/Latino; 6 Two or more races, non-Hispanic/Latino). Average age 32. 68 applicants, 82% accepted, 45 enrolled. In 2017, 83 master's awarded. *Degree requirements:* For master's, thesis or alternative, exit portfolio, oral presentation, internship, research project (depending on specialization). *Entrance requirements:* For master's, 3 letters of recommendation, NC Class A teacher license in related field, education statement of interest essay. Additional exam requirements/recommendations for international students: Required—TOEFL (minimum score 550 paper-based; 79 iBT), IELTS (minimum score 6.5). *Application deadline:* For fall admission, 5/15 for domestic students; for spring admission, 10/15 for domestic students; for summer admission, 3/15 for domestic students. Applications are processed on a rolling basis. Application fee: $75. Electronic applications accepted. *Expenses:* Tuition, state resident: full-time $4626; part-time $226.76 per credit hour. Tuition, nonresident: full-time $17,834; part-time $874.22 per credit hour. *Required fees:* $2124. Tuition and fees vary according to program. *Financial support:* Scholarships/grants and unspecified assistantships available. Financial award application deadline: 1/1; financial award applicants required to submit FAFSA. *Unit head:* Dr. Kathy Fox, Chair, 910-962-3240, Fax: 910-962-3988, E-mail: foxk@uncw.edu. *Application contact:* Dr. Elizabeth Crawford, Graduate Program Coordinator, 910-962-2916, Fax: 910-962-3988, E-mail: crawforde@uncw.edu. Website: http://www.uncw.edu/ed/eemls/index.html

The University of North Carolina Wilmington, Watson College of Education, Department of Educational Leadership, Wilmington, NC 28403-3297. Offers curriculum, instruction and supervision (M Ed); educational leadership and administration (Ed D), including curriculum and instruction; higher education (M Ed); school administration (MSA), including school administration. *Program availability:* Part-time, 100% online. *Faculty:* 14 full-time (11 women), 6 part-time/adjunct (4 women). *Students:* 39 full-time (24 women), 150 part-time (109 women); includes 56 minority (41 Black or African American, non-Hispanic/Latino; 7 American Indian or Alaska Native, non-Hispanic/Latino; 2 Asian, non-Hispanic/Latino; 4 Hispanic/Latino; 2 Native Hawaiian or other Pacific Islander, non-Hispanic/Latino), 1 international. Average age 36. 80 applicants, 74% accepted, 50 enrolled. In 2017, 53 master's, 20 doctorates awarded. *Degree requirements:* For master's, thesis or culminating project, e-Portfolio (for school administration); for doctorate, comprehensive exam, thesis/dissertation. *Entrance requirements:* For master's, GRE General Test, MAT, minimum B average in undergraduate work, 3 letters of recommendation, education statement of interest essay, autobiographical statement, NC Class A teacher licensure in related field,

minimum of 3 years' teaching experience; for doctorate, education statement of interest essay, master's degree in education field, 3 years of leadership experience. Additional exam requirements/recommendations for international students: Required—TOEFL (minimum score 550 paper-based; 79 iBT), IELTS (minimum score 6.5). *Application deadline:* For fall admission, 5/15 for domestic students; for spring admission, 10/15 for domestic students; for summer admission, 3/15 for domestic students. Applications are processed on a rolling basis. Application fee: $75. Electronic applications accepted. *Expenses:* Tuition, state resident: full-time $4626; part-time $226.76 per credit hour. Tuition, nonresident: full-time $17,834; part-time $874.22 per credit hour. *Required fees:* $2124. Tuition and fees vary according to program. *Financial support:* Scholarships/grants and unspecified assistantships available. Financial award application deadline: 1/1; financial award applicants required to submit FAFSA. *Unit head:* Dr. Marsha Carr, Interim Chair, 910-962-2913, Fax: 910-962-3609, E-mail: carrm@uncw.edu. *Application contact:* Dr. William Sterrett, Graduate Program Coordinator, 910-962-7995, E-mail: stewettw@uncw.edu.
Website: http://uncw.edu/ed/el/

University of North Dakota, Graduate School, College of Education and Human Development, Department of Educational Leadership, Grand Forks, ND 58202. Offers M Ed, Ed D, PhD, Ed S. *Accreditation:* NCATE. *Program availability:* Part-time, evening/weekend, online learning. *Degree requirements:* For master's and Ed S, comprehensive exam, thesis or alternative; for doctorate, comprehensive exam, thesis/dissertation, final exam. *Entrance requirements:* For master's, minimum GPA of 3.0; for doctorate, minimum GPA of 3.5. Additional exam requirements/recommendations for international students: Required—TOEFL (minimum score 550 paper-based; 79 iBT), IELTS (minimum score 6.5). Electronic applications accepted.

University of Northern Colorado, Graduate School, College of Education and Behavioral Sciences, Department of Leadership, Policy and Development: Higher Education and P-12 Education, Educational Leadership and Policy Studies Program, Greeley, CO 80639. Offers educational leadership (MA, Ed S); educational leadership and policy studies (Ed D). *Accreditation:* NCATE. *Program availability:* Part-time, evening/weekend, online learning. *Degree requirements:* For master's, comprehensive exam, thesis or alternative; for doctorate, comprehensive exam, thesis/dissertation; for Ed S, comprehensive exam, thesis. *Entrance requirements:* For master's, resume, interview; for doctorate, GRE General Test, resume, interview; for Ed S, resume. Electronic applications accepted.

University of Northern Colorado, Graduate School, College of Education and Behavioral Sciences, School of Teacher Education, Program in Educational Studies, Greeley, CO 80639. Offers Ed D. *Program availability:* Part-time, evening/weekend. Electronic applications accepted.

University of Northern Iowa, Graduate College, College of Education, Department of Educational Leadership and Postsecondary Education, MAE Program in Principalship, Cedar Falls, IA 50614. Offers MAE. *Program availability:* Part-time, evening/weekend. *Degree requirements:* For master's, comprehensive exam (for some programs), thesis or alternative, minimum of 1 year of successful teaching appropriate to the major. *Entrance requirements:* For master's, minimum GPA of 3.0. Additional exam requirements/recommendations for international students: Required—TOEFL (minimum score 500 paper-based; 61 iBT). Electronic applications accepted.

University of Northern Iowa, Graduate College, College of Education, Ed D Program in Education, Cedar Falls, IA 50614. Offers allied health, recreation, and community services (Ed D); curriculum and instruction (Ed D); educational leadership (Ed D). *Program availability:* Part-time, evening/weekend. *Degree requirements:* For doctorate, thesis/dissertation. *Entrance requirements:* For doctorate, GRE, minimum GPA of 3.0, master's degree. Additional exam requirements/recommendations for international students: Required—TOEFL (minimum score 500 paper-based; 61 iBT).

University of North Florida, College of Education and Human Services, Department of Leadership, School Counseling and Sport Management, Jacksonville, FL 32224. Offers counselor education (M Ed), including school counseling; educational leadership (M Ed, Ed D), including athletic administration (M Ed), educational leadership, educational technology (M Ed), instructional leadership (M Ed). *Program availability:* Part-time, evening/weekend. *Degree requirements:* For doctorate, thesis/dissertation. *Entrance requirements:* For master's, GRE General Test, minimum GPA of 3.0 in last 60 hours, interview, 3 letters of recommendation; for doctorate, GRE General Test, master's degree, interview, 3 letters of recommendation, writing sample. Additional exam requirements/recommendations for international students: Required—TOEFL (minimum score 500 paper-based). Electronic applications accepted. *Faculty research:* Counseling: ethics; lesbian, bisexual and transgender issues; educational leadership: school culture and climate; educational assessment and accountability; school safety and student discipline.

University of North Georgia, Doctor of Education Program in Higher Education Leadership and Practice, Dahlonega, GA 30597. Offers Ed D. *Program availability:* Part-time, evening/weekend, online only, 100% online. *Students:* 13 part-time (8 women); includes 2 minority (1 American Indian or Alaska Native, non-Hispanic/Latino; 1 Hispanic/Latino), 1 international. Average age 43. 35 applicants, 49% accepted, 13 enrolled. *Degree requirements:* For doctorate, thesis/dissertation. *Entrance requirements:* Additional exam requirements/recommendations for international students: Required—TOEFL (minimum score 550 paper-based; 79 iBT), IELTS (minimum score 6.5). *Application deadline:* For fall admission, 7/24 for domestic students. Application fee: $40. Electronic applications accepted. *Expenses:* Contact institution. *Financial support:* Application deadline: 3/17; applicants required to submit FAFSA. *Unit head:* Dr. Susan Brandenburg-Ayres, Dean, 706-864-1998, E-mail: susan.ayres@ung.edu. *Application contact:* Melinda Maxwell, Director of Graduate Admissions, 706-867-2077, E-mail: melinda.maxwell@ung.edu.
Website: https://ung.edu/teacher-education/graduate/doctor-of-education-with-a-major-in-higher-education-leadership-and-practice.php

University of North Georgia, Ed S in Educational Leadership Program, Dahlonega, GA 30597. Offers Certificate, Ed S. *Program availability:* Part-time, evening/weekend, blended/hybrid learning. *Faculty:* 1 (woman) full-time, 2 part-time/adjunct (1 woman). *Students:* 37 part-time (24 women); includes 1 minority (Asian, non-Hispanic/Latino). Average age 41. 30 applicants, 93% accepted, 18 enrolled. *Entrance requirements:* Additional exam requirements/recommendations for international students: Required—TOEFL (minimum score 550 paper-based; 79 iBT), IELTS (minimum score 6.5). *Application deadline:* For fall admission, 7/15 for domestic students. Application fee: $40. Electronic applications accepted. *Expenses:* Contact institution. *Financial support:* Application deadline: 3/17; applicants required to submit FAFSA. *Unit head:* Dr. Susan Brandenburg-Ayres, Dean, 706-864-1998, E-mail: susan.ayres@ung.edu. *Application contact:* Melinda Maxwell, Director of Graduate Admissions, 706-867-2077, E-mail: melinda.maxwell@ung.edu.
Website: https://ung.edu/graduate-admissions/programs/tier-2-eds.php

University of North Texas, Robert B. Toulouse School of Graduate Studies, Denton, TX 76203-5459. Offers accounting (MS); applied anthropology (MA, MS); applied behavior analysis (Certificate); applied geography (MA); applied technology and performance improvement (M Ed, MS); art education (MA); art history (MA); art museum education (Certificate); arts leadership (Certificate); audiology (Au D); behavior analysis (MS); behavioral science (PhD); biochemistry and molecular biology (MS); biology (MA, MS); biomedical engineering (MS); business analysis (MS); chemistry (MS); clinical health psychology (PhD); communication studies (MA, MS); computer engineering (MS); computer science (MS); counseling (M Ed, MS), including clinical mental health counseling (MS), college and university counseling, elementary school counseling, secondary school counseling; creative writing (MA); criminal justice (MS); curriculum and instruction (M Ed); decision sciences (MBA); design (MA, MFA), including fashion design (MFA), innovation studies, interior design (MFA); early childhood studies (MS); economics (MS); educational leadership (M Ed, Ed D); educational psychology (MS, PhD), including family studies (PhD), gifted and talented (MS), human development (MS), learning and cognition (MS), research, measurement and evaluation (MS); electrical engineering (MS); emergency management (MPA); engineering technology (MS); English (MA); English as a second language (MA); environmental science (MS); finance (MBA, MS); financial management (MPA); French (MA); health services management (MBA); higher education (M Ed, Ed D); history (MA, MS); hospitality management (MS); human resources management (MPA); information science (MS); information systems (PhD); information technologies (MBA); interdisciplinary studies (MA, MS); international studies (MA); international sustainable tourism (MS); jazz studies (MM); journalism (MA, MJ, Graduate Certificate), including interactive and virtual digital communication (Graduate Certificate), narrative journalism (Graduate Certificate), public relations (Graduate Certificate); kinesiology (MS); linguistics (MA); local government management (MPA); logistics (PhD); logistics and supply chain management (MBA); long-term care, senior housing, and aging services (MA); management (PhD); marketing (MBA); mathematics (MA, MS); mechanical and energy engineering (MS, PhD); music (MA), including ethnomusicology, music theory, musicology, performance; music composition (PhD); music education (MM Ed, PhD); nonprofit management (MPA); operations and supply chain management (MBA); performance (MM, DMA); philosophy (MA); political science (MA); professional and technical communication (MA); radio, television and film (MA, MFA); rehabilitation counseling (Certificate); sociology (MA); Spanish (MA); special education (M Ed); speech-language pathology (MA); strategic management (MBA); studio art (MFA); teaching (M Ed); MBA/MS. *Program availability:* Part-time, evening/weekend, online learning. Terminal master's awarded for partial completion of doctoral program. *Degree requirements:* For master's, variable foreign language requirement, comprehensive exam (for some programs), thesis (for some programs); for doctorate, variable foreign language requirement, comprehensive exam (for some programs), thesis/dissertation; for other advanced degree, variable foreign language requirement, comprehensive exam (for some programs). *Entrance requirements:* For master's and doctorate, GRE, GMAT. Additional exam requirements/recommendations for international students: Required—TOEFL (minimum score 550 paper-based; 79 iBT). Electronic applications accepted.

University of North Texas at Dallas, Graduate School, Dallas, TX 75241. Offers accounting (MBA); counseling (M Ed, MS); criminal justice (MS); curriculum and instruction (M Ed); educational administration (M Ed); human resources and organizational behavior (MBA); public leadership (MS); strategic management (MBA).

University of Oklahoma, Jeannine Rainbolt College of Education, Department of Educational Leadership and Policy Studies, Program in Educational Administration, Curriculum and Supervision, Norman, OK 73019. Offers M Ed, Ed D, PhD. *Accreditation:* NCATE. *Program availability:* Part-time, evening/weekend, blended/hybrid learning. *Students:* 28 full-time (23 women), 177 part-time (127 women); includes 66 minority (27 Black or African American, non-Hispanic/Latino; 14 American Indian or Alaska Native, non-Hispanic/Latino; 13 Hispanic/Latino; 12 Two or more races, non-Hispanic/Latino), 2 international. Average age 36. 91 applicants, 80% accepted, 61 enrolled. In 2017, 46 master's, 14 doctorates awarded. *Degree requirements:* For master's, comprehensive exam, thesis (for some programs); for doctorate, comprehensive exam, thesis/dissertation. *Entrance requirements:* For doctorate, GRE. Additional exam requirements/recommendations for international students: Required—TOEFL (minimum score 79 iBT) or IELTS (minimum score 6.5). *Application deadline:* Applications are processed on a rolling basis. Application fee: $50 ($100 for international students). Electronic applications accepted. *Expenses:* Tuition, state resident: full-time $5119; part-time $213.30 per credit hour. Tuition, nonresident: full-time $19,778; part-time $824.10 per credit hour. *Required fees:* $3458; $133.55 per credit hour. $126.50 per semester. *Financial support:* In 2017–18, 111 students received support. Fellowships, research assistantships, teaching assistantships, career-related internships or fieldwork, Federal Work-Study, institutionally sponsored loans, scholarships/grants, health care benefits, tuition waivers, and unspecified assistantships available. Support available to part-time students. Financial award application deadline: 6/1; financial award applicants required to submit FAFSA. *Faculty research:* Improvement science; leadership and ethics; education and social policy; gender and equity; organizational reform and change. *Unit head:* John Jones, Associate Professor, 405-325-4165, E-mail: jjones@ou.edu.
Website: http://www.ou.edu/education/elps

University of Oklahoma, Jeannine Rainbolt College of Education, Department of Instructional Leadership and Academic Curriculum, Norman, OK 73019. Offers instructional leadership and academic curriculum (M Ed, PhD), including biomedical education (PhD), early childhood education, elementary education, English education, instructional leadership, mathematics education, reading education, science education, social studies education, world languages education (M Ed); reading specialist (M Ed). *Accreditation:* NCATE. *Program availability:* Part-time. *Faculty:* 19 full-time (15 women), 1 (woman) part-time/adjunct. *Students:* 37 full-time (28 women), 121 part-time (98 women); includes 32 minority (7 Black or African American, non-Hispanic/Latino; 4 American Indian or Alaska Native, non-Hispanic/Latino; 5 Asian, non-Hispanic/Latino; 6 Hispanic/Latino; 1 Native Hawaiian or other Pacific Islander, non-Hispanic/Latino; 9 Two or more races, non-Hispanic/Latino), 12 international. Average age 35. 39 applicants, 77% accepted, 22 enrolled. In 2017, 49 master's, 12 doctorates awarded. Terminal master's awarded for partial completion of doctoral program. *Degree requirements:* For master's, comprehensive exam (for some programs), thesis (for some programs); for doctorate, comprehensive exam (for some programs), thesis/dissertation. *Entrance requirements:* For doctorate, GRE. Additional exam requirements/recommendations for international students: Required—TOEFL (minimum score 79 iBT) or IELTS (minimum score 6.5). Application fee: $50 ($100 for international students). Electronic applications accepted. *Expenses:* Tuition, state resident: full-time $5119; part-time $213.30 per credit hour. Tuition, nonresident: full-time $19,778; part-time $824.10 per credit hour. *Required fees:* $3458; $133.55 per credit hour. $126.50 per semester. *Financial support:* In 2017–18, 90 students received support, including 8 research assistantships (averaging $11,248 per year), 6 teaching assistantships (averaging $12,188 per year); fellowships, scholarships/grants, and unspecified assistantships also available. Financial award application deadline: 6/1; financial award applicants required to submit FAFSA. *Faculty research:* Teacher preparation; instruction; curriculum; learning; constructivist theory. Total annual research expenditures: $707,690. *Unit head:* Dr. Stacy Reeder, Chair, 405-325-1498, Fax: 405-325-4061, E-mail: reeder@ou.edu. *Application contact:* Anna Steele, Graduate Programs Officer, 405-325-4525, E-mail: anna.steele@ou.edu.
Website: http://www.ou.edu/education/ilac

University of Oregon, Graduate School, College of Education, Eugene, OR 97403. Offers communication disorders and sciences (MA, MS, PhD); counseling psychology (PhD); couples and family therapy (MS); critical and sociocultural studies in education (PhD); curriculum and teacher education (MA, MS); educational leadership (MS, D Ed, PhD); prevention science (M Ed, MS, PhD); school psychology (MS, PhD); special education (M Ed, MA, MS, PhD). *Program availability:* Part-time. Terminal master's awarded for partial completion of doctoral program. *Degree requirements:* For master's, exam, paper, or project; for doctorate, comprehensive exam, thesis/dissertation. *Entrance requirements:* Additional exam requirements/recommendations for international students: Required—TOEFL. *Faculty research:* Basic and applied research in teaching, learning and habilitation in all settings, schooling effectiveness.

University of Pennsylvania, Graduate School of Education, Division of Teaching, Learning, and Leadership, Program in Educational Leadership, Philadelphia, PA 19104. Offers MS Ed, Ed D, PhD. *Program availability:* Part-time. *Students:* Average age 36. 36 applicants, 6% accepted, 1 enrolled. In 2017, 1 doctorate awarded. *Entrance requirements:* For master's, GRE or MAT; for doctorate, GRE.

University of Pennsylvania, Graduate School of Education, Division of Teaching, Learning, and Leadership, Program in School Leadership, Philadelphia, PA 19104. Offers MS Ed. *Program availability:* Part-time, evening/weekend. *Students:* Average age 35. 87 applicants, 64% accepted, 46 enrolled. In 2017, 24 master's awarded. *Entrance requirements:* For master's, bachelor's degree. Additional exam requirements/recommendations for international students: Required—TOEFL, IELTS. *Application deadline:* Applications are processed on a rolling basis. Application fee: $75. Electronic applications accepted. *Financial support:* In 2017–18, 27 students received support. Scholarships/grants available. *Faculty research:* Governance issues in schools, teacher professional development, independent schools, leadership identification and development, curriculum innovation and design. *Unit head:* Dr. Earl Ball, Director, 215-573-7499. *Application contact:* Amara Rockar, Administrative Coordinator, 215-746-2718, E-mail: arockar@upenn.edu.
Website: http://www.gse.upenn.edu/tll/slp

University of Pennsylvania, Graduate School of Education, Division of Teaching, Learning, and Leadership, Program in Teaching, Learning, and Leadership, Philadelphia, PA 19104. Offers educational leadership (MS Ed); teaching and learning (MS Ed). *Program availability:* Part-time. *Students:* Average age 34. 240 applicants, 44% accepted, 71 enrolled. In 2017, 24 master's awarded.

University of Pennsylvania, Graduate School of Education, Mid-Career Doctoral Program in Educational Leadership, Philadelphia, PA 19104. Offers Ed D. *Program availability:* Evening/weekend. *Students:* Average age 43. 81 applicants, 49% accepted, 24 enrolled. In 2017, 19 doctorates awarded. *Degree requirements:* For doctorate, comprehensive exam, thesis/dissertation. *Entrance requirements:* For master's, master's degree. *Application deadline:* For summer admission, 2/1 priority date for domestic and international students. Application fee: $75. Electronic applications accepted. *Faculty research:* Educational leadership, district reform, team effectiveness, identity development and social identification, racial/ethnic socialization and negotiation. *Unit head:* Martha Williams, Program Coordinator, 215-746-6573, E-mail: marthaw@upenn.edu.
Website: http://www2.gse.upenn.edu/midcareer/

University of Pennsylvania, Graduate School of Education, Penn Chief Learning Officer (CLO) Executive Doctoral Program, Philadelphia, PA 19104. Offers Ed D. *Program availability:* Evening/weekend. *Students:* Average age 47. 43 applicants, 58% accepted, 24 enrolled. In 2017, 6 doctorates awarded. Terminal master's awarded for partial completion of doctoral program. *Degree requirements:* For doctorate, comprehensive exam, thesis/dissertation. *Entrance requirements:* For doctorate, bachelor's degree. *Application deadline:* For fall admission, 7/1 priority date for domestic and international students; for spring admission, 10/1 priority date for domestic and international students; for summer admission, 3/2 priority date for domestic and international students. Applications are processed on a rolling basis. Application fee: $75. Electronic applications accepted. *Faculty research:* Strategic leadership, workplace learning, business acumen, evidenced-best decision making, technology in the work place. *Unit head:* Elizabeth Ulivella, Associate Director, 215-573-0591, E-mail: ulivella@upenn.edu.
Website: http://www.pennclo.com/

University of Phoenix–Bay Area Campus, College of Education, San Jose, CA 95134-1805. Offers administration and supervision (MA Ed); adult education and training (MA Ed); early childhood education (MA Ed); education (Ed S); educational leadership (Ed D); elementary teacher education (MA Ed); higher education administration (PhD); secondary teacher education (MA Ed); special education (MA Ed); teacher leadership (MA Ed). *Program availability:* Evening/weekend, online learning. *Degree requirements:* For master's, thesis (for some programs). *Entrance requirements:* For master's, minimum undergraduate GPA of 2.5, 3 years of work experience. Additional exam requirements/recommendations for international students: Required—TOEFL (minimum score 550 paper-based; 79 iBT). Electronic applications accepted.

University of Phoenix–Hawaii Campus, College of Education, Honolulu, HI 96813-3800. Offers administration and supervision (MA Ed); curriculum and instruction (MA Ed); elementary education (MA Ed); secondary education (MA Ed); special education (MA Ed); teacher education for elementary licensure (MA Ed). *Program availability:* Evening/weekend. *Degree requirements:* For master's, thesis (for some programs). *Entrance requirements:* For master's, minimum undergraduate GPA of 2.5, 3 years of work experience. Additional exam requirements/recommendations for international students: Required—TOEFL (minimum score 550 paper-based; 79 iBT). Electronic applications accepted.

University of Phoenix–Las Vegas Campus, College of Education, Las Vegas, NV 89135. Offers administration and supervision (MA Ed); curriculum and instruction (MA Ed); school counseling (MSC); teacher education-elementary licensure (MA Ed). *Program availability:* Evening/weekend. *Degree requirements:* For master's, thesis (for some programs). *Entrance requirements:* For master's, minimum undergraduate GPA of 2.5, 3 years of work experience. Additional exam requirements/recommendations for international students: Required—TOEFL (minimum score 550 paper-based; 79 iBT). Electronic applications accepted.

University of Phoenix–Online Campus, College of Education, Phoenix, AZ 85034-7209. Offers administration and supervision (MAEd, Certificate); adult education and training (MAEd); curriculum and instruction (MAEd), including computer education, curriculum and instruction, English as a second language, language arts, mathematics, reading; early childhood education (MAEd); educational studies (MAEd); elementary teacher education (MAEd), including early childhood, elementary teacher education, high school middle level, middle level; principal licensure (Certificate); secondary teacher education (MAEd); special education (MAEd, Certificate); teacher education (MAEd), including middle level generalist; teacher education middle level mathematics (MAEd), including middle level mathematics; teacher education middle level science (MAEd), including middle level science; teacher education secondary mathematics (MAEd); teacher education secondary science (MAEd); teacher leadership (MAEd); teachers of English learners (Certificate); transition to teaching (Certificate), including

elementary education, secondary education. *Program availability:* Evening/weekend, online learning. *Entrance requirements:* Additional exam requirements/recommendations for international students: Required—TOEFL, TOEIC (Test of English as an International Communication), Berlitz Online English Proficiency Exam, PTE, or IELTS. Electronic applications accepted. *Expenses:* Contact institution.

University of Phoenix–Online Campus, School of Advanced Studies, Phoenix, AZ 85034-7209. Offers business administration (DBA); education (Ed S); educational leadership (Ed D), including curriculum and instruction, education technology, educational leadership; health administration (DHA); higher education administration (PhD); industrial/organizational psychology (PhD); nursing (PhD); organizational leadership (DM), including information systems and technology, organizational leadership. *Program availability:* Evening/weekend, online learning. *Degree requirements:* For doctorate, thesis/dissertation. *Entrance requirements:* Additional exam requirements/recommendations for international students: Required—TOEFL, TOEIC (Test of English as an International Communication), Berlitz Online English Proficiency Exam, PTE, or IELTS. Electronic applications accepted. *Expenses:* Contact institution.

University of Phoenix–Phoenix Campus, College of Education, Tempe, AZ 85282-2371. Offers administration and supervision (MA Ed); adult education and training (MA Ed); curriculum and instruction reading (MA Ed); early childhood education (MA Ed); education studies (MA Ed); elementary teacher education (MA Ed); secondary teacher education (MA Ed); special education (MA Ed); teacher leadership (MA Ed). *Program availability:* Evening/weekend, online learning. *Entrance requirements:* Additional exam requirements/recommendations for international students: Required—TOEFL, TOEIC (Test of English as an International Communication), Berlitz Online English Proficiency Exam, PTE, or IELTS. Electronic applications accepted. *Expenses:* Contact institution.

University of Pikeville, Patton College of Education, Pikeville, KY 41501. Offers teacher leader (MA). *Program availability:* Part-time, evening/weekend. *Faculty:* 10 part-time/adjunct (6 women). *Students:* 66 full-time (56 women), 15 part-time (11 women). Average age 35. In 2017, 25 master's awarded. *Degree requirements:* For master's, comprehensive exam. *Application deadline:* For fall admission, 8/15 for domestic students. Applications are processed on a rolling basis. Application fee: $50. *Expenses:* Contact institution. *Financial support:* Application deadline: 2/1; applicants required to submit FAFSA. *Unit head:* Dr. Coletta Parsley, Division Chair, 606-218-5318, E-mail: colettaparsley@upike.edu. *Application contact:* Fairy Coleman, Administrative Assistant, 606-218-5314, E-mail: fairycoleman@upike.edu.
Website: http://www.upike.edu/COE/

University of Pittsburgh, School of Education, Department of Administrative and Policy Studies, Program in School Leadership, Pittsburgh, PA 15260. Offers M Ed, Ed D, PhD. *Program availability:* Part-time, evening/weekend. *Degree requirements:* For master's, thesis; for doctorate, thesis/dissertation. *Entrance requirements:* For doctorate, GRE General Test. Additional exam requirements/recommendations for international students: Required—TOEFL (minimum score 80 iBT). Electronic applications accepted.

University of Portland, School of Education, Portland, OR 97203-5798. Offers education (MA, MAT); educational leadership (M Ed); English for speakers of other languages (M Ed); initial administrator licensure (M Ed); neuroeducation (M Ed, Ed D); organizational leadership and development (Ed D); reading (M Ed); school leadership and development (Ed D); special education (M Ed). M Ed also available through the Graduate Outreach Program for teachers residing in the Oregon and Washington state areas. *Accreditation:* NCATE. *Program availability:* Part-time, evening/weekend. *Entrance requirements:* For master's, minimum GPA of 3.0, teaching certificate, letters of recommendation, resume, statement of goals, official transcripts. Additional exam requirements/recommendations for international students: Required—TOEFL (minimum score 550 paper-based; 80 iBT), IELTS (minimum score 7). *Faculty research:* Multicultural education, supervision/leadership.

University of Prince Edward Island, Faculty of Education, Charlottetown, PE C1A 4P3, Canada. Offers educational studies (PhD); leadership in learning (M Ed). *Program availability:* Part-time. *Degree requirements:* For master's, thesis. *Entrance requirements:* For master's, 2 years of professional experience, bachelor of education, professional certificate. Additional exam requirements/recommendations for international students: Required—TOEFL (minimum score 550 paper-based; 80 iBT), Canadian Academic English Language Assessment, Michigan English Language Assessment Battery, Canadian Test of English for Scholars and Trainees. *Faculty research:* Distance learning, aboriginal communities and education leadership development, international development, immersion language learning.

University of Puerto Rico–Río Piedras, College of Education, Program in School Administration and Supervision, San Juan, PR 00931-3300. Offers M Ed, Ed D. *Program availability:* Part-time. *Degree requirements:* For master's, thesis; for doctorate, thesis/dissertation, internship. *Entrance requirements:* For master's, PAEG or GRE, minimum GPA of 3.0, letter of recommendation; for doctorate, GRE or PAEG, interview, master's degree, minimum GPA of 3.0, letter of recommendation.

University of Regina, Faculty of Graduate Studies and Research, Faculty of Education, Department of Educational Administration, Regina, SK S4S 0A2, Canada. Offers M Ed. *Program availability:* Part-time. *Faculty:* 4 full-time (2 women), 20 part-time/adjunct (11 women). *Students:* 4 full-time (3 women), 35 part-time (19 women). 35 applicants, 31% accepted. In 2017, 34 master's awarded. *Degree requirements:* For master's, thesis (for some programs), practicum, project, or thesis. *Entrance requirements:* For master's, bachelor's degree in education, 2 years of teaching or other relevant professional experience. Additional exam requirements/recommendations for international students: Required—TOEFL (minimum score 580 paper-based; 80 iBT), IELTS (minimum score 6.5), PTE (minimum score 59). *Application deadline:* For fall admission, 2/15 for domestic and international students; for winter admission, 10/15 for domestic and international students; for spring admission, 2/15 for domestic and international students. Application fee: $100. Electronic applications accepted. *Expenses:* $10,681. *Financial support:* In 2017–18, fellowships (averaging $6,000 per year), 10 teaching assistantships (averaging $2,562 per year) were awarded; research assistantships and scholarships/grants also available. Financial award application deadline: 6/15. *Faculty research:* Legal aspects of school administration, economics of education, education planning, politics of education, administrative behavior in education. *Unit head:* Dr. Paul Clarke, Associate Dean, Research and Graduate Programs in Education, 306-585-5353, Fax: 306-585-5330, E-mail: paul.clarke@uregina.ca. *Application contact:* Linda Jiang, Graduate Program Coordinator, 306-585-4506, Fax: 306-585-4880, E-mail: linda.jiang@uregina.ca.
Website: http://www.uregina.ca/education/

University of Rio Grande, Graduate School, Rio Grande, OH 45674. Offers athletic coaching leadership (M Ed); educational leadership (M Ed); integrated arts (M Ed); intervention specialist in early childhood (M Ed); intervention specialist in mild/moderate (M Ed). *Accreditation:* NCATE. *Program availability:* Part-time. *Degree requirements:* For master's, final research project, portfolio. *Entrance requirements:* For master's, minimum GPA of 2.7 in major, 2.5 overall. Additional exam requirements/recommendations for international students: Required—TOEFL. *Faculty research:* Interagency collaboration, reading and mathematics, learning styles, college access, literacy.

Educational Leadership and Administration

University of Rochester, Margaret Warner Graduate School of Education and Human Development, Doctoral Programs in Education, Rochester, NY 14627. Offers counseling (Ed D); educational administration (Ed D); educational policy and theory (PhD); higher education (PhD); human development in educational context (PhD); teaching, curriculum, and change (PhD).

University of Rochester, Margaret Warner Graduate School of Education and Human Development, Master's Program in School Leadership, Rochester, NY 14627. Offers MS.

University of St. Francis, College of Education, Joliet, IL 60435-6169. Offers educational leadership (MS, Ed D); elementary education (M Ed); reading (MS); secondary education (M Ed), including English education, math education, science education, social studies education, visual arts education; special education (M Ed); teaching and learning (MS); TESOL (Certificate). *Accreditation:* NCATE. *Program availability:* Part-time, evening/weekend, 100% online, blended/hybrid learning. *Faculty:* 11 full-time (8 women), 52 part-time/adjunct (36 women). *Students:* 39 full-time (32 women), 411 part-time (318 women); includes 106 minority (57 Black or African American, non-Hispanic/Latino; 8 Asian, non-Hispanic/Latino; 37 Hispanic/Latino; 4 Two or more races, non-Hispanic/Latino), 4 international. Average age 37. 277 applicants, 55% accepted, 137 enrolled. In 2017, 199 master's, 28 doctorates awarded. *Degree requirements:* For master's, comprehensive exam; for doctorate, thesis/dissertation. *Entrance requirements:* Additional exam requirements/recommendations for international students: Required—TOEFL (minimum score 550 paper-based; 79 iBT), IELTS (minimum score 6). *Application deadline:* Applications are processed on a rolling basis. Application fee: $30. Electronic applications accepted. Application fee is waived when completed online. *Expenses:* $365 to $748 per credit hour. *Financial support:* In 2017–18, 40 students received support. Scholarships/grants and unspecified assistantships available. Support available to part-time students. Financial award applicants required to submit FAFSA. *Unit head:* Dr. John Gambro, Dean, 815-740-3829, Fax: 815-740-2264, E-mail: jgambro@stfrancis.edu. *Application contact:* Sandra Sloka, Director of Admissions for Graduate and Degree Completion Programs, 800-735-7500, Fax: 815-740-3431, E-mail: ssloka@stfrancis.edu.
Website: http://www.stfrancis.edu/academics/college-of-education/

University of St. Thomas, College of Education, Leadership and Counseling, Department of Leadership, Policy and Administration, St. Paul, MN 55105-1096. Offers education leadership and administration (MA); educational leadership and learning (Ed D); executive coaching (Certificate); K-12 administration (Ed S); leadership in student affairs (MA). *Program availability:* Part-time, evening/weekend. Terminal master's awarded for partial completion of doctoral program. *Degree requirements:* For master's, thesis (for some programs); for doctorate, thesis/dissertation; for other advanced degree, thesis or alternative. *Entrance requirements:* For master's, minimum GPA of 3.0 or MAT; for doctorate, MAT, minimum graduate GPA of 3.5; for other advanced degree, minimum graduate GPA of 3.25 or MAT. Additional exam requirements/recommendations for international students: Required—TOEFL (minimum score 550 paper-based). *Application deadline:* For fall admission, 7/15 priority date for domestic and international students; for spring admission, 12/9 priority date for domestic and international students; for summer admission, 4/3 priority date for domestic and international students. Applications are processed on a rolling basis. Electronic applications accepted. *Expenses:* Contact institution. *Financial support:* Fellowships, research assistantships, institutionally sponsored loans, and scholarships/grants available. Support available to part-time students. Financial award application deadline: 8/1; financial award applicants required to submit FAFSA. *Application contact:* Jackie Grossklaus, Administrative Assistant II, 651-962-4885, Fax: 651-962-4169, E-mail: jmgrossklaus@stthomas.edu.

University of St. Thomas, School of Education and Human Services, Houston, TX 77006-4696. Offers all level education (M Ed); bilingual/dual language (M Ed); Catholic school teaching (M Ed); Catholic/private school leadership (M Ed); counselor education (M Ed); curriculum and instruction (M Ed); education (Ed D); educational leadership (M Ed); elementary teaching (M Ed); English as a second language (M Ed); exceptionality/educational diagnostician (M Ed); exceptionality/special education (M Ed); generalist (M Ed); reading (M Ed); secondary teaching (M Ed); teaching (MAT). *Accreditation:* TEAC. *Program availability:* Part-time, evening/weekend, online learning. *Faculty:* 33 full-time (22 women), 43 part-time/adjunct (26 women). *Students:* 119 full-time (97 women), 597 part-time (529 women); includes 478 minority (166 Black or African American, non-Hispanic/Latino; 29 Asian, non-Hispanic/Latino; 277 Hispanic/Latino; 2 Native Hawaiian or other Pacific Islander, non-Hispanic/Latino; 4 Two or more races, non-Hispanic/Latino), 19 international. Average age 36. 306 applicants, 91% accepted, 181 enrolled. In 2017, 328 master's awarded. *Degree requirements:* For master's, thesis, field experience. *Entrance requirements:* For master's, GRE or MAT if GPA is below 3.0, bachelor's degree; minimum GPA of 2.75 in bachelor's degree or last 60 credit hours; official transcripts from all institutions; goal statement of 250-300 words; 1 reference. Additional exam requirements/recommendations for international students: Required—TOEFL (minimum score 94 iBT), IELTS (minimum score 7), PTE (minimum score 53). *Application deadline:* Applications are processed on a rolling basis. Application fee: $35. Electronic applications accepted. *Expenses:* Contact institution. *Financial support:* In 2017–18, 27 students received support. Federal Work-Study, scholarships/grants, and state work-study, institutional employment available. Support available to part-time students. Financial award application deadline: 4/15; financial award applicants required to submit FAFSA. *Faculty research:* Leadership, diversity, personality traits, second language acquisition. *Unit head:* Dr. Paul C. Paese, Dean, 713-942-5999, Fax: 713-525-3871, E-mail: paesep@stthom.edu. *Application contact:* 713-525-3540, E-mail: education@stthom.edu.
Website: http://www.stthom.edu/Academics/School_of_Education_and_Human_Services/Index.aqf

University of San Diego, School of Leadership and Education Sciences, Department of Leadership Studies, San Diego, CA 92110-2492. Offers higher education leadership (MA); leadership studies (MA, PhD, Certificate); nonprofit leadership and management (MA). *Program availability:* Part-time, evening/weekend. *Faculty:* 10 full-time (5 women), 18 part-time/adjunct (7 women). *Students:* 53 full-time (34 women), 202 part-time (140 women); includes 118 minority (24 Black or African American, non-Hispanic/Latino; 16 Asian, non-Hispanic/Latino; 64 Hispanic/Latino; 1 Native Hawaiian or other Pacific Islander, non-Hispanic/Latino; 13 Two or more races, non-Hispanic/Latino), 23 international. Average age 34. 243 applicants, 73% accepted, 77 enrolled. In 2017, 53 master's, 15 doctorates awarded. *Degree requirements:* For master's, thesis (for some programs), international experience; for doctorate, comprehensive exam, thesis/dissertation, international experience. *Entrance requirements:* For master's, GRE (recommended with GPA less than 3.25); for doctorate, GRE (less than 5 years old), master's degree, minimum GPA of 3.5 (recommended), resume. Additional exam requirements/recommendations for international students: Required—TOEFL (minimum score 580 paper-based; 83 iBT), TWE. Application fee: $45. Electronic applications accepted. *Financial support:* In 2017–18, 204 students received support. Career-related internships or fieldwork, Federal Work-Study, institutionally sponsored loans, unspecified assistantships, and stipends available. Support available to part-time students. Financial award application deadline: 4/1; financial award applicants required

to submit FAFSA. *Faculty research:* Higher education administration policy and relations, organizational leadership, nonprofits and philanthropy, student affairs leadership. *Unit head:* Dr. Lea Hubbard, Graduate Program Director, 619-260-7818, E-mail: lhubbard@sandiego.edu. *Application contact:* Monica Mahon, Associate Director of Graduate Admissions, 619-260-4524, Fax: 619-260-4158, E-mail: grads@sandiego.edu.
Website: https://www.sandiego.edu/soles/leadership-studies/

University of San Diego, School of Leadership and Education Sciences, Department of Learning and Teaching, San Diego, CA 92110-2492. Offers curriculum and instruction (M Ed); inclusive learning (M Ed); literacy and digital learning (M Ed); school leadership (M Ed); special education (M Ed); STEAM (science, technology, engineering, arts, and mathematics) (M Ed); TESOL, literacy and culture (M Ed). *Program availability:* Part-time, evening/weekend. *Faculty:* 9 full-time (7 women), 30 part-time/adjunct (24 women). *Students:* 160 full-time (128 women), 221 part-time (176 women); includes 131 minority (10 Black or African American, non-Hispanic/Latino; 24 Asian, non-Hispanic/Latino; 83 Hispanic/Latino; 1 Native Hawaiian or other Pacific Islander, non-Hispanic/Latino; 13 Two or more races, non-Hispanic/Latino), 20 international. Average age 33. 398 applicants, 84% accepted, 196 enrolled. In 2017, 151 master's awarded. *Degree requirements:* For master's, thesis (for some programs), international experience. *Entrance requirements:* For master's, California Basic Educational Skills Test, California Subject Examination for Teachers. Additional exam requirements/recommendations for international students: Required—TOEFL (minimum score 580 paper-based; 83 iBT), TWE. *Application deadline:* Applications are processed on a rolling basis. Application fee: $45. Electronic applications accepted. *Financial support:* In 2017–18, 65 students received support. Career-related internships or fieldwork, Federal Work-Study, institutionally sponsored loans, and stipends available. Financial award application deadline: 4/1; financial award applicants required to submit FAFSA. *Faculty research:* Action research methodology, cultural studies, instructional theories and practices, second language acquisition, school reform. *Unit head:* Dr. Maya Kalyanpur, Chair, 619-260-7655, E-mail: mkalyanpur@sandiego.edu. *Application contact:* Monica Mahon, Associate Director of Graduate Admissions, 619-260-4524, Fax: 619-260-4158, E-mail: grads@sandiego.edu.
Website: http://www.sandiego.edu/soles/learning-and-teaching/

University of San Francisco, School of Education, Catholic Educational Leadership Program, San Francisco, CA 94117-1080. Offers Catholic school leadership (Ed D). *Program availability:* Part-time, evening/weekend. *Degree requirements:* For doctorate, thesis/dissertation. *Entrance requirements:* Additional exam requirements/recommendations for international students: Required—TOEFL, IELTS, PTE. Electronic applications accepted.

University of San Francisco, School of Education, Leadership Studies Program, San Francisco, CA 94117-1080. Offers MA, Ed D. *Program availability:* Part-time, evening/weekend. *Degree requirements:* For doctorate, thesis/dissertation. *Entrance requirements:* Additional exam requirements/recommendations for international students: Required—TOEFL, IELTS, PTE. Electronic applications accepted.

University of Saskatchewan, College of Graduate Studies and Research, College of Education, Department of Educational Administration, Saskatoon, SK S7N 5A2, Canada. Offers M Ed, PhD, Diploma. *Program availability:* Part-time. *Degree requirements:* For master's, thesis (for some programs); for doctorate, comprehensive exam (for some programs), thesis/dissertation. *Entrance requirements:* Additional exam requirements/recommendations for international students: Required—TOEFL (minimum score 80 iBT); Recommended—IELTS (minimum score 6.5). Electronic applications accepted.

The University of Scranton, Panuska College of Professional Studies, Department of Education, Program in Educational Administration, Scranton, PA 18510. Offers MS. *Accreditation:* NCATE. *Program availability:* Part-time, evening/weekend, online only, 100% online.

University of Sioux Falls, Fredrikson School of Education, Sioux Falls, SD 57105-1699. Offers educational administration (Ed S), including principal leadership, superintendent and district leadership; leadership in reading (M Ed); leadership in schools (M Ed); leadership in technology (M Ed); teaching (M Ed). Admission in summer only. *Accreditation:* NCATE. *Program availability:* Part-time, evening/weekend. *Degree requirements:* For master's, comprehensive exam (for some programs), research application project; for Ed S, comprehensive exam, portfolio. *Entrance requirements:* For master's, minimum GPA of 3.0, 1 year of teaching experience; for Ed S, minimum 3 years of teaching experience, minimum cumulative GPA of 3.5, 1 year of administrative experience. Additional exam requirements/recommendations for international students: Required—TOEFL. *Faculty research:* Reading, literacy, leadership.

University of South Africa, College of Human Sciences, Pretoria, South Africa. Offers adult education (M Ed); African languages (MA, PhD); African politics (MA, PhD); Afrikaans (MA, PhD); ancient history (MA, PhD); ancient Near Eastern studies (MA, PhD); anthropology (MA, PhD); applied linguistics (MA); Arabic (MA, PhD); archaeology (MA); art history (MA); Biblical archaeology (MA); Biblical studies (M Th, D Th, PhD); Christian spirituality (M Th, D Th); church history (M Th, D Th); classical studies (MA, PhD); clinical psychology (MA); communication (MA, PhD); comparative education (M Ed, Ed D); consulting psychology (D Admin, D Com, PhD); curriculum studies (M Ed, Ed D); development studies (M Admin, MA, D Admin, PhD); didactics (M Ed, Ed D); education (M Tech); education management (M Ed, Ed D); educational psychology (M Ed); English (MA); environmental education (M Ed); French (MA, PhD); German (MA, PhD); Greek (MA); guidance and counseling (M Ed); health studies (MA, PhD), including health sciences education (MA), health services management (MA), medical and surgical nursing science (critical care general) (MA), midwifery and neonatal nursing science (MA), trauma and emergency care (MA); history (MA, PhD); history of education (Ed D); inclusive education (M Ed, Ed D); information and communications technology policy and regulation (MA); information science (MA, MIS, PhD); international politics (MA, PhD); Islamic studies (MA, PhD); Italian (MA, PhD); Judaica (MA, PhD); linguistics (MA, PhD); mathematical education (M Ed); mathematics education (PhD); missiology (M Th, D Th); modern Hebrew (MA, PhD); musicology (MA, MMus, D Mus, PhD); natural science education (M Ed); New Testament (M Th, D Th); Old Testament (D Th); pastoral therapy (M Th, D Th); philosophy (MA); philosophy of education (M Ed, Ed D); politics (MA, PhD); Portuguese (MA, PhD); practical theology (M Th, D Th); psychology (MA, MS, PhD); psychology of education (M Ed, Ed D); public health (MA); religious studies (MA, D Th, PhD); Romance languages (MA); Russian (MA, PhD); Semitic languages (MA, PhD); social behavior studies in HIV/AIDS (MA); social science (mental health) (MA); social science in development studies (MA); social science in psychology (MA); social science in social work (MA); social science in sociology (MA); social work (MSW, DSW, PhD); socio-education (M Ed, Ed D); sociolinguistics (MA); sociology (MA, PhD); Spanish (MA, PhD); systematic theology (M Th, D Th); TESOL (teaching English to speakers of other languages) (MA); theological ethics (M Th, D Th); theory of literature (MA, PhD); urban ministries (D Th); urban ministry (M Th).

University of South Alabama, College of Education and Professional Studies, Department of Leadership and Teacher Education, Mobile, AL 36688. Offers art education (M Ed); early childhood education (M Ed); educational leadership (M Ed,

Ed D); elementary education (M Ed); reading education (M Ed); science education (M Ed); secondary education (M Ed); special education (M Ed). *Accreditation:* NCATE. *Program availability:* Part-time. *Faculty:* 15 full-time (11 women), 10 part-time/adjunct (6 women). *Students:* 203 full-time (154 women), 90 part-time (68 women); includes 73 minority (54 Black or African American, non-Hispanic/Latino; 3 American Indian or Alaska Native, non-Hispanic/Latino; 4 Asian, non-Hispanic/Latino; 10 Hispanic/Latino; 2 Two or more races, non-Hispanic/Latino). Average age 34. 134 applicants, 55% accepted, 57 enrolled. In 2017, 73 master's, 8 doctorates awarded. *Degree requirements:* For master's, comprehensive exam, thesis (for some programs); for doctorate, comprehensive exam, thesis/dissertation. *Entrance requirements:* For master's, GRE General Test or MAT, minimum GPA of 3.0; for doctorate, GRE, minimum graduate GPA of 3.25, 3 years of experience in field, 3 letters of recommendation, interview, official transcripts. Additional exam requirements/recommendations for international students: Required—TOEFL. *Application deadline:* For fall admission, 7/15 for domestic students, 6/15 for international students; for spring admission, 11/15 for domestic students, 11/1 for international students; for summer admission, 4/15 for domestic students, 4/1 for international students. Applications are processed on a rolling basis. Application fee: $35. Electronic applications accepted. *Expenses:* Tuition, state resident: full-time $10,104; part-time $421 per semester hour. Tuition, nonresident: full-time $20,208; part-time $842 per semester hour. *Financial support:* Fellowships, research assistantships, teaching assistantships, career-related internships or fieldwork, Federal Work-Study, institutionally sponsored loans, scholarships/grants, and unspecified assistantships available. Support available to part-time students. Financial award application deadline: 3/31; financial award applicants required to submit FAFSA. *Unit head:* Dr. Susan Santoli, Chair/Director of Graduate Studies, 251-380-2836, Fax: 251-380-2748, E-mail: ssantoli@southalabama.edu. Website: http://www.southalabama.edu/colleges/ceps/lte/index.html

University of South Carolina, The Graduate School, College of Education, Department of Educational Leadership and Policies, Program in Educational Administration, Columbia, SC 29208. Offers M Ed, PhD, Ed S. *Accreditation:* NCATE. *Program availability:* Part-time, evening/weekend, online learning. *Degree requirements:* For master's, comprehensive exam, thesis (for some programs), foreign language (MA); for doctorate, comprehensive exam, thesis/dissertation. *Entrance requirements:* For master's, GRE General Test or MAT, letter of reference, resume; for doctorate and Ed S, GRE General Test or MAT, interview, letter of intent, letter of reference, transcripts, resum&e. Electronic applications accepted.

University of South Dakota, Graduate School, School of Education, Division of Curriculum and Instruction, Vermillion, SD 57069. Offers American Indian education (Certificate); curriculum and instruction (Ed D, Ed S); elementary education (MA), including elementary education; English language learners (Certificate); literacy leadership and coaching (Certificate); reading interventionist (Certificate); science, technology and math pedagogy (Certificate); secondary education (MA), including secondary education; special education (MA), including special education; technology for education and training (MS), including technology for education and training. *Accreditation:* NCATE. *Program availability:* Part-time, online learning. *Degree requirements:* For master's and other advanced degree, comprehensive exam, thesis or alternative; for doctorate, comprehensive exam, thesis/dissertation. *Entrance requirements:* For master's, doctorate, and other advanced degree, GRE General Test, MAT, minimum GPA of 2.7. Additional exam requirements/recommendations for international students: Required—TOEFL (minimum score 550 paper-based; 79 iBT). *Application deadline:* Applications are processed on a rolling basis. Application fee: $35. Electronic applications accepted. *Financial support:* Research assistantships with partial tuition reimbursements, teaching assistantships with partial tuition reimbursements, career-related internships or fieldwork, Federal Work-Study, and unspecified assistantships available. Financial award applicants required to submit FAFSA. *Application contact:* Graduate School, 605-658-6140, Fax: 605-677-6118, E-mail: grad@usd.edu.
Website: http://www.usd.edu/ci

University of South Dakota, Graduate School, School of Education, Division of Educational Leadership, Vermillion, SD 57069. Offers educational administration (MA, Ed D, Ed S), including adult and higher education (MA, Ed D), curriculum director, director of special education (Ed D, Ed S), preK-12 principal, school district superintendent (Ed D, Ed S). *Accreditation:* NCATE. *Program availability:* Part-time, evening/weekend, 100% online, blended/hybrid learning. *Degree requirements:* For master's and Ed S, comprehensive exam, thesis or alternative; for doctorate, comprehensive exam, thesis/dissertation. *Entrance requirements:* For master's, GRE General Test, MAT, minimum GPA of 2.7; for doctorate, minimum GPA of 2.7. Additional exam requirements/recommendations for international students: Required—TOEFL (minimum score 550 paper-based; 79 iBT). *Application deadline:* Applications are processed on a rolling basis. Application fee: $35. Electronic applications accepted. *Financial support:* Research assistantships with partial tuition reimbursements, teaching assistantships with partial tuition reimbursements, Federal Work-Study, traineeships, and unspecified assistantships available. Financial award applicants required to submit FAFSA. *Application contact:* Graduate School, 605-658-6140, Fax: 605-677-6118, E-mail: grad@usd.edu.
Website: http://www.usd.edu/education/educational-administration

University of Southern California, Graduate School, Rossier School of Education, Doctor of Education Programs, Los Angeles, CA 90089. Offers educational psychology (Ed D); higher education administration (Ed D); K-12 leadership in urban school settings (Ed D); teacher education in multicultural societies (Ed D). *Program availability:* Part-time, evening/weekend. *Degree requirements:* For doctorate, thesis/dissertation. *Entrance requirements:* For doctorate, GRE. Additional exam requirements/recommendations for international students: Required—TOEFL (minimum score 100 iBT). Electronic applications accepted. *Faculty research:* Data-driven decision-making in K-12 schools and districts; examination of college and university leadership and management in U. S. and Asia; studies in facilitating student learning; organizational change and the role of leaders; leadership, diversity, learning and accountability.

University of Southern California, Graduate School, Rossier School of Education, Doctor of Philosophy in Education Programs, Los Angeles, CA 90089. Offers educational psychology (PhD); higher education administration and policy (PhD); K-12 policy and practice (PhD). *Degree requirements:* For doctorate, thesis/dissertation, 63 units; qualifying exam; dissertation proposal and defense. *Entrance requirements:* For doctorate, GRE. Additional exam requirements/recommendations for international students: Required—TOEFL (minimum score 100 iBT). Electronic applications accepted. *Faculty research:* Diversity in higher education, organizational change, educational psychology, policy and politics of educational reform, economics of education and education policy.

University of Southern Indiana, Graduate Studies, Pott College of Science, Engineering, and Education, Department of Teacher Education, Program in Educational Leadership, Evansville, IN 47712-3590. Offers administrative leadership (Ed D); pedagogical leadership (Ed D). *Program availability:* Part-time, evening/weekend. *Faculty:* 4 full-time (3 women), 2 part-time/adjunct (1 woman). *Entrance requirements:* For doctorate, GRE, master's degree transcript, essay, two letters of recommendation,

resume/curriculum vitae. Additional exam requirements/recommendations for international students: Required—TOEFL (minimum score 550 paper-based; 79 iBT), IELTS (minimum score 6). *Application deadline:* For fall admission, 4/15 for domestic students. Application fee: $40. *Expenses:* Tuition, state resident: full-time $9394. Tuition, nonresident: full-time $17,917. *Required fees:* $510. *Financial support:* Federal Work-Study, scholarships/grants, tuition waivers, and unspecified assistantships available. Financial award application deadline: 3/1; financial award applicants required to submit FAFSA. *Unit head:* Dr. Bonnie Beach, Associate Dean, 812-465-1620, E-mail: blbeach@usi.edu. *Application contact:* Dr. Mayola Rowser, Director, Graduate Studies, 812-465-7015, Fax: 812-464-1956, E-mail: mrowser@usi.edu.
Website: http://www.usi.edu/science/teacher-education/programs/doctor-of-education-edd/

University of Southern Indiana, Graduate Studies, Pott College of Science, Engineering, and Education, Department of Teacher Education, Program in School Administration and Leadership, Evansville, IN 47712-3590. Offers MSE. *Program availability:* Part-time, evening/weekend. *Faculty:* 4 full-time (3 women), 2 part-time/adjunct (1 woman). *Students:* 9 full-time (4 women), 3 part-time (all women); includes 1 minority (Black or African American, non-Hispanic/Latino). Average age 33. In 2017, 3 master's awarded. *Entrance requirements:* For master's, PRAXIS II, bachelor's degree with minimum cumulative GPA of 2.75 from college or university accredited by NCATE or comparable association; minimum GPA of 3.0 in all courses taken at graduate level at all schools attended; teaching license. Additional exam requirements/recommendations for international students: Required—TOEFL (minimum score 550 paper-based; 79 iBT), IELTS (minimum score 6). *Application deadline:* Applications are processed on a rolling basis. Application fee: $40. Electronic applications accepted. *Expenses:* Tuition, state resident: full-time $9394. Tuition, nonresident: full-time $17,917. *Required fees:* $510. *Financial support:* Federal Work-Study, scholarships/grants, tuition waivers (full and partial), and unspecified assistantships available. Financial award application deadline: 3/1; financial award applicants required to submit FAFSA. *Unit head:* Dr. Bonnie Beach, Associate Dean, 812-465-1620, E-mail: blbeach@usi.edu. *Application contact:* Dr. Mayola Rowser, Director, Graduate Studies, 812-465-7015, Fax: 812-464-1956, E-mail: mrowser@usi.edu.
Website: http://www.usi.edu/science/teacher-education/programs/mse

University of Southern Maine, College of Management and Human Service, School of Education and Human Development, Educational Leadership Program, Portland, ME 04103. Offers assistant principal (CGS); educational leadership (MS Ed, CAS). *Program availability:* Part-time, evening/weekend, online learning. *Degree requirements:* For master's, thesis or alternative, practicum, internship; for other advanced degree, thesis or alternative. *Entrance requirements:* For master's, three years of documented teaching; for other advanced degree, master's degree. Additional exam requirements/recommendations for international students: Required—TOEFL (minimum score 550 paper-based; 79 iBT). Electronic applications accepted. *Faculty research:* Teaching strategies, technology-enhanced leadership, school-community partnerships, workforce development, higher education.

University of Southern Mississippi, College of Education and Psychology, Department of Educational Research and Administration, Hattiesburg, MS 39406-0001. Offers educational administration (M Ed, Ed D, PhD, Ed S); educational administration and supervision (M Ed); educational studies and research (MS); higher education (Ed D); higher education administration (PhD); higher education: student affairs (M Ed); research, evaluation, statistics, assessment (PhD). *Students:* 30 full-time (23 women), 3 part-time (all women). 44 applicants, 91% accepted, 33 enrolled. *Degree requirements:* For master's and Ed S, comprehensive exam, thesis (for some programs); for doctorate, comprehensive exam, thesis/dissertation. *Entrance requirements:* For master's and doctorate, GRE General Test, minimum GPA of 2.75. Additional exam requirements/recommendations for international students: Required—TOEFL. *Application deadline:* For fall admission, 2/1 for domestic students, 3/1 for international students. Applications are processed on a rolling basis. Application fee: $60. *Expenses:* Tuition, state resident: full-time $3830. *Financial support:* Career-related internships or fieldwork, Federal Work-Study, and institutionally sponsored loans available. Financial award application deadline: 3/15; financial award applicants required to submit FAFSA. *Unit head:* Dr. Lilian Hill, Co-Chair, 601-266-4622.
Website: https://www.usm.edu/educational-research-administration

University of South Florida, College of Education, Department of Leadership, Counseling, Adult, Career and Higher Education, Tampa, FL 33620-9951. Offers adult education (MA, Ed D, PhD, Ed S); career and technical education (MA); career and workforce education (PhD); higher education/community college teaching (MA, Ed D, PhD); vocational education (Ed S). *Faculty:* 19 full-time (11 women). *Students:* 129 full-time (91 women), 274 part-time (187 women); includes 147 minority (71 Black or African American, non-Hispanic/Latino; 2 American Indian or Alaska Native, non-Hispanic/Latino; 9 Asian, non-Hispanic/Latino; 59 Hispanic/Latino; 6 Two or more races, non-Hispanic/Latino), 15 international. Average age 35. 158 applicants, 67% accepted, 83 enrolled. In 2017, 89 master's, 7 doctorates, 2 other advanced degrees awarded. Application fee: $30. *Total annual research expenditures:* $157,971. *Unit head:* Dr. Judith Ponticell, Chair, 813-974-4897, Fax: 813-974-5423, E-mail: jponticell@usf.edu.
Website: http://www.coedu.usf.edu/main/departments/ache/ache.html

University of South Florida, Innovative Education, Tampa, FL 33620-9951. Offers adult, career and higher education (Graduate Certificate), including college teaching, leadership in developing human resources, leadership in higher education; Africana studies (Graduate Certificate), including diasporas and health disparities, genocide and human rights; aging studies (Graduate Certificate), including gerontology; art research (Graduate Certificate), including museum studies; business foundations (Graduate Certificate); chemical and biomedical engineering (Graduate Certificate), including materials science and engineering, water, health and sustainability; child and family studies (Graduate Certificate), including positive behavior support; civil and industrial engineering (Graduate Certificate), including transportation systems analysis; community and family health (Graduate Certificate), including maternal and child health, social marketing and public health, violence and injury: prevention and intervention, women's health; criminology (Graduate Certificate), including criminal justice administration; data science for public administration (Graduate Certificate); digital humanities (Graduate Certificate); educational measurement and research (Graduate Certificate), including evaluation; English (Graduate Certificate), including comparative literary studies, creative writing, professional and technical communication; entrepreneurship (Graduate Certificate); environmental health (Graduate Certificate), including safety management; epidemiology and biostatistics (Graduate Certificate), including applied biostatistics, biostatistics, concepts and tools of epidemiology, epidemiology, epidemiology of infectious diseases; geography, environment and planning (Graduate Certificate), including community development, environmental policy and management, geographical information systems; geology (Graduate Certificate), including hydrogeology; global health (Graduate Certificate), including disaster management, global health and Latin American and Caribbean studies, global health practice, humanitarian assistance, infection control; government and international affairs (Graduate Certificate), including Cuban studies, globalization studies; health policy and management (Graduate Certificate), including health management and leadership,

Educational Leadership and Administration

public health policy and programs; hearing specialist: early intervention (Graduate Certificate); industrial and management systems engineering (Graduate Certificate), including systems engineering, technology management; information studies (Graduate Certificate), including school library media specialist; information systems/decision sciences (Graduate Certificate), including analytics and business intelligence; instructional technology (Graduate Certificate), including distance education, Florida digital/virtual educator, instructional design, multimedia design, Web design; internal medicine, bioethics and medical humanities (Graduate Certificate), including biomedical ethics; Latin American and Caribbean studies (Graduate Certificate); leadership for coastal resiliency planning (Graduate Certificate); mass communications (Graduate Certificate), including multimedia journalism; mathematics and statistics (Graduate Certificate), including mathematics; medicine (Graduate Certificate), including aging and neuroscience, bioinformatics, biotechnology, brain fitness and memory management, clinical investigation, hand and upper limb rehabilitation, health informatics, health sciences, integrative weight management, intellectual property, medicine and gender, metabolic and nutritional medicine, metabolic cardiology, pharmacy sciences; national and competitive intelligence (Graduate Certificate); nursing (Graduate Certificate), including simulation based academic fellowship in advanced pain management; psychological and social foundations (Graduate Certificate), including career counseling, college teaching, diversity in education, mental health counseling, school counseling; public affairs (Graduate Certificate), including nonprofit management, public management, research administration; public health (Graduate Certificate), including assessing chemical toxicity and public health risks, health equity, pharmacoepidemiology, public health generalist, toxicology, translational research in adolescent behavioral health; public health practices (Graduate Certificate), including planning for healthy communities; rehabilitation and mental health counseling (Graduate Certificate), including integrative mental health care, marriage and family therapy, rehabilitation technology; secondary education (Graduate Certificate), including ESOL, foreign language education: culture and content, foreign language education: professional; social work (Graduate Certificate), including geriatric social work/clinical gerontology; special education (Graduate Certificate), including autism spectrum disorder, disabilities education: severe/profound; world languages (Graduate Certificate), including teaching English as a second language (TESL) or foreign language. *Unit head:* Dr. Cynthia DeLuca, Associate Vice President and Assistant Vice Provost, 813-974-3077, Fax: 813-974-7061, E-mail: deluca@usf.edu. *Application contact:* Owen Hooper, Director, Summer and Alternative Calendar Programs, 813-974-6917, E-mail: hooper@usf.edu.
Website: http://www.usf.edu/innovative-education/

University of South Florida, St. Petersburg, College of Education, St. Petersburg, FL 33701. Offers educational leadership development (M Ed); elementary education (MA), including math/science; English education (MA); middle grades STEM education (MS); reading education (MA). *Program availability:* Part-time. *Degree requirements:* For master's, comprehensive exam, practicum, internship, comprehensive portfolio. *Entrance requirements:* For master's, State of Florida General Knowledge Test (GKT), Florida Teaching Certificate (for non-initial certification programs), letters of recommendation. Additional exam requirements/recommendations for international students: Required—TOEFL (minimum score 550 paper-based; 79 iBT); Recommended—IELTS. Electronic applications accepted.

University of South Florida Sarasota-Manatee, College of Liberal Arts and Social Sciences, Sarasota, FL 34243. Offers criminal justice (MA); education (MA); educational leadership (M Ed), including curriculum leadership, K-12 public school leadership, non-public/charter school leadership; elementary education (MAT); English education (MA); social work (MSW). *Program availability:* Part-time, 100% online, blended/hybrid learning. *Faculty:* 15 full-time (12 women), 8 part-time/adjunct (6 women). *Students:* 11 full-time (10 women), 43 part-time (37 women); includes 17 minority (7 Black or African American, non-Hispanic/Latino; 2 Asian, non-Hispanic/Latino; 8 Hispanic/Latino), 1 international. Average age 35. 62 applicants, 27% accepted, 14 enrolled. In 2017, 32 master's awarded. *Degree requirements:* For master's, comprehensive exam (for some programs). *Entrance requirements:* For master's, GRE. Additional exam requirements/recommendations for international students: Required—TOEFL (minimum score 550 paper-based; 79 iBT), IELTS (minimum score 6.5). *Application deadline:* For fall admission, 3/1 priority date for domestic students, 3/1 for international students; for spring admission, 10/1 priority date for domestic students, 10/1 for international students. Applications are processed on a rolling basis. Application fee: $30. Electronic applications accepted. *Expenses:* Tuition, state resident: full-time $8350; part-time $418 per credit hour. Tuition, nonresident: full-time $19,047; part-time $863 per credit hour. *Required fees:* $1689. Tuition and fees vary according to degree level and program. *Financial support:* In 2017–18, 1 student received support. Career-related internships or fieldwork, institutionally sponsored loans, scholarships/grants, health care benefits, and unspecified assistantships available. Support available to part-time students. Financial award application deadline: 3/1; financial award applicants required to submit FAFSA. *Faculty research:* Educational leadership, secondary education, elementary education, criminal justice, social work. *Total annual research expenditures:* $72,000. *Unit head:* Dr. Jane Rose, Dean, 941-359-4469, Fax: 941-359-4778, E-mail: jane.rose@sar.usf.edu. *Application contact:* Brandon Avery, Assistant Director, Admissions, 941-359-4331, E-mail: bavery@sar.usf.edu.

The University of Tampa, Programs in Education, Tampa, FL 33606-1490. Offers curriculum and instruction (M Ed); educational leadership (M Ed); instructional design and technology (MS). *Program availability:* Part-time, evening/weekend. *Faculty:* 5 full-time (4 women), 7 part-time/adjunct (5 women). *Students:* 41 full-time (27 women), 69 part-time (52 women); includes 20 minority (18 Black or African American, non-Hispanic/Latino; 2 Two or more races, non-Hispanic/Latino), 14 international. Average age 32. 126 applicants, 40% accepted, 29 enrolled. In 2017, 47 master's awarded. *Degree requirements:* For master's, capstone. *Entrance requirements:* For master's, GMAT or GRE, current Florida Professional Teaching Certificate, statement of eligibility for Florida Professional Teaching Certificate, or professional teaching certificate from another state; bachelor's degree in an area of education. Additional exam requirements/recommendations for international students: Required—TOEFL (minimum score 577 paper-based; 90 iBT), IELTS (minimum score 7.5). *Application deadline:* Applications are processed on a rolling basis. Application fee: $40. Electronic applications accepted. *Expenses:* Contact institution. *Financial support:* In 2017–18, 20 students received support. Career-related internships or fieldwork, scholarships/grants, and unspecified assistantships available. Financial award applicants required to submit FAFSA. *Faculty research:* Diversity in the classroom, technology integration, assessment methodologies, complex and ill-structured problem solving, communities of practice. *Unit head:* Dr. Antony Erben, Chair, 813-257-3414, E-mail: terben@ut.edu. *Application contact:* Chanelle Cox, Staff Assistant, Admissions for Graduate and Continuing Studies, 813-253-6249, E-mail: ccox@ut.edu.
Website: http://www.ut.edu/graduate/education/

The University of Tennessee, Graduate School, College of Education, Health and Human Sciences, Program in Education, Knoxville, TN 37996. Offers art education (MS); counseling education (PhD); cultural studies in education (PhD); curriculum (MS, Ed S); curriculum, educational research and evaluation (Ed D, PhD); early childhood education (PhD); early childhood special education (MS); education of deaf and hard of hearing (MS); educational administration and policy studies (Ed D, PhD); educational administration and supervision (Ed S); educational psychology (Ed D, PhD); elementary education (MS, Ed S); elementary teaching (MS); English education (MS, Ed S); exercise science (PhD); foreign language/ESL education (MS, Ed S); instructional technology (MS, Ed D, PhD, Ed S); literacy, language and ESL education (PhD); literacy, language education, and ESL education (Ed D); mathematics education (MS, Ed S); modified and comprehensive special education (MS); reading education (MS, Ed S); school counseling (Ed S); school psychology (PhD, Ed S); science education (MS, Ed S); secondary teaching (MS); social foundations (MS); social science education (MS, Ed S); socio-cultural foundations of sports and education (PhD); special education (Ed S); teacher education (Ed D, PhD). *Accreditation:* NCATE. *Program availability:* Part-time, evening/weekend. *Degree requirements:* For master's and Ed S, thesis optional; for doctorate, variable foreign language requirement, thesis/dissertation. *Entrance requirements:* For master's, minimum GPA of 2.7; for doctorate and Ed S, GRE General Test, minimum GPA of 2.7. Additional exam requirements/recommendations for international students: Required—TOEFL. Electronic applications accepted.

The University of Tennessee, Graduate School, College of Education, Health and Human Sciences, Program in Educational Administration and Policy Studies, Knoxville, TN 37996. Offers educational administration and policy studies (Ed D); educational administration and supervision (MS). *Accreditation:* NCATE. *Program availability:* Part-time, evening/weekend, online learning. *Degree requirements:* For master's, thesis optional. *Entrance requirements:* For master's, minimum GPA of 2.7. Additional exam requirements/recommendations for international students: Required—TOEFL. Electronic applications accepted.

The University of Tennessee at Chattanooga, Program in Learning and Leadership, Chattanooga, TN 37403. Offers educational leadership (Ed D, PhD). *Students:* 1 (woman) full-time, 86 part-time (49 women); includes 18 minority (12 Black or African American, non-Hispanic/Latino; 1 Asian, non-Hispanic/Latino; 3 Hispanic/Latino; 2 Two or more races, non-Hispanic/Latino). Average age 43. 19 applicants, 58% accepted, 11 enrolled. In 2017, 7 doctorates awarded. *Degree requirements:* For doctorate, thesis/dissertation, portfolio. *Entrance requirements:* For doctorate, GRE General Test, master's degree with minimum cumulative GPA of 3.0, two years of practical work experience in organizational environment. Additional exam requirements/recommendations for international students: Required—TOEFL (minimum score 550 paper-based; 79 iBT), IELTS (minimum score 6). *Application deadline:* For fall admission, 6/15 priority date for domestic students, 7/1 for international students; for spring admission, 11/1 priority date for domestic students, 11/1 for international students. Applications are processed on a rolling basis. Application fee: $35 ($40 for international students). Electronic applications accepted. *Expenses:* Tuition, state resident: full-time $8244; part-time $458 per credit hour. Tuition, nonresident: full-time $24,362; part-time $1353 per credit hour. *Required fees:* $1776; $487 per semester. Tuition and fees vary according to course load. *Financial support:* Research assistantships, career-related internships or fieldwork, scholarships/grants, and unspecified assistantships available. Support available to part-time students. Financial award application deadline: 7/1; financial award applicants required to submit FAFSA. *Faculty research:* Instructional design and development, curriculum inquiry/mapping, program evaluation, professional development and teacher training, fostering student diligence. *Total annual research expenditures:* $60,571. *Unit head:* Dr. David Rausch, Director, 423-425-5270, E-mail: utclead@utc.edu. *Application contact:* Dr. Joanne Romagni, Dean of the Graduate School, 423-425-4478, Fax: 423-425-5223, E-mail: joanne-romagni@utc.edu.
Website: https://www.utc.edu/doctorate-learning-leadership/index.php

The University of Tennessee at Chattanooga, School of Education, Chattanooga, TN 37403. Offers counseling (M Ed), including community counseling, school counseling; education (M Ed, Post-Master's Certificate), including elementary education (M Ed), school leadership (Post-Master's Certificate); elementary education (M Ed); learning and leadership (Ed D), including educational leadership; school leadership (Post-Master's Certificate); school leadership: principal licensure (Ed S); secondary education (M Ed); special education (M Ed). *Accreditation:* ACA; NCATE. *Program availability:* Part-time. *Students:* 43 full-time (30 women), 58 part-time (47 women); includes 18 minority (9 Black or African American, non-Hispanic/Latino; 1 Asian, non-Hispanic/Latino; 1 Hispanic/Latino; 7 Two or more races, non-Hispanic/Latino). Average age 31. 118 applicants, 75% accepted, 33 enrolled. In 2017, 59 master's, 7 other advanced degrees awarded. *Degree requirements:* For master's, comprehensive exam, thesis optional, culminating experience; for other advanced degree, internship. *Entrance requirements:* For master's, GRE General Test, PPST 1, teaching certificate; for other advanced degree, two letters of recommendation, graduate degree in education, teaching certificate with three years of experience. Additional exam requirements/recommendations for international students: Required—TOEFL (minimum score 550 paper-based; 79 iBT), IELTS (minimum score 6). *Application deadline:* For fall admission, 6/15 for domestic students, 7/1 for international students; for spring admission, 11/1 for domestic and international students. Applications are processed on a rolling basis. Application fee: $35 ($40 for international students). Electronic applications accepted. *Expenses:* Contact institution. *Financial support:* Research assistantships, teaching assistantships, career-related internships or fieldwork, institutionally sponsored loans, scholarships/grants, and unspecified assistantships available. Support available to part-time students. Financial award application deadline: 7/1; financial award applicants required to submit FAFSA. *Faculty research:* School counseling, community counseling, elementary and secondary education, school leadership and administration. *Total annual research expenditures:* $576,495. *Unit head:* Dr. Renee Murley, Director, 423-425-4684, Fax: 423-425-5380, E-mail: renee-murley@utc.edu. *Application contact:* Dr. Joanne Romagni, Dean of the Graduate School, 423-425-4478, Fax: 423-425-5223, E-mail: joanne-romagni@utc.edu.
Website: https://www.utc.edu/school-education/

The University of Tennessee at Martin, Graduate Programs, College of Education, Health and Behavioral Sciences, Program in Educational Leadership, Martin, TN 38238. Offers MS Ed. *Program availability:* Part-time, online only, 100% online. *Students:* 18 part-time (10 women); includes 2 minority (1 Black or African American, non-Hispanic/Latino; 1 Hispanic/Latino). Average age 35. 11 applicants, 18% accepted, 2 enrolled. In 2017, 5 master's awarded. *Degree requirements:* For master's, comprehensive exam. *Entrance requirements:* For master's, GRE General Test, minimum GPA of 2.5, letters of reference, teaching license, resume, teaching experience. Additional exam requirements/recommendations for international students: Required—TOEFL (minimum score 525 paper-based; 71 iBT). *Application deadline:* For fall admission, 7/27 priority date for domestic and international students; for spring admission, 12/17 priority date for domestic and international students; for summer admission, 5/10 priority date for domestic and international students. Applications are processed on a rolling basis. Application fee: $30 ($130 for international students). Electronic applications accepted. *Expenses:* Tuition, state resident: full-time $8658; part-time $481 per credit hour. Tuition, nonresident: full-time $14,418; part-time $801 per credit hour. *International tuition:* $22,602 full-time. *Required fees:* $1404; $79 per credit hour. Part-time tuition and fees vary according to course load. *Financial support:* In 2017–18, 2 students received support. Research assistantships with full tuition reimbursements available, teaching assistantships with full tuition reimbursements available, scholarships/grants, and tuition waivers (full and partial) available. Financial award application deadline: 2/1; financial award applicants required to submit FAFSA. *Unit head:* Cynthia West, Dean, 731-881-7125, Fax: 731-881-7975, E-mail: cwest@utm.edu. *Application contact:* Jolene L. Cunningham, Student Services Specialist, 731-881-7012, Fax: 731-881-7499, E-mail: jcunningham@utm.edu.

The University of Texas at Arlington, Graduate School, College of Education, Department of Educational Leadership and Policy Studies, Arlington, TX 76019. Offers educational leadership (PhD); higher education (M Ed); principal certification (M Ed). *Program availability:* Part-time, evening/weekend, online learning. *Degree requirements:* For master's, 2 field-based practica; for doctorate, comprehensive exam, thesis/dissertation, 2 research-based practica. *Entrance requirements:* For master's, GRE, 3 references, minimum undergraduate GPA of 3.0 in last 60 hours of course work; for doctorate, GRE, resume, statement of intent, 3 reference forms, applicable master's degree. *Faculty research:* Lived realities of students of color in K-16 contexts, K-16 faculty, K-16 policy and law, K-16 student access, K-16 student success.

The University of Texas at Austin, Graduate School, College of Education, Department of Educational Administration, Austin, TX 78712-1111. Offers M Ed, Ed D, PhD. *Degree requirements:* For doctorate, thesis/dissertation. *Entrance requirements:* For master's and doctorate, GRE General Test. Electronic applications accepted.

The University of Texas at Austin, Graduate School, College of Education, Department of Special Education, Austin, TX 78712-1111. Offers autism and developmental disabilities (Ed D, PhD); autism and developmental disability (M Ed, MA); early childhood special education (M Ed, MA, Ed D, PhD); learning disabilities (Ed D, PhD); learning disabilities/behavior disorders (M Ed, MA); multicultural special education (M Ed, MA, Ed D, PhD); rehabilitation counselor (M Ed); rehabilitation counselor education (Ed D, PhD); special education administration (Ed D, PhD). *Accreditation:* CORE. *Program availability:* Part-time, evening/weekend, online learning. *Degree requirements:* For master's, thesis or alternative; for doctorate, thesis/dissertation. *Entrance requirements:* For master's and doctorate, GRE General Test. *Faculty research:* Anchored instruction, reading disabilities, multicultural/bilingual.

The University of Texas at El Paso, Graduate School, College of Education, Department of Educational Leadership and Foundations, El Paso, TX 79968-0001. Offers educational administration (M Ed); educational leadership and administration (Ed D). *Program availability:* Part-time, evening/weekend. *Degree requirements:* For master's, thesis optional; for doctorate, thesis/dissertation. *Entrance requirements:* For doctorate, GRE General Test, minimum graduate GPA of 3.0. Additional exam requirements/recommendations for international students: Required—TOEFL. Electronic applications accepted.

The University of Texas at San Antonio, College of Education and Human Development, Department of Educational Leadership and Policy Studies, San Antonio, TX 78249-0617. Offers educational leadership (Ed D); educational leadership and policy studies (M Ed), including educational leadership, higher education administration. *Program availability:* Part-time. *Faculty:* 22 full-time (10 women), 11 part-time/adjunct (6 women). *Students:* 40 full-time (27 women), 289 part-time (202 women); includes 230 minority (37 Black or African American, non-Hispanic/Latino; 3 Asian, non-Hispanic/Latino; 185 Hispanic/Latino; 5 Two or more races, non-Hispanic/Latino), 4 international. Average age 35. 107 applicants, 87% accepted, 70 enrolled. In 2017, 147 master's, 18 doctorates awarded. *Degree requirements:* For master's, comprehensive exam, thesis or alternative; for doctorate, comprehensive exam, thesis/dissertation. *Entrance requirements:* For master's, transcripts, statement of purpose, resume or curriculum vitae; for doctorate, GRE General Test, minimum GPA of 3.5 in a master's program, resume, three letters of recommendation, statement of purpose. Additional exam requirements/recommendations for international students: Required—TOEFL (minimum score 550 paper-based; 79 iBT), IELTS (minimum score 6.5). *Application deadline:* For fall admission, 6/15 for domestic students, 3/1 for international students; for spring admission, 10/15 for domestic students, 9/15 for international students. Application fee: $50 ($90 for international students). Electronic applications accepted. *Expenses:* Tuition, state resident: full-time $5495. Tuition, nonresident: full-time $21,938. *Required fees:* $1915. Tuition and fees vary according to program. *Financial support:* Fellowships available. Financial award application deadline: 2/1. *Faculty research:* Urban and international school leadership, student success, college access, higher education policy, multiculturalism, minority student achievement. *Total annual research expenditures:* $90,372. *Unit head:* Dr. Enrique Aleman, Department Chair, 210-458-5411, E-mail: enrique.aleman@utsa.edu. *Application contact:* Elisha Reynolds, Student Development Specialist, 210-458-6620, Fax: 210-458-5848, E-mail: elisha.reynolds@utsa.edu.
Website: http://education.utsa.edu/educational_leadership_and_policy_studies/

The University of Texas at Tyler, College of Education and Psychology, Department of Educational Leadership, Tyler, TX 75799-0001. Offers M Ed. *Program availability:* Part-time, evening/weekend, online learning. *Degree requirements:* For master's, comprehensive exam, 2 years of teaching experience. *Entrance requirements:* For master's, GRE General Test. Additional exam requirements/recommendations for international students: Required—TOEFL. *Faculty research:* Effective schools, restructuring of schools, leadership.

The University of Texas of the Permian Basin, Office of Graduate Studies, School of Education, Program in Educational Leadership, Odessa, TX 79762-0001. Offers MA. *Degree requirements:* For master's, comprehensive exam (for some programs), thesis (for some programs). *Entrance requirements:* For master's, GRE General Test. Additional exam requirements/recommendations for international students: Required—TOEFL (minimum score 550 paper-based).

The University of Texas Rio Grande Valley, College of Education and P-16 Integration, Department of Organization and School Leadership, Edinburg, TX 78539. Offers educational leadership (M Ed, Ed D). *Program availability:* Part-time, evening/weekend. *Faculty:* 12. *Students:* 242. In 2017, 53 master's, 8 doctorates awarded. *Degree requirements:* For master's, comprehensive exam, thesis optional; for doctorate, comprehensive exam, thesis/dissertation. *Entrance requirements:* For master's, GRE, minimum GPA of 3.0 on undergraduate coursework; for doctorate, master's degree. Additional exam requirements/recommendations for international students: Required—TOEFL (minimum score 550 paper-based; 79 iBT), IELTS (minimum score 6.5). *Application deadline:* For fall admission, 4/15 for domestic students; for spring admission, 11/1 for domestic students; for summer admission, 3/1 for domestic students. Applications are processed on a rolling basis. Application fee: $50 ($75 for international students). Electronic applications accepted. *Expenses:* Tuition, state resident: full-time $5550; part-time $417 per credit hour. Tuition, nonresident: full-time $13,020; part-time $832 per credit hour. *Required fees:* $1169. *Financial support:* In 2017–18, research assistantships (averaging $15,000 per year) were awarded; teaching assistantships, career-related internships or fieldwork, institutionally sponsored loans, and scholarships/grants also available. Support available to part-time students. Financial award application deadline: 4/15; financial award applicants required to submit FAFSA. *Faculty research:* Leadership and gender studies, continuous improvement processes, leadership. *Unit head:* Dr. Velma Menchaca, Chair, 956-665-3436, E-mail: velma.menchaca@utrgv.edu. *Application contact:* Stephanie Ozuna, Graduate Student Recruiter, 956-665-3558, E-mail: stephanie.ozuna@utrgv.edu.

University of the Cumberlands, Graduate Programs in Education, Williamsburg, KY 40769-1372. Offers all grades (P-12) (M Ed); business and marketing (MA Ed, MAT); counselor education and supervision (Ed D); director of pupil personnel (Certificate); director of special education (Certificate); educational administration and supervision (Ed S); educational leadership (Ed D); elementary education (MA Ed, MAT); instructional leadership - principalship (MA Ed); instructional leadership - school principal (Certificate); middle school education (MA Ed, MAT); reading and writing (MA Ed); school counseling (MA Ed); school superintendent (Certificate); secondary education (MA Ed, MAT); special education (MAT); supervisor of instruction (Certificate); teacher leader (MA Ed). *Program availability:* Part-time, evening/weekend, online learning. *Degree requirements:* For master's, comprehensive exam. Electronic applications accepted.

University of the Pacific, Gladys L. Benerd School of Education, Stockton, CA 95211-0197. Offers curriculum and instruction (MA, Ed D); education (M Ed); educational administration and leadership (MA, Ed D); educational and school psychology (MA, Ed D); school psychology (Ed S); special education (MA); teacher education (MA). *Accreditation:* NCATE. *Faculty:* 19 full-time (12 women), 48 part-time/adjunct (39 women). *Students:* 141 full-time (115 women), 305 part-time (236 women); includes 219 minority (41 Black or African American, non-Hispanic/Latino; 44 Asian, non-Hispanic/Latino; 105 Hispanic/Latino; 2 Native Hawaiian or other Pacific Islander, non-Hispanic/Latino; 27 Two or more races, non-Hispanic/Latino), 7 international. Average age 33. 144 applicants, 83% accepted, 94 enrolled. In 2017, 231 master's, 8 doctorates awarded. *Degree requirements:* For doctorate, thesis/dissertation. *Entrance requirements:* For master's, GRE General Test; for doctorate, GRE General Test, GRE Subject Test. Additional exam requirements/recommendations for international students: Required—TOEFL. *Application deadline:* For fall admission, 3/1 priority date for domestic students; for spring admission, 10/15 for domestic students. Applications are processed on a rolling basis. Application fee: $75. *Financial support:* Teaching assistantships and institutionally sponsored loans available. Support available to part-time students. Financial award application deadline: 3/1; financial award applicants required to submit FAFSA. *Unit head:* Dr. Vanessa Sheared, Dean, 209-946-2683, E-mail: lwebster@pacific.edu. *Application contact:* Office of Graduate Admissions, 209-946-2344.

University of the Southwest, Graduate Programs, Hobbs, NM 88240-9129. Offers business administration (MBA); curriculum and instruction (MSE); curriculum and instruction: bilingual (MSE); curriculum and instruction: TESOL (MSE); early childhood education (MSE); educational administration (MSE); mental health counseling (MSE); school counseling (MSE); special education (MSE); sports management (MBA). *Program availability:* Part-time, evening/weekend, online learning. *Degree requirements:* For master's, comprehensive exam, thesis (for some programs). *Entrance requirements:* Additional exam requirements/recommendations for international students: Recommended—TOEFL. Electronic applications accepted.

University of the Virgin Islands, School of Education, St. Thomas, VI 00802. Offers creative leadership for innovation and change (PhD); educational leadership (MA); school counseling (MA); school psychology (Ed S). *Program availability:* Part-time, evening/weekend. *Degree requirements:* For master's, comprehensive exam, thesis or alternative; for doctorate, comprehensive exam, thesis/dissertation, qualifying examination; for Ed S, comprehensive exam. *Entrance requirements:* For master's, GRE, minimum GPA of 2.5, BA degree from accredited institution. Additional exam requirements/recommendations for international students: Required—TOEFL (minimum score 550 paper-based). Electronic applications accepted. *Expenses:* Contact institution.

The University of Toledo, College of Graduate Studies, Judith Herb College of Education, Department of Educational Foundations and Leadership, Toledo, OH 43606-3390. Offers educational administration and supervision (ME, DE, Ed S); educational psychology (ME, PhD); educational research and measurement (ME, PhD); educational sociology (PhD); educational theory and social foundations (ME); foundations of education (DE, PhD); history of education (PhD); philosophy of education (PhD). *Accreditation:* NCATE. *Program availability:* Part-time, evening/weekend. *Degree requirements:* For master's, comprehensive exam, thesis or alternative; for doctorate, comprehensive exam, thesis/dissertation; for Ed S, thesis optional. *Entrance requirements:* For master's, doctorate, and Ed S, minimum cumulative GPA of 2.7 for all previous academic work, letters of recommendation. Additional exam requirements/recommendations for international students: Required—TOEFL (minimum score 550 paper-based; 80 iBT). Electronic applications accepted.

University of Utah, Graduate School, College of Education, Department of Educational Leadership and Policy, Salt Lake City, UT 84084. Offers educational leadership and policy (Ed D, PhD), including higher education administration (Ed D); K-12 (Ed D); K-12 school administration (M Ed); K-12 teacher instructional leadership (M Ed); student affairs (M Ed); MPA/PhD. *Program availability:* Part-time, evening/weekend. *Faculty:* 10 full-time (7 women), 2 part-time/adjunct (both women). *Students:* 60 full-time (40 women), 185 part-time (124 women); includes 54 minority (14 Black or African American, non-Hispanic/Latino; 5 American Indian or Alaska Native, non-Hispanic/Latino; 5 Asian, non-Hispanic/Latino; 24 Hispanic/Latino; 2 Native Hawaiian or other Pacific Islander, non-Hispanic/Latino; 4 Two or more races, non-Hispanic/Latino), 1 international. Average age 35. 181 applicants, 69% accepted, 90 enrolled. In 2017, 64 master's, 6 doctorates awarded. *Degree requirements:* For master's, comprehensive exam (for some programs), internship, capstone; for doctorate, thesis/dissertation, qualifying exam. *Entrance requirements:* For master's, minimum undergraduate GPA of 3.0, valid bachelor's degree, 3 years' teaching or leadership experience, Level 1 or 2 UT educator's license (for K-12 programs only); for doctorate, GRE General Test (taken with five years of applying), minimum undergraduate GPA of 3.0, valid master's degree. Additional exam requirements/recommendations for international students: Required—TOEFL (minimum score 550 paper-based). *Application deadline:* For fall admission, 1/15 priority date for domestic and international students; for winter admission, 2/1 for domestic and international students; for spring admission, 11/1 priority date for domestic and international students; for summer admission, 3/1 priority date for domestic and international students. Applications are processed on a rolling basis. Application fee: $55 ($65 for international students). Electronic applications accepted. *Expenses:* Contact institution. *Financial support:* In 2017–18, 12 students received support, including 1 fellowship with full tuition reimbursement available (averaging $15,000 per year), 2 research assistantships with full tuition reimbursements available (averaging $15,000 per year), 6 teaching assistantships with full tuition reimbursements available (averaging $15,000 per year); career-related internships or fieldwork, scholarships/grants, health care benefits, and unspecified assistantships also available. Support available to part-time students. Financial award application deadline: 3/1; financial award applicants required to submit FAFSA. *Faculty research:* Education accountability, college student diversity, K-12 educational administration and school leadership, student affairs, higher education. *Unit head:* Dr. Gerardo Lopez, Chair, 801-581-6971, Fax: 801-585-6756, E-mail: gerardo.lopez@utah.edu. *Application contact:* Marilynn S. Howard, Academic Coordinator, 801-581-6714, Fax: 801-585-6756, E-mail: marilynn.howard@utah.edu.
Website: http://elp.utah.edu/

Educational Leadership and Administration

University of Vermont, Graduate College, College of Education and Social Services, Ed D Program in Educational Leadership and Policy Studies, Burlington, VT 05405-0160. Offers Ed D. *Accreditation:* NCATE. *Students:* 53 (36 women); includes 7 minority (3 Black or African American, non-Hispanic/Latino; 3 Hispanic/Latino; 1 Two or more races, non-Hispanic/Latino), 3 international. 24 applicants, 67% accepted, 13 enrolled. In 2017, 14 doctorates awarded. *Degree requirements:* For doctorate, thesis/dissertation. *Entrance requirements:* For doctorate, resume, writing sample. Additional exam requirements/recommendations for international students: Required—TOEFL (minimum score 550 paper-based, 90 iBT) or IELTS (6.5). *Application deadline:* For fall admission, 1/15 for domestic and international students. Application fee: $65. Electronic applications accepted. *Expenses:* Tuition, state resident: full-time $11,628; part-time $646 per credit. Tuition, nonresident: full-time $29,340; part-time $1630 per credit. *Required fees:* $1994; $10 per credit. Tuition and fees vary according to course load and program. *Financial support:* In 2017–18, 4 students received support, including 4 teaching assistantships with full tuition reimbursements available (averaging $20,000 per year); research assistantships and health care benefits also available. Financial award application deadline: 1/15. *Unit head:* Dr. Judith Aiken, Ed D Coordinator, 802-656-2936, E-mail: edd@uvm.edu.
Website: https://www.uvm.edu/cess/dlds/doctoral_programs

University of Vermont, Graduate College, College of Education and Social Services, PhD Program in Educational Leadership and Policy Studies, Burlington, VT 05405. Offers PhD. *Students:* 13 (9 women). 18 applicants, 44% accepted, 4 enrolled. In 2017, 5 doctorates awarded. *Degree requirements:* For doctorate, thesis/dissertation. *Entrance requirements:* For doctorate, GRE General Test, resume, writing sample. Additional exam requirements/recommendations for international students: Required—TOEFL (minimum iBT score of 90) or IELTS (6.5). *Application deadline:* For fall admission, 1/6 for domestic and international students. Application fee: $65. Electronic applications accepted. *Expenses:* Tuition, state resident: full-time $11,628; part-time $646 per credit. Tuition, nonresident: full-time $29,340; part-time $1630 per credit. *Required fees:* $1994; $10 per credit. Tuition and fees vary according to course load and program. *Financial support:* In 2017–18, 7 students received support, including 1 research assistantship with full tuition reimbursement available (averaging $20,000 per year), 6 teaching assistantships with full tuition reimbursements available (averaging $20,000 per year); health care benefits also available. Financial award application deadline: 1/6. *Unit head:* Dr. Kelly Clark Keefe, 802-656-2936, E-mail: cessphd@uvm.edu.
Website: https://www.uvm.edu/cess/dlds/doctoral/phd

University of Vermont, Graduate College, College of Education and Social Services, Program in Educational Leadership, Burlington, VT 05405. Offers educational leadership (M Ed), including community and organizational leadership, school leader with administrative endorsement. *Accreditation:* NCATE. *Students:* 17 (14 women), 1 international. 16 applicants, 100% accepted, 9 enrolled. In 2017, 8 master's awarded. *Degree requirements:* For master's, thesis or alternative. *Entrance requirements:* Additional exam requirements/recommendations for international students: Required—TOEFL (minimum score 550 paper-based, 90 iBT) or IELTS (6.5). *Application deadline:* For fall admission, 4/1 for domestic and international students; for spring admission, 11/15 for domestic and international students. Application fee: $65. Electronic applications accepted. *Expenses:* Tuition, state resident: full-time $11,628; part-time $646 per credit. Tuition, nonresident: full-time $29,340; part-time $1630 per credit. *Required fees:* $1994; $10 per credit. Tuition and fees vary according to course load and program. *Financial support:* Career-related internships or fieldwork and scholarships/grants available. Financial award application deadline: 3/1. *Unit head:* Dr. Kieran Killeen, 802-656-2936, E-mail: kieran.killeen@uvm.edu.
Website: https://www.uvm.edu/cess/dlds/leadership

University of Vermont, Graduate College, College of Education and Social Services, Program in Higher Education and Student Affairs Administration, Burlington, VT 05405-0305. Offers M Ed. *Accreditation:* NCATE. *Program availability:* Part-time. *Students:* 98 (68 women); includes 15 minority (6 Black or African American, non-Hispanic/Latino; 2 Asian, non-Hispanic/Latino; 5 Hispanic/Latino; 2 Two or more races, non-Hispanic/Latino), 7 international. 175 applicants, 33% accepted, 18 enrolled. In 2017, 16 master's awarded. *Degree requirements:* For master's, thesis or alternative. *Entrance requirements:* For master's, resume. Additional exam requirements/recommendations for international students: Required—TOEFL (minimum score 550 paper-based, 90 iBT) or IELTS (6.5). *Application deadline:* For fall admission, 12/1 for domestic and international students. Application fee: $65. Electronic applications accepted. *Expenses:* Tuition, state resident: full-time $11,628; part-time $646 per credit. Tuition, nonresident: full-time $29,340; part-time $1630 per credit. *Required fees:* $1994; $10 per credit. Tuition and fees vary according to course load and program. *Financial support:* In 2017–18, 27 students received support. Scholarships/grants, health care benefits, and unspecified assistantships available. Financial award application deadline: 12/1. *Unit head:* Dr. Deborah Hunter, 802-656-2030, E-mail: deborah.hunter@uvm.edu.
Website: https://www.uvm.edu/cess/dlds/hesa

University of Victoria, Faculty of Graduate Studies, Faculty of Education, Department of Educational Psychology and Leadership Studies, Victoria, BC V8W 2Y2, Canada. Offers aboriginal communities counseling (M Ed); counseling (M Ed, MA); educational psychology (M Ed, MA, PhD), including counseling psychology (M Ed, MA), leadership studies (PhD), learning and development (MA, PhD), measurement and evaluation, special education (M Ed, MA); leadership studies (M Ed, MA). *Program availability:* Part-time. *Degree requirements:* For master's, thesis (for some programs), comprehensive exam (M Ed); for doctorate, comprehensive exam, thesis/dissertation, candidacy exam. *Entrance requirements:* For master's, 2 years of work experience in a relevant field; for doctorate, GRE, 2 years of work experience in a relevant field, minimum B average. Additional exam requirements/recommendations for international students: Required—TOEFL (minimum score 575 paper-based), IELTS (minimum score 7). *Faculty research:* Learning and development (child, adolescent and adult), special education and exceptional children.

University of Virginia, Curry School of Education, Department of Leadership, Foundations and Policy, Program in Administration and Supervision, Charlottesville, VA 22903. Offers M Ed, Ed D, Ed S. *Students:* 11 part-time (5 women); includes 2 minority (both Hispanic/Latino). Average age 34. 34 applicants, 79% accepted, 25 enrolled. In 2017, 5 master's, 5 doctorates, 8 other advanced degrees awarded. *Entrance requirements:* For master's, doctorate, and Ed S, GRE General Test, letters of recommendation. *Application deadline:* Applications are processed on a rolling basis. Application fee: $60. Electronic applications accepted. *Financial support:* Fellowships, research assistantships, and teaching assistantships available. Financial award applicants required to submit FAFSA. *Unit head:* Pam Tucker, Program Coordinator, 434-924-7846, E-mail: pdtucker@virginia.edu. *Application contact:* E-mail: curry-admissions@virginia.edu.
Website: http://curry.virginia.edu/academics/areas-of-study/administration-supervision

University of Virginia, Curry School of Education, Program in Education, Charlottesville, VA 22903. Offers administration and supervision (PhD); applied developmental science (PhD); counselor education (PhD); curriculum and instruction (PhD); early childhood special education (MT); education evaluation (PhD); educational psychology (PhD); educational research (PhD); elementary education (MT); English education (MT, PhD); foreign language education (MT); higher education (PhD); instructional technology (PhD); kinesiology (MT, PhD); math education (PhD); reading education (PhD); research, statistics and evaluation (PhD); school psychology (PhD); science education (PhD); social studies education (MT, PhD); special education (PhD); world languages education (MT). *Students:* 431 full-time (353 women), 15 part-time (14 women); includes 100 minority (32 Black or African American, non-Hispanic/Latino; 33 Asian, non-Hispanic/Latino; 16 Hispanic/Latino; 19 Two or more races, non-Hispanic/Latino), 14 international. Average age 25. 264 applicants, 49% accepted, 83 enrolled. In 2017, 142 master's, 33 doctorates awarded. *Degree requirements:* For master's, comprehensive exam (for some programs), field project; for doctorate, comprehensive exam, thesis/dissertation. *Entrance requirements:* For doctorate, GRE General Test. Additional exam requirements/recommendations for international students: Required—TOEFL (minimum score 600 paper-based; 90 iBT), IELTS (minimum score 7). *Application deadline:* Applications are processed on a rolling basis. Application fee: $60. Electronic applications accepted. *Financial support:* Fellowships, research assistantships, and teaching assistantships available. Financial award application deadline: 1/5; financial award applicants required to submit FAFSA. *Unit head:* Robert C. Pianta, Dean, 434-924-3334, E-mail: pianta@virginia.edu. *Application contact:* E-mail: curry-admissions@virginia.edu.
Website: http://curry.virginia.edu/teacher-education

University of Washington, Graduate School, College of Education, Seattle, WA 98195. Offers curriculum and instruction (M Ed, Ed D, PhD), including educational technology, general curriculum (Ed D, PhD), language, literacy, and culture, mathematics education, multicultural education, reading and language arts education (Ed D), science education, social studies education, teaching and curriculum (M Ed); educational leadership and policy studies (M Ed, Ed D, PhD), including administration (Ed D), educational policy, organization, and leadership (M Ed, Ed D, PhD), higher education, leadership for learning (Ed D), social and cultural foundations of education (M Ed, PhD); educational psychology (M Ed, PhD), including educational psychology (PhD), human development and cognition (M Ed), learning sciences, measurement, statistics and research design (M Ed), school psychology (M Ed); instructional leadership (M Ed); intercollegiate athletic leadership (M Ed); special education (M Ed, Ed D, PhD), including early childhood special education (M Ed), emotional and behavioral disabilities (M Ed), learning disabilities (M Ed), low-incidence disabilities (M Ed), severe disabilities (M Ed), special education (Ed D, PhD); teacher education (MIT). *Accreditation:* APA. *Program availability:* Part-time, evening/weekend. *Degree requirements:* For master's, thesis optional; for doctorate, thesis/dissertation. *Entrance requirements:* For master's and doctorate, GRE General Test, minimum GPA of 3.0. Additional exam requirements/recommendations for international students: Required—TOEFL. Electronic applications accepted. *Faculty research:* School restructuring/effective schools, special education interventions, literacy and writing, technology, school partnerships, teacher preparation.

University of Washington, Bothell, Program in Education, Bothell, WA 98011. Offers education (M Ed); leadership development for educators (M Ed); secondary/middle level endorsement (M Ed). *Program availability:* Part-time, evening/weekend. *Degree requirements:* For master's, thesis. *Entrance requirements:* Additional exam requirements/recommendations for international students: Required—TOEFL. Electronic applications accepted. *Faculty research:* Multicultural education in citizenship education, intercultural education, knowledge and practice in the principalship, educational public policy, national board certification for teachers, teacher learning in literacy, technology and its impact on teaching and learning of mathematics, reading assessments, professional development in literacy education and mobility, digital media, education and class.

University of Washington, Tacoma, Graduate Programs, Program in Education, Tacoma, WA 98402-3100. Offers education (M Ed); educational administration (principal or program administrator certification) (M Ed); elementary education teacher certification (M Ed); elementary education/special education teacher certification (M Ed); secondary science or math teacher certification (M Ed). *Program availability:* Part-time, evening/weekend. *Degree requirements:* For master's, culminating project. *Entrance requirements:* For master's, WEST-B, WEST-E (teacher certification programs only), official sealed transcript from every college/university attended, personal goal statement, letters of recommendation, copy of valid teaching certificate. Additional exam requirements/recommendations for international students: Required—TOEFL (minimum score 580 paper-based; 92 iBT). Electronic applications accepted. *Faculty research:* Global learning communities for English/Chinese languages, evaluation of mathematics and reading intervention programs, response to intervention, school-wide behavioral and emotional support, mathematics education and culturally responsive mathematics education.

The University of West Alabama, School of Graduate Studies, College of Education, Program in Instructional Leadership, Livingston, AL 35470. Offers instructional leadership (M Ed, Ed S); teacher leader (Ed S). *Accreditation:* NCATE. *Program availability:* Part-time, evening/weekend, 100% online. *Faculty:* 6 full-time (5 women), 11 part-time/adjunct (5 women). *Students:* 398 (267 women); includes 124 minority (113 Black or African American, non-Hispanic/Latino; 3 American Indian or Alaska Native, non-Hispanic/Latino; 1 Asian, non-Hispanic/Latino; 4 Hispanic/Latino; 3 Two or more races, non-Hispanic/Latino). Average age 38. 158 applicants, 99% accepted, 95 enrolled. In 2017, 44 master's, 28 Ed Ss awarded. *Degree requirements:* For master's, comprehensive exam, thesis optional; for Ed S, comprehensive exam. *Entrance requirements:* For master's, GRE, valid Class B Professional Educator Certificate in a teaching field; verification of background clearance/fingerprints; transcripts documenting completion of bachelor's degree from regionally-accredited college or university with minimum GPA of 2.75. Additional exam requirements/recommendations for international students: Required—TOEFL (minimum score 500 paper-based; 61 iBT). *Application deadline:* Applications are processed on a rolling basis. Application fee: $40. Electronic applications accepted. *Expenses:* Tuition, state resident: part-time $371 per credit hour. Tuition, nonresident: part-time $742 per credit hour. *Required fees:* $130 per semester. *Financial support:* Teaching assistantships, Federal Work-Study, scholarships/grants, and unspecified assistantships available. Support available to part-time students. Financial award application deadline: 3/1; financial award applicants required to submit FAFSA. *Unit head:* Dr. Reenay Rogers, Chair of Instructional Leadership and Support, 205-652-5423, Fax: 205-652-3706, E-mail: rrogers@uwa.edu. *Application contact:* Dr. B. J. Kimbrough, Dean of Graduate Studies, 205-652-3647, Fax: 205-652-3670, E-mail: bkimbrough@uwa.edu.
Website: http://www.uwa.edu/medinstructionalleadership.aspx

University of West Florida, College of Education and Professional Studies, Department of Teacher Education and Educational Leadership, Program in Educational Leadership, Pensacola, FL 32514-5750. Offers M Ed. *Accreditation:* NCATE. *Program availability:* Part-time, evening/weekend, online learning. *Degree requirements:* For master's, thesis optional. *Entrance requirements:* For master's, GRE General Test or minimum GPA of 3.0. Additional exam requirements/recommendations for international students: Required—TOEFL (minimum score 550 paper-based).

University of West Florida, College of Education and Professional Studies, Ed D Programs, Specialization in Administrative and Leadership Studies, Pensacola, FL

32514-5750. Offers Ed D. *Degree requirements:* For doctorate, comprehensive exam, thesis/dissertation. *Entrance requirements:* For doctorate, GRE, MAT, or GMAT, letter of intent; writing sample; three letters of recommendation; two completed disposition assessment forms; written statement of goals; interview with admissions committee. Additional exam requirements/recommendations for international students: Required—TOEFL (minimum score 550 paper-based).

University of West Georgia, College of Education, Carrollton, GA 30118. Offers business education (M Ed); early childhood education (M Ed, Ed S); educational leadership (M Ed, Ed S); media (M Ed, Ed S); professional counseling (M Ed, Ed S); professional counseling and supervision (Ed D); reading instruction (M Ed); school improvement (Ed D); secondary education (M Ed); special education (M Ed, Ed S), including teaching (M Ed); speech language pathology (M Ed); teaching (MAT). *Accreditation:* NCATE. *Program availability:* Part-time, evening/weekend, 100% online, blended/hybrid learning. *Faculty:* 45 full-time (28 women). *Students:* 344 full-time (286 women), 1,243 part-time (1,039 women); includes 538 minority (456 Black or African American, non-Hispanic/Latino; 19 Asian, non-Hispanic/Latino; 46 Hispanic/Latino; 1 Native Hawaiian or other Pacific Islander, non-Hispanic/Latino; 16 Two or more races, non-Hispanic/Latino), 7 international. Average age 36. 685 applicants, 78% accepted, 429 enrolled. In 2017, 299 master's, 30 doctorates, 218 other advanced degrees awarded. *Entrance requirements:* Additional exam requirements/recommendations for international students: Required—TOEFL (minimum score 523 paper-based; 69 iBT); Recommended—IELTS (minimum score 6.5). *Application deadline:* For fall admission, 7/21 for domestic students, 6/1 for international students; for spring admission, 11/30 for domestic students, 10/15 for international students; for summer admission, 4/15 for domestic students, 3/30 for international students. Applications are processed on a rolling basis. Application fee: $40. Electronic applications accepted. Tuition and fees vary according to degree level and program. *Financial support:* Fellowships, research assistantships, teaching assistantships, career-related internships or fieldwork, Federal Work-Study, institutionally sponsored loans, scholarships/grants, and unspecified assistantships available. Support available to part-time students. Financial award application deadline: 4/1; financial award applicants required to submit FAFSA. *Unit head:* Dr. Diane Hoff, Dean, College of Education, 678-839-6570, Fax: 678-839-6098, E-mail: dhoff@westga.edu. *Application contact:* Dr. Toby Ziglar, Assistant Dean of the Graduate School, 678-839-1394, Fax: 678-839-1395, E-mail: graduate@westga.edu. Website: http://www.westga.edu/education/

University of Wisconsin–Madison, Graduate School, School of Education, Department of Educational Leadership and Policy Analysis, Madison, WI 53706-1380. Offers administration (Certificate); educational policy (MS, PhD); global higher education (MS). *Degree requirements:* For doctorate, thesis/dissertation. *Entrance requirements:* For master's and doctorate, GRE General Test. Electronic applications accepted.

University of Wisconsin–Milwaukee, Graduate School, School of Education, Department of Administrative Leadership, Milwaukee, WI 53201-0413. Offers administrative leadership (MS), including adult and continuing education leadership, educational administration and supervision, higher education administration; support services for online students in higher education (Graduate Certificate); teaching and learning in higher education (Graduate Certificate). *Program availability:* Part-time. *Students:* 33 full-time (19 women), 195 part-time (132 women); includes 53 minority (22 Black or African American, non-Hispanic/Latino; 4 American Indian or Alaska Native, non-Hispanic/Latino; 4 Asian, non-Hispanic/Latino; 2 Hispanic/Latino; 21 Two or more races, non-Hispanic/Latino), 1 international. Average age 35. 117 applicants, 75% accepted, 53 enrolled. In 2017, 61 master's, 14 other advanced degrees awarded. *Degree requirements:* For master's, comprehensive exam, thesis or alternative. *Entrance requirements:* For master's, GRE General Test. Additional exam requirements/recommendations for international students: Required—TOEFL (minimum score 550 paper-based; 79 iBT), IELTS (minimum score 6.5). *Application deadline:* For fall admission, 1/1 priority date for domestic students; for spring admission, 9/1 for domestic students. Application fee: $56 ($96 for international students). Electronic applications accepted. *Financial support:* In 2017–18, 2 fellowships were awarded; research assistantships, teaching assistantships, career-related internships or fieldwork, health care benefits, unspecified assistantships, and project assistantships also available. Support available to part-time students. Financial award application deadline: 4/15; financial award applicants required to submit FAFSA. *Unit head:* Alan Shoho, Dean, 414-229-4181, E-mail: shoho@uwm.edu. *Application contact:* General Information Contact, 414-229-4721, E-mail: soeinfo@uwm.edu. Website: http://uwm.edu/education/academics/administrative-leadership-department/

University of Wisconsin–Milwaukee, Graduate School, School of Education, Department of Exceptional Education, Milwaukee, WI 53201-0413. Offers autism spectrum disorders (Graduate Certificate); exceptional education (MS); transition for students with disabilities (Graduate Certificate); urban education (PhD), including adult, continuing and higher education leadership, art education, curriculum and instruction, exceptional education, mathematics education, multicultural studies, social foundations of education. *Program availability:* Part-time. *Students:* 45 full-time (34 women), 68 part-time (54 women); includes 46 minority (27 Black or African American, non-Hispanic/Latino; 7 Asian, non-Hispanic/Latino; 1 Hispanic/Latino; 11 Two or more races, non-Hispanic/Latino), 4 international. Average age 39. 43 applicants, 53% accepted, 19 enrolled. In 2017, 12 master's, 13 doctorates, 8 other advanced degrees awarded. *Entrance requirements:* Additional exam requirements/recommendations for international students: Required—TOEFL (minimum score 550 paper-based; 79 iBT), IELTS (minimum score 6.5). *Application deadline:* For fall admission, 1/1 priority date for domestic students; for spring admission, 9/1 for domestic students. Application fee: $56 ($96 for international students). Electronic applications accepted. *Financial support:* Fellowships, research assistantships, teaching assistantships, career-related internships or fieldwork, health care benefits, and unspecified assistantships available. Support available to part-time students. Financial award application deadline: 4/15; financial award applicants required to submit FAFSA. *Faculty research:* Emotional disturbance, hearing impairment, learning disabilities, mental retardation. *Application contact:* General Information Contact, 414-229-4721, E-mail: soeinfo@uwm.edu. Website: http://uwm.edu/education/academics/exceptional-edu-department/

University of Wisconsin–Oshkosh, Graduate Studies, College of Education and Human Services, Department of Educational Leadership and Human Services, Oshkosh, WI 54901. Offers educational leadership (MS). *Program availability:* Part-time, evening/weekend. *Degree requirements:* For master's, comprehensive exam, thesis optional. *Entrance requirements:* For master's, bachelor's degree in education or related field. Additional exam requirements/recommendations for international students: Required—TOEFL (minimum score 550 paper-based; 79 iBT). Electronic applications accepted. *Faculty research:* Supervision models, learning styles, total quality management, cooperative learning, school choice.

University of Wisconsin–Stevens Point, College of Professional Studies, School of Education, Program in Educational Administration, Stevens Point, WI 54481-3897. Offers MSE. Program offered jointly with University of Wisconsin–Superior. *Degree requirements:* For master's, comprehensive exam, thesis or alternative.

University of Wisconsin–Superior, Graduate Division, Department of Educational Administration, Superior, WI 54880-4500. Offers MSE, Ed S. Programs offered jointly with University of Wisconsin - Eau Claire, University of Wisconsin - Stevens Point. *Program availability:* Part-time, evening/weekend, online learning. *Degree requirements:* For master's, thesis or alternative, research project or position paper, written exam; for Ed S, thesis, internship, oral and written exams. *Entrance requirements:* For master's, GRE General Test or MAT, minimum GPA of 2.75, teaching license, 3 years of teaching experience; for Ed S, MAT, GRE, master's degree, 3 years of teaching experience, teaching license. *Faculty research:* Postsecondary disabilities, educational partnerships, K-12.

University of Wisconsin–Whitewater, School of Graduate Studies, College of Business and Economics, Program in School Business Management, Whitewater, WI 53190-1790. Offers MSE. *Program availability:* Part-time, evening/weekend, online learning. *Entrance requirements:* For master's, minimum GPA of 2.75. Additional exam requirements/recommendations for international students: Required—TOEFL (minimum score 550 paper-based; 80 iBT), IELTS (minimum score 6). Electronic applications accepted.

University of Wyoming, College of Education, Programs in Educational Leadership, Laramie, WY 82071. Offers MA, Ed D, Certificate. *Program availability:* Part-time, online learning. *Degree requirements:* For master's, thesis; for doctorate, comprehensive exam, thesis/dissertation; for Certificate, comprehensive exam, thesis, residency. *Entrance requirements:* For master's and Certificate, GRE; for doctorate, MA, 3 years' teaching experience. Additional exam requirements/recommendations for international students: Required—TOEFL (minimum score 520 paper-based). *Faculty research:* School leadership, leadership preparation, leadership skills.

Upper Iowa University, Master of Education Program, Fayette, IA 52142-1857. Offers early childhood (M Ed); English as a second language (M Ed); higher education (M Ed); instructional strategist (M Ed); reading (M Ed); teacher leadership (M Ed).

Ursuline College, School of Graduate and Professional Studies, Program in Educational Administration, Pepper Pike, OH 44124-4398. Offers MA. *Program availability:* Part-time. *Faculty:* 4 full-time (2 women), 9 part-time/adjunct (5 women). *Students:* 1 (woman) full-time, 61 part-time (40 women); includes 15 minority (all Black or African American, non-Hispanic/Latino). Average age 34. 16 applicants, 100% accepted, 15 enrolled. In 2017, 9 master's awarded. *Degree requirements:* For master's, thesis or alternative. *Entrance requirements:* For master's, minimum undergraduate GPA of 3.0, teaching certificate, professional experience. Additional exam requirements/recommendations for international students: Required—TOEFL (minimum score 500 paper-based; 80 iBT). *Application deadline:* For fall admission, 8/1 priority date for domestic students. Applications are processed on a rolling basis. Application fee: $25. Electronic applications accepted. *Expenses:* $657 per credit hour. *Financial support:* In 2017–18, 2 students received support. Scholarships/grants available. Support available to part-time students. Financial award application deadline: 3/1; financial award applicants required to submit FAFSA. *Faculty research:* Qualities of successful teachers, longevity of female superintendents. *Unit head:* Dr. James Connell, Director, 440-449-3413, Fax: 440-646-8328, E-mail: jconnell@ursuline.edu. *Application contact:* Melanie Steele, Director, Graduate Admission, 440-646-8146, Fax: 440-684-6138, E-mail: graduateadmissions@ursuline.edu.

Utah Valley University, Program in Education, Orem, UT 84058-5999. Offers educational technology (M Ed); elementary mathematics (M Ed); elementary STEM (M Ed); English as a second language (M Ed); reading (M Ed); teachers as leaders (M Ed). *Accreditation:* TEAC. *Program availability:* Part-time. *Degree requirements:* For master's, project. *Entrance requirements:* For master's, GRE, 3 letters of recommendation, interview, essay. Additional exam requirements/recommendations for international students: Required—TOEFL (minimum score 83 iBT). Electronic applications accepted. *Expenses:* Contact institution.

Valdosta State University, Department of Curriculum, Leadership, and Technology, Valdosta, GA 31698. Offers leadership (Ed D); P-12 school leadership (M Ed); performance-based leadership (Ed S). *Accreditation:* NCATE. *Program availability:* 100% online, blended/hybrid learning. *Degree requirements:* For master's, thesis (for some programs), comprehensive written and/or oral exams; for doctorate, thesis/dissertation, comprehensive written and/or oral exams; for Ed S, thesis, thesis. *Entrance requirements:* For master's and Ed S, GRE General Test or MAT; for doctorate, GRE General Test, minimum GPA of 3.5. Additional exam requirements/recommendations for international students: Required—TOEFL (minimum score 523 paper-based); Recommended—IELTS. *Application deadline:* For fall admission, 7/1 for domestic and international students; for spring admission, 11/15 for domestic and international students. Applications are processed on a rolling basis. Application fee: $45. Electronic applications accepted. *Expenses:* Contact institution. *Financial support:* Research assistantships with full tuition reimbursements, institutionally sponsored loans, scholarships/grants, and unspecified assistantships available. Support available to part-time students. Financial award application deadline: 7/1; financial award applicants required to submit FAFSA. *Faculty research:* Mentoring in higher education, contemporary issues in higher education. *Unit head:* Dr. Leon Pate, Department Head, 229-333-5633, E-mail: jlpate@valdosta.edu. *Application contact:* Dr. Leon Pate, Department Head, 229-333-5633, E-mail: jlpate@valdosta.edu. Website: http://www.valdosta.edu/academics/graduate-school/our-programs/leadership.php

Valparaiso University, Graduate School and Continuing Education, Programs in Education, Valparaiso, IN 46383. Offers initial licensure (M Ed), including Chinese teaching, elementary education, secondary education; instructional leadership (M Ed); school psychology (Ed S); secondary education (M Ed); M Ed/Ed S. *Accreditation:* NCATE. *Program availability:* Part-time, evening/weekend, online learning. *Entrance requirements:* For master's, GRE General Test, minimum GPA of 3.0. Additional exam requirements/recommendations for international students: Required—TOEFL (minimum score 550 paper-based; 80 iBT), IELTS (minimum score 6). Electronic applications accepted. *Expenses: Tuition:* Full-time $11,340; part-time $630 per credit hour. *Required fees:* $520; $250 per year. $125 per semester. Tuition and fees vary according to program and reciprocity agreements.

Vanderbilt University, Peabody College, Department of Leadership, Policy, and Organizations, Nashville, TN 37240-1001. Offers education policy (MPP); educational leadership and policy (Ed D); higher education (M Ed); higher education leadership and policy (Ed D); independent school leadership (M Ed); international education policy and management (M Ed); leadership and learning in organizations (Ed D); leadership and organizational performance (M Ed). *Program availability:* Part-time, on-campus immersion once every semester. *Faculty:* 30 full-time (15 women), 19 part-time/adjunct (6 women). *Students:* 141 full-time (105 women), 139 part-time (84 women); includes 66 minority (32 Black or African American, non-Hispanic/Latino; 13 Asian, non-Hispanic/Latino; 14 Hispanic/Latino; 1 Native Hawaiian or other Pacific Islander, non-Hispanic/Latino; 6 Two or more races, non-Hispanic/Latino), 25 international. Average age 30. 525 applicants, 66% accepted, 139 enrolled. In 2017, 109 master's, 22 doctorates awarded. *Degree requirements:* For master's, comprehensive exam, thesis optional; for doctorate, thesis/dissertation, qualifying exams, residency. *Entrance requirements:* For master's and doctorate, GRE General Test. Additional exam requirements/recommendations for international students: Required—TOEFL (minimum score 550

paper-based; 80 iBT). *Application deadline:* For fall admission, 12/31 priority date for domestic and international students; for spring admission, 11/1 priority date for domestic and international students. Applications are processed on a rolling basis. Application fee: $0. Electronic applications accepted. *Financial support:* Fellowships with partial tuition reimbursements, research assistantships with partial tuition reimbursements, teaching assistantships with partial tuition reimbursements, Federal Work-Study, institutionally sponsored loans, scholarships/grants, tuition waivers (partial), and unspecified assistantships available. Support available to part-time students. Financial award application deadline: 1/15; financial award applicants required to submit FAFSA. *Faculty research:* Financial aid policies, teacher labor markets, school choice, educational leadership, higher education access and equity. *Unit head:* Dr. Ellen B. Goldring, Chair, 615-322-8000, Fax: 615-343-7094, E-mail: ellen.b.goldring@vanderbilt.edu. *Application contact:* Rosie Moody, Educational Coordinator, 615-322-8019, Fax: 615-343-7094, E-mail: rosie.moody@vanderbilt.edu.
Website: http://peabody.vanderbilt.edu/departments/lpo/index.php

Vanderbilt University, Program in Leadership and Policy Studies, Nashville, TN 37240-1001. Offers higher education leadership and policy (PhD); K-12 educational leadership and policy (PhD). *Faculty:* 16 full-time (7 women). *Students:* 34 full-time (17 women), 1 part-time (0 women); includes 13 minority (2 Black or African American, non-Hispanic/Latino; 6 Asian, non-Hispanic/Latino; 3 Hispanic/Latino; 2 Two or more races, non-Hispanic/Latino). Average age 31. 104 applicants, 11% accepted, 4 enrolled. In 2017, 4 doctorates awarded. *Degree requirements:* For doctorate, comprehensive exam, thesis/dissertation, qualifying examinations. *Entrance requirements:* For doctorate, GRE General Test. Additional exam requirements/recommendations for international students: Required—TOEFL (minimum score 570 paper-based; 88 iBT). *Application deadline:* For fall admission, 12/1 for domestic and international students. Application fee: $0. Electronic applications accepted. *Expenses:* Contact institution. *Financial support:* Fellowships with full tuition reimbursements, research assistantships with full tuition reimbursements, teaching assistantships with full tuition reimbursements, Federal Work-Study, institutionally sponsored loans, scholarships/grants, traineeships, and health care benefits available. Financial award application deadline: 1/15; financial award applicants required to submit CSS PROFILE or FAFSA. *Faculty research:* Charter schooling, pay for performance, access and equity for immigrant and at-risk students, higher-education policy, race and ethnic relations, college student departure, college student success, and international comparisons. *Unit head:* Dr. Ron Zimmer, Director of Graduate Studies, 615-322-0722, Fax: 615-343-7094, E-mail: ronald.w.zimmer@vanderbilt.edu. *Application contact:* Rosie Moody, Admissions and Education Coordinator, 615-322-8019, Fax: 615-343-7094, E-mail: rosie.moody@vanderbilt.edu.
Website: http://peabody.vanderbilt.edu/departments/lpo/graduate_and_professional_programs/phd/index.php

Villanova University, Graduate School of Liberal Arts and Sciences, Department of Education and Counseling, Villanova, PA 19085-1699. Offers elementary school counseling (MS), including counseling and human relations; teacher leadership (MA). *Program availability:* Part-time, evening/weekend. *Faculty:* 24. *Students:* 80 full-time (58 women), 37 part-time (28 women); includes 15 minority (7 Black or African American, non-Hispanic/Latino; 2 Asian, non-Hispanic/Latino; 5 Hispanic/Latino; 1 Two or more races, non-Hispanic/Latino), 2 international. Average age 30. 62 applicants, 74% accepted, 32 enrolled. In 2017, 49 master's awarded. *Degree requirements:* For master's, comprehensive exam. *Entrance requirements:* For master's, GRE or MAT, minimum GPA of 3.0, statement of goals. *Application deadline:* For fall admission, 3/1 priority date for domestic students, 5/1 for international students; for spring admission, 11/15 priority date for domestic students, 10/15 for international students; for summer admission, 5/1 for domestic students. Applications are processed on a rolling basis. Application fee: $50. Electronic applications accepted. *Financial support:* Research assistantships, teaching assistantships, scholarships/grants, and unspecified assistantships available. Financial award applicants required to submit FAFSA. *Unit head:* Dr. Christopher Schmidt, Chairperson, 610-519-4618. *Application contact:* Dean, Graduate School of Liberal Arts and Sciences.
Website: http://www.education.villanova.edu/

Virginia Commonwealth University, Graduate School, School of Education, Doctoral Program in Education, Richmond, VA 23284-9005. Offers art education (PhD); counselor education and supervision (PhD); curriculum, culture and change (PhD); educational leadership (PhD); educational psychology (PhD); leadership (Ed D); research and evaluation (PhD); special education and disability leadership (PhD); sport leadership (PhD); urban services leadership (PhD). *Accreditation:* NCATE. *Program availability:* Part-time. *Degree requirements:* For doctorate, thesis/dissertation. *Entrance requirements:* For doctorate, GRE (for PhD), MAT (for Ed D), interview, master's degree, writing sample. Additional exam requirements/recommendations for international students: Required—TOEFL (minimum score 600 paper-based; 100 iBT). Electronic applications accepted.

Virginia Commonwealth University, Graduate School, School of Education, Program in Educational Leadership, Richmond, VA 23284-9005. Offers M Ed. *Entrance requirements:* Additional exam requirements/recommendations for international students: Required—TOEFL (minimum score 600 paper-based; 100 iBT); Recommended—IELTS. Electronic applications accepted.

Virginia Polytechnic Institute and State University, Graduate School, College of Liberal Arts and Human Sciences, Blacksburg, VA 24601. Offers career and technical education (MS Ed, Ed S); communication (MA); counselor education (MA); creative writing (MFA); curriculum and instruction (MA Ed, Ed S); educational leadership and policy studies (Ed S); educational research and evaluation (PhD); English (MA); social, political, ethical, and cultural thought (PhD); Ed D/PhD. *Faculty:* 411 full-time (213 women), 3 part-time/adjunct (all women). *Students:* 623 full-time (427 women), 431 part-time (278 women); includes 203 minority (115 Black or African American, non-Hispanic/Latino; 4 American Indian or Alaska Native, non-Hispanic/Latino; 29 Asian, non-Hispanic/Latino; 33 Hispanic/Latino; 2 Native Hawaiian or other Pacific Islander, non-Hispanic/Latino; 20 Two or more races, non-Hispanic/Latino), 87 international. Average age 34. 898 applicants, 50% accepted, 329 enrolled. In 2017, 314 master's, 102 doctorates awarded. *Degree requirements:* For master's, comprehensive exam (for some programs), thesis (for some programs); for doctorate, comprehensive exam (for some programs), thesis/dissertation (for some programs). *Entrance requirements:* For master's and doctorate, GRE/GMAT. Additional exam requirements/recommendations for international students: Required—TOEFL (minimum score 80 iBT). *Application deadline:* For fall admission, 8/1 for domestic students, 4/1 for international students; for spring admission, 1/1 for domestic students, 9/1 for international students. Applications are processed on a rolling basis. Application fee: $75. Electronic applications accepted. *Expenses:* Tuition, state resident: full-time $15,072; part-time $718.50 per credit hour. Tuition, nonresident: full-time $28,810; part-time $1448.25 per credit hour. *Required fees:* $2741; $502 per semester. Tuition and fees vary according to course load, campus/location and program. *Financial support:* In 2017–18, 19 research assistantships with full tuition reimbursements (averaging $19,611 per year), 226 teaching assistantships with full tuition reimbursements (averaging $16,220 per year) were awarded. Financial award application deadline: 3/1; financial award applicants

required to submit FAFSA. *Total annual research expenditures:* $7.9 million. *Unit head:* Dr. Rosemary Blieszner, Dean, 540-231-6779, Fax: 540-231-7157, E-mail: rmb@vt.edu. *Application contact:* Chelsea Blanchet, Executive Assistant, 540-231-6779, Fax: 540-231-7157, E-mail: bchels1@vt.edu.
Website: http://www.liberalarts.vt.edu/

Virginia State University, College of Graduate Studies, College of Education, Department of Administrative and Organizational Leadership, Petersburg, VA 23806-0001. Offers administration and supervision (M Ed). *Accreditation:* NCATE. *Degree requirements:* For master's, thesis optional.

Virginia State University, College of Graduate Studies, College of Education, Department of Doctoral Studies, Petersburg, VA 23806-0001. Offers educational administration and supervision (Ed D).

Virginia Theological Seminary, Graduate and Professional Programs, Alexandria, VA 22304. Offers Christian spirituality (D Min); educational leadership (D Ed Min, D Min); ministry development (D Min); theology (M Div, MA). *Accreditation:* ATS. *Program availability:* Part-time. *Degree requirements:* For master's, 2 foreign languages, thesis; for doctorate, thesis/dissertation. *Entrance requirements:* For master's and doctorate, GRE General Test.

Viterbo University, Graduate Programs in Education, La Crosse, WI 54601-4797. Offers cross-categorical special education (Certificate); director of instruction (Certificate); director of special education and pupil services (Certificate); early childhood (Certificate); education (MAE); literacy coaching (Certificate); PreK-12 principal/supervisor of special education (Certificate); principal (Certificate); reading specialist endorsement (Certificate); reading teacher (Certificate); reading teacher 5-12 endorsement (Certificate); reading teacher K-8 endorsement (Certificate); superintendent (Certificate); talented and gifted endorsement (Certificate); Wisconsin school business administrator (Certificate). Weekend courses available in summer. *Accreditation:* NCATE. *Program availability:* Part-time, evening/weekend. *Degree requirements:* For master's, comprehensive exam, thesis, 30 credits of course work. *Entrance requirements:* For master's, BS, transcripts, teaching license, written narrative. Electronic applications accepted. *Expenses:* Contact institution.

Walden University, Graduate Programs, Richard W. Riley College of Education and Leadership, Minneapolis, MN 55401. Offers adult education (Post-Master's Certificate); adult learning (Graduate Certificate); college teaching and learning (Graduate Certificate); community college leadership (Ed D); curriculum, instruction and assessment (Ed D, Ed S, Graduate Certificate); developmental education (Graduate Certificate); early childhood administration, management, and leadership (Graduate Certificate); early childhood education (Ed D, Ed S); early childhood public policy and advocacy (Graduate Certificate); early childhood studies (MS), including administration, management and leadership, early childhood public policy and advocacy, teaching adults in the early childhood field, teaching and diversity in early childhood education; education (MS, PhD), including adolescent literacy and learning (MS), curriculum, instruction, and assessment (grades K-12) (MS), curriculum, instruction, assessment, and evaluation (PhD), early childhood leadership and advocacy (PhD), early childhood special education (PhD), educational leadership (MS), educational leadership and administration (principal preparation) (MS), educational technology and design (PhD), elementary reading and literacy (PreK-6) (MS), elementary reading and mathematics (grades K-6) (MS), global and comparative education (PhD), higher education leadership management and policy (PhD), integrating technology in the classroom (grades K-12) (MS), learning, instruction and innovation (PhD), mathematics (grades 5-8) (MS), mathematics (grades K-6) (MS), mathematics and science (grades K-8) (MS), organizational research, assessment, and evaluation (PhD), reading and literacy with a reading K-12 endorsement (MS), reading literacy assessment and evaluation (PhD), science (grades K-8) (MS), special education (non-licensure) (grades K-12) (MS), teacher leadership (grades K-12) (MS), teaching English language learners (grades K-12) (MS); educational administration and leadership (Ed D); educational leadership and administration (principal preparation) (Ed S); educational technology (Ed D, Ed S, Post Master's Certificate); elementary reading and literacy (Graduate Certificate); engaging culturally diverse learners (Graduate Certificate); enrollment management and institutional marketing (Graduate Certificate); higher education (MS), including adult learning, college teaching and learning, enrollment management and institutional marketing, global higher education, leadership for student success, online and distance learning; higher education and adult learning (Ed D); higher education leadership and management (Ed D); higher education leadership for student success (Graduate Certificate); instructional design and technology (MS, Postbaccalaureate Certificate), including general program (MS), online learning (MS), training and performance improvement (MS); integrating technology in the classroom (Graduate Certificate); mathematics 5-8 (Graduate Certificate); mathematics K-6 (Graduate Certificate); online teaching for adult educators (Graduate Certificate); reading, literacy, and assessment (Ed D, Ed S); science K-8 (Graduate Certificate); special education (Ed D, Ed S, Graduate Certificate); special education (K-age 21) (MAT); teacher leadership (Graduate Certificate); teaching adults English as a second language (Graduate Certificate); teaching adults in the early childhood field (Graduate Certificate); teaching and diversity in early childhood education (Graduate Certificate); teaching English language learners (grades K-12) (Graduate Certificate); teaching K-12 students online (Graduate Certificate). *Accreditation:* NCATE. *Program availability:* Part-time, evening/weekend, online only, 100% online. *Degree requirements:* For doctorate, thesis/dissertation (for some programs), residency; for other advanced degree, residency (for some programs). *Entrance requirements:* For master's, bachelor's degree or higher; minimum GPA of 2.5; official transcripts; goal statement (for some programs); access to computer and Internet; for doctorate, master's degree or higher; three years of related professional or academic experience (preferred); minimum GPA of 3.0; goal statement and current resume (for select programs); official transcripts; access to computer and Internet; for other advanced degree, relevant work experience; access to computer and Internet. Additional exam requirements/recommendations for international students: Required—TOEFL (minimum score 550 paper-based, 79 iBT), IELTS (minimum score 6.5), Michigan English Language Assessment Battery (minimum score 82), or PTE (minimum score 53). Electronic applications accepted.

Waldorf University, Program in Organizational Leadership, Forest City, IA 50436. Offers criminal justice leadership (MA); emergency management leadership (MA); fire/rescue executive leadership (MA); human resource development (MA); public administration (MA); sport management (MA); teacher leader (MA).

Walla Walla University, Graduate Studies, School of Education and Psychology, College Place, WA 99324. Offers curriculum and instruction (M Ed, MAT); educational leadership (M Ed, MAT); literacy instruction (M Ed, MAT); special education (M Ed, MAT). *Program availability:* Part-time. *Entrance requirements:* For master's, GRE General Test, minimum GPA of 2.75. Additional exam requirements/recommendations for international students: Required—TOEFL (minimum score 550 paper-based; 79 iBT). *Application deadline:* For fall admission, 4/1 priority date for domestic students. Applications are processed on a rolling basis. Application fee: $50. Electronic applications accepted. *Financial support:* Research assistantships, teaching assistantships, Federal Work-Study, and tuition waivers (partial) available. Support available to part-time students. Financial award application deadline: 4/30; financial

award applicants required to submit FAFSA. *Faculty research:* Admissions/retention, instructional psychology, moral development, teaching of reading. *Unit head:* Dr. Debbie Muthersbaugh, Dean, 509-527-2212, Fax: 509-527-2248, E-mail: debbie.muthersbaugh@wallawalla.edu. *Application contact:* Dr. Joe G. Galusha, Dean of Graduate Studies, 509-527-2421, Fax: 509-527-2237, E-mail: joe.galusha@wallawalla.edu.
Website: https://wallawalla.edu/academics/areas-of-study/undergraduate-programs/education-and-psychology/

Washburn University, College of Arts and Sciences, Department of Education, Topeka, KS 66621. Offers curriculum and instruction (M Ed); educational leadership (M Ed); reading (M Ed); special education (M Ed). *Accreditation:* NCATE. *Program availability:* Part-time. *Degree requirements:* For master's, comprehensive exam, thesis or alternative, portfolio, comprehensive paper, or action research project. *Entrance requirements:* For master's, department exam, GRE General Test, or MAT, minimum GPA of 3.0 in graduate coursework or last 60 hours of undergraduate coursework. Additional exam requirements/recommendations for international students: Required—TOEFL (minimum score 80 iBT). *Faculty research:* Reading/literature/literacy, foundations, special education, diversity, teaching and technology.

Washington State University, College of Education, Department of Educational Leadership, Sports Studies, and Educational/Counseling Psychology, Pullman, WA 99164-2136. Offers counseling psychology (PhD); educational leadership (Ed M, MA, Ed D, PhD); educational psychology (MA, PhD); sport management (MA). Programs also offered at the Spokane, Tri-Cities, Vancouver and Global (online) campuses. *Program availability:* Part-time, online learning. *Degree requirements:* For master's, comprehensive exam (for some programs), thesis (for some programs), oral or written exam; for doctorate, comprehensive exam, thesis/dissertation, oral and written exam, internship. *Entrance requirements:* For master's and doctorate, GRE General Test, minimum GPA of 3.0, 3 letters of recommendation, transcripts showing all college or university course work, statement of professional objectives, current curriculum vitae/resume. Additional exam requirements/recommendations for international students: Required—TOEFL (minimum score 550 paper-based; 80 iBT). Electronic applications accepted. *Faculty research:* Multicultural counseling and career development, educational and psychological measurement issues, business decision-making process and power relationships, leadership practices and processes as suffused with and constituted by emotion work.

Washington State University, College of Education, Department of Teaching and Learning, Pullman, WA 99164-2132. Offers cultural studies and social thought in education (PhD); curriculum and instruction (Ed M, MA); English language learners (Ed M, MA); language, literacy and technology (PhD); literacy education (Ed M, MA); mathematics education (PhD); special education (Ed M, MA, PhD); teacher leadership (Ed D); teaching (MIT), including elementary education, secondary education. Programs offered at the Pullman, Spokane, Tri-cities, Vancouver and Global (online) campuses. *Program availability:* Part-time, online learning. *Degree requirements:* For master's, comprehensive exam, thesis, oral or written exam; for doctorate, comprehensive exam, thesis/dissertation, oral and written exam. *Entrance requirements:* For master's, GRE General Test, minimum GPA of 3.0, 3 letters of recommendation, letter of intent, transcripts, resume/curriculum vitae; for doctorate, GRE General Test, minimum GPA of 3.0, 3 letters of recommendation, letter of intent, transcripts, writing sample, resume/curriculum vitae. Additional exam requirements/recommendations for international students: Required—TOEFL (minimum score 550 paper-based; 80 iBT). Electronic applications accepted. *Faculty research:* Intersection of gender, youth cultures and schooling; examination of ideology of power in children's literature; early childhood special education; analyzing pre-service and in-service teacher development; second language acquisition.

Wayland Baptist University, Graduate Programs, Program in Education, Plainview, TX 79072-6998. Offers education administration (M Ed); education diagnostics (M Ed); education literacy (M Ed); elementary certification (M Ed); English (M Ed); English as a second language (M Ed); higher education administration (M Ed); human resources (M Ed); instructional leadership (M Ed); instructional technology (M Ed); leadership training and development (M Ed); science education (M Ed); secondary certification (M Ed); social studies (M Ed); special education (M Ed); sports administration and management (M Ed). *Program availability:* Part-time, evening/weekend, 100% online. *Faculty:* 33 full-time (17 women), 28 part-time/adjunct (17 women). *Students:* 16 full-time (13 women), 221 part-time (143 women); includes 97 minority (26 Black or African American, non-Hispanic/Latino; 1 American Indian or Alaska Native, non-Hispanic/Latino; 5 Asian, non-Hispanic/Latino; 54 Hispanic/Latino; 11 Two or more races, non-Hispanic/Latino), 1 international. Average age 39. 32 applicants, 97% accepted, 23 enrolled. In 2017, 78 master's awarded. *Degree requirements:* For master's, comprehensive exam, capstone course. *Entrance requirements:* For master's, GRE, GMAT or MAT. Additional exam requirements/recommendations for international students: Required—TOEFL (minimum score 500 paper-based; 61 iBT). *Application deadline:* Applications are processed on a rolling basis. Application fee: $50. Electronic applications accepted. *Expenses: Tuition:* Full-time $11,250; part-time $625 per credit hour. *Required fees:* $1200. *Financial support:* Federal Work-Study, institutionally sponsored loans, and scholarships/grants available. Support available to part-time students. Financial award application deadline: 5/1; financial award applicants required to submit FAFSA. *Unit head:* Dr. Gene Whitfill, Dean, 806-291-1047, Fax: 806-291-1951, E-mail: whitfillg@wbu.edu. *Application contact:* Amanda Stanton, Coordinator of Graduate Studies, 806-291-3423, Fax: 806-291-1950, E-mail: stanton@wbu.edu.

Waynesburg University, Graduate and Professional Studies, Canonsburg, PA 15370. Offers business (MBA), including energy management, finance, health systems, human resources, leadership, market development; counseling (MA), including addictions counseling, clinical mental health; counselor education and supervision (PhD); criminal investigation (MA); education (M Ed), including autism, curriculum and instruction, educational leadership, online teaching; nursing (MSN), including administration, education, informatics; nursing practice (DNP); special education (M Ed); technology (M Ed); MSN/MBA. *Accreditation:* AACN. *Program availability:* Part-time, evening/weekend. *Degree requirements:* For doctorate, thesis/dissertation. *Entrance requirements:* Additional exam requirements/recommendations for international students: Required—TOEFL. Electronic applications accepted.

Wayne State College, School of Education and Counseling, Department of Educational Foundations and Leadership, Program in Educational Administration, Wayne, NE 68787. Offers educational administration (Ed S); elementary administration (MSE); elementary and secondary administration (MSE); secondary administration (MSE). *Accreditation:* NCATE. *Program availability:* Part-time, evening/weekend. *Degree requirements:* For master's, comprehensive exam, thesis optional, research paper. *Entrance requirements:* For master's, GRE General Test, minimum GPA of 2.5; for Ed S, GRE General Test, minimum GPA of 3.2. Additional exam requirements/recommendations for international students: Required—TOEFL (minimum score 550 paper-based). Electronic applications accepted.

Wayne State University, College of Education, Division of Administrative and Organizational Studies, Detroit, MI 48202. Offers educational administration and supervision (Ed S); educational leadership (M Ed); educational leadership and policy studies (Ed D, PhD); educational technology (Certificate); learning design and technology (M Ed, Ed D, PhD, Ed S); online teaching (Certificate). *Program availability:* Part-time, 100% online, blended/hybrid learning. *Faculty:* 7. *Students:* 50 full-time (30 women), 266 part-time (184 women); includes 158 minority (130 Black or African American, non-Hispanic/Latino; 1 American Indian or Alaska Native, non-Hispanic/Latino; 5 Asian, non-Hispanic/Latino; 9 Hispanic/Latino; 1 Native Hawaiian or other Pacific Islander, non-Hispanic/Latino; 12 Two or more races, non-Hispanic/Latino), 9 international. Average age 39. 187 applicants, 31% accepted, 42 enrolled. In 2017, 48 master's, 17 doctorates, 47 other advanced degrees awarded. *Degree requirements:* For master's, thesis (for some programs); for doctorate, thesis/dissertation. *Entrance requirements:* For master's, baccalaureate degree from accredited U.S. institution or equivalent from college or university of government-recognized standing; minimum undergraduate GPA of 2.75 in upper-division coursework; personal statement; for doctorate, GRE (instructional design and technology), interview; curriculum vitae; three to four recommendations; master's degree (for educational leadership and policy studies); minimum graduate GPA of 3.5; autobiographical statement; research experience (for PhD program). Additional exam requirements/recommendations for international students: Required—TOEFL (minimum score 550 paper-based; 79 iBT); Recommended—IELTS (minimum score 6.5), TWE (minimum score 5.5). *Application deadline:* For fall admission, 6/1 priority date for domestic students, 5/1 priority date for international students; for winter admission, 10/1 priority date for domestic students, 9/1 priority date for international students; for spring admission, 2/1 priority date for domestic students, 1/1 priority date for international students. Applications are processed on a rolling basis. Application fee: $50. Electronic applications accepted. *Expenses:* Tuition, state resident: full-time $10,224; part-time $638.98 per credit hour. Tuition, nonresident: full-time $22,145; part-time $1384.04 per credit hour. Tuition and fees vary according to course load and program. *Financial support:* In 2017–18, 85 students received support, including 4 research assistantships with tuition reimbursements available (averaging $18,534 per year); fellowships with tuition reimbursements available, scholarships/grants, and unspecified assistantships also available. Support available to part-time students. Financial award applicants required to submit FAFSA. *Faculty research:* Total quality management, participatory management, administering educational technology, school improvement, principalship. *Unit head:* Dr. William Hill, Assistant Dean, 313-577-9316, E-mail: ad2107@wayne.edu. *Application contact:* Graduate Advisor, 313-577-1605, E-mail: askcoe@wayne.edu.
Website: http://coe.wayne.edu/aos/index.php

West Chester University of Pennsylvania, College of Education and Social Work, Department of Early and Middle Grades Education, West Chester, PA 19383. Offers applied studies in teaching and learning (M Ed); early childhood education (M Ed), including accomplished teacher, program administrator; grades 4-8 (Teaching Certificate); grades preK-4 (Teaching Certificate). *Accreditation:* NCATE. *Program availability:* Part-time, 100% online. *Students:* 21 full-time (17 women), 82 part-time (73 women); includes 17 minority (13 Black or African American, non-Hispanic/Latino; 4 Hispanic/Latino), 2 international. Average age 31. 52 applicants, 85% accepted, 27 enrolled. In 2017, 61 master's, 19 other advanced degrees awarded. *Degree requirements:* For master's, teacher research project, portfolio. *Entrance requirements:* For master's, certification (for applied studies in teaching and learning track); one year of full time teaching; minimum GPA of 3.0; for Teaching Certificate, math, social studies, or science concentration exams (for middle grades preparation), minimum GPA of 3.0. Additional exam requirements/recommendations for international students: Required—TOEFL or IELTS. *Application deadline:* For fall admission, 5/15 for international students; for spring admission, 10/15 for international students. Applications are processed on a rolling basis. Application fee: $50. Electronic applications accepted. *Expenses:* Tuition, state resident: full-time $9000; part-time $500 per credit. Tuition, nonresident: full-time $13,500; part-time $750 per credit. *Required fees:* $2959; $149.79 per credit. *Financial support:* Scholarships/grants and unspecified assistantships available. Financial award application deadline: 2/15; financial award applicants required to submit FAFSA. *Faculty research:* Cooperative learning, creative expression and critical thinking, teacher research, learning styles, middle school education. *Unit head:* Dr. Karen Johnson, Chair, 610-436-3545, Fax: 610-436-3102, E-mail: kjohnson@wcupa.edu. *Application contact:* Office of Graduate Studies and Extended Education, 610-436-2943, Fax: 610-436-2763, E-mail: gradstudy@wcupa.edu.
Website: http://www.wcupa.edu/education-socialWork/earlyMiddleGrades/

West Chester University of Pennsylvania, College of Education and Social Work, Program in Policy, Planning, and Administration, West Chester, PA 19383. Offers Ed D. *Program availability:* Part-time, evening/weekend, online only, 100% online. *Students:* 28 part-time (16 women); includes 3 minority (1 Black or African American, non-Hispanic/Latino; 1 Asian, non-Hispanic/Latino; 1 Hispanic/Latino). Average age 39. 36 applicants, 72% accepted, 14 enrolled. *Degree requirements:* For doctorate, comprehensive exam. *Entrance requirements:* For doctorate, GRE if master's GPA lower than 3.85, master's degree from regionally-accredited college or university, three letters of recommendation from education professionals, professional writing demonstration at time of application (waived for applicants who present GRE analytical writing score of 4.5 or higher), resume or curriculum vitae, interview (upon committee request). Additional exam requirements/recommendations for international students: Required—TOEFL or IELTS. *Application deadline:* For fall admission, 5/15 for international students; for spring admission, 10/15 for international students. Applications are processed on a rolling basis. Application fee: $50. Electronic applications accepted. *Expenses:* $625 per credit. *Financial support:* Application deadline: 2/15; applicants required to submit FAFSA. *Faculty research:* Literacy, special education, critical pedagogy, social and cultural foundations of education, educational technology. *Unit head:* Dr. Kenneth D. Witmer, Jr., Dean, 610-436-2321, Fax: 610-436-3102, E-mail: kwitmer@wcupa.edu. *Application contact:* Dr. Robert Haworth, Graduate Coordinator, 610-436-2246, E-mail: rhaworth@wcupa.edu.
Website: http://www.wcupa.edu/education-socialWork/doctorate/

Western Connecticut State University, Division of Graduate Studies, School of Professional Studies, Department of Education and Educational Psychology, Program in Instructional Leadership, Danbury, CT 06810-6885. Offers Ed D. *Program availability:* Part-time. *Degree requirements:* For doctorate, comprehensive exam, thesis/dissertation, completion of program in 6 years. *Entrance requirements:* For doctorate, GRE or MAT, resume, three recommendations (one in a supervisory capacity in an educational setting), satisfactory interview with WCSU representatives from the Ed D Admissions Committee. Additional exam requirements/recommendations for international students: Recommended—TOEFL (minimum score 550 paper-based; 79 iBT), IELTS (minimum score 6). *Expenses:* Contact institution. *Faculty research:* Differentiated instruction, the transition of teacher learning, teacher retention, relationship building through the evaluation process, leadership development.

Western Governors University, Teachers College, Salt Lake City, UT 84107. Offers curriculum and instruction (MS); educational leadership (MS); educational studies (MA); educational studies (5-12) (MA), including mathematics; elementary education (K-8) (MAT, Postbaccalaureate Certificate); elementary education (PreK-8) (MAT); English language learning (K-12) (MA); instructional design (MAT); learning and technology (M Ed, MA); management and innovation (M Ed); mathematics (5-12) (MAT, Postbaccalaureate Certificate); mathematics (5-9) (MAT, Postbaccalaureate Certificate);

Educational Leadership and Administration

mathematics education (5-12) (MA); mathematics education (5-9) (MA); mathematics education (K-6) (MA); measurement and evaluation (M Ed); science (5-12) (Postbaccalaureate Certificate); science (5-9) (MAT, Postbaccalaureate Certificate); science education (5-12) (MA), including biology, chemistry, geology, physics; science education (5-9) (MA); social science (5-12) (MAT, Postbaccalaureate Certificate); special education (MAT, MS). *Accreditation:* NCATE. *Program availability:* Evening/ weekend, online learning. *Degree requirements:* For master's, capstone project. *Entrance requirements:* For master's and Postbaccalaureate Certificate, Readiness Assessment, transcripts. Additional exam requirements/recommendations for international students: Required—TOEFL (minimum score 450 paper-based; 80 iBT). Electronic applications accepted. *Expenses:* Contact institution.

Western Illinois University, School of Graduate Studies, College of Education and Human Services, Department of Educational Studies, Program in College Student Personnel, Macomb, IL 61455-1390. Offers college student personnel (MS), including higher education leadership, student affairs. *Accreditation:* NCATE. *Program availability:* Part-time. *Students:* 59 full-time (41 women), 9 part-time (5 women); includes 19 minority (4 Black or African American, non-Hispanic/Latino; 10 Hispanic/Latino; 5 Two or more races, non-Hispanic/Latino), 2 international. Average age 24. 79 applicants, 82% accepted, 32 enrolled. In 2017, 27 master's awarded. *Degree requirements:* For master's, thesis or alternative. *Entrance requirements:* For master's, interview. Additional exam requirements/recommendations for international students: Required— TOEFL (minimum score 550 paper-based; 80 iBT). *Application deadline:* For fall admission, 1/5 priority date for domestic students. Application fee: $30. Electronic applications accepted. *Financial support:* Unspecified assistantships available. Financial award applicants required to submit FAFSA. *Unit head:* Dr. Tracy Davis, Coordinator, 309-298-1183. *Application contact:* Dr. Nancy Parsons, Associate Provost and Director of Graduate Studies, 309-298-1806, Fax: 309-298-2345, E-mail: grad-office@wiu.edu.
Website: http://wiu.edu/csp/

Western Illinois University, School of Graduate Studies, College of Education and Human Services, Department of Educational Studies, Program in Educational Leadership, Macomb, IL 61455-1390. Offers MS Ed, Ed D, Ed S. *Accreditation:* NCATE. *Program availability:* Part-time, evening/weekend. *Degree requirements:* For master's, thesis or alternative; for doctorate, comprehensive exam, thesis/dissertation, electronic portfolio. *Entrance requirements:* For master's and Ed S, interview; for doctorate, GRE General Test. Additional exam requirements/recommendations for international students: Required—TOEFL (minimum score 575 paper-based; 88 iBT). *Application deadline:* Applications are processed on a rolling basis. Application fee: $30. Electronic applications accepted. *Financial support:* Unspecified assistantships available. Financial award applicants required to submit FAFSA. *Unit head:* Dr. Eric Sheffield, Chairperson, 309-298-1183. *Application contact:* Dr. Nancy Parsons, Associate Provost and Director of Graduate Studies, 309-298-1806, Fax: 309-298-2345, E-mail: grad-office@wiu.edu.

Western Kentucky University, Graduate Studies, College of Education and Behavioral Sciences, Department of Educational Administration, Leadership, and Research, Bowling Green, KY 42101. Offers adult education (MAE); educational leadership (Ed D); school administration (Ed S); school principal (MAE). *Accreditation:* NCATE. *Program availability:* Part-time, evening/weekend. *Degree requirements:* For master's, comprehensive exam, thesis or applied project and oral defense; for Ed S, thesis. *Entrance requirements:* For master's, GRE General Test, minimum GPA of 2.75. Additional exam requirements/recommendations for international students: Required— TOEFL (minimum score 555 paper-based; 79 iBT). *Faculty research:* Principal internship, superintendent assessment, administrative leadership, group training for residential workers.

Western Michigan University, Graduate College, College of Education and Human Development, Department of Educational Leadership, Research and Technology, Kalamazoo, MI 49008. Offers educational leadership (MA, PhD, Ed S), including educational leadership (MA); educational technology (MA, Graduate Certificate); evaluation, measurement and research (MA, PhD); organizational learning and performance (MA).

Western New Mexico University, Graduate Division, School of Education, Silver City, NM 88062-0680. Offers bilingual education (MAT); educational leadership (MA); elementary education (MAT); reading (MAT); secondary education (MAT); special education (MAT); TESOL (teaching English to speakers of other languages) (MAT). *Accreditation:* NCATE. *Program availability:* Part-time, online learning. *Degree requirements:* For master's, comprehensive exam. *Entrance requirements:* For master's, minimum GPA of 3.0 in last 64 hours of undergraduate study. Additional exam requirements/recommendations for international students: Required—TOEFL (minimum score 550 paper-based; 79 iBT). Electronic applications accepted. *Faculty research:* International education, electronic reading assessment, developing STEM teachers.

Western State Colorado University, Graduate Programs in Education, Gunnison, CO 81231. Offers education administrator leadership (MA); reading leadership (MA); teacher leadership (MA). *Program availability:* Online learning. *Degree requirements:* For master's, capstone.

Western Washington University, Graduate School, Woodring College of Education, Department of Educational Leadership, Educational Administration Program, Bellingham, WA 98225-5996. Offers M Ed. *Accreditation:* NCATE. *Program availability:* Part-time. *Degree requirements:* For master's, comprehensive exam, thesis optional. *Entrance requirements:* For master's, GRE General Test or MAT, minimum GPA of 3.0 in last 60 semester hours or last 90 quarter hours, certification. Additional exam requirements/recommendations for international students: Required—TOEFL (minimum score 567 paper-based). Electronic applications accepted. *Faculty research:* Principal efficacy, collaborative school leadership, school/university partnerships, case study methodology, ethical leadership.

Western Washington University, Graduate School, Woodring College of Education, Department of Educational Leadership, Program in Student Affairs Administration, Bellingham, WA 98225-5996. Offers M Ed. *Accreditation:* NCATE. *Program availability:* Part-time. *Degree requirements:* For master's, comprehensive exam, thesis optional, research project. *Entrance requirements:* For master's, GRE General Test or MAT, minimum GPA of 3.0 in last 60 semester hours or last 90 quarter hours. Additional exam requirements/recommendations for international students: Required—TOEFL (minimum score 567 paper-based). Electronic applications accepted. *Faculty research:* Outcomes assessment, adult learning, best practices/student affairs, college health promotion, cultural pluralism.

West Liberty University, College of Education and Human Performance, West Liberty, WV 26074. Offers community education research and leadership (MA Ed); innovative instruction (MA Ed); leadership in disability services (MA Ed); leadership studies (MA Ed); multi-categorical special education (MA Ed); reading specialist (MA Ed); sports leadership and coaching (MA Ed). *Accreditation:* NCATE. *Program availability:* Part-time, evening/weekend. *Students:* 18 full-time (12 women), 74 part-time (60 women); includes 2 minority (1 Black or African American, non-Hispanic/Latino; 1 Native Hawaiian or other Pacific Islander, non-Hispanic/Latino). Average age 32. *Degree requirements:* For master's, capstone experience. *Entrance requirements:* For master's, minimum GPA of 2.5 or 3.0 (depending on track). Additional exam requirements/ recommendations for international students: Required—TOEFL. *Application deadline:* Applications are processed on a rolling basis. Application fee: $0. Electronic applications accepted. Tuition and fees vary according to course load and program. *Financial support:* Teaching assistantships and unspecified assistantships available. *Unit head:* Dr. Catherine Monteroso, Interim Dean, 304-336-8247, E-mail: cmonteroso@ westliberty.edu. *Application contact:* Sara Sweeney, Director, Office of Graduate Studies, 304-336-8545, E-mail: sara.sweeney@westliberty.edu.
Website: http://westliberty.edu/education/

Westminster College, Graduate School, Program in Educational Administration, New Wilmington, PA 16172-0001. Offers school principal K-12 (M Ed); school superintendent (M Ed). Application fee: $35. *Expenses: Tuition:* Part-time $454 per semester hour. *Required fees:* $235.50 per course. Tuition and fees vary according to course load. *Unit head:* Graduate School Director, 724-946-7031, Fax: 724-946-6158. *Application contact:* Graduate School Director, 724-946-7031, Fax: 724-946-6158.

West Texas A&M University, College of Education and Social Sciences, Department of Education, Program in Educational Leadership, Canyon, TX 79015. Offers M Ed. *Program availability:* Part-time, evening/weekend, online learning. *Degree requirements:* For master's, comprehensive exam, thesis optional. *Entrance requirements:* For master's, GRE General Test. Additional exam requirements/recommendations for international students: Required—TOEFL (minimum score 550 paper-based). Electronic applications accepted. *Faculty research:* Teacher quality, leadership, recruitment, retention.

West Virginia University, College of Education and Human Services, Morgantown, WV 26506. Offers audiology (Au D); autism spectrum disorder (MA); clinical rehabilitation and mental health counseling (MS); communication science and disorders (PhD); counseling (MA); counseling psychology (PhD); curriculum and instruction (Ed D); early childhood education (MA); early intervention (MA); education (PhD); educational leadership (MA, Ed D); educational leadership/public school administration (MA); educational psychology (MA, Ed D); elementary education (MA); gifted education (MA); higher education administration (MA, Ed D); higher education curriculum and teaching (MA); institutional design and technology (MA); instructional design and technology (Ed D); literacy education (MA); secondary education (MA); secondary education/ English (MA); special education (Ed D); speech pathology (MS). *Accreditation:* NCATE. *Program availability:* Part-time, evening/weekend, online learning. *Students:* 423 full-time (347 women), 367 part-time (316 women); includes 57 minority (14 Black or African American, non-Hispanic/Latino; 7 Asian, non-Hispanic/Latino; 20 Hispanic/Latino; 16 Two or more races, non-Hispanic/Latino), 13 international. *Degree requirements:* For master's, content exams; for doctorate, comprehensive exam, thesis/dissertation. *Entrance requirements:* Additional exam requirements/recommendations for international students: Required—TOEFL (minimum score 500 paper-based; 61 iBT). *Application deadline:* For fall admission, 8/1 for domestic students; for spring admission, 1/1 for domestic students; for summer admission, 5/1 for domestic students. Application fee: $60. Electronic applications accepted. *Expenses:* Tuition, state resident: full-time $9450. Tuition, nonresident: full-time $24,390. *Financial support:* Fellowships, research assistantships, teaching assistantships, career-related internships or fieldwork, Federal Work-Study, institutionally sponsored loans, health care benefits, tuition waivers (full and partial), and administrative assistantships available. Financial award applicants required to submit FAFSA. *Faculty research:* Internet training and integration for teachers, rural education, teacher preparation, organization of schools, evaluation of personnel. *Unit head:* Dr. Gypsy Denzine, Dean, 304-293-5703, Fax: 304-293-7565, E-mail: gypsy.denzine@mail.wvu.edu. *Application contact:* Dr. M. Cecil Smith, Associate Dean for Research and Graduate Education, 304-293-2174, Fax: 304-293-3802, E-mail: mcecil.smith@mail.wvu.edu.
Website: http://cehs.wvu.edu/

Wheeling Jesuit University, Department of Education, Wheeling, WV 26003-6295. Offers MEL. *Program availability:* Part-time, evening/weekend, online learning. *Degree requirements:* For master's, thesis. *Entrance requirements:* For master's, GRE or MAT, minimum GPA of 2.5, professional teaching certificate. Additional exam requirements/ recommendations for international students: Required—TOEFL (minimum score 600 paper-based; 100 iBT). Electronic applications accepted. Application fee is waived when completed online. *Faculty research:* Education leadership, school improvement, student achievement, leadership in special education.

Whittier College, Graduate Programs, Department of Education and Child Development, Program in Educational Administration, Whittier, CA 90608-0634. Offers MA Ed. *Program availability:* Part-time, evening/weekend. *Degree requirements:* For master's, thesis. *Entrance requirements:* For master's, GRE General Test, MAT. *Faculty research:* Candidate leadership development.

Whitworth University, School of Education, Graduate Studies in Education, Program in Administration, Spokane, WA 99251-0001. Offers M Ed. *Accreditation:* NCATE. *Program availability:* Part-time, evening/weekend. *Degree requirements:* For master's, comprehensive exam, internship, practicum, research project, or thesis. *Entrance requirements:* For master's, GRE General Test, MAT. *Faculty research:* Rural staff development.

Wichita State University, Graduate School, College of Education, Department of Counseling, Educational Leadership, Educational and School Psychology, Wichita, KS 67260. Offers counseling (M Ed); educational leadership (M Ed, Ed D); educational psychology (M Ed); school psychology (Ed S). *Accreditation:* NCATE. *Program availability:* Part-time, evening/weekend. Application fee: $50 ($65 for international students). *Unit head:* Dr. Jody Fiorini, Department Head, 316-978-3325, Fax: 316-978-3102, E-mail: jody.fiorini@wichita.edu. *Application contact:* Jordan Oleson, Admissions Coordinator, 316-978-3095, Fax: 316-978-3253, E-mail: jordan.oleson@wichita.edu.
Website: http://www.wichita.edu/cles

Widener University, School of Human Service Professions, Center for Education, Chester, PA 19013-5792. Offers adult education (M Ed); counseling in higher education (M Ed); counselor education (M Ed); early childhood education (M Ed); educational foundations (M Ed); educational leadership (M Ed); educational psychology (M Ed); elementary education (M Ed); English and language arts (M Ed); health education (M Ed); higher education leadership (Ed D); home and school visitor (M Ed); human sexuality (M Ed, PhD); mathematics education (M Ed); middle school education (M Ed); principalship (M Ed); reading and language arts (Ed D); reading education (M Ed); school administration (Ed D); science education (M Ed); social studies education (M Ed); special education (M Ed); technology education (M Ed). *Accreditation:* NCATE. *Program availability:* Part-time, evening/weekend. *Faculty:* 34 full-time (22 women), 37 part-time/adjunct (14 women). *Students:* 131 full-time (112 women), 244 part-time (179 women); includes 94 minority (58 Black or African American, non-Hispanic/Latino; 1 American Indian or Alaska Native, non-Hispanic/Latino; 1 Asian, non-Hispanic/Latino; 22 Hispanic/Latino; 12 Two or more races, non-Hispanic/Latino), 12 international. Average age 37. 140 applicants, 38% accepted, 26 enrolled. In 2017, 45 master's, 21 doctorates awarded. Terminal master's awarded for partial completion of doctoral program. *Degree requirements:* For doctorate, thesis/dissertation. *Entrance*

requirements: For master's, minimum GPA of 2.5; for doctorate, GRE or MAT, minimum GPA of 2.0 (undergraduate), 3.5 (graduate). *Application deadline:* Applications are processed on a rolling basis. Application fee: $25 ($300 for international students). Electronic applications accepted. *Expenses:* Contact institution. *Financial support:* Career-related internships or fieldwork, tuition waivers (full and partial), and unspecified assistantships available. Support available to part-time students. Financial award application deadline: 5/1. *Faculty research:* Reading and cognition, adult education, technology education, educational leadership, special education. *Unit head:* Dr. Shawn Fitzgerald, Dean, 610-499-4294, Fax: 610-499-4623, E-mail: smfitzgerald@widener.edu. *Application contact:* Megan Kuft, Director of Graduate Admissions, 610-499-4124, E-mail: gradprograms@widener.edu.
Website: http://www.widener.edu/academics/schools/eics

Wilkes University, College of Graduate and Professional Studies, School of Education, Wilkes-Barre, PA 18766-0002. Offers educational development and strategies (MS Ed); educational leadership (MS Ed, Ed D); effective teaching (MS Ed); instructional media (MS Ed); instructional technology (MS Ed); international school leadership (MS Ed); international teaching and learning (MS Ed); literacy specialist (MS Ed); middle level education (MS Ed); online teaching (MS Ed); school business leadership (MS Ed); special education (MS Ed); teaching English to speakers of other languages (MS Ed). *Program availability:* Part-time, evening/weekend, 100% online, blended/hybrid learning. *Students:* 76 full-time (57 women), 1,586 part-time (1,204 women); includes 82 minority (10 Black or African American, non-Hispanic/Latino; 12 Asian, non-Hispanic/Latino; 41 Hispanic/Latino; 1 Native Hawaiian or other Pacific Islander, non-Hispanic/Latino; 18 Two or more races, non-Hispanic/Latino). Average age 34. In 2017, 619 master's, 23 doctorates awarded. *Entrance requirements:* Additional exam requirements/recommendations for international students: Required—TOEFL (minimum score 550 paper-based; 79 iBT). *Application deadline:* Applications are processed on a rolling basis. Application fee: $45 ($65 for international students). Electronic applications accepted. *Expenses:* Contact institution. *Financial support:* Unspecified assistantships available. Financial award application deadline: 3/1; financial award applicants required to submit FAFSA. *Unit head:* Dr. Rhonda Rabbitt, Dean, 570-408-4680, Fax: 570-408-7872, E-mail: rhonda.rabbitt@wilkes.edu. *Application contact:* Stephanie Wasmanski, Associate Director of Graduate Admissions, 570-408-5535, Fax: 570-408-7846, E-mail: stephanie.wasmanski@wilkes.edu.
Website: http://www.wilkes.edu/academics/graduate-programs/masters-programs/graduate-education/index.aspx

William Paterson University of New Jersey, College of Education, Wayne, NJ 07470-8420. Offers curriculum and learning (M Ed); early childhood education (Certificate); educational leadership (M Ed); educational media specialist (Certificate); elementary education (MAT, Certificate); elementary education subject area (Certificate); higher education administration (MA); learning disabilities consultant (Certificate); literacy (M Ed); middle level education (M Ed); middle school education subject area (Certificate); professional counseling (M Ed); reading specialist (Certificate); school library media specialist (Certificate); school principal (Certificate); school supervisor (Certificate); secondary education (MAT); special education (M Ed); teacher of students with disabilities (Certificate). *Accreditation:* NCATE. *Program availability:* Part-time, evening/weekend. *Faculty:* 37 full-time (25 women), 21 part-time/adjunct (16 women). *Students:* 73 full-time (54 women), 480 part-time (409 women); includes 153 minority (48 Black or African American, non-Hispanic/Latino; 13 Asian, non-Hispanic/Latino; 81 Hispanic/Latino; 11 Two or more races, non-Hispanic/Latino), 1 international. Average age 35. 347 applicants, 87% accepted, 226 enrolled. In 2017, 136 master's awarded. *Degree requirements:* For master's, comprehensive exam, thesis (for some programs), exit interview (for some programs); practicum/internship; minimum GPA of 3.0 (for some programs); exit portfolio (for some programs). *Entrance requirements:* For master's, GRE/MAT, minimum GPA of 2.75; teaching certificate; essay; interview; 2 letters of recommendation; personal statement. Additional exam requirements/recommendations for international students: Required—TOEFL (minimum score 550 paper-based; 79 iBT), IELTS (minimum score 6). *Application deadline:* For fall admission, 6/1 for domestic students, 3/1 for international students; for spring admission, 11/1 for domestic students, 10/1 for international students. Applications are processed on a rolling basis. Application fee: $50. Electronic applications accepted. *Expenses:* Tuition, state resident: full-time $13,920; part-time $6264 per year. Tuition, nonresident: full-time $21,700; part-time $9765 per year. *Required fees:* $80; $36 per year. Tuition and fees vary according to course load, degree level and program. *Financial support:* In 2017–18, 8,416 students received support. Career-related internships or fieldwork, Federal Work-Study, scholarships/grants, and unspecified assistantships available. Support available to part-time students. Financial award application deadline: 3/15; financial award applicants required to submit FAFSA. *Faculty research:* Code switching and creative writing, language instruction, teacher evaluation, preschools, history of educational theories. *Total annual research expenditures:* $311,226. *Unit head:* Dr. Dorothy Feola, Dean, 973-720-2138, Fax: 973-720-3647, E-mail: feolad@wpunj.edu. *Application contact:* Liana Fornarotto, Director of Education Enrollment and Certification, 973-720-2206, Fax: 973-720-2989, E-mail: fornarottol@wpunj.edu.
Website: http://www.wpunj.edu/coe

William Woods University, Graduate and Adult Studies, Fulton, MO 65251-1098. Offers administration (M Ed, Ed S); athletic/activities administration (M Ed); curriculum and instruction (M Ed, Ed S); educational leadership (Ed D); equestrian education (M Ed); health management (MBA); human resources (MBA); leadership (MBA); marketing, advertising, and public relations (MBA); teaching and technology (M Ed). *Program availability:* Part-time, evening/weekend. *Degree requirements:* For master's, capstone course (MBA), action research (M Ed); for Ed S, field experience. *Entrance requirements:* Additional exam requirements/recommendations for international students: Required—TOEFL (minimum score 550 paper-based). Electronic applications accepted. *Expenses:* Contact institution.

Wilmington University, College of Education, New Castle, DE 19720-6491. Offers applied technology in education (M Ed); career and technical education (M Ed); educational leadership (Ed D); elementary and secondary school counseling (M Ed); elementary studies (M Ed); ESOL literacy (M Ed); higher education leadership (Ed D); instruction: gifted and talented (M Ed); instruction: teacher of reading (M Ed); instruction: teaching and learning (M Ed); organizational leadership (Ed D); school leadership (M Ed); secondary education (MAT); special education (M Ed). *Accreditation:* NCATE. *Program availability:* Part-time, evening/weekend. *Faculty:* 23 full-time (13 women), 162 part-time/adjunct (99 women). *Students:* 546 full-time (394 women), 960 part-time (732 women); includes 320 minority (241 Black or African American, non-Hispanic/Latino; 12 American Indian or Alaska Native, non-Hispanic/Latino; 11 Asian, non-Hispanic/Latino; 28 Hispanic/Latino; 3 Native Hawaiian or other Pacific Islander, non-Hispanic/Latino; 25 Two or more races, non-Hispanic/Latino), 7 international. Average age 34. 1,068 applicants, 64% accepted, 582 enrolled. In 2017, 430 master's, 59 doctorates awarded. *Entrance requirements:* For master's, 2 letters of recommendation, interview. Additional exam requirements/recommendations for international students: Required—TOEFL (minimum score 500 paper-based). *Application deadline:* For fall admission, 4/30 for domestic students. Applications are processed on a rolling basis. Application fee: $35. Electronic applications accepted. *Expenses: Tuition:* Part-time $466 per credit. *Required fees:* $25 per semester. Tuition and fees vary according to degree level and campus/location. *Financial support:* Applicants required to submit FAFSA. *Unit head:* Dr. John C. Gray, Dean, 302-295-1139. *Application contact:* Laura Morris, Director of Admissions, 877-967-5464, E-mail: infocenter@wilmu.edu.
Website: http://www.wilmu.edu/education/

Wingate University, Thayer School of Education, Wingate, NC 28174. Offers community college executive leadership (Ed D); educational leadership (MA Ed, Ed S); elementary education (MA Ed, MAT). *Accreditation:* NCATE. *Program availability:* Part-time, evening/weekend. *Degree requirements:* For master's, portfolio. *Entrance requirements:* For master's, GRE General Test or MAT, teaching certificate (MA Ed).

Winona State University, College of Education, Department of Leadership Education, Winona, MN 55987. Offers education leadership (MS, Ed S), including k-12 principal (Ed S); superintendent (Ed S); organizational leadership (MS); professional leadership (MS); sport management (MS). MS in sport management offered in cooperation with Department of Physical Education and Sport Science. *Accreditation:* NCATE. *Program availability:* Part-time, evening/weekend. *Degree requirements:* For master's, comprehensive exam, thesis optional; for Ed S, thesis optional.

Winthrop University, College of Education, Program in Educational Leadership, Rock Hill, SC 29733. Offers M Ed. *Students:* 132 full-time (108 women), 58 part-time (53 women); includes 57 minority (45 Black or African American, non-Hispanic/Latino; 1 American Indian or Alaska Native, non-Hispanic/Latino; 2 Asian, non-Hispanic/Latino; 6 Hispanic/Latino; 1 Native Hawaiian or other Pacific Islander, non-Hispanic/Latino; 2 Two or more races, non-Hispanic/Latino), 2 international. Average age 37. In 2017, 40 master's awarded. *Entrance requirements:* For master's, GRE General Test or MAT, 3 years of experience, South Carolina Class III Teaching Certificate, recommendations from current principal and district-level administrator. Additional exam requirements/recommendations for international students: Required—TOEFL (minimum score 550 paper-based; 79 iBT), IELTS (minimum score 6). *Application deadline:* For fall admission, 7/15 priority date for domestic students; for spring admission, 12/1 for domestic students. Applications are processed on a rolling basis. Application fee: $50. Electronic applications accepted. *Financial support:* Application deadline: 2/1; applicants required to submit FAFSA. *Unit head:* Dr. Walter Hart, Graduate Program Director, 803-323-4710, E-mail: hartw@winthrop.edu. *Application contact:* 800-411-7041, Fax: 803-323-2204, E-mail: gradschool@winthrop.edu.
Website: http://www.winthrop.edu/coe/edleadership

Wisconsin Lutheran College, College of Adult and Graduate Studies, Milwaukee, WI 53226-9942. Offers high performance instruction (MA Ed); instructional technology (MA Ed); leadership and innovation (MA Ed); science instruction (MA Ed).

Worcester State University, Graduate School, Department of Education, Program in Leadership and Administration, Worcester, MA 01602-2597. Offers M Ed. *Program availability:* Part-time. *Students:* 72 part-time (50 women); includes 7 minority (2 Black or African American, non-Hispanic/Latino; 1 American Indian or Alaska Native, non-Hispanic/Latino; 2 Hispanic/Latino; 2 Two or more races, non-Hispanic/Latino). Average age 40. 12 applicants, 100% accepted, 3 enrolled. In 2017, 28 master's awarded. *Degree requirements:* For master's, comprehensive exam (for some programs), thesis optional. *Entrance requirements:* For master's, GRE or MAT, MTEL Communication and Literacy exam, teaching license; essay explaining interest in becoming school administrator; 3 reference letters; at least 2 years of teaching experience. Additional exam requirements/recommendations for international students: Required—TOEFL (minimum score 550 paper-based; 79 iBT). *Application deadline:* For fall admission, 6/15 for domestic and international students; for spring admission, 11/1 for domestic and international students; for summer admission, 4/1 for domestic and international students. Applications are processed on a rolling basis. Application fee: $50. Electronic applications accepted. *Expenses:* Tuition, state resident: full-time $3042; part-time $169 per credit hour. Tuition, nonresident: full-time $3042; part-time $169 per credit hour. *Required fees:* $2754; $153 per credit hour. *Financial support:* Career-related internships or fieldwork, scholarships/grants, and unspecified assistantships available. Financial award application deadline: 3/1; financial award applicants required to submit FAFSA. *Unit head:* Dr. David Roach, Coordinator, 508-929-8788, E-mail: droach@worcester.edu. *Application contact:* Sara Grady, Associate Dean for Graduate Studies and Professional Development, 508-929-8130, E-mail: sara.grady@worcester.edu.

Wright State University, Graduate School, College of Education and Human Services, Department of Educational Leadership, Program in Advanced Educational Leadership, Dayton, OH 45435. Offers advanced curriculum and instruction (Ed S). *Accreditation:* NCATE. *Degree requirements:* For Ed S, thesis. *Entrance requirements:* For degree, GRE General Test, MAT. Additional exam requirements/recommendations for international students: Required—TOEFL.

Xavier University, College of Social Sciences, Health and Education, School of Education, Department of Educational Leadership and Human Resource Development, Cincinnati, OH 45207. Offers educational administration (M Ed); human resource development (MS). *Program availability:* Part-time, evening/weekend. *Degree requirements:* For master's, internship; for doctorate, comprehensive exam, thesis/dissertation. *Entrance requirements:* For master's, GRE or MAT, resume; 2 letters of recommendation; goal statement; official transcript; for doctorate, GRE, GMAT, LSAT or MAT, official transcript; 1,000-word goal statement; resume; 3 letters of recommendation. Additional exam requirements/recommendations for international students: Required—TOEFL (minimum score 550 paper-based; 79 iBT). Electronic applications accepted. Application fee is waived when completed online. *Expenses:* Contact institution.

Xavier University of Louisiana, Graduate School, Programs in Education, New Orleans, LA 70125. Offers counseling (MA); curriculum and instruction (MA); educational leadership (MA). *Accreditation:* NCATE. *Program availability:* Part-time, evening/weekend. *Degree requirements:* For master's, comprehensive exam, thesis or alternative. *Entrance requirements:* For master's, GRE General Test, MAT, minimum GPA of 2.5. Additional exam requirements/recommendations for international students: Required—TOEFL.

Yeshiva University, Azrieli Graduate School of Jewish Education and Administration, New York, NY 10033-4391. Offers MS, Ed D, Specialist. *Accreditation:* TEAC. *Program availability:* Part-time, evening/weekend. Terminal master's awarded for partial completion of doctoral program. *Degree requirements:* For master's, one foreign language, student teaching experience, comprehensive exam or thesis; for doctorate, one foreign language, comprehensive exam, thesis/dissertation, certifying exams, internship; for Specialist, one foreign language, comprehensive exam, certifying exams, internship. *Entrance requirements:* For master's, GRE General Test, BA in Jewish studies or equivalent; for doctorate and Specialist, GRE General Test, master's degree in Jewish education, 2 years of teaching experience. *Expenses:* Contact institution. *Faculty research:* Social patterns of American and Israeli Jewish population, special education, adult education, technology in education, return to religious values.

York College of Pennsylvania, Master of Education Program, York, PA 17403-3651. Offers educational leadership (M Ed); educational technology (M Ed); reading specialist (M Ed). *Program availability:* Part-time-only, evening/weekend. *Faculty:* 2 full-time (1 woman), 7 part-time/adjunct (3 women). *Students:* 87 part-time (62 women); includes 2 minority (1 Hispanic/Latino; 1 Two or more races, non-Hispanic/Latino), 1 international.

Average age 33. 57 applicants, 79% accepted, 39 enrolled. In 2017, 7 master's awarded. *Degree requirements:* For master's, comprehensive exam (for some programs), thesis (for some programs). *Entrance requirements:* For master's, PRAXIS, statement of applicant's professional and academic goals, 2 letters of recommendation, letter from current supervisor, official undergraduate and graduate transcript(s), copy of teaching certificate(s), current professional resume, interview. *Application deadline:* For fall admission, 7/15 priority date for domestic students; for spring admission, 11/15 priority date for domestic students; for summer admission, 4/15 priority date for domestic students. Applications are processed on a rolling basis. Application fee: $0. Electronic applications accepted. *Expenses:* $620 per credit. *Financial support:* Scholarships/grants available. Financial award applicants required to submit FAFSA. *Faculty research:* Classroom technology, assessment, educational leadership, professional development, literacy. *Unit head:* Dr. Joshua D. DeSantis, Director, Master of Education

Program, 717-815-1936, E-mail: jdesant1@ycp.edu. Website: https://www.ycp.edu/med

Youngstown State University, Graduate School, Beeghly College of Education, Department of Educational Foundations, Research, Technology, and Leadership, Youngstown, OH 44555-0001. Offers educational administration (MS Ed); educational leadership (Ed D). *Accreditation:* NCATE. *Program availability:* Part-time, evening/weekend. *Degree requirements:* For master's, comprehensive exam; for doctorate, comprehensive exam, thesis/dissertation. *Entrance requirements:* For master's, GRE, MAT, or teaching certificate; minimum GPA of 2.7; for doctorate, GRE General Test, GRE Subject Test, interview, minimum GPA of 3.5. Additional exam requirements/recommendations for international students: Required—TOEFL. *Faculty research:* Administrative theory, computer applications, education law, school and community relations, finance principalship.

Educational Measurement and Evaluation

American InterContinental University Online, Program in Education, Schaumburg, IL 60173. Offers curriculum and instruction (M Ed); educational assessment and evaluation (M Ed); instructional technology (M Ed); leadership of educational organizations (M Ed). *Accreditation:* TEAC. *Program availability:* Evening/weekend, online learning. *Entrance requirements:* Additional exam requirements/recommendations for international students: Required—TOEFL (minimum score 550 paper-based). Electronic applications accepted.

American University, School of Professional and Extended Studies, Washington, DC 20016-8030. Offers agile project management (MS); healthcare management (MS, Graduate Certificate); human resource analytics and management (MS, Graduate Certificate); instructional design and learning analytics (MS); measurement and evaluation (MS); project monitoring and evaluation (Graduate Certificate); sports analytics and management (MS, Graduate Certificate). *Program availability:* Part-time, evening/weekend, 100% online. *Faculty:* 27 full-time (13 women), 21 part-time/adjunct (10 women). *Students:* 17 full-time (8 women), 59 part-time (34 women); includes 9 minority (5 Black or African American, non-Hispanic/Latino; 2 Asian, non-Hispanic/Latino; 1 Hispanic/Latino; 1 Two or more races, non-Hispanic/Latino), 5 international. Average age 31. 55 applicants, 89% accepted, 38 enrolled. In 2017, 8 other advanced degrees awarded. *Entrance requirements:* For master's, official transcript(s), resume. Additional exam requirements/recommendations for international students: Required—TOEFL (minimum score 600 paper-based; 100 iBT). *Application deadline:* Applications are processed on a rolling basis. Application fee: $55. Electronic applications accepted. *Expenses:* Contact institution. *Financial support:* Applicants required to submit FAFSA. *Unit head:* Carola Weil, Dean, 202-885-5990, Fax: 202-895-4960, E-mail: weil@american.edu. *Application contact:* Emily Aronoff, Assistant Director for Recruitment and Admission, 202-895-4953, E-mail: aronoff@american.edu. Website: http://www.american.edu/spexs/

Arizona State University at the Tempe campus, Mary Lou Fulton Teachers College, Program in Educational Policy and Evaluation, Phoenix, AZ 85069. Offers PhD. Fall admission only. *Degree requirements:* For doctorate, comprehensive exam, thesis/dissertation, interactive Program of Study (iPOS) submitted before completing 50 percent of required credit hours. *Entrance requirements:* For doctorate, GRE, minimum GPA of 3.0 or equivalent in last 2 years of work leading to bachelor's degree, 3 letters of recommendation, personal statement, writing sample, curriculum vitae or resume. Additional exam requirements/recommendations for international students: Required—TOEFL, IELTS, or PTE. Electronic applications accepted. *Expenses:* Contact institution. *Faculty research:* Education policy analysis, school finance and quantitative methods, school improvement in ethnically, linguistically and economically diverse communities, parent/teacher engagement, school choice, accountability polices, school finance litigation, school segregation.

Ball State University, Graduate School, Teachers College, Department of Educational Psychology, Muncie, IN 47306. Offers educational psychology (MA, MS), including educational psychology (MA, MS, PhD); educational psychology (PhD), including educational psychology (MA, MS, PhD); gifted and talented education (Certificate); human development and learning (Certificate); instructional design and assessment (Certificate); neuropsychology (Certificate); quantitative psychology (MS); response to intervention (Certificate); school psychology (MA, PhD), including school psychology (MA, PhD, Ed S); school psychology (Ed S), including school psychology (MA, PhD, Ed S). *Program availability:* 100% online. *Faculty:* 24 full-time (15 women), 3 part-time/adjunct (all women). *Students:* 68 full-time (49 women), 122 part-time (106 women); includes 33 minority (16 Black or African American, non-Hispanic/Latino; 4 Asian, non-Hispanic/Latino; 7 Hispanic/Latino; 6 Two or more races, non-Hispanic/Latino), 3 international. Average age 32. 146 applicants, 42% accepted, 47 enrolled. In 2017, 49 master's, 8 doctorates, 20 other advanced degrees awarded. *Degree requirements:* For doctorate, thesis/dissertation; for other advanced degree, thesis. *Entrance requirements:* For master's, GRE General Test, minimum baccalaureate GPA of 2.75 or 3.0 in latter half of baccalaureate, professional goals and self-assessment; for doctorate, GRE General Test, minimum graduate GPA of 3.2; for other advanced degree, GRE General Test. Additional exam requirements/recommendations for international students: Required—TOEFL (minimum score 550 paper-based; 79 iBT), IELTS (minimum score 6.5). *Application deadline:* Applications are processed on a rolling basis. Application fee: $60. Electronic applications accepted. *Financial support:* In 2017–18, 40 students received support, including 29 research assistantships with partial tuition reimbursements available (averaging $12,276 per year), 3 teaching assistantships with partial tuition reimbursements available (averaging $11,167 per year); unspecified assistantships also available. Financial award application deadline: 3/1; financial award applicants required to submit FAFSA. *Unit head:* Dr. Jerell Cassady, Chairperson, 765-285-8503, E-mail: jccassady@bsu.edu. *Application contact:* Dr. Jerrell Cassady, Chairperson, 765-285-8503, Fax: 765-285-5455, E-mail: jccassady@bsu.edu. Website: http://www.bsu.edu/edpsych

Boston College, Lynch School of Education, Program in Educational Research, Measurement, and Evaluation, Chestnut Hill, MA 02467-3800. Offers applied statistics and psychometrics (MS); educational research methodology (M Ed); measurement, evaluation, statistics, and assessment (PhD). *Program availability:* Part-time, evening/weekend. *Students:* 34 full-time (22 women), 22 part-time (19 women); includes 11 minority (4 Black or African American, non-Hispanic/Latino; 2 Asian, non-Hispanic/Latino; 2 Hispanic/Latino; 3 Two or more races, non-Hispanic/Latino), 23 international. Average age 31. 57 applicants, 68% accepted, 20 enrolled. In 2017, 17 master's, 6 doctorates awarded. Terminal master's awarded for partial completion of doctoral program. *Degree requirements:* For master's, comprehensive exam; for doctorate, comprehensive exam,

thesis/dissertation. *Entrance requirements:* For master's, GRE General Test or MAT; for doctorate, GRE General Test. Additional exam requirements/recommendations for international students: Required—TOEFL (minimum score 100 iBT). *Application deadline:* For fall admission, 12/1 priority date for domestic and international students; for spring admission, 11/1 priority date for domestic and international students. Application fee: $65. Electronic applications accepted. *Financial support:* Research assistantships with full tuition reimbursements, teaching assistantships with partial tuition reimbursements, Federal Work-Study, scholarships/grants, and tuition waivers (full and partial) available. Support available to part-time students. Financial award applicants required to submit FAFSA. *Unit head:* Dr. Larry Ludlow, Department Chair, 617-552-4221, E-mail: ludlow@bc.edu. *Application contact:* Kimberly Rose, Graduate Admission Assistant, 617-552-4214, Fax: 617-552-0398, E-mail: roseki@bc.edu.

Brandeis University, Rabb School of Continuing Studies, Division of Graduate Professional Studies, Graduate Certificate in Learning Analytics Program, Waltham, MA 02454-9110. Offers Graduate Certificate. *Program availability:* Part-time-only, online only, 100% online. *Faculty:* 55 part-time/adjunct (18 women). *Students:* 1 (woman) part-time. Average age 37. *Entrance requirements:* For degree, three years of work experience; master's or doctoral degree in analytics, instructional design or a related field; master's degree from regionally-accredited U.S. institution or equivalent; official transcript(s) from every college or university attended; resume or curriculum vitae; statement of goals; letter of recommendation. Additional exam requirements/recommendations for international students: Required—TWE (minimum score 4.5), TOEFL (minimum scores: 600 paper-based, 100 iBT), IELTS (7), or PTE (68). *Application deadline:* For fall admission, 6/20 priority date for domestic and international students; for winter admission, 9/12 priority date for domestic and international students; for spring admission, 12/19 priority date for domestic and international students; for summer admission, 3/13 priority date for domestic and international students. Applications are processed on a rolling basis. Application fee: $75. Electronic applications accepted. *Expenses:* $1,178 per credit. *Financial support:* Applicants required to submit FAFSA. *Unit head:* Brian Salerno, Program Chair, 781-736-3443, E-mail: bsalerno@brandeis.edu. *Application contact:* Frances Stearns, Director of Student and Faculty Operations, 781-736-8785, E-mail: fstearns@brandeis.edu.

Brigham Young University, Graduate Studies, David O. McKay School of Education, Program in Educational Inquiry, Measurement, and Evaluation, Provo, UT 84602. Offers PhD. *Program availability:* Part-time, evening/weekend, online learning. *Faculty:* 10 full-time (4 women), 1 part-time/adjunct (0 women). *Students:* 20 full-time (9 women); includes 2 minority (1 Asian, non-Hispanic/Latino; 1 Hispanic/Latino). Average age 36. 13 applicants, 38% accepted, 4 enrolled. In 2017, 4 doctorates awarded. *Degree requirements:* For doctorate, comprehensive exam, thesis/dissertation. *Entrance requirements:* Additional exam requirements/recommendations for international students: Required—TOEFL. Electronic applications accepted. *Expenses:* Tuition: Full-time $6880; part-time $405 per credit hour. Tuition and fees vary according to course load, program and student's religious affiliation. *Financial support:* Fellowships, research assistantships, teaching assistantships, career-related internships or fieldwork, Federal Work-Study, institutionally sponsored loans, scholarships/grants, traineeships, health care benefits, tuition waivers, and unspecified assistantships available. Support available to part-time students. *Faculty research:* Educational research methods, structural equation modeling, quantitative methods, qualitative methods. *Unit head:* Dr. Richard R. Sudweeks, Program Coordinator, 801-422-7078, Fax: 801-422-0200, E-mail: richard_sudweeks@byu.edu. *Application contact:* Ashley C. Gordon, Program Manager, 801-422-4717, Fax: 801-422-0195, E-mail: eime@byu.edu. Website: http://education.byu.edu/eime

Cambridge College, School of Education, Boston, MA 02129. Offers autism specialist (M Ed); autism/behavior analyst (M Ed); behavior analyst (Post-Master's Certificate); behavioral management (M Ed); early childhood teacher (M Ed); education specialist in curriculum and instruction (CAGS); educational leadership (Ed D); elementary teacher (M Ed); English as a second language (M Ed, Certificate); general science (M Ed); health education (Post-Master's Certificate); health/family and consumer sciences (M Ed); history (M Ed); individualized (M Ed); information technology literacy (M Ed); instructional technology (M Ed); interdisciplinary studies (M Ed); library teacher (M Ed); literacy education (M Ed); mathematics (M Ed); mathematics specialist (Certificate); middle school mathematics and science (M Ed); school administration (M Ed, CAGS); school guidance counselor (M Ed); school nurse education (M Ed); school social worker/school adjustment counselor (M Ed); special education administrator (CAGS); special education/moderate disabilities (M Ed); teaching skills and methodologies (M Ed). *Program availability:* Part-time, evening/weekend, online learning. *Degree requirements:* For master's, thesis, internship/practicum (licensure program only); for doctorate, thesis/dissertation; for other advanced degree, thesis. *Entrance requirements:* For master's, interview, resume, documentation of licensure, 2 professional references; for doctorate, official transcripts, interview, resume, documentation of licensure (if any), written personal statement/essay, portfolio of scholarly and professional work, qualifying assessment, 2 professional references, health insurance, immunizations form; for other advanced degree, official transcripts, interview, resume, documentation of licensure (if any), written personal statement/essay, 2 professional references, health insurance, immunizations form. Additional exam requirements/recommendations for international students: Required—TOEFL (minimum score 550 paper-based; 79 iBT), Michigan English Language Assessment Battery (minimum score 85); Recommended—IELTS (minimum score 6). Electronic applications accepted. *Expenses:* Contact institution. *Faculty research:* Adult education, accelerated learning, mathematics education, brain compatible learning, special education and law.

Claremont Graduate University, Graduate Programs, School of Educational Studies, Claremont, CA 91711-6160. Offers Africana education (Certificate); education and policy (MA, PhD); higher education/student affairs (MA, PhD); human development (MA, PhD); public school administration (MA, PhD); quantitative evaluation (MA, PhD); special education (MA, PhD); teacher education (MA); teaching and learning (MA, PhD); urban leadership (PhD); MBA/PhD. PhD program offered jointly with San Diego State University. *Program availability:* Part-time. Terminal master's awarded for partial completion of doctoral program. *Entrance requirements:* For master's and doctorate, GRE General Test. Additional exam requirements/recommendations for international students: Required—TOEFL (minimum score 75 iBT). Electronic applications accepted. *Faculty research:* Education administration, K-12 and higher education, multicultural education, education policy, diversity in higher education, faculty issues.

Clemson University, Graduate School, College of Education, Department of Education and Human Development, Clemson, SC 29634. Offers counselor education (M Ed, Ed S), including mental health counseling, school counseling, student affairs (M Ed); learning sciences (PhD); literacy (M Ed); literacy, language and culture (PhD); special education (M Ed, MAT, PhD). *Program availability:* Part-time, evening/weekend, 100% online. *Faculty:* 32 full-time (22 women). *Students:* 445 full-time (355 women), 169 part-time (159 women); includes 126 minority (52 Black or African American, non-Hispanic/Latino; 16 Asian, non-Hispanic/Latino; 34 Hispanic/Latino; 24 Two or more races, non-Hispanic/Latino; 5 international. Average age 28. 401 applicants, 60% accepted, 135 enrolled. In 2017, 212 master's, 1 doctorate, 117 other advanced degrees awarded. *Degree requirements:* For master's, thesis (for some programs); for doctorate, comprehensive exam (for some programs), thesis/dissertation. *Entrance requirements:* For master's and doctorate, GRE General Test, unofficial transcripts, letters of recommendation. Additional exam requirements/recommendations for international students: Required—TOEFL (minimum score 80 iBT), IELTS (minimum score 7), PTE (minimum score 54). *Application deadline:* For fall admission, 3/1 priority date for domestic and international students; for spring admission, 10/1 priority date for domestic and international students. Applications are processed on a rolling basis. Application fee: $80 ($90 for international students). Electronic applications accepted. *Expenses:* $5,174 per semester full-time resident, $9,714 per semester full-time non-resident, $511 per credit hour part-time resident, $1,017 per credit hour part-time non-resident; $741 per credit hour online; other fees may apply per session. *Financial support:* In 2017–18, 84 students received support, including 9 fellowships with partial tuition reimbursements available (averaging $8,148 per year), 18 teaching assistantships with partial tuition reimbursements available (averaging $13,707 per year); career-related internships or fieldwork and unspecified assistantships also available. Financial award application deadline: 3/1. *Total annual research expenditures:* $1.2 million. *Unit head:* Dr. Debi Switzer, Department Chair, 864-656-5098, E-mail: debi@clemson.edu. *Application contact:* Julie Jones, Student Services Program Coordinator, 864-656-5096, E-mail: jgambre@clemson.edu.
Website: http://www.clemson.edu/education/departments/education-human-development/index.html

College of Saint Mary, Program in Education, Omaha, NE 68106. Offers assessment leadership (MSE); English as a second language (MSE). *Program availability:* Part-time. *Entrance requirements:* For master's, technology competency test or equivalent, minimum cumulative GPA of 3.0, teaching certificate, 2 letters of reference, resume.

Duquesne University, School of Education, Department of Educational Foundations and Leadership, Program in Educational Studies, Pittsburgh, PA 15282-0001. Offers educational studies (MS Ed); program evaluation (MS Ed). *Program availability:* Part-time, evening/weekend, 100% online. *Faculty:* 1 full-time (0 women). *Students:* 6 full-time (4 women), 13 part-time (10 women); includes 3 minority (all Black or African American, non-Hispanic/Latino), 11 international. Average age 37. 19 applicants, 95% accepted, 4 enrolled. In 2017, 5 master's awarded. *Degree requirements:* For master's, thesis optional. *Entrance requirements:* For master's, bachelor's degree. Additional exam requirements/recommendations for international students: Required—TOEFL (minimum score 550 paper-based), IELTS (minimum score 7). *Application deadline:* For fall admission, 8/15 for domestic students; for spring admission, 1/2 for domestic students. Applications are processed on a rolling basis. Application fee: $0. Electronic applications accepted. *Expenses:* $1,259 per credit. *Financial support:* Research assistantships available. Support available to part-time students. *Faculty research:* Online learning; impact of trauma on childhood and adolescent development; evaluation of educational programs; research in mathematics education; beliefs about classroom assessment. *Unit head:* Dr. Gibbs Kanyongo, Associate Professor, 412-396-5190, Fax: 412-396-5454, E-mail: kanyongo@duq.edu. *Application contact:* Kelly McGinley, Graduate Admissions Assistant, 412-396-1559, Fax: 412-396-5585, E-mail: mcginleyk@duq.edu.

Eastern Michigan University, Graduate School, College of Education, Department of Teacher Education, Programs in Educational Psychology and Assessment, Ypsilanti, MI 48197. Offers educational assessment (Graduate Certificate); learning technology and design (MA). *Accreditation:* NCATE. *Program availability:* Part-time, evening/weekend, online learning. *Students:* 4 full-time (all women), 26 part-time (24 women); includes 5 minority (3 Black or African American, non-Hispanic/Latino; 1 Hispanic/Latino; 1 Two or more races, non-Hispanic/Latino). Average age 32. 11 applicants, 82% accepted, 6 enrolled. In 2017, 9 master's, 1 other advanced degree awarded. *Degree requirements:* For master's, thesis or alternative. *Entrance requirements:* For master's, GRE. Additional exam requirements/recommendations for international students: Required—TOEFL. *Application deadline:* Applications are processed on a rolling basis. Application fee: $45. *Financial support:* Fellowships, research assistantships with full tuition reimbursements, teaching assistantships with full tuition reimbursements, career-related internships or fieldwork, Federal Work-Study, institutionally sponsored loans, scholarships/grants, tuition waivers (partial), and unspecified assistantships available. Support available to part-time students. Financial award applicants required to submit FAFSA. *Application contact:* Dr. Alane Starko, Coordinator, 734-487-3260, Fax: 734-487-2101, E-mail: astarko@emich.edu.

Florida State University, The Graduate School, College of Education, Department of Educational Leadership and Policy Studies, Tallahassee, FL 32306. Offers educational leadership and administration (Certificate); educational leadership and policy (MS, Ed D, PhD, Ed S), including education policy and evaluation (MS, Ed D, PhD), educational leadership and administration; foundations of education (MS, PhD), including history and philosophy of education, international and multicultural education; higher education (MS, PhD); institutional research (Certificate); program evaluation (Certificate). *Program availability:* Part-time, evening/weekend, 100% online, blended/hybrid learning, asynchronous, minimal on-campus study. *Faculty:* 19 full-time (15 women), 10 part-time/adjunct (7 women). *Students:* 151 full-time (105 women), 196 part-time (138 women); includes 127 minority (55 Black or African American, non-Hispanic/Latino; 4 Asian, non-Hispanic/Latino; 49 Hispanic/Latino; 19 Two or more races, non-Hispanic/Latino), 33 international. Average age 35. 229 applicants, 54% accepted, 66 enrolled. In 2017, 49 master's, 10 doctorates, 17 other advanced degrees awarded. *Degree requirements:* For master's, comprehensive exam, thesis optional; for doctorate, comprehensive exam, thesis/dissertation, diagnostic exam, preliminary exam, prospectus defense, dissertation defense. *Entrance requirements:* For master's, doctorate, and other advanced degree, GRE General Test, minimum GPA of 3.0. Additional exam requirements/recommendations for international students: Required—TOEFL (minimum score 550 paper-based, 80 iBT), IELTS (minimum score 6.5), Michigan English Language Assessment Battery (minimum score 77), or PTE (minimum score 55). Application fee: $30. Electronic applications accepted. *Financial support:* Fellowships, research assistantships, teaching assistantships, scholarships/grants, tuition waivers (full and partial), and unspecified assistantships available. Financial award application deadline: 1/15; financial award applicants required to submit FAFSA. *Faculty research:* Post-secondary success; leadership education; education policy; international education; multicultural education. *Unit head:* Dr. Robert A. Schwartz, Chair, 850-644-6885, Fax: 850-644-2725, E-mail: raschwartz@fsu.edu. *Application contact:* Linda Lyons, Academic Support Assistant, 850-644-7077, Fax: 850-644-1258, E-mail: ljlyons@fsu.edu.

Florida State University, The Graduate School, College of Education, Department of Educational Psychology and Learning Systems, Tallahassee, FL 32306. Offers counseling and human systems (PhD), including counseling psychology and school psychology; educational psychology (MS, PhD), including learning and cognition, sport psychology; human performance and technology (Certificate); instructional systems and learning technologies (MS, PhD); measurement and statistics (MS, PhD, Certificate); online instructional development (Certificate); MS/Ed S. *Program availability:* Part-time, evening/weekend, 100% online, blended/hybrid learning, asynchronous, minimal on-campus study. *Faculty:* 28 full-time (17 women), 12 part-time/adjunct (7 women). *Students:* 339 full-time (238 women), 136 part-time (93 women); includes 126 minority (47 Black or African American, non-Hispanic/Latino; 4 American Indian or Alaska Native, non-Hispanic/Latino; 7 Asian, non-Hispanic/Latino; 48 Hispanic/Latino; 20 Two or more races, non-Hispanic/Latino), 110 international. Average age 31. 419 applicants, 39% accepted, 82 enrolled. In 2017, 84 master's, 27 doctorates, 38 other advanced degrees awarded. Terminal master's awarded for partial completion of doctoral program. *Degree requirements:* For master's and Certificate, comprehensive exam, thesis optional; for doctorate, comprehensive exam, thesis/dissertation, diagnostic exam, preliminary exam, prospectus defense. *Entrance requirements:* For master's, doctorate, and Certificate, GRE General Test, minimum GPA of 3.0. Additional exam requirements/recommendations for international students: Required—TOEFL (minimum score 550 paper-based, 80 iBT), IELTS (minimum score 6.5) or Michigan English Language Assessment Battery (minimum score 77). Application fee: $30. Electronic applications accepted. *Financial support:* Fellowships, research assistantships, teaching assistantships, scholarships/grants, tuition waivers (full and partial), and unspecified assistantships available. Financial award application deadline: 1/15; financial award applicants required to submit FAFSA. *Faculty research:* Learning and cognition, counseling and school psychology, instructional systems, measurement and evaluation. *Unit head:* Dr. Betsy Becker, Chair, 850-644-4592, Fax: 850-644-8776, E-mail: bbecker@fsu.edu. *Application contact:* Deborah Kelly, Academic Program Specialist, 850-644-8046, Fax: 850-644-8781, E-mail: dhamkelly@fsu.edu.

Georgetown University, Master of Arts in Learning and Design Program, Washington, DC 20007. Offers MA. *Program availability:* Part-time, evening/weekend. *Students:* Average age 27. *Degree requirements:* For master's, design studio/capstone project, ePortfolio. *Entrance requirements:* For master's, GRE (recommended), personal/academic statement, writing sample, resume, 3 letters of recommendation (at least one professional and one faculty/professor). Additional exam requirements/recommendations for international students: Required—TOEFL (minimum score 550 paper-based; 80 iBT), IELTS (minimum score 7). *Application deadline:* For fall admission, 4/1 priority date for domestic students. Applications are processed on a rolling basis. Application fee: $90. Electronic applications accepted. *Financial support:* Scholarships/grants and unspecified assistantships available. Financial award application deadline: 4/1; financial award applicants required to submit FAFSA. *Unit head:* Dr. Edward J. Maloney, Founding Director. *Application contact:* Kimberly Luciano, Program Coordinator, 202-687-1882, E-mail: kl791@georgetown.edu.
Website: http://learninganddesign.georgetown.edu/

Georgia Southern University, Jack N. Averitt College of Graduate Studies, College of Education, Department of Curriculum, Foundations, and Reading, Statesboro, GA 30460. Offers curriculum studies (Ed D), including curriculum studies; evaluation, assessment, research, and learning (M Ed); reading education (M Ed, Ed S). *Accreditation:* NCATE. *Program availability:* Part-time, evening/weekend. *Faculty:* 22 full-time (13 women), 1 part-time/adjunct (0 women). *Students:* 29 full-time (22 women), 150 part-time (123 women); includes 47 minority (35 Black or African American, non-Hispanic/Latino; 2 Asian, non-Hispanic/Latino; 5 Hispanic/Latino; 5 Two or more races, non-Hispanic/Latino), 2 international. Average age 40. 7 applicants, 100% accepted, 7 enrolled. In 2017, 13 master's, 26 doctorates, 2 other advanced degrees awarded. *Degree requirements:* For master's, comprehensive exam; for doctorate, comprehensive exam, thesis/dissertation, exams. *Entrance requirements:* For master's, GRE General Test or MAT, minimum GPA of 2.5; for doctorate, GRE General Test or MAT, minimum GPA of 3.5, letters of reference, writing sample. Additional exam requirements/recommendations for international students: Required—TOEFL (minimum score 550 paper-based; 80 iBT), IELTS (minimum score 6). *Application deadline:* For fall admission, 3/1 priority date for domestic and international students; for spring admission, 10/1 priority date for domestic students, 10/1 for international students. Applications are processed on a rolling basis. Application fee: $50. Electronic applications accepted. *Expenses:* Tuition, state resident: full-time $4986; part-time $3324 per year. Tuition, nonresident: full-time $21,982; part-time $15,352 per year. *Required fees:* $2092; $1802 per credit hour. $901 per semester. Tuition and fees vary according to course load, campus/location and program. *Financial support:* In 2017–18, 7 students received support, including 1 research assistantship with full tuition reimbursement available (averaging $7,750 per year); fellowships, scholarships/grants, and unspecified assistantships also available. Financial award application deadline: 4/15; financial award applicants required to submit FAFSA. *Faculty research:* Curriculum theories, at-risk students, gifted female adolescents, cognitive mapping, faculty evaluation, learning environments, research methodology, social and cultural conditions of learning, preservice teacher education. *Unit head:* Dr. Kent Rittschof, Chair, 912-478-0698, Fax: 912-478-5382, E-mail: kent_r@georgiasouthern.edu. *Application contact:* Dr. Lydia Cross, Graduate Academic Services Center, 912-478-8664, E-mail: lcross@georgiasouthern.edu.
Website: http://coe.georgiasouthern.edu/cfr/

Georgia State University, College of Education and Human Development, Department of Educational Policy Studies, Program in Educational Research, Atlanta, GA 30302-3083. Offers MS, PhD. MS offered jointly with Department of Counseling and Psychological Services. *Accreditation:* NCATE. *Program availability:* Part-time. *Entrance requirements:* For master's and doctorate, GRE. *Application deadline:* Applications are processed on a rolling basis. Application fee: $50. Electronic applications accepted. *Expenses:* Tuition, state resident: full-time $7020. Tuition, nonresident: full-time $22,518. *Required fees:* $2128. Tuition and fees vary according to degree level and program. *Financial support:* Fellowships, research assistantships, teaching assistantships, career-related internships or fieldwork, scholarships/grants, health care benefits, tuition waivers (full), and unspecified assistantships available. Support available to part-time students. Financial award application deadline: 3/15. *Faculty research:* Program evaluation, item response

theory, quantitative research methodology, qualitative research methodology, gender and identity studies. *Unit head:* Dr. Janice Fournillier, Associate Professor, 404-413-8030, Fax: 404-413-8003, E-mail: jfournillier@gsu.edu. *Application contact:* Aishah Cowan, Administrative Academic Specialist, 404-413-8273, Fax: 404-413-8003, E-mail: acowan@gsu.edu.
Website: http://eps.education.gsu.edu/programs-courses/rms/educational-research-m-s/

Houston Baptist University, College of Education and Behavioral Sciences, Programs in Education, Houston, TX 77074-3298. Offers bilingual education (M Ed); counselor education (M Ed); curriculum and instruction (M Ed); curriculum and instruction (EC-6 bilingual) (M Ed); curriculum and instruction in all-level art, Spanish, music, or physical education (M Ed); curriculum and instruction in EC-6 and special education (EC-12) (M Ed); curriculum and instruction in instructional technology (M Ed); curriculum and instruction in mathematics, science, or social studies (4-8) (M Ed); curriculum and instruction with EC-6 generalist (M Ed); curriculum and instruction with English language arts and reading (4-8) (M Ed); educational administration (M Ed); educational diagnostician (M Ed); executive educational leadership (Ed D); higher education in business management (M Ed); higher education in Christian studies (M Ed); higher education in counseling (M Ed); higher education in educational technology (M Ed); reading (M Ed); special educational leadership (Ed D). *Program availability:* Part-time, evening/weekend, 100% online, blended/hybrid learning. *Students:* 83 full-time (65 women), 187 part-time (156 women); includes 189 minority (114 Black or African American, non-Hispanic/Latino; 2 American Indian or Alaska Native, non-Hispanic/Latino; 9 Asian, non-Hispanic/Latino; 58 Hispanic/Latino; 6 Two or more races, non-Hispanic/Latino; 7 international. Average age 36. 309 applicants, 31% accepted, 70 enrolled. In 2017, 92 master's awarded. *Degree requirements:* For master's, comprehensive exam; for doctorate, thesis/dissertation. *Entrance requirements:* For master's, minimum GPA of 2.75, two recommendations, resume, bachelor's degree conferred transcript; interview (for non-certified teachers); for doctorate, GRE, 5 letters of recommendation. Additional exam requirements/recommendations for international students: Required—TOEFL (minimum score 80 iBT), IELTS (minimum score 6.5). *Application deadline:* For fall admission, 8/1 for domestic students, 6/1 for international students; for spring admission, 1/1 for domestic students, 11/1 for international students; for summer admission, 5/1 for domestic students, 3/1 for international students. Applications are processed on a rolling basis. Application fee: $0 ($100 for international students). Electronic applications accepted. Application fee is waived when completed online. *Expenses:* $22,000 tuition; $4,500 fees (general, technology and parking). *Financial support:* In 2017–18, 59 students received support. Research assistantships, teaching assistantships, Federal Work-Study, and scholarships/grants available. Support available to part-time students. Financial award application deadline: 4/1; financial award applicants required to submit FAFSA. *Faculty research:* Autism and inclusion, integrating technology into instruction, school change and leadership trust. *Unit head:* Dr. Charlotte Fontenot, Director, Graduate Programs, 281-649-3078, Fax: 281-649-3361, E-mail: cfontenot@hbu.edu. *Application contact:* Kristy Wright, Administrative Assistant for Graduate Programs, 281-649-3094, Fax: 281-649-3361, E-mail: kwright@hbu.edu.
Website: http://www.hbu.edu/MED

Indiana University Bloomington, School of Education, Department of Counseling and Educational Psychology, Bloomington, IN 47405-1006. Offers counseling (MS, PhD, Ed S); counselor education (MS, Ed S); educational psychology (MS, PhD); inquiry methodology (PhD); learning and developmental sciences (MS, PhD); school psychology (PhD, Ed S). *Accreditation:* ACA (one or more programs are accredited); APA (one or more programs are accredited); NCATE. Terminal master's awarded for partial completion of doctoral program. *Degree requirements:* For master's, thesis optional; for doctorate, thesis/dissertation; for Ed S, comprehensive exam or project. *Entrance requirements:* For master's, doctorate, and Ed S, GRE General Test. Additional exam requirements/recommendations for international students: Required—TOEFL. Electronic applications accepted. *Faculty research:* Counseling psychology, inquiry methodology, school psychology, learning sciences, human development, educational psychology.

Indiana University Bloomington, School of Education, Program in Inquiry Methodology, Bloomington, IN 47405-7000. Offers PhD.

Iowa State University of Science and Technology, Department of Educational Leadership and Policy Studies, Ames, IA 50011. Offers counselor education (M Ed, MS); educational administration (M Ed, MS); educational leadership (PhD); higher education (M Ed, MS); organizational learning and human resource development (M Ed, MS); research and evaluation (MS); student affairs (MS). *Degree requirements:* For master's, thesis or alternative; for doctorate, thesis/dissertation. *Entrance requirements:* For master's and doctorate, GRE General Test. Additional exam requirements/recommendations for international students: Required—TOEFL (minimum score 560 paper-based; 83 iBT), IELTS (minimum score 6.5). Electronic applications accepted.

James Madison University, The Graduate School, College of Education, Program in Adult Education and Human Resource Development, Harrisonburg, VA 22801. Offers higher education (MS Ed); human resource management (MS Ed); individualized (MS Ed); instructional design (MS Ed); leadership and facilitation (MS Ed); program evaluation and measurement (MS Ed). *Accreditation:* NCATE. *Program availability:* Part-time, evening/weekend. *Students:* 11 full-time (7 women), 12 part-time (10 women); includes 7 minority (4 Black or African American, non-Hispanic/Latino; 1 Hispanic/Latino; 2 Two or more races, non-Hispanic/Latino), 1 international. Average age 30. In 2017, 3 master's awarded. Application fee: $55. Electronic applications accepted. *Expenses:* Tuition, state resident: full-time $10,512; part-time $438 per credit hour. Tuition, nonresident: full-time $28,358; part-time $1162 per credit hour. *Required fees:* $1128. *Financial support:* In 2017–18, 10 students received support. Teaching assistantships, Federal Work-Study, and 10 assistantships (averaging $7911) available. Financial award application deadline: 3/1; financial award applicants required to submit FAFSA. *Unit head:* Dr. Jane B. Thall, Department Head, 540-568-5531, E-mail: thalljb@jmu.edu. *Application contact:* Lynette D. Michael, Director of Graduate Admissions, 540-568-6131 Ext. 6395, Fax: 540-568-7860, E-mail: michaeld@jmu.edu.

James Madison University, The Graduate School, College of Health and Behavioral Studies, Program in Assessment and Measurement, Harrisonburg, VA 22801. Offers PhD. *Program availability:* Part-time. *Students:* 9 full-time (4 women), 2 part-time (both women); includes 2 minority (1 Black or African American, non-Hispanic/Latino; 1 Asian, non-Hispanic/Latino). Average age 30. In 2017, 6 doctorates awarded. Application fee: $55. Electronic applications accepted. *Expenses:* Tuition, state resident: full-time $10,512; part-time $438 per credit hour. Tuition, nonresident: full-time $28,358; part-time $1162 per credit hour. *Required fees:* $1128. *Financial support:* In 2017–18, 9 students received support, including 1 fellowship; Federal Work-Study, unspecified assistantships, and 9 doctoral assistantships (stipend varies) also available. Financial award application deadline: 3/1; financial award applicants required to submit FAFSA. *Unit head:* Dr. Deborah L. Bandalos, Graduate Program Director, 540-568-7132, E-mail: bandaldl@jmu.edu. *Application contact:* Lynette D. Michael, Director of Graduate Admissions and Student Records, 540-568-6131 Ext. 6395, Fax: 540-568-7860, E-mail: michaeld@jmu.edu.
Website: http://www.psyc.jmu.edu/assessment/

Kent State University, College of Education, Health and Human Services, School of Foundations, Leadership and Administration, Program in Evaluation and Measurement, Kent, OH 44242-0001. Offers M Ed, PhD. *Degree requirements:* For doctorate, comprehensive exam, thesis/dissertation. *Entrance requirements:* For master's, minimum GPA of 2.75, 2 letters of reference, goals statement; for doctorate, GRE, minimum GPA of 3.5 from master's degree, resume, 2 letters of reference, goal statement. Additional exam requirements/recommendations for international students: Required—TOEFL (minimum score 550 paper-based; 80 iBT). *Expenses:* Tuition, state resident: full-time $11,310; part-time $515 per credit hour. Tuition, nonresident: full-time $20,396; part-time $928 per credit hour. *International tuition:* $18,544 full-time.

Louisiana State University and Agricultural & Mechanical College, Graduate School, College of Human Sciences and Education, Department of Educational Theory, Policy and Practice, Baton Rouge, LA 70803. Offers counseling (M Ed, MA, Ed S); educational administration (M Ed, MA, PhD, Ed S); educational technology (MA); elementary education (M Ed, MAT); higher education (PhD); research methodology (PhD); secondary education (M Ed, MAT). *Accreditation:* ACA (one or more programs are accredited); NCATE. *Faculty:* 34 full-time (22 women). *Students:* 213 full-time (159 women), 228 part-time (178 women); includes 164 minority (123 Black or African American, non-Hispanic/Latino; 7 Asian, non-Hispanic/Latino; 27 Hispanic/Latino; 1 Native Hawaiian or other Pacific Islander, non-Hispanic/Latino; 6 Two or more races, non-Hispanic/Latino), 13 international. Average age 32. 231 applicants, 61% accepted, 82 enrolled. In 2017, 125 master's, 26 doctorates, 28 other advanced degrees awarded. *Financial support:* In 2017–18, 3 fellowships (averaging $12,129 per year), 2 research assistantships (averaging $16,019 per year), 96 teaching assistantships (averaging $16,061 per year) were awarded. *Total annual research expenditures:* $356,867.

Loyola University Chicago, School of Education, Program in Research Methods, Chicago, IL 60660. Offers MA, PhD, Certificate. PhD offered through the Graduate School. *Program availability:* Part-time, evening/weekend. *Faculty:* 4 full-time (3 women), 1 part-time/adjunct (0 women). *Students:* 8 full-time (6 women), 3 part-time (0 women); includes 1 minority (Hispanic/Latino), 1 international. Average age 35. 18 applicants, 33% accepted, 2 enrolled. In 2017, 1 master's, 7 doctorates awarded. *Degree requirements:* For master's, comprehensive exam (M Ed), thesis (MA); for doctorate, comprehensive exam, thesis/dissertation. *Entrance requirements:* For master's, GRE General Test, letters of recommendation, resume, minimum GPA of 3.0; for doctorate, GRE General Test, interview. Additional exam requirements/recommendations for international students: Required—TOEFL (minimum score 550 paper-based; 79 iBT). *Application deadline:* For fall admission, 12/1 for domestic and international students. Applications are processed on a rolling basis. Application fee: $50. Electronic applications accepted. Application fee is waived when completed online. *Expenses:* $949 per semester hour, $2,847 per course, $8,541-$11,388 full-time semester tuition; $432 per semester fees, $225 additional fees (first semester only). *Financial support:* In 2017–18, 2 research assistantships with full tuition reimbursements (averaging $14,000 per year), 10 teaching assistantships (averaging $4,000 per year) were awarded; institutionally sponsored loans, scholarships/grants, health care benefits, and unspecified assistantships also available. Support available to part-time students. Financial award application deadline: 2/1; financial award applicants required to submit FAFSA. *Faculty research:* Circular statistics, program evaluation, psychological measurement, infant attachment, adolescent development. *Unit head:* Dr. Leanne Kallemeyn, Program Chair, 312-915-6909, E-mail: lkallemeyn@luc.edu. *Application contact:* Mirtza Campbell, Information Contact, 312-915-8907, E-mail: mcampbell11@luc.edu.

McNeese State University, Doré School of Graduate Studies, Burton College of Education, Department of Education Professions, Lake Charles, LA 70609. Offers curriculum and instruction (M Ed), including academically gifted education, elementary education, reading, secondary education, special education; early childhood education grades PK-3 (Postbaccalaureate Certificate); educational leadership (M Ed, Ed S), including educational leadership, educational technology (Ed S); educational technology leadership (M Ed); elementary education (MAT); elementary education grades 1-5 (Postbaccalaureate Certificate); instructional technology (MS); middle school education grades 4-8 (Postbaccalaureate Certificate), including middle school education grades 4-8; multiple levels grades K-12 (Postbaccalaureate Certificate), including multiple levels grades K-12; school counseling (M Ed); school librarian (Postbaccalaureate Certificate); secondary education (MAT); secondary education grades 6-12 (Postbaccalaureate Certificate); special education (M Ed), including advanced professional, autism, educational diagnostician; special education - mild/moderate grades 1-12 (MAT); special education, mild/moderate for elementary education grades 1-5 (Postbaccalaureate Certificate). *Program availability:* Evening/weekend. *Entrance requirements:* For master's, GRE. *Application deadline:* For fall admission, 5/15 priority date for domestic and international students; for spring admission, 10/15 priority date for domestic and international students. Applications are processed on a rolling basis. Application fee: $20 ($30 for international students). *Financial support:* Application deadline: 5/1. *Unit head:* Dr. Deborah King, Department Head, 337-475-5437, Fax: 337-475-5402, E-mail: deborah@mcneese.edu. *Application contact:* Dr. Dustin M. Hebert, Director of Dore' School of Graduate Studies, 337-475-5396, Fax: 337-475-5397, E-mail: admissions@mcneese.edu.

Michigan State University, The Graduate School, College of Education, Department of Counseling, Educational Psychology and Special Education, East Lansing, MI 48824. Offers counseling (MA); educational psychology and educational technology (PhD); educational technology (MA); measurement and quantitative methods (PhD); rehabilitation counseling (MA); rehabilitation counselor education (PhD); school psychology (MA, PhD, Ed S); special education (MA, PhD). *Accreditation:* APA (one or more programs are accredited); CORE (one or more programs are accredited). *Program availability:* Part-time. *Entrance requirements:* Additional exam requirements/recommendations for international students: Required—TOEFL. Electronic applications accepted.

Missouri State University, Graduate College, College of Education, Department of Counseling, Leadership, and Special Education, Program in Counseling and Assessment, Springfield, MO 65897. Offers Ed S. *Program availability:* Part-time. *Faculty:* 8 full-time (5 women), 2 part-time/adjunct (both women). *Students:* 3 part-time (all women); includes 1 minority (Hispanic/Latino). Average age 28. 5 applicants. In 2017, 1 Ed S awarded. *Degree requirements:* For Ed S, comprehensive exam. *Entrance requirements:* For degree, GRE. Additional exam requirements/recommendations for international students: Required—TOEFL (minimum score 550 paper-based; 79 iBT), IELTS (minimum score 6). *Application deadline:* For fall admission, 2/1 for domestic and international students. Application fee: $35 ($50 for international students). Electronic applications accepted. *Expenses:* Tuition, state resident: full-time $2915; part-time $2021 per credit hour. Tuition, nonresident: full-time $5354; part-time $3647 per credit hour. *International tuition:* $11,992 full-time. *Required fees:* $173; $173 per credit hour. Tuition and fees vary according to class time, course level, course load, degree level, campus/location and program. *Financial support:* Federal Work-Study, institutionally sponsored loans, scholarships/grants, and unspecified assistantships available. Financial award application deadline: 3/31; financial award applicants required to submit FAFSA. *Unit head:* Dr. James Satterfield, Department Head, 417-836-5392, Fax: 417-

836-4918, E-mail: clse@missouristate.edu. *Application contact:* Stephanie Praschan, Director, Graduate Enrollment Management, 417-836-5330, Fax: 417-836-6200, E-mail: stephaniepraschan@missouristate.edu.
Website: http://education.missouristate.edu/assessment/

Missouri Western State University, Program in Assessment, St. Joseph, MO 64507-2294. Offers K-12 cross-categorical special education (MAS); TESOL (MAS, Graduate Certificate); writing (MAS). *Program availability:* Part-time. *Students:* 29 part-time (25 women); includes 1 minority (Black or African American, non-Hispanic/Latino). Average age 38. 8 applicants, 100% accepted, 4 enrolled. In 2017, 9 master's, 3 other advanced degrees awarded. *Entrance requirements:* For master's, minimum GPA of 2.75. Additional exam requirements/recommendations for international students: Recommended—TOEFL (minimum score 79 iBT), IELTS (minimum score 6). *Application deadline:* For fall admission, 7/15 for domestic and international students; for spring admission, 10/1 for domestic and international students; for summer admission, 3/15 for domestic students. Applications are processed on a rolling basis. Application fee: $45 ($50 for international students). Electronic applications accepted. *Expenses:* Tuition, state resident: full-time $6391; part-time $336 per credit hour. Tuition, nonresident: full-time $11,483; part-time $604 per credit hour. *Required fees:* $542; $99 per credit hour. $176 per semester. One-time fee: $45. Tuition and fees vary according to course load and program. *Financial support:* Scholarships/grants and unspecified assistantships available. Support available to part-time students. *Unit head:* Dr. Susan Bashinski, Director of Graduate Programs in Education, 816-271-5629, E-mail: sbashinski@missouriwestern.edu. *Application contact:* Dr. Benjamin D. Caldwell, Dean of the Graduate School, 816-271-4394, Fax: 816-271-4525, E-mail: graduate@missouriwestern.edu.
Website: https://www.missouriwestern.edu/masa/

Montclair State University, The Graduate School, College of Education and Human Services, Program Evaluation Certificate Program, Montclair, NJ 07043-1624. Offers Certificate.

New Mexico State University, College of Education, Department of Counseling and Educational Psychology, Las Cruces, NM 88003. Offers counseling psychology (PhD); educational diagnostics (MA), including counseling and guidance, educational diagnostics; school psychology (Ed S). *Accreditation:* ACA; APA (one or more programs are accredited); NCATE. *Program availability:* Part-time, evening/weekend. *Faculty:* 11 full-time (9 women), 3 part-time/adjunct (all women). *Students:* 80 full-time (57 women), 23 part-time (17 women); includes 68 minority (3 Black or African American, non-Hispanic/Latino; 3 American Indian or Alaska Native, non-Hispanic/Latino; 5 Asian, non-Hispanic/Latino; 56 Hispanic/Latino; 1 Two or more races, non-Hispanic/Latino), 1 international. Average age 31. 103 applicants, 59% accepted, 34 enrolled. In 2017, 18 master's, 5 doctorates, 6 other advanced degrees awarded. *Degree requirements:* For master's, comprehensive exam, thesis optional, internship; for doctorate, comprehensive exam, thesis/dissertation, internship; for Ed S, comprehensive exam, thesis or alternative, internship. *Entrance requirements:* For master's, doctorate, and Ed S, GRE General Test, minimum GPA of 3.0. Additional exam requirements/recommendations for international students: Required—TOEFL (minimum score 550 paper-based; 79 iBT), IELTS (minimum score 6.5). *Application deadline:* For fall admission, 12/15 for domestic and international students; for spring admission, 2/1 priority date for domestic students, 2/1 for international students. Application fee: $40 ($50 for international students). Electronic applications accepted. *Expenses:* Tuition, state resident: full-time $4390. Tuition, nonresident: full-time $15,309. *Required fees:* $853. *Financial support:* In 2017–18, 72 students received support, including 4 fellowships (averaging $4,390 per year), 2 research assistantships (averaging $15,197 per year), 25 teaching assistantships (averaging $14,416 per year); career-related internships or fieldwork, Federal Work-Study, scholarships/grants, traineeships, health care benefits, and unspecified assistantships also available. Support available to part-time students. Financial award application deadline: 3/1. *Faculty research:* Multicultural counseling and training, school and counseling psychology, social justice, integrated primary care behavioral health training, mental health disparities. *Total annual research expenditures:* $110,485. *Unit head:* Dr. Barbara Gormley, Department Head, 575-646-2121, Fax: 575-646-8035, E-mail: bgormley@nmsu.edu. *Application contact:* Norma Arrieta, Student Program Coordinator, 575-646-2121, Fax: 575-646-8035, E-mail: cep@nmsu.edu.
Website: http://cep.education.nmsu.edu

New Mexico State University, College of Education, Department of Curriculum and Instruction, Las Cruces, NM 88003. Offers bilingual education (MA); curriculum and instruction (MA, Ed D, PhD); early childhood education (MA); educational diagnostics (Ed S); language, literacy and culture (MA); learning design and technologies (MA); teaching (MAT), including dance, Spanish; teaching English to speakers of other languages (MA). *Accreditation:* NCATE. *Program availability:* Part-time, evening/weekend, 100% online. *Faculty:* 22 full-time (17 women), 7 part-time/adjunct (2 women). *Students:* 113 full-time (79 women), 194 part-time (138 women); includes 171 minority (15 Black or African American, non-Hispanic/Latino; 3 American Indian or Alaska Native, non-Hispanic/Latino; 4 Asian, non-Hispanic/Latino; 142 Hispanic/Latino; 7 Two or more races, non-Hispanic/Latino), 37 international. Average age 36. 106 applicants, 80% accepted, 56 enrolled. In 2017, 82 master's, 15 doctorates, 1 other advanced degree awarded. *Entrance requirements:* For master's, minimum cumulative GPA of 3.0; for doctorate, portfolio, minimum cumulative GPA of 3.0. Additional exam requirements/recommendations for international students: Required—TOEFL (minimum score 550 paper-based; 79 iBT), IELTS (minimum score 6.5). *Application deadline:* For fall admission, 12/15 priority date for domestic and international students; for spring admission, 11/1 for domestic students. Applications are processed on a rolling basis. Application fee: $40 ($50 for international students). Electronic applications accepted. *Expenses:* Tuition, state resident: full-time $4390. Tuition, nonresident: full-time $15,309. *Required fees:* $853. *Financial support:* In 2017–18, 97 students received support, including 2 fellowships (averaging $4,390 per year), 1 research assistantship (averaging $17,368 per year), 10 teaching assistantships (averaging $17,489 per year); career-related internships or fieldwork, Federal Work-Study, scholarships/grants, traineeships, health care benefits, and unspecified assistantships also available. Support available to part-time students. Financial award application deadline: 3/1. *Faculty research:* STEM education, bilingual and English as a second language education, critical pedagogy/multicultural education, learning design and technology, early childhood education. *Total annual research expenditures:* $13,518. *Unit head:* Dr. David Rutledge, Department Head, 575-646-5411, Fax: 575-646-5436, E-mail: rutledge@nmsu.edu. *Application contact:* Dr. David Rutledge, Associate Department Head for Graduate Programs, 575-646-5411, Fax: 575-646-5436, E-mail: rutledge@nmsu.edu.
Website: http://tpal.nmsu.edu/

North Carolina State University, Graduate School, College of Education, Department of Educational Leadership and Policy Studies, Program in Educational Research and Policy Analysis, Raleigh, NC 27695. Offers PhD. *Degree requirements:* For doctorate, thesis/dissertation. *Entrance requirements:* For doctorate, GRE General Test, minimum GPA of 3.0, interview, sample of work. Electronic applications accepted.

Ohio University, Graduate College, Gladys W. and David H. Patton College of Education and Human Services, Department of Educational Studies, Athens, OH 45701-2979. Offers computer education and technology (M Ed); educational administration (M Ed, Ed D); educational research and evaluation (M Ed, PhD); instructional technology (PhD). *Program availability:* Part-time, evening/weekend, online learning. *Degree requirements:* For master's, thesis or alternative; for doctorate, comprehensive exam, thesis/dissertation. *Entrance requirements:* For master's, GRE General Test (if GPA less than 2.9); for doctorate, GRE General Test, GRE Subject Test, minimum GPA of 2.9, work experience, 3 letters of reference, autobiography. Additional exam requirements/recommendations for international students: Required—TOEFL (minimum score 550 paper-based; 80 iBT) or IELTS (minimum score 6.5). Electronic applications accepted. *Faculty research:* Race, class and gender; computer programs; development and organization theory; evaluation/development of instruments, leadership.

Old Dominion University, Darden College of Education, Program in Educational Psychology and Program Evaluation, Norfolk, VA 23529. Offers education (PhD), including educational psychology, program evaluation. *Program availability:* Part-time, evening/weekend. *Faculty:* 4 full-time (2 women). *Students:* 6 full-time (all women), 4 part-time (all women); includes 3 minority (1 Black or African American, non-Hispanic/Latino; 1 Asian, non-Hispanic/Latino; 1 Hispanic/Latino), 1 international. Average age 38. 6 applicants, 50% accepted, 3 enrolled. *Degree requirements:* For doctorate, comprehensive exam, thesis/dissertation. *Entrance requirements:* Additional exam requirements/recommendations for international students: Required—TOEFL. *Application deadline:* Applications are processed on a rolling basis. Application fee: $50. Electronic applications accepted. *Expenses:* Contact institution. *Financial support:* In 2017–18, 5 students received support, including 4 fellowships with full tuition reimbursements available (averaging $15,000 per year), 10 research assistantships with full tuition reimbursements available (averaging $15,000 per year), 2 teaching assistantships with full tuition reimbursements available (averaging $15,000 per year); unspecified assistantships also available. Financial award application deadline: 2/1. *Faculty research:* Motivation, self-regulated learning, distance learning, calibration, STEM. *Total annual research expenditures:* $200,000. *Unit head:* Shana Pribesh, Graduate Program Director, 757-683-6684, E-mail: spribesh@odu.edu. *Application contact:* Nechell Bonds, Director of Admissions, 757-683-3685, Fax: 757-683-3255, E-mail: gradadmit@odu.edu.
Website: http://www.odu.edu/efl/academics/eppe

Rutgers University–New Brunswick, Graduate School of Education, Department of Educational Psychology, Program in Educational Statistics, Measurement and Evaluation, Piscataway, NJ 08854-8097. Offers Ed M. *Program availability:* Part-time, evening/weekend. *Entrance requirements:* For master's, GRE General Test, 3 letters of recommendation. Additional exam requirements/recommendations for international students: Required—TOEFL (minimum score 550 paper-based; 83 iBT). Electronic applications accepted. *Faculty research:* Program evaluation of student assessment, Type I error and power comparisons, test performance factors, theory building in participatory program evaluation, test validity in higher education admissions.

Seton Hall University, College of Education and Human Services, Department of Education Leadership, Management and Policy, South Orange, NJ 07079-2697. Offers college student personnel administration (MA); education research, assessment and program evaluation (PhD); higher education administration (Ed D, PhD); human resource training and development (MA); K–12 administration and supervision (Ed D, Exec Ed D, Ed S); K–12 leadership, management and policy (Ed D, Exec Ed D, Ed S). *Program availability:* Part-time, evening/weekend, blended/hybrid learning. *Degree requirements:* For master's, comprehensive exam, thesis or alternative; for doctorate, thesis/dissertation, oral exam, written exam; for Ed S, internship, research project. *Entrance requirements:* For master's, GRE or MAT, minimum GPA of 3.0; for doctorate, GRE or MAT, interview, minimum GPA of 3.5; for Ed S, GRE or MAT, minimum GPA of 3.5. Additional exam requirements/recommendations for international students: Required—TOEFL. *Expenses:* Contact institution.

Southern Connecticut State University, School of Graduate Studies, School of Education, Department of Educational Leadership, New Haven, CT 06515-1355. Offers educational leadership (Ed D, Diploma); research, statistics, and measurement (MS). *Program availability:* Part-time, evening/weekend. *Entrance requirements:* For degree, master's degree, minimum GPA of 3.0, writing sample. Electronic applications accepted.

Southwestern Oklahoma State University, College of Professional and Graduate Studies, School of Behavioral Sciences and Education, Specialization in School Psychometry, Weatherford, OK 73096-3098. Offers M Ed. M Ed distance learning degree program offered to Oklahoma residents only. *Accreditation:* NCATE. *Program availability:* Part-time, evening/weekend. *Degree requirements:* For master's, exam. *Entrance requirements:* For master's, GRE General Test or minimum undergraduate GPA of 3.0, portfolio. Additional exam requirements/recommendations for international students: Required—TOEFL.

Sul Ross State University, College of Professional Studies, Department of Education, Program in Educational Diagnostics, Alpine, TX 79832. Offers M Ed, Certificate. *Program availability:* Part-time, evening/weekend. *Degree requirements:* For master's, thesis optional. *Entrance requirements:* For master's, GMAT or GRE General Test, minimum GPA of 2.5 in last 60 hours of undergraduate work.

Sul Ross State University, Rio Grande College of Sul Ross State University, Alpine, TX 79832. Offers business administration (MBA); teacher education (M Ed), including bilingual education, counseling, educational diagnostics, elementary education, general education, reading, school administration, secondary education. *Program availability:* Part-time, evening/weekend, online learning. *Degree requirements:* For master's, comprehensive exam, thesis optional, minimum GPA of 3.0. *Entrance requirements:* For master's, GMAT or GRE General Test, minimum GPA of 2.5 in last 60 hours of undergraduate work. Additional exam requirements/recommendations for international students: Required—TOEFL.

Syracuse University, School of Education, Programs in Instructional Design, Development, and Evaluation, Syracuse, NY 13244. Offers MS, PhD, CAS. *Program availability:* Part-time. *Students:* Average age 34. *Degree requirements:* For master's, thesis or alternative; for doctorate, comprehensive exam, thesis/dissertation. *Entrance requirements:* For master's, GRE or MAT, baccalaureate degree from regionally-accredited college/university, statement of goals, three letters of recommendation, transcripts; for doctorate, GRE, master's degree in instructional design or equivalent, statement of goals, three letters of recommendation, transcripts; for CAS, GRE (recommended), master's degree in instructional design or equivalent, statement of goals, three letters of recommendation, transcripts. Additional exam requirements/recommendations for international students: Required—TOEFL (minimum score 100 iBT). *Application deadline:* For fall admission, 1/15 priority date for domestic and international students; for spring admission, 10/15 priority date for domestic and international students. Applications are processed on a rolling basis. Application fee: $75. Electronic applications accepted. *Financial support:* Fellowships with full tuition reimbursements, research assistantships, teaching assistantships, career-related internships or fieldwork, and scholarships/grants available. Financial award application

Educational Measurement and Evaluation

deadline: 1/15. *Faculty research:* Digital media production, technologies for instructional settings, strategies in educational project management, educational technology in international settings. *Unit head:* Dr. Jing Lei, Chair, 315-443-3703, E-mail: jlei@syr.edu. *Application contact:* Speranza Migliore, Graduate Admissions Recruiter, 315-443-2505, E-mail: gradrcrt@syr.edu.
Website: http://soe.syr.edu/academic/
Instructional_Design_Development_and_Evaluation/

Teachers College, Columbia University, Department of Human Development, New York, NY 10027-6696. Offers applied statistics (MS); cognitive studies in education (MA, Ed D, PhD); developmental psychology (MA, Ed D, PhD); educational psychology-human cognition and learning (Ed M, MA, Ed D, PhD); learning analytics (MS); measurement and evaluation (ME, Ed D, PhD); measurement, evaluation, and statistics (MA, MS, Ed D, PhD). *Program availability:* Part-time. *Students:* 155 full-time (105 women), 135 part-time (106 women); includes 93 minority (26 Black or African American, non-Hispanic/Latino; 44 Asian, non-Hispanic/Latino; 21 Hispanic/Latino; 2 Two or more races, non-Hispanic/Latino), 118 international. Average age 29. 459 applicants, 53% accepted, 100 enrolled. *Unit head:* Jim Corter, Chair, E-mail: jec34@tc.columbia.edu. *Application contact:* David Estrella, Director of Admission, 212-678-3305, E-mail: estrella@tc.columbia.edu.
Website: http://www.tc.columbia.edu/human-development/

Teachers College of San Joaquin, Master's Program in Education, Stockton, CA 95206. Offers early education (M Ed); educational inquiry (M Ed); educational leadership and school development (M Ed); science, technology, engineering, and mathematics (M Ed); special education (M Ed).

Tennessee Technological University, College of Graduate Studies, College of Education, Department of Curriculum and Instruction, Program in Exceptional Learning, Cookeville, TN 38505. Offers applied behavior analysis (PhD); literacy (PhD); program planning and evaluation (PhD); STEM education (PhD). *Program availability:* Part-time, evening/weekend. *Students:* 9 full-time (4 women), 32 part-time (24 women); includes 2 minority (1 Black or African American, non-Hispanic/Latino; 1 Two or more races, non-Hispanic/Latino), 4 international. 24 applicants, 54% accepted, 11 enrolled. In 2017, 10 doctorates awarded. *Degree requirements:* For doctorate, comprehensive exam, thesis/dissertation. *Entrance requirements:* For doctorate, GRE, minimum GPA of 3.0. Additional exam requirements/recommendations for international students: Required—TOEFL (minimum score 550 paper-based; 79 iBT), IELTS (minimum score 5.5), PTE (minimum score 53), or TOEIC (Test of English as an International Communication). *Application deadline:* For fall admission, 8/1 for domestic students, 5/1 for international students; for spring admission, 12/1 for domestic students, 10/1 for international students; for summer admission, 5/1 for domestic students, 2/1 for international students. Applications are processed on a rolling basis. Application fee: $35 ($40 for international students). Electronic applications accepted. *Expenses:* Tuition, state resident: full-time $9925; part-time $565 per credit hour. Tuition, nonresident: full-time $22,993; part-time $1291 per credit hour. *Financial support:* Fellowships, research assistantships, and teaching assistantships available. Financial award application deadline: 4/1. *Unit head:* Dr. Lisa Zagumny, Director, 931-372-3078, Fax: 931-372-3517, E-mail: lzagumny@tntech.edu. *Application contact:* Shelia K. Kendrick, Coordinator of Graduate Studies, 931-372-3808, Fax: 931-372-3497, E-mail: skendrick@tntech.edu.
Website: https://www.tntech.edu/education/elphd/

Texas A&M University–San Antonio, Department of Educator and Leadership Preparation, San Antonio, TX 78224. Offers bilingual education (MS); early childhood education (M Ed); educational administration (MA); reading specialization (MS); special education (M Ed), including educational diagnostician. *Program availability:* Part-time, evening/weekend, online learning. *Faculty:* 19 full-time (14 women), 8 part-time/adjunct (2 women). *Students:* 24 full-time (21 women), 188 part-time (143 women); includes 163 minority (7 Black or African American, non-Hispanic/Latino; 1 Asian, non-Hispanic/Latino; 149 Hispanic/Latino; 6 Two or more races, non-Hispanic/Latino), 1 international. Average age 36. 191 applicants, 62% accepted, 67 enrolled. In 2017, 70 master's awarded. *Degree requirements:* For master's, comprehensive exam, thesis or alternative. *Entrance requirements:* For master's, GRE (Quantitative and Verbal) or MAT. Additional exam requirements/recommendations for international students: Required—TOEFL (minimum score 550 paper-based; 79 iBT), IELTS (minimum score 6). *Application deadline:* For fall admission, 3/15 priority date for domestic and international students; for spring admission, 11/1 priority date for domestic and international students; for summer admission, 4/1 priority date for domestic and international students. Applications are processed on a rolling basis. Application fee: $35 ($50 for international students). Electronic applications accepted. *Expenses:* Tuition, state resident: full-time $3475; part-time $1930 per semester. Tuition, nonresident: full-time $10,945; part-time $6080 per semester. *Required fees:* $2148; $1412 per year. $706 per semester. Tuition and fees vary according to course load. *Financial support:* In 2017–18, 16 students received support. Research assistantships, Federal Work-Study, scholarships/grants, and tuition waivers available. Financial award application deadline: 3/15; financial award applicants required to submit FAFSA. *Faculty research:* Equity in education, biliteracy practices among Latina and immigrants, academic achievement of low socio-economic students, equity practices in instruction and educational leadership in diverse settings, racial identity development and multicultural education. *Unit head:* Dr. Debbie Vera, Department Chair. *Application contact:* Caitie Garza, Graduate Admissions Coordinator, 210-784-1300, E-mail: beajaguar@tamusa.edu.
Website: http://www.tamusa.edu/collegeofeducationandhumandevelopment/educatorleadershippreparation/index.html

Université Laval, Faculty of Education, Department of Foundations and Interventions in Education, Québec, QC G1K 7P4, Canada. Offers educational administration and evaluation (MA, PhD); educational practice (Diploma), including educational pedagogy, pedagogy management and development, school adaptation; orientation sciences (MA, PhD). *Degree requirements:* For doctorate, comprehensive exam, thesis/dissertation. Electronic applications accepted.

The University of Akron, Graduate School, College of Education, Department of Educational Foundations and Leadership, Program in Assessment and Evaluation, Akron, OH 44325. Offers MA, Certificate. *Program availability:* Online learning. *Students:* 3 full-time (all women), 20 part-time (19 women); includes 5 minority (all Black or African American, non-Hispanic/Latino). Average age 34. 9 applicants, 100% accepted, 9 enrolled. In 2017, 8 master's awarded. *Degree requirements:* For master's, project, culminating portfolio. *Entrance requirements:* Additional exam requirements/recommendations for international students: Required—TOEFL (minimum score 79 iBT), IELTS (minimum score 6.5). *Application deadline:* Applications are processed on a rolling basis. Application fee: $45 ($70 for international students). *Unit head:* Dr. Evonn Welton, Interim Department Chair, 330-972-6724, E-mail: ewelton@uakron.edu. *Application contact:* Kelly Chaff, College Program Specialist, 330-972-7028, E-mail: klchaff@uakron.edu.
Website: http://www.uakron.edu/education/academic-programs/graduate-programs.dot

University of Arkansas, Graduate School, College of Education and Health Professions, Department of Rehabilitation, Human Resources and Communication Disorders, Program in Educational Statistics and Research Methods, Fayetteville, AR 72701. Offers MS, PhD. In 2017, 2 doctorates awarded. *Application deadline:* For fall admission, 8/1 for domestic students, 4/1 for international students; for spring admission, 12/1 for domestic students, 10/1 for international students; for summer admission, 4/15 for domestic students, 3/1 for international students. Applications are processed on a rolling basis. Application fee: $60. Electronic applications accepted. *Expenses:* Tuition, state resident: full-time $3782. Tuition, nonresident: full-time $10,238. *Financial support:* In 2017–18, 14 research assistantships were awarded; fellowships and teaching assistantships also available. *Unit head:* Dr. Michael Hevel, Interim Department Head, 479-575-4924, Fax: 479-575-5119, E-mail: hevel@uark.edu. *Application contact:* Dr. Wen-Juo Lo, Graduate Coordinator, 479-575-6321, Fax: 479-575-6676, E-mail: wlo@uark.edu.
Website: https://esrm.uark.edu

The University of British Columbia, Faculty of Education, Department of Educational and Counseling Psychology, and Special Education, Vancouver, BC V6T 1Z4, Canada. Offers counseling psychology (M Ed, MA, PhD); guidance studies (Diploma); human development, learning and culture (M Ed, MA, PhD); measurement, evaluation, and research methodology (M Ed, MA, PhD); school psychology (M Ed, MA, PhD); special education (M Ed, MA, PhD, Diploma). *Program availability:* Part-time. *Degree requirements:* For master's, thesis (for some programs); for doctorate, comprehensive exam, thesis/dissertation. *Entrance requirements:* For master's, GRE General Test (for MA in counseling psychology); for doctorate, GRE General Test. Additional exam requirements/recommendations for international students: Required—TOEFL. Electronic applications accepted. *Expenses:* Contact institution. *Faculty research:* Women, family, social problems, career transition, stress and coping problems.

University of Calgary, Faculty of Graduate Studies, Werklund School of Education, Graduate Division of Educational Research, Calgary, AB T2N 1N4, Canada. Offers adult learning (M Ed, MA, Ed D, PhD); curriculum and learning (M Ed, MA, Ed D, PhD); educational leadership (M Ed, MA, Ed D, PhD); languages and diversity (M Ed, MA, Ed D, PhD); learning sciences (M Ed, MA, Ed D, PhD). Ed D in educational leadership offered via distance delivery. *Program availability:* Part-time, evening/weekend, online learning. *Degree requirements:* For master's, thesis (for some programs); for doctorate, thesis/dissertation, candidacy exam. *Entrance requirements:* For master's, minimum GPA of 3.0, 3 letters of reference; for doctorate, minimum GPA of 3.5, 3 letters of reference. Additional exam requirements/recommendations for international students: Required—TOEFL, IELTS. Electronic applications accepted. *Faculty research:* Curriculum, leadership, technology, contexts, gifted, second language teaching, work place and adult learning.

University of California, Riverside, Graduate Division, Graduate School of Education, Riverside, CA 92521. Offers applied behavior analysis (M Ed); diversity and equity (M Ed); education policy analysis and leadership (PhD); education specialist (Credential); education, society, and culture (MA, PhD); educational psychology (MA, PhD); general education (M Ed); higher education administration and policy (M Ed, PhD); multiple subject (Credential); research, evaluation, measurement and statistics (MA); school psychology (PhD); single subject (Credential); special education (M Ed, PhD); special education and autism (MA); TESOL (M Ed). *Faculty:* 29 full-time (16 women), 2 part-time/adjunct (1 woman). *Students:* 241 full-time (188 women). 396 applicants, 42% accepted, 166 enrolled. In 2017, 130 master's, 15 doctorates, 14 other advanced degrees awarded. Terminal master's awarded for partial completion of doctoral program. *Degree requirements:* For master's, comprehensive exams or thesis (MA), case study or analytical report (M Ed); for doctorate, comprehensive exam, thesis/dissertation, written and oral qualifying exams, college teaching practicum. *Entrance requirements:* For master's, GRE General Test (for MA); CBEST and CSET (for M Ed in general education only), UCR Extension TESOL certificate (for M Ed with TESOL emphasis only); for doctorate, GRE General Test, writing sample; for Credential, CBEST, CSET. Additional exam requirements/recommendations for international students: Required—TOEFL (minimum score 550 paper-based; 80 iBT), IELTS (minimum score 7). *Application deadline:* For fall admission, 9/1 for domestic students, 6/1 for international students; for winter admission, 11/15 for domestic students, 9/1 for international students; for spring admission, 3/1 for domestic students, 12/1 for international students. Applications are processed on a rolling basis. Application fee: $80 ($100 for international students). Electronic applications accepted. *Expenses:* Tuition, state resident: full-time $5746. Tuition, nonresident: full-time $10,780. Tuition and fees vary according to campus/location and program. *Financial support:* In 2017–18, 105 students received support, including 16 fellowships with full tuition reimbursements available (averaging $31,000 per year), 25 research assistantships with full tuition reimbursements available (averaging $31,000 per year), 10 teaching assistantships with full tuition reimbursements available (averaging $31,000 per year); career-related internships or fieldwork, Federal Work-Study, institutionally sponsored loans, scholarships/grants, and unspecified assistantships also available. Financial award application deadline: 12/15. *Faculty research:* Responsiveness to intervention, faculty core, response to intervention of English language learners, advanced modeling techniques, study on social capital, trust, and motivation. *Total annual research expenditures:* $1.7 million. *Unit head:* Thomas Smith, Dean, 951-827-4633, E-mail: thomas.smith@ucr.edu. *Application contact:* Heather Killeen, Graduate Program Coordinator, 951-827-6362, E-mail: heather.killeen@ucr.edu.
Website: http://www.education.ucr.edu/

University of Colorado Boulder, Graduate School, School of Education, Division of Research and Evaluation Methodology, Boulder, CO 80309. Offers PhD. *Accreditation:* NCATE. *Students:* 9 full-time (5 women), 1 (woman) part-time; all minorities (9 Black or African American, non-Hispanic/Latino; 1 Native Hawaiian or other Pacific Islander, non-Hispanic/Latino). Average age 34. 32 applicants, 16% accepted, 3 enrolled. In 2017, 1 doctorate awarded. *Degree requirements:* For doctorate, one foreign language, comprehensive exam, thesis/dissertation. *Entrance requirements:* For doctorate, GRE General Test, minimum undergraduate GPA of 2.75. *Application deadline:* For fall admission, 12/1 for domestic and international students; for spring admission, 9/1 for domestic and international students. Application fee: $60 ($80 for international students). Electronic applications accepted. Application fee is waived when completed online. *Financial support:* In 2017–18, 29 students received support, including 2 fellowships (averaging $25,112 per year), 9 research assistantships with full and partial tuition reimbursements available (averaging $33,297 per year), 1 teaching assistantship with full and partial tuition reimbursement available (averaging $5,050 per year); institutionally sponsored loans, scholarships/grants, health care benefits, and unspecified assistantships also available. Financial award application deadline: 2/15; financial award applicants required to submit FAFSA. *Application contact:* E-mail: edadvise@colorado.edu.
Website: http://www.colorado.edu/education/

University of Colorado Denver, School of Education and Human Development, Program in Educational Leadership and Innovation, Denver, CO 80217. Offers educational studies and research (PhD), including administrative leadership and policy, early childhood special education, math education, research, assessment and evaluation, science education, urban ecologies. *Program availability:* Part-time, evening/weekend. *Degree requirements:* For doctorate, comprehensive exam, thesis/

dissertation, 75 credit hours (for PhD). *Entrance requirements:* For doctorate, GRE or equivalent, resume or curriculum vitae, letters of recommendation, master's degree or equivalent, completion of basic or advanced statistics course with minimum B grade. Additional exam requirements/recommendations for international students: Required—TOEFL (minimum score 537 paper-based; 75 iBT); Recommended—IELTS (minimum score 6.5). Electronic applications accepted. *Expenses:* Contact institution. *Faculty research:* Administrative leadership and policy studies, early childhood education, research in diversity, paraprofessionals in education, urban schools lab.

University of Colorado Denver, School of Education and Human Development, Programs in Educational and School Psychology, Denver, CO 80217. Offers educational psychology (MA), including educational assessment, educational psychology, human development, human learning, research and evaluation; school psychology (Psy D, Ed S). MA program also offered in partnership with Boulder Journey School, Friends' School and Stanley British Primary School. *Program availability:* Part-time, evening/weekend. *Degree requirements:* For master's, comprehensive exam, 9 hours of core courses, embedded within a minimum of 36 to 38 hours of relevant coursework, including an educational psychology practicum, independent study project or thesis (recommended); for Ed S, comprehensive exam, minimum of 75 semester hours (61 hours of coursework, 6 of 500-hour practicum in field, and 8 of 1200-hour internship); PRAXIS II. *Entrance requirements:* For master's, GRE if undergraduate GPA below 2.75, resume, three letters of recommendation, transcripts; for Ed S, GRE, resume, letters of recommendation, transcripts. Additional exam requirements/recommendations for international students: Required—TOEFL (minimum score 537 paper-based; 75 iBT); Recommended—IELTS (minimum score 6.5). Electronic applications accepted. *Expenses:* Contact institution. *Faculty research:* Crisis response and intervention, school violence prevention, immigrant experience, educational environments for English language learners, culturally competent assessment and intervention, child and youth suicide.

University of Denver, Morgridge College of Education, Denver, CO 80208. Offers child, family and school psychology (MA, PhD, Ed S); counseling psychology (MA, PhD); curriculum and instruction (MA, Ed D, PhD); curriculum instruction and teaching (Certificate); early childhood special education (MA, Certificate); educational leadership and policy studies (MA, Ed D, PhD, Certificate); higher education (Ed D, PhD); library and information science (MLIS); research methods and statistics (MA, PhD). *Accreditation:* ALA; APA (one or more programs are accredited). *Program availability:* Part-time, evening/weekend, online learning. *Faculty:* 39 full-time (29 women), 60 part-time/adjunct (42 women). *Students:* 502 full-time (406 women), 361 part-time (267 women); includes 233 minority (54 Black or African American, non-Hispanic/Latino; 6 American Indian or Alaska Native, non-Hispanic/Latino; 25 Asian, non-Hispanic/Latino; 113 Hispanic/Latino; 35 Two or more races, non-Hispanic/Latino), 52 international. Average age 31. 1,167 applicants, 64% accepted, 415 enrolled. In 2017, 285 master's, 51 doctorates, 157 other advanced degrees awarded. Terminal master's awarded for partial completion of doctoral program. *Degree requirements:* For master's, comprehensive exam; for doctorate, 2 foreign languages, comprehensive exam, thesis/dissertation. *Entrance requirements:* For master's and doctorate, GRE General Test or GMAT. Additional exam requirements/recommendations for international students: Required—TOEFL (minimum score 550 paper-based; 80 iBT). *Application deadline:* Applications are processed on a rolling basis. Application fee: $65. Electronic applications accepted. *Expenses:* $31,935 per year full-time. *Financial support:* In 2017–18, 765 students received support, including 26 research assistantships with tuition reimbursements available (averaging $10,957 per year), 38 teaching assistantships with tuition reimbursements available (averaging $3,391 per year); career-related internships or fieldwork, Federal Work-Study, institutionally sponsored loans, scholarships/grants, and unspecified assistantships also available. Support available to part-time students. Financial award application deadline: 2/15; financial award applicants required to submit FAFSA. *Faculty research:* Early childhood education, educational leadership, access and opportunity to postsecondary education, marriage and family therapy, data management and archival research. *Unit head:* Dr. Karen Riley, Dean, 303-871-3665, Fax: 303-871-4456, E-mail: karen.riley@du.edu. *Application contact:* Jodi Dye, Director of Admissions, 303-871-2510, Fax: 303-871-4456, E-mail: jodi.dye@du.edu.
Website: http://morgridge.du.edu

University of Florida, Graduate School, College of Education, School of Human Development and Organizational Studies in Education, Gainesville, FL 32611. Offers counseling and counselor education (Ed D, PhD), including counseling and counselor education, marriage and family counseling, mental health counseling, school counseling and guidance; educational leadership (M Ed, MAE, Ed D, PhD, Ed S), including educational leadership (Ed D, PhD), educational policy (Ed D, PhD); higher education administration (Ed D, PhD), including education policy (Ed D), educational policy, higher education administration; marriage and family counseling (M Ed, MAE, Ed D, PhD, Ed S); mental health counseling (M Ed, MAE, Ed D, PhD, Ed S); research and evaluation methodology (M Ed, MAE, Ed D, PhD); school counseling and guidance (M Ed, MAE, Ed D, PhD, Ed S); student personnel in higher education (M Ed, MAE). *Accreditation:* ACA (one or more programs are accredited); NCATE. *Program availability:* Part-time, online learning. Terminal master's awarded for partial completion of doctoral program. *Degree requirements:* For master's, thesis optional; for doctorate, comprehensive exam, thesis/dissertation. *Entrance requirements:* For master's and doctorate, GRE General Test, minimum GPA of 3.0 (undergraduate), 3.5 (graduate); for Ed S, GRE General Test. Additional exam requirements/recommendations for international students: Required—TOEFL (minimum score 550 paper-based; 80 iBT), IELTS (minimum score 6). Electronic applications accepted.

University of Illinois at Chicago, College of Education, Department of Educational Psychology, Chicago, IL 60607-7128. Offers early childhood education (M Ed); educational psychology (PhD); measurement, evaluation, statistics, and assessment (M Ed); youth development (M Ed). *Program availability:* Part-time, online learning. *Faculty research:* Children's construction of morality, development of resilience in the face of enduring economical difficulties, cognition and cognitive development, test fairness.

The University of Iowa, Graduate College, College of Education, Department of Psychological and Quantitative Foundations, Iowa City, IA 52242-1316. Offers counseling psychology (PhD); educational measurement and statistics (MA, PhD); educational psychology (MA, PhD); school psychology (PhD, Ed S). *Accreditation:* APA. *Degree requirements:* For master's, thesis optional, exam; for doctorate, comprehensive exam, thesis/dissertation; for Ed S, exam. *Entrance requirements:* For master's, doctorate, and Ed S, GRE General Test, minimum GPA of 3.0. Additional exam requirements/recommendations for international students: Required—TOEFL (minimum score 550 paper-based; 81 iBT). Electronic applications accepted.

The University of Kansas, Graduate Studies, School of Education, Department of Educational Psychology, Program in Educational Psychology and Research, Lawrence, KS 66045. Offers MS Ed, PhD. *Program availability:* Part-time. *Students:* 40 full-time (21 women), 4 part-time (3 women); includes 5 minority (2 Black or African American, non-Hispanic/Latino; 2 Asian, non-Hispanic/Latino; 1 Hispanic/Latino), 20 international. Average age 32. 25 applicants, 76% accepted, 8 enrolled. In 2017, 7 master's, 3

doctorates awarded. *Entrance requirements:* For master's, GRE General Test, minimum GPA of 3.0, resume, statement of purpose, official transcripts, three recommendation letters; for doctorate, GRE General Test, resume, statement of purpose, official transcripts, three recommendation letters. *Application deadline:* For fall admission, 12/15 for domestic and international students. Application fee: $65 ($85 for international students). Electronic applications accepted. *Financial support:* Fellowships, research assistantships, teaching assistantships, career-related internships or fieldwork, institutionally sponsored loans, scholarships/grants, traineeships, health care benefits, tuition waivers (full and partial), and unspecified assistantships available. Support available to part-time students. Financial award application deadline: 12/15. *Faculty research:* Educational measurement, applied statistics, research design, program evaluation, learning and development. *Unit head:* Steven Wayne Lee, Chair, 785-864-9701, E-mail: swlee@ku.edu. *Application contact:* Penny Fritts, Admissions Coordinator, 785-864-9645, E-mail: fritts@ku.edu.
Website: http://www.soe.ku.edu/PRE/

University of Kentucky, Graduate School, College of Education, Program in Educational Policy Studies and Evaluation, Lexington, KY 40506-0032. Offers educational policy studies and evaluation (Ed D); higher education (MS Ed, PhD); social and philosophical studies (MS Ed). *Accreditation:* NCATE. Terminal master's awarded for partial completion of doctoral program. *Degree requirements:* For master's, comprehensive exam, thesis optional; for doctorate, comprehensive exam, thesis/dissertation. *Entrance requirements:* For master's, GRE General Test, minimum undergraduate GPA of 2.75; for doctorate, GRE General Test, minimum graduate GPA of 3.0. Additional exam requirements/recommendations for international students: Required—TOEFL (minimum score 550 paper-based). Electronic applications accepted. *Faculty research:* Studies in higher education; comparative and international education; evaluation of educational programs, policies, and reform; student, teacher, and faculty cultures; gender and education.

University of Louisville, Graduate School, College of Education and Human Development, Department of Counseling and Human Development, Louisville, KY 40292-0001. Offers counseling and personnel services (M Ed, PhD), including art therapy (M Ed), clinical mental health counseling (M Ed), college student personnel, counseling psychology, counselor education and supervision (PhD), educational psychology, measurement, and evaluation (PhD), school counseling (M Ed). *Accreditation:* APA; NCATE. *Program availability:* Part-time, evening/weekend. *Students:* 144 full-time (107 women), 63 part-time (44 women); includes 49 minority (32 Black or African American, non-Hispanic/Latino; 1 American Indian or Alaska Native, non-Hispanic/Latino; 3 Asian, non-Hispanic/Latino; 7 Hispanic/Latino; 6 Two or more races, non-Hispanic/Latino), 3 international. Average age 28. 178 applicants, 49% accepted, 51 enrolled. In 2017, 35 master's, 3 doctorates awarded. *Degree requirements:* For doctorate, comprehensive exam, thesis/dissertation. *Entrance requirements:* For master's and doctorate, GRE General Test. Application fee: $65. *Expenses:* Tuition, state resident: full-time $12,246; part-time $681 per credit hour. Tuition, nonresident: full-time $25,486; part-time $1417 per credit hour. *Required fees:* $196. Tuition and fees vary according to course load, program and reciprocity agreements. *Financial support:* Fellowships, research assistantships, teaching assistantships, career-related internships or fieldwork, Federal Work-Study, scholarships/grants, health care benefits, and unspecified assistantships available. Financial award application deadline: 6/1; financial award applicants required to submit FAFSA. *Faculty research:* Mental health services and under-served populations; health disparities and outcomes; well-being identity development; measurement and evaluation. *Total annual research expenditures:* $295,684. *Unit head:* Dr. Mark M. Leach, Interim Chair/Professor, 502-852-0588, Fax: 502-852-0629, E-mail: m.leach@louisville.edu. *Application contact:* Betty Hampton, Director of Graduate Student Services, 502-852-5597, Fax: 502-852-1465, E-mail: edadvise@louisville.edu.
Website: http://www.louisville.edu/education/departments/ecpy

University of Maryland, College Park, Academic Affairs, College of Education, Department of Human Development and Quantitative Methodology, College Park, MD 20742. Offers MA, Ed D, PhD. *Entrance requirements:* Additional exam requirements/recommendations for international students: Required—TOEFL.

University of Massachusetts Amherst, Graduate School, College of Education, Program in Education, Amherst, MA 01003. Offers bilingual, English as a second language, and multicultural education (M Ed, Ed S); child study and early education (M Ed); children, families and schools (Ed D, Ed S); early childhood and elementary teacher education (M Ed); educational leadership (M Ed); educational policy and leadership (Ed D); higher education (M Ed); international education (M Ed); language, literacy and culture (Ed D); learning, media and technology (M Ed, Ed S); mathematics, science, and learning technologies (Ed D); reading and writing (M Ed); research, educational measurement and psychometrics (Ed D); school counselor education (M Ed, Ed S); school psychology (Ed S); science education (Ed S); secondary teacher education (M Ed); social justice education (M Ed, Ed D, Ed S); special education (M Ed, Ed D, Ed S); teacher education and school improvement (Ed D, Ed S). *Accreditation:* NCATE. *Program availability:* Part-time, online learning. Terminal master's awarded for partial completion of doctoral program. *Degree requirements:* For doctorate, comprehensive exam, thesis/dissertation. *Entrance requirements:* Additional exam requirements/recommendations for international students: Required—TOEFL (minimum score 550 paper-based; 80 iBT), IELTS (minimum score 6.5). Electronic applications accepted.

University of Memphis, Graduate School, College of Education, Department of Counseling, Educational Psychology and Research, Memphis, TN 38152. Offers counseling (MS, Ed D), including clinical mental health counseling (MS), clinical rehabilitation counseling (MS), rehabilitation counseling (MS), school counseling (MS); counseling psychology (PhD); educational psychology and research (MS, PhD), including educational psychology, educational research. *Accreditation:* ACA (one or more programs are accredited); APA (one or more programs are accredited); CORE (one or more programs are accredited); NCATE. *Program availability:* Blended/hybrid learning. *Faculty:* 26 full-time (17 women), 8 part-time/adjunct (5 women). *Students:* 132 full-time (111 women), 87 part-time (66 women); includes 71 minority (51 Black or African American, non-Hispanic/Latino; 4 Asian, non-Hispanic/Latino; 10 Hispanic/Latino; 6 Two or more races, non-Hispanic/Latino), 5 international. Average age 31. 146 applicants, 49% accepted, 49 enrolled. In 2017, 39 master's, 13 doctorates awarded. *Degree requirements:* For master's, comprehensive exam, thesis or alternative, internship; for doctorate, comprehensive exam, thesis/dissertation, practicum, internship, residency, scholarly work. *Entrance requirements:* For master's, GRE General Test or MAT, minimum GPA of 2.5, letters of reference, interview; for doctorate, GRE General Test, master's degree or equivalent, letters of reference, interview, curriculum vitae, personal statement. Additional exam requirements/recommendations for international students: Required—TOEFL (minimum score 550 paper-based; 79 iBT). *Application deadline:* For fall admission, 10/1 priority date for domestic students; for spring admission, 4/1 priority date for domestic students. Applications are processed on a rolling basis. Application fee: $35 ($60 for international students). Electronic applications accepted. *Expenses:* Contact institution. *Financial support:* In 2017–18, 130 students received support, including 15 research assistantships with full tuition

reimbursements available (averaging $13,426 per year), 12 teaching assistantships with full tuition reimbursements available (averaging $11,976 per year); fellowships with full tuition reimbursements available, career-related internships or fieldwork, Federal Work-Study, scholarships/grants, and unspecified assistantships also available. Financial award application deadline: 2/1; financial award applicants required to submit FAFSA. *Faculty research:* Anger management, aging and disability, supervision, multicultural counseling. *Unit head:* Dr. Steve West, Chair, 901-678-2841, Fax: 901-678-5114, E-mail: slwest@memphis.edu. *Application contact:* Dr. Suzanne Lease, Interim Assistant Dean of Education and Graduate Programs, 901-678-4476, Fax: 901-678-4778, E-mail: slease@memphis.edu.
Website: http://www.memphis.edu/cepr/

University of Miami, Graduate School, School of Education and Human Development, Department of Educational and Psychological Studies, Program in Research, Measurement, and Evaluation, Coral Gables, FL 33124. Offers MS Ed, PhD. *Program availability:* Part-time, evening/weekend. Terminal master's awarded for partial completion of doctoral program. *Degree requirements:* For master's, comprehensive exam, thesis optional; for doctorate, thesis/dissertation, qualifying exam. *Entrance requirements:* For master's and doctorate, GRE General Test. Additional exam requirements/recommendations for international students: Required—TOEFL (minimum score 550 paper-based; 80 iBT); Recommended—IELTS (minimum score 6.5). Electronic applications accepted. *Faculty research:* Psychometric theory, computer-based testing, quantitative research methods.

University of Michigan–Dearborn, College of Education, Health, and Human Services, Master of Arts Program in Program Evaluation and Assessment, Dearborn, MI 48126. Offers MA. *Program availability:* Part-time, evening/weekend. *Faculty:* 4 full-time (3 women). *Students:* 3 part-time (all women); includes 1 minority (Two or more races, non-Hispanic/Latino). Average age 32. 5 applicants, 80% accepted, 1 enrolled. *Degree requirements:* For master's, essay. *Entrance requirements:* Additional exam requirements/recommendations for international students: Required—TOEFL (minimum score 560 paper-based; 84 iBT), IELTS (minimum score 6.5). *Application deadline:* For fall admission, 8/1 for domestic students, 5/1 for international students; for winter admission, 12/1 for domestic students, 9/1 for international students; for spring admission, 4/1 for domestic students, 1/1 for international students. Applications are processed on a rolling basis. Application fee: $60. Electronic applications accepted. *Expenses:* $683 per credit hour in-state; $1,176 per credit hour out-state. *Financial support:* In 2017–18, 1 student received support. Scholarships/grants available. Financial award application deadline: 3/1; financial award applicants required to submit FAFSA. *Faculty research:* Assessment and evaluation, research methodology, multiculturalism, urban education, pedagogy and interventions. *Unit head:* Dr. Stein Brunvand, Director, Master's Degree Programs, 313-583-6415, E-mail: sbrunvan@umich.edu. *Application contact:* Office of Graduate Studies, 313-583-6321, E-mail: umd-graduatestudies@umich.edu.
Website: https://umdearborn.edu/cehhs/graduate-programs/areas-study/ma-program-evaluation-and-assessment

University of Minnesota, Twin Cities Campus, Graduate School, College of Education and Human Development, Department of Educational Psychology, Program in Quantitative Methods in Education, Minneapolis, MN 55455-0213. Offers MA, PhD. *Students:* 22 full-time (10 women), 11 part-time (8 women); includes 9 minority (2 Black or African American, non-Hispanic/Latino; 3 Asian, non-Hispanic/Latino; 4 Hispanic/Latino), 9 international. Average age 34. 35 applicants, 26% accepted, 9 enrolled. In 2017, 1 master's, 6 doctorates awarded. *Financial support:* Fellowships, scholarships/grants, and unspecified assistantships available. Financial award application deadline: 12/1. *Unit head:* Dr. Geoffrey Maruyama, Chair, 612-624-1003, Fax: 612-625-5861, E-mail: geoff@umn.edu. *Application contact:* Dr. Ernest Davenport, Director of Graduate Studies, 612-624-1040, E-mail: lqr6576@umn.edu.
Website: http://www.cehd.umn.edu/edpsych/programs/qme/

University of Minnesota, Twin Cities Campus, Graduate School, College of Education and Human Development, Department of Organizational Leadership, Policy and Development, Program in Evaluation Studies, Minneapolis, MN 55455-0213. Offers MA, PhD. *Students:* 16 full-time (14 women), 18 part-time (13 women); includes 10 minority (4 Black or African American, non-Hispanic/Latino; 2 Asian, non-Hispanic/Latino; 1 Hispanic/Latino; 3 Two or more races, non-Hispanic/Latino), 4 international. Average age 41. 20 applicants, 35% accepted, 7 enrolled. In 2017, 4 master's, 2 doctorates awarded. Application fee: $75 ($95 for international students). *Unit head:* Dr. Heidi Barajas, Chair, 612-625-4823, E-mail: hbarajas@umn.edu. *Application contact:* Dr. Jeremy J. Hernandez, Director of Graduate Studies, 612-626-9377, E-mail: herna220@umn.edu.
Website: http://www.cehd.umn.edu/OLPD/grad-programs/ES/

University of Missouri–St. Louis, College of Education, Department of Education Sciences and Professional Programs, St. Louis, MO 63121. Offers adult and higher education (M Ed); educational psychology (M Ed), including character and citizenship education, research and program evaluation; program evaluation (Certificate); school psychology (Ed S). *Students:* 19 full-time (17 women), 13 part-time (12 women); includes 4 minority (2 Black or African American, non-Hispanic/Latino; 2 Hispanic/Latino). 16 applicants, 56% accepted, 9 enrolled. *Degree requirements:* For other advanced degree, comprehensive exam, thesis or alternative, internship. *Entrance requirements:* For degree, GRE General Test, 2-4 letters of recommendation, personal interview. Additional exam requirements/recommendations for international students: Required—IELTS (minimum score 6.5); Recommended—TOEFL (minimum score 550 paper-based; 79 iBT). *Application deadline:* For fall admission, 2/15 priority date for domestic students, 2/15 for international students. Application fee: $50 ($40 for international students). Electronic applications accepted. *Expenses:* Tuition, state resident: part-time $476.50 per credit hour. Tuition, nonresident: part-time $1169.70 per credit hour. *Financial support:* Application deadline: 4/1; applicants required to submit FAFSA. *Faculty research:* Child/adolescent psychology, quantitative and qualitative methodology, evaluation processes, measurement and assessment. *Unit head:* Dr. Donald Gouwens, Chairperson, 314-516-4773, Fax: 314-516-5784, E-mail: gouwensd@umsl.edu. *Application contact:* 314-516-5458, Fax: 314-516-6996, E-mail: gradadm@umsl.edu.
Website: https://coe.umsl.edu/dept/espp.html

University of Missouri–St. Louis, Graduate School, Program in Public Policy Administration, St. Louis, MO 63121. Offers local government management (MPPA, Certificate); nonprofit management and leadership (MPPA, Certificate); policy and program evaluation (MPPA, Certificate). *Accreditation:* NASPAA. *Program availability:* Part-time, evening/weekend. *Faculty:* 2 full-time (1 woman), 4 part-time/adjunct (3 women). *Students:* 9 full-time (5 women), 34 part-time (19 women); includes 10 minority (6 Black or African American, non-Hispanic/Latino; 2 Asian, non-Hispanic/Latino; 1 Hispanic/Latino; 1 Two or more races, non-Hispanic/Latino). 34 applicants, 79% accepted, 14 enrolled. *Degree requirements:* For master's, exit project. *Entrance requirements:* For master's, 3 letters of recommendation, personal statement. Additional exam requirements/recommendations for international students: Recommended—TOEFL (minimum score 550 paper-based), IELTS (minimum score 6.5). *Application deadline:* For fall admission, 7/1 priority date for domestic and international students; for

spring admission, 12/1 priority date for domestic and international students. Applications are processed on a rolling basis. Application fee: $50 ($40 for international students). Electronic applications accepted. *Expenses:* Tuition, state resident: part-time $476.50 per credit hour. Tuition, nonresident: part-time $1169.70 per credit hour. *Financial support:* Research assistantships with tuition reimbursements and career-related internships or fieldwork available. Financial award application deadline: 4/1; financial award applicants required to submit FAFSA. *Faculty research:* Urban policy, public finance, evaluation. *Unit head:* Daniel Sise, Interim Director, 314-516-6378, Fax: 314-516-5210, E-mail: sised@umsl.edu. *Application contact:* 314-516-5458, Fax: 314-516-6996, E-mail: gradadm@umsl.edu.
Website: http://www.umsl.edu/gradschool/ppa/

University of Nebraska–Lincoln, Graduate College, College of Education and Human Sciences, Department of Educational Psychology, Lincoln, NE 68588. Offers cognition, learning and development (MA); counseling psychology (MA); educational psychology (MA, Ed S); psychological studies in education (PhD), including cognition, learning and development, counseling psychology, quantitative, qualitative, and psychometric methods, school psychology; quantitative, qualitative, and psychometric methods (MA); school psychology (MA, Ed S). *Accreditation:* APA (one or more programs are accredited); NCATE. *Degree requirements:* For master's, thesis optional. *Entrance requirements:* For master's, GRE General Test. Additional exam requirements/recommendations for international students: Required—TOEFL (minimum score 500 paper-based). Electronic applications accepted. *Faculty research:* Measurement and assessment, metacognition, academic skills, child development, multicultural education and counseling.

The University of North Carolina at Chapel Hill, Graduate School, School of Education, Program in Education, Chapel Hill, NC 27599. Offers culture, curriculum and change (MA, PhD); early childhood, intervention and literacy (MA, PhD); educational psychology, measurement and evaluation (MA, PhD). *Accreditation:* NCATE. *Degree requirements:* For master's, thesis; for doctorate, comprehensive exam, thesis/dissertation. *Entrance requirements:* For master's, GRE General Test, minimum GPA of 3.0 during last 2 years of undergraduates course work; for doctorate, GRE General Test, minimum GPA of 3.0 during last 2 years of undergraduate course work. Additional exam requirements/recommendations for international students: Required—TOEFL (minimum score 550 paper-based). Electronic applications accepted.

The University of North Carolina at Greensboro, Graduate School, School of Education, Department of Educational Research Methodology, Greensboro, NC 27412-5001. Offers educational research, measurement and evaluation (PhD); MS/PhD. *Accreditation:* NCATE. *Degree requirements:* For doctorate, thesis/dissertation. *Entrance requirements:* For doctorate, GRE General Test. Additional exam requirements/recommendations for international students: Required—TOEFL. Electronic applications accepted.

University of Northern Colorado, Graduate School, College of Education and Behavioral Sciences, Department of Applied Statistics and Research Methods, Greeley, CO 80639. Offers MS, PhD. *Program availability:* Part-time. *Degree requirements:* For master's, comprehensive exam; for doctorate, comprehensive exam, thesis/dissertation. *Entrance requirements:* For master's, 3 letters of reference; for doctorate, GRE General Test, 3 letters of reference. Electronic applications accepted.

University of Northern Iowa, Graduate College, College of Education, Department of Educational Psychology and Foundations, MAE Program in Educational Psychology: Context and Techniques of Assessment, Cedar Falls, IA 50614. Offers MAE. *Entrance requirements:* For master's, GRE, official transcripts, statement of purpose, three reference letters, writing sample.

University of North Texas, Robert B. Toulouse School of Graduate Studies, Denton, TX 76203-5459. Offers accounting (MS); applied anthropology (MA, MS); applied behavior analysis (Certificate); applied geography (MA); applied technology and performance improvement (M Ed, MS); art education (MA); art history (MA); art museum education (Certificate); arts leadership (Certificate); audiology (Au D); behavior analysis (MS); behavioral science (PhD); biochemistry and molecular biology (MS); biology (MA, MS); biomedical engineering (MS); business analysis (MS); chemistry (MS); clinical health psychology (PhD); communication studies (MA, MS); computer engineering (MS); computer science (MS); counseling (M Ed, MS), including clinical mental health counseling (MS), college and university counseling, elementary school counseling, secondary school counseling; creative writing (MA); criminal justice (MS); curriculum and instruction (M Ed); decision sciences (MBA); design (MA, MFA), including fashion design (MFA), innovation studies, interior design (MFA); early childhood studies (MS); economics (MS); educational leadership (M Ed, Ed D); educational psychology (MS, PhD), including family studies (MS), gifted and talented (MS), human development (MS), learning and cognition (MS), research, measurement and evaluation (MS); electrical engineering (MS); emergency management (MPA); engineering technology (MS); English (MA); English as a second language (MA); environmental science (MS); finance (MBA, MS); financial management (MPA); French (MA); health services management (MBA); higher education (M Ed, Ed D); history (MA, MS); hospitality management (MS); human resources management (MPA); information science (MS); information systems (PhD); information technologies (MBA); interdisciplinary studies (MA, MS); international studies (MA); international sustainable tourism (MS); jazz studies (MM); journalism (MA, MJ, Graduate Certificate), including interactive and virtual digital communication (Graduate Certificate), narrative journalism (Graduate Certificate), public relations (Graduate Certificate); kinesiology (MS); linguistics (MA); local government management (MPA); logistics (PhD); logistics and supply chain management (MBA); long-term care, senior housing, and aging services (MA); management (PhD); marketing (MBA); mathematics (MA, MS); mechanical and energy engineering (MS, PhD); music (MA), including ethnomusicology, music theory, musicology, performance; music composition (PhD); music education (MM Ed, PhD); nonprofit management (MPA); operations and supply chain management (MBA); performance (MM, DMA); philosophy (MA); political science (MA); professional and technical communication (MA); radio, television and film (MA, MFA); rehabilitation counseling (Certificate); sociology (MA); Spanish (MA); special education (M Ed); speech-language pathology (MA); strategic management (MBA); studio art (MFA); teaching (M Ed); MBA/MS. *Program availability:* Part-time, evening/weekend, online learning. Terminal master's awarded for partial completion of doctoral program. *Degree requirements:* For master's, variable foreign language requirement, comprehensive exam (for some programs), thesis (for some programs); for doctorate, variable foreign language requirement, comprehensive exam (for some programs), thesis/dissertation; for other advanced degree, variable foreign language requirement, comprehensive exam (for some programs). *Entrance requirements:* For master's and doctorate, GRE, GMAT. Additional exam requirements/recommendations for international students: Required—TOEFL (minimum score 550 paper-based; 79 iBT). Electronic applications accepted.

University of Pennsylvania, Graduate School of Education, Division of Human Development and Quantitative Methods, Program in Quantitative Methods, Philadelphia, PA 19104. Offers M Phil, MS, PhD. *Program availability:* Part-time. *Students:* Average age 30. 6 applicants, 33% accepted, 2 enrolled. In 2017, 1 doctorate awarded. *Entrance requirements:* For master's, bachelor's degree. *Financial support:* In 2017–18, 20 students received support. Applicants required to submit FAFSA.

University of Pennsylvania, Graduate School of Education, Division of Human Development and Quantitative Methods, Program in Statistics, Measurement, Assessment, and Research Technology (SMART), Philadelphia, PA 19104. Offers MS. *Students:* Average age 25. 220 applicants, 34% accepted, 31 enrolled. In 2017, 21 master's awarded.

University of Pittsburgh, School of Education, Department of Psychology in Education, Program in Research Methodology, Pittsburgh, PA 15260. Offers M Ed, MA, PhD. *Program availability:* Part-time, evening/weekend. Terminal master's awarded for partial completion of doctoral program. *Degree requirements:* For master's, thesis; for doctorate, thesis/dissertation. *Entrance requirements:* For doctorate, GRE General Test. Additional exam requirements/recommendations for international students: Required—TOEFL. Electronic applications accepted.

University of Puerto Rico–Río Piedras, College of Education, Program in Educational Research and Evaluation, San Juan, PR 00931-3300. Offers M Ed. *Program availability:* Part-time. *Degree requirements:* For master's, thesis. *Entrance requirements:* For master's, PAEG or GRE, interview, minimum GPA of 3.0, letter of recommendation.

University of St. Thomas, School of Education and Human Services, Houston, TX 77006-4696. Offers all level education (M Ed); bilingual/dual language (M Ed); Catholic school teaching (M Ed); Catholic/private school leadership (M Ed); counselor education (M Ed); curriculum and instruction (M Ed); education (Ed D); educational leadership (M Ed); elementary teaching (M Ed); English as a second language (M Ed); exceptionality/educational diagnostician (M Ed); exceptionality/special education (M Ed); generalist (M Ed); reading (M Ed); secondary teaching (M Ed); teaching (MAT). *Accreditation:* TEAC. *Program availability:* Part-time, evening/weekend, online learning. *Faculty:* 33 full-time (22 women), 43 part-time/adjunct (26 women). *Students:* 119 full-time (97 women), 597 part-time (529 women); includes 478 minority (166 Black or African American, non-Hispanic/Latino; 29 Asian, non-Hispanic/Latino; 277 Hispanic/Latino; 2 Native Hawaiian or other Pacific Islander, non-Hispanic/Latino; 4 Two or more races, non-Hispanic/Latino), 19 international. Average age 36. 306 applicants, 91% accepted, 181 enrolled. In 2017, 328 master's awarded. *Degree requirements:* For master's, thesis, field experience. *Entrance requirements:* For master's, GRE or MAT if GPA is below 3.0, bachelor's degree; minimum GPA of 2.75 in bachelor's degree or last 60 credit hours; official transcripts from all institutions; goal statement of 250-300 words; 1 reference. Additional exam requirements/recommendations for international students: Required—TOEFL (minimum score 94 iBT), IELTS (minimum score 7), PTE (minimum score 53). *Application deadline:* Applications are processed on a rolling basis. Application fee: $35. Electronic applications accepted. *Expenses:* Contact institution. *Financial support:* In 2017–18, 27 students received support. Federal Work-Study, scholarships/grants, and state work-study, institutional employment available. Support available to part-time students. Financial award application deadline: 4/15; financial award applicants required to submit FAFSA. *Faculty research:* Leadership, diversity, personality traits, second language acquisition. *Unit head:* Dr. Paul C. Paese, Dean, 713-942-5999, Fax: 713-525-3871, E-mail: paesep@stthom.edu. *Application contact:* 713-525-3540, E-mail: education@stthom.edu.
Website: http://www.stthom.edu/Academics/
School_of_Education_and_Human_Services/Index.aqf

University of South Carolina, The Graduate School, College of Education, Department of Educational Studies, Program in Educational Psychology, Research, Columbia, SC 29208. Offers M Ed, PhD. *Accreditation:* NCATE. *Program availability:* Part-time. *Degree requirements:* For master's, comprehensive exam, thesis (for some programs); for doctorate, comprehensive exam, thesis/dissertation. *Entrance requirements:* For master's, GRE General Test; for doctorate, GRE General Test, interview. Electronic applications accepted. *Faculty research:* Problem solving, higher order thinking skills, psychometric research, methodology.

University of Southern Mississippi, College of Education and Psychology, Department of Educational Research and Administration, Hattiesburg, MS 39406-0001. Offers educational administration (M Ed, Ed D, PhD, Ed S); educational administration and supervision (M Ed); educational studies and research (MS); higher education (Ed D); higher education administration (PhD); higher education: student affairs (M Ed); research, evaluation, statistics, assessment (PhD). *Students:* 30 full-time (23 women), 3 part-time (all women). 44 applicants, 91% accepted, 33 enrolled. *Degree requirements:* For master's and Ed S, comprehensive exam, thesis (for some programs); for doctorate, comprehensive exam, thesis/dissertation. *Entrance requirements:* For master's and doctorate, GRE General Test, minimum GPA of 2.75. Additional exam requirements/recommendations for international students: Required—TOEFL. *Application deadline:* For fall admission, 2/1 for domestic students, 3/1 for international students. Applications are processed on a rolling basis. Application fee: $60. *Expenses:* Tuition, state resident: full-time $3830. *Financial support:* Career-related internships or fieldwork, Federal Work-Study, and institutionally sponsored loans available. Financial award application deadline: 3/15; financial award applicants required to submit FAFSA. *Unit head:* Dr. Lilian Hill, Co-Chair, 601-266-4622.
Website: https://www.usm.edu/educational-research-administration

University of South Florida, Innovative Education, Tampa, FL 33620-9951. Offers adult, career and higher education (Graduate Certificate), including college teaching, leadership in developing human resources, leadership in higher education; Africana studies (Graduate Certificate), including diasporas and health disparities, genocide and human rights; aging studies (Graduate Certificate), including gerontology; art research (Graduate Certificate), including museum studies; business foundations (Graduate Certificate); chemical and biomedical engineering (Graduate Certificate), including materials science and engineering, water, health and sustainability; child and family studies (Graduate Certificate), including positive behavior support; civil and industrial engineering (Graduate Certificate), including transportation systems analysis; community and family health (Graduate Certificate), including maternal and child health, social marketing and public health, violence and injury: prevention and intervention, women's health; criminology (Graduate Certificate), including criminal justice administration; data science for public administration (Graduate Certificate); digital humanities (Graduate Certificate); educational measurement and research (Graduate Certificate), including evaluation; English (Graduate Certificate), including comparative literary studies, creative writing, professional and technical communication; entrepreneurship (Graduate Certificate); environmental health (Graduate Certificate), including safety management; epidemiology and biostatistics (Graduate Certificate), including applied biostatistics, biostatistics, concepts and tools of epidemiology, epidemiology, epidemiology of infectious diseases; geography, environment and planning (Graduate Certificate), including community development, environmental policy and management, geographical information systems; geology (Graduate Certificate), including hydrogeology; global health (Graduate Certificate), including disaster management, global health and Latin American and Caribbean studies, global health practice, humanitarian assistance, infection control; government and international affairs (Graduate Certificate), including Cuban studies, globalization studies; health policy and management (Graduate Certificate), including health management and leadership, public health policy and programs; hearing specialist: early intervention (Graduate Certificate); industrial and management systems engineering (Graduate Certificate), including systems engineering, technology management; information studies (Graduate

Certificate), including school library media specialist; information systems/decision sciences (Graduate Certificate), including analytics and business intelligence; instructional technology (Graduate Certificate), including distance education, Florida digital/virtual educator, instructional design, multimedia design, Web design; internal medicine, bioethics and medical humanities (Graduate Certificate), including biomedical ethics; Latin American and Caribbean studies (Graduate Certificate); leadership for coastal resiliency planning (Graduate Certificate); mass communications (Graduate Certificate), including multimedia journalism; mathematics and statistics (Graduate Certificate), including mathematics; medicine (Graduate Certificate), including aging and neuroscience, bioinformatics, biotechnology, brain fitness and memory management, clinical investigation, hand and upper limb rehabilitation, health informatics, health sciences, integrative weight management, intellectual property, medicine and gender, metabolic and nutritional medicine, metabolic cardiology, pharmacy sciences; national and competitive intelligence (Graduate Certificate); nursing (Graduate Certificate), including simulation based academic fellowship in advanced pain management; psychological and social foundations (Graduate Certificate), including career counseling, college teaching, diversity in education, mental health counseling, school counseling; public affairs (Graduate Certificate), including nonprofit management, public management, research administration; public health (Graduate Certificate), including assessing chemical toxicity and public health risks, health equity, pharmacoepidemiology, public health generalist, toxicology, translational research in adolescent behavioral health; public health practices (Graduate Certificate), including planning for healthy communities; rehabilitation and mental health counseling (Graduate Certificate), including integrative mental health care, marriage and family therapy, rehabilitation technology; secondary education (Graduate Certificate), including ESOL, foreign language education: culture and content, foreign language education: professional; social work (Graduate Certificate), including geriatric social work/clinical gerontology; special education (Graduate Certificate), including autism spectrum disorder, disabilities education: severe/profound; world languages (Graduate Certificate), including teaching English as a second language (TESL) or foreign language. *Unit head:* Dr. Cynthia DeLuca, Associate Vice President and Assistant Vice Provost, 813-974-3077, Fax: 813-974-7061, E-mail: deluca@usf.edu. *Application contact:* Owen Hooper, Director, Summer and Alternative Calendar Programs, 813-974-6917, E-mail: hooper@usf.edu.
Website: http://www.usf.edu/innovative-education/

The University of Tennessee, Graduate School, College of Education, Health and Human Sciences, Program in Education, Knoxville, TN 37996. Offers art education (MS); counseling education (PhD); cultural studies in education (PhD); curriculum (MS, Ed S); curriculum, educational research and evaluation (Ed D, PhD); early childhood education (PhD); early childhood special education (MS); education of deaf and hard of hearing (MS); educational administration and policy studies (Ed D, PhD); educational administration and supervision (Ed S); educational psychology (Ed D, PhD); elementary education (MS, Ed S); elementary teaching (MS); English education (MS, Ed S); exercise science (PhD); foreign language/ESL education (MS, Ed S); instructional technology (MS, Ed D, PhD, Ed S); literacy, language and ESL education (PhD); literacy, language education, and ESL education (Ed D); mathematics education (MS, Ed S); modified and comprehensive special education (MS); reading education (MS, Ed S); school counseling (Ed S); school psychology (PhD, Ed S); science education (MS, Ed S); secondary teaching (MS); social foundations (MS); social science education (MS, Ed S); socio-cultural foundations of sports and education (PhD); special education (Ed S); teacher education (Ed D, PhD). *Accreditation:* NCATE. *Program availability:* Part-time, evening/weekend. *Degree requirements:* For master's and Ed S, thesis optional; for doctorate, variable foreign language requirement, thesis/dissertation. *Entrance requirements:* For master's, minimum GPA of 2.7; for doctorate and Ed S, GRE General Test, minimum GPA of 2.7. Additional exam requirements/recommendations for international students: Required—TOEFL. Electronic applications accepted.

The University of Texas at El Paso, Graduate School, College of Education, Department of Educational Psychology and Special Services, El Paso, TX 79968-0001. Offers educational diagnostics (M Ed); guidance and counseling (M Ed); special education (M Ed). *Program availability:* Part-time, evening/weekend. *Degree requirements:* For master's, thesis optional. *Entrance requirements:* For master's, minimum GPA of 3.0. Additional exam requirements/recommendations for international students: Required—TOEFL. Electronic applications accepted.

The University of Texas at San Antonio, College of Education and Human Development, Department of Educational Psychology, San Antonio, TX 78207. Offers applied behavior analysis (Certificate); educational psychology (MA), including applied educational psychology, behavior assessment and intervention, general educational psychology, program evaluation; language acquisition and bilingual psychoeducational assessment (Certificate); school psychology (MA). *Program availability:* Part-time. *Faculty:* 9 full-time (5 women), 1 (woman) part-time/adjunct. *Students:* 34 full-time (27 women), 40 part-time (35 women); includes 52 minority (5 Black or African American, non-Hispanic/Latino; 1 Asian, non-Hispanic/Latino; 43 Hispanic/Latino; 3 Two or more races, non-Hispanic/Latino). Average age 28. 46 applicants, 72% accepted, 23 enrolled. In 2017, 16 master's, 23 other advanced degrees awarded. *Degree requirements:* For master's, comprehensive exam, thesis (for some programs). *Entrance requirements:* For master's, GRE, bachelor's degree with 18 credit hours in field of study or in another appropriate field of study, two letters of recommendation, statement of purpose; for Certificate, 18 hours in psychology, sociology, education, or anything related (for applied behavioral analysis); minimum GPA of 2.7 in last 30 hours (for language acquisition and bilingual psychoeducational assessment). Additional exam requirements/recommendations for international students: Required—TOEFL (minimum score 550 paper-based; 79 iBT), IELTS (minimum score 6.5). *Application deadline:* For fall admission, 6/15 for domestic students, 3/1 for international students; for spring admission, 10/15 for domestic students, 9/15 for international students; for summer admission, 3/1 for international students. Applications are processed on a rolling basis. Application fee: $50 ($90 for international students). Electronic applications accepted. *Expenses:* Tuition, state resident: full-time $5495. Tuition, nonresident: full-time $21,938. *Required fees:* $1915. Tuition and fees vary according to program. *Financial support:* Research assistantships available. Financial award applicants required to submit FAFSA. *Faculty research:* Teacher consultation and culturally responsive school psychology practices, youth mentoring, cross-age peer mentoring, adolescent connectedness, pair counseling. *Total annual research expenditures:* $168,976. *Unit head:* Dr. Jeremy Sullivan, Department Chair, 210-458-2650, Fax: 210-458-2019, E-mail: jeremy.sullivan@utsa.edu.
Website: http://education.utsa.edu/educational_psychology

The University of Toledo, College of Graduate Studies, Judith Herb College of Education, Department of Educational Foundations and Leadership, Toledo, OH 43606-3390. Offers educational administration and supervision (ME, DE, Ed S); educational psychology (ME, PhD); educational research and measurement (ME, PhD); educational sociology (PhD); educational theory and social foundations (ME); foundations of education (DE, PhD); history of education (PhD); philosophy of education (PhD). *Accreditation:* NCATE. *Program availability:* Part-time, evening/weekend. *Degree requirements:* For master's, comprehensive exam, thesis or alternative; for doctorate, comprehensive exam, thesis/dissertation; for Ed S, thesis optional. *Entrance requirements:* For master's, doctorate, and Ed S, minimum cumulative GPA of 2.7 for all previous academic work, letters of recommendation. Additional exam requirements/recommendations for international students: Required—TOEFL (minimum score 550 paper-based; 80 iBT). Electronic applications accepted.

University of Victoria, Faculty of Graduate Studies, Faculty of Education, Department of Educational Psychology and Leadership Studies, Victoria, BC V8W 2Y2, Canada. Offers aboriginal communities counseling (M Ed); counseling (M Ed, MA); educational psychology (M Ed, MA, PhD), including counseling psychology (M Ed, MA), leadership studies (PhD), learning and development (MA, PhD), measurement and evaluation, special education (M Ed, MA); leadership studies (M Ed, MA). *Program availability:* Part-time. *Degree requirements:* For master's, thesis (for some programs), comprehensive exam (M Ed); for doctorate, comprehensive exam, thesis/dissertation, candidacy exam. *Entrance requirements:* For master's, 2 years of work experience in a relevant field; for doctorate, GRE, 2 years of work experience in a relevant field, minimum B average. Additional exam requirements/recommendations for international students: Required—TOEFL (minimum score 575 paper-based), IELTS (minimum score 7). *Faculty research:* Learning and development (child, adolescent and adult), special education and exceptional children.

University of Virginia, Curry School of Education, Department of Leadership, Foundations and Policy, Program in Educational Psychology, Charlottesville, VA 22903. Offers applied developmental science (M Ed); educational evaluation (M Ed); educational psychology (M Ed, Ed D, Ed S); educational research (Ed D); gifted education (M Ed); instructional technology (M Ed, Ed S); research statistics and evaluation (Ed D); school psychology (Ed D). *Students:* 36 full-time (29 women), 3 part-time (2 women); includes 14 minority (5 Black or African American, non-Hispanic/Latino; 4 Asian, non-Hispanic/Latino; 3 Hispanic/Latino; 2 Two or more races, non-Hispanic/Latino), 7 international. Average age 24. 85 applicants, 80% accepted, 37 enrolled. In 2017, 35 master's, 1 doctorate awarded. *Degree requirements:* For master's, comprehensive exam. *Entrance requirements:* For master's and doctorate, GRE General Test, 2 letters of recommendation. Additional exam requirements/recommendations for international students: Required—TOEFL (minimum score 600 paper-based; 90 iBT), IELTS (minimum score 7). *Application deadline:* Applications are processed on a rolling basis. Application fee: $60. Electronic applications accepted. *Financial support:* Fellowships, research assistantships, and teaching assistantships available. Financial award application deadline: 1/5; financial award applicants required to submit FAFSA. *Unit head:* Sara Rimm-Kaufman, Program Director, 434-982-2863, E-mail: serk@virginia.edu. *Application contact:* E-mail: curry-admissions@virginia.edu. Website: http://curry.virginia.edu/academics/areas-of-study/educational-psychology

University of Virginia, Curry School of Education, Program in Education, Charlottesville, VA 22903. Offers administration and supervision (PhD); applied developmental science (PhD); counselor education (PhD); curriculum and instruction (PhD); early childhood special education (MT); education evaluation (PhD); educational psychology (PhD); educational research (PhD); elementary education (MT); English education (MT, PhD); foreign language education (MT); higher education (PhD); instructional technology (PhD); kinesiology (MT, PhD); math education (PhD); reading education (PhD); research, statistics and evaluation (PhD); school psychology (PhD); science education (PhD); social studies education (MT, PhD); special education (PhD); world languages education (MT). *Students:* 431 full-time (353 women), 15 part-time (14 women); includes 100 minority (32 Black or African American, non-Hispanic/Latino; 33 Asian, non-Hispanic/Latino; 16 Hispanic/Latino; 19 Two or more races, non-Hispanic/Latino), 14 international. Average age 25. 264 applicants, 49% accepted, 83 enrolled. In 2017, 142 master's, 33 doctorates awarded. *Degree requirements:* For master's, comprehensive exam (for some programs), field project; for doctorate, comprehensive exam, thesis/dissertation. *Entrance requirements:* For doctorate, GRE General Test. Additional exam requirements/recommendations for international students: Required—TOEFL (minimum score 600 paper-based; 90 iBT), IELTS (minimum score 7). *Application deadline:* Applications are processed on a rolling basis. Application fee: $60. Electronic applications accepted. *Financial support:* Fellowships, research assistantships, and teaching assistantships available. Financial award application deadline: 1/5; financial award applicants required to submit FAFSA. *Unit head:* Robert C. Pianta, Dean, 434-924-3334, E-mail: pianta@virginia.edu. *Application contact:* E-mail: curry-admissions@virginia.edu. Website: http://curry.virginia.edu/teacher-education

University of Washington, Graduate School, College of Education, Program in Educational Psychology, Seattle, WA 98195. Offers educational psychology (PhD); human development and cognition (M Ed); learning sciences (M Ed, PhD); measurement, statistics and research design (M Ed); school psychology (M Ed). *Accreditation:* APA. *Degree requirements:* For master's, thesis optional; for doctorate, thesis/dissertation. *Entrance requirements:* For master's and doctorate, GRE General Test, minimum GPA of 3.0. Additional exam requirements/recommendations for international students: Required—TOEFL.

University of Wisconsin–Milwaukee, Graduate School, School of Education, Department of Educational Psychology, Milwaukee, WI 53201-0413. Offers children's mental health for school professionals (Graduate Certificate); counseling psychology (PhD); educational statistics and measurement (MS, PhD); learning and development (MS, PhD); multicultural knowledge of mental health practices (Graduate Certificate); school counseling (MS); school counseling (Graduate Certificate); school psychology (MS, PhD, Ed S). *Accreditation:* APA. *Program availability:* Part-time. *Students:* 170 full-time (132 women), 52 part-time (39 women); includes 51 minority (14 Black or African American, non-Hispanic/Latino; 1 American Indian or Alaska Native, non-Hispanic/Latino; 7 Asian, non-Hispanic/Latino; 7 Hispanic/Latino; 1 Native Hawaiian or other Pacific Islander, non-Hispanic/Latino; 21 Two or more races, non-Hispanic/Latino), 4 international. Average age 31. 304 applicants, 39% accepted, 83 enrolled. In 2017, 59 master's, 11 doctorates, 10 other advanced degrees awarded. *Degree requirements:* For master's, comprehensive exam, thesis; for doctorate, thesis/dissertation. *Entrance requirements:* For master's, minimum GPA of 3.0; for doctorate, GRE General Test, minimum GPA of 3.0. Additional exam requirements/recommendations for international students: Required—TOEFL (minimum score 550 paper-based; 79 iBT), IELTS (minimum score 6.5). *Application deadline:* For fall admission, 1/1 priority date for domestic students; for spring admission, 9/1 for domestic students. Application fee: $56 ($96 for international students). Electronic applications accepted. *Financial support:* Fellowships, research assistantships, teaching assistantships, career-related internships or fieldwork, health care benefits, unspecified assistantships, and project assistantships available. Support available to part-time students. Financial award application deadline: 4/15; financial award applicants required to submit FAFSA. *Application contact:* General Information Contact, 414-229-4721, E-mail: soeinfo@uwm.edu. Website: http://uwm.edu/education/academics/educational-psychology-department/

Utah State University, School of Graduate Studies, Emma Eccles Jones College of Education and Human Services, Department of Psychology, Logan, UT 84322. Offers clinical/counseling/school psychology (PhD); research and evaluation methodology (PhD); school counseling (MS); school psychology (MS). *Accreditation:* APA (one or

more programs are accredited). *Program availability:* Part-time, evening/weekend, online learning. Terminal master's awarded for partial completion of doctoral program. *Degree requirements:* For master's, thesis (for some programs); for doctorate, thesis/dissertation. *Entrance requirements:* For master's, GRE General Test (school psychology), MAT (school counseling), minimum GPA of 3.5; for doctorate, GRE General Test, minimum GPA of 3.5. Additional exam requirements/recommendations for international students: Required—TOEFL. *Faculty research:* Hearing loss detection in infancy, ADHD, eating disorders, domestic violence, neuropsychology, bilingual/Spanish speaking students/parents.

Utah State University, School of Graduate Studies, Emma Eccles Jones College of Education and Human Services, Doctoral Program in Education, Logan, UT 84322. Offers business information systems (Ed D, PhD); curriculum and instruction (Ed D, PhD); research and evaluation (PhD). *Degree requirements:* For doctorate, comprehensive exam, thesis/dissertation. *Entrance requirements:* For doctorate, GRE General Test, minimum GPA of 3.0, master's degree. Additional exam requirements/recommendations for international students: Required—TOEFL. Electronic applications accepted. *Faculty research:* Language and literacy development, math and science education, instructional technology, hearing problems/deafness, domestic violence and animal abuse.

Virginia Commonwealth University, Graduate School, School of Education, Doctoral Program in Education, Richmond, VA 23284-9005. Offers art education (PhD); counselor education and supervision (PhD); curriculum, culture and change (PhD); educational leadership (PhD); educational psychology (PhD); leadership (PhD); research and evaluation (PhD); special education and disability leadership (PhD); sport leadership (PhD); urban services leadership (PhD). *Accreditation:* NCATE. *Program availability:* Part-time. *Degree requirements:* For doctorate, thesis/dissertation. *Entrance requirements:* For doctorate, GRE (for PhD), MAT (for Ed D), interview, master's degree, writing sample. Additional exam requirements/recommendations for international students: Required—TOEFL (minimum score 600 paper-based; 100 iBT). Electronic applications accepted.

Virginia Polytechnic Institute and State University, Graduate School, College of Liberal Arts and Human Sciences, Blacksburg, VA 24061. Offers career and technical education (MS Ed, Ed S); communication (MA); counselor education (MA); creative writing (MFA); curriculum and instruction (MA Ed, Ed S); educational leadership and policy studies (Ed S); educational research and evaluation (PhD); English (MA); social, political, ethical, and cultural thought (PhD); Ed D/PhD. *Faculty:* 411 full-time (213 women), 3 part-time/adjunct (all women). *Students:* 623 full-time (427 women), 431 part-time (278 women); includes 203 minority (115 Black or African American, non-Hispanic/Latino; 4 American Indian or Alaska Native, non-Hispanic/Latino; 29 Asian, non-Hispanic/Latino; 33 Hispanic/Latino; 2 Native Hawaiian or other Pacific Islander, non-Hispanic/Latino; 20 Two or more races, non-Hispanic/Latino), 87 international. Average age 34. 898 applicants, 50% accepted, 329 enrolled. In 2017, 314 master's, 102 doctorates awarded. *Degree requirements:* For master's, comprehensive exam (for some programs), thesis (for some programs); for doctorate, comprehensive exam (for some programs), thesis/dissertation (for some programs). *Entrance requirements:* For master's and doctorate, GRE/GMAT. Additional exam requirements/recommendations for international students: Required—TOEFL (minimum score 80 iBT). *Application deadline:* For fall admission, 8/1 for domestic students, 4/1 for international students; for spring admission, 1/1 for domestic students, 9/1 for international students. Applications are processed on a rolling basis. Application fee: $75. Electronic applications accepted. *Expenses:* Tuition, state resident: full-time $15,072; part-time $718.50 per credit hour. Tuition, nonresident: full-time $28,810; part-time $1448.25 per credit hour. *Required fees:* $2741; $502 per semester. Tuition and fees vary according to course load, campus/location and program. *Financial support:* In 2017–18, 19 research assistantships with full tuition reimbursements (averaging $19,611 per year), 226 teaching assistantships with full tuition reimbursements (averaging $16,220 per year) were awarded. Financial award application deadline: 3/1; financial award applicants required to submit FAFSA. *Total annual research expenditures:* $7.9 million. *Unit head:* Dr. Rosemary Blieszner, Dean, 540-231-6779, Fax: 540-231-7157, E-mail: rmb@vt.edu. *Application contact:* Chelsea Blanchet, Executive Assistant, 540-231-6779, Fax: 540-231-7157, E-mail: bchels1@vt.edu. Website: http://www.liberalarts.vt.edu/

Walden University, Graduate Programs, Richard W. Riley College of Education and Leadership, Minneapolis, MN 55401. Offers adult education (Post-Master's Certificate); adult learning (Graduate Certificate); college teaching and learning (Graduate Certificate); community college leadership (Ed D); curriculum, instruction and assessment (Ed D, Ed S, Graduate Certificate); developmental education (Graduate Certificate); early childhood administration, management, and leadership (Graduate Certificate); early childhood education (Ed D, Ed S); early childhood public policy and advocacy (Graduate Certificate); early childhood studies (MS), including administration, management and leadership, early childhood public policy and advocacy, teaching adults in the early childhood field, teaching and diversity in early childhood education; education (MS, PhD), including adolescent literacy and learning (MS), curriculum, instruction, and assessment (grades K-12) (MS), curriculum, instruction, assessment, and evaluation (PhD), early childhood leadership and advocacy (PhD), early childhood special education (PhD), educational leadership (MS), educational leadership and administration (principal preparation) (MS), educational technology and design (PhD), elementary reading and literacy (PreK-6) (MS), elementary reading and mathematics (grades K-6) (MS), global and comparative education (PhD), higher education leadership management and policy (PhD), integrating technology in the classroom (grades K-12) (MS), learning, instruction and innovation (PhD), mathematics (grades 5-8) (MS), mathematics (grades K-6) (MS), mathematics and science (grades K-8) (MS), organizational research, assessment, and evaluation (PhD), reading and literacy with a reading K-12 endorsement (MS), reading literacy assessment and evaluation (PhD), science (grades K-8) (MS), special education (non-licensure) (grades K-12) (MS), teacher leadership (grades K-12) (MS), teaching English language learners (grades K-12) (MS); educational administration and leadership (Ed D); educational leadership and administration (principal preparation) (Ed S); educational technology (Ed D, Ed S, Post Master's Certificate); elementary reading and literacy (Graduate Certificate); engaging culturally diverse learners (Graduate Certificate); enrollment management and institutional marketing (Graduate Certificate); higher education (MS), including adult learning, college teaching and learning, enrollment management and institutional marketing, global higher education, leadership for student success, online and distance learning; higher education and adult learning (Ed D); higher education leadership and management (Ed D); higher education leadership for student success (Graduate Certificate); instructional design and technology (MS, Postbaccalaureate Certificate), including general program (MS), online learning (MS), training and performance improvement (MS); integrating technology in the classroom (Graduate Certificate); mathematics 5-8 (Graduate Certificate); mathematics K-6 (Graduate Certificate); online teaching for adult educators (Graduate Certificate); reading, literacy, and assessment (Ed D, Ed S); science K-8 (Graduate Certificate); special education (Ed D, Ed S, Graduate Certificate); special education (K-age 21) (MAT); teacher leadership (Graduate Certificate); teaching adults English as a second language (Graduate Certificate); teaching adults in the early childhood field (Graduate Certificate); teaching and diversity in early childhood education (Graduate Certificate); teaching English language learners (grades K-12) (Graduate Certificate); teaching K-12 students online (Graduate Certificate). *Accreditation:* NCATE. *Program availability:* Part-time, evening/weekend, online only, 100% online. *Degree requirements:* For doctorate, thesis/dissertation (for some programs), residency; for other advanced degree, residency (for some programs). *Entrance requirements:* For master's, bachelor's degree or higher; minimum GPA of 2.5; official transcripts; goal statement (for some programs); access to computer and Internet; for doctorate, master's degree or higher; three years of related professional or academic experience (preferred); minimum GPA of 3.0; goal statement and current resume (for select programs); official transcripts; access to computer and Internet; for other advanced degree, relevant work experience; access to computer and Internet. Additional exam requirements/recommendations for international students: Required—TOEFL (minimum score 550 paper-based, 79 iBT), IELTS (minimum score 6.5), Michigan English Language Assessment Battery (minimum score 82), or PTE (minimum score 53). Electronic applications accepted.

Washington University in St. Louis, The Graduate School, Department of Education, Program in Educational Research, St. Louis, MO 63130-4899. Offers PhD. *Entrance requirements:* For doctorate, GRE General Test. Additional exam requirements/recommendations for international students: Required—TOEFL. Electronic applications accepted.

Wayland Baptist University, Graduate Programs, Program in Education, Plainview, TX 79072-6998. Offers education administration (M Ed); education diagnostics (M Ed); education literacy (M Ed); elementary certification (M Ed); English (M Ed); English as a second language (M Ed); higher education administration (M Ed); human resources (M Ed); instructional leadership (M Ed); instructional technology (M Ed); leadership training and development (M Ed); science education (M Ed); secondary certification (M Ed); social studies (M Ed); special education (M Ed); sports administration and management (M Ed). *Program availability:* Part-time, evening/weekend, 100% online. *Faculty:* 33 full-time (17 women), 28 part-time/adjunct (17 women). *Students:* 16 full-time (13 women), 221 part-time (143 women); includes 97 minority (26 Black or African American, non-Hispanic/Latino; 1 American Indian or Alaska Native, non-Hispanic/Latino; 5 Asian, non-Hispanic/Latino; 54 Hispanic/Latino; 11 Two or more races, non-Hispanic/Latino), 1 international. Average age 39. 32 applicants, 97% accepted, 23 enrolled. In 2017, 78 master's awarded. *Degree requirements:* For master's, comprehensive exam, capstone course. *Entrance requirements:* For master's, GRE, GMAT or MAT. Additional exam requirements/recommendations for international students: Required—TOEFL (minimum score 500 paper-based; 61 iBT). *Application deadline:* Applications are processed on a rolling basis. Application fee: $50. Electronic applications accepted. *Expenses: Tuition:* Full-time $11,250; part-time $625 per credit hour. *Required fees:* $1200. *Financial support:* Federal Work-Study, institutionally sponsored loans, and scholarships/grants available. Support available to part-time students. Financial award application deadline: 5/1; financial award applicants required to submit FAFSA. *Unit head:* Dr. Gene Whitfill, Dean, 806-291-1047, Fax: 806-291-1951, E-mail: whitfillg@wbu.edu. *Application contact:* Amanda Stanton, Coordinator of Graduate Studies, 806-291-3423, Fax: 806-291-1950, E-mail: stanton@wbu.edu.

Wayne State University, College of Education, Division of Theoretical and Behavioral Foundations, Detroit, MI 48202. Offers applied behavior analysis (Certificate); counseling (M Ed, MA, Ed D, Ed S); counseling psychology (MA, PhD); education evaluation and research (M Ed, Ed D); educational psychology (M Ed, PhD), including learning and instruction sciences (PhD); rehabilitation counseling and community inclusion (MA); school and community psychology (MA, Certificate). *Accreditation:* ACA (one or more programs are accredited); CORE (one or more programs are accredited). *Program availability:* Evening/weekend. *Students:* Average age 32. 294 applicants, 34% accepted, 72 enrolled. In 2017, 87 master's, 12 doctorates, 14 other advanced degrees awarded. *Entrance requirements:* For master's, GRE, interview, personal statement, portfolio (art therapy); for doctorate, GRE, department-written exam, interview, curriculum vitae, references, master's degree in closely-related field with minimum GPA of 3.5, demonstration of counseling skills (for Ed D in counseling); for other advanced degree, master's degree in counseling and counseling license (for Ed S); good standing in school and community psychology MA program (for Certificate). Additional exam requirements/recommendations for international students: Required—TOEFL (minimum score 550 paper-based; 79 iBT), Michigan English Language Assessment Battery (minimum score 85), Recommended—IELTS (minimum score 6.5), TWE (minimum score 5.5). *Application deadline:* For fall admission, 6/1 priority date for domestic students, 5/1 priority date for international students; for winter admission, 10/1 priority date for domestic students, 9/1 priority date for international students; for spring admission, 2/1 priority date for domestic students, 1/1 priority date for international students. Applications are processed on a rolling basis. Application fee: $50. Electronic applications accepted. *Expenses:* Contact institution. *Financial support:* In 2017–18, 92 students received support, including 2 research assistantships with tuition reimbursements available (averaging $17,994 per year); fellowships, teaching assistantships, Federal Work-Study, scholarships/grants, health care benefits, and unspecified assistantships also available. Support available to part-time students. Financial award applicants required to submit FAFSA. *Faculty research:* Adolescents at risk, supervision of counseling. *Unit head:* Dr. Cheryl Somers, Assistant Dean, 313-577-1670, E-mail: c.somers@wayne.edu. *Application contact:* Janice Green, Assistant Dean, 313-577-1605, E-mail: jwgreen@wayne.edu. Website: http://coe.wayne.edu/tbf/index.php

Western Governors University, Teachers College, Salt Lake City, UT 84107. Offers curriculum and instruction (MS); educational leadership (MS); educational studies (MA); educational studies (5-12) (MA), including mathematics; elementary education (K-8) (MAT, Postbaccalaureate Certificate); elementary education (PreK-8) (MAT); English language learning (K-12) (MA); instructional design (MAT); learning and technology (M Ed, MA); management and innovation (M Ed); mathematics (5-12) (MAT, Postbaccalaureate Certificate); mathematics (5-9) (MAT, Postbaccalaureate Certificate); mathematics education (5-12) (MA); mathematics education (5-9) (MA); mathematics education (K-6) (MA); measurement and evaluation (M Ed); science (5-12) (Postbaccalaureate Certificate); science (5-9) (MAT, Postbaccalaureate Certificate); science education (5-12) (MA), including biology, chemistry, geology, physics; science education (5-9) (MA); social science (5-12) (MAT, Postbaccalaureate Certificate); special education (MAT, MS). *Accreditation:* NCATE. *Program availability:* Evening/weekend, online learning. *Degree requirements:* For master's, capstone project. *Entrance requirements:* For master's and Postbaccalaureate Certificate, Readiness Assessment, transcripts. Additional exam requirements/recommendations for international students: Required—TOEFL (minimum score 450 paper-based; 80 iBT). Electronic applications accepted. *Expenses:* Contact institution.

Western Michigan University, Graduate College, College of Education and Human Development, Department of Educational Leadership, Research and Technology, Kalamazoo, MI 49008. Offers educational leadership (MA, PhD, Ed S), including educational leadership (MA); educational technology (MA, Graduate Certificate); evaluation, measurement and research (MA, PhD); organizational learning and performance (MA).

Western Michigan University, Graduate College, College of Education and Human Development, Department of Interdisciplinary Education, Kalamazoo, MI 49008. Offers PhD.

West Texas A&M University, College of Education and Social Sciences, Department of Education, Program in Educational Diagnostician, Canyon, TX 79015. Offers M Ed. *Program availability:* Part-time, online learning. *Degree requirements:* For master's, comprehensive exam, thesis optional. *Entrance requirements:* For master's, GRE General Test, 3 years' teaching experience, competency in diagnosis and prescription. Additional exam requirements/recommendations for international students: Required—TOEFL (minimum score 550 paper-based). Electronic applications accepted. *Faculty research:* Teacher preparation through web-based instruction, developmental disabilities.

Wilkes University, College of Graduate and Professional Studies, School of Education, Wilkes-Barre, PA 18766-0002. Offers educational development and strategies (MS Ed); educational leadership (MS Ed, Ed D); effective teaching (MS Ed); instructional media (MS Ed); instructional technology (MS Ed); international school leadership (MS Ed); international teaching and learning (MS Ed); literacy specialist (MS Ed); middle level education (MS Ed); online teaching (MS Ed); school business leadership (MS Ed); special education (MS Ed); teaching English to speakers of other languages (MS Ed). *Program availability:* Part-time, evening/weekend, 100% online, blended/hybrid learning. *Students:* 76 full-time (57 women), 1,586 part-time (1,204 women); includes 82 minority (10 Black or African American, non-Hispanic/Latino; 12 Asian, non-Hispanic/Latino; 41 Hispanic/Latino; 1 Native Hawaiian or other Pacific Islander, non-Hispanic/Latino; 18 Two or more races, non-Hispanic/Latino). Average age 34. In 2017, 619 master's, 23 doctorates awarded. *Entrance requirements:* Additional exam requirements/recommendations for international students: Required—TOEFL (minimum score 550 paper-based; 79 iBT). *Application deadline:* Applications are processed on a rolling basis. Application fee: $45 ($65 for international students). Electronic applications accepted. *Expenses:* Contact institution. *Financial support:* Unspecified assistantships available. Financial award application deadline: 3/1; financial award applicants required to submit FAFSA. *Unit head:* Dr. Rhonda Rabbitt, Dean, 570-408-4680, Fax: 570-408-7872, E-mail: rhonda.rabbitt@wilkes.edu. *Application contact:* Stephanie Wasmanski, Associate Director of Graduate Admissions, 570-408-5535, Fax: 570-408-7846, E-mail: stephanie.wasmanski@wilkes.edu. Website: http://www.wilkes.edu/academics/graduate-programs/masters-programs/graduate-education/index.aspx

Educational Media/Instructional Technology

Adelphi University, Ruth S. Ammon School of Education, Program in Educational Technology, Garden City, NY 11530-0701. Offers MA. *Program availability:* Online learning. *Students:* 2 full-time (0 women), 7 part-time (5 women); includes 2 minority (1 Black or African American, non-Hispanic/Latino; 1 Two or more races, non-Hispanic/Latino). Average age 29. 14 applicants, 64% accepted, 3 enrolled. In 2017, 2 master's awarded. *Entrance requirements:* For master's, personal statement, two letters of reference, current resume or curriculum vitae. Additional exam requirements/recommendations for international students: Required—TOEFL (minimum score 550 paper-based; 80 iBT), IELTS (minimum score 6.5). *Unit head:* Dr. Jane Ashdown, Dean, 516-877-4065, E-mail: jashdown@adelphi.edu. *Application contact:* E-mail: graduateadmissions@adelphi.edu. Website: http://education-ci.adelphi.edu/educational-technology/

Alabama Agricultural and Mechanical University, School of Graduate Studies, College of Education, Humanities, and Behavioral Sciences, Department of Educational Leadership and Secondary Education, Huntsville, AL 35811. Offers biology (M Ed); business/marketing education (M Ed, Ed S); chemistry (M Ed); collaborative teacher secondary education (M Ed, Ed S); education (M Ed, Ed S); English language arts (M Ed); family/consumer science education (M Ed, Ed S); general science (M Ed); general social science (M Ed); mathematics (M Ed, Ed S); physics (M Ed, Ed S); technology education (M Ed). *Accreditation:* NCATE. *Program availability:* Evening/weekend. *Degree requirements:* For master's, comprehensive exam; for Ed S, thesis. *Entrance requirements:* For master's, GRE General Test. Additional exam requirements/recommendations for international students: Required—TOEFL (minimum score 500 paper-based; 61 iBT). Electronic applications accepted. *Faculty research:* World peace through education, computer-assisted instruction.

Alabama State University, College of Education, Department of Instructional Support Programs, Montgomery, AL 36101-0271. Offers applied technology (MS); counselor education (M Ed, MS, Ed S), including general counseling (MS, Ed S), school counseling (M Ed, Ed S); educational administration (M Ed, Ed D, PhD, Ed S), including educational administration (Ed S), educational leadership, policy and law (Ed D, PhD), instructional leadership (M Ed), teacher leadership (Ed S); library education media (M Ed, Ed S). *Program availability:* Part-time. *Faculty:* 11 full-time (6 women), 7 part-time/adjunct (5 women). *Students:* 35 full-time (20 women), 112 part-time (81 women); includes 139 minority (all Black or African American, non-Hispanic/Latino), 1 international. Average age 37. 48 applicants, 75% accepted, 16 enrolled. In 2017, 31 master's, 4 doctorates awarded. Terminal master's awarded for partial completion of doctoral program. *Degree requirements:* For master's, comprehensive exam; for Ed S, comprehensive exam, thesis. *Entrance requirements:* For master's, GRE General Test, MAT, writing competency test, bachelor's degree or its equivalent from accredited college or university with minimum GPA of 2.5; for Ed S, GRE General Test, MAT, writing competency test, minimum GPA of 3.25. Additional exam requirements/recommendations for international students: Required—TOEFL (minimum score 500 paper-based). *Application deadline:* For fall admission, 4/15 for domestic and international students; for spring admission, 11/15 for domestic and international students; for summer admission, 3/15 for domestic and international students. Applications are processed on a rolling basis. Application fee: $25. Electronic

Educational Media/Instructional Technology

applications accepted. *Expenses:* Contact institution. *Financial support:* In 2017–18, 3 students received support. Research assistantships and unspecified assistantships available. Financial award application deadline: 6/30; financial award applicants required to submit FAFSA. *Unit head:* Dr. Sonja Harrington, Chair, 334-229-8828, Fax: 334-229-6831, E-mail: sharrington@alasu.edu. *Application contact:* Dr. William Person, Dean of Graduate Studies, 334-229-4275, Fax: 334-229-4928, E-mail: wperson@alasu.edu. Website: http://www.alasu.edu/academics/colleges—departments/college-of-education/instructional-support-programs/index.aspx

Alverno College, School of Professional Studies - Education Division, Milwaukee, WI 53234-3922. Offers adaptive education (MA); administrative leadership (MA); adult education and organizational development (MA); adult educational and instructional design (MA); adult educational and instructional technology (MA); global connections in the humanities (MA); instructional leadership (MA); instructional technology for K-12 settings (MA); professional development (MA); reading education (MA); reading education with adaptive education (MA); science education (MA); special education (MA); teaching in alternative schools (MA). *Accreditation:* NCATE. *Program availability:* Part-time, evening/weekend. *Faculty:* 3 full-time (2 women), 23 part-time/adjunct (17 women). *Students:* 37 full-time (34 women), 68 part-time (65 women); includes 27 minority (16 Black or African American, non-Hispanic/Latino; 1 American Indian or Alaska Native, non-Hispanic/Latino; 1 Asian, non-Hispanic/Latino; 7 Hispanic/Latino; 2 Two or more races, non-Hispanic/Latino). Average age 35. 67 applicants, 100% accepted, 51 enrolled. In 2017, 68 master's awarded. *Degree requirements:* For master's, presentation/defense of proposal, conference presentation of inquiry projects. *Entrance requirements:* For master's, bachelor's degree in related field, communication samples from work setting, 3 letters of recommendation. Additional exam requirements/recommendations for international students: Required—TOEFL. *Application deadline:* For fall admission, 7/15 priority date for domestic and international students; for spring admission, 12/15 priority date for domestic and international students. Applications are processed on a rolling basis. Application fee: $0. Electronic applications accepted. *Expenses:* Contact institution. *Financial support:* Federal Work-Study and scholarships/grants available. Support available to part-time students. Financial award applicants required to submit FAFSA. *Faculty research:* Student self-assessment, self-reflection, integration of curriculum, identifying needs of students in strategic situations and designing appropriate classroom strategies. *Unit head:* Dr. Patricia Luebke, Dean, School of Professional Studies, 414-382-6368, Fax: 414-382-6354, E-mail: patricia.luebke@alverno.edu. *Application contact:* Katie Kipp, Graduate Admissions Counselor, 414-382-6045, Fax: 414-382-6354, E-mail: katie.kipp@alverno.edu.

American College of Education, Graduate Programs, Indianapolis, IN 46204. Offers curriculum and instruction (M Ed), including bilingual, ESL; educational leadership (M Ed); educational technology (M Ed).

American InterContinental University Online, Program in Education, Schaumburg, IL 60173. Offers curriculum and instruction (M Ed); educational assessment and evaluation (M Ed); instructional technology (M Ed); leadership of educational organizations (M Ed). *Accreditation:* TEAC. *Program availability:* Evening/weekend, online learning. *Entrance requirements:* Additional exam requirements/recommendations for international students: Required—TOEFL (minimum score 550 paper-based). Electronic applications accepted.

American University, School of Professional and Extended Studies, Washington, DC 20016-8030. Offers agile project management (MS); healthcare management (MS, Graduate Certificate); human resource analytics and management (MS, Graduate Certificate); instructional design and learning analytics (MS); measurement and evaluation (MS); project monitoring and evaluation (Graduate Certificate); sports analytics and management (MS, Graduate Certificate). *Program availability:* Part-time, evening/weekend, 100% online. *Faculty:* 27 full-time (13 women), 21 part-time/adjunct (10 women). *Students:* 17 full-time (8 women), 59 part-time (34 women); includes 9 minority (5 Black or African American, non-Hispanic/Latino; 2 Asian, non-Hispanic/Latino; 1 Hispanic/Latino; 1 Two or more races, non-Hispanic/Latino), 5 international. Average age 31. 55 applicants, 89% accepted, 38 enrolled. In 2017, 8 other advanced degrees awarded. *Entrance requirements:* For master's, official transcript(s), resume. Additional exam requirements/recommendations for international students: Required—TOEFL (minimum score 600 paper-based; 100 iBT). *Application deadline:* Applications are processed on a rolling basis. Application fee: $55. Electronic applications accepted. *Expenses:* Contact institution. *Financial support:* Applicants required to submit FAFSA. *Unit head:* Carola Weil, Dean, 202-885-5990, Fax: 202-895-4960, E-mail: weil@american.edu. *Application contact:* Emily Aronoff, Assistant Director for Recruitment and Admission, 202-895-4953, E-mail: aronoff@american.edu. Website: http://www.american.edu/spexs/

Antioch University New England, Graduate School, Department of Education, Experienced Educators Program, Keene, NH 03431-3552. Offers foundations of education (M Ed), including applied behavioral analysis, autism spectrum disorders, educating for sustainability, next-generation learning using technology, problem-based learning using critical skills, teacher leadership; principal certification (PMC). *Degree requirements:* For master's, thesis, practicum. *Entrance requirements:* For master's, previous course work and work experience in education. Additional exam requirements/recommendations for international students: Required—TOEFL (minimum score 550 paper-based). Electronic applications accepted. *Expenses:* Contact institution. *Faculty research:* Classroom action research, school restructuring, problem-based learning, brain-based learning.

Appalachian State University, Cratis D. Williams Graduate School, Department of Curriculum and Instruction, Boone, NC 28608. Offers curriculum specialist (MA); educational media (MA); elementary education (MA); middle grades education (MA), including language arts, mathematics, science, social studies. *Accreditation:* NCATE. *Program availability:* Part-time, evening/weekend, online learning. *Degree requirements:* For master's, comprehensive exam, thesis or alternative. *Entrance requirements:* For master's, GRE General Test or MAT, 3 letters of recommendation. Additional exam requirements/recommendations for international students: Required—TOEFL (minimum score 570 paper-based; 79 iBT), IELTS (minimum score 6.5). Electronic applications accepted. *Faculty research:* Media literacy, elementary teaching, curriculum development, online learning environments.

Appalachian State University, Cratis D. Williams Graduate School, Department of Leadership and Educational Studies, Boone, NC 28608. Offers educational administration (Ed S); educational media (MA); higher education (MA, Ed S); library science (MLS); school administration (MSA). *Program availability:* Part-time, evening/weekend, online learning. *Degree requirements:* For master's and Ed S, comprehensive exam, thesis optional. *Entrance requirements:* For master's and Ed S, GRE or MAT, 3 letters of recommendation. Additional exam requirements/recommendations for international students: Required—TOEFL (minimum score 570 paper-based; 79 iBT), IELTS (minimum score 6.5). Electronic applications accepted. *Faculty research:* Brain, learning and meditation; leadership of teaching and learning.

Arcadia University, School of Education, Glenside, PA 19038-3295. Offers art education (M Ed); computer education (CAS); curriculum (CAS); curriculum studies (M Ed); early childhood education (M Ed), including individualized, master teacher,

research in child development; educational leadership (M Ed, Ed D, CAS); elementary education (M Ed); English education (MA Ed); environmental education (MA Ed); instructional technology (M Ed); language arts (M Ed); library science (M Ed); mathematics education (M Ed, MA Ed); music education (MA Ed); psychology (MA Ed); reading (M Ed, CAS); science education (M Ed, CAS); secondary education (M Ed, CAS); special education (M Ed, Ed D, CAS); theater arts (MA Ed); written communication (MA Ed). *Accreditation:* NASAD. *Program availability:* Part-time, evening/weekend, online learning. Electronic applications accepted. *Expenses:* Contact institution.

Argosy University, Atlanta, College of Education, Atlanta, GA 30328. Offers educational leadership (MAEd, Ed D, Ed S), including higher education administration (Ed D), K-12 education (Ed D); teaching and learning (MAEd, Ed D, Ed S), including education technology (Ed D), higher education (Ed D), K-12 education (Ed D).

Argosy University, Orange County, College of Education, Orange, CA 92868. Offers community college executive leadership (Ed D); educational leadership (MA Ed, Ed D), including higher education administration (Ed D), K-12 education (Ed D); instructional leadership (MA Ed, Ed D), including education technology (Ed D), higher education (Ed D), K-12 education (Ed D); multiple subject teacher preparation (MA Ed), single subject teacher preparation (MA Ed).

Argosy University, Phoenix, College of Education, Phoenix, AZ 85021. Offers adult education and training (MA Ed); advanced educational administration (Ed D, Ed S); community college executive leadership (Ed D); educational administration (MA Ed); educational leadership (MA Ed, Ed D, Ed S), including education technology (Ed D), higher education administration (Ed D), K-12 education (Ed D); higher and postsecondary education (MA Ed); initial educational administration (Ed D, Ed S); school psychology (MA); teaching and learning (MA Ed, Ed D, Ed S), including education technology (Ed D), higher education (Ed D), K-12 education (Ed D).

Argosy University, Seattle, College of Education, Seattle, WA 98121. Offers adult education and training (MA Ed); community college executive leadership (Ed D); educational leadership (MA Ed, Ed D), including higher education administration (Ed D), K-12 education (Ed D); higher and postsecondary education (MA Ed); instructional leadership (MA Ed, Ed D), including education technology (Ed D), higher education (Ed D), K-12 education (Ed D).

Argosy University, Twin Cities, College of Education, Eagan, MN 55121. Offers advanced educational administration (Ed D, Ed S); educational leadership (MA Ed, Ed D, Ed S), including higher education administration (Ed D), K-12 education (Ed D); higher and postsecondary education (MA Ed); initial educational administration (Ed D, Ed S); instructional leadership (MA Ed, Ed D, Ed S), including education technology (Ed D), higher education (Ed D), K-12 education (Ed D).

Arizona State University at the Tempe campus, Mary Lou Fulton Teachers College, Program in Educational Technology, Phoenix, AZ 85069. Offers educational technology (M Ed); instructional design and performance improvement (Graduate Certificate); online teaching for grades K-12 (Graduate Certificate). *Program availability:* Part-time, evening/weekend, online learning. Terminal master's awarded for partial completion of doctoral program. *Degree requirements:* For master's, thesis or alternative, applied project, interactive Program of Study (iPOS) submitted before completing 50 percent of required credit hours. *Entrance requirements:* For master's, GRE (Verbal section) or MAT (for students with less than 3 years of professional experience as teacher, trainer or instructional designer), minimum GPA of 3.0 or equivalent in last 2 years of work leading to bachelor's degree, 3 letters of recommendation, personal statement, curriculum vitae or resume. Additional exam requirements/recommendations for international students: Required—TOEFL (minimum score 600 paper-based; 100 iBT). Electronic applications accepted. *Faculty research:* Virtual environments; innovative technologies; theory, design, and implementation of computer-based learning environments; impact of technology into curricula on student achievement/attitude; electronic portfolios for learning and assessment.

Arkansas Tech University, College of Education, Russellville, AR 72801. Offers college student personnel (MS); educational leadership (M Ed, Ed S); instructional technology (M Ed); school counseling and leadership (M Ed); school leadership (Ed D); special education K-12 (M Ed); strength and conditioning studies (MS); teaching (MAT); teaching, learning, and leadership (M Ed). *Accreditation:* NCATE. *Program availability:* Part-time, evening/weekend, 100% online, blended/hybrid learning. *Students:* 80 full-time (45 women), 433 part-time (328 women); includes 114 minority (81 Black or African American, non-Hispanic/Latino; 4 American Indian or Alaska Native, non-Hispanic/Latino; 1 Asian, non-Hispanic/Latino; 13 Hispanic/Latino; 15 Two or more races, non-Hispanic/Latino), 2 international. Average age 34. In 2017, 132 master's, 8 doctorates, 3 other advanced degrees awarded. *Degree requirements:* For master's, comprehensive exam, thesis optional, action research project; for doctorate, thesis/dissertation. *Entrance requirements:* Additional exam requirements/recommendations for international students: Required—TOEFL (minimum score 550 paper-based; 79 iBT), IELTS (minimum score 6.5), PTE (minimum score 58). *Application deadline:* For fall admission, 3/1 priority date for domestic students, 5/1 priority date for international students; for spring admission, 10/1 priority date for domestic and international students. Applications are processed on a rolling basis. Application fee: $40 ($90 for international students). Electronic applications accepted. *Expenses:* Tuition, state resident: full-time $6816; part-time $284 per credit hour. Tuition, nonresident: full-time $13,632; part-time $568 per credit hour. *Required fees:* $420 per semester. Tuition and fees vary according to course load. *Financial support:* In 2017–18, research assistantships with full and partial tuition reimbursements (averaging $4,800 per year), teaching assistantships with full and partial tuition reimbursements (averaging $4,800 per year) were awarded; career-related internships or fieldwork, Federal Work-Study, scholarships/grants, health care benefits, and unspecified assistantships also available. Support available to part-time students. Financial award application deadline: 4/15; financial award applicants required to submit FAFSA. *Unit head:* Dr. Mary Gunter, Dean, 479-964-3217, E-mail: mgunter@atu.edu. Website: http://www.atu.edu/education/

Auburn University, Graduate School, College of Education, Department of Educational Foundations, Leadership, and Technology, Auburn University, AL 36849. Offers adult education (PhD, Ed S); curriculum supervision (M Ed, PhD); higher education administration (PhD); library media (Ed S); school administration (M Ed, PhD). *Accreditation:* NCATE. *Program availability:* Part-time. *Faculty:* 30 full-time (17 women), 8 part-time/adjunct (5 women). *Students:* 139 full-time (94 women), 254 part-time (171 women); includes 109 minority (95 Black or African American, non-Hispanic/Latino; 1 American Indian or Alaska Native, non-Hispanic/Latino; 2 Asian, non-Hispanic/Latino; 4 Hispanic/Latino; 1 Native Hawaiian or other Pacific Islander, non-Hispanic/Latino; 6 Two or more races, non-Hispanic/Latino), 12 international. Average age 37. 216 applicants, 72% accepted, 94 enrolled. In 2017, 92 master's, 46 doctorates, 58 other advanced degrees awarded. *Degree requirements:* For master's, thesis (for some programs); for doctorate, thesis/dissertation; for Ed S, field project. *Entrance requirements:* For master's, doctorate, and Ed S, GRE General Test. *Application deadline:* Applications are processed on a rolling basis. Application fee: $50 ($60 for international students). Electronic applications accepted. *Expenses:* Tuition, state resident: full-time $10,974;

part-time $519 per credit hour. Tuition, nonresident: full-time $29,658; part-time $1557 per credit hour. *Required fees:* $816 per semester. Tuition and fees vary according to degree level and program. *Financial support:* Teaching assistantships and Federal Work-Study available. Support available to part-time students. Financial award application deadline: 3/15; financial award applicants required to submit FAFSA. *Unit head:* Dr. Sherida Downer, Head, 334-844-3060. *Application contact:* Dr. George Flowers, Dean of the Graduate School, 334-844-4700.
Website: http://www.education.auburn.edu/academic_departments/eflt/

Auburn University at Montgomery, College of Education, Department of Counselor, Leadership, and Special Education, Montgomery, AL 36124-4023. Offers counselor education (M Ed, Ed S), including clinical mental health counseling, school counseling; early childhood special education (M Ed); instructional leadership (M Ed, Ed S); special education/collaborative teacher (M Ed, Ed S). *Accreditation:* ACA; NCATE. *Program availability:* Part-time, evening/weekend. *Faculty:* 7 full-time (4 women), 2 part-time/adjunct (both women). *Students:* 27 full-time (23 women), 57 part-time (51 women); includes 40 minority (38 Black or African American, non-Hispanic/Latino; 2 Hispanic/Latino). Average age 34. 76 applicants, 72% accepted, 26 enrolled. In 2017, 37 master's awarded. *Degree requirements:* For master's and Ed S, comprehensive exam. *Entrance requirements:* For master's, GRE General Test or MAT, certification, BS in teaching; for Ed S, GRE General Test or MAT, certification. Additional exam requirements/recommendations for international students: Recommended—TOEFL (minimum score 500 paper-based; 61 iBT), IELTS (minimum score 5.5), TSE (minimum score 44). *Application deadline:* For fall admission, 7/15 for international students; for spring admission, 11/15 for international students; for summer admission, 4/15 for international students. Applications are processed on a rolling basis. Electronic applications accepted. *Expenses:* Tuition, state resident: full-time $6930; part-time $385 per credit hour. Tuition, nonresident: full-time $15,588; part-time $866 per credit hour. *Required fees:* $640. *Financial support:* Career-related internships or fieldwork and scholarships/grants available. Support available to part-time students. Financial award application deadline: 3/1; financial award applicants required to submit FAFSA. *Unit head:* Dr. Samuel Flynt, Head, 334-244-3835, Fax: 334-244-3101, E-mail: sflynt@aum.edu. *Application contact:* Dr. Rhonda Morton, Associate Dean/Graduate Coordinator, 334-244-3287, Fax: 334-244-3978, E-mail: rmorton@aum.edu.
Website: http://education.aum.edu/academic-departments/counselor-leadership-and-special-education

Auburn University at Montgomery, College of Education, Department of Curriculum, Instruction, and Technology, Montgomery, AL 36124-4023. Offers elementary education (M Ed, Ed S); instructional technology (Ed S); secondary education (M Ed). *Faculty:* 12 full-time (8 women), 8 part-time/adjunct (all women). *Students:* 43 full-time (34 women), 81 part-time (65 women); includes 39 minority (38 Black or African American, non-Hispanic/Latino; 1 Hispanic/Latino), 2 international. Average age 33. 99 applicants, 70% accepted, 37 enrolled. In 2017, 47 master's awarded. *Degree requirements:* For master's, comprehensive exam, thesis (for some programs). *Entrance requirements:* For master's, GRE or MAT. Additional exam requirements/recommendations for international students: Recommended—TOEFL (minimum score 500 paper-based; 61 iBT), IELTS (minimum score 5.5), TSE (minimum score 44). *Application deadline:* For fall admission, 7/15 for international students; for spring admission, 11/15 for international students; for summer admission, 4/15 for international students. Applications are processed on a rolling basis. Application fee: $25. Electronic applications accepted. *Expenses:* Tuition, state resident: full-time $6930; part-time $385 per credit hour. Tuition, nonresident: full-time $15,588; part-time $866 per credit hour. *Required fees:* $640. *Financial support:* Application deadline: 3/1; applicants required to submit FAFSA. *Unit head:* Dr. Kellie Shumack, Head, 334-244-3737, Fax: 334-244-3835, E-mail: kshumack@aum.edu. *Application contact:* Dr. Rhonda Morton, Associate Dean/Graduate Coordinator, 334-224-3287, Fax: 334-244-3978, E-mail: rmorton@aum.edu.
Website: http://education.aum.edu/academic-departments/curriculum-instruction-technology

Augustana University, MA in Education Program, Sioux Falls, SD 57197. Offers instructional strategies (MA); reading (MA); special populations (MA); STEM (MA); technology (MA). *Accreditation:* NCATE. *Program availability:* Part-time-only, evening/weekend, online only, 100% online. *Faculty:* 7 full-time (5 women), 6 part-time/adjunct (5 women). *Students:* 288 full-time (250 women); includes 20 minority (2 Black or African American, non-Hispanic/Latino; 2 American Indian or Alaska Native, non-Hispanic/Latino; 1 Asian, non-Hispanic/Latino; 11 Hispanic/Latino; 1 Native Hawaiian or other Pacific Islander, non-Hispanic/Latino; 3 Two or more races, non-Hispanic/Latino), 3 international. Average age 32. 47 applicants, 77% accepted, 35 enrolled. In 2017, 84 master's awarded. *Degree requirements:* For master's, thesis. *Entrance requirements:* For master's, appropriate bachelor's degree, minimum GPA of 3.0, teaching certificate. Additional exam requirements/recommendations for international students: Required—TOEFL (minimum score 550 paper-based). *Application deadline:* For fall admission, 8/1 for domestic and international students; for spring admission, 11/1 for domestic and international students; for summer admission, 4/1 for domestic and international students. Applications are processed on a rolling basis. Application fee: $60. Electronic applications accepted. *Expenses:* Contact institution. *Financial support:* Application deadline: 3/1; applicants required to submit FAFSA. *Faculty research:* Multicultural education, education of students with autism, well-being in school settings, factors that predict academic hopefulness. *Unit head:* Dr. Laurie Daily, Chair, 605-274-5211, E-mail: laurie.daily@augie.edu. *Application contact:* Julia Paulich, Graduate Coordinator, 605-274-4043, Fax: 605-274-4450, E-mail: graduate@augie.edu.
Website: http://www.augie.edu/master-arts-education

Augusta University, College of Education, Program in Educational Innovation, Augusta, GA 30912. Offers educational innovation (Ed D).

Aurora University, School of Education and Human Performance, Aurora, IL 60506-4892. Offers applied behavioral analysis (MS); bilingual-ESL education (MA); educational leadership with principal endorsement (MA); educational technology (MA); leadership in adult learning higher education (Ed D); leadership in curriculum and instruction (Ed D); leadership in educational administration (Ed D); reading instruction (MA); special education (MA). *Accreditation:* NCATE. *Program availability:* Part-time, evening/weekend. *Faculty:* 15 full-time (8 women), 39 part-time/adjunct (20 women). *Students:* 421 full-time (299 women), 142 part-time (89 women); includes 90 minority (25 Black or African American, non-Hispanic/Latino; 7 Asian, non-Hispanic/Latino; 50 Hispanic/Latino; 2 Native Hawaiian or other Pacific Islander, non-Hispanic/Latino; 6 Two or more races, non-Hispanic/Latino). Average age 37. 169 applicants, 95% accepted, 59 enrolled. In 2017, 175 master's, 36 doctorates awarded. *Degree requirements:* For master's, student teaching; for doctorate, comprehensive exam, thesis/dissertation. *Entrance requirements:* For master's, 2 years of teaching experience, valid teaching certificate, resume; for doctorate, appropriate master's degree, two references, curriculum vitae, personal statement, professional project, reflective essay. Additional exam requirements/recommendations for international students: Required—TOEFL (minimum score 550 paper-based; 79 iBT). *Application deadline:* For fall admission, 6/1 for international students; for spring admission, 10/1 for international students. Applications are processed on a rolling basis. Application fee: $0. Electronic applications

accepted. *Expenses:* Contact institution. *Financial support:* In 2017–18, 34 students received support. Federal Work-Study, scholarships/grants, and unspecified assistantships available. Support available to part-time students. Financial award applicants required to submit FAFSA. *Unit head:* Dr. Jen Buckley, Dean, School of Education and Human Performance, 630-844-1542, Fax: 630-844-6155, E-mail: jbuckley@aurora.edu. *Application contact:* Elizabeth Botica, Graduate Education Recruiter, 630-947-8918, E-mail: ebotica@aurora.edu.
Website: http://aurora.edu/education

Avila University, School of Professional Studies, Kansas City, MO 64145-1698. Offers executive leadership (MS); fundraising (MA); instructional design and technology (MA, MS); leadership coaching (MS); project management (MA); strategic human resources (MS). *Program availability:* Part-time-only, evening/weekend, 100% online, blended/hybrid learning. *Faculty:* 14 part-time/adjunct (8 women). *Students:* 85 full-time (61 women), 45 part-time (33 women); includes 42 minority (35 Black or African American, non-Hispanic/Latino; 2 Asian, non-Hispanic/Latino; 4 Hispanic/Latino; 1 Two or more races, non-Hispanic/Latino), 3 international. Average age 37. 63 applicants, 60% accepted, 29 enrolled. In 2017, 39 master's awarded. *Degree requirements:* For master's, thesis optional. *Entrance requirements:* For master's, 2 letters of recommendation, minimum GPA of 3.0 during last 60 hours, resume, statement of intent. Additional exam requirements/recommendations for international students: Required—TOEFL (minimum score 550 paper-based; 79 iBT). *Application deadline:* Applications are processed on a rolling basis. Application fee: $0. Electronic applications accepted. *Expenses:* Contact institution. *Financial support:* In 2017–18, 14 students received support. Unspecified assistantships available. Support available to part-time students. Financial award applicants required to submit FAFSA. *Unit head:* Kari Clevenger, Associate Dean/Director, 816-501-3675, Fax: 816-941-4650, E-mail: advantage@avila.edu. *Application contact:* Jessica Burson, Graduate Admission Advisor, 816-501-2482, Fax: 816-941-4650, E-mail: advantage@avila.edu.
Website: https://www.avila.edu/mrk/advantage-3

Azusa Pacific University, School of Education, Department of Teacher Education, Program in Educational Technology, Azusa, CA 91702-7000. Offers MA. *Program availability:* Part-time, evening/weekend, 100% online. *Degree requirements:* For master's, comprehensive exam, core exam, oral presentation. *Entrance requirements:* For master's, 12 units of course work in education, minimum GPA of 3.0. *Expenses:* Contact institution.

Azusa Pacific University, School of Education, Department of Teacher Education, Program in Learning and Technology, Azusa, CA 91702-7000. Offers MA Ed. *Program availability:* Online learning.

Baldwin Wallace University, Graduate Programs, School of Education, Leadership in Technology for Teaching and Learning Program, Berea, OH 44017-2088. Offers MA Ed. *Program availability:* Part-time, evening/weekend, 100% online. *Students:* 10 full-time (6 women), 7 part-time (2 women); includes 2 minority (1 Black or African American, non-Hispanic/Latino; 1 Two or more races, non-Hispanic/Latino). Average age 29. 9 applicants, 89% accepted, 6 enrolled. In 2017, 5 master's awarded. *Degree requirements:* For master's, capstone project. *Entrance requirements:* For master's, bachelor's degree in field, MAT or minimum GPA of 3.0. Additional exam requirements/recommendations for international students: Required—TOEFL (minimum score 550 paper-based; 79 iBT). *Application deadline:* For fall admission, 8/15 priority date for domestic students; for spring admission, 12/15 priority date for domestic students. Applications are processed on a rolling basis. Application fee: $25. Electronic applications accepted. Application fee is waived when completed online. *Expenses:* $721 per credit hour. *Financial support:* Career-related internships or fieldwork available. Financial award applicants required to submit FAFSA. *Faculty research:* No-cost software, online resources for building a classroom learning management system. *Unit head:* Dr. Susan Finelli-Genovese, Coordinator, 440-826-8064, Fax: 440-826-3779, E-mail: sfinelli@bw.edu. *Application contact:* Winnie W. Gerhardt, Director of Transfer, Adult and Graduate Admission, 440-826-2222, Fax: 440-826-3830, E-mail: admission@bw.edu.
Website: http://www.bw.edu/academics/master-of-arts-in-education/maed-technology-leadership/

Ball State University, Graduate School, Teachers College, Department of Educational Studies, Program in Curriculum and Educational Technology, Muncie, IN 47306. Offers MA. *Accreditation:* NCATE. *Program availability:* Part-time, online only, 100% online. *Students:* 3 full-time (all women), 42 part-time (32 women); includes 5 minority (3 Black or African American, non-Hispanic/Latino; 1 Hispanic/Latino; 1 Two or more races, non-Hispanic/Latino). Average age 33. 9 applicants, 78% accepted, 6 enrolled. In 2017, 24 master's awarded. *Entrance requirements:* For master's, minimum baccalaureate GPA of 2.75 or 3.0 in latter half of baccalaureate. Additional exam requirements/recommendations for international students: Required—TOEFL (minimum score 550 paper-based; 79 iBT), IELTS (minimum score 6.5). *Application deadline:* Applications are processed on a rolling basis. Application fee: $60. Electronic applications accepted. *Financial support:* Research assistantships with partial tuition reimbursements, teaching assistantships with partial tuition reimbursements, and unspecified assistantships available. Financial award application deadline: 3/1; financial award applicants required to submit FAFSA. *Unit head:* Dr. Ayesha Sadaf, Program Director, 785-285-4246, Fax: 785-285-5489, E-mail: sadaf@bsu.edu.
Website: http://www.bsu.edu/edstudies/

Ball State University, Graduate School, Teachers College, Department of Educational Studies, Program in Educational Studies, Muncie, IN 47306. Offers educational studies (PhD), including cultural and educational policy studies, curriculum, educational technology. *Program availability:* Part-time, blended/hybrid learning. *Students:* 8 full-time (4 women), 16 part-time (11 women); includes 4 minority (2 Black or African American, non-Hispanic/Latino; 1 Asian, non-Hispanic/Latino; 1 Two or more races, non-Hispanic/Latino), 3 international. Average age 43. 14 applicants, 57% accepted, 4 enrolled. In 2017, 3 doctorates awarded. *Degree requirements:* For doctorate, thesis/dissertation. *Entrance requirements:* For doctorate, GRE General Test, minimum graduate GPA of 3.2, curriculum vitae, writing sample, three letters of reference. Additional exam requirements/recommendations for international students: Required—TOEFL (minimum score 550 paper-based; 79 iBT), IELTS (minimum score 6.5). *Application deadline:* Applications are processed on a rolling basis. Application fee: $60. Electronic applications accepted. *Financial support:* Research assistantships with partial tuition reimbursements and teaching assistantships with partial tuition reimbursements available. Financial award application deadline: 3/1; financial award applicants required to submit FAFSA. *Faculty research:* Emerging curriculum trends, secondary teacher preparation, issues of equity and social justice in education, teacher technology integration, teaching for transformative understanding, teacher leadership, history of educational policy and practices, ethics and education. *Unit head:* Dr. Theresa Kruczek, Interim Chair, 765-285-8049, E-mail: tkruczek@bsu.edu.
Website: http://www.bsu.edu/edstudies

Barry University, School of Education, Graduate Certificate Programs, Miami Shores, FL 33161-6695. Offers advanced teaching and learning with technology (Certificate); distance education (Certificate); higher education technology integration (Certificate); human resources: not for profit and religious organizations (Certificate); K-12 technology integration (Certificate).

Educational Media/Instructional Technology

Barry University, School of Education, Program in Educational Technology Applications, Miami Shores, FL 33161-6695. Offers educational computing and technology (MS, Ed S). *Program availability:* Part-time, evening/weekend, online learning. *Degree requirements:* For master's and Ed S, comprehensive exam. *Entrance requirements:* For master's, GRE General Test or MAT, minimum GPA of 3.0; for Ed S, GRE General Test, minimum GPA of 3.0.

Barry University, School of Education, Program in Leadership and Education, Miami Shores, FL 33161-6695. Offers educational technology (PhD); exceptional student education (PhD); higher education administration (PhD); human resource development (PhD); leadership (PhD). *Program availability:* Part-time, evening/weekend. *Degree requirements:* For doctorate, thesis/dissertation. *Entrance requirements:* For doctorate, GRE General Test, minimum GPA of 3.25. Electronic applications accepted.

Barry University, School of Education, Program in Technology and TESOL, Miami Shores, FL 33161-6695. Offers MS, Ed S.

Bay Path University, Program in Higher Education Administration, Longmeadow, MA 01106-2292. Offers enrollment management (MS); general administration (MS); institutional advancement (MS); online teaching and program administration (MS). *Program availability:* Part-time, online only, 100% online. *Students:* 3 full-time (all women), 47 part-time (33 women); includes 19 minority (9 Black or African American, non-Hispanic/Latino; 8 Hispanic/Latino; 2 Two or more races, non-Hispanic/Latino). Average age 34. In 2017, 15 master's awarded. *Degree requirements:* For master's, 8 core courses (24 credits) and 4 elective courses (12 credits) for a total of 36 credits. *Application deadline:* Applications are processed on a rolling basis. Application fee: $45. Electronic applications accepted. Application fee is waived when completed online. *Expenses:* $760 per credit. *Financial support:* Unspecified assistantships available. Financial award applicants required to submit FAFSA. *Unit head:* Dr. Lauren Way, Program Director, 413-565-1193, E-mail: lway@baypath.edu. *Application contact:* Diane Ranaldi, Dean of Graduate Admissions, 413-565-1332, Fax: 413-565-1250, E-mail: dranaldi@baypath.edu.
Website: http://graduate.baypath.edu/Graduate-Programs/Programs-Online/MS-Programs/Higher-Education-Administration

Bellevue University, Graduate School, College of Professional Studies, Bellevue, NE 68005-3098. Offers instructional design and development (MS); justice administration and criminal management (MS); leadership (MA); organizational performance (MS); public administration (MPA); security management (MS).

Bloomsburg University of Pennsylvania, School of Graduate Studies, College of Science and Technology, Department of Instructional Technology, Bloomsburg, PA 17815-1301. Offers corporate instructional technology (MS); eLearning developer (Certificate). *Program availability:* Online learning. *Degree requirements:* For master's, thesis optional. *Entrance requirements:* For master's, minimum QPA of 2.8, 3 letters of recommendation, personal statement. Additional exam requirements/recommendations for international students: Required—TOEFL (minimum score 550 paper-based), IELTS. Electronic applications accepted. *Expenses:* Tuition, state resident: full-time $10,000; part-time $500 per credit hour. Tuition, nonresident: full-time $15,000; part-time $750 per credit hour. *Required fees:* $2484; $110.75 per credit hour. $75 per term. Tuition and fees vary according to program.

Boise State University, College of Education, Department of Educational Technology, Boise, ID 83725-0399. Offers educational technology (MET, MS, Ed D); online teaching (Graduate Certificate); school technology coordination (Graduate Certificate); technology integration (Graduate Certificate). *Accreditation:* NCATE. *Program availability:* Part-time, 100% online, blended/hybrid learning. *Faculty:* 27. *Students:* 13 full-time (7 women), 422 part-time (242 women); includes 41 minority (11 Black or African American, non-Hispanic/Latino; 1 American Indian or Alaska Native, non-Hispanic/Latino; 9 Asian, non-Hispanic/Latino; 17 Hispanic/Latino; 1 Native Hawaiian or other Pacific Islander, non-Hispanic/Latino; 2 Two or more races, non-Hispanic/Latino), 17 international. Average age 38. 192 applicants, 68% accepted, 72 enrolled. In 2017, 151 master's awarded. Terminal master's awarded for partial completion of doctoral program. *Degree requirements:* For master's, thesis optional; for doctorate, thesis/dissertation. *Entrance requirements:* For master's, minimum GPA of 3.0; for doctorate, GRE General Test. Additional exam requirements/recommendations for international students: Required—TOEFL (minimum score 550 paper-based; 80 iBT), IELTS (minimum score 6). *Application deadline:* For fall admission, 2/15 for domestic and international students; for spring admission, 9/15 for domestic and international students. Applications are processed on a rolling basis. Application fee: $65 ($95 for international students). Electronic applications accepted. *Expenses:* Tuition, state resident: full-time $6471; part-time $390 per credit. Tuition, nonresident: full-time $21,787; part-time $685 per credit. *Required fees:* $2283; $100 per term. Part-time tuition and fees vary according to course load and program. *Financial support:* Teaching assistantships, scholarships/grants, and unspecified assistantships available. Financial award application deadline: 3/1; financial award applicants required to submit FAFSA. *Unit head:* Dr. Brett Shelton, Department Chair, 208-426-3391, E-mail: brettshelton@boisestate.edu. *Application contact:* Dr. Ross Perkins, Admissions Coordinator, 208-426-4875, E-mail: edtechdoc@boisestate.edu.
Website: http://edtech.boisestate.edu/

Bowling Green State University, Graduate College, College of Education and Human Development, School of Teaching and Learning, Program in Classroom Technology, Bowling Green, OH 43403. Offers M Ed. *Accreditation:* NCATE. *Program availability:* Part-time, evening/weekend. *Degree requirements:* For master's, thesis or alternative. *Entrance requirements:* For master's, GRE General Test. Additional exam requirements/recommendations for international students: Required—TOEFL. Electronic applications accepted.

Brandman University, School of Education, Irvine, CA 92618. Offers curriculum and instruction (MAE); educational administration (MAE); educational leadership (MAE); educational leadership and administration (MA); elementary education (MAT); instructional technology: teaching the 21st century learner (MAE); leadership in early childhood education (MAE); organizational leadership (Ed D); school counseling (MA); secondary education (MAT); special education (MA); teaching and learning (MAE). *Expenses:* Tuition: Part-time $640 per credit hour. Tuition and fees vary according to degree level and program. *Unit head:* Dr. Christine G. Zeppos, Dean, 949-341-9948, E-mail: zeppos@brandman.edu. *Application contact:* Dr. Christine G. Zeppos, Dean, 949-341-9948, E-mail: zeppos@brandman.edu.
Website: https://www.brandman.edu/academic-programs/education

Bridgewater State University, College of Graduate Studies, College of Education and Allied Studies, Department of Secondary Education and Professional Programs, Program in Instructional Technology, Bridgewater, MA 02325. Offers M Ed. *Program availability:* Part-time, evening/weekend. *Entrance requirements:* For master's, GRE General Test or Massachusetts Test for Educator Licensure.

Brigham Young University, Graduate Studies, David O. McKay School of Education, Department of Instructional Psychology and Technology, Provo, UT 84602. Offers MS, PhD. *Faculty:* 10 full-time (1 woman). *Students:* 49 full-time (18 women), 27 part-time (11 women); includes 1 minority (Asian, non-Hispanic/Latino), 2 international. Average age 35. 46 applicants, 59% accepted, 21 enrolled. In 2017, 31 master's, 10 doctorates awarded. *Degree requirements:* For master's, thesis; for doctorate, comprehensive exam, thesis/dissertation. *Entrance requirements:* For master's and doctorate, GRE General Test. Additional exam requirements/recommendations for international students: Required—TOEFL. *Application deadline:* For fall and spring admission, 1/2 for domestic and international students. Application fee: $50. Electronic applications accepted. *Expenses:* Tuition: Full-time $6880; part-time $405 per credit hour. Tuition and fees vary according to course load, program and student's religious affiliation. *Financial support:* In 2017–18, 23 students received support, including 22 research assistantships with full and partial tuition reimbursements available (averaging $10,000 per year), 12 teaching assistantships with full and partial tuition reimbursements available (averaging $7,000 per year); career-related internships or fieldwork, scholarships/grants, tuition waivers (full and partial), and unspecified assistantships also available. Support available to part-time students. Financial award application deadline: 4/15. *Faculty research:* Interactive learning, learning theory, instructional designed development, research and evaluation, measurement. *Unit head:* Dr. Charles R. Graham, Department Chair, 801-422-4110, Fax: 801-422-0314, E-mail: charles.graham@byu.edu. *Application contact:* Michele Bray, Department Secretary, 801-422-2746, Fax: 801-422-0314, E-mail: michele_bray@byu.edu.
Website: http://education.byu.edu/ipt/

Brigham Young University, Graduate Studies, Ira A. Fulton College of Engineering and Technology, School of Technology, Provo, UT 84602. Offers construction management (MS); information technology (MS); manufacturing engineering technology (MS); technology and engineering education (MS). *Faculty:* 27 full-time (0 women), 12 part-time/adjunct (3 women). *Students:* 37 full-time (5 women); includes 5 minority (2 American Indian or Alaska Native, non-Hispanic/Latino; 2 Asian, non-Hispanic/Latino; 1 Hispanic/Latino), 1 international. Average age 28. 17 applicants, 65% accepted, 11 enrolled. In 2017, 8 master's awarded. *Degree requirements:* For master's, thesis. *Entrance requirements:* For master's, GRE General Test; GMAT or GRE (for construction management emphasis), minimum GPA of 3.0 in last 60 hours of course work. Additional exam requirements/recommendations for international students: Required—TOEFL (minimum score 580 paper-based; 85 iBT). *Application deadline:* For fall admission, 2/15 for domestic and international students; for winter admission, 9/10 for domestic students, 9/15 for international students; for spring admission, 2/15 for domestic and international students; for summer admission, 2/15 for domestic and international students. Application fee: $50. Electronic applications accepted. *Expenses:* Tuition: Full-time $6880; part-time $405 per credit hour. Tuition and fees vary according to course load, program and student's religious affiliation. *Financial support:* In 2017–18, 27 students received support, including 13 research assistantships (averaging $2,906 per year), 19 teaching assistantships (averaging $4,083 per year); scholarships/grants also available. Financial award application deadline: 1/15. *Faculty research:* Information assurance and security, HEI and databases, manufacturing materials, processes and systems, innovation in construction management scheduling and delivery methods. *Total annual research expenditures:* $307,681. *Unit head:* Dr. Barry M. Lunt, Director, 801-422-6300, Fax: 801-422-0490, E-mail: blunt@byu.edu. *Application contact:* Clifton Farnsworth, Graduate Coordinator, 801-422-6494, Fax: 801-422-0490, E-mail: clifton_farnsworth@byu.edu.
Website: http://www.et.byu.edu/sot/

Buffalo State College, State University of New York, The Graduate School, Faculty of Applied Science and Education, Department of Computer Information Systems, Program in Educational Computing, Buffalo, NY 14222-1095. Offers MS Ed. *Accreditation:* NCATE. *Program availability:* Part-time, evening/weekend. *Degree requirements:* For master's, thesis, project. *Entrance requirements:* Additional exam requirements/recommendations for international students: Required—TOEFL (minimum score 550 paper-based).

California Baptist University, Program in Education, Riverside, CA 92504-3206. Offers educational leadership (MS); educational leadership for faith-based institutions (MS); educational leadership for public institutions (MS); educational technology (MS); instructional computer applications (MS); international education (MS); leadership and adult learning (MS); leadership and organizational studies (MS); online teaching and learning (MS); reading (MS); science education (MA); special education in mild/moderate disabilities (MS); special education in moderate/severe disabilities (MS); teacher leadership (MS); teaching (MS); teaching and learning (MS). *Program availability:* Part-time, evening/weekend, 100% online, blended/hybrid learning. *Faculty:* 19 full-time (11 women), 36 part-time/adjunct (22 women). *Students:* 232 full-time (182 women), 315 part-time (247 women); includes 264 minority (33 Black or African American, non-Hispanic/Latino; 4 American Indian or Alaska Native, non-Hispanic/Latino; 11 Asian, non-Hispanic/Latino; 186 Hispanic/Latino; 7 Native Hawaiian or other Pacific Islander, non-Hispanic/Latino; 23 Two or more races, non-Hispanic/Latino). Average age 31. 217 applicants, 64% accepted, 129 enrolled. In 2017, 196 master's awarded. *Degree requirements:* For master's, comprehensive exam, project, or thesis. *Entrance requirements:* For master's, minimum undergraduate GPA of 2.75; 500-word essay; three letters of recommendation; two prerequisite courses completed with minimum C grade. Additional exam requirements/recommendations for international students: Required—TOEFL (minimum score 80 iBT). *Application deadline:* For fall admission, 8/1 priority date for domestic students, 7/1 for international students; for spring admission, 12/1 priority date for domestic students, 11/1 for international students. Applications are processed on a rolling basis. Application fee: $45. Electronic applications accepted. *Expenses:* Contact institution. *Financial support:* In 2017–18, 162 students received support. Federal Work-Study and scholarships/grants available. Financial award applicants required to submit CSS PROFILE or FAFSA. *Faculty research:* Leadership development, complexity theory, faith and learning, special education, social and philosophical contexts of education. *Unit head:* Dr. John Shoup, Dean, School of Education, 951-343-4516, E-mail: jshoup@calbaptist.edu. *Application contact:* Gavin Andrew, Graduate Admissions Counselor, 951-552-8437, E-mail: gandrew@calbaptist.edu.
Website: http://www.calbaptist.edu/mastersined/

California State University, East Bay, Office of Graduate Studies, College of Education and Allied Studies, Department of Teacher Education, Hayward, CA 94542-3000. Offers education (MS), including curriculum, early childhood education, educational technology and leadership, reading instruction. *Program availability:* Online learning. *Faculty:* 11 full-time (8 women), 56 part-time/adjunct (40 women). *Students:* 49 full-time (35 women), 15 part-time (13 women); includes 31 minority (5 Black or African American, non-Hispanic/Latino; 13 Asian, non-Hispanic/Latino; 11 Hispanic/Latino; 2 Two or more races, non-Hispanic/Latino), 7 international. Average age 31. 76 applicants, 82% accepted, 33 enrolled. In 2017, 83 master's awarded. *Degree requirements:* For master's, project or thesis. *Entrance requirements:* For master's, minimum GPA of 3.0 in field, 2.5 overall; teaching experience; baccalaureate degree; 3 letters of recommendation. Additional exam requirements/recommendations for international students: Required—TOEFL (minimum score 550 paper-based), IELTS. *Application deadline:* For fall admission, 6/1 for domestic and international students. Application fee: $55. Electronic applications accepted. *Financial support:* Career-related internships or fieldwork, Federal Work-Study, and institutionally sponsored loans available. Support available to part-time students. Financial award application deadline: 3/2; financial award applicants required to submit FAFSA. *Faculty research:* Online,

pedagogy, writing, learning, teaching. *Unit head:* Dr. Eric Engdahl, Chair, 510-885-4599, E-mail: eric.engdahl@csueastbay.edu. *Application contact:* Prof. Valerie Helgren-Lempesis, Education Graduate Advisor, 510-885-3006, Fax: 510-885-4632, E-mail: valerie.helgren-lempesis@csueastbay.edu.
Website: http://www20.csueastbay.edu/ceas/departments/ted/index.html

California State University, Fullerton, Graduate Studies, College of Education, Department of Elementary and Bilingual Education, Fullerton, CA 92831-3599. Offers bilingual/bicultural education (MS); educational technology (MS); elementary curriculum and instruction (MS). *Accreditation:* NCATE. *Program availability:* Part-time. *Faculty:* 10 full-time (7 women), 10 part-time/adjunct (8 women). *Students:* 224 full-time (194 women), 191 part-time (162 women); includes 218 minority (6 Black or African American, non-Hispanic/Latino; 1 American Indian or Alaska Native, non-Hispanic/Latino; 65 Asian, non-Hispanic/Latino; 127 Hispanic/Latino; 1 Native Hawaiian or other Pacific Islander, non-Hispanic/Latino; 18 Two or more races, non-Hispanic/Latino), 3 international. Average age 32. 272 applicants, 69% accepted, 170 enrolled. *Degree requirements:* For master's, comprehensive exam, project or thesis. *Entrance requirements:* For master's, minimum GPA of 2.5, teaching certificate. Application fee: $55. *Financial support:* Career-related internships or fieldwork, Federal Work-Study, institutionally sponsored loans, and scholarships/grants available. Support available to part-time students. Financial award application deadline: 3/1; financial award applicants required to submit FAFSA. *Faculty research:* Teacher training and tracking, model for improvement of teaching. *Unit head:* Lisa Kirtman, Chair, 657-278-4731. *Application contact:* Admissions/Applications, 657-278-2371.
Website: http://ed.fullerton.edu/EDEL/

California State University, Fullerton, Graduate Studies, College of Education, Program in Instructional Design and Technology, Fullerton, CA 92831-3599. Offers MS. *Program availability:* Part-time, online learning. *Faculty:* 4 part-time/adjunct (1 woman). *Students:* 1 (woman) full-time, 98 part-time (61 women); includes 48 minority (5 Black or African American, non-Hispanic/Latino; 1 American Indian or Alaska Native, non-Hispanic/Latino; 18 Asian, non-Hispanic/Latino; 19 Hispanic/Latino; 5 Two or more races, non-Hispanic/Latino), 2 international. Average age 35. 74 applicants, 84% accepted, 54 enrolled. Application fee: $55. *Financial support:* Career-related internships or fieldwork, Federal Work-Study, institutionally sponsored loans, and scholarships/grants available. Support available to part-time students. Financial award application deadline: 3/1; financial award applicants required to submit FAFSA. *Unit head:* Dr. Jo Ann Carter-Wells, Chair, 657-278-3357. *Application contact:* Admissions/Applications, 657-278-2371.
Website: http://ed.fullerton.edu/msidt/

California State University, Northridge, Graduate Studies, Michael D. Eisner College of Education, Department of Secondary Education, Northridge, CA 91330. Offers educational technology (MA); English education (MA); mathematics education (MA); secondary science education (MA); teaching and learning (MA). *Accreditation:* NCATE. *Program availability:* Part-time. *Students:* 9 full-time (5 women), 85 part-time (57 women); includes 37 minority (2 Black or African American, non-Hispanic/Latino; 12 Asian, non-Hispanic/Latino; 20 Hispanic/Latino; 1 Native Hawaiian or other Pacific Islander, non-Hispanic/Latino; 2 Two or more races, non-Hispanic/Latino), 1 international. Average age 37. 63 applicants, 78% accepted, 45 enrolled. *Degree requirements:* For master's, thesis optional. *Entrance requirements:* For master's, GRE General Test or minimum GPA of 3.0. Additional exam requirements/recommendations for international students: Required—TOEFL. *Application deadline:* For fall admission, 11/30 for domestic students. Application fee: $55. *Financial support:* Application deadline: 3/1. *Unit head:* Dr. Julie Gainsburg, Chair, 818-677-2580. *Application contact:* Dr. Michael Rivas, Graduate Advisor, 818-677-6792, E-mail: michael.rivas@csun.edu.
Website: http://www.csun.edu/eisner-education/secondary-education

California State University, Sacramento, College of Education, Graduate and Professional Studies in Education, Sacramento, CA 95819. Offers behavioral science and gender equity (MA); child development (MA); counseling (MS); curriculum and instruction (MA); education (Ed D), including K-12 and community college; education leadership and policy studies (MA), including higher education, PreK-12; education specialist (Ed S), including school psychology; educational technology (MA); language and literacy (MA); multicultural education (MA); school psychology (MA); special education (MA); workforce development advocacy (MA). *Program availability:* Part-time, evening/weekend, blended/hybrid learning. *Students:* 381 full-time (294 women), 135 part-time (101 women); includes 296 minority (44 Black or African American, non-Hispanic/Latino; 1 American Indian or Alaska Native, non-Hispanic/Latino; 94 Asian, non-Hispanic/Latino; 153 Hispanic/Latino; 4 Native Hawaiian or other Pacific Islander, non-Hispanic/Latino), 3 international. Average age 32. 553 applicants, 53% accepted, 292 enrolled. In 2017, 147 master's, 13 doctorates, 10 other advanced degrees awarded. *Degree requirements:* For master's, thesis or project; for doctorate, thesis/dissertation. *Entrance requirements:* For master's and doctorate, GRE. Additional exam requirements/recommendations for international students: Required—TOEFL (minimum score 550 paper-based; 80 iBT); Recommended—IELTS (minimum score 7), TSE. *Application deadline:* For fall admission, 2/15 for domestic students, 1/15 for international students. Applications are processed on a rolling basis. Application fee: $55. Electronic applications accepted. *Expenses:* Contact institution. *Financial support:* Career-related internships or fieldwork, Federal Work-Study, and scholarships/grants available. Support available to part-time students. Financial award application deadline: 3/1; financial award applicants required to submit FAFSA. *Unit head:* Dr. Elizabeth Liles, Chair, 916-278-5942, E-mail: coe@csus.edu. *Application contact:* Jose Martinez, Graduate Admissions Supervisor, 916-278-7871, E-mail: martinj@skymail.csus.edu.
Website: http://www.csus.edu/coe/academics/graduate/index.html

California State University, Stanislaus, College of Education, Kinesiology and Social Work, MA Program in Education, Turlock, CA 95382. Offers curriculum and instruction (MA), including education technology, elementary education, multilingual education, physical education, reading, secondary education, special education; school administration (MA); school counseling (MA). *Program availability:* Part-time, evening/weekend. *Degree requirements:* For master's, comprehensive exam (for some programs), thesis (for some programs). *Entrance requirements:* For master's, MAT, GRE, or CBEST (varies by concentration), 3 letters of recommendation, personal statement. Additional exam requirements/recommendations for international students: Required—TOEFL (minimum score 550 paper-based). Electronic applications accepted. *Faculty research:* Children's perspectives on historical events, method elementary schools dual language education, K-12 reading programs.

Cambridge College, School of Education, Boston, MA 02129. Offers autism specialist (M Ed); autism/behavior analyst (M Ed); behavior analyst (Post-Master's Certificate); behavioral management (M Ed); early childhood teacher (M Ed); education specialist in curriculum and instruction (CAGS); educational leadership (Ed D); elementary teacher (M Ed); English as a second language (M Ed, Certificate); general science (M Ed); health education (Post-Master's Certificate); health/family and consumer sciences (M Ed); history (M Ed); individualized (M Ed); information technology (M Ed); instructional technology (M Ed); interdisciplinary studies (M Ed); library teacher (M Ed); literacy education (M Ed); mathematics (M Ed); mathematics specialist (Certificate);

middle school mathematics and science (M Ed); school administration (M Ed, CAGS); school guidance counselor (M Ed); school nurse education (M Ed); school social worker/special adjustment counselor (M Ed); special education administrator (CAGS); special education/moderate disabilities (M Ed); teaching skills and methodologies (M Ed). *Program availability:* Part-time, evening/weekend, online learning. *Degree requirements:* For master's, thesis, internship/practicum (licensure program only); for doctorate, thesis/dissertation; for other advanced degree, thesis. *Entrance requirements:* For master's, interview, resume, documentation of licensure, 2 professional references; for doctorate, official transcripts, interview, resume, documentation of licensure (if any), written personal statement/essay, portfolio of scholarly and professional work, qualifying assessment, 2 professional references, health insurance, immunizations form; for other advanced degree, official transcripts, interview, resume, documentation of licensure (if any), written personal statement/essay, 2 professional references, health insurance, immunizations form. Additional exam requirements/recommendations for international students: Required—TOEFL (minimum score 550 paper-based; 79 iBT), Michigan English Language Assessment Battery (minimum score 85); Recommended—IELTS (minimum score 6). Electronic applications accepted. *Expenses:* Contact institution. *Faculty research:* Adult education, accelerated learning, mathematics education, brain compatible learning, special education and law.

Canisius College, Graduate Division, School of Education and Human Services, Department of Graduate Education and Leadership, Buffalo, NY 14208-1098. Offers business and marketing education (MS Ed); college student personnel (MS Ed); deaf education (MS Ed); deaf/adolescent education, grades 7-12 (MS Ed); deaf/childhood education, grades 1-6 (MS Ed); differentiated instruction (MS Ed); education administration (MS); educational administration (MS Ed); educational technologies (Certificate); gifted education extension (Certificate); literacy (MS Ed); reading (Certificate); school building leadership (MS Ed, Certificate); school district leadership (Certificate); teacher leader (Certificate); TESOL (MS Ed). *Accreditation:* NCATE. *Program availability:* Part-time, evening/weekend, 100% online, blended/hybrid learning. *Faculty:* 5 full-time (all women), 21 part-time/adjunct (16 women). *Students:* 85 full-time (67 women), 189 part-time (151 women); includes 31 minority (18 Black or African American, non-Hispanic/Latino; 3 American Indian or Alaska Native, non-Hispanic/Latino; 3 Asian, non-Hispanic/Latino; 4 Hispanic/Latino; 3 Two or more races, non-Hispanic/Latino), 1 international. Average age 31. 83 applicants, 96% accepted, 74 enrolled. In 2017, 94 master's, 47 other advanced degrees awarded. *Entrance requirements:* For master's, GRE (if cumulative GPA less than 2.7), transcripts, two letters of recommendation. Additional exam requirements/recommendations for international students: Required—TOEFL (minimum score 550 paper-based, 79 iBT), IELTS (minimum score 6.5), or CAEL (minimum score 70). *Application deadline:* Applications are processed on a rolling basis. Application fee: $0. Electronic applications accepted. *Expenses: Tuition:* Full-time $22,860; part-time $820 per credit. *Required fees:* $720; $25 per credit. $65 per semester. One-time fee: $425. *Financial support:* Career-related internships or fieldwork, Federal Work-Study, scholarships/grants, tuition waivers (partial), and unspecified assistantships available. Support available to part-time students. Financial award application deadline: 4/30; financial award applicants required to submit FAFSA. *Faculty research:* Asperger's disease, autism, private higher education, reading strategies. *Unit head:* Dr. Anne Marie Tryjankowski, Chair/Associate Professor of Graduate Education and Leadership, 716-888-3715, Fax: 716-888-3142, E-mail: tryjanka@canisius.edu.

Capella University, School of Education, Doctoral Programs in Education, Minneapolis, MN 55402. Offers curriculum and instruction (PhD); educational leadership and management (Ed D); instructional design for online learning (PhD); K-12 studies in education (PhD); leadership for higher education (PhD); leadership in educational administration (PhD); postsecondary and adult education (PhD); professional studies in education (PhD); reading and literacy (Ed D); special education leadership (PhD); training and performance improvement (PhD).

Capella University, School of Education, Master's Programs in Education, Minneapolis, MN 55402. Offers adult education (MS); curriculum and instruction (MS); early childhood education (MS); enrollment management (MS); higher education leadership and management (MS); instructional design for online learning (MS); integrative studies (MS); K-12 studies in education (MS); leadership in educational administration (MS); reading and literacy (MS); special education teaching (MS).

Caribbean University, Graduate School, Bayamón, PR 00960-0493. Offers administration and supervision (MA Ed); criminal justice (MA); curriculum and instruction (MA Ed, PhD), including elementary education (MA Ed), English education (MA Ed), history education (MA Ed), mathematics education (MA Ed), primary education (MA Ed), science education (MA Ed), Spanish education (MA Ed); educational technology in instructional systems (MA Ed); gerontology (MSN); human resources (MBA); museology, archiving and art history (MA Ed); neonatal pediatrics (MSN); physical education (MA Ed); special education (MA Ed). *Entrance requirements:* For master's, interview, minimum GPA of 2.5.

Central Michigan University, Central Michigan University Global Campus, Program in Education, Mount Pleasant, MI 48859. Offers college teaching (Graduate Certificate); community college (MA); curriculum and instruction (MA); educational technology (MA, DET); reading and literacy K-12 (MA); school principalship (MA), including charter school leadership; training and development (MA). *Accreditation:* TEAC. *Program availability:* Part-time, evening/weekend. *Entrance requirements:* For master's, minimum GPA of 2.7 in major. Additional exam requirements/recommendations for international students: Required—TOEFL. Electronic applications accepted.

Central Michigan University, College of Graduate Studies, College of Education and Human Services, Department of Educational Leadership, Mount Pleasant, MI 48859. Offers educational leadership (Ed D), including educational technology (Ed D, Ed S), higher education leadership, K-12 curriculum, K-12 leadership; general educational administration (Ed S), including administrative leadership K-12, educational technology (Ed D, Ed S), higher education administration, instructional leadership K-12; school principalship (MA), including charter school leadership, site-based leadership; student affairs administration (MA); teacher leadership (MA). *Program availability:* Part-time, evening/weekend. *Degree requirements:* For master's and Ed S, thesis or alternative; for doctorate, thesis/dissertation. *Entrance requirements:* For doctorate, GRE or MAT, master's degree, minimum GPA of 3.5, 3 years of professional education experience. Electronic applications accepted. *Faculty research:* Elementary administration, secondary administration, student achievement, in-service training, internships in administration.

Central Michigan University, College of Graduate Studies, College of Education and Human Services, Department of Teacher Education and Professional Development, Mount Pleasant, MI 48859. Offers educational technology (MA, Graduate Certificate); elementary education (MA), including classroom teaching, early childhood; reading and literacy K-12 (MA); secondary education (MA). *Program availability:* Part-time, evening/weekend. *Degree requirements:* For master's, thesis or alternative. Electronic applications accepted. *Faculty research:* Integrating literacy across the curriculum, science teaching and aesthetic learning in science, diversity education, educational technology, educational psychology and child development.

Educational Media/Instructional Technology

Chestnut Hill College, School of Graduate Studies, Program in Instructional Technology, Philadelphia, PA 19118-2693. Offers instructional technology (MS, CAS), including instructional design and e-learning, instructional design and e-learning with instructional technology specialist certification preparation. *Program availability:* Part-time, evening/weekend. *Degree requirements:* For master's, special project/internship. *Entrance requirements:* For master's, GRE General Test or MAT, letters of recommendation, writing sample. Additional exam requirements/recommendations for international students: Required—TOEFL (minimum score 500 paper-based), IELTS (minimum score 6.0), or TWE (minimum score 22). Electronic applications accepted. *Expenses:* Contact institution. *Faculty research:* Instructional design, learning management systems and related technologies, video as a teaching and learning tool, Web 2.0 technologies and virtual worlds as a learning tool, utilization of laptops and iPads in the classroom.

Clarion University of Pennsylvania, College of Business Administration and Information Sciences, MSLS Program in Information and Library Science, Clarion, PA 16214. Offers information and library science (MSLS); school library media (MSLS). *Program availability:* Part-time, evening/weekend, online only, 100% online. *Faculty:* 8 full-time (5 women), 6 part-time/adjunct (3 women). *Students:* 84 full-time (68 women), 253 part-time (212 women); includes 47 minority (20 Black or African American, non-Hispanic/Latino; 4 Asian, non-Hispanic/Latino; 16 Hispanic/Latino; 7 Two or more races, non-Hispanic/Latino), 1 international. Average age 33. 249 applicants, 87% accepted, 110 enrolled. In 2017, 139 master's awarded. *Entrance requirements:* For master's, minimum undergraduate QPA of 3.0. Additional exam requirements/recommendations for international students: Required—TOEFL (minimum score 550 paper-based, 80 iBT) or IELTS (7). *Application deadline:* For fall admission, 8/15 priority date for domestic students, 7/15 priority date for international students; for winter admission, 11/1 priority date for domestic students; for spring admission, 1/7 priority date for domestic students, 11/15 priority date for international students; for summer admission, 4/1 priority date for domestic students. Applications are processed on a rolling basis. Application fee: $40. Electronic applications accepted. *Expenses:* $655.05 per credit. *Financial support:* Career-related internships or fieldwork, scholarships/grants, and unspecified assistantships available. Support available to part-time students. Financial award application deadline: 3/1; financial award applicants required to submit FAFSA. *Unit head:* Linda Lillard, Department Chair, 814-393-2383, E-mail: llillard@clarion.edu. *Application contact:* Dana Bearer, Associate Director, Transfer, Adult, and Graduate Programs, 814-393-2337, Fax: 814-393-2772, E-mail: gradstudies@clarion.edu. Website: http://www.clarion.edu/academics/colleges-and-schools/college-of-business-administration-and-information-sciences/library-science/

Cleveland State University, College of Graduate Studies, College of Education and Human Services, Program in Urban Education, Specialization in Learning and Development, Cleveland, OH 44115. Offers PhD. *Program availability:* Part-time. *Faculty:* 17 full-time (9 women). *Students:* 2 full-time (both women), 14 part-time (12 women); includes 8 minority (6 Black or African American, non-Hispanic/Latino; 1 Asian, non-Hispanic/Latino; 1 Hispanic/Latino). Average age 47. 18 applicants, 28% accepted. In 2017, 3 doctorates awarded. *Entrance requirements:* For doctorate, GRE General Test (minimum score of 297 for combined Verbal and Quantitative exams, 4.0 preferred for Analytical Writing), minimum graduate GPA of 3.25 in educational psychology, school psychology and/or special education; curriculum vitae or resume; personal statement; 2 letters of recommendation. Additional exam requirements/recommendations for international students: Required—TOEFL (minimum score 550 paper-based; 78 iBT), IELTS (minimum score 6). Application fee: $40. Electronic applications accepted. *Financial support:* In 2017–18, 5 students received support. Research assistantships, teaching assistantships, and tuition waivers available. Support available to part-time students. Financial award application deadline: 4/1; financial award applicants required to submit FAFSA. *Faculty research:* Implications of human variability to instruction service delivery in educational and social agencies. *Unit head:* Dr. Graham Stead, Director, Doctoral Studies, 216-875-9869, E-mail: g.b.stead@csuohio.edu. *Application contact:* Rita M. Grabowski, Administrative Coordinator, 216-687-4697, Fax: 216-875-9697, E-mail: r.grabowski@csuohio.edu. Website: http://www.csuohio.edu/cehs/casal/programs-0

Coastal Carolina University, Spadoni College of Education, Conway, SC 29528-6054. Offers education (MAT); educational leadership (M Ed, Ed S); English for speakers of other languages (Certificate); instructional technology (M Ed, Ed S); language, literacy and culture (M Ed); learning and teaching (M Ed); online teaching and training (Certificate); special education (M Ed). *Accreditation:* NCATE. *Program availability:* Part-time, evening/weekend, 100% online, blended/hybrid learning. *Faculty:* 16 full-time (9 women), 22 part-time/adjunct (15 women). *Students:* 43 full-time (22 women), 345 part-time (290 women); includes 70 minority (51 Black or African American, non-Hispanic/Latino; 3 American Indian or Alaska Native, non-Hispanic/Latino; 3 Asian, non-Hispanic/Latino; 8 Hispanic/Latino; 1 Native Hawaiian or other Pacific Islander, non-Hispanic/Latino; 4 Two or more races, non-Hispanic/Latino). Average age 33. 288 applicants, 77% accepted, 157 enrolled. In 2017, 151 master's, 28 other advanced degrees awarded. *Degree requirements:* For master's and other advanced degree, comprehensive exam. *Entrance requirements:* For master's, GRE, GMAT, 2 letters of recommendation, evidence of teacher certification, official transcripts; for other advanced degree, official transcripts, 3 letters of reference, master's degree in related field with minimum overall cumulative GPA of 3.0. Additional exam requirements/recommendations for international students: Required—TOEFL (minimum score 550 paper-based; 79 iBT), IELTS (minimum score 6.5). *Application deadline:* For fall admission, 5/1 priority date for domestic and international students; for spring admission, 11/1 priority date for domestic and international students; for summer admission, 3/1 priority date for domestic and international students. Applications are processed on a rolling basis. Application fee: $45. Electronic applications accepted. *Expenses:* Tuition, state resident: full-time $5184; part-time $576 per credit hour. Tuition, nonresident: full-time $9369; part-time $1041 per credit hour. *Required fees:* $90; $5 per credit hour. *Financial support:* Fellowships, research assistantships, teaching assistantships, and tuition waivers available. Financial award application deadline: 3/1; financial award applicants required to submit FAFSA. *Unit head:* Dr. Edward Jadallah, Dean/Vice President for Online Education and Teaching Excellence, 843-349-2773, Fax: 843-349-2106, E-mail: ejadalla@coastal.edu. *Application contact:* Dr. James O. Luken, Associate Provost for Graduate Program/Vice-Dean of the Coastal Environment, 843-349-2235, Fax: 843-349-6444, E-mail: joluken@coastal.edu. Website: https://www.coastal.edu/education/

Coker College, Graduate Programs, Hartsville, SC 29550. Offers college athletic administration (MS); criminal and social justice policy (MS); curriculum and instructional technology (M Ed); literacy studies (M Ed); management and leadership (MS). *Program availability:* Part-time, 100% online. *Faculty:* 9 full-time (4 women), 3 part-time/adjunct (2 women). *Students:* 77 full-time (47 women), 9 part-time (4 women); includes 21 minority (15 Black or African American, non-Hispanic/Latino; 1 American Indian or Alaska Native, non-Hispanic/Latino; 1 Hispanic/Latino; 4 Two or more races, non-Hispanic/Latino), 1 international. Average age 30. *Degree requirements:* For master's, comprehensive exam, portfolio. *Entrance requirements:* For master's, GRE or GMAT, minimum overall GPA of 2.85 in bachelor's program, official transcripts, resume, three letters of recommendation, teacher licensure. *Application deadline:* Applications are processed

on a rolling basis. Application fee: $25. Electronic applications accepted. *Expenses:* Tuition: Full-time $14,424; part-time $601 per credit hour. *Required fees:* $176; $176 per credit hour. Tuition and fees vary according to course load and program. *Financial support:* Unspecified assistantships available. Financial award application deadline: 6/30; financial award applicants required to submit FAFSA. *Application contact:* Lacey Rice-Serafin, Director of Graduate Programs, 843-857-4128, E-mail: lriceserafin@coker.edu.

College of Mount Saint Vincent, School of Professional and Graduate Studies, Department of Teacher Education, Riverdale, NY 10471-1093. Offers instructional technology and global perspectives (Certificate); middle level education (Certificate); multicultural studies (Certificate); teaching English to speakers of other languages (MS Ed); urban and multicultural education (MS Ed). *Accreditation:* TEAC. *Program availability:* Part-time. *Degree requirements:* For master's, comprehensive exam. *Entrance requirements:* For master's, interview, New York teaching certificate. Additional exam requirements/recommendations for international students: Required—TOEFL.

The College of William and Mary, School of Education, Program in Education Policy, Planning, and Leadership, Williamsburg, VA 23187-8795. Offers curriculum and educational technology (PhD); curriculum leadership (Ed D, PhD); educational leadership (M Ed), including higher education administration (M Ed, Ed D, PhD), K-12 administration and supervision; educational policy, planning, and leadership (Ed D, PhD), including general education administration, gifted education administration, higher education administration (M Ed, Ed D, PhD). *Accreditation:* NCATE. *Program availability:* Part-time, evening/weekend. *Faculty:* 20 full-time (10 women), 21 part-time/adjunct (13 women). *Students:* 54 full-time (35 women), 172 part-time (113 women); includes 70 minority (42 Black or African American, non-Hispanic/Latino; 1 Asian, non-Hispanic/Latino; 19 Hispanic/Latino; 8 Two or more races, non-Hispanic/Latino), 3 international. Average age 39. 163 applicants, 71% accepted, 89 enrolled. In 2017, 23 master's, 37 doctorates awarded. *Degree requirements:* For doctorate, comprehensive exam, thesis/dissertation. *Entrance requirements:* For master's, GRE or MAT, minimum GPA 2.5; for doctorate, GRE or MAT, minimum GPA of 3.0. Additional exam requirements/recommendations for international students: Required—TOEFL (minimum score 100 iBT), IELTS (minimum score 7). *Application deadline:* For fall admission, 1/15 for domestic and international students. Application fee: $50. Electronic applications accepted. *Expenses:* $9,630 resident full-time, $535 resident part-time per credit hour; $25,920 nonresident full-time, $1,265 nonresident part-time per credit hour; $5,944 full-time fees. *Financial support:* In 2017–18, 59 students received support, including 1 fellowship (averaging $20,000 per year), 43 research assistantships (averaging $20,535 per year); scholarships/grants and unspecified assistantships also available. Support available to part-time students. Financial award application deadline: 1/15; financial award applicants required to submit FAFSA. *Faculty research:* Higher education policy, evaluation of teachers, program evaluation, civil rights and higher education, program evaluation. *Unit head:* Dr. Michael F. Dipaola, Department Chair, 757-221-2344, E-mail: mfdipa@wm.edu. *Application contact:* Dorothy Smith Osborne, Assistant Dean for Academic Programs and Student Services, 757-221-2317, E-mail: dsosbo@wm.edu. Website: http://education.wm.edu

Colorado Christian University, Program in Curriculum and Instruction, Lakewood, CO 80226. Offers corporate education (MACI); early childhood educator (MACI); elementary educator (MACI); instructional technology (MACI); master educator (MACI); online course developer (MACI); online teaching and learning (MACI); special education generalist (MACI). *Program availability:* Part-time, evening/weekend. *Degree requirements:* For master's, thesis optional, practicum. *Entrance requirements:* For master's, interviews, letters of recommendation. Additional exam requirements/recommendations for international students: Required—TOEFL. Electronic applications accepted. *Expenses:* Contact institution.

Colorado State University–Pueblo, College of Education, Engineering and Professional Studies, Education Program, Pueblo, CO 81001-4901. Offers art education (M Ed); foreign language education (M Ed); health and physical education (M Ed); instructional technology (M Ed); linguistically diverse education (M Ed); music education (M Ed); special education (M Ed). *Accreditation:* TEAC. *Program availability:* Part-time. *Degree requirements:* For master's, portfolio. *Entrance requirements:* For master's, 3 recommendations, teaching license. Additional exam requirements/recommendations for international students: Required—TOEFL (minimum score 500 paper-based). Electronic applications accepted. *Faculty research:* Portfolio assessment, math education, science education.

Concordia University, College of Education, Portland, OR 97211-6099. Offers career and technical education (M Ed); curriculum and instruction (M Ed), including adolescent literacy, career and technical education, e-learning/technology education, early childhood education, English for speakers of other languages, English language development, environmental education, mathematics, methods and curriculum, reading, science, teacher leadership, the inclusive classroom; early childhood (MAT); education leadership (Ed D); educational administration (M Ed); elementary education (MAT); secondary education (MAT); special education (M Ed); teacher leadership (Ed D). *Program availability:* Part-time, online learning. *Degree requirements:* For master's, comprehensive exam, work samples/portfolio. *Entrance requirements:* For master's, California Basic Educational Skills Test or PRAXIS I, minimum undergraduate GPA of 2.8, graduate 3.0; 2 letters of recommendation. Additional exam requirements/recommendations for international students: Required—TOEFL (minimum score 525 paper-based). Electronic applications accepted. *Faculty research:* Learner-centered classroom, brain-based learning, future of online learning.

Concordia University, School of Graduate Studies, Faculty of Arts and Science, Department of Education, Program in Educational Technology, Montréal, QC H3G 1M8, Canada. Offers MA. *Degree requirements:* For master's, one foreign language, thesis optional, internship. *Faculty research:* Instructional design and tele-education, educational cybernetics and systems analysis, media research and theory development, distance education.

Concordia University, School of Graduate Studies, Faculty of Arts and Science, Department of Education, Program in Instructional Technology, Montréal, QC H3G 1M8, Canada. Offers Diploma. *Entrance requirements:* For degree, BA in related field.

Concordia University Chicago, College of Graduate and Innovative Programs, Program in Educational Technology, River Forest, IL 60305-1499. Offers MA.

Concordia University Irvine, School of Education, Irvine, CA 92612-3299. Offers curriculum and instruction (MA); education and preliminary teaching credential (M Ed); educational administration and preliminary administrative services credential (MA); educational technology (MA); school counseling with pupil personnel services credential (MA). *Program availability:* Part-time, evening/weekend, online learning. *Degree requirements:* For master's, action research project. *Entrance requirements:* For master's, California Basic Educational Skills Test, California Subject Examinations for Teachers (M Ed and MA in educational administration and preliminary administrative services credential), official college transcript(s), signed statement of intent, two references, copy of credential. Additional exam requirements/recommendations for international students: Required—TOEFL. Electronic applications accepted. *Expenses:* Contact institution.

Concordia University, St. Paul, College of Education, St. Paul, MN 55104-5494. Offers classroom instruction (MA Ed), including K-12 reading; differentiated instruction (MA Ed); early childhood education (MA Ed); education (Ed D); educational leadership (MA Ed); educational technology (MA Ed, Certificate); K-12 principal licensure (Ed S); special education (MA Ed), including autism spectrum disorder, emotional and behavioral disorders, learning disabilities; superintendent (Ed S); teaching (MAT). *Accreditation:* NCATE. *Program availability:* Part-time, evening/weekend, 100% online, blended/hybrid learning. *Faculty:* 15 full-time (8 women), 86 part-time/adjunct (56 women). *Students:* 955 full-time (731 women), 42 part-time (28 women); includes 105 minority (35 Black or African American, non-Hispanic/Latino; 5 American Indian or Alaska Native, non-Hispanic/Latino; 31 Asian, non-Hispanic/Latino; 19 Hispanic/Latino; 15 Two or more races, non-Hispanic/Latino), 9 international. Average age 34. 409 applicants, 87% accepted, 347 enrolled. In 2017, 386 master's, 104 other advanced degrees awarded. *Degree requirements:* For master's, thesis (for some programs); for doctorate, thesis/dissertation, capstone projects; for other advanced degree, e-folio review of competencies. *Entrance requirements:* For master's, official transcripts from regionally-accredited institution stating the conferral of a bachelor's degree with minimum cumulative GPA of 3.0; personal statement; professional resume; practitioner in field through work or volunteerism; resume; for doctorate, minimum master's or specialist degree GPA of 3.25; transcript; writing sample; three letters of recommendation; current resume; on-campus interview; for other advanced degree, minimum master's or specialist degree GPA of 3.25; transcript; statement covering employment history and long-term academic and professional goals; two letters of recommendation; interview with program director. Additional exam requirements/recommendations for international students: Recommended—TOEFL (minimum score 547 paper-based; 78 iBT), IELTS (minimum score 6). *Application deadline:* For fall admission, 8/1 for domestic and international students; for spring admission, 12/1 for domestic and international students; for summer admission, 5/1 for domestic and international students. Applications are processed on a rolling basis. Application fee: $0. Electronic applications accepted. *Expenses:* $395 per credit (for MA in education); $440 per credit (for MAT); $615 per credit (for EdD). *Financial support:* In 2017–18, 105 students received support. Scholarships/grants and unspecified assistantships available. Financial award applicants required to submit FAFSA. *Faculty research:* Differentiated instruction in K-12 educational settings; educational leadership; effective online pedagogy in higher education; equine-assisted learning; faculty development in higher education. *Unit head:* Lonn Maly, Dean, 651-641-8203, E-mail: maly@csp.edu. *Application contact:* Amber Faletti, Director of Enrollment Management, 651-641-8838, Fax: 651-603-6320, E-mail: faletti@csp.edu.

Dakota State University, College of Education, Madison, SD 57042-1799. Offers educational technology (MSET). *Accreditation:* NCATE. *Program availability:* Part-time-only, evening/weekend, online only, 100% online. *Faculty:* 4 full-time (0 women). *Students:* 8 part-time (5 women). Average age 32. 3 applicants, 100% accepted, 2 enrolled. In 2017, 5 master's awarded. *Degree requirements:* For master's, thesis optional, portfolio. *Entrance requirements:* For master's, GRE General Test, demonstration of technology skills, minimum GPA of 2.7. *Application deadline:* For fall admission, 6/15 for domestic students; for spring admission, 11/15 for domestic students; for summer admission, 4/15 for domestic students. Applications are processed on a rolling basis. Application fee: $35. Electronic applications accepted. *Expenses:* Tuition, state resident: full-time $5749. Tuition, nonresident: full-time $10,733. *Required fees:* $715. Tuition and fees vary according to campus/location and reciprocity agreements. *Financial support:* Unspecified assistantships and administrative assistantships available. Financial award applicants required to submit FAFSA. *Faculty research:* Educational technology evaluation, computer-supported collaborative learning, cognitive theory and visual representation of the effects of ubiquitous wireless computing on student learning and productivity, accessible learning, pedagogies for exceptional children. *Unit head:* Dr. Crystal Pauli, Dean of College of Education, 605-256-5799. *Application contact:* Dr. Kevin Smith, Program Coordinator, 605-256-5175, Fax: 605-256-7300, E-mail: kevin.smith@dsu.edu. Website: http://dsu.edu/graduate-students/mset

Dallas Baptist University, Dorothy M. Bush College of Education, Program in Curriculum and Instruction, Dallas, TX 75211-9299. Offers Christian school administration (M Ed); distance learning (M Ed); English as a second language (M Ed); instructional technology (M Ed); professional life coaching (M Ed); special education (M Ed); supervision (M Ed). *Program availability:* Part-time, evening/weekend, online learning. *Application deadline:* Applications are processed on a rolling basis. Application fee: $25. Electronic applications accepted. Application fee is waived when completed online. *Expenses:* Tuition: Full-time $16,308; part-time $906 per credit hour. *Required fees:* $900; $450 per semester. Tuition and fees vary according to course load and degree level. *Unit head:* Dr. Neil Dugger, Dean, 214-333-5202, E-mail: neil@dbu.edu. *Application contact:* Dr. Deborah Tribble, Program Director, 214-333-5831, E-mail: debbiet@dbu.edu. Website: http://www3.dbu.edu/graduate/curriculum_instruction.asp

Delaware Valley University, Program in Educational Leadership, Doylestown, PA 18901-2697. Offers instruction, curriculum and technology (MS); school administration and leadership (MS). *Program availability:* Part-time, evening/weekend. *Entrance requirements:* For master's, minimum undergraduate GPA of 3.0.

DeSales University, Division of Liberal Arts and Social Sciences, Center Valley, PA 18034-9568. Offers criminal justice (MCJ); digital forensics (MCJ, Postbaccalaureate Certificate); education (M Ed), including instructional technology, secondary education, special education, teaching English to speakers of other languages; investigative forensics (MCJ, Postbaccalaureate Certificate). *Program availability:* Part-time, 100% online, blended/hybrid learning. *Faculty:* 5 full-time (3 women), 15 part-time/adjunct (9 women). *Students:* 54 full-time (36 women), 112 part-time (68 women); includes 23 minority (3 Black or African American, non-Hispanic/Latino; 1 Asian, non-Hispanic/Latino; 17 Hispanic/Latino; 2 Two or more races, non-Hispanic/Latino), 1 international. Average age 33. 114 applicants, 64% accepted, 41 enrolled. In 2017, 41 master's awarded. *Entrance requirements:* For master's, bachelor's degree from accredited institution, minimum undergraduate GPA of 3.0, personal statement showing potential of graduate work, three letters of recommendation, professional goal statement. Additional exam requirements/recommendations for international students: Required—TOEFL. *Application deadline:* Applications are processed on a rolling basis. Application fee: $50. Electronic applications accepted. *Expenses:* Tuition: Part-time $840 per credit. Full-time tuition and fees vary according to course load, degree level and program. *Financial support:* Applicants required to submit FAFSA. *Unit head:* Ronald Nordone, Dean of Graduate Education, 610-282-1100 Ext. 1289, E-mail: ronald.nordone@desales.edu. *Application contact:* Julia Ferraro, Director of Graduate Admissions, 610-282-1100 Ext. 1768, E-mail: gradadmissions@desales.edu.

DeVry University–Folsom Campus, Graduate Programs, Folsom, CA 95630. Offers accounting (M Acc); accounting and financial management (MAFM); business administration (MBA); curriculum leadership (M Ed); educational leadership (M Ed); educational technology (M Ed); higher education leadership (M Ed); human resource management (MHRM); information systems management (MISM); network and communications management (MNCM); project management (MPM); public administration (MPA).

Drexel University, Goodwin College of Professional Studies, School of Education, Philadelphia, PA 19104-2875. Offers applied behavior analysis (MS); creativity and innovation (MS); education improvement and transformation (MS); educational administration (MS); educational leadership and management (Ed D); educational leadership development and learning technologies (PhD); global and international education (MS); higher education (MS); human resources development (MS); learning technologies (MS); mathematics, learning and teaching (MS); special education (MS); teaching, learning and curriculum (MS). *Program availability:* Part-time, evening/weekend, online learning. *Degree requirements:* For doctorate, thesis/dissertation. *Entrance requirements:* For doctorate, GRE or GMAT. Additional exam requirements/recommendations for international students: Required—TOEFL, IELTS. Electronic applications accepted. Application fee is waived when completed online. *Expenses:* Contact institution. *Faculty research:* Leadership development, mathematics education, literacy, autism, educational technology.
See Display on page 654 and Close-Up on page 719.

Drexel University, Goodwin College of Professional Studies, School of Technology and Professional Studies, Philadelphia, PA 19104-2875. Offers construction management (MS); creativity and innovation (MS); engineering technology (MS); food science (MS); hospitality management (MS); professional studies: creativity studies (MS); professional studies: e-learning leadership (MS); professional studies: homeland security management (MS); project management (MS); property management (MS); sport management (MS). *Program availability:* Part-time, evening/weekend. *Entrance requirements:* Additional exam requirements/recommendations for international students: Required—TOEFL, IELTS. Electronic applications accepted. Application fee is waived when completed online.

Drury University, Master in Education Program, Springfield, MO 5802. Offers curriculum and instruction (M Ed), including elementary, middle school, secondary; gifted education (M Ed); instructional leadership (M Ed); instructional technology (M Ed); integrated learning (M Ed); online teaching (M Ed); special education (M Ed); special reading (M Ed). *Accreditation:* NCATE. *Program availability:* Part-time, evening/weekend, 100% online, blended/hybrid learning. *Entrance requirements:* For master's, GRE, bachelor's degree with minimum GPA of 2.75. Additional exam requirements/recommendations for international students: Recommended—TOEFL (minimum score 80 iBT), IELTS (minimum score 6.5). Electronic applications accepted. *Expenses:* Contact institution. *Faculty research:* Gifted students, instructional technology, autism, diversity and social justice.

Duquesne University, Graduate School of Liberal Arts, Department of Media, Pittsburgh, PA 15282-0001. Offers MS, Certificate. *Program availability:* Part-time, evening/weekend, blended/hybrid learning. *Faculty:* 10 full-time (2 women), 3 part-time/adjunct (0 women). *Students:* 25 full-time (13 women); includes 3 minority (2 Black or African American, non-Hispanic/Latino; 1 Two or more races, non-Hispanic/Latino), 12 international. Average age 26. 27 applicants, 78% accepted, 9 enrolled. In 2017, 16 master's awarded. *Entrance requirements:* For master's, GRE General Test, portfolio, writing sample. Additional exam requirements/recommendations for international students: Required—TOEFL. *Application deadline:* For fall admission, 8/1 for domestic students, 5/1 for international students; for spring admission, 11/1 for domestic students. Applications are processed on a rolling basis. Application fee: $0. Electronic applications accepted. *Expenses:* $1,259 per credit. *Financial support:* In 2017–18, 10 students received support, including 10 teaching assistantships with full tuition reimbursements available (averaging $8,000 per year); Federal Work-Study also available. Support available to part-time students. Financial award application deadline: 5/1. *Unit head:* Dr. Michael Dillon, Director, 412-396-6448, E-mail: dillonm@duq.edu. *Application contact:* Linda Rendulic, Assistant to the Dean, 412-396-6400, Fax: 412-396-5265, E-mail: rendulic@duq.edu. Website: http://www.duq.edu/academics/schools/liberal-arts/graduate-school/programs/media-arts-and-technology

Duquesne University, School of Education, Department of Instruction and Leadership, Program in Instructional Technology, Pittsburgh, PA 15282-0001. Offers MS Ed, Ed D, Post-Master's Certificate. *Program availability:* Part-time, evening/weekend, minimal on-campus study. *Faculty:* 3 full-time (1 woman). *Students:* 51 full-time (35 women), 11 part-time (6 women); includes 7 minority (4 Black or African American, non-Hispanic/Latino; 2 Asian, non-Hispanic/Latino; 1 Hispanic/Latino), 8 international. Average age 35. 41 applicants, 95% accepted, 16 enrolled. In 2017, 5 master's, 4 doctorates awarded. *Degree requirements:* For master's, thesis optional; for doctorate, thesis/dissertation. *Entrance requirements:* For master's, bachelor's degree; minimum GPA of 3.0 overall or on most recent 48 credits; for doctorate, GRE, master's degree; letter of interest; three letters of recommendation; electronic portfolio; for Post-Master's Certificate, bachelor's/master's degree. Additional exam requirements/recommendations for international students: Required—TOEFL (minimum score 550 paper-based), IELTS (minimum score 7). *Application deadline:* For fall admission, 9/1 for domestic students; for spring admission, 1/2 for domestic students. Applications are processed on a rolling basis. Application fee: $0. Electronic applications accepted. *Expenses:* $1,259 per credit. *Financial support:* Available to part-time students. *Faculty research:* Instructional technology in STEM; computational thinking; drag and drop programming; the advantages of individuals' processing speeds in different learning settings; different cognitive styles of problem solving. *Unit head:* Dr. David Carbonara, Assistant Professor/Director, 412-396-4039, Fax: 412-396-1997, E-mail: carbonara@duq.edu. *Application contact:* Kelly McGinley, Graduate Admissions Assistant, 412-396-1559, Fax: 412-396-5585, E-mail: mcginleyk@duq.edu. Website: http://www.duq.edu/academics/schools/education/graduate-programs/instructional-technology

East Carolina University, Graduate School, College of Education, Department of Mathematics, Science, and Instructional Technology Education, Greenville, NC 27858-4353. Offers distance learning and administration (Certificate); elementary mathematics education (Certificate); instructional technology (MA Ed, MS); mathematics education (MA Ed); science education (MA Ed, MAT); special endorsement in computer education (Certificate). *Program availability:* Part-time, evening/weekend. *Students:* 12 full-time (10 women), 202 part-time (153 women); includes 49 minority (31 Black or African American, non-Hispanic/Latino; 2 American Indian or Alaska Native, non-Hispanic/Latino; 2 Asian, non-Hispanic/Latino; 9 Hispanic/Latino; 5 Two or more races, non-Hispanic/Latino). Average age 38. 56 applicants, 100% accepted, 50 enrolled. In 2017, 76 master's, 30 other advanced degrees awarded. *Degree requirements:* For master's, comprehensive exam, thesis optional. *Entrance requirements:* For master's, GRE General Test or MAT, interview, minimum GPA of 2.5, bachelor's degree in related field, teaching license (MA Ed). Additional exam requirements/recommendations for international students: Required—TOEFL. *Application deadline:* For fall admission, 6/1 priority date for domestic students. Applications are processed on a rolling basis. Application fee: $75. *Expenses:* Tuition, state resident: full-time $4749; part-time $297 per credit hour. Tuition, nonresident: full-time $17,898; part-time $1119 per credit hour. *Required fees:* $2691; $224 per credit hour. Part-time tuition and fees vary according to course load and program. *Financial support:* Research assistantships, teaching assistantships, and Federal Work-Study available. Support available to part-time students. Financial award application deadline: 6/1. *Unit head:* Susan Ganter, Chair, 252-737-3001, E-mail: ganters@ecu.edu. Website: http://www.ecu.edu/cs-educ/msite/

Educational Media/Instructional Technology

East Carolina University, Graduate School, College of Education, Department of Special Education, Foundations, and Research, Greenville, NC 27858-4353. Offers assistive technology (Certificate); autism (Certificate); special education (MA Ed, MAT), including behavioral-emotional disabilities (MA Ed), intellectual disabilities (MA Ed), learning disabilities (MA Ed), low-incidence disabilities (MA Ed). *Program availability:* Part-time, evening/weekend, online learning. *Students:* 1 (woman) full-time, 61 part-time (56 women); includes 15 minority (8 Black or African American, non-Hispanic/Latino; 2 American Indian or Alaska Native, non-Hispanic/Latino; 1 Asian, non-Hispanic/Latino; 2 Hispanic/Latino; 2 Two or more races, non-Hispanic/Latino). Average age 31. 26 applicants, 92% accepted, 22 enrolled. In 2017, 10 master's, 6 other advanced degrees awarded. *Degree requirements:* For master's, comprehensive exam, thesis optional. *Entrance requirements:* For master's, GRE General Test or MAT, interview, bachelor's degree in related field, minimum GPA of 2.5, teaching license. Additional exam requirements/recommendations for international students: Required—TOEFL. *Application deadline:* For fall admission, 6/1 priority date for domestic students. Applications are processed on a rolling basis. Application fee: $75. *Expenses:* Tuition, state resident: full-time $4749; part-time $297 per credit hour. Tuition, nonresident: full-time $17,898; part-time $1119 per credit hour. *Required fees:* $2691; $224 per credit hour. Part-time tuition and fees vary according to course load and program. *Financial support:* Research assistantships, teaching assistantships, and Federal Work-Study available. Support available to part-time students. Financial award application deadline: 6/1; financial award applicants required to submit FAFSA. *Unit head:* Dr. Guili Zhang, Interim Chair, 252-328-4989, E-mail: zhangg@ecu.edu.
Website: http://www.ecu.edu/cs-educ/sefr/index.cfm

Eastern Connecticut State University, School of Education and Professional Studies/ Graduate Division, Program in Educational Technology, Willimantic, CT 06226-2295. Offers MS. *Program availability:* Part-time, evening/weekend, 100% online, blended/ hybrid learning. *Faculty:* 2 full-time (1 woman). *Students:* 6 part-time (2 women); includes 1 minority (Asian, non-Hispanic/Latino). Average age 42. 5 applicants, 80% accepted, 3 enrolled. In 2017, 8 master's awarded. *Degree requirements:* For master's, comprehensive exam, thesis or alternative, culminating portfolio. *Entrance requirements:* For master's, minimum GPA of 2.7, bachelor's degree from accredited institution. Additional exam requirements/recommendations for international students: Required—TOEFL (minimum score 550 paper-based; 79 iBT); Recommended—IELTS (minimum score 6). *Application deadline:* For fall admission, 7/6 priority date for domestic and international students; for spring admission, 11/3 priority date for domestic and international students. Applications are processed on a rolling basis. Application fee: $50. Electronic applications accepted. *Expenses: Tuition, area resident:* Full-time $12,252. Tuition, state resident: full-time $15,245; part-time $582 per credit hour. Tuition, nonresident: full-time $24,828; part-time $582 per credit hour. *Required fees:* $40 per semester. Full-time tuition and fees vary according to reciprocity agreements. *Financial support:* Research assistantships, teaching assistantships, career-related internships or fieldwork, institutionally sponsored loans, and unspecified assistantships available. Financial award application deadline: 3/1; financial award applicants required to submit FAFSA. *Unit head:* Dr. David Stoloff, Advisor, 860-465-5501, Fax: 860-465-5099, E-mail: stoloff@easternct.edu. *Application contact:* Paula Goyette, Graduate Division, School of Education and Professional Studies, 860-465-5292, Fax: 860-465-5710, E-mail: graduateadmissions@easternct.edu.

Eastern Michigan University, Graduate School, College of Education, Department of Teacher Education, Programs in Curriculum and Instruction, Ypsilanti, MI 48197. Offers advanced teaching and learning (MA); early literacy instruction (Graduate Certificate); instructional leadership (MA); learning, motivation and creativity (Graduate Certificate); literacy coaching (Graduate Certificate); online teaching (Certificate); secondary literacy instruction (Graduate Certificate); urban and diversity education (MA). *Students:* 1 full-time (0 women), 22 part-time (19 women); includes 6 minority (2 Black or African American, non-Hispanic/Latino; 1 Hispanic/Latino; 3 Two or more races, non-Hispanic/ Latino). Average age 31. 15 applicants, 67% accepted, 7 enrolled. In 2017, 15 master's, 1 other advanced degree awarded. Application fee: $45. *Application contact:* Dr. Virginia Harder, Graduate Coordinator/Advisor, 734-487-2729, Fax: 734-487-2101, E-mail: vharder1@emich.edu.

Eastern Michigan University, Graduate School, College of Education, Department of Teacher Education, Programs in Learning Technology and Design, Ypsilanti, MI 48197. Offers MA, Graduate Certificate. *Program availability:* Part-time, evening/weekend, online learning. *Students:* 23 part-time (17 women); includes 5 minority (3 Black or African American, non-Hispanic/Latino; 2 Hispanic/Latino). Average age 34. 12 applicants, 67% accepted, 2 enrolled. In 2017, 6 master's awarded. *Entrance requirements:* Additional exam requirements/recommendations for international students: Required—TOEFL. *Application deadline:* Applications are processed on a rolling basis. Application fee: $45. *Financial support:* Fellowships, research assistantships with full tuition reimbursements, teaching assistantships with full tuition reimbursements, career-related internships or fieldwork, Federal Work-Study, institutionally sponsored loans, scholarships/grants, tuition waivers (partial), and unspecified assistantships available. Support available to part-time students. Financial award applicants required to submit FAFSA. *Application contact:* Dr. Toni Stokes Jones, Coordinator, 734-487-3260, Fax: 734-487-2101, E-mail: tjones1@emich.edu.

Eastern New Mexico University, Graduate School, College of Education and Technology, Department of Curriculum and Instruction, Portales, NM 88130. Offers alternative licensure in elementary education (M Ed); bilingual education (M Ed); career and technical education (M Ed); educational technology (M Ed); elementary education (M Ed); English as a second language (M Ed); pedagogy and learning (M Ed); reading/ literacy (M Ed). *Program availability:* Part-time, online learning. *Degree requirements:* For master's, comprehensive exam, thesis optional. *Entrance requirements:* For master's, writing assessment, minimum GPA of 3.0, photocopy of teaching license, letter of recommendation. Additional exam requirements/recommendations for international students: Required—TOEFL (minimum score 550 paper-based; 79 iBT), IELTS (minimum score 6). *Application deadline:* For fall admission, 7/20 priority date for domestic students, 6/20 priority date for international students; for spring admission, 12/ 15 priority date for domestic students, 11/15 priority date for international students. Applications are processed on a rolling basis. Application fee: $10. Electronic applications accepted. *Financial support:* Applicants required to submit FAFSA. *Unit head:* Dr. Mary Daughrity, Graduate Coordinator, 575-562-2481, Fax: 575-562-2559, E-mail: mary.daughrity@enmu.edu. *Application contact:* Cheryl Reeves, Senior Secretary, 575-562-2443, E-mail: cheryl.reeves@enmu.edu.
Website: http://education.enmu.edu

East Stroudsburg University of Pennsylvania, Graduate and Extended Studies, College of Education, Department of Digital Media Technologies, East Stroudsburg, PA 18301-2999. Offers M Ed. *Program availability:* Part-time, evening/weekend, online learning. *Faculty:* 3 full-time (2 women), 2 part-time/adjunct (1 woman). *Students:* 8 full-time (4 women), 22 part-time (15 women); includes 3 minority (1 Black or African American, non-Hispanic/Latino; 2 Two or more races, non-Hispanic/Latino), 5 international. Average age 33. 26 applicants, 69% accepted, 14 enrolled. In 2017, 5 master's awarded. *Degree requirements:* For master's, comprehensive exam, comprehensive portfolio, internship. *Entrance requirements:* For master's, two letters of recommendation, portfolio or interview, minimum overall undergraduate QPA of 2.5. Additional exam requirements/recommendations for international students: Recommended—TOEFL (minimum score 560 paper-based; 83 iBT), IELTS. *Application deadline:* For fall admission, 7/31 priority date for domestic students, 6/30 priority date for international students; for spring admission, 11/30 for domestic students, 10/31 for international students. Applications are processed on a rolling basis. Application fee: $50. Electronic applications accepted. *Expenses:* Tuition, state resident: full-time $4500; part-time $3000 per credit. Tuition, nonresident: full-time $6750; part-time $4500 per credit. *Required fees:* $2642; $1756 per credit. $878 per semester. Tuition and fees vary according to course load, campus/location and program. *Financial support:* Research assistantships with tuition reimbursements, career-related internships or fieldwork, Federal Work-Study, and unspecified assistantships available. Support available to part-time students. Financial award application deadline: 3/1; financial award applicants required to submit FAFSA. *Unit head:* Dr. Richard Otto, Chair, 570-422-3763, Fax: 570-422-3876, E-mail: rotto@esu.edu. *Application contact:* Kevin Quintero, Associate Director, Graduate and Extended Studies, 570-422-3890, Fax: 570-422-2711, E-mail: kquintero@esu.edu.

East Tennessee State University, School of Graduate Studies, College of Education, Department of Curriculum and Instruction, Johnson City, TN 37614. Offers advanced studies in teaching and learning (M Ed), including childhood literacy; educational technology (M Ed), including educational communications and technology, school library media; elementary education (M Ed); reading (M Ed, MA), including reading education (MA), storytelling (MA); response to intervention (Post-Master's Certificate); school library professional (Post-Master's Certificate); secondary education (M Ed); STEAM K-12 education (Postbaccalaureate Certificate); storytelling (Postbaccalaureate Certificate); teacher education (MAT), including elementary education K-5, middle grades education 4-8, middle grades education 6-8, secondary education 6-12 and preK-12, secondary education K-12. *Accreditation:* NCATE. *Program availability:* Part-time, evening/weekend, online learning. *Degree requirements:* For master's, comprehensive exam, thesis optional, student teaching, practicum; for other advanced degree, field work (school library); culminating experience (storytelling). *Entrance requirements:* For master's, GRE, SAT, ACT, PRAXIS, minimum GPA of 3.0, interview, 3 letters of recommendation, background check; for other advanced degree, master's degree, TN teaching license. Additional exam requirements/recommendations for international students: Required—TOEFL (minimum score 550 paper-based; 79 iBT). *Application deadline:* For fall admission, 6/1 for domestic students, 4/29 for international students; for spring admission, 11/1 for domestic students, 4/29 for international students. Application fee: $55 ($65 for international students). Electronic applications accepted. *Financial support:* Research assistantships with full tuition reimbursements, teaching assistantships with tuition reimbursements, career-related internships or fieldwork, institutionally sponsored loans, scholarships/grants, and unspecified assistantships available. Financial award application deadline: 7/1; financial award applicants required to submit FAFSA. *Faculty research:* Critical thinking; curriculum development in reading, math, and science education; cultural diversity; cognitive processes; effective teaching strategies. *Unit head:* Dr. Karin Keith, Chair, 423-439-7598, Fax: 423-439-8362, E-mail: keithkj@etsu.edu. *Application contact:* Dr. Aimee Govett, Graduate Coordinator, 423-439-7804, Fax: 423-439-5624, E-mail: govett@etsu.edu.
Website: http://www.etsu.edu/coe/cuai/

Emporia State University, Department of Instructional Design and Technology, Emporia, KS 66801-5415. Offers elearning/online teaching (Certificate); teaching with technology (Certificate). *Accreditation:* NCATE. *Program availability:* Part-time, online only, 100% online. *Faculty:* 7 full-time (4 women). *Students:* 25 full-time (20 women), 40 part-time (30 women); includes 6 minority (2 Black or African American, non-Hispanic/ Latino; 2 Asian, non-Hispanic/Latino; 1 Hispanic/Latino; 1 Two or more races, non-Hispanic/Latino), 24 international. 26 applicants, 77% accepted, 11 enrolled. In 2017, 43 master's, 31 other advanced degrees awarded. *Degree requirements:* For master's, comprehensive exam (for some programs), thesis (for some programs), project. *Entrance requirements:* For master's, appropriate bachelor's degree, letters of recommendation. Additional exam requirements/recommendations for international students: Required—TOEFL (minimum score 520 paper-based; 68 iBT). *Application deadline:* For fall admission, 8/15 priority date for domestic students. Applications are processed on a rolling basis. Application fee: $30 ($75 for international students). Electronic applications accepted. *Expenses:* Tuition, state resident: full-time $6084; part-time $253.50 per credit hour. Tuition, nonresident: full-time $18,924; part-time $788.50 per credit hour. *Required fees:* $1943; $80.95 per credit hour. Tuition and fees vary according to campus/location. *Financial support:* In 2017–18, 7 teaching assistantships with full tuition reimbursements (averaging $6,295 per year) were awarded; Federal Work-Study, institutionally sponsored loans, health care benefits, and unspecified assistantships also available. Financial award application deadline: 3/15; financial award applicants required to submit FAFSA. *Unit head:* Dr. Zeni Colorado Resa, Chair, 620-341-5477, E-mail: jcolorad@emporia.edu. *Application contact:* Mary Sewell, Admissions Coordinator, 800-950-GRAD, Fax: 620-341-5909, E-mail: msewell@emporia.edu.
Website: http://www.emporia.edu/idt/

Fairfield University, Graduate School of Education and Allied Professions, Fairfield, CT 06824. Offers applied behavior analysis (ATC); applied psychology (MA); clinical mental health counseling (MA, CAS); educational technology (MA); elementary education (MA, CAS); family studies (MA); integration of spirituality and religion in counseling (ATC); marriage and family therapy (MA); reading and language development (Sixth Year Certificate); school counseling (MA, CAS); school psychology (MA, CAS); school-based marriage and family therapy (ATC); secondary education (MA); special education (MA, CAS); substance abuse counseling (ATC); teaching (Certificate); teaching and foundations (MA, CAS); TESOL, world languages, and bilingual education (MA, CAS). *Accreditation:* NCATE. *Program availability:* Part-time, evening/weekend. *Faculty:* 23 full-time (17 women), 39 part-time/adjunct (28 women). *Students:* 199 full-time (168 women), 251 part-time (206 women); includes 85 minority (21 Black or African American, non-Hispanic/Latino; 9 Asian, non-Hispanic/Latino; 49 Hispanic/Latino; 6 Two or more races, non-Hispanic/Latino), 4 international. Average age 32. 370 applicants, 56% accepted, 125 enrolled. In 2017, 136 master's, 28 other advanced degrees awarded. *Degree requirements:* For master's, comprehensive exam. *Entrance requirements:* For master's, minimum GPA of 3.0, 2 recommendations, resume. Additional exam requirements/recommendations for international students: Required—TOEFL (minimum score 550 paper-based; 84 iBT) or IELTS (minimum score 7.5). *Application deadline:* For fall admission, 2/15 for international students; for spring admission, 10/1 for international students. Application fee: $60. Electronic applications accepted. *Expenses:* $750 per credit hour. *Financial support:* In 2017–18, 34 students received support. Career-related internships or fieldwork and unspecified assistantships available. Support available to part-time students. Financial award applicants required to submit FAFSA. *Faculty research:* Reading and literacy, writing, social justice and inequality in education, addictions and mental health issues, therapeutic relationships and clinical supervision. *Unit head:* Dr. Robert D. Hannafin, Dean, 203-254-4250, Fax: 203-254-4241, E-mail: rhannafin@fairfield.edu. *Application contact:* Marianne Gumpper, Director of Graduate Admission, 203-254-4184, Fax: 203-254-4073, E-mail: gradadmis@fairfield.edu.
Website: http://www.fairfield.edu/gseap

Fairleigh Dickinson University, Florham Campus, University College: Arts, Sciences, and Professional Studies, Peter Sammartino School of Education, Madison, NJ 07940-1099. Offers education for certified teachers (MA, Certificate); educational leadership (MA); instructional technology (Certificate); literacy/reading (Certificate); teaching (MAT).

Fairleigh Dickinson University, Metropolitan Campus, University College: Arts, Sciences, and Professional Studies, Peter Sammartino School of Education, Teaneck, NJ 07666-1914. Offers dyslexia specialist (Certificate); education for certified teachers (MA); educational leadership (MA); instructional technology (Certificate); learning disabilities (MA); literacy/reading (Certificate); multilingual education (MA); teacher of the handicapped (Certificate); teaching (MAT). *Accreditation:* TEAC. *Program availability:* Part-time. *Degree requirements:* For master's, research project (MAT).

Fairmont State University, Programs in Education, Fairmont, WV 26554. Offers digital media, new literacies and learning (M Ed); education (MAT); exercise science, fitness and wellness (M Ed); professional studies (M Ed); reading (M Ed); special education (M Ed). *Accreditation:* NCATE. *Program availability:* Part-time, evening/weekend, 100% online. *Entrance requirements:* For master's, GRE. Additional exam requirements/recommendations for international students: Required—TOEFL (minimum score 80 iBT), IELTS (minimum score 6.5). Electronic applications accepted.

Florida Atlantic University, College of Education, Department of Teaching and Learning, Boca Raton, FL 33431-0991. Offers curriculum and instruction (M Ed), including art, biology, chemistry, English, French, German, mathematics, music, physics, Pre-K and primary education, reading, social sciences, Spanish; elementary education (M Ed); environmental education (M Ed); reading education (M Ed); social foundations of education (M Ed), including educational psychology, educational technology, multilingual education. *Accreditation:* NCATE. *Program availability:* Part-time, evening/weekend. *Faculty:* 13 full-time (10 women), 1 part-time/adjunct (0 women). *Students:* 26 full-time (22 women), 43 part-time (39 women); includes 19 minority (9 Black or African American, non-Hispanic/Latino; 1 Asian, non-Hispanic/Latino; 8 Hispanic/Latino; 1 Two or more races, non-Hispanic/Latino), 3 international. Average age 30. 91 applicants, 57% accepted, 33 enrolled. In 2017, 25 master's awarded. *Entrance requirements:* For master's, GRE General Test, minimum GPA of 3.0 in last 2 years of undergraduate course work. Additional exam requirements/recommendations for international students: Required—TOEFL (minimum score 500 paper-based; 61 iBT), IELTS (minimum score 6). *Application deadline:* For fall admission, 7/1 for domestic students, 2/15 for international students; for spring admission, 11/1 for domestic students, 7/15 for international students. Applications are processed on a rolling basis. Application fee: $30. *Expenses:* Tuition, state resident: full-time $7400; part-time $369.82 per credit. Tuition, nonresident: full-time $20,496; part-time $1042.81 per credit. *Financial support:* Fellowships with partial tuition reimbursements, research assistantships with partial tuition reimbursements, teaching assistantships with partial tuition reimbursements, career-related internships or fieldwork, scholarships/grants, and unspecified assistantships available. *Faculty research:* Technology, teaching English to speakers of other languages, math teaching, electronic portfolio assessment, global perspectives through social studies. *Unit head:* Dr. Barbara Ridener, Chairperson, 561-297-3588, E-mail: bridener@fau.edu. *Application contact:* Dr. Eliah Watlington, Associate Dean, 561-296-8520, Fax: 261-297-2991, E-mail: ewatling@fau.edu.
Website: http://www.coe.fau.edu/academicdepartments/tl/

Florida Institute of Technology, College of Science, Program in Educational Technology, Melbourne, FL 32901-6975. Offers MS. *Program availability:* Part-time. *Students:* Average age 31. *Degree requirements:* For master's, comprehensive exam (for some programs), thesis or oral final exam, 30 credit hours. *Entrance requirements:* For master's, resume, statement of objectives. Additional exam requirements/recommendations for international students: Required—TOEFL (minimum score 500 paper-based; 79 iBT). *Application deadline:* Applications are processed on a rolling basis. Electronic applications accepted. *Expenses: Tuition:* Part-time $1241 per credit hour. Part-time tuition and fees vary according to campus/location. *Financial support:* Applicants required to submit FAFSA. *Unit head:* Dr. Scott R. Tilley, Program Chair, 321-674-8126, E-mail: stilley@fit.edu. *Application contact:* Cheryl A. Brown, Associate Director of Graduate Admissions, 321-674-7581, Fax: 321-723-9468, E-mail: cbrown@fit.edu.
Website: http://www.fit.edu/programs/8115/ms-educational-technology#.VT_h8k10ypo

Florida International University, College of Arts, Sciences, and Education, Department of Leadership and Professional Studies, Miami, FL 33199. Offers adult education and human resource development (MS, Ed D); counseling (MS), including rehabilitation counseling, school counseling; counselor education (MS), including clinical mental health counseling; educational administration and supervision (Ed D); educational leadership (MS, Certificate, Ed S); higher education (Ed D); higher education administration (MS); international and comparative education (MS); recreation and sport management (MS), including recreation and sport management, recreational therapy; school psychology (Ed S); urban education (MS), including instruction in urban settings, learning technologies, multicultural/bilingual, multicultural/TESOL, urban education. *Program availability:* Part-time, evening/weekend. *Faculty:* 60 full-time (41 women), 112 part-time/adjunct (77 women). *Students:* 221 full-time (162 women), 301 part-time (239 women); includes 418 minority (127 Black or African American, non-Hispanic/Latino; 9 Asian, non-Hispanic/Latino; 271 Hispanic/Latino; 11 Two or more races, non-Hispanic/Latino), 10 international. Average age 31. 330 applicants, 55% accepted, 100 enrolled. In 2017, 181 master's, 6 doctorates awarded. *Degree requirements:* For doctorate, thesis/dissertation. *Entrance requirements:* For master's, minimum GPA of 3.0; for doctorate and other advanced degree, GRE General Test. Additional exam requirements/recommendations for international students: Required—TOEFL (minimum score 550 paper-based; 80 iBT), IELTS (minimum score 6.3). *Application deadline:* For fall admission, 6/1 priority date for domestic students, 4/1 for international students; for winter admission, 10/1 priority date for domestic students, 9/1 for international students; for spring admission, 3/1 priority date for domestic students, 2/1 for international students. Applications are processed on a rolling basis. Application fee: $30. Electronic applications accepted. *Expenses:* Tuition, state resident: full-time $8912; part-time $446 per credit hour. Tuition, nonresident: full-time $21,393; part-time $992 per credit hour. *Required fees:* $390; $195 per semester. *Financial support:* Fellowships, research assistantships with tuition reimbursements, teaching assistantships with tuition reimbursements, Federal Work-Study, and tuition waivers (full and partial) available. Support available to part-time students. Financial award applicants required to submit FAFSA. *Unit head:* Dr. Benjamin Baez, Chair, 305-348-3214, Fax: 305-348-1515, E-mail: benjamin.baez@fiu.edu. *Application contact:* Nanett Rojas, Assistant Director, Graduate Admissions, 305-348-7464, Fax: 305-348-7441, E-mail: gradadm@fiu.edu.
Website: http://education.fiu.edu

Florida International University, College of Arts, Sciences, and Education, Department of Teaching and Learning, Miami, FL 33199. Offers art education (MA, MS); curriculum and instruction (MS, Ed D, PhD, Ed S), including curriculum development (MS), elementary education (MS), English education (MS), learning technologies (MS), mathematics education (MS), modern language education (MS), physical education (MS), science education (MS), social studies education (MS), special education (MS);

early childhood education (MS); exceptional student education (Ed D); foreign language education (MS), including foreign language education, teaching English to speakers of other languages (TESOL); language, literacy and culture (PhD); mathematics, science, and learning technologies (PhD); physical education (MS), including sport and fitness; reading education (MS). *Program availability:* Part-time, evening/weekend. *Faculty:* 60 full-time (41 women), 112 part-time/adjunct (77 women). *Students:* 165 full-time (139 women), 191 part-time (148 women); includes 270 minority (56 Black or African American, non-Hispanic/Latino; 12 Asian, non-Hispanic/Latino; 191 Hispanic/Latino; 13 international. Average age 34. 238 applicants, 68% accepted, 107 enrolled. In 2017, 184 master's, 15 doctorates awarded. *Degree requirements:* For doctorate, comprehensive exam, thesis/dissertation. *Entrance requirements:* For master's, GRE General Test, Florida General Knowledge Test or Florida College Level Academic Skills Test; for doctorate and Ed S, GRE General Test. Additional exam requirements/recommendations for international students: Required—TOEFL (minimum score 550 paper-based; 80 iBT), IELTS (minimum score 6.3). *Application deadline:* For fall admission, 6/1 priority date for domestic students, 4/1 for international students; for winter admission, 10/1 priority date for domestic students, 9/1 for international students; for spring admission, 3/1 priority date for domestic students, 2/1 for international students. Applications are processed on a rolling basis. Application fee: $30. Electronic applications accepted. *Expenses:* Tuition, state resident: full-time $8912; part-time $446 per credit hour. Tuition, nonresident: full-time $21,393; part-time $992 per credit hour. *Required fees:* $390; $195 per semester. *Financial support:* Research assistantships with tuition reimbursements and teaching assistantships with tuition reimbursements available. *Unit head:* Dr. Lynn Miller, Chair, 305-348-2005, Fax: 305-348-2086, E-mail: lynne.miller@fiu.edu. *Application contact:* Nanett Rojas, Assistant Director, Graduate Admissions, 305-348-7464, E-mail: gradadm@fiu.edu.
Website: https://tl.fiu.edu/

Florida State University, The Graduate School, College of Education, Department of Educational Psychology and Learning Systems, Tallahassee, FL 32306. Offers counseling and human systems (PhD), including counseling psychology and school psychology; educational psychology (MS, PhD), including learning and cognition, sport psychology; human performance and technology (Certificate); instructional systems and learning technologies (MS, PhD); measurement and statistics (MS, PhD, Certificate); online instructional development (Certificate); MS/Ed S. *Program availability:* Part-time, evening/weekend, 100% online, blended/hybrid learning, asynchronous, minimal on-campus study. *Faculty:* 28 full-time (17 women), 12 part-time/adjunct (7 women). *Students:* 339 full-time (238 women), 136 part-time (93 women); includes 126 minority (47 Black or African American, non-Hispanic/Latino; 4 American Indian or Alaska Native, non-Hispanic/Latino; 7 Asian, non-Hispanic/Latino; 48 Hispanic/Latino; 20 Two or more races, non-Hispanic/Latino), 110 international. Average age 31. 419 applicants, 39% accepted, 82 enrolled. In 2017, 84 master's, 27 doctorates, 38 other advanced degrees awarded. Terminal master's awarded for partial completion of doctoral program. *Degree requirements:* For master's and Certificate, comprehensive exam, thesis optional; for doctorate, comprehensive exam, thesis/dissertation, diagnostic exam, preliminary exam, prospectus defense. *Entrance requirements:* For master's, doctorate, and Certificate, GRE General Test, minimum GPA of 3.0. Additional exam requirements/recommendations for international students: Required—TOEFL (minimum score 550 paper-based, 80 iBT), IELTS (minimum score 6.5) or Michigan English Language Assessment Battery (minimum score 77). Application fee: $30. Electronic applications accepted. *Financial support:* Fellowships, research assistantships, teaching assistantships, scholarships/grants, tuition waivers (full and partial), and unspecified assistantships available. Financial award application deadline: 1/15; financial award applicants required to submit FAFSA. *Faculty research:* Learning and cognition, counseling and school psychology, instructional systems, measurement and evaluation. *Unit head:* Dr. Betsy Becker, Chair, 850-644-4592, Fax: 850-644-8776, E-mail: bbecker@fsu.edu. *Application contact:* Deborah Kelly, Academic Program Specialist, 850-644-8046, Fax: 850-644-8781, E-mail: dhamkelly@fsu.edu.

Fontbonne University, Graduate Programs, St. Louis, MO 63105-3098. Offers accounting (MBA, MS); art (MA); art (K-12) (MAT); business (MBA); computer science (MS); deaf education (MA); early intervention in deaf education (MA); education (MA), including autism spectrum disorders, curriculum and instruction, diverse learners, early childhood education, reading, special education; elementary education (MAT); family and consumer sciences (MA), including multidisciplinary health communication studies; fine arts (MFA); instructional design and technology (MS); management and leadership (MM); middle school education (MAT); secondary education (MAT); special education (MAT); speech-language pathology (MS); supply chain management (MS); theatre (MA). *Program availability:* Part-time, evening/weekend, online learning. *Degree requirements:* For master's, comprehensive exam (for some programs), thesis (for some programs). *Entrance requirements:* Additional exam requirements/recommendations for international students: Required—TOEFL (minimum score 500 paper-based; 65 iBT). Electronic applications accepted.

Fort Hays State University, Graduate School, College of Education, Department of Technology Studies, Hays, KS 67601-4099. Offers instructional technology (MS). *Degree requirements:* For master's, comprehensive exam, thesis or alternative. *Entrance requirements:* Additional exam requirements/recommendations for international students: Required—TOEFL (minimum score 550 paper-based). Electronic applications accepted.

Framingham State University, Graduate Studies, Program in Curriculum and Instructional Technology, Framingham, MA 01701-9101. Offers M Ed. *Program availability:* Online learning. *Unit head:* Kim Cochrane, Visiting Associate Professor, E-mail: kcochrane1@framingham.edu. *Application contact:* 508-626-4550, Fax: 508-626-4030, E-mail: dgce@frc.mass.edu.

Franklin University, Instructional Design and Performance Technology Program, Columbus, OH 43215-5399. Offers MS.

Fresno Pacific University, Graduate Programs, School of Education, Program in Educational Technology, Fresno, CA 93702-4709. Offers MA. *Program availability:* Part-time, evening/weekend, online learning. *Degree requirements:* For master's, thesis or alternative. *Entrance requirements:* For master's, three references. Additional exam requirements/recommendations for international students: Required—TOEFL (minimum score 550 paper-based). *Expenses:* Contact institution.

Fresno Pacific University, Graduate Programs, School of Education, Program in School Library and Information Technology, Fresno, CA 93702-4709. Offers MA Ed. *Program availability:* Part-time, evening/weekend, online learning. *Degree requirements:* For master's, thesis or alternative. *Entrance requirements:* For master's, CBEST. Additional exam requirements/recommendations for international students: Required—TOEFL (minimum score 550 paper-based). Electronic applications accepted. *Expenses:* Contact institution.

Frostburg State University, College of Education, Department of Educational Professions, Program in Curriculum and Instruction, Frostburg, MD 21532. Offers curriculum and instruction (Ed D); educational technology (M Ed); elementary education (M Ed); secondary education (M Ed). *Program availability:* Part-time, evening/weekend.

Educational Media/Instructional Technology

Faculty: 2. *Students:* 45 part-time (33 women); includes 1 minority (Two or more races, non-Hispanic/Latino). Average age 34. 15 applicants, 93% accepted, 11 enrolled. In 2017, 5 master's, 1 doctorate awarded. *Degree requirements:* For master's, thesis or alternative. *Entrance requirements:* For master's, teaching certificate. Additional exam requirements/recommendations for international students: Required—TOEFL. *Application deadline:* For fall admission, 7/15 priority date for domestic students. Applications are processed on a rolling basis. Application fee: $45. Electronic applications accepted. *Expenses:* Tuition, state resident: part-time $433 per credit hour. Tuition, nonresident: part-time $557 per credit hour. *Required fees:* $121 per credit hour. $27 per term. *Financial support:* In 2017–18, 2 research assistantships with full tuition reimbursements (averaging $5,000 per year) were awarded. Financial award application deadline: 4/1; financial award applicants required to submit FAFSA. *Unit head:* Dr. Jennifer Rankin, Coordinator, 301-687-7010, E-mail: jerankin@frostburg.edu. *Application contact:* Vickie Mazer, Director, Graduate Services, 301-687-7053, Fax: 301-687-4597, E-mail: vmmazer@frostburg.edu.

Full Sail University, Education Media Design and Technology Master of Science Program - Online, Winter Park, FL 32792-7437. Offers MS. *Program availability:* Online learning. *Entrance requirements:* Additional exam requirements/recommendations for international students: Required—TOEFL (minimum score 550 paper-based; 79 iBT).

George Fox University, College of Education, Graduate Teaching and Leading Program, Newberg, OR 97132-2697. Offers administrative leadership (Ed S); continuing administrator license (Certificate); educational leadership (M Ed); educational technology (M Ed); English for speakers of other languages (M Ed); ESOL (Certificate); initial administrator license (Certificate); reading (M Ed, Certificate); special education (M Ed); teaching (MAT). *Accreditation:* NCATE. *Program availability:* Part-time, evening/weekend, online learning. *Degree requirements:* For master's, thesis (for some programs). *Entrance requirements:* For master's, minimum undergraduate GPA of 3.0 during previous 2 years of course work, resume, 3 professional recommendations on university forms, official transcripts. Additional exam requirements/recommendations for international students: Required—TOEFL (minimum score 577 paper-based; 90 iBT). Electronic applications accepted. *Expenses:* Contact institution.

George Mason University, College of Education and Human Development, Programs in Curriculum and Instruction, Fairfax, VA 22030. Offers advanced international baccalaureate (M Ed); assistive technology (M Ed); designing digital learning in schools (M Ed); early childhood education (M Ed); early childhood education for diverse learners (M Ed); elementary education (M Ed); English as a second language (M Ed); gifted child education (M Ed); history (M Ed); literacy (M Ed), including PK-12 classroom teachers, reading specialist; literacy leadership for diverse schools (M Ed), including K-12 reading; physical education (M Ed); science K-12 (M Ed); secondary education (M Ed), including biology, chemistry, earth science, English, history/social science, math, physics; special education (M Ed); teacher leadership (M Ed); teaching culturally, linguistically diverse and exceptional learners (M Ed); transformative teaching (M Ed). *Program availability:* Part-time, evening/weekend, 100% online, blended/hybrid learning. *Faculty:* 41 full-time (36 women), 45 part-time/adjunct (37 women). *Students:* 173 full-time (151 women), 729 part-time (611 women); includes 271 minority (65 Black or African American, non-Hispanic/Latino; 5 American Indian or Alaska Native, non-Hispanic/Latino; 88 Asian, non-Hispanic/Latino; 94 Hispanic/Latino; 1 Native Hawaiian or other Pacific Islander, non-Hispanic/Latino; 18 Two or more races, non-Hispanic/Latino, 28 international. Average age 32. 426 applicants, 91% accepted, 289 enrolled. In 2017, 349 master's awarded. *Degree requirements:* For master's, thesis. *Entrance requirements:* For master's, PRAXIS Core (for some programs), 2 letters of recommendation, interview, program goals statement; 9 hours of complete licensure endorsement requirements (for elementary education); minimum GPA of 3.0 in applicant's last 60 hours of undergraduate coursework (for secondary education); at least 1 year of teaching experience (for literacy). Additional exam requirements/recommendations for international students: Required—TOEFL (minimum score 575 paper-based; 88 iBT), IELTS (minimum score 6.5), PTE (minimum score 59). *Application deadline:* For fall admission, 4/2 priority date for domestic and international students; for spring admission, 11/1 for domestic and international students. Application fee: $75 ($80 for international students). Electronic applications accepted. *Expenses:* Tuition, state resident: full-time $11,228; part-time $459.50 per credit. Tuition, nonresident: full-time $30,932; part-time $1280.50 per credit. *Required fees:* $3252; $135.50 per credit. Part-time tuition and fees vary according to course load and program. *Financial support:* In 2017–18, 2 students received support, including 2 teaching assistantships; career-related internships or fieldwork, Federal Work-Study, scholarships/grants, unspecified assistantships, and health care benefits (for full-time research or teaching assistantship recipients) also available. Support available to part-time students. Financial award application deadline: 3/1; financial award applicants required to submit FAFSA. *Faculty research:* Teacher preparation and professional development; adaptive teaching; wonder in science teacher preparation; literacy (digital, adolescent); site based course instruction. *Unit head:* Rebecca Fox, Professor and Academic Program Coordinator, 703-993-4123, E-mail: rfox@gmu.edu. Website: http://gse.gmu.edu/programs/gsemasters

The George Washington University, Graduate School of Education and Human Development, Department of Educational Leadership, Program in Educational Technology Leadership, Washington, DC 20052. Offers MA Ed. *Accreditation:* NCATE. *Program availability:* Part-time, evening/weekend. *Students:* 4 full-time (3 women), 65 part-time (43 women); includes 19 minority (5 Black or African American, non-Hispanic/Latino; 1 American Indian or Alaska Native, non-Hispanic/Latino; 4 Asian, non-Hispanic/Latino; 5 Hispanic/Latino; 4 Two or more races, non-Hispanic/Latino, 1 international. Average age 35. 52 applicants, 90% accepted, 37 enrolled. In 2017, 22 master's awarded. *Degree requirements:* For master's, comprehensive exam, thesis or alternative. *Entrance requirements:* For master's, GRE General Test or MAT, minimum GPA of 2.75. *Application deadline:* For fall admission, 1/15 priority date for domestic students; for spring admission, 10/1 for domestic students. Applications are processed on a rolling basis. Application fee: $75. *Expenses:* Contact institution. *Financial support:* Fellowships, research assistantships, teaching assistantships, and career-related internships or fieldwork available. Financial award application deadline: 1/15. *Faculty research:* Interactive multimedia, distance education, federal technology policy. *Unit head:* Dr. Natalie Milman, Coordinator, 202-994-1884, E-mail: milman@gwu.edu. *Application contact:* Sarah Lang, Director of Graduate Admissions, 202-994-1447, Fax: 202-994-7207, E-mail: slang@gwu.edu.

The George Washington University, Graduate School of Education and Human Development, Department of Educational Leadership, Program in Instructional Design, Washington, DC 20052. Offers Graduate Certificate. *Students:* 15 part-time (14 women); includes 4 minority (1 Asian, non-Hispanic/Latino; 2 Hispanic/Latino; 1 Two or more races, non-Hispanic/Latino). Average age 41. 19 applicants, 79% accepted, 9 enrolled. In 2017, 9 Graduate Certificates awarded. *Expenses: Tuition:* Full-time $28,800; part-time $1655 per credit hour. *Required fees:* $45; $2.75 per credit hour. *Unit head:* Michael Feuer, Dean, 202-994-6161, E-mail: mjfeuer@gwu.edu. *Application contact:* Sarah Lang, Director of Graduate Admissions, 202-994-1447, Fax: 202-994-7207, E-mail: slang@gwu.edu. Website: http://gsehd.gwu.edu/instructional-design-certificate

The George Washington University, Graduate School of Education and Human Development, Department of Educational Leadership, Program in Integrating Technology into Education, Washington, DC 20052. Offers Graduate Certificate. *Students:* 1 applicant, 100% accepted. *Expenses: Tuition:* Full-time $28,800; part-time $1655 per credit hour. *Required fees:* $45; $2.75 per credit hour. *Unit head:* Dr. Natalie Milman, Coordinator, 202-994-1884, E-mail: nmilman@gwu.edu. *Application contact:* Sarah Lang, Director of Graduate Admissions, 202-994-1447, Fax: 202-994-7207, E-mail: slang@gwu.edu. Website: http://gsehd.gwu.edu/integrating-technology-education-certificate

The George Washington University, Graduate School of Education and Human Development, Department of Educational Leadership, Program in Leadership in Educational Technology, Washington, DC 20052. Offers Graduate Certificate. *Students:* 1 (woman) part-time. Average age 44. 1 applicant, 100% accepted. In 2017, 1 Graduate Certificate awarded. *Expenses: Tuition:* Full-time $28,800; part-time $1655 per credit hour. *Required fees:* $45; $2.75 per credit hour. *Unit head:* Dr. Natalie Milman, Coordinator, 202-994-1884, E-mail: nmilman@gwu.edu. *Application contact:* Sarah Lang, Director of Graduate Admissions, 202-994-1447, Fax: 202-994-7207, E-mail: slang@gwu.edu. Website: http://gsehd.gwu.edu/

The George Washington University, Graduate School of Education and Human Development, Department of Educational Leadership, Program in Multimedia Development, Washington, DC 20052. Offers Graduate Certificate. *Students:* 1 applicant, 100% accepted. *Expenses: Tuition:* Full-time $28,800; part-time $1655 per credit hour. *Required fees:* $45; $2.75 per credit hour. *Unit head:* Michael Feuer, Dean, 202-994-6161, E-mail: mjfeuer@gwu.edu. *Application contact:* Sarah Lang, Director of Graduate Admissions, 202-994-1447, Fax: 202-994-7207, E-mail: slang@gwu.edu. Website: http://gsehd.gwu.edu/multimedia-development-certificate

The George Washington University, Graduate School of Education and Human Development, Department of Educational Leadership, Program in Training and Educational Technology, Washington, DC 20052. Offers Graduate Certificate. *Students:* 1 (woman) part-time. Average age 36. 3 applicants, 67% accepted. *Expenses: Tuition:* Full-time $28,800; part-time $1655 per credit hour. *Required fees:* $45; $2.75 per credit hour. *Unit head:* Dr. Natalie Milman, Coordinator, 202-994-1884, E-mail: nmilman@gwu.edu. *Application contact:* Sarah Lang, Director of Graduate Admissions, 202-994-1447, Fax: 202-994-7207, E-mail: slang@gwu.edu. Website: http://gsehd.gwu.edu/training-and-educational-technology-certificate

Georgia College & State University, Graduate School, The John H. Lounsbury College of Education, Program in Instructional Technology, Milledgeville, GA 31061. Offers M Ed. *Program availability:* Part-time, evening/weekend, online only, 100% online. *Students:* 7 full-time (4 women), 23 part-time (18 women); includes 16 minority (14 Black or African American, non-Hispanic/Latino; 1 Hispanic/Latino; 1 Two or more races, non-Hispanic/Latino). Average age 35. 8 applicants, 100% accepted, 7 enrolled. In 2017, 1 master's awarded. *Degree requirements:* For master's, comprehensive exam, minimum GPA of 3.0, complete program within 6 years. *Entrance requirements:* For master's, minimum GPA of 2.75, level 4 Georgia Teacher certificate or eligibility, 2 professional recommendations, transcripts, proof of immunization. Additional exam requirements/recommendations for international students: Recommended—TOEFL. *Application deadline:* For fall admission, 7/1 priority date for domestic students, 4/1 priority date for international students; for spring admission, 11/1 priority date for domestic students, 9/1 priority date for international students; for summer admission, 4/1 priority date for domestic students. Applications are processed on a rolling basis. Application fee: $40. Electronic applications accepted. *Expenses:* $288 per credit hour full-time, $2,592 per semester; $343 per semester fees. *Financial support:* Applicants required to submit FAFSA. *Unit head:* Dr. Diane Gregg, Coordinator, 478-445-1505, E-mail: diane.gregg@gcsu.edu. *Application contact:* Shanda Brand, Graduate Admission Advisor, 478-445-1383, E-mail: shanda.brand@gcsu.edu. Website: http://www.gcsu.edu/education/proflearning/educational-technology-med

Georgia College & State University, Graduate School, The John H. Lounsbury College of Education, Program in Library Media, Milledgeville, GA 31061. Offers M Ed. *Program availability:* Part-time, evening/weekend, online only, 100% online. *Students:* 1 (woman) full-time, 9 part-time (8 women); includes 3 minority (2 Black or African American, non-Hispanic/Latino; 1 Hispanic/Latino). Average age 32. 3 applicants, 100% accepted, 2 enrolled. *Degree requirements:* For master's, comprehensive exam, minimum GPA of 3.0, complete program within 4 years, electronic portfolio presentation. *Entrance requirements:* For master's, 2 professional recommendations, transcripts, proof of immunization, minimum GPA of 2.75, 2 years' teaching experience with clear and renewable certificate. *Application deadline:* For fall admission, 7/1 priority date for domestic students; for spring admission, 11/1 priority date for domestic students; for summer admission, 4/1 priority date for domestic students. Applications are processed on a rolling basis. Application fee: $40. Electronic applications accepted. *Expenses:* $288 per credit hour full-time, $2,592 per semester; $343 per semester fees. *Financial support:* Application deadline: 3/1; applicants required to submit FAFSA. *Unit head:* Dr. Joseph Peters, Dean, College of Education, 478-445-2518, Fax: 478-445-6582, E-mail: joseph.peters@gcsu.edu. *Application contact:* Shanda Brand, Graduate Admissions Advisor, 478-445-1383, Fax: 478-445-6582, E-mail: shanda.brand@gcsu.edu.

Georgian Court University, School of Arts and Sciences, Lakewood, NJ 08701-2697. Offers applied behavior analysis (MA); autism spectrum disorders (Certificate); clinical mental health counseling (MA); criminal justice and human rights (MS); holistic health studies (MA, Certificate); homeland security (Certificate); instructional technology (CPC); mercy spirituality (Certificate); parish business management (Certificate); professional counselor (Certificate); school psychology (MA, Certificate); theology (MA, Certificate). *Program availability:* Part-time, evening/weekend. *Faculty:* 18 full-time (11 women), 8 part-time/adjunct (4 women). *Students:* 100 full-time (86 women), 92 part-time (67 women); includes 34 minority (9 Black or African American, non-Hispanic/Latino; 1 Asian, non-Hispanic/Latino; 20 Hispanic/Latino; 4 Two or more races, non-Hispanic/Latino), 2 international. Average age 34. 187 applicants, 56% accepted, 78 enrolled. In 2017, 58 master's, 20 other advanced degrees awarded. *Degree requirements:* For master's, comprehensive exam (for some programs), thesis (for some programs). *Entrance requirements:* For master's, GRE, GMAT, or NTE/PRAXIS, 3 letters of recommendation. Additional exam requirements/recommendations for international students: Required—TOEFL (minimum score 550 paper-based). *Application deadline:* For fall admission, 8/15 for domestic students, 5/1 for international students; for spring admission, 1/15 for domestic students, 10/1 for international students. Applications are processed on a rolling basis. Application fee: $40. Electronic applications accepted. *Expenses: Tuition:* Part-time $839 per credit. *Required fees:* $248 per semester. Tuition and fees vary according to campus/location and program. *Financial support:* Scholarships/grants, health care benefits, and unspecified assistantships available. Financial award application deadline: 4/15; financial award applicants required to submit FAFSA. *Unit head:* Dr. Mary Chinery, Dean, 732-987-2493, Fax: 732-987-2007, E-mail: mchinery@georgian.edu. *Application contact:* Patrick Givens, Director of Graduate and Professional Studies Admissions, 732-987-2736, Fax: 732-987-2000, E-mail: gps@georgian.edu. Website: https://georgian.edu/academics/school-of-arts-sciences/

Georgian Court University, School of Education, Lakewood, NJ 08701-2697. Offers administration and leadership (MA); autism spectrum disorders (Certificate); education (M Ed, MA, MAT); instructional technology (M Mat SE, Certificate). *Accreditation:* TEAC. *Program availability:* Part-time, evening/weekend. *Faculty:* 11 full-time (7 women), 40 part-time/adjunct (22 women). *Students:* 49 full-time (42 women), 472 part-time (388 women); includes 101 minority (42 Black or African American, non-Hispanic/Latino; 12 Asian, non-Hispanic/Latino; 44 Hispanic/Latino; 3 Two or more races, non-Hispanic/Latino). Average age 34. 412 applicants, 56% accepted, 153 enrolled. In 2017, 81 master's awarded. *Degree requirements:* For master's, comprehensive exam (for some programs), thesis (for some programs). *Entrance requirements:* For master's, GRE, GMAT or NTE/PRAXIS, 3 letters of recommendation. Additional exam requirements/recommendations for international students: Required—TOEFL (minimum score 550 paper-based). *Application deadline:* For fall admission, 8/15 priority date for domestic students, 5/1 for international students; for spring admission, 1/15 priority date for domestic students, 10/1 for international students. Applications are processed on a rolling basis. *Application fee:* $40. Electronic applications accepted. *Expenses: Tuition:* Part-time $839 per credit. *Required fees:* $248 per semester. Tuition and fees vary according to campus/location and program. *Financial support:* Scholarships/grants, health care benefits, and unspecified assistantships available. Financial award application deadline: 4/15; financial award applicants required to submit FAFSA. *Unit head:* Dr. Lynn DeCapua, Dean, 732-987-2729, E-mail: ldecapua@georgian.edu. *Application contact:* Patrick Givens, Director of Graduate and Professional Studies Admissions, 732-987-2736, Fax: 732-987-2000, E-mail: gps@georgian.edu.
Website: http://georgian.edu/academics/school-of-education/

Georgia Southern University, Jack N. Averitt College of Graduate Studies, College of Education, Department of Leadership, Technology, and Human Development, Program in Instructional Technology, Statesboro, GA 30460. Offers instructional technology (M Ed, Ed S); school library media (M Ed, Ed S). *Program availability:* Part-time, evening/weekend, online only, 100% online. *Students:* 7 full-time (5 women), 119 part-time (101 women); includes 40 minority (28 Black or African American, non-Hispanic/Latino; 1 American Indian or Alaska Native, non-Hispanic/Latino; 3 Asian, non-Hispanic/Latino; 4 Hispanic/Latino; 4 Two or more races, non-Hispanic/Latino). Average age 35. 48 applicants, 98% accepted, 22 enrolled. In 2017, 48 master's, 7 Ed Ss awarded. *Degree requirements:* For master's, portfolio, transition point assessments. *Entrance requirements:* For master's, minimum GPA of 2.5. Additional exam requirements/recommendations for international students: Required—TOEFL (minimum score 550 paper-based; 80 iBT), IELTS (minimum score 6). *Application deadline:* For fall admission, 8/16 for domestic students, 3/1 priority date for international students; for spring admission, 1/11 for domestic students, 10/1 for international students; for summer admission, 5/10 for domestic students. *Application fee:* $50. Electronic applications accepted. *Expenses:* Tuition, state resident: full-time $4986; part-time $3324 per year. Tuition, nonresident: full-time $21,982; part-time $15,352 per year. *Required fees:* $2092; $1802 per credit hour. $901 per semester. Tuition and fees vary according to course load, campus/location and program. *Financial support:* In 2017–18, 1 student received support. Research assistantships, teaching assistantships, career-related internships or fieldwork, and scholarships/grants available. Support available to part-time students. Financial award application deadline: 4/15; financial award applicants required to submit FAFSA. *Faculty research:* Online learning in higher education and K-12, instructional technology leadership, school library media programs, twenty-first century skills, instructional technology in the content areas. *Unit head:* Dr. Stephanie Jones, Program Director, 912-478-0275, Fax: 912-478-7104, E-mail: sjones@georgiasouthern.edu. *Application contact:* Dr. Lydia Cross, Coordinator for Graduate Academic Services Center, 912-478-8664, E-mail: lcross@georgiasouthern.edu.
Website: http://coe.georgiasouthern.edu/itec/

Georgia State University, College of Education and Human Development, Learning Technologies Division, Atlanta, GA 30302-3083. Offers instructional design and technology (MS); instructional technology (PhD). *Program availability:* Part-time, evening/weekend. *Faculty:* 7 full-time (3 women). *Students:* 17 full-time (12 women), 55 part-time (37 women); includes 40 minority (30 Black or African American, non-Hispanic/Latino; 3 Asian, non-Hispanic/Latino; 2 Hispanic/Latino; 5 Two or more races, non-Hispanic/Latino), 2 international. Average age 36. 41 applicants, 78% accepted, 22 enrolled. In 2017, 10 master's, 3 doctorates awarded. *Entrance requirements:* For master's, GRE General Test, minimum GPA of 2.5; for doctorate, GRE General Test or MAT, minimum GPA of 3.3. Additional exam requirements/recommendations for international students: Required—TOEFL. *Application fee:* $50. Electronic applications accepted. *Expenses:* Tuition, state resident: full-time $7020. Tuition, nonresident: full-time $22,518. *Required fees:* $2128. Tuition and fees vary according to degree level and program. *Financial support:* Federal Work-Study and institutionally sponsored loans available. *Unit head:* Dr. Paul A. Alberto, Interim Dean, 404-413-8100, Fax: 404-413-8103, E-mail: palberto@gsu.edu. *Application contact:* Nancy Keita, Director, Office of Academic Assistance and Graduate Admissions, 404-413-8001, E-mail: nkeita@gsu.edu.
Website: http://ltd.education.gsu.edu/

Goucher College, Graduate Programs in Education, Baltimore, MD 21204-2794. Offers at-risk and diverse learners (M Ed, Certificate); athletic program leadership and administration (M Ed, Certificate); elementary education (MAT); literacy strategies for content learning (M Ed); middle school (M Ed, Certificate); Montessori studies (M Ed); reading instruction (M Ed, Certificate); reducing student, classroom, and school disruption (M Ed); school improvement leadership (M Ed); secondary education (MAT); special education (MAT), including elementary education; special education for certified elementary and secondary teachers (M Ed); teacher as leader in technology (M Ed). *Program availability:* Part-time, evening/weekend. *Degree requirements:* For master's, thesis (M Ed), final presentation (MAT). *Entrance requirements:* For master's, minimum GPA of 3.0. Additional exam requirements/recommendations for international students: Required—TOEFL (minimum score 550 paper-based; 80 iBT), IELTS (minimum score 7). *Application deadline:* For fall admission, 9/1 for domestic students; for spring admission, 1/15 for domestic students. Applications are processed on a rolling basis. *Application fee:* $75. Electronic applications accepted. *Expenses:* Contact institution. *Financial support:* Career-related internships or fieldwork and unspecified assistantships available. Support available to part-time students. Financial award application deadline: 4/15; financial award applicants required to submit FAFSA. *Faculty research:* Urban education, middle school, school improvement, teacher education, at-risk student achievement. *Unit head:* Dr. Phyllis Sunshine, Assistant Provost, 410-337-6047, Fax: 410-337-6394, E-mail: psunshin@goucher.edu. *Application contact:* Carlton E. Surbeck, III, Director of Admissions, 410-337-6100, Fax: 410-337-6085, E-mail: admissions@goucher.edu.
Website: http://www.goucher.edu/graduate-programs/graduate-programs-in-education

Graceland University, Gleazer School of Education, Independence, MO 64050. Offers curriculum and instruction: collaborative learning and teaching (M Ed); differentiated instruction (M Ed); instructional leadership (M Ed); literacy instruction (M Ed); management in a quality classroom (M Ed); special education (M Ed); technology integration (M Ed). *Accreditation:* NCATE. *Program availability:* Part-time, 100% online. *Faculty:* 2 full-time (both women), 13 part-time/adjunct (10 women). *Students:* 117 full-time (102 women), 62 part-time (54 women); includes 8 minority (3 Black or African American, non-Hispanic/Latino; 1 Asian, non-Hispanic/Latino; 2 Hispanic/Latino; 1 Native Hawaiian or other Pacific Islander, non-Hispanic/Latino; 1 Two or more races, non-Hispanic/Latino), 1 international. Average age 35. 28 applicants, 100% accepted, 19 enrolled. In 2017, 64 master's awarded. *Degree requirements:* For master's, action research capstone. *Entrance requirements:* For master's, minimum GPA of 3.0, teaching certificate, current teaching contract and license, two letters of reference, statement of professional goals, verification of ongoing access to computer technology, including email and Internet. Additional exam requirements/recommendations for international students: Required—TOEFL (minimum score 550 paper-based; 79 iBT). *Application deadline:* For fall admission, 10/1 for domestic students; for winter admission, 11/15 for domestic students; for spring admission, 2/15 priority date for domestic students; for summer admission, 6/1 for domestic students. *Application fee:* $50. Electronic applications accepted. *Expenses:* Contact institution. *Financial support:* In 2017–18, 3 students received support. Tuition waivers available. Financial award applicants required to submit FAFSA. *Faculty research:* Literacy, technology, faculty mentoring, adult literacy, e-learning, online teaching. *Unit head:* Dr. Lee Bash, Interim Dean, 641-784-5072, E-mail: bash@graceland.edu. *Application contact:* Jeanette Calipetro, Admissions Representative, 816-423-4716, Fax: 816-833-2990, E-mail: jcali1@graceland.edu.
Website: http://www.graceland.edu/education

Grambling State University, School of Graduate Studies and Research, College of Education, Department of Educational Leadership, Grambling, LA 71245. Offers developmental education (MS, Ed D, PMC), including curriculum and instructional design (Ed D); English (MS); guidance and counseling (MS); higher education administration and management (Ed D); mathematics (MS); reading (MS); science (MS); student development and personnel services (Ed D); educational leadership (M Ed). *Program availability:* Part-time, evening/weekend. *Degree requirements:* For master's, comprehensive exam, thesis (for some programs); for doctorate, comprehensive exam, thesis/dissertation. *Entrance requirements:* For master's, GRE, minimum GPA of 2.5 on last degree; for doctorate, GRE (minimum score 1000, 500 on Verbal), master's degree, minimum GPA of 3.0 on last degree. Additional exam requirements/recommendations for international students: Required—TOEFL (minimum score 500 paper-based; 62 iBT). Electronic applications accepted.

Grand Canyon University, College of Education, Phoenix, AZ 85017-1097. Offers autism spectrum disorders (MA); curriculum and instruction (MA); early childhood education (M Ed); educational administration (M Ed); educational leadership (M Ed); elementary education (M Ed); gifted education (MA); instructional technology (MS); K-12 leadership (Ed S); reading (MA); secondary education (M Ed); secondary humanities education (M Ed); secondary STEM education (M Ed); special education (M Ed); teaching and learning (Ed D); teaching English to speakers of other languages (MA). *Program availability:* Part-time, evening/weekend, online learning. *Degree requirements:* For master's, publishable research paper (M Ed), e-portfolio. *Entrance requirements:* For master's, undergraduate degree from accredited, GCU-approved college, university, or program with minimum GPA 2.8. Additional exam requirements/recommendations for international students: Required—TOEFL (minimum score 550 paper-based; 79 iBT), IELTS (minimum score 6). Electronic applications accepted.

Grand Valley State University, College of Education, Program in Educational Technology, Allendale, MI 49401-9403. Offers M Ed. *Accreditation:* NCATE. *Program availability:* Part-time, evening/weekend, 100% online. *Students:* 2 full-time (1 woman), 40 part-time (29 women); includes 3 minority (1 Black or African American, non-Hispanic/Latino; 1 Hispanic/Latino; 1 Two or more races, non-Hispanic/Latino), 1 international. Average age 33. 13 applicants, 100% accepted, 7 enrolled. In 2017, 19 master's awarded. *Degree requirements:* For master's, project or thesis. *Entrance requirements:* For master's, GRE General Test or minimum GPA of 3.0, last 60 credits from regionally-accredited college/university, 3 letters of recommendation. Additional exam requirements/recommendations for international students: Required—TOEFL (minimum iBT score of 80), IELTS (6.5), or Michigan English Language Assessment Battery (77). *Application deadline:* Applications are processed on a rolling basis. *Application fee:* $30. Electronic applications accepted. *Expenses:* $652 per credit hour. *Financial support:* In 2017–18, 10 students received support, including 1 fellowship with full and partial tuition reimbursement available (averaging $8,000 per year); unspecified assistantships also available. *Unit head:* Dr. Sean Lancaster, Department Director, 616-331-6802, Fax: 616-331-6285, E-mail: lancasts@gvsu.edu. *Application contact:* Thomas Owens, Director, Student Information and Services Center, 616-331-6282, Fax: 616-331-6217, E-mail: owenst@gvsu.edu.

Grand Valley State University, College of Education, Programs in General Education, Allendale, MI 49401-9403. Offers adult and higher education (M Ed); early childhood education (M Ed); educational differentiation (M Ed); educational leadership (M Ed); educational technology integration (M Ed); elementary education (M Ed); middle level education (M Ed); school library media services (M Ed); secondary level education (M Ed); teaching English to speakers of other languages (M Ed). *Program availability:* Part-time, evening/weekend, 100% online, blended/hybrid learning. *Students:* 24 part-time (16 women). Average age 41. In 2017, 5 master's awarded. *Degree requirements:* For master's, project or thesis. *Entrance requirements:* For master's, GRE General Test or minimum GPA of 3.0, last 60 credits from regionally-accredited college/university, 3 letters of recommendation. Additional exam requirements/recommendations for international students: Required—TOEFL (minimum iBT score of 80), IELTS (6.5), or Michigan English Language Assessment Battery (77). *Application deadline:* Applications are processed on a rolling basis. *Application fee:* $30. Electronic applications accepted. *Expenses:* $652 per credit hour. *Financial support:* In 2017–18, 2 students received support, including 2 fellowships; career-related internships or fieldwork, Federal Work-Study, scholarships/grants, and unspecified assistantships also available. *Faculty research:* Effectiveness of technology in education, parental involvement, effective teaching, effective schools research. *Unit head:* Dr. David Bair, Department Director, 616-331-6489, Fax: 616-331-6489, E-mail: baird@gvsu.edu. *Application contact:* Thomas Owens, Director, Student Information and Services Center, 616-331-6282, Fax: 616-331-6217, E-mail: owenst@gvsu.edu.
Website: http://www.gvsu.edu/coe/

Harrisburg University of Science and Technology, Learning Technologies and Media Systems Program, Harrisburg, PA 17101. Offers games and simulations (MS); instructional design (MS); instructional development (MS); instructional technology (MS); integration and leadership (MS). *Program availability:* Part-time, evening/weekend. *Degree requirements:* For master's, thesis optional. *Entrance requirements:* Additional exam requirements/recommendations for international students: Required—TOEFL (minimum score 520 paper-based; 80 iBT); Recommended—IELTS (minimum score 6). Electronic applications accepted. *Faculty research:* User compatibility with technology, teaching and training, curriculum development, instructional design, gamification.

Harvard University, Extension School, Cambridge, MA 02138-3722. Offers applied sciences (CAS); biotechnology (ALM); educational technologies (ALM); educational technology (CET); English for graduate and professional studies (DGP); environmental management (ALM, CEM); information technology (ALM); journalism (ALM); liberal arts (ALM); management (ALM, CM); mathematics for teaching (ALM); museum studies

(ALM); premedical studies (Diploma); publication and communication (CPC). *Program availability:* Part-time, evening/weekend. *Degree requirements:* For master's, thesis. *Entrance requirements:* For master's, 3 completed graduate courses with grade of B or higher. Additional exam requirements/recommendations for international students: Required—TOEFL (minimum score 600 paper-based), TWE (minimum score 5). *Expenses:* Contact institution.

Harvard University, Harvard Graduate School of Education, Master's Programs in Education, Cambridge, MA 02138. Offers arts in education (Ed M); education policy and management (Ed M); higher education (Ed M); human development and psychology (Ed M); international education policy (Ed M); language and literacy (Ed M); learning and teaching (Ed M); mind, brain, and education (Ed M); prevention science and practice (Ed M); school leadership (Ed M); special studies (Ed M); teacher education (Ed M); technology, innovation, and education (Ed M). *Program availability:* Part-time. *Entrance requirements:* For master's, GRE General Test, statement of purpose, 3 letters of recommendation, resume, official transcripts. Additional exam requirements/recommendations for international students: Required—TOEFL (minimum score 613 paper-based; 104 iBT), TWE (minimum score 5). Electronic applications accepted. *Faculty research:* Learning and development, educational leadership and organizations, education policy analysis.

Hofstra University, School of Education, Programs in Teacher Education, Hempstead, NY 11549. Offers bilingual education (MA); bilingual extension (Advanced Certificate), including education/speech language pathology, intensive teacher institute; business education (MS Ed); curriculum studies (MS Ed); early childhood and childhood education (MS Ed); early childhood education (MA, MS Ed); educational technology (Advanced Certificate); elementary education (MA, MS Ed), including science, technology, engineering, and mathematics (STEM) (MA); English education (MS Ed); family and consumer science (MS Ed); fine arts and music education (Advanced Certificate); fine arts education (MS Ed); foreign language and TESOL (MS Ed); foreign language education (MA, MS Ed), including Arabic (MS Ed), biology, chemistry, Chinese (MS Ed), earth science, French, German, Italian (MS Ed), Mandarin (MS Ed), physics, Russian, Spanish; foundations of education (Advanced Certificate), including grades 5-6, grades 7-9; languages other than English and teaching English as a second language (MA); learning and teaching (Ed D), including applied linguistics, art education, arts and humanities, early childhood education, English education, human development, math education, math, science, and technology, multicultural education, physical education, science education, social studies education, special education; mathematics education (MA, MS Ed); music education (MA, MS Ed); science education (MA), including biology (MA, MS Ed), chemistry (MA, MS Ed), earth science (MA, MS Ed), physics (MA, MS Ed); secondary education (Advanced Certificate); social studies education (MA, MS Ed); teaching languages other than English and TESOL (MS Ed); technology for learning (MA); TESOL (MS Ed, Advanced Certificate); TESOL with specialization in STEM (MA); work based learning extension (Advanced Certificate). *Program availability:* Part-time, evening/weekend, blended/hybrid learning. *Students:* 119 full-time (83 women), 124 part-time (90 women); includes 54 minority (15 Black or African American, non-Hispanic/Latino; 9 Asian, non-Hispanic/Latino; 29 Hispanic/Latino; 1 Native Hawaiian or other Pacific Islander, non-Hispanic/Latino), 12 international. Average age 29. 205 applicants, 88% accepted, 93 enrolled. In 2017, 103 master's, 4 doctorates, 32 other advanced degrees awarded. *Degree requirements:* For master's, comprehensive exam, thesis (for some programs), exit project, student teaching, fieldwork, electronic portfolio, curriculum project, minimum GPA of 3.0; for doctorate, thesis/dissertation; for Advanced Certificate, 3 foreign languages, comprehensive exam (for some programs), thesis project. *Entrance requirements:* For master's, GRE, 2 letters of recommendation, portfolio, teacher certification (MA), interview, essay; for doctorate, GMAT, GRE, LSAT, or MAT; for Advanced Certificate, 2 letters of recommendation, essay, interview and/or portfolio, teaching certificate. Additional exam requirements/recommendations for international students: Required—TOEFL (minimum score 550 paper-based; 80 iBT). *Application deadline:* Applications are processed on a rolling basis. Application fee: $75. Electronic applications accepted. *Expenses: Tuition:* Full-time $1292. *Required fees:* $970. Tuition and fees vary according to program. *Financial support:* In 2017–18, 112 students received support, including 56 fellowships with full and partial tuition reimbursements available (averaging $4,998 per year), 2 research assistantships with full and partial tuition reimbursements available (averaging $8,753 per year); career-related internships or fieldwork, Federal Work-Study, institutionally sponsored loans, scholarships/grants, traineeships, tuition waivers (full and partial), and unspecified assistantships also available. Support available to part-time students. Financial award applicants required to submit FAFSA. *Faculty research:* Educational interventions that foster critical-thinking skills; teachers' attitudes about professional development; threats to teacher quality. *Unit head:* Dr. Eustace Thompson, Chairperson, 516-463-5749, Fax: 516-463-6275, E-mail: eustace.g.thompson@hofstra.edu. *Application contact:* Sunil Samuel, Assistant Vice President of Admissions, 516-463-4723, Fax: 516-463-4664, E-mail: graduateadmission@hofstra.edu.
Website: http://www.hofstra.edu/education/

Houston Baptist University, College of Education and Behavioral Sciences, Programs in Education, Houston, TX 77074-3298. Offers bilingual education (M Ed); counselor education (M Ed); curriculum and instruction (M Ed); curriculum and instruction (EC-6 bilingual) (M Ed); curriculum and instruction in all-level art, Spanish, music, or physical education (M Ed); curriculum and instruction in EC-6 and special education (EC-12) (M Ed); curriculum and instruction in instructional technology (M Ed); curriculum and instruction in mathematics, science, or social studies (4-8) (M Ed); curriculum and instruction with EC-6 generalist (M Ed); curriculum and instruction with English language arts and reading (4-8) (M Ed); educational administration (M Ed); educational diagnostician (M Ed); executive educational leadership (Ed D); higher education in business management (M Ed); higher education in Christian studies (M Ed); higher education in counseling (M Ed); higher education in educational technology (M Ed); reading (M Ed); special educational leadership (Ed D). *Program availability:* Part-time, evening/weekend, 100% online, blended/hybrid learning. *Students:* 83 full-time (65 women), 187 part-time (156 women); includes 189 minority (114 Black or African American, non-Hispanic/Latino; 2 American Indian or Alaska Native, non-Hispanic/Latino; 9 Asian, non-Hispanic/Latino; 58 Hispanic/Latino; 6 Two or more races, non-Hispanic/Latino), 7 international. Average age 36. 309 applicants, 31% accepted, 70 enrolled. In 2017, 92 master's awarded. *Degree requirements:* For master's, comprehensive exam; for doctorate, thesis/dissertation. *Entrance requirements:* For master's, minimum GPA of 2.75, two recommendations, resume, bachelor's degree conferred transcript; interview (for non-certified teachers); for doctorate, GRE, 5 letters of recommendation. Additional exam requirements/recommendations for international students: Required—TOEFL (minimum score 80 iBT), IELTS (minimum score 6.5). *Application deadline:* For fall admission, 8/1 for domestic students, 6/1 for international students; for spring admission, 1/1 for domestic students, 11/1 for international students; for summer admission, 5/1 for domestic students, 3/1 for international students. Applications are processed on a rolling basis. Application fee: $0 ($100 for international students). Electronic applications accepted. Application fee is waived when completed online. *Expenses:* $22,000 tuition; $4,500 fees (general, technology and parking). *Financial support:* In 2017–18, 59 students received support. Research assistantships, teaching assistantships, Federal Work-Study, and scholarships/grants available.

Support available to part-time students. Financial award application deadline: 4/1; financial award applicants required to submit FAFSA. *Faculty research:* Autism and inclusion, integrating technology into instruction, school change and leadership trust. *Unit head:* Dr. Charlotte Fontenot, Director, Graduate Programs, 281-649-3078, Fax: 281-649-3361, E-mail: cfontenot@hbu.edu. *Application contact:* Kristy Wright, Administrative Assistant for Graduate Programs, 281-649-3094, Fax: 281-649-3361, E-mail: kwright@hbu.edu.
Website: http://www.hbu.edu/MED

Idaho State University, Office of Graduate Studies, College of Education, Department of Organizational Learning and Performance, Pocatello, ID 83209. Offers human resource development (MS); instructional design (PhD); instructional technology (M Ed). *Program availability:* Part-time. *Degree requirements:* For master's, comprehensive exam, thesis optional, minimum 36 credits; for doctorate, comprehensive exam, thesis/dissertation (for some programs). *Entrance requirements:* For master's, GRE or MAT, bachelor's degree; for doctorate, GRE or MAT, master's degree. Additional exam requirements/recommendations for international students: Required—TOEFL (minimum score 550 paper-based; 80 iBT). Electronic applications accepted.

Indiana State University, College of Graduate and Professional Studies, Bayh College of Education, Department of Teaching and Learning, Terre Haute, IN 47809. Offers curriculum and instruction (M Ed, PhD); educational technology (MS). *Accreditation:* NCATE. *Degree requirements:* For doctorate, thesis/dissertation. *Entrance requirements:* For doctorate, GRE General Test. Electronic applications accepted. *Faculty research:* Discipline FERPA reading, teacher strengths and needs.

Indiana University Bloomington, School of Education, Department of Instructional Systems Technology, Bloomington, IN 47405-1006. Offers MS, PhD. *Program availability:* Online learning. Terminal master's awarded for partial completion of doctoral program. *Degree requirements:* For master's, thesis optional, portfolio; for doctorate, comprehensive exam, thesis/dissertation, dossier review. *Entrance requirements:* For master's and doctorate, GRE General Test, minimum GPA of 2.75. Additional exam requirements/recommendations for international students: Required—TOEFL. Electronic applications accepted. *Faculty research:* Instructional design and theory development, e-learning and distance education, systemic change, serious simulations and games, human performance improvement, technology integration in education.

Indiana University of Pennsylvania, School of Graduate Studies and Research, College of Education and Communications, Department of Adult and Community Education, Program in Adult and Community Education/Communications Technology, Indiana, PA 15705. Offers MA. *Program availability:* Part-time, evening/weekend. *Faculty:* 2 full-time (both women). *Students:* 1 (woman) full-time, 4 part-time (3 women), 4 international. Average age 31. 1 applicant. In 2017, 13 master's awarded. *Degree requirements:* For master's, thesis optional. *Entrance requirements:* For master's, 2 letters of recommendation, resume. Additional exam requirements/recommendations for international students: Required—TOEFL (minimum score 540 paper-based; 76 iBT). *Application deadline:* Applications are processed on a rolling basis. Application fee: $50. Electronic applications accepted. *Expenses:* Tuition, state resident: full-time $12,000; part-time $500 per credit. Tuition, nonresident: full-time $18,000; part-time $750 per credit. *Required fees:* $4073; $165.55 per credit. $64 per term. *Financial support:* In 2017–18, 11 research assistantships with tuition reimbursements (averaging $4,698 per year) were awarded; fellowships, teaching assistantships, career-related internships or fieldwork, Federal Work-Study, scholarships/grants, and unspecified assistantships also available. Support available to part-time students. Financial award application deadline: 4/15; financial award applicants required to submit FAFSA. *Unit head:* Prof. Jacqueline McGinty, Coordinator, 724-357-2470, E-mail: jacqueline.mcginty@iup.edu.
Website: http://www.iup.edu/aec

Indiana University of Pennsylvania, School of Graduate Studies and Research, College of Education and Communications, Department of Communications Media, Program in Communications Media and Instructional Technology, Indiana, PA 15705. Offers PhD. *Faculty:* 8 full-time (4 women). *Students:* 12 full-time (6 women), 38 part-time (15 women); includes 10 minority (4 Black or African American, non-Hispanic/Latino; 1 Asian, non-Hispanic/Latino; 3 Hispanic/Latino; 2 Two or more races, non-Hispanic/Latino), 5 international. Average age 39. 41 applicants, 41% accepted, 10 enrolled. In 2017, 10 doctorates awarded. Application fee: $50. *Expenses:* Contact institution. *Financial support:* In 2017–18, 2 fellowships with full tuition reimbursements (averaging $2,296 per year), 7 research assistantships with tuition reimbursements (averaging $5,769 per year), 3 teaching assistantships with partial tuition reimbursements (averaging $23,305 per year) were awarded. *Unit head:* Dr. Zachary Stiegler, Coordinator, 724-357-3219, E-mail: zachary.stiegler@iup.edu.
Website: http://www.iup.edu/commmedia/programs/phdcmit/

Indiana University South Bend, College of Liberal Arts and Sciences, South Bend, IN 46615. Offers advanced computer programming (Graduate Certificate); applied informatics (Graduate Certificate); applied mathematics and computer science (MS); behavior modification (Graduate Certificate); computer applications (Graduate Certificate); computer programming (Graduate Certificate); correctional management and supervision (Graduate Certificate); English (MA); health systems management (Graduate Certificate); international studies (Graduate Certificate); liberal studies (MLS); nonprofit management (Graduate Certificate); paralegal studies (Graduate Certificate); professional writing (Graduate Certificate); public affairs (MPA); public management (Graduate Certificate); social and cultural diversity (Graduate Certificate); strategic sustainability leadership (Graduate Certificate); technology for administration (Graduate Certificate). *Program availability:* Part-time, evening/weekend. *Degree requirements:* For master's, variable foreign language requirement, thesis (for some programs). *Entrance requirements:* For master's, minimum GPA of 3.0. Additional exam requirements/recommendations for international students: Required—TOEFL (minimum score 550 paper-based; 80 iBT). *Expenses:* Contact institution. *Faculty research:* Artificial intelligence, bioinformatics, English language and literature, creative writing, computer networks.

Instituto Tecnológico y de Estudios Superiores de Monterrey, Campus Central de Veracruz, Graduate Programs, Córdoba, Mexico. Offers administration (MA); administration of information technologies (MTI); computer sciences (MCC); education (MEE); educational institution administration (MAD); educational technology (MTE); electronic commerce (MCE); finance (MAF); humanistic studies (MEH); international business for Latin America (MNL); marketing (MMT); science (MCP). *Program availability:* Part-time, evening/weekend, online learning. *Degree requirements:* For master's, thesis (for some programs). *Entrance requirements:* For master's, PAEP College Board. Electronic applications accepted.

Instituto Tecnológico y de Estudios Superiores de Monterrey, Campus Ciudad de México, Virtual University Division, Ciudad de Mexico, Mexico. Offers administration of information technologies (MA); computer sciences (MA); education (MA, PhD); educational technology (MA); environmental engineering (MA); environmental systems (MA); humanistic studies (MA); industrial engineering (MA); international business for Latin America (MA); quality systems (MA); quality systems and productivity (MA). *Program availability:* Part-time, evening/weekend, online learning. *Entrance requirements:* For master's and doctorate, Instituto entrance exam. Additional exam requirements/recommendations for international students: Required—TOEFL.

Instituto Tecnológico y de Estudios Superiores de Monterrey, Campus Ciudad Juárez, Program in Educational Innovation, Ciudad Juárez, Mexico. Offers DE.

Instituto Tecnológico y de Estudios Superiores de Monterrey, Campus Ciudad Juárez, Program in Educational Technology, Ciudad Juárez, Mexico. Offers MTE.

Instituto Tecnológico y de Estudios Superiores de Monterrey, Campus Estado de México, Professional and Graduate Division, Estado de Mexico, Mexico. Offers administration of information technologies (MITA); architecture (M Arch); business administration (GMBA, MBA); computer sciences (MCS, PhD); education (M Ed); educational institution administration (MAD); educational technology and innovation (PhD); electronic commerce (MEC); environmental systems (MS); finance (MAF); humanistic studies (MHS); information sciences and knowledge management (MISKM); information systems (MS); manufacturing systems (MS); marketing (MEM); quality systems and productivity (MS); science and materials engineering (PhD); telecommunications management (MTM). *Program availability:* Part-time, online learning. *Degree requirements:* For master's, one foreign language, thesis (for some programs); for doctorate, one foreign language, thesis/dissertation. *Entrance requirements:* For master's, E-PAEP 500, interview; for doctorate, E-PAEP 500, research proposal. Additional exam requirements/recommendations for international students: Required—TOEFL (minimum score 550 paper-based). *Faculty research:* Surface treatments by plasmas, mechanical properties, robotics, graphical computing, mechatronics security protocols.

Instituto Tecnológico y de Estudios Superiores de Monterrey, Campus Irapuato, Graduate Programs, Irapuato, Mexico. Offers administration (MBA); administration of information technology (MAIT); administration of telecommunications (MAT); architecture (M Arch); computer science (MCS); education (M Ed); educational administration (MEA); educational innovation and technology (DEIT); educational technology (MET); electronic commerce (MBA); environmental administration and planning (MEAP); environmental systems (MES); finances (MBA); humanistic studies (MHS); international management for Latin American executives (MIMLAE); library and information science (MLIS); manufacturing quality management (MMQM); marketing research (MBA).

Inter American University of Puerto Rico, Metropolitan Campus, Graduate Programs, Program in Educational Computing, San Juan, PR 00919-1293. Offers MA. *Degree requirements:* For master's, comprehensive exam, portfolio. *Entrance requirements:* For master's, GRE or EXADEP, minimum GPA of 2.5. Electronic applications accepted. *Faculty research:* Effectiveness of multimedia, World Wide Web for distance learning.

Iowa State University of Science and Technology, Department of Education, Ames, IA 50011. Offers curriculum and instructional technology (M Ed, MS, PhD); elementary education (M Ed, MS); historical, philosophical, and comparative studies in education (M Ed, MS); special education (M Ed, MS, PhD). *Degree requirements:* For master's, thesis or alternative; for doctorate, thesis/dissertation. *Entrance requirements:* For master's and doctorate, GRE General Test. Additional exam requirements/recommendations for international students: Required—TOEFL (minimum score 560 paper-based; 83 iBT), IELTS (minimum score 6.5). Electronic applications accepted.

Jacksonville State University, College of Graduate Studies and Continuing Education, College of Education and Professional Studies, Program in Library Media, Jacksonville, AL 36265-1602. Offers MS Ed. *Program availability:* Part-time, evening/weekend. *Degree requirements:* For master's, comprehensive exam, thesis (for some programs). *Entrance requirements:* For master's, GRE General Test or MAT. Additional exam requirements/recommendations for international students: Required—TOEFL (minimum score 500 paper-based; 61 iBT). Electronic applications accepted.

James Madison University, The Graduate School, College of Education, Program in Education, Harrisonburg, VA 22807. Offers early childhood education (preK-3) (MAT); educational leadership (M Ed); educational technology (M Ed); elementary education (MAT); equity and cultural diversity (M Ed); inclusive early childhood education (MAT); K-8 mathematics specialist (M Ed); middle education (MAT); reading education (M Ed); secondary education (MAT); Spanish language and culture for educators (M Ed); TESOL (MAT). *Accreditation:* NCATE. *Program availability:* Part-time, evening/weekend. *Students:* 260 full-time (233 women), 158 part-time (100 women); includes 48 minority (10 Black or African American, non-Hispanic/Latino; 4 Asian, non-Hispanic/Latino; 26 Hispanic/Latino; 1 Native Hawaiian or other Pacific Islander, non-Hispanic/Latino; 7 Two or more races, non-Hispanic/Latino), 2 international. Average age 30. In 2017, 262 master's awarded. Application fee: $55. Electronic applications accepted. *Expenses:* Tuition, state resident: full-time $10,512; part-time $438 per credit hour. Tuition, nonresident: full-time $28,358; part-time $1162 per credit hour. *Required fees:* $1128. *Financial support:* In 2017–18, 23 students received support, including 1 teaching assistantship; career-related internships or fieldwork, Federal Work-Study, and 22 assistantships (averaging $7911) also available. Financial award application deadline: 3/1; financial award applicants required to submit FAFSA. *Unit head:* Dr. Phillip M. Wishon, Dean, 540-568-6572, E-mail: wishonpm@jmu.edu. *Application contact:* Lynette D. Michael, Director of Graduate Admissions, 540-568-6131 Ext. 6395, Fax: 540-568-7860, E-mail: michaeld@jmu.edu.
Website: http://www.jmu.edu/coe/index.shtml

Johns Hopkins University, School of Education, Master's Programs in Education, Baltimore, MD 21218. Offers counseling (MS), including clinical mental health counseling, school counseling; education (MS), including educational studies, gifted education, reading, school administration and supervision, technology for educators; elementary education (MAT); health professions (M Ed); intelligence analysis (MS); organizational leadership (MS); secondary education (MAT), including biology, chemistry, earth/space science, English, physics, social studies; special education (MS), including early childhood special education, general special education studies, mild to moderate disabilities, severe disabilities. *Program availability:* Part-time, evening/weekend, 100% online, blended/hybrid learning. *Degree requirements:* For master's, comprehensive exam (for some programs), portfolio, capstone project and/or internship; PRAXIS II (subject area assessments) for initial teacher preparation programs that lead to licensure. *Entrance requirements:* For master's, GRE (for full-time programs only); PRAXIS I/core or state-approved alternative (for initial teacher preparation programs that lead to licensure), minimum of bachelor's degree from regionally- or nationally-accredited institution; minimum GPA of 3.0 in all previous programs of study; official transcripts from all post-secondary institutions attended; essay; curriculum vitae/resume; letters of recommendation (3 for full-time programs, 2 for part-time programs); dispositions survey. Additional exam requirements/recommendations for international students: Required—TOEFL (minimum score 600 paper-based; 100 iBT), IELTS (minimum score 7). Electronic applications accepted. *Expenses:* Contact institution.

Johnson University, Graduate and Professional Programs, Knoxville, TN 37998-1001. Offers biblical interpretation (Graduate Certificate); business administration (MBA); Christian ministries (Graduate Certificate); clinical mental health counseling (MA); educational technology (MA); intercultural studies (MA); leadership (MBA); leadership studies (PhD); New Testament (MA); nonprofit management (MBA); school counseling (MA); spiritual formation and leadership (Graduate Certificate); strategic ministry (MA); teacher education (MA). *Program availability:* Part-time, evening/weekend, 100% online,

blended/hybrid learning. *Degree requirements:* For master's, variable foreign language requirement, comprehensive exam, thesis (for some programs), internships; for doctorate, variable foreign language requirement, comprehensive exam, thesis/dissertation, internships. *Entrance requirements:* For master's, PRAXIS (for MA in teacher education); MAT (for counseling); GRE or GMAT (for MBA), interview, 3 references, transcripts, essay, minimum GPA of 2.5 or 3.0 (depending on program); for doctorate, GRE or MAT (taken not less than 5 years prior), interview, 3 references, transcripts, essay, minimum GPA of 3.0; for Graduate Certificate, interview, 3 references, transcripts, essay, minimum GPA of 3.0. Additional exam requirements/recommendations for international students: Required—TOEFL (minimum score 527 paper-based; 71 iBT). Electronic applications accepted. *Expenses:* Contact institution.

Kansas State University, Graduate School, College of Education, Department of Curriculum and Instruction, Manhattan, KS 66506. Offers curriculum and instruction (Ed D, PhD); digital teaching and learning (MS); educational computing, design and online learning (MS); elementary/middle level curriculum and instruction (MS); online learning (Certificate); reading specialist endorsement (MS); reading/language arts (MS); teacher leader/school improvement (MS); teaching and learning (Certificate). *Accreditation:* NCATE. *Program availability:* Part-time, online learning. *Degree requirements:* For master's, comprehensive exam, portfolio, project, report or thesis; for doctorate, comprehensive exam, thesis/dissertation, preliminary exam; for Certificate, comprehensive exam, portfolio. *Entrance requirements:* For master's, minimum GPA of 3.0, 3 letters of recommendation; for doctorate, GRE, minimum GPA of 3.0, 3 letters of recommendation, evidence of scholarly writing; for Certificate, minimum GPA of 3.0, letters of recommendation. Additional exam requirements/recommendations for international students: Required—TOEFL (minimum score 550 paper-based; 80 iBT) or IELTS. Electronic applications accepted. *Faculty research:* Literacy and technology, critical race theory and diversity, achievement gaps, school improvement, teacher education.

Keiser University, Ed S in Instructional Design and Technology Program, Fort Lauderdale, FL 33309. Offers Ed S.
Website: https://www.keiseruniversity.edu/educational-specialist-in-instructional-design-and-technology-eds/

Keiser University, PhD in Instructional Design and Technology Program, Fort Lauderdale, FL 33309. Offers PhD.
Website: http://www.keiseruniversity.edu/graduateschool/instructional-design-andtechnology.php

Kennesaw State University, Leland and Clarice C. Bagwell College of Education, Program in Graduate Education, Kennesaw, GA 30144. Offers educational leadership (M Ed); educational leadership technology (M Ed); elementary and early childhood education (M Ed); instructional technology (M Ed); middle grades education (M Ed); reading (M Ed); secondary education (M Ed); special education (M Ed); teaching English to speakers of other languages (M Ed). *Accreditation:* NCATE. *Program availability:* Part-time. *Degree requirements:* For master's, thesis or alternative. *Entrance requirements:* For master's, GRE General Test, T-4 state certification, minimum GPA of 2.75. Additional exam requirements/recommendations for international students: Required—TOEFL (minimum score 550 paper-based; 80 iBT), IELTS (minimum score 6.5). Electronic applications accepted.

Kent State University, College of Education, Health and Human Services, School of Lifespan Development and Educational Sciences, Program in Instructional Technology, Kent, OH 44242-0001. Offers computer technology (M Ed); educational psychology (PhD), including instructional technology; general instructional technology (M Ed). *Accreditation:* NCATE. *Degree requirements:* For master's, thesis (for some programs). *Entrance requirements:* For master's, 2 letters of reference, goals statement, minimum GPA of 2.75. Additional exam requirements/recommendations for international students: Required—TOEFL (minimum score 550 paper-based; 80 iBT). *Expenses:* Tuition, state resident: full-time $11,310; part-time $515 per credit hour. Tuition, nonresident: full-time $20,396; part-time $928 per credit hour. *International tuition:* $18,544 full-time. *Faculty research:* Cooperative learning, aesthetics, computers in schools.

Kutztown University of Pennsylvania, College of Education, Program in Instructional Technology, Kutztown, PA 19530-0730. Offers M Ed. *Program availability:* Part-time, evening/weekend, 100% online, blended/hybrid learning. *Faculty:* 3 full-time (2 women). *Students:* 57 part-time (42 women); includes 3 minority (1 Black or African American, non-Hispanic/Latino; 2 Hispanic/Latino). Average age 34. 28 applicants, 93% accepted, 12 enrolled. In 2017, 8 master's awarded. *Degree requirements:* For master's, comprehensive exam. *Entrance requirements:* For master's, GRE or valid PA teaching certificate, 3 letters of recommendation. Additional exam requirements/recommendations for international students: Required—TOEFL (minimum score 550 paper-based, 79 iBT), IELTS (minimum score 6.5), or PTE (minimum score 53). *Application deadline:* For fall admission, 8/1 for domestic and international students; for spring admission, 12/1 for domestic and international students. Application fee: $35. Electronic applications accepted. *Expenses:* Tuition, state resident: part-time $500 per credit. Tuition, nonresident: part-time $750 per credit. *Required fees:* $115 per credit. One-time fee: $50 part-time. Tuition and fees vary according to degree level. *Financial support:* Career-related internships or fieldwork, Federal Work-Study, and unspecified assistantships available. Financial award application deadline: 3/1; financial award applicants required to submit FAFSA. *Unit head:* Dr. Andrea Harmer, Chairperson, 610-683-4301, Fax: 610-683-1326, E-mail: harmer@kutztown.edu.
Website: https://www.kutztown.edu/academics/graduate-programs/instructional-technology.htm

Lamar University, College of Graduate Studies, College of Education and Human Development, Department of Educational Leadership, Beaumont, TX 77701. Offers digital learning and leading (M Ed); education administration (M Ed); educational leadership (Ed D); educational technology (M Ed). *Program availability:* Part-time, evening/weekend. *Faculty:* 21 full-time (13 women), 10 part-time/adjunct (5 women). *Students:* 9 full-time (6 women), 1,576 part-time (1,093 women); includes 589 minority (242 Black or African American, non-Hispanic/Latino; 9 American Indian or Alaska Native, non-Hispanic/Latino; 17 Asian, non-Hispanic/Latino; 305 Hispanic/Latino; 16 Two or more races, non-Hispanic/Latino), 8 international. Average age 37. 1,961 applicants, 87% accepted, 264 enrolled. In 2017, 709 master's, 68 doctorates awarded. Terminal master's awarded for partial completion of doctoral program. *Degree requirements:* For master's, comprehensive exam, thesis optional; for doctorate, thesis/dissertation. *Entrance requirements:* For master's, GRE General Test, minimum GPA of 2.5; for doctorate, GRE. Additional exam requirements/recommendations for international students: Required—TOEFL (minimum score 550 paper-based; 79 iBT), IELTS (minimum score 6.5). *Application deadline:* For fall admission, 8/10 priority date for domestic students, 7/1 for international students; for spring admission, 1/5 priority date for domestic students, 12/1 for international students. Applications are processed on a rolling basis. Application fee: $25 ($50 for international students). Electronic applications accepted. *Expenses:* Contact institution. *Financial support:* In 2017–18, 3 fellowships (averaging $20,000 per year), 1 research assistantship with tuition reimbursement (averaging $6,500 per year) were awarded; teaching assistantships with tuition reimbursements, career-related internships or fieldwork, and scholarships/grants also available. Support available to part-time students. Financial award application

deadline: 4/1; financial award applicants required to submit FAFSA. *Faculty research:* School dropouts, suicide prevention in public school students, school climate and gifted performance, teacher evaluation. *Unit head:* Dr. Kaye Shelton, Director, 409-880-8689, Fax: 409-880-8685. *Application contact:* Deidre Mayer, Interim Director, Admissions and Academic Services, 409-880-8888, Fax: 409-880-7419, E-mail: gradmissions@ lamar.edu.
Website: http://education.lamar.edu/educational-leadership

La Salle University, School of Arts and Sciences, Program in Instructional Technology Management, Philadelphia, PA 19141-1199. Offers MS, Certificate. *Program availability:* Part-time, evening/weekend, online only, 100% online. *Faculty:* 3 part-time/adjunct (1 woman). *Students:* 1 (woman) full-time, 12 part-time (9 women); includes 9 minority (8 Black or African American, non-Hispanic/Latino; 1 Two or more races, non-Hispanic/ Latino). Average age 42. 4 applicants, 50% accepted, 2 enrolled. In 2017, 5 master's, 3 other advanced degrees awarded. *Degree requirements:* For master's, capstone project. *Entrance requirements:* For master's and Certificate, baccalaureate degree; two letters of recommendation; 3 years of professional experience in corporate training, human resources, information technology or business. Additional exam requirements/ recommendations for international students: Required—TOEFL. *Application deadline:* For fall admission, 8/15 priority date for domestic students; for spring admission, 12/15 priority date for domestic students; for summer admission, 4/15 priority date for domestic students. Applications are processed on a rolling basis. Application fee: $35. Electronic applications accepted. Application fee is waived when completed online. *Expenses:* Contact institution. *Financial support:* In 2017–18, 3 students received support. Scholarships/grants available. Support available to part-time students. Financial award application deadline: 8/31; financial award applicants required to submit FAFSA. *Unit head:* Margaret M. McCoey, Director, 215-951-1136, E-mail: mccoey@lasalle.edu. *Application contact:* Elizabeth Heenan, Director, Graduate and Adult Enrollment, 215-951-1100, Fax: 215-951-1462, E-mail: heenan@lasalle.edu.
Website: http://www.lasalle.edu/instructional-technology-management/

Lawrence Technological University, College of Arts and Sciences, Southfield, MI 48075-1058. Offers bioinformatics (Graduate Certificate); computer science (MS), including data science, big data, and data mining, intelligent systems; educational technology (MA), including robotics; instructional design, communication, and presentation (Graduate Certificate); integrated science (MA); science education (MA); technical and professional communication (MS, Graduate Certificate); writing for the digital age (Graduate Certificate). *Program availability:* Part-time, evening/weekend. *Faculty:* 6 full-time (2 women), 7 part-time/adjunct (3 women). *Students:* 34 part-time (15 women); includes 4 minority (1 Black or African American, non-Hispanic/Latino; 2 Asian, non-Hispanic/Latino; 1 Hispanic/Latino), 7 international. Average age 31. 84 applicants, 15% accepted, 10 enrolled. In 2017, 14 master's awarded. *Degree requirements:* For master's, thesis (for some programs). *Entrance requirements:* Additional exam requirements/recommendations for international students: Required—TOEFL (minimum score 550 paper-based; 79 iBT), IELTS (minimum score 6.5). *Application deadline:* For fall admission, 5/27 for international students; for spring admission, 10/8 for international students; for summer admission, 2/14 for international students. Applications are processed on a rolling basis. Application fee: $50. Electronic applications accepted. *Expenses: Tuition:* Full-time $15,274; part-time $1091 per credit. One-time fee: $150. *Financial support:* In 2017–18, 8 students received support. Scholarships/grants and tuition reduction available. Financial award application deadline: 4/1; financial award applicants required to submit FAFSA. *Faculty research:* Computer analysis of music, machine learning of literature and lyrics, customer sentiments and response analysis through social media, peta-scale computing in astronomical databases, early detection of diseases with pattern recognition. *Total annual research expenditures:* $242,460. *Unit head:* Glen Bauer, Interim Dean, 248-204-3532, Fax: 248-204-3518, E-mail: scidean@ ltu.edu. *Application contact:* Jane Rohrback, Director of Admissions, 248-204-3160, Fax: 248-204-2228, E-mail: admissions@ltu.edu.

Lehigh University, College of Education, Program in Teaching, Learning and Technology, Bethlehem, PA 18015. Offers elementary education (M Ed); instructional technology (MS); teaching, learning and technology (PhD); M Ed/MA. *Program availability:* Part-time. *Faculty:* 6 full-time (4 women), 3 part-time/adjunct (2 women). *Students:* 29 full-time (20 women), 61 part-time (41 women); includes 9 minority (1 Black or African American, non-Hispanic/Latino; 4 Asian, non-Hispanic/Latino; 3 Hispanic/ Latino; 1 Native Hawaiian or other Pacific Islander, non-Hispanic/Latino), 6 international. Average age 32. 75 applicants, 73% accepted, 15 enrolled. In 2017, 35 master's, 4 doctorates awarded. Terminal master's awarded for partial completion of doctoral program. *Degree requirements:* For doctorate, comprehensive exam, thesis/ dissertation, qualifying exam. *Entrance requirements:* For master's, minimum GPA of 3.0, 2 letters of recommendation, essay, transcript; for doctorate, GRE General Test, minimum graduate GPA of 3.0, writing sample, 2 letters of recommendation, essay, transcript. Additional exam requirements/recommendations for international students: Required—TOEFL (minimum iBT score of 93) or IELTS (6.5). *Application deadline:* For fall admission, 4/1 for domestic and international students; for summer admission, 4/1 for domestic and international students. Applications are processed on a rolling basis. Application fee: $65. Electronic applications accepted. *Expenses:* $565 per credit. *Financial support:* In 2017–18, 17 students received support, including 2 research assistantships with full and partial tuition reimbursements available (averaging $25,116 per year); fellowships and unspecified assistantships also available. Financial award application deadline: 1/31. *Faculty research:* Teaching and learning, K-16 curriculum development, Web-based learning, teaching and technology, language and literacy, teaching, learning with spatial technologies, visual instructional technologies, environmental science curriculum, multicultural issues, English language education, educational access and equity, English Language Learners with disabilities, integrated curriculum, augmented and virtual reality, STEM and agricultural education. *Total annual research expenditures:* $760,344. *Unit head:* Dr. Lynn Columba, Director, 610-758-3237, Fax: 610-758-3243, E-mail: hlc0@lehigh.edu. *Application contact:* Donna Toothman, Coordinator, 610-758-3230, Fax: 610-758-3243, E-mail: djt2@lehigh.edu.
Website: https://ed.lehigh.edu/academics/programs/instructional-technology

Lenoir-Rhyne University, Graduate Programs, School of Education, Program in Online Teaching and Instructional Design, Hickory, NC 28601. Offers MS. *Program availability:* Online learning. *Entrance requirements:* For master's, GRE or MAT, essay; minimum GPA of 2.7 undergraduate, 3.0 graduate. Additional exam requirements/ recommendations for international students: Required—TOEFL (minimum score 600 paper-based). Electronic applications accepted. *Expenses:* Contact institution.

Lesley University, Graduate School of Education, Cambridge, MA 02138-2790. Offers arts, community, and education (M Ed); autism studies (Certificate); curriculum and instruction (M Ed, CAGS); early childhood education (M Ed); ecological teaching and learning (MS); educational studies (PhD), including adult learning, educational leadership, individually designed; elementary education (M Ed); emergent technologies for educators (Certificate); ESLArts: language learning through the arts (M Ed); high school education (M Ed); individually designed (M Ed); integrated teaching through the arts (M Ed); literacy for K-8 classroom teachers (M Ed); mathematics education (M Ed); middle school education (M Ed); moderate disabilities (M Ed); online learning (Certificate); reading (CAGS); science in education (M Ed); severe disabilities (M Ed);

special needs (CAGS); specialist teacher of reading (M Ed); teacher of visual art (M Ed); technology in education (M Ed, CAGS). *Accreditation:* TEAC. *Program availability:* Part-time, evening/weekend, online learning. *Degree requirements:* For master's, practicum; for doctorate, thesis/dissertation. *Entrance requirements:* For master's, Massachusetts Tests for Educator Licensure (MTEL), transcripts, statement of purpose, recommendations; interview (for special education); for doctorate, GRE General Test, transcripts, statement of purpose, recommendations, interview, master's degree, resume; for other advanced degree, interview, master's degree. Additional exam requirements/recommendations for international students: Required—TOEFL (minimum score 550 paper-based; 80 iBT). Electronic applications accepted. *Faculty research:* Assessment in literacy, mathematics and science; autism spectrum disorders; instructional technology and online learning; multicultural education and English language learners.

Lewis University, College of Education, Program in Curriculum and Instruction: Technology Learning and Design, Romeoville, IL 60446. Offers M Ed. *Program availability:* Part-time, evening/weekend. *Students:* 1 (woman) full-time, 2 part-time (1 woman), 1 international. Average age 35. *Degree requirements:* For master's, departmental qualifying exam. *Entrance requirements:* For master's, writing exam, bachelor's degree, minimum GPA of 2.75, two letters of recommendation, interview. Additional exam requirements/recommendations for international students: Required— TOEFL (minimum score 550 paper-based; 79 iBT), IELTS (minimum score 6). *Application deadline:* For fall admission, 5/1 priority date for international students; for spring admission, 11/15 priority date for international students. Applications are processed on a rolling basis. Application fee: $40. Electronic applications accepted. Tuition and fees vary according to program. *Financial support:* Career-related internships or fieldwork, Federal Work-Study, institutionally sponsored loans, and unspecified assistantships available. Financial award application deadline: 5/1; financial award applicants required to submit FAFSA. *Unit head:* Dr. Seung Kim, Program Director, 815-838-0500, E-mail: kimse@lewisu.edu. *Application contact:* Kathy Lisak, Graduate Admission Counselor, 815-836-5610, E-mail: grad@lewisu.edu.

Lindenwood University, Graduate Programs, School of Education, St. Charles, MO 63301-1695. Offers behavioral analysis (MA); education (MA), including autism spectrum disorders, character education, early intervention in autism and sensory impairment, gifted, technology; educational administration (MA, Ed D, Ed S); English to speakers of other languages (MA); instructional leadership (Ed D, Ed S); library media (MA); professional counseling (MA); school administration (MA, Ed S); school counseling (MA); teaching (MA). *Program availability:* Part-time, evening/weekend, 100% online, blended/hybrid learning. *Faculty:* 47 full-time (31 women), 213 part-time/ adjunct (135 women). *Students:* 434 full-time (319 women), 1,292 part-time (989 women); includes 387 minority (313 Black or African American, non-Hispanic/Latino; 9 American Indian or Alaska Native, non-Hispanic/Latino; 13 Asian, non-Hispanic/Latino; 37 Hispanic/Latino; 1 Native Hawaiian or other Pacific Islander, non-Hispanic/Latino; 14 Two or more races, non-Hispanic/Latino), 20 international. Average age 36. 828 applicants, 61% accepted, 378 enrolled. In 2017, 431 master's, 63 doctorates, 94 other advanced degrees awarded. *Degree requirements:* For master's, thesis (for some programs), minimum GPA of 3.0; for doctorate, thesis/dissertation, minimum GPA of 3.0; for Ed S, comprehensive exam, project, minimum GPA of 3.0. *Entrance requirements:* For master's, interview, minimum undergraduate cumulative GPA of 3.0, writing sample, letter of recommendation; for doctorate, GRE, minimum graduate GPA of 3.4, resume, interview, writing sample, 4 letters of recommendation; for Ed S, master's degree in education, relevant work experience. Additional exam requirements/recommendations for international students: Required—TOEFL (minimum score 550 paper-based; 80 iBT); Recommended—IELTS (minimum score 6.5). *Application deadline:* For fall admission, 8/27 priority date for domestic and international students; for spring admission, 1/14 priority date for domestic and international students; for summer admission, 6/4 priority date for domestic and international students. Applications are processed on a rolling basis. Application fee: $30 ($100 for international students). Electronic applications accepted. *Expenses: Tuition:* Full-time $16,300; part-time $460 per credit. *Required fees:* $660; $330 per credit. Tuition and fees vary according to degree level and program. *Financial support:* In 2017–18, 1,615 students received support. Career-related internships or fieldwork, Federal Work-Study, institutionally sponsored loans, scholarships/grants, tuition waivers (partial), and unspecified assistantships available. Financial award application deadline: 6/30; financial award applicants required to submit FAFSA. *Unit head:* Dr. Anthony Scheffler, Dean, School of Education, 636-949-4618, Fax: 636-949-4197, E-mail: ascheffler@lindenwood.edu. *Application contact:* Kara Schilli, Director, Evening and Graduate Admissions, 636-949-4349, Fax: 636-949-4109, E-mail: adultadmissions@lindenwood.edu.
Website: http://www.lindenwood.edu/academics/academic-schools/school-of-education/

Lipscomb University, College of Education, Nashville, TN 37204-3951. Offers applied behavior analysis (MS, Certificate); coaching for learning (M Ed, Certificate, Ed S); educational leadership (M Ed, Ed S); English language learning (M Ed, Ed S); instructional coaching (M Ed, Certificate, Ed S); instructional practice (M Ed); learning organizations and strategic change (Ed D); literacy coaching (Certificate, Ed S); reading specialty (M Ed, Ed S); school counseling (M Ed, Ed S); special education (M Ed); teaching, learning, and leading (M Ed); technology integration (M Ed, Ed S); technology integration specialist (Certificate). *Accreditation:* NCATE. *Program availability:* Part-time, evening/weekend, 100% online. *Faculty:* 21 full-time (14 women), 42 part-time/adjunct (29 women). *Students:* 565 full-time (452 women), 59 part-time (45 women); includes 154 minority (102 Black or African American, non-Hispanic/Latino; 2 American Indian or Alaska Native, non-Hispanic/Latino; 8 Asian, non-Hispanic/Latino; 26 Hispanic/Latino; 16 Two or more races, non-Hispanic/Latino). Average age 32. 395 applicants, 54% accepted, 196 enrolled. In 2017, 162 master's, 30 doctorates, 54 other advanced degrees awarded. *Degree requirements:* For master's, comprehensive exam, portfolio, research project and presentation; for doctorate, practical capstone project in experiential setting. *Entrance requirements:* For master's, MAT (minimum score 31) or GRE General Test (minimum score 294), 2 reference letters, goals statement, writing sample, interview; for doctorate, MAT or GRE General Test, 3 reference letters, artifact of demonstrated academic excellence, written personal statements, interview. Additional exam requirements/recommendations for international students: Required—TOEFL (minimum score 570 paper-based; 80 iBT). *Application deadline:* For fall admission, 8/29 priority date for domestic students; for spring admission, 1/15 priority date for domestic students. Applications are processed on a rolling basis. Application fee: $50 ($75 for international students). Electronic applications accepted. *Expenses:* Contact institution. *Financial support:* Scholarships/grants, unspecified assistantships, and partnerships with local school districts available. Financial award applicants required to submit FAFSA. *Faculty research:* Facilitative learning styles, leadership, student assessment, interactive multimedia inclusion, learning organizations and strategic change. *Unit head:* Dr. Deborah Boyd, Director of Graduate Studies, 615-966-6263, E-mail: deborah.boyd@ lipscomb.edu. *Application contact:* Amanda Logsdon, Director of Enrollment and Outreach, 615-966-7199, E-mail: amanda.logsdon@lipscomb.edu.
Website: http://www.lipscomb.edu/education/graduate-programs

Long Island University–LIU Post, College of Education, Information and Technology, Brookville, NY 11548-1300. Offers adolescence education (MS); adolescence education 7-12 (MS); archives and records management (AC); art education (MS); childhood

education (MS); childhood education/literacy B-6 (MS); childhood education/special education (MS); clinical mental health counseling (MS, AC); early childhood education (MS); early childhood education/childhood education (MS); educational leadership (AC); educational technology (MS); information studies (PhD); interdisciplinary educational studies (Ed D); middle childhood education (MS); music education (MS); public library administration (AC); school counselor (MS); special education (MS Ed); speech-language pathology (MA); students with disabilities, 7-12 generalist (AC); TESOL (MA). *Accreditation:* TEAC. *Program availability:* Part-time, 100% online, blended/hybrid learning. *Faculty:* 40 full-time (26 women), 73 part-time/adjunct (38 women). *Students:* 472 full-time (400 women), 696 part-time (543 women); includes 254 minority (93 Black or African American, non-Hispanic/Latino; 46 Asian, non-Hispanic/Latino; 105 Hispanic/Latino; 10 Two or more races, non-Hispanic/Latino), 33 international. Average age 33. 917 applicants, 82% accepted, 357 enrolled. In 2017, 408 master's, 31 other advanced degrees awarded. Terminal master's awarded for partial completion of doctoral program. *Degree requirements:* For master's, variable foreign language requirement, comprehensive exam (for some programs), thesis optional; for doctorate, comprehensive exam, thesis/dissertation. *Entrance requirements:* For master's and AC, GRE (for some programs). Additional exam requirements/recommendations for international students: Required—TOEFL (minimum score 550 paper-based, 75 iBT), IELTS, or PTE. *Application deadline:* Applications are processed on a rolling basis. Application fee: $50. Electronic applications accepted. *Expenses: Tuition:* Full-time $21,618; part-time $1201 per credit. *Required fees:* $1840; $920 per term. Tuition and fees vary according to course load. *Financial support:* In 2017–18, 376 students received support. Career-related internships or fieldwork, Federal Work-Study, institutionally sponsored loans, scholarships/grants, tuition waivers (partial), and unspecified assistantships available. Support available to part-time students. Financial award application deadline: 2/15; financial award applicants required to submit FAFSA. *Faculty research:* Sleep; use of technology to develop executive function by students with disabilities; early childhood literacy development through play; social justice through education; using a structured protocol to discuss Bad News. *Unit head:* Dr. Albert Inserra, Dean, 516-299-2210, E-mail: albert.inserra@liu.edu. *Application contact:* Rita Langdon, Graduate Admissions, 516-299-2900, Fax: 516-299-2137, E-mail: postenroll@liu.edu.
Website: http://liu.edu/CWPost/Academics/College-of-Education-Information-and-Technology

Longwood University, College of Graduate and Professional Studies, College of Education and Human Services, Program in School Librarianship, Farmville, VA 23909. Offers M Ed. *Program availability:* Part-time, evening/weekend. *Degree requirements:* For master's, professional portfolio. *Entrance requirements:* For master's, PRAXIS I (for initial teaching licensure track), bachelor's degree from regionally-accredited institution, 2 recommendations, minimum 500-word personal essay, official transcripts, minimum GPA of 2.75, valid teaching license. Additional exam requirements/recommendations for international students: Required—TOEFL (minimum score 570 paper-based; 80 iBT), IELTS (minimum score 6.5). Electronic applications accepted. *Expenses:* Contact institution.

Louisiana State University and Agricultural & Mechanical College, Graduate School, College of Human Sciences and Education, Department of Educational Theory, Policy and Practice, Baton Rouge, LA 70803. Offers counseling (M Ed, MA, Ed S); educational administration (M Ed, MA, PhD, Ed S); educational technology (MA); elementary education (M Ed, MAT); higher education (PhD); research methodology (PhD); secondary education (M Ed, MAT). *Accreditation:* ACA (one or more programs are accredited); NCATE. *Faculty:* 34 full-time (22 women). *Students:* 213 full-time (159 women), 228 part-time (178 women); includes 164 minority (123 Black or African American, non-Hispanic/Latino; 7 Asian, non-Hispanic/Latino; 27 Hispanic/Latino; 1 Native Hawaiian or other Pacific Islander, non-Hispanic/Latino; 6 Two or more races, non-Hispanic/Latino), 13 international. Average age 32. 231 applicants, 61% accepted, 82 enrolled. In 2017, 125 master's, 26 doctorates, 28 other advanced degrees awarded. *Financial support:* In 2017–18, 3 fellowships (averaging $12,129 per year), 2 research assistantships (averaging $16,019 per year), 96 teaching assistantships (averaging $16,061 per year) were awarded. *Total annual research expenditures:* $356,867.

Loyola University Maryland, Graduate Programs, School of Education, Program in Educational Technology, Baltimore, MD 21210-2699. Offers M Ed, MA. *Program availability:* Part-time. *Faculty:* 36 full-time (27 women), 23 part-time/adjunct (15 women). *Students:* 1 (woman) full-time, 160 part-time (124 women); includes 47 minority (32 Black or African American, non-Hispanic/Latino; 7 Asian, non-Hispanic/Latino; 5 Hispanic/Latino; 3 Two or more races, non-Hispanic/Latino). Average age 32. *Degree requirements:* For master's, thesis. *Entrance requirements:* For master's, transcript, essay. Additional exam requirements/recommendations for international students: Required—TOEFL (minimum score 550 paper-based), IELTS (minimum score 7). Application fee: $60. Electronic applications accepted. *Expenses:* Contact institution. *Financial support:* Scholarships/grants available. Financial award application deadline: 4/15; financial award applicants required to submit FAFSA. *Unit head:* Dr. Kelly Keane, Director, 410-617-1552, E-mail: kjkeane@loyola.edu. *Application contact:* Office of Graduate Admission, 410-617-5020, E-mail: graduate@loyola.edu.

Manhattan College, Graduate Programs, School of Education and Health, Program in Instructional Design and Delivery, Riverdale, NY 10471. Offers MS. *Program availability:* Part-time, evening/weekend. *Faculty:* 1 (woman) full-time, 6 part-time/adjunct (3 women). *Students:* 14 full-time (12 women); includes 8 minority (4 Black or African American, non-Hispanic/Latino; 4 Hispanic/Latino). Average age 32. 16 applicants, 88% accepted, 14 enrolled. *Degree requirements:* For master's, thesis. *Entrance requirements:* For master's, GRE. *Application deadline:* For fall admission, 8/1 priority date for domestic students; for spring admission, 1/1 priority date for domestic students; for summer admission, 4/15 priority date for domestic students. Applications are processed on a rolling basis. Application fee: $105. Electronic applications accepted. *Expenses:* Contact institution. *Financial support:* In 2017–18, 2 students received support. Scholarships/grants, tuition waivers, and unspecified assistantships available. Financial award application deadline: 8/1; financial award applicants required to submit FAFSA. *Faculty research:* Simulations, gaming, adult technology integration, pre-service training, STEM integration into curriculum, Web 2.0 tool development. *Unit head:* Dr. Shawna Bushell, Director, 718-862-7147, E-mail: bushell@manhattan.edu. *Application contact:* William Bisset, Vice President for Enrollment, 718-862-7199, Fax: 718-862-8019, E-mail: william.bisset@manhattan.edu.
Website: http://manhattan.edu/academics/education/idd

Marconi International University, Graduate Programs, Pembroke Pines, FL 33028. Offers business administration (DBA); education leadership (Ed D); education leadership, management and emerging technologies (M Ed); international business administration (IMBA).

Marian University, School of Education, Fond du Lac, WI 54935-4699. Offers curriculum and instruction leadership (PhD); educational administration (PhD); educational leadership (MAE); educational technology (MAE); leadership studies (PhD); special education (MAE); teacher education (MAE). *Accreditation:* NCATE. *Program availability:* Part-time, evening/weekend, online learning. *Degree requirements:* For master's, exam, field-based experience project, portfolio; for doctorate, comprehensive

exam, thesis/dissertation, field-based experience. *Entrance requirements:* For master's, minimum GPA of 3.0, BA in education or related field, teaching license; for doctorate, GRE, MAT, resume, 2 writing samples, interview. Additional exam requirements/recommendations for international students: Required—TOEFL (minimum score 525 paper-based; 70 iBT). *Faculty research:* At-risk youth, multicultural issues, values in education, teaching/learning strategies.

Marlboro College, Graduate and Professional Studies, Program in Learning Design and Technology, Marlboro, VT 05344. Offers educational technology (Certificate); teaching with technology (MAT). *Program availability:* Part-time, evening/weekend, blended/hybrid learning. *Degree requirements:* For master's, 36 credits including capstone project. *Entrance requirements:* For master's, statement of intent, 2 letters of recommendation, transcripts. *Application deadline:* For fall admission, 7/1 priority date for domestic students; for winter admission, 11/1 priority date for domestic students; for spring admission, 3/1 priority date for domestic students. Applications are processed on a rolling basis. Application fee: $0. Electronic applications accepted. *Expenses:* $794 per credit ($664 for Vermont teachers). *Financial support:* Scholarships/grants available. Financial award application deadline: 8/5; financial award applicants required to submit FAFSA. *Unit head:* Caleb Clark, Chair, 802-258-9207, Fax: 802-258-9201, E-mail: cclark@gradschool.marlboro.edu. *Application contact:* Amanda Mehegan, Assistant Director of Graduate Admissions, 802-451-7505, Fax: 802-258-9201, E-mail: graduateadmissions@marlboro.edu.
Website: https://www.marlboro.edu/academics/graduate/mat

Martin Luther College, Graduate Studies, New Ulm, MN 56073. Offers early childhood director (MS Ed Admin); educational technology (MS Ed); instruction (MS Ed); leadership (MS Ed); principal (MS Ed Admin); special education (MS Ed). *Program availability:* Part-time, evening/weekend, online learning. *Faculty:* 8 full-time (1 woman), 21 part-time/adjunct (10 women). *Students:* 1 (woman) full-time, 81 part-time (28 women); includes 2 minority (1 Asian, non-Hispanic/Latino; 1 Two or more races, non-Hispanic/Latino), 2 international. Average age 37. 23 applicants, 100% accepted, 23 enrolled. In 2017, 25 master's awarded. *Degree requirements:* For master's, capstone project or comprehensive exam. *Entrance requirements:* For master's, undergraduate degree in education from an accredited college or university, minimum undergraduate GPA of 3.0. Additional exam requirements/recommendations for international students: Required—TOEFL (minimum score 550 paper-based; 80 iBT); Recommended—IELTS (minimum score 6.5). *Application deadline:* Applications are processed on a rolling basis. Application fee: $35. Electronic applications accepted. *Expenses:* $315 per credit. *Financial support:* In 2017–18, 4 students received support. Scholarships/grants available. Financial award application deadline: 9/1. *Faculty research:* Principal effectiveness, principal support, cognitive load in math instruction, reading strategies in multigrade classrooms, mentor provided professional development for new teachers. *Unit head:* John E. Meyer, Director of Graduate Studies, 507-354-8221 Ext. 398, E-mail: meyerjd@mlc-wels.edu.
Website: https://mlc-wels.edu/graduate-studies/

Marygrove College, Graduate Studies, Detroit, MI 48221-2599. Offers autism spectrum disorders (M Ed, Certificate); curriculum instruction and assessment (MAT); educational leadership (MA); educational technology (M Ed); effective teaching in the 21st century-classroom focus (MAT); effective teaching in the 21st century-technology focus (MAT); human resource management (MA, Certificate); mathematics 6-8 (MAT); mathematics K-5 (MAT); reading and literacy K-6 (MAT); reading specialist (M Ed); school administrator (Certificate); social justice (MA); special education (MAT); special education - learning disabilities (M Ed); teaching - pre-elementary education (M Ed); teaching - pre-secondary education (M Ed). *Program availability:* Part-time, evening/weekend, 100% online, blended/hybrid learning. *Students:* 163 full-time (123 women), 264 part-time (186 women). Average age 34. *Entrance requirements:* For master's, all official bachelor's transcripts. Additional exam requirements/recommendations for international students: Required—TOEFL (minimum score 550 paper-based; 80 iBT). *Application deadline:* Applications are processed on a rolling basis. Electronic applications accepted. *Expenses: Tuition:* Part-time $590 per credit hour. *Required fees:* $120 per semester. One-time fee: $25 part-time. *Financial support:* Applicants required to submit FAFSA. *Unit head:* Marygrove College Admissions, 313-927-1240, E-mail: info@marygrove.edu. *Application contact:* Marygrove College Admissions, 313-927-1240, E-mail: info@marygrove.edu.

Massachusetts College of Liberal Arts, Graduate Programs, North Adams, MA 01247-4100. Offers business (MBA); educational administration (M Ed); educational leadership (CAGS); instruction and curriculum (M Ed); instructional technology (M Ed); physical education and health (M Ed); reading (M Ed); special education (M Ed). *Program availability:* Part-time, evening/weekend. *Degree requirements:* For master's, thesis. *Entrance requirements:* For master's, writing sample.

McDaniel College, Graduate and Professional Studies, Program in School Librarianship, Westminster, MD 21157-4390. Offers MS. *Program availability:* Part-time, evening/weekend, online only, 100% online. *Faculty:* 1 (woman) full-time, 5 part-time/adjunct (all women). *Students:* 3 full-time (all women), 66 part-time (60 women); includes 3 minority (1 Black or African American, non-Hispanic/Latino; 2 Asian, non-Hispanic/Latino), 1 international. Average age 38. 10 applicants, 100% accepted, 9 enrolled. In 2017, 8 master's awarded. *Degree requirements:* For master's, comprehensive exam, thesis optional. *Entrance requirements:* For master's, PRAXIS, 3 recommendations, essay. Additional exam requirements/recommendations for international students: Required—TOEFL (minimum score 79 iBT), IELTS (minimum score 6). *Application deadline:* For fall admission, 6/1 priority date for domestic students; for spring admission, 11/1 priority date for domestic students; for summer admission, 3/1 priority date for domestic students. Applications are processed on a rolling basis. Application fee: $75. Electronic applications accepted. *Expenses: Tuition:* Full-time $11,760; part-time $490 per credit hour. Tuition and fees vary according to course load and program. *Financial support:* Career-related internships or fieldwork available. Financial award application deadline: 3/1; financial award applicants required to submit FAFSA. *Unit head:* Fax: 410-857-2515, E-mail: gradadms@mcdaniel.edu. *Application contact:* Crystal L. Perry, Assistant Director, Graduate Enrollment Management, 410-857-2516, Fax: 410-857-2515, E-mail: cperry@mcdaniel.edu.

McNeese State University, Doré School of Graduate Studies, Burton College of Education, Department of Education Professions, Program in Educational Leadership, Lake Charles, LA 70609. Offers educational leadership (M Ed, Ed S); educational technology (Ed S). *Program availability:* Evening/weekend. *Entrance requirements:* For master's, GRE, teaching certificate, 3 years of full-time teaching experience; for Ed S, teaching certificate, 3 years of teaching experience, 1 year of administration or supervision experience, master's degree with 12 semester hours in education. *Application deadline:* For fall admission, 5/15 priority date for domestic and international students; for spring admission, 10/15 priority date for domestic and international students. Applications are processed on a rolling basis. Application fee: $20 ($30 for international students). *Financial support:* Application deadline: 5/1. *Unit head:* Dr. Brett C. Welch, Director, 337-475-5405, Fax: 337-475-5272, E-mail: bwelch@mcneese.edu. *Application contact:* Dr. Dustin M. Hebert, Director of Dore' School of Graduate Studies, 337-475-5396, Fax: 337-475-5397, E-mail: admissions@mcneese.edu.

Educational Media/Instructional Technology

McNeese State University, Doré School of Graduate Studies, Burton College of Education, Department of Education Professions, Program in Educational Technology Leadership, Lake Charles, LA 70609. Offers M Ed. *Program availability:* Evening/weekend. *Entrance requirements:* For master's, GRE, teaching certificate. *Application deadline:* For fall admission, 5/15 priority date for domestic and international students; for spring admission, 10/15 priority date for domestic and international students. Applications are processed on a rolling basis. Application fee: $20 ($30 for international students). *Financial support:* Application deadline: 5/1. *Unit head:* Dr. Brett C. Welch, Director, 337-475-5405, Fax: 337-475-5272, E-mail: bwelch@mcneese.edu. *Application contact:* Dr. Dustin M. Hebert, Director of Doré' School of Graduate Studies, 337-475-5396, Fax: 337-475-5397, E-mail: admissions@mcneese.edu.

McNeese State University, Doré School of Graduate Studies, Burton College of Education, Department of Education Professions, Program in Instructional Technology, Lake Charles, LA 70609. Offers MS. *Program availability:* Evening/weekend. *Entrance requirements:* For master's, GRE. *Application deadline:* For fall admission, 5/15 priority date for domestic and international students; for spring admission, 10/15 priority date for domestic and international students. Applications are processed on a rolling basis. Application fee: $20 ($30 for international students). *Financial support:* Application deadline: 5/1. *Unit head:* Dr. Brett C. Welch, Director, 337-475-5405, Fax: 337-475-5272, E-mail: bwelch@mcneese.edu. *Application contact:* Dr. Dustin M. Hebert, Director of Doré' School of Graduate Studies, 337-475-5396, Fax: 337-475-5397, E-mail: admissions@mcneese.edu.

Memorial University of Newfoundland, School of Graduate Studies, Faculty of Education, St. John's, NL A1C 5S7, Canada. Offers counseling psychology (M Ed); curriculum, teaching, and learning studies (M Ed); education (PhD); educational leadership studies (M Ed, Graduate Diploma); information technology (M Ed); post-secondary studies (M Ed, Diploma), including health professional education (Diploma). *Program availability:* Part-time. *Degree requirements:* For master's, thesis optional, internship, paper folio, project; for doctorate, comprehensive exam, thesis/dissertation, thesis seminar, oral defense of thesis. *Entrance requirements:* For master's, undergraduate degree with at least 2nd class standing, 1-2 years of work experience; for doctorate, minimum A average in graduate course work, MA in education, 2 years of professional experience; for other advanced degree, 2nd class degree, 2 years of work experience with adult learners, appropriate academic qualifications and work experience in a health-related field. Electronic applications accepted. *Faculty research:* Critical thinking, literacy, cognitive studies and counseling, educational change, technology in instruction.

Michigan State University, The Graduate School, College of Education, Department of Counseling, Educational Psychology and Special Education, East Lansing, MI 48824. Offers counseling (MA); educational psychology and educational technology (PhD); educational technology (MA); measurement and quantitative methods (PhD); rehabilitation counseling (MA); rehabilitation counselor education (PhD); school psychology (MA, PhD, Ed S); special education (MA, PhD). *Accreditation:* APA (one or more programs are accredited); CORE (one or more programs are accredited). *Program availability:* Part-time. *Entrance requirements:* Additional exam requirements/recommendations for international students: Required—TOEFL. Electronic applications accepted.

MidAmerica Nazarene University, Professional and Graduate Studies in Education, Olathe, KS 66062-1899. Offers ESOL (M Ed); reading specialist (M Ed); technology enhanced teaching (M Ed). *Accreditation:* NCATE. *Program availability:* Part-time, evening/weekend, online only, 100% online. *Entrance requirements:* For master's, bachelor's degree from an accredited college or university, minimum undergraduate GPA of 3.0, valid teaching license. Additional exam requirements/recommendations for international students: Required—TOEFL (minimum score 81 iBT), IELTS (minimum score 6). Electronic applications accepted. *Expenses:* Contact institution.

Middle Tennessee State University, College of Graduate Studies, College of Education, Department of Educational Leadership, Program in Curriculum and Instruction, Murfreesboro, TN 37132. Offers curriculum and instruction (M Ed, Ed S); English as a second language (M Ed, Ed S); secondary education (M Ed); technology and curriculum design (Ed S). *Accreditation:* NCATE. *Program availability:* Part-time, evening/weekend, online learning. *Degree requirements:* For master's, comprehensive exam; for Ed S, comprehensive exam, thesis or alternative. *Entrance requirements:* For master's and Ed S, GRE, MAT or PRAXIS. Additional exam requirements/recommendations for international students: Required—TOEFL (minimum score 525 paper-based; 71 iBT) or IELTS (minimum score 6). Electronic applications accepted.

Midwestern State University, Billie Doris McAda Graduate School, West College of Education, Programs in Educational Leadership and Technology, Wichita Falls, TX 76308. Offers educational leadership (M Ed); educational technology (M Ed). *Program availability:* Part-time, evening/weekend. *Degree requirements:* For master's, comprehensive exam. *Entrance requirements:* For master's, GRE General Test or MAT. Additional exam requirements/recommendations for international students: Required—TOEFL (minimum score 550 paper-based). Electronic applications accepted. *Faculty research:* Role of the principal in the twenty-first century, culturally proficient leadership, human diversity, immigration, teacher collaboration.

Misericordia University, College of Health Sciences and Education, Program in Education, Dallas, PA 18612-1098. Offers instructional technology (MS); reading specialist (MS); special education (MS). *Program availability:* Part-time, evening/weekend. *Entrance requirements:* For master's, minimum undergraduate GPA of 3.0. Additional exam requirements/recommendations for international students: Required—TOEFL. Electronic applications accepted.

Mississippi State University, College of Education, Department of Instructional Systems and Workforce Development, Mississippi State, MS 39762. Offers instructional systems and workforce development (MSIT, PhD); technology (MST, Ed S). *Faculty:* 10 full-time (6 women). *Students:* 13 full-time (5 women), 45 part-time (34 women); includes 35 minority (34 Black or African American, non-Hispanic/Latino; 1 Two or more races, non-Hispanic/Latino), 1 international. Average age 37. 28 applicants, 68% accepted, 14 enrolled. In 2017, 4 master's, 6 doctorates, 4 other advanced degrees awarded. *Degree requirements:* For master's, thesis optional, comprehensive oral or written exam; for doctorate, thesis/dissertation, comprehensive oral and written exam; for Ed S, thesis, comprehensive written exam. *Entrance requirements:* For master's, GRE, minimum GPA of 2.75 on undergraduate work, 3.0 graduate; for doctorate, GRE, minimum GPA of 3.4 on graduate work; for Ed S, GRE, minimum GPA of 3.2, master's degree. Additional exam requirements/recommendations for international students: Required—TOEFL (minimum score 550 paper-based; 79 iBT); Recommended—IELTS (minimum score 6.5). *Application deadline:* For fall admission, 7/1 for domestic students, 5/1 for international students; for spring admission, 11/1 for domestic students, 9/1 for international students. Applications are processed on a rolling basis. Application fee: $60 ($80 for international students). Electronic applications accepted. *Expenses:* Tuition, state resident: full-time $8318; part-time $462.12 per credit hour. Tuition, nonresident: full-time $22,358; part-time $1242.12 per credit hour. *Required fees:* $110; $12.24 per credit hour. $6.12 per semester. *Financial support:* In 2017–18, 2 teaching assistantships with full tuition reimbursements (averaging $10,575 per year) were

awarded; Federal Work-Study, institutionally sponsored loans, scholarships/grants, and unspecified assistantships also available. Financial award application deadline: 4/1; financial award applicants required to submit FAFSA. *Faculty research:* Computer technology, nontraditional students, interactive video, instructional technology, educational leadership. *Unit head:* Dr. Trey Martindale, Associate Professor and Head, 662-325-7258, Fax: 662-325-7599, E-mail: tmartindale@colled.msstate.edu. *Application contact:* Angie Campbell, Admissions and Enrollment Assistant, 662-325-9514, E-mail: acampbell@grad.msstate.edu.
Website: http://www.iswd.msstate.edu

Missouri Southern State University, Program in Instructional Technology, Joplin, MO 64801-1595. Offers MS Ed. Program offered jointly with Northwest Missouri State University. *Degree requirements:* For master's, comprehensive exam, research paper. *Entrance requirements:* For master's, GRE (minimum combined score of 700), writing assessment, minimum overall undergraduate GPA of 3.0.

Missouri State University, Graduate College, College of Education, Department of Reading, Foundations, and Technology, Program in Educational Technology, Springfield, MO 65897. Offers MS Ed. *Program availability:* Part-time. *Faculty:* 16 full-time (11 women), 14 part-time/adjunct (13 women). *Students:* 10 full-time (9 women), 26 part-time (17 women); includes 1 minority (Hispanic/Latino), 6 international. Average age 27. 8 applicants, 88% accepted, 4 enrolled. In 2017, 16 master's awarded. *Degree requirements:* For master's, comprehensive exam, thesis or alternative. *Entrance requirements:* Additional exam requirements/recommendations for international students: Required—TOEFL (minimum score 550 paper-based; 79 iBT), IELTS (minimum score 6). *Application deadline:* For fall admission, 7/20 priority date for domestic students, 5/1 for international students; for spring admission, 12/20 priority date for domestic students, 9/1 for international students; for summer admission, 5/20 priority date for domestic students. Applications are processed on a rolling basis. Application fee: $35 ($50 for international students). Electronic applications accepted. *Expenses:* Tuition, state resident: full-time $2915; part-time $2021 per credit hour. Tuition, nonresident: full-time $5354; part-time $3647 per credit hour. *International tuition:* $11,992 full-time. *Required fees:* $173; $173 per credit hour. Tuition and fees vary according to class time, course level, course load, degree level, campus/location and program. *Financial support:* Federal Work-Study, institutionally sponsored loans, scholarships/grants, and unspecified assistantships available. Financial award application deadline: 3/31; financial award applicants required to submit FAFSA. *Unit head:* Dr. Emmett Sawyer, Interim Department Head, 417-836-6769, E-mail: rft@missouristate.edu. *Application contact:* Stephanie Praschan, Director, Graduate Enrollment Management, 417-836-5330, Fax: 417-836-6200, E-mail: stephaniepraschan@missouristate.edu.
Website: http://education.missouristate.edu/rft/

Molloy College, Graduate Education Program, Rockville Centre, NY 11571-5002. Offers adolescent education in biology (MS); adolescent special education (Advanced Certificate); bilingual extension (Advanced Certificate); childhood education (MS); childhood special education (Advanced Certificate); early childhood education (MS); educational technology (MS); English (MS); mathematics (MS); social studies (MS); Spanish (MS); special education on both childhood and adolescent levels (MS); teaching English to speakers of other languages (TESOL) in grades pre-K to 12 (MS); TESOL (Advanced Certificate). *Accreditation:* NCATE. *Program availability:* Part-time, evening/weekend. *Faculty:* 18 full-time (17 women), 11 part-time/adjunct (9 women). *Students:* 102 full-time (80 women), 217 part-time (167 women); includes 65 minority (16 Black or African American, non-Hispanic/Latino; 7 Asian, non-Hispanic/Latino; 38 Hispanic/Latino; 4 Two or more races, non-Hispanic/Latino), 1 international. Average age 41. 153 applicants, 68% accepted, 85 enrolled. In 2017, 95 master's, 3 other advanced degrees awarded. *Entrance requirements:* Additional exam requirements/recommendations for international students: Required—TOEFL (minimum score 550 paper-based; 79 iBT). *Application deadline:* Applications are processed on a rolling basis. Application fee: $60. Electronic applications accepted. *Expenses:* Tuition: Full-time $19,980; part-time $1110 per credit. *Required fees:* $1040. Tuition and fees vary according to course load and degree level. *Financial support:* Application deadline: 3/1; applicants required to submit FAFSA. *Faculty research:* English Language Learners; social emotional needs of students; gifted education; cultural diversity; collaborative teaching methods. *Unit head:* Joanne O'Brien, Associate Dean and Director of Graduate Education Programs, 516-323-3116, E-mail: jobrien@molloy.edu. *Application contact:* Jaclyn Machowicz, Assistant Director for Admissions, 516-323-4010, E-mail: jmachowicz@molloy.edu.

Montana State University Billings, College of Education, Department of Educational Theory and Practice, Option in Online Instructional Technologies, Billings, MT 59101. Offers M Ed. *Accreditation:* NCATE. *Program availability:* Part-time. *Degree requirements:* For master's, professional paper or thesis. *Entrance requirements:* For master's, GRE General Test or MAT, minimum GPA of 3.0. Additional exam requirements/recommendations for international students: Required—TOEFL (minimum score 79 iBT), IELTS (minimum score 6.5). *Application deadline:* For fall admission, 7/15 for domestic students; for spring admission, 12/1 for domestic students. Applications are processed on a rolling basis. Application fee: $40. Electronic applications accepted. *Expenses:* Tuition, state resident: full-time $11,740; part-time $7880 per year. Tuition, nonresident: full-time $32,200; part-time $24,140 per year. *Financial support:* Teaching assistantships with partial tuition reimbursements, career-related internships or fieldwork, Federal Work-Study, institutionally sponsored loans, scholarships/grants, tuition waivers (partial), and unspecified assistantships available. Support available to part-time students. Financial award application deadline: 5/1; financial award applicants required to submit FAFSA. *Unit head:* Dr. Cindy Dell, Chair, Educational Theory and Practice, 406-657-1614, E-mail: cdell@msbillings.edu. *Application contact:* Dr. Cindy Dell, Chair, Educational Theory and Practice, 406-657-1614, E-mail: cdell@msbillings.edu.
Website: http://www.msubillings.edu/grad/program-ed_technology.htm

Morehead State University, Graduate Programs, College of Education, Department of Foundational and Graduate Studies in Education, Morehead, KY 40351. Offers adult and higher education (MA, Ed S); certified professional counselor (Ed S); counseling P-12 (MA); curriculum and instruction (Ed S); educational technology (MA Ed); instructional leadership (Ed S); school administration (MA); school counseling (Ed S); teacher leader business and marketing content (MA Ed); teacher leader business and marketing technology (MA Ed); teacher leader educational technology (MA Ed); teacher leader English (MA Ed); teacher leader gifted education (MA Ed); teacher leader IECE certification (MA Ed); teacher leader interdisciplinary education P-5 (MA Ed); teacher leader middle grades (MA Ed); teacher leader non IECE certification (MA Ed); teacher leader reading/writing - non-certification (MA Ed); teacher leader reading/writing certification (MA Ed); teacher leader school communication - certification (MA Ed); teacher leader school communication - non-certification (MA Ed); teacher leader social studies (MA Ed); teacher leader special education (MA Ed). *Accreditation:* NCATE. *Program availability:* Part-time, evening/weekend. *Degree requirements:* For master's, thesis optional, oral and/or written comprehensive exams; for Ed S, thesis, oral exam. *Entrance requirements:* For master's, GRE General Test, minimum overall undergraduate GPA of 2.5; for Ed S, GRE General Test, interview, master's degree, minimum GPA of 3.5, work experience. Additional exam requirements/recommendations for international students: Required—TOEFL (minimum score 500 paper-based). Electronic applications accepted. *Faculty research:* Character education, school accountability, computer applications for school administrators.

Murray State University, College of Education and Human Services, Department of Educational Studies, Leadership and Counseling, Murray, KY 42071. Offers college advising (Certificate); education administration (MA Ed); human development and leadership (MS, Certificate); library media (MA Ed); middle school teacher leader (MA Ed); P-20 and community leadership (Ed D); postsecondary education administration (MA Ed); school counseling (MA Ed); school guidance and counseling (Ed S); secondary teacher leader (MA Ed). *Program availability:* Part-time, evening/weekend, 100% online, blended/hybrid learning. *Faculty:* 38 full-time (16 women), 3 part-time/adjunct (1 woman). *Students:* 45 full-time (22 women), 190 part-time (140 women); includes 33 minority (25 Black or African American, non-Hispanic/Latino; 4 Asian, non-Hispanic/Latino; 3 Hispanic/Latino; 1 Two or more races, non-Hispanic/Latino), 6 international. Average age 35. 87 applicants, 77% accepted, 51 enrolled. In 2017, 21 master's, 16 doctorates, 12 other advanced degrees awarded. *Entrance requirements:* For master's and other advanced degree, GRE or GMAT, minimum university GPA of 2.75. Additional exam requirements/recommendations for international students: Required—TOEFL (minimum score 527 paper-based; 71 iBT). *Application deadline:* Applications are processed on a rolling basis. Application fee: $40 ($50 for international students). Electronic applications accepted. *Expenses:* Tuition, state resident: full-time $9504. Tuition, nonresident: full-time $26,811. *International tuition:* $14,400 full-time. Tuition and fees vary according to course load, degree level and reciprocity agreements. *Financial support:* Federal Work-Study and unspecified assistantships available. Financial award applicants required to submit FAFSA. *Unit head:* Dr. Susana Bloomdahl, Chair, Department of Educational Studies, Leadership and Counseling, 270-809-6471, Fax: 270-809-3799, E-mail: sbloomdahl@murraystate.edu. *Application contact:* Kaitlyn Burzynski, Interim Assistant Director for Graduate Admission and Records, 270-809-5732, Fax: 270-809-3780, E-mail: msu.graduateadmissions@murraystate.edu.
Website: http://www.murraystate.edu/academics/CollegesDepartments/CollegeOfEducationandHumanServices/coehsacademicunits/EducationalStudiesLeadershipandCounseli

National Louis University, National College of Education, Chicago, IL 60603. Offers administration and supervision (M Ed, Ed D, CAS, Ed S); curriculum and instruction (M Ed, MS Ed, CAS); early childhood administration (M Ed, CAS); early childhood education (M Ed, MAT, MS Ed, CAS); education (Ed D); educational psychology/human learning and development (M Ed, MS Ed, CAS, Ed S); elementary education (MAT); interdisciplinary curriculum and instruction (M Ed); mathematics education (M Ed, MS Ed, CAS); middle grades education (MAT); reading and language (M Ed, MS Ed, CAS); school psychology (M Ed, Ed S); science education (M Ed, MS Ed, CAS); secondary education (MAT); special education (M Ed, MAT, CAS); technology in education (M Ed, CAS). *Accreditation:* NCATE. *Program availability:* Part-time, evening/weekend. *Degree requirements:* For doctorate, comprehensive exam, thesis/dissertation. *Entrance requirements:* For master's, MAT or GRE, minimum GPA of 3.0; for doctorate, GRE General Test, minimum GPA of 3.25, interview, resume, writing sample, 4 recommendations. Additional exam requirements/recommendations for international students: Required—TOEFL (minimum score 550 paper-based; 79 iBT).

National University, Academic Affairs, Sanford College of Education, La Jolla, CA 92037-1011. Offers advanced teaching practices (MS); applied behavior analysis (MS); applied school leadership (MS); e-teaching and learning (Certificate); education (MA); educational administration (MS); educational and instructional technology (MS); educational counseling (MS); higher education administration (MS); inspired teaching and learning (M Ed); school psychology (MS); special education (MA, MS). *Program availability:* Part-time, evening/weekend, 100% online, blended/hybrid learning. *Degree requirements:* For master's, thesis (for some programs). *Entrance requirements:* For master's, interview, minimum GPA of 2.5. Additional exam requirements/recommendations for international students: Required—TOEFL (minimum score 550 paper-based; 79 iBT), IELTS (minimum score 6). *Application deadline:* Applications are processed on a rolling basis. Application fee: $60 ($65 for international students). Electronic applications accepted. *Expenses: Tuition:* Part-time $430 per quarter hour. *Financial support:* Career-related internships or fieldwork, institutionally sponsored loans, scholarships/grants, and tuition waivers (partial) available. Support available to part-time students. Financial award application deadline: 6/30. *Faculty research:* Teacher education, special education, educational effectiveness, teaching abroad, school counseling. *Unit head:* Dr. Judy Mantle, Dean, 858-642-8320, E-mail: soe@nu.edu. *Application contact:* Brandon Jouganatos, Vice President for Enrollment Services, 800-628-8648, E-mail: advisor@nu.edu.
Website: http://www.nu.edu/OurPrograms/SchoolOfEducation.html

Nazareth College of Rochester, Graduate Studies, Department of Education, Program of Educational Technology, Rochester, NY 14618. Offers MS Ed. *Program availability:* Part-time, evening/weekend. *Entrance requirements:* For master's, minimum GPA of 3.0. Additional exam requirements/recommendations for international students: Required—TOEFL or IELTS.

New Jersey City University, Debra Cannon Partridge Wolfe College of Education, Department of Educational Technology, Jersey City, NJ 07305-1597. Offers educational technology (MA); educational technology leadership (Ed D). *Accreditation:* NCATE. *Program availability:* Part-time, evening/weekend, online learning. *Degree requirements:* For master's, internship. *Entrance requirements:* Additional exam requirements/recommendations for international students: Required—TOEFL (minimum score 79 iBT).

New York Institute of Technology, School of Interdisciplinary Studies and Education, Department of Instructional Technology, Old Westbury, NY 11568-8000. Offers emerging technologies for trainers (Advanced Certificate); instructional design for global e-learning (Advanced Certificate); instructional technology (MS), including educators, trainers; STEM education (Advanced Certificate). *Program availability:* Part-time, evening/weekend, 100% online, blended/hybrid learning. *Faculty:* 6 full-time (3 women), 6 part-time/adjunct (4 women). *Students:* 7 full-time (2 women), 105 part-time (73 women); includes 15 minority (5 Black or African American, non-Hispanic/Latino; 4 Asian, non-Hispanic/Latino; 4 Hispanic/Latino; 2 Two or more races, non-Hispanic/Latino), 1 international. Average age 33. 47 applicants, 83% accepted, 30 enrolled. In 2017, 53 master's, 13 other advanced degrees awarded. *Entrance requirements:* For master's, GRE (minimum combined score of 300) or MAT (minimum score of 400) within the last five years, bachelor's degree; minimum undergraduate GPA of 3.0; demonstrated proficiency in basic uses of instructional technologies; initial/provisional or permanent/professional NY state certification in any teaching area (for educators option); for Advanced Certificate, GRE or MAT (within last 5 years), BS; minimum undergraduate GPA of 3.0; demonstrated proficiency in basic uses of instructional technologies. Additional exam requirements/recommendations for international students: Required—TOEFL (minimum score 79 iBT), IELTS (minimum score 6). *Application deadline:* Applications are processed on a rolling basis. Application fee: $50. Electronic applications accepted. *Expenses:* $1,285 per credit plus fees. *Financial

support:* Career-related internships or fieldwork, scholarships/grants, health care benefits, tuition waivers (full and partial), and unspecified assistantships available. Support available to part-time students. Financial award application deadline: 2/15; financial award applicants required to submit FAFSA. *Faculty research:* Integration of information and communication technologies (ICTs) and media literacy education into learning environments; urban K-12 teachers' effective use of technology to enhance student achievement; instructional design and transdisciplinary curriculum studies for online instruction; STEM and computing partnerships for K-12 teachers; experiential, collaborative, and performance-based approaches to pedagogy and technology integration in the K-12 classroom. *Unit head:* Dr. Melda Yildiz, Department Chair, 516-686-1053, Fax: 516-686-7655, E-mail: myildiz@nyit.edu. *Application contact:* Alice Dolitsky, Director, Graduate Admissions, 516-686-7520, Fax: 516-686-1116, E-mail: nyitgrad@nyit.edu.
Website: http://www.nyit.edu/interdisciplinary/department_instructional_technology

New York Institute of Technology, School of Interdisciplinary Studies and Education, Department of School Leadership and Technology, Old Westbury, NY 11568-8000. Offers Advanced Diploma. *Program availability:* Part-time, evening/weekend, online only, 100% online. *Faculty:* 1 full-time (0 women), 6 part-time/adjunct (4 women). *Students:* 44 part-time (26 women); includes 8 minority (3 Black or African American, non-Hispanic/Latino; 4 Hispanic/Latino; 1 Two or more races, non-Hispanic/Latino). Average age 36. 13 applicants, 85% accepted, 7 enrolled. In 2017, 13 Advanced Diplomas awarded. *Degree requirements:* For Advanced Diploma, internship. *Entrance requirements:* For degree, master's degree with minimum cumulative GPA of 3.0; personal statement; at least 3 years of full-time teaching experience; professional NY state teacher certification; demonstration of computer competency; two letters of reference from school building or district administrator. Additional exam requirements/recommendations for international students: Required—TOEFL (minimum score 79 iBT), IELTS (minimum score 6). *Application deadline:* Applications are processed on a rolling basis. Application fee: $50. Electronic applications accepted. *Expenses:* $1,285 per credit plus fees. *Financial support:* Career-related internships or fieldwork, scholarships/grants, and unspecified assistantships available. Support available to part-time students. Financial award application deadline: 2/15; financial award applicants required to submit FAFSA. *Faculty research:* College readiness; school-community partnerships; administrator-school counselor relationships. *Unit head:* Dr. Robert Feirsen, Chair, 516-686-1169, E-mail: rfeirsen@nyit.edu. *Application contact:* Alice Dolitsky, Director, Graduate Admissions, 516-686-7520, Fax: 516-686-1116, E-mail: nyitgrad@nyit.edu.
Website: https://www.nyit.edu/programs/school_leadership_technology

New York University, Steinhardt School of Culture, Education, and Human Development, Department of Administration, Leadership, and Technology, Programs in Educational Communication and Technology, Brooklyn, NY 11201. Offers digital media design for learning (MA, Advanced Certificate); educational communication and technology (MS); games for learning (MS). *Program availability:* Part-time. *Students:* Average age 34. 110 applicants, 71% accepted, 31 enrolled. In 2017, 20 master's, 3 doctorates, 1 other advanced degree awarded. *Entrance requirements:* For doctorate, GRE General Test, interview; for Advanced Certificate, master's degree. Additional exam requirements/recommendations for international students: Required—TOEFL (minimum score 100 iBT). *Application deadline:* For fall admission, 12/1 priority date for domestic and international students; for spring admission, 10/1 for domestic and international students. Applications are processed on a rolling basis. Application fee: $75. Electronic applications accepted. *Expenses: Tuition:* Full-time $41,352; part-time $19,968 per year. *Required fees:* $2496; $1628 per unit. $814 per term. Tuition and fees vary according to course load and program. *Financial support:* Fellowships with full and partial tuition reimbursements, research assistantships with full and partial tuition reimbursements, teaching assistantships with partial tuition reimbursements, career-related internships or fieldwork, Federal Work-Study, institutionally sponsored loans, scholarships/grants, tuition waivers (partial), and unspecified assistantships available. Support available to part-time students. Financial award application deadline: 2/1; financial award applicants required to submit FAFSA. *Faculty research:* Digital design for learning, critical evaluation of games, multimedia, cognitive science, individual differences in multimedia learning, serious games. *Unit head:* Prof. Jan L. Plass, Director, 212-998-5520, Fax: 212-995-4047, E-mail: jan.plass@nyu.edu. *Application contact:* 212-998-5030, Fax: 212-995-4328, E-mail: steinhardt.gradadmissions@nyu.edu.
Website: http://steinhardt.nyu.edu/alt/ect

North Carolina Agricultural and Technical State University, School of Graduate Studies, School of Education, Department of Curriculum and Instruction, Greensboro, NC 27411. Offers elementary education (MA Ed); instructional technology (MS); reading education (MA Ed); teaching (MAT). *Accreditation:* NCATE. *Program availability:* Part-time, evening/weekend. *Degree requirements:* For master's, comprehensive exam, qualifying exam. *Entrance requirements:* For master's, GRE General Test, minimum GPA of 3.0.

North Carolina Central University, School of Education, Program in Educational Technology, Durham, NC 27707-3129. Offers MA. *Accreditation:* NCATE. *Program availability:* Part-time, evening/weekend. *Degree requirements:* For master's, comprehensive exam, thesis or alternative. *Entrance requirements:* For master's, GRE, minimum GPA of 3.0 in major, 2.5 overall. Additional exam requirements/recommendations for international students: Required—TOEFL. *Application deadline:* For fall admission, 8/1 for domestic students. Application fee: $30. *Expenses:* Tuition, state resident: full-time $2770; part-time $692.50 per credit hour. Tuition, nonresident: full-time $9247; part-time $2311.75 per credit hour. *Financial support:* Application deadline: 5/1; applicants required to submit FAFSA. *Unit head:* Dorothy M. Singleton, Interim Chair, 919-530-6689, E-mail: dsingleton@nccu.edu. *Application contact:* Dorothy M. Singleton, Interim Chair, 919-530-6689, E-mail: dsingleton@nccu.edu.

North Carolina State University, Graduate School, College of Education, Department of Curriculum and Instruction, Program in Instructional Technology, Raleigh, NC 27695. Offers M Ed, MS. *Entrance requirements:* For master's, MAT or GRE, minimum GPA of 3.0, 3 letters of reference.

North Carolina State University, Graduate School, College of Education, Department of Mathematics, Science, and Technology Education, Program in Technology Education, Raleigh, NC 27695. Offers M Ed, MS, Ed D. *Degree requirements:* For master's, thesis (for some programs); for doctorate, thesis/dissertation. *Entrance requirements:* For master's, GRE or MAT; for doctorate, GRE General Test or MAT, minimum GPA of 3.0, interview. Electronic applications accepted.

Northeastern State University, College of Education, Department of Curriculum and Instruction, Program in Library Media and Information Technology, Tahlequah, OK 74464-2399. Offers MS. *Students:* 1 (woman) full-time, 25 part-time (all women); includes 4 minority (1 Black or African American, non-Hispanic/Latino; 2 American Indian or Alaska Native, non-Hispanic/Latino; 1 Two or more races, non-Hispanic/Latino). Average age 39. In 2017, 19 master's awarded. *Entrance requirements:* Additional exam requirements/recommendations for international students: Required—TOEFL. *Application deadline:* For fall admission, 7/1 for domestic and international students; for spring admission, 11/1 for domestic and international students.

Applications are processed on a rolling basis. Application fee: $25. Electronic applications accepted. *Expenses:* Tuition, state resident: part-time $222 per credit hour. Tuition, nonresident: part-time $501.75 per credit hour. *Required fees:* $37.40 per credit hour. Tuition and fees vary according to degree level. *Unit head:* Dr. Kelli Carney, Program Chair, 918-449-6365, E-mail: carneyka@nsuok.edu. *Application contact:* Josh McCollum, Graduate Coordinator, 918-444-2093, E-mail: mccolluj@nsuok.edu. Website: http://academics.nsuok.edu/education/DegreePrograms/GraduatePrograms/LibraryMediaInformationTechnology.aspx

Northern Arizona University, College of Education, Department of Educational Specialties, Flagstaff, AZ 86011. Offers autism spectrum disorders (Certificate); bilingual/multicultural education (M Ed), including bilingual, ESL; career and technical education (M Ed, Certificate); educational technology (M Ed, Certificate); English as a second language (Certificate); positive behavior support (Certificate); special education (M Ed), including early childhood special education, mild/moderate disabilities. *Program availability:* Part-time, 100% online, blended/hybrid learning. *Faculty:* 31 full-time (19 women), 2 part-time/adjunct (1 woman). *Students:* 66 full-time (52 women), 203 part-time (147 women); includes 83 minority (20 Black or African American, non-Hispanic/Latino; 12 American Indian or Alaska Native, non-Hispanic/Latino; 5 Asian, non-Hispanic/Latino; 38 Hispanic/Latino; 3 Native Hawaiian or other Pacific Islander, non-Hispanic/Latino; 5 Two or more races, non-Hispanic/Latino), 6 international. Average age 37. 157 applicants, 94% accepted, 148 enrolled. In 2017, 119 master's, 26 Certificates awarded. *Degree requirements:* For master's, variable foreign language requirement, comprehensive exam (for some programs), thesis (for some programs); for Certificate, comprehensive exam (for some programs). *Entrance requirements:* Additional exam requirements/recommendations for international students: Required—TOEFL (minimum score 80 iBT), IELTS (minimum score 6.5). *Application deadline:* For fall admission, 3/1 for domestic and international students; for spring admission, 10/1 for domestic and international students. Applications are processed on a rolling basis. Application fee: $65. Electronic applications accepted. *Expenses:* Tuition, state resident: full-time $9240; part-time $458 per credit hour. Tuition, nonresident: full-time $21,588; part-time $1199 per credit hour. *Required fees:* $1021; $14 per credit hour. $646 per semester. Tuition and fees vary according to course load, campus/location and program. *Financial support:* In 2017–18, 11 students received support, including 1 fellowship with full and partial tuition reimbursement available (averaging $12,000 per year), 10 teaching assistantships with full and partial tuition reimbursements available (averaging $12,000 per year); Federal Work-Study, institutionally sponsored loans, health care benefits, tuition waivers (full and partial), and unspecified assistantships also available. Financial award application deadline: 2/1; financial award applicants required to submit FAFSA. *Unit head:* Dr. Shadow Armfield, Chair, 928-523-7651, Fax: 928-523-1929, E-mail: laura.sujo-montes@nau.edu. *Application contact:* Tina Sutton, Coordinator, Graduate College, 928-523-4348, Fax: 928-523-8950, E-mail: graduate@nau.edu.
Website: https://nau.edu/coe/Ed-Specialties/

Northern Illinois University, Graduate School, College of Education, Department of Educational Technology, Research and Assessment, De Kalb, IL 60115-2854. Offers educational research and evaluation (MS); instructional technology (MS Ed, Ed D). *Program availability:* Part-time, evening/weekend. *Faculty:* 13 full-time (7 women). *Students:* 71 full-time (39 women), 90 part-time (55 women); includes 30 minority (17 Black or African American, non-Hispanic/Latino; 5 Asian, non-Hispanic/Latino; 4 Hispanic/Latino; 4 Two or more races, non-Hispanic/Latino), 41 international. Average age 40. 39 applicants, 74% accepted, 10 enrolled. In 2017, 53 master's, 12 doctorates awarded. Terminal master's awarded for partial completion of doctoral program. *Degree requirements:* For master's, comprehensive exam, thesis optional; for doctorate, thesis/dissertation, candidacy exam, dissertation defense. *Entrance requirements:* For master's, GRE General Test or MAT, minimum GPA of 2.75; for doctorate, GRE General Test or MAT, minimum undergraduate GPA of 2.75, 3.2 graduate. Additional exam requirements/recommendations for international students: Required—TOEFL (minimum score 550 paper-based). *Application deadline:* For fall admission, 6/1 for domestic students, 5/1 for international students; for spring admission, 11/1 for domestic students, 10/1 for international students. Applications are processed on a rolling basis. Application fee: $40. Electronic applications accepted. *Financial support:* In 2017–18, 1 research assistantship with full tuition reimbursement, 39 teaching assistantships with full tuition reimbursements were awarded; fellowships with full tuition reimbursements, career-related internships or fieldwork, Federal Work-Study, scholarships/grants, tuition waivers (full), and unspecified assistantships also available. Support available to part-time students. Financial award applicants required to submit FAFSA. *Faculty research:* Distance education, Web-based training, copyright assessment during student teaching, instructional software. *Unit head:* Dr. Wei-Chen Hung, Chair, 815-753-9339, E-mail: etra@niu.edu. *Application contact:* Graduate School Office, 815-753-0395, E-mail: gradsch@niu.edu.
Website: http://www.cedu.niu.edu/etra/index.html

Northern State University, MS Ed Program in Instructional Design in E-learning, Aberdeen, SD 57401-7198. Offers MS Ed. *Program availability:* Part-time, online learning. *Degree requirements:* For master's, comprehensive exam, thesis optional. *Entrance requirements:* For master's, minimum GPA of 2.75. Additional exam requirements/recommendations for international students: Required—TOEFL (minimum score 550 paper-based; 78 iBT), IELTS (minimum score 6). Electronic applications accepted.

Northern State University, MS Program in Training and Development in E-learning, Aberdeen, SD 57401-7198. Offers MS. *Program availability:* Part-time, online learning. *Degree requirements:* For master's, comprehensive exam, thesis optional. *Entrance requirements:* For master's, minimum GPA of 2.75. Additional exam requirements/recommendations for international students: Required—TOEFL (minimum score 550 paper-based; 78 iBT), IELTS (minimum score 6). Electronic applications accepted.

Northwestern State University of Louisiana, Graduate Studies and Research, College of Education and Human Development, Program in Educational Technology Leadership, Natchitoches, LA 71497. Offers M Ed. *Degree requirements:* For master's, comprehensive exam, thesis (for some programs). *Entrance requirements:* For master's, GRE General Test. Additional exam requirements/recommendations for international students: Required—TOEFL. Electronic applications accepted.

Northwestern State University of Louisiana, Graduate Studies and Research, College of Education and Human Development, Programs in Educational Leadership and Instruction, Natchitoches, LA 71497. Offers counseling (Ed S); educational leadership (M Ed, Ed S); educational technology (Ed S); elementary teaching (Ed S); reading (Ed S); secondary teaching (Ed S); special education (Ed S). *Accreditation:* NASAD. *Degree requirements:* For master's, comprehensive exam, thesis (for some programs). *Entrance requirements:* For master's and Ed S, GRE General Test. Additional exam requirements/recommendations for international students: Required—TOEFL. Electronic applications accepted.

Northwestern University, The Graduate School, School of Education and Social Policy, Program in Learning Sciences, Evanston, IL 60208. Offers MA, PhD. Admissions and degrees offered through The Graduate School. Terminal master's awarded for partial completion of doctoral program. *Degree requirements:* For master's, thesis or

alternative, portfolio; for doctorate, thesis/dissertation, qualifying exam. *Entrance requirements:* For doctorate, GRE General Test. Additional exam requirements/recommendations for international students: Required—TOEFL (minimum score 600 paper-based; 100 iBT). Electronic applications accepted. *Expenses:* Contact institution. *Faculty research:* Technologically supported learning environments; inquiry-based learning in mathematics, science, and literacy; learning social contexts; cognitive models of learning and problem solving; changing roles for teachers involved in innovative design and practice.

Northwest Missouri State University, Graduate School, School of Computer Science and Information Systems, Maryville, MO 64468-6001. Offers applied computer science (MS); information systems (MS); instructional technology (MS). *Program availability:* Part-time. *Faculty:* 19 full-time (5 women). *Students:* 211 full-time (74 women), 64 part-time (20 women), 264 international. Average age 24. 395 applicants, 70% accepted, 75 enrolled. In 2017, 267 master's awarded. *Degree requirements:* For master's, comprehensive exam. *Entrance requirements:* For master's, GRE General Test, minimum GPA of 3.0. Additional exam requirements/recommendations for international students: Required—TOEFL (minimum score 550 paper-based). *Application deadline:* Applications are processed on a rolling basis. Application fee: $0 ($50 for international students). *Expenses:* Tuition, state resident: full-time $4551; part-time $252.86 per credit hour. Tuition, nonresident: full-time $9103; part-time $505.72 per credit hour. *Required fees:* $2453; $136.25 per credit hour. Tuition and fees vary according to course load and program. *Financial support:* Research assistantships, teaching assistantships with full tuition reimbursements, and unspecified assistantships available. Financial award application deadline: 4/1; financial award applicants required to submit FAFSA. *Unit head:* Dr. Carol Spradling, Director of School of Computer Science and Information Systems, 660-562-1588, Fax: 660-562-1963, E-mail: c_sprad@nwmissouri.edu. *Application contact:* Dr. Gregory Haddock, Dean of Graduate School, 660-562-1145, Fax: 660-562-1096, E-mail: gradsch@nwmissouri.edu.
Website: http://www.nwmissouri.edu/csis/

Nova Southeastern University, Abraham S. Fischler College of Education, Fort Lauderdale, FL 33314. Offers education (MS, Ed D, PhD, Ed S); instructional technology and distance education (MS); teaching and learning (MA). *Accreditation:* NCATE. *Program availability:* Part-time, evening/weekend, 100% online, blended/hybrid learning. *Faculty:* 94 full-time (58 women), 204 part-time/adjunct (145 women). *Students:* 1,513 full-time (1,199 women), 1,583 part-time (1,259 women); includes 2,373 minority (1,224 Black or African American, non-Hispanic/Latino; 5 American Indian or Alaska Native, non-Hispanic/Latino; 34 Asian, non-Hispanic/Latino; 1,057 Hispanic/Latino; 2 Native Hawaiian or other Pacific Islander, non-Hispanic/Latino; 51 Two or more races, non-Hispanic/Latino), 19 international. Average age 41. 1,753 applicants, 47% accepted, 581 enrolled. In 2017, 399 master's, 571 doctorates, 104 other advanced degrees awarded. *Degree requirements:* For master's, practicum, internship; for doctorate, thesis/dissertation; for Ed S, thesis, practicum, internship. *Entrance requirements:* For master's, MAT or GRE (for some programs), CLAST, PRAXIS I, CBEST, General Knowledge Test, teaching certification, minimum GPA of 2.5, verification of teaching, BS; for doctorate, MAT or GRE, master's degree, minimum cumulative GPA of 3.0; for Ed S, MAT or GRE, master's degree, teaching certificate, minimum GPA of 3.0. Additional exam requirements/recommendations for international students: Recommended—TOEFL (minimum score 550 paper-based; 79 iBT), IELTS (minimum score 6). *Application deadline:* Applications are processed on a rolling basis. Application fee: $50. Electronic applications accepted. *Expenses:* Contact institution. *Financial support:* In 2017–18, 67 students received support. Career-related internships or fieldwork and Federal Work-Study available. Support available to part-time students. Financial award application deadline: 4/15; financial award applicants required to submit FAFSA. *Faculty research:* STEM education, educational technology, principal training, quality of life. *Total annual research expenditures:* $50,000. *Unit head:* Dr. Kimberly Durham, Interim Dean, 954-262-8731, Fax: 954-262-3894, E-mail: durham@nova.edu. *Application contact:* Adriana Garay, Executive Director for Marketing, Recruitment and Admissions, 800-986-3223 Ext. 8500, E-mail: fserecruit@nova.edu.
Website: http://www.fischlerschool.nova.edu/

Ohio University, Graduate College, Gladys W. and David H. Patton College of Education and Human Services, Department of Educational Studies, Athens, OH 45701-2979. Offers computer education and technology (M Ed); educational administration (M Ed, Ed D); educational research and evaluation (M Ed, PhD); instructional technology (PhD). *Program availability:* Part-time, evening/weekend, online learning. *Degree requirements:* For master's, thesis or alternative; for doctorate, comprehensive exam, thesis/dissertation. *Entrance requirements:* For master's, GRE General Test (if GPA less than 2.9); for doctorate, GRE General Test, GRE Subject Test, minimum GPA of 2.9, work experience, 3 letters of reference, autobiography. Additional exam requirements/recommendations for international students: Required—TOEFL (minimum score 550 paper-based; 80 iBT) or IELTS (minimum score 6.5). Electronic applications accepted. *Faculty research:* Race, class and gender; computer programs; development and organization theory; evaluation/development of instruments, leadership.

Old Dominion University, Darden College of Education, Program in Elementary/Middle Education, Norfolk, VA 23529. Offers elementary education (Postbaccalaureate Certificate); instructional technology (MS Ed); library science (MS Ed). *Accreditation:* NCATE. *Program availability:* Part-time, evening/weekend, 100% online, blended/hybrid learning. *Faculty:* 21 full-time (19 women), 24 part-time/adjunct (22 women). *Students:* 134 full-time (127 women), 123 part-time (108 women); includes 60 minority (34 Black or African American, non-Hispanic/Latino; 1 American Indian or Alaska Native, non-Hispanic/Latino; 2 Asian, non-Hispanic/Latino; 15 Hispanic/Latino; 8 Two or more races, non-Hispanic/Latino). Average age 32. 213 applicants, 88% accepted, 172 enrolled. In 2017, 121 master's awarded. *Degree requirements:* For master's, comprehensive exam. *Entrance requirements:* For master's, GRE General Test or MAT; PRAXIS I, SAT or ACT, minimum GPA of 2.8. Additional exam requirements/recommendations for international students: Required—TOEFL (minimum score 600 paper-based). *Application deadline:* For fall admission, 6/1 priority date for domestic students; for winter admission, 11/1 priority date for domestic students; for spring admission, 3/1 priority date for domestic students. Applications are processed on a rolling basis. Application fee: $50. Electronic applications accepted. *Expenses:* Contact institution. *Financial support:* In 2017–18, 180 students received support. Unspecified assistantships available. Financial award application deadline: 2/15; financial award applicants required to submit FAFSA. *Faculty research:* Education pre-K to 6, school librarianship, reading, TESOL, literacy. *Unit head:* Dr. KaaVonia Hinton, Chair, Department of Teaching and Learning, 757-683-3284, Fax: 757-683-5862, E-mail: khintonj@odu.edu. *Application contact:* William Heffelfinger, Director of Graduate Admissions, 757-683-5554, Fax: 757-683-3255, E-mail: gradadmit@odu.edu.
Website: http://education.odu.edu/eci/

Old Dominion University, Darden College of Education, Program in Instructional Design and Technology, Norfolk, VA 23529. Offers PhD. *Program availability:* Part-time, evening/weekend, 100% online, blended/hybrid learning. *Faculty:* 3 full-time (2 women), 1 part-time/adjunct (0 women). *Students:* 3 full-time (all women), 40 part-time (29 women); includes 12 minority (8 Black or African American, non-Hispanic/Latino; 1

Asian, non-Hispanic/Latino; 1 Hispanic/Latino; 1 Native Hawaiian or other Pacific Islander, non-Hispanic/Latino; 1 Two or more races, non-Hispanic/Latino), 2 international. Average age 40. 30 applicants, 43% accepted, 13 enrolled. In 2017, 10 doctorates awarded. *Degree requirements:* For doctorate, comprehensive exam, thesis/dissertation. *Entrance requirements:* For doctorate, GRE, references, interview, essay of 500 words. Additional exam requirements/recommendations for international students: Required—TOEFL (minimum score 550 paper-based). *Application deadline:* For fall admission, 4/1 priority date for domestic students, 3/1 priority date for international students; for winter admission, 11/1 priority date for domestic students, 10/1 priority date for international students; for spring admission, 4/1 for domestic students, 2/1 priority date for international students. Applications are processed on a rolling basis. Application fee: $50. Electronic applications accepted. *Expenses:* Tuition, state resident: full-time $8928; part-time $496 per credit. Tuition, nonresident: full-time $22,482; part-time $1249 per credit. *Required fees:* $66 per semester. *Financial support:* In 2017–18, 4 students received support, including 3 research assistantships with full tuition reimbursements available (averaging $15,000 per year); career-related internships or fieldwork and unspecified assistantships also available. Financial award application deadline: 2/15; financial award applicants required to submit FAFSA. *Faculty research:* Instructional design, distance education, instructional strategies, human performance technology, simulation design. *Total annual research expenditures:* $2 million. *Unit head:* Dr. Jill E. Stefaniak, Graduate Program Director, 757-683-6696, Fax: 757-683-5227, E-mail: jstefani@odu.edu. *Application contact:* William Heffelfinger, Director of Graduate Admissions, 757-683-5554, Fax: 757-683-3255, E-mail: gradadmit@odu.edu. Website: http://education.odu.edu/eci/idt

Ottawa University, Graduate Studies-Arizona, Program in Education, Ottawa, KS 66067-3399. Offers community college counseling (MA); curriculum and instruction (MA); early childhood (MA); education intervention (MA); education leadership (MA); education technology (MA); Montessori early childhood education (MA); Montessori elementary education (MA); professional development (MA); school guidance counseling (MA); special education - cross categorical (MA). Programs offered in Mesa, Phoenix, Tempe and West Valley, AZ. *Accreditation:* NCATE. *Program availability:* Part-time. *Degree requirements:* For master's, thesis or alternative. *Entrance requirements:* For master's, minimum undergraduate GPA of 3.0, copy of current state certification or teaching license. Additional exam requirements/recommendations for international students: Required—TOEFL (minimum score 550 paper-based). Electronic applications accepted. *Expenses:* Contact institution.

Pace University, School of Education, New York, NY 10038. Offers adolescent education (MST), including biology, chemistry, earth science, English, foreign languages, mathematics, physics, social studies; childhood education (MST); early childhood development, learning and intervention (MST); educational technology studies (MS); inclusive adolescent education (MST), including biology, chemistry, earth science, English, foreign languages, mathematics, physics, social studies; integrated instruction for educational technology (Certificate); integrated instruction for literacy and technology (Certificate); literacy (MS Ed); special education (MS Ed). *Accreditation:* NCATE. *Program availability:* Part-time, evening/weekend, 100% online, blended/hybrid learning. *Faculty:* 19 full-time (13 women), 86 part-time/adjunct (49 women). *Students:* 91 full-time (76 women), 548 part-time (401 women); includes 247 minority (112 Black or African American, non-Hispanic/Latino; 2 American Indian or Alaska Native, non-Hispanic/Latino; 31 Asian, non-Hispanic/Latino; 93 Hispanic/Latino; 1 Native Hawaiian or other Pacific Islander, non-Hispanic/Latino; 8 Two or more races, non-Hispanic/Latino), 6 international. Average age 30. 188 applicants, 86% accepted, 114 enrolled. In 2017, 213 master's, 8 other advanced degrees awarded. *Degree requirements:* For master's and Certificate, certification exams. *Entrance requirements:* For master's, GRE (for initial certification programs only), teaching certificate (for MS Ed in literacy and special education programs only). Additional exam requirements/recommendations for international students: Required—TOEFL (minimum score 88 iBT), IELTS or PTE. *Application deadline:* For fall admission, 8/1 priority date for domestic students, 6/1 for international students; for spring admission, 12/1 priority date for domestic students, 10/1 for international students. Applications are processed on a rolling basis. Application fee: $70. Electronic applications accepted. *Expenses:* Contact institution. *Financial support:* In 2017–18, 17 students received support, including 17 research assistantships with partial tuition reimbursements available (averaging $6,020 per year); career-related internships or fieldwork, Federal Work-Study, scholarships/grants, and unspecified assistantships also available. Financial award application deadline: 9/1; financial award applicants required to submit FAFSA. *Faculty research:* STEM education, TESOL, teacher education, special education, language and literary development. *Total annual research expenditures:* $29,706. *Unit head:* Dr. Xiao-Lei Wang, Dean, School of Education, 914-773-3876, E-mail: xwang@pace.edu. *Application contact:* Susan Ford-Goldschein, Director of Graduate Admissions, 212-346-1531, Fax: 212-346-1585, E-mail: graduateadmission@pace.edu. Website: http://www.pace.edu/school-of-education

Penn State University Park, Graduate School, College of Education, Department of Learning and Performance Systems, University Park, PA 16802. Offers learning, design, and technology (M Ed, MS, PhD, Certificate); lifelong learning and adult education (M Ed, D Ed, PhD, Certificate); workforce education and development (M Ed, MS, PhD). *Unit head:* Dr. David H. Monk, Dean, 814-865-2523, Fax: 814-865-0555. *Application contact:* Lori Hawn, Director, Graduate Student Services, 814-865-1795, Fax: 814-863-4627, E-mail: l-gswww@lists.psu.edu. Website: http://ed.psu.edu/lps/dept-lps

Pepperdine University, Graduate School of Education and Psychology, Division of Education, Los Angeles, CA 90263. Offers administration and preliminary administrative services (MS); education (MA); educational leadership, administration, and policy (Ed D); global leadership and change (PhD); learning technologies (MA, Ed D); organizational leadership (Ed D); social entrepreneurship and change (MA); teaching (MA); teaching: TESOL (MA). *Program availability:* Part-time, evening/weekend, blended/hybrid learning. *Students:* 214 full-time (139 women), 327 part-time (216 women); includes 248 minority (113 Black or African American, non-Hispanic/Latino; 2 American Indian or Alaska Native, non-Hispanic/Latino; 48 Asian, non-Hispanic/Latino; 61 Hispanic/Latino; 6 Native Hawaiian or other Pacific Islander, non-Hispanic/Latino; 18 Two or more races, non-Hispanic/Latino), 49 international. Average age 39. 410 applicants, 91% accepted, 160 enrolled. In 2017, 151 master's, 88 doctorates awarded. *Degree requirements:* For doctorate, thesis/dissertation. *Entrance requirements:* For master's, GRE General Test; for doctorate, GRE General Test, MAT. Additional exam requirements/recommendations for international students: Required—TOEFL. *Application deadline:* Applications are processed on a rolling basis. Application fee: $55. Electronic applications accepted. *Expenses:* Contact institution. *Financial support:* Research assistantships, teaching assistantships, career-related internships or fieldwork, institutionally sponsored loans, and scholarships/grants available. Support available to part-time students. Financial award application deadline: 7/1; financial award applicants required to submit FAFSA. *Unit head:* Dr. Martine Jago, Associate Dean, Education Division, 310-568-2828, E-mail: martine.jago@pepperdine.edu. *Application contact:* Chris Costa, Director of Enrollment, 310-568-2850, E-mail: chris.costa@pepperdine.edu. Website: http://gsep.pepperdine.edu/masters-education/

Piedmont College, School of Education, Demorest, GA 30535. Offers art education (MA, MAT); curriculum and instruction (Ed D, Ed S); early childhood education (MA, MAT); instructional technology (MA); middle grades education (MA, MAT); music education (MA, MAT); secondary education (MA, MAT); special education (MA, MAT). *Program availability:* Part-time, evening/weekend. *Students:* 341 full-time (268 women), 682 part-time (571 women); includes 182 minority (136 Black or African American, non-Hispanic/Latino; 2 American Indian or Alaska Native, non-Hispanic/Latino; 11 Asian, non-Hispanic/Latino; 32 Hispanic/Latino; 1 Two or more races, non-Hispanic/Latino). Average age 37. 333 applicants, 77% accepted, 103 enrolled. In 2017, 292 master's, 9 doctorates, 318 other advanced degrees awarded. *Degree requirements:* For master's, thesis, field experience in the classroom teaching; for doctorate, thesis/dissertation. *Entrance requirements:* For master's, GRE General Test, MAT; for Ed S, minimum graduate GPA of 3.5, valid teaching certificate. Additional exam requirements/recommendations for international students: Required—TOEFL (minimum score 550 paper-based). *Application deadline:* For fall admission, 7/15 for domestic students; for spring admission, 12/1 for domestic students. Applications are processed on a rolling basis. Electronic applications accepted. *Expenses:* Tuition: Full-time $9360; part-time $520 per credit hour. *Required fees:* $200; $200 per year. $100 per term. *Financial support:* Career-related internships or fieldwork, Federal Work-Study, and unspecified assistantships available. Support available to part-time students. Financial award applicants required to submit FAFSA. *Unit head:* Dr. Don Gnecco, Dean, 706-778-3000 Ext. 1201, Fax: 706-776-9608, E-mail: dgnecco@piedmont.edu. *Application contact:* Kathleen Carter, Director of Graduate Enrollment Management, 706-778-8500 Ext. 1181, Fax: 706-778-0150, E-mail: kanderson@piedmont.edu.

Pittsburg State University, Graduate School, College of Education, Department of Teaching and Leadership, Program in Educational Technology, Pittsburg, KS 66762. Offers MS. *Accreditation:* NCATE. *Program availability:* Part-time, online only, 100% online. *Students:* 47. In 2017, 58 master's awarded. *Degree requirements:* For master's, thesis or alternative. *Entrance requirements:* For master's, PPST. Additional exam requirements/recommendations for international students: Required—TOEFL (minimum score 520 paper-based; 68 iBT), IELTS (minimum score 6), PTE (minimum score 47). *Application deadline:* For fall admission, 7/15 for domestic students, 6/1 for international students; for spring admission, 12/15 for domestic students, 10/15 for international students; for summer admission, 5/15 for domestic students, 4/1 for international students. Applications are processed on a rolling basis. Application fee: $35 ($60 for international students). Electronic applications accepted. *Expenses:* Contact institution. *Financial support:* In 2017–18, teaching assistantships (averaging $5,000 per year) were awarded; career-related internships or fieldwork, Federal Work-Study, and unspecified assistantships also available. Financial award application deadline: 2/1; financial award applicants required to submit FAFSA. *Unit head:* Dr. Brenda Roberts, Program Coordinator, 620-235-4498, Fax: 620-235-4520, E-mail: broberts@pittstate.edu. *Application contact:* Lisa Allen, Assistant Director of Graduate and Continuing Studies, 620-235-4218, Fax: 620-235-4219, E-mail: lallen@pittstate.edu.

Plymouth State University, College of Graduate Studies, Graduate Studies in Education, Program in Secondary Education, Plymouth, NH 03264-1595. Offers curriculum and instruction (M Ed); language education (M Ed); library media (M Ed); physical education (M Ed); social studies education (M Ed); special education (M Ed). *Program availability:* Part-time, evening/weekend. *Entrance requirements:* For master's, MAT.

Post University, Program in Education, Waterbury, CT 06723-2540. Offers curriculum and instruction (M Ed); education (M Ed); educational technology (M Ed); higher education administration (MS); learning design and technology (M Ed); online teaching (M Ed); teaching English to speakers of other languages (TESOL) (M Ed). *Program availability:* Online learning. *Entrance requirements:* For master's, resume. *Expenses:* Tuition: Part-time $730 per credit hour. Part-time tuition and fees vary according to degree level and program. *Application contact:* Veronica Montalvo, Vice President, Online Education Enrollment Management and Admissions, 203-596-6164, E-mail: vmontalvo@post.edu.

Purdue University, Graduate School, College of Education, Department of Curriculum and Instruction, West Lafayette, IN 47907. Offers agricultural and extension education (MS, MS Ed, PhD, Ed S); art education (PhD); career and technical education (MS Ed, PhD, Ed S); curriculum studies (MS Ed, PhD, Ed S); educational technology (MS Ed, PhD, Ed S); elementary education (MS Ed); family and consumer sciences education (MS Ed, PhD, Ed S); foreign language education (MS Ed, PhD, Ed S); industrial technology (PhD, Ed S); language arts (MS Ed, PhD, Ed S); literacy (MS Ed, PhD, Ed S); mathematics education (MS, MS Ed, PhD, Ed S); science education (MS, MS Ed, PhD, Ed S); social studies education (MS Ed, PhD, Ed S). *Accreditation:* NCATE. *Program availability:* Part-time, evening/weekend. *Faculty:* 37 full-time (27 women), 1 (woman) part-time/adjunct. *Students:* 78 full-time (50 women), 286 part-time (195 women); includes 68 minority (25 Black or African American, non-Hispanic/Latino; 3 American Indian or Alaska Native, non-Hispanic/Latino; 10 Asian, non-Hispanic/Latino; 22 Hispanic/Latino; 1 Native Hawaiian or other Pacific Islander, non-Hispanic/Latino; 7 Two or more races, non-Hispanic/Latino), 44 international. Average age 36. 150 applicants, 79% accepted, 73 enrolled. In 2017, 107 master's, 20 doctorates, 2 other advanced degrees awarded. *Degree requirements:* For master's, thesis optional; for doctorate, thesis/dissertation, oral and written exams; for Ed S, oral presentation, project. *Entrance requirements:* For master's, GRE General Test (if undergraduate GPA is below 3.0), minimum undergraduate GPA of 3.0 or equivalent; for doctorate, GRE General Test (minimum combined verbal and quantitative score of 1000, 300 for new scoring), minimum undergraduate GPA of 3.0 or equivalent; master's degree with minimum GPA of 3.0 or equivalent; for Ed S, GRE General Test (minimum combined verbal and quantitative score of 1000, 300 for new scoring), minimum undergraduate GPA of 3.0 or equivalent; master's degree. Additional exam requirements/recommendations for international students: Required—TOEFL (minimum score 550 paper-based; 77 iBT). *Application deadline:* For fall admission, 12/15 for domestic students, 3/1 for international students; for spring admission, 9/15 for domestic students, 8/1 for international students. Application fee: $60 ($75 for international students). Electronic applications accepted. *Financial support:* Fellowships with full tuition reimbursements, research assistantships with full tuition reimbursements, teaching assistantships with full tuition reimbursements, career-related internships or fieldwork, and tuition waivers (full) available. Support available to part-time students. Financial award application deadline: 3/1; financial award applicants required to submit FAFSA. *Faculty research:* Literacy acquisition and development, teacher beliefs and knowledge, recruitment and retention of underrepresented students, economic education, literacy discourse. *Unit head:* Janet M. Alsup, Head, 765-494-9667, E-mail: alsupj@purdue.edu. *Application contact:* Heather Brinkman, Graduate Contact, 765-494-2345, E-mail: hbrinkma@purdue.edu. Website: http://www.edci.purdue.edu/

Purdue University Global, School of Teacher Education, Davenport, IA 52807. Offers education (M Ed); secondary education (M Ed); teaching and learning (MA); teaching literacy and language: grades 6-12 (MA); teaching literacy and language: grades K-6 (MA); teaching mathematics: grades 6-8 (MA); teaching mathematics: grades 9-12 (MA); teaching mathematics: grades K-5 (MA); teaching science: grades 6-12 (MA);

teaching science: grades K-6 (MA); teaching students with special needs (MA); teaching with technology (MA). *Program availability:* Part-time, evening/weekend, online learning. *Entrance requirements:* Additional exam requirements/recommendations for international students: Required—TOEFL (minimum score 550 paper-based; 80 iBT).

Purdue University Northwest, Graduate Studies Office, School of Education, Program in Instructional Technology, Hammond, IN 46323-2094. Offers MS Ed. *Entrance requirements:* Additional exam requirements/recommendations for international students: Required—TOEFL.

Quinnipiac University, School of Education, Program in Instructional Design, Hamden, CT 06518-1940. Offers MS. *Program availability:* Part-time-only, evening/weekend, online only, 100% online. *Faculty:* 2 full-time (both women), 2 part-time/adjunct (0 women). *Students:* 1 (woman) full-time, 45 part-time (37 women); includes 7 minority (1 Black or African American, non-Hispanic/Latino; 4 Hispanic/Latino; 2 Two or more races, non-Hispanic/Latino). 16 applicants, 81% accepted, 11 enrolled. In 2017, 7 master's awarded. *Application deadline:* For fall admission, 8/15 for domestic students; for spring admission, 1/15 for domestic students. Applications are processed on a rolling basis. Application fee: $45. Electronic applications accepted. *Expenses:* Contact institution. *Financial support:* Federal Work-Study and unspecified assistantships available. Financial award application deadline: 6/1; financial award applicants required to submit FAFSA. *Unit head:* Ruth Schwartz, Director, 203-582-8419, E-mail: ruth.schwartz@qu.edu. *Application contact:* Quinnipiac University Online Admissions, 800-462-1944, Fax: 203-582-3443, E-mail: quonlineadmissions@qu.edu.
Website: https://quonline.quinnipiac.edu/online-programs/online-graduate-programs/ms-in-instructional-design/

Ramapo College of New Jersey, Master of Science in Educational Technology Program, Mahwah, NJ 07430-1680. Offers MS. *Program availability:* Part-time, evening/weekend. *Faculty:* 10 part-time/adjunct (4 women). *Students:* 2 full-time (both women), 124 part-time (95 women); includes 18 minority (3 Black or African American, non-Hispanic/Latino; 1 Asian, non-Hispanic/Latino; 14 Hispanic/Latino), 3 international. Average age 34. 50 applicants, 86% accepted, 29 enrolled. In 2017, 49 master's awarded. *Degree requirements:* For master's, capstone course. *Entrance requirements:* For master's, official transcript of baccalaureate degree from accredited institution with minimum recommended GPA of 3.0; personal statement; letter of recommendation; resume. Additional exam requirements/recommendations for international students: Required—TOEFL (minimum score 550 paper-based; 79 iBT); Recommended—IELTS (minimum score 6). *Application deadline:* For fall admission, 5/1 for domestic and international students; for spring admission, 12/1 for domestic and international students. Applications are processed on a rolling basis. Application fee: $65. Electronic applications accepted. *Expenses:* $690.60 per credit tuition, $56.95 per credit fees. *Financial support:* Career-related internships or fieldwork available. Financial award application deadline: 3/1; financial award applicants required to submit FAFSA. *Faculty research:* Integrating technology in the curriculum of K-12 learning environment. *Unit head:* Dr. Richard Russo, Director of the Master in Educational Technology Program, 201-684-7899, Fax: 201-684-6699, E-mail: rrusso@ramapo.edu. *Application contact:* M. Joyce Wilson, Administrative Assistant, 201-684-7721, Fax: 201-684-6699, E-mail: jwilson@ramapo.edu.
Website: http://www.ramapo.edu/mset/

Regent University, Graduate School, School of Education, Virginia Beach, VA 23464-9800. Offers education (M Ed, Ed D, PhD), including adult education (Ed D, PhD, Ed S), advanced educational leadership (Ed D, PhD, Ed S), character education (Ed D, PhD, Ed S), Christian education leadership (Ed D, PhD, Ed S), Christian school administration (M Ed), curriculum and instruction (Ed D, PhD, Ed S), curriculum and instruction - adult education (M Ed), curriculum and instruction - Christian school (M Ed), curriculum and instruction - gifted and talented (M Ed), curriculum and instruction - STEM education (M Ed), curriculum and instruction - teacher leader (M Ed), discipleship for ministry (M Ed), educational leadership (M Ed), educational psychology (Ed D, PhD, Ed S), educational technology and online learning (Ed D, PhD, Ed S), elementary education (M Ed), exceptional education executive leadership (Ed D, PhD, Ed S), higher education (Ed D, PhD, Ed S), higher education leadership and management (Ed D, PhD, Ed S), instructional design and technology (M Ed), K-12 school leadership (Ed D, PhD, Ed S), K-12 special education (M Ed), leadership in mathematics education (M Ed), reading specialist (M Ed), special education (Ed D, PhD, Ed S), student affairs (M Ed), TESOL - adult education (M Ed), TESOL - K-12 (M Ed); educational specialist (Ed S), including adult education (Ed D, PhD, Ed S), advanced educational leadership (Ed D, PhD, Ed S), character education (Ed D, PhD, Ed S), Christian education leadership (Ed D, PhD, Ed S), curriculum and instruction (Ed D, PhD, Ed S), educational psychology (Ed D, PhD, Ed S), educational technology and online learning (Ed D, PhD, Ed S), exceptional education executive leadership (Ed D, PhD, Ed S), higher education (Ed D, PhD, Ed S), higher education leadership and management (Ed D, PhD, Ed S), K-12 school leadership (Ed D, PhD, Ed S), special education (Ed D, PhD, Ed S). *Accreditation:* TEAC. *Program availability:* Part-time, evening/weekend, 100% online, blended/hybrid learning. *Faculty:* 22 full-time (10 women), 44 part-time/adjunct (32 women). *Students:* 80 full-time (59 women), 945 part-time (750 women); includes 432 minority (352 Black or African American, non-Hispanic/Latino; 4 American Indian or Alaska Native, non-Hispanic/Latino; 14 Asian, non-Hispanic/Latino; 43 Hispanic/Latino; 19 Two or more races, non-Hispanic/Latino), 12 international. Average age 40. 1,125 applicants, 49% accepted, 436 enrolled. In 2017, 316 master's, 24 doctorates awarded. *Degree requirements:* For master's, thesis or alternative; for doctorate, comprehensive exam, thesis/dissertation. *Entrance requirements:* For master's, Virginia Communication and Literacy Assessment (VCLA), PRAXIS, college transcripts, writing sample, interview; for doctorate, GRE, writing sample, resume, transcripts, interview. Additional exam requirements/recommendations for international students: Required—TOEFL (minimum score 577 paper-based). *Application deadline:* For fall admission, 4/1 priority date for domestic students; for spring admission, 10/15 priority date for domestic students. Applications are processed on a rolling basis. Application fee: $50. Electronic applications accepted. *Expenses:* Contact institution. *Financial support:* In 2017–18, 669 students received support, including 1 fellowship (averaging $10,000 per year); career-related internships or fieldwork, scholarships/grants, and unspecified assistantships also available. Support available to part-time students. *Faculty research:* Christian school administration, curriculum and instruction, educational technology and online learning, higher education, special education. *Unit head:* Dr. Donald Finn, Dean, 757-352-4278, Fax: 757-352-4318, E-mail: dfinn@regent.edu. *Application contact:* Heidi Cece, Assistant Vice President of Enrollment Management, 800-373-5504, Fax: 757-352-4381, E-mail: admissions@regent.edu.
Website: https://www.regent.edu/school-of-education/

Rockford University, Graduate Studies, Department of Education, Program in Instructional Strategies, Rockford, IL 61108-2393. Offers MAT. *Program availability:* Part-time, evening/weekend, online learning. *Degree requirements:* For master's, professional portfolio. *Entrance requirements:* For master's, GRE General Test, official transcripts, three letter of recommendation forms, essay. Additional exam requirements/recommendations for international students: Required—TOEFL (minimum score 550 paper-based; 79 iBT). Electronic applications accepted. *Expenses:* Contact institution.

Rowan University, Graduate School, College of Education, Department of Science, Technology, Engineering, Art and Math Education, Glassboro, NJ 08028-1701. Offers educational technology (CGS); STEM education (MA). *Program availability:* Part-time, evening/weekend. *Degree requirements:* For master's, thesis. *Entrance requirements:* For master's, GRE General Test. Additional exam requirements/recommendations for international students: Required—TOEFL. Electronic applications accepted. *Expenses:* Tuition, state resident: full-time $15,020; part-time $751 per semester hour. Tuition, nonresident: full-time $15,020; part-time $751 per semester hour. *Required fees:* $3158; $157.90 per semester hour. Tuition and fees vary according to course load, campus/location and program.

Saginaw Valley State University, College of Education, Program in Instructional Technology, University Center, MI 48710. Offers MA. *Program availability:* Part-time, evening/weekend. *Students:* 19 part-time (11 women); includes 2 minority (1 Hispanic/Latino; 1 Two or more races, non-Hispanic/Latino). Average age 33. 4 applicants, 100% accepted, 3 enrolled. In 2017, 13 master's awarded. *Degree requirements:* For master's, capstone course or thesis. *Entrance requirements:* For master's, minimum GPA of 3.0. Additional exam requirements/recommendations for international students: Required—TOEFL (minimum score 550 paper-based; 79 iBT). *Application deadline:* For fall admission, 7/15 for international students; for winter admission, 11/15 for international students; for spring admission, 4/15 for international students. Applications are processed on a rolling basis. Application fee: $30 ($90 for international students). Electronic applications accepted. *Expenses:* Tuition, state resident: full-time $10,156; part-time $564.20 per credit hour. Tuition, nonresident: full-time $19,336; part-time $1074.20 per credit hour. *Required fees:* $263; $14.60 per credit hour. Tuition and fees vary according to degree level and program. *Financial support:* Federal Work-Study and scholarships/grants available. Support available to part-time students. Financial award applicants required to submit FAFSA. *Unit head:* Dr. Carolyn Gilbreath, Associate Professor of Teaching Education, 989-749-4772, Fax: 989-964-4563, E-mail: cagilbre@svsu.edu. *Application contact:* Jenna Briggs, Director, Graduate and International Admissions, 989-964-6096, Fax: 989-964-2788, E-mail: gradadm@svsu.edu.

St. Cloud State University, School of Graduate Studies, School of Education, Center for Information Media, St. Cloud, MN 56301-4498. Offers MS. *Program availability:* Part-time, evening/weekend, online learning. *Degree requirements:* For master's, comprehensive exam, thesis or alternative. *Entrance requirements:* For master's, minimum overall GPA of 2.75 in previous undergraduate and graduate records or in last half of undergraduate work. Additional exam requirements/recommendations for international students: Required—Michigan English Language Assessment Battery; Recommended—TOEFL (minimum score 550 paper-based; 79 iBT), IELTS (minimum score 6.5). Electronic applications accepted.

St. John Fisher College, Ralph C. Wilson Jr. School of Education, Program in Library Media, Rochester, NY 14618-3597. Offers MS. *Program availability:* Evening/weekend, online only, 100% online. *Faculty:* 1 (woman) full-time, 1 (woman) part-time/adjunct. *Students:* 17 full-time (all women), 2 part-time (both women); includes 2 minority (both Black or African American, non-Hispanic/Latino). Average age 35. 24 applicants, 92% accepted, 19 enrolled. In 2017, 1 master's awarded. *Degree requirements:* For master's, practicum. *Entrance requirements:* For master's, teacher certification, 2 letters of recommendation, personal statement, current resume. Additional exam requirements/recommendations for international students: Required—TOEFL (minimum score 575 paper-based; 80 iBT). *Application deadline:* Applications are processed on a rolling basis. Application fee: $30. Electronic applications accepted. *Expenses:* Contact institution. *Financial support:* Scholarships/grants available. Financial award applicants required to submit FAFSA. *Unit head:* Dr. Michael Wischnowski, Dean, 585-385-7361, E-mail: mwischnowski@sjfc.edu. *Application contact:* Michelle Gosier, Associate Director of Transfer and Graduate Admissions, 585-385-8064, E-mail: mgosier@sjfc.edu.
Website: https://www.sjfc.edu/graduate-programs/ms-in-library-media/

Saint Leo University, Graduate Studies in Education, Saint Leo, FL 33574-6665. Offers educational leadership (M Ed), including Catholic school administration; exceptional student education (M Ed); instructional design (MS, Certificate); instructional leadership (M Ed); reading (M Ed, Certificate); school leadership (Ed S). *Program availability:* Part-time, evening/weekend, online only, 100% online. *Faculty:* 8 full-time (all women), 18 part-time/adjunct (11 women). *Students:* 1 (woman) full-time, 360 part-time (282 women); includes 95 minority (56 Black or African American, non-Hispanic/Latino; 1 American Indian or Alaska Native, non-Hispanic/Latino; 1 Asian, non-Hispanic/Latino; 31 Hispanic/Latino; 6 Two or more races, non-Hispanic/Latino), 1 international. Average age 37. 214 applicants, 69% accepted, 125 enrolled. In 2017, 158 master's, 5 other advanced degrees awarded. *Degree requirements:* For master's, appropriate State of Florida certification tests, internship. *Entrance requirements:* For master's, GRE (minimum score of 1000), MAT (minimum score of 410), or minimum undergraduate GPA of 3.0 in final 2 years, official transcripts, current resumé, 2 professional recommendations, personal statement, bachelor's degree from regionally-accredited university, valid professional teaching certificate; for other advanced degree, valid professional teaching certificate (for Ed S). Additional exam requirements/recommendations for international students: Required—TOEFL (minimum score 550 paper-based; 78 iBT). *Application deadline:* For fall admission, 7/1 priority date for domestic students, 7/1 for international students; for winter admission, 7/1 for international students; for spring admission, 11/1 priority date for domestic students. Applications are processed on a rolling basis. Application fee: $80. Electronic applications accepted. *Expenses:* $480 per credit (for M Ed), $670 per credit (for Ed S). *Financial support:* In 2017–18, 17 students received support. Career-related internships or fieldwork, scholarships/grants, health care benefits, and tuition remission for Saint Leo employees and their dependents available. Financial award application deadline: 3/1; financial award applicants required to submit FAFSA. *Faculty research:* Impact of partnerships with K-12 school and university programs. *Unit head:* Dr. Fern Aefsky, Director of Graduate Studies in Education, 352-588-8309, Fax: 352-588-8861, E-mail: kara.winkler@saintleo.edu. *Application contact:* Mark Russum, Assistant Vice President, Enrollment, 800-707-8846, Fax: 352-588-7873, E-mail: grad.admissions@saintleo.edu.
Website: https://www.saintleo.edu/education-master-degree

Saint Mary's University of Minnesota, Schools of Graduate and Professional Programs, Graduate School of Education, Learning Design and Technology Program, Winona, MN 55987-1399. Offers M Ed. *Program availability:* Online learning. *Unit head:* Nancy Van Erp, Associate Program Director, 320-260-5116, E-mail: nvanerp@smumn.edu. *Application contact:* James Callinan, Director of Admissions for Graduate and Professional Programs, 612-728-5158, Fax: 612-728-5121, E-mail: jcallina@smumn.edu.
Website: http://www.smumn.edu/graduate-home/areas-of-study/graduate-school-of-education/med-in-learning-design-technology

St. Thomas University, School of Leadership Studies, Institute for Education, Miami Gardens, FL 33054-6459. Offers earth/space science (Certificate); educational administration (MS, Certificate); educational leadership (Ed D); elementary education (MS); ESOL (Certificate); gifted education (Certificate); instructional technology (MS, Certificate); professional/studies (Certificate); reading (MS, Certificate); special education (MS). *Program availability:* Part-time, evening/weekend. *Degree* *requirements:* For master's, comprehensive exam; for doctorate, comprehensive exam, thesis/dissertation. *Entrance requirements:* For master's, interview, minimum GPA of 3.0 or GRE; for doctorate, GRE or MAT. Additional exam requirements/recommendations for international students: Required—TOEFL (minimum score 550 paper-based; 79 iBT). Electronic applications accepted.

Saint Vincent College, Program in Education, Latrobe, PA 15650-2690. Offers curriculum and instruction (MS); instructional design and technology (MS); school administration and supervision (MS); special education (MS). *Program availability:* Part-time, evening/weekend. *Degree requirements:* For master's, comprehensive exam. *Entrance requirements:* For master's, GRE (if undergraduate GPA less than 3.0). Additional exam requirements/recommendations for international students: Required—TOEFL (minimum score 550 paper-based). *Faculty research:* Assessment and instructional technology.

Saint Xavier University, Graduate Studies, School of Education, Chicago, IL 60655-3105. Offers counseling (MA); curriculum and instruction (MA); early childhood education (MA); educational administration (MA); elementary education (MA); individualized studies (MA), including educational technology, English as a second language (ESL), ISTEM (integrative science, technology, engineering, and math), science education; music education (MA); reading (MA); secondary education (MA); Spanish education (MA); special education (MA); teaching and leadership (MA). *Accreditation:* NCATE. *Program availability:* Part-time, evening/weekend. *Degree requirements:* For master's, thesis or project. *Entrance requirements:* For master's, minimum GPA of 3.0. *Expenses:* Contact institution.

Salem State University, School of Graduate Studies, Program in Library Media Studies, Salem, MA 01970-5353. Offers M Ed. *Accreditation:* NCATE. *Program availability:* Part-time, evening/weekend. *Entrance requirements:* For master's, GRE or MAT. Additional exam requirements/recommendations for international students: Required—TOEFL (minimum score 550 paper-based; 80 iBT) or IELTS (minimum score 5.5).

Samford University, Orlean Beeson School of Education, Birmingham, AL 35229. Offers educational leadership (MSE, Ed D); elementary education (MS Ed, MSE); gifted (MSE); instructional design and technology (MSE); instructional leadership (MSE, Ed S); secondary education (MSE); special education (MSE). *Accreditation:* NCATE. *Program availability:* Part-time, evening/weekend, 100% online, blended/hybrid learning. *Faculty:* 11 full-time (7 women), 22 part-time/adjunct (12 women). *Students:* 206 full-time (144 women), 102 part-time (75 women); includes 124 minority (113 Black or African American, non-Hispanic/Latino; 3 American Indian or Alaska Native, non-Hispanic/Latino; 3 Asian, non-Hispanic/Latino; 2 Hispanic/Latino; 3 Two or more races, non-Hispanic/Latino), 1 international. Average age 37. 134 applicants, 84% accepted, 76 enrolled. In 2017, 79 master's, 34 doctorates, 21 other advanced degrees awarded. *Degree requirements:* For master's and Ed S, comprehensive exam; for doctorate, comprehensive exam, thesis/dissertation. *Entrance requirements:* For master's, GRE, MAT, PRAXIS II, interview, transcripts, essay, recommendations, teaching certification; for doctorate, resume, transcripts, interview, essay; for Ed S, teaching certification, transcripts, essay, interview. Additional exam requirements/recommendations for international students: Required—TOEFL (minimum score 90 iBT), IELTS (minimum score 6.5). *Application deadline:* For fall admission, 7/15 for domestic and international students; for winter admission, 11/15 for domestic and international students; for spring admission, 11/15 for domestic and international students; for summer admission, 4/15 for domestic and international students. Application fee: $35. Electronic applications accepted. *Expenses:* $813 per credit hour, $100 School of Education fee, $175 technology fee. *Financial support:* In 2017–18, 220 students received support. Scholarships/grants and unspecified assistantships available. Financial award application deadline: 2/15; financial award applicants required to submit FAFSA. *Faculty research:* Principal leadership's and teacher organizational commitment mentoring, professional development, and middle grades leadership coaching and administrator effectiveness character development programs in schools teacher efficacy related STEM and professional growth. *Unit head:* Dr. Bonnie Rabe, Interim Dean, 205-726-2565, E-mail: brabe@samford.edu. *Application contact:* Brooke Karr, Graduate Admissions Office Coordinator, 205-729-2783, Fax: 205-726-4233, E-mail: kbgilrea@samford.edu.
Website: http://www.samford.edu/education/

San Diego State University, Graduate and Research Affairs, College of Education, Department of Educational Technology, San Diego, CA 92182. Offers educational technology (MA); educational technology and teaching and learning (Ed D). *Accreditation:* NCATE. *Program availability:* Evening/weekend. *Entrance requirements:* For master's, GRE General Test, letters of reference. Additional exam requirements/recommendations for international students: Required—TOEFL. Electronic applications accepted.

San Francisco State University, Division of Graduate Studies, College of Education, Department of Equity, Leadership Studies, and Instructional Technologies, Program in Instructional Technologies, San Francisco, CA 94132-1722. Offers MA. *Unit head:* Dr. Doris Flowers, Chair, 415-338-2614, Fax: 415-338-0568, E-mail: dflowers@sfsu.edu. *Application contact:* Dr. Patricia Donohue, Program Coordinator, 415-338-7833, Fax: 415-338-0568, E-mail: pdonohue@sfsu.edu.
Website: http://elsit.sfsu.edu/

Seattle Pacific University, Program in Digital Education Leadership, Seattle, WA 98119-1997. Offers M Ed. *Students:* 12 part-time (9 women); includes 2 minority (1 American Indian or Alaska Native, non-Hispanic/Latino; 1 Hispanic/Latino). Average age 37. 10 applicants, 80% accepted, 8 enrolled. In 2017, 4 master's awarded. *Application deadline:* For fall admission, 9/8 for domestic students. *Unit head:* Rick Eigenbrood, Dean, 206-281-2710, E-mail: eigend@spu.edu. *Application contact:* Graduate Center, 206-281-2091.
Website: http://spu.edu/academics/school-of-education/graduate-programs/masters-programs/digital-education

Seton Hall University, College of Education and Human Services, Department of Educational Studies, South Orange, NJ 07079-2697. Offers instructional design and technology (MA); special education (MA). *Program availability:* Part-time, evening/weekend, blended/hybrid learning. *Degree requirements:* For master's, comprehensive exam, capstone project. *Entrance requirements:* For master's, GRE or MAT, PRAXIS (for certification candidates), minimum GPA of 2.75. Electronic applications accepted. *Expenses:* Contact institution. *Faculty research:* Special education, applied behavioral analysis, educational technology.

Seton Hill University, Program in Innovative Instruction, Greensburg, PA 15601. Offers M Ed. *Program availability:* Part-time, evening/weekend. *Faculty:* 3 full-time (2 women), 3 part-time/adjunct (2 women). *Students:* 2 full-time (0 women), 18 part-time (14 women); includes 2 minority (1 Black or African American, non-Hispanic/Latino; 1 Hispanic/Latino). Average age 34. 21 applicants, 48% accepted, 9 enrolled. In 2017, 5 master's awarded. *Entrance requirements:* For master's, minimum GPA of 3.0. Additional exam requirements/recommendations for international students: Required—TOEFL. *Application deadline:* Applications are processed on a rolling basis. Application fee: $35. Electronic applications accepted. *Expenses: Tuition:* Part-time $734 per credit.

Tuition and fees vary according to class time, course level, course load and program. *Financial support:* In 2017–18, 7 students received support. Scholarships/grants, tuition waivers (partial), and unspecified assistantships available. Support available to part-time students. Financial award application deadline: 8/15; financial award applicants required to submit FAFSA. *Faculty research:* Use of technology for teaching and learning, problem-based theories in education and instruction. *Unit head:* E-mail: gadmit@setonhill.edu.
Website: https://www.setonhill.edu/academics/graduate-programs/innovative-instruction/

Simon Fraser University, Office of Graduate Studies and Postdoctoral Fellows, Faculty of Education, Program in Educational Technology and Learning Design, Burnaby, BC V5A 1S6, Canada. Offers M Ed, MA, PhD. *Program availability:* Part-time, evening/weekend. *Degree requirements:* For master's, comprehensive exam (for some programs), thesis (for some programs); for doctorate, comprehensive exam, thesis/dissertation. *Entrance requirements:* For master's, minimum GPA of 3.0 (on scale of 4.33) or 3.33 based on last 60 credits of undergraduate courses; for doctorate, minimum GPA of 3.5 (on scale of 4.33). Additional exam requirements/recommendations for international students: Recommended—TOEFL (minimum score 580 paper-based; 93 iBT), IELTS (minimum score 7), TWE (minimum score 5). *Faculty research:* Integration of technological applications in post-secondary education, problems in learning and teaching science, gaming and simulation for learning, adaptive software for researching and promoting self-regulated learning, design and use of online environments for learning.

Slippery Rock University of Pennsylvania, Graduate Studies (Recruitment), College of Education, Department of Special Education, Slippery Rock, PA 16057-1383. Offers autism (M Ed); master teacher (M Ed), including birth to grade 8, grades 7 to 12; special education (Ed D); supervision (M Ed); technology for online instruction (M Ed). *Accreditation:* NCATE. *Program availability:* Part-time, evening/weekend, 100% online. *Degree requirements:* For master's, thesis optional. *Entrance requirements:* For master's, minimum GPA of 3.0, official transcripts, teaching certification. Additional exam requirements/recommendations for international students: Required—TOEFL (minimum score 550 paper-based; 80 iBT). Electronic applications accepted. *Expenses:* Contact institution.

Southern Illinois University Edwardsville, Graduate School, School of Education, Health, and Human Behavior, Department of Educational Leadership, Program in Instructional Technology, Edwardsville, IL 62026. Offers MS Ed. *Accreditation:* NCATE. *Program availability:* Part-time, evening/weekend. *Degree requirements:* For master's, thesis or alternative, portfolio. *Entrance requirements:* Additional exam requirements/recommendations for international students: Required—TOEFL (minimum score 550 paper-based; 79 iBT), IELTS (minimum score 6.5). Electronic applications accepted.

Southern Illinois University Edwardsville, Graduate School, School of Education, Health, and Human Behavior, Department of Educational Leadership, Program in Web-Based Learning, Edwardsville, IL 62026. Offers Postbaccalaureate Certificate. *Program availability:* Part-time. *Entrance requirements:* Additional exam requirements/recommendations for international students: Required—TOEFL (minimum score 550 paper-based; 79 iBT), IELTS (minimum score 6.5). Electronic applications accepted.

Southern New Hampshire University, School of Education, Manchester, NH 03106-1045. Offers curriculum and instruction (M Ed), including dyslexia studies and language-based learning disabilities, educational leadership, reading, special education, technology integration; dyslexia studies and language-based learning disabilities (Certificate); early childhood and special education (M Ed); educational leadership (M Ed, Ed D); educational studies (M Ed); elementary and special education (M Ed); field based education (M Ed); higher education administration (MS); teaching English as a foreign language (MS). *Program availability:* Part-time, evening/weekend, online learning. *Degree requirements:* For master's, comprehensive exam (for some programs), thesis or alternative. *Entrance requirements:* For master's, PRAXIS I, minimum GPA of 2.75. Additional exam requirements/recommendations for international students: Required—TOEFL (minimum score 550 paper-based). *Application deadline:* Applications are processed on a rolling basis. Application fee: $40. Electronic applications accepted. *Expenses:* Contact institution. *Financial support:* Institutionally sponsored loans available. Financial award applicants required to submit FAFSA. *Unit head:* Raymond McNulty, Dean, 603-668-2211, Fax: 603-629-4673. *Application contact:* Office of Graduate Admission, 888-327-SNHU, Fax: 603-644-3144, E-mail: enroll@snhu.edu.

Southern University and Agricultural and Mechanical College, Graduate School, College of Education, Department of Curriculum and Instruction, Baton Rouge, LA 70813. Offers elementary education (M Ed); media (M Ed); secondary education (M Ed). *Degree requirements:* For master's, comprehensive exam, thesis optional. *Entrance requirements:* For master's, GMAT or GRE General Test. Additional exam requirements/recommendations for international students: Required—TOEFL (minimum score 525 paper-based).

Stanford University, Graduate School of Education, Program in Learning, Design, and Technology, Stanford, CA 94305-2004. Offers MA. Electronic applications accepted. *Expenses: Tuition:* Full-time $48,987; part-time $10,620 per quarter. One-time fee: $400. Tuition and fees vary according to program.

State University of New York College at Potsdam, School of Education and Professional Studies, Program in Information and Communication Technology, Potsdam, NY 13676. Offers educational technology specialist (MS Ed); organizational performance, leadership and technology (MS Ed). *Program availability:* Part-time, evening/weekend. *Degree requirements:* For master's, culminating experience. *Entrance requirements:* For master's, minimum GPA of 3.0 in last 60 hours of course work. Additional exam requirements/recommendations for international students: Required—TOEFL (minimum score 550 paper-based; 80 iBT), IELTS (minimum score 6). Electronic applications accepted.

State University of New York Empire State College, School for Graduate Studies, Programs in Education, Saratoga Springs, NY 12866-4391. Offers adult learning (MA); learning and emerging technologies (MA); teaching and learning (MAT); teaching and learning (M Ed). *Program availability:* Online learning.

Stockton University, Office of Graduate Studies, Program in Instructional Technology, Galloway, NJ 08205-9441. Offers MA. *Program availability:* Part-time, evening/weekend. *Faculty:* 3 full-time (2 women), 1 part-time/adjunct (0 women). *Students:* 2 full-time (1 woman), 35 part-time (23 women); includes 3 minority (1 Black or African American, non-Hispanic/Latino; 1 Asian, non-Hispanic/Latino; 1 Hispanic/Latino). Average age 35. 27 applicants, 93% accepted, 22 enrolled. In 2017, 23 master's awarded. *Entrance requirements:* For master's, GRE or MAT, minimum GPA of 3.0. Additional exam requirements/recommendations for international students: Required—TOEFL. *Application deadline:* For fall admission, 7/1 priority date for domestic students, 7/1 for international students; for spring admission, 12/1 for domestic students, 11/1 for international students. Applications are processed on a rolling basis. Application fee: $50. Electronic applications accepted. *Expenses:* Contact institution. *Financial support:* Fellowships, research assistantships, career-related internships or fieldwork, Federal Work-Study, scholarships/grants, and unspecified assistantships available. Support

available to part-time students. Financial award application deadline: 3/1; financial award applicants required to submit FAFSA. *Faculty research:* Ethics, digital imaging, virtual reality in the classroom, 3D art in multimedia, technology projects for job-skills training, community computing networks. *Unit head:* Dr. Doug Harvey, Director, 609-626-3640, E-mail: mait@stockton.edu. *Application contact:* Tara Williams, Assistant Director of Graduate Enrollment, 609-626-3640, Fax: 609-626-6050, E-mail: gradschool@stockton.edu.
Website: http://www.stockton.edu/grad

Stony Brook University, State University of New York, Graduate School, College of Engineering and Applied Sciences, Department of Technology and Society, Program in Educational Technology, Stony Brook, NY 11794. Offers MS. *Accreditation:* NCATE. *Entrance requirements:* For master's, GRE, minimum GPA of 3.0, statement of purpose. Additional exam requirements/recommendations for international students: Required—TOEFL (minimum score 85 iBT), IELTS (minimum score 6.5). *Application deadline:* For fall admission, 8/2 for domestic students, 4/15 for international students; for spring admission, 12/1 for domestic students, 10/5 for international students. Application fee: $100. Electronic applications accepted. *Expenses:* Contact institution. *Financial support:* Research assistantships and teaching assistantships available. *Unit head:* Dr. Wolf Schäfer, Interim Department Chair, 631-632-7924, E-mail: wolf.schafer@stonybrook.edu. *Application contact:* Marypat Taveras, Coordinator, 631-632-8762, Fax: 631-632-7809, E-mail: marypat.taveras@stonybrook.edu.
Website: https://www.stonybrook.edu/commcms/est/masters/msedtech

Stony Brook University, State University of New York, School of Professional Development, Stony Brook, NY 11794. Offers biology (MAT); chemistry (MAT); coaching (Graduate Certificate); earth science (MAT); educational computing (Graduate Certificate); educational leadership (Advanced Certificate); English (MAT); environmental management (MPS, Graduate Certificate); French (MAT); German (MAT); higher education administration (MA, Certificate); human resource management (MS, Graduate Certificate); industrial management (Graduate Certificate); information systems management (Graduate Certificate); Italian (MAT); liberal studies (MA); mathematics (MAT); operations research (Graduate Certificate); physics (MAT); school district business leadership (Advanced Certificate); social studies (MAT); Spanish (MAT). *Program availability:* Part-time, evening/weekend, online learning. *Faculty:* 3 full-time (2 women), 101 part-time/adjunct (45 women). *Students:* 190 full-time (126 women), 974 part-time (708 women); includes 255 minority (88 Black or African American, non-Hispanic/Latino; 2 American Indian or Alaska Native, non-Hispanic/Latino; 31 Asian, non-Hispanic/Latino; 113 Hispanic/Latino; 1 Native Hawaiian or other Pacific Islander, non-Hispanic/Latino; 20 Two or more races, non-Hispanic/Latino), 6 international. Average age 33. 411 applicants, 91% accepted, 288 enrolled. In 2017, 333 master's, 180 other advanced degrees awarded. *Entrance requirements:* Additional exam requirements/recommendations for international students: Required—TOEFL (minimum score 85 iBT). *Application deadline:* For fall admission, 1/15 for domestic students, 6/1 for international students; for spring admission, 10/1 for domestic and international students. Applications are processed on a rolling basis. Application fee: $100. *Expenses:* Contact institution. *Financial support:* Fellowships, research assistantships, teaching assistantships, and career-related internships or fieldwork available. Support available to part-time students. *Unit head:* Dr. Ken Lindblom, Dean, 631-632-7049, Fax: 631-632-9046, E-mail: kenneth.lindblom@stonybrook.edu. *Application contact:* Melissa Jordan, Assistant Dean, 631-632-7751, E-mail: melissa.jordan@stonybrook.edu.
Website: http://www.stonybrook.edu/spd/

Strayer University, Graduate Studies, Washington, DC 20005-2603. Offers accounting (MS); acquisition (MBA); business administration (MBA); communications technology (MS); educational management (M Ed); finance (MBA); health services administration (MHSA); hospitality and tourism management (MBA); human resource management (MBA); information systems (MS), including computer security management, decision support system management, enterprise resource management, network management, software engineering management, systems development management; management (MBA); management information systems (MS); marketing (MBA); professional accounting (MS), including accounting information systems, controllership, taxation; public administration (MPA); supply chain management (MBA); technology in education (M Ed). Programs also offered at campus locations in Birmingham, AL; Chamblee, GA; Cobb County, GA; Morrow, GA; White Marsh, MD; Charleston, SC; Columbia, SC; Greensboro, NC; Greenville, SC; Lexington, KY; Louisville, KY; Nashville, TN; North Raleigh, NC; Washington, DC. *Accreditation:* ACBSP. *Program availability:* Part-time, evening/weekend, online learning. *Degree requirements:* For master's, thesis. *Entrance requirements:* For master's, GMAT, GRE General Test, bachelor's degree from an accredited college or university, minimum undergraduate GPA of 2.75. Electronic applications accepted.

Syracuse University, School of Education, CAS Program in Educational Technology, Syracuse, NY 13244. Offers CAS. *Accreditation:* ACA. *Program availability:* Part-time. *Entrance requirements:* For degree, baccalaureate degree from regionally-accredited college/university, statement of goals, three recommendation letters, transcripts. Additional exam requirements/recommendations for international students: Required—TOEFL (minimum score 100 iBT). *Application deadline:* Applications are processed on a rolling basis. Application fee: $75. Electronic applications accepted. *Financial support:* Fellowships, research assistantships, teaching assistantships, career-related internships or fieldwork, and scholarships/grants available. Financial award application deadline: 1/15. *Faculty research:* Instructional design, learning with digital technologies, training and professional development, designing effective and efficient instruction, designing digital instruction. *Unit head:* Dr. Jing Lei, Chair, 315-443-3703, E-mail: takoszal@syr.edu. *Application contact:* Speranza Migliore, Graduate Admissions Recruiter, 315-443-2505, E-mail: gradrcrt@syr.edu.
Website: http://soe.syr.edu/academic/Instructional_Design_Development_and_Evaluation/graduate/certificates/default.aspx

Syracuse University, School of Education, MS Program in Instructional Technology, Syracuse, NY 13244. Offers MS. *Program availability:* Part-time. *Students:* Average age 25. In 2017, 2 master's awarded. *Entrance requirements:* For master's, GRE, baccalaureate degree from regionally-accredited college/university, initial New York State teaching certification, statement of goals, three letters of recommendation, transcripts. Additional exam requirements/recommendations for international students: Required—TOEFL (minimum score 100 iBT). *Application deadline:* For fall admission, 1/15 for domestic students, 1/15 priority date for international students. Application fee: $75. Electronic applications accepted. *Financial support:* Fellowships with full tuition reimbursements, research assistantships, teaching assistantships, career-related internships or fieldwork, and scholarships/grants available. Financial award application deadline: 1/15. *Unit head:* Dr. Jing Lei, Chair, 315-443-3703, E-mail: takoszal@syr.edu. *Application contact:* Speranza Migliore, Graduate Admissions Recruiter, 315-443-2505, E-mail: gradrcrt@syr.edu.
Website: http://soeweb.syr.edu/academic/Instructional_Design_Development_and_Evaluation/graduate/masters/instructional_technology/default.aspx

Syracuse University, School of Information Studies, CAS Program in School Media, Syracuse, NY 13244. Offers CAS. *Program availability:* Part-time, evening/weekend, online learning. *Entrance requirements:* For degree, MS in library and information science, letter of recommendation, personal statement, resume, official transcripts. Additional exam requirements/recommendations for international students: Required—TOEFL (minimum score 100 iBT). *Application deadline:* For fall admission, 1/1 priority date for domestic and international students; for spring admission, 10/15 priority date for domestic and international students; for summer admission, 2/1 priority date for domestic and international students. Applications are processed on a rolling basis. Application fee: $75. Electronic applications accepted. *Financial support:* Application deadline: 1/1. *Faculty research:* Managing a school library, literacy through school libraries, information technologies in educational organizations, information services to students with disabilities. *Unit head:* Prof. Caroline Haythornthwaite, Program Director, 315-443-2911, E-mail: igrad@syr.edu. *Application contact:* Susan Corieri, Director of Enrollment Management, 315-443-2575, E-mail: igrad@syr.edu.
Website: https://ischool.syr.edu/academics/graduate/cas/cas-school-media/

Syracuse University, School of Information Studies, MS Program in Library and Information Science: School Media, Syracuse, NY 13244. Offers MS. *Program availability:* Part-time, evening/weekend, online learning. *Students:* Average age 34. *Entrance requirements:* For master's, GRE General Test, personal statement, two letters of recommendation, resume. Additional exam requirements/recommendations for international students: Required—TOEFL (minimum score 100 iBT). *Application deadline:* For fall admission, 1/1 priority date for domestic and international students; for spring admission, 10/15 priority date for domestic and international students. Applications are processed on a rolling basis. Application fee: $75. Electronic applications accepted. *Financial support:* Fellowships with full tuition reimbursements, research assistantships with partial tuition reimbursements, and teaching assistantships with partial tuition reimbursements available. Financial award application deadline: 1/1. *Faculty research:* Collection management based on a unified media concept, use of information resources from a problem-solving perspective, digital literacy, curriculum consultation and technology innovation. *Unit head:* Prof. Caroline Haythornthwaite, Program Director, 315-443-2911, E-mail: igrad@syr.edu. *Application contact:* Susan Corieri, Director of Enrollment Management, 315-443-2575, E-mail: ischool@syr.edu.
Website: https://ischool.syr.edu/academics/graduate/masters-degrees/ms-library-information-science-school-media/

Tarleton State University, College of Graduate Studies, College of Education, Department of Curriculum and Instruction, Stephenville, TX 76402. Offers curriculum and instruction (M Ed); educational diagnostician (M Ed); elementary education (M Ed); instructional design and technology (M Ed); instructional leadership (M Ed); secondary education (M Ed); special education (M Ed); technology applications (M Ed); technology director (M Ed). *Program availability:* Part-time, evening/weekend. *Faculty:* 7 full-time (5 women), 4 part-time/adjunct (2 women). *Students:* 7 full-time (6 women), 156 part-time (137 women); includes 40 minority (11 Black or African American, non-Hispanic/Latino; 25 Hispanic/Latino; 4 Two or more races, non-Hispanic/Latino). Average age 38. 55 applicants, 96% accepted, 46 enrolled. In 2017, 33 master's awarded. *Degree requirements:* For master's, comprehensive exam, thesis (for some programs). *Entrance requirements:* For master's, GRE General Test, minimum GPA of 3.0. Additional exam requirements/recommendations for international students: Required—TOEFL (minimum score 550 paper-based; 80 iBT), IELTS (minimum score 6). *Application deadline:* For fall admission, 8/15 priority date for domestic students; for spring admission, 1/7 for domestic students. Applications are processed on a rolling basis. Application fee: $45 ($145 for international students). Electronic applications accepted. *Expenses:* Contact institution. *Financial support:* Research assistantships, teaching assistantships, career-related internships or fieldwork, Federal Work-Study, and institutionally sponsored loans available. Support available to part-time students. Financial award application deadline: 5/1; financial award applicants required to submit FAFSA. *Unit head:* Dr. Jordan Barkley, Dean, 254-968-9089, E-mail: jbarkley@tarleton.edu. *Application contact:* Information Contact, 254-968-9104, Fax: 254-968-9670, E-mail: gradoffice@tarleton.edu.
Website: http://www.tarleton.edu/cimasters/

Teachers College, Columbia University, Department of Mathematics, Science and Technology, New York, NY 10027-6696. Offers biology 7-12 (MA); chemistry 7-12 (MA); communication and education (MA, Ed D); computing in education (MA); earth science 7-12 (MA); instructional technology and media (Ed M, MA, Ed D); mathematics education (Ed M, MA, Ed D, Ed DCT, PhD); physics 7-12 (MA); science and dental education (MA); science education (Ed M, MS, Ed DCT, PhD); supervisor/teacher of science education (MA); technology specialist (MA). *Program availability:* Part-time, evening/weekend, online learning. *Students:* 187 full-time (129 women), 228 part-time (153 women); includes 143 minority (42 Black or African American, non-Hispanic/Latino; 64 Asian, non-Hispanic/Latino; 25 Hispanic/Latino; 12 Two or more races, non-Hispanic/Latino), 125 international. Average age 32. 484 applicants, 59% accepted, 141 enrolled. Terminal master's awarded for partial completion of doctoral program. *Degree requirements:* For doctorate, thesis/dissertation. *Unit head:* Prof. Erica Walker, Chair, E-mail: ewalker@tc.columbia.edu. *Application contact:* David Estrella, Director of Admission, 212-678-3305, E-mail: estrella@tc.columbia.edu.
Website: http://www.tc.columbia.edu/mathematics-science-and-technology/

Tennessee Technological University, College of Graduate Studies, College of Education, Department of Curriculum and Instruction, Program in Educational Technology, Cookeville, TN 38505. Offers MA, Ed S. *Program availability:* Part-time, evening/weekend. *Students:* 4 full-time (3 women), 22 part-time (19 women); includes 2 minority (both Two or more races, non-Hispanic/Latino). 12 applicants, 92% accepted, 6 enrolled. In 2017, 2 master's, 1 other advanced degree awarded. *Degree requirements:* For master's, comprehensive exam, thesis or alternative. *Entrance requirements:* For master's, MAT or GRE. Additional exam requirements/recommendations for international students: Required—TOEFL (minimum score 527 paper-based; 71 iBT), IELTS (minimum score 5.5), PTE (minimum score 48), or TOEIC (Test of English as an International Communication). *Application deadline:* For fall admission, 8/1 for domestic students, 5/1 for international students; for spring admission, 12/1 for domestic students, 10/1 for international students; for summer admission, 5/1 for domestic students, 2/1 for international students. Application fee: $35 ($40 for international students). Electronic applications accepted. *Expenses:* Tuition, state resident: full-time $565 per credit hour. Tuition, nonresident: full-time $22,993; part-time $1291 per credit hour. *Unit head:* Dr. Jeremy Wendt, Interim Chairperson, 931-372-3181, Fax: 931-372-6270, E-mail: jwendt@tntech.edu. *Application contact:* Shelia K. Kendrick, Coordinator of Graduate Studies, 931-372-3808, Fax: 931-372-3497, E-mail: skendrick@tntech.edu.

Texas A&M University, College of Education and Human Development, Department of Educational Psychology, College Station, TX 77843. Offers bilingual education (M Ed, MS); counseling psychology (PhD); educational psychology (M Ed, MS, PhD); educational technology (M Ed); school psychology (PhD); special education (M Ed, MS). *Accreditation:* APA (one or more programs are accredited). *Program availability:* Part-time, evening/weekend, blended/hybrid learning. *Faculty:* 45. *Students:* 165 full-time (131 women), 248 part-time (210 women); includes 144 minority (24 Black or African American, non-Hispanic/Latino; 3 American Indian or Alaska Native, non-Hispanic/Latino; 21 Asian, non-Hispanic/Latino; 84 Hispanic/Latino; 2 Native Hawaiian or other

Pacific Islander, non-Hispanic/Latino; 10 Two or more races, non-Hispanic/Latino), 45 international. Average age 33. 171 applicants, 44% accepted, 47 enrolled. In 2017, 141 master's, 28 doctorates awarded. *Degree requirements:* For master's, thesis optional; for doctorate, thesis/dissertation. *Entrance requirements:* For master's and doctorate, GRE General Test. Additional exam requirements/recommendations for international students: Required—TOEFL (minimum score 550 paper-based; 80 iBT), IELTS (minimum score 6), PTE (minimum score 53). *Application deadline:* For fall admission, 12/1 for domestic students; for spring admission, 10/15 for domestic students. Application fee: $50 ($90 for international students). Electronic applications accepted. *Expenses:* Contact institution. *Financial support:* In 2017–18, 210 students received support, including 4 fellowships with tuition reimbursements available (averaging $24,775 per year), 102 research assistantships with tuition reimbursements available (averaging $10,698 per year), 19 teaching assistantships with tuition reimbursements available (averaging $7,177 per year); career-related internships or fieldwork, institutionally sponsored loans, scholarships/grants, traineeships, health care benefits, tuition waivers (full and partial), and unspecified assistantships also available. Support available to part-time students. Financial award application deadline: 3/15; financial award applicants required to submit FAFSA. *Unit head:* Dr. Victor Willson, Department Head, 979-845-1394, E-mail: v-willson@tamu.edu. *Application contact:* Kristie Stramaski, Senior Academic Advisor, 979-845-1833, E-mail: epsyadvisor@tamu.edu. Website: http://epsy.tamu.edu

Texas A&M University–Commerce, College of Education and Human Services, Commerce, TX 75429. Offers counseling (M Ed, MS, PhD); early childhood education (M Ed, MS); educational administration (M Ed, MS, Ed D); educational psychology (PhD); educational technology leadership (M Ed, MS); educational technology library science (M Ed, MS); elementary education (M Ed); health, kinesiology and sports studies (MS); higher education (MS, Ed D); psychology (MS); reading (M Ed, MS); secondary education (M Ed, MS); social work (MSW); special education (M Ed, MS); supervision, curriculum and instruction-elementary education (Ed D); training and development (MS). *Program availability:* Part-time, evening/weekend, 100% online, blended/hybrid learning. *Faculty:* 91 full-time (51 women), 38 part-time/adjunct (31 women). *Students:* 400 full-time (310 women), 1,400 part-time (1,117 women); includes 724 minority (412 Black or African American, non-Hispanic/Latino; 8 American Indian or Alaska Native, non-Hispanic/Latino; 24 Asian, non-Hispanic/Latino; 220 Hispanic/Latino; 60 Two or more races, non-Hispanic/Latino), 18 international. Average age 37. 951 applicants, 46% accepted, 331 enrolled. In 2017, 564 master's, 24 doctorates awarded. *Degree requirements:* For master's, comprehensive exam, thesis optional, departmental qualifying exams (for some programs); for doctorate, comprehensive exam, thesis/dissertation, departmental qualifying exam; for SSP, comprehensive exam, thesis optional. *Entrance requirements:* For master's and doctorate, GRE General Test. Additional exam requirements/recommendations for international students: Required—TOEFL (minimum score 550 paper-based; 79 iBT), IELTS (minimum score 6). *Application deadline:* For fall admission, 6/1 priority date for international students; for spring admission, 10/15 priority date for international students; for summer admission, 3/15 priority date for international students. Applications are processed on a rolling basis. Application fee: $50. Electronic applications accepted. *Expenses:* Tuition, state resident: full-time $3630. Tuition, nonresident: full-time $11,100. *Required fees:* $2564. Tuition and fees vary according to course load, degree level and program. *Financial support:* In 2017–18, 84 students received support, including 40 research assistantships with partial tuition reimbursements available (averaging $10,800 per year), 12 teaching assistantships with partial tuition reimbursements available (averaging $13,000 per year); career-related internships or fieldwork, Federal Work-Study, institutionally sponsored loans, scholarships/grants, health care benefits, and unspecified assistantships also available. Financial award application deadline: 6/15; financial award applicants required to submit FAFSA. *Faculty research:* Cognitive and bilingual education, positive behavioral intervention, literacy, math readiness. *Total annual research expenditures:* $1.1 million. *Unit head:* Dr. Timothy Letzring, Dean, 903-886-5181, Fax: 903-886-5905, E-mail: tim.letzring@tamuc.edu. *Application contact:* Vicky Turner, Doctoral Degree and Special Programs Coordinator, 903-886-5167, E-mail: vicky.turner@tamuc.edu. Website: http://www.tamuc.edu/academics/graduateSchool/programs/education/default.aspx

Texas A&M University–Corpus Christi, College of Graduate Studies, College of Education and Human Development, Corpus Christi, TX 78412. Offers counseling (MS), including counseling; counselor education (PhD); curriculum and instruction (MS, PhD); early childhood education (MS); educational administration (MS); educational leadership (Ed D); elementary education (MS); instructional design and educational technology (MS); kinesiology (MS); reading (MS); secondary education (MS); special education (MS). *Program availability:* Part-time, evening/weekend, blended/hybrid learning. *Faculty:* 50 full-time (29 women), 29 part-time/adjunct (18 women). *Students:* 160 full-time (127 women), 366 part-time (293 women); includes 279 minority (40 Black or African American, non-Hispanic/Latino; 3 Asian, non-Hispanic/Latino; 228 Hispanic/Latino; 8 Two or more races, non-Hispanic/Latino), 18 international. Average age 35. 296 applicants, 65% accepted, 155 enrolled. In 2017, 103 master's, 27 doctorates awarded. *Degree requirements:* For master's, comprehensive exam, capstone; for doctorate, thesis/dissertation. *Entrance requirements:* For master's, GRE General Test, essay (300 words); for doctorate, GRE, essay, resume, 3-4 reference forms. *Application deadline:* For fall admission, 7/15 priority date for domestic students, 5/1 priority date for international students; for spring admission, 11/15 priority date for domestic students, 9/1 priority date for international students. Applications are processed on a rolling basis. Application fee: $50 ($70 for international students). Electronic applications accepted. *Expenses:* Tuition, state resident: full-time $3568; part-time $198.24 per credit hour. Tuition, nonresident: full-time $11,038; part-time $613.24 per credit hour. *Required fees:* $2129; $1422.58 per semester. Tuition and fees vary according to program. *Financial support:* Research assistantships, teaching assistantships, career-related internships or fieldwork, Federal Work-Study, institutionally sponsored loans, scholarships/grants, health care benefits, and unspecified assistantships available. Support available to part-time students. Financial award application deadline: 3/15; financial award applicants required to submit FAFSA. *Unit head:* Dr. David Scott, Dean, 361-825-2660, E-mail: david.scott@tamucc.edu. *Application contact:* Graduate Admissions Coordinator, 361-825-2177, Fax: 361-825-2755, E-mail: gradweb@tamucc.edu. Website: http://education.tamucc.edu/

Texas A&M University–Kingsville, College of Graduate Studies, College of Education and Human Performance, Department of Educational Leadership and Counseling, Program in Instructional Technology, Kingsville, TX 78363. Offers MS. *Program availability:* Part-time, evening/weekend. *Degree requirements:* For master's, variable foreign language requirement, comprehensive exam, thesis (for some programs). *Entrance requirements:* For master's, GRE, MAT, GMAT. Additional exam requirements/recommendations for international students: Required—TOEFL (minimum score 550 paper-based; 79 iBT). Electronic applications accepted.

Texas A&M University–Texarkana, Graduate Studies and Research, College of Education and Liberal Arts, Texarkana, TX 75503. Offers adult education (MS); curriculum and instruction (M Ed); education (MS); educational administration (M Ed); English (MA); instructional technology (MS); interdisciplinary studies (MA, MS); special

education (MS). *Program availability:* Part-time, evening/weekend. *Degree requirements:* For master's, comprehensive exam (for some programs), thesis optional. *Entrance requirements:* For master's, minimum GPA of 2.5 on last 60 hours of bachelor's degree. Additional exam requirements/recommendations for international students: Required—TOEFL. Electronic applications accepted.

Texas State University, The Graduate School, College of Education, Program in Educational Technology, San Marcos, TX 78666. Offers M Ed. *Program availability:* Part-time, evening/weekend. *Faculty:* 3 full-time (1 woman). *Students:* 5 full-time (4 women), 10 part-time (5 women); includes 6 minority (1 Black or African American, non-Hispanic/Latino; 4 Hispanic/Latino; 1 Two or more races, non-Hispanic/Latino), 1 international. Average age 36. 11 applicants, 55% accepted, 3 enrolled. In 2017, 7 master's awarded. *Degree requirements:* For master's, comprehensive exam. *Entrance requirements:* For master's, GRE (preferred), baccalaureate degree from regionally-accredited institution with minimum GPA of 2.75 in undergraduate work, statement of purpose. Additional exam requirements/recommendations for international students: Required—TOEFL (minimum score 550 paper-based; 78 iBT), IELTS (minimum score 6.5), TOEFL (minimum iBT scores: 22 listening, 22 reading, 24 speaking, 21 writing). *Application deadline:* For fall admission, 6/15 for domestic students, 6/1 for international students; for spring admission, 10/15 priority date for domestic students, 10/1 for international students; for summer admission, 4/15 for domestic students, 3/15 for international students. Applications are processed on a rolling basis. Application fee: $40 ($90 for international students). Electronic applications accepted. *Expenses:* Tuition, state resident: full-time $7868; part-time $3934 per semester. Tuition, nonresident: full-time $17,828; part-time $8914 per semester. *Required fees:* $2092; $1435 per semester. Tuition and fees vary according to course load. *Financial support:* In 2017–18, 7 students received support. Research assistantships, teaching assistantships, scholarships/grants, and unspecified assistantships available. Financial award application deadline: 3/1; financial award applicants required to submit FAFSA. *Faculty research:* University maker spaces: discovery, optimization and measurement impacts. *Unit head:* Dr. David Bynum, Graduate Advisor, 512-245-2038, Fax: 512-245-7911, E-mail: db15@txstate.edu. *Application contact:* Dr. Andrea Golato, Dean of Graduate School, 512-245-2581, Fax: 512-245-8365, E-mail: gradcollege@txstate.edu. Website: http://www.education.txstate.edu/ci/degrees-programs/graduate/edtech.html

Texas Tech University, Graduate School, College of Education, Department of Educational Psychology and Leadership, Lubbock, TX 79409. Offers counselor education (M Ed, PhD); educational leadership (M Ed, Ed D, PhD); educational psychology (M Ed, PhD); higher education (M Ed); higher education administration (Ed D); higher education research (PhD); instructional technology (M Ed, Ed D); special education (M Ed, Ed D, PhD). *Accreditation:* ACA; NCATE. *Program availability:* Part-time, evening/weekend. *Faculty:* 64 full-time (30 women), 6 part-time/adjunct (all women). *Students:* 263 full-time (193 women), 637 part-time (490 women); includes 307 minority (84 Black or African American, non-Hispanic/Latino; 3 American Indian or Alaska Native, non-Hispanic/Latino; 4 Asian, non-Hispanic/Latino; 193 Hispanic/Latino; 23 Two or more races, non-Hispanic/Latino), 48 international. Average age 36. 510 applicants, 47% accepted, 185 enrolled. In 2017, 209 master's, 64 doctorates awarded. Terminal master's awarded for partial completion of doctoral program. *Degree requirements:* For master's, comprehensive exam, thesis optional; for doctorate, comprehensive exam, thesis/dissertation. *Entrance requirements:* For master's, GRE (for some programs); for doctorate, GRE. Additional exam requirements/recommendations for international students: Required—TOEFL (minimum score 550 paper-based; 79 iBT). *Application deadline:* For fall admission, 6/1 priority date for domestic students, 1/15 priority date for international students; for spring admission, 9/1 priority date for domestic students, 6/15 priority date for international students. Applications are processed on a rolling basis. Application fee: $60. Electronic applications accepted. *Expenses:* Contact institution. *Financial support:* In 2017–18, 366 students received support, including 360 fellowships (averaging $3,231 per year), 63 research assistantships (averaging $11,899 per year); teaching assistantships, scholarships/grants, and unspecified assistantships also available. Support available to part-time students. Financial award application deadline: 1/3; financial award applicants required to submit FAFSA. *Faculty research:* Cognitive, motivational, and developmental processes in learning; counseling education; instructional technology; generic special education and sensory impairment; community college administration; K-12 school administration. *Total annual research expenditures:* $127,956. *Unit head:* Dr. Hansel Burley, Chair, 806-834-5135, Fax: 806-742-2179, E-mail: hansel.burley@ttu.edu. *Application contact:* Pam Smith, Admissions Advisor, 806-834-2969, Fax: 806-742-2179, E-mail: pam.smith@ttu.edu. Website: http://www.educ.ttu.edu/

Thomas Edison State University, Heavin School of Arts and Sciences, Program in Educational Technology and Online Learning, Trenton, NJ 08608. Offers educational technology and online learning (MA); online learning and teaching (Graduate Certificate). *Program availability:* Part-time, online learning. *Degree requirements:* For master's, practicum. *Entrance requirements:* Additional exam requirements/recommendations for international students: Required—TOEFL (minimum score 550 paper-based; 79 iBT). Electronic applications accepted.

Tiffin University, Program in Education, Tiffin, OH 44883-2161. Offers educational technology management (M Ed); higher education administration (M Ed). *Program availability:* Part-time, evening/weekend, online only, 100% online, blended/hybrid learning. *Entrance requirements:* Additional exam requirements/recommendations for international students: Required—TOEFL. Electronic applications accepted. *Expenses:* Contact institution.

Touro College, Graduate School of Education, New York, NY 10010. Offers education and special education (MS); instructional technology (MS); mathematics education (MS); school leadership (MS); teaching English to speakers of other languages (MS); teaching literacy (MS). *Accreditation:* TEAC. *Program availability:* Part-time, evening/weekend, online learning. *Faculty:* 52 full-time (34 women), 199 part-time/adjunct (136 women). *Students:* 756 full-time (686 women), 3,833 part-time (3,492 women). Average age 33. 1,422 applicants, 50% accepted, 675 enrolled. In 2017, 6 master's awarded. *Entrance requirements:* Additional exam requirements/recommendations for international students: Required—TOEFL (minimum score 83 iBT), IELTS (minimum score 6.5). *Application deadline:* For fall admission, 8/26 for domestic students, 7/15 for international students; for spring admission, 12/31 for domestic students, 12/15 for international students. Applications are processed on a rolling basis. Application fee: $50. *Financial support:* Federal Work-Study available. Financial award applicants required to submit FAFSA. *Faculty research:* Equity assistance, language development, specialty communications, Latin American studies and cultural sensitivity, behavior management techniques and strategies in special education. *Unit head:* Dr. Jacob Easley, III, Dean, 212-463-0400 Ext. 5561, Fax: 212-462-4889, E-mail: jeasley@touro.edu. *Application contact:* Sharmilee Hoopnarine, Admissions, 212-463-0400.

Touro College, Graduate School of Technology, New York, NY 10010. Offers information systems (MS); instructional technology (MS); Web and multimedia design (MA). *Faculty:* 18 part-time/adjunct (6 women). *Students:* 125 full-time (122 women), 177 part-time (163 women); includes 79 minority (39 Black or African American, non-Hispanic/Latino; 23 Asian, non-Hispanic/Latino; 14 Hispanic/Latino; 3 Two or more

Educational Media/Instructional Technology

races, non-Hispanic/Latino), 150 international. Average age 34. *Entrance requirements:* Additional exam requirements/recommendations for international students: Required—TOEFL (minimum score 83 iBT), IELTS (minimum score 6.5), PTE (minimum score 58). Application fee: $50. *Unit head:* Dr. Issac Herskowitz, Dean of the Graduate School of Technology, 202-463-0400 Ext. 5231, E-mail: issac.herskowitz@touro.edu. *Application contact:* Jack Romano, Program Director, 212-463-0400 Ext. 5462.
Website: http://www.touro.edu/gst/

Towson University, College of Education, Program in Instructional Technology, Towson, MD 21252-0001. Offers educational technology (MS); instructional design and development (MS); school library media (MS). *Program availability:* Part-time, evening/weekend. *Students:* 3 full-time (2 women), 82 part-time (68 women); includes 25 minority (20 Black or African American, non-Hispanic/Latino; 2 Asian, non-Hispanic/Latino; 1 Hispanic/Latino; 2 Two or more races, non-Hispanic/Latino). *Degree requirements:* For master's, thesis optional. *Entrance requirements:* For master's, minimum GPA of 3.0, technological literacy. Additional exam requirements/recommendations for international students: Required—TOEFL. *Application deadline:* For fall admission, 1/17 for domestic students, 5/15 for international students; for spring admission, 10/15 for domestic students, 12/1 for international students. Applications are processed on a rolling basis. Application fee: $45. Electronic applications accepted. *Expenses:* Tuition, state resident: full-time $7960; part-time $398 per unit. Tuition, nonresident: full-time $16,480; part-time $824 per unit. *Required fees:* $2600; $130 per year. $390 per term. *Financial support:* Application deadline: 4/1. *Unit head:* Dr. Gilda Martinez-Alba, Department Chair, 410-704-2576, E-mail: gmartinez@towson.edu. *Application contact:* Coverley Beidleman, Assistant Director of Graduate Admissions, 410-704-5630, Fax: 410-704-3030, E-mail: cbeidleman@towson.edu.
Website: https://www.towson.edu/coe/departments/edtech/grad/index.html

Trevecca Nazarene University, Graduate Instructional Design and Technology Program, Nashville, TN 37210-2877. Offers MS. *Program availability:* Online only. *Faculty:* 3 part-time/adjunct (2 women). *Students:* 10 full-time (9 women), 15 part-time (10 women); includes 8 minority (all Black or African American, non-Hispanic/Latino). Average age 39. *Degree requirements:* For master's, capstone. *Entrance requirements:* For master's, minimum GPA of 2.75, minimum math grade of C, minimum English composition grade of C. Additional exam requirements/recommendations for international students: Required—TOEFL (minimum score 550 paper-based; 80 iBT). *Application deadline:* Applications are processed on a rolling basis. Application fee: $0. Electronic applications accepted. *Expenses:* $395 per credit hour. *Financial support:* Applicants required to submit FAFSA. *Unit head:* 615-248-1529, E-mail: sgcsadmissions@trevecca.edu. *Application contact:* 844-TNU-GRAD, E-mail: sgcsadmissions@trevecca.edu.
Website: http://online.trevecca.edu/idt

Trident University International, College of Education, Program in Educational Leadership, Cypress, CA 90630. Offers e-learning leadership (MA Ed, PhD); educational leadership (MA Ed); higher education leadership (PhD); K-12 leadership (PhD). *Program availability:* Part-time, evening/weekend, online learning. *Degree requirements:* For doctorate, comprehensive exam, thesis/dissertation, defense of dissertation. *Entrance requirements:* For master's, minimum GPA of 2.5 (students with GPA 3.0 or greater may transfer up to 30% of graduate level credits); for doctorate, minimum GPA of 3.4, course work in research methods or statistics. Additional exam requirements/recommendations for international students: Required—TOEFL. Electronic applications accepted.

Université Laval, Faculty of Education, Department of Teaching and Learning Studies, Programs in Teaching Technology, Québec, QC G1K 7P4, Canada. Offers MA, PhD. Terminal master's awarded for partial completion of doctoral program. *Degree requirements:* For master's, thesis (for some programs); for doctorate, comprehensive exam, thesis/dissertation. *Entrance requirements:* For master's and doctorate, English exam (comprehension of written English), knowledge of French. Electronic applications accepted.

University at Albany, State University of New York, School of Education, Department of Educational Theory and Practice, Albany, NY 12222-0001. Offers curriculum and instruction (PhD, CAS); curriculum development and instructional technology (MS); general education studies (MS). *Program availability:* Part-time, evening/weekend, 100% online, blended/hybrid learning. *Faculty:* 13 full-time (6 women), 26 part-time/adjunct (18 women). *Students:* 80 full-time (58 women), 215 part-time (157 women); includes 29 minority (6 Black or African American, non-Hispanic/Latino; 8 Asian, non-Hispanic/Latino; 12 Hispanic/Latino; 3 Two or more races, non-Hispanic/Latino), 27 international. Average age 31. 197 applicants, 68% accepted, 120 enrolled. In 2017, 83 master's, 4 doctorates, 8 other advanced degrees awarded. *Degree requirements:* For doctorate, one foreign language, thesis/dissertation. *Entrance requirements:* For doctorate, GRE General Test. Additional exam requirements/recommendations for international students: Required—TOEFL (minimum score 550 paper-based). *Application deadline:* For fall admission, 2/1 for domestic students, 1/31 for international students. Application fee: $75. Electronic applications accepted. *Expenses:* Tuition, state resident: full-time $10,870; part-time $453 per credit hour. Tuition, nonresident: full-time $22,210; part-time $925 per credit hour. *Required fees:* $84.68 per credit hour. $508.06 per semester. Part-time tuition and fees vary according to course load and program. *Financial support:* Fellowships available. *Unit head:* Jianwei Zhang, Chair, 518-442-5006, E-mail: jzhang@albany.edu.

University at Buffalo, the State University of New York, Graduate School, Graduate School of Education, Department of Learning and Instruction, Buffalo, NY 14260. Offers biology education (Ed M, Certificate); chemistry education (Ed M, Certificate); childhood education (Ed M); childhood education with bilingual extension (Ed M); college teaching (Advanced Certificate); curriculum, instruction and the science of learning (PhD); early childhood education (Ed M); early childhood education with bilingual extension (Ed M); earth science education (Ed M, Certificate); education and technology (Ed M); education studies (Ed M); educational technology and new literacies (Certificate); educational technology and new literacies (Advanced Certificate); elementary education (Ed D); English education (Ed M, Certificate); English education studies (Ed M); English for speakers of other languages (Ed M); foreign and second language education (PhD); French education (Ed M, Certificate); German education (Ed M, Certificate); gifted education (Certificate); Latin education (Ed M, Certificate); literacy education studies (Ed M); literacy specialist (Ed M); literacy teaching and learning (Certificate); mathematics education (Ed M, Certificate); music education (Ed M, Certificate); music education studies (Ed M); music learning theory (Advanced Certificate); online education (Advanced Certificate); physics education (Ed M, Certificate); science and the public (Ed M); social studies education (Ed M, Certificate); Spanish education (Ed M, Certificate); special education (PhD); teaching English to speakers of other languages (Ed M). *Program availability:* Part-time, evening/weekend, 100% online. *Faculty:* 26 full-time (19 women), 74 part-time/adjunct (52 women). *Students:* 172 full-time (122 women), 325 part-time (226 women); includes 44 minority (25 Black or African American, non-Hispanic/Latino; 5 American Indian or Alaska Native, non-Hispanic/Latino; 14 Asian, non-Hispanic/Latino), 57 international. Average age 33. 316 applicants, 78% accepted, 174 enrolled. In 2017, 109 master's, 34 doctorates, 15 other advanced degrees awarded. *Degree requirements:* For master's, comprehensive exam; for doctorate, thesis/dissertation, research analysis exam, research experience.

Entrance requirements: For master's, letters of reference; for doctorate, GRE General Test or MAT, interview, writing sample, letters of recommendation. Additional exam requirements/recommendations for international students: Required—TOEFL (minimum score 600 paper-based; 96 iBT). *Application deadline:* For fall admission, 2/1 priority date for domestic and international students; for spring admission, 11/15 priority date for domestic students, 10/1 for international students. Applications are processed on a rolling basis. Application fee: $50. Electronic applications accepted. *Financial support:* In 2017–18, 42 fellowships (averaging $5,181 per year), 44 research assistantships with tuition reimbursements (averaging $10,908 per year) were awarded; teaching assistantships, career-related internships or fieldwork, Federal Work-Study, institutionally sponsored loans, scholarships/grants, tuition waivers (full and partial), and unspecified assistantships also available. Financial award application deadline: 2/28; financial award applicants required to submit FAFSA. *Faculty research:* Science assessment, foreign language teaching and learning, early learning, new literacies, gender and education. *Total annual research expenditures:* $413,233. *Unit head:* Dr. David Bruce, Chair, 716-645-4069, Fax: 716-645-3161, E-mail: gse-info@buffalo.edu. *Application contact:* Luann Zak, Admissions Assistant, 716-645-2110, Fax: 716-645-7937, E-mail: luannzak@buffalo.edu.
Website: http://gse.buffalo.edu/lai

University at Buffalo, the State University of New York, Graduate School, Graduate School of Education, Department of Library and Information Studies, Buffalo, NY 14260. Offers information and library science (MS); library and information studies (Certificate); school librarianship (MS). *Accreditation:* ALA (one or more programs are accredited). *Program availability:* Part-time, 100% online. *Faculty:* 9 full-time (6 women), 8 part-time/adjunct (6 women). *Students:* 42 full-time (32 women), 162 part-time (131 women); includes 11 minority (5 Black or African American, non-Hispanic/Latino; 2 American Indian or Alaska Native, non-Hispanic/Latino; 4 Asian, non-Hispanic/Latino), 2 international. Average age 34. 117 applicants, 91% accepted, 73 enrolled. In 2017, 62 master's, 1 other advanced degree awarded. *Degree requirements:* For master's, thesis optional; for Certificate, thesis. *Entrance requirements:* For master's, letters of recommendation. Additional exam requirements/recommendations for international students: Required—TOEFL (minimum score 550 paper-based; 79 iBT). *Application deadline:* For fall admission, 4/1 priority date for domestic and international students; for spring admission, 10/15 priority date for domestic students, 10/15 for international students. Applications are processed on a rolling basis. Application fee: $50. Electronic applications accepted. *Financial support:* In 2017–18, 16 fellowships (averaging $3,245 per year), 6 research assistantships with tuition reimbursements (averaging $10,222 per year) were awarded; teaching assistantships, Federal Work-Study, scholarships/grants, tuition waivers (full and partial), and unspecified assistantships also available. Support available to part-time students. Financial award application deadline: 3/1; financial award applicants required to submit FAFSA. *Faculty research:* Information-seeking behavior, thesauri, impact of technology, questioning behaviors, educational informatics. *Total annual research expenditures:* $56,553. *Unit head:* Dr. Heidi Julien, Chair, 716-645-1474, Fax: 716-645-3775, E-mail: heidijul@buffalo.edu. *Application contact:* Pat Glinski, Admissions Assistant, 716-645-2110, Fax: 716-645-7937, E-mail: gse-info@buffalo.edu.
Website: http://www.gse.buffalo.edu/lis/

The University of Akron, Graduate School, College of Education, Department of Educational Foundations and Leadership, Program in Instructional Technology, Akron, OH 44325. Offers MA. *Program availability:* Online learning. *Students:* 2 full-time (1 woman), 37 part-time (23 women); includes 6 minority (5 Black or African American, non-Hispanic/Latino; 1 Hispanic/Latino), 2 international. Average age 35. 16 applicants, 100% accepted, 16 enrolled. In 2017, 17 master's awarded. *Degree requirements:* For master's, electronic portfolio. *Entrance requirements:* Additional exam requirements/recommendations for international students: Required—TOEFL (minimum score 79 iBT), IELTS (minimum score 6.5). *Application deadline:* Applications are processed on a rolling basis. Application fee: $45 ($70 for international students). Electronic applications accepted. *Unit head:* Dr. Evonn Welton, Interim Department Chair, 330-972-6742, E-mail: ewelton@uakron.edu. *Application contact:* Kelly Chaff, College Program Specialist, 330-972-7028, E-mail: klchaff@uakron.edu.
Website: http://www.uakron.edu/education/academic-programs/graduate-programs.dot

University of Alaska Southeast, Graduate Programs, Program in Education, Juneau, AK 99801. Offers educational leadership (M Ed); elementary education (MAT); learning design and technology (M Ed); mathematics education (M Ed); reading specialist (M Ed); secondary education (MAT); special education (M Ed, MAT). *Accreditation:* NCATE. *Program availability:* Part-time, evening/weekend, online learning. *Degree requirements:* For master's, comprehensive exam or project, portfolio. *Entrance requirements:* For master's, PRAXIS, minimum GPA of 3.0, writing sample, letters of recommendation. Electronic applications accepted. *Faculty research:* Applied classroom research, culturally responsive practices, action research, teaching effectiveness.

University of Alberta, Faculty of Graduate Studies and Research, Department of Educational Psychology, Edmonton, AB T6G 2E1, Canada. Offers counseling psychology (M Ed, PhD); educational psychology (M Ed, PhD); instructional technology (M Ed); school counseling (M Ed); school psychology (M Ed, PhD); special education (M Ed, PhD); special education-deafness studies (M Ed); teaching English as a second language (M Ed). *Program availability:* Part-time. *Degree requirements:* For master's, thesis optional; for doctorate, comprehensive exam, thesis/dissertation. *Entrance requirements:* For master's and doctorate, minimum GPA of 3.0. Additional exam requirements/recommendations for international students: Required—TOEFL. *Faculty research:* Human learning, development and assessment.

University of Arkansas, Graduate School, College of Education and Health Professions, Department of Curriculum and Instruction, Program in Educational Technology, Fayetteville, AR 72701. Offers M Ed. *Accreditation:* NCATE. *Program availability:* Part-time, evening/weekend. In 2017, 12 master's awarded. *Entrance requirements:* For master's, GRE General Test, MAT or minimum GPA of 3.0. *Application deadline:* For fall admission, 8/1 for domestic students, 4/1 for international students; for spring admission, 12/1 for domestic students, 10/1 for international students; for summer admission, 4/15 for domestic students, 3/1 for international students. Applications are processed on a rolling basis. Application fee: $60. Electronic applications accepted. *Expenses:* Tuition, state resident: full-time $3782. Tuition, nonresident: full-time $10,238. *Financial support:* Fellowships with tuition reimbursements, research assistantships, teaching assistantships, career-related internships or fieldwork, and Federal Work-Study available. Support available to part-time students. Financial award application deadline: 4/1; financial award applicants required to submit FAFSA. *Unit head:* Dr. Derrick Mears, Program Coordinator, 479-575-5439, E-mail: dmears@uark.edu. *Application contact:* Dr. Cheryl Murphy, Graduate Coordinator, 479-575-5111, Fax: 479-575-6676, E-mail: cmurphy@uark.edu.
Website: https://etec.uark.edu

University of Arkansas at Little Rock, Graduate School, College of Education and Health Professions, Department of Educational Leadership, Program in Learning Systems Technology Education, Little Rock, AR 72204-1099. Offers M Ed. *Degree requirements:* For master's, comprehensive exam or defense of portfolio. *Faculty research:* Instructional program development, educational technology product development, educational technology management.

University of Central Arkansas, Graduate School, College of Education, Department of Leadership Studies, Program in Library Media and Information Technology, Conway, AR 72035-0001. Offers MS. *Program availability:* Part-time, evening/weekend, online learning. *Degree requirements:* For master's, comprehensive exam. *Entrance requirements:* For master's, GRE General Test, minimum GPA of 2.7. Additional exam requirements/recommendations for international students: Required—TOEFL (minimum score 550 paper-based). Electronic applications accepted.

University of Central Florida, College of Community Innovation and Education, Department of Learning Sciences and Educational Research, Program in Instructional Design and Technology, Orlando, FL 32816. Offers e-learning (Certificate); educational technology (Certificate); instructional design (Certificate); instructional design and technology (MA), including e-learning, educational technology, instructional systems; instructional design for simulations (Certificate). *Program availability:* Part-time. *Students:* 20 full-time (17 women), 114 part-time (85 women); includes 40 minority (12 Black or African American, non-Hispanic/Latino; 1 American Indian or Alaska Native, non-Hispanic/Latino; 5 Asian, non-Hispanic/Latino; 22 Hispanic/Latino), 1 international. Average age 37. 86 applicants, 90% accepted, 55 enrolled. In 2017, 36 master's, 14 other advanced degrees awarded. *Degree requirements:* For master's, thesis or alternative. *Entrance requirements:* For master's, letters of recommendation, resume. Additional exam requirements/recommendations for international students: Required—TOEFL. *Application deadline:* For fall admission, 7/15 for domestic students; for spring admission, 12/1 for domestic students. Application fee: $30. Electronic applications accepted. *Expenses:* Tuition, state resident: part-time $288.16 per credit hour. Tuition, nonresident: part-time $1073.31 per credit hour. Tuition and fees vary according to program. *Financial support:* In 2017–18, 4 students received support, including 1 fellowship with partial tuition reimbursement available (averaging $600 per year), 2 research assistantships with partial tuition reimbursements available (averaging $9,339 per year), 1 teaching assistantship with partial tuition reimbursement available (averaging $10,740 per year); health care benefits also available. Financial award application deadline: 3/1; financial award applicants required to submit FAFSA. *Unit head:* Dr. Richard Hartshorne, Program Coordinator, 407-823-1861, E-mail: richard.hartshorne@ucf.edu. *Application contact:* Associate Director, Graduate Admissions, 407-823-2766, Fax: 407-823-6442, E-mail: gradadmissions@ucf.edu. Website: https://edcollege.ucf.edu/insttech/

University of Central Florida, College of Community Innovation and Education, Education Doctoral Programs, Orlando, FL 32816. Offers curriculum and instruction (Ed D); education (PhD), including communication sciences and disorders, counselor education, early childhood education, elementary education, exceptional education, exercise physiology, higher education, instructional design and technology, mathematics education, methodology, measurement and analysis, reading education, science education, social science education, TESOL; educational leadership (Ed D). *Students:* 122 full-time (86 women), 129 part-time (88 women); includes 64 minority (24 Black or African American, non-Hispanic/Latino; 1 American Indian or Alaska Native, non-Hispanic/Latino; 9 Asian, non-Hispanic/Latino; 24 Hispanic/Latino; 6 Two or more races, non-Hispanic/Latino), 26 international. Average age 38. 195 applicants, 47% accepted, 72 enrolled. In 2017, 89 doctorates awarded. *Entrance requirements:* For doctorate, GRE, letters of recommendation, goal statement, resume, writing sample. Application fee: $30. Electronic applications accepted. *Expenses:* Tuition, state resident: part-time $288.16 per credit hour. Tuition, nonresident: part-time $1073.31 per credit hour. Tuition and fees vary according to program. *Financial support:* In 2017–18, 77 students received support, including 28 fellowships with partial tuition reimbursements available (averaging $5,733 per year), 29 research assistantships with partial tuition reimbursements available (averaging $10,230 per year), 54 teaching assistantships with partial tuition reimbursement available (averaging $11,614 per year); health care benefits also available. Financial award application deadline: 3/1; financial award applicants required to submit FAFSA. *Unit head:* Dr. Edward Robinson, Director of Doctoral Programs, 407-823-6106, E-mail: edward.robinson@ucf.edu. *Application contact:* Associate Director, Graduate Admissions, 407-823-2766, Fax: 407-823-6442, E-mail: gradadmissions@ucf.edu. Website: https://edcollege.ucf.edu/academic-programs/graduate/

University of Central Missouri, The Graduate School, Warrensburg, MO 64093. Offers accountancy (MA); accounting (MBA); applied mathematics (MS); aviation safety (MA); biology (MS); business administration (MBA); career and technical education leadership (MS); college student personnel administration (MS); communication (MA); computer science (MS); counseling (MS); criminal justice (MS); educational leadership (Ed D); educational technology (MS); elementary and early childhood education (MSE); English (MA); environmental studies (MA); finance (MBA); history (MA); human services/educational technology (Ed S); human services/learning resources (Ed S); human services/professional counseling (Ed S); industrial hygiene (MS); industrial management (MS); information systems (MBA); information technology (MS); kinesiology (MS); library science and information services (MS); literacy education (MSE); marketing (MBA); mathematics (MS); music (MA); occupational safety management (MS); psychology (MS); rural family nursing (MS); school administration (MSE); social gerontology (MS); sociology (MA); special education (MSE); speech language pathology (MS); superintendency (Ed S); teaching (MAT); teaching English as a second language (MA); technology (MS); technology management (PhD); theatre (MA). *Program availability:* Part-time, 100% online, blended/hybrid learning. *Faculty:* 337 full-time (145 women), 41 part-time/adjunct (28 women). *Students:* 785 full-time (398 women), 1,633 part-time (1,063 women); includes 231 minority (102 Black or African American, non-Hispanic/Latino; 4 American Indian or Alaska Native, non-Hispanic/Latino; 16 Asian, non-Hispanic/Latino; 52 Hispanic/Latino; 57 Two or more races, non-Hispanic/Latino), 692 international. Average age 30. In 2017, 2,605 master's, 122 other advanced degrees awarded. *Degree requirements:* For master's and Ed S, comprehensive exam (for some programs), thesis (for some programs). *Entrance requirements:* Additional exam requirements/recommendations for international students: Required—TOEFL (minimum score 550 paper-based; 79 iBT). *Application deadline:* For fall admission, 6/1 priority date for domestic and international students; for spring admission, 10/1 priority date for domestic and international students; for summer admission, 4/1 priority date for domestic and international students. Applications are processed on a rolling basis. Application fee: $30 ($75 for international students). Electronic applications accepted. *Expenses:* Tuition, state resident: full-time $8771; part-time $292.35 per credit hour. Tuition, nonresident: full-time $17,541; part-time $584.70 per credit hour. *Required fees:* $372; $24.78 per credit hour. *Financial support:* In 2017–18, 99 students received support. Research assistantships, teaching assistantships, career-related internships or fieldwork, Federal Work-Study, scholarships/grants, and administrative and laboratory assistantships available. Support available to part-time students. Financial award application deadline: 3/1; financial award applicants required to submit FAFSA. *Unit head:* Shellie Hewitt, Director of Graduate and International Student Services, 660-543-4621, Fax: 660-543-4778, E-mail: hewitt@ucmo.edu. *Application contact:* 660-543-4621, E-mail: admit_intl@ucmo.edu. Website: http://www.ucmo.edu/graduate/

University of Central Oklahoma, The Jackson College of Graduate Studies, College of Education and Professional Studies, Donna Nigh Department of Advanced Professional and Special Services, Edmond, OK 73034-5209. Offers educational leadership (M Ed); library media education (M Ed); reading (M Ed); school counseling (M Ed); special education (M Ed), including mild/moderate disabilities, severe-profound/multiple disabilities; speech-language pathology (MS). *Accreditation:* ASHA. *Program availability:* Part-time. *Faculty:* 17 full-time (12 women), 8 part-time/adjunct (4 women). *Students:* 73 full-time (65 women), 286 part-time (239 women); includes 91 minority (41 Black or African American, non-Hispanic/Latino; 8 American Indian or Alaska Native, non-Hispanic/Latino; 5 Asian, non-Hispanic/Latino; 20 Hispanic/Latino; 17 Two or more races, non-Hispanic/Latino), 3 international. Average age 35. 146 applicants, 83% accepted, 91 enrolled. In 2017, 128 master's awarded. *Degree requirements:* For master's, comprehensive exam (for some programs), thesis (for some programs). *Entrance requirements:* Additional exam requirements/recommendations for international students: Required—TOEFL (minimum score 550 paper-based; 79 iBT), IELTS (minimum score 6.5). *Application deadline:* For fall admission, 7/15 for international students; for spring admission, 11/15 for international students; for summer admission, 1/31 for domestic students. Applications are processed on a rolling basis. Application fee: $60. Electronic applications accepted. *Expenses:* Tuition, state resident: full-time $5375; part-time $268.75 per credit hour. Tuition, nonresident: full-time $13,295; part-time $664.75 per credit hour. *Required fees:* $626; $31.30 per credit hour. One-time fee: $50. Tuition and fees vary according to program. *Financial support:* In 2017–18, 74 students received support, including 1 research assistantship with partial tuition reimbursement available (averaging $2,958 per year), 1 teaching assistantship with partial tuition reimbursement available (averaging $5,915 per year); career-related internships or fieldwork, scholarships/grants, tuition waivers (partial), and unspecified assistantships also available. Financial award application deadline: 3/31; financial award applicants required to submit FAFSA. *Unit head:* Dr. Cheryl Evans, Chair, 405-974-5437, Fax: 405-974-3857. *Application contact:* Carlie Wellington, Assistant Director, CEPS Graduate Enrollment, 405-974-5105, Fax: 405-974-3851, E-mail: gradcoll@uco.edu. Website: http://sites.uco.edu/ceps/dept/Education-Programs/apss/index.asp

University of Colorado Denver, School of Education and Human Development, Information and Learning Technologies Program, Denver, CO 80217. Offers e-learning design and implementation (MA); instructional design and adult learning (MA); K-12 teaching (MA). *Program availability:* Part-time, evening/weekend, online learning. *Degree requirements:* For master's, comprehensive exam (for some programs), comprehensive exam or online portfolio; 30 credit hours. *Entrance requirements:* For master's, GRE or MAT (if GPA is below 2.75), resume, statement of intent, three letters of recommendation, transcripts from all colleges/universities previously attended. Additional exam requirements/recommendations for international students: Required—TOEFL (minimum score 537 paper-based; 75 iBT); Recommended—IELTS (minimum score 6.5). Electronic applications accepted. *Expenses:* Contact institution. *Faculty research:* Technology for educational management, instructional design foundations, e-learning, educational design.

University of Connecticut, Graduate School, Neag School of Education, Department of Educational Psychology, Cognition, Instruction, and Learning Technology Program, Storrs, CT 06269. Offers MA, PhD. *Degree requirements:* For master's, comprehensive exam; for doctorate, thesis/dissertation. *Entrance requirements:* For doctorate, GRE General Test. Additional exam requirements/recommendations for international students: Required—TOEFL (minimum score 550 paper-based). Electronic applications accepted.

University of Dayton, Department of Teacher Education, Dayton, OH 45469. Offers adolescence to young adult education (MS Ed); early childhood leadership and advocacy (MS Ed); interdisciplinary education (MS Ed), including visual arts; interdisciplinary education studies (MS Ed); leadership in educational systems (MS Ed); literacy (MS Ed); mathematics education (MS Ed); middle childhood education (MS Ed); multi-age education (MS Ed), including world languages; music education (MS Ed); teacher as leader (MS Ed); teacher education (MS Ed); technology-enhanced learning (MS Ed); trans-disciplinary early childhood education (MS Ed). *Program availability:* Part-time, 100% online. *Faculty:* 23 full-time (20 women), 41 part-time/adjunct (36 women). *Students:* 45 full-time (38 women), 68 part-time (57 women); includes 7 minority (3 Black or African American, non-Hispanic/Latino; 1 Hispanic/Latino; 3 Two or more races, non-Hispanic/Latino), 6 international. Average age 31. 106 applicants, 28% accepted. In 2017, 70 master's awarded. *Degree requirements:* For master's, variable foreign language requirement, thesis or alternative, internship (for teaching licensure or endorsement). *Entrance requirements:* For master's, GRE (minimum score of 149 verbal, 4 on writing) or MAT (minimum score of 396) if undergraduate GPA was under 2.75, minimum GPA of 2.75, 3 letters of recommendation, personal statement or resume, official transcripts. Additional exam requirements/recommendations for international students: Required—TOEFL (minimum score 550 paper-based; 80 iBT); Recommended—IELTS (minimum score 6.5). *Application deadline:* Applications are processed on a rolling basis. Application fee: $0 ($50 for international students). Electronic applications accepted. *Expenses:* Contact institution. *Financial support:* In 2017–18, 5 research assistantships with partial tuition reimbursements (averaging $9,640 per year) were awarded; teaching assistantships, career-related internships or fieldwork, institutionally sponsored loans, and unspecified assistantships also available. Financial award application deadline: 3/1; financial award applicants required to submit FAFSA. *Faculty research:* Social emotional learning, culturally responsive teaching, urban teaching, literacy, instructional strategies, pre-service teacher education preparation. *Unit head:* Dr. Connie L. Bowman, Chair, 937-229-3348, E-mail: cbowman1@udayton.edu. *Application contact:* Gina Seiter, Coordinator of Graduate Programs and Licensing, 937-229-3103, E-mail: gseiter1@udayton.edu. Website: https://www.udayton.edu/education/departments_and_programs/edt

The University of Findlay, Office of Graduate Admissions, Findlay, OH 45840. Offers applied security and analytics (MSAS); athletic training (MAT); business (MBA), including certified management accountant, certified public accountant, health care management, hospitality management; education (MA Ed, Ed D), including children's literature (MA Ed), curriculum and teaching (MA Ed), education (MA Ed), educational administration (MA Ed), human resource development (MA Ed), mathematics (MA Ed), reading (MA Ed), science education (MA Ed), superintendent (Ed D), teaching (Ed D), technology (MA Ed); environmental, safety, and health management (MSEM); health informatics (MS); occupational therapy (MOT); pharmacy (Pharm D); physical therapy (DPT); physician assistant (MPA); rhetoric and writing (MA); teaching English to speakers of other languages (TESOL) and applied linguistics (MA). *Program availability:* Part-time, evening/weekend, 100% online, blended/hybrid learning. *Students:* 688 full-time (430 women), 553 part-time (308 women), 170 international. Average age 28. In 2017, 366 master's, 137 doctorates awarded. *Degree requirements:* For master's, comprehensive exam (for some programs), thesis (for some programs), cumulative project, capstone project; for doctorate, thesis/dissertation (for some programs). *Entrance requirements:* For master's, GRE/GMAT, bachelor's degree from accredited institution, minimum undergraduate GPA of 2.5 in last 64 hours of course work; for doctorate, GRE, MAT, minimum cumulative GPA of 3.0. Additional exam requirements/recommendations for international students: Required—TOEFL (minimum score 79 iBT), IELTS (minimum score 7), PTE (minimum score 61). *Application deadline:* Applications are processed on a rolling basis. Electronic applications accepted. *Financial support:* In 2017–18, 10 research assistantships with partial tuition

reimbursements (averaging $7,200 per year), 35 teaching assistantships with partial tuition reimbursements (averaging $7,200 per year) were awarded; Federal Work-Study, institutionally sponsored loans, and unspecified assistantships also available. Financial award applicants required to submit FAFSA. *Unit head:* Christopher M. Harris, Director of Admissions, 419-434-4347, E-mail: harrisc1@findlay.edu. *Application contact:* Madeline Fauser Brennan, Graduate Admissions Counselor, 419-434-4636, Fax: 419-434-4898, E-mail: fauserbrennan@findlay.edu.
Website: http://www.findlay.edu/admissions/graduate/Pages/default.aspx

University of Georgia, College of Education, Department of Career and Information Studies, Athens, GA 30602. Offers learning, design, and technology (M Ed, PhD, Ed S), including instructional design and development (M Ed, Ed S); workforce education (MAT, Ed D), including business education (MAT). *Accreditation:* NCATE. *Entrance requirements:* For master's, GRE General Test, MAT; for doctorate, GRE General Test; for Ed S, GRE General Test or MAT. Electronic applications accepted.

University of Hartford, College of Education, Nursing, and Health Professions, Program in Educational Technology, West Hartford, CT 06117-1599. Offers M Ed. *Accreditation:* NCATE. *Program availability:* Part-time, evening/weekend. *Degree requirements:* For master's, comprehensive exam. *Entrance requirements:* For master's, interview, 2 letters of recommendation. Additional exam requirements/recommendations for international students: Required—TOEFL (minimum score 550 paper-based). Electronic applications accepted.

University of Hawaii at Manoa, Office of Graduate Education, College of Education, Department of Educational Technology, Honolulu, HI 96822. Offers M Ed. *Program availability:* Part-time. *Degree requirements:* For master's, thesis optional. *Entrance requirements:* Additional exam requirements/recommendations for international students: Required—TOEFL (minimum score 650 paper-based; 114 iBT), IELTS (minimum score 7). *Faculty research:* Distance education-interaction via electronic means.

University of Hawaii at Manoa, Office of Graduate Education, College of Education, PhD in Education Program, Honolulu, HI 96822. Offers curriculum and instruction (PhD); educational administration (PhD); educational foundations (PhD); educational policy studies (PhD); educational psychology (PhD); exceptionalities (PhD); kinesiology (PhD); learning design and technology (PhD). *Program availability:* Part-time, evening/weekend. *Degree requirements:* For doctorate, thesis/dissertation. *Entrance requirements:* For doctorate, GRE General Test, sample of written work. Additional exam requirements/recommendations for international students: Required—TOEFL (minimum score 600 paper-based; 100 iBT), IELTS (minimum score 7).

University of Houston–Clear Lake, School of Education, Program in Curriculum and Instruction, Houston, TX 77058-1002. Offers curriculum and instruction (MS); early childhood education (MS); reading (MS); school library and information science (MS). *Program availability:* Part-time, evening/weekend. *Degree requirements:* For master's, thesis (for some programs). *Entrance requirements:* For master's, GRE or minimum GPA of 3.0 in last 60 hours. Additional exam requirements/recommendations for international students: Required—TOEFL (minimum score 550 paper-based). Electronic applications accepted.

University of Houston–Clear Lake, School of Education, Program in Foundations and Professional Studies, Houston, TX 77058-1002. Offers counseling (MS); instructional technology (MS); multicultural studies (MS). *Program availability:* Part-time, evening/weekend. *Degree requirements:* For master's, thesis optional. *Entrance requirements:* For master's, GRE or minimum GPA of 3.0 in last 60 hours. Additional exam requirements/recommendations for international students: Required—TOEFL (minimum score 550 paper-based). Electronic applications accepted.

University of Houston–Victoria, School of Education, Health Professions and Human Development, Victoria, TX 77901-4450. Offers administration and supervision (M Ed); adult and higher education (M Ed); counselor education (M Ed); curriculum and instruction (M Ed); dyslexia education (Certificate); educational technology (M Ed); special education (M Ed). *Program availability:* Part-time, evening/weekend, online learning. *Degree requirements:* For master's, comprehensive exam, project or thesis. *Entrance requirements:* For master's, GRE General Test. Additional exam requirements/recommendations for international students: Required—TOEFL. Electronic applications accepted. *Faculty research:* Reading and language arts education, evaluation and diagnosis of special children's abilities.

University of Illinois at Springfield, Graduate Programs, College of Education and Human Services, Department of Educational Leadership, Springfield, IL 62703-5407. Offers chief school business official (CAS); educational leadership (MA, CAS); educational technology (Graduate Certificate); English as a second language (Graduate Certificate); higher education online pedagogy (Graduate Certificate); leadership and learning (Graduate Certificate); legal aspects of education (Graduate Certificate). *Program availability:* Part-time, evening/weekend, 100% online, blended/hybrid learning. *Faculty:* 4 full-time (1 woman), 14 part-time/adjunct (11 women). *Students:* 2 full-time (1 woman), 109 part-time (70 women); includes 15 minority (10 Black or African American, non-Hispanic/Latino; 1 American Indian or Alaska Native, non-Hispanic/Latino; 1 Asian, non-Hispanic/Latino; 3 Hispanic/Latino). Average age 35. 46 applicants, 57% accepted, 23 enrolled. In 2017, 30 master's, 5 other advanced degrees awarded. *Degree requirements:* For master's, capstone course. *Entrance requirements:* For master's, minimum undergraduate GPA of 3.0, valid Illinois Teaching License, minimum of two years of successful teaching experience, portfolio that includes letters of recommendation, interview. Additional exam requirements/recommendations for international students: Required—TOEFL (minimum score 500 paper-based; 61 iBT). *Application deadline:* Applications are processed on a rolling basis. Application fee: $60 ($75 for international students). Electronic applications accepted. *Expenses:* Tuition, state resident: full-time $7896; part-time $329 per credit hour. Tuition, nonresident: full-time $16,200; part-time $675 per credit hour. Tuition and fees vary according to program. *Financial support:* In 2017–18, research assistantships with full tuition reimbursements (averaging $10,249 per year), teaching assistantships with full tuition reimbursements (averaging $10,303 per year) were awarded; fellowships, career-related internships or fieldwork, Federal Work-Study, scholarships/grants, health care benefits, and unspecified assistantships also available. Support available to part-time students. Financial award application deadline: 11/15; financial award applicants required to submit FAFSA. *Unit head:* Dr. Scott Day, Program Administrator, 217-206-7520, Fax: 217-206-6775, E-mail: day.scott@uis.edu.
Website: http://www.uis.edu/edl/

The University of Kansas, Graduate Studies, School of Education, Department of Educational Leadership and Policy Studies, Program in Educational Technology, Lawrence, KS 66045. Offers MS Ed, PhD. *Program availability:* Part-time, evening/weekend. *Students:* 7 full-time (6 women), 12 part-time (10 women); includes 4 minority (1 American Indian or Alaska Native, non-Hispanic/Latino; 2 Asian, non-Hispanic/Latino; 1 Hispanic/Latino), 6 international. Average age 38. 16 applicants, 88% accepted, 5 enrolled. In 2017, 1,211 master's awarded. *Entrance requirements:* For master's, resume or electronic portfolio, official transcripts, statement of purpose, three letters of recommendation; for doctorate, GRE, resume or electronic portfolio, official transcripts, statement of purpose, three letters of recommendation, sample of academic writing.

Additional exam requirements/recommendations for international students: Required—TOEFL, IELTS. *Application deadline:* For fall admission, 6/1 priority date for domestic and international students; for spring admission, 11/1 for domestic and international students; for summer admission, 4/1 for domestic and international students. Application fee: $65 ($85 for international students). Electronic applications accepted. *Financial support:* Research assistantships, teaching assistantships, and unspecified assistantships available. Financial award application deadline: 2/21. *Unit head:* Dr. Susan B. Twombly, Chair, 785-864-9721, E-mail: stwombly@ku.edu. *Application contact:* Denise Brubaker, Admissions Coordinator, 785-864-4458, Fax: 785-864-4697, E-mail: elps@ku.edu.
Website: http://edtech.ku.edu/

University of Kentucky, Graduate School, College of Education, Program in Curriculum and Instruction, Lexington, KY 40506-0032. Offers curriculum and instruction (Ed D, PhD); elementary education (MA Ed); instructional system design (MS Ed); literacy (MA Ed); middle school education (MA Ed, MS Ed); secondary education (MA Ed, MS Ed). *Accreditation:* NCATE. *Degree requirements:* For master's, comprehensive exam, thesis optional; for doctorate, comprehensive exam, thesis/dissertation. *Entrance requirements:* For master's, GRE General Test, minimum undergraduate GPA of 2.75; for doctorate, GRE General Test, minimum graduate GPA of 3.0. Additional exam requirements/recommendations for international students: Required—TOEFL (minimum score 550 paper-based). Electronic applications accepted. *Faculty research:* Educational reform, multicultural education, classroom instructional practices, performance based assessment, primary school programs.

University of Maine, Graduate School, College of Education and Human Development, School of Kinesiology, Physical Education and Athletic Training, Orono, ME 04469. Offers classroom technology integrationist (CGS); education data specialist (CGS); educational technology coordinator (CGS); kinesiology and physical education (M Ed, MS); science education (M Ed, MS); STEM education (PhD). *Program availability:* Part-time, evening/weekend. *Faculty:* 3 full-time (0 women). *Students:* 10 full-time (3 women), 1 part-time (0 women); includes 2 minority (1 Black or African American, non-Hispanic/Latino; 1 Asian, non-Hispanic/Latino). Average age 24. 8 applicants, 100% accepted, 5 enrolled. In 2017, 6 master's awarded. *Degree requirements:* For master's, thesis (for some programs); for doctorate, comprehensive exam, thesis/dissertation. *Entrance requirements:* For master's, GRE General Test, MAT; for doctorate, GRE General Test. Additional exam requirements/recommendations for international students: Required—TOEFL. *Application deadline:* For fall admission, 1/15 for domestic students. Applications are processed on a rolling basis. Application fee: $65. Electronic applications accepted. *Expenses:* Tuition, state resident: full-time $7722; part-time $429 per credit hour. Tuition, nonresident: full-time $25,146; part-time $1397 per credit hour. *Required fees:* $1162; $581 per credit hour. *Financial support:* In 2017–18, 7 students received support, including 6 teaching assistantships with full tuition reimbursements available (averaging $15,200 per year); Federal Work-Study, scholarships/grants, and unspecified assistantships also available. Financial award application deadline: 3/1. *Faculty research:* Geriatric equilibrium, physical activity and technology, muscle cell metabolism, hormonal response to exercise. *Unit head:* Dr. Jim Artesani, Associate Dean of Accreditation and Graduate Affairs, 207-581-4061, Fax: 207-581-2423. *Application contact:* Scott G. Delcourt, Assistant Vice President for Graduate Studies and Senior Associate Dean, 207-581-3291, Fax: 207-581-3232, E-mail: graduate@maine.edu.
Website: http://umaine.edu/edhd/

University of Maine at Farmington, Graduate Programs in Education, Farmington, ME 04938. Offers early childhood education (MS Ed); educational leadership (MS Ed); instructional technology (M Ed). M Ed offered in collaboration with University of Maine and University of Southern Maine. *Accreditation:* NCATE. *Program availability:* Part-time-only, evening/weekend, 100% online, blended/hybrid learning. *Faculty:* 8 full-time (7 women), 2 part-time/adjunct (1 woman). *Students:* 106 part-time (92 women). Average age 36. 6 applicants, 100% accepted, 6 enrolled. In 2017, 29 master's awarded. *Degree requirements:* For master's, thesis, capstone research project. *Entrance requirements:* For master's, baccalaureate degree from accredited institution, valid teaching certificate or professional experience in education. Additional exam requirements/recommendations for international students: Required—TOEFL. *Application deadline:* For fall admission, 8/10 for domestic students; for spring admission, 1/5 for domestic students; for summer admission, 4/10 for domestic students. Applications are processed on a rolling basis. Application fee: $60. Electronic applications accepted. *Expenses:* Contact institution. *Financial support:* Applicants required to submit FAFSA. *Faculty research:* Teacher leadership, school improvement strategies, technology integration. *Unit head:* Dr. Johanna Prince, Director of Graduate Programs in Education, 207-778-7066, E-mail: gradstudies@maine.edu. *Application contact:* Valerie Soucie, Administrative Specialist, 207-778-7502, Fax: 207-778-8134, E-mail: gradstudies@maine.edu.
Website: http://www2.umf.maine.edu/gradstudies/

University of Maryland, Baltimore County, The Graduate School, College of Arts, Humanities and Social Sciences, Department of Education, Program in Instructional Systems Development, Halethorpe, MD 21227. Offers distance education (Graduate Certificate); instructional systems development (MA, Graduate Certificate), including distance education (Graduate Certificate); instructional technology (Graduate Certificate). *Program availability:* Part-time, evening/weekend, 100% online, blended/hybrid learning. *Faculty:* 2 full-time (0 women), 9 part-time/adjunct (3 women). *Students:* 4 full-time (2 women), 81 part-time (65 women); includes 29 minority (19 Black or African American, non-Hispanic/Latino; 4 Asian, non-Hispanic/Latino; 4 Hispanic/Latino; 2 Two or more races, non-Hispanic/Latino). Average age 41. 53 applicants, 96% accepted, 24 enrolled. In 2017, 27 master's, 60 other advanced degrees awarded. *Degree requirements:* For master's, comprehensive exam (for some programs), portfolio (for some programs). *Entrance requirements:* Additional exam requirements/recommendations for international students: Required—TOEFL (minimum score 99 iBT), GRE. *Application deadline:* For fall admission, 8/1 priority date for domestic students, 1/1 priority date for international students; for spring admission, 12/1 priority date for domestic students; for summer admission, 4/1 priority date for domestic students. Applications are processed on a rolling basis. Application fee: $50. Electronic applications accepted. *Expenses:* Required fees: $132. *Application deadline:* 2/14; applicants required to submit FAFSA. *Faculty research:* E-learning, distance education, instructional design. *Unit head:* Dr. Greg Williams, Graduate Program Director, 443-543-5447, Fax: 443-543-5096, E-mail: gregw@umbc.edu. *Application contact:* Renee Eisenhuth, Graduate Program Coordinator, 443-543-5446, Fax: 443-543-5096, E-mail: reisen@umbc.edu.
Website: http://isd.umbc.edu

University of Maryland, College Park, Academic Affairs, College of Education, Department of Education Policy and Leadership, College Park, MD 20742. Offers curriculum and educational communications (M Ed, MA, Ed D, PhD); social foundations of education (M Ed, MA, Ed D, PhD, CAGS). *Accreditation:* NCATE. *Program availability:* Part-time, evening/weekend, online learning. *Degree requirements:* For master's, thesis or alternative, internship and/or field experience; for doctorate, comprehensive exam, thesis/dissertation, practicum or internship. *Entrance* *requirements:* For master's, GRE General Test or MAT, minimum GPA of 3.0, scholarly writing sample, 3 letters of recommendation; for doctorate, GRE General Test or MAT, scholarly writing sample; minimum undergraduate GPA of 3.0, graduate 3.5. *Faculty research:* Educational technology, adult and higher education.

University of Maryland University College, The Graduate School, Program in Learning Design and Technology, Adelphi, MD 20783. Offers MS. *Program availability:* Part-time, evening/weekend. *Students:* 61 full-time (47 women); includes 27 minority (18 Black or African American, non-Hispanic/Latino; 1 Asian, non-Hispanic/Latino; 5 Hispanic/Latino; 3 Two or more races, non-Hispanic/Latino), 2 international. Average age 41. 31 applicants, 100% accepted, 15 enrolled. *Application deadline:* Applications are processed on a rolling basis. Application fee: $50. Electronic applications accepted. *Financial support:* Scholarships/grants available. Financial award application deadline: 6/1; financial award applicants required to submit FAFSA. *Unit head:* E-mail: graddean@umuc.edu. *Application contact:* Coordinator, Graduate Admissions, 800-888-8682, Fax: 240-684-2151, E-mail: newgrad@umuc.edu.
Website: http://www.umuc.edu/academic-programs/masters-degrees/learning-design-technology-ms.cfm

University of Massachusetts Amherst, Graduate School, College of Education, Program in Education, Amherst, MA 01003. Offers bilingual, English as a second language, and multicultural education (M Ed, Ed S); child study and early education (M Ed); children, families and schools (Ed D, Ed S); early childhood and elementary teacher education (M Ed); educational leadership (M Ed); educational policy and leadership (Ed D); higher education (M Ed); international education (M Ed); language, literacy and culture (Ed D); learning, media and technology (M Ed, Ed S); mathematics, science, and learning technologies (Ed D); reading and writing (M Ed); research, educational measurement and psychometrics (Ed D); school counselor education (M Ed, Ed S); school psychology (Ed S); science education (Ed S); secondary teacher education (M Ed); social justice education (M Ed, Ed D, Ed S); special education (M Ed, Ed D, Ed S); teacher education and school improvement (Ed D, Ed S). *Accreditation:* NCATE. *Program availability:* Part-time, online learning. Terminal master's awarded for partial completion of doctoral program. *Degree requirements:* For doctorate, comprehensive exam, thesis/dissertation. *Entrance requirements:* Additional exam requirements/recommendations for international students: Required—TOEFL (minimum score 550 paper-based; 80 iBT), IELTS (minimum score 6.5). Electronic applications accepted.

University of Massachusetts Boston, College of Advancing and Professional Studies, Program in Instructional Design, Boston, MA 02125-3393. Offers M Ed, Certificate. *Program availability:* Part-time, evening/weekend. *Students:* 5 full-time (3 women), 66 part-time (51 women); includes 4 minority (2 Black or African American, non-Hispanic/Latino; 2 Hispanic/Latino), 4 international. Average age 43. 21 applicants, 100% accepted, 19 enrolled. In 2017, 32 master's awarded. *Entrance requirements:* For master's, MAT, minimum GPA of 2.75. *Application deadline:* For fall admission, 3/1 for domestic students; for spring admission, 11/1 for domestic students. *Expenses:* Tuition, state resident: full-time $17,375. Tuition, nonresident: full-time $33,915. *Required fees:* $355. *Financial support:* Research assistantships, teaching assistantships, career-related internships or fieldwork, Federal Work-Study, and unspecified assistantships available. Support available to part-time students. Financial award application deadline: 3/1; financial award applicants required to submit FAFSA. *Faculty research:* Distance education, adult education. *Unit head:* 617-287-7749, E-mail: instructionaldesign@umb.edu. *Application contact:* Graduate Admissions Coordinator, 617-287-6400, Fax: 617-287-6236, E-mail: bos.gadm@dpc.umassp.edu.

University of Memphis, Graduate School, College of Education, Department of Instruction and Curriculum Leadership, Memphis, TN 38152. Offers advanced studies in teaching and learning (M Ed); applied behavior analysis (Graduate Certificate); autism studies (Graduate Certificate); early childhood education (MAT, MS, Ed D); elementary education (MAT); instruction and curriculum (MS, Ed D); instruction design and technology (MS, Ed D); instructional design and technology (Graduate Certificate); literacy, leadership, and coaching (Graduate Certificate); reading (MS, Ed D); school library information specialist (Graduate Certificate); secondary education (MAT); special education (MAT, MS, Ed D); STEM teacher leadership (Graduate Certificate); urban education (Graduate Certificate). *Accreditation:* NCATE (one or more programs are accredited). *Program availability:* Part-time. *Faculty:* 22 full-time (14 women), 14 part-time/adjunct (10 women). *Students:* 36 full-time (27 women), 351 part-time (271 women); includes 159 minority (132 Black or African American, non-Hispanic/Latino; 1 American Indian or Alaska Native, non-Hispanic/Latino; 7 Asian, non-Hispanic/Latino; 10 Hispanic/Latino; 9 Two or more races, non-Hispanic/Latino), 4 international. Average age 35. 170 applicants, 85% accepted, 111 enrolled. In 2017, 84 master's, 14 doctorates, 32 other advanced degrees awarded. Terminal master's awarded for partial completion of doctoral program. *Degree requirements:* For master's, comprehensive exam, thesis or alternative; for doctorate, comprehensive exam, thesis/dissertation. *Entrance requirements:* For master's, GRE General Test, PRAXIS, minimum GPA of 2.5, letters of reference; for doctorate, GRE General Test, GRE Subject Test, 2 years of teaching experience, letters of reference, statement of purpose, interview. Additional exam requirements/recommendations for international students: Required—TOEFL (minimum score 550 paper-based; 79 iBT). *Application deadline:* For fall admission, 4/1 priority date for domestic students; for spring admission, 10/1 priority date for domestic students; for summer admission, 2/1 priority date for domestic students. Applications are processed on a rolling basis. Application fee: $35 ($60 for international students). Electronic applications accepted. *Expenses:* Contact institution. *Financial support:* In 2017–18, 2 research assistantships with full tuition reimbursements (averaging $10,000 per year), 3 teaching assistantships with full tuition reimbursements (averaging $10,666 per year) were awarded; career-related internships or fieldwork, Federal Work-Study, institutionally sponsored loans, scholarships/grants, traineeships, and unspecified assistantships also available. Support available to part-time students. Financial award application deadline: 2/1; financial award applicants required to submit FAFSA. *Faculty research:* Effective urban teachers, preparation and retention of urban teachers, technology utilization in schools, field-based teacher preparation programs, effective use of online instruction. *Unit head:* Dr. Angiline Powell, Interim Chair, 901-678-3310, E-mail: apowell3@memphis.edu. *Application contact:* Dr. James Meindl, Coordinator of Graduate Studies, 901-678-3310, E-mail: jnmeindl@memphis.edu.
Website: http://www.memphis.edu/icl/

University of Michigan–Dearborn, College of Education, Health, and Human Services, Master of Arts Program in Educational Technology, Dearborn, MI 48162. Offers MA. *Program availability:* Part-time, evening/weekend, online only, 100% online. *Faculty:* 2 full-time (0 women), 2 part-time/adjunct (0 women). *Students:* 1 (woman) full-time, 23 part-time (16 women); includes 3 minority (2 Black or African American, non-Hispanic/Latino; 1 Hispanic/Latino). Average age 31. 6 applicants, 100% accepted, 6 enrolled. In 2017, 16 master's awarded. *Entrance requirements:* Additional exam requirements/recommendations for international students: Required—TOEFL (minimum score 560 paper-based; 84 iBT), IELTS (minimum score 6.5). *Application deadline:* For fall admission, 8/1 priority date for domestic students, 5/1 priority date for international students; for winter admission, 12/1 priority date for domestic students, 9/1 priority date for international students; for spring admission, 4/1 priority date for domestic students, 1/

1 priority date for international students. Applications are processed on a rolling basis. Application fee: $60. Electronic applications accepted. *Expenses:* $683 per credit hour in-state; $1,176 per credit hour out-state. *Financial support:* In 2017–18, 5 students received support. Scholarships/grants available. Financial award application deadline: 3/1; financial award applicants required to submit FAFSA. *Faculty research:* Technology integration, gamified learning, mobile technologies, instructional design, impact of technology on academic achievement. *Unit head:* Dr. Stein Brunvand, Director, Master's Programs, 313-583-6415, E-mail: sbrunvan@umich.edu. *Application contact:* Office of Graduate Studies, 313-583-6321, E-mail: umd-graduatestudies@umich.edu.
Website: http://umdearborn.edu/cehhs/cehhs_ma_ed_tech/

University of Michigan–Flint, School of Education and Human Services, Department of Education, Flint, MI 48502-1950. Offers curriculum and instruction (Ed S); early childhood education (MA); education (Ed D); educational leadership (Ed S); educational technology (MA), including curriculum and instruction, developer; literacy education (MA); secondary education with certification (MA). *Program availability:* Part-time, evening/weekend, 100% online, mixed mode format (for some programs). *Faculty:* 18 full-time (11 women), 26 part-time/adjunct (13 women). *Students:* 34 full-time (23 women), 192 part-time (137 women); includes 61 minority (46 Black or African American, non-Hispanic/Latino; 2 Asian, non-Hispanic/Latino; 5 Hispanic/Latino; 2 Native Hawaiian or other Pacific Islander, non-Hispanic/Latino; 6 Two or more races, non-Hispanic/Latino), 2 international. Average age 39. 124 applicants, 87% accepted, 81 enrolled. In 2017, 89 master's, 3 doctorates awarded. *Degree requirements:* For master's, thesis optional; for doctorate, thesis/dissertation. *Entrance requirements:* For master's, bachelor's degree from regionally-accredited institution, minimum overall undergraduate GPA of 3.0; for doctorate, Ed S; minimum overall graduate GPA of 3.3 (6.0 on a 9.0 scale) or equivalent; at least 3 years of work experience in a P-16 educational institution or in an education-related position; for Ed S, MA or MS in education-related field from accredited institution; minimum overall graduate GPA of 3.0 (6.0 on a 9.0 scale) or equivalent; at least 3 years of work experience in an educational setting. Additional exam requirements/recommendations for international students: Required—TOEFL (minimum score 84 iBT), IELTS (minimum score 6.5). *Application deadline:* For fall admission, 8/1 for domestic students, 5/1 for international students; for winter admission, 11/15 for domestic students, 9/15 for international students; for spring admission, 3/15 for domestic students, 1/15 for international students; for summer admission, 5/15 for domestic students. Applications are processed on a rolling basis. Application fee: $55. Electronic applications accepted. *Expenses:* Contact institution. *Financial support:* Federal Work-Study, scholarships/grants, and unspecified assistantships available. Financial award application deadline: 3/1; financial award applicants required to submit FAFSA. *Unit head:* Dr. Mary Jo Finney, Department Chair/Associate Professor, 810-766-6617, E-mail: mjfinney@umflint.edu. *Application contact:* Bradley T. Maki, Director of Graduate Admissions, 810-762-3171, Fax: 810-766-6789, E-mail: bmaki@umflint.edu.
Website: https://www.umflint.edu/education/graduate-programs

University of Minnesota, Twin Cities Campus, Graduate School, College of Education and Human Development, Department of Curriculum and Instruction, Minneapolis, MN 55455-0213. Offers art education (M Ed, MA, PhD); curriculum and instruction (M Ed, MA, PhD); elementary education (MA, PhD); English education (PhD); language and immersion education (Certificate); learning technologies (MA, PhD); literacy education (MA, PhD); second language education (MA, PhD); social studies education (MA, PhD); STEM education (MA, PhD); teaching (M Ed), including mathematics, science, social studies, teaching; teaching English to speakers of other languages (MA); technology enhanced learning (Certificate). *Faculty:* 37 full-time (21 women). *Students:* 401 full-time (282 women), 303 part-time (212 women); includes 139 minority (26 Black or African American, non-Hispanic/Latino; 4 American Indian or Alaska Native, non-Hispanic/Latino; 34 Asian, non-Hispanic/Latino; 45 Hispanic/Latino; 1 Native Hawaiian or other Pacific Islander, non-Hispanic/Latino; 29 Two or more races, non-Hispanic/Latino), 43 international. Average age 32. 596 applicants, 61% accepted, 330 enrolled. In 2017, 316 master's, 30 doctorates, 19 other advanced degrees awarded. Application fee: $75 ($95 for international students). *Financial support:* In 2017–18, 3 fellowships, 56 research assistantships with full tuition reimbursements (averaging $11,118 per year), 67 teaching assistantships with full tuition reimbursements (averaging $11,975 per year) were awarded. *Faculty research:* Teaching and learning; influence of cultural, linguistic, social, political, and technological factors on teaching, learning and educational research; relationship between educational practice and a democratic and just society; urban education; immigrant education, racial justice and education. *Total annual research expenditures:* $2.2 million. *Unit head:* Dr. Cynthia Lewis, Chair, 612-625-6313, E-mail: lewis@umn.edu. *Application contact:* Dr. Gillian Roehrig, Director of Graduate Studies, 612-625-0561, E-mail: roehr013@umn.edu.
Website: http://www.cehd.umn.edu/ci

University of Missouri, Office of Research and Graduate Studies, College of Education, School of Information Science and Learning Technologies, Columbia, MO 65211. Offers educational technology (M Ed, Ed S); information science and learning technology (PhD, Certificate); library science (MA). *Accreditation:* ALA (one or more programs are accredited). *Program availability:* Part-time, evening/weekend. *Entrance requirements:* For master's, GRE General Test or MAT, minimum GPA of 3.0. Additional exam requirements/recommendations for international students: Required—TOEFL (minimum score 540 paper-based; 76 iBT). Electronic applications accepted.

University of Nebraska at Kearney, College of Education, Department of Teacher Education, Kearney, NE 68849-0001. Offers curriculum and instruction (MA Ed), including early childhood education, elementary education, English as a second language, instructional effectiveness, reading/special education, secondary education; instructional technology (MS Ed), including information technology, instructional technology, school librarian; reading PK-12 (MA Ed); special education (MA Ed), including advanced practitioner: assistive technology specialist, advanced practitioner: behavioral interventionist, advanced practitioner: inclusive collaboration specialist, gifted, teacher education. *Program availability:* Part-time, evening/weekend, online only, 100% online. *Degree requirements:* For master's, comprehensive exam, thesis optional. *Entrance requirements:* For master's, portfolio or GRE. Additional exam requirements/recommendations for international students: Recommended—TOEFL (minimum score 550 paper-based; 79 iBT), IELTS (minimum score 6.5). Electronic applications accepted. *Expenses:* Contact institution.

University of Nevada, Las Vegas, Graduate College, College of Education, Department of Educational Psychology and Higher Education, Las Vegas, NV 89154-3002. Offers chief diversity officer in higher education (Certificate); college sport leadership (Certificate); educational psychology (M Ed, MS, PhD, Ed S); higher education (M Ed, PhD, Certificate); psychology/learning and technology (PhD), including learning and technology; workforce development/educational leadership (PhD); PhD/JD. *Program availability:* Part-time, evening/weekend, 100% online, blended/hybrid learning. *Faculty:* 22 full-time (15 women), 12 part-time/adjunct (8 women). *Students:* 95 full-time (73 women), 108 part-time (75 women); includes 72 minority (19 Black or African American, non-Hispanic/Latino; 9 Asian, non-Hispanic/Latino; 32 Hispanic/Latino; 12 Two or more races, non-Hispanic/Latino), 5 international. Average age 36. 86

Educational Media/Instructional Technology

applicants, 65% accepted, 44 enrolled. In 2017, 33 master's, 6 doctorates, 8 other advanced degrees awarded. *Degree requirements:* For master's, comprehensive exam (for some programs), thesis (for some programs); for doctorate, comprehensive exam, thesis/dissertation. *Entrance requirements:* For master's, GRE General Test or GMAT (for some programs), letters of recommendation; writing sample; bachelor's degree; for doctorate, GMAT or GRE General Test, writing exam; for other advanced degree, GRE General Test (for some programs). Additional exam requirements/recommendations for international students: Required—TOEFL (minimum score 550 paper-based; 80 iBT), IELTS (minimum score 7). Application fee: $60 ($95 for international students). Electronic applications accepted. *Expenses:* $275 per credit, $850 per course, $7,969 per year resident, $22,157 per year non-resident, $7,094 non-resident fee (7 credits or more), $1,307 annual health insurance fee. *Financial support:* In 2017–18, 49 students received support, including 31 research assistantships with partial tuition reimbursements available (averaging $15,769 per year), 18 teaching assistantships with partial tuition reimbursements available (averaging $19,486 per year); institutionally sponsored loans, scholarships/grants, health care benefits, and unspecified assistantships also available. Financial award application deadline: 3/15; financial award applicants required to submit FAFSA. *Faculty research:* Innovation and change in educational settings; educational policy, finance, and marketing; psycho-educational assessment; student retention, persistence, development, language, and culture; statistical modeling, program evaluation, qualitative and quantitative research methods. *Total annual research expenditures:* $470,161. *Unit head:* Dr. Alice Corkill, Chair/Professor, 702-895-4164, E-mail: alice.corkill@unlv.edu. *Application contact:* Dr. Steve McCafferty, Graduate Coordinator, 702-895-3245, Fax: 702-895-1658, E-mail: mccaffes@unlv.nevada.edu.
Website: http://education.unlv.edu/ephe/

University of New Hampshire, Graduate School, College of Health and Human Services, Department of Occupational Therapy, Durham, NH 03824. Offers assistive technology (Postbaccalaureate Certificate); occupational therapy (MS). *Accreditation:* AOTA. *Program availability:* Part-time. *Students:* 136 full-time (122 women), 7 part-time (all women); includes 5 minority (1 Black or African American, non-Hispanic/Latino; 2 Asian, non-Hispanic/Latino; 2 Hispanic/Latino), 2 international. Average age 24. 114 applicants, 67% accepted, 67 enrolled. In 2017, 62 master's, 7 other advanced degrees awarded. *Entrance requirements:* For master's, OT Course Prerequisite Verification Form. Additional exam requirements/recommendations for international students: Required—TOEFL (minimum score 550 paper-based; 80 iBT). *Application deadline:* For fall admission, 1/15 for domestic and international students. Application fee: $65. Electronic applications accepted. *Financial support:* In 2017–18, 4 students received support. Fellowships, research assistantships, teaching assistantships, career-related internships or fieldwork, Federal Work-Study, and scholarships/grants available. Support available to part-time students. Financial award application deadline: 2/15. *Unit head:* Lou Ann Griswold, Chair, 603-862-3416. *Application contact:* Deb Smith, Administrative Assistant, 603-862-3221, E-mail: deb.smith@unh.edu.
Website: http://www.chhs.unh.edu/ot

University of New Mexico, Graduate Studies, College of University Libraries and Learning Sciences, Albuquerque, NM 87131-2039. Offers organization, information and learning sciences (MA, PhD, Ed S). *Accreditation:* NCATE. *Program availability:* Part-time, evening/weekend, online learning. *Students:* Average age 45. 30 applicants, 80% accepted, 21 enrolled. In 2017, 19 master's, 4 doctorates awarded. *Degree requirements:* For master's, comprehensive exam, thesis or alternative; for doctorate, comprehensive exam, thesis/dissertation. *Entrance requirements:* For master's, minimum GPA of 3.0 in last 60 hours of course work, bachelor's degree; for doctorate, GRE General Test, MAT, master's degree, minimum GPA of 3.5. Additional exam requirements/recommendations for international students: Required—TOEFL. *Application deadline:* For fall admission, 3/15 for domestic and international students; for spring admission, 10/15 for domestic and international students. Application fee: $50. Electronic applications accepted. *Financial support:* Fellowships, research assistantships, teaching assistantships, and career-related internships or fieldwork available. Financial award application deadline: 3/1; financial award applicants required to submit FAFSA. *Faculty research:* Adult learning, distance education, instructional multimedia, organizational learning and development, transformational learning, workplace and learning environment factors that enhance learning and productivity, program and organization evaluation and reform, effects of technology on learning and problem solving. *Total annual research expenditures:* $50,371. *Unit head:* Dr. Charlotte Gunawardens, Program Director, 505-277-5046, Fax: 505-277-1427, E-mail: lani@unm.edu. *Application contact:* Linda Wood, Program Coordinator, 505-277-4131, Fax: 505-277-1427, E-mail: woodl@unm.edu.
Website: http://oils.unm.edu/

The University of North Carolina at Charlotte, Cato College of Education, Department of Educational Leadership, Charlotte, NC 28223-0001. Offers education research, measurement, and evaluation (PhD); educational leadership (Ed D); instructional systems technology (M Ed, Graduate Certificate); quantitative analysis (Graduate Certificate); school administration (MSA, Post-Master's Certificate); university and college teaching (Graduate Certificate). *Program availability:* Part-time, evening/weekend, 100% online, blended/hybrid learning. *Faculty:* 20 full-time (11 women), 16 part-time/adjunct (9 women). *Students:* 38 full-time (26 women), 257 part-time (163 women); includes 87 minority (64 Black or African American, non-Hispanic/Latino; 1 American Indian or Alaska Native, non-Hispanic/Latino; 7 Asian, non-Hispanic/Latino; 14 Hispanic/Latino; 1 Two or more races, non-Hispanic/Latino), 5 international. Average age 35. 155 applicants, 78% accepted, 103 enrolled. In 2017, 27 master's, 13 doctorates, 32 other advanced degrees awarded. *Degree requirements:* For master's, thesis or alternative, internship, capstone project; for doctorate, comprehensive exam (for some programs), thesis/dissertation, portfolio. *Entrance requirements:* For master's, GRE or MAT, bachelor's degree, or its U.S. equivalent, from regionally-accredited college or university; minimum overall GPA of 3.5 on all previous work beyond high school; statement of purpose (essay); at least three recommendation forms; for doctorate, GRE or MAT, bachelor's degree (or its U.S. equivalent) from regionally-accredited college or university; minimum overall GPA of 3.5 in master's degree program; for other advanced degree, bachelor's degree from regionally-accredited university; minimum GPA of 2.75 on all post-secondary work attempted; transcripts; personal statement outlining why the applicant seeks admission to the program. Additional exam requirements/recommendations for international students: Required—TOEFL (minimum score 523 paper-based, 70 iBT) or IELTS (6.5). *Application deadline:* For fall admission, 3/1 priority date for domestic and international students; for spring admission, 10/1 priority date for domestic and international students; for summer admission, 4/1 priority date for domestic and international students. Applications are processed on a rolling basis. Application fee: $75. Electronic applications accepted. *Expenses:* Tuition, state resident: full-time $4337. Tuition, nonresident: full-time $17,771. *Required fees:* $3211. Tuition and fees vary according to course load and program. *Financial support:* In 2017–18, 8 students received support, including 8 research assistantships (averaging $11,961 per year); career-related internships or fieldwork, institutionally sponsored loans, scholarships/grants, and unspecified assistantships also available. Support available to part-time students. Financial award application deadline: 3/1; financial award applicants required to submit FAFSA. *Total*

annual research expenditures: $1.9 million. *Unit head:* Dr. Claudia Flowers, Chair, 704-687-8862, E-mail: cpflower@uncc.edu. *Application contact:* Kathy B. Giddings, Director of Graduate Admissions, 704-687-5503, Fax: 704-687-1668, E-mail: gradadm@uncc.edu.
Website: http://edld.uncc.edu/

The University of North Carolina at Greensboro, Graduate School, School of Education, Department of Teacher Education and Higher Education, Greensboro, NC 27412-5001. Offers college teaching and adult learning (Certificate); curriculum and instruction (M Ed), including chemistry education, elementary education, English as a second language, French education, instructional technology, mathematics education, middle grades education, reading education, science education, social studies education, Spanish education; curriculum and teaching (PhD), including higher education, teacher education and development; English as a second language (Certificate); higher education (M Ed); supervision (M Ed). *Accreditation:* NCATE. *Program availability:* Part-time. *Degree requirements:* For doctorate, thesis/dissertation. *Entrance requirements:* For master's and doctorate, GRE General Test. Additional exam requirements/recommendations for international students: Required—TOEFL. Electronic applications accepted. *Faculty research:* Community college literacy program, middle school mathematics/computer mathematics.

The University of North Carolina Wilmington, Watson College of Education, Department of Instructional Technology, Foundations and Secondary Education, Wilmington, NC 28403-3297. Offers English as a second language (M Ed, MAT); instructional technology (MS); secondary education (M Ed, MAT). *Program availability:* Part-time, blended/hybrid learning. *Faculty:* 15 full-time (9 women). *Students:* 38 full-time (24 women), 90 part-time (63 women); includes 29 minority (12 Black or African American, non-Hispanic/Latino; 2 Asian, non-Hispanic/Latino; 10 Hispanic/Latino; 5 Two or more races, non-Hispanic/Latino). Average age 34. 51 applicants, 84% accepted, 30 enrolled. In 2017, 44 master's awarded. *Degree requirements:* For master's, thesis or research project/portfolio. *Entrance requirements:* For master's, GRE or MAT, education statement of interest essay, 3 letters of recommendation. Additional exam requirements/recommendations for international students: Required—TOEFL (minimum score 550 paper-based; 79 iBT), IELTS (minimum score 6.5). *Application deadline:* For fall admission, 5/15 for domestic students; for spring admission, 10/15 for domestic students; for summer admission, 3/15 for domestic students. Applications are processed on a rolling basis. Application fee: $75. Electronic applications accepted. *Expenses:* Tuition, state resident: full-time $4626; part-time $226.76 per credit hour. Tuition, nonresident: full-time $17,834; part-time $874.22 per credit hour. *Required fees:* $2124. Tuition and fees vary according to program. *Financial support:* Scholarships/grants and unspecified assistantships available. Financial award application deadline: 1/1; financial award applicants required to submit FAFSA. *Unit head:* Dr. Eleni Pappamihiel, Chair, 910-962-2746, Fax: 910-962-3609, E-mail: pappamihieln@uncw.edu. *Application contact:* Dr. Mahnaz Moallem, Graduate Coordinator, 910-962-4183, E-mail: moallemm@uncw.edu.
Website: http://www.uncw.edu/ed/itfse/

University of North Dakota, Graduate School, College of Education and Human Development, Program in Instructional Design and Technology, Grand Forks, ND 58202. Offers M Ed, MS. *Degree requirements:* For master's, comprehensive exam, thesis or alternative. *Entrance requirements:* For master's, minimum GPA of 3.0. Additional exam requirements/recommendations for international students: Required—TOEFL (minimum score 550 paper-based; 79 iBT), IELTS (minimum score 6.5). Electronic applications accepted.

University of Northern Iowa, Graduate College, College of Education, Department of Curriculum and Instruction, MA Program in Instructional Technology, Cedar Falls, IA 50614. Offers instructional technology (MA); performance and training technology (MA); school library endorsement (MA). *Degree requirements:* For master's, comprehensive exam, thesis or alternative. *Entrance requirements:* For master's, minimum GPA of 3.0. Additional exam requirements/recommendations for international students: Required—TOEFL (minimum score 500 paper-based; 61 iBT). Electronic applications accepted.

University of Northern Iowa, Graduate College, College of Education, Department of Curriculum and Instruction, MA Program in School Library Studies, Cedar Falls, IA 50614. Offers MA. *Program availability:* Part-time, evening/weekend. *Degree requirements:* For master's, comprehensive exam (for some programs), thesis or alternative, comprehensive portfolio. *Entrance requirements:* For master's, minimum GPA of 3.0. Additional exam requirements/recommendations for international students: Required—TOEFL (minimum score 500 paper-based; 61 iBT). Electronic applications accepted.

University of North Florida, College of Education and Human Services, Department of Leadership, School Counseling and Sport Management, Jacksonville, FL 32224. Offers counselor education (M Ed), including school counseling; educational leadership (M Ed, Ed D), including athletic administration (M Ed), educational leadership, educational technology (M Ed), instructional leadership (M Ed). *Program availability:* Part-time, evening/weekend. *Degree requirements:* For doctorate, thesis/dissertation. *Entrance requirements:* For master's, GRE General Test, minimum GPA of 3.0 in last 60 hours, interview, 3 letters of recommendation; for doctorate, GRE General Test, master's degree, interview, 3 letters of recommendation, writing sample. Additional exam requirements/recommendations for international students: Required—TOEFL (minimum score 500 paper-based). Electronic applications accepted. *Faculty research:* Counseling: ethics; lesbian, bisexual and transgender issues; educational leadership: school culture and climate; educational assessment and accountability; school safety and student discipline.

University of Oklahoma, Jeannine Rainbolt College of Education, Department of Educational Psychology, Program in Instructional Psychology and Technology, Norman, OK 73019. Offers educational psychology (M Ed); instructional design and technology (M Ed); instructional psychology and technology (PhD); integrating technology in teaching (M Ed). *Program availability:* Part-time. *Students:* 17 full-time (12 women), 32 part-time (24 women); includes 9 minority (1 Black or African American, non-Hispanic/Latino; 1 American Indian or Alaska Native, non-Hispanic/Latino; 3 Asian, non-Hispanic/Latino; 3 Hispanic/Latino; 1 Two or more races, non-Hispanic/Latino), 10 international. Average age 34. 16 applicants, 63% accepted, 8 enrolled. In 2017, 6 master's, 1 doctorate awarded. Terminal master's awarded for partial completion of doctoral program. *Degree requirements:* For doctorate, comprehensive exam, thesis/dissertation. *Entrance requirements:* For doctorate, GRE. Additional exam requirements/recommendations for international students: Required—TOEFL (minimum score 79 iBT) or IELTS (minimum score 6.5). *Application deadline:* Applications are processed on a rolling basis. Application fee: $50 ($100 for international students). Electronic applications accepted. *Expenses:* Tuition, state resident: full-time $5119; part-time $213.30 per credit hour. Tuition, nonresident: full-time $19,778; part-time $824.10 per credit hour. *Required fees:* $3458; $133.55 per credit hour. $126.50 per semester. *Financial support:* In 2017–18, 23 students received support. Fellowships with full and partial tuition reimbursements available, research assistantships with full and partial tuition reimbursements available, teaching assistantships with full and partial tuition reimbursements available, and scholarships/grants available. Financial award application deadline: 6/1; financial award applicants required to submit FAFSA. *Faculty* *research:* Social and cultural implications of technologies; girls interest in STEM; epistemic stance; qualitative and mixed-methods research; high-stakes assessments and related educational policy. *Unit head:* Dr. Nancy E. Marchand-Martella, Chair, Department of Educational Psychology, 405-325-0624, Fax: 405-325-6655, E-mail: nmarchand-martella@ou.edu. *Application contact:* Anna Steele, Graduate Programs Specialist, 405-325-4525, Fax: 405-325-7390, E-mail: jrcoe_gps@ou.edu. Website: http://www.ou.edu/education/edpy.html

University of Oklahoma, Price College of Business, Division of Management Information Systems, Norman, OK 73019. Offers digital technologies (Graduate Certificate); management of information technology (MS), including business analytics. *Program availability:* Part-time, evening/weekend. *Faculty:* 11 full-time (5 women). *Students:* 35 full-time (15 women), 13 part-time (7 women); includes 12 minority (2 Black or African American, non-Hispanic/Latino; 1 American Indian or Alaska Native, non-Hispanic/Latino; 3 Asian, non-Hispanic/Latino; 4 Hispanic/Latino; 2 Two or more races, non-Hispanic/Latino), 13 international. Average age 28. 24 applicants, 38% accepted, 8 enrolled. In 2017, 23 master's, 2 other advanced degrees awarded. *Degree requirements:* For master's, thesis optional. *Entrance requirements:* For master's and Graduate Certificate, GMAT or GRE, resume, statement of goals, 3 letters of recommendation. Additional exam requirements/recommendations for international students: Required—TOEFL (minimum score 100 iBT) or IELTS (minimum score 7). *Application deadline:* For fall admission, 6/15 for domestic students, 3/1 for international students; for spring admission, 10/1 for domestic students, 8/1 for international students. Applications are processed on a rolling basis. Application fee: $50 ($100 for international students). Electronic applications accepted. *Expenses:* Tuition, state resident: full-time $5119; part-time $213.30 per credit hour. Tuition, nonresident: full-time $19,778; part-time $824.10 per credit hour. *Required fees:* $3458; $133.55 per credit hour. $126.50 per semester. *Financial support:* In 2017–18, 40 students received support, including 2 research assistantships with partial tuition reimbursements available (averaging $16,864 per year), 8 teaching assistantships with partial tuition reimbursements available (averaging $11,121 per year); career-related internships or fieldwork, scholarships/grants, and unspecified assistantships also available. Support available to part-time students. Financial award application deadline: 6/1; financial award applicants required to submit FAFSA. *Faculty research:* Human-computer interaction and cognition; deception detection in IT-mediated contexts; social media use; computer-mediated collaboration and communication; meaning in discourse about IT and discourse through IT. *Total annual research expenditures:* $208,471. *Unit head:* Radhika Santhanam, Chair/Division Director, 405-325-0791, E-mail: radhika@ou.edu. *Application contact:* Jennifer Aragon, Academic Advisor, 405-325-2074, Fax: 405-325-7118, E-mail: jhardman@ou.edu.
Website: http://www.ou.edu/content/price/mis/mis_ms_in_mis.html

University of Pennsylvania, Graduate School of Education, Division of Teaching, Learning, and Leadership, Program in Learning Sciences and Technologies, Philadelphia, PA 19104. Offers MS Ed. *Students:* Average age 27. 60 applicants, 70% accepted, 10 enrolled. In 2017, 14 master's awarded.

University of Phoenix–Online Campus, School of Advanced Studies, Phoenix, AZ 85034-7209. Offers business administration (DBA); education (Ed S); educational leadership (Ed D), including curriculum and instruction, education technology, educational leadership; health administration (DHA); higher education administration (PhD); industrial/organizational psychology (PhD); nursing (PhD); organizational leadership (DM), including information systems and technology, organizational leadership. *Program availability:* Evening/weekend, online learning. *Degree requirements:* For doctorate, thesis/dissertation. *Entrance requirements:* Additional exam requirements/recommendations for international students: Required—TOEFL, TOEIC (Test of English as an International Communication), Berlitz Online English Proficiency Exam, PTE, or IELTS. Electronic applications accepted. *Expenses:* Contact institution.

University of Saint Joseph, Department of Education, West Hartford, CT 06117-2700. Offers curriculum and instruction (MA); elementary education (MAT); instructional technology (MA); literacy (MA); secondary education (MAT); TESOL (MA). *Program availability:* Part-time, evening/weekend. *Degree requirements:* For master's, comprehensive exam, thesis or alternative. *Entrance requirements:* For master's, 2 letters of recommendation. *Application deadline:* Applications are processed on a rolling basis. Application fee: $50. Electronic applications accepted. Application fee is waived when completed online. *Financial support:* Career-related internships or fieldwork and unspecified assistantships available. Support available to part-time students. Financial award applicants required to submit FAFSA.
Website: https://www.usj.edu/academics/schools/sasbe/education/

University of San Francisco, School of Education, Department of Learning and Instruction, San Francisco, CA 94117-1080. Offers digital technologies for teaching and learning (MA); learning and instruction (MA, Ed D); special education (MA, Ed D); teaching reading (MA). *Program availability:* Part-time, evening/weekend. *Degree requirements:* For doctorate, thesis/dissertation. *Entrance requirements:* Additional exam requirements/recommendations for international students: Required—TOEFL, IELTS, PTE. Electronic applications accepted.

University of San Francisco, School of Education, Department of Teacher Education, San Francisco, CA 94117-1080. Offers digital media and learning (MA); teaching (MA); teaching reading (MA); teaching urban education and social justice (MA). *Program availability:* Part-time. *Entrance requirements:* Additional exam requirements/recommendations for international students: Required—TOEFL, IELTS, PTE. Electronic applications accepted.

University of Sioux Falls, Fredrikson School of Education, Sioux Falls, SD 57105-1699. Offers educational administration (Ed S), including principal leadership, superintendent and district leadership; leadership in reading (M Ed); leadership in schools (M Ed); leadership in technology (M Ed); teaching (M Ed). Admission in summer only. *Accreditation:* NCATE. *Program availability:* Part-time, evening/weekend. *Degree requirements:* For master's, comprehensive exam (for some programs), research application project; for Ed S, comprehensive exam, portfolio. *Entrance requirements:* For master's, minimum GPA of 3.0, 1 year of teaching experience; for Ed S, minimum 3 years of teaching experience, minimum cumulative GPA of 3.5, 1 year of administrative experience. Additional exam requirements/recommendations for international students: Required—TOEFL. *Faculty research:* Reading, literacy, leadership.

University of South Africa, College of Human Sciences, Pretoria, South Africa. Offers adult education (M Ed); African languages (MA, PhD); African politics (MA, PhD); Afrikaans (MA, PhD); ancient history (MA, PhD); ancient Near Eastern studies (MA, PhD); anthropology (MA, PhD); applied linguistics (MA); Arabic (MA, PhD); archaeology (MA); art history (MA); Biblical archaeology (MA); Biblical studies (M Th, D Th); Christian spirituality (M Th, D Th); church history (M Th, D Th); classical studies (MA, PhD); clinical psychology (MA); communication (MA, PhD); comparative education (M Ed, Ed D); consulting psychology (D Admin, D Com, PhD); curriculum studies (M Ed, Ed D); development studies (M Admin, MA, D Admin, PhD); didactics (M Ed, Ed D); education (M Tech); education management (M Ed, Ed D); educational psychology (M Ed); English (MA); environmental education (M Ed); French (MA, PhD); German

(MA, PhD); Greek (MA); guidance and counseling (M Ed); health studies (MA, PhD), including health sciences education (MA), health services management (MA), medical and surgical nursing science (critical care general) (MA), midwifery and neonatal nursing science (MA), trauma and emergency care (MA); history (MA, PhD); history of education (Ed D); inclusive education (M Ed, Ed D); information and communications technology policy and regulation (MA); information science (MA, MIS, PhD); international politics (MA, PhD); Islamic studies (MA, PhD); Italian (MA, PhD); Judaica (MA, PhD); linguistics (MA, PhD); mathematical education (M Ed); mathematics education (MA); missiology (M Th, D Th); modern Hebrew (MA, PhD); musicology (MA, MMus, D Mus, PhD); natural science education (M Ed); New Testament (M Th, D Th); Old Testament (D Th); pastoral therapy (M Th, D Th); philosophy (MA); philosophy of education (M Ed, Ed D); politics (MA, PhD); Portuguese (MA, PhD); practical theology (M Th, D Th); psychology (MA, MS, PhD); psychology of education (M Ed, Ed D); public health (MA); religious studies (MA, D Th, PhD); Romance languages (MA); Russian (MA, PhD); Semitic languages (MA, PhD); social behavior studies in HIV/AIDS (MA); social science (mental health) (MA); social science in development studies (MA); social science in psychology (MA); social science in social work (MA); social science in sociology (MA); social work (MSW, DSW, PhD); socio-education (M Ed, Ed D); sociolinguistics (MA); sociology (MA, PhD); Spanish (MA, PhD); systematic theology (M Th, D Th); TESOL (teaching English to speakers of other languages) (MA); theological ethics (M Th, D Th); theory of literature (MA, PhD); urban ministries (D Th); urban ministry (M Th).

University of South Alabama, College of Education and Professional Studies, Department of Counseling and Instructional Sciences, Mobile, AL 36688. Offers clinical mental health counseling (MS); educational media (M Ed); educational media and technology (MS); instructional design and development (MS, PhD); instructional leadership (Ed S); school counseling (M Ed). *Accreditation:* NCATE. *Program availability:* Part-time. *Faculty:* 12 full-time (7 women), 10 part-time/adjunct (9 women). *Students:* 110 full-time (85 women), 39 part-time (32 women); includes 43 minority (33 Black or African American, non-Hispanic/Latino; 4 Asian, non-Hispanic/Latino; 5 Hispanic/Latino; 1 Two or more races, non-Hispanic/Latino), 5 international. Average age 34. 68 applicants, 53% accepted, 31 enrolled. In 2017, 32 master's, 9 doctorates, 10 other advanced degrees awarded. *Degree requirements:* For master's, comprehensive exam; for doctorate, comprehensive exam, thesis/dissertation. *Entrance requirements:* For master's, GRE General Test or MAT, minimum GPA of 3.0, three letters of recommendation; for doctorate, GRE, three letters of recommendation, master's degree in field or completion of prerequisites, resume. Additional exam requirements/recommendations for international students: Required—TOEFL (minimum score 525 paper-based; 71 iBT). *Application deadline:* For fall admission, 6/15 for domestic and international students; for spring admission, 12/1 for domestic students, 11/1 for international students; for summer admission, 4/1 for domestic and international students. Applications are processed on a rolling basis. Application fee: $35. Electronic applications accepted. *Expenses:* Tuition, state resident: full-time $10,104; part-time $421 per semester hour. Tuition, nonresident: full-time $20,208; part-time $842 per semester hour. *Financial support:* Fellowships, research assistantships, teaching assistantships, career-related internships or fieldwork, Federal Work-Study, institutionally sponsored loans, scholarships/grants, and unspecified assistantships available. Support available to part-time students. Financial award application deadline: 3/31; financial award applicants required to submit FAFSA. *Faculty research:* Agency counseling, rehabilitation counseling, school psychometry, juvenile delinquency, mixed methods research. *Unit head:* Dr. Tres Stefurak, Department Chair, 251-380-2734, Fax: 251-380-2713, E-mail: jstefurak@southalabama.edu. *Application contact:* Dr. James Van Haneghan, Graduate Coordinator, 251-380-2760, Fax: 251-380-2713, E-mail: jvanhane@southalabama.edu.
Website: http://www.southalabama.edu/colleges/ceps/cins/

University of South Carolina, The Graduate School, College of Education, Department of Educational Studies, Program in Educational Technology, Columbia, SC 29208. Offers M Ed. *Accreditation:* NCATE. *Program availability:* Part-time, online learning. *Degree requirements:* For master's, comprehensive exam. *Entrance requirements:* For master's, GRE or MAT, interview, letters of intent and reference.

University of South Carolina Aiken, Program in Educational Technology, Aiken, SC 29801. Offers M Ed. Program offered with University of South Carolina in Columbia. *Program availability:* Part-time, evening/weekend, online only, 100% online. *Faculty:* 2 full-time (0 women). *Students:* 1 (woman) part-time. Average age 30. 5 applicants. In 2017, 2 master's awarded. *Degree requirements:* For master's, culminating electronic portfolio, professional conference presentations. *Entrance requirements:* For master's, GRE or MAT. Additional exam requirements/recommendations for international students: Required—TOEFL (minimum score 551 paper-based, 80 iBT), IELTS (6), or PTE (53). *Application deadline:* Applications are processed on a rolling basis. Application fee: $45 ($100 for international students). Electronic applications accepted. *Expenses:* Tuition, state resident: full-time $13,254; part-time $552.25 per credit hour. Tuition, nonresident: full-time $28,368; part-time $1182.70 per credit hour. *Required fees:* $12 per credit hour. $25 per semester. Full-time tuition and fees vary according to course load. *Financial support:* Fellowships with partial tuition reimbursements, career-related internships or fieldwork, Federal Work-Study, scholarships/grants, tuition waivers (partial), and unspecified assistantships available. Support available to part-time students. Financial award application deadline: 3/1; financial award applicants required to submit FAFSA. *Faculty research:* Educational technology, instructional design, digital badges, e-learning, online and distance education, professional learning, and mobile learning, technology-enhanced learning environments, and curriculum development. *Total annual research expenditures:* $443,599. *Unit head:* Dr. Erin Besser, Educational Technology Program Coordinator, 803-641-3712, E-mail: erinbe@usca.edu. *Application contact:* Dan Robb, Associate Vice Chancellor for Enrollment Management, 803-641-3487, Fax: 803-641-3727, E-mail: danr@usca.edu.
Website: http://edtech.usca.edu/

University of South Dakota, Graduate School, School of Education, Division of Curriculum and Instruction, Program in Technology for Education and Training, Vermillion, SD 57069. Offers MS. *Program availability:* Part-time, evening/weekend, 100% online, blended/hybrid learning. *Degree requirements:* For master's, comprehensive exam, thesis or alternative. *Entrance requirements:* For master's, GRE, minimum GPA of 2.7. Additional exam requirements/recommendations for international students: Required—TOEFL (minimum score 550 paper-based; 79 iBT). *Application deadline:* Applications are processed on a rolling basis. Application fee: $35. Electronic applications accepted. *Financial support:* Research assistantships with partial tuition reimbursements, teaching assistantships with partial tuition reimbursements, career-related internships or fieldwork, Federal Work-Study, and unspecified assistantships available. Financial award applicants required to submit FAFSA. *Application contact:* Graduate School, 605-658-6140, Fax: 605-677-6118, E-mail: grad@usd.edu.
Website: http://www.usd.edu/ci

University of Southern Mississippi, College of Education and Psychology, Department of Curriculum, Instruction and Special Education, Hattiesburg, MS 39406-0001. Offers elementary education (M Ed, PhD); instructional technology (MS); instructional technology and design (PhD); secondary education (MAT); special education (M Ed, PhD). *Program availability:* Part-time, online learning. *Students:* 25

Educational Media/Instructional Technology

full-time (18 women), 5 part-time (3 women). 41 applicants, 59% accepted, 22 enrolled. *Degree requirements:* For master's, comprehensive exam, thesis (for some programs); for doctorate, comprehensive exam, thesis/dissertation. *Entrance requirements:* For master's, GRE General Test, MAT, minimum GPA of 3.0; for doctorate, GRE General Test, minimum GPA of 3.5. Additional exam requirements/recommendations for international students: Required—TOEFL, IELTS. *Application deadline:* For fall admission, 3/1 priority date for domestic students, 3/1 for international students; for spring admission, 1/10 priority date for domestic and international students. Applications are processed on a rolling basis. Application fee: $60. *Expenses:* Tuition, state resident: full-time $3830. *Financial support:* Research assistantships with tuition reimbursements, teaching assistantships with full tuition reimbursements, Federal Work-Study, institutionally sponsored loans, scholarships/grants, health care benefits, tuition waivers (partial), and unspecified assistantships available. Financial award application deadline: 3/15; financial award applicants required to submit FAFSA. *Faculty research:* Mathematical problem solving, integrative curriculum, writing process, teacher education models. *Unit head:* Dr. Jeff Hinton, Chair.
Website: https://www.usm.edu/elementary-special-technology-education

University of South Florida, Innovative Education, Tampa, FL 33620-9951. Offers adult, career and higher education (Graduate Certificate), including college teaching, leadership in developing human resources, leadership in higher education; Africana studies (Graduate Certificate), including diasporas and health disparities, genocide and human rights; aging studies (Graduate Certificate), including gerontology; art research (Graduate Certificate), including museum studies; business foundations (Graduate Certificate); chemical and biomedical engineering (Graduate Certificate), including materials science and engineering, water, health and sustainability; child and family studies (Graduate Certificate), including positive behavior support; civil and industrial engineering (Graduate Certificate), including transportation systems analysis; community and family health (Graduate Certificate), including maternal and child health, social marketing and public health, violence and injury: prevention and intervention, women's health; criminology (Graduate Certificate), including criminal justice administration; data science for public administration (Graduate Certificate); digital humanities (Graduate Certificate); educational measurement and research (Graduate Certificate), including evaluation; English (Graduate Certificate), including comparative literary studies, creative writing, professional and technical communication; entrepreneurship (Graduate Certificate); environmental health (Graduate Certificate), including safety management; epidemiology and biostatistics (Graduate Certificate), including applied biostatistics, biostatistics, concepts and tools of epidemiology, epidemiology, epidemiology of infectious diseases; geography, environment and planning (Graduate Certificate), including community development, environmental policy and management, geographical information systems; geology (Graduate Certificate), including hydrogeology; global health (Graduate Certificate), including disaster management, global health and Latin American and Caribbean studies, global health practice, humanitarian assistance, infection control; government and international affairs (Graduate Certificate), including Cuban studies, globalization studies; health policy and management (Graduate Certificate), including health management and leadership, public health policy and programs; hearing specialist: early intervention (Graduate Certificate); industrial and management systems engineering (Graduate Certificate), including systems engineering, technology management; information studies (Graduate Certificate), including school library media specialist; information systems/decision sciences (Graduate Certificate), including analytics and business intelligence; instructional technology (Graduate Certificate), including distance education, Florida digital/virtual educator, instructional design, multimedia design, Web design; internal medicine, bioethics and medical humanities (Graduate Certificate), including biomedical ethics; Latin American and Caribbean studies (Graduate Certificate); leadership for coastal resiliency planning (Graduate Certificate); mass communications (Graduate Certificate), including multimedia journalism; mathematics and statistics (Graduate Certificate), including mathematics; medicine (Graduate Certificate), including aging and neuroscience, bioinformatics, biotechnology, brain fitness and memory management, clinical investigation, hand and upper limb rehabilitation, health informatics, health sciences, integrative weight management, intellectual property, medicine and gender, metabolic and nutritional medicine, metabolic cardiology, pharmacy sciences; national and competitive intelligence (Graduate Certificate); nursing (Graduate Certificate), including simulation based academic fellowship in advanced pain management; psychological and social foundations (Graduate Certificate), including career counseling, college teaching, diversity in education, mental health counseling, school counseling; public affairs (Graduate Certificate), including nonprofit management, public management, research administration; public health (Graduate Certificate), including assessing chemical toxicity and public health risks, health equity, pharmacoepidemiology, public health generalist, toxicology, translational research in adolescent behavioral health; public health practices (Graduate Certificate), including planning for healthy communities; rehabilitation and mental health counseling (Graduate Certificate), including integrative mental health care, marriage and family therapy, rehabilitation technology; secondary education (Graduate Certificate), including ESOL, foreign language education: culture and content, foreign language education: professional; social work (Graduate Certificate), including geriatric social work/clinical gerontology; special education (Graduate Certificate), including autism spectrum disorder, disabilities education: severe/profound; world languages (Graduate Certificate), including teaching English as a second language (TESL) or foreign language. *Unit head:* Dr. Cynthia DeLuca, Associate Vice President and Assistant Vice Provost, 813-974-3077, Fax: 813-974-7061, E-mail: deluca@usf.edu. *Application contact:* Owen Hooper, Director, Summer and Alternative Calendar Programs, 813-974-6917, E-mail: hooper@usf.edu.
Website: http://www.usf.edu/innovative-education/

The University of Tampa, Programs in Education, Tampa, FL 33606-1490. Offers curriculum and instruction (M Ed); educational leadership (M Ed); instructional design and technology (MS). *Program availability:* Part-time, evening/weekend. *Faculty:* 5 full-time (4 women), 7 part-time/adjunct (5 women). *Students:* 41 full-time (27 women), 69 part-time (52 women); includes 20 minority (18 Black or African American, non-Hispanic/Latino; 2 Two or more races, non-Hispanic/Latino), 14 international. Average age 32. 126 applicants, 40% accepted, 29 enrolled. In 2017, 47 master's awarded. *Degree requirements:* For master's, capstone. *Entrance requirements:* For master's, GMAT or GRE, current Florida Professional Teaching Certificate, statement of eligibility for Florida Professional Teaching Certificate, or professional teaching certificate from another state; bachelor's degree in an area of education. Additional exam requirements/recommendations for international students: Required—TOEFL (minimum score 577 paper-based; 90 iBT), IELTS (minimum score 7.5). *Application deadline:* Applications are processed on a rolling basis. Application fee: $40. Electronic applications accepted. *Expenses:* Contact institution. *Financial support:* In 2017–18, 20 students received support. Career-related internships or fieldwork, scholarships/grants, and unspecified assistantships available. Financial award applicants required to submit FAFSA. *Faculty research:* Diversity in the classroom, technology integration, assessment methodologies, complex and ill-structured problem solving, communities of practice. *Unit head:* Dr. Antony Erben, Chair, 813-257-3414, E-mail: terben@ut.edu. *Application contact:* Chanelle Cox, Staff Assistant, Admissions for Graduate and Continuing Studies, 813-253-6249, E-mail: ccox@ut.edu.
Website: http://www.ut.edu/graduate/education/

The University of Tennessee, Graduate School, College of Education, Health and Human Sciences, Program in Education, Knoxville, TN 37996. Offers art education (MS); counseling education (PhD); cultural studies in education (PhD); curriculum (MS, Ed S); curriculum, educational research and evaluation (Ed D, PhD); early childhood education (PhD); early childhood special education (MS); education of deaf and hard of hearing (MS); educational administration and policy studies (Ed D, PhD); educational administration and supervision (Ed S); educational psychology (Ed D, PhD); elementary education (MS, Ed S); elementary teaching (MS); English education (MS, Ed S); exercise science (PhD); foreign language/ESL education (MS, Ed S); instructional technology (MS, Ed D, PhD, Ed S); literacy, language and ESL education (PhD); literacy, language education, and ESL education (Ed D); mathematics education (MS, Ed S); modified and comprehensive special education (MS); reading education (MS, Ed S); school counseling (Ed S); school psychology (PhD, Ed S); science education (MS, Ed S); secondary teaching (MS); social foundations (MS); social science education (MS, Ed S); socio-cultural foundations of sports and education (PhD); special education (Ed S); teacher education (Ed D, PhD). *Accreditation:* NCATE. *Program availability:* Part-time, evening/weekend. *Degree requirements:* For master's and Ed S, thesis optional; for doctorate, variable foreign language requirement, thesis/dissertation. *Entrance requirements:* For master's, minimum GPA of 2.7; for doctorate and Ed S, GRE General Test, minimum GPA of 2.7. Additional exam requirements/recommendations for international students: Required—TOEFL. Electronic applications accepted.

The University of Texas at Austin, Graduate School, College of Education, Department of Curriculum and Instruction, Austin, TX 78712-1111. Offers bilingual/bicultural education (M Ed, MA, PhD); cultural studies in education (M Ed, MA, PhD); early childhood education (M Ed, MA, PhD); language and literacy studies (M Ed, PhD); learning technologies (M Ed, MA, PhD); physical education (M Ed, MA, PhD). Terminal master's awarded for partial completion of doctoral program. *Degree requirements:* For doctorate, thesis/dissertation. *Entrance requirements:* For master's and doctorate, GRE General Test. Electronic applications accepted.

The University of Texas at San Antonio, College of Education and Human Development, Department of Interdisciplinary Learning and Teaching, San Antonio, TX 78249-0617. Offers education (MA), including curriculum and instruction, early childhood and elementary education, instructional technology, reading and literacy, special education; interdisciplinary learning and teaching (PhD). *Program availability:* Part-time, evening/weekend. *Faculty:* 24 full-time (16 women), 5 part-time/adjunct (3 women). *Students:* 73 full-time (57 women), 227 part-time (206 women); includes 179 minority (25 Black or African American, non-Hispanic/Latino; 10 Asian, non-Hispanic/Latino; 140 Hispanic/Latino; 1 Native Hawaiian or other Pacific Islander, non-Hispanic/Latino; 3 Two or more races, non-Hispanic/Latino), 7 international. Average age 34. 107 applicants, 88% accepted, 70 enrolled. In 2017, 103 master's, 5 doctorates awarded. *Degree requirements:* For master's, comprehensive exam, thesis optional, 36 hours of course work without thesis (33 with thesis); for doctorate, comprehensive exam, thesis/dissertation, minimum of 60 semester credit hours. *Entrance requirements:* For master's, bachelor's degree with minimum GPA of 3.0 in last 60 hours of coursework; 18 hours of undergraduate coursework in education or related field; for doctorate, GRE, transcripts from all colleges and universities attended, professional vitae demonstrating experience in work environment where education was primary professional emphasis, 3 letters of recommendation, statement of purpose, minimum GPA of 3.5. Additional exam requirements/recommendations for international students: Required—TOEFL (minimum score 550 paper-based; 79 iBT), IELTS (minimum score 6.5). *Application deadline:* For fall admission, 6/15 for domestic students, 3/1 for international students; for spring admission, 10/15 for domestic students, 9/15 for international students. Applications are processed on a rolling basis. Application fee: $50 ($90 for international students). Electronic applications accepted. *Expenses:* Tuition, state resident: full-time $5495. Tuition, nonresident: full-time $21,938. *Required fees:* $1915. Tuition and fees vary according to program. *Financial support:* Career-related internships or fieldwork, Federal Work-Study, and scholarships/grants available. Support available to part-time students. *Faculty research:* Explorations of science, learning and teaching, family involvement in early childhood, culturally-responsive literacy instruction in diverse settings, STEM education, autism spectrum disorder. *Total annual research expenditures:* $511,331. *Unit head:* Dr. Mari R. Cortez, Department Chair, 210-458-4414, Fax: 210-458-7281, E-mail: mari.cortez@utsa.edu. *Application contact:* Elizabeth Narvaez, Student Development Specialist, 210-458-7443, E-mail: elizabeth.narvaez@utsa.edu.
Website: http://education.utsa.edu/interdisciplinary_learning_and_teaching/

The University of Texas Rio Grande Valley, College of Education and P-16 Integration, Department of Teaching and Learning, Edinburg, TX 78539. Offers curriculum and instruction (M Ed, Ed D); educational technology (M Ed). *Program availability:* Part-time, evening/weekend. *Faculty:* 24. *Students:* 199. In 2017, 54 master's, 2 doctorates awarded. *Degree requirements:* For master's, comprehensive exam, thesis optional; for doctorate, comprehensive exam, thesis/dissertation. *Entrance requirements:* For master's, minimum GPA of 3.0. Additional exam requirements/recommendations for international students: Required—TOEFL (minimum score 550 paper-based; 79 iBT), IELTS (minimum score 6.5). *Application deadline:* For fall admission, 4/15 for domestic students; for spring admission, 11/1 for domestic students; for summer admission, 3/1 for domestic students. Applications are processed on a rolling basis. Application fee: $50 ($75 for international students). Electronic applications accepted. *Expenses:* Tuition, state resident: full-time $5550; part-time $417 per credit hour. Tuition, nonresident: full-time $13,020; part-time $832 per credit hour. *Required fees:* $1169. *Financial support:* Research assistantships, institutionally sponsored loans, scholarships/grants, and unspecified assistantships available. Financial award application deadline: 4/15; financial award applicants required to submit FAFSA. *Faculty research:* Teacher education, mathematics education, science education, educational technology, pedagogy. *Unit head:* Dr. James Jupp, Chair, 956-665-3401, E-mail: james.jupp@utrgv.edu. *Application contact:* Stephanie Ozuna, Graduate Student Recruiter, 956-665-3558, E-mail: stephanie.ozuna@utrgv.edu.

University of the Sacred Heart, Graduate Programs, Department of Education, Program in Instruction Systems and Education Technology, San Juan, PR 00914-0383. Offers M Ed. *Program availability:* Part-time, evening/weekend. *Degree requirements:* For master's, thesis. *Entrance requirements:* For master's, EXADEP, interview, minimum undergraduate GPA of 2.75.

The University of Toledo, College of Graduate Studies, Judith Herb College of Education, Department of Curriculum and Instruction, Toledo, OH 43606-3390. Offers art education (ME); career and technical education (ME, Ed S); curriculum and instruction (ME, PhD, Ed S); early childhood education (Ed S); education and anthropology (MAE); education and biology (MES); education and chemistry (MES); education and classics (MAE); education and economics (MAE); education and English (MAE); education and French (MAE); education and geology (MES); education and German (MAE); education and history (MAE); education and mathematics (MAE, MES); education and physics (MES); education and political science (MAE); education and sociology (MAE); education and Spanish (MAE); educational media (PhD); educational technology (ME); educational technology: virtual educator (Certificate); elementary education (PhD); English as a second language (MAE); gifted and talented education (PhD); middle childhood education (ME); secondary education (ME, PhD); special education (PhD). *Accreditation:* NCATE. *Program availability:* Part-time, evening/weekend. *Degree requirements:* For master's, comprehensive exam, thesis or alternative; for doctorate, comprehensive exam, thesis/dissertation; for other advanced degree, thesis optional. *Entrance requirements:* For master's, doctorate, and other advanced degree, minimum cumulative GPA of 2.7 for all previous academic work, letters of recommendation. Additional exam requirements/recommendations for international students: Required—TOEFL (minimum score 550 paper-based; 80 iBT). Electronic applications accepted.

University of Utah, Graduate School, College of Education, Department of Educational Psychology, Salt Lake City, UT 84112. Offers clinical mental health counseling (M Ed); counseling psychology (PhD); elementary education (M Ed); instructional design and educational technology (M Ed); instructional design and technology (MS); learning and cognition (MS, PhD); reading and literacy (M Ed, PhD); school counseling (M Ed); school psychology (M Ed, PhD, Ed S); statistics (M Stat). *Accreditation:* APA (one or more programs are accredited). *Faculty:* 19 full-time (9 women), 12 part-time/adjunct (8 women). *Students:* 122 full-time (95 women), 97 part-time (68 women); includes 26 minority (4 Asian, non-Hispanic/Latino; 16 Hispanic/Latino; 6 Two or more races, non-Hispanic/Latino), 7 international. Average age 31. 296 applicants, 27% accepted, 73 enrolled. In 2017, 65 master's, 15 doctorates awarded. Terminal master's awarded for partial completion of doctoral program. *Entrance requirements:* For master's and doctorate, GRE General Test, minimum GPA of 3.0. Additional exam requirements/recommendations for international students: Required—TOEFL (minimum score 80 iBT). *Application deadline:* For fall admission, 12/15 for domestic and international students; for winter admission, 11/1 for domestic and international students; for spring admission, 3/15 for domestic and international students. Application fee: $55 ($65 for international students). Electronic applications accepted. *Expenses:* Contact institution. *Financial support:* In 2017–18, 84 students received support, including 12 fellowships with full and partial tuition reimbursements available (averaging $17,000 per year), 16 research assistantships with full and partial tuition reimbursements available (averaging $15,500 per year), 39 teaching assistantships with full and partial tuition reimbursements available (averaging $15,500 per year); career-related internships or fieldwork, scholarships/grants, traineeships, health care benefits, and unspecified assistantships also available. Financial award application deadline: 4/1; financial award applicants required to submit FAFSA. *Faculty research:* Autism, computer technology and instruction, cognitive behavior, aging, group counseling. *Total annual research expenditures:* $620,935. *Unit head:* Dr. Anne E. Cook, Chair, 801-581-7148, Fax: 801-581-5566, E-mail: anne.cook@utah.edu. *Application contact:* JoLynn N. Yates, Academic Coordinator, 801-581-7148, Fax: 801-581-5566, E-mail: jo.yates@utah.edu. Website: http://www.ed.utah.edu/edps/

University of Virginia, Curry School of Education, Department of Leadership, Foundations and Policy, Program in Educational Psychology, Charlottesville, VA 22903. Offers applied developmental science (M Ed); educational evaluation (M Ed); educational psychology (M Ed, Ed D, Ed S); educational research (Ed D); gifted education (M Ed); instructional technology (M Ed, Ed S); research statistics and evaluation (Ed D); school psychology (Ed D). *Students:* 36 full-time (29 women), 3 part-time (2 women); includes 14 minority (5 Black or African American, non-Hispanic/Latino; 4 Asian, non-Hispanic/Latino; 3 Hispanic/Latino; 2 Two or more races, non-Hispanic/Latino), 7 international. Average age 24. 85 applicants, 80% accepted, 37 enrolled. In 2017, 35 master's, 1 doctorate awarded. *Degree requirements:* For master's, comprehensive exam. *Entrance requirements:* For master's and doctorate, GRE General Test, 2 letters of recommendation. Additional exam requirements/recommendations for international students: Required—TOEFL (minimum score 600 paper-based; 90 iBT), IELTS (minimum score 7). *Application deadline:* Applications are processed on a rolling basis. Application fee: $60. Electronic applications accepted. *Financial support:* Fellowships, research assistantships, and teaching assistantships available. Financial award application deadline: 1/5; financial award applicants required to submit FAFSA. *Unit head:* Sara Rimm-Kaufman, Program Director, 434-982-2863, E-mail: serk@virginia.edu. *Application contact:* E-mail: curry-admissions@virginia.edu. Website: http://curry.virginia.edu/academics/areas-of-study/educational-psychology

University of Virginia, Curry School of Education, Program in Education, Charlottesville, VA 22903. Offers administration and supervision (PhD); applied developmental science (PhD); counselor education (PhD); curriculum and instruction (PhD); early childhood special education (MT); education evaluation (PhD); educational psychology (PhD); educational research (PhD); elementary education (MT); English education (MT, PhD); foreign language education (MT); higher education (PhD); instructional technology (PhD); kinesiology (MT, PhD); math education (PhD); reading education (PhD); research, statistics and evaluation (PhD); school psychology (PhD); science education (PhD); social studies education (MT, PhD); special education (PhD); world languages education (MT). *Students:* 431 full-time (353 women), 15 part-time (14 women); includes 100 minority (32 Black or African American, non-Hispanic/Latino; 33 Asian, non-Hispanic/Latino; 16 Hispanic/Latino; 19 Two or more races, non-Hispanic/Latino), 14 international. Average age 25. 264 applicants, 49% accepted, 83 enrolled. In 2017, 142 master's, 33 doctorates awarded. *Degree requirements:* For master's, comprehensive exam (for some programs), field project; for doctorate, comprehensive exam, thesis/dissertation. *Entrance requirements:* For doctorate, GRE General Test. Additional exam requirements/recommendations for international students: Required—TOEFL (minimum score 600 paper-based; 90 iBT), IELTS (minimum score 7). *Application deadline:* Applications are processed on a rolling basis. Application fee: $60. Electronic applications accepted. *Financial support:* Fellowships, research assistantships, and teaching assistantships available. Financial award application deadline: 1/5; financial award applicants required to submit FAFSA. *Unit head:* Robert C. Pianta, Dean, 434-924-3334, E-mail: pianta@virginia.edu. *Application contact:* E-mail: curry-admissions@virginia.edu. Website: http://curry.virginia.edu/teacher-education

University of Washington, Graduate School, College of Education, Seattle, WA 98195. Offers curriculum and instruction (M Ed, Ed D, PhD), including educational technology, general curriculum (Ed D, PhD), language, literacy, and culture, mathematics education, multicultural education, reading and language arts education (Ed D), science education, social studies education, teaching and curriculum (M Ed); educational leadership and policy studies (M Ed, Ed D, PhD), including administration (Ed D), educational policy, organization, and leadership (M Ed, PhD), higher education, leadership for learning (Ed D), social and cultural foundations of education (M Ed, PhD); educational psychology (M Ed, PhD), including educational psychology (PhD), human development and cognition (M Ed), learning sciences, measurement, statistics and research design (M Ed), school psychology (M Ed); instructional leadership (M Ed); intercollegiate athletic leadership (M Ed); special education (M Ed, Ed D, PhD), including early childhood special education (M Ed), emotional and behavioral disabilities (M Ed), learning disabilities (M Ed), low-incidence disabilities (M Ed), severe disabilities (M Ed), special education (Ed D, PhD); teacher education (MIT). *Accreditation:* APA. *Program availability:* Part-time, evening/weekend. *Degree requirements:* For master's, thesis optional; for doctorate, thesis/dissertation. *Entrance requirements:* For master's and doctorate, GRE General Test, minimum GPA of 3.0. Additional exam requirements/

recommendations for international students: Required—TOEFL. Electronic applications accepted. *Faculty research:* School restructuring/effective schools, special education interventions, literacy and writing, technology, school partnerships, teacher preparation.

The University of West Alabama, School of Graduate Studies, College of Education, Program in Continuing Education, Livingston, AL 35470. Offers counseling and psychology (MSCE); general (MSCE); library media (MSCE). *Accreditation:* NCATE. *Program availability:* Part-time, evening/weekend, 100% online. *Faculty:* 13 full-time (11 women), 48 part-time/adjunct (36 women). *Students:* 195 (163 women); includes 137 minority (134 Black or African American, non-Hispanic/Latino; 1 American Indian or Alaska Native, non-Hispanic/Latino; 1 Native Hawaiian or other Pacific Islander, non-Hispanic/Latino; 1 Two or more races, non-Hispanic/Latino). Average age 34. 59 applicants, 100% accepted, 40 enrolled. In 2017, 103 master's awarded. *Degree requirements:* For master's, comprehensive exam, thesis optional. *Entrance requirements:* For master's, GRE, minimum GPA of 2.75. Additional exam requirements/recommendations for international students: Required—TOEFL (minimum score 500 paper-based; 61 iBT). *Application deadline:* Applications are processed on a rolling basis. Application fee: $40. Electronic applications accepted. *Expenses:* Tuition, state resident: part-time $371 per credit hour. Tuition, nonresident: part-time $742 per credit hour. *Required fees:* $130 per semester. *Financial support:* Teaching assistantships, Federal Work-Study, scholarships/grants, and unspecified assistantships available. Support available to part-time students. Financial award application deadline: 3/1; financial award applicants required to submit FAFSA. *Unit head:* Dr. Reenay Rogers, Chair of Instructional Leadership and Support, 205-652-5423, Fax: 205-652-3706, E-mail: rrogers@uwa.edu. *Application contact:* Dr. B. J. Kimbrough, Dean of Graduate Studies, 205-652-3647, Fax: 205-652-3670, E-mail: bkimbrough@uwa.edu.

The University of West Alabama, School of Graduate Studies, College of Education, Program in Library Media, Livingston, AL 35470. Offers learning, design, and technology (M Ed); library media (M Ed, Ed S). *Program availability:* Part-time, evening/weekend, 100% online. *Faculty:* 1 (woman) full-time, 6 part-time/adjunct (4 women). *Students:* 190 (180 women); includes 38 minority (31 Black or African American, non-Hispanic/Latino; 2 American Indian or Alaska Native, non-Hispanic/Latino; 5 Two or more races, non-Hispanic/Latino). Average age 37. 30 applicants, 93% accepted, 22 enrolled. In 2017, 58 master's, 9 Ed Ss awarded. *Degree requirements:* For master's, comprehensive exam, thesis optional; for Ed S, comprehensive exam. *Entrance requirements:* For master's, GRE, minimum GPA of 2.75, verification of background clearance/fingerprints, valid bachelor's-level Professional Educator Certificate in same teaching field. Additional exam requirements/recommendations for international students: Required—TOEFL (minimum score 500 paper-based; 61 iBT). *Application deadline:* Applications are processed on a rolling basis. Application fee: $40. Electronic applications accepted. *Expenses:* Tuition, state resident: part-time $371 per credit hour. Tuition, nonresident: part-time $742 per credit hour. *Required fees:* $130 per semester. *Financial support:* Teaching assistantships, Federal Work-Study, scholarships/grants, and unspecified assistantships available. Support available to part-time students. Financial award application deadline: 3/1; financial award applicants required to submit FAFSA. *Unit head:* Dr. Reenay Rogers, Chair of Instructional Leadership and Support, 205-652-5423, Fax: 205-652-3706, E-mail: rrogers@uwa.edu. *Application contact:* Dr. B. J. Kimbrough, Dean of Graduate Studies, 205-652-3647, Fax: 205-652-3670, E-mail: bkimbrough@uwa.edu.

University of West Florida, College of Education and Professional Studies, Department of Instructional, Workforce and Applied Technology, Pensacola, FL 32514-5750. Offers instructional design and technology (M Ed, Ed D), including instructional design and technology (M Ed), technology leadership (M Ed); network operations, performance and security (M Ed). *Entrance requirements:* For master's, GRE, GMAT, or MAT, letter of intent, names of references. Additional exam requirements/recommendations for international students: Required—TOEFL (minimum score 550 paper-based). Electronic applications accepted.

University of West Florida, College of Education and Professional Studies, Ed D Programs, Specialization in Instructional Design and Technology, Pensacola, FL 32514-5750. Offers Ed D. *Degree requirements:* For doctorate, comprehensive exam, thesis/dissertation. *Entrance requirements:* For doctorate, GRE, MAT, or GMAT, letter of intent; writing sample; three letters of recommendation; two completed disposition assessment forms; written statement of goals; interview with admissions committee. Additional exam requirements/recommendations for international students: Required—TOEFL (minimum score 550 paper-based).

University of West Georgia, College of Education, Carrollton, GA 30118. Offers business education (M Ed); early childhood education (M Ed, Ed S); educational leadership (M Ed, Ed S); media (M Ed, Ed S); professional counseling (M Ed, Ed S); professional counseling and supervision (Ed D); reading instruction (M Ed); school improvement (Ed D); secondary education (M Ed); special education (M Ed, Ed S), including teaching (M Ed); speech language pathology (M Ed); teaching (MAT). *Accreditation:* NCATE. *Program availability:* Part-time, evening/weekend, 100% online, blended/hybrid learning. *Faculty:* 45 full-time (28 women). *Students:* 344 full-time (286 women), 1,243 part-time (1,039 women); includes 538 minority (456 Black or African American, non-Hispanic/Latino; 19 Asian, non-Hispanic/Latino; 46 Hispanic/Latino; 1 Native Hawaiian or other Pacific Islander, non-Hispanic/Latino; 16 Two or more races, non-Hispanic/Latino), 7 international. Average age 36. 685 applicants, 78% accepted, 429 enrolled. In 2017, 299 master's, 30 doctorates, 218 other advanced degrees awarded. *Entrance requirements:* Additional exam requirements/recommendations for international students: Required—TOEFL (minimum score 523 paper-based; 69 iBT); Recommended—IELTS (minimum score 6.5). *Application deadline:* For fall admission, 7/21 for domestic students, 6/1 for international students; for spring admission, 11/30 for domestic students, 10/15 for international students; for summer admission, 4/15 for domestic students, 3/30 for international students. Applications are processed on a rolling basis. Application fee: $40. Electronic applications accepted. Tuition and fees vary according to degree level and program. *Financial support:* Fellowships, research assistantships, teaching assistantships, career-related internships or fieldwork, Federal Work-Study, institutionally sponsored loans, scholarships/grants, and unspecified assistantships available. Support available to part-time students. Financial award application deadline: 4/1; financial award applicants required to submit FAFSA. *Unit head:* Dr. Diane Hoff, Dean, College of Education, 678-839-6570, Fax: 678-839-6098, E-mail: dhoff@westga.edu. *Application contact:* Dr. Toby Ziglar, Assistant Dean of the Graduate School, 678-839-1394, Fax: 678-839-1395, E-mail: graduate@westga.edu. Website: http://www.westga.edu/education/

University of Wisconsin–Milwaukee, Graduate School, College of Health Sciences, Department of Occupational Science and Technology, Milwaukee, WI 53201-0413. Offers assistive technology and design (MS); disability and occupation (MS); ergonomics (MS); therapeutic recreation (MS). *Accreditation:* AOTA. *Students:* 86 full-time (74 women), 1 (woman) part-time; includes 6 minority (3 Asian, non-Hispanic/Latino; 1 Hispanic/Latino; 2 Two or more races, non-Hispanic/Latino), 1 international. Average age 27. 115 applicants, 30% accepted, 32 enrolled. In 2017, 22 master's awarded. *Degree requirements:* For master's, thesis or alternative. *Entrance requirements:* Additional exam requirements/recommendations for international students: Required—TOEFL (minimum score 550 paper-based; 79 iBT), IELTS

(minimum score 6.5). *Application deadline:* For fall admission, 1/1 priority date for domestic students; for spring admission, 9/1 for domestic students. Applications are processed on a rolling basis. Application fee: $56 ($75 for international students). *Financial support:* Fellowships, research assistantships, teaching assistantships, and unspecified assistantships available. Support available to part-time students. Financial award application deadline: 4/15. *Unit head:* Jay Kapellusch, PhD, Department Chair, 414-229-5292, Fax: 414-229-2619, E-mail: kap@uwm.edu. *Application contact:* Bhagwant S. Sindhu, PhD, Graduate Program Coordinator, 414-229-1180, Fax: 414-229-5100, E-mail: sindhu@uwm.edu.
Website: http://uwm.edu/healthsciences/academics/occupational-science-technology/

University of Wisconsin–Milwaukee, Graduate School, College of Health Sciences, Program in Assistive Technology and Accessible Design, Milwaukee, WI 53211. Offers assistive technology and accessible design (Graduate Certificate). *Accreditation:* NAACLS. *Program availability:* Part-time. *Students:* 2 part-time (both women). Average age 36. 5 applicants, 20% accepted. In 2017, 1 Graduate Certificate awarded. *Entrance requirements:* Additional exam requirements/recommendations for international students: Required—TOEFL (minimum score 550 paper-based; 79 iBT), IELTS (minimum score 6.5). *Application deadline:* For fall admission, 1/1 priority date for domestic students; for spring admission, 9/1 for domestic students. Applications are processed on a rolling basis. Application fee: $56 ($96 for international students). *Financial support:* Fellowships, research assistantships, teaching assistantships, career-related internships or fieldwork, and unspecified assistantships available. Support available to part-time students. Financial award application deadline: 4/15. *Application contact:* Michelle Silverman, Coordinator, 414-229-3556, E-mail: silverm2@uwm.edu.
Website: http://uwm.edu/healthsciences/academics/certificate-in-assistive-technology-accessible-design/

University of Wyoming, College of Education, Program in Instructional Technology, Laramie, WY 82071. Offers MS, Ed D, PhD. *Program availability:* Part-time, online learning. *Degree requirements:* For master's, thesis or alternative; for doctorate, comprehensive exam, thesis/dissertation. *Entrance requirements:* For master's, GRE, minimum GPA of 3.0; for doctorate, MS or MA, minimum GPA of 3.0. Additional exam requirements/recommendations for international students: Required—TOEFL. Electronic applications accepted. *Faculty research:* Web based instruction, instructional decision, adult education history, literacy in adults, international distance education.

Utah State University, School of Graduate Studies, Emma Eccles Jones College of Education and Human Services, Department of Instructional Technology and Learning Sciences, Logan, UT 84322. Offers M Ed, MS, PhD, Ed S. *Program availability:* Part-time, evening/weekend, online learning. Terminal master's awarded for partial completion of doctoral program. *Degree requirements:* For master's, thesis (for some programs); for doctorate, comprehensive exam, thesis/dissertation. *Entrance requirements:* For master's, GRE General Test or MAT, minimum GPA of 3.0, 3 recommendation letters; for doctorate, GRE General Test, minimum GPA of 3.0, 3 recommendation letters, transcripts, letter of intent; for Ed S, GRE General Test, GRE Subject Test, minimum GPA of 3.0. Additional exam requirements/recommendations for international students: Required—TOEFL (minimum score 550 paper-based). Electronic applications accepted. *Faculty research:* Interactive learning environments, computer-assisted instruction, learning, distance education, corporate training.

Utah Valley University, Program in Education, Orem, UT 84058-5999. Offers educational technology (M Ed); elementary mathematics (M Ed); elementary STEM (M Ed); English as a second language (M Ed); reading (M Ed); teachers as leaders (M Ed). *Accreditation:* TEAC. *Program availability:* Part-time. *Degree requirements:* For master's, project. *Entrance requirements:* For master's, GRE, 3 letters of recommendation, interview, essay. Additional exam requirements/recommendations for international students: Required—TOEFL (minimum score 83 iBT). Electronic applications accepted. *Expenses:* Contact institution.

Valley City State University, Online Graduate Programs, Valley City, ND 58072. Offers elementary education (M Ed); English education (M Ed); library and information technologies (M Ed); teaching (MAT); teaching and technology (M Ed); teaching English language learners (M Ed); technology education (M Ed). *Accreditation:* NCATE. *Program availability:* Part-time, evening/weekend, online only, 100% online. *Faculty:* 21 full-time (12 women), 15 part-time/adjunct (11 women). *Students:* 12 full-time (9 women), 138 part-time (99 women); includes 5 minority (3 Hispanic/Latino; 2 Two or more races, non-Hispanic/Latino). Average age 36. 13 applicants, 92% accepted, 12 enrolled. In 2017, 45 master's awarded. *Degree requirements:* For master's, action research report, comprehensive portfolio. *Entrance requirements:* For master's, GRE, MAT, PRAXIS II or National Teaching Board for Professional Standards (if GPA is less than 3.0). Additional exam requirements/recommendations for international students: Required—TOEFL (minimum score 525 paper-based; 71 iBT) Recommended—IELTS (minimum score 5.5). *Application deadline:* For fall admission, 7/21 for domestic and international students; for spring admission, 12/8 for domestic and international students; for summer admission, 5/5 for domestic and international students. Applications are processed on a rolling basis. Application fee: $35. Electronic applications accepted. *Expenses:* $384.21 per credit. *Financial support:* In 2017–18, 16 students received support. Scholarships/grants, tuition waivers (full and partial), and unspecified assistantships available. Financial award applicants required to submit FAFSA. *Faculty research:* Universal accessibility, instructional design and technology, gender communication, STEM education in K-12, English language learners. *Unit head:* Dr. Sheri Okland, Dean, 701-845-7184, E-mail: sheri.l.okland@vcsu.edu. *Application contact:* Misty Lindgren, Graduate Studies, 701-845-7303, Fax: 701-845-7190, E-mail: misty.lindgren@vcsu.edu.
Website: http://www.vcsu.edu/graduate

Virginia Commonwealth University, Graduate School, School of Education, Program in Adult Learning, Richmond, VA 23284-9005. Offers adult literacy (M Ed); human resource development (M Ed); teaching and learning with technology (M Ed). *Accreditation:* NCATE. *Program availability:* Part-time. *Entrance requirements:* For master's, GRE General Test or MAT. Additional exam requirements/recommendations for international students: Required—TOEFL (minimum score 600 paper-based; 100 iBT). Electronic applications accepted. *Faculty research:* Adult development and learning, program planning and evaluation.

Virginia Polytechnic Institute and State University, VT Online, Blacksburg, VA 24061. Offers advanced transportation systems (Certificate); aerospace engineering (MS); agricultural and life sciences (MSLFS); business information systems (Graduate Certificate); career and technical education (MS); civil engineering (MS); computer engineering (M Eng, MS); decision support systems (Graduate Certificate); eLearning leadership (MA); electrical engineering (M Eng, MS); engineering administration (MEA); environmental engineering (Certificate); environmental politics and policy (Graduate Certificate); environmental sciences and engineering (MS); foundations of political analysis (Graduate Certificate); health product risk management (Graduate Certificate); industrial and systems engineering (MS); information policy and society (Graduate Certificate); information security (Graduate Certificate); information technology (MIT); instructional technology (MA); integrative STEM education (MA Ed); liberal arts (Graduate Certificate); life sciences: health product risk management (MS); natural

resources (MNR, Graduate Certificate); networking (Graduate Certificate); nonprofit and nongovernmental organization management (Graduate Certificate); ocean engineering (MS); political science (MA); security studies (Graduate Certificate); software development (Graduate Certificate). *Expenses:* Tuition, state resident: full-time $15,072; part-time $718.50 per credit hour. Tuition, nonresident: full-time $28,810; part-time $1448.25 per credit hour. *Required fees:* $2741; $502 per semester. Tuition and fees vary according to course load, campus/location and program.

Walden University, Graduate Programs, Richard W. Riley College of Education and Leadership, Minneapolis, MN 55401. Offers adult education (Post-Master's Certificate); adult learning (Graduate Certificate); college teaching and learning (Graduate Certificate); community college leadership (Ed D); curriculum, instruction and assessment (Ed D, Ed S, Graduate Certificate); developmental education (Graduate Certificate); early childhood administration, management, and leadership (Graduate Certificate); early childhood education (Ed D, Ed S); early childhood public policy and advocacy (Graduate Certificate); early childhood studies (MS), including administration, management and leadership, early childhood public policy and advocacy, teaching adults in the early childhood field, teaching and diversity in early childhood education; education (MS, PhD), including adolescent literacy and learning (MS), curriculum, instruction, and assessment (grades K-12) (MS), curriculum, instruction, assessment, and evaluation (PhD), early childhood leadership and advocacy (PhD), early childhood special education (PhD), educational leadership (MS), educational leadership and administration (principal preparation) (MS), educational technology and design (PhD), elementary reading and literacy (PreK-6) (MS), elementary reading and mathematics (grades K-6) (MS), global and comparative education (PhD), higher education leadership management and policy (PhD), integrating technology in the classroom (grades K-12) (MS), learning, instruction and innovation (MS), mathematics (grades 5-8) (MS), mathematics (grades K-6) (MS), mathematics and science (grades K-8) (MS), organizational research, assessment, and evaluation (PhD), reading and literacy with a reading K-12 endorsement (MS), reading literacy assessment and evaluation (PhD), science (grades K-8) (MS), special education (non-licensure) (grades K-12) (MS), teacher leadership (grades K-12) (MS), teaching English language learners (grades K-12) (MS); educational administration and leadership (Ed D); educational leadership and administration (principal preparation) (Ed S); educational technology (Ed D, Ed S, Post Master's Certificate); elementary reading and literacy (Graduate Certificate); engaging culturally diverse learners (Graduate Certificate); enrollment management and institutional marketing (Graduate Certificate); higher education (MS), including adult learning, college teaching and learning, enrollment management and institutional marketing, global higher education, leadership for student success, online and distance learning; higher education and adult learning (Ed D); higher education leadership and management (Ed D); higher education leadership for student success (Graduate Certificate); instructional design and technology (MS, Postbaccalaureate Certificate), including general program (MS), online learning (MS), training and performance improvement (MS); integrating technology in the classroom (Graduate Certificate); mathematics 5-8 (Graduate Certificate); mathematics K-6 (Graduate Certificate); online teaching for adult educators (Graduate Certificate); reading, literacy, and assessment (Ed D, Ed S); science K-8 (Graduate Certificate); special education (Ed D, Ed S, Graduate Certificate); special education (K-age 21) (MAT); teacher leadership (Graduate Certificate); teaching adults English as a second language (Graduate Certificate); teaching adults in the early childhood field (Graduate Certificate); teaching and diversity in early childhood education (Graduate Certificate); teaching English language learners (grades K-12) (Graduate Certificate); teaching K-12 students online (Graduate Certificate). *Accreditation:* NCATE. *Program availability:* Part-time, evening/weekend, online only, 100% online. *Degree requirements:* For doctorate, thesis/dissertation (for some programs), residency; for other advanced degree, residency (for some programs). *Entrance requirements:* For master's, bachelor's degree or higher; minimum GPA of 2.5; official transcripts; goal statement (for some programs); access to computer and Internet; for doctorate, master's degree or higher; three years of related professional or academic experience (preferred); minimum GPA of 3.0; goal statement and current resume (for select programs); official transcripts; access to computer and Internet; for other advanced degree, relevant work experience; access to computer and Internet. Additional exam requirements/recommendations for international students: Required—TOEFL (minimum score 550 paper-based, 79 iBT), IELTS (minimum score 6.5), Michigan English Language Assessment Battery (minimum score 82), or PTE (minimum score 53). Electronic applications accepted.

Walden University, Graduate Programs, School of Psychology, Minneapolis, MN 55401. Offers clinical psychology (MS), including counseling, general program; forensic psychology (MS), including forensic psychology in the community, general program, mental health applications, program planning and evaluation in forensic settings, psychology and legal systems; industrial organizational (MS, PhD), including consulting psychology, forensic (MS), forensic psychology (PhD), general practice, leadership development and coaching (MS), organizational diversity and social change, research evaluation (PhD); online teaching in psychology (Post-Master's Certificate); organizational psychology and development (Postbaccalaureate Certificate); psychology (MS, PhD), including applied psychology (MS), clinical psychology (PhD), crisis management and response (MS), educational psychology, forensic psychology (PhD), general psychology (MS), general psychology research (PhD), general psychology teaching (PhD), health psychology, leadership development and coaching (MS), psychology of culture (MS), psychology, public administration, and social change (MS), social psychology, terrorism and security (MS); psychology respecialization (Post-Doctoral Certificate). *Program availability:* Part-time, evening/weekend, online only, 100% online. Terminal master's awarded for partial completion of doctoral program. *Degree requirements:* For master's, thesis optional; for doctorate, thesis/dissertation, residency. *Entrance requirements:* For master's, bachelor's degree or higher; minimum GPA of 2.5; official transcripts; goal statement (for some programs); access to computer and Internet; for doctorate, master's degree or higher; three years of related professional or academic experience (preferred); minimum GPA of 3.0; goal statement and current resume (for select programs); official transcripts; access to computer and Internet; for other advanced degree, relevant work experience; access to computer and Internet. Additional exam requirements/recommendations for international students: Required—TOEFL (minimum score 550 paper-based, 79 iBT), IELTS (minimum score 6.5), Michigan English Language Assessment Battery (minimum score 82) or PTE (minimum score 53). Electronic applications accepted.

Warner University, School of Education, Lake Wales, FL 33859. Offers curriculum and instruction (MAEd); elementary education (MAEd); science, technology, engineering, and mathematics (STEM) (MAEd). *Program availability:* Part-time, evening/weekend, online learning. *Degree requirements:* For master's, thesis, accomplished practices portfolio. *Entrance requirements:* For master's, minimum GPA of 3.0 in last 60 hours of undergraduate coursework; 2 letters of recommendation. Additional exam requirements/recommendations for international students: Required—TOEFL (minimum score 550 paper-based). Electronic applications accepted.

Wayland Baptist University, Graduate Programs, Program in Education, Plainview, TX 79072-6998. Offers education administration (M Ed); education diagnostics (M Ed); education literacy (M Ed); elementary certification (M Ed); English (M Ed); English as a second language (M Ed); higher education administration (M Ed); human resources

(M Ed); instructional leadership (M Ed); instructional technology (M Ed); leadership training and development (M Ed); science education (M Ed); secondary certification (M Ed); social studies (M Ed); special education (M Ed); sports administration and management (M Ed). *Program availability:* Part-time, evening/weekend, 100% online. *Faculty:* 33 full-time (17 women), 28 part-time/adjunct (17 women). *Students:* 16 full-time (13 women), 221 part-time (143 women); includes 97 minority (26 Black or African American, non-Hispanic/Latino; 1 American Indian or Alaska Native, non-Hispanic/Latino; 5 Asian, non-Hispanic/Latino; 54 Hispanic/Latino; 11 Two or more races, non-Hispanic/Latino), 1 international. Average age 39. 32 applicants, 97% accepted, 23 enrolled. In 2017, 78 master's awarded. *Degree requirements:* For master's, comprehensive exam, capstone course. *Entrance requirements:* For master's, GRE, GMAT or MAT. Additional exam requirements/recommendations for international students: Required—TOEFL (minimum score 500 paper-based; 61 iBT). *Application deadline:* Applications are processed on a rolling basis. Application fee: $50. Electronic applications accepted. *Expenses: Tuition:* Full-time $11,250; part-time $625 per credit hour. *Required fees:* $1200. *Financial support:* Federal Work-Study, institutionally sponsored loans, and scholarships/grants available. Support available to part-time students. Financial award application deadline: 5/1; financial award applicants required to submit FAFSA. *Unit head:* Dr. Gene Whitfill, Dean, 806-291-1047, Fax: 806-291-1951, E-mail: whitfillg@wbu.edu. *Application contact:* Amanda Stanton, Coordinator of Graduate Studies, 806-291-3423, Fax: 806-291-1950, E-mail: stanton@wbu.edu.

Waynesburg University, Graduate and Professional Studies, Canonsburg, PA 15370. Offers business (MBA), including energy management, finance, health systems, human resources, leadership, market development; counseling (MA), including addictions counseling, clinical mental health; counselor education and supervision (PhD); criminal investigation (MA); education (M Ed), including autism, curriculum and instruction, educational leadership, online teaching; nursing (MSN), including administration, education, informatics; nursing practice (DNP); special education (M Ed); technology (M Ed); MSN/MBA. *Accreditation:* AACN. *Program availability:* Part-time, evening/weekend. *Degree requirements:* For doctorate, thesis/dissertation. *Entrance requirements:* Additional exam requirements/recommendations for international students: Required—TOEFL. Electronic applications accepted.

Wayne State University, College of Education, Division of Administrative and Organizational Studies, Detroit, MI 48202. Offers educational administration and supervision (Ed S); educational leadership (M Ed); educational leadership and policy studies (Ed D, PhD); educational technology (Certificate); learning design and technology (M Ed, Ed D, PhD, Ed S); online teaching (Certificate). *Program availability:* Part-time, 100% online, blended/hybrid learning. *Faculty:* 7. *Students:* 50 full-time (30 women), 266 part-time (184 women); includes 158 minority (130 Black or African American, non-Hispanic/Latino; 1 American Indian or Alaska Native, non-Hispanic/Latino; 5 Asian, non-Hispanic/Latino; 9 Hispanic/Latino; 1 Native Hawaiian or other Pacific Islander, non-Hispanic/Latino; 12 Two or more races, non-Hispanic/Latino), 9 international. Average age 39. 187 applicants, 31% accepted, 42 enrolled. In 2017, 48 master's, 17 doctorates, 47 other advanced degrees awarded. *Degree requirements:* For master's, thesis (for some programs); for doctorate, thesis/dissertation. *Entrance requirements:* For master's, baccalaureate degree from accredited U.S. institution or equivalent from college or university of government-recognized standing; minimum undergraduate GPA of 2.75 in upper-division coursework; personal statement; for doctorate, GRE (instructional design and technology), interview; curriculum vitae; three to four recommendations; master's degree (for educational leadership and policy studies); minimum graduate GPA of 3.5; autobiographical statement; research experience (for PhD program). Additional exam requirements/recommendations for international students: Required—TOEFL (minimum score 550 paper-based; 79 iBT); Recommended—IELTS (minimum score 6.5), TWE (minimum score 5.5). *Application deadline:* For fall admission, 6/1 priority date for domestic students, 5/1 priority date for international students; for winter admission, 10/1 priority date for domestic students, 9/1 priority date for international students; for spring admission, 2/1 priority date for domestic students, 1/1 priority date for international students. Applications are processed on a rolling basis. Application fee: $50. Electronic applications accepted. *Expenses:* Tuition, state resident: full-time $10,224; part-time $638.98 per credit hour. Tuition, nonresident: full-time $22,145; part-time $1384.04 per credit hour. Tuition and fees vary according to course load and program. *Financial support:* In 2017–18, 85 students received support, including 4 research assistantships with tuition reimbursements available (averaging $18,534 per year); fellowships with tuition reimbursements available, scholarships/grants, and unspecified assistantships also available. Support available to part-time students. Financial award applicants required to submit FAFSA. *Faculty research:* Total quality management, participatory management, administering educational technology, school improvement, principalship. *Unit head:* Dr. William Hill, Assistant Dean, 313-577-9316, E-mail: ad2107@wayne.edu. *Application contact:* Graduate Advisor, 313-577-1605, E-mail: askcoe@wayne.edu.
Website: http://coe.wayne.edu/aos/index.php

Webster University, School of Education, Department of Multidisciplinary Studies, St. Louis, MO 63119-3194. Offers applied educational psychology (MA, Ed S); communication arts (MA); early childhood education (MA, MAT); education and innovation (MA); educational technology (MET); elementary education (MAT); mathematics for educators (MA); middle school education (MAT); multidisciplinary studies (MAT); multimodal literacy for global impact (MA); reading (MA); secondary school education (MAT); special education (MA, MAT); teaching English as a second language (MA); transformative learning in the global community (Ed S). *Program availability:* Part-time. *Entrance requirements:* For master's, minimum GPA of 2.5. Additional exam requirements/recommendations for international students: Required—TOEFL.

West Chester University of Pennsylvania, College of Education and Social Work, Department of Educational Foundations and Policy Studies, West Chester, PA 19383. Offers education for sustainability (Certificate); educational technology (Certificate); higher education policy and student affairs (MS); transformative education and social change (MS). *Program availability:* Part-time. *Students:* 35 full-time (21 women), 49 part-time (33 women); includes 15 minority (9 Black or African American, non-Hispanic/Latino; 1 Asian, non-Hispanic/Latino; 2 Hispanic/Latino; 3 Two or more races, non-Hispanic/Latino), 1 international. Average age 29. 77 applicants, 90% accepted, 51 enrolled. In 2017, 5 master's, 6 other advanced degrees awarded. *Degree requirements:* For master's, comprehensive exam (for some programs), thesis, 36 credits (42 credits for MS in higher education policy and student affairs). *Entrance requirements:* For master's, teaching certification (strongly recommended); for Certificate, minimum GPA of 3.0. Additional exam requirements/recommendations for international students: Required—TOEFL or IELTS. *Application deadline:* For fall admission, 5/15 for international students; for spring admission, 10/15 for international students. Applications are processed on a rolling basis. Application fee: $50. Electronic applications accepted. *Expenses:* Tuition, state resident: full-time $9000; part-time $500 per credit. Tuition, nonresident: full-time $13,500; part-time $750 per credit. *Required fees:* $2959; $149.79 per credit. *Financial support:* Scholarships/grants and unspecified assistantships available. Financial award application deadline: 2/15; financial award applicants required to submit FAFSA. *Faculty research:* Technology integration: preparing our teachers for the twenty-first century, critical pedagogy, education for

sustainability. *Unit head:* Dr. John Elmore, Chair, 610-436-6934, Fax: 610-436-3102, E-mail: jelmore@wcupa.edu. *Application contact:* Office of Graduate Studies and Extended Education, 610-436-2943, Fax: 610-436-2763, E-mail: gradstudy@wcupa.edu.
Website: http://www.wcupa.edu/education-socialWork/profsecedu/

West Chester University of Pennsylvania, College of Education and Social Work, Department of Special Education, West Chester, PA 19383. Offers autism (Certificate); special education (Teaching Certificate); special education (M Ed); universal design for learning and assistive technology (Certificate). *Accreditation:* NCATE. *Program availability:* Part-time, 100% online. *Students:* 13 full-time (11 women), 182 part-time (163 women); includes 13 minority (5 Black or African American, non-Hispanic/Latino; 4 Asian, non-Hispanic/Latino; 4 Two or more races, non-Hispanic/Latino). Average age 30. 101 applicants, 85% accepted, 61 enrolled. In 2017, 43 master's, 27 Certificates awarded. *Degree requirements:* For master's, minimum GPA of 3.0, action research; for other advanced degree, minimum GPA of 3.0; modified student teaching. *Entrance requirements:* For master's, GRE if GPA is below 3.0, two letters of recommendation; for other advanced degree, GRE if GPA is below 3.0. Additional exam requirements/recommendations for international students: Required—TOEFL or IELTS. *Application deadline:* For fall admission, 5/15 for international students; for spring admission, 10/15 for international students. Applications are processed on a rolling basis. Application fee: $50. Electronic applications accepted. *Expenses:* Tuition, state resident: full-time $9000; part-time $500 per credit. Tuition, nonresident: full-time $13,500; part-time $750 per credit. *Required fees:* $2959; $149.79 per credit. *Financial support:* Scholarships/grants and unspecified assistantships available. Financial award application deadline: 2/15; financial award applicants required to submit FAFSA. *Faculty research:* Instructional strategies for students with moderate to severe disabilities; family involvement for families of students with disabilities; instructional strategies for students with autism; math instruction for students with learning disabilities; transitions for students with disabilities; behavior management for students with behavior disorders. *Unit head:* Dr. Beatrice Adera, Interim Chairperson, 610-436-0040, Fax: 610-436-3102, E-mail: badera@wcupa.edu. *Application contact:* Dr. S. Christy Hicks, Graduate Coordinator, 610-436-3067, E-mail: shicks@wcupa.edu.
Website: http://www.wcupa.edu/education-socialWork/specialEducation/

Western Connecticut State University, Division of Graduate Studies, School of Professional Studies, Department of Education and Educational Psychology, Instructional Technology Option, Danbury, CT 06810-6885. Offers MS. *Program availability:* Part-time. *Degree requirements:* For master's, thesis or research project, completion of program in 6 years. *Entrance requirements:* For master's, minimum GPA of 2.8, teaching certificate. Additional exam requirements/recommendations for international students: Recommended—TOEFL (minimum score 550 paper-based; 79 iBT), IELTS (minimum score 6). *Expenses:* Tuition, state resident: full-time $6757; part-time $374 per credit hour. Tuition, nonresident: full-time $18,102; part-time $374 per credit hour. *Required fees:* $4994; $190 per credit hour. $60 per term. Tuition and fees vary according to degree level and program. *Faculty research:* Connectivism in education.

Western Governors University, Teachers College, Salt Lake City, UT 84107. Offers curriculum and instruction (MS); educational leadership (MS); educational studies (MA); educational studies (5-12) (MA), including mathematics; elementary education (K-8) (MAT, Postbaccalaureate Certificate); elementary education (PreK-8) (MAT); English language learning (K-12) (MA); instructional design (MAT); learning and technology (M Ed, MA); management and innovation (M Ed); mathematics (5-12) (MAT, Postbaccalaureate Certificate); mathematics (5-9) (MAT, Postbaccalaureate Certificate); mathematics education (5-12) (MA); mathematics education (5-9) (MA); mathematics education (K-6) (MA); measurement and evaluation (M Ed); science (5-12) (Postbaccalaureate Certificate); science (5-9) (MAT, Postbaccalaureate Certificate); science education (5-12) (MA), including biology, chemistry, geology, physics; science education (5-9) (MA); social science (5-12) (MAT, Postbaccalaureate Certificate); special education (MAT, MS). *Accreditation:* NCATE. *Program availability:* Evening/weekend, online learning. *Degree requirements:* For master's, capstone project. *Entrance requirements:* For master's and Postbaccalaureate Certificate, Readiness Assessment, transcripts. Additional exam requirements/recommendations for international students: Required—TOEFL (minimum score 450 paper-based; 80 iBT). Electronic applications accepted. *Expenses:* Contact institution.

Western Illinois University, School of Graduate Studies, College of Business and Technology, Program in Instructional Design and Technology, Macomb, IL 61455-1390. Offers educational technology specialist (Certificate); instructional design and technology (MS); instructional media development (Certificate); online and distance learning development (Certificate); technology integration in education (Certificate); workplace learning and performance (Certificate). *Program availability:* Part-time, online learning. *Students:* 8 full-time (4 women), 48 part-time (29 women); includes 4 minority (2 Black or African American, non-Hispanic/Latino; 1 Asian, non-Hispanic/Latino; 1 Hispanic/Latino), 2 international. Average age 35. 12 applicants, 83% accepted, 6 enrolled. In 2017, 18 master's awarded. *Degree requirements:* For master's, thesis or alternative. *Entrance requirements:* Additional exam requirements/recommendations for international students: Required—TOEFL (minimum score 550 paper-based; 80 iBT). *Application deadline:* Applications are processed on a rolling basis. Application fee: $30. Electronic applications accepted. *Financial support:* Teaching assistantships and unspecified assistantships available. Financial award applicants required to submit FAFSA. *Unit head:* Dr. Hoyet Hemphill, Chairperson, 309-298-1952. *Application contact:* Dr. Nancy Parsons, Associate Provost and Director of Graduate Studies, 309-298-1806, Fax: 309-298-2345, E-mail: grad-office@wiu.edu.
Website: http://wiu.edu/idt

Western Kentucky University, Graduate Studies, College of Education and Behavioral Sciences, School of Teacher Education, Bowling Green, KY 42101. Offers elementary education (MAE, Ed S); exceptional education: learning and behavioral disorders (MAE); exceptional education: moderate and severe disabilities (MAE); instructional design (MS); interdisciplinary early childhood education (MAE); library media education (MS); literacy education (MAE); middle grades education (MAE); secondary education (MAE, Ed S). *Program availability:* Part-time, evening/weekend, online learning. *Degree requirements:* For master's, comprehensive exam. *Entrance requirements:* For master's, GRE General Test. Additional exam requirements/recommendations for international students: Required—TOEFL (minimum score 555 paper-based; 79 iBT). *Faculty research:* Teacher preparation in moderate/severe disabilities.

Western Michigan University, Graduate College, College of Education and Human Development, Department of Educational Leadership, Research and Technology, Kalamazoo, MI 49008. Offers educational leadership (MA, PhD, Ed S), including educational leadership (MA); educational technology (MA, Graduate Certificate); evaluation, measurement and research (MA, PhD); organizational learning and performance (MA).

Western Oregon University, Graduate Programs, College of Education, Division of Teacher Education, Program in Information Technology, Monmouth, OR 97361. Offers MS Ed. *Accreditation:* NCATE. *Program availability:* Part-time, evening/weekend, online learning. *Degree requirements:* For master's, written exams. *Entrance requirements:* For master's, interview, minimum GPA of 3.0, teaching license. Additional exam requirements/recommendations for international students: Required—TOEFL (minimum score 550 paper-based; 79 iBT), IELTS (minimum score 6.5). *Faculty research:* Impact of technology on teaching and learning.

West Texas A&M University, College of Education and Social Sciences, Department of Education, Program in Instructional Design and Technology, Canyon, TX 79015. Offers M Ed. *Program availability:* Part-time, evening/weekend, 100% online. *Degree requirements:* For master's, comprehensive exam, thesis optional. *Entrance requirements:* For master's, GRE General Test, approval from the instructional technology admissions committee. Additional exam requirements/recommendations for international students: Required—TOEFL (minimum score 550 paper-based). Electronic applications accepted. *Faculty research:* Mathematics and science instruction, technology, developing online courses for freshmen, integrity of online courses.

West Virginia University, College of Education and Human Services, Morgantown, WV 26506. Offers audiology (Au D); autism spectrum disorder (MA); clinical rehabilitation and mental health counseling (MS); communication science and disorders (PhD); counseling (MA); counseling psychology (PhD); curriculum and instruction (Ed D); early childhood education (MA); early intervention (MA); education (PhD); educational leadership (MA, Ed D); educational leadership/public school administration (MA); educational psychology (MA, Ed D); elementary education (MA); gifted education (MA); higher education administration (MA, Ed D); higher education curriculum and teaching (MA); institutional design and technology (MA); instructional design and technology (Ed D); literacy education (MA); secondary education (MA); secondary education/English (MA); special education (Ed D); speech pathology (MS). *Accreditation:* NCATE. *Program availability:* Part-time, evening/weekend, online learning. *Students:* 423 full-time (347 women), 367 part-time (316 women); includes 57 minority (14 Black or African American, non-Hispanic/Latino; 7 Asian, non-Hispanic/Latino; 20 Hispanic/Latino; 16 Two or more races, non-Hispanic/Latino), 13 international. *Degree requirements:* For master's, content exams; for doctorate, comprehensive exam, thesis/dissertation. *Entrance requirements:* Additional exam requirements/recommendations for international students: Required—TOEFL (minimum score 500 paper-based; 61 iBT). *Application deadline:* For fall admission, 8/1 for domestic students; for spring admission, 1/1 for domestic students; for summer admission, 5/1 for domestic students. Application fee: $60. Electronic applications accepted. *Expenses:* Tuition, state resident: full-time $9450. Tuition, nonresident: full-time $24,390. *Financial support:* Fellowships, research assistantships, teaching assistantships, career-related internships or fieldwork, Federal Work-Study, institutionally sponsored loans, health care benefits, tuition waivers (full and partial), and administrative assistantships available. Financial award applicants required to submit FAFSA. *Faculty research:* Internet training and integration for teachers, rural education, teacher preparation, organization of schools, evaluation of personnel. *Unit head:* Dr. Gypsy Denzine, Dean, 304-293-5703, Fax: 304-293-7565, E-mail: gypsy.denzine@mail.wvu.edu. *Application contact:* Dr. M. Cecil Smith, Associate Dean for Research and Graduate Education, 304-293-2174, Fax: 304-293-3802, E-mail: mcecil.smith@mail.wvu.edu.
Website: http://cehs.wvu.edu/

Widener University, School of Human Service Professions, Center for Education, Chester, PA 19013-5792. Offers adult education (M Ed); counseling in higher education (M Ed); counselor education (M Ed); early childhood education (M Ed); educational foundations (M Ed); educational leadership (M Ed); educational psychology (M Ed); elementary education (M Ed); English and language arts (M Ed); health education (M Ed); higher education leadership (Ed D); home and school visitor (M Ed); human sexuality (M Ed, PhD); mathematics education (M Ed); middle school education (M Ed); principalship (M Ed); reading and language arts (Ed D); reading education (M Ed); school administration (Ed D); science education (M Ed); social studies education (M Ed); special education (M Ed); technology education (M Ed). *Accreditation:* NCATE. *Program availability:* Part-time, evening/weekend. *Faculty:* 34 full-time (22 women), 37 part-time/adjunct (14 women). *Students:* 131 full-time (112 women), 244 part-time (179 women); includes 94 minority (58 Black or African American, non-Hispanic/Latino; 1 American Indian or Alaska Native, non-Hispanic/Latino; 1 Asian, non-Hispanic/Latino; 22 Hispanic/Latino; 12 Two or more races, non-Hispanic/Latino), 12 international. Average age 37. 140 applicants, 38% accepted, 26 enrolled. In 2017, 45 master's, 21 doctorates awarded. Terminal master's awarded for partial completion of doctoral program. *Degree requirements:* For doctorate, thesis/dissertation. *Entrance requirements:* For master's, minimum GPA of 2.5; for doctorate, GRE or MAT, minimum GPA of 2.0 (undergraduate), 3.5 (graduate). *Application deadline:* Applications are processed on a rolling basis. Application fee: $25 ($300 for international students). Electronic applications accepted. *Expenses:* Contact institution. *Financial support:* Career-related internships or fieldwork, tuition waivers (full and partial), and unspecified assistantships available. Support available to part-time students. Financial award application deadline: 5/1. *Faculty research:* Reading and cognition, adult education, technology education, educational leadership, special education. *Unit head:* Dr. Shawn Fitzgerald, Dean, 610-499-4294, Fax: 610-499-4623, E-mail: smfitzgerald@widener.edu. *Application contact:* Megan Kuft, Director of Graduate Admissions, 610-499-4124, E-mail: gradprograms@widener.edu.
Website: http://www.widener.edu/academics/schools/eics

Wilkes University, College of Graduate and Professional Studies, School of Education, Wilkes-Barre, PA 18766-0002. Offers educational development and strategies (MS Ed); educational leadership (MS Ed, Ed D); effective teaching (MS Ed); instructional media (MS Ed); instructional technology (MS Ed); international school leadership (MS Ed); international teaching and learning (MS Ed); literacy specialist (MS Ed); middle level education (MS Ed); online teaching (MS Ed); school business leadership (MS Ed); special education (MS Ed); teaching English to speakers of other languages (MS Ed). *Program availability:* Part-time, evening/weekend, 100% online, blended/hybrid learning. *Students:* 76 full-time (57 women), 1,586 part-time (1,204 women); includes 82 minority (10 Black or African American, non-Hispanic/Latino; 12 Asian, non-Hispanic/Latino; 41 Hispanic/Latino; 1 Native Hawaiian or other Pacific Islander, non-Hispanic/Latino; 18 Two or more races, non-Hispanic/Latino). Average age 34. In 2017, 619 master's, 23 doctorates awarded. *Entrance requirements:* Additional exam requirements/recommendations for international students: Required—TOEFL (minimum score 550 paper-based; 79 iBT). *Application deadline:* Applications are processed on a rolling basis. Application fee: $45 ($65 for international students). Electronic applications accepted. *Expenses:* Contact institution. *Financial support:* Unspecified assistantships available. Financial award application deadline: 3/1; financial award applicants required to submit FAFSA. *Unit head:* Dr. Rhonda Rabbitt, Dean, 570-408-4680, Fax: 570-408-7872, E-mail: rhonda.rabbitt@wilkes.edu. *Application contact:* Stephanie Wasmanski, Associate Director of Graduate Admissions, 570-408-5535, Fax: 570-408-7846, E-mail: stephanie.wasmanski@wilkes.edu.
Website: http://www.wilkes.edu/academics/graduate-programs/masters-programs/graduate-education/index.aspx

William Paterson University of New Jersey, College of Education, Wayne, NJ 07470-8420. Offers curriculum and learning (M Ed); early childhood education (Certificate); educational leadership (M Ed); educational media specialist (Certificate); elementary education (MAT, Certificate); elementary education subject area (Certificate); higher education administration (MA); learning disabilities consultant (Certificate); literacy (M Ed); middle level education (M Ed); middle school education subject area (Certificate); professional counseling (M Ed); reading specialist (Certificate); school library media specialist (Certificate); school principal (Certificate); school supervisor (Certificate); secondary education (MAT); special education (M Ed); teacher of students with disabilities (Certificate). *Accreditation:* NCATE. *Program availability:* Part-time, evening/weekend. *Faculty:* 37 full-time (25 women), 21 part-time/adjunct (16 women). *Students:* 73 full-time (54 women), 480 part-time (409 women); includes 153 minority (48 Black or African American, non-Hispanic/Latino; 13 Asian, non-Hispanic/Latino; 81 Hispanic/Latino; 11 Two or more races, non-Hispanic/Latino), 1 international. Average age 35. 347 applicants, 87% accepted, 226 enrolled. In 2017, 136 master's awarded. *Degree requirements:* For master's, comprehensive exam, thesis (for some programs), exit interview (for some programs); practicum/internship; minimum GPA of 3.0 (for some programs); exit portfolio (for some programs). *Entrance requirements:* For master's, GRE/MAT, minimum GPA of 2.75; teaching certificate; essay; interview; 2 letters of recommendation; personal statement. Additional exam requirements/recommendations for international students: Required—TOEFL (minimum score 550 paper-based; 79 iBT), IELTS (minimum score 6). *Application deadline:* For fall admission, 6/1 for domestic students, 3/1 for international students; for spring admission, 11/1 for domestic students, 10/1 for international students. Applications are processed on a rolling basis. Application fee: $50. Electronic applications accepted. *Expenses:* Tuition, state resident: full-time $13,920; part-time $6264 per year. Tuition, nonresident: full-time $21,700; part-time $9765 per year. *Required fees:* $80; $36 per year. Tuition and fees vary according to course load, degree level and program. *Financial support:* In 2017–18, 8,416 students received support. Career-related internships or fieldwork, Federal Work-Study, scholarships/grants, and unspecified assistantships available. Support available to part-time students. Financial award application deadline: 3/15; financial award applicants required to submit FAFSA. *Faculty research:* Code switching and creative writing, language instruction, teacher evaluation, preschools, history of educational theories. *Total annual research expenditures:* $311,226. *Unit head:* Dr. Dorothy Feola, Dean, 973-720-2138, Fax: 973-720-3647, E-mail: feolad@wpunj.edu. *Application contact:* Liana Fornarotto, Director of Education Enrollment and Certification, 973-720-2206, Fax: 973-720-2989, E-mail: fornarottol@wpunj.edu.
Website: http://www.wpunj.edu/coe

William Woods University, Graduate and Adult Studies, Fulton, MO 65251-1098. Offers administration (M Ed, Ed S); athletic/activities administration (M Ed); curriculum and instruction (M Ed, Ed S); educational leadership (Ed D); equestrian education (M Ed); health management (MBA); human resources (MBA); leadership (MBA); marketing, advertising, and public relations (MBA); teaching and technology (M Ed). *Program availability:* Part-time, evening/weekend. *Degree requirements:* For master's, capstone course (MBA), action research (M Ed); for Ed S, field experience. *Entrance requirements:* Additional exam requirements/recommendations for international students: Required—TOEFL (minimum score 550 paper-based). Electronic applications accepted. *Expenses:* Contact institution.

Wilmington University, College of Education, New Castle, DE 19720-6491. Offers applied technology in education (M Ed); career and technical education (M Ed); educational leadership (Ed D); elementary and secondary school counseling (M Ed); elementary studies (M Ed); ESOL literacy (M Ed); higher education leadership (Ed D); instruction: gifted and talented (M Ed); instruction: teacher of reading (M Ed); instruction: teaching and learning (M Ed); organizational leadership (Ed D); school leadership (M Ed); secondary education (MAT); special education (M Ed). *Accreditation:* NCATE. *Program availability:* Part-time, evening/weekend. *Faculty:* 23 full-time (13 women), 162 part-time/adjunct (99 women). *Students:* 546 full-time (394 women), 960 part-time (732 women); includes 320 minority (241 Black or African American, non-Hispanic/Latino; 12 American Indian or Alaska Native, non-Hispanic/Latino; 11 Asian, non-Hispanic/Latino; 28 Hispanic/Latino; 3 Native Hawaiian or other Pacific Islander, non-Hispanic/Latino; 25 Two or more races, non-Hispanic/Latino), 7 international. Average age 34. 1,068 applicants, 64% accepted, 582 enrolled. In 2017, 430 master's, 59 doctorates awarded. *Entrance requirements:* For master's, 2 letters of recommendation, interview. Additional exam requirements/recommendations for international students: Required—TOEFL (minimum score 500 paper-based). *Application deadline:* For fall admission, 4/30 for domestic students. Applications are processed on a rolling basis. Application fee: $35. Electronic applications accepted. *Expenses: Tuition:* Part-time $466 per credit. *Required fees:* $25 per semester. Tuition and fees vary according to degree level and campus/location. *Financial support:* Applicants required to submit FAFSA. *Unit head:* Dr. John C. Gray, Dean, 302-295-1139. *Application contact:* Laura Morris, Director of Admissions, 877-967-5464, E-mail: infocenter@wilmu.edu.
Website: http://www.wilmu.edu/education/

Wilson College, Graduate Programs, Chambersburg, PA 17201-1285. Offers accounting (M Acc); choreography and visual art (MFA); education (M Ed); educational technology (MET); healthcare administration (MHA); humanities (MA), including art and culture, critical/cultural theory, English language and literature, women's studies; management (MSM); nursing (MSN), including nursing education, nursing leadership and management; special education (MSE). *Program availability:* Evening/weekend. *Degree requirements:* For master's, project. *Entrance requirements:* For master's, PRAXIS, minimum undergraduate cumulative GPA of 3.0, 2 letters of recommendation, current certification for eligibility to teach in grades K-12, resume, personal interview. Electronic applications accepted.

Wisconsin Lutheran College, College of Adult and Graduate Studies, Milwaukee, WI 53226-9942. Offers high performance instruction (MA Ed); instructional technology (MA Ed); leadership and innovation (MA Ed); science instruction (MA Ed).

Worcester Polytechnic Institute, Graduate Admissions, Program in Learning Sciences and Technologies, Worcester, MA 01609-2280. Offers MS, PhD. Program offered jointly between Department of Social Science and Policy Studies and Department of Computer Science. *Program availability:* Part-time, evening/weekend. *Students:* 10 full-time (6 women), 6 part-time (3 women); includes 3 minority (1 Hispanic/Latino; 2 Two or more races, non-Hispanic/Latino), 2 international. Average age 33. 11 applicants, 91% accepted, 6 enrolled. *Entrance requirements:* For master's and doctorate, GRE (strongly recommended), statement of purpose, brief sample of scholarly writing. Additional exam requirements/recommendations for international students: Required—TOEFL (minimum score 563 paper-based; 84 iBT), IELTS (minimum score 7). *Application deadline:* For fall admission, 1/1 for domestic and international students; for spring admission, 10/1 for domestic and international students. Applications are processed on a rolling basis. Application fee: $70. Electronic applications accepted. *Expenses: Tuition:* Full-time $26,226; part-time $1457 per credit. *Required fees:* $60; $30 per credit. One-time fee: $15. Tuition and fees vary according to course load. *Financial support:* Fellowships, research assistantships, teaching assistantships, career-related internships or fieldwork, health care benefits, and unspecified assistantships available. Financial award application deadline: 1/1. *Unit head:* Ivon Arroyo, Co-Director, 508-831-5296, E-mail: iarriyo@wpi.edu. *Application contact:* Tricia Desmarais, Administrative Assistant, 508-831-5296, Fax: 508-831-5896, E-mail: td@wpi.edu.
Website: https://www.wpi.edu/academics/departments/learning-sciences-technologies

York College of Pennsylvania, Master of Education Program, York, PA 17403-3651. Offers educational leadership (M Ed); educational technology (M Ed); reading specialist (M Ed). *Program availability:* Part-time-only, evening/weekend. *Faculty:* 2 full-time (1 woman), 7 part-time/adjunct (3 women). *Students:* 87 part-time (62 women); includes 2 minority (1 Hispanic/Latino; 1 Two or more races, non-Hispanic/Latino), 1 international. Average age 33. 57 applicants, 79% accepted, 39 enrolled. In 2017, 7 master's awarded. *Degree requirements:* For master's, comprehensive exam (for some programs), thesis (for some programs). *Entrance requirements:* For master's, PRAXIS, statement of applicant's professional and academic goals, 2 letters of recommendation, letter from current supervisor, official undergraduate and graduate transcript(s), copy of teaching certificate(s), current professional resume, interview. *Application deadline:* For fall admission, 7/15 priority date for domestic students; for spring admission, 11/15 priority date for domestic students; for summer admission, 4/15 priority date for domestic students. Applications are processed on a rolling basis. Application fee: $0. Electronic applications accepted. *Expenses:* $620 per credit. *Financial support:* Scholarships/grants available. Financial award applicants required to submit FAFSA. *Faculty*

research: Classroom technology, assessment, educational leadership, professional development, literacy. *Unit head:* Dr. Joshua D. DeSantis, Director, Master of Education Program, 717-815-1936, E-mail: jdesant1@ycp.edu.
Website: https://www.ycp.edu/med

Youngstown State University, Graduate School, Beeghly College of Education, Department of Teacher Education, Youngstown, OH 44555-0001. Offers adolescent/young adult education (MS Ed); content area concentration (MS Ed); early childhood education (MS Ed); educational technology (MS Ed); literacy (MS Ed); middle childhood education (MS Ed); special education (MS Ed), including gifted and talented education, special education. *Accreditation:* NCATE. *Program availability:* Part-time, evening/weekend. *Degree requirements:* For master's, comprehensive exam. *Entrance requirements:* For master's, GRE, MAT, or teaching certificate; minimum GPA of 2.7. Additional exam requirements/recommendations for international students: Required—TOEFL. *Faculty research:* Multicultural literacy, hands-on mathematics teaching, integrated instruction, reading comprehension, emergent curriculum.

Educational Policy

Alabama State University, College of Education, Department of Instructional Support Programs, Montgomery, AL 36101-0271. Offers applied technology (MS); counselor education (M Ed, MS, Ed S), including general counseling (MS, Ed S), school counseling (M Ed, Ed S); educational administration (M Ed, Ed D, PhD, Ed S), including educational administration (Ed S), educational leadership, policy and law (Ed D, PhD), instructional leadership (M Ed), teacher leadership (Ed S); library education media (M Ed, Ed S). *Program availability:* Part-time. *Faculty:* 11 full-time (6 women), 7 part-time/adjunct (5 women). *Students:* 35 full-time (20 women), 112 part-time (81 women); includes 139 minority (all Black or African American, non-Hispanic/Latino), 1 international. Average age 37. 48 applicants, 75% accepted, 16 enrolled. In 2017, 31 master's, 4 doctorates awarded. Terminal master's awarded for partial completion of doctoral program. *Degree requirements:* For master's, comprehensive exam; for Ed S, comprehensive exam, thesis. *Entrance requirements:* For master's, GRE General Test, MAT, writing competency test, bachelor's degree or its equivalent from accredited college or university with minimum GPA of 2.5; for Ed S, GRE General Test, MAT, writing competency test, minimum GPA of 3.25. Additional exam requirements/recommendations for international students: Required—TOEFL (minimum score 500 paper-based). *Application deadline:* For fall admission, 4/15 for domestic and international students; for spring admission, 11/15 for domestic and international students; for summer admission, 3/15 for domestic and international students. Applications are processed on a rolling basis. Application fee: $25. Electronic applications accepted. *Expenses:* Contact institution. *Financial support:* In 2017–18, 3 students received support. Research assistantships and unspecified assistantships available. Financial award application deadline: 6/30; financial award applicants required to submit FAFSA. *Unit head:* Dr. Sonja Harrington, Chair, 334-229-8828, Fax: 334-229-6831, E-mail: sharrington@alasu.edu. *Application contact:* Dr. William Person, Dean of Graduate Studies, 334-229-4275, Fax: 334-229-4928, E-mail: wperson@alasu.edu.
Website: http://www.alasu.edu/academics/colleges—departments/college-of-education/instructional-support-programs/index.aspx

American University of Beirut, Graduate Programs, Faculty of Arts and Sciences, 1107 2020, Lebanon. Offers anthropology (MA); Arab and Middle Eastern history (PhD); Arabic language and literature (MA, PhD); archaeology (MA); art history and curating (MA); biology (MS); cell and molecular biology (PhD); chemistry (MS); clinical psychology (MA); computational sciences (MS); computer science (MS); economics (MA); education (MA), including administration and policy studies, elementary education, mathematics education, psychology school guidance, psychology test and measurements, science education, teaching English as a foreign language; English language (MA); English literature (MA); environmental policy planning (MS); financial economics (MAFE); general psychology (MA); geology (MS); history (MA); Islamic studies (MA); mathematics (MA); media studies (MA); Middle East studies (MA); philosophy (MA); physics (MS); political studies (MA); public administration (MA); public policy and international affairs (MA); sociology (MA); theoretical physics (PhD). *Program availability:* Part-time. *Faculty:* 108 full-time (36 women), 5 part-time/adjunct (4 women). *Students:* 251 full-time (180 women), 233 part-time (172 women). Average age 26. 425 applicants, 65% accepted, 121 enrolled. In 2017, 47 master's, 2 doctorates awarded. *Degree requirements:* For master's, one foreign language, comprehensive exam, thesis (for some programs), project; for doctorate, one foreign language, comprehensive exam, thesis/dissertation. *Entrance requirements:* For master's, GRE General Test (for some programs); for doctorate, GRE General Test (GRE Subject Test for theoretical physics). Additional exam requirements/recommendations for international students: Required—TOEFL (minimum score 583 paper-based; 97 iBT), IELTS (minimum score 7). *Application deadline:* For fall admission, 2/8 for domestic students; for spring admission, 11/3 for domestic students. Application fee: $50. Electronic applications accepted. *Expenses:* Contact institution. *Financial support:* In 2017–18, 29 fellowships, 40 research assistantships were awarded; teaching assistantships, scholarships/grants, tuition waivers (full and partial), and unspecified assistantships also available. Financial award application deadline: 4/4. *Unit head:* Dr. Nadia Maria El Cheikh, Dean, Faculty of Arts and Sciences, 961-1-374374 Ext. 3800, Fax: 961-1-744461, E-mail: nmcheikh@aub.edu.lb. *Application contact:* Rima Rassi, Graduate Studies Officer, 961-1-350000 Ext. 3833, Fax: 961-1-744461, E-mail: rr46@aub.edu.lb.
Website: http://www.aub.edu.lb/fas/pages/default.aspx

Arizona State University at the Tempe campus, Mary Lou Fulton Teachers College, Program in Educational Policy and Evaluation, Phoenix, AZ 85069. Offers PhD. Fall admission only. *Degree requirements:* For doctorate, comprehensive exam, thesis/dissertation, interactive Program of Study (iPOS) submitted before completing 50 percent of required credit hours. *Entrance requirements:* For doctorate, GRE, minimum GPA of 3.0 or equivalent in last 2 years of work leading to bachelor's degree, 3 letters of recommendation, personal statement, writing sample, curriculum vitae or resume. Additional exam requirements/recommendations for international students: Required—TOEFL, IELTS, or PTE. Electronic applications accepted. *Expenses:* Contact institution. *Faculty research:* Education policy analysis, school finance and quantitative methods, school improvement in ethnically, linguistically and economically diverse communities, parent/teacher engagement, school choice, accountability polices, school finance litigation, school segregation.

Ball State University, Graduate School, Teachers College, Department of Educational Studies, Program in Educational Studies, Muncie, IN 47306. Offers educational studies (PhD), including cultural and educational policy studies, curriculum, educational technology. *Program availability:* Part-time, blended/hybrid learning. *Students:* 8 full-

time (4 women), 16 part-time (11 women); includes 4 minority (2 Black or African American, non-Hispanic/Latino; 1 Asian, non-Hispanic/Latino; 1 Two or more races, non-Hispanic/Latino), 3 international. Average age 43. 14 applicants, 57% accepted, 4 enrolled. In 2017, 3 doctorates awarded. *Degree requirements:* For doctorate, thesis/dissertation. *Entrance requirements:* For doctorate, GRE General Test, minimum graduate GPA of 3.2, curriculum vitae, writing sample, three letters of reference. Additional exam requirements/recommendations for international students: Required—TOEFL (minimum score 550 paper-based; 79 iBT), IELTS (minimum score 6.5). *Application deadline:* Applications are processed on a rolling basis. Application fee: $60. Electronic applications accepted. *Financial support:* Research assistantships with partial tuition reimbursements and teaching assistantships with partial tuition reimbursements available. Financial award application deadline: 3/1; financial award applicants required to submit FAFSA. *Faculty research:* Emerging curriculum trends, secondary teacher preparation, issues of equity and social justice in education, teacher technology integration, teaching for transformative understanding, teacher leadership, history of educational policy and practices, ethics and education. *Unit head:* Dr. Theresa Kruczek, Interim Chair, 765-285-8049, E-mail: tkruczek@bsu.edu.
Website: http://www.bsu.edu/edstudies

Brigham Young University, Graduate Studies, David O. McKay School of Education, Department of Educational Leadership and Foundations, Provo, UT 84602. Offers educational leadership and foundations (Ed D); educational leadership: education policy studies (M Ed); educational leadership: school leadership (M Ed). *Program availability:* Part-time, evening/weekend. *Faculty:* 12 full-time (2 women), 1 part-time/adjunct (0 women). *Students:* 31 full-time (25 women), 62 part-time (31 women); includes 8 minority (2 American Indian or Alaska Native, non-Hispanic/Latino; 1 Asian, non-Hispanic/Latino; 4 Hispanic/Latino; 1 Native Hawaiian or other Pacific Islander, non-Hispanic/Latino). Average age 42. 78 applicants, 49% accepted, 38 enrolled. In 2017, 29 master's, 10 doctorates awarded. Terminal master's awarded for partial completion of doctoral program. *Degree requirements:* For master's, comprehensive exam; for doctorate, comprehensive exam, thesis/dissertation, prospectus. *Entrance requirements:* For master's, GRE, LSAT, GMAT, or MAT, level 2 teaching license; for doctorate, GRE, LSAT, or GMAT, master's degree. Additional exam requirements/recommendations for international students: Required—TOEFL (minimum score 580 paper-based; 85 iBT). *Application deadline:* For fall admission, 5/1 for domestic and international students; for winter admission, 9/15 for domestic and international students; for spring admission, 1/15 for domestic and international students. Application fee: $50. Electronic applications accepted. *Expenses:* Contact institution. *Financial support:* In 2017–18, 38 students received support, including 19 research assistantships (averaging $2,100 per year); scholarships/grants also available. Financial award application deadline: 8/15. *Faculty research:* Inequality of educational opportunity, value of principals academies, role of trust in educational leadership, social networks in education, factors and indicators leading to the improvement of educational settings. *Unit head:* Pamela Hallam, Chair, 801-422-3600, Fax: 801-422-0196, E-mail: pam_hallam@byu.edu. *Application contact:* Michele Price, Department Secretary, 801-422-3813, Fax: 801-422-0196, E-mail: michele_price@byu.edu.
Website: http://education.byu.edu/edlf

California State University, Sacramento, College of Education, Graduate and Professional Studies in Education, Sacramento, CA 95819. Offers behavioral science and gender equity (MA); child development (MA); counseling (MS); curriculum and instruction (MA); education (Ed D), including K-12 and community college; education leadership and policy studies (MA), including higher education, PreK-12; education specialist (Ed S), including school psychology; educational technology (MA); language and literacy (MA); multicultural education (MA); school psychology (MA); special education (MA); workforce development advocacy (MA). *Program availability:* Part-time, evening/weekend, blended/hybrid learning. *Students:* 381 full-time (294 women), 135 part-time (101 women); includes 296 minority (44 Black or African American, non-Hispanic/Latino; 1 American Indian or Alaska Native, non-Hispanic/Latino; 94 Asian, non-Hispanic/Latino; 153 Hispanic/Latino; 4 Native Hawaiian or other Pacific Islander, non-Hispanic/Latino), 3 international. Average age 32. 553 applicants, 53% accepted, 292 enrolled. In 2017, 147 master's, 13 doctorates, 10 other advanced degrees awarded. *Degree requirements:* For master's, thesis or project; writing proficiency exam; for doctorate, thesis/dissertation. *Entrance requirements:* For master's and doctorate, GRE. Additional exam requirements/recommendations for international students: Required—TOEFL (minimum score 550 paper-based; 80 iBT); Recommended—IELTS (minimum score 7), TSE. *Application deadline:* For fall admission, 2/15 for domestic students, 1/15 for international students. Applications are processed on a rolling basis. Application fee: $55. Electronic applications accepted. *Expenses:* Contact institution. *Financial support:* Career-related internships or fieldwork, Federal Work-Study, and scholarships/grants available. Support available to part-time students. Financial award application deadline: 3/1; financial award applicants required to submit FAFSA. *Unit head:* Dr. Elizabeth Liles, Chair, 916-278-5942, E-mail: coe@csus.edu. *Application contact:* Jose Martinez, Graduate Admissions Supervisor, 916-278-7871, E-mail: martinj@skymail.csus.edu.
Website: http://www.csus.edu/coe/academics/graduate/index.html

Cleveland State University, College of Graduate Studies, College of Education and Human Services, Program in Urban Education, Specialization in Policy Studies, Cleveland, OH 44115. Offers PhD. *Program availability:* Part-time. *Faculty:* 6 full-time (1 woman). *Students:* 5 full-time (3 women), 15 part-time (8 women); includes 8 minority (7

Black or African American, non-Hispanic/Latino; 1 Hispanic/Latino), 1 international. Average age 46. 6 applicants, 33% accepted, 2 enrolled. In 2017, 3 doctorates awarded. *Entrance requirements:* For doctorate, GRE General Test (minimum score of 297 for combined Verbal and Quantitative exams, 4.0 preferred for Analytical Writing), minimum graduate GPA of 3.25, curriculum vitae or resume, personal statement, 2 letters of recommendation. Additional exam requirements/recommendations for international students: Required—TOEFL (minimum score 550 paper-based; 78 iBT), IELTS (minimum score 6). Application fee: $40. Electronic applications accepted. *Financial support:* In 2017–18, 5 students received support. Research assistantships, teaching assistantships, and tuition waivers (full and partial) available. Support available to part-time students. Financial award application deadline: 4/1; financial award applicants required to submit FAFSA. *Faculty research:* Historical, theoretical and practical aspects of educational policy formation; relationship of educational policy within the larger context of urban affairs, public policy, and school reform. *Unit head:* Dr. Graham Stead, Director, 216-875-9869, Fax: 216-875-9697, E-mail: g.b.stead@csuohio.edu. *Application contact:* Rita M. Grabowski, Administrative Coordinator, 216-687-4697, Fax: 216-875-9697, E-mail: r.grabowski@csuohio.edu.
Website: http://www.csuohio.edu/cehs/departments/DOC/ep_doc.html

The College of William and Mary, School of Education, Program in Education Policy, Planning, and Leadership, Williamsburg, VA 23187-8795. Offers curriculum and educational technology (PhD); curriculum leadership (Ed D, PhD); educational leadership (M Ed), including higher education administration (M Ed, Ed D, PhD), K-12 administration and supervision; educational policy, planning, and leadership (Ed D, PhD), including general education administration, gifted education administration, higher education administration (M Ed, Ed D, PhD). *Accreditation:* NCATE. *Program availability:* Part-time, evening/weekend. *Faculty:* 20 full-time (10 women), 21 part-time/adjunct (13 women). *Students:* 54 full-time (35 women), 172 part-time (113 women); includes 70 minority (42 Black or African American, non-Hispanic/Latino; 1 Asian, non-Hispanic/Latino; 19 Hispanic/Latino; 8 Two or more races, non-Hispanic/Latino), 3 international. Average age 39. 163 applicants, 71% accepted, 89 enrolled. In 2017, 23 master's, 37 doctorates awarded. *Degree requirements:* For doctorate, comprehensive exam, thesis/dissertation. *Entrance requirements:* For master's, GRE or MAT, minimum GPA of 2.5; for doctorate, GRE or MAT, minimum GPA of 3.0. Additional exam requirements/recommendations for international students: Required—TOEFL (minimum score 100 iBT), IELTS (minimum score 7). *Application deadline:* For fall admission, 1/15 for domestic and international students. Application fee: $50. Electronic applications accepted. *Expenses:* $9,630 resident full-time, $535 resident part-time per credit hour; $25,920 nonresident full-time, $1,265 nonresident part-time per credit hour; $5,944 full-time fees. *Financial support:* In 2017–18, 59 students received support, including 1 fellowship (averaging $20,000 per year), 43 research assistantships (averaging $20,535 per year); scholarships/grants and unspecified assistantships also available. Support available to part-time students. Financial award application deadline: 1/15; financial award applicants required to submit FAFSA. *Faculty research:* Higher education policy, evaluation of teachers, program evaluation, civil rights and higher education, program evaluation. *Unit head:* Dr. Michael F. Dipaola, Department Chair, 757-221-2344, E-mail: mfdipa@wm.edu. *Application contact:* Dorothy Smith Osborne, Assistant Dean for Academic Programs and Student Services, 757-221-2317, E-mail: dsosbo@wm.edu.
Website: http://education.wm.edu

Cornell University, Graduate School, Graduate Fields of Agriculture and Life Sciences, Field of Education, Ithaca, NY 14853. Offers adult and extension education (MPS, MS, PhD); learning, teaching, and social policy (MPS, MS, PhD); mathematics 7-12 (MS). Terminal master's awarded for partial completion of doctoral program. *Degree requirements:* For master's, thesis (MS); for doctorate, comprehensive exam, thesis/dissertation. *Entrance requirements:* For master's and doctorate, GRE General Test, sample of written work (recommended), 2 letters of recommendation. Additional exam requirements/recommendations for international students: Required—TOEFL (minimum score 550 paper-based; 77 iBT). Electronic applications accepted. *Faculty research:* Moral development and professional ethics, public issues education and community development, socio/political issues in public education, teacher education and curriculum in agricultural science and mathematics, extension research.

Eastern Michigan University, Graduate School, College of Arts and Sciences, Department of Sociology, Anthropology and Criminology, Program in Schools, Society and Violence, Ypsilanti, MI 48197. Offers MA. *Students:* 3 full-time (2 women), 5 part-time (3 women); includes 4 minority (all Black or African American, non-Hispanic/Latino). Average age 31. 5 applicants, 100% accepted, 2 enrolled. Application fee: $45. *Application contact:* Dr. Solage Simoes, Coordinator, 734-487-0012, Fax: 734-487-9666, E-mail: ssimoes@emich.edu.
Website: http://www.emich.edu/sac/

Florida State University, The Graduate School, College of Education, Department of Educational Leadership and Policy Studies, Tallahassee, FL 32306. Offers educational leadership and administration (Certificate); educational leadership and policy (MS, Ed D, PhD, Ed S), including education policy and evaluation (MS, Ed D, PhD), educational leadership and administration; foundations of education (MS, PhD), including history and philosophy of education, international and multicultural education; higher education (MS, PhD); institutional research (Certificate); program evaluation (Certificate). *Program availability:* Part-time, evening/weekend, 100% online, blended/hybrid learning, asynchronous, minimal on-campus study. *Faculty:* 19 full-time (15 women), 10 part-time/adjunct (7 women). *Students:* 151 full-time (105 women), 196 part-time (138 women); includes 127 minority (55 Black or African American, non-Hispanic/Latino; 4 Asian, non-Hispanic/Latino; 49 Hispanic/Latino; 19 Two or more races, non-Hispanic/Latino), 33 international. Average age 35. 229 applicants, 54% accepted, 66 enrolled. In 2017, 49 master's, 10 doctorates, 17 other advanced degrees awarded. *Degree requirements:* For master's, comprehensive exam, thesis optional; for doctorate, comprehensive exam, thesis/dissertation, diagnostic exam, preliminary exam, prospectus defense, dissertation defense. *Entrance requirements:* For master's, doctorate, and other advanced degree, GRE General Test, minimum GPA of 3.0. Additional exam requirements/recommendations for international students: Required—TOEFL (minimum score 550 paper-based, 80 iBT), IELTS (minimum score 6.5), Michigan English Language Assessment Battery (minimum score 77), or PTE (minimum score 55). Application fee: $30. Electronic applications accepted. *Financial support:* Fellowships, research assistantships, teaching assistantships, scholarships/grants, tuition waivers (full and partial), and unspecified assistantships available. Financial award application deadline: 1/15; financial award applicants required to submit FAFSA. *Faculty research:* Post-secondary success; leadership education; education policy; international education; multicultural education. *Unit head:* Dr. Robert A. Schwartz, Chair, 850-644-6885, Fax: 850-644-2725, E-mail: raschwartz@fsu.edu. *Application contact:* Linda Lyons, Academic Support Assistant, 850-644-7077, Fax: 850-644-1258, E-mail: ljlyons@fsu.edu.

The George Washington University, Graduate School of Education and Human Development, Department of Educational Leadership, Program in Educational Administration and Policy Studies, Washington, DC 20052. Offers education policy (Ed D); educational administration (Ed D). Ed D in educational administration offered at Newport News and Alexandria, VA. *Accreditation:* NCATE. *Students:* 3 full-time (1 woman), 104 part-time (75 women); includes 47 minority (36 Black or African American, non-Hispanic/Latino; 5 Asian, non-Hispanic/Latino; 4 Hispanic/Latino; 1 Native Hawaiian or other Pacific Islander, non-Hispanic/Latino; 1 Two or more races, non-Hispanic/Latino), 1 international. Average age 41. 45 applicants, 44% accepted. In 2017, 17 doctorates awarded. *Degree requirements:* For doctorate, comprehensive exam, thesis/dissertation. *Entrance requirements:* For doctorate, GRE General Test or MAT, interview, minimum GPA of 3.3. *Application deadline:* For fall admission, 1/15 priority date for domestic students; for spring admission, 10/1 for domestic students. Applications are processed on a rolling basis. Application fee: $75. *Expenses: Tuition:* Full-time $28,800; part-time $1655 per credit hour. *Required fees:* $45; $2.75 per credit hour. *Financial support:* In 2017–18, 9 students received support. Fellowships, research assistantships, teaching assistantships, career-related internships or fieldwork, Federal Work-Study, and tuition waivers (partial) available. Financial award application deadline: 1/15; financial award applicants required to submit FAFSA. *Unit head:* Michael Feuer, Dean, 202-994-6161, E-mail: mjfeuer@gwu.edu. *Application contact:* Sarah Lang, Director, Admissions and Marketing, 202-994-1447, Fax: 202-994-7207, E-mail: slang@gwu.edu.

The George Washington University, Graduate School of Education and Human Development, Department of Educational Leadership, Program in Education Policy Studies, Washington, DC 20052. Offers MA Ed. *Accreditation:* NCATE. *Students:* 19 full-time (15 women), 4 part-time (all women); includes 6 minority (2 Black or African American, non-Hispanic/Latino; 4 Hispanic/Latino), 4 international. Average age 26. 55 applicants, 71% accepted, 12 enrolled. In 2017, 9 master's awarded. *Entrance requirements:* For master's, GRE General Test or MAT, interview, minimum GPA of 2.75. *Application deadline:* For fall admission, 1/15 priority date for domestic students; for spring admission, 10/1 for domestic students. Applications are processed on a rolling basis. Application fee: $75. *Expenses: Tuition:* Full-time $28,800; part-time $1655 per credit hour. *Required fees:* $45; $2.75 per credit hour. *Financial support:* In 2017–18, 10 students received support. Fellowships, career-related internships or fieldwork, Federal Work-Study, and tuition waivers (partial) available. Financial award application deadline: 1/15. *Unit head:* Michael Feuer, Dean, 202-994-6161, E-mail: mjfeuer@gwu.edu. *Application contact:* Sarah Lang, Director of Graduate Admissions, 202-994-1447, Fax: 202-994-7207, E-mail: slang@gwu.edu.

The George Washington University, Graduate School of Education and Human Development, Department of Educational Leadership, Program in Higher Education Administration, Washington, DC 20052. Offers college teaching and academic leadership (MA Ed/HD, Ed S); general administration (MA Ed/HD, Ed S); higher education administration (Ed D); higher education finance (MA Ed/HD, Ed S); international education (MA Ed/HD, Ed S); policy (MA Ed/HD, Ed S); student affairs administration (MA Ed/HD, Ed S). *Accreditation:* NCATE. *Students:* 18 full-time (15 women), 65 part-time (44 women); includes 30 minority (17 Black or African American, non-Hispanic/Latino; 7 Asian, non-Hispanic/Latino; 5 Hispanic/Latino; 1 Two or more races, non-Hispanic/Latino), 2 international. Average age 32. 139 applicants, 76% accepted, 27 enrolled. In 2017, 34 master's, 9 doctorates, 1 other advanced degree awarded. *Degree requirements:* For master's and Ed S, comprehensive exam; for doctorate, comprehensive exam, thesis/dissertation. *Entrance requirements:* For master's, GRE General Test or MAT, minimum GPA of 2.75; for doctorate, GRE General Test or MAT, interview, minimum GPA of 3.3; for Ed S, GRE General Test or MAT, minimum GPA of 3.3. *Application deadline:* For fall admission, 1/15 priority date for domestic students; for spring admission, 10/1 for domestic students. Applications are processed on a rolling basis. Application fee: $75. *Expenses: Tuition:* Full-time $28,800; part-time $1655 per credit hour. *Required fees:* $45; $2.75 per credit hour. *Financial support:* In 2017–18, 17 students received support. Fellowships, research assistantships, career-related internships or fieldwork, Federal Work-Study, and tuition waivers (partial) available. Financial award application deadline: 1/15; financial award applicants required to submit FAFSA. *Faculty research:* Technology in higher education administration. *Unit head:* Michael Feuer, Dean, 202-994-6161, E-mail: mjfeuer@gwu.edu. *Application contact:* Sarah Lang, Director of Graduate Admissions, 202-994-1447, Fax: 202-994-7207, E-mail: slang@gwu.edu.

Georgia State University, College of Education and Human Development, Department of Educational Policy Studies, Atlanta, GA 30302-3083. Offers educational leadership (M Ed, Ed D, Ed S), including educational leadership, urban teacher leadership (M Ed); educational research (MS, PhD); social foundations of education (MS, PhD). *Program availability:* Part-time. *Faculty:* 20 full-time (14 women). *Students:* 55 full-time (40 women), 92 part-time (61 women); includes 81 minority (67 Black or African American, non-Hispanic/Latino; 2 Asian, non-Hispanic/Latino; 10 Hispanic/Latino; 2 Two or more races, non-Hispanic/Latino), 1 international. Average age 36. 68 applicants, 43% accepted, 22 enrolled. In 2017, 7 master's, 21 doctorates, 22 other advanced degrees awarded. *Entrance requirements:* For master's, GRE; for doctorate and Ed S, GRE, MAT. *Application deadline:* For fall admission, 1/15 for domestic and international students; for winter admission, 2/1 for domestic and international students; for spring admission, 10/1 for domestic and international students. Applications are processed on a rolling basis. Application fee: $50. Electronic applications accepted. *Expenses:* Tuition, state resident: full-time $7020. Tuition, nonresident: full-time $22,518. *Required fees:* $2128. Tuition and fees vary according to degree level and program. *Financial support:* In 2017–18, fellowships with full tuition reimbursements (averaging $23,000 per year), research assistantships with full tuition reimbursements (averaging $27,671 per year), teaching assistantships with full tuition reimbursements (averaging $2,300 per year) were awarded; career-related internships or fieldwork, institutionally sponsored loans, scholarships/grants, health care benefits, tuition waivers (full), and unspecified assistantships also available. Support available to part-time students. Financial award application deadline: 3/15. *Faculty research:* Social and cultural influences on schools, equity and social justice, research methodology, program evaluation, leadership and instruction in schools. *Unit head:* Dr. Bill Curlette, Chair, 404-413-8030, Fax: 404-413-8003, E-mail: wcurlette@gsu.edu. *Application contact:* Aishah Cowan, Administrative Academic Specialist, 404-413-8273, Fax: 404-413-8033, E-mail: acowan@gsu.edu.
Website: http://eps.education.gsu.edu/

Harvard University, Harvard Graduate School of Education, Master's Programs in Education, Cambridge, MA 02138. Offers arts in education (Ed M); education policy and management (Ed M); higher education (Ed M); human development and psychology (Ed M); international education policy (Ed M); language and literacy (Ed M); learning and teaching (Ed M); mind, brain, and education (Ed M); prevention science and practice (Ed M); school leadership (Ed M); special studies (Ed M); teacher education (Ed M); technology, innovation, and education (Ed M). *Program availability:* Part-time. *Entrance requirements:* For master's, GRE General Test, statement of purpose, 3 letters of recommendation, resume, official transcripts. Additional exam requirements/recommendations for international students: Required—TOEFL (minimum score 613 paper-based; 104 iBT), TWE (minimum score 5). Electronic applications accepted. *Faculty research:* Learning and development, educational leadership and organizations, education policy analysis.

Howard University, School of Education, Department of Educational Leadership and Policy Studies, Washington, DC 20059. Offers educational administration (Ed D); educational administration and supervision (M Ed, CAGS). *Program availability:* Part-time. *Degree requirements:* For master's, comprehensive exam, School Leaders Licensure Assessment, practicum; for doctorate, comprehensive exam, thesis/dissertation, internship; for CAGS, thesis. *Entrance requirements:* For master's, minimum GPA of 2.7; for doctorate, minimum GPA of 3.0. Additional exam requirements/recommendations for international students: Required—TOEFL (minimum score 550 paper-based; 79 iBT). Electronic applications accepted.

Illinois State University, Graduate School, College of Education, Department of Curriculum and Instruction, Normal, IL 61790. Offers curriculum and instruction (MS, MS Ed, Ed D); educational policies (Ed D); postsecondary education (Ed D); reading (MS Ed); supervision (Ed D). *Accreditation:* NCATE. *Degree requirements:* For master's, variable foreign language requirement, thesis or alternative; for doctorate, variable foreign language requirement, thesis/dissertation, 2 terms of residency, internship. *Entrance requirements:* For master's, GRE General Test, minimum GPA of 3.0 in last 60 hours of course work; for doctorate, GRE General Test. *Faculty research:* In-service and pre-service teacher education for teachers of English language learners; teachers for all children: developing a model for alternative, bilingual elementary certification for paraprofessionals in Illinois; Illinois Geographic Alliance, Connections Project.

Indiana University Bloomington, School of Education, Department of Educational Leadership and Policy Studies, Bloomington, IN 47405. Offers educational leadership (MS, Ed D, Ed S); higher education (Ed D, PhD); higher education and student affairs (MS); history and philosophy of education (MS); history, philosophy, and policy in education (PhD), including education policy studies, history of education, philosophy of education; international and comparative education (MS). *Accreditation:* NCATE. *Degree requirements:* For master's, thesis optional; for doctorate, comprehensive exam, thesis/dissertation; for Ed S, comprehensive exam or project. *Entrance requirements:* For master's, doctorate, and Ed S, GRE General Test. Additional exam requirements/recommendations for international students: Required—TOEFL (minimum score 79 iBT). Electronic applications accepted. *Faculty research:* Culturally engaging campus environments, school choice policy analysis, democracy and education in the national and international context, and principal leadership.

Johns Hopkins University, School of Education, Doctoral Programs in Education, Baltimore, MD 21218. Offers Ed D, PhD. *Program availability:* Part-time, evening/weekend, 100% online. *Degree requirements:* For doctorate, comprehensive exam, thesis/dissertation. *Entrance requirements:* For doctorate, GRE (for PhD only), master's degree from regionally- or nationally-accredited institution; minimum GPA of 3.0 in previous undergraduate and graduate studies (for Ed D only); official transcripts from all post-secondary institutions attended; three letters of recommendation; curriculum vitae/resume; personal statement; dispositions survey. Additional exam requirements/recommendations for international students: Required—TOEFL (minimum score 600 paper-based; 100 iBT), IELTS (minimum score 7). Electronic applications accepted. *Expenses:* Contact institution.

Loyola University Chicago, School of Education, Program in Cultural and Educational Policy Studies, Chicago, IL 60660. Offers M Ed, MA, PhD. PhD offered through the Graduate School. *Program availability:* Part-time, evening/weekend. *Faculty:* 4 full-time (2 women), 3 part-time/adjunct (0 women). *Students:* 39 full-time (27 women), 37 part-time (28 women); includes 31 minority (18 Black or African American, non-Hispanic/Latino; 1 Asian, non-Hispanic/Latino; 7 Hispanic/Latino; 1 Native Hawaiian or other Pacific Islander, non-Hispanic/Latino; 4 Two or more races, non-Hispanic/Latino), 6 international. Average age 30. 82 applicants, 57% accepted, 21 enrolled. In 2017, 13 master's, 4 doctorates awarded. *Degree requirements:* For master's, comprehensive exam (M Ed), thesis (MA); for doctorate, comprehensive exam, thesis/dissertation, oral candidacy exam. *Entrance requirements:* For master's, letters of recommendation, minimum GPA of 3.0; for doctorate, GRE General Test, interview, letter of recommendation, resume, minimum GPA of 3.0. Additional exam requirements/recommendations for international students: Required—TOEFL (minimum score 550 paper-based; 79 iBT). *Application deadline:* For fall admission, 12/1 for domestic and international students; for spring admission, 11/1 for domestic and international students. Applications are processed on a rolling basis. Application fee: $50. Electronic applications accepted. Application fee is waived when completed online. *Expenses:* $949 per semester hour, $2,847 per course, $8,541-$11,388 full-time semester tuition; $432 per semester fees, $225 additional fees (first semester only). *Financial support:* In 2017–18, 8 research assistantships with full tuition reimbursements (averaging $14,000 per year), 22 teaching assistantships (averaging $4,000 per year) were awarded; career-related internships or fieldwork, institutionally sponsored loans, scholarships/grants, health care benefits, and unspecified assistantships also available. Support available to part-time students. Financial award application deadline: 2/1; financial award applicants required to submit FAFSA. *Faculty research:* Politics of education, cultural foundations, policy studies, qualitative research methods, multicultural diversity. *Unit head:* Dr. Noah Sobe, Director, 312-915-6954, E-mail: nsobe@luc.edu. *Application contact:* Mirtza Campbell, Information Contact, 312-915-8907, E-mail: mcampbell11@luc.edu.

Marquette University, Graduate School, College of Education, Department of Educational Policy and Leadership, Milwaukee, WI 53201-1881. Offers college student personnel administration (M Ed); curriculum and instruction (MA); education (MA); educational administration (M Ed); educational policy and foundations (MA); elementary education (Certificate); literacy (MA); principal (Certificate); reading specialist (Certificate); reading teacher (Certificate); secondary education (Certificate); superintendent (Certificate). *Program availability:* Part-time, evening/weekend. Terminal master's awarded for partial completion of doctoral program. *Degree requirements:* For master's, comprehensive exam, thesis (for some programs); for doctorate, thesis/dissertation, qualifying exam. *Entrance requirements:* For master's, GRE General Test or MAT, official transcripts from all current and previous colleges/universities except Marquette, three letters of recommendation, statement of purpose; for doctorate, GRE General Test, MAT, sample of written work, official transcripts from all current and previous colleges/universities except Marquette, three letters of recommendation, statement of purpose, resume/curriculum vitae; for Certificate, GRE General Test or MAT, master's degree. Additional exam requirements/recommendations for international students: Required—TOEFL (minimum score 530 paper-based). *Expenses:* Contact institution. *Faculty research:* Leadership; social justice in education; development of lifelong learners; race, class, and schooling in historical perspective; urban teacher education.

Michigan State University, The Graduate School, College of Education, Program in Educational Policy, East Lansing, MI 48824. Offers PhD. *Entrance requirements:* Additional exam requirements/recommendations for international students: Required—TOEFL. Electronic applications accepted.

New York University, Steinhardt School of Culture, Education, and Human Development, Department of Humanities and Social Sciences in the Professions, Program in Sociology of Education, New York, NY 10012. Offers education policy (MA); social and cultural studies of education (MA); sociology of education (PhD). *Program availability:* Part-time. *Students:* Average age 26. 96 applicants, 45% accepted, 8 enrolled. In 2017, 24 master's, 2 doctorates awarded. *Entrance requirements:* For master's, letters of recommendation; for doctorate, GRE General Test, interview.

Additional exam requirements/recommendations for international students: Required—TOEFL (minimum score 100 iBT). *Application deadline:* For fall admission, 12/1 priority date for domestic and international students; for spring admission, 10/1 for domestic and international students. Applications are processed on a rolling basis. Application fee: $75. Electronic applications accepted. *Expenses: Tuition:* Full-time $41,352; part-time $19,968 per year. *Required fees:* $2496; $1628 per unit. $814 per term. Tuition and fees vary according to course load and program. *Financial support:* Fellowships with full and partial tuition reimbursements, Federal Work-Study, institutionally sponsored loans, scholarships/grants, and tuition waivers (partial) available. Support available to part-time students. Financial award application deadline: 2/1; financial award applicants required to submit FAFSA. *Faculty research:* Legal and institutional environments of schools; social inequality; high school reform and achievement; urban schooling, economics and education, educational policy. *Unit head:* Prof. Lisa Stulberg, Program Director, 212-992-9373, Fax: 212-995-4832, E-mail: lisa.stulberg@nyu.edu. *Application contact:* 212-998-5030, Fax: 212-995-4328, E-mail: steinhardt.gradadmissions@nyu.edu. Website: http://steinhardt.nyu.edu/humsocsci/sociology

Niagara University, Graduate Division of Education, Concentration in Educational Leadership, Niagara University, NY 14109. Offers leadership and policy (PhD); school building leader (MS Ed); school district business leader (Certificate); school district leader (MS Ed, Certificate). *Program availability:* Part-time, evening/weekend, 100% online. *Students:* 52 full-time (32 women), 149 part-time (105 women); includes 30 minority (16 Black or African American, non-Hispanic/Latino; 2 Asian, non-Hispanic/Latino; 7 Hispanic/Latino; 5 Two or more races, non-Hispanic/Latino), 45 international. Average age 38. In 2017, 21 master's, 10 doctorates, 18 other advanced degrees awarded. *Entrance requirements:* For master's, GRE General Test or MAT; for Certificate, GRE General Test and GRE Subject Test or MAT. Additional exam requirements/recommendations for international students: Required—TOEFL (minimum score 550 paper-based; 79 iBT), IELTS (minimum score 6). *Application deadline:* For fall admission, 8/1 for domestic students. Applications are processed on a rolling basis. Application fee: $30. *Expenses:* Contact institution. *Financial support:* In 2017–18, 1 research assistantship with tuition reimbursement was awarded; teaching assistantships with tuition reimbursements, career-related internships or fieldwork, Federal Work-Study, scholarships/grants, and unspecified assistantships also available. Support available to part-time students. Financial award application deadline: 4/15; financial award applicants required to submit FAFSA. *Unit head:* Dr. James Mills, Coordinator of Educational Leadership, 716-286-8553, E-mail: jmills@niagara.edu. *Application contact:* Evan Pierce, Associate Director, Graduate Studies, 716-286-8327, E-mail: epierce@niagara.edu. Website: http://www.niagara.edu/educational-leadership-online

Northwest Missouri State University, Graduate School, School of Education, Maryville, MO 64468-6001. Offers early childhood education (MS Ed); education leadership (MS Ed), including elementary, K-12, secondary; educational leadership (Ed S), including elementary school principalship, secondary school principalship, superintendency; educational leadership and policy analysis (Ed D); elementary education (MS Ed); elementary mathematics (MS Ed); higher education leadership (MS); middle school education (MS Ed); reading (MS Ed); special education (MS Ed); teacher leadership (MS Ed); teaching English language learners (MS Ed). *Accreditation:* NCATE. *Program availability:* Part-time. *Faculty:* 15 full-time (8 women). *Students:* 28 full-time (20 women), 170 part-time (114 women); includes 20 minority (7 Black or African American, non-Hispanic/Latino; 1 Asian, non-Hispanic/Latino; 8 Hispanic/Latino; 4 Two or more races, non-Hispanic/Latino). Average age 33. 168 applicants, 73% accepted, 114 enrolled. In 2017, 67 master's, 21 other advanced degrees awarded. *Degree requirements:* For master's, comprehensive exam; for Ed S, comprehensive exam, thesis. *Entrance requirements:* For master's, GRE General Test, writing sample; for Ed S, minimum graduate GPA of 3.25. Additional exam requirements/recommendations for international students: Required—TOEFL (minimum score 550 paper-based). *Application deadline:* For fall admission, 7/1 for domestic and international students; for spring admission, 11/15 for domestic and international students. Applications are processed on a rolling basis. Application fee: $0 ($50 for international students). Electronic applications accepted. *Expenses:* $389.11 per credit hour in-state tuition and fees, $641.97 out-of-state; $9,750 total cost (for online-based education program). *Financial support:* Research assistantships with full tuition reimbursements, teaching assistantships with full tuition reimbursements, and unspecified assistantships available. Financial award application deadline: 4/1; financial award applicants required to submit FAFSA. *Unit head:* Dr. Tim Wall, Director, 660-562-1179, E-mail: timwall@nwmissouri.edu. Website: https://www.nwmissouri.edu/education/index.htm

The Ohio State University, Graduate School, College of Education and Human Ecology, Department of Educational Studies, Columbus, OH 43210. Offers M Ed, MA, PhD, Ed S. *Accreditation:* NCATE. *Program availability:* Part-time. *Faculty:* 55. *Students:* 307 full-time (201 women), 157 part-time (114 women); includes 106 minority (61 Black or African American, non-Hispanic/Latino; 15 Asian, non-Hispanic/Latino; 17 Hispanic/Latino; 13 Two or more races, non-Hispanic/Latino), 48 international. Average age 32. In 2017, 115 master's, 36 doctorates, 1 other advanced degree awarded. *Degree requirements:* For master's, thesis optional; for doctorate, thesis/dissertation. *Entrance requirements:* For master's and doctorate, GRE General Test. Additional exam requirements/recommendations for international students: Required—TOEFL (minimum score 550 paper-based; 79 iBT), Michigan English Language Assessment Battery (minimum score 82); Recommended—IELTS (minimum score 7). *Application deadline:* For fall admission, 12/1 priority date for domestic and international students; for spring admission, 11/1 for domestic and international students; for summer admission, 3/1 for domestic and international students. Applications are processed on a rolling basis. Application fee: $60 ($70 for international students). Electronic applications accepted. *Financial support:* Fellowships with tuition reimbursements, research assistantships with tuition reimbursements, teaching assistantships with tuition reimbursements, Federal Work-Study, institutionally sponsored loans, and unspecified assistantships available. Support available to part-time students. *Unit head:* Dr. Eric Anderman, Chair and Professor, 614-688-5721, E-mail: anderman.1@osu.edu. *Application contact:* Graduate and Professional Admissions, 614-292-9444, E-mail: gpadmissions@osu.edu. Website: http://ehe.osu.edu/educational-studies/

Oregon State University, College of Education, Program in Education, Corvallis, OR 97331. Offers agricultural education (PhD); language equity and education policy (PhD); mathematics education (MS); science education (MS); science/mathematics education (PhD). *Program availability:* Part-time, 100% online, blended/hybrid learning. Terminal master's awarded for partial completion of doctoral program. *Degree requirements:* For master's, variable foreign language requirement, thesis (for some programs); for doctorate, variable foreign language requirement, thesis/dissertation. *Entrance requirements:* Additional exam requirements/recommendations for international students: Required—TOEFL (minimum score 575 paper-based). Application fee: $75 ($85 for international students). *Faculty research:* School administration, educational foundations, research methodology, education policy development, higher education administration. *Unit head:* Nick Cabot, Ecampus Counseling Lead, 541-737-8564, E-mail: cabotn@oregonstate.edu. *Application contact:* Nick Cabot, Ecampus Counseling Lead, 541-737-8564, E-mail: cabotn@oregonstate.edu.

Educational Policy

Penn State University Park, Graduate School, College of Education, Department of Education Policy Studies, University Park, PA 16802. Offers educational leadership (M Ed, D Ed, PhD, Certificate); educational theory and policy (MA, PhD); higher education (M Ed, D Ed, PhD). *Accreditation:* NCATE. *Program availability:* Online learning. *Unit head:* Dr. David H. Monk, Dean, 814-865-2523, Fax: 814-865-0555. *Application contact:* Lori Hawn, Director, Graduate Student Services, 814-865-1795, Fax: 814-863-4627, E-mail: l-gswww@lists.psu.edu.
Website: http://ed.psu.edu/eps

Rutgers University–Camden, Graduate School of Arts and Sciences, Department of Public Policy and Administration, Camden, NJ 08102. Offers education policy and leadership (MPA); international public service and development (MPA); public management (MPA); JD/MPA; MPA/MA. *Accreditation:* NASPAA. *Program availability:* Part-time, evening/weekend. *Degree requirements:* For master's, directed study, research workshop, 42 credits. *Entrance requirements:* For master's, GRE General Test, GMAT or LSAT, 3 letters of recommendation; resume. Additional exam requirements/recommendations for international students: Required—TOEFL (minimum score 550 paper-based), IELTS. Electronic applications accepted. *Faculty research:* Nonprofit management, county and municipal administration, health and human services, government communication, administrative law, educational finance.

Rutgers University–New Brunswick, Graduate School of Education, Doctoral Program in Education, New Brunswick, NJ 08901. Offers educational policy (PhD); educational psychology (PhD); literacy education (PhD); mathematics education (PhD). *Program availability:* Part-time. *Degree requirements:* For doctorate, thesis/dissertation, qualifying exam. *Entrance requirements:* For doctorate, GRE General Test, GRE Subject Test (mathematics education). Additional exam requirements/recommendations for international students: Required—TOEFL (minimum score 575 paper-based; 83 iBT). Electronic applications accepted. *Faculty research:* Literacy education, math education, educational psychology, educational policy, learning sciences.

Stanford University, Graduate School of Education, Program in Policy, Organization, and Leadership Studies, Stanford, CA 94305-2004. Offers MA, MA/MBA. *Degree requirements:* For master's, thesis (for some programs). *Entrance requirements:* For master's, GRE General Test. Electronic applications accepted. *Expenses: Tuition:* Full-time $48,987; part-time $10,620 per quarter. One-time fee: $400. Tuition and fees vary according to program.

Teachers College, Columbia University, Department of Education Policy and Social Analysis, New York, NY 10027-6696. Offers economics and education (Ed M, MA, PhD); education policy (Ed M, MA, Ed D, PhD); politics and education (Ed M, MA, Ed D, PhD); sociology and education (Ed M, MA, Ed D, PhD). *Students:* 144 full-time (109 women), 107 part-time (85 women); includes 100 minority (43 Black or African American, non-Hispanic/Latino; 17 Asian, non-Hispanic/Latino; 33 Hispanic/Latino; 7 Two or more races, non-Hispanic/Latino), 69 international. Average age 29. 524 applicants, 53% accepted, 104 enrolled. *Unit head:* Dr. Aaron Pallas, Chair, E-mail: amp155@tc.columbia.edu. *Application contact:* David Estrella, Director of Admissions, 212-678-3305, E-mail: estrella@tc.columbia.edu.
Website: http://www.tc.columbia.edu/education-policy-and-social-analysis/

Teachers College, Columbia University, Department of Organization and Leadership, New York, NY 10027-6696. Offers adult education guided intensive study (Ed D); adult learning and leadership (Ed M, MA, Ed D); educational leadership (Ed D); higher and postsecondary education (MA, Ed D); leadership, policy and politics (Ed D); nurse executive (MA, Ed D), including administration studies (MA), professional studies (MA); private school leadership (Ed M, MA); public school building leadership (Ed M, MA); social and organizational psychology (MA); urban education leaders (Ed D); MA/MBA. *Program availability:* Part-time, evening/weekend. *Students:* 342 full-time (244 women), 378 part-time (256 women); includes 288 minority (106 Black or African American, non-Hispanic/Latino; 69 Asian, non-Hispanic/Latino; 92 Hispanic/Latino; 21 Two or more races, non-Hispanic/Latino), 86 international. Average age 33. 1,063 applicants, 59% accepted, 405 enrolled. *Degree requirements:* For doctorate, thesis/dissertation. *Unit head:* Prof. Bill Baldwin, Chair, E-mail: wjb12@tc.columbia.edu. *Application contact:* David Estrella, Director of Admission, 212-678-3305, E-mail: estrella@tc.columbia.edu.

University at Albany, State University of New York, School of Education, Department of Educational Policy and Leadership, Albany, NY 12222-0001. Offers educational policy and leadership (MS, PhD); higher education (MS); international education management (CAS). *Program availability:* Evening/weekend. *Faculty:* 11 full-time (3 women), 13 part-time/adjunct (10 women). *Students:* 37 full-time (21 women), 93 part-time (51 women); includes 28 minority (14 Black or African American, non-Hispanic/Latino; 1 Asian, non-Hispanic/Latino; 11 Hispanic/Latino; 2 Two or more races, non-Hispanic/Latino), 21 international. Average age 32. 72 applicants, 71% accepted, 48 enrolled. In 2017, 11 master's, 7 doctorates, 12 other advanced degrees awarded. *Degree requirements:* For doctorate, one foreign language, thesis/dissertation. *Entrance requirements:* For doctorate, GRE General Test, GRE Subject Test. Additional exam requirements/recommendations for international students: Required—TOEFL (minimum score 550 paper-based). *Application deadline:* For fall admission, 2/1 for domestic students, 5/1 for international students; for spring admission, 9/1 for domestic students, 11/1 for international students. Applications are processed on a rolling basis. Application fee: $75. Electronic applications accepted. *Expenses:* Tuition, state resident: full-time $10,870; part-time $453 per credit hour. Tuition, nonresident: full-time $22,210; part-time $925 per credit hour. *Required fees:* $84.68 per credit hour. $508.06 per semester. Part-time tuition and fees vary according to course load and program. *Financial support:* Fellowships and career-related internships or fieldwork available. Financial award application deadline: 3/15. *Unit head:* Jason Lane, Chair, 518-442-5092, E-mail: jlane@albany.edu.
Website: http://www.albany.edu/epl/

University of Alberta, Faculty of Graduate Studies and Research, Department of Educational Policy Studies, Edmonton, AB T6G 2E1, Canada. Offers adult education (M Ed, Ed D, PhD); educational administration and leadership (M Ed, Ed D, PhD, Postgraduate Diploma); First Nations education (M Ed, Ed D, PhD); theoretical, cultural and international studies in education (M Ed, Ed D, PhD). *Degree requirements:* For master's, thesis (for some programs); for doctorate, thesis/dissertation. *Entrance requirements:* For master's, minimum GPA of 6.5 on a 9.0 scale; for doctorate, minimum GPA of 7.5 on a 9.0 scale. Additional exam requirements/recommendations for international students: Required—TOEFL (minimum score 580 paper-based). Electronic applications accepted.

University of Arkansas, Graduate School, College of Education and Health Professions, Department of Education Reform, Fayetteville, AR 72701. Offers education policy (PhD). In 2017, 4 doctorates awarded. *Application deadline:* For fall admission, 8/1 for domestic students, 4/1 for international students; for spring admission, 10/1 for international students; for summer admission, 4/15 for domestic students, 3/1 for international students. Applications are processed on a rolling basis. Application fee: $60. Electronic applications accepted. *Expenses:* Tuition, state resident: full-time $3782. Tuition, nonresident: full-time $10,238. *Financial support:* In 2017–18, 14 research assistantships were awarded; fellowships and teaching assistantships also available. *Unit head:* Dr. Jay Greene, Department Head, 479-575-3172, E-mail: jpg@

uark.edu. *Application contact:* Dr. Dirk C. van Raemdonck, Graduate Admissions, 479-575-5597, Fax: 479-575-6676, E-mail: dvanraem@uark.edu.
Website: http://edre.uark.edu/

The University of British Columbia, Faculty of Education, Department of Educational Studies, Vancouver, BC V6T 1Z1, Canada. Offers adult learning and education (M Ed); adult learning and global change (M Ed); curriculum and leadership (M Ed); educational administration and leadership (M Ed); educational leadership and policy (Ed D); educational studies (M Ed, MA, PhD); higher education (M Ed); society, culture and politics in education (M Ed). *Program availability:* Part-time, evening/weekend. Terminal master's awarded for partial completion of doctoral program. *Degree requirements:* For master's, thesis; for doctorate, comprehensive exam, thesis/dissertation. *Entrance requirements:* For master's, minimum B+ average, 4-year undergraduate degree, field-related experience; for doctorate, minimum B+ average, 4-year undergraduate degree, master's degree, field-related experience. Additional exam requirements/recommendations for international students: Required—TOEFL (minimum score 600 paper-based; 100 iBT) or IELTS (minimum score 6.5). Electronic applications accepted. *Expenses:* Contact institution. *Faculty research:* Educational leadership educational administration adult education politics in education, global change and adult learning.

University of California, Riverside, Graduate Division, Graduate School of Education, Riverside, CA 92521. Offers applied behavior analysis (M Ed); diversity and equity (M Ed); education policy analysis and leadership (PhD); education specialist (Credential); education, society, and culture (MA, PhD); educational psychology (MA, PhD); general education (M Ed); higher education administration and policy (M Ed, PhD); multiple subject (Credential); research, evaluation, measurement and statistics (MA); school psychology (PhD); single subject (Credential); special education (M Ed, PhD); special education and autism (MA); TESOL (M Ed). *Faculty:* 29 full-time (16 women), 2 part-time/adjunct (1 woman). *Students:* 241 full-time (188 women). 396 applicants, 42% accepted, 166 enrolled. In 2017, 130 master's, 15 doctorates, 14 other advanced degrees awarded. Terminal master's awarded for partial completion of doctoral program. *Degree requirements:* For master's, comprehensive exams or thesis (MA), case study or analytical report (M Ed); for doctorate, comprehensive exam, thesis/dissertation, written and oral qualifying exams, college teaching practicum. *Entrance requirements:* For master's, GRE General Test (for MA); CBEST and CSET (for M Ed in general education only); UCR Extension TESOL certificate (for M Ed with TESOL emphasis only); for doctorate, GRE General Test, writing sample; for Credential, CBEST, CSET. Additional exam requirements/recommendations for international students: Required—TOEFL (minimum score 550 paper-based; 80 iBT), IELTS (minimum score 7). *Application deadline:* For fall admission, 9/1 for domestic students, 6/1 for international students; for winter admission, 11/15 for domestic students, 9/1 for international students; for spring admission, 3/1 for domestic students, 12/1 for international students. Applications are processed on a rolling basis. Application fee: $80 ($100 for international students). Electronic applications accepted. *Expenses:* Tuition, state resident: full-time $5746. Tuition, nonresident: full-time $10,780. Tuition and fees vary according to campus/location and program. *Financial support:* In 2017–18, 105 students received support, including 16 fellowships with full tuition reimbursements available (averaging $31,000 per year), 25 research assistantships with full tuition reimbursements available (averaging $31,000 per year), 10 teaching assistantships with full tuition reimbursements available (averaging $31,000 per year); career-related internships or fieldwork, Federal Work-Study, institutionally sponsored loans, scholarships/grants, and unspecified assistantships also available. Financial award application deadline: 12/15. *Faculty research:* Responsiveness to intervention, faculty core, response to intervention of English language learners, advanced modeling techniques, study on social capital, trust, and motivation. *Total annual research expenditures:* $1.7 million. *Unit head:* Thomas Smith, Dean, 951-827-4633, E-mail: thomas.smith@ucr.edu. *Application contact:* Heather Killeen, Graduate Program Coordinator, 951-827-6362, E-mail: heather.killeen@ucr.edu.
Website: http://www.education.ucr.edu/

University of Colorado Boulder, Graduate School, School of Education, Division of Educational Foundations, Policy, and Practice, Boulder, CO 80309. Offers MA, PhD. *Students:* 35 full-time (20 women), 13 part-time (10 women); includes 24 minority (4 Black or African American, non-Hispanic/Latino; 2 Asian, non-Hispanic/Latino; 15 Hispanic/Latino; 3 Two or more races, non-Hispanic/Latino). Average age 31. 108 applicants, 44% accepted, 18 enrolled. In 2017, 8 master's, 1 doctorate awarded. *Entrance requirements:* For master's, minimum undergraduate GPA of 2.75. *Application deadline:* For fall admission, 12/1 for domestic and international students; for spring admission, 9/1 for domestic and international students. Application fee: $60 ($80 for international students). Electronic applications accepted. Application fee is waived when completed online. *Financial support:* In 2017–18, 100 students received support, including 27 fellowships (averaging $3,900 per year), 14 research assistantships with full and partial tuition reimbursements available (averaging $30,589 per year), 11 teaching assistantships with full and partial tuition reimbursements available (averaging $7,989 per year); institutionally sponsored loans, scholarships/grants, health care benefits, and unspecified assistantships also available. Financial award application deadline: 2/15; financial award applicants required to submit FAFSA. *Application contact:* E-mail: edadvise@colorado.edu.
Website: http://www.colorado.edu/education/

University of Colorado Denver, School of Education and Human Development, Program in Educational Leadership and Innovation, Denver, CO 80217. Offers educational studies and research (PhD), including administrative leadership and policy, early childhood special education, math education, research, assessment and evaluation, science education, urban ecologies. *Program availability:* Part-time, evening/weekend. *Degree requirements:* For doctorate, comprehensive exam, thesis/dissertation, 75 credit hours (for PhD). *Entrance requirements:* For doctorate, GRE or equivalent, resume or curriculum vitae, letters of recommendation, master's degree or equivalent, completion of basic or advanced statistics course with minimum B grade. Additional exam requirements/recommendations for international students: Required—TOEFL (minimum score 537 paper-based; 75 iBT); Recommended—IELTS (minimum score 6.5). Electronic applications accepted. *Expenses:* Contact institution. *Faculty research:* Administrative leadership and policy studies, early childhood education, research in diversity, paraprofessionals in education, urban schools lab.

University of Denver, Morgridge College of Education, Denver, CO 80208. Offers child, family and school psychology (MA, PhD, Ed S); counseling psychology (MA, PhD); curriculum and instruction (MA, Ed D, PhD); curriculum instruction and teaching (Certificate); early childhood special education (MA, Certificate); educational leadership and policy studies (MA, Ed D, PhD, Certificate); higher education (Ed D, PhD); library and information science (MLIS); research methods and statistics (MA, PhD). *Accreditation:* ALA; APA (one or more programs are accredited). *Program availability:* Part-time, evening/weekend, online learning. *Faculty:* 39 full-time (29 women), 60 part-time/adjunct (42 women). *Students:* 502 full-time (406 women), 361 part-time (267 women); includes 233 minority (54 Black or African American, non-Hispanic/Latino; 6 American Indian or Alaska Native, non-Hispanic/Latino; 25 Asian, non-Hispanic/Latino; 113 Hispanic/Latino; 35 Two or more races, non-Hispanic/Latino), 52 international. Average age 31. 1,167 applicants, 64% accepted, 415 enrolled. In 2017, 285 master's,

51 doctorates, 157 other advanced degrees awarded. Terminal master's awarded for partial completion of doctoral program. *Degree requirements:* For master's, comprehensive exam; for doctorate, 2 foreign languages, comprehensive exam, thesis/dissertation. *Entrance requirements:* For master's and doctorate, GRE General Test or GMAT. Additional exam requirements/recommendations for international students: Required—TOEFL (minimum score 550 paper-based; 80 iBT). *Application deadline:* Applications are processed on a rolling basis. Application fee: $65. Electronic applications accepted. *Expenses:* $31,935 per year full-time. *Financial support:* In 2017–18, 765 students received support, including 26 research assistantships with tuition reimbursements available (averaging $10,957 per year), 38 teaching assistantships with tuition reimbursements available (averaging $3,391 per year); career-related internships or fieldwork, Federal Work-Study, institutionally sponsored loans, scholarships/grants, and unspecified assistantships also available. Support available to part-time students. Financial award application deadline: 2/15; financial award applicants required to submit FAFSA. *Faculty research:* Early childhood education, educational leadership, access and opportunity to postsecondary education, marriage and family therapy, data management and archival research. *Unit head:* Dr. Karen Riley, Dean, 303-871-3665, Fax: 303-871-4456, E-mail: karen.riley@du.edu. *Application contact:* Jodi Dye, Director of Admissions, 303-871-2510, Fax: 303-871-4456, E-mail: jodi.dye@du.edu.
Website: http://morgridge.du.edu

University of Florida, Graduate School, College of Education, School of Human Development and Organizational Studies in Education, Gainesville, FL 32611. Offers counseling and counselor education (Ed D, PhD), including counseling and counselor education, marriage and family counseling, mental health counseling, school counseling and guidance; educational leadership (M Ed, MAE, Ed D, PhD, Ed S), including educational leadership (Ed D, PhD), educational policy (Ed D, PhD); higher education administration (Ed D, PhD), including education policy (Ed D), educational policy, higher education administration; marriage and family counseling (M Ed, MAE, Ed D, PhD, Ed S); mental health counseling (M Ed, MAE, Ed D, PhD, Ed S); research and evaluation methodology (M Ed, MAE, Ed D, PhD); school counseling and guidance (M Ed, MAE, Ed D, PhD, Ed S); student personnel in higher education (M Ed, MAE). *Accreditation:* ACA (one or more programs are accredited); NCATE. *Program availability:* Part-time, online learning. Terminal master's awarded for partial completion of doctoral program. *Degree requirements:* For master's, thesis optional; for doctorate, comprehensive exam, thesis/dissertation. *Entrance requirements:* For master's and doctorate, GRE General Test, minimum GPA of 3.0 (undergraduate), 3.5 (graduate); for Ed S, GRE General Test. Additional exam requirements/recommendations for international students: Required—TOEFL (minimum score 550 paper-based; 80 iBT), IELTS (minimum score 6). Electronic applications accepted.

University of Florida, Graduate School, College of Liberal Arts and Sciences, Department of Political Science, Gainesville, FL 32611. Offers educational policy (PhD); international development policy and administration (MA, Certificate); international relations (MA, MAT); political campaigning (MA, Certificate); political science (MA, PhD); public affairs (MA, Certificate); tropical conservation and development (MA, PhD); JD/MA. Terminal master's awarded for partial completion of doctoral program. *Degree requirements:* For master's, variable foreign language requirement, comprehensive exam (for some programs), thesis or alternative, internship (for some programs); for doctorate, variable foreign language requirement, comprehensive exam, thesis/dissertation. *Entrance requirements:* For master's and doctorate, GRE General Test (minimum score: 308 combined verbal/quantitative), minimum GPA of 3.5. Additional exam requirements/recommendations for international students: Required—TOEFL (minimum score 550 paper-based; 80 iBT), IELTS (minimum score 6). Electronic applications accepted. *Faculty research:* American electoral politics and political institutions, comparative democratization and development, theories of international relation, and political theory.

University of Georgia, College of Education, Department of Lifelong Education, Administration and Policy, Athens, GA 30602. Offers adult education (Ed D, Ed S); lifelong education, administration and policy (PhD). *Accreditation:* NCATE. *Entrance requirements:* For doctorate, GRE General Test; for Ed S, GRE General Test or MAT. Electronic applications accepted.

University of Hawaii at Manoa, Office of Graduate Education, College of Education, PhD in Education Program, Honolulu, HI 96822. Offers curriculum and instruction (PhD); educational administration (PhD); educational foundations (PhD); educational policy studies (PhD); educational psychology (PhD); exceptionalities (PhD); kinesiology (PhD); learning design and technology (PhD). *Program availability:* Part-time, evening/weekend. *Degree requirements:* For doctorate, thesis/dissertation. *Entrance requirements:* For doctorate, GRE General Test, sample of written work. Additional exam requirements/recommendations for international students: Required—TOEFL (minimum score 600 paper-based; 100 iBT), IELTS (minimum score 7).

University of Illinois at Chicago, College of Education, Department of Educational Policy Studies, Chicago, IL 60607-7128. Offers policy studies (M Ed); policy studies in urban education (PhD); urban education leadership (Ed D). *Faculty research:* Social foundations of education, educational organizations and leadership, education policy analysis, understanding and addressing educational problems in urban contexts.

University of Illinois at Urbana–Champaign, Graduate College, College of Education, Department of Education Policy, Organization, and Leadership, Champaign, IL 61820. Offers educational organization and leadership (Ed M, MS, Ed D, PhD, CAS); educational policy studies (Ed M, MA, PhD); human resource education (Ed M, MS, Ed D, PhD, CAS). *Program availability:* Part-time, online learning.

The University of Iowa, Graduate College, College of Education, Department of Educational Policy and Leadership Studies, Iowa City, IA 52242-1316. Offers educational leadership (MA, PhD, Ed S); higher education and student affairs (MA, PhD); schools, culture, and society (MA, PhD). *Degree requirements:* For master's and Ed S, exam; for doctorate, comprehensive exam, thesis/dissertation. *Entrance requirements:* For master's, doctorate, and Ed S, GRE General Test, minimum GPA of 3.0. Additional exam requirements/recommendations for international students: Required—TOEFL (minimum score 550 paper-based; 81 iBT). Electronic applications accepted.

The University of Kansas, Graduate Studies, School of Education, Department of Educational Leadership and Policy Studies, Education Leadership and Policy Program, Lawrence, KS 66045-3101. Offers policy studies (PhD); social and cultural studies in education (MSE). *Program availability:* Part-time, evening/weekend. *Students:* 128 full-time (70 women), 45 part-time (24 women); includes 37 minority (14 Black or African American, non-Hispanic/Latino; 2 American Indian or Alaska Native, non-Hispanic/Latino; 4 Asian, non-Hispanic/Latino; 8 Hispanic/Latino; 9 Two or more races, non-Hispanic/Latino), 30 international. Average age 38. 66 applicants, 68% accepted, 36 enrolled. In 2017, 23 doctorates awarded. *Entrance requirements:* For master's, minimum GPA of 3.0, resume or curriculum vitae, statement of purpose, official academic transcripts, three letters of recommendation; for doctorate, GRE General Test, minimum graduate GPA of 3.5, resume or curriculum vitae, statement of purpose, official academic transcripts, three letters of recommendation, writing sample. *Application*

deadline: For fall admission, 7/1 for domestic and international students; for spring admission, 11/1 for domestic and international students; for summer admission, 4/1 for domestic and international students. Application fee: $65 ($85 for international students). Electronic applications accepted. *Financial support:* Fellowships, research assistantships, teaching assistantships, scholarships/grants, and unspecified assistantships available. Financial award application deadline: 3/15. *Faculty research:* Historical and philosophical issues in education, education policy and leadership, higher education faculty, research on college students, education technology. *Unit head:* Dr. Susan B. Twombly, Chair, 785-864-9721, E-mail: stwombly@ku.edu. *Application contact:* Denise Brubaker, Admissions Coordinator, 785-864-7973, E-mail: brubaker@ku.edu.
Website: http://elps.soe.ku.edu/

University of Kentucky, Graduate School, College of Education, Program in Educational Policy Studies and Evaluation, Lexington, KY 40506-0032. Offers educational policy studies and evaluation (Ed D); higher education (MS Ed, PhD); social and philosophical studies (MS Ed). *Accreditation:* NCATE. Terminal master's awarded for partial completion of doctoral program. *Degree requirements:* For master's, comprehensive exam, thesis optional; for doctorate, comprehensive exam, thesis/dissertation. *Entrance requirements:* For master's, GRE General Test, minimum undergraduate GPA of 2.75; for doctorate, GRE General Test, minimum graduate GPA of 3.0. Additional exam requirements/recommendations for international students: Required—TOEFL (minimum score 550 paper-based). Electronic applications accepted. *Faculty research:* Studies in higher education; comparative and international education; evaluation of educational programs, policies, and reform; student, teacher, and faculty cultures; gender and education.

University of Maryland, Baltimore County, The Graduate School, College of Arts, Humanities and Social Sciences, School of Public Policy, Baltimore, MD 21250. Offers public policy (MPP, PhD), including economics (PhD), educational policy, emergency services (PhD), environmental policy (MPP), evaluation and analytical methods, health policy, policy history (PhD), public management, urban policy. *Program availability:* Part-time, evening/weekend. *Faculty:* 10 full-time (5 women). *Students:* 50 full-time (24 women), 69 part-time (37 women); includes 35 minority (17 Black or African American, non-Hispanic/Latino; 1 American Indian or Alaska Native, non-Hispanic/Latino; 8 Asian, non-Hispanic/Latino; 5 Hispanic/Latino; 1 Native Hawaiian or other Pacific Islander, non-Hispanic/Latino; 3 Two or more races, non-Hispanic/Latino), 6 international. Average age 37. 60 applicants, 68% accepted, 25 enrolled. In 2017, 15 master's, 3 doctorates awarded. Terminal master's awarded for partial completion of doctoral program. *Degree requirements:* For master's, thesis, policy analysis paper, internship for pre-service; for doctorate, comprehensive exam, thesis/dissertation, comprehensive and field qualifying exams. *Entrance requirements:* For master's, GRE General Test, 3 academic letters of reference, resume, official transcripts; for doctorate, GRE General Test, 3 academic letters of reference, resume, research paper, official transcripts. Additional exam requirements/recommendations for international students: Required—TOEFL (minimum score 550 paper-based; 80 iBT), IELTS (minimum score 6.5). *Application deadline:* For fall admission, 1/15 priority date for domestic students, 1/1 priority date for international students; for spring admission, 11/1 priority date for domestic students, 5/1 priority date for international students. Applications are processed on a rolling basis. Application fee: $50. Electronic applications accepted. *Expenses:* $28,061 in-state, $39,356 out-of-state to complete the degree (for MPP); $43,823 in-state, $61,508 out-of-state to complete the degree (for PhD). *Financial support:* In 2017–18, 26 students received support, including 26 research assistantships with full tuition reimbursements available (averaging $20,000 per year); Federal Work-Study, scholarships/grants, health care benefits, and unspecified assistantships also available. Financial award application deadline: 1/1; financial award applicants required to submit FAFSA. *Faculty research:* Education policy, health policy, urban and environmental policy, public management, evaluation and analytical method. *Unit head:* Dr. Susan Sterett, Director, 410-455-2140, Fax: 410-455-1172, E-mail: ssterett@umbc.edu. *Application contact:* Sally F. Helms, Administrator of Academic Affairs, 410-455-3202, Fax: 410-455-1172, E-mail: gradpubpol@umbc.edu.
Website: http://publicpolicy.umbc.edu/

University of Massachusetts Amherst, Graduate School, College of Education, Program in Education, Amherst, MA 01003. Offers bilingual, English as a second language, and multicultural education (M Ed, Ed S); child study and early education (M Ed); children, families and schools (Ed D, Ed S); early childhood and elementary teacher education (M Ed); educational leadership (M Ed); educational policy and leadership (Ed D); higher education (M Ed); international education (M Ed); language, literacy and culture (Ed D); learning, media and technology (M Ed, Ed S); mathematics, science, and learning technologies (Ed D); reading and writing (M Ed); research, educational measurement and psychometrics (Ed D); school counselor education (M Ed, Ed S); school psychology (Ed S); science education (Ed S); secondary teacher education (M Ed); social justice education (M Ed, Ed D, Ed S); special education (M Ed, Ed D, Ed S); teacher education and school improvement (Ed D, Ed S). *Accreditation:* NCATE. *Program availability:* Part-time, online learning. Terminal master's awarded for partial completion of doctoral program. *Degree requirements:* For doctorate, comprehensive exam, thesis/dissertation. *Entrance requirements:* Additional exam requirements/recommendations for international students: Required—TOEFL (minimum score 550 paper-based; 80 iBT), IELTS (minimum score 6.5). Electronic applications accepted.

University of Massachusetts Boston, College of Education and Human Development, Program in Urban Education, Leadership, and Policy Studies, Boston, MA 02125-3393. Offers Ed D, PhD. *Program availability:* Part-time, evening/weekend. *Faculty:* 13 full-time (8 women), 21 part-time/adjunct (12 women). *Students:* 7 full-time (all women), 32 part-time (22 women); includes 17 minority (6 Black or African American, non-Hispanic/Latino; 1 American Indian or Alaska Native, non-Hispanic/Latino; 8 Hispanic/Latino; 2 Two or more races, non-Hispanic/Latino), 3 international. Average age 36. 31 applicants, 45% accepted, 9 enrolled. In 2017, 3 doctorates awarded. *Entrance requirements:* For doctorate, GRE General Test or MAT, minimum GPA of 2.75. *Application deadline:* For fall admission, 3/15 for domestic students. Application fee: $25 ($40 for international students). *Expenses:* Tuition, state resident: full-time $17,375. Tuition, nonresident: full-time $33,915. *Required fees:* $355. *Financial support:* Research assistantships, teaching assistantships, career-related internships or fieldwork, Federal Work-Study, and unspecified assistantships available. Support available to part-time students. Financial award application deadline: 3/1; financial award applicants required to submit FAFSA. *Faculty research:* School reform, race and culture in schools, race and higher education, language, literacy and writing. *Unit head:* Dr. Tricia Kress, Director, 617-287-7646, E-mail: tricia.kress@umb.edu. *Application contact:* Graduate Admissions Coordinator, 617-287-6400, Fax: 617-287-6236, E-mail: bos.gadm@dpc.umassp.edu.

University of Massachusetts Dartmouth, Graduate School, College of Arts and Sciences, Department of Public Policy, North Dartmouth, MA 02747-2300. Offers educational policy (Graduate Certificate); environmental policy (Graduate Certificate); public management (Graduate Certificate); public policy (MPP). *Program availability:* Part-time, 100% online, blended/hybrid learning. *Faculty:* 4 full-time (0 women), 1 part-

Educational Policy

time/adjunct (0 women). *Students:* 6 full-time (2 women), 69 part-time (43 women); includes 18 minority (6 Black or African American, non-Hispanic/Latino; 2 Asian, non-Hispanic/Latino; 7 Hispanic/Latino; 3 Two or more races, non-Hispanic/Latino). Average age 36. 59 applicants, 95% accepted, 41 enrolled. In 2017, 10 master's, 18 other advanced degrees awarded. *Degree requirements:* For master's, e-portfolio. *Entrance requirements:* For master's, GRE or GMAT (waived if applicant has already earned a graduate degree from accredited school or if applicant has successfully completed the educational, environmental or public management certificate program), statement of purpose (minimum of 300 words), resume, 2 letters of recommendation, official transcripts; for Graduate Certificate, statement of purpose (minimum of 300 words), resume, official transcripts. Additional exam requirements/recommendations for international students: Required—TOEFL (minimum score 600 paper-based; 100 iBT). *Application deadline:* Applications are processed on a rolling basis. Application fee: $60. Electronic applications accepted. *Expenses:* Tuition, state resident: full-time $15,449; part-time $643.71 per credit. Tuition, nonresident: full-time $27,880; part-time $1161.67 per credit. *Required fees:* $405; $25.88 per credit. Tuition and fees vary according to course load and reciprocity agreements. *Financial support:* In 2017–18, 2 research assistantships (averaging $12,900 per year) were awarded; teaching assistantships, tuition waivers (full), and unspecified assistantships also available. Support available to part-time students. Financial award application deadline: 3/1; financial award applicants required to submit FAFSA. *Faculty research:* Environmental justice, sustainability, international trade and finance, corporate social responsibility, global governance. *Total annual research expenditures:* $6,000. *Unit head:* Chad McGuire, Graduate Program Director, Public Policy, 508-999-8520, E-mail: cmcguire@umassd.edu. *Application contact:* Steven Briggs, Director of Marketing and Recruitment for Graduate Studies, 508-999-8604, Fax: 508-999-8183, E-mail: graduate@umassd.edu.
Website: http://www.umassd.edu/cas/departmentsanddegreeprograms/publicpolicy/

University of Massachusetts Dartmouth, Graduate School, College of Arts and Sciences, School of Education, Department of Educational Leadership, North Dartmouth, MA 02747-2300. Offers educational leadership and policy studies (Ed D, PhD). *Program availability:* Part-time. *Faculty:* 4 full-time (0 women), 1 (woman) part-time/adjunct. *Students:* 11 full-time (9 women), 18 part-time (12 women); includes 11 minority (3 Black or African American, non-Hispanic/Latino; 1 American Indian or Alaska Native, non-Hispanic/Latino; 1 Asian, non-Hispanic/Latino; 4 Hispanic/Latino; 2 Two or more races, non-Hispanic/Latino), 1 international. Average age 42. 16 applicants, 88% accepted. In 2017, 9 doctorates awarded. *Degree requirements:* For doctorate, comprehensive exam, thesis/dissertation. *Entrance requirements:* For doctorate, GRE or GMAT, statement of purpose (minimum of 300 words), resume, 3 letters of recommendation, official transcripts, scholarly writing sample (minimum of 10 pages of writing). Additional exam requirements/recommendations for international students: Required—TOEFL (minimum score 600 paper-based; 100 iBT), IELTS (minimum score 6.5). *Application deadline:* For fall admission, 4/30 priority date for domestic students, 3/30 priority date for international students. Application fee: $60. Electronic applications accepted. *Expenses:* Tuition, state resident: full-time $15,449; part-time $643.71 per credit. Tuition, nonresident: full-time $27,880; part-time $1161.67 per credit. *Required fees:* $405; $25.88 per credit. Tuition and fees vary according to course load and reciprocity agreements. *Financial support:* In 2017–18, 2 fellowships (averaging $21,000 per year) were awarded; tuition waivers (full), unspecified assistantships, and doctoral support also available. Support available to part-time students. Financial award application deadline: 3/1; financial award applicants required to submit FAFSA. *Faculty research:* Sociology of education, critical theory, curriculum theory, globalization and education, urban education, teacher education. *Total annual research expenditures:* $99,000. *Unit head:* Amy Shapiro, Interim Dean, College of Arts and Sciences, 508-999-8352, E-mail: ashapiro@umassd.edu. *Application contact:* Steven Briggs, Director of Marketing and Recruitment for Graduate Studies, 508-999-8604, Fax: 508-999-8183, E-mail: graduate@umassd.edu.
Website: http://www.umassd.edu/educationalleadership

University of Minnesota, Twin Cities Campus, Graduate School, College of Education and Human Development, Department of Organizational Leadership, Policy and Development, Program in Education Policy and Leadership, Minneapolis, MN 55455-0213. Offers educational policy and leadership (MA, Ed D, PhD); leadership in education (M Ed). *Students:* 85 full-time (59 women), 87 part-time (55 women); includes 35 minority (11 Black or African American, non-Hispanic/Latino; 1 American Indian or Alaska Native, non-Hispanic/Latino; 7 Asian, non-Hispanic/Latino; 8 Hispanic/Latino; 8 Two or more races, non-Hispanic/Latino), 4 international. Average age 36. 141 applicants, 77% accepted, 84 enrolled. In 2017, 16 master's, 6 doctorates awarded. Application fee: $75 ($95 for international students). *Unit head:* Dr. Heidi Barajas, Chair, 612-625-4823, E-mail: hbarajas@umn.edu. *Application contact:* Dr. Jeremy J. Hernandez, Director of Graduate Studies, 612-626-9377, E-mail: herna220@umn.edu.
Website: http://www.cehd.umn.edu/OLPD/grad-programs/EPL/

University of Missouri–St. Louis, College of Education, Interdisciplinary Doctoral Programs, St. Louis, MO 63121. Offers counseling (PhD); educational leadership and policy studies (PhD); educational psychology (PhD); leadership in educational practice (Ed D); teaching-learning processes (PhD). *Faculty:* 50 full-time (29 women), 82 part-time/adjunct (66 women). *Students:* 131 full-time (98 women), 428 part-time (319 women); includes 174 minority (126 Black or African American, non-Hispanic/Latino; 3 American Indian or Alaska Native, non-Hispanic/Latino; 13 Asian, non-Hispanic/Latino; 27 Hispanic/Latino; 5 Two or more races, non-Hispanic/Latino), 11 international. 187 applicants, 84% accepted, 121 enrolled. *Degree requirements:* For doctorate, thesis/dissertation. *Entrance requirements:* For doctorate, GRE General Test, 3 letters of recommendation; personal interview. Additional exam requirements/recommendations for international students: Recommended—TOEFL (minimum score 550 paper-based; 79 iBT), IELTS (minimum score 6.5). *Application deadline:* For fall admission, 3/1 for domestic and international students; for spring admission, 10/1 for domestic and international students. Application fee: $50 ($40 for international students). Electronic applications accepted. *Expenses:* Tuition, state resident: part-time $476.50 per credit hour. Tuition, nonresident: part-time $1169.70 per credit hour. *Financial support:* Research assistantships and teaching assistantships available. Financial award application deadline: 4/1; financial award applicants required to submit FAFSA. *Faculty research:* Higher education law and policy, gender and higher education, student retention, lifelong learning orientation, school counselor's role in violence prevention. *Unit head:* Dr. Kathleen Haywood, Director of Graduate Studies, 314-516-5483, Fax: 314-516-5227, E-mail: kathleen_haywood@umsl.edu. *Application contact:* 314-516-5458, Fax: 314-516-6996, E-mail: gradadm@umsl.edu.

University of Mobile, Graduate Studies, Program in Education, Mobile, AL 36613. Offers education (MA); higher education leadership and policy (M Ed). *Program availability:* Part-time, 100% online. *Degree requirements:* For master's, comprehensive exam, thesis optional. *Entrance requirements:* For master's, GRE, Alabama teaching certificate. Additional exam requirements/recommendations for international students: Required—TOEFL (minimum score 550 paper-based; 80 iBT). *Application deadline:* For fall admission, 8/3 priority date for domestic students, 8/3 for international students; for spring admission, 12/23 priority date for domestic students, 12/3 priority date for international students. Applications are processed on a rolling basis. Application fee: $40 ($50 for international students). Electronic applications accepted. *Financial support:*

Application deadline: 8/1; applicants required to submit FAFSA. *Faculty research:* Retention, writing across the curriculum. *Unit head:* Dr. Carolyn D. Corliss, Dean, School of Education, 251-442-2276, Fax: 251-442-2523, E-mail: ccorliss@umobile.edu. *Application contact:* Brian Boyle, Director of Recruitment, 251-442-2727, Fax: 251-442-2523.
Website: http://umobile.edu/school-of-education/master-of-arts-in-education/

The University of North Carolina Wilmington, Watson College of Education, Department of Early Childhood, Elementary, Middle, Literacy and Special Education, Wilmington, NC 28403-3297. Offers educational leadership, policy, and advocacy (M Ed); elementary education (M Ed, MAT); language and literacy (M Ed); middle grades education (MAT). *Accreditation:* NCATE. *Program availability:* Part-time, blended/hybrid learning. *Faculty:* 22 full-time (15 women), 2 part-time/adjunct (both women). *Students:* 82 full-time (70 women), 91 part-time (84 women); includes 51 minority (33 Black or African American, non-Hispanic/Latino; 3 American Indian or Alaska Native, non-Hispanic/Latino; 1 Asian, non-Hispanic/Latino; 8 Hispanic/Latino; 6 Two or more races, non-Hispanic/Latino). Average age 32. 68 applicants, 82% accepted, 45 enrolled. In 2017, 83 master's awarded. *Degree requirements:* For master's, thesis or alternative, exit portfolio, oral presentation, internship, research project (depending on specialization). *Entrance requirements:* For master's, 3 letters of recommendations, NC Class A teacher license in related field, education statement of interest essay. Additional exam requirements/recommendations for international students: Required—TOEFL (minimum score 550 paper-based; 79 iBT), IELTS (minimum score 6.5). *Application deadline:* For fall admission, 5/15 for domestic students; for spring admission, 10/15 for domestic students; for summer admission, 3/15 for domestic students. Applications are processed on a rolling basis. Application fee: $75. Electronic applications accepted. *Expenses:* Tuition, state resident: full-time $4626; part-time $226.76 per credit hour. Tuition, nonresident: full-time $17,834; part-time $874.22 per credit hour. *Required fees:* $2124. Tuition and fees vary according to program. *Financial support:* Scholarships/grants and unspecified assistantships available. Financial award application deadline: 1/1; financial award applicants required to submit FAFSA. *Unit head:* Dr. Kathy Fox, Chair, 910-962-3240, Fax: 910-962-3988, E-mail: foxk@uncw.edu. *Application contact:* Dr. Elizabeth Crawford, Graduate Program Coordinator, 910-962-2916, Fax: 910-962-3988, E-mail: crawforde@uncw.edu.
Website: http://www.uncw.edu/ed/eemls/index.html

University of Northern Colorado, Graduate School, College of Education and Behavioral Sciences, Department of Leadership, Policy and Development: Higher Education and P-12 Education, Educational Leadership and Policy Studies Program, Greeley, CO 80639. Offers educational leadership (MA, Ed S); educational leadership and policy studies (Ed D). *Accreditation:* NCATE. *Program availability:* Part-time, evening/weekend, online learning. *Degree requirements:* For master's, comprehensive exam, thesis or alternative; for doctorate, comprehensive exam, thesis/dissertation; for Ed S, comprehensive exam, thesis. *Entrance requirements:* For master's, resume, interview; for doctorate, GRE General Test, resume, interview; for Ed S, resume. Electronic applications accepted.

University of Pennsylvania, Graduate School of Education, Division of Education Policy, Philadelphia, PA 19104. Offers MS Ed, PhD. *Program availability:* Part-time. *Students:* Average age 28. 250 applicants, 50% accepted, 34 enrolled. In 2017, 16 master's, 2 doctorates awarded. *Degree requirements:* For master's, thesis or alternative, research practicum; for doctorate, comprehensive exam, thesis/dissertation. *Entrance requirements:* For master's, GRE, bachelor's degree; for doctorate, GRE, bachelor's degree; master's degree (preferred). Additional exam requirements/recommendations for international students: Required—TOEFL, IELTS. *Application deadline:* For fall admission, 12/8 priority date for domestic and international students. Applications are processed on a rolling basis. Application fee: $75. Electronic applications accepted. *Financial support:* In 2017–18, 13 students received support. Fellowships, research assistantships, teaching assistantships, Federal Work-Study, scholarships/grants, and health care benefits available. *Faculty research:* Teachers and teaching policy, school reform, standards, and assessment, early childhood education, program evaluation and policy analysis, career and college readiness. *Unit head:* Krista Featherstone, Program Manager, 215-573-8075, E-mail: kfeat@upenn.edu.
Website: http://www.gse.upenn.edu/ep

University of Pittsburgh, School of Education, Learning Sciences and Policy Program, Pittsburgh, PA 15260. Offers PhD. *Program availability:* Part-time, evening/weekend. *Degree requirements:* For doctorate, comprehensive exam, thesis/dissertation. *Entrance requirements:* Additional exam requirements/recommendations for international students: Required—TOEFL (minimum score 550 paper-based; 80 iBT).

University of Rochester, Margaret Warner Graduate School of Education and Human Development, Doctoral Programs in Education, Rochester, NY 14627. Offers counseling (Ed D); educational administration (Ed D); educational policy and theory (PhD); higher education (PhD); human development in educational context (PhD); teaching, curriculum, and change (PhD).

University of Rochester, Margaret Warner Graduate School of Education and Human Development, Master's Program in Educational Policy, Rochester, NY 14627. Offers MS.

University of Southern California, Graduate School, Rossier School of Education, Doctor of Philosophy in Education Programs, Los Angeles, CA 90089. Offers educational psychology (PhD); higher education administration and policy (PhD); K-12 policy and practice (PhD). *Degree requirements:* For doctorate, thesis/dissertation, 63 units; qualifying exam; dissertation proposal and defense. *Entrance requirements:* For doctorate, GRE. Additional exam requirements/recommendations for international students: Required—TOEFL (minimum score 100 iBT). Electronic applications accepted. *Faculty research:* Diversity in higher education, organizational change, educational psychology, policy and politics of educational reform, economics of education and education policy.

The University of Texas at Arlington, Graduate School, College of Education, Department of Educational Leadership and Policy Studies, Arlington, TX 76019. Offers educational leadership (PhD); higher education (M Ed); principal certification (M Ed). *Program availability:* Part-time, evening/weekend, online learning. *Degree requirements:* For master's, 2 field-based practica; for doctorate, comprehensive exam, thesis/dissertation, 2 research-based practica. *Entrance requirements:* For master's, GRE, 3 references, minimum undergraduate GPA of 3.0 in last 60 hours of course work; for doctorate, GRE, resume, statement of intent, 3 reference forms, applicable master's degree. *Faculty research:* Lived realities of students of color in K-16 contexts, K-16 faculty, K-16 policy and law, K-16 student access, K-16 student success.

University of Utah, Graduate School, College of Education, Department of Educational Leadership and Policy, Salt Lake City, UT 84084. Offers educational leadership and policy (Ed D, PhD), including higher education administration (Ed D), K-12 (Ed D); K-12 school administration (M Ed); K-12 teacher instructional leadership (M Ed); student affairs (M Ed); MPA/PhD. *Program availability:* Part-time, evening/weekend. *Faculty:* 10 full-time (7 women), 2 part-time/adjunct (both women). *Students:* 60 full-time (40 women), 185 part-time (124 women); includes 54 minority (14 Black or African American, non-Hispanic/Latino; 5 American Indian or Alaska Native, non-Hispanic/

Latino; 5 Asian, non-Hispanic/Latino; 24 Hispanic/Latino; 2 Native Hawaiian or other Pacific Islander, non-Hispanic/Latino; 4 Two or more races, non-Hispanic/Latino), 1 international. Average age 35. 181 applicants, 69% accepted, 90 enrolled. In 2017, 64 master's, 6 doctorates awarded. *Degree requirements:* For master's, comprehensive exam (for some programs), internship, capstone; for doctorate, thesis/dissertation, qualifying exam. *Entrance requirements:* For master's, minimum undergraduate GPA of 3.0, valid bachelor's degree, 3 years' teaching or leadership experience, Level 1 or 2 UT educator's license (for K-12 programs only); for doctorate, GRE General Test (taken with five years of applying), minimum undergraduate GPA of 3.0, valid master's degree. Additional exam requirements/recommendations for international students: Required—TOEFL (minimum score 550 paper-based). *Application deadline:* For fall admission, 1/15 priority date for domestic and international students; for winter admission, 2/1 for domestic and international students; for spring admission, 11/1 priority date for domestic and international students; for summer admission, 3/1 priority date for domestic and international students. Applications are processed on a rolling basis. Application fee: $55 ($65 for international students). Electronic applications accepted. *Expenses:* Contact institution. *Financial support:* In 2017–18, 12 students received support, including 1 fellowship with full tuition reimbursement available (averaging $15,000 per year), 2 research assistantships with full tuition reimbursements available (averaging $15,000 per year), 6 teaching assistantships with full tuition reimbursements available (averaging $15,000 per year); career-related internships or fieldwork, scholarships/grants, health care benefits, and unspecified assistantships also available. Support available to part-time students. Financial award application deadline: 3/1; financial award applicants required to submit FAFSA. *Faculty research:* Education accountability, college student diversity, K-12 educational administration and school leadership, student affairs, higher education. *Unit head:* Dr. Gerardo Lopez, Chair, 801-581-6971, Fax: 801-585-6756, E-mail: gerardo.lopez@utah.edu. *Application contact:* Marilynn S. Howard, Academic Coordinator, 801-581-6714, Fax: 801-585-6756, E-mail: marilynn.howard@utah.edu.
Website: http://elp.utah.edu/

University of Vermont, Graduate College, College of Education and Social Services, PhD Program in Educational Leadership and Policy Studies, Burlington, VT 05405. Offers PhD. *Students:* 13 (9 women). 18 applicants, 44% accepted, 4 enrolled. In 2017, 5 doctorates awarded. *Degree requirements:* For doctorate, thesis/dissertation. *Entrance requirements:* For doctorate, GRE General Test, resume, writing sample. Additional exam requirements/recommendations for international students: Required—TOEFL (minimum iBT score of 90) or IELTS (6.5). *Application deadline:* For fall admission, 1/6 for domestic and international students. Application fee: $65. Electronic applications accepted. *Expenses:* Tuition, state resident: full-time $11,628; part-time $646 per credit. Tuition, nonresident: full-time $29,340; part-time $1630 per credit. *Required fees:* $1994; $10 per credit. Tuition and fees vary according to course load and program. *Financial support:* In 2017–18, 7 students received support, including 1 research assistantship with full tuition reimbursement available (averaging $20,000 per year), 6 teaching assistantships with full tuition reimbursements available (averaging $20,000 per year); health care benefits also available. Financial award application deadline: 1/6. *Unit head:* Dr. Kelly Clark Keefe, 802-656-2936, E-mail: cessphd@uvm.edu.
Website: https://www.uvm.edu/cess/dlds/doctoral/phd

University of Virginia, Curry School of Education, Department of Leadership, Foundations and Policy, Program in Educational Policy, Charlottesville, VA 22903. Offers PhD, PhD/MPP. *Entrance requirements:* For doctorate, GRE General Test, 2 letters of recommendation. Additional exam requirements/recommendations for international students: Required—TOEFL (minimum score 600 paper-based; 90 iBT), IELTS (minimum score 7). *Application deadline:* Applications are processed on a rolling basis. Application fee: $60. Electronic applications accepted. *Financial support:* Fellowships, research assistantships, and teaching assistantships available. Financial award application deadline: 1/5; financial award applicants required to submit FAFSA. *Unit head:* James H. Wyckoff, Director, Educational Policy PhD Program, 434-924-0842, E-mail: jhw4n@virginia.edu. *Application contact:* E-mail: curry-admissions@virginia.edu.
Website: http://curry.virginia.edu/academics/areas-of-study/education-policy

University of Washington, Graduate School, College of Education, Seattle, WA 98195. Offers curriculum and instruction (M Ed, Ed D, PhD), including educational technology, general curriculum (Ed D, PhD), language, literacy, and culture, mathematics education, multicultural education, reading and language arts education (Ed D), science education, social studies education, teaching and curriculum (M Ed); educational leadership and policy studies (M Ed, Ed D, PhD), including administration (Ed D), educational policy, organization, and leadership (M Ed, PhD), higher education, leadership for learning (Ed D), social and cultural foundations of education (M Ed, PhD); educational psychology (M Ed, PhD), including educational psychology (PhD), human development and cognition (M Ed), learning sciences, measurement, statistics and research design (M Ed), school psychology (M Ed); instructional leadership (M Ed); intercollegiate athletic leadership (M Ed); special education (M Ed, Ed D, PhD), including early childhood special education (M Ed), emotional and behavioral disabilities (M Ed), learning disabilities (M Ed), low-incidence disabilities (M Ed), severe disabilities (M Ed), special education (Ed D, PhD); teacher education (MIT). *Accreditation:* APA. *Program availability:* Part-time, evening/weekend. *Degree requirements:* For master's, thesis optional; for doctorate, thesis/dissertation. *Entrance requirements:* For master's and doctorate, GRE General Test, minimum GPA of 3.0. Additional exam requirements/recommendations for international students: Required—TOEFL. Electronic applications accepted. *Faculty research:* School restructuring/effective schools, special education interventions, literacy and writing, technology, school partnerships, teacher preparation.

The University of Western Ontario, Faculty of Graduate Studies, Social Sciences Division, Faculty of Education, Program in Educational Studies, London, ON N6A 5B8, Canada. Offers curriculum studies (M Ed); educational policy studies (M Ed); educational psychology/special education (M Ed). *Program availability:* Part-time. *Faculty research:* Reflective practice, gender and schooling, feminist pedagogy, narrative inquiry, second language, multiculturalism in Canada, education and law.

University of Wisconsin–Madison, Graduate School, School of Education, Department of Educational Leadership and Policy Analysis, Madison, WI 53706-1380. Offers administration (Certificate); educational policy (MS, PhD); global higher education (MS). *Degree requirements:* For doctorate, thesis/dissertation. *Entrance requirements:* For master's and doctorate, GRE General Test. Electronic applications accepted.

University of Wisconsin–Madison, Graduate School, School of Education, Department of Educational Policy Studies, Madison, WI 53706-1380. Offers MA, PhD. *Degree requirements:* For doctorate, thesis/dissertation. *Entrance requirements:* For master's and doctorate, GRE General Test. Electronic applications accepted.

University of Wisconsin–Milwaukee, Graduate School, School of Education, Department of Educational Policy and Community Studies, Milwaukee, WI 53201-0413. Offers cultural foundations of community engagement and education (MS), including alternative education, community engagement and partnerships, educational policy, race relations, youth work; educational policy (Graduate Certificate). *Program availability:* Part-time. *Students:* 8 full-time (6 women), 24 part-time (20 women);

includes 18 minority (9 Black or African American, non-Hispanic/Latino; 1 American Indian or Alaska Native, non-Hispanic/Latino; 2 Asian, non-Hispanic/Latino; 1 Hispanic/Latino; 5 Two or more races, non-Hispanic/Latino). Average age 35. 21 applicants, 67% accepted, 10 enrolled. In 2017, 11 master's awarded. *Entrance requirements:* Additional exam requirements/recommendations for international students: Required—TOEFL (minimum score 550 paper-based; 79 iBT), IELTS (minimum score 6.5). *Application deadline:* For fall admission, 1/1 priority date for domestic students; for spring admission, 9/1 for domestic students. Application fee: $56 ($96 for international students). Electronic applications accepted. *Financial support:* Fellowships with full tuition reimbursements, research assistantships, teaching assistantships, career-related internships or fieldwork, health care benefits, and unspecified assistantships available. Support available to part-time students. Financial award application deadline: 4/15; financial award applicants required to submit FAFSA. *Application contact:* General Information Contact, 414-229-4721, E-mail: soeinfo@uwm.edu.
Website: http://uwm.edu/education/academics/edu-policy-community-studies-department/

Vanderbilt University, Peabody College, Department of Leadership, Policy, and Organizations, Nashville, TN 37240-1001. Offers education policy (MPP); educational leadership and policy (Ed D); higher education (M Ed); higher education leadership and policy (Ed D); independent school leadership (M Ed); international education policy and management (M Ed); leadership and learning in organizations (Ed D); leadership and organizational performance (M Ed). *Program availability:* Part-time, on-campus immersion once every semester. *Faculty:* 30 full-time (15 women), 19 part-time/adjunct (6 women). *Students:* 141 full-time (105 women), 139 part-time (84 women); includes 66 minority (32 Black or African American, non-Hispanic/Latino; 13 Asian, non-Hispanic/Latino; 14 Hispanic/Latino; 1 Native Hawaiian or other Pacific Islander, non-Hispanic/Latino; 6 Two or more races, non-Hispanic/Latino), 25 international. Average age 30. 525 applicants, 66% accepted, 139 enrolled. In 2017, 109 master's, 22 doctorates awarded. *Degree requirements:* For master's, comprehensive exam, thesis optional; for doctorate, thesis/dissertation, qualifying exams, residency. *Entrance requirements:* For master's and doctorate, GRE General Test. Additional exam requirements/recommendations for international students: Required—TOEFL (minimum score 550 paper-based; 80 iBT). *Application deadline:* For fall admission, 12/31 priority date for domestic and international students; for spring admission, 11/1 priority date for domestic and international students. Applications are processed on a rolling basis. Application fee: $0. Electronic applications accepted. *Financial support:* Fellowships with partial tuition reimbursements, research assistantships with partial tuition reimbursements, teaching assistantships with partial tuition reimbursements, Federal Work-Study, institutionally sponsored loans, scholarships/grants, tuition waivers (partial), and unspecified assistantships available. Support available to part-time students. Financial award application deadline: 1/15; financial award applicants required to submit FAFSA. *Faculty research:* Financial aid policies, teacher labor markets, school choice, educational leadership, higher education access and equity. *Unit head:* Dr. Ellen B. Goldring, Chair, 615-322-8000, Fax: 615-343-7094, E-mail: ellen.b.goldring@vanderbilt.edu. *Application contact:* Rosie Moody, Educational Coordinator, 615-322-8019, Fax: 615-343-7094, E-mail: rosie.moody@vanderbilt.edu.
Website: http://peabody.vanderbilt.edu/departments/lpo/index.php

Virginia Polytechnic Institute and State University, Graduate School, College of Liberal Arts and Human Sciences, Blacksburg, VA 24061. Offers career and technical education (MS Ed, Ed S); communication (MA); counselor education (MA); creative writing (MFA); curriculum and instruction (MA Ed, Ed S); educational leadership and policy studies (Ed S); educational research and evaluation (PhD); English (MA); social, political, ethical, and cultural thought (PhD); Ed D/PhD. *Faculty:* 411 full-time (213 women), 3 part-time/adjunct (all women). *Students:* 623 full-time (427 women), 431 part-time (278 women); includes 203 minority (115 Black or African American, non-Hispanic/Latino; 4 American Indian or Alaska Native, non-Hispanic/Latino; 29 Asian, non-Hispanic/Latino; 33 Hispanic/Latino; 2 Native Hawaiian or other Pacific Islander, non-Hispanic/Latino; 20 Two or more races, non-Hispanic/Latino), 87 international. Average age 34. 898 applicants, 50% accepted, 329 enrolled. In 2017, 314 master's, 102 doctorates awarded. *Degree requirements:* For master's, comprehensive exam (for some programs), thesis (for some programs); for doctorate, comprehensive exam (for some programs), thesis/dissertation (for some programs). *Entrance requirements:* For master's and doctorate, GRE/GMAT. Additional exam requirements/recommendations for international students: Required—TOEFL (minimum score 80 iBT). *Application deadline:* For fall admission, 8/1 for domestic students, 4/1 for international students; for spring admission, 1/1 for domestic students, 9/1 for international students. Applications are processed on a rolling basis. Application fee: $75. Electronic applications accepted. *Expenses:* Tuition, state resident: full-time $15,072; part-time $718.50 per credit hour. Tuition, nonresident: full-time $28,810; part-time $1448.25 per credit hour. *Required fees:* $2741; $502 per semester. Tuition and fees vary according to course load, campus/location and program. *Financial support:* In 2017–18, 19 research assistantships with full tuition reimbursements (averaging $19,611 per year), 226 teaching assistantships with full tuition reimbursements (averaging $16,220 per year) were awarded. Financial award application deadline: 3/1; financial award applicants required to submit FAFSA. *Total annual research expenditures:* $7.9 million. *Unit head:* Dr. Rosemary Blieszner, Dean, 540-231-6779, Fax: 540-231-7157, E-mail: rmb@vt.edu. *Application contact:* Chelsea Blanchet, Executive Assistant, 540-231-6779, Fax: 540-231-7157, E-mail: bchels1@vt.edu.
Website: http://www.liberalarts.vt.edu/

Wayne State University, College of Education, Division of Administrative and Organizational Studies, Detroit, MI 48202. Offers educational administration and supervision (Ed S); educational leadership (M Ed); educational leadership and policy studies (Ed D, PhD); educational technology (Certificate); learning design and technology (M Ed, Ed D, PhD, Ed S); online teaching (Certificate). *Program availability:* Part-time, 100% online, blended/hybrid learning. *Faculty:* 7. *Students:* 50 full-time (30 women), 266 part-time (184 women); includes 158 minority (130 Black or African American, non-Hispanic/Latino; 1 American Indian or Alaska Native, non-Hispanic/Latino; 5 Asian, non-Hispanic/Latino; 9 Hispanic/Latino; 1 Native Hawaiian or other Pacific Islander, non-Hispanic/Latino; 12 Two or more races, non-Hispanic/Latino), 9 international. Average age 39. 187 applicants, 31% accepted, 42 enrolled. In 2017, 48 master's, 17 doctorates, 47 other advanced degrees awarded. *Degree requirements:* For master's, thesis (for some programs); for doctorate, thesis/dissertation. *Entrance requirements:* For master's, baccalaureate degree from accredited U.S. institution or equivalent from college or university of government-recognized standing; minimum undergraduate GPA of 2.75 in upper-division coursework; personal statement; for doctorate, GRE (instructional design and technology), interview; curriculum vitae; three to four recommendations; master's degree (for educational leadership and policy studies); minimum graduate GPA of 3.5; autobiographical statement; research experience (for PhD program). Additional exam requirements/recommendations for international students: Required—TOEFL (minimum score 550 paper-based; 79 iBT); Recommended—IELTS (minimum score 6.5), TWE (minimum score 5.5). *Application deadline:* For fall admission, 6/1 priority date for domestic students, 5/1 priority date for international students; for winter admission, 10/1 priority date for domestic students, 9/1 priority date for international students; for spring admission, 2/1 priority date for domestic

students, 1/1 priority date for international students. Applications are processed on a rolling basis. Application fee: $50. Electronic applications accepted. *Expenses:* Tuition, state resident: full-time $10,224; part-time $638.98 per credit hour. Tuition, nonresident: full-time $22,145; part-time $1384.04 per credit hour. Tuition and fees vary according to course load and program. *Financial support:* In 2017–18, 85 students received support, including 4 research assistantships with tuition reimbursements available (averaging $18,534 per year); fellowships with tuition reimbursements available, scholarships/grants, and unspecified assistantships also available. Support available to part-time students. Financial award applicants required to submit FAFSA. *Faculty research:* Total quality management, participatory management, administering educational technology, school improvement, principalship. *Unit head:* Dr. William Hill, Assistant Dean, 313-577-9316, E-mail: ad2107@wayne.edu. *Application contact:* Graduate Advisor, 313-577-1605, E-mail: askcoe@wayne.edu.
Website: http://coe.wayne.edu/aos/index.php

West Chester University of Pennsylvania, College of Education and Social Work, Department of Educational Foundations and Policy Studies, West Chester, PA 19383. Offers education for sustainability (Certificate); educational technology (Certificate); higher education policy and student affairs (MS); transformative education and social change (MS). *Program availability:* Part-time. *Students:* 35 full-time (21 women), 49 part-time (33 women); includes 15 minority (9 Black or African American, non-Hispanic/Latino; 1 Asian, non-Hispanic/Latino; 2 Hispanic/Latino; 3 Two or more races, non-Hispanic/Latino), 1 international. Average age 29. 77 applicants, 90% accepted, 51 enrolled. In 2017, 5 master's, 6 other advanced degrees awarded. *Degree requirements:* For master's, comprehensive exam (for some programs), thesis, 36 credits (42 credits for MS in higher education policy and student affairs). *Entrance requirements:* For master's, teaching certification (strongly recommended); for Certificate, minimum GPA of 3.0. Additional exam requirements/recommendations for international students: Required—TOEFL or IELTS. *Application deadline:* For fall admission, 5/15 for international students; for spring admission, 10/15 for international students. Applications are processed on a rolling basis. Application fee: $50. Electronic applications accepted. *Expenses:* Tuition, state resident: full-time $9000; part-time $500 per credit. Tuition, nonresident: full-time $13,500; part-time $750 per credit. *Required*

fees: $2959; $149.79 per credit. *Financial support:* Scholarships/grants and unspecified assistantships available. Financial award application deadline: 2/15; financial award applicants required to submit FAFSA. *Faculty research:* Technology integration: preparing our teachers for the twenty-first century, critical pedagogy, education for sustainability. *Unit head:* Dr. John Elmore, Chair, 610-436-6934, Fax: 610-436-3102, E-mail: jelmore@wcupa.edu. *Application contact:* Office of Graduate Studies and Extended Education, 610-436-2943, Fax: 610-436-2763, E-mail: gradstudy@wcupa.edu.
Website: http://www.wcupa.edu/education-socialWork/profsecedu/

West Chester University of Pennsylvania, College of Education and Social Work, Program in Policy, Planning, and Administration, West Chester, PA 19383. Offers Ed D. *Program availability:* Part-time, evening/weekend, online only, 100% online. *Students:* 28 part-time (16 women); includes 3 minority (1 Black or African American, non-Hispanic/Latino; 1 Asian, non-Hispanic/Latino; 1 Hispanic/Latino). Average age 39. 36 applicants, 72% accepted, 14 enrolled. *Degree requirements:* For doctorate, comprehensive exam. *Entrance requirements:* For doctorate, GRE if master's GPA lower than 3.85, master's degree from regionally-accredited college or university, three letters of recommendation from education professionals, professional writing demonstration at time of application (waived for applicants who present GRE analytical writing score of 4.5 or higher), resume or curriculum vitae, interview (upon committee request). Additional exam requirements/recommendations for international students: Required—TOEFL or IELTS. *Application deadline:* For fall admission, 5/15 for international students; for spring admission, 10/15 for international students. Applications are processed on a rolling basis. Application fee: $50. Electronic applications accepted. *Expenses:* $625 per credit. *Financial support:* Application deadline: 2/15; applicants required to submit FAFSA. *Faculty research:* Literacy, special education, critical pedagogy, social and cultural foundations of education, educational technology. *Unit head:* Dr. Kenneth D. Witmer, Jr., Dean, 610-436-2321, Fax: 610-436-3102, E-mail: kwitmer@wcupa.edu. *Application contact:* Dr. Robert Haworth, Graduate Coordinator, 610-436-2246, E-mail: rhaworth@wcupa.edu.
Website: http://www.wcupa.edu/education-socialWork/doctorate/

Educational Psychology

Alliant International University–Irvine, Shirley M. Hufstedler School of Education, Educational Psychology Programs, Irvine, CA 92606. Offers educational psychology (Psy D); pupil personnel services (Credential); school psychology (MA). *Program availability:* Part-time. *Degree requirements:* For doctorate, thesis/dissertation. *Entrance requirements:* For master's, minimum GPA of 2.5, letters of recommendation; for doctorate, interview, minimum GPA of 3.0, letters of recommendation. Additional exam requirements/recommendations for international students: Required—TOEFL (minimum score 550 paper-based; 80 iBT), TWE (minimum score 5). *Faculty research:* School-based mental health.

Alliant International University–Los Angeles, Shirley M. Hufstedler School of Education, Educational Psychology Programs, Alhambra, CA 91803. Offers educational psychology (Psy D); pupil personnel services (Credential); school psychology (MA). *Program availability:* Part-time. *Degree requirements:* For doctorate, comprehensive exam, thesis/dissertation. *Entrance requirements:* For master's, minimum GPA of 2.5, letters of recommendation; for doctorate, interview, minimum GPA of 3.0, letters of recommendation. Additional exam requirements/recommendations for international students: Required—TOEFL (minimum score 550 paper-based), TWE (minimum score 5). Electronic applications accepted. *Faculty research:* Early identification and intervention with high-risk preschoolers, pediatric neuropsychology, interpersonal violence, ADHD, learning theories.

Alliant International University–San Diego, Shirley M. Hufstedler School of Education, Educational Psychology Programs, San Diego, CA 92131. Offers educational psychology (Psy D); pupil personnel services (Credential); school neuropsychology (Certificate); school psychology (MA); school-based mental health (Certificate). *Program availability:* Part-time. *Degree requirements:* For doctorate, comprehensive exam, thesis/dissertation, internship. *Entrance requirements:* For master's, minimum GPA of 2.5, letters of recommendation; for doctorate, minimum GPA of 3.0, letters of recommendation. Additional exam requirements/recommendations for international students: Required—TOEFL (minimum score 550 paper-based; 80 iBT), TWE (minimum score 5). Electronic applications accepted. *Faculty research:* School-based mental health, pupil personnel services, childhood mood, school-based assessment.

Alliant International University–San Francisco, Shirley M. Hufstedler School of Education, Educational Psychology Programs, San Francisco, CA 94133. Offers educational psychology (Psy D); pupil personnel services (Credential); school psychology (MA). *Program availability:* Part-time. Terminal master's awarded for partial completion of doctoral program. *Degree requirements:* For doctorate, thesis/dissertation. *Entrance requirements:* For master's, minimum GPA of 3.0, letters of recommendation; for doctorate, interview, minimum GPA of 3.0, letters of recommendation. Additional exam requirements/recommendations for international students: Required—TOEFL (minimum score 550 paper-based), TWE (minimum score 5). Electronic applications accepted. *Faculty research:* Social skills, ADHD, cognitive functioning and learning, innovative teaching methods.

American International College, School of Business, Arts and Sciences, Springfield, MA 01109-3189. Offers accounting and taxation (MS); business administration (MBA); clinical psychology (MA); educational psychology (Ed D); forensic psychology (MS); general psychology (MA, CAGS); management (CAGS); resort and casino management (MBA, CAGS). *Program availability:* Part-time, evening/weekend. *Faculty:* 4 full-time (2 women), 25 part-time/adjunct (13 women). *Students:* 178 full-time (120 women), 24 part-time (20 women); includes 94 minority (42 Black or African American, non-Hispanic/Latino; 1 American Indian or Alaska Native, non-Hispanic/Latino; 4 Asian, non-Hispanic/Latino; 39 Hispanic/Latino; 8 Two or more races, non-Hispanic/Latino), 13 international. Average age 28. 155 applicants, 83% accepted, 71 enrolled. In 2017, 87 master's, 3 doctorates awarded. *Degree requirements:* For master's, practicum; for doctorate, comprehensive exam, thesis/dissertation, practicum. *Entrance requirements:* For master's, BS or BA, minimum undergraduate GPA of 2.75, 2 letters of recommendation, official transcripts, personal goal statement or essay; for doctorate, 3 letters of recommendation; BS or BA; minimum undergraduate GPA of 3.0 (3.25 recommended); official transcripts; personal goal statement or essay. Additional exam requirements/recommendations for international students: Required—TOEFL (minimum score 550 paper-based; 80 iBT). *Application deadline:* For fall admission, 8/15 for domestic and

international students; for spring admission, 12/15 for domestic and international students. Applications are processed on a rolling basis. Application fee: $50. *Expenses:* Contact institution. *Financial support:* In 2017–18, 6 students received support, including 6 research assistantships with full tuition reimbursements available (averaging $1,500 per year). Financial award application deadline: 4/1; financial award applicants required to submit FAFSA. *Faculty research:* Substance abuse, forensic psychology, special education. *Unit head:* Dr. Susanne Swanker, Dean, 413-205-3216, Fax: 413-205-3943, E-mail: susanne.swanker@aic.edu. *Application contact:* Kerry Barnes, Dean of Graduate Admissions, 413-205-3703, Fax: 413-205-3051, E-mail: kerry.barnes@aic.edu.
Website: http://www.aic.edu/school-of-business-arts-and-sciences/

Andrews University, School of Graduate Studies, School of Education, Department of Graduate Psychology and Counseling, Program in Educational and Developmental Psychology, Berrien Springs, MI 49104. Offers educational and developmental psychology (MA); educational psychology (Ed D, PhD). *Students:* 15 full-time (10 women), 4 part-time (3 women); includes 5 minority (3 Black or African American, non-Hispanic/Latino; 2 Hispanic/Latino), 9 international. Average age 39. 18 applicants, 50% accepted, 6 enrolled. In 2017, 8 master's, 4 doctorates awarded. *Degree requirements:* For master's, thesis optional. *Entrance requirements:* For master's, GRE. Additional exam requirements/recommendations for international students: Required—TOEFL (minimum score 550 paper-based). *Application deadline:* Applications are processed on a rolling basis. Application fee: $40. *Unit head:* Dr. Jimmy Kijai, Coordinator, 269-471-6240. *Application contact:* Justina Clayburn, Supervisor of Graduate Admission, 800-253-2874, Fax: 269-471-6321, E-mail: graduate@andrews.edu.

Ball State University, Graduate School, Teachers College, Department of Educational Psychology, Program in Educational Psychology, Muncie, IN 47306. Offers MA, MS, PhD. *Accreditation:* NCATE. *Program availability:* Part-time, 100% online. *Students:* 22 full-time (15 women), 69 part-time (61 women); includes 21 minority (8 Black or African American, non-Hispanic/Latino; 3 Asian, non-Hispanic/Latino; 4 Hispanic/Latino; 6 Two or more races, non-Hispanic/Latino), 2 international. Average age 34. 58 applicants, 33% accepted, 15 enrolled. In 2017, 40 master's, 1 doctorate awarded. *Entrance requirements:* For master's, GRE General Test (for MS only), minimum baccalaureate GPA of 2.75 or 3.0 in latter half of baccalaureate; for doctorate, GRE General Test, minimum graduate GPA of 3.2. Additional exam requirements/recommendations for international students: Required—TOEFL (minimum score 550 paper-based; 79 iBT), IELTS (minimum score 6.5). *Application deadline:* For fall admission, 7/15 for domestic students; for spring admission, 12/1 for domestic students; for summer admission, 4/1 for domestic students. Applications are processed on a rolling basis. Application fee: $60. Electronic applications accepted. *Financial support:* Research assistantships with partial tuition reimbursements and teaching assistantships with partial tuition reimbursements available. Financial award application deadline: 3/1; financial award applicants required to submit FAFSA. *Unit head:* Dr. Sharon Paulson, Chairperson, 765-285-8500, Fax: 765-285-5455, E-mail: spaulson@bsu.edu. *Application contact:* Dr. Jerrell Cassady, Graduate Advisor, 765-285-8522, Fax: 765-285-5455, E-mail: jccassady@bsu.edu.
Website: http://www.bsu.edu/edpsych

Ball State University, Graduate School, Teachers College, Department of Educational Psychology, Program in Quantitative Psychology, Muncie, IN 47306. Offers MS. *Program availability:* Online learning. *Students:* 6 full-time (1 woman), 4 part-time (3 women); includes 1 minority (Hispanic/Latino). Average age 25. 18 applicants, 44% accepted, 5 enrolled. *Entrance requirements:* For master's, official transcripts, minimum GPA of 2.75. Electronic applications accepted. *Financial support:* Application deadline: 3/1. *Unit head:* Dr. Sharon Paulson, Chairperson, 765-285-8500, Fax: 765-285-5455, E-mail: spaulson@bsu.edu. *Application contact:* Dr. Jerrell Cassady, Director, Graduate Programs, 765-285-8522, Fax: 765-285-5455, E-mail: jccassady@bsu.edu.

Baylor University, Graduate School, School of Education, Department of Educational Psychology, Waco, TX 76798. Offers applied behavior analysis (MS Ed); educational psychology (MA, MS Ed, PhD); exceptionalities (PhD); gifted and talented studies (MS Ed); learning and development (PhD); quantitative methods (MA); school psychology (Ed S). *Accreditation:* NCATE. *Faculty:* 11 full-time (6 women). *Students:* 45 full-time (41 women), 11 part-time (10 women); includes 16 minority (1 Black or African

American, non-Hispanic/Latino; 3 Asian, non-Hispanic/Latino; 10 Hispanic/Latino; 2 Two or more races, non-Hispanic/Latino; 4 international. Average age 29. 90 applicants, 33% accepted, 30 enrolled. In 2017, 24 master's, 1 doctorate, 7 other advanced degrees awarded. Terminal master's awarded for partial completion of doctoral program. *Degree requirements:* For master's, thesis optional; for doctorate, comprehensive exam, thesis/dissertation; for Ed S, comprehensive exam, thesis or alternative. *Entrance requirements:* For master's, GRE, minimum GPA of 3.0; for doctorate, GRE General Test, master's degree; for Ed S, GRE General Test. Additional exam requirements/recommendations for international students: Required—TOEFL (minimum score 550 paper-based; 80 iBT), IELTS (minimum score 6.5). *Application deadline:* For fall admission, 2/1 priority date for domestic and international students. Application fee: $80. Electronic applications accepted. *Financial support:* In 2017–18, 42 students received support, including 20 fellowships with full and partial tuition reimbursements available, 22 research assistantships with full and partial tuition reimbursements available; career-related internships or fieldwork, Federal Work-Study, institutionally sponsored loans, scholarships/grants, health care benefits, tuition waivers (full and partial), unspecified assistantships, and stipends also available. Financial award application deadline: 2/1; financial award applicants required to submit FAFSA. *Faculty research:* Individual differences, quantitative methods, gifted and talented, special education, school psychology, autism, applied behavior analysis, learning, human development. *Total annual research expenditures:* $300,000. *Unit head:* Dr. Susan K. Johnsen, Professor and Interim Chair, 254-710-6116, E-mail: susan_johnsen@baylor.edu. *Application contact:* Heather Tindle, Office Manager, 254-710-3112, E-mail: heather_tindle@baylor.edu.
Website: http://www.baylor.edu/soe/EDP/

Boston College, Lynch School of Education, Program in Applied Developmental and Educational Psychology, Chestnut Hill, MA 02467-3800. Offers MA, PhD. *Program availability:* Part-time, evening/weekend. *Students:* 34 full-time (32 women), 9 part-time (8 women); includes 6 minority (2 Black or African American, non-Hispanic/Latino; 2 Asian, non-Hispanic/Latino; 4 Hispanic/Latino; 1 Two or more races, non-Hispanic/Latino), 10 international. Average age 27. 97 applicants, 61% accepted, 20 enrolled. In 2017, 13 master's, 3 doctorates awarded. Terminal master's awarded for partial completion of doctoral program. *Degree requirements:* For master's, comprehensive exam; for doctorate, comprehensive exam, thesis/dissertation. *Entrance requirements:* For master's and doctorate, GRE General Test. Additional exam requirements/recommendations for international students: Required—TOEFL (minimum score 100 iBT). *Application deadline:* For fall admission, 12/1 priority date for domestic and international students; for spring admission, 11/1 for domestic and international students. Application fee: $65. Electronic applications accepted. *Financial support:* Fellowships with tuition reimbursements, research assistantships with tuition reimbursements, teaching assistantships with tuition reimbursements, career-related internships or fieldwork, Federal Work-Study, scholarships/grants, traineeships, health care benefits, tuition waivers (full and partial), and unspecified assistantships available. Support available to part-time students. Financial award applicants required to submit FAFSA. *Faculty research:* Cognitive learning and culture, effects of social policy reform on children and families, psychosocial trauma, human rights and international justice, positive youth development, children and adolescents living in poverty. *Unit head:* Dr. Rebekah Levine Coley, Chairperson, 617-552-6018, Fax: 617-552-4710. *Application contact:* Kimberly Rose, Graduate Admission Assistant, 617-552-4214, Fax: 617-552-0398, E-mail: roseki@bc.edu.

Brigham Young University, Graduate Studies, David O. McKay School of Education, Department of Instructional Psychology and Technology, Provo, UT 84602. Offers MS, PhD. *Faculty:* 10 full-time (1 woman). *Students:* 49 full-time (18 women), 27 part-time (11 women); includes 1 minority (Asian, non-Hispanic/Latino), 2 international. Average age 35. 46 applicants, 59% accepted, 21 enrolled. In 2017, 31 master's, 10 doctorates awarded. *Degree requirements:* For master's, thesis; for doctorate, comprehensive exam, thesis/dissertation. *Entrance requirements:* For master's and doctorate, GRE General Test. Additional exam requirements/recommendations for international students: Required—TOEFL. *Application deadline:* For fall and spring admission, 1/2 for domestic and international students. Application fee: $50. Electronic applications accepted. *Expenses: Tuition:* Full-time $6880; part-time $405 per credit hour. Tuition and fees vary according to course load, program and student's religious affiliation. *Financial support:* In 2017–18, 23 students received support, including 22 research assistantships with full and partial tuition reimbursements available (averaging $10,000 per year), 12 teaching assistantships with full and partial tuition reimbursements available (averaging $7,000 per year); career-related internships or fieldwork, scholarships/grants, tuition waivers (full and partial), and unspecified assistantships also available. Support available to part-time students. Financial award application deadline: 4/15. *Faculty research:* Interactive learning, learning theory, instructional designed development, research and evaluation, measurement. *Unit head:* Dr. Charles R. Graham, Department Chair, 801-422-4110, Fax: 801-422-0314, E-mail: charles.graham@byu.edu. *Application contact:* Michele Bray, Department Secretary, 801-422-2746, Fax: 801-422-0314, E-mail: michele_bray@byu.edu.
Website: http://education.byu.edu/ipt/

California Coast University, School of Education, Santa Ana, CA 92701. Offers administration (M Ed); curriculum and instruction (M Ed); educational administration (Ed D); educational psychology (Ed D); organizational leadership (Ed D). *Program availability:* Online learning.

California State University, Long Beach, Graduate Studies, College of Education, Department of Advanced Studies in Education and Counseling, Long Beach, CA 90840. Offers counseling (MS), including marriage and family therapy, school counseling, student development in higher education; education (MA, Ed D); educational administration (MA, Ed D); educational psychology (MA); special education (MS). *Program availability:* Part-time, evening/weekend. *Entrance requirements:* For master's, GRE General Test, minimum GPA of 2.75. Electronic applications accepted.

California State University, Northridge, Graduate Studies, Michael D. Eisner College of Education, Department of Educational Psychology and Counseling, Northridge, CA 91330. Offers counseling (MS), including career counseling, college counseling and student services, marriage and family therapy, school counseling, school psychology; educational psychology (MA Ed), including development, learning, and instruction, early childhood education. *Accreditation:* ACA (one or more programs are accredited); NCATE. *Program availability:* Part-time, evening/weekend. *Students:* 288 full-time (244 women), 84 part-time (76 women); includes 190 minority (13 Black or African American, non-Hispanic/Latino; 24 Asian, non-Hispanic/Latino; 139 Hispanic/Latino; 14 Two or more races, non-Hispanic/Latino), 11 international. Average age 29. 427 applicants, 34% accepted, 136 enrolled. In 2017, 103 master's awarded. *Entrance requirements:* For master's, GRE General Test or minimum GPA of 3.0. Additional exam requirements/recommendations for international students: Required—TOEFL. *Application deadline:* For fall admission, 11/30 for domestic students. Application fee: $55. *Financial support:* Scholarships/grants available. Support available to part-time students. Financial award application deadline: 3/1. *Unit head:* Dr. Alberto Restori, Chair, 818-677-2599. *Application contact:* 818-677-3755.
Website: http://www.csun.edu/eisner-education/educational-psychology-counseling

Capella University, Harold Abel School of Social and Behavioral Science, Doctoral Programs in Psychology, Minneapolis, MN 55402. Offers addiction psychology (PhD); clinical psychology (Psy D); educational psychology (PhD); general advanced studies in human behavior (PhD); general psychology (PhD); industrial/organizational psychology (PhD); school psychology (Psy D).

Capella University, Harold Abel School of Social and Behavioral Science, Master's Programs in Psychology, Minneapolis, MN 55402. Offers applied behavior analysis (MS); clinical psychology (MS); counseling psychology (MS); educational psychology (MS); evaluation, research, and measurement (MS); general advanced studies in human behavior (MS); general psychology (MS); industrial/organizational psychology (MS); leadership coaching psychology (MS); school psychology (MS); sport psychology (MS).

Chapman University, Donna Ford Attallah College of Educational Studies, Orange, CA 92866. Offers counseling (MA), including school counseling (MA, Credential); curriculum and instruction (MA), including elementary education, secondary education; education (PhD), including cultural and curricular studies, disability studies, leadership studies, school psychology (PhD, Credential); educational psychology (MA); leadership development (MA); multiple subjects (Credential), including Spanish/English bilingual; pupil personnel services (Credential), including school counseling (MA, Credential), school psychology (PhD, Credential); school psychology (Ed S); single subject (Credential); special education (MA, Credential), including mild/moderate (Credential), moderate/severe (Credential); teaching (MA), including elementary education, secondary education, secondary music education. *Accreditation:* TEAC. *Program availability:* Part-time, evening/weekend. *Faculty:* 32 full-time (18 women), 37 part-time/adjunct (26 women). *Students:* 170 full-time (140 women), 180 part-time (129 women); includes 164 minority (6 Black or African American, non-Hispanic/Latino; 38 Asian, non-Hispanic/Latino; 101 Hispanic/Latino; 1 Native Hawaiian or other Pacific Islander, non-Hispanic/Latino; 18 Two or more races, non-Hispanic/Latino), 10 international. Average age 28. 143 applicants, 63% accepted, 64 enrolled. In 2017, 126 master's, 18 doctorates awarded. *Application deadline:* Applications are processed on a rolling basis. Application fee: $60. Electronic applications accepted. *Expenses:* Contact institution. *Financial support:* Fellowships and scholarships/grants available. Financial award application deadline: 3/2; financial award applicants required to submit FAFSA. *Unit head:* Dr. Margaret Grogan, Dean, 714-516-5968, E-mail: grogan@chapman.edu. *Application contact:* Shannon McCance, Graduate Admission Counselor, 714-516-5236, E-mail: smccance@chapman.edu.
Website: http://www.chapman.edu/CES/

Clark Atlanta University, School of Education, Department of Counseling and Psychological Studies, Atlanta, GA 30314. Offers MA. *Accreditation:* ACA. *Program availability:* Part-time. *Faculty:* 4 full-time (2 women), 3 part-time/adjunct (2 women). *Students:* 35 full-time (26 women), 19 part-time (14 women); includes 45 minority (all Black or African American, non-Hispanic/Latino), 6 international. Average age 28. 35 applicants, 100% accepted, 20 enrolled. In 2017, 16 master's awarded. *Degree requirements:* For master's, comprehensive exam. *Entrance requirements:* For master's, GRE General Test, minimum undergraduate GPA of 2.6. Additional exam requirements/recommendations for international students: Required—TOEFL (minimum score 500 paper-based; 61 iBT). *Application deadline:* For fall admission, 4/1 for domestic and international students; for spring admission, 11/1 for domestic and international students. Applications are processed on a rolling basis. Application fee: $40 ($55 for international students). Electronic applications accepted. *Financial support:* Career-related internships or fieldwork, Federal Work-Study, scholarships/grants, and unspecified assistantships available. Support available to part-time students. Financial award application deadline: 4/30; financial award applicants required to submit FAFSA. *Unit head:* Dr. Ken Sanders, Chairperson, 404-880-8519, E-mail: ksanders1@cau.edu.

The College of Saint Rose, Graduate Studies, Thelma P. Lally School of Education, Educational and School Psychology Programs, Albany, NY 12203-1419. Offers educational psychology (MS Ed, Certificate); school psychology (MS Ed). *Students:* 35 full-time (31 women), 5 part-time (2 women); includes 3 minority (1 Black or African American, non-Hispanic/Latino; 1 Hispanic/Latino; 1 Two or more races, non-Hispanic/Latino), 1 international. Average age 25. 40 applicants, 75% accepted, 18 enrolled. In 2017, 20 master's awarded. *Entrance requirements:* For master's, minimum undergraduate GPA of 3.0. Additional exam requirements/recommendations for international students: Required—TOEFL (minimum score 550 paper-based; 80 iBT), IELTS (minimum score 6), PTE (minimum score 56). *Application deadline:* For fall admission, 2/15 priority date for domestic and international students. Applications are processed on a rolling basis. Application fee: $40. Electronic applications accepted. *Expenses: Tuition:* Full-time $7191; part-time $799 per credit hour. *Required fees:* $924; $462 per credit hour. Tuition and fees vary according to course load. *Financial support:* Career-related internships or fieldwork, scholarships/grants, tuition waivers (partial), and unspecified assistantships available. Support available to part-time students. Financial award application deadline: 4/15. *Unit head:* Dr. Andrew Shanock, Chair, 518-337-5694, E-mail: shanocka@strose.edu. *Application contact:* Cris Murray, Assistant Vice President for Graduate Recruitment and Enrollment, 518-485-3390, Fax: 518-458-5479, E-mail: grad@strose.edu.
Website: https://www.strose.edu/school-psychology/

Eastern Michigan University, Graduate School, College of Education, Department of Teacher Education, Programs in Educational Psychology and Assessment, Ypsilanti, MI 48197. Offers educational assessment (Graduate Certificate); learning technology and design (MA). *Accreditation:* NCATE. *Program availability:* Part-time, evening/weekend, online learning. *Students:* 4 full-time (all women), 26 part-time (24 women); includes 5 minority (3 Black or African American, non-Hispanic/Latino; 1 Hispanic/Latino; 1 Two or more races, non-Hispanic/Latino). Average age 32. 11 applicants, 82% accepted, 6 enrolled. In 2017, 9 master's, 1 other advanced degree awarded. *Degree requirements:* For master's, thesis or alternative. *Entrance requirements:* For master's, GRE. Additional exam requirements/recommendations for international students: Required—TOEFL. *Application deadline:* Applications are processed on a rolling basis. Application fee: $45. *Financial support:* Fellowships, research assistantships with full tuition reimbursements, teaching assistantships with full tuition reimbursements, career-related internships or fieldwork, Federal Work-Study, institutionally sponsored loans, scholarships/grants, tuition waivers (partial), and unspecified assistantships available. Support available to part-time students. Financial award applicants required to submit FAFSA. *Application contact:* Dr. Alane Starko, Coordinator, 734-487-3260, Fax: 734-487-2101, E-mail: astarko@emich.edu.

Edinboro University of Pennsylvania, Department of Counseling, School Psychology and Special Education, Edinboro, PA 16444. Offers counseling (MA), including art therapy, clinical mental health counseling, college counseling, rehabilitation counseling, school counseling; educational psychology (M Ed); school psychology (Ed S); special education (M Ed), including autism, behavior management. *Accreditation:* ACA. *Program availability:* Part-time, evening/weekend. *Degree requirements:* For master's, thesis or alternative, competency exam; for Ed S, thesis or alternative. *Entrance requirements:* For master's and Ed S, GRE or MAT, minimum QPA of 2.5. Electronic applications accepted.

Educational Psychology

Florida Atlantic University, College of Education, Department of Teaching and Learning, Boca Raton, FL 33431-0991. Offers curriculum and instruction (M Ed), including art, biology, chemistry, English, French, German, mathematics, music, physics, Pre-K and primary education, reading, social sciences, Spanish; elementary education (M Ed); environmental education (M Ed); reading education (M Ed); social foundations of education (M Ed), including educational psychology, educational technology, multilingual education. *Accreditation:* NCATE. *Program availability:* Part-time, evening/weekend. *Faculty:* 13 full-time (10 women), 1 part-time/adjunct (0 women). *Students:* 26 full-time (22 women), 43 part-time (39 women); includes 19 minority (9 Black or African American, non-Hispanic/Latino; 1 Asian, non-Hispanic/Latino; 8 Hispanic/Latino; 1 Two or more races, non-Hispanic/Latino), 3 international. Average age 30. 91 applicants, 57% accepted, 33 enrolled. In 2017, 25 master's awarded. *Entrance requirements:* For master's, GRE General Test, minimum GPA of 3.0 in last 2 years of undergraduate course work. Additional exam requirements/recommendations for international students: Required—TOEFL (minimum score 500 paper-based; 61 iBT), IELTS (minimum score 6). *Application deadline:* For fall admission, 7/1 for domestic students, 2/15 for international students; for spring admission, 11/1 for domestic students, 7/15 for international students. Applications are processed on a rolling basis. Application fee: $30. *Expenses:* Tuition, state resident: full-time $7400; part-time $369.82 per credit. Tuition, nonresident: full-time $20,496; part-time $1042.81 per credit. *Financial support:* Fellowships with partial tuition reimbursements, research assistantships with partial tuition reimbursements, teaching assistantships with partial tuition reimbursements, career-related internships or fieldwork, scholarships/grants, and unspecified assistantships available. *Faculty research:* Technology, teaching English to speakers of other languages, math teaching, electronic portfolio assessment, global perspectives through social studies. *Unit head:* Dr. Barbara Ridener, Chairperson, 561-297-3588, E-mail: bridener@fau.edu. *Application contact:* Dr. Eliah Watlington, Associate Dean, 561-296-8520, Fax: 261-297-2991, E-mail: ewatling@fau.edu.
Website: http://www.coe.fau.edu/academicdepartments/tl/

Florida State University, The Graduate School, College of Education, Department of Educational Psychology and Learning Systems, Tallahassee, FL 32306. Offers counseling and human systems (PhD), including counseling psychology and school psychology; educational psychology (MS, PhD), including learning and cognition, sport psychology; human performance and technology (Certificate); instructional systems and learning technologies (MS, PhD); measurement and statistics (MS, PhD, Certificate); online instructional development (Certificate); MS/Ed S. *Program availability:* Part-time, evening/weekend, 100% online, blended/hybrid learning, asynchronous, minimal on-campus study. *Faculty:* 28 full-time (17 women), 12 part-time/adjunct (7 women). *Students:* 339 full-time (238 women), 136 part-time (93 women); includes 126 minority (47 Black or African American, non-Hispanic/Latino; 4 American Indian or Alaska Native, non-Hispanic/Latino; 7 Asian, non-Hispanic/Latino; 48 Hispanic/Latino; 20 Two or more races, non-Hispanic/Latino), 110 international. Average age 31. 419 applicants, 39% accepted, 82 enrolled. In 2017, 84 master's, 27 doctorates, 38 other advanced degrees awarded. Terminal master's awarded for partial completion of doctoral program. *Degree requirements:* For master's and Certificate, comprehensive exam, thesis optional; for doctorate, comprehensive exam, thesis/dissertation, diagnostic exam, preliminary exam, prospectus defense. *Entrance requirements:* For master's, doctorate, and Certificate, GRE General Test, minimum GPA of 3.0. Additional exam requirements/recommendations for international students: Required—TOEFL (minimum score 550 paper-based, 80 iBT), IELTS (minimum score 6.5) or Michigan English Language Assessment Battery (minimum score 77). Application fee: $30. Electronic applications accepted. *Financial support:* Fellowships, research assistantships, teaching assistantships, scholarships/grants, tuition waivers (full and partial), and unspecified assistantships available. Financial award application deadline: 1/15; financial award applicants required to submit FAFSA. *Faculty research:* Learning and cognition, counseling and school psychology, instructional systems, measurement and evaluation. *Unit head:* Dr. Betsy Becker, Chair, 850-644-4592, Fax: 850-644-8776, E-mail: bbecker@fsu.edu. *Application contact:* Deborah Kelly, Academic Program Specialist, 850-644-8046, Fax: 850-644-8781, E-mail: dhamkelly@fsu.edu.

Fordham University, Graduate School of Arts and Sciences, Department of Psychology, Program in Psychometrics and Quantitative Psychology, New York, NY 10458. Offers PhD. *Students:* 10 full-time (8 women), 2 part-time (1 woman); includes 4 minority (2 Asian, non-Hispanic/Latino; 2 Hispanic/Latino), 6 international. Average age 33. 14 applicants, 50% accepted, 2 enrolled. In 2017, 1 doctorate awarded. *Degree requirements:* For doctorate, comprehensive exam, thesis/dissertation. *Entrance requirements:* For doctorate, GRE General Test. Additional exam requirements/recommendations for international students: Required—TOEFL (minimum score 600 paper-based). *Application deadline:* For fall admission, 12/14 for domestic students. Application fee: $70. Electronic applications accepted. *Financial support:* In 2017–18, 16 students received support, including 3 fellowships with tuition reimbursements available (averaging $25,870 per year), 1 research assistantship with tuition reimbursement available (averaging $24,130 per year), 2 teaching assistantships with tuition reimbursements available (averaging $7,950 per year); career-related internships or fieldwork, institutionally sponsored loans, tuition waivers (full and partial), and unspecified assistantships also available. Financial award application deadline: 12/14; financial award applicants required to submit FAFSA. *Faculty research:* Applications of Bayesian statistics, ethnic identity, hierarchical linear models. *Unit head:* Dr. Barry Rosenfeld, Department Chair, 718-817-3794, Fax: 718-817-3785, E-mail: rosenfeld@fordham.edu. *Application contact:* Bernadette Valentino-Morrison, Director of Graduate Admissions, 718-817-4419, Fax: 718-817-3566, E-mail: valentinomor@fordham.edu.

Fordham University, Graduate School of Education, Division of Psychological and Educational Services, New York, NY 10023. Offers counseling and personnel services (MSE); counseling psychology (PhD); school psychology (PhD). *Accreditation:* APA (one or more programs are accredited); NCATE. *Program availability:* Part-time, evening/weekend. Terminal master's awarded for partial completion of doctoral program. *Degree requirements:* For master's, comprehensive exam (for some programs); for doctorate, comprehensive exam (for some programs), thesis/dissertation. *Entrance requirements:* For doctorate, GRE General Test. Additional exam requirements/recommendations for international students: Required—TOEFL (minimum score 577 paper-based; 90 iBT), IELTS (minimum score 7). Electronic applications accepted.

George Mason University, College of Education and Human Development, Program in Educational Psychology, Fairfax, VA 22030. Offers assessment, evaluation, and testing (MS); data-driven decision-making for continuous improvement (Certificate); learning and decision-making in leadership (MS); learning, cognition, and motivation (MS); teacher preparation (MS). *Program availability:* Part-time. *Faculty:* 6 full-time (5 women), 4 part-time/adjunct (2 women). *Students:* 12 full-time (10 women), 31 part-time (26 women); includes 16 minority (8 Black or African American, non-Hispanic/Latino; 2 Asian, non-Hispanic/Latino; 4 Hispanic/Latino; 1 Native Hawaiian or other Pacific Islander, non-Hispanic/Latino; 1 Two or more races, non-Hispanic/Latino), 5 international. Average age 29. 35 applicants, 83% accepted, 19 enrolled. In 2017, 15 master's awarded. *Entrance requirements:* For master's, GRE, official transcripts; 3 letters of recommendation; expanded goals statement. Additional exam requirements/

recommendations for international students: Required—TOEFL (minimum score 575 paper-based; 80 iBT), IELTS (minimum score 6.5), PTE (minimum score 59). *Application deadline:* For fall admission, 4/2 priority date for domestic and international students; for spring admission, 11/1 priority date for domestic and international students. Application fee: $75 ($80 for international students). Electronic applications accepted. *Expenses:* Tuition, state resident: full-time $11,228; part-time $459.50 per credit. Tuition, nonresident: full-time $30,932; part-time $1280.50 per credit. *Required fees:* $3252; $135.50 per credit. Part-time tuition and fees vary according to course load and program. *Financial support:* In 2017–18, 1 student received support, including 1 research assistantship with tuition reimbursement available (averaging $12,480 per year); career-related internships or fieldwork, Federal Work-Study, scholarships/grants, unspecified assistantships, and health care benefits (for full-time research or teaching assistantship recipients) also available. Support available to part-time students. Financial award application deadline: 3/1; financial award applicants required to submit FAFSA. *Faculty research:* Learning, cognition, motivation measurement, evaluation assessment, educational policy. *Unit head:* Erin Peters-Burton, Academic Program Coordinator, 703-993-9695, Fax: 703-993-3678, E-mail: epeters1@gmu.edu. *Application contact:* Kim Howe, Office Manager, 703-993-3679, Fax: 703-993-3678, E-mail: khowe1@gmu.edu.
Website: http://gse.gmu.edu/programs/edpsych/

Georgia State University, College of Education and Human Development, Department of Educational Psychology, Special Education, and Communication Disorders, Program in Educational Psychology, Atlanta, GA 30302-3083. Offers MS, PhD. *Accreditation:* NCATE. *Program availability:* Part-time, evening/weekend, online learning. *Entrance requirements:* For master's and doctorate, GRE. *Application deadline:* Applications are processed on a rolling basis. Application fee: $50. Electronic applications accepted. *Expenses:* Tuition, state resident: full-time $7020. Tuition, nonresident: full-time $22,518. *Required fees:* $2128. Tuition and fees vary according to degree level and program. *Financial support:* Fellowships, research assistantships, teaching assistantships, institutionally sponsored loans, scholarships/grants, tuition waivers, and unspecified assistantships available. Financial award applicants required to submit FAFSA. *Faculty research:* Language and literacy, social emotional development, cognitive development, applied behavior analysis, motivation and metacognition. *Unit head:* Dr. Miles Anthony Irving, Program Coordinator, 404-413-3808, E-mail: iam@gsu.edu. *Application contact:* Sandy Vaughn, Senior Administrative Coordinator, 404-413-8318, E-mail: svaughn@gsu.edu.
Website: http://esc.education.gsu.edu/academics-and-admissions/educational-psychology/

The Graduate Center, City University of New York, Graduate Studies, Program in Educational Psychology, New York, NY 10016-4039. Offers PhD. *Accreditation:* APA. *Faculty:* 19 full-time (9 women). *Students:* 58 full-time (44 women), 1 (woman) part-time; includes 3 minority (1 Black or African American, non-Hispanic/Latino; 2 Hispanic/Latino), 1 international. Average age 36. 35 applicants, 26% accepted, 7 enrolled. In 2017, 10 doctorates awarded. *Degree requirements:* For doctorate, 2 foreign languages, thesis/dissertation. *Entrance requirements:* For doctorate, GRE General Test, interview, minimum GPA of 3.0. Additional exam requirements/recommendations for international students: Required—TOEFL. *Application deadline:* For fall admission, 1/15 for domestic students. Application fee: $125. Electronic applications accepted. *Financial support:* In 2017–18, 50 students received support, including 37 fellowships, 4 research assistantships, 2 teaching assistantships; career-related internships or fieldwork, Federal Work-Study, institutionally sponsored loans, and tuition waivers (full and partial) also available. Financial award application deadline: 2/1; financial award applicants required to submit FAFSA. *Unit head:* Dr. Bruce Homer, Executive Officer, 212-817-8286, Fax: 212-817-1516, E-mail: bhomer@gc.cuny.edu. *Application contact:* Les Gribben, Director of Admissions, 212-817-7470, Fax: 212-817-1624, E-mail: lgribben@gc.cuny.edu.

Harvard University, Harvard Graduate School of Education, Master's Programs in Education, Cambridge, MA 02138. Offers arts in education (Ed M); education policy and management (Ed M); higher education (Ed M); human development and psychology (Ed M); international education policy (Ed M); language and literacy (Ed M); learning and teaching (Ed M); mind, brain, and education (Ed M); prevention science and practice (Ed M); school leadership (Ed M); special studies (Ed M); teacher education (Ed M); technology, innovation, and education (Ed M). *Program availability:* Part-time. *Entrance requirements:* For master's, GRE General Test, statement of purpose, 3 letters of recommendation, resume, official transcripts. Additional exam requirements/recommendations for international students: Required—TOEFL (minimum score 613 paper-based; 104 iBT), TWE (minimum score 5). Electronic applications accepted. *Faculty research:* Learning and development, educational leadership and organizations, education policy analysis.

Holy Names University, Graduate Division, Department of Education, Oakland, CA 94619-1699. Offers educational therapy (Certificate); mild/moderate disabilities (Ed S); multiple subject teaching (Credential); single subject teaching (Credential); urban education: educational therapy (M Ed); urban education: K-12 education (M Ed); urban education: special education (M Ed). *Program availability:* Part-time. *Degree requirements:* For master's, comprehensive exam, research paper, thesis or project. *Entrance requirements:* For master's, minimum undergraduate GPA of 2.6 overall, 3.0 in major; personal statement; two recommendations; interview. Additional exam requirements/recommendations for international students: Required—TOEFL (minimum score 550 paper-based; 79 iBT). Electronic applications accepted. Application fee is waived when completed online. *Faculty research:* Cognitive development, language development, learning handicaps.

Howard University, School of Education, Department of Human Development and Psychoeducational Studies, Program in Educational Psychology, Washington, DC 20059-0002. Offers PhD. *Program availability:* Part-time. *Degree requirements:* For doctorate, one foreign language, comprehensive exam, thesis/dissertation, expository writing exam, internship. *Entrance requirements:* For doctorate, GRE General Test, minimum GPA of 3.4. Additional exam requirements/recommendations for international students: Required—TOEFL (minimum score 550 paper-based; 79 iBT). Electronic applications accepted.

Immaculata University, College of Graduate Studies, Department of Psychology, Immaculata, PA 19345. Offers clinical mental health counseling (MA); clinical psychology (Psy D); forensic psychology (Graduate Certificate); integrative psychotherapy (Graduate Certificate); neuropsychology (Graduate Certificate); psychodynamic psychotherapy (Graduate Certificate); psychological testing (Graduate Certificate); school counseling (MA, Graduate Certificate); school psychology (MA). *Accreditation:* APA. *Program availability:* Part-time, evening/weekend. Terminal master's awarded for partial completion of doctoral program. *Degree requirements:* For master's, comprehensive exam, thesis optional; for doctorate, comprehensive exam, thesis/dissertation. *Entrance requirements:* For master's, GRE General Test or MAT, minimum GPA of 3.0; for doctorate, GRE General Test or MAT, minimum GPA of 3.5. Additional exam requirements/recommendations for international students: Required—TOEFL, IELTS. Electronic applications accepted. *Faculty research:* Supervision ethics, psychology of teaching, gender.

Indiana University Bloomington, School of Education, Department of Counseling and Educational Psychology, Bloomington, IN 47405-1006. Offers counseling (MS, PhD, Ed S); counselor education (MS, Ed S); educational psychology (MS, PhD); inquiry methodology (PhD); learning and developmental sciences (MS, PhD); school psychology (PhD, Ed S). *Accreditation:* ACA (one or more programs are accredited); APA (one or more programs are accredited); NCATE. Terminal master's awarded for partial completion of doctoral program. *Degree requirements:* For master's, thesis optional; for doctorate, thesis/dissertation; for Ed S, comprehensive exam or project. *Entrance requirements:* For master's, doctorate, and Ed S, GRE General Test. Additional exam requirements/recommendations for international students: Required—TOEFL. Electronic applications accepted. *Faculty research:* Counseling psychology, inquiry methodology, school psychology, learning sciences, human development, educational psychology.

Indiana University of Pennsylvania, School of Graduate Studies and Research, College of Education and Communications, Department of Educational and School Psychology, Program in Educational Psychology, Indiana, PA 15705. Offers M Ed, Certificate. *Accreditation:* NCATE. *Program availability:* Part-time. *Faculty:* 7 full-time (3 women). *Students:* 8 full-time (7 women); includes 2 minority (1 Black or African American, non-Hispanic/Latino; 1 Two or more races, non-Hispanic/Latino). Average age 28. 15 applicants, 80% accepted, 8 enrolled. In 2017, 14 master's awarded. *Degree requirements:* For master's, thesis optional. *Entrance requirements:* For master's, GRE General Test, 2 letters of recommendation. Additional exam requirements/recommendations for international students: Required—TOEFL (minimum score 540 paper-based; 76 iBT). *Application deadline:* For fall admission, 2/1 priority date for domestic students. Application fee: $50. Electronic applications accepted. *Expenses:* Tuition, state resident: full-time $12,000; part-time $500 per credit. Tuition, nonresident: full-time $18,000; part-time $750 per credit. *Required fees:* $4073; $165.55 per credit. $64 per term. *Financial support:* In 2017–18, 9 research assistantships with tuition reimbursements (averaging $3,627 per year) were awarded; fellowships with full tuition reimbursements, teaching assistantships with partial tuition reimbursements, career-related internships or fieldwork, Federal Work-Study, scholarships/grants, and unspecified assistantships also available. Support available to part-time students. Financial award application deadline: 4/15; financial award applicants required to submit FAFSA. *Unit head:* Dr. Mark R. McGowan, Graduate Coordinator, 724-357-2174, E-mail: mmcgowan@iup.edu.
Website: http://www.iup.edu/schoolpsychology/grad/educational-psychology-med/default.aspx

Instituto Tecnologico de Santo Domingo, Graduate School, Area of Humanities and Social Sciences, Santo Domingo, Dominican Republic. Offers accounting (Certificate); adult education (Certificate); applied linguistics (MA); economics (MA); education (M Ed); educational psychology (MA, Certificate); gender and development (MA, Certificate); humanistic studies (MA); international marketing management (Certificate); international relations in the Caribbean basin (Certificate); intervention systems in family therapy (MA); linguistic and literary communication (Certificate); pedagogical support (MA); social science education (M Ed); sustainable human development (MA); terminal illness and death psychology (Certificate); youth and adult education (M Ed).

John Carroll University, Graduate Studies, Programs in Educational and School Psychology, University Heights, OH 44118. Offers educational psychology (M Ed, Ed S); school psychology (Ed S). *Accreditation:* NCATE. *Program availability:* Part-time, evening/weekend. *Faculty:* 9 full-time (5 women), 1 (woman) part-time/adjunct. *Students:* 28 full-time (26 women); includes 1 minority (Black or African American, non-Hispanic/Latino). Average age 24. In 2017, 20 master's, 13 Ed Ss awarded. *Degree requirements:* For master's, comprehensive exam, research essay or thesis (MA only). *Entrance requirements:* For master's, GRE General Test or MAT, minimum GPA of 2.75, degree in education or psychology, interview. *Application deadline:* For fall admission, 2/1 for domestic students; for spring admission, 10/15 for domestic students. Applications are processed on a rolling basis. Application fee: $25 ($35 for international students). Electronic applications accepted. *Expenses:* Tuition: Full-time $16,238; part-time $788 per credit hour. One-time fee: $200. Part-time tuition and fees vary according to course load and program. *Financial support:* Teaching assistantships, scholarships/grants, and unspecified assistantships available. Financial award application deadline: 3/1; financial award applicants required to submit FAFSA. *Unit head:* Dr. Catherine A. Rosemary, Chair, 216-397-4632, Fax: 216-397-3045. *Application contact:* Jennifer L. Tucker, Records Management Assistant, 216-397-1925, Fax: 216-397-1835, E-mail: jtucker@jcu.edu.

Kent State University, College of Education, Health and Human Services, School of Lifespan Development and Educational Sciences, Program in Educational Psychology, Kent, OH 44242-0001. Offers M Ed, MA. *Degree requirements:* For master's, thesis optional. *Entrance requirements:* For master's, 2 letters of reference, minimum GPA of 3.5, goals statement. Additional exam requirements/recommendations for international students: Required—TOEFL (minimum score 550 paper-based; 80 iBT). Electronic applications accepted. *Expenses:* Tuition, state resident: full-time $11,310; part-time $515 per credit hour. Tuition, nonresident: full-time $20,396; part-time $928 per credit hour. *International tuition:* $18,544 full-time.

La Sierra University, School of Education, Department of School Psychology and Counseling, Riverside, CA 92505. Offers counseling (MA); educational psychology (Ed S); school psychology (Ed S). *Program availability:* Part-time, evening/weekend. *Degree requirements:* For master's, thesis optional; for Ed S, practicum (educational psychology). *Entrance requirements:* For master's, California Basic Educational Skills Test, NTE, minimum GPA of 3.0; for Ed S, minimum GPA of 3.3. *Faculty research:* Equivalent score scales, self perception.

McGill University, Faculty of Graduate and Postdoctoral Studies, Faculty of Education, Department of Educational and Counseling Psychology, Montréal, QC H3A 2T5, Canada. Offers counseling psychology (MA, PhD); educational psychology (M Ed, MA, PhD); school/applied child psychology and applied developmental psychology (M Ed, MA, PhD, Diploma), including school psychology. *Accreditation:* APA.

Memorial University of Newfoundland, School of Graduate Studies, Faculty of Education, St. John's, NL A1C 5S7, Canada. Offers counseling psychology (M Ed); curriculum, teaching, and learning studies (M Ed); education (PhD); educational leadership studies (M Ed, Graduate Diploma); information technology (M Ed); post-secondary studies (M Ed, Diploma), including health professional education (Diploma). *Program availability:* Part-time. *Degree requirements:* For master's, thesis optional, internship, paper folio, project; for doctorate, comprehensive exam, thesis/dissertation, thesis seminar, oral defense of thesis. *Entrance requirements:* For master's, undergraduate degree with at least 2nd class standing, 1-2 years of work experience; for doctorate, minimum A average in graduate course work, MA in education, 2 years of professional experience; for other advanced degree, 2nd class degree, 2 years of work experience with adult learners, appropriate academic qualifications and work experience in a health-related field. Electronic applications accepted. *Faculty research:* Critical thinking, literacy, cognitive studies and counseling, educational change, technology in instruction.

Miami University, College of Education, Health and Society, Department of Educational Psychology, Oxford, OH 45056. Offers M Ed, MA, MS, Ed S. *Accreditation:* NCATE. *Students:* 55 full-time (47 women), 132 part-time (106 women); includes 28 minority (18 Black or African American, non-Hispanic/Latino; 3 Asian, non-Hispanic/Latino; 4 Hispanic/Latino; 3 Two or more races, non-Hispanic/Latino), 13 international. Average age 32. In 2017, 63 master's awarded. *Expenses:* Tuition, state resident: full-time $13,812; part-time $575 per credit hour. Tuition, nonresident: full-time $30,860; part-time $1286 per credit hour. *Unit head:* Dr. Raymond Witte, Chair and Professor, 513-529-6621, E-mail: edp@miamioh.edu. *Application contact:* 513-529-6621, E-mail: edp@miamioh.edu.
Website: http://www.MiamiOH.edu/EDP

Michigan School of Professional Psychology, MA and Psy D Programs in Clinical Psychology, Farmington Hills, MI 48334. Offers MA, Psy D. *Accreditation:* APA. *Program availability:* Part-time, evening/weekend. *Faculty:* 11 full-time (7 women), 21 part-time/adjunct (17 women). *Students:* 109 full-time (85 women), 64 part-time (51 women); includes 46 minority (30 Black or African American, non-Hispanic/Latino; 3 Asian, non-Hispanic/Latino; 2 Hispanic/Latino; 11 Two or more races, non-Hispanic/Latino), 1 international. Average age 31. 194 applicants, 47% accepted, 80 enrolled. In 2017, 37 master's, 16 doctorates awarded. *Degree requirements:* For master's, practicum; for doctorate, comprehensive exam, thesis/dissertation, internship, practicum. *Entrance requirements:* For master's, undergraduate degree from accredited institution with minimum GPA of 2.5; major in psychology, social work, or counseling; for doctorate, GRE General Test, undergraduate degree from accredited institution with minimum GPA of 2.5; graduate degree in psychology, social work, or counseling from accredited institution with minimum GPA of 3.25; graduate-level practicum. Additional exam requirements/recommendations for international students: Required—TOEFL (minimum score 550 paper-based; 79 iBT). *Application deadline:* For fall admission, 8/15 for domestic students. Applications are processed on a rolling basis. Application fee: $75. Electronic applications accepted. *Expenses:* $35,871 per academic year full-time tuition and fees (doctoral); $32,518 per academic year full-time tuition and fees (for master's). *Financial support:* In 2017–18, 12 students received support, including 1 research assistantship (averaging $8,566 per year), 5 teaching assistantships (averaging $14,436 per year); institutionally sponsored loans, scholarships/grants, and unspecified assistantships also available. Financial award application deadline: 8/30; financial award applicants required to submit FAFSA. *Faculty research:* Health psychology, trauma, multicultural, humanistic, applied behavior analysis. *Unit head:* Dr. Frances Brown, Program Director, 248-476-1122, Fax: 248-476-1125. *Application contact:* Carrie Hauser, Coordinator of Admissions and Student Engagement, 248-476-1122 Ext. 117, Fax: 248-476-1125, E-mail: chauser@mispp.edu.
Website: http://www.mispp.edu

Michigan State University, The Graduate School, College of Education, Department of Counseling, Educational Psychology and Special Education, East Lansing, MI 48824. Offers counseling (MA); educational psychology and educational technology (PhD); educational technology (MA); measurement and quantitative methods (PhD); rehabilitation counseling (MA); rehabilitation counselor education (PhD); school psychology (MA, PhD, Ed S); special education (MA, PhD). *Accreditation:* APA (one or more programs are accredited); CORE (one or more programs are accredited). *Program availability:* Part-time. *Entrance requirements:* Additional exam requirements/recommendations for international students: Required—TOEFL. Electronic applications accepted.

Mississippi State University, College of Education, Department of Counseling, Educational Psychology, and Foundations, Mississippi State, MS 39762. Offers clinical mental health (MS); college counseling (MS); counseling/mental health (PhD); counseling/school psychology (PhD); counselor education (Ed S); educational psychology/general educational psychology (PhD); educational psychology/school psychology (PhD); general educational psychology (MS); psychometry (MS); rehabilitation counseling (MS); school counseling (MS); school psychology (Ed S); student affairs (MS). *Accreditation:* ACA (one or more programs are accredited); APA; CORE (one or more programs are accredited); NCATE. *Program availability:* Part-time, blended/hybrid learning. *Faculty:* 21 full-time (14 women), 3 part-time/adjunct (2 women). *Students:* 106 full-time (85 women), 51 part-time (43 women); includes 55 minority (44 Black or African American, non-Hispanic/Latino; 1 American Indian or Alaska Native, non-Hispanic/Latino; 1 Asian, non-Hispanic/Latino; 5 Hispanic/Latino; 4 Two or more races, non-Hispanic/Latino), 5 international. Average age 29. 136 applicants, 55% accepted, 54 enrolled. In 2017, 50 master's, 7 doctorates, 10 other advanced degrees awarded. Terminal master's awarded for partial completion of doctoral program. *Degree requirements:* For master's, comprehensive exam, thesis optional; for doctorate, thesis/dissertation, comprehensive oral and written exam. *Entrance requirements:* For master's, GRE (taken within the last five years), BS with minimum GPA of 2.75 on last 60 hours; for doctorate, GRE, MS from CACREP- or CORE-accredited program in counseling; for Ed S, GRE, MS in counseling or related field, minimum GPA of 3.3 on all graduate work. Additional exam requirements/recommendations for international students: Required—TOEFL (minimum score 550 paper-based; 79 iBT); Recommended—IELTS (minimum score 6.5). *Application deadline:* For fall admission, 2/1 priority date for domestic and international students. Applications are processed on a rolling basis. Application fee: $60 ($80 for international students). Electronic applications accepted. *Expenses:* Tuition, state resident: full-time $8318; part-time $462.12 per credit hour. Tuition, nonresident: full-time $22,358; part-time $1242.12 per credit hour. *Required fees:* $110; $12.24 per credit hour. $6.12 per semester. *Financial support:* In 2017–18, 4 research assistantships (averaging $9,000 per year), 10 teaching assistantships with full tuition reimbursements (averaging $8,401 per year) were awarded; career-related internships or fieldwork, Federal Work-Study, institutionally sponsored loans, and unspecified assistantships also available. Financial award application deadline: 2/1; financial award applicants required to submit FAFSA. *Faculty research:* HIV/AIDS in college population, substance abuse in youth and college students, ADHD and conduct disorders in youth, assessment and identification of early childhood disabilities, assessment and vocational transition of the disabled. *Unit head:* Dr. David Morse, Professor and Head, 662-325-3426, Fax: 662-325-3263, E-mail: dmorse@colled.msstate.edu. *Application contact:* Marina Hunt, Admissions and Enrollment Assistant, 662-325-3363, E-mail: mhunt@grad.msstate.edu.
Website: http://www.cep.msstate.edu/

Mount Saint Vincent University, Graduate Programs, Faculty of Education, Program in Educational Psychology, Halifax, NS B3M 2J6, Canada. Offers education of the blind or visually impaired (M Ed, MA Ed); education of the deaf or hard of hearing (M Ed, MA Ed); educational psychology (MA-R); human relations (M Ed, MA Ed). *Program availability:* Part-time, evening/weekend, online learning. *Degree requirements:* For master's, thesis (for some programs). *Entrance requirements:* For master's, bachelor's degree in related field, 1 year of teaching experience. Electronic applications accepted. *Faculty research:* Personality measurement, values reasoning, aggression and sexuality, power and control, quantitative and qualitative research methodologies.

National Louis University, National College of Education, Chicago, IL 60603. Offers administration and supervision (M Ed, Ed D, CAS, Ed S); curriculum and instruction (M Ed, MS Ed, CAS); early childhood administration (M Ed, CAS); early childhood education (M Ed, MAT, MS Ed, CAS); education (Ed D); educational psychology/human learning and development (M Ed, MS Ed, CAS, Ed S); elementary education (MAT); interdisciplinary curriculum and instruction (M Ed); mathematics education (M Ed, MS Ed, CAS); middle grades education (MAT); reading and language (M Ed, MS Ed, CAS); school psychology (M Ed, Ed S); science education (M Ed, MS Ed, CAS); secondary education (MAT); special education (M Ed, MAT, CAS); technology in education (M Ed, CAS). *Accreditation:* NCATE. *Program availability:* Part-time, evening/weekend. *Degree requirements:* For doctorate, comprehensive exam, thesis/dissertation. *Entrance requirements:* For master's, MAT or GRE, minimum GPA of 3.0; for doctorate, GRE General Test, minimum GPA of 3.25, interview, resume, writing sample, 4 recommendations. Additional exam requirements/recommendations for international students: Required—TOEFL (minimum score 550 paper-based; 79 iBT).

New York University, Steinhardt School of Culture, Education, and Human Development, Department of Applied Psychology, Programs in Educational and Developmental Psychology, New York, NY 10012. Offers developmental psychology (PhD); human development and social intervention (MA); psychology and social intervention (PhD). *Accreditation:* APA (one or more programs are accredited). *Program availability:* Part-time. *Students:* Average age 27. 137 applicants, 26% accepted, 13 enrolled. In 2017, 16 master's, 4 doctorates awarded. *Entrance requirements:* For doctorate, GRE General Test, interview. Additional exam requirements/recommendations for international students: Required—TOEFL. *Application deadline:* For fall admission, 12/1 priority date for domestic and international students. Applications are processed on a rolling basis. Application fee: $75. Electronic applications accepted. *Expenses:* Tuition: Full-time $41,352; part-time $19,968 per year. *Required fees:* $2496; $1628 per unit. $814 per term. Tuition and fees vary according to course load and program. *Financial support:* Teaching assistantships with partial tuition reimbursements, career-related internships or fieldwork, Federal Work-Study, institutionally sponsored loans, and tuition waivers (partial) available. Support available to part-time students. Financial award application deadline: 2/1; financial award applicants required to submit FAFSA. *Faculty research:* Schools and communities, self-regulation and academic achievement, intervention and social change, trauma and resilience, cognition. *Unit head:* Prof. Clancy Blair, Director, 212-998-5853, Fax: 212-995-4358, E-mail: clancy.blair@nyu.edu. *Application contact:* 212-998-5030, Fax: 212-995-4328, E-mail: steinhardt.gradadmissions@nyu.edu.
Website: http://steinhardt.nyu.edu/appsych

Northern Arizona University, College of Education, Department of Educational Psychology, Flagstaff, AZ 86011. Offers clinical mental health counseling (MA); combined counseling/school psychology (PhD), including counseling psychology; counseling (M Ed), including school counseling, student affairs; human relations (M Ed); psychology of human development and learning (Graduate Certificate); school psychology (Ed S). *Program availability:* Part-time, 100% online, blended/hybrid learning. *Faculty:* 22 full-time (12 women), 6 part-time/adjunct (4 women). *Students:* 184 full-time (139 women), 175 part-time (131 women); includes 118 minority (14 Black or African American, non-Hispanic/Latino; 10 American Indian or Alaska Native, non-Hispanic/Latino; 5 Asian, non-Hispanic/Latino; 79 Hispanic/Latino; 1 Native Hawaiian or other Pacific Islander, non-Hispanic/Latino; 9 Two or more races, non-Hispanic/Latino), 9 international. Average age 33. 244 applicants, 44% accepted, 108 enrolled. In 2017, 147 master's, 4 doctorates awarded. Terminal master's awarded for partial completion of doctoral program. *Degree requirements:* For master's, variable foreign language requirement, comprehensive exam (for some programs), thesis (for some programs); for doctorate, variable foreign language requirement, comprehensive exam (for some programs), thesis/dissertation (for some programs); for other advanced degree, comprehensive exam (for some programs). *Entrance requirements:* Additional exam requirements/recommendations for international students: Required—TOEFL (minimum score 80 iBT), IELTS (minimum score 6.5). *Application deadline:* For fall admission, 12/1 for domestic and international students; for spring admission, 9/15 for domestic and international students. Applications are processed on a rolling basis. Application fee: $65. Electronic applications accepted. *Expenses:* Tuition, state resident: full-time $9240; part-time $458 per credit hour. Tuition, nonresident: full-time $21,588; part-time $1199 per credit hour. *Required fees:* $1021; $14 per credit hour. $646 per semester. Tuition and fees vary according to course load, campus/location and program. *Financial support:* In 2017–18, 62 students received support, including 1 fellowship with full and partial tuition reimbursement available (averaging $13,927 per year), 2 research assistantships with full and partial tuition reimbursements available (averaging $13,927 per year), 15 teaching assistantships with full and partial tuition reimbursements available (averaging $13,927 per year); institutionally sponsored loans, health care benefits, tuition waivers (full and partial), and unspecified assistantships also available. Financial award application deadline: 2/1; financial award applicants required to submit FAFSA. *Unit head:* Dr. Robert Horn, Chair, 928-523-0545, Fax: 928-523-9284, E-mail: robert.horn@nau.edu. *Application contact:* Hope DeMello, Administrative Assistant, 928-523-7103, Fax: 928-523-9284, E-mail: eps@nau.edu.
Website: https://nau.edu/coe/ed-psych/

Northern Illinois University, Graduate School, College of Education, Department of Leadership, Educational Psychology and Foundations, De Kalb, IL 60115-2854. Offers educational administration (MS Ed, Ed D, Ed S); educational psychology (MS Ed, Ed D); foundations of education (MS Ed); school business management (MS Ed). *Program availability:* Part-time, evening/weekend, online learning. *Faculty:* 23 full-time (12 women). *Students:* 11 full-time (7 women), 241 part-time (151 women); includes 42 minority (19 Black or African American, non-Hispanic/Latino; 3 Asian, non-Hispanic/Latino; 11 Hispanic/Latino; 9 Two or more races, non-Hispanic/Latino), 7 international. Average age 39. 76 applicants, 80% accepted, 26 enrolled. In 2017, 47 master's, 28 doctorates, 20 other advanced degrees awarded. *Degree requirements:* For master's, comprehensive exam, thesis optional; for doctorate, thesis/dissertation, candidacy exam, dissertation defense. *Entrance requirements:* For master's, minimum undergraduate GPA of 2.75; for doctorate, GRE General Test, minimum undergraduate GPA of 2.75, 3.2 graduate; for Ed S, GRE General Test, minimum GPA of 2.75 (undergraduate), 3.2 (graduate). Additional exam requirements/recommendations for international students: Required—TOEFL (minimum score 550 paper-based). *Application deadline:* For fall admission, 6/1 for domestic students, 5/1 for international students; for spring admission, 11/1 for domestic students, 10/1 for international students. Applications are processed on a rolling basis. Application fee: $40. Electronic applications accepted. *Financial support:* In 2017–18, 1 research assistantship with full tuition reimbursement, 2 teaching assistantships with full tuition reimbursements were awarded; fellowships with full tuition reimbursements, career-related internships or fieldwork, Federal Work-Study, scholarships/grants, tuition waivers (full), and staff assistantships also available. Support available to part-time students. Financial award applicants required to submit FAFSA. *Faculty research:* Interpersonal forgiveness, learner-centered education, psychedelic studies, senior theory, professional growth. *Unit head:* Carolyn V. Schee, Chair, 815-753-4404, E-mail: lepf@niu.edu. *Application contact:* Graduate School Office, 815-753-0395, E-mail: gradsch@niu.edu.
Website: http://cedu.niu.edu/LEPF/

Oklahoma State University, College of Education, Health and Aviation, School of Applied Health and Educational Psychology, Stillwater, OK 74078. Offers applied behavioral studies (Ed D); applied health and educational psychology (MS, PhD, Ed S).

Accreditation: APA (one or more programs are accredited). *Program availability:* Part-time. *Faculty:* 31 full-time (20 women), 9 part-time/adjunct (7 women). *Students:* 169 full-time (119 women), 158 part-time (102 women); includes 98 minority (29 Black or African American, non-Hispanic/Latino; 15 American Indian or Alaska Native, non-Hispanic/Latino; 5 Asian, non-Hispanic/Latino; 24 Hispanic/Latino; 25 Two or more races, non-Hispanic/Latino), 22 international. Average age 30. 140 applicants, 56% accepted, 69 enrolled. In 2017, 71 master's, 24 doctorates awarded. *Entrance requirements:* For master's and doctorate, GRE or GMAT. Additional exam requirements/recommendations for international students: Required—TOEFL (minimum score 550 paper-based; 79 iBT). *Application deadline:* For fall admission, 3/1 priority date for international students; for spring admission, 8/1 priority date for international students. Applications are processed on a rolling basis. Application fee: $40 ($75 for international students). Electronic applications accepted. *Expenses:* Tuition, state resident: full-time $4019; part-time $2679.60 per year. Tuition, nonresident: full-time $15,286; part-time $10,190.40 per year. *Required fees:* $2129; $1419 per unit. Tuition and fees vary according to program. *Financial support:* Research assistantships, teaching assistantships, career-related internships or fieldwork, Federal Work-Study, scholarships/grants, health care benefits, tuition waivers (partial), and unspecified assistantships available. Support available to part-time students. Financial award application deadline: 3/1; financial award applicants required to submit FAFSA. *Unit head:* Dr. Aric Warren, Head, 405-744-6040, Fax: 405-744-6779, E-mail: aric.warren@okstate.edu.
Website: http://education.okstate.edu/

Old Dominion University, Darden College of Education, Program in Educational Psychology and Program Evaluation, Norfolk, VA 23529. Offers education (PhD), including educational psychology, program evaluation. *Program availability:* Part-time, evening/weekend. *Faculty:* 4 full-time (2 women). *Students:* 6 full-time (all women), 4 part-time (all women); includes 3 minority (1 Black or African American, non-Hispanic/Latino; 1 Asian, non-Hispanic/Latino; 1 Hispanic/Latino), 1 international. Average age 38. 6 applicants, 50% accepted, 3 enrolled. *Degree requirements:* For doctorate, comprehensive exam, thesis/dissertation. *Entrance requirements:* Additional exam requirements/recommendations for international students: Required—TOEFL. *Application deadline:* Applications are processed on a rolling basis. Application fee: $50. Electronic applications accepted. *Expenses:* Contact institution. *Financial support:* In 2017–18, 5 students received support, including 4 fellowships with full tuition reimbursements available (averaging $15,000 per year), 10 research assistantships with full tuition reimbursements available (averaging $15,000 per year), 2 teaching assistantships with full tuition reimbursements available (averaging $15,000 per year); unspecified assistantships also available. Financial award application deadline: 2/1. *Faculty research:* Motivation, self-regulated learning, distance learning, calibration, STEM. *Total annual research expenditures:* $200,000. *Unit head:* Shana Pribesh, Graduate Program Director, 757-683-6684, E-mail: spribesh@odu.edu. *Application contact:* Nechell Bonds, Director of Admissions, 757-683-3685, Fax: 757-683-3255, E-mail: gradadmit@odu.edu.
Website: http://www.odu.edu/efl/academics/eppe

Penn State University Park, Graduate School, College of Education, Department of Educational Psychology, Counseling, and Special Education, University Park, PA 16802. Offers counselor education (M Ed, D Ed, PhD, Certificate); educational psychology (MS, PhD, Certificate); school psychology (M Ed, MS, PhD, Certificate); special education (M Ed, MS, PhD). *Unit head:* Dr. David H. Monk, Dean, 814-865-2523, Fax: 814-865-0555. *Application contact:* Lori Hawn, Director, Graduate Student Services, 814-865-1795, Fax: 814-863-4627, E-mail: l-gswww@lists.psu.edu.
Website: http://ed.psu.edu/epcse

Philadelphia College of Osteopathic Medicine, Graduate and Professional Programs, Department of Psychology, Philadelphia, PA 19131-1694. Offers applied behavior analysis (Certificate); clinical health psychology (Post-Doctoral Certificate); clinical neuropsychology (Post-Doctoral Certificate); clinical psychology (Psy D); educational psychology (PhD); mental health counseling (MS); organizational development and leadership (MS); psychology (Certificate); public health management and administration (MS); school psychology (MS, Psy D, Ed S). *Accreditation:* APA. *Faculty:* 19 full-time (11 women), 122 part-time/adjunct (58 women). *Students:* 487 (335 women); includes 138 minority (89 Black or African American, non-Hispanic/Latino; 4 American Indian or Alaska Native, non-Hispanic/Latino; 11 Asian, non-Hispanic/Latino; 12 Hispanic/Latino; 22 Two or more races, non-Hispanic/Latino). 298 applicants, 44% accepted, 100 enrolled. In 2017, 50 master's, 43 doctorates, 10 other advanced degrees awarded. Terminal master's awarded for partial completion of doctoral program. *Degree requirements:* For master's, comprehensive exam (for some programs), thesis (for some programs); for doctorate, comprehensive exam, thesis/dissertation. *Entrance requirements:* For master's, GRE or MAT, minimum GPA of 3.0; bachelor's degree from regionally-accredited college or university; for doctorate, PRAXIS II (for Psy D in school psychology), minimum undergraduate GPA of 3.0; for other advanced degree, GRE (for Ed S). Additional exam requirements/recommendations for international students: Required—TOEFL (minimum score 79 iBT). *Application deadline:* Applications are processed on a rolling basis. Application fee: $50. Electronic applications accepted. *Financial support:* In 2017–18, 28 teaching assistantships were awarded; Federal Work-Study, institutionally sponsored loans, and scholarships/grants also available. Financial award application deadline: 3/15; financial award applicants required to submit FAFSA. *Faculty research:* Adult and childhood anxiety and ADHD; coping with chronic illness; primary care psychology/integrated health care; applied behavior analysis; psychological, educational, and neuropsychological assessment. *Total annual research expenditures:* $533,489. *Unit head:* Dr. Robert DiTomasso, Chairman, 215-871-6442, Fax: 215-871-6458, E-mail: robertd@pcom.edu. *Application contact:* Johnathan Cox, Associate Director of Admissions, 215-871-6700, Fax: 215-871-6719, E-mail: johnathancox@pcom.edu.

Pontifical Catholic University of Puerto Rico, College of Education, Program in Educational Psychology, Ponce, PR 00717-0777. Offers M Ed. *Degree requirements:* For master's, comprehensive exam, thesis (for some programs). *Entrance requirements:* For master's, GRE, 2 letters of recommendation, interview, minimum GPA of 2.75.

Purdue University, Graduate School, College of Education, Department of Educational Studies, West Lafayette, IN 47907. Offers administration (MS Ed, PhD, Ed S); counseling and development (MS Ed, PhD); education of the gifted (MS Ed); educational psychology (MS Ed, PhD); foundations of education (MS Ed, PhD); higher education administration (MS Ed, PhD); special education (MS Ed, PhD). *Accreditation:* ACA (one or more programs are accredited); NCATE (one or more programs are accredited). *Program availability:* Part-time, evening/weekend. *Faculty:* 29 full-time (22 women), 1 part-time/adjunct (0 women). *Students:* 78 full-time (60 women), 226 part-time (162 women); includes 45 minority (16 Black or African American, non-Hispanic/Latino; 8 Asian, non-Hispanic/Latino; 15 Hispanic/Latino; 6 Two or more races, non-Hispanic/Latino), 45 international. Average age 32. 214 applicants, 53% accepted, 70 enrolled. In 2017, 38 master's, 20 doctorates, 4 other advanced degrees awarded. *Degree requirements:* For master's, thesis optional; for doctorate, thesis/dissertation, oral and written exams; for Ed S, oral presentation, project. *Entrance requirements:* For master's, GRE General Test (except for special education if undergraduate GPA is

higher than a 3.0), minimum undergraduate GPA of 3.0; for doctorate and Ed S, GRE General Test (minimum combined score of 1000, 300 for new scoring), minimum undergraduate GPA of 3.0. Additional exam requirements/recommendations for international students: Required—TOEFL (minimum score 550 paper-based; 77 iBT), TWE (minimum score 5). *Application deadline:* Applications are processed on a rolling basis. Application fee: $60 ($75 for international students). Electronic applications accepted. *Financial support:* Fellowships with full tuition reimbursements, research assistantships with full tuition reimbursements, teaching assistantships with full tuition reimbursements, career-related internships or fieldwork, and tuition waivers (full) available. Support available to part-time students. Financial award application deadline: 3/1; financial award applicants required to submit FAFSA. *Faculty research:* Motivation, learning disabilities, school learning, group processes, cognitive development. *Unit head:* F. Richard Olenchak, Head, 765-494-9170, E-mail: olenchak@purdue.edu. *Application contact:* Heather Brinkman, Graduate Contact, 765-494-2345, Fax: 765-494-5832, E-mail: hbrinkma@purdue.edu.
Website: http://www.edst.purdue.edu/

Regent University, Graduate School, School of Education, Virginia Beach, VA 23464-9800. Offers education (M Ed, Ed D, PhD), including adult education (Ed D, PhD, Ed S), advanced educational leadership (Ed D, PhD, Ed S), character education (Ed D, PhD, Ed S), Christian education leadership (Ed D, PhD, Ed S), Christian school administration (M Ed), curriculum and instruction (Ed D, PhD, Ed S), curriculum and instruction - adult education (M Ed), curriculum and instruction - Christian school (M Ed), curriculum and instruction - gifted and talented (M Ed), curriculum and instruction - STEM education (M Ed), curriculum and instruction - teacher leader (M Ed), discipleship for ministry (M Ed), educational leadership (M Ed), educational psychology (Ed D, PhD, Ed S), educational technology and online learning (Ed D, PhD, Ed S), elementary education (M Ed), exceptional education executive leadership (Ed D, PhD, Ed S), higher education (Ed D, PhD, Ed S), higher education leadership and management (Ed D, PhD, Ed S), instructional design and technology (M Ed), K-12 school leadership (Ed D, PhD, Ed S), K-12 special education (M Ed), leadership in mathematics education (M Ed), reading specialist (M Ed), special education (Ed D, PhD, Ed S), student affairs (M Ed), TESOL - adult education (M Ed), TESOL - K-12 (M Ed); educational specialist (Ed S), including adult education (Ed D, PhD, Ed S), advanced educational leadership (Ed D, PhD, Ed S), character education (Ed D, PhD, Ed S), Christian education leadership (Ed D, PhD, Ed S), curriculum and instruction (Ed D, PhD, Ed S), educational psychology (Ed D, PhD, Ed S), educational technology and online learning (Ed D, PhD, Ed S), exceptional education executive leadership (Ed D, PhD, Ed S), higher education (Ed D, PhD, Ed S), higher education leadership and management (Ed D, PhD, Ed S), K-12 school leadership (Ed D, PhD, Ed S), special education (Ed D, PhD, Ed S). *Accreditation:* TEAC. *Program availability:* Part-time, evening/weekend, 100% online, blended/hybrid learning. *Faculty:* 22 full-time (10 women), 44 part-time/adjunct (32 women). *Students:* 80 full-time (59 women), 945 part-time (750 women); includes 432 minority (352 Black or African American, non-Hispanic/Latino; 4 American Indian or Alaska Native, non-Hispanic/Latino; 14 Asian, non-Hispanic/Latino; 43 Hispanic/Latino; 19 Two or more races, non-Hispanic/Latino), 12 international. Average age 40. 1,125 applicants, 49% accepted, 436 enrolled. In 2017, 316 master's, 24 doctorates awarded. *Degree requirements:* For master's, thesis or alternative; for doctorate, comprehensive exam, thesis/dissertation. *Entrance requirements:* For master's, Virginia Communication and Literacy Assessment (VCLA), PRAXIS, college transcripts, writing sample, interview; for doctorate, GRE, writing sample, resume, transcripts, interview. Additional exam requirements/recommendations for international students: Required—TOEFL (minimum score 577 paper-based). *Application deadline:* For fall admission, 4/1 priority date for domestic students; for spring admission, 10/15 priority date for domestic students. Applications are processed on a rolling basis. Application fee: $50. Electronic applications accepted. *Expenses:* Contact institution. *Financial support:* In 2017–18, 669 students received support, including 1 fellowship (averaging $10,000 per year); career-related internships or fieldwork, scholarships/grants, and unspecified assistantships also available. Support available to part-time students. *Faculty research:* Christian school administration, curriculum and instruction, educational technology and online learning, higher education, special education. *Unit head:* Dr. Donald Finn, Dean, 757-352-4278, Fax: 757-352-4318, E-mail: dfinn@regent.edu. *Application contact:* Heidi Cece, Assistant Vice President of Enrollment Management, 800-373-5504, Fax: 757-352-4381, E-mail: admissions@regent.edu.
Website: https://www.regent.edu/school-of-education/

Rutgers University–New Brunswick, Graduate School of Education, Department of Educational Psychology, Program in Learning, Cognition and Development, Piscataway, NJ 08854-8097. Offers Ed M. *Program availability:* Part-time, evening/weekend. *Entrance requirements:* For master's, GRE General Test, 3 letters of recommendation. Additional exam requirements/recommendations for international students: Required—TOEFL (minimum score 550 paper-based; 83 iBT). Electronic applications accepted. *Faculty research:* Cognitive development, gender roles, cognition and instruction, peer learning, intimacy and early childhood.

Rutgers University–New Brunswick, Graduate School of Education, Doctoral Program in Education, New Brunswick, NJ 08901. Offers educational policy (PhD); educational psychology (PhD); literacy education (PhD); mathematics education (PhD). *Program availability:* Part-time. *Degree requirements:* For doctorate, thesis/dissertation, qualifying exam. *Entrance requirements:* For doctorate, GRE General Test, GRE Subject Test (mathematics education). Additional exam requirements/recommendations for international students: Required—TOEFL (minimum score 575 paper-based; 83 iBT). Electronic applications accepted. *Faculty research:* Literacy education, math education, educational psychology, educational policy, learning sciences.

Simon Fraser University, Office of Graduate Studies and Postdoctoral Fellows, Faculty of Education, Program in Educational Psychology, Burnaby, BC V5A 1S6, Canada. Offers M Ed, MA, PhD. *Program availability:* Part-time, evening/weekend. *Degree requirements:* For master's, comprehensive exam (for some programs), thesis (for some programs), project or thesis; for doctorate, comprehensive exam, thesis/dissertation. *Entrance requirements:* For master's, minimum GPA of 3.0 (on scale of 4.33) or 3.33 based on last 60 credits of undergraduate courses; for doctorate, GRE, minimum GPA of 3.5 (on scale of 4.33). Additional exam requirements/recommendations for international students: Recommended—TOEFL (minimum score 580 paper-based; 93 iBT), IELTS (minimum score 7), TWE (minimum score 5). Electronic applications accepted. *Faculty research:* Autism and social interaction; cultural and personal dimensions in psychological development; early childhood education; social and emotional development; historical emergence, practice, and ongoing development of the constructs of learning disabilities.

Southern Illinois University Carbondale, Graduate School, College of Education and Human Services, Department of Educational Psychology and Special Education, Program in Educational Psychology, Carbondale, IL 62901-4701. Offers MS Ed, PhD. *Accreditation:* NCATE. *Degree requirements:* For master's, thesis; for doctorate, thesis/dissertation. *Entrance requirements:* For master's, GRE General Test, minimum GPA of 2.7; for doctorate, minimum GPA of 3.25. Additional exam requirements/recommendations for international students: Required—TOEFL. *Faculty research:*

Career development, problem-solving, learning and instruction, cognitive development, family assessment.

State University of New York College at Oneonta, Graduate Programs, Division of Education, Department of Educational Psychology, Counseling and Special Education, Oneonta, NY 13820-4015. Offers school counselor K-12 (MS Ed, CAS); special education (MS Ed). *Accreditation:* NCATE. *Program availability:* Part-time, evening/weekend. *Degree requirements:* For master's, comprehensive exam. *Entrance requirements:* For master's, GRE General Test.

Teachers College, Columbia University, Department of Health and Behavior Studies, New York, NY 10027-6696. Offers applied behavior analysis (MA, PhD); applied educational psychology: school psychology (Ed M, PhD); behavioral nutrition (PhD), including nutrition (Ed D, PhD); community health education (MS); community nutrition education (Ed M), including community nutrition education; education of deaf and hard of hearing (MA, PhD); health education (MA, Ed D); hearing impairment (Ed D); intellectual disability/autism (MA, Ed D, PhD); nursing education (Ed D, Advanced Certificate); nutrition and education (MS); nutrition and exercise physiology (MS); nutrition and public health (MS); nutrition education (Ed D), including nutrition (Ed D, PhD); physical disabilities (Ed D); reading specialist (MA); severe or multiple disabilities (MA); special education (Ed M, MA, Ed D); teaching of sign language (MA). *Program availability:* Part-time, evening/weekend. *Students:* 245 full-time (226 women), 242 part-time (219 women); includes 167 minority (52 Black or African American, non-Hispanic/Latino; 2 American Indian or Alaska Native, non-Hispanic/Latino; 55 Asian, non-Hispanic/Latino; 48 Hispanic/Latino; 1 Native Hawaiian or other Pacific Islander, non-Hispanic/Latino; 9 Two or more races, non-Hispanic/Latino), 60 international. Average age 30. 480 applicants, 59% accepted, 157 enrolled. Terminal master's awarded for partial completion of doctoral program. *Unit head:* Prof. Dolores Perin, Chair, E-mail: dp111@tc.columbia.edu. *Application contact:* David Estrella, Director of Admission, 212-678-3305, E-mail: estrella@tc.columbia.edu.
Website: http://www.tc.columbia.edu/health-and-behavior-studies/

Teachers College, Columbia University, Department of Human Development, New York, NY 10027-6696. Offers applied statistics (MS); cognitive studies in education (MA, Ed D, PhD); developmental psychology (MA, Ed D, PhD); educational psychology-human cognition and learning (Ed M, MA, Ed D, PhD); learning analytics (MS); measurement and evaluation (ME, Ed D, PhD); measurement, evaluation, and statistics (MA, MS, Ed D, PhD). *Program availability:* Part-time. *Students:* 155 full-time (105 women), 135 part-time (106 women); includes 93 minority (26 Black or African American, non-Hispanic/Latino; 44 Asian, non-Hispanic/Latino; 21 Hispanic/Latino; 2 Two or more races, non-Hispanic/Latino), 118 international. Average age 29. 459 applicants, 53% accepted, 100 enrolled. *Unit head:* Jim Corter, Chair, E-mail: jec34@tc.columbia.edu. *Application contact:* David Estrella, Director of Admission, 212-678-3305, E-mail: estrella@tc.columbia.edu.
Website: http://www.tc.columbia.edu/human-development/

Temple University, College of Education, Department of Psychological Studies in Education, Philadelphia, PA 19122-6096. Offers applied behavior analysis (MS Ed); counseling psychology (Ed M), including agency counseling, school counseling; educational psychology (Ed M); school psychology (PhD, Ed S). *Accreditation:* APA (one or more programs are accredited). *Program availability:* Part-time, evening/weekend. *Faculty:* 25 full-time (12 women), 23 part-time/adjunct (11 women). *Students:* 255 full-time (191 women), 188 part-time (137 women); includes 136 minority (90 Black or African American, non-Hispanic/Latino; 1 American Indian or Alaska Native, non-Hispanic/Latino; 18 Asian, non-Hispanic/Latino; 14 Hispanic/Latino; 13 Two or more races, non-Hispanic/Latino), 28 international. 376 applicants, 51% accepted, 109 enrolled. In 2017, 129 master's, 27 doctorates, 21 other advanced degrees awarded. Terminal master's awarded for partial completion of doctoral program. *Degree requirements:* For master's, thesis or alternative; for doctorate, thesis/dissertation. *Entrance requirements:* Additional exam requirements/recommendations for international students: Required—TOEFL (minimum score 550 paper-based; 79 iBT). *Application deadline:* For fall admission, 12/15 for international students; for spring admission, 8/1 for international students. Application fee: $60. *Expenses:* Tuition, state resident: full-time $16,164; part-time $898 per credit hour. Tuition, nonresident: full-time $22,158; part-time $1231 per credit hour. *Required fees:* $890; $445 per semester. Full-time tuition and fees vary according to course load, degree level, campus/location and program. *Financial support:* Fellowships, research assistantships with full tuition reimbursements, and teaching assistantships with full tuition reimbursements available. Financial award application deadline: 1/15; financial award applicants required to submit FAFSA. *Unit head:* Dr. Catherine Fiorello, Chair, 215-204-6254, E-mail: catherine.fiorello@temple.edu.
Website: http://education.temple.edu/pse

Tennessee Technological University, College of Graduate Studies, College of Education, Department of Counseling and Psychology, Cookeville, TN 38505. Offers MA, Ed S. *Accreditation:* NCATE (one or more programs are accredited). *Program availability:* Part-time, evening/weekend. *Faculty:* 24 full-time (6 women). *Students:* 38 full-time (35 women), 31 part-time (27 women); includes 6 minority (3 Black or African American, non-Hispanic/Latino; 1 Asian, non-Hispanic/Latino; 1 Hispanic/Latino; 1 Two or more races, non-Hispanic/Latino). 41 applicants, 73% accepted, 16 enrolled. In 2017, 27 master's, 4 other advanced degrees awarded. *Degree requirements:* For master's and Ed S, comprehensive exam, thesis or alternative. *Entrance requirements:* For master's and Ed S, GRE. Additional exam requirements/recommendations for international students: Required—FLS International (completion of Level 18). *Application deadline:* For fall admission, 8/1 for domestic students, 5/1 for international students; for spring admission, 12/1 for domestic students, 10/1 for international students; for summer admission, 5/1 for domestic students, 2/1 for international students. Applications are processed on a rolling basis. Application fee: $35 ($40 for international students). Electronic applications accepted. *Expenses:* Tuition, state resident: full-time $9925; part-time $565 per credit hour. Tuition, nonresident: full-time $22,993; part-time $1291 per credit hour. *Financial support:* Fellowships, research assistantships, teaching assistantships, and career-related internships or fieldwork available. Financial award application deadline: 4/1. *Unit head:* Dr. Barry Stein, Chairperson, 931-372-3457, Fax: 931-372-6319, E-mail: bstein@tntech.edu. *Application contact:* Shelia K. Kendrick, Coordinator of Graduate Studies, 931-372-3808, Fax: 931-372-3497, E-mail: skendrick@tntech.edu.

Texas A&M University, College of Education and Human Development, Department of Educational Psychology, College Station, TX 77843. Offers bilingual education (M Ed, MS); counseling psychology (PhD); educational psychology (M Ed, MS, PhD); educational technology (M Ed); school psychology (PhD); special education (M Ed, MS). *Accreditation:* APA (one or more programs are accredited). *Program availability:* Part-time, evening/weekend, blended/hybrid learning. *Faculty:* 45. *Students:* 165 full-time (131 women), 248 part-time (210 women); includes 144 minority (24 Black or African American, non-Hispanic/Latino; 3 American Indian or Alaska Native, non-Hispanic/Latino; 21 Asian, non-Hispanic/Latino; 84 Hispanic/Latino; 2 Native Hawaiian or other Pacific Islander, non-Hispanic/Latino; 10 Two or more races, non-Hispanic/Latino), 45 international. Average age 33. 171 applicants, 44% accepted, 47 enrolled. In 2017, 141 master's, 28 doctorates awarded. *Degree requirements:* For master's, thesis optional;

for doctorate, thesis/dissertation. *Entrance requirements:* For master's and doctorate, GRE General Test. Additional exam requirements/recommendations for international students: Required—TOEFL (minimum score 550 paper-based; 80 iBT), IELTS (minimum score 6), PTE (minimum score 53). *Application deadline:* For fall admission, 12/1 for domestic students; for spring admission, 10/15 for domestic students. Application fee: $50 ($90 for international students). Electronic applications accepted. *Expenses:* Contact institution. *Financial support:* In 2017–18, 210 students received support, including 4 fellowships with tuition reimbursements available (averaging $24,775 per year), 102 research assistantships with tuition reimbursements available (averaging $10,698 per year), 19 teaching assistantships with tuition reimbursements available (averaging $7,177 per year); career-related internships or fieldwork, institutionally sponsored loans, scholarships/grants, traineeships, health care benefits, tuition waivers (full and partial), and unspecified assistantships also available. Support available to part-time students. Financial award application deadline: 3/15; financial award applicants required to submit FAFSA. *Unit head:* Dr. Victor Willson, Department Head, 979-845-1394, E-mail: v-willson@tamu.edu. *Application contact:* Kristie Stramaski, Senior Academic Advisor, 979-845-1833, E-mail: epsyadvisor@tamu.edu. Website: http://epsy.tamu.edu.

Texas A&M University–Central Texas, Graduate Studies and Research, Killeen, TX 76549. Offers accounting (MS); business administration (MBA); clinical mental health counseling (MS); criminal justice (MCJ); curriculum and instruction (M Ed); educational administration (M Ed); educational psychology - experimental psychology (MS); history (MA); human resource management (MS); information systems (MS); liberal studies (MS); management and leadership (MS); marriage and family therapy (MS); mathematics (MS); political science (MA); school counseling (M Ed); school psychology (Ed S).

Texas A&M University–Commerce, College of Education and Human Services, Commerce, TX 75429. Offers counseling (M Ed, MS, PhD); early childhood education (M Ed, MS); educational administration (M Ed, MS, Ed D); educational psychology (PhD); educational technology leadership (M Ed, MS); educational technology library science (M Ed, MS); elementary education (M Ed); health, kinesiology and sports studies (MS); higher education (MS, Ed D); psychology (MS); reading (M Ed, MS); secondary education (M Ed, MS); social work (MSW); special education (M Ed, MS); supervision, curriculum and instruction-elementary education (Ed D); training and development (MS). *Program availability:* Part-time, evening/weekend, 100% online, blended/hybrid learning. *Faculty:* 91 full-time (51 women), 38 part-time/adjunct (31 women). *Students:* 400 full-time (310 women) 1,400 part-time (1,117 women); includes 724 minority (412 Black or African American, non-Hispanic/Latino; 8 American Indian or Alaska Native, non-Hispanic/Latino; 24 Asian, non-Hispanic/Latino; 220 Hispanic/Latino; 60 Two or more races, non-Hispanic/Latino), 18 international. Average age 37. 951 applicants, 46% accepted, 331 enrolled. In 2017, 564 master's, 24 doctorates awarded. *Degree requirements:* For master's, comprehensive exam, thesis optional, departmental qualifying exams (for some programs); for doctorate, comprehensive exam, thesis/dissertation, departmental qualifying exam; for SSP, comprehensive exam, thesis optional. *Entrance requirements:* For master's and doctorate, GRE General Test. Additional exam requirements/recommendations for international students: Required—TOEFL (minimum score 550 paper-based; 79 iBT), IELTS (minimum score 6). *Application deadline:* For fall admission, 6/1 priority date for international students; for spring admission, 10/15 priority date for international students; for summer admission, 3/15 priority date for international students. Applications are processed on a rolling basis. Application fee: $50. Electronic applications accepted. *Expenses:* Tuition, state resident: full-time $3630. Tuition, nonresident: full-time $11,100. *Required fees:* $2564. Tuition and fees vary according to course load, degree level and program. *Financial support:* In 2017–18, 84 students received support, including 40 research assistantships with partial tuition reimbursements available (averaging $10,800 per year), 12 teaching assistantships with partial tuition reimbursements available (averaging $13,000 per year); career-related internships or fieldwork, Federal Work-Study, institutionally sponsored loans, scholarships/grants, health care benefits, and unspecified assistantships also available. Financial award application deadline: 6/15; financial award applicants required to submit FAFSA. *Faculty research:* Cognitive and bilingual education, positive behavioral intervention, literacy, math readiness. *Total annual research expenditures:* $1.1 million. *Unit head:* Dr. Timothy Letzring, Dean, 903-886-5181, Fax: 903-886-5905, E-mail: tim.letzring@tamuc.edu. *Application contact:* Vicky Turner, Doctoral Degree and Special Programs Coordinator, 903-886-5167, E-mail: vicky.turner@tamuc.edu. Website: http://www.tamuc.edu/academics/graduateSchool/programs/education/default.aspx

Texas Tech University, Graduate School, College of Education, Department of Educational Psychology and Leadership, Lubbock, TX 79409. Offers counselor education (M Ed, PhD); educational leadership (M Ed, Ed D, PhD); educational psychology (M Ed, PhD); higher education (M Ed); higher education administration (Ed D); higher education research (PhD); instructional technology (M Ed, Ed D); special education (M Ed, Ed D, PhD). *Accreditation:* ACA; NCATE. *Program availability:* Part-time, evening/weekend. *Faculty:* 64 full-time (30 women), 6 part-time/adjunct (all women). *Students:* 263 full-time (193 women), 637 part-time (490 women); includes 307 minority (84 Black or African American, non-Hispanic/Latino; 3 American Indian or Alaska Native, non-Hispanic/Latino; 4 Asian, non-Hispanic/Latino; 193 Hispanic/Latino; 23 Two or more races, non-Hispanic/Latino), 48 international. Average age 36. 510 applicants, 47% accepted, 185 enrolled. In 2017, 209 master's, 64 doctorates awarded. Terminal master's awarded for partial completion of doctoral program. *Degree requirements:* For master's, comprehensive exam, thesis optional; for doctorate, comprehensive exam, thesis/dissertation. *Entrance requirements:* For master's, GRE (for some programs); for doctorate, GRE. Additional exam requirements/recommendations for international students: Required—TOEFL (minimum score 550 paper-based; 79 iBT). *Application deadline:* For fall admission, 6/1 priority date for domestic students, 1/15 priority date for international students; for spring admission, 9/1 priority date for domestic students, 6/15 priority date for international students. Applications are processed on a rolling basis. Application fee: $60. Electronic applications accepted. *Expenses:* Contact institution. *Financial support:* In 2017–18, 366 students received support, including 360 fellowships (averaging $3,231 per year), 63 research assistantships (averaging $11,899 per year); teaching assistantships, scholarships/grants, and unspecified assistantships also available. Support available to part-time students. Financial award application deadline: 1/3; financial award applicants required to submit FAFSA. *Faculty research:* Cognitive, motivational, and developmental processes in learning; counseling education; instructional technology; generic special education and sensory impairment; community college administration; K-12 school administration. *Total annual research expenditures:* $127,956. *Unit head:* Dr. Hansel Burley, Chair, 806-834-5135, Fax: 806-742-2179, E-mail: hansel.burley@ttu.edu. *Application contact:* Pam Smith, Admissions Advisor, 806-834-2969, Fax: 806-742-2179, E-mail: pam.smith@ttu.edu. Website: http://www.educ.ttu.edu/

Universidad de Iberoamerica, Graduate School, San Jose, Costa Rica. Offers clinical neuropsychology (PhD); clinical psychology (M Psych); educational psychology (M Psych); forensic psychology (M Psych); hospital management (MHA); intensive care nursing (MN); medicine (MD).

Université de Moncton, Faculty of Education, Graduate Studies in Education, Moncton, NB E1A 3E9, Canada. Offers educational psychology (M Ed, MA Ed); guidance (M Ed, MA Ed); school administration (M Ed, MA Ed); teaching (M Ed, MA Ed). *Program availability:* Part-time. *Degree requirements:* For master's, proficiency in English and French. *Entrance requirements:* For master's, minimum GPA of 3.0. *Faculty research:* Guidance, ethnolinguistic vitality, children's rights, ecological education, entrepreneurship.

Université de Montréal, Faculty of Education, Department of Psychopedagogy and Andragogy, Montréal, QC H3C 3J7, Canada. Offers M Ed, MA, PhD, DESS. *Program availability:* Part-time, evening/weekend. Terminal master's awarded for partial completion of doctoral program. *Degree requirements:* For master's, thesis (for some programs); for doctorate, thesis/dissertation, general exam. *Entrance requirements:* For doctorate, MA or M Ed. Electronic applications accepted.

Université du Québec à Trois-Rivières, Graduate Programs, Program in Psychoeducation, Trois-Rivières, QC G9A 5H7, Canada. Offers M Ed, PhD. M Ed offered jointly with Université du Québec en Outaouais. *Entrance requirements:* For master's, appropriate bachelor's degree, proficiency in French. *Faculty research:* Troubled youth intervention.

Université du Québec en Outaouais, Graduate Programs, Program in Psychoeducation, Gatineau, QC J8X 3X7, Canada. Offers M Ed, MA. *Program availability:* Part-time. *Degree requirements:* For master's, thesis (for some programs). *Entrance requirements:* For master's, appropriate bachelor's degree, proficiency in French.

Université Laval, Faculty of Education, Department of Teaching and Learning Studies, Programs in Educational Psychology, Québec, QC G1K 7P4, Canada. Offers MA, PhD. Terminal master's awarded for partial completion of doctoral program. *Degree requirements:* For master's, thesis (for some programs); for doctorate, comprehensive exam, thesis/dissertation. *Entrance requirements:* For master's and doctorate, English exam (comprehension of written English), knowledge of French. Electronic applications accepted. *Faculty research:* Emotional, social, and cognitive development; learning and motivation in school; language development; reading acquisition; computer and learning strategies.

University at Buffalo, the State University of New York, Graduate School, Graduate School of Education, Department of Counseling, School, and Educational Psychology, Buffalo, NY 14260. Offers applied statistical analysis (Advanced Certificate); counseling/school psychology (PhD); counselor education (PhD); education studies (Ed M); educational psychology (MA, PhD); mental health counseling (MS, Certificate); mindful counseling for wellness and engagement (Advanced Certificate); rehabilitation counseling (MS, Advanced Certificate); school counseling (Ed M, Certificate). *Accreditation:* CORE (one or more programs are accredited). *Program availability:* Part-time, 100% online. *Faculty:* 21 full-time (11 women), 53 part-time/adjunct (41 women). *Students:* 173 full-time (140 women), 138 part-time (116 women); includes 32 minority (25 Black or African American, non-Hispanic/Latino; 2 American Indian or Alaska Native, non-Hispanic/Latino; 2 Asian, non-Hispanic/Latino; 3 Hispanic/Latino), 16 international. Average age 32. 328 applicants, 59% accepted, 143 enrolled. In 2017, 74 master's, 12 doctorates, 39 other advanced degrees awarded. *Degree requirements:* For master's, comprehensive exam (for some programs), thesis (for some programs); for doctorate, comprehensive exam, thesis/dissertation. *Entrance requirements:* For master's, GRE General Test, interview, letters of reference; for doctorate, GRE General Test, interview, letters of reference, writing sample. Additional exam requirements/recommendations for international students: Required—TOEFL (minimum score 79 iBT). *Application deadline:* For fall admission, 2/1 priority date for domestic and international students. Application fee: $50. Electronic applications accepted. *Financial support:* In 2017–18, 22 fellowships (averaging $7,823 per year), 41 research assistantships with tuition reimbursements (averaging $10,876 per year) were awarded; teaching assistantships, career-related internships or fieldwork, Federal Work-Study, institutionally sponsored loans, scholarships/grants, tuition waivers (full and partial), and unspecified assistantships also available. Financial award application deadline: 2/1; financial award applicants required to submit FAFSA. *Faculty research:* Multicultural counseling, class size effects, good work in counseling, eating disorders, outcome assessment, change agents and therapeutic factors in group counseling. *Total annual research expenditures:* $1.3 million. *Unit head:* Dr. Jeremy Finn, Chair, 716-645-1126, Fax: 716-645-6616, E-mail: finn@buffalo.edu. *Application contact:* Baylee Richards, Recruitment and Student Services Coordinator, 716-645-2110, Fax: 716-645-7937, E-mail: gse-info@buffalo.edu. Website: http://gse.buffalo.edu/csep

University of Alberta, Faculty of Graduate Studies and Research, Department of Educational Psychology, Edmonton, AB T6G 2E1, Canada. Offers counseling psychology (M Ed, PhD); educational psychology (M Ed, PhD); instructional technology (M Ed); school counseling (M Ed); school psychology (M Ed, PhD); special education (M Ed, PhD); special education-deafness studies (M Ed); teaching English as a second language (M Ed). *Program availability:* Part-time. *Degree requirements:* For master's, thesis optional; for doctorate, comprehensive exam, thesis/dissertation. *Entrance requirements:* For master's and doctorate, minimum GPA of 3.0. Additional exam requirements/recommendations for international students: Required—TOEFL. *Faculty research:* Human learning, development and assessment.

The University of Arizona, College of Education, Department of Educational Psychology, Tucson, AZ 85721. Offers educational psychology (MA, PhD); educational research methodology (Certificate); motivating learning environments (Certificate). *Accreditation:* APA (one or more programs are accredited). *Program availability:* Part-time. Terminal master's awarded for partial completion of doctoral program. *Degree requirements:* For master's, comprehensive exam (for some programs), thesis optional; for doctorate, comprehensive exam, thesis/dissertation. *Entrance requirements:* For master's, minimum GPA of 3.0, 3 letters of recommendation, 500-word professional writing sample; for doctorate, GRE General Test, minimum GPA of 3.0, 3 letters of recommendation, statement of purpose, 500-word professional writing sample. Additional exam requirements/recommendations for international students: Required—TOEFL (minimum score 600 paper-based). Electronic applications accepted. *Faculty research:* School reform, motivational learning in classroom settings, measurement and evaluation of learning outcomes, student resilience, preadolescent and adolescent development.

University of California, Davis, Graduate Studies, Graduate Group in Education, Davis, CA 95616. Offers education (MA, Ed D); instructional studies (PhD); psychological studies (PhD); sociocultural studies (PhD). Ed D offered jointly with California State University, Fresno. Terminal master's awarded for partial completion of doctoral program. *Degree requirements:* For master's, comprehensive exam (for some programs), thesis (for some programs); for doctorate, thesis/dissertation. *Entrance requirements:* For master's and doctorate, GRE. Additional exam requirements/recommendations for international students: Required—TOEFL (minimum score 550 paper-based). Electronic applications accepted. *Faculty research:* Language and literacy, mathematics education, science education, teacher development, school psychology.

University of California, Riverside, Graduate Division, Graduate School of Education, Riverside, CA 92521. Offers applied behavior analysis (M Ed); diversity and equity (M Ed); education policy analysis and leadership (PhD); education specialist (Credential); education, society, and culture (MA, PhD); educational psychology (MA, PhD); general education (M Ed); higher education administration and policy (M Ed, PhD); multiple subject (Credential); research, evaluation, measurement and statistics (MA); school psychology (PhD); single subject (Credential); special education (M Ed, PhD); special education and autism (MA); TESOL (M Ed). *Faculty:* 29 full-time (16 women), 2 part-time/adjunct (1 woman). *Students:* 241 full-time (188 women). 396 applicants, 42% accepted, 166 enrolled. In 2017, 130 master's, 15 doctorates, 14 other advanced degrees awarded. Terminal master's awarded for partial completion of doctoral program. *Degree requirements:* For master's, comprehensive exams or thesis (MA), case study or analytical report (M Ed); for doctorate, comprehensive exam, thesis/dissertation, written and oral qualifying exams, college teaching practicum. *Entrance requirements:* For master's, GRE General Test (for MA); CBEST and CSET (for M Ed in general education only), UCR Extension TESOL certificate (for M Ed with TESOL emphasis only); for doctorate, GRE General Test, writing sample; for Credential, CBEST, CSET. Additional exam requirements/recommendations for international students: Required—TOEFL (minimum score 550 paper-based; 80 iBT), IELTS (minimum score 7). *Application deadline:* For fall admission, 9/1 for domestic students, 6/1 for international students; for winter admission, 11/15 for domestic students, 9/1 for international students; for spring admission, 3/1 for domestic students, 12/1 for international students. Applications are processed on a rolling basis. Application fee: $80 ($100 for international students). Electronic applications accepted. *Expenses:* Tuition, state resident: full-time $5746. Tuition, nonresident: full-time $10,780. Tuition and fees vary according to campus/location and program. *Financial support:* In 2017–18, 105 students received support, including 16 fellowships with full tuition reimbursements available (averaging $31,000 per year), 25 research assistantships with full tuition reimbursements available (averaging $31,000 per year), 10 teaching assistantships with full tuition reimbursements available (averaging $31,000 per year); career-related internships or fieldwork, Federal Work-Study, institutionally sponsored loans, scholarships/grants, and unspecified assistantships also available. Financial award application deadline: 12/15. *Faculty research:* Responsiveness to intervention, faculty core, response to intervention of English language learners, advanced modeling techniques, study on social capital, trust, and motivation. *Total annual research expenditures:* $1.7 million. *Unit head:* Thomas Smith, Dean, 951-827-4633, E-mail: thomas.smith@ucr.edu. *Application contact:* Heather Killeen, Graduate Program Coordinator, 951-827-6362, E-mail: heather.killeen@ucr.edu.
Website: http://www.education.ucr.edu/

University of Colorado Boulder, Graduate School, School of Education, Division of Educational and Psychological Studies, Boulder, CO 80309. Offers MA, PhD. *Accreditation:* NCATE. *Students:* 19 full-time (14 women), 5 part-time (1 woman); includes 11 minority (6 Black or African American, non-Hispanic/Latino; 4 Hispanic/Latino; 1 Native Hawaiian or other Pacific Islander, non-Hispanic/Latino), 1 international. Average age 32. 57 applicants, 21% accepted, 4 enrolled. In 2017, 4 master's, 2 doctorates awarded. Terminal master's awarded for partial completion of doctoral program. *Degree requirements:* For master's, comprehensive exam, thesis or alternative; for doctorate, one foreign language, comprehensive exam, thesis/dissertation. *Entrance requirements:* For master's, GRE General Test or MAT, minimum undergraduate GPA of 2.75; for doctorate, GRE General Test. *Application deadline:* For fall admission, 12/1 for domestic and international students; for spring admission, 9/1 for domestic and international students. Application fee: $60 ($80 for international students). Electronic applications accepted. Application fee is waived when completed online. *Financial support:* In 2017–18, 57 students received support, including 17 fellowships (averaging $5,081 per year), 12 research assistantships with full and partial tuition reimbursements available (averaging $31,498 per year), 6 teaching assistantships with full and partial tuition reimbursements available (averaging $10,004 per year); institutionally sponsored loans, scholarships/grants, health care benefits, and unspecified assistantships also available. Financial award application deadline: 2/15; financial award applicants required to submit FAFSA. *Application contact:* E-mail: edadvise@colorado.edu.
Website: http://www.colorado.edu/education/

University of Colorado Denver, School of Education and Human Development, Programs in Educational and School Psychology, Denver, CO 80217. Offers educational psychology (MA), including educational assessment, educational psychology, human development, human learning, research and evaluation; school psychology (Psy D, Ed S). MA program also offered in partnership with Boulder Journey School, Friends' School and Stanley British Primary School. *Program availability:* Part-time, evening/weekend. *Degree requirements:* For master's, comprehensive exam, 9 hours of core courses, embedded within a minimum of 36 to 38 hours of relevant coursework, including an educational psychology practicum, independent study project or thesis (recommended); for Ed S, comprehensive exam, minimum of 75 semester hours (61 hours of coursework, 6 of 500-hour practicum in field, and 8 of 1200-hour internship); PRAXIS II. *Entrance requirements:* For master's, GRE if undergraduate GPA below 2.75, resume, three letters of recommendation, transcripts; for Ed S, GRE, resume, letters of recommendation, transcripts. Additional exam requirements/recommendations for international students: Required—TOEFL (minimum score 537 paper-based; 75 iBT); Recommended—IELTS (minimum score 6.5). Electronic applications accepted. *Expenses:* Contact institution. *Faculty research:* Crisis response and intervention, school violence prevention, immigrant experience, educational environments for English language learners, culturally competent assessment and intervention, child and youth suicide.

University of Connecticut, Graduate School, Neag School of Education, Department of Educational Psychology, Storrs, CT 06269. Offers cognition and instruction (MA, PhD). *Degree requirements:* For master's, comprehensive exam; for doctorate, thesis/dissertation. *Entrance requirements:* For doctorate, GRE General Test. Additional exam requirements/recommendations for international students: Required—TOEFL (minimum score 550 paper-based). Electronic applications accepted.

University of Georgia, College of Education, Department of Educational Psychology, Athens, GA 30602. Offers educational psychology (Ed S). *Accreditation:* NCATE. *Entrance requirements:* For degree, GRE General Test or MAT. Electronic applications accepted.

University of Hawaii at Manoa, Office of Graduate Education, College of Education, Department of Educational Psychology, Honolulu, HI 96822. Offers M Ed, PhD. *Program availability:* Part-time. *Degree requirements:* For master's, thesis optional; for doctorate, comprehensive exam, thesis/dissertation. *Entrance requirements:* Additional exam requirements/recommendations for international students: Required—TOEFL (minimum score 600 paper-based; 100 iBT), IELTS (minimum score 7). *Faculty research:* Human learning and development, measurement, research methods, statistics.

University of Hawaii at Manoa, Office of Graduate Education, College of Education, PhD in Education Program, Honolulu, HI 96822. Offers curriculum and instruction (PhD); educational administration (PhD); educational foundations (PhD); educational policy studies (PhD); educational psychology (PhD); exceptionalities (PhD); kinesiology (PhD); learning design and technology (PhD). *Program availability:* Part-time, evening/weekend. *Degree requirements:* For doctorate, thesis/dissertation. *Entrance requirements:* For doctorate, GRE General Test, sample of written work. Additional exam requirements/recommendations for international students: Required—TOEFL (minimum score 600 paper-based; 100 iBT), IELTS (minimum score 7).

University of Houston, College of Education, Department of Educational Psychology, Houston, TX 77204. Offers administration and supervision - higher education (M Ed); counseling (M Ed); counseling psychology (PhD); educational psychology (M Ed); school psychology (PhD); school psychology and individual differences (PhD); special education (M Ed). *Accreditation:* NCATE. *Program availability:* Part-time, evening/weekend, online learning. *Degree requirements:* For master's, comprehensive exam or thesis; for doctorate, comprehensive exam, thesis/dissertation. *Entrance requirements:* For master's, GRE, transcripts, 3 letters of recommendation, curriculum vita, goal statement; for doctorate, GRE, transcripts, 3 letters of recommendation, curriculum vita, goal statement, writing sample, interview. Additional exam requirements/recommendations for international students: Required—TOEFL (minimum score 550 paper-based; 79 iBT), IELTS (minimum score 6.5). Electronic applications accepted. *Faculty research:* Evidence-based assessment and intervention, multicultural issues in psychology, social and cultural context of learning, systemic barriers to college, motivational aspects of self-regulated learning.

University of Illinois at Chicago, College of Education, Department of Educational Psychology, Chicago, IL 60607-7128. Offers early childhood education (M Ed); educational psychology (PhD); measurement, evaluation, statistics, and assessment (M Ed); youth development (M Ed). *Program availability:* Part-time, online learning. *Faculty research:* Children's construction of morality, development of resilience in the face of enduring economical difficulties, cognition and cognitive development, test fairness.

University of Illinois at Urbana–Champaign, Graduate College, College of Education, Department of Educational Psychology, Champaign, IL 61820. Offers Ed M, MA, MS, PhD, CAS. *Accreditation:* APA (one or more programs are accredited). *Program availability:* Part-time, online learning.

The University of Iowa, Graduate College, College of Education, Department of Psychological and Quantitative Foundations, Iowa City, IA 52242-1316. Offers counseling psychology (PhD); educational measurement and statistics (MA, PhD); educational psychology (MA, PhD); school psychology (PhD, Ed S). *Accreditation:* APA. *Degree requirements:* For master's, thesis optional, exam; for doctorate, comprehensive exam, thesis/dissertation; for Ed S, exam. *Entrance requirements:* For master's, doctorate, and Ed S, GRE General Test, minimum GPA of 3.0. Additional exam requirements/recommendations for international students: Required—TOEFL (minimum score 550 paper-based; 81 iBT). Electronic applications accepted.

The University of Kansas, Graduate Studies, School of Education, Department of Educational Psychology, Program in Educational Psychology and Research, Lawrence, KS 66045. Offers MS Ed, PhD. *Program availability:* Part-time. *Students:* 40 full-time (21 women), 4 part-time (3 women); includes 5 minority (2 Black or African American, non-Hispanic/Latino; 2 Asian, non-Hispanic/Latino; 1 Hispanic/Latino), 20 international. Average age 32. 25 applicants, 76% accepted, 8 enrolled. In 2017, 7 master's, 3 doctorates awarded. *Entrance requirements:* For master's, GRE General Test, minimum GPA of 3.0, resume, statement of purpose, official transcripts, three recommendation letters; for doctorate, GRE General Test, resume, statement of purpose, official transcripts, three recommendation letters. *Application deadline:* For fall admission, 12/15 for domestic and international students. Application fee: $65 ($85 for international students). Electronic applications accepted. *Financial support:* Fellowships, research assistantships, teaching assistantships, career-related internships or fieldwork, institutionally sponsored loans, scholarships/grants, traineeships, health care benefits, tuition waivers (full and partial), and unspecified assistantships available. Support available to part-time students. Financial award application deadline: 12/15. *Faculty research:* Educational measurement, applied statistics, research design, program evaluation, learning and development. *Unit head:* Steven Wayne Lee, Chair, 785-864-9701, E-mail: swlee@ku.edu. *Application contact:* Penny Fritts, Admissions Coordinator, 785-864-9645, E-mail: fritts@ku.edu.
Website: http://www.soe.ku.edu/PRE/

University of Kentucky, Graduate School, College of Education, Program in Educational and Counseling Psychology, Lexington, KY 40506-0032. Offers counseling psychology (MS, PhD, Ed S); educational psychology (MS, PhD); school psychology (PhD, Ed S). *Accreditation:* APA (one or more programs are accredited); NCATE. *Degree requirements:* For doctorate, comprehensive exam, thesis/dissertation; for Ed S, comprehensive exam. *Entrance requirements:* For doctorate, GRE General Test, minimum graduate GPA of 3.0; for Ed S, GRE General Test. Additional exam requirements/recommendations for international students: Required—TOEFL (minimum score 550 paper-based). Electronic applications accepted.

University of Louisville, Graduate School, College of Education and Human Development, Department of Counseling and Human Development, Louisville, KY 40292-0001. Offers counseling and personnel services (M Ed, PhD), including art therapy (M Ed), clinical mental health counseling (M Ed), college student personnel, counseling psychology, counselor education and supervision (PhD), educational psychology, measurement, and evaluation (PhD), school counseling (M Ed). *Accreditation:* APA; NCATE. *Program availability:* Part-time, evening/weekend. *Students:* 144 full-time (107 women), 63 part-time (44 women); includes 49 minority (32 Black or African American, non-Hispanic/Latino; 1 American Indian or Alaska Native, non-Hispanic/Latino; 3 Asian, non-Hispanic/Latino; 7 Hispanic/Latino; 6 Two or more races, non-Hispanic/Latino), 3 international. Average age 28. 178 applicants, 49% accepted, 51 enrolled. In 2017, 35 master's, 3 doctorates awarded. *Degree requirements:* For doctorate, comprehensive exam, thesis/dissertation. *Entrance requirements:* For master's and doctorate, GRE General Test. Application fee: $65. *Expenses:* Tuition, state resident: full-time $12,246; part-time $681 per credit hour. Tuition, nonresident: full-time $25,486; part-time $1417 per credit hour. *Required fees:* $196. Tuition and fees vary according to course load, program and reciprocity agreements. *Financial support:* Fellowships, research assistantships, teaching assistantships, career-related internships or fieldwork, Federal Work-Study, scholarships/grants, health care benefits, and unspecified assistantships available. Financial award application deadline: 6/1; financial award applicants required to submit FAFSA. *Faculty research:* Mental health services and under-served populations; health disparities and outcomes; well-being identity development; measurement and evaluation. *Total annual research expenditures:* $295,684. *Unit head:* Dr. Mark M. Leach, Interim Chair/Professor, 502-852-0588, Fax: 502-852-0629, E-mail: m.leach@louisville.edu. *Application contact:* Betty Hampton, Director of Graduate Student Services, 502-852-5597, Fax: 502-852-1465, E-mail: edadvise@louisville.edu.
Website: http://www.louisville.edu/education/departments/ecpy

The University of Manchester, School of Education, Manchester, United Kingdom. Offers counseling (D Couns); counseling psychology (D Couns); education (M Phil, Ed D, PhD); educational and child psychology (Ed D); educational psychology (Ed D).

Educational Psychology

University of Manitoba, Faculty of Graduate Studies, Faculty of Education, Department of Educational Administration, Foundations and Psychology, Winnipeg, MB R3T 2N2, Canada. Offers adult and post-secondary education (M Ed); educational administration (M Ed); guidance and counseling (M Ed); inclusive special education (M Ed); social foundations of education (M Ed). *Degree requirements:* For master's, thesis or alternative.

University of Memphis, Graduate School, College of Education, Department of Counseling, Educational Psychology and Research, Memphis, TN 38152. Offers counseling (MS, Ed D), including clinical mental health counseling (MS), clinical rehabilitation counseling (MS), rehabilitation counseling (MS), school counseling (MS); counseling psychology (PhD); educational psychology and research (MS, PhD), including educational psychology, educational research. *Accreditation:* ACA (one or more programs are accredited); APA (one or more programs are accredited); CORE (one or more programs are accredited); NCATE. *Program availability:* Blended/hybrid learning. *Faculty:* 26 full-time (17 women), 8 part-time/adjunct (5 women). *Students:* 132 full-time (111 women), 87 part-time (66 women); includes 71 minority (51 Black or African American, non-Hispanic/Latino; 4 Asian, non-Hispanic/Latino; 10 Hispanic/Latino; 6 Two or more races, non-Hispanic/Latino), 5 international. Average age 31. 146 applicants, 49% accepted, 49 enrolled. In 2017, 39 master's, 13 doctorates awarded. *Degree requirements:* For master's, comprehensive exam, thesis or alternative, internship; for doctorate, comprehensive exam, thesis/dissertation, practicum, internship, residency, scholarly work. *Entrance requirements:* For master's, GRE General Test or MAT, minimum GPA of 2.5, letters of reference, interview; for doctorate, GRE General Test, master's degree or equivalent, letters of reference, interview, curriculum vitae, personal statement. Additional exam requirements/recommendations for international students: Required—TOEFL (minimum score 550 paper-based; 79 iBT). *Application deadline:* For fall admission, 10/1 priority date for domestic students; for spring admission, 4/1 priority date for domestic students. Applications are processed on a rolling basis. Application fee: $35 ($60 for international students). Electronic applications accepted. *Expenses:* Contact institution. *Financial support:* In 2017–18, 130 students received support, including 15 research assistantships with full tuition reimbursements available (averaging $13,426 per year), 12 teaching assistantships with full tuition reimbursements available (averaging $11,976 per year); fellowships with full tuition reimbursements available, career-related internships or fieldwork, Federal Work-Study, scholarships/grants, and unspecified assistantships also available. Financial award application deadline: 2/1; financial award applicants required to submit FAFSA. *Faculty research:* Anger management, aging and disability, supervision, multicultural counseling. *Unit head:* Dr. Steve West, Chair, 901-678-2841, Fax: 901-678-5114, E-mail: slwest@memphis.edu. *Application contact:* Dr. Suzanne Lease, Interim Assistant Dean of Education and Graduate Programs, 901-678-4476, Fax: 901-678-4778, E-mail: slease@memphis.edu.
Website: http://www.memphis.edu/cepr/

University of Minnesota, Twin Cities Campus, Graduate School, College of Education and Human Development, Department of Educational Psychology, Minneapolis, MN 55455-0213. Offers autism spectrum disorder (Certificate); counseling and student personnel psychology (MA); early childhood special education (M Ed); psychological foundations of education (MA, PhD); quantitative methods in education (MA, PhD); school psychology (MA, PhD, Ed S); special education (M Ed, MA, PhD); talent development and gifted education (Certificate). *Accreditation:* APA (one or more programs are accredited). *Faculty:* 30 full-time (15 women). *Students:* 250 full-time (185 women), 63 part-time (49 women); includes 49 minority (6 Black or African American, non-Hispanic/Latino; 19 Asian, non-Hispanic/Latino; 14 Hispanic/Latino; 10 Two or more races, non-Hispanic/Latino), 36 international. Average age 29. 264 applicants, 45% accepted, 110 enrolled. In 2017, 94 master's, 18 doctorates, 10 other advanced degrees awarded. Application fee: $75 ($95 for international students). *Financial support:* In 2017–18, 22 fellowships, 63 research assistantships (averaging $14,194 per year), 37 teaching assistantships (averaging $10,351 per year) were awarded. *Faculty research:* Achievement gap; autism; behavioral and social-emotional development; improving skills in mathematics, reading, and comprehension; measuring and analyzing student change. *Total annual research expenditures:* $6 million. *Unit head:* Dr. Geoffrey Maruyama, Chair, 612-624-1003, Fax: 612-625-5861, E-mail: geoff@umn.edu. *Application contact:* Dr. Ernest Davenport, Director of Graduate Studies, 612-624-1040, E-mail: lqr6576@umn.edu.
Website: http://www.cehd.umn.edu/EdPsych

University of Missouri, Office of Research and Graduate Studies, College of Education, Department of Educational, School, and Counseling Psychology, Columbia, MO 65211. Offers counseling psychology (M Ed, MA, PhD, Ed S); educational psychology (M Ed, MA, PhD, Ed S); learning and instruction (M Ed); school psychology (M Ed, MA, PhD, Ed S). *Accreditation:* APA (one or more programs are accredited). *Program availability:* Part-time. *Degree requirements:* For doctorate, thesis/dissertation. *Entrance requirements:* For master's, doctorate, and Ed S, GRE General Test, minimum GPA of 3.0. Additional exam requirements/recommendations for international students: Required—TOEFL (minimum score 580 paper-based; 92 iBT). Electronic applications accepted.

University of Missouri–St. Louis, College of Education, Interdisciplinary Doctoral Programs, St. Louis, MO 63121. Offers counseling (PhD); educational leadership and policy studies (PhD); educational psychology (PhD); leadership in educational practice (Ed D); teaching-learning processes (PhD). *Faculty:* 50 full-time (29 women), 82 part-time/adjunct (66 women). *Students:* 131 full-time (98 women), 428 part-time (319 women); includes 174 minority (126 Black or African American, non-Hispanic/Latino; 3 American Indian or Alaska Native, non-Hispanic/Latino; 13 Asian, non-Hispanic/Latino; 27 Hispanic/Latino; 5 Two or more races, non-Hispanic/Latino), 11 international. 187 applicants, 84% accepted, 121 enrolled. *Degree requirements:* For doctorate, thesis/dissertation. *Entrance requirements:* For doctorate, GRE General Test, 3 letters of recommendation; personal interview. Additional exam requirements/recommendations for international students: Recommended—TOEFL (minimum score 550 paper-based; 79 iBT), IELTS (minimum score 6.5). *Application deadline:* For fall admission, 3/1 for domestic and international students; for spring admission, 10/1 for domestic and international students. Application fee: $50 ($40 for international students). Electronic applications accepted. *Expenses:* Tuition, state resident: part-time $476.50 per credit hour. Tuition, nonresident: part-time $1169.70 per credit hour. *Financial support:* Research assistantships and teaching assistantships available. Financial award application deadline: 4/1; financial award applicants required to submit FAFSA. *Faculty research:* Higher education law and policy, gender and higher education, student retention, lifelong learning orientation, school counselor's role in violence prevention. *Unit head:* Dr. Kathleen Haywood, Director of Graduate Studies, 314-516-5483, Fax: 314-516-5227, E-mail: kathleen_haywood@umsl.edu. *Application contact:* 314-516-5458, Fax: 314-516-6996, E-mail: gradadm@umsl.edu.

University of Nebraska–Lincoln, Graduate College, College of Education and Human Sciences, Department of Educational Psychology, Lincoln, NE 68588. Offers cognition, learning and development (MA); counseling psychology (MA); educational psychology (MA, Ed S); psychological studies in education (PhD), including cognition, learning and development, counseling psychology, quantitative, qualitative, and psychometric

methods, school psychology; quantitative, qualitative, and psychometric methods (MA); school psychology (MA, Ed S). *Accreditation:* APA (one or more programs are accredited); NCATE. *Degree requirements:* For master's, thesis optional. *Entrance requirements:* For master's, GRE General Test. Additional exam requirements/recommendations for international students: Required—TOEFL (minimum score 500 paper-based). Electronic applications accepted. *Faculty research:* Measurement and assessment, metacognition, academic skills, child development, multicultural education and counseling.

University of Nevada, Reno, Graduate School, College of Education, Department of Counseling and Educational Psychology, Reno, NV 89557. Offers M Ed, MA, MS, Ed D, PhD, Ed S. *Accreditation:* ACA (one or more programs are accredited); NCATE. Terminal master's awarded for partial completion of doctoral program. *Degree requirements:* For master's, comprehensive exam, thesis optional; for doctorate, comprehensive exam, thesis/dissertation, qualifying exam. *Entrance requirements:* For master's, GRE, minimum GPA of 2.75; for doctorate, GRE, minimum GPA of 3.0. Additional exam requirements/recommendations for international students: Required—TOEFL (minimum score 500 paper-based; 61 iBT), IELTS (minimum score 6). Electronic applications accepted. *Faculty research:* Marriage and family counseling, substance abuse attitudes of teachers, current supply of counseling educators, HIV-positive services for patients, family counseling for youth at risk.

University of New Mexico, Graduate Studies, College of Education, Program in Educational Psychology, Albuquerque, NM 87131. Offers MA, PhD. *Accreditation:* NCATE. *Program availability:* Part-time, evening/weekend. *Faculty:* 6 full-time (2 women). *Students:* 7 full-time (4 women), 17 part-time (14 women); includes 10 minority (1 Black or African American, non-Hispanic/Latino; 4 American Indian or Alaska Native, non-Hispanic/Latino; 4 Hispanic/Latino; 1 Two or more races, non-Hispanic/Latino). Average age 37. 1 applicant, 100% accepted, 1 enrolled. In 2017, 4 master's, 4 doctorates awarded. Terminal master's awarded for partial completion of doctoral program. *Degree requirements:* For master's, comprehensive exam (for some programs), thesis (for some programs); for doctorate, comprehensive exam, thesis/dissertation. *Entrance requirements:* For master's, GRE General Test or MAT, minimum GPA of 3.0 in last 2 years of undergraduate study, 3 letters of reference, interview with 3 faculty; for doctorate, GRE General Test or MAT, minimum GPA of 3.0 in last 2 years of undergraduate study, 3 letters of reference, interview with 3 faculty, writing sample. Additional exam requirements/recommendations for international students: Required—TOEFL. *Application deadline:* For fall admission, 3/1 for domestic and international students; for spring admission, 10/1 for domestic and international students. Application fee: $50. Electronic applications accepted. *Financial support:* Teaching assistantships and unspecified assistantships available. Financial award application deadline: 3/1; financial award applicants required to submit FAFSA. *Faculty research:* Measurement and assessment, cognitive strategies, accountability, motivation, instructional technology, educational research, human lifespan development, beliefs. *Unit head:* Dr. Jay Parkes, Department Chair, 505-277-3320, Fax: 505-277-8361, E-mail: edpsy@unm.edu. *Application contact:* Cynthia Salas, Department Administrator, 505-277-4535, Fax: 505-277-8361, E-mail: divbse@unm.edu.
Website: https://coe.unm.edu/departments-programs/ifce/educational-psychology/

The University of North Carolina at Chapel Hill, Graduate School, School of Education, Program in Education, Chapel Hill, NC 27599. Offers culture, curriculum and change (MA, PhD); early childhood, intervention and literacy (MA, PhD); educational psychology, measurement and evaluation (MA, PhD). *Accreditation:* NCATE. *Degree requirements:* For master's, thesis; for doctorate, comprehensive exam, thesis/dissertation. *Entrance requirements:* For master's, GRE General Test, minimum GPA of 3.0 during last 2 years of undergraduates course work; for doctorate, GRE General Test, minimum GPA of 3.0 during last 2 years of undergraduate course work. Additional exam requirements/recommendations for international students: Required—TOEFL (minimum score 550 paper-based). Electronic applications accepted.

University of Northern Colorado, Graduate School, College of Education and Behavioral Sciences, School of Psychological Sciences, Greeley, CO 80639. Offers educational psychology (MA, PhD). *Program availability:* Part-time. *Degree requirements:* For master's, comprehensive exam, thesis or alternative; for doctorate, comprehensive exam, thesis/dissertation. *Entrance requirements:* For master's and doctorate, GRE General Test, letters of recommendation. Electronic applications accepted.

University of Northern Iowa, Graduate College, College of Education, Department of Educational Psychology and Foundations, MAE Program in Educational Psychology: Professional Development for Teachers, Cedar Falls, IA 50614. Offers MAE. *Program availability:* Online learning.

University of North Texas, Robert B. Toulouse School of Graduate Studies, Denton, TX 76203-5459. Offers accounting (MS); applied anthropology (MA, MS); applied behavior analysis (Certificate); applied geography (MA); applied technology and performance improvement (M Ed, MS); art education (MA); art history (MA); art museum education (Certificate); arts leadership (Certificate); audiology (Au D); behavior analysis (MS); behavioral science (PhD); biochemistry and molecular biology (MS); biology (MA, MS); biomedical engineering (MS); business analysis (MS); chemistry (MS); clinical health psychology (PhD); communication studies (MA, MS); computer engineering (MS); computer science (MS); counseling (M Ed, MS), including clinical mental health counseling (MS), college and university counseling, elementary school counseling, secondary school counseling; creative writing (MA); criminal justice (MS); curriculum and instruction (M Ed); decision sciences (MBA); design (MA, MFA), including fashion design (MFA), innovation studies, interior design (MFA); early childhood studies (MS); economics (MS); educational leadership (M Ed, Ed D); educational psychology (MS, PhD), including family studies (MS), gifted and talented (MS), human development (MS), learning and cognition (MS), research, measurement and evaluation (MS); electrical engineering (MS); emergency management (MPA); engineering technology (MS); English (MA); English as a second language (MA); environmental science (MS); finance (MBA, MS); financial management (MPA); French (MA); health services management (MBA); higher education (M Ed, Ed D); history (MA, MS); hospitality management (MS); human resources management (MPA); information science (MS); information systems (PhD); information technologies (MBA); interdisciplinary studies (MA, MS); international studies (MA); international sustainable tourism (MS); jazz studies (MM); journalism (MA, MJ, Graduate Certificate), including interactive and virtual digital communication (Graduate Certificate), narrative journalism (Graduate Certificate), public relations (Graduate Certificate); kinesiology (MS); linguistics (MA); local government management (MPA); logistics (PhD); logistics and supply chain management (MBA); long-term care, senior housing, and aging services (MA); management (PhD); marketing (MBA); mathematics (MA, MS); mechanical and energy engineering (MS, PhD); music (MA), including ethnomusicology, music theory, musicology, performance; music composition (PhD); music education (MM Ed, PhD); nonprofit management (MPA); operations and supply chain management (MBA); performance (MM, DMA); philosophy (MA); political science (MA); professional and technical communication (MA); radio, television and film (MA, MFA); rehabilitation counseling (Certificate); sociology (MA); Spanish (MA); special education (M Ed); speech-language pathology (MA); strategic management (MBA); studio art (MFA); teaching (M Ed); MBA/MS. *Program availability:* Part-time, evening/weekend, online learning. Terminal master's awarded for partial completion of doctoral program. *Degree requirements:* For master's, variable foreign language requirement, comprehensive exam (for some programs), thesis (for some programs); for doctorate, variable foreign language requirement, comprehensive exam (for some programs), thesis/dissertation; for other advanced degree, variable foreign language requirement, comprehensive exam (for some programs). *Entrance requirements:* For master's and doctorate, GRE, GMAT. Additional exam requirements/recommendations for international students: Required—TOEFL (minimum score 550 paper-based; 79 iBT). Electronic applications accepted.

University of Oklahoma, Jeannine Rainbolt College of Education, Department of Educational Psychology, Program in Instructional Psychology and Technology, Norman, OK 73019. Offers educational psychology (M Ed); instructional design and technology (M Ed); instructional psychology and technology (PhD); integrating technology in teaching (M Ed). *Program availability:* Part-time. *Students:* 17 full-time (12 women), 32 part-time (24 women); includes 9 minority (1 Black or African American, non-Hispanic/Latino; 1 American Indian or Alaska Native, non-Hispanic/Latino; 3 Asian, non-Hispanic/Latino; 3 Hispanic/Latino; 1 Two or more races, non-Hispanic/Latino), 10 international. Average age 34. 16 applicants, 63% accepted, 8 enrolled. In 2017, 6 master's, 1 doctorate awarded. Terminal master's awarded for partial completion of doctoral program. *Degree requirements:* For doctorate, comprehensive exam, thesis/dissertation. *Entrance requirements:* For doctorate, GRE. Additional exam requirements/recommendations for international students: Required—TOEFL (minimum score 79 iBT) or IELTS (minimum score 6.5). *Application deadline:* Applications are processed on a rolling basis. Application fee: $50 ($100 for international students). Electronic applications accepted. *Expenses:* Tuition, state resident: full-time $5119; part-time $213.30 per credit hour. Tuition, nonresident: full-time $19,778; part-time $824.10 per credit hour. *Required fees:* $3458; $133.55 per credit hour. $126.50 per semester. *Financial support:* In 2017–18, 23 students received support. Fellowships with full and partial tuition reimbursements available, research assistantships with full and partial tuition reimbursements available, teaching assistantships with full and partial tuition reimbursements available, and scholarships/grants available. Financial award application deadline: 6/1; financial award applicants required to submit FAFSA. *Faculty research:* Social and cultural implications of technologies; girls interest in STEM; epistemic stance; qualitative and mixed-methods research; high-stakes assessments and related educational policy. *Unit head:* Dr. Nancy E. Marchand-Martella, Chair, Department of Educational Psychology, 405-325-0624, Fax: 405-325-6655, E-mail: nmarchand-martella@ou.edu. *Application contact:* Anna Steele, Graduate Programs Specialist, 405-325-4525, Fax: 405-325-7390, E-mail: jrcoe_gps@ou.edu.
Website: http://www.ou.edu/education/edpy.html

University of Regina, Faculty of Graduate Studies and Research, Faculty of Education, Department of Educational Psychology, Regina, SK S4S 0A2, Canada. Offers M Ed. *Program availability:* Part-time. *Faculty:* 5 full-time (2 women), 20 part-time/adjunct (11 women). *Students:* 21 full-time (18 women), 63 part-time (51 women). 56 applicants, 36% accepted. In 2017, 6 master's awarded. *Degree requirements:* For master's, thesis (for some programs), practicum, project, or thesis. *Entrance requirements:* For master's, bachelor's degree in education. Additional exam requirements/recommendations for international students: Required—TOEFL (minimum score 580 paper-based; 80 iBT), IELTS (minimum score 6.5), PTE (minimum score 59). *Application deadline:* For fall admission, 2/15 for domestic and international students; for winter admission, 10/15 for domestic and international students; for spring admission, 2/15 for domestic and international students. Application fee: $100. Electronic applications accepted. *Expenses:* $10,681. *Financial support:* In 2017–18, fellowships (averaging $6,000 per year), 10 teaching assistantships (averaging $2,562 per year) were awarded; research assistantships, career-related internships or fieldwork, and scholarships/grants also available. Financial award application deadline: 6/15. *Faculty research:* Theories of counseling, psychology of learning, aptitude and achievement analysis, education and vocational guidance, resilience: re-conceptualizing PRAXIS. *Unit head:* Dr. Paul Clarke, Dean, Research and Graduate Programs, 306-585-5353, Fax: 306-585-5330, E-mail: paul.clarke@uregina.ca. *Application contact:* Linda Jiang, Graduate Program Coordinator, 306-585-4506, Fax: 306-585-5387, E-mail: edgrad@uregina.ca.
Website: http://www.uregina.ca/education/

University of Saskatchewan, College of Graduate Studies and Research, College of Education, Department of Educational Psychology and Special Education, Saskatoon, SK S7N 5A2, Canada. Offers M Ed, PhD, Diploma. *Degree requirements:* For master's, thesis (for some programs); for doctorate, comprehensive exam (for some programs), thesis/dissertation. *Entrance requirements:* Additional exam requirements/recommendations for international students: Required—TOEFL (minimum score 80 iBT); Recommended—IELTS (minimum score 6.5). Electronic applications accepted.

University of South Africa, College of Human Sciences, Pretoria, South Africa. Offers adult education (M Ed); African languages (MA, PhD); African politics (MA, PhD); Afrikaans (MA, PhD); ancient history (MA, PhD); ancient Near Eastern studies (MA, PhD); anthropology (MA, PhD); applied linguistics (MA); Arabic (MA, PhD); archaeology (MA); art history (MA); Biblical archaeology (MA); Biblical studies (M Th, D Th, PhD); Christian spirituality (M Th, D Th); church history (M Th, D Th); classical studies (MA, PhD); clinical psychology (MA); communication (MA, PhD); comparative education (M Ed, Ed D); consulting psychology (D Admin, D Com, PhD); curriculum studies (M Ed, Ed D); development studies (M Admin, MA, D Admin, PhD); didactics (M Ed, Ed D); education (M Tech); education management (M Ed, Ed D); educational psychology (M Ed); English (MA); environmental education (M Ed); French (MA, PhD); German (MA, PhD); Greek (MA); guidance and counseling (M Ed); health studies (MA, PhD), including health sciences education (MA), health services management (MA), medical and surgical nursing science (critical care general) (MA), midwifery and neonatal nursing science (MA), trauma and emergency care (MA); history (MA, PhD); history of education (Ed D); inclusive education (M Ed, Ed D); information and communications technology policy and regulation (MA); information science (MA, MIS, PhD); international politics (MA, PhD); Islamic studies (MA, PhD); Italian (MA, PhD); Judaica (MA, PhD); linguistics (MA, PhD); mathematical education (M Ed); mathematics education (MA); missiology (M Th, D Th); modern Hebrew (MA, PhD); musicology (MA, MMus, D Mus, PhD); natural science education (M Ed); New Testament (M Th, D Th); Old Testament (D Th); pastoral therapy (M Th, D Th); philosophy (MA); philosophy of education (M Ed, Ed D); politics (MA, PhD); Portuguese (MA, PhD); practical theology (M Th, D Th); psychology (MA, MS, PhD); psychology of education (M Ed, Ed D); public health (MA); religious studies (MA, D Th, PhD); Romance languages (MA); Russian (MA, PhD); Semitic languages (MA, PhD); social behavior studies in HIV/AIDS (MA); social science (mental health) (MA); social science in development studies (MA); social science in psychology (MA); social science in social work (MA); social science in sociology (MA); social work (MSW, DSW, PhD); socio-education (M Ed, Ed D); sociolinguistics (MA); sociology (MA, PhD); Spanish (MA, PhD); systematic theology (M Th, D Th); TESOL (teaching English to speakers of other languages) (MA); theological ethics (M Th, D Th); theory of literature (MA, PhD); urban ministries (D Th); urban ministry (M Th).

University of South Carolina, The Graduate School, College of Education, Department of Educational Studies, Program in Educational Psychology, Research, Columbia, SC 29208. Offers M Ed, PhD. *Accreditation:* NCATE. *Program availability:* Part-time. *Degree requirements:* For master's, comprehensive exam, thesis (for some programs);

for doctorate, comprehensive exam, thesis/dissertation. *Entrance requirements:* For master's, GRE General Test; for doctorate, GRE General Test, interview. Electronic applications accepted. *Faculty research:* Problem solving, higher order thinking skills, psychometric research, methodology.

University of South Dakota, Graduate School, School of Education, Division of Counseling and Psychology in Education, Vermillion, SD 57069. Offers counseling (MA, PhD, Ed S); human development and educational psychology (MA, PhD, Ed S); mental health counseling (Certificate); school psychology (PhD, Ed S). *Accreditation:* ACA (one or more programs are accredited); NCATE. *Program availability:* Part-time. *Degree requirements:* For master's and other advanced degree, comprehensive exam, thesis or alternative; for doctorate, comprehensive exam, thesis/dissertation. *Entrance requirements:* For master's and doctorate, GRE General Test, minimum GPA of 3.0. Additional exam requirements/recommendations for international students: Required—TOEFL (minimum score 550 paper-based; 79 iBT). *Application deadline:* Applications are processed on a rolling basis. Application fee: $35. Electronic applications accepted. *Financial support:* Research assistantships with partial tuition reimbursements, teaching assistantships with partial tuition reimbursements, career-related internships or fieldwork, Federal Work-Study, and unspecified assistantships available. Financial award applicants required to submit FAFSA. *Application contact:* Graduate School, 605-658-6140, Fax: 605-677-6118.
Website: http://www.usd.edu/cpe

University of Southern California, Graduate School, Rossier School of Education, Doctor of Education Programs, Los Angeles, CA 90089. Offers educational psychology (Ed D); higher education administration (Ed D); K-12 leadership in urban school settings (Ed D); teacher education in multicultural societies (Ed D). *Program availability:* Part-time, evening/weekend. *Degree requirements:* For doctorate, thesis/dissertation. *Entrance requirements:* For doctorate, GRE. Additional exam requirements/recommendations for international students: Required—TOEFL (minimum score 100 iBT). Electronic applications accepted. *Faculty research:* Data-driven decision-making in K-12 schools and districts; examination of college and university leadership and management in U. S. and Asia; studies in facilitating student learning; organizational change and the role of leaders; leadership, diversity, learning and accountability.

University of Southern California, Graduate School, Rossier School of Education, Doctor of Philosophy in Education Programs, Los Angeles, CA 90089. Offers educational psychology (PhD); higher education administration and policy (PhD); K-12 policy and practice (PhD). *Degree requirements:* For doctorate, thesis/dissertation, 63 units; qualifying exam; dissertation proposal and defense. *Entrance requirements:* For doctorate, GRE. Additional exam requirements/recommendations for international students: Required—TOEFL (minimum score 100 iBT). Electronic applications accepted. *Faculty research:* Diversity in higher education, organizational change, educational psychology, policy and politics of educational reform, economics of education and education policy.

University of Southern Maine, College of Management and Human Service, School of Education and Human Development, Program in Educational Psychology, Portland, ME 04103. Offers applied behavior analysis (MS, CGS). *Program availability:* Part-time, evening/weekend. *Entrance requirements:* For master's, GRE or MAT. Additional exam requirements/recommendations for international students: Required—TOEFL (minimum score 550 paper-based; 79 iBT). Electronic applications accepted. *Faculty research:* Applied behavior analysis, functional behavioral analysis, positive behavioral interventions and supports.

University of South Florida, College of Education, Department of Educational and Psychological Studies, Tampa, FL 33620-9951. Offers college student affairs (M Ed); counselor education (MA, PhD, Ed S); interdisciplinary education (PhD); school psychology (PhD, Ed S). *Faculty:* 28 full-time (13 women). *Students:* 115 full-time (77 women), 107 part-time (80 women); includes 59 minority (29 Black or African American, non-Hispanic/Latino; 6 Asian, non-Hispanic/Latino; 18 Hispanic/Latino; 1 Native Hawaiian or other Pacific Islander, non-Hispanic/Latino; 5 Two or more races, non-Hispanic/Latino), 23 international. Average age 33. 163 applicants, 72% accepted, 84 enrolled. In 2017, 46 master's, 5 doctorates, 1 other advanced degree awarded. Application fee: $30. *Faculty research:* College student affairs, counselor education, educational psychology, school psychology, social foundations. *Total annual research expenditures:* $9 million. *Unit head:* Dr. Barabara Shircliff, Chair, 813-974-4001, E-mail: shirclif@usf.edu.

The University of Tennessee, Graduate School, College of Education, Health and Human Sciences, Department of Educational Psychology and Counseling, Knoxville, TN 37996. Offers adult education (MS); applied educational psychology (MS); collaborative learning (Ed D); college student personnel (MS); mental health counseling (MS); rehabilitation counseling (MS); school counseling (MS). *Accreditation:* ACA (one or more programs are accredited); CORE (one or more programs are accredited); NCATE. *Program availability:* Part-time, evening/weekend. *Degree requirements:* For master's, thesis optional. *Entrance requirements:* For master's, GRE General Test, minimum GPA of 2.7. Additional exam requirements/recommendations for international students: Required—TOEFL. Electronic applications accepted.

The University of Tennessee, Graduate School, College of Education, Health and Human Sciences, Program in Education, Knoxville, TN 37996. Offers art education (MS); counseling education (PhD); cultural studies in education (PhD); curriculum (MS, Ed S); curriculum, educational research and evaluation (Ed D, PhD); early childhood education (PhD); early childhood special education (MS); education of deaf and hard of hearing (MS); educational administration and policy studies (Ed D, PhD); educational administration and supervision (Ed S); educational psychology (Ed D, PhD); elementary education (MS, Ed S); elementary teaching (MS); English education (MS, Ed S); exercise science (PhD); foreign language/ESL education (MS, Ed S); instructional technology (MS, Ed D, PhD, Ed S); literacy, language and ESL education (PhD); literacy, language education, and ESL education (Ed D); mathematics education (MS, Ed S); modified and comprehensive special education (MS); reading education (MS, Ed S); school counseling (Ed S); school psychology (PhD, Ed S); science education (MS, Ed S); secondary teaching (MS); social foundations (MS); social science education (MS, Ed S); socio-cultural foundations of sports and education (PhD); special education (Ed S); teacher education (Ed D, PhD). *Accreditation:* NCATE. *Program availability:* Part-time, evening/weekend. *Degree requirements:* For master's and Ed S, thesis optional; for doctorate, variable foreign language requirement, thesis/dissertation. *Entrance requirements:* For master's, minimum GPA of 2.7; for doctorate and Ed S, GRE General Test, minimum GPA of 2.7. Additional exam requirements/recommendations for international students: Required—TOEFL. Electronic applications accepted.

The University of Texas at Austin, Graduate School, College of Education, Department of Educational Psychology, Austin, TX 78712-1111. Offers academic educational psychology (M Ed, MA); counseling psychology (PhD); counselor education (M Ed); human development, culture and learning sciences (PhD); program evaluation (MA); quantitative methods (M Ed, MA, PhD); school psychology (MA, PhD). *Accreditation:* APA (one or more programs are accredited). *Degree requirements:* For master's, thesis optional; for doctorate, thesis/dissertation. *Entrance requirements:* For master's and doctorate, GRE General Test, 3 letters of recommendation. Additional exam requirements/recommendations for international students: Required—TOEFL.

Educational Psychology

The University of Texas at El Paso, Graduate School, College of Education, Department of Educational Psychology and Special Services, El Paso, TX 79968-0001. Offers educational diagnostics (M Ed); guidance and counseling (M Ed); special education (M Ed). *Program availability:* Part-time, evening/weekend. *Degree requirements:* For master's, thesis optional. *Entrance requirements:* For master's, minimum GPA of 3.0. Additional exam requirements/recommendations for international students: Required—TOEFL. Electronic applications accepted.

The University of Texas at San Antonio, College of Education and Human Development, Department of Educational Psychology, San Antonio, TX 78207. Offers applied behavior analysis (Certificate); educational psychology (MA), including applied educational psychology, behavior assessment and intervention, general educational psychology, program evaluation; language acquisition and bilingual psychoeducational assessment (Certificate); school psychology (MA). *Program availability:* Part-time. *Faculty:* 9 full-time (5 women), 1 (woman) part-time/adjunct. *Students:* 34 full-time (27 women), 40 part-time (35 women); includes 52 minority (5 Black or African American, non-Hispanic/Latino; 1 Asian, non-Hispanic/Latino; 43 Hispanic/Latino; 3 Two or more races, non-Hispanic/Latino). Average age 28. 46 applicants, 72% accepted, 23 enrolled. In 2017, 16 master's, 23 other advanced degrees awarded. *Degree requirements:* For master's, comprehensive exam, thesis (for some programs). *Entrance requirements:* For master's, GRE, bachelor's degree with 18 credit hours in field of study or in another appropriate field of study, two letters of recommendation, statement of purpose; for Certificate, 18 hours in psychology, sociology, education, or anything related (for applied behavioral analysis); minimum GPA of 2.7 in last 30 hours (for language acquisition and bilingual psychoeducational assessment). Additional exam requirements/ recommendations for international students: Required—TOEFL (minimum score 550 paper-based; 79 iBT), IELTS (minimum score 6.5). *Application deadline:* For fall admission, 6/15 for domestic students, 3/1 for international students; for spring admission, 10/15 for domestic students, 9/15 for international students; for summer admission, 3/1 for international students. Applications are processed on a rolling basis. Application fee: $50 ($90 for international students). Electronic applications accepted. *Expenses:* Tuition, state resident: full-time $5495. Tuition, nonresident: full-time $21,938. *Required fees:* $1915. Tuition and fees vary according to program. *Financial support:* Research assistantships available. Financial award applicants required to submit FAFSA. *Faculty research:* Teacher consultation and culturally responsive school psychology practices, youth mentoring, cross-age peer mentoring, adolescent connectedness, pair counseling. *Total annual research expenditures:* $168,976. *Unit head:* Dr. Jeremy Sullivan, Department Chair, 210-458-2650, Fax: 210-458-2019, E-mail: jeremy.sullivan@utsa.edu.
Website: http://education.utsa.edu/educational_psychology

The University of Texas Rio Grande Valley, College of Education and P-16 Integration, Department of Human Development and School Services, Edinburg, TX 78539. Offers early childhood education (M Ed); early childhood special education (M Ed); school psychology (MA); special education (M Ed). *Program availability:* Part-time, evening/weekend. *Faculty:* 14. *Students:* 131. In 2017, 164 master's awarded. *Degree requirements:* For master's, comprehensive exam (for some programs). *Entrance requirements:* For master's, minimum GPA of 3.0. Additional exam requirements/recommendations for international students: Required—TOEFL (minimum score 550 paper-based; 79 iBT), IELTS (minimum score 6.5). *Application deadline:* For fall admission, 4/15 for domestic students; for spring admission, 11/1 for domestic students; for summer admission, 3/1 for domestic students. Applications are processed on a rolling basis. Application fee: $50 ($75 for international students). Electronic applications accepted. *Expenses:* Tuition, state resident: full-time $5550; part-time $417 per credit hour. Tuition, nonresident: full-time $13,020; part-time $832 per credit hour. *Required fees:* $1169. *Financial support:* Research assistantships, career-related internships or fieldwork, institutionally sponsored loans, and scholarships/grants available. Financial award application deadline: 4/15; financial award applicants required to submit FAFSA. *Faculty research:* Special education, assessment practice, behavior interventions, mental retardation, early childhood. *Unit head:* Dr. John Lowdermilk, Chair, 956-665-3466, E-mail: john.lowdermilk@utrgv.edu. *Application contact:* Stephanie Ozuna, Graduate Student Recruiter, 956-665-3661, E-mail: stephanie.ozuna@utrgv.edu.

University of the Pacific, Gladys L. Benerd School of Education, Stockton, CA 95211-0197. Offers curriculum and instruction (MA, Ed D); education (M Ed); educational administration and leadership (MA, Ed D); educational and school psychology (MA, Ed D); school psychology (Ed S); special education (MA); teacher education (MA). *Accreditation:* NCATE. *Faculty:* 19 full-time (12 women), 48 part-time/adjunct (39 women). *Students:* 141 full-time (115 women), 305 part-time (236 women); includes 219 minority (41 Black or African American, non-Hispanic/Latino; 44 Asian, non-Hispanic/Latino; 105 Hispanic/Latino; 2 Native Hawaiian or other Pacific Islander, non-Hispanic/Latino; 27 Two or more races, non-Hispanic/Latino), 7 international. Average age 33. 144 applicants, 83% accepted, 94 enrolled. In 2017, 231 master's, 8 doctorates awarded. *Degree requirements:* For doctorate, thesis/dissertation. *Entrance requirements:* For master's, GRE General Test; for doctorate, GRE General Test, GRE Subject Test. Additional exam requirements/recommendations for international students: Required—TOEFL. *Application deadline:* For fall admission, 3/1 priority date for domestic students; for spring admission, 10/15 for domestic students. Applications are processed on a rolling basis. Application fee: $75. *Financial support:* Teaching assistantships and institutionally sponsored loans available. Support available to part-time students. Financial award application deadline: 3/1; financial award applicants required to submit FAFSA. *Unit head:* Dr. Vanessa Sheared, Dean, 209-946-2683, E-mail: lwebster@pacific.edu. *Application contact:* Office of Graduate Admissions, 209-946-2344.

The University of Toledo, College of Graduate Studies, Judith Herb College of Education, Department of Educational Foundations and Leadership, Toledo, OH 43606-3390. Offers educational administration and supervision (ME, DE, Ed S); educational psychology (ME, PhD); educational research and measurement (ME, PhD); educational sociology (PhD); educational theory and social foundations (ME); foundations of education (DE, PhD); history of education (PhD); philosophy of education (PhD). *Accreditation:* NCATE. *Program availability:* Part-time, evening/weekend. *Degree requirements:* For master's, comprehensive exam, thesis or alternative; for doctorate, comprehensive exam, thesis/dissertation; for Ed S, thesis optional. *Entrance requirements:* For master's, doctorate, and Ed S, minimum cumulative GPA of 2.7 for all previous academic work, letters of recommendation. Additional exam requirements/recommendations for international students: Required—TOEFL (minimum score 550 paper-based; 80 iBT). Electronic applications accepted.

University of Utah, Graduate School, College of Education, Department of Educational Psychology, Salt Lake City, UT 84112. Offers clinical mental health counseling (M Ed); counseling psychology (PhD); elementary education (M Ed); instructional design and educational technology (M Ed); instructional design and technology (MS); learning and cognition (MS, PhD); reading and literacy (M Ed, PhD); school counseling (M Ed); school psychology (M Ed, PhD, Ed S); statistics (M Stat). *Accreditation:* APA (one or more programs are accredited). *Faculty:* 19 full-time (9 women), 12 part-time/adjunct (8 women). *Students:* 122 full-time (95 women), 97 part-time (68 women); includes 26 minority (4 Asian, non-Hispanic/Latino; 16 Hispanic/Latino; 6 Two or more races, non-Hispanic/Latino), 7 international. Average age 31. 296 applicants, 27% accepted, 73 enrolled. In 2017, 65 master's, 15 doctorates awarded. Terminal master's awarded for partial completion of doctoral program. *Entrance requirements:* For master's and doctorate, GRE General Test, minimum GPA of 3.0. Additional exam requirements/ recommendations for international students: Required—TOEFL (minimum score 80 iBT). *Application deadline:* For fall admission, 12/15 for domestic and international students; for winter admission, 11/1 for domestic and international students; for spring admission, 3/15 for domestic and international students. Application fee: $55 ($65 for international students). Electronic applications accepted. *Expenses:* Contact institution. *Financial support:* In 2017–18, 84 students received support, including 12 fellowships with full and partial tuition reimbursements available (averaging $17,000 per year), 16 research assistantships with full and partial tuition reimbursements available (averaging $15,500 per year), 39 teaching assistantships with full and partial tuition reimbursements available (averaging $15,500 per year); career-related internships or fieldwork, scholarships/grants, traineeships, health care benefits, and unspecified assistantships also available. Financial award application deadline: 4/1; financial award applicants required to submit FAFSA. *Faculty research:* Autism, computer technology and instruction, cognitive behavior, aging, group counseling. *Total annual research expenditures:* $620,935. *Unit head:* Dr. Anne E. Cook, Chair, 801-581-7148, Fax: 801-581-5566, E-mail: anne.cook@utah.edu. *Application contact:* JoLynn N. Yates, Academic Coordinator, 801-581-7148, Fax: 801-581-5566, E-mail: jo.yates@utah.edu. Website: http://www.ed.utah.edu/edps/

University of Victoria, Faculty of Graduate Studies, Faculty of Education, Department of Educational Psychology and Leadership Studies, Victoria, BC V8W 2Y2, Canada. Offers aboriginal communities counseling (M Ed); counseling (M Ed, MA); educational psychology (M Ed, MA, PhD), including counseling psychology (M Ed, MA), leadership studies (PhD), learning and development (MA, PhD), measurement and evaluation, special education (M Ed, MA); leadership studies (M Ed, MA). *Program availability:* Part-time. *Degree requirements:* For master's, thesis (for some programs), comprehensive exam (M Ed); for doctorate, comprehensive exam, thesis/dissertation, candidacy exam. *Entrance requirements:* For master's, 2 years of work experience in a relevant field; for doctorate, GRE, 2 years of work experience in a relevant field, minimum B average. Additional exam requirements/recommendations for international students: Required—TOEFL (minimum score 575 paper-based), IELTS (minimum score 7). *Faculty research:* Learning and development (child, adolescent and adult), special education and exceptional children.

University of Virginia, Curry School of Education, Department of Leadership, Foundations and Policy, Program in Educational Psychology, Charlottesville, VA 22903. Offers applied developmental science (M Ed); educational evaluation (M Ed); educational psychology (M Ed, Ed D, Ed S); educational research (Ed D); gifted education (M Ed); instructional technology (M Ed, Ed S); research statistics and evaluation (Ed D); school psychology (Ed D). *Students:* 36 full-time (29 women), 3 part-time (2 women); includes 14 minority (5 Black or African American, non-Hispanic/Latino; 4 Asian, non-Hispanic/Latino; 3 Hispanic/Latino; 2 Two or more races, non-Hispanic/Latino), 7 international. Average age 24. 85 applicants, 80% accepted, 37 enrolled. In 2017, 35 master's, 1 doctorate awarded. *Degree requirements:* For master's, comprehensive exam. *Entrance requirements:* For master's and doctorate, GRE General Test, 2 letters of recommendation. Additional exam requirements/ recommendations for international students: Required—TOEFL (minimum score 600 paper-based; 90 iBT), IELTS (minimum score 7). *Application deadline:* Applications are processed on a rolling basis. Application fee: $60. Electronic applications accepted. *Financial support:* Fellowships, research assistantships, and teaching assistantships available. Financial award application deadline: 1/5; financial award applicants required to submit FAFSA. *Unit head:* Sara Rimm-Kaufman, Program Director, 434-982-2863, E-mail: serk@virginia.edu. *Application contact:* E-mail: curry-admissions@virginia.edu. Website: http://curry.virginia.edu/academics/areas-of-study/educational-psychology

University of Virginia, Curry School of Education, Program in Education, Charlottesville, VA 22903. Offers administration and supervision (PhD); applied developmental science (PhD); counselor education (PhD); curriculum and instruction (PhD); early childhood special education (MT); education evaluation (PhD); educational psychology (PhD); educational research (PhD); elementary education (MT); English education (MT, PhD); foreign language education (MT); higher education (PhD); instructional technology (PhD); kinesiology (MT, PhD); math education (PhD); reading education (PhD); research, statistics and evaluation (PhD); school psychology (PhD); science education (PhD); social studies education (MT, PhD); special education (PhD); world languages education (MT). *Students:* 431 full-time (353 women), 15 part-time (14 women); includes 100 minority (32 Black or African American, non-Hispanic/Latino; 33 Asian, non-Hispanic/Latino; 16 Hispanic/Latino; 19 Two or more races, non-Hispanic/Latino), 14 international. Average age 25. 264 applicants, 49% accepted, 83 enrolled. In 2017, 142 master's, 33 doctorates awarded. *Degree requirements:* For master's, comprehensive exam (for some programs), field project; for doctorate, comprehensive exam, thesis/dissertation. *Entrance requirements:* For doctorate, GRE General Test. Additional exam requirements/recommendations for international students: Required—TOEFL (minimum score 600 paper-based; 90 iBT), IELTS (minimum score 7). *Application deadline:* Applications are processed on a rolling basis. Application fee: $60. Electronic applications accepted. *Financial support:* Fellowships, research assistantships, and teaching assistantships available. Financial award application deadline: 1/5; financial award applicants required to submit FAFSA. *Unit head:* Robert C. Pianta, Dean, 434-924-3334, E-mail: pianta@virginia.edu. *Application contact:* E-mail: curry-admissions@virginia.edu. Website: http://curry.virginia.edu/teacher-education

University of Washington, Graduate School, College of Education, Program in Educational Psychology, Seattle, WA 98195. Offers educational psychology (PhD); human development and cognition (M Ed); learning sciences (M Ed, PhD); measurement, statistics and research design (M Ed); school psychology (M Ed). *Accreditation:* APA. *Degree requirements:* For master's, thesis optional; for doctorate, thesis/dissertation. *Entrance requirements:* For master's and doctorate, GRE General Test, minimum GPA of 3.0. Additional exam requirements/recommendations for international students: Required—TOEFL.

The University of Western Ontario, Faculty of Graduate Studies, Social Sciences Division, Faculty of Education, Program in Educational Studies, London, ON N6A 5B8, Canada. Offers curriculum studies (M Ed); educational policy studies (M Ed); educational psychology/special education (M Ed). *Program availability:* Part-time. *Faculty research:* Reflective practice, gender and schooling, feminist pedagogy, narrative inquiry, second language, multiculturalism in Canada, education and law.

University of Wisconsin–Madison, Graduate School, School of Education, Department of Educational Psychology, Madison, WI 53706-1380. Offers MS, PhD. *Accreditation:* APA (one or more programs are accredited). *Degree requirements:* For doctorate, thesis/dissertation. *Entrance requirements:* For master's and doctorate, GRE General Test. Electronic applications accepted.

University of Wisconsin–Milwaukee, Graduate School, School of Education, Department of Educational Psychology, Milwaukee, WI 53201-0413. Offers children's

mental health for school professionals (Graduate Certificate); counseling psychology (PhD); educational statistics and measurement (MS, PhD); learning and development (MS, PhD); multicultural knowledge of mental health practices (Graduate Certificate); school counseling (MS); school counseling (Graduate Certificate); school psychology (MS, PhD, Ed S). *Accreditation:* APA. *Program availability:* Part-time. *Students:* 170 full-time (132 women), 52 part-time (39 women); includes 51 minority (14 Black or African American, non-Hispanic/Latino; 1 American Indian or Alaska Native, non-Hispanic/Latino; 7 Asian, non-Hispanic/Latino; 7 Hispanic/Latino; 1 Native Hawaiian or other Pacific Islander, non-Hispanic/Latino; 21 Two or more races, non-Hispanic/Latino), 4 international. Average age 31. 304 applicants, 39% accepted, 83 enrolled. In 2017, 59 master's, 11 doctorates, 10 other advanced degrees awarded. *Degree requirements:* For master's, comprehensive exam, thesis; for doctorate, thesis/dissertation. *Entrance requirements:* For master's, minimum GPA of 3.0; for doctorate, GRE General Test, minimum GPA of 3.0. Additional exam requirements/recommendations for international students: Required—TOEFL (minimum score 550 paper-based; 79 iBT), IELTS (minimum score 6.5). *Application deadline:* For fall admission, 1/1 priority date for domestic students; for spring admission, 9/1 for domestic students. Application fee: $56 ($96 for international students). Electronic applications accepted. *Financial support:* Fellowships, research assistantships, teaching assistantships, career-related internships or fieldwork, health care benefits, unspecified assistantships, and project assistantships available. Support available to part-time students. Financial award application deadline: 4/15; financial award applicants required to submit FAFSA. *Application contact:* General Information Contact, 414-229-4721, E-mail: soeinfo@uwm.edu.
Website: http://uwm.edu/education/academics/educational-psychology-department/

Virginia Commonwealth University, Graduate School, School of Education, Doctoral Program in Education, Richmond, VA 23284-9005. Offers art education (PhD); counselor education and supervision (PhD); curriculum, culture and change (PhD); educational leadership (PhD); educational psychology (PhD); leadership (Ed D); research and evaluation (PhD); special education and disability leadership (PhD); sport leadership (PhD); urban services leadership (PhD). *Accreditation:* NCATE. *Program availability:* Part-time. *Degree requirements:* For doctorate, thesis/dissertation. *Entrance requirements:* For doctorate, GRE (for PhD), MAT (for Ed D), interview, master's degree, writing sample. Additional exam requirements/recommendations for international students: Required—TOEFL (minimum score 600 paper-based; 100 iBT). Electronic applications accepted.

Walden University, Graduate Programs, School of Psychology, Minneapolis, MN 55401. Offers clinical psychology (MS), including counseling, general program; forensic psychology (MS), including forensic psychology in the community, general program, mental health applications, program planning and evaluation in forensic settings, psychology and legal systems; industrial organizational (MS, PhD), including consulting psychology, forensic (MS), forensic psychology (PhD), general practice, leadership development and coaching (MS), organizational diversity and social change, research evaluation (PhD); online teaching in psychology (Post-Master's Certificate); organizational psychology and development (Postbaccalaureate Certificate); psychology (MS, PhD), including applied psychology (MS), clinical psychology (PhD), crisis management and response (MS), educational psychology, forensic psychology (PhD), general psychology (MS), general psychology research (PhD), general psychology teaching (PhD), health psychology, leadership development and coaching (MS), psychology of culture (MS), psychology, public administration, and social change (MS), social psychology, terrorism and security (MS); psychology respecialization (Post-Doctoral Certificate). *Program availability:* Part-time, evening/weekend, online only, 100% online. Terminal master's awarded for partial completion of doctoral program. *Degree requirements:* For master's, thesis optional; for doctorate, thesis/dissertation, residency. *Entrance requirements:* For master's, bachelor's degree or higher; minimum GPA of 2.5; official transcripts; goal statement (for some programs); access to computer and Internet; for doctorate, master's degree or higher; three years of related professional or academic experience (preferred); minimum GPA of 3.0; goal statement and current resume (for select programs); official transcripts; access to computer and Internet; for other advanced degree, relevant work experience; access to computer and Internet. Additional exam requirements/recommendations for international students: Required—TOEFL (minimum score 550 paper-based, 79 iBT), IELTS (minimum score 6.5), Michigan English Language Assessment Battery (minimum score 82), or PTE (minimum score 53). Electronic applications accepted.

Washington State University, College of Education, Department of Educational Leadership, Sports Studies, and Educational/Counseling Psychology, Pullman, WA 99164-2136. Offers counseling psychology (PhD); educational leadership (Ed M, MA, Ed D, PhD); educational psychology (MA, PhD); sport management (MA). Programs also offered at the Spokane, Tri-Cities, Vancouver and Global (online) campuses. *Program availability:* Part-time, online learning. *Degree requirements:* For master's, comprehensive exam (for some programs), thesis (for some programs), oral or written exam; for doctorate, comprehensive exam, thesis/dissertation, oral and written exam, internship. *Entrance requirements:* For master's and doctorate, GRE General Test, minimum GPA of 3.0, 3 letters of recommendation, transcripts showing all college or university course work, statement of professional objectives, current curriculum vitae/resume. Additional exam requirements/recommendations for international students: Required—TOEFL (minimum score 550 paper-based; 80 iBT). Electronic applications accepted. *Faculty research:* Multicultural counseling and career development, educational and psychological measurement issues, business decision-making process and power relationships, leadership practices and processes as suffused with and constituted by emotion work.

Wayne State University, College of Education, Division of Theoretical and Behavioral Foundations, Detroit, MI 48202. Offers applied behavior analysis (Certificate); counseling (M Ed, MA, Ed D, Ed S); counseling psychology (MA, PhD); education evaluation and research (M Ed, Ed D); educational psychology (M Ed, PhD), including learning and instruction sciences (PhD); rehabilitation counseling and community inclusion (MA); school and community psychology (MA, Certificate). *Accreditation:* ACA (one or more programs are accredited); CORE (one or more programs are accredited). *Program availability:* Evening/weekend. *Students:* Average age 32. 294 applicants, 34% accepted, 72 enrolled. In 2017, 87 master's, 12 doctorates, 14 other advanced degrees awarded. *Entrance requirements:* For master's, GRE, interview, personal statement, portfolio (art therapy); for doctorate, GRE, department-written exam, interview, curriculum vitae, references, master's degree in closely-related field with minimum GPA of 3.5, demonstration of counseling skills (for Ed D in counseling); for other advanced degree, master's degree in counseling and counseling license (for Ed S); good standing in school and community psychology MA program (for Certificate). Additional exam requirements/recommendations for international students: Required—TOEFL (minimum score 550 paper-based; 79 iBT), Michigan English Language Assessment Battery

(minimum score 85); Recommended—IELTS (minimum score 6.5), TWE (minimum score 5.5). *Application deadline:* For fall admission, 6/1 priority date for domestic students, 5/1 priority date for international students; for winter admission, 10/1 priority date for domestic students, 9/1 priority date for international students; for spring admission, 2/1 priority date for domestic students, 1/1 priority date for international students. Applications are processed on a rolling basis. Application fee: $50. Electronic applications accepted. *Expenses:* Contact institution. *Financial support:* In 2017–18, 92 students received support, including 2 research assistantships with tuition reimbursements available (averaging $17,994 per year); fellowships, teaching assistantships, Federal Work-Study, scholarships/grants, health care benefits, and unspecified assistantships also available. Support available to part-time students. Financial award applicants required to submit FAFSA. *Faculty research:* Adolescents at risk, supervision of counseling. *Unit head:* Dr. Cheryl Somers, Assistant Dean, 313-577-1670, E-mail: c.somers@wayne.edu. *Application contact:* Janice Green, Assistant Dean, 313-577-1605, E-mail: jwgreen@wayne.edu.
Website: http://coe.wayne.edu/tbf/index.php

Webster University, School of Education, Department of Multidisciplinary Studies, St. Louis, MO 63119-3194. Offers applied educational psychology (MA, Ed S); communication arts (MA); early childhood education (MA, MAT); education and innovation (MA); educational technology (MET); elementary education (MAT); mathematics for educators (MA); middle school education (MAT); multidisciplinary studies (MAT); multimodal literacy for global impact (MA); reading (MA); secondary school education (MA, MAT); special education (MA, MAT); teaching English as a second language (MA); transformative learning in the global community (Ed S). *Program availability:* Part-time. *Entrance requirements:* For master's, minimum GPA of 2.5. Additional exam requirements/recommendations for international students: Required—TOEFL.

West Virginia University, College of Education and Human Services, Morgantown, WV 26506. Offers audiology (Au D); autism spectrum disorder (MA); clinical rehabilitation and mental health counseling (MS); communication science and disorders (PhD); counseling (MA); counseling psychology (PhD); curriculum and instruction (Ed D); early childhood education (MA); early intervention (MA); education (PhD); educational leadership (MA, Ed D); educational leadership/public school administration (MA); educational psychology (MA, Ed D); elementary education (MA); gifted education (MA); higher education administration (MA, Ed D); higher education curriculum and teaching (MA); institutional design and technology (MA); instructional design and technology (Ed D); literacy education (MA); secondary education (MA); secondary education/English (MA); special education (Ed D); speech pathology (MS). *Accreditation:* NCATE. *Program availability:* Part-time, evening/weekend, online learning. *Students:* 423 full-time (347 women), 367 part-time (316 women); includes 57 minority (14 Black or African American, non-Hispanic/Latino; 7 Asian, non-Hispanic/Latino; 20 Hispanic/Latino; 16 Two or more races, non-Hispanic/Latino), 13 international. *Degree requirements:* For master's, content exams; for doctorate, comprehensive exam, thesis/dissertation. *Entrance requirements:* Additional exam requirements/recommendations for international students: Required—TOEFL (minimum score 500 paper-based; 61 iBT). *Application deadline:* For fall admission, 8/1 for domestic students; for spring admission, 1/1 for domestic students; for summer admission, 5/1 for domestic students. Application fee: $60. Electronic applications accepted. *Expenses:* Tuition, state resident: full-time $9450. Tuition, nonresident: full-time $24,390. *Financial support:* Fellowships, research assistantships, teaching assistantships, career-related internships or fieldwork, Federal Work-Study, institutionally sponsored loans, health care benefits, tuition waivers (full and partial), and administrative assistantships available. Financial award applicants required to submit FAFSA. *Faculty research:* Internet training and integration for teachers, rural education, teacher preparation, organization of schools, evaluation of personnel. *Unit head:* Dr. Gypsy Denzine, Dean, 304-293-5703, Fax: 304-293-7565, E-mail: gypsy.denzine@mail.wvu.edu. *Application contact:* Dr. M. Cecil Smith, Associate Dean for Research and Graduate Education, 304-293-2174, Fax: 304-293-3802, E-mail: mcecil.smith@mail.wvu.edu.
Website: http://cehs.wvu.edu/

Wichita State University, Graduate School, College of Education, Department of Counseling, Educational Leadership, Educational and School Psychology, Wichita, KS 67260. Offers counseling (M Ed); educational leadership (M Ed, Ed D); educational psychology (M Ed); school psychology (Ed S). *Accreditation:* NCATE. *Program availability:* Part-time, evening/weekend. Application fee: $50 ($65 for international students). *Unit head:* Dr. Jody Fiorini, Department Head, 316-978-3325, Fax: 316-978-3102, E-mail: jody.fiorini@wichita.edu. *Application contact:* Jordan Oleson, Admissions Coordinator, 316-978-3095, Fax: 316-978-3253, E-mail: jordan.oleson@wichita.edu.
Website: http://www.wichita.edu/cles

Widener University, School of Human Service Professions, Center for Education, Chester, PA 19013-5792. Offers adult education (M Ed); counseling in higher education (M Ed); counselor education (M Ed); early childhood education (M Ed); educational foundations (M Ed); educational leadership (M Ed); educational psychology (M Ed); elementary education (M Ed); English and language arts (M Ed); health education (M Ed); higher education leadership (Ed D); home and school visitor (M Ed); human sexuality (M Ed, PhD); mathematics education (M Ed); middle school education (M Ed); principalship (M Ed); reading and language arts (Ed D); reading education (M Ed); school administration (Ed D); science education (M Ed); social studies education (M Ed); special education (M Ed); technology education (M Ed). *Accreditation:* NCATE. *Program availability:* Part-time, evening/weekend. *Faculty:* 34 full-time (22 women), 37 part-time/adjunct (14 women). *Students:* 131 full-time (112 women), 244 part-time (179 women); includes 94 minority (58 Black or African American, non-Hispanic/Latino; 1 American Indian or Alaska Native, non-Hispanic/Latino; 1 Asian, non-Hispanic/Latino; 22 Hispanic/Latino; 12 Two or more races, non-Hispanic/Latino), 12 international. Average age 37. 140 applicants, 38% accepted, 26 enrolled. In 2017, 45 master's, 21 doctorates awarded. Terminal master's awarded for partial completion of doctoral program. *Degree requirements:* For doctorate, thesis/dissertation. *Entrance requirements:* For master's, minimum GPA of 2.5; for doctorate, GRE or MAT, minimum GPA of 2.0 (undergraduate), 3.5 (graduate). *Application deadline:* Applications are processed on a rolling basis. Application fee: $25 ($300 for international students). Electronic applications accepted. *Expenses:* Contact institution. *Financial support:* Career-related internships or fieldwork, tuition waivers (full and partial), and unspecified assistantships available. Support available to part-time students. Financial award application deadline: 5/1. *Faculty research:* Reading and cognition, adult education, technology education, educational leadership, special education. *Unit head:* Dr. Shawn Fitzgerald, Dean, 610-499-4294, Fax: 610-499-4623, E-mail: smfitzgerald@widener.edu. *Application contact:* Megan Kuft, Director of Graduate Admissions, 610-499-4124, E-mail: gradprograms@widener.edu.
Website: http://www.widener.edu/academics/schools/eics

Foundations and Philosophy of Education

Antioch University New England, Graduate School, Department of Education, Experienced Educators Program, Keene, NH 03431-3552. Offers foundations of education (M Ed), including applied behavioral analysis, autism spectrum disorders, educating for sustainability, next-generation learning using technology, problem-based learning using critical skills, teacher leadership; principal certification (PMC). *Degree requirements:* For master's, thesis, practicum. *Entrance requirements:* For master's, previous course work and work experience in education. Additional exam requirements/recommendations for international students: Required—TOEFL (minimum score 550 paper-based). Electronic applications accepted. *Expenses:* Contact institution. *Faculty research:* Classroom action research, school restructuring, problem-based learning, brain-based learning.

Arkansas State University, Graduate School, College of Education and Behavioral Science, School of Teacher Education and Leadership, State University, AR 72467. Offers community college administration (SCCT); curriculum and instruction (MSE); early childhood education (MSE); early childhood services (MS); educational leadership (MSE, Ed D, Ed S); educational theory and practice (MSE); middle level education (MAT, MSE); reading (MSE, Ed S); special education - gifted, talented, and creative (MSE); special education - instructional specialist grades 4-12 (MSE); special education - instructional specialist grades P-4 (MSE); special education, K-12 (MSE). *Accreditation:* NCATE. *Program availability:* Part-time, online learning. *Degree requirements:* For master's, comprehensive exam, thesis or alternative; for doctorate, comprehensive exam, thesis/dissertation; for other advanced degree, comprehensive exam. *Entrance requirements:* For master's, GRE General Test or MAT, appropriate bachelor's degree, official transcripts, immunization records, letters of reference, interview; for doctorate, GRE General Test or MAT, interview, master's degree, letters of reference, official transcript, personal statement, writing sample, immunization records; for other advanced degree, GRE General Test or MAT, interview, master's degree, official transcript, immunization records, letters of reference, 3 years of teaching experience, teaching license. Additional exam requirements/recommendations for international students: Required—TOEFL (minimum score 550 paper-based; 79 iBT), IELTS (minimum score 6), PTE (minimum score 56). Electronic applications accepted.

Ball State University, Graduate School, Teachers College, Department of Educational Studies, Program in Educational Studies, Muncie, IN 47306. Offers educational studies (PhD), including cultural and educational policy studies; curriculum, educational technology. *Program availability:* Part-time, blended/hybrid learning. *Students:* 8 full-time (4 women), 16 part-time (11 women); includes 4 minority (2 Black or African American, non-Hispanic/Latino; 1 Asian, non-Hispanic/Latino; 1 Two or more races, non-Hispanic/Latino), 3 international. Average age 43. 14 applicants, 57% accepted, 4 enrolled. In 2017, 3 doctorates awarded. *Degree requirements:* For doctorate, thesis/dissertation. *Entrance requirements:* For doctorate, GRE General Test, minimum graduate GPA of 3.2, curriculum vitae, writing sample, three letters of reference. Additional exam requirements/recommendations for international students: Required—TOEFL (minimum score 550 paper-based; 79 iBT), IELTS (minimum score 6.5). *Application deadline:* Applications are processed on a rolling basis. Application fee: $60. Electronic applications accepted. *Financial support:* Research assistantships with partial tuition reimbursements and teaching assistantships with partial tuition reimbursements available. Financial award application deadline: 3/1; financial award applicants required to submit FAFSA. *Faculty research:* Emerging curriculum trends, secondary teacher preparation, issues of equity and social justice in education, teacher technology integration, teaching for transformative understanding, teacher leadership, history of educational policy and practices, ethics and education. *Unit head:* Dr. Theresa Kruczek, Interim Chair, 765-285-8049, E-mail: tkruczek@bsu.edu.
Website: http://www.bsu.edu/edstudies

Bank Street College of Education, Graduate School, Studies in Education Program, New York, NY 10025. Offers Ed M, MS Ed. *Degree requirements:* For master's, thesis. *Entrance requirements:* For master's, interview, essays. Additional exam requirements/recommendations for international students: Required—TOEFL (minimum score 600 paper-based; 100 iBT), IELTS (minimum score 7). Electronic applications accepted.

Binghamton University, State University of New York, Graduate School, College of Community and Public Affairs, Department of Teaching, Learning and Educational Leadership, Program in Educational Theory and Practice, Binghamton, NY 13902-6000. Offers Ed D. *Program availability:* Part-time. *Students:* 5 full-time (4 women), 84 part-time (67 women); includes 8 minority (3 Black or African American, non-Hispanic/Latino; 1 American Indian or Alaska Native, non-Hispanic/Latino; 1 Asian, non-Hispanic/Latino; 2 Hispanic/Latino; 1 Two or more races, non-Hispanic/Latino), 4 international. Average age 42. 35 applicants, 94% accepted, 23 enrolled. In 2017, 5 doctorates awarded. *Degree requirements:* For doctorate, thesis/dissertation. *Entrance requirements:* For doctorate, GRE General Test. Additional exam requirements/recommendations for international students: Required—TOEFL (minimum score 550 paper-based; 80 iBT). *Application deadline:* For fall admission, 2/1 priority date for domestic and international students. Application fee: $75. Electronic applications accepted. *Financial support:* In 2017–18, 11 students received support, including 1 fellowship with full tuition reimbursement available (averaging $15,500 per year), 3 teaching assistantships with full tuition reimbursements available (averaging $15,500 per year); career-related internships or fieldwork, Federal Work-Study, institutionally sponsored loans, scholarships/grants, health care benefits, tuition waivers (full and partial), and unspecified assistantships also available. Financial award applicants required to submit FAFSA. *Unit head:* Dr. Susan Strehle, Dean, 607-777-7329, E-mail: sstrehle@binghamton.edu. *Application contact:* Ben Balkaya, Assistant Dean and Director, 607-777-2151, Fax: 607-777-2501, E-mail: balkaya@binghamton.edu.
Website: http://www2.binghamton.edu/gse/doctoral-program/index.html

Brigham Young University, Graduate Studies, David O. McKay School of Education, Department of Educational Leadership and Foundations, Provo, UT 84602. Offers educational leadership and foundations (Ed D); educational leadership: education policy studies (M Ed); educational leadership: school leadership (M Ed). *Program availability:* Part-time, evening/weekend. *Faculty:* 12 full-time (2 women), 1 part-time/adjunct (0 women). *Students:* 31 full-time (25 women), 62 part-time (31 women); includes 8 minority (2 American Indian or Alaska Native, non-Hispanic/Latino; 1 Asian, non-Hispanic/Latino; 4 Hispanic/Latino; 1 Native Hawaiian or other Pacific Islander, non-Hispanic/Latino). Average age 42. 78 applicants, 49% accepted, 38 enrolled. In 2017, 29 master's, 10 doctorates awarded. Terminal master's awarded for partial completion of doctoral program. *Degree requirements:* For master's, comprehensive exam; for doctorate, comprehensive exam, thesis/dissertation, prospectus. *Entrance requirements:* For master's, GRE, LSAT, GMAT, or MAT, level 2 teaching license; for doctorate, GRE, LSAT, or GMAT, master's degree. Additional exam requirements/recommendations for international students: Required—TOEFL (minimum score 580 paper-based; 85 iBT). *Application deadline:* For fall admission, 5/1 for domestic and

international students; for winter admission, 9/15 for domestic and international students; for spring admission, 1/15 for domestic and international students. Application fee: $50. Electronic applications accepted. *Expenses:* Contact institution. *Financial support:* In 2017–18, 38 students received support, including 19 research assistantships (averaging $2,100 per year); scholarships/grants also available. Financial award application deadline: 8/15. *Faculty research:* Inequality of educational opportunity, value of principals academies, role of trust in educational leadership, social networks in education, factors and indicators leading to the improvement of educational settings. *Unit head:* Pamela Hallam, Chair, 801-422-3600, Fax: 801-422-0196, E-mail: pam_hallam@byu.edu. *Application contact:* Michele Price, Department Secretary, 801-422-3813, Fax: 801-422-0196, E-mail: michele_price@byu.edu.
Website: http://education.byu.edu/edlf/

Chicago State University, School of Graduate and Professional Studies, College of Education, Department of Educational Leadership, Curriculum and Foundations, Program in Curriculum and Instruction, Chicago, IL 60628. Offers instructional foundations (MS Ed), including adult education, elementary education, secondary education. *Degree requirements:* For master's, comprehensive exam, thesis optional. *Entrance requirements:* For master's, minimum GPA of 2.75. *Application deadline:* For fall admission, 7/1 for domestic students; for spring admission, 11/10 for domestic students. Application fee: $25. *Unit head:* Dr. Cathryn Busch, Chairperson. *Application contact:* Anika Miller, Graduate Studies Office, 773-995-2404, E-mail: g-studies1@csu.edu.

Columbia University, Graduate School of Arts and Sciences, New York, NY 10027. Offers African-American studies (MA); American studies (MA); anthropology (MA, PhD); art history and archaeology (MA, PhD); astronomy (PhD); biological sciences (PhD); biotechnology (MA); chemical physics (PhD); chemistry (PhD); classical studies (MA, PhD); classics (MA, PhD); climate and society (MA); conservation biology (MA); earth and environmental sciences (PhD); East Asia: regional studies (MA); East Asian languages and cultures (MA, PhD); ecology, evolution and environmental biology (MA), including conservation biology; ecology, evolution, and environmental biology (PhD), including ecology and evolutionary biology, evolutionary primatology; economics (MA, PhD); English and comparative literature (MA, PhD); French and Romance philology (MA, PhD); Germanic languages (MA, PhD); global French studies (MA); global thought (MA); Hispanic cultural studies (MA); history (PhD); history and literature (MA); human rights studies (MA); Islamic studies (MA); Italian (MA, PhD); Japanese pedagogy (MA); Jewish studies (MA); Latin America and the Caribbean: regional studies (MA); Latin American and Iberian cultures (PhD); mathematics (MA, PhD), including finance (MA); medieval and Renaissance studies (MA); Middle Eastern, South Asian, and African studies (MA, PhD); modern art: critical and curatorial studies (MA); modern European studies (MA); museum anthropology (MA); music (DMA, PhD); oral history (MA); philosophical foundations of physics (MA); philosophy (MA, PhD); physics (PhD); political science (MA, PhD); psychology (PhD); quantitative methods in the social sciences (MA); religion (MA, PhD); Russia, Eurasia and East Europe: regional studies (MA); Russian translation (MA); Slavic cultures (MA); Slavic languages (MA, PhD); sociology (MA, PhD); South Asian studies (MA); statistics (MA, PhD); theatre (PhD). Dual-degree programs require admission to both Graduate School of Arts and Sciences and another Columbia school. *Program availability:* Part-time. Terminal master's awarded for partial completion of doctoral program. *Degree requirements:* For master's, variable foreign language requirement, comprehensive exam (for some programs), thesis (for some programs); for doctorate, variable foreign language requirement, comprehensive exam (for some programs), thesis/dissertation. *Entrance requirements:* For master's and doctorate, GRE General Test, GRE Subject Test (for some programs). Additional exam requirements/recommendations for international students: Required—TOEFL, IELTS. Electronic applications accepted. *Expenses: Tuition:* Full-time $44,864; part-time $1704 per credit. *Required fees:* $2370 per semester. One-time fee: $105.

Curry College, Graduate Studies, Program in Education, Milton, MA 02186-9984. Offers elementary education (M Ed); foundations (non-license) (M Ed); reading (M Ed, Certificate); special education (M Ed). *Program availability:* Part-time, evening/weekend. *Degree requirements:* For master's, project or thesis. *Entrance requirements:* For master's, interview, recommendations, resume, written statement. Additional exam requirements/recommendations for international students: Required—TOEFL (minimum score 550 paper-based; 80 iBT). *Expenses:* Contact institution. *Faculty research:* Classroom trauma, therapeutic writing, inclusionary practices.

DePaul University, College of Education, Chicago, IL 60614. Offers bilingual-bicultural education (M Ed, MA); counseling (M Ed, MA), including clinical mental health counseling, college student development, school counseling; curriculum studies (M Ed, MA, Ed D); early childhood education (M Ed, MA, Ed D); educational leadership (M Ed, MA, Ed D), including Catholic leadership (M Ed, MA), general (M Ed, MA), higher education (M Ed, MA), physical education (M Ed, MA), principal preparation (M Ed); teacher preparation (M Ed); elementary education (M Ed, MA); middle grades education (M Ed); middle school mathematics education (MS); reading specialist (M Ed, MA); secondary education (M Ed, MA); social and cultural foundations in education (M Ed, MA); special education (M Ed); sport, fitness and recreation leadership (MS); value-creating education for global citizenship (M Ed); world languages education (M Ed, MA). *Program availability:* Part-time, evening/weekend, online learning. *Degree requirements:* For doctorate, thesis/dissertation. *Application deadline:* Applications are processed on a rolling basis. Application fee: $40. Electronic applications accepted. *Financial support:* Application deadline: 12/31; applicants required to submit FAFSA. *Unit head:* Dr. Paul Zionts, Dean, 773-325-7713, Fax: 773-325-7713, E-mail: pzionts@depaul.edu. *Application contact:* Dr. Paul Zionts, Dean, 773-325-7581, Fax: 773-325-7713, E-mail: pzionts@depaul.edu.
Website: http://education.depaul.edu

Duquesne University, School of Education, Department of Educational Foundations and Leadership, Program in Educational Studies, Pittsburgh, PA 15282-0001. Offers educational studies (MS Ed); program evaluation (MS Ed). *Program availability:* Part-time, evening/weekend, 100% online. *Faculty:* 1 full-time (0 women). *Students:* 6 full-time (4 women), 13 part-time (10 women); includes 3 minority (all Black or African American, non-Hispanic/Latino), 11 international. Average age 37. 19 applicants, 95% accepted, 4 enrolled. In 2017, 5 master's awarded. *Degree requirements:* For master's, thesis optional. *Entrance requirements:* For master's, bachelor's degree. Additional exam requirements/recommendations for international students: Required—TOEFL (minimum score 550 paper-based), IELTS (minimum score 7). *Application deadline:* For fall admission, 8/15 for domestic students; for spring admission, 1/2 for domestic students. Applications are processed on a rolling basis. Application fee: $0. Electronic applications accepted. *Expenses:* $1,259 per credit. *Financial support:* Research assistantships available. Support available to part-time students. *Faculty research:* Online learning; impact of trauma on childhood and adolescent development; evaluation of educational programs;

research in mathematics education; beliefs about classroom assessment. *Unit head:* Dr. Gibbs Kanyongo, Associate Professor, 412-396-5190, Fax: 412-396-5454, E-mail: kanyongog@duq.edu. *Application contact:* Kelly McGinley, Graduate Admissions Assistant, 412-396-1559, Fax: 412-396-5585, E-mail: mcginleyk@duq.edu.

Eastern Michigan University, Graduate School, College of Education, Department of Teacher Education, Program in Social Foundations, Ypsilanti, MI 48197. Offers MA. *Accreditation:* NCATE. *Program availability:* Part-time, evening/weekend, online learning. *Students:* 14 part-time (10 women); includes 3 minority (1 Hispanic/Latino; 2 Two or more races, non-Hispanic/Latino), 1 international. Average age 30. 6 applicants, 100% accepted, 6 enrolled. In 2017, 3 master's awarded. *Entrance requirements:* For master's, GRE. Additional exam requirements/recommendations for international students: Required—TOEFL. *Application deadline:* Applications are processed on a rolling basis. Application fee: $45. *Financial support:* Fellowships, research assistantships with full tuition reimbursements, teaching assistantships with full tuition reimbursements, career-related internships or fieldwork, Federal Work-Study, institutionally sponsored loans, scholarships/grants, tuition waivers (partial), and unspecified assistantships available. Support available to part-time students. Financial award applicants required to submit FAFSA. *Application contact:* Dr. Paul Ramsey, Coordinator, 734-487-3260, Fax: 734-487-2101, E-mail: pramsey1@emich.edu.

Eastern Washington University, Graduate Studies, College of Arts, Letters and Education, Department of Education, Program in Educational Foundations, Cheney, WA 99004-2431. Offers M Ed. *Students:* 1 (woman) full-time, 3 part-time (all women). Average age 37. In 2017, 1 master's awarded. *Degree requirements:* For master's, comprehensive exam. *Entrance requirements:* For master's, minimum GPA of 3.0. Additional exam requirements/recommendations for international students: Required—TOEFL (minimum score 580 paper-based; 92 iBT), IELTS (minimum score 7). *Application deadline:* For fall admission, 4/1 priority date for domestic students; for spring admission, 1/15 for domestic students. Applications are processed on a rolling basis. *Expenses:* Tuition, state resident: full-time $11,191; part-time $373.06 per credit. Tuition, nonresident: full-time $25,995; part-time $866.52 per credit. *Financial support:* In 2017–18, teaching assistantships with partial tuition reimbursements (averaging $7,000 per year) were awarded; career-related internships or fieldwork, Federal Work-Study, institutionally sponsored loans, scholarships/grants, health care benefits, tuition waivers (partial), and unspecified assistantships also available. Support available to part-time students. Financial award application deadline: 2/1; financial award applicants required to submit FAFSA. *Unit head:* Dr. Vince Aleccia, Program Coordinator, 509-359-7024, E-mail: valeccia@ewu.edu.

Fairfield University, Graduate School of Education and Allied Professions, Fairfield, CT 06824. Offers applied behavior analysis (ATC); applied psychology (MA); clinical mental health counseling (MA, CAS); educational technology (MA); elementary education (MA, CAS); family studies (MA); integration of spirituality and religion in counseling (ATC); marriage and family therapy (MA); reading and language development (Sixth Year Certificate); school counseling (MA, CAS); school psychology (MA, CAS); school-based marriage and family therapy (ATC); secondary education (MA); special education (MA, CAS); substance abuse counseling (ATC); teaching (Certificate); teaching and foundations (MA, CAS); TESOL, world languages, and bilingual education (MA, CAS). *Accreditation:* NCATE. *Program availability:* Part-time, evening/weekend. *Faculty:* 23 full-time (17 women), 39 part-time/adjunct (28 women). *Students:* 199 full-time (168 women), 251 part-time (206 women); includes 85 minority (21 Black or African American, non-Hispanic/Latino; 9 Asian, non-Hispanic/Latino; 49 Hispanic/Latino; 6 Two or more races, non-Hispanic/Latino), 4 international. Average age 32. 370 applicants, 56% accepted, 125 enrolled. In 2017, 136 master's, 28 other advanced degrees awarded. *Degree requirements:* For master's, comprehensive exam. *Entrance requirements:* For master's, minimum GPA of 3.0, 2 recommendations, resume. Additional exam requirements/recommendations for international students: Required—TOEFL (minimum score 550 paper-based; 84 iBT) or IELTS (minimum score 7.5). *Application deadline:* For fall admission, 2/15 for international students; for spring admission, 10/1 for international students. Application fee: $60. Electronic applications accepted. *Expenses:* $750 per credit hour. *Financial support:* In 2017–18, 34 students received support. Career-related internships or fieldwork and unspecified assistantships available. Support available to part-time students. Financial award applicants required to submit FAFSA. *Faculty research:* Reading and literacy, writing, social justice and inequality in education, addictions and mental health issues, therapeutic relationships and clinical supervision. *Unit head:* Dr. Robert D. Hannafin, Dean, 203-254-4250, Fax: 203-254-4241, E-mail: rhannafin@fairfield.edu. *Application contact:* Marianne Gumpper, Director of Graduate Admission, 203-254-4184, Fax: 203-254-4073, E-mail: gradadmis@fairfield.edu.
Website: http://www.fairfield.edu/gseap

Fairleigh Dickinson University, Metropolitan Campus, University College: Arts, Sciences, and Professional Studies, School of Computer Sciences and Engineering, Program in Mathematical Foundation, Teaneck, NJ 07666-1914. Offers MS.

Florida Atlantic University, College of Education, Department of Teaching and Learning, Boca Raton, FL 33431-0991. Offers curriculum and instruction (M Ed), including art, biology, chemistry, English, French, German, mathematics, music, physics, Pre-K and primary education, reading, social sciences, Spanish; elementary education (M Ed); environmental education (M Ed); reading education (M Ed); social foundations of education (M Ed), including educational psychology, educational technology, multilingual education. *Accreditation:* NCATE. *Program availability:* Part-time, evening/weekend. *Faculty:* 13 full-time (10 women), 1 part-time/adjunct (0 women). *Students:* 26 full-time (22 women), 43 part-time (39 women); includes 19 minority (9 Black or African American, non-Hispanic/Latino; 1 Asian, non-Hispanic/Latino; 8 Hispanic/Latino; 1 Two or more races, non-Hispanic/Latino), 3 international. Average age 30. 91 applicants, 57% accepted, 33 enrolled. In 2017, 25 master's awarded. *Entrance requirements:* For master's, GRE General Test, minimum GPA of 3.0 in last 2 years of undergraduate course work. Additional exam requirements/recommendations for international students: Required—TOEFL (minimum score 500 paper-based; 61 iBT), IELTS (minimum score 6). *Application deadline:* For fall admission, 7/1 for domestic students, 2/15 for international students; for spring admission, 11/1 for domestic students, 7/15 for international students. Applications are processed on a rolling basis. Application fee: $30. *Expenses:* Tuition, state resident: full-time $7400; part-time $369.82 per credit. Tuition, nonresident: full-time $20,496; part-time $1042.81 per credit. *Financial support:* Fellowships with partial tuition reimbursements, research assistantships with partial tuition reimbursements, teaching assistantships with partial tuition reimbursements, career-related internships or fieldwork, scholarships/grants, and unspecified assistantships available. *Faculty research:* Technology, teaching English to speakers of other languages, math teaching, electronic portfolio assessment, global perspectives through social studies. *Unit head:* Dr. Barbara Ridener, Chairperson, 561-297-3588, E-mail: bridener@fau.edu. *Application contact:* Dr. Eliah Watlington, Associate Dean, 561-296-8520, Fax: 261-297-2991, E-mail: ewatling@fau.edu.
Website: http://www.coe.fau.edu/academicdepartments/tl/

Florida State University, The Graduate School, College of Education, Department of Educational Leadership and Policy Studies, Tallahassee, FL 32306. Offers educational leadership and administration (Certificate); educational leadership and policy (MS, Ed D, PhD, Ed S), including education policy and evaluation (MS, Ed D, PhD), educational leadership and administration; foundations of education (MS, PhD), including history and philosophy of education, international and multicultural education; higher education (MS, PhD); institutional research (Certificate); program evaluation (Certificate). *Program availability:* Part-time, evening/weekend, 100% online, blended/hybrid learning, asynchronous, minimal on-campus study. *Faculty:* 19 full-time (15 women), 10 part-time/adjunct (7 women). *Students:* 151 full-time (105 women), 196 part-time (138 women); includes 127 minority (55 Black or African American, non-Hispanic/Latino; 4 Asian, non-Hispanic/Latino; 49 Hispanic/Latino; 19 Two or more races, non-Hispanic/Latino), 33 international. Average age 35. 229 applicants, 54% accepted, 66 enrolled. In 2017, 49 master's, 10 doctorates, 17 other advanced degrees awarded. *Degree requirements:* For master's, comprehensive exam, thesis optional; for doctorate, comprehensive exam, thesis/dissertation, diagnostic exam, preliminary exam, prospectus defense, dissertation defense. *Entrance requirements:* For master's, doctorate, and other advanced degree, GRE General Test, minimum GPA of 3.0. Additional exam requirements/recommendations for international students: Required—TOEFL (minimum score 550 paper-based, 80 iBT), IELTS (minimum score 6.5), Michigan English Language Assessment Battery (minimum score 77), or PTE (minimum score 55). Application fee: $30. Electronic applications accepted. *Financial support:* Fellowships, research assistantships, teaching assistantships, scholarships/grants, tuition waivers (full and partial), and unspecified assistantships available. Financial award application deadline: 1/15; financial award applicants required to submit FAFSA. *Faculty research:* Post-secondary success; leadership education; education policy; international education; multicultural education. *Unit head:* Dr. Robert A. Schwartz, Chair, 850-644-6885, Fax: 850-644-2725, E-mail: raschwartz@fsu.edu. *Application contact:* Linda Lyons, Academic Support Assistant, 850-644-7077, Fax: 850-644-1258, E-mail: ljlyons@fsu.edu.

Georgia State University, College of Education and Human Development, Department of Educational Policy Studies, Program in Social Foundations of Education, Atlanta, GA 30302-3083. Offers MS, PhD. *Accreditation:* NCATE. *Program availability:* Part-time. *Entrance requirements:* For master's and doctorate, GRE. *Application deadline:* Applications are processed on a rolling basis. Application fee: $50. Electronic applications accepted. *Expenses:* Tuition, state resident: full-time $7020. Tuition, nonresident: full-time $22,518. *Required fees:* $2128. Tuition and fees vary according to degree level and program. *Financial support:* Fellowships, research assistantships, teaching assistantships, career-related internships or fieldwork, institutionally sponsored loans, scholarships/grants, health care benefits, tuition waivers, and unspecified assistantships available. Financial award application deadline: 3/15. *Faculty research:* Social and cultural influences on schools, globalization and the workforce, history of women teachers in the U.S., school-corporate nexus, curriculum transformation for equity and inclusion. *Unit head:* Dr. Richard Lakes, Professor, 404-413-8030, Fax: 404-413-8003, E-mail: rlakes@gsu.edu. *Application contact:* Aishah Cowan, Administrative Academic Specialist, 404-413-8273, Fax: 404-413-8033, E-mail: acowan@gsu.edu.
Website: http://eps.education.gsu.edu/programs-courses/social-foundations-education/ms-sfd/

Harvard University, Extension School, Cambridge, MA 02138-3722. Offers applied sciences (CAS); biotechnology (ALM); educational technologies (ALM); educational technology (CET); English for graduate and professional studies (DGP); environmental management (ALM, CEM); information technology (ALM); journalism (ALM); liberal arts (ALM); management (ALM, CM); mathematics for teaching (ALM); museum studies (ALM); premedical studies (Diploma); publication and communication (CPC). *Program availability:* Part-time, evening/weekend. *Degree requirements:* For master's, thesis. *Entrance requirements:* For master's, 3 completed graduate courses with grade of B or higher. Additional exam requirements/recommendations for international students: Required—TOEFL (minimum score 600 paper-based), TWE (minimum score 5). *Expenses:* Contact institution.

Indiana University Bloomington, School of Education, Department of Educational Leadership and Policy Studies, Bloomington, IN 47405. Offers educational leadership (MS, Ed D, Ed S); higher education (Ed D, PhD); higher education and student affairs (MS); history and philosophy of education (MS); history, philosophy, and policy in education (PhD), including education policy studies, history of education, philosophy of education; international and comparative education (MS). *Accreditation:* NCATE. *Degree requirements:* For master's, thesis optional; for doctorate, comprehensive exam, thesis/dissertation; for Ed S, comprehensive exam or project. *Entrance requirements:* For master's, doctorate, and Ed S, GRE General Test. Additional exam requirements/recommendations for international students: Required—TOEFL (minimum score 79 iBT). Electronic applications accepted. *Faculty research:* Culturally engaging campus environments, school choice policy analysis, democracy and education in the national and international context, and principal leadership.

Indiana University Bloomington, University Graduate School, College of Arts and Sciences, School of Global and International Studies, Department of East Asian Languages and Cultures, Bloomington, IN 47408. Offers Chinese (MA, PhD); Chinese language pedagogy (MA); East Asian studies (MA); Japanese (MA, PhD); Japanese language pedagogy (MA). *Program availability:* Part-time. *Degree requirements:* For master's, one foreign language, thesis; for doctorate, 2 foreign languages, comprehensive exam, thesis/dissertation. *Entrance requirements:* Additional exam requirements/recommendations for international students: Required—TOEFL (minimum score 93 iBT). Electronic applications accepted. *Faculty research:* Modern East Asian history; politics and society; traditional Chinese thought and society; medieval and premodern Japanese history, literature and society; modern Chinese and Japanese film and literature; Chinese, Japanese, Korean language and linguistics.

Iowa State University of Science and Technology, Department of Education, Ames, IA 50011. Offers curriculum and instructional technology (M Ed, MS, PhD); elementary education (M Ed, MS); historical, philosophical, and comparative studies in education (M Ed, MS); special education (M Ed, MS, PhD). *Degree requirements:* For master's, thesis or alternative; for doctorate, thesis/dissertation. *Entrance requirements:* For master's and doctorate, GRE General Test. Additional exam requirements/recommendations for international students: Required—TOEFL (minimum score 560 paper-based; 83 iBT), IELTS (minimum score 6.5). Electronic applications accepted.

Kent State University, College of Education, Health and Human Services, School of Foundations, Leadership and Administration, Program in Cultural Foundations, Kent, OH 44242-0001. Offers M Ed, MA, PhD. *Accreditation:* NCATE. *Degree requirements:* For master's, thesis optional; for doctorate, comprehensive exam, thesis/dissertation. *Entrance requirements:* For master's, minimum GPA of 2.75, 2 letters of reference, goal statement; for doctorate, GRE General Test, minimum GPA of 3.5, master's degree, resume, interview, goal statement, 2 letters of reference. Additional exam requirements/recommendations for international students: Required—TOEFL (minimum score 550 paper-based; 80 iBT). Electronic applications accepted. *Expenses:* Tuition, state resident: full-time $11,310; part-time $515 per credit hour. Tuition, nonresident: full-time $20,396; part-time $928 per credit hour. *International tuition:* $18,544 full-time. *Faculty research:* Public politics, intercultural communication and training, research paradigms, comparative and international education.

Marquette University, Graduate School, College of Education, Department of Educational Policy and Leadership, Milwaukee, WI 53201-1881. Offers college student personnel administration (M Ed); curriculum and instruction (MA); education (MA); educational administration (M Ed); educational policy and foundations (MA); elementary education (Certificate); literacy (MA); principal (Certificate); reading specialist (Certificate); reading teacher (Certificate); secondary education (Certificate); superintendent (Certificate). *Program availability:* Part-time, evening/weekend. Terminal master's awarded for partial completion of doctoral program. *Degree requirements:* For master's, comprehensive exam, thesis (for some programs); for doctorate, thesis/ dissertation, qualifying exam. *Entrance requirements:* For master's, GRE General Test or MAT, official transcripts from all current and previous colleges/universities except Marquette, three letters of recommendation, statement of purpose; for doctorate, GRE General Test, MAT, sample of written work, official transcripts from all current and previous colleges/universities except Marquette, three letters of recommendation, statement of purpose, resume/curriculum vitae; for Certificate, GRE General Test or MAT, master's degree. Additional exam requirements/recommendations for international students: Required—TOEFL (minimum score 530 paper-based). *Expenses:* Contact institution. *Faculty research:* Leadership; social justice in education; development of lifelong learners; race, class, and schooling in historical perspective; urban teacher education.

McGill University, Faculty of Graduate and Postdoctoral Studies, Faculty of Education, Department of Integrated Studies in Education, Montréal, QC H3A 2T5, Canada. Offers culture and values in education (MA, PhD); curriculum studies (MA); educational leadership (MA, Certificate); educational studies (PhD); integrated studies in education (M Ed); second language education (MA, PhD).

Mount Saint Vincent University, Graduate Programs, Faculty of Education, Program in Educational Foundations, Halifax, NS B3M 2J6, Canada. Offers M Ed, MA Ed, MA-R. *Program availability:* Part-time, evening/weekend. *Degree requirements:* For master's, thesis (for some programs). *Entrance requirements:* For master's, bachelor's degree in related field, minimum B average. Electronic applications accepted. *Faculty research:* Research paradigms, moral aspects of education and teaching, private/independent schools, theory of critical thinking, teachers as workers and as agents of social change.

New York University, Steinhardt School of Culture, Education, and Human Development, Department of Humanities and Social Sciences in the Professions, Program in History of Education, New York, NY 10012. Offers MA, PhD. *Program availability:* Part-time. *Students:* Average age 27. 11 applicants, 55% accepted, 3 enrolled. In 2017, 1 master's awarded. *Entrance requirements:* For doctorate, GRE General Test, interview. Additional exam requirements/recommendations for international students: Required—TOEFL (minimum score 100 iBT). *Application deadline:* For fall admission, 12/1 priority date for domestic and international students; for spring admission, 10/1 for domestic and international students. Applications are processed on a rolling basis. Application fee: $75. Electronic applications accepted. *Expenses: Tuition:* Full-time $41,352; part-time $19,968 per year. *Required fees:* $2496; $1628 per unit. $814 per term. Tuition and fees vary according to course load and program. *Financial support:* Fellowships with full and partial tuition reimbursements, Federal Work-Study, institutionally sponsored loans, scholarships/grants, and tuition waivers (partial) available. Support available to part-time students. Financial award application deadline: 2/1; financial award applicants required to submit FAFSA. *Faculty research:* American educational thought, democratic community and education, twentieth century history of education, Jewish history. *Unit head:* Dr. Jonathan L. Zimmerman, Director, 212-998-5049, Fax: 212-995-4832, E-mail: jlzimm@aol.com. *Application contact:* 212-998-5030, Fax: 212-995-4328, E-mail: steinhardt.gradadmissions@nyu.edu.
Website: http://steinhardt.nyu.edu/humsocsci/history

Northern Arizona University, College of Education, Department of Educational Leadership, Flagstaff, AZ 86011. Offers community college teaching and learning (Graduate Certificate); educational leadership (M Ed, Ed D), including community college/ higher education (M Ed), educational foundations (M Ed), instructional leadership K-12 school leadership (M Ed), principal certification K-12 (M Ed); principal (Graduate Certificate); superintendent (Graduate Certificate). *Program availability:* Part-time. *Faculty:* 24 full-time (10 women), 1 (woman) part-time/adjunct. *Students:* 193 full-time (128 women), 648 part-time (425 women); includes 329 minority (54 Black or African American, non-Hispanic/Latino; 63 American Indian or Alaska Native, non-Hispanic/Latino; 10 Asian, non-Hispanic/Latino; 169 Hispanic/Latino; 1 Native Hawaiian or other Pacific Islander, non-Hispanic/Latino; 32 Two or more races, non-Hispanic/Latino), 2 international. Average age 38. 298 applicants, 98% accepted, 291 enrolled. In 2017, 252 master's, 12 doctorates, 48 other advanced degrees awarded. *Degree requirements:* For master's, comprehensive exam, thesis (for some programs); for doctorate, comprehensive exam, thesis/ dissertation; for Graduate Certificate, comprehensive exam (for some programs). *Entrance requirements:* Additional exam requirements/recommendations for international students: Required—TOEFL (minimum score 80 iBT), IELTS (minimum score 6.5). *Application deadline:* For fall admission, 3/1 for domestic and international students; for spring admission, 10/1 for domestic and international students. Applications are processed on a rolling basis. Application fee: $65. Electronic applications accepted. *Expenses:* Tuition, state resident: full-time $9240; part-time $458 per credit hour. Tuition, nonresident: full-time $21,588; part-time $1199 per credit hour. *Required fees:* $1021; $14 per credit hour. $646 per semester. Tuition and fees vary according to course load, campus/location and program. *Financial support:* In 2017–18, 1 student received support. Institutionally sponsored loans, health care benefits, tuition waivers (partial), and unspecified assistantships available. Financial award application deadline: 2/1; financial award applicants required to submit FAFSA. *Unit head:* Dr. Michael Schwanenberger, Chair, 928-523-3202, Fax: 928-523-1929, E-mail: michael.schwanenberger@nau.edu. *Application contact:* Jennifer Offutt, Administrative Assistant, 928-523-3202, Fax: 928-523-1929, E-mail: jennifer.offutt@nau.edu.
Website: https://nau.edu/coe/Ed-Leadership/

Northern Illinois University, Graduate School, College of Education, Department of Leadership, Educational Psychology and Foundations, De Kalb, IL 60115-2854. Offers educational administration (MS Ed, Ed D, Ed S); educational psychology (MS Ed, Ed D); foundations of education (MS Ed); school business management (MS Ed). *Program availability:* Part-time, evening/weekend, online learning. *Faculty:* 23 full-time (12 women). *Students:* 11 full-time (7 women), 241 part-time (151 women); includes 42 minority (19 Black or African American, non-Hispanic/Latino; 3 Asian, non-Hispanic/ Latino; 11 Hispanic/Latino; 9 Two or more races, non-Hispanic/Latino), 7 international. Average age 39. 76 applicants, 80% accepted, 26 enrolled. In 2017, 47 master's, 28 doctorates, 20 other advanced degrees awarded. *Degree requirements:* For master's, comprehensive exam, thesis optional; for doctorate, thesis/dissertation, candidacy exam, dissertation defense. *Entrance requirements:* For master's, minimum undergraduate GPA of 2.75; for doctorate, GRE General Test, minimum undergraduate GPA of 2.75, 3.2 graduate; for Ed S, GRE General Test, minimum GPA of 2.75 (undergraduate), 3.2 (graduate). Additional exam requirements/recommendations for international students: Required—TOEFL (minimum score 550 paper-based). *Application deadline:* For fall admission, 6/1 for domestic students, 5/1 for international students; for spring admission, 11/1 for domestic students, 10/1 for international

students. Applications are processed on a rolling basis. Application fee: $40. Electronic applications accepted. *Financial support:* In 2017–18, 1 research assistantship with full tuition reimbursement, 2 teaching assistantships with full tuition reimbursements were awarded; fellowships with full tuition reimbursements, career-related internships or fieldwork, Federal Work-Study, scholarships/grants, tuition waivers (full), and staff assistantships also available. Support available to part-time students. Financial award applicants required to submit FAFSA. *Faculty research:* Interpersonal forgiveness, learner-centered education, psychedelic studies, senior theory, professional growth. *Unit head:* Carolyn V. Schee, Chair, 815-753-4404, E-mail: lepf@niu.edu. *Application contact:* Graduate School Office, 815-753-0395, E-mail: gradsch@niu.edu.
Website: http://cedu.niu.edu/LEPF/

Northern Vermont University–Johnson, Program in Education, Johnson, VT 05656. Offers applied behavior analysis (MA Ed); curriculum and instruction (MA Ed); foundations of education (MA Ed); special education (MA Ed). *Program availability:* Part-time. *Faculty:* 5 full-time (3 women), 4 part-time/adjunct (3 women). *Students:* 3 full-time (all women), 36 part-time (30 women). In 2017, 23 master's awarded. *Degree requirements:* For master's, thesis or alternative, exit interview. *Entrance requirements:* For master's, interview. Additional exam requirements/recommendations for international students: Required—TOEFL. *Application deadline:* For fall admission, 5/1 for domestic students, 2/1 for international students. Applications are processed on a rolling basis. Electronic applications accepted. *Expenses:* Tuition, state resident: part-time $572 per credit hour. Tuition, nonresident: part-time $832 per credit hour. *Financial support:* Scholarships/grants and unspecified assistantships available. Financial award application deadline: 3/1; financial award applicants required to submit FAFSA. *Unit head:* Dr. Kathleen Brinegar, Chair, Department of Education, 802-635-1472, Fax: 802-635-1465, E-mail: kathleen.brinegar@jsc.edu. *Application contact:* Catherine H. Higley, Administrative Assistant, 800-635-2356 Ext. 1244, Fax: 802-635-1248, E-mail: catherine.higley@jsc.edu.
Website: http://www.jsc.edu/academics/education/majors-and-minors/master-of-arts-in-education/

Penn State University Park, Graduate School, College of Education, Department of Education Policy Studies, University Park, PA 16802. Offers educational leadership (M Ed, D Ed, PhD, Certificate); educational theory and policy (MA, PhD); higher education (M Ed, D Ed, PhD). *Accreditation:* NCATE. *Program availability:* Online learning. *Unit head:* Dr. David H. Monk, Dean, 814-865-2523, Fax: 814-865-0555. *Application contact:* Lori Hawn, Director, Graduate Student Services, 814-865-1795, Fax: 814-863-4627, E-mail: l-gswww@lists.psu.edu.
Website: http://ed.psu.edu/eps

Purdue University, Graduate School, College of Education, Department of Educational Studies, West Lafayette, IN 47907. Offers administration (MS Ed, PhD, Ed S); counseling and development (MS Ed, PhD); education of the gifted (MS Ed); educational psychology (MS Ed, PhD); foundations of education (MS Ed, PhD); higher education administration (MS Ed, PhD); special education (MS Ed, PhD). *Accreditation:* ACA (one or more programs are accredited); NCATE (one or more programs are accredited). *Program availability:* Part-time, evening/weekend. *Faculty:* 29 full-time (22 women), 1 part-time/adjunct (0 women). *Students:* 78 full-time (60 women), 226 part-time (162 women); includes 45 minority (16 Black or African American, non-Hispanic/ Latino; 8 Asian, non-Hispanic/Latino; 15 Hispanic/Latino; 6 Two or more races, non-Hispanic/Latino), 45 international. Average age 32. 214 applicants, 53% accepted, 70 enrolled. In 2017, 38 master's, 20 doctorates, 4 other advanced degrees awarded. *Degree requirements:* For master's, thesis optional; for doctorate, thesis/dissertation, oral and written exams; for Ed S, oral presentation, project. *Entrance requirements:* For master's, GRE General Test (except for special education if undergraduate GPA is higher than a 3.0), minimum undergraduate GPA of 3.0; for doctorate and Ed S, GRE General Test (minimum combined score of 1000, 300 for new scoring), minimum undergraduate GPA of 3.0. Additional exam requirements/recommendations for international students: Required—TOEFL (minimum score 550 paper-based; 77 iBT), TWE (minimum score 5). *Application deadline:* Applications are processed on a rolling basis. Application fee: $60 ($75 for international students). Electronic applications accepted. *Financial support:* Fellowships with full tuition reimbursements, research assistantships with full tuition reimbursements, teaching assistantships with full tuition reimbursements, career-related internships or fieldwork, and tuition waivers (full) available. Support available to part-time students. Financial award application deadline: 3/1; financial award applicants required to submit FAFSA. *Faculty research:* Motivation, learning disabilities, school learning, group processes, cognitive development. *Unit head:* F. Richard Olenchak, Head, 765-494-9170, E-mail: olenchak@purdue.edu. *Application contact:* Heather Brinkman, Graduate Contact, 765-494-2345, Fax: 765-494-5832, E-mail: hbrinkma@purdue.edu.
Website: http://www.edst.purdue.edu/

Rutgers University–New Brunswick, Graduate School of Education, Department of Educational Theory, Policy and Administration, Program in Social and Philosophical Foundations of Education, Piscataway, NJ 08854-8097. Offers Ed M, Ed D. *Program availability:* Part-time, evening/weekend. *Degree requirements:* For doctorate, thesis/ dissertation, qualifying exam. *Entrance requirements:* For master's, GRE General Test; for doctorate, GRE General Test, writing sample. Additional exam requirements/ recommendations for international students: Required—TOEFL. Electronic applications accepted. *Faculty research:* Anthropology, history, sociology, philosophy, comparative education.

Saint Louis University, Graduate Programs, School of Education, Department of Educational Studies, St. Louis, MO 63103. Offers curriculum and instruction (MA, Ed D, PhD); educational foundations (MA, Ed D, PhD); special education (MA); teaching (MAT). *Accreditation:* NCATE. *Program availability:* Part-time. *Degree requirements:* For master's, comprehensive exam; for doctorate, comprehensive exam, thesis/dissertation, preliminary oral and written exams. *Entrance requirements:* For master's, GRE General Test or MAT, letters of recommendation, resume; for doctorate, GRE General Test, letters of recommendation, resumé, goal statement, transcripts. Additional exam requirements/recommendations for international students: Required—TOEFL (minimum score 525 paper-based). Electronic applications accepted. *Faculty research:* Teacher preparation, multicultural issues, children with special needs, qualitative research in education, inclusion.

Simon Fraser University, Office of Graduate Studies and Postdoctoral Fellows, Faculty of Education, Programs in Curriculum and Instruction, Burnaby, BC V5A 1S6, Canada. Offers curriculum and instruction (M Ed); curriculum and instruction foundations (M Ed, MA); curriculum theory and implementation (PhD); educational practice (M Ed); philosophy of education (PhD). *Degree requirements:* For master's, comprehensive exam (for some programs), thesis (for some programs); for doctorate, comprehensive exam, thesis/dissertation. *Entrance requirements:* For master's, minimum GPA of 3.0 (on scale of 4.33) or 3.33 based on last 60 credits of undergraduate courses; for doctorate, minimum GPA of 3.5 (on scale of 4.33). Additional exam requirements/recommendations for international students: Recommended—TOEFL (minimum score 580 paper-based; 93 iBT), IELTS (minimum score 7), TWE (minimum score 5). Electronic applications accepted. *Faculty research:* Philosophy of education, applied and comparative epistemology, ethics and moral education, critical multicultural practices.

Southern Illinois University Edwardsville, Graduate School, School of Education, Health, and Human Behavior, Department of Educational Leadership, Program in Learning, Culture, and Society, Edwardsville, IL 62026. Offers MS Ed. *Program availability:* Part-time, evening/weekend. *Degree requirements:* For master's, thesis or alternative, project, oral defense. *Entrance requirements:* Additional exam requirements/recommendations for international students: Required—TOEFL (minimum score 550 paper-based; 79 iBT), IELTS (minimum score 6.5). Electronic applications accepted.

Spring Hill College, Graduate Programs, Program in Education, Mobile, AL 36608-1791. Offers early childhood education (MAT, MS Ed); educational theory (MS Ed); elementary education (MAT, MS Ed); secondary education (MAT, MS Ed). *Program availability:* Part-time. *Faculty:* 2 full-time (both women). *Students:* 15 part-time (14 women); includes 6 minority (5 Black or African American, non-Hispanic/Latino; 1 Hispanic/Latino). Average age 30. In 2017, 5 master's awarded. *Degree requirements:* For master's, comprehensive exam, completion of program within 6 calendar years of entrance into graduate studies at Spring Hill; documentation of course field assignments (MS) or completion of internship (MAT). *Entrance requirements:* For master's, GRE, MAT, or PRAXIS (varies by program), bachelor's degree with minimum undergraduate GPA of 3.0; class B certificate (for MS); minimum number of hours in specific fields (for MAT). Additional exam requirements/recommendations for international students: Required—TOEFL (minimum score 550 paper-based; 80 iBT), IELTS (minimum score 6.5), CPE or CAE (minimum score C), Michigan English Language Assessment Battery (minimum score 90). *Application deadline:* For fall admission, 8/1 priority date for domestic and international students; for spring admission, 12/1 priority date for domestic and international students. Applications are processed on a rolling basis. Application fee: $25 ($35 for international students). Electronic applications accepted. *Expenses:* Contact institution. *Financial support:* Applicants required to submit FAFSA. *Unit head:* Dr. Lori P. Aultman, Chair of Education, 251-380-3473, Fax: 251-460-2184, E-mail: laultman@shc.edu. *Application contact:* Robert Stewart, Vice President of Enrollment, 251-380-3030, Fax: 251-460-2186, E-mail: rstewart@shc.edu. Website: http://ug.shc.edu/graduate-degrees/master-science-education/

Syracuse University, School of Education, CAS Program in Instructional Design Foundations, Syracuse, NY 13244. Offers CAS. *Program availability:* Part-time. *Entrance requirements:* For degree, baccalaureate degree from regionally-accredited college/university, statement of goals, three recommendation letters, transcripts. *Application deadline:* Applications are processed on a rolling basis. Application fee: $75. Electronic applications accepted. *Financial support:* Fellowships, research assistantships, teaching assistantships, career-related internships or fieldwork, and scholarships/grants available. Financial award application deadline: 1/15. *Unit head:* Dr. Jing Lei, Chair, 315-443-3703, E-mail: takoszal@syr.edu. *Application contact:* Speranza Migliore, Graduate Admissions Recruiter, 315-443-2505, E-mail: gradrcrt@syr.edu. Website: http://soe.syr.edu/academic/Instructional_Design_Development_and_Evaluation/graduate/certificates/default.aspx

Syracuse University, School of Education, Programs in Cultural Foundations of Education, Syracuse, NY 13244. Offers MS, PhD, CAS. *Program availability:* Part-time. In 2017, 4 master's, 4 doctorates awarded. *Degree requirements:* For master's, thesis or alternative; for doctorate, comprehensive exam, thesis/dissertation. *Entrance requirements:* For master's, baccalaureate degree from regionally-accredited college/university, writing sample; for doctorate, GRE, master's degree (preferred); writing sample; interview (recommended); personal statement. Additional exam requirements/recommendations for international students: Required—TOEFL (minimum score 100 iBT). *Application deadline:* For fall admission, 1/15 priority date for domestic and international students. Applications are processed on a rolling basis. Application fee: $75. Electronic applications accepted. *Financial support:* Fellowships with full tuition reimbursements, research assistantships, teaching assistantships, career-related internships or fieldwork, and scholarships/grants available. Financial award application deadline: 1/15; financial award applicants required to submit FAFSA. *Faculty research:* Gender and education, history of women's education, the role of science in liberal education, student attrition, inequality in education. *Unit head:* Dr. Barbara Applebaum, Chair, 315-443-3343, E-mail: bappleba@syr.edu. *Application contact:* Speranza Migliore, Graduate Admissions Recruiter, 315-443-2505, E-mail: gradrcrt@syr.edu. Website: http://soe.syr.edu/academic/cultural_foundations_of_education/

Teachers College, Columbia University, Department of Arts and Humanities, New York, NY 10027. Offers applied linguistics (MA, Ed D); art and art education (Ed M, MA, Ed D, Ed DCT); arts administration (MA); bilingual and bicultural education (MA); global competence (Certificate); history and education (Ed D, PhD); music and music education (Ed DCT); philosophy and education (MA, Ed D, PhD); social studies education (Ed M, PhD); teaching English to speakers of other languages (Ed M); teaching of English and English education (Ed M, MA, Ed D, PhD), including English education (Ed M, Ed D, PhD), teaching of English (MA); teaching of social studies (MA); TESOL (MA, Ed D). *Program availability:* Part-time, evening/weekend. *Students:* 391 full-time (305 women), 418 part-time (283 women); includes 246 minority (62 Black or African American, non-Hispanic/Latino; 3 American Indian or Alaska Native, non-Hispanic/Latino; 94 Asian, non-Hispanic/Latino; 75 Hispanic/Latino; 12 Two or more races, non-Hispanic/Latino), 209 international. Average age 30. 1,053 applicants, 60% accepted, 334 enrolled. Terminal master's awarded for partial completion of doctoral program. *Financial support:* Fellowships, research assistantships, teaching assistantships, career-related internships or fieldwork, Federal Work-Study, institutionally sponsored loans, tuition waivers (full and partial), and unspecified assistantships available. Support available to part-time students. *Unit head:* Prof. William Gaudelli, Department Chair, E-mail: gaudelli@tc.columbia.edu. *Application contact:* David Estrella, Director of Admissions, 212-678-3305, Fax: 212-678-4171, E-mail: estrella@tc.columbia.edu.

University at Buffalo, the State University of New York, Graduate School, Graduate School of Education, Department of Educational Leadership and Policy, Buffalo, NY 14260. Offers economics and education policy analysis (MA); education studies (Ed M); educational administration (Ed M, Ed D, PhD); educational culture, policy and society (PhD); higher education administration (Ed M, PhD); school building leadership (Certificate); school business and human resource administration (Certificate); school district business leadership (Certificate); school district leadership (Certificate). *Program availability:* Part-time, evening/weekend. *Faculty:* 16 full-time (10 women), 9 part-time/adjunct (6 women). *Students:* 65 full-time (44 women), 125 part-time (82 women); includes 29 minority (23 Black or African American, non-Hispanic/Latino; 3 Asian, non-Hispanic/Latino; 3 Hispanic/Latino), 19 international. Average age 35. 153 applicants, 75% accepted, 59 enrolled. In 2017, 45 master's, 4 doctorates, 23 other advanced degrees awarded. *Degree requirements:* For master's, comprehensive exam (for some programs), thesis optional; for doctorate, comprehensive exam, thesis/dissertation. *Entrance requirements:* For master's, interview, letters of reference; for doctorate, GRE General Test or MAT, writing sample, letters of reference. Additional exam requirements/recommendations for international students: Required—TOEFL (minimum score 550 paper-based; 79 iBT). *Application deadline:* For fall admission, 2/1 priority date for domestic students, 2/1 for international students; for spring admission, 11/15 priority date for domestic students, 10/1 for international students. Applications are

processed on a rolling basis. Application fee: $50. Electronic applications accepted. *Financial support:* In 2017–18, 18 fellowships (averaging $5,673 per year), 34 research assistantships with tuition reimbursements (averaging $12,055 per year) were awarded; career-related internships or fieldwork, Federal Work-Study, institutionally sponsored loans, scholarships/grants, health care benefits, tuition waivers (full and partial), and unspecified assistantships also available. Financial award application deadline: 3/15; financial award applicants required to submit FAFSA. *Faculty research:* College access and choice, school leadership preparation and practice, public policy, curriculum and pedagogy, comparative and international education. *Total annual research expenditures:* $637,951. *Unit head:* Dr. Janina C. Brutt-Griffler, Chair, 716-645-2471, Fax: 716-645-2481, E-mail: bruttg@buffalo.edu. *Application contact:* Veronica Kase, Admission Assistant, 716-645-2110, Fax: 716-645-7937, E-mail: vakase@buffalo.edu. Website: http://gse.buffalo.edu/elp

The University of British Columbia, Faculty of Education, Department of Educational Studies, Vancouver, BC V6T 1Z1, Canada. Offers adult learning and education (M Ed); adult learning and global change (M Ed); curriculum and leadership (M Ed); educational administration and leadership (M Ed); educational leadership and policy (Ed D); educational studies (M Ed, MA, PhD); higher education (M Ed); society, culture and politics in education (M Ed). *Program availability:* Part-time, evening/weekend. Terminal master's awarded for partial completion of doctoral program. *Degree requirements:* For master's, thesis; for doctorate, comprehensive exam, thesis/dissertation. *Entrance requirements:* For master's, minimum B+ average, 4-year undergraduate degree, field-related experience; for doctorate, minimum B+ average, 4-year undergraduate degree, master's degree, field-related experience. Additional exam requirements/recommendations for international students: Required—TOEFL (minimum score 600 paper-based; 100 iBT) or IELTS (minimum score 6.5). Electronic applications accepted. *Expenses:* Contact institution. *Faculty research:* Educational leadership educational administration adult education politics in education, global change and adult learning.

University of California, Riverside, Graduate Division, Graduate School of Education, Riverside, CA 92521. Offers applied behavior analysis (M Ed); diversity and equity (M Ed); education policy analysis and leadership (PhD); education specialist (Credential); education, society, and culture (MA, PhD); educational psychology (MA, PhD); general education (M Ed); higher education administration and policy (M Ed, PhD); multiple subject (Credential); research, evaluation, measurement and statistics (MA); school psychology (PhD); single subject (Credential); special education (M Ed, PhD); special education and autism (MA); TESOL (M Ed). *Faculty:* 29 full-time (16 women), 2 part-time/adjunct (1 woman). *Students:* 241 full-time (188 women). 396 applicants, 42% accepted, 166 enrolled. In 2017, 130 master's, 15 doctorates, 14 other advanced degrees awarded. Terminal master's awarded for partial completion of doctoral program. *Degree requirements:* For master's, comprehensive exams or thesis (MA), case study or analytical report (M Ed); for doctorate, comprehensive exam, thesis/dissertation, written and oral qualifying exams, college teaching practicum. *Entrance requirements:* For master's, GRE General Test (for MA); CBEST and CSET (for M Ed in general education only), UCR Extension TESOL certificate (for M Ed with TESOL emphasis only); for doctorate, GRE General Test, writing sample; for Credential, CBEST, CSET. Additional exam requirements/recommendations for international students: Required—TOEFL (minimum score 550 paper-based; 80 iBT), IELTS (minimum score 7). *Application deadline:* For fall admission, 9/1 for domestic students, 6/1 for international students; for winter admission, 11/15 for domestic students, 9/1 for international students; for spring admission, 3/1 for domestic students, 12/1 for international students. Applications are processed on a rolling basis. Application fee: $80 ($100 for international students). Electronic applications accepted. *Expenses:* Tuition, state resident: full-time $5746. Tuition, nonresident: full-time $10,780. Tuition and fees vary according to campus/location and program. *Financial support:* In 2017–18, 105 students received support, including 16 fellowships with full tuition reimbursements available (averaging $31,000 per year), 25 research assistantships with full tuition reimbursements available (averaging $31,000 per year), 10 teaching assistantships with full tuition reimbursements available (averaging $31,000 per year); career-related internships or fieldwork, Federal Work-Study, institutionally sponsored loans, scholarships/grants, and unspecified assistantships also available. Financial award application deadline: 12/15. *Faculty research:* Responsiveness to intervention, faculty core, response to intervention of English language learners, advanced modeling techniques, study on social capital, trust, and motivation. *Total annual research expenditures:* $1.7 million. *Unit head:* Thomas Smith, Dean, 951-827-4633, E-mail: thomas.smith@ucr.edu. *Application contact:* Heather Killeen, Graduate Program Coordinator, 951-827-6362, E-mail: heather.killeen@ucr.edu. Website: http://www.education.ucr.edu/

University of Central Oklahoma, The Jackson College of Graduate Studies, College of Liberal Arts, Department of Political Science, Edmond, OK 73034-5209. Offers political science (MA), including international affairs; public administration (MPA), including public and nonprofit management, urban management. *Program availability:* Part-time. *Faculty:* 11 full-time (4 women), 1 part-time/adjunct (0 women). *Students:* 42 full-time (21 women), 58 part-time (26 women); includes 33 minority (14 Black or African American, non-Hispanic/Latino; 3 American Indian or Alaska Native, non-Hispanic/Latino; 10 Hispanic/Latino; 6 Two or more races, non-Hispanic/Latino), 18 international. Average age 32. 127 applicants, 84% accepted, 29 enrolled. In 2017, 32 master's awarded. *Degree requirements:* For master's, comprehensive exam (for some programs), thesis (for some programs). *Entrance requirements:* For master's, 18 undergraduate hours in political science. Additional exam requirements/recommendations for international students: Required—TOEFL (minimum score 550 paper-based; 79 iBT), IELTS (minimum score 6.5). *Application deadline:* For fall admission, 7/15 for international students; for spring admission, 11/15 for international students. Applications are processed on a rolling basis. Application fee: $60. Electronic applications accepted. *Expenses:* Tuition, state resident: full-time $5375; part-time $268.75 per credit hour. Tuition, nonresident: full-time $13,295; part-time $664.75 per credit hour. *Required fees:* $626; $31.30 per credit hour. One-time fee: $50. Tuition and fees vary according to program. *Financial support:* In 2017–18, 20 students received support, including 3 research assistantships with partial tuition reimbursements available (averaging $3,943 per year), 4 teaching assistantships with partial tuition reimbursements available (averaging $7,394 per year); career-related internships or fieldwork, scholarships/grants, tuition waivers (partial), and unspecified assistantships also available. Financial award application deadline: 3/31; financial award applicants required to submit FAFSA. *Unit head:* Dr. Lou Furmanski, Department Chair, 405-974-5540, Fax: 405-974-3823. *Application contact:* Dr. Jan Hardt, Graduate Advisor, 405-974-5840, Fax: 405-974-3823, E-mail: gradcoll@uco.edu. Website: http://sites.uco.edu/la/political-science/index.asp

University of Cincinnati, Graduate School, College of Education, Criminal Justice, and Human Services, School of Education, Program in Educational Studies, Cincinnati, OH 45221. Offers M Ed, PhD. *Accreditation:* NCATE. *Program availability:* Part-time. *Degree requirements:* For master's, thesis optional; for doctorate, comprehensive exam, thesis/dissertation. *Entrance requirements:* For master's, GRE General Test; for doctorate, GRE General Test, GRE Subject Test. Additional exam requirements/recommendations for international students: Required—TOEFL (minimum score 520 paper-based), OEPT 3. Electronic applications accepted. *Expenses:* Tuition, area resident: Full-time $14,468.

Foundations and Philosophy of Education

Tuition, state resident: full-time $14,968; part-time $754 per credit hour. Tuition, nonresident: full-time $24,210; part-time $1311 per credit hour. *International tuition:* $26,460 full-time. *Required fees:* $3958; $84 per credit hour. One-time fee: $85 full-time. Tuition and fees vary according to course load, degree level and program.

University of Hawaii at Manoa, Office of Graduate Education, College of Education, Department of Educational Foundations, Honolulu, HI 96822. Offers M Ed. *Program availability:* Part-time, evening/weekend. *Degree requirements:* For master's, thesis optional. *Entrance requirements:* Additional exam requirements/recommendations for international students: Required—TOEFL (minimum score 580 paper-based; 92 iBT), IELTS (minimum score 5). *Faculty research:* Multicultural-ethnic education, comparative education, educational policy, interdisciplinary inquiry, moral/political education.

University of Hawaii at Manoa, Office of Graduate Education, College of Education, PhD in Education Program, Honolulu, HI 96822. Offers curriculum and instruction (PhD); educational administration (PhD); educational foundations (PhD); educational policy studies (PhD); educational psychology (PhD); exceptionalities (PhD); kinesiology (PhD); learning design and technology (PhD). *Program availability:* Part-time, evening/weekend. *Degree requirements:* For doctorate, thesis/dissertation. *Entrance requirements:* For doctorate, GRE General Test, sample of written work. Additional exam requirements/recommendations for international students: Required—TOEFL (minimum score 600 paper-based; 100 iBT), IELTS (minimum score 7).

University of Houston, College of Education, Department of Educational Leadership and Cultural Studies, Houston, TX 77204. Offers administration and supervision (M Ed, Ed D); higher education (M Ed); historical, social, and cultural foundations of education (M Ed). *Accreditation:* NCATE. *Program availability:* Part-time, evening/weekend. *Degree requirements:* For master's, comprehensive exam or thesis; for doctorate, comprehensive exam, thesis/dissertation. *Entrance requirements:* For master's, GRE General Test, minimum cumulative GPA of 2.6, 3 letters of recommendation, resume/vitae, goal statement; for doctorate, GRE General Test, minimum cumulative GPA of 2.6, 3 letters of recommendation, resume/vitae, goal statement, writing sample, interview. Additional exam requirements/recommendations for international students: Required—TOEFL (minimum score 550 paper-based; 79 iBT). Electronic applications accepted. *Faculty research:* Change, supervision, multiculturalism, evaluation, policy.

University of Houston–Clear Lake, School of Education, Program in Foundations and Professional Studies, Houston, TX 77058-1002. Offers counseling (MS); instructional technology (MS); multicultural studies (MS). *Program availability:* Part-time, evening/weekend. *Degree requirements:* For master's, thesis optional. *Entrance requirements:* For master's, GRE or minimum GPA of 3.0 in last 60 hours. Additional exam requirements/recommendations for international students: Required—TOEFL (minimum score 550 paper-based). Electronic applications accepted.

The University of Iowa, Graduate College, College of Education, Department of Educational Policy and Leadership Studies, Program in Schools, Culture, and Society, Iowa City, IA 52242-1316. Offers MA, PhD. *Degree requirements:* For master's, thesis optional, exam; for doctorate, comprehensive exam, thesis/dissertation. *Entrance requirements:* For master's and doctorate, GRE General Test, minimum GPA of 3.0. Additional exam requirements/recommendations for international students: Required—TOEFL (minimum score 550 paper-based; 81 iBT). Electronic applications accepted.

The University of Iowa, Graduate College, College of Education, Department of Psychological and Quantitative Foundations, Iowa City, IA 52242-1316. Offers counseling psychology (PhD); educational measurement and statistics (MA, PhD); educational psychology (MA, PhD); school psychology (PhD, Ed S). *Accreditation:* APA. *Degree requirements:* For master's, thesis optional, exam; for doctorate, comprehensive exam, thesis/dissertation; for Ed S, exam. *Entrance requirements:* For master's, doctorate, and Ed S, GRE General Test, minimum GPA of 3.0. Additional exam requirements/recommendations for international students: Required—TOEFL (minimum score 550 paper-based; 81 iBT). Electronic applications accepted.

University of Manitoba, Faculty of Graduate Studies, Faculty of Education, Department of Educational Administration, Foundations and Psychology, Winnipeg, MB R3T 2N2, Canada. Offers adult and post-secondary education (M Ed); educational administration (M Ed); guidance and counseling (M Ed); inclusive special education (M Ed); social foundations of education (M Ed). *Degree requirements:* For master's, thesis or alternative.

University of Maryland, College Park, Academic Affairs, College of Education, Department of Education Policy and Leadership, College Park, MD 20742. Offers curriculum and educational communications (M Ed, MA, Ed D, PhD); social foundations of education (M Ed, MA, Ed D, PhD, CAGS). *Accreditation:* NCATE. *Program availability:* Part-time, evening/weekend, online learning. *Degree requirements:* For master's, thesis or alternative, internship and/or field experience; for doctorate, comprehensive exam, thesis/dissertation, practicum or internship. *Entrance requirements:* For master's, GRE General Test or MAT, minimum GPA of 3.0, scholarly writing sample, 3 letters of recommendation; for doctorate, GRE General Test or MAT, scholarly writing sample; minimum undergraduate GPA of 3.0, graduate 3.5. *Faculty research:* Educational technology, adult and higher education.

University of Minnesota, Twin Cities Campus, Graduate School, College of Education and Human Development, Department of Educational Psychology, Program in Psychological Foundations of Education, Minneapolis, MN 55455-0213. Offers MA, PhD. *Students:* 23 full-time (15 women), 2 part-time (0 women); includes 5 minority (3 Asian, non-Hispanic/Latino; 2 Two or more races, non-Hispanic/Latino), 7 international. Average age 25. 37 applicants, 27% accepted, 10 enrolled. In 2017, 8 master's, 2 doctorates awarded. Application fee: $75 ($95 for international students). *Unit head:* Dr. Geoffrey Maruyama, Chair, 612-625-5861, Fax: 612-624-8241, E-mail: geoff@umn.edu. *Application contact:* Dr. Ernest Davenport, Director of Graduate Studies, 612-624-1040, E-mail: lqr6576@umn.edu.
Website: http://www.cehd.umn.edu/EdPsych/programs/Foundations/

University of New Mexico, Graduate Studies, College of Education, Program in Language, Literacy and Sociocultural Studies, Albuquerque, NM 87131. Offers American Indian education (MA); bilingual education (MA, PhD); educational linguistics (PhD); educational thought and sociocultural studies (MA, PhD); literacy/language arts (MA, PhD); social studies (MA); TESOL (MA, PhD). *Faculty:* 16 full-time (10 women), 4 part-time/adjunct (all women). *Students:* 56 full-time (34 women), 129 part-time (97 women); includes 93 minority (7 Black or African American, non-Hispanic/Latino; 15 American Indian or Alaska Native, non-Hispanic/Latino; 9 Asian, non-Hispanic/Latino; 56 Hispanic/Latino; 6 Two or more races, non-Hispanic/Latino), 44 international. Average age 40. 61 applicants, 38% accepted, 23 enrolled. In 2017, 36 master's, 4 doctorates awarded. *Degree requirements:* For master's, comprehensive exam, thesis optional; for doctorate, comprehensive exam, thesis/dissertation, research skills. *Entrance requirements:* For master's, letter of intent, 3 letters of recommendation, resume, BA/BS, department demographic form, transcripts; for doctorate, writing sample, letter of intent, 3 letters of recommendation, resume, BA/BS, MA, department demographic form, transcripts. Additional exam requirements/recommendations for international students: Required—TOEFL. *Application deadline:* For fall admission, 12/1 for domestic and international students; for spring admission, 9/15 for domestic and international students. Application fee: $50. Electronic applications accepted. *Financial support:* Fellowships, research assistantships, teaching assistantships, career-related internships or fieldwork, institutionally sponsored loans, scholarships/grants, and unspecified assistantships available. Support available to part-time students. Financial award application deadline: 3/1; financial award applicants required to submit FAFSA. *Faculty research:* School reform, professional development, history of education, Native American education, politics of education, feminism and issues of sexual identity, critical race theory, bilingualism, literacy reading, adolescent literature, second language acquisition, critical theory and schooling, indigenous languages. *Unit head:* Dr. Lois M. Meyer, Chair, 505-277-7244, Fax: 505-277-8362, E-mail: lsmeyer@unm.edu. *Application contact:* Debra Schaffer, Administrative Assistant, 505-277-0437, Fax: 505-277-8362, E-mail: schaffer@unm.edu.
Website: http://coe.unm.edu/departments-programs/llss/index.html

University of Pennsylvania, Graduate School of Education, Division of Literacy, Culture, and International Education, Program in Education, Culture and Society, Philadelphia, PA 19104. Offers MS Ed, PhD. *Students:* Average age 29. 187 applicants, 32% accepted, 30 enrolled. In 2017, 11 master's, 4 doctorates awarded.

University of Pittsburgh, School of Education, Department of Administrative and Policy Studies, Program in Social and Comparative Analysis in Education, Pittsburgh, PA 15260. Offers M Ed, MA, Ed D, PhD. *Program availability:* Evening/weekend. *Degree requirements:* For master's, thesis; for doctorate, thesis/dissertation. *Entrance requirements:* For doctorate, GRE General Test. Additional exam requirements/recommendations for international students: Required—TOEFL (minimum score 80 iBT). Electronic applications accepted.

University of Rochester, Margaret Warner Graduate School of Education and Human Development, Doctoral Programs in Education, Rochester, NY 14627. Offers counseling (Ed D); educational administration (Ed D); educational policy and theory (PhD); higher education (PhD); human development in educational context (PhD); teaching, curriculum, and change (PhD).

University of Saskatchewan, College of Graduate Studies and Research, College of Education, Department of Educational Foundations, Saskatoon, SK S7N 5A2, Canada. Offers M Ed, MC Ed, PhD, Diploma. *Program availability:* Part-time. *Degree requirements:* For master's, thesis (for some programs); for doctorate, comprehensive exam (for some programs), thesis/dissertation. *Entrance requirements:* Additional exam requirements/recommendations for international students: Required—TOEFL (minimum score 80 iBT); Recommended—IELTS (minimum score 6.5). Electronic applications accepted. *Faculty research:* Indian and northern education, adult and continuing education, international education.

University of South Africa, College of Human Sciences, Pretoria, South Africa. Offers adult education (M Ed); African languages (MA, PhD); African politics (MA, PhD); Afrikaans (MA, PhD); ancient history (MA, PhD); ancient Near Eastern studies (MA, PhD); anthropology (MA, PhD); applied linguistics (MA); Arabic (MA, PhD); archaeology (MA); art history (MA); Biblical archaeology (MA); Biblical studies (M Th, D Th, PhD); Christian spirituality (M Th, D Th); church history (M Th, D Th); classical studies (MA, PhD); clinical psychology (MA); communication (MA, PhD); comparative education (M Ed, Ed D); consulting psychology (D Admin, D Com, PhD); curriculum studies (M Ed, Ed D); development studies (M Admin, MA, D Admin, PhD); didactics (M Ed, Ed D); education (M Tech); education management (M Ed, Ed D); educational psychology (M Ed); English (MA); environmental education (M Ed); French (MA, PhD); German (MA, PhD); Greek (MA); guidance and counseling (M Ed); health studies (MA, PhD), including health sciences education (MA), health services management (MA), medical and surgical nursing science (critical care general) (MA), midwifery and neonatal nursing science (MA), trauma and emergency care (MA); history (MA, PhD); history of education (Ed D); inclusive education (M Ed, Ed D); information and communications technology policy and regulation (MA); information science (MA, MIS, PhD); international politics (MA, PhD); Islamic studies (MA, PhD); Italian (MA, PhD); Judaica (MA, PhD); linguistics (MA, PhD); mathematical education (M Ed); mathematics education (MA); missiology (M Th, D Th); modern Hebrew (MA, PhD); musicology (MA, MMus, D Mus, PhD); natural science education (M Ed); New Testament (M Th, D Th); Old Testament (D Th); pastoral therapy (M Th, D Th); philosophy (MA); philosophy of education (M Ed, Ed D); politics (MA, PhD); Portuguese (MA, PhD); practical theology (M Th, D Th); psychology (MA, MS, PhD); psychology of education (M Ed, Ed D); public health (MA); religious studies (MA, D Th, PhD); Romance languages (MA); Russian (MA, PhD); Semitic languages (MA, PhD); social behavior studies in HIV/AIDS (MA); social science (mental health) (MA); social science in development studies (MA); social science in psychology (MA); social science in social work (MA); social science in sociology (MA); social work (MSW, DSW, PhD); socio-education (M Ed, Ed D); sociolinguistics (MA); sociology (MA, PhD); Spanish (MA, PhD); systematic theology (M Th, D Th); TESOL (teaching English to speakers of other languages) (MA); theological ethics (M Th, D Th); theory of literature (MA, PhD); urban ministries (D Th); urban ministry (M Th).

University of South Carolina, The Graduate School, College of Education, Department of Educational Studies, Program in Foundations in Education, Columbia, SC 29208. Offers PhD. *Accreditation:* NCATE. *Program availability:* Part-time. *Degree requirements:* For doctorate, comprehensive exam, thesis/dissertation. *Entrance requirements:* For doctorate, GRE General Test or MAT, interview. Electronic applications accepted. *Faculty research:* Oral history, educational biography, home schooling, international education.

The University of Tennessee, Graduate School, College of Education, Health and Human Sciences, Program in Education, Knoxville, TN 37996. Offers art education (MS); counseling education (PhD); cultural studies in education (PhD); curriculum (MS, Ed S); curriculum, educational research and evaluation (Ed D, PhD); early childhood education (PhD); early childhood special education (MS); education of deaf and hard of hearing (MS); educational administration and policy studies (Ed D, PhD); educational administration and supervision (Ed S); educational psychology (Ed D, PhD); elementary education (MS, Ed S); elementary teaching (MS); English education (MS, Ed S); exercise science (PhD); foreign language/ESL education (MS, Ed S); instructional technology (MS, Ed D, PhD, Ed S); literacy, language and ESL education (PhD); literacy, language education, and ESL education (Ed D); mathematics education (MS, Ed S); modified and comprehensive special education (MS); reading education (MS, Ed S); school counseling (Ed S); school psychology (PhD, Ed S); science education (MS, Ed S); secondary teaching (MS); social foundations (MS); social science education (MS, Ed S); socio-cultural foundations of sports and education (PhD); special education (Ed S); teacher education (Ed D, PhD). *Accreditation:* NCATE. *Program availability:* Part-time, evening/weekend. *Degree requirements:* For master's and Ed S, thesis optional; for doctorate, variable foreign language requirement, thesis/dissertation. *Entrance requirements:* For master's, minimum GPA of 2.7; for doctorate and Ed S, GRE General Test, minimum GPA of 2.7. Additional exam requirements/recommendations for international students: Required—TOEFL. Electronic applications accepted.

The University of Texas of the Permian Basin, Office of Graduate Studies, School of Education, Program in Professional Education, Odessa, TX 79762-0001. Offers MA. *Degree requirements:* For master's, comprehensive exam (for some programs), thesis (for some programs). *Entrance requirements:* For master's, GRE General Test. Additional exam requirements/recommendations for international students: Required—TOEFL (minimum score 550 paper-based).

The University of Toledo, College of Graduate Studies, Judith Herb College of Education, Department of Educational Foundations and Leadership, Toledo, OH 43606-3390. Offers educational administration and supervision (ME, DE, Ed S); educational psychology (ME, PhD); educational research and measurement (ME, PhD); educational sociology (ME, PhD); educational theory and social foundations (ME); foundations of education (DE, PhD); history of education (PhD); philosophy of education (PhD). *Accreditation:* NCATE. *Program availability:* Part-time, evening/weekend. *Degree requirements:* For master's, comprehensive exam, thesis or alternative; for doctorate, comprehensive exam, thesis/dissertation; for Ed S, thesis optional. *Entrance requirements:* For master's, doctorate, and Ed S, minimum cumulative GPA of 2.7 for all previous academic work, letters of recommendation. Additional exam requirements/recommendations for international students: Required—TOEFL (minimum score 550 paper-based; 80 iBT). Electronic applications accepted.

University of Utah, Graduate School, College of Education, Department of Education, Culture, and Society, Salt Lake City, UT 84112. Offers M Ed, MA, MS, PhD. *Program availability:* Evening/weekend. *Faculty:* 10 full-time (8 women), 1 part-time/adjunct (0 women). *Students:* 43 full-time (24 women), 47 part-time (30 women); includes 50 minority (6 Black or African American, non-Hispanic/Latino; 2 Asian, non-Hispanic/Latino; 38 Hispanic/Latino; 4 Two or more races, non-Hispanic/Latino), 2 international. Average age 34. 41 applicants, 61% accepted, 20 enrolled. In 2017, 25 master's, 7 doctorates awarded. Terminal master's awarded for partial completion of doctoral program. *Entrance requirements:* For master's, minimum GPA of 3.0; for doctorate, minimum GPA of 3.5. Additional exam requirements/recommendations for international students: Required—TOEFL (minimum score 650 paper-based; 114 iBT). *Application deadline:* For fall admission, 2/1 priority date for domestic and international students. Application fee: $55 ($65 for international students). Electronic applications accepted. *Financial support:* In 2017–18, 8 students received support, including 5 fellowships with full tuition reimbursements available (averaging $13,500 per year), 3 research assistantships with full tuition reimbursements available (averaging $13,500 per year), 8 teaching assistantships with full tuition reimbursements available (averaging $15,000 per year); scholarships/grants, health care benefits, tuition waivers (full and partial), and unspecified assistantships also available. Financial award application deadline: 4/1; financial award applicants required to submit FAFSA. *Faculty research:* History, philosophy and sociology of education, language, culture and curriculum. *Total annual research expenditures:* $6,404. *Unit head:* Dr. Edward Buendía, Department Chair, 801-587-7803, E-mail: ed.buendia@utah.edu. *Application contact:* Amy Suzanne Wright, Academic Program Support Specialist, 801-587-7814, E-mail: amy.wright@utah.edu. Website: http://ecs.utah.edu/

University of Victoria, Faculty of Graduate Studies, Faculty of Education, Department of Curriculum and Instruction, Victoria, BC V8W 2Y2, Canada. Offers art education (M Ed, PhD); curriculum studies (M Ed, MA, PhD); early childhood education (M Ed, PhD); educational studies (PhD); language and literacy (M Ed, MA, PhD); mathematics (M Ed, MA, PhD); music education (M Ed, MA, PhD); science (M Ed, MA, PhD); social studies (M Ed, MA); social, cultural and foundational studies (MA, PhD); technology and environmental education (PhD). *Program availability:* Part-time. *Degree requirements:* For master's, thesis, project (M Ed); for doctorate, comprehensive exam, thesis/dissertation. *Entrance requirements:* For master's, minimum B average. Additional exam requirements/recommendations for international students: Required—TOEFL (minimum score 575 paper-based), IELTS (minimum score 7). Electronic applications accepted. *Faculty research:* Elementary and secondary English, language arts, curriculum theory and practice, educational media and technology, educational administration and leadership, history and philosophy of education.

University of Washington, Graduate School, College of Education, Seattle, WA 98195. Offers curriculum and instruction (M Ed, Ed D, PhD), including educational technology, general curriculum (Ed D, PhD), language, literacy, and culture, mathematics education, multicultural education, reading and language arts education (Ed D), science education, social studies education, teaching and curriculum (M Ed); educational leadership and policy studies (M Ed, Ed D, PhD), including administration (Ed D), educational policy, organization, and leadership (M Ed, PhD), higher education, leadership for learning (Ed D), social and cultural foundations of education (M Ed, PhD); educational psychology (M Ed, PhD), including educational psychology (PhD), human development and cognition (M Ed), learning sciences, measurement, statistics and research design (M Ed), school psychology (M Ed); instructional leadership (M Ed); intercollegiate athletic leadership (M Ed); special education (M Ed, Ed D, PhD), including early childhood special education (M Ed), emotional and behavioral disabilities (M Ed), learning disabilities (M Ed), low-incidence disabilities (M Ed), severe disabilities (M Ed), special education (Ed D, PhD); teacher education (MIT). *Accreditation:* APA. *Program availability:* Part-time, evening/weekend. *Degree requirements:* For master's, thesis optional; for doctorate, thesis/dissertation. *Entrance requirements:* For master's and doctorate, GRE General Test, minimum GPA of 3.0. Additional exam requirements/recommendations for international students: Required—TOEFL. Electronic applications accepted. *Faculty research:* School restructuring/effective schools, special education interventions, literacy and writing, technology, school partnerships, teacher preparation.

University of Wisconsin–Milwaukee, Graduate School, School of Education, Department of Educational Policy and Community Studies, Milwaukee, WI 53201-0413. Offers cultural foundations of community engagement and education (MS), including alternative education, community engagement and partnerships, educational policy, race relations, youth work; educational policy (Graduate Certificate). *Program availability:* Part-time. *Students:* 8 full-time (6 women), 24 part-time (20 women); includes 18 minority (9 Black or African American, non-Hispanic/Latino; 1 American Indian or Alaska Native, non-Hispanic/Latino; 2 Asian, non-Hispanic/Latino; 1 Hispanic/Latino; 5 Two or more races, non-Hispanic/Latino). Average age 35. 21 applicants, 67% accepted, 10 enrolled. In 2017, 11 master's awarded. *Entrance requirements:* Additional exam requirements/recommendations for international students: Required—TOEFL (minimum score 550 paper-based; 79 iBT), IELTS (minimum score 6.5). *Application deadline:* For fall admission, 1/1 priority date for domestic students; for spring admission, 9/1 for domestic students. Application fee: $56 ($96 for international students). Electronic applications accepted. *Financial support:* Fellowships with full tuition reimbursements, research assistantships, teaching assistantships, career-related internships or fieldwork, health care benefits, and unspecified assistantships available. Support available to part-time students. Financial award application deadline: 4/15; financial award applicants required to submit FAFSA. *Application contact:* General Information Contact, 414-229-4721, E-mail: soeinfo@uwm.edu. Website: http://uwm.edu/education/academics/edu-policy-community-studies-department/

University of Wisconsin–Milwaukee, Graduate School, School of Education, Department of Exceptional Education, Milwaukee, WI 53201-0413. Offers autism spectrum disorders (Graduate Certificate); exceptional (MS); transition for students with disabilities (Graduate Certificate); urban education (PhD), including adult, continuing and higher education leadership, art education, curriculum and instruction, exceptional education, mathematics education, multicultural studies, social foundations of education. *Program availability:* Part-time. *Students:* 45 full-time (34 women), 68 part-time (54 women); includes 46 minority (27 Black or African American, non-Hispanic/

Latino; 7 Asian, non-Hispanic/Latino; 1 Hispanic/Latino; 11 Two or more races, non-Hispanic/Latino), 4 international. Average age 39. 43 applicants, 53% accepted, 19 enrolled. In 2017, 12 master's, 13 doctorates, 8 other advanced degrees awarded. *Entrance requirements:* Additional exam requirements/recommendations for international students: Required—TOEFL (minimum score 550 paper-based; 79 iBT), IELTS (minimum score 6.5). *Application deadline:* For fall admission, 1/1 priority date for domestic students; for spring admission, 9/1 for domestic students. Application fee: $56 ($96 for international students). Electronic applications accepted. *Financial support:* Fellowships, research assistantships, teaching assistantships, career-related internships or fieldwork, health care benefits, and unspecified assistantships available. Support available to part-time students. Financial award application deadline: 4/15; financial award applicants required to submit FAFSA. *Faculty research:* Emotional disturbance, hearing impairment, learning disabilities, mental retardation. *Application contact:* General Information Contact, 414-229-4721, E-mail: soeinfo@uwm.edu. Website: http://uwm.edu/education/academics/exceptional-edu-department/

Wayne State University, College of Education, Division of Theoretical and Behavioral Foundations, Detroit, MI 48202. Offers applied behavior analysis (Certificate); counseling (M Ed, MA, Ed D, Ed S); counseling psychology (MA, PhD); education evaluation and research (M Ed, Ed D); educational psychology (M Ed, PhD), including learning and instruction sciences (PhD); rehabilitation counseling and community inclusion (MA); school and community psychology (MA, Certificate). *Accreditation:* ACA (one or more programs are accredited); CORE (one or more programs are accredited). *Program availability:* Evening/weekend. *Students:* Average age 32. 294 applicants, 34% accepted, 72 enrolled. In 2017, 87 master's, 12 doctorates, 14 other advanced degrees awarded. *Entrance requirements:* For master's, GRE, interview, personal statement, portfolio (art therapy); for doctorate, GRE, department-written exam, interview, curriculum vitae, references, master's degree in closely-related field with minimum GPA of 3.5, demonstration of counseling skills (for Ed D in counseling); for other advanced degree, master's degree in counseling and counseling license (for Ed S); good standing in school and community psychology MA program (for Certificate). Additional exam requirements/recommendations for international students: Required—TOEFL (minimum score 550 paper-based; 79 iBT), Michigan English Language Assessment Battery (minimum score 85); Recommended—IELTS (minimum score 6.5), TWE (minimum score 5.5). *Application deadline:* For fall admission, 6/1 priority date for domestic students, 5/1 priority date for international students; for winter admission, 10/1 priority date for domestic students, 9/1 priority date for international students; for spring admission, 2/1 priority date for domestic students, 1/1 priority date for international students. Applications are processed on a rolling basis. Application fee: $50. Electronic applications accepted. *Expenses:* Contact institution. *Financial support:* In 2017–18, 92 students received support, including 2 research assistantships with tuition reimbursements available (averaging $17,994 per year); fellowships, teaching assistantships, Federal Work-Study, scholarships/grants, health care benefits, and unspecified assistantships also available. Support available to part-time students. Financial award applicants required to submit FAFSA. *Faculty research:* Adolescents at risk, supervision of counseling. *Unit head:* Dr. Cheryl Somers, Assistant Dean, 313-577-1670, E-mail: c.somers@wayne.edu. *Application contact:* Janice Green, Assistant Dean, 313-577-1605, E-mail: jwgreen@wayne.edu. Website: http://coe.wayne.edu/tbf/index.php

West Chester University of Pennsylvania, College of Education and Social Work, Department of Educational Foundations and Policy Studies, West Chester, PA 19383. Offers education for sustainability (Certificate); educational technology (Certificate); higher education policy and student affairs (MS); transformative education and social change (MS). *Program availability:* Part-time. *Students:* 35 full-time (21 women), 49 part-time (33 women); includes 15 minority (9 Black or African American, non-Hispanic/Latino; 1 Asian, non-Hispanic/Latino; 2 Hispanic/Latino; 3 Two or more races, non-Hispanic/Latino), 1 international. Average age 29. 77 applicants, 90% accepted, 51 enrolled. In 2017, 5 master's, 6 other advanced degrees awarded. *Degree requirements:* For master's, comprehensive exam (for some programs), thesis, 36 credits (42 credits for MS in higher education policy and student affairs). *Entrance requirements:* For master's, teaching certification (strongly recommended); for Certificate, minimum GPA of 3.0. Additional exam requirements/recommendations for international students: Required—TOEFL or IELTS. *Application deadline:* For fall admission, 5/15 for international students; for spring admission, 10/15 for international students. Applications are processed on a rolling basis. Application fee: $50. Electronic applications accepted. *Expenses:* Tuition, state resident: full-time $9000; part-time $500 per credit. Tuition, nonresident: full-time $13,500; part-time $750 per credit. *Required fees:* $2959; $149.79 per credit. *Financial support:* Scholarships/grants and unspecified assistantships available. Financial award application deadline: 2/15; financial award applicants required to submit FAFSA. *Faculty research:* Technology integration: preparing our teachers for the twenty-first century, critical pedagogy, education for sustainability. *Unit head:* Dr. John Elmore, Chair, 610-436-6934, Fax: 610-436-3102, E-mail: jelmore@wcupa.edu. *Application contact:* Office of Graduate Studies and Extended Education, 610-436-2943, Fax: 610-436-2763, E-mail: gradstudy@wcupa.edu. Website: http://www.wcupa.edu/education-socialWork/profsecedu/

Western Illinois University, School of Graduate Studies, College of Education and Human Services, Department of Educational Studies, Program in Educational and Interdisciplinary Studies, Macomb, IL 61455-1390. Offers educational and interdisciplinary studies (MS Ed); teaching English to speakers of other languages (Certificate). *Accreditation:* NCATE. *Program availability:* Part-time. *Students:* 6 full-time (all women), 29 part-time (25 women); includes 4 minority (1 Asian, non-Hispanic/Latino; 2 Hispanic/Latino; 1 Two or more races, non-Hispanic/Latino), 2 international. Average age 42. 15 applicants, 73% accepted, 10 enrolled. In 2017, 15 master's, 10 Certificates awarded. *Degree requirements:* For master's, thesis or alternative. *Entrance requirements:* For master's, minimum GPA of 2.75, interview. Additional exam requirements/recommendations for international students: Required—TOEFL (minimum score 550 paper-based; 80 iBT). *Application deadline:* Applications are processed on a rolling basis. Application fee: $30. Electronic applications accepted. *Financial support:* In 2017–18, 1 research assistantship with full tuition reimbursement (averaging $7,544 per year) was awarded; unspecified assistantships also available. Financial award applicants required to submit FAFSA. *Unit head:* Dr. Greg Montalvo, Interim Chairperson, 309-298-1183. *Application contact:* Dr. Nancy Parsons, Associate Provost and Director of Graduate Studies, 309-298-1806, Fax: 309-298-2345, E-mail: grad-office@wiu.edu. Website: http://www.wiu.edu/coehs/es/programs/eis/eis.php

Widener University, School of Human Service Professions, Center for Education, Chester, PA 19013-5792. Offers adult education (M Ed); counseling in higher education (M Ed); counselor education (M Ed); early childhood education (M Ed); educational foundations (M Ed); educational leadership (M Ed); educational psychology (M Ed); elementary education (M Ed); English and language arts (M Ed); health education (M Ed); higher education leadership (Ed D); home and school visitor (M Ed); human sexuality (M Ed, PhD); mathematics education (M Ed); middle school education (M Ed); principalship (M Ed); reading and language arts (Ed D); reading education (M Ed); school administration (Ed D); science education (M Ed); social studies education

Foundations and Philosophy of Education

(M Ed); special education (M Ed); technology education (M Ed). *Accreditation:* NCATE. *Program availability:* Part-time, evening/weekend. *Faculty:* 34 full-time (22 women), 37 part-time/adjunct (14 women). *Students:* 131 full-time (112 women), 244 part-time (179 women); includes 94 minority (58 Black or African American, non-Hispanic/Latino; 1 American Indian or Alaska Native, non-Hispanic/Latino; 1 Asian, non-Hispanic/Latino; 22 Hispanic/Latino; 12 Two or more races, non-Hispanic/Latino), 12 international. Average age 37. 140 applicants, 38% accepted, 26 enrolled. In 2017, 45 master's, 21 doctorates awarded. Terminal master's awarded for partial completion of doctoral program. *Degree requirements:* For doctorate, thesis/dissertation. *Entrance requirements:* For master's, minimum GPA of 2.5; for doctorate, GRE or MAT, minimum GPA of 2.0 (undergraduate), 3.5 (graduate). *Application deadline:* Applications are processed on a rolling basis. Application fee: $25 ($300 for international students). Electronic applications accepted. *Expenses:* Contact institution. *Financial support:* Career-related internships or fieldwork, tuition waivers (full and partial), and unspecified assistantships available. Support available to part-time students. Financial award application deadline: 5/1. *Faculty research:* Reading and cognition, adult education, technology education, educational leadership, special education. *Unit head:* Dr. Shawn Fitzgerald, Dean, 610-499-4294, Fax: 610-499-4623, E-mail: smfitzgerald@widener.edu. *Application contact:* Megan Kuft, Director of Graduate Admissions, 610-499-4124, E-mail: gradprograms@widener.edu.
Website: http://www.widener.edu/academics/schools/eics

William Paterson University of New Jersey, College of Humanities and Social Sciences, Wayne, NJ 07470-8420. Offers applied sociology (MA); assessment and evaluation research (Certificate); bilingual education (Certificate); clinical and counseling psychology (MA); clinical psychology (Psy D); creative and professional writing (MFA); English (MA); history (MA); public policy and international affairs (MA); teaching English as a second language (Certificate). *Program availability:* Part-time. *Faculty:* 36 full-time

(21 women), 10 part-time/adjunct (5 women). *Students:* 62 full-time (44 women), 102 part-time (71 women); includes 76 minority (12 Black or African American, non-Hispanic/Latino; 8 Asian, non-Hispanic/Latino; 50 Hispanic/Latino; 6 Two or more races, non-Hispanic/Latino), 6 international. Average age 33. 156 applicants, 51% accepted, 52 enrolled. In 2017, 39 master's awarded. *Degree requirements:* For master's, thesis (for some programs), internship (for some programs). *Entrance requirements:* For master's, GRE/MAT, minimum GPA of 3.0; 2 letters of recommendation; writing sample/personal statement. Additional exam requirements/recommendations for international students: Required—TOEFL (minimum score 550 paper-based; 79 iBT), IELTS (minimum score 6). *Application deadline:* For fall admission, 6/1 for domestic students, 3/1 for international students; for spring admission, 11/1 for domestic students, 10/1 for international students. Applications are processed on a rolling basis. Application fee: $50. Electronic applications accepted. *Expenses:* Tuition, state resident: full-time $13,920; part-time $6264 per year. Tuition, nonresident: full-time $21,700; part-time $9765 per year. *Required fees:* $80; $36 per year. Tuition and fees vary according to course load, degree level and program. *Financial support:* In 2017–18, 3,480 students received support. Career-related internships or fieldwork, Federal Work-Study, scholarships/grants, and unspecified assistantships available. Support available to part-time students. Financial award application deadline: 3/15; financial award applicants required to submit FAFSA. *Faculty research:* Relationship violence, work-family balance, social development of Japan, theories justifying war, reactions to trauma. *Total annual research expenditures:* $32,300. *Unit head:* Dr. Kara Rabbitt, Dean, 973-720-2180, Fax: 973-720-2955, E-mail: rabbittk@wpunj.edu. *Application contact:* Tinu Adeniran, Associate Director, Graduate Admissions, 973-720-2764, Fax: 973-720-2035, E-mail: adenirant@wpunj.edu.
Website: http://www.wpunj.edu/cohss

International and Comparative Education

The American University in Cairo, Graduate School of Education, Cairo, Egypt. Offers educational leadership (MA); international and comparative education (MA). *Program availability:* Part-time, evening/weekend. *Faculty:* 9 full-time (6 women). *Students:* 6 full-time (4 women), 77 part-time (65 women). Average age 33. 40 applicants, 48% accepted, 11 enrolled. In 2017, 24 master's awarded. *Degree requirements:* For master's, thesis. *Entrance requirements:* Additional exam requirements/recommendations for international students: Required—TOEFL (minimum score 450 paper-based; 45 iBT), IELTS (minimum score 5). *Application deadline:* For fall admission, 2/1 priority date for domestic and international students; for spring admission, 10/15 priority date for domestic and international students. Applications are processed on a rolling basis. Application fee: $85. Electronic applications accepted. *Financial support:* Fellowships with partial tuition reimbursements, teaching assistantships, career-related internships or fieldwork, scholarships/grants, tuition waivers (partial), and unspecified assistantships available. Financial award application deadline: 3/10. *Faculty research:* Educational reform. *Unit head:* Dr. Ted Purinton, Dean, 20-2-2615-1490, E-mail: tedpurinton@aucegypt.edu. *Application contact:* Maha Hegazi, Director for Graduate Admissions, 20-2-2615-1462, E-mail: mahahegazi@aucegypt.edu.
Website: http://www.aucegypt.edu/GSE/Pages/default.aspx

Andrews University, School of Graduate Studies, College of Arts and Sciences, Department of Behavioral Science, Berrien Springs, MI 49104. Offers international development (MSCID), including community and international development. *Faculty:* 10 full-time (2 women), 1 part-time/adjunct (0 women). *Students:* 18 full-time (13 women), 3 part-time (all women); includes 7 minority (3 Black or African American, non-Hispanic/Latino; 2 Asian, non-Hispanic/Latino; 2 Hispanic/Latino), 12 international. Average age 31. 29 applicants, 62% accepted, 6 enrolled. In 2017, 11 master's awarded. *Entrance requirements:* For master's, GRE. Additional exam requirements/recommendations for international students: Required—TOEFL (minimum score 550 paper-based). *Application deadline:* Applications are processed on a rolling basis. Application fee: $40. *Faculty research:* Risk behaviors. *Unit head:* Dr. Duane C. McBride, Chair, 269-471-3152. *Application contact:* Justina Clayburn, Supervisor of Graduate Admission, 800-253-2874, Fax: 269-471-6321, E-mail: graduate@andrews.edu.

Boston College, Lynch School of Education, Program in International Higher Education, Chestnut Hill, MA 02467-3800. Offers MA. *Students:* 10 full-time (5 women), 7 part-time (5 women); includes 2 minority (both Asian, non-Hispanic/Latino), 10 international. Average age 27. 44 applicants, 59% accepted, 11 enrolled. In 2017, 1 master's awarded. *Application deadline:* Applications are processed on a rolling basis. Application fee: $65. *Unit head:* Hans de Wit, Director, 617-552-4236. *Application contact:* Laura E. Rumbley, Coordinator, 617-552-4185.

Bowling Green State University, Graduate College, College of Education and Human Development, School of Educational Foundations, Leadership and Policy, Program in Cross-Cultural and International Education, Bowling Green, OH 43403. Offers MA. *Program availability:* Part-time. *Degree requirements:* For master's, thesis or alternative. *Entrance requirements:* For master's, GRE General Test. Additional exam requirements/recommendations for international students: Required—TOEFL.

California Baptist University, Program in Education, Riverside, CA 92504-3206. Offers educational leadership (MS); educational leadership for faith-based institutions (MS); educational leadership for public institutions (MS); educational technology (MS); instructional computer applications (MS); international education (MS); leadership and adult learning (MS); leadership and organizational studies (MS); online teaching and learning (MS); reading (MS); science education (MA); special education in mild/moderate disabilities (MS); special education in moderate/severe disabilities (MS); teacher leadership (MS); teaching (MS); teaching and learning (MS). *Program availability:* Part-time, evening/weekend, 100% online, blended/hybrid learning. *Faculty:* 19 full-time (11 women), 36 part-time/adjunct (22 women). *Students:* 232 full-time (182 women), 315 part-time (247 women); includes 264 minority (33 Black or African American, non-Hispanic/Latino; 4 American Indian or Alaska Native, non-Hispanic/Latino; 11 Asian, non-Hispanic/Latino; 186 Hispanic/Latino; 7 Native Hawaiian or other Pacific Islander, non-Hispanic/Latino; 23 Two or more races, non-Hispanic/Latino). Average age 31. 217 applicants, 64% accepted, 129 enrolled. In 2017, 196 master's awarded. *Degree requirements:* For master's, comprehensive exam, project, or thesis. *Entrance requirements:* For master's, minimum undergraduate GPA of 2.75; 500-word essay; three letters of recommendation; two prerequisite courses completed with minimum C grade. Additional exam requirements/recommendations for international students: Required—TOEFL (minimum score 80 iBT). *Application deadline:* For fall admission, 8/1 priority date for domestic students, 7/1 for international students; for

spring admission, 12/1 priority date for domestic students, 11/1 for international students. Applications are processed on a rolling basis. Application fee: $45. Electronic applications accepted. *Expenses:* Contact institution. *Financial support:* In 2017–18, 162 students received support. Federal Work-Study and scholarships/grants available. Financial award applicants required to submit CSS PROFILE or FAFSA. *Faculty research:* Leadership development, complexity theory, faith and learning, special education, social and philosophical contexts of education. *Unit head:* Dr. John Shoup, Dean, School of Education, 951-343-4516, E-mail: jshoup@calbaptist.edu. *Application contact:* Gavin Andrew, Graduate Admissions Counselor, 951-552-8437, E-mail: gandrew@calbaptist.edu.
Website: http://www.calbaptist.edu/mastersined/

California State University, Dominguez Hills, College of Extended and International Education, Carson, CA 90747-0001. Offers MA, MS. *Program availability:* Part-time, evening/weekend, online learning. *Degree requirements:* For master's, thesis. *Entrance requirements:* Additional exam requirements/recommendations for international students: Required—TOEFL. Electronic applications accepted. *Expenses:* Contact institution.

The College of New Jersey, Office of Graduate and Advancing Education, Office of Global Programs, Program in Overseas Education, Ewing, NJ 08628. Offers M Ed, Certificate. *Program availability:* Part-time. *Degree requirements:* For master's, comprehensive exam. *Entrance requirements:* For master's, GRE, minimum GPA of 3.0 in field or 2.75 overall; for Certificate, previous master's degree or higher. Additional exam requirements/recommendations for international students: Required—TOEFL. Electronic applications accepted.

Drexel University, Goodwin College of Professional Studies, School of Education, Philadelphia, PA 19104-2875. Offers applied behavior analysis (MS); creativity and innovation (MS); education improvement and transformation (MS); educational administration (MS); educational leadership and management (Ed D); educational leadership development and learning technologies (PhD); global and international education (MS); higher education (MS); human resources development (MS); learning technologies (MS); mathematics, learning and teaching (MS); special education (MS); teaching, learning and curriculum (MS). *Program availability:* Part-time, evening/weekend, online learning. *Degree requirements:* For doctorate, thesis/dissertation. *Entrance requirements:* For doctorate, GRE or GMAT. Additional exam requirements/recommendations for international students: Required—TOEFL, IELTS. Electronic applications accepted. Application fee is waived when completed online. *Expenses:* Contact institution. *Faculty research:* Leadership development, mathematics education, literacy, autism, educational technology.

See Display on page 654 and Close-Up on page 719.

East Carolina University, Graduate School, Thomas Harriot College of Arts and Sciences, Program in International Studies, Greenville, NC 27858-4353. Offers international studies (MA); international teaching (Certificate). *Program availability:* Part-time. *Students:* 13 full-time (9 women), 3 part-time (1 woman); includes 5 minority (3 Black or African American, non-Hispanic/Latino; 2 Hispanic/Latino), 2 international. Average age 27. 8 applicants, 100% accepted, 7 enrolled. In 2017, 5 master's, 2 other advanced degrees awarded. *Degree requirements:* For master's, comprehensive exam, thesis optional, international field experience. *Entrance requirements:* For master's, GRE General Test, MAT or GMAT. Additional exam requirements/recommendations for international students: Recommended—TOEFL (minimum score 78 iBT), IELTS (minimum score 6.5). *Application deadline:* For fall admission, 7/1 priority date for domestic and international students; for spring admission, 11/15 priority date for domestic and international students; for summer admission, 3/15 priority date for domestic and international students. Applications are processed on a rolling basis. Application fee: $75. Electronic applications accepted. *Expenses:* Tuition, state resident: full-time $4749; part-time $297 per credit hour. Tuition, nonresident: full-time $17,898; part-time $1119 per credit hour. *Required fees:* $2691; $224 per credit hour. Part-time tuition and fees vary according to course load and program. *Financial support:* Research assistantships with partial tuition reimbursements available. Financial award application deadline: 3/1. *Unit head:* Dr. David L. Smith, Director, 252-328-5554, E-mail: smithdav@ecu.edu. *Application contact:* Dean of Graduate School, 252-328-6012, Fax: 252-328-6071, E-mail: gradschool@ecu.edu.
Website: http://www.ecu.edu/cs-cas/international/maisindex.cfm

Florida International University, College of Arts, Sciences, and Education, Department of Leadership and Professional Studies, Miami, FL 33199. Offers adult education and human resource development (MS, Ed D); counseling (MS), including

rehabilitation counseling, school counseling; counselor education (MS), including clinical mental health counseling; educational administration and supervision (Ed D); educational leadership (MS, Certificate, Ed S); higher education (Ed D); higher education administration (MS); international and comparative education (MS); recreation and sport management (MS), including recreation and sport management, recreational therapy; school psychology (Ed S); urban education (MS), including instruction in urban settings, learning technologies, multicultural/bilingual, multicultural/TESOL, urban education. *Program availability:* Part-time, evening/weekend. *Faculty:* 60 full-time (41 women), 112 part-time/adjunct (77 women). *Students:* 221 full-time (162 women), 301 part-time (239 women); includes 418 minority (127 Black or African American, non-Hispanic/Latino; 9 Asian, non-Hispanic/Latino; 271 Hispanic/Latino; 11 Two or more races, non-Hispanic/Latino), 10 international. Average age 31. 330 applicants, 55% accepted, 100 enrolled. In 2017, 181 master's, 6 doctorates awarded. *Degree requirements:* For doctorate, thesis/dissertation. *Entrance requirements:* For master's, minimum GPA of 3.0; for doctorate and other advanced degree, GRE General Test. Additional exam requirements/recommendations for international students: Required—TOEFL (minimum score 550 paper-based; 80 iBT), IELTS (minimum score 6.3). *Application deadline:* For fall admission, 6/1 priority date for domestic students, 4/1 for international students; for winter admission, 10/1 priority date for domestic students, 9/1 for international students; for spring admission, 3/1 priority date for domestic students, 2/1 for international students. Applications are processed on a rolling basis. Application fee: $30. Electronic applications accepted. *Expenses:* Tuition, state resident: full-time $8912; part-time $446 per credit hour. Tuition, nonresident: full-time $21,393; part-time $992 per credit hour. *Required fees:* $390; $195 per semester. *Financial support:* Fellowships, research assistantships with tuition reimbursements, teaching assistantships with tuition reimbursements, Federal Work-Study, and tuition waivers (full and partial) available. Support available to part-time students. Financial award applicants required to submit FAFSA. *Unit head:* Dr. Benjamin Baez, Chair, 305-348-3214, Fax: 305-348-1515, E-mail: benjamin.baez@fiu.edu. *Application contact:* Nanett Rojas, Assistant Director, Graduate Admissions, 305-348-7464, Fax: 305-348-7441, E-mail: gradadm@fiu.edu.
Website: http://education.fiu.edu

Florida State University, The Graduate School, College of Education, Department of Educational Leadership and Policy Studies, Tallahassee, FL 32306. Offers educational leadership and administration (Certificate); educational leadership and policy (MS, Ed D, PhD, Ed S), including education policy and evaluation (MS, Ed D, PhD), educational leadership and administration; foundations of education (MS, PhD), including history and philosophy of education, international and multicultural education; higher education (MS, PhD); institutional research (Certificate); program evaluation (Certificate). *Program availability:* Part-time, evening/weekend, 100% online, blended/hybrid learning, asynchronous, minimal on-campus study. *Faculty:* 19 full-time (15 women), 10 part-time/adjunct (7 women). *Students:* 151 full-time (105 women), 196 part-time (138 women); includes 127 minority (55 Black or African American, non-Hispanic/Latino; 4 Asian, non-Hispanic/Latino; 49 Hispanic/Latino; 19 Two or more races, non-Hispanic/Latino), 33 international. Average age 35. 229 applicants, 54% accepted, 66 enrolled. In 2017, 49 master's, 10 doctorates, 17 other advanced degrees awarded. *Degree requirements:* For master's, comprehensive exam, thesis optional; for doctorate, comprehensive exam, thesis/dissertation, diagnostic exam, preliminary exam, prospectus defense, dissertation defense. *Entrance requirements:* For master's, doctorate, and other advanced degree, GRE General Test, minimum GPA of 3.0. Additional exam requirements/recommendations for international students: Required—TOEFL (minimum score 550 paper-based, 80 iBT), IELTS (minimum score 6.5), Michigan English Language Assessment Battery (minimum score 77), or PTE (minimum score 55). Application fee: $30. Electronic applications accepted. *Financial support:* Fellowships, research assistantships, teaching assistantships, scholarships/grants, tuition waivers (full and partial), and unspecified assistantships available. Financial award application deadline: 1/15; financial award applicants required to submit FAFSA. *Faculty research:* Post-secondary success; leadership education; education policy; international education; multicultural education. *Unit head:* Dr. Robert A. Schwartz, Chair, 850-644-6885, Fax: 850-644-2725, E-mail: raschwartz@fsu.edu. *Application contact:* Linda Lyons, Academic Support Assistant, 850-644-7077, Fax: 850-644-1258, E-mail: ljlyons@fsu.edu.

Gallaudet University, The Graduate School, Washington, DC 20002-3625. Offers American Sign Language/English bilingual early childhood deaf education: birth to 5 (Certificate); audiology (Au D); clinical psychology (PhD); deaf and hard of hearing infants, toddlers, and their families (Certificate); deaf education (MA, Ed S); deaf history (Certificate); deaf studies (Certificate); educating deaf students with disabilities (Certificate); education: teacher preparation (MA), including deaf education, early childhood education and deaf education, elementary education and deaf education, secondary education and deaf education; educational neuroscience (PhD); hearing, speech and language sciences (MS, PhD); international development (MA); interpretation (MA, PhD), including combined interpreting practice and research (MA), interpreting research (MA); linguistics (MA, PhD); mental health counseling (MA); peer mentoring (Certificate); public administration (MPA); school counseling (MA); school psychology (Psy S); sign language teaching (MA); social work (MSW); speech-language pathology (MS). *Program availability:* Part-time. Terminal master's awarded for partial completion of doctoral program. *Degree requirements:* For master's, comprehensive exam (for some programs), thesis optional; for doctorate, comprehensive exam, thesis/dissertation. *Entrance requirements:* For master's and doctorate, GRE General Test or MAT, letters of recommendation, interviews, goals statement, American Sign Language proficiency interview, written English competency. Additional exam requirements/recommendations for international students: Required—TOEFL. Electronic applications accepted. *Faculty research:* Signing math dictionaries, telecommunications access, cancer genetics, linguistics, visual language and visual learning, integrated quantum materials, deaf legal discourse, advance recruitment and retention in geosciences.

The George Washington University, Graduate School of Education and Human Development, Department of Educational Leadership, Program in Higher Education Administration, Washington, DC 20052. Offers college teaching and academic leadership (MA Ed/HD, Ed S); general administration (MA Ed/HD, Ed S); higher education administration (Ed D); higher education finance (MA Ed/HD, Ed S); international education (MA Ed/HD, Ed S); policy (MA Ed/HD, Ed S); student affairs administration (MA Ed/HD, Ed S). *Accreditation:* NCATE. *Students:* 18 full-time (15 women), 65 part-time (44 women); includes 30 minority (17 Black or African American, non-Hispanic/Latino; 7 Asian, non-Hispanic/Latino; 5 Hispanic/Latino; 1 Two or more races, non-Hispanic/Latino), 2 international. Average age 32. 139 applicants, 76% accepted, 27 enrolled. In 2017, 34 master's, 9 doctorates, 1 other advanced degree awarded. *Degree requirements:* For master's and Ed S, comprehensive exam; for doctorate, comprehensive exam, thesis/dissertation. *Entrance requirements:* For master's, GRE General Test or MAT, minimum GPA of 2.75; for doctorate, GRE General Test or MAT, interview, minimum GPA of 3.3; for Ed S, GRE General Test or MAT, minimum GPA of 3.3. *Application deadline:* For fall admission, 1/15 priority date for domestic students; for spring admission, 10/1 for domestic students. Applications are processed on a rolling basis. Application fee: $75. *Expenses:* Tuition: Full-time $28,800; part-time $1655 per credit hour. *Required fees:* $45; $2.75 per credit hour. *Financial support:* In 2017–18, 17 students received support. Fellowships, research

assistantships, career-related internships or fieldwork, Federal Work-Study, and tuition waivers (partial) available. Financial award application deadline: 1/15; financial award applicants required to submit FAFSA. *Faculty research:* Technology in higher education administration. *Unit head:* Michael Feuer, Dean, 202-994-6161, E-mail: mjfeuer@gwu.edu. *Application contact:* Sarah Lang, Director of Graduate Admissions, 202-994-1447, Fax: 202-994-7207, E-mail: slang@gwu.edu.

The George Washington University, Graduate School of Education and Human Development, Department of Educational Leadership, Program in International Education, Washington, DC 20052. Offers MA Ed. *Accreditation:* NCATE. *Students:* 44 full-time (33 women), 36 part-time (33 women); includes 25 minority (9 Black or African American, non-Hispanic/Latino; 8 Asian, non-Hispanic/Latino; 3 Hispanic/Latino; 5 Two or more races, non-Hispanic/Latino), 17 international. Average age 27. 142 applicants, 83% accepted, 32 master's awarded. *Entrance requirements:* For master's, GRE General Test or MAT, minimum GPA of 2.75. *Application deadline:* For fall admission, 1/15 priority date for domestic students; for spring admission, 10/1 for domestic students. Applications are processed on a rolling basis. Application fee: $75. *Expenses:* Tuition: Full-time $28,800; part-time $1655 per credit hour. *Required fees:* $45; $2.75 per credit hour. *Financial support:* In 2017–18, 13 students received support. Fellowships, research assistantships, career-related internships or fieldwork, Federal Work-Study, and tuition waivers available. Financial award application deadline: 1/15; financial award applicants required to submit FAFSA. *Faculty research:* Education and development. *Unit head:* Dr. William K. Cummings, Coordinator, 202-994-4698, E-mail: wkcum@gwu.edu. *Application contact:* Sarah Lang, Director of Graduate Admissions, 202-994-1447, Fax: 202-994-7207, E-mail: slang@gwu.edu.

Harvard University, Harvard Graduate School of Education, Master's Programs in Education, Cambridge, MA 02138. Offers arts in education (Ed M); education policy and management (Ed M); higher education (Ed M); human development and psychology (Ed M); international education policy (Ed M); language and literacy (Ed M); learning and teaching (Ed M); mind, brain, and education (Ed M); prevention science and practice (Ed M); school leadership (Ed M); special studies (Ed M); teacher education (Ed M); technology, innovation, and education (Ed M). *Program availability:* Part-time. *Entrance requirements:* For master's, GRE General Test, statement of purpose, 3 letters of recommendation, resume, official transcripts. Additional exam requirements/recommendations for international students: Required—TOEFL (minimum score 613 paper-based; 104 iBT), TWE (minimum score 5). Electronic applications accepted. *Faculty research:* Learning and development, educational leadership and organizations, education policy analysis.

Indiana University Bloomington, School of Education, Department of Educational Leadership and Policy Studies, Bloomington, IN 47405. Offers educational leadership (MS, Ed D, Ed S); higher education (Ed D, PhD); higher education and student affairs (MS); history and philosophy of education (MS); history, philosophy, and policy in education (PhD), including education policy studies, history of education, philosophy of education; international and comparative education (MS). *Accreditation:* NCATE. *Degree requirements:* For master's, thesis optional; for doctorate, comprehensive exam, thesis/dissertation; for Ed S, comprehensive exam or project. *Entrance requirements:* For master's, doctorate, and Ed S, GRE General Test. Additional exam requirements/recommendations for international students: Required—TOEFL (minimum score 79 iBT). Electronic applications accepted. *Faculty research:* Culturally engaging campus environments, school choice policy analysis, democracy and education in the national and international context, and principal leadership.

Louisiana State University and Agricultural & Mechanical College, Graduate School, College of Human Sciences and Education, School of Human Resource Education and Workforce Development, Baton Rouge, LA 70803. Offers agriculture and extension education and youth development (MS, PhD); career and technical education (MS, PhD); comprehensive vocational education (MS, PhD); extension and international education (MS, PhD); human resource and leadership development (MS, PhD); industrial education (MS); vocational agriculture education (MS, PhD); vocational business education (MS); vocational home economics education (MS). *Accreditation:* NCATE. *Faculty:* 11 full-time (6 women). *Students:* 102 full-time (71 women), 130 part-time (92 women); includes 89 minority (63 Black or African American, non-Hispanic/Latino; 3 American Indian or Alaska Native, non-Hispanic/Latino; 8 Asian, non-Hispanic/Latino; 14 Hispanic/Latino; 1 Two or more races, non-Hispanic/Latino), 6 international. Average age 35. 98 applicants, 69% accepted, 52 enrolled. In 2017, 94 master's, 15 doctorates awarded. *Financial support:* In 2017–18, 1 fellowship (averaging $18,238 per year), 16 teaching assistantships (averaging $15,341 per year) were awarded. *Total annual research expenditures:* $1,998.

Loyola University Chicago, School of Education, Program in Higher Education, Chicago, IL 60660. Offers higher education (M Ed, PhD); international higher education (M Ed). PhD offered through the Graduate School. *Accreditation:* NCATE. *Program availability:* Part-time, blended/hybrid learning. *Faculty:* 4 full-time (2 women), 10 part-time/adjunct (9 women). *Students:* 78 full-time (50 women), 22 part-time (15 women); includes 54 minority (18 Black or African American, non-Hispanic/Latino; 10 Asian, non-Hispanic/Latino; 22 Hispanic/Latino; 4 Two or more races, non-Hispanic/Latino), 1 international. Average age 28. 275 applicants, 63% accepted, 57 enrolled. In 2017, 33 master's, 7 doctorates awarded. *Degree requirements:* For master's, comprehensive exam; for doctorate, comprehensive exam, thesis/dissertation. *Entrance requirements:* For master's, letters of recommendation, minimum GPA of 3.0, resume, transcripts; for doctorate, GMAT, GRE General Test, or MAT, 5 years of higher education work experience, interview. Additional exam requirements/recommendations for international students: Required—TOEFL (minimum score 550 paper-based; 79 iBT). *Application deadline:* For fall admission, 12/1 for domestic and international students. Applications are processed on a rolling basis. Application fee: $50. Electronic applications accepted. Application fee is waived when completed online. *Expenses:* $949 per semester hour, $2,847 per course, $8,541-$11,388 full-time semester tuition; $432 per semester fees, $225 additional fees (first semester only). *Financial support:* In 2017–18, 37 fellowships with partial tuition reimbursements, 42 research assistantships with full tuition reimbursements (averaging $14,000 per year), 23 teaching assistantships with full tuition reimbursements (averaging $4,000 per year) were awarded; career-related internships or fieldwork, institutionally sponsored loans, scholarships/grants, traineeships, health care benefits, and unspecified assistantships also available. Support available to part-time students. Financial award application deadline: 2/1; financial award applicants required to submit FAFSA. *Faculty research:* Church-affiliated higher education, enrollment management, academic programs, program evaluation/quality. *Unit head:* Dr. Bridget Kelly, Director, 312-915-6855, Fax: 312-915-6660, E-mail: bkelly4@luc.edu. *Application contact:* Mirtza Campbell, Information Contact, 312-915-8907, E-mail: mcampbell11@luc.edu.

Middlebury Institute of International Studies at Monterey, Graduate School of International Policy and Management, Program in International Education Management, Monterey, CA 93940-2691. Offers MA. *Degree requirements:* For master's, one foreign language, practicum. *Entrance requirements:* For master's, minimum GPA of 3.0, proficiency in a foreign language. Additional exam requirements/recommendations for international students: Required—TOEFL (minimum score 550 paper-based; 80 iBT). Electronic applications accepted. Application fee is waived when completed online.

International and Comparative Education

Morehead State University, Graduate Programs, College of Education, Department of Curriculum and Instruction, Morehead, KY 40351. Offers curriculum and instruction (Ed S); elementary education (MA Ed), including elementary education, international education, middle school education, reading; secondary education (MA Ed); special education (MA Ed); teaching (MAT). *Program availability:* Part-time, evening/weekend. *Degree requirements:* For master's, comprehensive exam, thesis optional; for Ed S, thesis, oral exam. *Entrance requirements:* For master's, GRE General Test, minimum GPA of 2.75, teaching certificate; for Ed S, GRE General Test, interview, master's degree, minimum GPA of 3.5, work experience. Additional exam requirements/recommendations for international students: Required—TOEFL (minimum score 500 paper-based). Electronic applications accepted. *Faculty research:* Communicative competence of learning-disabled students, teaching social studies in elementary schools, ungraded primary school organization, study skills.

New York University, Steinhardt School of Culture, Education, and Human Development, Department of Humanities and Social Sciences in the Professions, Program in International Education, New York, NY 10012. Offers MA, PhD, Advanced Certificate. *Program availability:* Part-time. *Students:* Average age 36. 220 applicants, 64% accepted, 38 enrolled. In 2017, 45 master's, 6 doctorates, 6 other advanced degrees awarded. *Entrance requirements:* For doctorate, GRE General Test, interview; for Advanced Certificate, master's degree. Additional exam requirements/recommendations for international students: Required—TOEFL (minimum score 100 iBT). *Application deadline:* For fall admission, 12/1 priority date for domestic and international students; for spring admission, 10/1 for domestic and international students. Applications are processed on a rolling basis. *Application fee:* $75. Electronic applications accepted. *Expenses: Tuition:* Full-time $41,352; part-time $19,968 per year. *Required fees:* $2496; $1628 per unit. $814 per term. Tuition and fees vary according to course load and program. *Financial support:* Fellowships with full and partial tuition reimbursements, career-related internships or fieldwork, Federal Work-Study, institutionally sponsored loans, and scholarships/grants available. Support available to part-time students. Financial award application deadline: 2/1; financial award applicants required to submit FAFSA. *Faculty research:* Civic education, ethnic identity among students and teachers, comparative education, education during emergencies, cross-cultural exchange. *Unit head:* Dr. Philip M. Hosay, Director, 212-998-5496, Fax: 212-995-4832, E-mail: pmh2@nyu.edu. *Application contact:* 212-998-5030, Fax: 212-995-4328, E-mail: steinhardt.gradadmissions@nyu.edu.
Website: http://steinhardt.nyu.edu/humsocsci/international

St. John's University, The School of Education, Department of Curriculum and Instruction, PhD in Curriculum and Instruction Program, Queens, NY 11439. Offers early childhood (PhD); global education (PhD); STEM education (PhD); teaching, learning, and knowing (PhD). *Program availability:* Part-time-only. *Degree requirements:* For doctorate, comprehensive exam, thesis/dissertation. *Entrance requirements:* For doctorate, teacher certification (or equivalent), at least three years' teaching experience or the equivalent in informal learning environments, master's degree. Additional exam requirements/recommendations for international students: Required—TOEFL. *Application deadline:* Applications are processed on a rolling basis. Application fee: $70. Electronic applications accepted. *Expenses: Tuition:* Full-time $44,280; part-time $1230 per credit. *Required fees:* $340; $340 per credit. Tuition and fees vary according to course load, degree level and program. *Financial support:* Fellowships, research assistantships, and scholarships/grants available. Support available to part-time students. Financial award application deadline: 2/1; financial award applicants required to submit FAFSA. *Faculty research:* Literacies, early childhood, STEM, school culture, global education. *Unit head:* Dr. Sandra Schamroth Abrams, PhD Program Director, 718-990-8313, E-mail: abramss@stjohns.edu. *Application contact:* Dr. Sandra Schamroth Abrams, PhD Program Director, 718-990-8313, E-mail: abramss@stjohns.edu.
Website: https://www.stjohns.edu/academics/schools-and-colleges/school-education/programs-and-majors/phd-curriculum-and-instruction

SIT Graduate Institute, Graduate Programs, Master's Programs in Intercultural Service, Leadership, and Management, Master's Program in International Education, Brattleboro, VT 05302-0676. Offers MA.

Stanford University, Graduate School of Education, Program in International Comparative Education, Stanford, CA 94305-2004. Offers MA, PhD. *Expenses: Tuition:* Full-time $48,987; part-time $10,620 per quarter. One-time fee: $400. Tuition and fees vary according to program.

Teachers College, Columbia University, Department of International and Transcultural Studies, New York, NY 10027-6696. Offers anthropology and education (MA, Ed D, PhD); applied anthropology (PhD); comparative and international education (MA, Ed D, PhD); international educational development (Ed M, MA, Ed D, PhD). *Program availability:* Part-time. *Students:* 150 full-time (120 women), 143 part-time (116 women); includes 95 minority (22 Black or African American, non-Hispanic/Latino; 33 Asian, non-Hispanic/Latino; 29 Hispanic/Latino; 11 Two or more races, non-Hispanic/Latino), 116 international. Average age 29. 433 applicants, 59% accepted, 120 enrolled. *Degree requirements:* For doctorate, thesis/dissertation. *Unit head:* Prof. Herve Varenne, Chair, 212-678-3190, E-mail: varenne@tc.columbia.edu. *Application contact:* David Estrella, Director of Admission, 212-678-3305, E-mail: estrella@tc.columbia.edu.

University at Albany, State University of New York, School of Education, Department of Educational Policy and Leadership, Albany, NY 12222-0001. Offers educational policy and leadership (MS, PhD); higher education (MS); international education management (CAS). *Program availability:* Evening/weekend. *Faculty:* 11 full-time (3 women), 13 part-time/adjunct (10 women). *Students:* 37 full-time (21 women), 93 part-time (51 women); includes 28 minority (14 Black or African American, non-Hispanic/Latino; 1 Asian, non-Hispanic/Latino; 11 Hispanic/Latino; 2 Two or more races, non-Hispanic/Latino), 21 international. Average age 32. 72 applicants, 71% accepted, 48 enrolled. In 2017, 11 master's, 7 doctorates, 12 other advanced degrees awarded. *Degree requirements:* For doctorate, one foreign language, thesis/dissertation. *Entrance requirements:* For doctorate, GRE General Test, GRE Subject Test. Additional exam requirements/recommendations for international students: Required—TOEFL (minimum score 550 paper-based). *Application deadline:* For fall admission, 2/1 for domestic students, 5/1 for international students; for spring admission, 9/1 for domestic students, 11/1 for international students. Applications are processed on a rolling basis. Application fee: $75. Electronic applications accepted. *Expenses:* Tuition, state resident: full-time $10,870; part-time $453 per credit hour. Tuition, nonresident: full-time $22,210; part-time $925 per credit hour. *Required fees:* $84.68 per credit hour. $508.06 per semester. Part-time tuition and fees vary according to course load and program. *Financial support:* Fellowships and career-related internships or fieldwork available. Financial award application deadline: 3/15. *Unit head:* Jason Lane, Chair, 518-442-5092, E-mail: jlane@albany.edu.
Website: http://www.albany.edu/epl/

University of Bridgeport, School of Education, Department of Education, Bridgeport, CT 06604. Offers education (MS); educational management (Ed D, Diploma), including intermediate administrator or supervisor (Diploma), leadership (Ed D); elementary education (MS, Diploma), including early childhood education, elementary education; middle school education (MS); music education (MS); remedial reading and language

arts (Diploma); secondary education (MS, Diploma), including computer specialist (Diploma), international education (Diploma), reading specialist, secondary education. *Program availability:* Part-time, evening/weekend. *Degree requirements:* For master's, final exam, final project, or thesis; for doctorate, comprehensive exam, thesis/dissertation; for Diploma, thesis or alternative, final project. *Entrance requirements:* For master's, minimum undergraduate QPA of 2.67; for doctorate, GRE, MAT; for Diploma, GRE General Test or MAT, minimum graduate QPA of 3.0. Additional exam requirements/recommendations for international students: Recommended—TOEFL (minimum score 550 paper-based; 80 iBT), IELTS (minimum score 6.5). Electronic applications accepted. *Expenses:* Contact institution.

University of Massachusetts Amherst, Graduate School, College of Education, Program in Education, Amherst, MA 01003. Offers bilingual, English as a second language, and multicultural education (M Ed, Ed S); child study and early education (M Ed); children, families and schools (Ed D, Ed S); early childhood and elementary teacher education (M Ed); educational leadership (M Ed); educational policy and leadership (Ed D); higher education (M Ed); international education (M Ed); language, literacy and culture (Ed D); learning, media and technology (M Ed, Ed S); mathematics, science, and learning technologies (Ed D); reading and writing (M Ed); research, educational measurement and psychometrics (Ed D); school counselor education (M Ed, Ed S); school psychology (Ed S); science education (Ed S); secondary teacher education (M Ed); social justice education (M Ed, Ed D, Ed S); special education (M Ed, Ed D, Ed S); teacher education and school improvement (Ed D, Ed S). *Accreditation:* NCATE. *Program availability:* Part-time, online learning. Terminal master's awarded for partial completion of doctoral program. *Degree requirements:* For doctorate, comprehensive exam, thesis/dissertation. *Entrance requirements:* Additional exam requirements/recommendations for international students: Required—TOEFL (minimum score 550 paper-based; 80 iBT), IELTS (minimum score 6.5). Electronic applications accepted.

University of Minnesota, Twin Cities Campus, Graduate School, College of Education and Human Development, Department of Organizational Leadership, Policy and Development, Program in Comparative and International Development Education, Minneapolis, MN 55455-0213. Offers MA, PhD. *Students:* 55 full-time (42 women), 45 part-time (28 women); includes 19 minority (9 Black or African American, non-Hispanic/Latino; 5 Asian, non-Hispanic/Latino; 4 Hispanic/Latino; 1 Two or more races, non-Hispanic/Latino), 17 international. Average age 37. 101 applicants, 34% accepted, 32 enrolled. In 2017, 11 master's, 7 doctorates awarded. Application fee: $75 ($95 for international students). *Unit head:* Dr. Frances Vavrus, Chair, 612-624-1006, Fax: 612-624-3377, E-mail: vavru003@umn.edu. *Application contact:* Dr. Jeremy J. Hernandez, Director of Graduate Studies, 612-626-9377, E-mail: herna220@umn.edu.
Website: http://www.cehd.umn.edu/OLPD/grad-programs/CIDE/

University of Pennsylvania, Graduate School of Education, Division of Literacy, Culture, and International Education, Program in International Educational Development, Philadelphia, PA 19104. Offers MS Ed. *Students:* Average age 26. 159 applicants, 60% accepted, 33 enrolled. In 2017, 26 master's awarded.

University of Pittsburgh, School of Education, Department of Administrative and Policy Studies, Program in Social and Comparative Analysis in Education, Pittsburgh, PA 15260. Offers M Ed, MA, Ed D, PhD. *Program availability:* Evening/weekend. *Degree requirements:* For master's, thesis; for doctorate, thesis/dissertation. *Entrance requirements:* For doctorate, GRE General Test. Additional exam requirements/recommendations for international students: Required—TOEFL (minimum score 80 iBT). Electronic applications accepted.

University of San Francisco, School of Education, Department of International and Multicultural Education, San Francisco, CA 94117-1080. Offers MA, Ed D. *Program availability:* Part-time, evening/weekend. *Degree requirements:* For doctorate, thesis/dissertation. *Entrance requirements:* Additional exam requirements/recommendations for international students: Required—TOEFL, IELTS, PTE. Electronic applications accepted.

University of South Africa, College of Human Sciences, Pretoria, South Africa. Offers adult education (M Ed); African languages (MA, PhD); African politics (MA, PhD); Afrikaans (MA, PhD); ancient history (MA, PhD); ancient Near Eastern studies (MA, PhD); anthropology (MA, PhD); applied linguistics (MA); Arabic (MA, PhD); archaeology (MA); art history (MA); Biblical archaeology (MA); Biblical studies (M Th, D Th, PhD); Christian spirituality (M Th, D Th); church history (M Th, D Th); classical studies (MA, PhD); clinical psychology (MA); communication (MA, PhD); comparative education (M Ed, Ed D); consulting psychology (D Admin, D Com, PhD); curriculum studies (M Ed, Ed D); development studies (M Admin, MA, D Admin, PhD); didactics (M Ed, Ed D); education (M Tech); education management (M Ed, Ed D); educational psychology (M Ed); English (MA); environmental education (M Ed); French (MA, PhD); German (MA, PhD); Greek (MA); guidance and counseling (M Ed); health studies (MA, PhD), including health sciences education (MA), health services management (MA), medical and surgical nursing science (critical care general) (MA), midwifery and neonatal nursing science (MA), trauma and emergency care (MA); history (MA, PhD); history of education (Ed D); inclusive education (M Ed, Ed D); information and communications technology policy and regulation (MA); information science (MA, MIS, PhD); international politics (MA, PhD); Islamic studies (MA, PhD); Italian (MA, PhD); Judaica (MA, PhD); linguistics (MA, PhD); mathematical education (M Ed); mathematics education (MA); missiology (M Th, D Th); modern Hebrew (MA, PhD); musicology (MA, MMus, D Mus, PhD); natural science education (M Ed); New Testament (M Th, D Th); Old Testament (D Th); pastoral therapy (M Th, D Th); philosophy (MA); philosophy of education (M Ed, Ed D); politics (MA, PhD); Portuguese (MA, PhD); practical theology (M Th, D Th); psychology (MA, MS, PhD); psychology of education (M Ed, Ed D); public health (MA); religious studies (MA, D Th, PhD); Romance languages (MA); Russian (MA, PhD); Semitic languages (MA, PhD); social behavior studies in HIV/AIDS (MA); social science (mental health) (MA); social science in development studies (MA); social science in psychology (MA); social science in social work (MA); social science in sociology (MA); social work (MSW, DSW, PhD); socio-education (M Ed, Ed D); sociolinguistics (MA); sociology (MA, PhD); Spanish (MA, PhD); systematic theology (M Th, D Th); TESOL (teaching English to speakers of other languages) (MA); theological ethics (M Th, D Th); theory of literature (MA, PhD); urban ministries (D Th); urban ministry (M Th).

University of Wisconsin–Madison, Graduate School, School of Education, Department of Educational Leadership and Policy Analysis, Madison, WI 53706-1380. Offers administration (Certificate); educational policy (MS, PhD); global higher education (MS). *Degree requirements:* For doctorate, thesis/dissertation. *Entrance requirements:* For master's and doctorate, GRE General Test. Electronic applications accepted.

Vanderbilt University, Peabody College, Department of Leadership, Policy, and Organizations, Nashville, TN 37240-1001. Offers education policy (MPP); educational leadership and policy (Ed D); higher education (M Ed); higher education leadership and policy (Ed D); independent school leadership (M Ed); international education policy and management (M Ed); leadership and learning in organizations (Ed D); leadership and organizational performance (M Ed). *Program availability:* Part-time, on-campus immersion once every semester. *Faculty:* 30 full-time (15 women), 19 part-time/adjunct (6 women). *Students:* 141 full-time (105 women), 139 part-time (84 women); includes 66

minority (32 Black or African American, non-Hispanic/Latino; 13 Asian, non-Hispanic/Latino; 14 Hispanic/Latino; 1 Native Hawaiian or other Pacific Islander, non-Hispanic/Latino; 6 Two or more races, non-Hispanic/Latino), 25 international. Average age 30. 525 applicants, 66% accepted, 139 enrolled. In 2017, 109 master's, 22 doctorates awarded. *Degree requirements:* For master's, comprehensive exam, thesis optional; for doctorate, thesis/dissertation, qualifying exams, residency. *Entrance requirements:* For master's and doctorate, GRE General Test. Additional exam requirements/recommendations for international students: Required—TOEFL (minimum score 550 paper-based; 80 iBT). *Application deadline:* For fall admission, 12/31 priority date for domestic and international students; for spring admission, 11/1 priority date for domestic and international students. Applications are processed on a rolling basis. Application fee: $0. Electronic applications accepted. *Financial support:* Fellowships with partial tuition reimbursements, research assistantships with partial tuition reimbursements, teaching assistantships with partial tuition reimbursements, Federal Work-Study, institutionally sponsored loans, scholarships/grants, tuition waivers (partial), and unspecified assistantships available. Support available to part-time students. Financial award application deadline: 1/15; financial award applicants required to submit FAFSA. *Faculty research:* Financial aid policies, teacher labor markets, school choice, educational leadership, higher education access and equity. *Unit head:* Dr. Ellen B. Goldring, Chair, 615-322-8000, Fax: 615-343-7094, E-mail: ellen.b.goldring@vanderbilt.edu. *Application contact:* Rosie Moody, Educational Coordinator, 615-322-8019, Fax: 615-343-7094, E-mail: rosie.moody@vanderbilt.edu.
Website: http://peabody.vanderbilt.edu/departments/lpo/index.php

Walden University, Graduate Programs, Richard W. Riley College of Education and Leadership, Minneapolis, MN 55401. Offers adult education (Post-Master's Certificate); adult learning (Graduate Certificate); college teaching and learning (Graduate Certificate); community college leadership (Ed D); curriculum, instruction and assessment (Ed D, Ed S, Graduate Certificate); developmental education (Graduate Certificate); early childhood administration, management, and leadership (Graduate Certificate); early childhood education (Ed D, Ed S); early childhood public policy and advocacy (Graduate Certificate); early childhood studies (MS), including administration, management and leadership, early childhood public policy and advocacy, teaching adults in the early childhood field, teaching and diversity in early childhood education; education (MS, PhD), including adolescent literacy and learning (MS), curriculum, instruction, and assessment (grades K-12) (MS), curriculum, instruction, assessment, and evaluation (PhD), early childhood leadership and advocacy (PhD), early childhood special education (PhD), educational leadership (MS), educational leadership and administration (principal preparation) (MS), educational technology and design (PhD), elementary reading and literacy (PreK-6) (MS), elementary reading and mathematics (grades K-6) (MS), global and comparative education (PhD), higher education leadership management and policy (PhD), integrating technology in the classroom (grades K-12) (MS), learning, instruction and innovation (PhD), mathematics (grades 5-8) (MS), mathematics (grades K-6) (MS), mathematics and science (grades K-8) (MS), organizational research, assessment, and evaluation (PhD), reading and literacy with a reading K-12 endorsement (MS), reading literacy assessment and evaluation (PhD), science (grades K-8) (MS), special education (non-licensure) (grades K-12) (MS), teacher leadership (grades K-12) (MS), teaching English language learners (grades K-12) (MS); educational administration and leadership (Ed D); educational leadership and administration (principal preparation) (Ed S); educational technology (Ed D, Ed S, Post Master's Certificate); elementary reading and literacy (Graduate Certificate); engaging culturally diverse learners (Graduate Certificate); enrollment management and institutional marketing (Graduate Certificate); higher education (MS), including adult learning, college teaching and learning, enrollment management and institutional marketing, global higher education, leadership for student success, online and distance learning; higher education and adult learning (Ed D); higher education leadership and management (Ed D); higher education leadership for student success (Graduate Certificate); instructional design and technology (MS, Postbaccalaureate Certificate), including general program (MS), online learning (MS), training and performance improvement (MS); integrating technology in the classroom (Graduate Certificate); mathematics 5-8 (Graduate Certificate); mathematics K-6 (Graduate Certificate); online teaching for adult educators (Graduate Certificate); reading, literacy, and assessment (Ed D, Ed S); science K-8 (Graduate Certificate); special education (Ed D, Ed S, Graduate Certificate); special education (K-age 21) (MAT); teacher leadership (Graduate Certificate); teaching adults English as a second language (Graduate Certificate); teaching adults in the early childhood field (Graduate Certificate); teaching and diversity in early childhood education (Graduate Certificate); teaching English language learners (grades K-12) (Graduate Certificate); teaching K-12 students online (Graduate Certificate). *Accreditation:* NCATE. *Program availability:* Part-time, evening/weekend, online only, 100% online. *Degree requirements:* For doctorate, thesis/dissertation (for some programs), residency (for other advanced degree, residency (for some programs). *Entrance requirements:* For master's, bachelor's degree or higher; minimum GPA of 2.5; official transcripts; goal statement (for some programs); access to computer and Internet; for doctorate, master's degree or higher; three years of related professional or academic experience (preferred); minimum GPA of 3.0; goal statement and current resume (for select programs); official transcripts; access to computer and Internet; for other advanced degree, relevant work experience; access to computer and Internet. Additional exam requirements/recommendations for international students: Required—TOEFL (minimum score 550 paper-based, 79 iBT), IELTS (minimum score 6.5), Michigan English Language Assessment Battery (minimum score 82), or PTE (minimum score 53). Electronic applications accepted.

Wilkes University, College of Graduate and Professional Studies, School of Education, Wilkes-Barre, PA 18766-0002. Offers educational development and strategies (MS Ed); educational leadership (MS Ed, Ed D); effective teaching (MS Ed); instructional media (MS Ed); instructional technology (MS Ed); international school leadership (MS Ed); international teaching and learning (MS Ed); literacy specialist (MS Ed); middle level education (MS Ed); online teaching (MS Ed); school business leadership (MS Ed); special education (MS Ed); teaching English to speakers of other languages (MS Ed). *Program availability:* Part-time, evening/weekend, 100% online, blended/hybrid learning. *Students:* 76 full-time (57 women), 1,586 part-time (1,204 women); includes 82 minority (10 Black or African American, non-Hispanic/Latino; 12 Asian, non-Hispanic/Latino; 41 Hispanic/Latino; 1 Native Hawaiian or other Pacific Islander, non-Hispanic/Latino; 18 Two or more races, non-Hispanic/Latino). Average age 34. In 2017, 619 master's, 23 doctorates awarded. *Entrance requirements:* Additional exam requirements/recommendations for international students: Required—TOEFL (minimum score 550 paper-based; 79 iBT). *Application deadline:* Applications are processed on a rolling basis. Application fee: $45 ($65 for international students). Electronic applications accepted. *Expenses:* Contact institution. *Financial support:* Unspecified assistantships available. Financial award application deadline: 3/1; financial award applicants required to submit FAFSA. *Unit head:* Dr. Rhonda Rabbitt, Dean, 570-408-4680, Fax: 570-408-7872, E-mail: rhonda.rabbitt@wilkes.edu. *Application contact:* Stephanie Wasmanski, Associate Director of Graduate Admissions, 570-408-5535, Fax: 570-408-7846, E-mail: stephanie.wasmanski@wilkes.edu.
Website: http://www.wilkes.edu/academics/graduate-programs/masters-programs/graduate-education/index.aspx

Student Affairs

Adler University, Graduate Programs, MA in Counseling Program: Specialization in Student Affairs and College Counseling, Chicago, IL 60602. Offers MAC. *Program availability:* Part-time, evening/weekend, online learning. *Entrance requirements:* For master's, baccalaureate degree, minimum GPA of 3.0, interview, official transcripts.

Alfred University, Graduate School, Division of Education, Alfred, NY 14802-1205. Offers college student development (MS Ed); literacy (MS Ed). *Accreditation:* TEAC. *Program availability:* Part-time. *Entrance requirements:* For master's, Liberal Arts and Sciences Test (LAST), Assessment of Teaching Skills (written) (ATS-W), Content Specialty Test (CST). Additional exam requirements/recommendations for international students: Required—TOEFL (minimum score 590 paper-based; 90 iBT), IELTS (minimum score 6.5). Electronic applications accepted.

Alliant International University–Los Angeles, Shirley M. Hufstedler School of Education, Educational Psychology Programs, Alhambra, CA 91803. Offers educational psychology (Psy D); pupil personnel services (Credential); school psychology (MA). *Program availability:* Part-time. *Degree requirements:* For doctorate, comprehensive exam, thesis/dissertation. *Entrance requirements:* For master's, minimum GPA of 2.5, letters of recommendation; for doctorate, interview, minimum GPA of 3.0, letters of recommendation. Additional exam requirements/recommendations for international students: Required—TOEFL (minimum score 550 paper-based), TWE (minimum score 5). Electronic applications accepted. *Faculty research:* Early identification and intervention with high-risk preschoolers, pediatric neuropsychology, interpersonal violence, ADHD, learning theories.

Alliant International University–San Diego, Shirley M. Hufstedler School of Education, Educational Psychology Programs, San Diego, CA 92131. Offers educational psychology (Psy D); pupil personnel services (Credential); school neuropsychology (Certificate); school psychology (MA); school-based mental health (Certificate). *Program availability:* Part-time. *Degree requirements:* For doctorate, comprehensive exam, thesis/dissertation, internship. *Entrance requirements:* For master's, minimum GPA of 2.5, letters of recommendation; for doctorate, minimum GPA of 3.0, letters of recommendation. Additional exam requirements/recommendations for international students: Required—TOEFL (minimum score 550 paper-based; 80 iBT), TWE (minimum score 5). Electronic applications accepted. *Faculty research:* School-based mental health, pupil personnel services, childhood mood, school-based assessment.

Appalachian State University, Cratis D. Williams Graduate School, Department of Human Development and Psychological Counseling, Boone, NC 28608. Offers clinical mental health counseling (MA); college student development (MA); marriage and family therapy (MA); school counseling (MA). *Accreditation:* AAMFT/COAMFTE; ACA; NCATE. *Program availability:* Part-time. *Degree requirements:* For master's, comprehensive exam (for some programs), thesis optional, internships. *Entrance requirements:* For master's, GRE General Test, 3 letters of recommendation. Additional exam requirements/recommendations for international students: Required—TOEFL (minimum score 570 paper-based; 79 iBT), IELTS (minimum score 6.5). Electronic applications accepted. *Faculty research:* Multicultural counseling, addictions counseling, play therapy, expressive arts, child and adolescent therapy, sexual abuse counseling.

Arkansas State University, Graduate School, College of Education and Behavioral Science, Department of Psychology and Counseling, State University, AR 72467. Offers clinical mental health counseling (Graduate Certificate); college student personnel services (MS); dyslexia therapy (Graduate Certificate); psychological science (MS); psychology and counseling (Ed S); rehabilitation counseling (MRC); school counseling (MSE); student affairs (Graduate Certificate). *Accreditation:* ACA (one or more programs are accredited); CORE (one or more programs are accredited); NCATE. *Program availability:* Part-time. *Degree requirements:* For master's and other advanced degree, comprehensive exam, thesis or alternative. *Entrance requirements:* For master's, GRE General Test or MAT (for MSE), appropriate bachelor's degree, interview, letters of reference, official transcripts, immunization records, written statement, 2-3 page autobiography; for other advanced degree, GRE General Test, interview, master's degree, letters of reference, official transcript, personal statement, immunization records. Additional exam requirements/recommendations for international students: Required—TOEFL (minimum score 550 paper-based; 79 iBT), IELTS (minimum score 6), PTE (minimum score 56). Electronic applications accepted.

Arkansas Tech University, College of Education, Russellville, AR 72801. Offers college student personnel (MS); educational leadership (M Ed, Ed S); instructional technology (M Ed); school counseling and leadership (M Ed); school leadership (Ed D); special education K-12 (M Ed); strength and conditioning studies (MS); teaching (MAT); teaching, learning, and leadership (M Ed). *Accreditation:* NCATE. *Program availability:* Part-time, evening/weekend, 100% online, blended/hybrid learning. *Students:* 80 full-time (45 women), 433 part-time (328 women); includes 114 minority (81 Black or African American, non-Hispanic/Latino; 4 American Indian or Alaska Native, non-Hispanic/Latino; 1 Asian, non-Hispanic/Latino; 13 Hispanic/Latino; 15 Two or more races, non-Hispanic/Latino), 2 international. Average age 34. In 2017, 132 master's, 8 doctorates, 3 other advanced degrees awarded. *Degree requirements:* For master's, comprehensive exam, thesis optional, action research project; for doctorate, thesis/dissertation. *Entrance requirements:* Additional exam requirements/recommendations for international students: Required—TOEFL (minimum score 550 paper-based; 79 iBT), IELTS (minimum score 6.5), PTE (minimum score 58). *Application deadline:* For fall admission, 3/1 priority date for domestic students, 5/1 priority date for international students; for spring admission, 10/1 priority date for domestic and international students. Applications are processed on a rolling basis. Application fee: $40 ($90 for international students). Electronic applications accepted. *Expenses:* Tuition, state resident: full-time $6816; part-time $284 per credit hour. Tuition, nonresident: full-time $13,632; part-time $568 per credit hour. *Required fees:* $420 per semester. Tuition and fees vary according to course load. *Financial support:* In 2017–18, research assistantships with full and

partial tuition reimbursements (averaging $4,800 per year), teaching assistantships with full and partial tuition reimbursements (averaging $4,800 per year) were awarded; career-related internships or fieldwork, Federal Work-Study, scholarships/grants, health care benefits, and unspecified assistantships also available. Support available to part-time students. Financial award application deadline: 4/15; financial award applicants required to submit FAFSA. *Unit head:* Dr. Mary Gunter, Dean, 479-964-3217, E-mail: mgunter@atu.edu.
Website: http://www.atu.edu/education/

Binghamton University, State University of New York, Graduate School, College of Community and Public Affairs, Department of Student Affairs Administration, Binghamton, NY 13902-6000. Offers MS. *Program availability:* Part-time. *Faculty:* 4 full-time (3 women). *Students:* 50 full-time (30 women), 14 part-time (10 women); includes 19 minority (7 Black or African American, non-Hispanic/Latino; 3 Asian, non-Hispanic/Latino; 4 Hispanic/Latino; 5 Two or more races, non-Hispanic/Latino), 2 international. Average age 27. 75 applicants, 89% accepted, 31 enrolled. In 2017, 16 master's awarded. *Degree requirements:* For master's, comprehensive exam. *Entrance requirements:* For master's, GRE General Test. Additional exam requirements/recommendations for international students: Required—TOEFL (minimum score 80 iBT). *Application deadline:* For fall admission, 4/15 priority date for domestic and international students; for spring admission, 11/15 priority date for domestic and international students. Application fee: $75. Electronic applications accepted. *Financial support:* In 2017–18, 34 students received support. Fellowships, career-related internships or fieldwork, Federal Work-Study, institutionally sponsored loans, scholarships/grants, health care benefits, and unspecified assistantships available. Financial award applicants required to submit FAFSA. *Unit head:* Brianna King, Director of Student Admissions, 607-777-2719, E-mail: bking@binghamton.edu. *Application contact:* Ben Balkaya, Assistant Dean and Director, 607-777-2151, Fax: 607-777-2501, E-mail: balkaya@binghamton.edu.
Website: http://www2.binghamton.edu/ccpa/student-affairs-administration/

Bloomsburg University of Pennsylvania, School of Graduate Studies, College of Education, Department of Teaching and Learning, Program in Educational Leadership, Bloomsburg, PA 17815-1301. Offers college student affairs (M Ed); PreK-12 curriculum and instruction (M Ed); PreK-12 school counseling (M Ed); PreK-12 school principal (M Ed). *Degree requirements:* For master's, practicum. *Entrance requirements:* For master's, 3 letters of recommendation, resume, minimum QPA of 3.0, personal statement, interview. Additional exam requirements/recommendations for international students: Required—TOEFL, IELTS. Electronic applications accepted. *Expenses:* Tuition, state resident: full-time $10,000; part-time $500 per credit hour. Tuition, nonresident: full-time $15,000; part-time $750 per credit hour. *Required fees:* $2484; $110.75 per credit hour. $75 per term. Tuition and fees vary according to program.

Bob Jones University, Graduate Programs, Greenville, SC 29614. Offers accountancy (MS); Bible (MA); Bible translation (MA); Biblical studies (Certificate); broadcast management (MS); business administration (MBA); church history (MA, PhD); church ministries (MA); church music (MM); cinema and video production (MA); counseling (MS); curriculum and instruction (Ed D); divinity (M Div); dramatic production (MA); educational leadership (MS, Ed D, Ed S); elementary education (M Ed, MAT); English (M Ed, MA, MAT); fine arts (MA); graphic design (MA); history (M Ed, MA); illustration (MA); interpretative speech (MA); mathematics (M Ed, MAT); medical missions (Certificate); ministry (MM, D Min); multi-categorical special education (M Ed, MAT); music (M Ed); New Testament interpretation (PhD); Old Testament interpretation (PhD); orchestral instrument performance (MM); organ performance (MM); pastoral studies (MA); personnel services (MS, Ed S); piano pedagogy (MM); piano performance (MM); platform arts (MA); radio and television broadcasting (MS); rhetoric and public address (MA); secondary education (M Ed); studio art (MA); teaching Bible (MA); theology (MA, PhD); voice performance (MM); youth ministries (MA); M Div/MM.

Bowling Green State University, Graduate College, College of Education and Human Development, Department of Higher Education and Student Affairs, Program in College Student Personnel, Bowling Green, OH 43403. Offers MA. *Program availability:* Part-time. *Degree requirements:* For master's, thesis or alternative. *Entrance requirements:* For master's, GRE General Test, interview. Additional exam requirements/recommendations for international students: Required—TOEFL. Electronic applications accepted. *Faculty research:* Adult learning, legal issues, moral and ethical development.

Bucknell University, Graduate Studies, College of Arts and Sciences, Department of Education, Lewisburg, PA 17837. Offers college student personnel (MS Ed). *Program availability:* Part-time. *Degree requirements:* For master's, comprehensive exam (for some programs), thesis or alternative. *Entrance requirements:* For master's, GRE General Test, minimum GPA of 3.0. Additional exam requirements/recommendations for international students: Required—TOEFL (minimum score 600 paper-based).

Buffalo State College, State University of New York, The Graduate School, Faculty of Applied Science and Education, Department of Educational Foundations, Program in Student Personnel Administration, Buffalo, NY 14222-1095. Offers MS. *Degree requirements:* For master's, comprehensive exam. *Entrance requirements:* For master's, minimum GPA of 2.75 in last 60 hours of undergraduate course work. Additional exam requirements/recommendations for international students: Required—TOEFL (minimum score 550 paper-based).

California State University, Bakersfield, Division of Graduate Studies, School of Social Sciences and Education, Program in Counseling, Bakersfield, CA 93311. Offers school counseling (MS); student affairs (MS). *Accreditation:* NCATE. *Faculty:* 2 full-time (both women), 7 part-time/adjunct (6 women). *Students:* 64 full-time (52 women), 5 part-time (3 women); includes 55 minority (1 Black or African American, non-Hispanic/Latino; 1 American Indian or Alaska Native, non-Hispanic/Latino; 2 Asian, non-Hispanic/Latino; 51 Hispanic/Latino), 1 international. Average age 27. 74 applicants, 59% accepted, 38 enrolled. In 2017, 35 master's awarded. *Degree requirements:* For master's, thesis or alternative, culminating projects. *Entrance requirements:* For master's, CBEST (for school counseling). *Application deadline:* Applications are processed on a rolling basis. Application fee: $55. *Expenses:* Tuition, state resident: full-time $7176; part-time $4164 per year. *Financial support:* In 2017–18, fellowships (averaging $1,850 per year) were awarded; Federal Work-Study, scholarships/grants, and tuition waivers (full and partial) also available. Financial award application deadline: 3/2; financial award applicants required to submit FAFSA. *Unit head:* Dr. Karen Haas, Director, 661-654-6214, Fax: 661-654-2479, E-mail: khaas8@csub.edu. *Application contact:* Julia Bavier, Admissions and Graduation Advisor, 661-654-3193, Fax: 661-654-2479, E-mail: jbavier@csub.edu.
Website: https://www.csub.edu/psychology/mscounselingpsych/index.html

California State University, Fresno, Division of Research and Graduate Studies, Kremen School of Education and Human Development, Department of Counselor Education and Rehabilitation, Program in Student Affairs and College Counseling, Fresno, CA 93740-8027. Offers MS. *Accreditation:* NCATE. *Program availability:* Part-time, evening/weekend. *Degree requirements:* For master's, thesis or alternative. *Entrance requirements:* For master's, GRE General Test, MAT, minimum GPA of 3.0. Additional exam requirements/recommendations for international students: Required—TOEFL. Electronic applications accepted.

California State University, Long Beach, Graduate Studies, College of Education, Department of Advanced Studies in Education and Counseling, Long Beach, CA 90840. Offers counseling (MS), including marriage and family therapy, school counseling, student development in higher education; education (MA, Ed D); educational administration (MA, Ed D); educational psychology (MA); special education (MS). *Program availability:* Part-time, evening/weekend. *Entrance requirements:* For master's, GRE General Test, minimum GPA of 2.75. Electronic applications accepted.

Canisius College, Graduate Division, School of Education and Human Services, Department of Graduate Education and Leadership, Buffalo, NY 14208-1098. Offers business and marketing education (MS Ed); college student personnel (MS Ed); deaf education (MS Ed); deaf/adolescent education, grades 7-12 (MS Ed); deaf/childhood education, grades 1-6 (MS Ed); differentiated instruction (MS Ed); education administration (MS); educational leadership (MS Ed); educational technologies (Certificate); gifted education extension (Certificate); literacy (MS Ed); reading (Certificate); school building leadership (MS Ed, Certificate); school district leadership (Certificate); teacher leader (Certificate); TESOL (MS Ed). *Accreditation:* NCATE. *Program availability:* Part-time, evening/weekend, 100% online, blended/hybrid learning. *Faculty:* 5 full-time (all women), 21 part-time/adjunct (16 women). *Students:* 85 full-time (67 women), 189 part-time (151 women); includes 31 minority (18 Black or African American, non-Hispanic/Latino; 3 American Indian or Alaska Native, non-Hispanic/Latino; 3 Asian, non-Hispanic/Latino; 4 Hispanic/Latino; 3 Two or more races, non-Hispanic/Latino), 1 international. Average age 31. 83 applicants, 96% accepted, 74 enrolled. In 2017, 94 master's, 47 other advanced degrees awarded. *Entrance requirements:* For master's, GRE (if cumulative GPA less than 2.7), transcripts, two letters of recommendation. Additional exam requirements/recommendations for international students: Required—TOEFL (minimum score 550 paper-based, 79 iBT), IELTS (minimum score 6.5), or CAEL (minimum score 70). *Application deadline:* Applications are processed on a rolling basis. Application fee: $0. Electronic applications accepted. *Expenses: Tuition:* Full-time $22,860; part-time $820 per credit. *Required fees:* $720; $25 per credit. $65 per semester. One-time fee: $425. *Financial support:* Career-related internships or fieldwork, Federal Work-Study, scholarships/grants, tuition waivers (partial), and unspecified assistantships available. Support available to part-time students. Financial award application deadline: 4/30; financial award applicants required to submit FAFSA. *Faculty research:* Asperger's disease, autism, private higher education, reading strategies. *Unit head:* Dr. Anne Marie Tryjankowski, Chair/Associate Professor of Graduate Education and Leadership, 716-888-3715, Fax: 716-888-3142, E-mail: tryjanka@canisius.edu.

Cardinal Stritch University, College of Education and Leadership, Department of Education, Milwaukee, WI 53217-3985. Offers educational leadership (MS); higher education student affairs leadership (MS); leadership for the advancement of learning and service (Ed D, PhD); leadership for the advancement of learning and service in higher education (Ed D, PhD); teaching (MAT); urban education (MA). *Accreditation:* NCATE. *Program availability:* Part-time, evening/weekend, 100% online, blended/hybrid learning. *Students:* 73 full-time (57 women), 332 part-time (220 women); includes 113 minority (59 Black or African American, non-Hispanic/Latino; 2 American Indian or Alaska Native, non-Hispanic/Latino; 10 Asian, non-Hispanic/Latino; 38 Hispanic/Latino; 1 Native Hawaiian or other Pacific Islander, non-Hispanic/Latino; 3 Two or more races, non-Hispanic/Latino), 7 international. Average age 35. 137 applicants, 97% accepted, 104 enrolled. In 2017, 135 master's, 28 doctorates awarded. *Degree requirements:* For master's, comprehensive exam, thesis (for some programs), research project, faculty recommendation; for doctorate, thesis/dissertation, practica, field experience. *Entrance requirements:* For master's, 2 letters of recommendation, minimum GPA of 3.0; for doctorate, minimum GPA of 3.5 in master's coursework, 3 letters of recommendation. Additional exam requirements/recommendations for international students: Required—TOEFL (minimum score 550 paper-based; 79 iBT), IELTS (minimum score 6.5). *Application deadline:* For fall admission, 7/15 priority date for domestic students; for spring admission, 12/15 priority date for domestic students. Applications are processed on a rolling basis. Application fee: $0. Electronic applications accepted. *Expenses:* Tuition varies by program. *Financial support:* Fellowships, research assistantships with partial tuition reimbursements, career-related internships or fieldwork, Federal Work-Study, and scholarships/grants available. Financial award applicants required to submit FAFSA. *Application contact:* 800-347-8822 Ext. 4042, E-mail: admissions@stritch.edu.

Carlow University, College of Leadership and Social Change, Program in Student Affairs, Pittsburgh, PA 15213-3165. Offers MA. *Program availability:* Part-time, evening/weekend. *Students:* 2 full-time (both women), 3 part-time (all women); includes 3 minority (2 Black or African American, non-Hispanic/Latino; 1 Asian, non-Hispanic/Latino). Average age 37. 6 applicants, 100% accepted, 3 enrolled. *Entrance requirements:* For master's, personal essay; resume or curriculum vitae; two recommendations; official transcripts; interview; minimum undergraduate GPA of 3.0. Additional exam requirements/recommendations for international students: Required—TOEFL (minimum score 550 paper-based). *Application deadline:* Applications are processed on a rolling basis. Electronic applications accepted. *Expenses: Tuition:* Full-time $12,103; part-time $825 per credit hour. Tuition and fees vary according to program. *Financial support:* Application deadline: 4/1; applicants required to submit FAFSA. *Unit head:* Dr. Harriet Schwartz, Chair, 412-578-8720, E-mail: hlschwartz@carlow.edu. *Application contact:* 412-578-6059, Fax: 412-578-6321, E-mail: gradstudies@carlow.edu.
Website: http://www.carlow.edu/MA_studentaffairs.aspx

Carlow University, College of Leadership and Social Change, Program in Student Affairs/Professional Counseling, Pittsburgh, PA 15213-3165. Offers MA/MS. *Program availability:* Part-time, evening/weekend. *Students:* 14 full-time (12 women), 2 part-time (1 woman); includes 8 minority (6 Black or African American, non-Hispanic/Latino; 1 Hispanic/Latino; 1 Two or more races, non-Hispanic/Latino). Average age 33. 11 applicants, 82% accepted, 6 enrolled. *Entrance requirements:* Additional exam requirements/recommendations for international students: Required—TOEFL (minimum score 550 paper-based). *Application deadline:* Applications are processed on a rolling basis. Electronic applications accepted. *Expenses: Tuition:* Full-time $12,103; part-time $825 per credit hour. Tuition and fees vary according to program. *Financial support:* Application deadline: 4/1; applicants required to submit FAFSA. *Unit head:* Dr. Harriet Schwartz, Chair, 412-578-8720, E-mail: hlschwartz@carlow.edu. *Application contact:* 412-578-6059, Fax: 412-578-6321, E-mail: gradstudies@carlow.edu.

Central Michigan University, College of Graduate Studies, College of Education and Human Services, Department of Educational Leadership, Mount Pleasant, MI 48859. Offers educational leadership (Ed D), including educational technology (Ed D, Ed S), higher education leadership, K-12 curriculum, K-12 leadership; general educational administration (Ed S), including administrative leadership K-12, educational technology (Ed D, Ed S), higher education administration, instructional leadership K-12; school principalship (MA), including charter school leadership, site-based leadership; student affairs administration (MA); teacher leadership (MA). *Program availability:* Part-time, evening/weekend. *Degree requirements:* For master's and Ed S, thesis or alternative; for doctorate, thesis/dissertation. *Entrance requirements:* For doctorate, GRE or MAT, master's degree, minimum GPA of 3.5, 3 years of professional education experience. Electronic applications accepted. *Faculty research:* Elementary administration, secondary administration, student achievement, in-service training, internships in administration.

The Citadel, The Military College of South Carolina, Citadel Graduate College, Zucker Family School of Education, Charleston, SC 29409. Offers elementary/secondary school administration and supervision (M Ed); elementary/secondary school counseling (M Ed); interdisciplinary STEM education (M Ed, Graduate Certificate); middle grades (MAT), including English, mathematics, science, social studies; physical education (grades K-12) (MAT); school superintendency (Ed S); secondary education (MAT), including biology, English, mathematics, social studies; student affairs (Graduate Certificate); student affairs and college counseling (M Ed). *Accreditation:* NCATE. *Program availability:* Part-time, evening/weekend, 100% online, blended/hybrid learning. *Degree requirements:* For master's, comprehensive exam (for some programs). *Entrance requirements:* For master's, GRE (minimum combined verbal and quantitative score of 290) or MAT (minimum score 396). Additional exam requirements/recommendations for international students: Required—TOEFL (minimum score 550 paper-based; 79 iBT). Electronic applications accepted. *Expenses:* Tuition, state resident: part-time $587 per credit hour. Tuition, nonresident: part-time $988 per credit hour. *Required fees:* $90 per term.

Claremont Graduate University, Graduate Programs, School of Educational Studies, Claremont, CA 91711-6160. Offers Africana education (Certificate); education and policy (MA, PhD); higher education/student affairs (MA, PhD); human development (MA, PhD); public school administration (MA, PhD); quantitative evaluation (MA, PhD); special education (MA, PhD); teacher education (MA); teaching and learning (MA, PhD); urban leadership (MA, PhD); MBA/PhD. PhD program offered jointly with San Diego State University. *Program availability:* Part-time. Terminal master's awarded for partial completion of doctoral program. *Entrance requirements:* For master's and doctorate, GRE General Test. Additional exam requirements/recommendations for international students: Required—TOEFL (minimum score 75 iBT). Electronic applications accepted. *Faculty research:* Education administration, K-12 and higher education, multicultural education, education policy, diversity in higher education, faculty issues.

Clemson University, Graduate School, College of Education, Department of Educational and Organizational Leadership Development, Clemson, SC 29634. Offers administration and supervision (M Ed, Ed S); athletic leadership (MS, Certificate); education systems improvement science (Ed D); educational leadership (PhD), including higher education, P-12; human resource development (MHRD), including human resource development; leadership (Certificate); student affairs (M Ed). *Program availability:* Part-time, evening/weekend, 100% online. *Faculty:* 21 full-time (14 women), 1 part-time/adjunct (0 women). *Students:* 55 full-time (32 women), 285 part-time (169 women); includes 89 minority (71 Black or African American, non-Hispanic/Latino; 1 American Indian or Alaska Native, non-Hispanic/Latino; 1 Asian, non-Hispanic/Latino; 13 Hispanic/Latino; 3 Two or more races, non-Hispanic/Latino), 2 international. Average age 35. 216 applicants, 69% accepted, 100 enrolled. In 2017, 58 master's, 16 doctorates, 20 other advanced degrees awarded. *Degree requirements:* For master's, thesis (for some programs); for doctorate, comprehensive exam, thesis/dissertation. *Entrance requirements:* For master's, doctorate, and other advanced degree, GRE General Test, unofficial transcripts, letters of recommendation. Additional exam requirements/recommendations for international students: Required—TOEFL (minimum score 80 iBT), IELTS (minimum score 7), PTE (minimum score 54). *Application deadline:* For fall admission, 3/1 priority date for domestic and international students; for spring admission, 10/1 priority date for domestic and international students. Applications are processed on a rolling basis. Application fee: $80 ($90 for international students). Electronic applications accepted. *Expenses:* $5,174 per semester full-time resident, $9,714 per semester full-time non-resident, $511 per credit hour part-time resident, $1,017 per credit hour part-time non-resident; $741 per credit hour online; other fees may apply per session. *Financial support:* In 2017–18, 20 students received support, including 4 fellowships with partial tuition reimbursements available (averaging $8,750 per year), 1 research assistantship with partial tuition reimbursement available (averaging $9,378 per year); career-related internships or fieldwork and unspecified assistantships also available. Financial award application deadline: 3/1. *Total annual research expenditures:* $31,201. *Unit head:* Dr. Roy Jones, Interim Department Chair, 864-656-7915, E-mail: royj@clemson.edu. *Application contact:* Alison Search, Student Services Program Coordinator, 864-250-8880, E-mail: alisonp@clemson.edu. Website: http://www.clemson.edu/education/departments/educational-organizational-leadership-development/index.html

Clemson University, Graduate School, College of Education, Department of Education and Human Development, Clemson, SC 29634. Offers counselor education (M Ed, Ed S), including mental health counseling, school counseling, student affairs (M Ed); learning sciences (PhD); literacy (M Ed); literacy, language and culture (PhD); special education (M Ed, MAT, PhD); teacher education (M Ed). *Program availability:* Part-time, evening/weekend, 100% online. *Faculty:* 32 full-time (22 women). *Students:* 445 full-time (355 women), 169 part-time (159 women); includes 126 minority (52 Black or African American, non-Hispanic/Latino; 16 Asian, non-Hispanic/Latino; 34 Hispanic/Latino; 24 Two or more races, non-Hispanic/Latino), 5 international. Average age 28. 401 applicants, 60% accepted, 135 enrolled. In 2017, 212 master's, 1 doctorate, 117 other advanced degrees awarded. *Degree requirements:* For master's, thesis (for some programs); for doctorate, comprehensive exam (for some programs), thesis/dissertation. *Entrance requirements:* For master's and doctorate, GRE General Test, unofficial transcripts, letters of recommendation. Additional exam requirements/recommendations for international students: Required—TOEFL (minimum score 80 iBT), IELTS (minimum score 7), PTE (minimum score 54). *Application deadline:* For fall admission, 3/1 priority date for domestic and international students; for spring admission, 10/1 priority date for domestic and international students. Applications are processed on a rolling basis. Application fee: $80 ($90 for international students). Electronic applications accepted. *Expenses:* $5,174 per semester full-time resident, $9,714 per semester full-time non-resident, $511 per credit hour part-time resident, $1,017 per credit hour part-time non-resident; $741 per credit hour online; other fees may apply per session. *Financial support:* In 2017–18, 84 students received support, including 9 fellowships with partial tuition reimbursements available (averaging $8,148 per year), 18 teaching assistantships with partial tuition reimbursements available (averaging $13,707 per year); career-related internships or fieldwork and unspecified assistantships also available. Financial award application deadline: 3/1. *Total annual research expenditures:* $1.2 million. *Unit head:* Dr. Debi Switzer, Department Chair, 864-656-5098, E-mail: debi@clemson.edu. *Application contact:* Julie Jones, Student Services Program Coordinator, 864-656-5096, E-mail: jgambre@clemson.edu. Website: http://www.clemson.edu/education/departments/education-human-development/index.html

The College of Saint Rose, Graduate Studies, Thelma P. Lally School of Education, Program in College Student Services Administration, Albany, NY 12203-1419. Offers MS Ed. *Accreditation:* NCATE. *Program availability:* Part-time, evening/weekend. *Students:* 9 full-time (4 women), 5 part-time (3 women); includes 6 minority (2 Black or African American, non-Hispanic/Latino; 1 Asian, non-Hispanic/Latino; 3 Hispanic/Latino). Average age 25. 7 applicants, 100% accepted, 6 enrolled. In 2017, 6 master's awarded. *Degree requirements:* For master's, comprehensive exam or thesis. *Entrance requirements:* For master's, interview, minimum undergraduate GPA of 3.0, 9 hours of psychology coursework. Additional exam requirements/recommendations for international students: Required—TOEFL (minimum score 550 paper-based; 80 iBT),

IELTS (minimum score 6), PTE (minimum score 56). *Application deadline:* For fall admission, 4/1 for domestic and international students; for spring admission, 10/15 priority date for domestic and international students; for summer admission, 3/15 for domestic and international students. Applications are processed on a rolling basis. Application fee: $40. Electronic applications accepted. *Expenses:* Tuition: Full-time $7191; part-time $799 per credit hour. *Required fees:* $924; $462 per credit hour. Tuition and fees vary according to course load. *Financial support:* Career-related internships or fieldwork, scholarships/grants, tuition waivers (partial), and unspecified assistantships available. Support available to part-time students. Financial award application deadline: 4/15. *Unit head:* Claudia Lingertat-Putnam, Department Chair, 518-337-4311, E-mail: lingertc@strose.edu. *Application contact:* Cris Murray, Assistant Vice President for Graduate Recruitment and Enrollment, 518-485-3390, Fax: 518-458-5479, E-mail: grad@strose.edu.
Website: https://www.strose.edu/academics/agraduate-programs/college-student-services-administration-ms/

Colorado State University, College of Health and Human Sciences, School of Education, Fort Collins, CO 80523-1588. Offers adult education and training (M Ed); counseling and career development (MA); education and human resources (M Ed); education, equity, and transformation (PhD); higher education leadership (PhD); organizational learning, performance, and change (M Ed, PhD); student affairs in higher education (MS). *Accreditation:* ACA; TEAC. *Program availability:* Part-time, online only, 100% online, blended/hybrid learning. *Faculty:* 33 full-time (23 women), 19 part-time/adjunct (11 women). *Students:* 74 full-time (53 women), 548 part-time (357 women); includes 151 minority (37 Black or African American, non-Hispanic/Latino; 4 American Indian or Alaska Native, non-Hispanic/Latino; 14 Asian, non-Hispanic/Latino; 71 Hispanic/Latino; 25 Two or more races, non-Hispanic/Latino), 16 international. Average age 37. 456 applicants, 31% accepted, 123 enrolled. In 2017, 177 master's, 22 doctorates awarded. *Degree requirements:* For master's, thesis optional, professional portfolio or capstone project; for doctorate, comprehensive exam, thesis/dissertation. *Entrance requirements:* For master's, bachelor's degree; minimum GPA of 3.0 in last degree earned; for doctorate, GRE; GRE or GMAT (for organizational learning, performance and change only), master's degree; minimum GPA of 3.0 in last degree earned. Additional exam requirements/recommendations for international students: Required—TOEFL (minimum score 550 paper-based; 80 iBT), IELTS (minimum score 6.5), PTE (minimum score 58). *Application deadline:* Applications are processed on a rolling basis. Application fee: $60 ($70 for international students). Electronic applications accepted. *Expenses:* Contact institution. *Financial support:* In 2017–18, 4 students received support, including 8 research assistantships with full and partial tuition reimbursements available (averaging $12,758 per year), 4 teaching assistantships with full and partial tuition reimbursements available (averaging $14,256 per year); fellowships with full and partial tuition reimbursements available, Federal Work-Study, scholarships/grants, tuition waivers (full and partial), and unspecified assistantships also available. Financial award applicants required to submit FAFSA. *Faculty research:* Diversity, equity, and inclusion; STEM education; higher education; occupational learning, performance, and change; teacher education. *Total annual research expenditures:* $312,562. *Unit head:* Dr. Louise Jennings, Co-Director, 970-491-6317, Fax: 970-491-1317, E-mail: louise.jennings@colostate.edu. *Application contact:* Kelli Clark, Graduate Programs Coordinator, 970-491-2093, Fax: 970-491-1317, E-mail: kelli.clark@colostate.edu.
Website: http://www.soe.chhs.colostate.edu/

Dallas Baptist University, Gary Cook School of Leadership, Program in Higher Education, Dallas, TX 75211-9299. Offers leadership studies (M Ed); student affairs leadership (M Ed), including community college leadership, distance learning, interdisciplinary studies, student affairs leadership. *Program availability:* Part-time, evening/weekend. *Application deadline:* Applications are processed on a rolling basis. Application fee: $25. Electronic applications accepted. Application fee is waived when completed online. *Expenses: Tuition:* Full-time $16,308; part-time $906 per credit hour. *Required fees:* $900; $450 per semester. Tuition and fees vary according to course load and degree level. *Unit head:* Dr. Jack Goodyear, Dean, 214-333-5595, Fax: 214-333-6809, E-mail: jackg@dbu.edu. *Application contact:* Dr. Sena Baker, Program Director, 214-333-6850, E-mail: sena@dbu.edu.
Website: http://www4.dbu.edu/leadership/hied/

DePaul University, College of Education, Chicago, IL 60614. Offers bilingual-bicultural education (M Ed, MA); counseling (M Ed, MA), including clinical mental health counseling, college student development, school counseling; curriculum studies (M Ed, MA, Ed D); early childhood education (M Ed, MA, Ed D); educational leadership (M Ed, MA, Ed D), including Catholic leadership (M Ed, MA), general (M Ed, MA), higher education (M Ed, MA), physical education (M Ed, MA), principal preparation (M Ed); teacher preparation (M Ed); elementary education (M Ed, MA); middle grades education (M Ed); middle school mathematics education (MS); reading specialist (M Ed, MA); secondary education (M Ed, MA); social and cultural foundations in education (M Ed, MA); special education (M Ed); sport, fitness and recreation leadership (MS); value-creating education for global citizenship (M Ed); world languages education (M Ed, MA). *Program availability:* Part-time, evening/weekend, online learning. *Degree requirements:* For doctorate, thesis/dissertation. *Application deadline:* Applications are processed on a rolling basis. Application fee: $40. Electronic applications accepted. *Financial support:* Application deadline: 12/31; applicants required to submit FAFSA. *Unit head:* Dr. Paul Zionts, Dean, 773-325-7581, Fax: 773-325-7713, E-mail: pzionts@depaul.edu. *Application contact:* Dr. Paul Zionts, Dean, 773-325-7581, Fax: 773-325-7713, E-mail: pzionts@depaul.edu.
Website: http://education.depaul.edu

Eastern Illinois University, Graduate School, College of Education and Professional Studies, Department of Counseling and Higher Education, Charleston, IL 61920. Offers college student affairs (MS); counseling (MS). *Accreditation:* ACA; NCATE. *Program availability:* Part-time, evening/weekend. *Degree requirements:* For master's, comprehensive exam (for some programs), thesis (for some programs). *Entrance requirements:* For master's, GMAT or GRE. Additional exam requirements/recommendations for international students: Required—TOEFL (minimum score 500 paper-based; 61 iBT), IELTS (minimum score 6). *Application deadline:* For fall admission, 5/15 for domestic and international students; for spring admission, 10/15 for domestic and international students. Applications are processed on a rolling basis. Application fee: $30. Electronic applications accepted. *Financial support:* Research assistantships with full tuition reimbursements, career-related internships or fieldwork, Federal Work-Study, and unspecified assistantships available. Support available to part-time students. Financial award application deadline: 3/1; financial award applicants required to submit FAFSA. *Unit head:* Richard Roberts, Chair, 217-581-2400, Fax: 217-581-7800, E-mail: rlroberts@eiu.edu. *Application contact:* Richard Roberts, Chair, 217-581-2400, Fax: 217-581-7800, E-mail: rlroberts@eiu.edu.
Website: https://www.eiu.edu/che/

Eastern Michigan University, Graduate School, Academic and Student Affairs Division, Ypsilanti, MI 48197. Offers individualized studies (MA, MS); integrated marketing communications (MS). *Students:* 4 full-time (2 women), 36 part-time (25 women); includes 6 minority (2 Asian, non-Hispanic/Latino; 1 Hispanic/Latino; 3 Two or

Student Affairs

more races, non-Hispanic/Latino). Average age 35. 64 applicants, 84% accepted, 26 enrolled. In 2017, 1 master's awarded. *Entrance requirements:* Additional exam requirements/recommendations for international students: Required—TOEFL. Application fee: $45. *Unit head:* Dr. Wade Tornquist, Interim Dean, 734-487-0042, Fax: 734-487-0050, E-mail: wade.tornquist@emich.edu. *Application contact:* Graduate Admissions, 734-487-2400, Fax: 734-487-6559, E-mail: graduate.admissions@emich.edu.

Eastern Michigan University, Graduate School, College of Education, Department of Leadership and Counseling, Programs in Educational Leadership, Ypsilanti, MI 48197. Offers community college leadership (Graduate Certificate); educational leadership (MA, Ed D, SPA); higher education/general administration (MA); higher education/student affairs (MA); K-12 administration (MA); K-12 basic administration (Post Master's Certificate). *Program availability:* Part-time, evening/weekend, online learning. *Students:* 50 full-time (34 women), 286 part-time (186 women); includes 108 minority (85 Black or African American, non-Hispanic/Latino; 3 American Indian or Alaska Native, non-Hispanic/Latino; 1 Asian, non-Hispanic/Latino; 12 Hispanic/Latino; 7 Two or more races, non-Hispanic/Latino), 2 international. Average age 40. 200 applicants, 72% accepted, 76 enrolled. In 2017, 88 master's, 22 doctorates, 28 other advanced degrees awarded. *Degree requirements:* For master's, portfolio. *Entrance requirements:* For doctorate, GRE. Additional exam requirements/recommendations for international students: Required—TOEFL. *Application deadline:* For winter admission, 2/1 for domestic and international students. Applications are processed on a rolling basis. Application fee: $45. *Financial support:* Fellowships, research assistantships with full tuition reimbursements, teaching assistantships with full tuition reimbursements, career-related internships or fieldwork, Federal Work-Study, institutionally sponsored loans, scholarships/grants, tuition waivers (partial), and unspecified assistantships available. Support available to part-time students. *Application contact:* Dr. Jaclynn Tracy, Coordinator of Advising, Programs in Educational Leadership, 734-487-0255, Fax: 734-487-4608, E-mail: jtracy@emich.edu.

Fresno Pacific University, Graduate Programs, School of Education, Division of Pupil Personnel Services, Fresno, CA 93702-4709. Offers board certified associate behavior analyst (Certificate); school counseling (MA); school psychology (MA). *Program availability:* Part-time. *Degree requirements:* For master's, thesis or alternative. *Entrance requirements:* Additional exam requirements/recommendations for international students: Required—TOEFL (minimum score 550 paper-based).

George Mason University, College of Humanities and Social Sciences, Higher Education Program, Fairfax, VA 22030. Offers higher education administration (Certificate); higher education and student development (MA). *Faculty:* 4 full-time (all women), 1 part-time/adjunct (0 women). *Students:* 1 full-time (0 women), 13 part-time (7 women); includes 4 minority (2 Black or African American, non-Hispanic/Latino; 1 Asian, non-Hispanic/Latino; 1 Hispanic/Latino). Average age 43. 6 applicants, 50% accepted, 3 enrolled. In 2017, 3 other advanced degrees awarded. *Degree requirements:* For master's, thesis optional, practicum; for Certificate, practicum. *Entrance requirements:* For master's and Certificate, transcript, resume, writing sample, goals statement, 3 letters of recommendation. Additional exam requirements/recommendations for international students: Required—TOEFL (minimum score 575 paper-based; 88 iBT), IELTS (minimum score 6.5), PTE (minimum score 59). *Application deadline:* For fall admission, 3/1 for domestic and international students; for spring admission, 10/15 for domestic and international students. Application fee: $75 ($80 for international students). Electronic applications accepted. *Expenses:* Tuition, state resident: full-time $11,228; part-time $459.50 per credit. Tuition, nonresident: full-time $30,932; part-time $1280.50 per credit. *Required fees:* $3252; $135.50 per credit. Part-time tuition and fees vary according to course load and program. *Financial support:* Career-related internships or fieldwork, Federal Work-Study, and scholarships/grants available. Support available to part-time students. Financial award application deadline: 3/1; financial award applicants required to submit FAFSA. *Faculty research:* Multicultural issues, leadership, assessment, scholarship of teaching and learning, learning analytics. *Total annual research expenditures:* $24,019. *Unit head:* Jan Arminio, Director, 703-993-2064, Fax: 703-993-2307, E-mail: jarminio@gmu.edu. *Application contact:* Katie Richards, Administrative Coordinator, 703-993-2310, Fax: 703-993-2307, E-mail: kricha22@gmu.edu.
Website: http://highered.gmu.edu/

The George Washington University, Graduate School of Education and Human Development, Department of Educational Leadership, Program in Higher Education Administration, Washington, DC 20052. Offers college teaching and academic leadership (MA Ed/HD, Ed S); general administration (MA Ed/HD, Ed S); higher education administration (Ed D); higher education finance (MA Ed/HD, Ed S); international education (MA Ed/HD, Ed S); policy (MA Ed/HD, Ed S); student affairs administration (MA Ed/HD, Ed S). *Accreditation:* NCATE. *Students:* 18 full-time (15 women), 65 part-time (44 women); includes 30 minority (17 Black or African American, non-Hispanic/Latino; 7 Asian, non-Hispanic/Latino; 5 Hispanic/Latino; 1 Two or more races, non-Hispanic/Latino), 2 international. Average age 32. 139 applicants, 76% accepted, 27 enrolled. In 2017, 34 master's, 9 doctorates, 1 other advanced degree awarded. *Degree requirements:* For master's and Ed S, comprehensive exam; for doctorate, comprehensive exam, thesis/dissertation. *Entrance requirements:* For master's, GRE General Test or MAT, minimum GPA of 2.75; for doctorate, GRE General Test or MAT, interview, minimum GPA of 3.3; for Ed S, GRE General Test or MAT, minimum GPA of 3.3. *Application deadline:* For fall admission, 1/15 priority date for domestic students; for spring admission, 10/1 for domestic students. Applications are processed on a rolling basis. Application fee: $75. *Expenses:* Tuition: Full-time $28,800; part-time $1655 per credit hour. *Required fees:* $45; $2.75 per credit hour. *Financial support:* In 2017–18, 17 students received support. Fellowships, research assistantships, career-related internships or fieldwork, Federal Work-Study, and tuition waivers (partial) available. Financial award application deadline: 1/15; financial award applicants required to submit FAFSA. *Faculty research:* Technology in higher education administration. *Unit head:* Michael Feuer, 202-994-6161, E-mail: mjfeuer@gwu.edu. *Application contact:* Sarah Lang, Director of Graduate Admissions, 202-994-1447, Fax: 202-994-7207, E-mail: slang@gwu.edu.

Grambling State University, School of Graduate Studies and Research, College of Education, Department of Educational Leadership, Grambling, LA 71245. Offers developmental education (MS, Ed D, PMC), including curriculum and instructional design (Ed D), English (MS), guidance and counseling (MS), higher education administration and management (Ed D), mathematics (MS), reading (MS), science (MS), student development and personnel services (Ed D); educational leadership (M Ed). *Program availability:* Part-time, evening/weekend. *Degree requirements:* For master's, comprehensive exam, thesis (for some programs); for doctorate, comprehensive exam, thesis/dissertation. *Entrance requirements:* For master's, GRE, minimum GPA of 2.5 on last degree; for doctorate, GRE (minimum score 1000, 500 on Verbal), master's degree, minimum GPA of 3.0 on last degree. Additional exam requirements/recommendations for international students: Required—TOEFL (minimum score 500 paper-based; 62 iBT). Electronic applications accepted.

Hampton University, School of Liberal Arts and Education, Program in Counseling, Hampton, VA 23668. Offers college student development (MA); community agency

counseling (MA); counseling (Ed S); counselor education and supervision (PhD); pastoral counseling (MA); school counseling (MA). *Accreditation:* ACA; NCATE. *Program availability:* Part-time, evening/weekend, online learning. *Students:* 30 full-time (28 women), 15 part-time (13 women); includes 39 minority (all Black or African American, non-Hispanic/Latino), 1 international. Average age 33. 28 applicants, 25% accepted, 3 enrolled. In 2017, 16 master's awarded. *Degree requirements:* For master's, comprehensive exam; for doctorate, comprehensive exam, thesis/dissertation. *Entrance requirements:* For master's, GRE General Test, personal statement, two letters of recommendation; for doctorate, GRE General Test, personal statement, writing sample, three letters of recommendation; for Ed S, personal statement, two letters of recommendation. Additional exam requirements/recommendations for international students: Required—TOEFL (minimum score 525 paper-based) or IELTS (6.5). *Application deadline:* For fall admission, 6/1 priority date for domestic students, 4/1 priority date for international students; for winter admission, 9/1 priority date for international students; for spring admission, 11/1 priority date for domestic students, 9/1 for international students; for summer admission, 4/1 priority date for domestic students, 2/1 priority date for international students. Applications are processed on a rolling basis. Application fee: $35. Electronic applications accepted. *Expenses: Tuition:* Full-time $22,630; part-time $575 per semester hour. *Required fees:* $70. Tuition and fees vary according to program. *Financial support:* Fellowships, research assistantships, teaching assistantships, career-related internships or fieldwork, Federal Work-Study, institutionally sponsored loans, and scholarships/grants available. Support available to part-time students. Financial award application deadline: 6/30; financial award applicants required to submit FAFSA. *Faculty research:* Personality development, temperament, post-traumatic stress disorder, continuum of normal to abnormal personality. *Unit head:* Dr. Richard Mason, Chairperson, 757-728-6160, E-mail: richard.mason@hamptonu.edu.
Website: http://edhd.hamptonu.edu/counseling/

Illinois State University, Graduate School, College of Education, Department of Educational Administration and Foundations, Program in College Student Personnel Administration, Normal, IL 61790. Offers MS.

Indiana State University, College of Graduate and Professional Studies, Bayh College of Education, Department of Educational Leadership, Terre Haute, IN 47809. Offers educational administration (PhD); higher education leadership (PhD); K-12 district leadership (PhD); school administration (Ed S); school administration and supervision (M Ed); student affairs and higher education (MS). *Accreditation:* NCATE. *Program availability:* Part-time, evening/weekend. Terminal master's awarded for partial completion of doctoral program. *Degree requirements:* For master's, thesis; for doctorate, thesis/dissertation. *Entrance requirements:* For master's, GRE General Test, minimum undergraduate GPA of 2.5; for doctorate, GRE General Test, minimum undergraduate GPA of 3.5; for Ed S, GRE General Test, minimum graduate GPA of 3.25. Electronic applications accepted.

Indiana University Bloomington, School of Education, Department of Educational Leadership and Policy Studies, Bloomington, IN 47405. Offers educational leadership (MS, Ed D, Ed S); higher education (Ed D, PhD); higher education and student affairs (MS); history and philosophy of education (MS); history, philosophy, and policy in education (PhD), including education policy studies, history of education, philosophy of education; international and comparative education (MS). *Accreditation:* NCATE. *Degree requirements:* For master's, thesis optional; for doctorate, comprehensive exam, thesis/dissertation; for Ed S, comprehensive exam or project. *Entrance requirements:* For master's, doctorate, and Ed S, GRE General Test. Additional exam requirements/recommendations for international students: Required—TOEFL (minimum score 79 iBT). Electronic applications accepted. *Faculty research:* Culturally engaging campus environments, school choice policy analysis, democracy and education in the national and international context, and principal leadership.

Indiana University of Pennsylvania, School of Graduate Studies and Research, College of Education and Communications, Department of Student Affairs in Higher Education, Indiana, PA 15705. Offers MA. *Accreditation:* NCATE. *Program availability:* Part-time. *Faculty:* 3 full-time (1 woman), 1 (woman) part-time/adjunct. *Students:* 44 full-time (25 women), 3 part-time (2 women); includes 11 minority (9 Black or African American, non-Hispanic/Latino; 1 Asian, non-Hispanic/Latino; 1 Hispanic/Latino), 3 international. Average age 24. 80 applicants, 78% accepted, 23 enrolled. In 2017, 23 master's awarded. *Degree requirements:* For master's, comprehensive exam, thesis optional. *Entrance requirements:* For master's, resume, interview, 2 letters of recommendation, writing sample, minimum GPA of 2.8. Additional exam requirements/recommendations for international students: Required—TOEFL (minimum score 540 paper-based). *Application deadline:* For fall admission, 1/15 priority date for domestic students. Application fee: $50. Electronic applications accepted. *Expenses:* Contact institution. *Financial support:* In 2017–18, 21 research assistantships with tuition reimbursements (averaging $5,445 per year) were awarded; fellowships, career-related internships or fieldwork, Federal Work-Study, scholarships/grants, and unspecified assistantships also available. Support available to part-time students. Financial award application deadline: 4/15; financial award applicants required to submit FAFSA. *Unit head:* Dr. John Wesley Lowery, Chairperson, 724-357-4545, E-mail: jlowery@iup.edu.
Website: http://www.iup.edu/sahe

Iowa State University of Science and Technology, Department of Educational Leadership and Policy Studies, Ames, IA 50011. Offers counselor education (M Ed, MS); educational administration (M Ed, MS); educational leadership (PhD); higher education (M Ed, MS); organizational learning and human resource development (M Ed, MS); research and evaluation (MS); student affairs (MS). *Degree requirements:* For master's, thesis or alternative; for doctorate, thesis/dissertation. *Entrance requirements:* For master's and doctorate, GRE General Test. Additional exam requirements/recommendations for international students: Required—TOEFL (minimum score 560 paper-based; 83 iBT), IELTS (minimum score 6.5). Electronic applications accepted.

Kansas State University, Graduate School, College of Education, Department of Special Education, Counseling and Student Affairs, Manhattan, KS 66506. Offers academic advising (MS, Certificate); counseling and student development (MS), including college student development, school counseling; special education (MS, Ed D); special education, counseling, and student affairs (PhD). *Accreditation:* ACA; NCATE. *Program availability:* Part-time, online learning. *Degree requirements:* For master's, comprehensive exam; for doctorate, comprehensive exam, thesis/dissertation. *Entrance requirements:* For master's, minimum undergraduate GPA of 3.0; for doctorate, GRE General Test, minimum GPA of 3.0 in last 60 hours. Additional exam requirements/recommendations for international students: Required—TOEFL. Electronic applications accepted. *Faculty research:* Counseling supervision, academic advising, career development, student development, universal design for learning, autism, learning disabilities.

Kent State University, College of Education, Health and Human Services, School of Foundations, Leadership and Administration, Program in Higher Education and Student Personnel, Kent, OH 44242-0001. Offers M Ed. *Accreditation:* NCATE. *Program availability:* Part-time, evening/weekend. *Entrance requirements:* For master's, GRE if undergraduate GPA is below 3.0, resume, interview, 2 letters of recommendation, goals statement. Additional exam requirements/recommendations for international students:

Required—TOEFL (minimum score 550 paper-based; 80 iBT). Electronic applications accepted. *Expenses:* Tuition, state resident: full-time $11,310; part-time $515 per credit hour. Tuition, nonresident: full-time $20,396; part-time $928 per credit hour. *International tuition:* $18,544 full-time. *Faculty research:* History/sociology of higher education, organization and administration in higher education.

Lewis & Clark College, Graduate School of Education and Counseling, Department of Educational Leadership, Program in Educational Leadership, Portland, OR 97219-7899. Offers educational administration (M Ed, Ed S); educational leadership (Ed D); student affairs administration (MA). *Program availability:* Part-time, evening/weekend. *Degree requirements:* For doctorate, thesis/dissertation. *Entrance requirements:* For master's, minimum undergraduate GPA of 2.75, Oregon teaching or personnel service license, three years of successful teaching and/or personnel service experience in the public schools or regionally-accredited private schools; for doctorate, master's degree plus minimum of 14 degree-applicable, post-master's semester credits; minimum undergraduate GPA of 2.75. Additional exam requirements/recommendations for international students: Required—TOEFL (minimum score 575 paper-based). Electronic applications accepted.

Lewis University, College of Arts and Sciences, Program in Organizational Leadership, Romeoville, IL 60446. Offers higher education/student services (MA); non-profit management (MA); organizational and leadership coaching (MA); organizational management (MA); training and development (MA). *Program availability:* Part-time, evening/weekend, 100% online, blended/hybrid learning. *Students:* 16 full-time (11 women), 154 part-time (115 women); includes 49 minority (27 Black or African American, non-Hispanic/Latino; 1 American Indian or Alaska Native, non-Hispanic/Latino; 4 Asian, non-Hispanic/Latino; 12 Hispanic/Latino; 5 Two or more races, non-Hispanic/Latino), 4 international. Average age 37. *Entrance requirements:* For master's, bachelor's degree, personal statement, minimum GPA of 3.0, letters of recommendation. Additional exam requirements/recommendations for international students: Required—TOEFL (minimum score 550 paper-based; 79 iBT), IELTS (minimum score 6). *Application deadline:* For fall admission, 5/1 priority date for international students; for spring admission, 11/15 priority date for international students. Applications are processed on a rolling basis. Application fee: $40. Electronic applications accepted. Tuition and fees vary according to program. *Financial support:* Federal Work-Study, tuition waivers, and unspecified assistantships available. Financial award application deadline: 5/1; financial award applicants required to submit FAFSA. *Unit head:* Dr. Lesley Page, Chair of Organizational Leadership, 815-838-0500, E-mail: page@lewisu.edu. *Application contact:* Kathy Lisak, Graduate Admission Counselor, 815-836-5610, E-mail: grad@lewisu.edu.

Manhattan College, Graduate Programs, School of Education and Health, Program in School Counseling, Riverdale, NY 10471. Offers bilingual pupil personnel services (Professional Diploma); school counseling (MA, Professional Diploma). *Program availability:* Part-time, evening/weekend. *Faculty:* 2 full-time (both women), 11 part-time/adjunct (7 women). *Students:* 50 full-time (35 women), 15 part-time (11 women); includes 40 minority (14 Black or African American, non-Hispanic/Latino; 2 Asian, non-Hispanic/Latino; 24 Hispanic/Latino). Average age 30. 41 applicants, 95% accepted, 39 enrolled. In 2017, 38 master's, 11 other advanced degrees awarded. *Degree requirements:* For master's, thesis, internship. *Entrance requirements:* For master's, minimum GPA of 3.0. Additional exam requirements/recommendations for international students: Required—TOEFL. *Application deadline:* For fall admission, 7/1 priority date for domestic students; for spring admission, 12/20 priority date for domestic students. Applications are processed on a rolling basis. Application fee: $75. Electronic applications accepted. *Expenses:* $925 per credit; $110 registration fee per semester; $180 per semester services fee; $170 per semester information fee; $400 graduation fee. *Financial support:* Federal Work-Study, health care benefits, and unspecified assistantships available. Financial award application deadline: 2/1; financial award applicants required to submit FAFSA. *Faculty research:* Cognitive development, college and career readiness, group counseling, cultural attitudes, bullying, family social environments. *Unit head:* Dr. Corine Fitzpatrick, Director, 718-862-7497, Fax: 718-862-7472, E-mail: corine.fitzpatrick@manhattan.edu. *Application contact:* Suzana Pavisic, Director of Graduate Admissions, 718-862-7825, Fax: 718-862-8019, E-mail: spavisic01@manhattan.edu.

Marquette University, Graduate School, College of Education, Department of Educational Policy and Leadership, Milwaukee, WI 53201-1881. Offers college student personnel administration (M Ed); curriculum and instruction (MA); education (MA); educational administration (M Ed); educational policy and foundations (MA); elementary education (Certificate); literacy (MA); principal (Certificate); reading specialist (Certificate); reading teacher (Certificate); secondary education (Certificate); superintendent (Certificate). *Program availability:* Part-time, evening/weekend. Terminal master's awarded for partial completion of doctoral program. *Degree requirements:* For master's, comprehensive exam, thesis (for some programs); for doctorate, thesis/dissertation, qualifying exam. *Entrance requirements:* For master's, GRE General Test or MAT, official transcripts from all current and previous colleges/universities except Marquette, three letters of recommendation, statement of purpose; for doctorate, GRE General Test, MAT, sample of written work, official transcripts from all current and previous colleges/universities except Marquette, three letters of recommendation, statement of purpose, resume/curriculum vitae; for Certificate, GRE General Test or MAT, master's degree. Additional exam requirements/recommendations for international students: Required—TOEFL (minimum score 530 paper-based). *Expenses:* Contact institution. *Faculty research:* Leadership; social justice in education; development of lifelong learners; race, class, and schooling in historical perspective; urban teacher education.

Merrimack College, School of Education and Social Policy, North Andover, MA 01845-5800. Offers community engagement (M Ed), including community organizations, higher education, PreK-12 education; criminology and criminal justice (MS); curriculum and instruction (M Ed); early childhood education (M Ed); educational leadership (CAGS), including instructional leadership; elementary education (M Ed); English as a second language (PreK-6) (M Ed); high school education (M Ed); higher education (M Ed), including leadership and organizational development, student affairs; middle school education (M Ed); moderate disabilities (PreK-8) (M Ed); school counseling (M Ed). *Program availability:* Part-time, evening/weekend, 100% online courses with immersion events and in-classroom practicum close to home. *Faculty:* 15 full-time, 36 part-time/adjunct. *Students:* 212 full-time (175 women), 121 part-time (101 women); includes 42 minority (6 Black or African American, non-Hispanic/Latino; 6 Asian, non-Hispanic/Latino; 27 Hispanic/Latino; 3 Two or more races, non-Hispanic/Latino), 3 international. Average age 27. 420 applicants, 84% accepted, 250 enrolled. In 2017, 177 master's awarded. *Degree requirements:* For master's, practicum, portfolio, and state test (for licensure track); capstone (for higher education, curriculum and instruction, and community engagement tracks); for CAGS, capstone. *Entrance requirements:* For master's, Massachusetts Teacher Education Licensure (MTEL), official transcripts from other colleges, resume, personal statement, 2 letters of recommendation. Additional exam requirements/recommendations for international students: Required—TOEFL (minimum score 84 iBT), IELTS (minimum score 6.5), PTE (minimum score 56). *Application deadline:* For fall admission, 8/24 for domestic students, 7/30 for

international students; for spring admission, 1/10 for domestic students, 12/10 for international students; for summer admission, 5/10 for domestic students, 4/10 for international students. Applications are processed on a rolling basis. Application fee: $0. Electronic applications accepted. *Expenses:* Contact institution. *Financial support:* Fellowships with full tuition reimbursements, career-related internships or fieldwork, scholarships/grants, and health care benefits available. Support available to part-time students. Financial award application deadline: 5/1; financial award applicants required to submit FAFSA. *Application contact:* Alyssa Orlando, Graduate Admissions Counselor, 978-837-3563, E-mail: orlandoaf@merrimack.edu. Website: http://www.merrimack.edu/academics/graduate/education/

Messiah College, Program in Higher Education, Mechanicsburg, PA 17055. Offers college athletics management (MA); self-designed concentration (MA); student affairs (MA). *Program availability:* Part-time. Electronic applications accepted. *Faculty research:* College athletics management, assessment and student learning outcomes, the life and legacy of Ernest L. Boyer, common learning, student affairs practice.

Miami University, College of Education, Health and Society, Department of Educational Leadership, Oxford, OH 45056. Offers educational leadership (Ed D, PhD); school leadership (M Ed); student affairs in higher education (MS, PhD); transformative education (M Ed). *Accreditation:* NCATE. *Students:* 83 full-time (57 women), 138 part-time (91 women); includes 50 minority (22 Black or African American, non-Hispanic/Latino; 1 American Indian or Alaska Native, non-Hispanic/Latino; 10 Asian, non-Hispanic/Latino; 10 Hispanic/Latino; 7 Two or more races, non-Hispanic/Latino), 11 international. Average age 35. In 2017, 50 master's, 12 doctorates awarded. *Expenses:* Tuition, state resident: full-time $13,812; part-time $575 per credit hour. Tuition, nonresident: full-time $30,860; part-time $1286 per credit hour. *Unit head:* Dr. Kathleen Knight Abowitz, Chair and Professor, 513-529-6848, E-mail: knightk2@miamioh.edu. *Application contact:* Dr. Thomas Poetter, Professor and Director of Graduate Studies, 513-529-6825, E-mail: poettets@miamioh.edu. Website: http://www.MiamiOH.edu/EDL

Minnesota State University Mankato, College of Graduate Studies and Research, College of Education, Department of Counseling and Student Personnel, Mankato, MN 56001. Offers college student affairs (MS); counselor education and supervision (Ed D); mental health counseling (MS); professional school counseling (K-12) (MS). *Accreditation:* ACA (one or more programs are accredited); NCATE. *Degree requirements:* For master's, comprehensive exam, thesis or alternative. *Entrance requirements:* For master's, GRE General Test or MAT (if GPA less than 3.0 for last 2 years), minimum GPA of 3.0 during previous 2 years, 3 letters of reference. Additional exam requirements/recommendations for international students: Required—TOEFL. Electronic applications accepted.

Mississippi State University, College of Education, Department of Counseling, Educational Psychology, and Foundations, Mississippi State, MS 39762. Offers clinical mental health (MS); college counseling (MS); counseling/mental health (PhD); counseling/school psychology (PhD); counselor education (Ed S); educational psychology/general educational psychology (PhD); educational psychology/school psychology (PhD); general educational psychology (MS); psychometry (MS); rehabilitation counseling (MS); school counseling (MS); school psychology (Ed S); student affairs (MS). *Accreditation:* ACA (one or more programs are accredited); APA; CORE (one or more programs are accredited); NCATE. *Program availability:* Part-time, blended/hybrid learning. *Faculty:* 21 full-time (14 women), 3 part-time/adjunct (2 women). *Students:* 106 full-time (85 women), 51 part-time (43 women); includes 55 minority (44 Black or African American, non-Hispanic/Latino; 1 American Indian or Alaska Native, non-Hispanic/Latino; 1 Asian, non-Hispanic/Latino; 5 Hispanic/Latino; 4 Two or more races, non-Hispanic/Latino), 5 international. Average age 29. 136 applicants, 55% accepted, 54 enrolled. In 2017, 50 master's, 7 doctorates, 10 other advanced degrees awarded. Terminal master's awarded for partial completion of doctoral program. *Degree requirements:* For master's, comprehensive exam, thesis optional; for doctorate, thesis/dissertation, comprehensive oral and written exam. *Entrance requirements:* For master's, GRE (taken within the last five years), BS with minimum GPA of 2.75 on last 60 hours; for doctorate, GRE, MS from CACREP- or CORE-accredited program in counseling; for Ed S, GRE, MS in counseling or related field, minimum GPA of 3.3 on all graduate work. Additional exam requirements/recommendations for international students: Required—TOEFL (minimum score 550 paper-based; 79 iBT); Recommended—IELTS (minimum score 6.5). *Application deadline:* For fall admission, 2/1 priority date for domestic and international students. Applications are processed on a rolling basis. Application fee: $60 ($80 for international students). Electronic applications accepted. *Expenses:* Tuition, state resident: full-time $8318; part-time $462.12 per credit hour. Tuition, nonresident: full-time $22,358; part-time $1242.12 per credit hour. *Required fees:* $110; $12.24 per credit hour. $6.12 per semester. *Financial support:* In 2017–18, 4 research assistantships (averaging $9,000 per year), 10 teaching assistantships with full tuition reimbursements (averaging $8,401 per year) were awarded; career-related internships or fieldwork, Federal Work-Study, institutionally sponsored loans, and unspecified assistantships also available. Financial award application deadline: 2/1; financial award applicants required to submit FAFSA. *Faculty research:* HIV/AIDS in college population, substance abuse in youth and college students, ADHD and conduct disorders in youth, assessment and identification of early childhood disabilities, assessment and vocational transition of the disabled. *Unit head:* Dr. David Morse, Professor and Head, 662-325-3426, Fax: 662-325-3263, E-mail: dmorse@colled.msstate.edu. *Application contact:* Marina Hunt, Admissions and Enrollment Assistant, 662-325-3363, E-mail: mhunt@grad.msstate.edu. Website: http://www.cep.msstate.edu/

Mississippi State University, College of Education, Educational Leadership Program, Mississippi State, MS 39762. Offers community college education (MAT); community college leadership (PhD); higher education leadership (PhD); P-12 school leadership (PhD); school administration (MS, Ed S); student affairs and higher education (MS); workforce education leadership (MS). MS in workforce education leadership held jointly with Alcorn State University. *Faculty:* 12 full-time (9 women). *Students:* 62 full-time (33 women), 149 part-time (93 women); includes 94 minority (79 Black or African American, non-Hispanic/Latino; 5 American Indian or Alaska Native, non-Hispanic/Latino; 4 Hispanic/Latino; 1 Native Hawaiian or other Pacific Islander, non-Hispanic/Latino; 5 Two or more races, non-Hispanic/Latino). Average age 36. 95 applicants, 79% accepted, 64 enrolled. In 2017, 41 master's, 32 doctorates, 7 other advanced degrees awarded. *Degree requirements:* For master's and Ed S, comprehensive exam, thesis; for doctorate, comprehensive exam, thesis/dissertation. *Entrance requirements:* For master's, GRE, minimum GPA of 2.75 in junior and senior courses; for doctorate, GRE, minimum GPA of 3.4 on previous graduate work; for Ed S, GRE, minimum GPA of 3.2, master's degree. Additional exam requirements/recommendations for international students: Required—TOEFL (minimum score 550 paper-based; 79 iBT); Recommended—IELTS (minimum score 6.5). *Application deadline:* For fall admission, 7/1 for domestic students, 5/1 for international students; for spring admission, 11/1 for domestic students, 9/1 for international students. Application fee: $60 ($80 for international students). Electronic applications accepted. *Expenses:* Tuition, state resident: full-time $8318; part-time $462.12 per credit hour. Tuition, nonresident: full-time $22,358; part-time $1242.12 per credit hour. *Required fees:* $110; $12.24 per credit

hour. $6.12 per semester. *Financial support:* In 2017–18, 1 research assistantship with full tuition reimbursement (averaging $10,879 per year) was awarded; Federal Work-Study, institutionally sponsored loans, and unspecified assistantships also available. Financial award application deadline: 4/1; financial award applicants required to submit FAFSA. *Unit head:* Dr. Eric Moyen, Associate Professor and Head, 662-325-0969, Fax: 662-325-0975, E-mail: em1621@msstate.edu. *Application contact:* Nathan Drake, Admissions and Enrollment Assistant, 662-325-3804, E-mail: ndrake@grad.msstate.edu.
Website: http://www.educationalleadership.msstate.edu/

Missouri State University, Graduate College, College of Education, Department of Counseling, Leadership, and Special Education, Program in Student Affairs in Higher Education, Springfield, MO 65897. Offers MS. *Program availability:* Part-time. *Faculty:* 6 full-time (4 women). *Students:* 22 full-time (18 women), 5 part-time (4 women); includes 8 minority (3 Black or African American, non-Hispanic/Latino; 1 Asian, non-Hispanic/Latino; 1 Hispanic/Latino; 3 Two or more races, non-Hispanic/Latino), 2 international. Average age 23. 17 applicants, 76% accepted, 4 enrolled. In 2017, 16 master's awarded. *Degree requirements:* For master's, comprehensive exam, thesis or alternative. *Entrance requirements:* For master's, GRE, statement of purpose; three references. Additional exam requirements/recommendations for international students: Required—TOEFL (minimum score 550 paper-based; 79 iBT), IELTS (minimum score 6). *Application deadline:* For fall admission, 2/1 priority date for domestic students, 2/1 for international students. Applications are processed on a rolling basis. Application fee: $35 ($50 for international students). Electronic applications accepted. *Expenses:* Tuition, state resident: full-time $2915; part-time $2021 per credit hour. Tuition, nonresident: full-time $5354; part-time $3647 per credit hour. *International tuition:* $11,992 full-time. *Required fees:* $173; $173 per credit hour. Tuition and fees vary according to class time, course level, course load, degree level, campus/location and program. *Financial support:* Federal Work-Study, institutionally sponsored loans, scholarships/grants, and unspecified assistantships available. Financial award application deadline: 3/31; financial award applicants required to submit FAFSA. *Unit head:* Dr. James Satterfield, Department Head, 417-836-5392, E-mail: clse@missouristate.edu. *Application contact:* Stephanie Praschan, Director, Graduate Enrollment Management, 417-836-5330, Fax: 417-836-6200, E-mail: stephaniepraschan@missouristate.edu.
Website: http://education.missouristate.edu/edadmin/MSEDSA.htm

Monmouth University, Graduate Studies, School of Education, West Long Branch, NJ 07764-1898. Offers applied behavior analysis (Certificate); autism (Certificate); director of school counseling services (Post-Master's Certificate); early childhood (M Ed); educational leadership (Ed D); elementary education (MAT), including elementary level, secondary level; English as a second language (M Ed); learning disabilities teacher-consultant (Post-Master's Certificate); literacy (MS Ed); school counseling (MS Ed); special education (MS Ed), including autism, learning disabilities teacher-consultant, teacher of students with disabilities, teaching in inclusive settings; speech-language pathology (MS Ed); student affairs and college counseling (MS Ed); supervisor (Post-Master's Certificate); teaching English to speakers of other languages (Certificate). *Accreditation:* NCATE. *Program availability:* Part-time, evening/weekend, 100% online, blended/hybrid learning. *Faculty:* 23 full-time (19 women), 33 part-time/adjunct (25 women). *Students:* 175 full-time (163 women), 168 part-time (142 women); includes 54 minority (10 Black or African American, non-Hispanic/Latino; 4 Asian, non-Hispanic/Latino; 32 Hispanic/Latino; 8 Two or more races, non-Hispanic/Latino). Average age 27. In 2017, 160 master's, 3 other advanced degrees awarded. *Entrance requirements:* For master's, GRE taken within last 5 years (for MS Ed in speech-language pathology); SAT (minimum combined score of 1660 in 3 sections), ACT (23), GRE (minimum score of 4.0 on analytical writing section and minimum combined score of 310 on quantitative and verbal sections), or passing scores on 3 parts of Core Academic Skills Educators, minimum GPA of 3.0 in major; 2 letters of recommendation (for some programs); resume, personal statement or essay (depending on program). Additional exam requirements/recommendations for international students: Required—TOEFL (minimum score 550 paper-based; 79 iBT), IELTS (minimum score 6), Michigan English Language Assessment Battery (minimum score 77) or Certificate of Advanced English (minimum score 160). *Application deadline:* For fall admission, 7/15 priority date for domestic students, 7/1 for international students; for spring admission, 12/1 priority date for domestic students, 11/1 for international students; for summer admission, 5/1 for domestic students. Applications are processed on a rolling basis. Application fee: $50. Electronic applications accepted. *Expenses:* Tuition: Full-time $21,366; part-time $7122 per credit. *Required fees:* $700; $175 per term. *Financial support:* In 2017–18, 125 students received support. Institutionally sponsored loans, scholarships/grants, and unspecified assistantships available. Support available to part-time students. Financial award applicants required to submit FAFSA. *Faculty research:* Multicultural literacy, science and mathematics teaching strategies, teacher as reflective practitioner, children with disabilities. *Unit head:* Dr. John E. Henning, Dean, 732-263-5513, Fax: 732-263-5277. *Application contact:* Laurie Kuhn, Associate Director of Graduate Admission, 732-571-3452, Fax: 732-263-5123, E-mail: gradadm@monmouth.edu.
Website: http://www.monmouth.edu/academics/schools/education/default.asp

Morgan State University, School of Graduate Studies, School of Education and Urban Studies, Department of Advanced Studies, Leadership and Policy, Program in Higher Education Administration, Baltimore, MD 21251. Offers higher education (PhD); higher education and student affairs administration (MA). *Degree requirements:* For doctorate, comprehensive exam, thesis/dissertation. *Entrance requirements:* For doctorate, GRE General Test or MAT, minimum GPA of 3.0. *Application deadline:* For fall admission, 2/1 priority date for domestic students; for spring admission, 10/1 priority date for domestic students. Applications are processed on a rolling basis. Application fee: $0. *Expenses:* Tuition, state resident: part-time $433 per credit. Tuition, nonresident: part-time $851 per credit. *Required fees:* $81.50 per credit. *Financial support:* Application deadline: 2/1. *Unit head:* Dr. Sean Robinson, Admissions Coordinator, E-mail: sean.robinson@morgan.edu. *Application contact:* Dr. Dean Campbell, Graduate Recruitment Specialist, 443-885-3185, Fax: 443-885-8226, E-mail: dean.campbell@morgan.edu.

New York University, Steinhardt School of Culture, Education, and Human Development, Department of Administration, Leadership, and Technology, Program in Higher Education (PhD); higher education administration (Ed D); higher education and student affairs (MA). *Accreditation:* TEAC. *Program availability:* Part-time. *Students:* Average age 36. 222 applicants, 18% accepted, 34 enrolled. In 2017, 52 master's, 10 doctorates awarded. *Entrance requirements:* For master's, interview, 2 letters of recommendation; for doctorate, GRE General Test, interview. Additional exam requirements/recommendations for international students: Required—TOEFL (minimum score 100 iBT). *Application deadline:* For fall admission, 12/1 priority date for domestic and international students; for spring admission, 10/1 for domestic and international students. Applications are processed on a rolling basis. Application fee: $75. Electronic applications accepted. *Expenses:* Tuition: Full-time $41,352; part-time $19,968 per year. *Required fees:* $2496; $1628 per unit. $814 per term. Tuition and fees vary according to course load and program. *Financial support:* Fellowships with full and partial tuition reimbursements, career-related internships or fieldwork, Federal Work-Study, institutionally sponsored loans, scholarships/grants, tuition waivers (partial), and

unspecified assistantships available. Support available to part-time students. Financial award application deadline: 2/1; financial award applicants required to submit FAFSA. *Faculty research:* Organizational theory and culture, systemic change, leadership development, access, equity and diversity. *Unit head:* Prof. Ann Marcus, Director, 212-998-5276, Fax: 212-995-4041, E-mail: alm1@nyu.edu. *Application contact:* 212-998-5030, Fax: 212-995-4328, E-mail: steinhardt.gradadmissions@nyu.edu.
Website: http://steinhardt.nyu.edu/alt/highered

Northern Arizona University, College of Education, Department of Educational Psychology, Flagstaff, AZ 86011. Offers clinical mental health counseling (MA); combined counseling/school psychology (PhD), including counseling psychology; counseling (M Ed), including school counseling, student affairs; human relations (M Ed); psychology of human development and learning (Graduate Certificate); school psychology (Ed S). *Program availability:* Part-time, 100% online, blended/hybrid learning. *Faculty:* 22 full-time (12 women), 6 part-time/adjunct (4 women). *Students:* 184 full-time (139 women), 175 part-time (131 women); includes 118 minority (14 Black or African American, non-Hispanic/Latino; 10 American Indian or Alaska Native, non-Hispanic/Latino; 5 Asian, non-Hispanic/Latino; 79 Hispanic/Latino; 1 Native Hawaiian or other Pacific Islander, non-Hispanic/Latino; 9 Two or more races, non-Hispanic/Latino), 9 international. Average age 33. 244 applicants, 44% accepted, 108 enrolled. In 2017, 147 master's, 4 doctorates awarded. Terminal master's awarded for partial completion of doctoral program. *Degree requirements:* For master's, variable foreign language requirement, comprehensive exam (for some programs), thesis (for some programs); for doctorate, variable foreign language requirement, comprehensive exam (for some programs), thesis/dissertation (for some programs); for other advanced degree, comprehensive exam (for some programs). *Entrance requirements:* Additional exam requirements/recommendations for international students: Required—TOEFL (minimum score 80 iBT), IELTS (minimum score 6.5). *Application deadline:* For fall admission, 12/1 for domestic and international students; for spring admission, 9/15 for domestic and international students. Applications are processed on a rolling basis. Application fee: $65. Electronic applications accepted. *Expenses:* Tuition, state resident: full-time $9240; part-time $458 per credit hour. Tuition, nonresident: full-time $21,588; part-time $1199 per credit hour. *Required fees:* $1021; $14 per credit hour. $646 per semester. Tuition and fees vary according to course load, campus/location and program. *Financial support:* In 2017–18, 62 students received support, including 1 fellowship with full and partial tuition reimbursement available (averaging $13,927 per year), 2 research assistantships with full and partial tuition reimbursements available (averaging $13,927 per year), 15 teaching assistantships with full and partial tuition reimbursements available (averaging $13,927 per year); institutionally sponsored loans, health care benefits, tuition waivers (full and partial), and unspecified assistantships also available. Financial award application deadline: 2/1; financial award applicants required to submit FAFSA. *Unit head:* Dr. Robert Horn, Chair, 928-523-0545, Fax: 928-523-9284, E-mail: robert.horn@nau.edu. *Application contact:* Hope DeMello, Administrative Assistant, 928-523-7103, Fax: 928-523-9284, E-mail: eps@nau.edu.
Website: https://nau.edu/coe/ed-psych/

Northwestern State University of Louisiana, Graduate Studies and Research, College of Education and Human Development, Program in Student Affairs in Higher Education, Natchitoches, LA 71497. Offers MA. *Accreditation:* NCATE. *Degree requirements:* For master's, comprehensive exam, thesis or alternative. *Entrance requirements:* For master's, GRE General Test, GRE Subject Test, minimum undergraduate GPA of 2.5. Additional exam requirements/recommendations for international students: Required—TOEFL. Electronic applications accepted.

Nova Southeastern University, College of Arts, Humanities, and Social Sciences, Fort Lauderdale, FL 33314-7796. Offers advanced conflict resolution practice (Graduate Certificate); child protection (MHS); college student affairs (MS); conflict analysis and resolution (MS, PhD); criminal justice (MS, PhD); cross-disciplinary studies (MA); developmental disabilities (MS); family studies (Graduate Certificate); family systems health care (Graduate Certificate); family therapy (MS, PhD); marriage and family therapy (DMFT); peace studies (Graduate Certificate); qualitative research (Graduate Certificate); solution focused coaching (Graduate Certificate). *Accreditation:* AAMFT/COAMFTE (one or more programs are accredited). *Program availability:* Part-time, evening/weekend, 100% online, blended/hybrid learning. *Faculty:* 29 full-time (18 women), 27 part-time/adjunct (21 women). *Students:* 303 full-time (238 women), 903 part-time (677 women); includes 689 minority (385 Black or African American, non-Hispanic/Latino; 4 American Indian or Alaska Native, non-Hispanic/Latino; 31 Asian, non-Hispanic/Latino; 234 Hispanic/Latino; 1 Native Hawaiian or other Pacific Islander, non-Hispanic/Latino; 34 Two or more races, non-Hispanic/Latino), 60 international. Average age 37. 624 applicants, 61% accepted, 285 enrolled. In 2017, 277 master's, 62 doctorates, 25 other advanced degrees awarded. *Degree requirements:* For master's, thesis optional, comprehensive exams, portfolios (for some programs), table-top exams (for some programs); for doctorate, comprehensive exam, thesis/dissertation, qualifying exams, portfolios (for some programs). *Entrance requirements:* For master's, interview, minimum GPA of 3.0, writing sample; for doctorate, interview, minimum GPA of 3.5, master's degree in related field, writing sample; for Graduate Certificate, minimum GPA of 3.0. Additional exam requirements/recommendations for international students: Required—TOEFL. *Application deadline:* For fall admission, 5/17 priority date for domestic and international students; for winter admission, 12/1 priority date for domestic and international students; for spring admission, 4/1 priority date for domestic and international students. Applications are processed on a rolling basis. Application fee: $50. Electronic applications accepted. *Expenses:* Contact institution. *Financial support:* In 2017–18, 170 students received support. Career-related internships or fieldwork, Federal Work-Study, scholarships/grants, and unspecified assistantships available. Financial award application deadline: 4/1; financial award applicants required to submit CSS PROFILE. *Faculty research:* Conflict resolution, family therapy, peace research, international conflict, multi-disciplinary studies, college student affairs, national security affairs, health care conflict resolution, family systems health care, advanced family systems, qualitative research, solution-focused coaching. *Unit head:* Dr. Honggang Yang, Dean, 954-262-3016, Fax: 954-262-3968, E-mail: yangh@nova.edu. *Application contact:* Marcia Arango, Student Recruitment Coordinator, 954-262-3006, Fax: 954-262-3968, E-mail: marango@nsu.nova.edu.
Website: http://cahss.nova.edu/

Ohio University, Graduate College, Gladys W. and David H. Patton College of Education and Human Services, Department of Counseling and Higher Education, Athens, OH 45701-2979. Offers college student personnel (M Ed); community/agency counseling (M Ed); counselor education (PhD); higher education (PhD); rehabilitation counseling (M Ed); school counseling (M Ed). *Accreditation:* ACA; CORE. *Program availability:* Part-time, evening/weekend. *Degree requirements:* For master's, comprehensive exam (for some programs), thesis or alternative; for doctorate, comprehensive exam, thesis/dissertation. *Entrance requirements:* For master's, GRE General Test or MAT (if GPA less than 2.9), 3 letters of reference; for doctorate, GRE General Test, work experience, minimum GPA of 3.4. Additional exam requirements/recommendations for international students: Required—TOEFL (minimum score 550 paper-based; 80 iBT) or IELTS (minimum score 6.5). Electronic applications accepted. *Faculty research:* Youth violence, gender studies, student affairs, chemical dependency, disabilities issues.

Oregon State University, College of Liberal Arts, Program in College Student Services Administration, Corvallis, OR 97331. Offers Ed M, MS. *Entrance requirements:* For master's, minimum GPA of 3.0 in last 90 hours of course work. Additional exam requirements/recommendations for international students: Required—TOEFL (minimum score 80 iBT), IELTS (minimum score 6.5). *Application deadline:* For fall admission, 12/15 for domestic students. Application fee: $75 ($85 for international students). *Unit head:* Dr. Larry Roper, Director, 541-737-3759, E-mail: larry.roper@oregonstate.edu. *Application contact:* Dr. Larry Roper, Director, 541-737-3759, E-mail: larry.roper@oregonstate.edu.

Providence University College & Theological Seminary, Theological Seminary, Otterburne, MB R0A 1G0, Canada. Offers children's ministry (Certificate); Christian studies (MA, Certificate); counseling (MA); cross-cultural discipleship (Certificate); divinity (M Div); educational studies (MA), including counseling psychology, educational ministries, student development, teaching English to speakers of other languages, training teachers of English to speakers of other languages; global studies (MA); lay counseling (Diploma); ministry (D Min); teaching English to speakers of other languages (Certificate); theological studies (MA); training teacher of English to speakers of other languages (Certificate); youth ministry (Certificate). *Accreditation:* ATS. *Program availability:* Part-time. *Degree requirements:* For master's, variable foreign language requirement, thesis (for some programs); for doctorate, thesis/dissertation. *Entrance requirements:* Additional exam requirements/recommendations for international students: Recommended—TOEFL (minimum score 550 paper-based). *Faculty research:* Studies in Isaiah, theology of sin.

Purdue University Global, School of Higher Education Studies, Davenport, IA 52807. Offers college administration and leadership (MS); college teaching and learning (MS); student services (MS). *Program availability:* Part-time, evening/weekend, online learning. *Entrance requirements:* Additional exam requirements/recommendations for international students: Required—TOEFL (minimum score 550 paper-based; 80 iBT).

Quincy University, Master of Science in Education Counseling Program, Quincy, IL 62301-2699. Offers clinical mental health counseling (MS Ed); college student personnel (MS Ed); school counseling (MS Ed). *Program availability:* Part-time, evening/weekend. *Degree requirements:* For master's, comprehensive exam, practicum, internship. *Entrance requirements:* For master's, MAT or GRE. Additional exam requirements/recommendations for international students: Required—TOEFL (minimum score 550 paper-based; 79 iBT). *Application deadline:* Applications are processed on a rolling basis. Application fee: $25. Electronic applications accepted. *Expenses:* Tuition: Part-time $450 per credit hour. *Financial support:* Applicants required to submit FAFSA. *Unit head:* Dr. Kenneth Oliver, Director, 217-228-5432 Ext. 3113, E-mail: oliveke@quincy.edu. *Application contact:* Office of Admissions, 217-228-5210, Fax: 217-228-5479, E-mail: admissions@quincy.edu.
Website: http://www.quincy.edu/academics/graduate-programs/counseling/

Regent University, Graduate School, School of Education, Virginia Beach, VA 23464-9800. Offers education (M Ed, Ed D, PhD), including adult education (Ed D, PhD, Ed S), advanced educational leadership (Ed D, PhD, Ed S), character education (Ed D, PhD, Ed S), Christian education leadership (Ed D, PhD, Ed S), Christian school administration (M Ed), curriculum and instruction (Ed D, PhD, Ed S), curriculum and instruction - adult education (M Ed), curriculum and instruction - Christian school (M Ed), curriculum and instruction - gifted and talented (M Ed), curriculum and instruction - STEM education (M Ed), curriculum and instruction - teacher leader (M Ed), discipleship for ministry (M Ed), educational leadership (M Ed), educational psychology (Ed D, PhD, Ed S), educational technology and online learning (Ed D, PhD, Ed S), elementary education (M Ed), exceptional education executive leadership (Ed D, PhD, Ed S), higher education (Ed D, PhD, Ed S), higher education leadership and management (Ed D, PhD, Ed S), instructional design and technology (M Ed), K-12 school leadership (Ed D, PhD, Ed S), K-12 special education (M Ed), leadership in mathematics education (M Ed), reading specialist (M Ed), special education (Ed D, PhD, Ed S), student affairs (M Ed), TESOL - adult education (M Ed), TESOL - K-12 (M Ed); educational specialist (Ed S), including adult education (Ed D, PhD, Ed S), advanced educational leadership (Ed D, PhD, Ed S), character education (Ed D, PhD, Ed S), Christian education leadership (Ed D, PhD, Ed S), curriculum and instruction (Ed D, PhD, Ed S), educational psychology (Ed D, PhD, Ed S), educational technology and online learning (Ed D, PhD, Ed S), exceptional education executive leadership (Ed D, PhD, Ed S), higher education (Ed D, PhD, Ed S), higher education leadership and management (Ed D, PhD, Ed S), K-12 school leadership (Ed D, PhD, Ed S), special education (Ed D, PhD, Ed S). *Accreditation:* TEAC. *Program availability:* Part-time, evening/weekend, 100% online, blended/hybrid learning. *Faculty:* 22 full-time (10 women), 44 part-time/adjunct (32 women). *Students:* 80 full-time (59 women), 945 part-time (750 women); includes 432 minority (352 Black or African American, non-Hispanic/Latino; 4 American Indian or Alaska Native, non-Hispanic/Latino; 14 Asian, non-Hispanic/Latino; 43 Hispanic/Latino; 19 Two or more races, non-Hispanic/Latino), 12 international. Average age 40. 1,125 applicants, 49% accepted, 436 enrolled. In 2017, 316 master's, 24 doctorates awarded. *Degree requirements:* For master's, thesis or alternative; for doctorate, comprehensive exam, thesis/dissertation. *Entrance requirements:* For master's, Virginia Communication and Literacy Assessment (VCLA), PRAXIS, college transcripts, writing sample, interview; for doctorate, GRE, writing sample, resume, transcripts, interview. Additional exam requirements/recommendations for international students: Required—TOEFL (minimum score 577 paper-based). *Application deadline:* For fall admission, 4/1 priority date for domestic students; for spring admission, 10/15 priority date for domestic students. Applications are processed on a rolling basis. Application fee: $50. Electronic applications accepted. *Expenses:* Contact institution. *Financial support:* In 2017–18, 669 students received support, including 1 fellowship (averaging $10,000 per year); career-related internships or fieldwork, scholarships/grants, and unspecified assistantships also available. Support available to part-time students. *Faculty research:* Christian school administration, curriculum and instruction, educational technology and online learning, higher education, special education. *Unit head:* Dr. Donald Finn, Dean, 757-352-4278, Fax: 757-352-4318, E-mail: dfinn@regent.edu. *Application contact:* Heidi Cece, Assistant Vice President of Enrollment Management, 800-373-5504, Fax: 757-352-4381, E-mail: admissions@regent.edu.
Website: https://www.regent.edu/school-of-education/

Rutgers University–New Brunswick, Graduate School of Education, Department of Educational Psychology, Program in College Student Affairs, Piscataway, NJ 08854-8097. Offers Ed M. *Accreditation:* ACA. *Degree requirements:* For master's, comprehensive exam. *Entrance requirements:* For master's, GRE General Test, 3 letters of recommendation, resume. Additional exam requirements/recommendations for international students: Required—TOEFL (minimum score 550 paper-based; 83 iBT). Electronic applications accepted. *Faculty research:* Higher education equality, Latino college student experience.

St. Cloud State University, School of Graduate Studies, School of Education, Department of Educational Leadership and Higher Education, Program in College Counseling and Student Development, St. Cloud, MN 56301-4498. Offers MS. *Degree requirements:* For master's, comprehensive exam, thesis or alternative. *Entrance requirements:* For master's, GRE General Test, minimum GPA of 2.75. Additional exam requirements/recommendations for international students: Required—Michigan English

Language Assessment Battery; Recommended—TOEFL (minimum score 550 paper-based), IELTS (minimum score 6.5). Electronic applications accepted.

St. Edward's University, School of Education, Master of Arts in College Student Development Program, Austin, TX 78704. Offers MA. *Program availability:* Part-time-only, evening/weekend. *Students:* 20 part-time (15 women); includes 11 minority (3 Black or African American, non-Hispanic/Latino; 6 Hispanic/Latino; 2 Two or more races, non-Hispanic/Latino). Average age 34. 22 applicants, 45% accepted, 6 enrolled. In 2017, 8 master's awarded. *Entrance requirements:* Additional exam requirements/recommendations for international students: Required—TOEFL, IELTS. *Application deadline:* For fall admission, 6/1 priority date for domestic and international students; for spring admission, 10/1 priority date for domestic and international students. Applications are processed on a rolling basis. Application fee: $50. Electronic applications accepted. *Expenses:* Tuition: Full-time $26,406; part-time $1467 per hour. *Required fees:* $75 per trimester. Full-time tuition and fees vary according to course load and program. *Unit head:* Dr. Richard A. Parsells, Program Director/Associate Professor of Organizational Studies, 512-637-1978, E-mail: richp@stedwards.edu. *Application contact:* Dave Bralower, Director of Graduate Admission, 512-233-1424, E-mail: davidcb@stedwards.edu.

Saint Louis University, Graduate Programs, School of Education and Graduate Programs, Department of Educational Leadership and Higher Education, St. Louis, MO 63103. Offers Catholic school leadership (MA); educational administration (MA, Ed D, PhD, Ed S); higher education (MA, Ed D, PhD); student personnel administration (MA). *Accreditation:* NCATE. *Program availability:* Part-time. *Degree requirements:* For master's, comprehensive written and oral exam; for doctorate, comprehensive exam, thesis/dissertation, preliminary oral and written exams. *Entrance requirements:* For master's, GRE General Test, MAT, LSAT, GMAT or MCAT, letters of recommendation, resume; for doctorate and Ed S, GRE General Test, LSAT, GMAT or MCAT, letters of recommendation, resumé, goal statement, transcripts. Additional exam requirements/recommendations for international students: Required—TOEFL (minimum score 525 paper-based). Electronic applications accepted. *Faculty research:* Superintendent of schools, school finance, school facilities, student personal administration, building leadership.

Seton Hall University, College of Education and Human Services, Department of Education Leadership, Management and Policy, Program in College Student Personnel Administration, South Orange, NJ 07079-2697. Offers MA. *Program availability:* Part-time, evening/weekend. *Entrance requirements:* For master's, GRE or MAT (within past 5 years), minimum GPA of 3.0. Additional exam requirements/recommendations for international students: Required—TOEFL.

Shippensburg University of Pennsylvania, School of Graduate Studies, College of Education and Human Services, Department of Counseling, Shippensburg, PA 17257-2299. Offers college counseling (MS); college student personnel (MS); counselor education and supervision (Ed D); mental health counseling (MS); school counseling (M Ed). *Accreditation:* ACA (one or more programs are accredited); NCATE. *Program availability:* Part-time, evening/weekend, blended/hybrid learning. *Faculty:* 9 full-time (3 women), 1 part-time/adjunct (0 women). *Students:* 75 full-time (64 women), 49 part-time (40 women); includes 28 minority (17 Black or African American, non-Hispanic/Latino; 1 Asian, non-Hispanic/Latino; 7 Hispanic/Latino; 3 Two or more races, non-Hispanic/Latino), 3 international. Average age 29. 94 applicants, 54% accepted, 41 enrolled. In 2017, 56 master's awarded. *Degree requirements:* For master's, fieldwork, research project, internship, candidacy; for doctorate, thesis/dissertation, practicum, internship. *Entrance requirements:* For master's, GRE or MAT (for MS if GPA is less than 2.75), minimum GPA of 2.75 (3.0 for M Ed), resume, 3 letter of recommendation forms, one year of relevant work experience, on-campus interview, autobiographical statement; for doctorate, master's degree in counseling or related discipline; resume; three recommendation letters (1 each from employer, clinical supervisor, and prior graduate school faculty member); personal essay; interview with department chair. Additional exam requirements/recommendations for international students: Required—TOEFL (minimum score 550 paper-based, 68 iBT) or IELTS (minimum score 6). *Application deadline:* Applications are processed on a rolling basis. Application fee: $45. Electronic applications accepted. *Expenses:* Tuition, state resident: part-time $500 per credit. Tuition, nonresident: part-time $750 per credit. *Required fees:* $145 per credit. *Financial support:* In 2017–18, 54 students received support. Career-related internships or fieldwork, scholarships/grants, unspecified assistantships, and resident hall director and student payroll positions available. Support available to part-time students. Financial award application deadline: 3/1; financial award applicants required to submit FAFSA. *Unit head:* Dr. Kurt L. Kraus, Departmental Chair and Program Coordinator, 717-477-1603, Fax: 717-477-4056, E-mail: klkrau@ship.edu. *Application contact:* Maya T. Mapp, Director of Admissions, 717-477-1231, Fax: 717-477-4016, E-mail: mtmapp@ship.edu. Website: http://www.ship.edu/counsel/

Slippery Rock University of Pennsylvania, Graduate Studies (Recruitment), College of Education, Department of Counseling and Development, Slippery Rock, PA 16057-1383. Offers clinical mental health (MA); school counseling (M Ed); student affairs in higher education (MA); student affairs in higher education with college counseling (MA). *Accreditation:* ACA (one or more programs are accredited); NCATE. *Program availability:* Part-time, evening/weekend. *Degree requirements:* For master's, comprehensive exam, thesis (for some programs). *Entrance requirements:* For master's, GRE General Test or MAT, official transcripts, personal statement, three letters of recommendation, interview. Additional exam requirements/recommendations for international students: Required—TOEFL (minimum score 550 paper-based; 80 iBT). Electronic applications accepted. *Expenses:* Contact institution.

Southern Arkansas University–Magnolia, School of Graduate Studies, Magnolia, AR 71753. Offers agriculture (MS); business administration (MBA), including agribusiness, social entrepreneurship, supply chain management; clinical and mental health counseling (MS); computer and information sciences (MS), including cyber security and privacy, data science, information technology; gifted and talented (M Ed), including curriculum and instruction, educational administration and supervision, gifted and talented P-8/7-12, instructional specialist P-4; higher, adult and lifelong education (M Ed); kinesiology (M Ed), including coaching; library media and information specialist (M Ed); public administration (MPA); school counseling K-12 (M Ed); student affairs and college counseling (M Ed); teaching (MAT). *Accreditation:* NCATE. *Program availability:* Part-time, 100% online, blended/hybrid learning. *Faculty:* 36 full-time (20 women), 31 part-time/adjunct (12 women). *Students:* 242 full-time (89 women), 889 part-time (459 women); includes 167 minority (143 Black or African American, non-Hispanic/Latino; 7 American Indian or Alaska Native, non-Hispanic/Latino; 7 Asian, non-Hispanic/Latino; 3 Hispanic/Latino; 7 Two or more races, non-Hispanic/Latino), 562 international. Average age 28. 400 applicants, 100% accepted, 239 enrolled. In 2017, 875 master's awarded. *Degree requirements:* For master's, comprehensive exam (for some programs), thesis optional. *Entrance requirements:* For master's, GRE, MAT or GMAT, minimum GPA of 2.5. Additional exam requirements/recommendations for international students: Required—TOEFL (minimum score 550 paper-based), IELTS (minimum score 6). *Application deadline:* For fall admission, 7/20 for domestic students, 7/10 for international students; for spring admission, 12/1 for domestic students, 11/15 for international students; for summer admission, 4/1 for domestic students, 5/1 for international students. Applications are

processed on a rolling basis. Application fee: $25 ($50 for international students). Electronic applications accepted. *Expenses:* Tuition, state resident: full-time $6038. Tuition, nonresident: full-time $8558. *Required fees:* $804. One-time fee: $110 full-time. Tuition and fees vary according to course load. *Financial support:* Career-related internships or fieldwork, Federal Work-Study, scholarships/grants, tuition waivers (full), and unspecified assistantships available. Financial award applicants required to submit FAFSA. *Faculty research:* Alternative certification for teachers, supervision of instruction, instructional leadership, counseling. *Unit head:* Dr. Kim Bloss, Dean, School of Graduate Studies, 870-235-4150, Fax: 870-235-5227, E-mail: kkbloss@saumag.edu. *Application contact:* Shrijana Malakar, Admissions Specialist, 870-235-4150, Fax: 870-235-5227, E-mail: smalakar@saumag.edu.
Website: http://www.saumag.edu/graduate

Southern Illinois University Edwardsville, Graduate School, School of Education, Health, and Human Behavior, Department of Educational Leadership, Program in College Student Personnel Administration, Edwardsville, IL 62026. Offers MS Ed. *Program availability:* Part-time, evening/weekend. *Degree requirements:* For master's, thesis or alternative, research project. *Entrance requirements:* Additional exam requirements/recommendations for international students: Required—TOEFL (minimum score 550 paper-based; 79 iBT), IELTS (minimum score 6.5). Electronic applications accepted.

Springfield College, Graduate Programs, Programs in Psychology, Springfield, MA 01109-3797. Offers athletic counseling (MS, CAGS); clinical mental health counseling (M Ed, CAGS); counseling psychology (Psy D); general counseling (M Ed); industrial/organizational psychology (M Ed, CAGS); school counseling (M Ed, CAGS); student personnel administration in higher education (M Ed, CAGS). *Accreditation:* APA. *Program availability:* Part-time. *Students:* 192 applicants, 65% accepted, 64 enrolled. In 2017, 56 master's, 5 doctorates awarded. *Degree requirements:* For master's, research project, portfolio; for doctorate, dissertation project, 1500 hours of counseling psychology practicum, full-year internship. *Entrance requirements:* For doctorate, GRE. Additional exam requirements/recommendations for international students: Required—TOEFL (minimum score 550 paper-based); Recommended—IELTS (minimum score 7). *Application deadline:* For fall admission, 1/15 priority date for domestic students, 1/15 for international students; for winter admission, 11/1 for domestic and international students; for spring admission, 11/1 for domestic and international students. Applications are processed on a rolling basis. Application fee: $50. Electronic applications accepted. *Financial support:* Fellowships with partial tuition reimbursements, teaching assistantships with partial tuition reimbursements, career-related internships or fieldwork, Federal Work-Study, institutionally sponsored loans, scholarships/grants, and unspecified assistantships available. Financial award application deadline: 3/1; financial award applicants required to submit FAFSA. *Unit head:* Dr. Allison Cumming-McCann, Chair, 413-748-3025, Fax: 413-748-3854, E-mail: acumming@springfield.edu. *Application contact:* Anne Griffin, Director of Graduate Admissions, 413-748-3225, E-mail: agriffin2@springfield.edu.
Website: http://springfield.edu/programs

State University of New York at Plattsburgh, School of Education, Health, and Human Services, Department of Counselor Education, Plattsburgh, NY 12901-2681. Offers clinical mental health counseling (MS, Advanced Certificate); school counselor (MS Ed, CAS); student affairs counseling (MS). *Accreditation:* ACA (one or more programs are accredited); TEAC. *Program availability:* Part-time. *Entrance requirements:* For master's, GRE General Test or MAT, minimum GPA of 2.8. Additional exam requirements/recommendations for international students: Required—TOEFL. *Faculty research:* Campus violence, program accreditation, substance abuse, vocational assessment, group counseling, divorce.

Syracuse University, School of Education, MS Program in Student Affairs Counseling, Syracuse, NY 13244. Offers MS. *Program availability:* Part-time. *Students:* Average age 28. *Entrance requirements:* For master's, GRE or MAT, baccalaureate degree from regionally-accredited college/university, three letters of recommendation, personal statement, transcripts, interview. Additional exam requirements/recommendations for international students: Required—TOEFL (minimum score 100 iBT). *Application deadline:* For fall admission, 6/15 priority date for domestic and international students; for spring admission, 10/15 priority date for domestic and international students; for summer admission, 1/15 priority date for domestic and international students. Applications are processed on a rolling basis. Application fee: $75. Electronic applications accepted. *Financial support:* Fellowships with full tuition reimbursements, research assistantships, teaching assistantships, career-related internships or fieldwork, and scholarships/grants available. Financial award application deadline: 1/15. *Faculty research:* Group work in counseling, theories of counseling and psychotherapy, social and cultural dimensions of counseling, life-span human development, assessment in counseling. *Unit head:* Dr. Derek Seward, Professor/Chair of the Department of Counseling and Human Service, 315-443-2266, E-mail: dxseward@syr.edu. *Application contact:* Speranza Migliore, Graduate Admissions Recruiter, 315-443-2505, E-mail: gradrcrt@syr.edu.
Website: http://soe.syr.edu/academic/counseling_and_human_services/graduate/masters/student_affairs_counseling/default.aspx

Texas State University, The Graduate College, College of Education, Program in Student Affairs in Higher Education, San Marcos, TX 78666. Offers M Ed. *Accreditation:* ACA. *Program availability:* Part-time, evening/weekend. *Faculty:* 7 full-time (5 women), 3 part-time/adjunct (1 woman). *Students:* 38 full-time (27 women); includes 23 minority (5 Black or African American, non-Hispanic/Latino; 3 Asian, non-Hispanic/Latino; 11 Hispanic/Latino; 4 Two or more races, non-Hispanic/Latino). Average age 24. 43 applicants, 65% accepted, 16 enrolled. In 2017, 18 master's awarded. *Degree requirements:* For master's, comprehensive exam. *Entrance requirements:* For master's, GRE General Test (minimum preferred score of 295 [150 verbal, 145 quantitative], 4 analytical writing), baccalaureate degree from regionally-accredited institution with minimum GPA of 3.0 in last 60 hours of undergraduate course work, resume, statement of purpose, 3 letters of recommendation. Additional exam requirements/recommendations for international students: Required—TOEFL (minimum score 550 paper-based; 78 iBT), IELTS (minimum score 6.5). *Application deadline:* For fall admission, 1/15 for domestic and international students. Applications are processed on a rolling basis. Application fee: $40 ($90 for international students). Electronic applications accepted. *Expenses:* Tuition, state resident: full-time $7868; part-time $3934 per semester. Tuition, nonresident: full-time $17,828; part-time $8914 per semester. *Required fees:* $2092; $1435 per semester. Tuition and fees vary according to course load. *Financial support:* In 2017–18, 33 students received support, including 35 teaching assistantships (averaging $11,609 per year); research assistantships, career-related internships or fieldwork, Federal Work-Study, institutionally sponsored loans, scholarships/grants, and unspecified assistantships also available. Support available to part-time students. Financial award application deadline: 3/1; financial award applicants required to submit FAFSA. *Unit head:* Dr. Paige Haber-Curran, Graduate Advisor, 512-245-7628, Fax: 512-245-8872, E-mail: ph31@txstate.edu. *Application contact:* Dr. Andrea Golato, Dean of Graduate School, 512-245-2581, Fax: 512-245-8365, E-mail: gradcollege@txstate.edu.
Website: http://www.gradcollege.txstate.edu/programs/sahe.html

University of Arkansas at Little Rock, Graduate School, College of Education and Health Professions, Department of Educational Leadership, Program in Higher Education, Little Rock, AR 72204-1099. Offers administration (MA); college student affairs (MA); health professions teaching and learning (MA); higher education (Ed D); two-year college teaching (MA). *Degree requirements:* For doctorate, comprehensive exam, oral defense of dissertation, residency. *Entrance requirements:* For master's, GRE General Test or MAT, interview, minimum graduate GPA of 3.0; for doctorate, GRE General Test, interview, minimum graduate GPA of 3.5, teaching certificate, three years of work experience.

University of Bridgeport, School of Arts and Sciences, Department of Counseling, Bridgeport, CT 06604. Offers clinical mental health counseling (MS); college student personnel (MS); community counseling (MS); human resource development (MS); human service (MS). *Program availability:* Part-time, evening/weekend. *Degree requirements:* For master's, thesis, project. *Entrance requirements:* Additional exam requirements/recommendations for international students: Recommended—TOEFL (minimum score 550 paper-based; 80 iBT), IELTS (minimum score 6.5). Electronic applications accepted. *Expenses:* Contact institution.

University of Central Arkansas, Graduate School, College of Education, Department of Leadership Studies, Program in College Student Personnel, Conway, AR 72035-0001. Offers MS. *Degree requirements:* For master's, comprehensive exam, thesis. *Entrance requirements:* For master's, GRE General Test, minimum GPA of 2.7. Additional exam requirements/recommendations for international students: Required—TOEFL (minimum score 550 paper-based). Electronic applications accepted. *Expenses:* Contact institution.

University of Central Florida, College of Community Innovation and Education, Department of Educational Leadership and Higher Education, Orlando, FL 32816. Offers career and technical education (MA); educational leadership (M Ed, MA, Ed S); higher education/college teaching and leadership (MA); higher education/student personnel (MA). *Program availability:* Part-time, evening/weekend. *Students:* 86 full-time (65 women), 233 part-time (184 women); includes 136 minority (66 Black or African American, non-Hispanic/Latino; 1 American Indian or Alaska Native, non-Hispanic/Latino; 4 Asian, non-Hispanic/Latino; 59 Hispanic/Latino; 6 Two or more races, non-Hispanic/Latino). Average age 31. 235 applicants, 82% accepted, 113 enrolled. In 2017, 114 master's, 16 other advanced degrees awarded. *Degree requirements:* For master's, thesis or alternative; for Ed S, thesis or alternative, final exam. *Entrance requirements:* For master's, GRE General Test; for Ed S, GRE General Test, minimum GPA of 3.0, resume, letters of recommendation. Additional exam requirements/recommendations for international students: Required—TOEFL. *Application deadline:* For fall admission, 6/20 for domestic students; for spring admission, 9/20 for domestic students. Application fee: $30. Electronic applications accepted. *Expenses:* Tuition, state resident: part-time $288.16 per credit hour. Tuition, nonresident: part-time $1073.31 per credit hour. Tuition and fees vary according to program. *Financial support:* In 2017–18, 12 students received support, including 2 fellowships with partial tuition reimbursements available (averaging $3,000 per year), 10 research assistantships with partial tuition reimbursements available (averaging $8,387 per year), 2 teaching assistantships with partial tuition reimbursements available (averaging $12,166 per year); career-related internships or fieldwork, Federal Work-Study, institutionally sponsored loans, health care benefits, tuition waivers (partial), and unspecified assistantships also available. Financial award application deadline: 3/1; financial award applicants required to submit FAFSA. *Unit head:* Dr. Kenneth Murray, Program Coordinator, 407-832-1468, E-mail: kenneth.murray@ucf.edu. *Application contact:* Associate Director, Graduate Admissions, 407-823-2766, Fax: 407-823-6442, E-mail: gradadmissions@ucf.edu.
Website: https://ccie.ucf.edu/elhe/

University of Central Missouri, The Graduate School, Warrensburg, MO 64093. Offers accountancy (MA); accounting (MBA); applied mathematics (MS); aviation safety (MA); biology (MS); business administration (MBA); career and technical education leadership (MS); college student personnel administration (MS); communication (MA); computer science (MS); counseling (MS); criminal justice (MS); educational leadership (Ed D); educational technology (MS); elementary and early childhood education (MSE); English (MA); environmental studies (MA); finance (MBA); history (MA); human services/educational technology (Ed S); human services/learning resources (Ed S); human services/professional counseling (Ed S); industrial hygiene (MS); industrial management (MS); information systems (MBA); information technology (MS); kinesiology (MS); library science and information services (MS); literacy education (MSE); marketing (MBA); mathematics (MS); music (MA); occupational safety management (MS); psychology (MS); rural family nursing (MS); school administration (MSE); social gerontology (MS); sociology (MA); special education (MSE); speech language pathology (MS); superintendency (Ed S); teaching (MAT); teaching English as a second language (MA); technology (MS); technology management (PhD); theatre (MA). *Program availability:* Part-time, 100% online, blended/hybrid learning. *Faculty:* 337 full-time (145 women), 41 part-time/adjunct (28 women). *Students:* 785 full-time (398 women), 1,633 part-time (1,063 women); includes 231 minority (102 Black or African American, non-Hispanic/Latino; 4 American Indian or Alaska Native, non-Hispanic/Latino; 16 Asian, non-Hispanic/Latino; 52 Hispanic/Latino; 57 Two or more races, non-Hispanic/Latino), 692 international. Average age 30. In 2017, 2,605 master's, 122 other advanced degrees awarded. *Degree requirements:* For master's and Ed S, comprehensive exam (for some programs), thesis (for some programs). *Entrance requirements:* Additional exam requirements/recommendations for international students: Required—TOEFL (minimum score 550 paper-based; 79 iBT). *Application deadline:* For fall admission, 6/1 priority date for domestic and international students; for spring admission, 10/1 priority date for domestic and international students; for summer admission, 4/1 priority date for domestic and international students. Applications are processed on a rolling basis. Application fee: $30 ($75 for international students). Electronic applications accepted. *Expenses:* Tuition, state resident: full-time $8771; part-time $292.35 per credit hour. Tuition, nonresident: full-time $17,541; part-time $584.70 per credit hour. *Required fees:* $372; $24.78 per credit hour. *Financial support:* In 2017–18, 99 students received support. Research assistantships, teaching assistantships, career-related internships or fieldwork, Federal Work-Study, scholarships/grants, and administrative and laboratory assistantships available. Support available to part-time students. Financial award application deadline: 3/1; financial award applicants required to submit FAFSA. *Unit head:* Shellie Hewitt, Director of Graduate and International Student Services, 660-543-4621, Fax: 660-543-4778, E-mail: hewitt@ucmo.edu. *Application contact:* 660-543-4621, E-mail: admit_intl@ucmo.edu.
Website: http://www.ucmo.edu/graduate/

University of Central Oklahoma, The Jackson College of Graduate Studies, College of Education and Professional Studies, Department of Adult Education and Safety Science, Edmond, OK 73034-5209. Offers adult and higher education (M Ed), including interdisciplinary studies, student personnel, training. *Program availability:* Part-time. *Faculty:* 9 full-time (4 women), 8 part-time/adjunct (4 women). *Students:* 25 full-time (14 women), 85 part-time (61 women); includes 43 minority (25 Black or African American, non-Hispanic/Latino; 2 American Indian or Alaska Native, non-Hispanic/Latino; 1 Asian, non-Hispanic/Latino; 10 Hispanic/Latino; 5 Two or more races, non-Hispanic/Latino), 4 international. Average age 34. 49 applicants, 78% accepted, 23 enrolled. In 2017, 40

master's awarded. *Degree requirements:* For master's, comprehensive exam (for some programs), thesis (for some programs). *Entrance requirements:* Additional exam requirements/recommendations for international students: Required—TOEFL (minimum score 550 paper-based; 79 iBT), IELTS (minimum score 6.5). *Application deadline:* For fall admission, 7/15 for international students; for spring admission, 11/15 for international students. Applications are processed on a rolling basis. Application fee: $60. Electronic applications accepted. *Expenses:* Tuition, state resident: full-time $5375; part-time $268.75 per credit hour. Tuition, nonresident: full-time $13,295; part-time $664.75 per credit hour. *Required fees:* $626; $31.30 per credit hour. One-time fee: $50. Tuition and fees vary according to program. *Financial support:* In 2017–18, 38 students received support, including 1 research assistantship with partial tuition reimbursement available (averaging $2,958 per year); teaching assistantships, career-related internships or fieldwork, scholarships/grants, tuition waivers (partial), and unspecified assistantships also available. Financial award application deadline: 3/31; financial award applicants required to submit FAFSA. *Unit head:* Dr. Candy Sebert, Chair, 405-974-5741, Fax: 405-974-3809. *Application contact:* Carlie Wellington, Assistant Director, CEPS Graduate Enrollment, 405-974-5105, Fax: 405-974-3851, E-mail: gradcoll@uco.edu.
Website: http://sites.uco.edu/ceps/dept/Professional-Studies-Programs/aess/index.asp

University of Dayton, Department of Counselor Education and Human Services, Dayton, OH 45469. Offers clinical mental health counseling (MS Ed); college student personnel (MS Ed); higher education administration (MS Ed); human services (MS Ed); school counseling (MS Ed); school psychology (MS Ed, Ed S). *Accreditation:* ACA; NCATE. *Program availability:* Part-time. *Faculty:* 11 full-time (6 women), 34 part-time/adjunct (24 women). *Students:* 194 full-time (153 women), 83 part-time (68 women); includes 58 minority (37 Black or African American, non-Hispanic/Latino; 2 Asian, non-Hispanic/Latino; 9 Hispanic/Latino; 10 Two or more races, non-Hispanic/Latino), 3 international. Average age 30. 426 applicants, 28% accepted. In 2017, 107 master's, 6 Ed Ss awarded. *Degree requirements:* For master's, thesis (for some programs); for Ed S, thesis (for some programs), professional portfolio. *Entrance requirements:* For master's, MAT or GRE (if GPA less than 2.75), essays (for some programs). Additional exam requirements/recommendations for international students: Required—TOEFL (minimum score 550 paper-based; 80 iBT). *Application deadline:* For fall admission, 1/10 priority date for domestic and international students; for spring admission, 9/10 priority date for domestic and international students; for summer admission, 11/10 priority date for domestic and international students. Application fee: $0 ($50 for international students). Electronic applications accepted. *Expenses:* Contact institution. *Financial support:* In 2017–18, 5 research assistantships with partial tuition reimbursements (averaging $9,950 per year) were awarded; career-related internships or fieldwork, institutionally sponsored loans, and unspecified assistantships also available. Financial award application deadline: 3/1; financial award applicants required to submit FAFSA. *Faculty research:* Student school bonding, traumatic brain injuries, wellness and counseling, creativity in education. *Unit head:* Dr. Alan Demmitt, Chair, 937-229-3644, Fax: 937-229-1055, E-mail: ademmitt1@udayton.edu. *Application contact:* Kathleen Brown, Administrative Assistant, 937-229-3644, Fax: 937-229-1055, E-mail: kbrown1@udayton.edu.
Website: https://www.udayton.edu/education/departments_and_programs/edc/

University of Florida, Graduate School, College of Education, School of Human Development and Organizational Studies in Education, Gainesville, FL 32611. Offers counseling and counselor education (Ed D, PhD), including counseling and counselor education, marriage and family counseling, mental health counseling, school counseling and guidance; educational leadership (M Ed, MAE, Ed D, PhD, Ed S), including educational leadership (Ed D, PhD), educational policy (Ed D, PhD); higher education administration (Ed D, PhD), including education policy (Ed D), educational policy, higher education administration; marriage and family counseling (M Ed, MAE, Ed D, PhD, Ed S); mental health counseling (M Ed, MAE, Ed D, PhD, Ed S); research and evaluation methodology (M Ed, MAE, Ed D, PhD); school counseling and guidance (M Ed, MAE, Ed D, PhD, Ed S); student personnel in higher education (M Ed, MAE). *Accreditation:* ACA (one or more programs are accredited); NCATE. *Program availability:* Part-time, online learning. Terminal master's awarded for partial completion of doctoral program. *Degree requirements:* For master's, thesis optional; for doctorate, comprehensive exam, thesis/dissertation. *Entrance requirements:* For master's and doctorate, GRE General Test, minimum GPA of 3.0 (undergraduate), 3.5 (graduate); for Ed S, GRE General Test. Additional exam requirements/recommendations for international students: Required—TOEFL (minimum score 550 paper-based; 80 iBT), IELTS (minimum score 6). Electronic applications accepted.

University of Georgia, College of Education, Department of Counseling and Human Development Services, Athens, GA 30602. Offers college student affairs administration (M Ed, PhD); professional school counseling (Ed S). *Accreditation:* ACA (one or more programs are accredited); APA (one or more programs are accredited); NCATE. *Degree requirements:* For master's, thesis (MA); for doctorate, variable foreign language requirement, thesis/dissertation. *Entrance requirements:* For master's, GRE General Test or MAT; for doctorate, GRE General Test. Electronic applications accepted.

The University of Iowa, Graduate College, College of Education, Department of Educational Policy and Leadership Studies, Program in Higher Education and Student Affairs, Iowa City, IA 52242-1316. Offers MA, PhD. *Degree requirements:* For master's, exam; for doctorate, comprehensive exam, thesis/dissertation. *Entrance requirements:* For master's and doctorate, GRE General Test, minimum GPA of 3.0. Additional exam requirements/recommendations for international students: Required—TOEFL (minimum score 550 paper-based; 81 iBT). Electronic applications accepted.

University of La Verne, LaFetra College of Education, Program in Social Justice Higher Education Administration, La Verne, CA 91750-4443. Offers MA. *Program availability:* Part-time. *Faculty:* 1 full-time (0 women). *Students:* 8 part-time (5 women); includes 4 minority (all Hispanic/Latino). Average age 24. *Entrance requirements:* Additional exam requirements/recommendations for international students: Required—TOEFL (minimum score 550 paper-based; 80 iBT), IELTS (minimum score 6.5). *Application deadline:* Applications are processed on a rolling basis. Application fee: $50. Electronic applications accepted. Tuition and fees vary according to program. *Financial support:* Federal Work-Study and scholarships/grants available. Financial award applicants required to submit FAFSA. *Unit head:* Issac Carter, Chair, 909-448-4185, E-mail: icarter@laverne.edu. *Application contact:* Christy Ranells, Associate Director of Graduate Admission, 909-448-4644, Fax: 909-971-2295, E-mail: cranells@laverne.edu.
Website: https://education.laverne.edu/sjhe/

University of Louisville, Graduate School, College of Education and Human Development, Department of Counseling and Human Development, Louisville, KY 40292-0001. Offers counseling and personnel services (M Ed, PhD), including art therapy (M Ed), clinical mental health counseling (M Ed), college student personnel, counseling psychology, counselor education and supervision (PhD), educational psychology, measurement, and evaluation (PhD), school counseling (M Ed). *Accreditation:* APA; NCATE. *Program availability:* Part-time, evening/weekend. *Students:* 144 full-time (107 women), 63 part-time (44 women); includes 49 minority (32 Black or African American, non-Hispanic/Latino; 1 American Indian or Alaska Native, non-Hispanic/Latino; 3 Asian, non-Hispanic/Latino; 7 Hispanic/Latino; 6 Two or more

races, non-Hispanic/Latino), 3 international. Average age 28. 178 applicants, 49% accepted, 51 enrolled. In 2017, 35 master's, 3 doctorates awarded. *Degree requirements:* For doctorate, comprehensive exam, thesis/dissertation. *Entrance requirements:* For master's and doctorate, GRE General Test. Application fee: $65. *Expenses:* Tuition, state resident: full-time $12,246; part-time $681 per credit hour. Tuition, nonresident: full-time $25,486; part-time $1417 per credit hour. *Required fees:* $196. Tuition and fees vary according to course load, program and reciprocity agreements. *Financial support:* Fellowships, research assistantships, teaching assistantships, career-related internships or fieldwork, Federal Work-Study, scholarships/grants, health care benefits, and unspecified assistantships available. Financial award application deadline: 6/1; financial award applicants required to submit FAFSA. *Faculty research:* Mental health services and under-served populations; health disparities and outcomes; well-being identity development; measurement and evaluation. *Total annual research expenditures:* $295,684. *Unit head:* Dr. Mark M. Leach, Interim Chair/Professor, 502-852-0588, Fax: 502-852-0629, E-mail: m.leach@louisville.edu. *Application contact:* Betty Hampton, Director of Graduate Student Services, 502-852-5597, Fax: 502-852-1465, E-mail: edadvise@louisville.edu.
Website: http://www.louisville.edu/education/departments/ecpy

University of Maryland, College Park, Academic Affairs, College of Education, Department of Counseling, Higher Education and Special Education, College Park, MD 20742. Offers college student personnel (M Ed, MA); college student personnel administration (PhD); community counseling (CAGS); community/career counseling (M Ed, MA); counseling and personnel services (M Ed, MA, PhD), including art therapy (M Ed), college student personnel (M Ed), counseling and personnel services (PhD), counseling psychology (M Ed), mental health counseling (M Ed), school counseling (M Ed); counseling psychology (PhD); counselor education (PhD); rehabilitation counseling (M Ed, MA, AGSC); school counseling (M Ed, MA); school psychology (M Ed, MA, PhD). *Accreditation:* APA (one or more programs are accredited); NCATE. *Program availability:* Part-time, evening/weekend, online learning. *Degree requirements:* For master's, thesis (for some programs); for doctorate, thesis/dissertation. *Entrance requirements:* For master's, GRE General Test or MAT, minimum GPA of 3.0, 3 letters of recommendation; for doctorate, GRE General Test or MAT, minimum GPA of 3.5, 3 letters of recommendation. Additional exam requirements/recommendations for international students: Required—TOEFL. Electronic applications accepted. *Faculty research:* Educational psychology, counseling, health.

University of Minnesota, Twin Cities Campus, Graduate School, College of Education and Human Development, Department of Educational Psychology, Program in Counseling and Student Personnel Psychology, Minneapolis, MN 55455-0213. Offers MA. *Students:* 69 full-time (51 women), 7 part-time (4 women); includes 10 minority (3 Asian, non-Hispanic/Latino; 4 Hispanic/Latino; 3 Two or more races, non-Hispanic/Latino), 8 international. Average age 27. 71 applicants, 52% accepted, 36 enrolled. In 2017, 36 master's awarded. Application fee: $75 ($95 for international students). *Unit head:* Dr. Geoffrey Maruyama, Chair, 612-624-1003, Fax: 612-625-5861, E-mail: geoff@umn.edu. *Application contact:* Dr. Ernest Davenport, Director of Graduate Studies, 612-624-1040, E-mail: lqr6576@umn.edu.
Website: http://www.cehd.umn.edu/EdPsych/Programs/CSPP/default.html

University of Nebraska at Kearney, College of Education, Department of Counseling and School Psychology, Kearney, NE 68849-0001. Offers clinical mental health counseling (MS Ed); school counseling (MS Ed), including elementary, secondary; school psychology (Ed S); student affairs (MS Ed). *Accreditation:* ACA; NCATE. *Program availability:* Part-time, evening/weekend, 100% online. *Degree requirements:* For master's, comprehensive exam, thesis optional; for Ed S, thesis. *Entrance requirements:* For master's and Ed S, personal statement, recommendations, resume, interview. Additional exam requirements/recommendations for international students: Recommended—TOEFL (minimum score 550 paper-based; 79 iBT), IELTS (minimum score 6.5). Electronic applications accepted. *Faculty research:* Multicultural counseling and diversity issues, team decision-making, adult development, women's issues, brief therapy.

University of Northern Colorado, Graduate School, College of Education and Behavioral Sciences, Department of Leadership, Policy and Development: Higher Education and P-12 Education, Program in Higher Education and Student Affairs Leadership, Greeley, CO 80639. Offers MA, PhD. *Program availability:* Part-time. *Entrance requirements:* For doctorate, GRE General Test, transcripts, 3 letters of recommendation. Electronic applications accepted.

University of Northern Iowa, Graduate College, College of Education, Department of Educational Leadership and Postsecondary Education, MA Program in Postsecondary Education: Student Affairs, Cedar Falls, IA 50614. Offers MA. *Degree requirements:* For master's, comprehensive exam, thesis or alternative. *Entrance requirements:* For master's, minimum GPA of 3.0. Additional exam requirements/recommendations for international students: Required—TOEFL (minimum score 500 paper-based; 61 iBT). Electronic applications accepted.

University of Oklahoma, Jeannine Rainbolt College of Education, Department of Educational Leadership and Policy Studies, Program in Adult and Higher Education, Norman, OK 73019. Offers adult and higher education (M Ed, PhD), including adult and workforce (M Ed), community college administration (M Ed), institutional research (M Ed), intercollegiate athletics administration (M Ed), student affairs (M Ed). *Accreditation:* NCATE. *Program availability:* Part-time, evening/weekend. *Students:* 110 full-time (69 women), 69 part-time (42 women); includes 66 minority (29 Black or African American, non-Hispanic/Latino; 10 American Indian or Alaska Native, non-Hispanic/Latino; 2 Asian, non-Hispanic/Latino; 13 Hispanic/Latino; 12 Two or more races, non-Hispanic/Latino), 5 international. Average age 29. 102 applicants, 60% accepted, 58 enrolled. In 2017, 70 master's, 1 doctorate awarded. Terminal master's awarded for partial completion of doctoral program. *Degree requirements:* For master's, comprehensive exam, thesis optional; for doctorate, comprehensive exam, thesis/dissertation. *Entrance requirements:* For doctorate, GRE. Additional exam requirements/recommendations for international students: Required—TOEFL (minimum score 79 iBT) or IELTS (minimum score 6.5). *Application deadline:* For fall admission, 10/1 for domestic and international students; for spring admission, 4/1 for domestic and international students. Application fee: $50 ($100 for international students). Electronic applications accepted. *Expenses:* Tuition, state resident: full-time $5119; part-time $213.30 per credit hour. Tuition, nonresident: full-time $19,778; part-time $824.10 per credit hour. *Required fees:* $3458; $133.55 per credit hour. $126.50 per semester. *Financial support:* In 2017–18, 148 students received support. Fellowships, research assistantships, teaching assistantships, career-related internships or fieldwork, Federal Work-Study, institutionally sponsored loans, scholarships/grants, traineeships, health care benefits, tuition waivers, and unspecified assistantships available. Support available to part-time students. Financial award application deadline: 6/1; financial award applicants required to submit FAFSA. *Faculty research:* Education and social policy; gender and equity; collegiate athletics; higher education and student affairs; adult learning and workforce development. *Unit head:* Doo Hun Lim, Associate Professor, 405-325-7941, E-mail: dhlim@ou.edu.
Website: http://www.ou.edu/education/elps/graduate-programs/adult-and-higher-education-masters.html

University of Rhode Island, Graduate School, College of Health Sciences, Department of Human Development and Family Studies, Kingston, RI 02881. Offers college student personnel (MS); human development and family studies (MS); marriage and family therapy (MS). *Accreditation:* AAMFT/COAMFTE. *Program availability:* Part-time. *Faculty:* 16 full-time (11 women). *Students:* 47 full-time (35 women), 12 part-time (10 women); includes 13 minority (4 Black or African American, non-Hispanic/Latino; 1 American Indian or Alaska Native, non-Hispanic/Latino; 4 Asian, non-Hispanic/Latino; 3 Hispanic/Latino; 1 Two or more races, non-Hispanic/Latino), 2 international. 91 applicants, 43% accepted, 29 enrolled. In 2017, 24 master's awarded. *Entrance requirements:* Additional exam requirements/recommendations for international students: Required—TOEFL. *Application deadline:* For fall admission, 1/15 for domestic and international students. Application fee: $65. Electronic applications accepted. *Expenses:* Tuition, state resident: full-time $12,706; part-time $786 per credit. Tuition, nonresident: full-time $25,216; part-time $1401 per credit. *Required fees:* $1598; $45 per credit. One-time fee: $30 part-time. *Financial support:* In 2017–18, 1 research assistantship (averaging $4,431 per year), 4 teaching assistantships (averaging $10,128 per year) were awarded. Financial award application deadline: 1/15; financial award applicants required to submit FAFSA. *Unit head:* Dr. Karen McCurdy, Chair, 401-874-5960, Fax: 401-874-4020, E-mail: kmccurdy@uri.edu.
Website: http://www.uri.edu/hss/hdf/

University of Rochester, Margaret Warner Graduate School of Education and Human Development, Master's Program in Higher Education, Rochester, NY 14627. Offers higher education (MS); higher education student affairs (MS).

University of St. Thomas, College of Education, Leadership and Counseling, Department of Leadership, Policy and Administration, St. Paul, MN 55105-1096. Offers education leadership and administration (MA); educational leadership and learning (Ed D); executive coaching (Certificate); K-12 administration (Ed S); leadership in student affairs (MA). *Program availability:* Part-time, evening/weekend. Terminal master's awarded for partial completion of doctoral program. *Degree requirements:* For master's, thesis (for some programs); for doctorate, thesis/dissertation; for other advanced degree, thesis or alternative. *Entrance requirements:* For master's, minimum GPA of 3.0 or MAT; for doctorate, MAT, minimum graduate GPA of 3.5; for other advanced degree, minimum graduate GPA of 3.25 or MAT. Additional exam requirements/recommendations for international students: Required—TOEFL (minimum score 550 paper-based). *Application deadline:* For fall admission, 7/15 priority date for domestic and international students; for spring admission, 12/9 priority date for domestic and international students; for summer admission, 4/3 priority date for domestic and international students. Applications are processed on a rolling basis. Electronic applications accepted. *Expenses:* Contact institution. *Financial support:* Fellowships, research assistantships, institutionally sponsored loans, and scholarships/grants available. Support available to part-time students. Financial award application deadline: 8/1; financial award applicants required to submit FAFSA. *Application contact:* Jackie Grossklaus, Administrative Assistant II, 651-962-4885, Fax: 651-962-4169, E-mail: jmgrossklaus@stthomas.edu.

University of South Carolina, The Graduate School, College of Education, Department of Educational Leadership and Policies, Program in Higher Education and Student Affairs, Columbia, SC 29208. Offers M Ed. *Accreditation:* NCATE. *Program availability:* Part-time. *Degree requirements:* For master's, comprehensive exam, thesis (for some programs). *Entrance requirements:* For master's, GRE General Test or MAT, letters of reference. Electronic applications accepted. *Faculty research:* Minorities in higher education, community college transfer problem, federal role in educational research.

University of Southern California, Graduate School, Rossier School of Education, Master's Programs in Education, Los Angeles, CA 90089-4038. Offers educational counseling (ME); marriage, family and child counseling (MMFT); postsecondary administration and student affairs [PASA] (ME); school counseling (ME); teaching (online) (MAT); teaching and teaching credential (MAT); teaching English to speakers of other languages (MAT). *Program availability:* Part-time, evening/weekend, online learning. *Degree requirements:* For master's, thesis optional. *Entrance requirements:* For master's, GRE (for all programs except MAT). Additional exam requirements/recommendations for international students: Required—TOEFL (minimum score 100 iBT). Electronic applications accepted. *Faculty research:* College access and equity, preparing teachers for culturally diverse populations, sociocultural basis of learning as mediated by instruction with focus on reading and literacy in English learners, social and political aspects of teaching and learning English, school counselor development and training.

University of Southern Mississippi, College of Education and Psychology, Department of Educational Research and Administration, Hattiesburg, MS 39406-0001. Offers educational administration (M Ed, Ed D, PhD, Ed S); educational administration and supervision (M Ed); educational studies and research (MS); higher education (Ed D); higher education administration (PhD); higher education: student affairs (M Ed); research, evaluation, statistics, assessment (PhD). *Students:* 30 full-time (23 women), 3 part-time (all women). 44 applicants, 91% accepted, 33 enrolled. *Degree requirements:* For master's and Ed S, comprehensive exam, thesis (for some programs); for doctorate, comprehensive exam, thesis/dissertation. *Entrance requirements:* For master's and doctorate, GRE General Test, minimum GPA of 2.75. Additional exam requirements/recommendations for international students: Required—TOEFL. *Application deadline:* For fall admission, 2/1 for domestic students, 3/1 for international students. Applications are processed on a rolling basis. Application fee: $60. *Expenses:* Tuition, state resident: full-time $3830. *Financial support:* Career-related internships or fieldwork, Federal Work-Study, and institutionally sponsored loans available. Financial award application deadline: 3/15; financial award applicants required to submit FAFSA. *Unit head:* Dr. Lilian Hill, Co-Chair, 601-266-4622.
Website: https://www.usm.edu/educational-research-administration

University of South Florida, College of Education, Department of Educational and Psychological Studies, Tampa, FL 33620-9951. Offers college student affairs (M Ed); counselor education (MA, PhD, Ed S); interdisciplinary education (PhD, Ed S); school psychology (PhD, Ed S). *Faculty:* 28 full-time (13 women). *Students:* 115 full-time (77 women), 107 part-time (80 women); includes 59 minority (29 Black or African American, non-Hispanic/Latino; 6 Asian, non-Hispanic/Latino; 18 Hispanic/Latino; 1 Native Hawaiian or other Pacific Islander, non-Hispanic/Latino; 5 Two or more races, non-Hispanic/Latino), 23 international. Average age 33. 163 applicants, 72% accepted, 84 enrolled. In 2017, 46 master's, 5 doctorates, 1 other advanced degree awarded. Application fee: $30. *Faculty research:* College student affairs, counselor education, educational psychology, school psychology, social foundations. *Total annual research expenditures:* $9 million. *Unit head:* Dr. Barabara Shircliff, Chair, 813-974-4001, E-mail: shirclif@usf.edu.

The University of Tennessee, Graduate School, College of Education, Health and Human Sciences, Department of Educational Psychology and Counseling, Program in College Student Personnel, Knoxville, TN 37996. Offers MS. *Accreditation:* NCATE. *Program availability:* Part-time. *Degree requirements:* For master's, thesis optional. *Entrance requirements:* For master's, GRE General Test, minimum GPA of 2.7. Additional exam requirements/recommendations for international students: Required—TOEFL. Electronic applications accepted.

The University of Tennessee at Martin, Graduate Programs, College of Education, Health and Behavioral Sciences, Program in Counseling, Martin, TN 38238. Offers addictions counseling (MS Ed); community counseling (MS Ed); school counseling (MS Ed); student affairs and college counseling (MS Ed). *Accreditation:* NCATE. *Program availability:* Part-time, online only, 100% online. *Students:* 17 full-time (15 women), 54 part-time (51 women); includes 7 minority (6 Black or African American, non-Hispanic/Latino; 1 Two or more races, non-Hispanic/Latino). Average age 34. 35 applicants, 54% accepted, 12 enrolled. In 2017, 14 master's awarded. *Degree requirements:* For master's, comprehensive exam. *Entrance requirements:* For master's, GRE General Test, minimum GPA of 2.5, resume, letters of reference. Additional exam requirements/recommendations for international students: Required—TOEFL (minimum score 525 paper-based; 71 iBT). *Application deadline:* For fall admission, 7/27 priority date for domestic and international students; for spring admission, 12/17 priority date for domestic and international students; for summer admission, 5/10 priority date for domestic and international students. Applications are processed on a rolling basis. Application fee: $30 ($130 for international students). Electronic applications accepted. *Expenses:* Tuition, state resident: full-time $8658; part-time $481 per credit hour. Tuition, nonresident: full-time $14,418; part-time $801 per credit hour. *International tuition:* $22,602 full-time. *Required fees:* $1404; $79 per credit hour. Part-time tuition and fees vary according to course load. *Financial support:* In 2017–18, 14 students received support, including 1 research assistantship with full tuition reimbursement available (averaging $7,540 per year), 2 teaching assistantships with full tuition reimbursements available (averaging $6,283 per year); scholarships/grants and tuition waivers (full and partial) also available. Financial award application deadline: 2/1; financial award applicants required to submit FAFSA. *Unit head:* Cynthia West, Dean, 731-881-7125, Fax: 731-881-7975, E-mail: cwest@utm.edu. *Application contact:* Jolene L. Cunningham, Student Services Specialist, 731-881-7012, Fax: 731-881-7499, E-mail: jcunningham@utm.edu.

University of the Cumberlands, Graduate Programs in Education, Williamsburg, KY 40769-1372. Offers all grades (P-12) (M Ed); business and marketing (MA Ed, MAT); counselor education and supervision (Ed D); director of pupil personnel (Certificate); director of special education (Certificate); educational administration and supervision (Ed S); educational leadership (Ed D); elementary education (MA Ed, MAT); instructional leadership - principalship (MA Ed); instructional leadership - school principal (Certificate); middle school education (MA Ed, MAT); reading and writing (MA Ed); school counseling (MA Ed); school superintendent (Certificate); secondary education (MA Ed, MAT); special education (MAT); supervisor of instruction (Certificate); teacher leader (MA Ed). *Program availability:* Part-time, evening/weekend, online learning. *Degree requirements:* For master's, comprehensive exam. Electronic applications accepted.

University of Utah, Graduate School, College of Education, Department of Educational Leadership and Policy, Salt Lake City, UT 84084. Offers educational leadership and policy (Ed D, PhD), including higher education administration (Ed D), K-12 (Ed D); K-12 school administration (M Ed); K-12 teacher instructional leadership (M Ed); student affairs (M Ed); MPA/PhD. *Program availability:* Part-time, evening/weekend. *Faculty:* 10 full-time (7 women), 2 part-time/adjunct (both women). *Students:* 60 full-time (40 women), 185 part-time (124 women); includes 54 minority (14 Black or African American, non-Hispanic/Latino; 5 American Indian or Alaska Native, non-Hispanic/Latino; 5 Asian, non-Hispanic/Latino; 24 Hispanic/Latino; 2 Native Hawaiian or other Pacific Islander, non-Hispanic/Latino; 4 Two or more races, non-Hispanic/Latino), 1 international. Average age 35. 181 applicants, 69% accepted, 90 enrolled. In 2017, 64 master's, 6 doctorates awarded. *Degree requirements:* For master's, comprehensive exam (for some programs), internship, capstone; for doctorate, thesis/dissertation, qualifying exam. *Entrance requirements:* For master's, minimum undergraduate GPA of 3.0, valid bachelor's degree, 3 years' teaching or leadership experience, Level 1 or 2 UT educator's license (for K-12 programs only); for doctorate, GRE General Test (taken with five years of applying), minimum undergraduate GPA of 3.0, valid master's degree. Additional exam requirements/recommendations for international students: Required—TOEFL (minimum score 550 paper-based). *Application deadline:* For fall admission, 1/15 priority date for domestic and international students; for winter admission, 2/1 for domestic and international students; for spring admission, 11/1 priority date for domestic and international students; for summer admission, 3/1 priority date for domestic and international students. Applications are processed on a rolling basis. Application fee: $55 ($65 for international students). Electronic applications accepted. *Expenses:* Contact institution. *Financial support:* In 2017–18, 12 students received support, including 1 fellowship with full tuition reimbursement available (averaging $15,000 per year), 2 research assistantships with full tuition reimbursements available (averaging $15,000 per year), 6 teaching assistantships with full tuition reimbursements available (averaging $15,000 per year); career-related internships or fieldwork, scholarships/grants, health care benefits, and unspecified assistantships also available. Support available to part-time students. Financial award application deadline: 3/1; financial award applicants required to submit FAFSA. *Faculty research:* Education accountability, college student diversity, K-12 educational administration and school leadership, student affairs, higher education. *Unit head:* Dr. Gerardo Lopez, Chair, 801-581-6971, Fax: 801-585-6756, E-mail: gerardo.lopez@utah.edu. *Application contact:* Marilynn S. Howard, Academic Coordinator, 801-581-6714, Fax: 801-585-6756, E-mail: marilynn.howard@utah.edu.
Website: http://elp.utah.edu/

University of Virginia, Curry School of Education, Department of Leadership, Foundations and Policy, Program in Higher Education, Charlottesville, VA 22903. Offers higher education (Ed S); student affairs practice (M Ed). *Students:* 38 full-time (21 women), 29 part-time (16 women); includes 18 minority (12 Black or African American, non-Hispanic/Latino; 1 Asian, non-Hispanic/Latino; 4 Hispanic/Latino; 1 Two or more races, non-Hispanic/Latino), 2 international. Average age 28. 22 applicants, 55% accepted, 11 enrolled. In 2017, 52 master's awarded. *Entrance requirements:* For master's, doctorate, and Ed S, GRE General Test, 2 letters of recommendation. Additional exam requirements/recommendations for international students: Required—TOEFL (minimum score 600 paper-based; 90 iBT), IELTS (minimum score 7). *Application deadline:* Applications are processed on a rolling basis. Application fee: $60. Electronic applications accepted. *Financial support:* Fellowships, research assistantships, and teaching assistantships available. Financial award applicants required to submit FAFSA. *Unit head:* Cristian Steinmetz, Program Coordinator, 434-924-3180, E-mail: highered@virginia.edu. *Application contact:* E-mail: curry-admissions@virginia.edu.
Website: http://curry.virginia.edu/academics/areas-of-study/higher-education

The University of West Alabama, School of Graduate Studies, College of Education, Program in Student Affairs in Higher Education, Livingston, AL 35470. Offers M Ed. *Program availability:* Part-time, evening/weekend, 100% online. *Faculty:* 1 (woman) full-time, 3 part-time/adjunct (2 women). *Students:* 79 (53 women); includes 47 minority (45 Black or African American, non-Hispanic/Latino; 2 Hispanic/Latino). Average age 32. 34 applicants, 97% accepted, 29 enrolled. In 2017, 4 master's awarded. *Degree requirements:* For master's, comprehensive exam. *Entrance requirements:* For master's, GRE, minimum GPA of 2.75, criminal background check. Additional exam requirements/recommendations for international students: Required—TOEFL (minimum score 500 paper-based; 61 iBT). *Application deadline:* Applications are processed on a rolling basis. Application fee: $40. Electronic applications accepted. *Expenses:* Tuition, state resident: part-time $371 per credit hour. Tuition, nonresident: part-time $742 per credit hour. *Required fees:* $130 per semester. *Financial support:* Teaching assistantships, Federal Work-Study, scholarships/grants, and unspecified assistantships available. Support available to part-time students. Financial award application deadline: 3/1; financial award applicants required to submit FAFSA. *Unit head:* Dr. Reenay Rogers, Chair of Instructional Leadership and Support, 205-652-5423, E-mail: rrogers@uwa.edu. *Application contact:* Dr. B.J. Kimbrough, Dean of Graduate Studies, 205-652-3647, Fax: 205-652-3670, E-mail: bkimbrough@uwa.edu.

University of West Florida, College of Education and Professional Studies, Department of Research and Advanced Studies, Program in College Student Affairs Administration, Pensacola, FL 32514-5750. Offers M Ed. *Program availability:* Part-time, evening/weekend. *Degree requirements:* For master's, internship. *Entrance requirements:* For master's, GRE General Test, minimum GPA of 3.0. Additional exam requirements/recommendations for international students: Required—TOEFL (minimum score 550 paper-based).

University of Wisconsin–La Crosse, College of Liberal Studies, Department of Student Affairs Administration, La Crosse, WI 54601-3742. Offers MS Ed, Ed D. *Program availability:* Part-time, evening/weekend, 100% online, blended/hybrid learning. *Students:* 31 full-time (25 women), 57 part-time (42 women); includes 14 minority (3 Black or African American, non-Hispanic/Latino; 1 American Indian or Alaska Native, non-Hispanic/Latino; 2 Asian, non-Hispanic/Latino; 4 Hispanic/Latino; 4 Two or more races, non-Hispanic/Latino), 1 international. Average age 27. 121 applicants, 51% accepted, 47 enrolled. In 2017, 45 master's awarded. *Degree requirements:* For master's, comprehensive exam (for some programs), thesis optional, electronic portfolio, applied research project. *Entrance requirements:* For master's, bachelor's degree from accredited institution, minimum GPA of 2.85, resume, essay, 2 references. Additional exam requirements/recommendations for international students: Required—TOEFL (minimum score 550 paper-based; 79 iBT). *Application deadline:* For fall admission, 2/1 priority date for domestic and international students. Electronic applications accepted. *Financial support:* Research assistantships with partial tuition reimbursements, Federal Work-Study, scholarships/grants, and health care benefits available. Support available to part-time students. Financial award application deadline: 3/15; financial award applicants required to submit FAFSA. *Faculty research:* Persistence; developing positive social justice behaviors in heterosexual white college men; equity; diversity; inclusion in higher education at both interpersonal and institutional levels; expanding student affairs administration research and practice beyond the traditional, majority, or dominant student experience; underrepresented students at historically white institutions; college men and masculinities; Latina/o college student leadership; ethnic cultural centers at HWIs. *Unit head:* Dr. Jodie Rindt, Department Chair, 608-785-6450, E-mail: jrindt@uwlax.edu. *Application contact:* Brandon Schaller, Senior Graduate Student Status Examiner, 608-785-8941, E-mail: admissions@uwlax.edu.
Website: http://www.uwlax.edu/saa/

University of Wyoming, College of Education, Programs in Counselor Education, Laramie, WY 82071. Offers community mental health (MS); counselor education and supervision (PhD); school counseling (MS); student affairs (MS). *Accreditation:* ACA (one or more programs are accredited). *Degree requirements:* For master's, comprehensive exam (for some programs), thesis optional; for doctorate, thesis/dissertation, video demonstration. *Entrance requirements:* For master's, interview, background check; for doctorate, video tape session, interview, writing sample, master's degree, background check. Additional exam requirements/recommendations for international students: Required—TOEFL. *Faculty research:* Wyoming SAGE photovoice project; accountable school counseling programs; GLBT issues; addictions; play therapy-early childhood mental health.

Virginia Commonwealth University, Graduate School, School of Education, Program in Counselor Education, Richmond, VA 23284-9005. Offers college student development and counseling (M Ed); school counseling (M Ed). *Accreditation:* ACA; NCATE. *Entrance requirements:* For master's, GRE General Test or MAT. Additional exam requirements/recommendations for international students: Required—TOEFL (minimum score 600 paper-based; 100 iBT). Electronic applications accepted.

Walsh University, Graduate Programs, Program in Counseling and Human Development, North Canton, OH 44720-3396. Offers clinical mental health counseling (MA); school counseling (MA); student affairs in higher education (MA). *Accreditation:* ACA. *Program availability:* Part-time, evening/weekend. *Degree requirements:* For master's, comprehensive exam, internship, practicum. *Entrance requirements:* For master's, GRE (minimum score of 145 verbal and 146 quantitative) or MAT (minimum score of 397), interview, minimum GPA of 3.0, writing sample, reference forms, notarized affidavit of good moral conduct. Additional exam requirements/recommendations for international students: Required—TOEFL (minimum score 500 paper-based; 61 iBT). Electronic applications accepted. Application fee is waived when completed online. *Expenses:* Contact institution. *Faculty research:* Supervision of clinical mental health, clinical mental health practice/issues, clinical mental health skills development, advocacy, teaching and professional development, career development, refugee development in US, supervision in student affairs, offender treatment, domestic violence issues, alcohol and drug treatment issues, Professional identity and advocacy in school counseling, Efficacy in counseling clinic.

West Chester University of Pennsylvania, College of Education and Social Work, Department of Counselor Education, West Chester, PA 19383. Offers clinical mental health counseling (MS); counseling (Certificate); higher education counseling (Post Master's Certificate); higher education counseling/student affairs (MS, Certificate); school counseling (M Ed). *Accreditation:* ACA; NCATE. *Program availability:* Part-time, evening/weekend. *Students:* 134 full-time (110 women), 40 part-time (32 women); includes 38 minority (17 Black or African American, non-Hispanic/Latino; 2 Asian, non-Hispanic/Latino; 11 Hispanic/Latino; 8 Two or more races, non-Hispanic/Latino), 1 international. Average age 27. 177 applicants, 58% accepted, 58 enrolled. In 2017, 79 master's, 1 other advanced degree awarded. *Degree requirements:* For master's, comprehensive exam. *Entrance requirements:* For master's, minimum GPA of 3.0, three letters of reference. Additional exam requirements/recommendations for international students: Required—TOEFL or IELTS. *Application deadline:* For fall admission, 5/15 for international students; for spring admission, 10/15 for international students. Applications are processed on a rolling basis. Application fee: $50. Electronic applications accepted. *Expenses:* Tuition, state resident: full-time $9000; part-time $500 per credit. Tuition, nonresident: full-time $13,500; part-time $750 per credit. *Required fees:* $2959; $149.79 per credit. *Financial support:* Scholarships/grants and unspecified assistantships available. Financial award application deadline: 2/15; financial award applicants required to submit FAFSA. *Faculty research:* Bullying in the schools, adolescent cognitive development, counseling pedagogy, motivational interviewing. *Unit head:* Dr. Eric Owens, Chair, 610-425-7412, E-mail: eowens@wcupa.edu. *Application contact:* Dr. Cheryl Neale-McFall, Graduate Coordinator, 610-436-2559, Fax: 610-425-7432, E-mail: cneale-mcfall@wcupa.edu.
Website: http://www.wcupa.edu/education-socialWork/counselorEducation/

West Chester University of Pennsylvania, College of Education and Social Work, Department of Educational Foundations and Policy Studies, West Chester, PA 19383. Offers education for sustainability (Certificate); educational technology (Certificate); higher education policy and student affairs (MS); transformative education and social change (MS). *Program availability:* Part-time. *Students:* 35 full-time (21 women), 49 part-time (33 women); includes 15 minority (9 Black or African American, non-Hispanic/Latino; 1 Asian, non-Hispanic/Latino; 2 Hispanic/Latino; 3 Two or more races, non-Hispanic/Latino), 1 international. Average age 29. 77 applicants, 90% accepted, 51 enrolled. In 2017, 5 master's, 6 other advanced degrees awarded. *Degree requirements:* For master's, comprehensive exam (for some programs), thesis, 36 credits (42 credits for MS in higher education policy and student affairs). *Entrance requirements:* For master's, teaching certification (strongly recommended); for Certificate, minimum GPA of 3.0. Additional exam requirements/recommendations for international students: Required—TOEFL or IELTS. *Application deadline:* For fall admission, 5/15 for international students; for spring admission, 10/15 for international students. Applications are processed on a rolling basis. Application fee: $50. Electronic applications accepted. *Expenses:* Tuition, state resident: full-time $9000; part-time $500 per credit. Tuition, nonresident: full-time $13,500; part-time $750 per credit. *Required fees:* $2959; $149.79 per credit. *Financial support:* Scholarships/grants and unspecified assistantships available. Financial award application deadline: 2/15; financial award applicants required to submit FAFSA. *Faculty research:* Technology integration: preparing our teachers for the twenty-first century, critical pedagogy, education for sustainability. *Unit head:* Dr. John Elmore, Chair, 610-436-6934, Fax: 610-436-3102, E-mail: jelmore@wcupa.edu. *Application contact:* Office of Graduate Studies and Extended Education, 610-436-2943, Fax: 610-436-2763, E-mail: gradstudy@wcupa.edu.
Website: http://www.wcupa.edu/education-socialWork/profsecedu/

Western Illinois University, School of Graduate Studies, College of Education and Human Services, Department of Educational Studies, Program in College Student Personnel, Macomb, IL 61455-1390. Offers college student personnel (MS), including higher education leadership, student affairs. *Accreditation:* NCATE. *Program availability:* Part-time. *Students:* 59 full-time (41 women), 9 part-time (5 women); includes 19 minority (4 Black or African American, non-Hispanic/Latino; 10 Hispanic/Latino; 5 Two or more races, non-Hispanic/Latino), 2 international. Average age 24. 79 applicants, 82% accepted, 32 enrolled. In 2017, 27 master's awarded. *Degree requirements:* For master's, thesis or alternative. *Entrance requirements:* For master's, interview. Additional exam requirements/recommendations for international students: Required—TOEFL (minimum score 550 paper-based; 80 iBT). *Application deadline:* For fall admission, 1/5 priority date for domestic students. Application fee: $30. Electronic applications accepted. *Financial support:* Unspecified assistantships available. Financial award applicants required to submit FAFSA. *Unit head:* Dr. Tracy Davis, Coordinator, 309-298-1183. *Application contact:* Dr. Nancy Parsons, Associate Provost and Director of Graduate Studies, 309-298-1806, Fax: 309-298-2345, E-mail: grad-office@wiu.edu.
Website: http://wiu.edu/csp/

Western Kentucky University, Graduate Studies, College of Education and Behavioral Sciences, Department of Counseling and Student Affairs, Bowling Green, KY 42101. Offers counseling (MA Ed), including marriage and family therapy, mental health counseling; school counseling (P-12) (MA Ed); student affairs in higher education (MA Ed). *Accreditation:* ACA; NCATE. *Program availability:* Part-time, evening/weekend. *Degree requirements:* For master's, comprehensive exam, thesis optional. *Entrance requirements:* For master's, GRE General Test. Additional exam requirements/recommendations for international students: Required—TOEFL (minimum score 555 paper-based; 79 iBT). *Faculty research:* Counselor education, research for residential workers.

William James College, Graduate Programs, Newton, MA 02459. Offers applied psychology in higher education student personnel administration (MA); clinical psychology (Psy D); counseling psychology (MA); counseling psychology and community mental health (MA); counseling psychology and global mental health (MA); executive coaching (Graduate Certificate); forensic and counseling psychology (MA); leadership psychology (Psy D); organizational psychology (MA); primary care psychology (MA); respecialization in clinical psychology (Certificate); school psychology (Psy D); MA/CAGS. *Accreditation:* APA. *Degree requirements:* For master's, comprehensive exam (for some programs); for doctorate, thesis/dissertation (for some programs). Electronic applications accepted.

SOKA UNIVERSITY OF AMERICA
Graduate School, Masters of Arts in Educational Leadership and Societal Changes

 For more information, visit http://petersons.to/sokaueducation

Programs of Study

The educational leader of tomorrow requires a new kind of preparation for a new kind of world, global in scope, all-inclusive in depth and breadth, calling out for meaningful, broad-based societal change focused on harnessing the values of peace.

Soka University of America's (SUA) Master of Arts (M.A.) program in Educational Leadership and Societal Change examines the broad landscape of modern institutions and structures, including but not limited to schools and colleges. It casts a wide interdisciplinary net to bring new light to bear on the symbiotic relationship between value-creating educational leadership and the transformation of society itself. Embedded in the curriculum are also the practical skills and abilities as well as the professional research tools needed by effective educational leaders to develop the knowledge, skills, and dispositions necessary to create learning environments that value diversity, continual knowledge acquisition, instructional leadership, innovative and ethical decision-making, and the successful achievement of all school-aged youth.

In the course of their studies, students will analyze past and present models of administrative leadership for their effectiveness in promoting equality of educational opportunity and greater workplace democracy and gain foundational knowledge of the historical and philosophical underpinnings of education. Students will learn to utilize networks and coalitions for broad-based initiative and reforms in addition to promoting meaningful collaboration among and between parents, and school administrators.

A Master of Arts in Educational Leadership and Societal Change is a degree with international and comparative dimensions that provides broad knowledge, cultural sensitivity, and perspective that is in demand. A Soka graduate-level education can help prepare and place students in a variety of industries. The desire to pursue a doctorate, become an educational leader, work in civil service or for a nonprofit organization, work in government, make a difference in the growing for-profit sector in education, or desire to start a school are some of the reasons students choose this program.

The M.A. in Educational Leadership and Societal Change is a full-time, two-year program (39 semester credits). The University's full-time learning environment provides students support for professional development opportunities, engagement with visiting distinguished scholars and practitioners, a summer research grant providing a field experience in a real-world leadership setting, and a residential living and learning experience including off-campus housing opportunities for students with dependents or special circumstances.

Students study and conduct research into the historical roots of educational policies and problems as well as on the relationship between educational philosophies and practices and contemporary social, political, economic and cultural developments. Related areas of study include comparative and international education, multicultural education, educational psychology, gender and education, school administration policy and practice, and educational law.

Regular semester-long courses are taught in a traditional graduate seminar format in which students read and discuss both common and individual readings, pursue a research project under the direction of a professor/mentor, and provide regular progress reports to the class as a whole for commentary and input. Courses include a fieldwork component, including a summer-long research internship that provides students with hands-on opportunities to shadow administrators, analyze organizational dynamics, and evaluate curriculum. Under the supervision of a principal professor, students integrate their fieldwork and educational research to produce a master's thesis for graduation.

Financial Aid

Soka University of America is committed to being a partner in helping students meet the costs of their education and investing its resources to ensure the success of its students. The Office of Financial Aid works with students to ensure that a Soka education is accessible to all students who are admitted. In an effort to promote greater diversity and access, SUA has designed a comprehensive merit and need-based financial aid program that ensures the fair distribution of institutional, state, and federal funds.

Soka's M.A. program is affordable. Financial aid in the form of grants and scholarships is available up to the full cost of tuition. Loan programs are also available to domestic and international students.

Cost of Study

For the 2018–19 academic year, the cost of tuition for domestic students is $31,310. Books and supplies are estimated at $1,916. Costs for transportation and personal expenses vary by student.

Living and Housing Costs

Soka University of America recognizes the value of establishing a culture of learning throughout the university campus. As a residential campus, Soka students are provided with distinctive accommodations within a unique setting. Soka's residence halls are a dynamic environment offering living and learning opportunities for residents to share intellectual and educational goals and grow through community engagement, interpersonal relationships, and social interaction within a diverse community.

Single graduate students may live in suite-style housing accommodations in the residence hall community. Graduate student housing is a designated floor in a residence hall community shared with undergraduate students. Graduate students will be matched with another student from the program. Soka University does not have on-campus accommodations for married students or students with families.

The cost of on-campus room and board is $12,530 for the 2018–19 academic year.

Student Group

The program offers a small, select, international community of inquiry, diverse in age and experience with a student/faculty ratio of 7:1.

Location

Soka University of America is a 103 acre campus located in south Orange County, California in the City of Aliso Viejo (between San Diego and Los Angeles). The campus is just 9 miles from the beach and located in the heart of Southern California's abundance of cultural, educational, sporting, and adventure opportunities.

The University

The Soka University of America Graduate School strives to provide an academic setting that nurtures men and women from a variety of cultures and national backgrounds, who seek to learn from shared experiences. The School also seeks to develop critical thinking and learning and to foster a commitment to lifelong learning. To this end, the School emphasizes small class sizes that cultivate close and informal relationship between teachers and students, rigorous academic endeavors, free and open dialogue, and an appreciation for human diversity.

Faculty

Soka University's high-caliber faculty enjoys working closely with students. With a low student/faculty ratio, the faculty can work individually with students to see how far they can go in exploring new concepts and learning opportunities.

Program Director John H. Heffron, Ph.D., is a Professor of Educational History and Culture. He is also the author of Leadership for Development: What Globalization Demands of Leaders Seeking Change and Toward a Cybernetic Pedagogy: The Cognitive Revolution and the Classroom, 1948–Present.

Applying

The student seeking admission to the M.A. program is expected to have completed a bachelor's degree from an accredited college or university with at least a B average or the equivalent of an undergraduate level education (normally 16 years of pre- and postsecondary education) from a foreign institution. The Graduate

School Faculty Admission Committee will review applications to the program. Applicants will be admitted to the program based on ability to complete a rigorous program of academic study successfully; strong writing skills; clear professional and scholarly goals; and strong evidence of the ability to work cooperatively, influence group opinion, and facilitate task completion. There are some differences in the application process for domestic and international applicants. Additional information and a complete admission checklist is available at http://www.soka.edu/gradadmission.

The application deadline for the M.A. program is February 15. Students can apply by visiting http://admissions.soka.edu/apply.

Correspondence and Information

Soka University of America
Office of Graduate Admission
1 University Drive
Aliso Viejo, California 92656
Phone: 949-480-4111
E-mail: grad_admissions@soka.edu
Website: www.soka.edu
www.soka.edu/gradadmission
www.soka.edu/maprogram

Section 24
Instructional Levels

This section contains a directory of institutions offering graduate work in instructional levels. Additional information about programs listed in the directory may be obtained by writing directly to the dean of a graduate school or chair of a department at the address given in the directory.

For programs offering related work, see also in this book *Administration, Instruction, and Theory; Education; Leisure Studies and Recreation; Physical Education and Kinesiology; Special Focus;* and *Subject Areas.* In other guides in this series:

Graduate Programs in the Humanities, Arts & Social Sciences
See *Psychology and Counseling (School Psychology)*
Graduate Programs in the Biological/Biomedical Sciences and Health-Related Medical Professions
See *Health-Related Professions*

CONTENTS

Adult Education

Alverno College, School of Professional Studies - Education Division, Milwaukee, WI 53234-3922. Offers adaptive education (MA); administrative leadership (MA); adult education and organizational development (MA); adult educational and instructional design (MA); adult educational and instructional technology (MA); global connections in the humanities (MA); instructional leadership (MA); instructional technology for K-12 settings (MA); professional development (MA); reading education (MA); reading education with adaptive education (MA); science education (MA); special education (MA); teaching in alternative schools (MA). *Accreditation:* NCATE. *Program availability:* Part-time, evening/weekend. *Faculty:* 3 full-time (2 women), 23 part-time/adjunct (17 women). *Students:* 37 full-time (34 women), 68 part-time (65 women); includes 27 minority (16 Black or African American, non-Hispanic/Latino; 1 American Indian or Alaska Native, non-Hispanic/Latino; 1 Asian, non-Hispanic/Latino; 7 Hispanic/Latino; 2 Two or more races, non-Hispanic/Latino). Average age 35. 67 applicants, 100% accepted, 51 enrolled. In 2017, 68 master's awarded. *Degree requirements:* For master's, presentation/defense of proposal, conference presentation of inquiry projects. *Entrance requirements:* For master's, bachelor's degree in related field, communication samples from work setting, 3 letters of recommendation. Additional exam requirements/recommendations for international students: Required—TOEFL. *Application deadline:* For fall admission, 7/15 priority date for domestic and international students; for spring admission, 12/15 priority date for domestic and international students. Applications are processed on a rolling basis. Application fee: $0. Electronic applications accepted. *Expenses:* Contact institution. *Financial support:* Federal Work-Study and scholarships/grants available. Support available to part-time students. Financial award applicants required to submit FAFSA. *Faculty research:* Student self-assessment, self-reflection, integration of curriculum, identifying needs of students in strategic situations and designing appropriate classroom strategies. *Unit head:* Dr. Patricia Luebke, Dean, School of Professional Studies, 414-382-6368, Fax: 414-382-6354, E-mail: patricia.luebke@alverno.edu. *Application contact:* Katie Kipp, Graduate Admissions Counselor, 414-382-6045, Fax: 414-382-6354, E-mail: katie.kipp@alverno.edu.

Antioch University Seattle, Program in Education, Seattle, WA 98121. Offers adult education (MA); drama therapy (MA); individualized studies (MA); leadership in edible education (MA); teaching (MAT); urban environmental education (MA). *Program availability:* Part-time, evening/weekend. *Students:* 58 full-time (40 women), 15 part-time (12 women); includes 12 minority (2 Asian, non-Hispanic/Latino; 6 Hispanic/Latino; 4 Two or more races, non-Hispanic/Latino). Average age 36. *Degree requirements:* For master's, comprehensive exam (for some programs), thesis. *Entrance requirements:* For master's, WEST-B, WEST-E, current resume, transcripts of undergraduate degree and coursework (or for highest degree completed), two letters of recommendation, proof of fingerprinting and background check, moral character with fitness statement of understanding, documentation of 40 hours' experience in school classroom(s). *Application deadline:* Applications are processed on a rolling basis. *Expenses:* Contact institution. *Financial support:* Research assistantships, Federal Work-Study, scholarships/grants, and unspecified assistantships available. Financial award application deadline: 6/15. *Faculty research:* Visual thinking and science education, K-8 equity and engaged pedagogy in science education, K-12 inquiry-based mathematics education, education in prisons and other institutions of confinement. *Unit head:* Ed Mikel, Interim Dean, 206-268-4617, E-mail: emikel@antioch.edu. *Application contact:* Eileen Knight, Recruitment and Admissions Director, 206-268-4200, E-mail: eknight@antioch.edu.
Website: https://www.antioch.edu/seattle/degrees-programs/education-degrees/

Argosy University, Chicago, College of Education, Chicago, IL 60601. Offers adult education and training (MA Ed); community college executive leadership (Ed D); educational leadership (MA Ed, Ed D, Ed S), including district leadership (Ed D), higher education administration (Ed D), K-12 education (Ed D); instructional leadership (Ed D, Ed S), including higher education (Ed D), K-12 education (Ed D). *Program availability:* Online learning.

Argosy University, Hawai`i, College of Education, Honolulu, HI 96813. Offers adult education and training (MAEd); educational leadership (Ed D), including higher education administration, K-12 education; instructional leadership (Ed D), including higher education, K-12 education; school psychology (MA).

Argosy University, Phoenix, College of Education, Phoenix, AZ 85021. Offers adult education and training (MA Ed); advanced educational administration (Ed D, Ed S); community college executive leadership (Ed D); educational administration (MA Ed); educational leadership (MA Ed, Ed D, Ed S), including education technology (Ed D), higher education administration (Ed D), K-12 education (Ed D); higher and postsecondary education (MA Ed); initial educational administration (Ed D, Ed S); school psychology (MA); teaching and learning (MA Ed, Ed D, Ed S), including education technology (Ed D), higher education (Ed D), K-12 education (Ed D).

Argosy University, Seattle, College of Education, Seattle, WA 98121. Offers adult education and training (MA Ed); community college executive leadership (Ed D); educational leadership (MA Ed, Ed D), including higher education administration (Ed D), K-12 education (Ed D); higher and postsecondary education (MA Ed); instructional leadership (MA Ed, Ed D), including education technology (Ed D), higher education (Ed D), K-12 education (Ed D).

Athabasca University, Centre for Interdisciplinary Studies, Athabasca, AB T9S 3A3, Canada. Offers adult education (MA); community studies (MA); cultural studies (MA); educational studies (MA); global change (MA); heritage resource management (Postbaccalaureate Certificate); legislative drafting (Postbaccalaureate Certificate); work, organization, and leadership (MA). *Program availability:* Part-time, evening/weekend, online learning. *Degree requirements:* For master's, project. *Entrance requirements:* Additional exam requirements/recommendations for international students: Required—TOEFL (minimum score 560 paper-based). Electronic applications accepted. *Faculty research:* Women's history, literature and culture studies, sustainable development, labor and education.

Auburn University, Graduate School, College of Education, Department of Educational Foundations, Leadership, and Technology, Auburn University, AL 36849. Offers adult education (PhD, Ed S); curriculum supervision (M Ed, PhD); higher education administration (PhD); library media (Ed S); school administration (M Ed, PhD). *Accreditation:* NCATE. *Program availability:* Part-time. *Faculty:* 30 full-time (17 women), 8 part-time/adjunct (5 women). *Students:* 139 full-time (94 women), 254 part-time (171 women); includes 109 minority (95 Black or African American, non-Hispanic/Latino; 1 American Indian or Alaska Native, non-Hispanic/Latino; 2 Asian, non-Hispanic/Latino; 4 Hispanic/Latino; 1 Native Hawaiian or other Pacific Islander, non-Hispanic/Latino; 6 Two or more races, non-Hispanic/Latino), 12 international. Average age 37. 216 applicants, 72% accepted, 94 enrolled. In 2017, 92 master's, 46 doctorates, 58 other advanced degrees awarded. *Degree requirements:* For master's, thesis (for some programs); for doctorate, thesis/dissertation; for Ed S, field project. *Entrance requirements:* For master's, doctorate, and Ed S, GRE General Test. *Application deadline:* Applications are processed on a rolling basis. Application fee: $50 ($60 for international students). Electronic applications accepted. *Expenses:* Tuition, state resident: full-time $10,974; part-time $519 per credit hour. Tuition, nonresident: full-time $29,658; part-time $1557 per credit hour. *Required fees:* $816 per semester. Tuition and fees vary according to degree level and program. *Financial support:* Teaching assistantships and Federal Work-Study available. Support available to part-time students. Financial award application deadline: 3/15; financial award applicants required to submit FAFSA. *Unit head:* Dr. Sherida Downer, Head, 334-844-3060. *Application contact:* Dr. George Flowers, Dean of the Graduate School, 334-844-4700.
Website: http://www.education.auburn.edu/academic_departments/eflt/

Aurora University, School of Education and Human Performance, Aurora, IL 60506-4892. Offers applied behavioral analysis (MS); bilingual-ESL education (MA); educational leadership with principal endorsement (MA); educational technology (MA); leadership in adult learning higher education (Ed D); leadership in curriculum and instruction (Ed D); leadership in educational administration (Ed D); reading instruction (MA); special education (MA). *Accreditation:* NCATE. *Program availability:* Part-time, evening/weekend. *Faculty:* 15 full-time (8 women), 39 part-time/adjunct (20 women). *Students:* 421 full-time (299 women), 142 part-time (89 women); includes 90 minority (25 Black or African American, non-Hispanic/Latino; 7 Asian, non-Hispanic/Latino; 50 Hispanic/Latino; 2 Native Hawaiian or other Pacific Islander, non-Hispanic/Latino; 6 Two or more races, non-Hispanic/Latino). Average age 37. 169 applicants, 95% accepted, 59 enrolled. In 2017, 175 master's, 36 doctorates awarded. *Degree requirements:* For master's, student teaching; for doctorate, comprehensive exam, thesis/dissertation. *Entrance requirements:* For master's, 2 years of teaching experience, valid teaching certificate, resume; for doctorate, appropriate master's degree, two references, curriculum vitae, personal statement, professional project, reflective essay. Additional exam requirements/recommendations for international students: Required—TOEFL (minimum score 550 paper-based; 79 iBT). *Application deadline:* For fall admission, 6/1 for international students; for spring admission, 10/1 for international students. Applications are processed on a rolling basis. Application fee: $0. Electronic applications accepted. *Expenses:* Contact institution. *Financial support:* In 2017–18, 34 students received support. Federal Work-Study, scholarships/grants, and unspecified assistantships available. Support available to part-time students. Financial award applicants required to submit FAFSA. *Unit head:* Dr. Jen Buckley, Dean, School of Education and Human Performance, 630-844-1542, Fax: 630-844-6155, E-mail: jbuckley@aurora.edu. *Application contact:* Elizabeth Botica, Graduate Education Recruiter, 630-947-8918, E-mail: ebotica@aurora.edu.
Website: http://aurora.edu/education

Ball State University, Graduate School, Teachers College, Department of Educational Studies, Program in Adult Education, Muncie, IN 47306. Offers adult and community education (MA); adult, higher and community education (Ed D). *Accreditation:* NCATE. *Program availability:* Part-time, 100% online, blended/hybrid learning. *Students:* 30 full-time (22 women), 101 part-time (77 women); includes 26 minority (19 Black or African American, non-Hispanic/Latino; 6 Hispanic/Latino; 1 Two or more races, non-Hispanic/Latino), 2 international. Average age 39. 53 applicants, 77% accepted, 34 enrolled. In 2017, 23 master's, 4 doctorates awarded. *Degree requirements:* For doctorate, thesis/dissertation. *Entrance requirements:* For master's, minimum baccalaureate GPA of 2.75 or 3.0 in latter half of baccalaureate; for doctorate, GRE General Test, minimum graduate GPA of 3.2. Additional exam requirements/recommendations for international students: Required—TOEFL (minimum score 550 paper-based; 79 iBT), IELTS (minimum score 6.5). *Application deadline:* Applications are processed on a rolling basis. Application fee: $60. Electronic applications accepted. *Financial support:* Research assistantships with partial tuition reimbursements, teaching assistantships with partial tuition reimbursements, and unspecified assistantships available. Financial award application deadline: 3/1; financial award applicants required to submit FAFSA. *Faculty research:* Community education, executive development for public services. *Unit head:* Dr. Theresa Kruczek, Interim Chair, 765-285-8049, E-mail: tkruczek@bsu.edu.
Website: http://www.bsu.edu/edstudies

Buffalo State College, State University of New York, The Graduate School, Faculty of Applied Science and Education, Department of Educational Foundations, Program in Adult Education, Buffalo, NY 14222-1095. Offers adult education (MS, Certificate); human resources development (Certificate). *Program availability:* Part-time, evening/weekend, online learning. *Degree requirements:* For master's, comprehensive exam. *Entrance requirements:* Additional exam requirements/recommendations for international students: Required—TOEFL (minimum score 550 paper-based).

California Baptist University, Program in Education, Riverside, CA 92504-3206. Offers educational leadership (MS); educational leadership for faith-based institutions (MS); educational leadership for public institutions (MS); educational technology (MS); instructional computer applications (MS); international education (MS); leadership and adult learning (MS); leadership and organizational studies (MS); online teaching and learning (MS); reading (MS); science education (MA); special education in mild/moderate disabilities (MS); special education in moderate/severe disabilities (MS); teacher leadership (MS); teaching (MS); teaching and learning (MS). *Program availability:* Part-time, evening/weekend, 100% online, blended/hybrid learning. *Faculty:* 19 full-time (11 women), 36 part-time/adjunct (22 women). *Students:* 232 full-time (182 women), 315 part-time (247 women); includes 264 minority (33 Black or African American, non-Hispanic/Latino; 4 American Indian or Alaska Native, non-Hispanic/Latino; 11 Asian, non-Hispanic/Latino; 186 Hispanic/Latino; 7 Native Hawaiian or other Pacific Islander, non-Hispanic/Latino; 23 Two or more races, non-Hispanic/Latino). Average age 31. 217 applicants, 64% accepted, 129 enrolled. In 2017, 196 master's awarded. *Degree requirements:* For master's, comprehensive exam, project, or thesis. *Entrance requirements:* For master's, minimum undergraduate GPA of 2.75; 500-word essay; three letters of recommendation; two prerequisite courses completed with minimum C grade. Additional exam requirements/recommendations for international students: Required—TOEFL (minimum score 80 iBT). *Application deadline:* For fall admission, 8/1 priority date for domestic students, 7/1 for international students; for spring admission, 12/1 priority date for domestic students, 11/1 for international students. Applications are processed on a rolling basis. Application fee: $45. Electronic applications accepted. *Expenses:* Contact institution. *Financial support:* In 2017–18, 162 students received support. Federal Work-Study and scholarships/grants available. Financial award applicants required to submit CSS PROFILE or FAFSA. *Faculty research:* Leadership development, complexity theory, faith and learning, special education, social and philosophical contexts of education. *Unit head:* Dr. John Shoup, Dean, School of Education, 951-343-4516, E-mail: jshoup@calbaptist.edu. *Application contact:* Gavin Andrew, Graduate Admissions Counselor, 951-552-8437, E-mail: gandrew@calbaptist.edu.
Website: http://www.calbaptist.edu/mastersined/

California Baptist University, Program in Leadership and Adult Learning, Riverside, CA 92504-3206. Offers MA. *Program availability:* Part-time, evening/weekend. *Faculty:* 1 full-time (0 women). *Degree requirements:* For master's, CCCAOE professional training or leadership tactics. *Entrance requirements:* For master's, minimum undergraduate GPA of 2.75, bachelor's degree transcripts, three letters of recommendation, essay, resume. Additional exam requirements/recommendations for international students: Required—TOEFL (minimum score 80 iBT). *Application deadline:* For fall admission, 8/1 priority date for domestic students, 7/1 priority date for international students; for spring admission, 12/1 priority date for domestic students, 11/1 priority date for international students. Applications are processed on a rolling basis. Application fee: $45. Electronic applications accepted. *Expenses:* Contact institution. *Financial support:* Applicants required to submit CSS PROFILE or FAFSA. *Unit head:* Dr. John Shoup, Dean, School of Education, 951-343-4205, E-mail: jshoup@calbaptist.edu.

Capella University, School of Education, Doctoral Programs in Education, Minneapolis, MN 55402. Offers curriculum and instruction (PhD); educational leadership and management (Ed D); instructional design for online learning (PhD); K-12 studies in education (PhD); leadership for higher education (PhD); leadership in educational administration (PhD); postsecondary and adult education (PhD); professional studies in education (PhD); reading and literacy (Ed D); special education leadership (PhD); training and performance improvement (PhD).

Capella University, School of Education, Master's Programs in Education, Minneapolis, MN 55402. Offers adult education (MS); curriculum and instruction (MS); early childhood education (MS); enrollment management (MS); higher education leadership and management (MS); instructional design for online learning (MS); integrative studies (MS); K-12 studies in education (MS); leadership in educational administration (MS); reading and literacy (MS); special education teaching (MS).

Carroll University, Graduate Programs in Education, Waukesha, WI 53186-5593. Offers adult and continuing education (M Ed); educational leadership (MS); PK-12 (M Ed). *Program availability:* Part-time, evening/weekend. *Degree requirements:* For master's, thesis. *Entrance requirements:* For master's, minimum undergraduate GPA of 2.5 in related field. Additional exam requirements/recommendations for international students: Required—TOEFL. Electronic applications accepted. *Faculty research:* Qualitative research methods, whole language approaches to teaching, the writing process, multicultural education, gifted/talented learners.

Chicago State University, School of Graduate and Professional Studies, College of Education, Department of Educational Leadership, Curriculum and Foundations, Program in Curriculum and Instruction, Chicago, IL 60628. Offers instructional foundations (MS Ed), including adult education, elementary education, secondary education. *Degree requirements:* For master's, comprehensive exam, thesis optional. *Entrance requirements:* For master's, minimum GPA of 2.75. *Application deadline:* For fall admission, 7/1 for domestic students; for spring admission, 11/10 for domestic students. Application fee: $25. *Unit head:* Dr. Cathryn Busch, Chairperson. *Application contact:* Anika Miller, Graduate Studies Office, 773-995-2404, E-mail: g-studies1@csu.edu.

Cleveland State University, College of Graduate Studies, College of Education and Human Services, Department of Counseling, Administration, Supervision and Adult Learning (CASAL), Cleveland, OH 44115. Offers adult learning and development (M Ed); counselor education (PhD); early childhood mental health counseling (Certificate); educational administration and supervision (M Ed). *Accreditation:* ACA (one or more programs are accredited). *Program availability:* Part-time, evening/weekend. *Faculty:* 15 full-time (8 women), 19 part-time/adjunct (10 women). *Students:* 121 full-time (98 women), 272 part-time (198 women); includes 127 minority (106 Black or African American, non-Hispanic/Latino; 1 American Indian or Alaska Native, non-Hispanic/Latino; 4 Asian, non-Hispanic/Latino; 11 Hispanic/Latino; 5 Two or more races, non-Hispanic/Latino), 8 international. Average age 33. 57 applicants, 93% accepted, 51 enrolled. In 2017, 99 master's awarded. *Degree requirements:* For master's, comprehensive exam (for some programs), thesis optional, internship. *Entrance requirements:* For master's, GRE General Test or MAT, letter of recommendation and minimum GPA of 2.75 (for counseling); 2 letters of recommendation and interviews (for organizational leadership). Additional exam requirements/recommendations for international students: Required—TOEFL (minimum score 550 paper-based; 78 iBT), IELTS (minimum score 6). *Application deadline:* For fall admission, 6/21 for domestic students, 5/15 for international students; for spring admission, 8/31 for domestic students, 11/1 for international students. Application fee: $40. Electronic applications accepted. *Financial support:* In 2017–18, 19 students received support, including 10 research assistantships with tuition reimbursements available (averaging $11,882 per year), 5 teaching assistantships with tuition reimbursements available (averaging $11,882 per year); scholarships/grants and unspecified assistantships also available. Support available to part-time students. *Faculty research:* Education law, career development, bullying, psychopharmacology, counseling and spirituality. *Total annual research expenditures:* $225,821. *Unit head:* Dr. R. Elliott Ingersoll, Chair/Professor, 216-687-4582, Fax: 216-687-5378, E-mail: r.ingersoll@csuohio.edu. *Application contact:* Deborah L. Brown, Interim Assistant Director, Graduate Admissions, 216-523-7572, Fax: 216-687-5400, E-mail: d.l.brown@csuohio.edu.
Website: http://www.csuohio.edu/cehs/departments/CASAL/casal_dept.html

Cleveland State University, College of Graduate Studies, College of Education and Human Services, Program in Urban Education, Specialization in Adult, Continuing, and Higher Education, Cleveland, OH 44115. Offers PhD. *Program availability:* Part-time. *Faculty:* 4 full-time (3 women). *Students:* 6 full-time (4 women), 7 part-time (6 women); includes 3 minority (all Black or African American, non-Hispanic/Latino). Average age 41. In 2017, 2 doctorates awarded. *Entrance requirements:* For doctorate, GRE General Test (minimum score of 297 for combined Verbal and Quantitative exams, 4.0 preferred for Analytical Writing), minimum graduate GPA of 3.25, curriculum vitae or resume, personal statement, 2 letters of recommendation. Additional exam requirements/recommendations for international students: Required—TOEFL (minimum score 550 paper-based; 78 iBT), IELTS (minimum score 6). Application fee: $40. Electronic applications accepted. *Financial support:* In 2017–18, 2 students received support. Research assistantships, teaching assistantships, and tuition waivers (full) available. Support available to part-time students. Financial award application deadline: 4/1; financial award applicants required to submit FAFSA. *Faculty research:* Adult education research, practice in diverse contexts. *Unit head:* Dr. Graham Stead, Director, Doctoral Studies, 216-875-9869, E-mail: g.b.stead@csuohio.edu. *Application contact:* Rita M. Grabowski, Administrative Coordinator, 216-687-4697, Fax: 216-875-9697, E-mail: r.grabowski@csuohio.edu.
Website: http://www.csuohio.edu/cehs/departments/DOC/III_doc.html

Colorado State University, College of Health and Human Sciences, School of Education, Fort Collins, CO 80523-1588. Offers adult education and training (M Ed); counseling and career development (MA); education and human resources (M Ed); education, equity, and transformation (MA); higher education leadership (PhD); organizational learning, performance, and change (M Ed, PhD); student affairs in higher education (MS). *Accreditation:* ACA; TEAC. *Program availability:* Part-time, online only, 100% online, blended/hybrid learning. *Faculty:* 33 full-time (23 women), 19 part-time/adjunct (11 women). *Students:* 74 full-time (53 women), 548 part-time (357 women); includes 151 minority (37 Black or African American, non-Hispanic/Latino; 4 American Indian or Alaska Native, non-Hispanic/Latino; 14 Asian, non-Hispanic/Latino; 71 Hispanic/Latino; 25 Two or more races, non-Hispanic/Latino), 16 international. Average age 37. 456 applicants, 31% accepted, 123 enrolled. In 2017, 177 master's, 22 doctorates awarded. *Degree requirements:* For master's, thesis optional, professional portfolio or capstone project; for doctorate, comprehensive exam, thesis/dissertation. *Entrance requirements:* For master's, bachelor's degree; minimum GPA of 3.0 in last degree earned; for doctorate, GRE; GRE or GMAT (for organizational learning, performance and change only), master's degree; minimum GPA of 3.0 in last degree earned. Additional exam requirements/recommendations for international students: Required—TOEFL (minimum score 550 paper-based; 80 iBT), IELTS (minimum score 6.5), PTE (minimum score 58). *Application deadline:* Applications are processed on a rolling basis. Application fee: $60 ($70 for international students). Electronic applications accepted. *Expenses:* Contact institution. *Financial support:* In 2017–18, 4 students received support, including 8 research assistantships with full and partial tuition reimbursements available (averaging $12,758 per year), 4 teaching assistantships with full and partial tuition reimbursements available (averaging $14,256 per year); fellowships with full and partial tuition reimbursements available, Federal Work-Study, scholarships/grants, tuition waivers (full and partial), and unspecified assistantships also available. Financial award applicants required to submit FAFSA. *Faculty research:* Diversity, equity, and inclusion; STEM education; higher education; occupational learning, performance, and change; teacher education. *Total annual research expenditures:* $312,562. *Unit head:* Dr. Louise Jennings, Co-Director, 970-491-6317, Fax: 970-491-1317, E-mail: louise.jennings@colostate.edu. *Application contact:* Kelli Clark, Graduate Programs Coordinator, 970-491-2093, Fax: 970-491-1317, E-mail: kelli.clark@colostate.edu.
Website: http://www.soe.chhs.colostate.edu/

Concordia University, School of Graduate Studies, Faculty of Arts and Science, Department of Education, Program in Adult Education, Montréal, QC H3G 1M8, Canada. Offers Certificate, Diploma. *Degree requirements:* For other advanced degree, internship. *Entrance requirements:* For degree, interview. *Faculty research:* Staff development, human relations training, adult learning, professional development, learning in the workplace.

Concordia University, School of Graduate Studies, Faculty of Arts and Science, Department of Education, Program in Educational Studies, Montréal, QC H3G 1M8, Canada. Offers MA. *Degree requirements:* For master's, one foreign language, thesis optional. *Faculty research:* Social aspects of microtechnology, gender and education, minorities and immigrants in Canadian education, professional development, political education.

Coppin State University, Division of Graduate Studies, Division of Education, Department of Adult and General Education, Baltimore, MD 21216-3698. Offers MS. *Program availability:* Part-time, evening/weekend. *Degree requirements:* For master's, thesis optional, research paper, internship. *Entrance requirements:* For master's, GRE or PRAXIS, minimum GPA of 2.5, interview, resume, references.

Cornell University, Graduate School, Graduate Fields of Agriculture and Life Sciences, Field of Education, Ithaca, NY 14853. Offers adult and extension education (MPS, MS, PhD); learning, teaching, and social policy (MPS, MS, PhD); mathematics 7-12 (MS). Terminal master's awarded for partial completion of doctoral program. *Degree requirements:* For master's, thesis (MS); for doctorate, comprehensive exam, thesis/dissertation. *Entrance requirements:* For master's and doctorate, GRE General Test, sample of written work (recommended), 2 letters of recommendation. Additional exam requirements/recommendations for international students: Required—TOEFL (minimum score 550 paper-based; 77 iBT). Electronic applications accepted. *Faculty research:* Moral development and professional ethics, public issues education and community development, socio/political issues in public education, teacher education and curriculum in agricultural science and mathematics, extension research.

Dallas Theological Seminary, Graduate Programs, Dallas, TX 75204-6499. Offers adult education (Th M); apologetics (Th M); Bible backgrounds (Th M); Bible translation (Th M); Biblical and theological studies (Certificate); biblical counseling (Th M); biblical exegesis and linguistics (MA); biblical exposition (PhD); biblical studies (MA); Biblical theology (Th M); children's education (Th M); Christian education (MA, D Min); Christian leadership (MA); cross-cultural ministries (MA); educational administration (Th M); educational leadership (Th M); evangelism and discipleship (Th M); exposition of Biblical books (Th M); family life education (Th M); general studies (Th M); Hebrew and cognate studies (Th M); hermeneutics (Th M); historical theology (Th M); homiletics (Th M); intercultural ministries (Th M); Jesus studies (Th M); leadership studies (Th M); media and communication (MA); media arts (Th M); ministry (D Min); ministry with women (Th M); New Testament studies (Th M, PhD); Old Testament studies (Th M, PhD); parachurch ministries (Th M); pastoral care and counseling (Th M); pastoral theology and practice (Th M); philosophy (Th M); sacred theology (STM); spiritual formation (Th M); systematic theology (Th M); teaching in Christian institutions (Th M); theological studies (PhD); urban ministries (Th M); worship studies (Th M); youth education (Th M). *Program availability:* Part-time, online learning. *Degree requirements:* For master's, variable foreign language requirement, thesis (for some programs); for doctorate, 2 foreign languages, thesis/dissertation. *Entrance requirements:* For master's, GRE or MAT (if minimum undergraduate cumulative GPA is below 2.5 or undergraduate degree is unaccredited). Additional exam requirements/recommendations for international students: Required—TOEFL (minimum score 575 paper-based; 85 iBT), TWE. Electronic applications accepted.

Delaware State University, Graduate Programs, College of Education, Health and Public Policy, Program in Adult Literacy and Basic Education, Dover, DE 19901-2277. Offers MA. *Entrance requirements:* Additional exam requirements/recommendations for international students: Required—TOEFL (minimum score 550 paper-based). Electronic applications accepted.

DePaul University, School for New Learning, Chicago, IL 60604. Offers applied professional studies (MA); applied technology (MS); educating adults (MA). *Program availability:* Part-time, evening/weekend. *Degree requirements:* For master's, thesis or alternative. *Entrance requirements:* For master's, resume, interview, official transcript. *Application deadline:* Applications are processed on a rolling basis. Application fee: $25. Electronic applications accepted. *Financial support:* Applicants required to submit FAFSA. *Unit head:* Dr. Don Opitz, Interim Dean, 312-362-8512, Fax: 312-362-8809. *Application contact:* Russ Rogers, Director, Graduate Programs, 312-362-8512, Fax: 312-362-8809, E-mail: rrogers@depaul.edu.
Website: http://snl.depaul.edu/

East Carolina University, Graduate School, College of Education, Department of Interdisciplinary Professions, Greenville, NC 27858-4353. Offers adult education (MA Ed); business and marketing education (MA Ed); community college instruction (Certificate); counselor education (MS); education in the healthcare professions (Certificate); library science (MLS); student affairs in higher education (Certificate); vocational education (MS). *Accreditation:* ACA; NCATE. *Program availability:* Part-time, evening/weekend. *Students:* 97 full-time (77 women), 392 part-time (344 women);

Adult Education

includes 107 minority (73 Black or African American, non-Hispanic/Latino; 6 American Indian or Alaska Native, non-Hispanic/Latino; 5 Asian, non-Hispanic/Latino; 11 Hispanic/Latino; 12 Two or more races, non-Hispanic/Latino). Average age 36. 148 applicants, 97% accepted, 116 enrolled. In 2017, 148 master's, 23 other advanced degrees awarded. *Degree requirements:* For master's, comprehensive exam, thesis optional. *Entrance requirements:* For master's, GRE General Test or MAT, interview, minimum GPA of 2.5, bachelor's degree in related field, teaching license (MA Ed). Additional exam requirements/recommendations for international students: Required—TOEFL. *Application deadline:* For fall admission, 5/15 priority date for domestic students. Applications are processed on a rolling basis. Application fee: $75. *Expenses:* Tuition, state resident: full-time $4749; part-time $297 per credit hour. Tuition, nonresident: full-time $17,898; part-time $1119 per credit hour. *Required fees:* $2691; $224 per credit hour. Part-time tuition and fees vary according to course load and program. *Financial support:* Research assistantships with partial tuition reimbursements, teaching assistantships with partial tuition reimbursements, and Federal Work-Study available. Support available to part-time students. Financial award application deadline: 6/1. *Unit head:* Dr. Vivian W. Mott, Chair, 252-328-6177, Fax: 252-328-4368, E-mail: mottv@ecu.edu.
Website: http://www.ecu.edu/cs-educ/idp/index.cfm

Eastern Washington University, Graduate Studies, College of Arts, Letters and Education, Department of Education, Program in Adult Education, Cheney, WA 99004-2431. Offers M Ed. *Students:* 9 full-time (7 women), 7 part-time (4 women); includes 1 minority (Hispanic/Latino), 1 international. Average age 43. 8 applicants, 100% accepted, 7 enrolled. In 2017, 3 master's awarded. *Degree requirements:* For master's, comprehensive exam, thesis or alternative. *Entrance requirements:* For master's, minimum GPA of 3.0. Additional exam requirements/recommendations for international students: Required—PTE (minimum score 63), TOEFL (minimum score 580 paper-based, 92 iBT) or IELTS (7). *Application deadline:* For fall admission, 4/1 priority date for domestic students; for spring admission, 1/15 for domestic students. Applications are processed on a rolling basis. Application fee: $75. *Expenses:* Contact institution. *Financial support:* Teaching assistantships with partial tuition reimbursements, career-related internships or fieldwork, Federal Work-Study, institutionally sponsored loans, scholarships/grants, health care benefits, tuition waivers (partial), and unspecified assistantships available. Support available to part-time students. Financial award application deadline: 2/1; financial award applicants required to submit FAFSA. *Unit head:* Dr. Vince Aleccia, Program Coordinator, 509-359-6492, E-mail: valeccia@ewu.edu.

Edgewood College, School of Education, Madison, WI 53711-1997. Offers adult learning (MA Ed); director of special education and pupil services (Certificate); education (MA Ed); teaching and learning (MA Ed). *Accreditation:* NCATE (one or more programs are accredited). *Program availability:* Part-time, evening/weekend. *Faculty:* 13 full-time (9 women), 15 part-time/adjunct (10 women). *Students:* 157 full-time (106 women), 188 part-time (133 women); includes 65 minority (26 Black or African American, non-Hispanic/Latino; 1 American Indian or Alaska Native, non-Hispanic/Latino; 8 Asian, non-Hispanic/Latino; 23 Hispanic/Latino; 7 Two or more races, non-Hispanic/Latino), 14 international. Average age 37. In 2017, 68 master's, 34 doctorates awarded. *Degree requirements:* For master's, practicum, research project; for doctorate, comprehensive exam, thesis/dissertation. *Entrance requirements:* For master's, minimum GPA of 2.75, 2 letters of recommendation, personal statement; for doctorate, resume, letter of intent, 2 letters of recommendation, interview, writing sample. Additional exam requirements/recommendations for international students: Required—TOEFL (minimum score 525 paper-based; 72 iBT). *Application deadline:* For fall admission, 8/15 for domestic students, 5/1 for international students; for spring admission, 1/8 for domestic students, 11/1 for international students. Applications are processed on a rolling basis. Application fee: $30. Electronic applications accepted. *Financial support:* Applicants required to submit FAFSA. *Faculty research:* Urban high schools, transgender students, literacy pedagogy, funds of knowledge, English language learners. *Unit head:* Dr. Timothy D. Slekar, Dean, 608-663-2293, E-mail: tslekar@edgewood.edu. *Application contact:* Joann Eastman, Admissions Counselor, 608-663-3250, Fax: 608-663-2214, E-mail: gps@edgewood.edu.
Website: https://www.edgewood.edu/academics/schools/school-of-education

Florida Agricultural and Mechanical University, Division of Graduate Studies, Research, and Continuing Education, College of Education, Department of Educational Leadership and Human Services, Tallahassee, FL 32307-3200. Offers administration and supervision (M Ed, MS, PhD); adult education (M Ed, MS); educational leadership (PhD); guidance and counseling (M Ed, MS). *Accreditation:* NCATE. *Degree requirements:* For master's, thesis (for some programs); for doctorate, thesis/dissertation. *Entrance requirements:* For master's, GRE General Test, minimum GPA of 3.0. Additional exam requirements/recommendations for international students: Required—TOEFL.

Florida Atlantic University, College of Education, Department of Educational Leadership and Research Methodology, Boca Raton, FL 33431-0991. Offers adult and community education (M Ed, PhD, Ed S); educational leadership (M Ed, PhD, Ed S); higher education (M Ed, PhD); K-12 school leadership (M Ed, PhD, Ed S). *Accreditation:* NCATE. *Program availability:* Part-time, evening/weekend, online learning. *Faculty:* 22 full-time (12 women), 13 part-time/adjunct (8 women). *Students:* 98 full-time (55 women), 240 part-time (162 women); includes 165 minority (94 Black or African American, non-Hispanic/Latino; 4 Asian, non-Hispanic/Latino; 60 Hispanic/Latino; 7 Two or more races, non-Hispanic/Latino), 6 international. Average age 36. 205 applicants, 61% accepted, 105 enrolled. In 2017, 67 master's, 15 doctorates, 8 other advanced degrees awarded. *Degree requirements:* For doctorate, comprehensive exam, thesis/dissertation, departmental qualifying exam; for Ed S, departmental qualifying exam. *Entrance requirements:* For master's, GRE General Test, minimum GPA of 3.0 during previous 2 years; for doctorate, GRE General Test, minimum GPA of 3.5; for Ed S, GRE General Test. Additional exam requirements/recommendations for international students: Required—TOEFL (minimum score 500 paper-based; 61 iBT), IELTS (minimum score 6). *Application deadline:* For fall admission, 7/1 for domestic students, 2/15 for international students; for spring admission, 9/15 for domestic students, 7/15 for international students. Applications are processed on a rolling basis. Application fee: $30. Electronic applications accepted. *Expenses:* Tuition, state resident: full-time $7400; part-time $369.82 per credit. Tuition, nonresident: full-time $20,496; part-time $1042.81 per credit. *Financial support:* Fellowships, research assistantships, teaching assistantships, career-related internships or fieldwork, and tuition waivers (partial) available. *Faculty research:* Self-directed learning, school reform issues, legal issues, mentoring, school leadership. *Unit head:* Dr. Robert E. Shockley, Chair, 561-297-3550, Fax: 561-297-3618, E-mail: shockley@fau.edu. *Application contact:* Kathy DuBois, Senior Secretary, 561-297-3550, Fax: 561-297-3618, E-mail: edleadership@fau.edu.
Website: http://www.coe.fau.edu/academicdepartments/el/

Florida International University, College of Arts, Sciences, and Education, Department of Leadership and Professional Studies, Miami, FL 33199. Offers adult education and human resource development (MS, Ed D); counseling (MS), including rehabilitation counseling, school counseling; counselor education (MS), including clinical

mental health counseling; educational administration and supervision (Ed D); educational leadership (MS, Certificate, Ed S); higher education (Ed D); higher education administration (MS); international and comparative education (MS); recreation and sport management (MS), including recreation and sport management, recreational therapy; school psychology (Ed S); urban education (MS), including instruction in urban settings, learning technologies, multicultural/bilingual, multicultural/TESOL, urban education. *Program availability:* Part-time, evening/weekend. *Faculty:* 60 full-time (41 women), 112 part-time/adjunct (77 women). *Students:* 221 full-time (162 women), 301 part-time (239 women); includes 418 minority (127 Black or African American, non-Hispanic/Latino; 9 Asian, non-Hispanic/Latino; 271 Hispanic/Latino; 11 Two or more races, non-Hispanic/Latino), 10 international. Average age 33. 330 applicants, 55% accepted, 100 enrolled. In 2017, 181 master's, 6 doctorates awarded. *Degree requirements:* For doctorate, thesis/dissertation. *Entrance requirements:* For master's, minimum GPA of 3.0; for doctorate and other advanced degree, GRE General Test. Additional exam requirements/recommendations for international students: Required—TOEFL (minimum score 550 paper-based; 80 iBT), IELTS (minimum score 6.3). *Application deadline:* For fall admission, 6/1 priority date for domestic students, 4/1 for international students; for winter admission, 10/1 priority date for domestic students, 9/1 for international students; for spring admission, 3/1 priority date for domestic students, 2/1 for international students. Applications are processed on a rolling basis. Application fee: $30. Electronic applications accepted. *Expenses:* Tuition, state resident: full-time $8912; part-time $446 per credit hour. Tuition, nonresident: full-time $21,393; part-time $992 per credit hour. *Required fees:* $390; $195 per semester. *Financial support:* Fellowships, research assistantships with tuition reimbursements, teaching assistantships with tuition reimbursements, Federal Work-Study, and tuition waivers (full and partial) available. Support available to part-time students. Financial award applicants required to submit FAFSA. *Unit head:* Dr. Benjamin Baez, Chair, 305-348-3214, Fax: 305-348-1515, E-mail: benjamin.baez@fiu.edu. *Application contact:* Nanett Rojas, Assistant Director, Graduate Admissions, 305-348-7464, Fax: 305-348-7441, E-mail: gradadm@fiu.edu.
Website: http://education.fiu.edu

The George Washington University, Graduate School of Education and Human Development, Department of Human and Organizational Learning, Program in Design and Assessment of Adult Learning, Washington, DC 20052. Offers Graduate Certificate. *Entrance requirements:* For degree, two letters of recommendation, resume, statement of purpose. Electronic applications accepted. *Expenses:* Tuition: Full-time $28,800; part-time $1655 per credit hour. *Required fees:* $45; $2.75 per credit hour. *Unit head:* Michael Feuer, Dean, 202-994-6161, E-mail: mjfeuer@gwu.edu. *Application contact:* Sarah Lang, Director of Graduate Admissions, 202-994-1447, Fax: 202-994-7207, E-mail: slang@gwu.edu.
Website: http://gsehd.gwu.edu/

Georgia Southern University–Armstrong Campus, College of Graduate Studies, Department of Secondary, Adult, and Physical Education, Savannah, GA 31419-1997. Offers adolescent and adult education (Certificate); adult education and community leadership (M Ed); curriculum and instruction (M Ed); secondary education (MAT). *Program availability:* Part-time, evening/weekend, online learning. *Faculty:* 8 full-time (all women), 4 part-time/adjunct (3 women). *Students:* 19 full-time (16 women), 106 part-time (60 women); includes 41 minority (31 Black or African American, non-Hispanic/Latino; 1 Asian, non-Hispanic/Latino; 3 Hispanic/Latino; 6 Two or more races, non-Hispanic/Latino), 1 international. Average age 33. 83 applicants, 48% accepted, 40 enrolled. In 2017, 43 master's, 1 other advanced degree awarded. *Degree requirements:* For master's, comprehensive exam (for some programs), thesis (for some programs), capstone project (for M Ed). *Entrance requirements:* For master's, edTPA (for MAT). Additional exam requirements/recommendations for international students: Required—TOEFL (minimum score 523 paper-based). *Application deadline:* For fall admission, 6/30 priority date for domestic students, 5/1 priority date for international students; for spring admission, 11/15 priority date for domestic students, 9/15 priority date for international students; for summer admission, 4/15 priority date for domestic students, 9/15 for international students. Applications are processed on a rolling basis. Application fee: $30. Electronic applications accepted. *Expenses:* Tuition, state resident: part-time $211 per credit hour. Tuition, nonresident: part-time $782 per credit hour. *Required fees:* $737 per semester. Tuition and fees vary according to course load, degree level, campus/location and program. *Financial support:* In 2017–18, research assistantships with full tuition reimbursements (averaging $5,000 per year) were awarded; career-related internships or fieldwork, Federal Work-Study, scholarships/grants, and unspecified assistantships also available. Support available to part-time students. Financial award application deadline: 3/15; financial award applicants required to submit FAFSA. *Faculty research:* Quality of teacher leadership, classroom management and first year teachers; edTPA preparation and success of candidates; social justice issues related to educational preparation; recruitment of STEM teachers. *Unit head:* Dr. Amelia Adkins, Department Head, 912-344-2562, E-mail: amee.adkins@armstrong.edu. *Application contact:* McKenzie Peterman, Graduate Admissions Specialist, 912-478-5678, Fax: 912-478-0740, E-mail: mpeterman@georgiasouthern.edu.
Website: http://www.armstrong.edu/Education/adolescent_adult_education2/aaed_welcome

Grand Valley State University, College of Education, Programs in General Education, Allendale, MI 49401-9403. Offers adult and higher education (M Ed); early childhood education (M Ed); educational differentiation (M Ed); educational leadership (M Ed); educational technology integration (M Ed); elementary education (M Ed); middle level education (M Ed); school library media services (M Ed); secondary level education (M Ed); teaching English to speakers of other languages (M Ed). *Program availability:* Part-time, evening/weekend, 100% online, blended/hybrid learning. *Students:* 24 part-time (16 women). Average age 41. In 2017, 5 master's awarded. *Degree requirements:* For master's, project or thesis. *Entrance requirements:* For master's, GRE General Test or minimum GPA of 3.0, last 60 credits from regionally-accredited college/university, 3 letters of recommendation. Additional exam requirements/recommendations for international students: Required—TOEFL (minimum iBT score of 80), IELTS (6.5), or Michigan English Language Assessment Battery (77). *Application deadline:* Applications are processed on a rolling basis. Application fee: $30. Electronic applications accepted. *Expenses:* $652 per credit hour. *Financial support:* In 2017–18, 2 students received support, including 2 fellowships; career-related internships or fieldwork, Federal Work-Study, scholarships/grants, and unspecified assistantships also available. *Faculty research:* Effectiveness of technology in education, parental involvement, effective teaching, effective schools research. *Unit head:* Dr. David Bair, Department Director, 616-331-6489, Fax: 616-331-6489, E-mail: baird@gvsu.edu. *Application contact:* Thomas Owens, Director, Student Information and Services Center, 616-331-6282, Fax: 616-331-6217, E-mail: owenst@gvsu.edu.
Website: http://www.gvsu.edu/coe/

Indiana University of Pennsylvania, School of Graduate Studies and Research, College of Education and Communications, Department of Adult and Community Education, Program in Adult and Community Education, Indiana, PA 15705. Offers MA. *Program availability:* Part-time, online learning. *Faculty:* 2 full-time (both women). *Students:* 4 full-time (3 women), 14 part-time (10 women); includes 6 minority (all Black or African American, non-Hispanic/Latino). Average age 35. 10 applicants, 90% accepted, 6 enrolled. In 2017, 8 master's awarded. *Degree requirements:* For master's, thesis optional. *Entrance requirements:* For master's, goal statement, letters of recommendation, official transcripts. Additional exam requirements/recommendations for international students: Required—TOEFL (minimum score 540 paper-based; 76 iBT). *Application deadline:* Applications are processed on a rolling basis. Application fee: $50. Electronic applications accepted. *Expenses:* Tuition, state resident: full-time $12,000; part-time $500 per credit. Tuition, nonresident: full-time $18,000; part-time $750 per credit. *Required fees:* $4073; $165.55 per credit. $64 per term. *Financial support:* In 2017–18, 3 research assistantships with tuition reimbursements (averaging $1,000 per year) were awarded; career-related internships or fieldwork, Federal Work-Study, scholarships/grants, and unspecified assistantships also available. Support available to part-time students. Financial award application deadline: 4/15; financial award applicants required to submit FAFSA. *Unit head:* Prof. Jacqueline McGinty, Coordinator, 724-357-2470, E-mail: jacqueline.mcginty@iup.edu. Website: http://www.iup.edu/grad/ace/default.aspx

Indiana University of Pennsylvania, School of Graduate Studies and Research, College of Education and Communications, Department of Adult and Community Education, Program in Adult and Community Education/Communications Technology, Indiana, PA 15705. Offers MA. *Program availability:* Part-time, evening/weekend. *Faculty:* 2 full-time (both women). *Students:* 1 (woman) full-time, 4 part-time (3 women), 4 international. Average age 31. 1 applicant. In 2017, 13 master's awarded. *Degree requirements:* For master's, thesis optional. *Entrance requirements:* For master's, 2 letters of recommendation, resume. Additional exam requirements/recommendations for international students: Required—TOEFL (minimum score 540 paper-based; 76 iBT). *Application deadline:* Applications are processed on a rolling basis. Application fee: $50. Electronic applications accepted. *Expenses:* Tuition, state resident: full-time $12,000; part-time $500 per credit. Tuition, nonresident: full-time $18,000; part-time $750 per credit. *Required fees:* $4073; $165.55 per credit. $64 per term. *Financial support:* In 2017–18, 11 research assistantships with tuition reimbursements (averaging $4,698 per year) were awarded; fellowships, teaching assistantships, career-related internships or fieldwork, Federal Work-Study, scholarships/grants, and unspecified assistantships also available. Support available to part-time students. Financial award application deadline: 4/15; financial award applicants required to submit FAFSA. *Unit head:* Prof. Jacqueline McGinty, Coordinator, 724-357-2470, E-mail: jacqueline.mcginty@iup.edu. Website: http://www.iup.edu/aec

Instituto Tecnologico de Santo Domingo, Graduate School, Area of Humanities and Social Sciences, Santo Domingo, Dominican Republic. Offers accounting (Certificate); adult education (Certificate); applied linguistics (MA); economics (MA); education (M Ed); educational psychology (MA, Certificate); gender and development (MA, Certificate); humanistic studies (MA); international marketing management (Certificate); international relations in the Caribbean basin (Certificate); intervention systems in family therapy (MA); linguistic and literary communication (Certificate); pedagogical support (MA); social science education (M Ed); sustainable human development (MA); terminal illness and death psychology (Certificate); youth and adult education (M Ed).

Kansas State University, Graduate School, College of Education, Department of Educational Leadership, Manhattan, KS 66506. Offers adult learning (Certificate); educational leadership (MS, Ed D, PhD); leadership dynamics for adult learners (Certificate); qualitative research (Certificate); social justice education (Certificate); teaching English as a second language for adult learners (Certificate). *Accreditation:* NCATE. *Program availability:* Online learning. *Degree requirements:* For master's, comprehensive exam; for doctorate, comprehensive exam, thesis/dissertation. *Entrance requirements:* For master's, minimum undergraduate GPA of 3.0; for doctorate, MAT (for educational administration); GRE General Test (for adult education), minimum GPA of 3.0 in last 60 hours. Additional exam requirements/recommendations for international students: Required—TOEFL. Electronic applications accepted. *Faculty research:* Educational law, school finance, school facilities, organizational leadership, adult learning, distance learning/education.

Lesley University, Graduate School of Education, Cambridge, MA 02138-2790. Offers arts, community, and education (M Ed); autism studies (Certificate); curriculum and instruction (M Ed, CAGS); early childhood education (M Ed); ecological teaching and learning (MS); educational studies (PhD), including adult learning, educational leadership, individually designed; elementary education (M Ed); emergent technologies for educators (Certificate); ESLArts: language learning through the arts (M Ed); high school education (M Ed); individually designed (M Ed); integrated teaching through the arts (M Ed); literacy for K-8 classroom teachers (M Ed); mathematics education (M Ed); middle school education (M Ed); moderate disabilities (M Ed); online learning (Certificate); reading (CAGS); science in education (M Ed); severe disabilities (M Ed); special needs (CAGS); specialist teacher of reading (M Ed); teacher of visual art (M Ed); technology in education (M Ed, CAGS). *Accreditation:* TEAC. *Program availability:* Part-time, evening/weekend, online learning. *Degree requirements:* For master's, practicum; for doctorate, thesis/dissertation. *Entrance requirements:* For master's, Massachusetts Tests for Educator Licensure (MTEL), transcripts, statement of purpose, recommendations; interview (for special education); for doctorate, GRE General Test, transcripts, statement of purpose, recommendations, interview, master's degree, resume; for other advanced degree, interview, master's degree. Additional exam requirements/recommendations for international students: Required—TOEFL (minimum score 550 paper-based; 80 iBT). Electronic applications accepted. *Faculty research:* Assessment in literacy, mathematics and science; autism spectrum disorders; instructional technology and online learning; multicultural education and English language learners.

Marshall University, Academic Affairs Division, College of Education and Professional Development, Program in Adult and Continuing Education, Huntington, WV 25755. Offers MS. *Accreditation:* NCATE. *Program availability:* Evening/weekend. *Students:* 18 full-time (9 women), 45 part-time (28 women); includes 9 minority (4 Black or African American, non-Hispanic/Latino; 1 Asian, non-Hispanic/Latino; 3 Hispanic/Latino; 1 Two or more races, non-Hispanic/Latino). Average age 42. In 2017, 18 master's awarded. *Degree requirements:* For master's, thesis optional, comprehensive assessment. Application fee: $40. *Unit head:* Dr. Michael Cunningham, Program Coordinator, 304-746-1902, E-mail: mcunningham@marshall.edu. *Application contact:* Graduate Admission.

Memorial University of Newfoundland, School of Graduate Studies, Faculty of Education, St. John's, NL A1C 5S7, Canada. Offers counseling psychology (M Ed); curriculum, teaching, and learning studies (M Ed); education (PhD); educational leadership studies (M Ed, Graduate Diploma); information technology (M Ed); post-secondary studies (M Ed, Diploma), including health professional education (Diploma). *Program availability:* Part-time. *Degree requirements:* For master's, thesis optional, internship, paper folio, project; for doctorate, comprehensive exam, thesis/dissertation, thesis seminar, oral defense of thesis. *Entrance requirements:* For master's, undergraduate degree with at least 2nd class standing, 1-2 years of work experience; for doctorate, minimum A average in graduate course work, MA in education, 2 years of professional experience; for other advanced degree, 2nd class degree, 2 years of work experience with adult learners, appropriate academic qualifications and work experience

in a health-related field. Electronic applications accepted. *Faculty research:* Critical thinking, literacy, cognitive studies and counseling, educational change, technology in instruction.

Merrimack College, School of Education and Social Policy, North Andover, MA 01845-5800. Offers community engagement (M Ed), including community organizations, higher education, PreK-12 education; criminology and criminal justice (MS); curriculum and instruction (M Ed); early childhood education (M Ed); educational leadership (CAGS), including instructional leadership; elementary education (M Ed); English as a second language (PreK-6) (M Ed); high school education (M Ed); higher education (M Ed), including leadership and organizational development, student affairs; middle school education (M Ed); moderate disabilities (PreK-8) (M Ed); school counseling (M Ed). *Program availability:* Part-time, evening/weekend, 100% online courses with immersion events and in-classroom practicum close to home. *Faculty:* 15 full-time, 36 part-time/adjunct. *Students:* 212 full-time (175 women), 121 part-time (101 women); includes 42 minority (6 Black or African American, non-Hispanic/Latino; 6 Asian, non-Hispanic/Latino; 27 Hispanic/Latino; 3 Two or more races, non-Hispanic/Latino), 3 international. Average age 27. 420 applicants, 84% accepted, 250 enrolled. In 2017, 177 master's awarded. *Degree requirements:* For master's, practicum, portfolio, and state test (for licensure track); capstone (for higher education, curriculum and instruction, and community engagement tracks); for CAGS, capstone. *Entrance requirements:* For master's, Massachusetts Teacher Education Licensure (MTEL), official transcripts from other colleges, resume, personal statement, 2 letters of recommendation. Additional exam requirements/recommendations for international students: Required—TOEFL (minimum score 84 iBT), IELTS (minimum score 6.5), PTE (minimum score 56). *Application deadline:* For fall admission, 8/24 for domestic students, 7/30 for international students; for spring admission, 1/10 for domestic students, 12/10 for international students; for summer admission, 5/10 for domestic students, 4/10 for international students. Applications are processed on a rolling basis. Application fee: $0. Electronic applications accepted. *Expenses:* Contact institution. *Financial support:* Fellowships with full tuition reimbursements, career-related internships or fieldwork, scholarships/grants, and health care benefits available. Support available to part-time students. Financial award application deadline: 5/1; financial award applicants required to submit FAFSA. *Application contact:* Alyssa Orlando, Graduate Admissions Counselor, 978-837-3563, E-mail: orlandoaf@merrimack.edu. Website: http://www.merrimack.edu/academics/graduate/education/

Michigan State University, The Graduate School, College of Education, Department of Educational Administration, East Lansing, MI 48824. Offers higher, adult and lifelong education (MA, PhD); K–12 educational administration (MA, PhD, Ed S); student affairs administration (MA). *Program availability:* Part-time. *Entrance requirements:* Additional exam requirements/recommendations for international students: Required—TOEFL. Electronic applications accepted.

Montana State University, The Graduate School, College of Education, Health, and Human Development, Department of Education, Bozeman, MT 59717. Offers adult and higher education (Ed D); curriculum and instruction (M Ed, Ed D), including professional educator (M Ed); technology education (M Ed); education (M Ed), including adult and higher education, educational leadership, school counseling; educational leadership (Ed D, Ed S). *Accreditation:* TEAC. *Program availability:* Part-time, online learning. *Degree requirements:* For master's, comprehensive exam; for doctorate, comprehensive exam, thesis/dissertation. *Entrance requirements:* For master's, GRE, 3 letters of reference, essays, BA transcripts; for doctorate, GRE, MAT, 3 letters of reference, essay, BA and M Ed transcripts; for Ed S, PRAXIS. Additional exam requirements/recommendations for international students: Required—TOEFL (minimum score 550 paper-based). Electronic applications accepted. *Faculty research:* Critical literacy; standards-based education; school Improvement, organizational change, leadership in rural education, leadership in Indian education; student Learning; multicultural/culturally responsive education for social justice Native American indigenous education, community-centered education teacher preparation.

Morehead State University, Graduate Programs, College of Education, Department of Foundational and Graduate Studies in Education, Morehead, KY 40351. Offers adult and higher education (MA, Ed S); certified professional counselor (Ed S); counseling P-12 (MA); curriculum and instruction (Ed S); educational technology (MA Ed); instructional leadership (Ed S); school administration (MA); school counseling (Ed S); teacher leader business and marketing content (MA Ed); teacher leader business and marketing technology (MA Ed); teacher leader educational technology (MA Ed); teacher leader English (MA Ed); teacher leader gifted education (MA Ed); teacher leader IECE certification (MA Ed); teacher leader interdisciplinary education P-5 (MA Ed); teacher leader middle grades (MA Ed); teacher leader non IECE certification (MA Ed); teacher leader reading/writing - non-certification (MA Ed); teacher leader reading/writing certification (MA Ed); teacher leader school communication - certification (MA Ed); teacher leader school communication - non-certification (MA Ed); teacher leader social studies (MA Ed); teacher leader special education (MA Ed). *Accreditation:* NCATE. *Program availability:* Part-time, evening/weekend. *Degree requirements:* For master's, thesis optional, oral and/or written comprehensive exams; for Ed S, thesis, oral exam. *Entrance requirements:* For master's, GRE General Test, minimum overall undergraduate GPA of 2.5; for Ed S, GRE General Test, interview, master's degree, minimum GPA of 3.5, work experience. Additional exam requirements/recommendations for international students: Required—TOEFL (minimum score 500 paper-based). Electronic applications accepted. *Faculty research:* Character education, school accountability, computer applications for school administrators.

Mount Saint Vincent University, Graduate Programs, Faculty of Education, Program in Adult Education, Halifax, NS B3M 2J6, Canada. Offers M Ed, MA Ed, MA-R. *Program availability:* Part-time, evening/weekend, online learning. *Degree requirements:* For master's, thesis (for some programs), practicum. *Entrance requirements:* For master's, bachelor's degree in related field, minimum B average. Electronic applications accepted.

National Louis University, College of Arts and Sciences, Chicago, IL 60603. Offers adult education (Ed D); counseling and human services (MS); language and academic development (M Ed, Certificate); psychology (MA, PhD, Certificate); public policy (MA); written communication (MS, Certificate). *Program availability:* Part-time, evening/weekend, online learning. *Degree requirements:* For master's and Certificate, comprehensive exam (for some programs), thesis (for some programs); for doctorate, thesis/dissertation. *Entrance requirements:* For master's, MAT or GRE, 3 professional or academic references, interview, minimum GPA of 3.0; for doctorate, GRE General Test, MAT, or Watson-Glaser Critical Thinking Appraisal, three professional or academic references, statement of academic and professional goals, 3 years of experience in field, interview, master's degree, resume, writing sample; for Certificate, GRE, MAT, or Watson-Glaser Critical Thinking Appraisal, three professional or academic references, statement of academic and professional goals, interview, minimum GPA of 3.0. Additional exam requirements/recommendations for international students: Required—Department of Language Studies Assessment or TOEFL (minimum score 550 paper-based; 79 iBT). Electronic applications accepted.

North Carolina Agricultural and Technical State University, School of Graduate Studies, School of Education, Department of Human Development and Services, Greensboro, NC 27411. Offers adult education (MS); counseling (MS); school

Adult Education

administration (MS). *Accreditation:* ACA. *Program availability:* Part-time, evening/weekend. *Degree requirements:* For master's, comprehensive exam, thesis, qualifying exam. *Entrance requirements:* For master's, GRE General Test, minimum GPA of 3.0.

North Carolina State University, Graduate School, College of Education, Department of Adult and Higher Education, Program in Adult and Community College Education, Raleigh, NC 27695. Offers M Ed, MS, Ed D. *Degree requirements:* For master's, thesis (for some programs); for doctorate, thesis/dissertation. *Entrance requirements:* For master's and doctorate, GRE or MAT. Electronic applications accepted.

North Dakota State University, College of Graduate and Interdisciplinary Studies, College of Human Development and Education, School of Education, Fargo, ND 58102. Offers agricultural education (M Ed, MS), including agricultural education; counselor education (M Ed, MS, PhD), including clinical mental health counseling (M Ed, MS); counselor education and supervision (PhD); school counseling (M Ed, MS); curriculum and instruction (M Ed, MS); education (PhD); educational leadership (M Ed, MS, Ed S); family and consumer sciences education (M Ed, MS); history education (M Ed, MS); institutional analysis (Ed D); mathematics education (M Ed, MS); music education (M Ed, MS); occupational and adult education (Ed D); science education (M Ed, MS). *Accreditation:* NCATE. *Program availability:* Part-time, evening/weekend, online learning. *Degree requirements:* For master's, comprehensive exam; for doctorate, thesis/dissertation; for Ed S, thesis. *Entrance requirements:* For degree, GRE General Test, master's degree, minimum GPA of 3.25. Additional exam requirements/recommendations for international students: Required—TOEFL.

Northern Illinois University, Graduate School, College of Education, Department of Counseling, Adult and Higher Education, De Kalb, IL 60115-2854. Offers adult and higher education (MS Ed, Ed D); counseling (MS Ed, Ed D). *Accreditation:* ACA. *Program availability:* Part-time, evening/weekend. *Faculty:* 19 full-time (11 women), 2 part-time/adjunct (1 woman). *Students:* 114 full-time (80 women), 215 part-time (156 women); includes 136 minority (74 Black or African American, non-Hispanic/Latino; 2 American Indian or Alaska Native, non-Hispanic/Latino; 11 Asian, non-Hispanic/Latino; 37 Hispanic/Latino; 12 Two or more races, non-Hispanic/Latino), 8 international. Average age 36. 124 applicants, 77% accepted, 49 enrolled. In 2017, 67 master's, 16 doctorates awarded. Terminal master's awarded for partial completion of doctoral program. *Degree requirements:* For master's, comprehensive exam, thesis optional; for doctorate, thesis/dissertation, candidacy exam, dissertation defense. *Entrance requirements:* For master's, GRE General Test or MAT, minimum undergraduate GPA of 2.75, interview (for counseling); for doctorate, GRE General Test, minimum undergraduate GPA of 2.75, 3.2 graduate; interview (for counseling). Additional exam requirements/recommendations for international students: Required—TOEFL (minimum score 550 paper-based). *Application deadline:* For fall admission, 6/1 for domestic students, 5/1 for international students; for spring admission, 11/1 for domestic students, 10/1 for international students. Applications are processed on a rolling basis. Application fee: $40. Electronic applications accepted. *Financial support:* In 2017–18, 15 research assistantships with full tuition reimbursements, 7 teaching assistantships with full tuition reimbursements were awarded; fellowships with full tuition reimbursements, career-related internships or fieldwork, Federal Work-Study, scholarships/grants, tuition waivers (full), and staff assistantships also available. Support available to part-time students. Financial award applicants required to submit FAFSA. *Unit head:* Dr. Suzanne Degges-White, Interim Chair, 815-753-1448, E-mail: cahe@niu.edu. *Application contact:* Graduate School Office, 815-753-0395, E-mail: gradsch@niu.edu. Website: http://www.cedu.niu.edu/cahe/index.html

Northwestern Oklahoma State University, School of Professional Studies, Program in Adult Education Management and Administration, Alva, OK 73717-2799. Offers M Ed. *Program availability:* Part-time. *Degree requirements:* For master's, thesis optional, portfolio. *Entrance requirements:* For master's, GRE and MAT, minimum GPA of 2.75.

Northwestern State University of Louisiana, Graduate Studies and Research, College of Education and Human Development, Program in Adult and Continuing Education, Natchitoches, LA 71497. Offers MA. *Degree requirements:* For master's, comprehensive exam, thesis or alternative. *Entrance requirements:* For master's, GRE General Test, minimum undergraduate GPA of 2.5. Additional exam requirements/recommendations for international students: Required—TOEFL. Electronic applications accepted.

Oregon State University, College of Education, Program in Adult and Higher Education, Corvallis, OR 97331. Offers Ed M, Ed D, PhD. *Accreditation:* NCATE. *Program availability:* Part-time, blended/hybrid learning. *Entrance requirements:* For master's, minimum GPA of 3.0 in last 90 hours. Additional exam requirements/recommendations for international students: Required—TOEFL (minimum score 575 paper-based). *Application deadline:* For fall admission, 3/15 for domestic students. Applications are processed on a rolling basis. Application fee: $75 ($85 for international students). *Unit head:* Dr. Erich N. Pitcher, Program Lead, 541-737-3574. *Application contact:* Dr. Erich N. Pitcher, Program Lead, 541-737-3574. Website: http://education.oregonstate.edu/adult-education-masters-degree-program

Penn State Harrisburg, Graduate School, School of Behavioral Sciences and Education, Middletown, PA 17057. Offers adult education in the health and medical professions (Certificate); applied behavior analysis (MA); applied clinical psychology (MA); applied psychological research (MA); community psychology and social change (MA); English as a second language (ESL) program specialist and leadership (Certificate); health education (M Ed); lifelong learning and adult education (M Ed, D Ed); literacy education (M Ed); literacy leadership (Certificate); psychology: applications in clinical psychology (Certificate); psychology: health psychology (Certificate); teaching and curriculum (M Ed); training and development (M Ed, Certificate). *Program availability:* Part-time, evening/weekend. *Unit head:* Dr. Mukund S. Kulkarni, Chancellor, 717-948-6105, Fax: 717-948-6452. *Application contact:* Robert W. Coffman, Jr., Director of Enrollment Management, Recruitment and Admissions, 717-948-6250, Fax: 717-948-6325, E-mail: hbgadmit@psu.edu. Website: https://harrisburg.psu.edu/behavioral-sciences-and-education/

Penn State University Park, Graduate School, College of Education, Department of Learning and Performance Systems, University Park, PA 16802. Offers learning, design, and technology (M Ed, MS, PhD, Certificate); lifelong learning and adult education (M Ed, D Ed, PhD, Certificate); workforce education and development (M Ed, MS, PhD). *Unit head:* Dr. David H. Monk, Dean, 814-865-2523, Fax: 814-865-0555. *Application contact:* Lori Hawn, Director, Graduate Student Services, 814-865-1795, Fax: 814-863-4627, E-mail: l-gswww@lists.psu.edu. Website: http://ed.psu.edu/lps/dept-lps

Plymouth State University, College of Graduate Studies, Graduate Studies in Education, Program in Learning, Leadership and Community, Plymouth, NH 03264-1595. Offers Ed D. *Degree requirements:* For doctorate, thesis/dissertation.

Point Park University, School of Arts and Sciences, Department of Education, Pittsburgh, PA 15222-1984. Offers adult learning and training (MA); athletic coaching (M Ed); curriculum and instruction (MA); educational administration (MA); leadership and administration (Ed D); secondary education (M Ed); special education grades 7-12 (M Ed); special education PreK-grade 8 (M Ed). *Program availability:* Part-time, evening/weekend, 100% online, blended/hybrid learning. *Degree requirements:* For master's,

comprehensive exam (for some programs), thesis or alternative. *Entrance requirements:* For master's, minimum GPA of 3.0, resume, 2 letters of recommendation. Additional exam requirements/recommendations for international students: Required—TOEFL. Electronic applications accepted.

Regent University, Graduate School, School of Education, Virginia Beach, VA 23464-9800. Offers education (M Ed, Ed D, PhD), including adult education (Ed D, PhD, Ed S), advanced educational leadership (Ed D, PhD, Ed S), character education (Ed D, PhD, Ed S), Christian education leadership (Ed D, PhD, Ed S), Christian school administration (M Ed), curriculum and instruction (Ed D, PhD, Ed S), curriculum and instruction - adult education (M Ed), curriculum and instruction - Christian school (M Ed), curriculum and instruction - gifted and talented (M Ed), curriculum and instruction - STEM education (M Ed), curriculum and instruction - teacher leader (M Ed), discipleship for ministry (M Ed), educational leadership (M Ed), educational psychology (Ed D, PhD, Ed S), educational technology and online learning (Ed D, PhD, Ed S), elementary education (M Ed), exceptional education executive leadership (Ed D, PhD, Ed S), higher education (Ed D, PhD, Ed S), higher education leadership and management (Ed D, PhD, Ed S), instructional design and technology (M Ed), K-12 school leadership (Ed D, PhD, Ed S), K-12 special education (M Ed), leadership in mathematics education (M Ed), reading specialist (M Ed), special education (Ed D, PhD, Ed S), student affairs (M Ed), TESOL - adult education (M Ed), TESOL - K-12 (M Ed); educational specialist (Ed S), including adult education (Ed D, PhD, Ed S), advanced educational leadership (Ed D, PhD, Ed S), character education (Ed D, PhD, Ed S), Christian education leadership (Ed D, PhD, Ed S), curriculum and instruction (Ed D, PhD, Ed S), educational psychology (Ed D, PhD, Ed S), educational technology and online learning (Ed D, PhD, Ed S), exceptional education executive leadership (Ed D, PhD, Ed S), higher education (Ed D, PhD, Ed S), higher education leadership and management (Ed D, PhD, Ed S), K-12 school leadership (Ed D, PhD, Ed S), special education (Ed D, PhD, Ed S). *Accreditation:* TEAC. *Program availability:* Part-time, evening/weekend, 100% online, blended/hybrid learning. *Faculty:* 22 full-time (10 women), 44 part-time/adjunct (32 women). *Students:* 80 full-time (59 women), 945 part-time (750 women); includes 439 minority (352 Black or African American, non-Hispanic/Latino; 4 American Indian or Alaska Native, non-Hispanic/Latino; 14 Asian, non-Hispanic/Latino; 43 Hispanic/Latino; 19 Two or more races, non-Hispanic/Latino), 12 international. Average age 40. 1,125 applicants, 49% accepted, 436 enrolled. In 2017, 316 master's, 24 doctorates awarded. *Degree requirements:* For master's, thesis or alternative; for doctorate, comprehensive exam, thesis/dissertation. *Entrance requirements:* For master's, Virginia Communication and Literacy Assessment (VCLA), PRAXIS, college transcripts, writing sample, interview; for doctorate, GRE, writing sample, resume, transcripts, interview. Additional exam requirements/recommendations for international students: Required—TOEFL (minimum score 577 paper-based). *Application deadline:* For fall admission, 4/1 priority date for domestic students; for spring admission, 10/15 priority date for domestic students. Applications are processed on a rolling basis. Application fee: $50. Electronic applications accepted. *Expenses:* Contact institution. *Financial support:* In 2017–18, 669 students received support, including 1 fellowship (averaging $10,000 per year); career-related internships or fieldwork, scholarships/grants, and unspecified assistantships also available. Support available to part-time students. *Faculty research:* Christian school administration, curriculum and instruction, educational technology and online learning, higher education, special education. *Unit head:* Dr. Donald Finn, Dean, 757-352-4278, Fax: 757-352-4318, E-mail: dfinn@regent.edu. *Application contact:* Heidi Cece, Assistant Vice President of Enrollment Management, 800-373-5504, Fax: 757-352-4381, E-mail: admissions@regent.edu. Website: https://www.regent.edu/school-of-education/

St. Francis Xavier University, Graduate Studies, Department of Adult Education, Antigonish, NS B2G 2W5, Canada. Offers adult education (M Ad Ed); community development (M Ad Ed). *Program availability:* Part-time, online learning. *Degree requirements:* For master's, thesis. *Entrance requirements:* For master's, minimum undergraduate B average, 2 years of work experience in field. Additional exam requirements/recommendations for international students: Required—TOEFL (minimum score 580 paper-based). *Faculty research:* Adult learning and development, religious education, women's issues, literacy, action research.

Saint Joseph's College of Maine, Master of Science in Education Program, Standish, ME 04084. Offers adult education and training (MS Ed); Catholic school leadership (MS Ed); health care educator (MS Ed); school educator (MS Ed). Program available by correspondence. *Program availability:* Part-time, online learning. Electronic applications accepted.

San Francisco State University, Division of Graduate Studies, College of Education, Department of Equity, Leadership Studies, and Instructional Technologies, Program in Adult Education, San Francisco, CA 94132-1722. Offers MA. *Accreditation:* NCATE. *Unit head:* Dr. Doris Flowers, Chair, 415-338-2614, Fax: 415-338-0568, E-mail: dflowers@sfsu.edu. *Application contact:* Dr. Ming Yeh Lee, Graduate Coordinator, 415-338-1061, Fax: 415-338-0568, E-mail: mylee@sfsu.edu. Website: http://elsit.sfsu.edu/

Seattle University, College of Education, Program in Adult Education and Training, Seattle, WA 98122-1090. Offers M Ed, MA, Certificate. *Accreditation:* NCATE. *Program availability:* Part-time, evening/weekend. *Faculty:* 1 (woman) full-time, 2 part-time/adjunct (1 woman). *Students:* 20 part-time (15 women); includes 8 minority (1 Black or African American, non-Hispanic/Latino; 1 American Indian or Alaska Native, non-Hispanic/Latino; 3 Asian, non-Hispanic/Latino; 3 Hispanic/Latino). Average age 36. 10 applicants, 70% accepted, 6 enrolled. In 2017, 10 master's awarded. *Degree requirements:* For master's, comprehensive exam. *Entrance requirements:* For master's, GRE, MAT, or minimum GPA of 3.0; 1 year of related experience. Additional exam requirements/recommendations for international students: Required—TOEFL. *Application deadline:* For fall admission, 8/20 priority date for domestic students; for winter admission, 11/20 for domestic students; for spring admission, 2/20 for domestic students. Applications are processed on a rolling basis. Application fee: $55. *Expenses: Tuition:* Full-time $12,960. *Required fees:* $570. Tuition and fees vary according to program. *Financial support:* Career-related internships or fieldwork and Federal Work-Study available. Support available to part-time students. Financial award applicants required to submit FAFSA. *Unit head:* Dr. Carol Weaver, Director, 206-296-5908, E-mail: cweaver@seattleu.edu. *Application contact:* Janet Shandley, Associate Dean of Graduate Admissions, 206-296-5900, Fax: 206-298-5656, E-mail: grad_admissions@seattleu.edu. Website: https://www.seattleu.edu/education/adulted/

Southern Arkansas University–Magnolia, School of Graduate Studies, Magnolia, AR 71753. Offers agriculture (MS); business administration (MBA), including agribusiness, social entrepreneurship, supply chain management; clinical and mental health counseling (MS); computer and information sciences (MS), including cyber security and privacy, data science, information technology; gifted and talented (M Ed), including curriculum and instruction, educational administration and supervision, gifted and talented P-8/7-12, instructional specialist P-4; higher, adult and lifelong education (M Ed); kinesiology (M Ed), including coaching; library media and information specialist (M Ed); public administration (MPA); school counseling K-12 (M Ed); student affairs and college counseling (M Ed); teaching (MAT). *Accreditation:* NCATE. *Program availability:*

Part-time, 100% online, blended/hybrid learning. *Faculty:* 36 full-time (20 women), 31 part-time/adjunct (12 women). *Students:* 242 full-time (89 women), 889 part-time (459 women); includes 167 minority (143 Black or African American, non-Hispanic/Latino; 7 American Indian or Alaska Native, non-Hispanic/Latino; 7 Asian, non-Hispanic/Latino; 3 Hispanic/Latino; 7 Two or more races, non-Hispanic/Latino), 562 international. Average age 28. 400 applicants, 100% accepted, 239 enrolled. In 2017, 875 master's awarded. *Degree requirements:* For master's, comprehensive exam (for some programs), thesis optional. *Entrance requirements:* For master's, GRE, MAT or GMAT, minimum GPA of 2.5. Additional exam requirements/recommendations for international students: Required—TOEFL (minimum score 550 paper-based), IELTS (minimum score 6). *Application deadline:* For fall admission, 7/20 for domestic students, 7/10 for international students; for spring admission, 12/1 for domestic students, 11/15 for international students; for summer admission, 4/1 for domestic students, 5/1 for international students. Applications are processed on a rolling basis. Application fee: $25 ($50 for international students). Electronic applications accepted. *Expenses:* Tuition, state resident: full-time $6038. Tuition, nonresident: full-time $8558. *Required fees:* $804. One-time fee: $110 full-time. Tuition and fees vary according to course load. *Financial support:* Career-related internships or fieldwork, Federal Work-Study, scholarships/grants, tuition waivers (full), and unspecified assistantships available. Financial award applicants required to submit FAFSA. *Faculty research:* Alternative certification for teachers, supervision of instruction, instructional leadership, counseling. *Unit head:* Dr. Kim Bloss, Dean, School of Graduate Studies, 870-235-4150, Fax: 870-235-5227, E-mail: kkbloss@saumag.edu. *Application contact:* Shrijana Malakar, Admissions Specialist, 870-235-4150, Fax: 870-235-5227, E-mail: smalakar@saumag.edu.
Website: http://www.saumag.edu/graduate

State University of New York Empire State College, School for Graduate Studies, Programs in Education, Saratoga Springs, NY 12866-4391. Offers adult learning (MA); learning and emerging technologies (MA); teaching (MAT); teaching and learning (M Ed). *Program availability:* Online learning.

Teachers College, Columbia University, Department of Organization and Leadership, New York, NY 10027-6696. Offers adult education guided intensive study (Ed D); adult learning and leadership (Ed M, MA, Ed D); educational leadership (Ed D); higher and postsecondary education (MA, Ed D); leadership, policy and politics (Ed D); nurse executive (MA, Ed D), including administration studies (MA), professorial studies (MA); private school leadership (Ed M, MA); public school building leadership (Ed M, MA); social and organizational psychology (MA); urban education leaders (Ed D); MA/MBA. *Program availability:* Part-time, evening/weekend. *Students:* 342 full-time (244 women), 378 part-time (256 women); includes 288 minority (106 Black or African American, non-Hispanic/Latino; 69 Asian, non-Hispanic/Latino; 92 Hispanic/Latino; 21 Two or more races, non-Hispanic/Latino), 86 international. Average age 33. 1,063 applicants, 59% accepted, 405 enrolled. *Degree requirements:* For doctorate, thesis/dissertation. *Unit head:* Prof. Bill Baldwin, Chair, E-mail: wjb12@tc.columbia.edu. *Application contact:* David Estrella, Director of Admission, 212-678-3305, E-mail: estrella@tc.columbia.edu.

Texas A&M University–Kingsville, College of Graduate Studies, College of Education and Human Performance, Department of Educational Leadership and Counseling, Program in Adult Education, Kingsville, TX 78363. Offers M Ed. Program offered jointly with Texas A&M University. *Program availability:* Part-time, evening/weekend. *Degree requirements:* For master's, variable foreign language requirement, comprehensive exam, thesis (for some programs). *Entrance requirements:* For master's, GRE, MAT, GMAT. Additional exam requirements/recommendations for international students: Required—TOEFL (minimum score 550 paper-based; 79 iBT). Electronic applications accepted. *Faculty research:* Continuing education efforts in south Texas, adult education methodologies.

Texas A&M University–Texarkana, Graduate Studies and Research, College of Education and Liberal Arts, Texarkana, TX 75503. Offers adult education (MS); curriculum and instruction (M Ed); education (MS); educational administration (M Ed); English (MA); instructional technology (MS); interdisciplinary studies (MA, MS); special education (MS). *Program availability:* Part-time, evening/weekend. *Degree requirements:* For master's, comprehensive exam (for some programs), thesis optional. *Entrance requirements:* For master's, minimum GPA of 2.5 on last 60 hours of bachelor's degree. Additional exam requirements/recommendations for international students: Required—TOEFL. Electronic applications accepted.

Texas State University, The Graduate College, College of Education, Program in Adult Education, San Marcos, TX 78666. Offers MA. *Program availability:* Faculty: 5 full-time (4 women), 4 part-time/adjunct (all women). *Students:* 3 full-time (0 women), 16 part-time (14 women); includes 13 minority (3 Black or African American, non-Hispanic/Latino; 2 Asian, non-Hispanic/Latino; 8 Hispanic/Latino). Average age 41. 13 applicants, 69% accepted, 7 enrolled. In 2017, 7 master's awarded. *Degree requirements:* For master's, comprehensive exam, thesis optional, internship practicum. *Entrance requirements:* For master's, baccalaureate degree from regionally-accredited university; minimum GPA of 2.75 on last 60 undergraduate semester hours of letter-grade work earned at four-year college or university before receipt of bachelor's degree (plus any previously completed graduate work); 3 letters of recommendation; writing sample addressing current adult education issue. Additional exam requirements/recommendations for international students: Required—TOEFL (minimum score 78 iBT), IELTS (minimum score 6.5). *Application deadline:* For fall admission, 2/15 priority date for domestic and international students; for spring admission, 10/15 for domestic students, 10/1 for international students; for summer admission, 4/15 for domestic and international students. Applications are processed on a rolling basis. Application fee: $40 ($90 for international students). Electronic applications accepted. *Expenses:* Tuition, state resident: full-time $7868; part-time $3934 per semester. Tuition, nonresident: full-time $17,828; part-time $8914 per semester. *Required fees:* $2092; $1435 per semester. Tuition and fees vary according to course load. *Financial support:* In 2017–18, 8 students received support. Research assistantships, teaching assistantships, scholarships/grants, and unspecified assistantships available. Financial award application deadline: 3/1; financial award applicants required to submit FAFSA. *Unit head:* Dr. Clarena Larrotta, Graduate Advisor, 512-245-2531, E-mail: cl24@txstate.edu. *Application contact:* Dr. Andrea Golato, Dean of Graduate School, 512-245-2581, Fax: 512-245-8365, E-mail: gradcollege@txstate.edu.
Website: http://www.gradcollege.txstate.edu/programs/adult-ed.html

Texas State University, The Graduate College, College of Education, Program in Adult, Professional and Community Education, San Marcos, TX 78666. Offers PhD. *Program availability:* Part-time. *Faculty:* 5 full-time (4 women), 4 part-time/adjunct (all women). *Students:* 24 full-time (19 women), 38 part-time (26 women); includes 40 minority (16 Black or African American, non-Hispanic/Latino; 2 Asian, non-Hispanic/Latino; 21 Hispanic/Latino; 1 Two or more races, non-Hispanic/Latino), 2 international. Average age 40. 49 applicants, 39% accepted, 9 enrolled. In 2017, 8 doctorates awarded. *Degree requirements:* For doctorate, comprehensive exam, thesis/dissertation. *Entrance requirements:* For doctorate, baccalaureate and master's degrees from regionally-accredited institution with minimum GPA of 3.5 in all related graduate course work; 3 complete recommendation forms addressing professional and academic background; statement of purpose including rationale for doctoral degree; interview with

program faculty. Additional exam requirements/recommendations for international students: Required—TOEFL (minimum score 550 paper-based; 78 iBT), IELTS (minimum score 6.5). *Application deadline:* For fall admission, 2/1 for domestic and international students. Applications are processed on a rolling basis. Application fee: $40 ($90 for international students). Electronic applications accepted. *Expenses:* Tuition, state resident: full-time $7868; part-time $3934 per semester. Tuition, nonresident: full-time $17,828; part-time $8914 per semester. *Required fees:* $2092; $1435 per semester. Tuition and fees vary according to course load. *Financial support:* In 2017–18, 39 students received support, including 10 research assistantships (averaging $23,651 per year); teaching assistantships, career-related internships or fieldwork, Federal Work-Study, institutionally sponsored loans, and scholarships/grants also available. Support available to part-time students. Financial award application deadline: 3/1; financial award applicants required to submit FAFSA. *Unit head:* Dr. Joellen Coryell, PhD Program Director, 512-245-2531, Fax: 512-245-8872, E-mail: jc59@txstate.edu. *Application contact:* Dr. Andrea Golato, Dean of Graduate School, 512-245-2531, Fax: 512-245-8365, E-mail: gradcollege@txstate.edu.
Website: http://www.gradcollege.txstate.edu/programs/apce-phd.html

Trident University International, College of Education, Program in Education, Cypress, CA 90630. Offers adult education (MA Ed); aviation education (MA Ed); children's literacy development (MA Ed); e-learning (MA Ed); early childhood education (MA Ed); enrollment management (MA Ed); higher education (MA Ed); teaching and instruction (MA Ed); training and development (MA Ed). *Program availability:* Part-time, evening/weekend, online learning. *Degree requirements:* For master's, capstone project with integrative paper. *Entrance requirements:* For master's, minimum GPA of 2.5 (students with GPA 3.0 or greater may transfer up to 30% of graduate level credits). Additional exam requirements/recommendations for international students: Required—TOEFL (minimum score 525 paper-based). Electronic applications accepted.

Troy University, Graduate School, College of Education, Program in Adult Education, Troy, AL 36082. Offers MS. *Program availability:* Part-time, evening/weekend. *Faculty:* 7 full-time (4 women), 1 (woman) part-time/adjunct. *Students:* 12 full-time (9 women), 75 part-time (46 women); includes 35 minority (33 Black or African American, non-Hispanic/Latino; 1 American Indian or Alaska Native, non-Hispanic/Latino; 1 Two or more races, non-Hispanic/Latino). Average age 39. 38 applicants, 92% accepted, 17 enrolled. In 2017, 42 master's awarded. *Degree requirements:* For master's, comprehensive exam, capstone course or thesis. *Entrance requirements:* For master's, GRE (minimum score of 850 on old exam or 290 on new exam), GMAT (minimum score of 380), or MAT (minimum score of 385), bachelor's degree; minimum undergraduate GPA of 2.5 or 3.0 on last 30 semester hours, letter of recommendation. Additional exam requirements/recommendations for international students: Required—TOEFL (minimum score 523 paper-based; 70 iBT), IELTS (minimum score 6). *Application deadline:* Applications are processed on a rolling basis. Application fee: $50. Electronic applications accepted. *Expenses:* Tuition, state resident: part-time $417 per credit hour. Tuition, nonresident: part-time $834 per credit hour. *Required fees:* $42 per credit hour. $50 per semester. Tuition and fees vary according to campus/location. *Financial support:* Fellowships, career-related internships or fieldwork, and scholarships/grants available. Support available to part-time students. Financial award applicants required to submit FAFSA. *Unit head:* Dr. Jan Oliver, Chair, Leadership Development and Professional Studies, 334-670-3546, Fax: 670-808-6666, E-mail: oliverj@troy.edu. *Application contact:* Jessica A. Kimbro, Director of Graduate Admissions, 334-670-3178, E-mail: jacord@troy.edu.

Troy University, Graduate School, College of Education, Program in Postsecondary Education, Troy, AL 36082. Offers MS Ed. *Accreditation:* NCATE. *Program availability:* Part-time, evening/weekend. *Faculty:* 8 full-time (7 women). *Students:* 1 (woman) full-time; minority (Black or African American, non-Hispanic/Latino). Average age 53. In 2017, 15 master's awarded. *Degree requirements:* For master's, comprehensive exam (for some programs), thesis (for some programs), thesis or comprehensive exam. *Entrance requirements:* For master's, GRE (minimum score of 850 on old exam or 290 on new exam), GMAT (minimum score of 380), or MAT (minimum score of 385), bachelor's degree; minimum undergraduate GPA of 2.5 or 3.0 on last 30 semester hours, letter of recommendation. Additional exam requirements/recommendations for international students: Required—TOEFL (minimum score 523 paper-based; 70 iBT), IELTS (minimum score 6). *Application deadline:* Applications are processed on a rolling basis. Application fee: $50. Electronic applications accepted. *Expenses:* Tuition, state resident: part-time $417 per credit hour. Tuition, nonresident: part-time $834 per credit hour. *Required fees:* $42 per credit hour. $50 per semester. Tuition and fees vary according to campus/location. *Financial support:* Fellowships, career-related internships or fieldwork, and scholarships/grants available. Support available to part-time students. Financial award applicants required to submit FAFSA. *Unit head:* Dr. Ruth Busby, Chair, Teacher Education, 334-670-3546, Fax: 334-808-6666, E-mail: rsbusby@troy.edu. *Application contact:* Jessica A. Kimbro, Director of Graduate Admissions, 334-670-3178, E-mail: jacord@troy.edu.

Universidad del Este, Graduate School, Carolina, PR 00984. Offers accounting (MBA); adult education (M Ed); agribusiness (MBA); criminal justice and criminology (MA); curriculum and instruction - early education (M Ed); curriculum and instruction - elementary (M Ed); curriculum and instruction - English (M Ed); curriculum and instruction - Spanish (M Ed); human resources (MBA); information security management (MBA); information technology and Web business development (MBA); management (MBA); public policy (MPA); social work (MA), including clinical social work; special education (M Ed); strategic leadership (MBA).

Universidad Metropolitana, School of Education, Program in Teaching of Physical Education, San Juan, PR 00928-1150. Offers teaching of adult physical education (M Ed); teaching of elementary physical education (M Ed); teaching of secondary physical education (M Ed). *Degree requirements:* For master's, thesis or alternative. *Entrance requirements:* For master's, EXADEP, interview. Electronic applications accepted.

University of Alberta, Faculty of Graduate Studies and Research, Department of Educational Policy Studies, Edmonton, AB T6G 2E1, Canada. Offers adult education (M Ed, Ed D, PhD); educational administration and leadership (M Ed, Ed D, PhD, Postgraduate Diploma); First Nations education (M Ed, Ed D, PhD); theoretical, cultural and international studies in education (M Ed, Ed D, PhD). *Degree requirements:* For master's, thesis (for some programs); for doctorate, thesis/dissertation. *Entrance requirements:* For master's, minimum GPA of 6.5 on a 9.0 scale; for doctorate, minimum GPA of 7.5 on a 9.0 scale. Additional exam requirements/recommendations for international students: Required—TOEFL (minimum score 580 paper-based). Electronic applications accepted.

University of Arkansas, Graduate School, College of Education and Health Professions, Department of Rehabilitation, Human Resources and Communication Disorders, Adult and Lifelong Learning Program, Fayetteville, AR 72701. Offers M Ed, Ed D. *Program availability:* Part-time, evening/weekend, online learning. In 2017, 5 master's, 2 doctorates awarded. *Application deadline:* For fall admission, 8/1 for domestic students, 4/1 for international students; for spring admission, 12/1 for domestic students, 10/1 for international students; for summer admission, 4/15 for domestic students, 3/1 for international students. Applications are processed on a rolling basis.

Adult Education

Application fee: $60. Electronic applications accepted. *Expenses:* Tuition, state resident: full-time $3782. Tuition, nonresident: full-time $10,238. *Financial support:* Fellowships, research assistantships, teaching assistantships, career-related internships or fieldwork, and Federal Work-Study available. Support available to part-time students. Financial award application deadline: 4/1; financial award applicants required to submit FAFSA. *Unit head:* Dr. Kenda Grover, Program Coordinator, 479-575-2675, Fax: 479-575-3319, E-mail: kgrover@uark.edu. *Application contact:* Dr. Kenda Grover, Graduate Coordinator, 479-575-4758, E-mail: kgrover@uark.edu. Website: http://rhrc.uark.edu

University of Arkansas at Little Rock, Graduate School, College of Education and Health Professions, Department of Counseling, Adult and Rehabilitation Education, Program in Adult Education, Little Rock, AR 72204-1099. Offers M Ed. *Accreditation:* NCATE. *Program availability:* Part-time, online learning. *Degree requirements:* For master's, comprehensive exam. *Entrance requirements:* For master's, minimum GPA of 2.75. *Faculty research:* Adult literacy, volunteer training, in-services education.

The University of British Columbia, Faculty of Education, Department of Educational Studies, Vancouver, BC V6T 1Z1, Canada. Offers adult learning and education (M Ed); adult learning and global change (M Ed); curriculum and leadership (M Ed); educational administration and leadership (M Ed); educational leadership and policy (Ed D); educational studies (M Ed, MA, PhD); higher education (M Ed); society, culture and politics in education (M Ed). *Program availability:* Part-time, evening/weekend. Terminal master's awarded for partial completion of doctoral program. *Degree requirements:* For master's, thesis; for doctorate, comprehensive exam, thesis/dissertation. *Entrance requirements:* For master's, minimum B+ average, 4-year undergraduate degree, field-related experience; for doctorate, minimum B+ average, 4-year undergraduate degree, master's degree, field-related experience. Additional exam requirements/recommendations for international students: Required—TOEFL (minimum score 600 paper-based; 100 iBT) or IELTS (minimum score 6.5). Electronic applications accepted. *Expenses:* Contact institution. *Faculty research:* Educational leadership educational administration adult education politics in education, global change and adult learning.

University of Calgary, Faculty of Graduate Studies, Werklund School of Education, Graduate Division of Educational Research, Calgary, AB T2N 1N4, Canada. Offers adult learning (M Ed, MA, Ed D, PhD); curriculum and learning (M Ed, MA, Ed D, PhD); educational leadership (M Ed, MA, Ed D, PhD); languages and diversity (M Ed, MA, Ed D, PhD); learning sciences (M Ed, MA, Ed D, PhD). Ed D in educational leadership offered via distance delivery. *Program availability:* Part-time, evening/weekend, online learning. *Degree requirements:* For master's, thesis (for some programs); for doctorate, thesis/dissertation, candidacy exam. *Entrance requirements:* For master's, minimum GPA of 3.0, 3 letters of reference; for doctorate, minimum GPA of 3.5, 3 letters of reference. Additional exam requirements/recommendations for international students: Required—TOEFL, IELTS. Electronic applications accepted. *Faculty research:* Curriculum, leadership, technology, contexts, gifted, second language teaching, work place and adult learning.

University of Central Arkansas, Graduate School, College of Education, Department of Leadership Studies, Conway, AR 72035-0001. Offers college student personnel (MS); district-level administration (PMC); educational leadership - district level (Ed S); instructional technology (MS); library media and information technology (MS); school counseling (MS); school leadership (MS); school-based leadership adult education program administration (PMC); school-based leadership building administration (PMC); school-based leadership curriculum administration (PMC); school-based leadership gifted and talented program administration (PMC); school-based leadership special education program administration (PMC). *Accreditation:* NCATE. *Program availability:* Part-time, evening/weekend, online learning. *Degree requirements:* For master's and other advanced degree, comprehensive exam. *Entrance requirements:* For master's, GRE. Additional exam requirements/recommendations for international students: Required—TOEFL (minimum score 80 iBT). Electronic applications accepted. *Expenses:* Contact institution.

University of Central Oklahoma, The Jackson College of Graduate Studies, College of Education and Professional Studies, Department of Adult Education and Safety Science, Edmond, OK 73034-5209. Offers adult and higher education (M Ed), including interdisciplinary studies, student personnel, training. *Program availability:* Part-time. *Faculty:* 9 full-time (4 women), 8 part-time/adjunct (4 women). *Students:* 25 full-time (14 women), 85 part-time (61 women); includes 43 minority (25 Black or African American, non-Hispanic/Latino; 2 American Indian or Alaska Native, non-Hispanic/Latino; 1 Asian, non-Hispanic/Latino; 10 Hispanic/Latino; 5 Two or more races, non-Hispanic/Latino), 4 international. Average age 34. 49 applicants, 78% accepted, 23 enrolled. In 2017, 40 master's awarded. *Degree requirements:* For master's, comprehensive exam (for some programs), thesis (for some programs). *Entrance requirements:* Additional exam requirements/recommendations for international students: Required—TOEFL (minimum score 550 paper-based; 79 iBT), IELTS (minimum score 6.5). *Application deadline:* For fall admission, 7/15 for international students; for spring admission, 11/15 for international students. Applications are processed on a rolling basis. Application fee: $60. Electronic applications accepted. *Expenses:* Tuition, state resident: full-time $5375; part-time $268.75 per credit hour. Tuition, nonresident: full-time $13,295; part-time $664.75 per credit hour. *Required fees:* $626; $31.30 per credit hour. One-time fee: $50. Tuition and fees vary according to program. *Financial support:* In 2017–18, 38 students received support, including 1 research assistantship with partial tuition reimbursement available (averaging $2,958 per year); teaching assistantships, career-related internships or fieldwork, scholarships/grants, tuition waivers (partial), and unspecified assistantships also available. Financial award application deadline: 3/31; financial award applicants required to submit FAFSA. *Unit head:* Dr. Candy Sebert, Chair, 405-974-5741, Fax: 405-974-3809. *Application contact:* Carlie Wellington, Assistant Director, CEPS Graduate Enrollment, 405-974-5105, Fax: 405-974-3851, E-mail: gradcoll@uco.edu. Website: http://sites.uco.edu/ceps/dept/Professional-Studies-Programs/aess/index.asp

University of Colorado Denver, School of Education and Human Development, Information and Learning Technologies Program, Denver, CO 80217. Offers e-learning design and implementation (MA); instructional design and adult learning (MA); K-12 teaching (MA). *Program availability:* Part-time, evening/weekend, online learning. *Degree requirements:* For master's, comprehensive exam (for some programs), comprehensive exam or online portfolio; 30 credit hours. *Entrance requirements:* For master's, GRE or MAT (if GPA is below 2.75), resume, statement of intent, three letters of recommendation, transcripts from all colleges/universities previously attended. Additional exam requirements/recommendations for international students: Required—TOEFL (minimum score 537 paper-based; 75 iBT); Recommended—IELTS (minimum score 6.5). Electronic applications accepted. *Expenses:* Contact institution. *Faculty research:* Technology for educational management, instructional design foundations, e-learning, educational design.

University of Connecticut, Graduate School, Neag School of Education, Department of Educational Leadership, Field of Adult Learning, Storrs, CT 06269. Offers MA, Certificate. *Accreditation:* NCATE. Terminal master's awarded for partial completion of doctoral program. *Degree requirements:* For master's, comprehensive exam, thesis or alternative. *Entrance requirements:* For master's, GRE General Test. Additional exam

requirements/recommendations for international students: Required—TOEFL (minimum score 550 paper-based). Electronic applications accepted.

University of Georgia, College of Education, Department of Lifelong Education, Administration and Policy, Athens, GA 30602. Offers adult education (Ed D, Ed S); lifelong education, administration and policy (PhD). *Accreditation:* NCATE. *Entrance requirements:* For doctorate, GRE General Test; for Ed S, GRE General Test or MAT. Electronic applications accepted.

University of Houston–Victoria, School of Education, Health Professions and Human Development, Victoria, TX 77901-4450. Offers administration and supervision (M Ed); adult and higher education (M Ed); counselor education (M Ed); curriculum and instruction (M Ed); dyslexia education (Certificate); educational technology (M Ed); special education (M Ed). *Program availability:* Part-time, evening/weekend, online learning. *Degree requirements:* For master's, comprehensive exam, project or thesis. *Entrance requirements:* For master's, GRE General Test. Additional exam requirements/recommendations for international students: Required—TOEFL. Electronic applications accepted. *Faculty research:* Reading and language arts education, evaluation and diagnosis of special children's abilities.

University of Manitoba, Faculty of Graduate Studies, Faculty of Education, Department of Educational Administration, Foundations and Psychology, Winnipeg, MB R3T 2N2, Canada. Offers adult and post-secondary education (M Ed); educational administration (M Ed); guidance and counseling (M Ed); inclusive special education (M Ed); social foundations of education (M Ed). *Degree requirements:* For master's, thesis or alternative.

University of Memphis, Graduate School, College of Education, Department of Leadership, Memphis, TN 38152. Offers adult education (Ed D); community college teaching and leadership (Graduate Certificate); community education (Ed D); educational leadership (Ed D); higher education (Ed D); leadership (MS); policy studies (Ed D); school administration and supervision (MS); student personnel (MS). *Accreditation:* NCATE. *Program availability:* Part-time, evening/weekend, online learning. *Faculty:* 9 full-time (5 women), 6 part-time/adjunct (2 women). *Students:* 13 full-time (9 women), 154 part-time (96 women). Average age 35. 54 applicants, 93% accepted, 44 enrolled. In 2017, 19 master's, 26 doctorates, 4 other advanced degrees awarded. *Degree requirements:* For master's, comprehensive exam, thesis optional; for doctorate, comprehensive exam, thesis/dissertation. *Entrance requirements:* For master's, GRE, resume, letters of reference, statement of professional goals, current teacher certification, sample work, interview; for doctorate, GRE, resume, letters of reference, statement of professional goals, interview. Additional exam requirements/recommendations for international students: Required—TOEFL (minimum score 550 paper-based; 79 iBT). *Application deadline:* For fall admission, 6/15 for domestic students; for spring admission, 9/15 for domestic students; for summer admission, 2/15 for domestic students. Application fee: $35 ($60 for international students). Electronic applications accepted. *Expenses:* Contact institution. *Financial support:* In 2017–18, 70 students received support, including 4 research assistantships with full tuition reimbursements available (averaging $14,700 per year); teaching assistantships, Federal Work-Study, scholarships/grants, and unspecified assistantships also available. Financial award application deadline: 2/1; financial award applicants required to submit FAFSA. *Faculty research:* School improvement, social justice, online learning, adult learning, diversity. *Unit head:* Dr. Reginald Green, Interim Chair, 901-678-3445, E-mail: rlgreen1@memphis.edu. Website: http://www.memphis.edu/lead

University of Minnesota, Twin Cities Campus, Graduate School, College of Education and Human Development, Department of Organizational Leadership, Policy and Development, Minneapolis, MN 55455-0213. Offers adult literacy (Certificate); comparative and international development education (MA, PhD); disability policy and services (Certificate); education policy and leadership (M Ed, MA, Ed D, PhD), including educational policy and leadership (MA, Ed D, PhD), leadership in education (M Ed); evaluation studies (MA, PhD); higher education (MA, Ed D, PhD), including higher education (MA, PhD), multicultural college teaching and learning (MA); human resource development (M Ed, MA, Ed D, PhD, Certificate); PK-12 administrative licensure (Certificate); private college leadership (Certificate); professional development (Certificate); program evaluation (Certificate); technical education (Certificate); undergraduate multicultural teaching and learning (Certificate). *Faculty:* 32 full-time (14 women). *Students:* 289 full-time (210 women), 251 part-time (157 women); includes 114 minority (41 Black or African American, non-Hispanic/Latino; 4 American Indian or Alaska Native, non-Hispanic/Latino; 27 Asian, non-Hispanic/Latino; 22 Hispanic/Latino; 1 Native Hawaiian or other Pacific Islander, non-Hispanic/Latino; 19 Two or more races, non-Hispanic/Latino), 77 international. Average age 36. 419 applicants, 58% accepted, 204 enrolled. In 2017, 79 master's, 36 doctorates, 49 other advanced degrees awarded. Application fee: $75 ($95 for international students). *Financial support:* In 2017–18, 2 fellowships, 30 research assistantships with full tuition reimbursements (averaging $9,944 per year), 27 teaching assistantships with full tuition reimbursements (averaging $10,036 per year) were awarded; scholarships/grants also available. *Faculty research:* Organizational issues in schools, universities, and other organizations; international education and development; program evaluation and research on applied evaluation methods; international human resource development and change; gender and race/ethnicity in relation to learning and leadership. *Total annual research expenditures:* $930,589. *Unit head:* Dr. Heidi Barajas, Chair, 612-625-4823, Fax: 612-624-3377, E-mail: hbarajas@umn.edu. *Application contact:* Dr. Jeremy J. Hernandez, Coordinator of Graduate Studies, 612-626-9377, E-mail: herna220@umn.edu. Website: http://www.cehd.umn.edu/olpd/

University of Missouri, Office of Research and Graduate Studies, College of Education, Department of Educational Leadership and Policy Analysis, Columbia, MO 65211. Offers education administration (M Ed, MA, Ed D, PhD, Ed S); higher and adult education (M Ed, MA, Ed D, PhD, Ed S). *Program availability:* Part-time. *Degree requirements:* For doctorate, variable foreign language requirement, comprehensive exam (for some programs), thesis/dissertation. *Entrance requirements:* For master's, doctorate, and Ed S, minimum GPA of 3.0. Additional exam requirements/recommendations for international students: Required—TOEFL (minimum score 500 paper-based; 61 iBT), IELTS (minimum score 5.5). Electronic applications accepted.

University of Missouri–St. Louis, College of Education, Department of Education Sciences and Professional Programs, St. Louis, MO 63121. Offers adult and higher education (M Ed); educational psychology (M Ed), including character and citizenship education, research and program evaluation; program evaluation (Certificate); school psychology (Ed S). *Students:* 19 full-time (17 women), 13 part-time (12 women); includes 4 minority (2 Black or African American, non-Hispanic/Latino; 2 Hispanic/Latino). 16 applicants, 56% accepted, 9 enrolled. *Degree requirements:* For other advanced degree, comprehensive exam, thesis or alternative, internship. *Entrance requirements:* For degree, GRE General Test, 2-4 letters of recommendation, personal interview. Additional exam requirements/recommendations for international students: Required—IELTS (minimum score 6.5); Recommended—TOEFL (minimum score 550 paper-based; 79 iBT). *Application deadline:* For fall admission, 2/15 priority date for domestic students, 2/15 for international students. Application fee: $50 ($40 for international students). Electronic applications accepted. *Expenses:* Tuition, state

resident: part-time $476.50 per credit hour. Tuition, nonresident: part-time $1169.70 per credit hour. *Financial support:* Application deadline: 4/1; applicants required to submit FAFSA. *Faculty research:* Child/adolescent psychology, quantitative and qualitative methodology, evaluation processes, measurement and assessment. *Unit head:* Dr. Donald Gouwens, Chairperson, 314-516-4773, Fax: 314-516-5784, E-mail: gouwensd@umsl.edu. *Application contact:* 314-516-5458, Fax: 314-516-6996, E-mail: gradadm@umsl.edu.
Website: https://coe.umsl.edu/dept/espp.html

University of Nebraska–Lincoln, Graduate College, College of Education and Human Sciences, Department of Teaching, Learning and Teacher Education, Lincoln, NE 68588. Offers adult and continuing education (MA); educational studies (Ed D, PhD), including special education (Ed D); teaching, learning and teacher education (M Ed, MA, MST, Ed D, PhD); vocational and adult education (M Ed, MA). *Accreditation:* NCATE. *Degree requirements:* For master's, thesis optional. *Entrance requirements:* Additional exam requirements/recommendations for international students: Required—TOEFL (minimum score 550 paper-based). Electronic applications accepted. *Faculty research:* Teacher education, instructional leadership, literacy education, technology, improvement of school curriculum.

The University of North Carolina at Greensboro, Graduate School, School of Education, Department of Teacher Education and Higher Education, Greensboro, NC 27412-5001. Offers college teaching and adult learning (Certificate); curriculum and instruction (M Ed), including chemistry education, elementary education, English as a second language, French education, instructional technology, mathematics education, middle grades education, reading education, science education, social studies education, Spanish education; curriculum and teaching (PhD), including higher education, teacher education and development; English as a second language (Certificate); higher education (M Ed); supervision (M Ed). *Accreditation:* NCATE. *Program availability:* Part-time. *Degree requirements:* For doctorate, thesis/dissertation. *Entrance requirements:* For master's and doctorate, GRE General Test. Additional exam requirements/recommendations for international students: Required—TOEFL. Electronic applications accepted. *Faculty research:* Community college literacy program, middle school mathematics/computer mathematics.

University of North Florida, College of Education and Human Services, Department of Foundations and Secondary Education, Jacksonville, FL 32224. Offers adult learning (M Ed); professional education (M Ed). *Accreditation:* NCATE. *Program availability:* Part-time, evening/weekend. *Entrance requirements:* For master's, GRE General Test, minimum GPA of 3.0 in last 60 hours, interview, 3 letters of recommendation. Additional exam requirements/recommendations for international students: Required—TOEFL (minimum score 500 paper-based; 61 iBT). Electronic applications accepted. *Faculty research:* Using children's literature to enhance metalinguistic awareness, education, oral language diagnosis of middle-schoolers, science inquiry teaching and learning.

University of Oklahoma, Jeannine Rainbolt College of Education, Department of Educational Leadership and Policy Studies, Program in Adult and Higher Education, Norman, OK 73019. Offers adult and higher education (M Ed, PhD), including adult and workforce (M Ed), community college administration (M Ed), institutional research (M Ed), intercollegiate athletics administration (M Ed), student affairs (M Ed). *Accreditation:* NCATE. *Program availability:* Part-time, evening/weekend. *Students:* 110 full-time (69 women), 69 part-time (42 women); includes 66 minority (29 Black or African American, non-Hispanic/Latino; 10 American Indian or Alaska Native, non-Hispanic/Latino; 2 Asian, non-Hispanic/Latino; 13 Hispanic/Latino; 12 Two or more races, non-Hispanic/Latino), 5 international. Average age 29. 102 applicants, 60% accepted, 58 enrolled. In 2017, 70 master's, 1 doctorate awarded. Terminal master's awarded for partial completion of doctoral program. *Degree requirements:* For master's, comprehensive exam, thesis optional; for doctorate, comprehensive exam, thesis/dissertation. *Entrance requirements:* For doctorate, GRE. Additional exam requirements/recommendations for international students: Required—TOEFL (minimum score 79 iBT) or IELTS (minimum score 6.5). *Application deadline:* For fall admission, 10/1 for domestic and international students; for spring admission, 4/1 for domestic and international students. Application fee: $50 ($100 for international students). Electronic applications accepted. *Expenses:* Tuition, state resident: full-time $5119; part-time $213.30 per credit hour. Tuition, nonresident: full-time $19,778; part-time $824.10 per credit hour. *Required fees:* $3458; $133.55 per credit hour. $126.50 per semester. *Financial support:* In 2017–18, 148 students received support. Fellowships, research assistantships, teaching assistantships, career-related internships or fieldwork, Federal Work-Study, institutionally sponsored loans, scholarships/grants, traineeships, health care benefits, tuition waivers, and unspecified assistantships available. Support available to part-time students. Financial award application deadline: 6/1; financial award applicants required to submit FAFSA. *Faculty research:* Education and social policy; gender and equity; collegiate athletics; higher education and student affairs; adult learning and workforce development. *Unit head:* Doo Hun Lim, Associate Professor, 405-325-7941, E-mail: dhlim@ou.edu.
Website: http://www.ou.edu/education/elps/graduate-programs/adult-and-higher-education-masters.html

University of Phoenix–Bay Area Campus, College of Education, San Jose, CA 95134-1805. Offers administration and supervision (MA Ed); adult education and training (MA Ed); early childhood education (MA Ed); education (Ed S); educational leadership (Ed D); elementary teacher education (MA Ed); higher education administration (PhD); secondary teacher education (MA Ed); special education (MA Ed); teacher leadership (MA Ed). *Program availability:* Evening/weekend, online learning. *Degree requirements:* For master's, thesis (for some programs). *Entrance requirements:* For master's, minimum undergraduate GPA of 2.5, 3 years of work experience. Additional exam requirements/recommendations for international students: Required—TOEFL (minimum score 550 paper-based; 79 iBT). Electronic applications accepted.

University of Phoenix–Online Campus, College of Education, Phoenix, AZ 85034-7209. Offers administration and supervision (MAEd, Certificate); adult education and training (MAEd); curriculum and instruction (MAEd), including computer education, curriculum and instruction, English as a second language, language arts, mathematics, reading; early childhood education (MAEd); educational studies (MAEd); elementary teacher education (MAEd), including early childhood, elementary teacher education, high school middle level, middle level; principal licensure (Certificate); secondary teacher education (MAEd); special education (MAEd, Certificate); teacher education (MAEd), including middle level generalist; teacher education middle level mathematics (MAEd), including middle level mathematics; teacher education middle level science (MAEd), including middle level science; teacher education secondary mathematics (MAEd); teacher education secondary science (MAEd); teacher leadership (MAEd); teachers of English learners (Certificate); transition to teaching (Certificate), including elementary education, secondary education. *Program availability:* Evening/weekend, online learning. *Entrance requirements:* Additional exam requirements/recommendations for international students: Required—TOEFL, TOEIC (Test of English as an International Communication), Berlitz Online English Proficiency Exam, PTE, or IELTS. Electronic applications accepted. *Expenses:* Contact institution.

University of Phoenix–Phoenix Campus, College of Education, Tempe, AZ 85282-2371. Offers administration and supervision (MA Ed); adult education and training

(MA Ed); curriculum and instruction reading (MA Ed); early childhood education (MA Ed); education studies (MA Ed); elementary teacher education (MA Ed); secondary teacher education (MA Ed); special education (MA Ed); teacher leadership (MA Ed). *Program availability:* Evening/weekend, online learning. *Entrance requirements:* Additional exam requirements/recommendations for international students: Required—TOEFL, TOEIC (Test of English as an International Communication), Berlitz Online English Proficiency Exam, PTE, or IELTS. Electronic applications accepted. *Expenses:* Contact institution.

University of Phoenix–Sacramento Valley Campus, College of Education, Sacramento, CA 95833-4334. Offers adult education (MA Ed); curriculum instruction (MA Ed); elementary teacher education (MA Ed); secondary teacher education (MA Ed); teacher education (Certificate). *Program availability:* Evening/weekend. *Degree requirements:* For master's, thesis (for some programs). *Entrance requirements:* For master's, 3 years of work experience, minimum undergraduate GPA of 2.5. Additional exam requirements/recommendations for international students: Required—TOEFL (minimum score 550 paper-based; 79 iBT). Electronic applications accepted.

University of Regina, Faculty of Graduate Studies and Research, Faculty of Education, Department of Adult Education, Regina, SK S4S 0A2, Canada. Offers MA Ed. *Program availability:* Part-time (2 women). *Students:* 3 full-time (all women), 23 part-time (19 women). 13 applicants, 31% accepted. In 2017, 1 master's awarded. *Degree requirements:* For master's, thesis (for some programs), practicum, project, or thesis. *Entrance requirements:* For master's, bachelor's degree in education, 2 years of teaching or other relevant professional experience. Additional exam requirements/recommendations for international students: Required—TOEFL (minimum score 580 paper-based; 80 iBT), IELTS (minimum score 6.5), PTE (minimum score 59). *Application deadline:* For fall admission, 2/15 for domestic and international students; for winter admission, 10/15 for domestic and international students; for spring admission, 2/15 for domestic students. Application fee: $100. Electronic applications accepted. *Expenses:* $10,681. *Financial support:* In 2017–18, 2 fellowships (averaging $6,000 per year), 2 teaching assistantships (averaging $2,501 per year) were awarded; research assistantships and scholarships/grants also available. Financial award application deadline: 6/15. *Unit head:* Dr. Paul Clarke, Associate Dean, Research and Graduate Programs in Education, 306-585-5031, Fax: 306-585-5387, E-mail: paul.clarke@uregina.ca. *Application contact:* Linda Jiang, Graduate Program Coordinator, 306-585-4506, Fax: 306-585-5387, E-mail: edgrad@uregina.ca.
Website: http://www.uregina.ca/education/

University of South Africa, College of Human Sciences, Pretoria, South Africa. Offers adult education (M Ed); African languages (MA, PhD); African politics (MA, PhD); Afrikaans (MA, PhD); ancient history (MA, PhD); ancient Near Eastern studies (MA, PhD); anthropology (MA, PhD); applied linguistics (MA); Arabic (MA, PhD); archaeology (MA); art history (MA); Biblical archaeology (MA); Biblical studies (M Th, D Th, PhD); Christian spirituality (M Th, D Th); church history (M Th, D Th); classical studies (MA, PhD); clinical psychology (MA); communication (MA, PhD); comparative education (M Ed, Ed D); consulting psychology (D Admin, D Com, PhD); curriculum studies (M Ed, Ed D); development studies (M Admin, MA, D Admin, PhD); didactics (M Ed, Ed D); education (M Tech); education management (M Ed, Ed D); educational psychology (M Ed); English (MA); environmental education (M Ed); French (MA, PhD); German (MA, PhD); Greek (MA); guidance and counseling (M Ed); health studies (MA, PhD), including health sciences education (MA), health services management (MA), medical and surgical nursing science (critical care general) (MA), midwifery and neonatal nursing science (MA), trauma and emergency care (MA); history (MA, PhD); history of education (Ed D); inclusive education (M Ed, Ed D); information and communications technology policy and regulation (MA); information science (MA, MIS, PhD); international politics (MA, PhD); Islamic studies (MA, PhD); Italian (MA, PhD); Judaica (MA); linguistics (MA, PhD); mathematical education (M Ed); mathematics education (MA); missiology (M Th, D Th); modern Hebrew (MA, PhD); musicology (MA, MMus, D Mus, PhD); natural science education (M Ed); New Testament (M Th, D Th); Old Testament (D Th); pastoral therapy (M Th, D Th); philosophy (MA); philosophy of education (M Ed, Ed D); politics (MA, PhD); Portuguese (MA, PhD); practical theology (M Th, D Th); psychology (MA, MS, PhD); psychology of education (M Ed, Ed D); public health (MA); religious studies (MA, D Th, PhD); Romance languages (MA); Russian (MA, PhD); Semitic languages (MA, PhD); social behavior studies in HIV/AIDS (MA); social science (mental health) (MA); social science in development studies (MA); social science in psychology (MA); social science in social work (MA); social science in sociology (MA); social work (MSW, DSW, PhD); socio-education (M Ed, Ed D); sociolinguistics (MA); sociology (MA, PhD); Spanish (MA, PhD); systematic theology (M Th, D Th); TESOL (teaching English to speakers of other languages) (MA); theological ethics (M Th, D Th); theory of literature (MA, PhD); urban ministries (D Th); urban ministry (M Th).

University of South Dakota, Graduate School, School of Education, Division of Educational Leadership, Vermillion, SD 57069. Offers educational administration (MA, Ed D, Ed S), including adult and higher education (MA, Ed D), curriculum director, director of special education (Ed D, Ed S), preK-12 principal, school district superintendent (Ed D, Ed S). *Accreditation:* NCATE. *Program availability:* Part-time, evening/weekend, 100% online, blended/hybrid learning. *Degree requirements:* For master's and Ed S, comprehensive exam, thesis or alternative; for doctorate, comprehensive exam, thesis/dissertation. *Entrance requirements:* For master's, GRE General Test, MAT, minimum GPA of 2.7; for doctorate, minimum GPA of 2.7. Additional exam requirements/recommendations for international students: Required—TOEFL (minimum score 550 paper-based; 79 iBT). *Application deadline:* Applications are processed on a rolling basis. Application fee: $35. Electronic applications accepted. *Financial support:* Research assistantships with partial tuition reimbursements, teaching assistantships with partial tuition reimbursements, Federal Work-Study, traineeships, and unspecified assistantships available. Financial award applicants required to submit FAFSA. *Application contact:* Graduate School, 605-658-6140, Fax: 605-677-6118, E-mail: grad@usd.edu.
Website: http://www.usd.edu/education/educational-administration

University of Southern Maine, College of Management and Human Service, School of Education and Human Development, Program in Adult Education, Portland, ME 04103. Offers adult and higher education (MS); adult learning (CAS). *Accreditation:* TEAC. *Program availability:* Part-time, evening/weekend, online learning. *Degree requirements:* For master's and CAS, thesis or alternative. *Entrance requirements:* For master's, interview; for CAS, master's degree. Additional exam requirements/recommendations for international students: Required—TOEFL (minimum score 550 paper-based; 79 iBT). Electronic applications accepted. *Faculty research:* Older learners, lifelong learning institutes, teaching and learning in later age.

University of South Florida, College of Education, Department of Leadership, Counseling, Adult, Career and Higher Education, Tampa, FL 33620-9951. Offers adult education (MA, Ed D, PhD, Ed S); career and technical education (MA); career and workforce education (PhD); higher education/community college teaching (MA, Ed D, PhD); vocational education (Ed S). *Faculty:* 19 full-time (11 women). *Students:* 129 full-time (91 women), 274 part-time (187 women); includes 147 minority (71 Black or African American, non-Hispanic/Latino; 2 American Indian or Alaska Native, non-Hispanic/Latino; 9 Asian, non-Hispanic/Latino; 59 Hispanic/Latino; 6 Two or more races, non-

Adult Education

Hispanic/Latino), 15 international. Average age 35. 158 applicants, 67% accepted, 83 enrolled. In 2017, 89 master's, 7 doctorates, 2 other advanced degrees awarded. Application fee: $30. *Total annual research expenditures:* $157,971. *Unit head:* Dr. Judith Ponticell, Chair, 813-974-4897, Fax: 813-974-5423, E-mail: jponticell@usf.edu. Website: http://www.coedu.usf.edu/main/departments/ache/ache.html

University of South Florida, Innovative Education, Tampa, FL 33620-9951. Offers adult, career and higher education (Graduate Certificate), including college teaching, leadership in developing human resources, leadership in higher education; Africana studies (Graduate Certificate), including diasporas and health disparities, genocide and human rights; aging studies (Graduate Certificate), including gerontology; art research (Graduate Certificate), including museum studies; business foundations (Graduate Certificate); chemical and biomedical engineering (Graduate Certificate), including materials science and engineering, water, health and sustainability; child and family studies (Graduate Certificate), including positive behavior support; civil and industrial engineering (Graduate Certificate), including transportation systems analysis; community and family health (Graduate Certificate), including maternal and child health, social marketing and public health, violence and injury: prevention and intervention, women's health; criminology (Graduate Certificate), including criminal justice administration; data science for public administration (Graduate Certificate); digital humanities (Graduate Certificate); educational measurement and research (Graduate Certificate), including evaluation; English (Graduate Certificate), including comparative literary studies, creative writing, professional and technical communication, entrepreneurship (Graduate Certificate); environmental health (Graduate Certificate), including safety management; epidemiology and biostatistics (Graduate Certificate), including applied biostatistics, biostatistics, concepts and tools of epidemiology, epidemiology, epidemiology of infectious diseases; geography, environment and planning (Graduate Certificate), including community development, environmental policy and management, geographical information systems; geology (Graduate Certificate), including hydrogeology; global health (Graduate Certificate), including disaster management, global health and Latin American and Caribbean studies, global health practice, humanitarian assistance, infection control; government and international affairs (Graduate Certificate), including Cuban studies, globalization studies; health policy and management (Graduate Certificate), including health management and leadership, public health policy and programs; hearing specialist: early intervention (Graduate Certificate); industrial and management systems engineering (Graduate Certificate), including systems engineering, technology management; information studies (Graduate Certificate), including school library media specialist; information systems/decision sciences (Graduate Certificate), including analytics and business intelligence; instructional technology (Graduate Certificate), including distance education, Florida digital/virtual educator, instructional design, multimedia design, Web design; internal medicine, bioethics and medical humanities (Graduate Certificate), including biomedical ethics; Latin American and Caribbean studies (Graduate Certificate); leadership for coastal resiliency planning (Graduate Certificate); mass communications (Graduate Certificate), including multimedia journalism; mathematics and statistics (Graduate Certificate), including mathematics; medicine (Graduate Certificate), including aging and neuroscience, bioinformatics, biotechnology, brain fitness and memory management, clinical investigation, hand and upper limb rehabilitation, health informatics, health sciences, integrative weight management, intellectual property, medicine and gender, metabolic and nutritional medicine, metabolic cardiology, pharmacy sciences; national and competitive intelligence (Graduate Certificate), including simulation based academic fellowship in advanced pain management; psychological and social foundations (Graduate Certificate), including career counseling, college teaching, diversity in education, mental health counseling, school counseling; public affairs (Graduate Certificate), including nonprofit management, public management, research administration; public health (Graduate Certificate), including assessing chemical toxicity and public health risks, health equity, pharmacoepidemiology, public health generalist, toxicology, translational research in adolescent behavioral health; public health practices (Graduate Certificate), including planning for healthy communities; rehabilitation and mental health counseling (Graduate Certificate), including integrative mental health care, marriage and family therapy, rehabilitation technology; secondary education (Graduate Certificate), including ESOL, foreign language education: culture and content, foreign language education: professional; social work (Graduate Certificate), including geriatric social work/clinical gerontology; special education (Graduate Certificate), including autism spectrum disorder, disabilities education: severe/profound; world languages (Graduate Certificate), including teaching English as a second language (TESL) or foreign language. *Unit head:* Dr. Cynthia DeLuca, Associate Vice President and Assistant Vice Provost, 813-974-3077, Fax: 813-974-7061, E-mail: deluca@usf.edu. *Application contact:* Owen Hooper, Director, Summer and Alternative Calendar Programs, 813-974-6917, E-mail: hooper@usf.edu.
Website: http://www.usf.edu/innovative-education/

The University of Tennessee, Graduate School, College of Education, Health and Human Sciences, Department of Educational Psychology and Counseling, Knoxville, TN 37996. Offers adult education (MS); applied educational psychology (MS); collaborative learning (Ed D); college student personnel (MS); mental health counseling (MS); rehabilitation counseling (MS); school counseling (MS). *Accreditation:* ACA (one or more programs are accredited); CORE (one or more programs are accredited); NCATE. *Program availability:* Part-time, evening/weekend. *Degree requirements:* For master's, thesis optional. *Entrance requirements:* For master's, GRE General Test, minimum GPA of 2.7. Additional exam requirements/recommendations for international students: Required—TOEFL. Electronic applications accepted.

University of the District of Columbia, College of Arts and Sciences, Program in Adult Education, Washington, DC 20008-1175. Offers Graduate Certificate.

The University of West Alabama, School of Graduate Studies, College of Education, Program in Continuing Education, Livingston, AL 35470. Offers counseling and psychology (MSCE); general (MSCE); library media (MSCE). *Accreditation:* NCATE. *Program availability:* Part-time, evening/weekend, 100% online. *Faculty:* 13 full-time (11 women), 48 part-time/adjunct (36 women). *Students:* 195 (163 women); includes 137 minority (134 Black or African American, non-Hispanic/Latino; 1 American Indian or Alaska Native, non-Hispanic/Latino; 1 Native Hawaiian or other Pacific Islander, non-Hispanic/Latino; 1 Two or more races, non-Hispanic/Latino). Average age 34. 59 applicants, 100% accepted, 40 enrolled. In 2017, 103 master's awarded. *Degree requirements:* For master's, comprehensive exam, thesis optional. *Entrance requirements:* For master's, GRE, minimum GPA of 2.75. Additional exam requirements/ recommendations for international students: Required—TOEFL (minimum score 500 paper-based; 61 iBT). *Application deadline:* Applications are processed on a rolling basis. Application fee: $40. Electronic applications accepted. *Expenses:* Tuition, state resident: part-time $371 per credit hour. Tuition, nonresident: part-time $742 per credit hour. *Required fees:* $130 per semester. *Financial support:* Teaching assistantships, Federal Work-Study, scholarships/grants, and unspecified assistantships available. Support available to part-time students. Financial award application deadline: 3/1; financial award applicants required to submit FAFSA. *Unit head:* Dr. Reenay Rogers, Chair of Instructional Leadership and Support, 205-652-5423, Fax: 205-652-3706,

E-mail: rrogers@uwa.edu. *Application contact:* Dr. B. J. Kimbrough, Dean of Graduate Studies, 205-652-3647, Fax: 205-652-3670, E-mail: bkimbrough@uwa.edu.

University of Wisconsin–Milwaukee, Graduate School, College of Letters and Science, Department of Linguistics, Milwaukee, WI 53201-0413. Offers linguistics (MA, PhD), including teaching English to speakers of other languages (MA); teaching English to speakers of other languages, adult- and university-level (Graduate Certificate). *Students:* 19 full-time (5 women), 12 part-time (11 women); includes 1 minority (Two or more races, non-Hispanic/Latino), 18 international. Average age 33. 47 applicants, 34% accepted, 12 enrolled. In 2017, 4 master's, 2 other advanced degrees awarded. Electronic applications accepted. *Unit head:* Hamid Ouali, Department Chair, 414-229-1113, E-mail: ouali@uwm.edu. *Application contact:* General Information Contact, 414-229-4982, Fax: 414-229-6967, E-mail: gradschool@uwm.edu.
Website: http://www4.uwm.edu/letsci/linguistics/

University of Wisconsin–Milwaukee, Graduate School, School of Education, Department of Administrative Leadership, Milwaukee, WI 53201-0413. Offers administrative leadership (MS), including adult and continuing education leadership, educational administration and supervision, higher education administration; support services for online students in higher education (Graduate Certificate); teaching and learning in higher education (Graduate Certificate). *Program availability:* Part-time. *Students:* 33 full-time (19 women), 195 part-time (132 women); includes 53 minority (22 Black or African American, non-Hispanic/Latino; 4 American Indian or Alaska Native, non-Hispanic/Latino; 4 Asian, non-Hispanic/Latino; 2 Hispanic/Latino; 21 Two or more races, non-Hispanic/Latino), 1 international. Average age 35. 117 applicants, 75% accepted, 53 enrolled. In 2017, 61 master's, 14 other advanced degrees awarded. *Degree requirements:* For master's, comprehensive exam, thesis or alternative. *Entrance requirements:* For master's, GRE General Test. Additional exam requirements/ recommendations for international students: Required—TOEFL (minimum score 550 paper-based; 79 iBT), IELTS (minimum score 6.5). *Application deadline:* For fall admission, 1/1 priority date for domestic students; for spring admission, 9/1 for domestic students. Application fee: $56 ($96 for international students). Electronic applications accepted. *Financial support:* In 2017–18, 2 fellowships were awarded; research assistantships, teaching assistantships, career-related internships or fieldwork, health care benefits, unspecified assistantships, and project assistantships also available. Support available to part-time students. Financial award application deadline: 4/15; financial award applicants required to submit FAFSA. *Unit head:* Alan Shoho, Dean, 414-229-4181, E-mail: shoho@uwm.edu. *Application contact:* General Information Contact, 414-229-4721, E-mail: soeinfo@uwm.edu.
Website: http://uwm.edu/education/academics/administrative-leadership-department/

University of Wisconsin–Milwaukee, Graduate School, School of Education, Department of Exceptional Education, Milwaukee, WI 53201-0413. Offers autism spectrum disorders (Graduate Certificate); exceptional education (MS); transition for students with disabilities (Graduate Certificate); urban education (PhD), including adult, continuing and higher education leadership, art education, curriculum and instruction, exceptional education, mathematics education, multicultural studies, social foundations of education. *Program availability:* Part-time. *Students:* 45 full-time (34 women), 68 part-time (54 women); includes 46 minority (27 Black or African American, non-Hispanic/ Latino; 7 Asian, non-Hispanic/Latino; 1 Hispanic/Latino; 11 Two or more races, non-Hispanic/Latino), 4 international. Average age 39. 43 applicants, 53% accepted, 19 enrolled. In 2017, 12 master's, 13 doctorates, 8 other advanced degrees awarded. *Entrance requirements:* Additional exam requirements/recommendations for international students: Required—TOEFL (minimum score 550 paper-based; 79 iBT), IELTS (minimum score 6.5). *Application deadline:* For fall admission, 1/1 priority date for domestic students; for spring admission, 9/1 for domestic students. Application fee: $56 ($96 for international students). Electronic applications accepted. *Financial support:* Fellowships, research assistantships, teaching assistantships, career-related internships or fieldwork, health care benefits, and unspecified assistantships available. Support available to part-time students. Financial award application deadline: 4/15; financial award applicants required to submit FAFSA. *Faculty research:* Emotional disturbance, hearing impairment, learning disabilities, mental retardation. *Application contact:* General Information Contact, 414-229-4721, E-mail: soeinfo@uwm.edu.
Website: http://uwm.edu/education/academics/exceptional-edu-department/

University of Wisconsin–Platteville, School of Graduate Studies, College of Liberal Arts and Education, School of Education, Platteville, WI 53818-3099. Offers adult education (MSE). *Accreditation:* NCATE. *Program availability:* Part-time, evening/weekend. *Students:* 41 full-time (32 women), 109 part-time (82 women); includes 14 minority (12 Black or African American, non-Hispanic/Latino; 1 Asian, non-Hispanic/Latino; 1 Hispanic/Latino). 37 applicants, 86% accepted, 25 enrolled. In 2017, 62 master's awarded. *Degree requirements:* For master's, thesis or alternative. *Entrance requirements:* Additional exam requirements/recommendations for international students: Required—TOEFL (minimum score 550 paper-based; 79 iBT), IELTS (minimum score 6.5). *Application deadline:* For fall admission, 9/1 for domestic students, 7/1 for international students; for spring admission, 1/1 for domestic students, 11/15 for international students. Applications are processed on a rolling basis. Application fee: $56. Electronic applications accepted. *Financial support:* Research assistantships with partial tuition reimbursements, career-related internships or fieldwork, Federal Work-Study, institutionally sponsored loans, scholarships/grants, and unspecified assistantships available. Support available to part-time students. Financial award applicants required to submit FAFSA. *Unit head:* Dr. Dominic Barraclough, Interim Director, 608-342-1131, Fax: 608-342-1133, E-mail: education@uwplatt.edu. *Application contact:* Dee Dunbar, School of Graduate Studies, 608-342-1322, Fax: 608-342-1454, E-mail: gradstudies@uwplatt.edu.
Website: http://www.uwplatt.edu/

Virginia Commonwealth University, Graduate School, School of Education, Program in Adult Learning, Richmond, VA 23284-9005. Offers adult literacy (M Ed); human resource development (M Ed); teaching and learning with technology (M Ed). *Accreditation:* NCATE. *Program availability:* Part-time. *Entrance requirements:* For master's, GRE General Test or MAT. Additional exam requirements/recommendations for international students: Required—TOEFL (minimum score 600 paper-based; 100 iBT). Electronic applications accepted. *Faculty research:* Adult development and learning, program planning and evaluation.

Walden University, Graduate Programs, Richard W. Riley College of Education and Leadership, Minneapolis, MN 55401. Offers adult education (Post-Master's Certificate); adult learning (Graduate Certificate); college teaching and learning (Graduate Certificate); community college leadership (Ed D); curriculum, instruction and assessment (Ed D, Ed S, Graduate Certificate); developmental education (Graduate Certificate); early childhood administration, management, and leadership (Graduate Certificate); early childhood education (Ed D, Ed S); early childhood public policy and advocacy (Graduate Certificate); early childhood studies (MS), including administration, management and leadership, early childhood public policy and advocacy, teaching adults in the early childhood field, teaching and diversity in early childhood education; education (MS, PhD), including adolescent literacy and learning (MS), curriculum, instruction, and assessment (grades K-12) (MS), curriculum, instruction, assessment, and evaluation (PhD), early childhood leadership and advocacy (PhD), early childhood special education (PhD), educational leadership (MS), educational leadership and administration (principal preparation) (MS), educational technology and design (PhD), elementary reading and literacy (PreK-6) (MS), elementary reading and mathematics (grades K-6) (MS), global and comparative education (PhD), higher education leadership management and policy (PhD), integrating technology in the classroom (grades K-12) (MS), learning, instruction and innovation (PhD), mathematics (grades 5-8) (MS), mathematics (grades K-6) (MS), mathematics and science (grades K-8) (MS), organizational research, assessment, and evaluation (PhD), reading and literacy with a reading K-12 endorsement (MS), reading literacy assessment and evaluation (PhD), science (grades K-8) (MS), special education (non-licensure) (grades K-12) (MS), teacher leadership (grades K-12) (MS), teaching English language learners (grades K-12) (MS); educational administration and leadership (Ed D); educational leadership and administration (principal preparation) (Ed S); educational technology (Ed D, Ed S, Post Master's Certificate); elementary reading and literacy (Graduate Certificate); engaging culturally diverse learners (Graduate Certificate); enrollment management and institutional marketing (Graduate Certificate); higher education (MS), including adult learning, college teaching and learning, enrollment management and institutional marketing, global higher education, leadership for student success, online and distance learning; higher education and adult learning (Ed D); higher education leadership and management (Ed D); higher education leadership for student success (Graduate Certificate); instructional design and technology (MS, Postbaccalaureate Certificate), including general program (MS), online learning (MS), training and performance improvement (MS); integrating technology in the classroom (Graduate Certificate); mathematics 5-8 (Graduate Certificate); mathematics K-6 (Graduate Certificate); online teaching for adult educators (Graduate Certificate); reading, literacy, and assessment (Ed D, Ed S); science K-8 (Graduate Certificate); special education (Ed D, Ed S, Graduate Certificate); special education (K-age 21) (MAT); teacher leadership (Graduate Certificate); teaching adults English as a second language (Graduate Certificate); teaching adults in the early childhood field (Graduate Certificate); teaching and diversity in early childhood education (Graduate Certificate); teaching English language learners (grades K-12) (Graduate Certificate); teaching K-12 students online (Graduate Certificate). *Accreditation:* NCATE. *Program availability:* Part-time, evening/weekend, online only, 100% online. *Degree requirements:* For doctorate, thesis/dissertation (for some programs), residency (for other advanced degree, residency (for some programs). *Entrance requirements:* For master's, bachelor's degree or higher; minimum GPA of 2.5; official transcripts; goal statement (for some programs); access to computer and Internet; for doctorate, master's degree or higher; three years of related professional or academic experience (preferred); minimum GPA of 3.0; goal statement and current resume (for select programs); official transcripts; access to computer and Internet; for other advanced degree, relevant work experience; access to computer and Internet. Additional exam requirements/recommendations for international students: Required—TOEFL (minimum score 550 paper-based, 79 iBT), IELTS (minimum score 6.5), Michigan English Language Assessment Battery (minimum score 82), or PTE (minimum score 53). Electronic applications accepted.

Western Kentucky University, Graduate Studies, College of Education and Behavioral Sciences, Department of Educational Administration, Leadership, and Research, Bowling Green, KY 42101. Offers adult education (MAE); educational leadership (Ed D); school administration (Ed S); school principal (MAE). *Accreditation:* NCATE. *Program availability:* Part-time, evening/weekend. *Degree requirements:* For master's,

comprehensive exam, thesis or applied project and oral defense; for Ed S, thesis. *Entrance requirements:* For master's, GRE General Test, minimum GPA of 2.75. Additional exam requirements/recommendations for international students: Required—TOEFL (minimum score 555 paper-based; 79 iBT). *Faculty research:* Principal internship, superintendent assessment, administrative leadership, group training for residential workers.

Western Washington University, Graduate School, Woodring College of Education, Department of Educational Leadership, Program in Continuing and College Education, Bellingham, WA 98225-5996. Offers M Ed. *Program availability:* Part-time, evening/weekend, online learning. *Degree requirements:* For master's, comprehensive exam, thesis optional. *Entrance requirements:* For master's, GRE General Test or MAT, minimum GPA of 3.0 in last 60 semester hours or last 90 quarter hours. Additional exam requirements/recommendations for international students: Required—TOEFL (minimum score 567 paper-based). Electronic applications accepted. *Faculty research:* Transfer of learning, postsecondary faculty development, action research as professional development, literacy education in community colleges, adult education in the Middle East, distance learning tools for graduate students.

Widener University, School of Human Service Professions, Center for Education, Chester, PA 19013-5792. Offers adult education (M Ed); counseling in higher education (M Ed); counselor education (M Ed); early childhood education (M Ed); educational foundations (M Ed); educational leadership (M Ed); educational psychology (M Ed); elementary education (M Ed); English and language arts (M Ed); health education (M Ed); higher education leadership (Ed D); home and school visitor (M Ed); human sexuality (M Ed, PhD); mathematics education (M Ed); middle school education (M Ed); principalship (M Ed); reading and language arts (Ed D); reading education (M Ed); school administration (Ed D); science education (M Ed); social studies education (M Ed); special education (M Ed); technology education (M Ed). *Accreditation:* NCATE. *Program availability:* Part-time, evening/weekend. *Faculty:* 34 full-time (22 women), 37 part-time/adjunct (14 women). *Students:* 131 full-time (112 women), 244 part-time (179 women); includes 94 minority (58 Black or African American, non-Hispanic/Latino; 1 American Indian or Alaska Native, non-Hispanic/Latino; 1 Asian, non-Hispanic/Latino; 22 Hispanic/Latino; 12 Two or more races, non-Hispanic/Latino), 12 international. Average age 37. 140 applicants, 38% accepted, 26 enrolled. In 2017, 45 master's, 21 doctorates awarded. Terminal master's awarded for partial completion of doctoral program. *Degree requirements:* For doctorate, thesis/dissertation. *Entrance requirements:* For master's, minimum GPA of 2.5; for doctorate, GRE or MAT, minimum GPA of 2.0 (undergraduate), 3.5 (graduate). *Application deadline:* Applications are processed on a rolling basis. Application fee: $25 ($300 for international students). Electronic applications accepted. *Expenses:* Contact institution. *Financial support:* Career-related internships or fieldwork, tuition waivers (full and partial), and unspecified assistantships available. Support available to part-time students. Financial award application deadline: 5/1. *Faculty research:* Reading and cognition, adult education, technology education, educational leadership, special education. *Unit head:* Dr. Shawn Fitzgerald, Dean, 610-499-4294, Fax: 610-499-4623, E-mail: smfitzgerald@widener.edu. *Application contact:* Megan Kuft, Director of Graduate Admissions, 610-499-4124, E-mail: gradprograms@widener.edu.
Website: http://www.widener.edu/academics/schools/eics

Community College Education

Argosy University, Chicago, College of Education, Chicago, IL 60601. Offers adult education and training (MA Ed); community college executive leadership (Ed D); educational leadership (MA Ed, Ed D, Ed S), including district leadership (Ed D), higher education administration (Ed D), K-12 education (Ed D); instructional leadership (Ed D, Ed S), including higher education (Ed D), K-12 education (Ed D). *Program availability:* Online learning.

Argosy University, Los Angeles, College of Education, Los Angeles, CA 90045. Offers community college executive leadership (Ed D); educational leadership (MA Ed, Ed D), including higher education administration (Ed D), K-12 education (Ed D); instructional leadership (MA Ed, Ed D), including higher education (Ed D), K-12 education (Ed D); multiple subject teacher preparation (MA Ed), single subject teacher preparation (MA Ed).

Argosy University, Northern Virginia, College of Education, Arlington, VA 22209. Offers community college executive leadership (Ed D); educational leadership (MA Ed, Ed D, Ed S), including higher education administration (Ed D), K-12 education (Ed D); instructional leadership (MA Ed, Ed D, Ed S), including higher education (Ed D), K-12 education (Ed D).

Argosy University, Orange County, College of Education, Orange, CA 92868. Offers community college executive leadership (Ed D); educational leadership (MA Ed, Ed D), including higher education administration (Ed D), K-12 education (Ed D); instructional leadership (MA Ed, Ed D), including education technology (Ed D), higher education (Ed D), K-12 education (Ed D); multiple subject teacher preparation (MA Ed), single subject teacher preparation (MA Ed).

Argosy University, Phoenix, College of Education, Phoenix, AZ 85021. Offers adult education and training (MA Ed); advanced educational administration (Ed D, Ed S); community college executive leadership (Ed D); educational administration (MA Ed); educational leadership (MA Ed, Ed D, Ed S), including education technology (Ed D), higher education administration (Ed D), K-12 education (Ed D); higher and postsecondary education (MA Ed); initial educational administration (Ed D, Ed S); school psychology (MA); teaching and learning (MA Ed, Ed D, Ed S), including education technology (Ed D), higher education (Ed D), K-12 education (Ed D).

Argosy University, Seattle, College of Education, Seattle, WA 98121. Offers adult education and training (MA Ed); community college executive leadership (Ed D); educational leadership (MA Ed, Ed D), including higher education administration (Ed D), K-12 education (Ed D); higher and postsecondary education (MA Ed); instructional leadership (MA Ed, Ed D), including education technology (Ed D), higher education (Ed D), K-12 education (Ed D).

Argosy University, Tampa, College of Education, Tampa, FL 33607. Offers community college executive leadership (Ed D); educational leadership (MA Ed, Ed D, Ed S), including higher education administration (Ed D), K-12 education (Ed D); school counseling (MA); teaching and learning (MA Ed, Ed D, Ed S), including higher education (Ed D), K-12 education (Ed D).

Arkansas State University, Graduate School, College of Education and Behavioral Science, School of Teacher Education and Leadership, State University, AR 72467. Offers community college administration (SCCT); curriculum and instruction (MSE); early childhood education (MSE); early childhood services (MS); educational leadership (MSE, Ed D, Ed S); educational theory and practice (MSE); middle level education (MAT, MSE); reading (MSE, Ed S); special education - gifted, talented, and creative (MSE); special education - instructional specialist grades 4-12 (MSE); special education - instructional specialist grades P-4 (MSE); special education, K-12 (MSE). *Accreditation:* NCATE. *Program availability:* Part-time, online learning. *Degree requirements:* For master's, comprehensive exam, thesis or alternative; for doctorate, comprehensive exam, thesis/dissertation; for other advanced degree, comprehensive exam. *Entrance requirements:* For master's, GRE General Test or MAT, appropriate bachelor's degree, official transcripts, immunization records, letters of reference, interview; for doctorate, GRE General Test or MAT, interview, master's degree, letters of reference, official transcript, personal statement, writing sample, immunization records; for other advanced degree, GRE General Test or MAT, interview, master's degree, official transcript, immunization records, letters of reference, 3 years of teaching experience, teaching license. Additional exam requirements/recommendations for international students: Required—TOEFL (minimum score 550 paper-based; 79 iBT), IELTS (minimum score 6), PTE (minimum score 56). Electronic applications accepted.

California State University, San Bernardino, Graduate Studies, College of Education, Program in Educational Leadership: Community College Specialization, San Bernardino, CA 92407. Offers MA. *Program availability:* Part-time, evening/weekend. *Students:* 14 full-time (8 women), 10 part-time (6 women); includes 10 minority (1 Asian, non-Hispanic/Latino; 8 Hispanic/Latino; 1 Two or more races, non-Hispanic/Latino), 1 international. Average age 39. 15 applicants, 67% accepted, 8 enrolled. *Degree requirements:* For master's, thesis optional. *Entrance requirements:* Additional exam requirements/recommendations for international students: Required—TOEFL. *Application deadline:* For fall admission, 7/17 for domestic students. Application fee: $55. *Unit head:* Dr. Jay Fiene, Dean, 909-537-7621, E-mail: jfiene@csusb.edu. *Application contact:* Dr. Dorota Huizinga, Dean of Graduate Studies, 909-537-3064, E-mail: dorota.huizinga@csusb.edu.

California State University, Stanislaus, College of Education, Kinesiology and Social Work, Doctor of Education in Educational Leadership Programs, Turlock, CA 95382. Offers community college leadership (Ed D); P-12 leadership (Ed D). *Program availability:* Part-time, evening/weekend. *Degree requirements:* For doctorate, thesis/dissertation. *Entrance requirements:* For doctorate, GRE, minimum GPA of 3.0, 3 letters of reference, interview, personal statement. Additional exam requirements/recommendations for international students: Required—TOEFL (minimum score 550 paper-based). Electronic applications accepted.

Central Michigan University, Central Michigan University Global Campus, Program in Education, Mount Pleasant, MI 48859. Offers college teaching (Graduate Certificate); community college (MA); curriculum and instruction (MA); educational technology (MA, DET); reading and literacy K-12 (MA); school principalship (MA), including charter

Community College Education

school leadership; training and development (MA). *Accreditation:* TEAC. *Program availability:* Part-time, evening/weekend. *Entrance requirements:* For master's, minimum GPA of 2.7 in major. Additional exam requirements/recommendations for international students: Required—TOEFL. Electronic applications accepted.

Drew University, Caspersen School of Graduate Studies, Madison, NJ 07940-1493. Offers conflict resolution and leadership (Certificate), including community leadership, moderation, peace building; education (M Ed); finance (MA); history and culture (MA, PhD), including American history, book history, British history, European history, Holocaust and genocide (M Litt, MA, D Litt, PhD), intellectual history, Irish history, print culture, public history; K-12 education (MAT), including art, biology, chemistry, elementary education, English, French, Italian, math, secondary education, special education, teacher of students with disabilities; liberal studies (M Litt, D Litt), including history, Holocaust and genocide (M Litt, MA, D Litt, PhD), Irish/Irish-American studies, literature (M Litt, MMH, D Litt, DMH, CMH), religion, spirituality, teaching in the two-year college, writing; medical humanities (MMH, DMH, CMH), including arts, health, healthcare, literature (M Litt, MMH, D Litt, DMH, CMH), scientific research; poetry (MFA). *Program availability:* Part-time, evening/weekend. *Faculty:* 4 full-time (2 women), 29 part-time/adjunct (15 women). *Students:* 77 full-time (42 women), 175 part-time (114 women); includes 39 minority (12 Black or African American, non-Hispanic/Latino; 6 Asian, non-Hispanic/Latino; 16 Hispanic/Latino; 5 Two or more races, non-Hispanic/Latino), 11 international. Average age 41. 126 applicants, 75% accepted, 52 enrolled. In 2017, 38 master's, 23 doctorates, 35 other advanced degrees awarded. Terminal master's awarded for partial completion of doctoral program. *Degree requirements:* For master's and other advanced degree, thesis (for some programs); for doctorate, one foreign language, comprehensive exam (for some programs); thesis/dissertation. *Entrance requirements:* For master's, PRAXIS Core and Subject Area tests (for MAT), GRE/GMAT (for M Fin), resume, transcripts, writing sample, personal statement, letters of recommendation; for doctorate, GRE (PhD in history and culture), resume, transcripts, writing sample, personal statement, letters of recommendation; for other advanced degree, resume, transcripts, personal statement. Additional exam requirements/recommendations for international students: Required—TOEFL (minimum score 587 paper-based; 80 iBT), IELTS (minimum score 6), TWE (minimum score 4). *Application deadline:* For fall admission, 8/1 for domestic students, 6/1 for international students; for spring admission, 12/1 for domestic students, 10/1 for international students. Applications are processed on a rolling basis. Application fee: $35. Electronic applications accepted. *Financial support:* Fellowships, research assistantships, teaching assistantships, career-related internships or fieldwork, Federal Work-Study, scholarships/grants, and unspecified assistantships available. Support available to part-time students. Financial award applicants required to submit FAFSA. *Faculty research:* Irish history and culture, conflict resolution and leadership. *Application contact:* Leanne Horinko, Director of Caspersen Admissions, 973-408-3280, E-mail: gradm@drew.edu. Website: http://www.drew.edu/caspersen

East Carolina University, Graduate School, Thomas Harriot College of Arts and Sciences, Department of English, Greenville, NC 27858-4353. Offers creative writing (MA); English studies (MA); linguistics (MA); literature (MA); multicultural and transnational literatures (MA, Certificate); professional communication (Certificate); rhetoric and composition (MA); rhetoric, writing, and professional communication (PhD); teaching English in the two-year college (Certificate); teaching English to speakers of other languages (MA, Certificate); technical and professional communication (MA). *Program availability:* Part-time, evening/weekend, online learning. *Students:* 40 full-time (27 women), 74 part-time (57 women); includes 33 minority (23 Black or African American, non-Hispanic/Latino; 2 Asian, non-Hispanic/Latino; 4 Hispanic/Latino; 4 Two or more races, non-Hispanic/Latino). Average age 35. 36 applicants, 94% accepted, 25 enrolled. In 2017, 23 master's, 4 doctorates, 24 other advanced degrees awarded. *Degree requirements:* For master's, comprehensive exam, thesis optional; for doctorate, comprehensive exam, thesis/dissertation. *Entrance requirements:* For master's, GRE General Test or MAT; for doctorate, GRE General Test or MAT, writing samples. Additional exam requirements/recommendations for international students: Recommended—TOEFL (minimum score 78 iBT), IELTS (minimum score 6.5), TWE. *Application deadline:* For fall admission, 7/31 priority date for domestic students, 2/1 priority date for international students; for spring admission, 11/30 priority date for domestic students, 10/1 priority date for international students. Applications are processed on a rolling basis. Application fee: $75. Electronic applications accepted. *Expenses:* Tuition, state resident: full-time $4749; part-time $297 per credit hour. Tuition, nonresident: full-time $17,898; part-time $1119 per credit hour. *Required fees:* $2691; $224 per credit hour. Part-time tuition and fees vary according to course load and program. *Financial support:* Research assistantships with partial tuition reimbursements, teaching assistantships with partial tuition reimbursements, and Federal Work-Study available. Support available to part-time students. Financial award application deadline: 3/1. *Faculty research:* Technical and professional communication, rhetoric/composition, multicultural and transnational literature, creative writing, film studies. *Unit head:* Dr. Marianne Montgomery, Chair, 252-328-6687, E-mail: montgomerym@ecu.edu. *Application contact:* Dean of Graduate School, 252-328-6012, Fax: 252-328-6071, E-mail: gradschool@ecu.edu. Website: http://www.ecu.edu/cs-cas/engl/

East Carolina University, Graduate School, Thomas Harriot College of Arts and Sciences, Department of Mathematics, Greenville, NC 27858-4353. Offers mathematics (MA), including mathematics in the community college, statistics. *Program availability:* Part-time, evening/weekend. *Students:* 12 full-time (4 women), 2 part-time (both women); includes 2 minority (1 Asian, non-Hispanic/Latino; 1 Hispanic/Latino), 2 international. Average age 27. 7 applicants, 100% accepted, 6 enrolled. In 2017, 3 master's awarded. *Degree requirements:* For master's, comprehensive exam, thesis or alternative. *Entrance requirements:* For master's, GRE General Test or MAT. Additional exam requirements/recommendations for international students: Recommended—TOEFL (minimum score 78 iBT), IELTS (minimum score 6.5). *Application deadline:* For fall admission, 6/1 priority date for domestic students, 2/1 priority date for international students; for spring admission, 10/15 priority date for domestic students, 10/1 priority date for international students. Applications are processed on a rolling basis. Application fee: $75. Electronic applications accepted. *Expenses:* Tuition, state resident: full-time $4749; part-time $297 per credit hour. Tuition, nonresident: full-time $17,898; part-time $1119 per credit hour. *Required fees:* $2691; $224 per credit hour. Part-time tuition and fees vary according to course load and program. *Financial support:* Research assistantships with partial tuition reimbursements and teaching assistantships with partial tuition reimbursements available. Financial award application deadline: 3/1. *Faculty research:* Complex analysis, financial and actuarial mathematics, mathematical biology, mathematics education, operations research. *Unit head:* Dr. Johannes H. Hattingh, Chair, 252-328-6461, E-mail: hattinghj@ecu.edu. *Application contact:* Dean of Graduate School, 252-328-6012, Fax: 252-328-6071, E-mail: gradschool@ecu.edu. Website: http://www.ecu.edu/cs-cas/math/

Eastern Michigan University, Graduate School, College of Education, Department of Leadership and Counseling, Programs in Educational Leadership, Ypsilanti, MI 48197. Offers community college leadership (Graduate Certificate); educational leadership (MA, Ed D, SPA); higher education/general administration (MA); higher education/student affairs (MA); K-12 administration (MA); K-12 basic administration (Post Master's

Certificate). *Program availability:* Part-time, evening/weekend, online learning. *Students:* 50 full-time (34 women), 286 part-time (186 women); includes 108 minority (85 Black or African American, non-Hispanic/Latino; 3 American Indian or Alaska Native, non-Hispanic/Latino; 1 Asian, non-Hispanic/Latino; 12 Hispanic/Latino; 7 Two or more races, non-Hispanic/Latino), 2 international. Average age 40. 200 applicants, 72% accepted, 76 enrolled. In 2017, 88 master's, 22 doctorates, 28 other advanced degrees awarded. *Degree requirements:* For master's, portfolio. *Entrance requirements:* For doctorate, GRE. Additional exam requirements/recommendations for international students: Required—TOEFL. *Application deadline:* For winter admission, 2/1 for domestic and international students. Applications are processed on a rolling basis. Application fee: $45. *Financial support:* Fellowships, research assistantships with full tuition reimbursements, teaching assistantships with full tuition reimbursements, career-related internships or fieldwork, Federal Work-Study, institutionally sponsored loans, scholarships/grants, tuition waivers (partial), and unspecified assistantships available. Support available to part-time students. *Application contact:* Dr. Jaclynn Tracy, Coordinator of Advising, Programs in Educational Leadership, 734-487-0255, Fax: 734-487-4608, E-mail: jtracy@emich.edu.

Elizabeth City State University, Department of Mathematics and Computer Science, Master of Science in Mathematics Program, Elizabeth City, NC 27909-7806. Offers applied mathematics (MS); community college teaching (MS); mathematics education (MS); remote sensing (MS). *Program availability:* Part-time, evening/weekend. *Faculty:* 7 full-time (2 women). *Students:* 25 part-time (13 women); includes 19 minority (all Black or African American, non-Hispanic/Latino). Average age 25. 5 applicants, 80% accepted, 4 enrolled. In 2017, 18 master's awarded. *Degree requirements:* For master's, thesis. *Entrance requirements:* For master's, MAT and/or GRE, minimum GPA of 3.0, 3 letters of recommendation, two official transcripts from all undergraduate/graduate schools attended, typewritten one-page request for entry into program that includes description of student's educational preparation. Additional exam requirements/recommendations for international students: Required—TOEFL (minimum score 550 paper-based, 80 iBT) or IELTS (minimum score 6.5). *Application deadline:* For fall admission, 7/15 priority date for domestic and international students; for spring admission, 11/15 priority date for domestic and international students; for summer admission, 3/15 priority date for domestic and international students. Applications are processed on a rolling basis. Application fee: $30. Electronic applications accepted. Tuition and fees vary according to course load and program. *Financial support:* In 2017–18, 22 students received support, including 3 research assistantships (averaging $19,000 per year), 2 teaching assistantships (averaging $18,000 per year); scholarships/grants and tuition waivers also available. Financial award application deadline: 6/30; financial award applicants required to submit FAFSA. *Faculty research:* Oceanic temperature effects, mathematics strategies in elementary schools, multimedia, Antarctic temperature mapping, computer networks, water quality, remote sensing, polar ice, satellite imagery. *Total annual research expenditures:* $25,000. *Unit head:* Dr. Kenneth L. Jones, Chair, 252-335-3858, E-mail: kljones@ecsu.edu. *Application contact:* Dr. Sharon D. Raynor, Director, Graduate Education Program, 252-335-3945, E-mail: sdraynor@ecsu.edu. Website: http://www.ecsu.edu/academics/mathsciencetechnology/

Ferris State University, Extended and International Operations, Big Rapids, MI 49307. Offers community college leadership (Ed D). *Program availability:* Evening/weekend, blended/hybrid learning. *Faculty:* 25 part-time/adjunct (15 women). *Students:* 103 full-time (72 women), 2 part-time (0 women); includes 29 minority (19 Black or African American, non-Hispanic/Latino; 1 Asian, non-Hispanic/Latino; 9 Hispanic/Latino). Average age 46. 41 applicants, 73% accepted, 27 enrolled. In 2017, 11 doctorates awarded. *Degree requirements:* For doctorate, thesis/dissertation, e-portfolio demonstrating completion of program outcomes. *Entrance requirements:* For doctorate, master's degree with minimum GPA of 3.25, fierce commitment to the mission of community colleges, essay, writing samples. *Application deadline:* For fall admission, 12/15 for domestic and international students; for winter admission, 1/27 for domestic and international students; for spring admission, 4/15 for domestic students, 4/18 for international students. Applications are processed on a rolling basis. Application fee: $0. Electronic applications accepted. *Expenses:* Contact institution. *Financial support:* In 2017–18, 4 teaching assistantships (averaging $1,000 per year) were awarded. Financial award application deadline: 5/1; financial award applicants required to submit FAFSA. *Faculty research:* Community college leadership. *Unit head:* Dr. Roberta Teahen, Director, 231-591-3805, E-mail: robertateahen@ferris.edu. *Application contact:* Megan Biller, Coordinator, 231-591-2710, Fax: 231-591-3539, E-mail: meganbiller@ferris.edu.

Lenoir-Rhyne University, Graduate Programs, School of Education, Program in Community College Administration, Hickory, NC 28601. Offers MA. *Program availability:* Online learning. *Entrance requirements:* For master's, GRE or MAT, official transcripts, essay, resume. Electronic applications accepted. *Expenses:* Contact institution.

Marymount University, School of Arts and Sciences, Program in English and the Humanities, Arlington, VA 22207-4299. Offers English and humanities (MA); teaching English at the community college (Certificate). *Program availability:* Part-time, evening/weekend. *Faculty:* 3 full-time (0 women). *Students:* 2 full-time (both women), 10 part-time (6 women); includes 5 minority (2 Black or African American, non-Hispanic/Latino; 1 Asian, non-Hispanic/Latino; 1 Hispanic/Latino; 1 Two or more races, non-Hispanic/Latino). Average age 34. 8 applicants, 100% accepted, 5 enrolled. In 2017, 7 master's, 1 other advanced degree awarded. *Degree requirements:* For master's, thesis, capstone. *Entrance requirements:* For master's, 2 letters of recommendation, resume, bachelor's degree in English or other humanities discipline, writing sample of 8-10 pages. Additional exam requirements/recommendations for international students: Required—TOEFL (minimum score 600 paper-based; 96 iBT), IELTS (minimum score 6.5). *Application deadline:* Applications are processed on a rolling basis. Application fee: $40. Electronic applications accepted. *Expenses: Tuition:* Full-time $17,550; part-time $975 per credit hour. *Required fees:* $198; $11 per credit hour. One-time fee: $250. Tuition and fees vary according to program. *Financial support:* In 2017–18, 1 student received support, including 1 research assistantship with full and partial tuition reimbursement available (averaging $11,700 per year); teaching assistantships with full and partial tuition reimbursements available, career-related internships or fieldwork, Federal Work-Study, scholarships/grants, and unspecified assistantships also available. Support available to part-time students. Financial award application deadline: 3/1; financial award applicants required to submit FAFSA. *Unit head:* Dr. David Brown, Director, English and the Humanities, 703-284-5762, Fax: 703-284-3859, E-mail: david.brown@marymount.edu. *Application contact:* Francesca Reed, Director, Graduate Admissions, 703-284-5901, Fax: 703-527-3815, E-mail: grad.admissions@marymount.edu. Website: http://www.marymount.edu/Academics/School-of-Arts-Sciences/Graduate-Programs/English-Humanities-(M-A-)

Mississippi State University, College of Education, Educational Leadership Program, Mississippi State, MS 39762. Offers community college education (MAT); community college leadership (PhD); higher education leadership (PhD); P-12 school leadership (PhD); school administration (MS, Ed S); student affairs and higher education (MS); workforce education leadership (MS). MS in workforce education leadership held jointly with Alcorn State University. *Faculty:* 12 full-time (9 women). *Students:* 62 full-time (33 women), 149 part-time (93 women); includes 94 minority (79 Black or African American, non-Hispanic/Latino; 5 American Indian or Alaska Native, non-Hispanic/Latino; 4 Hispanic/Latino; 1 Native Hawaiian or other Pacific Islander, non-Hispanic/Latino; 5 Two or more races, non-Hispanic/Latino). Average age 36. 95 applicants, 79% accepted, 64 enrolled. In 2017, 41 master's, 32 doctorates, 7 other advanced degrees awarded. *Degree requirements:* For master's and Ed S, comprehensive exam, thesis; for doctorate, comprehensive exam, thesis/dissertation. *Entrance requirements:* For master's, GRE, minimum GPA of 2.75 in junior and senior courses; for doctorate, GRE, minimum GPA of 3.4 on previous graduate work; for Ed S, GRE, minimum GPA of 3.2, master's degree. Additional exam requirements/recommendations for international students: Required—TOEFL (minimum score 550 paper-based; 79 iBT); Recommended—IELTS (minimum score 6.5). *Application deadline:* For fall admission, 7/1 for domestic students, 5/1 for international students; for spring admission, 11/1 for domestic students, 9/1 for international students. Application fee: $60 ($80 for international students). Electronic applications accepted. *Expenses:* Tuition, state resident: full-time $8318; part-time $462.12 per credit hour. Tuition, nonresident: full-time $22,358; part-time $1242.12 per credit hour. *Required fees:* $110; $12.24 per credit hour. $6.12 per semester. *Financial support:* In 2017–18, 1 research assistantship with full tuition reimbursement (averaging $10,879 per year) was awarded; Federal Work-Study, institutionally sponsored loans, and unspecified assistantships also available. Financial award application deadline: 4/1; financial award applicants required to submit FAFSA. *Unit head:* Dr. Eric Moyen, Associate Professor and Head, 662-325-0969, Fax: 662-325-0975, E-mail: em1621@msstate.edu. *Application contact:* Nathan Drake, Admissions and Enrollment Assistant, 662-325-3804, E-mail: ndrake@grad.msstate.edu. Website: http://www.educationalleadership.msstate.edu/

Morgan State University, School of Graduate Studies, School of Education and Urban Studies, Department of Advanced Studies, Leadership and Policy, Program in Community College Leadership, Baltimore, MD 21251. Offers Ed D. *Accreditation:* NCATE. *Program availability:* Part-time, evening/weekend. *Degree requirements:* For doctorate, comprehensive exam, thesis/dissertation. *Entrance requirements:* For doctorate, GRE General Test or MAT. Additional exam requirements/recommendations for international students: Required—TOEFL (minimum score 550 paper-based). *Application deadline:* For fall admission, 2/1 priority date for domestic students; for spring admission, 10/1 priority date for domestic students. Applications are processed on a rolling basis. Application fee: $0. *Expenses:* Tuition, state resident: part-time $433 per credit. Tuition, nonresident: part-time $851 per credit. *Required fees:* $81.50 per credit. *Financial support:* Application deadline: 2/1. *Faculty research:* Multicultural education, cooperative learning, psychology of cognition. *Unit head:* Carolyn Anderson, Interim Director, 443-885-4497, Fax: 443-885-8231, E-mail: carolyn.anderson@morgan.edu. *Application contact:* Dr. Dean Campbell, Graduate Recruitment Specialist, 443-885-3185, Fax: 443-885-8226, E-mail: dean.campbell@morgan.edu.

National American University, Roueche Graduate Center, Austin, TX 78731. Offers accounting (MBA); aviation management (MBA, MM); care coordination (MSN); community college leadership (Ed D); criminal justice (MM); e-marketing (MBA, MM); health care administration (MBA, MM); higher education (MM); human resources management (MBA, MM); information technology management (MBA, MM); international business (MBA); leadership (EMBA); management (MBA); nursing administration (MSN); nursing education (MSN); nursing informatics (MSN); operations and configuration management (MBA, MM); project and process management (MBA, MM). Master's programs offered online through the Harold D. Buckingham Graduate School. *Program availability:* Part-time, evening/weekend, online learning. *Entrance requirements:* For master's, minimum undergraduate GPA of 2.75. Additional exam requirements/recommendations for international students: Required—TOEFL, TWE. Electronic applications accepted. *Faculty research:* Tourism, finance, marketing.

North Carolina State University, Graduate School, College of Education, Department of Adult and Higher Education, Program in Adult and Community College Education, Raleigh, NC 27695. Offers M Ed, MS, Ed D. *Degree requirements:* For master's, thesis (for some programs); for doctorate, thesis/dissertation. *Entrance requirements:* For master's and doctorate, GRE or MAT. Electronic applications accepted.

Northern Arizona University, College of Education, Department of Educational Leadership, Flagstaff, AZ 86011. Offers community college teaching and learning (Graduate Certificate); educational leadership (M Ed, Ed D), including community college/higher education (M Ed), educational foundations (M Ed), instructional leadership K-12 school leadership (M Ed), principal certification K-12 (M Ed); principal (Graduate Certificate); superintendent (Graduate Certificate). *Program availability:* Part-time. *Faculty:* 24 full-time (10 women), 1 (woman) part-time/adjunct. *Students:* 193 full-time (128 women), 648 part-time (425 women); includes 329 minority (54 Black or African American, non-Hispanic/Latino; 63 American Indian or Alaska Native, non-Hispanic/Latino; 10 Asian, non-Hispanic/Latino; 169 Hispanic/Latino; 1 Native Hawaiian or other Pacific Islander, non-Hispanic/Latino; 32 Two or more races, non-Hispanic/Latino), 2 international. Average age 38. 298 applicants, 98% accepted, 291 enrolled. In 2017, 252 master's, 12 doctorates, 48 other advanced degrees awarded. *Degree requirements:* For master's, comprehensive exam, thesis (for some programs); for doctorate, comprehensive exam, thesis/dissertation; for Graduate Certificate, comprehensive exam (for some programs). *Entrance requirements:* Additional exam requirements/recommendations for international students: Required—TOEFL (minimum score 80 iBT), IELTS (minimum score 6.5). *Application deadline:* For fall admission, 3/1 for domestic and international students; for spring admission, 10/1 for domestic and international students. Applications are processed on a rolling basis. Application fee: $65. Electronic applications accepted. *Expenses:* Tuition, state resident: full-time $9240; part-time $458 per credit hour. Tuition, nonresident: full-time $21,588; part-time $1199 per credit hour. *Required fees:* $1021; $14 per credit hour. $646 per semester. Tuition and fees vary according to course load, campus/location and program. *Financial support:* In 2017–18, 1 student received support. Institutionally sponsored loans, health care benefits, tuition waivers (partial), and unspecified assistantships available. Financial award application deadline: 2/1; financial award applicants required to submit FAFSA. *Unit head:* Dr. Michael Schwanenberger, Chair, 928-523-3202, Fax: 928-523-1929, E-mail: michael.schwanenberger@nau.edu. *Application contact:* Jennifer Offutt, Administrative Assistant, 928-523-3202, Fax: 928-523-1929, E-mail: jennifer.offutt@nau.edu. Website: https://nau.edu/coe/Ed-Leadership/

Old Dominion University, Darden College of Education, Doctoral Program in Community College Leadership, Norfolk, VA 23529. Offers PhD. *Program availability:* Evening/weekend, online only, 100% online, blended/hybrid learning. *Faculty:* 6 full-time (2 women), 1 (woman) part-time/adjunct. *Students:* 46 part-time (24 women); includes 10 minority (8 Black or African American, non-Hispanic/Latino; 1 Hispanic/Latino; 1 Two or more races, non-Hispanic/Latino). Average age 46. 32 applicants, 56% accepted, 16 enrolled. In 2017, 18 doctorates awarded. *Degree requirements:* For doctorate, comprehensive exam, thesis/dissertation, internship. *Entrance requirements:* For doctorate, GRE, master's degree, writing sample, 3 letters of reference, resume, essay, interview with faculty. Additional exam requirements/recommendations for international students: Required—TOEFL (minimum score 600 paper-based). *Application deadline:* For spring admission, 2/1 for domestic students, 2/1 priority date for international students. Application fee: $50. Electronic applications accepted. *Expenses:* Tuition, state resident:

full-time $8928; part-time $496 per credit. Tuition, nonresident: full-time $22,482; part-time $1249 per credit. *Required fees:* $66 per semester. *Financial support:* In 2017–18, 12 fellowships with partial tuition reimbursements (averaging $1,500 per year), 1 research assistantship with full tuition reimbursement (averaging $15,000 per year) were awarded; career-related internships or fieldwork and unspecified assistantships also available. Financial award application deadline: 4/15. *Faculty research:* Rural community colleges, inter-institutional collaboration in higher education. *Unit head:* Dr. Chris Glass, Graduate Program Director, 757-683-4118, Fax: 757-683-5756, E-mail: ccl@odu.edu. Website: http://education.odu.edu/efl/academics/ccl

Old Dominion University, Darden College of Education, Programs in STEM Education and Professional Studies, Norfolk, VA 23529. Offers community college teaching (MS); human resources training (PhD); technology education (PhD). *Accreditation:* NCATE (one or more programs are accredited). *Program availability:* Part-time, evening/weekend, mix of synchronous and asynchronous study. *Faculty:* 6 full-time (2 women). *Students:* 10 full-time (7 women), 35 part-time (24 women); includes 22 minority (18 Black or African American, non-Hispanic/Latino; 1 American Indian or Alaska Native, non-Hispanic/Latino; 2 Hispanic/Latino; 1 Two or more races, non-Hispanic/Latino), 1 international. Average age 41. 3 applicants, 100% accepted, 3 enrolled. In 2017, 4 master's, 3 doctorates awarded. Terminal master's awarded for partial completion of doctoral program. *Degree requirements:* For master's, comprehensive exam, thesis optional, writing exam, candidacy exam; for doctorate, comprehensive exam, thesis/dissertation, writing exam, candidacy exam. *Entrance requirements:* For master's, GRE General Test or MAT, minimum GPA of 2.8, 2 letters of reference; for doctorate, GRE, minimum GPA of 3.0, 3 letters of reference. Additional exam requirements/recommendations for international students: Required—TOEFL. *Application deadline:* For fall admission, 6/1 priority date for domestic students, 6/1 for international students; for winter admission, 11/1 priority date for domestic students, 11/1 for international students; for spring admission, 3/1 priority date for domestic students, 3/1 for international students. Applications are processed on a rolling basis. Application fee: $50. Electronic applications accepted. *Expenses:* Tuition, state resident: full-time $8928; part-time $496 per credit. Tuition, nonresident: full-time $22,482; part-time $1249 per credit. *Required fees:* $66 per semester. *Financial support:* In 2017–18, 3 students received support, including 2 teaching assistantships with partial tuition reimbursements available (averaging $15,000 per year). Financial award application deadline: 2/15; financial award applicants required to submit FAFSA. *Faculty research:* Training and development, STEM education, visualization, leadership, technology literacy. *Total annual research expenditures:* $1 million. *Unit head:* Dr. Petros Katsioloudis, Department Chair, 757-683-5323, E-mail: pkatsiol@odu.edu. Website: http://education.odu.edu/ots/

University of Arkansas at Little Rock, Graduate School, College of Education and Health Professions, Department of Educational Leadership, Program in Higher Education, Little Rock, AR 72204-1099. Offers administration (MA); college student affairs (MA); health professions teaching and learning (MA); higher education (Ed D); two-year college teaching (MA). *Degree requirements:* For doctorate, comprehensive exam, oral defense of dissertation, residency. *Entrance requirements:* For master's, GRE General Test or MAT, interview, minimum graduate GPA of 3.0; for doctorate, GRE General Test, interview, minimum graduate GPA of 3.5, teaching certificate, three years of work experience.

University of Central Florida, College of Community Innovation and Education, Department of Educational Leadership and Higher Education, Orlando, FL 32816. Offers career and technical education (MA); educational leadership (M Ed, MA, Ed S); higher education/college teaching and leadership (MA); higher education/student personnel (MA). *Program availability:* Part-time, evening/weekend. *Students:* 86 full-time (65 women), 233 part-time (184 women); includes 136 minority (66 Black or African American, non-Hispanic/Latino; 1 American Indian or Alaska Native, non-Hispanic/Latino; 4 Asian, non-Hispanic/Latino; 59 Hispanic/Latino; 6 Two or more races, non-Hispanic/Latino). Average age 31. 235 applicants, 82% accepted, 113 enrolled. In 2017, 114 master's, 16 other advanced degrees awarded. *Degree requirements:* For master's, thesis or alternative; for Ed S, thesis or alternative, final exam. *Entrance requirements:* For master's, GRE General Test; for Ed S, GRE General Test, minimum GPA of 3.0, resume, letters of recommendation. Additional exam requirements/recommendations for international students: Required—TOEFL. *Application deadline:* For fall admission, 6/20 for domestic students; for spring admission, 9/20 for domestic students. Application fee: $30. Electronic applications accepted. *Expenses:* Tuition, state resident: part-time $288.16 per credit hour. Tuition, nonresident: part-time $1073.31 per credit hour. Tuition and fees vary according to program. *Financial support:* In 2017–18, 12 students received support, including 2 fellowships with partial tuition reimbursements available (averaging $3,000 per year), 10 research assistantships with partial tuition reimbursements available (averaging $8,387 per year), 2 teaching assistantships with partial tuition reimbursements available (averaging $12,166 per year); career-related internships or fieldwork, Federal Work-Study, institutionally sponsored loans, health care benefits, tuition waivers (partial), and unspecified assistantships also available. Financial award application deadline: 3/1; financial award applicants required to submit FAFSA. *Unit head:* Dr. Kenneth Murray, Program Coordinator, 407-832-1468, E-mail: kenneth.murray@ucf.edu. *Application contact:* Associate Director, Graduate Admissions, 407-823-2766, Fax: 407-823-6442, E-mail: gradadmissions@ucf.edu. Website: https://ccie.ucf.edu/elhe/

University of Memphis, Graduate School, College of Education, Department of Leadership, Memphis, TN 38152. Offers adult education (Ed D); community college teaching and leadership (Graduate Certificate); community education (Ed D); educational leadership (Ed D); higher education (Ed D); leadership (MS); policy studies (Ed D); school administration and supervision (MS); student personnel (MS). *Accreditation:* NCATE. *Program availability:* Part-time, evening/weekend, online learning. *Faculty:* 9 full-time (5 women), 6 part-time/adjunct (2 women). *Students:* 13 full-time (9 women), 154 part-time (96 women). Average age 35. 54 applicants, 93% accepted, 44 enrolled. In 2017, 19 master's, 26 doctorates, 4 other advanced degrees awarded. *Degree requirements:* For master's, comprehensive exam, thesis optional; for doctorate, comprehensive exam, thesis/dissertation. *Entrance requirements:* For master's, GRE, resume, letters of reference, statement of professional goals, current teacher certification, sample work, interview; for doctorate, GRE, resume, letters of reference, statement of professional goals, interview. Additional exam requirements/recommendations for international students: Required—TOEFL (minimum score 550 paper-based; 79 iBT). *Application deadline:* For fall admission, 6/15 for domestic students; for spring admission, 9/15 for domestic students; for summer admission, 2/15 for domestic students. Application fee: $35 ($60 for international students). Electronic applications accepted. *Expenses:* Contact institution. *Financial support:* In 2017–18, 70 students received support, including 4 research assistantships with full tuition reimbursements available (averaging $14,700 per year); teaching assistantships, Federal Work-Study, scholarships/grants, and unspecified assistantships also available. Financial award application deadline: 2/1; financial award applicants required to submit FAFSA. *Faculty research:* School improvement, social justice, online learning, adult learning, diversity. *Unit head:* Dr. Reginald Green, Interim Chair, 901-678-3445, E-mail: rlgreen1@memphis.edu. Website: http://www.memphis.edu/lead

University of Northern Iowa, Graduate College, College of Humanities, Arts and Sciences, Department of Mathematics, MA Program in Mathematics, Cedar Falls, IA 50614. Offers community college teaching (MA); mathematics (MA); secondary teaching (MA).

University of South Florida, College of Education, Department of Leadership, Counseling, Adult, Career and Higher Education, Tampa, FL 33620-9951. Offers adult education (MA, Ed D, PhD, Ed S); career and technical education (MA); career and workforce education (PhD); higher education/community college teaching (MA, Ed D, PhD); vocational education (Ed S). *Faculty:* 19 full-time (11 women). *Students:* 129 full-time (91 women), 274 part-time (187 women); includes 147 minority (71 Black or African American, non-Hispanic/Latino; 2 American Indian or Alaska Native, non-Hispanic/

Latino; 9 Asian, non-Hispanic/Latino; 59 Hispanic/Latino; 6 Two or more races, non-Hispanic/Latino), 15 international. Average age 35. 158 applicants, 67% accepted, 83 enrolled. In 2017, 89 master's, 7 doctorates, 2 other advanced degrees awarded. Application fee: $30. *Total annual research expenditures:* $157,971. *Unit head:* Dr. Judith Ponticell, Chair, 813-974-4897, Fax: 813-974-5423, E-mail: jponticell@usf.edu. Website: http://www.coedu.usf.edu/main/departments/ache/ache.html

Wingate University, Thayer School of Education, Wingate, NC 28174. Offers community college executive leadership (Ed D); educational leadership (MA Ed, Ed S); elementary education (MA Ed, MAT). *Accreditation:* NCATE. *Program availability:* Part-time, evening/weekend. *Degree requirements:* For master's, portfolio. *Entrance requirements:* For master's, GRE General Test or MAT, teaching certificate (MA Ed).

Early Childhood Education

Alabama Agricultural and Mechanical University, School of Graduate Studies, College of Education, Humanities, and Behavioral Sciences, Department of Reading, Elementary, Early Childhood and Special Education, Huntsville, AL 35811. Offers early childhood education (MS Ed, Ed S); elementary education (MS Ed, Ed S); reading/literacy (PhD); special education collaborative teacher training (MS Ed, Ed S). *Accreditation:* NCATE. *Program availability:* Evening/weekend. *Degree requirements:* For master's, comprehensive exam; for Ed S, thesis. *Entrance requirements:* For master's, GRE General Test. Additional exam requirements/recommendations for international students: Required—TOEFL (minimum score 500 paper-based; 61 iBT). Electronic applications accepted. *Faculty research:* Multicultural education, learning styles, diagnostic-prescriptive instruction.

Alabama State University, College of Education, Department of Curriculum and Instruction, Montgomery, AL 36101-0271. Offers early childhood education (M Ed, Ed S); elementary education (M Ed, Ed S); secondary education (M Ed, Ed S), including biology education, English language arts education (M Ed), history education, math education, music education (M Ed), reading education (M Ed), social science education; special education (M Ed). *Program availability:* Part-time. *Faculty:* 7 full-time (4 women), 7 part-time/adjunct (4 women). *Students:* 43 full-time (35 women), 71 part-time (62 women); includes 112 minority (111 Black or African American, non-Hispanic/Latino; 1 Two or more races, non-Hispanic/Latino). Average age 22. 47 applicants, 66% accepted, 19 enrolled. In 2017, 21 master's, 13 Ed Ss awarded. *Degree requirements:* For master's, comprehensive exam, thesis optional; for Ed S, comprehensive exam, thesis. *Entrance requirements:* For master's, GRE General Test, MAT, writing competency test; for Ed S, writing competency test, GRE, MAT. Additional exam requirements/recommendations for international students: Required—TOEFL (minimum score 500 paper-based). *Application deadline:* For fall admission, 4/15 for domestic and international students; for spring admission, 11/15 for domestic and international students; for summer admission, 3/15 for domestic and international students. Applications are processed on a rolling basis. Application fee: $25. Electronic applications accepted. *Expenses:* Tuition, state resident: part-time $412 per credit hour. Tuition, nonresident: part-time $824 per credit hour. *Required fees:* $685 per semester. *Financial support:* Research assistantships available. Financial award application deadline: 6/30; financial award applicants required to submit FAFSA. *Unit head:* Dr. Joyce Johnson, Acting Chairperson, 334-229-4485, Fax: 334-229-5603, E-mail: jjohnson@alasu.edu. *Application contact:* Dr. William Person, Dean of Graduate Studies, 334-229-4274, Fax: 334-229-4928, E-mail: wperson@alasu.edu.
Website: http://www.alasu.edu/academics/colleges—departments/college-of-education/curriculum—instruction/index.aspx

Albany State University, College of Education, Albany, GA 31705-2717. Offers early childhood education (M Ed); educational leadership (Ed S); health and physical education (M Ed); middle grades education (M Ed); school counseling (M Ed); special education (M Ed). *Accreditation:* NCATE. *Program availability:* Part-time, evening/weekend, online learning. *Degree requirements:* For master's, comprehensive exam, internship, GACE Content Exam. *Entrance requirements:* For master's, GRE or MAT. Electronic applications accepted. *Faculty research:* GACE preparation, STEM (science, technology, engineering, and mathematics), technology education, special education, professional teacher development, health implications liberation philosophy, NET-Q, learning community, disabled or at-risk students.

Albright College, Graduate Division, Reading, PA 19612-5234. Offers early childhood education (MS); elementary education (MS); English as a second language (MA); general education (MA); special education (MS). *Program availability:* Part-time, evening/weekend. *Degree requirements:* For master's, thesis. *Entrance requirements:* For master's, GRE General Test or MAT, minimum undergraduate GPA of 3.0, 2 letters of recommendation, interview. Additional exam requirements/recommendations for international students: Recommended—TOEFL (minimum score 525 paper-based). Electronic applications accepted.

American International College, School of Education, Springfield, MA 01109-3189. Offers early childhood education (M Ed, CAGS); education (MA, Ed D), including counseling psychology (MA), educational leadership and supervision (Ed D), professional counseling and supervision (Ed D), teaching and learning (Ed D); elementary education (M Ed, CAGS); middle education/secondary education (M Ed, CAGS); moderate disabilities (M Ed, CAGS); reading specialist (M Ed, CAGS); school adjustment counseling (MAEP, CAGS); school guidance counseling (MAEP, CAGS); school leadership (M Ed, CAGS). *Program availability:* Evening/weekend. *Faculty:* 1 (woman) full-time, 151 part-time/adjunct (95 women). *Students:* 1,082 full-time (910 women), 143 part-time (113 women); includes 109 minority (19 Black or African American, non-Hispanic/Latino; 2 American Indian or Alaska Native, non-Hispanic/Latino; 10 Asian, non-Hispanic/Latino; 58 Hispanic/Latino; 1 Native Hawaiian or other Pacific Islander, non-Hispanic/Latino; 19 Two or more races, non-Hispanic/Latino). Average age 34. 537 applicants, 77% accepted, 327 enrolled. In 2017, 486 master's, 112 other advanced degrees awarded. *Degree requirements:* For master's and CAGS, practicum/culminating experience. *Entrance requirements:* For master's, Communication and Literacy portion of the Massachusetts Tests for Education Licensure, graduate of accredited four-year college with minimum B- average in undergraduate course work; for CAGS, M Ed or master's degree in field related to licensure from accredited institution. *Application deadline:* Applications are processed on a rolling basis. Application fee: $50. Electronic applications accepted. *Expenses:* $439 per credit, $30 per term registration fee, $100 graduation fee, $110 technology fee. *Financial support:* Applicants required to submit FAFSA. *Unit head:* Sylvia Mason, Dean, 413-205-1743, Fax: 413-205-3943, E-mail: sylvia.mason@aic.edu. *Application contact:* Kerry Barnes, Dean of Graduate Admissions, 413-205-3703, Fax: 413-205-

3051, E-mail: kerry.barnes@aic.edu.
Website: http://www.aic.edu/school-of-education/

Anna Maria College, Graduate Division, Program in Education, Paxton, MA 01612. Offers early childhood education (M Ed); education (CAGS); elementary education (M Ed); English language arts (M Ed); visual arts (M Ed). *Program availability:* Part-time, evening/weekend. *Entrance requirements:* For master's, bachelor's degree in liberal arts or sciences, minimum GPA of 3.0. Additional exam requirements/recommendations for international students: Required—TOEFL (minimum score 500 paper-based). Electronic applications accepted.

Antioch University New England, Graduate School, Department of Education, Integrated Learning Program, Keene, NH 03431-3552. Offers early childhood education (M Ed); elementary education (M Ed), including arts and humanities, science and environmental education; special education (M Ed). *Degree requirements:* For master's, internship. *Entrance requirements:* For master's, previous course work or work experience in education. Additional exam requirements/recommendations for international students: Required—TOEFL (minimum score 550 paper-based). Electronic applications accepted. *Expenses:* Contact institution. *Faculty research:* Problem-based learning, place-based education, mathematics education, democratic classrooms, art education.

Arcadia University, School of Education, Glenside, PA 19038-3295. Offers art education (M Ed); computer education (CAS); curriculum (CAS); curriculum studies (M Ed); early childhood education (M Ed), including individualized, master teacher, research in child development; educational leadership (M Ed, Ed D, CAS); elementary education (M Ed); English education (MA Ed); environmental education (MA Ed); instructional technology (M Ed); language arts (M Ed); library science (M Ed); mathematics education (M Ed, MA Ed); music education (MA Ed); psychology (MA Ed); reading (M Ed, CAS); science education (M Ed, CAS); secondary education (M Ed, CAS); special education (M Ed, Ed D, CAS); theater arts (MA Ed); written communication (MA Ed). *Accreditation:* NASAD. *Program availability:* Part-time, evening/weekend, online learning. Electronic applications accepted. *Expenses:* Contact institution.

Arkansas State University, Graduate School, College of Education and Behavioral Science, School of Teacher Education and Leadership, State University, AR 72467. Offers community college administration (SCCT); curriculum and instruction (MSE); early childhood education (MSE); early childhood services (MS); educational leadership (MSE, Ed D, Ed S); educational theory and practice (MSE); middle level education (MAT, MSE); reading (MSE, Ed S); special education - gifted, talented, and creative (MSE); special education - instructional specialist grades 4-12 (MSE); special education - instructional specialist grades P-4 (MSE); special education, K-12 (MSE). *Accreditation:* NCATE. *Program availability:* Part-time, online learning. *Degree requirements:* For master's, comprehensive exam, thesis or alternative; for doctorate, comprehensive exam, thesis/dissertation; for other advanced degree, comprehensive exam. *Entrance requirements:* For master's, GRE General Test or MAT, appropriate bachelor's degree, official transcripts, immunization records, letters of reference, interview; for doctorate, GRE General Test or MAT, interview, master's degree, letters of reference, official transcript, personal statement, writing sample, immunization records; for other advanced degree, GRE General Test or MAT, interview, master's degree, official transcript, immunization records, letters of reference, 3 years of teaching experience, teaching license. Additional exam requirements/recommendations for international students: Required—TOEFL (minimum score 550 paper-based; 79 iBT), IELTS (minimum score 6), PTE (minimum score 56). Electronic applications accepted.

Auburn University at Montgomery, College of Education, Department of Counselor, Leadership, and Special Education, Montgomery, AL 36124-4023. Offers counselor education (M Ed, Ed S), including clinical mental health counseling, school counseling; early childhood special education (M Ed); instructional leadership (M Ed, Ed S); special education/collaborative teacher (M Ed, Ed S). *Accreditation:* ACA; NCATE. *Program availability:* Part-time, evening/weekend. *Faculty:* 7 full-time (4 women), 2 part-time/adjunct (both women). *Students:* 27 full-time (23 women), 57 part-time (51 women); includes 40 minority (38 Black or African American, non-Hispanic/Latino; 2 Hispanic/Latino). Average age 34. 76 applicants, 72% accepted, 26 enrolled. In 2017, 37 master's awarded. *Degree requirements:* For master's and Ed S, comprehensive exam. *Entrance requirements:* For master's, GRE General Test or MAT, certification, BS in teaching; for Ed S, GRE General Test or MAT, certification. Additional exam requirements/recommendations for international students: Recommended—TOEFL (minimum score 500 paper-based; 61 iBT), IELTS (minimum score 5.5), TSE (minimum score 44). *Application deadline:* For fall admission, 7/15 for international students; for spring admission, 11/15 for international students; for summer admission, 4/15 for international students. Applications are processed on a rolling basis. Electronic applications accepted. *Expenses:* Tuition, state resident: full-time $6930; part-time $385 per credit hour. Tuition, nonresident: full-time $15,588; part-time $866 per credit hour. *Required fees:* $640. *Financial support:* Career-related internships or fieldwork and scholarships/grants available. Support available to part-time students. Financial award application deadline: 3/1; financial award applicants required to submit FAFSA. *Unit head:* Dr. Samuel Flynt, Head, 334-244-3835, Fax: 334-244-3101, E-mail: sflynt@aum.edu. *Application contact:* Dr. Rhonda Morton, Associate Dean/Graduate Coordinator, 334-244-3287, Fax: 334-244-3978, E-mail: rmorton@aum.edu.
Website: http://education.aum.edu/academic-departments/counselor-leadership-and-special-education

Avila University, School of Education, Kansas City, MO 64145-1698. Offers advanced classroom management (MA); art K-12 (Teaching Certificate); educational technology (MA, Certificate); elementary education (Teaching Certificate); English as a second

language (MA); English language learners (Advanced Certificate); middle school (Teaching Certificate); physical education K-12 (Teaching Certificate); secondary education (Teaching Certificate); special education (Teaching Certificate); special reading (Advanced Certificate); teaching and learning (MA). *Program availability:* Part-time, evening/weekend, online learning. *Faculty:* 6 full-time (5 women), 9 part-time/adjunct (8 women). *Students:* 81 full-time (63 women), 20 part-time (11 women); includes 14 minority (8 Black or African American, non-Hispanic/Latino; 2 Asian, non-Hispanic/Latino; 3 Hispanic/Latino; 1 Two or more races, non-Hispanic/Latino), 4 international. Average age 35. 92 applicants, 62% accepted, 40 enrolled. In 2017, 24 master's awarded. *Entrance requirements:* For master's, minimum GPA of 3.0, writing sample, recommendation, interview; for other advanced degree, foreign language. Additional exam requirements/recommendations for international students: Required—TOEFL (minimum score 580 paper-based; 92 iBT). *Application deadline:* Applications are processed on a rolling basis. Electronic applications accepted. *Expenses:* Contact institution. *Financial support:* In 2017–18, 14 students received support. Unspecified assistantships available. Financial award applicants required to submit FAFSA. *Unit head:* Dr. Stacy Keith, Director of Graduate Education, 816-501-2446, Fax: 816-501-2915, E-mail: stacy.keith@avila.edu. *Application contact:* Cory Roup, Graduate Education Enrollment and Academic Advisor, 816-501-2464, E-mail: cory.roup@avila.edu.
Website: https://www.avila.edu/academics/graduate-studies/grad-education

Bank Street College of Education, Graduate School, Program in Early Childhood Education, New York, NY 10025. Offers MS Ed. *Degree requirements:* For master's, thesis. *Entrance requirements:* For master's, interview, essays. Additional exam requirements/recommendations for international students: Required—TOEFL (minimum score 600 paper-based; 100 iBT), IELTS (minimum score 7). Electronic applications accepted. *Faculty research:* Play in early childhood settings, early childhood learning environments, family-teacher interaction, child-centered education, developmental interaction.

Bank Street College of Education, Graduate School, Program in Infant and Family Development and Early Intervention, New York, NY 10025. Offers infant and family development (MS Ed); infant and family early childhood special and general education (MS Ed); infant and family/early childhood special education (Ed M). *Degree requirements:* For master's, thesis. *Entrance requirements:* For master's, interview, essays. Additional exam requirements/recommendations for international students: Required—TOEFL (minimum score 600 paper-based; 100 iBT), IELTS (minimum score 7). Electronic applications accepted. *Faculty research:* Early intervention, early attachment practice in infant and toddler childcare, parenting skills in adolescents.

Bank Street College of Education, Graduate School, Program in Reading and Literacy, New York, NY 10025. Offers advanced literacy specialization (Ed M); reading and literacy (MS Ed); teaching literacy (MS Ed); teaching literacy and childhood general education (MS Ed). *Degree requirements:* For master's, thesis. *Entrance requirements:* For master's, interview, essays. Additional exam requirements/recommendations for international students: Required—TOEFL (minimum score 600 paper-based; 100 iBT), IELTS (minimum score 7). Electronic applications accepted. *Faculty research:* Language development, children's literature, whole language, the reading and writing processes, reading difficulties in multicultural classrooms.

Bank Street College of Education, Graduate School, Programs in Educational Leadership, New York, NY 10025. Offers early childhood leadership (MS Ed); educational leadership (MS Ed); leadership for educational change (Ed M, MS Ed); leadership in community-based learning (MS Ed); leadership in mathematics education (MS Ed); leadership in museum education (MS Ed); leadership in the arts: creative writing (MS Ed); leadership in the arts: visual arts (MS Ed). *Degree requirements:* For master's, thesis. *Entrance requirements:* For master's, interview, essays, minimum of 2 years experience as a classroom teacher. Additional exam requirements/recommendations for international students: Required—TOEFL (minimum score 600 paper-based; 100 iBT), IELTS (minimum score 7). Electronic applications accepted. *Faculty research:* Leadership in urban schools, leadership in small schools, mathematics in elementary schools, professional development in early childhood, leadership in arts education, leadership in special education, museum leadership, community-based leadership.

Barry University, School of Education, Program in Curriculum and Instruction, Miami Shores, FL 33161-6695. Offers accomplished teacher (Ed S); culture, language and literacy (TESOL) (PhD); curriculum evaluation and research (PhD); early childhood (Ed S); early childhood education (PhD); elementary (Ed S); elementary education (PhD); ESOL (Ed S); gifted (Ed S); Montessori (Ed S); PKP/elementary (Ed S); reading (Ed S); reading, language and cognition (PhD). *Entrance requirements:* For doctorate, GRE, minimum GPA of 3.25.

Barry University, School of Education, Program in Montessori Education, Miami Shores, FL 33161-6695. Offers MS, Ed S. *Program availability:* Part-time, evening/weekend. *Degree requirements:* For master's, comprehensive exam, practicum; for Ed S, practicum. *Entrance requirements:* For master's, GRE General Test or MAT, minimum GPA of 3.0; for Ed S, GRE General Test, minimum GPA of 3.0. Electronic applications accepted.

Barry University, School of Education, Program in Pre-Kindergarten and Primary Education, Miami Shores, FL 33161-6695. Offers pre-k/primary (MS); pre-k/primary/ESOL (MS). *Program availability:* Part-time, evening/weekend. *Degree requirements:* For master's, comprehensive exam, practicum. *Entrance requirements:* For master's, GRE General Test or MAT, minimum GPA of 3.0. Electronic applications accepted.

Bayamón Central University, Graduate Programs, Program in Education, Bayamón, PR 00960-1725. Offers administration and supervision (MA Ed); commercial education (MA Ed); elementary education (K–3) (MA Ed); family counseling (Graduate Certificate); guidance and counseling (MA Ed); pre-elementary teacher (MA Ed); rehabilitation counseling (MA Ed); special education (MA Ed), including attention deficit disorder, education of the autistic, learning disabilities. *Program availability:* Part-time, evening/weekend. *Degree requirements:* For master's, comprehensive exam. *Entrance requirements:* For master's, EXADEP, bachelor's degree in education or related field.

Berry College, Graduate Programs, Graduate Programs in Education, Program in Early Childhood Education, Mount Berry, GA 30149-0159. Offers M Ed, MAT. *Accreditation:* NCATE. *Program availability:* Part-time. In 2017, 1 master's awarded. *Degree requirements:* For master's, thesis, portfolio, oral exams. *Entrance requirements:* For master's, GRE General Test or MAT, minimum GPA of 2.5. Additional exam requirements/recommendations for international students: Required—TOEFL (minimum score 550 paper-based). *Application deadline:* For fall admission, 7/20 for domestic students, 5/1 for international students; for spring admission, 12/1 for domestic students, 10/1 for international students. Applications are processed on a rolling basis. Application fee: $25 ($30 for international students). *Expenses:* $8,370 full-time tuition plus $176 fees per year; $465 per credit hour part-time tuition. *Financial support:* Research assistantships with full tuition reimbursements, scholarships/grants, tuition waivers, and unspecified assistantships available. Support available to part-time students. Financial award application deadline: 3/1; financial award applicants required to submit FAFSA. *Unit head:* Dr. Jacqueline McDowell, Dean, 706-236-1717, Fax: 706-238-5827, E-mail:

jmcdowell@berry.edu. *Application contact:* Brett Kennedy, Assistant Vice President of Enrollment Management, 706-236-2215, Fax: 706-290-2178, E-mail: admissions@berry.edu.
Website: http://www.berry.edu/academics/education/graduate/

Binghamton University, State University of New York, Graduate School, College of Community and Public Affairs, Department of Teaching, Learning and Educational Leadership, Program in Childhood and Early Childhood Education, Binghamton, NY 13902-6000. Offers MS Ed. *Accreditation:* TEAC. *Program availability:* Part-time, evening/weekend. *Entrance requirements:* For master's, GRE General Test. Additional exam requirements/recommendations for international students: Required—TOEFL (minimum score 550 paper-based; 80 iBT). *Application deadline:* For fall admission, 2/1 priority date for domestic and international students. Application fee: $75. Electronic applications accepted. *Financial support:* Career-related internships or fieldwork, Federal Work-Study, institutionally sponsored loans, scholarships/grants, health care benefits, tuition waivers (full and partial), and unspecified assistantships available. Financial award applicants required to submit FAFSA. *Unit head:* Dr. Susan Strehle, Dean, 607-777-7329, E-mail: sstrehle@binghamton.edu. *Application contact:* Ben Balkaya, Assistant Dean and Director, 607-777-2151, Fax: 607-777-2501, E-mail: balkaya@binghamton.edu.

Biola University, School of Education, La Mirada, CA 90639-0001. Offers curriculum and instruction (Certificate); early childhood (MA Ed, MAT); multiple subject (MAT); single subject (MAT); special education (MA Ed, MAT, Certificate). *Program availability:* Part-time, evening/weekend, online learning. *Faculty:* 16. *Students:* 67 full-time (52 women), 164 part-time (142 women); includes 97 minority (8 Black or African American, non-Hispanic/Latino; 1 American Indian or Alaska Native, non-Hispanic/Latino; 51 Asian, non-Hispanic/Latino; 30 Hispanic/Latino; 7 Two or more races, non-Hispanic/Latino), 4 international. 164 applicants, 87% accepted, 116 enrolled. In 2017, 25 master's awarded. *Entrance requirements:* For master's, CBEST, CSET, GRE (waived if cumulative GPA is 3.5 or above or if CBEST and all CSET subtests are passed). Additional exam requirements/recommendations for international students: Required—TOEFL (minimum score 100 iBT). *Application deadline:* For fall admission, 7/1 for domestic students, 6/1 for international students; for spring admission, 12/1 for domestic students; for summer admission, 5/1 for domestic students. Applications are processed on a rolling basis. Application fee: $65. Electronic applications accepted. *Financial support:* Scholarships/grants available. Support available to part-time students. Financial award applicants required to submit FAFSA. *Faculty research:* Early childhood education, elementary education, special education, curriculum development, teacher preparation. *Unit head:* Dr. June Hetzel, Dean, 562-903-4715. *Application contact:* Graduate Admissions Office, 562-903-4752, E-mail: graduate.admissions@biola.edu.
Website: http://education.biola.edu/

Bloomsburg University of Pennsylvania, School of Graduate Studies, College of Education, Department of Teaching and Learning, Program in Early Childhood Education, Bloomsburg, PA 17815-1301. Offers M Ed. *Accreditation:* NCATE. *Degree requirements:* For master's, thesis, practicum, student teaching. *Entrance requirements:* For master's, MAT, GRE, minimum QPA of 3.0, valid teaching certificate, U.S. citizenship. Additional exam requirements/recommendations for international students: Required—TOEFL, IELTS. Electronic applications accepted. *Expenses:* Tuition, state resident: full-time $10,000; part-time $500 per credit hour. Tuition, nonresident: full-time $15,000; part-time $750 per credit hour. *Required fees:* $2484; $110.75 per credit hour. $75 per term. Tuition and fees vary according to program.

Boise State University, College of Education, Department of Early and Special Education, Boise, ID 83725-0399. Offers early and special education (M Ed). *Accreditation:* NCATE. *Program availability:* Part-time. *Faculty:* 14. *Students:* 29 full-time (27 women), 13 part-time (10 women); includes 4 minority (2 Asian, non-Hispanic/Latino; 1 Hispanic/Latino; 1 Native Hawaiian or other Pacific Islander, non-Hispanic/Latino). Average age 38. 18 applicants, 33% accepted, 3 enrolled. In 2017, 10 master's awarded. *Degree requirements:* For master's, thesis optional. *Entrance requirements:* For master's, minimum GPA of 3.0. Additional exam requirements/recommendations for international students: Required—TOEFL (minimum score 587 paper-based; 95 iBT), IELTS (minimum score 6.5). *Application deadline:* For fall admission, 3/31 for domestic and international students. Application fee: $65 ($95 for international students). Electronic applications accepted. *Expenses:* Tuition, state resident: full-time $6471; part-time $390 per credit. Tuition, nonresident: full-time $21,787; part-time $685 per credit. *Required fees:* $2283; $100 per term. Part-time tuition and fees vary according to course load and program. *Financial support:* Scholarships/grants and unspecified assistantships available. Financial award application deadline: 3/31; financial award applicants required to submit FAFSA. *Unit head:* Dr. Deb Carter, Department Chair, 208-426-2804, E-mail: debcarter@boisestate.edu. *Application contact:* Dr. Carrie Semmelroth, Graduate Coordinator, 208-426-2818, E-mail: carriesemmelroth@boisestate.edu.
Website: http://education.boisestate.edu/spedecs/

Boston College, Lynch School of Education, Program in Early Childhood Education, Chestnut Hill, MA 02467-3800. Offers M Ed. *Accreditation:* TEAC. *Program availability:* Part-time, evening/weekend. *Degree requirements:* For master's, comprehensive exam. *Entrance requirements:* For master's, GRE General Test or MAT. Additional exam requirements/recommendations for international students: Required—TOEFL (minimum score 550 paper-based; 79 iBT). Electronic applications accepted. *Faculty research:* Early childhood testing and assessment, selective attention abilities in children, problem-solving, dual language learning and literacy.

Brandman University, School of Education, Irvine, CA 92618. Offers curriculum and instruction (MAE); educational administration (MAE); educational leadership (MAE); educational leadership and administration (MA); elementary education (MAT); instructional technology: teaching the 21st century learner (MAE); leadership in early childhood education (MAE); organizational leadership (Ed D); school counseling (MA); secondary education (MAT); special education (MA); teaching and learning (MAE). *Expenses:* Tuition: Part-time $640 per credit hour. Tuition and fees vary according to degree level and program. *Unit head:* Dr. Christine G. Zeppos, Dean, 949-341-9948, E-mail: zeppos@brandman.edu. *Application contact:* Dr. Christine G. Zeppos, Dean, 949-341-9948, E-mail: zeppos@brandman.edu.
Website: https://www.brandman.edu/academic-programs/education

Brenau University, Sydney O. Smith Graduate School, College of Education, Gainesville, GA 30501. Offers early childhood (Ed S); early childhood education (M Ed, MAT); middle grades (Ed S); middle grades education (M Ed, MAT); secondary education (MAT); special education (M Ed, MAT). *Accreditation:* NCATE. *Program availability:* Part-time, evening/weekend, online learning. *Degree requirements:* For master's, thesis optional, comprehensive exam or applied research project, effective portfolio; for Ed S, thesis, applied research project. *Entrance requirements:* For master's, GRE, MAT, interview, minimum GPA of 3.0, 3 references, writing samples; for Ed S, GRE, MAT, master's degree, minimum GPA of 3.0, writing sample, letters of reference. Additional exam requirements/recommendations for international students: Required—TOEFL (minimum score 500 paper-based; 61 iBT); Recommended—IELTS (minimum score 5). Electronic applications accepted. *Expenses:* Contact institution.

Early Childhood Education

Bridgewater State University, College of Graduate Studies, College of Education and Allied Studies, Department of Elementary and Early Childhood Education, Program in Early Childhood Education, Bridgewater, MA 02325. Offers M Ed. *Accreditation:* NCATE. *Program availability:* Part-time, evening/weekend. *Entrance requirements:* For master's, GRE General Test or Massachusetts Test for Educator Licensure.

Brooklyn College of the City University of New York, School of Education, Program in Early Childhood Education, Brooklyn, NY 11210-2889. Offers art teacher (K-12) (MA); birth-grade 2 (MS Ed). *Program availability:* Part-time, evening/weekend. *Entrance requirements:* For master's, LAST, bachelor's degree in early childhood education, resume, 2 letters of recommendation, essay. Additional exam requirements/recommendations for international students: Required—TOEFL (minimum score 500 paper-based; 61 iBT). Electronic applications accepted. *Faculty research:* Children's narrations, language acquisition, culture and education.

Brooklyn College of the City University of New York, School of Education, Program in Special Education, Brooklyn, NY 11210-2889. Offers autism spectrum disorders (AC); teacher of students with disabilities (MS Ed), including adolescence education, childhood education, early childhood education. *Program availability:* Part-time. *Entrance requirements:* For master's, LAST, interview; previous course work in education and psychology; minimum GPA of 3.0 in education, 2.8 overall; resume, 2 letters of recommendation; essay. Additional exam requirements/recommendations for international students: Required—TOEFL (minimum score 500 paper-based; 61 iBT). Electronic applications accepted. *Faculty research:* School reform, conflict resolution, curriculum for inclusive settings, urban issues in special education.

Buffalo State College, State University of New York, The Graduate School, Faculty of Applied Science and Education, Department of Elementary Education and Reading, Program in Elementary Education, Buffalo, NY 14222-1095. Offers childhood education (grades 1-6) (MS Ed); early childhood and childhood curriculum and instruction (MS Ed); early childhood education (birth-grade 2) (MS Ed). *Accreditation:* NCATE. *Program availability:* Part-time. *Degree requirements:* For master's, thesis or project. *Entrance requirements:* For master's, minimum GPA of 2.5 in last 60 hours, New York teaching certificate. Additional exam requirements/recommendations for international students: Required—TOEFL (minimum score 550 paper-based).

Cabrini University, Academic Affairs, Radnor, PA 19087. Offers accounting (M Acc); autism spectrum disorder (M Ed); biological sciences (MS), including civic leadership; criminology and criminal justice (MA); curriculum, instruction, and assessment (M Ed); educational leadership (M Ed, Ed D), including curriculum and instructional leadership (Ed D), preK-12 leadership (Ed D); English as a second language (M Ed); organizational leadership (DBA, PhD); preK to 4 (M Ed); reading specialist (M Ed); secondary education (M Ed), including biology, chemistry, English, English/communication, mathematics, social studies; special education grades 7-12 (M Ed); special education preK-8 (M Ed); teaching and learning (M Ed). *Program availability:* Part-time, evening/weekend. *Faculty:* 23 full-time (17 women), 46 part-time/adjunct (38 women). *Students:* 60 full-time (35 women), 559 part-time (435 women); includes 93 minority (66 Black or African American, non-Hispanic/Latino; 1 American Indian or Alaska Native, non-Hispanic/Latino; 8 Asian, non-Hispanic/Latino; 15 Hispanic/Latino; 3 Two or more races, non-Hispanic/Latino), 4 international. Average age 33. 290 applicants, 82% accepted, 154 enrolled. In 2017, 283 master's awarded. *Degree requirements:* For master's, comprehensive exam (for some programs), thesis (for some programs); for doctorate, comprehensive exam (for some programs), thesis/dissertation. *Entrance requirements:* For master's, professional resume, personal statement, two recommendations, official transcripts; for doctorate, official transcripts, minimum master's GPA of 3.0, two recommendations, interview with admissions committee. Additional exam requirements/recommendations for international students: Required—TOEFL (minimum score 80 iBT). *Application deadline:* For fall admission, 8/26 for domestic students, 8/1 for international students; for winter admission, 1/13 for domestic students, 12/20 for international students; for spring admission, 1/13 for domestic students, 12/20 for international students; for summer admission, 5/20 for domestic students, 4/30 for international students. Applications are processed on a rolling basis. Application fee: $50. Electronic applications accepted. Application fee is waived when completed online. *Expenses:* Contact institution. *Financial support:* In 2017–18, 1,459 students received support. Tuition waivers and unspecified assistantships available. Financial award application deadline: 5/1; financial award applicants required to submit FAFSA. *Unit head:* Dr. Maliha Zaman, 610-902-8502, Fax: 610-902-8797, E-mail: msz37@cabrini.edu. *Application contact:* Diane Greenwood, Director of Graduate Admissions, 610-902-8291, E-mail: diane.l.greenwood@cabrini.edu.
Website: http://cabrini.edu/graduate

California State University, Dominguez Hills, College of Education, Division of Teacher Education, Program in Special Education, Carson, CA 90747-0001. Offers early childhood special education (MA). *Program availability:* Part-time, evening/weekend. *Degree requirements:* For master's, comprehensive exam, thesis or alternative. *Entrance requirements:* For master's, minimum GPA of 2.75 in last 60 units, 3 letters of recommendation. Additional exam requirements/recommendations for international students: Required—TOEFL.

California State University, East Bay, Office of Graduate Studies, College of Education and Allied Studies, Department of Teacher Education, Hayward, CA 94542-3000. Offers education (MS), including curriculum, early childhood education, educational technology and leadership, reading instruction. *Program availability:* Online learning. *Faculty:* 11 full-time (8 women), 56 part-time/adjunct (40 women). *Students:* 49 full-time (35 women), 15 part-time (13 women); includes 31 minority (5 Black or African American, non-Hispanic/Latino; 13 Asian, non-Hispanic/Latino; 11 Hispanic/Latino; 2 Two or more races, non-Hispanic/Latino), 7 international. Average age 31. 76 applicants, 82% accepted, 33 enrolled. In 2017, 83 master's awarded. *Degree requirements:* For master's, project or thesis. *Entrance requirements:* For master's, minimum GPA of 3.0 in field, 2.5 overall; teaching experience; baccalaureate degree; 3 letters of recommendation. Additional exam requirements/recommendations for international students: Required—TOEFL (minimum score 550 paper-based), IELTS. *Application deadline:* For fall admission, 6/1 for domestic and international students. Application fee: $55. Electronic applications accepted. *Financial support:* Career-related internships or fieldwork, Federal Work-Study, and institutionally sponsored loans available. Support available to part-time students. Financial award application deadline: 3/2; financial award applicants required to submit FAFSA. *Faculty research:* Online, pedagogy, writing, learning, teaching. *Unit head:* Dr. Eric Engdahl, Chair, 510-885-4599, E-mail: eric.engdahl@csueastbay.edu. *Application contact:* Prof. Valerie Helgren-Lempesis, Education Graduate Advisor, 510-885-3006, Fax: 510-885-4632, E-mail: valerie.helgren-lempesis@csueastbay.edu.
Website: http://www20.csueastbay.edu/ceas/departments/ted/index.html

California State University, Fresno, Division of Research and Graduate Studies, Kremen School of Education and Human Development, Department of Literacy, Early, Bilingual, and Special Education, Fresno, CA 93740-8027. Offers education (MA), including early childhood education, reading/language arts; special education (MA). *Accreditation:* NCATE. *Program availability:* Part-time, evening/weekend. *Degree requirements:* For master's, thesis or alternative. *Entrance requirements:* For master's, GRE General Test, MAT, minimum GPA of 2.75. Additional exam requirements/

recommendations for international students: Required—TOEFL. Electronic applications accepted. *Faculty research:* Reading recovery, monitoring/tutoring programs, character and academics, professional ethics, low-performing partnership schools.

California State University, Northridge, Graduate Studies, Michael D. Eisner College of Education, Department of Educational Psychology and Counseling, Northridge, CA 91330. Offers counseling (MS), including career counseling, college counseling and student services, marriage and family therapy, school counseling, school psychology; educational psychology (MA Ed), including development, learning, and instruction, early childhood education. *Accreditation:* ACA (one or more programs are accredited); NCATE. *Program availability:* Part-time, evening/weekend. *Students:* 288 full-time (244 women), 84 part-time (76 women); includes 190 minority (13 Black or African American, non-Hispanic/Latino; 24 Asian, non-Hispanic/Latino; 139 Hispanic/Latino; 14 Two or more races, non-Hispanic/Latino), 11 international. Average age 29. 427 applicants, 34% accepted, 136 enrolled. In 2017, 103 master's awarded. *Entrance requirements:* For master's, GRE General Test or minimum GPA of 3.0. Additional exam requirements/recommendations for international students: Required—TOEFL. *Application deadline:* For fall admission, 11/30 for domestic students. Application fee: $55. *Financial support:* Scholarships/grants available. Support available to part-time students. Financial award application deadline: 3/1. *Unit head:* Dr. Alberto Restori, Chair, 818-677-2599. *Application contact:* 818-677-3755.
Website: http://www.csun.edu/eisner-education/educational-psychology-counseling

California State University, Sacramento, College of Education, Graduate and Professional Studies in Education, Sacramento, CA 95819. Offers behavioral science and gender equity (MA); child development (MA); counseling (MS); curriculum and instruction (MA); education (Ed D), including K-12 and community college; education leadership and policy studies (MA), including higher education, PreK-12; education specialist (Ed S), including school psychology; educational technology (MA); language and literacy (MA); multicultural education (MA); school psychology (MA); special education (MA); workforce development advocacy (MA). *Program availability:* Part-time, evening/weekend, blended/hybrid learning. *Students:* 381 full-time (294 women), 135 part-time (101 women); includes 296 minority (44 Black or African American, non-Hispanic/Latino; 1 American Indian or Alaska Native, non-Hispanic/Latino; 94 Asian, non-Hispanic/Latino; 153 Hispanic/Latino; 4 Native Hawaiian or other Pacific Islander, non-Hispanic/Latino), 3 international. Average age 32. 553 applicants, 53% accepted, 292 enrolled. In 2017, 147 master's, 13 doctorates, 10 other advanced degrees awarded. *Degree requirements:* For master's, thesis or project; writing proficiency exam; for doctorate, thesis/dissertation. *Entrance requirements:* For master's and doctorate, GRE. Additional exam requirements/recommendations for international students: Required—TOEFL (minimum score 550 paper-based; 80 iBT); Recommended—IELTS (minimum score 7), TSE. *Application deadline:* For fall admission, 2/15 for domestic students, 1/15 for international students. Applications are processed on a rolling basis. Application fee: $55. Electronic applications accepted. *Expenses:* Contact institution. *Financial support:* Career-related internships or fieldwork, Federal Work-Study, and scholarships/grants available. Support available to part-time students. Financial award application deadline: 3/1; financial award applicants required to submit FAFSA. *Unit head:* Dr. Elizabeth Liles, Chair, 916-278-5942, E-mail: coe@csus.edu. *Application contact:* Jose Martinez, Graduate Admissions Supervisor, 916-278-7871, E-mail: martinj@skymail.csus.edu.
Website: http://www.csus.edu/coe/academics/graduate/index.html

California University of Pennsylvania, School of Graduate Studies and Research, College of Education and Human Services, Department of Childhood Education, California, PA 15419-1394. Offers early childhood education (M Ed); elementary education (M Ed); STEM education (M Ed). *Accreditation:* NCATE. *Program availability:* Part-time, evening/weekend. *Degree requirements:* For master's, comprehensive exam, thesis optional. *Entrance requirements:* For master's, MAT, PRAXIS, minimum GPA of 3.0, state police clearances. Additional exam requirements/recommendations for international students: Required—TOEFL (minimum score 550 paper-based; 80 iBT). *Application deadline:* For fall admission, 8/1 priority date for domestic and international students; for spring admission, 5/1 priority date for domestic and international students. Applications are processed on a rolling basis. Application fee: $25. Electronic applications accepted. *Financial support:* Applicants required to submit FAFSA. *Faculty research:* English as a second language, adult literacy, emerging literacy, diagnosis and remediation, phonemic awareness. *Unit head:* Dr. Diane H. Nettles, Department Chair, 724-938-4497, E-mail: nettles@calu.edu. *Application contact:* Suzanne G. Powers, Director of Graduate Admissions and Recruitment, 724-938-4029, Fax: 724-938-5712, E-mail: powers_s@cup.edu.
Website: http://www.calu.edu/academics/graduate-programs/elementary/

Cambridge College, School of Education, Boston, MA 02129. Offers autism specialist (M Ed); autism/behavior analyst (M Ed); behavior analyst (Post-Master's Certificate); behavioral management (M Ed); early childhood teacher (M Ed); education specialist in curriculum and instruction (CAGS); educational leadership (Ed D); elementary teacher (M Ed); English as a second language (M Ed, Certificate); general science (M Ed); health education (Post-Master's Certificate); health/family and consumer sciences (M Ed); history (M Ed); individualized (M Ed); information technology literacy (M Ed); instructional technology (M Ed); interdisciplinary studies (M Ed); library teacher (M Ed); literacy education (M Ed); mathematics (M Ed); mathematics specialist (Certificate); middle school mathematics and science (M Ed); school administration (M Ed, CAGS); school guidance counselor (M Ed); school nurse education (M Ed); school social worker/school adjustment counselor (M Ed); special education administrator (CAGS); special education/moderate disabilities (M Ed); teaching skills and methodologies (M Ed). *Program availability:* Part-time, evening/weekend, online learning. *Degree requirements:* For master's, thesis, internship/practicum (licensure program only); for doctorate, thesis/dissertation; for other advanced degree, thesis. *Entrance requirements:* For master's, interview, resume, documentation of licensure, 2 professional references; for doctorate, official transcripts, interview, resume, documentation of licensure (if any), written personal statement/essay, portfolio of scholarly and professional work, qualifying assessment, 2 professional references, health insurance, immunizations form; for other advanced degree, official transcripts, interview, resume, documentation of licensure (if any), written personal statement/essay, 2 professional references, health insurance, immunizations form. Additional exam requirements/recommendations for international students: Required—TOEFL (minimum score 550 paper-based; 79 iBT), Michigan English Language Assessment Battery (minimum score 85); Recommended—IELTS (minimum score 6). Electronic applications accepted. *Expenses:* Contact institution. *Faculty research:* Adult education, accelerated learning, mathematics education, brain compatible learning, special education and law.

Canisius College, Graduate Division, School of Education and Human Services, Department of Teacher Education, Buffalo, NY 14208-1098. Offers adolescence education (MS Ed); childhood education (MS Ed); general education (MS Ed); special education (MS), including adolescence special education, advanced special education, childhood education grade 1-6, childhood special education. *Program availability:* Part-time, evening/weekend, 100% online, blended/hybrid learning. *Faculty:* 8 full-time (7 women), 9 part-time/adjunct (7 women). *Students:* 52 full-time (44 women), 32 part-time (24 women); includes 8 minority (5 Black or African American, non-Hispanic/Latino; 1 Hispanic/Latino; 2 Two or more races, non-Hispanic/Latino), 1 international. Average

age 25. 59 applicants, 97% accepted, 47 enrolled. In 2017, 34 master's awarded. *Degree requirements:* For master's, research project or thesis, project internship. *Entrance requirements:* For master's, GRE (if cumulative GPA less than 2.7), transcripts, letters of recommendation. Additional exam requirements/recommendations for international students: Required—TOEFL (minimum score 550 paper-based, 79 iBT), IELTS (minimum score 6.5), or CAEL (minimum score 70). *Application deadline:* Applications are processed on a rolling basis. Application fee: $0. Electronic applications accepted. *Expenses: Tuition:* Full-time $22,860; part-time $820 per credit. *Required fees:* $720; $25 per credit. $65 per semester. One-time fee: $425. *Financial support:* Career-related internships or fieldwork, Federal Work-Study, scholarships/grants, tuition waivers (partial), and unspecified assistantships available. Support available to part-time students. Financial award application deadline: 4/30; financial award applicants required to submit FAFSA. *Unit head:* Dr. Michele A. Marable, Chair/Professor, 716-888-2317, E-mail: marablem@canisius.edu.
Website: http://www.canisius.edu/academics/graduate/

Capella University, School of Education, Master's Programs in Education, Minneapolis, MN 55402. Offers adult education (MS); curriculum and instruction (MS); early childhood education (MS); enrollment management (MS); higher education leadership and management (MS); instructional design for online learning (MS); integrative studies (MS); K-12 studies in education (MS); leadership in educational administration (MS); reading and literacy (MS); special education teaching (MS).

Caribbean University, Graduate School, Bayamón, PR 00960-0493. Offers administration and supervision (MA Ed); criminal justice (MA); curriculum and instruction (MA Ed, PhD), including elementary education (MA Ed), English education (MA Ed), history education (MA Ed), mathematics education (MA Ed), primary education (MA Ed), science education (MA Ed), Spanish education (MA Ed); educational technology in instructional systems (MA Ed); gerontology (MSN); human resources (MBA); museology, archiving and art history (MA Ed); neonatal pediatrics (MSN); physical education (MA Ed); special education (MA Ed). *Entrance requirements:* For master's, interview, minimum GPA of 2.5.

Carlow University, College of Learning and Innovation, Program in Early Childhood Education, Pittsburgh, PA 15213-3165. Offers M Ed. *Program availability:* Part-time, evening/weekend. *Students:* 5 full-time (4 women), 4 part-time (all women); includes 3 minority (2 Black or African American, non-Hispanic/Latino; 1 Asian, non-Hispanic/Latino). Average age 31. 5 applicants, 100% accepted, 5 enrolled. In 2017, 4 master's awarded. *Entrance requirements:* For master's, personal essay; resume or curriculum vitae; two recommendations; official transcripts; interview; minimum undergraduate GPA of 3.0. Additional exam requirements/recommendations for international students: Required—TOEFL (minimum score 550 paper-based). *Application deadline:* Applications are processed on a rolling basis. Electronic applications accepted. *Expenses: Tuition:* Full-time $12,103; part-time $825 per credit hour. Tuition and fees vary according to program. *Financial support:* Application deadline: 4/1; applicants required to submit FAFSA. *Faculty research:* Understanding children's play, infant and toddler development, effects of violence on children, supervision and staff development. *Unit head:* Dr. Rae Ann Hirsh, Program Director, 412-578-6014, E-mail: rahirsh@carlow.edu. *Application contact:* 412-578-6059, E-mail: gradstudies@carlow.edu.
Website: http://www.carlow.edu/Early_Childhood_MEd.aspx

Carlow University, College of Learning and Innovation, Program in Education, Pittsburgh, PA 15213-3165. Offers early childhood education (M Ed); education (M Ed); online instructional design and technology (Certificate); special education (M Ed), including early childhood. *Program availability:* Part-time, evening/weekend, 100% online, blended/hybrid learning. *Students:* 44 full-time (41 women), 14 part-time (13 women); includes 12 minority (8 Black or African American, non-Hispanic/Latino; 1 Asian, non-Hispanic/Latino; 3 Two or more races, non-Hispanic/Latino). Average age 31. 16 applicants, 100% accepted, 12 enrolled. In 2017, 22 master's, 1 Certificate awarded. *Entrance requirements:* For master's, personal essay; resume or curriculum vitae; two recommendations; official transcripts; interview; minimum undergraduate GPA of 3.0. Additional exam requirements/recommendations for international students: Required—TOEFL (minimum score 550 paper-based). *Application deadline:* Applications are processed on a rolling basis. Electronic applications accepted. *Expenses: Tuition:* Full-time $12,103; part-time $825 per credit hour. Tuition and fees vary according to program. *Financial support:* Application deadline: 4/1; applicants required to submit FAFSA. *Unit head:* Dr. Keeley Baronak, Chair, Department of Education, 412-578-6135, Fax: 412-578-8816, E-mail: kobaronak@carlow.edu. *Application contact:* 412-578-6059, E-mail: gradstudies@carlow.edu.
Website: http://www.carlow.edu/education.aspx

Carroll University, Graduate Programs in Education, Waukesha, WI 53186-5593. Offers adult and continuing education (M Ed); educational leadership (MS); PK-12 (M Ed). *Program availability:* Part-time, evening/weekend. *Degree requirements:* For master's, thesis. *Entrance requirements:* For master's, minimum undergraduate GPA of 2.5 in related field. Additional exam requirements/recommendations for international students: Required—TOEFL. Electronic applications accepted. *Faculty research:* Qualitative research methods, whole language approaches to teaching, the writing process, multicultural education, gifted/talented learners.

The Catholic University of America, School of Arts and Sciences, Department of Education, Washington, DC 20064. Offers Catholic school leadership (MA); education (Certificate); secondary education (MA); special education (MA), including early childhood, non-categorical. *Accreditation:* NCATE. *Program availability:* Part-time. *Faculty:* 8 full-time (7 women), 3 part-time/adjunct (all women). *Students:* 9 full-time (all women), 25 part-time (14 women); includes 2 minority (both Hispanic/Latino), 4 international. Average age 39. 24 applicants, 63% accepted, 9 enrolled. In 2017, 9 master's awarded. *Degree requirements:* For master's, comprehensive exam, thesis or alternative; for Certificate, action research project. *Entrance requirements:* For master's, GRE General Test or MAT, statement of purpose, official copies of academic transcripts, three letters of recommendation, interview; for Certificate, PRAXIS I, statement of purpose, official copies of academic transcripts, three letters of recommendation, interview. Additional exam requirements/recommendations for international students: Required—TOEFL (minimum score 550 paper-based; 80 iBT). *Application deadline:* For fall admission, 7/15 priority date for domestic students, 7/1 for international students; for spring admission, 11/15 priority date for domestic students, 11/1 for international students. Applications are processed on a rolling basis. Application fee: $55. Electronic applications accepted. *Expenses:* Contact institution. *Financial support:* Fellowships, research assistantships, teaching assistantships, Federal Work-Study, scholarships/grants, tuition waivers (full and partial), and unspecified assistantships available. Financial award application deadline: 2/1; financial award applicants required to submit FAFSA. *Faculty research:* Special education, early childhood education, educational psychology, Catholic school administration, leadership and policy studies, counseling, curriculum and instruction. *Unit head:* Dr. Agnes Cave, Chair, 202-319-5805, Fax: 202-319-5815, E-mail: cave@cua.edu. *Application contact:* Dr. Steven Brown, Director of Graduate Admissions, 202-319-5057, Fax: 202-319-6533, E-mail: cua-admissions@cua.edu.
Website: http://education.cua.edu/

Central Connecticut State University, School of Graduate Studies, School of Education and Professional Studies, Department of Literacy, Elementary, and Early Childhood Education, New Britain, CT 06050-4010. Offers MS, AC, Sixth Year Certificate. *Program availability:* Part-time, evening/weekend. *Faculty:* 7 full-time (6 women), 1 (woman) part-time/adjunct. *Students:* 9 full-time (7 women), 109 part-time (101 women); includes 7 minority (1 Black or African American, non-Hispanic/Latino; 5 Hispanic/Latino; 1 Two or more races, non-Hispanic/Latino). Average age 31. 49 applicants, 73% accepted, 26 enrolled. In 2017, 44 master's, 10 other advanced degrees awarded. *Degree requirements:* For master's, comprehensive exam, thesis or alternative; for other advanced degree, qualifying exam. *Entrance requirements:* For master's, minimum undergraduate GPA of 2.7, teacher certification, interview, essay, letters of recommendation; for other advanced degree, master's degree, essay, teacher certification, interview, letters of recommendation. Additional exam requirements/recommendations for international students: Required—TOEFL (minimum score 550 paper-based; 79 iBT); Recommended—IELTS (minimum score 6.5). *Application deadline:* For fall admission, 8/1 for domestic students, 5/1 for international students; for spring admission, 11/1 for domestic and international students. Applications are processed on a rolling basis. Application fee: $50. Electronic applications accepted. *Expenses: Tuition, area resident:* Full-time $6757. Tuition, state resident: full-time $9750; part-time $374 per credit. Tuition, nonresident: full-time $18,102; part-time $374 per credit. *Required fees:* $4635; $255 per credit. *Financial support:* In 2017–18, 6 students received support. Career-related internships or fieldwork, Federal Work-Study, scholarships/grants, and unspecified assistantships available. Support available to part-time students. Financial award application deadline: 3/1. *Faculty research:* Developmental, clinical, and administrative aspects of reading and language arts instruction. *Unit head:* Dr. Helen Abadiano, Chair, 860-832-2175, E-mail: abadiano@ccsu.edu. *Application contact:* Patricia Gardner, Associate Director of Graduate Studies, 860-832-2350, Fax: 860-832-2362.
Website: http://www.ccsu.edu/leece/index.html

Central Michigan University, College of Graduate Studies, College of Education and Human Services, Department of Teacher Education and Professional Development, Mount Pleasant, MI 48859. Offers educational technology (MA, Graduate Certificate); elementary education (MA), including classroom teaching, early childhood; reading and literacy K-12 (MA); secondary education (MA). *Program availability:* Part-time, evening/weekend. *Degree requirements:* For master's, thesis or alternative. Electronic applications accepted. *Faculty research:* Integrating literacy across the curriculum, science teaching and aesthetic learning in science, diversity education, educational technology, educational psychology and child development.

Chaminade University of Honolulu, Office of Professional and Continuing Education, Program in Education, Honolulu, HI 96816-1578. Offers child development (M Ed); early childhood education (Montessori) (MAT); early childhood education (PK-3) (MAT); educational leadership (M Ed); elementary education (MAT); instructional leadership (M Ed); Montessori (M Ed); secondary education (MAT); special education (MAT); teacher leader (M Ed). *Program availability:* Part-time, evening/weekend, 100% online, blended/hybrid learning. *Faculty:* 7 full-time (3 women), 8 part-time/adjunct (6 women). *Students:* 86 full-time (68 women), 88 part-time (64 women); includes 113 minority (7 Black or African American, non-Hispanic/Latino; 2 American Indian or Alaska Native, non-Hispanic/Latino; 46 Asian, non-Hispanic/Latino; 7 Hispanic/Latino; 51 Native Hawaiian or other Pacific Islander, non-Hispanic/Latino), 6 international. Average age 34. 61 applicants, 98% accepted, 49 enrolled. In 2017, 91 master's awarded. *Degree requirements:* For master's, thesis or alternative. *Entrance requirements:* For master's, PRAXIS (for MAT), minimum GPA of 2.75 (for M Ed), 3.0 (for MAT); 2 letters of recommendation, resume, writing sample (for MAT). Additional exam requirements/recommendations for international students: Required—TOEFL (minimum score 550 paper-based; 79 iBT). *Application deadline:* Applications are processed on a rolling basis. Application fee: $40. Electronic applications accepted. *Expenses:* $780 per credit hour plus $93 fee per online class. *Financial support:* Applicants required to submit FAFSA. *Unit head:* Dr. Dale Fryxell, Dean, 808-739-4652, Fax: 808-739-4607, E-mail: edu-office@chaminade.edu. *Application contact:* 808-735-4755, E-mail: gradserv@chaminade.edu.
Website: https://education.chaminade.edu/

Champlain College, Graduate Studies, Burlington, VT 05402-0670. Offers business (MBA); digital forensic science (MS); early childhood education (M Ed); emergent media (MFA, MS); executive leadership (MS); health care administration (MS); information security operations (MS); law (MS); mediation and applied conflict studies (MS). MS in emergent media program held in Shanghai. *Program availability:* Part-time, online learning. *Degree requirements:* For master's, capstone project. *Entrance requirements:* Additional exam requirements/recommendations for international students: Required—TOEFL (minimum score 550 paper-based; 80 iBT). Electronic applications accepted.

Chatham University, Program in Education, Pittsburgh, PA 15232-2826. Offers early childhood education (MAT); elementary education (MAT); environmental education (K-12) (MAT); secondary art (MAT); secondary biology education (MAT); secondary chemistry education (MAT); secondary English education (MAT); secondary math education (MAT); secondary physics education (MAT); secondary social studies education (MAT); special education (MAT). *Faculty:* 1 (woman) full-time, 15 part-time/adjunct (13 women). *Students:* 31 full-time (23 women), 3 part-time (1 woman); includes 9 minority (8 Black or African American, non-Hispanic/Latino; 1 Hispanic/Latino). Average age 30. 25 applicants, 60% accepted, 9 enrolled. In 2017, 23 master's awarded. *Degree requirements:* For master's, thesis, teaching experience. *Entrance requirements:* For master's, minimum GPA of 3.0, sample of written work, recommendation letters. Additional exam requirements/recommendations for international students: Required—TOEFL (minimum score 600 paper-based; 100 iBT), IELTS (minimum score 7), TWE. *Application deadline:* For fall admission, 4/1 priority date for domestic and international students; for spring admission, 11/1 priority date for domestic students, 10/1 priority date for international students. Applications are processed on a rolling basis. Application fee: $45. Electronic applications accepted. Application fee is waived when completed online. *Expenses: Tuition:* Full-time $16,740; part-time $930 per credit. *Required fees:* $486; $27 per credit. $243 per semester. *Financial support:* Career-related internships or fieldwork available. Financial award applicants required to submit FAFSA. *Faculty research:* Gifted education, environmental education, technology in education, writing as learning, class size and achievement. *Application contact:* Katie Noel, Assistant Director of Graduate Admission, 412-365-2758, Fax: 412-365-1609, E-mail: gradadmissions@chatham.edu.
Website: http://www.chatham.edu/mat

Chestnut Hill College, School of Graduate Studies, Department of Education, Program in Early Education, Philadelphia, PA 19118-2693. Offers early education (M Ed), including Montessori certificate preparation, preK-4 education, preK-4 education and special education preK-8. *Program availability:* Part-time, evening/weekend. *Degree requirements:* For master's, thesis optional. *Entrance requirements:* For master's, PRAXIS I or proof of teaching certification, writing sample, letters of recommendation, 6 graduate credits with minimum B grade or minimum undergraduate GPA of 3.0. Additional exam requirements/recommendations for international students: Required—TOEFL (minimum score 500 paper-based), IELTS (minimum score 6.0), or TWE (minimum score 22). Electronic applications accepted. *Expenses:* Contact institution. *Faculty research:* Gender issues, early childhood education standardized testing.

Early Childhood Education

Chestnut Hill College, School of Graduate Studies, Department of Education, Program in Reading, Philadelphia, PA 19118-2693. Offers reading specialist (M Ed), including K-12, special education 7-12, special education PreK-8. *Program availability:* Part-time, evening/weekend. *Degree requirements:* For master's, thesis optional. *Entrance requirements:* Additional exam requirements/recommendations for international students: Required—TOEFL (minimum score 500 paper-based) or IELTS (minimum score 6). Electronic applications accepted. *Expenses:* Contact institution. *Faculty research:* Inclusive education, cultural issues in education.

Chicago State University, School of Graduate and Professional Studies, College of Education, Department of Special Education, Early Childhood Education and Bilingual Education, Program in Early Childhood Education, Chicago, IL 60628. Offers MAT, MS Ed. *Accreditation:* NCATE. *Entrance requirements:* For master's, minimum GPA of 2.75. *Application deadline:* For fall admission, 7/1 for domestic students; for spring admission, 11/10 for domestic students. Application fee: $25. *Unit head:* Dr. Timothy E. Harrington, Chairperson, E-mail: cvalenci@csu.edu. *Application contact:* Daphne G. Townsend, Admissions and Records Officer II, 773-995-2404, Fax: 773-995-3671, E-mail: g-studies1@csu.edu.

The Citadel, The Military College of South Carolina, Citadel Graduate College, Zucker Family School of Education, Charleston, SC 29409. Offers elementary/secondary school administration and supervision (M Ed); elementary/secondary school counseling (M Ed); interdisciplinary STEM education (M Ed); literacy education (M Ed, Graduate Certificate); middle grades (MAT), including English, mathematics, science, social studies; physical education (grades K-12) (MAT); school superintendency (Ed S); secondary education (MAT), including biology, English, mathematics, social studies; student affairs (Graduate Certificate); student affairs and college counseling (M Ed). *Accreditation:* NCATE. *Program availability:* Part-time, evening/weekend, 100% online, blended/hybrid learning. *Degree requirements:* For master's, comprehensive exam (for some programs). *Entrance requirements:* For master's, GRE (minimum combined verbal and quantitative score of 290) or MAT (minimum score 396). Additional exam requirements/recommendations for international students: Required—TOEFL (minimum score 550 paper-based; 79 iBT). Electronic applications accepted. *Expenses:* Tuition, state resident: part-time $587 per credit hour. Tuition, nonresident: part-time $988 per credit hour. *Required fees:* $90 per term.

City College of the City University of New York, Graduate School, School of Education, Department of Teaching, Learning and Culture, New York, NY 10031-9198. Offers bilingual education (MS); childhood education (MS); early childhood education (MS); educational theatre (MS); literacy (MS); TESOL (MS). *Accreditation:* NCATE. *Degree requirements:* For master's, thesis. *Entrance requirements:* For master's, Liberal Arts and Sciences Test (LAST), Content Specialty Test (CST). Additional exam requirements/recommendations for international students: Required—TOEFL.

Clarion University of Pennsylvania, College of Arts, Education and Sciences, Master of Education Program, Clarion, PA 16214. Offers curriculum and instruction (M Ed); early childhood (M Ed); math education (M Ed); reading (M Ed); science education (M Ed); special education (M Ed); technology (M Ed). *Accreditation:* NCATE. *Program availability:* Part-time, evening/weekend, online only, 100% online, blended/hybrid learning. *Faculty:* 6 full-time (3 women). *Students:* 11 full-time (all women), 101 part-time (82 women); includes 4 minority (2 Black or African American, non-Hispanic/Latino; 1 Hispanic/Latino; 1 Two or more races, non-Hispanic/Latino). Average age 30. 80 applicants, 98% accepted, 33 enrolled. In 2017, 52 master's awarded. *Degree requirements:* For master's, comprehensive exam, thesis, or portfolio. *Entrance requirements:* For master's, minimum QPA of 3.0. Additional exam requirements/recommendations for international students: Required—TOEFL (minimum score 550 paper-based, 80 iBT) or IELTS (7). *Application deadline:* For fall admission, 8/15 priority date for domestic students; 7/15 priority date for international students; for winter admission, 11/1 priority date for domestic students; for spring admission, 1/7 priority date for domestic students, 11/15 priority date for international students; for summer admission, 4/1 priority date for domestic students. Applications are processed on a rolling basis. Application fee: $40. Electronic applications accepted. *Expenses:* $655.05 per credit. *Financial support:* Career-related internships or fieldwork and scholarships/grants available. Support available to part-time students. Financial award application deadline: 3/1; financial award applicants required to submit FAFSA. *Unit head:* Dr. John McCullough, Chair, Department of Education, 814-393-2404, Fax: 814-393-2446, E-mail: gradstudies@clarion.edu. *Application contact:* Dana Bearer, Associate Director for Transfer, Adult, and Graduate Programs, 814-393-2337, Fax: 814-393-2722, E-mail: gradstudies@clarion.edu.

Clarkson University, Program in Education, Schenectady, NY 12308. Offers adolescence education 7-12 (MAT); teaching of English to speakers of other languages (MAT); technology education K-12 (MAT). *Accreditation:* TEAC. *Faculty:* 3 full-time (all women), 23 part-time/adjunct (14 women). *Students:* 22 full-time (13 women), 12 part-time (8 women); includes 4 minority (1 Black or African American, non-Hispanic/Latino; 3 Asian, non-Hispanic/Latino), 6 international. 39 applicants, 72% accepted, 21 enrolled. In 2017, 28 master's awarded. *Degree requirements:* For master's, thesis (for some programs), thesis or project. *Entrance requirements:* For master's, GRE, minimum undergraduate GPA of 3.0. Additional exam requirements/recommendations for international students: Required—TOEFL (minimum score 550 paper-based, 80 iBT) or IELTS (6.5). *Application deadline:* Applications are processed on a rolling basis. Application fee: $50. Electronic applications accepted. *Expenses:* Contact institution. *Financial support:* Scholarships/grants available. *Unit head:* Dr. Catherine Snyder, Chair of Education, 518-631-9870, E-mail: csnyder@clarkson.edu. *Application contact:* Dan Capogna, Director of Graduate Admissions, 518-631-9910, E-mail: graduate@clarkson.edu.
Website: https://www.clarkson.edu/academics/graduate

Clemson University, Graduate School, College of Education, Department of Educational and Organizational Leadership Development, Clemson, SC 29634. Offers administration and supervision (M Ed, Ed S); athletic leadership (MS, Certificate); education systems improvement science (Ed D); educational leadership (PhD), including higher education, P-12; human resource development (MHRD), including human resource development; leadership (Certificate); student affairs (M Ed). *Program availability:* Part-time, evening/weekend, 100% online. *Faculty:* 21 full-time (14 women), 1 part-time/adjunct (0 women). *Students:* 55 full-time (32 women), 285 part-time (169 women); includes 89 minority (71 Black or African American, non-Hispanic/Latino; 1 American Indian or Alaska Native, non-Hispanic/Latino; 1 Asian, non-Hispanic/Latino; 13 Hispanic/Latino; 3 Two or more races, non-Hispanic/Latino), 2 international. Average age 35. 216 applicants, 69% accepted, 100 enrolled. In 2017, 58 master's, 16 doctorates, 20 other advanced degrees awarded. *Degree requirements:* For master's, thesis (for some programs); for doctorate, comprehensive exam, thesis/dissertation. *Entrance requirements:* For master's, doctorate, and other advanced degree, GRE General Test, unofficial transcripts, letters of recommendation. Additional exam requirements/recommendations for international students: Required—TOEFL (minimum score 80 iBT), IELTS (minimum score 7), PTE (minimum score 54). *Application deadline:* For fall admission, 3/1 priority date for domestic and international students; for spring admission, 10/1 priority date for domestic and international students. Applications are processed on a rolling basis. Application fee: $80 ($90 for international students).

Electronic applications accepted. *Expenses:* $5,174 per semester full-time resident, $9,714 per semester full-time non-resident, $511 per credit hour part-time resident, $1,017 per credit hour part-time non-resident; $741 per credit hour online; other fees may apply per session. *Financial support:* In 2017–18, 20 students received support, including 4 fellowships with partial tuition reimbursements available (averaging $8,750 per year), 1 research assistantship with partial tuition reimbursement available (averaging $9,378 per year); career-related internships or fieldwork and unspecified assistantships also available. Financial award application deadline: 3/1. *Total annual research expenditures:* $31,201. *Unit head:* Dr. Roy Jones, Interim Department Chair, 864-656-7915, E-mail: royj@clemson.edu. *Application contact:* Alison Search, Student Services Program Coordinator, 864-250-8880, E-mail: alisonp@clemson.edu.
Website: http://www.clemson.edu/education/departments/educational-organizational-leadership-development/index.html

Cleveland State University, College of Graduate Studies, College of Education and Human Services, Department of Teacher Education, Cleveland, OH 44115. Offers art education (M Ed); early childhood education (M Ed); foreign language education (M Ed); middle childhood mathematics and science education (M Ed); special education (M Ed), including mild/moderate disabilities, moderate/intensive disabilities; teaching English to speakers of other languages (M Ed). *Program availability:* Part-time, evening/weekend. *Faculty:* 19 full-time (14 women), 32 part-time/adjunct (27 women). *Students:* 80 full-time (60 women), 361 part-time (277 women); includes 119 minority (86 Black or African American, non-Hispanic/Latino; 5 Asian, non-Hispanic/Latino; 16 Hispanic/Latino; 12 Two or more races, non-Hispanic/Latino), 20 international. Average age 34. 177 applicants, 55% accepted, 68 enrolled. In 2017, 137 master's awarded. *Degree requirements:* For master's, comprehensive exam (for some programs), thesis or alternative. *Entrance requirements:* For master's, GRE General Test or MAT, minimum GPA of 2.75. Additional exam requirements/recommendations for international students: Required—TOEFL (minimum score 550 paper-based; 78 iBT), IELTS (minimum score 6). *Application deadline:* For fall admission, 7/1 priority date for domestic students, 5/15 for international students; for spring admission, 11/15 for domestic students, 11/1 for international students; for summer admission, 4/1 for domestic students, 3/15 for international students. Applications are processed on a rolling basis. Application fee: $30. *Financial support:* In 2017–18, 13 research assistantships with full tuition reimbursements (averaging $15,845 per year) were awarded; tuition waivers (partial) and unspecified assistantships also available. Financial award application deadline: 2/15; financial award applicants required to submit FAFSA. *Faculty research:* Early childhood education, literacy education, special education: mild/moderate, moderate/intensive, early childhood intervention specialist), teaching English to speakers of other languages (TESOL). *Total annual research expenditures:* $275,907. *Unit head:* Dr. Tachelle Banks, Department Chairperson, 216-687-4600, Fax: 216-687-5379, E-mail: t.i.banks@csuohio.edu. *Application contact:* Rosalyn Adams, Administrative Coordinator, 216-523-7139, Fax: 216-687-5491, E-mail: r.m.adams@csuohio.edu.
Website: http://www.csuohio.edu/cehs/te/te

The College at Brockport, State University of New York, School of Education, Health, and Human Services, Department of Education and Human Development, Program in Childhood Curriculum Specialist, Brockport, NY 14420-2997. Offers MS Ed. *Accreditation:* NCATE. *Program availability:* Part-time. In 2017, 2 master's awarded. *Degree requirements:* For master's, thesis or alternative. *Entrance requirements:* For master's, minimum GPA of 3.0, letters of recommendation, statement of objectives, current resume. Additional exam requirements/recommendations for international students: Required—TOEFL (minimum score 550 paper-based; 79 iBT), IELTS (minimum score 6.5). *Application deadline:* For fall admission, 3/15 priority date for domestic and international students; for spring admission, 10/15 priority date for domestic and international students. Application fee: $80. Electronic applications accepted. *Expenses:* Tuition, state resident: full-time $10,870; part-time $453 per credit hour. Tuition, nonresident: full-time $22,210. *Required fees:* $988; $246 per semester. *Financial support:* Federal Work-Study, scholarships/grants, and unspecified assistantships available. Support available to part-time students. Financial award application deadline: 3/15; financial award applicants required to submit FAFSA. *Unit head:* Dr. Sue Robb, Chairperson, 585-395-5935, Fax: 585-395-2172, E-mail: srobb@brockport.edu. *Application contact:* Anne Walton, Coordinator of Certification and Graduate Advisement, 585-395-2326, Fax: 585-395-2172, E-mail: awalton@brockport.edu.
Website: https://www.brockport.edu/academics/education_human_development/department.html

College of Charleston, Graduate School, School of Education, Health, and Human Performance, Department of Elementary and Early Childhood Education, Program in Early Childhood Education, Charleston, SC 29424-0001. Offers MAT. *Accreditation:* NCATE. *Program availability:* Part-time, evening/weekend. *Degree requirements:* For master's, thesis or alternative, written qualifying exam, student teaching experience (MAT). *Entrance requirements:* For master's, GRE, minimum GPA of 2.5, 2 letters of recommendation. Additional exam requirements/recommendations for international students: Required—TOEFL (minimum score 81 iBT). Electronic applications accepted. *Faculty research:* Teacher education and creative arts, integrated curriculum, multicultural awareness, teaching models, cooperative learning.

The College of New Jersey, Office of Graduate and Advancing Education, School of Education, Department of Elementary and Early Childhood Education, Program in Early Childhood Education, Ewing, NJ 08628. Offers M Ed, MAT. *Program availability:* Part-time. *Entrance requirements:* For master's, GRE, minimum GPA of 3.0 in field or 2.75 overall. Additional exam requirements/recommendations for international students: Required—TOEFL. Electronic applications accepted.

The College of New Rochelle, Graduate School, Division of Education, Program in Childhood Education/Early Childhood Education, New Rochelle, NY 10805-2308. Offers childhood education (MS Ed); early childhood education (MS Ed). *Program availability:* Part-time. *Degree requirements:* For master's, comprehensive exam (for some programs), thesis (for some programs), practicum. *Entrance requirements:* For master's, interview, minimum GPA of 3.0 in field, 2.7 overall. *Expenses: Tuition:* Full-time $17,406. *Required fees:* $1120.

College of Saint Elizabeth, Program in Education, Morristown, NJ 07960-6989. Offers assistive technology (Certificate); education (MA); ESL (Certificate); Holocaust/genocide education (Certificate); middle school science (Certificate); online teaching in the 21st century (Certificate); teaching (Certificate), including K-12, K-6, teacher of students with disabilities. *Program availability:* Part-time. *Faculty:* 3 full-time (2 women), 8 part-time/adjunct (6 women). *Students:* 1 (woman) full-time, 34 part-time (29 women); includes 1 minority (Hispanic/Latino). Average age 32. 25 applicants, 100% accepted, 24 enrolled. In 2017, 23 master's awarded. *Degree requirements:* For master's and Certificate, thesis. *Entrance requirements:* For master's, certification. Additional exam requirements/recommendations for international students: Required—TOEFL (minimum score 550 paper-based; 79 iBT), IELTS (minimum score 6.5). *Application deadline:* For fall admission, 5/1 for international students. Applications are processed on a rolling basis. Application fee: $35. Electronic applications accepted. Application fee is waived when completed online. *Financial support:* Career-related internships or fieldwork, scholarships/grants, and unspecified assistantships available. Financial award

applicants required to submit FAFSA. *Unit head:* Dr. Joseph Ciccone, 973-290-4383, Fax: 973-290-4389, E-mail: jciccone@cse.edu. *Application contact:* Lori J. Fragoso, Director of Graduate and Continuing Studies Admissions, 973-290-4413, Fax: 973-290-4710, E-mail: apply@cse.edu.
Website: http://www.cse.edu/academics/prof-studies/education/

The College of Saint Rose, Graduate Studies, Thelma P. Lally School of Education, Programs in Special Education, Albany, NY 12203-1419. Offers adolescence education/special education (MS Ed); childhood education/special education (MS Ed); childhood special education (MS Ed); early childhood special education (MS Ed); special education (Certificate); special education professional (MS Ed). *Accreditation:* NCATE. *Students:* 8 full-time (5 women), 13 part-time (11 women), 1 international. Average age 27. 11 applicants, 82% accepted, 5 enrolled. In 2017, 15 master's awarded. *Degree requirements:* For master's, comprehensive exam (for some programs), thesis or alternative, research project. *Entrance requirements:* For master's, minimum undergraduate GPA of 3.0. Additional exam requirements/recommendations for international students: Required—TOEFL (minimum score 550 paper-based; 80 iBT), IELTS (minimum score 6), PTE (minimum score 56). *Application deadline:* For fall admission, 4/1 priority date for domestic and international students; for spring admission, 10/15 for domestic and international students; for summer admission, 3/15 priority date for domestic and international students. Applications are processed on a rolling basis. Application fee: $40. Electronic applications accepted. *Expenses: Tuition:* Full-time $7191; part-time $799 per credit hour. *Required fees:* $924; $462 per credit hour. Tuition and fees vary according to course load. *Financial support:* Career-related internships or fieldwork, scholarships/grants, tuition waivers (partial), and unspecified assistantships available. Support available to part-time students. Financial award application deadline: 4/15. *Unit head:* Franics Ihle, Chair, 518-337-4885, E-mail: ihlef@strose.edu. *Application contact:* Cris Murray, Assistant Vice President for Graduate Recruitment and Enrollment, 518-485-3390, E-mail: grad@strose.edu.
Website: https://www.strose.edu/special-education/

The College of Saint Rose, Graduate Studies, Thelma P. Lally School of Education, Teacher Education Programs, Albany, NY 12203-1419. Offers adolescence education (MS Ed, Advanced Certificate); adolescence education/special education (Advanced Certificate); childhood education (MS Ed); curriculum and instruction (MS Ed); early childhood education (MS Ed). *Students:* 69 full-time (60 women), 21 part-time (16 women); includes 7 minority (4 Black or African American, non-Hispanic/Latino; 2 Hispanic/Latino; 1 Two or more races, non-Hispanic/Latino), 1 international. Average age 27. 46 applicants, 52% accepted, 23 enrolled. In 2017, 43 master's awarded. *Entrance requirements:* For master's, minimum undergraduate GPA of 3.0. Additional exam requirements/recommendations for international students: Required—TOEFL (minimum score 550 paper-based; 80 iBT), IELTS (minimum score 6), PTE (minimum score 56). *Application deadline:* For fall admission, 4/1 priority date for domestic and international students; for spring admission, 10/15 priority date for domestic and international students; for summer admission, 3/15 priority date for domestic and international students. Applications are processed on a rolling basis. Application fee: $40. Electronic applications accepted. *Expenses: Tuition:* Full-time $7191; part-time $799 per credit hour. *Required fees:* $924; $462 per credit hour. Tuition and fees vary according to course load. *Financial support:* Career-related internships or fieldwork, scholarships/grants, tuition waivers (partial), and unspecified assistantships available. Support available to part-time students. Financial award application deadline: 4/15. *Unit head:* Dr. Drey Martone, Chair, 518-454-5262, E-mail: martoned@strose.edu. *Application contact:* Cris Murray, Assistant Vice President for Graduate Recruitment and Enrollment, 518-485-3390, Fax: 518-458-5479, E-mail: grad@strose.edu.
Website: https://www.strose.edu/academics/schools/school-of-education/

College of Staten Island of the City University of New York, Graduate Programs, School of Education, Program in Special Education, Staten Island, NY 10314-6600. Offers special education (MS Ed), including adolescence (grades 7-12, grades 1-6. *Program availability:* Part-time, evening/weekend. *Faculty:* 3 full-time, 8 part-time/adjunct. *Students:* 144. 73 applicants, 73% accepted, 41 enrolled. In 2017, 39 master's awarded. *Degree requirements:* For master's, comprehensive exam, fieldwork; ten three-credit required courses and one elective for a total of 11 courses (33 credits) or 14 three-credit required courses and a three- to six-credit, field-based requirement for a total of 45-48 credits; research project. *Entrance requirements:* For master's, GRE General Test or an approved equivalent examination, BA/BS or 36 approved credits with minimum GPA of 3.0, 2 letters of recommendations, 1-2 page statement of experience. Additional exam requirements/recommendations for international students: Required—TOEFL (minimum score 550 paper-based; 79 iBT), IELTS (minimum score 6.5). *Application deadline:* For fall admission, 4/25 for domestic and international students; for spring admission, 11/25 for domestic and international students. Applications are processed on a rolling basis. Application fee: $125. Electronic applications accepted. *Expenses: Tuition:* Tuition, state resident: full-time $10,450; part-time $440 per credit. Tuition, nonresident: full-time $19,320; part-time $440 per credit. *Required fees:* $181.10 per semester. Tuition and fees vary according to program. *Faculty research:* Disabilities studies, social justice, arts-based research on disabilities, assessment of students with disabilities, technological pedagogical and content knowledge (TPACK) in special education teachers, juvenile justice. *Unit head:* Diane Brescia, 718-982-3877, E-mail: diane.brescia@csi.cuny.edu. *Application contact:* Sasha Spence, Associate Director for Graduate Admissions, 718-982-2019, Fax: 718-982-2500, E-mail: sasha.spence@csi.cuny.edu.
Website: https://www.csi.cuny.edu/sites/default/files/pdf/admissions/grad/pdf/Education%20Fact%20Sheet.pdf

Colorado Christian University, Program in Curriculum and Instruction, Lakewood, CO 80226. Offers corporate education (MACI); early childhood educator (MACI); elementary educator (MACI); instructional technology (MACI); master educator (MACI); online course developer (MACI); online teaching and learning (MACI); special education generalist (MACI). *Program availability:* Part-time, evening/weekend. *Degree requirements:* For master's, thesis optional, practicum. *Entrance requirements:* For master's, interviews, letters of recommendation. Additional exam requirements/recommendations for international students: Required—TOEFL. Electronic applications accepted. *Expenses:* Contact institution.

Columbia International University, Columbia Graduate School, Columbia, SC 29203. Offers Bible teaching (MABT); counseling (MACN); early childhood and elementary education (MAT); educational administration (M Ed); educational leadership (PhD); instruction and learning (M Ed); teaching English as a foreign language (Certificate); teaching English as a foreign language and intercultural studies (MATF). *Program availability:* Part-time, evening/weekend, online learning. *Degree requirements:* For master's, internships, professional project. *Entrance requirements:* For master's, MAT; GRE (for some programs), minimum GPA of 2.7. Additional exam requirements/recommendations for international students: Required—TOEFL. Electronic applications accepted.

Columbus State University, Graduate Studies, College of Education and Health Professions, Department of Teacher Education, Columbus, GA 31907-5645. Offers curriculum and instruction in accomplished teaching (M Ed); early childhood education (M Ed, MAT, Ed S); middle grades education (M Ed, MAT, Ed S); secondary education (M Ed, MAT, Ed S), including biology (MAT), chemistry (MAT), earth and space science (MAT), English/language arts, general science (M Ed), history (MAT), mathematics,

science (Ed S), social science (M Ed, Ed S); special education (M Ed, MAT, Ed S), including general curriculum (M Ed, MAT); teacher leadership (M Ed). *Accreditation:* NCATE. *Program availability:* Part-time, evening/weekend, 100% online, blended/hybrid learning. *Faculty:* 19 full-time (12 women), 24 part-time/adjunct (18 women). *Students:* 99 full-time (76 women), 181 part-time (143 women); includes 109 minority (94 Black or African American, non-Hispanic/Latino; 1 American Indian or Alaska Native, non-Hispanic/Latino; 1 Asian, non-Hispanic/Latino; 6 Hispanic/Latino; 7 Two or more races, non-Hispanic/Latino). Average age 34. 136 applicants, 63% accepted, 56 enrolled. In 2017, 119 master's, 8 other advanced degrees awarded. *Degree requirements:* For Ed S, thesis or alternative. *Entrance requirements:* For master's, GRE General Test, minimum undergraduate GPA of 2.75; for Ed S, GRE General Test, minimum undergraduate GPA of 2.75, graduate 3.0. Additional exam requirements/recommendations for international students: Required—TOEFL (minimum score 550 paper-based; 79 iBT). *Application deadline:* For fall admission, 6/30 for domestic students, 5/1 for international students; for spring admission, 11/1 for domestic and international students; for summer admission, 3/1 for domestic and international students. Applications are processed on a rolling basis. Application fee: $50. Electronic applications accepted. *Expenses: Tuition,* state resident: full-time $3708; part-time $2472 per year. Tuition, nonresident: full-time $14,418; part-time $9612 per year. *International tuition:* $19,218 full-time. *Required fees:* $1605. Tuition and fees vary according to program. *Financial support:* In 2017–18, 45 students received support, including 9 research assistantships with partial tuition reimbursements available (averaging $3,000 per year); career-related internships or fieldwork, Federal Work-Study, institutionally sponsored loans, scholarships/grants, tuition waivers (partial), and unspecified assistantships also available. Support available to part-time students. Financial award application deadline: 5/1; financial award applicants required to submit FAFSA. *Unit head:* Dr. Jan Burcham, Department Chair, 706-507-8519, Fax: 706-568-3134, E-mail: burcham_jan@columbusstate.edu. *Application contact:* Catrina Smith-Edmond, Assistant Director for Graduate and Global Admission, 706-507-8824, Fax: 706-568-5091, E-mail: smithedmond_catrina@columbusstate.edu.
Website: http://te.columbusstate.edu/

Concordia University, College of Education, Portland, OR 97211-6099. Offers career and technical education (M Ed); curriculum and instruction (M Ed), including adolescent literacy, career and technical education, e-learning/technology education, early childhood education, English for speakers of other languages, English language development, environmental education, mathematics, methods and curriculum, reading, science, teacher leadership, the inclusive classroom; early childhood (MAT); education leadership (Ed D); educational administration (M Ed); elementary education (MAT); secondary education (MAT); special education (M Ed); teacher leadership (Ed D). *Program availability:* Part-time, online learning. *Degree requirements:* For master's, comprehensive exam, work samples/portfolio. *Entrance requirements:* For master's, California Basic Educational Skills Test or PRAXIS I, minimum undergraduate GPA of 2.8, graduate 3.0; 2 letters of recommendation. Additional exam requirements/recommendations for international students: Required—TOEFL (minimum score 525 paper-based). Electronic applications accepted. *Faculty research:* Learner-centered classroom, brain-based learning, future of online learning.

Concordia University Chicago, College of Education, Program in Early Childhood Education, River Forest, IL 60305-1499. Offers MA, Ed D. *Program availability:* Part-time, evening/weekend. *Degree requirements:* For master's, comprehensive exam, thesis. *Entrance requirements:* For master's, minimum GPA of 2.9; for doctorate, MAT or GRE, minimum graduate GPA of 3.5. Additional exam requirements/recommendations for international students: Required—TOEFL (minimum score 550 paper-based). Electronic applications accepted. *Faculty research:* Child care training project, "Children in Worship" project, ethical development of children.

Concordia University Chicago, College of Education, Program in Teaching, River Forest, IL 60305-1499. Offers early childhood education (MAT); elementary education (MAT); secondary education (MAT). *Degree requirements:* For master's, thesis or alternative. *Entrance requirements:* For master's, minimum GPA of 2.9. Additional exam requirements/recommendations for international students: Required—TOEFL (minimum score 550 paper-based). Electronic applications accepted.

Concordia University, Nebraska, Graduate Programs in Education, Program in Early Childhood Education, Seward, NE 68434. Offers M Ed. *Accreditation:* NCATE. *Program availability:* Part-time. *Degree requirements:* For master's, comprehensive exam, thesis or alternative. *Entrance requirements:* For master's, GRE, MAT, or NTE, minimum GPA of 3.0, BS in education or equivalent. Additional exam requirements/recommendations for international students: Required—TOEFL.

Concordia University, St. Paul, College of Education, St. Paul, MN 55104-5494. Offers classroom instruction (MA Ed), including K-12 reading; differentiated instruction (MA Ed); early childhood education (MA Ed); education (Ed D); educational leadership (MA Ed); educational technology (MA Ed, Certificate); K-12 principal licensure (Ed S); special education (MA Ed), including autism spectrum disorder, emotional and behavioral disorders, learning disabilities; superintendent (Ed S); teaching (MAT). *Accreditation:* NCATE. *Program availability:* Part-time, evening/weekend, 100% online, blended/hybrid learning. *Faculty:* 15 full-time (8 women), 86 part-time/adjunct (56 women). *Students:* 955 full-time (731 women), 42 part-time (28 women); includes 105 minority (35 Black or African American, non-Hispanic/Latino; 5 American Indian or Alaska Native, non-Hispanic/Latino; 31 Asian, non-Hispanic/Latino; 19 Hispanic/Latino; 15 Two or more races, non-Hispanic/Latino), 9 international. Average age 34. 409 applicants, 87% accepted, 347 enrolled. In 2017, 386 master's, 104 other advanced degrees awarded. *Degree requirements:* For master's, thesis (for some programs); for doctorate, thesis/dissertation, capstone projects; for other advanced degree, e-folio review of competencies. *Entrance requirements:* For master's, official transcripts from regionally-accredited institution stating the conferral of a bachelor's degree with minimum cumulative GPA of 3.0; personal statement; professional resume; practitioner in field through work or volunteerism; resume; for doctorate, minimum master's or specialist degree GPA of 3.25; transcript; writing sample; three letters of recommendation; current resume; on-campus interview; for other advanced degree, minimum master's or specialist degree GPA of 3.25; transcript; statement covering employment history and long-term academic and professional goals; two letters of recommendation; interview with program director. Additional exam requirements/recommendations for international students: Recommended—TOEFL (minimum score 547 paper-based; 78 iBT), IELTS (minimum score 6). *Application deadline:* For fall admission, 8/1 for domestic and international students; for spring admission, 12/1 for domestic and international students; for summer admission, 5/1 for domestic and international students. Applications are processed on a rolling basis. Application fee: $0. Electronic applications accepted. *Expenses:* $395 per credit (for MA in education); $440 per credit (for MAT); $615 per credit (for EdD). *Financial support:* In 2017–18, 105 students received support. Scholarships/grants and unspecified assistantships available. Financial award applicants required to submit FAFSA. *Faculty research:* Differentiated instruction in K-12 educational settings; educational leadership; effective online pedagogy in higher education; equine-assisted learning; faculty development in higher education. *Unit head:* Lonn Maly, Dean, 651-641-8203, E-mail: maly@csp.edu. *Application contact:* Amber Faletti, Director of Enrollment Management, 651-641-8838, Fax: 651-603-6320, E-mail: faletti@csp.edu.

Early Childhood Education

Concordia University Wisconsin, Graduate Programs, Department of Education, Program in Early Childhood, Mequon, WI 53097-2402. Offers MS Ed. *Degree requirements:* For master's, comprehensive exam, thesis or alternative. *Entrance requirements:* For master's, minimum GPA of 3.0, teaching license. Additional exam requirements/recommendations for international students: Required—TOEFL.

Daemen College, Education Department, Amherst, NY 14226-3592. Offers adolescence education (MS); childhood education (MS); childhood special education (MS); childhood special-alternative certification (MS); early childhood special-alternative certification (MS). *Accreditation:* TEAC. *Program availability:* Part-time. *Degree requirements:* For master's, thesis optional, research thesis in lieu of comprehensive exam; completion of degree within 5 years. *Entrance requirements:* For master's, 2 letters of recommendation (professional and character), proof of initial certificate of license for professional programs, resume. Additional exam requirements/recommendations for international students: Required—TOEFL (minimum score 500 paper-based; 63 iBT), IELTS (minimum score 5.5). Electronic applications accepted. *Faculty research:* Transition for students with disabilities, early childhood special education, traumatic brain injury (TBI), reading assessment.

Dallas Baptist University, Dorothy M. Bush College of Education, Program in Educational Leadership, Dallas, TX 75211-9299. Offers charter school administration (M Ed); educational leadership (M Ed); educational leadership K-12 (Ed D). *Program availability:* Part-time, evening/weekend, online learning. *Application deadline:* Applications are processed on a rolling basis. Application fee: $25. Electronic applications accepted. Application fee is waived when completed online. *Expenses: Tuition:* Full-time $16,308; part-time $906 per credit hour. *Required fees:* $900; $450 per semester. Tuition and fees vary according to course load and degree level. *Unit head:* Dr. Neil Dugger, Dean, 214-333-5202, E-mail: neil@dbu.edu. *Application contact:* Dr. Carolyn Spain, Program Director, 214-333-5217, E-mail: carolyns@dbu.edu. Website: http://www3.dbu.edu/graduate/education.asp

Dallas Baptist University, Dorothy M. Bush College of Education, Teaching Program, Dallas, TX 75211-9299. Offers distance learning (MAT); early childhood through grade 6 certification (MAT); early childhood-12 (MAT); elementary (MAT); English as a second language (MAT); Montessori (MAT); multisensory (MAT); secondary (MAT). *Program availability:* Part-time, evening/weekend. *Application deadline:* Applications are processed on a rolling basis. Application fee: $25. Electronic applications accepted. Application fee is waived when completed online. *Expenses: Tuition:* Full-time $16,308; part-time $906 per credit hour. *Required fees:* $900; $450 per semester. Tuition and fees vary according to course load and degree level. *Unit head:* Dr. Neil Dugger, Dean, 214-333-5202, E-mail: neil@dbu.edu. *Application contact:* Dr. DeAnna Jenkins, Program Director, 214-333-5402, E-mail: deannaj@dbu.edu. Website: http://www3.dbu.edu/graduate/mat.asp

DePaul University, College of Education, Chicago, IL 60614. Offers bilingual-bicultural education (M Ed, MA); counseling (M Ed, MA), including clinical mental health counseling, college student development, school counseling; curriculum studies (M Ed, MA, Ed D); early childhood education (M Ed, MA, Ed D); educational leadership (M Ed, MA, Ed D), including Catholic leadership (M Ed, MA), general (M Ed, MA), higher education (M Ed, MA), physical education (M Ed, MA), principal preparation (M Ed), teacher preparation (M Ed); elementary education (M Ed, MA); middle grades education (M Ed); middle school mathematics education (MS); reading specialist (M Ed, MA); secondary education (M Ed, MA); social and cultural foundations in education (M Ed, MA); special education (M Ed); sport, fitness and recreation leadership (MS); value-creating education for global citizenship (M Ed); world languages education (M Ed, MA). *Program availability:* Part-time, evening/weekend, online learning. *Degree requirements:* For doctorate, thesis/dissertation. *Application deadline:* Applications are processed on a rolling basis. Application fee: $40. Electronic applications accepted. *Financial support:* Application deadline: 12/31; applicants required to submit FAFSA. *Unit head:* Dr. Paul Zionts, Dean, 773-325-7713, Fax: 773-325-7713, E-mail: pzionts@depaul.edu. *Application contact:* Dr. Paul Zionts, Dean, 773-325-7713, Fax: 773-325-7713, E-mail: pzionts@depaul.edu. Website: http://education.depaul.edu

Dominican University, School of Education, River Forest, IL 60305-1099. Offers child life studies (MS); early childhood education (MS); education (MAT); elementary education (MA Ed); English as a second language (MA Ed); reading (MA Ed); secondary education (MAT); special education (MS). *Accreditation:* NCATE. *Program availability:* Part-time, evening/weekend, 100% online, blended/hybrid learning. *Faculty:* 8 full-time (6 women), 42 part-time/adjunct (38 women). *Students:* 5 full-time (all women), 261 part-time (206 women); includes 45 minority (16 Black or African American, non-Hispanic/Latino; 1 American Indian or Alaska Native, non-Hispanic/Latino; 5 Asian, non-Hispanic/Latino; 18 Hispanic/Latino; 5 Two or more races, non-Hispanic/Latino), 1 international. Average age 32. 95 applicants, 98% accepted, 72 enrolled. In 2017, 206 master's awarded. *Entrance requirements:* For master's, Illinois Test of Basic Skills. Additional exam requirements/recommendations for international students: Required—TOEFL (minimum score 550 paper-based; 79 iBT). *Application deadline:* Applications are processed on a rolling basis. Application fee: $25. *Expenses:* Contact institution. *Financial support:* Career-related internships or fieldwork, scholarships/grants, tuition waivers (partial), and unspecified assistantships available. Support available to part-time students. Financial award application deadline: 8/15; financial award applicants required to submit FAFSA. *Faculty research:* Governance of private education institutions, reading and language arts, inclusion, organizational planning, leadership and vision. *Unit head:* Dr. Colleen Reardon, Interim Executive Director, School of Education, 708-524-6643, Fax: 708-524-6665, E-mail: creardon@dom.edu. *Application contact:* Benjamin Mueller, Senior Graduate Marketing and Recruitment Coordinator, 708-524-6456, Fax: 708-524-6665, E-mail: bmueller@dom.edu. Website: http://educate.dom.edu/

Duquesne University, School of Education, Department of Instruction and Leadership, Program in Early Level (PreK-4) Education, Pittsburgh, PA 15282-0001. Offers MS Ed. *Program availability:* Part-time, evening/weekend. *Faculty:* 3 full-time (2 women). *Students:* 25 full-time (23 women), 6 part-time (5 women); includes 2 minority (1 Black or African American, non-Hispanic/Latino; 1 Asian, non-Hispanic/Latino), 1 international. Average age 30. 30 applicants, 97% accepted, 12 enrolled. In 2017, 10 master's awarded. *Degree requirements:* For master's, thesis optional. *Entrance requirements:* For master's, bachelor's degree; minimum GPA of 3.0 overall or on most recent 48 credits. Additional exam requirements/recommendations for international students: Required—TOEFL (minimum score 550 paper-based), IELTS (minimum score 7). *Application deadline:* For fall admission, 9/1 for domestic students; for spring admission, 1/2 for domestic students. Applications are processed on a rolling basis. Application fee: $0. Electronic applications accepted. *Expenses:* $1,259 per credit. *Faculty research:* How young students perceive moral learning; using storytelling for moral learning; faith and character development in young students; early literacy development; engaging parents and families. *Unit head:* Dr. Julia Williams, Assistant Professor, 412-396-6098, Fax: 412-396-5388, E-mail: williamsj@duq.edu. *Application contact:* Kelly McGinley, Graduate Admissions Assistant, 412-396-1559, Fax: 412-396-5585, E-mail: mcginleyk@duq.edu. Website: http://www.duq.edu/academics/schools/education/graduate-programs/ms-early-level-prek-4

East Carolina University, Graduate School, College of Health and Human Performance, Department of Human Development and Family Science, Greenville, NC 27858-4353. Offers birth through kindergarten education (MA Ed); human development and family science (MS); marriage and family therapy (MS); medical family therapy (PhD). *Accreditation:* AAMFT/COAMFTE. *Program availability:* Part-time. *Students:* 73 full-time (69 women), 24 part-time (21 women); includes 20 minority (14 Black or African American, non-Hispanic/Latino; 3 American Indian or Alaska Native, non-Hispanic/Latino; 2 Hispanic/Latino; 1 Native Hawaiian or other Pacific Islander, non-Hispanic/Latino), 2 international. Average age 28. 98 applicants, 50% accepted, 35 enrolled. In 2017, 26 master's, 3 doctorates awarded. *Degree requirements:* For master's, comprehensive exam, thesis optional. *Entrance requirements:* Additional exam requirements/recommendations for international students: Recommended—TOEFL (minimum score 78 iBT), IELTS (minimum score 6.5). *Application deadline:* For fall admission, 1/15 for domestic students; for spring admission, 10/15 for domestic students. Applications are processed on a rolling basis. Application fee: $75. *Expenses:* Tuition, state resident: full-time $4749; part-time $297 per credit hour. Tuition, nonresident: full-time $17,898; part-time $1119 per credit hour. *Required fees:* $2691; $224 per credit hour. Part-time tuition and fees vary according to course load and program. *Financial support:* Research assistantships, teaching assistantships, career-related internships or fieldwork, Federal Work-Study, institutionally sponsored loans, and scholarships/grants available. Support available to part-time students. Financial award application deadline: 6/1. *Faculty research:* Child care quality, mental health delivery systems for children, family violence. *Unit head:* Dr. Sharon Ballard, Interim Chair, 252-328-1356, E-mail: ballards@ecu.edu. Website: https://hhp.ecu.edu/hdfs/

Eastern Connecticut State University, School of Education and Professional Studies/Graduate Division, Program in Early Childhood Education, Willimantic, CT 06226-2295. Offers MS. *Accreditation:* NCATE. *Program availability:* Part-time, evening/weekend. *Faculty:* 12 full-time (7 women), 13 part-time/adjunct (9 women). *Students:* 12 full-time (9 women), 17 part-time (all women); includes 2 minority (1 Black or African American, non-Hispanic/Latino; 1 Two or more races, non-Hispanic/Latino). Average age 31. 8 applicants, 88% accepted, 6 enrolled. In 2017, 5 master's awarded. *Degree requirements:* For master's, thesis optional. *Entrance requirements:* For master's, PRAXIS I, GRE, SAT, ACT, or PAA and PRAXIS II, minimum GPA of 3.0, bachelor's degree from accredited institution. Additional exam requirements/recommendations for international students: Required—TOEFL (minimum score 550 paper-based; 79 iBT); Recommended—IELTS (minimum score 6). *Application deadline:* For fall admission, 7/6 priority date for domestic and international students; for spring admission, 11/3 priority date for domestic and international students. Applications are processed on a rolling basis. Application fee: $50. Electronic applications accepted. *Expenses: Tuition, area resident:* Full-time $12,252. Tuition, state resident: full-time $15,245; part-time $582 per credit hour. Tuition, nonresident: full-time $24,828; part-time $582 per credit hour. *Required fees:* $40 per semester. Full-time tuition and fees vary according to reciprocity agreements. *Financial support:* In 2017–18, 1 student received support. Research assistantships, teaching assistantships, career-related internships or fieldwork, institutionally sponsored loans, and unspecified assistantships available. Financial award application deadline: 3/1; financial award applicants required to submit FAFSA. *Unit head:* Dr. Jeffrey Trawick-Smith, Advisor, 860-465-5232, Fax: 860-465-5099, E-mail: trawick@easternct.edu. *Application contact:* Paula Goyette, Graduate Division, School of Education and Professional Studies, 860-465-5292, Fax: 860-465-4538, E-mail: graduateadmissions@easternct.edu.

Eastern Illinois University, Graduate School, College of Education and Professional Studies, Department of Early Childhood, Elementary and Middle Level Education, Charleston, IL 61920. Offers curriculum and instruction (MS Ed). *Accreditation:* NCATE. *Program availability:* Part-time, evening/weekend. *Degree requirements:* For master's, comprehensive exam (for some programs), thesis (for some programs). *Entrance requirements:* For master's, GMAT or GRE. Additional exam requirements/recommendations for international students: Required—TOEFL (minimum score 500 paper-based; 61 iBT), IELTS (minimum score 6). *Application deadline:* For fall admission, 5/15 for domestic and international students; for spring admission, 10/15 for domestic and international students. Applications are processed on a rolling basis. Application fee: $30. Electronic applications accepted. *Financial support:* Research assistantships with full tuition reimbursements, teaching assistantships with full tuition reimbursements, career-related internships or fieldwork, Federal Work-Study, and unspecified assistantships available. Support available to part-time students. Financial award application deadline: 3/1; financial award applicants required to submit FAFSA. *Unit head:* Jeanne E. Okrasinski, Chair, 217-581-5728, Fax: 217-581-6300, E-mail: jeokrasinski@eiu.edu. *Application contact:* Jeanne E. Okrasinski, Chair, 217-581-5728, Fax: 217-581-6300, E-mail: jeokrasinski@eiu.edu. Website: http://www.eiu.edu/elegrad/

Eastern Michigan University, Graduate School, College of Education, Department of Teacher Education, Program in Early Childhood Education, Ypsilanti, MI 48197. Offers MA. *Accreditation:* NCATE. *Program availability:* Part-time, evening/weekend. *Students:* 30 part-time (all women); includes 4 minority (2 Black or African American, non-Hispanic/Latino; 1 Hispanic/Latino; 1 Two or more races, non-Hispanic/Latino). Average age 34. 15 applicants, 80% accepted, 6 enrolled. In 2017, 17 master's awarded. *Degree requirements:* For master's, thesis optional. *Entrance requirements:* For master's, GRE. Additional exam requirements/recommendations for international students: Required—TOEFL. *Application deadline:* Applications are processed on a rolling basis. Application fee: $45. *Financial support:* Fellowships and teaching assistantships available. Support available to part-time students. Financial award applicants required to submit FAFSA. *Application contact:* Dr. Brigid Beaubien, Coordinator, 734-487-3260, Fax: 734-487-2101, E-mail: brigid.beaubien@emich.edu.

Eastern Nazarene College, Adult and Graduate Studies, Division of Teacher Education, Quincy, MA 02170. Offers administration (M Ed); early childhood education (M Ed, Certificate); elementary education (M Ed, Certificate); English as a second language (Certificate); instructional enrichment and development (Certificate); middle school education (M Ed, Certificate); moderate special needs education (Certificate); principal (Certificate); program development and supervision (Certificate); secondary education (M Ed, Certificate); special education administrator (Certificate); special needs (M Ed); supervisor (Certificate); teacher of reading (M Ed, Certificate). M Ed also available through weekend program for administration, special needs, and teacher of reading only. *Program availability:* Part-time, evening/weekend. *Entrance requirements:* Additional exam requirements/recommendations for international students: Required—TOEFL (minimum score 550 paper-based).

Eastern New Mexico University, Graduate School, College of Education and Technology, Department of Educational Studies, Program in Special Education, Portales, NM 88130. Offers early childhood special education (M Sp Ed); general special education (M Sp Ed); gifted education pedagogy (M Ed); special education pedagogy (M Ed). *Program availability:* Part-time. *Degree requirements:* For master's, comprehensive exam, thesis optional. *Entrance requirements:* For master's, writing assessment, minimum GPA of 3.0, letter of recommendation, photocopy of teaching license or confirmation of entrance into alternative licensure program, special education license or minimum 30 hours of undergraduate course work. Additional exam requirements/recommendations for international students: Required—TOEFL (minimum score 550 paper-based; 79 iBT), IELTS (minimum score 6). *Application deadline:* For fall admission, 7/20 priority date for domestic students, 6/20 priority date for international students; for spring admission, 12/15 priority date for domestic students, 11/15 priority date for international students. Applications are processed on a rolling basis. Application fee: $10. Electronic applications accepted. *Financial support:* Applicants required to submit FAFSA. *Unit head:* Dr. Rebecca Davis, Graduate Coordinator, 575-392-6840, E-mail: rebecca.davis@enmu.edu. *Application contact:* Cheryl Reeves, Senior Secretary, 575-562-2443, Fax: 575-562-2559, E-mail: cheryl.reeves@enmu.edu.

Eastern University, Graduate Education Programs, St. Davids, PA 19087-3696. Offers ESL program specialist (K-12) (Certificate); general supervisor (PreK-12) (Certificate); health and physical education (K-12) (Certificate); middle level (4-8) (Certificate); multicultural education (M Ed); music (K-12) (Certificate); Pre K-4 (Certificate); Pre K-4 with special education (Certificate); reading (M Ed); reading specialist (K-12) (Certificate); reading supervisor (K-12) (Certificate); school counseling (MA, CAGS); school principalship (preK-12) (Certificate); school psychology (MS, CAGS); secondary biology education (7-12) (Certificate); secondary chemistry education (7-12) (Certificate); secondary communication education (7-12) (Certificate); secondary English education (7-12) (Certificate); secondary math education (7-12) (Certificate); secondary social studies education (7-12) (Certificate); special education (M Ed); special education (7-12) (Certificate); special education (Pre K-8) (Certificate); special education supervisor (K-12) (Certificate); TESOL (M Ed); world language (Certificate), including Spanish. *Program availability:* Part-time, evening/weekend, online learning. *Students:* 46 full-time (40 women), 115 part-time (93 women); includes 65 minority (42 Black or African American, non-Hispanic/Latino; 3 Asian, non-Hispanic/Latino; 14 Hispanic/Latino; 6 Two or more races, non-Hispanic/Latino), 1 international. Average age 32. In 2017, 72 master's awarded. *Entrance requirements:* Additional exam requirements/recommendations for international students: Required—TOEFL. *Application deadline:* Applications are processed on a rolling basis. Application fee: $35. Electronic applications accepted. Application fee is waived when completed online. *Expenses:* Contact institution. *Unit head:* Michael Dziedziak, Executive Director of Enrollment, 800-452-0996, E-mail: gpsadmissions@eastern.edu. Website: https://www.eastern.edu/academics/programs/education-department-graduate-programs/graduate-programs

Eastern Washington University, Graduate Studies, College of Arts, Letters and Education, Department of Education, Program in Early Childhood Education, Cheney, WA 99004-2431. Offers M Ed. *Students:* 5 full-time (all women), 1 (woman) part-time; includes 1 minority (Hispanic/Latino). Average age 34. 7 applicants, 14% accepted, 1 enrolled. In 2017, 3 master's awarded. *Degree requirements:* For master's, comprehensive exam, thesis (for some programs). *Entrance requirements:* For master's, GRE, minimum GPA of 3.0. Additional exam requirements/recommendations for international students: Required—TOEFL (minimum score 580 paper-based; 92 iBT), IELTS (minimum score 7), PTE (minimum score 63). *Application deadline:* Applications are processed on a rolling basis. Application fee: $75. Electronic applications accepted. *Expenses:* Tuition, state resident: full-time $11,191; part-time $373.06 per credit. Tuition, nonresident: full-time $25,995; part-time $866.52 per credit. *Financial support:* Application deadline: 2/1; applicants required to submit FAFSA. *Unit head:* Dr. Allison Wilson, Program Coordinator, 509-359-7021, E-mail: awilson28@ewu.edu.

East Stroudsburg University of Pennsylvania, Graduate and Extended Studies, College of Education, Department of Early Childhood and Elementary Education, East Stroudsburg, PA 18301-2999. Offers M Ed. *Program availability:* Part-time, evening/weekend, online learning. *Faculty:* 1 (woman) full-time. *Students:* 2 full-time (both women), 6 part-time (all women). Average age 40. 9 applicants, 78% accepted, 4 enrolled. In 2017, 2 master's awarded. *Degree requirements:* For master's, comprehensive exam, professional portfolio, curriculum project or action research. *Entrance requirements:* For master's, PRAXIS/teacher certification, letter of recommendation, Pennsylvania Department of Education requirements. Additional exam requirements/recommendations for international students: Recommended—TOEFL (minimum score 560 paper-based; 83 iBT), IELTS. *Application deadline:* For fall admission, 7/31 priority date for domestic students, 6/30 priority date for international students; for spring admission, 11/30 for domestic students, 10/31 for international students. Applications are processed on a rolling basis. Application fee: $50. Electronic applications accepted. *Expenses:* Tuition, state resident: full-time $4500; part-time $3000 per credit. Tuition, nonresident: full-time $6750; part-time $4500 per credit. *Required fees:* $2642; $1756 per credit. $878 per semester. Tuition and fees vary according to course load, campus/location and program. *Financial support:* Research assistantships with tuition reimbursements, Federal Work-Study, and unspecified assistantships available. Support available to part-time students. Financial award application deadline: 3/1; financial award applicants required to submit FAFSA. *Unit head:* Andrew Whitehead, Chair, 570-422-3356, Fax: 570-422-3942, E-mail: awhitehead@esu.edu. *Application contact:* Kevin Quintero, Associate Director, Graduate and Extended Studies, 570-422-3890, Fax: 570-422-2711, E-mail: kquintero@esu.edu.

East Tennessee State University, School of Graduate Studies, College of Education, Department of Early Childhood Education, Johnson City, TN 37614. Offers early childhood education (MA, PhD); early childhood education emergent inquiry (Postbaccalaureate Certificate). *Degree requirements:* For master's, thesis optional, practicum; for doctorate, comprehensive exam, thesis/dissertation, research apprenticeship and at least one of the additional apprenticeship options, oral exam. *Entrance requirements:* For master's, GRE, PRAXIS, ACT, SAT, minimum undergraduate GPA of 3.0; for doctorate, GRE, resume, 4 letters of recommendation, personal essay that includes written statement of career and educational goals, master's degree in early childhood or related field, interview; for Postbaccalaureate Certificate, bachelor or master's degree in early childhood or related field, 2 letters of recommendation. Additional exam requirements/recommendations for international students: Required—TOEFL (minimum score 550 paper-based; 79 iBT). *Application deadline:* For fall admission, 6/1 for domestic students, 4/29 for international students; for spring admission, 11/1 for domestic students, 9/29 for international students. Application fee: $55 ($65 for international students). Electronic applications accepted. *Unit head:* Pamela Evanshen, Chair, 423-439-7694, E-mail: evanshep@etsu.edu. *Application contact:* Dr. Amy Malkus, Graduate Program Coordinator, 423-463-0841, E-mail: malkus@etsu.edu.
Website: http://www.etsu.edu/coe/eced/

East Tennessee State University, School of Graduate Studies, College of Education, Department of Educational Foundations and Special Education, Johnson City, TN 37614. Offers community leadership (Post-Master's Certificate), including early childhood special education (M Ed, Post-Master's Certificate), high incidence disabilities (M Ed, Post-Master's Certificate), low incidence disabilities (M Ed, Post-Master's Certificate); special education (M Ed, Post-Master's Certificate), including advanced studies in special education (M Ed), early childhood special education, high incidence disabilities, low incidence disabilities. *Program availability:* Part-time. *Degree requirements:* For master's, thesis (for some programs), practicum, residency, or thesis.

Entrance requirements: For master's, PRAXIS I or Tennessee teaching license (for special education only), minimum GPA of 3.0 (or complete probationary period with no grade lower than B for first 9 graduate hours for early childhood education), 2-page essay outlining past experience with individuals with disabilities and goals for acquiring an advanced degree in special education; for Post-Master's Certificate, bachelor's or master's degree in early childhood or related field; two years of experience working with young children (preferred). Additional exam requirements/recommendations for international students: Required—TOEFL (minimum score 550 paper-based; 79 iBT). *Application deadline:* For fall admission, 3/15 for domestic and international students. Application fee: $55 ($65 for international students). *Financial support:* Fellowships with full tuition reimbursements, research assistantships with full tuition reimbursements, teaching assistantships with full tuition reimbursements, career-related internships or fieldwork, institutionally sponsored loans, scholarships/grants, and unspecified assistantships available. Financial award application deadline: 7/1; financial award applicants required to submit FAFSA. *Faculty research:* Teaching students with significant disabilities, problem-solving in toddlers, children and their development and learning, connecting classroom environment to student engagement in PreK-3, bilingual education in Ecuador, positive discipline/behavior support programs, early childhood relationships, international and comparative special education. *Unit head:* Dr. Cathy Galyon-Keramidas, Chair, 423-439-7688, E-mail: galyonkerami@etsu.edu. *Application contact:* Dr. Cynthia Chambers, Graduate Program Coordinator, 423-439-7586, Fax: 423-439-5624, E-mail: chamberc@etsu.edu.
Website: http://www.etsu.edu/coe/efse/

Edinboro University of Pennsylvania, Department of Early Childhood and Reading, Edinboro, PA 16444. Offers arts infusion (Graduate Certificate); early childhood education (M Ed); reading (M Ed); reading specialist (Graduate Certificate). *Program availability:* Part-time, evening/weekend. *Degree requirements:* For master's, thesis or alternative, competency exam; for Graduate Certificate, thesis or alternative. *Entrance requirements:* For master's and Graduate Certificate, GRE or MAT, minimum QPA of 2.5. Electronic applications accepted.

Elms College, Division of Education, Chicopee, MA 01013-2839. Offers early childhood education (MAT); education (M Ed, CAGS); elementary education (MAT); English as a second language (MAT); reading (MAT); secondary education (MAT), including biology education, English education, Spanish education; special education (MAT). *Program availability:* Part-time, evening/weekend. *Faculty:* 4 full-time (all women), 8 part-time/adjunct (7 women). *Students:* 6 full-time (4 women), 127 part-time (107 women); includes 8 minority (2 Asian, non-Hispanic/Latino; 6 Hispanic/Latino). Average age 33. 42 applicants, 88% accepted, 36 enrolled. In 2017, 50 master's, 6 other advanced degrees awarded. *Degree requirements:* For master's, thesis (for some programs). *Entrance requirements:* For master's, Massachusetts Educators Certification Test, minimum GPA of 3.0; for CAGS, master's degree in education. Additional exam requirements/recommendations for international students: Required—TOEFL. *Application deadline:* For fall admission, 7/1 priority date for domestic students; for spring admission, 11/1 priority date for domestic students. Applications are processed on a rolling basis. Application fee: $30. *Expenses: Tuition:* Full-time $13,860; part-time $770 per credit hour. *Required fees:* $200. Tuition and fees vary according to degree level and program. *Financial support:* In 2017–18, 2 teaching assistantships with partial tuition reimbursements were awarded. Financial award applicants required to submit FAFSA. *Unit head:* Dr. Mary Janeczek, Chair, Division of Education, 413-594-2761, Fax: 413-592-4871, E-mail: janeczeke@elms.edu. *Application contact:* School of Graduate and Professional Studies, 413-265-2445, E-mail: graduateeducation@elms.edu.

Emporia State University, Program in Early Childhood Education, Emporia, KS 66801-5415. Offers MS. *Accreditation:* NCATE. *Program availability:* Part-time, online learning. *Faculty:* 30 full-time (24 women), 1 part-time/adjunct (0 women). *Students:* 2 full-time (both women), 48 part-time (all women); includes 2 minority (both Hispanic/Latino). 12 applicants, 50% accepted, 4 enrolled. In 2017, 23 master's awarded. *Degree requirements:* For master's, comprehensive exam or thesis, practicum. *Entrance requirements:* For master's, GRE General Test or MAT, essay exam, appropriate bachelor's degree, letters of recommendation. Additional exam requirements/recommendations for international students: Required—TOEFL (minimum score 520 paper-based; 68 iBT). *Application deadline:* For fall admission, 8/15 priority date for domestic students. Applications are processed on a rolling basis. Application fee: $30 ($75 for international students). Electronic applications accepted. *Expenses:* Tuition, state resident: full-time $6084; part-time $253.50 per credit hour. Tuition, nonresident: full-time $18,924; part-time $788.50 per credit hour. *Required fees:* $1943; $80.95 per credit hour. Tuition and fees vary according to campus/location. *Financial support:* In 2017–18, 4 research assistantships (averaging $7,344 per year), 4 teaching assistantships (averaging $7,344 per year) were awarded; Federal Work-Study, institutionally sponsored loans, health care benefits, and unspecified assistantships also available. Financial award application deadline: 3/15; financial award applicants required to submit FAFSA. *Unit head:* Dr. Matt Siemears, Chair, 620-341-6057, E-mail: mseimear@emporia.edu. *Application contact:* Mary Sewell, Admissions Coordinator, 800-950-GRAD, Fax: 620-341-5909, E-mail: msewell@emporia.edu.

Endicott College, Van Loan School of Graduate and Professional Studies, Program in Early Childhood and Elementary Education, Beverly, MA 01915-2096. Offers early childhood and elementary education (M Ed); early childhood education (M Ed); elementary education (M Ed). *Program availability:* Part-time, evening/weekend, 100% online, blended/hybrid learning. *Faculty:* 4 full-time (3 women), 12 part-time/adjunct (10 women). *Students:* 14 full-time (13 women), 9 part-time (8 women). Average age 31. 5 applicants, 100% accepted, 5 enrolled. In 2017, 13 master's awarded. *Degree requirements:* For master's, comprehensive exam, thesis, practicum. *Entrance requirements:* For master's, MAT or GRE, Massachusetts Tests for Educator Licensure (MTEL), Massachusetts teaching certificate, 2 professional letters of recommendation, personal statement. Additional exam requirements/recommendations for international students: Required—TOEFL. *Application deadline:* Applications are processed on a rolling basis. Application fee: $50. Electronic applications accepted. *Expenses:* Contact institution. *Financial support:* Career-related internships or fieldwork available. Financial award applicants required to submit FAFSA. *Unit head:* Dr. Aubry Threlkeld, Director of Graduate Licensure Programs, 978-232-2408, E-mail: athrelke@endicott.edu. *Application contact:* Ian Menchini, Director, Graduate Enrollment and Advising, 978-232-5292, E-mail: imenchin@endicott.edu.
Website: https://vanloan.endicott.edu/programs-of-study/masters-programs/educator-preparation-program/early-childhood-education-program

Endicott College, Van Loan School of Graduate and Professional Studies, Program in Integrative Education, Beverly, MA 01915-2096. Offers M Ed. Program offered in conjunction with The Institute for Educational Studies (TIES). *Program availability:* Part-time, online only, 100% online. *Faculty:* 1 full-time (0 women). *Students:* 33 full-time (31 women); includes 1 minority (Hispanic/Latino). Average age 35. 15 applicants, 100% accepted, 13 enrolled. In 2017, 16 master's awarded. *Degree requirements:* For master's, thesis. *Entrance requirements:* For master's, undergraduate transcript. Additional exam requirements/recommendations for international students: Required—TOEFL. *Application deadline:* Applications are processed on a rolling basis. Application fee: $50. Electronic applications accepted. *Expenses:* Contact institution. *Financial*

Early Childhood Education

support: Tuition waivers (partial) available. Financial award applicants required to submit FAFSA. *Faculty research:* Neurophenomenology, autopoiesis, systems view. *Unit head:* Dr. Phil Snow Gang, Academic Dean, 888-722-4547, Fax: 978-232-3000, E-mail: ties@endicott.edu. *Application contact:* Ian Menchini, Director, Graduate Enrollment and Advising, 978-232-5292, E-mail: imenchin@endicott.edu. Website: https://vanloan.endicott.edu/programs-of-study/masters-programs/montessori-integrative-education-program-med

Erikson Institute, Erikson Institute, Chicago, IL 60654. Offers child development (MS); early childhood education (M Ed, MS, PhD). PhD offered through the Graduate School. *Accreditation:* NCA. *Degree requirements:* For master's, comprehensive exam, internship; for doctorate, one foreign language, comprehensive exam, thesis/dissertation. *Entrance requirements:* For master's, experience working with young children, interview; for doctorate, GRE General Test, interview. *Faculty research:* Early childhood development, cognitive development, sociocultural contexts, early childhood education, family and culture, early literacy.

Erikson Institute, Academic Programs, Program in Early Childhood Education, Chicago, IL 60654. Offers MS. *Degree requirements:* For master's, comprehensive exam. *Entrance requirements:* For master's, 3 letters of recommendation, minimum GPA of 2.75. Additional exam requirements/recommendations for international students: Required—TOEFL.

Fairleigh Dickinson University, Florham Campus, University College: Arts, Sciences, and Professional Studies, Peter Sammartino School of Education, Program in Education for Certified Teachers, Madison, NJ 07940-1099. Offers PreK - 3 certification (MA).

Fairleigh Dickinson University, Florham Campus, University College: Arts, Sciences, and Professional Studies, Peter Sammartino School of Education, Program in Teaching, Madison, NJ 07940-1099. Offers PreK - 3 certification (MAT).

Fairleigh Dickinson University, Metropolitan Campus, University College: Arts, Sciences, and Professional Studies, Peter Sammartino School of Education, Program in Education for Certified Teachers, Teaneck, NJ 07666-1914. Offers PreK - 3 certification (MA).

Fairleigh Dickinson University, Metropolitan Campus, University College: Arts, Sciences, and Professional Studies, Peter Sammartino School of Education, Program in Teaching, Teaneck, NJ 07666-1914. Offers PreK - 3 certification (MAT).

Fielding Graduate University, Graduate Programs, School of Leadership Studies, Programs in Infant and Early Childhood Development, Santa Barbara, CA 93105-3814. Offers infant and early childhood development (MA, PhD, Graduate Certificate), including early childhood development: education, mental health, and disruptive behaviors (MA), infant mental health and neurodevelopment (MA), reflective practice and supervision (Graduate Certificate). *Program availability:* Part-time, evening/weekend, 100% online, blended/hybrid learning. *Faculty:* 1 (woman) full-time, 28 part-time/adjunct (22 women). *Students:* 84 full-time (79 women), 1 (woman) part-time; includes 33 minority (12 Black or African American, non-Hispanic/Latino; 2 American Indian or Alaska Native, non-Hispanic/Latino; 3 Asian, non-Hispanic/Latino; 10 Hispanic/Latino; 6 Two or more races, non-Hispanic/Latino), 1 international. Average age 45. 17 applicants, 94% accepted, 14 enrolled. In 2017, 9 doctorates awarded. Terminal master's awarded for partial completion of doctoral program. *Degree requirements:* For master's, thesis or alternative, capstone; for doctorate, comprehensive exam, thesis/dissertation. *Entrance requirements:* For master's and Graduate Certificate, bachelor's degree from regionally-accredited U.S. institution or equivalent; for doctorate, bachelor's or master's degree from regionally-accredited U.S. institution or equivalent, curriculum vitae, statement of purpose, critical thinking writing sample, 2 letters of recommendation, official transcript. *Application deadline:* For fall admission, 7/16 for domestic and international students; for spring admission, 11/1 for domestic and international students; for summer admission, 3/1 for domestic and international students. Application fee: $75. Electronic applications accepted. *Expenses:* Contact institution. *Financial support:* Research assistantships, teaching assistantships, and scholarships/grants available. Support available to part-time students. Financial award applicants required to submit FAFSA. *Unit head:* Dr. Barbra Mink, Program Director, E-mail: bmink@fielding.edu. *Application contact:* Enrollment Coordinator, 800-340-1099 Ext. 4098, Fax: 805-687-9793, E-mail: hodadmission@fielding.edu. Website: http://www.fielding.edu/our-programs/school-of-leadership-studies/phd-infant-early-childhood-development/

Fitchburg State University, Division of Graduate and Continuing Education, Program in Early Childhood Education, Fitchburg, MA 01420-2697. Offers M Ed. *Accreditation:* NCATE. *Program availability:* Part-time, evening/weekend. *Students:* 19 full-time (all women), 15 part-time (all women); includes 1 minority (Hispanic/Latino). Average age 33. 10 applicants, 100% accepted, 9 enrolled. In 2017, 9 master's awarded. *Entrance requirements:* Additional exam requirements/recommendations for international students: Required—TOEFL (minimum score 550 paper-based; 79 iBT). *Application deadline:* For fall admission, 7/15 for international students; for spring admission, 12/1 for international students. Applications are processed on a rolling basis. Application fee: $50. Electronic applications accepted. *Expenses:* Contact institution. *Financial support:* In 2017–18, research assistantships with partial tuition reimbursements (averaging $5,500 per year) were awarded; Federal Work-Study, scholarships/grants, and unspecified assistantships also available. Support available to part-time students. Financial award application deadline: 3/1; financial award applicants required to submit FAFSA. *Unit head:* Dr. Lyndsey Benharris, Chair, 978-665-3539, Fax: 978-665-3658, E-mail: gce@fitchburgstate.edu. *Application contact:* Jinawa McNeil, Director of Admissions, 978-665-3140, Fax: 978-665-4540, E-mail: admissions@fitchburgstate.edu. Website: http://www.fitchburgstate.edu

Five Towns College, Graduate Programs, Dix Hills, NY 11746-6055. Offers childhood education (MS Ed); composition and arranging (DMA); jazz/commercial music (MM); music education (MM, DMA); music history and literature (DMA); music performance (DMA). *Program availability:* Part-time. *Faculty:* 12 full-time (3 women), 6 part-time/adjunct (0 women). *Students:* 18 full-time (7 women), 6 part-time (2 women); includes 9 minority (3 Black or African American, non-Hispanic/Latino; 4 Asian, non-Hispanic/Latino; 1 Hispanic/Latino; 1 Two or more races, non-Hispanic/Latino), 1 international. Average age 35. 63 applicants, 11% accepted, 7 enrolled. In 2017, 4 master's, 2 doctorates awarded. *Degree requirements:* For master's, thesis, exams, major composition or capstone project, recital; for doctorate, comprehensive exam, thesis/dissertation, final oral exam. *Entrance requirements:* For master's, audition (for MM); New York state teaching certification (for MS Ed); personal statement, two letters of recommendation; for doctorate, 3 letters of recommendation, audition, essay. Additional exam requirements/recommendations for international students: Required—TOEFL (minimum score 520 paper-based; 85 iBT); Recommended—IELTS (minimum score 7). *Application deadline:* For fall admission, 9/1 for domestic and international students; for spring admission, 1/25 for domestic and international students. Applications are processed on a rolling basis. Application fee: $50. Electronic applications accepted. *Financial support:* Fellowships with tuition reimbursements, teaching assistantships with tuition reimbursements, and tuition waivers (partial) available. Financial award applicants required to submit FAFSA. *Faculty research:* Teaching methods, teaching

strategies and techniques, analysis of modern music, jazz. *Application contact:* Ronnie MacDonald, Director of Admissions, 631-656-2110, Fax: 631-656-2172, E-mail: admissions@ftc.edu. Website: http://www.ftc.edu

Florida Atlantic University, College of Education, Department of Curriculum, Culture, and Educational Inquiry, Boca Raton, FL 33431-0991. Offers curriculum and instruction (M Ed, PhD, Ed S); early childhood education (M Ed); multicultural education (M Ed); TESOL and bilingual education (MA). *Program availability:* Part-time, evening/weekend. *Faculty:* 10 full-time (8 women), 2 part-time/adjunct (both women). *Students:* 15 full-time (13 women), 81 part-time (65 women); includes 28 minority (11 Black or African American, non-Hispanic/Latino; 3 Asian, non-Hispanic/Latino; 12 Hispanic/Latino; 2 Two or more races, non-Hispanic/Latino), 3 international. Average age 36. 54 applicants, 37% accepted, 14 enrolled. In 2017, 23 master's, 5 doctorates, 4 other advanced degrees awarded. *Entrance requirements:* Additional exam requirements/recommendations for international students: Required—TOEFL (minimum score 500 paper-based; 61 iBT), IELTS (minimum score 6). *Application deadline:* For fall admission, 7/1 for domestic students, 2/15 for international students; for spring admission, 11/1 for domestic students, 7/15 for international students. Application fee: $30. *Expenses:* Tuition, state resident: full-time $7400; part-time $369.82 per credit. Tuition, nonresident: full-time $20,496; part-time $1042.81 per credit. *Faculty research:* Multicultural education, early intervention strategies, family literacy, religious diversity in schools, early childhood curriculum. *Unit head:* Dr. Dilys Schoorman, Chair, 561-297-3965, E-mail: dschoorm@fau.edu. *Application contact:* Dr. Eliah Watlington, Associate Dean, 561-296-8520, Fax: 261-297-2991, E-mail: ewatling@fau.edu. Website: http://www.coe.fau.edu/academicdepartments/ccei

Florida Atlantic University, College of Education, Department of Teaching and Learning, Boca Raton, FL 33431-0991. Offers curriculum and instruction (M Ed), including art, biology, chemistry, English, French, German, mathematics, music, physics, Pre-K and primary education, reading, social sciences, Spanish; elementary education (M Ed); environmental education (M Ed); reading education (M Ed); social foundations of education (M Ed), including educational psychology, educational technology, multilingual education. *Accreditation:* NCATE. *Program availability:* Part-time, evening/weekend. *Faculty:* 13 full-time (10 women), 1 part-time/adjunct (0 women). *Students:* 26 full-time (22 women), 43 part-time (39 women); includes 19 minority (9 Black or African American, non-Hispanic/Latino; 1 Asian, non-Hispanic/Latino; 8 Hispanic/Latino; 1 Two or more races, non-Hispanic/Latino), 3 international. Average age 30. 91 applicants, 57% accepted, 33 enrolled. In 2017, 25 master's awarded. *Entrance requirements:* For master's, GRE General Test, minimum GPA of 3.0 in last 2 years of undergraduate course work. Additional exam requirements/recommendations for international students: Required—TOEFL (minimum score 500 paper-based; 61 iBT), IELTS (minimum score 6). *Application deadline:* For fall admission, 7/1 for domestic students, 2/15 for international students; for spring admission, 11/1 for domestic students, 7/15 for international students. Applications are processed on a rolling basis. Application fee: $30. *Expenses:* Tuition, state resident: full-time $7400; part-time $369.82 per credit. Tuition, nonresident: full-time $20,496; part-time $1042.81 per credit. *Financial support:* Fellowships with partial tuition reimbursements, research assistantships with partial tuition reimbursements, teaching assistantships with partial tuition reimbursements, career-related internships or fieldwork, scholarships/grants, and unspecified assistantships available. *Faculty research:* Technology, teaching English to speakers of other languages, math teaching, electronic portfolio assessment, global perspectives through social studies. *Unit head:* Dr. Barbara Ridener, Chairperson, 561-297-3588, E-mail: bridener@fau.edu. *Application contact:* Dr. Eliah Watlington, Associate Dean, 561-296-8520, Fax: 261-297-2991, E-mail: ewatling@fau.edu. Website: http://www.coe.fau.edu/academicdepartments/tl/

Florida International University, College of Arts, Sciences, and Education, Department of Teaching and Learning, Miami, FL 33199. Offers art education (MA, MS); curriculum and instruction (MS, Ed D, PhD, Ed S), including curriculum development (MS), elementary education (MS), English education (MS), learning technologies (MS), mathematics education (MS), modern language education (MS), physical education (MS), science education (MS), social studies education (MS), special education (MS); early childhood education (MS); exceptional student education (Ed D); foreign language education (MS), including foreign language education, teaching English to speakers of other languages (TESOL); language, literacy and culture (PhD); mathematics, science, and learning technologies (PhD); physical education (MS), including sport and fitness; reading education (MS). *Program availability:* Part-time, evening/weekend. *Faculty:* 60 full-time (41 women), 112 part-time/adjunct (77 women). *Students:* 165 full-time (139 women), 191 part-time (148 women); includes 270 minority (56 Black or African American, non-Hispanic/Latino; 12 Asian, non-Hispanic/Latino; 191 Hispanic/Latino; 11 Two or more races, non-Hispanic/Latino), 13 international. Average age 34. 238 applicants, 68% accepted, 107 enrolled. In 2017, 184 master's, 15 doctorates awarded. *Degree requirements:* For doctorate, comprehensive exam, thesis/dissertation. *Entrance requirements:* For master's, GRE General Test, Florida General Knowledge Test or Florida College Level Academic Skills Test; for doctorate and Ed S, GRE General Test. Additional exam requirements/recommendations for international students: Required—TOEFL (minimum score 550 paper-based; 80 iBT), IELTS (minimum score 6.3). *Application deadline:* For fall admission, 6/1 priority date for domestic students, 4/1 for international students; for winter admission, 10/1 priority date for domestic students, 9/1 for international students; for spring admission, 3/1 priority date for domestic students, 2/1 for international students. Applications are processed on a rolling basis. Application fee: $30. Electronic applications accepted. *Expenses:* Tuition, state resident: full-time $8912; part-time $446 per credit hour. Tuition, nonresident: full-time $21,393; part-time $992 per credit hour. *Required fees:* $390; $195 per semester. *Financial support:* Research assistantships with tuition reimbursements and teaching assistantships with tuition reimbursements available. *Unit head:* Dr. Lynn Miller, Chair, 305-348-2005, Fax: 305-348-2086, E-mail: lynne.miller@fiu.edu. *Application contact:* Nanett Rojas, Assistant Director, Graduate Admissions, 305-348-7464, Fax: 305-348-7441, E-mail: gradadm@fiu.edu. Website: https://tl.fiu.edu/

Florida State University, The Graduate School, College of Education, School of Teacher Education, Tallahassee, FL 32306-4450. Offers curriculum and instruction (MS, PhD, Ed S), including early childhood education, elementary education, English education, foreign and second language education, mathematics education, reading and language arts, science education, social science education, special education, visual disabilities education (MS); teaching English to speakers of other languages (Certificate). *Program availability:* Part-time, evening/weekend, 100% online, blended/hybrid learning, asynchronous, minimal on-campus study. *Faculty:* 41 full-time (33 women), 21 part-time/adjunct (18 women). *Students:* 133 full-time (93 women), 84 part-time (69 women); includes 48 minority (20 Black or African American, non-Hispanic/Latino; 2 Asian, non-Hispanic/Latino; 19 Hispanic/Latino; 7 Two or more races, non-Hispanic/Latino), 52 international. Average age 31. 146 applicants, 56% accepted, 52 enrolled. In 2017, 91 master's, 7 doctorates, 1 other advanced degree awarded. Terminal master's awarded for partial completion of doctoral program. *Degree requirements:* For master's and other advanced degree, comprehensive exam, thesis

optional; for doctorate, comprehensive exam, thesis/dissertation, diagnostic exam, preliminary exam, prospectus defense, dissertation defense. *Entrance requirements:* For master's, doctorate, and other advanced degree, GRE General Test, minimum upper-division GPA of 3.0. Additional exam requirements/recommendations for international students: Required—TOEFL (minimum score 550 paper-based, 80 iBT), Michigan English Language Assessment Battery (minimum score 77), IELTS (minimum score 6.5) or PTE (minimum score 55). Application fee: $30. Electronic applications accepted. *Financial support:* Fellowships, research assistantships, teaching assistantships, scholarships/grants, tuition waivers (full and partial), and unspecified assistantships available. Financial award application deadline: 1/15; financial award applicants required to submit FAFSA. *Faculty research:* Identifying effective intervention strategies to improve reading skills; improving literacy teaching and learning through technology; understanding of student sense making, problem solving, the history and structure of STEM disciplines, and teacher education to support the development of ambitious instruction that supports the STEM learning of all students; examining practices of international education; identifying ways to support the professional development of teachers. *Unit head:* Dr. Sherry Southerland, Professor/Department Chair, 850-644-6885, Fax: 850-644-2725, E-mail: ssoutherland@admin.fsu.edu. *Application contact:* Britni DeZerga, Academic Program Specialist, 850-644-2122, Fax: 850-644-7736, E-mail: bpurvis@fsu.edu.
Website: http://education.fsu.edu

Fontbonne University, Graduate Programs, St. Louis, MO 63105-3098. Offers accounting (MBA, MS); art (MA); art (K-12) (MAT); business (MBA); computer science (MS); deaf education (MA); early intervention in deaf education (MA); education (MA), including autism spectrum disorders, curriculum and instruction, diverse learners, early childhood education, reading, special education; elementary education (MAT); family and consumer sciences (MA), including multidisciplinary health communication studies; fine arts (MFA); instructional design and technology (MS); management and leadership (MM); middle school education (MAT); secondary education (MAT); special education (MAT); speech-language pathology (MS); supply chain management (MS); theatre (MA). *Program availability:* Part-time, evening/weekend, online learning. *Degree requirements:* For master's, comprehensive exam (for some programs), thesis (for some programs). *Entrance requirements:* Additional exam requirements/recommendations for international students: Required—TOEFL (minimum score 500 paper-based; 65 iBT). Electronic applications accepted.

Fordham University, Graduate School of Education, Division of Curriculum and Teaching, New York, NY 10023. Offers curriculum and teaching (MSE); early childhood education (MSE); elementary education (MST); special education (MSE, Adv C); teaching English as a second language (MSE). *Accreditation:* NCATE. *Program availability:* Part-time, evening/weekend. *Degree requirements:* For Adv C, thesis. *Entrance requirements:* Additional exam requirements/recommendations for international students: Required—TOEFL (minimum score 577 paper-based; 90 iBT), IELTS (minimum score 7). Electronic applications accepted.

Framingham State University, Graduate Studies, Program in Early Childhood Education, Framingham, MA 01701-9101. Offers M Ed. *Unit head:* Dr. Valerie Hytholt, Program Coordinator and Advisor, E-mail: vhytholt@framingham.edu. *Application contact:* Graduate Office, 508-626-4550, Fax: 508-626-4030, E-mail: dgce@frc.mass.edu.

Furman University, Graduate Division, Department of Education, Greenville, SC 29613. Offers curriculum and instruction (MA); early childhood education (MA); educational leadership (Ed S); English as a second language (MA); literacy (MA); school leadership (MA); special education (MA). *Accreditation:* NCATE. *Program availability:* Part-time, online learning. *Degree requirements:* For master's, comprehensive exam (for some programs), thesis or alternative. *Entrance requirements:* For master's, PRAXIS II. *Faculty research:* Literacy, pedagogy and practice, social justice, advanced leadership, achievement in high poverty schools.

Gallaudet University, The Graduate School, Washington, DC 20002-3625. Offers American Sign Language/English bilingual early childhood deaf education: birth to 5 (Certificate); audiology (Au D); clinical psychology (PhD); deaf and hard of hearing infants, toddlers, and their families (Certificate); deaf education (MA, Ed S); deaf history (Certificate); deaf studies (Certificate); educating deaf students with disabilities (Certificate); education: teacher preparation (MA), including deaf education, early childhood education and deaf education, elementary education and deaf education, secondary education and deaf education; educational neuroscience (PhD); hearing, speech and language sciences (MS, PhD); international development (MA); interpretation (MA, PhD), including combined interpreting practice and research (MA), interpreting research (MA); linguistics (MA, PhD); mental health counseling (MA); peer mentoring (Certificate); public administration (MPA); school counseling (MA); school psychology (Psy S); sign language teaching (MA); social work (MSW); speech-language pathology (MS). *Program availability:* Part-time. Terminal master's awarded for partial completion of doctoral program. *Degree requirements:* For master's, comprehensive exam (for some programs), thesis optional; for doctorate, comprehensive exam, thesis/dissertation. *Entrance requirements:* For master's and doctorate, GRE General Test or MAT, letters of recommendation, interviews, goals statement, American Sign Language proficiency interview, written English competency. Additional exam requirements/recommendations for international students: Required—TOEFL. Electronic applications accepted. *Faculty research:* Signing math dictionaries, telecommunications access, cancer genetics, linguistics, visual language and visual learning, integrated quantum materials, deaf legal discourse, advance recruitment and retention in geosciences.

Gateway Seminary, Graduate and Professional Programs, Ontario, CA 91761-8642. Offers divinity (M Div); early childhood education (Certificate); education leadership (MAEL, Diploma); ministry (D Min); theological studies (MTS); theology (Th M); youth ministry (Certificate). *Accreditation:* ACIPE; ATS. *Program availability:* Part-time, evening/weekend. *Degree requirements:* For master's, thesis (for some programs); for doctorate, 2 foreign languages, thesis/dissertation. *Entrance requirements:* For doctorate, MAT. Additional exam requirements/recommendations for international students: Required—TOEFL (minimum score 550 paper-based). Electronic applications accepted.

George Mason University, College of Education and Human Development, Programs in Curriculum and Instruction, Fairfax, VA 22030. Offers advanced international baccalaureate (M Ed); assistive technology (M Ed); designing digital learning in schools (M Ed); early childhood education (M Ed); early childhood education for diverse learners (M Ed); elementary education (M Ed); English as a second language (M Ed); gifted child education (M Ed); history (M Ed); literacy (M Ed), including PK-12 classroom teachers, reading specialist; literacy leadership for diverse schools (M Ed), including K-12 reading; physical education (M Ed); science K-12 (M Ed); secondary education (M Ed), including biology, chemistry, earth science, English, history/social science, math, physics; special education (M Ed); teacher leadership (M Ed); teaching culturally, linguistically diverse and exceptional learners (M Ed); transformative teaching (M Ed). *Program availability:* Part-time, evening/weekend, 100% online, blended/hybrid learning. *Faculty:* 41 full-time (36 women), 45 part-time/adjunct (37 women). *Students:* 173 full-time (151 women), 729 part-time (611 women); includes 271 minority (65 Black or African American, non-Hispanic/Latino; 5 American Indian or Alaska Native, non-Hispanic/Latino; 88 Asian,

non-Hispanic/Latino; 94 Hispanic/Latino; 1 Native Hawaiian or other Pacific Islander, non-Hispanic/Latino; 18 Two or more races, non-Hispanic/Latino), 28 international. Average age 32. 426 applicants, 91% accepted, 289 enrolled. In 2017, 349 master's awarded. *Degree requirements:* For master's, thesis. *Entrance requirements:* For master's, PRAXIS Core (for some programs), 2 letters of recommendation, interview, program goals statement; 9 hours of complete licensure endorsement requirements (for elementary education); minimum GPA of 3.0 in applicant's last 60 hours of undergraduate coursework (for secondary education); at least 1 year of teaching experience (for literacy). Additional exam requirements/recommendations for international students: Required—TOEFL (minimum score 575 paper-based; 88 iBT), IELTS (minimum score 6.5), PTE (minimum score 59). *Application deadline:* For fall admission, 4/2 priority date for domestic and international students; for spring admission, 11/1 for domestic and international students. Application fee: $75 ($80 for international students). Electronic applications accepted. *Expenses:* Tuition, state resident: part-time $11,228; part-time $459.50 per credit. Tuition, nonresident: full-time $30,932; part-time $1280.50 per credit. *Required fees:* $3252; $135.50 per credit. Part-time tuition and fees vary according to course load and program. *Financial support:* In 2017–18, 2 students received support, including 2 teaching assistantships; career-related internships or fieldwork, Federal Work-Study, scholarships/grants, unspecified assistantships, and health care benefits (for full-time research or teaching assistantship recipients) also available. Support available to part-time students. Financial award application deadline: 3/1; financial award applicants required to submit FAFSA. *Faculty research:* Teacher preparation and professional development; adaptive teaching; wonder in science teacher preparation; literacy (digital, adolescent); site based course instruction. *Unit head:* Rebecca Fox, Professor and Academic Program Coordinator, 703-993-4123, E-mail: rfox@gmu.edu.
Website: http://gse.gmu.edu/programs/gsemasters

The George Washington University, Graduate School of Education and Human Development, Department of Special Education and Disability Studies, Program in Early Childhood Special Education, Washington, DC 20052. Offers infant special education (MA Ed/HD). *Accreditation:* NCATE. *Students:* 16 full-time (all women), 5 part-time (all women); includes 3 minority (1 Black or African American, non-Hispanic/Latino; 1 Asian, non-Hispanic/Latino; 1 Two or more races, non-Hispanic/Latino), 13 international. Average age 27. 33 applicants, 73% accepted, 11 enrolled. In 2017, 16 master's awarded. *Entrance requirements:* For master's, GRE General Test or MAT, minimum GPA of 2.75. *Application deadline:* For fall admission, 1/15 priority date for domestic students; for spring admission, 10/1 for domestic students. Applications are processed on a rolling basis. Application fee: $75. *Expenses: Tuition:* Full-time $28,800; part-time $1655 per credit hour. *Required fees:* $45; $2.75 per credit hour. *Financial support:* In 2017–18, 19 students received support. Fellowships, career-related internships or fieldwork, Federal Work-Study, and tuition waivers (full) available. Financial award application deadline: 1/15; financial award applicants required to submit FAFSA. *Faculty research:* Computer-assisted instruction and learning, disabled learner assessment of preschool, handicapped children. *Unit head:* Dr. Marian H. Jarrett, Faculty Coordinator, 202-994-1509, E-mail: mjarrett@gwu.edu. *Application contact:* Sarah Lang, Director of Graduate Admissions, 202-994-1447, Fax: 202-994-7207, E-mail: slang@gwu.edu.

Georgia College & State University, Graduate School, The John H. Lounsbury College of Education, Program in Early Childhood Education, Milledgeville, GA 31061. Offers M Ed. *Accreditation:* NCATE. *Program availability:* Part-time, evening/weekend. *Students:* 11 part-time (all women); includes 1 minority (Black or African American, non-Hispanic/Latino). Average age 32. In 2017, 12 master's awarded. *Degree requirements:* For master's, minimum GPA of 3.0, complete program within 6 years. *Entrance requirements:* For master's, 2 professional recommendations, transcript, T-4 certificate, verification of immunization; minimum GPA of 2.75 or 3 successful years' teaching experience. *Application deadline:* For fall admission, 7/1 priority date for domestic students; for spring admission, 11/1 priority date for domestic students; for summer admission, 4/1 priority date for domestic students. Applications are processed on a rolling basis. Application fee: $40. Electronic applications accepted. *Expenses:* $288 per credit hour full-time in-state, $2,592 per semester, $1,011 fees: $1,027 per credit hour out-of-state, $9,243 per semester. *Financial support:* Application deadline: 3/1; applicants required to submit FAFSA. *Unit head:* Dr. Joseph Peters, Dean, College of Education, 478-445-2518, Fax: 478-445-6582, E-mail: joseph.peters@gcsu.edu. *Application contact:* Shanda Brand, Graduate Coordinator, 478-445-1383, E-mail: shanda.brand@gcsu.edu.
Website: http://gcsu.edu/education/teached/early-childhood-education-med

Georgia Southern University, Jack N. Averitt College of Graduate Studies, College of Education, Department of Teaching and Learning, Program in Early Childhood Education, Statesboro, GA 30460. Offers early childhood (M Ed, MAT, Ed S). *Accreditation:* NCATE. *Program availability:* Part-time, evening/weekend, online only, 100% online. *Students:* 38 full-time (all women), 31 part-time (all women); includes 14 minority (11 Black or African American, non-Hispanic/Latino; 2 Hispanic/Latino; 1 Two or more races, non-Hispanic/Latino). Average age 29. 18 applicants, 94% accepted, 12 enrolled. In 2017, 21 master's, 15 other advanced degrees awarded. *Degree requirements:* For master's, portfolio, transition point assessments, exit assessment; for Ed S, field based research projects, assessments. *Entrance requirements:* For master's, minimum cumulative GPA of 2.5. Additional exam requirements/recommendations for international students: Required—TOEFL (minimum score 550 paper-based; 80 iBT), IELTS (minimum score 6). *Application deadline:* For fall admission, 3/15 priority date for domestic and international students; for spring admission, 10/1 priority date for domestic students, 10/1 for international students; for summer admission, 3/1 priority date for domestic students, 3/1 for international students. Applications are processed on a rolling basis. Application fee: $50. Electronic applications accepted. *Expenses:* Tuition, state resident: full-time $4986; part-time $3324 per year. Tuition, nonresident: full-time $21,982; part-time $15,352 per year. *Required fees:* $2092; $1802 per credit hour. $901 per semester. Tuition and fees vary according to course load, campus/location and program. *Financial support:* In 2017–18, 3 students received support. Career-related internships or fieldwork, Federal Work-Study, and scholarships/grants available. Support available to part-time students. Financial award application deadline: 4/15; financial award applicants required to submit FAFSA. *Faculty research:* Technology, effective instructional strategies, multiculturalism, children's literature, school violence. *Unit head:* Dr. Bruce Field, Department Chair, 912-478-0210, Fax: 912-478-0026. *Application contact:* Dr. Lydia Cross, Coordinator for Graduate Academic Services Center, 912-478-8664, E-mail: lcross@georgiasouthern.edu.
Website: http://coe.georgiasouthern.edu/eced

Georgia Southern University–Armstrong Campus, College of Graduate Studies, Department of Childhood and Exceptional Student Education, Savannah, GA 31419-1997. Offers early childhood education (M Ed, MAT); reading (Certificate); special education (M Ed, MAT); special education transition specialist (Certificate). *Accreditation:* NCATE. *Program availability:* Part-time, evening/weekend. *Faculty:* 14 full-time (11 women), 1 (woman) part-time/adjunct. *Students:* 7 full-time (6 women), 214 part-time (195 women); includes 79 minority (63 Black or African American, non-Hispanic/Latino; 3 Asian, non-Hispanic/Latino; 6 Hispanic/Latino; 7 Two or more races, non-Hispanic/Latino). Average age 34. 159 applicants, 50% accepted, 69 enrolled. In 2017, 72 master's, 3 other advanced degrees awarded. *Degree requirements:* For

Early Childhood Education

master's, portfolio. *Entrance requirements:* For master's, MAT, Georgia Assessment for the Certification of Educators. Additional exam requirements/recommendations for international students: Required—TOEFL (minimum score 523 paper-based; 70 iBT). *Application deadline:* For fall admission, 7/1 priority date for domestic students, 5/1 priority date for international students; for spring admission, 11/15 priority date for domestic students, 9/15 priority date for international students; for summer admission, 4/15 priority date for domestic students, 9/15 for international students. Applications are processed on a rolling basis. Application fee: $30. Electronic applications accepted. *Expenses:* Tuition, state resident: part-time $211 per credit hour. Tuition, nonresident: part-time $782 per credit hour. *Required fees:* $737 per semester. Tuition and fees vary according to course load, degree level, campus/location and program. *Financial support:* In 2017–18, research assistantships with full tuition reimbursements (averaging $5,000 per year) were awarded; career-related internships or fieldwork, Federal Work-Study, and scholarships/grants also available. Support available to part-time students. Financial award application deadline: 3/15; financial award applicants required to submit FAFSA. *Faculty research:* Literacy, instructional design, poetry, working with local schools. *Unit head:* Dr. John Hobe, Department Head, 912-344-2619, Fax: 912-344-3443, E-mail: john.hobe@armstrong.edu. *Application contact:* McKenzie Peterman, Assistant Director of Graduate Admissions, 912-344-2503, Fax: 912-344-3417, E-mail: graduate@armstrong.edu.
Website: https://www.armstrong.edu/academic-departments/education-ceed

Georgia Southwestern State University, School of Education, Americus, GA 31709-4693. Offers early childhood education (M Ed, Ed S); middle grades education (Ed S); middle grades language arts (M Ed); middle grades mathematics (M Ed); special education (M Ed). *Accreditation:* NCATE. *Faculty:* 17 full-time (7 women), 7 part-time/adjunct (all women). *Students:* 221 full-time (206 women), 5 part-time (all women); includes 70 minority (all Black or African American, non-Hispanic/Latino). Average age 35. In 2017, 89 master's, 94 Ed Ss awarded. *Degree requirements:* For master's, minimum cumulative GPA of 3.0; maximum of 6 credit hours with C grade; no courses with D grade; degree completed within 7 calendar years; for Ed S, minimum GPA of 3.25 in all courses with no grade less than a B; degree must be completed within 7 calendar years from date of initial enrollment in graduate work. *Entrance requirements:* For master's, undergraduate degree from accredited institution; professional Georgia Teaching Certificate or eligibility; minimum undergraduate GPA of 2.75 as reported on official final transcripts from all accredited institutions attended; 2 confidential Administrative Recommendation Forms; for Ed S, master's degree from accredited college or university; professional Georgia Teaching Certificate or eligibility; minimum graduate GPA of 3.0 as reported on official final graduate transcripts from all accredited institutions attended; 2 confidential Administrative Recommendation Forms. *Application deadline:* For summer admission, 4/15 for domestic students. Application fee: $25. Electronic applications accepted. *Expenses:* $257 per credit hour for online courses plus fees which vary according to number of enrolled credit hours. *Financial support:* Application deadline: 6/1; applicants required to submit FAFSA. *Unit head:* Dr. Rachel Abbott, Dean, 229-931-2145. *Application contact:* Whitney Ford, Admissions Specialist, Office of Graduate Admissions, 800-338-0082, Fax: 229-931-2983.
Website: https://gsw.edu/Academics/Schools-and-Departments/School-of-Education/index

Georgia State University, College of Education and Human Development, Department of Early Childhood Education, Atlanta, GA 30302-3083. Offers early childhood and elementary education (PhD); early childhood education (M Ed, Ed S); mathematics education (M Ed); urban education (M Ed). *Accreditation:* NCATE. *Program availability:* Part-time, evening/weekend. *Faculty:* 27 full-time (22 women). *Students:* 74 full-time (68 women), 22 part-time (21 women); includes 49 minority (41 Black or African American, non-Hispanic/Latino; 4 Asian, non-Hispanic/Latino; 2 Hispanic/Latino; 2 Two or more races, non-Hispanic/Latino), 3 international. Average age 30. 49 applicants, 65% accepted, 25 enrolled. In 2017, 27 master's, 3 doctorates awarded. *Entrance requirements:* For master's, GRE, undergraduate diploma; for doctorate and Ed S, GRE, master's degree. *Application deadline:* Applications are processed on a rolling basis. Application fee: $50. Electronic applications accepted. *Expenses:* Tuition, state resident: full-time $7020. Tuition, nonresident: full-time $22,518. *Required fees:* $2128. Tuition and fees vary according to degree level and program. *Financial support:* In 2017–18, fellowships with full tuition reimbursements (averaging $24,000 per year), research assistantships with full tuition reimbursements (averaging $4,000 per year), teaching assistantships with full tuition reimbursements (averaging $2,000 per year) were awarded; career-related internships or fieldwork, Federal Work-Study, institutionally sponsored loans, scholarships/grants, traineeships, health care benefits, tuition waivers (partial), and unspecified assistantships also available. Support available to part-time students. Financial award applicants required to submit FAFSA. *Faculty research:* Teacher development; language arts/literacy education; mathematics education; intersection of science, urban, and multicultural education; diversity in education. *Unit head:* Dr. Barbara Meyers, Department Chair, 404-413-8021, Fax: 404-413-8023, E-mail: barbara@gsu.edu. *Application contact:* Elaine King Jones, Administrative Curriculum Specialist, 404-413-8234, Fax: 404-413-8023, E-mail: ekjones@gsu.edu.
Website: http://ecee.education.gsu.edu/

Georgia State University, College of Education and Human Development, Department of Educational Psychology, Special Education, and Communication Disorders, Program in Education of Students with Exceptionalities, Atlanta, GA 30302-3083. Offers autism spectrum disorders (PhD); behavior disorders (PhD); communication disorders (PhD); early childhood special education (PhD); learning disabilities (PhD); mental retardation (PhD); orthopedic impairments (PhD); sensory impairments (PhD). *Accreditation:* NCATE. *Program availability:* Part-time, evening/weekend. Application fee: $50. Electronic applications accepted. *Expenses:* Tuition, state resident: full-time $7020. Tuition, nonresident: full-time $22,518. *Required fees:* $2128. Tuition and fees vary according to degree level and program. *Financial support:* Fellowships, research assistantships, scholarships/grants, health care benefits, and unspecified assistantships available. *Faculty research:* Academic and behavioral supports for students with emotional/behavior disorders; academic interventions for learning disabilities; cultural, socioeconomic, and linguistic diversity; language and literacy development, disorders, and instruction. *Unit head:* Dr. Kristine Jolivette, Associate Professor, 404-413-8040, Fax: 404-413-8043, E-mail: kjolivette@gsu.edu. *Application contact:* Sandy Vaughn, Senior Administrative Coordinator, 404-413-8318, Fax: 404-413-8043, E-mail: svaughn@gsu.edu.
Website: http://esc.education.gsu.edu/academics-and-admissions/special-education/education-of-students-with-exceptionalities-ph-d/

Georgia State University, College of Education and Human Development, Department of Educational Psychology, Special Education, and Communication Disorders, Program in Multiple and Severe Disabilities, Atlanta, GA 30302-3083. Offers early childhood special education (M Ed); special education adapted curriculum (intellectual disabilities) (M Ed); special education deaf education (M Ed); special education general and adapted curriculum (autism spectrum disorders) (M Ed); special education physical and health disabilities (orthopedic impairments) (M Ed). *Accreditation:* NCATE. *Program availability:* Part-time. *Entrance requirements:* For master's, GRE. Application fee: $50. Electronic applications accepted. *Expenses:* Tuition, state resident: full-time $7020.

Tuition, nonresident: full-time $22,518. *Required fees:* $2128. Tuition and fees vary according to degree level and program. *Financial support:* Fellowships, research assistantships, teaching assistantships, scholarships/grants, health care benefits, and unspecified assistantships available. *Faculty research:* Literacy, language, behavioral supports. *Unit head:* Dr. Kathryn Wolff Heller, Professor, 404-413-8040, E-mail: kheller@gsu.edu. *Application contact:* Sandy Vaughn, Senior Administrative Coordinator, 404-413-8318, Fax: 404-413-8043, E-mail: svaughn@gsu.edu.

Gordon College, Graduate Education Program, Wenham, MA 01984-1899. Offers early childhood (M Ed); educational leadership (M Ed, Ed S); elementary education (M Ed); English as a second language (M Ed, Ed S); math specialist (M Ed); mathematics specialist (Ed S); middle school education (M Ed); moderate disabilities (M Ed); Montessori education (M Ed); reading (M Ed, Ed S); secondary education (M Ed). *Program availability:* Part-time, evening/weekend. *Faculty:* 23 full-time (17 women), 32 part-time/adjunct (23 women). *Students:* 68 full-time (50 women), 114 part-time (99 women); includes 24 minority (2 Black or African American, non-Hispanic/Latino; 8 Asian, non-Hispanic/Latino; 13 Hispanic/Latino; 1 Two or more races, non-Hispanic/Latino), 10 international. Average age 34. 248 applicants, 100% accepted, 182 enrolled. In 2017, 99 master's, 16 Ed Ss awarded. *Degree requirements:* For master's, action research or clinical experience (for most programs); for Ed S, action research or clinical experience (for some programs). *Entrance requirements:* For master's, minimum undergraduate GPA of 3.0; 2 official undergraduate transcripts; professional resume; 3 recommendation letters (one professional reference, one academic reference, one personal reference); 500-700 word statement of purpose; for Ed S, minimum master's GPA of 3.3; 2 official transcripts from undergraduate and graduate schools; professional resume; 3 recommendation letters (one professional reference, one academic reference, one personal reference); 500-700 word statement of purpose. Additional exam requirements/recommendations for international students: Required—TOEFL (minimum score 550 paper-based, 80 iBT) or IELTS (minimum score 6.5). *Application deadline:* Applications are processed on a rolling basis. Application fee: $75. *Expenses:* $325 per credit tuition; $75 per semester administrative fee. *Financial support:* Applicants required to submit FAFSA. *Faculty research:* Reading, early childhood development, English language learners, universal design for learning. *Unit head:* Dr. Janet Arndt, Director of Graduate Studies, 978-867-4355, Fax: 978-867-4663. *Application contact:* Julie Lenocker, Program Administrator, 978-867-4322, Fax: 978-867-4663, E-mail: graduate-education@gordon.edu.
Website: http://www.gordon.edu/graduate

Governors State University, College of Education, Program in Early Childhood Education, University Park, IL 60484. Offers MA. *Accreditation:* NCATE. *Program availability:* Part-time. *Faculty:* 20 full-time (12 women), 40 part-time/adjunct (28 women). *Students:* 1 (woman) full-time, 1 part-time (0 women); includes 1 minority (Black or African American, non-Hispanic/Latino). Average age 35. *Application deadline:* For fall admission, 4/1 for domestic students. Applications are processed on a rolling basis. Application fee: $50. Electronic applications accepted. *Expenses:* Tuition, state resident: full-time $8472; part-time $353 per credit hour. Tuition, nonresident: full-time $16,944; part-time $706 per credit hour. *Required fees:* $1824; $76 per credit hour. $38 per term. Tuition and fees vary according to course load, degree level and program. *Financial support:* Application deadline: 5/1; applicants required to submit FAFSA. *Unit head:* Timothy Harrington, Chair, Division of Education, 708-534-5000 Ext. 4361, E-mail: tharrington2@govst.edu.

Grand Canyon University, College of Education, Phoenix, AZ 85017-1097. Offers autism spectrum disorders (MA); curriculum and instruction (MA); early childhood education (M Ed); educational administration (M Ed); educational leadership (M Ed); elementary education (M Ed); gifted education (MA); instructional technology (MS); K-12 leadership (Ed S); reading (MA); secondary education (M Ed); secondary humanities education (M Ed); secondary STEM education (M Ed); special education (M Ed); teaching and learning (Ed D); teaching English to speakers of other languages (MA). *Program availability:* Part-time, evening/weekend, online learning. *Degree requirements:* For master's, publishable research paper (M Ed), e-portfolio. *Entrance requirements:* For master's, undergraduate degree from accredited, GCU-approved college, university, or program with minimum GPA 2.8. Additional exam requirements/recommendations for international students: Required—TOEFL (minimum score 550 paper-based; 79 iBT), IELTS (minimum score 6). Electronic applications accepted.

Grand Valley State University, College of Education, Program in Special Education, Allendale, MI 49401-9403. Offers cognitive impairment (M Ed); early childhood developmental delay (M Ed); emotional impairment (M Ed); learning disabilities (M Ed); special education (M Ed). *Accreditation:* NCATE. *Program availability:* Part-time, evening/weekend. *Students:* 3 full-time (1 woman), 68 part-time (54 women); includes 4 minority (2 Hispanic/Latino; 2 Two or more races, non-Hispanic/Latino), 4 international. Average age 33. 8 applicants, 100% accepted, 3 enrolled. In 2017, 32 master's awarded. *Degree requirements:* For master's, project or thesis. *Entrance requirements:* For master's, GRE General Test or minimum GPA of 3.0, last 60 credits from regionally-accredited college/university, 3 letters of recommendation. Additional exam requirements/recommendations for international students: Required—TOEFL (minimum iBT score of 80), IELTS (6.5), or Michigan English Language Assessment Battery (77). *Application deadline:* Applications are processed on a rolling basis. Application fee: $30. Electronic applications accepted. *Expenses:* $652 per credit hour. *Financial support:* In 2017–18, 10 students received support, including 10 fellowships; career-related internships or fieldwork, Federal Work-Study, scholarships/grants, and unspecified assistantships also available. *Faculty research:* Evaluation of special education program effects, adaptive behavior assessment, language development, writing disorders, comparative effects of presentation methods. *Unit head:* Dr. Amy Schelling, Director of Special Education, 616-331-6243, Fax: 616-331-6294, E-mail: schellia@gvsu.edu. *Application contact:* Thomas Owens, Director, Student Information and Services Center, 616-331-6282, Fax: 616-331-6217, E-mail: owenst@gvsu.edu.

Grand Valley State University, College of Education, Programs in General Education, Allendale, MI 49401-9403. Offers adult and higher education (M Ed); early childhood education (M Ed); educational differentiation (M Ed); educational leadership (M Ed); educational technology integration (M Ed); elementary education (M Ed); middle level education (M Ed); school library media services (M Ed); secondary level education (M Ed); teaching English to speakers of other languages (M Ed). *Program availability:* Part-time, evening/weekend, 100% online, blended/hybrid learning. *Students:* 24 part-time (16 women). Average age 41. In 2017, 5 master's awarded. *Degree requirements:* For master's, project or thesis. *Entrance requirements:* For master's, GRE General Test or minimum GPA of 3.0, last 60 credits from regionally-accredited college/university, 3 letters of recommendation. Additional exam requirements/recommendations for international students: Required—TOEFL (minimum iBT score of 80), IELTS (6.5), or Michigan English Language Assessment Battery (77). *Application deadline:* Applications are processed on a rolling basis. Application fee: $30. Electronic applications accepted. *Expenses:* $652 per credit hour. *Financial support:* In 2017–18, 2 students received support, including 2 fellowships; career-related internships or fieldwork, Federal Work-Study, scholarships/grants, and unspecified assistantships also available. *Faculty research:* Effectiveness of technology in education, parental involvement, effective teaching, effective schools research. *Unit head:* Dr. David Bair, Department Director,

616-331-6489, Fax: 616-331-6489, E-mail: baird@gvsu.edu. *Application contact:* Thomas Owens, Director, Student Information and Services Center, 616-331-6282, Fax: 616-331-6217, E-mail: owenst@gvsu.edu.
Website: http://www.gvsu.edu/coe/

Hampton University, School of Liberal Arts and Education, Program in Teaching, Hampton, VA 23668. Offers biology education 6-12 (MT); English education 6-12 (MT); mathematics education 6-12 (MT); music education PreK-12 (MT). *Program availability:* Part-time. *Students:* 5 full-time (4 women); all minorities (all Black or African American, non-Hispanic/Latino). Average age 23. 6 applicants, 67% accepted, 1 enrolled. In 2017, 7 master's awarded. *Entrance requirements:* For master's, GRE General Test. Additional exam requirements/recommendations for international students: Required—TOEFL (minimum score 525 paper-based) or IELTS (6.5). *Application deadline:* For fall admission, 6/1 priority date for domestic students, 4/1 for international students; for spring admission, 11/1 priority date for domestic students, 9/1 for international students; for summer admission, 4/1 priority date for domestic students, 2/1 priority date for international students. Applications are processed on a rolling basis. Application fee: $35. Electronic applications accepted. *Expenses: Tuition:* Full-time $22,630; part-time $575 per semester hour. *Required fees:* $70. Tuition and fees vary according to program. *Financial support:* Application deadline: 6/30; applicants required to submit FAFSA. *Unit head:* Dr. Martha Jallim-Hall, Program Coordinator, 757-727-5793.

Harding University, Cannon-Clary College of Education, Searcy, AR 72149-0001. Offers advanced studies in teaching and learning (M Ed); art (MSE); behavioral science (MSE); counseling (MS, Ed S); early childhood special education (M Ed, MSE); education (MSE); educational leadership (M Ed, Ed S); elementary education (M Ed); English (MSE); French (MSE); history/social science (MSE); kinesiology (MSE); math (MSE); reading (M Ed); secondary education (M Ed); Spanish (MSE); teaching (MAT); teaching English as a second language (MSE). *Accreditation:* NCATE. *Program availability:* Part-time, evening/weekend. *Faculty:* 22 full-time (9 women), 51 part-time/adjunct (37 women). *Students:* 135 full-time (95 women), 316 part-time (231 women); includes 77 minority (46 Black or African American, non-Hispanic/Latino; 7 American Indian or Alaska Native, non-Hispanic/Latino; 4 Asian, non-Hispanic/Latino; 9 Hispanic/Latino; 11 Two or more races, non-Hispanic/Latino), 11 international. Average age 34. 128 applicants, 87% accepted, 111 enrolled. In 2017, 153 master's, 24 other advanced degrees awarded. *Degree requirements:* For master's, comprehensive exam (for some programs), thesis optional, portfolio(s); for Ed S, comprehensive exam, portfolio, project. *Entrance requirements:* For master's, GRE, MAT, PRAXIS; for Ed S, MAT or GRE. Additional exam requirements/recommendations for international students: Required—TOEFL (minimum score 550 paper-based; 79 iBT). *Application deadline:* For fall admission, 8/1 for domestic and international students; for spring admission, 1/1 for domestic and international students. Applications are processed on a rolling basis. Application fee: $35. Tuition and fees vary according to course load, degree level, campus/location and program. *Financial support:* In 2017–18, 33 students received support. Unspecified assistantships available. *Faculty research:* Reading, comprehension, school violence, educational technology, behavior, college choice, differentiated instruction, brain-based teaching. *Unit head:* Dr. Clara Carroll, Chair, 501-279-4501, Fax: 501-279-4083, E-mail: ccarroll@harding.edu. *Application contact:* Information Contact, 501-279-4315, E-mail: gradstudiesedu@harding.edu.
Website: http://www.harding.edu/education

Hebrew College, Shoolman Graduate School of Jewish Education, Newton Centre, MA 02459. Offers early childhood Jewish education (Certificate); Jewish day school education (Certificate); Jewish education (MJ Ed); Jewish family education (Certificate); Jewish special education (Certificate); Jewish youth education, informal education and camping (Certificate). *Program availability:* Part-time, evening/weekend, online learning. *Degree requirements:* For master's, one foreign language. *Entrance requirements:* For master's, GRE, interview. Additional exam requirements/recommendations for international students: Required—TOEFL.

Henderson State University, Graduate Studies, Teachers College, Department of Advanced Instructional Studies, Arkadelphia, AR 71999-0001. Offers developmental therapy (MSE); dyslexia therapy (Graduate Certificate); education (MAT); educational technology leadership (Graduate Certificate); English as a second language (MSE, Graduate Certificate); instructional facilitator (MSE, Graduate Certificate); middle level education (MAT); special education (K-12) (MAT, MSE); special education/early childhood (MAT). *Accreditation:* NCATE. *Program availability:* Part-time. *Entrance requirements:* For master's, GRE General Test or MAT, minimum GPA of 2.7, teacher certification. Additional exam requirements/recommendations for international students: Required—TOEFL (minimum score 600 paper-based); Recommended—IELTS (minimum score 6.5).

Hofstra University, School of Education, Programs in Teacher Education, Hempstead, NY 11549. Offers bilingual education (MA); bilingual extension (Advanced Certificate), including education/speech language pathology, intensive teacher institute; business education (MS Ed); curriculum studies (MS Ed); early childhood and childhood education (MS Ed); early childhood education (MA, MS Ed); educational technology (Advanced Certificate); elementary education (MA, MS Ed), including science, technology, engineering, and mathematics (STEM) (MA); English education (MS Ed); family and consumer science (MS Ed); fine arts and music education (Advanced Certificate); fine arts education (MS Ed); foreign language and TESOL (MS Ed); foreign language education (MA, MS Ed), including Arabic (MS Ed), biology, chemistry, Chinese (MS Ed), earth science, French, German, Italian (MS Ed), Mandarin (MS Ed), physics, Russian, Spanish; foundations of education (Advanced Certificate), including grades 5-6, grades 7-9; languages other than English and teaching English as a second language (MA); learning and teaching (Ed D), including applied linguistics, art education, arts and humanities, early childhood education, English education, human development, math education, math, science, and technology, multicultural education, physical education, science education, social studies education, special education; mathematics education (MA, MS Ed); music education (MA, MS Ed); science education (MA), including biology (MA, MS Ed), chemistry (MA, MS Ed), earth science (MA, MS Ed), physics (MA, MS Ed); secondary education (Advanced Certificate); social studies education (MA, MS Ed); teaching languages other than English and TESOL (MS Ed); technology for learning (MA); TESOL (MS Ed, Advanced Certificate); TESOL with specialization in STEM (MA); work based learning extension (Advanced Certificate). *Program availability:* Part-time, evening/weekend, blended/hybrid learning. *Students:* 119 full-time (83 women), 124 part-time (90 women); includes 54 minority (15 Black or African American, non-Hispanic/Latino; 9 Asian, non-Hispanic/Latino; 29 Hispanic/Latino; 1 Native Hawaiian or other Pacific Islander, non-Hispanic/Latino), 12 international. Average age 29. 205 applicants, 88% accepted, 93 enrolled. In 2017, 103 master's, 4 doctorates, 32 other advanced degrees awarded. *Degree requirements:* For master's, comprehensive exam, thesis (for some programs), exit project, student teaching, fieldwork, electronic portfolio, curriculum project, minimum GPA of 3.0; for doctorate, thesis/dissertation; for Advanced Certificate, 3 foreign languages, comprehensive exam (for some programs), thesis project. *Entrance requirements:* For master's, GRE, 2 letters of recommendation, portfolio, teacher certification (MA), interview, essay; for doctorate, GMAT, GRE, LSAT, or MAT; for Advanced Certificate, 2 letters of recommendation, essay, interview and/or portfolio, teaching certificate. Additional exam requirements/recommendations for

international students: Required—TOEFL (minimum score 550 paper-based; 80 iBT). *Application deadline:* Applications are processed on a rolling basis. Application fee: $75. Electronic applications accepted. *Expenses: Tuition:* Full-time $1292. *Required fees:* $970. Tuition and fees vary according to program. *Financial support:* In 2017–18, 112 students received support, including 56 fellowships with full and partial tuition reimbursements available (averaging $4,998 per year), 2 research assistantships with full and partial tuition reimbursements available (averaging $8,753 per year); career-related internships or fieldwork, Federal Work-Study, institutionally sponsored loans, scholarships/grants, traineeships, tuition waivers (full and partial), and unspecified assistantships also available. Support available to part-time students. Financial award applicants required to submit FAFSA. *Faculty research:* Educational interventions that foster critical-thinking skills; teachers' attitudes about professional development; threats to teacher quality. *Unit head:* Dr. Eustace Thompson, Chairperson, 516-463-5749, Fax: 516-463-6275, E-mail: eustace.g.thompson@hofstra.edu. *Application contact:* Sunil Samuel, Assistant Vice President of Admissions, 516-463-4723, Fax: 516-463-4664, E-mail: graduateadmission@hofstra.edu.
Website: http://www.hofstra.edu/education/

Hofstra University, School of Education, Specialized Programs in Education, Hempstead, NY 11549. Offers applied behavior analysis (Advanced Certificate); childhood special education (MS Ed); early childhood special education (MS Ed, Advanced Certificate); educational and policy leadership (Ed D); educational leadership (Advanced Certificate), including school building leader/school district business leader; educational leadership and policy studies (MS Ed), including K-12; elementary special education (MS Ed); gifted education (Advanced Certificate), including school building leader/school district business leader; health education (MS); health professions pedagogy and leadership (MS); higher education leadership and policy studies (MS Ed); inclusive early childhood special education (MS Ed); inclusive elementary special education (MS Ed); inclusive secondary special education (MS Ed); literacy studies (MA, MS Ed, Ed D, Advanced Certificate), including birth-grade 6 (MS Ed, Advanced Certificate), grades 5-12 (MS Ed, Advanced Certificate), literacy studies (Ed D); pedagogy for health professions (Advanced Certificate); physical education (MS Ed); school district business leader (Advanced Certificate); secondary education generalist - students with disabilities 7-12 (MS Ed), including students with disabilities 7-12; secondary special education generalist (MS Ed), including extension in secondary education; special education (MS Ed, Advanced Certificate); special education assessment and diagnosis (Advanced Certificate); special education early childhood intervention (MS Ed); special education: international perspectives (MS Ed); teaching students with severe or multiple disabilities (Advanced Certificate). *Program availability:* Part-time, evening/weekend, blended/hybrid learning. *Students:* 148 full-time (110 women), 249 part-time (188 women); includes 105 minority (54 Black or African American, non-Hispanic/Latino; 1 American Indian or Alaska Native, non-Hispanic/Latino; 13 Asian, non-Hispanic/Latino; 35 Hispanic/Latino; 1 Native Hawaiian or other Pacific Islander, non-Hispanic/Latino; 1 Two or more races, non-Hispanic/Latino), 1 international. Average age 32. 228 applicants, 93% accepted, 132 enrolled. In 2017, 97 master's, 22 doctorates, 31 other advanced degrees awarded. *Degree requirements:* For master's, one foreign language, comprehensive exam (for some programs), thesis (for some programs), electronic portfolio, capstone course, internship, practicum, student teaching, seminars, minimum GPA 3.0; for doctorate, one foreign language, comprehensive exam, thesis/dissertation, qualifying hearing. *Entrance requirements:* For master's, GRE, interview, letters of recommendation, portfolio, essay, certification; for doctorate, GRE or MAT, interview, resume, essay, master's degree, 3 letters of recommendation, writing sample; for Advanced Certificate, GRE, interview, letters of recommendation, essay, professional experience, resume, master's degree. Additional exam requirements/recommendations for international students: Required—TOEFL (minimum score 550 paper-based; 80 iBT). *Application deadline:* Applications are processed on a rolling basis. Application fee: $75. Electronic applications accepted. *Expenses: Tuition:* Full-time $1292. *Required fees:* $970. Tuition and fees vary according to program. *Financial support:* In 2017–18, 225 students received support, including 118 fellowships with full and partial tuition reimbursements available (averaging $3,887 per year), 12 research assistantships with full and partial tuition reimbursements available (averaging $7,215 per year); career-related internships or fieldwork, Federal Work-Study, institutionally sponsored loans, scholarships/grants, traineeships, tuition waivers (full and partial), and unspecified assistantships also available. Support available to part-time students. Financial award applicants required to submit FAFSA. *Faculty research:* Collaborative teaching and learning; language and culture; new media literacies; applied behavior analysis; K-12 leadership development. *Unit head:* Dr. Elfreda Blue, Chairperson, 516-463-5762, Fax: 516-463-6184, E-mail: elfreda.blue@hofstra.edu. *Application contact:* Sunil Samuel, Assistant Vice President of Admissions, 516-463-4723, Fax: 516-463-4664, E-mail: graduateadmission@hofstra.edu.
Website: http://www.hofstra.edu/education/

Holy Family University, Graduate and Professional Programs, School of Education, Master of Education Programs, Philadelphia, PA 19114. Offers early elementary education (PreK-Grade 4) (M Ed); education leadership (M Ed); general education (M Ed); reading specialist (M Ed); special education (M Ed); TESOL and literacy (M Ed). *Program availability:* Part-time. *Degree requirements:* For master's, thesis optional. Electronic applications accepted. *Expenses: Tuition:* Full-time $13,518; part-time $9012 per credit hour. Tuition and fees vary according to degree level and program.

Hunter College of the City University of New York, Graduate School, School of Education, Department of Curriculum and Teaching, New York, NY 10065-5085. Offers bilingual education (MS); early childhood education (MS); educational supervision and administration (Ed D, AC), including administration and supervision (AC), instructional leadership (Ed D); elementary education (MS); teaching English as a second language (MA). *Degree requirements:* For master's, thesis; for AC, portfolio review. *Entrance requirements:* For degree, minimum B average in graduate course work, teaching certificate, minimum 3 years of full-time teaching experience, interview, 2 letters of support. Additional exam requirements/recommendations for international students: Required—TOEFL, TWE. *Faculty research:* Teacher opportunity corps (mentor program for first-year teachers), adult literacy, student literacy corporation.

Indiana University–Purdue University Indianapolis, School of Education, Indianapolis, IN 46202-5155. Offers curriculum and instruction (MS); early childhood (MS); educational leadership (MS, Certificate); English as a second language (Certificate); kindergarten (Certificate); language education (MS); reading (Certificate); school counseling (MS); special education (MS, Certificate). *Program availability:* Part-time, evening/weekend. Terminal master's awarded for partial completion of doctoral program. *Degree requirements:* For master's, thesis optional. *Entrance requirements:* For master's, GRE General Test, minimum GPA of 2.5; for Certificate, official transcripts. Additional exam requirements/recommendations for international students: Required—TOEFL (minimum score 60 iBT), IELTS (minimum score 5.5). Electronic applications accepted. *Expenses:* Contact institution. *Faculty research:* Educational policies and school leaders' responses to these; issues of intersectionality in the experiences of African American lesbian, gay, and bisexual students attending historically black colleges and universities and those who belong to black Greek-letter organizations; students' experiential knowledge and their evolving disciplinary-specific literacy and understanding; innovative program development; urban ESL teacher preparation; target-based instructional coaching.

Early Childhood Education

Inter American University of Puerto Rico, Guayama Campus, Department of Education and Social Sciences, Guayama, PR 00785. Offers early childhood education (0-4 years) (M Ed); elementary education (M Ed). *Program availability:* Part-time. *Entrance requirements:* For master's, GRE, MAT, EXADEP, letters of recommendation, minimum GPA of 2.5. Electronic applications accepted.

Iona College, School of Arts and Science, Department of Education, New Rochelle, NY 10801-1890. Offers adolescence education: biology (MS Ed, MST); adolescence education: English (MS Ed); adolescence education: mathematics (MST); adolescence education: social studies (MS Ed, MST); adolescence education: Spanish (MS Ed); adolescence special education 5-12 (MST); childhood and special education (MST); early childhood and childhood (MST); educational leadership (MS Ed). *Accreditation:* NCATE. *Program availability:* Part-time, evening/weekend. *Faculty:* 7 full-time (5 women), 2 part-time/adjunct (1 woman). *Students:* 23 full-time (18 women), 26 part-time (19 women); includes 12 minority (4 Black or African American, non-Hispanic/Latino; 8 Hispanic/Latino). Average age 26. 33 applicants, 97% accepted, 20 enrolled. In 2017, 31 master's awarded. *Degree requirements:* For master's, thesis or alternative. *Entrance requirements:* For master's, minimum GPA of 3.0, NY State teaching certificate and bachelor's degree (for MS Ed). Additional exam requirements/recommendations for international students: Required—TOEFL (minimum score 550 paper-based; 80 iBT), IELTS (minimum score 6.5). *Application deadline:* For fall admission, 8/1 priority date for domestic students, 5/1 priority date for international students; for spring admission, 1/1 priority date for domestic students, 9/1 priority date for international students. Applications are processed on a rolling basis. Electronic applications accepted. Tuition and fees vary according to program. *Financial support:* In 2017–18, 16 students received support. Unspecified assistantships available. Support available to part-time students. Financial award application deadline: 4/15; financial award applicants required to submit FAFSA. *Faculty research:* Engaging teacher educators in scientific process, cross-national comparisons of mathematics teaching, questioning strategies in the classroom, research methods, literacy development. *Unit head:* Margaret Smith, PhD, Chair, 914-633-2210, Fax: 914-633-2608, E-mail: msmith@iona.edu. *Application contact:* Richard McMahon, Coordinator, Graduate School of Education, 914-633-2552, E-mail: rmcmahon@iona.edu.
Website: http://www.iona.edu/Academics/School-of-Arts-Science/Departments/Education/Graduate-Programs.aspx

Jackson State University, Graduate School, College of Education and Human Development, Department of Elementary and Early Childhood Education, Jackson, MS 39217. Offers early childhood education (MS Ed, Ed D); elementary education (MS Ed, Ed S); reading education (MS Ed). *Accreditation:* NCATE. *Program availability:* Part-time, evening/weekend, 100% online, blended/hybrid learning. Terminal master's awarded for partial completion of doctoral program. *Degree requirements:* For master's, comprehensive exam, thesis or alternative; for doctorate, comprehensive exam, thesis/dissertation. *Entrance requirements:* For master's, GRE General Test; for doctorate, MAT, teaching experience. Additional exam requirements/recommendations for international students: Required—TOEFL (minimum score 520 paper-based; 67 iBT). Electronic applications accepted. *Expenses:* Contact institution.

Jacksonville State University, College of Graduate Studies and Continuing Education, College of Education and Professional Studies, Program in Early Childhood Education, Jacksonville, AL 36265-1602. Offers MS Ed. *Accreditation:* NCATE. *Program availability:* Part-time, evening/weekend. *Degree requirements:* For master's, comprehensive exam, thesis (for some programs). *Entrance requirements:* For master's, GRE General Test or MAT. Additional exam requirements/recommendations for international students: Required—TOEFL (minimum score 500 paper-based; 61 iBT). Electronic applications accepted.

James Madison University, The Graduate School, College of Education, Program in Early Childhood Education, Harrisonburg, VA 22807. Offers MAT. *Accreditation:* NCATE. *Program availability:* Part-time. *Students:* Average age 27. *Entrance requirements:* For master's, GRE General Test or MAT, PRAXIS I and II, 2-3 page written statement, faculty interview, minimum undergraduate GPA of 2.75. Additional exam requirements/recommendations for international students: Required—TOEFL. *Application deadline:* For fall admission, 5/1 priority date for domestic students; for spring admission, 9/1 priority date for domestic students. Applications are processed on a rolling basis. Application fee: $55. Electronic applications accepted. *Expenses:* Tuition, state resident: full-time $10,512; part-time $438 per credit hour. Tuition, nonresident: full-time $28,358; part-time $1162 per credit hour. *Required fees:* $1128. *Financial support:* Career-related internships or fieldwork and unspecified assistantships available. Financial award application deadline: 3/1; financial award applicants required to submit FAFSA. *Unit head:* Dr. Martha Ross, Academic Unit Head, 540-568-6255. *Application contact:* Lynette M. Bible, Director of Graduate Admissions, 540-568-6395, Fax: 540-568-7860, E-mail: biblelm@jmu.edu.

James Madison University, The Graduate School, College of Education, Program in Education, Harrisonburg, VA 22807. Offers early childhood education (preK-3) (MAT); educational leadership (M Ed); educational technology (M Ed); elementary education (MAT); equity and cultural diversity (M Ed); inclusive early childhood education (MAT); K-8 mathematics specialist (M Ed); middle education (MAT); reading education (M Ed); secondary education (MAT); Spanish language and culture for educators (M Ed); TESOL (MAT). *Accreditation:* NCATE. *Program availability:* Part-time, evening/weekend. *Students:* 260 full-time (233 women), 158 part-time (100 women); includes 48 minority (10 Black or African American, non-Hispanic/Latino; 4 Asian, non-Hispanic/Latino; 26 Hispanic/Latino; 1 Native Hawaiian or other Pacific Islander, non-Hispanic/Latino; 7 Two or more races, non-Hispanic/Latino), 2 international. Average age 30. In 2017, 262 master's awarded. Application fee: $55. Electronic applications accepted. *Expenses:* Tuition, state resident: full-time $10,512; part-time $438 per credit hour. Tuition, nonresident: full-time $28,358; part-time $1162 per credit hour. *Required fees:* $1128. *Financial support:* In 2017–18, 23 students received support, including 1 teaching assistantship; career-related internships or fieldwork, Federal Work-Study, and 22 assistantships (averaging $7911) also available. Financial award application deadline: 3/1; financial award applicants required to submit FAFSA. *Unit head:* Dr. Phillip M. Wishon, Dean, 540-568-6572, E-mail: wishonpm@jmu.edu. *Application contact:* Lynette D. Michael, Director of Graduate Admissions, 540-568-6131 Ext. 6395, Fax: 540-568-7860, E-mail: michaeld@jmu.edu.
Website: http://www.jmu.edu/coe/index.shtml

Johns Hopkins University, School of Education, Master's Programs in Education, Baltimore, MD 21218. Offers counseling (MS), including clinical mental health counseling, school counseling; education (MS), including educational studies, gifted education, reading, school administration and supervision, technology for educators; elementary education (MAT); health professions (M Ed); intelligence analysis (MS); organizational leadership (MS); secondary education (MAT), including biology, chemistry, earth/space science, English, physics, social studies; special education (MS), including early childhood special education, general special education studies, mild to moderate disabilities, severe disabilities. *Program availability:* Part-time, evening/weekend, 100% online, blended/hybrid learning. *Degree requirements:* For master's, comprehensive exam (for some programs), portfolio, capstone project and/or internship; PRAXIS II (subject area assessments) for initial teacher preparation programs that lead

to licensure. *Entrance requirements:* For master's, GRE (for full-time programs only); PRAXIS I/core or state-approved alternative (for initial teacher preparation programs that lead to licensure), minimum of bachelor's degree from regionally- or nationally-accredited institution; minimum GPA of 3.0 in all previous programs of study; official transcripts from all post-secondary institutions attended; essay; curriculum vitae/resume; letters of recommendation (3 for full-time programs, 2 for part-time programs); dispositions survey. Additional exam requirements/recommendations for international students: Required—TOEFL (minimum score 600 paper-based; 100 iBT), IELTS (minimum score 7). Electronic applications accepted. *Expenses:* Contact institution.

Jose Maria Vargas University, Program in Preschool Education, Pembroke Pines, FL 33026. Offers MS.

Kansas State University, Graduate School, College of Human Ecology, School of Family Studies and Human Services, Manhattan, KS 66506-1403. Offers applied family sciences (MS); communication sciences and disorders (MS); conflict resolution (Graduate Certificate); couple and family therapy (MS); early childhood education (MS); family and community service (MS); life-span human development (MS); personal financial planning (MS, PhD, Graduate Certificate); youth development (MS, Graduate Certificate). *Accreditation:* AAMFT/COAMFTE; ASHA. *Program availability:* Part-time, online learning. *Degree requirements:* For master's, comprehensive exam (for some programs), thesis optional. *Entrance requirements:* For master's, GRE, minimum GPA of 3.0 in last 2 years (60 semester hours) of undergraduate study; for doctorate, GRE. Additional exam requirements/recommendations for international students: Required—TOEFL (minimum score 600 paper-based). Electronic applications accepted. *Faculty research:* Health and security of military families, training in and evaluation of professional human services (marriage and couple therapy, family life education, treatment of speech and swallowing disorders, financial therapy), disorders of communication and swallowing, family and relationship development and health, financial decision-making.

Kean University, College of Education, Program in Early Childhood Education, Union, NJ 07083. Offers administration in early childhood and family studies (MA); advanced curriculum and teaching (MA); classroom instruction - P-3 certification (MA). *Accreditation:* NCATE. *Program availability:* Part-time. *Faculty:* 13 full-time (7 women). *Students:* 4 full-time (2 women), 10 part-time (all women); includes 6 minority (3 Asian, non-Hispanic/Latino; 3 Hispanic/Latino). Average age 30. 4 applicants, 75% accepted, 3 enrolled. In 2017, 5 master's awarded. *Entrance requirements:* For master's, GRE General Test, PRAXIS Early Childhood Content Knowledge (for some programs), minimum GPA of 3.0, 2 letters of recommendation, teacher certification (for some programs), personal statement, official transcripts, resume. Additional exam requirements/recommendations for international students: Required—TOEFL (minimum score 550 paper-based; 79 iBT), IELTS (minimum score 6.5). *Application deadline:* For fall admission, 6/30 for domestic and international students; for spring admission, 12/1 for domestic and international students. Applications are processed on a rolling basis. Application fee: $75. Electronic applications accepted. *Expenses:* Tuition, state resident: full-time $13,419; part-time $653 per credit. Tuition, nonresident: full-time $18,188; part-time $801 per credit. *Required fees:* $3382; $154 per credit. Tuition and fees vary according to course level, course load, degree level and program. *Financial support:* Scholarships/grants and unspecified assistantships available. Financial award applicants required to submit FAFSA. *Unit head:* Dr. Jennifer Chen, Program Coordinator, 908-737-3809, E-mail: jchen@kean.edu. *Application contact:* Brittany Gerstenhaber, Admissions Counselor, 908-737-7100, E-mail: gradadmissions@kean.edu.

Kennesaw State University, Leland and Clarice C. Bagwell College of Education, Program in Graduate Education, Kennesaw, GA 30144. Offers educational leadership (M Ed); educational leadership technology (M Ed); elementary and early childhood education (M Ed); instructional technology (M Ed); middle grades education (M Ed); reading (M Ed); secondary education (M Ed); special education (M Ed); teaching English to speakers of other languages (M Ed). *Accreditation:* NCATE. *Program availability:* Part-time. *Degree requirements:* For master's, thesis or alternative. *Entrance requirements:* For master's, GRE General Test, T-4 state certification, minimum GPA of 2.75. Additional exam requirements/recommendations for international students: Required—TOEFL (minimum score 550 paper-based; 80 iBT), IELTS (minimum score 6.5). Electronic applications accepted.

Kent State University, College of Education, Health and Human Services, School of Lifespan Development and Educational Sciences, Program in Special Education, Kent, OH 44242-0001. Offers deaf education (M Ed); early childhood education (M Ed); educational interpreter K-12 (M Ed); general special education (M Ed); mild/moderate intervention (M Ed); special education (PhD, Ed S); transition to work (M Ed). *Accreditation:* NCATE. *Degree requirements:* For doctorate, comprehensive exam, thesis/dissertation. *Entrance requirements:* For master's, minimum undergraduate GPA of 2.75, moral character form, 2 letters of reference, goals statement; for doctorate and Ed S, GRE General Test, goals statement, 2 letters of reference, interview, resume. Additional exam requirements/recommendations for international students: Required—TOEFL (minimum score 550 paper-based; 80 iBT). Electronic applications accepted. *Expenses:* Tuition, state resident: full-time $11,310; part-time $515 per credit hour. Tuition, nonresident: full-time $20,396; part-time $928 per credit hour. *International tuition:* $18,544 full-time. *Faculty research:* Social/emotional needs of gifted, inclusion transition services, early intervention/ecobehavioral assessments, applied behavioral analysis.

Kent State University, College of Education, Health and Human Services, School of Teaching, Learning and Curriculum Studies, Program in Early Childhood Education, Kent, OH 44242-0001. Offers M Ed, MA, MAT. *Accreditation:* NCATE. *Degree requirements:* For master's, thesis (for some programs). *Entrance requirements:* For master's, GRE General Test (for licensure), 2 letters of reference, goals statement. Additional exam requirements/recommendations for international students: Required—TOEFL (minimum score 550 paper-based; 80 iBT). Electronic applications accepted. *Expenses:* Tuition, state resident: full-time $11,310; part-time $515 per credit hour. Tuition, nonresident: full-time $20,396; part-time $928 per credit hour. *International tuition:* $18,544 full-time. *Faculty research:* Parent-child relationships, professional preparation, curriculum and assessment.

Keuka College, Program in Childhood Education/Literacy, Keuka Park, NY 14478. Offers literacy 5-12 (MS); literacy B-6 (MS). *Degree requirements:* For master's, thesis, capstone project/student-led research project. *Entrance requirements:* For master's, GRE, minimum GPA of 3.0; 3 letters of recommendation (2 academic and one from cooperating teacher from student teaching or other professional). Additional exam requirements/recommendations for international students: Required—TOEFL (minimum score 550 paper-based). Electronic applications accepted. *Expenses:* Contact institution. *Faculty research:* Marginalized populations, international literacy, teacher assessment.

Keystone College, Program in Early Childhood Education Leadership, La Plume, PA 18440. Offers M Ed. *Program availability:* Part-time, blended/hybrid learning. *Faculty:* 1 (woman) full-time, 4 part-time/adjunct (all women). *Students:* 49 part-time (all women); includes 24 minority (6 Black or African American, non-Hispanic/Latino; 1 American

Indian or Alaska Native, non-Hispanic/Latino; 17 Hispanic/Latino). 23 applicants, 83% accepted, 18 enrolled. In 2017, 19 master's awarded. *Degree requirements:* For master's, thesis or alternative. *Entrance requirements:* For master's, GRE, college transcripts, resume or curriculum vitae, current clearances. Additional exam requirements/recommendations for international students: Required—TOEFL (minimum score 80 iBT) or IELTS (minimum score 6.5). *Application deadline:* For fall admission, 8/1 for domestic students; for spring admission, 12/1 for domestic students; for summer admission, 5/1 for domestic students. Applications are processed on a rolling basis. Application fee: $0. Electronic applications accepted. *Expenses:* $650 per credit. *Financial support:* Unspecified assistantships available. Financial award application deadline: 5/1; financial award applicants required to submit FAFSA. *Unit head:* Fran Langan, PhD, Dean, School of Professional Studies, 570-945-8472, E-mail: fran.langan@keystone.edu. *Application contact:* Jennifer Sekol, Director of Admissions, 570-945-8117, Fax: 570-945-7916, E-mail: jennifer.sekol@keystone.edu.

Lander University, Graduate Studies, Greenwood, SC 29649-2099. Offers clinical nurse leader (MSN); emergency management (MS); Montessori education (M Ed); teaching and learning (M Ed). *Accreditation:* NCATE. *Program availability:* Part-time, online learning. *Degree requirements:* For master's, comprehensive exam, thesis or alternative. *Entrance requirements:* For master's, GRE General Test. Additional exam requirements/recommendations for international students: Required—TOEFL (minimum score 550 paper-based). Electronic applications accepted.

La Salle University, School of Arts and Sciences, Program in Education, Philadelphia, PA 19141-1199. Offers autism spectrum disorders (MA, Certificate); bilingual/bicultural studies (MA); classroom management (MA); dual early childhood and special education (MA); dual middle-level science and math and special education (MA); education (MA); English (MA); English as a second language (Certificate); history (MA); instructional coach (Certificate); instructional leadership (MA); reading specialist (MA, Certificate); secondary education (MA); special education (MA, Certificate). *Program availability:* Part-time, evening/weekend. *Faculty:* 5 full-time (4 women), 8 part-time/adjunct (5 women). *Students:* 2 full-time (1 woman), 110 part-time (81 women); includes 23 minority (11 Black or African American, non-Hispanic/Latino; 1 Asian, non-Hispanic/Latino; 7 Hispanic/Latino; 4 Two or more races, non-Hispanic/Latino). Average age 33. 137 applicants, 70% accepted, 63 enrolled. In 2017, 148 master's awarded. *Degree requirements:* For master's, comprehensive exam. *Entrance requirements:* For master's, MAT or GRE, 2 letters of recommendation; for Certificate, GMAT or GRE, 2 letters of recommendation. Additional exam requirements/recommendations for international students: Required—TOEFL. *Application deadline:* For fall admission, 8/15 priority date for domestic students, 7/15 for international students; for spring admission, 12/15 priority date for domestic students, 11/15 for international students; for summer admission, 4/15 priority date for domestic students, 3/15 for international students. Applications are processed on a rolling basis. Application fee: $35. Electronic applications accepted. Application fee is waived when completed online. *Expenses:* Contact institution. *Financial support:* In 2017–18, 19 students received support. Scholarships/grants available. Support available to part-time students. Financial award application deadline: 8/31; financial award applicants required to submit FAFSA. *Unit head:* Dr. Greer Richardson, Director, 215-951-1806, Fax: 215-951-1843, E-mail: graded@lasalle.edu. *Application contact:* Elizabeth Heenan, Director, Graduate and Adult Enrollment, 215-951-1100, Fax: 215-951-1462, E-mail: heenan@lasalle.edu. Website: http://www.lasalle.edu/grad-education-programs/

Lee University, Program in Education, Cleveland, TN 37320-3450. Offers art (MAT); curriculum and instruction (M Ed, Ed S); early childhood (MAT); educational leadership (M Ed, Ed S); elementary education (MAT); English and math (MAT); English and science (MAT); English and social studies (MAT); higher education administration (MS); history (MAT); history and economics (MAT); math and science (MAT); math and social studies (MAT); middle grades (MAT); science and social studies (MASW); secondary education (MAT); Spanish (MAT); special education (M Ed, MAT); TESOL (MAT). *Accreditation:* NCATE. *Program availability:* Part-time. *Faculty:* 15 full-time (7 women), 8 part-time/adjunct (3 women). *Students:* 28 full-time (21 women), 77 part-time (48 women); includes 12 minority (7 Black or African American, non-Hispanic/Latino; 2 Hispanic/Latino; 3 Two or more races, non-Hispanic/Latino), 1 international. Average age 31. 35 applicants, 83% accepted, 22 enrolled. In 2017, 54 master's, 4 other advanced degrees awarded. *Degree requirements:* For master's, variable foreign language requirement, thesis optional, internship. *Entrance requirements:* For master's, MAT or GRE General Test, minimum undergraduate GPA of 2.75, 3 letters of recommendation, interview, writing sample, official transcripts, background check; for Ed S, minimum undergraduate and master's GPA of 2.75, official transcripts for undergraduate and master's degrees. Additional exam requirements/recommendations for international students: Required—TOEFL (minimum score 61 iBT). *Application deadline:* For fall admission, 6/1 priority date for domestic and international students; for spring admission, 11/1 priority date for domestic and international students; for summer admission, 4/1 priority date for domestic and international students. Applications are processed on a rolling basis. Application fee: $25. Electronic applications accepted. *Expenses:* Tuition: Full-time $12,780; part-time $710 per credit hour. *Required fees:* $60; $60 per term. Tuition and fees vary according to program. *Financial support:* In 2017–18, 32 students received support. Career-related internships or fieldwork, Federal Work-Study, institutionally sponsored loans, scholarships/grants, and unspecified assistantships available. Financial award application deadline: 3/1; financial award applicants required to submit FAFSA. *Unit head:* Dr. William Kamm, Director, 423-614-8544, E-mail: wkamm@leeuniversity.edu. *Application contact:* Crystal Keeter, Graduate Education Secretary, 423-614-8544, E-mail: ckeeter@leeuniversity.edu. Website: http://www.leeuniversity.edu/academics/graduate/education

Lehigh University, College of Education, Program in Educational Leadership, Bethlehem, PA 18015. Offers curriculum and instruction (Certificate); educational leadership (M Ed, Ed D); K-12 principal (Certificate); superintendent letter (Certificate). *Program availability:* Part-time, evening/weekend, online learning. *Faculty:* 5 full-time (2 women), 7 part-time/adjunct (3 women). *Students:* 6 full-time (5 women), 111 part-time (70 women); includes 14 minority (1 Black or African American, non-Hispanic/Latino; 1 Asian, non-Hispanic/Latino; 12 Hispanic/Latino), 6 international. Average age 34. 82 applicants, 67% accepted, 9 enrolled. In 2017, 52 master's, 9 Certificates awarded. Terminal master's awarded for partial completion of doctoral program. *Degree requirements:* For master's, thesis (for some programs); for doctorate, comprehensive exam, thesis/dissertation. *Entrance requirements:* For master's, minimum undergraduate GPA of 3.0, essay, transcripts, 2 letters of recommendation; for doctorate, GRE General Test or MAT, minimum graduate GPA of 3.6, 2 letters of recommendation, essay, transcript; for Certificate, minimum undergraduate GPA of 3.0. Additional exam requirements/recommendations for international students: Required—TOEFL (minimum score 600 paper-based, 93 iBT) or IELTS. *Application deadline:* For fall admission, 1/15 for domestic and international students; for spring admission, 12/1 for domestic and international students; for summer admission, 5/1 for domestic and international students. Applications are processed on a rolling basis. Application fee: $65. Electronic applications accepted. *Expenses:* $565 per credit; $225 internship fee. *Financial support:* In 2017–18, 18 students received support, including 3 research assistantships (averaging $8,092 per year); fellowships and unspecified assistantships also available. Financial award application deadline: 1/31; financial award applicants

required to submit FAFSA. *Faculty research:* Supervision of instruction, middle-level education, organizational change, leadership preparation and development, international school leadership, urban school leadership, comparative education, social justice, education and human services, social network, principal leadership, policy implementation, teacher evaluation, teaching quality. *Unit head:* Dr. Floyd D. Beachum, Director, 610-758-5955, Fax: 610-758-3227, E-mail: fdb209@lehigh.edu. *Application contact:* Kristi Ball, Coordinator, 610-758-3250, Fax: 610-758-6223, E-mail: kmb618@lehigh.edu.
Website: https://ed.lehigh.edu/academics/programs/educational-leadership

Lehman College of the City University of New York, School of Education, Department of Early Childhood and Elementary Education, Program in Early Childhood Education, Bronx, NY 10468-1589. Offers MS Ed. *Accreditation:* NCATE. *Program availability:* Part-time, evening/weekend. *Entrance requirements:* For master's, minimum GPA of 2.7. *Faculty research:* TV programming, literacy, children's trauma conceptualization.

Le Moyne College, Department of Education, Syracuse, NY 13214. Offers adolescent education (MS Ed, MST); adolescent education/special education (MS Ed, MST); adolescent English (MST), including grades 7-12; adolescent English/special education (MST), including grades 7-12; adolescent foreign language (MST), including grades 7-12; adolescent history (MST), including grades 7-12; childhood education (MS Ed); childhood education/special education (MS Ed); elementary education (MS Ed); general education (MS Ed); inclusive childhood education (MST); literacy education (MS Ed), including birth to grade 6, grades 5-12; school building leader (MS Ed); school building leadership (CAS); school district business leader (MS Ed, CAS); school district leader (MS Ed); school district leadership (CAS); secondary education (MS Ed); special education (MS Ed); teaching English to speakers of other languages (MS Ed); urban studies (MS Ed). *Accreditation:* TEAC. *Program availability:* Part-time, evening/weekend. *Faculty:* 7 full-time (5 women), 20 part-time/adjunct (12 women). *Students:* 30 full-time (19 women), 126 part-time (93 women); includes 15 minority (7 Black or African American, non-Hispanic/Latino; 1 American Indian or Alaska Native, non-Hispanic/Latino; 1 Asian, non-Hispanic/Latino; 6 Hispanic/Latino), 4 international. Average age 29. 139 applicants, 65% accepted, 76 enrolled. In 2017, 82 master's, 43 CASs awarded. *Degree requirements:* For master's, thesis. *Entrance requirements:* For master's, bachelor's degree with minimum undergraduate GPA of 3.0, 2 letters of recommendation, transcripts. Additional exam requirements/recommendations for international students: Required—TOEFL (minimum score 550 paper-based; 79 iBT); Recommended—IELTS (minimum score 6.5). *Application deadline:* For fall admission, 4/1 priority date for domestic and international students; for spring admission, 10/1 priority date for domestic and international students; for summer admission, 3/1 priority date for domestic and international students. Applications are processed on a rolling basis. Application fee: $50. Electronic applications accepted. *Expenses:* $700 per credit hour. *Financial support:* In 2017–18, 30 students received support. Career-related internships or fieldwork, scholarships/grants, and health care benefits available. Support available to part-time students. Financial award applicants required to submit FAFSA. *Faculty research:* Minority teachers, special education, multiculturalism, literacy, technology, media literacy learning, autism, school district organization, service-learning, higher level problem solving, teacher leadership. *Unit head:* Dr. Stephen C. Fleury, Chair, Department of Education, 315-445-4376, Fax: 315-445-4744, E-mail: fleurysc@lemoyne.edu. *Application contact:* Kristen P. Richards, Senior Director of Enrollment Management, 315-445-5444, Fax: 315-445-6092, E-mail: trapaskp@lemoyne.edu.
Website: http://www.lemoyne.edu/education

Lesley University, Graduate School of Education, Cambridge, MA 02138-2790. Offers arts, community, and education (M Ed); autism studies (Certificate); curriculum and instruction (M Ed, CAGS); early childhood education (M Ed); ecological teaching and learning (MS); educational studies (PhD), including adult learning, educational leadership, individually designed; elementary education (M Ed); emergent technologies for educators (Certificate); ESLArts: language learning through the arts (M Ed); high school education (M Ed); individually designed; integrated teaching through the arts (M Ed); literacy for K-8 classroom teachers (M Ed); mathematics education (M Ed); middle school education (M Ed); moderate disabilities (M Ed); online learning (Certificate); reading (CAGS); science in education (M Ed); severe disabilities (M Ed); special needs (CAGS); specialist teacher of reading (M Ed); teacher of visual art (M Ed); technology in education (M Ed, CAGS). *Accreditation:* TEAC. *Program availability:* Part-time, evening/weekend, online learning. *Degree requirements:* For master's, practicum; for doctorate, thesis/dissertation. *Entrance requirements:* For master's, Massachusetts Tests for Educator Licensure (MTEL), transcripts, statement of purpose, recommendations; interview (for special education); for doctorate, GRE General Test, transcripts, statement of purpose, recommendations, interview, master's degree, resume; for other advanced degree, interview, master's degree. Additional exam requirements/recommendations for international students: Required—TOEFL (minimum score 550 paper-based; 80 iBT). Electronic applications accepted. *Faculty research:* Assessment in literacy, mathematics and science; autism spectrum disorders; instructional technology and online learning; multicultural education and English language learners.

Lewis University, College of Education, Program in Early Childhood Special Education, Romeoville, IL 60446. Offers MA. *Program availability:* Part-time. *Students:* 9 full-time (8 women), 7 part-time (all women); includes 5 minority (all Hispanic/Latino). Average age 32. *Degree requirements:* For master's, comprehensive exam. *Entrance requirements:* For master's, writing exam, Test of Academic Proficiency/Basic Skills Test/ACT/SAT, bachelor's degree, minimum undergraduate GPA of 2.75, two letters of recommendation, professional educator license, interview. Additional exam requirements/recommendations for international students: Required—TOEFL (minimum score 550 paper-based; 79 iBT), IELTS (minimum score 6). *Application deadline:* For fall admission, 5/1 priority date for international students; for spring admission, 11/1 priority date for international students. Application fee: $40. Electronic applications accepted. Tuition and fees vary according to program. *Financial support:* Federal Work-Study and unspecified assistantships available. Financial award application deadline: 5/1; financial award applicants required to submit FAFSA. *Unit head:* Dr. Pamela Jessee, Dean, 815-836-5316, E-mail: jesseepa@lewisu.edu. *Application contact:* Linda Campbell, Graduate Admission Counselor, 815-836-5704, Fax: 815-836-5578, E-mail: campbelli@lewisu.edu.
Website: http://www.lewisu.edu/academics/grad-education/earlychildhood/index.htm

Lincoln University, Graduate Programs, Philadelphia, PA 19104. Offers counseling (MSC); early childhood education (M Ed), including PreK-4; early childhood education and special education (M Ed), including principal certification; finance (MBA); human resources management (MBA); human services delivery (MAHS). *Program availability:* Part-time, evening/weekend. *Faculty:* 9 full-time (3 women), 25 part-time/adjunct (15 women). *Students:* 196 full-time (138 women), 68 part-time (46 women); includes 236 minority (227 Black or African American, non-Hispanic/Latino; 1 American Indian or Alaska Native, non-Hispanic/Latino; 7 Hispanic/Latino; 1 Two or more races, non-Hispanic/Latino), 3 international. Average age 34. 120 applicants, 100% accepted, 95 enrolled. In 2017, 126 master's awarded. *Degree*

Early Childhood Education

requirements: For master's, comprehensive exam, thesis or alternative, capstone, grant proposal. *Entrance requirements:* For master's, official academic transcript(s), letters of recommendation, personal statement, resume, supervisor's evaluation form. Additional exam requirements/recommendations for international students: Recommended—TOEFL (minimum score 500 paper-based; 71 iBT), IELTS. *Application deadline:* For fall admission, 8/1 priority date for domestic students, 7/1 priority date for international students; for spring admission, 12/1 priority date for domestic students, 10/1 for international students. Applications are processed on a rolling basis. Application fee: $50. Electronic applications accepted. *Expenses:* Contact institution. *Financial support:* Scholarships/grants available. Financial award application deadline: 6/30; financial award applicants required to submit FAFSA. *Unit head:* Dr. Patricia Pierce Ramsey, Provost, 484-365-7437, Fax: 484-365-8108, E-mail: provost@lincoln.edu. *Application contact:* Jernice Lea, Director, University City Student Services and Admissions, 215-590-8231, Fax: 215-387-3859, E-mail: jlea@lincoln.edu.
Website: http://www.lincoln.edu/admissions/graduate-admissions

London Metropolitan University, Graduate Programs, London, United Kingdom. Offers applied psychology (M Sc); architecture (MA); biomedical science (M Sc); blood science (M Sc); cancer pharmacology (M Sc); computer networking and cyber security (M Sc); computing and information systems (M Sc); conference interpreting (MA); counter-terrorism studies (M Sc); creative, digital and professional writing (MA); crime, violence and prevention (M Sc); criminology (M Sc); curating contemporary art (MA); data analytics (MA); digital media (MA); early childhood studies (MA); education (MA, Ed D); financial services law, regulation and compliance (LL M); food science (M Sc); forensic psychology (M Sc); health and social care management and policy (M Sc); human nutrition (M Sc); human resource management (MA); human rights and international conflict (MA); information technology (M Sc); intelligence and security studies (M Sc); international oil, gas and energy law (LL M); international relations (MA); interpreting (MA); learning and teaching in higher education (MA); legal practice (LL M); media and entertainment law (LL M); organizational and consumer psychology (M Sc); psychological therapy (M Sc); psychology of mental health (M Sc); public health (M Sc); public policy and management (MPA); security studies (M Sc); social work (M Sc); spatial planning and urban design (MA); sports therapy (M Sc); supporting older children and young people with dyslexia (MA); teaching languages (MA), including Arabic, English; translation (MA); woman and child abuse (MA).

Long Island University–Brentwood Campus, Graduate Programs, Brentwood, NY 11717. Offers childhood education (MS), including grades 1-6; childhood education/literacy B-6 (MS); childhood education/special education (grades 1-6) (MS); clinical mental health counseling (MS, Advanced Certificate); criminal justice (MS); early childhood education (MS); educational leadership (MS Ed); family nurse practitioner (MS, Advanced Certificate); health administration (MPA); library and information science (MS); literacy (B-6) (MS Ed); school counselor (MS, Advanced Certificate); social work (MSW); special education (MS Ed); students with disabilities generalist (grades 7-12) (Advanced Certificate). *Program availability:* Part-time. *Faculty:* 14 full-time (9 women), 22 part-time/adjunct (11 women). *Students:* 111 full-time (89 women), 47 part-time (34 women); includes 35 minority (8 Black or African American, non-Hispanic/Latino; 1 American Indian or Alaska Native, non-Hispanic/Latino; 3 Asian, non-Hispanic/Latino; 22 Hispanic/Latino; 1 Two or more races, non-Hispanic/Latino), 1 international. Average age 30. 110 applicants, 82% accepted, 63 enrolled. In 2017, 58 master's, 5 other advanced degrees awarded. *Entrance requirements:* For master's and Advanced Certificate, GRE. Additional exam requirements/recommendations for international students: Required—TOEFL or IELTS. *Application deadline:* Applications are processed on a rolling basis. Application fee: $50. Electronic applications accepted. *Expenses:* Tuition: Full-time $21,168; part-time $1201 per credit. *Required fees:* $1840; $920 per term. Tuition and fees vary according to course load. *Financial support:* In 2017–18, 121 students received support. Scholarships/grants available. Support available to part-time students. Financial award application deadline: 2/15; financial award applicants required to submit FAFSA. *Unit head:* Dr. Abby Van Vlerah, Dean and Chief Operating Officer, 631-299-3831, E-mail: abagail.vanvlerah@liu.edu. *Application contact:* Scott Aug, Associate Director of Enrollment Management, 631-287-8506, E-mail: scott.aug@liu.edu.
Website: http://liu.edu/brentwood

Long Island University–Hudson, Graduate School, Purchase, NY 10577. Offers autism (Advanced Certificate); bilingual education (Advanced Certificate); childhood education (MS Ed); crisis management (Advanced Certificate); early childhood education (MS Ed); educational leadership (MS Ed); health administration (MPA); literacy (MS Ed); marriage and family therapy (MS); mental health counseling (MS, Advanced Certificate), including credentialed alcoholism and substance abuse counselor (MS); middle childhood and adolescence education (MS Ed); pharmaceutics (MS), including cosmetic science, industrial pharmacy; public administration (MPA); school counseling (MS Ed, Advanced Certificate); school psychology (MS Ed); special education (MS Ed); TESOL (MS Ed); TESOL (all grades) (Advanced Certificate). *Program availability:* Part-time, evening/weekend. *Faculty:* 8 full-time (6 women), 41 part-time/adjunct (24 women). *Students:* 69 full-time (54 women), 249 part-time (200 women); includes 102 minority (29 Black or African American, non-Hispanic/Latino; 1 American Indian or Alaska Native, non-Hispanic/Latino; 9 Asian, non-Hispanic/Latino; 62 Hispanic/Latino; 1 Native Hawaiian or other Pacific Islander, non-Hispanic/Latino). Average age 33. 153 applicants, 96% accepted, 103 enrolled. In 2017, 138 master's, 36 other advanced degrees awarded. *Entrance requirements:* Additional exam requirements/recommendations for international students: Required—TOEFL. *Application deadline:* Applications are processed on a rolling basis. Application fee: $50. Electronic applications accepted. *Expenses:* Contact institution. *Financial support:* In 2017–18, 32 students received support. Scholarships/grants available. Support available to part-time students. Financial award application deadline: 2/15; financial award applicants required to submit FAFSA. *Unit head:* Dr. Sylvia Blake, Dean and Chief Operating Officer, 914-831-2700, E-mail: westchester@liu.edu. *Application contact:* Dr. Sylvia Blake, Dean and Chief Operating Officer, 914-831-2700, E-mail: westchester@liu.edu.

Long Island University–LIU Brooklyn, School of Education, Brooklyn, NY 11201-8423. Offers adolescence urban education (MS Ed); applied behavior analysis (Advanced Certificate); bilingual education (Advanced Certificate); bilingual education in urban setting (MS Ed); bilingual school counselor (MS Ed, Advanced Certificate); childhood urban education (MS Ed); childhood/early childhood education (MS Ed); childhood/early childhood urban education (MS Ed); early childhood urban education (MS Ed, Advanced Certificate); educational leadership (Advanced Certificate); marriage and family therapy (MS, Advanced Certificate); mental health counseling (MS, Advanced Certificate); school building district leader (Advanced Certificate); school counselor (MS Ed, Advanced Certificate); school psychologist (MS Ed); teaching students with disabilities (MS Ed); teaching urban children with disabilities (MS Ed); TESOL (MS Ed, Advanced Certificate). *Accreditation:* TEAC. *Program availability:* Part-time, evening/weekend, 100% online. *Faculty:* 14 full-time (12 women), 42 part-time/adjunct (32 women). *Students:* 140 full-time (130 women), 563 part-time (414 women); includes 417 minority (183 Black or African American, non-Hispanic/Latino; 1 American Indian or Alaska Native, non-Hispanic/Latino; 32 Asian, non-Hispanic/Latino; 187 Hispanic/Latino; 14 Two or more races, non-Hispanic/Latino), 10 international. Average

age 31. 449 applicants, 82% accepted, 264 enrolled. In 2017, 408 master's, 31 other advanced degrees awarded. *Entrance requirements:* For master's, GRE. Additional exam requirements/recommendations for international students: Required—TOEFL (minimum score 527 paper-based, 75 iBT), IELTS, or PTE. *Application deadline:* Applications are processed on a rolling basis. Application fee: $50. Electronic applications accepted. *Expenses: Tuition:* Full-time $21,618; part-time $1201 per credit. *Required fees:* $1840; $920 per term. Tuition and fees vary according to course load. *Financial support:* In 2017–18, 58 students received support. Career-related internships or fieldwork, Federal Work-Study, scholarships/grants, and unspecified assistantships available. Support available to part-time students. Financial award application deadline: 2/15; financial award applicants required to submit FAFSA. *Faculty research:* Diversity issues in education and mental health care, inclusion - disability studies, sustainability, teacher professional development. *Unit head:* Dean, 718-488-1055, E-mail: bkln-admissions@liu.edu. *Application contact:* Bayu Sutrisno, Graduate Admissions Counselor, 718-488-1011, Fax: 718-780-6110, E-mail: bkln-admissions@liu.edu.
Website: http://www.liu.edu/Brooklyn/Academics/School-of-Education

Long Island University–LIU Post, College of Education, Information and Technology, Brookville, NY 11548-1300. Offers adolescence education (MS); adolescence education 7-12 (MS); archives and records management (AC); art education (MS); childhood education (MS); childhood education/literacy B-6 (MS); childhood education/special education (MS); clinical mental health counseling (MS, AC); early childhood education (MS); early childhood education/childhood education (MS); educational leadership (AC); educational technology (MS); information studies (PhD); interdisciplinary educational studies (Ed D); middle childhood education (MS); music education (MS); public library administration (AC); school counselor (MS); special education (MS Ed); speech-language pathology (MA); students with disabilities, 7-12 generalist (AC); TESOL (MA). *Accreditation:* TEAC. *Program availability:* Part-time, 100% online, blended/hybrid learning. *Faculty:* 40 full-time (26 women), 73 part-time/adjunct (38 women). *Students:* 472 full-time (400 women), 696 part-time (543 women); includes 254 minority (93 Black or African American, non-Hispanic/Latino; 46 Asian, non-Hispanic/Latino; 105 Hispanic/Latino; 10 Two or more races, non-Hispanic/Latino), 33 international. Average age 33. 917 applicants, 82% accepted, 357 enrolled. In 2017, 408 master's, 31 other advanced degrees awarded. Terminal master's awarded for partial completion of doctoral program. *Degree requirements:* For master's, variable foreign language requirement, comprehensive exam (for some programs), thesis optional; for doctorate, comprehensive exam, thesis/dissertation. *Entrance requirements:* For master's and AC, GRE (for some programs). Additional exam requirements/recommendations for international students: Required—TOEFL (minimum score 550 paper-based, 75 iBT), IELTS, or PTE. *Application deadline:* Applications are processed on a rolling basis. Application fee: $50. Electronic applications accepted. *Expenses: Tuition:* Full-time $21,618; part-time $1201 per credit. *Required fees:* $1840; $920 per term. Tuition and fees vary according to course load. *Financial support:* In 2017–18, 376 students received support. Career-related internships or fieldwork, Federal Work-Study, institutionally sponsored loans, scholarships/grants, tuition waivers (partial), and unspecified assistantships available. Support available to part-time students. Financial award application deadline: 2/15; financial award applicants required to submit FAFSA. *Faculty research:* Sleep; use of technology to develop executive function by students with disabilities; early childhood literacy development through play; social justice through education; using a structured protocol to discuss Bad News. *Unit head:* Dr. Albert Inserra, Dean, 516-299-2210, E-mail: albert.inserra@liu.edu. *Application contact:* Rita Langdon, Graduate Admissions, 516-299-2900, Fax: 516-299-2137, E-mail: post-enroll@liu.edu.
Website: http://liu.edu/CWPost/Academics/College-of-Education-Information-and-Technology

Long Island University–Riverhead, Graduate Programs, Riverhead, NY 11901. Offers applied behavior analysis (Advanced Certificate); childhood education (MS), including grades 1-6; cybersecurity policy (Advanced Certificate); homeland security management (MS, Advanced Certificate); literacy education (MS); literacy education B-6 (MS); teaching students with disabilities (MS), including grades 1-6; TESOL (Advanced Certificate). *Accreditation:* TEAC. *Program availability:* Part-time. *Faculty:* 4 full-time (1 woman), 11 part-time/adjunct (5 women). *Students:* 17 full-time (14 women), 58 part-time (36 women); includes 14 minority (4 Black or African American, non-Hispanic/Latino; 1 American Indian or Alaska Native, non-Hispanic/Latino; 1 Asian, non-Hispanic/Latino; 6 Hispanic/Latino; 2 Two or more races, non-Hispanic/Latino). Average age 32. 68 applicants, 79% accepted, 26 enrolled. In 2017, 30 master's, 7 other advanced degrees awarded. *Entrance requirements:* Additional exam requirements/recommendations for international students: Required—TOEFL or IELTS. *Application deadline:* Applications are processed on a rolling basis. Application fee: $50. Electronic applications accepted. *Expenses:* Contact institution. *Financial support:* In 2017–18, 53 students received support. Scholarships/grants available. Support available to part-time students. Financial award application deadline: 2/15; financial award applicants required to submit FAFSA. *Unit head:* Dr. Abagail VanVlerah, Dean and Chief Operating Officer, 631-299-3831, E-mail: abagail.vanvlerah@liu.edu. *Application contact:* Jean Conroy, Associate Dean, 631-287-8301, E-mail: jean.conroy@liu.edu.

Louisiana Tech University, Graduate School, College of Education, Ruston, LA 71272. Offers counseling and guidance (MA), including clinical mental health counseling, human services, orientation and mobility; counseling psychology (PhD); curriculum and instruction (M Ed); cyber education (Graduate Certificate); dynamics of domestic and family violence (Graduate Certificate); early childhood education - PreK-3 (MAT); educational leadership (M Ed, Ed D); elementary education and special education mild/moderate grades 1-5 (MAT); higher education administration (Graduate Certificate); industrial/organizational psychology (MA, PhD); kinesiology (MS); middle school education (MAT), including mathematics; orientation and mobility (Graduate Certificate); rehabilitation teaching for the blind (Graduate Certificate); secondary education (MAT), including agriculture, biology, business, chemistry, English; special education: visually impaired (MAT); teacher leader education (Graduate Certificate); visual impairments - blind education (Graduate Certificate). *Accreditation:* NCATE. *Program availability:* Part-time. *Faculty:* 28 full-time (16 women), 23 part-time/adjunct (22 women). *Students:* 269 full-time (192 women), 194 part-time (150 women); includes 127 minority (94 Black or African American, non-Hispanic/Latino; 2 American Indian or Alaska Native, non-Hispanic/Latino; 6 Asian, non-Hispanic/Latino; 16 Hispanic/Latino; 1 Native Hawaiian or other Pacific Islander, non-Hispanic/Latino; 8 Two or more races, non-Hispanic/Latino), 8 international. Average age 34. 226 applicants, 74% accepted, 60 enrolled. In 2017, 5 master's, 2 doctorates, 1 other advanced degree awarded. *Degree requirements:* For master's, thesis; for doctorate, thesis/dissertation. *Entrance requirements:* For master's and doctorate, GRE General Test. Additional exam requirements/recommendations for international students: Required—TOEFL (minimum score 550 paper-based; 80 iBT), IELTS (minimum score 6.5). *Application deadline:* For fall admission, 9/1 priority date for domestic students, 6/1 for international students; for winter admission, 11/1 priority date for domestic students, 9/1 for international students; for spring admission, 2/1 priority date for domestic students, 12/1 for international students; for summer admission, 5/1 priority date for domestic students, 3/1 for international students. Application fee: $40. Electronic applications accepted. *Expenses:* Tuition, state resident: full-time $5146. Tuition, nonresident: full-time $10,147. *International tuition:* $10,267 full-time. *Required*

fees: $2273. *Financial support:* In 2017–18, 40 students received support, including 23 research assistantships (averaging $10,346 per year), 15 teaching assistantships (averaging $6,887 per year); fellowships and career-related internships or fieldwork also available. Financial award application deadline: 2/1. *Faculty research:* Blindness and the best methods for increasing independence for individuals who are blind or visually impaired; educating and investigating factors contributing to improvements in human performance across the lifespan and a reduction in injury rates during training. *Total annual research expenditures:* $2.1 million. *Unit head:* Dr. Don Schillinger, Dean, 318-257-3712, E-mail: dschill@latech.edu. *Application contact:* Dr. Dawn Basinger, Associate Dean of Academic Affairs, 318-257-2977, Fax: 318-257-2379, E-mail: dbasing@latech.edu.
Website: http://education.latech.edu/

Loyola University Maryland, Graduate Programs, School of Education, Program in Montessori Education, Baltimore, MD 21210-2699. Offers elementary education (M Ed); Montessori education (CAS). *Accreditation:* NCATE. *Degree requirements:* For master's, thesis. *Entrance requirements:* For master's, essay, transcripts. Additional exam requirements/recommendations for international students: Required—TOEFL (minimum score 550 paper-based), IELTS (minimum score 7). *Application deadline:* For fall admission, 5/1 priority date for domestic students, 5/1 for international students. Applications are processed on a rolling basis. Application fee: $60. *Expenses:* Contact institution. *Financial support:* Scholarships/grants available. Financial award application deadline: 4/15; financial award applicants required to submit FAFSA. *Unit head:* Jack Rice, Director, 410-617-2308, E-mail: jhrice@loyola.edu. *Application contact:* Office of Graduate Admission, 410-617-5020, E-mail: graduate@loyola.edu.
Website: https://www.loyola.edu/school-education/academics/graduate/montessori

Lynn University, Donald E. and Helen L. Ross College of Education, Boca Raton, FL 33431-5598. Offers educational leadership (M Ed, Ed D), including K-12 (Ed D), school administration K-12 (M Ed); exceptional student education (M Ed), including school administration K-12. *Program availability:* Part-time, evening/weekend, online learning. *Faculty:* 6 full-time (4 women), 4 part-time/adjunct (3 women). *Students:* 31 full-time (23 women), 62 part-time (42 women); includes 32 minority (20 Black or African American, non-Hispanic/Latino; 1 American Indian or Alaska Native, non-Hispanic/Latino; 10 Hispanic/Latino; 1 Two or more races, non-Hispanic/Latino), 3 international. Average age 36. 46 applicants, 78% accepted, 30 enrolled. In 2017, 24 master's, 22 doctorates awarded. *Degree requirements:* For master's, comprehensive exam, thesis (for some programs), completion of degree in maximum of four calendar years; minimum cumulative GPA of 3.0 and B grade or higher in each course; orientation seminar (one credit); minimum of 40 credits; FTCE ESE K-12 Exam; for doctorate, thesis/dissertation, mid-program review; minimum cumulative GPA of 3.25 and B grade or higher in each course. *Entrance requirements:* For master's, bachelor's degree from accredited institution, minimum undergraduate GPA of 3.0, official undergraduate and graduate transcripts of all academic coursework attempted, current résumé, statement of professional goals, writing sample, two recent letters of recommendation; for doctorate, professional practice statement that identifies applicant's goals and explains how Lynn's program will help attain them, official transcript showing conferral of master's degree, two letters of recommendation from previous professors or employers, current resume, interview. Additional exam requirements/recommendations for international students: Required—TOEFL (minimum score 550 paper-based; 80 iBT), IELTS (minimum score 6.5). *Application deadline:* For fall admission, 8/18 for domestic students, 8/4 for international students; for spring admission, 12/15 for domestic students, 12/1 for international students; for summer admission, 4/17 for domestic students, 4/3 for international students. Applications are processed on a rolling basis. Application fee: $45. Electronic applications accepted. *Expenses:* $740 per credit (for master's degrees); $850 per credit (for EdD). *Financial support:* Career-related internships or fieldwork, Federal Work-Study, scholarships/grants, tuition waivers (partial), and unspecified assistantships available. Support available to part-time students. Financial award application deadline: 3/1; financial award applicants required to submit FAFSA. *Faculty research:* Student achievement, students with learning differences, teacher and student retention, student motivation and cognition, neuroscience leadership and learning. *Unit head:* Dr. Kathleen Weigel, Dean, College of Education, 561-237-7441, E-mail: kweigel@lynn.edu. *Application contact:* Steven Pruitt, Director of Graduate and Undergraduate Evening Admission, 561-237-7834, Fax: 561-237-7100, E-mail: spruitt@lynn.edu.
Website: http://www.lynn.edu/academics/colleges/education

Manhattan College, Graduate Programs, School of Education and Health, Program in Special Education, Riverdale, NY 10471. Offers adolescence education students with disabilities generalist extension in English or math or social studies - grades 7-12 (MS Ed); bilingual education (Advanced Certificate); dual childhood/students with disabilities - grades 1-6 (MS Ed); students with disabilities - grades 1-6 (MS Ed). *Program availability:* Part-time, evening/weekend. *Degree requirements:* For master's, thesis, internship (if not certified). *Entrance requirements:* For master's, GRE, minimum GPA of 3.0. Additional exam requirements/recommendations for international students: Required—TOEFL (minimum score 550 paper-based; 80 iBT), IELTS (minimum score 6). Electronic applications accepted. Application fee is waived when completed online. *Expenses:* Contact institution.

Manhattanville College, School of Education, Jump Start Program, Purchase, NY 10577-2132. Offers childhood education and special education (grades 1-6) (MPS); early childhood education (birth-grade 2) (MAT); education (Advanced Certificate); English and special education (grades 5-12) (MPS); mathematics and special education (grades 5-12) (MPS); science and special education (grades 5-12) (MPS); social studies and special education (grades 5-12) (MPS); Spanish (grades 7-12) (MAT); TESOL (all grades) (MPS). *Program availability:* Part-time, evening/weekend. *Faculty:* 10 full-time (7 women), 39 part-time/adjunct (27 women). *Students:* 3 full-time (2 women), 40 part-time (24 women); includes 11 minority (3 Black or African American, non-Hispanic/Latino; 6 Hispanic/Latino; 1 Native Hawaiian or other Pacific Islander, non-Hispanic/Latino; 1 Two or more races, non-Hispanic/Latino). Average age 33. 25 applicants, 60% accepted, 7 enrolled. In 2017, 17 master's, 2 other advanced degrees awarded. *Degree requirements:* For master's, comprehensive exam (for some programs), thesis (for some programs), student teaching, research seminars, portfolios, internships, writing assessment; for Advanced Certificate, comprehensive exam (for some programs). *Entrance requirements:* For master's, GRE or MAT (for programs leading to certification), minimum GPA of 3.0, 2 letters of recommendation, interview, essay (2-3 page personal statement that describes reasons for choosing teaching or educational leadership as profession and philosophy of education), proof of immunization (for those born after 1957). Additional exam requirements/recommendations for international students: Required—TOEFL (minimum score 600 paper-based; 110 iBT); Recommended—IELTS (minimum score 8). *Application deadline:* Applications are processed on a rolling basis. Application fee: $75. Electronic applications accepted. *Expenses:* $915 per credit. *Financial support:* Teaching assistantships, career-related internships or fieldwork, Federal Work-Study, institutionally sponsored loans, scholarships/grants, and unspecified assistantships available. Financial award application deadline: 3/15; financial award applicants required to submit FAFSA. *Faculty research:* Early childhood and technology, professional development schools and community schools, students with emotional difficulties, literacy and adolescents,

mindfulness, changing suburbs institute, and community schools, studying the effects of the environment on special populations, the most difficult cases, students who are presented with multiple challenges: learning, behavioral and ACE experiences who see criminal behavior as a way to cope; working on giving them the tools they need to succeed. *Unit head:* Dr. Shelly Wepner, Dean, 914-323-3153, E-mail: shelly.wepner@mville.edu. *Application contact:* Alissa Wilson, Director, Graduate Admissions, 914-323-3150, Fax: 914-694-1732, E-mail: edschool@mville.edu.
Website: http://www.mville.edu/programs/jump-start

Manhattanville College, School of Education, Program in Childhood Education, Purchase, NY 10577-2132. Offers childhood education (grades 1-6) (MAT, MPS); early childhood (birth - grade 2) (MAT); special education: childhood (grades 1-6) (MPS, Certificate); special education: early childhood (birth - grade 2) and childhood (grades 1-6) (Certificate); special education: early childhood and childhood (birth - grade 6) (MPS). *Program availability:* Part-time, evening/weekend. *Faculty:* 3 full-time (all women), 7 part-time/adjunct (5 women). *Students:* 7 full-time (all women), 28 part-time (23 women); includes 8 minority (2 Black or African American, non-Hispanic/Latino; 6 Hispanic/Latino). Average age 29. 27 applicants, 93% accepted, 22 enrolled. In 2017, 13 master's awarded. *Degree requirements:* For master's, comprehensive exam (for some programs), thesis (for some programs), student teaching, research seminars, portfolios, internships, writing assessment; for Certificate, comprehensive exam (for some programs). *Entrance requirements:* For master's, GRE or MAT (for programs leading to certification), minimum GPA of 3.0, 2 letters of recommendation, interview, essay (2-3 page personal statement that describes reasons for choosing teaching or educational leadership as profession and philosophy of education), proof of immunization (for those born after 1957). Additional exam requirements/recommendations for international students: Required—TOEFL (minimum score 600 paper-based; 110 iBT); Recommended—IELTS (minimum score 8). *Application deadline:* Applications are processed on a rolling basis. Application fee: $75. Electronic applications accepted. *Expenses:* $915 per credit. *Financial support:* Teaching assistantships, career-related internships or fieldwork, Federal Work-Study, institutionally sponsored loans, scholarships/grants, and unspecified assistantships available. Financial award application deadline: 3/15; financial award applicants required to submit FAFSA. *Faculty research:* Early childhood and technology, professional development schools and community schools. *Unit head:* Dr. Shelly Wepner, Dean, 914-323-3153, Fax: 914-323-5493, E-mail: shelly.wepner@mville.edu. *Application contact:* Alissa Wilson, Director, Graduate Admissions, 914-323-3150, Fax: 914-694-1732, E-mail: edschool@mville.edu.
Website: http://www.mville.edu/programs/childhood-education

Manhattanville College, School of Education, Program in Early Childhood Education, Purchase, NY 10577-2132. Offers childhood education (grades 1-6) (MAT); early childhood and special education (birth-grade 2) (MPS); early childhood education (birth-grade 2) (MAT); special education (birth-grade 2) (MPS); special education (birth-grade 6) (MPS); special education: early childhood (birth - grade 2) and childhood (grades 1-6) (Certificate); special education: early childhood (birth-grade 2) (Certificate). *Program availability:* Part-time, evening/weekend. *Faculty:* 2 full-time (both women), 3 part-time/adjunct (all women). *Students:* 7 full-time (all women), 22 part-time (21 women); includes 1 minority (Hispanic/Latino). Average age 29. 21 applicants, 81% accepted, 12 enrolled. In 2017, 10 master's awarded. *Degree requirements:* For master's, comprehensive exam (for some programs), thesis (for some programs), student teaching, research seminars, portfolios, internships, writing assessment; for Certificate, comprehensive exam (for some programs). *Entrance requirements:* For master's, GRE or MAT (for programs leading to certification), minimum GPA of 3.0, 2 letters of recommendation, interview, essay (2-3 page personal statement that describes reasons for choosing teaching or educational leadership as profession and philosophy of education), proof of immunization (for those born after 1957). Additional exam requirements/recommendations for international students: Required—TOEFL (minimum score 600 paper-based; 110 iBT); Recommended—IELTS (minimum score 8). *Application deadline:* Applications are processed on a rolling basis. Application fee: $75. Electronic applications accepted. *Expenses:* $915 per credit. *Financial support:* Teaching assistantships, career-related internships or fieldwork, Federal Work-Study, institutionally sponsored loans, scholarships/grants, and unspecified assistantships available. Financial award application deadline: 3/15; financial award applicants required to submit FAFSA. *Faculty research:* Early childhood and technology. *Unit head:* Dr. Shelly Wepner, Dean, 914-323-3153, Fax: 914-323-5493, E-mail: shelly.wepner@mville.edu. *Application contact:* Alissa Wilson, Director, Graduate Admissions, 914-323-3150, Fax: 914-694-1732, E-mail: edschool@mville.edu.
Website: http://www.mville.edu/programs/early-childhood-education

Manhattanville College, School of Education, Program in Literacy Education, Purchase, NY 10577-2132. Offers literacy (birth-grade 6) and special education childhood (grades 1-6) (MPS); literacy 5-12 (MPS); literacy specialist (birth-grade 6) (MPS); literacy specialist (grades 5-12) (MPS); science of reading: multisensory instruction (Advanced Certificate). *Program availability:* Part-time, evening/weekend. *Faculty:* 4 full-time (all women), 8 part-time/adjunct (5 women). *Students:* 1 (woman) full-time, 21 part-time (20 women). Average age 31. 12 applicants, 92% accepted, 8 enrolled. In 2017, 7 master's, 3 Advanced Certificates awarded. *Degree requirements:* For master's, comprehensive exam (for some programs), thesis (for some programs), student teaching, research seminars, portfolios, internships, writing assessment; for Advanced Certificate, comprehensive exam (for some programs). *Entrance requirements:* For master's, GRE or MAT (for programs leading to certification), minimum GPA of 3.0, 2 letters of recommendation, interview, essay (2-3 page personal statement that describes reasons for choosing teaching or educational leadership as profession and philosophy of education), proof of immunization (for those born after 1957). Additional exam requirements/recommendations for international students: Required—TOEFL (minimum score 600 paper-based; 110 iBT); Recommended—IELTS (minimum score 8). *Application deadline:* Applications are processed on a rolling basis. Application fee: $75. Electronic applications accepted. *Expenses:* $915 per credit. *Financial support:* Teaching assistantships, career-related internships or fieldwork, Federal Work-Study, institutionally sponsored loans, scholarships/grants, and unspecified assistantships available. Financial award application deadline: 3/15; financial award applicants required to submit FAFSA. *Faculty research:* Power of story for literacy development, English learners. *Total annual research expenditures:* $800. *Unit head:* Dr. Shelly Wepner, Dean, 914-323-3153, Fax: 914-323-5493, E-mail: shelly.wepner@mville.edu. *Application contact:* Alissa Wilson, Director, Graduate Admissions, 914-323-3150, Fax: 914-694-1732, E-mail: edschool@mville.edu.
Website: http://www.mville.edu/programs/literacy-education

Manhattanville College, School of Education, Program in Special Education, Purchase, NY 10577-2132. Offers childhood (grades 1-6) (MPS); childhood education (grades 1-6) and special education (MPS); early childhood (birth-grade 2) (MPS); early childhood (birth-grade 2) and special education (MPS); early childhood and childhood (birth-grade 6) (MPS); English (5-9 and 7-12) (MPS); grades 7-12 generalist (MPS); literacy (birth-grade 6) and special education childhood (grades 1-6) (MPS); literacy 5-12 (MPS); mathematics (5-9 and 7-12) (MPS); science (biology or chemistry 5-9 and 7-12) (MPS); social studies (5-9 and 7-12) (MPS); special education: childhood (grades 1-6) (Certificate); special education: early childhood (birth-grade 2) and childhood (grades 1-

Early Childhood Education

6) (Certificate); special education: early childhood (birth-grade 2) (Certificate); special education: grades 7-12 generalist (Certificate). *Program availability:* Part-time, evening/weekend. *Faculty:* 5 full-time (3 women), 24 part-time/adjunct (16 women). *Students:* 77 full-time (69 women), 154 part-time (132 women); includes 33 minority (9 Black or African American, non-Hispanic/Latino; 2 Asian, non-Hispanic/Latino; 22 Hispanic/Latino), 1 international. Average age 28. 87 applicants, 77% accepted, 57 enrolled. In 2017, 86 master's, 2 Certificates awarded. *Degree requirements:* For master's, comprehensive exam (for some programs), thesis (for some programs), student teaching, research seminars, portfolios, internships, writing assessment; for Certificate, comprehensive exam (for some programs). *Entrance requirements:* For master's, GRE or MAT (for programs leading to certification), minimum GPA of 3.0, 2 letters of recommendation, interview, essay (2-3 page personal statement that describes reasons for choosing teaching or educational leadership as profession and philosophy of education), proof of immunization (for those born after 1957). Additional exam requirements/recommendations for international students: Required—TOEFL (minimum score 600 paper-based; 110 iBT); Recommended—IELTS (minimum score 8). *Application deadline:* Applications are processed on a rolling basis. Application fee: $75. Electronic applications accepted. *Expenses:* $915 per credit. *Financial support:* Teaching assistantships, career-related internships or fieldwork, Federal Work-Study, institutionally sponsored loans, scholarships/grants, and unspecified assistantships available. Financial award application deadline: 3/15; financial award applicants required to submit FAFSA. *Faculty research:* Students with emotional difficulties, literacy and adolescents, mindfulness, studying the effects of the environment on special populations, the most difficult cases, students who are presented with multiple challenges: learning, behavioral and ACE experiences who see criminal behavior as a way to cope; working on giving them the tools they need to succeed emotionally and cognitively despite the odds stacked against them. *Unit head:* Dr. Shelly Wepner, Dean, 914-323-3153, Fax: 914-323-5493, E-mail: shelly.wepner@mville.edu. *Application contact:* Alissa Wilson, Director, Graduate Admissions, 914-323-3150, Fax: 914-694-1732, E-mail: edschool@mville.edu.
Website: http://www.mville.edu/programs/special-education

Martin Luther College, Graduate Studies, New Ulm, MN 56073. Offers early childhood director (MS Ed Admin); educational technology (MS Ed); instruction (MS Ed); leadership (MS Ed); principal (MS Ed Admin); special education (MS Ed). *Program availability:* Part-time, evening/weekend, online learning. *Faculty:* 8 full-time (1 woman), 21 part-time/adjunct (10 women). *Students:* 1 (woman) full-time, 81 part-time (28 women); includes 2 minority (1 Asian, non-Hispanic/Latino; 1 Two or more races, non-Hispanic/Latino), 2 international. Average age 37. 23 applicants, 100% accepted, 23 enrolled. In 2017, 25 master's awarded. *Degree requirements:* For master's, capstone project or comprehensive exam. *Entrance requirements:* For master's, undergraduate degree in education from an accredited college or university, minimum undergraduate GPA of 3.0. Additional exam requirements/recommendations for international students: Required—TOEFL (minimum score 550 paper-based; 80 iBT); Recommended—IELTS (minimum score 6.5). *Application deadline:* Applications are processed on a rolling basis. Application fee: $35. Electronic applications accepted. *Expenses:* $315 per credit. *Financial support:* In 2017–18, 4 students received support. Scholarships/grants available. Financial award application deadline: 9/1. *Faculty research:* Principal effectiveness, principal support, cognitive load in math instruction, reading strategies in multigrade classrooms, mentor provided professional development for new teachers. *Unit head:* John E. Meyer, Director of Graduate Studies, 507-354-8221 Ext. 398, E-mail: meyerjd@mlc-wels.edu.
Website: https://mlc-wels.edu/graduate-studies/

Marygrove College, Graduate Studies, Detroit, MI 48221-2599. Offers autism spectrum disorders (M Ed, Certificate); curriculum instruction and assessment (MAT); educational leadership (MA); educational technology (M Ed); effective teaching in the 21st century-classroom focus (MAT); effective teaching in the 21st century-technology focus (MAT); human resource management (MA, Certificate); mathematics 6-8 (MAT); mathematics K-5 (MAT); reading and literacy K-6 (MAT); reading specialist (M Ed); school administrator (Certificate); social justice (MA); special education (MAT); special education - learning disabilities (M Ed); teaching - pre-elementary education (M Ed); teaching - pre-secondary education (M Ed). *Program availability:* Part-time, evening/weekend, 100% online, blended/hybrid learning. *Students:* 163 full-time (123 women), 264 part-time (186 women). Average age 34. *Entrance requirements:* For master's, all official bachelor's transcripts. Additional exam requirements/recommendations for international students: Required—TOEFL (minimum score 550 paper-based; 80 iBT). *Application deadline:* Applications are processed on a rolling basis. Electronic applications accepted. *Expenses: Tuition:* Part-time $590 per credit hour. *Required fees:* $120 per semester. One-time fee: $25 part-time. *Financial support:* Applicants required to submit FAFSA. *Unit head:* Marygrove College Admissions, 313-927-1240, E-mail: info@marygrove.edu. *Application contact:* Marygrove College Admissions, 313-927-1240, E-mail: info@marygrove.edu.

Maryville University of Saint Louis, School of Education, St. Louis, MO 63141-7299. Offers early childhood education (MA Ed); educational leadership (Ed D); elementary education (MA Ed); higher education leadership (Ed D); literacy specialist (MA Ed); middle grades education (MA Ed); secondary teaching and inquiry (MA Ed); teacher as leader (MA Ed, Ed D). *Accreditation:* NCATE. *Program availability:* Part-time, 100% online, blended/hybrid learning. *Faculty:* 20 full-time (14 women), 19 part-time/adjunct (13 women). *Students:* 6 full-time (4 women), 337 part-time (250 women); includes 101 minority (85 Black or African American, non-Hispanic/Latino; 4 Asian, non-Hispanic/Latino; 8 Hispanic/Latino; 4 Two or more races, non-Hispanic/Latino), 3 international. Average age 38. In 2017, 34 master's, 67 doctorates awarded. *Degree requirements:* For master's, thesis, project. *Entrance requirements:* For master's, minimum cumulative GPA of 3.0, 3 professional recommendations, essays, interview with program faculty; for doctorate, minimum GPA of 3.0, 3 professional recommendations, essay, interview, on-site writing sample. Additional exam requirements/recommendations for international students: Required—TOEFL (minimum score 550 paper-based). *Application deadline:* Applications are processed on a rolling basis. Electronic applications accepted. *Expenses:* Contact institution. *Financial support:* Career-related internships or fieldwork, Federal Work-Study, tuition waivers (partial), and professional educator discounts available. Financial award application deadline: 4/1; financial award applicants required to submit FAFSA. *Faculty research:* Collaboration with public schools, pre-service program development, mathematics, diversity, literacy. *Unit head:* Dr. Cathy Bear, Dean, 314-529-9692, Fax: 314-529-9921, E-mail: cbear@maryville.edu. *Application contact:* Stacey Ruffin, Coordinator of Clinical Experiences and Graduate Programs, 314-529-9542, Fax: 314-529-9921, E-mail: teachered@maryville.edu.
Website: http://www.maryville.edu/ed/graduate-programs/

Marywood University, Academic Affairs, Reap College of Education and Human Development, Department of Education, Program in Early Childhood Intervention, Scranton, PA 18509-1598. Offers MS. *Accreditation:* NCATE. *Program availability:* Part-time. Electronic applications accepted. *Faculty research:* Montessori education, developmentally-appropriate practice, child care environment.

McNeese State University, Doré School of Graduate Studies, Burton College of Education, Department of Education Professions, Program in Early Childhood Education Grades PK-3, Lake Charles, LA 70609. Offers Postbaccalaureate Certificate. *Entrance requirements:* For degree, PRAXIS, 2 letters of recommendation, autobiography. *Application deadline:* For fall admission, 5/15 priority date for domestic and international students; for spring admission, 10/15 priority date for domestic and international students. Applications are processed on a rolling basis. Application fee: $30 for international students). *Financial support:* Application deadline: 5/1. *Unit head:* Dr. Veronica Faye White, Head, 337-475-5400, Fax: 337-475-5272, E-mail: vfwhite@mcneese.edu. *Application contact:* Dr. Dustin M. Hebert, Director of Doré School of Graduate Studies, 337-475-5396, Fax: 337-475-5397, E-mail: admissions@mcneese.edu.

Mercer University, Graduate Studies, Cecil B. Day Campus, Tift College of Education (Atlanta), Atlanta, GA 30341. Offers curriculum and instruction (PhD); early childhood education (M Ed, MAT, Ed S); educational leadership (PhD), including higher education leadership, P-12 school leadership; educational leadership P-12 (M Ed, Ed S); higher education leadership (M Ed); independent and charter school leadership (M Ed); middle grades education (M Ed, MAT); secondary education (M Ed, MAT); teacher leadership (Ed S). *Accreditation:* NCATE. *Program availability:* Part-time, evening/weekend. *Faculty:* 30 full-time (18 women), 34 part-time/adjunct (27 women). *Students:* 159 full-time (131 women), 284 part-time (229 women); includes 264 minority (232 Black or African American, non-Hispanic/Latino; 1 American Indian or Alaska Native, non-Hispanic/Latino; 9 Asian, non-Hispanic/Latino; 18 Hispanic/Latino; 4 Two or more races, non-Hispanic/Latino), 2 international. Average age 35. In 2017, 137 master's, 22 doctorates, 40 other advanced degrees awarded. *Degree requirements:* For master's and Ed S, research project; for doctorate, comprehensive exam, thesis/dissertation. *Entrance requirements:* For master's, GRE or MAT, minimum undergraduate GPA of 2.75; for doctorate, GRE; for Ed S, GRE or MAT, minimum GPA of 3.25; 3 years of certified teaching experience (for educational leadership and teacher leadership). Additional exam requirements/recommendations for international students: Required—TOEFL (minimum score 80 iBT). *Application deadline:* For fall admission, 8/1 for domestic and international students; for spring admission, 12/1 for domestic and international students; for summer admission, 5/1 for domestic and international students. Applications are processed on a rolling basis. Application fee: $25 ($50 for international students). Electronic applications accepted. *Expenses:* Contact institution. *Financial support:* Federal Work-Study and unspecified assistantships available. Support available to part-time students. Financial award application deadline: 5/1; financial award applicants required to submit FAFSA. *Faculty research:* Educational technology, multicultural and minority issues in education, educational leadership (P-12 and higher education), school discipline and school bullying, standards-based mathematics education. *Unit head:* Dr. Scott Davis, Dean, 478-301-2110, Fax: 478-301-5576.
Website: http://education.mercer.edu/

Mercer University, Graduate Studies, Macon Campus, Tift College of Education (Macon), Macon, GA 31207. Offers curriculum and instruction (PhD); early childhood education (M Ed, Ed S); educational leadership (M Ed, PhD, Ed S), including higher education (PhD), P-12; higher education leadership (M Ed); independent and charter school leadership (M Ed); secondary education (MAT), including STEM; teacher leadership (Ed S). *Accreditation:* NCATE. *Program availability:* Part-time, evening/weekend, 100% online, blended/hybrid learning. *Faculty:* 13 full-time (8 women), 1 part-time/adjunct (0 women). *Students:* 33 full-time (18 women), 51 part-time (37 women); includes 49 minority (44 Black or African American, non-Hispanic/Latino; 2 Asian, non-Hispanic/Latino; 2 Hispanic/Latino; 1 Two or more races, non-Hispanic/Latino), 1 international. Average age 32. In 2017, 22 master's, 17 doctorates awarded. *Degree requirements:* For master's, research project report; for doctorate, comprehensive exam, thesis/dissertation. *Entrance requirements:* For master's, GRE or MAT, minimum GPA of 2.75; for doctorate, GRE, minimum GPA of 3.5; interview; writing sample; 3 recommendations; for Ed S, GRE or MAT, minimum GPA of 3.5 (for teacher leadership), 3.0 (for educational leadership). Additional exam requirements/recommendations for international students: Required—TOEFL (minimum score 80 iBT). *Application deadline:* For fall admission, 8/1 for domestic and international students; for spring admission, 12/1 for domestic and international students. Applications are processed on a rolling basis. Application fee: $35. Electronic applications accepted. *Expenses:* Contact institution. *Financial support:* Federal Work-Study, institutionally sponsored loans, and unspecified assistantships available. Support available to part-time students. Financial award application deadline: 5/1; financial award applicants required to submit FAFSA. *Faculty research:* Teacher effectiveness, specific learning disabilities, inclusion. *Unit head:* Dr. Scott Davis, Dean, 478-301-2110, Fax: 478-301-5576, E-mail: davis_ds@mercer.edu.
Website: http://education.mercer.edu/

Mercy College, School of Education, Program in Early Childhood Education, Dobbs Ferry, NY 10522-1189. Offers MS. *Program availability:* Part-time, evening/weekend, blended/hybrid learning. *Students:* 91 full-time (88 women), 175 part-time (171 women); includes 144 minority (51 Black or African American, non-Hispanic/Latino; 1 American Indian or Alaska Native, non-Hispanic/Latino; 10 Asian, non-Hispanic/Latino; 80 Hispanic/Latino; 1 Native Hawaiian or other Pacific Islander, non-Hispanic/Latino; 1 Two or more races, non-Hispanic/Latino). Average age 32. 117 applicants, 40% accepted, 28 enrolled. In 2017, 221 master's awarded. *Degree requirements:* For master's, comprehensive exam (for some programs). *Entrance requirements:* For master's, GRE, resume, undergraduate transcript. Additional exam requirements/recommendations for international students: Required—TOEFL (minimum score 600 paper-based; 100 iBT), IELTS (minimum score 8). *Application deadline:* For fall admission, 8/1 for international students. Applications are processed on a rolling basis. Application fee: $40. Electronic applications accepted. *Expenses: Tuition:* Full-time $15,426; part-time $857 per credit hour. *Required fees:* $630; $158 per term. Tuition and fees vary according to course load, degree level and program. *Financial support:* Career-related internships or fieldwork, Federal Work-Study, scholarships/grants, and unspecified assistantships available. Support available to part-time students. Financial award applicants required to submit FAFSA. *Unit head:* Dr. Rose Rudnitski, Dean for the School of Education, 914-674-7447, Fax: 914-674-7352, E-mail: rrudnitski@mercy.edu. *Application contact:* Allison Gurdineer, Senior Director of Admissions, 877-637-2946, Fax: 914-674-7382, E-mail: admissions@mercy.edu.
Website: https://www.mercy.edu/degrees-programs/ms-early-childhood-education-birth-grade-2

Merrimack College, School of Education and Social Policy, North Andover, MA 01845-5800. Offers community engagement (M Ed), including community organizations, higher education, PreK-12 education; criminology and criminal justice (MS); curriculum and instruction (M Ed); early childhood education (M Ed); educational leadership (CAGS), including instructional leadership; elementary education (M Ed); English as a second language (PreK-6) (M Ed); high school education (M Ed); higher education (M Ed), including leadership and organizational development, student affairs; middle school education (M Ed); moderate disabilities (PreK-8) (M Ed); school counseling (M Ed). *Program availability:* Part-time, evening/weekend, 100% online courses with immersion events and in-classroom practicum close to home. *Faculty:* 15 full-time, 36 part-time/adjunct. *Students:* 212 full-time (175 women), 121 part-time (101 women); includes 42 minority (6 Black or African American, non-Hispanic/Latino; 6 Asian, non-Hispanic/Latino; 27 Hispanic/Latino; 3 Two or more races, non-Hispanic/Latino), 3 international.

Average age 27. 420 applicants, 84% accepted, 250 enrolled. In 2017, 177 master's awarded. *Degree requirements:* For master's, practicum, portfolio, and state test (for licensure track); capstone (for higher education, curriculum and instruction, and community engagement tracks); for CAGS, capstone. *Entrance requirements:* For master's, Massachusetts Teacher Education Licensure (MTEL), official transcripts from other colleges, resume, personal statement, 2 letters of recommendation. Additional exam requirements/recommendations for international students: Required—TOEFL (minimum score 84 iBT), IELTS (minimum score 6.5), PTE (minimum score 56). *Application deadline:* For fall admission, 8/24 for domestic students, 7/30 for international students; for spring admission, 1/10 for domestic students, 12/10 for international students; for summer admission, 5/10 for domestic students, 4/10 for international students. Applications are processed on a rolling basis. Application fee: $0. Electronic applications accepted. *Expenses:* Contact institution. *Financial support:* Fellowships with full tuition reimbursements, career-related internships or fieldwork, scholarships/grants, and health care benefits available. Support available to part-time students. Financial award application deadline: 5/1; financial award applicants required to submit FAFSA. *Application contact:* Alyssa Orlando, Graduate Admissions Counselor, 978-837-3563, E-mail: orlandoaf@merrimack.edu.
Website: http://www.merrimack.edu/academics/graduate/education/

Middle Tennessee State University, College of Graduate Studies, College of Education, Department of Elementary and Special Education, Major in Curriculum and Instruction, Murfreesboro, TN 37132. Offers early childhood education (M Ed); elementary education (M Ed, Ed S); middle school education (M Ed). *Accreditation:* NCATE. *Program availability:* Part-time, evening/weekend, online learning. *Degree requirements:* For master's, comprehensive exam; for Ed S, comprehensive exam, thesis or alternative. *Entrance requirements:* For master's and Ed S, GRE, MAT or PRAXIS. Additional exam requirements/recommendations for international students: Required—TOEFL (minimum score 525 paper-based; 71 iBT) or IELTS (minimum score 6). Electronic applications accepted.

Millersville University of Pennsylvania, College of Graduate Studies and Adult Learning, College of Education and Human Services, Department of Early, Middle, and Exceptional Education, Program in Early Childhood Education, Millersville, PA 17551-0302. Offers early childhood education (M Ed), including preK-4. *Program availability:* Part-time, evening/weekend. *Faculty:* 9 full-time (4 women), 11 part-time/adjunct (8 women). *Students:* 6 full-time (5 women), 24 part-time (19 women); includes 3 minority (1 Black or African American, non-Hispanic/Latino; 2 Hispanic/Latino). Average age 32. 20 applicants, 100% accepted, 12 enrolled. In 2017, 8 master's awarded. *Degree requirements:* For master's, comprehensive exam, thesis optional. *Entrance requirements:* For master's, teaching certificate (unless enrolled in post baccalaureate certification concurrently). Additional exam requirements/recommendations for international students: Required—TOEFL (minimum score 80 iBT), IELTS (minimum score 6.5), PTE (minimum score 60). *Application deadline:* Applications are processed on a rolling basis. Application fee: $40. Electronic applications accepted. *Expenses:* $500 per credit resident tuition and fees; $750 per credit non-resident tuition and fees; $114.75 per credit general fee (maximum of 12 credits); technology fee $27 per credit (resident), $39 per credit (non-resident). *Financial support:* In 2017–18, 2 students received support. Unspecified assistantships available. Financial award application deadline: 3/15; financial award applicants required to submit FAFSA. *Faculty research:* Play-based pedagogy, early childhood teacher preparation, child development, STEM integration. *Unit head:* Dr. Marcia Nell, Department Chair, 717-871-7344, E-mail: marcia.nell@millersville.edu. *Application contact:* Dr. Victor S. DeSantis, Dean of College of Graduate Studies and Adult Learning/Associate Provost for Civic and Community Engagement, 717-871-7619, Fax: 717-871-7954, E-mail: victor.desantis@millersville.edu.
Website: http://www.millersville.edu/academics/eled/graduate-programs/early-childhood-education.php#MasterofEducationDegreeinEarlyChildhoodEducation

Milligan College, Area of Education, Milligan College, TN 37682. Offers combined preK-3/K-5 education (M Ed); educational leadership (Ed D, Ed S); K-5 education (M Ed); middle grades education (M Ed); preK-3 education (M Ed); preK-3 special education (M Ed); secondary education (M Ed). *Accreditation:* NCATE. *Program availability:* Part-time. *Faculty:* 6 full-time (4 women), 3 part-time/adjunct (2 women). *Students:* 27 full-time (20 women), 20 part-time (11 women); includes 2 minority (1 Hispanic/Latino; 1 Two or more races, non-Hispanic/Latino), 1 international. Average age 34. 17 applicants, 35% accepted, 6 enrolled. In 2017, 21 master's awarded. *Degree requirements:* For master's, thesis, portfolio, research project; for doctorate, thesis/dissertation, portfolio, research project. *Entrance requirements:* For master's, MAT, GRE General Test, ACT, SAT, or PRAXIS, undergraduate degree and supporting transcripts, professional recommendations, interview; for doctorate, MAT or GRE, master's degree and supporting transcripts, demonstrated scholastic ability, recognized leadership role within education, professional recommendations, essay/personal statement, portfolio (professional development plan, evidence of ability, knowledge and qualities), interview. Additional exam requirements/recommendations for international students: Required—TOEFL (minimum score 550 paper-based, 79 iBT) or IELTS (6.5). *Application deadline:* For fall admission, 8/1 priority date for domestic students, 6/1 for international students; for spring admission, 11/15 priority date for domestic students, 12/1 for international students; for summer admission, 4/1 for domestic students. Applications are processed on a rolling basis. Application fee: $30. Electronic applications accepted. *Expenses:* $360 per hour tuition (M Ed), $475 per hour (Ed D and Ed S), $325 per semester tech/activity fees. *Financial support:* Scholarships/grants available. Financial award application deadline: 12/1; financial award applicants required to submit FAFSA. *Faculty research:* Assessment; school mental health; literacy; technology; educator preparation. *Unit head:* Dr. Angela Hilton-Prillhart, Area Chair of Education, 423-461-8769, Fax: 423-461-3103, E-mail: anhilton-prillhart@milligan.edu. *Application contact:* Melissa Dillow, Graduate Admissions Recruiter, Education, 423-461-8306, Fax: 423-461-8982, E-mail: msdillow@milligan.edu.
Website: http://www.Milligan.edu/GPS

Mills College, Graduate Studies, Program in Infant Mental Health, Oakland, CA 94613-1000. Offers MA. *Program availability:* Part-time. *Faculty:* 2 full-time (both women). *Students:* 6 full-time (all women), 3 part-time (2 women); includes 3 minority (2 Hispanic/Latino; 1 Two or more races, non-Hispanic/Latino), 1 international. Average age 28. 15 applicants, 67% accepted, 6 enrolled. In 2017, 9 master's awarded. *Entrance requirements:* For master's, bachelor's degree, preferably in psychology, and the following prerequisite courses: fundamentals of psychology, developmental psychology, psychopathology, analytical methods/statistics, and research methods; three letters of recommendation; statement of purpose essay. Additional exam requirements/recommendations for international students: Required—TOEFL (minimum score 550 paper-based; 80 iBT) or IELTS (minimum score 6). *Application deadline:* For fall admission, 12/31 priority date for domestic students, 12/15 for international students. Applications are processed on a rolling basis. Electronic applications accepted. *Expenses: Tuition:* Full-time $33,480; part-time $1000 per credit. *Required fees:* $1479. Tuition and fees vary according to program. *Financial support:* In 2017–18, 7 students received support, including 7 fellowships with tuition reimbursements available (averaging $3,661 per year); teaching assistantships with tuition reimbursements available and scholarships/grants also available. Financial award application deadline:

2/1; financial award applicants required to submit FAFSA. *Faculty research:* Development and sequelae of attachment in children and adults in normative and clinical/risk populations, identifying the mental health needs of young children who have experienced extraordinary traumatic situations during critical points in their early development, examining the effects of early childhood trauma, work on helping professionals' psychological well-being. *Unit head:* Linda Perez, Professor of Education, 510-430-2328, Fax: 510-430-2159, E-mail: lmperez@mills.edu. *Application contact:* Robynne Lofton, Director of Admissions, 510-430-3295, Fax: 510-430-2159, E-mail: grad-admission@mills.edu.
Website: http://www.mills.edu/imh/

Mississippi State University, College of Education, Department of Curriculum, Instruction and Special Education, Mississippi State, MS 39762. Offers early childhood education (PhD); elementary education (MS, PhD, Ed S), including early childhood education (MS), general elementary education (MS), middle level education (MS); general curriculum and instruction (PhD); reading education (PhD); secondary education (MAT, MS, PhD, Ed S); special education (MAT, MS, PhD, Ed S). *Accreditation:* NCATE. *Program availability:* Part-time, evening/weekend. *Faculty:* 22 full-time (16 women), 1 (woman) part-time/adjunct. *Students:* 38 full-time (26 women), 170 part-time (131 women); includes 46 minority (37 Black or African American, non-Hispanic/Latino; 4 American Indian or Alaska Native, non-Hispanic/Latino; 2 Hispanic/Latino; 1 Native Hawaiian or other Pacific Islander, non-Hispanic/Latino; 2 Two or more races, non-Hispanic/Latino), 4 international. Average age 32. 88 applicants, 53% accepted, 39 enrolled. In 2017, 68 master's, 4 doctorates, 5 other advanced degrees awarded. *Degree requirements:* For master's, comprehensive exam; for doctorate, thesis/dissertation; for Ed S, comprehensive exam, thesis or alternative. *Entrance requirements:* For master's, GRE, minimum GPA of 2.75 in junior and senior year, eligibility for initial teacher certification; for doctorate, GRE, minimum GPA of 3.4 on previous graduate work; for Ed S, GRE, minimum GPA of 3.2 on master's degree. Additional exam requirements/recommendations for international students: Required—TOEFL (minimum score 550 paper-based; 79 iBT); Recommended—IELTS (minimum score 6.5). *Application deadline:* For fall admission, 3/1 priority date for domestic students, 5/1 for international students; for spring admission, 9/1 priority date for domestic students, 9/1 for international students. Applications are processed on a rolling basis. Application fee: $60 ($80 for international students). Electronic applications accepted. *Expenses: Tuition,* state resident: full-time $8318; part-time $462.12 per credit hour. Tuition, nonresident: full-time $22,358; part-time $1242.12 per credit hour. *Required fees:* $110; $12.24 per credit hour. $6.12 per semester. *Financial support:* In 2017–18, 6 research assistantships with partial tuition reimbursements (averaging $11,307 per year) were awarded; Federal Work-Study, institutionally sponsored loans, scholarships/grants, and unspecified assistantships also available. Financial award application deadline: 4/1; financial award applicants required to submit FAFSA. *Faculty research:* Early childhood education, reading, rural schools, multicultural education, use of technology in instruction. *Unit head:* Dr. Linda Cornelious, Professor and Interim Head, 662-325-3747, Fax: 662-325-7857, E-mail: lcornelious@colled.msstate.edu. *Application contact:* Laken Drinker, Admissions and Enrollment Assistant, 662-325-8951, E-mail: ldrinker@grad.msstate.edu.
Website: http://www.cise.msstate.edu/

Mississippi State University, College of Education, Educational Leadership Program, Mississippi State, MS 39762. Offers community college education (MAT); community college leadership (PhD); higher education leadership (PhD); P-12 school leadership (PhD); school administration (MS, Ed S); student affairs and higher education (MS); workforce education leadership (MS). MS in workforce education leadership held jointly with Alcorn State University. *Faculty:* 12 full-time (9 women). *Students:* 62 full-time (33 women), 149 part-time (93 women); includes 94 minority (79 Black or African American, non-Hispanic/Latino; 5 American Indian or Alaska Native, non-Hispanic/Latino; 4 Hispanic/Latino; 1 Native Hawaiian or other Pacific Islander, non-Hispanic/Latino; 5 Two or more races, non-Hispanic/Latino). Average age 36. 95 applicants, 79% accepted, 64 enrolled. In 2017, 41 master's, 32 doctorates, 7 other advanced degrees awarded. *Degree requirements:* For master's and Ed S, comprehensive exam, thesis; for doctorate, comprehensive exam, thesis/dissertation. *Entrance requirements:* For master's, GRE, minimum GPA of 2.75 in junior and senior courses; for doctorate, GRE, minimum GPA of 3.4 on previous graduate work; for Ed S, GRE, minimum GPA of 3.2, master's degree. Additional exam requirements/recommendations for international students: Required—TOEFL (minimum score 550 paper-based; 79 iBT); Recommended—IELTS (minimum score 6.5). *Application deadline:* For fall admission, 7/1 for domestic students, 5/1 for international students; for spring admission, 11/1 for domestic students, 9/1 for international students. Application fee: $60 ($80 for international students). Electronic applications accepted. *Expenses: Tuition,* state resident: full-time $8318; part-time $462.12 per credit hour. Tuition, nonresident: full-time $22,358; part-time $1242.12 per credit hour. *Required fees:* $110; $12.24 per credit hour. $6.12 per semester. *Financial support:* In 2017–18, 1 research assistantship with full tuition reimbursement (averaging $10,879 per year) was awarded; Federal Work-Study, institutionally sponsored loans, and unspecified assistantships also available. Financial award application deadline: 4/1; financial award applicants required to submit FAFSA. *Unit head:* Dr. Eric Moyen, Associate Professor and Head, 662-325-0969, Fax: 662-325-0975, E-mail: em1621@msstate.edu. *Application contact:* Nathan Drake, Admissions and Enrollment Assistant, 662-325-3804, E-mail: ndrake@grad.msstate.edu.
Website: http://www.educationalleadership.msstate.edu/

Missouri Southern State University, Program in Early Childhood Education, Joplin, MO 64801-1595. Offers MS Ed. Program offered jointly with Northwest Missouri State University. *Accreditation:* NCATE. *Entrance requirements:* For master's, GRE, minimum cumulative undergraduate GPA of 2.5.

Missouri State University, Graduate College, College of Education, Department of Childhood Education and Family Studies, Springfield, MO 65897. Offers early childhood and family development (MS); elementary education (MS Ed). *Program availability:* Part-time. *Faculty:* 11 full-time (8 women), 2 part-time/adjunct (both women). *Students:* 18 full-time (16 women), 94 part-time (89 women); includes 13 minority (5 Black or African American, non-Hispanic/Latino; 3 Asian, non-Hispanic/Latino; 2 Hispanic/Latino; 3 Two or more races, non-Hispanic/Latino), 2 international. Average age 25. 73 applicants, 56% accepted, 27 enrolled. In 2017, 62 master's awarded. *Degree requirements:* For master's, comprehensive exam. *Entrance requirements:* For master's, GRE, minimum GPA of 3.0. Additional exam requirements/recommendations for international students: Required—TOEFL (minimum score 550 paper-based; 79 iBT), IELTS (minimum score 6). *Application deadline:* For fall admission, 7/20 priority date for domestic students, 5/1 for international students; for spring admission, 12/20 priority date for domestic students, 9/1 for international students; for summer admission, 5/20 priority date for domestic students. Applications are processed on a rolling basis. Application fee: $35 ($50 for international students). Electronic applications accepted. *Expenses:* Tuition, state resident: full-time $2915; part-time $2021 per credit hour. Tuition, nonresident: full-time $5354; part-time $3647 per credit hour. *International tuition:* $11,992 full-time. *Required fees:* $173; $173 per credit hour. Tuition and fees vary according to class time, course level, course load, degree level, campus/location and program. *Financial support:* Federal Work-Study, institutionally sponsored loans, scholarships/grants, and

Early Childhood Education

unspecified assistantships available. Financial award application deadline: 3/31; financial award applicants required to submit FAFSA. *Faculty research:* Infant development, play advocacy, building mathematical concepts. *Unit head:* Dr. Denise Cunningham, Department Head, 417-836-8915, Fax: 417-836-8900, E-mail: cefs@missouristate.edu. *Application contact:* Stephanie Praschan, Director, Graduate Enrollment Management, 417-836-5330, Fax: 417-836-6200, E-mail: stephaniepraschan@missouristate.edu.
Website: http://education.missouristate.edu/cefs/

Missouri Western State University, Program in Assessment, St. Joseph, MO 64507-2294. Offers K-12 cross-categorical special education (MAS); TESOL (MAS, Graduate Certificate); writing (MAS). *Program availability:* Part-time. *Students:* 29 part-time (25 women); includes 1 minority (Black or African American, non-Hispanic/Latino). Average age 38. 8 applicants, 100% accepted, 4 enrolled. In 2017, 9 master's, 3 other advanced degrees awarded. *Entrance requirements:* For master's, minimum GPA of 2.75. Additional exam requirements/recommendations for international students: Recommended—TOEFL (minimum score 79 iBT), IELTS (minimum score 6). *Application deadline:* For fall admission, 7/15 for domestic and international students; for spring admission, 10/1 for domestic and international students; for summer admission, 3/15 for domestic students. Applications are processed on a rolling basis. Application fee: $45 ($50 for international students). Electronic applications accepted. *Expenses:* Tuition, state resident: full-time $6391; part-time $336 per credit hour. Tuition, nonresident: full-time $11,483; part-time $604 per credit hour. *Required fees:* $542; $99 per credit hour. $176 per semester. One-time fee: $45. Tuition and fees vary according to course load and program. *Financial support:* Scholarships/grants and unspecified assistantships available. Support available to part-time students. *Unit head:* Dr. Susan Bashinski, Director of Graduate Programs in Education, 816-271-5629, E-mail: sbashinski@missouriwestern.edu. *Application contact:* Dr. Benjamin D. Caldwell, Dean of the Graduate School, 816-271-4394, Fax: 816-271-4525, E-mail: graduate@missouriwestern.edu.
Website: https://www.missouriwestern.edu/masa/

Molloy College, Graduate Education Program, Rockville Centre, NY 11571-5002. Offers adolescent education in biology (MS); adolescent special education (Advanced Certificate); bilingual extension (Advanced Certificate); childhood education (MS); childhood special education (Advanced Certificate); early childhood education (MS); educational technology (MS); English (MS); mathematics (MS); social studies (MS); Spanish (MS); special education on both childhood and adolescent levels (MS); teaching English to speakers of other languages (TESOL) in grades pre-K to 12 (MS); TESOL (Advanced Certificate). *Accreditation:* NCATE. *Program availability:* Part-time, evening/weekend. *Faculty:* 18 full-time (17 women), 11 part-time/adjunct (9 women). *Students:* 102 full-time (80 women), 217 part-time (167 women); includes 65 minority (16 Black or African American, non-Hispanic/Latino; 7 Asian, non-Hispanic/Latino; 38 Hispanic/Latino; 4 Two or more races, non-Hispanic/Latino), 1 international. Average age 41. 153 applicants, 68% accepted, 85 enrolled. In 2017, 95 master's, 3 other advanced degrees awarded. *Entrance requirements:* Additional exam requirements/recommendations for international students: Required—TOEFL (minimum score 550 paper-based; 79 iBT). *Application deadline:* Applications are processed on a rolling basis. Application fee: $60. Electronic applications accepted. *Expenses:* Tuition: Full-time $19,980; part-time $1110 per credit. *Required fees:* $1040. Tuition and fees vary according to course load and degree level. *Financial support:* Application deadline: 3/1; applicants required to submit FAFSA. *Faculty research:* English Language Learners; social emotional needs of students; gifted education; cultural diversity; collaborative teaching methods. *Unit head:* Joanne O'Brien, Associate Dean and Director of Graduate Education Programs, 516-323-3116, E-mail: jobrien@molloy.edu. *Application contact:* Jaclyn Machowicz, Assistant Director for Admissions, 516-323-4010, E-mail: jmachowicz@molloy.edu.

Monmouth University, Graduate Studies, School of Education, West Long Branch, NJ 07764-1898. Offers applied behavior analysis (Certificate); autism (Certificate); director of school counseling services (Post-Master's Certificate); early childhood (M Ed); educational leadership (Ed D); elementary education (MAT), including elementary level, secondary level; English as a second language (M Ed); learning disabilities teacher-consultant (Post-Master's Certificate); literacy (MS Ed); school counseling (MS Ed); special education (MS Ed), including autism, learning disabilities teacher-consultant, teacher of students with disabilities, teaching in inclusive settings; speech-language pathology (MS Ed); student affairs and college counseling (MS Ed); supervisor (Post-Master's Certificate); teaching English to speakers of other languages (Certificate). *Accreditation:* NCATE. *Program availability:* Part-time, evening/weekend, 100% online, blended/hybrid learning. *Faculty:* 23 full-time (19 women), 33 part-time/adjunct (25 women). *Students:* 175 full-time (163 women), 168 part-time (142 women); includes 54 minority (10 Black or African American, non-Hispanic/Latino; 4 Asian, non-Hispanic/Latino; 32 Hispanic/Latino; 8 Two or more races, non-Hispanic/Latino). Average age 27. In 2017, 160 master's, 3 other advanced degrees awarded. *Entrance requirements:* For master's, GRE taken within last 5 years (for MS Ed in speech-language pathology); SAT (minimum combined score of 1660 in 3 sections), ACT (23), GRE (minimum score of 4.0 on analytical writing section and minimum combined score of 310 on quantitative and verbal sections), or passing scores on 3 parts of Core Academic Skills Educators, minimum GPA of 3.0 in major; 2 letters of recommendation (for some programs); resume, personal statement or essay (depending on program). Additional exam requirements/recommendations for international students: Required—TOEFL (minimum score 550 paper-based; 79 iBT), IELTS (minimum score 6), Michigan English Language Assessment Battery (minimum score 77) or Certificate of Advanced English (minimum score 160). *Application deadline:* For fall admission, 7/15 priority date for domestic students, 7/1 for international students; for spring admission, 12/1 priority date for domestic students, 11/1 for international students; for summer admission, 5/1 for domestic students. Applications are processed on a rolling basis. Application fee: $50. Electronic applications accepted. *Expenses: Tuition:* Full-time $21,366; part-time $7122 per credit. *Required fees:* $700; $175 per term. *Financial support:* In 2017–18, 125 students received support. Institutionally sponsored loans, scholarships/grants, and unspecified assistantships available. Support available to part-time students. Financial award applicants required to submit FAFSA. *Faculty research:* Multicultural literacy, science and mathematics teaching strategies, teacher as reflective practitioner, children with disabilities. *Unit head:* Dr. John E. Henning, Dean, 732-263-5513, Fax: 732-263-5277. *Application contact:* Laurie Kuhn, Associate Director of Graduate Admission, 732-571-3452, Fax: 732-263-5123, E-mail: gradadm@monmouth.edu.
Website: http://www.monmouth.edu/academics/schools/education/default.asp

Mount St. Joseph University, Graduate Education Program, Cincinnati, OH 45233-1670. Offers adolescent to young adult education (MA); dyslexia (Certificate); inclusive early childhood education (MA); middle childhood education (MA); multicultural special education (MA); reading science (MA). *Accreditation:* TEAC. *Program availability:* Part-time, evening/weekend, 100% online, blended/hybrid learning. *Faculty:* 6 full-time (5 women), 11 part-time/adjunct (8 women). *Students:* 37 full-time (30 women), 91 part-time (83 women); includes 13 minority (11 Black or African American, non-Hispanic/Latino; 1 Hispanic/Latino; 1 Two or more races, non-Hispanic/Latino). Average age 34. In 2017, 79 master's awarded. *Degree requirements:* For master's, comprehensive exam, thesis, research project, student teaching, clinical and field-based experiences.

Entrance requirements: For master's, GRE (if GPA is below 3.0), letter of intent, 2 referrals, background check, interview, resume, minimum undergraduate GPA of 3.0. Additional exam requirements/recommendations for international students: Required—TOEFL (minimum score 560 paper-based; 83 iBT). *Application deadline:* Applications are processed on a rolling basis. Application fee: $50. Electronic applications accepted. *Expenses:* $600 per credit hour. *Financial support:* Applicants required to submit FAFSA. *Faculty research:* Foreign and second language learning problems/reading disabilities, multicultural/bilingual special education, science education, pedagogical content knowledge, early childhood, response to intervention. *Unit head:* Dr. Laura Saylor, Dean, 513-244-3263, E-mail: laura.saylor@msj.edu. *Application contact:* Mary Brigham, Assistant Director of Graduate Recruitment, 513-244-4233, Fax: 513-244-4629, E-mail: mary.brigham@msj.edu.
Website: http://www.msj.edu/academics/graduate-programs/master-of-arts-initial-teacher-licensure-programs/

Murray State University, College of Education and Human Services, Department of Early Childhood and Elementary Education, Murray, KY 42071. Offers elementary teacher leader (MA Ed); interdisciplinary early childhood education (MA Ed), including elementary education (MA Ed, Ed S), reading and writing; teacher education and professional development (Ed S), including elementary education (MA Ed, Ed S). *Accreditation:* NCATE. *Program availability:* Part-time. *Faculty:* 17 full-time (16 women), 1 (woman) part-time/adjunct. *Students:* 10 full-time (all women), 91 part-time (87 women); includes 7 minority (4 Black or African American, non-Hispanic/Latino; 1 Hispanic/Latino; 2 Two or more races, non-Hispanic/Latino). Average age 33. 27 applicants, 89% accepted, 19 enrolled. In 2017, 35 master's awarded. *Entrance requirements:* For master's and Ed S, GRE or GMAT, minimum university GPA of 2.75. Additional exam requirements/recommendations for international students: Required—TOEFL (minimum score 527 paper-based; 71 iBT). *Application deadline:* Applications are processed on a rolling basis. Application fee: $40 ($50 for international students). Electronic applications accepted. *Expenses:* Tuition, state resident: full-time $9504. Tuition, nonresident: full-time $26,811. *International tuition:* $14,400 full-time. Tuition and fees vary according to course load, degree level and reciprocity agreements. *Financial support:* Federal Work-Study and unspecified assistantships available. Financial award applicants required to submit FAFSA. *Unit head:* Dr. Jacqueline Hansen, Chair, Department of Early Childhood and Elementary Education, 270-809-2500, Fax: 270-809-3799, E-mail: jhansen@murraystate.edu. *Application contact:* Kaitlyn Burzynski, Interim Assistant Director for Graduate Admission and Records, 270-809-5732, Fax: 270-809-3780, E-mail: msu.graduateadmissions@murraystate.edu.
Website: http://www.murraystate.edu/academics/CollegesDepartments/CollegeOfEducationandHumanServices/coehsacademicunits/EarlyChildhoodandElementaryEducation/in

National Louis University, National College of Education, Chicago, IL 60603. Offers administration and supervision (M Ed, Ed D, CAS, Ed S); curriculum and instruction (M Ed, MS Ed, CAS); early childhood administration (M Ed, CAS); early childhood education (M Ed, MAT, MS Ed, CAS); education (Ed D); educational psychology/human learning and development (M Ed, MS Ed, CAS, Ed S); elementary education (MAT); interdisciplinary curriculum and instruction (M Ed); mathematics education (M Ed, MS Ed, CAS); middle grades education (MAT); reading and language (M Ed, MS Ed, CAS); school psychology (M Ed, Ed S); science education (M Ed, MS Ed, CAS); secondary education (MAT); special education (M Ed, MAT, CAS); technology in education (M Ed, CAS). *Accreditation:* NCATE. *Program availability:* Part-time, evening/weekend. *Degree requirements:* For doctorate, comprehensive exam, thesis/dissertation. *Entrance requirements:* For master's, MAT or GRE, minimum GPA of 3.0; for doctorate, GRE General Test, minimum GPA of 3.25, interview, resume, writing sample, 4 recommendations. Additional exam requirements/recommendations for international students: Required—TOEFL (minimum score 550 paper-based; 79 iBT).

Nazareth College of Rochester, Graduate Studies, Department of Education, Program in Inclusive Early Childhood Education, Rochester, NY 14618. Offers MS Ed. *Accreditation:* TEAC. *Program availability:* Part-time, evening/weekend. *Entrance requirements:* For master's, minimum GPA of 3.0. Additional exam requirements/recommendations for international students: Required—TOEFL or IELTS.

New Jersey City University, Debra Cannon Partridge Wolfe College of Education, Department of Early Childhood Education, Jersey City, NJ 07305-1597. Offers MAT. *Accreditation:* TEAC. *Program availability:* Part-time, evening/weekend. *Entrance requirements:* Additional exam requirements/recommendations for international students: Required—TOEFL (minimum score 79 iBT).

New Mexico State University, College of Education, Department of Curriculum and Instruction, Las Cruces, NM 88003. Offers bilingual education (MA); curriculum and instruction (MA, Ed D, PhD); early childhood education (MA); educational diagnostics (Ed S); language, literacy and culture (MA); learning design and technologies (MA); teaching (MAT), including dance, Spanish; teaching English to speakers of other languages (MA). *Accreditation:* NCATE. *Program availability:* Part-time, evening/weekend, 100% online. *Faculty:* 22 full-time (17 women), 7 part-time/adjunct (2 women). *Students:* 113 full-time (79 women), 194 part-time (138 women); includes 171 minority (15 Black or African American, non-Hispanic/Latino; 3 American Indian or Alaska Native, non-Hispanic/Latino; 4 Asian, non-Hispanic/Latino; 142 Hispanic/Latino; 7 Two or more races, non-Hispanic/Latino), 37 international. Average age 36. 106 applicants, 80% accepted, 56 enrolled. In 2017, 82 master's, 15 doctorates, 1 other advanced degree awarded. *Entrance requirements:* For master's, minimum cumulative GPA of 3.0; for doctorate, portfolio, minimum cumulative GPA of 3.0. Additional exam requirements/recommendations for international students: Required—TOEFL (minimum score 550 paper-based; 79 iBT), IELTS (minimum score 6.5). *Application deadline:* For fall admission, 12/15 priority date for domestic and international students; for spring admission, 11/1 for domestic students. Applications are processed on a rolling basis. Application fee: $40 ($50 for international students). Electronic applications accepted. *Expenses:* Tuition, state resident: full-time $4390. Tuition, nonresident: full-time $15,309. *Required fees:* $853. *Financial support:* In 2017–18, 97 students received support, including 2 fellowships (averaging $4,390 per year), 1 research assistantship (averaging $17,368 per year), 10 teaching assistantships (averaging $17,489 per year); career-related internships or fieldwork, Federal Work-Study, scholarships/grants, traineeships, health care benefits, and unspecified assistantships also available. Support available to part-time students. Financial award application deadline: 3/1. *Faculty research:* STEM education, bilingual and English as a second language education, critical pedagogy/multicultural education, learning design and technology, early childhood education. *Total annual research expenditures:* $13,518. *Unit head:* Dr. David Rutledge, Department Head, 575-646-5411, Fax: 575-646-5436, E-mail: rutledge@nmsu.edu. *Application contact:* Dr. David Rutledge, Associate Department Head for Graduate Programs, 575-646-5411, Fax: 575-646-5436, E-mail: rutledge@nmsu.edu.
Website: http://tpal.nmsu.edu/

New Mexico State University, College of Education, Department of Educational Leadership and Administration, Las Cruces, NM 88003. Offers educational administration (MA), including community college and university administration, PK-12 public school administration; educational leadership (Ed D, PhD). *Accreditation:* NCATE. *Program*

availability: Part-time-only, evening/weekend, blended/hybrid learning. *Faculty:* 6 full-time (5 women), 2 part-time/adjunct (1 woman). *Students:* 11 full-time (10 women), 124 part-time (88 women); includes 93 minority (2 Black or African American, non-Hispanic/Latino; 8 American Indian or Alaska Native, non-Hispanic/Latino; 3 Asian, non-Hispanic/Latino; 78 Hispanic/Latino; 1 Native Hawaiian or other Pacific Islander, non-Hispanic/Latino; 1 Two or more races, non-Hispanic/Latino), 1 international. Average age 41. 29 applicants, 28% accepted, 8 enrolled. In 2017, 26 master's, 9 doctorates awarded. *Degree requirements:* For master's, comprehensive exam, internship; for doctorate, comprehensive exam, thesis/dissertation, internship. *Entrance requirements:* For doctorate, minimum GPA of 3.0, master's degree. Additional exam requirements/recommendations for international students: Required—TOEFL (minimum score 550 paper-based; 79 iBT), IELTS (minimum score 6.5). *Application deadline:* For spring admission, 11/15 for domestic and international students. Application fee: $40 ($50 for international students). Electronic applications accepted. *Expenses:* Tuition, state resident: full-time $4390. Tuition, nonresident: full-time $15,309. *Required fees:* $853. *Financial support:* In 2017–18, 21 students received support, including 4 research assistantships (averaging $17,489 per year), 1 teaching assistantship (averaging $8,684 per year); career-related internships or fieldwork, Federal Work-Study, scholarships/grants, traineeships, health care benefits, and unspecified assistantships also available. Support available to part-time students. Financial award application deadline: 3/1. *Faculty research:* Leadership in pk-12 and postsecondary education, community college administration, distance education administration, leadership for social justice, educational change. *Total annual research expenditures:* $2,456. *Unit head:* Dr. Azadeh Osanloo, Department Head, 575-646-5976, Fax: 575-646-4767, E-mail: azadeh@nmsu.edu. *Application contact:* Denise Rodriguez-Strawn, Program Coordinator, 575-646-3825, Fax: 575-646-4767, E-mail: edmandev@nmsu.edu.
Website: http://ela.nmsu.edu/

New York Institute of Technology, School of Interdisciplinary Studies and Education, Department of Teacher Education, Old Westbury, NY 11568-8000. Offers adolescence education (MS), including math (MAT, MS), science; adolescent education (MAT), including biology, chemistry, English, math (MAT, MS), social studies; childhood education (MS); early childhood (MS). *Program availability:* Part-time, evening/weekend, 100% online, blended/hybrid learning. *Faculty:* 2 full-time (both women), 7 part-time/adjunct (3 women). *Students:* 46 full-time (44 women), 30 part-time (22 women); includes 23 minority (8 Black or African American, non-Hispanic/Latino; 6 Asian, non-Hispanic/Latino; 8 Hispanic/Latino; 1 Two or more races, non-Hispanic/Latino), 2 international. Average age 29. 39 applicants, 72% accepted, 15 enrolled. In 2017, 14 master's awarded. *Entrance requirements:* For master's, GRE or MAT, BS or equivalent; minimum cumulative undergraduate GPA of 3.0; NY state provisional or initial certification (for MS in adolescence education); BS with major in biology, chemistry, economics, English, history, life sciences, math, physics, or psychology (for MS in childhood, early childhood education, and MAT); interview; personal statement. Additional exam requirements/recommendations for international students: Required—TOEFL (minimum score 79 iBT), IELTS (minimum score 6). *Application deadline:* Applications are processed on a rolling basis. Application fee: $50. Electronic applications accepted. *Expenses:* $1,285 per credit plus fees. *Financial support:* Career-related internships or fieldwork, Federal Work-Study, scholarships/grants, tuition waivers (full and partial), and unspecified assistantships available. Support available to part-time students. Financial award application deadline: 2/15; financial award applicants required to submit FAFSA. *Faculty research:* Evolving definition of new literacies and its impact on teaching and learning (twenty-first century skills), new literacies practices in teacher education, teachers' professional development, English language and literacy learning through mobile learning, teaching reading to culturally and linguistically diverse children. *Unit head:* Dr. Hui-Yin Hsu, Department Chair, 516-686-1322, Fax: 516-686-7655, E-mail: hhsu02@nyit.edu. *Application contact:* Alice Dolitsky, Director, Graduate Admissions, 516-686-7520, Fax: 516-686-1116, E-mail: nyitgrad@nyit.edu.
Website: http://www.nyit.edu/interdisciplinary/department_teacher_education

New York University, Steinhardt School of Culture, Education, and Human Development, Department of Teaching and Learning, Program in Early Childhood and Childhood Education, New York, NY 10012. Offers childhood education (MA); early childhood education (MA); early childhood education/early childhood special education (MA). *Accreditation:* TEAC. *Program availability:* Part-time. *Faculty:* 9 full-time (all women). *Students:* 59 full-time (55 women), 24 part-time (22 women); includes 25 minority (3 Black or African American, non-Hispanic/Latino; 15 Asian, non-Hispanic/Latino; 5 Hispanic/Latino; 2 Two or more races, non-Hispanic/Latino), 8 international. Average age 28. 91 applicants, 68% accepted, 15 enrolled. In 2017, 57 master's awarded. *Degree requirements:* For master's, thesis (for some programs). *Entrance requirements:* Additional exam requirements/recommendations for international students: Required—TOEFL (minimum score 100 iBT). *Application deadline:* For fall admission, 12/1 priority date for domestic and international students; for spring admission, 10/1 for domestic and international students. Applications are processed on a rolling basis. Application fee: $75. Electronic applications accepted. *Expenses: Tuition:* Full-time $41,352; part-time $19,968 per year. *Required fees:* $2496; $1628 per unit. $814 per term. Tuition and fees vary according to course load and program. *Financial support:* Fellowships with full and partial tuition reimbursements, career-related internships or fieldwork, Federal Work-Study, institutionally sponsored loans, scholarships/grants, tuition waivers (partial), and unspecified assistantships available. Support available to part-time students. Financial award application deadline: 2/1; financial award applicants required to submit FAFSA. *Faculty research:* Teacher evaluation and beliefs about teaching, early literacy development, language arts, child development and education, cultural differences. *Unit head:* 212-998-5460, Fax: 212-995-4049. *Application contact:* 212-998-5030, Fax: 212-995-4328, E-mail: steinhardt.gradadmissions@nyu.edu.
Website: http://steinhardt.nyu.edu/teachlearn/childhood

New York University, Steinhardt School of Culture, Education, and Human Development, Department of Teaching and Learning, Program in Special Education, New York, NY 10012-1019. Offers childhood (MA); early childhood (MA). *Accreditation:* TEAC. *Program availability:* Part-time. *Students:* Average age 25. 101 applicants, 81% accepted, 12 enrolled. In 2017, 8 master's awarded. *Entrance requirements:* Additional exam requirements/recommendations for international students: Required—TOEFL (minimum score 100 iBT). *Application deadline:* For fall admission, 12/1 priority date for domestic and international students. Applications are processed on a rolling basis. Application fee: $75. Electronic applications accepted. *Expenses: Tuition:* Full-time $41,352; part-time $19,968 per year. *Required fees:* $2496; $1628 per unit. $814 per term. Tuition and fees vary according to course load and program. *Financial support:* Career-related internships or fieldwork, Federal Work-Study, institutionally sponsored loans, scholarships/grants, tuition waivers (partial) available. Support available to part-time students. Financial award application deadline: 2/1; financial award applicants required to submit FAFSA. *Faculty research:* Special education referrals, attention deficit disorders in children, mainstreaming, curriculum-based assessment and program implementation, special education policy. *Unit head:* Prof. Joan Rosenberg, Director, 212-998-5554, Fax: 212-995-4049, E-mail: joanrosenberg@nyu.edu. *Application contact:* 212-998-5030, Fax: 212-995-4328, E-mail: steinhardt.gradadmissions@nyu.edu.
Website: http://steinhardt.nyu.edu/teachlearn/special/ma

Niagara University, Graduate Division of Education, Concentration in Teacher Education, Niagara University, NY 14109. Offers early childhood and childhood education (MS Ed, Certificate); early childhood special education (MS); middle and adolescence education (MS Ed); special education (MS Ed), including 1-6, 7-12; special education (grades 1-12) (Certificate); teaching English to speakers of other languages (MS Ed, Certificate). *Accreditation:* NCATE. *Students:* 105 full-time (79 women), 109 part-time (88 women); includes 20 minority (9 Black or African American, non-Hispanic/Latino; 2 American Indian or Alaska Native, non-Hispanic/Latino; 1 Asian, non-Hispanic/Latino; 5 Hispanic/Latino; 3 Two or more races, non-Hispanic/Latino), 35 international. Average age 28. In 2017, 86 master's, 18 other advanced degrees awarded. *Entrance requirements:* For master's, GRE General Test or Academic Literacy Skills Test (ALST). Additional exam requirements/recommendations for international students: Required—TOEFL (minimum score 550 paper-based; 79 iBT), IELTS (minimum score 6). *Application deadline:* For fall admission, 8/1 for domestic students. Applications are processed on a rolling basis. Application fee: $30. *Expenses:* Contact institution. *Financial support:* Research assistantships with tuition reimbursements, teaching assistantships with tuition reimbursements, career-related internships or fieldwork, Federal Work-Study, scholarships/grants, and unspecified assistantships available. Financial award application deadline: 4/15; financial award applicants required to submit FAFSA. *Unit head:* Dr. Chandra Foote, Dean, College of Education, 716-286-8549, E-mail: cjf@niagara.edu. *Application contact:* Evan Pierce, Associate Director, Graduate Studies, 716-286-8327, E-mail: epierce@niagara.edu.
Website: http://www.niagara.edu/teacher-education

Norfolk State University, School of Graduate Studies, School of Education, Department of Early Childhood and Elementary Education, Norfolk, VA 23504. Offers early childhood education (MAT); pre-elementary education (MA). *Accreditation:* NCATE. *Program availability:* Part-time. *Degree requirements:* For master's, comprehensive exam, thesis or alternative. *Entrance requirements:* For master's, PRAXIS I and II, minimum GPA of 2.5, letters of recommendation, interview. *Faculty research:* Parent involvement in education.

North Carolina Agricultural and Technical State University, School of Graduate Studies, School of Agriculture and Environmental Sciences, Department of Family and Consumer Sciences, Greensboro, NC 27411. Offers child development early education and family studies (MAT); family and consumer sciences (MAT); food and nutrition (MS). *Program availability:* Part-time, evening/weekend. *Degree requirements:* For master's, comprehensive exam, thesis or alternative, qualifying exam. *Entrance requirements:* For master's, GRE General Test, minimum GPA of 2.6.

Northeastern Illinois University, College of Graduate Studies and Research, Daniel L. Goodwin College of Education, Program in Early Childhood Education, Chicago, IL 60625. Offers MAT. *Entrance requirements:* For master's, bachelor's degree from accredited college or university; minimum undergraduate GPA of 3.0; three professional references. Electronic applications accepted. *Expenses:* Tuition, state resident: full-time $7274; part-time $404.11 per credit hour. Tuition, nonresident: full-time $14,548; part-time $808.23 per credit hour. *Required fees:* $1284. *Unit head:* Dr. Ngoc-Diep Nguyen, Department Chair, 773-442-6197, E-mail: n-nguyen8@neiu.edu. *Application contact:* Martha Narvaez, Graduate Admission Representative, 773-442-6006, E-mail: m-narvaez@neiu.edu.

Northeastern State University, College of Education, Department of Curriculum and Instruction, Program in Early Childhood Education, Tahlequah, OK 74464-2399. Offers M Ed. *Program availability:* Part-time, evening/weekend. *Faculty:* 4 full-time (all women). *Students:* 1 (woman) full-time, 21 part-time (all women); includes 5 minority (1 Black or African American, non-Hispanic/Latino; 2 American Indian or Alaska Native, non-Hispanic/Latino; 1 Hispanic/Latino; 1 Two or more races, non-Hispanic/Latino), 1 international. Average age 34. In 2017, 2 master's awarded. *Degree requirements:* For master's, thesis. *Entrance requirements:* For master's, GRE or MAT, minimum GPA of 2.5. Additional exam requirements/recommendations for international students: Required—TOEFL. *Application deadline:* For fall admission, 6/1 priority date for domestic students. Applications are processed on a rolling basis. Application fee: $25. Electronic applications accepted. *Expenses:* Tuition, state resident: part-time $222 per credit hour. Tuition, nonresident: part-time $501.75 per credit hour. *Required fees:* $37.40 per credit hour. Tuition and fees vary according to degree level. *Financial support:* Teaching assistantships and Federal Work-Study available. Financial award application deadline: 3/1. *Unit head:* Dr. Anita Ede, Program Chair, 918-449-6523, E-mail: edear@nsuok.edu. *Application contact:* Josh McCollum, Graduate Coordinator, 918-444-2093, E-mail: mccolluj@nsuok.edu.
Website: https://academics.nsuok.edu/education/EducationHome/COEDepartments/CurriculumInstruction.aspx

Northern Arizona University, College of Education, Department of Educational Specialties, Flagstaff, AZ 86011. Offers autism spectrum disorders (Certificate); bilingual/multicultural education (M Ed), including bilingual, ESL; career and technical education (M Ed, Certificate); educational technology (M Ed, Certificate); English as a second language (Certificate); positive behavior support (Certificate); special education (M Ed), including early childhood special education, mild/moderate disabilities. *Program availability:* Part-time, 100% online, blended/hybrid learning. *Faculty:* 31 full-time (19 women), 2 part-time/adjunct (1 woman). *Students:* 66 full-time (52 women), 203 part-time (147 women); includes 83 minority (20 Black or African American, non-Hispanic/Latino; 12 American Indian or Alaska Native, non-Hispanic/Latino; 5 Asian, non-Hispanic/Latino; 38 Hispanic/Latino; 3 Native Hawaiian or other Pacific Islander, non-Hispanic/Latino; 5 Two or more races, non-Hispanic/Latino), 6 international. Average age 37. 157 applicants, 94% accepted, 148 enrolled. In 2017, 119 master's, 26 Certificates awarded. *Degree requirements:* For master's, variable foreign language requirement, comprehensive exam (for some programs), thesis (for some programs); for Certificate, comprehensive exam (for some programs). *Entrance requirements:* Additional exam requirements/recommendations for international students: Required—TOEFL (minimum score 80 iBT), IELTS (minimum score 6.5). *Application deadline:* For fall admission, 3/1 for domestic and international students; for spring admission, 10/1 for domestic and international students. Applications are processed on a rolling basis. Application fee: $65. Electronic applications accepted. *Expenses:* Tuition, state resident: full-time $9240; part-time $458 per credit hour. Tuition, nonresident: full-time $21,588; part-time $1199 per credit hour. *Required fees:* $1021; $14 per credit hour. $646 per semester. Tuition and fees vary according to course load, campus/location and program. *Financial support:* In 2017–18, 11 students received support, including 1 fellowship with full and partial tuition reimbursement available (averaging $12,000 per year), 10 teaching assistantships with full and partial tuition reimbursements available (averaging $12,000 per year); Federal Work-Study, institutionally sponsored loans, health care benefits, tuition waivers (full and partial), and unspecified assistantships also available. Financial award application deadline: 2/1; financial award applicants required to submit FAFSA. *Unit head:* Dr. Shadow Armfield, Chair, 928-523-7651, Fax: 928-523-1929, E-mail: laura.sujo-montes@nau.edu. *Application contact:* Tina Sutton, Coordinator, Graduate College, 928-523-4348, Fax: 928-523-8950, E-mail: graduate@nau.edu.
Website: https://nau.edu/coe/Ed-Specialties/

Early Childhood Education

Northern Arizona University, College of Education, Department of Teaching and Learning, Flagstaff, AZ 86011. Offers curriculum and instruction (Ed D); early childhood education (M Ed); elementary education (M Ed); secondary education (M Ed). *Program availability:* Part-time, 100% online, blended/hybrid learning. *Faculty:* 28 full-time (24 women), 1 (woman) part-time/adjunct. *Students:* 82 full-time (71 women), 181 part-time (167 women); includes 87 minority (19 Black or African American, non-Hispanic/Latino; 11 American Indian or Alaska Native, non-Hispanic/Latino; 4 Asian, non-Hispanic/Latino; 47 Hispanic/Latino; 1 Native Hawaiian or other Pacific Islander, non-Hispanic/Latino; 5 Two or more races, non-Hispanic/Latino), 7 international. Average age 36. 106 applicants, 95% accepted, 99 enrolled. In 2017, 79 master's, 5 doctorates awarded. *Degree requirements:* For master's, variable foreign language requirement, comprehensive exam (for some programs), thesis (for some programs); for doctorate, variable foreign language requirement, comprehensive exam (for some programs), thesis/dissertation (for some programs). *Entrance requirements:* Additional exam requirements/recommendations for international students: Required—TOEFL (minimum score 80 iBT), IELTS (minimum score 6.5). *Application deadline:* For fall admission, 2/15 for domestic and international students; for spring admission, 9/15 for domestic and international students. Applications are processed on a rolling basis. Application fee: $65. Electronic applications accepted. *Expenses:* Tuition, state resident: full-time $9240; part-time $458 per credit hour. Tuition, nonresident: full-time $21,588; part-time $1199 per credit hour. *Required fees:* $1021; $14 per credit hour. $646 per semester. Tuition and fees vary according to course load, campus/location and program. *Financial support:* In 2017–18, 5 students received support, including 1 research assistantship with full and partial tuition reimbursement available (averaging $13,500 per year), 4 teaching assistantships with full and partial tuition reimbursements available (averaging $13,500 per year); institutionally sponsored loans, health care benefits, tuition waivers (full and partial), and unspecified assistantships also available. Financial award application deadline: 2/1; financial award applicants required to submit FAFSA. *Unit head:* Dr. Pamela Powell, Chair, 928-523-5644, Fax: 928-523-1929, E-mail: pamela.powell@nau.edu. *Application contact:* Tina Sutton, Coordinator, Graduate College, 928-523-4348, Fax: 928-523-8950, E-mail: graduate@nau.edu. Website: https://nau.edu/coe/Teaching-and-Learning/

Northern Illinois University, Graduate School, College of Education, Department of Special and Early Education, De Kalb, IL 60115-2854. Offers curriculum and instruction (MS Ed); early childhood education (MS Ed); elementary education (MS Ed); special education (MS Ed). *Program availability:* Part-time, evening/weekend. *Faculty:* 22 full-time (14 women), 2 part-time/adjunct (both women). *Students:* 40 full-time (33 women), 79 part-time (65 women); includes 16 minority (5 Black or African American, non-Hispanic/Latino; 3 Asian, non-Hispanic/Latino; 6 Hispanic/Latino; 2 Two or more races, non-Hispanic/Latino). Average age 32. 48 applicants, 83% accepted, 25 enrolled. In 2017, 58 master's awarded. *Degree requirements:* For master's, comprehensive exam, thesis optional. *Entrance requirements:* For master's, GRE General Test or MAT, minimum undergraduate GPA of 2.75. Additional exam requirements/recommendations for international students: Required—TOEFL (minimum score 550 paper-based). *Application deadline:* For fall admission, 6/1 for domestic students, 5/1 for international students; for spring admission, 11/1 for domestic students, 10/1 for international students. Applications are processed on a rolling basis. Application fee: $40. Electronic applications accepted. *Financial support:* In 2017–18, 17 research assistantships with full tuition reimbursements were awarded; fellowships with full tuition reimbursements, teaching assistantships with full tuition reimbursements, career-related internships or fieldwork, Federal Work-Study, scholarships/grants, tuition waivers (full), and unspecified assistantships also available. Support available to part-time students. Financial award applicants required to submit FAFSA. *Faculty research:* Teacher certification, stress reduction during student teaching, teaching history, portfolios in student teaching. *Unit head:* Gregory Conderman, Chair, 815-753-1619, E-mail: seed@niu.edu. *Application contact:* Gail Myers, Clerk, Graduate Advising, 815-753-0381, E-mail: gmyers@niu.edu. Website: http://www.cedu.niu.edu/seed/

Northwestern College, Program in Education, Orange City, IA 51041-1996. Offers early childhood (M Ed); master teacher (M Ed); teacher leadership (M Ed, Graduate Certificate). *Program availability:* Online learning.

Northwestern State University of Louisiana, Graduate Studies and Research, College of Education and Human Development, Program in Early Childhood Education, Natchitoches, LA 71497. Offers early childhood education and teaching (M Ed, MAT). *Degree requirements:* For master's, comprehensive exam, thesis or alternative. *Entrance requirements:* For master's, GRE General Test. Additional exam requirements/recommendations for international students: Required—TOEFL. Electronic applications accepted.

Northwest Missouri State University, Graduate School, School of Education, Maryville, MO 64468-6001. Offers early childhood education (MS Ed); education leadership (MS Ed), including elementary, K-12, secondary; educational leadership (Ed S), including elementary school principalship, secondary school principalship, superintendency; educational leadership and policy analysis (Ed D); elementary education (MS Ed); elementary mathematics (MS Ed); higher education leadership (MS); middle school education (MS Ed); reading (MS Ed); special education (MS Ed); teacher leadership (MS Ed); teaching English language learners (MS Ed). *Accreditation:* NCATE. *Program availability:* Part-time. *Faculty:* 15 full-time (8 women). *Students:* 28 full-time (20 women), 170 part-time (114 women); includes 20 minority (7 Black or African American, non-Hispanic/Latino; 1 Asian, non-Hispanic/Latino; 8 Hispanic/Latino; 4 Two or more races, non-Hispanic/Latino). Average age 33. 168 applicants, 73% accepted, 114 enrolled. In 2017, 67 master's, 21 other advanced degrees awarded. *Degree requirements:* For master's, comprehensive exam; for Ed S, comprehensive exam, thesis. *Entrance requirements:* For master's, GRE General Test, writing sample; for Ed S, minimum graduate GPA of 3.25. Additional exam requirements/recommendations for international students: Required—TOEFL (minimum score 550 paper-based). *Application deadline:* For fall admission, 7/1 for domestic and international students; for spring admission, 11/15 for domestic and international students. Applications are processed on a rolling basis. Application fee: $0 ($50 for international students). Electronic applications accepted. *Expenses:* $389.11 per credit hour in-state tuition and fees, $641.97 out-of-state; $9,750 total cost (for online-based education program). *Financial support:* Research assistantships with full tuition reimbursements, teaching assistantships with full tuition reimbursements, and unspecified assistantships available. Financial award application deadline: 4/1; financial award applicants required to submit FAFSA. *Unit head:* Dr. Tim Wall, Director, 660-562-1179, E-mail: timwall@nwmissouri.edu. Website: https://www.nwmissouri.edu/education/index.htm

Oakland University, Graduate Study and Lifelong Learning, School of Education and Human Services, Department of Human Development and Child Studies, Program in Early Childhood Education, Rochester, MI 48309-4401. Offers early childhood education (M Ed, PhD); early education and intervention (Ed S). *Accreditation:* TEAC. *Degree requirements:* For doctorate, thesis/dissertation. *Entrance requirements:* For master's, minimum GPA of 3.0; for doctorate, GRE General Test, minimum GPA of 3.0. Additional exam requirements/recommendations for international students: Required—TOEFL

(minimum score 550 paper-based). *Expenses:* Tuition, state resident: full-time $16,950; part-time $706.25 per credit. Tuition, nonresident: full-time $24,648; part-time $1027 per credit.

Oklahoma City University, Petree College of Arts and Sciences, Oklahoma City, OK 73106-1402. Offers applied behavioral studies (M Ed); applied sociology: nonprofit leadership (MA); creative writing (MFA); criminology (MS); early childhood education (M Ed); elementary education (M Ed); general studies (MLA); leadership/management (MLA); moving image arts (MFA); professional counseling (M Ed); teaching (MA); teaching English to speakers of other languages (MA). *Program availability:* Part-time, evening/weekend. *Faculty:* 6 full-time (2 women), 16 part-time/adjunct (10 women). *Students:* 84 full-time (61 women), 32 part-time (23 women); includes 31 minority (13 Black or African American, non-Hispanic/Latino; 3 American Indian or Alaska Native, non-Hispanic/Latino; 1 Asian, non-Hispanic/Latino; 9 Hispanic/Latino; 5 Two or more races, non-Hispanic/Latino), 30 international. Average age 34. 192 applicants, 67% accepted, 57 enrolled. In 2017, 65 master's awarded. *Degree requirements:* For master's, capstone/practicum. *Entrance requirements:* For master's, bachelor's degree from accredited institution with minimum GPA of 3.0, essay, recommendation letters. Additional exam requirements/recommendations for international students: Required—TOEFL (minimum score 550 paper-based; 80 iBT). *Application deadline:* Applications are processed on a rolling basis. Application fee: $50. Electronic applications accepted. *Expenses:* $8,580. *Financial support:* In 2017–18, 19 students received support. Federal Work-Study, institutionally sponsored loans, scholarships/grants, and tuition waivers (full and partial) available. Support available to part-time students. Financial award application deadline: 6/1; financial award applicants required to submit FAFSA. *Unit head:* Dr. Amy Cataldi, Dean, 405-208-5446, Fax: 405-208-5447, E-mail: acataldi@okcu.edu. *Application contact:* Michael Harrington, Director of Graduate Admissions, 800-633-7242, Fax: 405-208-5356, E-mail: gadmissions@okcu.edu. Website: https://www.okcu.edu/artsci/home

Old Dominion University, Darden College of Education, Program in Early Childhood Education, Norfolk, VA 23529. Offers MS Ed, PhD. *Accreditation:* NCATE. *Program availability:* Part-time, evening/weekend. *Students:* Average age 37. 5 applicants, 80% accepted, 4 enrolled. In 2017, 6 master's, 1 doctorate awarded. *Degree requirements:* For master's, comprehensive exam, written exams; for doctorate, comprehensive exam, thesis/dissertation. *Entrance requirements:* For master's, GRE General Test, PRAXIS I, minimum undergraduate GPA of 2.8; for doctorate, GRE General Test. Additional exam requirements/recommendations for international students: Required—TOEFL. *Application deadline:* For fall admission, 6/1 for domestic students; for winter admission, 11/1 for domestic students; for spring admission, 3/1 for domestic students. Applications are processed on a rolling basis. Application fee: $50. *Expenses:* Tuition, state resident: full-time $8928; part-time $496 per credit. Tuition, nonresident: full-time $22,482; part-time $1249 per credit. *Required fees:* $66 per semester. *Financial support:* In 2017–18, fellowships with full tuition reimbursements (averaging $15,000 per year), 2 research assistantships (averaging $9,000 per year), 2 teaching assistantships with full tuition reimbursements (averaging $15,000 per year) were awarded. Financial award application deadline: 2/15; financial award applicants required to submit FAFSA. *Faculty research:* Creativity, informal learning environment, children's thinking, early childhood teacher professional development, integrated curriculum. *Unit head:* Dr. Angela Eckhoff, Graduate Program Director, 757-683-3284, Fax: 757-683-5862, E-mail: aeckhoff@odu.edu. *Application contact:* William Heffelfinger, Director of Graduate Admissions, 757-683-5554, Fax: 757-683-3255, E-mail: gradadmit@odu.edu. Website: http://www.odu.edu/academics/programs/masters/early-childhood-education

Old Dominion University, Darden College of Education, Program in Special Education, Norfolk, VA 23529. Offers adapted curriculum K-12 (MS Ed); early childhood special education (MS Ed); general curriculum K-12 (MS Ed); special education (PhD). *Accreditation:* NCATE. *Program availability:* Part-time, evening/weekend, 100% online, blended/hybrid learning. *Faculty:* 13 full-time (10 women), 10 part-time/adjunct (7 women). *Students:* 39 full-time (35 women), 67 part-time (57 women); includes 30 minority (17 Black or African American, non-Hispanic/Latino; 4 Asian, non-Hispanic/Latino; 5 Two or more races, non-Hispanic/Latino), 7 international. Average age 33. 65 applicants, 40% accepted, 26 enrolled. In 2017, 24 master's, 1 doctorate awarded. *Degree requirements:* For master's, comprehensive exam, thesis or alternative, VCLA; for doctorate, comprehensive exam, thesis/dissertation. *Entrance requirements:* For master's, GRE General Test or MAT, PRAXIS Core Academic Skills for Educator Tests, minimum GPA of 2.8; for doctorate, GRE General Test or MAT. Additional exam requirements/recommendations for international students: Recommended—TOEFL (minimum score 550 paper-based). *Application deadline:* For fall admission, 6/1 priority date for domestic and international students; for winter admission, 11/1 priority date for domestic and international students; for spring admission, 3/1 priority date for domestic and international students. Applications are processed on a rolling basis. Application fee: $55. Electronic applications accepted. Application fee is waived when completed online. *Expenses:* $45,000 (for MS Ed); $90,000 (for PhD). *Financial support:* In 2017–18, 50 students received support, including 1 research assistantship (averaging $5,000 per year), 3 teaching assistantships with full tuition reimbursements available (averaging $15,000 per year); fellowships, scholarships/grants, and unspecified assistantships also available. Support available to part-time students. Financial award application deadline: 2/15; financial award applicants required to submit FAFSA. *Faculty research:* Inclusion, autism spectrum disorder, functional behavioral assessment, infant, preschool, and school-age children and youth with disabilities, distance learning. *Total annual research expenditures:* $3.6 million. *Unit head:* Dr. Sabra Gear, Graduate Program Director, 757-683-4383, Fax: 757-683-4129, E-mail: sgear@odu.edu. *Application contact:* William Heffelfinger, Director of Graduate Admissions, 757-683-5554, Fax: 757-683-3255, E-mail: gradadmit@odu.edu. Website: https://www.odu.edu/cdse/academics/sped

Ottawa University, Graduate Studies-Arizona, Program in Education, Ottawa, KS 66067-3399. Offers community college counseling (MA); curriculum and instruction (MA); early childhood (MA); education intervention (MA); education leadership (MA); education technology (MA); Montessori early childhood education (MA); Montessori elementary education (MA); professional development (MA); school guidance counseling (MA); special education - cross categorical (MA). Programs offered in Mesa, Phoenix, Tempe and West Valley, AZ. *Accreditation:* NCATE. *Program availability:* Part-time. *Degree requirements:* For master's, thesis or alternative. *Entrance requirements:* For master's, minimum undergraduate GPA of 3.0, copy of current state certification or teaching license. Additional exam requirements/recommendations for international students: Required—TOEFL (minimum score 550 paper-based). Electronic applications accepted. *Expenses:* Contact institution.

Pace University, School of Education, New York, NY 10038. Offers adolescent education (MST), including biology, chemistry, earth science, English, foreign languages, mathematics, physics, social studies; childhood education (MST); early childhood development, learning and intervention (MST); educational technology studies (MS); inclusive adolescent education (MST), including biology, chemistry, earth science, English, foreign languages, mathematics, physics, social studies; integrated instruction for educational technology (Certificate); integrated instruction for literacy and technology (Certificate); literacy (MS Ed); special education (MS Ed). *Accreditation:* NCATE. *Program availability:* Part-time, evening/weekend, 100% online, blended/hybrid learning. *Faculty:* 19 full-time (13 women), 86 part-time/adjunct (49 women). *Students:* 91 full-time (76 women), 548 part-time (401 women); includes 247 minority (112 Black or African American, non-Hispanic/Latino; 2 American Indian or Alaska Native, non-Hispanic/Latino; 31 Asian, non-Hispanic/Latino; 93 Hispanic/Latino; 1 Native Hawaiian or other Pacific Islander, non-Hispanic/Latino; 8 Two or more races, non-Hispanic/Latino), 6 international. Average age 30. 188 applicants, 86% accepted, 114 enrolled. In 2017, 213 master's, 8 other advanced degrees awarded. *Degree requirements:* For master's and Certificate, certification exams. *Entrance requirements:* Required—GRE (for initial certification programs only), teaching certificate (for MS Ed in literacy and special education programs only). Additional exam requirements/recommendations for international students: Required—TOEFL (minimum score 88 iBT), IELTS or PTE. *Application deadline:* For fall admission, 8/1 priority date for domestic students, 6/1 for international students; for spring admission, 12/1 priority date for domestic students, 10/1 for international students. Applications are processed on a rolling basis. Application fee: $70. Electronic applications accepted. *Expenses:* Contact institution. *Financial support:* In 2017–18, 17 students received support, including 17 research assistantships with partial tuition reimbursements available (averaging $6,020 per year); career-related internships or fieldwork, Federal Work-Study, scholarships/grants, and unspecified assistantships also available. Financial award application deadline: 9/1; financial award applicants required to submit FAFSA. *Faculty research:* STEM education, TESOL, teacher education, special education, language and literary development. *Total annual research expenditures:* $29,706. *Unit head:* Dr. Xiao-Lei Wang, Dean, School of Education, 914-773-3876, E-mail: xwang@pace.edu. *Application contact:* Susan Ford-Goldschein, Director of Graduate Admissions, 212-346-1531, Fax: 212-346-1585, E-mail: graduateadmission@pace.edu. Website: http://www.pace.edu/school-of-education

Pacific Oaks College, Graduate School, Program in Early Childhood Education, Pasadena, CA 91103. Offers MA. *Program availability:* Part-time, online learning.

Pacific University, College of Education, Forest Grove, OR 97116-1797. Offers early childhood education (MAT); education (MAE); elementary education (MAT); ESOL (MAT); high school education (MAT); middle school education (MAT); special education (MAT); speech-language pathology (MS); STEM education (MAT); talented and gifted (M Ed); visual function in learning (M Ed). *Accreditation:* ASHA; NCATE. *Program availability:* Part-time, evening/weekend. *Degree requirements:* For master's, research project. *Entrance requirements:* For master's, California Basic Educational Skills Test, PRAXIS II, minimum undergraduate GPA of 2.75, 3.0 graduate. Additional exam requirements/recommendations for international students: Required—TOEFL. Electronic applications accepted. *Expenses:* Contact institution. *Faculty research:* Defining a culturally competent classroom, technology in the K-12 classroom, Socratic seminars, social studies education.

Piedmont College, School of Education, Demorest, GA 30535. Offers art education (MA, MAT); curriculum and instruction (Ed D, Ed S); early childhood education (MA, MAT); instructional technology (MA); middle grades education (MA, MAT); music education (MA, MAT); secondary education (MA, MAT); special education (MA, MAT). *Program availability:* Part-time, evening/weekend. *Students:* 341 full-time (268 women), 682 part-time (571 women); includes 182 minority (136 Black or African American, non-Hispanic/Latino; 2 American Indian or Alaska Native, non-Hispanic/Latino; 11 Asian, non-Hispanic/Latino; 32 Hispanic/Latino; 1 Two or more races, non-Hispanic/Latino). Average age 37. 333 applicants, 77% accepted, 103 enrolled. In 2017, 292 master's, 9 doctorates, 318 other advanced degrees awarded. *Degree requirements:* For master's, thesis, field experience in the classroom teaching; for doctorate, thesis/dissertation. *Entrance requirements:* For master's, GRE General Test, MAT; for Ed S, minimum graduate GPA of 3.5, valid teaching certificate. Additional exam requirements/recommendations for international students: Required—TOEFL (minimum score 550 paper-based). *Application deadline:* For fall admission, 7/15 for domestic students; for spring admission, 12/1 for domestic students. Applications are processed on a rolling basis. Electronic applications accepted. *Expenses:* Tuition: Full-time $9360; part-time $520 per credit hour. *Required fees:* $200; $200 per year. $100 per term. *Financial support:* Career-related internships or fieldwork, Federal Work-Study, and unspecified assistantships available. Support available to part-time students. Financial award applicants required to submit FAFSA. *Unit head:* Dr. Don Gnecco, Dean, 706-778-3000 Ext. 1201, Fax: 706-776-9608, E-mail: dgnecco@piedmont.edu. *Application contact:* Kathleen Carter, Director of Graduate Enrollment Management, 706-778-8500 Ext. 1181, Fax: 706-778-0150, E-mail: kanderson@piedmont.edu.

Pontificia Universidad Catolica Madre y Maestra, Graduate School, Faculty of Sciences and Humanities, Santiago, Dominican Republic. Offers architecture (M Arch), including architecture of interiors, architecture of tourist lodgings, landscaping; early childhood education (M Ed).

Prescott College, Graduate Programs, Program in Education, Prescott, AZ 86301. Offers early childhood education (MA); early childhood special education (MA); education (MA); elementary education (MA); environmental education leadership and administration (MA); equine-assisted learning (MA); school guidance counseling (MA); secondary education (MA); special education: learning disabilities (MA); special education: mental retardation (MA); special education: serious emotional disabilities (MA); student-directed independent study (MA); sustainability education (PhD). *Program availability:* Part-time, online learning. *Degree requirements:* For master's, thesis, fieldwork or internship, practicum; for doctorate, thesis/dissertation. *Entrance requirements:* For master's, 2 letters of recommendation, resume; for doctorate, 3 letters of recommendation, resume, official transcripts, personal statement, program proposal. Additional exam requirements/recommendations for international students: Required—TOEFL (minimum score 500 paper-based). Electronic applications accepted.

Queens College of the City University of New York, Division of Education, Department of Educational and Community Programs, Queens, NY 11367-1597. Offers bilingual pupil personnel (AC); counselor education (MS Ed); mental health counseling (MS); school building leader (AC); school district leader (AC); school psychologist (MS Ed); special education-childhood education (AC); special education-early childhood (MS Ed); teacher of special education 1-6 (MS Ed); teacher of special education birth-2 (MS Ed); teaching students with disabilities, grades 7-12 (MS Ed, AC). *Program availability:* Part-time. *Faculty:* 20 full-time (14 women), 63 part-time/adjunct (37 women). *Students:* 105 full-time (94 women), 423 part-time (350 women); includes 241 minority (40 Black or African American, non-Hispanic/Latino; 2 American Indian or Alaska Native, non-Hispanic/Latino; 50 Asian, non-Hispanic/Latino; 142 Hispanic/Latino; 1 Native Hawaiian or other Pacific Islander, non-Hispanic/Latino; 6 Two or more races, non-Hispanic/Latino), 5 international. Average age 28. 515 applicants, 57% accepted, 230 enrolled. In 2017, 163 master's, 74 other advanced degrees awarded. *Degree requirements:* For master's, research project; for AC, internship. *Entrance requirements:* For master's, minimum GPA of 3.0. Additional exam requirements/recommendations for international students: Required—TOEFL, IELTS. *Application deadline:* For fall admission, 3/1 for domestic students. Applications are processed on a rolling basis. Application fee: $125. Electronic applications accepted. *Financial support:* Career-related internships or fieldwork available. Financial award application deadline: 4/1;

financial award applicants required to submit FAFSA. *Unit head:* Dr. Emilia Lopez, Chair, 718-997-5250, E-mail: emilia.lopez@qc.cuny.edu. *Application contact:* Elizabeth D'Amico-Ramirez, Assistant Director of Graduate Admissions, 718-997-5203, E-mail: elizabeth.damicoramirez@qc.cuny.edu.

Queens College of the City University of New York, Division of Education, Department of Elementary and Early Childhood Education, Queens, NY 11367-1597. Offers bilingual education (MAT, MS Ed, AC); childhood education (MAT, MS Ed); early childhood education birth-2 (MAT, MS Ed, AC); literacy education birth-grade 6 (MS Ed, AC). *Program availability:* Part-time, evening/weekend. *Students:* 112 full-time (98 women), 342 part-time (312 women); includes 243 minority (39 Black or African American, non-Hispanic/Latino; 87 Asian, non-Hispanic/Latino; 110 Hispanic/Latino; 7 Two or more races, non-Hispanic/Latino), 12 international. Average age 29. *Degree requirements:* For master's, research project. *Entrance requirements:* For master's, minimum GPA of 3.0. Additional exam requirements/recommendations for international students: Required—TOEFL, IELTS. *Application deadline:* For fall admission, 4/1 for domestic students. Applications are processed on a rolling basis. Application fee: $125. Electronic applications accepted. *Financial support:* Career-related internships or fieldwork available. Financial award application deadline: 4/1; financial award applicants required to submit FAFSA. *Unit head:* Daisuke Akiba, Chair, 718-997-5300, E-mail: daisuke.akiba@qc.cuny.edu. *Application contact:* Elizabeth D'Amico-Ramirez, Assistant Director of Graduate Admissions, 718-997-5203, E-mail: elizabeth.damicoramirez@qc.cuny.edu.

Radford University, College of Graduate Studies and Research, Program in Education, Radford, VA 24142. Offers early childhood education (MS); mathematics education (MS). *Accreditation:* NCATE. *Program availability:* Part-time, evening/weekend. *Faculty:* 18 full-time (13 women), 9 part-time/adjunct (7 women). *Students:* 33 full-time (26 women), 61 part-time (47 women); includes 11 minority (2 Black or African American, non-Hispanic/Latino; 2 Asian, non-Hispanic/Latino; 6 Hispanic/Latino; 1 Two or more races, non-Hispanic/Latino). Average age 31. 28 applicants, 100% accepted, 22 enrolled. In 2017, 33 master's awarded. *Degree requirements:* For master's, comprehensive exam. *Entrance requirements:* For master's, GRE (waived for any applicant with advanced degree), minimum GPA of 3.0, 2 letters of professional reference, personal statement, resume, official transcripts. Additional exam requirements/recommendations for international students: Required—TOEFL (minimum score 550 paper-based; 79 iBT), IELTS (minimum score 6.5). *Application deadline:* For fall admission, 2/15 priority date for domestic students, 12/1 for international students; for spring admission, 7/1 for international students. Applications are processed on a rolling basis. Application fee: $50. Electronic applications accepted. *Expenses:* Tuition, state resident: full-time $8336; part-time $347 per credit hour. Tuition, nonresident: full-time $16,862; part-time $702 per credit hour. *Required fees:* $3220; $135 per credit hour. Tuition and fees vary according to course load and program. *Financial support:* In 2017–18, 7 students received support, including 1 research assistantship (averaging $10,000 per year); career-related internships or fieldwork, scholarships/grants, and unspecified assistantships also available. Support available to part-time students. Financial award application deadline: 3/1; financial award applicants required to submit FAFSA. *Unit head:* Dr. Wendy Eckenrod-Green, Coordinator, 540-831-5302, E-mail: stel@radford.edu. Website: http://www.radford.edu/content/cehd/home/teacher-ed/programs/education-master.html

Regent University, Graduate School, School of Education, Virginia Beach, VA 23464-9800. Offers education (M Ed, Ed D, PhD), including adult education (Ed D, PhD, Ed S), advanced educational leadership (Ed D, PhD, Ed S), character education (Ed D, PhD, Ed S), Christian education leadership (Ed D, PhD, Ed S), Christian school administration (M Ed), curriculum and instruction (Ed D, PhD, Ed S), curriculum and instruction - adult education (M Ed), curriculum and instruction - Christian school (M Ed), curriculum and instruction - gifted and talented (M Ed), curriculum and instruction - STEM education (M Ed), curriculum and instruction - teacher leader (M Ed), discipleship for ministry (M Ed), educational leadership (M Ed), educational psychology (Ed D, PhD, Ed S), educational technology and online learning (Ed D, PhD, Ed S), elementary education (M Ed), exceptional education executive leadership (Ed D, PhD, Ed S), higher education (Ed D, PhD, Ed S), higher education leadership and management (Ed D, PhD, Ed S), instructional design and technology (M Ed), K-12 school leadership (Ed D, PhD, Ed S), K-12 special education (M Ed), leadership in mathematics education (M Ed), reading specialist (M Ed), special education (Ed D, PhD, Ed S), student affairs (M Ed), TESOL - adult education (M Ed), TESOL - K-12 (M Ed); educational specialist (Ed S), including adult education (Ed D, PhD, Ed S), advanced educational leadership (Ed D, PhD, Ed S), character education (Ed D, PhD, Ed S), Christian education leadership (Ed D, PhD, Ed S), curriculum and instruction (Ed D, PhD, Ed S), educational psychology (Ed D, PhD, Ed S), educational technology and online learning (Ed D, PhD, Ed S), exceptional education executive leadership (Ed D, PhD, Ed S), higher education (Ed D, PhD, Ed S), higher education leadership and management (Ed D, PhD, Ed S), K-12 school leadership (Ed D, PhD, Ed S), special education (Ed D, PhD, Ed S). *Accreditation:* TEAC. *Program availability:* Part-time, evening/weekend, 100% online, blended/hybrid learning. *Faculty:* 22 full-time (10 women), 44 part-time/adjunct (32 women). *Students:* 80 full-time (59 women), 945 part-time (750 women); includes 432 minority (352 Black or African American, non-Hispanic/Latino; 4 American Indian or Alaska Native, non-Hispanic/Latino; 14 Asian, non-Hispanic/Latino; 43 Hispanic/Latino; 19 Two or more races, non-Hispanic/Latino), 12 international. Average age 40. 1,125 applicants, 49% accepted, 436 enrolled. In 2017, 316 master's, 24 doctorates awarded. *Degree requirements:* For master's, thesis or alternative; for doctorate, comprehensive exam, thesis/dissertation. *Entrance requirements:* For master's, Virginia Communication and Literacy Assessment (VCLA), PRAXIS, college transcripts, writing sample, interview; for doctorate, GRE, writing sample, resume, transcripts, interview. Additional exam requirements/recommendations for international students: Required—TOEFL (minimum score 577 paper-based). *Application deadline:* For fall admission, 4/1 priority date for domestic students; for spring admission, 10/15 priority date for domestic students. Applications are processed on a rolling basis. Application fee: $50. Electronic applications accepted. *Expenses:* Contact institution. *Financial support:* In 2017–18, 669 students received support, including 1 fellowship (averaging $10,000 per year); career-related internships or fieldwork, scholarships/grants, and unspecified assistantships also available. Support available to part-time students. *Faculty research:* Christian school administration, curriculum and instruction, educational technology and online learning, higher education, special education. *Unit head:* Dr. Donald Finn, Dean, 757-352-4278, Fax: 757-352-4318, E-mail: dfinn@regent.edu. *Application contact:* Heidi Cece, Assistant Vice President of Enrollment Management, 800-373-5504, Fax: 757-352-4381, E-mail: admissions@regent.edu. Website: https://www.regent.edu/school-of-education/

Reinhardt University, Price School of Education, Waleska, GA 30183-2981. Offers M Ed, MAT. *Program availability:* Part-time, evening/weekend, online learning. *Degree requirements:* For master's, comprehensive exam. *Entrance requirements:* For master's, GACE, background check. Additional exam requirements/recommendations for international students: Required—TOEFL. Electronic applications accepted.

Early Childhood Education

Rhode Island College, School of Graduate Studies, Feinstein School of Education and Human Development, Department of Elementary Education, Providence, RI 02908-1991. Offers early childhood education (M Ed); elementary education (M Ed, MAT); reading (M Ed). *Accreditation:* NCATE. *Program availability:* Part-time, evening/weekend. *Faculty:* 9. *Students:* 19 full-time (18 women), 24 part-time (23 women). Average age 33. In 2017, 21 master's awarded. *Degree requirements:* For master's, comprehensive exam (for some programs), comprehensive assessment. *Entrance requirements:* For master's, GRE General Test or MAT, PRAXIS II (elementary content knowledge), undergraduate transcripts; minimum undergraduate GPA of 3.0; 3 letters of recommendation. Additional exam requirements/recommendations for international students: Recommended—TOEFL (minimum score 550 paper-based; 79 iBT). *Application deadline:* For fall admission, 3/1 for domestic students; for spring admission, 11/1 for domestic students. Applications are processed on a rolling basis. Application fee: $50. Electronic applications accepted. *Expenses:* Tuition, state resident: full-time $9768; part-time $407 per credit. Tuition, nonresident: full-time $19,008; part-time $792 per credit. *Required fees:* $696; $29 per credit. One-time fee: $200 full-time; $100 part-time. Tuition and fees vary according to course load. *Financial support:* Teaching assistantships with full tuition reimbursements, Federal Work-Study, scholarships/grants, and health care benefits available. Support available to part-time students. Financial award application deadline: 5/15; financial award applicants required to submit FAFSA. *Unit head:* Dr. Carolyn Obel-Omia, Chair, 401-456-8016. *Application contact:* Graduate Studies, 401-456-8700.
Website: http://www.ric.edu/elementaryEducation/

Rivier University, School of Graduate Studies, Department of Education, Nashua, NH 03060. Offers curriculum and instruction (M Ed); early childhood education (M Ed); educational administration (M Ed); educational studies (M Ed); elementary education (M Ed); elementary education and general special education (M Ed); emotional and behavioral disorders (M Ed); general social education (M Ed); leadership and learning (Ed D, CAGS); learning disabilities (M Ed); learning disabilities and reading (M Ed); mental health counseling (MA); reading (M Ed); school counseling (M Ed). *Program availability:* Part-time, evening/weekend. *Degree requirements:* For master's, comprehensive exam (for some programs), internships. *Entrance requirements:* For master's, GRE General Test or MAT.

Roberts Wesleyan College, Graduate Teacher Education Programs, Rochester, NY 14624-1997. Offers adolescence and special education (M Ed); childhood and special education (M Ed); literacy education (M Ed); special education (M Ed). *Program availability:* Part-time, evening/weekend. *Degree requirements:* For master's, thesis. Electronic applications accepted.

Rockford University, Graduate Studies, Department of Education, Program in Early Childhood Education, Rockford, IL 61108-2393. Offers MAT. *Program availability:* Part-time, evening/weekend. *Degree requirements:* For master's, thesis optional. *Entrance requirements:* For master's, GRE General Test, basic skills test (for students seeking certification), 3 letters of recommendation. Additional exam requirements/recommendations for international students: Required—TOEFL. Electronic applications accepted.

Roosevelt University, Graduate Division, College of Education, Program in Teaching and Learning, Chicago, IL 60605. Offers early childhood education (MA). *Program availability:* Part-time, evening/weekend. *Students:* 15 part-time (13 women); includes 5 minority (3 Black or African American, non-Hispanic/Latino; 2 Hispanic/Latino). Average age 31. 4 applicants, 100% accepted, 4 enrolled. In 2017, 14 master's awarded. *Application deadline:* Applications are processed on a rolling basis. Application fee: $40. Electronic applications accepted. *Financial support:* Scholarships/grants available. *Application contact:* Laura Lag, Associate Dean for Graduate Admission, 312-853-4753, E-mail: llag@roosevelt.edu.
Website: https://www.roosevelt.edu/academics/programs/masters-in-teaching-and-learning-ma

Rutgers University–New Brunswick, Graduate School of Education, Department of Learning and Teaching, Program in Early Childhood/Elementary Education, Piscataway, NJ 08854-8097. Offers Ed M, Ed D. *Program availability:* Part-time. Terminal master's awarded for partial completion of doctoral program. *Degree requirements:* For master's, comprehensive exam (for some programs); for doctorate, thesis/dissertation, qualifying exam. *Entrance requirements:* For master's, GRE General Test, minimum GPA of 3.0; for doctorate, GRE General Test, minimum GPA of 3.5. Additional exam requirements/recommendations for international students: Required—TOEFL. Electronic applications accepted.

Saginaw Valley State University, College of Education, Program in Early Childhood Education, University Center, MI 48710. Offers MAT. *Accreditation:* NCATE. *Program availability:* Part-time, evening/weekend. *Students:* 2 full-time (both women), 45 part-time (all women); includes 5 minority (2 Black or African American, non-Hispanic/Latino; 1 Hispanic/Latino; 2 Two or more races, non-Hispanic/Latino), 1 international. Average age 33. 14 applicants, 100% accepted, 9 enrolled. In 2017, 28 master's awarded. *Degree requirements:* For master's, capstone course. *Entrance requirements:* For master's, minimum GPA of 3.0, teaching certificate. Additional exam requirements/recommendations for international students: Required—TOEFL (minimum score 550 paper-based; 79 iBT). *Application deadline:* For fall admission, 7/15 for international students; for winter admission, 11/15 for international students; for spring admission, 4/15 for international students. Applications are processed on a rolling basis. Application fee: $30 ($90 for international students). Electronic applications accepted. *Expenses:* Tuition, state resident: full-time $10,156; part-time $564.20 per credit hour. Tuition, nonresident: full-time $19,336; part-time $1074.20 per credit hour. *Required fees:* $263; $14.60 per credit hour. Tuition and fees vary according to degree level and program. *Financial support:* Federal Work-Study and scholarships/grants available. Support available to part-time students. Financial award applicants required to submit FAFSA. *Unit head:* Dr. Mary Harmon, Dean, 989-964-4057, Fax: 989-964-4563, E-mail: coeconnect@svsu.edu. *Application contact:* Jenna Briggs, Director, Graduate and International Admissions, 989-964-6096, Fax: 989-964-2788, E-mail: gradadm@svsu.edu.

St. Ambrose University, School of Education, Davenport, IA 52803-2898. Offers early childhood education (M Ed); educational administration (M Ed). *Accreditation:* TEAC. *Program availability:* Part-time, evening/weekend, online learning. *Degree requirements:* For master's, comprehensive exam. *Entrance requirements:* For master's, GRE General Test or MAT, minimum GPA of 2.75. Additional exam requirements/recommendations for international students: Required—TOEFL. Electronic applications accepted. *Faculty research:* Disabilities and postsecondary career avenues, self-determination.

St. Bonaventure University, School of Graduate Studies, School of Education, Literacy Programs, St. Bonaventure, NY 14778-2284. Offers adolescent literacy 5-12 (MS Ed); childhood literacy B-6 (MS Ed). *Accreditation:* NCATE. *Program availability:* Part-time, evening/weekend. *Faculty:* 2 part-time/adjunct (both women). *Students:* 7 full-time (all women), 3 part-time (1 woman); includes 2 minority (1 Black or African American, non-Hispanic/Latino; 1 Hispanic/Latino). Average age 23. 3 applicants, 100% accepted, 3 enrolled. In 2017, 13 master's awarded. *Degree requirements:* For master's, comprehensive exam, thesis optional, minimum cumulative GPA of 3.0, clinical practicum, literacy coaching internship, electronic portfolio. *Entrance requirements:* For master's, GRE or MAT, teaching certificate in matching area in-hand or pending, transcripts from all previous colleges, minimum GPA of 3.0, 2 references, interview, writing sample. Additional exam requirements/recommendations for international students: Required—TOEFL (minimum score 550 paper-based; 80 iBT). *Application deadline:* For fall admission, 6/15 priority date for domestic students, 2/1 for international students; for spring admission, 11/15 priority date for domestic students, 7/1 for international students. Applications are processed on a rolling basis. Application fee: $0. Electronic applications accepted. *Expenses:* $733 per credit hour, $100 graduation fee. *Financial support:* Federal Work-Study, scholarships/grants, health care benefits, and unspecified assistantships available. Support available to part-time students. Financial award application deadline: 4/15; financial award applicants required to submit FAFSA. *Unit head:* Dr. Lisa Buenaventura, Interim Program Director, 716-375-2394, Fax: 716-375-2360, E-mail: lbuenave@sbu.edu. *Application contact:* Bruce Campbell, Director of Graduate Admissions, 716-375-2429, Fax: 716-375-4015, E-mail: gradsch@sbu.edu.
Website: http://www.sbu.edu/academics/schools/education/graduate-degrees-certificates/msed-in-childhood-literacy

St. Catherine University, Graduate Programs, Program in Education - Montessori Education, St. Paul, MN 55105. Offers MA. *Program availability:* Part-time, evening/weekend, online learning. *Students:* 27 full-time (26 women), 9 part-time (all women); includes 4 minority (1 Black or African American, non-Hispanic/Latino; 1 Asian, non-Hispanic/Latino; 1 Hispanic/Latino; 1 Two or more races, non-Hispanic/Latino), 3 international. Average age 35. In 2017, 14 master's awarded. Tuition and fees vary according to program. *Unit head:* Teresa Ripple, Director, Montessori Programs, 651-690-6227, Fax: 651-690-6024, E-mail: tmripple@stkate.edu.

St. John's University, The School of Education, Department of Curriculum and Instruction, PhD in Curriculum and Instruction Program, Queens, NY 11439. Offers early childhood (PhD); global education (PhD); STEM education (PhD); teaching, learning, and knowing (PhD). *Program availability:* Part-time-only. *Degree requirements:* For doctorate, comprehensive exam, thesis/dissertation. *Entrance requirements:* For doctorate, teacher certification (or equivalent), at least three years' teaching experience or the equivalent in informal learning environments, master's degree. Additional exam requirements/recommendations for international students: Required—TOEFL. *Application deadline:* Applications are processed on a rolling basis. Application fee: $70. Electronic applications accepted. *Expenses:* Tuition: Full-time $44,280; part-time $1230 per credit. *Required fees:* $340; $340 per credit. Tuition and fees vary according to course load, degree level and program. *Financial support:* Fellowships, research assistantships, and scholarships/grants available. Support available to part-time students. Financial award application deadline: 2/1; financial award applicants required to submit FAFSA. *Faculty research:* Literacies, early childhood, STEM, school culture, global education. *Unit head:* Dr. Sandra Schamroth Abrams, PhD Program Director, 718-990-8313, E-mail: abramss@stjohns.edu. *Application contact:* Dr. Sandra Schamroth Abrams, PhD Program Director, 718-990-8313, E-mail: abramss@stjohns.edu.
Website: https://www.stjohns.edu/academics/schools-and-colleges/school-education/programs-and-majors/phd-curriculum-and-instruction

St. John's University, The School of Education, Department of Curriculum and Instruction, Program in Early Childhood Education, Queens, NY 11439. Offers MS Ed. *Program availability:* Part-time, evening/weekend, online learning. *Students:* 3 full-time (all women), 11 part-time (10 women); includes 9 minority (3 Black or African American, non-Hispanic/Latino; 4 Asian, non-Hispanic/Latino; 1 Hispanic/Latino; 1 Two or more races, non-Hispanic/Latino), 2 international. Average age 30. 6 applicants, 67% accepted, 3 enrolled. In 2017, 6 master's awarded. *Degree requirements:* For master's, thesis. *Entrance requirements:* For master's, GRE, MAT, or PRAXIS, statement of goals (personal essay), official undergraduate transcripts, initial teaching certification. Additional exam requirements/recommendations for international students: Required—TOEFL, IELTS. *Application deadline:* For fall admission, 8/17 for domestic students; for summer admission, 5/15 for domestic and international students. Application fee: $70. Electronic applications accepted. *Expenses:* Tuition: Full-time $44,280; part-time $1230 per credit. *Required fees:* $340; $340 per credit. Tuition and fees vary according to course load, degree level and program. *Financial support:* Fellowships, research assistantships, scholarships/grants, and unspecified assistantships available. Support available to part-time students. Financial award application deadline: 2/1; financial award applicants required to submit FAFSA. *Faculty research:* Improving children's learning in math, science and technology; health and nutrition education to prevent obesity; oral language and literacy development in diverse populations; multicultural and international education; special needs and inclusive education. *Unit head:* Dr. Daniel Ness, Chair, 718-990-2717, E-mail: nessd@stjohns.edu. *Application contact:* Dr. Daniel Ness, Chair, 718-990-2717, E-mail: nessd@stjohns.edu.
Website: https://www.stjohns.edu/academics/schools-and-colleges/school-education/programs-and-majors/early-childhood-education-master-science-education

St. John's University, The School of Education, Department of Education Specialties, Program in Teaching English to Speakers of Other Languages and Bilingual Education, Queens, NY 11439. Offers bilingual education (Adv C); childhood education and teaching English to speakers of other languages (MS Ed); teaching English to speakers of other languages (MS Ed, Adv C). *Students:* 21 full-time (19 women), 83 part-time (73 women); includes 39 minority (4 Black or African American, non-Hispanic/Latino; 9 Asian, non-Hispanic/Latino; 24 Hispanic/Latino; 2 Two or more races, non-Hispanic/Latino), 8 international. Average age 32. 54 applicants, 91% accepted, 35 enrolled. In 2017, 47 master's, 71 Adv Cs awarded. *Degree requirements:* For Adv C, one foreign language. *Entrance requirements:* For master's, GRE, MAT, or PRAXIS, statement of goals (personal essay), official undergraduate transcripts, initial teaching certification; for Adv C, initial teaching certification, first master's transcripts, statement of purpose. Additional exam requirements/recommendations for international students: Required—TOEFL, IELTS. *Application deadline:* For fall admission, 8/17 for domestic and international students; for summer admission, 5/15 for domestic and international students. Application fee: $70. Electronic applications accepted. *Expenses:* Tuition: Full-time $44,280; part-time $1230 per credit. *Required fees:* $340; $340 per credit. Tuition and fees vary according to course load, degree level and program. *Financial support:* Fellowships, research assistantships, scholarships/grants, and unspecified assistantships available. Support available to part-time students. Financial award application deadline: 2/1; financial award applicants required to submit FAFSA. *Faculty research:* Second language learning and academic achievement, heritage language education, assessing the progress of English language learners toward English acquisition, dual language acquisition, study of English Creoles and dialects of other English's, literacy development for ESL learners; investigating Caribbean and Creole language and culture, education law. *Unit head:* Dr. John Spiridakis, Chair, 718-990-5591, E-mail: spiridaj@stjohns.edu. *Application contact:* Dr. John Spiridakis, Chair, 718-990-5591, E-mail: spiridaj@stjohns.edu.
Website: https://www.stjohns.edu/academics/schools-and-colleges/school-education/programs-and-majors/tesol-master-science-education

St. Joseph's College, Long Island Campus, Programs in Education, Field of Infant/Toddler Early Childhood Special Education, Patchogue, NY 11772-2399. Offers MA.

Program availability: Part-time, evening/weekend. *Faculty:* 6 full-time (5 women), 5 part-time/adjunct (all women). *Students:* 31 full-time (30 women), 95 part-time (87 women); includes 19 minority (1 Black or African American, non-Hispanic/Latino; 1 Asian, non-Hispanic/Latino; 17 Hispanic/Latino). Average age 27. 83 applicants, 77% accepted, 53 enrolled. In 2017, 7 master's awarded. *Entrance requirements:* For master's, official transcripts, two letters of recommendation, resume, copies of all teaching certificates, completed medical form. Additional exam requirements/recommendations for international students: Recommended—TOEFL (minimum score 550 paper-based; 79 iBT), IELTS (minimum score 7). *Application deadline:* Applications are processed on a rolling basis. Application fee: $25. Electronic applications accepted. *Expenses: Tuition:* Full-time $17,550; part-time $975 per credit. *Required fees:* $362. *Financial support:* In 2017–18, 32 students received support. Applicants required to submit FAFSA. *Unit head:* Katherine Granelli, Director of MA in Infant/Toddler Early Childhood Special Education, 631-687-1217, E-mail: kgranelli@sjcny.edu.

Saint Joseph's University, College of Arts and Sciences, Graduate Programs in Education, Philadelphia, PA 19131-1395. Offers curriculum supervisor (Certificate); educational leadership (MS, Ed D); elementary education (MS, Certificate); elementary/middle school education (Certificate); organizational development and leadership (MS); principal (Certificate); professional education (MS); reading specialist (MS, Certificate); reading supervisor (Certificate); secondary education (MS, Certificate); special education (MS); special education 7-12 (Certificate); special education PK-8 (Certificate); superintendent's letter of eligibility (Certificate); supervisor of special education (Certificate); teacher of the deaf and hard of hearing (Certificate). *Program availability:* Part-time, evening/weekend, blended/hybrid learning. *Faculty:* 18 full-time (16 women), 63 part-time/adjunct (44 women). *Students:* 79 full-time (60 women), 793 part-time (604 women); includes 179 minority (125 Black or African American, non-Hispanic/Latino; 5 American Indian or Alaska Native, non-Hispanic/Latino; 15 Asian, non-Hispanic/Latino; 27 Hispanic/Latino; 1 Native Hawaiian or other Pacific Islander, non-Hispanic/Latino; 6 Two or more races, non-Hispanic/Latino), 12 international. Average age 34. 375 applicants, 75% accepted, 189 enrolled. In 2017, 340 master's, 13 doctorates, 3 other advanced degrees awarded. *Degree requirements:* For master's, thesis or alternative; for doctorate, comprehensive exam, thesis/dissertation. *Entrance requirements:* For master's, 2 letters of recommendation, minimum GPA of 3.0, official transcripts, personal statement; for doctorate, GRE, master's degree from accredited institution, minimum graduate GPA of 3.5, computer competence, interview with program director. Additional exam requirements/recommendations for international students: Required—TOEFL (minimum score 550 paper-based; 80 iBT), IELTS (minimum score 6.5), PTE (minimum score 60). *Application deadline:* For fall admission, 7/15 for international students; for spring admission, 11/1 for international students. Applications are processed on a rolling basis. Application fee: $35. Electronic applications accepted. *Expenses:* Contact institution. *Financial support:* Scholarships/grants and unspecified assistantships available. Financial award application deadline: 5/1; financial award applicants required to submit FAFSA. *Faculty research:* Factors predicting early mathematics skills for low income children, early child care and development, preschool quality, parent communication and home-school collaboration issues, education of terminally ill children, preparing literacy teachers for urban schools. *Unit head:* Dr. John Vacca, Associate Dean, 610-660-3131, E-mail: gradcas@sju.edu. *Application contact:* Graduate Admissions, College of Arts and Sciences, 610-660-3131, E-mail: gradcas@sju.edu.
Website: https://sites.sju.edu/graduate-programs/

Saint Mary's College of California, Kalmanovitz School of Education, Program in Early Childhood Education, Moraga, CA 94575. Offers supervision and leadership (MA). *Program availability:* Part-time, evening/weekend. *Degree requirements:* For master's, thesis or alternative. *Entrance requirements:* For master's, interview, minimum GPA of 3.0.

Saint Mary's College of California, Kalmanovitz School of Education, Program in Montessori Education, Moraga, CA 94575. Offers MA. *Degree requirements:* For master's, thesis or project. *Entrance requirements:* For master's, writing proficiency exam.

Saint Xavier University, Graduate Studies, School of Education, Chicago, IL 60655-3105. Offers counseling (MA); curriculum and instruction (MA); early childhood education (MA); educational administration (MA); elementary education (MA); individualized studies (MA), including educational technology, English as a second language (ESL), ISTEM (integrative science, technology, engineering, and math), science education; music education (MA); reading (MA); secondary education (MA); Spanish education (MA); special education (MA); teaching and leadership (MA). *Accreditation:* NCATE. *Program availability:* Part-time, evening/weekend. *Degree requirements:* For master's, thesis or project. *Entrance requirements:* For master's, minimum GPA of 3.0. *Expenses:* Contact institution.

Salem State University, School of Graduate Studies, Program in Early Childhood Education, Salem, MA 01970-5353. Offers M Ed. *Accreditation:* NCATE. *Program availability:* Part-time, evening/weekend. *Entrance requirements:* For master's, GRE or MAT. Additional exam requirements/recommendations for international students: Required—TOEFL (minimum score 550 paper-based; 80 iBT) or IELTS (minimum score 5.5).

San Francisco State University, Division of Graduate Studies, College of Education, Department of Elementary Education, Program in Early Childhood Education, San Francisco, CA 94132-1722. Offers MA. *Accreditation:* NCATE. *Unit head:* Dr. Josephine Arce, Chair, 415-338-7636, Fax: 415-338-0567, E-mail: jarce@sfsu.edu. *Application contact:* Dr. Daniel Meier, MA Program Coordinator, 415-338-3417, Fax: 415-338-0567, E-mail: dmeier@sfsu.edu.
Website: https://eed.sfsu.edu/

San Francisco State University, Division of Graduate Studies, College of Education, Department of Special Education, San Francisco, CA 94132-1722. Offers augmentative and alternative communication (AC); autism spectrum (AC); early childhood special education (AC); education specialist (Credential); orientation and mobility (Credential); special education (MA, PhD), including early childhood special education (MA), mild to moderate disabilities (MA), moderate to severe disabilities (MA), orientation and mobility (MA), visual impairments (MA). PhD offered jointly with University of California, Berkeley. *Accreditation:* NCATE. *Unit head:* Dr. Yvonne Bui, Chair, 415-338-2503, Fax: 415-338-0566, E-mail: ybui@sfsu.edu. *Application contact:* Jeanne Oh, Academic Office Coordinator, 415-338-2501, Fax: 415-338-0566, E-mail: joh2@sfsu.edu.
Website: http://sped.sfsu.edu/home

San Ignacio University, Graduate Programs, Doral, FL 33178. Offers business administration (MBA), including human resources management, international business, marketing management; education (M Ed), including early childhood education, educational leadership, special education; hospitality management (MA), including gastronomy and restaurant management, tourism management.

Shaw University, Department of Education, Raleigh, NC 27601-2399. Offers curriculum and instruction (MS), including early childhood education. *Program availability:* Part-time, evening/weekend. *Degree requirements:* For master's, comprehensive exam, thesis, practicum/internship, PRAXIS II. *Entrance requirements:* For master's, GRE

General Test, letters of recommendation. Additional exam requirements/recommendations for international students: Required—TOEFL (minimum score 500 paper-based). Electronic applications accepted. *Faculty research:* Multicultural education, instructional technology.

Shenandoah University, School of Education and Leadership, Winchester, VA 22601. Offers administration and supervision (Certificate); administrative leadership (D Ed); early childhood literacy (MS); educational administration (MS); elementary school teacher education (Certificate); emphasis in teaching (MSE); health and physical education (Certificate); individualized focus (MS, MSE); literacy education (MS); middle school teacher education (Certificate); organizational leadership (MS, D Prof); reading licensure (MS, Certificate); reading non-licensure (MS); secondary school teacher education (Certificate); special education (MSE); writing (MS). *Accreditation:* TEAC. *Program availability:* Part-time, evening/weekend. *Faculty:* 8 full-time (7 women), 22 part-time/adjunct (16 women). *Students:* 16 full-time (14 women), 221 part-time (167 women); includes 32 minority (17 Black or African American, non-Hispanic/Latino; 1 American Indian or Alaska Native, non-Hispanic/Latino; 6 Asian, non-Hispanic/Latino; 5 Hispanic/Latino; 1 Native Hawaiian or other Pacific Islander, non-Hispanic/Latino; 2 Two or more races, non-Hispanic/Latino), 3 international. Average age 38. 81 applicants, 99% accepted, 63 enrolled. In 2017, 53 master's, 11 doctorates, 49 other advanced degrees awarded. *Degree requirements:* For master's, comprehensive exam (for some programs), thesis (for some programs); for doctorate, comprehensive exam, thesis/dissertation. *Entrance requirements:* For degree, PRAXIS Academic Core, SAT/ACT, PRAXIS Academic Core Math, or VCLA, three letters of recommendation, writing sample, undergraduate degree. Additional exam requirements/recommendations for international students: Required—TOEFL (minimum score 550 paper-based, 79 iBT) or IELTS (6.5). *Application deadline:* For fall admission, 5/1 priority date for domestic students, 5/1 for international students; for spring admission, 10/15 priority date for domestic students, 10/15 for international students; for summer admission, 3/15 priority date for domestic students, 3/15 for international students. Application fee: $30. Electronic applications accepted. *Expenses:* $15,600 tuition plus $1,296 fees (technology and student services). *Financial support:* In 2017–18, 26 students received support. Scholarships/grants and unspecified assistantships available. Financial award applicants required to submit FAFSA. *Faculty research:* Mentoring, behavior support for students, teacher change agency, educational technology in pedagogy, literacy education. *Unit head:* Jill Lindsey, PhD, Director, 540-535-7324, Fax: 540-665-4726, E-mail: jlindsey@su.edu. *Application contact:* Andrew Woodall, Executive Director of Recruitment and Admissions, 540-665-4581, Fax: 540-665-4627, E-mail: admit@su.edu.
Website: http://www.su.edu/education/

Shippensburg University of Pennsylvania, School of Graduate Studies, College of Education and Human Services, Department of Teacher Education, Shippensburg, PA 17257-2299. Offers curriculum and instruction (M Ed), including biology, early childhood education, elementary education, geography/earth science, history, mathematics, middle school education, modern languages; reading (M Ed). *Accreditation:* NCATE. *Program availability:* Part-time, evening/weekend, 100% online, blended/hybrid learning. *Faculty:* 13 full-time (8 women), 1 (woman) part-time/adjunct. *Students:* 10 full-time (7 women), 94 part-time (81 women); includes 10 minority (3 Black or African American, non-Hispanic/Latino; 2 Asian, non-Hispanic/Latino; 5 Hispanic/Latino), 1 international. Average age 34. 71 applicants, 86% accepted, 35 enrolled. In 2017, 23 master's awarded. *Degree requirements:* For master's, comprehensive exam (for some programs), thesis optional, practicum or internship; capstone seminar (for some programs). *Entrance requirements:* For master's, MAT or GRE (if GPA less than 2.75), interview, 3 letters of reference, questionnaire of teaching background and future goals, resume. Additional exam requirements/recommendations for international students: Required—TOEFL (minimum score 550 paper-based, 68 iBT) or IELTS (minimum score 6). *Application deadline:* For fall admission, 4/1 priority date for domestic students, 4/30 for international students; for spring admission, 9/1 priority date for domestic students, 9/30 for international students; for summer admission, 2/1 priority date for domestic students. Applications are processed on a rolling basis. Application fee: $45. Electronic applications accepted. *Expenses:* Tuition, state resident: part-time $500 per credit. Tuition, nonresident: part-time $750 per credit. *Required fees:* $145 per credit. *Financial support:* In 2017–18, 1 student received support. Career-related internships or fieldwork, scholarships/grants, unspecified assistantships, and resident hall director and student payroll positions available. Support available to part-time students. Financial award application deadline: 3/1; financial award applicants required to submit FAFSA. *Unit head:* Dr. Christine A. Royce, Chairperson, 717-477-1688, Fax: 717-477-4046, E-mail: caroyc@ship.edu. *Application contact:* Maya T. Mapp, Director of Admissions, 717-477-1231, Fax: 717-477-4016, E-mail: mtmapp@ship.edu.
Website: http://www.ship.edu/teacher/

Siena Heights University, Graduate College, Adrian, MI 49221-1796. Offers clinical mental health counseling (MA); educational leadership (Specialist); leadership (MA), including health care leadership, organizational leadership; teacher education (MA), including early childhood education, early childhood education: Montessori, education leadership: principal, elementary education: reading K-12, leadership: higher education, secondary education: reading K-12, special education: cognitive impairment, special education: learning disabilities. *Program availability:* Part-time, evening/weekend. *Degree requirements:* For master's, thesis, presentation. *Entrance requirements:* For master's, minimum GPA of 3.0, current resume, essay, all post-secondary transcripts, 3 letters of reference, conviction disclosure form; copy of teaching certificate (for some education programs); for Specialist, master's degree, minimum GPA of 3.0, current resume, essay, all post-secondary transcripts, 3 letters of reference, conviction disclosure form; copy of teaching certificate (for some education programs). Electronic applications accepted.

Sonoma State University, School of Education, Rohnert Park, CA 94928. Offers administrative services (Credential); curriculum, teaching, and learning (MA); early childhood education (MA); education specialist (Credential); educational leadership (MA); multiple subject (Credential); reading and literacy (MA, Credential); single subject (Credential); special education (MA). *Accreditation:* NCATE. *Program availability:* Part-time, evening/weekend. *Entrance requirements:* For master's, minimum GPA of 2.5. Additional exam requirements/recommendations for international students: Required—TOEFL (minimum score 500 paper-based). Application fee: $55. *Financial support:* Fellowships, research assistantships, career-related internships or fieldwork, and Federal Work-Study available. Support available to part-time students. Financial award application deadline: 3/2; financial award applicants required to submit FAFSA. *Unit head:* Dr. Carlos Ayala, Dean, 707-664-4412, E-mail: carlos.ayala@sonoma.edu. *Application contact:* Dr. Karen Grady, Coordinator of Graduate Studies, 707-664-3328, E-mail: karen.grady@sonoma.edu.
Website: http://www.sonoma.edu/education/

South Carolina State University, College of Graduate and Professional Studies, Department of Education, Orangeburg, SC 29117-0001. Offers early childhood education (MAT); education (M Ed); elementary education (M Ed, MAT); English (MAT); general science/biology (MAT); mathematics (MAT); secondary education (M Ed), including biology education, business education, counselor education, English education, home economics education, industrial education, mathematics education, science education, social studies education; special education (M Ed), including emotionally handicapped, learning disabilities, mentally handicapped. *Accreditation:* NCATE. *Program availability:* Part-time, evening/weekend. *Faculty:* 11 full-time (6 women), 4 part-time/adjunct (2 women). *Students:* 26 full-time (18 women), 22 part-time (17 women); includes 41 minority (all Black or African American, non-Hispanic/Latino), 1 international. Average age 33. 25 applicants, 100% accepted, 19 enrolled. In 2017, 6 master's awarded. *Degree requirements:* For master's, thesis optional, departmental qualifying exam. *Entrance requirements:* For master's, GRE General Test, NTE, interview, teaching certificate. *Application deadline:* For fall admission, 6/15 priority date for domestic students, 6/15 for international students; for spring admission, 11/1 for domestic and international students. Application fee: $25. Electronic applications accepted. *Expenses:* Tuition, state resident: full-time $9388; part-time $607 per credit hour. Tuition, nonresident: full-time $19,968; part-time $1194 per credit hour. *Required fees:* $766; $766 per credit hour. *Financial support:* Fellowships, career-related internships or fieldwork, Federal Work-Study, and scholarships/grants available. Financial award application deadline: 6/1. *Unit head:* Dr. Charlie Spell, Interim Chair, Department of Education, 803-536-8963, Fax: 803-516-4568, E-mail: cspell@scsu.edu. *Application contact:* Curtis Foskey, Coordinator of Graduate Studies, 803-536-8419, Fax: 803-536-8812, E-mail: cfoskey@scsu.edu.

Southern New Hampshire University, School of Education, Manchester, NH 03106-1045. Offers curriculum and instruction (M Ed), including dyslexia studies and language-based learning disabilities, educational leadership, reading, special education, technology integration; dyslexia studies and language-based learning disabilities (Certificate); early childhood and special education (M Ed); educational leadership (M Ed, Ed D); educational studies (M Ed); elementary and special education (M Ed); field based education (M Ed); higher education administration (MS); teaching English as a foreign language (MS). *Program availability:* Part-time, evening/weekend, online learning. *Degree requirements:* For master's, comprehensive exam (for some programs), thesis or alternative. *Entrance requirements:* For master's, PRAXIS I, minimum GPA of 2.75. Additional exam requirements/recommendations for international students: Required—TOEFL (minimum score 550 paper-based). *Application deadline:* Applications are processed on a rolling basis. Application fee: $40. Electronic applications accepted. *Expenses:* Contact institution. *Financial support:* Institutionally sponsored loans available. Financial award applicants required to submit FAFSA. *Unit head:* Raymond McNulty, Dean, 603-668-2211, Fax: 603-629-4673. *Application contact:* Office of Graduate Admission, 888-327-SNHU, Fax: 603-644-3144, E-mail: enroll@snhu.edu.

Southern Oregon University, Graduate Studies, School of Education, Ashland, OR 97520. Offers elementary education (MA Ed, MS Ed), including classroom teacher, early childhood, handicapped learner, reading, supervision; secondary education (MA Ed, MS Ed), including classroom teacher, handicapped learner, reading, supervision; teaching (MAT). *Program availability:* Online learning. *Degree requirements:* For master's, thesis optional. *Entrance requirements:* For master's, GRE General Test, minimum cumulative GPA of 3.0 in the last 90 quarter credits (60 semester credits) of undergraduate coursework. Additional exam requirements/recommendations for international students: Required—TOEFL (minimum score 540 paper-based; 76 iBT), IELTS (minimum score 6), ELPT (minimum score 964) or ELS (minimum score 112). Electronic applications accepted.

Southwestern College, Education Programs, Winfield, KS 67156-2499. Offers curriculum and instruction (M Ed); early childhood education (M Ed); educational leadership (Ed D), including higher education leadership, PK-12 education leadership; special education (M Ed), including high-incidence disabilities, low-incidence disabilities; teaching (MA). *Accreditation:* NCATE. *Program availability:* Part-time, evening/weekend, 100% online, blended/hybrid learning. *Faculty:* 6 full-time (5 women), 12 part-time/adjunct (10 women). *Students:* 12 full-time (10 women), 77 part-time (51 women); includes 12 minority (5 Black or African American, non-Hispanic/Latino; 2 American Indian or Alaska Native, non-Hispanic/Latino; 1 Asian, non-Hispanic/Latino; 3 Hispanic/Latino; 1 Native Hawaiian or other Pacific Islander, non-Hispanic/Latino), 10 international. Average age 39. 29 applicants, 86% accepted, 18 enrolled. In 2017, 52 master's, 11 doctorates awarded. *Degree requirements:* For master's, practicum, portfolio; for doctorate, thesis/dissertation, professional portfolio. *Entrance requirements:* For master's, baccalaureate degree, minimum GPA of 3.0, valid teaching certificate (for special education); for doctorate, GRE if no master's degree, baccalaureate degree with minimum GPA of 3.25 and current teaching experience, or master's degree with minimum GPA of 3.5. Additional exam requirements/recommendations for international students: Required—TOEFL (minimum score 550 paper-based; 80 iBT). *Application deadline:* Applications are processed on a rolling basis. Application fee: $40. Electronic applications accepted. *Expenses:* $577 per credit hour, $509 online (for master's programs); $609 per credit hour (for doctorate program). *Financial support:* In 2017–18, 9 students received support. Unspecified assistantships and employee tuition waivers available. Financial award applicants required to submit FAFSA. *Unit head:* Dana Pentz, Director of Education Operations, 620-229-6253, E-mail: dana.pentz@sckans.edu. *Application contact:* Dennis Russell, Director of Admissions and Student Services, 888-684-5335 Ext. 3372, Fax: 888-684-5218, E-mail: dennis.russell@sckans.edu. Website: http://www.sckans.edu/graduate/education-med/

Southwestern Oklahoma State University, College of Professional and Graduate Studies, School of Behavioral Sciences and Education, Specialization in Early Childhood Education, Weatherford, OK 73096-3098. Offers M Ed. M Ed distance learning degree program offered to Oklahoma residents only. *Accreditation:* NCATE. *Program availability:* Part-time, evening/weekend. *Degree requirements:* For master's, exam. *Entrance requirements:* For master's, GRE General Test or minimum undergraduate GPA of 3.0. Additional exam requirements/recommendations for international students: Required—TOEFL.

Southwest Minnesota State University, Department of Education, Marshall, MN 56258. Offers ESL (MS); math (MS); reading (MS); special education (MS), including developmental disabilities, early childhood education, emotional behavioral disorders, learning disabilities; teaching, learning and leadership (MS). *Program availability:* Part-time, evening/weekend, online learning. *Entrance requirements:* Additional exam requirements/recommendations for international students: Required—TOEFL or IELTS; Recommended—TOEFL (minimum score 550 paper-based; 80 iBT), IELTS.

Springfield College, Graduate Programs, Programs in Education, Springfield, MA 01109-3797. Offers early childhood education (M Ed); educational studies (M Ed); elementary education (M Ed); secondary education (M Ed); special education (M Ed, CAGS). *Program availability:* Part-time, evening/weekend. *Students:* 18 applicants, 72% accepted, 12 enrolled. In 2017, 22 master's awarded. *Entrance requirements:* For master's, Massachusetts Tests for Educator Licensure (MTEL). Additional exam requirements/recommendations for international students: Required—TOEFL (minimum score 550 paper-based); Recommended—IELTS (minimum score 7). *Application deadline:* For fall admission, 1/15 for domestic and international students; for winter admission, 11/1 for domestic and international students; for spring admission, 11/1 for domestic and international students. Applications are processed on a rolling basis. Application fee: $50. Electronic applications accepted. *Expenses:* Contact institution.

Financial support: Fellowships with partial tuition reimbursements, teaching assistantships with partial tuition reimbursements, career-related internships or fieldwork, Federal Work-Study, institutionally sponsored loans, scholarships/grants, and unspecified assistantships available. Financial award application deadline: 3/1; financial award applicants required to submit FAFSA. *Unit head:* Linda Davis-Delano, Director of Education Preparation and Licensure, 413-748-3295, E-mail: ldelano@springfield.edu. *Application contact:* Anne Griffin, Director of Graduate Admissions, 413-748-3225, Fax: 413-748-3694, E-mail: agriffin2@springfield.edu.
Website: http://springfield.edu/wtp

Spring Hill College, Graduate Programs, Program in Education, Mobile, AL 36608-1791. Offers early childhood education (MAT, MS Ed); educational theory (MS Ed); elementary education (MAT, MS Ed); secondary education (MAT, MS Ed). *Program availability:* Part-time. *Faculty:* 2 full-time (both women). *Students:* 15 part-time (14 women); includes 6 minority (5 Black or African American, non-Hispanic/Latino; 1 Hispanic/Latino). Average age 30. In 2017, 5 master's awarded. *Degree requirements:* For master's, comprehensive exam, completion of program within 6 calendar years of entrance into graduate studies at Spring Hill; documentation of course field assignments (MS) or completion of internship (MAT). *Entrance requirements:* For master's, GRE, MAT, or PRAXIS (varies by program), bachelor's degree with minimum undergraduate GPA of 3.0; class B certificate (for MS); minimum number of hours in specific fields (for MAT). Additional exam requirements/recommendations for international students: Required—TOEFL (minimum score 550 paper-based; 80 iBT), IELTS (minimum score 6.5), CPE or CAE (minimum score C), Michigan English Language Assessment Battery (minimum score 90). *Application deadline:* For fall admission, 8/1 priority date for domestic and international students; for spring admission, 12/1 priority date for domestic and international students. Applications are processed on a rolling basis. Application fee: $25 ($35 for international students). Electronic applications accepted. *Expenses:* Contact institution. *Financial support:* Applicants required to submit FAFSA. *Unit head:* Dr. Lori P. Aultman, Chair of Education, 251-380-3473, Fax: 251-460-2184, E-mail: laultman@shc.edu. *Application contact:* Robert Stewart, Vice President of Enrollment, 251-380-3030, Fax: 251-460-2186, E-mail: rstewart@shc.edu.
Website: http://ug.shc.edu/graduate-degrees/master-science-education/

State University of New York at Fredonia, College of Education, Fredonia, NY 14063-1136. Offers curriculum and instruction (MS Ed); literacy education (MS Ed), including birth-grade 12, grades 5-12; TESOL (MS Ed). *Accreditation:* NCATE. *Program availability:* Part-time. *Faculty:* 11 full-time (9 women), 1 part-time/adjunct (0 women). *Students:* Average age 29. 60 applicants, 97% accepted, 39 enrolled. In 2017, 33 master's awarded. *Degree requirements:* For master's, thesis. *Entrance requirements:* For master's, GRE, minimum undergraduate GPA of 3.0. Additional exam requirements/recommendations for international students: Required—TOEFL (minimum score 79 iBT), IELTS (minimum score 6.5). *Application deadline:* For fall admission, 4/1 priority date for domestic and international students; for spring admission, 11/1 priority date for domestic students, 11/1 for international students. Applications are processed on a rolling basis. Application fee: $75. Electronic applications accepted. *Expenses:* Tuition, state resident: full-time $8154. Tuition, nonresident: full-time $16,650. *Required fees:* $1209. *Financial support:* In 2017–18, 4 teaching assistantships with full and partial tuition reimbursements (averaging $7,075 per year) were awarded. Financial award application deadline: 3/15; financial award applicants required to submit FAFSA. *Faculty research:* Positive behavioral intervention and support (PBIS), place-based science education, peer support for education, primary source material for social studies education, policies and practices in learning English language. *Unit head:* Dr. Christine Givner, Dean, 716-673-3311, E-mail: christine.givner@fredonia.edu. *Application contact:* Wendy S. Dunst, Interim Graduate Recruitment and Admissions Associate, 716-673-3808, Fax: 716-673-3712, E-mail: wendy.dunst@fredonia.edu.
Website: http://www.fredonia.edu/coe/

State University of New York at New Paltz, Graduate and Extended Learning School, School of Education, Department of Educational Studies and Leadership, Program in Special Education, New Paltz, NY 12561. Offers adolescence special education (7-12) (MS Ed); adolescence special education and literacy (MS Ed); childhood special education (1-6) (MS Ed); childhood special education and literacy (MS Ed); early childhood special education (B-2) (MS Ed). *Accreditation:* NCATE. *Program availability:* Part-time, evening/weekend. *Faculty:* 3 full-time (2 women). *Students:* 11 full-time (7 women), 37 part-time (31 women); includes 4 minority (1 Asian, non-Hispanic/Latino; 3 Hispanic/Latino). 29 applicants, 93% accepted, 24 enrolled. In 2017, 28 master's awarded. *Entrance requirements:* For master's, minimum GPA of 3.0 (3.2 for special education and literacy programs), New York state teaching certificate. Additional exam requirements/recommendations for international students: Required—TOEFL (minimum score 550 paper-based; 80 iBT), IELTS (minimum score 6.5). *Application deadline:* For fall admission, 3/15 priority date for domestic students, 3/15 for international students; for spring admission, 11/1 for domestic and international students. Application fee: $50. Electronic applications accepted. *Financial support:* Application deadline: 8/1. *Unit head:* Dr. Jane Sileo, Coordinator, 845-257-2835, E-mail: sileoj@newpaltz.edu. *Application contact:* Vika Shock, Director of Graduate Admissions, 845-257-3286, E-mail: gradschool@newpaltz.edu.
Website: http://www.newpaltz.edu/schoolofed/department-of-teaching—learning/special_ed.html

State University of New York at New Paltz, Graduate and Extended Learning School, School of Education, Program in Early Childhood and Childhood Education, New Paltz, NY 12561. Offers childhood education 1-6 (MS Ed, MST), including childhood education 1-6 (MST), early childhood B-2 (MS Ed). *Accreditation:* NCATE. *Program availability:* Part-time, evening/weekend. *Faculty:* 12 full-time (9 women), 4 part-time/adjunct (3 women). *Students:* 44 full-time (40 women), 63 part-time (56 women); includes 16 minority (4 Black or African American, non-Hispanic/Latino; 10 Hispanic/Latino; 2 Two or more races, non-Hispanic/Latino). 48 applicants, 75% accepted, 34 enrolled. In 2017, 56 master's awarded. *Degree requirements:* For master's, comprehensive exam (for some programs), portfolio. *Entrance requirements:* For master's, GRE or MAT (for MST), minimum GPA of 3.0 (3.2 for literacy and special education), New York state teaching certificate (for MS Ed). Additional exam requirements/recommendations for international students: Required—TOEFL (minimum score 550 paper-based; 80 iBT), IELTS (minimum score 6.5). *Application deadline:* For fall admission, 4/1 for domestic and international students; for spring admission, 11/1 priority date for domestic and international students; for summer admission, 4/15 priority date for domestic and international students. Applications are processed on a rolling basis. Application fee: $50. Electronic applications accepted. *Financial support:* Application deadline: 8/1. *Faculty research:* Multi-sensory teaching methods, volunteer tutoring programs for struggling readers, school readiness and transition, math/science/technology, university-school partnerships. *Unit head:* Dr. Aaron Isabelle, Chair, 845-257-2837, E-mail: isabella@newpaltz.edu. *Application contact:* Vika Shock, Assistant Director of Graduate Admissions, 845-257-3285, Fax: 845-257-3284, E-mail: gradschool@newpaltz.edu.
Website: http://www.newpaltz.edu/elementaryed/

State University of New York at Oswego, Graduate Studies, School of Education, Department of Curriculum and Instruction, Oswego, NY 13126. Offers adolescence education (MST); art education (MAT); childhood education (MST); curriculum and instruction (MS Ed); literacy education (MS Ed); special education (MS Ed). *Program availability:* Part-time, evening/weekend. *Degree requirements:* For master's, comprehensive exam (for some programs), thesis optional. *Entrance requirements:* For master's, GRE General Test, minimum GPA of 2.7, provisional teaching certificate. Additional exam requirements/recommendations for international students: Required—TOEFL (minimum score 560 paper-based). *Faculty research:* Classroom applications for microcomputers; classroom questioning, wait-time, and achievement; values clarification and academic achievement.

State University of New York at Plattsburgh, School of Education, Health, and Human Services, Program in Early Childhood Education, Plattsburgh, NY 12901-2681. Offers early childhood birth-grade 6 (Advanced Certificate).

State University of New York College at Cortland, Graduate Studies, School of Education, Program in Childhood Education, Cortland, NY 13045. Offers MST. *Accreditation:* NCATE.

State University of New York College at Potsdam, School of Education and Professional Studies, Program in Special Education, Potsdam, NY 13676. Offers adolescence (grades 7-12); childhood (grades 1-6) (MS Ed); early childhood (birth-grade 2) (MS Ed). *Accreditation:* NCATE. *Program availability:* Part-time. *Degree requirements:* For master's, culminating experience. *Entrance requirements:* For master's, minimum GPA of 3.0 in last 60 hours of course work. Additional exam requirements/recommendations for international students: Required—TOEFL (minimum score 550 paper-based; 80 iBT), IELTS (minimum score 6). Electronic applications accepted.

Stephen F. Austin State University, Graduate School, College of Education, Department of Elementary Education, Program in Early Childhood Education, Nacogdoches, TX 75962. Offers M Ed. *Accreditation:* NCATE. *Degree requirements:* For master's, comprehensive exam. *Entrance requirements:* For master's, GRE General Test. Additional exam requirements/recommendations for international students: Required—TOEFL (minimum score 550 paper-based).

Syracuse University, School of Education, MS Program in Early Childhood Special Education, Syracuse, NY 13244. Offers MS. *Program availability:* Part-time. *Entrance requirements:* For master's, GRE, baccalaureate degree from regionally-accredited college/university, strong teacher and/or employer recommendations, personal statement, experience working with children. Additional exam requirements/recommendations for international students: Required—TOEFL (minimum score 100 iBT). *Application deadline:* For fall admission, 1/15 priority date for domestic and international students; for spring admission, 10/15 priority date for domestic and international students; for summer admission, 1/15 priority date for domestic and international students. Applications are processed on a rolling basis. Application fee: $75. Electronic applications accepted. *Financial support:* Fellowships with full tuition reimbursements, research assistantships, teaching assistantships, career-related internships or fieldwork, and scholarships/grants available. Financial award application deadline: 1/15; financial award applicants required to submit FAFSA. *Faculty research:* Teaching children with diverse backgrounds and abilities, home-based itinerant teaching, early childhood special education, general preschool teaching, teacher consulting. *Unit head:* Dr. Benjamin Dotger, Department Chair, 315-443-2685, E-mail: bdotger@syr.edu. *Application contact:* Speranza Migliore, Graduate Admissions Recruiter, 315-443-2505, E-mail: gradrcrt@syr.edu. Website: http://soe.syr.edu/academic/teaching_and_leadership/graduate/masters/early_childhood_special_education/default.aspx

Teachers College, Columbia University, Department of Curriculum and Teaching, New York, NY 10027-6696. Offers curriculum and teaching (Ed M, MA, Ed D); curriculum and teaching: elementary education (MA); curriculum and teaching: secondary education (MA); early childhood education (MA, Ed D); early childhood education: special education (MA); elementary education-gifted extension (MA); elementary inclusive education (MA); gifted education (MA); literacy specialist (MA); secondary inclusive education (MA); special inclusive elementary education (MA). *Program availability:* Part-time, evening/weekend. *Students:* 196 full-time (181 women), 181 part-time (161 women); includes 141 minority (45 Black or African American, non-Hispanic/Latino; 2 American Indian or Alaska Native, non-Hispanic/Latino; 45 Asian, non-Hispanic/Latino; 35 Hispanic/Latino; 14 Two or more races, non-Hispanic/Latino), 37 international. Average age 30. 509 applicants, 72% accepted, 155 enrolled. Terminal master's awarded for partial completion of doctoral program. *Degree requirements:* For doctorate, thesis/dissertation. *Unit head:* Prof. Daniel Friedrich, Chair, E-mail: friedrich@exchange.tc.columbia.edu. *Application contact:* David Estrella, Director of Admission, 212-678-3305, Fax: 212-678-4171, E-mail: estrella@tc.columbia.edu.

Teachers College of San Joaquin, Master's Program in Education, Stockton, CA 95206. Offers early education (M Ed); educational inquiry (M Ed); educational leadership and school development (M Ed); science, technology, engineering, and mathematics (M Ed); special education (M Ed).

Tennessee Technological University, College of Graduate Studies, College of Education, Department of Curriculum and Instruction, Program in Early Childhood Education, Cookeville, TN 38505. Offers MA, Ed S. *Accreditation:* NCATE. *Program availability:* Part-time, evening/weekend. *Faculty:* 2 full-time (both women). *Students:* 2 full-time (both women), 11 part-time (all women); includes 3 minority (2 Black or African American, non-Hispanic/Latino; 1 Hispanic/Latino), 2 international. 10 applicants, 90% accepted, 8 enrolled. In 2017, 2 master's awarded. *Degree requirements:* For master's and Ed S, comprehensive exam, thesis or alternative. *Entrance requirements:* For master's and Ed S, MAT or GRE. Additional exam requirements/recommendations for international students: Required—TOEFL (minimum score 527 paper-based; 71 iBT), IELTS (minimum score 5.5), PTE (minimum score 48), or TOEIC (Test of English as an International Communication). *Application deadline:* For fall admission, 8/1 priority date for domestic students, 5/1 for international students; for spring admission, 12/1 for domestic students, 10/1 for international students; for summer admission, 5/1 for domestic students, 2/1 for international students. Application fee: $35 ($40 for international students). Electronic applications accepted. *Expenses:* Tuition, state resident: full-time $9925; part-time $565 per credit hour. Tuition, nonresident: full-time $22,993; part-time $1291 per credit hour. *Financial support:* Fellowships, research assistantships, teaching assistantships, and career-related internships or fieldwork available. Financial award application deadline: 4/1. *Unit head:* Dr. Jeremy Wendt, Interim Chairperson, 931-372-3181, Fax: 931-372-6270, E-mail: jwendt@tntech.edu. *Application contact:* Shelia K. Kendrick, Coordinator of Graduate Studies, 931-372-3808, Fax: 931-372-3497, E-mail: skendrick@tntech.edu.

Texas A&M University–Commerce, College of Education and Human Services, Commerce, TX 75429. Offers counseling (M Ed, MS, PhD); early childhood education (M Ed, MS); educational administration (M Ed, MS, Ed D); educational psychology (PhD); educational technology leadership (M Ed, MS); educational technology library science (M Ed, MS); elementary education (M Ed); health, kinesiology and sports studies (MS); higher education (MS, Ed D); psychology (MS); reading (M Ed, MS); secondary education (M Ed, MS); social work (MSW); special education (M Ed, MS); supervision, curriculum and instruction-elementary education (Ed D); training and development (MS). *Program availability:* Part-time, evening/weekend, 100% online, blended/hybrid learning. *Faculty:* 91 full-time (51 women), 38 part-time/adjunct (31

women). *Students:* 400 full-time (310 women), 1,400 part-time (1,117 women); includes 724 minority (412 Black or African American, non-Hispanic/Latino; 8 American Indian or Alaska Native, non-Hispanic/Latino; 24 Asian, non-Hispanic/Latino; 220 Hispanic/Latino; 60 Two or more races, non-Hispanic/Latino), 18 international. Average age 37. 951 applicants, 46% accepted, 331 enrolled. In 2017, 564 master's, 24 doctorates awarded. *Degree requirements:* For master's, comprehensive exam, thesis optional, departmental qualifying exams (for some programs); for doctorate, comprehensive exam, thesis/dissertation, departmental qualifying exam; for SSP, comprehensive exam, thesis optional. *Entrance requirements:* For master's and doctorate, GRE General Test. Additional exam requirements/recommendations for international students: Required—TOEFL (minimum score 550 paper-based; 79 iBT), IELTS (minimum score 6). *Application deadline:* For fall admission, 6/1 priority date for international students; for spring admission, 10/15 priority date for international students; for summer admission, 3/15 priority date for international students. Applications are processed on a rolling basis. Application fee: $50. Electronic applications accepted. *Expenses:* Tuition, state resident: full-time $3630. Tuition, nonresident: full-time $11,100. *Required fees:* $2564. Tuition and fees vary according to course load, degree level and program. *Financial support:* In 2017–18, 84 students received support, including 40 research assistantships with partial tuition reimbursements available (averaging $10,800 per year), 12 teaching assistantships with partial tuition reimbursements available (averaging $13,000 per year); career-related internships or fieldwork, Federal Work-Study, institutionally sponsored loans, scholarships/grants, health care benefits, and unspecified assistantships also available. Financial award application deadline: 6/15; financial award applicants required to submit FAFSA. *Faculty research:* Cognitive and bilingual education, positive behavioral intervention, literacy, math readiness. *Total annual research expenditures:* $1.1 million. *Unit head:* Dr. Timothy Letzring, Dean, 903-886-5181, Fax: 903-886-5905, E-mail: tim.letzring@tamuc.edu. *Application contact:* Vicky Turner, Doctoral Degree and Special Programs Coordinator, 903-886-5167, E-mail: vicky.turner@tamuc.edu. Website: http://www.tamuc.edu/academics/graduateSchool/programs/education/default.aspx

Texas A&M University–Commerce, College of Humanities, Social Sciences and Arts, Commerce, TX 75429. Offers applied criminology (MS); applied linguistics (MA, MS); art (MA, MFA); computational linguistics (Graduate Certificate); creative writing (Graduate Certificate); criminal justice management (Graduate Certificate); criminal justice studies (Graduate Certificate); English (MA, MS, PhD); film studies (Graduate Certificate); history (MA, MS); history of Christianity (Graduate Certificate); Holocaust studies (Graduate Certificate); homeland security (Graduate Certificate); music education (MM); music performance (MM); political science (MA, MS); public history (Graduate Certificate); sociology (MS); Spanish (MA); studies in children's and adolescent literature and culture (Graduate Certificate); teaching English to speakers of other languages (Graduate Certificate); theater (MA); world history (Graduate Certificate). *Program availability:* Part-time. *Faculty:* 56 full-time (26 women), 10 part-time/adjunct (5 women). *Students:* 133 full-time (85 women), 439 part-time (311 women); includes 204 minority (79 Black or African American, non-Hispanic/Latino; 4 American Indian or Alaska Native, non-Hispanic/Latino; 9 Asian, non-Hispanic/Latino; 98 Hispanic/Latino; 14 Two or more races, non-Hispanic/Latino), 26 international. Average age 36. 261 applicants, 50% accepted, 113 enrolled. In 2017, 105 master's, 5 doctorates awarded. *Degree requirements:* For master's, one foreign language, comprehensive exam, thesis (for some programs); for doctorate, one foreign language, comprehensive exam, thesis/dissertation, departmental qualifying exam. *Entrance requirements:* For master's and doctorate, GRE General Test. Additional exam requirements/recommendations for international students: Required—TOEFL (minimum score 550 paper-based; 79 iBT), IELTS (minimum score 6). *Application deadline:* Applications are processed on a rolling basis. Application fee: $50. Electronic applications accepted. *Expenses:* Contact institution. *Financial support:* In 2017–18, 43 students received support, including 9 research assistantships with partial tuition reimbursements available (averaging $9,000 per year), 68 teaching assistantships with partial tuition reimbursements available (averaging $9,000 per year); Federal Work-Study, institutionally sponsored loans, scholarships/grants, health care benefits, and unspecified assistantships also available. Financial award application deadline: 5/1; financial award applicants required to submit FAFSA. *Unit head:* Dr. William F. Kuracina, Interim Dean, 903-886-5166, Fax: 903-886-5774, E-mail: william.kuracina@tamuc.edu. *Application contact:* Vicky Turner, Doctoral Degree and Special Programs Coordinator, 903-886-5167, E-mail: vicky.turner@tamuc.edu. Website: http://www.tamuc.edu/academics/graduateSchool/programs/humanitiesSocialScienceArts/default.aspx

Texas A&M University–Corpus Christi, College of Graduate Studies, College of Education and Human Development, Corpus Christi, TX 78412. Offers counseling (MS), including counseling; counselor education (PhD); curriculum and instruction (MS, PhD); early childhood education (MS); educational administration (MS); educational leadership (Ed D); elementary education (MS); instructional design and educational technology (MS); kinesiology (MS); reading (MS); secondary education (MS); special education (MS). *Program availability:* Part-time, evening/weekend, blended/hybrid learning. *Faculty:* 50 full-time (29 women), 29 part-time/adjunct (18 women). *Students:* 160 full-time (127 women), 366 part-time (293 women); includes 279 minority (40 Black or African American, non-Hispanic/Latino; 3 Asian, non-Hispanic/Latino; 228 Hispanic/Latino; 8 Two or more races, non-Hispanic/Latino), 18 international. Average age 35. 296 applicants, 65% accepted, 155 enrolled. In 2017, 103 master's, 27 doctorates awarded. *Degree requirements:* For master's, comprehensive exam, capstone; for doctorate, thesis/dissertation. *Entrance requirements:* For master's, GRE General Test, essay (300 words); for doctorate, GRE, essay, resume, 3-4 reference forms. *Application deadline:* For fall admission, 7/15 priority date for domestic students, 5/1 priority date for international students; for spring admission, 11/15 priority date for domestic students, 9/1 priority date for international students. Applications are processed on a rolling basis. Application fee: $50 ($70 for international students). Electronic applications accepted. *Expenses:* Tuition, state resident: full-time $3568; part-time $198.24 per credit hour. Tuition, nonresident: full-time $11,038; part-time $613.24 per credit hour. *Required fees:* $2129; $1422.58 per semester. Tuition and fees vary according to program. *Financial support:* Research assistantships, teaching assistantships, career-related internships or fieldwork, Federal Work-Study, institutionally sponsored loans, scholarships/grants, health care benefits, and unspecified assistantships available. Support available to part-time students. Financial award application deadline: 3/15; financial award applicants required to submit FAFSA. *Unit head:* Dr. David Scott, Dean, 361-825-2660, E-mail: david.scott@tamucc.edu. *Application contact:* Graduate Admissions Coordinator, 361-825-2177, Fax: 361-825-2755, E-mail: gradweb@tamucc.edu. Website: http://education.tamucc.edu/

Texas A&M University–Kingsville, College of Graduate Studies, College of Education and Human Performance, Department of Teacher and Bilingual Education, Program in Early Childhood Education, Kingsville, TX 78363. Offers M Ed. *Program availability:* Part-time, evening/weekend. *Degree requirements:* For master's, variable foreign language requirement, comprehensive exam, thesis (for some programs). *Entrance requirements:* For master's, GRE, MAT, GMAT. Additional exam requirements/recommendations for international students: Required—TOEFL (minimum score 550 paper-based; 79 iBT). Electronic applications accepted.

Early Childhood Education

Texas A&M University–San Antonio, Department of Educator and Leadership Preparation, San Antonio, TX 78224. Offers bilingual education (MS); early childhood education (M Ed); educational administration (MA); reading specialization (MS); special education (M Ed), including educational diagnostician. *Program availability:* Part-time, evening/weekend, online learning. *Faculty:* 19 full-time (14 women), 8 part-time/adjunct (2 women). *Students:* 24 full-time (21 women), 188 part-time (143 women); includes 163 minority (7 Black or African American, non-Hispanic/Latino; 1 Asian, non-Hispanic/Latino; 149 Hispanic/Latino; 6 Two or more races, non-Hispanic/Latino), 1 international. Average age 36. 191 applicants, 62% accepted, 67 enrolled. In 2017, 70 master's awarded. *Degree requirements:* For master's, comprehensive exam, thesis or alternative. *Entrance requirements:* For master's, GRE (Quantitative and Verbal) or MAT. Additional exam requirements/recommendations for international students: Required—TOEFL (minimum score 550 paper-based; 79 iBT), IELTS (minimum score 6). *Application deadline:* For fall admission, 3/15 priority date for domestic and international students; for spring admission, 11/1 priority date for domestic and international students; for summer admission, 4/1 priority date for domestic and international students. Applications are processed on a rolling basis. Application fee: $35 ($50 for international students). Electronic applications accepted. *Expenses:* Tuition, state resident: full-time $3475; part-time $1930 per semester. Tuition, nonresident: full-time $10,945; part-time $6080 per semester. *Required fees:* $2148; $1412 per year. $706 per semester. Tuition and fees vary according to course load. *Financial support:* In 2017–18, 16 students received support. Research assistantships, Federal Work-Study, scholarships/grants, and tuition waivers available. Financial award application deadline: 3/15; financial award applicants required to submit FAFSA. *Faculty research:* Equity in education, biliteracy practices among Latina and immigrants, academic achievement of low socio-economic students, equity practices in instruction and educational leadership in diverse settings, racial identity development and multicultural education. *Unit head:* Dr. Debbie Vera, Department Chair. *Application contact:* Caitie Garza, Graduate Admissions Coordinator, 210-784-1300, E-mail: beajaguar@tamusa.edu.
Website: http://www.tamusa.edu/collegeofeducationandhumandevelopment/educatorleadershippreparation/index.html

Texas State University, The Graduate College, College of Education, Program in Reading Education, San Marcos, TX 78666. Offers early childhood-12 reading specialist (M Ed). *Program availability:* Part-time, evening/weekend. *Faculty:* 10 full-time (9 women), 2 part-time/adjunct (1 woman). *Students:* 1 (woman) full-time, 24 part-time (23 women); includes 12 minority (all Hispanic/Latino). Average age 37. 4 applicants, 75% accepted. In 2017, 7 master's awarded. *Degree requirements:* For master's, comprehensive exam. *Entrance requirements:* For master's, baccalaureate degree from regionally-accredited institution with minimum GPA of 3.0 in last 60 hours of course work, statement of purpose, official teaching certificate. Additional exam requirements/recommendations for international students: Required—IELTS, TOEFL (minimum iBT scores: 22 listening, 22 reading, 24 speaking, 21 writing). *Application deadline:* For fall admission, 2/15 priority date for domestic and international students; for spring admission, 10/15 priority date for domestic students, 10/1 for international students; for summer admission, 4/15 for domestic students, 3/15 for international students. Applications are processed on a rolling basis. Application fee: $40 ($90 for international students). Electronic applications accepted. *Expenses:* Tuition, state resident: full-time $7868; part-time $3934 per semester. Tuition, nonresident: full-time $17,828; part-time $8914 per semester. *Required fees:* $2092; $1435 per semester. Tuition and fees vary according to course load. *Financial support:* In 2017–18, 15 students received support, including 1 research assistantship (averaging $12,152 per year); teaching assistantships, career-related internships or fieldwork, Federal Work-Study, institutionally sponsored loans, scholarships/grants, and unspecified assistantships also available. Support available to part-time students. Financial award application deadline: 3/1; financial award applicants required to submit FAFSA. *Faculty research:* Impact of developmental integrated reading and writing. *Total annual research expenditures:* $64,880. *Unit head:* Dr. Jane Saunders, Graduate Advisor, 512-245-1512, Fax: 512-245-8365, E-mail: js99@txstate.edu. *Application contact:* Dr. Andrea Golato, Dean of Graduate School, 512-245-2581, Fax: 512-245-8365, E-mail: gradcollege@txstate.edu.
Website: http://www.education.txstate.edu/ci/degrees-certifications/graduate/reading.html

Texas Woman's University, Graduate School, College of Professional Education, Department of Family Sciences, Denton, TX 76204. Offers child development (MS); child life (MS); counseling and development (MS); early childhood development and education (PhD); early childhood education (M Ed); family studies (MS, PhD); family therapy (MS, PhD). *Accreditation:* ACA (one or more programs are accredited). *Program availability:* Part-time, evening/weekend. *Faculty:* 24 full-time (19 women), 17 part-time/adjunct (15 women). *Students:* 153 full-time (146 women), 237 part-time (220 women); includes 169 minority (81 Black or African American, non-Hispanic/Latino; 9 Asian, non-Hispanic/Latino; 68 Hispanic/Latino; 11 Two or more races, non-Hispanic/Latino), 10 international. Average age 32. 235 applicants, 55% accepted, 87 enrolled. In 2017, 77 master's, 15 doctorates awarded. Terminal master's awarded for partial completion of doctoral program. *Degree requirements:* For master's, comprehensive exam (for some programs), thesis, professional paper, or coursework; practicums (for some programs); for doctorate, comprehensive exam, thesis/dissertation. *Entrance requirements:* For master's, GRE with preferred minimum score 147 Verbal, 144 Quantitative, 4.0 Analytical (for MS in child development and M Ed), minimum GPA of 3.0 (3.25 for family therapy), 3 letters of recommendations (1 for child life), letter of intent, curriculum vitae/resume, interview, writing sample; for doctorate, GRE (preferred minimum score 147 Verbal, 144 Quantitative, 4.0 Analytical), minimum GPA of 3.5 (3.35 for family studies) on all prior graduate work, curriculum vitae/resume, letter of intent. Additional exam requirements/recommendations for international students: Required—TOEFL (minimum score 550 paper-based; 79 iBT); Recommended—IELTS (minimum score 6.5), TSE (minimum score 53). *Application deadline:* For fall admission, 3/1 priority date for domestic and international students; for spring admission, 11/1 priority date for domestic students, 7/1 priority date for international students. Applications are processed on a rolling basis. Application fee: $50 ($75 for international students). Electronic applications accepted. *Expenses:* $7,520 per year full-time in-state; $16,820 per year full-time out-of-state. *Financial support:* In 2017–18, 104 students received support, including 12 teaching assistantships (averaging $22,972 per year); career-related internships or fieldwork, Federal Work-Study, institutionally sponsored loans, scholarships/grants, traineeships, health care benefits, and unspecified assistantships also available. Support available to part-time students. Financial award application deadline: 3/1; financial award applicants required to submit FAFSA. *Faculty research:* Parenting/parent education, play therapy, healthy relationships, child development, technology integration. *Unit head:* Dr. Jerry Whitworth, Interim Chair, 940-898-2685, Fax: 940-898-2676, E-mail: famsci@twu.edu. *Application contact:* Korie Hawkins, Associate Director of Admissions, Graduate Recruitment, 940-898-3188, Fax: 940-898-3081, E-mail: admissions@twu.edu.
Website: http://www.twu.edu/family-sciences/

Theological University of the Caribbean, Graduate Programs, Saint Just, PR 00978-0901. Offers childhood and adolescent education (MA); counseling and pastoral care (MA); ministry (D Min); missions (MA).

Towson University, College of Education, Program in Early Childhood Education, Towson, MD 21252-0001. Offers M Ed, CAS. *Accreditation:* NCATE. *Program availability:* Part-time, evening/weekend. *Students:* 7 full-time (6 women), 104 part-time (102 women); includes 18 minority (12 Black or African American, non-Hispanic/Latino; 3 Asian, non-Hispanic/Latino; 2 Hispanic/Latino; 1 Two or more races, non-Hispanic/Latino), 1 international. *Degree requirements:* For master's, thesis optional. *Entrance requirements:* For master's, bachelor's degree with minimum GPA of 3.0, resume, teacher certification, work experience or course work in early childhood education; for CAS, master's degree in early childhood education or related field from nationally-accredited institution; minimum overall GPA of 3.75 for graduate work; resume; 3 letters of recommendation. *Application deadline:* For fall admission, 1/17 for domestic students, 5/15 for international students; for spring admission, 10/15 for domestic students, 12/1 for international students. Applications are processed on a rolling basis. Application fee: $45. Electronic applications accepted. *Expenses:* Tuition, state resident: full-time $7960; part-time $398 per unit. Tuition, nonresident: full-time $16,480; part-time $824 per unit. *Required fees:* $2600; $130 per year. $390 per term. *Financial support:* Application deadline: 4/1. *Unit head:* Dr. Janese Daniels, Department Chair, 410-704-4832, E-mail: ecedgrad@towson.edu. *Application contact:* Coverley Beidleman, Assistant Director of Graduate Admissions, 410-704-5630, Fax: 410-704-3030, E-mail: cbeidleman@towson.edu.
Website: http://www.towson.edu/coe/departments/earlychildhood/grad/earlychildhood/index.html

Towson University, College of Education, Program in Teaching, Towson, MD 21252-0001. Offers early childhood education (MAT); elementary education (MAT); secondary education (MAT); special education (MAT). *Students:* 64 full-time (44 women), 48 part-time (34 women); includes 16 minority (5 Black or African American, non-Hispanic/Latino; 5 Asian, non-Hispanic/Latino; 5 Hispanic/Latino; 1 Two or more races, non-Hispanic/Latino). *Entrance requirements:* For master's, ACT, GRE, PRAXIS I or SAT, 2 letters of reference, resume, minimum GPA of 3.0, essay. *Application deadline:* For fall admission, 1/17 for domestic students, 5/15 for international students; for spring admission, 10/15 for domestic students, 12/1 for international students. Applications are processed on a rolling basis. Application fee: $45. Electronic applications accepted. *Expenses:* Tuition, state resident: full-time $7960; part-time $398 per unit. Tuition, nonresident: full-time $16,480; part-time $824 per unit. *Required fees:* $2600; $130 per year. $390 per term. *Financial support:* Application deadline: 4/1. *Unit head:* Dr. Pamela Wruble, Graduate Program Director, 410-704-4935, E-mail: pwruble@towson.edu. *Application contact:* Coverley Beidleman, Assistant Director of Graduate Admissions, 410-704-5630, Fax: 410-704-3030, E-mail: grads@towson.edu.
Website: https://www.towson.edu/coe/departments/teaching/

Trident University International, College of Education, Program in Education, Cypress, CA 90630. Offers adult education (MA Ed); aviation education (MA Ed); children's literacy development (MA Ed); e-learning (MA Ed); early childhood education (MA Ed); enrollment management (MA Ed); higher education (MA Ed); teaching and instruction (MA Ed); training and development (MA Ed). *Program availability:* Part-time, evening/weekend, online learning. *Degree requirements:* For master's, capstone project with integrative paper. *Entrance requirements:* For master's, minimum GPA of 2.5 (students with GPA 3.0 or greater may transfer up to 30% of graduate level credits). Additional exam requirements/recommendations for international students: Required—TOEFL (minimum score 525 paper-based). Electronic applications accepted.

Trinity Washington University, School of Education, Washington, DC 20017-1094. Offers clinical mental health counseling (MA); early childhood education (MAT); educating for change (M Ed); educational administration (MSA); elementary education (MAT); reading (M Ed); school counseling (MA); secondary education (MAT), including English, social studies; special education (MAT). *Accreditation:* NCATE. *Program availability:* Part-time, evening/weekend. *Degree requirements:* For master's, thesis (for some programs), capstone project(s). *Entrance requirements:* For master's, PRAXIS I, minimum GPA of 2.8. Additional exam requirements/recommendations for international students: Required—TOEFL (minimum score 550 paper-based). *Faculty research:* Technology, literacy, special education, organizations, inclusion models.

Troy University, Graduate School, College of Education, Program in Early Childhood Education, Troy, AL 36082. Offers MS, Ed S. *Program availability:* Part-time, evening/weekend, 100% online, blended/hybrid learning. *Faculty:* 1 (woman) full-time, 1 (woman) part-time/adjunct. *Students:* 1 (woman) full-time, 2 part-time (both women); includes 1 minority (Black or African American, non-Hispanic/Latino). Average age 34. 1 applicant, 100% accepted, 1 enrolled. In 2017, 6 master's awarded. *Entrance requirements:* For master's, GRE (minimum score of 850 on old exam or 290 on new exam), GMAT (minimum score of 380), or MAT (minimum score of 385), bachelor's degree; minimum undergraduate GPA of 2.5 or 3.0 on last 30 semester hours, letter of recommendation. Additional exam requirements/recommendations for international students: Required—TOEFL (minimum score 523 paper-based; 70 iBT), IELTS (minimum score 6). *Application deadline:* Applications are processed on a rolling basis. Application fee: $50. Electronic applications accepted. *Expenses:* Tuition, state resident: part-time $417 per credit hour. Tuition, nonresident: part-time $834 per credit hour. *Required fees:* $42 per credit hour. $50 per semester. Tuition and fees vary according to campus/location. *Financial support:* Fellowships, career-related internships or fieldwork, and scholarships/grants available. Support available to part-time students. Financial award applicants required to submit FAFSA. *Unit head:* Dr. Ruth Busby, Chair, Teacher Education, 334-670-3546, Fax: 334-808-6666, E-mail: rsbusby@troy.edu. *Application contact:* Jessica A. Kimbro, Director of Graduate Admissions, 334-670-3178, E-mail: jacord@troy.edu.

Universidad del Turabo, Graduate Programs, Programs in Education, Program in Teaching at Primary Level, Gurabo, PR 00778-3030. Offers M Ed. *Entrance requirements:* For master's, GRE, EXADEP, GMAT, interview, official transcript, essay, recommendation letters. Electronic applications accepted.

University at Buffalo, the State University of New York, Graduate School, Graduate School of Education, Department of Learning and Instruction, Buffalo, NY 14260. Offers biology education (Ed M, Certificate); chemistry education (Ed M, Certificate); childhood education (Ed M); childhood education with bilingual extension (Ed M); college teaching (Advanced Certificate); curriculum, instruction and the science of learning (PhD); early childhood education (Ed M); early childhood education with bilingual extension (Ed M); earth science education (Ed M, Certificate); education and technology (Ed M); education studies (Ed M); educational technology and new literacies (Certificate); educational technology and new literacies (Advanced Certificate); elementary education (Ed D); English education (Ed M, Certificate); English education studies (Ed M); English for speakers of other languages (Ed M); foreign and second language education (PhD); French education (Ed M, Certificate); German education (Ed M, Certificate); gifted education (Certificate); Latin education (Ed M, Certificate); literacy education studies (Ed M); literacy specialist (Ed M); literacy teaching and learning (Certificate); mathematics education (Ed M, Certificate); music education (Ed M, Certificate); music education studies (Ed M); music learning theory (Advanced Certificate); music education (Advanced Certificate); physics education (Ed M, Certificate); science and the public (Ed M); social studies education (Ed M, Certificate); Spanish education (Ed M, Certificate); special education (PhD); teaching English to speakers of other languages

(Ed M). *Program availability:* Part-time, evening/weekend, 100% online. *Faculty:* 26 full-time (19 women), 74 part-time/adjunct (52 women). *Students:* 172 full-time (122 women), 325 part-time (226 women); includes 44 minority (25 Black or African American, non-Hispanic/Latino; 5 American Indian or Alaska Native, non-Hispanic/Latino; 14 Asian, non-Hispanic/Latino; 57 international. Average age 33. 316 applicants, 78% accepted, 174 enrolled. In 2017, 109 master's, 34 doctorates, 15 other advanced degrees awarded. *Degree requirements:* For master's, comprehensive exam; for doctorate, thesis/dissertation, research analysis exam, research experience. *Entrance requirements:* For master's, letters of reference; for doctorate, GRE General Test or MAT, interview, writing sample, letters of recommendation. Additional exam requirements/recommendations for international students: Required—TOEFL (minimum score 600 paper-based; 96 iBT). *Application deadline:* For fall admission, 2/1 priority date for domestic and international students; for spring admission, 11/15 priority date for domestic students, 10/1 for international students. Applications are processed on a rolling basis. Application fee: $50. Electronic applications accepted. *Financial support:* In 2017–18, 42 fellowships (averaging $5,181 per year), 44 research assistantships with tuition reimbursements (averaging $10,908 per year) were awarded; teaching assistantships, career-related internships or fieldwork, Federal Work-Study, institutionally sponsored loans, scholarships/grants, tuition waivers (full and partial), and unspecified assistantships also available. Financial award application deadline: 2/28; financial award applicants required to submit FAFSA. *Faculty research:* Science assessment, foreign language teaching and learning, early learning, new literacies, gender and education. *Total annual research expenditures:* $413,233. *Unit head:* Dr. David Bruce, Chair, 716-645-4069, Fax: 716-645-3161, E-mail: gse-info@buffalo.edu. *Application contact:* Luann Zak, Admissions Assistant, 716-645-2110, Fax: 716-645-7937, E-mail: luannzak@buffalo.edu.
Website: http://gse.buffalo.edu/lai

The University of Alabama at Birmingham, School of Education, Program in Early Childhood Education, Birmingham, AL 35294. Offers MA Ed, PhD. *Accreditation:* NCATE. *Degree requirements:* For master's, comprehensive exam, thesis optional; for doctorate, thesis/dissertation. *Entrance requirements:* For master's, GRE General Test or MAT; for doctorate, GRE General Test, MAT, minimum GPA of 3.25, at least 3 years' teaching experience, essay, recommendations, interview. Electronic applications accepted.

University of Alaska Anchorage, College of Education, Program in Special Education, Anchorage, AK 99508. Offers early childhood special education (M Ed); special education (M Ed, Certificate). *Program availability:* Part-time. *Degree requirements:* For master's, comprehensive exam (for some programs), thesis or alternative. *Entrance requirements:* For master's, GRE or MAT, interview, minimum GPA of 2.75. Additional exam requirements/recommendations for international students: Required—TOEFL (minimum score 550 paper-based). *Faculty research:* Mild disabilities, substance abuse issues for educators, partnerships to improve at-risk youth, analysis of planning models for teachers in special education.

University of Arkansas, Graduate School, College of Education and Health Professions, Department of Curriculum and Instruction, Program in Childhood Education, Fayetteville, AR 72701. Offers MAT. *Accreditation:* NCATE. In 2017, 68 master's awarded. *Application deadline:* For fall admission, 8/1 for domestic students, 4/1 for international students; for spring admission, 12/1 for domestic students, 10/1 for international students; for summer admission, 4/15 for domestic students, 3/1 for international students. Applications are processed on a rolling basis. Application fee: $60. Electronic applications accepted. *Expenses:* Tuition, state resident: full-time $3782. Tuition, nonresident: full-time $10,238. *Financial support:* Fellowships, research assistantships, and teaching assistantships available. *Unit head:* Dr. Heather D. Kindall, Program Coordinator, 479-575-2516, E-mail: hkindall@uark.edu. *Application contact:* Dr. Heather Kindall, Graduate Coordinator, 479-575-2516, Fax: 479-575-6676, E-mail: hkindall@uark.edu.
Website: http://cied.uark.edu/

University of Bridgeport, School of Education, Department of Education, Bridgeport, CT 06604. Offers education (MS); educational management (Ed D, Diploma), including intermediate administrator or supervisor (Diploma), leadership (Ed D); elementary education (MS, Diploma), including early childhood education, elementary education; middle school education (MS); music education (MS); remedial reading and language arts (Diploma); secondary education (MS, Diploma), including computer specialist (Diploma), international education (Diploma), reading specialist, secondary education. *Program availability:* Part-time, evening/weekend. *Degree requirements:* For master's, final exam, final project, or thesis; for doctorate, comprehensive exam, thesis/dissertation; for Diploma, thesis or alternative, final project. *Entrance requirements:* For master's, minimum undergraduate QPA of 2.67; for doctorate, GRE, MAT; for Diploma, GRE General Test or MAT, minimum graduate QPA of 3.0. Additional exam requirements/recommendations for international students: Recommended—TOEFL (minimum score 550 paper-based; 80 iBT), IELTS (minimum score 6.5). Electronic applications accepted. *Expenses:* Contact institution.

University of Central Florida, College of Community Innovation and Education, Education Doctoral Programs, Orlando, FL 32816. Offers curriculum and instruction (Ed D); education (PhD), including communication sciences and disorders, counselor education, early childhood education, elementary education, exceptional education, exercise physiology, higher education, instructional design and technology, mathematics education, methodology, measurement and analysis, reading education, science education, social science education, TESOL; educational leadership (Ed D). *Students:* 122 full-time (86 women), 129 part-time (88 women); includes 64 minority (24 Black or African American, non-Hispanic/Latino; 1 American Indian or Alaska Native, non-Hispanic/Latino; 9 Asian, non-Hispanic/Latino; 24 Hispanic/Latino; 6 Two or more races, non-Hispanic/Latino), 26 international. Average age 38. 195 applicants, 47% accepted, 72 enrolled. In 2017, 89 doctorates awarded. *Entrance requirements:* For doctorate, GRE, letters of recommendation, goal statement, resume, writing sample. Application fee: $30. Electronic applications accepted. *Expenses:* Tuition, state resident: part-time $288.16 per credit hour. Tuition, nonresident: part-time $1073.31 per credit hour. Tuition and fees vary according to program. *Financial support:* In 2017–18, 77 students received support, including 28 fellowships with partial tuition reimbursements available (averaging $5,733 per year), 29 research assistantships with partial tuition reimbursements available (averaging $10,230 per year), 54 teaching assistantships with partial tuition reimbursements available (averaging $11,614 per year); health care benefits also available. Financial award application deadline: 3/1; financial award applicants required to submit FAFSA. *Unit head:* Dr. Edward Robinson, Director of Doctoral Programs, 407-823-6106, E-mail: edward.robinson@ucf.edu. *Application contact:* Associate Director, Graduate Admissions, 407-823-2766, Fax: 407-823-6442, E-mail: gradadmissions@ucf.edu.
Website: https://edcollege.ucf.edu/academic-programs/graduate/

University of Central Missouri, The Graduate School, Warrensburg, MO 64093. Offers accountancy (MA); accounting (MBA); applied mathematics (MS); aviation safety (MA); biology (MS); business administration (MBA); career and technical education leadership (MS); college student personnel administration (MS); communication (MA); computer science (MS); counseling (MS); criminal justice (MS); educational leadership (Ed D);

educational technology (MS); elementary and early childhood education (MSE); English (MA); environmental studies (MA); finance (MBA); history (MA); human services/educational technology (Ed S); human services/learning resources (Ed S); human services/professional counseling (Ed S); industrial hygiene (MS); industrial management (MS); information systems (MBA); information technology (MS); kinesiology (MS); library science and information services (MS); literacy education (MSE); marketing (MBA); mathematics (MS); music (MA); occupational safety management (MS); psychology (MS); rural family nursing (MS); school administration (MSE); social gerontology (MS); sociology (MA); special education (MSE); speech language pathology (MS); superintendency (Ed S); teaching (MAT); teaching English as a second language (MA); technology (MS); technology management (PhD); theatre (MA). *Program availability:* Part-time, 100% online, blended/hybrid learning. *Faculty:* 337 full-time (145 women), 41 part-time/adjunct (28 women). *Students:* 785 full-time (398 women), 1,633 part-time (1,063 women); includes 231 minority (102 Black or African American, non-Hispanic/Latino; 4 American Indian or Alaska Native, non-Hispanic/Latino; 16 Asian, non-Hispanic/Latino; 52 Hispanic/Latino; 57 Two or more races, non-Hispanic/Latino), 692 international. Average age 30. In 2017, 2,605 master's, 122 other advanced degrees awarded. *Degree requirements:* For master's and Ed S, comprehensive exam (for some programs), thesis (for some programs). *Entrance requirements:* Additional exam requirements/recommendations for international students: Required—TOEFL (minimum score 550 paper-based; 79 iBT). *Application deadline:* For fall admission, 6/1 priority date for domestic and international students; for spring admission, 10/1 priority date for domestic and international students; for summer admission, 4/1 priority date for domestic and international students. Applications are processed on a rolling basis. Application fee: $30 ($75 for international students). Electronic applications accepted. *Expenses:* Tuition, state resident: full-time $8771; part-time $292.35 per credit hour. Tuition, nonresident: full-time $17,541; part-time $584.70 per credit hour. *Required fees:* $372; $24.78 per credit hour. *Financial support:* In 2017–18, 99 students received support. Research assistantships, teaching assistantships, career-related internships or fieldwork, Federal Work-Study, scholarships/grants, and administrative and laboratory assistantships available. Support available to part-time students. Financial award application deadline: 3/1; financial award applicants required to submit FAFSA. *Unit head:* Shellie Hewitt, Director of Graduate and International Student Services, 660-543-4621, Fax: 660-543-4778, E-mail: hewitt@ucmo.edu. *Application contact:* 660-543-4621, E-mail: admit_intl@ucmo.edu.
Website: http://www.ucmo.edu/graduate/

University of Central Oklahoma, The Jackson College of Graduate Studies, College of Education and Professional Studies, Department of Curriculum and Instruction, Edmond, OK 73034-5209. Offers bilingual education/teaching English as a second language (M Ed); early childhood education (M Ed); elementary education (M Ed). *Program availability:* Part-time. *Faculty:* 14 full-time (12 women), 4 part-time/adjunct (3 women). *Students:* 25 full-time (21 women), 67 part-time (60 women); includes 33 minority (8 Black or African American, non-Hispanic/Latino; 3 American Indian or Alaska Native, non-Hispanic/Latino; 2 Asian, non-Hispanic/Latino; 4 Two or more races, non-Hispanic/Latino), 14 international. Average age 33. 44 applicants, 93% accepted, 31 enrolled. In 2017, 27 master's awarded. *Degree requirements:* For master's, comprehensive exam (for some programs), thesis optional. *Entrance requirements:* Additional exam requirements/recommendations for international students: Required—TOEFL (minimum score 550 paper-based; 79 iBT), IELTS (minimum score 6.5). *Application deadline:* For fall admission, 7/15 for international students; for spring admission, 11/15 for international students. Applications are processed on a rolling basis. Application fee: $60. Electronic applications accepted. *Expenses:* Tuition, state resident: full-time $5375; part-time $268.75 per credit hour. Tuition, nonresident: full-time $13,295; part-time $664.75 per credit hour. *Required fees:* $626; $31.30 per credit hour. One-time fee: $50. Tuition and fees vary according to program. *Financial support:* In 2017–18, 13 students received support. Research assistantships, teaching assistantships, career-related internships or fieldwork, Federal Work-Study, scholarships/grants, tuition waivers (partial), and unspecified assistantships available. Financial award application deadline: 3/31; financial award applicants required to submit FAFSA. *Unit head:* Dr. Paulette Shreck, Chair, 405-974-5721, Fax: 405-974-3858. *Application contact:* Carlie Wellington, Assistant Director, CEPS Graduate Enrollment, 405-974-5105, Fax: 405-974-3851, E-mail: gradcoll@uco.edu.

University of Colorado Denver, School of Education and Human Development, Early Childhood Education Program, Denver, CO 80217. Offers early childhood education (MA); special education (MA). *Accreditation:* NCATE. *Program availability:* Part-time, evening/weekend, online learning. *Degree requirements:* For master's, comprehensive exam, fieldwork, practica, 40 credit hours. *Entrance requirements:* For master's, GRE or MAT (if GPA is below 2.75), minimum GPA of 2.75, resume, three letters of recommendation, documented experience with young children, transcripts from all previous colleges/universities attended. Additional exam requirements/recommendations for international students: Required—TOEFL (minimum score 537 paper-based; 75 iBT); Recommended—IELTS (minimum score 6.5). Electronic applications accepted. *Expenses:* Contact institution. *Faculty research:* Early childhood growth and development, faculty development, adult learning, gender and equity issues, research methodology.

University of Colorado Denver, School of Education and Human Development, Program in Educational Leadership and Innovation, Denver, CO 80217. Offers educational studies and research (PhD), including administrative leadership and policy, early childhood special education, math education, research, assessment and evaluation, science education, urban ecologies. *Program availability:* Part-time, evening/weekend. *Degree requirements:* For doctorate, comprehensive exam, thesis/dissertation, 75 credit hours (for PhD). *Entrance requirements:* For doctorate, GRE or equivalent, resume or curriculum vitae, letters of recommendation, master's degree or equivalent, completion of basic or advanced statistics course with minimum B grade. Additional exam requirements/recommendations for international students: Required—TOEFL (minimum score 537 paper-based; 75 iBT); Recommended—IELTS (minimum score 6.5). Electronic applications accepted. *Expenses:* Contact institution. *Faculty research:* Administrative leadership and policy studies, early childhood education, research in diversity, paraprofessionals in education, urban schools lab.

University of Dayton, Department of Teacher Education, Dayton, OH 45469. Offers adolescence to young adult education (MS Ed); early childhood leadership and advocacy (MS Ed); interdisciplinary education (MS Ed), including visual arts; interdisciplinary education studies (MS Ed); leadership in educational systems (MS Ed); literacy (MS Ed); mathematics education (MS Ed); middle childhood education (MS Ed); multi-age education (MS Ed), including world languages; music education (MS Ed); teacher as leader (MS Ed); teacher education (MS Ed); technology-enhanced learning (MS Ed); trans-disciplinary early childhood education (MS Ed). *Program availability:* Part-time, 100% online. *Faculty:* 23 full-time (20 women), 41 part-time/adjunct (36 women). *Students:* 45 full-time (38 women), 68 part-time (57 women); includes 7 minority (3 Black or African American, non-Hispanic/Latino; 1 Hispanic/Latino; 3 Two or more races, non-Hispanic/Latino), 6 international. Average age 31. 106 applicants, 28% accepted. In 2017, 70 master's awarded. *Degree requirements:* For master's, variable foreign language requirement, thesis or alternative, internship (for teaching licensure or

Early Childhood Education

endorsement). *Entrance requirements:* For master's, GRE (minimum score of 149 verbal, 4 on writing) or MAT (minimum score of 396) if undergraduate GPA was under 2.75, minimum GPA of 2.75, 3 letters of recommendation, personal statement or resume, official transcripts. Additional exam requirements/recommendations for international students: Required—TOEFL (minimum score 550 paper-based; 80 iBT); Recommended—IELTS (minimum score 6.5). *Application deadline:* Applications are processed on a rolling basis. Application fee: $0 ($50 for international students). Electronic applications accepted. *Expenses:* Contact institution. *Financial support:* In 2017–18, 5 research assistantships with partial tuition reimbursements (averaging $9,640 per year) were awarded; teaching assistantships, career-related internships or fieldwork, institutionally sponsored loans, and unspecified assistantships also available. Financial award application deadline: 3/1; financial award applicants required to submit FAFSA. *Faculty research:* Social emotional learning, culturally responsive teaching, urban teaching, literacy, instructional strategies, pre-service teacher education preparation. *Unit head:* Dr. Connie L. Bowman, Chair, 937-229-3348, E-mail: cbowman1@udayton.edu. *Application contact:* Gina Seiter, Coordinator of Graduate Programs and Licensing, 937-229-3103, E-mail: gseiter1@udayton.edu.
Website: https://www.udayton.edu/education/departments_and_programs/edt

University of Denver, Morgridge College of Education, Denver, CO 80208. Offers child, family and school psychology (MA, PhD, Ed S); counseling psychology (MA, PhD); curriculum and instruction (MA, Ed D, PhD); curriculum instruction and teaching (Certificate); early childhood special education (MA, Certificate); educational leadership and policy studies (MA, Ed D, PhD, Certificate); higher education (Ed D, PhD); library and information science (MLIS); research methods and statistics (MA, PhD). *Accreditation:* ALA; APA (one or more programs are accredited). *Program availability:* Part-time, evening/weekend, online learning. *Faculty:* 39 full-time (29 women), 60 part-time/adjunct (42 women). *Students:* 502 full-time (406 women), 361 part-time (267 women); includes 233 minority (54 Black or African American, non-Hispanic/Latino; 6 American Indian or Alaska Native, non-Hispanic/Latino; 25 Asian, non-Hispanic/Latino; 113 Hispanic/Latino; 35 Two or more races, non-Hispanic/Latino), 52 international. Average age 31. 1,167 applicants, 64% accepted, 415 enrolled. In 2017, 285 master's, 51 doctorates, 157 other advanced degrees awarded. Terminal master's awarded for partial completion of doctoral program. *Degree requirements:* For master's, comprehensive exam; for doctorate, 2 foreign languages, comprehensive exam, thesis/dissertation. *Entrance requirements:* For master's and doctorate, GRE General Test or GMAT. Additional exam requirements/recommendations for international students: Required—TOEFL (minimum score 550 paper-based; 80 iBT). *Application deadline:* Applications are processed on a rolling basis. Application fee: $65. Electronic applications accepted. *Expenses:* $31,935 per year full-time. *Financial support:* In 2017–18, 765 students received support, including 26 research assistantships with tuition reimbursements available (averaging $10,957 per year), 38 teaching assistantships with tuition reimbursements available (averaging $3,391 per year); career-related internships or fieldwork, Federal Work-Study, institutionally sponsored loans, scholarships/grants, and unspecified assistantships also available. Support available to part-time students. Financial award application deadline: 2/15; financial award applicants required to submit FAFSA. *Faculty research:* Early childhood education, educational leadership, access and opportunity to postsecondary education, marriage and family therapy, data management and archival research. *Unit head:* Dr. Karen Riley, Dean, 303-871-3665, Fax: 303-871-4456, E-mail: karen.riley@du.edu. *Application contact:* Jodi Dye, Director of Admissions, 303-871-2510, Fax: 303-871-4456, E-mail: jodi.dye@du.edu.
Website: http://morgridge.du.edu

University of Florida, Graduate School, College of Education, School of Special Education, School Psychology and Early Childhood Studies, Gainesville, FL 32611. Offers early childhood education (M Ed, MAE); school psychology (M Ed, MAE, Ed D, PhD, Ed S); special education (M Ed, MAE, Ed D, PhD, Ed S). *Accreditation:* NCATE. *Program availability:* Part-time, evening/weekend, online learning. *Degree requirements:* For master's, comprehensive exam (for some programs), thesis (MAE); for doctorate, comprehensive exam, thesis/dissertation. *Entrance requirements:* For master's and doctorate, GRE General Test, minimum GPA of 3.0; for Ed S, GRE General Test. Additional exam requirements/recommendations for international students: Required—TOEFL (minimum score 550 paper-based; 80 iBT), IELTS (minimum score 6). Electronic applications accepted. *Faculty research:* Teacher quality/teacher education, early childhood, autism, academic and behavioral assessment and interventions.

University of Hartford, College of Education, Nursing, and Health Professions, Program in Early Childhood Education, West Hartford, CT 06117-1599. Offers M Ed. *Accreditation:* NCATE. *Program availability:* Part-time, evening/weekend. *Degree requirements:* For master's, comprehensive exam. *Entrance requirements:* For master's, PRAXIS I or waiver, interview, 2 letters of recommendation. Additional exam requirements/recommendations for international students: Required—TOEFL (minimum score 550 paper-based). Electronic applications accepted.

University of Hawaii at Manoa, Office of Graduate Education, College of Education, Department of Curriculum Studies, Program in Early Childhood Education, Honolulu, HI 96822. Offers M Ed. *Accreditation:* NCATE. *Program availability:* Part-time. *Degree requirements:* For master's, thesis optional. *Entrance requirements:* Additional exam requirements/recommendations for international students: Required—TOEFL (minimum score 580 paper-based; 92 iBT), IELTS (minimum score 5).

University of Houston–Clear Lake, School of Education, Program in Curriculum and Instruction, Houston, TX 77058-1002. Offers curriculum and instruction (MS); early childhood education (MS); reading (MS); school library and information science (MS). *Program availability:* Part-time, evening/weekend. *Degree requirements:* For master's, thesis (for some programs). *Entrance requirements:* For master's, GRE or minimum GPA of 3.0 in last 60 hours. Additional exam requirements/recommendations for international students: Required—TOEFL (minimum score 550 paper-based). Electronic applications accepted.

University of Illinois at Chicago, College of Education, Department of Educational Psychology, Chicago, IL 60607-7128. Offers early childhood education (M Ed); educational psychology (PhD); measurement, evaluation, statistics, and assessment (M Ed); youth development (M Ed). *Program availability:* Part-time, online learning. *Faculty research:* Children's construction of morality, development of resilience in the face of enduring economical difficulties, cognition and cognitive development, test fairness.

The University of Kansas, Graduate Studies, School of Education, Department of Special Education, Lawrence, KS 66045. Offers autism spectrum disorder (Certificate); early childhood unified (MS Ed); special and inclusive education leadership (Certificate); special education (PhD). *Accreditation:* NCATE. *Program availability:* Part-time, online learning. *Students:* 68 full-time (57 women), 333 part-time (296 women); includes 59 minority (20 Black or African American, non-Hispanic/Latino; 2 American Indian or Alaska Native, non-Hispanic/Latino; 14 Asian, non-Hispanic/Latino; 7 Hispanic/Latino; 1 Native Hawaiian or other Pacific Islander, non-Hispanic/Latino; 15 Two or more races, non-Hispanic/Latino), 23 international. Average age 34. 261 applicants, 70% accepted, 150 enrolled. In 2017, 140 master's, 4 doctorates, 28 other advanced degrees awarded. *Entrance requirements:* For master's, minimum GPA of 3.0, official transcripts, 3 letters of reference, professional resume; for doctorate, GRE General Test, official transcripts,

3 letters of reference, professional resume, professional writing sample. Application fee: $65 ($85 for international students). Electronic applications accepted. *Financial support:* Fellowships, research assistantships, teaching assistantships, Federal Work-Study, scholarships/grants, and unspecified assistantships available. Support available to part-time students. Financial award application deadline: 2/21; financial award applicants required to submit FAFSA. *Faculty research:* Autism spectrum disorders, learning disabilities research, leadership development, qualitative research and evaluation. *Unit head:* Elizabeth B. Kozleski, Chair, 785-864-0556, E-mail: elizabeth.kozleski@ku.edu. *Application contact:* Graduate Admission Contact, 785-864-4342, E-mail: specialeduadm@ku.edu.
Website: http://specialedu.ku.edu/

University of Kentucky, Graduate School, College of Education, Program in Special Education, Lexington, KY 40506-0032. Offers early childhood (MS Ed); rehabilitation counseling (MRC, PhD); special education (MS Ed, PhD). *Accreditation:* CORE; NCATE. Terminal master's awarded for partial completion of doctoral program. *Degree requirements:* For master's, comprehensive exam, thesis optional; for doctorate, comprehensive exam, thesis/dissertation. *Entrance requirements:* For master's, GRE General Test, minimum undergraduate GPA of 2.75; for doctorate, GRE General Test, minimum graduate GPA of 3.0. Additional exam requirements/recommendations for international students: Required—TOEFL (minimum score 550 paper-based). Electronic applications accepted. *Faculty research:* Applied behavior analysis applications in special education, single subject research design in classroom settings, transition research across life span, rural special education personnel.

University of Louisville, Graduate School, College of Education and Human Development, Departments of Early Childhood and Elementary Education, Middle and Secondary Education, and Special Education, Louisville, KY 40292-0001. Offers art education (MAT); autism and applied behavior analysis (Certificate); curriculum and instruction (PhD); early elementary education (MAT); exercise physiology (MS); health and physical education (MAT); health professions education (Certificate); higher education (MA); human resources and organization development (MS); instructional technology (M Ed); interdisciplinary early childhood education (MAT); middle school education (MAT); music education (MAT); secondary education (MAT); special education (MAT); sport administration (MS); teacher leadership (M Ed). *Program availability:* Part-time, evening/weekend. *Students:* 114 full-time (73 women), 173 part-time (114 women); includes 49 minority (19 Black or African American, non-Hispanic/Latino; 5 Asian, non-Hispanic/Latino; 13 Hispanic/Latino; 12 Two or more races, non-Hispanic/Latino), 7 international. Average age 29. 132 applicants, 73% accepted, 57 enrolled. In 2017, 70 master's, 2 doctorates, 2 other advanced degrees awarded. *Application deadline:* For spring admission, 1/1 priority date for international students. Application fee: $65. *Expenses:* Tuition, state resident: full-time $12,246; part-time $681 per credit hour. Tuition, nonresident: full-time $25,486; part-time $1417 per credit hour. *Required fees:* $196. Tuition and fees vary according to course load, program and reciprocity agreements. *Financial support:* Application deadline: 6/1; applicants required to submit FAFSA. *Faculty research:* STEM teaching and learning; content literacy for English language learners; social justice in teacher education; adolescent literacy; mathematics teacher development. *Total annual research expenditures:* $1.7 million. *Unit head:* Dr. Ann E. Larson, Dean, College of Education and Human Development, 502-852-6411, Fax: 502-852-1464, E-mail: ann@louisville.edu. *Application contact:* Betty Hampton, Director of Graduate Student Services, 502-852-5597, Fax: 502-852-1465, E-mail: edadvise@louisville.edu.
Website: http://louisville.edu/delphi

University of Maine, Graduate School, College of Education and Human Development, School of Learning and Teaching, Orono, ME 04469. Offers counselor education (M Ed, MA, MS, CAS); early childhood teacher (CGS); education (PhD), including counselor education, literacy education, prevention and intervention studies; elementary education (M Ed, CAS); individualized education (M Ed); literacy education (CAS); response to intervention for behavior (CGS); secondary education (M Ed, CAS); social studies education (M Ed); special education (M Ed, CAS). *Program availability:* Part-time. *Faculty:* 21 full-time (12 women), 37 part-time/adjunct (29 women). *Students:* 84 full-time (73 women), 190 part-time (165 women); includes 19 minority (1 Black or African American, non-Hispanic/Latino; 9 American Indian or Alaska Native, non-Hispanic/Latino; 2 Asian, non-Hispanic/Latino; 4 Hispanic/Latino; 3 Two or more races, non-Hispanic/Latino), 4 international. Average age 38. 141 applicants, 94% accepted, 91 enrolled. In 2017, 74 master's, 3 doctorates, 36 other advanced degrees awarded. *Degree requirements:* For master's, thesis (for some programs); for doctorate, comprehensive exam, thesis/dissertation. *Entrance requirements:* For master's, GRE General Test, MAT. Additional exam requirements/recommendations for international students: Required—TOEFL (minimum score 550 paper-based; 80 iBT), IELTS (minimum score 6.5). *Application deadline:* For fall admission, 2/1 priority date for domestic students. Applications are processed on a rolling basis. Application fee: $65. Electronic applications accepted. *Expenses:* Tuition, state resident: full-time $7722; part-time $429 per credit hour. Tuition, nonresident: full-time $25,146; part-time $1397 per credit hour. *Required fees:* $1162; $581 per credit hour. *Financial support:* In 2017–18, 14 students received support, including 11 teaching assistantships (averaging $15,200 per year); Federal Work-Study, scholarships/grants, and unspecified assistantships also available. Financial award application deadline: 3/1. *Faculty research:* Gender and leadership, virtual reality, using writing to improve performance in athletics, digital citizenship, professional development for special and general education. *Total annual research expenditures:* $5 million. *Unit head:* Dr. Jim Artesani, Associate Dean of Accreditation and Graduate Affairs, 207-581-4061. *Application contact:* Scott G. Delcourt, Assistant Vice President for Graduate Studies and Senior Associate Dean, 207-581-3291, Fax: 207-581-3232, E-mail: graduate@maine.edu.
Website: http://umaine.edu/edhd

University of Maine at Farmington, Graduate Programs in Education, Farmington, ME 04938. Offers early childhood education (MS Ed); educational leadership (MS Ed); instructional technology (M Ed). M Ed offered in collaboration with University of Maine and University of Southern Maine. *Accreditation:* NCATE. *Program availability:* Part-time-only, evening/weekend, 100% online, blended/hybrid learning. *Faculty:* 8 full-time (7 women), 2 part-time/adjunct (1 woman). *Students:* 106 part-time (92 women). Average age 36. 6 applicants, 100% accepted, 6 enrolled. In 2017, 29 master's awarded. *Degree requirements:* For master's, thesis, capstone research project. *Entrance requirements:* For master's, baccalaureate degree from accredited institution, valid teaching certificate or professional experience in education. Additional exam requirements/recommendations for international students: Required—TOEFL. *Application deadline:* For fall admission, 8/10 for domestic students; for spring admission, 1/5 for domestic students; for summer admission, 4/10 for domestic students. Applications are processed on a rolling basis. Application fee: $60. Electronic applications accepted. *Expenses:* Contact institution. *Financial support:* Applicants required to submit FAFSA. *Faculty research:* Teacher leadership, school improvement strategies, technology integration. *Unit head:* Dr. Johanna Prince, Director of Graduate Programs in Education, 207-778-7066, E-mail: gradstudies@maine.edu. *Application contact:* Valerie Soucie, Administrative Specialist, 207-778-7502, Fax: 207-778-8134, E-mail: gradstudies@maine.edu.
Website: http://www2.umf.maine.edu/gradstudies/

University of Maryland, Baltimore County, The Graduate School, College of Arts, Humanities and Social Sciences, Department of Education, Program in Teaching, Baltimore, MD 21250. Offers early childhood education (MAT); elementary education (MAT); teaching (MAT), including art, biology, chemistry, choral music, classical foreign language, dance, earth/space science, English, instrumental music, mathematics, modern foreign language, physical science, physics, social studies, theatre. *Program availability:* Part-time, evening/weekend. *Faculty:* 24 full-time (18 women), 25 part-time/adjunct (19 women). *Students:* 41 full-time (34 women), 27 part-time (18 women); includes 26 minority (6 Black or African American, non-Hispanic/Latino; 9 Asian, non-Hispanic/Latino; 7 Hispanic/Latino; 1 Native Hawaiian or other Pacific Islander, non-Hispanic/Latino; 3 Two or more races, non-Hispanic/Latino), 2 international. Average age 30. 54 applicants, 83% accepted, 35 enrolled. In 2017, 50 master's awarded. *Degree requirements:* For master's, comprehensive exam (for some programs), thesis (for some programs). *Entrance requirements:* For master's, PRAXIS Core Examination or GRE (minimum score of 1000), minimum GPA of 3.0. Additional exam requirements/recommendations for international students: Required—TOEFL. *Application deadline:* For fall admission, 6/1 for domestic and international students; for spring admission, 11/1 for domestic and international students. Applications are processed on a rolling basis. Application fee: $50. Electronic applications accepted. *Expenses: Required fees:* $132. *Financial support:* In 2017–18, 8 students received support, including teaching assistantships with tuition reimbursements available (averaging $12,000 per year); career-related internships or fieldwork, Federal Work-Study, scholarships/grants, tuition waivers, and unspecified assistantships also available. Financial award application deadline: 3/15. *Faculty research:* STEM teacher education, culturally sensitive pedagogy, ESOL/bilingual education, early childhood education, language, literacy and culture. *Total annual research expenditures:* $100,000. *Unit head:* Dr. Susan M. Blunck, Graduate Program Director, 410-455-2869, Fax: 410-455-3986, E-mail: blunck@umbc.edu. *Application contact:* Cheryl Johnson, MAT Program Specialist, 410-455-3388, E-mail: blackwel@umbc.edu.
Website: http://www.umbc.edu/education/

University of Massachusetts Amherst, Graduate School, College of Education, Program in Education, Amherst, MA 01003. Offers bilingual, English as a second language, and multicultural education (M Ed, Ed S); child study and early education (M Ed); children, families and schools (Ed D, Ed S); early childhood and elementary teacher education (M Ed); educational leadership (M Ed); educational policy and leadership (Ed D); higher education (M Ed); international education (M Ed); language, literacy and culture (Ed D); learning, media and technology (M Ed, Ed S); mathematics, science, and learning technologies (Ed D); reading and writing (M Ed); research, educational measurement and psychometrics (Ed D); school counselor education (M Ed, Ed S); school psychology (Ed S); science education (Ed S); secondary teacher education (M Ed); social justice education (M Ed, Ed D, Ed S); special education (M Ed, Ed D, Ed S); teacher education and school improvement (Ed D, Ed S). *Accreditation:* NCATE. *Program availability:* Part-time, online learning. Terminal master's awarded for partial completion of doctoral program. *Degree requirements:* For doctorate, comprehensive exam, thesis/dissertation. *Entrance requirements:* Additional exam requirements/recommendations for international students: Required—TOEFL (minimum score 550 paper-based; 80 iBT), IELTS (minimum score 6.5). Electronic applications accepted.

University of Massachusetts Boston, College of Education and Human Development, Program in Early Childhood Education and Care, Boston, MA 02125-3393. Offers PhD. *Students:* 9 full-time (8 women); includes 1 minority (Hispanic/Latino), 4 international. Average age 32. 11 applicants, 45% accepted, 4 enrolled. *Application deadline:* For fall admission, 2/1 for domestic students. *Expenses:* Tuition, state resident: full-time $17,375. Tuition, nonresident: full-time $33,915. *Required fees:* $355. *Unit head:* Dr. Anne Douglass, Program Director, 617-287-5000. *Application contact:* Graduate Admissions Coordinator, 617-287-6400, Fax: 617-287-6236, E-mail: bos.gadm@dpc.umassp.edu.

University of Memphis, Graduate School, College of Education, Department of Instruction and Curriculum Leadership, Memphis, TN 38152. Offers advanced studies in teaching and learning (M Ed); applied behavior analysis (Graduate Certificate); autism studies (Graduate Certificate); early childhood education (MAT, MS, Ed D); elementary education (MAT); instruction and curriculum (MS, Ed D); instruction design and technology (MS, Ed D); instructional design and technology (Graduate Certificate); literacy, leadership, and coaching (Graduate Certificate); reading (MS, Ed D); school library information specialist (Graduate Certificate); secondary education (MAT); special education (MAT, MS, Ed D); STEM teacher leadership (Graduate Certificate); urban education (Graduate Certificate). *Accreditation:* NCATE (one or more programs are accredited). *Program availability:* Part-time. *Faculty:* 22 full-time (14 women), 14 part-time/adjunct (10 women). *Students:* 36 full-time (27 women), 351 part-time (271 women); includes 159 minority (132 Black or African American, non-Hispanic/Latino; 1 American Indian or Alaska Native, non-Hispanic/Latino; 7 Asian, non-Hispanic/Latino; 10 Hispanic/Latino; 9 Two or more races, non-Hispanic/Latino), 4 international. Average age 35. 170 applicants, 85% accepted, 111 enrolled. In 2017, 84 master's, 14 doctorates, 32 other advanced degrees awarded. Terminal master's awarded for partial completion of doctoral program. *Degree requirements:* For master's, comprehensive exam, thesis or alternative; for doctorate, comprehensive exam, thesis/dissertation. *Entrance requirements:* For master's, GRE General Test, PRAXIS, minimum GPA of 2.5, letters of reference; for doctorate, GRE General Test, GRE Subject Test, 2 years of teaching experience, letters of reference, statement of purpose, interview. Additional exam requirements/recommendations for international students: Required—TOEFL (minimum score 550 paper-based; 79 iBT). *Application deadline:* For fall admission, 4/1 priority date for domestic students; for spring admission, 10/1 priority date for domestic students; for summer admission, 2/1 priority date for domestic students. Applications are processed on a rolling basis. Application fee: $35 ($60 for international students). Electronic applications accepted. *Expenses:* Contact institution. *Financial support:* In 2017–18, 2 research assistantships with full tuition reimbursements (averaging $10,000 per year), 3 teaching assistantships with full tuition reimbursements (averaging $10,666 per year) were awarded; career-related internships or fieldwork, Federal Work-Study, institutionally sponsored loans, scholarships/grants, traineeships, and unspecified assistantships also available. Support available to part-time students. Financial award application deadline: 2/1; financial award applicants required to submit FAFSA. *Faculty research:* Effective urban teachers, preparation and retention of urban teachers, technology utilization in schools, field-based teacher preparation programs, effective use of online instruction. *Unit head:* Dr. Angiline Powell, Interim Chair, 901-678-3310, E-mail: apowell3@memphis.edu. *Application contact:* Dr. James Meindl, Coordinator of Graduate Studies, 901-678-3310, E-mail: jnmeindl@memphis.edu.
Website: http://www.memphis.edu/icl/

University of Miami, Graduate School, School of Education and Human Development, Department of Teaching and Learning, Program in Early Childhood Special Education, Coral Gables, FL 33124. Offers MS Ed, Ed S. *Program availability:* Part-time, evening/weekend. *Degree requirements:* For master's, electronic portfolio. *Entrance requirements:* For master's, GRE General Test. Additional exam requirements/recommendations for international students: Required—TOEFL (minimum score 550 paper-based; 80 iBT); Recommended—IELTS (minimum score 6.5). Electronic applications accepted.

University of Michigan–Dearborn, College of Education, Health, and Human Services, Master of Arts Program in Early Childhood Education, Dearborn, MI 48126. Offers MA. *Program availability:* Part-time, evening/weekend. *Faculty:* 2 full-time (both women), 2 part-time/adjunct (both women). *Students:* 1 (woman) full-time, 18 part-time (all women); includes 7 minority (5 Black or African American, non-Hispanic/Latino; 2 Hispanic/Latino). Average age 33. 12 applicants, 67% accepted, 4 enrolled. In 2017, 5 master's awarded. *Entrance requirements:* Additional exam requirements/recommendations for international students: Required—TOEFL (minimum score 560 paper-based; 84 iBT), IELTS (minimum score 6.5). *Application deadline:* For fall admission, 8/1 priority date for domestic students, 5/1 for international students; for winter admission, 12/1 priority date for domestic students, 9/1 for international students; for spring admission, 4/1 priority date for domestic students, 1/1 for international students. Applications are processed on a rolling basis. Application fee: $60. Electronic applications accepted. *Expenses:* $683 per credit hour in-state; $1,176 per credit hour out-state. *Financial support:* In 2017–18, 5 students received support. Career-related internships or fieldwork and scholarships/grants available. Financial award application deadline: 3/1; financial award applicants required to submit FAFSA. *Faculty research:* Place based education, curriculum development, early childhood learning and development, literacy, multicultural education. *Unit head:* Dr. Stein Brunvand, Director, Master's Programs, 313-583-6415, E-mail: sbrunvan@umich.edu. *Application contact:* Office of Graduate Studies, 313-583-6321, E-mail: umd-graduatestudies@umich.edu.
Website: http://umdearborn.edu/cehhs/cehhs_maeced/

University of Michigan–Flint, School of Education and Human Services, Department of Education, Flint, MI 48502-1950. Offers curriculum and instruction (MA); early childhood education (MA); education (Ed D); educational leadership (Ed S); educational technology (MA), including curriculum and instruction, developer; literacy education (MA); secondary education with certification (MA). *Program availability:* Part-time, evening/weekend, 100% online, mixed mode format (for some programs). *Faculty:* 18 full-time (11 women), 26 part-time/adjunct (13 women). *Students:* 34 full-time (23 women), 192 part-time (137 women); includes 61 minority (46 Black or African American, non-Hispanic/Latino; 2 Asian, non-Hispanic/Latino; 5 Hispanic/Latino; 2 Native Hawaiian or other Pacific Islander, non-Hispanic/Latino; 6 Two or more races, non-Hispanic/Latino), 2 international. Average age 39. 124 applicants, 87% accepted, 81 enrolled. In 2017, 89 master's, 3 doctorates awarded. *Degree requirements:* For master's, thesis optional; for doctorate, thesis/dissertation. *Entrance requirements:* For master's, bachelor's degree from regionally-accredited institution, minimum overall undergraduate GPA of 3.0; for doctorate, Ed S; minimum overall graduate GPA of 3.3 (6.0 on a 9.0 scale) or equivalent; at least 3 years of work experience in a P-16 educational institution or in an education-related position; for Ed S, MA or MS in education-related field from accredited institution; minimum overall graduate GPA of 3.0 (6.0 on a 9.0 scale) or equivalent; at least 3 years of work experience in an educational setting. Additional exam requirements/recommendations for international students: Required—TOEFL (minimum score 84 iBT), IELTS (minimum score 6.5). *Application deadline:* For fall admission, 8/1 for domestic students, 5/1 for international students; for winter admission, 11/15 for domestic students, 9/15 for international students; for spring admission, 3/15 for domestic students, 1/15 for international students; for summer admission, 5/15 for domestic students. Applications are processed on a rolling basis. Application fee: $55. Electronic applications accepted. *Expenses:* Contact institution. *Financial support:* Federal Work-Study, scholarships/grants, and unspecified assistantships available. Financial award application deadline: 3/1; financial award applicants required to submit FAFSA. *Unit head:* Dr. Mary Jo Finney, Department Chair/Associate Professor, 810-766-6617, E-mail: mjfinney@umflint.edu. *Application contact:* Bradley T. Maki, Director of Graduate Admissions, 810-762-3171, Fax: 810-766-6789, E-mail: bmaki@umflint.edu.
Website: https://www.umflint.edu/education/graduate-programs

University of Minnesota, Twin Cities Campus, Graduate School, College of Education and Human Development, Department of Educational Psychology, Minneapolis, MN 55455-0213. Offers autism spectrum disorder (Certificate); counseling and student personnel psychology (MA); early childhood special education (M Ed); psychological foundations of education (MA, PhD); quantitative methods in education (MA, PhD); school psychology (MA, PhD, Ed S); special education (M Ed, MA, PhD); talent development and gifted education (Certificate). *Accreditation:* APA (one or more programs are accredited). *Faculty:* 30 full-time (15 women). *Students:* 250 full-time (185 women), 63 part-time (49 women); includes 49 minority (6 Black or African American, non-Hispanic/Latino; 19 Asian, non-Hispanic/Latino; 14 Hispanic/Latino; 10 Two or more races, non-Hispanic/Latino), 36 international. Average age 29. 264 applicants, 45% accepted, 110 enrolled. In 2017, 94 master's, 18 doctorates, 10 other advanced degrees awarded. Application fee: $75 ($95 for international students). *Financial support:* In 2017–18, 22 fellowships, 63 research assistantships (averaging $14,194 per year), 37 teaching assistantships (averaging $10,351 per year) were awarded. *Faculty research:* Achievement gap; autism; behavioral and social-emotional development; improving skills in mathematics, reading, and comprehension; measuring and analyzing student change. *Total annual research expenditures:* $6 million. *Unit head:* Dr. Geoffrey Maruyama, Chair, 612-624-1003, Fax: 612-625-5861, E-mail: geoff@umn.edu. *Application contact:* Dr. Ernest Davenport, Director of Graduate Studies, 612-624-1040, E-mail: lqr6576@umn.edu.
Website: http://www.cehd.umn.edu/EdPsych

University of Minnesota, Twin Cities Campus, Graduate School, College of Education and Human Development, Institute of Child Development, Minneapolis, MN 55455-0213. Offers applied child and adolescent development (MA); child psychology (PhD); early childhood education (M Ed). *Program availability:* Online learning. *Faculty:* 15 full-time (8 women). *Students:* 55 full-time (49 women), 12 part-time (all women); includes 17 minority (5 Black or African American, non-Hispanic/Latino; 3 Asian, non-Hispanic/Latino; 6 Hispanic/Latino; 3 Two or more races, non-Hispanic/Latino), 2 international. Average age 27. 120 applicants, 25% accepted, 30 enrolled. In 2017, 41 master's, 9 doctorates awarded. Application fee: $75 ($95 for international students). *Financial support:* In 2017–18, 21 fellowships, 17 research assistantships with full tuition reimbursements (averaging $16,246 per year), 19 teaching assistantships with full tuition reimbursements (averaging $14,389 per year) were awarded. *Faculty research:* Developmental affective and cognitive neuroscience; developmental psychopathology; intervention and prevention science; social and emotional development; cognitive, language, and perceptual development. *Total annual research expenditures:* $7.5 million. *Unit head:* Dr. Megan Gunnar, Director, 612-624-2713, E-mail: gunnar@umn.edu. *Application contact:* Dr. Kathleen Thomas, Director of Graduate Studies, 612-625-3389, E-mail: thoma114@umn.edu.
Website: http://www.cehd.umn.edu/ICD

University of Mississippi, Graduate School, School of Education, University, MS 38677. Offers counselor education (M Ed, PhD); counselor education - play therapy (Ed S); early childhood (M Ed); educational leadership K-12 (M Ed, Ed D, PhD, Ed S); elementary education (M Ed, Ed D, Ed S); higher education/student personnel (Ed D, PhD); literacy education (M Ed); math education (Ed D); secondary education (M Ed,

Early Childhood Education

PhD, Ed S); special education (M Ed, PhD, Ed S); teacher corporations (MA); teacher education (MA). *Accreditation:* NCATE. *Faculty:* 65 full-time (40 women), 25 part-time/adjunct (5 women). *Students:* 185 full-time (148 women), 410 part-time (310 women); includes 193 minority (168 Black or African American, non-Hispanic/Latino; 7 Asian, non-Hispanic/Latino; 14 Hispanic/Latino; 4 Two or more races, non-Hispanic/Latino), 7 international. Average age 33. In 2017, 176 master's, 20 doctorates, 37 other advanced degrees awarded. *Entrance requirements:* For master's, GRE General Test, minimum GPA of 3.0; for doctorate, GRE General Test. Additional exam requirements/recommendations for international students: Required—TOEFL. *Application deadline:* For fall admission, 3/1 for domestic students; for spring admission, 10/1 for domestic students; for summer admission, 3/1 for domestic students. Applications are processed on a rolling basis. Application fee: $50. Electronic applications accepted. *Financial support:* Scholarships/grants available. Financial award application deadline: 3/1; financial award applicants required to submit FAFSA. *Unit head:* Dr. David Rock, Dean, 662-915-7063, Fax: 662-915-7249, E-mail: soe@olemiss.edu. *Application contact:* Dr. Joe Sumrall, Professor of Elementary Education, 662-915-7350, E-mail: soe@olemiss.edu.

University of Missouri, Office of Research and Graduate Studies, College of Education, Department of Learning, Teaching and Curriculum, Columbia, MO 65211. Offers agricultural education (M Ed, PhD, Ed S); art education (M Ed, PhD, Ed S); business and office education (M Ed, PhD, Ed S); early childhood education (M Ed, PhD, Ed S); elementary education (M Ed, PhD, Ed S); English education (M Ed, PhD, Ed S); foreign language education (M Ed, PhD, Ed S); health education and promotion (M Ed, PhD); learning and instruction (M Ed); marketing education (M Ed, PhD, Ed S); mathematics education (M Ed, PhD, Ed S); music education (M Ed, PhD, Ed S); reading education (M Ed, PhD, Ed S); science education (M Ed, PhD, Ed S); social studies education (M Ed, PhD, Ed S); vocational education (M Ed, PhD, Ed S). *Program availability:* Part-time. Terminal master's awarded for partial completion of doctoral program. *Degree requirements:* For doctorate, thesis/dissertation. *Entrance requirements:* For master's and Ed S, GRE General Test or MAT, minimum GPA of 3.0; for doctorate, GRE General Test, minimum GPA of 3.0. Additional exam requirements/recommendations for international students: Required—TOEFL (minimum score 600 paper-based; 100 iBT). Electronic applications accepted.

University of Missouri–St. Louis, College of Education, Department of Educator Preparation, Innovation and Research, St. Louis, MO 63121. Offers elementary education (M Ed), including early childhood, general, reading; secondary education (M Ed), including curriculum and instruction, general, middle level education, reading, teaching English to speakers of other languages (TESOL); special education (M Ed), including autism and developmental disabilities, early childhood special education. *Program availability:* Part-time, evening/weekend. *Students:* 75 full-time (63 women), 462 part-time (363 women); includes 127 minority (85 Black or African American, non-Hispanic/Latino; 2 American Indian or Alaska Native, non-Hispanic/Latino; 8 Asian, non-Hispanic/Latino; 24 Hispanic/Latino; 8 Two or more races, non-Hispanic/Latino), 1 international. 247 applicants, 92% accepted, 153 enrolled. *Degree requirements:* For master's, comprehensive exam. *Entrance requirements:* Additional exam requirements/recommendations for international students: Recommended—TOEFL (minimum score 550 paper-based; 79 iBT), IELTS (minimum score 6.5). *Application deadline:* For fall admission, 7/1 priority date for domestic and international students; for spring admission, 12/1 priority date for domestic and international students. Application fee: $50 ($40 for international students). Electronic applications accepted. *Expenses:* Tuition, state resident: part-time $476.50 per credit hour. Tuition, nonresident: part-time $1169.70 per credit hour. *Financial support:* Application deadline: 4/1; applicants required to submit FAFSA. *Unit head:* Dr. Gayle Wilkinson, Chair, 314-516-5791. *Application contact:* 314-516-5458, Fax: 314-516-6996, E-mail: gadadm@umsl.edu. Website: https://coe.umsl.edu/dept/epir.html

University of Montana, Graduate School, Phyllis J. Washington College of Education and Human Sciences, Department of Teaching and Learning, Missoula, MT 59812. Offers curriculum and instruction (M Ed, Ed D); early childhood education (M Ed); education (MA); teaching and learning (PhD). *Program availability:* Part-time. *Degree requirements:* For doctorate, thesis/dissertation. *Entrance requirements:* For master's, GRE General Test. Additional exam requirements/recommendations for international students: Required—TOEFL.

University of Nebraska at Kearney, College of Education, Department of Teacher Education, Kearney, NE 68849-0001. Offers curriculum and instruction (MA Ed), including early childhood education, elementary education, English as a second language, instructional effectiveness, reading/special education, secondary education; instructional technology (MS Ed), including information technology, instructional technology, school librarian; reading PK-12 (MA Ed); special education (MA Ed), including advanced practitioner: assistive technology specialist, advanced practitioner: behavioral interventionist, advanced practitioner: inclusive collaboration specialist, gifted, teacher education. *Program availability:* Part-time, evening/weekend, online only, 100% online. *Degree requirements:* For master's, comprehensive exam, thesis optional. *Entrance requirements:* For master's, portfolio or GRE. Additional exam requirements/recommendations for international students: Recommended—TOEFL (minimum score 550 paper-based; 79 iBT), IELTS (minimum score 6.5). Electronic applications accepted. *Expenses:* Contact institution.

University of Nebraska–Lincoln, Graduate College, College of Education and Human Sciences, Department of Child, Youth and Family Studies, Lincoln, NE 68588. Offers child development/early childhood education (MS, PhD); child, youth and family studies (MS); family and consumer sciences education (MS, PhD); family financial planning (MS); family science (MS, PhD); gerontology (PhD); human sciences (PhD), including child, youth and family studies, gerontology, medical family therapy; marriage and family therapy (MS); medical family therapy (PhD); youth development (MS). *Accreditation:* AAMFT/COAMFTE (one or more programs are accredited). *Program availability:* Online learning. *Degree requirements:* For master's, thesis optional. *Entrance requirements:* For master's, GRE. Additional exam requirements/recommendations for international students: Required—TOEFL (minimum score 550 paper-based). Electronic applications accepted. *Faculty research:* Marriage and family therapy, child development/early childhood education, family financial management.

University of Nevada, Las Vegas, Graduate College, College of Education, Department of Educational and Clinical Studies, Las Vegas, NV 89154-3066. Offers addiction studies (Advanced Certificate); counselor education (M Ed, MS), including clinical mental health (MS), school counseling (M Ed); early childhood education (M Ed); early childhood special education (Certificate), including infancy, preschool; English language learning (M Ed); mental health counseling (Advanced Certificate); special education (M Ed, PhD); PhD/JD. *Program availability:* Part-time. *Faculty:* 18 full-time (9 women), 28 part-time/adjunct (22 women). *Students:* 281 full-time (230 women), 193 part-time (148 women); includes 211 minority (54 Black or African American, non-Hispanic/Latino; 2 American Indian or Alaska Native, non-Hispanic/Latino; 28 Asian, non-Hispanic/Latino; 95 Hispanic/Latino; 4 Native Hawaiian or other Pacific Islander, non-Hispanic/Latino; 28 Two or more races, non-Hispanic/Latino), 13 international. Average age 34. 262 applicants, 76% accepted, 161 enrolled. In 2017, 204 master's, 8 doctorates, 1 other advanced degree awarded. *Degree requirements:* For master's,

comprehensive exam (for some programs); for doctorate, comprehensive exam, thesis/dissertation; for other advanced degree, final project. *Entrance requirements:* For master's, bachelor's degree; letter of recommendation; statement of purpose; for doctorate, GRE General Test, statement of purpose; writing sample; 3 letters of recommendation. Additional exam requirements/recommendations for international students: Required—TOEFL (minimum score 550 paper-based; 80 iBT), IELTS (minimum score 7). Application fee: $60 ($95 for international students). Electronic applications accepted. *Expenses:* $275 per credit, $850 per course, $7,969 per year resident, $22,157 per year non-resident, $7,094 non-resident fee (7 credits or more), $1,307 annual health insurance fee. *Financial support:* In 2017–18, 35 students received support, including 10 research assistantships with full tuition reimbursements available (averaging $13,775 per year), 25 teaching assistantships with full tuition reimbursements available (averaging $17,140 per year); institutionally sponsored loans, scholarships/grants, health care benefits, and unspecified assistantships also available. Financial award application deadline: 3/15; financial award applicants required to submit FAFSA. *Faculty research:* Multicultural issues in counseling, academic interventions for students with disabilities, establishment of pro-social skills in young children with severe disabilities, inclusive strategies for students with disabilities, language and literacy for English language learners. *Total annual research expenditures:* $1.1 million. *Unit head:* Dr. Monica Brown, Interim Department Chair/Professor, 702-895-3167, Fax: 702-895-3205, E-mail: monica.brown@unlv.edu. *Application contact:* Dr. Joseph Morgan, Graduate Coordinator, 702-895-3329, Fax: 702-895-3205, E-mail: joseph.morgan@unlv.edu.
Website: http://education.unlv.edu/ecs/

University of New England, College of Graduate and Professional Studies, Portland, ME 04005-9526. Offers advanced educational leadership (CAGS); applied nutrition (MS); career and technical education (MS Ed); curriculum and instruction (MS Ed); education (CAGS, Post-Master's Certificate); educational leadership (MS Ed, Ed D); generalist (MS Ed); health informatics (MS, Graduate Certificate); inclusion education (MS Ed); literacy K-12 (MS Ed); medical education leadership (MMEL); public health (MPH); public health (Graduate Certificate); reading specialist (MS Ed); social work (MSW). *Program availability:* Part-time, evening/weekend, online only, 100% online. *Faculty:* 125 part-time/adjunct (94 women). *Students:* 1,403 full-time (1,128 women), 594 part-time (475 women); includes 474 minority (332 Black or African American, non-Hispanic/Latino; 13 American Indian or Alaska Native, non-Hispanic/Latino; 83 Asian, non-Hispanic/Latino; 27 Hispanic/Latino; 11 Native Hawaiian or other Pacific Islander, non-Hispanic/Latino; 8 Two or more races, non-Hispanic/Latino). Average age 35. 3,153 applicants, 41% accepted, 990 enrolled. In 2017, 307 master's, 59 doctorates, 124 other advanced degrees awarded. *Application deadline:* Applications are processed on a rolling basis. Electronic applications accepted. Tuition and fees vary according to degree level, program and student level. *Financial support:* Application deadline: 5/1; applicants required to submit FAFSA. *Unit head:* Dr. Martha Wilson, Associate Provost for Online Worldwide Learning/Dean of the College of Graduate and Professional Studies, 207-221-4985, E-mail: mwilson13@une.edu.
Website: http://online.une.edu

University of New Hampshire, Graduate School, College of Liberal Arts, Department of Education, Program in Early Childhood Education, Durham, NH 03824. Offers early childhood education (M Ed); early childhood education: special needs (M Ed). *Program availability:* Part-time. *Students:* 4 full-time (3 women), 6 part-time (all women). Average age 32. 9 applicants, 78% accepted, 4 enrolled. In 2017, 13 master's awarded. *Entrance requirements:* For master's, PRAXIS, Department of Education background check. Additional exam requirements/recommendations for international students: Required—TOEFL (minimum score 550 paper-based; 80 iBT). *Application deadline:* For fall admission, 3/1 priority date for domestic students, 3/1 for international students; for spring admission, 11/1 for domestic students. Application fee: $65. Electronic applications accepted. *Financial support:* In 2017–18, 4 students received support. Fellowships, research assistantships, teaching assistantships, career-related internships or fieldwork, Federal Work-Study, scholarships/grants, and tuition waivers (full and partial) available. Support available to part-time students. Financial award application deadline: 2/15. *Unit head:* Leslie Couse, Chair, 603-862-0638, E-mail: education.department@unh.edu. *Application contact:* Cindy Glidden, Department Coordinator, 603-862-2381, E-mail: education.department@unh.edu.
Website: http://cola.unh.edu/education

University of New Mexico, Graduate Studies, College of Education, Program in Multicultural Teacher and Childhood Education, Albuquerque, NM 87131-2039. Offers Ed D, PhD. *Accreditation:* NCATE. *Program availability:* Part-time. *Faculty:* 1 part-time/adjunct (0 women). *Students:* 2 full-time (0 women), 10 part-time (7 women); includes 5 minority (4 Hispanic/Latino; 1 Two or more races, non-Hispanic/Latino). Average age 47. 5 applicants, 20% accepted. In 2017, 1 doctorate awarded. *Degree requirements:* For doctorate, comprehensive exam, thesis/dissertation. *Entrance requirements:* For doctorate, GRE, master's degree, minimum GPA of 3.0, 3 years of teaching experience, 3-5 letters of reference, letter of intent, professional writing sample. Additional exam requirements/recommendations for international students: Required—TOEFL (minimum score 550 paper-based). *Application deadline:* For fall admission, 1/15 priority date for domestic students, 1/15 for international students; for spring admission, 10/30 for domestic and international students. Application fee: $50. Electronic applications accepted. *Financial support:* Fellowships, research assistantships, teaching assistantships with partial tuition reimbursements, scholarships/grants, and unspecified assistantships available. Financial award application deadline: 3/1; financial award applicants required to submit FAFSA. *Faculty research:* Teacher education, clinical preparation, reflective practice, science education, mathematics education, social justice, technology education, media literacy. *Unit head:* Dr. Cheryl Torrez, Department Chair, 505-277-9611, Fax: 505-277-0455, E-mail: ted@unm.edu. *Application contact:* Robert Romero, Program Coordinator, 505-277-0513, Fax: 505-277-0455, E-mail: ted@unm.edu.
Website: https://coe.unm.edu/departments-programs/ifce/ecme/

The University of North Carolina at Chapel Hill, Graduate School, School of Education, Master of Education Program for Experienced Teachers: Early Childhood Intervention and Family Support, Chapel Hill, NC 27599. Offers M Ed. *Accreditation:* NCATE. *Program availability:* Part-time. *Degree requirements:* For master's, comprehensive exam. *Entrance requirements:* For master's, minimum GPA of 3.0 during last 2 years of undergraduate course work. Electronic applications accepted.

The University of North Carolina at Chapel Hill, Graduate School, School of Education, Program in Education, Chapel Hill, NC 27599. Offers culture, curriculum and change (MA, PhD); early childhood, intervention and literacy (MA, PhD); educational psychology, measurement and evaluation (MA, PhD). *Accreditation:* NCATE. *Degree requirements:* For master's, thesis; for doctorate, comprehensive exam, thesis/dissertation. *Entrance requirements:* For master's, GRE General Test, minimum GPA of 3.0 during last 2 years of undergraduate course work; for doctorate, GRE General Test, minimum GPA of 3.0 during last 2 years of undergraduate course work. Additional exam requirements/recommendations for international students: Required—TOEFL (minimum score 550 paper-based). Electronic applications accepted.

The University of North Carolina at Charlotte, Cato College of Education, Interdisciplinary Education Programs, Charlotte, NC 28223-0001. Offers art education (Graduate Certificate); child and family development: early childhood education (MAT); curriculum and instruction (PhD); elementary education (MAT); foreign language education (MAT); middle grades education (MAT); secondary education (MAT); special education (MAT); teaching (Graduate Certificate); teaching English as a second language (MAT); theatre education (Graduate Certificate). *Program availability:* Part-time, 100% online, blended/hybrid learning. *Students:* 86 full-time (63 women), 533 part-time (423 women); includes 229 minority (169 Black or African American, non-Hispanic/Latino; 1 American Indian or Alaska Native, non-Hispanic/Latino; 7 Asian, non-Hispanic/Latino; 39 Hispanic/Latino; 13 Two or more races, non-Hispanic/Latino), 13 international. Average age 32. 382 applicants, 91% accepted, 253 enrolled. In 2017, 182 master's, 10 doctorates, 172 other advanced degrees awarded. *Degree requirements:* For master's, thesis or alternative, research project/portfolio. *Entrance requirements:* For master's, GRE or MAT, bachelor's degree, or its U.S. equivalent, from regionally-accredited college or university; minimum overall GPA of 3.0 on all previous work beyond high school; statement of purpose (essay); at least three recommendation forms; for doctorate, GRE or MAT, bachelor's degree (or its U.S. equivalent) from regionally-accredited college or university; minimum overall GPA of 3.5 in master's degree program; for Graduate Certificate, bachelor's degree from regionally-accredited university; minimum GPA of 2.75 on all post-secondary work attempted; transcripts; personal statement outlining why the applicant seeks admission to the program. Additional exam requirements/recommendations for international students: Required—TOEFL (minimum score 523 paper-based, 70 iBT) or IELTS (6.5). *Application deadline:* For fall admission, 3/1 priority date for domestic and international students; for spring admission, 10/1 priority date for domestic and international students; for summer admission, 4/1 priority date for domestic and international students. Applications are processed on a rolling basis. Application fee: $75. Electronic applications accepted. *Expenses:* Tuition, state resident: full-time $4337. Tuition, nonresident: full-time $17,771. *Required fees:* $3211. Tuition and fees vary according to course load and program. *Financial support:* Career-related internships or fieldwork, institutionally sponsored loans, scholarships/grants, and unspecified assistantships available. Support available to part-time students. Financial award application deadline: 3/1; financial award applicants required to submit FAFSA. *Unit head:* Dr. Ellen McIntyre, Dean, 704-687-8722, E-mail: ellen.mcintyre@uncc.edu. *Application contact:* Kathy B. Giddings, Director of Graduate Admissions, 704-687-5503, Fax: 704-687-1668, E-mail: gradadm@uncc.edu.
Website: http://education.uncc.edu/academic-programs

The University of North Carolina at Greensboro, Graduate School, School of Education, Department of Specialized Education Services, Greensboro, NC 27412-5001. Offers cross-categorical special education (M Ed); interdisciplinary studies in special education (M Ed); leadership early care and education (Certificate); special education (M Ed, PhD). *Degree requirements:* For master's, thesis or alternative. *Entrance requirements:* For master's, GRE General Test. Additional exam requirements/recommendations for international students: Required—TOEFL. Electronic applications accepted.

The University of North Carolina Wilmington, Watson College of Education, Department of Early Childhood, Elementary, Middle, Literacy and Special Education, Wilmington, NC 28403-3297. Offers educational leadership, policy, and advocacy (M Ed); elementary education (M Ed, MAT); language and literacy (M Ed); middle grades education (MAT). *Accreditation:* NCATE. *Program availability:* Part-time, blended/hybrid learning. *Faculty:* 22 full-time (15 women), 2 part-time/adjunct (both women). *Students:* 82 full-time (70 women), 91 part-time (84 women); includes 51 minority (33 Black or African American, non-Hispanic/Latino; 3 American Indian or Alaska Native, non-Hispanic/Latino; 1 Asian, non-Hispanic/Latino; 8 Hispanic/Latino; 6 Two or more races, non-Hispanic/Latino). Average age 32. 68 applicants, 82% accepted, 45 enrolled. In 2017, 83 master's awarded. *Degree requirements:* For master's, thesis or alternative, exit portfolio, oral presentation, internship, research project (depending on specialization). *Entrance requirements:* For master's, 3 letters of recommendations, NC Class A teacher license in related field, education statement of interest essay. Additional exam requirements/recommendations for international students: Required—TOEFL (minimum score 550 paper-based; 79 iBT), IELTS (minimum score 6.5). *Application deadline:* For fall admission, 5/15 for domestic students; for spring admission, 10/15 for domestic students; for summer admission, 3/15 for domestic students. Applications are processed on a rolling basis. Application fee: $75. Electronic applications accepted. *Expenses:* Tuition, state resident: full-time $4626; part-time $226.76 per credit hour. Tuition, nonresident: full-time $17,834; part-time $874.22 per credit hour. *Required fees:* $2124. Tuition and fees vary according to program. *Financial support:* Scholarships/grants and unspecified assistantships available. Financial award application deadline: 1/1; financial award applicants required to submit FAFSA. *Unit head:* Dr. Kathy Fox, Chair, 910-962-3240, Fax: 910-962-3988, E-mail: foxk@uncw.edu. *Application contact:* Dr. Elizabeth Crawford, Graduate Program Coordinator, 910-962-2916, Fax: 910-962-3988, E-mail: crawforde@uncw.edu.
Website: http://www.uncw.edu/ed/eemls/index.html

University of North Dakota, Graduate School, College of Education and Human Development, Program in Early Childhood Education, Grand Forks, ND 58202. Offers MS. *Accreditation:* NCATE. *Program availability:* Part-time. *Degree requirements:* For master's, comprehensive exam, thesis or alternative. *Entrance requirements:* For master's, minimum GPA of 3.0. Additional exam requirements/recommendations for international students: Required—TOEFL (minimum score 550 paper-based; 79 iBT), IELTS (minimum score 6.5). Electronic applications accepted.

University of Northern Iowa, Graduate College, College of Education, Department of Curriculum and Instruction, MAE Program in Early Childhood Education, Cedar Falls, IA 50614. Offers MAE. *Degree requirements:* For master's, comprehensive exam, thesis or alternative. *Entrance requirements:* For master's, minimum GPA of 3.0. Additional exam requirements/recommendations for international students: Required—TOEFL (minimum score 500 paper-based; 61 iBT). Electronic applications accepted.

University of North Georgia, Program in Early Childhood Education, Dahlonega, GA 30597. Offers M Ed. *Program availability:* Part-time, blended/hybrid learning. *Faculty:* 13 full-time (10 women), 6 part-time/adjunct (5 women). *Students:* 8 part-time (all women); includes 3 minority (all Hispanic/Latino). Average age 29. In 2017, 19 master's awarded. *Degree requirements:* For master's, content field capstone. *Entrance requirements:* For master's, GRE or MAT (exempt with GPA 3.0 or higher), renewable teaching certificate. Additional exam requirements/recommendations for international students: Required—TOEFL (minimum score 550 paper-based; 79 iBT), IELTS (minimum score 6.5). *Application deadline:* For summer admission, 5/15 for domestic students. Application fee: $40. Electronic applications accepted. *Expenses:* Tuition, state resident: full-time $2025. Tuition, nonresident: full-time $8082. Tuition and fees vary according to course load, degree level and program. *Financial support:* Application deadline: 3/17; applicants required to submit FAFSA. *Unit head:* Dr. Susan Brandenburg-Ayers, Dean, College of Education, 706-864-1998, E-mail: susan.ayers@ung.edu. *Application contact:* Melinda Maxwell, Director of Graduate Admissions, 706-867-2077, E-mail: melinda.maxwell@ung.edu.
Website: https://ung.edu/teacher-education/graduate/master-of-education.php

University of North Texas, Robert B. Toulouse School of Graduate Studies, Denton, TX 76203-5459. Offers accounting (MS); applied anthropology (MA, MS); applied behavior analysis (Certificate); applied geography (MA); applied technology and performance improvement (M Ed, MS); art education (M Ed); art history (MA); art museum education (Certificate); arts leadership (Certificate); audiology (Au D); behavior analysis (MS); behavioral science (PhD); biochemistry and molecular biology (MS); biology (MA, MS); biomedical engineering (MS); business analysis (Certificate); chemistry (MS); clinical health psychology (PhD); communication studies (MA, MS); computer engineering (MS); computer science (MS); counseling (M Ed, MS), including clinical mental health counseling (MS), college and university counseling, elementary school counseling, secondary school counseling; creative writing (MA); criminal justice (MS); curriculum and instruction (M Ed); decision sciences (MBA); design (MA, MFA), including fashion design (MFA), innovation studies, interior design (MFA); early childhood studies (MS); economics (MS); educational leadership (M Ed, Ed D); educational psychology (MS, PhD), including family studies (MS), gifted and talented (MS), human development (MS), learning and cognition (MS), research, measurement and evaluation (MS); electrical engineering (MS); emergency management (MPA); engineering technology (MS); English (MA); English as a second language (MA); environmental science (MS); finance (MBA, MS); financial management (MPA); French (MA); health services management (MBA); higher education (M Ed, Ed D); history (MA, MS); hospitality management (MS); human resources management (MPA); information science (MS); information systems (PhD); information technologies (MBA); interdisciplinary studies (MA, MS); international studies (MA); international sustainable tourism (MS); jazz studies (MM); journalism (MA, MJ, Graduate Certificate), including interactive and virtual digital communication (Graduate Certificate), narrative journalism (Graduate Certificate), public relations (Graduate Certificate); kinesiology (MS); linguistics (MA); local government management (MPA); logistics (PhD); logistics and supply chain management (MBA); long-term care, senior housing, and aging services (MA); management (PhD); marketing (MBA); mathematics (MA, MS); mechanical and energy engineering (MS, PhD); music (MA), including ethnomusicology, music theory, musicology, performance; music composition (PhD); music education (MM Ed, PhD); nonprofit management (MPA); operations and supply chain management (MBA); performance (MM, DMA); philosophy (MA); political science (MA); professional and technical communication (MA); radio, television and film (MA, MFA); rehabilitation counseling (Certificate); sociology (MA); Spanish (MA); special education (M Ed); speech-language pathology (MA); strategic management (MBA); studio art (MFA); teaching (M Ed); MBA/MS. *Program availability:* Part-time, evening/weekend, online learning. Terminal master's awarded for partial completion of doctoral program. *Degree requirements:* For master's, variable foreign language requirement, comprehensive exam (for some programs), thesis (for some programs); for doctorate, variable foreign language requirement, comprehensive exam (for some programs), thesis/dissertation; for other advanced degree, variable foreign language requirement, comprehensive exam (for some programs). *Entrance requirements:* For master's and doctorate, GRE, GMAT. Additional exam requirements/recommendations for international students: Required—TOEFL (minimum score 550 paper-based; 79 iBT). Electronic applications accepted.

University of Oklahoma, Jeannine Rainbolt College of Education, Department of Instructional Leadership and Academic Curriculum, Norman, OK 73019. Offers instructional leadership and academic curriculum (M Ed, PhD), including biomedical education (PhD), early childhood education, elementary education, English education, instructional leadership, mathematics education, reading education, science education, social studies education, world languages education (M Ed); reading specialist (M Ed). *Accreditation:* NCATE. *Program availability:* Part-time. *Faculty:* 19 full-time (15 women), 1 (woman) part-time/adjunct. *Students:* 37 full-time (28 women), 121 part-time (98 women); includes 32 minority (7 Black or African American, non-Hispanic/Latino; 4 American Indian or Alaska Native, non-Hispanic/Latino; 5 Asian, non-Hispanic/Latino; 6 Hispanic/Latino; 1 Native Hawaiian or other Pacific Islander, non-Hispanic/Latino; 9 Two or more races, non-Hispanic/Latino), 12 international. Average age 35. 39 applicants, 77% accepted, 22 enrolled. In 2017, 49 master's, 12 doctorates awarded. Terminal master's awarded for partial completion of doctoral program. *Degree requirements:* For master's, comprehensive exam (for some programs); for doctorate, comprehensive exam (for some programs), thesis/dissertation. *Entrance requirements:* For doctorate, GRE. Additional exam requirements/recommendations for international students: Required—TOEFL (minimum score 79 iBT) or IELTS (minimum score 6.5). Application fee: $50 ($100 for international students). Electronic applications accepted. *Expenses:* Tuition, state resident: full-time $5119; part-time $213.30 per credit hour. Tuition, nonresident: full-time $19,778; part-time $824.10 per credit hour. *Required fees:* $3458; $133.55 per credit hour. $126.50 per semester. *Financial support:* In 2017–18, 90 students received support, including 8 research assistantships (averaging $11,248 per year), 6 teaching assistantships (averaging $12,188 per year); fellowships, scholarships/grants, and unspecified assistantships also available. Financial award application deadline: 6/1; financial award applicants required to submit FAFSA. *Faculty research:* Teacher preparation; instruction; curriculum; learning; constructivist theory. *Total annual research expenditures:* $707,690. *Unit head:* Dr. Stacy Reeder, Chair, 405-325-1498, Fax: 405-325-4061, E-mail: reeder@ou.edu. *Application contact:* Anna Steele, Graduate Programs Officer, 405-325-4525, E-mail: anna.steele@ou.edu.
Website: http://www.ou.edu/education/ilac

University of Phoenix–Bay Area Campus, College of Education, San Jose, CA 95134-1805. Offers administration and supervision (MA Ed); adult education and training (MA Ed); early childhood education (MA Ed); education (Ed S); educational leadership (Ed D); elementary teacher education (MA Ed); higher education administration (PhD); secondary teacher education (MA Ed); special education (MA Ed); teacher leadership (MA Ed). *Program availability:* Evening/weekend, online learning. *Degree requirements:* For master's, thesis (for some programs). *Entrance requirements:* For master's, minimum undergraduate GPA of 2.5, 3 years of work experience. Additional exam requirements/recommendations for international students: Required—TOEFL (minimum score 550 paper-based; 79 iBT). Electronic applications accepted.

University of Phoenix–Online Campus, College of Education, Phoenix, AZ 85034-7209. Offers administration and supervision (MAEd, Certificate); adult education and training (MAEd); curriculum and instruction (MAEd), including computer education, curriculum and instruction, English as a second language, language arts, mathematics, reading; early childhood education (MAEd); educational studies (MAEd); elementary teacher education (MAEd), including early childhood, elementary teacher education, high school middle level, middle level; principal licensure (Certificate); secondary teacher education (MAEd); special education (MAEd, Certificate); teacher education (MAEd), including middle level generalist; teacher education middle level mathematics (MAEd), including middle level mathematics; teacher education middle level science (MAEd), including middle level science; teacher education secondary mathematics (MAEd); teacher education secondary science (MAEd); teacher leadership (MAEd); teachers of English learners (Certificate); transition to teaching (Certificate), including elementary education, secondary education. *Program availability:* Evening/weekend, online learning. *Entrance requirements:* Additional exam requirements/recommendations for international students: Required—TOEFL, TOEIC (Test of English as an International Communication), Berlitz Online English Proficiency Exam, PTE, or IELTS. Electronic applications accepted. *Expenses:* Contact institution.

Early Childhood Education

University of Phoenix–Phoenix Campus, College of Education, Tempe, AZ 85282-2371. Offers administration and supervision (MA Ed); adult education and training (MA Ed); curriculum and instruction reading (MA Ed); early childhood education (MA Ed); education studies (MA Ed); elementary teacher education (MA Ed); secondary teacher education (MA Ed); special education (MA Ed); teacher leadership (MA Ed). *Program availability:* Evening/weekend, online learning. *Entrance requirements:* Additional exam requirements/recommendations for international students: Required—TOEFL, TOEIC (Test of English as an International Communication), Berlitz Online English Proficiency Exam, PTE, or IELTS. Electronic applications accepted. *Expenses:* Contact institution.

University of Pittsburgh, School of Education, Department of Instruction and Learning, Program in Early Childhood Education, Pittsburgh, PA 15260. Offers M Ed. *Program availability:* Part-time, evening/weekend. *Degree requirements:* For master's, thesis. *Entrance requirements:* For master's, PRAXIS I. Additional exam requirements/recommendations for international students: Required—TOEFL. Electronic applications accepted.

University of Puerto Rico–Río Piedras, College of Education, Program in Early Child Education, San Juan, PR 00931-3300. Offers M Ed. *Program availability:* Part-time. *Degree requirements:* For master's, thesis. *Entrance requirements:* For master's, EXADEP, GRE General Test or PAEG, interview, minimum GPA of 3.0, letter of recommendation.

University of South Alabama, College of Education and Professional Studies, Department of Leadership and Teacher Education, Mobile, AL 36688. Offers art education (M Ed); early childhood education (M Ed); educational leadership (M Ed, Ed D); elementary education (M Ed); reading education (M Ed); science education (M Ed); secondary education (M Ed); special education (M Ed). *Accreditation:* NCATE. *Program availability:* Part-time. *Faculty:* 15 full-time (11 women), 10 part-time/adjunct (6 women). *Students:* 203 full-time (154 women), 90 part-time (68 women); includes 73 minority (54 Black or African American, non-Hispanic/Latino; 3 American Indian or Alaska Native, non-Hispanic/Latino; 4 Asian, non-Hispanic/Latino; 10 Hispanic/Latino; 2 Two or more races, non-Hispanic/Latino). Average age 34. 134 applicants, 55% accepted, 57 enrolled. In 2017, 73 master's, 8 doctorates awarded. *Degree requirements:* For master's, comprehensive exam, thesis (for some programs); for doctorate, comprehensive exam, thesis/dissertation. *Entrance requirements:* For master's, GRE General Test or MAT, minimum GPA of 3.0; for doctorate, GRE, minimum graduate GPA of 3.25, 3 years of experience in field, 3 letters of recommendation, interview, official transcripts. Additional exam requirements/recommendations for international students: Required—TOEFL. *Application deadline:* For fall admission, 7/15 for domestic students, 6/15 for international students; for spring admission, 11/15 for domestic students, 11/1 for international students; for summer admission, 4/15 for domestic students, 4/1 for international students. Applications are processed on a rolling basis. Application fee: $35. Electronic applications accepted. *Expenses:* Tuition, state resident: full-time $10,104; part-time $421 per semester hour. Tuition, nonresident: full-time $20,208; part-time $842 per semester hour. *Financial support:* Fellowships, research assistantships, teaching assistantships, career-related internships or fieldwork, Federal Work-Study, institutionally sponsored loans, scholarships/grants, and unspecified assistantships available. Support available to part-time students. Financial award application deadline: 3/31; financial award applicants required to submit FAFSA. *Unit head:* Dr. Susan Santoli, Chair/Director of Graduate Studies, 251-380-2836, Fax: 251-380-2748, E-mail: ssantoli@southalabama.edu. Website: http://www.southalabama.edu/colleges/ceps/lte/index.html

University of South Carolina, The Graduate School, College of Education, Department of Instruction and Teacher Education, Program in Early Childhood Education, Columbia, SC 29208. Offers M Ed, Ed D, PhD. *Accreditation:* NCATE. *Degree requirements:* For master's, comprehensive exam; for doctorate, one foreign language, comprehensive exam, thesis/dissertation. *Entrance requirements:* For master's, GRE General Test, MAT, interview; for doctorate, GRE General Test, MAT, interview, teaching experience. *Faculty research:* Parent involvement, play, multicultural education, global education.

University of South Carolina Upstate, Graduate Programs, Spartanburg, SC 29303-4999. Offers early childhood education (M Ed); elementary education (M Ed); informatics (MS); special education: visual impairment (M Ed). *Accreditation:* NCATE. *Program availability:* Part-time, evening/weekend. *Degree requirements:* For master's, professional portfolio. *Entrance requirements:* For master's, GRE General Test or MAT, interview, minimum undergraduate GPA of 2.5, teaching certificate, 2 letters of recommendation. *Faculty research:* Promoting university diversity awareness, rough and tumble play, social justice education, American Indian literatures and cultures, diversity and multicultural education, science teaching strategy.

University of South Dakota, Graduate School, School of Education, Division of Curriculum and Instruction, Program in Elementary Education, Vermillion, SD 57069. Offers elementary education (MA), including early childhood education, English language learning, reading specialist/literacy coach, science, technology and math (STEM). *Accreditation:* NCATE. *Program availability:* Part-time, 100% online, blended/hybrid learning. *Degree requirements:* For master's, comprehensive exam, thesis or alternative. *Entrance requirements:* For master's, GRE General Test, MAT, minimum GPA of 2.7. Additional exam requirements/recommendations for international students: Required—TOEFL (minimum score 550 paper-based; 79 iBT). *Application deadline:* Applications are processed on a rolling basis. Application fee: $35. Electronic applications accepted. *Financial support:* Research assistantships with partial tuition reimbursements, teaching assistantships with partial tuition reimbursements, career-related internships or fieldwork, Federal Work-Study, and unspecified assistantships available. Financial award applicants required to submit FAFSA. *Application contact:* Graduate School, 605-658-6140, Fax: 605-677-6118, E-mail: grad@usd.edu. Website: http://www.usd.edu/ci

University of South Dakota, Graduate School, School of Education, Division of Curriculum and Instruction, Program in Special Education, Vermillion, SD 57069. Offers special education (MA), including advanced specialist in disabilities, early childhood special education, multicategorical special education K-12. *Accreditation:* NCATE. *Program availability:* Part-time, online learning. *Degree requirements:* For master's, comprehensive exam, thesis or alternative. *Entrance requirements:* For master's, GRE General Test, MAT, minimum GPA of 2.7. Additional exam requirements/recommendations for international students: Required—TOEFL (minimum score 550 paper-based; 79 iBT). *Application deadline:* Applications are processed on a rolling basis. Application fee: $35. Electronic applications accepted. *Financial support:* Research assistantships with partial tuition reimbursements, teaching assistantships with partial tuition reimbursements, career-related internships or fieldwork, Federal Work-Study, and unspecified assistantships available. Financial award applicants required to submit FAFSA. *Application contact:* Graduate School, 605-658-6140, Fax: 605-677-6118, E-mail: grad@usd.edu. Website: http://www.usd.edu/ci

University of South Dakota, Graduate School, School of Education, Division of Educational Leadership, Vermillion, SD 57069. Offers educational administration (MA, Ed D, Ed S), including adult and higher education (MA, Ed D), curriculum director,

director of special education (Ed D, Ed S), preK-12 principal, school district superintendent (Ed D, Ed S). *Accreditation:* NCATE. *Program availability:* Part-time, evening/weekend, 100% online, blended/hybrid learning. *Degree requirements:* For master's and Ed S, comprehensive exam, thesis or alternative; for doctorate, comprehensive exam, thesis/dissertation. *Entrance requirements:* For master's, GRE General Test, MAT, minimum GPA of 2.7; for doctorate, minimum GPA of 2.7. Additional exam requirements/recommendations for international students: Required—TOEFL (minimum score 550 paper-based; 79 iBT). *Application deadline:* Applications are processed on a rolling basis. Application fee: $35. Electronic applications accepted. *Financial support:* Research assistantships with partial tuition reimbursements, teaching assistantships with partial tuition reimbursements, Federal Work-Study, traineeships, and unspecified assistantships available. Financial award applicants required to submit FAFSA. *Application contact:* Graduate School, 605-658-6140, Fax: 605-677-6118, E-mail: grad@usd.edu. Website: http://www.usd.edu/education/educational-administration

University of South Florida, College of Education, Department of Teaching and Learning, Tampa, FL 33620-9951. Offers early childhood education (M Ed, MA, PhD); elementary education (MA, MAT, PhD); reading/language arts (MA, PhD, Ed S). *Accreditation:* NCATE. *Faculty:* 37 full-time (28 women). *Students:* 219 full-time (174 women), 302 part-time (217 women); includes 135 minority (65 Black or African American, non-Hispanic/Latino; 3 American Indian or Alaska Native, non-Hispanic/Latino; 12 Asian, non-Hispanic/Latino; 49 Hispanic/Latino; 6 Two or more races, non-Hispanic/Latino), 63 international. Average age 35. 195 applicants, 84% accepted, 138 enrolled. In 2017, 77 master's, 13 doctorates awarded. Application fee: $30. *Total annual research expenditures:* $940,639. *Unit head:* Dr. Denisse Thompson, Chair, 813-974-4110. Website: http://www.coedu.usf.edu/main/departments/ce/ce.html

The University of Tennessee, Graduate School, College of Education, Health and Human Sciences, Department of Child and Family Studies, Knoxville, TN 37996. Offers child and family studies (MS); early childhood education (MS). *Program availability:* Part-time. *Degree requirements:* For master's, thesis or alternative. *Entrance requirements:* For master's, GRE General Test, minimum GPA of 2.7. Additional exam requirements/recommendations for international students: Required—TOEFL. Electronic applications accepted.

The University of Tennessee, Graduate School, College of Education, Health and Human Sciences, Program in Education, Knoxville, TN 37996. Offers art education (MS); counseling education (PhD); cultural studies in education (PhD); curriculum (MS, Ed S); curriculum, educational research and evaluation (Ed D, PhD); early childhood education (PhD); early childhood special education (MS); education of deaf and hard of hearing (MS); educational administration and policy studies (Ed D, PhD); educational administration and supervision (Ed S); educational psychology (Ed D, PhD); elementary education (MS, Ed S); elementary teaching (MS); English education (MS, Ed S); exercise science (PhD); foreign language/ESL education (MS, Ed S); instructional technology (MS, Ed D, PhD, Ed S); literacy, language and ESL education (PhD); literacy, language education, and ESL education (Ed D); mathematics education (MS, Ed S); modified and comprehensive special education (MS); reading education (MS, Ed S); school counseling (Ed S); school psychology (PhD, Ed S); science education (MS, Ed S); secondary teaching (MS); social foundations (MS); social science education (MS, Ed S); socio-cultural foundations of sports and education (PhD); special education (Ed S); teacher education (Ed D, PhD). *Accreditation:* NCATE. *Program availability:* Part-time, evening/weekend. *Degree requirements:* For master's and Ed S, thesis optional; for doctorate, variable foreign language requirement, thesis/dissertation. *Entrance requirements:* For master's, minimum GPA of 2.7; for doctorate and Ed S, GRE General Test, minimum GPA of 2.7. Additional exam requirements/recommendations for international students: Required—TOEFL. Electronic applications accepted.

The University of Texas at Austin, Graduate School, College of Education, Department of Curriculum and Instruction, Austin, TX 78712-1111. Offers bilingual/bicultural education (M Ed, MA, PhD); cultural studies in education (M Ed, MA, PhD); early childhood education (M Ed, MA, PhD); language and literacy studies (M Ed, PhD); learning technologies (M Ed, MA, PhD); physical education (M Ed, MA, PhD). Terminal master's awarded for partial completion of doctoral program. *Degree requirements:* For doctorate, thesis/dissertation. *Entrance requirements:* For master's and doctorate, GRE General Test. Electronic applications accepted.

The University of Texas at Austin, Graduate School, College of Education, Department of Special Education, Austin, TX 78712-1111. Offers autism and developmental disabilities (Ed D, PhD); autism and developmental disability (M Ed, MA); early childhood special education (M Ed, MA, Ed D, PhD); learning disabilities (Ed D, PhD); learning disabilities/behavior disorders (M Ed, MA); multicultural special education (M Ed, MA, Ed D, PhD); rehabilitation counselor (M Ed); rehabilitation counselor education (Ed D, PhD); special education administration (Ed D, PhD). *Accreditation:* CORE. *Program availability:* Part-time, evening/weekend, online learning. *Degree requirements:* For master's, thesis or alternative; for doctorate, thesis/dissertation. *Entrance requirements:* For master's and doctorate, GRE General Test. *Faculty research:* Anchored instruction, reading disabilities, multicultural/bilingual.

The University of Texas at San Antonio, College of Education and Human Development, Department of Interdisciplinary Learning and Teaching, San Antonio, TX 78249-0617. Offers education (MA), including curriculum and instruction, early childhood and elementary education, instructional technology, reading and literacy, special education; interdisciplinary learning and teaching (PhD). *Program availability:* Part-time, evening/weekend. *Faculty:* 24 full-time (16 women), 5 part-time/adjunct (3 women). *Students:* 73 full-time (57 women), 227 part-time (206 women); includes 179 minority (25 Black or African American, non-Hispanic/Latino; 10 Asian, non-Hispanic/Latino; 140 Hispanic/Latino; 1 Native Hawaiian or other Pacific Islander, non-Hispanic/Latino; 3 Two or more races, non-Hispanic/Latino), 7 international. Average age 34. 107 applicants, 88% accepted, 70 enrolled. In 2017, 103 master's, 5 doctorates awarded. *Degree requirements:* For master's, comprehensive exam, thesis optional, 36 hours of course work without thesis (33 with thesis); for doctorate, comprehensive exam, thesis/dissertation, minimum of 60 semester credit hours. *Entrance requirements:* For master's, bachelor's degree with minimum GPA of 3.0 in last 60 hours of coursework; 18 hours of undergraduate coursework in education or related field; for doctorate, GRE, transcripts from all colleges and universities attended, professional vitae demonstrating experience in work environment where education was primary professional emphasis, 3 letters of recommendation, statement of purpose, minimum GPA of 3.5. Additional exam requirements/recommendations for international students: Required—TOEFL (minimum score 550 paper-based; 79 iBT), IELTS (minimum score 6.5). *Application deadline:* For fall admission, 6/15 for domestic students, 3/1 for international students; for spring admission, 10/15 for domestic students, 9/15 for international students. Applications are processed on a rolling basis. Application fee: $50 ($90 for international students). Electronic applications accepted. *Expenses:* Tuition, state resident: full-time $5495. Tuition, nonresident: full-time $21,938. *Required fees:* $1915. Tuition and fees vary according to program. *Financial support:* Career-related internships or fieldwork, Federal Work-Study, and scholarships/grants available. Support available to part-time

students. *Faculty research:* Explorations of science, learning and teaching, family involvement in early childhood, culturally-responsive literacy instruction in diverse settings, STEM education, autism spectrum disorder. *Total annual research expenditures:* $511,331. *Unit head:* Dr. Mari R. Cortez, Department Chair, 210-458-4414, Fax: 210-458-7281, E-mail: mari.cortez@utsa.edu. *Application contact:* Elizabeth Narvaez, Student Development Specialist, 210-458-7443, E-mail: elizabeth.narvaez@utsa.edu.
Website: http://education.utsa.edu/interdisciplinary_learning_and_teaching/

The University of Texas at Tyler, College of Education and Psychology, School of Education, Tyler, TX 75799-0001. Offers early childhood education (M Ed, MA); reading (M Ed, MA); special education (M Ed, MA). *Program availability:* Part-time, evening/weekend. *Degree requirements:* For master's, comprehensive exam, thesis (for some programs), research project. *Entrance requirements:* For master's, GRE General Test. Additional exam requirements/recommendations for international students: Required—TOEFL. Electronic applications accepted. *Faculty research:* Improving quality in childcare settings, play and creativity, teacher interactions, effects of modeling on early childhood teachers, biofeedback, literacy instruction.

The University of Texas of the Permian Basin, Office of Graduate Studies, School of Education, Program in Early Childhood Education, Odessa, TX 79762-0001. Offers MA. *Degree requirements:* For master's, comprehensive exam (for some programs), thesis (for some programs). *Entrance requirements:* For master's, GRE General Test. Additional exam requirements/recommendations for international students: Required—TOEFL (minimum score 550 paper-based).

The University of Texas Rio Grande Valley, College of Education and P-16 Integration, Department of Human Development and School Services, Edinburg, TX 78539. Offers early childhood education (M Ed); early childhood special education (M Ed); school psychology (MA); special education (M Ed). *Program availability:* Part-time, evening/weekend. *Faculty:* 14. *Students:* 131. In 2017, 164 master's awarded. *Degree requirements:* For master's, comprehensive exam (for some programs). *Entrance requirements:* For master's, minimum GPA of 3.0. Additional exam requirements/recommendations for international students: Required—TOEFL (minimum score 550 paper-based; 79 iBT), IELTS (minimum score 6.5). *Application deadline:* For fall admission, 4/15 for domestic students; for spring admission, 11/1 for domestic students; for summer admission, 3/1 for domestic students. Applications are processed on a rolling basis. Application fee: $50 ($75 for international students). Electronic applications accepted. *Expenses:* Tuition, state resident: full-time $5550; part-time $417 per credit hour. Tuition, nonresident: full-time $13,020; part-time $832 per credit hour. *Required fees:* $1169. *Financial support:* Research assistantships, career-related internships or fieldwork, institutionally sponsored loans, and scholarships/grants available. Financial award application deadline: 4/15; financial award applicants required to submit FAFSA. *Faculty research:* Special education, assessment practice, behavior interventions, mental retardation, early childhood. *Unit head:* Dr. John Lowdermilk, Chair, 956-665-3466, E-mail: john.lowdermilk@utrgv.edu. *Application contact:* Stephanie Ozuna, Graduate Student Recruiter, 956-665-3661, E-mail: stephanie.ozuna@utrgv.edu.

University of the District of Columbia, College of Arts and Sciences, Program in Early Childhood Education, Washington, DC 20008-1175. Offers MA. *Accreditation:* NCATE. *Program availability:* Part-time. *Degree requirements:* For master's, comprehensive exam, research paper. *Entrance requirements:* For master's, GRE General Test, writing proficiency exam, minimum GPA of 3.0.

University of the Sacred Heart, Graduate Programs, Department of Education, San Juan, PR 00914-0383. Offers early childhood education (M Ed); information technology and multimedia (Certificate); instruction systems and education technology (M Ed); including English, information technology and multimedia, instructional design, mathematics, Spanish. *Program availability:* Part-time, evening/weekend. *Degree requirements:* For master's, thesis. *Entrance requirements:* For master's, EXADEP, minimum undergraduate GPA of 2.75, interview.

University of the Southwest, Graduate Programs, Hobbs, NM 88240-9129. Offers business administration (MBA); curriculum and instruction (MSE); curriculum and instruction: bilingual (MSE); curriculum and instruction: TESOL (MSE); early childhood education (MSE); educational administration (MSE); mental health counseling (MSE); school counseling (MSE); special education (MSE); sports management (MBA). *Program availability:* Part-time, evening/weekend, online learning. *Degree requirements:* For master's, comprehensive exam, thesis (for some programs). *Entrance requirements:* Additional exam requirements/recommendations for international students: Recommended—TOEFL. Electronic applications accepted.

The University of Toledo, College of Graduate Studies, Judith Herb College of Education, Department of Curriculum and Instruction, Toledo, OH 43606-3390. Offers art education (ME); career and technical education (ME, Ed S); curriculum and instruction (ME, PhD, Ed S); early childhood education (Ed S); education and anthropology (MAE); education and biology (MES); education and chemistry (MES); education and classics (MAE); education and economics (MAE); education and English (MAE); education and French (MAE); education and geology (MES); education and German (MAE); education and history (MAE); education and mathematics (MAE, MES); education and physics (MES); education and political science (MAE); education and sociology (MAE); education and Spanish (MAE); educational media (PhD); educational technology (ME); educational technology: virtual educator (Certificate); elementary education (PhD); English as a second language (MAE); gifted and talented education (PhD); middle childhood education (ME); secondary education (ME, PhD); special education (PhD). *Accreditation:* NCATE. *Program availability:* Part-time, evening/weekend. *Degree requirements:* For master's, comprehensive exam, thesis or alternative; for doctorate, comprehensive exam, thesis/dissertation; for other advanced degree, thesis optional. *Entrance requirements:* For master's, doctorate, and other advanced degree, minimum cumulative GPA of 2.7 for all previous academic work, letters of recommendation. Additional exam requirements/recommendations for international students: Required—TOEFL (minimum score 550 paper-based; 80 iBT). Electronic applications accepted.

The University of Toledo, College of Graduate Studies, Judith Herb College of Education, Department of Early Childhood, Physical and Special Education, Toledo, OH 43606-3390. Offers early childhood education (ME); physical education (ME); special education (ME). *Program availability:* Part-time. *Degree requirements:* For master's, thesis. *Entrance requirements:* For master's, minimum cumulative GPA of 2.7 for all previous academic work, letters of recommendation. Additional exam requirements/recommendations for international students: Required—TOEFL (minimum score 550 paper-based; 80 iBT). Electronic applications accepted.

University of Utah, Graduate School, College of Education, Department of Special Education, Salt Lake City, UT 84112. Offers board certified behavior analyst (M Ed, MS, PhD); deaf and hard of hearing (M Ed); deaf/blind (M Ed, MS); early childhood deaf and hard of hearing (MS); early childhood special education (M Ed, MS, PhD); early childhood vision impairments (M Ed); mild/moderate disabilities (M Ed, MS, PhD); severe disabilities (M Ed, MS, PhD); visual impairment (M Ed, MS). *Program availability:* Part-time, evening/weekend, 100% online, blended/hybrid learning. *Faculty:* 9 full-time

(6 women), 8 part-time/adjunct (7 women). *Students:* 45 full-time (41 women), 26 part-time (24 women); includes 6 minority (4 Asian, non-Hispanic/Latino; 2 Hispanic/Latino). Average age 31. 30 applicants, 97% accepted, 28 enrolled. In 2017, 29 master's awarded. Terminal master's awarded for partial completion of doctoral program. *Degree requirements:* For master's, comprehensive exam, thesis (for some programs), qualifying exam; for doctorate, thesis/dissertation, qualifying exam. *Entrance requirements:* For master's, GRE, minimum GPA of 3.0; for doctorate, GRE General Test, minimum GPA of 3.5. Additional exam requirements/recommendations for international students: Required—TOEFL (minimum score 600 paper-based; 100 iBT); Recommended—IELTS (minimum score 7). *Application deadline:* For fall admission, 3/1 for domestic and international students; for spring admission, 11/1 for domestic and international students; for summer admission, 5/16 for domestic and international students. Application fee: $55 ($65 for international students). Electronic applications accepted. *Financial support:* In 2017–18, 22 students received support, including 33 fellowships with partial tuition reimbursements available (averaging $4,350 per year), 3 teaching assistantships with tuition reimbursements available (averaging $10,000 per year); career-related internships or fieldwork and health care benefits also available. Support available to part-time students. Financial award application deadline: 3/1; financial award applicants required to submit FAFSA. *Faculty research:* Inclusive education, positive behavior support, reading, instruction and intervention strategies. *Total annual research expenditures:* $139,750. *Unit head:* Dr. Robert E. O'Neill, Chair, 801-581-8121, Fax: 801-585-6476, E-mail: rob.oneill@utah.edu. *Application contact:* Patty Davis, Academic Advisor, 801-581-4764, Fax: 801-585-6476, E-mail: patty.davis@utah.edu.
Website: http://special-ed.utah.edu/

University of Vermont, Graduate College, College of Education and Social Services, Program in Early Childhood Special Education, Burlington, VT 05405. Offers M Ed. *Program availability:* Part-time, evening/weekend. *Entrance requirements:* Additional exam requirements/recommendations for international students: Required—TOEFL (minimum iBT score of 90) or IELTS (6.5). *Application deadline:* For fall admission, 2/15 for domestic and international students; for spring admission, 11/1 for domestic and international students. Application fee: $65. Electronic applications accepted. *Expenses:* Tuition, state resident: full-time $11,628; part-time $646 per credit. Tuition, nonresident: full-time $29,340; part-time $1630 per credit. *Required fees:* $1994; $10 per credit. Tuition and fees vary according to course load and program. *Financial support:* Scholarships/grants available. *Unit head:* Dr. Michael Giancreco, Coordinator, 802-656-2936, E-mail: ecse_grad@uvm.edu.
Website: https://www.uvm.edu/cess/doe/med_earlychild_specialed

University of Vermont, Graduate College, College of Education and Social Services, Program in Special Education, Grades K-12, Burlington, VT 05405. Offers M Ed. *Accreditation:* NCATE. *Degree requirements:* For master's, thesis or alternative. *Entrance requirements:* For master's, license (or eligible for licensure). Additional exam requirements/recommendations for international students: Required—TOEFL (minimum score 550 paper-based, 90 iBT) or IELTS (6.5). *Application deadline:* For fall admission, 2/15 for domestic and international students; for spring admission, 11/1 for domestic and international students. Application fee: $65. Electronic applications accepted. *Expenses:* Tuition, state resident: full-time $11,628; part-time $646 per credit. Tuition, nonresident: full-time $29,340; part-time $1630 per credit. *Required fees:* $1994; $10 per credit. Tuition and fees vary according to course load and program. *Financial support:* In 2017–18, 4 students received support. Research assistantships, teaching assistantships, career-related internships or fieldwork, and scholarships/grants available. Financial award application deadline: 3/1. *Unit head:* Dr. Michael Giangreco, Program Coordinator, 802-656-1144, E-mail: michael.giangreco@uvm.edu. *Application contact:* Roman Vogel, Graduate Program Support, 802-656-2936, E-mail: special.education@uvm.edu.
Website: https://www.uvm.edu/cess/doe/masters_education_special_education_k_12th_grade

University of Victoria, Faculty of Graduate Studies, Faculty of Education, Department of Curriculum and Instruction, Victoria, BC V8W 2Y2, Canada. Offers art education (M Ed, MA, PhD); curriculum studies (M Ed, MA, PhD); early childhood education (M Ed, PhD); educational studies (PhD); language and literacy (M Ed, MA, PhD); mathematics (M Ed, MA, PhD); music education (M Ed, MA, PhD); science (M Ed, MA, PhD); social studies (M Ed, MA); social, cultural and foundational studies (MA, PhD); technology and environmental education (PhD). *Program availability:* Part-time. *Degree requirements:* For master's, thesis, project (M Ed); for doctorate, comprehensive exam, thesis/dissertation. *Entrance requirements:* For master's, minimum B average. Additional exam requirements/recommendations for international students: Required—TOEFL (minimum score 575 paper-based), IELTS (minimum score 7). Electronic applications accepted. *Faculty research:* Elementary and secondary English, language arts, curriculum theory and practice, educational media and technology, educational administration and leadership, history and philosophy of education.

University of Virginia, Curry School of Education, Program in Education, Charlottesville, VA 22903. Offers administration and supervision (PhD); applied developmental science (PhD); counselor education (PhD); curriculum and instruction (PhD); early childhood special education (MT); education evaluation (PhD); educational psychology (PhD); educational research (PhD); elementary education (MT); English education (MT, PhD); foreign language education (MT); higher education (PhD); instructional technology (PhD); kinesiology (MT, PhD); math education (PhD); reading education (PhD); research, statistics and evaluation (PhD); school psychology (PhD); science education (PhD); social studies education (MT, PhD); special education (PhD); world languages education (MT). *Students:* 431 full-time (353 women), 15 part-time (14 women); includes 100 minority (32 Black or African American, non-Hispanic/Latino; 33 Asian, non-Hispanic/Latino; 16 Hispanic/Latino; 19 Two or more races, non-Hispanic/Latino), 14 international. Average age 25. 264 applicants, 49% accepted, 83 enrolled. In 2017, 142 master's, 33 doctorates awarded. *Degree requirements:* For master's, comprehensive exam (for some programs), field project; for doctorate, comprehensive exam, thesis/dissertation. *Entrance requirements:* For doctorate, GRE General Test. Additional exam requirements/recommendations for international students: Required—TOEFL (minimum score 600 paper-based; 90 iBT), IELTS (minimum score 7). *Application deadline:* Applications are processed on a rolling basis. Application fee: $60. Electronic applications accepted. *Financial support:* Fellowships, research assistantships, and teaching assistantships available. Financial award application deadline: 1/5; financial award applicants required to submit FAFSA. *Unit head:* Robert C. Pianta, Dean, 434-924-3334, E-mail: pianta@virginia.edu. *Application contact:* E-mail: curry-admissions@virginia.edu.
Website: http://curry.virginia.edu/teacher-education

The University of West Alabama, School of Graduate Studies, College of Education, Program in Early Childhood Education, Livingston, AL 35470. Offers early childhood development (M Ed); early childhood education P-3 (M Ed, Ed S). *Accreditation:* NCATE. *Program availability:* Part-time, evening/weekend, 100% online. *Faculty:* 6 full-time (all women), 23 part-time/adjunct (18 women). *Students:* 102 (101 women); includes 37 minority (36 Black or African American, non-Hispanic/Latino; 1 Two or more races, non-Hispanic/Latino). Average age 33. 30 applicants, 93% accepted, 22 enrolled.

Early Childhood Education

In 2017, 11 master's, 13 Ed Ss awarded. *Degree requirements:* For master's, comprehensive exam, thesis optional; for Ed S, comprehensive exam. *Entrance requirements:* For master's, GRE, minimum GPA of 2.75, verification of background clearance/fingerprints, valid bachelor's-level Professional Educator Certificate in same teaching field. Additional exam requirements/recommendations for international students: Required—TOEFL (minimum score 500 paper-based; 61 iBT). *Application deadline:* Applications are processed on a rolling basis. Application fee: $40. Electronic applications accepted. *Expenses:* Tuition, state resident: part-time $371 per credit hour. Tuition, nonresident: part-time $742 per credit hour. *Required fees:* $130 per semester. *Financial support:* Teaching assistantships, Federal Work-Study, scholarships/grants, and unspecified assistantships available. Support available to part-time students. Financial award application deadline: 3/1; financial award applicants required to submit FAFSA. *Unit head:* Dr. Jodie Winship, Chair of Teaching and Learning, 205-652-5415, Fax: 205-652-3706, E-mail: jwinship@uwa.edu. *Application contact:* Dr. B. J. Kimbrough, Dean of Graduate Studies, 205-652-3647, Fax: 205-652-3670, E-mail: bkimbrough@uwa.edu.

University of West Georgia, College of Education, Carrollton, GA 30118. Offers business education (M Ed); early childhood education (M Ed, Ed S); educational leadership (M Ed, Ed S); media (M Ed, Ed S); professional counseling (M Ed, Ed S); professional counseling and supervision (Ed D); reading instruction (M Ed); school improvement (Ed D); secondary education (M Ed); special education (M Ed, Ed S), including teaching (M Ed); speech language pathology (M Ed); teaching (MAT). *Accreditation:* NCATE. *Program availability:* Part-time, evening/weekend, 100% online, blended/hybrid learning. *Faculty:* 45 full-time (28 women). *Students:* 344 full-time (286 women), 1,243 part-time (1,039 women); includes 538 minority (456 Black or African American, non-Hispanic/Latino; 19 Asian, non-Hispanic/Latino; 46 Hispanic/Latino; 1 Native Hawaiian or other Pacific Islander, non-Hispanic/Latino; 16 Two or more races, non-Hispanic/Latino), 7 international. Average age 36. 685 applicants, 78% accepted, 429 enrolled. In 2017, 299 master's, 30 doctorates, 218 other advanced degrees awarded. *Entrance requirements:* Additional exam requirements/recommendations for international students: Required—TOEFL (minimum score 523 paper-based; 69 iBT); Recommended—IELTS (minimum score 6.5). *Application deadline:* For fall admission, 7/21 for domestic students, 6/1 for international students; for spring admission, 11/30 for domestic students, 10/15 for international students; for summer admission, 4/15 for domestic students, 3/30 for international students. Applications are processed on a rolling basis. Application fee: $40. Electronic applications accepted. Tuition and fees vary according to degree level and program. *Financial support:* Fellowships, research assistantships, teaching assistantships, career-related internships or fieldwork, Federal Work-Study, institutionally sponsored loans, scholarships/grants, and unspecified assistantships available. Support available to part-time students. Financial award application deadline: 4/1; financial award applicants required to submit FAFSA. *Unit head:* Dr. Diane Hoff, Dean, College of Education, 678-839-6570, Fax: 678-839-6098, E-mail: dhoff@westga.edu. *Application contact:* Dr. Toby Ziglar, Assistant Dean of the Graduate School, 678-839-1394, Fax: 678-839-1395, E-mail: graduate@westga.edu. Website: http://www.westga.edu/education/

University of Wisconsin–Milwaukee, Graduate School, School of Education, Department of Curriculum and Instruction, Milwaukee, WI 53201-0413. Offers curriculum and instruction (MS), including cross-curricular focus, early childhood education, English education, mathematics education, middle childhood/early adolescence education, reading education, science education, urban social studies education. *Program availability:* Part-time. *Students:* 17 full-time (13 women), 45 part-time (39 women); includes 13 minority (2 Black or African American, non-Hispanic/Latino; 3 Asian, non-Hispanic/Latino; 1 Hispanic/Latino; 7 Two or more races, non-Hispanic/Latino). Average age 33. 32 applicants, 66% accepted, 16 enrolled. In 2017, 26 master's awarded. *Entrance requirements:* Additional exam requirements/recommendations for international students: Required—TOEFL (minimum score 550 paper-based; 79 iBT), IELTS (minimum score 6.5). *Application deadline:* For fall admission, 1/1 priority date for domestic students; for spring admission, 9/1 for domestic students. Application fee: $56 ($96 for international students). Electronic applications accepted. *Financial support:* Fellowships, research assistantships, teaching assistantships, career-related internships or fieldwork, health care benefits, unspecified assistantships, and project assistantships available. Support available to part-time students. Financial award application deadline: 4/15; financial award applicants required to submit FAFSA. *Application contact:* General Information Contact, 414-229-4721, E-mail: soeinfo@uwm.edu. Website: http://uwm.edu/education/academics/curriculum-instruction-department/

University of Wisconsin–Oshkosh, Graduate Studies, College of Education and Human Services, Department of Special Education, Oshkosh, WI 54901. Offers cross-categorical (MSE); early childhood: exceptional education needs (MSE); non-licensure (MSE). *Program availability:* Part-time, evening/weekend. *Degree requirements:* For master's, comprehensive exam (for some programs), thesis or alternative, field report. *Entrance requirements:* For master's, interview, minimum GPA of 3.0, teaching license, letters of recommendation. Additional exam requirements/recommendations for international students: Required—TOEFL (minimum score 550 paper-based; 79 iBT). Electronic applications accepted. *Faculty research:* Private agency contributions to the disabled, graduation requirements for exceptional education needs students, direct instruction in spelling for learning disabled, effects of behavioral parent training, secondary education programming issues.

Upper Iowa University, Master of Education Program, Fayette, IA 52142-1857. Offers early childhood (M Ed); English as a second language (M Ed); higher education (M Ed); instructional strategist (M Ed); reading (M Ed); teacher leadership (M Ed).

Ursuline College, School of Graduate and Professional Studies, Master Apprenticeship Program, Pepper Pike, OH 44124-4398. Offers adolescent to young adult education (MA); early childhood education (MA); middle childhood education (MA); special education (MA). *Accreditation:* NCATE. *Faculty:* 1 full-time (0 women), 6 part-time/adjunct (all women). *Students:* 19 full-time (16 women); includes 4 minority (all Black or African American, non-Hispanic/Latino). Average age 32. In 2017, 18 master's awarded. *Degree requirements:* For master's, comprehensive exam. *Entrance requirements:* For master's, minimum undergraduate GPA of 3.0. Additional exam requirements/recommendations for international students: Required—TOEFL (minimum score 500 paper-based). *Application deadline:* For fall admission, 8/1 priority date for domestic students. Applications are processed on a rolling basis. Application fee: $25. Electronic applications accepted. *Expenses:* Contact institution. *Financial support:* Application deadline: 3/1; applicants required to submit FAFSA. *Faculty research:* Longevity of female superintendents, expectations of student teacher mentors, qualities of successful student teachers, literacy preparation of K-12 student teachers. *Unit head:* Dr. Mary Jo Cherry, Director, 440-646-8147, Fax: 440-646-8328, E-mail: mcherry@ursuline.edu. *Application contact:* Melanie Steele, Director of Graduate Admission, 440-646-8146, Fax: 440-684-6138, E-mail: graduateadmissions@ursuline.edu. Website: http://www.ursuline.edu/Academics/Graduate_Professional/Masters_Programs/MAP/index.html

Virginia Commonwealth University, Graduate School, School of Education, Program in Special Education, Richmond, VA 23284-9005. Offers early childhood (M Ed); general

education (M Ed); severe disabilities (M Ed). *Accreditation:* NCATE. *Degree requirements:* For master's, comprehensive exam. *Entrance requirements:* For master's, GRE General Test or MAT. Additional exam requirements/recommendations for international students: Required—TOEFL (minimum score 600 paper-based; 100 iBT). Electronic applications accepted.

Virginia Commonwealth University, Graduate School, School of Education, Program in Teaching and Learning, Richmond, VA 23284-9005. Offers early and elementary education (MT). *Accreditation:* NCATE. *Program availability:* Part-time. *Entrance requirements:* For master's, GRE General Test or MAT. Additional exam requirements/recommendations for international students: Required—TOEFL (minimum score 600 paper-based; 100 iBT). Electronic applications accepted.

Viterbo University, Graduate Programs in Education, La Crosse, WI 54601-4797. Offers cross-categorical special education (Certificate); director of instruction (Certificate); director of special education and pupil services (Certificate); early childhood (Certificate); education (MAE); literacy coaching (Certificate); PreK-12 principal/supervisor of special education (Certificate); principal (Certificate); reading specialist endorsement (Certificate); reading teacher (Certificate); reading teacher 5-12 endorsement (Certificate); reading teacher K-8 endorsement (Certificate); superintendent (Certificate); talented and gifted endorsement (Certificate); Wisconsin school business administrator (Certificate). Weekend courses available in summer. *Accreditation:* NCATE. *Program availability:* Part-time, evening/weekend. *Degree requirements:* For master's, comprehensive exam, thesis, 30 credits of course work. *Entrance requirements:* For master's, BS, transcripts, teaching license, written narrative. Electronic applications accepted. *Expenses:* Contact institution.

Wagner College, Division of Graduate Studies, Education Department, Program in Early Childhood Education/Students with Disabilities (Birth-Grade 2), Staten Island, NY 10301-4495. Offers MS Ed. *Program availability:* Part-time, evening/weekend. *Faculty:* 4 full-time (3 women), 1 (woman) part-time/adjunct. *Students:* 7 full-time (all women), 1 (woman) part-time; includes 2 minority (1 Asian, non-Hispanic/Latino; 1 Two or more races, non-Hispanic/Latino). Average age 23. 2 applicants, 50% accepted, 1 enrolled. In 2017, 4 master's awarded. *Degree requirements:* For master's, thesis. *Entrance requirements:* For master's, minimum GPA of 3.0, valid initial NY State Certificate or equivalent, interview, recommendations. Additional exam requirements/recommendations for international students: Recommended—TOEFL (minimum score 550 paper-based; 79 iBT), IELTS (minimum score 6.5). *Application deadline:* For fall admission, 4/15 priority date for domestic and international students; for spring admission, 10/15 priority date for domestic and international students. Applications are processed on a rolling basis. Application fee: $60. Electronic applications accepted. *Expenses:* $1,140 per credit. *Financial support:* Unspecified assistantships and alumni fellowship available. Financial award application deadline: 4/15; financial award applicants required to submit FAFSA. *Unit head:* Dr. Jason Fitzgerald, Department Chair, 718-420-4129, Fax: 718-390-3456, E-mail: jason.fitzgerald@wagner.edu. *Application contact:* Patricia Clancy, Assistant Director of Enrollment, 718-420-4464, Fax: 718-390-3105, E-mail: patricia.clancy@wagner.edu. Website: http://www.wagner.edu/education

Walden University, Graduate Programs, Richard W. Riley College of Education and Leadership, Minneapolis, MN 55401. Offers adult education (Post-Master's Certificate); adult learning (Graduate Certificate); college teaching and learning (Graduate Certificate); community college leadership (Ed D); curriculum, instruction and assessment (Ed D, Ed S, Graduate Certificate); developmental education (Graduate Certificate); early childhood administration, management, and leadership (Graduate Certificate); early childhood education (Ed D, Ed S); early childhood public policy and advocacy (Graduate Certificate); early childhood studies (MS), including administration, management and leadership, early childhood public policy and advocacy, teaching adults in the early childhood field, teaching and diversity in early childhood education; education (MS, PhD), including adolescent literacy and learning (MS), curriculum, instruction, and assessment (grades K-12) (MS), curriculum, instruction, assessment, and evaluation (PhD), early childhood leadership and advocacy (PhD), early childhood special education (PhD), educational leadership (MS), educational leadership and administration (principal preparation) (MS), educational technology and design (PhD), elementary reading and literacy (PreK-6) (MS), elementary reading and mathematics (grades K-6) (MS), global and comparative education (PhD), higher education leadership management and policy (PhD), integrating technology in the classroom (grades K-12) (MS), learning, instruction and innovation (PhD), mathematics (grades 5-8) (MS), mathematics (grades K-6) (MS), mathematics and science (grades K-8) (MS), organizational research, assessment, and evaluation (PhD), reading and literacy with a reading K-12 endorsement (MS), reading literacy assessment and evaluation (PhD), science (grades K-8) (MS), special education (non-licensure) (grades K-12) (MS), teacher leadership (grades K-12) (MS), teaching English language learners (grades K-12) (MS); educational administration and leadership (Ed D); educational leadership and administration (principal preparation) (Ed S); educational technology (Ed D, Ed S, Post Master's Certificate); elementary reading and literacy (Graduate Certificate); engaging culturally diverse learners (Graduate Certificate); enrollment management and institutional marketing (Graduate Certificate); higher education (MS), including adult learning, college teaching and learning, enrollment management and institutional marketing, global higher education, leadership for student success, online and distance learning; higher education and adult learning (Ed D); higher education leadership and management (Ed D); higher education leadership for student success (Graduate Certificate); instructional design and technology (MS, Postbaccalaureate Certificate), including general program (MS), online learning (MS), training and performance improvement (MS); integrating technology in the classroom (Graduate Certificate); mathematics 5-8 (Graduate Certificate); mathematics K-6 (Graduate Certificate); online teaching for adult educators (Graduate Certificate); reading, literacy, and assessment (Ed D, Ed S); science K-8 (Graduate Certificate); special education (Ed D, Ed S, Graduate Certificate); special education (K-age 21) (MAT); teacher leadership (Graduate Certificate); teaching adults English as a second language (Graduate Certificate); teaching adults in the early childhood field (Graduate Certificate); teaching and diversity in early childhood education (Graduate Certificate); teaching English language learners (grades K-12) (Graduate Certificate); teaching K-12 students online (Graduate Certificate). *Accreditation:* NCATE. *Program availability:* Part-time, evening/weekend, online only, 100% online. *Degree requirements:* For doctorate, thesis/dissertation (for some programs), residency; for other advanced degree, residency (for some programs). *Entrance requirements:* For master's, bachelor's degree or higher; minimum GPA of 2.5; official transcripts; goal statement (for some programs); access to computer and Internet; for doctorate, master's degree or higher; three years of related professional or academic experience (preferred); minimum GPA of 3.0; goal statement and current resume (for select programs); official transcripts; access to computer and Internet; for other advanced degree, relevant work experience; access to computer and Internet. Additional exam requirements/recommendations for international students: Required—TOEFL (minimum score 550 paper-based, 79 iBT), IELTS (minimum score 6.5), Michigan English Language Assessment Battery (minimum score 82), or PTE (minimum score 53). Electronic applications accepted.

Wayne State College, School of Education and Counseling, Department of Educational Foundations and Leadership, Program in Curriculum and Instruction, Wayne, NE 68787. Offers alternative education (MSE); business and information technology education (MSE); communication arts education (MSE); early childhood education (MSE); elementary education (MSE); English as a second language (MSE); English education (MSE); family and consumer sciences education (MSE); industrial technology and vocational education (MSE); learning communities (MSE); mathematics education (MSE); music education (MSE); science education (MSE); social science education (MSE). *Accreditation:* NCATE. *Program availability:* Part-time, evening/weekend. *Degree requirements:* For master's, comprehensive exam, thesis optional. *Entrance requirements:* For master's, GRE General Test. Additional exam requirements/recommendations for international students: Required—TOEFL (minimum score 550 paper-based).

Wayne State University, College of Education, Division of Teacher Education, Detroit, MI 48202. Offers art education (M Ed); bilingual/bicultural education (Certificate); curriculum and instruction (Ed D, PhD, Ed S), including English as a second language (MAT, Ed D, Ed S), K-12 curriculum (PhD); elementary education (MAT), including bilingual/bicultural education (M Ed, MAT), early childhood education (M Ed, MAT), English as a second language (MAT, Ed D, Ed S), foreign language education, science education (M Ed, MAT), special education (M Ed, MAT); elementary mathematics specialist (Certificate); English as a second language (Certificate); reading (M Ed, Ed S); reading, language and literature (Ed D); secondary education (MAT), including bilingual/bicultural education (M Ed, MAT), early childhood education (M Ed, MAT), English as a second language (MAT, Ed D, Ed S), English education, foreign language education, mathematics education (M Ed, MAT), science education (M Ed, MAT), social studies education (M Ed, MAT); special education (MAT), including career and technical education; teaching and learning (M Ed), including bilingual/bicultural education (M Ed, MAT), early childhood education, foreign language, mathematics education (M Ed, MAT), science education (M Ed, MAT), social studies education (M Ed, MAT), special education (M Ed, MAT). *Program availability:* Part-time, blended/hybrid learning. *Faculty:* 22. *Students:* 126 full-time (96 women), 317 part-time (258 women); includes 134 minority (95 Black or African American, non-Hispanic/Latino; 1 American Indian or Alaska Native, non-Hispanic/Latino; 8 Asian, non-Hispanic/Latino; 17 Hispanic/Latino; 1 Native Hawaiian or other Pacific Islander, non-Hispanic/Latino; 12 Two or more races, non-Hispanic/Latino), 13 international. Average age 37. 260 applicants, 33% accepted, 57 enrolled. In 2017, 111 master's, 13 doctorates, 7 other advanced degrees awarded. *Degree requirements:* For master's, essay or project (for some M Ed programs), professional field experience (for MAT programs); for doctorate, thesis/dissertation. *Entrance requirements:* For master's, Michigan Test for Teacher Certification (for most programs), verification of participation in group work with children (for MAT programs), Michigan State Police criminal background check; for doctorate, minimum undergraduate GPA of 3.0, graduate 3.5; interview; curriculum vitae; references; master's degree (for most programs). Additional exam requirements/recommendations for international students: Required—TOEFL (minimum score 550 paper-based; 79 iBT), TWE (minimum score 5.5); Recommended—IELTS (minimum score 6.5). *Application deadline:* For fall admission, 6/1 priority date for domestic students, 5/1 priority date for international students; for winter admission, 10/1 priority date for domestic students, 9/1 priority date for international students; for spring admission, 2/1 priority date for domestic students, 1/1 priority date for international students. Applications are processed on a rolling basis. Application fee: $50. Electronic applications accepted. *Expenses:* Tuition, state resident: full-time $10,224; part-time $638.98 per credit hour. Tuition, nonresident: full-time $22,145; part-time $1384.04 per credit hour. Tuition and fees vary according to course load and program. *Financial support:* In 2017–18, 78 students received support, including 4 fellowships (averaging $13,500 per year), 1 research assistantship with tuition reimbursement available (averaging $16,000 per year); Federal Work-Study, scholarships/grants, and unspecified assistantships also available. Support available to part-time students. Financial award applicants required to submit FAFSA. *Faculty research:* Improving students' skill achievement in mathematics, improving elementary children's understanding of informational text, teachers' use of their pedagogical and mathematical knowledge in the interactive work of teaching, the intersection of identity construction in teaching and learning, identifying effective methods of literacy instruction and assessments for bilingual students in elementary language arts classrooms. *Unit head:* Dr. Thomas Edwards, Interim Associate Dean for Teacher Education, 313-577-3886, E-mail: t.g.edwards@wayne.edu. *Application contact:* 313-577-0902, E-mail: askcoe@wayne.edu.
Website: http://coe.wayne.edu/ted/index.php

Webster University, School of Education, Department of Multidisciplinary Studies, St. Louis, MO 63119-3194. Offers applied educational psychology (MA, Ed S); communication arts (MA); early childhood education (MA, MAT); education and innovation (MA); educational technology (MET); elementary education (MAT); mathematics for educators (MA); middle school education (MAT); multidisciplinary studies (MAT); multimodal literacy for global impact (MA); reading (MA); secondary school education (MAT); special education (MA, MAT); teaching English as a second language (MA); transformative learning in the global community (Ed S). *Program availability:* Part-time. *Entrance requirements:* For master's, minimum GPA of 2.5. Additional exam requirements/recommendations for international students: Required—TOEFL.

Wesleyan College, Department of Education, Program in Early Childhood Education, Macon, GA 31210-4462. Offers MA. *Program availability:* Part-time. *Degree requirements:* For master's, thesis or alternative, practicum, professional portfolio. *Entrance requirements:* For master's, GRE or MAT, interview, teaching certificate, 3 letters of recommendation. Additional exam requirements/recommendations for international students: Required—TOEFL.

West Chester University of Pennsylvania, College of Education and Social Work, Department of Early and Middle Grades Education, West Chester, PA 19383. Offers applied studies in teaching and learning (M Ed); early childhood education (M Ed), including accomplished teacher, program administrator; grades 4-8 (Teaching Certificate); grades preK-4 (Teaching Certificate). *Accreditation:* NCATE. *Program availability:* Part-time, 100% online. *Students:* 21 full-time (17 women), 82 part-time (73 women); includes 17 minority (13 Black or African American, non-Hispanic/Latino; 4 Hispanic/Latino), 2 international. Average age 31. 52 applicants, 85% accepted, 27 enrolled. In 2017, 61 master's, 19 other advanced degrees awarded. *Degree requirements:* For master's, teacher research project, portfolio. *Entrance requirements:* For master's, certification (for applied studies in teaching and learning track); one year of full time teaching; minimum GPA of 3.0; for Teaching Certificate, math, social studies, or science concentration exams (for middle grades preparation), minimum GPA of 3.0. Additional exam requirements/recommendations for international students: Required—TOEFL or IELTS. *Application deadline:* For fall admission, 5/15 for international students; for spring admission, 10/15 for international students. Applications are processed on a rolling basis. Application fee: $50. Electronic applications accepted. *Expenses:* Tuition, state resident: full-time $9000; part-time $500 per credit. Tuition, nonresident: full-time $13,500; part-time $750 per credit. *Required fees:* $2959; $149.79 per credit. *Financial support:* Scholarships/grants and unspecified assistantships

available. Financial award application deadline: 2/15; financial award applicants required to submit FAFSA. *Faculty research:* Cooperative learning, creative expression and critical thinking, teacher research, learning styles, middle school education. *Unit head:* Dr. Karen Johnson, Chair, 610-436-3545, Fax: 610-436-3102, E-mail: kjohnson@wcupa.edu. *Application contact:* Office of Graduate Studies and Extended Education, 610-436-2943, Fax: 610-436-2763, E-mail: gradstudy@wcupa.edu.
Website: http://www.wcupa.edu/education-socialWork/earlyMiddleGrades/

Western Kentucky University, Graduate Studies, College of Education and Behavioral Sciences, School of Teacher Education, Bowling Green, KY 42101. Offers elementary education (MAE, Ed S); exceptional education: learning and behavioral disorders (MAE); exceptional education: moderate and severe disabilities (MAE); instructional design (MS); interdisciplinary early childhood education (MAE); library media education (MS); literacy education (MAE); middle grades education (MAE); secondary education (MAE, Ed S). *Program availability:* Part-time, evening/weekend, online learning. *Degree requirements:* For master's, comprehensive exam. *Entrance requirements:* For master's, GRE General Test. Additional exam requirements/recommendations for international students: Required—TOEFL (minimum score 555 paper-based; 79 iBT). *Faculty research:* Teacher preparation in moderate/severe disabilities.

Western Oregon University, Graduate Programs, College of Education, Division of Special Education, Program in Early Childhood Special Education, Monmouth, OR 97361. Offers MS Ed. *Accreditation:* NCATE. *Program availability:* Part-time, evening/weekend. *Degree requirements:* For master's, thesis optional, written exam, portfolio. *Entrance requirements:* For master's, CBEST, PRAXIS or GRE General Test, minimum GPA of 3.0, teaching license. Additional exam requirements/recommendations for international students: Required—TOEFL (minimum score 550 paper-based; 79 iBT), IELTS (minimum score 6.5). *Faculty research:* High school through university articulation, career development for early childhood educators professional collaboration/cooperation.

Westfield State University, College of Graduate and Continuing Education, Department of Education, Program in Early Childhood Education, Westfield, MA 01086. Offers M Ed. *Accreditation:* NCATE. *Program availability:* Part-time, evening/weekend. *Students:* 5 full-time (all women), 18 part-time (all women); includes 1 minority (Asian, non-Hispanic/Latino). Average age 24. 7 applicants, 100% accepted, 6 enrolled. In 2017, 8 master's awarded. *Degree requirements:* For master's, comprehensive exam, practicum. *Entrance requirements:* For master's, GRE General Test or MAT, minimum undergraduate GPA of 2.8. Additional exam requirements/recommendations for international students: Recommended—TOEFL (minimum score 550 paper-based; 79 iBT). *Application deadline:* For fall admission, 7/1 for domestic students; for spring admission, 11/1 for domestic students; for summer admission, 4/1 for domestic students. Applications are processed on a rolling basis. Application fee: $50. *Expenses:* Tuition, state resident: part-time $332 per credit. Tuition, nonresident: part-time $332 per credit. *Required fees:* $75 per semester. Tuition and fees vary according to program. *Financial support:* Unspecified assistantships and SOS scholarships (for education majors only) available. Financial award application deadline: 3/1; financial award applicants required to submit FAFSA. *Unit head:* Dr. Laura Baker, Department Chair, 413-572-5324, E-mail: lbaker@westfield.ma.edu. *Application contact:* Shelly Henrichon, Coordinator of College of Graduate and Continuing Education Admissions, 413-572-8022, Fax: 413-572-5227, E-mail: mhenrichon@westfield.ma.edu.
Website: http://www.westfield.ma.edu/academics/degrees/education-graduate-programs

Westminster College, Graduate School, Program in Educational Administration, New Wilmington, PA 16172-0001. Offers school principal K-12 (M Ed); school superintendent (M Ed). Application fee: $35. *Expenses: Tuition:* Part-time $454 per semester hour. *Required fees:* $235.50 per course. Tuition and fees vary according to course load. *Unit head:* Graduate School Director, 724-946-7031, Fax: 724-946-6158. *Application contact:* Graduate School Director, 724-946-7031, Fax: 724-946-6158.

West Virginia University, College of Education and Human Services, Morgantown, WV 26506. Offers audiology (Au D); autism spectrum disorder (MA); clinical rehabilitation and mental health counseling (MS); communication science and disorders (PhD); counseling (MA); counseling psychology (PhD); curriculum and instruction (Ed D); early childhood education (MA); early intervention (MA); education (PhD); educational leadership (MA, Ed D); educational leadership/public school administration (MA); educational psychology (MA, Ed D); elementary education (MA); gifted education (MA); higher education administration (MA, Ed D); higher education curriculum and teaching (MA); institutional design and technology (MA); instructional design and technology (Ed D); literacy education (MA); secondary education (MA); secondary education/English (MA); special education (MA); speech pathology (MS). *Accreditation:* NCATE. *Program availability:* Part-time, evening/weekend, online learning. *Students:* 423 full-time (347 women), 367 part-time (316 women); includes 57 minority (14 Black or African American, non-Hispanic/Latino; 7 Asian, non-Hispanic/Latino; 20 Hispanic/Latino; 16 Two or more races, non-Hispanic/Latino), 13 international. *Degree requirements:* For master's, content exams; for doctorate, comprehensive exam, thesis/dissertation. *Entrance requirements:* Additional exam requirements/recommendations for international students: Required—TOEFL (minimum score 500 paper-based; 61 iBT). *Application deadline:* For fall admission, 8/1 for domestic students; for spring admission, 1/1 for domestic students; for summer admission, 5/1 for domestic students. Application fee: $60. Electronic applications accepted. *Expenses:* Tuition, state resident: full-time $9450. Tuition, nonresident: full-time $24,390. *Financial support:* Fellowships, research assistantships, teaching assistantships, career-related internships or fieldwork, Federal Work-Study, institutionally sponsored loans, health care benefits, tuition waivers (full and partial), and administrative assistantships available. Financial award applicants required to submit FAFSA. *Faculty research:* Internet training and integration for teachers, rural education, teacher preparation, organization of schools, evaluation of personnel. *Unit head:* Dr. Gypsy Denzine, Dean, 304-293-5703, Fax: 304-293-7565, E-mail: gypsy.denzine@mail.wvu.edu. *Application contact:* Dr. M. Cecil Smith, Associate Dean for Research and Graduate Education, 304-293-2174, Fax: 304-293-3802, E-mail: mcecil.smith@mail.wvu.edu.
Website: http://cehs.wvu.edu/

Wichita State University, Graduate School, College of Education, Department of Curriculum and Instruction, Wichita, KS 67260. Offers learning and instructional design (M Ed); special education (M Ed), including early childhood (M Ed, MAT), gifted, high incidence, low incidence; teaching (MAT), including early childhood (M Ed, MAT), middle level/secondary, transition to teaching. *Accreditation:* NCATE. *Program availability:* Part-time, evening/weekend, 100% online, blended/hybrid learning. *Entrance requirements:* For master's, MAT, minimum GPA of 2.75. *Unit head:* Dr. Kimberly McDowell, Department Head, 316-978-3322, E-mail: kim.mcdowell@wichita.edu. *Application contact:* Jordan Oleson, Admission Coordinator, 316-978-3095, Fax: 316-978-3253, E-mail: jordan.oleson@wichita.edu.

Widener University, School of Human Service Professions, Center for Education, Chester, PA 19013-5792. Offers adult education (M Ed); counseling in higher education (M Ed); counselor education (M Ed); early childhood education (M Ed); educational foundations (M Ed); educational leadership (M Ed); educational psychology (M Ed); elementary education (M Ed); English and language arts (M Ed); health education

(M Ed); higher education leadership (Ed D); home and school visitor (M Ed); human sexuality (M Ed, PhD); mathematics education (M Ed); middle school education (M Ed); principalship (M Ed); reading and language arts (Ed D); reading education (M Ed); school administration (Ed D); science education (M Ed); social studies education (M Ed); special education (M Ed); technology education (M Ed). *Accreditation:* NCATE. *Program availability:* Part-time, evening/weekend. *Faculty:* 34 full-time (22 women), 37 part-time/adjunct (14 women). *Students:* 131 full-time (112 women), 244 part-time (179 women); includes 94 minority (58 Black or African American, non-Hispanic/Latino; 1 American Indian or Alaska Native, non-Hispanic/Latino; 1 Asian, non-Hispanic/Latino; 22 Hispanic/Latino; 12 Two or more races, non-Hispanic/Latino), 12 international. Average age 37. 140 applicants, 38% accepted, 26 enrolled. In 2017, 45 master's, 21 doctorates awarded. Terminal master's awarded for partial completion of doctoral program. *Degree requirements:* For doctorate, thesis/dissertation. *Entrance requirements:* For master's, minimum GPA of 2.5; for doctorate, GRE or MAT, minimum GPA of 2.0 (undergraduate), 3.5 (graduate). *Application deadline:* Applications are processed on a rolling basis. Application fee: $25 ($300 for international students). Electronic applications accepted. *Expenses:* Contact institution. *Financial support:* Career-related internships or fieldwork, tuition waivers (full and partial), and unspecified assistantships available. Support available to part-time students. Financial award application deadline: 5/1. *Faculty research:* Reading and cognition, adult education, technology education, educational leadership, special education. *Unit head:* Dr. Shawn Fitzgerald, Dean, 610-499-4294, Fax: 610-499-4623, E-mail: smfitzgerald@widener.edu. *Application contact:* Megan Kuft, Director of Graduate Admissions, 610-499-4124, E-mail: gradprograms@widener.edu.
Website: http://www.widener.edu/academics/schools/eics

William Paterson University of New Jersey, College of Education, Wayne, NJ 07470-8420. Offers curriculum and learning (M Ed); early childhood education (Certificate); educational leadership (M Ed); educational media specialist (Certificate); elementary education (MAT, Certificate); elementary education subject area (Certificate); higher education administration (MA); learning disabilities consultant (Certificate); literacy (M Ed); middle level education (M Ed); middle school education subject area (Certificate); professional counseling (M Ed); reading specialist (Certificate); school library media specialist (Certificate); school principal (Certificate); school supervisor (Certificate); secondary education (MAT); special education (M Ed); teacher of students with disabilities (Certificate). *Accreditation:* NCATE. *Program availability:* Part-time, evening/weekend. *Faculty:* 37 full-time (25 women), 21 part-time/adjunct (16 women). *Students:* 73 full-time (54 women), 480 part-time (409 women); includes 153 minority (48 Black or African American, non-Hispanic/Latino; 13 Asian, non-Hispanic/Latino; 81 Hispanic/Latino; 11 Two or more races, non-Hispanic/Latino), 1 international. Average age 35. 347 applicants, 87% accepted, 226 enrolled. In 2017, 136 master's awarded. *Degree requirements:* For master's, comprehensive exam, thesis (for some programs), exit interview (for some programs); practicum/internship; minimum GPA of 3.0 (for some programs); exit portfolio (for some programs). *Entrance requirements:* For master's, GRE/MAT, minimum GPA of 2.75; teaching certificate; essay; interview; 2 letters of recommendation; personal statement. Additional exam requirements/recommendations for international students: Required—TOEFL (minimum score 550 paper-based; 79 iBT), IELTS (minimum score 6). *Application deadline:* For fall admission, 6/1 for domestic students, 3/1 for international students; for spring admission, 11/1 for domestic students, 10/1 for international students. Applications are processed on a rolling basis. Application fee: $50. Electronic applications accepted. *Expenses:* Tuition, state resident: full-time $13,920; part-time $6264 per year. Tuition, nonresident: full-time $21,700; part-time $9765 per year. *Required fees:* $80; $36 per year. Tuition and fees vary according to course load, degree level and program. *Financial support:* In 2017–18, 8,416 students

received support. Career-related internships or fieldwork, Federal Work-Study, scholarships/grants, and unspecified assistantships available. Support available to part-time students. Financial award application deadline: 3/15; financial award applicants required to submit FAFSA. *Faculty research:* Code switching and creative writing, language instruction, teacher evaluation, preschools, history of educational theories. *Total annual research expenditures:* $311,226. *Unit head:* Dr. Dorothy Feola, Dean, 973-720-2138, Fax: 973-720-3647, E-mail: feolad@wpunj.edu. *Application contact:* Liana Fornarotto, Director of Education Enrollment and Certification, 973-720-2206, Fax: 973-720-2989, E-mail: fornarottol@wpunj.edu.
Website: http://www.wpunj.edu/coe

Worcester State University, Graduate School, Department of Education, Program in Early Childhood Education, Worcester, MA 01602-2597. Offers M Ed, Postbaccalaureate Certificate. *Program availability:* Part-time, evening/weekend. *Students:* 2 full-time (both women), 12 part-time (all women); includes 1 minority (Hispanic/Latino). Average age 34. 12 applicants, 83% accepted, 8 enrolled. In 2017, 12 master's, 13 other advanced degrees awarded. *Degree requirements:* For master's, comprehensive exam (for some programs), thesis optional, research project. *Entrance requirements:* For master's, GRE General Test or MAT, initial license or its equivalent in early childhood education. Additional exam requirements/recommendations for international students: Required—TOEFL (minimum score 550 paper-based; 79 iBT), IELTS. *Application deadline:* For fall admission, 6/15 for domestic and international students; for spring admission, 11/1 for domestic and international students; for summer admission, 4/1 for domestic and international students. Applications are processed on a rolling basis. Application fee: $50. Electronic applications accepted. *Expenses:* Tuition, state resident: full-time $3042; part-time $169 per credit hour. Tuition, nonresident: full-time $3042; part-time $169 per credit hour. *Required fees:* $2754; $153 per credit hour. *Financial support:* Career-related internships or fieldwork, scholarships/grants, and unspecified assistantships available. Financial award application deadline: 3/1; financial award applicants required to submit FAFSA. *Unit head:* Dr. Carol Donnelly, Coordinator, 508-929-8667, E-mail: cdonnelly@worcester.edu. *Application contact:* Sara Grady, Associate Dean of Graduate Studies and Professional Development, 508-929-8130, E-mail: sara.grady@worcester.edu.

Xavier University, College of Social Sciences, Health and Education, School of Education, Department of Childhood Education and Literacy, Cincinnati, OH 45207. Offers children's multicultural literature (M Ed); elementary education (M Ed); Montessori education (M Ed); reading (M Ed). *Program availability:* Part-time. *Degree requirements:* For master's, comprehensive exam, thesis, 30 semester hours. *Entrance requirements:* For master's, GRE, MAT, official transcript; 3 letters of recommendation (for Montessori education); resume; statement of purpose. Additional exam requirements/recommendations for international students: Required—TOEFL (minimum score 550 paper-based; 79 iBT). Electronic applications accepted. Application fee is waived when completed online. *Expenses:* Contact institution. *Faculty research:* Multicultural literacy/fluency, early literacy development, writing/creative and across curriculum, assessment of reading abilities.

Youngstown State University, Graduate School, Beeghly College of Education, Department of Teacher Education, Program in Early Childhood Education, Youngstown, OH 44555-0001. Offers MS Ed. *Accreditation:* NCATE. *Program availability:* Part-time, evening/weekend. *Degree requirements:* For master's, comprehensive exam. *Entrance requirements:* For master's, GRE, MAT, or teaching certificate; minimum GPA of 2.7. Additional exam requirements/recommendations for international students: Required—TOEFL.

Elementary Education

Acacia University, American Graduate School of Education, Tempe, AZ 85284. Offers educational administration (M Ed); elementary education (MA); English as a second language (M Ed); secondary education (MA); special education (M Ed).

Adelphi University, Ruth S. Ammon School of Education, Program in Childhood Education, Garden City, NY 11530-0701. Offers MA. *Program availability:* Part-time, evening/weekend. *Students:* 45 full-time (41 women), 9 part-time (5 women); includes 12 minority (4 Asian, non-Hispanic/Latino; 8 Hispanic/Latino). Average age 25. 34 applicants, 38% accepted, 7 enrolled. In 2017, 11 master's awarded. *Entrance requirements:* For master's, 2 letters of recommendation, resume. Additional exam requirements/recommendations for international students: Required—TOEFL (minimum score 550 paper-based; 80 iBT), IELTS (minimum score 6.5). *Application deadline:* For fall admission, 4/1 for international students; for spring admission, 11/1 for international students. Application fee: $50. Electronic applications accepted. *Expenses:* Contact institution. *Financial support:* Research assistantships, teaching assistantships, career-related internships or fieldwork, institutionally sponsored loans, scholarships/grants, traineeships, and unspecified assistantships available. Support available to part-time students. Financial award application deadline: 2/15; financial award applicants required to submit FAFSA. *Faculty research:* Diversity; parental involvement; teacher education; psychoanalytic understanding of racial formation; relationships between ideology, language, culture and individual subject formation. *Unit head:* Dr. Carl Mirra, Director, 516-877-4137, E-mail: mirra@adelphi.edu. *Application contact:* E-mail: graduateadmissions@adelphi.edu.

Alabama Agricultural and Mechanical University, School of Graduate Studies, College of Education, Humanities, and Behavioral Sciences, Department of Reading, Elementary, Early Childhood and Special Education, Huntsville, AL 35811. Offers early childhood education (MS Ed, Ed S); elementary education (MS Ed, Ed S); reading/literacy (PhD); special education collaborative teacher training (MS Ed, Ed S). *Accreditation:* NCATE. *Program availability:* Evening/weekend. *Degree requirements:* For master's, comprehensive exam; for Ed S, thesis. *Entrance requirements:* For master's, GRE General Test. Additional exam requirements/recommendations for international students: Required—TOEFL (minimum score 500 paper-based; 61 iBT). Electronic applications accepted. *Faculty research:* Multicultural education, learning styles, diagnostic-prescriptive instruction.

Alabama State University, College of Education, Department of Curriculum and Instruction, Montgomery, AL 36101-0271. Offers early childhood education (M Ed, Ed S); elementary education (M Ed, Ed S); secondary education (M Ed, Ed S), including biology education, English language arts education (M Ed), history education, math education, music education (M Ed), reading education (M Ed), social science education; special education (M Ed). *Program availability:* Part-time. *Faculty:* 7 full-time (4 women), 7 part-time/adjunct (4 women). *Students:* 43 full-time (35 women), 71 part-time (62

women); includes 112 minority (111 Black or African American, non-Hispanic/Latino; 1 Two or more races, non-Hispanic/Latino). Average age 22. 47 applicants, 66% accepted, 19 enrolled. In 2017, 21 master's, 13 Ed Ss awarded. *Degree requirements:* For master's, comprehensive exam, thesis optional; for Ed S, comprehensive exam, thesis. *Entrance requirements:* For master's, GRE General Test, MAT, writing competency test; for Ed S, writing competency test, GRE, MAT. Additional exam requirements/recommendations for international students: Required—TOEFL (minimum score 500 paper-based). *Application deadline:* For fall admission, 4/15 for domestic and international students; for spring admission, 11/15 for domestic and international students; for summer admission, 3/15 for domestic and international students. Applications are processed on a rolling basis. Application fee: $25. Electronic applications accepted. *Expenses:* Tuition, state resident: part-time $412 per credit hour. Tuition, nonresident: part-time $824 per credit hour. *Required fees:* $685 per semester. *Financial support:* Research assistantships available. Financial award application deadline: 6/30; financial award applicants required to submit FAFSA. *Unit head:* Dr. Joyce Johnson, Acting Chairperson, 334-229-4485, Fax: 334-229-5603, E-mail: jjohnson@alasu.edu. *Application contact:* Dr. William Person, Dean of Graduate Studies, 334-229-4274, Fax: 334-229-4928, E-mail: wperson@alasu.edu.
Website: http://www.alasu.edu/academics/colleges—departments/college-of-education/curriculum—instruction/index.aspx

Alaska Pacific University, Graduate Programs, Education Department, Program in Teaching, Anchorage, AK 99508-4672. Offers teaching (K-8) (MAT). *Degree requirements:* For master's, research project. *Entrance requirements:* For master's, GRE or MAT, PRAXIS, minimum GPA of 3.0.

Albright College, Graduate Division, Reading, PA 19612-5234. Offers early childhood education (MS); elementary education (MS); English as a second language (MA); general education (MA); special education (MS). *Program availability:* Part-time, evening/weekend. *Degree requirements:* For master's, thesis. *Entrance requirements:* For master's, GRE General Test or MAT, minimum undergraduate GPA of 3.0, 2 letters of recommendation, interview. Additional exam requirements/recommendations for international students: Recommended—TOEFL (minimum score 525 paper-based). Electronic applications accepted.

Alcorn State University, School of Graduate Studies, School of Psychology and Education, Lorman, MS 39096-7500. Offers agricultural education (MS Ed); elementary education (MS Ed, Ed S); guidance and counseling (MS Ed); industrial education (MS Ed); secondary education (MS Ed), including health and physical education; special education (MS Ed). *Accreditation:* NCATE. *Degree requirements:* For master's, thesis optional.

American International College, School of Education, Springfield, MA 01109-3189. Offers early childhood education (M Ed, CAGS); education (MA, Ed D), including

counseling psychology (MA), educational leadership and supervision (Ed D); professional counseling and supervision (Ed D), teaching and learning (Ed D); elementary education (M Ed, CAGS); middle education/secondary education (M Ed, CAGS); moderate disabilities (M Ed, CAGS); reading specialist (M Ed, CAGS); school adjustment counseling (MAEP, CAGS); school guidance counseling (MAEP, CAGS); school leadership (M Ed, CAGS). *Program availability:* Evening/weekend. *Faculty:* 1 (woman) full-time, 151 part-time/adjunct (95 women). *Students:* 1,082 full-time (910 women), 143 part-time (113 women); includes 109 minority (19 Black or African American, non-Hispanic/Latino; 2 American Indian or Alaska Native, non-Hispanic/Latino; 10 Asian, non-Hispanic/Latino; 58 Hispanic/Latino; 1 Native Hawaiian or other Pacific Islander, non-Hispanic/Latino; 19 Two or more races, non-Hispanic/Latino). Average age 34. 537 applicants, 77% accepted, 327 enrolled. In 2017, 486 master's, 112 other advanced degrees awarded. *Degree requirements:* For master's and CAGS, practicum/culminating experience. *Entrance requirements:* For master's, Communication and Literacy portion of the Massachusetts Tests for Education Licensure, graduate of accredited four-year college with minimum B- average in undergraduate course work; for CAGS, M Ed or master's degree in field related to licensure from accredited institution. *Application deadline:* Applications are processed on a rolling basis. Application fee: $50. Electronic applications accepted. *Expenses:* $439 per credit, $30 per term registration fee, $100 graduation fee, $110 technology fee. *Financial support:* Applicants required to submit FAFSA. *Unit head:* Sylvia Mason, Dean, 413-205-1743, Fax: 413-205-3943, E-mail: sylvia.mason@aic.edu. *Application contact:* Kerry Barnes, Dean of Graduate Admissions, 413-205-3703, Fax: 413-205-3051, E-mail: kerry.barnes@aic.edu.
Website: http://www.aic.edu/school-of-education/

American University of Beirut, Graduate Programs, Faculty of Arts and Sciences, 1107 2020, Lebanon. Offers anthropology (MA); Arab and Middle Eastern history (PhD); Arabic language and literature (MA, PhD); archaeology (MA); art history and curating (MA); biology (MS); cell and molecular biology (PhD); chemistry (MS); clinical psychology (MA); computational sciences (MS); computer science (MS); economics (MA); education (MA), including administration and policy studies, elementary education, mathematics education, psychology school guidance, psychology test and measurements, science education, teaching English as a foreign language; English language (MA); English literature (MA); environmental policy planning (MS); financial economics (MAFE); general psychology (MA); geology (MS); history (MA); Islamic studies (MA); mathematics (MS); media studies (MA); Middle East studies (MA); philosophy (MA); physics (MS); political studies (MA); public administration (MA); public policy and international affairs (MA); sociology (MA); theoretical physics (PhD). *Program availability:* Part-time. *Faculty:* 108 full-time (36 women), 5 part-time/adjunct (4 women). *Students:* 251 full-time (180 women), 233 part-time (172 women). Average age 26. 425 applicants, 65% accepted, 121 enrolled. In 2017, 47 master's, 2 doctorates awarded. *Degree requirements:* For master's, one foreign language, comprehensive exam, thesis (for some programs), project; for doctorate, one foreign language, comprehensive exam, thesis/dissertation. *Entrance requirements:* For master's, GRE General Test (for some programs); for doctorate, GRE General Test (GRE Subject Test for theoretical physics). Additional exam requirements/recommendations for international students: Required—TOEFL (minimum score 583 paper-based; 97 iBT), IELTS (minimum score 7). *Application deadline:* For fall admission, 2/8 for domestic students; for spring admission, 11/3 for domestic students. Application fee: $50. Electronic applications accepted. *Expenses:* Contact institution. *Financial support:* In 2017–18, 29 fellowships, 40 research assistantships were awarded; teaching assistantships, scholarships/grants, tuition waivers (full and partial), and unspecified assistantships also available. Financial award application deadline: 4/4. *Unit head:* Dr. Nadia Maria El Cheikh, Dean, Faculty of Arts and Sciences, 961-1-374374 Ext. 3800, Fax: 961-1-744461, E-mail: nmcheikh@aub.edu.lb. *Application contact:* Rima Rassi, Graduate Studies Officer, 961-1-350000 Ext. 3833, Fax: 961-1-744461, E-mail: rr46@aub.edu.lb.
Website: http://www.aub.edu.lb/fas/pages/default.aspx

American University of Puerto Rico, Program in Education, Bayamon, PR 00960-2037. Offers art education (M Ed); elementary education 4-6 (M Ed); elementary education K-3 (M Ed); general science education (M Ed); physical education (M Ed); special education (M Ed). *Program availability:* Part-time, evening/weekend. *Faculty:* 15 part-time/adjunct (7 women). *Students:* 22 full-time (18 women), 54 part-time (42 women); all minorities (all Hispanic/Latino). Average age 33. 22 applicants, 86% accepted, 19 enrolled. In 2017, 53 master's awarded. *Entrance requirements:* For master's, EXADEP, GRE, or MAT, 2 letters of recommendation, minimum GPA of 2.5. *Application deadline:* For fall admission, 8/1 for domestic students; for winter admission, 10/18 for domestic students; for spring admission, 3/15 for domestic students. Applications are processed on a rolling basis. Application fee: $25. Tuition and fees vary according to course load and degree level. *Financial support:* In 2017–18, 79 students received support, including 76 fellowships (averaging $400 per year), 55 teaching assistantships (averaging $1,741 per year). Financial award applicants required to submit FAFSA. *Unit head:* Prof. Bolivar Ramirez-Carlo, III, Dean of Faculty, 787-620-2040 Ext. 2010, Fax: 787-620-2958, E-mail: bramirez@aupr.edu. *Application contact:* Keren I. Llanos-Figueroa, Information Contact, 787-620-2040 Ext. 2021, Fax: 787-785-7377, E-mail: oficnaadmisiones@aupr.edu.

Anderson University, College of Education, Anderson, SC 29621-4035. Offers administration and supervision (M Ed); education (M Ed); elementary education (MAT). *Accreditation:* NCATE. *Program availability:* 100% online. *Expenses:* Contact institution. *Financial support:* Tuition waivers available. Financial award application deadline: 3/1; financial award applicants required to submit FAFSA. *Unit head:* Dr. Mark Butler, Dean, 864-231-2042. *Application contact:* Mallory Knight, Graduate Admission Counselor, 864-231-2182, Fax: 864-231-2115, E-mail: malloryknight@andersonuniversity.edu.
Website: https://www.andersonuniversity.edu/education

Andrews University, School of Graduate Studies, School of Education, Department of Teaching, Learning, and Curriculum, Berrien Springs, MI 49104. Offers curriculum and instruction (MA, Ed D, PhD, Ed S); elementary education (MAT); secondary education (MAT), including biology, education, English, English as a second language, French, history, physics; teacher education (MAT). *Faculty:* 7 full-time (5 women). *Students:* 14 full-time (8 women), 7 part-time (6 women); includes 5 minority (all Black or African American, non-Hispanic/Latino), 9 international. Average age 39. 29 applicants, 31% accepted, 4 enrolled. In 2017, 5 master's, 3 doctorates awarded. *Entrance requirements:* For master's, GRE Subject Test. Additional exam requirements/recommendations for international students: Required—TOEFL (minimum score 550 paper-based). *Application deadline:* For fall admission, 8/15 for domestic students. Applications are processed on a rolling basis. Application fee: $40. *Unit head:* Dr. Lee C. Davidson, Chair, 269-471-6364. *Application contact:* Justina Clayburn, Supervisor of Graduate Admission, 800-253-2874, Fax: 269-471-6321, E-mail: graduate@andrews.edu.

Anna Maria College, Graduate Division, Program in Education, Paxton, MA 01612. Offers early childhood education (M Ed); education (CAGS); elementary education (M Ed); English language arts (M Ed); visual arts (M Ed). *Program availability:* Part-time, evening/weekend. *Entrance requirements:* For master's, bachelor's degree in liberal arts or sciences, minimum GPA of 3.0. Additional exam requirements/recommendations for

international students: Required—TOEFL (minimum score 500 paper-based). Electronic applications accepted.

Antioch University New England, Graduate School, Department of Education, Integrated Learning Program, Keene, NH 03431-3552. Offers early childhood education (M Ed); elementary education (M Ed), including arts and humanities, science and environmental education; special education (M Ed). *Degree requirements:* For master's, internship. *Entrance requirements:* For master's, previous course work or work experience in education. Additional exam requirements/recommendations for international students: Required—TOEFL (minimum score 550 paper-based). Electronic applications accepted. *Expenses:* Contact institution. *Faculty research:* Problem-based learning, place-based education, mathematics education, democratic classrooms, art education.

Antioch University New England, Graduate School, Department of Education, Waldorf Teacher Training Program, Keene, NH 03431-3552. Offers elementary education (M Ed, Certificate). *Degree requirements:* For master's, thesis (for some programs), internship. *Entrance requirements:* For master's, foundation studies in anthroposophy or equivalent. Additional exam requirements/recommendations for international students: Required—TOEFL (minimum score 550 paper-based). Electronic applications accepted. *Expenses:* Contact institution. *Faculty research:* Teacher renewal, early childhood education, collaborative leadership.

Appalachian State University, Cratis D. Williams Graduate School, Department of Curriculum and Instruction, Boone, NC 28608. Offers curriculum specialist (MA); educational media (MA); elementary education (MA); middle grades education (MA), including language arts, mathematics, science, social studies. *Accreditation:* NCATE. *Program availability:* Part-time, evening/weekend, online learning. *Degree requirements:* For master's, comprehensive exam, thesis or alternative. *Entrance requirements:* For master's, GRE General Test or MAT, 3 letters of recommendation. Additional exam requirements/recommendations for international students: Required—TOEFL (minimum score 570 paper-based; 79 iBT), IELTS (minimum score 6.5). Electronic applications accepted. *Faculty research:* Media literacy, elementary teaching, curriculum development, online learning environments.

Aquinas College, School of Education, Nashville, TN 37205-2005. Offers elementary education (MAT); secondary education (MAT); teaching and learning (M Ed).

Arcadia University, School of Education, Glenside, PA 19038-3295. Offers art education (M Ed); computer education (CAS); curriculum (CAS); curriculum studies (M Ed); early childhood education (M Ed), including individualized, master teacher, research in child development; educational leadership (M Ed, Ed D, CAS); elementary education (M Ed); English education (MA Ed); environmental education (MA Ed); instructional technology (M Ed); language arts (M Ed); library science (M Ed); mathematics education (M Ed, MA Ed); music education (MA Ed); psychology (MA Ed); reading (M Ed, CAS); science education (M Ed, CAS); secondary education (M Ed, CAS); special education (M Ed, Ed D, CAS); theater arts (MA Ed); written communication (MA Ed). *Accreditation:* NASAD. *Program availability:* Part-time, evening/weekend, online learning. Electronic applications accepted. *Expenses:* Contact institution.

Argosy University, Atlanta, College of Education, Atlanta, GA 30328. Offers educational leadership (MAEd, Ed D, Ed S), including higher education administration (Ed D), K-12 education (Ed D); teaching and learning (MAEd, Ed D, Ed S), including education technology (Ed D), higher education (Ed D), K-12 education (Ed D).

Argosy University, Chicago, College of Education, Chicago, IL 60601. Offers adult education and training (MA Ed); community college executive leadership (Ed D); educational leadership (MA Ed, Ed D, Ed S), including district leadership (Ed D), higher education administration (Ed D); K-12 education (Ed D); instructional leadership (Ed D, Ed S), including higher education (Ed D), K-12 education (Ed D). *Program availability:* Online learning.

Argosy University, Hawai`i, College of Education, Honolulu, HI 96813. Offers adult education and training (MA Ed); educational leadership (Ed D), including higher education administration, K-12 education; instructional leadership (Ed D), including higher education, K-12 education; school psychology (MA).

Argosy University, Los Angeles, College of Education, Los Angeles, CA 90045. Offers community college executive leadership (Ed D); educational leadership (MA Ed, Ed D), including higher education administration (Ed D), K-12 education (Ed D); instructional leadership (MA Ed, Ed D), including higher education (Ed D), K-12 education (Ed D); multiple subject teacher preparation (MA Ed); single subject teacher preparation (MA Ed).

Argosy University, Northern Virginia, College of Education, Arlington, VA 22209. Offers community college executive leadership (Ed D); educational leadership (MA Ed, Ed D, Ed S), including higher education administration (Ed D), K-12 education (Ed D); instructional leadership (MA Ed, Ed D, Ed S), including higher education (Ed D), K-12 education (Ed D).

Argosy University, Orange County, College of Education, Orange, CA 92868. Offers community college executive leadership (Ed D); educational leadership (MA Ed, Ed D), including higher education administration (Ed D), K-12 education (Ed D); instructional leadership (MA Ed, Ed D), including education technology (Ed D), higher education (Ed D), K-12 education (Ed D), multiple subject teacher preparation (MA Ed), single subject teacher preparation (MA Ed).

Argosy University, Phoenix, College of Education, Phoenix, AZ 85021. Offers adult education and training (MA Ed); advanced educational administration (Ed D, Ed S); community college executive leadership (Ed D); educational administration (MA Ed); educational leadership (MA Ed, Ed D, Ed S), including education technology (Ed D), higher education administration (Ed D), K-12 education (Ed D); higher and postsecondary education (MA Ed); initial educational administration (Ed D, Ed S); school psychology (MA); teaching and learning (MA Ed, Ed D, Ed S), including education technology (Ed D), higher education (Ed D), K-12 education (Ed D).

Argosy University, Seattle, College of Education, Seattle, WA 98121. Offers adult education and training (MA Ed); community college executive leadership (Ed D); educational leadership (MA Ed, Ed D), including higher education administration (Ed D), K-12 education (Ed D); higher and postsecondary education (MA Ed); instructional leadership (MA Ed, Ed D), including education technology (Ed D), higher education (Ed D), K-12 education (Ed D).

Argosy University, Tampa, College of Education, Tampa, FL 33607. Offers community college executive leadership (Ed D); educational leadership (MA Ed, Ed D, Ed S), including higher education administration (Ed D), K-12 education (Ed D); school counseling (MA); teaching and learning (MA Ed, Ed D, Ed S), including higher education (Ed D), K-12 education (Ed D).

Argosy University, Twin Cities, College of Education, Eagan, MN 55121. Offers advanced educational administration (Ed D, Ed S); educational leadership (MA Ed, Ed D, Ed S), including higher education administration (Ed D), K-12 education (Ed D); higher and postsecondary education (MA Ed); initial educational administration (Ed D, Ed S); instructional leadership (MA Ed, Ed D, Ed S), including education technology (Ed D), higher education (Ed D), K-12 education (Ed D).

Elementary Education

Arizona State University at the Tempe campus, Mary Lou Fulton Teachers College, Program in Curriculum and Instruction, Phoenix, AZ 85069. Offers curriculum and instruction (M Ed, MA); elementary education (M Ed); physical education (MPE); secondary education (M Ed). *Program availability:* Part-time, evening/weekend, online learning. Terminal master's awarded for partial completion of doctoral program. *Degree requirements:* For master's, thesis or alternative, applied project, interactive Program of Study (iPOS) submitted before completing 50 percent of required credit hours. *Entrance requirements:* For master's, GRE or GMAT (for some programs), minimum GPA of 3.0 or equivalent in last 2 years of work leading to bachelor's degree, 3 letters of recommendation, personal statement describing research and career goals, curriculum vitae or resume, IVP fingerprint clearance card (for those seeking Arizona certification). Additional exam requirements/recommendations for international students: Required—TOEFL, IELTS, or PTE. Electronic applications accepted. *Expenses:* Contact institution. *Faculty research:* Early childhood, media and computers, elementary education, secondary education, English education, bilingual education, language and literacy, science education, engineering education, exercise and wellness education.

Arkansas State University, Graduate School, College of Education and Behavioral Science, School of Teacher Education and Leadership, State University, AR 72467. Offers community college administration (SCCT); curriculum and instruction (MSE); early childhood education (MSE); early childhood services (MS); educational leadership (MSE, Ed D, Ed S); educational theory and practice (MSE); middle level education (MAT, MSE); reading (MSE, Ed S); special education - gifted, talented, and creative (MSE); special education - instructional specialist grades 4-12 (MSE); special education - instructional specialist grades P-4 (MSE); special education, K-12 (MSE). *Accreditation:* NCATE. *Program availability:* Part-time, online learning. *Degree requirements:* For master's, comprehensive exam, thesis or alternative; for doctorate, comprehensive exam, thesis/dissertation; for other advanced degree, comprehensive exam. *Entrance requirements:* For master's, GRE General Test or MAT, appropriate bachelor's degree, official transcripts, immunization records, letters of reference, interview; for doctorate, GRE General Test or MAT, interview, master's degree, letters of reference, official transcript, personal statement, writing sample, immunization records; for other advanced degree, GRE General Test or MAT, interview, master's degree, official transcript, immunization records, letters of reference, 3 years of teaching experience, teaching license. Additional exam requirements/recommendations for international students: Required—TOEFL (minimum score 550 paper-based; 79 iBT), IELTS (minimum score 6), PTE (minimum score 56). Electronic applications accepted.

Arkansas Tech University, College of Education, Russellville, AR 72801. Offers college student personnel (MS); educational leadership (M Ed, Ed S); instructional technology (M Ed); school counseling and leadership (M Ed); school leadership (Ed D); special education K-12 (M Ed); strength and conditioning studies (MS); teaching (MAT); teaching, learning, and leadership (M Ed). *Accreditation:* NCATE. *Program availability:* Part-time, evening/weekend, 100% online, blended/hybrid learning. *Students:* 80 full-time (45 women), 433 part-time (328 women); includes 114 minority (81 Black or African American, non-Hispanic/Latino; 4 American Indian or Alaska Native, non-Hispanic/Latino; 1 Asian, non-Hispanic/Latino; 13 Hispanic/Latino; 15 Two or more races, non-Hispanic/Latino), 2 international. Average age 34. In 2017, 132 master's, 8 doctorates, 3 other advanced degrees awarded. *Degree requirements:* For master's, comprehensive exam, thesis optional, action research project; for doctorate, thesis/dissertation. *Entrance requirements:* Additional exam requirements/recommendations for international students: Required—TOEFL (minimum score 550 paper-based; 79 iBT), IELTS (minimum score 6.5), PTE (minimum score 58). *Application deadline:* For fall admission, 3/1 priority date for domestic students, 5/1 priority date for international students; for spring admission, 10/1 priority date for domestic and international students. Applications are processed on a rolling basis. Application fee: $40 ($90 for international students). Electronic applications accepted. *Expenses:* Tuition, state resident: full-time $6816; part-time $284 per credit hour. Tuition, nonresident: full-time $13,632; part-time $568 per credit hour. *Required fees:* $420 per semester. Tuition and fees vary according to course load. *Financial support:* In 2017–18, research assistantships with full and partial tuition reimbursements (averaging $4,800 per year), teaching assistantships with full and partial tuition reimbursements (averaging $4,800 per year) were awarded; career-related internships or fieldwork, Federal Work-Study, scholarships/grants, health care benefits, and unspecified assistantships also available. Support available to part-time students. Financial award application deadline: 4/15; financial award applicants required to submit FAFSA. *Unit head:* Dr. Mary Gunter, Dean, 479-964-3217, E-mail: mgunter@atu.edu.
Website: http://www.atu.edu/education/

Auburn University at Montgomery, College of Education, Department of Curriculum, Instruction, and Technology, Montgomery, AL 36124-4023. Offers elementary education (M Ed, Ed S); instructional technology (Ed S); secondary education (M Ed). *Faculty:* 12 full-time (8 women), 8 part-time/adjunct (all women). *Students:* 43 full-time (34 women), 81 part-time (65 women); includes 39 minority (38 Black or African American, non-Hispanic/Latino; 1 Hispanic/Latino), 2 international. Average age 33. 99 applicants, 70% accepted, 37 enrolled. In 2017, 47 master's awarded. *Degree requirements:* For master's, comprehensive exam, thesis (for some programs). *Entrance requirements:* For master's, GRE or MAT. Additional exam requirements/recommendations for international students: Recommended—TOEFL (minimum score 500 paper-based; 61 iBT), IELTS (minimum score 5.5), TSE (minimum score 44). *Application deadline:* For fall admission, 7/15 for international students; for spring admission, 11/15 for international students; for summer admission, 4/15 for international students. Applications are processed on a rolling basis. Application fee: $25. Electronic applications accepted. *Expenses:* Tuition, state resident: full-time $6930; part-time $385 per credit hour. Tuition, nonresident: full-time $15,588; part-time $866 per credit hour. *Required fees:* $640. *Financial support:* Application deadline: 3/1; applicants required to submit FAFSA. *Unit head:* Dr. Kellie Shumack, Head, 334-244-3737, Fax: 334-244-3835, E-mail: kshumack@aum.edu. *Application contact:* Dr. Rhonda Morton, Associate Dean/Graduate Coordinator, 334-224-3287, Fax: 334-244-3978, E-mail: rmorton@aum.edu.
Website: http://education.aum.edu/academic-departments/curriculum-instruction-technology

Augusta University, College of Education, Program in Curriculum and Instruction, Augusta, GA 30912. Offers curriculum and instruction (Ed S); elementary education (MAT); foreign language education (MAT); instruction (M Ed); middle grades education (MAT); music education (MAT); secondary education (MAT); special education (MAT). *Degree requirements:* For master's, thesis, portfolio. *Entrance requirements:* For master's, GRE, MAT, minimum GPA of 2.5.

Austin Peay State University, College of Graduate Studies, College of Education, Department of Educational Specialties, Clarksville, TN 37044. Offers administration and supervision (Ed S); counseling and guidance (Ed S); curriculum and instruction (MA Ed); education leadership (MA Ed); elementary education (Ed S); reading (MA Ed); secondary education (Ed S). *Program availability:* Part-time, evening/weekend, online learning. *Faculty:* 15 full-time (9 women), 5 part-time/adjunct (4 women). *Students:* 73 full-time (54 women), 139 part-time (106 women); includes 49 minority (23 Black or African American, non-Hispanic/Latino; 4 Asian, non-Hispanic/Latino; 12 Hispanic/Latino; 10 Two or more races, non-Hispanic/Latino), 1 international. Average age 35. 72

applicants, 96% accepted, 42 enrolled. In 2017, 94 master's, 12 Ed Ss awarded. *Degree requirements:* For master's, comprehensive exam, thesis optional. *Entrance requirements:* For master's, GRE General Test, MAT, minimum undergraduate GPA of 2.75. Additional exam requirements/recommendations for international students: Required—TOEFL (minimum score 500 paper-based). *Application deadline:* For fall admission, 8/8 priority date for domestic students. Applications are processed on a rolling basis. Application fee: $45 ($50 for international students). Electronic applications accepted. *Expenses:* Tuition, state resident: full-time $7686; part-time $427 per credit hour. Tuition, nonresident: full-time $20,268; part-time $1126 per credit hour. *Required fees:* $1529; $76.45 per credit hour. *Financial support:* Research assistantships with full tuition reimbursements, career-related internships or fieldwork, Federal Work-Study, institutionally sponsored loans, scholarships/grants, and unspecified assistantships available. Support available to part-time students. Financial award application deadline: 4/1; financial award applicants required to submit FAFSA. *Unit head:* Dr. Moniqueka Gold, Chair, 931-221-7696, Fax: 931-221-7252, E-mail: goldm@apsu.edu. *Application contact:* Megan Mitchell, Coordinator of Graduate Admissions, 800-859-4723, Fax: 931-221-7641, E-mail: gradadmissions@apsu.edu.

Avila University, School of Education, Kansas City, MO 64145-1698. Offers advanced classroom management (MA); art K-12 (Teaching Certificate); educational technology (MA, Certificate); elementary education (Teaching Certificate); English as a second language (MA); English language learners (Advanced Certificate); middle school (Teaching Certificate); physical education K-12 (Teaching Certificate); secondary education (Teaching Certificate); special education (Teaching Certificate); special reading (Advanced Certificate); teaching and learning (MA). *Program availability:* Part-time, evening/weekend, online learning. *Faculty:* 6 full-time (5 women), 9 part-time/adjunct (8 women). *Students:* 81 full-time (63 women), 20 part-time (11 women); includes 14 minority (8 Black or African American, non-Hispanic/Latino; 2 Asian, non-Hispanic/Latino; 3 Hispanic/Latino; 1 Two or more races, non-Hispanic/Latino), 4 international. Average age 35. 92 applicants, 62% accepted, 40 enrolled. In 2017, 24 master's awarded. *Entrance requirements:* For master's, minimum GPA of 3.0, writing sample, recommendation, interview; for other advanced degree, foreign language. Additional exam requirements/recommendations for international students: Required—TOEFL (minimum score 580 paper-based; 92 iBT). *Application deadline:* Applications are processed on a rolling basis. Electronic applications accepted. *Expenses:* Contact institution. *Financial support:* In 2017–18, 14 students received support. Unspecified assistantships available. Financial award applicants required to submit FAFSA. *Unit head:* Dr. Stacy Keith, Director of Graduate Education, 816-501-2446, Fax: 816-501-2915, E-mail: stacy.keith@avila.edu. *Application contact:* Cory Roup, Graduate Education Enrollment and Academic Advisor, 816-501-2464, E-mail: cory.roup@avila.edu.
Website: https://www.avila.edu/academics/graduate-studies/grad-education

Ball State University, Graduate School, College of Sciences and Humanities, Department of Mathematical Sciences, Muncie, IN 47306. Offers actuarial science (MA); elementary mathematics teacher leadership (Certificate); mathematics (MA, MS), including mathematics; mathematics education (MA), including mathematics education; middle school mathematics education (Certificate); post-secondary foundational mathematics teaching (MA, Certificate); statistical modeling (Certificate); statistics (MA, MS), including statistics. *Program availability:* Part-time, 100% online, blended/hybrid learning. *Faculty:* 13 full-time (5 women), 1 part-time/adjunct (0 women). *Students:* 26 full-time (7 women), 71 part-time (47 women); includes 11 minority (5 Black or African American, non-Hispanic/Latino; 4 Asian, non-Hispanic/Latino; 1 Hispanic/Latino; 1 Two or more races, non-Hispanic/Latino), 19 international. Average age 33. 106 applicants, 82% accepted, 35 enrolled. In 2017, 46 master's, 2 other advanced degrees awarded. *Entrance requirements:* For master's, minimum baccalaureate GPA of 2.75 or 3.0 in latter half of baccalaureate. Additional exam requirements/recommendations for international students: Required—TOEFL (minimum score 550 paper-based; 79 iBT), IELTS (minimum score 6.5). *Application deadline:* Applications are processed on a rolling basis. Application fee: $60. Electronic applications accepted. *Financial support:* In 2017–18, 23 students received support, including 23 teaching assistantships with partial tuition reimbursements available (averaging $13,022 per year); unspecified assistantships also available. Financial award application deadline: 3/1; financial award applicants required to submit FAFSA. *Faculty research:* Differential equations. *Unit head:* Dr. Michael Karls, Chairperson/Professor, 765-285-8640, Fax: 765-285-1721, E-mail: mkarls@bsu.edu.
Website: http://www.bsu.edu/math

Ball State University, Graduate School, Teachers College, Department of Elementary Education, Muncie, IN 47306. Offers early childhood administration (Certificate); elementary education (MAE, Ed D, PhD); enhanced teaching practices for elementary teachers (Certificate); literacy instruction (Certificate). *Accreditation:* NCATE. *Program availability:* Part-time, 100% online. *Faculty:* 11 full-time (all women), 2 part-time/adjunct (both women). *Students:* 17 full-time (15 women), 193 part-time (189 women); includes 31 minority (21 Black or African American, non-Hispanic/Latino; 1 Asian, non-Hispanic/Latino; 3 Hispanic/Latino; 6 Two or more races, non-Hispanic/Latino), 1 international. Average age 36. 152 applicants, 79% accepted, 83 enrolled. In 2017, 53 master's, 1 doctorate, 12 other advanced degrees awarded. *Entrance requirements:* For master's, minimum baccalaureate GPA of 2.75 or 3.0 in latter half of baccalaureate; for doctorate, GRE General Test, minimum graduate GPA of 3.2. Additional exam requirements/recommendations for international students: Required—TOEFL (minimum score 550 paper-based; 79 iBT), IELTS (minimum score 6.5). *Application deadline:* For fall admission, 7/15 for domestic students; for spring admission, 11/15 for domestic students; for summer admission, 4/15 for domestic students. Applications are processed on a rolling basis. Application fee: $60. Electronic applications accepted. *Financial support:* In 2017–18, 11 students received support, including 5 research assistantships with partial tuition reimbursements available (averaging $7,831 per year), 4 teaching assistantships with partial tuition reimbursements available (averaging $8,723 per year). Financial award application deadline: 3/1; financial award applicants required to submit FAFSA. *Unit head:* Dr. Pat Clark, Chairperson, 765-285-8564, Fax: 765-285-8793, E-mail: pclark@bsu.edu.
Website: http://www.bsu.edu/elementaryeducation/

Bank Street College of Education, Graduate School, Program in Elementary/Childhood Education, New York, NY 10025. Offers early childhood and elementary/childhood education (MS Ed); elementary/childhood education (MS Ed). *Degree requirements:* For master's, thesis. *Entrance requirements:* For master's, interview, essays. Additional exam requirements/recommendations for international students: Required—TOEFL (minimum score 600 paper-based; 100 iBT), IELTS (minimum score 7). Electronic applications accepted. *Faculty research:* Social studies in the elementary grades, urban education, experiential learning, child-centered classrooms.

Barry University, School of Education, Program in Curriculum and Instruction, Miami Shores, FL 33161-6695. Offers accomplished teacher (Ed S); culture, language and literacy (TESOL) (PhD); curriculum evaluation and research (PhD); early childhood (Ed S); early childhood education (PhD); elementary (Ed S); elementary education (PhD); ESOL (Ed S); gifted (Ed S); Montessori (Ed S); PKP/elementary (Ed S); reading (Ed S); reading, language and cognition (PhD). *Entrance requirements:* For doctorate, GRE, minimum GPA of 3.25.

Barry University, School of Education, Program in Elementary Education, Miami Shores, FL 33161-6695. Offers elementary education (MS); elementary education/ESOL (MS). *Program availability:* Part-time, evening/weekend. *Degree requirements:* For master's, comprehensive exam, practicum. *Entrance requirements:* For master's, GRE General Test or MAT, minimum GPA of 3.0. Electronic applications accepted.

Barton College, Program in Elementary Education, Wilson, NC 27893-7000. Offers M Ed. *Entrance requirements:* For master's, MAT or GRE taken within last five years, bachelor's degree from accredited college or university, minimum GPA of 3.0 for undergraduate work (recommended), official transcript, one year of teaching experience, copy of recognized teaching license in elementary education, personal statement, recommendation form from current employer or administrator, interview. Additional exam requirements/recommendations for international students: Required—TOEFL (minimum score 550 paper-based). Electronic applications accepted.

Bayamón Central University, Graduate Programs, Program in Education, Bayamón, PR 00960-1725. Offers administration and supervision (MA Ed); commercial education (MA Ed); elementary education (K–3) (MA Ed); family counseling (Graduate Certificate); guidance and counseling (MA Ed); pre-elementary teacher (MA Ed); rehabilitation counseling (MA Ed); special education (MA Ed), including attention deficit disorder, education of the autistic, learning disabilities. *Program availability:* Part-time, evening/weekend. *Degree requirements:* For master's, comprehensive exam. *Entrance requirements:* For master's, EXADEP, bachelor's degree in education or related field.

Bellarmine University, Annsley Frazier Thornton School of Education, Louisville, KY 40205. Offers education and district leadership (Ed D); education and social change (PhD); elementary education (MA Ed, MAT); leadership in higher education (PhD); middle school education (MA Ed, MAT); principalship (Ed S); reading and writing (MA Ed); secondary education (MAT); teacher leadership (MA Ed). *Accreditation:* NCATE. *Program availability:* Part-time, evening/weekend. *Faculty:* 19 full-time (10 women), 36 part-time/adjunct (29 women). *Students:* 34 full-time (27 women), 204 part-time (158 women); includes 60 minority (43 Black or African American, non-Hispanic/Latino; 7 Asian, non-Hispanic/Latino; 7 Hispanic/Latino; 3 Two or more races, non-Hispanic/Latino). Average age 33. In 2017, 50 master's, 8 doctorates, 42 other advanced degrees awarded. *Degree requirements:* For master's, comprehensive exam (for some programs), thesis (for some programs); for doctorate, comprehensive exam (for some programs), thesis/dissertation; for Ed S, comprehensive exam (for some programs). *Entrance requirements:* For master's, GRE, baccalaureate degree from accredited institution; minimum cumulative GPA of 2.75; recommendations from employers, supervisors, or professors attesting to applicant's potential as graduate student; statement of intent to pursue graduate degree; for doctorate, GRE, minimum GPA of 3.5 in all graduate coursework; baccalaureate and master's degrees in education or fields directly relevant to education; three letters of recommendation; two essays (no more than 1,000 words each); resume or curriculum vitae; interview; for Ed S, master's degree in education; valid teaching certificate; three years of experience in teaching; three recommendations; minimum GPA of 3.0 in all graduate work; interview; essays; personal goal statement. Additional exam requirements/recommendations for international students: Required—TOEFL (minimum score 550 paper-based, 6 iBT), IELTS (minimum score 6), or Michigan English Language Assessment Battery. *Application deadline:* For fall admission, 8/1 priority date for domestic and international students; for spring admission, 12/1 priority date for domestic and international students; for summer admission, 4/10 priority date for domestic and international students. Applications are processed on a rolling basis. Application fee: $40. Electronic applications accepted. Tuition and fees vary according to program. *Financial support:* Scholarships/grants available. Financial award applicants required to submit FAFSA. *Faculty research:* Literacy, service-learning, dispositions, educational technology, special education. *Unit head:* Dr. Elizabeth Dinkins, Interim Dean, 502-272-7958, Fax: 502-272-8189, E-mail: edinkins@bellarmine.edu. *Application contact:* Sarah Schuble, Senior Graduate Admissions Recruiter, 502-272-8271, Fax: 502-272-8002, E-mail: sschuble@bellarmine.edu.
Website: http://www.bellarmine.edu/education/graduate

Benedictine University, Graduate Programs, Program in Education, Lisle, IL 60532. Offers curriculum and instruction and collaborative teaching (M Ed); elementary education (MA Ed); leadership and administration (M Ed); reading and literacy (M Ed); secondary education (MA Ed); special education (MA Ed). *Program availability:* Part-time, evening/weekend. *Degree requirements:* For master's, comprehensive exam, thesis (for some programs). *Entrance requirements:* For master's, GRE or MAT. Additional exam requirements/recommendations for international students: Required—TOEFL (minimum score 550 paper-based). Electronic applications accepted. *Expenses:* Contact institution.

Bethel University, Graduate School, St. Paul, MN 55112-6999. Offers business administration (MBA); classroom management (Certificate); counseling (MA); K-12 education (MA); leadership (Ed D); leadership foundations (Certificate); nurse educator (MS, Certificate); nurse-midwifery (MS); physician assistant (MS); special education (MA); strategic leadership (MA); teaching (MA); teaching and learning (Certificate). *Program availability:* Part-time, evening/weekend, 100% online, blended/hybrid learning. *Faculty:* 22 full-time (16 women), 70 part-time/adjunct (44 women). *Students:* 611 full-time (431 women), 393 part-time (249 women); includes 176 minority (82 Black or African American, non-Hispanic/Latino; 4 American Indian or Alaska Native, non-Hispanic/Latino; 31 Asian, non-Hispanic/Latino; 39 Hispanic/Latino; 2 Native Hawaiian or other Pacific Islander, non-Hispanic/Latino; 18 Two or more races, non-Hispanic/Latino), 9 international. Average age 36. 668 applicants, 42% accepted, 223 enrolled. In 2017, 287 master's, 30 doctorates, 172 other advanced degrees awarded. *Degree requirements:* For master's, comprehensive exam (for some programs), thesis (for some programs); for doctorate, comprehensive exam, thesis/dissertation. *Entrance requirements:* Additional exam requirements/recommendations for international students: Required—TOEFL (minimum score 550 paper-based, 80 iBT) or IELTS. *Application deadline:* Applications are processed on a rolling basis. Application fee: $0. Electronic applications accepted. *Expenses:* Contact institution. *Financial support:* Teaching assistantships, career-related internships or fieldwork, and scholarships/grants available. Support available to part-time students. Financial award applicants required to submit FAFSA. *Unit head:* Dr. Randy Bergen, Associate Provost, 651-635-8000, Fax: 651-635-8004, E-mail: r-bergen@bethel.edu. *Application contact:* Director of Admissions, 651-635-8000, Fax: 651-635-8004, E-mail: gs@bethel.edu.
Website: https://www.bethel.edu/graduate/

Blue Mountain College, Program in Elementary Education, Blue Mountain, MS 38610. Offers M Ed. *Program availability:* Part-time, evening/weekend. *Faculty:* 2 part-time/adjunct (1 woman). *Students:* 1 (woman) part-time. Average age 28. 2 applicants, 100% accepted. In 2017, 5 master's awarded. *Degree requirements:* For master's, comprehensive exam. *Entrance requirements:* For master's, PRAXIS, GRE or MAT, official transcripts; bachelor's degree in a field of education from accredited university or college; teaching certificate; three recommendations. Additional exam requirements/recommendations for international students: Required—TOEFL (minimum score 550 paper-based). *Application deadline:* For fall admission, 7/15 priority date for domestic students; for spring admission, 12/1 priority date for domestic students; for summer admission, 5/1 priority date for domestic students. Applications are processed on a rolling

basis. Electronic applications accepted. *Expenses: Tuition:* Full-time $6030; part-time $335 per semester hour. *Required fees:* $790; $790 per semester hour. *Financial support:* Scholarships/grants available. Financial award application deadline: 6/30; financial award applicants required to submit FAFSA. *Unit head:* Dr. Jenetta R. Waddell, Dean of Graduate Studies, 662-685-4771 Ext. 118, Fax: 662-815-2919, E-mail: jwaddell@bmc.edu. *Application contact:* Jean Harrington, Administrative Assistant, Department of Education, 662-685-4771 Ext. 238, Fax: 662-815-2919, E-mail: jharrington@bmc.edu.
Website: http://www.bmc.edu/master_of_education.asp

Bob Jones University, Graduate Programs, Greenville, SC 29614. Offers accountancy (MS); Bible (MA); Bible translation (MA); Biblical counseling (Certificate); broadcast management (MS); business administration (MBA); church history (MA, PhD); church ministries (MA); church music (MA); cinema and video production (MA); counseling (MS); curriculum and instruction (Ed D); divinity (M Div); dramatic production (MA); educational leadership (MS, Ed D, Ed S); elementary education (M Ed, MAT); English (M Ed, MA, MAT); fine arts (MA); graphic design (MA); history (M Ed, MA); illustration (MA); interpretative speech (MA); mathematics (M Ed, MAT); medical missions (Certificate); ministry (MM, D Min); multi-categorical special education (M Ed, MAT); music (M Ed); New Testament interpretation (PhD); Old Testament interpretation (PhD); orchestral instrument performance (MM); organ performance (MM); pastoral studies (MA); personnel services (MS, Ed S); piano pedagogy (MM); piano performance (MM); platform arts (MA); radio and television broadcasting (MS); rhetoric and public address (MA); secondary education (M Ed); studio art (MA); teaching Bible (MA); theology (MA, PhD); voice performance (MM); youth ministries (MA); M Div/MM.

Boston College, Lynch School of Education, Program in Elementary Education, Chestnut Hill, MA 02467-3800. Offers M Ed, MAT. *Accreditation:* TEAC. *Program availability:* Part-time, evening/weekend. *Students:* 12 full-time (8 women), 1 (woman) part-time; includes 5 minority (4 Black or African American, non-Hispanic/Latino; 1 Hispanic/Latino). Average age 24. 43 applicants, 84% accepted, 9 enrolled. In 2017, 14 master's awarded. *Degree requirements:* For master's, comprehensive exam. *Entrance requirements:* For master's, GRE General Test or MAT. Additional exam requirements/recommendations for international students: Required—TOEFL (minimum score 100 iBT). *Application deadline:* For fall admission, 12/1 priority date for domestic and international students; for spring admission, 11/1 priority date for domestic and international students. Application fee: $65. Electronic applications accepted. *Financial support:* Federal Work-Study, scholarships/grants, and tuition waivers (full and partial) available. Financial award applicants required to submit FAFSA. *Unit head:* Dr. Susan Bruce, Chairperson, 617-552-4214, Fax: 617-552-0398. *Application contact:* Kimberly Rose, Graduate Admission Assistant, 617-552-4214, Fax: 617-552-0398, E-mail: roseki@bc.edu.

Bowie State University, Graduate Programs, Program in Elementary Education, Bowie, MD 20715-9465. Offers M Ed. *Accreditation:* NCATE. *Program availability:* Part-time, evening/weekend. *Degree requirements:* For master's, comprehensive exam, thesis optional, research paper. *Entrance requirements:* For master's, minimum GPA of 2.5, teaching certificate, teaching experience. Electronic applications accepted.

Brandeis University, Graduate School of Arts and Sciences, Program in Education, Waltham, MA 02454-9110. Offers Jewish day schools (MAT); public elementary education (MAT); secondary education (MAT), including Bible, biology, chemistry, Chinese, English, history, Jewish day schools, math, physics; teacher leadership (Ed M, AGC). *Faculty:* 4 full-time (2 women), 11 part-time/adjunct (10 women). *Students:* 21 full-time (19 women), 38 part-time (33 women); includes 5 minority (1 Black or African American, non-Hispanic/Latino; 3 Asian, non-Hispanic/Latino; 1 Hispanic/Latino), 8 international. Average age 34. 93 applicants, 78% accepted, 55 enrolled. In 2017, 43 master's, 10 other advanced degrees awarded. *Degree requirements:* For master's, thesis or alternative, internship; research project. *Entrance requirements:* For master's, GRE General Test or MAT, transcripts, letters of recommendation, resume, statement of purpose. Additional exam requirements/recommendations for international students: Required—PTE (minimum score 68), TOEFL (minimum score 600 paper-based, 100 iBT) or IELTS (7). *Application deadline:* For fall admission, 12/1 priority date for domestic students. Applications are processed on a rolling basis. Application fee: $75. Electronic applications accepted. *Expenses:* $32,440 (MAT), $17,520 (M Ed), $23,360 (AGS); $88 fees. *Financial support:* In 2017–18, 61 students received support. Scholarships/grants available. Financial award application deadline: 4/15; financial award applicants required to submit FAFSA. *Faculty research:* Teacher education, education, teaching, elementary education, secondary education, Jewish education, English, history, biology, chemistry, physics, math, Chinese, Bible/Tanakh. *Unit head:* Marya Levenson, Director, 781-736-2002, E-mail: mlevenso@brandeis.edu. *Application contact:* Manuel Tuan, Department Coordinator, 781-736-2002, E-mail: tuan@brandeis.edu.
Website: http://www.brandeis.edu/gsas/programs/education.html

Brandman University, School of Education, Irvine, CA 92618. Offers curriculum and instruction (MAE); educational administration (MAE); educational leadership (MAE); educational leadership and administration (MAE); elementary education (MAT); instructional technology: teaching the 21st century learner (MAE); leadership in early childhood education (MAE); organizational leadership (Ed D); school counseling (MA); secondary education (MAT); special education (MAE); teaching and learning (MAE). *Expenses: Tuition:* Part-time $640 per credit hour. Tuition and fees vary according to degree level and program. *Unit head:* Dr. Christine G. Zeppos, Dean, 949-341-9948, E-mail: zeppos@brandman.edu. *Application contact:* Dr. Christine G. Zeppos, Dean, 949-341-9948, E-mail: zeppos@brandman.edu.
Website: http://www.brandman.edu/academic-programs/education

Bridgewater State University, College of Graduate Studies, College of Education and Allied Studies, Department of Elementary and Early Childhood Education, Program in Elementary Education, Bridgewater, MA 02325. Offers M Ed. *Accreditation:* NCATE. *Program availability:* Part-time, evening/weekend. *Entrance requirements:* For master's, GRE General Test or Massachusetts Test for Educator Licensure.

Brooklyn College of the City University of New York, School of Education, Program in Childhood Education, Brooklyn, NY 11210-2889. Offers bilingual education (MS Ed); liberal arts (MS Ed); mathematics (MS Ed); science and environmental education (MS Ed). *Program availability:* Part-time, evening/weekend. *Entrance requirements:* For master's, LAST, interview, previous course work in education, writing sample, resume, 2 letters of recommendation. Additional exam requirements/recommendations for international students: Required—TOEFL (minimum score 500 paper-based; 61 iBT). Electronic applications accepted. *Faculty research:* Emotional intelligence, multiculturalism, arts immersion, the Holocaust.

Brooklyn College of the City University of New York, School of Education, Program in Special Education, Brooklyn, NY 11210-2889. Offers autism spectrum disorders (AC); teacher of students with disabilities (MS Ed), including adolescence education, childhood education, early childhood education. *Program availability:* Part-time. *Entrance requirements:* For master's, LAST, interview; previous course work in education and psychology; minimum GPA of 3.0 in education, 2.8 overall; resume, 2 letters of recommendation; essay. Additional exam requirements/recommendations for international students: Required—TOEFL (minimum score 500 paper-based; 61 iBT). Electronic applications accepted. *Faculty research:* School reform, conflict resolution, curriculum for inclusive settings, urban issues in special education.

Elementary Education

Brown University, Graduate School, Department of Education, Providence, RI 02912. Offers teaching (MAT), including elementary education, English, history/social studies, science, secondary education; urban education policy (AM). *Degree requirements:* For master's, student teaching, portfolio. *Entrance requirements:* For master's, GRE General Test, letters of recommendation, interview. Additional exam requirements/recommendations for international students: Recommended—TOEFL.

Buffalo State College, State University of New York, The Graduate School, Faculty of Applied Science and Education, Department of Elementary Education and Reading, Program in Elementary Education, Buffalo, NY 14222-1095. Offers childhood education (grades 1-6) (MS Ed); early childhood and childhood curriculum and instruction (MS Ed); early childhood education (birth-grade 2) (MS Ed). *Accreditation:* NCATE. *Program availability:* Part-time. *Degree requirements:* For master's, thesis or project. *Entrance requirements:* For master's, minimum GPA of 2.5 in last 60 hours, New York teaching certificate. Additional exam requirements/recommendations for international students: Required—TOEFL (minimum score 550 paper-based).

Cabrini University, Academic Affairs, Radnor, PA 19087. Offers accounting (M Acc); autism spectrum disorder (M Ed); biological sciences (MS), including civic leadership; criminology and criminal justice (MA); curriculum, instruction, and assessment (M Ed); educational leadership (M Ed, Ed D), including curriculum and instructional leadership (Ed D), preK-12 leadership (Ed D); English as a second language (M Ed); organizational leadership (DBA, PhD); preK to 4 (M Ed); reading specialist (M Ed); secondary education (M Ed), including biology, chemistry, English, English/communication, mathematics, social studies; special education grades 7-12 (M Ed); special education preK-8 (M Ed); teaching and learning (M Ed). *Program availability:* Part-time, evening/weekend. *Faculty:* 23 full-time (17 women), 46 part-time/adjunct (38 women). *Students:* 60 full-time (35 women), 559 part-time (435 women); includes 93 minority (66 Black or African American, non-Hispanic/Latino; 1 American Indian or Alaska Native, non-Hispanic/Latino; 8 Asian, non-Hispanic/Latino; 15 Hispanic/Latino; 3 Two or more races, non-Hispanic/Latino), 4 international. Average age 33. 290 applicants, 82% accepted, 154 enrolled. In 2017, 283 master's awarded. *Degree requirements:* For master's, comprehensive exam (for some programs), thesis (for some programs); for doctorate, comprehensive exam (for some programs), thesis/dissertation. *Entrance requirements:* For master's, professional resume, personal statement, two recommendations, official transcripts; for doctorate, official transcripts, minimum master's GPA of 3.0, two recommendations, interview with admissions committee. Additional exam requirements/recommendations for international students: Required—TOEFL (minimum score 80 iBT). *Application deadline:* For fall admission, 8/26 for domestic students, 8/1 for international students; for winter admission, 1/13 for domestic students, 12/20 for international students; for spring admission, 1/13 for domestic students, 12/20 for international students; for summer admission, 5/20 for domestic students, 4/30 for international students. Applications are processed on a rolling basis. Application fee: $50. Electronic applications accepted. Application fee is waived when completed online. *Expenses:* Contact institution. *Financial support:* In 2017–18, 1,459 students received support. Tuition waivers and unspecified assistantships available. Financial award application deadline: 5/1; financial award applicants required to submit FAFSA. *Unit head:* Dr. Maliha Zaman, 610-902-8502, Fax: 610-902-8797, E-mail: msz37@cabrini.edu. *Application contact:* Diane Greenwood, Director of Graduate Admissions, 610-902-8291, E-mail: diane.l.greenwood@cabrini.edu.
Website: http://cabrini.edu/graduate

California Lutheran University, Graduate Studies, Graduate School of Education, Thousand Oaks, CA 91360-2787. Offers counseling and guidance (MS), including college student personnel, counseling and guidance; educational leadership (MA, Ed D), including educational leadership (K-12) (Ed D), higher education leadership (Ed D); special education (MS); teacher leadership (M Ed); teaching (M Ed). *Accreditation:* NCATE. *Program availability:* Part-time, evening/weekend. *Faculty:* 21 full-time (18 women), 40 part-time/adjunct (27 women). *Students:* 390 full-time (303 women), 61 part-time (51 women); includes 228 minority (6 Black or African American, non-Hispanic/Latino; 2 American Indian or Alaska Native, non-Hispanic/Latino; 13 Asian, non-Hispanic/Latino; 186 Hispanic/Latino; 1 Native Hawaiian or other Pacific Islander, non-Hispanic/Latino; 20 Two or more races, non-Hispanic/Latino). Average age 31. 201 applicants, 76% accepted, 121 enrolled. In 2017, 129 master's, 19 doctorates awarded. *Degree requirements:* For master's, comprehensive exam or thesis; for doctorate, thesis/dissertation. *Entrance requirements:* For master's, GRE General Test, interview, minimum GPA of 3.0. *Application deadline:* For fall admission, 7/1 priority date for domestic students; for spring admission, 11/1 priority date for domestic students; for summer admission, 4/1 priority date for domestic students. Applications are processed on a rolling basis. Application fee: $50. Electronic applications accepted. *Expenses:* Tuition: Full-time $15,000. Full-time tuition and fees vary according to degree level and program. *Unit head:* Dr. Michael Hillis, Dean, 805-493-3421. *Application contact:* 805-493-3325, Fax: 805-493-3861, E-mail: clugrad@callutheran.edu.

California State University, Fullerton, Graduate Studies, College of Education, Department of Elementary and Bilingual Education, Fullerton, CA 92831-3599. Offers bilingual/bicultural education (MS); educational technology (MS); elementary curriculum and instruction (MS). *Accreditation:* NCATE. *Program availability:* Part-time. *Faculty:* 10 full-time (7 women), 10 part-time/adjunct (8 women). *Students:* 224 full-time (194 women), 191 part-time (162 women); includes 218 minority (6 Black or African American, non-Hispanic/Latino; 1 American Indian or Alaska Native, non-Hispanic/Latino; 65 Asian, non-Hispanic/Latino; 127 Hispanic/Latino; 1 Native Hawaiian or other Pacific Islander, non-Hispanic/Latino; 18 Two or more races, non-Hispanic/Latino), 3 international. Average age 32. 272 applicants, 69% accepted, 170 enrolled. *Degree requirements:* For master's, comprehensive exam, project or thesis. *Entrance requirements:* For master's, minimum GPA of 2.5, teaching certificate. Application fee: $55. *Financial support:* Career-related internships or fieldwork, Federal Work-Study, institutionally sponsored loans, and scholarships/grants available. Support available to part-time students. Financial award application deadline: 3/1; financial award applicants required to submit FAFSA. *Faculty research:* Teacher training and tracking, model for improvement of teaching. *Unit head:* Lisa Kirtman, Chair, 657-278-4731. *Application contact:* Admissions/Applications, 657-278-2371.
Website: http://ed.fullerton.edu/EDEL/

California State University, Long Beach, Graduate Studies, College of Education, Department of Teacher Education, Long Beach, CA 90840. Offers elementary education (MA); secondary education (MA). *Program availability:* Part-time, evening/weekend. *Degree requirements:* For master's, comprehensive exam or thesis. *Entrance requirements:* For master's, GRE General Test, minimum GPA of 2.75. Electronic applications accepted. *Faculty research:* Teacher stress and burnout, new teacher induction.

California State University, Los Angeles, Graduate Studies, Charter College of Education, Division of Curriculum and Instruction, Los Angeles, CA 90032-8530. Offers elementary teaching (MA). *Program availability:* Part-time, evening/weekend. *Entrance requirements:* For master's, minimum GPA of 2.75 in last 90 units of course work, teaching certificate. Additional exam requirements/recommendations for international students: Required—TOEFL (minimum score 500 paper-based). Electronic applications accepted. *Faculty research:* Media, language arts, mathematics, computers, drug-free schools.

California State University, Northridge, Graduate Studies, Michael D. Eisner College of Education, Department of Elementary Education, Northridge, CA 91330. Offers curriculum and instruction (MA); language and literacy (MA); multilingual/multicultural education (MA). *Accreditation:* NCATE. *Program availability:* Part-time, evening/weekend. *Students:* 3 full-time (all women), 62 part-time (56 women); includes 37 minority (7 Asian, non-Hispanic/Latino; 26 Hispanic/Latino; 4 Two or more races, non-Hispanic/Latino). Average age 30. 42 applicants, 50% accepted, 19 enrolled. In 2017, 103 master's awarded. *Degree requirements:* For master's, comprehensive exam. *Entrance requirements:* For master's, GRE General Test or minimum GPA of 3.0. Additional exam requirements/recommendations for international students: Required—TOEFL. *Application deadline:* For fall admission, 11/30 for domestic students. Application fee: $55. Financial Work-Study available. Financial award application deadline: 3/1. *Unit head:* Dr. Joyce Burstein, Chair, 818-677-2621.
Website: http://www.csun.edu/eisner-education/elementary-education

California State University, Sacramento, College of Education, Graduate and Professional Studies in Education, Sacramento, CA 95819. Offers behavioral science and gender equity (MA); child development (MA); counseling (MS); curriculum and instruction (MA); education (Ed D), including K-12 and community college; education leadership and policy studies (MA), including higher education, PreK-12; education specialist (Ed S), including school psychology; educational technology (MA); language and literacy (MA); multicultural education (MA); school psychology (MA); special education (MA); workforce development advocacy (MA). *Program availability:* Part-time, evening/weekend, blended/hybrid learning. *Students:* 381 full-time (294 women), 135 part-time (101 women); includes 296 minority (44 Black or African American, non-Hispanic/Latino; 1 American Indian or Alaska Native, non-Hispanic/Latino; 94 Asian, non-Hispanic/Latino; 153 Hispanic/Latino; 4 Native Hawaiian or other Pacific Islander, non-Hispanic/Latino), 3 international. Average age 32. 553 applicants, 53% accepted, 292 enrolled. In 2017, 147 master's, 13 doctorates, 10 other advanced degrees awarded. *Degree requirements:* For master's, thesis or project; writing proficiency exam; for doctorate, thesis/dissertation. *Entrance requirements:* For master's and doctorate, GRE. Additional exam requirements/recommendations for international students: Required—TOEFL (minimum score 550 paper-based; 80 iBT); Recommended—IELTS (minimum score 7), TSE. *Application deadline:* For fall admission, 2/15 for domestic students, 1/15 for international students. Applications are processed on a rolling basis. Application fee: $55. Electronic applications accepted. *Expenses:* Contact institution. *Financial support:* Career-related internships or fieldwork, Federal Work-Study, and scholarships/grants available. Support available to part-time students. Financial award application deadline: 3/1; financial award applicants required to submit FAFSA. *Unit head:* Dr. Elizabeth Liles, Chair, 916-278-5942, E-mail: coe@csus.edu. *Application contact:* Jose Martinez, Graduate Admissions Supervisor, 916-278-7871, E-mail: martinj@skymail.csus.edu.
Website: http://www.csus.edu/coe/academics/graduate/index.html

California State University, Stanislaus, College of Education, Kinesiology and Social Work, MA Program in Education, Turlock, CA 95382. Offers curriculum and instruction (MA), including education technology, elementary education, multilingual education, physical education, reading, secondary education, special education; school administration (MA); school counseling (MA). *Program availability:* Part-time, evening/weekend. *Degree requirements:* For master's, comprehensive exam (for some programs), thesis (for some programs). *Entrance requirements:* For master's, MAT, GRE, or CBEST (varies by concentration), 3 letters of recommendation, personal statement. Additional exam requirements/recommendations for international students: Required—TOEFL (minimum score 550 paper-based). Electronic applications accepted. *Faculty research:* Children's perspectives on historical events, method elementary schools dual language education, K-12 reading programs.

California University of Pennsylvania, School of Graduate Studies and Research, College of Education and Human Services, Department of Childhood Education, California, PA 15419-1394. Offers early childhood education (M Ed); elementary education (M Ed); STEM education (M Ed). *Accreditation:* NCATE. *Program availability:* Part-time, evening/weekend. *Degree requirements:* For master's, comprehensive exam, thesis optional. *Entrance requirements:* For master's, MAT, PRAXIS, minimum GPA of 3.0, state police clearances. Additional exam requirements/recommendations for international students: Required—TOEFL (minimum score 550 paper-based; 80 iBT). *Application deadline:* For fall admission, 8/1 priority date for domestic and international students; for spring admission, 5/1 priority date for domestic and international students. Applications are processed on a rolling basis. Application fee: $25. Electronic applications accepted. *Financial support:* Applicants required to submit FAFSA. *Faculty research:* English as a second language, adult literacy, emerging literacy, diagnosis and remediation, phonemic awareness. *Unit head:* Dr. Diane H. Nettles, Department Chair, 724-938-4497, E-mail: nettles@calu.edu. *Application contact:* Suzanne C. Powers, Director of Graduate Admissions and Recruitment, 724-938-4029, Fax: 724-938-5712, E-mail: powers_s@cup.edu.
Website: http://www.calu.edu/academics/graduate-programs/elementary/

Calvary University, Graduate School and Seminary, Kansas City, MO 64147. Offers Bible and theology (MS); Biblical counseling (MA); education (MS), including administration and leadership, Christian education, curriculum and instruction, elementary education; organizational development (MS); pastoral studies (M Div); worship arts (MS). *Program availability:* Part-time, evening/weekend. *Faculty:* 6 full-time (2 women), 2 part-time/adjunct (1 woman). *Students:* 11 full-time (3 women), 29 part-time (15 women); includes 12 minority (4 Black or African American, non-Hispanic/Latino; 1 American Indian or Alaska Native, non-Hispanic/Latino; 6 Asian, non-Hispanic/Latino; 1 Native Hawaiian or other Pacific Islander, non-Hispanic/Latino). Average age 39. *Degree requirements:* For master's, variable foreign language requirement, comprehensive exam, thesis or alternative. *Entrance requirements:* For master's, minimum GPA of 2.5, BA or BS, doctrine agreement. Additional exam requirements/recommendations for international students: Required—TOEFL (minimum score 550 paper-based). *Application deadline:* Applications are processed on a rolling basis. Application fee: $0. Electronic applications accepted. *Expenses:* Contact institution. *Financial support:* Scholarships/grants available. Financial award application deadline: 11/5; financial award applicants required to submit FAFSA. *Unit head:* Dr. Thomas Baurain, Director of Seminary, 816-322-0110 Ext. 1502, Fax: 816-331-4474, E-mail: thomas.baurain@calvary.edu. *Application contact:* Ann Rogers, Admissions Office Assistant, 800-326-3960 Ext. 1321, Fax: 816-331-4474, E-mail: admissions@calvary.edu.
Website: http://www.calvary.edu

Cambridge College, School of Education, Boston, MA 02129. Offers autism specialist (M Ed); autism/behavior analyst (M Ed); behavior analyst (Post-Master's Certificate); behavioral management (M Ed); early childhood teacher (M Ed); education specialist in curriculum and instruction (CAGS); educational leadership (Ed D); elementary teacher (M Ed); English as a second language (M Ed, Certificate); general science (M Ed); health education (Post-Master's Certificate); health/family and consumer sciences (M Ed); history (M Ed); individualized (M Ed); information technology literacy (M Ed); instructional technology (M Ed); interdisciplinary studies (M Ed); library teacher (M Ed); literacy education (M Ed); mathematics (M Ed); mathematics specialist (Certificate);

middle school mathematics and science (M Ed); school administration (M Ed, CAGS); school guidance counselor (M Ed); school nurse education (M Ed); school social worker/school adjustment counselor (M Ed); special education administrator (CAGS); special education/moderate disabilities (M Ed); teaching skills and methodologies (M Ed). *Program availability:* Part-time, evening/weekend, online learning. *Degree requirements:* For master's, thesis, internship/practicum (licensure program only); for doctorate, thesis/dissertation; for other advanced degree, thesis. *Entrance requirements:* For master's, interview, resume, documentation of licensure, 2 professional references; for doctorate, official transcripts, interview, resume, documentation of licensure (if any), written personal statement/essay, portfolio of scholarly and professional work, qualifying assessment, 2 professional references, health insurance, immunizations form; for other advanced degree, official transcripts, interview, resume, documentation of licensure (if any), written personal statement/essay, 2 professional references, health insurance, immunizations form. Additional exam requirements/recommendations for international students: Required—TOEFL (minimum score 550 paper-based; 79 iBT), Michigan English Language Assessment Battery (minimum score 85); Recommended—IELTS (minimum score 6). Electronic applications accepted. *Expenses:* Contact institution. *Faculty research:* Adult education, accelerated learning, mathematics education, brain compatible learning, special education and law.

Campbell University, Graduate and Professional Programs, School of Education, Buies Creek, NC 27506. Offers elementary education (M Ed); interdisciplinary studies (M Ed); middle grades education (M Ed); physical education (M Ed); school administration (MSA); school counseling (M Ed); secondary education (M Ed). *Accreditation:* NCATE. *Program availability:* Part-time, evening/weekend. *Degree requirements:* For master's, comprehensive exam. *Entrance requirements:* For master's, GRE General Test, minimum GPA of 2.7. *Faculty research:* Spiritual values and wellness issues in counseling, stress and professional burnout among counselors, thinking strategies, leadership, adaptive technology.

Canisius College, Graduate Division, School of Education and Human Services, Department of Graduate Education and Leadership, Buffalo, NY 14208-1098. Offers business and marketing education (MS Ed); college student personnel (MS Ed); deaf education (MS Ed); deaf/adolescent education, grades 7-12 (MS Ed); deaf/childhood education, grades 1-6 (MS Ed); differentiated instruction (MS Ed); education administration (MS); educational administration (MS Ed); educational technologies (Certificate); gifted education extension (Certificate); literacy (MS Ed); reading (Certificate); school building leadership (MS Ed, Certificate); school district leadership (Certificate); teacher leader (Certificate); TESOL (MS Ed). *Accreditation:* NCATE. *Program availability:* Part-time, evening/weekend, 100% online, blended/hybrid learning. *Faculty:* 5 full-time (all women), 21 part-time/adjunct (16 women). *Students:* 85 full-time (67 women), 189 part-time (151 women); includes 31 minority (18 Black or African American, non-Hispanic/Latino; 3 American Indian or Alaska Native, non-Hispanic/Latino; 3 Asian, non-Hispanic/Latino; 4 Hispanic/Latino; 3 Two or more races, non-Hispanic/Latino), 1 international. Average age 31. 83 applicants, 96% accepted, 74 enrolled. In 2017, 94 master's, 47 other advanced degrees awarded. *Entrance requirements:* For master's, GRE (if cumulative GPA less than 2.7), transcripts, two letters of recommendation. Additional exam requirements/recommendations for international students: Required—TOEFL (minimum score 550 paper-based, 79 iBT), IELTS (minimum score 6.5), or CAEL (minimum score 70). *Application deadline:* Applications are processed on a rolling basis. Application fee: $0. Electronic applications accepted. *Expenses: Tuition:* Full-time $22,860; part-time $820 per credit. *Required fees:* $720; $25 per credit. $65 per semester. One-time fee: $425. *Financial support:* Career-related internships or fieldwork, Federal Work-Study, scholarships/grants, tuition waivers (partial), and unspecified assistantships available. Support available to part-time students. Financial award application deadline: 4/30; financial award applicants required to submit FAFSA. *Faculty research:* Asperger's disease, autism, private higher education, reading strategies. *Unit head:* Dr. Anne Marie Tryjankowski, Chair/Associate Professor of Graduate Education and Leadership, 716-888-3715, Fax: 716-888-3142, E-mail: tryjanka@canisius.edu.

Capella University, School of Education, Doctoral Programs in Education, Minneapolis, MN 55402. Offers curriculum and instruction (PhD); educational leadership and management (Ed D); instructional design for online learning (PhD); K-12 studies in education (PhD); leadership for higher education (PhD); leadership in educational administration (PhD); postsecondary and adult education (PhD); professional studies in education (PhD); reading and literacy (Ed D); special education leadership (PhD); training and performance improvement (PhD).

Capella University, School of Education, Master's Programs in Education, Minneapolis, MN 55402. Offers adult education (MS); curriculum and instruction (MS); early childhood education (MS); enrollment management (MS); higher education leadership and management (MS); instructional design for online learning (MS); integrative studies (MS); K-12 studies in education (MS); leadership in educational administration (MS); reading and literacy (MS); special education teaching (MS).

Caribbean University, Graduate School, Bayamón, PR 00960-0493. Offers administration and supervision (MA Ed); criminal justice (MA); curriculum and instruction (MA Ed, PhD), including elementary education (MA Ed), English education (MA Ed), history education (MA Ed), mathematics education (MA Ed), primary education (MA Ed), science education (MA Ed), Spanish education (MA Ed); educational technology in instructional systems (MA Ed); gerontology (MSN); human resources (MBA); museology, archiving and art history (MA Ed); neonatal pediatrics (MSN); physical education (MA Ed); special education (MA Ed). *Entrance requirements:* For master's, interview, minimum GPA of 2.5.

Carroll University, Graduate Programs in Education, Waukesha, WI 53186-5593. Offers adult and continuing education (M Ed); educational leadership (MS); PK-12 (M Ed). *Program availability:* Part-time, evening/weekend. *Degree requirements:* For master's, thesis. *Entrance requirements:* For master's, minimum undergraduate GPA of 2.5 in related field. Additional exam requirements/recommendations for international students: Required—TOEFL. Electronic applications accepted. *Faculty research:* Qualitative research methods, whole language approaches to teaching, the writing process, multicultural education, gifted/talented learners.

Carson-Newman University, Graduate Program in Education, Jefferson City, TN 37760. Offers curriculum and instruction (M Ed); educational leadership (M Ed); elementary education (MAT); school counseling (MS); secondary education (MAT); teaching English as a second language (MATESL). *Accreditation:* NCATE. *Program availability:* Part-time, evening/weekend, 100% online, blended/hybrid learning. *Faculty:* 20 full-time (11 women), 16 part-time/adjunct (13 women). *Students:* 63 full-time (37 women), 488 part-time (362 women); includes 60 minority (46 Black or African American, non-Hispanic/Latino; 2 American Indian or Alaska Native, non-Hispanic/Latino; 1 Asian, non-Hispanic/Latino; 5 Hispanic/Latino; 1 Native Hawaiian or other Pacific Islander, non-Hispanic/Latino; 5 Two or more races, non-Hispanic/Latino), 29 international. Average age 35. 204 applicants, 100% accepted, 188 enrolled. In 2017, 211 master's awarded. *Degree requirements:* For master's, thesis or alternative. *Entrance requirements:* For master's, PRAXIS II or GRE with minimum score of 290 on the verbal and quantitative components (for MAT), minimum GPA of 3.0 in major, 2.5 overall. Additional exam requirements/recommendations for international students:

Recommended—TOEFL (minimum score 79 iBT), IELTS (minimum score 6.5), TSE (minimum score 53). *Application deadline:* For fall admission, 7/15 priority date for domestic students. Applications are processed on a rolling basis. Application fee: $50. *Expenses: Tuition:* Full-time $10,516; part-time $478 per credit hour. *Required fees:* $240; $120 per semester. One-time fee: $150. *Financial support:* Federal Work-Study and unspecified assistantships available. Financial award applicants required to submit FAFSA. *Unit head:* Dr. Kim Hawkins, Chair, 865-471-3314, E-mail: khawkins@cn.edu. *Application contact:* Nilma Stewart, Graduate Admissions and Services Adviser, 865-471-3230, Fax: 865-471-3875, E-mail: adults@cn.edu. Website: http://www.cn.edu/adult-graduate-studies

Catawba College, Department of Teacher Education, Salisbury, NC 28144-2488. Offers STEM education (M Ed). *Accreditation:* NCATE. *Program availability:* Part-time-only. *Faculty:* 3 full-time (2 women), 4 part-time/adjunct (3 women). *Students:* 14 part-time (13 women); includes 1 minority (Black or African American, non-Hispanic/Latino). Average age 30. 7 applicants, 100% accepted, 7 enrolled. *Degree requirements:* For master's, portfolio. *Entrance requirements:* For master's, NTE, PRAXIS II, minimum undergraduate GPA of 3.0, valid teaching license, official transcripts, 3 references, essay, interview, practicing teacher. *Application deadline:* For spring admission, 10/1 for domestic students. Applications are processed on a rolling basis. Application fee: $25. Electronic applications accepted. *Expenses:* $190 per semester hour; $25 per semester parking fee. *Financial support:* In 2017–18, 12 students received support. Scholarships/grants and free tuition (for Rowan-Salisbury teachers only) available. Financial award application deadline: 10/1. *Unit head:* Dr. Kimberly Creamer, Director, Graduate Program, 704-637-4462, Fax: 704-637-4732, E-mail: kcreamer14@catawba.edu. *Application contact:* Jane V. Snider, Administrative Assistant, 704-637-4461, Fax: 704-637-4732, E-mail: jvsnider@catawba.edu. Website: http://catawba.edu/academics/schools/education/teacher-education/

Centenary College of Louisiana, Graduate Programs, Department of Education, Shreveport, LA 71104. Offers elementary education (MAT); secondary education (MAT). *Program availability:* Part-time, evening/weekend. *Degree requirements:* For master's, comprehensive exam. *Entrance requirements:* For master's, PRAXIS I and II (for MAT), undergraduate degree, minimum GPA of 2.5. *Expenses:* Contact institution. *Faculty research:* Teachers as advocates for teachers, portfolio assessment, disabled readers.

Central Connecticut State University, School of Graduate Studies, School of Education and Professional Studies, Department of Literacy, Elementary, and Early Childhood Education, New Britain, CT 06050-4010. Offers MS, AC, Sixth Year Certificate. *Program availability:* Part-time, evening/weekend. *Faculty:* 7 full-time (6 women), 1 (woman) part-time/adjunct. *Students:* 9 full-time (7 women), 109 part-time (101 women); includes 7 minority (1 Black or African American, non-Hispanic/Latino; 5 Hispanic/Latino; 1 Two or more races, non-Hispanic/Latino). Average age 31. 49 applicants, 73% accepted, 26 enrolled. In 2017, 44 master's, 10 other advanced degrees awarded. *Degree requirements:* For master's, comprehensive exam, thesis or alternative; for other advanced degree, qualifying exam. *Entrance requirements:* For master's, minimum undergraduate GPA of 2.7, teacher certification, interview, essay, letters of recommendation; for other advanced degree, master's degree, essay, teacher certification, interview, letters of recommendation. Additional exam requirements/recommendations for international students: Required—TOEFL (minimum score 550 paper-based; 79 iBT); Recommended—IELTS (minimum score 6.5). *Application deadline:* For fall admission, 8/1 for domestic students, 5/1 for international students; for spring admission, 11/1 for domestic and international students. Applications are processed on a rolling basis. Application fee: $50. Electronic applications accepted. *Expenses: Tuition, area resident:* Full-time $6757. Tuition, state resident: full-time $9750; part-time $374 per credit. Tuition, nonresident: full-time $18,102; part-time $374 per credit. *Required fees:* $4635; $255 per credit. *Financial support:* In 2017–18, 6 students received support. Career-related internships or fieldwork, Federal Work-Study, scholarships/grants, and unspecified assistantships available. Support available to part-time students. Financial award application deadline: 3/1. *Faculty research:* Developmental, clinical, and administrative aspects of reading and language arts instruction. *Unit head:* Dr. Helen Abadiano, Chair, 860-832-2175, E-mail: abadiano@ccsu.edu. *Application contact:* Patricia Gardner, Associate Director of Graduate Studies, 860-832-2350, Fax: 860-832-2362. Website: http://www.ccsu.edu/leece/index.html

Central Michigan University, Central Michigan University Global Campus, Program in Educational Leadership, Mount Pleasant, MI 48859. Offers K-12 leadership (Ed D). *Program availability:* Part-time, evening/weekend. *Entrance requirements:* Additional exam requirements/recommendations for international students: Required—TOEFL. Electronic applications accepted.

Central Michigan University, College of Graduate Studies, College of Education and Human Services, Department of Teacher Education and Professional Development, Mount Pleasant, MI 48859. Offers educational technology (MA, Graduate Certificate); elementary education (MA), including classroom teaching, early childhood; reading and literacy K-12 (MA); secondary education (MA). *Program availability:* Part-time, evening/weekend. *Degree requirements:* For master's, thesis or alternative. Electronic applications accepted. *Faculty research:* Integrating literacy across the curriculum, science teaching and aesthetic learning in science, diversity education, educational technology, educational psychology and child development.

Chadron State College, School of Professional and Graduate Studies, Department of Education, Chadron, NE 69337. Offers business (MA Ed); community counseling (MA Ed); educational administration (MS Ed, Sp Ed); elementary education (MS Ed); history (MA Ed); language and literature (MA Ed); secondary administration (MS Ed); secondary education (MS Ed). *Accreditation:* NCATE. *Program availability:* Part-time, evening/weekend, online learning. *Degree requirements:* For master's, thesis optional. *Entrance requirements:* For master's, GRE General Test, GRE Writing Test, minimum GPA of 2.75 or 12 graduate hours at CSC with minimum GPA of 3.25. Additional exam requirements/recommendations for international students: Required—TOEFL. Electronic applications accepted. *Faculty research:* Rural education, technology, mental health.

Chaminade University of Honolulu, Office of Professional and Continuing Education, Program in Education, Honolulu, HI 96816-1578. Offers child development (M Ed); early childhood education (Montessori) (MAT); early childhood education (PK-3) (MAT); educational leadership (M Ed); elementary education (MAT); instructional leadership (M Ed); Montessori (M Ed); secondary education (MAT); special education (MAT); teacher leader (M Ed). *Program availability:* Part-time, evening/weekend, 100% online, blended/hybrid learning. *Faculty:* 7 full-time (3 women), 8 part-time/adjunct (6 women). *Students:* 86 full-time (68 women), 88 part-time (64 women); includes 113 minority (7 Black or African American, non-Hispanic/Latino; 2 American Indian or Alaska Native, non-Hispanic/Latino; 46 Asian, non-Hispanic/Latino; 7 Hispanic/Latino; 51 Native Hawaiian or other Pacific Islander, non-Hispanic/Latino), 6 international. Average age 34. 61 applicants, 98% accepted, 49 enrolled. In 2017, 91 master's awarded. *Degree requirements:* For master's, thesis or alternative. *Entrance requirements:* For master's, PRAXIS (for MAT), minimum GPA of 2.75 (for M Ed), 3.0 (for MAT); 2 letters of recommendation, resume, writing sample (for MAT). Additional exam requirements/recommendations for international students: Required—TOEFL (minimum score 550

Elementary Education

paper-based; 79 iBT). *Application deadline:* Applications are processed on a rolling basis. Application fee: $40. Electronic applications accepted. *Expenses:* $780 per credit hour plus $93 fee per online class. *Financial support:* Applicants required to submit FAFSA. *Unit head:* Dr. Dale Fryxell, Dean, 808-739-4652, Fax: 808-739-4607, E-mail: edu-office@chaminade.edu. *Application contact:* 808-735-4755, E-mail: gradserv@chaminade.edu.
Website: https://education.chaminade.edu/

Chapman University, Donna Ford Attallah College of Educational Studies, Orange, CA 92866. Offers counseling (MA), including school counseling (MA, Credential); curriculum and instruction (MA), including elementary education, secondary education; education (PhD), including cultural and curricular studies, disability studies, leadership studies, school psychology (PhD, Credential); educational psychology (MA); leadership development (MA); multiple subjects (Credential), including Spanish/English bilingual; pupil personnel services (Credential), including school counseling (MA, Credential), school psychology (PhD, Credential); school psychology (Ed S); single subject (Credential); special education (MA, Credential), including mild/moderate (Credential), moderate/severe (Credential); teaching (MA), including elementary education, secondary education, secondary music education. *Accreditation:* TEAC. *Program availability:* Part-time, evening/weekend. *Faculty:* 32 full-time (18 women), 37 part-time/adjunct (26 women). *Students:* 170 full-time (140 women), 180 part-time (129 women); includes 164 minority (6 Black or African American, non-Hispanic/Latino; 38 Asian, non-Hispanic/Latino; 101 Hispanic/Latino; 1 Native Hawaiian or other Pacific Islander, non-Hispanic/Latino; 18 Two or more races, non-Hispanic/Latino), 10 international. Average age 28. 143 applicants, 63% accepted, 64 enrolled. In 2017, 126 master's, 18 doctorates awarded. *Application deadline:* Applications are processed on a rolling basis. Application fee: $60. Electronic applications accepted. *Expenses:* Contact institution. *Financial support:* Fellowships and scholarships/grants available. Financial award application deadline: 3/2; financial award applicants required to submit FAFSA. *Unit head:* Dr. Margaret Grogan, Dean, 714-516-5968, E-mail: grogan@chapman.edu. *Application contact:* Shannon McCance, Graduate Admission Counselor, 714-516-5236, E-mail: smccance@chapman.edu.
Website: http://www.chapman.edu/CES/

Charleston Southern University, College of Education, Charleston, SC 29423-8087. Offers elementary administration and supervision (M Ed); elementary education (M Ed); secondary administration and supervision (M Ed). *Accreditation:* NCATE. *Program availability:* Part-time, evening/weekend. *Degree requirements:* For master's, thesis optional. *Entrance requirements:* For master's, GRE or MAT. Additional exam requirements/recommendations for international students: Required—TOEFL (minimum score 550 paper-based; 79 iBT). *Application deadline:* Applications are processed on a rolling basis. Application fee: $40. Electronic applications accepted. *Expenses:* Contact institution. *Financial support:* Research assistantships with full tuition reimbursements, career-related internships or fieldwork, and Federal Work-Study available. Financial award application deadline: 4/15; financial award applicants required to submit FAFSA. *Unit head:* Dr. George Metz, Dean, 843-863-7765, Fax: 843-863-7784, E-mail: gmetz@csuniv.edu.
Website: http://www.csuniv.edu/education/

Chatham University, Program in Education, Pittsburgh, PA 15232-2826. Offers early childhood education (MAT); elementary education (MAT); environmental education (K-12) (MAT); secondary art (MAT); secondary biology education (MAT); secondary chemistry education (MAT); secondary English education (MAT); secondary math education (MAT); secondary physics education (MAT); secondary social studies education (MAT); special education (MAT). *Faculty:* 1 (woman) full-time, 15 part-time/adjunct (13 women). *Students:* 31 full-time (23 women), 3 part-time (1 woman); includes 9 minority (8 Black or African American, non-Hispanic/Latino; 1 Hispanic/Latino). Average age 30. 25 applicants, 60% accepted, 9 enrolled. In 2017, 23 master's awarded. *Degree requirements:* For master's, thesis, teaching experience. *Entrance requirements:* For master's, minimum GPA of 3.0, sample of written work, recommendation letters. Additional exam requirements/recommendations for international students: Required—TOEFL (minimum score 600 paper-based; 100 iBT), IELTS (minimum score 7), TWE. *Application deadline:* For fall admission, 4/1 priority date for domestic and international students; for spring admission, 11/1 priority date for domestic students, 10/1 priority date for international students. Applications are processed on a rolling basis. Application fee: $45. Electronic applications accepted. Application fee is waived when completed online. *Expenses: Tuition:* Full-time $16,740; part-time $930 per credit. *Required fees:* $486; $27 per credit. $243 per semester. *Financial support:* Career-related internships or fieldwork available. Financial award applicants required to submit FAFSA. *Faculty research:* Gifted education, environmental education, technology in education, writing as learning, class size and achievement. *Application contact:* Katie Noel, Assistant Director of Graduate Admission, 412-365-2758, Fax: 412-365-1609, E-mail: gradadmissions@chatham.edu.
Website: http://www.chatham.edu/mat

Chestnut Hill College, School of Graduate Studies, Department of Education, Program in Elementary/Middle Education, Philadelphia, PA 19118-2693. Offers M Ed. *Program availability:* Part-time, evening/weekend. *Degree requirements:* For master's, thesis optional. *Entrance requirements:* For master's, PRAXIS I or proof of teaching certification, letters of recommendation, writing sample, 6 graduate credits with minimum B grade if undergraduate GPA less than 3.0. Additional exam requirements/recommendations for international students: Required—TOEFL (minimum score 500 paper-based), IELTS (minimum score 6.0), or TWE (minimum score 22). Electronic applications accepted. *Expenses:* Contact institution. *Faculty research:* Inclusive education, cultural issues in education.

Cheyney University of Pennsylvania, Graduate Programs, Program in Elementary Education, Cheyney, PA 19319. Offers M Ed. *Program availability:* Part-time, evening/weekend. *Degree requirements:* For master's, thesis. *Entrance requirements:* For master's, GRE General Test, MAT, minimum GPA of 2.75. Electronic applications accepted.

Chicago State University, School of Graduate and Professional Studies, College of Education, Department of Educational Leadership, Curriculum and Foundations, Program in Curriculum and Instruction, Chicago, IL 60628. Offers instructional foundations (MS Ed), including adult education, elementary education, secondary education. *Degree requirements:* For master's, comprehensive exam, thesis optional. *Entrance requirements:* For master's, minimum GPA of 2.75. *Application deadline:* For fall admission, 7/1 for domestic students; for spring admission, 11/10 for domestic students. Application fee: $25. *Unit head:* Dr. Cathryn Busch, Chairperson. *Application contact:* Anika Miller, Graduate Studies Office, 773-995-2404, E-mail: g-studies1@csu.edu.

Chicago State University, School of Graduate and Professional Studies, College of Education, Department of Reading, Elementary Education, Library Information and Media Studies, Program in Elementary Education, Chicago, IL 60628. Offers MAT. *Accreditation:* NCATE. *Degree requirements:* For master's, comprehensive exam, thesis optional. *Entrance requirements:* For master's, minimum GPA of 3.0 in last 60 hours. *Application deadline:* For fall admission, 7/1 for domestic students; for spring admission, 11/10 for domestic students. Application fee: $25. *Unit head:* Dr. Margaret Kelly,

Chairperson, 773-995-2059, E-mail: mkelly@csu.edu. *Application contact:* Anika Miller, Graduate Studies Office, 773-995-2404, E-mail: g-studies1@csu.edu.

City University of Seattle, Graduate Division, Albright School of Education, Seattle, WA 98121. Offers administrator certification (Certificate); curriculum and instruction (M Ed); elementary education (MIT); guidance and counseling (M Ed); leadership (M Ed); reading and literacy (M Ed); school counseling (M Ed); special education (MIT); superintendent certification (Certificate). *Program availability:* Part-time, evening/weekend, online learning. *Degree requirements:* For master's, comprehensive exam (for some programs), thesis (for some programs). *Entrance requirements:* For master's, baccalaureate degree or equivalent from an accredited or otherwise recognized institution. Additional exam requirements/recommendations for international students: Required—TOEFL (minimum score 567 paper-based; 87 iBT); Recommended—IELTS. Electronic applications accepted. *Expenses:* Contact institution.

Clemson University, Graduate School, College of Education, Department of Educational and Organizational Leadership Development, Clemson, SC 29634. Offers administration and supervision (M Ed, Ed S); athletic leadership (MS, Certificate); education systems improvement science (Ed D); educational leadership (PhD), including higher education, P-12; human resource development (MHRD), including human resource development; leadership (Certificate); student affairs (M Ed). *Program availability:* Part-time, evening/weekend, 100% online. *Faculty:* 21 full-time (14 women), 1 part-time/adjunct (0 women). *Students:* 55 full-time (32 women), 285 part-time (169 women); includes 89 minority (71 Black or African American, non-Hispanic/Latino; 1 American Indian or Alaska Native, non-Hispanic/Latino; 1 Asian, non-Hispanic/Latino; 13 Hispanic/Latino; 3 Two or more races, non-Hispanic/Latino), 2 international. Average age 35. 216 applicants, 69% accepted, 100 enrolled. In 2017, 58 master's, 16 doctorates, 20 other advanced degrees awarded. *Degree requirements:* For master's, thesis (for some programs); for doctorate, comprehensive exam, thesis/dissertation. *Entrance requirements:* For master's, doctorate, and other advanced degree, GRE General Test, unofficial transcripts, letters of recommendation. Additional exam requirements/recommendations for international students: Required—TOEFL (minimum score 80 iBT), IELTS (minimum score 7), PTE (minimum score 54). *Application deadline:* For fall admission, 3/1 priority date for domestic and international students; for spring admission, 10/1 priority date for domestic and international students. Applications are processed on a rolling basis. Application fee: $80 ($90 for international students). Electronic applications accepted. *Expenses:* $5,174 per semester full-time resident, $9,714 per semester full-time non-resident, $511 per credit hour part-time resident, $1,017 per credit hour part-time non-resident; $741 per credit hour online; other fees may apply per session. *Financial support:* In 2017–18, 20 students received support, including 4 fellowships with partial tuition reimbursements available (averaging $8,750 per year), 1 research assistantship with partial tuition reimbursement available (averaging $9,378 per year); career-related internships or fieldwork and unspecified assistantships also available. Financial award application deadline: 3/1. *Total annual research expenditures:* $31,201. *Unit head:* Dr. Roy Jones, Interim Department Chair, 864-656-7915, E-mail: royj@clemson.edu. *Application contact:* Alison Search, Student Services Program Coordinator, 864-250-8880, E-mail: alisonp@clemson.edu.
Website: http://www.clemson.edu/education/departments/educational-organizational-leadership-development/index.html

College of Charleston, Graduate School, School of Education, Health, and Human Performance, Department of Elementary and Early Childhood Education, Program in Elementary Education, Charleston, SC 29424-0001. Offers MAT. *Accreditation:* NCATE. *Program availability:* Part-time, evening/weekend. *Degree requirements:* For master's, thesis or alternative, written qualifying exam, student teaching experience. *Entrance requirements:* For master's, GRE, 2 letters of recommendation. Additional exam requirements/recommendations for international students: Required—TOEFL (minimum score 81 iBT). Electronic applications accepted.

The College of New Jersey, Office of Graduate and Advancing Education, School of Education, Department of Elementary and Early Childhood Education, Program in Elementary Education, Ewing, NJ 08628. Offers M Ed, MAT. *Accreditation:* NCATE. *Program availability:* Part-time. *Degree requirements:* For master's, comprehensive exam. *Entrance requirements:* For master's, GRE General Test, minimum GPA of 3.0 in field or 2.75 overall. Additional exam requirements/recommendations for international students: Required—TOEFL. Electronic applications accepted.

The College of New Rochelle, Graduate School, Division of Education, Program in Childhood Education/Early Childhood Education, New Rochelle, NY 10805-2308. Offers childhood education (MS Ed); early childhood education (MS Ed). *Program availability:* Part-time. *Degree requirements:* For master's, comprehensive exam (for some programs), thesis (for some programs), practicum. *Entrance requirements:* For master's, interview, minimum GPA of 3.0 in field, 2.7 overall. *Expenses: Tuition:* Full-time $17,406. *Required fees:* $1120.

College of Saint Elizabeth, Program in Education, Morristown, NJ 07960-6989. Offers assistive technology (Certificate); education (MA); ESL (Certificate); Holocaust/genocide education (Certificate); middle school science (Certificate); online teaching in the 21st century (Certificate); teaching (Certificate), including K-12, K-6, teacher of students with disabilities. *Program availability:* Part-time. *Faculty:* 3 full-time (2 women), 8 part-time/adjunct (6 women). *Students:* 1 (woman) full-time, 34 part-time (29 women); includes 1 minority (Hispanic/Latino). Average age 32. 25 applicants, 100% accepted, 24 enrolled. In 2017, 23 master's awarded. *Degree requirements:* For master's and Certificate, thesis. *Entrance requirements:* For master's, certification. Additional exam requirements/recommendations for international students: Required—TOEFL (minimum score 550 paper-based; 79 iBT), IELTS (minimum score 6.5). *Application deadline:* For fall admission, 5/1 for international students. Applications are processed on a rolling basis. Application fee: $35. Electronic applications accepted. Application fee is waived when completed online. *Financial support:* Career-related internships or fieldwork, scholarships/grants, and unspecified assistantships available. Financial award applicants required to submit FAFSA. *Unit head:* Dr. Joseph Ciccone, 973-290-4383, Fax: 973-290-4389, E-mail: jciccone@cse.edu. *Application contact:* Lori J. Fragoso, Director of Graduate and Continuing Studies Admissions, 973-290-4413, Fax: 973-290-4710, E-mail: apply@cse.edu.
Website: http://www.cse.edu/academics/prof-studies/education/

College of St. Joseph, Graduate Programs, Division of Education, Program in Elementary Education, Rutland, VT 05701-3899. Offers M Ed. *Program availability:* Part-time, evening/weekend. *Degree requirements:* For master's, comprehensive exam. *Entrance requirements:* For master's, PRAXIS I (for initial licensure), official college transcripts; 2 letters of reference; minimum GPA of 3.0 (initial licensure) or 2.7 (nonlicensure); interview. Additional exam requirements/recommendations for international students: Required—TOEFL (minimum score 550 paper-based). Electronic applications accepted.

College of Staten Island of the City University of New York, Graduate Programs, School of Education, Program in Childhood Education, Staten Island, NY 10314-6600. Offers childhood (MS Ed). *Program availability:* Part-time, evening/weekend. *Faculty:* 4 part-time/adjunct (3 women). *Students:* 64. 27 applicants, 48% accepted, 10 enrolled. In 2017, 23 master's awarded. *Degree requirements:* For master's, educational research

project. *Entrance requirements:* For master's, GRE General Test or approved equivalent examination, relevant bachelor's degree, letters of recommendation, one- or two-page personal statement. Additional exam requirements/recommendations for international students: Required—TOEFL (minimum score 550 paper-based; 79 iBT), IELTS (minimum score 6.5). *Application deadline:* For fall admission, 4/25 for domestic and international students; for spring admission, 11/25 for domestic and international students. Applications are processed on a rolling basis. Application fee: $125. Electronic applications accepted. *Expenses:* Tuition, state resident: full-time $10,450; part-time $440 per credit. Tuition, nonresident: full-time $19,320; part-time $440 per credit. *Required fees:* $181.10 per semester. Tuition and fees vary according to program. *Faculty research:* Preservice teacher preparation, music integration, music education through children's songs, literacy, emergent bilingual. *Unit head:* Diane Brescia, 718-982-3877, E-mail: diane.brescia@csi.cuny.edu. *Application contact:* Sasha Spence, Associate Director for Graduate Admissions, 718-982-2019, Fax: 718-982-2500, E-mail: sasha.spence@csi.cuny.edu.
Website: https://www.csi.cuny.edu/sites/default/files/pdf/admissions/grad/pdf/Education%20Fact%20Sheet.pdf

College of Staten Island of the City University of New York, Graduate Programs, School of Education, Program in Special Education, Staten Island, NY 10314-6600. Offers special education (MS Ed), including adolescence generalist: grades 7-12, grades 1-6. *Program availability:* Part-time, evening/weekend. *Faculty:* 3 full-time, 6 part-time/adjunct. *Students:* 144. 73 applicants, 73% accepted, 41 enrolled. In 2017, 39 master's awarded. *Degree requirements:* For master's, comprehensive exam, fieldwork; ten three-credit required courses and one elective for a total of 11 courses (33 credits) or 14 three-credit required courses and a three- to six-credit, field-based requirement for a total of 45-48 credits; research project. *Entrance requirements:* For master's, GRE General Test or an approved equivalent examination, BA/BS or 36 approved credits with minimum GPA of 3.0, 2 letters of recommendations, 1-2 page statement of experience. Additional exam requirements/recommendations for international students: Required—TOEFL (minimum score 550 paper-based; 79 iBT), IELTS (minimum score 6.5). *Application deadline:* For fall admission, 4/25 for domestic and international students; for spring admission, 11/25 for domestic and international students. Applications are processed on a rolling basis. Application fee: $125. Electronic applications accepted. *Expenses:* Tuition, state resident: full-time $10,450; part-time $440 per credit. Tuition, nonresident: full-time $19,320; part-time $440 per credit. *Required fees:* $181.10 per semester. Tuition and fees vary according to program. *Faculty research:* Disabilities studies, social justice, arts-based research on disabilities, assessment of students with disabilities, technological pedagogical and content knowledge (TPACK) in special education teachers, juvenile justice. *Unit head:* Diane Brescia, 718-982-3877, E-mail: diane.brescia@csi.cuny.edu. *Application contact:* Sasha Spence, Associate Director for Graduate Admissions, 718-982-2019, Fax: 718-982-2500, E-mail: sasha.spence@csi.cuny.edu.
Website: https://www.csi.cuny.edu/sites/default/files/pdf/admissions/grad/pdf/Education%20Fact%20Sheet.pdf

The College of William and Mary, School of Education, Program in Curriculum and Instruction, Williamsburg, VA 23187-8795. Offers elementary education (MA Ed); English as a second language/bilingual education (MA Ed); gifted education (MA Ed); literacy leadership (MA Ed); math specialist (MA Ed); secondary education (MA Ed), including English, foreign language, math, science, social studies; special education (MA Ed). *Accreditation:* NCATE. *Program availability:* Part-time. *Faculty:* 23 full-time (16 women), 40 part-time/adjunct (32 women). *Students:* 85 full-time (63 women), 16 part-time (15 women); includes 18 minority (5 Black or African American, non-Hispanic/Latino; 4 Asian, non-Hispanic/Latino; 7 Hispanic/Latino; 2 Two or more races, non-Hispanic/Latino), 1 international. Average age 27. 152 applicants, 83% accepted, 90 enrolled. In 2017, 67 master's awarded. *Degree requirements:* For master's, project. *Entrance requirements:* For master's, GRE, MAT, PRAXIS Core Academic Skills for Educators, minimum GPA of 2.5. Additional exam requirements/recommendations for international students: Required—TOEFL (minimum score 100 iBT), IELTS (minimum score 7). *Application deadline:* For fall admission, 1/15 for domestic and international students; for spring admission, 10/1 for domestic and international students. Application fee: $50. Electronic applications accepted. *Expenses:* $9,630 resident full-time, $535 resident part-time per credit hour; $25,920 nonresident full-time, $1,265 nonresident part-time per credit hour; $5,944 full-time fees. *Financial support:* In 2017–18, 35 students received support, including 7 research assistantships (averaging $6,678 per year); scholarships/grants and unspecified assistantships also available. Financial award application deadline: 1/15; financial award applicants required to submit FAFSA. *Faculty research:* Educational technology, professional development and evaluation, inclusive education, rural education, education policy. *Unit head:* Dr. Jeremy D. Stoddard, Department Chair, 757-221-2348, E-mail: jdstod@wm.edu. *Application contact:* Dorothy Smith Osborne, Assistant Dean for Academic Programs and Student Services, 757-221-2317, E-mail: dsosbo@wm.edu.
Website: http://education.wm.edu

Colorado Christian University, Program in Curriculum and Instruction, Lakewood, CO 80226. Offers corporate education (MACI); early childhood educator (MACI); elementary educator (MACI); instructional technology (MACI); master educator (MACI); online course developer (MACI); online teaching and learning (MACI); special education generalist (MACI). *Program availability:* Part-time, evening/weekend. *Degree requirements:* For master's, thesis optional, practicum. *Entrance requirements:* For master's, interviews, letters of recommendation. Additional exam requirements/recommendations for international students: Required—TOEFL. Electronic applications accepted. *Expenses:* Contact institution.

The Colorado College, Education Department, Program in Elementary Education, Colorado Springs, CO 80903-3294. Offers elementary school teaching (MAT). *Degree requirements:* For master's, thesis, internship. Electronic applications accepted.

Columbia College, Graduate Programs, Education Division, Columbia, SC 29203-5998. Offers divergent learning (M Ed); higher education administration (M Ed). *Accreditation:* NCATE. *Program availability:* Part-time, evening/weekend, online learning. *Degree requirements:* For master's, thesis. *Entrance requirements:* For master's, GRE General Test, MAT, 2 recommendations, current South Carolina teaching certificate, minimum GPA of 3.2. *Application deadline:* For fall admission, 8/22 for domestic students. Application fee: $50. Electronic applications accepted. *Expenses:* Contact institution. *Financial support:* Available to part-time students. Application deadline: 7/1; applicants required to submit FAFSA. *Application contact:* Myles Hacking, Associate Dean of Admissions, 803-786-3871, Fax: 803-786-3674, E-mail: mhacking@columbiasc.edu.

Columbia International University, Columbia Graduate School, Columbia, SC 29203. Offers Bible teaching (MABT); counseling (MACN); early childhood and elementary education (MAT); educational administration (M Ed); educational leadership (PhD); instruction and learning (M Ed); teaching English as a foreign language (Certificate); teaching English as a foreign language and intercultural studies (MATF). *Program availability:* Part-time, evening/weekend, online learning. *Degree requirements:* For master's, internships, professional project. *Entrance requirements:* For master's, MAT; GRE (for some programs), minimum GPA of 2.7. Additional exam requirements/

recommendations for international students: Required—TOEFL. Electronic applications accepted.

Concordia University, College of Education, Portland, OR 97211-6099. Offers career and technical education (M Ed); curriculum and instruction (M Ed), including adolescent literacy, career and technical education, e-learning/technology education, early childhood education, English for speakers of other languages, English language development, environmental education, mathematics, methods and curriculum, reading, science, teacher leadership, the inclusive classroom; early childhood (MAT); education leadership (Ed D); educational administration (M Ed); elementary education (MAT); secondary education (MAT); special education (M Ed); teacher leadership (Ed D). *Program availability:* Part-time, online learning. *Degree requirements:* For master's, comprehensive exam, work samples/portfolio. *Entrance requirements:* For master's, California Basic Educational Skills Test or PRAXIS I, minimum undergraduate GPA of 2.8, graduate 3.0; 2 letters of recommendation. Additional exam requirements/recommendations for international students: Required—TOEFL (minimum score 525 paper-based). Electronic applications accepted. *Faculty research:* Learner-centered classroom, brain-based learning, future of online learning.

Concordia University Chicago, College of Education, Program in Teaching, River Forest, IL 60305-1499. Offers early childhood education (MAT); elementary education (MAT); secondary education (MAT). *Degree requirements:* For master's, thesis or alternative. *Entrance requirements:* For master's, minimum GPA of 2.9. Additional exam requirements/recommendations for international students: Required—TOEFL (minimum score 550 paper-based). Electronic applications accepted.

Concordia University, Nebraska, Graduate Programs in Education, Program in Educational Administration, Seward, NE 68434. Offers elementary and secondary education (M Ed); elementary education (M Ed); secondary education (M Ed). *Accreditation:* NCATE. *Program availability:* Part-time. *Degree requirements:* For master's, thesis or alternative. *Entrance requirements:* For master's, GRE, MAT, or NTE, BS in education or equivalent, minimum GPA of 3.0.

Converse College, Program in Elementary Education, Spartanburg, SC 29302. Offers M Ed, MAT. *Program availability:* Part-time. *Degree requirements:* For master's, capstone paper. *Entrance requirements:* For master's, NTE or PRAXIS II (M Ed), minimum GPA of 2.75, 2 recommendations. *Application deadline:* For fall admission, 8/1 for domestic and international students; for winter admission, 11/15 for domestic and international students; for spring admission, 1/15 for domestic and international students. Applications are processed on a rolling basis. Application fee: $40. Electronic applications accepted. *Financial support:* Available to part-time students. Applicants required to submit FAFSA. *Unit head:* Dean of Graduate Studies and Distance Education, 864-596-9082, E-mail: lienne.medford@converse.edu. *Application contact:* 864-596-9404, E-mail: graduate@converse.edu.

Creighton University, Graduate School, College of Arts and Sciences, Department of Education, Program in Teaching, Omaha, NE 68178-0001. Offers elementary teaching (M Ed); secondary teaching (M Ed). *Program availability:* Part-time. *Faculty:* 10 full-time (5 women). *Students:* 8 full-time (6 women), 22 part-time (17 women); includes 1 minority (Asian, non-Hispanic/Latino). Average age 26. In 2017, 23 master's awarded. *Degree requirements:* For master's, portfolio. *Entrance requirements:* For master's, 3 letters of recommendation, 2 writing samples. Additional exam requirements/recommendations for international students: Required—TOEFL (minimum score 90 iBT). *Application deadline:* For fall admission, 7/1 priority date for domestic students, 3/1 priority date for international students; for winter admission, 12/1 priority date for domestic students, 6/1 priority date for international students; for spring admission, 3/1 priority date for domestic and international students; for summer admission, 3/1 for domestic and international students. Application fee: $50. Electronic applications accepted. Part-time tuition and fees vary according to course load, degree level, campus/location and program. *Financial support:* Scholarships/grants and tuition waivers (partial) available. Support available to part-time students. Financial award applicants required to submit FAFSA. *Unit head:* Dr. Debra Ponec, Director, 402-280-2557, E-mail: dlponec@creighton.edu. *Application contact:* Lindsay Johnson, Director of Graduate and Adult Recruitment, 402-280-2703, Fax: 402-280-2423, E-mail: gradschool@creighton.edu.

Curry College, Graduate Studies, Program in Education, Milton, MA 02186-9984. Offers elementary education (M Ed); foundations (non-license) (M Ed); reading (M Ed, Certificate); special education (M Ed). *Program availability:* Part-time, evening/weekend. *Degree requirements:* For master's, project or thesis. *Entrance requirements:* For master's, interview, recommendations, resume, written statement. Additional exam requirements/recommendations for international students: Required—TOEFL (minimum score 550 paper-based; 80 iBT). *Expenses:* Contact institution. *Faculty research:* Classroom trauma, therapeutic writing, inclusionary practices.

Dallas Baptist University, Dorothy M. Bush College of Education, Teaching Program, Dallas, TX 75211-9299. Offers distance learning (MAT); early childhood through grade 6 certification (MAT); early childhood-12 (MAT); elementary (MAT); English as a second language (MAT); Montessori (MAT); multisensory (MAT); secondary (MAT). *Program availability:* Part-time, evening/weekend. *Application deadline:* Applications are processed on a rolling basis. Application fee: $25. Electronic applications accepted. Application fee is waived when completed online. *Expenses:* Tuition: Full-time $16,308; part-time $906 per credit hour. *Required fees:* $900; $450 per semester. Tuition and fees vary according to course load and degree level. *Unit head:* Dr. Neil Dugger, Dean, 214-333-5202, E-mail: neil@dbu.edu. *Application contact:* Dr. DeAnna Jenkins, Program Director, 214-333-5402, E-mail: deannaj@dbu.edu.
Website: http://www3.dbu.edu/graduate/mat.asp

Delta State University, Graduate Programs, College of Education, Division of Teacher Education, Leadership, and Research, Program in Professional Studies, Cleveland, MS 38733-0001. Offers counselor education (Ed D); elementary education (Ed D); higher education (Ed D). *Program availability:* Part-time, evening/weekend. *Degree requirements:* For doctorate, thesis/dissertation. *Entrance requirements:* For doctorate, GRE General Test.

Delta State University, Graduate Programs, College of Education, Division of Teacher Education, Leadership, and Research, Programs in Elementary Education, Cleveland, MS 38733-0001. Offers M Ed, MAT, Ed S. *Accreditation:* NCATE. *Program availability:* Part-time, evening/weekend. *Degree requirements:* For master's, thesis optional. *Entrance requirements:* For master's, GRE General Test; for Ed S, master's degree, teaching certificate.

DePaul University, College of Education, Chicago, IL 60614. Offers bilingual-bicultural education (M Ed, MA); counseling (M Ed, MA), including clinical mental health counseling, college student development, school counseling; curriculum studies (M Ed, MA, Ed D); early childhood education (M Ed, MA, Ed D); educational leadership (M Ed, MA, Ed D), including Catholic leadership (M Ed, MA), general (M Ed, MA), higher education (M Ed, MA), physical education (M Ed, MA), principal preparation (M Ed, MA), teacher preparation (M Ed); elementary education (M Ed, MA); middle grades education (M Ed); middle school mathematics education (MS); reading specialist (M Ed, MA); secondary education (M Ed, MA); social and cultural foundations in education (M Ed, MA); special education (M Ed); sport, fitness and recreation leadership (MS); value-

Elementary Education

creating education for global citizenship (M Ed); world languages education (M Ed, MA). *Program availability:* Part-time, evening/weekend, online learning. *Degree requirements:* For doctorate, thesis/dissertation. *Application deadline:* Applications are processed on a rolling basis. Application fee: $40. Electronic applications accepted. *Financial support:* Application deadline: 12/31; applicants required to submit FAFSA. *Unit head:* Dr. Paul Zionts, Dean, 773-325-7581, Fax: 773-325-7713, E-mail: pzionts@depaul.edu. *Application contact:* Dr. Paul Zionts, Dean, 773-325-7581, Fax: 773-325-7713, E-mail: pzionts@depaul.edu.
Website: http://education.depaul.edu

Dominican College, Division of Teacher Education, Orangeburg, NY 10962-1210. Offers education/teaching of individuals with multiple disabilities (MS Ed). *Program availability:* Part-time, evening/weekend, online learning. *Faculty:* 2 full-time (1 woman), 7 part-time/adjunct (all women). *Students:* 3 full-time (all women), 48 part-time (30 women); includes 9 minority (1 Black or African American, non-Hispanic/Latino; 1 Asian, non-Hispanic/Latino; 7 Hispanic/Latino). In 2017, 18 master's awarded. *Degree requirements:* For master's, comprehensive exam (for some programs), thesis. *Entrance requirements:* For master's, 3 letters of recommendation (written by former or current work supervisors or instructors), interview. Additional exam requirements/recommendations for international students: Required—TOEFL (minimum score 90 iBT). *Application deadline:* Applications are processed on a rolling basis. *Expenses: Tuition:* Part-time $900 per credit. One-time fee: $200. Tuition and fees vary according to degree level and program. *Financial support:* Application deadline: 2/1; applicants required to submit FAFSA. *Unit head:* Dr. Mike Kelly, Director, 845-848-4090, Fax: 845-359-7802, E-mail: mike.kelly@dc.edu. *Application contact:* Christina Lifshey, Assistant Director of Graduate Admissions, 845-848-7908 Ext. 15, Fax: 845-365-3150, E-mail: admissions@dc.edu.

Dominican University, School of Education, River Forest, IL 60305-1099. Offers child life studies (MS); early childhood education (MS); education (MAT); elementary education (MA Ed); English as a second language (MA Ed); reading (MA Ed); secondary education (MAT); special education (MS). *Accreditation:* NCATE. *Program availability:* Part-time, evening/weekend, 100% online, blended/hybrid learning. *Faculty:* 8 full-time (6 women), 42 part-time/adjunct (38 women). *Students:* 5 full-time (all women), 261 part-time (206 women); includes 45 minority (16 Black or African American, non-Hispanic/Latino; 1 American Indian or Alaska Native, non-Hispanic/Latino; 5 Asian, non-Hispanic/Latino; 18 Hispanic/Latino; 5 Two or more races, non-Hispanic/Latino), 1 international. Average age 32. 95 applicants, 98% accepted, 72 enrolled. In 2017, 206 master's awarded. *Entrance requirements:* For master's, Illinois Test of Basic Skills. Additional exam requirements/recommendations for international students: Required—TOEFL (minimum score 550 paper-based; 79 iBT). *Application deadline:* Applications are processed on a rolling basis. Application fee: $25. *Expenses:* Contact institution. *Financial support:* Career-related internships or fieldwork, scholarships/grants, tuition waivers (partial), and unspecified assistantships available. Support available to part-time students. Financial award application deadline: 8/15; financial award applicants required to submit FAFSA. *Faculty research:* Governance of private education institutions, reading and language arts, inclusion, organizational planning, leadership and vision. *Unit head:* Dr. Colleen Reardon, Interim Executive Director, School of Education, 708-524-6643, Fax: 708-524-6665, E-mail: creardon@dom.edu. *Application contact:* Benjamin Mueller, Senior Graduate Marketing and Recruitment Coordinator, 708-524-6456, Fax: 708-524-6665, E-mail: bmueller@dom.edu.
Website: http://educate.dom.edu/

Drew University, Caspersen School of Graduate Studies, Madison, NJ 07940-1493. Offers conflict resolution and leadership (Certificate), including community leadership, moderation, peace building; education (M Ed); finance (MA); history and culture (MA, PhD), including American history, book history, British history, European history, Holocaust and genocide (M Litt, MA, D Litt, PhD), intellectual history, Irish history, print culture, public history; K-12 education (MAT), including art, biology, chemistry, elementary education, English, French, Italian, math, secondary education, special education, teacher of students with disabilities; liberal studies (M Litt, D Litt), including history, Holocaust and genocide (M Litt, MA, D Litt, PhD), Irish/Irish-American studies, literature (M Litt, MMH, D Litt, DMH, CMH), religion, spirituality, teaching in the two-year college, writing; medical humanities (MMH, DMH, CMH), including arts, health, healthcare, literature (M Litt, MMH, D Litt, DMH, CMH), scientific research; poetry (MFA). *Program availability:* Part-time, evening/weekend. *Faculty:* 4 full-time (2 women), 29 part-time/adjunct (15 women). *Students:* 77 full-time (42 women), 175 part-time (114 women); includes 39 minority (12 Black or African American, non-Hispanic/Latino; 6 Asian, non-Hispanic/Latino; 16 Hispanic/Latino; 5 Two or more races, non-Hispanic/Latino), 11 international. Average age 41. 126 applicants, 75% accepted, 52 enrolled. In 2017, 38 master's, 23 doctorates, 35 other advanced degrees awarded. Terminal master's awarded for partial completion of doctoral program. *Degree requirements:* For master's and other advanced degree, thesis (for some programs); for doctorate, one foreign language, comprehensive exam (for some programs), thesis/dissertation. *Entrance requirements:* For master's, PRAXIS Core and Subject Area tests (for MAT), GRE/GMAT (for M Fin), resume, transcripts, writing sample, personal statement, letters of recommendation; for doctorate, GRE (PhD in history and culture), resume, transcripts, writing sample, personal statement, letters of recommendation; for other advanced degree, resume, transcripts, personal statement. Additional exam requirements/recommendations for international students: Required—TOEFL (minimum score 587 paper-based; 80 iBT), IELTS (minimum score 6), TWE (minimum score 4). *Application deadline:* For fall admission, 8/1 for domestic students, 6/1 for international students; for spring admission, 12/1 for domestic students, 10/1 for international students. Applications are processed on a rolling basis. Application fee: $35. Electronic applications accepted. *Financial support:* Fellowships, research assistantships, teaching assistantships, career-related internships or fieldwork, Federal Work-Study, scholarships/grants, and unspecified assistantships available. Support available to part-time students. Financial award applicants required to submit FAFSA. *Faculty research:* Irish history and culture, conflict resolution and leadership. *Application contact:* Leanne Horinko, Director of Caspersen Admissions, 973-408-3280, E-mail: gradm@drew.edu.
Website: http://www.drew.edu/caspersen

Drury University, Master in Education Program, Springfield, MO 5802. Offers curriculum and instruction (M Ed), including elementary, middle school, secondary; gifted education (M Ed); instructional leadership (M Ed); instructional technology (M Ed); integrated learning (M Ed); online teaching (M Ed); special education (M Ed); special reading (M Ed). *Accreditation:* NCATE. *Program availability:* Part-time, evening/weekend, 100% online, blended/hybrid learning. *Entrance requirements:* For master's, GRE, bachelor's degree with minimum GPA of 2.75. Additional exam requirements/recommendations for international students: Recommended—TOEFL (minimum score 80 iBT), IELTS (minimum score 6.5). Electronic applications accepted. *Expenses:* Contact institution. *Faculty research:* Gifted students, instructional technology, autism, diversity and social justice.

Duquesne University, School of Education, Department of Instruction and Leadership, Program in Secondary Education, Pittsburgh, PA 15282-0001. Offers biology (MS Ed); chemistry (MS Ed); English (MS Ed); K-12 education (MS Ed), including Latin;

mathematics (MS Ed); physics (MS Ed); social studies (MS Ed). *Program availability:* Part-time, evening/weekend. *Faculty:* 5 full-time (4 women). *Students:* 22 full-time (10 women); includes 3 minority (2 Black or African American, non-Hispanic/Latino; 1 Two or more races, non-Hispanic/Latino). Average age 26. 8 applicants, 100% accepted, 5 enrolled. In 2017, 9 master's awarded. *Entrance requirements:* For master's, two letters of recommendation, letter of intent, interview, bachelor's degree. Additional exam requirements/recommendations for international students: Required—TOEFL (minimum score 550 paper-based), IELTS (minimum score 7). *Application deadline:* For fall admission, 9/1 for domestic students; for spring admission, 1/2 for domestic students. Applications are processed on a rolling basis. Application fee: $0. Electronic applications accepted. *Expenses:* $1,259 per credit. *Financial support:* Research assistantships and Federal Work-Study available. Support available to part-time students. *Faculty research:* Factors that create highly effective teachers; how to best support teachers to support students in reform-oriented environments; urban education; models of teacher leadership; improving instruction in mathematics/science/social studies/English. *Unit head:* Dr. Melissa Boston, Associate Dean for Teacher Education/Professor, 412-396.6109, Fax: 412-396-5585, E-mail: bostonm@duq.edu. *Application contact:* Kelly McGinley, Graduate Admissions Assistant, 412-396-1559, Fax: 412-396-5585, E-mail: mcginleyk@duq.edu.
Website: http://www.duq.edu/academics/schools/education/graduate-programs-education/ms-ed-secondary-education

D'Youville College, Department of Education, Buffalo, NY 14201-1084. Offers educational leadership (Ed D); elementary education (MS Ed); secondary education (MS Ed); special education (MS Ed). *Program availability:* Part-time, evening/weekend. *Degree requirements:* For master's, one foreign language, comprehensive exam, project or thesis. *Entrance requirements:* For master's, GRE (if GPA less than 2.75), minimum GPA of 3.0. Additional exam requirements/recommendations for international students: Required—TOEFL (minimum score 500 paper-based). Electronic applications accepted. *Faculty research:* Developmental disabilities, multiculturalism, early childhood education.

East Carolina University, Graduate School, College of Education, Department of Elementary and Middle Grades Education, Greenville, NC 27858-4353. Offers elementary education (MA Ed, MAT); middle grades education (MA Ed, MAT). *Accreditation:* NCATE. *Program availability:* Part-time, evening/weekend, online learning. *Students:* 13 full-time (12 women), 27 part-time (26 women); includes 9 minority (5 Black or African American, non-Hispanic/Latino; 1 Asian, non-Hispanic/Latino; 2 Hispanic/Latino; 1 Two or more races, non-Hispanic/Latino). Average age 29. 39 applicants, 97% accepted, 31 enrolled. In 2017, 11 master's awarded. *Degree requirements:* For master's, comprehensive exam, thesis optional. *Entrance requirements:* For master's, GRE or MAT, minimum GPA of 2.5, bachelor's degree in related field, teaching license (MA Ed). Additional exam requirements/recommendations for international students: Required—TOEFL. *Application deadline:* For fall admission, 6/1 priority date for domestic students. Applications are processed on a rolling basis. Application fee: $75. *Expenses:* Tuition, state resident: full-time $4749; part-time $297 per credit hour. Tuition, nonresident: full-time $17,898; part-time $1119 per credit hour. *Required fees:* $2691; $224 per credit hour. Part-time tuition and fees vary according to course load and program. *Financial support:* Federal Work-Study available. Support available to part-time students. Financial award application deadline: 3/1. *Unit head:* Dr. Ann Bullock, Chair, 252-328-1126, E-mail: bullockv@ecu.edu.
Website: http://www.ecu.edu/cs-educ/elmid/index.cfm

East Carolina University, Graduate School, College of Education, Department of Mathematics, Science, and Instructional Technology Education, Greenville, NC 27858-4353. Offers distance learning and administration (Certificate); elementary mathematics education (Certificate); instructional technology (MA Ed, MS); mathematics education (MA Ed); science education (MA Ed, MAT); special endorsement in computer education (Certificate). *Program availability:* Part-time, evening/weekend. *Students:* 12 full-time (10 women), 202 part-time (153 women); includes 49 minority (31 Black or African American, non-Hispanic/Latino; 2 American Indian or Alaska Native, non-Hispanic/Latino; 2 Asian, non-Hispanic/Latino; 9 Hispanic/Latino; 5 Two or more races, non-Hispanic/Latino). Average age 38. 56 applicants, 100% accepted, 50 enrolled. In 2017, 76 master's, 30 other advanced degrees awarded. *Degree requirements:* For master's, comprehensive exam, thesis optional. *Entrance requirements:* For master's, GRE General Test or MAT, interview, minimum GPA of 2.5, bachelor's degree in related field, teaching license (MA Ed). Additional exam requirements/recommendations for international students: Required—TOEFL. *Application deadline:* For fall admission, 6/1 priority date for domestic students. Applications are processed on a rolling basis. Application fee: $75. *Expenses:* Tuition, state resident: full-time $4749; part-time $297 per credit hour. Tuition, nonresident: full-time $17,898; part-time $1119 per credit hour. *Required fees:* $2691; $224 per credit hour. Part-time tuition and fees vary according to course load and program. *Financial support:* Research assistantships, teaching assistantships, and Federal Work-Study available. Support available to part-time students. Financial award application deadline: 6/1. *Unit head:* Susan Ganter, Chair, 252-737-3001, E-mail: ganters@ecu.edu.
Website: http://www.ecu.edu/cs-educ/msite/

Eastern Connecticut State University, School of Education and Professional Studies/Graduate Division, Program in Elementary Education, Willimantic, CT 06226-2295. Offers MS. *Accreditation:* NCATE. *Program availability:* Part-time, evening/weekend. *Faculty:* 9 full-time (5 women), 12 part-time/adjunct (9 women). *Students:* 36 full-time (30 women), 11 part-time (7 women); includes 13 minority (1 Black or African American, non-Hispanic/Latino; 1 Asian, non-Hispanic/Latino; 5 Hispanic/Latino; 1 Native Hawaiian or other Pacific Islander, non-Hispanic/Latino; 5 Two or more races, non-Hispanic/Latino). Average age 26. 20 applicants, 70% accepted, 12 enrolled. In 2017, 10 master's awarded. *Degree requirements:* For master's, comprehensive exam or thesis. *Entrance requirements:* For master's, PRAXIS I, PRAXIS II, GRE, minimum GPA of 3.0, bachelor's degree from accredited institution. Additional exam requirements/recommendations for international students: Required—TOEFL (minimum score 550 paper-based; 79 iBT); Recommended—IELTS (minimum score 6). *Application deadline:* For fall admission, 7/6 priority date for domestic and international students; for spring admission, 11/3 priority date for domestic and international students. Applications are processed on a rolling basis. Application fee: $50. Electronic applications accepted. *Expenses: Tuition, area resident:* Full-time $12,252. Tuition, state resident: full-time $15,245; part-time $582 per credit hour. Tuition, nonresident: full-time $24,828; part-time $582 per credit hour. *Required fees:* $40 per semester. Full-time tuition and fees vary according to reciprocity agreements. *Financial support:* Research assistantships, teaching assistantships, career-related internships or fieldwork, institutionally sponsored loans, and unspecified assistantships available. Financial award application deadline: 3/1; financial award applicants required to submit FAFSA. *Unit head:* Dr. Ann Anderberg, Advisor, 860-465-0109, Fax: 860-465-4538, E-mail: anderberga@easternct.edu. *Application contact:* Paula Goyette, Graduate Division, School of Education and Professional Studies, 860-465-5292, Fax: 860-465-4538, E-mail: graduateadmissions@easternct.edu.

Eastern Illinois University, Graduate School, College of Education and Professional Studies, Department of Early Childhood, Elementary and Middle Level Education,

Charleston, IL 61920. Offers curriculum and instruction (MS Ed). *Accreditation:* NCATE. *Program availability:* Part-time, evening/weekend. *Degree requirements:* For master's, comprehensive exam (for some programs), thesis (for some programs). *Entrance requirements:* For master's, GMAT or GRE. Additional exam requirements/recommendations for international students: Required—TOEFL (minimum score 500 paper-based; 61 iBT), IELTS (minimum score 6). *Application deadline:* For fall admission, 5/15 for domestic and international students; for spring admission, 10/15 for domestic and international students. Applications are processed on a rolling basis. Application fee: $30. Electronic applications accepted. *Financial support:* Research assistantships with full tuition reimbursements, teaching assistantships with full tuition reimbursements, career-related internships or fieldwork, Federal Work-Study, and unspecified assistantships available. Support available to part-time students. Financial award application deadline: 3/1; financial award applicants required to submit FAFSA. *Unit head:* Jeanne E. Okrasinski, Chair, 217-581-5728, Fax: 217-581-6300, E-mail: jeokrasinski@eiu.edu. *Application contact:* Jeanne E. Okrasinski, Chair, 217-581-5728, Fax: 217-581-6300, E-mail: jeokrasinski@eiu.edu.
Website: http://www.eiu.edu/elegrad/

Eastern Illinois University, Graduate School, College of Liberal Arts and Sciences, Department of Mathematics and Computer Science, Charleston, IL 61920. Offers elementary/middle school mathematics education (MA); mathematics (MA); secondary mathematics education (MA). *Program availability:* Part-time, evening/weekend. *Degree requirements:* For master's, comprehensive exam (for some programs), thesis (for some programs). *Entrance requirements:* For master's, GMAT or GRE. Additional exam requirements/recommendations for international students: Required—TOEFL (minimum score 500 paper-based; 61 iBT), IELTS (minimum score 6). *Application deadline:* For fall admission, 5/15 for domestic and international students; for spring admission, 10/15 for domestic and international students. Applications are processed on a rolling basis. Application fee: $30. Electronic applications accepted. *Financial support:* Teaching assistantships with full tuition reimbursements, career-related internships or fieldwork, Federal Work-Study, and unspecified assistantships available. Support available to part-time students. Financial award application deadline: 3/1; financial award applicants required to submit FAFSA. *Unit head:* Marshall B. Lassak, Chair, 217-581-6450, Fax: 217-581-6284, E-mail: mblassak@eiu.edu. *Application contact:* Peter S. Wiles, Graduate Coordinator, 217-581-6275, Fax: 217-581-6284, E-mail: pswiles@eiu.edu.
Website: http://www.eiu.edu/mathgrad/

Eastern Kentucky University, The Graduate School, College of Education, Department of Curriculum and Instruction, Richmond, KY 40475-3102. Offers elementary education (MA Ed), including early elementary education, reading; library science (MA Ed); music education (MA Ed); secondary and higher education (MA Ed), including secondary education; teaching (MAT). *Accreditation:* NCATE. *Program availability:* Part-time. *Degree requirements:* For master's, portfolio is part of exam. *Entrance requirements:* For master's, GRE General Test, PRAXIS II (KY), minimum GPA of 2.5. *Faculty research:* Technology in education, reading instruction, e-portfolios, induction to teacher education, dispositions of teachers.

Eastern Nazarene College, Adult and Graduate Studies, Division of Teacher Education, Quincy, MA 02170. Offers administration (M Ed); early childhood education (M Ed, Certificate); elementary education (M Ed, Certificate); English as a second language (Certificate); instructional enrichment and development (Certificate); middle school education (M Ed, Certificate); moderate special needs education (Certificate); principal (Certificate); program development and supervision (Certificate); secondary education (M Ed, Certificate); special education administrator (Certificate); special needs (M Ed); supervisor (Certificate); teacher of reading (M Ed, Certificate). M Ed also available through weekend program for administration, special needs, and teacher of reading only. *Program availability:* Part-time, evening/weekend. *Entrance requirements:* Additional exam requirements/recommendations for international students: Required—TOEFL (minimum score 550 paper-based).

Eastern New Mexico University, Graduate School, College of Education and Technology, Department of Curriculum and Instruction, Portales, NM 88130. Offers alternative licensure in elementary education (M Ed); bilingual education (M Ed); career and technical education (M Ed); educational technology (M Ed); elementary education (M Ed); English as a second language (M Ed); pedagogy and learning (M Ed); reading/literacy (M Ed). *Program availability:* Part-time, online learning. *Degree requirements:* For master's, comprehensive exam, thesis optional. *Entrance requirements:* For master's, writing assessment, minimum GPA of 3.0, photocopy of teaching license, letter of recommendation. Additional exam requirements/recommendations for international students: Required—TOEFL (minimum score 550 paper-based; 79 iBT), IELTS (minimum score 6). *Application deadline:* For fall admission, 7/20 priority date for domestic students, 6/20 priority date for international students; for spring admission, 12/15 priority date for domestic students, 11/15 priority date for international students. Applications are processed on a rolling basis. Application fee: $10. Electronic applications accepted. *Financial support:* Applicants required to submit FAFSA. *Unit head:* Dr. Mary Daughrity, Graduate Coordinator, 575-562-2481, Fax: 575-562-2559, E-mail: mary.daughrity@enmu.edu. *Application contact:* Cheryl Reeves, Senior Secretary, 575-562-2443, E-mail: cheryl.reeves@enmu.edu.
Website: http://education.enmu.edu.

Eastern Oregon University, Master of Arts in Teaching Program, La Grande, OR 97850. Offers elementary education (MAT); secondary education (MAT). *Faculty:* 12 full-time (9 women), 4 part-time/adjunct (1 woman). *Students:* 53 full-time (41 women), 2 part-time (both women); includes 6 minority (5 Hispanic/Latino; 1 Two or more races, non-Hispanic/Latino), 1 international. Average age 29. In 2017, 32 master's awarded. *Degree requirements:* For master's, thesis. *Entrance requirements:* For master's, NTE. *Application deadline:* For fall admission, 3/1 for domestic students. Applications are processed on a rolling basis. Electronic applications accepted. *Expenses:* $404.50 per credit. *Financial support:* In 2017–18, 24 students received support. Federal Work-Study, scholarships/grants, and tuition waivers (full and partial) available. Support available to part-time students. *Unit head:* Dr. Danny Ray Mielke, Dean of College of Business and Education, 541-962-3399, Fax: 541-962-3701, E-mail: dmeilke@eou.edu. *Application contact:* Janet Frye, Administrative Support, MAT/MS Graduate Admission, 541-962-3772, Fax: 541-962-3701, E-mail: jfrye@eou.edu.
Website: https://www.eou.edu/cobe/ed/mat/

Eastern University, Graduate Education Programs, St. Davids, PA 19087-3696. Offers ESL program specialist (K-12) (Certificate); general supervisor (PreK-12) (Certificate); health and physical education (K-12) (Certificate); middle level (4-8) (Certificate); multicultural education (M Ed); music (K-12) (Certificate); Pre K-4 (Certificate); Pre K-4 with special education (Certificate); reading (M Ed); reading specialist (K-12) (Certificate); reading supervisor (K-12) (Certificate); school counseling (MA, CAGS); school principalship (preK-12) (Certificate); school psychology (MS, CAGS); secondary biology education (7-12) (Certificate); secondary chemistry education (7-12) (Certificate); secondary communication education (7-12) (Certificate); secondary English education (7-12) (Certificate); secondary math education (7-12) (Certificate); secondary social studies education (7-12) (Certificate); special education (M Ed); special education (7-12) (Certificate); special education (Pre K-8) (Certificate); special education supervisor (K-12) (Certificate); TESOL (M Ed); world language (Certificate),

including Spanish. *Program availability:* Part-time, evening/weekend, online learning. *Students:* 46 full-time (40 women), 115 part-time (93 women); includes 65 minority (42 Black or African American, non-Hispanic/Latino; 3 Asian, non-Hispanic/Latino; 14 Hispanic/Latino; 6 Two or more races, non-Hispanic/Latino), 1 international. Average age 32. In 2017, 72 master's awarded. *Entrance requirements:* Additional exam requirements/recommendations for international students: Required—TOEFL. *Application deadline:* Applications are processed on a rolling basis. Application fee: $35. Electronic applications accepted. Application fee is waived when completed online. *Expenses:* Contact institution. *Unit head:* Michael Dziedziak, Executive Director of Enrollment, 800-452-0996, E-mail: gpsadmissions@eastern.edu.
Website: https://www.eastern.edu/academics/programs/education-department-graduate-programs/graduate-programs

Eastern Washington University, Graduate Studies, College of Arts, Letters and Education, Department of Education, Cheney, WA 99004-2431. Offers adult education (M Ed); curriculum development (M Ed); early childhood education (M Ed); educational foundations (M Ed); educational leadership (M Ed); literacy (M Ed); teaching K-8 (M Ed). *Program availability:* Part-time. *Faculty:* 13. *Students:* 32 full-time (25 women), 36 part-time (25 women); includes 5 minority (all Hispanic/Latino), 4 international. Average age 37. 38 applicants, 55% accepted, 18 enrolled. In 2017, 24 master's awarded. *Degree requirements:* For master's, comprehensive exam. *Entrance requirements:* For master's, minimum GPA of 3.0. Additional exam requirements/recommendations for international students: Required—TOEFL (minimum score 580 paper-based; 92 iBT), IELTS (minimum score 7), PTE (minimum score 63). *Application deadline:* For fall admission, 4/1 priority date for domestic students; for spring admission, 1/15 for domestic students. Applications are processed on a rolling basis. Application fee: $75. Electronic applications accepted. *Expenses:* Tuition, state resident: full-time $11,191; part-time $373.06 per credit. Tuition, nonresident: full-time $25,995; part-time $866.52 per credit. *Financial support:* Teaching assistantships with partial tuition reimbursements, career-related internships or fieldwork, Federal Work-Study, institutionally sponsored loans, scholarships/grants, health care benefits, tuition waivers (partial), and unspecified assistantships available. Support available to part-time students. Financial award application deadline: 2/1; financial award applicants required to submit FAFSA. *Unit head:* Dr. Tara Haskins, Education Department Chair/Associate Professor of Literacy, 509-359-2831, E-mail: thaskins@ewu.edu. *Application contact:* Dr. Robin Showalter, Graduate Program Coordinator, 509-359-6492, E-mail: rshowalter@ewu.edu.
Website: http://www.ewu.edu/CALE/Programs/Education.xml

East Stroudsburg University of Pennsylvania, Graduate and Extended Studies, College of Education, Department of Early Childhood and Elementary Education, East Stroudsburg, PA 18301-2999. Offers M Ed. *Program availability:* Part-time, evening/weekend, online learning. *Faculty:* 1 (woman) full-time. *Students:* 2 full-time (both women), 6 part-time (all women). Average age 40. 9 applicants, 78% accepted, 4 enrolled. In 2017, 2 master's awarded. *Degree requirements:* For master's, comprehensive exam, professional portfolio, curriculum project or action research. *Entrance requirements:* For master's, PRAXIS/teacher certification, letter of recommendation, Pennsylvania Department of Education requirements. Additional exam requirements/recommendations for international students: Recommended—TOEFL (minimum score 560 paper-based; 83 iBT), IELTS. *Application deadline:* For fall admission, 7/31 priority date for domestic students, 6/30 priority date for international students; for spring admission, 11/30 for domestic students, 10/31 for international students. Applications are processed on a rolling basis. Application fee: $50. Electronic applications accepted. *Expenses:* Tuition, state resident: full-time $4500; part-time $3000 per credit. Tuition, nonresident: full-time $6750; part-time $4500 per credit. *Required fees:* $2642; $1756 per credit. $878 per semester. Tuition and fees vary according to course load, campus/location and program. *Financial support:* Research assistantships with tuition reimbursements, Federal Work-Study, and unspecified assistantships available. Support available to part-time students. Financial award application deadline: 3/1; financial award applicants required to submit FAFSA. *Unit head:* Andrew Whitehead, Chair, 570-422-3356, Fax: 570-422-3942, E-mail: awhitehead@esu.edu. *Application contact:* Kevin Quintero, Associate Director, Graduate and Extended Studies, 570-422-3890, Fax: 570-422-2711, E-mail: kquintero@esu.edu.

East Tennessee State University, School of Graduate Studies, College of Education, Department of Curriculum and Instruction, Johnson City, TN 37614. Offers advanced studies in teaching and learning (M Ed), including childhood literacy; educational technology (M Ed), including educational communications and technology, school library media; elementary education (M Ed); reading (M Ed, MA), including reading education (MA), storytelling (MA); response to intervention (Post-Master's Certificate); school library professional (Post-Master's Certificate); secondary education (M Ed); STEAM K-12 education (Postbaccalaureate Certificate); storytelling (Postbaccalaureate Certificate); teacher education (MAT), including elementary education K-5, middle grades education 4-8, middle grades education 6-8, secondary education 6-12 and preK-12, secondary education K-12. *Accreditation:* NCATE. *Program availability:* Part-time, evening/weekend, online learning. *Degree requirements:* For master's, comprehensive exam, thesis optional, student teaching, practicum; for other advanced degree, field work (school library); culminating experience (storytelling). *Entrance requirements:* For master's, GRE, SAT, ACT, PRAXIS, minimum GPA of 3.0, interview, 3 letters of recommendation, background check; for other advanced degree, master's degree, TN teaching license. Additional exam requirements/recommendations for international students: Required—TOEFL (minimum score 550 paper-based; 79 iBT). *Application deadline:* For fall admission, 6/1 for domestic students, 4/29 for international students; for spring admission, 11/1 for domestic students, 4/29 for international students. Application fee: $55 ($65 for international students). Electronic applications accepted. *Financial support:* Research assistantships with full tuition reimbursements, teaching assistantships with tuition reimbursements, career-related internships or fieldwork, institutionally sponsored loans, scholarships/grants, and unspecified assistantships available. Financial award application deadline: 7/1; financial award applicants required to submit FAFSA. *Faculty research:* Critical thinking; curriculum development in reading, math, and science education; cultural diversity; cognitive processes; effective teaching strategies. *Unit head:* Dr. Karin Keith, Chair, 423-439-7598, Fax: 423-439-8362, E-mail: keithkj@etsu.edu. *Application contact:* Dr. Aimee Govett, Graduate Coordinator, 423-439-7804, Fax: 423-439-5624, E-mail: govett@etsu.edu.
Website: http://www.etsu.edu/coe/cuai/

Elizabeth City State University, Department of Education, Psychology and Health, Master of Education in Elementary Education Program, Elizabeth City, NC 27909-7806. Offers M Ed. *Accreditation:* NCATE. *Program availability:* Part-time, evening/weekend. *Faculty:* 4 full-time (3 women), 1 (woman) part-time/adjunct. *Students:* 2 full-time (both women), 12 part-time (10 women); includes 6 minority (5 Black or African American, non-Hispanic/Latino; 1 Two or more races, non-Hispanic/Latino). Average age 35. 27 applicants, 81% accepted, 14 enrolled. In 2017, 3 master's awarded. *Degree requirements:* For master's, comprehensive exam (for some programs), thesis or alternative, electronic transformational teaching project. *Entrance requirements:* For master's, GRE and/or MAT, minimum GPA of 2.5, 3 letters of recommendation, 2 official

Elementary Education

transcripts from all undergraduate/graduate schools attended, teacher license, typewritten 2-page essay specifying educational philosophy. Additional exam requirements/recommendations for international students: Required—TOEFL (minimum score 550 paper-based, 80 iBT) or IELTS (minimum score 6.5). *Application deadline:* For fall admission, 7/15 priority date for domestic and international students; for spring admission, 11/15 priority date for domestic and international students; for summer admission, 3/15 priority date for domestic and international students. Applications are processed on a rolling basis. Application fee: $30. Electronic applications accepted. Application fee is waived when completed online. Tuition and fees vary according to course load and program. *Financial support:* Scholarships/grants available. Financial award application deadline: 6/30; financial award applicants required to submit FAFSA. *Faculty research:* Diverse learners, disproportionality, inclusionary classrooms, international curriculum development. *Unit head:* Dr. Sharon D. Raynor, Director, Graduate Education Program, 252-335-3945, E-mail: sdraynor@ecsu.edu. *Application contact:* Dr. Sharon D. Raynor, Director, Graduate Education Program, 252-335-3945, E-mail: sdraynor@ecsu.edu.

Elms College, Division of Education, Chicopee, MA 01013-2839. Offers early childhood education (MAT); education (M Ed, CAGS); elementary education (MAT); English as a second language (MAT); reading (MAT); secondary education (MAT), including biology education, English education, Spanish education; special education (MAT). *Program availability:* Part-time, evening/weekend. *Faculty:* 4 full-time (all women), 8 part-time/ adjunct (7 women). *Students:* 6 full-time (4 women), 127 part-time (107 women); includes 8 minority (2 Asian, non-Hispanic/Latino; 6 Hispanic/Latino). Average age 33. 42 applicants, 88% accepted, 36 enrolled. In 2017, 50 master's, 6 other advanced degrees awarded. *Degree requirements:* For master's, thesis (for some programs). *Entrance requirements:* For master's, Massachusetts Educators Certification Test, minimum GPA of 3.0; for CAGS, master's degree in education. Additional exam requirements/recommendations for international students: Required—TOEFL. *Application deadline:* For fall admission, 7/1 priority date for domestic students; for spring admission, 11/1 priority date for domestic students. Applications are processed on a rolling basis. Application fee: $30. *Expenses: Tuition:* Full-time $13,860; part-time $770 per credit hour. *Required fees:* $200. Tuition and fees vary according to degree level and program. *Financial support:* In 2017–18, 2 teaching assistantships with partial tuition reimbursements were awarded. Financial award applicants required to submit FAFSA. *Unit head:* Dr. Mary Janeczek, Chair, Division of Education, 413-594-2761, Fax: 413-592-4871, E-mail: janeczeke@elms.edu. *Application contact:* School of Graduate and Professional Studies, 413-265-2445, E-mail: graduateeducaion@elms.edu.

Elon University, Program in Education, Elon, NC 27244-2010. Offers elementary education (M Ed); gifted education (M Ed); special education (M Ed). *Accreditation:* NCATE. *Program availability:* Part-time. *Faculty:* 8 full-time (6 women), 2 part-time/ adjunct (both women). *Students:* 24 part-time (22 women); includes 13 minority (2 Black or African American, non-Hispanic/Latino; 2 Asian, non-Hispanic/Latino; 8 Hispanic/ Latino; 1 Two or more races, non-Hispanic/Latino). Average age 23. 29 applicants, 69% accepted, 16 enrolled. In 2017, 10 master's awarded. *Entrance requirements:* For master's, GRE, MAT. Additional exam requirements/recommendations for international students: Required—TOEFL (minimum score 550 paper-based; 79 iBT). *Application deadline:* For fall admission, 5/1 for domestic students. Applications are processed on a rolling basis. Application fee: $50. Electronic applications accepted. *Financial support:* Federal Work-Study and scholarships/grants available. Support available to part-time students. Financial award application deadline: 6/1; financial award applicants required to submit FAFSA. *Faculty research:* Teaching reading to low-achieving second and third graders, pre- and post-student teaching attitudes, children's writing, whole language methodology, critical creative thinking. *Unit head:* Dr. Ann Bullock, Dean of the School of Education/Professor, 336-278-5900, E-mail: abullock9@elon.edu. *Application contact:* Art Fadde, Director of Graduate Admissions, 800-334-8448 Ext. 3, Fax: 336-278-7699, E-mail: afadde@elon.edu.
Website: http://www.elon.edu/med

Emporia State University, Program in Instructional Specialist, Emporia, KS 66801-5415. Offers elementary subject matter (MS); reading (MS). *Accreditation:* NCATE. *Program availability:* Part-time. *Faculty:* 30 full-time (24 women), 1 part-time/adjunct (0 women). *Students:* 2 full-time (1 woman), 88 part-time (80 women); includes 3 minority (1 Black or African American, non-Hispanic/Latino; 1 Asian, non-Hispanic/Latino; 1 Two or more races, non-Hispanic/Latino). 14 applicants, 93% accepted, 11 enrolled. In 2017, 15 master's awarded. *Degree requirements:* For master's, comprehensive exam or thesis, practicum. *Entrance requirements:* For master's, GRE General Test or MAT, essay exam, appropriate bachelor's degree, letters of recommendation. Additional exam requirements/recommendations for international students: Required—TOEFL (minimum score 520 paper-based; 68 iBT). *Application deadline:* For fall admission, 8/15 priority date for domestic students. Applications are processed on a rolling basis. Application fee: $30 ($75 for international students). Electronic applications accepted. *Expenses:* Tuition, state resident: full-time $6084; part-time $253.50 per credit hour. Tuition, nonresident: full-time $18,924; part-time $788.50 per credit hour. *Required fees:* $1943; $80.95 per credit hour. Tuition and fees vary according to campus/location. *Financial support:* Federal Work-Study, institutionally sponsored loans, health care benefits, and unspecified assistantships available. Financial award application deadline: 3/15; financial award applicants required to submit FAFSA. *Unit head:* Dr. Matt Siemears, Chair, 620-341-6057, E-mail: msiemear@emporia.edu. *Application contact:* Mary Sewell, Admissions Coordinator, 800-950-GRAD, Fax: 620-341-5909, E-mail: msewell@emporia.edu.

Endicott College, Van Loan School of Graduate and Professional Studies, Program in Early Childhood and Elementary Education, Beverly, MA 01915-2096. Offers early childhood and elementary education (M Ed); early childhood education (M Ed); elementary education (M Ed). *Program availability:* Part-time, evening/weekend, 100% online, blended/hybrid learning. *Faculty:* 4 full-time (3 women), 12 part-time/adjunct (10 women). *Students:* 14 full-time (13 women), 9 part-time (8 women). Average age 31. 5 applicants, 100% accepted, 5 enrolled. In 2017, 13 master's awarded. *Degree requirements:* For master's, comprehensive exam, thesis, practicum. *Entrance requirements:* For master's, MAT or GRE, Massachusetts Tests for Educator Licensure (MTEL), Massachusetts teaching certificate, 2 professional letters of recommendation, personal statement. Additional exam requirements/recommendations for international students: Required—TOEFL. *Application deadline:* Applications are processed on a rolling basis. Application fee: $50. Electronic applications accepted. *Expenses:* Contact institution. *Financial support:* Career-related internships or fieldwork available. Financial award applicants required to submit FAFSA. *Unit head:* Dr. Aubry Threlkeld, Director of Graduate Licensure Programs, 978-232-2408, E-mail: athrelke@endicott.edu. *Application contact:* Ian Menchini, Director, Graduate Enrollment and Advising, 978-232-5292, E-mail: imenchin@endicott.edu.
Website: https://vanloan.endicott.edu/programs-of-study/masters-programs/educator-preparation-program/early-childhood-education-program

Fairfield University, Graduate School of Education and Allied Professions, Fairfield, CT 06824. Offers applied behavior analysis (ATC); applied psychology (MA); clinical mental health counseling (MA, CAS); educational technology (MA); elementary education (MA, CAS); family studies (MA); integration of spirituality and religion in counseling (ATC);

marriage and family therapy (MA); reading and language development (Sixth Year Certificate); school counseling (MA, CAS); school psychology (MA, CAS); school-based marriage and family therapy (ATC); secondary education (MA); special education (MA, CAS); substance abuse counseling (ATC); teaching (Certificate); teaching and foundations (MA, CAS); TESOL, world languages, and bilingual education (MA, CAS). *Accreditation:* NCATE. *Program availability:* Part-time, evening/weekend. *Faculty:* 23 full-time (17 women), 39 part-time/adjunct (28 women). *Students:* 199 full-time (168 women), 251 part-time (206 women); includes 85 minority (21 Black or African American, non-Hispanic/Latino; 9 Asian, non-Hispanic/Latino; 49 Hispanic/Latino; 6 Two or more races, non-Hispanic/Latino), 4 international. Average age 32. 370 applicants, 56% accepted, 125 enrolled. In 2017, 136 master's, 28 other advanced degrees awarded. *Degree requirements:* For master's, comprehensive exam. *Entrance requirements:* For master's, minimum GPA of 3.0, 2 recommendations, resume. Additional exam requirements/recommendations for international students: Required—TOEFL (minimum score 550 paper-based; 84 iBT) or IELTS (minimum score 7.5). *Application deadline:* For fall admission, 2/15 for international students; for spring admission, 10/1 for international students. Application fee: $60. Electronic applications accepted. *Expenses:* $750 per credit hour. *Financial support:* In 2017–18, 34 students received support. Career-related internships or fieldwork and unspecified assistantships available. Support available to part-time students. Financial award applicants required to submit FAFSA. *Faculty research:* Reading and literacy, writing, social justice and inequality in education, addictions and mental health issues, therapeutic relationships and clinical supervision. *Unit head:* Dr. Robert D. Hannafin, Dean, 203-254-4250, Fax: 203-254-4241, E-mail: rhannafin@fairfield.edu. *Application contact:* Marianne Gumpper, Director of Graduate Admission, 203-254-4184, Fax: 203-254-4073, E-mail: gradadmis@fairfield.edu.
Website: http://www.fairfield.edu/gseap

Faulkner University, College of Education, Montgomery, AL 36109-3398. Offers counseling (MS); curriculum and instruction (M Ed); elementary education (M Ed); school counseling (M Ed). *Program availability:* Part-time, evening/weekend, 100% online, blended/hybrid learning. *Faculty:* 13 full-time (8 women), 6 part-time/adjunct (1 woman). *Students:* 140 full-time (107 women), 16 part-time (13 women); includes 97 minority (92 Black or African American, non-Hispanic/Latino; 1 American Indian or Alaska Native, non-Hispanic/Latino; 1 Asian, non-Hispanic/Latino; 3 Hispanic/Latino). Average age 37. 92 applicants, 55% accepted, 48 enrolled. In 2017, 51 master's awarded. *Degree requirements:* For master's, 5+ hours in clinical training (for MS, M Ed in school counseling). *Entrance requirements:* For master's, MAT (minimum score of 370) or GRE (minimum score of 280) taken within last five years, bachelor's degree from regionally-accredited college or university; official transcripts from all colleges and universities attended; three letters of recommendation; goal statement (approximately 600 words); minimum cumulative GPA of 2.75 in undergraduate courses, 3.0 in graduate courses. Additional exam requirements/recommendations for international students: Required—TOEFL (minimum score 500 paper-based). *Application deadline:* For fall admission, 8/1 for domestic students; for spring admission, 12/1 for domestic students; for summer admission, 5/1 for domestic students. Application fee: $35. Electronic applications accepted. *Expenses:* Contact institution. *Financial support:* Applicants required to submit FAFSA. *Unit head:* Dr. Leslie S. Cowell, Dean, College of Education, 334-386-7224, Fax: 334-386-7194, E-mail: lcowell@faulkner.edu. *Application contact:* Rebecca L. Horn, Director, Graduate Education, 334-386-7264, Fax: 334-386-7194, E-mail: rhorn@faulkner.edu.
Website: https://www.faulkner.edu/graduate/graduate_academics/

Fayetteville State University, Graduate School, Programs in Middle Grades, Secondary, Special and Elementary Education, Fayetteville, NC 28301-4298. Offers middle grades (MA Ed); sociology (MA Ed); special education (MA Ed), including behavioral-emotional handicaps, mentally handicapped, specific training disability. *Accreditation:* NCATE. *Program availability:* Part-time, evening/weekend. *Faculty:* 8 full-time (5 women). *Students:* 14 full-time (7 women), 8 part-time (6 women); includes 16 minority (13 Black or African American, non-Hispanic/Latino; 1 Asian, non-Hispanic/Latino; 2 Hispanic/Latino). Average age 35. 10 applicants, 80% accepted, 7 enrolled. In 2017, 9 master's awarded. *Degree requirements:* For master's, comprehensive exam, internship. *Entrance requirements:* Additional exam requirements/recommendations for international students: Required—TOEFL. *Application deadline:* For fall admission, 4/15 for domestic students; for spring admission, 10/15 for domestic students. Applications are processed on a rolling basis. Application fee: $40. Electronic applications accepted. *Expenses:* Tuition, state resident: full-time $8604. Tuition, nonresident: full-time $19,669. *Financial support:* Application deadline: 3/1; applicants required to submit FAFSA. *Faculty research:* Students with disabilities and selected leadership behaviors, new vision for professional development, gifted and talented students, emotional and behavioral disabilities, professional development for high school biology teachers. *Unit head:* Dr. Cynthia Shamberger, Chair of Middle Grades, Secondary and Specialized Subjects, 910-672-1181, Fax: 910-672-1941, E-mail: cshamber@uncfsu.edu. *Application contact:* Debra D. Brown, Administrative Support Associate, 910-672-1181, Fax: 910-672-1596, E-mail: ddbrown@uncfsu.edu.

Fitchburg State University, Division of Graduate and Continuing Education, Program in Elementary Education, Fitchburg, MA 01420-2697. Offers M Ed. *Accreditation:* NCATE. *Program availability:* Part-time, evening/weekend. *Students:* 18 full-time (16 women), 3 part-time (all women). Average age 31. 5 applicants, 100% accepted, 2 enrolled. In 2017, 7 master's awarded. *Entrance requirements:* Additional exam requirements/recommendations for international students: Required—TOEFL (minimum score 550 paper-based; 79 iBT). *Application deadline:* For fall admission, 7/15 for international students; for spring admission, 12/1 for international students. Applications are processed on a rolling basis. Application fee: $50. Electronic applications accepted. *Expenses:* Contact institution. *Financial support:* In 2017–18, research assistantships with partial tuition reimbursements (averaging $5,500 per year) were awarded; Federal Work-Study, scholarships/grants, and unspecified assistantships also available. Support available to part-time students. Financial award application deadline: 3/1; financial award applicants required to submit FAFSA. *Unit head:* Dr. Lyndsey Benharris, Chair, 978-665-3539, Fax: 978-665-3658, E-mail: gce@fitchburgstate.edu. *Application contact:* Jinawa McNeil, Director of Admissions, 978-665-3140, Fax: 978-665-4540, E-mail: admissions@fitchburgstate.edu.

Florida Agricultural and Mechanical University, Division of Graduate Studies, Research, and Continuing Education, College of Education, Department of Elementary Education, Tallahassee, FL 32307-3200. Offers M Ed, MS. *Accreditation:* NCATE. *Degree requirements:* For master's, thesis (for some programs). *Entrance requirements:* For master's, GRE General Test, minimum GPA of 3.0. Additional exam requirements/ recommendations for international students: Required—TOEFL.

Florida Atlantic University, College of Education, Department of Teaching and Learning, Boca Raton, FL 33431-0991. Offers curriculum and instruction (M Ed), including art, biology, chemistry, English, French, German, mathematics, music, physics, Pre-K and primary education, reading, social sciences, Spanish; elementary education (M Ed); environmental education (M Ed); reading education (M Ed); social foundations of education (M Ed), including educational psychology, educational technology, multilingual education. *Accreditation:* NCATE. *Program availability:* Part-

time, evening/weekend. *Faculty:* 13 full-time (10 women), 1 part-time/adjunct (0 women). *Students:* 26 full-time (22 women), 43 part-time (39 women); includes 19 minority (9 Black or African American, non-Hispanic/Latino; 1 Asian, non-Hispanic/Latino; 8 Hispanic/Latino; 1 Two or more races, non-Hispanic/Latino), 3 international. Average age 30. 91 applicants, 57% accepted, 33 enrolled. In 2017, 25 master's awarded. *Entrance requirements:* For master's, GRE General Test, minimum GPA of 3.0 in last 2 years of undergraduate course work. Additional exam requirements/recommendations for international students: Required—TOEFL (minimum score 500 paper-based; 61 iBT), IELTS (minimum score 6). *Application deadline:* For fall admission, 7/1 for domestic students, 2/15 for international students; for spring admission, 11/1 for domestic students, 7/15 for international students. Applications are processed on a rolling basis. Application fee: $30. *Expenses:* Tuition, state resident: full-time $7400; part-time $369.82 per credit. Tuition, nonresident: full-time $20,496; part-time $1042.81 per credit. *Financial support:* Fellowships with partial tuition reimbursements, research assistantships with partial tuition reimbursements, teaching assistantships with partial tuition reimbursements, career-related internships or fieldwork, scholarships/grants, and unspecified assistantships available. *Faculty research:* Technology, teaching English to speakers of other languages, math teaching, electronic portfolio assessment, global perspectives through social studies. *Unit head:* Dr. Barbara Ridener, Chairperson, 561-297-3588, E-mail: bridener@fau.edu. *Application contact:* Dr. Eliah Watlington, Associate Dean, 561-296-8520, Fax: 261-297-2991, E-mail: ewatling@fau.edu.
Website: http://www.coe.fau.edu/academicdepartments/tl/

Florida Gulf Coast University, College of Education, Program in Curriculum and Instruction, Fort Myers, FL 33965-6565. Offers elementary education (M Ed); English education (M Ed); English speakers of other languages endorsement (M Ed); gifted education (M Ed); mathematics education (M Ed); middle school education (M Ed); reading education (M Ed); science education (M Ed); social science education (M Ed); special education (M Ed). *Program availability:* Part-time, evening/weekend, online learning. *Faculty:* 27 full-time (19 women), 44 part-time/adjunct (30 women). *Students:* 3 full-time (all women), 16 part-time (14 women); includes 4 minority (2 Black or African American, non-Hispanic/Latino; 2 Hispanic/Latino). Average age 30. 6 applicants, 100% accepted, 5 enrolled. In 2017, 4 master's awarded. *Degree requirements:* For master's, final project or portfolio. *Entrance requirements:* For master's, GRE General Test, MAT, minimum undergraduate GPA of 3.0 in last 2 years. Additional exam requirements/recommendations for international students: Required—TOEFL (minimum score 550 paper-based). *Application deadline:* For fall admission, 2/15 priority date for domestic students, 5/1 for international students; for spring admission, 12/1 for domestic students, 9/15 for international students. Applications are processed on a rolling basis. Application fee: $30. Electronic applications accepted. *Expenses:* Tuition, state resident: part-time $290 per credit hour. Tuition, nonresident: part-time $1173 per credit hour. *Required fees:* $127 per credit hour. Tuition and fees vary according to course load. *Financial support:* In 2017–18, 2 students received support. Application deadline: 6/30; applicants required to submit FAFSA. *Faculty research:* Internet in schools, technology in pre-service and in-service teacher training. *Unit head:* Dr. Vickie Johnston, Instructor, 239-590-7754, Fax: 239-590-7801, E-mail: vjohnston@fgcu.edu. *Application contact:* Keiana Desmore, Adviser/Counselor, 239-590-7759, Fax: 239-590-7801, E-mail: kdesmore@fgcu.edu.
Website: http://coe.fgcu.edu/c-imed/

Florida Institute of Technology, College of Science, Program in Elementary Science Education, Melbourne, FL 32901-6975. Offers M Ed. *Program availability:* Part-time. *Students:* Average age 25. 2 applicants. *Degree requirements:* For master's, comprehensive exam, thesis or alternative, 30 credit hours, minimum GPA of 3.0. *Entrance requirements:* For master's, minimum GPA of 3.0, 3 letters of recommendation, resume, statement of objectives. Additional exam requirements/recommendations for international students: Required—TOEFL (minimum score 550 paper-based; 79 iBT). *Application deadline:* Applications are processed on a rolling basis. Electronic applications accepted. *Expenses: Tuition:* Part-time $1241 per credit hour. Part-time tuition and fees vary according to campus/location. *Financial support:* Applicants required to submit FAFSA. *Unit head:* Dr. Kastro Hamed, Department Head, 321-674-7206, E-mail: khamed@fit.edu. *Application contact:* Cheryl A. Brown, Associate Director of Graduate Admissions, 321-674-7581, Fax: 321-723-9468, E-mail: cbrown@fit.edu.
Website: http://www.fit.edu/programs/8118/med-elementary-science-education#.VT_jIU0ypo

Florida International University, College of Arts, Sciences, and Education, Department of Teaching and Learning, Miami, FL 33199. Offers art education (MA, MS); curriculum and instruction (MS, Ed D, PhD, Ed S), including curriculum development (MS), elementary education (MS), English education (MS), learning technologies (MS), mathematics education (MS), modern language education (MS), physical education (MS), science education (MS), social studies education (MS), special education (MS), early childhood education (MS); exceptional student education (Ed D); foreign language education (MS), including foreign language education, teaching English to speakers of other languages (TESOL); language, literacy and culture (PhD); mathematics, science, and learning technologies (PhD); physical education (MS), including sport and fitness; reading education (MS). *Program availability:* Part-time, evening/weekend. *Faculty:* 60 full-time (41 women), 112 part-time/adjunct (77 women). *Students:* 165 full-time (139 women), 191 part-time (148 women); includes 270 minority (56 Black or African American, non-Hispanic/Latino; 12 Asian, non-Hispanic/Latino; 191 Hispanic/Latino; 11 Two or more races, non-Hispanic/Latino), 13 international. Average age 34. 238 applicants, 68% accepted, 107 enrolled. In 2017, 184 master's, 15 doctorates awarded. *Degree requirements:* For doctorate, comprehensive exam, thesis/dissertation. *Entrance requirements:* For master's, GRE General Test, Florida General Knowledge Test or Florida College Level Academic Skills Test; for doctorate and Ed S, GRE General Test. Additional exam requirements/recommendations for international students: Required—TOEFL (minimum score 550 paper-based; 80 iBT), IELTS (minimum score 6.3). *Application deadline:* For fall admission, 6/1 priority date for domestic students, 4/1 for international students; for winter admission, 10/1 priority date for domestic students, 9/1 for international students; for spring admission, 3/1 priority date for domestic students, 2/1 for international students. Applications are processed on a rolling basis. Application fee: $30. Electronic applications accepted. *Expenses:* Tuition, state resident: full-time $8912; part-time $446 per credit hour. Tuition, nonresident: full-time $21,393; part-time $992 per credit hour. *Required fees:* $390; $195 per semester. *Financial support:* Research assistantships with tuition reimbursements and teaching assistantships with tuition reimbursements available. *Unit head:* Dr. Lynn Miller, Chair, 305-348-2005, Fax: 305-348-2086, E-mail: lynne.miller@fiu.edu. *Application contact:* Nanett Rojas, Assistant Director, Graduate Admissions, 305-348-7464, Fax: 305-348-7441, E-mail: gradadm@fiu.edu.
Website: https://tl.fiu.edu/

Florida Memorial University, School of Education, Miami-Dade, FL 33054. Offers elementary education (MS); exceptional student education (MS); reading (MS). *Degree requirements:* For master's, comprehensive exam or thesis, field and clinical experiences, exit exam. *Entrance requirements:* For master's, GRE, CLAST, PRAXIS I, baccalaureate or graduate degree with minimum GPA of 3.0 in last 60 hours, 3

recommendations. Additional exam requirements/recommendations for international students: Recommended—TOEFL.

Florida State University, The Graduate School, College of Education, School of Teacher Education, Tallahassee, FL 32306-4450. Offers curriculum and instruction (MS, PhD, Ed S), including early childhood education, elementary education, English education, foreign and second language education, mathematics education, reading and language arts, science education, social science education, special education, visual disabilities education (MS); teaching English to speakers of other languages (Certificate). *Program availability:* Part-time, evening/weekend, 100% online, blended/hybrid learning, asynchronous, minimal on-campus study. *Faculty:* 41 full-time (33 women), 21 part-time/adjunct (18 women). *Students:* 133 full-time (93 women), 84 part-time (69 women); includes 48 minority (20 Black or African American, non-Hispanic/Latino; 2 Asian, non-Hispanic/Latino; 19 Hispanic/Latino; 7 Two or more races, non-Hispanic/Latino), 52 international. Average age 31. 146 applicants, 56% accepted, 52 enrolled. In 2017, 91 master's, 7 doctorates, 1 other advanced degree awarded. Terminal master's awarded for partial completion of doctoral program. *Degree requirements:* For master's and other advanced degree, comprehensive exam, thesis optional; for doctorate, comprehensive exam, thesis/dissertation, diagnostic exam, preliminary exam, prospectus defense, dissertation defense. *Entrance requirements:* For master's, doctorate, and other advanced degree, GRE General Test, minimum upper-division GPA of 3.0. Additional exam requirements/recommendations for international students: Required—TOEFL (minimum score 550 paper-based, 80 iBT), Michigan English Language Assessment Battery (minimum score 77), IELTS (minimum score 6.5) or PTE (minimum score 55). Application fee: $30. Electronic applications accepted. *Financial support:* Fellowships, research assistantships, teaching assistantships, scholarships/grants, tuition waivers (full and partial), and unspecified assistantships available. Financial award application deadline: 1/15; financial award applicants required to submit FAFSA. *Faculty research:* Identifying effective intervention strategies to improve reading skills; improving literacy teaching and learning through technology; understanding of student sense making, problem solving, the history and structure of STEM disciplines, and teacher education to support the development of ambitious instruction that supports the STEM learning of all students; examining practices of international education; identifying ways to support the professional development of teachers. *Unit head:* Dr. Sherry Southerland, Professor/Department Chair, 850-644-6885, Fax: 850-644-2725, E-mail: ssoutherland@admin.fsu.edu. *Application contact:* Britni DeZerga, Academic Program Specialist, 850-644-2122, Fax: 850-644-7736, E-mail: bpurvis@fsu.edu.
Website: http://education.fsu.edu

Fontbonne University, Graduate Programs, St. Louis, MO 63105-3098. Offers accounting (MBA, MS); art (MA); art (K-12) (MAT); business (MBA); computer science (MS); deaf education (MA); early intervention in deaf education (MA); education (MA), including autism spectrum disorders, curriculum and instruction, diverse learners, early childhood education, reading, special education; elementary education (MAT); family and consumer sciences (MA), including multidisciplinary health communication studies; fine arts (MFA); instructional design and technology (MS); management and leadership (MM); middle school education (MAT); secondary education (MAT); special education (MAT); speech-language pathology (MS); supply chain management (MS); theatre (MA). *Program availability:* Part-time, evening/weekend, online learning. *Degree requirements:* For master's, comprehensive exam (for some programs), thesis (for some programs). *Entrance requirements:* Additional exam requirements/recommendations for international students: Required—TOEFL (minimum score 500 paper-based; 65 iBT). Electronic applications accepted.

Fordham University, Graduate School of Education, Division of Curriculum and Teaching, New York, NY 10023. Offers curriculum and teaching (MSE); early childhood education (MSE); elementary education (MST); special education (MSE, Adv C); teaching English as a second language (MSE). *Accreditation:* NCATE. *Program availability:* Part-time, evening/weekend. *Degree requirements:* For Adv C, thesis. *Entrance requirements:* Additional exam requirements/recommendations for international students: Required—TOEFL (minimum score 577 paper-based; 90 iBT), IELTS (minimum score 7). Electronic applications accepted.

Framingham State University, Graduate Studies, Program in Elementary Education, Framingham, MA 01701-9101. Offers M Ed. *Unit head:* Sandra Shaw, Program Advisor, 508-626-4573, Fax: 508-626-5734, E-mail: sshaw1@framingham.edu. *Application contact:* Graduate Office, 508-626-4550, Fax: 508-626-4030, E-mail: dgce@frc.mass.edu.

Franklin Pierce University, Graduate and Professional Studies, Rindge, NH 03461-0060. Offers curriculum and instruction (M Ed); elementary education (MS Ed); emerging network technologies (Graduate Certificate); energy and sustainability studies (MBA, Graduate Certificate); health administration (MBA, Graduate Certificate); human resource management (MBA, Graduate Certificate); information technology (MBA); leadership (MBA); nursing education (MS); nursing leadership (MS); physical therapy (DPT); physician assistant studies (MPAS); special education (M Ed); sports management (MBA). *Accreditation:* APTA. *Program availability:* Part-time, 100% online, blended/hybrid learning. *Degree requirements:* For master's, concentrated original research projects; student teaching; fieldwork and/or internship; leadership project; PRAXIS I and II (for M Ed); for doctorate, concentrated original research projects, clinical fieldwork and/or internship, leadership project. *Entrance requirements:* For master's, minimum GPA of 2.5, 3 letters of recommendation; competencies in accounting, economics, statistics, and computer skills through life experience or undergraduate coursework (for MBA); certification/e-portfolio, minimum C grade in all education courses (for M Ed); license to practice as RN (for MS); for doctorate, GRE, 80 hours of observation/work in PT settings; completion of anatomy, chemistry, physics, and statistics; minimum GPA of 3.0. Additional exam requirements/recommendations for international students: Required—TOEFL (minimum score 550 paper-based; 61 iBT). Electronic applications accepted. *Faculty research:* Evidence-based practice in sports physical therapy, human resource management in economic crisis, leadership in nursing, innovation in sports facility management, differentiated learning and understanding by design.

Frostburg State University, College of Education, Department of Educational Professions, Program in Curriculum and Instruction, Frostburg, MD 21532. Offers curriculum and instruction (Ed D); educational technology (M Ed); elementary education (M Ed); secondary education (M Ed). *Program availability:* Part-time, evening/weekend. *Faculty:* 2. *Students:* 45 part-time (33 women); includes 1 minority (Two or more races, non-Hispanic/Latino). Average age 34. 15 applicants, 93% accepted, 11 enrolled. In 2017, 5 master's, 1 doctorate awarded. *Degree requirements:* For master's, thesis or alternative. *Entrance requirements:* For master's, teaching certificate. Additional exam requirements/recommendations for international students: Required—TOEFL. *Application deadline:* For fall admission, 7/15 priority date for domestic students. Applications are processed on a rolling basis. Application fee: $45. Electronic applications accepted. *Expenses:* Tuition, state resident: part-time $433 per credit hour. Tuition, nonresident: part-time $557 per credit hour. *Required fees:* $121 per credit hour. $27 per term. *Financial support:* In 2017–18, 2 research assistantships with full tuition reimbursements (averaging $5,000 per year) were awarded. Financial award application

Elementary Education

deadline: 4/1; financial award applicants required to submit FAFSA. *Unit head:* Dr. Jennifer Rankin, Coordinator, 301-687-7010, E-mail: jerankin@frostburg.edu. *Application contact:* Vickie Mazer, Director, Graduate Services, 301-687-7053, Fax: 301-687-4597, E-mail: vmmazer@frostburg.edu.

Frostburg State University, College of Education, Department of Educational Professions, Program in Elementary Teaching, Frostburg, MD 21532. Offers MAT. *Accreditation:* NCATE. *Students:* 8 full-time (5 women); includes 1 minority (Two or more races, non-Hispanic/Latino). Average age 28. 35 applicants, 66% accepted, 10 enrolled. In 2017, 5 master's awarded. *Degree requirements:* For master's, thesis or alternative, PRAXIS II. *Entrance requirements:* For master's, PRAXIS I, entry portfolio. Additional exam requirements/recommendations for international students: Required—TOEFL. *Application deadline:* For fall admission, 7/15 priority date for domestic students. Applications are processed on a rolling basis. Application fee: $45. Electronic applications accepted. *Expenses:* Tuition, state resident: part-time $433 per credit hour. Tuition, nonresident: part-time $557 per credit hour. *Required fees:* $121 per credit hour. $27 per term. *Financial support:* In 2017–18, 1 research assistantship with full tuition reimbursement (averaging $5,000 per year) was awarded. Financial award application deadline: 4/1; financial award applicants required to submit FAFSA. *Unit head:* Yvonne Belt, Coordinator, 301-687-4294. *Application contact:* Vickie Mazer, Director, Graduate Services, 301-687-7053, Fax: 301-687-4597, E-mail: vmmazer@frostburg.edu.

Gallaudet University, The Graduate School, Washington, DC 20002-3625. Offers American Sign Language/English bilingual early childhood deaf education: birth to 5 (Certificate); audiology (Au D); clinical psychology (PhD); deaf and hard of hearing infants, toddlers, and their families (Certificate); deaf education (MA, Ed S); deaf history (Certificate); deaf studies (Certificate); educating deaf students with disabilities (Certificate); education: teacher preparation (MA), including deaf education, early childhood education and deaf education, elementary education and deaf education, secondary education and deaf education; educational neuroscience (PhD); hearing, speech and language sciences (MS, PhD); international development (MA); interpretation (MA, PhD), including combined interpreting practice and research (MA), interpreting research (MA); linguistics (MA, PhD); mental health counseling (MA); peer mentoring (Certificate); public administration (MPA); school counseling (MA); school psychology (Psy S); sign language teaching (MA); social work (MSW); speech-language pathology (MS). *Program availability:* Part-time. Terminal master's awarded for partial completion of doctoral program. *Degree requirements:* For master's, comprehensive exam (for some programs), thesis optional; for doctorate, comprehensive exam, thesis/dissertation. *Entrance requirements:* For master's and doctorate, GRE General Test or MAT, letters of recommendation, interviews, goals statement, American Sign Language proficiency interview, written English competency. Additional exam requirements/recommendations for international students: Required—TOEFL. Electronic applications accepted. *Faculty research:* Signing math dictionaries, telecommunications access, cancer genetics, linguistics, visual language and visual learning, integrated quantum materials, deaf legal discourse, advance recruitment and retention in geosciences.

George Mason University, College of Education and Human Development, Programs in Curriculum and Instruction, Fairfax, VA 22030. Offers advanced international baccalaureate (M Ed); assistive technology (M Ed); designing digital learning in schools (M Ed); early childhood education (M Ed); early childhood education for diverse learners (M Ed); elementary education (M Ed); English as a second language (M Ed); gifted child education (M Ed); history (M Ed); literacy (M Ed), including PK-12 classroom teachers, reading specialist; literacy leadership for diverse schools (M Ed), including K-12 reading; physical education (M Ed); science K-12 (M Ed); secondary education (M Ed), including biology, chemistry, earth science, English, history/social science, math, physics; special education (M Ed); teacher leadership (M Ed); teaching culturally, linguistically diverse and exceptional learners (M Ed); transformative teaching (M Ed). *Program availability:* Part-time, evening/weekend, 100% online, blended/hybrid learning. *Faculty:* 41 full-time (36 women), 45 part-time/adjunct (37 women). *Students:* 173 full-time (151 women), 729 part-time (611 women); includes 271 minority (65 Black or African American, non-Hispanic/Latino; 5 American Indian or Alaska Native, non-Hispanic/Latino; 88 Asian, non-Hispanic/Latino; 94 Hispanic/Latino; 1 Native Hawaiian or other Pacific Islander, non-Hispanic/Latino; 18 Two or more races, non-Hispanic/Latino; 28 international. Average age 32. 426 applicants, 91% accepted, 289 enrolled. In 2017, 349 master's awarded. *Degree requirements:* For master's, thesis. *Entrance requirements:* For master's, PRAXIS Core (for some programs), 2 letters of recommendation, interview, program goals statement; 9 hours of complete licensure endorsement requirements (for elementary education); minimum GPA of 3.0 in applicant's last 60 hours of undergraduate coursework (for secondary education); at least 1 year of teaching experience (for literacy). Additional exam requirements/recommendations for international students: Required—TOEFL (minimum score 575 paper-based; 88 iBT), IELTS (minimum score 6.5), PTE (minimum score 59). *Application deadline:* For fall admission, 4/2 priority date for domestic and international students; for spring admission, 11/1 for domestic and international students. Application fee: $75 ($80 for international students). Electronic applications accepted. *Expenses:* Tuition, state resident: full-time $11,228; part-time $459.50 per credit. Tuition, nonresident: full-time $30,932; part-time $1280.50 per credit. *Required fees:* $3252; $135.50 per credit. Part-time tuition and fees vary according to course load and program. *Financial support:* In 2017–18, 2 students received support, including 2 teaching assistantships; career-related internships or fieldwork, Federal Work-Study, scholarships/grants, unspecified assistantships, and health care benefits (for full-time research or teaching assistantship recipients) also available. Support available to part-time students. Financial award application deadline: 3/1; financial award applicants required to submit FAFSA. *Faculty research:* Teacher preparation and professional development; adaptive teaching; wonder in science teacher preparation; literacy (digital, adolescent); site based course instruction. *Unit head:* Rebecca Fox, Professor and Academic Program Coordinator, 703-993-4123, E-mail: rfox@gmu.edu.
Website: http://gse.gmu.edu/programs/gsemasters

The George Washington University, Graduate School of Education and Human Development, Department of Curriculum and Pedagogy, Program in Elementary Education, Washington, DC 20052. Offers MA Ed/HD. *Accreditation:* NCATE. *Program availability:* Part-time. *Students:* 17 full-time (15 women), 6 part-time (3 women); includes 7 minority (4 Black or African American, non-Hispanic/Latino; 1 Asian, non-Hispanic/Latino; 2 Hispanic/Latino), 1 international. Average age 27. 47 applicants, 79% accepted, 20 enrolled. In 2017, 14 master's awarded. *Entrance requirements:* For master's, GRE General Test or MAT, minimum GPA of 2.75. *Application deadline:* For fall admission, 1/15 priority date for domestic students; for spring admission, 10/1 for domestic students. Applications are processed on a rolling basis. Application fee: $75. *Expenses:* Tuition: Full-time $28,800; part-time $1655 per credit hour. *Required fees:* $45; $2.75 per credit hour. *Financial support:* In 2017–18, 20 students received support. Fellowships, career-related internships or fieldwork, Federal Work-Study, and tuition waivers (partial) available. Financial award application deadline: 1/15; financial award applicants required to submit FAFSA. *Faculty research:* Issues in teacher training. *Unit head:* Dr. Sylvan S. Beck, Director, 202-994-3365, E-mail: sbeck@gwu.edu. *Application contact:* Sarah Lang, Director of Graduate Admissions, 202-994-1447, Fax: 202-994-7207, E-mail: slang@gwu.edu.

Georgia State University, College of Education and Human Development, Department of Early Childhood Education, Atlanta, GA 30302-3083. Offers early childhood and elementary education (PhD); early childhood education (M Ed, Ed S); mathematics education (M Ed); urban education (M Ed). *Accreditation:* NCATE. *Program availability:* Part-time, evening/weekend. *Faculty:* 27 full-time (22 women). *Students:* 74 full-time (68 women), 22 part-time (21 women); includes 49 minority (41 Black or African American, non-Hispanic/Latino; 4 Asian, non-Hispanic/Latino; 2 Hispanic/Latino; 2 Two or more races, non-Hispanic/Latino), 3 international. Average age 30. 49 applicants, 65% accepted, 25 enrolled. In 2017, 27 master's, 3 doctorates awarded. *Entrance requirements:* For master's, GRE, undergraduate diploma; for doctorate and Ed S, GRE, master's degree. *Application deadline:* Applications are processed on a rolling basis. Application fee: $50. Electronic applications accepted. *Expenses:* Tuition, state resident: full-time $7020. Tuition, nonresident: full-time $22,518. *Required fees:* $2128. Tuition and fees vary according to degree level and program. *Financial support:* In 2017–18, fellowships with full tuition reimbursements (averaging $24,000 per year), research assistantships with tuition reimbursements (averaging $4,000 per year), teaching assistantships with full tuition reimbursements (averaging $2,000 per year) were awarded; career-related internships or fieldwork, Federal Work-Study, institutionally sponsored loans, scholarships/grants, traineeships, health care benefits, tuition waivers (partial), and unspecified assistantships also available. Support available to part-time students. Financial award applicants required to submit FAFSA. *Faculty research:* Teacher development; language arts/literacy education; mathematics education; intersection of science, urban, and multicultural education; diversity in education. *Unit head:* Dr. Barbara Meyers, Department Chair, 404-413-8021, Fax: 404-413-8023, E-mail: barbara@gsu.edu. *Application contact:* Elaine King Jones, Administrative Curriculum Specialist, 404-413-8234, Fax: 404-413-8023, E-mail: ekjones@gsu.edu. Website: http://ecee.education.gsu.edu.

Gonzaga University, School of Education, Spokane, WA 99258. Offers clinical mental health counseling (MA); educational leadership (M Ed, Ed D); elementary education (MIT); marriage and family counseling (MA); school counseling (MA); secondary education (MIT); special education (M Ed, MIT); sport and athletic administration (MA). *Accreditation:* NCATE. *Program availability:* Part-time, evening/weekend, 100% online, blended/hybrid learning. *Faculty:* 16 full-time (11 women), 31 part-time/adjunct (19 women). *Students:* 108 full-time (90 women), 225 part-time (140 women); includes 34 minority (4 Black or African American, non-Hispanic/Latino; 2 American Indian or Alaska Native, non-Hispanic/Latino; 5 Asian, non-Hispanic/Latino; 18 Hispanic/Latino; 5 Two or more races, non-Hispanic/Latino), 114 international. Average age 31. 367 applicants, 74% accepted, 160 enrolled. In 2017, 175 master's awarded. *Degree requirements:* For master's, comprehensive exam. *Entrance requirements:* For master's, GRE, MAT, and/or Washington Educator Skills Test-Basic (WEST-B), Washington Educator Skills Test-Endorsements (WEST-E), official transcripts from all colleges or universities attended, interview, two letters of recommendation, resume, essay, minimum GPA of 3.0. Additional exam requirements/recommendations for international students: Required—TOEFL (minimum score 580 paper-based, 88 iBT) or IELTS (minimum score 6.5). *Application deadline:* Applications are processed on a rolling basis. Application fee: $50. Electronic applications accepted. *Expenses:* $990 per credit. *Financial support:* In 2017–18, 51 students received support. Scholarships/grants and unspecified assistantships available. Support available to part-time students. Financial award applicants required to submit FAFSA. *Unit head:* Dr. Vincent Alfonso, Dean, 509-313-3594, Fax: 509-313-5821, E-mail: alfonso@gonzaga.edu. *Application contact:* Meg Martens, Graduate Admissions Program Specialist, 509-313-4314, E-mail: martens@gonzaga.edu. Website: https://www.gonzaga.edu/school-of-education

Gordon College, Graduate Education Program, Wenham, MA 01984-1899. Offers early childhood (M Ed); educational leadership (M Ed, Ed S); elementary education (M Ed); English as a second language (M Ed, Ed S); math specialist (M Ed); mathematics specialist (Ed S); middle school education (M Ed); moderate disabilities (M Ed); Montessori education (M Ed); reading (M Ed, Ed S); secondary education (M Ed). *Program availability:* Part-time, evening/weekend. *Faculty:* 23 full-time (17 women), 32 part-time/adjunct (23 women). *Students:* 68 full-time (50 women), 114 part-time (99 women); includes 24 minority (2 Black or African American, non-Hispanic/Latino; 8 Asian, non-Hispanic/Latino; 13 Hispanic/Latino; 1 Two or more races, non-Hispanic/Latino), 10 international. Average age 34. 248 applicants, 100% accepted, 182 enrolled. In 2017, 99 master's, 16 Ed Ss awarded. *Degree requirements:* For master's, action research or clinical experience (for most programs); for Ed S, action research or clinical experience (for some programs). *Entrance requirements:* For master's, minimum undergraduate GPA of 3.0; 2 official undergraduate transcripts; professional resume; 3 recommendation letters (one professional reference, one academic reference, one personal reference); 500-700 word statement of purpose; for Ed S, minimum master's GPA of 3.3; 2 official transcripts from undergraduate and graduate schools; professional resume; 3 recommendation letters (one professional reference, one academic reference, one personal reference); 500-700 word statement of purpose. Additional exam requirements/recommendations for international students: Required—TOEFL (minimum score 550 paper-based, 80 iBT) or IELTS (minimum score 6.5). *Application deadline:* Applications are processed on a rolling basis. Application fee: $75. *Expenses:* $325 per credit tuition; $75 per semester administrative fee. *Financial support:* Applicants required to submit FAFSA. *Faculty research:* Reading, early childhood development, English language learners, universal design for learning. *Unit head:* Dr. Janet Arndt, Director of Graduate Studies, 978-867-4355, Fax: 978-867-4663. *Application contact:* Julie Lenocker, Program Administrator, 978-867-4322, Fax: 978-867-4663, E-mail: graduate-education@gordon.edu. Website: http://www.gordon.edu/graduate

Goucher College, Graduate Programs in Education, Baltimore, MD 21204-2794. Offers at-risk and diverse learners (M Ed, Certificate); athletic program leadership and administration (M Ed, Certificate); elementary education (MAT); literacy strategies for content learning (M Ed); middle school (M Ed, Certificate); Montessori studies (M Ed); reading instruction (M Ed, Certificate); reducing student, classroom, and school disruption (M Ed); school improvement leadership (M Ed); secondary education (MAT); special education (MAT), including elementary education; special education for certified elementary and secondary teachers (M Ed); teacher as leader in technology (M Ed). *Program availability:* Part-time, evening/weekend. *Degree requirements:* For master's, thesis (M Ed), final presentation (MAT). *Entrance requirements:* For master's, minimum GPA of 3.0. Additional exam requirements/recommendations for international students: Required—TOEFL (minimum score 550 paper-based; 80 iBT), IELTS (minimum score 7). *Application deadline:* For fall admission, 9/1 for domestic students; for spring admission, 1/15 for domestic students. Applications are processed on a rolling basis. Application fee: $75. Electronic applications accepted. *Expenses:* Contact institution. *Financial support:* Career-related internships or fieldwork and unspecified assistantships available. Support available to part-time students. Financial award application deadline: 4/15; financial award applicants required to submit FAFSA. *Faculty research:* Urban education, middle school, school improvement, teacher education, at-risk student achievement. *Unit head:* Dr. Phyllis Sunshine, Assistant Provost, 410-337-6047, Fax: 410-337-6394, E-mail: psunshin@goucher.edu. *Application contact:* Carlton E. Surbeck, III, Director of Admissions, 410-337-6100, Fax: 410-337-6085, E-mail: admissions@goucher.edu. Website: http://www.goucher.edu/graduate-programs/graduate-programs-in-education

Grand Canyon University, College of Education, Phoenix, AZ 85017-1097. Offers autism spectrum disorders (MA); curriculum and instruction (MA); early childhood education (M Ed); educational administration (M Ed); educational leadership (M Ed); elementary education (M Ed); gifted education (MA); instructional technology (MS); K-12 leadership (Ed S); reading (MA); secondary education (M Ed); secondary humanities education (M Ed); secondary STEM education (M Ed); special education (M Ed); teaching and learning (Ed D); teaching English to speakers of other languages (MA). *Program availability:* Part-time, evening/weekend, online learning. *Degree requirements:* For master's, publishable research paper (M Ed), e-portfolio. *Entrance requirements:* For master's, undergraduate degree from accredited, GCU-approved college, university, or program with minimum GPA 2.8. Additional exam requirements/recommendations for international students: Required—TOEFL (minimum score 550 paper-based; 79 iBT), IELTS (minimum score 6). Electronic applications accepted.

Grand Valley State University, College of Education, Programs in General Education, Allendale, MI 49401-9403. Offers adult and higher education (M Ed); early childhood education (M Ed); educational differentiation (M Ed); educational leadership (M Ed); educational technology integration (M Ed); elementary education (M Ed); middle level education (M Ed); school library media services (M Ed); secondary level education (M Ed); teaching English to speakers of other languages (M Ed). *Program availability:* Part-time, evening/weekend, 100% online, blended/hybrid learning. *Students:* 24 part-time (16 women). Average age 41. In 2017, 5 master's awarded. *Degree requirements:* For master's, project or thesis. *Entrance requirements:* For master's, GRE General Test or minimum GPA of 3.0, last 60 credits from regionally-accredited college/university, 3 letters of recommendation. Additional exam requirements/recommendations for international students: Required—TOEFL (minimum iBT score of 80), IELTS (6.5), or Michigan English Language Assessment Battery (77). *Application deadline:* Applications are processed on a rolling basis. Application fee: $30. Electronic applications accepted. *Expenses:* $652 per credit hour. *Financial support:* In 2017–18, 2 students received support, including 2 fellowships; career-related internships or fieldwork, Federal Work-Study, scholarships/grants, and unspecified assistantships also available. *Faculty research:* Effectiveness of technology in education, parental involvement, effective teaching, effective schools research. *Unit head:* Dr. David Bair, Department Director, 616-331-6489, Fax: 616-331-6489, E-mail: baird@gvsu.edu. *Application contact:* Thomas Owens, Director, Student Information and Services Center, 616-331-6282, Fax: 616-331-6217, E-mail: owenst@gvsu.edu.
Website: http://www.gvsu.edu/coe/

Greensboro College, Program in Education, Greensboro, NC 27401-1875. Offers elementary education (M Ed); special education (M Ed). *Program availability:* Part-time, evening/weekend. *Degree requirements:* For master's, thesis. *Entrance requirements:* For master's, GRE, teacher license, 2 years of teaching experience, 2 letters of recommendation. Additional exam requirements/recommendations for international students: Required—TOEFL (minimum score 550 paper-based). Electronic applications accepted.

Greenville University, Program in Education, Greenville, IL 62246-0159. Offers education (MAT); elementary education (MAE); secondary education (MAE). *Degree requirements:* For master's, thesis (for some programs). *Entrance requirements:* For master's, GRE, Illinois Basic Skills Test, teacher certification. Electronic applications accepted.

Harding University, Cannon-Clary College of Education, Searcy, AR 72149-0001. Offers advanced studies in teaching and learning (M Ed); art (MSE); behavioral science (MSE); counseling (MS, Ed S); early childhood special education (M Ed, MSE); education (MSE); educational leadership (M Ed, Ed S); elementary education (M Ed); English (MSE); French (MSE); history/social science (MSE); kinesiology (MSE); math (MSE); reading (M Ed); secondary education (MSE); Spanish (MSE); teaching (MAT); teaching English as a second language (MSE). *Accreditation:* NCATE. *Program availability:* Part-time, evening/weekend. *Faculty:* 22 full-time (9 women), 51 part-time/adjunct (37 women). *Students:* 135 full-time (95 women), 316 part-time (231 women); includes 77 minority (46 Black or African American, non-Hispanic/Latino; 7 American Indian or Alaska Native, non-Hispanic/Latino; 4 Asian, non-Hispanic/Latino; 9 Hispanic/Latino; 11 Two or more races, non-Hispanic/Latino), 11 international. Average age 34. 128 applicants, 87% accepted, 111 enrolled. In 2017, 153 master's, 24 other advanced degrees awarded. *Degree requirements:* For master's, comprehensive exam (for some programs), thesis optional, portfolio(s); for Ed S, comprehensive exam, portfolio, project. *Entrance requirements:* For master's, GRE, MAT, PRAXIS; for Ed S, MAT or GRE. Additional exam requirements/recommendations for international students: Required—TOEFL (minimum score 550 paper-based; 79 iBT). *Application deadline:* For fall admission, 8/1 for domestic and international students; for spring admission, 1/1 for domestic and international students. Applications are processed on a rolling basis. Application fee: $35. Tuition and fees vary according to course load, degree level, campus/location and program. *Financial support:* In 2017–18, 33 students received support. Unspecified assistantships available. *Faculty research:* Reading, comprehension, school violence, educational technology, behavior, college choice, differentiated instruction, brain-based teaching. *Unit head:* Dr. Clara Carroll, Chair, 501-279-4501, Fax: 501-279-4083, E-mail: ccarroll@harding.edu. *Application contact:* Information Contact, 501-279-4315, E-mail: gradstudiesedu@harding.edu.
Website: http://www.harding.edu/education

Hawai'i Pacific University, College of Professional Studies, Program in Elementary Education, Honolulu, HI 96813. Offers M Ed. *Accreditation:* TEAC. *Program availability:* Part-time, evening/weekend. *Faculty:* 4 full-time (3 women), 6 part-time/adjunct (3 women). *Students:* 11 full-time (6 women); includes 6 minority (1 Black or African American, non-Hispanic/Latino; 2 Asian, non-Hispanic/Latino; 2 Hispanic/Latino; 1 Two or more races, non-Hispanic/Latino). Average age 40. 10 applicants, 80% accepted, 6 enrolled. In 2017, 8 master's awarded. *Entrance requirements:* For master's, minimum undergraduate GPA of 3.0, background check, interview. Additional exam requirements/recommendations for international students: Recommended—TOEFL (minimum score 550 paper-based; 80 iBT), IELTS (minimum score 6), TWE (minimum score 5). *Application deadline:* For fall admission, 1/15 priority date for domestic students; for spring admission, 10/15 priority date for domestic students. Applications are processed on a rolling basis. Application fee: $50. Electronic applications accepted. *Expenses: Tuition:* Full-time $18,000; part-time $1000 per credit. *Required fees:* $200; $26 per credit. Tuition and fees vary according to course load and program. *Financial support:* In 2017–18, 2 students received support. Career-related internships or fieldwork, Federal Work-Study, scholarships/grants, tuition waivers (partial), and unspecified assistantships available. Financial award application deadline: 3/1; financial award applicants required to submit FAFSA. *Unit head:* Dr. Roger Kiyomura, Director, 808-544-1477, E-mail: rkiyomura@hpu.edu. *Application contact:* Danny Lam, Assistant Director of Graduate Admissions, 808-544-1135, E-mail: graduate@hpu.edu.
Website: https://www.hpu.edu/cps/education/me-elementary.html

High Point University, Norcross Graduate School, High Point, NC 27268. Offers athletic training (MSAT); business administration (MBA); educational leadership (M Ed, Ed D); elementary education (M Ed, MAT); pharmacy (Pharm D); physical therapy (DPT); physician assistant studies (MPAS); secondary mathematics (M Ed, MAT); special education (M Ed); strategic communication (MA). *Accreditation:* NCATE.

Program availability: Part-time, evening/weekend. *Degree requirements:* For master's, comprehensive exam (for some programs), thesis (for some programs). *Entrance requirements:* For master's, GMAT (MBA), GRE, MAT, minimum GPA of 3.0. Additional exam requirements/recommendations for international students: Required—TOEFL (minimum score 550 paper-based). Electronic applications accepted.

Hofstra University, School of Education, Programs in Teacher Education, Hempstead, NY 11549. Offers bilingual education (MA); bilingual extension (Advanced Certificate), including education/speech language pathology, intensive teacher institute; business education (MS Ed); curriculum studies (MS Ed); early childhood and childhood education (MS Ed); early childhood education (MA, MS Ed); educational technology (Advanced Certificate); elementary education (MA, MS Ed), including science, technology, engineering, and mathematics (STEM) (MA); English education (MS Ed); family and consumer science (MS Ed); fine arts and music education (Advanced Certificate); fine arts education (MS Ed); foreign language and TESOL (MS Ed); foreign language education (MA, MS Ed), including Arabic (MS Ed), biology, chemistry, Chinese (MS Ed), earth science, French, German, Italian (MS Ed), Mandarin (MS Ed), physics, Russian, Spanish; foundations of education (Advanced Certificate), including grades 5-6, grades 7-9; languages other than English and teaching English as a second language (MA); learning and teaching (Ed D), including applied linguistics, art education, arts and humanities, early childhood education, English education, human development, math education, math, science, and technology, multicultural education, physical education, science education, social studies education, special education; mathematics education (MA, MS Ed); music education (MA, MS Ed); science education (MA), including biology (MA, MS Ed), chemistry (MA, MS Ed), earth science (MA, MS Ed), physics (MA, MS Ed); secondary education (Advanced Certificate); social studies education (MA, MS Ed); teaching languages other than English and TESOL (MS Ed); technology for learning (MA); TESOL (MS Ed, Advanced Certificate); TESOL with specialization in STEM (MA); work based learning extension (Advanced Certificate). *Program availability:* Part-time, evening/weekend, blended/hybrid learning. *Students:* 119 full-time (83 women), 124 part-time (90 women); includes 54 minority (15 Black or African American, non-Hispanic/Latino; 9 Asian, non-Hispanic/Latino; 29 Hispanic/Latino; 1 Native Hawaiian or other Pacific Islander, non-Hispanic/Latino), 12 international. Average age 29. 205 applicants, 88% accepted, 93 enrolled. In 2017, 103 master's, 4 doctorates, 32 other advanced degrees awarded. *Degree requirements:* For master's, comprehensive exam, thesis, exit project, student teaching, fieldwork, electronic portfolio, curriculum project, minimum GPA of 3.0; for doctorate, thesis/dissertation; for Advanced Certificate, 3 foreign languages, comprehensive exam (for some programs), thesis project. *Entrance requirements:* For master's, GRE, 2 letters of recommendation, portfolio, teacher certification (MA), interview, essay; for doctorate, GMAT, GRE, LSAT, or MAT; for Advanced Certificate, 2 letters of recommendation, essay, interview and/or portfolio, teaching certificate. Additional exam requirements/recommendations for international students: Required—TOEFL (minimum score 550 paper-based; 80 iBT). *Application deadline:* Applications are processed on a rolling basis. Application fee: $75. Electronic applications accepted. *Expenses: Tuition:* Full-time $1292. *Required fees:* $970. Tuition and fees vary according to program. *Financial support:* In 2017–18, 112 students received support, including 56 fellowships with full and partial tuition reimbursements available (averaging $4,998 per year), 2 research assistantships with full and partial tuition reimbursements available (averaging $8,753 per year); career-related internships or fieldwork, Federal Work-Study, institutionally sponsored loans, scholarships/grants, traineeships, tuition waivers (full and partial), and unspecified assistantships also available. Support available to part-time students. Financial award applicants required to submit FAFSA. *Faculty research:* Educational interventions that foster critical-thinking skills; teachers' attitudes about professional development; threats to teacher quality. *Unit head:* Dr. Eustace Thompson, Chairperson, 516-463-5749, Fax: 516-463-6275, E-mail: eustace.g.thompson@hofstra.edu. *Application contact:* Sunil Samuel, Assistant Vice President of Admissions, 516-463-4723, Fax: 516-463-4664, E-mail: graduateadmission@hofstra.edu.
Website: http://www.hofstra.edu/education/

Hofstra University, School of Education, Specialized Programs in Education, Hempstead, NY 11549. Offers applied behavior analysis (Advanced Certificate); childhood special education (MS Ed); early childhood special education (MS Ed, Advanced Certificate); educational and policy leadership (Ed D); educational leadership (Advanced Certificate), including school building leader/school district business leader; educational leadership and policy studies (MS Ed), including K-12; elementary special education (MS Ed); gifted education (Advanced Certificate), including school building leader/school district business leader; health education (MS); health professions pedagogy and leadership (MS); higher education leadership and policy studies (MS Ed); inclusive early childhood special education (MS Ed); inclusive elementary special education (MS Ed); inclusive secondary special education (MS Ed); literacy studies (MA, MS Ed, Ed D, Advanced Certificate), including birth-grade 6 (MS Ed, Advanced Certificate), grades 5-12 (MS Ed, Advanced Certificate); literacy studies (Ed D); pedagogy for health professions (Advanced Certificate); physical education (MS); school district business leader (Advanced Certificate); secondary education generalist - students with disabilities 7-12 (MS Ed), including students with disabilities 7-12; secondary special education generalist (MS Ed), including extension in secondary education; special education (MS Ed, Advanced Certificate); special education assessment and diagnosis (Advanced Certificate); special education early childhood intervention (MS Ed); special education: international perspectives (MS Ed); teaching students with severe or multiple disabilities (Advanced Certificate). *Program availability:* Part-time, evening/weekend, blended/hybrid learning. *Students:* 148 full-time (110 women), 249 part-time (188 women); includes 105 minority (54 Black or African American, non-Hispanic/Latino; 1 American Indian or Alaska Native, non-Hispanic/Latino; 13 Asian, non-Hispanic/Latino; 35 Hispanic/Latino; 1 Native Hawaiian or other Pacific Islander, non-Hispanic/Latino; 1 Two or more races, non-Hispanic/Latino), 1 international. Average age 32. 228 applicants, 93% accepted, 132 enrolled. In 2017, 97 master's, 22 doctorates, 31 other advanced degrees awarded. *Degree requirements:* For master's, one foreign language, comprehensive exam (for some programs), thesis (for some programs), electronic portfolio, capstone course, internship, practicum, student teaching, seminars, minimum GPA of 3.0; for doctorate, one foreign language, comprehensive exam, thesis/dissertation, qualifying hearing. *Entrance requirements:* For master's, GRE, interview, letters of recommendation, portfolio, essay, certification; for doctorate, GRE or MAT, interview, resume, essay, master's degree, 3 letters of recommendation, writing sample; for Advanced Certificate, GRE, interview, letters of recommendation, essay, professional experience, resume, master's degree. Additional exam requirements/recommendations for international students: Required—TOEFL (minimum score 550 paper-based; 80 iBT). *Application deadline:* Applications are processed on a rolling basis. Application fee: $75. Electronic applications accepted. *Expenses: Tuition:* Full-time $1292. *Required fees:* $970. Tuition and fees vary according to program. *Financial support:* In 2017–18, 225 students received support, including 118 fellowships with full and partial tuition reimbursements available (averaging $3,887 per year), 12 research assistantships with full and partial tuition reimbursements available (averaging $7,215 per year); career-related internships or fieldwork, Federal Work-Study, institutionally sponsored loans, scholarships/grants, traineeships, tuition waivers (full and partial), and unspecified assistantships also available. Support available to part-time students. Financial award applicants required to submit FAFSA. *Faculty research:*

Collaborative teaching and learning; language and culture; new media literacies; applied behavior analysis; K-12 leadership development. *Unit head:* Dr. Elfreda Blue, Chairperson, 516-463-5762, Fax: 516-463-6184, E-mail: elfreda.blue@hofstra.edu. *Application contact:* Sunil Samuel, Assistant Vice President of Admissions, 516-463-4723, Fax: 516-463-4664, E-mail: graduateadmission@hofstra.edu. Website: http://www.hofstra.edu/education/

Holy Family University, Graduate and Professional Programs, School of Education, Master of Education Programs, Philadelphia, PA 19114. Offers early elementary education (PreK-Grade 4) (M Ed); education leadership (M Ed); general education (M Ed); reading specialist (M Ed); special education (M Ed); TESOL and literacy (M Ed). *Program availability:* Part-time. *Degree requirements:* For master's, thesis optional. Electronic applications accepted. *Expenses: Tuition:* Full-time $13,518; part-time $9012 per credit hour. Tuition and fees vary according to degree level and program.

Hood College, Graduate School, Department of Education, Frederick, MD 21701-8575. Offers curriculum and instruction (MS), including elementary education, elementary science and mathematics education, secondary education, special education, education, multidisciplinary studies (MS); educational leadership (MS, Certificate); reading specialization (MS); STEM education (Certificate). *Accreditation:* NCATE. *Program availability:* Part-time-only, evening/weekend. *Faculty:* 6 full-time (4 women), 35 part-time/adjunct (27 women). *Students:* 3 full-time (all women), 329 part-time (265 women); includes 62 minority (35 Black or African American, non-Hispanic/Latino; 4 Asian, non-Hispanic/Latino; 14 Hispanic/Latino; 9 Two or more races, non-Hispanic/Latino), 3 international. Average age 33. 76 applicants, 100% accepted, 63 enrolled. In 2017, 53 master's, 58 other advanced degrees awarded. *Degree requirements:* For master's, action research project, portfolio (for reading specialization); for Certificate, STEM capstone activity. *Entrance requirements:* For master's, minimum GPA of 2.75, teaching certification, writing sample during interview, letter of recommendation from principal (for educational leadership program only). Additional exam requirements/recommendations for international students: Required—TOEFL (minimum score 575 paper-based; 89 iBT), IELTS (minimum score 6.5). *Application deadline:* For fall admission, 8/15 priority date for domestic students, 8/5 for international students; for spring admission, 12/1 priority date for domestic students, 12/1 for international students; for summer admission, 5/1 priority date for domestic students, 4/15 for international students. Applications are processed on a rolling basis. Application fee: $35. Electronic applications accepted. *Expenses:* $465 per credit plus $110 comprehensive fee per semester. *Financial support:* Tuition waivers (partial) and unspecified assistantships available. Financial award applicants required to submit FAFSA. *Faculty research:* Leadership, action research, brain research, learning styles. *Unit head:* Dr. April M. Boulton, Dean of the Graduate School, 301-696-3612, E-mail: gofurther@hood.edu. *Application contact:* Jan Marcus, Assistant Director of Graduate Admissions, 301-696-3600, E-mail: gofurther@hood.edu. Website: http://www.hood.edu/academics/education/index.html

Hope International University, School of Graduate and Professional Studies, Program in Education, Fullerton, CA 92831-3138. Offers education administration (MA); elementary education (ME); secondary education (ME). *Program availability:* Part-time, evening/weekend. *Degree requirements:* For master's, comprehensive exam (for some programs), thesis. *Entrance requirements:* For master's, minimum GPA of 3.0, 2 references. Additional exam requirements/recommendations for international students: Required—TOEFL (minimum score 550 paper-based; 86 iBT); Recommended—IELTS (minimum score 6.5). Electronic applications accepted. *Expenses:* Contact institution. *Faculty research:* Distance education.

Houston Baptist University, School of Humanities, Program in Liberal Arts, Houston, TX 77074-3298. Offers education (EC-12 art, music, physical education, or Spanish) (MLA); education (EC-6 generalist) (MLA); general liberal arts (MLA); specialization in education (4-8 or 7-12) (MLA). *Program availability:* Part-time, evening/weekend. *Students:* 11 full-time (7 women), 13 part-time (9 women); includes 12 minority (5 Black or African American, non-Hispanic/Latino; 2 Asian, non-Hispanic/Latino; 5 Hispanic/Latino). Average age 31. 26 applicants, 73% accepted, 12 enrolled. In 2017, 15 master's awarded. *Entrance requirements:* For master's, minimum GPA of 2.5, essay/personal statement, resume, bachelor's degree transcript. Additional exam requirements/recommendations for international students: Required—TOEFL (minimum score 80 iBT), IELTS (minimum score 6.5). *Application deadline:* For fall admission, 8/1 for domestic students, 6/1 for international students; for spring admission, 1/1 for domestic students, 11/1 for international students; for summer admission, 5/1 for domestic students, 3/1 for international students. Applications are processed on a rolling basis. Application fee: $0 ($100 for international students). Electronic applications accepted. Application fee is waived when completed online. *Expenses:* $18,000 tuition; $4,500 fees (general, technology and parking). *Financial support:* In 2017–18, 12 students received support. Federal Work-Study and scholarships/grants available. Support available to part-time students. Financial award application deadline: 4/1; financial award applicants required to submit FAFSA. *Unit head:* Dr. Collin Garbarino, Graduate Programs Director, 281-649-3679, E-mail: cgarbarino@hbu.edu. *Application contact:* Kathy Holston, Administrative Assistant to the Dean, 281-649-3404, E-mail: kholston@hbu.edu. Website: http://www.hbu.edu/mla

Howard University, School of Education, Department of Curriculum and Instruction, Program in Elementary Education, Washington, DC 20059-0002. Offers M Ed. *Accreditation:* NCATE. *Degree requirements:* For master's, comprehensive exam, expository writing exam, internships, seminar paper. *Entrance requirements:* For master's, PRAXIS I, GRE, minimum GPA of 2.7. Additional exam requirements/recommendations for international students: Required—TOEFL (minimum score 550 paper-based; 79 iBT). Electronic applications accepted.

Hunter College of the City University of New York, Graduate School, School of Education, Department of Curriculum and Teaching and Department of Educational Foundations and Counseling, Program in Elementary Education, New York, NY 10065-5085. Offers MS. *Accreditation:* NCATE. *Degree requirements:* For master's, thesis, integrative seminar, New York State Teacher Certification Exams, student teaching. *Entrance requirements:* For master's, minimum undergraduate GPA of 2.8, writing sample. Additional exam requirements/recommendations for international students: Required—TOEFL, TWE. *Faculty research:* Urban education, multicultural education, gifted education, educational technology, cultural cognition.

Huntington University, Graduate School, Huntington, IN 46750-1299. Offers adolescent and young adult education (M Ed); business administration (MBA); counseling (MA), including licensed mental health counselor; early adolescent education (M Ed); elementary education (M Ed); global youth ministry (MA); occupational therapy (OTD); organizational leadership (MA); pastoral leadership (MA); TESOL education (M Ed). *Program availability:* Part-time, online learning. *Faculty:* 17 full-time (10 women), 14 part-time/adjunct (4 women). *Students:* 221 full-time (163 women), 22 part-time (13 women). *Degree requirements:* For master's, comprehensive exam (for some programs), thesis (for some programs). *Entrance requirements:* For master's, GRE (for counseling and education students only); for doctorate, GRE (for occupational therapy students). Additional exam requirements/recommendations for international students: Required—TOEFL (minimum score 85 iBT), IELTS (minimum score 6.5). *Application deadline:* For fall admission, 7/1 for domestic students, 5/1 for international students; for

winter admission, 10/1 for domestic students, 9/1 for international students; for spring admission, 11/30 for domestic students, 10/30 for international students. Applications are processed on a rolling basis. Application fee: $30. Electronic applications accepted. *Expenses:* Contact institution. *Financial support:* Scholarships/grants and unspecified assistantships available. Support available to part-time students. Financial award application deadline: 8/1; financial award applicants required to submit FAFSA. *Faculty research:* Leadership, educational technology trends, evangelism, youth ministry, mental health. *Unit head:* Michael Wanous, Vice President for Academic Affairs, 260-359-4008, Fax: 260-359-4126, E-mail: mwanous@huntington.edu. *Application contact:* Evan Bennett, Assistant Director of Graduate Admissions, 260-359-4111, Fax: 260-359-4126, E-mail: graduate@huntington.edu. Website: http://www.huntington.edu/graduate

Idaho State University, Office of Graduate Studies, College of Education, Department of Teaching and Educational Studies, Pocatello, ID 83209-8059. Offers deaf education (M Ed); elementary education (M Ed); human exceptionality (M Ed); literacy (M Ed); music education (M Ed); secondary education (M Ed). *Program availability:* Part-time. *Degree requirements:* For master's, comprehensive exam, thesis (for some programs), oral thesis defense or written comprehensive exam and oral exam. *Entrance requirements:* For master's, GRE or MAT, minimum undergraduate GPA of 3.0, bachelor's degree, professional experience in an educational context. Additional exam requirements/recommendations for international students: Required—TOEFL (minimum score 550 paper-based; 80 iBT). Electronic applications accepted. *Faculty research:* Literacy, school psychology, special education.

Indiana University Bloomington, School of Education, Department of Curriculum and Instruction, Bloomington, IN 47405-7000. Offers art education (MS, Ed D, PhD); curriculum studies (Ed D, PhD); elementary education (MS, Ed D, PhD, Ed S); mathematics education (MS, Ed D, PhD); science education (MS, Ed D, PhD); secondary education (MS, Ed D, PhD); social studies education (MS, PhD); special education (PhD, Ed S). *Accreditation:* NCATE. *Program availability:* Part-time, evening/weekend. Terminal master's awarded for partial completion of doctoral program. *Degree requirements:* For doctorate, thesis/dissertation; for Ed S, comprehensive exam or project. *Entrance requirements:* For master's, doctorate, and Ed S, GRE General Test. Electronic applications accepted.

Indiana University Northwest, School of Education, Gary, IN 46408. Offers educational leadership (MS Ed); elementary education (MS Ed); K-12 online teaching (Graduate Certificate); secondary education (MS Ed). *Accreditation:* NCATE. *Program availability:* Part-time, evening/weekend. *Entrance requirements:* For master's, GRE General Test or MAT, minimum GPA of 3.0. Electronic applications accepted. *Expenses:* Contact institution.

Indiana University–Purdue University Fort Wayne, College of Education and Public Policy, Department of Educational Studies, Fort Wayne, IN 46805-1499. Offers elementary education (MS Ed); secondary education (MS Ed). *Accreditation:* NCATE. *Program availability:* Part-time. *Entrance requirements:* For master's, minimum GPA of 2.5, three professional letters of recommendation. Additional exam requirements/recommendations for international students: Required—TOEFL (minimum score 550 paper-based; 79 iBT). *Faculty research:* International faculty, gender in Burmese refugee narratives, planning effective instruction.

Indiana University South Bend, School of Education, South Bend, IN 46615. Offers addiction counseling (MS Ed); alcohol and drug counseling (Graduate Certificate); clinical mental health counseling (MS Ed); educational leadership (MS Ed); elementary education (MS Ed); marriage, couple, and family counseling (MS Ed); school counseling (MS Ed); secondary education (MS Ed); special education (MAT, MS Ed), including intense intervention (MS Ed), mild intervention (MS Ed). *Accreditation:* NCATE. *Program availability:* Part-time, evening/weekend. *Degree requirements:* For master's, thesis or alternative, exit project. *Entrance requirements:* For master's, letters of recommendation, GRE or minimum GPA of 3.0. Additional exam requirements/recommendations for international students: Required—TOEFL. Electronic applications accepted. *Expenses:* Contact institution. *Faculty research:* Professional dispositions, early childhood literacy, online learning, program assessments, problem-based learning.

Indiana University Southeast, School of Education, New Albany, IN 47150. Offers counselor education (MS Ed); elementary education (MS Ed); secondary education (MS Ed). *Accreditation:* NCATE. *Program availability:* Part-time, evening/weekend. *Entrance requirements:* For master's, minimum undergraduate GPA of 2.5, graduate 3.0. Electronic applications accepted. *Faculty research:* Learning styles, technology, constructivism, group process, innovative math strategies.

Inter American University of Puerto Rico, Aguadilla Campus, Graduate School, Aguadilla, PR 00605. Offers accounting (MBA); counseling psychology specializing in family (MS); criminal justice (MA); educative management and leadership (MA); elementary education (M Ed); finance (MBA); human resources (MBA); industrial management (MBA); management information systems (MBA); marketing (MBA). *Program availability:* Part-time, evening/weekend. *Degree requirements:* For master's, comprehensive exam. *Entrance requirements:* For master's, EXADEP, 2 letters of recommendation, minimum GPA of 2.5. Electronic applications accepted.

Inter American University of Puerto Rico, Arecibo Campus, Programs in Education, Arecibo, PR 00614-4050. Offers administration and educational supervision (MA Ed); counseling and guidance (MA Ed); curriculum and teaching (MA Ed), including biology education, English as a second language, history education, math education, Spanish; elementary education (MA Ed). *Accreditation:* TEAC. *Degree requirements:* For master's, comprehensive exam, thesis optional. *Entrance requirements:* For master's, GRE, EXADEP, bachelor's degree in education or teaching license (administration and supervision) or courses in education and psychology (counseling and guidance), minimum GPA of 2.5 in last 60 credits.

Inter American University of Puerto Rico, Barranquitas Campus, Program in Education, Barranquitas, PR 00794. Offers curriculum and teaching (M Ed), including biology, English as a second language, history, Spanish; educational leadership and management (MA); elementary education (M Ed); information and library service technology (M Ed); special education (MA). *Accreditation:* TEAC. *Program availability:* Part-time, evening/weekend. *Faculty:* 1 full-time (0 women), 3 part-time/adjunct (2 women). *Students:* 17 full-time (16 women), 2 part-time (both women); all minorities (all Hispanic/Latino). Average age 34. 9 applicants, 89% accepted, 8 enrolled. In 2017, 5 master's awarded. *Degree requirements:* For master's, 2 foreign languages, comprehensive exam, thesis (for some programs). *Entrance requirements:* For master's, GRE or EXADEP, bachelor's degree or its equivalent from accredited institution, official academic transcript from institution that conferred bachelor's degree, minimum GPA of 2.5, two recommendation letters, interview (for some programs), essay (for some programs). *Application deadline:* Applications are processed on a rolling basis. Application fee: $31. Electronic applications accepted. *Expenses:* $3,392 full-time tuition plus $652 fees. *Financial support:* Applicants required to submit FAFSA. *Unit head:* Juan A. Negron-Berrios, PhD, Chancellor, 787-857-3600 Ext. 2002, Fax: 787-857-2125, E-mail: janegron@br.inter.edu. *Application contact:* Aramilda Cartagena-Santiago, Dean of Students, 787-857-3600 Ext. 2009, Fax: 787-857-2125, E-mail: aramildacartagena@br.inter.edu.

Inter American University of Puerto Rico, Guayama Campus, Department of Education and Social Sciences, Guayama, PR 00785. Offers early childhood education (0-4 years) (M Ed); elementary education (M Ed). *Program availability:* Part-time. *Entrance requirements:* For master's, GRE, MAT, EXADEP, letters of recommendation, minimum GPA of 2.5. Electronic applications accepted.

Inter American University of Puerto Rico, Metropolitan Campus, Graduate Programs, Program in Elementary Education, San Juan, PR 00919-1293. Offers MA. *Degree requirements:* For master's, comprehensive exam. *Entrance requirements:* For master's, GRE or EXADEP, interview. Electronic applications accepted.

Inter American University of Puerto Rico, Ponce Campus, Graduate School, Mercedita, PR 00715-1602. Offers accounting (MBA); biology (M Ed); chemistry (M Ed); criminal justice (MA); elementary education (M Ed); English as a Second Language (M Ed); finance (MBA); history (M Ed); human resources (MBA); marketing (MBA); mathematics (M Ed); Spanish (M Ed). *Entrance requirements:* For master's, minimum GPA of 2.5.

Inter American University of Puerto Rico, San Germán Campus, Graduate Studies Center, Program in Elementary Education, San Germán, PR 00683-5008. Offers MA. *Program availability:* Part-time, evening/weekend. *Degree requirements:* For master's, comprehensive exam. *Entrance requirements:* For master's, GRE General Test or EXADEP, minimum GPA of 3.0.

Iowa State University of Science and Technology, Department of Education, Ames, IA 50011. Offers curriculum and instructional technology (M Ed, MS, PhD); elementary education (M Ed, MS); historical, philosophical, and comparative studies in education (M Ed, MS); special education (M Ed, MS, PhD). *Degree requirements:* For master's, thesis or alternative; for doctorate, thesis/dissertation. *Entrance requirements:* For master's and doctorate, GRE General Test. Additional exam requirements/recommendations for international students: Required—TOEFL (minimum score 560 paper-based; 83 iBT), IELTS (minimum score 6.5). Electronic applications accepted.

Ithaca College, School of Humanities and Sciences, Program in Childhood Education, Ithaca, NY 14850. Offers MS. *Program availability:* Part-time. *Faculty:* 11 full-time (7 women), 1 part-time/adjunct (0 women). *Students:* 5 full-time (4 women); includes 1 minority (Two or more races, non-Hispanic/Latino). Average age 26. 11 applicants, 64% accepted, 5 enrolled. In 2017, 13 master's awarded. *Degree requirements:* For master's, thesis or alternative, student teaching. *Entrance requirements:* Additional exam requirements/recommendations for international students: Required—TOEFL (minimum score 550 paper-based; 80 iBT). *Application deadline:* For fall admission, 3/19 for domestic and international students. Applications are processed on a rolling basis. Application fee: $40. Electronic applications accepted. *Expenses:* Contact institution. *Financial support:* In 2017–18, 5 students received support, including 6 research assistantships (averaging $11,709 per year); career-related internships or fieldwork, Federal Work-Study, scholarships/grants, and unspecified assistantships also available. Support available to part-time students. Financial award application deadline: 3/1; financial award applicants required to submit FAFSA. *Unit head:* Dr. Peter Martin, Chair, 607-274-1076, Fax: 607-274-1263, E-mail: pmartin@ithaca.edu. *Application contact:* Nicole Eversley Bradwell, Director, Office of Admission, 607-274-3124, Fax: 607-274-1263, E-mail: admission@ithaca.edu.
Website: http://www.ithaca.edu/gradprograms/education/programs/childhooded/

Jackson State University, Graduate School, College of Education and Human Development, Department of Elementary and Early Childhood Education, Jackson, MS 39217. Offers early childhood education (MS Ed, Ed D); elementary education (MS Ed, Ed S); reading education (MS Ed). *Accreditation:* NCATE. *Program availability:* Part-time, evening/weekend, 100% online, blended/hybrid learning. Terminal master's awarded for partial completion of doctoral program. *Degree requirements:* For master's, comprehensive exam, thesis or alternative; for doctorate, comprehensive exam, thesis/dissertation. *Entrance requirements:* For master's, GRE General Test; for doctorate, MAT, teaching experience. Additional exam requirements/recommendations for international students: Required—TOEFL (minimum score 520 paper-based; 67 iBT). Electronic applications accepted. *Expenses:* Contact institution.

Jacksonville State University, College of Graduate Studies and Continuing Education, College of Education and Professional Studies, Program in Elementary Education, Jacksonville, AL 36265-1602. Offers MS Ed. *Accreditation:* NCATE. *Program availability:* Part-time, evening/weekend. *Degree requirements:* For master's, comprehensive exam, thesis (for some programs). *Entrance requirements:* For master's, GRE General Test or MAT. Additional exam requirements/recommendations for international students: Required—TOEFL (minimum score 500 paper-based; 61 iBT). Electronic applications accepted.

James Madison University, The Graduate School, College of Education, Program in Education, Harrisonburg, VA 22807. Offers early childhood education (preK-3) (MAT); educational leadership (M Ed); educational technology (M Ed); elementary education (MAT); equity and cultural diversity (M Ed); inclusive early childhood education (MAT); K-8 mathematics specialist (M Ed); middle education (MAT); reading education (M Ed); secondary education (MAT); Spanish language and culture for educators (M Ed); TESOL (MAT). *Accreditation:* NCATE. *Program availability:* Part-time, evening/weekend. *Students:* 260 full-time (233 women), 158 part-time (100 women); includes 48 minority (10 Black or African American, non-Hispanic/Latino; 4 Asian, non-Hispanic/Latino; 26 Hispanic/Latino; 1 Native Hawaiian or other Pacific Islander, non-Hispanic/Latino; 7 Two or more races, non-Hispanic/Latino), 2 international. Average age 30. In 2017, 262 master's awarded. Application fee: $55. Electronic applications accepted. *Expenses:* Tuition, state resident: full-time $10,512; part-time $438 per credit hour. Tuition, nonresident: full-time $28,358; part-time $1162 per credit hour. *Required fees:* $1128. *Financial support:* In 2017–18, 23 students received support, including 1 teaching assistantship; career-related internships or fieldwork, Federal Work-Study, and 22 assistantships (averaging $7911) also available. Financial award application deadline: 3/1; financial award applicants required to submit FAFSA. *Unit head:* Dr. Phillip M. Wishon, Dean, 540-568-6572, E-mail: wishonpm@jmu.edu. *Application contact:* Lynette D. Michael, Director of Graduate Admissions, 540-568-6131 Ext. 6395, Fax: 540-568-7860, E-mail: michaeld@jmu.edu.
Website: http://www.jmu.edu/coe/index.shtml

James Madison University, The Graduate School, College of Education, Program in Elementary Education, Harrisonburg, VA 22807. Offers MAT. *Students:* Average age 27. *Entrance requirements:* For master's, GRE General Test, PRAXIS II, minimum undergraduate GPA of 2.75, 2-page essay, interview. Additional exam requirements/recommendations for international students: Required—TOEFL. *Application deadline:* For fall admission, 5/1 for domestic students; for spring admission, 9/1 for domestic students. Applications are processed on a rolling basis. Application fee: $55. Electronic applications accepted. *Expenses:* Tuition, state resident: full-time $10,512; part-time $438 per credit hour. Tuition, nonresident: full-time $28,358; part-time $1162 per credit hour. *Required fees:* $1128. *Unit head:* Dr. Martha Ross, Academic Unit Head, 540-568-6255. *Application contact:* Lynette M. Bible, Director of Graduate Admissions, 540-568-6395, Fax: 540-568-7860, E-mail: biblelm@jmu.edu.

Johns Hopkins University, School of Education, Master's Programs in Education, Baltimore, MD 21218. Offers counseling (MS), including clinical mental health counseling, school counseling; education (MS), including educational studies, gifted education, reading, school administration and supervision, technology for educators; elementary education (MAT); health professions (M Ed); intelligence analysis (MS); organizational leadership (MS); secondary education (MAT), including biology, chemistry, earth/space science, English, physics, social studies; special education (MS), including early childhood special education, general special education studies, mild to moderate disabilities, severe disabilities. *Program availability:* Part-time, evening/weekend, 100% online, blended/hybrid learning. *Degree requirements:* For master's, comprehensive exam (for some programs), portfolio, capstone project and/or internship; PRAXIS II (subject area assessments) for initial teacher preparation programs that lead to licensure. *Entrance requirements:* For master's, GRE (for full-time programs only); PRAXIS I/core or state-approved alternative (for initial teacher preparation programs that lead to licensure), minimum of bachelor's degree from regionally- or nationally-accredited institution; minimum GPA of 3.0 in all previous programs of study; official transcripts from all post-secondary institutions attended; essay; curriculum vitae/resume; letters of recommendation (3 for full-time programs, 2 for part-time programs); dispositions survey. Additional exam requirements/recommendations for international students: Required—TOEFL (minimum score 600 paper-based; 100 iBT), IELTS (minimum score 7). Electronic applications accepted. *Expenses:* Contact institution.

Johnson & Wales University, Graduate Studies, MAT Program in Teacher Education, Providence, RI 02903-3703. Offers business education and secondary special education (MAT); culinary arts education (MAT); elementary education and elementary special education (MAT). *Program availability:* Part-time, evening/weekend. *Entrance requirements:* For master's, MAT, minimum GPA of 2.75. Additional exam requirements/recommendations for international students: Required—TOEFL (minimum score 550 paper-based) or IELTS (recommended). *Application deadline:* For fall admission, 8/21 priority date for domestic students, 6/15 priority date for international students; for winter admission, 11/15 priority date for domestic students, 10/1 priority date for international students. Applications are processed on a rolling basis. Application fee: $0. *Expenses:* Tuition: Full-time $12,636; part-time $702 per credit hour. *Financial support:* Unspecified assistantships available. Financial award application deadline: 5/1. *Faculty research:* Secondary education, student teaching, educational reform, evaluation procedures. *Unit head:* Karen Swoboda, Director, 401-598-1922, Fax: 401-598-1125. *Application contact:* Graduate School Admissions, 401-598-1015, Fax: 401-598-1286, E-mail: gradadm@jwu.edu.

Kansas State University, Graduate School, College of Education, Department of Curriculum and Instruction, Manhattan, KS 66506. Offers curriculum and instruction (Ed D, PhD); digital teaching and learning (MS); educational computing, design and online learning (MS); elementary/middle level curriculum and instruction (MS); online learning (Certificate); reading specialist endorsement (MS); reading/language arts (MS); teacher leader/school improvement (MS); teaching and learning (Certificate). *Accreditation:* NCATE. *Program availability:* Part-time, online learning. *Degree requirements:* For master's, comprehensive exam, portfolio, project, report or thesis; for doctorate, comprehensive exam, thesis/dissertation, preliminary exam; for Certificate, comprehensive exam, portfolio. *Entrance requirements:* For master's, minimum GPA of 3.0, 3 letters of recommendation; for doctorate, GRE, minimum GPA of 3.0, 3 letters of recommendation, evidence of scholarly writing; for Certificate, minimum GPA of 3.0, letters of recommendation. Additional exam requirements/recommendations for international students: Required—TOEFL (minimum score 550 paper-based; 80 iBT) or IELTS. Electronic applications accepted. *Faculty research:* Literacy and technology, critical race theory and diversity, achievement gaps, school improvement, teacher education.

Kennesaw State University, Leland and Clarice C. Bagwell College of Education, Program in Graduate Education, Kennesaw, GA 30144. Offers educational leadership (M Ed); educational leadership technology (M Ed); elementary and early childhood education (M Ed); instructional technology (M Ed); middle grades education (M Ed); reading (M Ed); secondary education (M Ed); special education (M Ed); teaching English to speakers of other languages (M Ed). *Accreditation:* NCATE. *Program availability:* Part-time. *Degree requirements:* For master's, thesis or alternative. *Entrance requirements:* For master's, GRE General Test, T-4 state certification, minimum GPA of 2.75. Additional exam requirements/recommendations for international students: Required—TOEFL (minimum score 550 paper-based; 80 iBT), IELTS (minimum score 6.5). Electronic applications accepted.

Keuka College, Program in Childhood Education/Literacy, Keuka Park, NY 14478. Offers literacy 5-12 (MS); literacy B-6 (MS). *Degree requirements:* For master's, thesis, capstone project/student-led research project. *Entrance requirements:* For master's, GRE, minimum GPA of 3.0; 3 letters of recommendation (2 academic and one from cooperating teacher from student teaching or other professional). Additional exam requirements/recommendations for international students: Required—TOEFL (minimum score 550 paper-based). Electronic applications accepted. *Expenses:* Contact institution. *Faculty research:* Marginalized populations, international literacy, teacher assessment.

Kutztown University of Pennsylvania, College of Education, Program in Elementary Education, Kutztown, PA 19530-0730. Offers M Ed. *Accreditation:* NCATE. *Program availability:* Part-time, evening/weekend. *Faculty:* 10 full-time (9 women). *Students:* 4 full-time (2 women), 52 part-time (47 women); includes 6 minority (2 Black or African American, non-Hispanic/Latino; 1 Asian, non-Hispanic/Latino; 2 Hispanic/Latino; 1 Two or more races, non-Hispanic/Latino), 1 international. Average age 32. 52 applicants, 79% accepted, 29 enrolled. In 2017, 16 master's awarded. *Degree requirements:* For master's, comprehensive exam, thesis optional, comprehensive project. *Entrance requirements:* For master's, GRE General Test, PA teaching certificate in elementary education, 3 letters of recommendation. Additional exam requirements/recommendations for international students: Required—TOEFL (minimum score 550 paper-based, 79 iBT), IELTS (minimum score 6.5), or PTE (minimum score 53). *Application deadline:* For fall admission, 8/1 for domestic and international students; for spring admission, 12/1 for domestic and international students. Application fee: $35. Electronic applications accepted. *Expenses:* Tuition, state resident: part-time $500 per credit. Tuition, nonresident: part-time $750 per credit. *Required fees:* $115 per credit. One-time fee: $50 part-time. Tuition and fees vary according to degree level. *Financial support:* Career-related internships or fieldwork, Federal Work-Study, and unspecified assistantships available. Financial award application deadline: 3/1; financial award applicants required to submit FAFSA. *Faculty research:* Whole language, middle schools, cooperative learning discussion techniques, oral reading techniques, hemisphericity. *Unit head:* Dr. Tracy Keyes, Department Chair, 610-683-4286, Fax: 610-683-1327, E-mail: keyes@kutztown.edu.
Website: https://www.kutztown.edu/academics/graduate-programs/elementary-education.htm

Lake Forest College, Master of Arts in Teaching Program, Lake Forest, IL 60045. Offers elementary education (MAT); K-12 French (MAT); K-12 music (MAT); K-12 Spanish (MAT); K-12 visual art (MAT); secondary biology (MAT); secondary chemistry (MAT); secondary English (MAT); secondary history (MAT); secondary mathematics (MAT). *Degree requirements:* For master's, comprehensive exam, portfolio. *Entrance requirements:* For master's, GRE.

Lancaster Bible College, Graduate School, Lancaster, PA 17601-5036. Offers adult ministries (MA); Bible (MA); children and family ministry (MA); church planting (MA); consulting resource teacher (M Ed); elementary school counseling (M Ed); leadership (PhD); leadership studies (MA); marriage and family counseling (MA); mental health counseling (MA); pastoral studies (MA); secondary school counseling (M Ed); sports ministry (MA); student ministry (MA); town and country ministry (MA). *Program availability:* Part-time, evening/weekend. *Degree requirements:* For master's, comprehensive exam (for some programs), thesis (for some programs). *Entrance requirements:* For master's, bachelor's degree with a minimum of 30 credits of course work in Bible, minimum undergraduate GPA of 3.0, interview. Additional exam requirements/recommendations for international students: Required—TOEFL.

Langston University, School of Education and Behavioral Sciences, Langston, OK 73050. Offers bilingual/multicultural (M Ed); elementary education (M Ed); English as a second language (M Ed); rehabilitation counseling (M Sc); urban education (M Ed). *Accreditation:* CORE; NCATE (one or more programs are accredited). *Program availability:* Part-time. *Degree requirements:* For master's, comprehensive exam, thesis optional. *Entrance requirements:* For master's, GRE, writing skills test, minimum GPA of 2.5, 3 letters of recommendation. Additional exam requirements/recommendations for international students: Required—TOEFL, TWE. *Faculty research:* Bilingual/multicultural education, financing post-secondary education.

Lasell College, Graduate and Professional Studies in Education, Newton, MA 02466-2709. Offers curriculum, leadership, and inclusion (M Ed); elementary education (M Ed); special education (M Ed), including moderate disabilities; teaching bilingual/English learners with disabilities (Graduate Certificate). *Program availability:* Part-time-only, evening/weekend, blended/hybrid learning. *Faculty:* 3 full-time (all women), 5 part-time/adjunct (4 women). *Students:* 8 full-time (7 women), 43 part-time (38 women); includes 4 minority (2 Asian, non-Hispanic/Latino; 1 Hispanic/Latino; 1 Two or more races, non-Hispanic/Latino), 1 international. Average age 28. 23 applicants, 74% accepted, 10 enrolled. In 2017, 15 master's awarded. *Degree requirements:* For master's, minimum GPA of 3.0; practicum. *Entrance requirements:* For master's, Massachusetts Tests for Educator Licensure (MTEL) Curriculum and Literacy foundations of reading and writing subtest, one-page personal statement, 2 letters of recommendation, resume, bachelor's degree transcript. Additional exam requirements/recommendations for international students: Required—TOEFL (minimum score 550 paper-based, 79 iBT) or IELTS (minimum score 6). *Application deadline:* For fall admission, 8/31 priority date for domestic students, 6/30 priority date for international students; for spring admission, 12/31 priority date for domestic students, 10/31 priority date for international students. Applications are processed on a rolling basis. Electronic applications accepted. *Expenses:* $600 per credit. *Financial support:* Federal Work-Study, scholarships/grants, and tuition discounts available. Support available to part-time students. Financial award application deadline: 8/31; financial award applicants required to submit FAFSA. *Faculty research:* Inclusion, English language learners, literacy, and urban education; teacher inquiry; universal design for learning, deaf-blindness, and visual impairments; social and emotional learning; educational law, applied behavior analysis, and classroom management. *Unit head:* Eric Turner, Vice President of Graduate and Professional Studies, 617-243-2071, Fax: 617-243-2450, E-mail: gradinfo@lasell.edu. *Application contact:* Adrienne Franciosi, Director of Graduate Enrollment, 617-243-2214, Fax: 617-243-2450, E-mail: gradinfo@lasell.edu.
Website: http://www.lasell.edu/academics/graduate-and-professional-studies/programs-of-study/master-of-education.html

Lee University, Program in Education, Cleveland, TN 37320-3450. Offers art (MAT); curriculum and instruction (M Ed, Ed S); early childhood (MAT); educational leadership (M Ed, Ed S); elementary education (MAT); English and math (MAT); English and science (MAT); English and social studies (MAT); higher education administration (MS); history (MAT); history and economics (MAT); math and science (MAT); math and social studies (MAT); middle grades (MAT); science and social studies (MASW); secondary education (MAT); Spanish (MAT); special education (M Ed, MAT); TESOL (MAT). *Accreditation:* NCATE. *Program availability:* Part-time. *Faculty:* 15 full-time (9 women), 8 part-time/adjunct (3 women). *Students:* 28 full-time (21 women), 77 part-time (48 women); includes 12 minority (7 Black or African American, non-Hispanic/Latino; 2 Hispanic/Latino; 3 Two or more races, non-Hispanic/Latino), 1 international. Average age 31. 35 applicants, 83% accepted, 22 enrolled. In 2017, 54 master's, 4 other advanced degrees awarded. *Degree requirements:* For master's, variable foreign language requirement, thesis optional, internship. *Entrance requirements:* For master's, MAT or GRE General Test, minimum undergraduate GPA of 2.75, 3 letters of recommendation, interview, writing sample, official transcripts, background check; for Ed S, minimum undergraduate and master's GPA of 2.75, official transcripts for undergraduate and master's degrees. Additional exam requirements/recommendations for international students: Required—TOEFL (minimum score 61 iBT). *Application deadline:* For fall admission, 6/1 priority date for domestic and international students; for spring admission, 11/1 priority date for domestic and international students; for summer admission, 4/1 priority date for domestic and international students. Applications are processed on a rolling basis. Application fee: $25. Electronic applications accepted. *Expenses: Tuition:* Full-time $12,780; part-time $710 per credit hour. *Required fees:* $60; $60 per term. Tuition and fees vary according to program. *Financial support:* In 2017–18, 32 students received support. Career-related internships or fieldwork, Federal Work-Study, institutionally sponsored loans, scholarships/grants, and unspecified assistantships available. Financial award application deadline: 3/1; financial award applicants required to submit FAFSA. *Unit head:* Dr. William Kamm, Director, 423-614-8544, E-mail: wkamm@leeuniversity.edu. *Application contact:* Crystal Keeter, Graduate Education Secretary, 423-614-8544, E-mail: ckeeter@leeuniversity.edu.
Website: http://www.leeuniversity.edu/academics/graduate/education

Lehigh University, College of Education, Program in Teaching, Learning and Technology, Bethlehem, PA 18015. Offers elementary education (M Ed); instructional technology (MS); teaching, learning and technology (PhD); M Ed/MA. *Program availability:* Part-time. *Faculty:* 6 full-time (4 women), 3 part-time/adjunct (2 women). *Students:* 29 full-time (20 women), 61 part-time (41 women); includes 9 minority (1 Black or African American, non-Hispanic/Latino; 4 Asian, non-Hispanic/Latino; 3 Hispanic/Latino; 1 Native Hawaiian or other Pacific Islander, non-Hispanic/Latino), 6 international. Average age 32. 75 applicants, 73% accepted, 15 enrolled. In 2017, 35 master's, 4 doctorates awarded. Terminal master's awarded for partial completion of doctoral program. *Degree requirements:* For doctorate, comprehensive exam, thesis/dissertation, qualifying exam. *Entrance requirements:* For master's, minimum GPA of 3.0, 2 letters of recommendation, essay, transcript; for doctorate, GRE General Test, minimum graduate GPA of 3.0, writing sample, 2 letters of recommendation, essay, transcript. Additional exam requirements/recommendations for international students: Required—TOEFL (minimum iBT score of 93) or IELTS (6.5). *Application deadline:* For fall admission, 4/1 for domestic and international students; for summer admission, 4/1 for domestic and international students. Applications are processed on a rolling basis. Application fee: $65. Electronic applications accepted. *Expenses:* $565 per credit. *Financial support:* In 2017–18, 17 students received support, including 2 research assistantships with full and partial tuition reimbursements available (averaging $25,116 per year); fellowships and unspecified assistantships also available. Financial award application deadline: 1/31. *Faculty research:* Teaching and learning, K-16 curriculum

development, Web-based learning, teaching and technology, language and literacy, teaching, learning with spatial technologies, visual instructional technologies, environmental science curriculum, multicultural issues, English language education, educational access and equity, English Language Learners with disabilities, integrated curriculum, augmented and virtual reality, STEM and agricultural education. *Total annual research expenditures:* $760,344. *Unit head:* Dr. Lynn Columba, Director, 610-758-3237, Fax: 610-758-3243, E-mail: hlc0@lehigh.edu. *Application contact:* Donna Toothman, Coordinator, 610-758-3230, Fax: 610-758-3243, E-mail: djt2@lehigh.edu. Website: https://ed.lehigh.edu/academics/programs/instructional-technology

Lehman College of the City University of New York, School of Education, Department of Early Childhood and Elementary Education, Program in Elementary Education, Bronx, NY 10468-1589. Offers MS Ed. *Accreditation:* NCATE. *Program availability:* Part-time, evening/weekend. *Degree requirements:* For master's, thesis. *Entrance requirements:* For master's, minimum GPA of 3.0. *Faculty research:* POS network, emotional and intellectual learning, realistic picture books.

Le Moyne College, Department of Education, Syracuse, NY 13214. Offers adolescent education (MS Ed, MST); adolescent education/special education (MS Ed, MST); adolescent English (MST), including grades 7-12; adolescent English/special education (MST), including grades 7-12; adolescent foreign language (MST), including grades 7-12; adolescent history (MST), including grades 7-12; childhood education (MS Ed); childhood education/special education (MS Ed); elementary education (MS Ed); general education (MS Ed); inclusive childhood education (MST); literacy education (MS Ed), including birth to grade 6, grades 5-12; school building leader (MS Ed); school building leadership (CAS); school district business leader (MS Ed, CAS); school district leader (MS Ed); school district leadership (CAS); secondary education (MS Ed); special education (MS Ed); teaching English to speakers of other languages (MS Ed); urban studies (MS Ed). *Accreditation:* TEAC. *Program availability:* Part-time, evening/weekend. *Faculty:* 7 full-time (5 women), 20 part-time/adjunct (12 women). *Students:* 30 full-time (19 women), 126 part-time (93 women); includes 15 minority (7 Black or African American, non-Hispanic/Latino; 1 American Indian or Alaska Native, non-Hispanic/Latino; 1 Asian, non-Hispanic/Latino; 6 Hispanic/Latino), 4 international. Average age 29. 139 applicants, 65% accepted, 76 enrolled. In 2017, 82 master's, 43 CASs awarded. *Degree requirements:* For master's, thesis. *Entrance requirements:* For master's, bachelor's degree with minimum undergraduate GPA of 3.0, 2 letters of recommendation, transcripts. Additional exam requirements/recommendations for international students: Required—TOEFL (minimum score 550 paper-based; 79 iBT); Recommended—IELTS (minimum score 6.5). *Application deadline:* For fall admission, 4/1 priority date for domestic and international students; for spring admission, 10/1 priority date for domestic and international students; for summer admission, 3/1 priority date for domestic and international students. Applications are processed on a rolling basis. Application fee: $50. Electronic applications accepted. *Expenses:* $700 per credit hour. *Financial support:* In 2017–18, 30 students received support. Career-related internships or fieldwork, scholarships/grants, and health care benefits available. Support available to part-time students. Financial award applicants required to submit FAFSA. *Faculty research:* Minority teachers, special education, multiculturalism, literacy, technology, media literacy learning, autism, school district organization, service-learning, higher level problem solving, teacher leadership. *Unit head:* Dr. Stephen C. Fleury, Chair, Department of Education, 315-445-4376, Fax: 315-445-4744, E-mail: fleurysc@lemoyne.edu. *Application contact:* Kristen P. Richards, Senior Director of Enrollment Management, 315-445-5444, Fax: 315-445-6092, E-mail: trapaskp@lemoyne.edu.
Website: http://www.lemoyne.edu/education

Lesley University, Graduate School of Education, Cambridge, MA 02138-2790. Offers arts, community, and education (M Ed); autism studies (Certificate); curriculum and instruction (M Ed, CAGS); early childhood education (M Ed); ecological teaching and learning (MS); educational studies (PhD), including adult learning, educational leadership, individually designed; elementary education (M Ed); emergent technologies for educators (Certificate); ESLArts: language learning through the arts (M Ed); high school education (M Ed); individually designed (M Ed); integrated teaching through the arts (M Ed); literacy for K-8 classroom teachers (M Ed); mathematics education (M Ed); middle school education (M Ed); moderate disabilities (M Ed); online learning (Certificate); reading (CAGS); science in education (M Ed); severe disabilities (M Ed); special needs (CAGS); specialist teacher of reading (M Ed); teacher of visual art (M Ed); technology in education (M Ed, CAGS). *Accreditation:* TEAC. *Program availability:* Part-time, evening/weekend, online learning. *Degree requirements:* For master's, practicum; for doctorate, thesis/dissertation. *Entrance requirements:* For master's, Massachusetts Tests for Educator Licensure (MTEL), transcripts, statement of purpose, recommendations; interview (for special education); for doctorate, GRE General Test, transcripts, statement of purpose, recommendations, interview, master's degree, resume; for other advanced degree, interview, master's degree. Additional exam requirements/recommendations for international students: Required—TOEFL (minimum score 550 paper-based; 80 iBT). Electronic applications accepted. *Faculty research:* Assessment in literacy, mathematics and science; autism spectrum disorders; instructional technology and online learning; multicultural education and English language learners.

Lewis & Clark College, Graduate School of Education and Counseling, Department of Teacher Education, Program in Elementary Education, Portland, OR 97219-7899. Offers MAT. *Accreditation:* NCATE. *Entrance requirements:* For master's, minimum undergraduate GPA of 2.75; history of work, either volunteer or paid, with children in grades K-6. Additional exam requirements/recommendations for international students: Required—TOEFL (minimum score 575 paper-based). Electronic applications accepted. *Faculty research:* Classroom ethnography, assessing student learning, reading, moral development, language arts.

Lewis University, College of Education, Program in Elementary Education, Romeoville, IL 60446. Offers MA. *Program availability:* Part-time. *Students:* 12 full-time (9 women), 18 part-time (13 women); includes 9 minority (1 Black or African American, non-Hispanic/Latino; 1 Asian, non-Hispanic/Latino; 7 Hispanic/Latino). Average age 31. *Degree requirements:* For master's, comprehensive exam, departmental qualifying exam. *Entrance requirements:* For master's, writing exam, Test of Academic Proficiency/Basic Skills Test/ACT/SAT, bachelor's degree, minimum undergraduate GPA of 2.75, two letter of recommendation. Additional exam requirements/recommendations for international students: Required—TOEFL (minimum score 550 paper-based; 80 iBT), IELTS (minimum score 6). *Application deadline:* For fall admission, 5/1 priority date for international students; for spring admission, 11/15 priority date for international students. Applications are processed on a rolling basis. Application fee: $40. Electronic applications accepted. Tuition and fees vary according to program. *Financial support:* Federal Work-Study, scholarships/grants, and unspecified assistantships available. Financial award application deadline: 5/1; financial award applicants required to submit FAFSA. *Unit head:* Dr. Ann O'Brien, 815-838-0500, E-mail: obrienan@lewisu.edu. *Application contact:* Kathy Lisak, Graduate Admission Counselor, 815-838-5610, E-mail: grad@lewisu.edu.

Liberty University, School of Education, Lynchburg, VA 24515. Offers curriculum and instruction (Ed D, Ed S), including elementary education, middle grades education,

secondary education, special education; educational leadership (Ed D); gifted education (Certificate); math specialist (M Ed); middle grades (MAT, Certificate); reading specialist (M Ed); school leadership (Certificate); secondary education (MAT); sport management (MS), including coaching and athletic administration, outdoor adventure sport, sport administration, tourism. *Accreditation:* NCATE. *Program availability:* Part-time, online learning. *Students:* 1,966 full-time (1,428 women), 3,484 part-time (2,528 women); includes 1,323 minority (1,026 Black or African American, non-Hispanic/Latino; 29 American Indian or Alaska Native, non-Hispanic/Latino; 49 Asian, non-Hispanic/Latino; 100 Hispanic/Latino; 9 Native Hawaiian or other Pacific Islander, non-Hispanic/Latino; 110 Two or more races, non-Hispanic/Latino), 58 international. Average age 37. 3,748 applicants, 58% accepted, 1167 enrolled. In 2017, 656 master's, 110 doctorates, 316 other advanced degrees awarded. *Degree requirements:* For doctorate, comprehensive exam, thesis/dissertation. *Entrance requirements:* For master's, GRE General Test or MAT (if taken in or before 1999), 2 letters of recommendation, minimum undergraduate GPA of 3.0, curriculum vitae; for doctorate and other advanced degree, GRE General Test or MAT (if taken before 1999), minimum master's GPA of 3.0, 3 years of teaching experience. Additional exam requirements/recommendations for international students: Required—TOEFL (minimum score 600 paper-based; 100 iBT). *Application deadline:* For fall admission, 6/1 for domestic students; for spring admission, 11/1 for domestic students. Applications are processed on a rolling basis. Application fee: $50. Electronic applications accepted. *Expenses:* Contact institution. *Financial support:* Federal Work-Study and tuition waivers (partial) available. *Faculty research:* Self-determination, character education, bibliotherapy, learning styles, distance education. *Unit head:* Dr. Heather Schoffstall, Dean, 434-582-2445, Fax: 434-582-2468, E-mail: awgunter@liberty.edu. *Application contact:* Jay Bridge, Director of Graduate Admissions, 800-424-9595, Fax: 800-628-7977, E-mail: gradadmissions@liberty.edu.
Website: http://www.liberty.edu/academics/education/graduate/

Lincoln University, Graduate Studies, Jefferson City, MO 65101. Offers business administration (MBA), including accounting, management, management information systems, public administration/policy; elementary teaching (M Ed); environmental science (MS); guidance and counseling (M Ed), including community/agency counseling, elementary school, secondary school; higher education (MA); history (MA); integrated agricultural systems (MS); middle school (M Ed); natural sciences (MS); secondary teaching (M Ed); sociology (MA); sociology/criminal justice (MA). *Program availability:* Part-time, evening/weekend, 100% online, blended/hybrid learning. *Students:* 40 full-time (23 women), 64 part-time (32 women); includes 33 minority (30 Black or African American, non-Hispanic/Latino; 2 Hispanic/Latino; 1 Two or more races, non-Hispanic/Latino), 12 international. Average age 33. 48 applicants, 81% accepted, 22 enrolled. In 2017, 46 master's awarded. *Degree requirements:* For master's, comprehensive exam, thesis optional. *Entrance requirements:* For master's, GRE, MAT, or GMAT, minimum GPA of 2.75 overall, 3.0 in courses related to specialization; 3 letters of recommendation; minimum C average in English composition; personal statement of purpose. Additional exam requirements/recommendations for international students: Required—TOEFL (minimum score 500 paper-based; 61 iBT), IELTS (minimum score 5.5), Michigan English Language Assessment Battery (minimum score 80). *Application deadline:* For fall admission, 7/1 priority date for domestic students, 5/1 priority date for international students; for spring admission, 11/1 priority date for domestic students, 10/1 priority date for international students; for summer admission, 6/1 priority date for domestic students. Applications are processed on a rolling basis. Application fee: $30. Electronic applications accepted. *Expenses:* Tuition, state resident: part-time $291 per credit hour. Tuition, nonresident: part-time $541.50 per credit hour. *Financial support:* In 2017–18, 2 fellowships with tuition reimbursements, 3 research assistantships with tuition reimbursements were awarded; Federal Work-Study, scholarships/grants, and unspecified assistantships also available. Support available to part-time students. Financial award application deadline: 3/1; financial award applicants required to submit FAFSA. *Unit head:* Dr. Debra F. Greene, Interim Provost, 573-681-5247, Fax: 573-681-5106, E-mail: gradschool@lincolnu.edu. *Application contact:* Irasema Steck, Administrative Assistant, 573-681-5247, Fax: 573-681-5106, E-mail: gradschool@lincolnu.edu.
Website: http://www.lincolnu.edu/web/graduate-studies/graduate-studies

Lock Haven University of Pennsylvania, College of Liberal Arts and Education, Lock Haven, PA 17745-2390. Offers alternative education (M Ed); educational leadership (M Ed); teaching and learning (M Ed). *Accreditation:* NCATE. *Program availability:* Part-time, evening/weekend, online learning. *Degree requirements:* For master's, thesis. *Entrance requirements:* For master's, minimum undergraduate GPA of 3.0. Additional exam requirements/recommendations for international students: Required—TOEFL. Electronic applications accepted.

Long Island University–Brentwood Campus, Graduate Programs, Brentwood, NY 11717. Offers childhood education (MS), including grades 1-6; childhood education/literacy B-6 (MS); childhood education/special education (grades 1-6) (MS); clinical mental health counseling (MS, Advanced Certificate); criminal justice (MS); early childhood education (MS); educational leadership (MS Ed); family nurse practitioner (MS, Advanced Certificate); health administration (MPA); library and information science (MS); literacy (B-6) (MS Ed); school counselor (MS, Advanced Certificate); social work (MSW); special education (MS Ed); students with disabilities generalist (grades 7-12) (Advanced Certificate). *Program availability:* Part-time. *Faculty:* 14 full-time (9 women), 22 part-time/adjunct (11 women). *Students:* 111 full-time (89 women), 47 part-time (34 women); includes 35 minority (8 Black or African American, non-Hispanic/Latino; 1 American Indian or Alaska Native, non-Hispanic/Latino; 3 Asian, non-Hispanic/Latino; 22 Hispanic/Latino; 1 Two or more races, non-Hispanic/Latino), 1 international. Average age 30. 110 applicants, 82% accepted, 63 enrolled. In 2017, 58 master's, 5 other advanced degrees awarded. *Entrance requirements:* For master's and Advanced Certificate, GRE. Additional exam requirements/recommendations for international students: Required—TOEFL or IELTS. *Application deadline:* Applications are processed on a rolling basis. Application fee: $50. Electronic applications accepted. *Expenses:* Tuition: Full-time $21,168; part-time $1201 per credit. *Required fees:* $1840; $920 per term. Tuition and fees vary according to course load. *Financial support:* In 2017–18, 121 students received support. Scholarships/grants available. Support available to part-time students. Financial award application deadline: 2/15; financial award applicants required to submit FAFSA. *Unit head:* Dr. Abby Van Vlerah, Dean and Chief Operating Officer, 631-299-3831, E-mail: abagail.vanvlerah@liu.edu. *Application contact:* Scott Aug, Associate Director of Enrollment Management, 631-287-8506, E-mail: scott.aug@liu.edu.
Website: http://liu.edu/brentwood

Long Island University–Hudson, Graduate School, Purchase, NY 10577. Offers autism (Advanced Certificate); bilingual education (Advanced Certificate); childhood education (MS Ed); crisis management (Advanced Certificate); early childhood education (MS Ed); educational leadership (MS Ed); health administration (MPA); literacy (MS Ed); marriage and family therapy (MS); mental health counseling (MS, Advanced Certificate), including credentialed alcoholism and substance abuse counselor (MS); middle childhood and adolescence education (MS Ed); pharmaceutics (MS), including cosmetic science, industrial pharmacy; public administration (MPA); school counseling (MS Ed, Advanced Certificate); school psychology (MS Ed); special education (MS Ed); TESOL (MS Ed); TESOL (all grades) (Advanced Certificate).

Program availability: Part-time, evening/weekend. *Faculty:* 8 full-time (6 women), 41 part-time/adjunct (24 women). *Students:* 69 full-time (54 women), 249 part-time (200 women); includes 102 minority (29 Black or African American, non-Hispanic/Latino; 1 American Indian or Alaska Native, non-Hispanic/Latino; 9 Asian, non-Hispanic/Latino; 62 Hispanic/Latino; 1 Native Hawaiian or other Pacific Islander, non-Hispanic/Latino). Average age 33. 153 applicants, 96% accepted, 103 enrolled. In 2017, 138 master's, 36 other advanced degrees awarded. *Entrance requirements:* Additional exam requirements/recommendations for international students: Required—TOEFL. *Application deadline:* Applications are processed on a rolling basis. Application fee: $50. Electronic applications accepted. *Expenses:* Contact institution. *Financial support:* In 2017–18, 32 students received support. Scholarships/grants available. Support available to part-time students. Financial award application deadline: 2/15; financial award applicants required to submit FAFSA. *Unit head:* Dr. Sylvia Blake, Dean and Chief Operating Officer, 914-831-2700, E-mail: westchester@liu.edu. *Application contact:* Dr. Sylvia Blake, Dean and Chief Operating Officer, 914-831-2700, E-mail: westchester@liu.edu.

Long Island University–Riverhead, Graduate Programs, Riverhead, NY 11901. Offers applied behavior analysis (Advanced Certificate); childhood education (MS), including grades 1-6; cybersecurity policy (Advanced Certificate); homeland security management (MS, Advanced Certificate); literacy education (MS); literacy education B-6 (MS); teaching students with disabilities (MS), including grades 1-6; TESOL (Advanced Certificate). *Accreditation:* TEAC. *Program availability:* Part-time. *Faculty:* 4 full-time (1 woman), 11 part-time/adjunct (5 women). *Students:* 17 full-time (14 women), 58 part-time (36 women); includes 14 minority (4 Black or African American, non-Hispanic/Latino; 1 American Indian or Alaska Native, non-Hispanic/Latino; 1 Asian, non-Hispanic/Latino; 6 Hispanic/Latino; 2 Two or more races, non-Hispanic/Latino). Average age 32. 68 applicants, 79% accepted, 26 enrolled. In 2017, 30 master's, 7 other advanced degrees awarded. *Entrance requirements:* Additional exam requirements/recommendations for international students: Required—TOEFL or IELTS. *Application deadline:* Applications are processed on a rolling basis. Application fee: $50. Electronic applications accepted. *Expenses:* Contact institution. *Financial support:* In 2017–18, 53 students received support. Scholarships/grants available. Support available to part-time students. Financial award application deadline: 2/15; financial award applicants required to submit FAFSA. *Unit head:* Dr. Abagail VanVlerah, Dean and Chief Operating Officer, 631-299-3831, E-mail: abagail.vanvlerah@liu.edu. *Application contact:* Jean Conroy, Associate Dean, 631-287-8301, E-mail: jean.conroy@liu.edu.

Longwood University, College of Graduate and Professional Studies, College of Education and Human Services, Farmville, VA 23909. Offers education (MS), including algebra and middle school mathematics, counselor education, elementary and middle school mathematics, elementary education, elementary education initial licensure, health and physical education, special education general curriculum, special education initial licensure; reading, literacy and learning (M Ed); school librarianship (M Ed); social work and communication sciences and disorders (MS), including communication sciences and disorders. *Accreditation:* NCATE. *Program availability:* Part-time, evening/weekend. *Degree requirements:* For master's, comprehensive exam (for some programs), thesis optional, professional portfolio, internship, clinical experience, or practicum. *Entrance requirements:* For master's, PRAXIS I (for initial teaching licensure programs); GRE (for some programs), bachelor's degree from regionally-accredited institution, 2 recommendations (3 for some programs), minimum 500-word personal essay, official transcripts, minimum GPA of 2.75, valid teaching license (for some programs). Additional exam requirements/recommendations for international students: Required—TOEFL (minimum score 570 paper-based), IELTS (minimum score 6.5). Electronic applications accepted. *Expenses:* Contact institution.

Louisiana State University and Agricultural & Mechanical College, Graduate School, College of Human Sciences and Education, Department of Educational Theory, Policy and Practice, Baton Rouge, LA 70803. Offers counseling (M Ed, MA, Ed S); educational administration (M Ed, MA, PhD, Ed S); educational technology (MA); elementary education (M Ed, MAT); higher education (PhD); research methodology (PhD); secondary education (M Ed, MAT). *Accreditation:* ACA (one or more programs are accredited); NCATE. *Faculty:* 34 full-time (22 women). *Students:* 213 full-time (159 women), 228 part-time (178 women); includes 164 minority (123 Black or African American, non-Hispanic/Latino; 7 Asian, non-Hispanic/Latino; 27 Hispanic/Latino; 1 Native Hawaiian or other Pacific Islander, non-Hispanic/Latino; 6 Two or more races, non-Hispanic/Latino), 13 international. Average age 32. 231 applicants, 61% accepted, 82 enrolled. In 2017, 125 master's, 26 doctorates, 28 other advanced degrees awarded. *Financial support:* In 2017–18, 3 fellowships (averaging $12,129 per year), 2 research assistantships (averaging $16,019 per year), 96 teaching assistantships (averaging $16,061 per year) were awarded. *Total annual research expenditures:* $356,867.

Louisiana Tech University, Graduate School, College of Education, Ruston, LA 71272. Offers counseling and guidance (MA), including clinical mental health counseling, human services, orientation and mobility; counseling psychology (PhD); curriculum and instruction (M Ed); cyber education (Graduate Certificate); dynamics of domestic and family violence (Graduate Certificate); early childhood education - PreK-3 (MAT); educational leadership (M Ed, Ed D); elementary education and special education mild/moderate grades 1-5 (MAT); higher education administration (Graduate Certificate); industrial/organizational psychology (MA, PhD); kinesiology (MS); middle school education (MAT), including mathematics; orientation and mobility (Graduate Certificate); rehabilitation teaching for the blind (Graduate Certificate); secondary education (MAT), including agriculture, biology, business, chemistry, English; special education: visually impaired (MAT); teacher leader education (Graduate Certificate); visual impairments - blind education (Graduate Certificate). *Accreditation:* NCATE. *Program availability:* Part-time. *Faculty:* 28 full-time (16 women), 23 part-time/adjunct (22 women). *Students:* 269 full-time (192 women), 194 part-time (150 women); includes 127 minority (94 Black or African American, non-Hispanic/Latino; 2 American Indian or Alaska Native, non-Hispanic/Latino; 6 Asian, non-Hispanic/Latino; 16 Hispanic/Latino; 1 Native Hawaiian or other Pacific Islander, non-Hispanic/Latino; 8 Two or more races, non-Hispanic/Latino), 8 international. Average age 34. 226 applicants, 74% accepted, 60 enrolled. In 2017, 5 master's, 2 doctorates, 1 other advanced degree awarded. *Degree requirements:* For master's, thesis; for doctorate, thesis/dissertation. *Entrance requirements:* For master's and doctorate, GRE General Test. Additional exam requirements/recommendations for international students: Required—TOEFL (minimum score 550 paper-based; 80 iBT), IELTS (minimum score 6.5). *Application deadline:* For fall admission, 9/1 priority date for domestic students, 6/1 for international students; for winter admission, 11/1 priority date for domestic students, 9/1 for international students; for spring admission, 2/1 priority date for domestic students, 12/1 for international students; for summer admission, 5/1 priority date for domestic students, 3/1 for international students. Application fee: $40. Electronic applications accepted. *Expenses:* Tuition, state resident: full-time $5146. Tuition, nonresident: full-time $10,147. International tuition: $10,267 full-time. *Required fees:* $2273. *Financial support:* In 2017–18, 40 students received support, including 23 research assistantships (averaging $10,346 per year), 15 teaching assistantships (averaging $6,887 per year); fellowships and career-related internships or fieldwork also available. Financial award application deadline: 2/1. *Faculty research:* Blindness and the best methods for increasing independence for individuals who are blind or visually impaired; educating and investigating factors contributing to improvements in human

performance across the lifespan and a reduction in injury rates during training. *Total annual research expenditures:* $2.1 million. *Unit head:* Dr. Don Schillinger, Dean, 318-257-3712, E-mail: dschill@latech.edu. *Application contact:* Dr. Dawn Basinger, Associate Dean of Academic Affairs, 318-257-2977, Fax: 318-257-2379, E-mail: dbasing@latech.edu.
Website: http://education.latech.edu/

Loyola Marymount University, School of Education, Program in Elementary Education, Los Angeles, CA 90045-2659. Offers MA. *Unit head:* Dr. Liza Mastrippolito, Assistant Director, Department of Elementary and Secondary Education, 310-568-6697, E-mail: smastrip@lmu.edu. *Application contact:* Chake H. Kouyoumjian, Associate Dean of Graduate Studies, 310-338-2721, Fax: 310-338-6086, E-mail: graduateinfo@lmu.edu.
Website: http://soe.lmu.edu/academics/elementaryeducation

Loyola University Chicago, School of Education, Program in Teaching and Learning, Chicago, IL 60660. Offers elementary education (M Ed); English language teaching and learning (M Ed); secondary education (M Ed); special education (M Ed). *Accreditation:* NCATE. *Faculty:* 18 full-time (12 women), 33 part-time/adjunct (29 women). *Students:* 19 full-time (13 women), 20 part-time (17 women); includes 7 minority (1 Black or African American, non-Hispanic/Latino; 2 Asian, non-Hispanic/Latino; 4 Hispanic/Latino). Average age 27. 129 applicants, 48% accepted, 28 enrolled. In 2017, 38 master's awarded. *Degree requirements:* For master's, comprehensive exam. *Entrance requirements:* For master's, Illinois Basic Skills Test, 3 letters of recommendation, minimum GPA of 3.0, resume. Additional exam requirements/recommendations for international students: Required—TOEFL (minimum score 550 paper-based; 79 iBT). *Application deadline:* For summer admission, 3/1 priority date for domestic and international students. *Application fee:* $50. Electronic applications accepted. Application fee is waived when completed online. *Expenses:* $949 per semester hour, $2,847 per course, $8,541-$11,388 full-time semester tuition; $432 per semester fees, $225 additional fees (first semester only). *Financial support:* In 2017–18, 12 fellowships with partial tuition reimbursements were awarded; institutionally sponsored loans, scholarships/grants, and unspecified assistantships also available. Support available to part-time students. Financial award application deadline: 2/1; financial award applicants required to submit FAFSA. *Faculty research:* Positive behavior support, school reform, school improvement. *Unit head:* Dr. Hank Bohanon, Program Chair, 312-915-7009, E-mail: hbohano@luc.edu. *Application contact:* Mirtza Campbell, Information Contact, 312-915-8907, E-mail: mcampbell11@luc.edu.

Loyola University Maryland, Graduate Programs, School of Education, Master of Arts in Teaching Program, Baltimore, MD 21210-2699. Offers elementary education (MAT); secondary education (MAT). *Program availability:* Part-time. *Faculty:* 36 full-time (27 women), 23 part-time/adjunct (15 women). *Students:* 11 full-time (8 women), 149 part-time (133 women); includes 58 minority (43 Black or African American, non-Hispanic/Latino; 4 Asian, non-Hispanic/Latino; 7 Hispanic/Latino; 1 Native Hawaiian or other Pacific Islander, non-Hispanic/Latino; 3 Two or more races, non-Hispanic/Latino). Average age 32. *Entrance requirements:* For master's, essay, 2 letters of recommendation, resume, transcript. Additional exam requirements/recommendations for international students: Required—TOEFL (minimum score 550 paper-based), IELTS (minimum score 7). *Application deadline:* For spring admission, 11/1 for domestic students. Applications are processed on a rolling basis. Application fee: $60. Electronic applications accepted. *Expenses:* Contact institution. *Financial support:* Scholarships/grants available. Financial award application deadline: 4/15; financial award applicants required to submit FAFSA. *Application contact:* Brandon Gumabon, 410-617-2559, E-mail: bggumabon@loyola.edu.
Website: http://www.loyola.edu/soe/academics/graduate/mat.aspx

Loyola University Maryland, Graduate Programs, School of Education, Program in Montessori Education, Baltimore, MD 21210-2699. Offers elementary education (M Ed); Montessori education (CAS). *Accreditation:* NCATE. *Degree requirements:* For master's, thesis. *Entrance requirements:* For master's, essay, transcripts. Additional exam requirements/recommendations for international students: Required—TOEFL (minimum score 550 paper-based), IELTS (minimum score 7). *Application deadline:* For fall admission, 5/1 priority date for domestic students, 5/1 for international students. Applications are processed on a rolling basis. Application fee: $60. *Expenses:* Contact institution. *Financial support:* Scholarships/grants available. Financial award application deadline: 4/15; financial award applicants required to submit FAFSA. *Unit head:* Jack Rice, Director, 410-617-2308, E-mail: jhrice@loyola.edu. *Application contact:* Office of Graduate Admission, 410-617-5020, E-mail: graduate@loyola.edu.
Website: https://www.loyola.edu/school-education/academics/graduate/montessori

Manhattan College, Graduate Programs, School of Education and Health, Program in Special Education, Riverdale, NY 10471. Offers adolescence education students with disabilities generalist extension in English or math or social studies - grades 7-12 (MS Ed); bilingual education (Advanced Certificate); dual childhood/students with disabilities - grades 1-6 (MS Ed); students with disabilities - grades 1-6 (MS Ed). *Program availability:* Part-time, evening/weekend. *Degree requirements:* For master's, thesis, internship (if not certified). *Entrance requirements:* For master's, GRE, minimum GPA of 3.0. Additional exam requirements/recommendations for international students: Required—TOEFL (minimum score 550 paper-based; 80 iBT), IELTS (minimum score 6). Electronic applications accepted. Application fee is waived when completed online. *Expenses:* Contact institution.

Manhattanville College, School of Education, Jump Start Program, Purchase, NY 10577-2132. Offers childhood education and special education (grades 1-6) (MPS); early childhood education (birth-grade 2) (MAT); education (Advanced Certificate); English and special education (grades 5-12) (MPS); mathematics and special education (grades 5-12) (MPS); science and special education (grades 5-12) (MPS); social studies and special education (grades 5-12) (MPS); Spanish (grades 7-12) (MAT); TESOL (all grades) (MPS). *Program availability:* Part-time, evening/weekend. *Faculty:* 10 full-time (7 women), 39 part-time/adjunct (27 women). *Students:* 3 full-time (2 women), 40 part-time (24 women); includes 11 minority (3 Black or African American, non-Hispanic/Latino; 6 Hispanic/Latino; 1 Native Hawaiian or other Pacific Islander, non-Hispanic/Latino; 1 Two or more races, non-Hispanic/Latino). Average age 33. 25 applicants, 60% accepted, 7 enrolled. In 2017, 17 master's, 2 other advanced degrees awarded. *Degree requirements:* For master's, comprehensive exam (for some programs), thesis (for some programs), student teaching, research seminars, portfolios, internships, writing assessment; for Advanced Certificate, comprehensive exam (for some programs). *Entrance requirements:* For master's, GRE or MAT (for programs leading to certification), minimum GPA of 3.0, 2 letters of recommendation, interview, essay (2-3 page personal statement that describes reasons for choosing teaching or educational leadership as profession and philosophy of education), proof of immunization (for those born after 1957). Additional exam requirements/recommendations for international students: Required—TOEFL (minimum score 600 paper-based; 110 iBT); Recommended—IELTS (minimum score 8). *Application deadline:* Applications are processed on a rolling basis. Application fee: $75. Electronic applications accepted. *Expenses:* $915 per credit. *Financial support:* Teaching assistantships, career-related internships or fieldwork, Federal Work-Study, institutionally sponsored loans, scholarships/grants, and unspecified assistantships available. Financial award application deadline: 3/15; financial award applicants required to submit FAFSA. *Faculty*

research: Early childhood and technology, professional development schools and community schools, students with emotional difficulties, literacy and adolescents, mindfulness, changing suburbs institute, and community schools, studying the effects of the environment on special populations, the most difficult cases, students who are presented with multiple challenges: learning, behavioral and ACE experiences who see criminal behavior as a way to cope; working on giving them the tools they need to succeed. *Unit head:* Dr. Shelly Wepner, Dean, 914-323-3153, E-mail: shelly.wepner@mville.edu. *Application contact:* Alissa Wilson, Director, Graduate Admissions, 914-323-3150, Fax: 914-694-1732, E-mail: edschool@mville.edu.
Website: http://www.mville.edu/programs/jump-start

Manhattanville College, School of Education, Program in Childhood Education, Purchase, NY 10577-2132. Offers childhood education (grades 1-6) (MAT, MPS); early childhood (birth - grade 2) (MAT); special education: childhood (grades 1-6) (MPS, Certificate); special education: early childhood (birth - grade 2) and childhood (grades 1-6) (Certificate); special education: early childhood and childhood (birth - grade 6) (MPS). *Program availability:* Part-time, evening/weekend. *Faculty:* 3 full-time (all women), 7 part-time/adjunct (5 women). *Students:* 7 full-time (all women), 28 part-time (23 women); includes 8 minority (2 Black or African American, non-Hispanic/Latino; 6 Hispanic/Latino). Average age 29. 27 applicants, 93% accepted, 22 enrolled. In 2017, 13 master's awarded. *Degree requirements:* For master's, comprehensive exam (for some programs), thesis (for some programs), student teaching, research seminars, portfolios, internships, writing assessment; for Certificate, comprehensive exam (for some programs). *Entrance requirements:* For master's, GRE or MAT (for programs leading to certification), minimum GPA of 3.0, 2 letters of recommendation, interview, essay (2-3 page personal statement that describes reasons for choosing teaching or educational leadership as profession and philosophy of education), proof of immunization (for those born after 1957). Additional exam requirements/recommendations for international students: Required—TOEFL (minimum score 600 paper-based; 110 iBT); Recommended—IELTS (minimum score 8). *Application deadline:* Applications are processed on a rolling basis. Application fee: $75. Electronic applications accepted. *Expenses:* $915 per credit. *Financial support:* Teaching assistantships, career-related internships or fieldwork, Federal Work-Study, institutionally sponsored loans, scholarships/grants, and unspecified assistantships available. Financial award application deadline: 3/15; financial award applicants required to submit FAFSA. *Faculty research:* Early childhood and technology, professional development schools and community schools. *Unit head:* Dr. Shelly Wepner, Dean, 914-323-3153, Fax: 914-323-5493, E-mail: shelly.wepner@mville.edu. *Application contact:* Alissa Wilson, Director, Graduate Admissions, 914-323-3150, Fax: 914-694-1732, E-mail: edschool@mville.edu.
Website: http://www.mville.edu/programs/childhood-education

Manhattanville College, School of Education, Program in Literacy Education, Purchase, NY 10577-2132. Offers literacy (birth-grade 6) and special education childhood (grades 1-6) (MPS); literacy 5-12 (MPS); literacy specialist (birth-grade 6) (MPS); literacy specialist (grades 5-12) (MPS); science of reading: multisensory instruction (Advanced Certificate). *Program availability:* Part-time, evening/weekend. *Faculty:* 4 full-time (all women), 8 part-time/adjunct (5 women). *Students:* 1 (woman) full-time, 21 part-time (20 women). Average age 31. 12 applicants, 92% accepted, 8 enrolled. In 2017, 7 master's, 3 Advanced Certificates awarded. *Degree requirements:* For master's, comprehensive exam (for some programs), thesis (for some programs), student teaching, research seminars, portfolios, internships, writing assessment; for Advanced Certificate, comprehensive exam (for some programs). *Entrance requirements:* For master's, GRE or MAT (for programs leading to certification), minimum GPA of 3.0, 2 letters of recommendation, interview, essay (2-3 page personal statement that describes reasons for choosing teaching or educational leadership as profession and philosophy of education), proof of immunization (for those born after 1957). Additional exam requirements/recommendations for international students: Required—TOEFL (minimum score 600 paper-based; 110 iBT); Recommended—IELTS (minimum score 8). *Application deadline:* Applications are processed on a rolling basis. Application fee: $75. Electronic applications accepted. *Expenses:* $915 per credit. *Financial support:* Teaching assistantships, career-related internships or fieldwork, Federal Work-Study, institutionally sponsored loans, scholarships/grants, and unspecified assistantships available. Financial award application deadline: 3/15; financial award applicants required to submit FAFSA. *Faculty research:* Power of story for literacy development, English learners. *Total annual research expenditures:* $800. *Unit head:* Dr. Shelly Wepner, Dean, 914-323-3153, Fax: 914-323-5493, E-mail: shelly.wepner@mville.edu. *Application contact:* Alissa Wilson, Director, Graduate Admissions, 914-323-3150, Fax: 914-694-1732, E-mail: edschool@mville.edu.
Website: http://www.mville.edu/programs/literacy-education

Manhattanville College, School of Education, Program in Special Education, Purchase, NY 10577-2132. Offers childhood (grades 1-6) (MPS); childhood education (grades 1-6) and special education (MPS); early childhood (birth-grade 2) (MPS); early childhood (birth-grade 2) and special education (MPS); early childhood and childhood (birth-grade 6) (MPS); English (5-9 and 7-12) (MPS); grades 7-12 generalist (MPS); literacy (birth-grade 6) and special education childhood (grades 1-6) (MPS); literacy 5-12 (MPS); mathematics (5-9 and 7-12) (MPS); science (biology or chemistry 5-9 and 7-12) (MPS); social studies (5-9 and 7-12) (MPS); special education: childhood (grades 1-6) (Certificate); special education: early childhood (birth-grade 2) and childhood (grades 1-6) (Certificate); special education: early childhood (birth-grade 2) (Certificate); special education: grades 7-12 generalist (Certificate). *Program availability:* Part-time, evening/weekend. *Faculty:* 5 full-time (3 women), 24 part-time/adjunct (16 women). *Students:* 77 full-time (69 women), 154 part-time (132 women); includes 33 minority (9 Black or African American, non-Hispanic/Latino; 2 Asian, non-Hispanic/Latino; 22 Hispanic/Latino), 1 international. Average age 28. 87 applicants, 77% accepted, 57 enrolled. In 2017, 86 master's, 2 Certificates awarded. *Degree requirements:* For master's, comprehensive exam (for some programs), thesis (for some programs), student teaching, research seminars, portfolios, internships, writing assessment; for Certificate, comprehensive exam (for some programs). *Entrance requirements:* For master's, GRE or MAT (for programs leading to certification), minimum GPA of 3.0, 2 letters of recommendation, interview, essay (2-3 page personal statement that describes reasons for choosing teaching or educational leadership as profession and philosophy of education), proof of immunization (for those born after 1957). Additional exam requirements/recommendations for international students: Required—TOEFL (minimum score 600 paper-based; 110 iBT); Recommended—IELTS (minimum score 8). *Application deadline:* Applications are processed on a rolling basis. Application fee: $75. Electronic applications accepted. *Expenses:* $915 per credit. *Financial support:* Teaching assistantships, career-related internships or fieldwork, Federal Work-Study, institutionally sponsored loans, scholarships/grants, and unspecified assistantships available. Financial award application deadline: 3/15; financial award applicants required to submit FAFSA. *Faculty research:* Students with emotional difficulties, literacy and adolescents, mindfulness, studying the effects of the environment on special populations, the most difficult cases, students who are presented with multiple challenges: learning, behavioral and ACE experiences who see criminal behavior as a way to cope; working on giving them the tools they need to succeed emotionally and cognitively despite the odds stacked against them. *Unit head:* Dr. Shelly Wepner, Dean,

914-323-3153, Fax: 914-323-5493, E-mail: shelly.wepner@mville.edu. *Application contact:* Alissa Wilson, Director, Graduate Admissions, 914-323-3150, Fax: 914-694-1732, E-mail: edschool@mville.edu.
Website: http://www.mville.edu/programs/special-education

Mansfield University of Pennsylvania, Graduate Studies, Department of Education and Special Education, Mansfield, PA 16933. Offers elementary education (M Ed); secondary education (MS); special education (M Ed). *Accreditation:* NCATE (one or more programs are accredited). *Program availability:* Part-time, evening/weekend, online learning. *Degree requirements:* For master's, comprehensive exam, thesis optional. *Entrance requirements:* For master's, minimum GPA of 3.0. Additional exam requirements/recommendations for international students: Required—TOEFL (minimum score 550 paper-based). Electronic applications accepted.

Marquette University, Graduate School, College of Education, Department of Educational Policy and Leadership, Milwaukee, WI 53201-1881. Offers college student personnel administration (M Ed); curriculum and instruction (MA); education (MA); educational administration (M Ed); educational policy and foundations (MA); elementary education (Certificate); literacy (MA); principal (Certificate); reading specialist (Certificate); reading teacher (Certificate); secondary education (Certificate); superintendent (Certificate). *Program availability:* Part-time, evening/weekend. Terminal master's awarded for partial completion of doctoral program. *Degree requirements:* For master's, comprehensive exam, thesis (for some programs); for doctorate, thesis/dissertation, qualifying exam. *Entrance requirements:* For master's, GRE General Test or MAT, official transcripts from all current and previous colleges/universities except Marquette, three letters of recommendation, statement of purpose; for doctorate, GRE General Test, MAT, sample of written work, official transcripts from all current and previous colleges/universities except Marquette, three letters of recommendation, statement of purpose, resume/curriculum vitae; for Certificate, GRE General Test or MAT, master's degree. Additional exam requirements/recommendations for international students: Required—TOEFL (minimum score 530 paper-based). *Expenses:* Contact institution. *Faculty research:* Leadership; social justice in education; development of lifelong learners; race, class, and schooling in historical perspective; urban teacher education.

Mars Hill University, Adult and Graduate Studies, Mars Hill, NC 28754. Offers elementary education (K-6) (M Ed). *Degree requirements:* For master's, project.

Mary Baldwin University, Graduate Studies, Program in Teaching, Staunton, VA 24401-3610. Offers elementary education (MAT); middle grades education (MAT). *Accreditation:* TEAC.

Marygrove College, Graduate Studies, Detroit, MI 48221-2599. Offers autism spectrum disorders (M Ed, Certificate); curriculum instruction and assessment (MAT); educational leadership (MA); educational technology (M Ed); effective teaching in the 21st century-classroom focus (MAT); effective teaching in the 21st century-technology focus (MAT); human resource management (MA, Certificate); mathematics 6-8 (MAT); mathematics K-5 (MAT); reading and literacy K-6 (MAT); reading specialist (M Ed); school administrator (Certificate); social justice (MA); special education (MAT); special education - learning disabilities (M Ed); teaching - pre-elementary education (M Ed); teaching - pre-secondary education (M Ed). *Program availability:* Part-time, evening/weekend, 100% online, blended/hybrid learning. *Students:* 163 full-time (123 women), 264 part-time (186 women). Average age 34. *Entrance requirements:* For master's, all official bachelor's transcripts. Additional exam requirements/recommendations for international students: Required—TOEFL (minimum score 550 paper-based; 80 iBT). *Application deadline:* Applications are processed on a rolling basis. Electronic applications accepted. *Expenses: Tuition:* Part-time $590 per credit hour. *Required fees:* $120 per semester. One-time fee: $25 part-time. *Financial support:* Applicants required to submit FAFSA. *Unit head:* Marygrove College Admissions, 313-927-1240, E-mail: info@marygrove.edu. *Application contact:* Marygrove College Admissions, 313-927-1240, E-mail: info@marygrove.edu.

Marymount University, School of Education and Human Services, Program in Education, Arlington, VA 22207-4299. Offers curriculum and instruction (M Ed); elementary education (M Ed); professional studies (M Ed); secondary education (M Ed); special education: general curriculum (M Ed). *Accreditation:* NCATE. *Program availability:* Part-time, evening/weekend. *Faculty:* 7 full-time (all women), 10 part-time/adjunct (7 women). *Students:* 51 full-time (40 women), 92 part-time (61 women); includes 33 minority (9 Black or African American, non-Hispanic/Latino; 9 Asian, non-Hispanic/Latino; 10 Hispanic/Latino; 5 Two or more races, non-Hispanic/Latino), 11 international. Average age 34. 39 applicants, 97% accepted, 30 enrolled. In 2017, 72 master's awarded. *Degree requirements:* For master's, thesis or alternative, capstone/internship. *Entrance requirements:* For master's, GRE or MAT and PRAXIS I or SAT/ACT and Virginia Communication and Literacy Assessment (VCLA), 2 letters of recommendation, resume, interview, minimum undergraduate GPA of 2.75 or 3.25 in the last 60 hours. Additional exam requirements/recommendations for international students: Required—TOEFL (minimum score 600 paper-based; 96 iBT), IELTS (minimum score 6.5). *Application deadline:* Applications are processed on a rolling basis. Application fee: $40. Electronic applications accepted. *Expenses:* $715 per credit. *Financial support:* In 2017–18, 7 students received support, including 2 teaching assistantships with full and partial tuition reimbursements available (averaging $14,520 per year); career-related internships or fieldwork, Federal Work-Study, scholarships/grants, and unspecified assistantships also available. Support available to part-time students. Financial award application deadline: 3/1; financial award applicants required to submit FAFSA. *Unit head:* Dr. Lisa Turissini, Chair, Education, 703-526-1668, Fax: 703-284-1631, E-mail: lisa.turissini@marymount.edu. *Application contact:* Francesca Reed, Director, Graduate Admissions, 703-284-5901, Fax: 703-527-3815, E-mail: grad.admissions@marymount.edu.
Website: http://www.marymount.edu/Academics/School-of-Education-Human-Services/Graduate-Programs/Education-(M-Ed-)

Maryville University of Saint Louis, School of Education, St. Louis, MO 63141-7299. Offers early childhood education (MA Ed); educational leadership (Ed D); elementary education (MA Ed); higher education leadership (Ed D); literacy specialist (MA Ed); middle grades education (MA Ed); secondary teaching and inquiry (MA Ed); teacher as leader (MA Ed, Ed D). *Accreditation:* NCATE. *Program availability:* Part-time, 100% online, blended/hybrid learning. *Faculty:* 20 full-time (14 women), 19 part-time/adjunct (13 women). *Students:* 6 full-time (4 women), 337 part-time (250 women); includes 101 minority (85 Black or African American, non-Hispanic/Latino; 4 Asian, non-Hispanic/Latino; 8 Hispanic/Latino; 4 Two or more races, non-Hispanic/Latino), 3 international. Average age 38. In 2017, 34 master's, 67 doctorates awarded. *Degree requirements:* For master's, thesis, project. *Entrance requirements:* For master's, minimum cumulative GPA of 3.0, 3 professional recommendations, essays, interview with program faculty; for doctorate, minimum GPA of 3.0, 3 professional recommendations, essay, interview, on-site writing sample. Additional exam requirements/recommendations for international students: Required—TOEFL (minimum score 550 paper-based). *Application deadline:* Applications are processed on a rolling basis. Electronic applications accepted. *Expenses:* Contact institution. *Financial support:* Career-related internships or fieldwork, Federal Work-Study, tuition waivers (partial), and professional educator discounts available. Financial award application deadline: 4/1; financial award applicants

required to submit FAFSA. *Faculty research:* Collaboration with public schools, pre-service program development, mathematics, diversity, literacy. *Unit head:* Dr. Cathy Bear, Dean, 314-529-9692, Fax: 314-529-9921, E-mail: cbear@maryville.edu. *Application contact:* Stacey Ruffin, Coordinator of Clinical Experiences and Graduate Programs, 314-529-9542, Fax: 314-529-9921, E-mail: teachered@maryville.edu.
Website: http://www.maryville.edu/ed/graduate-programs/

Marywood University, Academic Affairs, Reap College of Education and Human Development, Department of Education, Program in PK-4 Education, Scranton, PA 18509-1598. Offers MAT. *Accreditation:* NCATE. *Program availability:* Part-time. Electronic applications accepted.

McDaniel College, Graduate and Professional Studies, Program in Elementary and Secondary Education, Westminster, MD 21157-4390. Offers elementary education (MS); elementary STEM instructional leader (Postbaccalaureate Certificate); equity and excellence in education (Postbaccalaureate Certificate); learning technology specialist (Postbaccalaureate Certificate); secondary education (MS). *Accreditation:* NCATE. *Program availability:* Part-time, evening/weekend. *Faculty:* 3 full-time (2 women), 27 part-time/adjunct (22 women). *Students:* 16 full-time (8 women), 148 part-time (114 women); includes 30 minority (17 Black or African American, non-Hispanic/Latino; 5 Asian, non-Hispanic/Latino; 7 Hispanic/Latino; 1 Two or more races, non-Hispanic/Latino), 1 international. Average age 34. 34 applicants, 97% accepted, 18 enrolled. In 2017, 24 master's, 47 other advanced degrees awarded. *Degree requirements:* For master's, comprehensive exam (for some programs), thesis optional. *Entrance requirements:* For master's, PRAXIS, 2 references. Additional exam requirements/recommendations for international students: Required—TOEFL (minimum score 79 iBT), IELTS (minimum score 6). *Application deadline:* For fall admission, 6/1 priority date for domestic students; for spring admission, 11/1 priority date for domestic students; for summer admission, 3/1 priority date for domestic students. Applications are processed on a rolling basis. Application fee: $75. Electronic applications accepted. *Expenses: Tuition:* Full-time $11,760; part-time $490 per credit hour. Tuition and fees vary according to course load and program. *Financial support:* Application deadline: 3/1; applicants required to submit FAFSA. *Unit head:* Fax: 410-857-2515, E-mail: gradadms@mcdaniel.edu. *Application contact:* Penny Pfeiffer, Senior Graduate Enrollment Management Specialist, 410-857-2513, Fax: 410-857-2515, E-mail: ppfeiffer@mcdaniel.edu.

McNeese State University, Doré School of Graduate Studies, Burton College of Education, Department of Education Professions, Program in Curriculum and Instruction, Lake Charles, LA 70609. Offers academically gifted education (M Ed); elementary education (M Ed); reading (M Ed); secondary education (M Ed); special education (M Ed). *Program availability:* Evening/weekend. *Entrance requirements:* For master's, GRE, teaching certificate. *Application deadline:* For fall admission, 5/15 priority date for domestic and international students; for spring admission, 10/15 priority date for domestic and international students. Applications are processed on a rolling basis. Application fee: $20 ($30 for international students). *Financial support:* Application deadline: 5/1. *Unit head:* Dr. Brett C. Welch, Director, 337-475-5405, Fax: 337-475-5272, E-mail: bwelch@mcneese.edu. *Application contact:* Dr. Dustin M. Hebert, Director of Dore' School of Graduate Studies, 337-475-5396, Fax: 337-475-5397, E-mail: admissions@mcneese.edu.

McNeese State University, Doré School of Graduate Studies, Burton College of Education, Department of Education Professions, Program in Elementary Education, Lake Charles, LA 70609. Offers MAT. *Program availability:* Evening/weekend. *Degree requirements:* For master's, comprehensive exam, field experiences. *Entrance requirements:* For master's, GRE General Test, PRAXIS I and II, autobiography, two letters of recommendation. *Application deadline:* For fall admission, 5/15 priority date for domestic and international students; for spring admission, 10/15 priority date for domestic and international students. Applications are processed on a rolling basis. Application fee: $20 ($30 for international students). *Financial support:* Application deadline: 5/1. *Unit head:* Dr. Brett C Welch, Director, 337-475-5405, Fax: 337-475-5272, E-mail: bwelch@mcneese.edu. *Application contact:* Dr. Dustin M Hebert, Director of Dore' School of Graduate Studies, 337-475-5396, Fax: 337-475-5397, E-mail: admissions@mcneese.edu.
Website: http://www.mcneese.edu/gep/master-of-arts-in-teaching-in-elementary-educati

McNeese State University, Doré School of Graduate Studies, Burton College of Education, Department of Education Professions, Program in Elementary Education Grades 1-5, Lake Charles, LA 70609. Offers Postbaccalaureate Certificate. *Entrance requirements:* For degree, PRAXIS, 2 letters of recommendation, autobiography. *Application deadline:* For fall admission, 5/15 priority date for domestic and international students; for spring admission, 10/15 priority date for domestic and international students. Applications are processed on a rolling basis. Application fee: $20 ($30 for international students). *Financial support:* Application deadline: 5/1. *Unit head:* Dr. Veronica Faye White, Head, 337-475-5400, Fax: 337-475-5272, E-mail: vfwhite@mcneese.edu. *Application contact:* Dr. Dustin M. Hebert, Director of Dore' School of Graduate Studies, 337-475-5396, Fax: 337-475-5397, E-mail: admissions@mcneese.edu.

Medaille College, Program in Education, Buffalo, NY 14214-2695. Offers adolescent education (MS Ed); curriculum and instruction (MS Ed); education preparation (MS Ed); literacy (MS Ed); special education (MS). *Accreditation:* TEAC. *Program availability:* Part-time, evening/weekend. *Degree requirements:* For master's, comprehensive exam (for some programs), thesis or alternative. *Entrance requirements:* For master's, minimum undergraduate GPA of 2.7. Additional exam requirements/recommendations for international students: Required—TOEFL (minimum score 550 paper-based). Electronic applications accepted. *Faculty research:* Curriculum planning, truancy, tracking minority students, curriculum design, mentoring students.

Mercy College, School of Education, Program in Childhood Education, Dobbs Ferry, NY 10522-1189. Offers MS. *Program availability:* Part-time, evening/weekend, blended/hybrid learning. *Students:* 24 full-time (22 women), 43 part-time (33 women); includes 33 minority (15 Black or African American, non-Hispanic/Latino; 3 Asian, non-Hispanic/Latino; 13 Hispanic/Latino; 2 Two or more races, non-Hispanic/Latino). Average age 32. 60 applicants, 45% accepted, 13 enrolled. In 2017, 23 master's awarded. *Degree requirements:* For master's, comprehensive exam (for some programs), thesis (for some programs). *Entrance requirements:* For master's, GRE, resume, undergraduate transcript. Additional exam requirements/recommendations for international students: Required—TOEFL (minimum score 600 paper-based; 100 iBT), IELTS (minimum score 8). *Application deadline:* For fall admission, 8/1 for international students. Applications are processed on a rolling basis. Application fee: $40. Electronic applications accepted. *Expenses: Tuition:* Full-time $15,426; part-time $857 per credit hour. *Required fees:* $630; $158 per term. Tuition and fees vary according to course load, degree level and program. *Financial support:* Career-related internships or fieldwork, Federal Work-Study, scholarships/grants, and unspecified assistantships available. Financial award applicants required to submit FAFSA. *Unit head:* Dr. Rose Rudnitski, Dean for the School of Education, 914-674-7447 Ext. 914, Fax: 914-674-7352, E-mail: rrudnitski@mercy.edu. *Application contact:* Allison Gurdineer, Senior Director of Admissions, 877-637-2946, Fax: 914-674-7382, E-mail: admissions@mercy.edu.
Website: https://www.mercy.edu/degrees-programs/ms-childhood-education-grade-1-6

Elementary Education

Meredith College, School of Education, Health and Human Sciences, Raleigh, NC 27607-5298. Offers academically and intellectually gifted (M Ed); elementary education (M Ed, MAT); English as a second language (M Ed, MAT); health and physical education (MAT); nutrition, health and human performance (MS, Postbaccalaureate Certificate), including dietetic internship (Postbaccalaureate Certificate), nutrition (MS); psychology (MA), including industrial/organizational psychology; reading (M Ed); special education (MAT); special education (general curriculum) (M Ed). *Accreditation:* NCATE. *Program availability:* Part-time, evening/weekend. *Students:* 25 full-time (24 women), 22 part-time (all women); includes 13 minority (8 Black or African American, non-Hispanic/Latino; 1 American Indian or Alaska Native, non-Hispanic/Latino; 1 Asian, non-Hispanic/Latino; 3 Hispanic/Latino). Average age 31. 57 applicants, 54% accepted, 31 enrolled. In 2017, 14 master's awarded. *Degree requirements:* For master's, thesis optional. *Entrance requirements:* For master's, GRE General Test or MAT, minimum GPA of 2.5, teaching license, recommendations. Additional exam requirements/recommendations for international students: Required—TOEFL. *Application deadline:* For fall admission, 7/1 priority date for domestic students; for spring admission, 11/1 priority date for domestic students. Applications are processed on a rolling basis. Application fee: $50. Electronic applications accepted. *Expenses:* Contact institution. *Financial support:* Career-related internships or fieldwork, institutionally sponsored loans, and tuition waivers (partial) available. Support available to part-time students. Financial award application deadline: 2/15; financial award applicants required to submit FAFSA. *Unit head:* Dr. Monica McKinney, Graduate Program Manager, 919-760-8056, Fax: 919-760-2303, E-mail: mckinneym@meredith.edu.
Website: https://www.meredith.edu/school-of-education-health-and-human-sciences

Merrimack College, School of Education and Social Policy, North Andover, MA 01845-5800. Offers community engagement (M Ed), including community organizations, higher education, PreK-12 education; criminology and criminal justice (MS); curriculum and instruction (M Ed); early childhood education (M Ed); educational leadership (CAGS), including instructional leadership; elementary education (M Ed); English as a second language (PreK-6) (M Ed); high school education (M Ed); higher education (M Ed), including leadership and organizational development, student affairs; middle school education (M Ed); moderate disabilities (PreK-8) (M Ed); school counseling (M Ed). *Program availability:* Part-time, evening/weekend, 100% online courses with immersion events and in-classroom practicum close to home. *Faculty:* 15 full-time, 36 part-time/adjunct. *Students:* 212 full-time (175 women), 121 part-time (101 women); includes 42 minority (6 Black or African American, non-Hispanic/Latino; 6 Asian, non-Hispanic/Latino; 27 Hispanic/Latino; 3 Two or more races, non-Hispanic/Latino), 3 international. Average age 27. 420 applicants, 84% accepted, 250 enrolled. In 2017, 177 master's awarded. *Degree requirements:* For master's, practicum, portfolio, and state test (for licensure track); capstone (for higher education, curriculum and instruction, and community engagement tracks); for CAGS, capstone. *Entrance requirements:* For master's, Massachusetts Teacher Education Licensure (MTEL), official transcripts from other colleges, resume, personal statement, 2 letters of recommendation. Additional exam requirements/recommendations for international students: Required—TOEFL (minimum score 84 iBT), IELTS (minimum score 6.5), PTE (minimum score 56). *Application deadline:* For fall admission, 8/24 for domestic students, 7/30 for international students; for spring admission, 1/10 for domestic students, 12/10 for international students; for summer admission, 5/10 for domestic students, 4/10 for international students. Applications are processed on a rolling basis. Application fee: $0. Electronic applications accepted. *Expenses:* Contact institution. *Financial support:* Fellowships with full tuition reimbursements, career-related internships or fieldwork, scholarships/grants, and health care benefits available. Support available to part-time students. Financial award application deadline: 5/1; financial award applicants required to submit FAFSA. *Application contact:* Alyssa Orlando, Graduate Admissions Counselor, 978-837-3563, E-mail: orlandoaf@merrimack.edu.
Website: http://www.merrimack.edu/academics/graduate/education/

Metropolitan College of New York, Program in Childhood/Special Education, New York, NY 10006. Offers dual childhood 1-6 special education (MS). *Accreditation:* NCATE. *Students:* 22 full-time (16 women), 1 (woman) part-time; includes 21 minority (15 Black or African American, non-Hispanic/Latino; 6 Hispanic/Latino). Average age 36. 44 applicants, 30% accepted, 10 enrolled. In 2017, 16 master's awarded. *Entrance requirements:* For master's, GRE or MAT, minimum GPA of 3.0, 2 letters of reference, interview, resume. Additional exam requirements/recommendations for international students: Required—TOEFL (minimum score 550 paper-based; 80 iBT), IELTS (minimum score 6.5). *Application deadline:* Applications are processed on a rolling basis. Application fee: $45. Electronic applications accepted. *Expenses:* $807 per semester credit, $395 fee per semester. *Financial support:* Career-related internships or fieldwork, Federal Work-Study, institutionally sponsored loans, and scholarships/grants available. Financial award application deadline: 8/15; financial award applicants required to submit FAFSA. *Faculty research:* Classroom management, learner autonomy, teacher research, math and gender, intelligence. *Unit head:* Dr. Patrick Ianniello, Director, 212-343-1234 Ext. 2424, E-mail: pianniello@metropolitan.edu. *Application contact:* Steebo Varghese, Associate Director of Admissions, 212-343-1234 Ext. 2708, E-mail: svarghese@mcny.edu.
Website: https://www.mcny.edu/academics/audrey-cohen-school-human-services-education/master-science-education-dual-childhood-grades-1-6special-education/

Metropolitan State University of Denver, School of Education, Denver, CO 80204. Offers elementary education (MAT); special education (MAT). *Expenses:* Contact institution.

Middle Tennessee State University, College of Graduate Studies, College of Education, Department of Elementary and Special Education, Major in Curriculum and Instruction, Murfreesboro, TN 37132. Offers early childhood education (M Ed); elementary education (M Ed, Ed S); middle school education (M Ed). *Accreditation:* NCATE. *Program availability:* Part-time, evening/weekend, online learning. *Degree requirements:* For master's, comprehensive exam; for Ed S, comprehensive exam, thesis or alternative. *Entrance requirements:* For master's and Ed S, GRE, MAT or PRAXIS. Additional exam requirements/recommendations for international students: Required—TOEFL (minimum score 525 paper-based; 71 iBT) or IELTS (minimum score 6). Electronic applications accepted.

Milligan College, Area of Education, Milligan College, TN 37682. Offers combined preK-3/K-5 education (M Ed); educational leadership (Ed D, Ed S); K-5 education (M Ed); middle grades education (M Ed); preK-3 education (M Ed); preK-3 special education (M Ed); secondary education (M Ed). *Accreditation:* NCATE. *Program availability:* Part-time. *Faculty:* 6 full-time (4 women), 3 part-time/adjunct (2 women). *Students:* 27 full-time (20 women), 20 part-time (11 women); includes 2 minority (1 Hispanic/Latino; 1 Two or more races, non-Hispanic/Latino), 1 international. Average age 34. 17 applicants, 35% accepted, 6 enrolled. In 2017, 21 master's awarded. *Degree requirements:* For master's, thesis, portfolio, research project; for doctorate, thesis/dissertation, portfolio, research project. *Entrance requirements:* For master's, MAT, GRE General Test, ACT, SAT, or PRAXIS, undergraduate degree and supporting transcripts, professional recommendations, interview; for doctorate, MAT or GRE, master's degree and supporting transcripts, demonstrated scholastic ability, recognized leadership role within education, professional recommendations, essay/personal statement, portfolio (professional development plan, evidence of ability, knowledge and qualities), interview. Additional exam requirements/recommendations for international students: Required—TOEFL (minimum score 550 paper-based, 79 iBT) or IELTS (6.5). *Application deadline:* For fall admission, 8/1 priority date for domestic students, 6/1 for international students; for spring admission, 11/15 priority date for domestic students, 12/1 for international students; for summer admission, 4/1 for domestic students. Applications are processed on a rolling basis. Application fee: $0. Electronic applications accepted. *Expenses:* $360 per hour tuition (M Ed), $475 per hour (Ed D and Ed S); $325 per semester tech/activity fees. *Financial support:* Scholarships/grants available. Financial award application deadline: 12/1; financial award applicants required to submit FAFSA. *Faculty research:* Assessment; school mental health; literacy; technology; educator preparation. *Unit head:* Dr. Angela Hilton-Prillhart, Area Chair of Education, 423-461-8769, Fax: 423-461-3103, E-mail: anhilton-prillhart@milligan.edu. *Application contact:* Melissa Dillow, Graduate Admissions Recruiter, Education, 423-461-8306, Fax: 423-461-8982, E-mail: msdillow@milligan.edu.
Website: http://www.Milligan.edu/GPS

Minot State University, Graduate School, Teacher Education and Human Performance Department, Minot, ND 58707-0002. Offers elementary education (M Ed). *Accreditation:* NCATE. *Degree requirements:* For master's, thesis. *Entrance requirements:* For master's, 2 years of teaching experience, bachelor's degree in education, minimum GPA of 2.75. Additional exam requirements/recommendations for international students: Required—TOEFL (minimum score 79 iBT), IELTS (minimum score 6).

Mississippi College, Graduate School, School of Education, Department of Teacher Education and Leadership, Clinton, MS 39058. Offers art (M Ed); biological science (M Ed); business education (M Ed); computer science (M Ed); dyslexia therapy (M Ed); educational leadership (M Ed, Ed D, Ed S); elementary education (M Ed, Ed S); English (M Ed); higher education administration (MS); mathematics (M Ed); secondary education (M Ed); social studies (history) (M Ed); teaching arts (M Ed). *Program availability:* Part-time, online learning. *Degree requirements:* For master's, comprehensive exam, thesis optional. *Entrance requirements:* For master's, NTE. Additional exam requirements/recommendations for international students: Recommended—TOEFL, IELTS. Electronic applications accepted.

Mississippi State University, College of Education, Department of Curriculum, Instruction and Special Education, Mississippi State, MS 39762. Offers early childhood education (PhD); elementary education (MS, PhD, Ed S), including early childhood education (MS), general elementary education (MS), middle level education (MS); general curriculum and instruction (PhD); reading education (PhD); secondary education (MAT, MS, PhD, Ed S); special education (MAT, MS, PhD, Ed S). *Accreditation:* NCATE. *Program availability:* Part-time, evening/weekend. *Faculty:* 22 full-time (16 women), 1 (woman) part-time/adjunct. *Students:* 38 full-time (26 women), 170 part-time (131 women); includes 46 minority (37 Black or African American, non-Hispanic/Latino; 4 American Indian or Alaska Native, non-Hispanic/Latino; 2 Hispanic/Latino; 1 Native Hawaiian or other Pacific Islander, non-Hispanic/Latino; 2 Two or more races, non-Hispanic/Latino), 4 international. Average age 32. 88 applicants, 53% accepted, 39 enrolled. In 2017, 68 master's, 4 doctorates, 5 other advanced degrees awarded. *Degree requirements:* For master's, comprehensive exam; for doctorate, thesis/dissertation; for Ed S, comprehensive exam, thesis or alternative. *Entrance requirements:* For master's, GRE, minimum GPA of 2.75 in junior and senior year, eligibility for initial teacher certification; for doctorate, GRE, minimum GPA of 3.4 on previous graduate work; for Ed S, GRE, minimum GPA of 3.2 on master's degree. Additional exam requirements/recommendations for international students: Required—TOEFL (minimum score 550 paper-based; 79 iBT); Recommended—IELTS (minimum score 6.5). *Application deadline:* For fall admission, 3/1 priority date for domestic students, 5/1 for international students; for spring admission, 9/1 priority date for domestic students, 9/1 for international students. Applications are processed on a rolling basis. Application fee: $60 ($80 for international students). Electronic applications accepted. *Expenses:* Tuition, state resident: full-time $8318; part-time $462.12 per credit hour. Tuition, nonresident: full-time $22,358; part-time $1242.12 per credit hour. *Required fees:* $110; $12.24 per credit hour. $6.12 per semester. *Financial support:* In 2017–18, 6 research assistantships with partial tuition reimbursements (averaging $11,307 per year) were awarded; Federal Work-Study, institutionally sponsored loans, scholarships/grants, and unspecified assistantships also available. Financial award application deadline: 4/1; financial award applicants required to submit FAFSA. *Faculty research:* Early childhood education, reading, rural schools, multicultural education, use of technology in instruction. *Unit head:* Dr. Linda Cornelious, Professor and Interim Head, 662-325-3747, Fax: 662-325-7857, E-mail: lcornelious@colled.msstate.edu. *Application contact:* Laken Drinker, Admissions and Enrollment Assistant, 662-325-8951, E-mail: ldrinker@grad.msstate.edu.
Website: http://www.cise.msstate.edu/

Missouri State University, Graduate College, College of Education, Department of Childhood Education and Family Studies, Program in Elementary Education, Springfield, MO 65897. Offers MS Ed. *Program availability:* Part-time, evening/weekend, 100% online, blended/hybrid learning. *Faculty:* 22 full-time (1 woman), 11 part-time/adjunct (6 women). *Students:* 10 full-time (8 women), 46 part-time (42 women); includes 5 minority (3 Black or African American, non-Hispanic/Latino; 1 Asian, non-Hispanic/Latino; 1 Hispanic/Latino). Average age 25. 25 applicants, 76% accepted, 9 enrolled. In 2017, 44 master's awarded. *Degree requirements:* For master's, comprehensive exam, thesis or alternative. *Entrance requirements:* For master's, GRE (if GPA less than 3.0), minimum GPA of 2.75, teaching certificate. Additional exam requirements/recommendations for international students: Required—TOEFL (minimum score 550 paper-based; 79 iBT), IELTS (minimum score 6). *Application deadline:* For fall admission, 7/20 priority date for domestic students, 5/1 for international students; for spring admission, 12/20 priority date for domestic students, 9/1 for international students; for summer admission, 5/20 priority date for domestic students. Applications are processed on a rolling basis. Application fee: $35 ($50 for international students). Electronic applications accepted. *Expenses:* Tuition, state resident: full-time $2915; part-time $2021 per credit hour. Tuition, nonresident: full-time $5354; part-time $3647 per credit hour. International tuition: $11,992 full-time. *Required fees:* $173; $173 per credit hour. Tuition and fees vary according to class time, course level, course load, degree level, campus/location and program. *Financial support:* Federal Work-Study, institutionally sponsored loans, and scholarships/grants available. Financial award application deadline: 3/31; financial award applicants required to submit FAFSA. *Unit head:* Dr. Denise Cunningham, Department Head, 417-836-8915, E-mail: cefs@missouristate.edu. *Application contact:* Stephanie Praschan, Director, Graduate Enrollment Management, 417-836-5300, Fax: 417-836-6200, E-mail: stephaniepraschan@missouristate.edu.
Website: http://education.missouristate.edu/ele/

Missouri State University, Graduate College, College of Education, Department of Counseling, Leadership, and Special Education, Program in Educational Administration, Springfield, MO 65897. Offers elementary principal (MS Ed, Ed S); secondary principal (MS Ed, Ed S); superintendent (Ed S). *Program availability:* Part-time, evening/weekend. *Faculty:* 5 full-time (2 women), 1 part-time/adjunct (0 women). *Students:* 8 full-time (4 women), 60 part-time (42 women); includes 7 minority (1 American Indian or Alaska Native, non-Hispanic/Latino; 4 Hispanic/Latino; 2 Two or more races, non-Hispanic/Latino). Average age 26. 46 applicants, 98% accepted, 31 enrolled. In 2017, 18 master's,

8 Ed Ss awarded. *Degree requirements:* For master's and Ed S, comprehensive exam, thesis or alternative. *Entrance requirements:* For master's, minimum GPA of 2.75; for Ed S, GRE General Test, MAT, minimum GPA of 2.75. Additional exam requirements/recommendations for international students: Required—TOEFL (minimum score 550 paper-based; 79 iBT), IELTS (minimum score 6). *Application deadline:* For fall admission, 7/20 priority date for domestic students, 5/1 for international students; for spring admission, 12/20 priority date for domestic students, 9/1 for international students; for summer admission, 5/20 priority date for domestic students. Applications are processed on a rolling basis. Application fee: $35 ($50 for international students). Electronic applications accepted. *Expenses:* Tuition, state resident: full-time $2915; part-time $2021 per credit hour. Tuition, nonresident: full-time $5354; part-time $3647 per credit hour. *International tuition:* $11,992 full-time. *Required fees:* $173; $173 per credit hour. Tuition and fees vary according to class time, course level, course load, degree level, campus/location and program. *Financial support:* Career-related internships or fieldwork, Federal Work-Study, institutionally sponsored loans, scholarships/grants, and unspecified assistantships available. Financial award applicants required to submit FAFSA. *Unit head:* Dr. James Satterfield, Department Head, 417-836-5392, Fax: 417-836-4918, E-mail: clse@missouristate.edu. *Application contact:* Stephanie Praschan, Director, Graduate Enrollment Management, 417-836-5330, Fax: 417-836-6200, E-mail: stephaniepraschan@missouristate.edu.
Website: http://education.missouristate.edu/edadmin

Monmouth University, Graduate Studies, School of Education, West Long Branch, NJ 07764-1898. Offers applied behavior analysis (Certificate); autism (Certificate); director of school counseling services (Post-Master's Certificate); early childhood (M Ed); educational leadership (Ed D); elementary education (MAT), including elementary level, secondary level; English as a second language (M Ed); learning disabilities teacher-consultant (Post-Master's Certificate); literacy (MS Ed); school counseling (MS Ed); special education (MS Ed), including autism, learning disabilities teacher-consultant, teacher of students with disabilities, teaching in inclusive settings; speech-language pathology (MS Ed); student affairs and college counseling (MS Ed); supervisor (Post-Master's Certificate); teaching English to speakers of other languages (Certificate). *Accreditation:* NCATE. *Program availability:* Part-time, evening/weekend, 100% online, blended/hybrid learning. *Faculty:* 23 full-time (19 women), 33 part-time/adjunct (25 women). *Students:* 175 full-time (163 women), 168 part-time (142 women); includes 54 minority (10 Black or African American, non-Hispanic/Latino; 4 Asian, non-Hispanic/Latino; 32 Hispanic/Latino; 8 Two or more races, non-Hispanic/Latino). Average age 27. In 2017, 160 master's, 3 other advanced degrees awarded. *Entrance requirements:* For master's, GRE taken within last 5 years (for MS Ed in speech-language pathology); SAT (minimum combined score of 1660 in 3 sections), ACT (23), GRE (minimum score of 4.0 on analytical writing section and minimum combined score of 310 on quantitative and verbal sections), or passing scores on 3 parts of Core Academic Skills Educators, minimum GPA of 3.0 in major; 2 letters of recommendation (for some programs); resume, personal statement or essay (depending on program). Additional exam requirements/recommendations for international students: Required—TOEFL (minimum score 550 paper-based; 79 iBT), IELTS (minimum score 6), Michigan English Language Assessment Battery (minimum score 77) or Certificate of Advanced English (minimum score 160). *Application deadline:* For fall admission, 7/15 priority date for domestic students, 7/1 for international students; for spring admission, 12/1 priority date for domestic students, 11/1 for international students; for summer admission, 5/1 for domestic students. Applications are processed on a rolling basis. Application fee: $50. Electronic applications accepted. *Expenses: Tuition:* Full-time $21,366; part-time $7122 per credit. *Required fees:* $700; $175 per term. *Financial support:* In 2017–18, 125 students received support. Institutionally sponsored loans, scholarships/grants, and unspecified assistantships available. Support available to part-time students. Financial award applicants required to submit FAFSA. *Faculty research:* Multicultural literacy, science and mathematics teaching strategies, teacher as reflective practitioner, children with disabilities. *Unit head:* Dr. John E. Henning, Dean, 732-263-5513, Fax: 732-263-5277. *Application contact:* Laurie Kuhn, Associate Director of Graduate Admission, 732-571-3452, Fax: 732-263-5123, E-mail: gradadm@monmouth.edu.
Website: http://www.monmouth.edu/academics/schools/education/default.asp

Montana State University Billings, College of Education, Department of Educational Theory and Practice, Option in Curriculum and Instruction, Billings, MT 59101. Offers K-8 elementary education (M Ed); secondary education (M Ed). *Accreditation:* NCATE. *Program availability:* Part-time. *Degree requirements:* For master's, thesis or professional paper and/or field experience. *Entrance requirements:* For master's, GRE General Test or MAT, minimum GPA of 3.0. Additional exam requirements/recommendations for international students: Required—TOEFL (minimum score 79 iBT), IELTS (minimum score 6.5). *Application deadline:* Applications are processed on a rolling basis. Application fee: $40. Electronic applications accepted. *Expenses:* Tuition, state resident: full-time $11,740; part-time $7880 per year. Tuition, nonresident: full-time $32,200; part-time $24,140 per year. *Financial support:* Teaching assistantships with partial tuition reimbursements, career-related internships or fieldwork, Federal Work-Study, institutionally sponsored loans, scholarships/grants, tuition waivers (partial), and unspecified assistantships available. Support available to part-time students. Financial award application deadline: 5/1; financial award applicants required to submit FAFSA. *Faculty research:* Social studies education, science education. *Unit head:* Dr. Cindy Dell, Chair, Educational Theory and Practice, 406-657-1614, Fax: 406-657-2807, E-mail: cdell@msubillings.edu. *Application contact:* Dr. Cindy Dell, Chair, Educational Theory and Practice, 406-657-1614, Fax: 406-657-2807, E-mail: cdell@msubillings.edu.
Website: http://www.msubillings.edu/grad/program-med_curric_and_instruct.htm

Morehead State University, Graduate Programs, College of Education, Department of Curriculum and Instruction, Morehead, KY 40351. Offers curriculum and instruction (Ed S); elementary education (MA Ed), including elementary education, international education, middle school education, reading; secondary education (MA Ed); special education (MA Ed); teaching (MAT). *Program availability:* Part-time, evening/weekend. *Degree requirements:* For master's, comprehensive exam, thesis optional; for Ed S, thesis, oral exam. *Entrance requirements:* For master's, GRE General Test, minimum GPA of 2.75, teaching certificate; for Ed S, GRE General Test, interview, master's degree, minimum GPA of 3.5, work experience. Additional exam requirements/recommendations for international students: Required—TOEFL (minimum score 500 paper-based). Electronic applications accepted. *Faculty research:* Communicative competence of learning-disabled students, teaching social studies in elementary schools, ungraded primary school organization, study skills.

Morehead State University, Graduate Programs, College of Education, Department of Foundational and Graduate Studies in Education, Morehead, KY 40351. Offers adult and higher education (MA, Ed S); certified professional counselor (Ed S); counseling P-12 (MA); curriculum and instruction (Ed S); educational technology (MA Ed); instructional leadership (Ed S); school administration (MA); school counseling (Ed S); teacher leader business and marketing content (MA Ed); teacher leader business and marketing technology (MA Ed); teacher leader educational technology (MA Ed); teacher leader English (MA Ed); teacher leader gifted education (MA Ed); teacher leader IECE certification (MA Ed); teacher leader interdisciplinary education P-5 (MA Ed); teacher leader middle grades (MA Ed); teacher leader non IECE certification (MA Ed); teacher leader reading/writing - non-certification (MA Ed); teacher leader reading/writing

certification (MA Ed); teacher leader school communication - certification (MA Ed); teacher leader school communication - non-certification (MA Ed); teacher leader social studies (MA Ed); teacher leader special education (MA Ed). *Accreditation:* NCATE. *Program availability:* Part-time, evening/weekend. *Degree requirements:* For master's, thesis optional, oral and/or written comprehensive exams; for Ed S, thesis, oral exam. *Entrance requirements:* For master's, GRE General Test, minimum overall undergraduate GPA of 2.5; for Ed S, GRE General Test, interview, master's degree, minimum GPA of 3.5, work experience. Additional exam requirements/recommendations for international students: Required—TOEFL (minimum score 500 paper-based). Electronic applications accepted. *Faculty research:* Character education, school accountability, computer applications for school administrators.

Morgan State University, School of Graduate Studies, School of Education and Urban Studies, MAT Program, Baltimore, MD 21251. Offers elementary education (MAT). *Program availability:* Part-time. *Entrance requirements:* For master's, GRE General Test or MAT. *Application deadline:* For fall admission, 2/1 priority date for domestic students; for spring admission, 10/1 priority date for domestic students. Applications are processed on a rolling basis. Application fee: $0. *Expenses:* Tuition, state resident: part-time $433 per credit. Tuition, nonresident: part-time $851 per credit. *Required fees:* $81.50 per credit. *Financial support:* Application deadline: 4/1. *Faculty research:* Multicultural education, cooperative learning, psychology of cognition. *Unit head:* Dr. Flossie Windley, Graduate Coordinator, 443-885-1982, E-mail: fwindley@moac.morgan.edu. *Application contact:* Dr. Dean Campbell, Graduate Recruitment Specialist, 443-885-3185, Fax: 443-885-8226, E-mail: dean.campbell@morgan.edu.

Mount Saint Vincent University, Graduate Programs, Faculty of Education, Program in Elementary Education, Halifax, NS B3M 2J6, Canada. Offers M Ed, MA Ed, MA-R. *Program availability:* Part-time, evening/weekend, online learning. *Degree requirements:* For master's, thesis (for some programs). *Entrance requirements:* For master's, bachelor's degree in education, 1 year of teaching experience. Electronic applications accepted. *Faculty research:* Curriculum theory, mathematics education, philosophy in teacher education, science education, literacy education.

Murray State University, College of Education and Human Services, Department of Early Childhood and Elementary Education, Murray, KY 42071. Offers elementary teacher leader (MA Ed); interdisciplinary early childhood education (MA Ed), including elementary education (MA Ed, Ed S), reading and writing; teacher education and professional development (Ed S), including elementary education (MA Ed, Ed S). *Accreditation:* NCATE. *Program availability:* Part-time. *Faculty:* 17 full-time (16 women), 1 (woman) part-time/adjunct. *Students:* 10 full-time (all women), 91 part-time (87 women); includes 7 minority (4 Black or African American, non-Hispanic/Latino; 1 Hispanic/Latino; 2 Two or more races, non-Hispanic/Latino). Average age 33. 27 applicants, 89% accepted, 19 enrolled. In 2017, 35 master's awarded. *Entrance requirements:* For master's and Ed S, GRE or GMAT, minimum university GPA of 2.75. Additional exam requirements/recommendations for international students: Required—TOEFL (minimum score 527 paper-based; 71 iBT). *Application deadline:* Applications are processed on a rolling basis. Application fee: $40 ($50 for international students). Electronic applications accepted. *Expenses:* Tuition, state resident: full-time $9504. Tuition, nonresident: full-time $26,811. *International tuition:* $14,400 full-time. Tuition and fees vary according to course load, degree level and reciprocity agreements. *Financial support:* Federal Work-Study and unspecified assistantships available. Financial award applicants required to submit FAFSA. *Unit head:* Dr. Jacqueline Hansen, Chair, Department of Early Childhood and Elementary Education, 270-809-2500, Fax: 270-809-3799, E-mail: jhansen@murraystate.edu. *Application contact:* Kaitlyn Burzynski, Interim Assistant Director for Graduate Admission and Records, 270-809-5732, Fax: 270-809-3780, E-mail: msu.graduateadmissions@murraystate.edu.
Website: http://www.murraystate.edu/academics/CollegesDepartments/CollegeOfEducationandHumanServices/coehsacademicunits/EarlyChildhoodandElementaryEducation/in

National Louis University, National College of Education, Chicago, IL 60603. Offers administration and supervision (M Ed, Ed D, CAS, Ed S); curriculum and instruction (M Ed, MS Ed, CAS); early childhood administration (M Ed, CAS); early childhood education (M Ed, MAT, MS Ed, CAS); education (Ed D); educational psychology/human learning and development (M Ed, MS Ed, CAS, Ed S); elementary education (MAT); interdisciplinary curriculum and instruction (M Ed); mathematics education (M Ed, MS Ed, CAS); middle grades education (MAT); reading and language (M Ed, MS Ed, CAS); school psychology (M Ed, Ed S); science education (M Ed, MS Ed, CAS); secondary education (MAT); special education (M Ed, MAT, CAS); technology in education (M Ed, CAS). *Accreditation:* NCATE. *Program availability:* Part-time, evening/weekend. *Degree requirements:* For doctorate, comprehensive exam, thesis/dissertation. *Entrance requirements:* For master's, MAT or GRE, minimum GPA of 3.0; for doctorate, GRE General Test, minimum GPA of 3.25, interview, resume, writing sample, 4 recommendations. Additional exam requirements/recommendations for international students: Required—TOEFL (minimum score 550 paper-based; 79 iBT).

Nazareth College of Rochester, Graduate Studies, Department of Education, Program in Inclusive Childhood Education, Rochester, NY 14618. Offers MS Ed. *Accreditation:* TEAC. *Program availability:* Part-time, evening/weekend. *Entrance requirements:* For master's, minimum GPA of 3.0. Additional exam requirements/recommendations for international students: Required—TOEFL or IELTS.

Neumann University, Graduate Program in Education, Aston, PA 19014-1298. Offers education (MS), including administrative certification (school principal PK-12), autism, early elementary education, secondary education, special education. *Program availability:* Part-time, evening/weekend, 100% online, blended/hybrid learning. *Faculty:* 6 full-time (5 women), 16 part-time/adjunct (7 women). *Students:* 68 full-time (56 women), 108 part-time (93 women); includes 36 minority (28 Black or African American, non-Hispanic/Latino; 3 Hispanic/Latino; 5 Two or more races, non-Hispanic/Latino). Average age 33. 83 applicants, 69% accepted, 36 enrolled. In 2017, 114 master's awarded. *Entrance requirements:* For master's, official transcripts from all institutions attended, letter of intent, three professional references, copy of any teaching certifications. Additional exam requirements/recommendations for international students: Required—TOEFL (minimum score 70 iBT). *Application deadline:* Applications are processed on a rolling basis. Application fee: $0. Electronic applications accepted. *Expenses:* $700 per credit hour (for on-campus master's-level education courses); $480 per credit hour (for online or off-campus master's-level education courses). *Financial support:* Scholarships/grants and health care benefits available. Support available to part-time students. Financial award application deadline: 3/15; financial award applicants required to submit FAFSA. *Unit head:* Dr. Stephanie Smith-Budhai, Director of Graduate Education, 610-358-4249, E-mail: budhais@neumann.edu. *Application contact:* Dr. Erika K. Davis, Director of Adult and Graduate Admissions, 800-9-NEUMANN Ext. 5208, Fax: 610-361-2548, E-mail: gradadultadmiss@neumann.edu.
Website: https://www.neumann.edu/academics/grad/education/index.asp

New Jersey City University, Debra Cannon Partridge Wolfe College of Education, Department of Elementary and Secondary Education, Jersey City, NJ 07305-1597. Offers elementary education (MAT); secondary education (MAT). *Program availability:* Part-time, evening/weekend. *Entrance requirements:* Additional exam requirements/recommendations for international students: Required—TOEFL (minimum score 79 iBT).

Elementary Education

New York Institute of Technology, School of Interdisciplinary Studies and Education, Department of Teacher Education, Old Westbury, NY 11568-8000. Offers adolescence education (MS), including math (MAT, MS); science; adolescent education (MAT), including biology, chemistry, English, math (MAT, MS), social studies; childhood education (MS); early childhood (MS). *Program availability:* Part-time, evening/weekend, 100% online, blended/hybrid learning. *Faculty:* 2 full-time (both women), 7 part-time/adjunct (3 women). *Students:* 46 full-time (44 women), 30 part-time (22 women); includes 23 minority (8 Black or African American, non-Hispanic/Latino; 6 Asian, non-Hispanic/Latino; 8 Hispanic/Latino; 1 Two or more races, non-Hispanic/Latino), 2 international. Average age 29. 39 applicants, 72% accepted, 15 enrolled. In 2017, 14 master's awarded. *Entrance requirements:* For master's, GRE or MAT, BS or equivalent; minimum cumulative undergraduate GPA of 3.0; NY state provisional or initial certification (for MS in adolescence education); BS with major in biology, chemistry, economics, English, history, life sciences, math, physics, or psychology (for MS in childhood, early childhood education, and MAT); interview; personal statement. Additional exam requirements/recommendations for international students: Required—TOEFL (minimum score 79 iBT), IELTS (minimum score 6). *Application deadline:* Applications are processed on a rolling basis. Application fee: $50. Electronic applications accepted. *Expenses:* $1,285 per credit plus fees. *Financial support:* Career-related internships or fieldwork, Federal Work-Study, scholarships/grants, tuition waivers (full and partial), and unspecified assistantships available. Support available to part-time students. Financial award application deadline: 2/15; financial award applicants required to submit FAFSA. *Faculty research:* Evolving definition of new literacies and its impact on teaching and learning (twenty-first century skills), new literacies practices in teacher education, teachers' professional development, English language and literacy learning through mobile learning, teaching reading to culturally and linguistically diverse children. *Unit head:* Dr. Hui-Yin Hsu, Department Chair, 516-686-1322, Fax: 516-686-7655, E-mail: hhsu02@nyit.edu. *Application contact:* Alice Dolitsky, Director, Graduate Admissions, 516-686-7520, Fax: 516-686-1116, E-mail: nyitgrad@nyit.edu.
Website: http://www.nyit.edu/interdisciplinary/department_teacher_education

New York University, Steinhardt School of Culture, Education, and Human Development, Department of Teaching and Learning, Program in Early Childhood and Childhood Education, New York, NY 10012. Offers childhood education (MA); early childhood education (MA); early childhood education/early childhood special education (MA). *Accreditation:* TEAC. *Program availability:* Part-time. *Faculty:* 9 full-time (all women). *Students:* 59 full-time (55 women), 24 part-time (22 women); includes 25 minority (3 Black or African American, non-Hispanic/Latino; 15 Asian, non-Hispanic/Latino; 5 Hispanic/Latino; 2 Two or more races, non-Hispanic/Latino), 8 international. Average age 28. 91 applicants, 68% accepted, 15 enrolled. In 2017, 57 master's awarded. *Degree requirements:* For master's, thesis (for some programs). *Entrance requirements:* Additional exam requirements/recommendations for international students: Required—TOEFL (minimum score 100 iBT). *Application deadline:* For fall admission, 12/1 priority date for domestic and international students; for spring admission, 10/1 for domestic and international students. Applications are processed on a rolling basis. Application fee: $75. Electronic applications accepted. *Expenses: Tuition:* Full-time $41,352; part-time $19,968 per year. *Required fees:* $2496; $1628 per unit. $814 per term. Tuition and fees vary according to course load and program. *Financial support:* Fellowships with full and partial tuition reimbursements, career-related internships or fieldwork, Federal Work-Study, institutionally sponsored loans, scholarships/grants, tuition waivers (partial), and unspecified assistantships available. Support available to part-time students. Financial award application deadline: 2/1; financial award applicants required to submit FAFSA. *Faculty research:* Teacher evaluation and beliefs about teaching, early literacy development, language arts, child development and education, cultural differences. *Unit head:* 212-998-5460, Fax: 212-995-4049. *Application contact:* 212-998-5030, Fax: 212-995-4328, E-mail: steinhardt.gradadmissions@nyu.edu.
Website: http://steinhardt.nyu.edu/teachlearn/childhood

Niagara University, Graduate Division of Education, Concentration in Teacher Education, Niagara University, NY 14109. Offers early childhood and childhood education (MS Ed, Certificate); early childhood special education (MS); middle and adolescence education (MS Ed); special education (MS Ed), including 1-6, 7-12; special education (grades 1-12) (Certificate); teaching English to speakers of other languages (MS Ed, Certificate). *Accreditation:* NCATE. *Students:* 105 full-time (79 women), 109 part-time (88 women); includes 20 minority (9 Black or African American, non-Hispanic/Latino; 2 American Indian or Alaska Native, non-Hispanic/Latino; 1 Asian, non-Hispanic/Latino; 5 Hispanic/Latino; 3 Two or more races, non-Hispanic/Latino), 35 international. Average age 28. In 2017, 86 master's, 18 other advanced degrees awarded. *Entrance requirements:* For master's, GRE General Test or Academic Literacy Skills Test (ALST). Additional exam requirements/recommendations for international students: Required—TOEFL (minimum score 550 paper-based; 79 iBT), IELTS (minimum score 6). *Application deadline:* For fall admission, 8/1 for domestic students. Applications are processed on a rolling basis. Application fee: $30. *Expenses:* Contact institution. *Financial support:* Research assistantships with tuition reimbursements, teaching assistantships with tuition reimbursements, career-related internships or fieldwork, Federal Work-Study, scholarships/grants, and unspecified assistantships available. Financial award application deadline: 4/15; financial award applicants required to submit FAFSA. *Unit head:* Dr. Chandra Foote, Dean, College of Education, 716-286-8549, E-mail: cjf@niagara.edu. *Application contact:* Evan Pierce, Associate Director, Graduate Studies, 716-286-8327, E-mail: epierce@niagara.edu.
Website: http://www.niagara.edu/teacher-education

Nicholls State University, Graduate Studies, College of Education, Department of Teacher Education, Thibodaux, LA 70310. Offers curriculum and instruction (M Ed); educational leadership (M Ed); elementary education (MAT); human performance education (MAT); middle school education (MAT); secondary education (MAT). *Accreditation:* NCATE. *Program availability:* Part-time, evening/weekend, online learning. *Degree requirements:* For master's, comprehensive exam, portfolio. *Entrance requirements:* For master's, GRE General Test, teaching license. Electronic applications accepted.

North Carolina Agricultural and Technical State University, School of Graduate Studies, School of Education, Department of Curriculum and Instruction, Program in Elementary Education, Greensboro, NC 27411. Offers MA Ed. *Accreditation:* NCATE. *Program availability:* Part-time, evening/weekend. *Degree requirements:* For master's, comprehensive exam, research project or comprehensive portfolio. *Entrance requirements:* For master's, GRE General Test, minimum GPA of 3.0.

North Carolina State University, Graduate School, College of Education, Department of Elementary Education, Raleigh, NC 27695. Offers M Ed. *Entrance requirements:* For master's, MAT or GRE, 3 letters of reference.

Northeastern Illinois University, College of Graduate Studies and Research, Daniel L. Goodwin College of Education, MAT Program in Elementary Education, Chicago, IL 60625. Offers MAT. *Expenses:* Tuition, state resident: full-time $7274; part-time $404.11 per credit hour. Tuition, nonresident: full-time $14,548; part-time $808.23 per credit hour. *Required fees:* $1284. *Unit head:* Dr. Ngoc-Diep Nguyen, Department Chair, 773-442-6197, E-mail: n-nguyen8@neiu.edu. *Application contact:* Martha Narvaez, Graduate Admission Representative, 773-442-6006, E-mail: m-narvaez@neiu.edu.

Northeastern University, College of Professional Studies, Boston, MA 02115-5096. Offers applied nutrition (MS); college athletics administration (MSL); commerce and economic development (MS); corporate and organizational communication (MS); criminal justice (MS); digital media (MPS); elearning and instructional design (M Ed); elementary education (MAT); geographic information technology (MPS); global studies and international relations (MS); higher education administration (M Ed); homeland security (MA); human services (MS); informatics (MPS); leadership (MS); learning analytics (M Ed); learning and instruction (M Ed); nonprofit management (MS); professional sports administration (MSL); project management (MS); regulatory affairs for drugs, biologics, and medical devices (MS); respiratory care leadership (MS); special education (M Ed); technical communication (MS). *Program availability:* Part-time, evening/weekend, 100% online, blended/hybrid learning. *Faculty:* 82 full-time (51 women), 853 part-time/adjunct (366 women). *Students:* 5,278 part-time (3,230 women). In 2017, 1,586 master's awarded. *Application deadline:* Applications are processed on a rolling basis. Application fee: $0. Electronic applications accepted. *Expenses:* Contact institution. *Financial support:* Applicants required to submit FAFSA. *Unit head:* Dr. Mary Loeffelholz, Dean of the College of Professional Studies. *Application contact:* E-mail: cpsadmissions@northeastern.edu.
Website: https://cps.northeastern.edu/

Northern Arizona University, College of Education, Department of Teaching and Learning, Flagstaff, AZ 86011. Offers curriculum and instruction (Ed D); early childhood education (M Ed); elementary education (M Ed); secondary education (M Ed). *Program availability:* Part-time, 100% online, blended/hybrid learning. *Faculty:* 28 full-time (24 women), 1 (woman) part-time/adjunct. *Students:* 82 full-time (71 women), 181 part-time (167 women); includes 87 minority (19 Black or African American, non-Hispanic/Latino; 11 American Indian or Alaska Native, non-Hispanic/Latino; 4 Asian, non-Hispanic/Latino; 47 Hispanic/Latino; 1 Native Hawaiian or other Pacific Islander, non-Hispanic/Latino; 5 Two or more races, non-Hispanic/Latino), 7 international. Average age 36. 106 applicants, 95% accepted, 99 enrolled. In 2017, 79 master's, 5 doctorates awarded. *Degree requirements:* For master's, variable foreign language requirement, comprehensive exam (for some programs), thesis (for some programs); for doctorate, variable foreign language requirement, comprehensive exam (for some programs), thesis/dissertation (for some programs). *Entrance requirements:* Additional exam requirements/recommendations for international students: Required—TOEFL (minimum score 80 iBT), IELTS (minimum score 6.5). *Application deadline:* For fall admission, 2/15 for domestic and international students; for spring admission, 9/15 for domestic and international students. Applications are processed on a rolling basis. Application fee: $65. Electronic applications accepted. *Expenses:* Tuition, state resident: full-time $9240; part-time $458 per credit hour. Tuition, nonresident: full-time $21,588; part-time $1199 per credit hour. *Required fees:* $1021; $14 per credit hour. $646 per semester. Tuition and fees vary according to course load, campus/location and program. *Financial support:* In 2017–18, 5 students received support, including 1 research assistantship with full and partial tuition reimbursement available (averaging $13,500 per year), 4 teaching assistantships with full and partial tuition reimbursements available (averaging $13,500 per year); institutionally sponsored loans, health care benefits, tuition waivers (full and partial), and unspecified assistantships also available. Financial award application deadline: 2/1; financial award applicants required to submit FAFSA. *Unit head:* Dr. Pamela Powell, Chair, 928-523-5644, Fax: 928-523-1929, E-mail: pamela.powell@nau.edu. *Application contact:* Tina Sutton, Coordinator, Graduate College, 928-523-4348, Fax: 928-523-8950, E-mail: graduate@nau.edu.
Website: https://nau.edu/coe/Teaching-and-Learning/

Northern Illinois University, Graduate School, College of Education, Department of Special and Early Education, De Kalb, IL 60115-2854. Offers curriculum and instruction (MS Ed); early childhood education (MS Ed); elementary education (MS Ed); special education (MS Ed). *Program availability:* Part-time, evening/weekend. *Faculty:* 22 full-time (14 women), 2 part-time/adjunct (both women). *Students:* 40 full-time (33 women), 79 part-time (65 women); includes 16 minority (5 Black or African American, non-Hispanic/Latino; 3 Asian, non-Hispanic/Latino; 6 Hispanic/Latino; 2 Two or more races, non-Hispanic/Latino). Average age 32. 48 applicants, 83% accepted, 25 enrolled. In 2017, 58 master's awarded. *Degree requirements:* For master's, comprehensive exam, thesis optional. *Entrance requirements:* For master's, GRE General Test or MAT, minimum undergraduate GPA of 2.75. Additional exam requirements/recommendations for international students: Required—TOEFL (minimum score 550 paper-based). *Application deadline:* For fall admission, 6/1 for domestic students, 5/1 for international students; for spring admission, 11/1 for domestic students, 10/1 for international students. Applications are processed on a rolling basis. Application fee: $40. Electronic applications accepted. *Financial support:* In 2017–18, 17 research assistantships with full tuition reimbursements were awarded; fellowships with full tuition reimbursements, teaching assistantships with full tuition reimbursements, career-related internships or fieldwork, Federal Work-Study, scholarships/grants, tuition waivers (full), and unspecified assistantships also available. Support available to part-time students. Financial award applicants required to submit FAFSA. *Faculty research:* Teacher certification, stress reduction during student teaching, teaching history, portfolios in student teaching. *Unit head:* Gregory Conderman, Chair, 815-753-1619, E-mail: seed@niu.edu. *Application contact:* Gail Myers, Clerk, Graduate Advising, 815-753-0381, E-mail: gmyers@niu.edu.
Website: http://www.cedu.niu.edu/seed/

Northwest Christian University, School of Education and Counseling, Eugene, OR 97401-3745. Offers clinical mental health counseling (MA); elementary teaching (MAT); English for speakers of other languages (MAT); physical education (MAT); school counseling (MA); secondary teaching (MAT); special education (MAT). *Program availability:* Part-time, evening/weekend, online learning. *Faculty:* 9 full-time (4 women), 14 part-time/adjunct (10 women). *Students:* 77 full-time (60 women), 44 part-time (30 women); includes 19 minority (4 Black or African American, non-Hispanic/Latino; 1 American Indian or Alaska Native, non-Hispanic/Latino; 3 Asian, non-Hispanic/Latino; 2 Hispanic/Latino; 1 Native Hawaiian or other Pacific Islander, non-Hispanic/Latino; 8 Two or more races, non-Hispanic/Latino). Average age 34. In 2017, 58 master's awarded. *Degree requirements:* For master's, thesis (for some programs). *Entrance requirements:* For master's, GRE or MAT, minimum undergraduate GPA of 3.0, interview, 2-3 page statement of purpose, two letters of recommendation, resume, background check. Additional exam requirements/recommendations for international students: Required—TOEFL (minimum score 550 paper-based; 80 iBT). *Application deadline:* Applications are processed on a rolling basis. Electronic applications accepted. *Expenses:* $640 to $660 per credit tuition, $90 per semester technology fee. *Financial support:* Applicants required to submit FAFSA. *Unit head:* Elizabeth Wosley-George, Director, 541-349-7465, Fax: 541-684-7310, E-mail: ewosleygeorge@nwcu.edu. *Application contact:* Billy Dorsch, Admission Counselor for Graduate Studies, 541-684-7279, Fax: 541-349-5281, E-mail: wdorsch@nwcu.edu.

Northwestern Oklahoma State University, School of Professional Studies, Program in Elementary Education, Alva, OK 73717-2799. Offers M Ed. *Accreditation:* NCATE. *Program availability:* Part-time. *Degree requirements:* For master's, thesis optional, portfolio. *Entrance requirements:* For master's, GRE General Test or MAT, minimum GPA of 2.75.

Northwestern State University of Louisiana, Graduate Studies and Research, College of Education and Human Development, Program in Elementary Education, Natchitoches, LA 71497. Offers MAT. *Degree requirements:* For master's, comprehensive exam, thesis or alternative. *Entrance requirements:* For master's, GRE General Test, minimum undergraduate GPA of 2.5. Additional exam requirements/recommendations for international students: Required—TOEFL. Electronic applications accepted.

Northwestern State University of Louisiana, Graduate Studies and Research, College of Education and Human Development, Programs in Educational Leadership and Instruction, Natchitoches, LA 71497. Offers counseling (Ed S); educational leadership (M Ed, Ed S); educational technology (Ed S); elementary teaching (Ed S); reading (Ed S); secondary teaching (Ed S); special education (Ed S). *Accreditation:* NASAD. *Degree requirements:* For master's, comprehensive exam, thesis (for some programs). *Entrance requirements:* For master's and Ed S, GRE General Test. Additional exam requirements/recommendations for international students: Required—TOEFL. Electronic applications accepted.

Northwestern University, The Graduate School, School of Education and Social Policy, Education and Social Policy Program, Evanston, IL 60035. Offers elementary teaching (MS); secondary teaching (MS); teacher leadership (MS). *Program availability:* Part-time, evening/weekend. *Degree requirements:* For master's, research project. *Entrance requirements:* For master's, GRE General Test, Illinois State Board of Education Basic Skills Exam (secondary and elementary), bachelor's degree. Additional exam requirements/recommendations for international students: Recommended—TOEFL. Electronic applications accepted. *Faculty research:* Cultural context and literacy, philosophy of education and interpretive discussion, productivity, enhancing research and teaching, motivation, new and junior faculty issues, professional development for K-12 teachers to improve math and science teaching, female/underrepresented students/faculty in STEM disciplines.

Northwest Missouri State University, Graduate School, School of Education, Maryville, MO 64468-6001. Offers early childhood education (MS Ed); education leadership (MS Ed), including elementary, K-12, secondary; educational leadership (Ed S), including elementary school principalship, secondary school principalship, superintendency; educational leadership and policy analysis (Ed D); elementary education (MS Ed); elementary mathematics (MS Ed); higher education leadership (MS); middle school education (MS Ed); reading (MS Ed); special education (MS Ed); teacher leadership (MS Ed); teaching English language learners (MS Ed). *Accreditation:* NCATE. *Program availability:* Part-time. *Faculty:* 15 full-time (8 women). *Students:* 28 full-time (20 women), 170 part-time (114 women); includes 20 minority (7 Black or African American, non-Hispanic/Latino; 1 Asian, non-Hispanic/Latino; 8 Hispanic/Latino; 4 Two or more races, non-Hispanic/Latino). Average age 33. 168 applicants, 73% accepted, 114 enrolled. In 2017, 67 master's, 21 other advanced degrees awarded. *Degree requirements:* For master's, comprehensive exam; for Ed S, comprehensive exam, thesis. *Entrance requirements:* For master's, GRE General Test, writing sample; for Ed S, minimum graduate GPA of 3.25. Additional exam requirements/recommendations for international students: Required—TOEFL (minimum score 550 paper-based). *Application deadline:* For fall admission, 7/1 for domestic and international students; for spring admission, 11/15 for domestic and international students. Applications are processed on a rolling basis. Application fee: $0 ($50 for international students). Electronic applications accepted. *Expenses:* $389.11 per credit hour in-state tuition and fees, $641.97 out-of-state; $9,750 total cost (for online-based education program). *Financial support:* Research assistantships with full tuition reimbursements, teaching assistantships with full tuition reimbursements, and unspecified assistantships available. Financial award application deadline: 4/1; financial award applicants required to submit FAFSA. *Unit head:* Dr. Tim Wall, Director, 660-562-1179, E-mail: timwall@nwmissouri.edu.
Website: https://www.nwmissouri.edu/education/index.htm

Nyack College, School of Education, Nyack, NY 10960. Offers childhood education (MS); childhood special education (MS); TESOL (MAT, MS). *Program availability:* Part-time, evening/weekend, 100% online, blended/hybrid learning. *Students:* 22 full-time (20 women), 27 part-time (23 women); includes 23 minority (10 Black or African American, non-Hispanic/Latino; 1 American Indian or Alaska Native, non-Hispanic/Latino; 1 Asian, non-Hispanic/Latino; 10 Hispanic/Latino; 1 Two or more races, non-Hispanic/Latino), 2 international. Average age 34. In 2017, 25 master's awarded. *Degree requirements:* For master's, comprehensive exam, clinical experience. *Entrance requirements:* For master's, GRE, transcripts, autobiography and statement on reasons for pursuing graduate study in education, recommendations, 6 credits of language, evidence of computer literacy, introductory course in psychology. Additional exam requirements/recommendations for international students: Required—TOEFL (minimum score 550 paper-based; 80 iBT), GRE. *Application deadline:* Applications are processed on a rolling basis. Application fee: $30. Electronic applications accepted. *Expenses:* $725 per credit. *Financial support:* Scholarships/grants available. Financial award applicants required to submit FAFSA. *Unit head:* Dr. JoAnn Looney, Dean, 845-675-4538. *Application contact:* Emma Chery, Admissions Associate, 845-770-5708, E-mail: admissions.grad@nyack.edu.
Website: http://www.nyack.edu/edu

Oakland University, Graduate Study and Lifelong Learning, School of Education and Human Services, Department of Teacher Development and Educational Studies, Rochester, MI 48309-4401. Offers educational studies (M Ed); elementary education (MAT); secondary education (MAT); teaching and learning (Graduate Certificate). *Entrance requirements:* For master's, minimum GPA of 3.0. Electronic applications accepted. *Expenses:* Tuition, state resident: full-time $16,950; part-time $706.25 per credit. Tuition, nonresident: full-time $24,648; part-time $1027 per credit.

Oklahoma City University, Petree College of Arts and Sciences, Oklahoma City, OK 73106-1402. Offers applied behavioral studies (M Ed); applied sociology: nonprofit leadership (MA); creative writing (MFA); criminology (MS); early childhood education (M Ed); elementary education (M Ed); general studies (MLA); leadership/management (MLA); moving image arts (MFA); professional counseling (M Ed); teaching (MA); teaching English to speakers of other languages (MA). *Program availability:* Part-time, evening/weekend. *Faculty:* 6 full-time (2 women), 16 part-time/adjunct (10 women). *Students:* 84 full-time (61 women), 32 part-time (23 women); includes 31 minority (13 Black or African American, non-Hispanic/Latino; 3 American Indian or Alaska Native, non-Hispanic/Latino; 1 Asian, non-Hispanic/Latino; 9 Hispanic/Latino; 5 Two or more races, non-Hispanic/Latino), 30 international. Average age 34. 192 applicants, 67% accepted, 57 enrolled. In 2017, 65 master's awarded. *Degree requirements:* For master's, capstone/practicum. *Entrance requirements:* For master's, bachelor's degree from accredited institution with minimum GPA of 3.0, essay, recommendation letters. Additional exam requirements/recommendations for international students: Required—TOEFL (minimum score 550 paper-based; 80 iBT). *Application deadline:* Applications are processed on a rolling basis. Application fee: $50. Electronic applications accepted. *Expenses:* $8,580. *Financial support:* In 2017-18, 19 students received support. Federal Work-Study, institutionally sponsored loans, scholarships/grants, and tuition waivers (full and partial) available. Support available to part-time students. Financial award application deadline: 6/1; financial award applicants required to submit FAFSA.

Unit head: Dr. Amy Cataldi, Dean, 405-208-5446, Fax: 405-208-5447, E-mail: acataldi@okcu.edu. *Application contact:* Michael Harrington, Director of Graduate Admissions, 800-633-7242, Fax: 405-208-5356, E-mail: gadmissions@okcu.edu.
Website: https://www.okcu.edu/artsci/home

Old Dominion University, Darden College of Education, Program in Elementary/Middle Education, Norfolk, VA 23529. Offers elementary education (Postbaccalaureate Certificate); instructional technology (MS Ed); library science (MS Ed). *Accreditation:* NCATE. *Program availability:* Part-time, evening/weekend, 100% online, blended/hybrid learning. *Faculty:* 21 full-time (19 women), 24 part-time/adjunct (22 women). *Students:* 134 full-time (127 women), 123 part-time (108 women); includes 60 minority (34 Black or African American, non-Hispanic/Latino; 1 American Indian or Alaska Native, non-Hispanic/Latino; 2 Asian, non-Hispanic/Latino; 15 Hispanic/Latino; 8 Two or more races, non-Hispanic/Latino). Average age 32. 213 applicants, 88% accepted, 172 enrolled. In 2017, 121 master's awarded. *Degree requirements:* For master's, comprehensive exam. *Entrance requirements:* For master's, GRE General Test or MAT; PRAXIS I, SAT or ACT, minimum GPA of 2.8. Additional exam requirements/recommendations for international students: Required—TOEFL (minimum score 600 paper-based). *Application deadline:* For fall admission, 6/1 priority date for domestic students; for winter admission, 11/1 priority date for domestic students; for spring admission, 3/1 priority date for domestic students. Applications are processed on a rolling basis. Application fee: $50. Electronic applications accepted. *Expenses:* Contact institution. *Financial support:* In 2017-18, 180 students received support. Unspecified assistantships available. Financial award application deadline: 2/15; financial award applicants required to submit FAFSA. *Faculty research:* Education pre-K to 6, school librarianship, reading, TESOL, literacy. *Unit head:* Dr. KaaVonia Hinton, Chair, Department of Teaching and Learning, 757-683-3284, Fax: 757-683-5862, E-mail: khintonj@odu.edu. *Application contact:* William Heffelfinger, Director of Graduate Admissions, 757-683-5554, Fax: 757-683-3255, E-mail: gradadmit@odu.edu.
Website: http://education.odu.edu/eci/

Olivet Nazarene University, Graduate School, Division of Education, Program in Elementary Education, Bourbonnais, IL 60914. Offers MAT. *Accreditation:* NCATE. *Program availability:* Evening/weekend. *Degree requirements:* For master's, thesis or alternative.

Oregon State University, College of Education, Program in Teaching, Corvallis, OR 97331. Offers clinically based elementary education (MAT); elementary education (MAT); language arts (MAT); mathematics (MAT); music education (MAT); science (MAT); social studies (MAT). *Program availability:* Part-time, blended/hybrid learning. *Entrance requirements:* For master's, CBEST. Additional exam requirements/recommendations for international students: Required—TOEFL (minimum score 575 paper-based). *Application deadline:* For fall admission, 12/1 for domestic students. Application fee: $60. *Expenses:* Contact institution. *Unit head:* Jordon Zardinejad, 541-322-3118, E-mail: jordon.zardinejad@osucascades.edu. *Application contact:* Jordon Zardinejad, 541-322-3118, E-mail: jordon.zardinejad@osucascades.edu.
Website: http://education.oregonstate.edu/mat

Ottawa University, Graduate Studies-Arizona, Program in Education, Ottawa, KS 66067-3399. Offers community college counseling (MA); curriculum and instruction (MA); early childhood (MA); education intervention (MA); education leadership (MA); education technology (MA); Montessori early childhood education (MA); Montessori elementary education (MA); professional development (MA); school guidance counseling (MA); special education - cross categorical (MA). Programs offered in Mesa, Phoenix, Tempe and West Valley, AZ. *Accreditation:* NCATE. *Program availability:* Part-time. *Degree requirements:* For master's, thesis or alternative. *Entrance requirements:* For master's, minimum undergraduate GPA of 3.0, copy of current state certification or teaching license. Additional exam requirements/recommendations for international students: Required—TOEFL (minimum score 550 paper-based). Electronic applications accepted. *Expenses:* Contact institution.

Pace University, School of Education, New York, NY 10038. Offers adolescent education (MST), including biology, chemistry, earth science, English, foreign languages, mathematics, physics, social studies; childhood education (MST); early childhood development, learning and intervention (MST); educational technology studies (MS); inclusive adolescent education (MST), including biology, chemistry, earth science, English, foreign languages, mathematics, physics, social studies; integrated instruction for educational technology (Certificate); integrated instruction for literacy and technology (Certificate); literacy (MS Ed); special education (MS Ed). *Accreditation:* NCATE. *Program availability:* Part-time, evening/weekend, 100% online, blended/hybrid learning. *Faculty:* 19 full-time (13 women), 86 part-time/adjunct (49 women). *Students:* 91 full-time (76 women), 548 part-time (401 women); includes 247 minority (112 Black or African American, non-Hispanic/Latino; 2 American Indian or Alaska Native, non-Hispanic/Latino; 31 Asian, non-Hispanic/Latino; 93 Hispanic/Latino; 1 Native Hawaiian or other Pacific Islander, non-Hispanic/Latino; 8 Two or more races, non-Hispanic/Latino), 6 international. Average age 30. 188 applicants, 86% accepted, 114 enrolled. In 2017, 213 master's, 8 other advanced degrees awarded. *Degree requirements:* For master's and Certificate, certification exams. *Entrance requirements:* For master's, GRE (for initial certification programs only), teaching certificate (for MS Ed in literacy and special education programs only). Additional exam requirements/recommendations for international students: Required—TOEFL (minimum score 88 iBT), IELTS or PTE. *Application deadline:* For fall admission, 8/1 priority date for domestic students, 6/1 for international students; for spring admission, 12/1 priority date for domestic students, 10/1 for international students. Applications are processed on a rolling basis. Application fee: $70. Electronic applications accepted. *Expenses:* Contact institution. *Financial support:* In 2017-18, 17 students received support, including 17 research assistantships with partial tuition reimbursements available (averaging $6,020 per year); career-related internships or fieldwork, Federal Work-Study, scholarships/grants, and unspecified assistantships also available. Financial award application deadline: 9/1; financial award applicants required to submit FAFSA. *Faculty research:* STEM education, TESOL, teacher education, special education, language and literary development. *Total annual research expenditures:* $29,706. *Unit head:* Dr. Xiao-Lei Wang, Dean, School of Education, 914-773-3876, E-mail: xwang@pace.edu. *Application contact:* Susan Ford-Goldschein, Director of Graduate Admissions, 212-346-1531, Fax: 212-346-1585, E-mail: graduateadmission@pace.edu.
Website: http://www.pace.edu/school-of-education

Pacific Union College, Education Department, Angwin, CA 94508-9707. Offers education (M Ed); elementary teaching (MAT); secondary teaching (MAT). *Program availability:* Part-time. *Faculty:* 3 full-time (1 woman), 1 (woman) part-time/adjunct. *Students:* 3 full-time (2 women), 4 part-time (2 women); includes 1 minority (Black or African American, non-Hispanic/Latino). Average age 45. 4 applicants, 100% accepted, 4 enrolled. In 2017, 1 master's awarded. *Degree requirements:* For master's, thesis, action research project, field experiences. *Entrance requirements:* For master's, GRE General Test, two interviews, teaching credential, letters of recommendation, essay. *Application deadline:* For fall admission, 8/30 for domestic and international students; for summer admission, 6/1 for domestic and international students. Applications are processed on a rolling basis. Application fee: $0. *Expenses:* $29,469 per year, $9,823 per quarter. *Financial support:* Scholarships/grants available. Support available to part-

Elementary Education

time students. Financial award application deadline: 9/25. *Unit head:* Prof. Thomas Lee, Department Chair, 707-965-6646, Fax: 707-965-6645, E-mail: tdlee@puc.edu. *Application contact:* Cherith Mundy, Credential Analyst, 707-965-6643, Fax: 707-965-6645, E-mail: teachingcredentials@puc.edu.
Website: http://www.puc.edu/academics/departments/education/

Pacific University, College of Education, Forest Grove, OR 97116-1797. Offers early childhood education (MAT); education (MAE); elementary education (MAT); ESOL (MAT); high school education (MAT); middle school education (MAT); special education (MAT); speech-language pathology (MS); STEM education (MAT); talented and gifted (M Ed); visual function in learning (M Ed). *Accreditation:* ASHA; NCATE. *Program availability:* Part-time, evening/weekend. *Degree requirements:* For master's, research project. *Entrance requirements:* For master's, California Basic Educational Skills Test, PRAXIS II, minimum undergraduate GPA of 2.75, 3.0 graduate. Additional exam requirements/recommendations for international students: Required—TOEFL. Electronic applications accepted. *Expenses:* Contact institution. *Faculty research:* Defining a culturally competent classroom, technology in the K-12 classroom, Socratic seminars, social studies education.

Pfeiffer University, Program in Elementary Education, Misenheimer, NC 28109-0960. Offers MAT, MS. *Accreditation:* NCATE. *Entrance requirements:* For master's, GRE, MAT, minimum GPA of 2.75.

Plymouth State University, College of Graduate Studies, Graduate Studies in Education, Program in Elementary Education, Plymouth, NH 03264-1595. Offers M Ed. *Accreditation:* NCATE. *Program availability:* Part-time, evening/weekend. *Degree requirements:* For master's, capstone project. *Entrance requirements:* For master's, MAT, minimum GPA of 3.0.

Point Park University, School of Arts and Sciences, Department of Education, Pittsburgh, PA 15222-1984. Offers adult learning and training (MA); athletic coaching (M Ed); curriculum and instruction (MA); educational administration (MA); leadership and administration (Ed D); secondary education (M Ed); special education grades 7-12 (M Ed); special education PreK-grade 8 (M Ed). *Program availability:* Part-time, evening/weekend, 100% online, blended/hybrid learning. *Degree requirements:* For master's, comprehensive exam (for some programs), thesis or alternative. *Entrance requirements:* For master's, minimum GPA of 3.0, resume, 2 letters of recommendation. Additional exam requirements/recommendations for international students: Required—TOEFL. Electronic applications accepted.

Prescott College, Graduate Programs, Program in Education, Prescott, AZ 86301. Offers early childhood education (MA); early childhood special education (MA); education (MA); elementary education (MA); environmental education leadership and administration (MA); equine-assisted learning (MA); school guidance counseling (MA); secondary education (MA); special education: learning disabilities (MA); special education: mental retardation (MA); special education: serious emotional disabilities (MA); student-directed independent study (MA); sustainability education (PhD). *Program availability:* Part-time, online learning. *Degree requirements:* For master's, thesis, fieldwork or internship, practicum; for doctorate, thesis/dissertation. *Entrance requirements:* For master's, 2 letters of recommendation, resume; for doctorate, 3 letters of recommendation, resume, official transcripts, personal statement, program proposal. Additional exam requirements/recommendations for international students: Required—TOEFL (minimum score 500 paper-based). Electronic applications accepted.

Providence College, Program in Special Education, Providence, RI 02918. Offers special education (M Ed), including elementary teaching, secondary teaching. *Program availability:* Part-time, evening/weekend. *Degree requirements:* For master's, comprehensive exam, portfolio. *Entrance requirements:* Additional exam requirements/recommendations for international students: Required—TOEFL (minimum score 577 paper-based; 90 iBT).

Providence College, Programs in Administration, Providence, RI 02918. Offers elementary administration (M Ed); secondary administration (M Ed). *Program availability:* Part-time, evening/weekend. *Degree requirements:* For master's, comprehensive exam, portfolio. *Entrance requirements:* Additional exam requirements/recommendations for international students: Required—TOEFL (minimum score 577 paper-based; 90 iBT).

Purdue University, Graduate School, College of Education, Department of Curriculum and Instruction, West Lafayette, IN 47907. Offers agricultural and extension education (MS, MS Ed, PhD, Ed S); art education (PhD); career and technical education (MS Ed, PhD, Ed S); curriculum studies (MS Ed, PhD, Ed S); educational technology (MS Ed, PhD, Ed S); elementary education (MS Ed); family and consumer sciences education (MS Ed, PhD, Ed S); foreign language education (MS Ed, PhD, Ed S); industrial technology (PhD, Ed S); language arts (MS Ed, PhD, Ed S); literacy (MS Ed, PhD, Ed S); mathematics education (MS, MS Ed, PhD, Ed S); science education (MS, MS Ed, PhD, Ed S); social studies education (MS Ed, PhD, Ed S). *Accreditation:* NCATE. *Program availability:* Part-time, evening/weekend. *Faculty:* 37 full-time (27 women), 1 (woman) part-time/adjunct. *Students:* 78 full-time (50 women), 286 part-time (195 women); includes 68 minority (25 Black or African American, non-Hispanic/Latino; 3 American Indian or Alaska Native, non-Hispanic/Latino; 10 Asian, non-Hispanic/Latino; 22 Hispanic/Latino; 1 Native Hawaiian or other Pacific Islander, non-Hispanic/Latino; 7 Two or more races, non-Hispanic/Latino), 44 international. Average age 36. 150 applicants, 79% accepted, 73 enrolled. In 2017, 107 master's, 20 doctorates, 2 other advanced degrees awarded. *Degree requirements:* For master's, thesis optional; for doctorate, thesis/dissertation, oral and written exams; for Ed S, oral presentation, project. *Entrance requirements:* For master's, GRE General Test (if undergraduate GPA is below 3.0), minimum undergraduate GPA of 3.0 or equivalent; for doctorate, GRE General Test (minimum combined verbal and quantitative score of 1000, 300 for new scoring), minimum undergraduate GPA of 3.0 or equivalent; master's degree with minimum GPA of 3.0 or equivalent; for Ed S, GRE General Test (minimum combined verbal and quantitative score of 1000, 300 for new scoring), minimum undergraduate GPA of 3.0 or equivalent; master's degree. Additional exam requirements/recommendations for international students: Required—TOEFL (minimum score 550 paper-based; 77 iBT). *Application deadline:* For fall admission, 12/15 for domestic students, 3/1 for international students; for spring admission, 9/15 for domestic students, 8/1 for international students. Application fee: $60 ($75 for international students). Electronic applications accepted. *Financial support:* Fellowships with full tuition reimbursements, research assistantships with full tuition reimbursements, teaching assistantships with full tuition reimbursements, career-related internships or fieldwork, and tuition waivers (full) available. Support available to part-time students. Financial award application deadline: 3/1; financial award applicants required to submit FAFSA. *Faculty research:* Literacy acquisition and development, teacher beliefs and knowledge, recruitment and retention of underrepresented students, economic education, literacy discourse. *Unit head:* Janet M. Alsup, Head, 765-494-9667, E-mail: alsupj@purdue.edu. *Application contact:* Heather Brinkman, Graduate Contact, 765-494-2345, E-mail: hbrinkma@purdue.edu.
Website: http://www.edci.purdue.edu/

Queens College of the City University of New York, Division of Education, Department of Elementary and Early Childhood Education, Queens, NY 11367-1597.

Offers bilingual education (MAT, MS Ed, AC); childhood education (MAT, MS Ed); early childhood education birth-2 (MAT, MS Ed, AC); literacy education birth-grade 6 (MS Ed, AC). *Program availability:* Part-time, evening/weekend. *Students:* 112 full-time (98 women), 342 part-time (312 women); includes 243 minority (39 Black or African American, non-Hispanic/Latino; 87 Asian, non-Hispanic/Latino; 110 Hispanic/Latino; 7 Two or more races, non-Hispanic/Latino), 12 international. Average age 29. *Degree requirements:* For master's, research project. *Entrance requirements:* For master's, minimum GPA of 3.0. Additional exam requirements/recommendations for international students: Required—TOEFL, IELTS. *Application deadline:* For fall admission, 4/1 for domestic students. Applications are processed on a rolling basis. Application fee: $125. Electronic applications accepted. *Financial support:* Career-related internships or fieldwork available. Financial award application deadline: 4/1; financial award applicants required to submit FAFSA. *Unit head:* Daisuke Akiba, Chair, 718-997-5300, E-mail: daisuke.akiba@qc.cuny.edu. *Application contact:* Elizabeth D'Amico-Ramirez, Assistant Director of Graduate Admissions, 718-997-5203, E-mail: elizabeth.damicoramirez@qc.cuny.edu.

Queens University of Charlotte, Wayland H. Cato, Jr. School of Education, Charlotte, NC 28274-0002. Offers educational leadership (MA); K-6 (MAT); literacy K-12 (M Ed). *Accreditation:* NCATE. *Program availability:* Part-time, evening/weekend, online learning. *Degree requirements:* For master's, comprehensive exam. *Entrance requirements:* For master's, GRE General Test. *Expenses:* Contact institution.

Quinnipiac University, School of Education, Program in Elementary Education, Hamden, CT 06518-1940. Offers MAT. *Accreditation:* NCATE. *Faculty:* 8 full-time (5 women), 27 part-time/adjunct (19 women). *Students:* 51 full-time (50 women), 1 (woman) part-time; includes 2 minority (1 Black or African American, non-Hispanic/Latino; 1 American Indian or Alaska Native, non-Hispanic/Latino), 1 international. 47 applicants, 94% accepted, 38 enrolled. In 2017, 39 master's awarded. *Entrance requirements:* For master's, PRAXIS I or PRAXIS Core Academic Skills Exam, minimum GPA of 3.0, interview. *Application deadline:* For fall admission, 5/1 priority date for domestic students. Applications are processed on a rolling basis. Application fee: $45. Electronic applications accepted. *Financial support:* Career-related internships or fieldwork, Federal Work-Study, and unspecified assistantships available. Financial award application deadline: 6/1; financial award applicants required to submit FAFSA. *Faculty research:* Multicultural and urban education/leadership, challenges of teaching diverse learners, scholarship of teaching and learning, technology and teaching, humor and education. *Unit head:* Mordechai Gordon, Program Director, 203-582-8442, E-mail: mordechai.gordon@qu.edu. *Application contact:* Office of Graduate Admissions, 203-582-8672, Fax: 203-582-3443, E-mail: graduate@qu.edu.
Website: http://www.qu.edu/gradeducation

Regent University, Graduate School, School of Education, Virginia Beach, VA 23464-9800. Offers education (M Ed, Ed D, PhD), including adult education (Ed D, PhD, Ed S), advanced educational leadership (Ed D, PhD, Ed S), character education (Ed D, PhD, Ed S), Christian education leadership (Ed D, PhD, Ed S), Christian school administration (M Ed), curriculum and instruction (Ed D, PhD, Ed S), curriculum and instruction - adult education (M Ed), curriculum and instruction - Christian school (M Ed), curriculum and instruction - gifted and talented (M Ed), curriculum and instruction - STEM education (M Ed), curriculum and instruction - teacher leader (M Ed), discipleship for ministry (M Ed), educational leadership (M Ed), educational psychology (Ed D, PhD, Ed S), educational technology and online learning (Ed D, PhD, Ed S), elementary education (M Ed), exceptional education executive leadership (Ed D, PhD, Ed S), higher education (Ed D, PhD, Ed S), higher education leadership and management (Ed D, PhD, Ed S), instructional design and technology (M Ed), K-12 school leadership (Ed D, PhD, Ed S), K-12 special education (M Ed), leadership in mathematics education (M Ed), reading specialist (M Ed), special education (Ed D, PhD, Ed S), student affairs (M Ed), TESOL - adult education (M Ed), TESOL - K-12 (M Ed); educational specialist (Ed S), including adult education (Ed D, PhD, Ed S), advanced educational leadership (Ed D, PhD, Ed S), character education (Ed D, PhD, Ed S), Christian education leadership (Ed D, PhD, Ed S), curriculum and instruction (Ed D, PhD, Ed S), educational psychology (Ed D, PhD, Ed S), educational technology and online learning (Ed D, PhD, Ed S), exceptional education executive leadership (Ed D, PhD, Ed S), higher education (Ed D, PhD, Ed S), higher education leadership and management (Ed D, PhD, Ed S), K-12 school leadership (Ed D, PhD, Ed S), special education (Ed D, PhD, Ed S). *Accreditation:* TEAC. *Program availability:* Part-time, evening/weekend, 100% online, blended/hybrid learning. *Faculty:* 22 full-time (10 women), 44 part-time/adjunct (32 women). *Students:* 80 full-time (59 women), 945 part-time (750 women); includes 432 minority (352 Black or African American, non-Hispanic/Latino; 4 American Indian or Alaska Native, non-Hispanic/Latino; 14 Asian, non-Hispanic/Latino; 43 Hispanic/Latino; 19 Two or more races, non-Hispanic/Latino), 12 international. Average age 40. 1,125 applicants, 49% accepted, 436 enrolled. In 2017, 316 master's, 24 doctorates awarded. *Degree requirements:* For master's, thesis or alternative; for doctorate, comprehensive exam, thesis/dissertation. *Entrance requirements:* For master's, Virginia Communication and Literacy Assessment (VCLA), PRAXIS, college transcripts, writing sample, interview; for doctorate, GRE, writing sample, resume, transcripts, interview. Additional exam requirements/recommendations for international students: Required—TOEFL (minimum score 577 paper-based). *Application deadline:* For fall admission, 4/1 priority date for domestic students; for spring admission, 10/15 priority date for domestic students. Applications are processed on a rolling basis. Application fee: $50. Electronic applications accepted. *Expenses:* Contact institution. *Financial support:* In 2017–18, 669 students received support, including 1 fellowship (averaging $10,000 per year); career-related internships or fieldwork, scholarships/grants, and unspecified assistantships also available. Support available to part-time students. *Faculty research:* Christian school administration, curriculum and instruction, educational technology and online learning, higher education, special education. *Unit head:* Dr. Donald Finn, Dean, 757-352-4278, Fax: 757-352-4318, E-mail: dfinn@regent.edu. *Application contact:* Heidi Cece, Assistant Vice President of Enrollment Management, 800-373-5504, Fax: 757-352-4381, E-mail: admissions@regent.edu.
Website: https://www.regent.edu/school-of-education/

Regis College, Department of Education, Weston, MA 02493. Offers elementary teacher (M Ed); higher education leadership (Ed D); special education (M Ed). *Program availability:* Part-time, evening/weekend. *Degree requirements:* For doctorate, thesis/dissertation, capstone project. *Entrance requirements:* For master's, GRE or MAT, personal statement, recommendations, resume/curriculum vitae, official transcripts, interview; for doctorate, personal statement, recommendations, resume/curriculum vitae, official transcripts, presentation/interview. Additional exam requirements/recommendations for international students: Required—TOEFL (minimum score 560 paper-based; 79 iBT); Recommended—IELTS (minimum score 6.5). *Application deadline:* Applications are processed on a rolling basis. Application fee: $65. Electronic applications accepted. *Financial support:* Federal Work-Study, scholarships/grants, and unspecified assistantships available. Financial award applicants required to submit FAFSA. *Unit head:* Dr. Priscilla Boerger, Department Chair/Graduate Program Director, 781-768-7422, E-mail: priscilla.boerger@regiscollege.edu.

Regis University, College of Contemporary Liberal Studies, Denver, CO 80221-1099. Offers creative writing (MFA); criminology (M Sc); curriculum, instruction and assessment (M Ed); education - teacher leadership (M Ed); educational leadership (M Ed); elementary education (M Ed); literacy (Certificate); reading (M Ed); secondary education (M Ed); special education (M Ed); teacher academic leadership (Certificate); teacher leadership (MA); teacher/educational leadership (M Ed); teaching the linguistically diverse (M Ed). *Program availability:* Part-time, evening/weekend, 100% online, blended/hybrid learning. *Degree requirements:* For master's, thesis (for some programs). *Entrance requirements:* For master's, official transcript reflecting baccalaureate degree awarded from regionally-accredited college or university, work experience, resume, letters of recommendation. Additional exam requirements/recommendations for international students: Required—TOEFL (minimum score 550 paper-based; 82 iBT). Electronic applications accepted. *Expenses:* Contact institution.

Rhode Island College, School of Graduate Studies, Feinstein School of Education and Human Development, Department of Elementary Education, Providence, RI 02908-1991. Offers early childhood education (M Ed); elementary education (M Ed, MAT); reading (M Ed). *Accreditation:* NCATE. *Program availability:* Part-time, evening/weekend. *Faculty:* 9. *Students:* 19 full-time (18 women), 24 part-time (23 women). Average age 33. In 2017, 21 master's awarded. *Degree requirements:* For master's, comprehensive exam (for some programs), comprehensive assessment. *Entrance requirements:* For master's, GRE General Test or MAT, PRAXIS II (elementary content knowledge), undergraduate transcripts; minimum undergraduate GPA of 3.0; 3 letters of recommendation. Additional exam requirements/recommendations for international students: Recommended—TOEFL (minimum score 550 paper-based; 79 iBT). *Application deadline:* For fall admission, 3/1 for domestic students; for spring admission, 11/1 for domestic students. Applications are processed on a rolling basis. Application fee: $50. Electronic applications accepted. *Expenses:* Tuition, state resident: full-time $9768; part-time $407 per credit. Tuition, nonresident: full-time $19,008; part-time $792 per credit. *Required fees:* $696; $29 per credit. One-time fee: $200 full-time; $100 part-time. Tuition and fees vary according to course load. *Financial support:* Teaching assistantships with full tuition reimbursements, Federal Work-Study, scholarships/grants, and health care benefits available. Support available to part-time students. Financial award application deadline: 5/15; financial award applicants required to submit FAFSA. *Unit head:* Dr. Carolyn Obel-Omia, Chair, 401-456-8016. *Application contact:* Graduate Studies, 401-456-8700.
Website: http://www.ric.edu/elementaryEducation/

Rider University, College of Education and Human Services, Teacher Certification Program, Lawrenceville, NJ 08648-3001. Offers bilingual education (Certificate); business education (Certificate); early childhood education (Certificate); elementary education (Certificate); English as a second language (Certificate); English education (Certificate); mathematics education (Certificate); science education (Certificate); secondary education (Certificate); social studies education (Certificate); world languages (Certificate), including French, German, Spanish. *Program availability:* Part-time, online learning. *Degree requirements:* For Certificate, internship, professional portfolio. *Entrance requirements:* For degree, PRAXIS, resume. Additional exam requirements/recommendations for international students: Required—TOEFL (minimum score 550 paper-based). Electronic applications accepted. *Faculty research:* Conceptual foundations for optimal development of creativity; creative theory, cognitive processes in mathematics learning, teacher collaboration.

Rivier University, School of Graduate Studies, Department of Education, Nashua, NH 03060. Offers curriculum and instruction (M Ed); early childhood education (M Ed); educational administration (M Ed); educational studies (M Ed); elementary education (M Ed); elementary education and general special education (M Ed); emotional and behavioral disorders (M Ed); general social education (M Ed); leadership and learning (Ed D, CAGS); learning disabilities (M Ed); learning disabilities and reading (M Ed); mental health counseling (MA); reading (M Ed); school counseling (M Ed). *Program availability:* Part-time, evening/weekend. *Degree requirements:* For master's, comprehensive exam (for some programs), internships. *Entrance requirements:* For master's, GRE General Test or MAT.

Rockford University, Graduate Studies, Department of Education, Program in Elementary Education, Rockford, IL 61108-2393. Offers MAT. *Program availability:* Part-time, evening/weekend. *Degree requirements:* For master's, thesis optional. *Entrance requirements:* For master's, GRE General Test, basic skills test (for students seeking certification), 3 letters of recommendation. Additional exam requirements/recommendations for international students: Required—TOEFL (minimum score 550 paper-based; 79 iBT). Electronic applications accepted.

Rollins College, Hamilton Holt School, Graduate Education Programs, Winter Park, FL 32789-4499. Offers elementary education (M Ed, MAT). *Program availability:* Part-time, evening/weekend. *Faculty:* 5 full-time (3 women), 1 part-time/adjunct (0 women). *Students:* 10 full-time (7 women), 4 part-time (3 women); includes 5 minority (2 Black or African American, non-Hispanic/Latino; 1 American Indian or Alaska Native, non-Hispanic/Latino; 2 Hispanic/Latino), 1 international. Average age 31. In 2017, 6 master's awarded. *Degree requirements:* For master's, comprehensive exam, Professional Education Test (PED) and Subject Area Examination (SAE) of the Florida Teacher Certification Examinations (FTCE), successful review of the Expanded Teacher Education Portfolio (ETEP). *Entrance requirements:* For master's, General Knowledge Test of the Florida Teacher Certification Examination (FTCE), official transcripts, letter(s) of recommendation, essay. Additional exam requirements/recommendations for international students: Required—TOEFL (minimum score 550 paper-based; 80 iBT). *Application deadline:* For fall admission, 8/11 for domestic students; for spring admission, 12/10 for domestic students. Applications are processed on a rolling basis. Application fee: $50. *Expenses:* $1,575 per course. *Financial support:* Scholarships/grants and unspecified assistantships available. Support available to part-time students. Financial award applicants required to submit FAFSA. *Unit head:* Dr. H. James McLaughlin, Department Chair, 407-646-2242, E-mail: hmclaughlin@rollins.edu. *Application contact:* 407-646-1568, Fax: 407-975-6430.

Roosevelt University, Graduate Division, College of Education, Program in Elementary Education, Chicago, IL 60605. Offers MA. *Students:* 8 full-time (7 women), 7 part-time (6 women); includes 6 minority (4 Black or African American, non-Hispanic/Latino; 2 Hispanic/Latino), 1 international. Average age 28. 12 applicants, 100% accepted, 6 enrolled. In 2017, 10 master's awarded. *Application deadline:* Applications are processed on a rolling basis. Application fee: $40. Electronic applications accepted. *Financial support:* Scholarships/grants and unspecified assistantships available. *Application contact:* Laura Lag, Associate Dean for Graduate Admission, 312-853-4753, E-mail: llag@roosevelt.edu.
Website: https://www.roosevelt.edu/academics/programs/masters-in-elementary-education-ma

Rosemont College, Schools of Graduate and Professional Studies, Graduate Education PreK-4 Program, Rosemont, PA 19010-1699. Offers elementary certification (MA); PreK-4 (MA). *Program availability:* Part-time, evening/weekend. *Degree requirements:* For master's, thesis optional. *Entrance requirements:* For master's, minimum college GPA of 3.0, 3 letters of recommendation. Additional exam requirements/recommendations for international students: Required—TOEFL. Electronic applications accepted. Application fee is waived when completed online.

Rutgers University–New Brunswick, Graduate School of Education, Department of Learning and Teaching, Program in Early Childhood/Elementary Education, Piscataway, NJ 08854-8097. Offers Ed M, Ed D. *Program availability:* Part-time. Terminal master's awarded for partial completion of doctoral program. *Degree requirements:* For master's, comprehensive exam (for some programs); for doctorate, thesis/dissertation, qualifying exam. *Entrance requirements:* For master's, GRE General Test, minimum GPA of 3.0; for doctorate, GRE General Test, minimum GPA of 3.5. Additional exam requirements/recommendations for international students: Required—TOEFL. Electronic applications accepted.

Sage Graduate School, Esteves School of Education, Program in Childhood Education/Literacy, Troy, NY 12180-4115. Offers MS. *Program availability:* Part-time, evening/weekend. *Faculty:* 2 full-time (both women), 8 part-time/adjunct (4 women). *Students:* 11 full-time (all women). Average age 28. 13 applicants, 15% accepted, 1 enrolled. In 2017, 1 master's awarded. *Degree requirements:* For master's, thesis optional. *Entrance requirements:* For master's, GRE (minimum scores: Verbal Reasoning 145, Quantitative Reasoning 145, Analytical Writing 3.5) or MAT (minimum score: 350), bachelor's degree in a liberal arts or science area, minimum cumulative GPA of 3.0. Additional exam requirements/recommendations for international students: Required—TOEFL (minimum score 550 paper-based). *Application deadline:* Applications are processed on a rolling basis. Application fee: $30. Electronic applications accepted. Tuition and fees vary according to degree level and program. *Financial support:* Fellowships, research assistantships, scholarships/grants, and unspecified assistantships available. Financial award application deadline: 3/1; financial award applicants required to submit FAFSA. *Unit head:* Dr. John Pelizza, Interim Dean, Esteves School of Education, 518-244-2051, Fax: 518-244-2334, E-mail: pelizj@sage.edu. *Application contact:* Dr. Kathleen Gormley, Chair and Professor of Education, 518-244-2403, Fax: 518-244-2334, E-mail: gormlk@sage.edu.

Sage Graduate School, Esteves School of Education, Program in Childhood Special Education, Troy, NY 12180-4115. Offers MS Ed. *Accreditation:* NCATE. *Program availability:* Part-time, evening/weekend. *Faculty:* 2 full-time (both women), 8 part-time/adjunct (4 women). *Students:* 3 full-time (2 women), 8 part-time (all women); includes 2 minority (1 Black or African American, non-Hispanic/Latino; 1 Asian, non-Hispanic/Latino). Average age 25. 12 applicants, 33% accepted, 3 enrolled. In 2017, 2 master's awarded. *Degree requirements:* For master's, thesis optional. *Entrance requirements:* For master's, bachelor's degree in a liberal arts or sciences area or the equivalent. Additional exam requirements/recommendations for international students: Required—TOEFL (minimum score 550 paper-based). *Application deadline:* Applications are processed on a rolling basis. Application fee: $30. Electronic applications accepted. Tuition and fees vary according to degree level and program. *Financial support:* Fellowships, research assistantships, scholarships/grants, and unspecified assistantships available. Financial award application deadline: 3/1; financial award applicants required to submit FAFSA. *Faculty research:* Effective behavioral strategies for classroom instruction. *Unit head:* Dr. John Pelizza, Interim Dean, Esteves School of Education, 518-244-2051, Fax: 518-244-2334, E-mail: pelizj@sage.edu. *Application contact:* Tracey McLeod, Chair and Assistant Professor, 518-244-3132, Fax: 518-244-2334, E-mail: mcleot@sage.edu.

St. John Fisher College, Ralph C. Wilson Jr. School of Education, Program in Childhood Education/Special Education, Rochester, NY 14618-3597. Offers childhood education (MS); childhood education/special education (Certificate). *Program availability:* Part-time, evening/weekend. *Faculty:* 5 full-time (3 women), 6 part-time/adjunct (5 women). *Students:* 22 full-time (19 women), 8 part-time (all women); includes 4 minority (1 Black or African American, non-Hispanic/Latino; 1 Asian, non-Hispanic/Latino; 1 Hispanic/Latino; 1 Two or more races, non-Hispanic/Latino). Average age 26. 33 applicants, 70% accepted, 14 enrolled. In 2017, 17 master's awarded. *Degree requirements:* For master's, field experience, student teaching. *Entrance requirements:* For master's, LAST, 2 letters of recommendation, personal statement, current resume. Additional exam requirements/recommendations for international students: Required—TOEFL (minimum score 575 paper-based; 80 iBT). *Application deadline:* Applications are processed on a rolling basis. Application fee: $30. Electronic applications accepted. *Expenses:* Contact institution. *Financial support:* Scholarships/grants available. Financial award applicants required to submit FAFSA. *Faculty research:* Professional development, science assessment, multi-cultural, educational technology. *Unit head:* Dr. Susan Hildenbrand, Program Director, 585-385-7297, E-mail: shildenbrand@sjfc.edu. *Application contact:* Michelle Gosier, Associate Director of Transfer and Graduate Admissions, 585-385-8064, E-mail: mgosier@sjfc.edu.
Website: https://www.sjfc.edu/graduate-programs/ms-in-childhood-special-education/

St. John's University, The School of Education, Department of Curriculum and Instruction, Program in Childhood Education, Queens, NY 11439. Offers MS Ed. *Program availability:* Part-time, evening/weekend. *Students:* 7 full-time (5 women), 10 part-time (8 women); includes 2 minority (1 Black or African American, non-Hispanic/Latino; 1 Asian, non-Hispanic/Latino), 2 international. Average age 32. 17 applicants, 88% accepted, 4 enrolled. In 2017, 12 master's awarded. *Degree requirements:* For master's, thesis. *Entrance requirements:* For master's, GRE, MAT, or PRAXIS, statement of goals (personal essay), official undergraduate transcripts, initial teaching certification. Additional exam requirements/recommendations for international students: Required—TOEFL, IELTS. *Application deadline:* For fall admission, 8/17 for domestic and international students; for summer admission, 5/15 for domestic and international students. Application fee: $70. Electronic applications accepted. *Expenses:* Tuition: Full-time $44,280; part-time $1230 per credit. *Required fees:* $340; $340 per credit. Tuition and fees vary according to course load, degree level and program. *Financial support:* Fellowships, research assistantships, scholarships/grants, and unspecified assistantships available. Support available to part-time students. Financial award application deadline: 2/1; financial award applicants required to submit FAFSA. *Faculty research:* Self-determination in the special education setting; parent, teacher, and student views on testing in elementary school; children's play; children's acquisition of STEM related subjects; the politics of preschool. *Unit head:* Dr. Daniel Ness, Chair, 718-990-2717, E-mail: nessd@stjohns.edu. *Application contact:* Dr. Daniel Ness, Chair, 718-990-2717, E-mail: nessd@stjohns.edu.
Website: https://www.stjohns.edu/academics/schools-and-colleges/school-education/programs-and-majors/childhood-education-master-science-education

Saint Joseph's University, College of Arts and Sciences, Graduate Programs in Education, Philadelphia, PA 19131-1395. Offers curriculum supervisor (Certificate); educational leadership (MS, Ed D); elementary education (MS, Certificate); elementary/middle school education (Certificate); organizational development and leadership (MS); principal (Certificate); professional education (MS); reading specialist (MS, Certificate); reading supervisor (Certificate); secondary education (MS, Certificate); special education (MS); special education 7-12 (Certificate); special education PK-8 (Certificate); superintendent's letter of eligibility (Certificate); supervisor of special education (Certificate); teacher of the deaf and hard of hearing (Certificate). *Program availability:* Part-time, evening/weekend, blended/hybrid learning. *Faculty:* 18 full-time (16 women), 63 part-time/adjunct (44 women). *Students:* 79 full-time (60 women), 793 part-time (604 women); includes 179 minority (125 Black or African American, non-Hispanic/Latino; 5 American Indian or Alaska Native, non-Hispanic/Latino; 15 Asian,

non-Hispanic/Latino; 27 Hispanic/Latino; 1 Native Hawaiian or other Pacific Islander, non-Hispanic/Latino; 6 Two or more races, non-Hispanic/Latino; 12 international. Average age 34. 375 applicants, 75% accepted, 189 enrolled. In 2017, 340 master's, 13 doctorates, 3 other advanced degrees awarded. *Degree requirements:* For master's, thesis or alternative; for doctorate, comprehensive exam, thesis/dissertation. *Entrance requirements:* For master's, 2 letters of recommendation, minimum GPA of 3.0, official transcripts, personal statement; for doctorate, GRE, master's degree from accredited institution, minimum graduate GPA of 3.5, computer competence, interview with program director. Additional exam requirements/recommendations for international students: Required—TOEFL (minimum score 550 paper-based; 80 iBT), IELTS (minimum score 6.5), PTE (minimum score 60). *Application deadline:* For fall admission, 7/15 for international students; for spring admission, 11/1 for international students. Applications are processed on a rolling basis. Application fee: $35. Electronic applications accepted. *Expenses:* Contact institution. *Financial support:* Scholarships/grants and unspecified assistantships available. Financial award application deadline: 5/1; financial award applicants required to submit FAFSA. *Faculty research:* Factors predicting early mathematics skills for low income children, early child care and development, preschool quality, parent communication and home-school collaboration issues, education of terminally ill children, preparing literacy teachers for urban schools. *Unit head:* Dr. John Vacca, Associate Dean, Education, 610-660-3131, E-mail: gradcas@sju.edu. *Application contact:* Graduate Admissions, College of Arts and Sciences, 610-660-3131, E-mail: gradcas@sju.edu.
Website: https://sites.sju.edu/education/graduate-programs/

Saint Mary's University of Minnesota, Schools of Graduate and Professional Programs, Graduate School of Education, Instruction Program, Winona, MN 55987-1399. Offers MA. *Unit head:* Delores Roethke, Director, 612-238-4511, E-mail: droethke@smumn.edu. *Application contact:* James Callinan, Director of Admissions for Graduate and Professional Programs, 612-728-5158, Fax: 612-728-5121, E-mail: jcallina@smumn.edu.
Website: http://www.smumn.edu/graduate-home/areas-of-study/graduate-school-of-education/ma-in-instruction

Saint Peter's University, Graduate Programs in Education, Program in Teaching, Jersey City, NJ 07306-5997. Offers 6-8 middle school education (MA Ed, Certificate); K-12 secondary education (MA Ed, Certificate); K-5 elementary education (MA Ed, Certificate). *Program availability:* Part-time, evening/weekend. *Degree requirements:* For master's, comprehensive exam. *Entrance requirements:* For master's, GRE or MAT. Additional exam requirements/recommendations for international students: Required—TOEFL. Electronic applications accepted.

St. Thomas Aquinas College, Division of Teacher Education, Sparkill, NY 10976. Offers adolescence education (MST); childhood and special education (MST); childhood education (MST); educational leadership (MS Ed); reading (MS Ed, PMC); special education (MS Ed, PMC); teaching (MS Ed), including elementary education, middle school education, secondary education. *Accreditation:* NCATE. *Program availability:* Part-time, evening/weekend. *Degree requirements:* For master's, comprehensive exam, comprehensive professional portfolio; for PMC, action research project. *Entrance requirements:* For master's, New York State Qualifying Exam, GRE General Test or minimum GPA of 3.0, teaching certificate; for PMC, GRE General Test or minimum GPA of 3.0. Electronic applications accepted. *Faculty research:* Computer applications in education, adolescent special education students, literacy development, inclusive practices for special education students.

St. Thomas University, School of Leadership Studies, Institute for Education, Miami Gardens, FL 33054-6459. Offers earth/space science (Certificate); educational administration (MS, Certificate); educational leadership (Ed D); elementary education (MS); ESOL (Certificate); gifted education (Certificate); instructional technology (MS, Certificate); professional/studies (Certificate); reading (MS, Certificate); special education (MS). *Program availability:* Part-time, evening/weekend. *Degree requirements:* For master's, comprehensive exam; for doctorate, comprehensive exam, thesis/dissertation. *Entrance requirements:* For master's, interview, minimum GPA of 3.0 or GRE; for doctorate, GRE or MAT. Additional exam requirements/recommendations for international students: Required—TOEFL (minimum score 550 paper-based; 79 iBT). Electronic applications accepted.

Saint Xavier University, Graduate Studies, School of Education, Chicago, IL 60655-3105. Offers counseling (MA); curriculum and instruction (MA); early childhood education (MA); educational administration (MA); elementary education (MA); individualized studies (MA), including educational technology, English as a second language (ESL), ISTEM (integrative science, technology, engineering, and math), science education; music education (MA); reading (MA); secondary education (MA); Spanish education (MA); special education (MA); teaching and leadership (MA). *Accreditation:* NCATE. *Program availability:* Part-time, evening/weekend. *Degree requirements:* For master's, thesis or project. *Entrance requirements:* For master's, minimum GPA of 3.0. *Expenses:* Contact institution.

Salem College, Graduate Studies, Winston-Salem, NC 27101. Offers art education (MAT); elementary education (M Ed, MAT); language and literacy (M Ed); middle school education (MAT); organ (MM); piano (MM); school counseling (M Ed); second language studies (MAT); secondary education (MAT); special education (M Ed, MAT). *Accreditation:* NCATE. *Program availability:* Part-time, evening/weekend, online learning. *Faculty:* 8 full-time (all women), 11 part-time/adjunct (8 women). In 2017, 17 master's awarded. *Degree requirements:* For master's, practicum (MAT), action research project (M Ed). *Entrance requirements:* For master's, minimum GPA of 3.0, two academic/professional recommendations, acceptable criminal background check. Additional exam requirements/recommendations for international students: Recommended—TOEFL. *Application deadline:* For fall admission, 8/1 for domestic students, 7/15 for international students; for spring admission, 1/15 for domestic students; for summer admission, 5/1 for domestic students. Applications are processed on a rolling basis. Application fee: $30. Electronic applications accepted. *Expenses: Tuition:* Part-time $440 per semester hour. *Financial support:* Scholarships/grants available. Support available to part-time students. Financial award applicants required to submit FAFSA. *Faculty research:* Teacher professional development, adolescent literacy, instructional technology. *Application contact:* Sheryl Long, Director, 336-721-2658, Fax: 336-917-5384, E-mail: sheryl.long@salem.edu.
Website: http://www.salem.edu

Salem State University, School of Graduate Studies, Program in Elementary Education, Salem, MA 01970-5353. Offers M Ed. *Accreditation:* NCATE. *Program availability:* Part-time, evening/weekend. *Entrance requirements:* For master's, GRE or MAT. Additional exam requirements/recommendations for international students: Required—TOEFL (minimum score 550 paper-based; 80 iBT) or IELTS (minimum score 5.5).

Salem State University, School of Graduate Studies, Program in Spanish, Salem, MA 01970-5353. Offers MAT. *Program availability:* Part-time, evening/weekend. *Entrance requirements:* For master's, GRE or MAT. Additional exam requirements/recommendations for international students: Required—TOEFL (minimum score 550 paper-based; 80 iBT) or IELTS (minimum score 5.5).

Samford University, Orlean Beeson School of Education, Birmingham, AL 35229. Offers educational leadership (MSE, Ed D); elementary education (MS Ed, MSE); gifted (MSE); instructional design and technology (MSE); instructional leadership (MSE, Ed S); secondary education (MSE); special education (MSE). *Accreditation:* NCATE. *Program availability:* Part-time, evening/weekend, 100% online, blended/hybrid learning. *Faculty:* 11 full-time (7 women), 22 part-time/adjunct (12 women). *Students:* 206 full-time (144 women), 102 part-time (75 women); includes 124 minority (113 Black or African American, non-Hispanic/Latino; 3 American Indian or Alaska Native, non-Hispanic/Latino; 3 Asian, non-Hispanic/Latino; 2 Hispanic/Latino; 3 Two or more races, non-Hispanic/Latino), 1 international. Average age 37. 134 applicants, 84% accepted, 76 enrolled. In 2017, 79 master's, 34 doctorates, 21 other advanced degrees awarded. *Degree requirements:* For master's and Ed S, comprehensive exam; for doctorate, comprehensive exam, thesis/dissertation. *Entrance requirements:* For master's, GRE, MAT, PRAXIS II, interview, transcripts, essay, recommendations, teaching certification; for doctorate, resume, transcripts, interview, essay; for Ed S, teaching certification, transcripts, essay, interview. Additional exam requirements/recommendations for international students: Required—TOEFL (minimum score 90 iBT), IELTS (minimum score 6.5). *Application deadline:* For fall admission, 7/15 for domestic and international students; for winter admission, 11/15 for domestic and international students; for spring admission, 11/15 for domestic and international students; for summer admission, 4/15 for domestic and international students. Application fee: $35. Electronic applications accepted. *Expenses:* $813 per credit hour, $100 School of Education fee, $175 technology fee. *Financial support:* In 2017–18, 220 students received support. Scholarships/grants and unspecified assistantships available. Financial award application deadline: 2/15; financial award applicants required to submit FAFSA. *Faculty research:* Principal leadership's and teacher organizational commitment mentoring, professional development, and middle grades leadership coaching and administrator effectiveness character development programs in schools teacher efficacy related STEM and professional growth. *Unit head:* Dr. Bonnie Rabe, Interim Dean, 205-726-2565, E-mail: brabe@samford.edu. *Application contact:* Brooke Karr, Graduate Admissions Office Coordinator, 205-729-2783, Fax: 205-726-4233, E-mail: kbgilrea@samford.edu.
Website: http://www.samford.edu/education/

San Diego State University, Graduate and Research Affairs, College of Education, School of Teacher Education, Program in Elementary Curriculum and Instruction, San Diego, CA 92182. Offers MA. *Accreditation:* NCATE. *Program availability:* Evening/weekend. *Entrance requirements:* For master's, GRE General Test, letters of reference. Additional exam requirements/recommendations for international students: Required—TOEFL. Electronic applications accepted.

San Francisco State University, Division of Graduate Studies, College of Education, Department of Elementary Education, Program in Elementary Education, San Francisco, CA 94132-1722. Offers MA. *Accreditation:* NCATE. *Unit head:* Dr. Josephine Arce, Chair, 415-338-7636, Fax: 415-338-0567, E-mail: jarce@sfsu.edu. *Application contact:* Dr. Stephanie Sisk-Hilton, MA Program Coordinator, 415-338-3442, Fax: 415-338-0567, E-mail: stephsh@sfsu.edu.
Website: https://eed.sfsu.edu/

San Jose State University, Graduate Studies and Research, Connie L. Lurie College of Education, San Jose, CA 95192-0071. Offers child and adolescent development (MA); education (MA), including counseling and student personnel, curriculum and instruction, speech pathology; educational leadership (MA, Ed D), including administration and supervision (MA), educational leadership (MA); elementary education (MA), including curriculum and instruction. *Accreditation:* NCATE. *Program availability:* Part-time, evening/weekend. *Faculty:* 29 full-time (22 women), 47 part-time/adjunct (40 women). *Students:* 414 full-time (339 women), 115 part-time (93 women); includes 340 minority (14 Black or African American, non-Hispanic/Latino; 87 Asian, non-Hispanic/Latino; 176 Hispanic/Latino; 64 Two or more races, non-Hispanic/Latino), 9 international. Average age 30. 654 applicants, 34% accepted, 161 enrolled. In 2017, 286 master's, 7 doctorates awarded. Terminal master's awarded for partial completion of doctoral program. *Degree requirements:* For master's, project or theses, graduate writing assessment; for doctorate, thesis/dissertation. *Entrance requirements:* For master's, GRE General Test (for some programs). Additional exam requirements/recommendations for international students: Required—TOEFL (minimum score 550 paper-based; 80 iBT), IELTS (minimum score 6.5), PTE (minimum score 53). *Application deadline:* For fall admission, 2/1 for domestic and international students. Applications are processed on a rolling basis. Application fee: $55. Electronic applications accepted. *Expenses:* Tuition, state resident: full-time $7176. Tuition, nonresident: full-time $16,680. Tuition and fees vary according to course load and program. *Financial support:* In 2017–18, 4 research assistantships with partial tuition reimbursements (averaging $2,500 per year) were awarded; fellowships, career-related internships or fieldwork, Federal Work-Study, scholarships/grants, traineeships, and tuition waivers (full and partial) also available. Support available to part-time students. Financial award application deadline: 4/28; financial award applicants required to submit FAFSA. *Faculty research:* Equity and social justice in public education, interdisciplinary practices, teacher training, and effective pedagogy, clinical efficacy, typical and atypical development in children. *Unit head:* Dr. Paul Cascella, Interim Dean, 408-924-3600, Fax: 408-924-3713, E-mail: paul.cascella@sjsu.edu.
Website: http://www.sjsu.edu/education/

Seton Hill University, Master of Arts Program in Elementary/Middle Level Education, Greensburg, PA 15601. Offers MA. *Program availability:* Part-time, evening/weekend, blended/hybrid learning. *Entrance requirements:* For master's, teacher's certification, 3 letters of recommendation, personal statement, transcripts, resume. Additional exam requirements/recommendations for international students: Required—TOEFL (minimum score 600 paper-based; 100 iBT), IELTS (minimum score 6.5). *Application deadline:* Applications are processed on a rolling basis. Application fee: $0. Electronic applications accepted. *Expenses: Tuition:* Part-time $734 per credit. Tuition and fees vary according to class time, course level, course load and program. *Financial support:* Federal Work-Study, scholarships/grants, and tuition discounts available. Financial award application deadline: 8/15; financial award applicants required to submit FAFSA.
Website: https://www.setonhill.edu/academics/graduate-programs/elementary-middle-level-education-ma/

Shenandoah University, School of Education and Leadership, Winchester, VA 22601. Offers administration and supervision (Certificate); administrative leadership (D Ed); early childhood literacy (MS); educational administration (MSE); elementary school teacher education (Certificate); emphasis in teaching (MSE); health and physical education (Certificate); individualized focus (MS, MSE); literacy education (MS); middle school teacher education (Certificate); organizational leadership (MS, D Prof); reading licensure (MS, Certificate); reading non-licensure (MS); secondary school teacher education (Certificate); special education (MSE); writing (MS). *Accreditation:* TEAC. *Program availability:* Part-time, evening/weekend. *Faculty:* 8 full-time (7 women), 22 part-time/adjunct (16 women). *Students:* 16 full-time (14 women), 221 part-time (167 women); includes 32 minority (17 Black or African American, non-Hispanic/Latino; 1 American Indian or Alaska Native, non-Hispanic/Latino; 6 Asian, non-Hispanic/Latino; 5 Hispanic/Latino; 1 Native Hawaiian or other Pacific Islander, non-Hispanic/Latino; 2 Two

or more races, non-Hispanic/Latino), 3 international. Average age 38. 81 applicants, 99% accepted, 63 enrolled. In 2017, 53 master's, 11 doctorates, 49 other advanced degrees awarded. *Degree requirements:* For master's, comprehensive exam (for some programs), thesis (for some programs); for doctorate, comprehensive exam, thesis/dissertation. *Entrance requirements:* For degree, PRAXIS Academic Core, SAT/ACT, PRAXIS Academic Core Math, or VCLA, three letters of recommendation, writing sample, undergraduate degree. Additional exam requirements/recommendations for international students: Required—TOEFL (minimum score 550 paper-based, 79 iBT) or IELTS (6.5). *Application deadline:* For fall admission, 5/1 priority date for domestic students, 5/1 for international students; for spring admission, 10/15 priority date for domestic students, 10/15 for international students; for summer admission, 3/15 priority date for domestic students, 3/15 for international students. Application fee: $30. Electronic applications accepted. *Expenses:* $15,600 tuition plus $1,296 fees (technology and student services). *Financial support:* In 2017–18, 26 students received support. Scholarships/grants and unspecified assistantships available. Financial award applicants required to submit FAFSA. *Faculty research:* Mentoring, behavior support for students, teacher change agency, educational technology in pedagogy, literacy education. *Unit head:* Jill Lindsey, PhD, Director, 540-535-7324, Fax: 540-665-4726, E-mail: jlindsey@su.edu. *Application contact:* Andrew Woodall, Executive Director of Recruitment and Admissions, 540-665-4581, Fax: 540-665-4627, E-mail: admit@su.edu.
Website: http://www.su.edu/education/

Shippensburg University of Pennsylvania, School of Graduate Studies, College of Education and Human Services, Department of Teacher Education, Shippensburg, PA 17257-2299. Offers curriculum and instruction (M Ed), including biology, early childhood education, elementary education, geography/earth science, history, mathematics, middle school education, modern languages; reading (M Ed). *Accreditation:* NCATE. *Program availability:* Part-time, evening/weekend, 100% online, blended/hybrid learning. *Faculty:* 13 full-time (8 women), 1 (woman) part-time/adjunct. *Students:* 10 full-time (7 women), 94 part-time (81 women); includes 10 minority (3 Black or African American, non-Hispanic/Latino; 2 Asian, non-Hispanic/Latino; 5 Hispanic/Latino), 1 international. Average age 34. 71 applicants, 86% accepted, 35 enrolled. In 2017, 23 master's awarded. *Degree requirements:* For master's, comprehensive exam (for some programs), thesis optional, practicum or internship; capstone seminar (for some programs). *Entrance requirements:* For master's, MAT or GRE (if GPA less than 2.75), interview, 3 letters of reference, questionnaire of teaching background and future goals, resume. Additional exam requirements/recommendations for international students: Required—TOEFL (minimum score 550 paper-based, 68 iBT) or IELTS (minimum score 6). *Application deadline:* For fall admission, 4/1 priority date for domestic students, 4/30 for international students; for spring admission, 9/1 priority date for domestic students, 9/30 for international students; for summer admission, 2/1 priority date for domestic students. Applications are processed on a rolling basis. Application fee: $45. Electronic applications accepted. *Expenses:* Tuition, state resident: part-time $500 per credit. Tuition, nonresident: part-time $750 per credit. *Required fees:* $145 per credit. *Financial support:* In 2017–18, 1 student received support. Career-related internships or fieldwork, scholarships/grants, unspecified assistantships, and resident hall director and student payroll positions available. Support available to part-time students. Financial award application deadline: 3/1; financial award applicants required to submit FAFSA. *Unit head:* Dr. Christine A. Royce, Chairperson, 717-477-1688, Fax: 717-477-4046, E-mail: caroyc@ship.edu. *Application contact:* Maya T. Mapp, Director of Admissions, 717-477-1231, Fax: 717-477-4016, E-mail: mtmapp@ship.edu.
Website: http://www.ship.edu/teacher/

Siena Heights University, Graduate College, Adrian, MI 49221-1796. Offers clinical mental health counseling (MA); educational leadership (Specialist); leadership (MA), including health care leadership, organizational leadership; teacher education (MA), including early childhood education, early childhood education: Montessori, education leadership: principal, elementary education: reading K-12, leadership: higher education, secondary education: reading K-12, special education: cognitive impairment, special education: learning disabilities. *Program availability:* Part-time, evening/weekend. *Degree requirements:* For master's, thesis, presentation. *Entrance requirements:* For master's, minimum GPA of 3.0, current resume, essay, all post-secondary transcripts, 3 letters of reference, conviction disclosure form; copy of teaching certificate (for some education programs); for Specialist, master's degree, minimum GPA of 3.0, current resume, essay, all post-secondary transcripts, 3 letters of reference, conviction disclosure form; copy of teaching certificate (for some education programs). Electronic applications accepted.

Sierra Nevada College, Teacher Education Program, Incline Village, NV 89451. Offers advanced teaching and leadership (M Ed); elementary education (MAT); secondary education (MAT). *Program availability:* Part-time, evening/weekend, online learning. *Degree requirements:* For master's, comprehensive exam, thesis, PRAXIS I and II. *Entrance requirements:* For master's, 2 letters of recommendation, minimum GPA of 3.0. Electronic applications accepted.

Simmons College, College of Arts and Sciences, Boston, MA 02115. Offers English (MA); gender/cultural studies (MA); history (MA); public health (MPH); public policy (MPP). *Program availability:* Part-time. *Faculty:* 19 full-time (13 women), 2 part-time/adjunct (both women). *Students:* 4 full-time (3 women), 39 part-time (34 women); includes 11 minority (7 Black or African American, non-Hispanic/Latino; 1 Hispanic/Latino; 3 Two or more races, non-Hispanic/Latino). Average age 26. 99 applicants, 57% accepted, 27 enrolled. In 2017, 23 master's awarded. Terminal master's awarded for partial completion of doctoral program. *Degree requirements:* For master's, thesis optional. *Entrance requirements:* For master's, GRE, bachelor's degree from accredited college or university; minimum B average (preferred). Additional exam requirements/recommendations for international students: Required—TOEFL (minimum score 600 paper-based; 100 iBT). *Application deadline:* For fall admission, 8/1 for domestic and international students; for spring admission, 12/15 for domestic and international students; for summer admission, 5/1 for domestic and international students. Applications are processed on a rolling basis. Application fee: $35. Electronic applications accepted. *Expenses:* $1,052 per credit, $55 activity fee per semester. *Financial support:* In 2017–18, 4 fellowships with partial tuition reimbursements, 22 teaching assistantships with partial tuition reimbursements were awarded; scholarships/grants and unspecified assistantships also available. Support available to part-time students. Financial award applicants required to submit FAFSA. *Faculty research:* Film and media studies, postcolonial literature, critical theory, arts and culture. *Unit head:* Dr. Leanne Doherty, Dean, 617-521-2581, E-mail: leanne.doherty@simmons.edu. *Application contact:* Patricia Flaherty, Director, Graduate Studies Admission, 617-521-3902, Fax: 617-521-3058, E-mail: gsa@simmons.edu.
Website: http://www.simmons.edu/gradstudies/

Simmons College, School of Social Work, Boston, MA 02115. Offers behavior analysis (MS, PhD, Ed S); education (MS Ed); social work (MSW, PhD); special education (MS Ed), including moderate and severe disabilities; teaching (MAT), including elementary education; MSW/MBA. *Accreditation:* CSWE (one or more programs are accredited). *Program availability:* Part-time, 100% online, blended/hybrid learning. *Faculty:* 57 full-time (47 women), 48 part-time/adjunct (36 women). *Students:* 878 full-

time (757 women), 979 part-time (869 women); includes 468 minority (213 Black or African American, non-Hispanic/Latino; 1 American Indian or Alaska Native, non-Hispanic/Latino; 45 Asian, non-Hispanic/Latino; 152 Hispanic/Latino; 3 Native Hawaiian or other Pacific Islander, non-Hispanic/Latino; 54 Two or more races, non-Hispanic/Latino), 12 international. Average age 30. 1,521 applicants, 74% accepted, 545 enrolled. In 2017, 611 master's, 7 doctorates, 1 other advanced degree awarded. Terminal master's awarded for partial completion of doctoral program. *Degree requirements:* For master's, thesis (for some programs); for doctorate, comprehensive exam (for some programs), thesis/dissertation (for some programs). *Entrance requirements:* For master's, GRE, MAT, Massachusetts Tests for Education Licensure (for different programs), minimum grade of B in introductory statistics course within five years prior to entering program, resume, transcripts, three letters of recommendation, personal statement; for doctorate, GRE, BCBA Analyst Exam. Additional exam requirements/recommendations for international students: Required—TOEFL (minimum score 600 paper-based; 100 iBT). *Application deadline:* For fall admission, 8/1 for domestic students; for spring admission, 12/15 for domestic students; for summer admission, 5/1 for domestic students. Applications are processed on a rolling basis. Application fee: $35. Electronic applications accepted. *Expenses:* $1,001 per credit hour, $3,003 per course, $55 activity fee per semester. *Financial support:* In 2017–18, 12 fellowships with partial tuition reimbursements were awarded; scholarships/grants and unspecified assistantships also available. Support available to part-time students. Financial award applicants required to submit FAFSA. *Unit head:* Dr. Cheryl Parks, Dean, 617-521-3293, E-mail: cheryl.parks@simmons.edu. *Application contact:* Carlos D. Frontado, Director of Admissions, 617-521-3920, Fax: 617-521-3980, E-mail: ssw@simmons.edu.
Website: http://www.simmons.edu/ssw/

Sinte Gleska University, Graduate Education Program, Mission, SD 57555. Offers elementary education (M Ed). *Program availability:* Part-time, evening/weekend. *Degree requirements:* For master's, thesis. *Entrance requirements:* For master's, 2 years of experience in elementary education, minimum GPA of 2.5, South Dakota elementary education certification. *Faculty research:* American Indian graduate education, teaching of Native American students.

Slippery Rock University of Pennsylvania, Graduate Studies (Recruitment), College of Education, Department of Elementary Education and Early Childhood, Slippery Rock, PA 16057-1383. Offers instructional coach (M Ed); K-12 reading (M Ed); K-12 science and math (M Ed); reading specialist (M Ed). *Accreditation:* NCATE. *Program availability:* Part-time, evening/weekend, online only, 100% online. *Degree requirements:* For master's, comprehensive exam (for some programs), thesis optional. *Entrance requirements:* For master's, minimum GPA of 3.0, resume, teaching certification, transcripts, letters of recommendation (depending on program). Additional exam requirements/recommendations for international students: Required—TOEFL (minimum score 550 paper-based; 80 iBT). Electronic applications accepted. *Expenses:* Contact institution.

Smith College, Graduate and Special Programs, Department of Education and Child Study, Program in Elementary Education, Northampton, MA 01063. Offers elementary education (MAT); middle school education (MAT). *Program availability:* Part-time. *Students:* 5 full-time (all women), 3 part-time (2 women). Average age 24. 15 applicants, 93% accepted, 8 enrolled. In 2017, 9 master's awarded. *Entrance requirements:* Additional exam requirements/recommendations for international students: Required—TOEFL (minimum score 595 paper-based; 97 iBT), IELTS. *Application deadline:* For fall admission, 4/15 for domestic students, 1/15 priority date for international students; for spring admission, 12/1 for domestic students. Applications are processed on a rolling basis. Application fee: $60. *Expenses:* Contact institution. *Financial support:* In 2017–18, 8 students received support, including 1 fellowship with full tuition reimbursement available; scholarships/grants and human resources employee benefit also available. Support available to part-time students. Financial award application deadline: 4/15; financial award applicants required to submit FAFSA. *Unit head:* Alan Rudnitsky, Graduate Student Adviser, 413-585-3261, E-mail: arudnits@smith.edu. *Application contact:* Ruth Morgan, Program Assistant, 413-585-3050, Fax: 413-585-3054, E-mail: gradstdy@smith.edu.
Website: http://www.smith.edu/educ/

South Carolina State University, College of Graduate and Professional Studies, Department of Education, Orangeburg, SC 29117-0001. Offers early childhood education (MAT); education (M Ed); elementary education (M Ed, MAT); English (MAT); general science/biology (MAT); mathematics (MAT); secondary education (M Ed), including biology education, business education, counselor education, English education, home economics education, industrial education, mathematics education, science education, social studies education; special education (M Ed), including emotionally handicapped, learning disabilities, mentally handicapped. *Accreditation:* NCATE. *Program availability:* Part-time, evening/weekend. *Faculty:* 11 full-time (6 women), 4 part-time/adjunct (2 women). *Students:* 26 full-time (18 women), 22 part-time (17 women); includes 41 minority (all Black or African American, non-Hispanic/Latino), 1 international. Average age 33. 25 applicants, 100% accepted, 19 enrolled. In 2017, 6 master's awarded. *Degree requirements:* For master's, thesis optional, departmental qualifying exam. *Entrance requirements:* For master's, GRE General Test, NTE, interview, teaching certificate. *Application deadline:* For fall admission, 6/15 priority date for domestic students, 6/15 for international students; for spring admission, 11/1 for domestic and international students. Application fee: $25. Electronic applications accepted. *Expenses:* Tuition, state resident: full-time $9388; part-time $607 per credit hour. Tuition, nonresident: full-time $19,968; part-time $1194 per credit hour. *Required fees:* $766; $766 per credit hour. *Financial support:* Fellowships, career-related internships or fieldwork, Federal Work-Study, and scholarships/grants available. Financial award application deadline: 6/1. *Unit head:* Dr. Charlie Spell, Interim Chair, Department of Education, 803-536-8963, Fax: 803-516-4568, E-mail: cspell@scsu.edu. *Application contact:* Curtis Foskey, Coordinator of Graduate Studies, 803-536-8419, Fax: 803-536-8812, E-mail: cfoskey@scsu.edu.

Southeastern Louisiana University, College of Education, Department of Teaching and Learning, Hammond, LA 70402. Offers curriculum and instruction (M Ed); elementary education (MAT); special education (M Ed); special education: early interventionist (MAT). *Accreditation:* NCATE. *Program availability:* Part-time, evening/weekend. *Faculty:* 14 full-time (all women), 2 part-time/adjunct (1 woman). *Students:* 19 full-time (16 women), 115 part-time (104 women); includes 13 minority (3 Black or African American, non-Hispanic/Latino; 5 Hispanic/Latino; 5 Two or more races, non-Hispanic/Latino), 1 international. Average age 37. 55 applicants, 45% accepted, 18 enrolled. In 2017, 29 master's awarded. *Degree requirements:* For master's, comprehensive exam (for some programs), thesis (for some programs), action research project, oral defense of research project, portfolio, teaching certificate, minimum cumulative GPA of 3.0. *Entrance requirements:* For master's, GRE (verbal and quantitative), PRAXIS (for MAT), Prospective Education Candidate (PEC) self-assessment survey; competency on a technology performance assessment in education or three-hour graduate-level technology course; orientation seminar. Additional exam requirements/recommendations for international students: Required—TOEFL (minimum score 500 paper-based; 61 iBT). *Application deadline:* For fall admission, 7/15 priority date for domestic students, 6/1 priority date for international students; for spring

Elementary Education

admission, 12/1 priority date for domestic students, 10/1 priority date for international students. Applications are processed on a rolling basis. Application fee: $20 ($30 for international students). Electronic applications accepted. *Expenses:* Tuition, state resident: full-time $6684. Tuition, nonresident: full-time $19,162. *Required fees:* $2088. *Financial support:* In 2017–18, 5 students received support. Research assistantships, teaching assistantships, career-related internships or fieldwork, Federal Work-Study, institutionally sponsored loans, scholarships/grants, and unspecified assistantships available. Support available to part-time students. Financial award application deadline: 5/1; financial award applicants required to submit FAFSA. *Faculty research:* Teacher in services, STEM, educational technology, pre-service teacher education. *Unit head:* Dr. Colleen Klein-Ezell, Department Head, 985-549-2221, Fax: 985-549-5009, E-mail: colleen.klein-ezell@southeastern.edu. *Application contact:* Amanda Harper, Graduate Admissions Analyst, 985-549-5620, Fax: 985-549-5632, E-mail: admissions@southeastern.edu.
Website: http://www.southeastern.edu/acad_research/depts/teach_lrn/index.html

Southeastern University, College of Education, Lakeland, FL 33801-6099. Offers curriculum and instruction (Ed D); educational leadership (M Ed); elementary education (M Ed); exceptional student education (M Ed); exceptional student education/educational therapy (M Ed); kinesiology (M Ed); organizational leadership (Ed D); reading education (M Ed); teaching English to speakers of other languages (M Ed). *Faculty:* 8 full-time (5 women), 12 part-time/adjunct (7 women). *Students:* 139 full-time (109 women), 225 part-time (172 women); includes 107 minority (57 Black or African American, non-Hispanic/Latino; 2 Asian, non-Hispanic/Latino; 48 Hispanic/Latino), 4 international. Average age 40. Application fee: $50. Electronic applications accepted. *Unit head:* James A. Anderson, Dean, 863-667-5366, E-mail: jaanderson2@seu.edu. Website: http://www.seu.edu/education/

Southeast Missouri State University, School of Graduate Studies, Department of Educational Leadership and Counseling, Cape Girardeau, MO 63701-4799. Offers counseling (MA, Ed S), including career counseling (MA), counseling education (Ed S), mental health counseling (MA), school counseling (MA); educational administration (MA, Ed D, Ed S), including educational administration (Ed S), educational leadership (Ed D), elementary administration (MA), higher education administration (MA), secondary administration (MA), teacher leadership (MA, Ed S). *Accreditation:* NCATE. *Program availability:* Part-time, evening/weekend, online only, 100% online. *Faculty:* 11 full-time (7 women), 6 part-time/adjunct (3 women). *Students:* 75 full-time (54 women), 233 part-time (159 women); includes 30 minority (22 Black or African American, non-Hispanic/Latino; 3 American Indian or Alaska Native, non-Hispanic/Latino; 4 Asian, non-Hispanic/Latino; 1 Two or more races, non-Hispanic/Latino), 14 international. Average age 32. 131 applicants, 100% accepted, 131 enrolled. In 2017, 80 master's, 35 other advanced degrees awarded. *Degree requirements:* For master's and Ed S, comprehensive exam, thesis or alternative, paper; for doctorate, comprehensive exam, thesis/dissertation. *Entrance requirements:* For master's, minimum GPA of 3.5; for doctorate, minimum GPA of 3.7. Additional exam requirements/recommendations for international students: Required—TOEFL (minimum score 550 paper-based; 79 iBT), IELTS (minimum score 6), PTE (minimum score 53). *Application deadline:* For fall admission, 8/1 for domestic students, 6/1 for international students; for spring admission, 11/21 for domestic students, 10/1 for international students; for summer admission, 5/15 for domestic students. Applications are processed on a rolling basis. Application fee: $270.35 per credit hour in-state tuition, $33.40 per credit hour fees. *Financial support:* In 2017–18, 28 students received support. Career-related internships or fieldwork, Federal Work-Study, scholarships/grants, traineeships, tuition waivers (full), and unspecified assistantships available. Financial award application deadline: 6/30; financial award applicants required to submit FAFSA. *Faculty research:* Mental health counseling; technology in the classroom; administration and student success; school counseling; social justice in leadership and higher education; career counseling; leadership, equity, and social justice in P-12 schools and higher education; gender identity and queer youth; building level and district level leadership; school culture and climate; higher education; equity and social justice; organizational analysis and program planning; global leadership. *Unit head:* Dr. C. P. Gause, Professor/Department Chair, 573-651-2137, Fax: 573-986-6512, E-mail: cgause@semo.edu.
Website: http://www.semo.edu/eduleadcounsel/

Southeast Missouri State University, School of Graduate Studies, Department of Elementary, Early and Special Education, Program in Elementary Education, Cape Girardeau, MO 63701-4799. Offers MA. *Accreditation:* NCATE. *Program availability:* Part-time, evening/weekend, online only, 100% online. *Faculty:* 11 full-time (9 women), 1 (woman) part-time/adjunct. *Students:* 51 part-time (47 women); includes 1 minority (Hispanic/Latino). Average age 32. 14 applicants, 100% accepted, 14 enrolled. In 2017, 14 master's awarded. *Degree requirements:* For master's, comprehensive exam, action research project and presentation. *Entrance requirements:* For master's, state licensure exam or GRE, minimum GPA of 2.75; teaching certificate. Additional exam requirements/recommendations for international students: Required—TOEFL (minimum score 95 iBT), IELTS (minimum score 7), PTE. *Application deadline:* For fall admission, 8/1 for domestic students, 6/1 for international students; for spring admission, 11/21 for domestic students, 10/1 for international students; for summer admission, 5/15 for domestic students. Applications are processed on a rolling basis. Application fee: $30 ($40 for international students). Electronic applications accepted. *Expenses:* $270.35 per credit hour in-state tuition, $33.40 per credit hour fees. *Financial support:* In 2017–18, 3 students received support. Career-related internships or fieldwork, Federal Work-Study, scholarships/grants, traineeships, tuition waivers (full), and unspecified assistantships available. Financial award application deadline: 6/30; financial award applicants required to submit FAFSA. *Faculty research:* Instructional technology, field and clinical experiences, teacher candidate professional dispositions, family engagement in P-12 schools, learning communities. *Unit head:* Dr. Julie Ray, Department of Elementary, Early, and Special Education Chair/Professor, 573-651-2444, E-mail: jaray@semo.edu. *Application contact:* Dr. Min Zou, Assistant Professor, 573-651-2122, E-mail: mzou@semo.edu.
Website: http://www.semo.edu/eese/

Southern Connecticut State University, School of Graduate Studies, School of Education, Department of Elementary Education, New Haven, CT 06515-1355. Offers classroom teacher specialist (Diploma); educational coach (Diploma); elementary education (MS). *Accreditation:* NCATE. *Program availability:* Part-time, evening/weekend. *Degree requirements:* For master's, thesis or alternative. *Entrance requirements:* For master's, interview, minimum QPA of 2.5; for Diploma, master's degree. Electronic applications accepted.

Southern New Hampshire University, School of Education, Manchester, NH 03106-1045. Offers curriculum and instruction (M Ed), including dyslexia studies and language-based learning disabilities, educational leadership, reading, special education, technology integration; dyslexia studies and language-based learning disabilities (Certificate); early childhood and special education (M Ed); educational leadership (M Ed, Ed D); educational studies (M Ed); elementary and special education (M Ed); field based education (M Ed); higher education administration (MS); teaching English as a foreign. language (MS). *Program availability:* Part-time, evening/weekend, online learning. *Degree requirements:*

For master's, comprehensive exam (for some programs), thesis or alternative. *Entrance requirements:* For master's, PRAXIS I, minimum GPA of 2.75. Additional exam requirements/recommendations for international students: Required—TOEFL (minimum score 550 paper-based). *Application deadline:* Applications are processed on a rolling basis. Application fee: $40. Electronic applications accepted. *Expenses:* Contact institution. *Financial support:* Institutionally sponsored loans available. Financial award applicants required to submit FAFSA. *Unit head:* Raymond McNulty, Dean, 603-668-2211, Fax: 603-629-4673. *Application contact:* Office of Graduate Admission, 888-327-SNHU, Fax: 603-644-3144, E-mail: enroll@snhu.edu.

Southern Oregon University, Graduate Studies, School of Education, Ashland, OR 97520. Offers elementary education (MA Ed, MS Ed), including classroom teacher, early childhood, handicapped learner, reading, supervision; secondary education (MA Ed, MS Ed), including classroom teacher, handicapped learner, reading, supervision; teaching (MAT). *Program availability:* Online learning. *Degree requirements:* For master's, thesis optional. *Entrance requirements:* For master's, GRE General Test, minimum cumulative GPA of 3.0 in the last 90 quarter credits (60 semester credits) of undergraduate coursework. Additional exam requirements/recommendations for international students: Required—TOEFL (minimum score 540 paper-based; 76 iBT), IELTS (minimum score 6), ELPT (minimum score 964) or ELS (minimum score 112). Electronic applications accepted.

Southern University and Agricultural and Mechanical College, Graduate School, College of Education, Department of Curriculum and Instruction, Baton Rouge, LA 70813. Offers elementary education (M Ed); media (M Ed); secondary education (M Ed). *Degree requirements:* For master's, comprehensive exam, thesis optional. *Entrance requirements:* For master's, GMAT or GRE General Test. Additional exam requirements/recommendations for international students: Required—TOEFL (minimum score 525 paper-based).

Southwestern College, Education Programs, Winfield, KS 67156-2499. Offers curriculum and instruction (M Ed); early childhood education (M Ed); educational leadership (Ed D), including higher education leadership, PK-12 education leadership; special education (M Ed), including high-incidence disabilities, low-incidence disabilities; teaching (MA). *Accreditation:* NCATE. *Program availability:* Part-time, evening/weekend, 100% online, blended/hybrid learning. *Faculty:* 6 full-time (5 women), 12 part-time/adjunct (10 women). *Students:* 12 full-time (10 women), 77 part-time (51 women); includes 12 minority (5 Black or African American, non-Hispanic/Latino; 2 American Indian or Alaska Native, non-Hispanic/Latino; 1 Asian, non-Hispanic/Latino; 3 Hispanic/Latino; 1 Native Hawaiian or other Pacific Islander, non-Hispanic/Latino), 10 international. Average age 39. 29 applicants, 86% accepted, 18 enrolled. In 2017, 52 master's, 11 doctorates awarded. *Degree requirements:* For master's, practicum, portfolio; for doctorate, thesis/dissertation, professional portfolio. *Entrance requirements:* For master's, baccalaureate degree, minimum GPA of 3.0, valid teaching certificate (for special education); for doctorate, GRE if no master's degree, baccalaureate degree with minimum GPA of 3.25 and current teaching experience, or master's degree with minimum GPA of 3.5. Additional exam requirements/recommendations for international students: Required—TOEFL (minimum score 550 paper-based; 80 iBT). *Application deadline:* Applications are processed on a rolling basis. Application fee: $40. Electronic applications accepted. *Expenses:* $577 per credit hour, $509 online (for master's programs); $609 per credit hour (for doctorate program). *Financial support:* In 2017–18, 9 students received support. Unspecified assistantships and employee tuition waivers available. Financial award applicants required to submit FAFSA. *Unit head:* Dana Pentz, Director of Education Operations, 620-229-6253, E-mail: dana.pentz@sckans.edu. *Application contact:* Dennis Russell, Director of Admissions and Student Services, 888-684-5335 Ext. 3372, Fax: 888-684-5218, E-mail: dennis.russell@sckans.edu.
Website: http://www.sckans.edu/graduate/education-med/

Southwestern Oklahoma State University, College of Professional and Graduate Studies, School of Behavioral Sciences and Education, Specialization in Elementary Education, Weatherford, OK 73096-3098. Offers M Ed. M Ed distance learning degree program offered to Oklahoma residents only. *Accreditation:* NCATE. *Program availability:* Part-time, evening/weekend. *Degree requirements:* For master's, exam. *Entrance requirements:* For master's, GRE General Test or minimum undergraduate GPA of 3.0. Additional exam requirements/recommendations for international students: Required—TOEFL.

Spalding University, Graduate Studies, College of Education, Programs in Education, Louisville, KY 40203-2188. Offers art teacher education (MAT); business teacher education (MAT); elementary school education (MAT); foreign language (MAT); high school education (MAT); middle school education (MAT); secondary education (MAT); special education (learning and behavioral disorders) (MAT); student guidance counselor (MA); teacher leader (M Ed). *Accreditation:* NCATE. *Program availability:* Part-time, evening/weekend. *Entrance requirements:* For master's, GRE General Test or MAT, interview, letters of recommendation, resume. Additional exam requirements/recommendations for international students: Required—TOEFL (minimum score 535 paper-based). Electronic applications accepted. *Faculty research:* Instructional technology, achievement gap, classroom management, assessment.

Springfield College, Graduate Programs, Programs in Education, Springfield, MA 01109-3797. Offers early childhood education (M Ed); educational studies (M Ed); elementary education (M Ed); secondary education (M Ed); special education (M Ed, CAGS). *Program availability:* Part-time, evening/weekend. *Students:* 18 applicants, 72% accepted, 12 enrolled. In 2017, 22 master's awarded. *Entrance requirements:* For master's, Massachusetts Tests for Educator Licensure (MTEL). Additional exam requirements/recommendations for international students: Required—TOEFL (minimum score 550 paper-based); Recommended—IELTS (minimum score 7). *Application deadline:* For fall admission, 1/15 for domestic and international students; for winter admission, 11/1 for domestic and international students; for spring admission, 11/1 for domestic and international students. Applications are processed on a rolling basis. Application fee: $50. Electronic applications accepted. *Expenses:* Contact institution. *Financial support:* Fellowships with partial tuition reimbursements, teaching assistantships with partial tuition reimbursements, career-related internships or fieldwork, Federal Work-Study, institutionally sponsored loans, scholarships/grants, and unspecified assistantships available. Financial award application deadline: 3/1; financial award applicants required to submit FAFSA. *Unit head:* Linda Davis-Delano, Director of Education Preparation and Licensure, 413-748-3295, E-mail: ldelano@springfield.edu. *Application contact:* Anne Griffin, Director of Graduate Admissions, 413-748-3225, Fax: 413-748-3694, E-mail: agriffin2@springfield.edu.
Website: http://springfield.edu/wtp

Spring Hill College, Graduate Programs, Program in Education, Mobile, AL 36608-1791. Offers early childhood education (MAT, MS Ed); educational theory (MS Ed); elementary education (MAT, MS Ed); secondary education (MAT, MS Ed). *Program availability:* Part-time. *Faculty:* 2 full-time (both women). *Students:* 15 part-time (14 women); includes 6 minority (5 Black or African American, non-Hispanic/Latino; 1 Hispanic/Latino). Average age 30. In 2017, 5 master's awarded. *Degree requirements:* For master's, comprehensive exam, completion of program within 6 calendar years of entrance into graduate studies at Spring Hill; documentation of course field assignments (MS) or completion of internship (MAT). *Entrance requirements:* For master's, GRE,

MAT, or PRAXIS (varies by program), bachelor's degree with minimum undergraduate GPA of 3.0; class B certificate (for MS); minimum number of hours in specific fields (for MAT). Additional exam requirements/recommendations for international students: Required—TOEFL (minimum score 550 paper-based; 80 iBT), IELTS (minimum score 6.5), CPE or CAE (minimum score C), Michigan English Language Assessment Battery (minimum score 90). *Application deadline:* For fall admission, 8/1 priority date for domestic and international students; for spring admission, 12/1 priority date for domestic and international students. Applications are processed on a rolling basis. Application fee: $25 ($35 for international students). Electronic applications accepted. *Expenses:* Contact institution. *Financial support:* Applicants required to submit FAFSA. *Unit head:* Dr. Lori P. Aultman, Chair of Education, 251-380-3473, Fax: 251-460-2184, E-mail: laultman@shc.edu. *Application contact:* Robert Stewart, Vice President of Enrollment, 251-380-3030, Fax: 251-460-2186, E-mail: rstewart@shc.edu. Website: http://ug.shc.edu/graduate-degrees/master-science-education/

Stanford University, Graduate School of Education, Teacher Education Program, Stanford, CA 94305-2004. Offers elementary education (MAE); secondary education (MAE). *Degree requirements:* For master's, thesis. *Entrance requirements:* For master's, GRE General Test. Electronic applications accepted. *Expenses: Tuition:* Full-time $48,987; part-time $10,620 per quarter. One-time fee: $400. Tuition and fees vary according to program.

State University of New York at New Paltz, Graduate and Extended Learning School, School of Education, Program in Early Childhood and Childhood Education, New Paltz, NY 12561. Offers childhood education 1-6 (MS Ed, MST), including childhood education 1-6 (MST), early childhood B-2 (MS Ed). *Accreditation:* NCATE. *Program availability:* Part-time, evening/weekend. *Faculty:* 12 full-time (9 women), 4 part-time/adjunct (3 women). *Students:* 44 full-time (40 women), 63 part-time (56 women); includes 16 minority (4 Black or African American, non-Hispanic/Latino; 10 Hispanic/Latino; 2 Two or more races, non-Hispanic/Latino). 48 applicants, 75% accepted, 34 enrolled. In 2017, 56 master's awarded. *Degree requirements:* For master's, comprehensive exam (for some programs), portfolio. *Entrance requirements:* For master's, GRE or MAT (for MST), minimum GPA of 3.0 (3.2 for literacy and special education), New York state teaching certificate (for MS Ed). Additional exam requirements/recommendations for international students: Required—TOEFL (minimum score 550 paper-based; 80 iBT), IELTS (minimum score 6.5). *Application deadline:* For fall admission, 4/1 for domestic and international students; for spring admission, 11/1 priority date for domestic and international students; for summer admission, 4/15 priority date for domestic and international students. Applications are processed on a rolling basis. Application fee: $50. Electronic applications accepted. *Financial support:* Application deadline: 8/1. *Faculty research:* Multi-sensory teaching methods, volunteer tutoring programs for struggling readers, school readiness and transition, math/science/technology, university-school partnerships. *Unit head:* Dr. Aaron Isabelle, Chair, 845-257-2837, E-mail: isabella@newpaltz.edu. *Application contact:* Vika Shock, Assistant Director of Graduate Admissions, 845-257-3285, Fax: 845-257-3284, E-mail: gradschool@newpaltz.edu. Website: http://www.newpaltz.edu/elementaryed/

State University of New York at Oswego, Graduate Studies, School of Education, Department of Curriculum and Instruction, Oswego, NY 13126. Offers adolescence education (MST); art education (MAT); childhood education (MST); curriculum and instruction (MS Ed); literacy education (MS Ed); special education (MS Ed). *Program availability:* Part-time, evening/weekend. *Degree requirements:* For master's, comprehensive exam (for some programs), thesis optional. *Entrance requirements:* For master's, GRE General Test, minimum GPA of 2.7, provisional teaching certificate. Additional exam requirements/recommendations for international students: Required—TOEFL (minimum score 560 paper-based). *Faculty research:* Classroom applications for microcomputers; classroom questioning, wait-time, and achievement; values clarification and academic achievement.

State University of New York at Plattsburgh, School of Education, Health, and Human Services, Program in Early Childhood Education, Plattsburgh, NY 12901-2681. Offers early childhood birth-grade 6 (Advanced Certificate).

State University of New York at Plattsburgh, School of Education, Health, and Human Services, Program in Teacher Education: Adolescence Education, Plattsburgh, NY 12901-2681. Offers adolescence education (MST); biology 7-12 (MST); chemistry 7-12 (MST); earth science 7-12 (MST); English 7-12 (MST); French 7-12 (MST); mathematics 7-12 (MST); physics 7-12 (MST); social studies 7-12 (MST); Spanish 7-12 (MST). *Accreditation:* TEAC. *Program availability:* Part-time, evening/weekend. *Entrance requirements:* For master's, minimum GPA of 2.75. Additional exam requirements/recommendations for international students: Required—TOEFL.

State University of New York at Plattsburgh, School of Education, Health, and Human Services, Program in Teacher Education: Childhood Education, Plattsburgh, NY 12901-2681. Offers childhood education (grades 1-6) (MST). *Accreditation:* TEAC. *Program availability:* Part-time, evening/weekend. *Entrance requirements:* For master's, minimum GPA of 2.75. Additional exam requirements/recommendations for international students: Required—TOEFL.

State University of New York College at Oneonta, Graduate Programs, Division of Education, Department of Elementary Education and Reading, Oneonta, NY 13820-4015. Offers childhood education (MS Ed); literacy education (MS Ed). *Accreditation:* NCATE. *Program availability:* Part-time, evening/weekend. *Entrance requirements:* For master's, GRE General Test.

State University of New York College at Potsdam, School of Education and Professional Studies, Program in Curriculum and Instruction, Potsdam, NY 13676. Offers childhood education (MST); curriculum and instruction (MS Ed). *Accreditation:* NCATE. *Program availability:* Online learning. *Degree requirements:* For master's, thesis (for some programs). *Entrance requirements:* For master's, minimum GPA of 2.75 in last 60 credit hours of undergraduate study. Additional exam requirements/recommendations for international students: Required—TOEFL (minimum score 550 paper-based; 80 iBT), IELTS (minimum score 6). Electronic applications accepted.

State University of New York College at Potsdam, School of Education and Professional Studies, Program in Special Education, Potsdam, NY 13676. Offers adolescence (grades 7-12) (MS Ed); childhood (grades 1-6) (MS Ed); early childhood (birth-grade 2) (MS Ed). *Accreditation:* NCATE. *Program availability:* Part-time. *Degree requirements:* For master's, culminating experience. *Entrance requirements:* For master's, minimum GPA of 3.0 in last 60 hours of course work. Additional exam requirements/recommendations for international students: Required—TOEFL (minimum score 550 paper-based; 80 iBT), IELTS (minimum score 6). Electronic applications accepted.

Stephen F. Austin State University, Graduate School, College of Education, Department of Elementary Education, Program in Elementary Education, Nacogdoches, TX 75962. Offers M Ed. *Accreditation:* NCATE. *Degree requirements:* For master's, comprehensive exam. *Entrance requirements:* For master's, GRE General Test. Additional exam requirements/recommendations for international students: Required—TOEFL.

Sul Ross State University, Rio Grande College of Sul Ross State University, Alpine, TX 79832. Offers business administration (MBA); teacher education (M Ed), including bilingual education, counseling, educational diagnostics, elementary education, general

education, reading, school administration, secondary education. *Program availability:* Part-time, evening/weekend, online learning. *Degree requirements:* For master's, comprehensive exam, thesis optional, minimum GPA of 3.0. *Entrance requirements:* For master's, GMAT or GRE General Test, minimum GPA of 2.5 in last 60 hours of undergraduate work. Additional exam requirements/recommendations for international students: Required—TOEFL.

Tarleton State University, College of Graduate Studies, College of Education, Department of Curriculum and Instruction, Stephenville, TX 76402. Offers curriculum and instruction (M Ed); educational diagnostician (M Ed); elementary education (M Ed); instructional design and technology (M Ed); instructional leadership (M Ed); secondary education (M Ed); special education (M Ed); technology applications (M Ed); technology director (M Ed). *Program availability:* Part-time, evening/weekend. *Faculty:* 7 full-time (5 women), 4 part-time/adjunct (2 women). *Students:* 7 full-time (6 women), 156 part-time (137 women); includes 40 minority (11 Black or African American, non-Hispanic/Latino; 25 Hispanic/Latino; 4 Two or more races, non-Hispanic/Latino). Average age 38. 55 applicants, 96% accepted, 46 enrolled. In 2017, 33 master's awarded. *Degree requirements:* For master's, comprehensive exam, thesis (for some programs). *Entrance requirements:* For master's, GRE General Test, minimum GPA of 3.0. Additional exam requirements/recommendations for international students: Required—TOEFL (minimum score 550 paper-based; 80 iBT), IELTS (minimum score 6). *Application deadline:* For fall admission, 8/15 priority date for domestic students; for spring admission, 1/7 for domestic students. Applications are processed on a rolling basis. Application fee: $45 ($145 for international students). Electronic applications accepted. *Expenses:* Contact institution. *Financial support:* Research assistantships, teaching assistantships, career-related internships or fieldwork, Federal Work-Study, and institutionally sponsored loans available. Support available to part-time students. Financial award application deadline: 5/1; financial award applicants required to submit FAFSA. *Unit head:* Dr. Jordan Barkley, Dean, 254-968-9099, E-mail: jbarkley@tarleton.edu. *Application contact:* Information Contact, 254-968-9104, Fax: 254-968-9670, E-mail: gradoffice@tarleton.edu. Website: http://www.tarleton.edu/cimasters/

Teachers College, Columbia University, Department of Curriculum and Teaching, New York, NY 10027-6696. Offers curriculum and teaching (Ed M, MA, Ed D); curriculum and teaching: elementary education (MA); curriculum and teaching: secondary education (MA); early childhood education (MA, Ed D); early childhood education: special education (MA); elementary education-gifted extension (MA); elementary inclusive education (MA); gifted education (MA); literacy specialist (MA); secondary inclusive education (MA); special inclusive elementary education (MA). *Program availability:* Part-time, evening/weekend. *Students:* 196 full-time (181 women), 181 part-time (161 women); includes 141 minority (45 Black or African American, non-Hispanic/Latino; 2 American Indian or Alaska Native, non-Hispanic/Latino; 45 Asian, non-Hispanic/Latino; 35 Hispanic/Latino; 14 Two or more races, non-Hispanic/Latino), 37 international. Average age 30. 509 applicants, 72% accepted, 155 enrolled. Terminal master's awarded for partial completion of doctoral program. *Degree requirements:* For doctorate, thesis/dissertation. *Unit head:* Prof. Daniel Friedrich, Chair, E-mail: friedrich@exchange.tc.columbia.edu. *Application contact:* David Estrella, Director of Admission, 212-678-3305, Fax: 212-678-4171, E-mail: estrella@tc.columbia.edu.

Tennessee State University, The School of Graduate Studies and Research, College of Education, Department of Teaching and Learning, Nashville, TN 37209-1561. Offers curriculum and instruction (M Ed, Ed D); elementary education (M Ed); special education (M Ed). *Accreditation:* NCATE. *Degree requirements:* For doctorate, thesis/dissertation. *Entrance requirements:* For master's, GRE General Test, GRE Subject Test, or MAT, minimum GPA of 2.5; for doctorate, GRE General Test, GRE Subject Test, or MAT, minimum GPA of 3.25. Electronic applications accepted. *Faculty research:* Multicultural education, teacher education reform, whole language, interactive video teaching, English as a second language.

Tennessee Technological University, College of Graduate Studies, College of Education, Department of Curriculum and Instruction, Program in Elementary Education, Cookeville, TN 38505. Offers MA and Ed S. *Accreditation:* NCATE. *Program availability:* Part-time, evening/weekend. *Faculty:* 8 full-time (2 women). *Students:* 8 full-time (all women), 13 part-time (11 women); includes 1 minority (Black or African American, non-Hispanic/Latino). 6 applicants, 67% accepted, 3 enrolled. In 2017, 6 master's awarded. *Degree requirements:* For master's and Ed S, comprehensive exam, thesis or alternative. *Entrance requirements:* For master's and Ed S, MAT or GRE. Additional exam requirements/recommendations for international students: Required—TOEFL (minimum score 527 paper-based; 71 iBT), IELTS (minimum score 5.5), PTE (minimum score 48), or TOEIC (Test of English as an International Communication). *Application deadline:* For fall admission, 8/1 for domestic students, 5/1 for international students; for spring admission, 12/1 for domestic students, 10/1 for international students; for summer admission, 5/1 for domestic students, 2/1 for international students. Applications are processed on a rolling basis. Application fee: $35 ($40 for international students). Electronic applications accepted. *Expenses:* Tuition, state resident: full-time $9925; part-time $565 per credit hour. Tuition, nonresident: full-time $22,993; part-time $1291 per credit hour. *Financial support:* Fellowships, research assistantships, teaching assistantships, and career-related internships or fieldwork available. Financial award application deadline: 4/1. *Faculty research:* Educational television art program. *Unit head:* Dr. Jeremy Wendt, Interim Chairperson, 931-372-3181, Fax: 931-372-6270, E-mail: jwendt@tntech.edu. *Application contact:* Shelia K. Kendrick, Coordinator of Graduate Studies, 931-372-3808, Fax: 931-372-3497, E-mail: skendrick@tntech.edu.

Tennessee Technological University, College of Graduate Studies, College of Education, Department of Exercise Science, Physical Education and Wellness, Cookeville, TN 38505. Offers adapted physical education (MA); elementary/middle school physical education (MA); lifetime wellness (MA); sport management (MA). *Accreditation:* NCATE. *Program availability:* Part-time, online learning. *Faculty:* 7 full-time (0 women). *Students:* 17 full-time (8 women), 34 part-time (14 women); includes 10 minority (5 Black or African American, non-Hispanic/Latino; 1 Asian, non-Hispanic/Latino; 2 Hispanic/Latino; 2 Two or more races, non-Hispanic/Latino). 35 applicants, 71% accepted, 23 enrolled. In 2017, 28 master's awarded. *Degree requirements:* For master's, comprehensive exam, thesis or alternative. *Entrance requirements:* For master's, MAT or GRE. Additional exam requirements/recommendations for international students: Required—TOEFL (minimum score 527 paper-based; 71 iBT), IELTS (minimum score 5.5), PTE (minimum score 48), or TOEIC (Test of English as an International Communication). *Application deadline:* For fall admission, 8/1 for domestic students, 5/1 for international students; for spring admission, 12/1 for domestic students, 10/1 for international students; for summer admission, 5/1 for domestic students, 2/1 for international students. Applications are processed on a rolling basis. Application fee: $35 ($40 for international students). Electronic applications accepted. *Expenses:* Tuition, state resident: full-time $9925; part-time $565 per credit hour. Tuition, nonresident: full-time $22,993; part-time $1291 per credit hour. *Financial support:* Fellowships, research assistantships, teaching assistantships, and career-related internships or fieldwork available. Financial award application deadline: 4/1. *Unit head:* Dr. Christy Killman, Chairperson, 931-372-3467, Fax: 931-372-6319, E-mail: ckillman@tntech.edu. *Application contact:* Shelia K. Kendrick, Coordinator of Graduate Studies, 931-372-3808, Fax: 931-372-3497, E-mail: skendrick@tntech.edu.

Elementary Education

Texas A&M University–Commerce, College of Education and Human Services, Commerce, TX 75429. Offers counseling (M Ed, MS, PhD); early childhood education (M Ed, MS); educational administration (M Ed, MS, Ed D); educational psychology (PhD); educational technology leadership (M Ed, MS); educational technology library science (M Ed, MS); elementary education (M Ed); health, kinesiology and sports studies (MS); higher education (MS, Ed D); psychology (MS); reading (M Ed, MS); secondary education (M Ed, MS); social work (MSW); special education (M Ed, MS); supervision, curriculum and instruction-elementary education (Ed D); training and development (MS). *Program availability:* Part-time, evening/weekend, 100% online, blended/hybrid learning. *Faculty:* 91 full-time (51 women), 38 part-time/adjunct (31 women). *Students:* 400 full-time (310 women), 1,400 part-time (1,117 women); includes 724 minority (412 Black or African American, non-Hispanic/Latino; 8 American Indian or Alaska Native, non-Hispanic/Latino; 24 Asian, non-Hispanic/Latino; 220 Hispanic/Latino; 60 Two or more races, non-Hispanic/Latino), 18 international. Average age 37. 951 applicants, 46% accepted, 331 enrolled. In 2017, 564 master's, 24 doctorates awarded. *Degree requirements:* For master's, comprehensive exam, thesis optional, departmental qualifying exams (for some programs); for doctorate, comprehensive exam, thesis/dissertation, departmental qualifying exam; for SSP, comprehensive exam, thesis optional. *Entrance requirements:* For master's and doctorate, GRE General Test. Additional exam requirements/recommendations for international students: Required—TOEFL (minimum score 550 paper-based; 79 iBT), IELTS (minimum score 6). *Application deadline:* For fall admission, 6/1 priority date for international students; for spring admission, 10/15 priority date for international students; for summer admission, 3/15 priority date for international students. Applications are processed on a rolling basis. Application fee: $50. Electronic applications accepted. *Expenses:* Tuition, state resident: full-time $3630. Tuition, nonresident: full-time $11,100. *Required fees:* $2564. Tuition and fees vary according to course load, degree level and program. *Financial support:* In 2017–18, 84 students received support, including 40 research assistantships with partial tuition reimbursements available (averaging $10,800 per year), 12 teaching assistantships with partial tuition reimbursements available (averaging $13,000 per year); career-related internships or fieldwork, Federal Work-Study, institutionally sponsored loans, scholarships/grants, health care benefits, and unspecified assistantships also available. Financial award application deadline: 6/15; financial award applicants required to submit FAFSA. *Faculty research:* Cognitive and bilingual education, positive behavioral intervention, literacy, math readiness. *Total annual research expenditures:* $1.1 million. *Unit head:* Dr. Timothy Letzring, Dean, 903-886-5181, Fax: 903-886-5905, E-mail: tim.letzring@tamuc.edu. *Application contact:* Vicky Turner, Doctoral Degree and Special Programs Coordinator, 903-886-5167, E-mail: vicky.turner@tamuc.edu.
Website: http://www.tamuc.edu/academics/graduateSchool/programs/education/default.aspx

Texas A&M University–Commerce, College of Humanities, Social Sciences and Arts, Commerce, TX 75429. Offers applied criminology (MS); applied linguistics (MA, MS); art (MA, MFA); computational linguistics (Graduate Certificate); creative writing (Graduate Certificate); criminal justice management (Graduate Certificate); criminal justice studies (Graduate Certificate); English (MA, MS, PhD); film studies (Graduate Certificate); history (MA, MS); history of Christianity (Graduate Certificate); Holocaust studies (Graduate Certificate); homeland security (Graduate Certificate); music education (MM); music performance (MM); political science (MA, MS); public history (Graduate Certificate); sociology (MS); Spanish (MA); studies in children's and adolescent literature and culture (Graduate Certificate); teaching English to speakers of other languages (Graduate Certificate); theater (MA, MS); world history (Graduate Certificate). *Program availability:* Part-time. *Faculty:* 56 full-time (26 women), 10 part-time/adjunct (5 women). *Students:* 133 full-time (85 women), 439 part-time (311 women); includes 204 minority (79 Black or African American, non-Hispanic/Latino; 4 American Indian or Alaska Native, non-Hispanic/Latino; 9 Asian, non-Hispanic/Latino; 98 Hispanic/Latino; 14 Two or more races, non-Hispanic/Latino), 26 international. Average age 36. 261 applicants, 50% accepted, 113 enrolled. In 2017, 105 master's, 5 doctorates awarded. *Degree requirements:* For master's, one foreign language, comprehensive exam, thesis (for some programs); for doctorate, one foreign language, comprehensive exam, thesis/dissertation, departmental qualifying exam. *Entrance requirements:* For master's and doctorate, GRE General Test. Additional exam requirements/recommendations for international students: Required—TOEFL (minimum score 550 paper-based; 79 iBT), IELTS (minimum score 6). *Application deadline:* Applications are processed on a rolling basis. Application fee: $50. Electronic applications accepted. *Expenses:* Contact institution. *Financial support:* In 2017–18, 43 students received support, including 9 research assistantships with partial tuition reimbursements available (averaging $9,000 per year), 68 teaching assistantships with partial tuition reimbursements available (averaging $9,000 per year); Federal Work-Study, institutionally sponsored loans, scholarships/grants, health care benefits, and unspecified assistantships also available. Financial award application deadline: 5/1; financial award applicants required to submit FAFSA. *Unit head:* Dr. William F. Kuracina, Interim Dean, 903-886-5166, Fax: 903-886-5774, E-mail: william.kuracina@tamuc.edu. *Application contact:* Vicky Turner, Doctoral Degree and Special Programs Coordinator, 903-886-5167, E-mail: vicky.turner@tamuc.edu.
Website: http://www.tamuc.edu/academics/graduateSchool/programs/humanitiesSocialScienceArts/default.aspx

Texas A&M University–Corpus Christi, College of Graduate Studies, College of Education and Human Development, Program in Elementary Education, Corpus Christi, TX 78412. Offers MS. *Program availability:* Part-time, evening/weekend, online learning. *Students:* 8 full-time (7 women), 16 part-time (13 women); includes 23 minority (1 Black or African American, non-Hispanic/Latino; 22 Hispanic/Latino). Average age 33. 22 applicants, 45% accepted, 8 enrolled. In 2017, 9 master's awarded. *Degree requirements:* For master's, comprehensive exam, capstone experience. *Entrance requirements:* For master's, minimum GPA of 3.0 in last 60 hours. Additional exam requirements/recommendations for international students: Required—TOEFL (minimum score 550 paper-based; 79 iBT), IELTS (minimum score 6.5). *Application deadline:* For fall admission, 8/19 priority date for domestic students, 7/26 priority date for international students; for spring admission, 1/13 priority date for domestic students, 12/20 priority date for international students; for summer admission, 5/25 priority date for domestic students, 5/1 priority date for international students. Applications are processed on a rolling basis. Application fee: $50 ($70 for international students). Electronic applications accepted. *Expenses:* Tuition, state resident: full-time $3568; part-time $198.24 per credit hour. Tuition, nonresident: full-time $11,038; part-time $613.24 per credit hour. *Required fees:* $2129; $1422.58 per semester. Tuition and fees vary according to program. *Financial support:* Research assistantships, teaching assistantships, career-related internships or fieldwork, Federal Work-Study, institutionally sponsored loans, scholarships/grants, health care benefits, and unspecified assistantships available. Support available to part-time students. Financial award application deadline: 3/15; financial award applicants required to submit FAFSA. *Unit head:* Dr. Carmen Tejeda-Delgado, Associate Professor/Chair, 361-825-2860, E-mail: carmen.tejeda-delgado@tamucc.edu. *Application contact:* Graduate Admissions Coordinator, 361-825-2177, Fax: 361-825-2755, E-mail: gradweb@tamucc.edu.
Website: http://macprogram.tamucc.edu/

Texas State University, The Graduate College, College of Education, Program in Elementary Education, San Marcos, TX 78666. Offers M Ed, MA. *Program availability:* Part-time, evening/weekend. *Faculty:* 12 full-time (8 women), 9 part-time/adjunct (8 women). *Students:* 70 full-time (62 women), 73 part-time (68 women); includes 62 minority (16 Black or African American, non-Hispanic/Latino; 9 Asian, non-Hispanic/Latino; 34 Hispanic/Latino; 3 Two or more races, non-Hispanic/Latino), 4 international. Average age 31. 72 applicants, 69% accepted, 25 enrolled. In 2017, 82 master's awarded. *Degree requirements:* For master's, comprehensive exam, thesis (for some programs). *Entrance requirements:* For master's, baccalaureate degree from regionally-accredited institution with minimum GPA of 2.75 in last 60 hours of course work. Additional exam requirements/recommendations for international students: Required—TOEFL (minimum score 550 paper-based; 78 iBT), IELTS (minimum score 6.5), TOEFL (minimum iBT scores: 22 listening, 22 reading, 24 speaking, 21 writing). *Application deadline:* For fall admission, 2/15 priority date for domestic and international students; for spring admission, 10/15 for domestic students, 10/1 for international students; for summer admission, 4/15 for domestic students, 3/15 for international students. Applications are processed on a rolling basis. Application fee: $40 ($90 for international students). Electronic applications accepted. *Expenses:* Tuition, state resident: full-time $7868; part-time $3934 per semester. Tuition, nonresident: full-time $17,828; part-time $8914 per semester. *Required fees:* $2092; $1435 per semester. Tuition and fees vary according to course load. *Financial support:* In 2017–18, 88 students received support, including 1 research assistantship (averaging $12,150 per year), 18 teaching assistantships (averaging $17,350 per year); career-related internships or fieldwork, Federal Work-Study, institutionally sponsored loans, scholarships/grants, and unspecified assistantships also available. Support available to part-time students. Financial award application deadline: 3/1; financial award applicants required to submit FAFSA. *Faculty research:* Latin America: a region of human and physical contrast. *Total annual research expenditures:* $1,303. *Unit head:* Dr. Cheryll Dennis, Graduate Advisor, 512-716-4533, Fax: 512-245-7911, E-mail: elemedgrad@txstate.edu. *Application contact:* Dr. Andrea Golato, Dean of Graduate School, 512-245-2581, Fax: 512-245-8365, E-mail: gradcollege@txstate.edu.
Website: http://www.education.txstate.edu/ci/degrees-programs/graduate/elementary-education.html

Texas State University, The Graduate College, College of Education, Program in Elementary Education - Bilingual/Bicultural, San Marcos, TX 78666. Offers M Ed, MA. *Program availability:* Part-time. *Faculty:* 4 full-time (2 women), 2 part-time/adjunct (both women). *Students:* 3 full-time (2 women), 3 part-time (all women); includes 5 minority (all Hispanic/Latino), 1 international. Average age 36. 6 applicants, 67% accepted, 2 enrolled. In 2017, 7 master's awarded. *Degree requirements:* For master's, comprehensive exam, thesis (for some programs). *Entrance requirements:* For master's, baccalaureate degree from regionally-accredited institution with minimum GPA of 2.75 in last 60 hours of course work; meeting with bilingual coordinator to ensure proficiency in written and spoken Spanish; statement of purpose; three letters of recommendation. Additional exam requirements/recommendations for international students: Required—TOEFL (minimum score 550 paper-based; 78 iBT), IELTS (minimum score 6.5). *Application deadline:* For fall admission, 2/15 priority date for domestic and international students; for spring admission, 10/15 for domestic students, 10/1 for international students; for summer admission, 4/15 for domestic students, 3/15 for international students. Applications are processed on a rolling basis. Application fee: $40 ($90 for international students). Electronic applications accepted. *Expenses:* Tuition, state resident: full-time $7868; part-time $3934 per semester. Tuition, nonresident: full-time $17,828; part-time $8914 per semester. *Required fees:* $2092; $1435 per semester. Tuition and fees vary according to course load. *Financial support:* In 2017–18, 5 students received support. Research assistantships, teaching assistantships, career-related internships or fieldwork, Federal Work-Study, institutionally sponsored loans, scholarships/grants, and unspecified assistantships available. Support available to part-time students. Financial award application deadline: 3/1; financial award applicants required to submit FAFSA. *Unit head:* Dr. Mary Esther Huerta, Graduate Advisor, 512-245-3099, Fax: 512-245-7911, E-mail: mh75@txstate.edu. *Application contact:* Dr. Andrea Golato, Dean of Graduate School, 512-245-2581, Fax: 512-245-8365, E-mail: gradcollege@txstate.edu.
Website: http://www.gradcollege.txstate.edu/programs/bilingual-bicultural.html

Texas State University, The Graduate College, College of Education, Program in Reading Education, San Marcos, TX 78666. Offers early childhood-12 reading specialist (M Ed). *Program availability:* Part-time, evening/weekend. *Faculty:* 10 full-time (9 women), 2 part-time/adjunct (1 woman). *Students:* 1 (woman) full-time, 24 part-time (23 women); includes 12 minority (all Hispanic/Latino). Average age 37. 4 applicants, 75% accepted. In 2017, 7 master's awarded. *Degree requirements:* For master's, comprehensive exam. *Entrance requirements:* For master's, baccalaureate degree from regionally-accredited institution with minimum GPA of 3.0 in last 60 hours of course work, statement of purpose, official teaching certificate. Additional exam requirements/recommendations for international students: Required—IELTS, TOEFL (minimum iBT scores: 22 listening, 22 reading, 24 speaking, 21 writing). *Application deadline:* For fall admission, 2/15 priority date for domestic and international students; for spring admission, 10/15 priority date for domestic students, 10/1 for international students; for summer admission, 4/15 for domestic students, 3/15 for international students. Applications are processed on a rolling basis. Application fee: $40 ($90 for international students). Electronic applications accepted. *Expenses:* Tuition, state resident: full-time $7868; part-time $3934 per semester. Tuition, nonresident: full-time $17,828; part-time $8914 per semester. *Required fees:* $2092; $1435 per semester. Tuition and fees vary according to course load. *Financial support:* In 2017–18, 15 students received support, including 1 research assistantship (averaging $12,152 per year); teaching assistantships, career-related internships or fieldwork, Federal Work-Study, institutionally sponsored loans, scholarships/grants, and unspecified assistantships also available. Support available to part-time students. Financial award application deadline: 3/1; financial award applicants required to submit FAFSA. *Faculty research:* Impact of developmental integrated reading and writing. *Total annual research expenditures:* $64,880. *Unit head:* Dr. Jane Saunders, Graduate Advisor, 512-245-1512, Fax: 512-245-8365, E-mail: js99@txstate.edu. *Application contact:* Dr. Andrea Golato, Dean of Graduate School, 512-245-2581, Fax: 512-245-8365, E-mail: gradcollege@txstate.edu.
Website: http://www.education.txstate.edu/ci/degrees-certifications/graduate/reading.html

Texas Tech University, Graduate School, College of Education, Department of Curriculum and Instruction, Lubbock, TX 79409. Offers bilingual education (M Ed); curriculum and instruction (M Ed); elementary education (M Ed); language/literacy education (M Ed); multidisciplinary science (MS); secondary education (M Ed). *Accreditation:* NCATE. *Program availability:* Part-time, evening/weekend, online learning. *Faculty:* 22 full-time (14 women), 2 part-time/adjunct (1 woman). *Students:* 64 full-time (50 women), 247 part-time (205 women); includes 100 minority (26 Black or African American, non-Hispanic/Latino; 1 American Indian or Alaska Native, non-Hispanic/Latino; 11 Asian, non-Hispanic/Latino; 54 Hispanic/Latino; 8 Two or more races, non-Hispanic/Latino), 39 international. Average age 39. 157 applicants, 56% accepted, 71 enrolled. In 2017, 20 master's, 21 doctorates awarded. Terminal master's awarded for partial completion of doctoral program. *Degree requirements:* For master's,

comprehensive exam (for some programs), thesis optional; for doctorate, comprehensive exam, thesis/dissertation. *Entrance requirements:* For master's, bachelor's degree; resume; letter of intent; academic writing sample; 2 letters of recommendation; for doctorate, GRE, master's degree; resume; letter of intent; academic writing sample; 3 letters of recommendation. Additional exam requirements/recommendations for international students: Required—TOEFL (minimum score 550 paper-based; 79 iBT). *Application deadline:* For fall admission, 6/1 priority date for domestic students, 1/15 priority date for international students; for spring admission, 9/1 priority date for domestic students, 6/15 priority date for international students. Applications are processed on a rolling basis. Application fee: $60. Electronic applications accepted. *Expenses:* Contact institution. *Financial support:* In 2017–18, 96 students received support, including 92 fellowships (averaging $3,321 per year), 37 research assistantships (averaging $12,336 per year); teaching assistantships, Federal Work-Study, institutionally sponsored loans, scholarships/grants, health care benefits, and unspecified assistantships also available. Support available to part-time students. Financial award application deadline: 2/1; financial award applicants required to submit FAFSA. *Faculty research:* Teacher education, curriculum studies, bilingual education, science and math education, language and literacy education. *Total annual research expenditures:* $107,999. *Unit head:* Dr. Fanni Liu Coward, Interim Chairperson, 806-834-4475, Fax: 806-742-2179, E-mail: fanni.coward@ttu.edu. *Application contact:* Brianna Sanchez, Coordinator, 806-834-2353, Fax: 806-742-2179, E-mail: brianna.sanchez@ttu.edu.
Website: http://www.educ.ttu.edu

Towson University, College of Education, Program in Elementary Education, Towson, MD 21252-0001. Offers M Ed. *Accreditation:* NCATE. *Program availability:* Part-time, evening/weekend. *Students:* 6 part-time (all women); includes 2 minority (1 Black or African American, non-Hispanic/Latino; 1 Hispanic/Latino). *Entrance requirements:* For master's, minimum GPA of 3.0, bachelor's degree in education, teaching certification or eligibility for certification. *Application deadline:* For fall admission, 1/17 for domestic students, 5/15 for international students; for spring admission, 10/15 for domestic students, 12/1 for international students. Applications are processed on a rolling basis. Application fee: $45. Electronic applications accepted. *Expenses:* Tuition, state resident: full-time $7960; part-time $398 per unit. Tuition, nonresident: full-time $16,480; part-time $824 per unit. *Required fees:* $2600; $130 per year. $390 per term. *Financial support:* Application deadline: 4/1. *Unit head:* Dr. Todd Kenreich, Graduate Program Director, 410-704-4956, E-mail: scedmed@towson.edu. *Application contact:* Coverley Beidleman, Assistant Director of Graduate Admissions, 410-704-5630, Fax: 410-704-3030, E-mail: cbeidleman@towson.edu.
Website: http://www.towson.edu/coe/departments/grad/elementary/

Towson University, College of Education, Program in Teaching, Towson, MD 21252-0001. Offers early childhood education (MAT); elementary education (MAT); secondary education (MAT); special education (MAT). *Students:* 64 full-time (44 women), 48 part-time (34 women); includes 16 minority (5 Black or African American, non-Hispanic/Latino; 5 Asian, non-Hispanic/Latino; 5 Hispanic/Latino; 1 Two or more races, non-Hispanic/Latino). *Entrance requirements:* For master's, ACT, GRE, PRAXIS I or SAT, 2 letters of reference, resume, minimum GPA of 3.0, essay. *Application deadline:* For fall admission, 1/17 for domestic students, 5/15 for international students; for spring admission, 10/15 for domestic students, 12/1 for international students. Applications are processed on a rolling basis. Application fee: $45. Electronic applications accepted. *Expenses:* Tuition, state resident: full-time $7960; part-time $398 per unit. Tuition, nonresident: full-time $16,480; part-time $824 per unit. *Required fees:* $2600; $130 per year. $390 per term. *Financial support:* Application deadline: 4/1. *Unit head:* Dr. Pamela Wruble, Graduate Program Director, 410-704-4935, E-mail: pwruble@towson.edu. *Application contact:* Coverley Beidleman, Assistant Director of Graduate Admissions, 410-704-5630, Fax: 410-704-3030, E-mail: grads@towson.edu.
Website: https://www.towson.edu/coe/departments/teaching/

Trevecca Nazarene University, Graduate Education Program, Nashville, TN 37210-2877. Offers accountability and instructional leadership (Ed S); curriculum and instruction for Christian school educators (M Ed); curriculum and instruction K-12 (M Ed); educational leadership (M Ed); English second language (M Ed); library and information science (MLI Sc); special education: visual impairments (M Ed); teaching (MAT), including teaching 6-12, teaching K-5. *Accreditation:* NCATE. *Program availability:* Part-time, evening/weekend, online learning. *Faculty:* 8 full-time (6 women), 22 part-time/adjunct (18 women). *Students:* 150 full-time (114 women), 3 part-time (1 woman); includes 54 minority (49 Black or African American, non-Hispanic/Latino; 4 Hispanic/Latino; 1 Two or more races, non-Hispanic/Latino). Average age 36. In 2017, 57 master's, 4 other advanced degrees awarded. *Degree requirements:* For master's, comprehensive exam, exit assessment/e-portfolio. *Entrance requirements:* For master's, GRE or MAT; PRAXIS (for MAT), minimum GPA of 3.0, official transcript from regionally-accredited institution, references, interview, writing sample, at least 3 years' successful teaching experience (for M Ed in educational leadership); for Ed S, GRE or MAT, master's degree with minimum GPA of 3.0, official transcript from regionally accredited institution, at least 3 years' successful teaching experience, interview, writing sample, background and fingerprinting check, recommendations. Additional exam requirements/recommendations for international students: Required—TOEFL (minimum score 550 paper-based). *Application deadline:* Applications are processed on a rolling basis. Electronic applications accepted. *Expenses:* Contact institution. *Financial support:* Applicants required to submit FAFSA. *Unit head:* Dr. Suzie Harris, Dean, School of Education, 615-248-1201, Fax: 615-248-1597, E-mail: admissions_ged@trevecca.edu. *Application contact:* 844-TNU-GRAD, E-mail: sgcsadmissions@trevecca.edu.
Website: http://www.trevecca.edu/soe

Trinity Washington University, School of Education, Washington, DC 20017-1094. Offers clinical mental health counseling (MA); early childhood education (MAT); educating for change (M Ed); educational administration (MSA); elementary education (MAT); reading (M Ed); school counseling (MA); secondary education (MAT), including English, social studies; special education (MAT). *Accreditation:* NCATE. *Program availability:* Part-time, evening/weekend. *Degree requirements:* For master's, thesis (for some programs), capstone project(s). *Entrance requirements:* For master's, PRAXIS I, minimum GPA of 2.8. Additional exam requirements/recommendations for international students: Required—TOEFL (minimum score 550 paper-based). *Faculty research:* Technology, literacy, special education, organizations, inclusion models.

Troy University, Graduate School, College of Education, Program in K–6 Elementary and Collaborative Education, Troy, AL 36082. Offers MS, Ed S. *Accreditation:* NCATE. *Program availability:* Part-time, evening/weekend. *Faculty:* 5 full-time (3 women), 6 part-time/adjunct (5 women). *Students:* 33 full-time (29 women), 38 part-time (33 women); includes 23 minority (21 Black or African American, non-Hispanic/Latino; 1 American Indian or Alaska Native, non-Hispanic/Latino; 1 Hispanic/Latino). Average age 29. 30 applicants, 77% accepted, 17 enrolled. In 2017, 36 master's, 10 other advanced degrees awarded. *Degree requirements:* For master's, comprehensive exam, thesis. *Entrance requirements:* For master's, GRE (minimum score of 850 on old exam or 290 on new exam), GMAT (minimum score of 380), or MAT (minimum score of 385), bachelor's degree; minimum undergraduate GPA of 2.5 or 3.0 on last 30 semester hours, letter of recommendation; for Ed S, GRE (minimum score of 850 on old exam or

286 on new exam) or GMAT (minimum score of 380), Alabama Class A certificate or equivalent, master's degree, minimum graduate GPA of 3.0. Additional exam requirements/recommendations for international students: Required—TOEFL (minimum score 523 paper-based; 70 iBT), IELTS (minimum score 5.5). *Application deadline:* Applications are processed on a rolling basis. Application fee: $50. Electronic applications accepted. *Expenses:* Tuition, state resident: part-time $417 per credit hour. Tuition, nonresident: part-time $834 per credit hour. *Required fees:* $42 per credit hour. $50 per semester. Tuition and fees vary according to campus/location. *Financial support:* Fellowships, career-related internships or fieldwork, and scholarships/grants available. Support available to part-time students. Financial award applicants required to submit FAFSA. *Unit head:* Dr. Ruth Busby, Chair, Teacher Education, 334-670-3546, Fax: 334-670-6666, E-mail: rbusby@troy.edu. *Application contact:* Jessica A. Kimbro, Director of Graduate Admissions, 334-670-3178, E-mail: jacord@troy.edu.

Tufts University, Graduate School of Arts and Sciences, Department of Education, Program in Education, Medford, MA 02155. Offers educational studies (MA); elementary education (MAT); middle and secondary education (MAT); museum education (MA); secondary education (MA); STEM education (MS, PhD). *Program availability:* Part-time. *Students:* 50 full-time (38 women), 9 part-time (8 women); includes 9 minority (2 Black or African American, non-Hispanic/Latino; 2 Asian, non-Hispanic/Latino; 4 Hispanic/Latino; 1 Two or more races, non-Hispanic/Latino), 4 international. Average age 28. 120 applicants, 71% accepted, 49 enrolled. In 2017, 51 master's awarded. *Degree requirements:* For master's, thesis optional. *Entrance requirements:* For master's, GRE General Test, portfolio (for art education only); for doctorate, GRE General Test, writing sample. Additional exam requirements/recommendations for international students: Required—TOEFL (minimum score 550 paper-based; 80 iBT), IELTS (minimum score 6.5). *Application deadline:* For fall admission, 1/2 for domestic and international students; for spring admission, 10/15 for domestic and international students. Applications are processed on a rolling basis. Application fee: $85. Electronic applications accepted. *Expenses:* Contact institution. *Financial support:* Research assistantships, teaching assistantships, Federal Work-Study, scholarships/grants, and tuition waivers (full and partial) available. Support available to part-time students. Financial award application deadline: 1/2. *Unit head:* Dr. David Hammer, Graduate Program Director, 617-627-2396. *Application contact:* Office of Graduate Admissions, 617-627-3395, E-mail: gradadmissions@tufts.edu.

Union College, Graduate Programs, Department of Education, Program in Elementary Education, Barbourville, KY 40906-1499. Offers MA. *Degree requirements:* For master's, thesis optional. *Entrance requirements:* For master's, GRE General Test, NTE.

Universidad del Este, Graduate School, Carolina, PR 00984. Offers accounting (MBA); adult education (M Ed); agribusiness (MBA); criminal justice and criminology (MA); curriculum and instruction - early education (M Ed); curriculum and instruction - elementary (M Ed); curriculum and instruction - English (M Ed); curriculum and instruction - Spanish (M Ed); human resources (MBA); information security management (MBA); information technology and Web business development (MBA); management (MBA); public policy (MPA); social work (MA), including clinical social work; special education (M Ed); strategic leadership (MBA).

Universidad Metropolitana, School of Education, Program in Teaching of Physical Education, San Juan, PR 00928-1150. Offers teaching of adult physical education (M Ed); teaching of elementary physical education (M Ed); teaching of secondary physical education (M Ed). *Degree requirements:* For master's, thesis or alternative. *Entrance requirements:* For master's, EXADEP, interview. Electronic applications accepted.

Université de Sherbrooke, Faculty of Education, Program in Elementary Education, Sherbrooke, QC J1K 2R1, Canada. Offers M Ed, Diploma. *Program availability:* Part-time, evening/weekend. *Degree requirements:* For master's, thesis.

University at Buffalo, the State University of New York, Graduate School, Graduate School of Education, Department of Learning and Instruction, Buffalo, NY 14260. Offers biology education (Ed M, Certificate); chemistry education (Ed M, Certificate); childhood education (Ed M); childhood education with bilingual extension (Ed M); college teaching (Advanced Certificate); curriculum, instruction and the science of learning (PhD); early childhood education (Ed M); early childhood education with bilingual extension (Ed M); earth science education (Ed M, Certificate); education and technology (Ed M); education studies (Ed M); educational technology and new literacies (Certificate); educational technology and new literacies (Advanced Certificate); elementary education (Ed D); English education (Ed M, Certificate); English education studies (Ed M); English for speakers of other languages (Ed M); foreign and second language education (PhD); French education (Ed M, Certificate); German education (Ed M, Certificate); gifted education (Certificate); Latin education (Ed M, Certificate); literacy education studies (Ed M); literacy specialist (Ed M); literacy teaching and learning (Certificate); mathematics education (Ed M, Certificate); music education (Ed M, Certificate); music education studies (Ed M); music learning theory (Advanced Certificate); online education (Advanced Certificate); physics education (Ed M, Certificate); science and the public (Ed M); social studies education (Ed M, Certificate); Spanish education (Ed M, Certificate); special education (PhD); teaching English to speakers of other languages (Ed M). *Program availability:* Part-time, evening/weekend, 100% online. *Faculty:* 26 full-time (19 women), 74 part-time/adjunct (52 women). *Students:* 172 full-time (122 women), 325 part-time (226 women); includes 44 minority (25 Black or African American, non-Hispanic/Latino; 5 American Indian or Alaska Native, non-Hispanic/Latino; 14 Asian, non-Hispanic/Latino), 57 international. Average age 33. 316 applicants, 78% accepted, 174 enrolled. In 2017, 109 master's, 34 doctorates, 15 other advanced degrees awarded. *Degree requirements:* For master's, comprehensive exam; for doctorate, thesis/dissertation, research analysis exam, research experience. *Entrance requirements:* For master's, letters of reference; for doctorate, GRE General Test or MAT, interview, writing sample, letters of recommendation. Additional exam requirements/recommendations for international students: Required—TOEFL (minimum score 600 paper-based; 96 iBT). *Application deadline:* For fall admission, 2/1 priority date for domestic and international students; for spring admission, 11/15 priority date for domestic students, 10/1 for international students. Applications are processed on a rolling basis. Application fee: $50. Electronic applications accepted. *Financial support:* In 2017–18, 42 fellowships (averaging $5,181 per year), 44 research assistantships with tuition reimbursements (averaging $10,908 per year) were awarded; teaching assistantships, career-related internships or fieldwork, Federal Work-Study, institutionally sponsored loans, scholarships/grants, tuition waivers (full and partial), and unspecified assistantships also available. Financial award application deadline: 2/28; financial award applicants required to submit FAFSA. *Faculty research:* Science assessment, foreign language teaching and learning, early learning, new literacies, gender and education. *Total annual research expenditures:* $413,233. *Unit head:* Dr. David Bruce, Chair, 716-645-4069, Fax: 716-645-3161, E-mail: gse-info@buffalo.edu. *Application contact:* Luann Zak, Admissions Assistant, 716-645-2110, Fax: 716-645-7937, E-mail: luannzak@buffalo.edu.
Website: http://gse.buffalo.edu/lai

The University of Akron, Graduate School, College of Education, Department of Curricular and Instructional Studies, Program in Elementary Education - Literacy Option,

Elementary Education

Akron, OH 44325. Offers MA. *Accreditation:* NCATE. *Students:* 4 full-time (3 women), 17 part-time (16 women); includes 2 minority (both Black or African American, non-Hispanic/Latino), 3 international. Average age 37. 2 applicants, 100% accepted, 2 enrolled. In 2017, 19 master's awarded. *Degree requirements:* For master's, comprehensive exam, thesis optional. *Entrance requirements:* For master's, valid teaching license. Additional exam requirements/recommendations for international students: Required—TOEFL (minimum score 79 iBT), IELTS (minimum score 6.5). *Application deadline:* Applications are processed on a rolling basis. Application fee: $45 ($70 for international students). Electronic applications accepted. *Unit head:* Dr. Evonn Welton, Interim Department Chair, 330-972-6742, E-mail: ewelton@uakron.edu. *Application contact:* Kelly Chaff, College Program Specialist, 330-972-7028, E-mail: klchaff@uakron.edu.
Website: http://www.uakron.edu/education/academic-programs/graduate-programs.dot

The University of Alabama, Graduate School, College of Education, Department of Curriculum and Instruction, Tuscaloosa, AL 35487. Offers elementary education (MA, Ed D, PhD, Ed S); secondary education (MA, Ed D, PhD, Ed S). *Program availability:* Part-time, evening/weekend, 100% online, blended/hybrid learning. *Faculty:* 22 full-time (13 women), 6 part-time/adjunct (4 women). *Students:* 62 full-time (42 women), 94 part-time (67 women); includes 19 minority (9 Black or African American, non-Hispanic/Latino; 1 American Indian or Alaska Native, non-Hispanic/Latino; 3 Asian, non-Hispanic/Latino; 3 Hispanic/Latino; 3 Two or more races, non-Hispanic/Latino), 21 international. Average age 34. 85 applicants, 64% accepted, 44 enrolled. In 2017, 55 master's, 9 doctorates, 13 other advanced degrees awarded. *Degree requirements:* For master's, comprehensive exam, thesis (for some programs); for doctorate, comprehensive exam, thesis/dissertation; for Ed S, comprehensive exam, thesis. *Entrance requirements:* For master's and Ed S, MAT and/or GRE; for doctorate, GRE. Additional exam requirements/recommendations for international students: Recommended—TOEFL (minimum score 550 paper-based), IELTS (minimum score 6.5). *Application deadline:* For fall admission, 7/15 priority date for domestic students, 1/15 priority date for international students; for spring admission, 11/15 priority date for domestic students, 6/1 priority date for international students; for summer admission, 5/1 priority date for domestic students, 3/1 priority date for international students. Applications are processed on a rolling basis. Application fee: $50 ($60 for international students). Electronic applications accepted. *Financial support:* In 2017–18, 18 students received support, including research assistantships with tuition reimbursements available (averaging $13,140 per year), teaching assistantships with tuition reimbursements available (averaging $13,140 per year); institutionally sponsored loans, traineeships, and unspecified assistantships also available. Financial award application deadline: 12/31; financial award applicants required to submit FAFSA. *Faculty research:* Teacher education, diversity, integration of curriculum, technology, pedagogical content knowledge. *Total annual research expenditures:* $145,886. *Unit head:* Dr. Cynthia Camille Sunal, Chair, 205-348-8264, Fax: 205-348-9863, E-mail: cvsunal@ua.edu. *Application contact:* Dr. Kathy S. Wetzel, Assistant Dean for Student Services, 205-348-1154, Fax: 205-348-0080, E-mail: kwetzel@bamaed.ua.edu.
Website: http://courseleaf.ua.edu/education/curriculumandinstruction/

The University of Alabama at Birmingham, School of Education, Program in Elementary Education, Birmingham, AL 35294. Offers MA Ed. *Accreditation:* NCATE. *Program availability:* Part-time, online learning. *Degree requirements:* For master's, thesis optional. *Entrance requirements:* For master's, GRE General Test or MAT. Electronic applications accepted.

University of Alaska Southeast, Graduate Programs, Program in Education, Juneau, AK 99801. Offers educational leadership (M Ed); elementary education (MAT); learning design and technology (M Ed); mathematics education (M Ed); reading specialist (M Ed); secondary education (MAT); special education (M Ed, MAT). *Accreditation:* NCATE. *Program availability:* Part-time, evening/weekend, online learning. *Degree requirements:* For master's, comprehensive exam or project, portfolio. *Entrance requirements:* For master's, PRAXIS, minimum GPA of 3.0, writing sample, letters of recommendation. Electronic applications accepted. *Faculty research:* Applied classroom research, culturally responsive practices, action research, teaching effectiveness.

University of Alberta, Faculty of Graduate Studies and Research, Department of Elementary Education, Edmonton, AB T6G 2E1, Canada. Offers M Ed, Ed D, PhD. *Program availability:* Part-time, evening/weekend, online learning. *Degree requirements:* For master's, thesis (for some programs); for doctorate, thesis/dissertation. *Entrance requirements:* For master's and doctorate, 1 year of teaching experience, minimum GPA of 6.5 on a 9.0 scale. *Faculty research:* Literacy education, early childhood education, teacher education, curriculum studies, instructional studies.

The University of Arizona, College of Education, Department of Teaching, Learning and Sociocultural Studies, Program in Teaching and Teacher Education, Tucson, AZ 85721. Offers M Ed, MA, PhD. *Program availability:* Part-time, evening/weekend. *Degree requirements:* For master's, thesis optional; for doctorate, comprehensive exam, thesis/dissertation. *Entrance requirements:* For master's, writing sample, 1 year of teaching experience, 3 letters of recommendation; for doctorate, GRE General Test (minimum score 1000), minimum GPA of 3.5, 2 years of teaching experience, 3 letters of recommendation, writing sample. Additional exam requirements/recommendations for international students: Required—TOEFL (minimum score 550 paper-based; 79 iBT). Electronic applications accepted. *Faculty research:* Staff development, science education, environmental education, math education.

University of Arkansas at Pine Bluff, School of Education, Pine Bluff, AR 71601-2799. Offers elementary education (M Ed); secondary education (M Ed), including English education, mathematics education, science education, social studies education; teaching (MAT). *Accreditation:* NCATE. *Program availability:* Part-time, evening/weekend. *Degree requirements:* For master's, comprehensive exam. *Entrance requirements:* For master's, GRE, minimum GPA of 2.75, NTE or Standard Arkansas Teaching Certificate. *Faculty research:* Teacher certification, accreditation, assessment, standards, portfolio development, rehabilitation, technology.

University of Bridgeport, School of Education, Department of Education, Bridgeport, CT 06604. Offers education (MS); educational management (Ed D, Diploma), including intermediate administrator or supervisor (Diploma), leadership (Ed D); elementary education (MS, Diploma), including early childhood education, elementary education; middle school education (MS); music education (MS); remedial reading and language arts (Diploma); secondary education (MS, Diploma), including computer specialist (Diploma), international education (Diploma), reading specialist, secondary education. *Program availability:* Part-time, evening/weekend. *Degree requirements:* For master's, final exam, final project, or thesis; for doctorate, comprehensive exam, thesis/dissertation; for Diploma, thesis or alternative, final project. *Entrance requirements:* For master's, minimum undergraduate QPA of 2.67; for doctorate, GRE, MAT; for Diploma, GRE General Test or MAT, minimum graduate QPA of 3.0. Additional exam requirements/recommendations for international students: Recommended—TOEFL (minimum score 550 paper-based; 80 iBT), IELTS (minimum score 6.5). Electronic applications accepted. *Expenses:* Contact institution.

University of California, Irvine, School of Education, Irvine, CA 92697. Offers educational administration (Ed D); educational administration and leadership (Ed D); elementary and secondary education (MAT). *Program availability:* Part-time, evening/weekend. *Students:* 210 full-time (157 women), 1 (woman) part-time; includes 104 minority (1 Black or African American, non-Hispanic/Latino; 46 Asian, non-Hispanic/Latino; 39 Hispanic/Latino; 1 Native Hawaiian or other Pacific Islander, non-Hispanic/Latino; 17 Two or more races, non-Hispanic/Latino), 20 international. Average age 27. 451 applicants, 46% accepted, 147 enrolled. In 2017, 130 master's, 7 doctorates awarded. *Entrance requirements:* For master's, GRE, minimum GPA of 3.0; for doctorate, GRE General Test, minimum GPA of 3.0. Additional exam requirements/recommendations for international students: Required—TOEFL (minimum score 550 paper-based). *Application deadline:* For fall admission, 1/2 priority date for domestic students, 1/2 for international students. Application fee: $105 ($125 for international students). Electronic applications accepted. *Financial support:* Fellowships, research assistantships with full tuition reimbursements, institutionally sponsored loans, traineeships, health care benefits, and unspecified assistantships available. Financial award application deadline: 3/1; financial award applicants required to submit FAFSA. *Faculty research:* Education technology, learning theory, social theory, cultural diversity, postmodernism. *Unit head:* Richard Arum, Dean, 949-824-2534, E-mail: richard.arum@uci.edu. *Application contact:* Denise Earley, Assistant Director of Student Affairs, 949-824-4022, E-mail: denise.earley@uci.edu.
Website: http://education.uci.edu/

University of Central Florida, College of Community Innovation and Education, Education Doctoral Programs, Orlando, FL 32816. Offers curriculum and instruction (Ed D); education (PhD), including communication sciences and disorders, counselor education, early childhood education, elementary education, exceptional education, exercise physiology, higher education, instructional design and technology, mathematics education, methodology, measurement and analysis, reading education, science education, social science education, TESOL; educational leadership (Ed D). *Students:* 122 full-time (86 women), 129 part-time (88 women); includes 64 minority (24 Black or African American, non-Hispanic/Latino; 1 American Indian or Alaska Native, non-Hispanic/Latino; 9 Asian, non-Hispanic/Latino; 24 Hispanic/Latino; 6 Two or more races, non-Hispanic/Latino), 26 international. Average age 38. 195 applicants, 47% accepted, 72 enrolled. In 2017, 89 doctorates awarded. *Entrance requirements:* For doctorate, GRE, letters of recommendation, goal statement, resume, writing sample. Application fee: $30. Electronic applications accepted. *Expenses:* Tuition, state resident: part-time $288.16 per credit hour. Tuition, nonresident: part-time $1073.31 per credit hour. Tuition and fees vary according to program. *Financial support:* In 2017–18, 77 students received support, including 28 fellowships with partial tuition reimbursements available (averaging $5,733 per year), 29 research assistantships with partial tuition reimbursements available (averaging $10,230 per year), 54 teaching assistantships with partial tuition reimbursements available (averaging $11,614 per year); health care benefits also available. Financial award application deadline: 3/1; financial award applicants required to submit FAFSA. *Unit head:* Dr. Edward Robinson, Director of Doctoral Programs, 407-823-6106, E-mail: edward.robinson@ucf.edu. *Application contact:* Associate Director, Graduate Admissions, 407-823-2766, Fax: 407-823-6442, E-mail: gradadmissions@ucf.edu.
Website: https://edcollege.ucf.edu/academic-programs/graduate/

University of Central Florida, College of Community Innovation and Education, School of Teacher Education, Program in Elementary Education, Orlando, FL 32816. Offers M Ed, MA. *Accreditation:* NCATE. *Students:* 16 full-time (all women), 32 part-time (31 women); includes 16 minority (4 Black or African American, non-Hispanic/Latino; 3 Asian, non-Hispanic/Latino; 9 Hispanic/Latino). Average age 28. 24 applicants, 63% accepted, 11 enrolled. In 2017, 22 master's awarded. *Degree requirements:* For master's, thesis or alternative. *Entrance requirements:* For master's, Florida Professional Teaching Certificate in subject area or professional teaching certificate. Additional exam requirements/recommendations for international students: Required—TOEFL. *Application deadline:* For fall admission, 7/15 for domestic students; for spring admission, 12/1 for domestic students; for summer admission, 4/15 for domestic students. Application fee: $30. Electronic applications accepted. *Expenses:* Tuition, state resident: part-time $288.16 per credit hour. Tuition, nonresident: part-time $1073.31 per credit hour. Tuition and fees vary according to program. *Financial support:* In 2017–18, 1 student received support, including 1 teaching assistantship with partial tuition reimbursement available (averaging $9,086 per year); career-related internships or fieldwork, Federal Work-Study, institutionally sponsored loans, tuition waivers (partial), and unspecified assistantships also available. Financial award application deadline: 3/1; financial award applicants required to submit FAFSA. *Unit head:* Dr. Robert Everett, Program Coordinator, 407-823-5788, E-mail: robert.everett@ucf.edu. *Application contact:* Associate Director, Graduate Admissions, 321-823-2766, Fax: 407-823-6442, E-mail: gradadmissions@ucf.edu.
Website: https://edcollege.ucf.edu/academic-programs/graduate/elementary-education/#ma

University of Central Missouri, The Graduate School, Warrensburg, MO 64093. Offers accountancy (MA); accounting (MBA); applied mathematics (MS); aviation safety (MA); biology (MS); business administration (MBA); career and technical education leadership (MS); college student personnel administration (MS); communication (MA); computer science (MS); counseling (MS); criminal justice (MS); educational leadership (Ed D); educational technology (MS); elementary and early childhood education (MSE); English (MA); environmental studies (MA); finance (MBA); history (MA); human services/educational technology (Ed S); human services/learning resources (Ed S); human services/professional counseling (Ed S); industrial hygiene (MS); industrial management (MS); information systems (MBA); information technology (MS); kinesiology (MS); library science and information services (MS); literacy education (MSE); marketing (MBA); mathematics (MS); music (MA); occupational safety management (MS); psychology (MS); rural family nursing (MS); school administration (MS); social gerontology (MS); sociology (MA); special education (MSE); speech language pathology (MS); superintendency (Ed S); teaching (MAT); teaching English as a second language (MA); technology (MS); technology management (PhD); theatre (MA). *Program availability:* Part-time, 100% online, blended/hybrid learning. *Faculty:* 337 full-time (145 women), 41 part-time/adjunct (28 women). *Students:* 785 full-time (398 women), 1,633 part-time (1,063 women); includes 231 minority (102 Black or African American, non-Hispanic/Latino; 4 American Indian or Alaska Native, non-Hispanic/Latino; 16 Asian, non-Hispanic/Latino; 52 Hispanic/Latino; 57 Two or more races, non-Hispanic/Latino), 692 international. Average age 30. In 2017, 2,605 master's, 122 other advanced degrees awarded. *Degree requirements:* For master's and Ed S, comprehensive exam (for some programs), thesis (for some programs). *Entrance requirements:* Additional exam requirements/recommendations for international students: Required—TOEFL (minimum score 550 paper-based; 79 iBT). *Application deadline:* For fall admission, 6/1 priority date for domestic and international students; for spring admission, 10/1 priority date for domestic and international students; for summer admission, 4/1 priority date for domestic and international students. Applications are processed on a rolling basis. Application fee: $30 ($75 for international students). Electronic applications accepted. *Expenses:* Tuition, state resident: full-time $8771; part-time $292.35 per credit hour. Tuition, nonresident: full-time $17,541; part-time $584.70 per credit hour. *Required fees:* $372; $24.78 per credit hour. *Financial support:* In 2017–18, 99 students received support. Research assistantships, teaching assistantships, career-related internships or

fieldwork, Federal Work-Study, scholarships/grants, and administrative and laboratory assistantships available. Support available to part-time students. Financial award application deadline: 3/1; financial award applicants required to submit FAFSA. *Unit head:* Shellie Hewitt, Director of Graduate and International Student Services, 660-543-4621, Fax: 660-543-4778, E-mail: hewitt@ucmo.edu. *Application contact:* 660-543-4621, E-mail: admit_intl@ucmo.edu.
Website: http://www.ucmo.edu/graduate/

University of Central Oklahoma, The Jackson College of Graduate Studies, College of Education and Professional Studies, Department of Curriculum and Instruction, Edmond, OK 73034-5209. Offers bilingual education/teaching English as a second language (M Ed); early childhood education (M Ed); elementary education (M Ed). *Program availability:* Part-time. *Faculty:* 14 full-time (12 women), 4 part-time/adjunct (3 women). *Students:* 25 full-time (21 women), 67 part-time (60 women); includes 33 minority (8 Black or African American, non-Hispanic/Latino; 3 American Indian or Alaska Native, non-Hispanic/Latino; 2 Asian, non-Hispanic/Latino; 16 Hispanic/Latino; 4 Two or more races, non-Hispanic/Latino), 14 international. Average age 33. 44 applicants, 93% accepted, 31 enrolled. In 2017, 27 master's awarded. *Degree requirements:* For master's, comprehensive exam (for some programs), thesis optional. *Entrance requirements:* Additional exam requirements/recommendations for international students: Required—TOEFL (minimum score 550 paper-based; 79 iBT), IELTS (minimum score 6.5). *Application deadline:* For fall admission, 7/15 for international students; for spring admission, 11/15 for international students. Applications are processed on a rolling basis. Application fee: $60. Electronic applications accepted. *Expenses:* Tuition, state resident: full-time $5375; part-time $268.75 per credit hour. Tuition, nonresident: full-time $13,295; part-time $664.75 per credit hour. *Required fees:* $626; $31.30 per credit hour. One-time fee: $50. Tuition and fees vary according to program. *Financial support:* In 2017–18, 13 students received support. Research assistantships, teaching assistantships, career-related internships or fieldwork, Federal Work-Study, scholarships/grants, tuition waivers (partial), and unspecified assistantships available. Financial award application deadline: 3/31; financial award applicants required to submit FAFSA. *Unit head:* Dr. Paulette Shreck, Chair, 405-974-5721, Fax: 405-974-3858. *Application contact:* Carlie Wellington, Assistant Director, CEPS Graduate Enrollment, 405-974-5105, Fax: 405-974-3851, E-mail: gradcoll@uco.edu.

University of Colorado Denver, School of Education and Human Development, Information and Learning Technologies Program, Denver, CO 80217. Offers e-learning design and implementation (MA); instructional design and adult learning (MA); K-12 teaching (MA). *Program availability:* Part-time, evening/weekend, online learning. *Degree requirements:* For master's, comprehensive exam (for some programs), comprehensive exam or online portfolio; 30 credit hours. *Entrance requirements:* For master's, GRE or MAT (if GPA is below 2.75), resume, statement of intent, three letters of recommendation, transcripts from all colleges/universities previously attended. Additional exam requirements/recommendations for international students: Required—TOEFL (minimum score 537 paper-based; 75 iBT); Recommended—IELTS (minimum score 6.5). Electronic applications accepted. *Expenses:* Contact institution. *Faculty research:* Technology for educational management, instructional design foundations, e-learning, educational design.

University of Colorado Denver, School of Education and Human Development, Teacher Education Programs, Denver, CO 80217. Offers elementary linguistically diverse education (MA); elementary math and science education (MA); elementary math education (MA); elementary reading and writing (MA); elementary science education (MA); secondary English education (MA); secondary linguistically diverse education (MA); secondary math education (MA); secondary reading and writing (MA); secondary science education (MA); special education (MA). *Accreditation:* NCATE. *Program availability:* Part-time, evening/weekend. *Degree requirements:* For master's, comprehensive exam. *Entrance requirements:* For master's, GRE or MAT (for those with GPA below 2.75), transcripts, resume, letters of recommendation. Additional exam requirements/recommendations for international students: Required—TOEFL (minimum score 537 paper-based; 75 iBT); Recommended—IELTS (minimum score 6.5). Electronic applications accepted. *Expenses:* Contact institution. *Faculty research:* Linguistically diverse education/ESL, elementary reading and writing, elementary teacher education, secondary teacher education, special education.

University of Connecticut, Graduate School, Neag School of Education, Department of Curriculum and Instruction, Program in Elementary Education, Storrs, CT 06269. Offers MA, PhD. *Accreditation:* NCATE. Terminal master's awarded for partial completion of doctoral program. *Degree requirements:* For master's, comprehensive exam, thesis or alternative; for doctorate, thesis/dissertation. *Entrance requirements:* For doctorate, GRE General Test. Additional exam requirements/recommendations for international students: Required—TOEFL (minimum score 550 paper-based). Electronic applications accepted.

University of Dayton, Department of Teacher Education, Dayton, OH 45469. Offers adolescence to young adult education (MS Ed); early childhood leadership and advocacy (MS Ed); interdisciplinary education (MS Ed), including visual arts; interdisciplinary education studies (MS Ed); leadership in educational systems (MS Ed); literacy (MS Ed); mathematics education (MS Ed); middle childhood education (MS Ed); multi-age education (MS Ed), including world languages; music education (MS Ed); teacher as leader (MS Ed); teacher education (MS Ed); technology-enhanced learning (MS Ed); trans-disciplinary early childhood education (MS Ed). *Program availability:* Part-time, 100% online. *Faculty:* 23 full-time (20 women), 41 part-time/adjunct (36 women). *Students:* 45 full-time (38 women), 68 part-time (57 women); includes 7 minority (3 Black or African American, non-Hispanic/Latino; 1 Hispanic/Latino; 3 Two or more races, non-Hispanic/Latino), 6 international. Average age 31. 106 applicants, 28% accepted. In 2017, 70 master's awarded. *Degree requirements:* For master's, variable foreign language requirement, thesis or alternative, internship (for teaching licensure or endorsement). *Entrance requirements:* For master's, GRE (minimum score of 149 verbal, 4 on writing) or MAT (minimum score of 396) if undergraduate GPA was under 2.75, minimum GPA of 2.75, 3 letters of recommendation, personal statement or resume, official transcripts. Additional exam requirements/recommendations for international students: Required—TOEFL (minimum score 550 paper-based; 80 iBT); Recommended—IELTS (minimum score 6.5). *Application deadline:* Applications are processed on a rolling basis. Application fee: $0 ($50 for international students). Electronic applications accepted. *Expenses:* Contact institution. *Financial support:* In 2017–18, 5 research assistantships with partial tuition reimbursements (averaging $9,640 per year) were awarded; teaching assistantships, career-related internships or fieldwork, institutionally sponsored loans, and unspecified assistantships also available. Financial award application deadline: 3/1; financial award applicants required to submit FAFSA. *Faculty research:* Social emotional learning, culturally responsive teaching, urban teaching, literacy, instructional strategies, pre-service teacher education preparation. *Unit head:* Dr. Connie L. Bowman, Chair, 937-229-3348, E-mail: cbowman1@udayton.edu. *Application contact:* Gina Seiter, Coordinator of Graduate Programs and Licensing, 937-229-3103, E-mail: gseiter1@udayton.edu.
Website: https://www.udayton.edu/education/departments_and_programs/edt

University of Florida, Graduate School, College of Education, School of Teaching and Learning, Gainesville, FL 32611. Offers curriculum and instruction (M Ed, MAE, Ed D, PhD, Ed S); elementary education (M Ed, MAE); English education (M Ed, MAE); mathematics education (M Ed, MAE); reading education (M Ed, MAE); science education (M Ed, MAE); social studies education (M Ed, MAE). *Accreditation:* NCATE. *Program availability:* Part-time, evening/weekend, online learning. Terminal master's awarded for partial completion of doctoral program. *Degree requirements:* For master's, comprehensive exam (for some programs), thesis (for some programs); for doctorate, comprehensive exam (for some programs), thesis/dissertation (for some programs). *Entrance requirements:* For master's and doctorate, GRE General Test, minimum GPA of 3.0; for Ed S, GRE General Test. Additional exam requirements/recommendations for international students: Required—TOEFL (minimum score 550 paper-based; 80 iBT), IELTS (minimum score 6). Electronic applications accepted. *Faculty research:* STEM education; curriculum; teaching and teacher education; languages and literacy; schools, culture, and society; theories and processes of learning.

University of Hartford, College of Education, Nursing, and Health Professions, Program in Elementary and Special Education, West Hartford, CT 06117-1599. Offers elementary education (M Ed). *Accreditation:* NCATE. *Program availability:* Part-time, evening/weekend. *Degree requirements:* For master's, comprehensive exam. *Entrance requirements:* For master's, PRAXIS I or waiver, interview, 2 letters of recommendation. Additional exam requirements/recommendations for international students: Required—TOEFL (minimum score 550 paper-based). Electronic applications accepted.

University of Illinois at Chicago, College of Education, Department of Curriculum and Instruction, Chicago, IL 60607-7128. Offers curriculum studies (PhD); elementary education (M Ed); secondary education (M Ed). *Program availability:* Part-time, evening/weekend. *Degree requirements:* For doctorate, thesis/dissertation. *Entrance requirements:* For master's, minimum GPA of 2.75; for doctorate, GRE General Test, minimum GPA of 2.75. Additional exam requirements/recommendations for international students: Required—TOEFL. Electronic applications accepted. *Faculty research:* Curriculum theory, curriculum development, research on teaching, curriculum and context, reading/literacy.

University of Indianapolis, Graduate Programs, School of Education, Indianapolis, IN 46227-3697. Offers art education (MAT); biology (MAT); chemistry (MAT); curriculum and instruction (MA); earth sciences (MAT); education (MA, MAT); educational leadership (MA); elementary education (MA); English (MAT); French (MAT); math (MAT); physical education (MAT); physics (MAT); secondary education (MA), including art education, education, English education, social studies education; social studies (MAT); Spanish (MAT). *Accreditation:* NCATE. *Program availability:* Part-time, evening/weekend. *Entrance requirements:* For master's, GRE Subject Test, PRAXIS I, minimum GPA of 2.5, 3 letters of recommendation, interview. Additional exam requirements/recommendations for international students: Required—TOEFL (minimum score 550 paper-based). *Faculty research:* Assessment of teacher education, perceptions of prospective teachers by parents.

The University of Iowa, Graduate College, College of Education, Department of Teaching and Learning, Program in Education, Iowa City, IA 52242-1316. Offers art education (MA); developmental reading (MA); elementary education (MA); English education (MA, MAT); foreign and second language education (MAT); foreign language education (MA); foreign language/ESL education (PhD); language, literacy and culture (PhD); mathematics education (MA, MAT, PhD); music education (MM, PhD); science education (MA); secondary education (MA); social studies (MA, PhD). *Degree requirements:* For master's, thesis optional, exam; for doctorate, comprehensive exam, thesis/dissertation. *Entrance requirements:* For master's and doctorate, GRE General Test, minimum GPA of 3.0. Additional exam requirements/recommendations for international students: Required—TOEFL (minimum score 550 paper-based; 81 iBT). Electronic applications accepted.

University of Kentucky, Graduate School, College of Education, Program in Curriculum and Instruction, Lexington, KY 40506-0032. Offers curriculum and instruction (Ed D, PhD); elementary education (MA Ed); instructional system design (MS Ed); literacy (MA Ed); middle school education (MA Ed, MS Ed); secondary education (MA Ed, MS Ed). *Accreditation:* NCATE. *Degree requirements:* For master's, comprehensive exam, thesis optional; for doctorate, comprehensive exam, thesis/dissertation. *Entrance requirements:* For master's, GRE General Test, minimum undergraduate GPA of 2.75; for doctorate, GRE General Test, minimum graduate GPA of 3.0. Additional exam requirements/recommendations for international students: Required—TOEFL (minimum score 550 paper-based). Electronic applications accepted. *Faculty research:* Educational reform, multicultural education, classroom instructional practices, performance based assessment, primary school programs.

University of La Verne, Regional and Online Campuses, Graduate Programs, High Desert Campus, Victorville, CA 92392. Offers business administration for experienced professionals (MBA); educational (special emphasis) (M Ed); educational counseling (MS); leadership and management (MS); multiple subject (elementary) (Credential); preliminary administrative services (Credential); pupil personnel services (Credential); single subject (secondary) (Credential). *Students:* 7 full-time (3 women), 16 part-time (12 women); includes 14 minority (3 Black or African American, non-Hispanic/Latino; 1 American Indian or Alaska Native, non-Hispanic/Latino; 1 Asian, non-Hispanic/Latino; 9 Hispanic/Latino). Average age 41. In 2017, 9 master's awarded. *Application deadline:* Applications are processed on a rolling basis. Application fee: $50. *Expenses:* Contact institution. *Financial support:* Application deadline: 3/2; applicants required to submit FAFSA. *Unit head:* Juli Roberts, Regional Campus Director, 760-955-6448, Fax: 760-843-9505, E-mail: jroberts@laverne.edu. *Application contact:* Admissions, 760-955-6440, Fax: 760-955-6443, E-mail: hdcv@laverne.edu.
Website: https://laverne.edu/locations/

University of La Verne, Regional and Online Campuses, Graduate Programs, Kern County Campus, Bakersfield, CA 93301. Offers business administration for experienced professionals (MBA-EP); education (special emphasis) (M Ed); educational counseling (MS); educational leadership (M Ed); health administration (MHA); leadership and management (MS); mild/moderate education specialist (Credential); multiple subject (elementary) (Credential); organizational leadership (Ed D); preliminary administrative services (Credential); single subject (secondary) (Credential); special education studies (MS). *Program availability:* Part-time, evening/weekend. *Students:* Average age 36. In 2017, 3 master's awarded. *Application deadline:* Applications are processed on a rolling basis. Application fee: $50. *Expenses:* Contact institution. *Financial support:* Institutionally sponsored loans available. Financial award application deadline: 3/2; financial award applicants required to submit FAFSA. *Unit head:* Nora Dominguez, Regional Campus Director, 661-861-6802, E-mail: ndominguez@laverne.edu. *Application contact:* Rebecca Murillo, Associate Director of Admissions, 661-861-6807, E-mail: rmurillo@laverne.edu.
Website: https://laverne.edu/locations/

University of La Verne, Regional and Online Campuses, Graduate Programs, Ventura County/Point Mugu Naval Air Station Campuses, Oxnard, CA 93036. Offers business administration for experienced professionals (MS); educational counseling (MS); educational leadership (M Ed); leadership and management (MS); multiple subject

Elementary Education

(elementary) (Credential); pupil personnel services (Credential); single subject (secondary) (Credential). *Program availability:* Part-time, evening/weekend. *Students:* Average age 38. In 2017, 19 master's awarded. Application fee: $50. *Expenses:* Contact institution. *Financial support:* Institutionally sponsored loans available. Financial award application deadline: 3/2; financial award applicants required to submit FAFSA. *Unit head:* Kitt Vincent, Senior Executive Director, 805-788-6202, E-mail: kvincent@laverne.edu. *Application contact:* Mike Stadler, Assistant Director/Academic Advisor, 805-986-6909, E-mail: mstadler3@laverne.edu.
Website: https://laverne.edu/locations/

University of Louisiana at Monroe, Graduate School, College of Arts, Education, and Sciences, School of Education, Program in Elementary Education, Monroe, LA 71209-0001. Offers MAT. *Accreditation:* NCATE. *Program availability:* Part-time, evening/weekend. *Faculty:* 11 full-time (7 women). *Students:* 3 full-time (all women), 10 part-time (all women); includes 2 minority (both Black or African American, non-Hispanic/Latino). Average age 28. 7 applicants, 29% accepted, 2 enrolled. In 2017, 2 master's awarded. *Degree requirements:* For master's, thesis optional. *Entrance requirements:* For master's, GRE General Test, minimum GPA of 2.5. Additional exam requirements/recommendations for international students: Required—TOEFL (minimum score 500 paper-based; 61 iBT). *Application deadline:* For fall admission, 8/24 for domestic students, 7/1 for international students; for winter admission, 12/14 priority date for domestic students; for spring admission, 1/19 for domestic students, 11/1 for international students. Applications are processed on a rolling basis. Application fee: $20 ($30 for international students). Electronic applications accepted. *Expenses:* Tuition, state resident: full-time $6489; part-time $479 per hour. Tuition, nonresident: full-time $12,100; part-time $479 per hour. *Required fees:* $8860; $802 per hour. $3273 per semester. *Financial support:* Career-related internships or fieldwork, Federal Work-Study, and unspecified assistantships available. Financial award application deadline: 4/1; financial award applicants required to submit FAFSA. *Faculty research:* Student attitudes.

University of Louisville, Graduate School, College of Education and Human Development, Departments of Early Childhood and Elementary Education, Middle and Secondary Education, and Special Education, Louisville, KY 40292-0001. Offers art education (MAT); autism and applied behavior analysis (Certificate); curriculum and instruction (PhD); early elementary education (MAT); exercise physiology (MS); health and physical education (MAT); health professions education (Certificate); higher education (MA); human resources and organization development (MS); instructional technology (M Ed); interdisciplinary early childhood education (MAT); middle school education (MAT); music education (MAT); secondary education (MAT); special education (MAT); sport administration (MS); teacher leadership (M Ed). *Program availability:* Part-time, evening/weekend. *Students:* 114 full-time (73 women), 173 part-time (114 women); includes 49 minority (19 Black or African American, non-Hispanic/Latino; 5 Asian, non-Hispanic/Latino; 13 Hispanic/Latino; 12 Two or more races, non-Hispanic/Latino), 7 international. Average age 29. 132 applicants, 73% accepted, 57 enrolled. In 2017, 70 master's, 2 doctorates, 2 other advanced degrees awarded. *Application deadline:* For spring admission, 1/1 priority date for international students. Application fee: $65. *Expenses:* Tuition, state resident: full-time $12,246; part-time $681 per credit hour. Tuition, nonresident: full-time $25,486; part-time $1417 per credit hour. *Required fees:* $196. Tuition and fees vary according to course load, program and reciprocity agreements. *Financial support:* Application deadline: 6/1; applicants required to submit FAFSA. *Faculty research:* STEM teaching and learning; content literacy for English language learners; social justice in teacher education; adolescent literacy; mathematics teacher development. *Total annual research expenditures:* $1.7 million. *Unit head:* Dr. Ann E. Larson, Dean, College of Education and Human Development, 502-852-6411, Fax: 502-852-1464, E-mail: ann@louisville.edu. *Application contact:* Betty Hampton, Director of Graduate Student Services, 502-852-5597, Fax: 502-852-1465, E-mail: edadvise@louisville.edu.
Website: http://louisville.edu/delphi

University of Mary Hardin-Baylor, Graduate Studies in Education, Belton, TX 76513. Offers curriculum and instruction (M Ed); educational administration (M Ed, Ed D), including higher education (Ed D); leadership in nursing education (Ed D), P-12 (Ed D). *Program availability:* Part-time, evening/weekend. *Faculty:* 12 full-time (8 women), 5 part-time/adjunct (2 women). *Students:* 29 full-time (20 women), 79 part-time (55 women); includes 53 minority (35 Black or African American, non-Hispanic/Latino; 17 Hispanic/Latino; 1 Two or more races, non-Hispanic/Latino), 1 international. Average age 39. 15 applicants, 80% accepted, 10 enrolled. In 2017, 47 master's, 16 doctorates awarded. *Degree requirements:* For master's, comprehensive exam; for doctorate, thesis/dissertation. *Entrance requirements:* For master's, minimum GPA of 3.0, interview; for doctorate, minimum GPA of 3.5, interview, essay, resume, employment verification, 3 letters of recommendation. Additional exam requirements/recommendations for international students: Required—TOEFL (minimum score 60 iBT), IELTS (minimum score 4.5). *Application deadline:* For fall admission, 6/1 for domestic students, 4/30 priority date for international students; for spring admission, 11/1 for domestic students, 9/30 priority date for international students. Applications are processed on a rolling basis. Application fee: $35 ($135 for international students). Electronic applications accepted. *Expenses:* $920 per credit hour. *Financial support:* In 2017–18, 90 students received support. Federal Work-Study and scholarships for some active duty military personnel available. Support available to part-time students. Financial award application deadline: 6/1; financial award applicants required to submit FAFSA. *Faculty research:* Motivational orientation of preservice teachers. *Unit head:* Dr. Craig Hammonds, Director, Graduate Programs in Education, 254-295-4189, E-mail: rhammonds@umhb.edu. *Application contact:* Sharon Aguilera, Assistant Director, Graduate Admissions, 254-295-4835, E-mail: saguilera@umhb.edu.
Website: https://go.umhb.edu/graduate/education/home

University of Maryland, Baltimore County, The Graduate School, College of Arts, Humanities and Social Sciences, Department of Education, Program in Teaching, Baltimore, MD 21250. Offers early childhood education (MAT); elementary education (MAT); teaching (MAT), including art, biology, chemistry, choral music, classical foreign language, dance, earth/space science, English, instrumental music, mathematics, modern foreign language, physical science, physics, social studies, theatre. *Program availability:* Part-time, evening/weekend. *Faculty:* 24 full-time (18 women), 25 part-time/adjunct (19 women). *Students:* 41 full-time (34 women), 27 part-time (18 women); includes 26 minority (6 Black or African American, non-Hispanic/Latino; 9 Asian, non-Hispanic/Latino; 7 Hispanic/Latino; 1 Native Hawaiian or other Pacific Islander, non-Hispanic/Latino; 3 Two or more races, non-Hispanic/Latino), 2 international. Average age 30. 54 applicants, 83% accepted, 35 enrolled. In 2017, 50 master's awarded. *Degree requirements:* For master's, comprehensive exam (for some programs), thesis (for some programs). *Entrance requirements:* For master's, PRAXIS Core Examination or GRE (minimum score of 1000), minimum GPA of 3.0. Additional exam requirements/recommendations for international students: Required—TOEFL. *Application deadline:* For fall admission, 6/1 for domestic and international students; for spring admission, 11/1 for domestic and international students. Applications are processed on a rolling basis. Application fee: $50. Electronic applications accepted. *Expenses:* Required fees: $132. *Financial support:* In 2017–18, 8 students received support, including teaching assistantships with tuition reimbursements available (averaging $12,000 per year);

career-related internships or fieldwork, Federal Work-Study, scholarships/grants, tuition waivers, and unspecified assistantships also available. Financial award application deadline: 3/15. *Faculty research:* STEM teacher education, culturally sensitive pedagogy, ESOL/bilingual education, early childhood education, language, literacy and culture. *Total annual research expenditures:* $100,000. *Unit head:* Dr. Susan M. Blunck, Graduate Program Director, 410-455-2869, Fax: 410-455-3986, E-mail: blunck@umbc.edu. *Application contact:* Cheryl Johnson, MAT Program Specialist, 410-455-3388, E-mail: blackwel@umbc.edu.
Website: http://www.umbc.edu/education/

University of Mary Washington, College of Education, Fredericksburg, VA 22401. Offers education (M Ed); elementary education (MS). *Program availability:* Part-time, evening/weekend. *Degree requirements:* For master's, one foreign language, comprehensive exam (for some programs). *Entrance requirements:* For master's, PRAXIS Core Academic Skills for Educators (Reading; Writing; Math or Virginia Department of Education accepted equivalent). Additional exam requirements/recommendations for international students: Required—TOEFL (minimum score 570 paper-based; 88 iBT), IELTS (minimum score 6.5). Electronic applications accepted. Application fee is waived when completed online. *Expenses:* Contact institution.

University of Massachusetts Amherst, Graduate School, College of Education, Program in Education, Amherst, MA 01003. Offers bilingual, English as a second language, and multicultural education (M Ed, Ed S); child study and early education (M Ed); children, families and schools (Ed D, Ed S); early childhood and elementary teacher education (M Ed); educational leadership (M Ed); educational policy and leadership (Ed D); higher education (M Ed); international education (M Ed); language, literacy and culture (Ed D); learning, media and technology (M Ed, Ed S); mathematics, science, and learning technologies (Ed D); reading and writing (M Ed); research, educational measurement and psychometrics (Ed D); school counselor education (M Ed, Ed S); school psychology (Ed S); science education (Ed S); secondary teacher education (M Ed); social justice education (M Ed, Ed D, Ed S); special education (M Ed, Ed D, Ed S); teacher education and school improvement (Ed D, Ed S). *Accreditation:* NCATE. *Program availability:* Part-time, online learning. Terminal master's awarded for partial completion of doctoral program. *Degree requirements:* For doctorate, comprehensive exam, thesis/dissertation. *Entrance requirements:* Additional exam requirements/recommendations for international students: Required—TOEFL (minimum score 550 paper-based; 80 iBT), IELTS (minimum score 6.5). Electronic applications accepted.

University of Memphis, Graduate School, College of Education, Department of Instruction and Curriculum Leadership, Memphis, TN 38152. Offers advanced studies in teaching and learning (M Ed); applied behavior analysis (Graduate Certificate); autism studies (Graduate Certificate); early childhood education (MAT, MS, Ed D); elementary education (MAT); instruction and curriculum (MS, Ed D); instruction design and technology (MS, Ed D); instructional design and technology (Graduate Certificate); literacy, leadership, and coaching (Graduate Certificate); reading (MS, Ed D); school library information specialist (Graduate Certificate); secondary education (MAT); special education (MAT, MS, Ed D); STEM teacher leadership (Graduate Certificate); urban education (Graduate Certificate). *Accreditation:* NCATE (one or more programs are accredited). *Program availability:* Part-time. *Faculty:* 22 full-time (14 women), 14 part-time/adjunct (10 women). *Students:* 36 full-time (27 women), 351 part-time (271 women); includes 159 minority (132 Black or African American, non-Hispanic/Latino; 1 American Indian or Alaska Native, non-Hispanic/Latino; 7 Asian, non-Hispanic/Latino; 10 Hispanic/Latino; 9 Two or more races, non-Hispanic/Latino), 4 international. Average age 35. 170 applicants, 85% accepted, 111 enrolled. In 2017, 84 master's, 14 doctorates, 32 other advanced degrees awarded. Terminal master's awarded for partial completion of doctoral program. *Degree requirements:* For master's, comprehensive exam, thesis or alternative; for doctorate, comprehensive exam, thesis/dissertation. *Entrance requirements:* For master's, GRE General Test, PRAXIS, minimum GPA of 2.5, letters of reference; for doctorate, GRE General Test, GRE Subject Test, 2 years of teaching experience, letters of reference, statement of purpose, interview. Additional exam requirements/recommendations for international students: Required—TOEFL (minimum score 550 paper-based; 79 iBT). *Application deadline:* For fall admission, 4/1 priority date for domestic students; for spring admission, 10/1 priority date for domestic students; for summer admission, 2/1 priority date for domestic students. Applications are processed on a rolling basis. Application fee: $35 ($60 for international students). Electronic applications accepted. *Expenses:* Contact institution. *Financial support:* In 2017–18, 2 research assistantships with full tuition reimbursements (averaging $10,000 per year), 3 teaching assistantships with full tuition reimbursements (averaging $10,666 per year) were awarded; career-related internships or fieldwork, Federal Work-Study, institutionally sponsored loans, scholarships/grants, traineeships, and unspecified assistantships also available. Support available to part-time students. Financial award application deadline: 2/1; financial award applicants required to submit FAFSA. *Faculty research:* Effective urban teachers, preparation and retention of urban teachers, technology utilization in schools, field-based teacher preparation programs, effective use of online instruction. *Unit head:* Dr. Angiline Powell, Interim Chair, 901-678-3310, E-mail: apowell3@memphis.edu. *Application contact:* Dr. James Meindl, Coordinator of Graduate Studies, 901-678-3310, E-mail: jnmeindl@memphis.edu.
Website: http://www.memphis.edu/icl/

University of Minnesota, Twin Cities Campus, Graduate School, College of Education and Human Development, Department of Curriculum and Instruction, Program in Teaching, Minneapolis, MN 55455-0213. Offers teaching (M Ed), including arts in education, elementary education, English education, mathematics, science, second language education, social studies. *Students:* 251 full-time (180 women), 136 part-time (82 women); includes 68 minority (16 Black or African American, non-Hispanic/Latino; 15 Asian, non-Hispanic/Latino; 17 Hispanic/Latino; 20 Two or more races, non-Hispanic/Latino), 9 international. Average age 28. 341 applicants, 72% accepted, 229 enrolled. In 2017, 263 master's awarded. Application fee: $75 ($95 for international students). *Unit head:* Dr. Cynthia Lewis, Chair, 612-625-6313, Fax: 612-624-8277, E-mail: lewis@umn.edu. *Application contact:* Dr. Kendall King, Director of Graduate Studies, 612-625-3692, E-mail: roehr013@umn.edu.
Website: http://www.cehd.umn.edu/ci/

University of Mississippi, Graduate School, School of Education, University, MS 38677. Offers counselor education (M Ed, PhD); counselor education - play therapy (Ed S); early childhood (M Ed); educational leadership K-12 (M Ed, Ed D, PhD, Ed S); elementary education (M Ed, Ed D, Ed S); higher education/student personnel (Ed D, PhD); literacy education (M Ed); math education (Ed D); secondary education (M Ed, PhD, Ed S); special education (M Ed, PhD, Ed S); teacher corporations (MA); teacher education (MA). *Accreditation:* NCATE. *Faculty:* 65 full-time (40 women), 25 part-time/adjunct (5 women). *Students:* 185 full-time (148 women), 410 part-time (310 women); includes 193 minority (168 Black or African American, non-Hispanic/Latino; 7 Asian, non-Hispanic/Latino; 14 Hispanic/Latino; 4 Two or more races, non-Hispanic/Latino), 7 international. Average age 33. In 2017, 176 master's, 20 doctorates, 37 other advanced degrees awarded. *Entrance requirements:* For master's, GRE General Test, minimum GPA of 3.0; for doctorate, GRE General Test. Additional exam requirements/recommendations for international students: Required—TOEFL. *Application deadline:*

For fall admission, 3/1 for domestic students; for spring admission, 10/1 for domestic students; for summer admission, 3/1 for domestic students. Applications are processed on a rolling basis. Application fee: $50. Electronic applications accepted. *Financial support:* Scholarships/grants available. Financial award application deadline: 3/1; financial award applicants required to submit FAFSA. *Unit head:* Dr. David Rock, Dean, 662-915-7063, Fax: 662-915-7249, E-mail: soe@olemiss.edu. *Application contact:* Dr. Joe Sumrall, Professor of Elementary Education, 662-915-7350, E-mail: soe@olemiss.edu.

University of Missouri, Office of Research and Graduate Studies, College of Education, Department of Learning, Teaching and Curriculum, Columbia, MO 65211. Offers agricultural education (M Ed, PhD, Ed S); art education (M Ed, PhD, Ed S); business and office education (M Ed, PhD, Ed S); early childhood education (M Ed, PhD, Ed S); elementary education (M Ed, PhD, Ed S); English education (M Ed, PhD, Ed S); foreign language education (M Ed, PhD, Ed S); health education and promotion (M Ed, PhD); learning and instruction (M Ed); marketing education (M Ed, PhD, Ed S); mathematics education (M Ed, PhD, Ed S); music education (M Ed, PhD, Ed S); reading education (M Ed, PhD, Ed S); science education (M Ed, PhD, Ed S); social studies education (M Ed, PhD, Ed S); vocational education (M Ed, PhD, Ed S). *Program availability:* Part-time. Terminal master's awarded for partial completion of doctoral program. *Degree requirements:* For doctorate, thesis/dissertation. *Entrance requirements:* For master's and Ed S, GRE General Test or MAT, minimum GPA of 3.0; for doctorate, GRE General Test, minimum GPA of 3.0. Additional exam requirements/recommendations for international students: Required—TOEFL (minimum score 600 paper-based; 100 iBT). Electronic applications accepted.

University of Missouri–St. Louis, College of Education, Department of Educator Preparation, Innovation and Research, St. Louis, MO 63121. Offers elementary education (M Ed), including early childhood, general, reading; secondary education (M Ed), including curriculum and instruction, general, middle level education, reading, teaching English to speakers of other languages (TESOL); special education (M Ed), including autism and developmental disabilities, early childhood special education. *Program availability:* Part-time, evening/weekend. *Students:* 75 full-time (63 women), 462 part-time (363 women); includes 127 minority (85 Black or African American, non-Hispanic/Latino; 2 American Indian or Alaska Native, non-Hispanic/Latino; 8 Asian, non-Hispanic/Latino; 24 Hispanic/Latino; 8 Two or more races, non-Hispanic/Latino), 1 international. 247 applicants, 92% accepted, 153 enrolled. *Degree requirements:* For master's, comprehensive exam. *Entrance requirements:* Additional exam requirements/recommendations for international students: Recommended—TOEFL (minimum score 550 paper-based; 79 iBT), IELTS (minimum score 6.5). *Application deadline:* For fall admission, 7/1 priority date for domestic and international students; for spring admission, 12/1 priority date for domestic and international students. Application fee: $50 ($40 for international students). Electronic applications accepted. *Expenses:* Tuition, state resident: part-time $476.50 per credit hour. Tuition, nonresident: part-time $1169.70 per credit hour. *Financial support:* Application deadline: 4/1; applicants required to submit FAFSA. *Unit head:* Dr. Gayle Wilkinson, Chair, 314-516-5791. *Application contact:* 314-516-5458, Fax: 314-516-6996, E-mail: gadadm@umsl.edu. Website: https://coe.umsl.edu/dept/epir.html

University of Montevallo, College of Education, Program in Elementary Education, Montevallo, AL 35115. Offers M Ed. *Accreditation:* NCATE. *Program availability:* Part-time. *Students:* 5 full-time (all women), 19 part-time (18 women); includes 3 minority (2 Black or African American, non-Hispanic/Latino; 1 Two or more races, non-Hispanic/Latino). *Entrance requirements:* For master's, GRE General Test, MAT, minimum undergraduate GPA of 2.5. Additional exam requirements/recommendations for international students: Required—TOEFL (minimum score 550 paper-based). *Application deadline:* For fall admission, 7/15 for domestic students; for spring admission, 11/15 for domestic students. Application fee: $30. *Expenses:* Tuition, state resident: full-time $9888. Tuition, nonresident: full-time $21,144. *Required fees:* $1920. *Financial support:* Federal Work-Study, scholarships/grants, and unspecified assistantships available. *Unit head:* Dr. Charlotte Daughhetee, Interim Dean, 205-665-6360, E-mail: daughc@montevallo.edu. *Application contact:* Colleen Kennedy, Graduate Program Assistant, 205-665-6350, E-mail: ckennedy@montevallo.edu. Website: https://www.montevallo.edu/academics/colleges/college-of-education/

University of Nebraska at Kearney, College of Education, Department of Teacher Education, Kearney, NE 68849-0001. Offers curriculum and instruction (MA Ed), including early childhood education, elementary education, English as a second language, instructional effectiveness, reading/special education, secondary education; instructional technology (MS Ed), including information technology, instructional technology, school librarian; reading PK-12 (MA Ed); special education (MA Ed), including advanced practitioner: assistive technology specialist, advanced practitioner: behavioral interventionist, advanced practitioner: inclusive collaboration specialist, gifted, teacher education. *Program availability:* Part-time, evening/weekend, online only, 100% online. *Degree requirements:* For master's, comprehensive exam, thesis optional. *Entrance requirements:* For master's, portfolio or GRE. Additional exam requirements/recommendations for international students: Recommended—TOEFL (minimum score 550 paper-based; 79 iBT), IELTS (minimum score 6.5). Electronic applications accepted. *Expenses:* Contact institution.

University of Nebraska at Omaha, Graduate Studies, College of Education, Department of Teacher Education, Program in Elementary Education, Omaha, NE 68182. Offers MS. *Accreditation:* NCATE. *Program availability:* Part-time, evening/weekend. *Degree requirements:* For master's, comprehensive exam (for some programs), thesis (for some programs). *Entrance requirements:* For master's, minimum GPA of 3.0, transcripts. Additional exam requirements/recommendations for international students: Required—TOEFL, IELTS, PTE. Electronic applications accepted.

University of Nevada, Las Vegas, Graduate College, College of Education, Department of Teaching and Learning, Las Vegas, NV 89154-3005. Offers curriculum and instruction (M Ed, MS, Ed D, PhD, Ed S), including teacher education (PhD); elementary teaching (Certificate); online teaching and training (Certificate); secondary teaching (Certificate); social justice studies (Certificate); teaching and learning (PhD). *Program availability:* Part-time, evening/weekend. *Faculty:* 27 full-time (13 women), 10 part-time/adjunct (8 women). *Students:* 315 full-time (222 women), 244 part-time (161 women); includes 226 minority (58 Black or African American, non-Hispanic/Latino; 2 American Indian or Alaska Native, non-Hispanic/Latino; 24 Asian, non-Hispanic/Latino; 104 Hispanic/Latino; 2 Native Hawaiian or other Pacific Islander, non-Hispanic/Latino; 36 Two or more races, non-Hispanic/Latino), 10 international. Average age 35. 234 applicants, 89% accepted, 174 enrolled. In 2017, 153 master's, 16 doctorates, 3 other advanced degrees awarded. *Degree requirements:* For master's, comprehensive exam (for some programs), thesis (for some programs); for doctorate, comprehensive exam, thesis/dissertation, defense of dissertation; for other advanced degree, comprehensive exam (for some programs), oral presentation of special project or professional paper. *Entrance requirements:* For master's, bachelor's degree with minimum GPA 2.75; for doctorate, GRE General Test, master's degree with minimum GPA of 3.0; statement of purpose; demonstration of oral communication skills; 3 letters of recommendation; for other advanced degree, PRAXIS Core (for some programs); PRAXIS II (for some

programs), bachelor's degree (for some programs). Additional exam requirements/recommendations for international students: Required—TOEFL (minimum score 550 paper-based; 80 iBT), IELTS (minimum score 7). *Application deadline:* For fall admission, 6/1 for domestic students, 5/1 for international students; for spring admission, 11/1 for domestic students, 10/1 for international students; for summer admission, 3/15 for domestic students. Application fee: $60 ($95 for international students). *Expenses:* $275 per credit, $850 per course, $7,969 per year resident, $22,157 per year non-resident, $7,094 non-resident fee (7 credits or more), $1,307 annual health insurance fee. *Financial support:* In 2017–18, 36 students received support, including 13 research assistantships with full tuition reimbursements available (averaging $18,065 per year), 23 teaching assistantships with full tuition reimbursements available (averaging $19,564 per year); institutionally sponsored loans, scholarships/grants, health care benefits, and unspecified assistantships also available. Financial award application deadline: 3/15; financial award applicants required to submit FAFSA. *Faculty research:* Content area and critical literacy, education in content areas, teacher education, STEM education, immersive environments/simulations/games. *Total annual research expenditures:* $1.1 million. *Unit head:* Dr. Emily Lin, Chair/Professor, 702-895-6407, Fax: 702-895-4898, E-mail: emily.lin@unlv.edu. *Application contact:* Dr. Travis Olson, Graduate Coordinator, 702-895-0471, Fax: 702-895-4898, E-mail: travis.olson@unlv.edu. Website: http://tl.unlv.edu/

University of Nevada, Reno, Graduate School, College of Education, Department of Curriculum, Teaching and Learning, Program in Elementary Education, Reno, NV 89557. Offers M Ed, MA, MS. *Degree requirements:* For master's, thesis optional. *Entrance requirements:* For master's, GRE General Test, minimum GPA of 2.75. Additional exam requirements/recommendations for international students: Required—TOEFL (minimum score 500 paper-based; 61 iBT), IELTS (minimum score 6). Electronic applications accepted. *Faculty research:* Child development, educational trends.

University of New Hampshire, Graduate School, College of Liberal Arts, Department of Education, Program in Elementary Education, Durham, NH 03824. Offers M Ed. *Program availability:* Part-time. *Students:* 12 full-time (11 women), 17 part-time (16 women). Average age 26. 12 applicants, 75% accepted, 8 enrolled. In 2017, 35 master's awarded. *Entrance requirements:* For master's, PRAXIS. Additional exam requirements/recommendations for international students: Required—TOEFL (minimum score 550 paper-based; 80 iBT). *Application deadline:* For fall admission, 4/15 for domestic and international students; for spring admission, 11/1 for domestic students; for summer admission, 4/15 for domestic students. Application fee: $65. Electronic applications accepted. *Financial support:* In 2017–18, 7 students received support, including 1 teaching assistantship; fellowships, research assistantships, career-related internships or fieldwork, Federal Work-Study, scholarships/grants, and tuition waivers (full and partial) also available. Support available to part-time students. Financial award application deadline: 2/15. *Unit head:* Paula Salvio, Chair, 603-862-0024, E-mail: education.department@unh.edu. *Application contact:* Cindy Glidden, Department Coordinator, 603-862-2311, E-mail: education.department@unh.edu. Website: http://cola.unh.edu/education

University of New Hampshire, Graduate School Manchester Campus, Manchester, NH 03101. Offers business administration (MBA); cybersecurity policy and risk management (MS); educational administration and supervision (Ed S); educational studies (M Ed); elementary education (M Ed); information technology (MS); public administration (MPA); public health (MPH, Certificate); secondary education (M Ed, MAT); social work (MSW); substance use disorders (Certificate). *Program availability:* Part-time, evening/weekend. *Students:* 13 full-time (6 women), 17 part-time (0 women); includes 7 minority (1 Black or African American, non-Hispanic/Latino; 4 Asian, non-Hispanic/Latino; 1 Hispanic/Latino; 1 Two or more races, non-Hispanic/Latino), 10 international. Average age 33. 42 applicants, 71% accepted, 8 enrolled. In 2017, 4 master's awarded. *Entrance requirements:* Additional exam requirements/recommendations for international students: Required—TOEFL (minimum score 550 paper-based; 80 iBT). *Application deadline:* For fall admission, 6/1 for domestic students, 4/1 for international students; for spring admission, 12/1 for domestic students. Application fee: $65. Electronic applications accepted. *Financial support:* Fellowships, research assistantships, teaching assistantships, Federal Work-Study, scholarships/grants, health care benefits, and unspecified assistantships available. Support available to part-time students. Financial award application deadline: 2/15; financial award applicants required to submit FAFSA. *Unit head:* Candice Morey, Educational Programs Coordinator, 603-641-4313, E-mail: unhm.gradcenter@unh.edu. Website: http://www.gradschool.unh.edu/manchester/

University of New Mexico, Graduate Studies, College of Education, Program in Elementary Education, Albuquerque, NM 87131-2039. Offers math, science, and educational technology (MA). *Program availability:* Part-time. *Students:* Average age 33. 39 applicants, 79% accepted, 26 enrolled. In 2017, 71 master's awarded. *Degree requirements:* For master's, comprehensive exam, thesis optional. *Entrance requirements:* For master's, minimum overall GPA of 3.0, some experience working with students, NMTA or teacher's license, 3 letters of reference, letter of intent. Additional exam requirements/recommendations for international students: Required—TOEFL (minimum score 550 paper-based). *Application deadline:* For fall admission, 2/15 for domestic students; for spring admission, 10/1 for domestic students. Application fee: $50. Electronic applications accepted. *Financial support:* Fellowships, career-related internships or fieldwork, scholarships/grants, and unspecified assistantships available. Financial award application deadline: 4/15; financial award applicants required to submit FAFSA. *Faculty research:* Elementary education, science education, technology education, reflective practice, teacher education. *Unit head:* Dr. Cheryl Torrez, Chair, 505-277-0911, Fax: 505-277-0455, E-mail: ted@unm.edu. *Application contact:* Lea Briggs, Administrative Assistant, 505-277-9439, Fax: 505-277-0455, E-mail: ted@unm.edu. Website: http://coe.unm.edu/departments-programs/teelp/elementary-education/index.html

University of North Alabama, College of Education, Department of Elementary Education, Program in Elementary Education, Florence, AL 35632-0001. Offers MA Ed, Ed S. *Accreditation:* NCATE. *Program availability:* Part-time, 100% online. *Faculty:* 5 full-time (all women), 3 part-time/adjunct (1 woman). *Students:* 8 full-time (7 women), 61 part-time (58 women); includes 11 minority (9 Black or African American, non-Hispanic/Latino; 2 Two or more races, non-Hispanic/Latino). Average age 30. 22 applicants, 82% accepted, 14 enrolled. In 2017, 40 master's, 5 Ed Ss awarded. *Degree requirements:* For master's, comprehensive exam. *Entrance requirements:* For master's, GRE, MAT, or NTE, minimum GPA of 2.5, Alabama Class B Certificate or equivalent, teaching experience. Additional exam requirements/recommendations for international students: Required—TOEFL (minimum score 79 iBT), IELTS (minimum score 6), PTE (minimum score 54). *Application deadline:* Applications are processed on a rolling basis. Application fee: $50 ($100 for international students). Electronic applications accepted. *Expenses:* Tuition, state resident: full-time $7824; part-time $5943 per year. Tuition, nonresident: full-time $15,648; part-time $11,736 per year. *Required fees:* $3064; $2298 per unit. Tuition and fees vary according to course load and reciprocity agreements. *Financial support:* In 2017–18, 6 students received support. Federal Work-Study,

Elementary Education

scholarships/grants, and unspecified assistantships available. Financial award application deadline: 2/1; financial award applicants required to submit FAFSA. *Unit head:* Dr. Donna Lefort, Dean, College of Education and Human Sciences, 256-765-4252, E-mail: dpjacobs@una.edu. *Application contact:* Hillary N. Coats, Graduate Admissions Coordinator, 256-765-4447, E-mail: graduate@una.edu. Website: https://www.una.edu/education/departments/elementary-education.html

The University of North Carolina at Charlotte, Cato College of Education, Department of Reading and Elementary Education, Charlotte, NC 28223-0001. Offers elementary education (M Ed, Graduate Certificate); elementary mathematics education (Graduate Certificate); reading education (M Ed). *Program availability:* Part-time, evening/weekend, 100% online, blended/hybrid learning. *Faculty:* 26 full-time (13 women), 1 part-time/adjunct (0 women). *Students:* 4 full-time (all women), 52 part-time (all women); includes 12 minority (8 Black or African American, non-Hispanic/Latino; 1 American Indian or Alaska Native, non-Hispanic/Latino; 2 Hispanic/Latino; 1 Two or more races, non-Hispanic/Latino). Average age 29. 26 applicants, 100% accepted, 21 enrolled. In 2017, 18 master's, 2 other advanced degrees awarded. *Degree requirements:* For master's, thesis or alternative, capstone project. *Entrance requirements:* For master's, GRE or MAT, three letters of recommendation, official transcripts, academic and professional goals statement, valid teacher's license, bachelor's degree in elementary education; NC A-level license or its equivalent in another state (for reading education). Additional exam requirements/recommendations for international students: Required—TOEFL (minimum score 523 paper-based, 70 iBT) or IELTS (6.5). *Application deadline:* For fall admission, 3/1 priority date for domestic students, 3/1 for international students; for spring admission, 10/1 priority date for domestic students, 10/1 for international students; for summer admission, 4/1 priority date for domestic students, 4/1 for international students. Applications are processed on a rolling basis. Application fee: $75. Electronic applications accepted. *Expenses:* Tuition, state resident: full-time $4337. Tuition, nonresident: full-time $17,771. *Required fees:* $3211. Tuition and fees vary according to course load and program. *Financial support:* In 2017–18, 4 students received support, including 4 research assistantships (averaging $15,000 per year); career-related internships or fieldwork, institutionally sponsored loans, scholarships/grants, and unspecified assistantships also available. Support available to part-time students. Financial award application deadline: 3/1; financial award applicants required to submit FAFSA. *Total annual research expenditures:* $163,549. *Unit head:* Dr. Mike Putman, Chair, 704-687-8019, E-mail: michael.putman@uncc.edu. *Application contact:* Kathy B. Giddings, Director of Graduate Admissions, 704-687-5503, Fax: 704-687-1668, E-mail: gradadm@uncc.edu. Website: http://reel.uncc.edu/

The University of North Carolina at Greensboro, Graduate School, School of Education, Department of Teacher Education and Higher Education, Program in Curriculum and Teaching, Greensboro, NC 27412-5001. Offers higher education (PhD); teacher education and development (PhD). *Accreditation:* NCATE. *Degree requirements:* For doctorate, comprehensive exam, thesis/dissertation. *Entrance requirements:* For doctorate, GRE General Test. Additional exam requirements/recommendations for international students: Required—TOEFL. Electronic applications accepted.

The University of North Carolina at Pembroke, The Graduate School, School of Education, Program in Elementary Education, Pembroke, NC 28372-1510. Offers MA Ed, MAT. *Accreditation:* NCATE. *Program availability:* Part-time, evening/weekend, online learning. *Degree requirements:* For master's, comprehensive exam, thesis optional. *Entrance requirements:* For master's, GRE General Test or MAT, minimum GPA of 3.0 in major, 2.5 overall; teaching license; two years of full-time teaching experience (recommended). Additional exam requirements/recommendations for international students: Required—TOEFL. *Application deadline:* For fall admission, 7/15 priority date for domestic and international students; for spring admission, 12/1 priority date for domestic and international students. Applications are processed on a rolling basis. Application fee: $45 ($60 for international students). *Financial support:* Application deadline: 4/15; applicants required to submit FAFSA. *Unit head:* Dr. Lisa Mitchell, Program Director, 910-775-4412, Fax: 910-521-6165, E-mail: lisa.mitchell@uncp.edu.

The University of North Carolina Wilmington, Watson College of Education, Department of Early Childhood, Elementary, Middle, Literacy and Special Education, Wilmington, NC 28403-3297. Offers educational leadership, policy, and advocacy (M Ed); elementary education (M Ed, MAT); language and literacy (M Ed); middle grades education (MAT). *Accreditation:* NCATE. *Program availability:* Part-time, blended/hybrid learning. *Faculty:* 22 full-time (15 women), 2 part-time/adjunct (both women). *Students:* 82 full-time (70 women), 91 part-time (84 women); includes 51 minority (33 Black or African American, non-Hispanic/Latino; 3 American Indian or Alaska Native, non-Hispanic/Latino; 1 Asian, non-Hispanic/Latino; 8 Hispanic/Latino; 6 Two or more races, non-Hispanic/Latino). Average age 32. 68 applicants, 82% accepted, 45 enrolled. In 2017, 83 master's awarded. *Degree requirements:* For master's, thesis or alternative, exit portfolio, oral presentation, internship, research project (depending on specialization). *Entrance requirements:* For master's, 3 letters of recommendation, NC Class A teacher license in related field, education statement of interest essay. Additional exam requirements/recommendations for international students: Required—TOEFL (minimum score 550 paper-based; 79 iBT), IELTS (minimum score 6.5). *Application deadline:* For fall admission, 5/15 for domestic students; for spring admission, 10/15 for domestic students; for summer admission, 3/15 for domestic students. Applications are processed on a rolling basis. Application fee: $75. Electronic applications accepted. *Expenses:* Tuition, state resident: full-time $4626; part-time $226.76 per credit hour. Tuition, nonresident: full-time $17,834; part-time $874.22 per credit hour. *Required fees:* $2124. Tuition and fees vary according to program. *Financial support:* Scholarships/grants and unspecified assistantships available. Financial award application deadline: 1/1; financial award applicants required to submit FAFSA. *Unit head:* Dr. Kathy Fox, Chair, 910-962-3240, Fax: 910-962-3988, E-mail: foxk@uncw.edu. *Application contact:* Dr. Elizabeth Crawford, Graduate Program Coordinator, 910-962-2916, Fax: 910-962-3988, E-mail: crawforde@uncw.edu. Website: http://www.uncw.edu/ed/eemls/index.html

University of North Dakota, Graduate School, College of Education and Human Development, Program in Elementary Education, Grand Forks, ND 58202. Offers M Ed, MS. *Accreditation:* NCATE. *Program availability:* Part-time, online learning. *Degree requirements:* For master's, comprehensive exam, thesis or alternative. *Entrance requirements:* For master's, minimum GPA of 3.0. Additional exam requirements/recommendations for international students: Required—TOEFL (minimum score 550 paper-based; 79 iBT), IELTS (minimum score 6.5). Electronic applications accepted. *Faculty research:* Whole language, multicultural education, child-focused learning, experiential science, cooperative learning.

University of Northern Colorado, Graduate School, College of Education and Behavioral Sciences, School of Teacher Education, Program in Elementary Education, Greeley, CO 80639. Offers MAT. *Accreditation:* NCATE. *Program availability:* Part-time, evening/weekend. *Degree requirements:* For master's, comprehensive exam, thesis or alternative. *Entrance requirements:* For master's, GRE General Test. Electronic applications accepted.

University of Northern Iowa, Graduate College, College of Education, Department of Curriculum and Instruction, MAE Program in Elementary Education, Cedar Falls, IA 50614. Offers MAE. *Program availability:* Part-time, evening/weekend. *Degree requirements:* For master's, comprehensive exam, thesis or alternative. *Entrance requirements:* For master's, minimum GPA 3.0. Additional exam requirements/recommendations for international students: Required—TOEFL (minimum score 500 paper-based; 61 iBT).

University of North Florida, College of Education and Human Services, Department of Childhood Education, Literacy, and TESOL, Jacksonville, FL 32224. Offers literacy (M Ed); professional education (M Ed); TESOL (M Ed). *Accreditation:* NCATE. *Program availability:* Part-time, evening/weekend. *Entrance requirements:* For master's, GRE General Test, minimum GPA of 3.0 in last 60 hours, 3 letters of recommendation, interview. Additional exam requirements/recommendations for international students: Required—TOEFL (minimum score 500 paper-based). Electronic applications accepted. *Faculty research:* Social context of and processes in learning, inter-disciplinary instruction, cross-cultural conflict resolution, the Vygotskian perspective on literacy diagnosis and instruction, performance poetry and teaching the language arts through drama.

University of Oklahoma, Jeannine Rainbolt College of Education, Department of Instructional Leadership and Academic Curriculum, Norman, OK 73019. Offers instructional leadership and academic curriculum (M Ed, PhD), including biomedical education (PhD), early childhood education, elementary education, English education, instructional leadership, mathematics education, reading education, science education, social studies education, world languages education (M Ed); reading specialist (M Ed). *Accreditation:* NCATE. *Program availability:* Part-time. *Faculty:* 19 full-time (15 women), 1 (woman) part-time/adjunct. *Students:* 37 full-time (28 women), 121 part-time (98 women); includes 32 minority (7 Black or African American, non-Hispanic/Latino; 4 American Indian or Alaska Native, non-Hispanic/Latino; 5 Asian, non-Hispanic/Latino; 6 Hispanic/Latino; 1 Native Hawaiian or other Pacific Islander, non-Hispanic/Latino; 9 Two or more races, non-Hispanic/Latino), 12 international. Average age 35. 39 applicants, 77% accepted, 22 enrolled. In 2017, 49 master's, 12 doctorates awarded. Terminal master's awarded for partial completion of doctoral program. *Degree requirements:* For master's, comprehensive exam (for some programs), thesis (for some programs); for doctorate, comprehensive exam (for some programs), thesis/dissertation. *Entrance requirements:* For doctorate, GRE. Additional exam requirements/recommendations for international students: Required—TOEFL (minimum score 79 iBT) or IELTS (minimum score 6.5). Application fee: $50 ($100 for international students). Electronic applications accepted. *Expenses:* Tuition, state resident: full-time $5119; part-time $213.30 per credit hour. Tuition, nonresident: full-time $19,778; part-time $824.10 per credit hour. *Required fees:* $3458; $133.55 per credit hour. $126.50 per semester. *Financial support:* In 2017–18, 90 students received support, including 8 research assistantships (averaging $11,248 per year), 6 teaching assistantships (averaging $12,188 per year); fellowships, scholarships/grants, and unspecified assistantships also available. Financial award application deadline: 6/1; financial award applicants required to submit FAFSA. *Faculty research:* Teacher preparation; instruction; curriculum; learning; constructivist theory. *Total annual research expenditures:* $707,690. *Unit head:* Dr. Stacy Reeder, Chair, 405-325-1498, Fax: 405-325-4061, E-mail: reeder@ou.edu. *Application contact:* Anna Steele, Graduate Programs Officer, 405-325-4525, E-mail: anna.steele@ou.edu. Website: http://www.ou.edu/education/ilac

University of Pennsylvania, Graduate School of Education, Division of Teaching, Learning, and Leadership, Teacher Education Program, Philadelphia, PA 19104. Offers elementary education (MS Ed); secondary education (MS Ed). *Students:* Average age 25. 123 applicants, 81% accepted. In 2017, 60 master's awarded. *Degree requirements:* For master's, thesis or alternative, student teaching, portfolio. *Entrance requirements:* For master's, GRE, bachelor's degree. Additional exam requirements/recommendations for international students: Required—TOEFL, IELTS. *Application deadline:* For summer admission, 6/1 priority date for domestic students, 6/1 for international students. Applications are processed on a rolling basis. Application fee: $75. Electronic applications accepted. *Financial support:* In 2017–18, 53 students received support. Federal Work-Study and scholarships/grants available. Financial award applicants required to submit FAFSA. *Faculty research:* Teacher competencies, social justice teaching, teacher practitioner inquiry. *Unit head:* Maureen Cotterill, Program Manager, 215-898-7364. Website: http://www2.gse.upenn.edu/tep/

University of Phoenix–Bay Area Campus, College of Education, San Jose, CA 95134-1805. Offers administration and supervision (MA Ed); adult education and training (MA Ed); early childhood education (MA Ed); education (Ed S); educational leadership (Ed D); elementary teacher education (MA Ed); higher education administration (PhD); secondary teacher education (MA Ed); special education (MA Ed); teacher leadership (MA Ed). *Program availability:* Evening/weekend, online learning. *Degree requirements:* For master's, thesis (for some programs). *Entrance requirements:* For master's, minimum undergraduate GPA of 2.5, 3 years of work experience. Additional exam requirements/recommendations for international students: Required—TOEFL (minimum score 550 paper-based; 79 iBT). Electronic applications accepted.

University of Phoenix–Central Valley Campus, College of Education, Fresno, CA 93720-1552. Offers curriculum and instruction (MA Ed); curriculum and instruction-computer education (MA Ed); elementary teacher education (MA Ed); secondary teacher education (MA Ed).

University of Phoenix–Hawaii Campus, College of Education, Honolulu, HI 96813-3800. Offers administration and supervision (MA Ed); curriculum and instruction (MA Ed); elementary education (MA Ed); secondary education (MA Ed); special education (MA Ed); teacher education for elementary licensure (MA Ed). *Program availability:* Evening/weekend. *Degree requirements:* For master's, thesis (for some programs). *Entrance requirements:* For master's, minimum undergraduate GPA of 2.5, 3 years of work experience. Additional exam requirements/recommendations for international students: Required—TOEFL (minimum score 550 paper-based; 79 iBT). Electronic applications accepted.

University of Phoenix–Las Vegas Campus, College of Education, Las Vegas, NV 89135. Offers administration and supervision (MA Ed); curriculum and instruction (MA Ed); school counseling (MSC); teacher education-elementary licensure (MA Ed). *Program availability:* Evening/weekend. *Degree requirements:* For master's, thesis (for some programs). *Entrance requirements:* For master's, minimum undergraduate GPA of 2.5, 3 years of work experience. Additional exam requirements/recommendations for international students: Required—TOEFL (minimum score 550 paper-based; 79 iBT). Electronic applications accepted.

University of Phoenix–Online Campus, College of Education, Phoenix, AZ 85034-7209. Offers administration and supervision (MAEd, Certificate); adult education and training (MAEd); curriculum and instruction (MAEd), including computer education, curriculum and instruction, English as a second language, language arts, mathematics, reading; early childhood education (MAEd); educational studies (MAEd); elementary teacher education (MAEd), including early childhood, elementary teacher education, high school middle level, middle level; principal licensure (Certificate); secondary teacher education (MAEd); special education (MAEd, Certificate); teacher education (MAEd), including middle level generalist; teacher education middle level mathematics (MAEd), including middle level mathematics; teacher education middle level science (MAEd), including middle level science; teacher education secondary mathematics (MAEd); teacher education secondary science (MAEd); teacher leadership (MAEd); teachers of English learners (Certificate); transition to teaching (Certificate), including elementary education, secondary education. *Program availability:* Evening/weekend, online learning. *Entrance requirements:* Additional exam requirements/recommendations for international students: Required—TOEFL, TOEIC (Test of English as an International Communication), Berlitz Online English Proficiency Exam, PTE, or IELTS. Electronic applications accepted. *Expenses:* Contact institution.

University of Phoenix–Phoenix Campus, College of Education, Tempe, AZ 85282-2371. Offers administration and supervision (MA Ed); adult education and training (MA Ed); curriculum and instruction reading (MA Ed); early childhood education (MA Ed); education studies (MA Ed); elementary teacher education (MA Ed); secondary teacher education (MA Ed); special education (MA Ed); teacher leadership (MA Ed). *Program availability:* Evening/weekend, online learning. *Entrance requirements:* Additional exam requirements/recommendations for international students: Required—TOEFL, TOEIC (Test of English as an International Communication), Berlitz Online English Proficiency Exam, PTE, or IELTS. Electronic applications accepted. *Expenses:* Contact institution.

University of Phoenix–Sacramento Valley Campus, College of Education, Sacramento, CA 95833-4334. Offers adult education (MA Ed); curriculum instruction (MA Ed); elementary teacher education (MA Ed); secondary teacher education (MA Ed); teacher education (Certificate). *Program availability:* Evening/weekend. *Degree requirements:* For master's, thesis (for some programs). *Entrance requirements:* For master's, 3 years of work experience, minimum undergraduate GPA of 2.5. Additional exam requirements/recommendations for international students: Required—TOEFL (minimum score 550 paper-based; 79 iBT). Electronic applications accepted.

University of Phoenix–San Diego Campus, College of Education, San Diego, CA 92123. Offers curriculum and instruction (MA Ed), including computer education, curriculum and instruction, English as a second language; elementary teacher education (MA Ed); secondary teacher education (MA Ed). *Program availability:* Evening/weekend. *Degree requirements:* For master's, thesis (for some programs). *Entrance requirements:* For master's, 3 years of work experience, minimum undergraduate GPA of 3.0. Additional exam requirements/recommendations for international students: Required—TOEFL (minimum score 550 paper-based; 79 iBT). Electronic applications accepted.

University of Pittsburgh, School of Education, Department of Instruction and Learning, Program in Elementary Education, Pittsburgh, PA 15260. Offers M Ed, MAT. *Degree requirements:* For master's, thesis. *Entrance requirements:* For master's, PRAXIS I. Additional exam requirements/recommendations for international students: Required—TOEFL. Electronic applications accepted.

University of Puget Sound, School of Education, Program in Teaching, Tacoma, WA 98416. Offers elementary education (MAT); secondary education (MAT). *Accreditation:* NASM. *Degree requirements:* For master's, project. *Entrance requirements:* For master's, WEST-E or NES, WEST-B or ACT/SAT, two education foundation prerequisite courses; minor in content area (for secondary education). Additional exam requirements/recommendations for international students: Required—TOEFL (minimum score 550 paper-based; 90 iBT). Electronic applications accepted. *Expenses:* Contact institution. *Faculty research:* Pre-service teacher learning, public school partnerships and professional development, creating equitable classrooms, literacy development, teaching social studies.

University of St. Francis, College of Education, Joliet, IL 60435-6169. Offers educational leadership (MS, Ed D); elementary education (M Ed); reading (MS); secondary education (M Ed), including English education, math education, science education, social studies education, visual arts education; special education (M Ed); teaching and learning (MS); TESOL (Certificate). *Accreditation:* NCATE. *Program availability:* Part-time, evening/weekend, 100% online, blended/hybrid learning. *Faculty:* 11 full-time (8 women), 52 part-time/adjunct (36 women). *Students:* 39 full-time (32 women), 411 part-time (318 women); includes 106 minority (57 Black or African American, non-Hispanic/Latino; 8 Asian, non-Hispanic/Latino; 37 Hispanic/Latino; 4 Two or more races, non-Hispanic/Latino). Average age 37. 277 applicants, 55% accepted, 137 enrolled. In 2017, 199 master's, 28 doctorates awarded. *Degree requirements:* For master's, comprehensive exam; for doctorate, thesis/dissertation. *Entrance requirements:* Additional exam requirements/recommendations for international students: Required—TOEFL (minimum score 550 paper-based; 79 iBT), IELTS (minimum score 6). *Application deadline:* Applications are processed on a rolling basis. Application fee: $30. Electronic applications accepted. Application fee is waived when completed online. *Expenses:* $365 to $748 per credit hour. *Financial support:* In 2017–18, 40 students received support. Scholarships/grants and unspecified assistantships available. Support available to part-time students. Financial award applicants required to submit FAFSA. *Unit head:* Dr. John Gambro, Dean, 815-740-3829, Fax: 815-740-2264, E-mail: jgambro@stfrancis.edu. *Application contact:* Sandra Sloka, Director of Admissions for Graduate and Degree Completion Programs, 800-735-7500, Fax: 815-740-3431, E-mail: ssloka@stfrancis.edu.
Website: http://www.stfrancis.edu/academics/college-of-education/

University of Saint Joseph, Department of Education, West Hartford, CT 06117-2700. Offers curriculum and instruction (MA); elementary education (MAT); instructional technology (MA); literacy (MA); secondary education (MAT); TESOL (MA). *Program availability:* Part-time, evening/weekend. *Degree requirements:* For master's, comprehensive exam, thesis or alternative. *Entrance requirements:* For master's, 2 letters of recommendation. *Application deadline:* Applications are processed on a rolling basis. Application fee: $50. Electronic applications accepted. Application fee is waived when completed online. *Financial support:* Career-related internships or fieldwork and unspecified assistantships available. Support available to part-time students. Financial award applicants required to submit FAFSA.
Website: https://www.usj.edu/academics/schools/sasbe/education/

University of Saint Mary, Graduate Programs, Program in Elementary Education, Leavenworth, KS 66048-5082. Offers MA. *Program availability:* Part-time, evening/weekend. *Entrance requirements:* For master's, PPST, minimum GPA of 2.75, interview, essay, two letters of reference. Electronic applications accepted. *Expenses:* Contact institution.

University of St. Thomas, School of Education and Human Services, Houston, TX 77006-4696. Offers all level education (M Ed); bilingual/dual language (M Ed); Catholic school teaching (M Ed); Catholic/private school leadership (M Ed); counselor education (M Ed); curriculum and instruction (M Ed); educational leadership (Ed D); educational leadership (M Ed); elementary teaching (M Ed); English as a second language (M Ed); exceptionality/educational diagnostician (M Ed); exceptionality/special education (M Ed); generalist (M Ed); reading (M Ed); secondary teaching (M Ed); teaching (MAT). *Accreditation:* TEAC. *Program availability:* Part-time, evening/weekend, online learning. *Faculty:* 33 full-time (22 women), 43 part-time/adjunct (26 women). *Students:* 119 full-time (97 women), 597 part-time (529 women); includes 478 minority (166 Black or

African American, non-Hispanic/Latino; 29 Asian, non-Hispanic/Latino; 277 Hispanic/Latino; 2 Native Hawaiian or other Pacific Islander, non-Hispanic/Latino; 4 Two or more races, non-Hispanic/Latino), 19 international. Average age 36. 306 applicants, 91% accepted, 181 enrolled. In 2017, 328 master's awarded. *Degree requirements:* For master's, thesis, field experience. *Entrance requirements:* For master's, GRE or MAT if GPA is below 3.0, bachelor's degree; minimum GPA of 2.75 in bachelor's degree or last 60 credit hours; official transcripts from all institutions; goal statement of 250-300 words; 1 reference. Additional exam requirements/recommendations for international students: Required—TOEFL (minimum score 94 iBT), IELTS (minimum score 7), PTE (minimum score 53). *Application deadline:* Applications are processed on a rolling basis. Application fee: $35. Electronic applications accepted. *Expenses:* Contact institution. *Financial support:* In 2017–18, 27 students received support. Federal Work-Study, scholarships/grants, and state work-study, institutional employment available. Support available to part-time students. Financial award application deadline: 4/15; financial award applicants required to submit FAFSA. *Faculty research:* Leadership, diversity, personality traits, second language acquisition. *Unit head:* Dr. Paul C. Paese, Dean, 713-942-5999, Fax: 713-525-3871, E-mail: paesep@stthom.edu. *Application contact:* 713-525-3540, E-mail: education@stthom.edu.
Website: http://www.stthom.edu/Academics/School_of_Education_and_Human_Services/Index.aqf

University of South Alabama, College of Education and Professional Studies, Department of Leadership and Teacher Education, Mobile, AL 36688. Offers art education (M Ed); early childhood education (M Ed); educational leadership (M Ed, Ed D); elementary education (M Ed); reading education (M Ed); science education (M Ed); secondary education (M Ed); special education (M Ed). *Accreditation:* NCATE. *Program availability:* Part-time. *Faculty:* 15 full-time (11 women), 10 part-time/adjunct (6 women). *Students:* 203 full-time (154 women), 90 part-time (68 women); includes 73 minority (54 Black or African American, non-Hispanic/Latino; 3 American Indian or Alaska Native, non-Hispanic/Latino; 4 Asian, non-Hispanic/Latino; 10 Hispanic/Latino; 2 Two or more races, non-Hispanic/Latino). Average age 34. 134 applicants, 55% accepted, 57 enrolled. In 2017, 73 master's, 8 doctorates awarded. *Degree requirements:* For master's, comprehensive exam, thesis (for some programs); for doctorate, comprehensive exam, thesis/dissertation. *Entrance requirements:* For master's, GRE General Test or MAT, minimum GPA of 3.0; for doctorate, GRE, minimum graduate GPA of 3.25, 3 years of experience in field, 3 letters of recommendation, interview, official transcripts. Additional exam requirements/recommendations for international students: Required—TOEFL. *Application deadline:* For fall admission, 7/15 for domestic students, 6/15 for international students; for spring admission, 11/15 for domestic students, 11/1 for international students; for summer admission, 4/15 for domestic students, 4/1 for international students. Applications are processed on a rolling basis. Application fee: $35. Electronic applications accepted. *Expenses:* Tuition: state resident: full-time $10,104; part-time $421 per semester hour. Tuition, nonresident: full-time $20,208; part-time $842 per semester hour. *Financial support:* Fellowships, research assistantships, teaching assistantships, career-related internships or fieldwork, Federal Work-Study, institutionally sponsored loans, scholarships/grants, and unspecified assistantships available. Support available to part-time students. Financial award application deadline: 3/31; financial award applicants required to submit FAFSA. *Unit head:* Dr. Susan Santoli, Chair/Director of Graduate Studies, 251-380-2836, Fax: 251-380-2748, E-mail: ssantoli@southalabama.edu.
Website: http://www.southalabama.edu/colleges/ceps/lte/index.html

University of South Carolina, The Graduate School, College of Education, Department of Instruction and Teacher Education, Program in Elementary Education, Columbia, SC 29208. Offers MAT, Ed D, PhD. *Accreditation:* NCATE. *Degree requirements:* For master's, comprehensive exam; for doctorate, one foreign language, comprehensive exam, thesis/dissertation. *Entrance requirements:* For master's, GRE General Test, MAT, interview, letters of reference, resume; for doctorate, GRE General Test, MAT, interview, letters of reference, letters of intent, resum&e, transcript. *Faculty research:* Children's conception of science, whole language, middle school curriculum.

University of South Carolina Upstate, Graduate Programs, Spartanburg, SC 29303-4999. Offers early childhood education (M Ed); elementary education (M Ed); informatics (MS); special education: visual impairment (M Ed). *Accreditation:* NCATE. *Program availability:* Part-time, evening/weekend. *Degree requirements:* For master's, professional portfolio. *Entrance requirements:* For master's, GRE General Test or MAT, interview, minimum undergraduate GPA of 2.5, teaching certificate, 2 letters of recommendation. *Faculty research:* Promoting university diversity awareness, rough and tumble play, social justice education, American Indian literatures and cultures, diversity and multicultural education, science teaching strategy.

University of South Dakota, Graduate School, School of Education, Division of Curriculum and Instruction, Program in Elementary Education, Vermillion, SD 57069. Offers elementary education (MA), including early childhood education, English language learning, reading specialist/literacy coach, science, technology and math (STEM). *Accreditation:* NCATE. *Program availability:* Part-time, 100% online, blended/hybrid learning. *Degree requirements:* For master's, comprehensive exam, thesis or alternative. *Entrance requirements:* For master's, GRE General Test, MAT, minimum GPA of 2.7. Additional exam requirements/recommendations for international students: Required—TOEFL (minimum score 550 paper-based; 79 iBT). *Application deadline:* Applications are processed on a rolling basis. Application fee: $35. Electronic applications accepted. *Financial support:* Research assistantships with partial tuition reimbursements, teaching assistantships with partial tuition reimbursements, career-related internships or fieldwork, Federal Work-Study, and unspecified assistantships available. Financial award applicants required to submit FAFSA. *Application contact:* Graduate School, 605-658-6140, Fax: 605-677-6118, E-mail: grad@usd.edu.
Website: http://www.usd.edu/ci

University of Southern Indiana, Graduate Studies, Pott College of Science, Engineering, and Education, Department of Teacher Education, Program in Elementary Education, Evansville, IN 47712-3590. Offers MSE. *Accreditation:* NCATE. *Program availability:* Part-time, evening/weekend. *Faculty:* 4 full-time (3 women), 2 part-time/adjunct (1 woman). *Students:* 4 full-time (all women), 4 part-time (all women). Average age 36. In 2017, 6 master's awarded. *Entrance requirements:* For master's, PRAXIS II, bachelor's degree with minimum cumulative GPA of 2.75 from college or university accredited by NCATE or comparable association; minimum GPA of 3.0 in all courses taken at graduate level at all schools attended; teaching license. Additional exam requirements/recommendations for international students: Required—TOEFL (minimum score 550 paper-based; 79 iBT), IELTS (minimum score 6). *Application deadline:* For fall admission, 7/1 priority date for domestic students. Applications are processed on a rolling basis. Application fee: $40. Electronic applications accepted. *Expenses:* Tuition, state resident: full-time $9394. Tuition, nonresident: full-time $17,917. *Required fees:* $510. *Financial support:* Fellowships, Federal Work-Study, scholarships/grants, tuition waivers (full and partial), and unspecified assistantships available. Financial award application deadline: 3/1; financial award applicants required to submit FAFSA. *Unit head:* Dr. Bonnie Beach, Associate Dean, 812-465-1620, E-mail: blbeach@usi.edu. *Application contact:* Dr. Mayola Rowser, Director, Graduate Studies, 812-465-7015, Fax: 812-464-1956, E-mail: mrowser@usi.edu.
Website: http://www.usi.edu/science/teacher-education/programs/mse

Elementary Education

University of Southern Mississippi, College of Education and Psychology, Department of Curriculum, Instruction and Special Education, Hattiesburg, MS 39406-0001. Offers elementary education (M Ed, PhD); instructional technology (MS); instructional technology and design (PhD); secondary education (MAT); special education (M Ed, PhD). *Program availability:* Part-time, online learning. *Students:* 25 full-time (18 women), 5 part-time (3 women). 41 applicants, 59% accepted, 22 enrolled. *Degree requirements:* For master's, comprehensive exam, thesis (for some programs); for doctorate, comprehensive exam, thesis/dissertation. *Entrance requirements:* For master's, GRE General Test, MAT, minimum GPA of 3.0; for doctorate, GRE General Test, minimum GPA of 3.5. Additional exam requirements/recommendations for international students: Required—TOEFL, IELTS. *Application deadline:* For fall admission, 3/1 priority date for domestic students, 3/1 for international students; for spring admission, 1/10 priority date for domestic and international students. Applications are processed on a rolling basis. Application fee: $60. *Expenses:* Tuition, state resident: full-time $3830. *Financial support:* Research assistantships with tuition reimbursements, teaching assistantships with full tuition reimbursements, Federal Work-Study, institutionally sponsored loans, scholarships/grants, health care benefits, tuition waivers (partial), and unspecified assistantships available. Financial award application deadline: 3/15; financial award applicants required to submit FAFSA. *Faculty research:* Mathematical problem solving, integrative curriculum, writing process, teacher education models. *Unit head:* Dr. Jeff Hinton, Chair.
Website: https://www.usm.edu/elementary-special-technology-education

University of South Florida, College of Education, Department of Teaching and Learning, Tampa, FL 33620-9951. Offers early childhood education (M Ed, MA, PhD); elementary education (MA, MAT, PhD); reading/language arts (MA, PhD, Ed S). *Accreditation:* NCATE. *Faculty:* 37 full-time (28 women). *Students:* 219 full-time (174 women), 302 part-time (217 women); includes 135 minority (65 Black or African American, non-Hispanic/Latino; 3 American Indian or Alaska Native, non-Hispanic/Latino; 12 Asian, non-Hispanic/Latino; 49 Hispanic/Latino; 6 Two or more races, non-Hispanic/Latino), 63 international. Average age 35. 195 applicants, 84% accepted, 138 enrolled. In 2017, 77 master's, 13 doctorates awarded. Application fee: $30. *Total annual research expenditures:* $940,639. *Unit head:* Dr. Denisse Thompson, Chair, 813-974-4110.
Website: http://www.coedu.usf.edu/main/departments/ce/ce.html

University of South Florida, St. Petersburg, College of Education, St. Petersburg, FL 33701. Offers educational leadership development (M Ed); elementary education (MA), including math/science; English education (MA); middle grades STEM education (MS); reading education (MA). *Program availability:* Part-time. *Degree requirements:* For master's, comprehensive exam, practicum, internship, comprehensive portfolio. *Entrance requirements:* For master's, State of Florida General Knowledge Test (GKT), Florida Teaching Certificate (for non-initial certification programs), letters of recommendation. Additional exam requirements/recommendations for international students: Required—TOEFL (minimum score 550 paper-based; 79 iBT), Recommended—IELTS. Electronic applications accepted.

University of South Florida Sarasota-Manatee, College of Liberal Arts and Social Sciences, Sarasota, FL 34243. Offers criminal justice (MA); education (MA); educational leadership (M Ed), including curriculum leadership, K-12 public school leadership, non-public/charter school leadership; elementary education (MAT); English education (MA); social work (MSW). *Program availability:* Part-time, 100% online, blended/hybrid learning. *Faculty:* 15 full-time (12 women), 8 part-time/adjunct (6 women). *Students:* 11 full-time (10 women), 43 part-time (37 women); includes 17 minority (7 Black or African American, non-Hispanic/Latino; 2 Asian, non-Hispanic/Latino; 8 Hispanic/Latino), 1 international. Average age 35. 62 applicants, 27% accepted, 14 enrolled. In 2017, 32 master's awarded. *Degree requirements:* For master's, comprehensive exam (for some programs). *Entrance requirements:* For master's, GRE. Additional exam requirements/recommendations for international students: Required—TOEFL (minimum score 550 paper-based; 79 iBT), IELTS (minimum score 6.5). *Application deadline:* For fall admission, 3/1 priority date for domestic students, 3/1 for international students; for spring admission, 10/1 priority date for domestic students, 10/1 for international students. Applications are processed on a rolling basis. Application fee: $30. Electronic applications accepted. *Expenses:* Tuition, state resident: full-time $8350; part-time $418 per credit hour. Tuition, nonresident: full-time $19,047; part-time $863 per credit hour. *Required fees:* $1689. Tuition and fees vary according to degree level and program. *Financial support:* In 2017–18, 1 student received support. Career-related internships or fieldwork, institutionally sponsored loans, scholarships/grants, health care benefits, and unspecified assistantships available. Support available to part-time students. Financial award application deadline: 3/1; financial award applicants required to submit FAFSA. *Faculty research:* Educational leadership, secondary education, elementary education, criminal justice, social work. *Total annual research expenditures:* $72,000. *Unit head:* Dr. Jane Rose, Dean, 941-359-4469, Fax: 941-359-4778, E-mail: jane.rose@sar.usf.edu. *Application contact:* Brandon Avery, Assistant Director, Admissions, 941-359-4331, E-mail: bavery@sar.usf.edu.

The University of Tennessee, Graduate School, College of Education, Health and Human Sciences, Program in Education, Knoxville, TN 37996. Offers art education (MS); counseling education (PhD); cultural studies in education (PhD); curriculum (MS, Ed S); curriculum, educational research and evaluation (Ed D, PhD); early childhood education (PhD); early childhood special education (MS); education of deaf and hard of hearing (MS); educational administration and policy studies (Ed D, PhD); educational administration and supervision (Ed S); educational psychology (Ed D, PhD); elementary education (MS, Ed S); elementary teaching (MS); English education (MS, Ed S); exercise science (PhD); foreign language/ESL education (MS, Ed S); instructional technology (MS, Ed D, PhD, Ed S); literacy, language and ESL education (PhD); literacy, language education, and ESL education (Ed D); mathematics education (MS, Ed S); modified and comprehensive special education (MS); reading education (MS, Ed S); school counseling (Ed S); school psychology (PhD, Ed S); science education (MS, Ed S); secondary teaching (MS); social foundations (MS); social science education (MS, Ed S); socio-cultural foundations of sports and education (PhD); special education (Ed S); teacher education (Ed D, PhD). *Accreditation:* NCATE. *Program availability:* Part-time, evening/weekend. *Degree requirements:* For master's and Ed S, thesis optional; for doctorate, variable foreign language requirement, thesis/dissertation. *Entrance requirements:* For master's, minimum GPA of 2.7; for doctorate and Ed S, GRE General Test, minimum GPA of 2.7. Additional exam requirements/recommendations for international students: Required—TOEFL. Electronic applications accepted.

The University of Tennessee at Chattanooga, School of Education, Chattanooga, TN 37403. Offers counseling (M Ed), including community counseling, school counseling; education (M Ed, Post-Master's Certificate), including elementary education (M Ed); school leadership (Post-Master's Certificate); elementary education (M Ed); learning and leadership (Ed D), including educational leadership; school leadership (Post-Master's Certificate); school leadership: principal licensure (Ed S); secondary education (M Ed); special education (M Ed). *Accreditation:* ACA; NCATE. *Program availability:* Part-time. *Students:* 43 full-time (30 women), 58 part-time (47 women); includes 18 minority (9 Black or African American, non-Hispanic/Latino; 1 Asian, non-Hispanic/

Latino; 1 Hispanic/Latino; 7 Two or more races, non-Hispanic/Latino). Average age 31. 118 applicants, 75% accepted, 33 enrolled. In 2017, 59 master's, 7 other advanced degrees awarded. *Degree requirements:* For master's, comprehensive exam, thesis optional, culminating experience; for other advanced degree, internship. *Entrance requirements:* For master's, GRE General Test, PPST 1, teaching certificate; for other advanced degree, two letters of recommendation, graduate degree in education, teaching certificate with three years of experience. Additional exam requirements/recommendations for international students: Required—TOEFL (minimum score 550 paper-based; 79 iBT), IELTS (minimum score 6). *Application deadline:* For fall admission, 6/15 for domestic students, 7/1 for international students; for spring admission, 11/1 for domestic and international students. Applications are processed on a rolling basis. Application fee: $35 ($40 for international students). Electronic applications accepted. *Expenses:* Contact institution. *Financial support:* Research assistantships, teaching assistantships, career-related internships or fieldwork, institutionally sponsored loans, scholarships/grants, and unspecified assistantships available. Support available to part-time students. Financial award application deadline: 7/1; financial award applicants required to submit FAFSA. *Faculty research:* School counseling, community counseling, elementary and secondary education, school leadership and administration. *Total annual research expenditures:* $576,495. *Unit head:* Dr. Renee Murley, Director, 423-425-4684, Fax: 423-425-5380, E-mail: renee-murley@utc.edu. *Application contact:* Dr. Joanne Romagni, Dean of the Graduate School, 423-425-4478, Fax: 423-425-5223, E-mail: joanne-romagni@utc.edu.
Website: https://www.utc.edu/school-education/

The University of Tennessee at Martin, Graduate Programs, College of Education, Health and Behavioral Sciences, Program in Teaching, Martin, TN 38238. Offers curriculum and instruction (MS Ed), including 7-12, K-6; initial licensure (MS Ed), including elementary education, secondary education; initial licensure K-12 (MS Ed), including physical education, special education; interdisciplinary (MS Ed). *Program availability:* Part-time, online only, 100% online. *Students:* 20 full-time (17 women), 92 part-time (66 women); includes 20 minority (14 Black or African American, non-Hispanic/Latino; 2 Hispanic/Latino; 4 Two or more races, non-Hispanic/Latino). Average age 32. 79 applicants, 70% accepted, 38 enrolled. In 2017, 14 master's awarded. *Entrance requirements:* Additional exam requirements/recommendations for international students: Required—TOEFL (minimum score 525 paper-based; 71 iBT). *Application deadline:* For fall admission, 7/27 for domestic and international students; for spring admission, 12/17 for domestic and international students; for summer admission, 5/10 for domestic and international students. Applications are processed on a rolling basis. Electronic applications accepted. *Expenses:* Tuition, state resident: full-time $8658; part-time $481 per credit hour. Tuition, nonresident: full-time $14,418; part-time $801 per credit hour. *International tuition:* $22,602 full-time. *Required fees:* $1404; $79 per credit hour. Part-time tuition and fees vary according to course load. *Financial support:* In 2017–18, 26 students received support, including 1 research assistantship with full tuition reimbursement available (averaging $6,283 per year), 5 teaching assistantships with full tuition reimbursements available (averaging $7,001 per year); scholarships/grants and tuition waivers also available. Financial award applicants required to submit FAFSA. *Faculty research:* Special education, science/math/technology, school reform, reading. *Unit head:* Cynthia West, Dean, 731-881-7125, Fax: 731-881-7975, E-mail: cwest@utm.edu. *Application contact:* Jolene L. Cunningham, Student Services Specialist, 731-881-7012, Fax: 731-881-7499, E-mail: jcunningham@utm.edu.

The University of Texas Rio Grande Valley, College of Education and P-16 Integration, Department of Teaching and Learning, Edinburg, TX 78539. Offers curriculum and instruction (M Ed, Ed D); educational technology (M Ed). *Program availability:* Part-time, evening/weekend. *Faculty:* 24. *Students:* 199. In 2017, 54 master's, 2 doctorates awarded. *Degree requirements:* For master's, comprehensive exam, thesis optional; for doctorate, comprehensive exam, thesis/dissertation. *Entrance requirements:* For master's, minimum GPA 3.0. Additional exam requirements/recommendations for international students: Required—TOEFL (minimum score 550 paper-based; 79 iBT), IELTS (minimum score 6.5). *Application deadline:* For fall admission, 4/15 for domestic students; for spring admission, 11/1 for domestic students; for summer admission, 3/1 for domestic students. Applications are processed on a rolling basis. Application fee: $50 ($75 for international students). *Expenses:* Tuition, state resident: full-time $5550; part-time $417 per credit hour. Tuition, nonresident: full-time $13,020; part-time $832 per credit hour. *Required fees:* $1169. *Financial support:* Research assistantships, institutionally sponsored loans, scholarships/grants, and unspecified assistantships available. Financial award application deadline: 4/15; financial award applicants required to submit FAFSA. *Faculty research:* Teacher education, mathematics education, science education, educational technology, pedagogy. *Unit head:* Dr. James Jupp, Chair, 956-665-3401, E-mail: james.jupp@utrgv.edu. *Application contact:* Stephanie Ozuna, Graduate Student Recruiter, 956-665-3558, E-mail: stephanie.ozuna@utrgv.edu.

University of the Cumberlands, Graduate Programs in Education, Williamsburg, KY 40769-1372. Offers all grades (P-12) (M Ed); business and marketing (MA Ed, MAT); counselor education and supervision (Ed D); director of pupil personnel (Certificate); director of special education (Certificate); educational administration and supervision (Ed S); educational leadership (Ed D); elementary education (MA Ed, MAT); instructional leadership - principalship (MA Ed); instructional leadership - school principal (Certificate); middle school education (MA Ed, MAT); reading and writing (MA Ed); school counseling (MA Ed); school superintendent (Certificate); secondary education (MA Ed, MAT); special education (MAT); supervisor of instruction (Certificate); teacher leader (MA Ed). *Program availability:* Part-time, evening/weekend, online learning. *Degree requirements:* For master's, comprehensive exam. Electronic applications accepted.

University of the District of Columbia, College of Arts and Sciences, Program in Teaching, Washington, DC 20008-1175. Offers elementary education (MAT); middle school mathematics (MAT); secondary English language arts (MAT); secondary social studies (MAT).

The University of Toledo, College of Graduate Studies, Judith Herb College of Education, Department of Curriculum and Instruction, Toledo, OH 43606-3390. Offers art education (ME); career and technical education (ME, Ed S); curriculum and instruction (ME, PhD, Ed S); early childhood education (Ed S); education and anthropology (MAE); education and biology (MES); education and chemistry (MES); education and classics (MAE); education and economics (MAE); education and English (MAE); education and French (MAE); education and geology (MES); education and German (MAE); education and history (MAE); education and mathematics (MAE, MES); education and physics (MES); education and political science (MAE); education and sociology (MAE); education and Spanish (MAE); educational media (PhD); educational technology (ME); educational technology: virtual educator (Certificate); elementary education (PhD); English as a second language (MAE); gifted and talented education (PhD); middle childhood education (ME); secondary education (ME, PhD); special education (PhD). *Accreditation:* NCATE. *Program availability:* Part-time, evening/weekend. *Degree requirements:* For master's, comprehensive exam, thesis or alternative; for doctorate, comprehensive exam, thesis/dissertation; for other advanced degree, thesis optional. *Entrance requirements:* For master's, doctorate, and other advanced degree, minimum cumulative GPA of 2.7 for all previous academic work, letters of recommendation. Additional exam requirements/recommendations for international students: Required—TOEFL (minimum score 550 paper-based; 80 iBT). Electronic applications accepted.

University of Utah, Graduate School, College of Education, Department of Educational Leadership and Policy, Salt Lake City, UT 84084. Offers educational leadership and policy (Ed D, PhD), including higher education administration (Ed D); K-12 (Ed D); K-12 school administration (M Ed); K-12 teacher instructional leadership (M Ed); student affairs (M Ed); MPA/PhD. *Program availability:* Part-time, evening/weekend. *Faculty:* 10 full-time (7 women), 2 part-time/adjunct (both women). *Students:* 60 full-time (40 women), 185 part-time (124 women); includes 54 minority (14 Black or African American, non-Hispanic/Latino; 5 American Indian or Alaska Native, non-Hispanic/Latino; 5 Asian, non-Hispanic/Latino; 24 Hispanic/Latino; 2 Native Hawaiian or other Pacific Islander, non-Hispanic/Latino; 4 Two or more races, non-Hispanic/Latino), 1 international. Average age 35. 181 applicants, 69% accepted, 90 enrolled. In 2017, 64 master's, 6 doctorates awarded. *Degree requirements:* For master's, comprehensive exam (for some programs); internship, capstone; for doctorate, thesis/dissertation, qualifying exam. *Entrance requirements:* For master's, minimum undergraduate GPA of 3.0, valid bachelor's degree, 3 years' teaching or leadership experience, Level 1 or 2 UT educator's license (for K-12 programs only); for doctorate, GRE General Test (taken with five years of applying), minimum undergraduate GPA of 3.0, valid master's degree. Additional exam requirements/recommendations for international students: Required—TOEFL (minimum score 550 paper-based). *Application deadline:* For fall admission, 1/15 priority date for domestic and international students; for winter admission, 2/1 for domestic and international students; for spring admission, 11/1 priority date for domestic and international students; for summer admission, 3/1 priority date for domestic and international students. Applications are processed on a rolling basis. Application fee: $55 ($65 for international students). Electronic applications accepted. *Expenses:* Contact institution. *Financial support:* In 2017–18, 12 students received support, including 1 fellowship with full tuition reimbursement available (averaging $15,000 per year), 2 research assistantships with full tuition reimbursements available (averaging $15,000 per year), 6 teaching assistantships with full tuition reimbursements available (averaging $15,000 per year); career-related internships or fieldwork, scholarships/grants, health care benefits, and unspecified assistantships also available. Support available to part-time students. Financial award application deadline: 3/1; financial award applicants required to submit FAFSA. *Faculty research:* Education accountability, college student diversity, K-12 educational administration and school leadership, student affairs, higher education. *Unit head:* Dr. Gerardo Lopez, Chair, 801-581-6971, Fax: 801-585-6756, E-mail: gerardo.lopez@utah.edu. *Application contact:* Marilynn S. Howard, Academic Coordinator, 801-581-6714, Fax: 801-585-6756, E-mail: marilynn.howard@utah.edu. Website: http://elp.utah.edu/

University of Utah, Graduate School, College of Education, Department of Educational Psychology, Salt Lake City, UT 84112. Offers clinical mental health counseling (M Ed); counseling psychology (PhD); elementary education (M Ed); instructional design and educational technology (M Ed); instructional design and technology (MS); learning and cognition (MS, PhD); reading and literacy (M Ed, PhD); school counseling (M Ed); school psychology (M Ed, PhD, Ed S); statistics (M Stat). *Accreditation:* APA (one or more programs are accredited). *Faculty:* 19 full-time (9 women), 12 part-time/adjunct (8 women). *Students:* 122 full-time (95 women), 97 part-time (68 women); includes 26 minority (4 Asian, non-Hispanic/Latino; 16 Hispanic/Latino; 6 Two or more races, non-Hispanic/Latino), 7 international. Average age 31. 296 applicants, 27% accepted, 73 enrolled. In 2017, 65 master's, 15 doctorates awarded. Terminal master's awarded for partial completion of doctoral program. *Entrance requirements:* For master's and doctorate, GRE General Test, minimum GPA of 3.0. Additional exam requirements/recommendations for international students: Required—TOEFL (minimum score 80 iBT). *Application deadline:* For fall admission, 12/15 for domestic and international students; for winter admission, 11/1 for domestic and international students; for spring admission, 3/15 for domestic and international students. Application fee: $55 ($65 for international students). Electronic applications accepted. *Expenses:* Contact institution. *Financial support:* In 2017–18, 84 students received support, including 12 fellowships with full and partial tuition reimbursements available (averaging $17,000 per year), 16 research assistantships with full and partial tuition reimbursements available (averaging $15,500 per year), 39 teaching assistantships with full and partial tuition reimbursements available (averaging $15,500 per year); career-related internships or fieldwork, scholarships/grants, traineeships, health care benefits, and unspecified assistantships also available. Financial award application deadline: 4/1; financial award applicants required to submit FAFSA. *Faculty research:* Autism, computer technology and instruction, cognitive behavior, aging, group counseling. *Total annual research expenditures:* $620,935. *Unit head:* Dr. Anne E. Cook, Chair, 801-581-7148, Fax: 801-581-5566, E-mail: anne.cook@utah.edu. *Application contact:* JoLynn N. Yates, Academic Coordinator, 801-581-7148, Fax: 801-581-5566, E-mail: jo.yates@utah.edu. Website: http://www.ed.utah.edu/edps/

University of Vermont, Graduate College, College of Education and Social Services, Program in Special Education, Grades K-12, Burlington, VT 05405. Offers M Ed. *Accreditation:* NCATE. *Degree requirements:* For master's, thesis or alternative. *Entrance requirements:* For master's, license (or eligible for licensure). Additional exam requirements/recommendations for international students: Required—TOEFL (minimum score 550 paper-based, 90 iBT) or IELTS (6.5). *Application deadline:* For fall admission, 2/15 for domestic and international students; for spring admission, 11/1 for domestic and international students. Application fee: $65. Electronic applications accepted. *Expenses:* Tuition, state resident: full-time $11,628; part-time $646 per credit. Tuition, nonresident: full-time $29,340; part-time $1630 per credit. *Required fees:* $1994; $10 per credit. Tuition and fees vary according to course load and program. *Financial support:* In 2017–18, 4 students received support. Research assistantships, teaching assistantships, career-related internships or fieldwork, and scholarships/grants available. Financial award application deadline: 3/1. *Unit head:* Dr. Michael Giangreco, Program Coordinator, 802-656-1144, E-mail: michael.giangreco@uvm.edu. *Application contact:* Roman Vogel, Graduate Program Support, 802-656-2936, E-mail: special.education@uvm.edu. Website: https://www.uvm.edu/cess/doe/masters_education_special_education_k_12th_grade

University of Virginia, Curry School of Education, Department of Curriculum, Instruction, and Special Education, Program in Curriculum and Instruction, Charlottesville, VA 22903. Offers curriculum and instruction (M Ed, Ed S); elementary education (M Ed, Ed D); English education (M Ed, Ed D); foreign language education (M Ed); mathematics education (M Ed, Ed D); science education (Ed D); social studies education (M Ed); MBA/M Ed. *Program availability:* 100% online. *Students:* 38 full-time (31 women), 15 part-time (12 women); includes 6 minority (2 Asian, non-Hispanic/Latino; 2 Hispanic/Latino; 2 Two or more races, non-Hispanic/Latino), 2 international. Average age 32. 92 applicants, 64% accepted, 47 enrolled. In 2017, 47 master's, 9 doctorates, 8 other advanced degrees awarded. *Degree requirements:* For master's, comprehensive exam (for some programs); for doctorate, comprehensive exam, thesis/dissertation; for Ed S, comprehensive exam. *Entrance requirements:* For master's, doctorate, and Ed S, GRE General Test, 2 letters of recommendation. Additional exam requirements/recommendations for international students: Required—TOEFL (minimum

score 600 paper-based; 90 iBT), IELTS (minimum score 7). *Application deadline:* Applications are processed on a rolling basis. Application fee: $60. Electronic applications accepted. *Financial support:* Fellowships with tuition reimbursements, research assistantships with tuition reimbursements, and teaching assistantships with tuition reimbursements available. Financial award application deadline: 1/5; financial award applicants required to submit FAFSA. *Unit head:* Susan Mintz, Program Area Director, 434-924-3128, E-mail: slm4r@virginia.edu. *Application contact:* E-mail: curry-admissions@virginia.edu. Website: http://curry.virginia.edu/academics/areas-of-study/curriculum-teaching-learning

University of Virginia, Curry School of Education, Program in Education, Charlottesville, VA 22903. Offers administration and supervision (PhD); applied developmental science (PhD); counselor education (PhD); curriculum and instruction (PhD); early childhood special education (MT); education evaluation (PhD); educational psychology (PhD); educational research (PhD); elementary education (MT); English education (MT, PhD); foreign language education (MT); higher education (PhD); instructional technology (PhD); kinesiology (MT, PhD); math education (PhD); reading education (PhD); research, statistics and evaluation (PhD); school psychology (PhD); science education (PhD); social studies education (MT, PhD); special education (PhD); world languages education (MT). *Students:* 431 full-time (353 women), 15 part-time (14 women); includes 100 minority (32 Black or African American, non-Hispanic/Latino; 33 Asian, non-Hispanic/Latino; 16 Hispanic/Latino; 19 Two or more races, non-Hispanic/Latino), 14 international. Average age 25. 264 applicants, 49% accepted, 83 enrolled. In 2017, 142 master's, 33 doctorates awarded. *Degree requirements:* For master's, comprehensive exam (for some programs), field project; for doctorate, comprehensive exam, thesis/dissertation. *Entrance requirements:* For doctorate, GRE General Test. Additional exam requirements/recommendations for international students: Required—TOEFL (minimum score 600 paper-based; 90 iBT), IELTS (minimum score 7). *Application deadline:* Applications are processed on a rolling basis. Application fee: $60. Electronic applications accepted. *Financial support:* Fellowships, research assistantships, and teaching assistantships available. Financial award application deadline: 1/5; financial award applicants required to submit FAFSA. *Unit head:* Robert C. Pianta, Dean, 434-924-3334, E-mail: pianta@virginia.edu. *Application contact:* E-mail: curry-admissions@virginia.edu. Website: http://curry.virginia.edu/teacher-education

University of Washington, Tacoma, Graduate Programs, Program in Education, Tacoma, WA 98402-3100. Offers education (M Ed); educational administration (principal or program administrator certification) (M Ed); elementary education teacher certification (M Ed); elementary education/special education teacher certification (M Ed); secondary science or math teacher certification (M Ed). *Program availability:* Part-time, evening/weekend. *Degree requirements:* For master's, culminating project. *Entrance requirements:* For master's, WEST-B, WEST-E (teacher certification programs only), official sealed transcript from every college/university attended, personal goal statement, letters of recommendation, copy of valid teaching certificate. Additional exam requirements/recommendations for international students: Required—TOEFL (minimum score 580 paper-based; 92 iBT). Electronic applications accepted. *Faculty research:* Global learning communities for English/Chinese languages, evaluation of mathematics and reading intervention programs, response to intervention, school-wide behavioral and emotional support, mathematics education and culturally responsive mathematics education.

The University of West Alabama, School of Graduate Studies, College of Education, Program in Elementary Education, Livingston, AL 35470. Offers elementary education (Ed S); elementary education K-6 (M Ed). *Accreditation:* NCATE. *Program availability:* Part-time, evening/weekend, 100% online. *Faculty:* 7 full-time (all women), 25 part-time/adjunct (20 women). *Students:* 356 (340 women); includes 113 minority (105 Black or African American, non-Hispanic/Latino; 3 American Indian or Alaska Native, non-Hispanic/Latino; 1 Hispanic/Latino; 4 Two or more races, non-Hispanic/Latino). Average age 32. 107 applicants, 96% accepted, 87 enrolled. In 2017, 94 master's, 41 Ed Ss awarded. *Degree requirements:* For master's, comprehensive exam, thesis optional; for Ed S, comprehensive exam. *Entrance requirements:* For master's, GRE, minimum GPA of 2.75, verification of background clearance/fingerprints, valid bachelor's-level Professional Educator Certificate in same teaching field. Additional exam requirements/recommendations for international students: Required—TOEFL (minimum score 500 paper-based; 61 iBT). *Application deadline:* Applications are processed on a rolling basis. Application fee: $40. Electronic applications accepted. *Expenses:* Tuition, state resident: part-time $371 per credit hour. Tuition, nonresident: part-time $742 per credit hour. *Required fees:* $130 per semester. *Financial support:* Teaching assistantships, Federal Work-Study, and unspecified assistantships available. Support available to part-time students. Financial award application deadline: 3/1; financial award applicants required to submit FAFSA. *Unit head:* Dr. Jodie Winship, Chair of Teaching and Learning, 205-652-5415, Fax: 205-652-3706, E-mail: jwinship@uwa.edu. *Application contact:* Dr. B. J. Kimbrough, Dean of Graduate Studies, 205-652-3647, Fax: 205-652-3670, E-mail: bkimbrough@uwa.edu. Website: http://www.uwa.edu/elementaryeducationk6.aspx

University of West Florida, College of Education and Professional Studies, Department of Teacher Education and Educational Leadership, Program in Curriculum and Instruction, Pensacola, FL 32514-5750. Offers elementary education (M Ed); middle level education (M Ed); secondary education (M Ed). *Program availability:* Part-time, evening/weekend. *Entrance requirements:* For master's, GRE (minimum score 450 verbal) or MAT (minimum score 396) if bachelor's GPA less than 3.0, state teaching certification; letter of intent; two professional references. Additional exam requirements/recommendations for international students: Required—TOEFL (minimum score 550 paper-based).

University of Wisconsin–Milwaukee, Graduate School, School of Education, Department of Curriculum and Instruction, Milwaukee, WI 53201-0413. Offers curriculum and instruction (MS), including cross-curricular focus, early childhood education, English education, mathematics education, middle childhood/early adolescence education, reading education, science education, urban social studies education. *Program availability:* Part-time. *Students:* 17 full-time (13 women), 45 part-time (39 women); includes 13 minority (2 Black or African American, non-Hispanic/Latino; 3 Asian, non-Hispanic/Latino; 1 Hispanic/Latino; 7 Two or more races, non-Hispanic/Latino). Average age 33. 32 applicants, 66% accepted, 16 enrolled. In 2017, 26 master's awarded. *Entrance requirements:* Additional exam requirements/recommendations for international students: Required—TOEFL (minimum score 550 paper-based; 79 iBT), IELTS (minimum score 6.5). *Application deadline:* For fall admission, 1/1 priority date for domestic students; for spring admission, 9/1 for domestic students. Application fee: $56 ($96 for international students). Electronic applications accepted. *Financial support:* Fellowships, research assistantships, teaching assistantships, career-related internships or fieldwork, health care benefits, unspecified assistantships, and project assistantships available. Support available to part-time students. Financial award application deadline: 4/15; financial award applicants required to submit FAFSA. *Application contact:* General Information Contact, 414-229-4721, E-mail: soeinfo@uwm.edu. Website: http://uwm.edu/education/academics/curriculum-instruction-department/

Elementary Education

University of Wisconsin–River Falls, Outreach and Graduate Studies, College of Education and Professional Studies, Department of Teacher Education, River Falls, WI 54022. Offers elementary education (MSE); professional development shared inquiry communities (MSE); reading (MSE). *Program availability:* Part-time. *Degree requirements:* For master's, comprehensive exam, thesis or alternative. *Entrance requirements:* For master's, minimum GPA of 2.75. Additional exam requirements/recommendations for international students: Required—TOEFL (minimum score 500 paper-based; 65 iBT), IELTS (minimum score 5.5). Electronic applications accepted.

University of Wisconsin–Stevens Point, College of Fine Arts and Communication, Department of Music, Stevens Point, WI 54481-3897. Offers elementary/secondary (MM Ed); studio pedagogy (MM Ed); Suzuki talent education (MM Ed). *Accreditation:* NASM. *Program availability:* Part-time. *Degree requirements:* For master's, thesis or alternative. *Entrance requirements:* For master's, teaching certificate. *Faculty research:* Music education, music composition, music performance.

University of Wisconsin–Stevens Point, College of Professional Studies, School of Education, Program in Elementary Education, Stevens Point, WI 54481-3897. Offers MSE. *Program availability:* Part-time. *Degree requirements:* For master's, comprehensive exam, thesis or alternative. *Entrance requirements:* For master's, teacher certification, minimum undergraduate GPA of 3.0. Additional exam requirements/recommendations for international students: Required—TOEFL (minimum score 523 paper-based). *Faculty research:* Gifted education, early childhood special education, curriculum and instruction, standards-based education.

Utah State University, School of Graduate Studies, Emma Eccles Jones College of Education and Human Services, Program in Elementary Education, Logan, UT 84322. Offers M Ed, MA, MS. *Program availability:* Part-time, online learning. *Degree requirements:* For master's, comprehensive exam (for some programs), thesis (for some programs). *Entrance requirements:* For master's, GRE General Test or MAT, minimum GPA of 3.0, teaching certificate, 3 recommendations, 1 year teaching department record. Additional exam requirements/recommendations for international students: Required—TOEFL. *Faculty research:* Teacher education, supervision, gifted and talented education, language arts/writing, early childhood education.

Utah Valley University, Program in Education, Orem, UT 84058-5999. Offers educational technology (M Ed); elementary mathematics (M Ed); elementary STEM (M Ed); English as a second language (M Ed); reading (M Ed); teachers as leaders (M Ed). *Accreditation:* TEAC. *Program availability:* Part-time. *Degree requirements:* For master's, project. *Entrance requirements:* For master's, GRE, 3 letters of recommendation, interview, essay. Additional exam requirements/recommendations for international students: Required—TOEFL (minimum score 83 iBT). Electronic applications accepted. *Expenses:* Contact institution.

Valdosta State University, Department of Elementary Education, Valdosta, GA 31698. Offers M Ed. *Accreditation:* ASHA; NCATE. *Program availability:* Part-time, evening/weekend, blended/hybrid learning. *Degree requirements:* For master's, thesis (for some programs), comprehensive written and/or oral exams. *Entrance requirements:* For master's, GRE General Test or MAT, minimum GPA of 2.75. Additional exam requirements/recommendations for international students: Required—TOEFL (minimum score 523 paper-based); Recommended—IELTS. *Application deadline:* For fall and spring admission, 7/1 for domestic and international students. Applications are processed on a rolling basis. Application fee: $45. Electronic applications accepted. *Expenses:* Contact institution. *Financial support:* Research assistantships with full tuition reimbursements, institutionally sponsored loans, scholarships/grants, and unspecified assistantships available. Support available to part-time students. Financial award application deadline: 7/1; financial award applicants required to submit FAFSA. *Application contact:* Julia Stokes, Administrative Secretary, 229-333-5929, Fax: 229-245-3853, E-mail: jdstokes@valdosta.edu.
Website: http://www.valdosta.edu/colleges/education/early-childhood-and-special-education/welcome.php

Valley City State University, Online Graduate Programs, Valley City, ND 58072. Offers elementary education (M Ed); English education (M Ed); library and information technologies (M Ed); teaching (MAT); teaching and technology (M Ed); teaching English language learners (M Ed); technology education (M Ed). *Accreditation:* NCATE. *Program availability:* Part-time, evening/weekend, online only, 100% online. *Faculty:* 21 full-time (12 women), 15 part-time/adjunct (11 women). *Students:* 12 full-time (9 women), 138 part-time (99 women); includes 5 minority (3 Hispanic/Latino; 2 Two or more races, non-Hispanic/Latino). Average age 36. 13 applicants, 92% accepted, 12 enrolled. In 2017, 45 master's awarded. *Degree requirements:* For master's, action research report, comprehensive portfolio. *Entrance requirements:* For master's, GRE, MAT, PRAXIS II or National Teaching Board for Professional Standards (if GPA is less than 3.0). Additional exam requirements/recommendations for international students: Required—TOEFL (minimum score 525 paper-based; 71 iBT); Recommended—IELTS (minimum score 5.5). *Application deadline:* For fall admission, 7/21 for domestic and international students; for spring admission, 12/8 for domestic and international students; for summer admission, 5/5 for domestic and international students. Applications are processed on a rolling basis. Application fee: $35. Electronic applications accepted. *Expenses:* $384.21 per credit. *Financial support:* In 2017–18, 16 students received support. Scholarships/grants, tuition waivers (full and partial), and unspecified assistantships available. Financial award applicants required to submit FAFSA. *Faculty research:* Universal accessibility, instructional design and technology, gender communication, STEM education in K-12, English language learners. *Unit head:* Dr. Sheri Okland, Dean, 701-845-7184, E-mail: sheri.l.okland@vcsu.edu. *Application contact:* Misty Lindgren, Graduate Studies, 701-845-7303, Fax: 701-845-7190, E-mail: misty.lindgren@vcsu.edu.
Website: http://www.vcsu.edu/graduate

Valparaiso University, Graduate School and Continuing Education, Programs in Education, Valparaiso, IN 46383. Offers initial licensure (M Ed), including Chinese teaching, elementary education, secondary education; instructional leadership (M Ed); school psychology (Ed S); secondary education (M Ed); M Ed/Ed S. *Accreditation:* NCATE. *Program availability:* Part-time, evening/weekend, online learning. *Entrance requirements:* For master's, GRE General Test, minimum GPA of 3.0. Additional exam requirements/recommendations for international students: Required—TOEFL (minimum score 550 paper-based; 80 iBT), IELTS (minimum score 6). Electronic applications accepted. *Expenses: Tuition:* Full-time $11,340; part-time $630 per credit hour. *Required fees:* $520; $250 per year. $125 per semester. Tuition and fees vary according to program and reciprocity agreements.

Vanderbilt University, Peabody College, Department of Teaching and Learning, Nashville, TN 37240-1001. Offers elementary education (M Ed); English language learners (M Ed); learning and design (M Ed); learning, diversity, and urban studies (M Ed); reading education (M Ed); secondary education (M Ed). *Accreditation:* NCATE. *Program availability:* Part-time. *Faculty:* 43 full-time (32 women), 28 part-time/adjunct (25 women). *Students:* 139 full-time (110 women), 35 part-time (23 women); includes 31 minority (18 Black or African American, non-Hispanic/Latino; 1 American Indian or Alaska Native, non-Hispanic/Latino; 6 Asian, non-Hispanic/Latino; 4 Hispanic/Latino; 2 Two or more races, non-Hispanic/Latino), 44 international. Average age 26. 510 applicants, 69% accepted, 113 enrolled. In 2017, 87 master's awarded. *Degree requirements:* For master's, comprehensive exam, thesis optional. *Entrance requirements:* For master's, GRE General Test, MAT. Additional exam requirements/recommendations for international students: Required—TOEFL (minimum score 550 paper-based; 80 iBT). *Application deadline:* For fall admission, 12/31 priority date for domestic and international students; for spring admission, 11/1 priority date for domestic and international students. Applications are processed on a rolling basis. Application fee: $0. Electronic applications accepted. *Financial support:* Fellowships with partial tuition reimbursements, research assistantships with partial tuition reimbursements, teaching assistantships with partial tuition reimbursements, Federal Work-Study, institutionally sponsored loans, scholarships/grants, tuition waivers (partial), and unspecified assistantships available. Support available to part-time students. Financial award application deadline: 1/15; financial award applicants required to submit FAFSA. *Faculty research:* Children's learning and development in core conceptual domains (STEM, English language arts, social studies); classroom discourse structures that teachers can learn and use to support students' learning and development K-6; intervention and design-based research on educational improvement at classroom, school, and district levels; design-based and learning sciences research on relations between learning in schools and other settings. *Unit head:* Dr. Deborah Rowe, Chair, 615-322-8100, Fax: 615-322-8999, E-mail: deborah.w.rowe@vanderbilt.edu. *Application contact:* Angela Saylor, Educational Coordinator, 615-322-8092, Fax: 615-322-8999, E-mail: angela.saylor@vanderbilt.edu.

Virginia Commonwealth University, Graduate School, School of Education, Program in Teaching and Learning, Richmond, VA 23284-9005. Offers early and elementary education (MT). *Accreditation:* NCATE. *Program availability:* Part-time. *Entrance requirements:* For master's, GRE General Test or MAT. Additional exam requirements/recommendations for international students: Required—TOEFL (minimum score 600 paper-based; 100 iBT). Electronic applications accepted.

Wagner College, Division of Graduate Studies, Education Department, Program in Childhood Education/Students with Disabilities, Staten Island, NY 10301-4495. Offers childhood education (MS Ed). *Program availability:* Part-time, evening/weekend. *Faculty:* 4 full-time (all women), 1 part-time/adjunct (0 women). *Students:* 3 full-time (all women), 5 part-time (4 women); includes 3 minority (1 Black or African American, non-Hispanic/Latino; 1 Asian, non-Hispanic/Latino; 1 Hispanic/Latino). Average age 27. 11 applicants, 45% accepted, 2 enrolled. In 2017, 8 master's awarded. *Degree requirements:* For master's, thesis (for some programs), passage of New York State certification exams before student teaching. *Entrance requirements:* For master's, GRE, minimum GPA of 3.0, interview, recommendations. Additional exam requirements/recommendations for international students: Required—TOEFL (minimum score 550 paper-based; 79 iBT), IELTS (minimum score 6.5). *Application deadline:* For fall admission, 2/15 priority date for domestic and international students. Applications are processed on a rolling basis. Application fee: $60. Electronic applications accepted. *Expenses:* $1,140 per credit. *Financial support:* Unspecified assistantships available. Financial award applicants required to submit FAFSA. *Unit head:* Dr. Jason Fitzgerald, Department Chair, 718-420-4129, Fax: 718-390-3456, E-mail: jason.fitzgerald@wagner.edu. *Application contact:* Patricia Clancy, Assistant Director of Enrollment, 718-420-4464, Fax: 718-390-3105, E-mail: patricia.clancy@wagner.edu.
Website: http://www.wagner.edu/education

Walden University, Graduate Programs, Richard W. Riley College of Education and Leadership, Minneapolis, MN 55401. Offers adult education (Post-Master's Certificate); adult learning (Graduate Certificate); college teaching and learning (Graduate Certificate); community college leadership (Ed D); curriculum, instruction and assessment (Ed D, Ed S, Graduate Certificate); developmental education (Graduate Certificate); early childhood administration, management, and leadership (Graduate Certificate); early childhood education (Ed D, Ed S); early childhood public policy and advocacy (Graduate Certificate); early childhood studies (MS), including administration, management and leadership, early childhood public policy and advocacy, teaching adults in the early childhood field, teaching and diversity in early childhood education; education (MS, PhD), including adolescent literacy and learning (MS), curriculum, instruction, and assessment (grades K-12) (MS), curriculum, instruction, assessment, and evaluation (PhD), early childhood leadership and advocacy (PhD), early childhood special education (PhD), educational leadership (MS), educational leadership and administration (principal preparation) (MS), educational technology and design (PhD), elementary reading and literacy (PreK-6) (MS), elementary reading and mathematics (grades K-6) (MS), global and comparative education (PhD), higher education leadership management and policy (PhD), integrating technology in the classroom (grades K-12) (MS), learning, instruction and innovation (PhD), mathematics (grades 5-8) (MS), mathematics (grades K-6) (MS), mathematics and science (grades K-8) (MS), organizational research, assessment, and evaluation (PhD), reading and literacy with a reading K-12 endorsement (MS), reading literacy assessment and evaluation (PhD), science (grades K-8) (MS), special education (non-licensure) (grades K-12) (MS), teacher leadership (grades K-12) (MS), teaching English language learners (grades K-12) (MS); educational administration and leadership (Ed D); educational leadership and administration (principal preparation) (Ed S); educational technology (Ed D, Ed S, Post Master's Certificate); elementary reading and literacy (Graduate Certificate); engaging culturally diverse learners (Graduate Certificate); enrollment management and institutional marketing (Graduate Certificate); higher education (MS), including adult learning, college teaching and learning, enrollment management and institutional marketing, global higher education, leadership for student success, online and distance learning; higher education and adult learning (Ed D); higher education leadership and management (Ed D); higher education leadership for student success (Graduate Certificate); instructional design and technology (MS, Postbaccalaureate Certificate), including general program (MS), online learning (MS), training and performance improvement (MS); integrating technology in the classroom (Graduate Certificate); mathematics 5-8 (Graduate Certificate); mathematics K-6 (Graduate Certificate); online teaching for adult educators (Graduate Certificate); reading, literacy, and assessment (Ed D, Ed S); science K-8 (Graduate Certificate); special education (Ed D, Ed S, Graduate Certificate); special education (K-age 21) (MAT); teacher leadership (Graduate Certificate); teaching adults English as a second language (Graduate Certificate); teaching adults in the early childhood field (Graduate Certificate); teaching and diversity in early childhood education (Graduate Certificate); teaching English language learners (grades K-12) (Graduate Certificate); teaching K-12 students online (Graduate Certificate). *Accreditation:* NCATE. *Program availability:* Part-time, evening/weekend, online only, 100% online. *Degree requirements:* For doctorate, thesis/dissertation (for some programs), residency; for other advanced degree, residency (for some programs). *Entrance requirements:* For master's, bachelor's degree or higher; minimum GPA of 2.5; official transcripts; goal statement (for some programs); access to computer and Internet; for doctorate, master's degree or higher; three years of related professional or academic experience (preferred); minimum GPA of 3.0; goal statement and current resume (for select programs); official transcripts; access to computer and Internet; for other advanced degree, relevant work experience; access to computer and Internet. Additional exam requirements/recommendations for international students: Required—TOEFL (minimum score 550 paper-based, 79 iBT), IELTS (minimum score 6.5), Michigan English Language Assessment Battery (minimum score 82), or PTE (minimum score 53). Electronic applications accepted.

Warner University, School of Education, Lake Wales, FL 33859. Offers curriculum and instruction (MAEd); elementary education (MAEd); science, technology, engineering, and mathematics (STEM) (MAEd). *Program availability:* Part-time, evening/weekend, online learning. *Degree requirements:* For master's, thesis, accomplished practices portfolio. *Entrance requirements:* For master's, minimum GPA of 3.0 in last 60 hours of undergraduate coursework; 2 letters of recommendation. Additional exam requirements/recommendations for international students: Required—TOEFL (minimum score 550 paper-based). Electronic applications accepted.

Washington State University, College of Education, Department of Teaching and Learning, Pullman, WA 99164-2132. Offers cultural studies and social thought in education (PhD); curriculum and instruction (Ed M, MA); English language learners (Ed M, MA); language, literacy and technology (PhD); literacy education (Ed M, MA); mathematics education (Ed M, MA, PhD); special education (Ed M, MA, PhD); teacher leadership (Ed D); teaching (MIT), including elementary education, secondary education. Programs offered at the Pullman, Spokane, Tri-cities, Vancouver and Global (online) campuses. *Program availability:* Part-time, online learning. *Degree requirements:* For master's, comprehensive exam, thesis, oral or written exam; for doctorate, comprehensive exam, thesis/dissertation, oral and written exam. *Entrance requirements:* For master's, GRE General Test, minimum GPA of 3.0, 3 letters of recommendation, letter of intent, transcripts, resume/curriculum vitae; for doctorate, GRE General Test, minimum GPA of 3.0, 3 letters of recommendation, letter of intent, transcripts, writing sample, resume/curriculum vitae. Additional exam requirements/recommendations for international students: Required—TOEFL (minimum score 550 paper-based; 80 iBT). Electronic applications accepted. *Faculty research:* Intersection of gender, youth cultures and schooling; examination of ideology of power in children's literature; early childhood special education; analyzing pre-service and in-service teacher development; second language acquisition.

Washington University in St. Louis, The Graduate School, Department of Education, Program in Elementary Education, St. Louis, MO 63130-4899. Offers MA Ed. *Degree requirements:* For master's, thesis or alternative. *Entrance requirements:* For master's, GRE General Test or MAT. Additional exam requirements/recommendations for international students: Required—TOEFL. Electronic applications accepted.

Wayland Baptist University, Graduate Programs, Program in Education, Plainview, TX 79072-6998. Offers education administration (M Ed); education diagnostics (M Ed); education literacy (M Ed); elementary certification (M Ed); English (M Ed); English as a second language (M Ed); higher education administration (M Ed); human resources (M Ed); instructional leadership (M Ed); instructional technology (M Ed); leadership training and development (M Ed); science education (M Ed); secondary certification (M Ed); social studies (M Ed); special education (M Ed); sports administration and management (M Ed). *Program availability:* Part-time, evening/weekend, 100% online. *Faculty:* 33 full-time (17 women), 28 part-time/adjunct (17 women). *Students:* 16 full-time (13 women), 221 part-time (143 women); includes 97 minority (26 Black or African American, non-Hispanic/Latino; 1 American Indian or Alaska Native, non-Hispanic/Latino; 5 Asian, non-Hispanic/Latino; 54 Hispanic/Latino; 11 Two or more races, non-Hispanic/Latino), 1 international. Average age 39. 32 applicants, 97% accepted, 23 enrolled. In 2017, 78 master's awarded. *Degree requirements:* For master's, comprehensive exam, capstone course. *Entrance requirements:* For master's, GRE, GMAT or MAT. Additional exam requirements/recommendations for international students: Required—TOEFL (minimum score 500 paper-based; 61 iBT). *Application deadline:* Applications are processed on a rolling basis. Application fee: $50. Electronic applications accepted. *Expenses: Tuition:* Full-time $11,250; part-time $625 per credit hour. *Required fees:* $1200. *Financial support:* Federal Work-Study, institutionally sponsored loans, and scholarships/grants available. Support available to part-time students. Financial award application deadline: 5/1; financial award applicants required to submit FAFSA. *Unit head:* Dr. Gene Whitfill, Dean, 806-291-1047, Fax: 806-291-1951, E-mail: whitfillg@wbu.edu. *Application contact:* Amanda Stanton, Coordinator of Graduate Studies, 806-291-3423, Fax: 806-291-1950, E-mail: stanton@wbu.edu.

Wayne State College, School of Education and Counseling, Department of Educational Foundations and Leadership, Program in Curriculum and Instruction, Wayne, NE 68787. Offers alternative education (MSE); business and information technology education (MSE); communication arts education (MSE); early childhood education (MSE); elementary education (MSE); English as a second language (MSE); English education (MSE); family and consumer sciences education (MSE); industrial technology and vocational education (MSE); learning communities (MSE); mathematics education (MSE); music education (MSE); science education (MSE); social science education (MSE). *Accreditation:* NCATE. *Program availability:* Part-time, evening/weekend. *Degree requirements:* For master's, comprehensive exam, thesis optional. *Entrance requirements:* For master's, GRE General Test. Additional exam requirements/recommendations for international students: Required—TOEFL (minimum score 550 paper-based).

Wayne State University, College of Education, Division of Teacher Education, Detroit, MI 48202. Offers art education (M Ed); bilingual/bicultural education (Certificate); curriculum and instruction (Ed D, PhD, Ed S), including English as a second language (MAT, Ed D, Ed S), K-12 curriculum (PhD); elementary education (MAT), including bilingual/bicultural education (M Ed, MAT), early childhood education (M Ed, MAT), English as a second language (MAT, Ed D, Ed S), foreign language education, science education (M Ed, MAT), special education (M Ed, MAT); elementary mathematics specialist (Certificate); English as a second language (Certificate); reading (M Ed, Ed S); reading, language and literature (Ed D); secondary education (MAT), including bilingual/bicultural education (M Ed, MAT), early childhood education (M Ed, MAT), English as a second language (MAT, Ed D, Ed S), English education, foreign language education, mathematics education (M Ed, MAT), science education (M Ed, MAT), social studies education (M Ed, MAT); special education (MAT), including career and technical education; teaching and learning (M Ed), including bilingual/bicultural education (M Ed, MAT), early childhood education (M Ed, MAT), elementary education, foreign language, mathematics education (M Ed, MAT), science education (M Ed, MAT), social studies education (M Ed, MAT), special education (M Ed, MAT). *Program availability:* Part-time, blended/hybrid learning. *Faculty:* 22. *Students:* 126 full-time (96 women), 317 part-time (258 women); includes 134 minority (95 Black or African American, non-Hispanic/Latino; 1 American Indian or Alaska Native, non-Hispanic/Latino; 8 Asian, non-Hispanic/Latino; 17 Hispanic/Latino; 1 Native Hawaiian or other Pacific Islander, non-Hispanic/Latino; 12 Two or more races, non-Hispanic/Latino), 13 international. Average age 37. 260 applicants, 33% accepted, 57 enrolled. In 2017, 111 master's, 13 doctorates, 7 other advanced degrees awarded. *Degree requirements:* For master's, essay or project (for some M Ed programs), professional field experience (for MAT programs); for doctorate, thesis/dissertation. *Entrance requirements:* For master's, Michigan Test for Teacher Certification (for most programs), verification of participation in group work with children (for MAT programs), Michigan State Police criminal background check; for doctorate, minimum undergraduate GPA of 3.0, graduate 3.5; interview; curriculum vitae; references; master's degree (for most programs). Additional exam requirements/recommendations for international students: Required—TOEFL (minimum score 550 paper-based; 79 iBT), TWE (minimum score 5.5); Recommended—IELTS (minimum score 6.5). *Application deadline:* For fall admission, 6/1 priority date for domestic students, 5/1 priority date for international students; for winter admission, 10/1 priority date for domestic students, 9/1 priority date for international students; for spring admission, 2/1 priority date for domestic students, 1/1 priority date for international students. Applications are processed on a rolling basis. Application fee: $50. Electronic applications accepted. *Expenses:* Tuition, state resident: full-time $10,224; part-time $638.98 per credit hour. Tuition, nonresident: full-time $22,145; part-time $1384.04 per credit hour. Tuition and fees vary according to course load and program. *Financial support:* In 2017–18, 78 students received support, including 4 fellowships (averaging $13,500 per year), 1 research assistantship with tuition reimbursement available (averaging $16,000 per year); Federal Work-Study, scholarships/grants, and unspecified assistantships also available. Support available to part-time students. Financial award applicants required to submit FAFSA. *Faculty research:* Improving students' skill achievement in mathematics, improving elementary children's understanding of informational text, teachers' use of their pedagogical and mathematical knowledge in the interactive work of teaching, the intersection of identity construction in teaching and learning, identifying effective methods of literacy instruction and assessments for bilingual students in elementary language arts classrooms. *Unit head:* Dr. Thomas Edwards, Interim Associate Dean for Teacher Education, 313-577-3886, E-mail: t.g.edwards@wayne.edu. *Application contact:* 313-577-0902, E-mail: askcoe@wayne.edu.
Website: http://coe.wayne.edu/ted/index.php

Webster University, School of Education, Department of Multidisciplinary Studies, St. Louis, MO 63119-3194. Offers applied educational psychology (MA, Ed S); communication arts (MA); early childhood education (MA, MAT); education and innovation (MA); educational technology (MET); elementary education (MAT); mathematics for educators (MA); middle school education (MAT); multidisciplinary studies (MAT); multimodal literacy for global impact (MA); reading (MA); secondary school education (MAT); special education (MA, MAT); teaching English as a second language (MA); transformative learning in the global community (Ed S). *Program availability:* Part-time. *Entrance requirements:* For master's, minimum GPA of 2.5. Additional exam requirements/recommendations for international students: Required—TOEFL.

Western Governors University, Teachers College, Salt Lake City, UT 84107. Offers curriculum and instruction (MS); educational leadership (MS); educational studies (MA); educational studies (5-12) (MA), including mathematics; elementary education (K-8) (MAT, Postbaccalaureate Certificate); elementary education (PreK-8) (MAT); English language learning (K-12) (MA); instructional design (MAT); learning and technology (M Ed, MA); management and innovation (M Ed); mathematics (5-12) (MAT, Postbaccalaureate Certificate); mathematics (5-9) (MAT, Postbaccalaureate Certificate); mathematics education (5-12) (MA); mathematics education (5-9) (MA); mathematics education (K-6) (MA); measurement and evaluation (M Ed); science (5-12) (Postbaccalaureate Certificate); science (5-9) (MAT, Postbaccalaureate Certificate); science education (5-12) (MA), including biology, chemistry, geology, physics; science education (5-9) (MA); social science (5-12) (MAT, Postbaccalaureate Certificate); special education (MAT, MS). *Accreditation:* NCATE. *Program availability:* Evening/weekend, online learning. *Degree requirements:* For master's, capstone project. *Entrance requirements:* For master's and Postbaccalaureate Certificate, Readiness Assessment, transcripts. Additional exam requirements/recommendations for international students: Required—TOEFL (minimum score 450 paper-based; 80 iBT). Electronic applications accepted. *Expenses:* Contact institution.

Western Kentucky University, Graduate Studies, College of Education and Behavioral Sciences, School of Teacher Education, Bowling Green, KY 42101. Offers elementary education (MAE, Ed S); exceptional education: learning and behavioral disorders (MAE); exceptional education: moderate and severe disabilities (MAE); instructional design (MS); interdisciplinary early childhood education (MAE); library media education (MS); literacy education (MAE); middle grades education (MAE); secondary education (MAE, Ed S). *Program availability:* Part-time, evening/weekend, online learning. *Degree requirements:* For master's, comprehensive exam. *Entrance requirements:* For master's, GRE General Test. Additional exam requirements/recommendations for international students: Required—TOEFL (minimum score 555 paper-based; 79 iBT). *Faculty research:* Teacher preparation in moderate/severe disabilities.

Western New Mexico University, Graduate Division, School of Education, Silver City, NM 88062-0680. Offers bilingual education (MAT); educational leadership (MA); elementary education (MAT); reading (MAT); secondary education (MAT); special education (MAT); TESOL (teaching English to speakers of other languages) (MAT). *Accreditation:* NCATE. *Program availability:* Part-time, online learning. *Degree requirements:* For master's, comprehensive exam. *Entrance requirements:* For master's, minimum GPA of 3.0 in last 64 hours of undergraduate study. Additional exam requirements/recommendations for international students: Required—TOEFL (minimum score 550 paper-based; 79 iBT). Electronic applications accepted. *Faculty research:* International education, electronic reading assessment, developing STEM teachers.

Western Washington University, Graduate School, Woodring College of Education, Department of Elementary Education, Bellingham, WA 98225-5996. Offers M Ed. *Accreditation:* NCATE. *Program availability:* Part-time. *Degree requirements:* For master's, comprehensive exam, thesis optional. *Entrance requirements:* For master's, GRE General Test or MAT, minimum GPA of 3.0 in last 60 semester hours or last 90 quarter hours, elementary teaching certificate. Additional exam requirements/recommendations for international students: Required—TOEFL (minimum score 567 paper-based). Electronic applications accepted. *Faculty research:* Teacher learning through National Board certification.

Westfield State University, College of Graduate and Continuing Education, Department of Education, Program in Elementary Education, Westfield, MA 01086. Offers M Ed. *Accreditation:* NCATE. *Program availability:* Part-time, evening/weekend. *Students:* 1 (woman) full-time, 25 part-time (20 women). Average age 30. 8 applicants, 100% accepted, 5 enrolled. In 2017, 11 master's awarded. *Degree requirements:* For master's, comprehensive exam, practicum. *Entrance requirements:* For master's, GRE General Test or MAT, minimum undergraduate GPA of 2.8. Additional exam requirements/recommendations for international students: Recommended—TOEFL (minimum score 550 paper-based; 79 iBT). *Application deadline:* For fall admission, 7/1 for domestic students; for spring admission, 10/1 for domestic students; for summer admission, 4/1 for domestic students. Applications are processed on a rolling basis. Application fee: $50. *Expenses:* Tuition, state resident: part-time $332 per credit. Tuition, nonresident: part-time $332 per credit. *Required fees:* $75 per semester. Tuition and fees vary according to program. *Financial support:* Unspecified assistantships and SOS scholarships (for education majors only) available. Financial award application deadline: 3/1; financial award applicants required to submit FAFSA. *Unit head:* Dr. Laura Baker, Department Chair, 413-572-5324, E-mail: lbaker@westfield.ma.edu. *Application contact:* Shelly Henrichon, Coordinator of College of Graduate and Continuing Education Admissions, 413-572-8022, Fax: 413-572-5227, E-mail: mhenrichon@westfield.ma.edu.
Website: http://www.westfield.ma.edu/academics/degrees/education-graduate-programs

SECTION 24: INSTRUCTIONAL LEVELS

Elementary Education

West Virginia University, College of Education and Human Services, Morgantown, WV 26506. Offers audiology (Au D); autism spectrum disorder (MA); clinical rehabilitation and mental health counseling (MS); communication science and disorders (PhD); counseling (MA); counseling psychology (PhD); curriculum and instruction (Ed D); early childhood education (MA); early intervention (MA); education (PhD); educational leadership (MA, Ed D); educational leadership/public school administration (MA); educational psychology (MA, Ed D); elementary education (MA); gifted education (MA); higher education administration (MA, Ed D); higher education curriculum and teaching (MA); institutional design and technology (MA); instructional design and technology (Ed D); literacy education (MA); secondary education (MA); secondary education/ English (MA); special education (Ed D); speech pathology (MS). *Accreditation:* NCATE. *Program availability:* Part-time, evening/weekend, online learning. *Students:* 423 full-time (347 women), 367 part-time (316 women); includes 57 minority (14 Black or African American, non-Hispanic/Latino; 7 Asian, non-Hispanic/Latino; 20 Hispanic/Latino; 16 Two or more races, non-Hispanic/Latino), 13 international. *Degree requirements:* For master's, content exams; for doctorate, comprehensive exam, thesis/dissertation. *Entrance requirements:* Additional exam requirements/recommendations for international students: Required—TOEFL (minimum score 500 paper-based; 61 iBT). *Application deadline:* For fall admission, 8/1 for domestic students; for spring admission, 1/1 for domestic students; for summer admission, 5/1 for domestic students. Application fee: $60. Electronic applications accepted. *Expenses:* Tuition, state resident: full-time $9450. Tuition, nonresident: full-time $24,390. *Financial support:* Fellowships, research assistantships, teaching assistantships, career-related internships or fieldwork, Federal Work-Study, institutionally sponsored loans, health care benefits, tuition waivers (full and partial), and administrative assistantships available. Financial award applicants required to submit FAFSA. *Faculty research:* Internet training and integration for teachers, rural education, teacher preparation, organization of schools, evaluation of personnel. *Unit head:* Dr. Gypsy Denzine, Dean, 304-293-5703, Fax: 304-293-7565, E-mail: gypsy.denzine@mail.wvu.edu. *Application contact:* Dr. M. Cecil Smith, Associate Dean for Research and Graduate Education, 304-293-2174, Fax: 304-293-3802, E-mail: mcecil.smith@mail.wvu.edu.
Website: http://cehs.wvu.edu/

Wheaton College, Graduate School, Department of Education, Wheaton, IL 60187-5593. Offers elementary education (MAT); secondary education (MAT). *Accreditation:* NCATE. *Faculty:* 1 full-time (0 women), 1 part-time/adjunct (0 women). *Students:* 24 full-time (13 women); includes 4 minority (3 Asian, non-Hispanic/Latino; 1 Hispanic/Latino), 1 international. Average age 24. 18 applicants, 100% accepted, 17 enrolled. In 2017, 11 master's awarded. *Degree requirements:* For master's, thesis or alternative. *Entrance requirements:* For master's, GRE General Test or MAT. Additional exam requirements/recommendations for international students: Required—TOEFL (minimum score 550 paper-based; 80 iBT), IELTS (minimum score 6.5). *Application deadline:* For fall admission, 5/1 for domestic students, 1/1 for international students; for spring admission, 11/1 for domestic students. Applications are processed on a rolling basis. Application fee: $30. Electronic applications accepted. *Expenses: Tuition:* Full-time $19,800; part-time $825 per credit hour. Tuition and fees vary according to degree level and program. *Financial support:* Career-related internships or fieldwork and Federal Work-Study available. Financial award application deadline: 3/1; financial award applicants required to submit FAFSA. *Unit head:* Dr. Paul Egeland, Chair, 630-752-5041, E-mail: education.dept@wheaton.edu. *Application contact:* Director of Graduate Admissions, 630-752-5195, Fax: 630-752-7047, E-mail: graduate.admissions@wheaton.edu.
Website: https://www.wheaton.edu/academics/programs/education/master-of-arts-in-teaching/

Whittier College, Graduate Programs, Department of Education and Child Development, Program in Elementary Education, Whittier, CA 90608-0634. Offers MA Ed. *Program availability:* Part-time, evening/weekend. *Degree requirements:* For master's, thesis. *Entrance requirements:* For master's, GRE General Test, MAT.

Whitworth University, School of Education, Graduate Studies in Education, Spokane, WA 99251-0001. Offers administration (M Ed); counseling (M Ed), including school counselors, social agency/church setting; elementary education (M Ed); gifted and talented (MAT); secondary education (M Ed); special education (MAT); teaching (MIT). *Accreditation:* NCATE. *Program availability:* Part-time, evening/weekend. *Degree requirements:* For master's, comprehensive exam, thesis (for some programs). *Entrance requirements:* For master's, GRE General Test, MAT. Additional exam requirements/recommendations for international students: Required—TOEFL. *Faculty research:* Rural program development, mainstreaming, special needs learners.

Widener University, School of Human Service Professions, Center for Education, Chester, PA 19013-5792. Offers adult education (M Ed); counseling in higher education (M Ed); counselor education (M Ed); early childhood education (M Ed); educational foundations (M Ed); educational leadership (M Ed); educational psychology (M Ed); elementary education (M Ed); English and language arts (M Ed); health education (M Ed); higher education leadership (Ed D); home and school visitor (M Ed); human sexuality (M Ed, PhD); mathematics education (M Ed); middle school education (M Ed); principalship (M Ed); reading and language arts (Ed D); reading education (M Ed); school administration (Ed D); science education (M Ed); social studies education (M Ed); special education (M Ed); technology education (M Ed). *Accreditation:* NCATE. *Program availability:* Part-time, evening/weekend. *Faculty:* 34 full-time (22 women), 37 part-time/adjunct (14 women). *Students:* 131 full-time (112 women), 244 part-time (179 women); includes 94 minority (58 Black or African American, non-Hispanic/Latino; 1 American Indian or Alaska Native, non-Hispanic/Latino; 1 Asian, non-Hispanic/Latino; 22 Hispanic/Latino; 12 Two or more races, non-Hispanic/Latino), 12 international. Average age 37. 140 applicants, 38% accepted, 26 enrolled. In 2017, 45 master's, 21 doctorates awarded. Terminal master's awarded for partial completion of doctoral program. *Degree requirements:* For doctorate, thesis/dissertation. *Entrance requirements:* For master's, minimum GPA of 2.5; for doctorate, GRE or MAT, minimum GPA of 2.0 (undergraduate), 3.5 (graduate). *Application deadline:* Applications are processed on a rolling basis. Application fee: $25 ($300 for international students). Electronic applications accepted. *Financial support:* Career-related internships or fieldwork, tuition waivers (full and partial), and unspecified assistantships available. Support available to part-time students. Financial award application deadline: 5/1. *Faculty research:* Reading and cognition, adult education, technology education, educational leadership, special education. *Unit head:* Dr. Shawn Fitzgerald, Dean, 610-499-4294, Fax: 610-499-4623, E-mail: smfitzgerald@widener.edu. *Application contact:* Megan Kuft, Director of Graduate Admissions, 610-499-4124, E-mail: gradprograms@widener.edu.
Website: http://www.widener.edu/academics/schools/eics

William Carey University, School of Education, Hattiesburg, MS 39401. Offers art education (M Ed); art of teaching (M Ed); elementary education (M Ed, Ed S); English education (M Ed); gifted education (M Ed); history and social science (M Ed); mild/moderate disabilities (M Ed); secondary education (M Ed). *Accreditation:* NCATE. *Program availability:* Part-time. *Degree requirements:* For master's, comprehensive exam. *Entrance requirements:* For master's, GRE, MAT, minimum GPA of 2.5, Class A teacher's license. Additional exam requirements/recommendations for international students: Required—TOEFL (minimum score 550 paper-based).

William Paterson University of New Jersey, College of Education, Wayne, NJ 07470-8420. Offers curriculum and learning (M Ed); early childhood education (Certificate); educational leadership (M Ed); educational media specialist (Certificate); elementary education (MAT, Certificate); elementary education subject area (Certificate); higher education administration (MA); learning disabilities consultant (Certificate); literacy (M Ed); middle level education (M Ed); middle school education subject area (Certificate); professional counseling (M Ed); reading specialist (Certificate); school library media specialist (Certificate); school principal (Certificate); school supervisor (Certificate); secondary education (MAT); special education (M Ed); teacher of students with disabilities (Certificate). *Accreditation:* NCATE. *Program availability:* Part-time, evening/weekend. *Faculty:* 37 full-time (25 women), 21 part-time/adjunct (16 women). *Students:* 73 full-time (54 women), 480 part-time (409 women); includes 153 minority (48 Black or African American, non-Hispanic/Latino; 13 Asian, non-Hispanic/Latino; 81 Hispanic/Latino; 11 Two or more races, non-Hispanic/Latino), 1 international. Average age 35. 347 applicants, 87% accepted, 226 enrolled. In 2017, 136 master's awarded. *Degree requirements:* For master's, comprehensive exam, thesis (for some programs), exit interview (for some programs); practicum/internship; minimum GPA of 3.0 (for some programs); exit portfolio (for some programs). *Entrance requirements:* For master's, GRE/MAT, minimum GPA of 2.75; teaching certificate; essay; interview; 2 letters of recommendation; personal statement. Additional exam requirements/recommendations for international students: Required—TOEFL (minimum score 550 paper-based; 79 iBT), IELTS (minimum score 6). *Application deadline:* For fall admission, 6/1 for domestic students, 3/1 for international students; for spring admission, 11/1 for domestic students, 10/1 for international students. Applications are processed on a rolling basis. Application fee: $50. Electronic applications accepted. *Expenses:* Tuition, state resident: full-time $13,920; part-time $6264 per year. Tuition, nonresident: full-time $21,700; part-time $9765 per year. *Required fees:* $80; $36 per year. Tuition and fees vary according to course load, degree level and program. *Financial support:* In 2017–18, 8,416 students received support. Career-related internships or fieldwork, Federal Work-Study, scholarships/grants, and unspecified assistantships available. Support available to part-time students. Financial award application deadline: 3/15; financial award applicants required to submit FAFSA. *Faculty research:* Code switching and creative writing, language instruction, teacher evaluation, preschools, history of educational theories. *Total annual research expenditures:* $311,226. *Unit head:* Dr. Dorothy Feola, Dean, 973-720-2138, Fax: 973-720-3647, E-mail: feolad@wpunj.edu. *Application contact:* Liana Fornarotto, Director of Education Enrollment and Certification, 973-720-2206, Fax: 973-720-2989, E-mail: fornarottol@wpunj.edu.
Website: http://www.wpunj.edu/coe

Wilmington University, College of Education, New Castle, DE 19720-6491. Offers applied technology in education (M Ed); career and technical education (M Ed); educational leadership (Ed D); elementary and secondary school counseling (M Ed); elementary studies (M Ed); ESOL literacy (M Ed); higher education leadership (Ed D); instruction: gifted and talented (M Ed); instruction: teacher of reading (M Ed); instruction: teaching and learning (M Ed); organizational leadership (Ed D); school leadership (M Ed); secondary education (MAT); special education (M Ed). *Accreditation:* NCATE. *Program availability:* Part-time, evening/weekend. *Faculty:* 23 full-time (13 women), 162 part-time/adjunct (99 women). *Students:* 546 full-time (394 women), 960 part-time (732 women); includes 320 minority (241 Black or African American, non-Hispanic/Latino; 12 American Indian or Alaska Native, non-Hispanic/Latino; 11 Asian, non-Hispanic/Latino; 28 Hispanic/Latino; 3 Native Hawaiian or other Pacific Islander, non-Hispanic/Latino; 25 Two or more races, non-Hispanic/Latino), 7 international. Average age 34. 1,068 applicants, 64% accepted, 582 enrolled. In 2017, 430 master's, 59 doctorates awarded. *Entrance requirements:* For master's, 2 letters of recommendation, interview. Additional exam requirements/recommendations for international students: Required—TOEFL (minimum score 500 paper-based). *Application deadline:* For fall admission, 4/30 for domestic students. Applications are processed on a rolling basis. Application fee: $35. Electronic applications accepted. *Expenses: Tuition:* Part-time $466 per credit. *Required fees:* $25 per semester. Tuition and fees vary according to degree level and campus/location. *Financial support:* Applicants required to submit FAFSA. *Unit head:* Dr. John C. Gray, Dean, 302-295-1139. *Application contact:* Laura Morris, Director of Admissions, 877-967-5464, E-mail: infocenter@wilmu.edu.
Website: http://www.wilmu.edu/education/

Wilson College, Graduate Programs, Chambersburg, PA 17201-1285. Offers accounting (M Acc); choreography and visual art (MFA); education (M Ed); educational technology (MET); healthcare administration (MHA); humanities (MA), including art and culture, critical/cultural theory, English language and literature, women's studies; management (MSM); nursing (MSN), including nursing education, nursing leadership and management; special education (MSE). *Program availability:* Evening/weekend. *Degree requirements:* For master's, project. *Entrance requirements:* For master's, PRAXIS, minimum undergraduate cumulative GPA of 3.0, 2 letters of recommendation, current certification for eligibility to teach in grades K-12, resume, personal interview. Electronic applications accepted.

Wingate University, Thayer School of Education, Wingate, NC 28174. Offers community college executive leadership (Ed D); educational leadership (MA Ed, Ed S); elementary education (MA Ed, MAT). *Accreditation:* NCATE. *Program availability:* Part-time, evening/weekend. *Degree requirements:* For master's, portfolio. *Entrance requirements:* For master's, GRE General Test or MAT, teaching certificate (MA Ed).

Worcester State University, Graduate School, Department of Education, Program in Elementary Education, Worcester, MA 01602-2597. Offers M Ed, Postbaccalaureate Certificate. *Program availability:* Part-time, evening/weekend. *Students:* 1 (woman) full-time, 17 part-time (all women). Average age 26. 10 applicants, 90% accepted, 7 enrolled. In 2017, 9 master's, 36 other advanced degrees awarded. *Degree requirements:* For master's, comprehensive exam (for some programs), thesis optional. *Entrance requirements:* For master's, GRE General Test or MAT, elementary teaching certificate. Additional exam requirements/recommendations for international students: Required—TOEFL (minimum score 550 paper-based; 79 iBT). *Application deadline:* For fall admission, 6/15 for domestic and international students; for spring admission, 11/1 for domestic and international students; for summer admission, 4/1 for domestic and international students. Applications are processed on a rolling basis. Application fee: $50. Electronic applications accepted. *Expenses:* Tuition, state resident: full-time $3042; part-time $169 per credit hour. Tuition, nonresident: full-time $3042; part-time $169 per credit hour. *Required fees:* $2754; $153 per credit hour. *Financial support:* Career-related internships or fieldwork, scholarships/grants, and unspecified assistantships available. Financial award application deadline: 3/1; financial award applicants required to submit FAFSA. *Faculty research:* Contemporary elementary education, social studies in the elementary school. *Unit head:* Dr. Christina Kaniu, Coordinator, 508-929-8753, E-mail: cbebas@worcester.edu. *Application contact:* Sara Grady, Associate Dean of Graduate Studies and Professional Development, 508-929-8130, Fax: 508-929-8100, E-mail: sara.grady@worcester.edu.

Wright State University, Graduate School, College of Education and Human Services, Department of Teacher Education, Programs in Classroom Teacher Education, Dayton,

OH 45435. Offers M Ed, MA. *Accreditation:* NCATE. *Degree requirements:* For master's, thesis (for some programs). *Entrance requirements:* For master's, GRE General Test, MAT, PRAXIS II. Additional exam requirements/recommendations for international students: Required—TOEFL.

Xavier University, College of Social Sciences, Health and Education, School of Education, Department of Childhood Education and Literacy, Cincinnati, OH 45207. Offers children's multicultural literature (M Ed); elementary education (M Ed); Montessori education (M Ed); reading (M Ed). *Program availability:* Part-time. *Degree requirements:* For master's, comprehensive exam, thesis, 30 semester hours. *Entrance requirements:* For master's, GRE, MAT, official transcript; 3 letters of recommendation (for Montessori education); resume; statement of purpose. Additional exam requirements/recommendations for international students: Required—TOEFL (minimum score 550 paper-based; 79 iBT). Electronic applications accepted. Application fee is waived when completed online. *Expenses:* Contact institution. *Faculty research:* Multicultural literacy/fluency, early literacy development, writing/creative and across curriculum, assessment of reading abilities.

Higher Education

Abilene Christian University, College of Graduate and Professional Studies, Program in Higher Education, Addison, TX 75001. Offers conflict management (M Ed); enrollment management (M Ed). *Program availability:* Part-time, online only. *Faculty:* 1 full-time (0 women). *Students:* 34 full-time (24 women), 16 part-time (12 women); includes 21 minority (15 Black or African American, non-Hispanic/Latino; 1 American Indian or Alaska Native, non-Hispanic/Latino; 2 Asian, non-Hispanic/Latino; 3 Hispanic/Latino). 24 applicants, 67% accepted, 11 enrolled. In 2017, 28 master's awarded. *Degree requirements:* For master's, internship, capstone. *Entrance requirements:* Additional exam requirements/recommendations for international students: Required—TOEFL (minimum score 80 iBT), IELTS (minimum score 6), PTE. *Application deadline:* For fall admission, 8/15 priority date for domestic students; for winter admission, 10/1 priority date for domestic students; for spring admission, 12/15 priority date for domestic students; for summer admission, 4/15 for domestic students. Applications are processed on a rolling basis. Application fee: $50. Electronic applications accepted. *Expenses:* $726 per hour. *Financial support:* In 2017–18, 2 students received support. Scholarships/grants available. Financial award application deadline: 4/1; financial award applicants required to submit FAFSA. *Unit head:* Dr. Jason Morris, Graduate Director, 325-674-2830, Fax: 325-674-2123, E-mail: morrisj@acu.edu. *Application contact:* Graduate Advisor, 855-219-7300, E-mail: gradonline@acu.edu.
Website: http://www.acu.edu/online/academics/higher-education.html

Alliant International University–San Diego, Shirley M. Hufstedler School of Education, Educational Leadership Programs, San Diego, CA 92131. Offers educational administration (MA); educational leadership and management (K-12) (Ed D); higher education (Ed D, Certificate); preliminary administrative services (Credential). *Program availability:* Part-time. *Degree requirements:* For doctorate, comprehensive exam, thesis/dissertation. *Entrance requirements:* For master's, minimum GPA of 2.5, letters of recommendation; for doctorate, minimum GPA of 3.0, letters of recommendation. Additional exam requirements/recommendations for international students: Required—TOEFL (minimum score 550 paper-based; 80 iBT), TWE (minimum score 5). Electronic applications accepted. *Faculty research:* Global education, women and international educational opportunities.

Alliant International University–San Francisco, Shirley M. Hufstedler School of Education, Educational Leadership Programs, San Francisco, CA 94133. Offers community college administration (Ed D); educational administration; educational leadership and management (K-12) (Ed D); higher education (Ed D); preliminary administrative services (Credential). *Program availability:* Part-time. *Degree requirements:* For doctorate, comprehensive exam, thesis/dissertation. *Entrance requirements:* For master's and doctorate, minimum GPA of 3.0, letters of recommendation. Additional exam requirements/recommendations for international students: Required—TOEFL (minimum score 550 paper-based; 80 iBT), TWE (minimum score 5). Electronic applications accepted. *Faculty research:* Leadership in higher education, community colleges.

Andrews University, School of Graduate Studies, School of Education, Department of Leadership and Educational Administration, Berrien Springs, MI 49104. Offers educational administration and leadership (MA, Ed D, PhD, Ed S); higher education administration (MA, Ed D, PhD, Ed S); leadership (MA, Ed D, PhD, Ed S). *Faculty:* 6 full-time (2 women). *Students:* 41 full-time (21 women), 46 part-time (23 women); includes 32 minority (13 Black or African American, non-Hispanic/Latino; 4 Asian, non-Hispanic/Latino; 12 Hispanic/Latino; 3 Two or more races, non-Hispanic/Latino), 22 international. Average age 48. 58 applicants, 59% accepted, 15 enrolled. In 2017, 6 master's, 7 doctorates, 4 other advanced degrees awarded. *Degree requirements:* For doctorate, thesis/dissertation. *Entrance requirements:* For master's, GRE. Additional exam requirements/recommendations for international students: Required—TOEFL (minimum score 550 paper-based). *Application deadline:* Applications are processed on a rolling basis. Application fee: $40. *Unit head:* Dr. Robson Marinho, Chair, 269-471-3487. *Application contact:* Justina Clayburn, Supervisor of Graduate Admission, 800-253-2874, Fax: 269-471-6321, E-mail: graduate@andrews.edu.

Angelo State University, College of Graduate Studies and Research, College of Education, Department of Curriculum and Instruction, San Angelo, TX 76909. Offers curriculum and instruction (MA); educational administration (M Ed); guidance and counseling (M Ed); student development and leadership in higher education (M Ed). *Program availability:* Part-time, evening/weekend, online learning. *Students:* 405 full-time (332 women), 449 part-time (380 women); includes 291 minority (98 Black or African American, non-Hispanic/Latino; 3 American Indian or Alaska Native, non-Hispanic/Latino; 3 Asian, non-Hispanic/Latino; 178 Hispanic/Latino; 9 Two or more races, non-Hispanic/Latino), 1 international. Average age 35. *Application deadline:* For fall admission, 7/15 priority date for domestic students, 6/10 for international students; for spring admission, 12/1 priority date for domestic students, 11/1 for international students. Application fee: $40 ($50 for international students). *Expenses:* Tuition, state resident: full-time $3856. Tuition, nonresident: full-time $11,324. *Required fees:* $2650. *Unit head:* Dr. Jim Summerlin, Chair, 325-942-2647, Fax: 325-942-2039, E-mail: james.summerlin@angelo.edu. *Application contact:* Lesley Casarez, Graduate Advisor, 325-486-6775, E-mail: lesley.casarez@angelo.edu.
Website: http://www.angelo.edu/dept/ci/

Appalachian State University, Cratis D. Williams Graduate School, Department of Leadership and Educational Studies, Boone, NC 28608. Offers educational administration (Ed S); educational media (MA); higher education (MA, Ed S); library science (MLS); school administration (MSA). *Program availability:* Part-time, evening/weekend, online learning. *Degree requirements:* For master's and Ed S, comprehensive exam, thesis optional. *Entrance requirements:* For master's and Ed S, GRE or MAT, 3 letters of recommendation. Additional exam requirements/recommendations for international students: Required—TOEFL (minimum score 570 paper-based; 79 iBT), IELTS (minimum score 6.5). Electronic applications accepted. *Faculty research:* Brain, learning and meditation; leadership of teaching and learning.

Argosy University, Atlanta, College of Education, Atlanta, GA 30328. Offers educational leadership (MAEd, Ed D, Ed S), including higher education administration (Ed D), K-12 education (Ed D); teaching and learning (MAEd, Ed D, Ed S), including education technology (Ed D), higher education (Ed D), K-12 education (Ed D).

Argosy University, Chicago, College of Education, Chicago, IL 60601. Offers adult education and training (MA Ed); community college executive leadership (Ed D); educational leadership (MA Ed, Ed D, Ed S), including district leadership (Ed D), higher education administration (Ed D), K-12 education (Ed D); instructional leadership (Ed D, Ed S), including higher education (Ed D), K-12 education (Ed D). *Program availability:* Online learning.

Argosy University, Hawai`i, College of Education, Honolulu, HI 96813. Offers adult education and training (MAEd); educational leadership (Ed D), including higher education administration, K-12 education; instructional leadership (Ed D), including higher education, K-12 education; school psychology (MA).

Argosy University, Los Angeles, College of Education, Los Angeles, CA 90045. Offers community college executive leadership (Ed D); educational leadership (MA Ed, Ed D), including higher education administration (Ed D), K-12 education (Ed D); instructional leadership (MA Ed, Ed D), including higher education (Ed D), K-12 education (Ed D), multiple subject teacher preparation (MA Ed), single subject teacher preparation (MA Ed).

Argosy University, Northern Virginia, College of Education, Arlington, VA 22209. Offers community college executive leadership (Ed D); educational leadership (MA Ed, Ed D, Ed S), including higher education administration (Ed D), K-12 education (Ed D); instructional leadership (MA Ed, Ed D, Ed S), including higher education (Ed D), K-12 education (Ed D).

Argosy University, Orange County, College of Education, Orange, CA 92868. Offers community college executive leadership (Ed D); educational leadership (MA Ed, Ed D), including higher education administration (Ed D), K-12 education (Ed D); instructional leadership (MA Ed, Ed D), including education technology (Ed D), higher education (Ed D), K-12 education (Ed D), multiple subject teacher preparation (MA Ed), single subject teacher preparation (MA Ed).

Argosy University, Phoenix, College of Education, Phoenix, AZ 85021. Offers adult education and training (MA Ed); advanced educational administration (Ed D, Ed S); community college executive leadership (Ed D); educational administration (MA Ed); educational leadership (MA Ed, Ed D, Ed S), including education technology (Ed D), higher education administration (Ed D), K-12 education (Ed D); higher and postsecondary education (MA Ed); initial educational administration (Ed D, Ed S); school psychology (MA); teaching and learning (MA Ed, Ed D, Ed S), including education technology (Ed D), higher education (Ed D), K-12 education (Ed D).

Argosy University, Seattle, College of Education, Seattle, WA 98121. Offers adult education and training (MA Ed); community college executive leadership (Ed D); educational leadership (MA Ed, Ed D), including higher education administration (Ed D), K-12 education (Ed D); higher and postsecondary education (MA Ed); instructional leadership (MA Ed, Ed D), including education technology (Ed D), higher education (Ed D), K-12 education (Ed D).

Argosy University, Tampa, College of Education, Tampa, FL 33607. Offers community college executive leadership (Ed D); educational leadership (MA Ed, Ed D, Ed S), including higher education administration (Ed D), K-12 education (Ed D); school counseling (MA); teaching and learning (MA Ed, Ed D, Ed S), including higher education (Ed D), K-12 education (Ed D).

Argosy University, Twin Cities, College of Education, Eagan, MN 55121. Offers advanced educational administration (Ed D, Ed S); educational leadership (MA Ed, Ed D, Ed S), including higher education administration (Ed D), K-12 education (Ed D); higher and postsecondary education (MA Ed); initial educational administration (Ed D, Ed S); instructional leadership (MA Ed, Ed D, Ed S), including education technology (Ed D), higher education (Ed D), K-12 education (Ed D).

Arizona State University at the Tempe campus, Mary Lou Fulton Teachers College, Program in Higher and Post-Secondary Education, Phoenix, AZ 85069. Offers M Ed. *Program availability:* Part-time, evening/weekend. *Degree requirements:* For master's, thesis or alternative, applied project, interactive Program of Study (iPOS) submitted before completing 50 percent of required credit hours. *Entrance requirements:* For master's, minimum GPA of 3.0 or equivalent in last 2 years of work leading to bachelor's degree, 3 letters of recommendation, personal statement describing research and career goals, curriculum vitae or resume. Additional exam requirements/recommendations for international students: Required—TOEFL, IELTS, or PTE. Electronic applications accepted.

Auburn University, Graduate School, College of Education, Department of Educational Foundations, Leadership, and Technology, Auburn University, AL 36849. Offers adult education (PhD, Ed S); curriculum supervision (M Ed, PhD); higher education administration (PhD); library media (Ed S); school administration (M Ed, PhD). *Accreditation:* NCATE. *Program availability:* Part-time. *Faculty:* 30 full-time (17 women), 8 part-time/adjunct (5 women). *Students:* 139 full-time (94 women), 254 part-time (171 women); includes 109 minority (95 Black or African American, non-Hispanic/Latino; 1 American Indian or Alaska Native, non-Hispanic/Latino; 2 Asian, non-Hispanic/Latino; 4 Hispanic/Latino; 1 Native Hawaiian or other Pacific Islander, non-Hispanic/Latino; 6 Two or more races, non-Hispanic/Latino), 12 international. Average age 37. 216 applicants, 72% accepted, 94 enrolled. In 2017, 92 master's, 46 doctorates, 58 other advanced degrees awarded. *Degree requirements:* For master's, thesis (for some programs); for doctorate, thesis/dissertation; for Ed S, field project. *Entrance requirements:* For master's, doctorate, and Ed S, GRE General Test. *Application deadline:* Applications are processed on a rolling basis. Application fee: $50 ($60 for international students). Electronic applications accepted. *Expenses:* Tuition, state resident: full-time $10,974; part-time $519 per credit hour. Tuition, nonresident: full-time $29,658; part-time $1557

per credit hour. *Required fees:* $816 per semester. Tuition and fees vary according to degree level and program. *Financial support:* Teaching assistantships and Federal Work-Study available. Support available to part-time students. Financial award application deadline: 3/15; financial award applicants required to submit FAFSA. *Unit head:* Dr. Sherida Downer, Head, 334-844-3060. *Application contact:* Dr. George Flowers, Dean of the Graduate School, 334-844-4700.
Website: http://www.education.auburn.edu/academic_departments/eflt/

Azusa Pacific University, School of Behavioral and Applied Sciences, Department of Higher Education, Azusa, CA 91702-7000. Offers college counseling and student development (MS); higher education (PhD); higher education leadership (Ed D).

Ball State University, Graduate School, Teachers College, Department of Educational Studies, Program in Adult Education, Muncie, IN 47306. Offers adult and community education (MA); adult, higher and community education (Ed D). *Accreditation:* NCATE. *Program availability:* Part-time, 100% online, blended/hybrid learning. *Students:* 30 full-time (22 women), 101 part-time (77 women); includes 26 minority (19 Black or African American, non-Hispanic/Latino; 6 Hispanic/Latino; 1 Two or more races, non-Hispanic/Latino), 2 international. Average age 39. 53 applicants, 77% accepted, 34 enrolled. In 2017, 23 master's, 4 doctorates awarded. *Degree requirements:* For doctorate, thesis/dissertation. *Entrance requirements:* For master's, minimum baccalaureate GPA of 2.75 or 3.0 in latter half of baccalaureate; for doctorate, GRE General Test, minimum graduate GPA of 3.2. Additional exam requirements/recommendations for international students: Required—TOEFL (minimum score 550 paper-based; 79 iBT), IELTS (minimum score 6.5). *Application deadline:* Applications are processed on a rolling basis. Application fee: $60. Electronic applications accepted. *Financial support:* Research assistantships with partial tuition reimbursements, teaching assistantships with partial tuition reimbursements, and unspecified assistantships available. Financial award application deadline: 3/1; financial award applicants required to submit FAFSA. *Faculty research:* Community education, executive development for public services. *Unit head:* Dr. Theresa Kruczek, Interim Chair, 765-285-8049, E-mail: tkruczek@bsu.edu.
Website: http://www.bsu.edu/edstudies

Ball State University, Graduate School, Teachers College, Department of Educational Studies, Program in Student Affairs Administration in Higher Education, Muncie, IN 47306. Offers MA. *Accreditation:* NCATE. *Students:* 42 full-time (24 women), 1 (woman) part-time; includes 14 minority (8 Black or African American, non-Hispanic/Latino; 1 Asian, non-Hispanic/Latino; 4 Hispanic/Latino; 1 Two or more races, non-Hispanic/Latino). Average age 23. 156 applicants, 20% accepted, 31 enrolled. In 2017, 30 master's awarded. *Entrance requirements:* For master's, GRE General Test, minimum baccalaureate GPA of 2.75 or 3.0 in latter half of baccalaureate, resume, three professional references. Additional exam requirements/recommendations for international students: Required—TOEFL (minimum score 550 paper-based; 79 iBT), IELTS (minimum score 6.5). *Application deadline:* For fall admission, 1/1 priority date for domestic students. Applications are processed on a rolling basis. Application fee: $60. Electronic applications accepted. *Financial support:* Teaching assistantships with partial tuition reimbursements and unspecified assistantships available. Financial award application deadline: 3/1; financial award applicants required to submit FAFSA. *Unit head:* Dr. Theresa Kruczek, Interim Chair, 765-285-8049, E-mail: tkruczek@bsu.edu.
Website: http://www.bsu.edu/edstudies

Barry University, School of Education, Program in Higher Education Administration, Miami Shores, FL 33161-6695. Offers MS. *Program availability:* Part-time, evening/weekend. *Degree requirements:* For master's, comprehensive exam. *Entrance requirements:* For master's, GRE General Test or MAT, minimum GPA of 3.0. Electronic applications accepted.

Barry University, School of Education, Program in Leadership and Education, Miami Shores, FL 33161-6695. Offers educational technology (PhD); exceptional student education (PhD); higher education administration (PhD); human resource development (PhD); leadership (PhD). *Program availability:* Part-time, evening/weekend. *Degree requirements:* For doctorate, thesis/dissertation. *Entrance requirements:* For doctorate, GRE General Test, minimum GPA of 3.25. Electronic applications accepted.

Baruch College of the City University of New York, Austin W. Marxe School of Public and International Affairs, Program in Higher Education Administration, New York, NY 10010-5585. Offers MS Ed. *Program availability:* Part-time, evening/weekend. *Entrance requirements:* For master's, GRE General Test. Additional exam requirements/recommendations for international students: Required—TOEFL. Electronic applications accepted. *Expenses:* Contact institution.

Bay Path University, Program in Higher Education Administration, Longmeadow, MA 01106-2292. Offers enrollment management (MS); general administration (MS); institutional advancement (MS); online teaching and program administration (MS). *Program availability:* Part-time, online only, 100% online. *Students:* 3 full-time (all women), 47 part-time (33 women); includes 19 minority (9 Black or African American, non-Hispanic/Latino; 8 Hispanic/Latino; 2 Two or more races, non-Hispanic/Latino). Average age 34. In 2017, 15 master's awarded. *Degree requirements:* For master's, 8 core courses (24 credits) and 4 elective courses (12 credits) for a total of 36 credits. *Application deadline:* Applications are processed on a rolling basis. Application fee: $45. Electronic applications accepted. Application fee is waived when completed online. *Expenses:* $760 per credit. *Financial support:* Unspecified assistantships available. Financial award applicants required to submit FAFSA. *Unit head:* Dr. Lauren Way, Program Director, 413-565-1193, E-mail: lway@baypath.edu. *Application contact:* Diane Ranaldi, Dean of Graduate Admissions, 413-565-1332, Fax: 413-565-1250, E-mail: dranaldi@baypath.edu.
Website: http://graduate.baypath.edu/Graduate-Programs/Programs-Online/MS-Programs/Higher-Education-Administration

Bay Path University, Program in Strategic Fundraising and Philanthropy, Longmeadow, MA 01106-2292. Offers higher education fundraising (MS); nonprofit fundraising (MS). *Program availability:* Part-time, 100% online. *Students:* 2 full-time (both women), 9 part-time (7 women); includes 2 minority (1 Black or African American, non-Hispanic/Latino; 1 Native Hawaiian or other Pacific Islander, non-Hispanic/Latino). Average age 36. In 2017, 4 master's awarded. *Degree requirements:* For master's, 36 hours of coursework including portfolio. *Application deadline:* Applications are processed on a rolling basis. Application fee: $45. Electronic applications accepted. Application fee is waived when completed online. *Expenses:* $675 per credit. *Financial support:* Unspecified assistantships available. Financial award applicants required to submit FAFSA. *Unit head:* Silvia de Haas-Phillips, Program Director, E-mail: sdphillips@baypath.edu. *Application contact:* Diane Ranaldi, Dean of Graduate Admissions, 413-565-1332, Fax: 413-565-1250, E-mail: dranaldi@baypath.edu.
Website: http://graduate.baypath.edu/Graduate-Programs/Programs-On-Campus/MS-Programs/Strategic-Fundraising-and-Philanthropy

Bellarmine University, Annsley Frazier Thornton School of Education, Louisville, KY 40205. Offers education and district leadership (Ed D); education and social change (PhD); elementary education (MA Ed, MAT); leadership in higher education (PhD); middle school education (MA Ed, MAT); principalship (Ed S); reading and writing (MA Ed); secondary education (MAT); teacher leadership (MA Ed). *Accreditation:* NCATE. *Program availability:* Part-time, evening/weekend. *Faculty:* 19 full-time (10

women), 36 part-time/adjunct (29 women). *Students:* 34 full-time (27 women), 204 part-time (158 women); includes 60 minority (43 Black or African American, non-Hispanic/Latino; 7 Asian, non-Hispanic/Latino; 7 Hispanic/Latino; 3 Two or more races, non-Hispanic/Latino). Average age 33. In 2017, 50 master's, 8 doctorates, 42 other advanced degrees awarded. *Degree requirements:* For master's, comprehensive exam (for some programs), thesis (for some programs); for doctorate, comprehensive exam (for some programs), thesis/dissertation; for Ed S, comprehensive exam (for some programs). *Entrance requirements:* For master's, GRE, baccalaureate degree from accredited institution; minimum cumulative GPA of 2.75; recommendations from employers, supervisors, or professors attesting to applicant's potential as graduate student; statement of intent to pursue graduate degree; for doctorate, GRE, minimum GPA of 3.5 in all graduate coursework; baccalaureate and master's degrees in education or fields directly relevant to education; three letters of recommendation; two essays (no more than 1,000 words each); resume or curriculum vitae; interview; for Ed S, master's degree in education; valid teaching certificate; three years of experience in teaching; three recommendations; minimum GPA of 3.0 in all graduate work; interview; essays; personal goal statement. Additional exam requirements/recommendations for international students: Required—TOEFL (minimum score 550 paper-based, 68 iBT), IELTS (minimum score 6), or Michigan English Language Assessment Battery. *Application deadline:* For fall admission, 8/1 priority date for domestic and international students; for spring admission, 12/1 priority date for domestic and international students; for summer admission, 4/10 priority date for domestic and international students. Applications are processed on a rolling basis. Application fee: $40. Electronic applications accepted. Tuition and fees vary according to program. *Financial support:* Scholarships/grants available. Financial award applicants required to submit FAFSA. *Faculty research:* Literacy, service-learning, dispositions, educational technology, special education. *Unit head:* Dr. Elizabeth Dinkins, Interim Dean, 502-272-7958, Fax: 502-272-8189, E-mail: edinkins@bellarmine.edu. *Application contact:* Sarah Schuble, Senior Graduate Admissions Recruiter, 502-272-8271, Fax: 502-272-8002, E-mail: sschuble@bellarmine.edu.
Website: http://www.bellarmine.edu/education/graduate

Benedictine University, Graduate Programs, Program in Higher Education and Organizational Change, Lisle, IL 60532. Offers Ed D.

Boston College, Lynch School of Education, Program in Higher Education, Chestnut Hill, MA 02467-3800. Offers MA, PhD, JD/MA, MBA/MA. *Accreditation:* TEAC. *Program availability:* Part-time, evening/weekend. *Students:* 52 full-time (32 women), 57 part-time (45 women); includes 20 minority (2 Black or African American, non-Hispanic/Latino; 6 Asian, non-Hispanic/Latino; 8 Hispanic/Latino; 4 Two or more races, non-Hispanic/Latino), 4 international. Average age 28. 164 applicants, 60% accepted, 45 enrolled. In 2017, 43 master's, 6 doctorates awarded. Terminal master's awarded for partial completion of doctoral program. *Degree requirements:* For master's, comprehensive exam; for doctorate, comprehensive exam, thesis/dissertation. *Entrance requirements:* For master's, GRE General Test or MAT; for doctorate, GRE General Test. Additional exam requirements/recommendations for international students: Required—TOEFL (minimum score 100 iBT). *Application deadline:* For fall admission, 12/1 priority date for domestic and international students; for spring admission, 11/1 priority date for domestic and international students. Application fee: $65. Electronic applications accepted. *Financial support:* Research assistantships with full tuition reimbursements, Federal Work-Study, scholarships/grants, tuition waivers (full and partial), and unspecified assistantships available. Support available to part-time students. Financial award applicants required to submit FAFSA. *Application contact:* Kimberly Rose, Graduate Admission Assistant, 617-552-4214, Fax: 617-552-0398, E-mail: roseki@bc.edu.

Boston College, Lynch School of Education, Program in International Higher Education, Chestnut Hill, MA 02467-3800. Offers MA. *Students:* 10 full-time (5 women), 7 part-time (5 women); includes 2 minority (both Asian, non-Hispanic/Latino), 10 international. Average age 27. 44 applicants, 59% accepted, 11 enrolled. In 2017, 1 master's awarded. *Application deadline:* Applications are processed on a rolling basis. Application fee: $65. *Unit head:* Hans de Wit, Director, 617-552-4236. *Application contact:* Laura E. Rumbley, Coordinator, 617-552-4185.

Bowling Green State University, Graduate College, College of Education and Human Development, Department of Higher Education and Student Affairs, Program in Higher Education Administration, Bowling Green, OH 43403. Offers PhD. *Accreditation:* NCATE. *Program availability:* Part-time. *Degree requirements:* For doctorate, comprehensive exam, thesis/dissertation. *Entrance requirements:* For doctorate, GRE General Test. Additional exam requirements/recommendations for international students: Required—TOEFL. Electronic applications accepted. *Faculty research:* Adult learners, legal issues, intellectual development.

California Baptist University, Program in Higher Education Leadership and Student Development, Riverside, CA 92504-3206. Offers MS. *Program availability:* Part-time, evening/weekend. *Faculty:* 9 full-time (3 women), 4 part-time/adjunct (1 woman). *Students:* 30 master's (21 women); includes 19 minority (6 Black or African American, non-Hispanic/Latino; 13 Hispanic/Latino), 1 international. Average age 29. 22 applicants, 77% accepted, 15 enrolled. In 2017, 3 master's awarded. *Entrance requirements:* For master's, minimum cumulative GPA of 2.75, three letters of recommendation, current resume, 500-word comprehensive essay. Additional exam requirements/recommendations for international students: Required—TOEFL (minimum score 80 iBT). *Application deadline:* For fall admission, 8/1 priority date for domestic students, 7/1 for international students; for spring admission, 12/1 priority date for domestic students, 11/1 for international students. Applications are processed on a rolling basis. Application fee: $45. Electronic applications accepted. *Expenses:* Contact institution. *Financial support:* In 2017–18, 5 students received support. Federal Work-Study and scholarships/grants available. Financial award applicants required to submit CSS PROFILE or FAFSA. *Faculty research:* Sociology of education, student retention, women in academic leadership, curriculum and instruction, global education. *Unit head:* Dr. John Shoup, Dean, School of Education, 951-343-4205, E-mail: jshoup@calbaptist.edu. *Application contact:* David Little, Graduate Admissions Counselor, 951-552-8093, E-mail: dlittle@calbaptist.edu.
Website: http://www.calbaptist.edu/academics/schools-colleges/school-education/programs/graduate/master-science-higher-education-leadership-and-student-develop

California Lutheran University, Graduate Studies, Graduate School of Education, Thousand Oaks, CA 91360-2787. Offers counseling and guidance (MS), including college student personnel, counseling and guidance; educational leadership (MA, Ed D), including educational leadership (K-12) (Ed D), higher education leadership (Ed D); special education (MS); teacher leadership (M Ed); teaching (M Ed). *Accreditation:* NCATE. *Program availability:* Part-time, evening/weekend. *Faculty:* 21 full-time (18 women), 40 part-time/adjunct (27 women). *Students:* 390 full-time (303 women), 61 part-time (51 women); includes 228 minority (6 Black or African American, non-Hispanic/Latino; 2 American Indian or Alaska Native, non-Hispanic/Latino; 13 Asian, non-Hispanic/Latino; 186 Hispanic/Latino; 1 Native Hawaiian or other Pacific Islander, non-Hispanic/Latino; 20 Two or more races, non-Hispanic/Latino). Average age 31. 201 applicants, 76% accepted, 121 enrolled. In 2017, 129 master's, 19 doctorates awarded. *Degree requirements:* For master's, comprehensive exam or thesis; for doctorate, thesis/dissertation. *Entrance requirements:* For master's, GRE General Test, interview, minimum GPA of 3.0. *Application deadline:* For fall admission, 7/1 priority date for domestic students; for spring admission, 11/1 priority date for domestic students; for summer admission, 4/1 priority date for domestic students. Applications are processed on a rolling basis. Application fee: $50. Electronic applications accepted. *Expenses: Tuition:* Full-time $15,000. Full-time tuition and fees vary according to degree level and program. *Unit head:* Dr. Michael Hillis, Dean, 805-493-3421. *Application contact:* 805-493-3325, Fax: 805-493-3861, E-mail: clugrad@callutheran.edu.

California State University, Long Beach, Graduate Studies, College of Education, Department of Advanced Studies in Education and Counseling, Long Beach, CA 90840. Offers counseling (MS), including marriage and family therapy, school counseling, student development in higher education; education (MA, Ed D); educational administration (MA, Ed D); educational psychology (MA); special education (MS). *Program availability:* Part-time, evening/weekend. *Entrance requirements:* For master's, GRE General Test, minimum GPA of 2.75. Electronic applications accepted.

California State University, Sacramento, College of Education, Graduate and Professional Studies in Education, Sacramento, CA 95819. Offers behavioral science and gender equity (MA); child development (MA); counseling (MS); curriculum and instruction (MA); education (Ed D), including K-12 and community college; education leadership and policy studies (MA), including higher education, PreK-12; education specialist (Ed S), including school psychology; educational technology (MA); language and literacy (MA); multicultural education (MA); school psychology (MA); special education (MA); workforce development advocacy (MA). *Program availability:* Part-time, evening/weekend, blended/hybrid learning. *Students:* 381 full-time (294 women), 135 part-time (101 women); includes 296 minority (44 Black or African American, non-Hispanic/Latino; 1 American Indian or Alaska Native, non-Hispanic/Latino; 94 Asian, non-Hispanic/Latino; 153 Hispanic/Latino; 4 Native Hawaiian or other Pacific Islander, non-Hispanic/Latino; 3 international. Average age 32. 553 applicants, 53% accepted, 292 enrolled. In 2017, 147 master's, 13 doctorates, 10 other advanced degrees awarded. *Degree requirements:* For master's, thesis or project; writing proficiency exam; for doctorate, thesis/dissertation. *Entrance requirements:* For master's and doctorate, GRE. Additional exam requirements/recommendations for international students: Required—TOEFL (minimum score 550 paper-based; 80 iBT); Recommended—IELTS (minimum score 7), TSE. *Application deadline:* For fall admission, 2/15 for domestic students, 1/15 for international students. Applications are processed on a rolling basis. Application fee: $55. Electronic applications accepted. *Expenses:* Contact institution. *Financial support:* Career-related internships or fieldwork, Federal Work-Study, and scholarships/grants available. Support available to part-time students. Financial award application deadline: 3/1; financial award applicants required to submit FAFSA. *Unit head:* Dr. Elizabeth Liles, Chair, 916-278-5942, E-mail: coe@csus.edu. *Application contact:* Jose Martinez, Graduate Admissions Supervisor, 916-278-7871, E-mail: martinj@skymail.csus.edu.
Website: http://www.csus.edu/coe/academics/graduate/index.html

Capella University, School of Education, Doctoral Programs in Education, Minneapolis, MN 55402. Offers curriculum and instruction (PhD); educational leadership and management (Ed D); instructional design for online learning (PhD); K-12 studies in education (PhD); leadership for higher education (PhD); leadership in educational administration (PhD); postsecondary and adult education (PhD); professional studies in education (PhD); reading and literacy (Ed D); special education leadership (PhD); training and performance improvement (PhD).

Capella University, School of Education, Master's Programs in Education, Minneapolis, MN 55402. Offers adult education (MS); curriculum and instruction (MS); early childhood education (MS); enrollment management (MS); higher education leadership and management (MS); instructional design for online learning (MS); integrative studies (MS); K-12 studies in education (MS); leadership in educational administration (MS); reading and literacy (MS); special education teaching (MS).

Cardinal Stritch University, College of Education and Leadership, Department of Education, Milwaukee, WI 53217-3985. Offers educational leadership (MS); higher education student affairs leadership (MS); leadership for the advancement of learning and service (Ed D, PhD); leadership for the advancement of learning and service in higher education (Ed D, PhD); teaching (MAT); urban education (MA). *Accreditation:* NCATE. *Program availability:* Part-time, evening/weekend, 100% online, blended/hybrid learning. *Students:* 73 full-time (57 women), 332 part-time (220 women); includes 113 minority (59 Black or African American, non-Hispanic/Latino; 2 American Indian or Alaska Native, non-Hispanic/Latino; 10 Asian, non-Hispanic/Latino; 38 Hispanic/Latino; 1 Native Hawaiian or other Pacific Islander, non-Hispanic/Latino; 3 Two or more races, non-Hispanic/Latino; 7 international. Average age 35. 137 applicants, 97% accepted, 104 enrolled. In 2017, 135 master's, 28 doctorates awarded. *Degree requirements:* For master's, comprehensive exam, thesis (for some programs), research project, faculty recommendation; for doctorate, thesis/dissertation, practica, field experience. *Entrance requirements:* For master's, 2 letters of recommendation, minimum GPA of 3.0; for doctorate, minimum GPA of 3.5 in master's coursework, 3 letters of recommendation. Additional exam requirements/recommendations for international students: Required—TOEFL (minimum score 550 paper-based; 79 iBT), IELTS (minimum score 6.5). *Application deadline:* For fall admission, 7/15 priority date for domestic students; for spring admission, 12/15 priority date for domestic students. Applications are processed on a rolling basis. Application fee: $0. Electronic applications accepted. *Expenses:* Tuition varies by program. *Financial support:* Fellowships, research assistantships with partial tuition reimbursements, career-related internships or fieldwork, Federal Work-Study, and scholarships/grants available. Financial award applicants required to submit FAFSA. *Application contact:* 800-347-8822 Ext. 4042, E-mail: admissions@stritch.edu.

Central Michigan University, Central Michigan University Global Campus, Program in Education, Mount Pleasant, MI 48859. Offers college teaching (Graduate Certificate); community college (MA); curriculum and instruction (MA); educational technology (MA, DET); reading and literacy K-12 (MA); school principalship (MA), including charter school leadership; training and development (MA). *Accreditation:* TEAC. *Program availability:* Part-time, evening/weekend. *Entrance requirements:* For master's, minimum GPA of 2.7 in major. Additional exam requirements/recommendations for international students: Required—TOEFL. Electronic applications accepted.

Central Michigan University, College of Graduate Studies, College of Education and Human Services, Department of Educational Leadership, Mount Pleasant, MI 48859. Offers educational leadership (Ed D), including educational technology (Ed D, Ed S), higher education leadership, K-12 curriculum, K-12 leadership; general educational administration (Ed S), including administrative leadership K-12, educational technology (Ed D, Ed S), higher education administration, instructional leadership K-12; school principalship (MA), including charter school leadership, site-based leadership; student affairs administration (MA); teacher leadership (MA). *Program availability:* Part-time, evening/weekend. *Degree requirements:* For master's and Ed S, thesis or alternative; for doctorate, thesis/dissertation. *Entrance requirements:* For doctorate, GRE or MAT, master's degree, minimum GPA of 3.5, 3 years of professional education experience. Electronic applications accepted. *Faculty research:* Elementary administration, secondary administration, student achievement, in-service training, internships in administration.

Central Washington University, School of Graduate Studies and Research, College of Education and Professional Studies, Department of Curriculum, Supervision, and Educational Leadership, Ellensburg, WA 98926. Offers higher education (M Ed); master teacher (M Ed). *Program availability:* Part-time. *Degree requirements:* For master's, comprehensive exam (for some programs), thesis or alternative. *Entrance requirements:* For master's, 1 year of contracted teaching experience. Additional exam requirements/recommendations for international students: Required—TOEFL (minimum score 550 paper-based; 79 iBT), IELTS (minimum score 6.5). *Application deadline:* For fall admission, 2/1 for domestic students; for winter admission, 10/1 for domestic students; for spring admission, 1/1 for domestic students. Applications are processed on a rolling basis. Application fee: $50. Electronic applications accepted. *Financial support:* Application deadline: 3/1; applicants required to submit FAFSA. *Unit head:* Traci Pantano, Chair, 509-963-2661, E-mail: traci.seely@cwu.edu. *Application contact:* Justine Eason, Admissions Program Coordinator, 509-963-3103, Fax: 509-963-1799, E-mail: masters@cwu.edu.
Website: http://www.cwu.edu/~edfoundations/

Chicago State University, School of Graduate and Professional Studies, College of Education, Department of Educational Leadership, Curriculum and Foundations, Program in Educational Leadership, Chicago, IL 60628. Offers educational leadership (Ed D); higher education administration (MA); principal preparation (MA). *Accreditation:* NCATE. *Degree requirements:* For master's, comprehensive exam, thesis optional. *Entrance requirements:* For master's, minimum GPA of 2.75. *Application deadline:* For fall admission, 7/1 for domestic students; for spring admission, 11/10 for domestic students. Application fee: $25. *Unit head:* Dr. Athanase Gahungu, Program Facilitator, 773-995-2086, E-mail: agahungu@csu.edu. *Application contact:* Anika Miller, Graduate Studies Office, 773-995-2404, E-mail: g-studies1@csu.edu.

Claremont Graduate University, Graduate Programs, School of Educational Studies, Claremont, CA 91711-6160. Offers Africana education (Certificate); education and policy (MA, PhD); higher education/student affairs (MA, PhD); human development (MA, PhD); public school administration (MA, PhD); quantitative evaluation (MA, PhD); special education (MA, PhD); teacher education (MA); teaching and learning (MA, PhD); urban leadership (PhD); MBA/PhD. PhD program offered jointly with San Diego State University. *Program availability:* Part-time. Terminal master's awarded for partial completion of doctoral program. *Entrance requirements:* For master's and doctorate, GRE General Test. Additional exam requirements/recommendations for international students: Required—TOEFL (minimum score 75 iBT). Electronic applications accepted. *Faculty research:* Education administration, K-12 and higher education, multicultural education, education policy, diversity in higher education, faculty issues.

Clemson University, Graduate School, College of Education, Department of Educational and Organizational Leadership Development, Clemson, SC 29634. Offers administration and supervision (M Ed, Ed S); athletic leadership (MS, Certificate); education systems improvement science (Ed D); educational leadership (PhD), including higher education, P-12; human resource development (MHRD), including human resource development; leadership (Certificate); student affairs (M Ed). *Program availability:* Part-time, evening/weekend, 100% online. *Faculty:* 21 full-time (14 women), 1 part-time/adjunct (0 women). *Students:* 55 full-time (32 women), 285 part-time (169 women); includes 89 minority (71 Black or African American, non-Hispanic/Latino; 1 American Indian or Alaska Native, non-Hispanic/Latino; 1 Asian, non-Hispanic/Latino; 13 Hispanic/Latino; 3 Two or more races, non-Hispanic/Latino), 2 international. Average age 35. 216 applicants, 69% accepted, 100 enrolled. In 2017, 58 master's, 16 doctorates, 20 other advanced degrees awarded. *Degree requirements:* For master's, thesis (for some programs); for doctorate, comprehensive exam, thesis/dissertation. *Entrance requirements:* For master's, doctorate, and other advanced degree, GRE General Test, unofficial transcripts, letters of recommendation. Additional exam requirements/recommendations for international students: Required—TOEFL (minimum score 80 iBT), IELTS (minimum score 7), PTE (minimum score 54). *Application deadline:* For fall admission, 3/1 priority date for domestic and international students; for spring admission, 10/1 priority date for domestic and international students. Applications are processed on a rolling basis. Application fee: $80 ($90 for international students). Electronic applications accepted. *Expenses:* $5,174 per semester full-time resident, $9,714 per semester full-time non-resident, $511 per credit hour part-time resident, $1,017 per credit hour part-time non-resident; $741 per credit hour online; other fees may apply per session. *Financial support:* In 2017–18, 20 students received support, including 4 fellowships with partial tuition reimbursements available (averaging $8,750 per year), 1 research assistantship with partial tuition reimbursement available (averaging $9,378 per year); career-related internships or fieldwork and unspecified assistantships also available. Financial award application deadline: 3/1. *Total annual research expenditures:* $31,201. *Unit head:* Dr. Roy Jones, Interim Department Chair, 864-656-7915, E-mail: royj@clemson.edu. *Application contact:* Alison Search, Student Services Program Coordinator, 864-250-8880, E-mail: alisonp@clemson.edu.
Website: http://www.clemson.edu/education/departments/educational-organizational-leadership-development/index.html

Cleveland State University, College of Graduate Studies, College of Education and Human Services, Program in Urban Education, Specialization in Adult, Continuing, and Higher Education, Cleveland, OH 44115. Offers PhD. *Program availability:* Part-time. *Faculty:* 4 full-time (3 women). *Students:* 6 full-time (4 women), 7 part-time (6 women); includes 3 minority (all Black or African American, non-Hispanic/Latino). Average age 41. In 2017, 2 doctorates awarded. *Entrance requirements:* For doctorate, GRE General Test (minimum score of 297 for combined Verbal and Quantitative exams, 4.0 preferred for Analytical Writing), minimum graduate GPA of 3.25, curriculum vitae or resume, personal statement, 2 letters of recommendation. Additional exam requirements/recommendations for international students: Required—TOEFL (minimum score 550 paper-based; 78 iBT), IELTS (minimum score 6). Application fee: $40. Electronic applications accepted. *Financial support:* In 2017–18, 2 students received support. Research assistantships, teaching assistantships, and tuition waivers (full) available. Support available to part-time students. Financial award application deadline: 4/1; financial award applicants required to submit FAFSA. *Faculty research:* Adult education research, practice in diverse contexts. *Unit head:* Dr. Graham Stead, Director, Doctoral Studies, 216-875-9869, E-mail: g.b.stead@csuohio.edu. *Application contact:* Rita M. Grabowski, Administrative Coordinator, 216-687-4697, Fax: 216-875-9697, E-mail: r.grabowski@csuohio.edu.
Website: http://www.csuohio.edu/cehs/departments/DOC/III_doc.html

College of Saint Elizabeth, Department of Educational Leadership, Morristown, NJ 07960-6989. Offers educational leadership (MA, Ed D), including higher education (Ed D), Pre-K to 12th grade (Ed D); supervisor (Certificate). *Program availability:* Part-time. *Faculty:* 3 full-time (0 women), 8 part-time/adjunct (3 women). *Students:* 4 full-time (3 women), 74 part-time (51 women); includes 34 minority (20 Black or African American, non-Hispanic/Latino; 2 Asian, non-Hispanic/Latino; 11 Hispanic/Latino; 1 Two or more races, non-Hispanic/Latino). Average age 44. 33 applicants, 97% accepted, 28 enrolled. In 2017, 15 master's, 6 doctorates awarded. *Degree requirements:* For master's, thesis or alternative; for doctorate, thesis/dissertation. *Entrance requirements:* For master's, baccalaureate degree with minimum GPA of 2.75, standard teaching certificate, three years of exemplary certified teaching experience, writing sample, two letters of

recommendation from school(s) of employment, personal interview (for educational leadership); for doctorate, MA in educational leadership or related field; leadership experience including certification as principal and/or supervisor; letter of recommendation from college/university professor attesting to candidate's ability to perform a high level of academic work in the program; for Certificate, MA in education; certification; baccalaureate degree with minimum GPA of 2.75; personal written statement; two letters of recommendation; official transcripts from all colleges attended. Additional exam requirements/recommendations for international students: Required—TOEFL (minimum score 550 paper-based; 79 iBT), IELTS (minimum score 6.5). *Application deadline:* For fall admission, 5/1 for international students. Applications are processed on a rolling basis. Application fee: $35. Electronic applications accepted. Application fee is waived when completed online. *Expenses:* Contact institution. *Financial support:* Career-related internships or fieldwork, scholarships/grants, and unspecified assistantships available. Financial award applicants required to submit FAFSA. *Unit head:* Dr. Joseph Ciccone, Program Chair, 973-290-4383, Fax: 973-290-4389, E-mail: jciccone@cse.edu. *Application contact:* Lori J. Fragoso, Director of Graduate and Continuing Studies Admissions, 973-290-4413, Fax: 973-290-4710, E-mail: apply@cse.edu.
Website: http://www.cse.edu/academics/prof-studies/education/

The College of Saint Rose, Graduate Studies, Thelma P. Lally School of Education, Programs in Higher Education Leadership and Administration, Albany, NY 12203-1419. Offers MS Ed, Advanced Certificate. *Program availability:* Part-time, evening/weekend. *Students:* 2 full-time (1 woman), 10 part-time (3 women); includes 1 minority (Hispanic/Latino), 1 international. Average age 29. 8 applicants, 63% accepted, 3 enrolled. In 2017, 9 master's, 2 Advanced Certificates awarded. *Degree requirements:* For master's, capstone seminar. *Entrance requirements:* For master's, resume, letter of recommendation. Additional exam requirements/recommendations for international students: Required—TOEFL (minimum score 550 paper-based; 80 iBT), IELTS (minimum score 6), PTE (minimum score 56). *Application deadline:* For fall admission, 4/1 priority date for domestic and international students; for spring admission, 10/15 priority date for domestic and international students; for summer admission, 3/15 priority date for domestic and international students. Applications are processed on a rolling basis. Application fee: $40. Electronic applications accepted. *Expenses: Tuition:* Full-time $7191; part-time $799 per credit hour. *Required fees:* $924; $462 per credit hour. Tuition and fees vary according to course load. *Financial support:* Scholarships/grants, tuition waivers (partial), and unspecified assistantships available. Support available to part-time students. Financial award application deadline: 4/15. *Unit head:* Dr. Margaret McLane, Interim Provost and Vice President for Academic Affairs, 518-454-5160, E-mail: mclanem@strose.edu. *Application contact:* Cris Murray, Assistant Vice President for Graduate Recruitment and Enrollment, 518-454-5136, Fax: 518-458-5479, E-mail: grad@strose.edu.
Website: https://www.strose.edu/higher-education-leadership-and-administration/

Colorado State University, College of Health and Human Sciences, School of Education, Fort Collins, CO 80523-1588. Offers adult education and training (M Ed); counseling and career development (MA); education and human resources (M Ed); education, equity, and transformation (PhD); higher education leadership (PhD); organizational learning, performance, and change (M Ed, PhD); student affairs in higher education (MS). *Accreditation:* ACA; TEAC. *Program availability:* Part-time, online only, 100% online, blended/hybrid learning. *Faculty:* 33 full-time (23 women), 19 part-time/adjunct (11 women). *Students:* 74 full-time (53 women), 548 part-time (357 women); includes 151 minority (37 Black or African American, non-Hispanic/Latino; 4 American Indian or Alaska Native, non-Hispanic/Latino; 14 Asian, non-Hispanic/Latino; 71 Hispanic/Latino; 25 Two or more races, non-Hispanic/Latino), 16 international. Average age 37. 456 applicants, 31% accepted, 123 enrolled. In 2017, 177 master's, 22 doctorates awarded. *Degree requirements:* For master's, thesis optional, professional portfolio or capstone project; for doctorate, comprehensive exam, thesis/dissertation. *Entrance requirements:* For master's, bachelor's degree; minimum GPA of 3.0 in last degree earned; for doctorate, GRE; GRE or GMAT (for organizational learning, performance and change only), master's degree; minimum GPA of 3.0 in last degree earned. Additional exam requirements/recommendations for international students: Required—TOEFL (minimum score 550 paper-based; 80 iBT), IELTS (minimum score 6.5), PTE (minimum score 58). *Application deadline:* Applications are processed on a rolling basis. Application fee: $60 ($70 for international students). Electronic applications accepted. *Expenses:* Contact institution. *Financial support:* In 2017–18, 4 students received support, including 8 research assistantships with full and partial tuition reimbursements available (averaging $12,758 per year), 4 teaching assistantships with full and partial tuition reimbursements available (averaging $14,256 per year); fellowships with full and partial tuition reimbursements available, Federal Work-Study, scholarships/grants, tuition waivers (full and partial), and unspecified assistantships also available. Financial award applicants required to submit FAFSA. *Faculty research:* Diversity, equity, and inclusion; STEM education; higher education; occupational learning, performance, and change; teacher education. *Total annual research expenditures:* $312,562. *Unit head:* Dr. Louise Jennings, Co-Director, 970-491-6317, Fax: 970-491-1317, E-mail: louise.jennings@colostate.edu. *Application contact:* Kelli Clark, Graduate Programs Coordinator, 970-491-2093, Fax: 970-491-1317, E-mail: kelli.clark@colostate.edu.
Website: http://www.soe.chhs.colostate.edu/

Columbia College, Graduate Programs, Education Division, Columbia, SC 29203-5998. Offers divergent learning (M Ed); higher education administration (M Ed). *Accreditation:* NCATE. *Program availability:* Part-time, evening/weekend, online learning. *Degree requirements:* For master's, thesis. *Entrance requirements:* For master's, GRE General Test, MAT, 2 recommendations, current South Carolina teaching certificate, minimum GPA of 3.2. *Application deadline:* For fall admission, 8/22 for domestic students. Application fee: $50. Electronic applications accepted. *Expenses:* Contact institution. *Financial support:* Available to part-time students. Application deadline: 7/1; applicants required to submit FAFSA. *Application contact:* Myles Hacking, Associate Dean of Admissions, 803-786-3871, Fax: 803-786-3674, E-mail: mhacking@columbiasc.edu.

Columbus State University, Graduate Studies, College of Education and Health Professions, Department of Counseling, Foundations, and Leadership, Columbus, GA 31907-5645. Offers clinical mental health counseling (MS); curriculum and leadership (Ed D), including curriculum, educational leadership, higher education (M Ed, Ed D); educational leadership (M Ed, Ed S), including higher education (M Ed, Ed D); school counseling (M Ed, Ed S). *Accreditation:* ACA; NCATE. *Program availability:* Part-time, evening/weekend, 100% online, blended/hybrid learning. *Faculty:* 18 full-time (8 women), 20 part-time/adjunct (10 women). *Students:* 248 full-time (166 women), 308 part-time (236 women); includes 315 minority (278 Black or African American, non-Hispanic/Latino; 11 Asian, non-Hispanic/Latino; 15 Hispanic/Latino; 1 Native Hawaiian or other Pacific Islander, non-Hispanic/Latino; 10 Two or more races, non-Hispanic/Latino), 2 international. Average age 39. 155 applicants, 38% accepted, 40 enrolled. In 2017, 41 master's, 18 doctorates, 110 other advanced degrees awarded. *Degree requirements:* For master's, thesis, exit exam; for doctorate, comprehensive exam, thesis/dissertation; for Ed S, thesis or alternative. *Entrance requirements:* For master's, GRE General Test, minimum undergraduate GPA of 2.75; for doctorate, GRE General Test, minimum graduate GPA of 3.5, four years of professional service; for Ed S, GRE

General Test, minimum undergraduate GPA of 2.75, graduate 3.0. Additional exam requirements/recommendations for international students: Required—TOEFL (minimum score 550 paper-based; 79 iBT). *Application deadline:* For fall admission, 6/30 for domestic and international students; for spring admission, 11/1 for domestic and international students; for summer admission, 3/1 for domestic and international students. Applications are processed on a rolling basis. Application fee: $50. Electronic applications accepted. *Expenses:* Tuition, state resident: full-time $3708; part-time $2472 per year. Tuition, nonresident: full-time $14,418; part-time $9612 per year. *International tuition:* $19,218 full-time. *Required fees:* $1605. Tuition and fees vary according to program. *Financial support:* In 2017–18, 34 students received support, including 14 research assistantships with partial tuition reimbursements available (averaging $3,000 per year); career-related internships or fieldwork, Federal Work-Study, institutionally sponsored loans, scholarships/grants, tuition waivers (partial), and unspecified assistantships also available. Support available to part-time students. Financial award application deadline: 5/1; financial award applicants required to submit FAFSA. *Unit head:* Dr. Tom Hackett, Department Chair, 706-507-8968, Fax: 706-569-3134, E-mail: hackett_paul@columbusstate.edu. *Application contact:* Catrina Smith-Edmond, Assistant Director for Graduate and Global Admission, 706-507-8824, Fax: 706-568-5091, E-mail: smithedmond_catrina@columbusstate.edu.
Website: http://cfl.columbusstate.edu/

Dallas Baptist University, Gary Cook School of Leadership, Program in Educational Leadership, Dallas, TX 75211-9299. Offers higher education leadership (Ed D), including educational ministry leadership, general leadership, higher education leadership. *Program availability:* Part-time. *Degree requirements:* For doctorate, thesis/dissertation. *Application deadline:* Applications are processed on a rolling basis. Application fee: $25. Electronic applications accepted. Application fee is waived when completed online. *Expenses: Tuition:* Full-time $16,308; part-time $906 per credit hour. *Required fees:* $900; $450 per semester. Tuition and fees vary according to course load and degree level. *Unit head:* Dr. Jack Goodyear, Dean, 214-333-5595, E-mail: jackg@dbu.edu. *Application contact:* Dr. Ozzie Ingram, Program Director, 214-333-6875, E-mail: ozzie@dbu.edu.
Website: http://www4.dbu.edu/leadership/education-leadership-ed-d

Dallas Baptist University, Gary Cook School of Leadership, Program in Higher Education, Dallas, TX 75211-9299. Offers leadership studies (M Ed); student affairs leadership (M Ed), including community college leadership, distance learning, interdisciplinary studies, student affairs leadership. *Program availability:* Part-time, evening/weekend. *Application deadline:* Applications are processed on a rolling basis. Application fee: $25. Electronic applications accepted. Application fee is waived when completed online. *Expenses: Tuition:* Full-time $16,308; part-time $906 per credit hour. *Required fees:* $900; $450 per semester. Tuition and fees vary according to course load and degree level. *Unit head:* Dr. Jack Goodyear, Dean, 214-333-5595, Fax: 214-333-6809, E-mail: jackg@dbu.edu. *Application contact:* Dr. Sena Baker, Program Director, 214-333-6850, E-mail: sena@dbu.edu.
Website: http://www4.dbu.edu/leadership/hied/

Dallas Baptist University, Professional Development Program, Dallas, TX 75211-9299. Offers accounting (MA); church leadership (MA); communication (MA); counseling (MA); criminal justice (MA); English as a second language (MA); finance (MA); higher education (MA); leadership studies (MA); management (MA). *Program availability:* Part-time, evening/weekend. *Application deadline:* Applications are processed on a rolling basis. Application fee: $25. Electronic applications accepted. Application fee is waived when completed online. *Expenses: Tuition:* Full-time $16,308; part-time $906 per credit hour. *Required fees:* $900; $450 per semester. Tuition and fees vary according to course load and degree level. *Unit head:* Jared Ingram, Program Director, 214-333-5584, E-mail: jaredi@dbu.edu. *Application contact:* Bobby Soto, Director of Admissions, 214-333-5242, E-mail: bobby@dbu.edu.
Website: http://www3.dbu.edu/graduate/mapd.asp

Delta State University, Graduate Programs, College of Education, Division of Teacher Education, Leadership, and Research, Program in Professional Studies, Cleveland, MS 38733-0001. Offers counselor education (Ed D); elementary education (Ed D); higher education (Ed D). *Program availability:* Part-time, evening/weekend. *Degree requirements:* For doctorate, thesis/dissertation. *Entrance requirements:* For doctorate, GRE General Test.

DePaul University, College of Education, Chicago, IL 60614. Offers bilingual-bicultural education (M Ed, MA); counseling (M Ed, MA), including clinical mental health counseling, college student development, school counseling; curriculum studies (M Ed, MA, Ed D); early childhood education (M Ed, MA, Ed D); educational leadership (M Ed, MA, Ed D), including Catholic leadership (M Ed, MA), general (M Ed, MA), higher education (M Ed, MA), physical education (M Ed, MA), principal preparation (M Ed); teacher preparation (M Ed); elementary education (M Ed, MA); middle grades education (M Ed); middle school mathematics education (MS); reading specialist (M Ed, MA); secondary education (M Ed, MA); social and cultural foundations in education (M Ed, MA); special education (M Ed); sport, fitness and recreation leadership (MS); value-creating education for global citizenship (M Ed); world languages education (M Ed, MA). *Program availability:* Part-time, evening/weekend, online learning. *Degree requirements:* For doctorate, thesis/dissertation. *Application deadline:* Applications are processed on a rolling basis. Application fee: $40. Electronic applications accepted. *Financial support:* Application deadline: 12/31; applicants required to submit FAFSA. *Unit head:* Dr. Paul Zionts, Dean, 773-325-7581, Fax: 773-325-7713, E-mail: pzionts@depaul.edu. *Application contact:* Dr. Paul Zionts, Dean, 773-325-7581, Fax: 773-325-7713, E-mail: pzionts@depaul.edu.
Website: http://education.depaul.edu

DeVry University–Folsom Campus, Graduate Programs, Folsom, CA 95630. Offers accounting (M Acc); accounting and financial management (MAFM); business administration (MBA); curriculum leadership (M Ed); educational leadership (M Ed); educational technology (M Ed); higher education leadership (M Ed); human resource management (MHRM); information systems management (MISM); network and communications management (MNCM); project management (MPM); public administration (MPA).

Drexel University, Goodwin College of Professional Studies, School of Education, Philadelphia, PA 19104-2875. Offers applied behavior analysis (MS); creativity and innovation (MS); education improvement and transformation (MS); educational administration (MS); educational leadership and management (Ed D); educational leadership development and learning technologies (PhD); global and international education (MS); higher education (MS); human resources development (MS); learning technologies (MS); mathematics, learning and teaching (MS); special education (MS); teaching, learning and curriculum (MS). *Program availability:* Part-time, evening/weekend, online learning. *Degree requirements:* For doctorate, thesis/dissertation. *Entrance requirements:* For doctorate, GRE or GMAT. Additional exam requirements/recommendations for international students: Required—TOEFL, IELTS. Electronic applications accepted. Application fee is waived when completed online. *Expenses:* Contact institution. *Faculty research:* Leadership development, mathematics education, literacy, autism, educational technology.

See Display on page 654 and Close-Up on page 719.

East Carolina University, Graduate School, College of Education, Department of Interdisciplinary Professions, Greenville, NC 27858-4353. Offers adult education (MA Ed); business and marketing education (MA Ed); community college instruction (Certificate); counselor education (MS); education in the healthcare professions (Certificate); library science (MLS); student affairs in higher education (Certificate); vocational education (MS). *Accreditation:* ACA; NCATE. *Program availability:* Part-time, evening/weekend. *Students:* 97 full-time (77 women), 392 part-time (344 women); includes 107 minority (73 Black or African American, non-Hispanic/Latino; 6 American Indian or Alaska Native, non-Hispanic/Latino; 5 Asian, non-Hispanic/Latino; 11 Hispanic/Latino; 12 Two or more races, non-Hispanic/Latino). Average age 36. 148 applicants, 97% accepted, 116 enrolled. In 2017, 148 master's, 23 other advanced degrees awarded. *Degree requirements:* For master's, comprehensive exam, thesis optional. *Entrance requirements:* For master's, GRE General Test or MAT, interview, minimum GPA of 2.5, bachelor's degree in related field, teaching license (MA Ed). Additional exam requirements/recommendations for international students: Required—TOEFL. *Application deadline:* For fall admission, 5/15 priority date for domestic students. Applications are processed on a rolling basis. Application fee: $75. *Expenses:* Tuition, state resident: full-time $4749; part-time $297 per credit hour. Tuition, nonresident: full-time $17,898; part-time $1119 per credit hour. *Required fees:* $2691; $224 per credit hour. Part-time tuition and fees vary according to course load and program. *Financial support:* Research assistantships with partial tuition reimbursements, teaching assistantships with partial tuition reimbursements, and Federal Work-Study available. Support available to part-time students. Financial award application deadline: 6/1. *Unit head:* Dr. Vivian W. Mott, Chair, 252-328-6177, Fax: 252-328-4368, E-mail: mottv@ecu.edu.
Website: http://www.ecu.edu/cs-educ/idp/index.cfm

Eastern Kentucky University, The Graduate School, College of Education, Department of Curriculum and Instruction, Program in Secondary and Higher Education, Richmond, KY 40475-3102. Offers secondary education (MA Ed), including agricultural education, art education, biological sciences education, business education, English education, geography education, history education, home economics education, industrial education, mathematical sciences education, physical education, school health education. *Accreditation:* NCATE. *Program availability:* Part-time. *Entrance requirements:* For master's, GRE General Test, minimum GPA of 2.5.

Eastern Michigan University, Graduate School, College of Education, Department of Leadership and Counseling, Programs in Educational Leadership, Ypsilanti, MI 48197. Offers community college leadership (Graduate Certificate); educational leadership (MA, Ed D, SPA); higher education/general administration (MA); higher education/student affairs (MA); K-12 administration (MA); K-12 basic administration (Post Master's Certificate). *Program availability:* Part-time, evening/weekend, online learning. *Students:* 50 full-time (34 women), 286 part-time (186 women); includes 108 minority (85 Black or African American, non-Hispanic/Latino; 3 American Indian or Alaska Native, non-Hispanic/Latino; 1 Asian, non-Hispanic/Latino; 12 Hispanic/Latino; 7 Two or more races, non-Hispanic/Latino), 2 international. Average age 40. 200 applicants, 72% accepted, 76 enrolled. In 2017, 88 master's, 22 doctorates, 28 other advanced degrees awarded. *Degree requirements:* For master's, portfolio. *Entrance requirements:* For doctorate, GRE. Additional exam requirements/recommendations for international students: Required—TOEFL. *Application deadline:* For winter admission, 2/1 for domestic and international students. Applications are processed on a rolling basis. Application fee: $45. *Financial support:* Fellowships, research assistantships with full tuition reimbursements, teaching assistantships with full tuition reimbursements, career-related internships or fieldwork, Federal Work-Study, institutionally sponsored loans, scholarships/grants, tuition waivers (partial), and unspecified assistantships available. Support available to part-time students. *Application contact:* Dr. Jaclynn Tracy, Coordinator of Advising, Programs in Educational Leadership, 734-487-0255, Fax: 734-487-4608, E-mail: jtracy@emich.edu.

Fitchburg State University, Division of Graduate and Continuing Education, Program in Educational Leadership and Management, Fitchburg, MA 01420-2697. Offers education technology (Certificate); educational leadership and management (M Ed, CAGS); higher education administration (CAGS); school principal (M Ed, CAGS); supervisor/director (M Ed, CAGS). *Accreditation:* NCATE. *Program availability:* Part-time, evening/weekend. *Students:* 15 full-time (12 women), 23 part-time (17 women). Average age 39. 9 applicants, 100% accepted, 8 enrolled. In 2017, 4 master's, 6 CAGSs awarded. *Entrance requirements:* Additional exam requirements/recommendations for international students: Required—TOEFL (minimum score 550 paper-based; 79 iBT). *Application deadline:* For fall admission, 7/15 for international students; for spring admission, 12/1 for international students. Applications are processed on a rolling basis. Application fee: $50. Electronic applications accepted. *Expenses:* Contact institution. *Financial support:* In 2017–18, research assistantships with partial tuition reimbursements (averaging $5,500 per year) were awarded; Federal Work-Study, scholarships/grants, and unspecified assistantships also available. Support available to part-time students. Financial award application deadline: 3/1; financial award applicants required to submit FAFSA. *Unit head:* Dr. Janna Heiligenstein, Chair, 978-665-3477, Fax: 978-665-3658, E-mail: gce@fitchburgstate.edu. *Application contact:* Jinawa McNeil, Director of Admissions, 978-665-3140, Fax: 978-665-4540, E-mail: admissions@fitchburgstate.edu.
Website: http://www.fitchburgstate.edu

Florida Atlantic University, College of Education, Department of Educational Leadership and Research Methodology, Boca Raton, FL 33431-0991. Offers adult and community education (M Ed, PhD, Ed S); educational leadership (M Ed, PhD, Ed S); higher education (M Ed, PhD); K-12 school leadership (M Ed, PhD, Ed S). *Accreditation:* NCATE. *Program availability:* Part-time, evening/weekend, online learning. *Faculty:* 22 full-time (12 women), 13 part-time/adjunct (8 women). *Students:* 98 full-time (55 women), 240 part-time (162 women); includes 165 minority (94 Black or African American, non-Hispanic/Latino; 4 Asian, non-Hispanic/Latino; 60 Hispanic/Latino; 7 Two or more races, non-Hispanic/Latino), 6 international. Average age 36. 205 applicants, 61% accepted, 105 enrolled. In 2017, 67 master's, 15 doctorates, 8 other advanced degrees awarded. *Degree requirements:* For doctorate, comprehensive exam, thesis/dissertation, departmental qualifying exam; for Ed S, departmental qualifying exam. *Entrance requirements:* For master's, GRE General Test, minimum GPA of 3.0 during previous 2 years; for doctorate, GRE General Test, minimum GPA of 3.5; for Ed S, GRE General Test. Additional exam requirements/recommendations for international students: Required—TOEFL (minimum score 500 paper-based; 61 iBT), IELTS (minimum score 6). *Application deadline:* For fall admission, 7/1 for domestic students, 2/15 for international students; for spring admission, 9/15 for domestic students, 7/15 for international students. Applications are processed on a rolling basis. Application fee: $30. Electronic applications accepted. *Expenses:* Tuition, state resident: full-time $7400; part-time $369.82 per credit. Tuition, nonresident: full-time $20,496; part-time $1042.81 per credit. *Financial support:* Fellowships, research assistantships, teaching assistantships, career-related internships or fieldwork, and tuition waivers (partial) available. *Faculty research:* Self-directed learning, school reform issues, legal issues, mentoring, school leadership. *Unit head:* Dr. Robert E. Shockley, Chair, 561-297-3550, Fax: 561-297-3618, E-mail: shockley@fau.edu. *Application contact:* Kathy DuBois,

Senior Secretary, 561-297-3550, Fax: 561-297-3618, E-mail: edleadership@fau.edu.
Website: http://www.coe.fau.edu/academicdepartments/el/

Florida International University, College of Arts, Sciences, and Education, Department of Leadership and Professional Studies, Miami, FL 33199. Offers adult education and human resource development (MS, Ed D); counseling (MS), including rehabilitation counseling, school counseling; counselor education (MS), including clinical mental health counseling; educational administration and supervision (Ed D); educational leadership (MS, Certificate, Ed S); higher education (Ed D); higher education administration (MS); international and comparative education (MS); recreation and sport management (MS), including recreation and sport management, recreational therapy; school psychology (Ed S); urban education (MS), including instruction in urban settings, learning technologies, multicultural/bilingual, multicultural/TESOL, urban education. *Program availability:* Part-time, evening/weekend. *Faculty:* 60 full-time (41 women), 112 part-time/adjunct (77 women). *Students:* 221 full-time (162 women), 301 part-time (239 women); includes 418 minority (127 Black or African American, non-Hispanic/Latino; 9 Asian, non-Hispanic/Latino; 271 Hispanic/Latino; 11 Two or more races, non-Hispanic/Latino), 10 international. Average age 31. 330 applicants, 55% accepted, 100 enrolled. In 2017, 181 master's, 6 doctorates awarded. *Degree requirements:* For doctorate, thesis/dissertation. *Entrance requirements:* For master's, minimum GPA of 3.0; for doctorate and other advanced degree, GRE General Test. Additional exam requirements/recommendations for international students: Required—TOEFL (minimum score 550 paper-based; 80 iBT), IELTS (minimum score 6.3). *Application deadline:* For fall admission, 6/1 priority date for domestic students, 4/1 for international students; for winter admission, 10/1 priority date for domestic students, 9/1 for international students; for spring admission, 3/1 priority date for domestic students, 2/1 for international students. Applications are processed on a rolling basis. Application fee: $30. Electronic applications accepted. *Expenses:* Tuition, state resident: full-time $8912; part-time $446 per credit hour. Tuition, nonresident: full-time $21,393; part-time $992 per credit hour. *Required fees:* $390; $195 per semester. *Financial support:* Fellowships, research assistantships with tuition reimbursements, teaching assistantships with tuition reimbursements, Federal Work-Study, and tuition waivers (full and partial) available. Support available to part-time students. Financial award applicants required to submit FAFSA. *Unit head:* Dr. Benjamin Baez, Chair, 305-348-3214, Fax: 305-348-1515, E-mail: benjamin.baez@fiu.edu. *Application contact:* Nanett Rojas, Assistant Director, Graduate Admissions, 305-348-7464, Fax: 305-348-7441, E-mail: gradadm@fiu.edu.
Website: http://education.fiu.edu

Florida State University, The Graduate School, College of Education, Department of Educational Leadership and Policy Studies, Tallahassee, FL 32306. Offers educational leadership and administration (Certificate); educational leadership and policy (MS, Ed D, PhD, Ed S), including education policy and evaluation (MS, Ed D, PhD), educational leadership and administration; foundations of education (MS, PhD), including history and philosophy of education, international and multicultural education; higher education (MS, PhD); institutional research (Certificate); program evaluation (Certificate). *Program availability:* Part-time, evening/weekend, 100% online, blended/hybrid learning, asynchronous, minimal on-campus study. *Faculty:* 19 full-time (15 women), 10 part-time/adjunct (7 women). *Students:* 151 full-time (105 women), 196 part-time (138 women); includes 127 minority (55 Black or African American, non-Hispanic/Latino; 4 Asian, non-Hispanic/Latino; 49 Hispanic/Latino; 19 Two or more races, non-Hispanic/Latino), 33 international. Average age 35. 229 applicants, 54% accepted, 66 enrolled. In 2017, 49 master's, 10 doctorates, 17 other advanced degrees awarded. *Degree requirements:* For master's, comprehensive exam, thesis optional; for doctorate, comprehensive exam, thesis/dissertation, diagnostic exam, preliminary exam, prospectus defense, dissertation defense. *Entrance requirements:* For master's, doctorate, and other advanced degree, GRE General Test, minimum GPA of 3.0. Additional exam requirements/recommendations for international students: Required—TOEFL (minimum score 550 paper-based, 80 iBT), IELTS (minimum score 6.5), Michigan English Language Assessment Battery (minimum score 77), or PTE (minimum score 55). Application fee: $30. Electronic applications accepted. *Financial support:* Fellowships, research assistantships, teaching assistantships, scholarships/grants, tuition waivers (full and partial), and unspecified assistantships available. Financial award application deadline: 1/15; financial award applicants required to submit FAFSA. *Faculty research:* Post-secondary success; leadership education; education policy; international education; multicultural education. *Unit head:* Dr. Robert A. Schwartz, Chair, 850-644-6885, Fax: 850-644-2725, E-mail: raschwartz@fsu.edu. *Application contact:* Linda Lyons, Academic Support Assistant, 850-644-7077, Fax: 850-644-1258, E-mail: ljlyons@fsu.edu.

Geneva College, Master of Arts in Higher Education Program, Beaver Falls, PA 15010-3599. Offers campus ministry (MA); college teaching (MA); educational leadership (MA); student affairs administration (MA). *Program availability:* Part-time, evening/weekend, blended/hybrid learning. *Faculty:* 1 full-time (0 women), 6 part-time/adjunct (1 woman). *Students:* 44 full-time (27 women), 10 part-time (6 women); includes 8 minority (5 Black or African American, non-Hispanic/Latino; 2 Hispanic/Latino; 1 Two or more races, non-Hispanic/Latino), 1 international. Average age 27. 40 applicants, 75% accepted, 21 enrolled. In 2017, 18 master's awarded. *Degree requirements:* For master's, 36 hours (27 in core courses) including a capstone research project. *Entrance requirements:* For master's, minimum GPA of 3.0, writing sample, 3 letters of recommendation, essay on motivation for participation in the program. Additional exam requirements/recommendations for international students: Required—TOEFL. *Application deadline:* Applications are processed on a rolling basis. Application fee: $0. Electronic applications accepted. *Expenses:* $655 per credit. *Financial support:* Unspecified assistantships available. Financial award application deadline: 8/1; financial award applicants required to submit FAFSA. *Faculty research:* Learning theories, church-related higher education, organizational culture, sexual assault and transgender students at Christian colleges, emerging technology in higher education. *Unit head:* Dr. Keith Martel, Program Director, 724-847-6884, Fax: 724-847-6107, E-mail: hed@geneva.edu. *Application contact:* Allison Davis, Assistant Director, 724-847-6510, Fax: 724-847-6696, E-mail: hed@geneva.edu.
Website: http://www.geneva.edu/page/higher_ed

George Mason University, College of Education and Human Development, Program in Education, Fairfax, VA 22030. Offers higher education (PhD). *Faculty:* 61 full-time (43 women), 1 part-time/adjunct (0 women). *Students:* 96 full-time (75 women), 239 part-time (180 women); includes 89 minority (42 Black or African American, non-Hispanic/Latino; 1 American Indian or Alaska Native, non-Hispanic/Latino; 18 Asian, non-Hispanic/Latino; 19 Hispanic/Latino; 9 Two or more races, non-Hispanic/Latino), 34 international. Average age 39. 114 applicants, 47% accepted, 34 enrolled. In 2017, 40 doctorates awarded. *Degree requirements:* For doctorate, thesis/dissertation, portfolio review. *Entrance requirements:* For doctorate, GRE (no more than 5 years old), resume; official transcripts from graduate and undergraduate institutions; 3 letters of recommendation; goal statement of 750-1000 words. Additional exam requirements/recommendations for international students: Required—TOEFL (minimum score 575 paper-based; 88 iBT), IELTS, PTE (minimum score 59). *Application deadline:* For fall admission, 1/15 for domestic and international students; for spring admission, 10/1 for domestic and international students. Application fee: $75 ($80 for international students). Electronic applications accepted. *Expenses:* Tuition, state resident: full-time $11,228; part-time $459.50 per credit. Tuition, nonresident: full-time $30,932; part-time $1280.50 per credit. *Required fees:* $3252; $135.50 per credit. Part-time tuition and fees vary according to course load and program. *Financial support:* In 2017–18, 86 students received support, including 5 fellowships (averaging $6,080 per year), 70 research assistantships with tuition reimbursements available (averaging $14,380 per year), 28 teaching assistantships with tuition reimbursements available (averaging $4,827 per year); career-related internships or fieldwork, Federal Work-Study, unspecified assistantships, and health care benefits (for full-time research or teaching assistantship recipients) also available. Support available to part-time students. Financial award application deadline: 3/1; financial award applicants required to submit FAFSA. *Unit head:* Anastasia Kitsantis, Director, 703-993-2688, E-mail: akitsant@gmu.edu. *Application contact:* Nicole Mariam, Graduate Admissions Coordinator, 703-993-3832, Fax: 703-993-2020, E-mail: nwhite5@gmu.edu.

George Mason University, College of Humanities and Social Sciences, Department of English, Fairfax, VA 22030. Offers college teaching (Certificate), including higher education pedagogy; creative writing (MFA), including fiction, nonfiction writing, poetry; English (MA), including cultural studies, linguistics, literature, professional writing and rhetoric, teaching of writing and literature; English pedagogy (Certificate); folklore studies (Certificate); linguistics (PhD); writing and rhetoric (PhD). *Program availability:* Part-time. *Faculty:* 78 full-time (40 women), 45 part-time/adjunct (30 women). *Students:* 120 full-time (84 women), 116 part-time (94 women); includes 43 minority (13 Black or African American, non-Hispanic/Latino; 8 Asian, non-Hispanic/Latino; 14 Hispanic/Latino; 1 Native Hawaiian or other Pacific Islander, non-Hispanic/Latino; 7 Two or more races, non-Hispanic/Latino), 19 international. Average age 32. 224 applicants, 61% accepted, 68 enrolled. In 2017, 60 master's, 1 doctorate, 17 other advanced degrees awarded. *Degree requirements:* For master's, thesis (for some programs), proficiency in a foreign language by course work or translation test; for doctorate, comprehensive exam, thesis/dissertation, 2 papers. *Entrance requirements:* For master's, official transcripts; expanded goals statement; writing sample; portfolio; 2 letters of recommendation; resume; for doctorate, GRE (for linguistics), expanded goals statement; 2 letters of recommendation (writing and rhetoric); 3 letters of recommendation (linguistics); writing sample; introductory course in linguistics; official transcripts; master's degree in relevant field; for Certificate, official transcripts; expanded goals statement; 2 letters of recommendation; writing sample; resume. Additional exam requirements/recommendations for international students: Required—TOEFL (minimum score 575 paper-based; 88 iBT), IELTS (minimum score 6.5), PTE (minimum score 59). *Application deadline:* For fall admission, 3/15 for domestic and international students; for spring admission, 10/15 for domestic and international students. Application fee: $75 ($80 for international students). Electronic applications accepted. *Expenses:* Tuition, state resident: full-time $11,228; part-time $459.50 per credit. Tuition, nonresident: full-time $30,932; part-time $1280.50 per credit. *Required fees:* $3252; $135.50 per credit. Part-time tuition and fees vary according to course load and program. *Financial support:* In 2017–18, 84 students received support, including 9 research assistantships with tuition reimbursements available (averaging $17,199 per year), 76 teaching assistantships with tuition reimbursements available (averaging $11,917 per year); career-related internships or fieldwork, Federal Work-Study, scholarships/grants, unspecified assistantships, and health care benefits (for full-time research or teaching assistantship recipients) also available. Support available to part-time students. Financial award application deadline: 3/1; financial award applicants required to submit FAFSA. *Faculty research:* Literature, professional writing and editing, writing of fiction or poetry. *Total annual research expenditures:* $68,592. *Unit head:* Debra Lattanzi-Shutika, Chair, 703-993-1170, Fax: 703-993-1161, E-mail: dshutika@gmu.edu. *Application contact:* Alex Walsh, Graduate Admissions Coordinator, 703-993-1185, Fax: 703-993-1161, E-mail: awalsh7@gmu.edu.
Website: http://english.gmu.edu

George Mason University, College of Humanities and Social Sciences, Higher Education Program, Fairfax, VA 22030. Offers higher education administration (Certificate); higher education and student development (MA). *Faculty:* 4 full-time (all women), 1 part-time/adjunct (0 women). *Students:* 1 full-time (0 women), 13 part-time (7 women); includes 4 minority (2 Black or African American, non-Hispanic/Latino; 2 Asian, non-Hispanic/Latino; 1 Hispanic/Latino). Average age 43. 6 applicants, 50% accepted, 3 enrolled. In 2017, 3 other advanced degrees awarded. *Degree requirements:* For master's, thesis optional, practicum; for Certificate, practicum. *Entrance requirements:* For master's and Certificate, transcript, resume, writing sample, goals statement, 3 letters of recommendation. Additional exam requirements/recommendations for international students: Required—TOEFL (minimum score 575 paper-based; 88 iBT), IELTS (minimum score 6.5), PTE (minimum score 59). *Application deadline:* For fall admission, 3/1 for domestic and international students; for spring admission, 10/15 for domestic and international students. Application fee: $75 ($80 for international students). Electronic applications accepted. *Expenses:* Tuition, state resident: full-time $11,228; part-time $459.50 per credit. Tuition, nonresident: full-time $30,932; part-time $1280.50 per credit. *Required fees:* $3252; $135.50 per credit. Part-time tuition and fees vary according to course load and program. *Financial support:* Career-related internships or fieldwork, Federal Work-Study, and scholarships/grants available. Support available to part-time students. Financial award application deadline: 3/1; financial award applicants required to submit FAFSA. *Faculty research:* Multicultural issues, leadership, assessment, scholarship of teaching and learning, learning analytics. *Total annual research expenditures:* $24,019. *Unit head:* Jan Arminio, Director, 703-993-2064, Fax: 703-993-2307, E-mail: jarminio@gmu.edu. *Application contact:* Katie Richards, Administrative Coordinator, 703-993-2310, Fax: 703-993-2307, E-mail: kricha22@gmu.edu.
Website: http://highered.gmu.edu/

George Mason University, College of Humanities and Social Sciences, Interdisciplinary Studies Program, Fairfax, VA 22030. Offers computational social science (MAIS); energy and sustainability (MAIS); folklore studies (MAIS); higher education (MAIS); individualized studies (MAIS); religion, culture, and values (MAIS); social entrepreneurship (MAIS); social justice and human rights (MAIS); war and the military in society (MAIS); women and gender studies (MAIS). *Faculty:* 10 full-time (3 women), 15 part-time/adjunct (7 women). *Students:* 29 full-time (23 women), 76 part-time (50 women); includes 39 minority (18 Black or African American, non-Hispanic/Latino; 6 Asian, non-Hispanic/Latino; 11 Hispanic/Latino; 4 Two or more races, non-Hispanic/Latino), 7 international. Average age 32. 71 applicants, 90% accepted, 29 enrolled. In 2017, 23 master's awarded. *Degree requirements:* For master's, thesis or alternative, experiential learning (for some programs). *Entrance requirements:* Additional exam requirements/recommendations for international students: Required—TOEFL (minimum score 575 paper-based; 88 iBT), IELTS (minimum score 6.5), PTE (minimum score 59). *Application deadline:* For fall admission, 3/1 for domestic and international students; for spring admission, 10/15 for domestic and international students. Application fee: $75 ($80 for international students). Electronic applications accepted. *Expenses:* Tuition, state resident: full-time $11,228; part-time $459.50 per credit. Tuition, nonresident: full-time $30,932; part-time $1280.50 per credit. *Required fees:* $3252; $135.50 per credit. Part-time tuition and fees vary according to course load and program. *Financial support:* In 2017–18, 9 students received support, including 2

research assistantships with tuition reimbursements available, 7 teaching assistantships with tuition reimbursements available (averaging $8,599 per year); career-related internships or fieldwork, Federal Work-Study, scholarships/grants, unspecified assistantships, and health care benefits (for full-time research or teaching assistantship recipients) also available. Support available to part-time students. Financial award application deadline: 3/1; financial award applicants required to submit FAFSA. *Faculty research:* Combined English and folklore, religious and cultural studies (Christianity and Muslim society). *Unit head:* Meredith H. Lair, Director, 703-993-2159, Fax: 703-993-1251, E-mail: mlair@gmu.edu. *Application contact:* Morgan Fisher, Graduate Coordinator, 703-993-8762, E-mail: mfisherb@gmu.edu.
Website: http://mais.gmu.edu

The George Washington University, Graduate School of Education and Human Development, Department of Educational Leadership, Program in Higher Education Administration, Washington, DC 20052. Offers college teaching and academic leadership (MA Ed/HD, Ed S); general administration (MA Ed/HD, Ed S); higher education administration (Ed D); higher education finance (MA Ed/HD, Ed S); international education (MA Ed/HD, Ed S); policy (MA Ed/HD, Ed S); student affairs administration (MA Ed/HD, Ed S). *Accreditation:* NCATE. *Students:* 18 full-time (15 women), 65 part-time (44 women); includes 30 minority (8 Black or African American, non-Hispanic/Latino; 7 Asian, non-Hispanic/Latino; 5 Hispanic/Latino; 1 Two or more races, non-Hispanic/Latino), 2 international. Average age 32. 139 applicants, 76% accepted, 27 enrolled. In 2017, 34 master's, 9 doctorates, 1 other advanced degree awarded. *Degree requirements:* For master's and Ed S, comprehensive exam; for doctorate, comprehensive exam, thesis/dissertation. *Entrance requirements:* For master's, GRE General Test or MAT, minimum GPA of 2.75; for doctorate, GRE General Test or MAT, interview, minimum GPA of 3.3; for Ed S, GRE General Test or MAT, minimum GPA of 3.3. *Application deadline:* For fall admission, 1/15 priority date for domestic students; for spring admission, 10/1 for domestic students. Applications are processed on a rolling basis. Application fee: $75. *Expenses:* Tuition: Full-time $28,800; part-time $1655 per credit hour. *Required fees:* $45; $2.75 per credit hour. *Financial support:* In 2017–18, 17 students received support. Fellowships, research assistantships, career-related internships or fieldwork, Federal Work-Study, and tuition waivers (partial) available. Financial award application deadline: 1/15; financial award applicants required to submit FAFSA. *Faculty research:* Technology in higher education administration. *Unit head:* Michael Feuer, Dean, 202-994-6161, E-mail: mjfeuer@gwu.edu. *Application contact:* Sarah Lang, Director of Graduate Admissions, 202-994-1447, Fax: 202-994-7207, E-mail: slang@gwu.edu.

Georgia Southern University, Jack N. Averitt College of Graduate Studies, College of Education, Department of Leadership, Technology, and Human Development, Program in Higher Education, Statesboro, GA 30460. Offers educational leadership (Ed D); higher education administration (M Ed). *Accreditation:* NCATE. *Program availability:* Part-time, evening/weekend. *Students:* 1 part-time (0 women). Average age 38. In 2017, 7 master's awarded. *Degree requirements:* For master's, portfolio, practicum, transition point assessments; for doctorate, comprehensive exam, thesis/dissertation. *Entrance requirements:* For master's, minimum GPA of 2.5. Additional exam requirements/recommendations for international students: Required—TOEFL (minimum score 550 paper-based; 80 iBT), IELTS (minimum score 6). *Application deadline:* For fall admission, 4/1 priority date for domestic students, 3/1 for international students; for spring admission, 10/1 for domestic and international students. Applications are processed on a rolling basis. Application fee: $50. Electronic applications accepted. *Expenses:* Tuition, state resident: full-time $4986; part-time $3324 per year. Tuition, nonresident: full-time $21,982; part-time $15,352 per year. *Required fees:* $2092; $1802 per credit hour. $901 per semester. Tuition and fees vary according to course load, campus/location and program. *Financial support:* In 2017–18, 1 student received support. Research assistantships with partial tuition reimbursements available, teaching assistantships with partial tuition reimbursements available, career-related internships or fieldwork, Federal Work-Study, scholarships/grants, and unspecified assistantships available. Support available to part-time students. Financial award application deadline: 4/15; financial award applicants required to submit FAFSA. *Faculty research:* Global issues in higher education, leadership and identity development in higher education, student affairs. *Unit head:* Dr. Daniel Calhoun, Program Coordinator, 912-478-1428, Fax: 912-478-7140, E-mail: dwcalhoun@georgiasouthern.edu. *Application contact:* Dr. Lydia Cross, Coordinator for Graduate Academic Services Center, 912-478-8664, E-mail: lcross@georgiasouthern.edu.
Website: http://coe.georgiasouthern.edu/edld/

Georgia Southern University, Jack N. Averitt College of Graduate Studies, College of Education, Department of Leadership, Technology, and Human Development, Program in Higher Education Administration, Statesboro, GA 30458. Offers M Ed. *Program availability:* Part-time, evening/weekend. *Students:* 29 full-time (22 women), 150 part-time (123 women); includes 47 minority (35 Black or African American, non-Hispanic/Latino; 2 Asian, non-Hispanic/Latino; 5 Hispanic/Latino; 5 Two or more races, non-Hispanic/Latino), 2 international. Average age 40. In 2017, 56 master's awarded. *Entrance requirements:* For master's, GRE, minimum GPA of 2.5. Additional exam requirements/recommendations for international students: Required—TOEFL (minimum score 550 paper-based; 80 iBT), IELTS (minimum score 6). *Application deadline:* For fall admission, 4/1 for domestic students; for spring admission, 11/1 for domestic students. Application fee: $50. Electronic applications accepted. *Expenses:* Tuition, state resident: full-time $4986; part-time $3324 per year. Tuition, nonresident: full-time $21,982; part-time $15,352 per year. *Required fees:* $2092; $1802 per credit hour. $901 per semester. Tuition and fees vary according to course load, campus/location and program. *Financial support:* In 2017–18, 16 students received support, including 3 fellowships with full tuition reimbursements available (averaging $7,750 per year). Financial award application deadline: 4/20; financial award applicants required to submit FAFSA. *Faculty research:* Higher education administration, student affairs. *Unit head:* Dr. Daniel Calhoun, Program Director, 912-478-1428, Fax: 912-478-7104, E-mail: dwcalhoun@georgiasouthern.edu.

Grambling State University, School of Graduate Studies and Research, College of Education, Department of Educational Leadership, Grambling, LA 71245. Offers developmental education (MS, Ed D, PMC), including curriculum and instructional design (Ed D), English (MS), guidance and counseling (MS), higher education administration and management (Ed D), mathematics (MS), reading (MS), science (MS), student development and personnel services (Ed D); educational leadership (M Ed). *Program availability:* Part-time, evening/weekend. *Degree requirements:* For master's, comprehensive exam, thesis (for some programs); for doctorate, comprehensive exam, thesis/dissertation. *Entrance requirements:* For master's, GRE, minimum GPA of 2.5 on last degree; for doctorate, GRE (minimum score 1000, 500 on Verbal), master's degree, minimum GPA of 3.0 on last degree. Additional exam requirements/recommendations for international students: Required—TOEFL (minimum score 500 paper-based; 62 iBT). Electronic applications accepted.

Grand Valley State University, College of Education, Program in College Student Affairs Leadership, Allendale, MI 49401-9403. Offers M Ed. *Students:* 72 full-time (47 women), 4 part-time (3 women); includes 23 minority (11 Black or African American, non-Hispanic/Latino; 2 American Indian or Alaska Native, non-Hispanic/Latino; 1 Asian, non-Hispanic/Latino; 7 Hispanic/Latino; 2 Two or more races, non-Hispanic/Latino), 2 international. Average age 24. In 2017, 28 master's awarded. *Degree requirements:* For master's, project or thesis. *Entrance requirements:* For master's, GRE General Test or minimum GPA of 3.0, last 60 credits from regionally-accredited college/university, 3 letters of recommendation. Additional exam requirements/recommendations for international students: Required—TOEFL (minimum iBT score of 80), IELTS (6.5), or Michigan English Language Assessment Battery (77). *Application deadline:* Applications are processed on a rolling basis. Application fee: $30. Electronic applications accepted. *Expenses:* $652 per credit hour. *Financial support:* In 2017–18, 65 students received support, including 12 fellowships, 25 research assistantships with full and partial tuition reimbursements available (averaging $9,000 per year); unspecified assistantships also available. *Faculty research:* Adult learners, diversity and multiculturalism. *Unit head:* Dr. Jay Cooper, Department Director, 616-331-0336, Fax: 616-331-6422, E-mail: cooperj@gvsu.edu. *Application contact:* Dr. Karyn Rabourn, Graduate Program Director, 616-331-6250, Fax: 616-331-6422, E-mail: rabournk@gvsu.edu.

Grand Valley State University, College of Education, Program in Higher Education, Allendale, MI 49401-9403. Offers M Ed. *Program availability:* Part-time. *Students:* 11 full-time (7 women), 36 part-time (24 women); includes 15 minority (6 Black or African American, non-Hispanic/Latino; 2 Asian, non-Hispanic/Latino; 4 Hispanic/Latino; 3 Two or more races, non-Hispanic/Latino), 1 international. Average age 33. 113 applicants, 93% accepted, 11 enrolled. In 2017, 15 master's awarded. *Degree requirements:* For master's, project or thesis. *Entrance requirements:* For master's, minimum undergraduate GPA of 3.0 or GRE General Test, last 60 credits from regionally-accredited college/university, 3 letters of recommendation. Additional exam requirements/recommendations for international students: Required—TOEFL (minimum iBT score of 80), IELTS (6.5), or Michigan English Language Assessment Battery (77). *Application deadline:* Applications are processed on a rolling basis. Application fee: $30. Electronic applications accepted. *Expenses:* $652 per credit hour. *Financial support:* In 2017–18, 10 students received support, including 7 fellowships; research assistantships and unspecified assistantships also available. *Unit head:* Dr. Jay Cooper, Director, Educational Leadership and Counseling, 616-331-0336, Fax: 616-331-6422, E-mail: cooperj@gvsu.edu. *Application contact:* Thomas Owens, Director, Student Information and Services Center, 616-331-6282, Fax: 616-331-6217, E-mail: owenst@gvsu.edu. Website: http://www.gvsu.edu/grad/highered/

Grand Valley State University, College of Education, Programs in General Education, Allendale, MI 49401-9403. Offers adult and higher education (M Ed); early childhood education (M Ed); educational differentiation (M Ed); educational leadership (M Ed); educational technology integration (M Ed); elementary education (M Ed); middle level education (M Ed); school library media services (M Ed); secondary level education (M Ed); teaching English to speakers of other languages (M Ed). *Program availability:* Part-time, evening/weekend, 100% online, blended/hybrid learning. *Students:* 24 part-time (16 women). Average age 41. In 2017, 5 master's awarded. *Degree requirements:* For master's, project or thesis. *Entrance requirements:* For master's, GRE General Test or minimum GPA of 3.0, last 60 credits from regionally-accredited college/university, 3 letters of recommendation. Additional exam requirements/recommendations for international students: Required—TOEFL (minimum iBT score of 80), IELTS (6.5), or Michigan English Language Assessment Battery (77). *Application deadline:* Applications are processed on a rolling basis. Application fee: $30. Electronic applications accepted. *Expenses:* $652 per credit hour. *Financial support:* In 2017–18, 2 students received support, including 2 fellowships; career-related internships or fieldwork, Federal Work-Study, scholarships/grants, and unspecified assistantships also available. *Faculty research:* Effectiveness of technology in education, parental involvement, effective teaching, effective schools research. *Unit head:* Dr. David Bair, Department Director, 616-331-6489, Fax: 616-331-6489, E-mail: baird@gvsu.edu. *Application contact:* Thomas Owens, Director, Student Information and Services Center, 616-331-6282, Fax: 616-331-6217, E-mail: owenst@gvsu.edu. Website: http://www.gvsu.edu/coe/

Hardin-Simmons University, Graduate School, Irvin School of Education, Program in Education Leadership, Abilene, TX 79698-0001. Offers educational leadership in superintendency (Ed D); higher education leadership (Ed D). *Program availability:* Part-time. *Faculty:* 3 full-time (all women), 3 part-time/adjunct (1 woman). *Students:* 32 part-time (27 women); includes 3 minority (all Hispanic/Latino), 1 international. Average age 39. 12 applicants, 100% accepted, 6 enrolled. In 2017, 1 doctorate awarded. *Entrance requirements:* For doctorate, minimum master's GPA of 3.5; resume or curriculum vitae; three recommendations from doctoral degree holder, employer/supervisor, and professional colleague. Additional exam requirements/recommendations for international students: Required—TOEFL (minimum score 550 paper-based; 79 iBT), TWE (minimum score 5). *Application deadline:* For fall admission, 7/15 priority date for domestic students, 4/1 for international students; for spring admission, 1/5 priority date for domestic students, 8/1 for international students. Applications are processed on a rolling basis. Application fee: $50 ($150 for international students). Electronic applications accepted. *Expenses: Tuition:* Full-time $13,500; part-time $750 per semester hour. *Required fees:* $220 per term. One-time fee: $50. Tuition and fees vary according to course load, campus/location and program. *Financial support:* In 2017–18, 22 students received support. Fellowships and scholarships/grants available. Support available to part-time students. Financial award application deadline: 6/30; financial award applicants required to submit FAFSA. *Unit head:* Dr. Mary Christopher, Program Director, 325-670-1510, Fax: 325-670-5859, E-mail: leadership@hsutx.edu. *Application contact:* Dr. Nancy Kucinski, Dean of Graduate Studies, 325-670-1298, Fax: 325-670-1564, E-mail: gradoff@hsutx.edu. Website: http://www.hsutx.edu/doctorateinleadership

Hofstra University, School of Education, Specialized Programs in Education, Hempstead, NY 11549. Offers applied behavior analysis (Advanced Certificate); childhood special education (MS Ed); early childhood special education (MS Ed, Advanced Certificate); educational and policy leadership (Ed D); educational leadership (Advanced Certificate), including school building leader/school district business leader; educational leadership and policy studies (MS Ed), including K-12; elementary special education (MS Ed); gifted education (Advanced Certificate), including school building leader/school district business leader; health education (MS); health professions pedagogy and leadership (MS); higher education leadership and policy studies (MS Ed); inclusive early childhood special education (MS Ed); inclusive elementary special education (MS Ed); inclusive secondary special education (MS Ed); literacy studies (MA, MS Ed, Ed D, Advanced Certificate), including birth-grade 6 (MS Ed, Advanced Certificate), grades 5-12 (MS Ed, Advanced Certificate), literacy studies (Ed D); pedagogy for health professions (Advanced Certificate); physical education (MS); school district business leader (Advanced Certificate); secondary education generalist - students with disabilities 7-12 (MS Ed), including students with disabilities 7-12; secondary special education generalist (MS Ed), including extension in secondary education; special education (MS Ed, Advanced Certificate); special education assessment and diagnosis (Advanced Certificate); special education early childhood intervention (MS Ed); special education: international perspectives (MS Ed); teaching students with severe or multiple disabilities (Advanced Certificate). *Program availability:* Part-time, evening/weekend, blended/hybrid learning. *Students:* 148 full-time (110 women), 249 part-time (188 women); includes 105 minority (54 Black or African American, non-Hispanic/Latino; 1 American Indian or Alaska

Native, non-Hispanic/Latino; 13 Asian, non-Hispanic/Latino; 35 Hispanic/Latino; 1 Native Hawaiian or other Pacific Islander, non-Hispanic/Latino; 1 Two or more races, non-Hispanic/Latino), 1 international. Average age 32. 228 applicants, 93% accepted, 132 enrolled. In 2017, 97 master's, 22 doctorates, 31 other advanced degrees awarded. *Degree requirements:* For master's, one foreign language, comprehensive exam (for some programs), thesis (for some programs), electronic portfolio, capstone course, internship, practicum, student teaching, seminars, minimum GPA of 3.0; for doctorate, one foreign language, comprehensive exam, thesis/dissertation, qualifying hearing. *Entrance requirements:* For master's, GRE, interview, letters of recommendation, portfolio, essay, certification; for doctorate, GRE or MAT, interview, resume, essay, master's degree, 3 letters of recommendation, writing sample; for Advanced Certificate, GRE, interview, letters of recommendation, essay, professional experience, resume, master's degree. Additional exam requirements/recommendations for international students: Required—TOEFL (minimum score 550 paper-based; 80 iBT). *Application deadline:* Applications are processed on a rolling basis. Application fee: $75. Electronic applications accepted. *Expenses: Tuition:* Full-time $1292. *Required fees:* $970. Tuition and fees vary according to program. *Financial support:* In 2017–18, 225 students received support, including 118 fellowships with full and partial tuition reimbursements available (averaging $3,887 per year), 12 research assistantships with full and partial tuition reimbursements available (averaging $7,215 per year); career-related internships or fieldwork, Federal Work-Study, institutionally sponsored loans, scholarships/grants, traineeships, tuition waivers (full and partial), and unspecified assistantships also available. Support available to part-time students. Financial award applicants required to submit FAFSA. *Faculty research:* Collaborative teaching and learning; language and culture; new media literacies; applied behavior analysis; K-12 leadership development. *Unit head:* Dr. Elfreda Blue, Chairperson, 516-463-5762, Fax: 516-463-6184, E-mail: elfreda.blue@hofstra.edu. *Application contact:* Sunil Samuel, Assistant Vice President of Admissions, 516-463-4723, Fax: 516-463-4664, E-mail: graduateadmission@hofstra.edu. Website: http://www.hofstra.edu/education/

Houston Baptist University, College of Education and Behavioral Sciences, Programs in Education, Houston, TX 77074-3298. Offers bilingual education (M Ed); counselor education (M Ed); curriculum and instruction (M Ed); curriculum and instruction (EC-6 bilingual) (M Ed); curriculum and instruction in all-level art, Spanish, music, or physical education (M Ed); curriculum and instruction in EC-6 and special education (EC-12) (M Ed); curriculum and instruction in instructional technology (M Ed); curriculum and instruction in mathematics, science, or social studies (4-8) (M Ed); curriculum and instruction with EC-6 generalist (M Ed); curriculum and instruction with English language arts and reading (4-8) (M Ed); educational administration (M Ed); educational diagnostician (M Ed); executive educational leadership (Ed D); higher education in business management (M Ed); higher education in Christian studies (M Ed); higher education in counseling (M Ed); higher education in educational technology (M Ed); reading (M Ed); special educational leadership (Ed D). *Program availability:* Part-time, evening/weekend, 100% online, blended/hybrid learning. *Students:* 83 full-time (65 women), 187 part-time (156 women); includes 189 minority (114 Black or African American, non-Hispanic/Latino; 2 American Indian or Alaska Native, non-Hispanic/Latino; 9 Asian, non-Hispanic/Latino; 58 Hispanic/Latino; 6 Two or more races, non-Hispanic/Latino), 7 international. Average age 36. 309 applicants, 31% accepted, 70 enrolled. In 2017, 92 master's awarded. *Degree requirements:* For master's, comprehensive exam; for doctorate, thesis/dissertation. *Entrance requirements:* For master's, minimum GPA of 2.75, two recommendations, resume, bachelor's degree conferred transcript; interview (for non-certified teachers); for doctorate, GRE, 5 letters of recommendation. Additional exam requirements/recommendations for international students: Required—TOEFL (minimum score 80 iBT), IELTS (minimum score 6.5). *Application deadline:* For fall admission, 8/1 for domestic students, 6/1 for international students; for spring admission, 1/1 for domestic students, 11/1 for international students; for summer admission, 5/1 for domestic students, 3/1 for international students. Applications are processed on a rolling basis. Application fee: $0 ($100 for international students). Electronic applications accepted. Application fee is waived when completed online. *Expenses:* $22,000 tuition; $4,500 fees (general, technology and parking). *Financial support:* In 2017–18, 59 students received support. Research assistantships, teaching assistantships, Federal Work-Study, and scholarships/grants available. Support available to part-time students. Financial award application deadline: 4/1; financial award applicants required to submit FAFSA. *Faculty research:* Autism and inclusion, integrating technology into instruction, school change and leadership trust. *Unit head:* Dr. Charlotte Fontenot, Director, Graduate Programs, 281-649-3078, Fax: 281-649-3361, E-mail: cfontenot@hbu.edu. *Application contact:* Kristy Wright, Administrative Assistant for Graduate Programs, 281-649-3094, Fax: 281-649-3361, E-mail: kwright@hbu.edu. Website: http://www.hbu.edu/MED

Illinois State University, Graduate School, College of Education, Department of Curriculum and Instruction, Normal, IL 61790. Offers curriculum and instruction (MS, MS Ed, Ed D); educational policies (Ed D); postsecondary education (Ed D); reading (MS Ed); supervision (Ed D). *Accreditation:* NCATE. *Degree requirements:* For master's, variable foreign language requirement, thesis or alternative; for doctorate, variable foreign language requirement, thesis/dissertation, 2 terms of residency, internship. *Entrance requirements:* For master's, GRE General Test, minimum GPA of 3.0 in last 60 hours of course work; for doctorate, GRE General Test. *Faculty research:* In-service and pre-service teacher education for teachers of English language learners; teachers for all children; developing a model for alternative, bilingual elementary certification for paraprofessionals in Illinois; Illinois Geographic Alliance, Connections Project.

Indiana State University, College of Graduate and Professional Studies, Bayh College of Education, Department of Educational Leadership, Terre Haute, IN 47809. Offers educational administration (PhD); higher education leadership (PhD); K-12 district leadership (PhD); school administration (Ed S); school administration and supervision (M Ed); student affairs and higher education (MS). *Accreditation:* NCATE. *Program availability:* Part-time, evening/weekend. Terminal master's awarded for partial completion of doctoral program. *Degree requirements:* For master's, thesis; for doctorate, thesis/dissertation. *Entrance requirements:* For master's, GRE General Test, minimum undergraduate GPA of 2.5; for doctorate, GRE General Test, minimum undergraduate GPA of 3.5; for Ed S, GRE General Test, minimum graduate GPA of 3.25. Electronic applications accepted.

Indiana University Bloomington, School of Education, Department of Educational Leadership and Policy Studies, Bloomington, IN 47405. Offers educational leadership (MS, Ed D, Ed S); higher education (Ed D, PhD); higher education and student affairs (MS); history and philosophy of education (MS); history, philosophy, and policy in education (PhD), including education policy studies, history of education, philosophy of education; international and comparative education (MS). *Accreditation:* NCATE. *Degree requirements:* For master's, thesis optional; for doctorate, comprehensive exam, thesis/dissertation; for Ed S, comprehensive exam or project. *Entrance requirements:* For master's, doctorate, and Ed S, GRE General Test. Additional exam requirements/recommendations for international students: Required—TOEFL (minimum score 79 iBT). Electronic applications accepted. *Faculty research:* Culturally engaging campus environments, school choice policy analysis, democracy and education in the national and international context, and principal leadership.

Indiana University of Pennsylvania, School of Graduate Studies and Research, College of Education and Communications, Department of Student Affairs in Higher Education, Indiana, PA 15705. Offers MA. *Accreditation:* NCATE. *Program availability:* Part-time. *Faculty:* 3 full-time (1 woman), 1 (woman) part-time/adjunct. *Students:* 44 full-time (25 women), 3 part-time (2 women); includes 11 minority (9 Black or African American, non-Hispanic/Latino; 1 Asian, non-Hispanic/Latino; 1 Hispanic/Latino), 3 international. Average age 24. 80 applicants, 78% accepted, 23 enrolled. In 2017, 23 master's awarded. *Degree requirements:* For master's, comprehensive exam, thesis optional. *Entrance requirements:* For master's, resume, interview, 2 letters of recommendation, writing sample, minimum GPA of 2.8. Additional exam requirements/recommendations for international students: Required—TOEFL (minimum score 540 paper-based). *Application deadline:* For fall admission, 1/15 priority date for domestic students. Application fee: $50. Electronic applications accepted. *Expenses:* Contact institution. *Financial support:* In 2017–18, 21 research assistantships with tuition reimbursements (averaging $5,445 per year) were awarded; fellowships, career-related internships or fieldwork, Federal Work-Study, scholarships/grants, and unspecified assistantships also available. Support available to part-time students. Financial award application deadline: 4/15; financial award applicants required to submit FAFSA. *Unit head:* Dr. John Wesley Lowery, Chairperson, 724-357-4545, E-mail: jlowery@iup.edu. *Website:* http://www.iup.edu/sahe

Indiana Wesleyan University, Graduate School, College of Arts and Sciences, Marion, IN 46953. Offers addictions counseling (MS); clinical mental health counseling (MS); community counseling (MS); marriage and family therapy (MS); school counseling (MS); student development counseling and administration (MS). *Accreditation:* ACA. *Program availability:* Part-time. *Degree requirements:* For master's, thesis or alternative. *Entrance requirements:* For master's, GRE General Test. Additional exam requirements/recommendations for international students: Required—TOEFL. Electronic applications accepted. *Expenses:* Contact institution. *Faculty research:* Community counseling, multicultural counseling, addictions.

Inter American University of Puerto Rico, Metropolitan Campus, Graduate Programs, Program in Higher Education Administration, San Juan, PR 00919-1293. Offers MA. *Degree requirements:* For master's, comprehensive exam. *Entrance requirements:* For master's, GRE or EXADEP, interview. Electronic applications accepted.

Iowa State University of Science and Technology, Department of Educational Leadership and Policy Studies, Ames, IA 50011. Offers counselor education (M Ed, MS); educational administration (M Ed, MS); educational leadership (PhD); higher education (M Ed, MS); organizational learning and human resource development (M Ed, MS); research and evaluation (MS); student affairs (MS). *Degree requirements:* For master's, thesis or alternative; for doctorate, thesis/dissertation. *Entrance requirements:* For master's and doctorate, GRE General Test. Additional exam requirements/recommendations for international students: Required—TOEFL (minimum score 560 paper-based; 83 iBT), IELTS (minimum score 6.5). Electronic applications accepted.

Jackson State University, Graduate School, College of Education and Human Development, Department of Educational Leadership, Jackson, MS 39217. Offers education administration and supervision (Ed S); educational administration and supervision (MS Ed, PhD); higher education (Ed S). *Accreditation:* NCATE. *Program availability:* Part-time, evening/weekend, online only, 100% online, blended/hybrid learning. *Degree requirements:* For master's and Ed S, comprehensive exam, thesis; for doctorate, comprehensive exam, thesis/dissertation. *Entrance requirements:* For master's, GRE General Test; for doctorate, MAT, GRE, teaching experience. Additional exam requirements/recommendations for international students: Required—TOEFL (minimum score 520 paper-based; 67 iBT). Electronic applications accepted. *Expenses:* Contact institution.

James Madison University, The Graduate School, College of Education, Program in Adult Education and Human Resource Development, Harrisonburg, VA 22801. Offers higher education (MS Ed); human resource management (MS Ed); individualized (MS Ed); instructional design (MS Ed); leadership and facilitation (MS Ed); program evaluation and measurement (MS Ed). *Accreditation:* NCATE. *Program availability:* Part-time, evening/weekend. *Students:* 11 full-time (7 women), 12 part-time (10 women); includes 7 minority (4 Black or African American, non-Hispanic/Latino; 1 Hispanic/Latino; 2 Two or more races, non-Hispanic/Latino), 1 international. Average age 30. In 2017, 3 master's awarded. Application fee: $55. Electronic applications accepted. *Expenses:* Tuition, state resident: full-time $10,512; part-time $438 per credit hour. Tuition, nonresident: full-time $28,358; part-time $1162 per credit hour. *Required fees:* $1128. *Financial support:* In 2017–18, 10 students received support. Teaching assistantships, Federal Work-Study, and 10 assistantships (averaging $7911) available. Financial award application deadline: 3/1; financial award applicants required to submit FAFSA. *Unit head:* Dr. Jane B. Thall, Department Head, 540-568-5531, E-mail: thalljb@jmu.edu. *Application contact:* Lynette D. Michael, Director of Graduate Admissions, 540-568-6131 Ext. 6395, Fax: 540-568-7860, E-mail: michaeld@jmu.edu.

Johnson University, Graduate and Professional Programs, Knoxville, TN 37998-1001. Offers biblical interpretation (Graduate Certificate); business administration (MBA); Christian ministries (Graduate Certificate); clinical mental health counseling (MA); educational technology (MA); intercultural studies (MA); leadership (MBA); leadership studies (PhD); New Testament (MA); nonprofit management (MBA); school counseling (MA); spiritual formation and leadership (Graduate Certificate); strategic ministry (MA); teacher education (MA). *Program availability:* Part-time, evening/weekend, 100% online, blended/hybrid learning. *Degree requirements:* For master's, variable foreign language requirement, comprehensive exam, thesis (for some programs), internships; for doctorate, variable foreign language requirement, comprehensive exam, thesis/dissertation, internships. *Entrance requirements:* For master's, PRAXIS (for MA in teacher education); MAT (for counseling); GRE or GMAT (for MBA), interview, 3 references, transcripts, essay, minimum GPA of 2.5 or 3.0 (depending on program); for doctorate, GRE or MAT (taken not less than 5 years prior), interview, 3 references, transcripts, essay, minimum GPA of 3.0; for Graduate Certificate, interview, 3 references, transcripts, essay, minimum GPA of 3.0. Additional exam requirements/recommendations for international students: Required—TOEFL (minimum score 527 paper-based; 71 iBT). Electronic applications accepted. *Expenses:* Contact institution.

Kent State University, College of Education, Health and Human Services, School of Foundations, Leadership and Administration, Program in Higher Education, Kent, OH 44242-0001. Offers PhD, Ed S. *Accreditation:* NCATE. *Program availability:* Part-time, evening/weekend. *Degree requirements:* For doctorate, comprehensive exam, thesis/dissertation. *Entrance requirements:* For doctorate, GRE General Test, 2 letters of reference, resume, interview, goals statement. Additional exam requirements/recommendations for international students: Required—TOEFL (minimum score 550 paper-based; 80 iBT). Electronic applications accepted. *Expenses:* Tuition, state resident: full-time $11,310; part-time $515 per credit hour. Tuition, nonresident: full-time $20,396; part-time $928 per credit hour. *International tuition:* $18,544 full-time. *Faculty research:* Leadership.

Kent State University, College of Education, Health and Human Services, School of Foundations, Leadership and Administration, Program in Higher Education and Student Personnel, Kent, OH 44242-0001. Offers M Ed. *Accreditation:* NCATE. *Program availability:* Part-time, evening/weekend. *Entrance requirements:* For master's, GRE if

undergraduate GPA is below 3.0, resume, interview, 2 letters of recommendation, goals statement. Additional exam requirements/recommendations for international students: Required—TOEFL (minimum score 550 paper-based; 80 iBT). Electronic applications accepted. *Expenses:* Tuition, state resident: full-time $11,310; part-time $515 per credit hour. Tuition, nonresident: full-time $20,396; part-time $928 per credit hour. *International tuition:* $18,544 full-time. *Faculty research:* History/sociology of higher education, organization and administration in higher education.

Lee University, Program in Education, Cleveland, TN 37320-3450. Offers art (MAT); curriculum and instruction (M Ed, Ed S); early childhood (MAT); educational leadership (M Ed, Ed S); elementary education (MAT); English and math (MAT); English and science (MAT); English and social studies (MAT); higher education administration (MS); history (MAT); history and economics (MAT); math and science (MAT); math and social studies (MAT); middle grades (MAT); science and social studies (MASW); secondary education (MAT); Spanish (MAT); special education (M Ed, MAT; TESOL (MAT). *Accreditation:* NCATE. *Program availability:* Part-time. *Faculty:* 15 full-time (7 women), 8 part-time/adjunct (3 women). *Students:* 28 full-time (21 women), 77 part-time (48 women); includes 12 minority (7 Black or African American, non-Hispanic/Latino; 2 Hispanic/Latino; 3 Two or more races, non-Hispanic/Latino), 1 international. Average age 31. 35 applicants, 83% accepted, 22 enrolled. In 2017, 54 master's, 4 other advanced degrees awarded. *Degree requirements:* For master's, variable foreign language requirement, thesis optional, internship. *Entrance requirements:* For master's, MAT or GRE General Test, minimum undergraduate GPA of 2.75, 3 letters of recommendation, interview, writing sample, official transcripts, background check; for Ed S, minimum undergraduate and master's GPA of 2.75, official transcripts for undergraduate and master's degrees. Additional exam requirements/recommendations for international students: Required—TOEFL (minimum score 61 iBT). *Application deadline:* For fall admission, 6/1 priority date for domestic and international students; for spring admission, 11/1 priority date for domestic and international students; for summer admission, 4/1 priority date for domestic and international students. Applications are processed on a rolling basis. Application fee: $25. Electronic applications accepted. *Expenses: Tuition:* Full-time $12,780; part-time $710 per credit hour. *Required fees:* $60; $60 per term. Tuition and fees vary according to program. *Financial support:* In 2017–18, 32 students received support. Career-related internships or fieldwork, Federal Work-Study, institutionally sponsored loans, scholarships/grants, and unspecified assistantships available. Financial award application deadline: 3/1; financial award applicants required to submit FAFSA. *Unit head:* Dr. William Kamm, Director, 423-614-8544, E-mail: wkamm@leeuniversity.edu. *Application contact:* Crystal Keeter, Graduate Education Secretary, 423-614-8544, E-mail: ckeeter@leeuniversity.edu. *Website:* http://www.leeuniversity.edu/academics/graduate/education

Lewis University, College of Arts and Sciences, Program in Organizational Leadership, Romeoville, IL 60446. Offers higher education/student services (MA); non-profit management (MA); organizational and leadership coaching (MA); organizational management (MA); training and development (MA). *Program availability:* Part-time, evening/weekend, 100% online, blended/hybrid learning. *Students:* 16 full-time (11 women), 154 part-time (115 women); includes 49 minority (27 Black or African American, non-Hispanic/Latino; 1 American Indian or Alaska Native, non-Hispanic/Latino; 4 Asian, non-Hispanic/Latino; 12 Hispanic/Latino; 5 Two or more races, non-Hispanic/Latino), 4 international. Average age 37. *Entrance requirements:* For master's, bachelor's degree, personal statement, minimum GPA of 3.0, letters of recommendation. Additional exam requirements/recommendations for international students: Required—TOEFL (minimum score 550 paper-based; 79 iBT), IELTS (minimum score 6). *Application deadline:* For fall admission, 5/1 priority date for international students; for spring admission, 11/15 priority date for international students. Applications are processed on a rolling basis. Application fee: $40. Electronic applications accepted. Tuition and fees vary according to program. *Financial support:* Federal Work-Study, tuition waivers, and unspecified assistantships available. Financial award application deadline: 5/1; financial award applicants required to submit FAFSA. *Unit head:* Dr. Lesley Page, Chair of Organizational Leadership, 815-838-0500, E-mail: pagele@lewisu.edu. *Application contact:* Kathy Lisak, Graduate Admission Counselor, 815-836-5610, E-mail: grad@lewisu.edu.

Lincoln Memorial University, Carter and Moyers School of Education, Harrogate, TN 37752-1901. Offers administration and supervision (M Ed, Ed S); counseling and guidance (M Ed); curriculum and instruction (M Ed, Ed D, Ed S); English (M Ed); executive leadership (Ed D); higher education administration (Ed D); human resource development (Ed D); leadership and administration (Ed D). *Program availability:* Part-time, evening/weekend, online learning. *Degree requirements:* For master's, comprehensive exam, thesis optional; for Ed S, comprehensive exam. *Entrance requirements:* For master's, PRAXIS, NTE, GRE, MAT, letters of recommendation; for Ed S, graduate transcripts. Additional exam requirements/recommendations for international students: Recommended—TOEFL. *Faculty research:* Brain compatible teaching and learning; poverty in Appalachia; leadership for change; ethics, moral responsibility and social justice; human and organizational learning.

Lincoln University, Graduate Studies, Jefferson City, MO 65101. Offers business administration (MBA), including accounting, management, management information systems, public administration/policy; elementary teaching (M Ed); environmental science (MS); guidance and counseling (M Ed), including community/agency counseling, elementary school, secondary school; higher education (MA); history (MA); integrated agricultural systems (MS); middle school (M Ed); natural sciences (MS); secondary teaching (M Ed); sociology (MA); sociology/criminal justice (MA). *Program availability:* Part-time, evening/weekend, 100% online, blended/hybrid learning. *Students:* 40 full-time (23 women), 64 part-time (32 women); includes 33 minority (30 Black or African American, non-Hispanic/Latino; 2 Hispanic/Latino; 1 Two or more races, non-Hispanic/Latino), 12 international. Average age 33. 48 applicants, 81% accepted, 22 enrolled. In 2017, 46 master's awarded. *Degree requirements:* For master's, comprehensive exam, thesis optional. *Entrance requirements:* For master's, GRE, MAT, or GMAT, minimum GPA of 2.75 overall, 3.0 in courses related to specialization; 3 letters of recommendation; minimum C average in English composition; personal statement of purpose. Additional exam requirements/recommendations for international students: Required—TOEFL (minimum score 500 paper-based; 61 iBT), IELTS (minimum score 5.5), Michigan English Language Assessment Battery (minimum score 80). *Application deadline:* For fall admission, 7/1 priority date for domestic students, 5/1 priority date for international students; for spring admission, 11/1 priority date for domestic students, 10/1 priority date for international students; for summer admission, 6/1 priority date for domestic students. Applications are processed on a rolling basis. Application fee: $30. Electronic applications accepted. *Expenses:* Tuition, state resident: part-time $291 per credit hour. Tuition, nonresident: part-time $541.50 per credit hour. *Financial support:* In 2017–18, 2 fellowships with tuition reimbursements, 3 research assistantships with tuition reimbursements were awarded; Federal Work-Study, scholarships/grants, and unspecified assistantships also available. Support available to part-time students. Financial award application deadline: 3/1; financial award applicants required to submit FAFSA. *Unit head:* Dr. Debra F. Greene, Interim Provost, 573-681-5247, Fax: 573-681-5106, E-mail: gradschool@lincolnu.edu. *Application contact:* Irasema Steck, Administrative Assistant, 573-681-5247, Fax: 573-681-5106, E-mail: gradschool@lincolnu.edu. *Website:* http://www.lincolnu.edu/web/graduate-studies/graduate-studies

London Metropolitan University, Graduate Programs, London, United Kingdom. Offers applied psychology (M Sc); architecture (MA); biomedical science (M Sc); blood science (M Sc); cancer pharmacology (M Sc); computer networking and cyber security (M Sc); computing and information systems (M Sc); conference interpreting (MA); counter-terrorism studies (M Sc); creative, digital and professional writing (MA); crime, violence and prevention (MA); criminology (M Sc); curating contemporary art (MA); data analytics (M Sc); digital media (MA); early childhood studies (MA); education (MA, Ed D); financial services law, regulation and compliance (LL M); food science (M Sc); forensic psychology (M Sc); health and social care management and policy (M Sc); human nutrition (M Sc); human resource management (MA); human rights and international conflict (MA); information technology (M Sc); intelligence and security studies (M Sc); international oil, gas and energy law (LL M); international relations (MA); interpreting (MA); learning and teaching in higher education (M Sc); legal practice (LL M); media and entertainment law (LL M); organizational and consumer psychology (M Sc); psychological therapy (M Sc); psychology of mental health (M Sc); public health (M Sc); public policy and management (MPA); security studies (M Sc); social work (M Sc); spatial planning and urban design (MA); sports therapy (M Sc); supporting older children and young people with dyslexia (MA); teaching languages (MA), including Arabic, English; translation (MA); woman and child abuse (MA).

Louisiana State University and Agricultural & Mechanical College, Graduate School, College of Human Sciences and Education, Department of Educational Theory, Policy and Practice, Baton Rouge, LA 70803. Offers counseling (M Ed, MA, Ed S); educational administration (M Ed, MA, PhD, Ed S); educational technology (MA); elementary education (M Ed, MAT); higher education (PhD); research methodology (PhD); secondary education (M Ed, MAT). *Accreditation:* ACA (one or more programs are accredited); NCATE. *Faculty:* 34 full-time (22 women). *Students:* 213 full-time (159 women), 228 part-time (178 women); includes 164 minority (123 Black or African American, non-Hispanic/Latino; 7 Asian, non-Hispanic/Latino; 27 Hispanic/Latino; 1 Native Hawaiian or other Pacific Islander, non-Hispanic/Latino; 6 Two or more races, non-Hispanic/Latino), 13 international. Average age 32. 231 applicants, 61% accepted, 82 enrolled. In 2017, 125 master's, 26 doctorates, 28 other advanced degrees awarded. *Financial support:* In 2017–18, 3 fellowships (averaging $12,129 per year), 2 research assistantships (averaging $16,019 per year), 96 teaching assistantships (averaging $16,061 per year) were awarded. *Total annual research expenditures:* $356,867.

Louisiana Tech University, Graduate School, College of Education, Ruston, LA 71272. Offers counseling and guidance (MA), including clinical mental health counseling, human services, orientation and mobility; counseling psychology (PhD); curriculum and instruction (M Ed); cyber education (Graduate Certificate); dynamics of domestic and family violence (Graduate Certificate); early childhood education - PreK-3 (MAT); educational leadership (M Ed, Ed D); elementary education and special education mild/moderate grades 1-5 (MAT); higher education administration (Graduate Certificate); industrial/organizational psychology (MA, PhD); kinesiology (MS); middle school education (MAT), including mathematics; orientation and mobility (Graduate Certificate); rehabilitation teaching for the blind (Graduate Certificate); secondary education (MAT), including agriculture, biology, business, chemistry, English; special education: visually impaired (MAT); teacher leader education (Graduate Certificate); visual impairments - blind education (Graduate Certificate). *Accreditation:* NCATE. *Program availability:* Part-time. *Faculty:* 28 full-time (16 women), 23 part-time/adjunct (22 women). *Students:* 269 full-time (192 women), 194 part-time (150 women); includes 127 minority (94 Black or African American, non-Hispanic/Latino; 2 American Indian or Alaska Native, non-Hispanic/Latino; 6 Asian, non-Hispanic/Latino; 16 Hispanic/Latino; 1 Native Hawaiian or other Pacific Islander, non-Hispanic/Latino; 8 Two or more races, non-Hispanic/Latino), 8 international. Average age 34. 226 applicants, 74% accepted, 60 enrolled. In 2017, 5 master's, 2 doctorates, 1 other advanced degree awarded. *Degree requirements:* For master's, thesis; for doctorate, thesis/dissertation. *Entrance requirements:* For master's and doctorate, GRE General Test. Additional exam requirements/recommendations for international students: Required—TOEFL (minimum score 550 paper-based; 80 iBT), IELTS (minimum score 6.5). *Application deadline:* For fall admission, 9/1 priority date for domestic students, 6/1 for international students; for winter admission, 11/1 priority date for domestic students, 9/1 for international students; for spring admission, 2/1 priority date for domestic students, 12/1 for international students; for summer admission, 5/1 priority date for domestic students, 3/1 for international students. Application fee: $40. Electronic applications accepted. *Expenses:* Tuition, state resident: full-time $5146. Tuition, nonresident: full-time $10,147. *International tuition:* $10,267 full-time. *Required fees:* $2273. *Financial support:* In 2017–18, 40 students received support, including 23 research assistantships (averaging $10,346 per year), 15 teaching assistantships (averaging $6,887 per year); fellowships and career-related internships or fieldwork also available. Financial award application deadline: 2/1. *Faculty research:* Blindness and the best methods for increasing independence for individuals who are blind or visually impaired; educating and investigating factors contributing to improvements in human performance across the lifespan and a reduction in injury rates during training. *Total annual research expenditures:* $2.1 million. *Unit head:* Dr. Don Schillinger, Dean, 318-257-3712, E-mail: dschill@latech.edu. *Application contact:* Dr. Dawn Basinger, Associate Dean of Academic Affairs, 318-257-2977, Fax: 318-257-2379, E-mail: dbasing@latech.edu.
Website: http://education.latech.edu/

Loyola Marymount University, School of Education, Program in Higher Education Administration, Los Angeles, CA 90045-2659. Offers MA. *Unit head:* Dr. Elizabeth Stoddard, Director, Higher Education, 310-338-1967, E-mail: elizabeth.stoddard@lmu.edu. *Application contact:* Chake H. Kouyoumjian, Associate Dean of Graduate Studies, 310-338-2721, Fax: 310-338-6086, E-mail: graduateinfo@lmu.edu.
Website: http://soe.lmu.edu/academics/highereducationadministration

Loyola University Chicago, School of Education, Program in Higher Education, Chicago, IL 60660. Offers higher education (M Ed, PhD); international higher education (M Ed). PhD offered through the Graduate School. *Accreditation:* NCATE. *Program availability:* Part-time, blended/hybrid learning. *Faculty:* 4 full-time (2 women), 10 part-time/adjunct (9 women). *Students:* 78 full-time (50 women), 22 part-time (15 women); includes 54 minority (18 Black or African American, non-Hispanic/Latino; 10 Asian, non-Hispanic/Latino; 22 Hispanic/Latino; 4 Two or more races, non-Hispanic/Latino), 1 international. Average age 28. 275 applicants, 63% accepted, 57 enrolled. In 2017, 33 master's, 7 doctorates awarded. *Degree requirements:* For master's, comprehensive exam; for doctorate, comprehensive exam, thesis/dissertation. *Entrance requirements:* For master's, letters of recommendation, minimum GPA of 3.0, resume, transcripts; for doctorate, GMAT, GRE General Test, or MAT, 5 years of higher education work experience, interview. Additional exam requirements/recommendations for international students: Required—TOEFL (minimum score 550 paper-based; 79 iBT). *Application deadline:* For fall admission, 12/1 for domestic and international students. Applications are processed on a rolling basis. Application fee: $50. Electronic applications accepted. Application fee is waived when completed online. *Expenses:* $949 per semester hour, $2,847 per course, $8,541-$11,388 full-time semester tuition; $432 per semester fees, $225 additional fees (first semester only). *Financial support:* In 2017–18, 37 fellowships with partial tuition reimbursements, 42 research assistantships with full tuition reimbursements (averaging $14,000 per year), 23 teaching assistantships with full tuition reimbursements (averaging $4,000 per year) were awarded; career-related

internships or fieldwork, institutionally sponsored loans, scholarships/grants, traineeships, health care benefits, and unspecified assistantships also available. Support available to part-time students. Financial award application deadline: 2/1; financial award applicants required to submit FAFSA. *Faculty research:* Church-affiliated higher education, enrollment management, academic programs, program evaluation/quality. *Unit head:* Dr. Bridget Kelly, Director, 312-915-6855, Fax: 312-915-6660, E-mail: bkelly4@luc.edu. *Application contact:* Mirtza Campbell, Information Contact, 312-915-8907, E-mail: mcampbell11@luc.edu.

Maryville University of Saint Louis, School of Education, St. Louis, MO 63141-7299. Offers early childhood education (MA Ed); educational leadership (Ed D); elementary education (MA Ed); higher education leadership (Ed D); literacy specialist (MA Ed); middle grades education (MA Ed); secondary teaching and inquiry (MA Ed); teacher as leader (MA Ed, Ed D). *Accreditation:* NCATE. *Program availability:* Part-time, 100% online, blended/hybrid learning. *Faculty:* 20 full-time (14 women), 19 part-time/adjunct (13 women). *Students:* 6 full-time (4 women), 337 part-time (250 women); includes 101 minority (85 Black or African American, non-Hispanic/Latino; 4 Asian, non-Hispanic/Latino; 8 Hispanic/Latino; 4 Two or more races, non-Hispanic/Latino), 3 international. Average age 38. In 2017, 34 master's, 67 doctorates awarded. *Degree requirements:* For master's, thesis, project. *Entrance requirements:* For master's, minimum cumulative GPA of 3.0, 3 professional recommendations, essays, interview with program faculty; for doctorate, minimum GPA of 3.0, 3 professional recommendations, essay, interview, on-site writing sample. Additional exam requirements/recommendations for international students: Required—TOEFL (minimum score 550 paper-based). *Application deadline:* Applications are processed on a rolling basis. Electronic applications accepted. *Expenses:* Contact institution. *Financial support:* Career-related internships or fieldwork, Federal Work-Study, tuition waivers (partial), and professional educator discounts available. Financial award application deadline: 4/1; financial award applicants required to submit FAFSA. *Faculty research:* Collaboration with public schools, pre-service program development, mathematics, diversity, literacy. *Unit head:* Dr. Cathy Bear, Dean, 314-529-9692, Fax: 314-529-9921, E-mail: cbear@maryville.edu. *Application contact:* Stacey Ruffin, Coordinator of Clinical Experiences and Graduate Programs, 314-529-9542, Fax: 314-529-9921, E-mail: teachered@maryville.edu.
Website: http://www.maryville.edu/ed/graduate-programs/

Marywood University, Academic Affairs, Center for Interdisciplinary Studies, Scranton, PA 18509-1598. Offers human development (PhD), including educational administration, health promotion, higher education administration, instructional leadership, social work. *Program availability:* Part-time. Electronic applications accepted. *Expenses:* Contact institution.

Marywood University, Academic Affairs, Reap College of Education and Human Development, Department of Education, Program in Higher Education Administration, Scranton, PA 18509-1598. Offers MS. *Program availability:* Part-time, evening/weekend. Electronic applications accepted. *Faculty research:* Integrated thematic instruction.

McKendree University, Graduate Programs, Programs in Education, Lebanon, IL 62254-1299. Offers curriculum design and instruction (Ed D, Ed S); educational administration and leadership (MA Ed); educational studies (MA Ed); higher education administrative services (MA Ed); music education (MA Ed); reading (MA Ed); special education (MA Ed); teacher leadership (MA Ed); teaching certification (MA Ed). *Accreditation:* NCATE. *Program availability:* Part-time, evening/weekend, online learning. *Entrance requirements:* For master's, official transcripts from all institutions previously attended, minimum GPA of 3.0, resume, references; for doctorate, GRE (within the past 5 years), master's degree in education and Ed S, or the equivalent, from regionally-accredited institution; official transcripts from all institutions previously attended; curriculum vitae/resume; essay/personal statement; two years of teaching/professional experience; for Ed S, GRE (within the past 5 years), master's degree in education from regionally-accredited institution of higher education; official transcripts from all institutions previously attended; curriculum vitae/resume; essay/personal statement; two years of teaching/professional experience. Additional exam requirements/recommendations for international students: Required—TOEFL. Electronic applications accepted.

Mercer University, Graduate Studies, Cecil B. Day Campus, Tift College of Education (Atlanta), Atlanta, GA 30341. Offers curriculum and instruction (PhD); early childhood education (M Ed, MAT, Ed S); educational leadership (PhD), including higher education leadership, P-12 school leadership; educational leadership P-12 (M Ed, Ed S); higher education leadership (M Ed); independent and charter school leadership (M Ed); middle grades education (M Ed, MAT); secondary education (M Ed, MAT); teacher leadership (Ed S). *Accreditation:* NCATE. *Program availability:* Part-time, evening/weekend. *Faculty:* 30 full-time (18 women), 34 part-time/adjunct (27 women). *Students:* 159 full-time (131 women), 284 part-time (229 women); includes 264 minority (232 Black or African American, non-Hispanic/Latino; 1 American Indian or Alaska Native, non-Hispanic/Latino; 9 Asian, non-Hispanic/Latino; 18 Hispanic/Latino; 4 Two or more races, non-Hispanic/Latino), 2 international. Average age 35. In 2017, 137 master's, 22 doctorates, 40 other advanced degrees awarded. *Degree requirements:* For master's and Ed S, research project; for doctorate, comprehensive exam, thesis/dissertation. *Entrance requirements:* For master's, GRE or MAT, minimum undergraduate GPA of 2.75; for doctorate, GRE; for Ed S, GRE or MAT, minimum GPA of 3.25; 3 years of certified teaching experience (for educational leadership and teacher leadership). Additional exam requirements/recommendations for international students: Required—TOEFL (minimum score 80 iBT). *Application deadline:* For fall admission, 8/1 for domestic and international students; for spring admission, 12/1 for domestic and international students; for summer admission, 5/1 for domestic and international students. Applications are processed on a rolling basis. Application fee: $25 ($50 for international students). Electronic applications accepted. *Expenses:* Contact institution. *Financial support:* Federal Work-Study and unspecified assistantships available. Support available to part-time students. Financial award application deadline: 5/1; financial award applicants required to submit FAFSA. *Faculty research:* Educational technology, multicultural and minority issues in education, educational leadership (P-12 and higher education), school discipline and school bullying, standards-based mathematics education. *Unit head:* Dr. Scott Davis, Dean, 478-301-2110, Fax: 478-301-5576.
Website: http://education.mercer.edu/

Mercer University, Graduate Studies, Macon Campus, Tift College of Education (Macon), Macon, GA 31207. Offers curriculum and instruction (PhD); early childhood education (M Ed, Ed S); educational leadership (M Ed, PhD, Ed S), including higher education (PhD), P-12; higher education leadership (M Ed); independent and charter school leadership (M Ed); secondary education (MAT), including STEM; teacher leadership (Ed S). *Accreditation:* NCATE. *Program availability:* Part-time, evening/weekend, 100% online, blended/hybrid learning. *Faculty:* 13 full-time (8 women), 1 part-time/adjunct (0 women). *Students:* 33 full-time (18 women), 51 part-time (37 women); includes 49 minority (44 Black or African American, non-Hispanic/Latino; 2 Asian, non-Hispanic/Latino; 2 Hispanic/Latino; 1 Two or more races, non-Hispanic/Latino), 1 international. Average age 32. In 2017, 22 master's, 17 doctorates awarded. *Degree requirements:* For master's, research project report; for doctorate, comprehensive exam, thesis/dissertation. *Entrance requirements:* For master's, GRE or MAT, minimum GPA of 2.75; for doctorate, GRE, minimum GPA of 3.5; interview; writing sample; 3 recommendations; for Ed S, GRE or MAT, minimum GPA of 3.5 (for teacher leadership), 3.0 (for educational leadership). Additional exam requirements/recommendations for international students: Required—TOEFL (minimum score 80 iBT). *Application deadline:* For fall admission, 8/1 for domestic and international students; for spring admission, 12/1 for domestic and international students. Applications are processed on a rolling basis. Application fee: $35. Electronic applications accepted. *Expenses:* Contact institution. *Financial support:* Federal Work-Study, institutionally sponsored loans, and unspecified assistantships available. Support available to part-time students. Financial award application deadline: 5/1; financial award applicants required to submit FAFSA. *Faculty research:* Teacher effectiveness, specific learning disabilities, inclusion. *Unit head:* Dr. Scott Davis, Dean, 478-301-2110, Fax: 478-301-5576, E-mail: davis_ds@mercer.edu. Website: http://education.mercer.edu/

Mercyhurst University, Graduate Studies, Program in Organizational Leadership, Erie, PA 16546. Offers accounting (MS); higher education administration (MS); human resources (MS); organizational leadership (MS, Certificate); sports leadership (MS); strategy and innovation (MS). *Program availability:* Part-time, evening/weekend. *Degree requirements:* For master's, thesis. *Entrance requirements:* For master's, GRE General Test or MAT, interview, resume, essay, three professional references, transcripts. Additional exam requirements/recommendations for international students: Required—TOEFL (minimum score 80 iBT), IELTS (minimum score 6.5). Electronic applications accepted. *Faculty research:* Leadership training, organizational communication, leadership pedagogy.

Merrimack College, School of Education and Social Policy, North Andover, MA 01845-5800. Offers community engagement (M Ed), including community organizations, higher education, PreK-12 education; criminology and criminal justice (MS); curriculum and instruction (M Ed); early childhood education (M Ed); educational leadership (CAGS), including instructional leadership; elementary education (M Ed); English as a second language (PreK-6) (M Ed); high school education (M Ed); higher education (M Ed), including leadership and organizational development, student affairs; middle school education (M Ed); moderate disabilities (PreK-8) (M Ed); school counseling (M Ed). *Program availability:* Part-time, evening/weekend, 100% online courses with immersion events and in-classroom practicum close to home. *Faculty:* 15 full-time, 36 part-time/adjunct. *Students:* 212 full-time (175 women), 121 part-time (101 women); includes 42 minority (6 Black or African American, non-Hispanic/Latino; 6 Asian, non-Hispanic/Latino; 27 Hispanic/Latino; 3 Two or more races, non-Hispanic/Latino), 3 international. Average age 27. 420 applicants, 84% accepted, 250 enrolled. In 2017, 177 master's awarded. *Degree requirements:* For master's, practicum, portfolio, and state test (for licensure track); capstone (for higher education, curriculum and instruction, and community engagement tracks); for CAGS, capstone. *Entrance requirements:* For master's, Massachusetts Teacher Education Licensure (MTEL), official transcripts from other colleges, resume, personal statement, 2 letters of recommendation. Additional exam requirements/recommendations for international students: Required—TOEFL (minimum score 84 iBT), IELTS (minimum score 6.5), PTE (minimum score 56). *Application deadline:* For fall admission, 8/24 for domestic students, 7/30 for international students; for spring admission, 1/10 for domestic students, 12/10 for international students; for summer admission, 5/10 for domestic students, 4/10 for international students. Applications are processed on a rolling basis. Application fee: $0. Electronic applications accepted. *Expenses:* Contact institution. *Financial support:* Fellowships with full tuition reimbursements, career-related internships or fieldwork, scholarships/grants, and health care benefits available. Support available to part-time students. Financial award application deadline: 5/1; financial award applicants required to submit FAFSA. *Application contact:* Alyssa Orlando, Graduate Admissions Counselor, 978-837-3563, E-mail: orlandoaf@merrimack.edu. Website: http://www.merrimack.edu/academics/graduate/education/

Messiah College, Program in Higher Education, Mechanicsburg, PA 17055. Offers college athletics management (MA); self-designed concentration (MA); student affairs (MA). *Program availability:* Part-time. Electronic applications accepted. *Faculty research:* College athletics management, assessment and student learning outcomes, the life and legacy of Ernest L. Boyer, common learning, student affairs practice.

Michigan State University, The Graduate School, College of Education, Department of Educational Administration, East Lansing, MI 48824. Offers higher, adult and lifelong education (MA, PhD); K–12 educational administration (MA, PhD, Ed S); student affairs administration (MA). *Program availability:* Part-time. *Entrance requirements:* Additional exam requirements/recommendations for international students: Required—TOEFL. Electronic applications accepted.

Minnesota State University Mankato, College of Graduate Studies and Research, College of Social and Behavioral Sciences, Department of Sociology and Corrections, Mankato, MN 56001. Offers sociology (MA); sociology: college teaching (MA); sociology: corrections (MS); sociology: human services planning and administration (MS). *Program availability:* Part-time. *Degree requirements:* For master's, comprehensive exam, thesis or alternative. *Entrance requirements:* For master's, minimum GPA of 3.0 during previous 2 years, 3 letters of reference, resume. Additional exam requirements/recommendations for international students: Required—TOEFL. Electronic applications accepted.

Mississippi College, Graduate School, School of Education, Department of Teacher Education and Leadership, Clinton, MS 39058. Offers art (M Ed); biological science (M Ed); business education (M Ed); computer science (M Ed); dyslexia therapy (M Ed); educational leadership (M Ed, Ed D, Ed S); elementary education (M Ed, Ed S); English (M Ed); higher education administration (MS); mathematics (M Ed); secondary education (M Ed); social studies (history) (M Ed); teaching arts (M Ed). *Program availability:* Part-time, online learning. *Degree requirements:* For master's, comprehensive exam, thesis optional. *Entrance requirements:* For master's, NTE. Additional exam requirements/recommendations for international students: Recommended—TOEFL, IELTS. Electronic applications accepted.

Mississippi College, Graduate School, School of Education, Program in Higher Education Administration, Clinton, MS 39058. Offers MS. *Program availability:* Part-time, online learning. *Degree requirements:* For master's, comprehensive exam, thesis optional. *Entrance requirements:* For master's, GRE or GMAT, minimum GPA of 3.0. Additional exam requirements/recommendations for international students: Recommended—TOEFL, IELTS.

Mississippi State University, College of Education, Educational Leadership Program, Mississippi State, MS 39762. Offers community college education (MAT); community college leadership (PhD); higher education leadership (PhD); P-12 school leadership (PhD); school administration (MS, Ed S); student affairs and higher education (MS); workforce education leadership (MS). MS in workforce education leadership held jointly with Alcorn State University. *Faculty:* 12 full-time (9 women). *Students:* 62 full-time (33 women), 149 part-time (93 women); includes 94 minority (79 Black or African American, non-Hispanic/Latino; 5 American Indian or Alaska Native, non-Hispanic/Latino; 4 Hispanic/Latino; 1 Native Hawaiian or other Pacific Islander, non-Hispanic/Latino; 5 Two or more races, non-Hispanic/Latino). Average age 36. 95 applicants, 79% accepted, 64

enrolled. In 2017, 41 master's, 32 doctorates, 7 other advanced degrees awarded. *Degree requirements:* For master's and Ed S, comprehensive exam, thesis; for doctorate, comprehensive exam, thesis/dissertation. *Entrance requirements:* For master's, GRE, minimum GPA of 2.75 in junior and senior courses; for doctorate, GRE, minimum GPA of 3.4 on previous graduate work; for Ed S, GRE, minimum GPA of 3.2, master's degree. Additional exam requirements/recommendations for international students: Required—TOEFL (minimum score 550 paper-based; 79 iBT); Recommended—IELTS (minimum score 6.5). *Application deadline:* For fall admission, 7/1 for domestic students, 5/1 for international students; for spring admission, 11/1 for domestic students, 9/1 for international students. Application fee: $60 ($80 for international students). Electronic applications accepted. *Expenses:* Tuition, state resident: full-time $8318; part-time $462.12 per credit hour. Tuition, nonresident: full-time $22,358; part-time $1242.12 per credit hour. *Required fees:* $110; $12.24 per credit hour. $6.12 per semester. *Financial support:* In 2017–18, 1 research assistantship with full tuition reimbursement (averaging $10,879 per year) was awarded; Federal Work-Study, institutionally sponsored loans, and unspecified assistantships also available. Financial award application deadline: 4/1; financial award applicants required to submit FAFSA. *Unit head:* Dr. Eric Moyen, Associate Professor and Head, 662-325-0969, Fax: 662-325-0975, E-mail: em1621@msstate.edu. *Application contact:* Nathan Drake, Admissions and Enrollment Assistant, 662-325-3804, E-mail: ndrake@grad.msstate.edu. Website: http://www.educationalleadership.msstate.edu/

Missouri State University, Graduate College, College of Education, Department of Counseling, Leadership, and Special Education, Program in Student Affairs in Higher Education, Springfield, MO 65897. Offers MS. *Program availability:* Part-time. *Faculty:* 6 full-time (4 women). *Students:* 22 full-time (18 women), 5 part-time (4 women); includes 8 minority (3 Black or African American, non-Hispanic/Latino; 1 Asian, non-Hispanic/Latino; 1 Hispanic/Latino; 3 Two or more races, non-Hispanic/Latino), 2 international. Average age 23. 17 applicants, 76% accepted, 4 enrolled. In 2017, 16 master's awarded. *Degree requirements:* For master's, comprehensive exam, thesis or alternative. *Entrance requirements:* For master's, GRE, statement of purpose; three references. Additional exam requirements/recommendations for international students: Required—TOEFL (minimum score 550 paper-based; 79 iBT), IELTS (minimum score 6). *Application deadline:* For fall admission, 2/1 priority date for domestic students, 2/1 for international students. Applications are processed on a rolling basis. Application fee: $35 ($50 for international students). Electronic applications accepted. *Expenses:* Tuition, state resident: full-time $2915; part-time $2021 per credit hour. Tuition, nonresident: full-time $5354; part-time $3647 per credit hour. *International tuition:* $11,992 full-time. *Required fees:* $173; $173 per credit hour. Tuition and fees vary according to class time, course level, course load, degree level, campus/location and program. *Financial support:* Federal Work-Study, institutionally sponsored loans, scholarships/grants, and unspecified assistantships available. Financial award application deadline: 3/31; financial award applicants required to submit FAFSA. *Unit head:* Dr. James Satterfield, Department Head, 417-836-5392, E-mail: clse@missouristate.edu. *Application contact:* Stephanie Praschan, Director, Graduate Enrollment Management, 417-836-5330, Fax: 417-836-6200, E-mail: stephaniepraschan@missouristate.edu. Website: http://education.missouristate.edu/edadmin/MSEDSA.htm

Montana State University, The Graduate School, College of Education, Health, and Human Development, Department of Education, Bozeman, MT 59717. Offers adult and higher education (Ed D); curriculum and instruction (M Ed, Ed D), including professional educator (M Ed); technology education (M Ed); education (M Ed), including adult and higher education, educational leadership, school counseling; educational leadership (Ed D, Ed S). *Accreditation:* TEAC. *Program availability:* Part-time, online learning. *Degree requirements:* For master's, comprehensive exam; for doctorate, comprehensive exam, thesis/dissertation. *Entrance requirements:* For master's, GRE, 3 letters of reference, essays, BA transcripts; for doctorate, GRE, MAT, 3 letters of reference, essay, BA and M Ed transcripts; for Ed S, PRAXIS. Additional exam requirements/recommendations for international students: Required—TOEFL (minimum score 550 paper-based). Electronic applications accepted. *Faculty research:* Critical literacy; standards-based education; school Improvement, organizational change, leadership in rural education, leadership in Indian education; student Learning; multicultural/culturally responsive education for social justice Native American indigenous education, community-centered education teacher preparation.

Morehead State University, Graduate Programs, College of Education, Department of Foundational and Graduate Studies in Education, Morehead, KY 40351. Offers adult and higher education (MA, Ed S); certified professional counselor (Ed S); counseling P-12 (MA); curriculum and instruction (Ed S); educational technology (MA Ed); instructional leadership (Ed S); school administration (MA); school counseling (Ed S); teacher leader business and marketing content (MA Ed); teacher leader business and marketing technology (MA Ed); teacher leader educational technology (MA Ed); teacher leader English (MA Ed); teacher leader gifted education (MA Ed); teacher leader IECE certification (MA Ed); teacher leader interdisciplinary education P-5 (MA Ed); teacher leader middle grades (MA Ed); teacher leader non IECE certification (MA Ed); teacher leader reading/writing - non-certification (MA Ed); teacher leader reading/writing certification (MA Ed); teacher leader school communication - certification (MA Ed); teacher leader school communication - non-certification (MA Ed); teacher leader social studies (MA Ed); teacher leader special education (MA Ed). *Accreditation:* NCATE. *Program availability:* Part-time, evening/weekend. *Degree requirements:* For master's, thesis optional, oral and/or written comprehensive exams; for Ed S, thesis, oral exam. *Entrance requirements:* For master's, GRE General Test, minimum overall undergraduate GPA of 2.5; for Ed S, GRE General Test, interview, master's degree, minimum GPA of 3.5, work experience. Additional exam requirements/recommendations for international students: Required—TOEFL (minimum score 500 paper-based). Electronic applications accepted. *Faculty research:* Character education, school accountability, computer applications for school administrators.

Morgan State University, School of Graduate Studies, School of Education and Urban Studies, Department of Advanced Studies, Leadership and Policy, Program in Higher Education Administration, Baltimore, MD 21251. Offers higher education (PhD); higher education and student affairs administration (MA). *Degree requirements:* For doctorate, comprehensive exam, thesis/dissertation. *Entrance requirements:* For doctorate, GRE General Test or MAT, minimum GPA of 3.0. *Application deadline:* For fall admission, 2/1 priority date for domestic students; for spring admission, 10/1 priority date for domestic students. Applications are processed on a rolling basis. Application fee: $0. *Expenses:* Tuition, state resident: part-time $433 per credit. Tuition, nonresident: part-time $851 per credit. *Required fees:* $81.50 per credit. *Financial support:* Application deadline: 2/1. *Unit head:* Dr. Sean Robinson, Admissions Coordinator, E-mail: sean.robinson@morgan.edu. *Application contact:* Dr. Dean Campbell, Graduate Recruitment Specialist, 443-885-3185, Fax: 443-885-8226, E-mail: dean.campbell@morgan.edu.

National American University, Roueche Graduate Center, Austin, TX 78731. Offers accounting (MBA); aviation management (MBA, MM); care coordination (MSN); community college leadership (Ed D); criminal justice (MM); e-marketing (MBA, MM); health care administration (MBA, MM); higher education (MM); human resources management (MBA, MM); information technology management (MBA, MM); international business (MBA); leadership (EMBA); management (MBA); nursing administration (MSN); nursing education (MSN); nursing informatics (MSN); operations and configuration management (MBA, MM); project and process management (MBA, MM). Master's programs offered online through the Harold D. Buckingham Graduate School. *Program availability:* Part-time, evening/weekend, online learning. *Entrance requirements:* For master's, minimum undergraduate GPA of 2.75. Additional exam requirements/recommendations for international students: Required—TOEFL, TWE. Electronic applications accepted. *Faculty research:* Tourism, finance, marketing.

National University, Academic Affairs, Sanford College of Education, La Jolla, CA 92037-1011. Offers advanced teaching practices (MS); applied behavior analysis (MS); applied school leadership (MS); e-teaching and learning (Certificate); education (MA); educational administration (MS); educational and instructional technology (MS); educational counseling (MS); higher education administration (MS); inspired teaching and learning (M Ed); school psychology (MS); special education (MA, MS). *Program availability:* Part-time, evening/weekend, 100% online, blended/hybrid learning. *Degree requirements:* For master's, thesis (for some programs). *Entrance requirements:* For master's, interview, minimum GPA of 2.5. Additional exam requirements/ recommendations for international students: Required—TOEFL (minimum score 550 paper-based; 79 iBT), IELTS (minimum score 6). *Application deadline:* Applications are processed on a rolling basis. Application fee: $60 ($65 for international students). Electronic applications accepted. *Expenses: Tuition:* Part-time $430 per quarter hour. *Financial support:* Career-related internships or fieldwork, institutionally sponsored loans, scholarships/grants, and tuition waivers (partial) available. Support available to part-time students. Financial award application deadline: 6/30. *Faculty research:* Teacher education, special education, educational effectiveness, teaching abroad, school counseling. *Unit head:* Dr. Judy Mantle, Dean, 858-642-8320, E-mail: soe@ nu.edu. *Application contact:* Brandon Jouganatos, Vice President for Enrollment Services, 800-628-8648, E-mail: advisor@nu.edu.
Website: http://www.nu.edu/OurPrograms/SchoolOfEducation.html

New England College, Program in Education, Henniker, NH 03242-3293. Offers higher education administration (MS, Ed D); K-12 leadership (Ed D); literacy and language arts (M Ed); meeting the needs of all learners/special education (M Ed); teacher leadership/ school reform (M Ed). *Program availability:* Part-time, evening/weekend.

New Mexico State University, College of Education, Department of Educational Leadership and Administration, Las Cruces, NM 88003. Offers educational administration (MA), including community college and university administration, PK-12 public school administration; educational leadership (Ed D, PhD). *Accreditation:* NCATE. *Program availability:* Part-time-only, evening/weekend, blended/hybrid learning. *Faculty:* 6 full-time (5 women), 2 part-time/adjunct (1 woman). *Students:* 11 full-time (10 women), 124 part-time (88 women); includes 93 minority (2 Black or African American, non-Hispanic/Latino; 8 American Indian or Alaska Native, non-Hispanic/ Latino; 3 Asian, non-Hispanic/Latino; 78 Hispanic/Latino; 1 Native Hawaiian or other Pacific Islander, non-Hispanic/Latino; 1 Two or more races, non-Hispanic/Latino), 1 international. Average age 41. 29 applicants, 28% accepted, 8 enrolled. In 2017, 26 master's, 9 doctorates awarded. *Degree requirements:* For master's, comprehensive exam, internship; for doctorate, comprehensive exam, thesis/dissertation, internship. *Entrance requirements:* For doctorate, minimum GPA of 3.0, master's degree. Additional exam requirements/recommendations for international students: Required—TOEFL (minimum score 550 paper-based; 79 iBT), IELTS (minimum score 6.5). *Application deadline:* For spring admission, 11/15 for domestic and international students. Application fee: $40 ($50 for international students). Electronic applications accepted. *Expenses:* Tuition, state resident: full-time $4390. Tuition, nonresident: full-time $15,309. *Required fees:* $853. *Financial support:* In 2017–18, 21 students received support, including 4 research assistantships (averaging $17,489 per year), 1 teaching assistantship (averaging $8,684 per year); career-related internships or fieldwork, Federal Work-Study, scholarships/grants, traineeships, health care benefits, and unspecified assistantships also available. Support available to part-time students. Financial award application deadline: 3/1. *Faculty research:* Leadership in pk-12 and postsecondary education, community college administration, distance education administration, leadership for social justice, educational change. *Total annual research expenditures:* $2,456. *Unit head:* Dr. Azadeh Osanloo, Department Head, 575-646-5976, Fax: 575-646-4767, E-mail: azadeh@nmsu.edu. *Application contact:* Denise Rodriguez-Strawn, Program Coordinator, 575-646-3825, Fax: 575-646-4767, E-mail: edmandev@nmsu.edu.
Website: http://ela.nmsu.edu/

New York University, Steinhardt School of Culture, Education, and Human Development, Department of Administration, Leadership, and Technology, Program in Higher Education, New York, NY 10012. Offers higher and postsecondary education (PhD); higher education administration (Ed D); higher education and student affairs (MA). *Accreditation:* TEAC. *Program availability:* Part-time. *Students:* Average age 36. 222 applicants, 18% accepted, 34 enrolled. In 2017, 52 master's, 10 doctorates awarded. *Entrance requirements:* For master's, interview, 2 letters of recommendation; for doctorate, GRE General Test, interview. Additional exam requirements/ recommendations for international students: Required—TOEFL (minimum score 100 iBT). *Application deadline:* For fall admission, 12/1 priority date for domestic and international students; for spring admission, 10/1 for domestic and international students. Applications are processed on a rolling basis. Application fee: $75. Electronic applications accepted. *Expenses: Tuition:* Full-time $41,352; part-time $19,968 per year. *Required fees:* $2496; $1628 per unit. $814 per term. Tuition and fees vary according to course load and program. *Financial support:* Fellowships with full and partial tuition reimbursements, career-related internships or fieldwork, Federal Work-Study, institutionally sponsored loans, scholarships/grants, tuition waivers (partial), and unspecified assistantships available. Support available to part-time students. Financial award application deadline: 2/1; financial award applicants required to submit FAFSA. *Faculty research:* Organizational theory and culture, systemic change, leadership development, access, equity and diversity. *Unit head:* Prof. Ann Marcus, Director, 212-998-5276, Fax: 212-995-4041, E-mail: alm1@nyu.edu. *Application contact:* 212-998-5030, Fax: 212-995-4328, E-mail: steinhardt.gradadmissions@nyu.edu.
Website: http://steinhardt.nyu.edu/alt/highered

New York University, Steinhardt School of Culture, Education, and Human Development, Department of Music and Performing Arts Professions, Program in Educational Theatre, New York, NY 10012. Offers educational theatre and English 7-12 (MA); educational theatre and social studies 7-12 (MA); educational theatre in colleges and communities (MA, Ed D, PhD); educational theatre, all grades (MA). *Program availability:* Part-time. *Students:* Average age 28. 90 applicants, 76% accepted, 37 enrolled. In 2017, 47 master's, 5 doctorates awarded. *Entrance requirements:* For master's, audition; for doctorate, GRE General Test, interview. Additional exam requirements/recommendations for international students: Required—TOEFL (minimum score 100 iBT). *Application deadline:* For fall admission, 12/1 priority date for domestic and international students; for spring admission, 10/1 for domestic and international students. Applications are processed on a rolling basis. Application fee: $75. Electronic applications accepted. *Expenses: Tuition:* Full-time $41,352; part-time $19,968 per year.

Required fees: $2496; $1628 per unit. $814 per term. Tuition and fees vary according to course load and program. *Financial support:* Teaching assistantships with partial tuition reimbursements, career-related internships or fieldwork, Federal Work-Study, institutionally sponsored loans, and scholarships/grants available. Support available to part-time students. Financial award application deadline: 2/1; financial award applicants required to submit FAFSA. *Faculty research:* Theatre for young audiences, drama in education, applied theatre, arts education assessment, reflective praxis. *Unit head:* Prof. David Montgomery, Director, 212-998-5869, Fax: 212-995-4043, E-mail: dm635@ nyu.edu. *Application contact:* 212-998-5030, Fax: 212-995-4328, E-mail: steinhardt.gradadmissions@nyu.edu.
Website: http://steinhardt.nyu.edu/music/edtheatre

North Carolina State University, Graduate School, College of Education, Department of Adult and Higher Education, Program in Higher Education Administration, Raleigh, NC 27695. Offers M Ed, MS, Ed D. *Degree requirements:* For master's, thesis (for some programs); for doctorate, thesis/dissertation. *Entrance requirements:* For master's and doctorate, GRE General Test or MAT, minimum GPA of 3.0 in major. Electronic applications accepted.

North Dakota State University, College of Graduate and Interdisciplinary Studies, Program in College Teaching, Fargo, ND 58102. Offers Certificate. *Entrance requirements:* For degree, minimum cumulative GPA of 3.0. Electronic applications accepted.

Northeastern University, College of Professional Studies, Boston, MA 02115-5096. Offers applied nutrition (MS); college athletics administration (MSL); commerce and economic development (MS); corporate and organizational communication (MS); criminal justice (MS); digital media (MPS); elearning and instructional design (M Ed); elementary education (MAT); geographic information technology (MPS); global studies and international relations (MS); higher education administration (M Ed); homeland security (MA); human services (MS); informatics (MPS); leadership (MS); learning analytics (M Ed); learning and instruction (M Ed); nonprofit management (MS); professional sports administration (MSL); project management (MS); regulatory affairs for drugs, biologics, and medical devices (MS); respiratory care leadership (MS); special education (M Ed); technical communication (MS). *Program availability:* Part-time, evening/weekend, 100% online, blended/hybrid learning. *Faculty:* 82 full-time (51 women), 853 part-time/adjunct (366 women). *Students:* 5,278 part-time (3,230 women). In 2017, 1,586 master's awarded. *Application deadline:* Applications are processed on a rolling basis. Application fee: $0. Electronic applications accepted. *Expenses:* Contact institution. *Financial support:* Applicants required to submit FAFSA. *Unit head:* Dr. Mary Loeffelholz, Dean of the College of Professional Studies. *Application contact:* E-mail: cpsadmissions@northeastern.edu.
Website: https://cps.northeastern.edu/

Northern Arizona University, College of Education, Department of Educational Leadership, Flagstaff, AZ 86011. Offers community college teaching and learning (Graduate Certificate); educational leadership (M Ed, Ed D), including community college/higher education (M Ed), educational foundations (M Ed), instructional leadership K-12 school leadership (M Ed), principal certification K-12 (M Ed); principal (Graduate Certificate); superintendent (Graduate Certificate). *Program availability:* Part-time. *Faculty:* 24 full-time (10 women), 1 (woman) part-time/adjunct. *Students:* 193 full-time (128 women), 648 part-time (425 women); includes 329 minority (54 Black or African American, non-Hispanic/Latino; 63 American Indian or Alaska Native, non-Hispanic/Latino; 10 Asian, non-Hispanic/Latino; 169 Hispanic/Latino; 1 Native Hawaiian or other Pacific Islander, non-Hispanic/Latino; 32 Two or more races, non-Hispanic/ Latino), 2 international. Average age 38. 298 applicants, 98% accepted, 291 enrolled. In 2017, 252 master's, 12 doctorates, 48 other advanced degrees awarded. *Degree requirements:* For master's, comprehensive exam, thesis (for some programs); for doctorate, comprehensive exam, thesis/dissertation; for Graduate Certificate, comprehensive exam (for some programs). *Entrance requirements:* Additional exam requirements/recommendations for international students: Required—TOEFL (minimum score 80 iBT), IELTS (minimum score 6.5). *Application deadline:* For fall admission, 3/1 for domestic and international students; for spring admission, 10/1 for domestic and international students. Applications are processed on a rolling basis. Application fee: $65. Electronic applications accepted. *Expenses:* Tuition, state resident: full-time $9240; part-time $458 per credit hour. Tuition, nonresident: full-time $21,588; part-time $1199 per credit hour. *Required fees:* $1021; $14 per credit hour. $646 per semester. Tuition and fees vary according to course load, campus/location and program. *Financial support:* In 2017–18, 1 student received support. Institutionally sponsored loans, health care benefits, tuition waivers (partial), and unspecified assistantships available. Financial award application deadline: 2/1; financial award applicants required to submit FAFSA. *Unit head:* Dr. Michael Schwanenberger, Chair, 928-523-3202, Fax: 928-523-1929, E-mail: michael.schwanenberger@nau.edu. *Application contact:* Jennifer Offutt, Administrative Assistant, 928-523-3202, Fax: 928-523-1929, E-mail: jennifer.offutt@ nau.edu.
Website: https://nau.edu/coe/Ed-Leadership

Northern Illinois University, Graduate School, College of Education, Department of Counseling, Adult and Higher Education, De Kalb, IL 60115-2854. Offers adult and higher education (MS Ed, Ed D); counseling (MS Ed, Ed D). *Accreditation:* ACA. *Program availability:* Part-time, evening/weekend. *Faculty:* 19 full-time (11 women), 2 part-time/adjunct (1 woman). *Students:* 114 full-time (80 women), 215 part-time (156 women); includes 136 minority (74 Black or African American, non-Hispanic/Latino; 2 American Indian or Alaska Native, non-Hispanic/Latino; 11 Asian, non-Hispanic/Latino; 37 Hispanic/Latino; 12 Two or more races, non-Hispanic/Latino), 8 international. Average age 36. 124 applicants, 77% accepted, 49 enrolled. In 2017, 67 master's, 16 doctorates awarded. Terminal master's awarded for partial completion of doctoral program. *Degree requirements:* For master's, comprehensive exam, thesis optional; for doctorate, thesis/dissertation, candidacy exam, dissertation defense. *Entrance requirements:* For master's, GRE General Test or MAT, minimum undergraduate GPA of 2.75, interview (for counseling); for doctorate, GRE General Test, minimum undergraduate GPA of 2.75, 3.2 graduate; interview (for counseling). Additional exam requirements/recommendations for international students: Required—TOEFL (minimum score 550 paper-based). *Application deadline:* For fall admission, 6/1 for domestic students, 5/1 for international students; for spring admission, 11/1 for domestic students, 10/1 for international students. Applications are processed on a rolling basis. Application fee: $40. Electronic applications accepted. *Financial support:* In 2017–18, 15 research assistantships with full tuition reimbursements, 7 teaching assistantships with full tuition reimbursements were awarded; fellowships with full tuition reimbursements, career-related internships or fieldwork, Federal Work-Study, scholarships/grants, tuition waivers (full), and staff assistantships also available. Support available to part-time students. Financial award applicants required to submit FAFSA. *Unit head:* Dr. Suzanne Degges-White, Interim Chair, 815-753-1448, E-mail: cahe@niu.edu. *Application contact:* Graduate School Office, 815-753-0395, E-mail: gradsch@niu.edu.
Website: http://www.cedu.niu.edu/cahe/index.html

Northwest Missouri State University, Graduate School, School of Education, Maryville, MO 64468-6001. Offers early childhood education (MS Ed); education leadership (MS Ed), including elementary, K-12, secondary; educational leadership

Higher Education

(Ed S), including elementary school principalship, secondary school principalship, superintendency; educational leadership and policy analysis (Ed D); elementary education (MS Ed); elementary mathematics (MS Ed); higher education leadership (MS); middle school education (MS Ed); reading (MS Ed); special education (MS Ed); teacher leadership (MS Ed); teaching English language learners (MS Ed). *Accreditation:* NCATE. *Program availability:* Part-time. *Faculty:* 15 full-time (8 women). *Students:* 28 full-time (20 women), 170 part-time (114 women); includes 20 minority (7 Black or African American, non-Hispanic/Latino; 1 Asian, non-Hispanic/Latino; 8 Hispanic/Latino; 4 Two or more races, non-Hispanic/Latino. Average age 33. 168 applicants, 73% accepted, 114 enrolled. In 2017, 67 master's, 21 other advanced degrees awarded. *Degree requirements:* For master's, comprehensive exam; for Ed S, comprehensive exam, thesis. *Entrance requirements:* For master's, GRE General Test, writing sample; for Ed S, minimum graduate GPA of 3.25. Additional exam requirements/recommendations for international students: Required—TOEFL (minimum score 550 paper-based). *Application deadline:* For fall admission, 7/1 for domestic and international students; for spring admission, 11/15 for domestic and international students. Applications are processed on a rolling basis. Application fee: $0 ($50 for international students). Electronic applications accepted. *Expenses:* $389.11 per credit hour in-state tuition and fees, $641.97 out-of-state; $9,750 total cost (for online-based education program). *Financial support:* Research assistantships with full tuition reimbursements, teaching assistantships with full tuition reimbursements, and unspecified assistantships available. Financial award application deadline: 4/1; financial award applicants required to submit FAFSA. *Unit head:* Dr. Tim Wall, Director, 660-562-1179, E-mail: timwall@nwmissouri.edu.
Website: https://www.nwmissouri.edu/education/index.htm

Oakland University, Graduate Study and Lifelong Learning, School of Education and Human Services, Department of Organizational Leadership, Rochester, MI 48309-4401. Offers educational leadership (M Ed, PhD); higher education (Certificate); school administration (Ed S). *Entrance requirements:* Additional exam requirements/recommendations for international students: Required—TOEFL (minimum score 550 paper-based). *Expenses:* Tuition, state resident: full-time $16,950; part-time $706.25 per credit. Tuition, nonresident: full-time $24,648; part-time $1027 per credit.

Ohio University, Graduate College, Gladys W. and David H. Patton College of Education and Human Services, Department of Counseling and Higher Education, Athens, OH 45701-2979. Offers college student personnel (M Ed); community/agency counseling (M Ed); counselor education (PhD); higher education (PhD); rehabilitation counseling (M Ed); school counseling (M Ed). *Accreditation:* ACA; CORE. *Program availability:* Part-time, evening/weekend. *Degree requirements:* For master's, comprehensive exam (for some programs), thesis or alternative; for doctorate, comprehensive exam, thesis/dissertation. *Entrance requirements:* For master's, GRE General Test or MAT (if GPA less than 2.9), 3 letters of reference; for doctorate, GRE General Test, work experience, minimum GPA of 3.4. Additional exam requirements/recommendations for international students: Required—TOEFL (minimum score 550 paper-based; 80 iBT) or IELTS (minimum score 6.5). Electronic applications accepted. *Faculty research:* Youth violence, gender studies, student affairs, chemical dependency, disabilities issues.

Oklahoma State University, College of Education, Health and Aviation, School of Educational Studies, Stillwater, OK 74078. Offers higher education (Ed D). *Program availability:* Part-time. *Faculty:* 28 full-time (15 women), 31 part-time/adjunct (8 women). *Students:* 66 full-time (38 women), 232 part-time (120 women); includes 85 minority (20 Black or African American, non-Hispanic/Latino; 18 American Indian or Alaska Native, non-Hispanic/Latino; 3 Asian, non-Hispanic/Latino; 21 Hispanic/Latino; 2 Native Hawaiian or other Pacific Islander, non-Hispanic/Latino; 21 Two or more races, non-Hispanic/Latino), 5 international. Average age 38. 110 applicants, 83% accepted, 80 enrolled. In 2017, 42 master's, 25 doctorates awarded. *Entrance requirements:* For master's and doctorate, GRE or GMAT. Additional exam requirements/recommendations for international students: Required—TOEFL (minimum score 550 paper-based; 79 iBT). *Application deadline:* For fall admission, 3/1 priority date for international students; for spring admission, 8/1 priority date for international students. Applications are processed on a rolling basis. Application fee: $40 ($75 for international students). Electronic applications accepted. *Expenses:* Tuition, state resident: full-time $4019; part-time $2679.60 per year. Tuition, nonresident: full-time $15,286; part-time $10,190.40 per year. *Required fees:* $2129; $1419 per unit. Tuition and fees vary according to program. *Financial support:* Research assistantships, teaching assistantships, career-related internships or fieldwork, Federal Work-Study, scholarships/grants, health care benefits, tuition waivers (partial), and unspecified assistantships available. Support available to part-time students. Financial award application deadline: 3/1; financial award applicants required to submit FAFSA. *Unit head:* Dr. Jesse Mendez, Head, 405-744-9447, Fax: 405-744-7758, E-mail: jesse.perez.mendez@okstate.edu.
Website: http://education.okstate.edu/

Old Dominion University, Darden College of Education, Doctoral Program in Higher Education, Norfolk, VA 23529. Offers PhD. *Program availability:* Part-time, online learning. *Faculty:* 5 full-time (2 women), 8 part-time/adjunct (2 women). *Students:* 6 full-time (4 women), 20 part-time (15 women); includes 12 minority (8 Black or African American, non-Hispanic/Latino; 1 Asian, non-Hispanic/Latino; 2 Hispanic/Latino; 1 Two or more races, non-Hispanic/Latino). Average age 36. 16 applicants, 50% accepted, 6 enrolled. In 2017, 5 doctorates awarded. *Degree requirements:* For doctorate, comprehensive exam, thesis/dissertation. *Entrance requirements:* For doctorate, GRE, master's degree, minimum graduate GPA of 3.5. Additional exam requirements/recommendations for international students: Required—TOEFL. *Application deadline:* For spring admission, 2/1 for domestic and international students. Application fee: $50. Electronic applications accepted. *Expenses:* Tuition, state resident: full-time $8928; part-time $496 per credit. Tuition, nonresident: full-time $22,482; part-time $1249 per credit. *Required fees:* $66 per semester. *Financial support:* In 2017–18, 2 fellowships with tuition reimbursements (averaging $15,000 per year), research assistantships with full tuition reimbursements (averaging $15,000 per year), 6 teaching assistantships with full tuition reimbursements (averaging $15,000 per year) were awarded; career-related internships or fieldwork, tuition waivers (full), and unspecified assistantships also available. Financial award application deadline: 2/1. *Faculty research:* Law leadership, student development, research administration, international higher education administration, academic integrity, leadership. *Unit head:* Dr. Chris Glass, Graduate Program Director, 757-683-4118, E-mail: hied@odu.edu.

Old Dominion University, Darden College of Education, Programs in Higher Education, Norfolk, VA 23529. Offers MS Ed, Ed S. *Program availability:* Part-time. *Faculty:* 6 full-time (2 women), 6 part-time/adjunct (3 women). *Students:* 31 full-time (23 women), 15 part-time (10 women); includes 17 minority (8 Black or African American, non-Hispanic/Latino; 2 American Indian or Alaska Native, non-Hispanic/Latino; 2 Asian, non-Hispanic/Latino; 3 Hispanic/Latino; 2 Two or more races, non-Hispanic/Latino), 5 international. Average age 28. 59 applicants, 47% accepted, 16 enrolled. In 2017, 19 master's, 3 Ed Ss awarded. *Degree requirements:* For master's, comprehensive exam. *Entrance requirements:* For master's, GRE; for Ed S, GRE, 2 letters of reference, minimum GPA of 3.5, master's degree. Additional exam requirements/recommendations for international students: Required—TOEFL. *Application deadline:* For fall admission, 2/1 priority date for domestic and international students; for winter admission, 10/1 for

domestic and international students; for spring admission, 2/1 for domestic and international students. Application fee: $50. Electronic applications accepted. *Expenses:* Tuition, state resident: full-time $8928; part-time $496 per credit. Tuition, nonresident: full-time $22,482; part-time $1249 per credit. *Required fees:* $66 per semester. *Financial support:* Research assistantships with partial tuition reimbursements, career-related internships or fieldwork, scholarships/grants, and unspecified assistantships available. *Faculty research:* Law leadership, student development, research administration, international higher education administration. *Unit head:* Dr. Chris Glass, Graduate Program Director, 757-683-4118, E-mail: hied@odu.edu. *Application contact:* William Heffelfinger, Director of Graduate Admissions, 757-683-5554, Fax: 757-683-3255, E-mail: gradadmit@odu.edu.
Website: http://education.odu.edu/efl/academics/hied

Oral Roberts University, School of Education, Tulsa, OK 74171. Offers Christian school administration (K-12) (MA Ed, Ed D); college and higher education administration (Ed D); curriculum and instruction (MA Ed); initial teaching with alternative licensure (MAT); initial teaching with licensure (MAT); public school administration (K-12) (MA Ed, Ed D). *Accreditation:* NCATE. *Program availability:* Part-time, online learning. *Faculty:* 7 full-time (2 women), 6 part-time/adjunct (2 women). *Students:* 344 full-time (223 women); includes 117 minority (93 Black or African American, non-Hispanic/Latino; 7 American Indian or Alaska Native, non-Hispanic/Latino; 11 Asian, non-Hispanic/Latino; 6 Hispanic/Latino). 80 applicants, 94% accepted, 65 enrolled. In 2017, 14 master's, 4 doctorates awarded. *Degree requirements:* For master's, comprehensive exam, thesis optional; for doctorate, comprehensive exam, thesis/dissertation. *Entrance requirements:* For master's, GRE General Test or MAT (minimum score in 80th percentile or higher); Oklahoma general education or subject area test (for MAT), minimum GPA of 3.0, bachelor's degree from regionally-accredited institution; for doctorate, minimum GPA of 3.0, master's degree from regionally-accredited institution. *Application deadline:* Applications are processed on a rolling basis. Application fee: $35. Electronic applications accepted. Application fee is waived when completed online. *Expenses:* Contact institution. *Financial support:* Fellowships and scholarships/grants available. Financial award application deadline: 3/15. *Faculty research:* Teacher effectiveness, college success in high achieving African-Americans, professional development practices. *Unit head:* Dr. Patrick Otto, Chair of Graduate School of Education, 918-495-7087, E-mail: jotto@oru.edu. *Application contact:* Audrey Ripley, Enrollment Counselor, 918-495-6375, E-mail: aripley@oru.edu.

Oregon State University, College of Education, Program in Adult and Higher Education, Corvallis, OR 97331. Offers Ed M, Ed D, PhD. *Accreditation:* NCATE. *Program availability:* Part-time, blended/hybrid learning. *Entrance requirements:* For master's, minimum GPA of 3.0 in last 90 hours. Additional exam requirements/recommendations for international students: Required—TOEFL (minimum score 575 paper-based). *Application deadline:* For fall admission, 3/15 for domestic students. Applications are processed on a rolling basis. Application fee: $75 ($85 for international students). *Unit head:* Dr. Erich N. Pitcher, Program Lead, 541-737-3574. *Application contact:* Dr. Erich N. Pitcher, Program Lead, 541-737-3574.
Website: http://education.oregonstate.edu/adult-education-masters-degree-program

Penn State University Park, Graduate School, College of Education, Department of Education Policy Studies, University Park, PA 16802. Offers educational leadership (M Ed, D Ed, PhD, Certificate); educational theory and policy (MA, PhD); higher education (M Ed, D Ed, PhD). *Accreditation:* NCATE. *Program availability:* Online learning. *Unit head:* Dr. David H. Monk, Dean, 814-865-2523, Fax: 814-865-0555. *Application contact:* Lori Hawn, Director, Graduate Student Services, 814-865-1795, Fax: 814-863-4627, E-mail: l-gswww@lists.psu.edu.
Website: http://ed.psu.edu/eps

Phillips Theological Seminary, Programs in Theology, Tulsa, OK 74116. Offers administration of church agencies (M Div); campus ministry (M Div); church-related social work (M Div); college and seminary teaching (M Div); global mission work (M Div); institutional chaplaincy (M Div); ministerial vocations in Christian education (M Div); ministry (D Min), including parish ministry, pastoral counseling, practices of ministry; ministry and culture (MAMC), including Christian education, congregational leadership, history and practice of Christian spirituality, theology, ethics, and culture; ministry of music (M Div); pastoral care and counseling (M Div); pastoral ministry (M Div); theological studies (MTS). *Accreditation:* ATS. *Program availability:* Part-time, online learning. *Degree requirements:* For master's, thesis (for some programs); for doctorate, thesis/dissertation. *Entrance requirements:* For master's, minimum GPA of 2.5; for doctorate, M Div, minimum GPA of 3.0. *Faculty research:* Biblical studies, historical studies, theology and culture, practical theology, theology and film.

Plymouth State University, College of Graduate Studies, Graduate Studies in Education, Certificate of Advanced Graduate Studies Programs, Plymouth, NH 03264-1595. Offers clinical mental health counseling (CAGS); educational leadership (CAGS); higher education (CAGS); school psychology (CAGS). *Program availability:* Part-time, evening/weekend.

Plymouth State University, College of Graduate Studies, Graduate Studies in Education, Program in Higher Education, Plymouth, NH 03264-1595. Offers Ed D.

Purdue University, Graduate School, College of Education, Department of Educational Studies, West Lafayette, IN 47907. Offers administration (MS Ed, PhD, Ed S); counseling and development (MS Ed, PhD); education of the gifted (MS Ed); educational psychology (MS Ed, PhD); foundations of education (MS Ed, PhD); higher education administration (MS Ed, PhD); special education (MS Ed, PhD). *Accreditation:* ACA (one or more programs are accredited); NCATE (one or more programs are accredited). *Program availability:* Part-time, evening/weekend. *Faculty:* 29 full-time (22 women), 1 part-time/adjunct (0 women). *Students:* 78 full-time (60 women), 226 part-time (162 women); includes 45 minority (16 Black or African American, non-Hispanic/Latino; 8 Asian, non-Hispanic/Latino; 15 Hispanic/Latino; 6 Two or more races, non-Hispanic/Latino), 45 international. Average age 32. 214 applicants, 53% accepted, 70 enrolled. In 2017, 38 master's, 20 doctorates, 4 other advanced degrees awarded. *Degree requirements:* For master's, thesis optional; for doctorate, thesis/dissertation, oral and written exams; for Ed S, oral presentation, project. *Entrance requirements:* For master's, GRE General Test (except for special education if undergraduate GPA is higher than a 3.0), minimum undergraduate GPA of 3.0; for doctorate and Ed S, GRE General Test (minimum combined score of 1000, 300 for new scoring), minimum undergraduate GPA of 3.0. Additional exam requirements/recommendations for international students: Required—TOEFL (minimum score 550 paper-based; 77 iBT), TWE (minimum score 5). *Application deadline:* Applications are processed on a rolling basis. Application fee: $60 ($75 for international students). Electronic applications accepted. *Financial support:* Fellowships with full tuition reimbursements, research assistantships with full tuition reimbursements, teaching assistantships with full tuition reimbursements, career-related internships or fieldwork, and tuition waivers (full) available. Support available to part-time students. Financial award application deadline: 3/1; financial award applicants required to submit FAFSA. *Faculty research:* Motivation, learning disabilities, school learning, group processes, cognitive development. *Unit head:* F. Richard Olenchak, Head, 765-494-9170, E-mail: olenchak@purdue.edu. *Application contact:* Heather Brinkman, Graduate Contact, 765-494-2345, Fax: 765-494-5832, E-mail: hbrinkma@purdue.edu.
Website: http://www.edst.purdue.edu/

Purdue University Global, School of Higher Education Studies, Davenport, IA 52807. Offers college administration and leadership (MS); college teaching and learning (MS); student services (MS). *Program availability:* Part-time, evening/weekend, online learning. *Entrance requirements:* Additional exam requirements/recommendations for international students: Required—TOEFL (minimum score 550 paper-based; 80 iBT).

Regent University, Graduate School, School of Education, Virginia Beach, VA 23464-9800. Offers education (M Ed, Ed D, PhD), including adult education (Ed D, PhD, Ed S); advanced educational leadership (Ed D, PhD, Ed S); character education (Ed D, PhD, Ed S); Christian education leadership (Ed D, PhD, Ed S); Christian school administration (M Ed); curriculum and instruction (Ed D, PhD, Ed S); curriculum and instruction - adult education (M Ed); curriculum and instruction - Christian school (M Ed); curriculum and instruction - gifted and talented (M Ed); curriculum and instruction - STEM education (M Ed); curriculum and instruction - teacher leader (M Ed); discipleship for ministry (M Ed); educational leadership (M Ed); educational psychology (Ed D, PhD, Ed S); educational technology and online learning (Ed D, PhD, Ed S); elementary education (M Ed); exceptional education executive leadership (Ed D, PhD, Ed S); higher education (Ed D, PhD, Ed S); higher education leadership and management (Ed D, PhD, Ed S); instructional design and technology (M Ed); K-12 school leadership (Ed D, PhD, Ed S); K-12 special education (M Ed); leadership in mathematics education (M Ed); reading specialist (M Ed); special education (Ed D, PhD, Ed S); student affairs (M Ed); TESOL - adult education (M Ed); TESOL - K-12 (M Ed); educational specialist (Ed S), including adult education (Ed D, PhD, Ed S); advanced educational leadership (Ed D, PhD, Ed S); character education (Ed D, PhD, Ed S); Christian education leadership (Ed D, PhD, Ed S); curriculum and instruction (Ed D, PhD, Ed S); educational psychology (Ed D, PhD, Ed S); educational technology and online learning (Ed D, PhD, Ed S); exceptional education executive leadership (Ed D, PhD, Ed S); higher education (Ed D, PhD, Ed S); higher education leadership and management (Ed D, PhD, Ed S); K-12 school leadership (Ed D, PhD, Ed S); special education (Ed D, PhD, Ed S). *Accreditation:* TEAC. *Program availability:* Part-time, evening/weekend, 100% online, blended/hybrid learning. *Faculty:* 22 full-time (10 women), 44 part-time/adjunct (32 women). *Students:* 80 full-time (59 women), 945 part-time (750 women); includes 432 minority (352 Black or African American, non-Hispanic/Latino; 4 American Indian or Alaska Native, non-Hispanic/Latino; 14 Asian, non-Hispanic/Latino; 43 Hispanic/Latino; 19 Two or more races, non-Hispanic/Latino), 12 international. Average age 40. 1,125 applicants, 49% accepted, 436 enrolled. In 2017, 316 master's, 24 doctorates awarded. *Degree requirements:* For master's, thesis or alternative; for doctorate, comprehensive exam, thesis/dissertation. *Entrance requirements:* For master's, Virginia Communication and Literacy Assessment (VCLA), PRAXIS, college transcripts, writing sample, interview; for doctorate, GRE, writing sample, resume, transcripts, interview. Additional exam requirements/recommendations for international students: Required—TOEFL (minimum score 577 paper-based). *Application deadline:* For fall admission, 4/1 priority date for domestic students; for spring admission, 10/15 priority date for domestic students. Applications are processed on a rolling basis. Application fee: $50. Electronic applications accepted. *Expenses:* Contact institution. *Financial support:* In 2017–18, 669 students received support, including 1 fellowship (averaging $10,000 per year); career-related internships or fieldwork, scholarships/grants, and unspecified assistantships also available. Support available to part-time students. *Faculty research:* Christian school administration, curriculum and instruction, educational technology and online learning, higher education, special education. *Unit head:* Dr. Donald Finn, Dean, 757-352-4278, Fax: 757-352-4318, E-mail: dfinn@regent.edu. *Application contact:* Heidi Cece, Assistant Vice President of Enrollment Management, 800-373-5504, Fax: 757-352-4381, E-mail: admissions@regent.edu.
Website: https://www.regent.edu/school-of-education/

Regis College, Department of Education, Weston, MA 02493. Offers elementary teacher (M Ed); higher education leadership (Ed D); special education (M Ed). *Program availability:* Part-time, evening/weekend. *Degree requirements:* For doctorate, thesis/dissertation, capstone project. *Entrance requirements:* For master's, GRE or MAT, personal statement, recommendations, resume/curriculum vitae, official transcripts, interview; for doctorate, personal statement, recommendations, resume/curriculum vitae, official transcripts, presentation/interview. Additional exam requirements/recommendations for international students: Required—TOEFL (minimum score 560 paper-based; 79 iBT); Recommended—IELTS (minimum score 6.5). *Application deadline:* Applications are processed on a rolling basis. Application fee: $65. Electronic applications accepted. *Financial support:* Federal Work-Study, scholarships/grants, and unspecified assistantships available. Financial award applicants required to submit FAFSA. *Unit head:* Dr. Priscilla Boerger, Department Chair/Graduate Program Director, 781-768-7422, E-mail: priscilla.boerger@regiscollege.edu.

Robert Morris University, School of Education and Social Sciences, Moon Township, PA 15108-1189. Offers business education (MS); counseling psychology (MS); education (Postbaccalaureate Certificate); higher education (MS); instructional leadership (MS), including education; instructional management and leadership (PhD); literacy (MS); special education (MS). *Accreditation:* TEAC. *Program availability:* Part-time, evening/weekend, online learning. *Faculty:* 18 full-time (10 women), 5 part-time/adjunct (2 women). *Students:* 151 part-time (90 women); includes 23 minority (12 Black or African American, non-Hispanic/Latino; 2 Asian, non-Hispanic/Latino; 2 Hispanic/Latino; 7 Two or more races, non-Hispanic/Latino), 4 international. Average age 34. 51 applicants, 39% accepted, 10 enrolled. In 2017, 31 master's, 16 doctorates awarded. *Degree requirements:* For doctorate, thesis/dissertation. *Entrance requirements:* Additional exam requirements/recommendations for international students: Required—TOEFL (minimum score 550 paper-based; 79 iBT). *Application deadline:* For fall admission, 7/1 priority date for domestic and international students; for spring admission, 11/1 priority date for domestic and international students. Applications are processed on a rolling basis. Application fee: $35. Electronic applications accepted. *Expenses:* $890 per credit tuition, $80 per credit university fee. *Unit head:* Dr. George Semich, Acting Dean, 412-397-6032, Fax: 412-397-6044, E-mail: semich@rmu.edu. *Application contact:* E-mail: graduateadmissions@rmu.edu.
Website: http://www.rmu.edu/web/cms/schools/sess/

Robert Morris University Illinois, Morris Graduate School of Management, Chicago, IL 60605. Offers accounting (MBA); accounting/finance (MBA); business analytics (MIS); health care administration (MM); higher education administration (MM); human performance (MS); human resource management (MBA); information security (MIS); information systems management (MIS); law enforcement administration (MM); management (MBA); management/finance (MBA); management/human resource management (MBA); sports administration (MM). *Program availability:* Part-time, evening/weekend. *Faculty:* 2 full-time (0 women), 26 part-time/adjunct (8 women). *Students:* 186 full-time (108 women), 114 part-time (57 women); includes 167 minority (88 Black or African American, non-Hispanic/Latino; 15 Asian, non-Hispanic/Latino; 62 Hispanic/Latino; 1 Native Hawaiian or other Pacific Islander, non-Hispanic/Latino; 1 Two or more races, non-Hispanic/Latino), 18 international. Average age 32. 157 applicants, 78% accepted, 72 enrolled. In 2017, 191 master's awarded. *Entrance requirements:* For master's, official transcripts and letters of recommendation (for some programs); written personal statement. Additional exam requirements/recommendations for international students: Required—TOEFL (minimum score 550 paper-based). *Application deadline:* Applications are processed on a rolling basis. Application fee: $20 ($100 for international

students). Electronic applications accepted. *Expenses: Tuition:* Full-time $17,100; part-time $2850 per course. *Financial support:* In 2017–18, 381 students received support. Federal Work-Study, scholarships/grants, and unspecified assistantships available. Support available to part-time students. Financial award applicants required to submit FAFSA. *Unit head:* Kayed Akkawi, Dean, 312-935-6050, Fax: 312-935-6020, E-mail: kakkawi@robertmorris.edu. *Application contact:* Mark Daugherty, Director of Admissions, 312-935-4814, Fax: 312-935-6020, E-mail: mdaugherty@robertmorris.edu.

Rowan University, Graduate School, College of Education, Department of Educational Services and Leadership, Program in Higher Education Administration, Glassboro, NJ 08028-1701. Offers MA. *Accreditation:* NCATE. *Program availability:* Part-time, evening/weekend. *Degree requirements:* For master's, comprehensive exam, thesis. *Entrance requirements:* For master's, GRE General Test, minimum GPA of 2.8, 2 years of teaching experience. Additional exam requirements/recommendations for international students: Required—TOEFL. Electronic applications accepted. *Expenses:* Tuition, state resident: full-time $15,020; part-time $751 per semester hour. Tuition, nonresident: full-time $15,020; part-time $751 per semester hour. *Required fees:* $3158; $157.90 per semester hour. Tuition and fees vary according to course load, campus/location and program.

St. Cloud State University, School of Graduate Studies, School of Education, Department of Educational Leadership and Higher Education, Program in Higher Education Administration, St. Cloud, MN 56301-4498. Offers MS, Ed D.

Saint Louis University, Graduate Programs, School of Education and Graduate Programs, Department of Educational Leadership and Higher Education, St. Louis, MO 63103. Offers Catholic school leadership (MA); educational administration (MA, Ed D, PhD, Ed S); higher education (MA, Ed D, PhD); student personnel administration (MA). *Accreditation:* NCATE. *Program availability:* Part-time. *Degree requirements:* For master's, comprehensive written and oral exam; for doctorate, comprehensive exam, thesis/dissertation, preliminary oral and written exams. *Entrance requirements:* For master's, GRE General Test, MAT, LSAT, GMAT or MCAT, letters of recommendation, resume; for doctorate and Ed S, GRE General Test, LSAT, GMAT or MCAT, letters of recommendation, resumé, goal statement, transcripts. Additional exam requirements/recommendations for international students: Required—TOEFL (minimum score 525 paper-based). Electronic applications accepted. *Faculty research:* Superintendent of schools, school finance, school facilities, student personal administration, building leadership.

Saint Peter's University, Graduate Programs in Education, Program in Higher Education, Jersey City, NJ 07306-5997. Offers Ed D. *Degree requirements:* For doctorate, comprehensive exam, thesis/dissertation, qualifying examination, internship. *Entrance requirements:* For doctorate, GRE or MAT (taken within the last 5 years), official transcripts from all previously attended postsecondary institutions; bachelor's degree; master's degree; three letters of recommendation; essay; current resume; personal interview.

Salem State University, School of Graduate Studies, Program in Higher Education in Student Affairs, Salem, MA 01970-5353. Offers M Ed. *Program availability:* Part-time, evening/weekend. *Entrance requirements:* For master's, GRE or MAT. Additional exam requirements/recommendations for international students: Required—TOEFL (minimum score 550 paper-based; 80 iBT) or IELTS (minimum score 5.5).

Sam Houston State University, College of Education, Department of Educational Leadership, Huntsville, TX 77341. Offers administration (M Ed); developmental education administration (Ed D); educational leadership (Ed D); higher education administration (MA); higher education leadership (Ed D); instructional leadership (M Ed, MA). *Program availability:* Part-time, evening/weekend, online learning. *Degree requirements:* For master's, comprehensive exam (for some programs), thesis (for some programs); for doctorate, comprehensive exam, thesis/dissertation. *Entrance requirements:* For master's, GRE General Test, references, personal essay, resume, professional statement; for doctorate, GRE General Test, master's degree, references, personal essay, resume. Additional exam requirements/recommendations for international students: Required—TOEFL (minimum score 550 paper-based; 79 iBT), IELTS (minimum score 6.5). Electronic applications accepted.

San Diego State University, Graduate and Research Affairs, College of Education, Department of Administration, Rehabilitation and Post-Secondary Education, San Diego, CA 92182. Offers educational leadership in post-secondary education (MA); rehabilitation counseling (MS), including deafness. *Program availability:* Evening/weekend, online learning. *Degree requirements:* For master's, comprehensive exam (for some programs), thesis (for some programs). *Entrance requirements:* For master's, GRE General Test, letters of reference. Additional exam requirements/recommendations for international students: Required—TOEFL. Electronic applications accepted. *Faculty research:* Rehabilitation in cultural diversity, distance learning technology.

Seton Hall University, College of Education and Human Services, Department of Education Leadership, Management and Policy, Program in Higher Education Administration, South Orange, NJ 07079-2697. Offers Ed D, PhD. *Accreditation:* NCATE. *Program availability:* Part-time, evening/weekend. *Degree requirements:* For doctorate, comprehensive exam, thesis/dissertation, internship. *Entrance requirements:* For doctorate, GRE or MAT, interview, minimum GPA of 3.5. Additional exam requirements/recommendations for international students: Required—TOEFL.

Shippensburg University of Pennsylvania, School of Graduate Studies, College of Arts and Sciences, Department of Sociology and Anthropology, Shippensburg, PA 17257-2299. Offers organizational development and leadership (MS), including business, higher education structure and policy, historical administration, leadership in society, management information systems, public organizations. *Program availability:* Part-time, evening/weekend. *Faculty:* 4 full-time (2 women). *Students:* 14 full-time (6 women), 19 part-time (11 women); includes 7 minority (4 Black or African American, non-Hispanic/Latino; 2 Hispanic/Latino; 1 Two or more races, non-Hispanic/Latino), 1 international. Average age 26. 31 applicants, 81% accepted, 15 enrolled. In 2017, 22 master's awarded. *Degree requirements:* For master's, capstone experience including internship. *Entrance requirements:* For master's, interview (if GPA less than 2.75), current resume, personal goals statement. Additional exam requirements/recommendations for international students: Required—TOEFL (minimum score 550 paper-based, 68 iBT) or IELTS (minimum score 6). *Application deadline:* For fall admission, 4/30 for domestic students; for spring admission, 9/30 for international students. Applications are processed on a rolling basis. Application fee: $45. Electronic applications accepted. *Expenses:* Tuition, state resident: part-time $500 per credit. Tuition, nonresident: part-time $750 per credit. *Required fees:* $145 per credit. *Financial support:* In 2017–18, 12 students received support. Career-related internships or fieldwork, scholarships/grants, unspecified assistantships, and resident hall director and student payroll positions available. Support available to part-time students. Financial award application deadline: 3/1; financial award applicants required to submit FAFSA. *Unit head:* Dr. Barbara J. Denison, Departmental Chair and Program Coordinator, 717-477-1735, Fax: 717-477-4011, E-mail: bjdeni@ship.edu. *Application contact:* Maya T. Mapp, Director of Admissions, 717-477-1231, Fax: 717-477-4016, E-mail: mtmapp@ship.edu.
Website: http://www.ship.edu/odl/

Higher Education

Siena Heights University, Graduate College, Adrian, MI 49221-1796. Offers clinical mental health counseling (MA); educational leadership (Specialist); leadership (MA), including health care leadership, organizational leadership; teacher education (MA), including early childhood education, early childhood education: Montessori, education leadership: principal, elementary education: reading K-12, leadership: higher education, secondary education: reading K-12, special education: cognitive impairment, special education: learning disabilities. *Program availability:* Part-time, evening/weekend. *Degree requirements:* For master's, thesis, presentation. *Entrance requirements:* For master's, minimum GPA of 3.0, current resume, essay, all post-secondary transcripts, 3 letters of reference, conviction disclosure form; copy of teaching certificate (for some education programs); for Specialist, master's degree, minimum GPA of 3.0, current resume, essay, all post-secondary transcripts, 3 letters of reference, conviction disclosure form; copy of teaching certificate (for some education programs). Electronic applications accepted.

Southeast Missouri State University, School of Graduate Studies, Department of Educational Leadership and Counseling, Program in Educational Administration, Cape Girardeau, MO 63701-4799. Offers educational leadership (Ed D); higher education administration (MA); secondary administration (MA); teacher leadership (MA, Ed S). *Accreditation:* NCATE. *Program availability:* Part-time, evening/weekend, online only, 100% online. *Faculty:* 7 full-time (4 women), 4 part-time/adjunct (1 woman). *Students:* 45 full-time (31 women), 203 part-time (133 women); includes 24 minority (18 Black or African American, non-Hispanic/Latino; 1 American Indian or Alaska Native, non-Hispanic/Latino; 4 Asian, non-Hispanic/Latino; 1 Two or more races, non-Hispanic/Latino), 13 international. Average age 32. 105 applicants, 100% accepted, 105 enrolled. In 2017, 29 master's, 31 other advanced degrees awarded. *Degree requirements:* For master's and Ed S, comprehensive exam, thesis or alternative, paper; for doctorate, comprehensive exam, thesis/dissertation. *Entrance requirements:* For master's, minimum GPA of 3.5; for doctorate, GRE, interview; for Ed S, minimum GPA of 3.7. Additional exam requirements/recommendations for international students: Required—TOEFL (minimum score 550 paper-based; 79 iBT), IELTS (minimum score 6), PTE (minimum score 53). *Application deadline:* For fall admission, 8/1 for domestic students, 6/1 for international students; for spring admission, 11/21 for domestic students, 10/1 for international students; for summer admission, 5/15 for domestic students. Applications are processed on a rolling basis. Application fee: $30 ($40 for international students). Electronic applications accepted. *Expenses:* $270.35 per credit hour in-state tuition, $33.40 per credit hour fees. *Financial support:* In 2017–18, 22 students received support. Career-related internships or fieldwork, Federal Work-Study, scholarships/grants, traineeships, tuition waivers (full), and unspecified assistantships available. Financial award application deadline: 6/30; financial award applicants required to submit FAFSA. *Faculty research:* Learning and technology; leadership, equity and social justice in P-12 schools and higher education; school culture; leadership and academic achievement; school leadership and student success. *Unit head:* Dr. C. P. Gause, Professor/Chair, 573-651-2137, Fax: 573-986-6512, E-mail: cgause@semo.edu. *Application contact:* Dr. Lisa Bertrand, Professor/Coordinator, 573-651-5080, Fax: 573-986-6512, E-mail: lbertrand@semo.edu.
Website: http://www.semo.edu/eduleadcounsel/

Southern Arkansas University–Magnolia, School of Graduate Studies, Magnolia, AR 71753. Offers agriculture (MS); business administration (MBA), including agribusiness, social entrepreneurship, supply chain management; clinical and mental health counseling (MS); computer and information sciences (MS), including cyber security and privacy, data science, information technology; gifted and talented (M Ed), including curriculum and instruction, educational administration and supervision, gifted and talented P-8/7-12, instructional specialist P-4; higher, adult and lifelong education (M Ed); kinesiology (M Ed), including coaching; library media and information specialist (M Ed); public administration (MPA); school counseling K-12 (M Ed); student affairs and college counseling (M Ed); teaching (MAT). *Accreditation:* NCATE. *Program availability:* Part-time, 100% online, blended/hybrid learning. *Faculty:* 36 full-time (20 women), 31 part-time/adjunct (12 women). *Students:* 242 full-time (89 women), 889 part-time (459 women); includes 167 minority (143 Black or African American, non-Hispanic/Latino; 7 American Indian or Alaska Native, non-Hispanic/Latino; 7 Asian, non-Hispanic/Latino; 3 Hispanic/Latino; 7 Two or more races, non-Hispanic/Latino), 562 international. Average age 28. 400 applicants, 100% accepted, 239 enrolled. In 2017, 875 master's awarded. *Degree requirements:* For master's, comprehensive exam (for some programs), thesis optional. *Entrance requirements:* For master's, GRE, MAT or GMAT, minimum GPA of 2.5. Additional exam requirements/recommendations for international students: Required—TOEFL (minimum score 550 paper-based), IELTS (minimum score 6). *Application deadline:* For fall admission, 7/20 for domestic students, 7/10 for international students; for spring admission, 12/1 for domestic students, 11/15 for international students; for summer admission, 4/1 for domestic students, 5/1 for international students. Applications are processed on a rolling basis. Application fee: $25 ($50 for international students). Electronic applications accepted. *Expenses:* Tuition, state resident: full-time $6038. Tuition, nonresident: full-time $8558. *Required fees:* $804. One-time fee: $110 full-time. Tuition and fees vary according to course load. *Financial support:* Career-related internships or fieldwork, Federal Work-Study, scholarships/grants, tuition waivers (full), and unspecified assistantships available. Financial award applicants required to submit FAFSA. *Faculty research:* Alternative certification for teachers, supervision of instruction, instructional leadership, counseling. *Unit head:* Dr. Kim Bloss, Dean, School of Graduate Studies, 870-235-4150, Fax: 870-235-5227, E-mail: kkbloss@saumag.edu. *Application contact:* Shrijana Malakar, Admissions Specialist, 870-235-4150, Fax: 870-235-5227, E-mail: smalakar@saumag.edu.
Website: http://www.saumag.edu/graduate

Southern Illinois University Carbondale, Graduate School, College of Education and Human Services, Department of Educational Administration and Higher Education, Program in Higher Education, Carbondale, IL 62901-4701. Offers education (MS Ed). *Accreditation:* NCATE. *Program availability:* Part-time. *Degree requirements:* For master's, thesis. *Entrance requirements:* For master's, GRE General Test or MAT, minimum GPA of 2.7. Additional exam requirements/recommendations for international students: Required—TOEFL. *Faculty research:* Student affairs administration, international education, community college teaching.

Southern Illinois University Edwardsville, Graduate School, College of Arts and Sciences, Department of Mathematics and Statistics, Program in Postsecondary Mathematics Education, Edwardsville, IL 62026. Offers MS. *Program availability:* Part-time. *Degree requirements:* For master's, thesis (for some programs), special project. *Entrance requirements:* Additional exam requirements/recommendations for international students: Required—TOEFL (minimum score 550 paper-based, 79 iBT), IELTS (minimum score 6.5), Michigan Test of English Language Proficiency or PTE. Electronic applications accepted.

Southern New Hampshire University, School of Education, Manchester, NH 03106-1045. Offers curriculum and instruction (M Ed), including dyslexia studies and language-based learning disabilities, educational leadership, reading, special education, technology integration; dyslexia studies and language-based learning disabilities (Certificate); early childhood and special education (M Ed); educational leadership (M Ed, Ed D); educational studies (M Ed); elementary and special education (M Ed); field based education (M Ed); higher education administration (MS); teaching English as a foreign language (MS). *Program availability:* Part-time, evening/weekend, online learning. *Degree requirements:* For master's, comprehensive exam (for some programs), thesis or alternative. *Entrance requirements:* For master's, PRAXIS I, minimum GPA of 2.75. Additional exam requirements/recommendations for international students: Required—TOEFL (minimum score 550 paper-based). *Application deadline:* Applications are processed on a rolling basis. Application fee: $40. Electronic applications accepted. *Expenses:* Contact institution. *Financial support:* Institutionally sponsored loans available. Financial award applicants required to submit FAFSA. *Unit head:* Raymond McNulty, Dean, 603-668-2211, Fax: 603-629-4673. *Application contact:* Office of Graduate Admission, 888-327-SNHU, Fax: 603-644-3144, E-mail: enroll@snhu.edu.

Southwestern College, Education Programs, Winfield, KS 67156-2499. Offers curriculum and instruction (M Ed); early childhood education (M Ed); educational leadership (Ed D), including higher education leadership, PK-12 education leadership; special education (M Ed), including high-incidence disabilities, low-incidence disabilities; teaching (MA). *Accreditation:* NCATE. *Program availability:* Part-time, evening/weekend, 100% online, blended/hybrid learning. *Faculty:* 6 full-time (5 women), 12 part-time/adjunct (10 women). *Students:* 12 full-time (10 women), 77 part-time (51 women); includes 12 minority (5 Black or African American, non-Hispanic/Latino; 2 American Indian or Alaska Native, non-Hispanic/Latino; 1 Asian, non-Hispanic/Latino; 3 Hispanic/Latino; 1 Native Hawaiian or other Pacific Islander, non-Hispanic/Latino), 10 international. Average age 39. 29 applicants, 86% accepted, 18 enrolled. In 2017, 52 master's, 11 doctorates awarded. *Degree requirements:* For master's, practicum, portfolio; for doctorate, thesis/dissertation, professional portfolio. *Entrance requirements:* For master's, baccalaureate degree, minimum GPA of 3.0, valid teaching certificate (for special education); for doctorate, GRE if no master's degree, baccalaureate degree with minimum GPA of 3.25 and current teaching experience, or master's degree with minimum GPA of 3.5. Additional exam requirements/recommendations for international students: Required—TOEFL (minimum score 550 paper-based; 80 iBT). *Application deadline:* Applications are processed on a rolling basis. Application fee: $40. Electronic applications accepted. *Expenses:* $577 per credit hour, $509 online (for master's programs); $609 per credit hour (for doctorate program). *Financial support:* In 2017–18, 9 students received support. Unspecified assistantships and employee tuition waivers available. Financial award applicants required to submit FAFSA. *Unit head:* Dana Pentz, Director of Education Operations, 620-229-6253, E-mail: dana.pentz@sckans.edu. *Application contact:* Dennis Russell, Director of Admissions and Student Services, 888-684-5335 Ext. 3372, Fax: 888-684-5218, E-mail: dennis.russell@sckans.edu.
Website: http://www.sckans.edu/graduate/education-med

Springfield College, Graduate Programs, Programs in Psychology, Springfield, MA 01109-3797. Offers athletic counseling (MS, CAGS); clinical mental health counseling (M Ed, CAGS); counseling psychology (Psy D); general counseling (M Ed); industrial/organizational psychology (M Ed, CAGS); school counseling (M Ed, CAGS); student personnel administration in higher education (M Ed, CAGS). *Accreditation:* APA. *Program availability:* Part-time. *Students:* 192 applicants, 65% accepted, 64 enrolled. In 2017, 56 master's, 5 doctorates awarded. *Degree requirements:* For master's, research project, portfolio; for doctorate, dissertation project, 1500 hours of counseling psychology practicum, full-year internship. *Entrance requirements:* For doctorate, GRE. Additional exam requirements/recommendations for international students: Required—TOEFL (minimum score 550 paper-based); Recommended—IELTS (minimum score 7). *Application deadline:* For fall admission, 1/15 priority date for domestic students, 1/15 for international students; for winter admission, 11/1 for domestic and international students; for spring admission, 11/1 for domestic and international students. Applications are processed on a rolling basis. Application fee: $50. Electronic applications accepted. *Financial support:* Fellowships with partial tuition reimbursements, teaching assistantships with partial tuition reimbursements, career-related internships or fieldwork, Federal Work-Study, institutionally sponsored loans, scholarships/grants, and unspecified assistantships available. Financial award application deadline: 3/1; financial award applicants required to submit FAFSA. *Unit head:* Dr. Allison Cumming-McCann, Chair, 413-748-3025, Fax: 413-748-3854, E-mail: acumming@springfield.edu. *Application contact:* Anne Griffin, Director of Graduate Admissions, 413-748-3225, E-mail: agriffin2@springfield.edu.
Website: http://springfield.edu/programs

Stony Brook University, State University of New York, School of Professional Development, Stony Brook, NY 11794. Offers biology (MAT); chemistry (MAT); coaching (Graduate Certificate); earth science (MAT); educational computing (Graduate Certificate); educational leadership (Advanced Certificate); English (MAT); environmental management (MPS, Graduate Certificate); French (MAT); German (MAT); higher education administration (MA, Certificate); human resource management (MS, Graduate Certificate); industrial management (Graduate Certificate); information systems management (Graduate Certificate); Italian (MAT); liberal studies (MA); mathematics (MAT); operations research (Graduate Certificate); physics (MAT); school district business leadership (Advanced Certificate); social studies (MAT); Spanish (MAT). *Program availability:* Part-time, evening/weekend, online learning. *Faculty:* 3 full-time (2 women), 101 part-time/adjunct (45 women). *Students:* 190 full-time (126 women), 974 part-time (708 women); includes 255 minority (88 Black or African American, non-Hispanic/Latino; 2 American Indian or Alaska Native, non-Hispanic/Latino; 31 Asian, non-Hispanic/Latino; 113 Hispanic/Latino; 1 Native Hawaiian or other Pacific Islander, non-Hispanic/Latino; 20 Two or more races, non-Hispanic/Latino), 6 international. Average age 33. 411 applicants, 91% accepted, 288 enrolled. In 2017, 333 master's, 180 other advanced degrees awarded. *Entrance requirements:* Additional exam requirements/recommendations for international students: Required—TOEFL (minimum score 85 iBT). *Application deadline:* For fall admission, 1/15 for domestic students, 6/1 for international students; for spring admission, 10/1 for domestic and international students. Applications are processed on a rolling basis. Application fee: $100. *Expenses:* Contact institution. *Financial support:* Fellowships, research assistantships, teaching assistantships, and career-related internships or fieldwork available. Support available to part-time students. *Unit head:* Dr. Ken Lindblom, Dean, 631-632-7049, Fax: 631-632-9046, E-mail: kenneth.lindblom@stonybrook.edu. *Application contact:* Melissa Jordan, Assistant Dean, 631-632-7751, E-mail: melissa.jordan@stonybrook.edu.
Website: http://www.stonybrook.edu/spd/

Syracuse University, College of Arts and Sciences, Program in College Science Teaching, Syracuse, NY 13244. Offers PhD. *Program availability:* Part-time. *Degree requirements:* For doctorate, thesis/dissertation. *Entrance requirements:* For doctorate, GRE General Test, three letters of recommendation, personal statement, transcripts, scholarly writing sample. Additional exam requirements/recommendations for international students: Required—TOEFL (minimum score 100 iBT). *Application deadline:* For fall admission, 2/1 priority date for domestic and international students. Applications are processed on a rolling basis. Application fee: $75. Electronic applications accepted. *Financial support:* Fellowships with full tuition reimbursements, research assistantships with tuition reimbursements, teaching assistantships with tuition reimbursements, and scholarships/grants available. Financial award application

deadline: 1/15; financial award applicants required to submit FAFSA. *Faculty research:* Philosophy of science, methods of teaching science in higher education, research focused on the problems of college teaching, curriculum development. *Unit head:* Dr. John W. Tillotson, Department Chairperson, 315-443-9137, E-mail: jwtillot@syr.edu. *Application contact:* Heather Thompson, Administrative Assistant, Earth Sciences and Science Teaching, 315-443-2672, E-mail: hethomps@syr.edu.
Website: http://sciteach.syr.edu/academics/program-science-teaching-phd.html

Syracuse University, School of Education, Programs in Higher Education, Syracuse, NY 13244. Offers MS, PhD. *Program availability:* Part-time. *Students:* Average age 30. *Degree requirements:* For master's, thesis or alternative; for doctorate, comprehensive exam, thesis/dissertation. *Entrance requirements:* For master's, baccalaureate degree from regionally-accredited college/university, experience in student affairs or higher education, personal statement, resume, transcripts, three letters of recommendation; for doctorate, GRE, master's degree in higher education, student affairs, or related area; three years of work experience in higher education, student affairs, related area, or college teaching; strong writing skills; transcripts, three letters of recommendation. Additional exam requirements/recommendations for international students: Required—TOEFL (minimum score 100 iBT). *Application deadline:* For fall admission, 2/1 priority date for domestic and international students; for spring admission, 10/15 priority date for domestic and international students. Applications are processed on a rolling basis. Application fee: $75. Electronic applications accepted. *Financial support:* Fellowships with full tuition reimbursements, research assistantships, teaching assistantships, career-related internships or fieldwork, and scholarships/grants available. Financial award application deadline: 1/15. *Faculty research:* Student culture, college student personnel development, programming advising, policy-making, faculty roles on behalf of students from diverse groups. *Unit head:* Dr. Dawn Johnson, Associate Professor/Chair, 315-443-3130, E-mail: drjohn02@syr.edu. *Application contact:* Speranza Migliore, Graduate Admissions Recruiter, 315-443-2505, E-mail: gradrcrt@syr.edu.
Website: http://soe.syr.edu/academic/higher_education/

Taylor University, Master of Arts in Higher Education Program, Upland, IN 46989-1001. Offers MA. *Accreditation:* NCATE. *Program availability:* Part-time. *Degree requirements:* For master's, thesis. *Entrance requirements:* For master's, resume, official transcripts, three references, interview. *Application deadline:* For fall admission, 1/31 for domestic students, 12/31 for international students. Applications are processed on a rolling basis. Application fee: $100. *Expenses:* $635 per credit hour. *Financial support:* Fellowships, scholarships/grants, and unspecified assistantships available. Financial award applicants required to submit FAFSA. *Unit head:* Dr. Tim Herrmann, Chair, 765-998-5142, E-mail: tmherrmann@taylor.edu. *Application contact:* Dr. Tim Herrmann, Chair, 765-998-5142, E-mail: tmherrmann@taylor.edu.
Website: http://www.taylor.edu/mahe

Teachers College, Columbia University, Department of Organization and Leadership, New York, NY 10027-6696. Offers adult education guided intensive study (Ed D); adult learning and leadership (Ed M, MA, Ed D); educational leadership (Ed D); higher and postsecondary education (MA, Ed D); leadership, policy and politics (Ed D); nurse executive (MA, Ed D), including administration studies (MA), professorial studies (MA); private school leadership (Ed M, MA); public school building leadership (Ed M, MA); social and organizational psychology (MA); urban education leaders (Ed D); MA/MBA. *Program availability:* Part-time, evening/weekend. *Students:* 342 full-time (244 women), 378 part-time (256 women); includes 288 minority (106 Black or African American, non-Hispanic/Latino; 69 Asian, non-Hispanic/Latino; 92 Hispanic/Latino; 21 Two or more races, non-Hispanic/Latino), 86 international. Average age 33. 1,063 applicants, 59% accepted, 405 enrolled. *Degree requirements:* For doctorate, thesis/dissertation. *Unit head:* Prof. Bill Baldwin, Chair, E-mail: wjb12@tc.columbia.edu. *Application contact:* David Estrella, Director of Admission, 212-678-3305, E-mail: estrella@tc.columbia.edu.

Texas A&M University–Commerce, College of Education and Human Services, Commerce, TX 75429. Offers counseling (M Ed, MS, PhD); early childhood education (M Ed, MS); educational administration (M Ed, MS, Ed D); educational psychology (PhD); educational technology leadership (M Ed, MS); educational technology library science (M Ed, MS); elementary education (M Ed); health, kinesiology and sports studies (MS); higher education (MS, Ed D); psychology (MS); reading (M Ed, MS); secondary education (M Ed, MS); social work (MSW); special education (M Ed, MS); supervision, curriculum and instruction-elementary education (Ed D); training and development (MS). *Program availability:* Part-time, evening/weekend, 100% online, blended/hybrid learning. *Faculty:* 91 full-time (51 women), 38 part-time/adjunct (31 women). *Students:* 400 full-time (310 women), 1,400 part-time (1,117 women); includes 724 minority (412 Black or African American, non-Hispanic/Latino; 8 American Indian or Alaska Native, non-Hispanic/Latino; 24 Asian, non-Hispanic/Latino; 220 Hispanic/Latino; 60 Two or more races, non-Hispanic/Latino), 18 international. Average age 37. 951 applicants, 46% accepted, 331 enrolled. In 2017, 564 master's, 24 doctorates awarded. *Degree requirements:* For master's, comprehensive exam, thesis optional, departmental qualifying exams (for some programs); for doctorate, comprehensive exam, thesis/dissertation, departmental qualifying exam; for SSP, comprehensive exam, thesis optional. *Entrance requirements:* For master's and doctorate, GRE General Test. Additional exam requirements/recommendations for international students: Required—TOEFL (minimum score 550 paper-based; 79 iBT), IELTS (minimum score 6). *Application deadline:* For fall admission, 6/1 priority date for international students; for spring admission, 10/15 priority date for international students; for summer admission, 3/15 priority date for international students. Applications are processed on a rolling basis. Application fee: $50. Electronic applications accepted. *Expenses:* Tuition, state resident: full-time $3630. Tuition, nonresident: full-time $11,100. *Required fees:* $2564. Tuition and fees vary according to course load, degree level and program. *Financial support:* In 2017–18, 84 students received support, including 40 research assistantships with partial tuition reimbursements available (averaging $10,800 per year), 12 teaching assistantships with partial tuition reimbursements available (averaging $13,000 per year); career-related internships or fieldwork, Federal Work-Study, institutionally sponsored loans, scholarships/grants, health care benefits, and unspecified assistantships also available. Financial award application deadline: 6/15; financial award applicants required to submit FAFSA. *Faculty research:* Cognitive and bilingual education, positive behavioral intervention, literacy, math readiness. *Total annual research expenditures:* $1.1 million. *Unit head:* Dr. Timothy Letzring, Dean, 903-886-5181, Fax: 903-886-5905, E-mail: tim.letzring@tamuc.edu. *Application contact:* Vicky Turner, Doctoral Degree and Special Programs Coordinator, 903-886-5167, E-mail: vicky.turner@tamuc.edu.
Website: http://www.tamuc.edu/academics/graduateSchool/programs/education/default.aspx

Texas Southern University, College of Education, Department of Educational Administration and Foundation, Houston, TX 77004-4584. Offers educational administration (M Ed, Ed D). *Program availability:* Part-time, evening/weekend. *Degree requirements:* For master's, comprehensive exam; for doctorate, comprehensive exam, thesis/dissertation. *Entrance requirements:* For master's, GRE General Test, minimum GPA of 2.5; for doctorate, GRE General Test or MAT, master's degree, minimum B+ average. Additional exam requirements/recommendations for international students: Required—TOEFL. Electronic applications accepted.

Texas State University, The Graduate College, College of Education, Program in Student Affairs in Higher Education, San Marcos, TX 78666. Offers M Ed. *Accreditation:* ACA. *Program availability:* Part-time, evening/weekend. *Faculty:* 7 full-time (5 women), 3 part-time/adjunct (1 woman). *Students:* 38 full-time (27 women); includes 23 minority (5 Black or African American, non-Hispanic/Latino; 3 Asian, non-Hispanic/Latino; 11 Hispanic/Latino; 4 Two or more races, non-Hispanic/Latino). Average age 24. 43 applicants, 65% accepted, 16 enrolled. In 2017, 18 master's awarded. *Degree requirements:* For master's, comprehensive exam. *Entrance requirements:* For master's, GRE General Test (minimum preferred score of 295 [150 verbal, 145 quantitative], 4 analytical writing), baccalaureate degree from regionally-accredited institution with minimum GPA of 3.0 in last 60 hours of undergraduate course work, resume, statement of purpose, 3 letters of recommendation. Additional exam requirements/recommendations for international students: Required—TOEFL (minimum score 550 paper-based; 78 iBT), IELTS (minimum score 6.5). *Application deadline:* For fall admission, 1/15 for domestic and international students. Applications are processed on a rolling basis. Application fee: $40 ($90 for international students). Electronic applications accepted. *Expenses:* Tuition, state resident: full-time $7868; part-time $3934 per semester. Tuition, nonresident: full-time $17,828; part-time $8914 per semester. *Required fees:* $2092; $1435 per semester. Tuition and fees vary according to course load. *Financial support:* In 2017–18, 33 students received support, including 35 teaching assistantships (averaging $11,609 per year); research assistantships, career-related internships or fieldwork, Federal Work-Study, institutionally sponsored loans, scholarships/grants, and unspecified assistantships also available. Support available to part-time students. Financial award application deadline: 3/1; financial award applicants required to submit FAFSA. *Unit head:* Dr. Paige Haber-Curran, Graduate Advisor, 512-245-7628, Fax: 512-245-8872, E-mail: ph31@txstate.edu. *Application contact:* Dr. Andrea Golato, Dean of Graduate School, 512-245-2581, Fax: 512-245-8365, E-mail: gradcollege@txstate.edu.
Website: http://www.gradcollege.txstate.edu/programs/sahe.html

Texas Tech University, Graduate School, College of Education, Department of Educational Psychology and Leadership, Lubbock, TX 79409. Offers counselor education (M Ed, PhD); educational leadership (M Ed, Ed D, PhD); educational psychology (M Ed, PhD); higher education (M Ed); higher education administration (Ed D); higher education research (PhD); instructional technology (M Ed, Ed D); special education (M Ed, Ed D, PhD). *Accreditation:* ACA; NCATE. *Program availability:* Part-time, evening/weekend. *Faculty:* 64 full-time (30 women), 6 part-time/adjunct (all women). *Students:* 263 full-time (193 women), 637 part-time (490 women); includes 307 minority (84 Black or African American, non-Hispanic/Latino; 3 American Indian or Alaska Native, non-Hispanic/Latino; 4 Asian, non-Hispanic/Latino; 193 Hispanic/Latino; 23 Two or more races, non-Hispanic/Latino), 48 international. Average age 36. 510 applicants, 47% accepted, 185 enrolled. In 2017, 209 master's, 64 doctorates awarded. Terminal master's awarded for partial completion of doctoral program. *Degree requirements:* For master's, comprehensive exam, thesis optional; for doctorate, comprehensive exam, thesis/dissertation. *Entrance requirements:* For master's, GRE (for some programs); for doctorate, GRE. Additional exam requirements/recommendations for international students: Required—TOEFL (minimum score 550 paper-based; 79 iBT). *Application deadline:* For fall admission, 6/1 priority date for domestic students, 1/15 priority date for international students; for spring admission, 9/1 priority date for domestic students, 6/15 priority date for international students. Applications are processed on a rolling basis. Application fee: $60. Electronic applications accepted. *Expenses:* Contact institution. *Financial support:* In 2017–18, 366 students received support, including 360 fellowships (averaging $3,231 per year), 63 research assistantships (averaging $11,899 per year); teaching assistantships, scholarships/grants, and unspecified assistantships also available. Support available to part-time students. Financial award application deadline: 1/3; financial award applicants required to submit FAFSA. *Faculty research:* Cognitive, motivational, and developmental processes in learning; counseling education; instructional technology; generic special education and sensory impairment; community college administration; K-12 school administration. *Total annual research expenditures:* $127,956. *Unit head:* Dr. Hansel Burley, Chair, 806-834-5135, Fax: 806-742-2179, E-mail: hansel.burley@ttu.edu. *Application contact:* Pam Smith, Admissions Advisor, 806-834-2969, Fax: 806-742-2179, E-mail: pam.smith@ttu.edu.
Website: http://www.educ.ttu.edu/

Tiffin University, Program in Education, Tiffin, OH 44883-2161. Offers educational technology management (M Ed); higher education administration (M Ed). *Program availability:* Part-time, evening/weekend, online only, 100% online, blended/hybrid learning. *Entrance requirements:* Additional exam requirements/recommendations for international students: Required—TOEFL. Electronic applications accepted. *Expenses:* Contact institution.

Trident University International, College of Education, Program in Education, Cypress, CA 90630. Offers adult education (MA Ed); aviation education (MA Ed); children's literacy development (MA Ed); e-learning (MA Ed); early childhood education (MA Ed); enrollment management (MA Ed); higher education (MA Ed); teaching and instruction (MA Ed); training and development (MA Ed). *Program availability:* Part-time, evening/weekend, online learning. *Degree requirements:* For master's, capstone project with integrative paper. *Entrance requirements:* For master's, minimum GPA of 2.5 (students with GPA 3.0 or greater may transfer up to 30% of graduate level credits). Additional exam requirements/recommendations for international students: Required—TOEFL (minimum score 525 paper-based). Electronic applications accepted.

Trident University International, College of Education, Program in Educational Leadership, Cypress, CA 90630. Offers e-learning leadership (MA Ed, PhD); educational leadership (MA Ed); higher education leadership (PhD); K-12 leadership (PhD). *Program availability:* Part-time, evening/weekend, online learning. *Degree requirements:* For doctorate, comprehensive exam, thesis/dissertation, defense of dissertation. *Entrance requirements:* For master's, minimum GPA of 2.5 (students with GPA 3.0 or greater may transfer up to 30% of graduate level credits); for doctorate, minimum GPA of 3.4, course work in research methods or statistics. Additional exam requirements/recommendations for international students: Required—TOEFL. Electronic applications accepted.

Union University, School of Education, Jackson, TN 38305-3697. Offers education (M Ed, MA Ed); education administration generalist (Ed S); educational leadership (Ed D); educational supervision (Ed S); higher education (Ed D). M Ed also available at Germantown campus. *Accreditation:* NCATE. *Program availability:* Part-time, evening/weekend, online learning. *Degree requirements:* For master's, thesis (for some programs), capstone research course (for MA Ed); performance exhibition (for M Ed); for doctorate, comprehensive exam, thesis/dissertation; for Ed S, thesis or alternative. *Entrance requirements:* For master's, MAT, PRAXIS II or GRE, minimum GPA of 3.0, teaching license (for M Ed only), writing sample; for doctorate, GRE, minimum graduate GPA of 3.2, writing sample; for Ed S, PRAXIS II, minimum graduate GPA of 3.2, writing sample. Additional exam requirements/recommendations for international students: Required—TOEFL (minimum score 560 paper-based; 80 iBT). Electronic applications accepted. *Expenses:* Contact institution. *Faculty research:* Mathematics education, brain compatible learning, transformational teaching, cognitive strategy development, instructional technology.

Higher Education

Universidad Central del Este, Graduate School, San Pedro de Macoris, Dominican Republic. Offers environmental engineering (ME); financial management (M Ad); higher education (M Ed), including higher education management, higher education pedagogy; human resources (M Ad). *Entrance requirements:* For master's, letters of recommendation.

Université de Sherbrooke, Faculty of Education, Program in Postsecondary Education Training, Sherbrooke, QC J1K 2R1, Canada. Offers M Ed, Diploma. *Degree requirements:* For master's, thesis.

University at Albany, State University of New York, School of Education, Department of Educational Policy and Leadership, Albany, NY 12222-0001. Offers educational policy and leadership (MS, Ed D); higher education (MS); international education management (CAS). *Program availability:* Evening/weekend. *Faculty:* 11 full-time (3 women), 13 part-time/adjunct (10 women). *Students:* 37 full-time (21 women), 93 part-time (51 women); includes 28 minority (14 Black or African American, non-Hispanic/Latino; 1 Asian, non-Hispanic/Latino; 11 Hispanic/Latino; 2 Two or more races, non-Hispanic/Latino), 21 international. Average age 32. 72 applicants, 71% accepted, 48 enrolled. In 2017, 11 master's, 7 doctorates, 12 other advanced degrees awarded. *Degree requirements:* For doctorate, one foreign language, thesis/dissertation. *Entrance requirements:* For doctorate, GRE General Test, GRE Subject Test. Additional exam requirements/recommendations for international students: Required—TOEFL (minimum score 550 paper-based). *Application deadline:* For fall admission, 2/1 for domestic students, 5/1 for international students; for spring admission, 9/1 for domestic students, 11/1 for international students. Applications are processed on a rolling basis. Application fee: $75. Electronic applications accepted. *Expenses:* Tuition, state resident: full-time $10,870; part-time $453 per credit hour. Tuition, nonresident: full-time $22,210; part-time $925 per credit hour. *Required fees:* $84.68 per credit hour. $508.06 per semester. Part-time tuition and fees vary according to course load and program. *Financial support:* Fellowships and career-related internships or fieldwork available. Financial award application deadline: 3/15. *Unit head:* Jason Lane, Chair, 518-442-5092, E-mail: jlane@albany.edu.
Website: http://www.albany.edu/epl/

University at Buffalo, the State University of New York, Graduate School, Graduate School of Education, Department of Educational Leadership and Policy, Buffalo, NY 14260. Offers economics and education policy analysis (MA); education studies (Ed M); educational administration (Ed M, Ed D, PhD); educational culture, policy and society (PhD); higher education administration (Ed M, PhD); school building leadership (Certificate); school business and human resource administration (Certificate); school district business leadership (Certificate); school district leadership (Certificate). *Program availability:* Part-time, evening/weekend. *Faculty:* 16 full-time (10 women), 9 part-time/adjunct (6 women). *Students:* 65 full-time (44 women), 125 part-time (82 women); includes 29 minority (23 Black or African American, non-Hispanic/Latino; 3 Asian, non-Hispanic/Latino; 3 Hispanic/Latino), 19 international. Average age 35. 153 applicants, 75% accepted, 59 enrolled. In 2017, 45 master's, 4 doctorates, 23 other advanced degrees awarded. *Degree requirements:* For master's, comprehensive exam (for some programs), thesis optional; for doctorate, comprehensive exam, thesis/dissertation. *Entrance requirements:* For master's, interview, letters of reference; for doctorate, GRE General Test or MAT, writing sample, letters of reference. Additional exam requirements/recommendations for international students: Required—TOEFL (minimum score 550 paper-based; 79 iBT). *Application deadline:* For fall admission, 2/1 priority date for domestic students, 2/1 for international students; for spring admission, 11/15 priority date for domestic students, 10/1 for international students. Applications are processed on a rolling basis. Application fee: $50. Electronic applications accepted. *Financial support:* In 2017–18, 18 fellowships (averaging $5,673 per year), 34 research assistantships with tuition reimbursements (averaging $12,055 per year) were awarded; career-related internships or fieldwork, Federal Work-Study, institutionally sponsored loans, scholarships/grants, health care benefits, tuition waivers (full and partial), and unspecified assistantships also available. Financial award application deadline: 3/15; financial award applicants required to submit FAFSA. *Faculty research:* College access and choice, school leadership preparation and practice, public policy, curriculum and pedagogy, comparative and international education. *Total annual research expenditures:* $637,951. *Unit head:* Dr. Janina C. Brutt-Griffler, Chair, 716-645-2471, Fax: 716-645-2481, E-mail: bruttg@buffalo.edu. *Application contact:* Veronica Kase, Admission Assistant, 716-645-2110, Fax: 716-645-7937, E-mail: vakase@buffalo.edu.
Website: http://gse.buffalo.edu/elp

The University of Akron, Graduate School, College of Education, Department of Educational Foundations and Leadership, Program in Higher Education Administration, Akron, OH 44325. Offers MA, MS. *Accreditation:* NCATE. *Students:* 8 full-time (4 women), 10 part-time (8 women); includes 2 minority (1 Black or African American, non-Hispanic/Latino; 1 Hispanic/Latino). Average age 34. 8 applicants, 63% accepted, 3 enrolled. In 2017, 20 master's awarded. *Degree requirements:* For master's, comprehensive exam. *Entrance requirements:* For master's, GRE (if an applicant's GPA is between 2.75 and 2.99), minimum GPA of 2.75, declaration of intent that includes statement of professional goals and reasons for choosing the field of higher education administration and The University of Akron. Additional exam requirements/recommendations for international students: Required—TOEFL (minimum score 79 iBT), IELTS (minimum score 6.5). *Application deadline:* Applications are processed on a rolling basis. Application fee: $45 ($70 for international students). Electronic applications accepted. *Financial support:* Research assistantships and teaching assistantships available. *Unit head:* Dr. Evonn Welton, Interim Department Chair, 330-972-6742, E-mail: ewelton@uakron.edu. *Application contact:* Kelly Chaff, College Program Specialist, 330-972-7028, E-mail: klchaff@uakron.edu.
Website: http://www.uakron.edu/education/academic-programs/graduate-programs.dot

The University of Alabama, Graduate School, College of Education, Department of Educational Leadership, Policy, and Technology Studies, Higher Education Administration Program, Tuscaloosa, AL 35487. Offers MA, Ed D, PhD. *Program availability:* Evening/weekend, 100% online. *Students:* 8 full-time (2 women), 22 part-time (13 women); includes 5 minority (3 Black or African American, non-Hispanic/Latino; 1 American Indian or Alaska Native, non-Hispanic/Latino; 1 Two or more races, non-Hispanic/Latino). Average age 36. 31 applicants, 58% accepted, 16 enrolled. In 2017, 9 master's awarded. Terminal master's awarded for partial completion of doctoral program. *Degree requirements:* For master's, capstone seminar; for doctorate, comprehensive exam, thesis/dissertation. *Entrance requirements:* For master's, GRE or MAT, minimum GPA of 3.0; for doctorate, GRE (for PhD), GRE or MAT (for Ed D), master's degree, minimum GPA of 3.0. Additional exam requirements/recommendations for international students: Required—TOEFL. *Application deadline:* For fall admission, 1/15 priority date for domestic and international students. Application fee: $60 ($75 for international students). Electronic applications accepted. *Financial support:* In 2017–18, research assistantships with full tuition reimbursements (averaging $11,900 per year) were awarded; career-related internships or fieldwork, scholarships/grants, health care benefits, and unspecified assistantships also available. *Faculty research:* College teaching and learning, faculty-administration relations, community colleges, organizational change, student affairs. *Unit head:* Dr. Karri Holley, Coordinator and Associate Professor, 205-348-7825, Fax: 205-348-2161, E-mail: kaholley@ua.edu.

Application contact: Donna Smith, Administrative Assistant, 205-348-6871, Fax: 205-348-2161, E-mail: dbsmith@ua.edu.
Website: http://education.ua.edu/academics/elpts/hea/

The University of Arizona, College of Education, Department of Educational Policy Studies and Practice, Program in Higher Education, Tucson, AZ 85721. Offers MA, PhD. *Program availability:* Part-time. Terminal master's awarded for partial completion of doctoral program. *Degree requirements:* For master's, comprehensive exam, thesis; for doctorate, comprehensive exam, thesis/dissertation. *Entrance requirements:* For master's, GRE General Test or MAT, minimum undergraduate GPA of 3.0; for doctorate, GRE General Test or MAT, minimum undergraduate GPA of 3.0, graduate 3.5. Additional exam requirements/recommendations for international students: Required—TOEFL (minimum score 550 paper-based; 79 iBT). Electronic applications accepted. *Faculty research:* Technology transfer, higher education policy, finance, curricular change.

University of Arkansas, Graduate School, College of Education and Health Professions, Department of Rehabilitation, Human Resources and Communication Disorders, Program in Higher Education, Fayetteville, AR 72701. Offers M Ed, Ed D, Ed S. *Accreditation:* NCATE. *Program availability:* Part-time, evening/weekend. In 2017, 26 master's, 5 doctorates awarded. *Degree requirements:* For master's, thesis optional; for doctorate, thesis/dissertation. *Entrance requirements:* For master's, GRE General Test, MAT or minimum GPA of 3.0; for doctorate, GRE General Test or MAT. *Application deadline:* For fall admission, 8/1 for domestic students, 4/1 for international students; for spring admission, 12/1 for domestic students, 10/1 for international students; for summer admission, 4/15 for domestic students, 3/1 for international students. Applications are processed on a rolling basis. Application fee: $60. Electronic applications accepted. *Expenses:* Tuition, state resident: full-time $3782. Tuition, nonresident: full-time $10,238. *Financial support:* In 2017–18, 30 research assistantships, 1 teaching assistantship were awarded; fellowships with tuition reimbursements, career-related internships or fieldwork, and Federal Work-Study also available. Support available to part-time students. Financial award application deadline: 4/1; financial award applicants required to submit FAFSA. *Unit head:* Dr. John Murry, Program Coordinator, 479-575-3802, Fax: 479-575-3319, E-mail: jmurry@uark.edu. *Application contact:* Dr. John Murry, Graduate Coordinator, 479-575-7332, E-mail: jmurry@uark.edu.
Website: http://hied.uark.edu

University of Arkansas at Little Rock, Graduate School, College of Education and Health Professions, Department of Educational Leadership, Program in Higher Education, Little Rock, AR 72204-1099. Offers administration (MA); college student affairs (MA); health professions teaching and learning (MA); higher education (Ed D); two-year college teaching (MA). *Degree requirements:* For doctorate, comprehensive exam, oral defense of dissertation, residency. *Entrance requirements:* For master's, GRE General Test or MAT, interview, minimum graduate GPA of 3.0; for doctorate, GRE General Test, interview, minimum graduate GPA of 3.5, teaching certificate, three years of work experience.

The University of British Columbia, Faculty of Education, Department of Educational Studies, Vancouver, BC V6T 1Z1, Canada. Offers adult learning and education (M Ed); adult learning and global change (M Ed); curriculum and leadership (M Ed); educational administration and leadership (M Ed); educational leadership and policy (Ed D); educational studies (M Ed, MA, PhD); higher education (M Ed); society, culture and politics in education (M Ed). *Program availability:* Part-time, evening/weekend. Terminal master's awarded for partial completion of doctoral program. *Degree requirements:* For master's, thesis; for doctorate, comprehensive exam, thesis/dissertation. *Entrance requirements:* For master's, minimum B+ average, 4-year undergraduate degree, field-related experience; for doctorate, minimum B+ average, 4-year undergraduate degree, master's degree, field-related experience. Additional exam requirements/recommendations for international students: Required—TOEFL (minimum score 600 paper-based; 100 iBT) or IELTS (minimum score 6.5). Electronic applications accepted. *Expenses:* Contact institution. *Faculty research:* Educational leadership educational administration adult education politics in education, global change and adult learning.

University of California, Riverside, Graduate Division, Graduate School of Education, Riverside, CA 92521. Offers applied behavior analysis (M Ed); diversity and equity (M Ed); education policy analysis and leadership (PhD); education specialist (Credential); education, society, and culture (MA, PhD); educational psychology (MA, PhD); general education (M Ed); higher education administration and policy (M Ed, PhD); multiple subject (Credential); research, evaluation, measurement and statistics (MA); school psychology (PhD); single subject (Credential); special education (M Ed, PhD); special education and autism (MA); TESOL (M Ed). *Faculty:* 29 full-time (16 women), 2 part-time/adjunct (1 woman). *Students:* 241 full-time (188 women). 396 applicants, 42% accepted, 166 enrolled. In 2017, 130 master's, 15 doctorates, 14 other advanced degrees awarded. Terminal master's awarded for partial completion of doctoral program. *Degree requirements:* For master's, comprehensive exams or thesis (MA), case study or analytical report (M Ed); for doctorate, comprehensive exam, thesis/dissertation, written and oral qualifying exams, college teaching practicum. *Entrance requirements:* For master's, GRE General Test (for MA); CBEST and CSET (for M Ed in general education only), UCR Extension TESOL certificate (for M Ed with TESOL emphasis only); for doctorate, GRE General Test, writing sample; for Credential, CBEST, CSET. Additional exam requirements/recommendations for international students: Required—TOEFL (minimum score 550 paper-based; 80 iBT), IELTS (minimum score 7). *Application deadline:* For fall admission, 9/1 for domestic students, 6/1 for international students; for winter admission, 11/15 for domestic students, 9/1 for international students; for spring admission, 3/1 for domestic students, 12/1 for international students. Applications are processed on a rolling basis. Application fee: $80 ($100 for international students). Electronic applications accepted. *Expenses:* Tuition, state resident: full-time $5746. Tuition, nonresident: full-time $10,780. Tuition and fees vary according to campus/location and program. *Financial support:* In 2017–18, 105 students received support, including 16 fellowships with full tuition reimbursements available (averaging $31,000 per year), 25 research assistantships with full tuition reimbursements available (averaging $31,000 per year), 10 teaching assistantships with full tuition reimbursements available (averaging $31,000 per year); career-related internships or fieldwork, Federal Work-Study, institutionally sponsored loans, scholarships/grants, and unspecified assistantships also available. Financial award application deadline: 12/15. *Faculty research:* Responsiveness to intervention, faculty core, response to intervention of English language learners, advanced modeling techniques, study on social capital, trust, and motivation. *Total annual research expenditures:* $1.7 million. *Unit head:* Thomas Smith, Dean, 951-827-4633, E-mail: thomas.smith@ucr.edu. *Application contact:* Heather Killeen, Graduate Program Coordinator, 951-827-6362, E-mail: heather.killeen@ucr.edu.
Website: http://www.education.ucr.edu/

University of Central Florida, College of Community Innovation and Education, Department of Educational Leadership and Higher Education, Orlando, FL 32816. Offers career and technical education (MA); educational leadership (M Ed, MA, Ed S); higher education/college teaching and leadership (MA); higher education/student personnel (MA). *Program availability:* Part-time, evening/weekend. *Students:* 86 full-time

(65 women), 233 part-time (184 women); includes 136 minority (66 Black or African American, non-Hispanic/Latino; 1 American Indian or Alaska Native, non-Hispanic/Latino; 4 Asian, non-Hispanic/Latino; 59 Hispanic/Latino; 6 Two or more races, non-Hispanic/Latino). Average age 31. 235 applicants, 82% accepted, 113 enrolled. In 2017, 114 master's, 16 other advanced degrees awarded. *Degree requirements:* For master's, thesis or alternative; for Ed S, thesis or alternative, final exam. *Entrance requirements:* For master's, GRE General Test; for Ed S, GRE General Test, minimum GPA of 3.0, resume, letters of recommendation. Additional exam requirements/recommendations for international students: Required—TOEFL. *Application deadline:* For fall admission, 6/20 for domestic students; for spring admission, 9/20 for domestic students. Application fee: $30. Electronic applications accepted. *Expenses:* Tuition, state resident: part-time $288.16 per credit hour. Tuition, nonresident: part-time $1073.31 per credit hour. Tuition and fees vary according to program. *Financial support:* In 2017–18, 12 students received support, including 2 fellowships with partial tuition reimbursements available (averaging $3,000 per year), 10 research assistantships with partial tuition reimbursements available (averaging $8,387 per year), 2 teaching assistantships with partial tuition reimbursements available (averaging $12,166 per year); career-related internships or fieldwork, Federal Work-Study, institutionally sponsored loans, health care benefits, tuition waivers (partial), and unspecified assistantships also available. Financial award application deadline: 3/1; financial award applicants required to submit FAFSA. *Unit head:* Dr. Kenneth Murray, Program Coordinator, 407-832-1468, E-mail: kenneth.murray@ucf.edu. *Application contact:* Associate Director, Graduate Admissions, 407-823-2766, Fax: 407-823-6442, E-mail: gradadmissions@ucf.edu. Website: https://ccie.ucf.edu/elhe/

University of Central Florida, College of Community Innovation and Education, Education Doctoral Programs, Orlando, FL 32816. Offers curriculum and instruction (Ed D); education (PhD), including communication sciences and disorders, counselor education, early childhood education, elementary education, exceptional education, exercise physiology, higher education, instructional design and technology, mathematics education, methodology, measurement and analysis, reading education, science education, social science education, TESOL; educational leadership (Ed D). *Students:* 122 full-time (86 women), 129 part-time (88 women); includes 64 minority (24 Black or African American, non-Hispanic/Latino; 1 American Indian or Alaska Native, non-Hispanic/Latino; 9 Asian, non-Hispanic/Latino; 24 Hispanic/Latino; 6 Two or more races, non-Hispanic/Latino), 26 international. Average age 38. 195 applicants, 47% accepted, 72 enrolled. In 2017, 89 doctorates awarded. *Entrance requirements:* For doctorate, GRE, letters of recommendation, goal statement, resume, writing sample. Application fee: $30. Electronic applications accepted. *Expenses:* Tuition, state resident: part-time $288.16 per credit hour. Tuition, nonresident: part-time $1073.31 per credit hour. Tuition and fees vary according to program. *Financial support:* In 2017–18, 77 students received support, including 28 fellowships with partial tuition reimbursements available (averaging $5,733 per year), 29 research assistantships with partial tuition reimbursements available (averaging $10,230 per year), 54 teaching assistantships with partial tuition reimbursements available (averaging $11,614 per year); health care benefits also available. Financial award application deadline: 3/1; financial award applicants required to submit FAFSA. *Unit head:* Dr. Edward Robinson, Director of Doctoral Programs, 407-823-6106, E-mail: edward.robinson@ucf.edu. *Application contact:* Associate Director, Graduate Admissions, 407-823-2766, Fax: 407-823-6442, E-mail: gradadmissions@ucf.edu. Website: https://edcollege.ucf.edu/academic-programs/graduate/

University of Connecticut, Graduate School, Neag School of Education, Department of Educational Leadership, Field of Higher Education and Student Affairs, Storrs, CT 06269. Offers MA. *Accreditation:* NCATE. *Degree requirements:* For master's, comprehensive exam, thesis or alternative. *Entrance requirements:* Additional exam requirements/recommendations for international students: Required—TOEFL (minimum score 550 paper-based). Electronic applications accepted.

University of Delaware, College of Education and Human Development, School of Education, Newark, DE 19716. Offers education (PhD); educational leadership (Ed D); higher education (M Ed); instruction (MI); reading (M Ed); school leadership (M Ed); school psychology (MA, Ed S); teaching English as a second language (TESL) (MA). *Accreditation:* NCATE. *Program availability:* Part-time, evening/weekend. Terminal master's awarded for partial completion of doctoral program. *Degree requirements:* For master's, comprehensive exam (for some programs), thesis (for some programs); for doctorate, comprehensive exam (for some programs), thesis/dissertation. *Entrance requirements:* For master's and doctorate, GRE, 3 letters of recommendation. Additional exam requirements/recommendations for international students: Required—TOEFL (minimum score 600 paper-based). Electronic applications accepted. *Faculty research:* Teacher education; curriculum theory and development; community based education models, educational leadership.

University of Denver, Morgridge College of Education, Denver, CO 80208. Offers child, family and school psychology (MA, PhD, Ed S); counseling psychology (MA, PhD); curriculum and instruction (MA, Ed D, PhD); curriculum instruction and teaching (Certificate); early childhood special education (MA, Certificate); educational leadership and policy studies (MA, Ed D, PhD, Certificate); higher education (Ed D, PhD); library and information science (MLIS); research methods and statistics (MA, PhD). *Accreditation:* ALA; APA (one or more programs are accredited). *Program availability:* Part-time, evening/weekend, online learning. *Faculty:* 39 full-time (29 women), 60 part-time/adjunct (42 women). *Students:* 502 full-time (406 women), 361 part-time (267 women); includes 233 minority (54 Black or African American, non-Hispanic/Latino; 6 American Indian or Alaska Native, non-Hispanic/Latino; 25 Asian, non-Hispanic/Latino; 113 Hispanic/Latino; 35 Two or more races, non-Hispanic/Latino), 52 international. Average age 31. 1,167 applicants, 64% accepted, 415 enrolled. In 2017, 285 master's, 51 doctorates, 157 other advanced degrees awarded. Terminal master's awarded for partial completion of doctoral program. *Degree requirements:* For master's, comprehensive exam; for doctorate, 2 foreign languages, comprehensive exam, thesis/dissertation. *Entrance requirements:* For master's and doctorate, GRE General Test or GMAT. Additional exam requirements/recommendations for international students: Required—TOEFL (minimum score 550 paper-based; 80 iBT). *Application deadline:* Applications are processed on a rolling basis. Application fee: $65. Electronic applications accepted. *Expenses:* $31,935 per year full-time. *Financial support:* In 2017–18, 765 students received support, including 26 research assistantships with tuition reimbursements available (averaging $10,957 per year), 38 teaching assistantships with tuition reimbursements available (averaging $3,391 per year); career-related internships or fieldwork, Federal Work-Study, institutionally sponsored loans, scholarships/grants, and unspecified assistantships also available. Support available to part-time students. Financial award application deadline: 2/15; financial award applicants required to submit FAFSA. *Faculty research:* Early childhood education, educational leadership, access and opportunity to postsecondary education, marriage and family therapy, data management and archival research. *Unit head:* Dr. Karen Riley, Dean, 303-871-3665, Fax: 303-871-4456, E-mail: karen.riley@du.edu. *Application contact:* Jodi Dye, Director of Admissions, 303-871-2510, Fax: 303-871-4456, E-mail: jodi.dye@du.edu. Website: http://morgridge.du.edu

University of Florida, Graduate School, College of Education, School of Human Development and Organizational Studies in Education, Gainesville, FL 32611. Offers counseling and counselor education (Ed D, PhD), including counseling and counselor education, marriage and family counseling, mental health counseling, school counseling and guidance; educational leadership (M Ed, MAE, Ed D, PhD, Ed S), including educational leadership (Ed D, PhD), educational policy (Ed D, PhD); higher education administration (Ed D, PhD), including education policy (Ed D), educational policy, higher education administration; marriage and family counseling (M Ed, MAE, Ed D, PhD, Ed S); mental health counseling (M Ed, MAE, Ed D, PhD, Ed S); research and evaluation methodology (M Ed, MAE, Ed D, PhD); school counseling and guidance (M Ed, MAE, Ed D, PhD, Ed S); student personnel in higher education (M Ed, MAE). *Accreditation:* ACA (one or more programs are accredited); NCATE. *Program availability:* Part-time, online learning. Terminal master's awarded for partial completion of doctoral program. *Degree requirements:* For master's, thesis optional; for doctorate, comprehensive exam, thesis/dissertation. *Entrance requirements:* For master's and doctorate, GRE General Test, minimum GPA of 3.0 (undergraduate), 3.5 (graduate); for Ed S, GRE General Test. Additional exam requirements/recommendations for international students: Required—TOEFL (minimum score 550 paper-based; 80 iBT), IELTS (minimum score 6). Electronic applications accepted.

University of Georgia, College of Education, Program in Higher Education, Athens, GA 30602. Offers M Ed, Ed D, PhD. *Accreditation:* NCATE. *Degree requirements:* For doctorate, thesis/dissertation. *Entrance requirements:* For doctorate, GRE General Test. Electronic applications accepted.

University of Houston, College of Education, Department of Educational Leadership and Cultural Studies, Houston, TX 77204. Offers administration and supervision (M Ed, Ed D); higher education (M Ed); historical, social, and cultural foundations of education (M Ed). *Accreditation:* NCATE. *Program availability:* Part-time, evening/weekend. *Degree requirements:* For master's, comprehensive exam or thesis; for doctorate, comprehensive exam, thesis/dissertation. *Entrance requirements:* For master's, GRE General Test, minimum cumulative GPA of 2.6, 3 letters of recommendation, resume/vitae, goal statement; for doctorate, GRE General Test, minimum cumulative GPA of 2.6, 3 letters of recommendation, resume/vitae, goal statement, writing sample, interview. Additional exam requirements/recommendations for international students: Required—TOEFL (minimum score 550 paper-based; 79 iBT). Electronic applications accepted. *Faculty research:* Change, supervision, multiculturalism, evaluation, policy.

University of Houston, College of Education, Department of Educational Psychology, Houston, TX 77204. Offers administration and supervision - higher education (M Ed); counseling (M Ed); counseling psychology (PhD); educational psychology (M Ed); school psychology (PhD); school psychology and individual differences (PhD); special education (M Ed). *Accreditation:* NCATE. *Program availability:* Part-time, evening/weekend, online learning. *Degree requirements:* For master's, comprehensive exam or thesis; for doctorate, comprehensive exam, thesis/dissertation. *Entrance requirements:* For master's, GRE, transcripts, 3 letters of recommendation, curriculum vita, goal statement; for doctorate, GRE, transcripts, 3 letters of recommendation, curriculum vita, goal statement, writing sample, interview. Additional exam requirements/recommendations for international students: Required—TOEFL (minimum score 550 paper-based; 79 iBT), IELTS (minimum score 6.5). Electronic applications accepted. *Faculty research:* Evidence-based assessment and intervention, multicultural issues in psychology, social and cultural context of learning, systemic barriers to college, motivational aspects of self-regulated learning.

University of Houston–Victoria, School of Education, Health Professions and Human Development, Victoria, TX 77901-4450. Offers administration and supervision (M Ed); adult and higher education (M Ed); counselor education (M Ed); curriculum and instruction (M Ed); dyslexia education (Certificate); educational technology (M Ed); special education (M Ed). *Program availability:* Part-time, evening/weekend, online learning. *Degree requirements:* For master's, comprehensive exam, project or thesis. *Entrance requirements:* For master's, GRE General Test. Additional exam requirements/recommendations for international students: Required—TOEFL. Electronic applications accepted. *Faculty research:* Reading and language arts education, evaluation and diagnosis of special children's abilities.

University of Illinois at Springfield, Graduate Programs, College of Education and Human Services, Department of Educational Leadership, Springfield, IL 62703-5407. Offers chief school business official (CAS); educational leadership (MA, CAS); educational technology (Graduate Certificate); English as a second language (Graduate Certificate); higher education online pedagogy (Graduate Certificate); leadership and learning (Graduate Certificate); legal aspects of education (Graduate Certificate). *Program availability:* Part-time, evening/weekend, 100% online, blended/hybrid learning. *Faculty:* 4 full-time (1 woman), 14 part-time/adjunct (11 women). *Students:* 2 full-time (1 woman), 109 part-time (70 women); includes 15 minority (10 Black or African American, non-Hispanic/Latino; 1 American Indian or Alaska Native, non-Hispanic/Latino; 1 Asian, non-Hispanic/Latino; 3 Hispanic/Latino). Average age 35. 46 applicants, 57% accepted, 23 enrolled. In 2017, 30 master's, 5 other advanced degrees awarded. *Degree requirements:* For master's, capstone course. *Entrance requirements:* For master's, minimum undergraduate GPA of 3.0, valid Illinois Teaching License, minimum of two years of successful teaching experience, portfolio that includes letters of recommendation, interview. Additional exam requirements/recommendations for international students: Required—TOEFL (minimum score 500 paper-based; 61 iBT). *Application deadline:* Applications are processed on a rolling basis. Application fee: $60 ($75 for international students). Electronic applications accepted. *Expenses:* Tuition, state resident: full-time $7896; part-time $329 per credit hour. Tuition, nonresident: full-time $16,200; part-time $675 per credit hour. Tuition and fees vary according to program. *Financial support:* In 2017–18, research assistantships with full tuition reimbursements (averaging $10,249 per year), teaching assistantships with full tuition reimbursements (averaging $10,303 per year) were awarded; fellowships, career-related internships or fieldwork, Federal Work-Study, scholarships/grants, health care benefits, and unspecified assistantships also available. Support available to part-time students. Financial award application deadline: 11/15; financial award applicants required to submit FAFSA. *Unit head:* Dr. Scott Day, Program Administrator, 217-206-7520, Fax: 217-206-6775, E-mail: day.scott@uis.edu. Website: http://www.uis.edu/edl/

The University of Iowa, Graduate College, College of Education, Department of Educational Policy and Leadership Studies, Program in Higher Education and Student Affairs, Iowa City, IA 52242-1316. Offers MA, PhD. *Degree requirements:* For master's, exam; for doctorate, comprehensive exam, thesis/dissertation. *Entrance requirements:* For master's and doctorate, GRE General Test, minimum GPA of 3.0. Additional exam requirements/recommendations for international students: Required—TOEFL (minimum score 550 paper-based; 81 iBT). Electronic applications accepted.

The University of Kansas, Graduate Studies, School of Education, Department of Educational Leadership and Policy Studies, Program in Higher Education Administration, Lawrence, KS 66045-3101. Offers MS Ed, Ed D, PhD. *Program availability:* Part-time, evening/weekend. *Students:* 51 full-time (37 women), 14 part-time (13 women); includes 19 minority (6 Black or African American, non-Hispanic/Latino; 1 American Indian or Alaska Native, non-Hispanic/Latino; 1 Asian, non-Hispanic/Latino; 7

Hispanic/Latino; 4 Two or more races, non-Hispanic/Latino). Average age 26. 79 applicants, 87% accepted, 35 enrolled. In 2017, 32 master's awarded. *Entrance requirements:* For master's, minimum GPA of 3.0, resume, statement of purpose, official transcript, three letters of recommendation; for doctorate, GRE General Test, minimum graduate GPA of 3.5, resume, statement of purpose, official transcripts, three letters of recommendation, writing sample; minimum of three years of professional experience in higher education or related organization and master's degree (preferred for Ed D). *Application deadline:* For fall admission, 7/1 for domestic and international students; for spring admission, 11/1 for domestic and international students; for summer admission, 3/1 for domestic and international students. Application fee: $65 ($85 for international students). Electronic applications accepted. *Financial support:* Fellowships, career-related internships or fieldwork, scholarships/grants, and unspecified assistantships available. Financial award application deadline: 1/3; financial award applicants required to submit FAFSA. *Faculty research:* Higher education policy, faculty issues, research on college students, financial aid, access to higher education. *Unit head:* Dr. Susan B. Twombly, Chair, 785-864-9721, Fax: 785-864-4697, E-mail: stwombly@ku.edu. *Application contact:* Denise Brubaker, Admissions Coordinator, 785-864-7973, Fax: 785-864-4697, E-mail: brubaker@ku.edu.

University of Kentucky, Graduate School, College of Education, Program in Educational Policy Studies and Evaluation, Lexington, KY 40506-0032. Offers educational policy studies and evaluation (Ed D); higher education (MS Ed, PhD); social and philosophical studies (MS Ed). *Accreditation:* NCATE. Terminal master's awarded for partial completion of doctoral program. *Degree requirements:* For master's, comprehensive exam, thesis optional; for doctorate, comprehensive exam, thesis/dissertation. *Entrance requirements:* For master's, GRE General Test, minimum undergraduate GPA of 2.75; for doctorate, GRE General Test, minimum graduate GPA of 3.0. Additional exam requirements/recommendations for international students: Required—TOEFL (minimum score 550 paper-based). Electronic applications accepted. *Faculty research:* Studies in higher education; comparative and international education; evaluation of educational programs, policies, and reform; student, teacher, and faculty cultures; gender and education.

University of La Verne, LaFetra College of Education, Program in Social Justice Higher Education Administration, La Verne, CA 91750-4443. Offers MA. *Program availability:* Part-time. *Faculty:* 1 full-time (0 women). *Students:* 8 part-time (5 women); includes 4 minority (all Hispanic/Latino). Average age 24. *Entrance requirements:* Additional exam requirements/recommendations for international students: Required—TOEFL (minimum score 550 paper-based; 80 iBT), IELTS (minimum score 6.5). *Application deadline:* Applications are processed on a rolling basis. Application fee: $50. Electronic applications accepted. Tuition and fees vary according to program. *Financial support:* Federal Work-Study and scholarships/grants available. Financial award applicants required to submit FAFSA. *Unit head:* Issac Carter, Chair, 909-448-4185, E-mail: icarter@laverne.edu. *Application contact:* Christy Ranells, Associate Director of Graduate Admission, 909-448-4644, Fax: 909-971-2295, E-mail: cranells@laverne.edu. Website: https://education.laverne.edu/sjhe/

University of Louisville, Graduate School, College of Education and Human Development, Department of Educational Leadership, Evaluation and Organizational Development, Louisville, KY 40292-0001. Offers educational leadership and organizational development (Ed D, PhD), including evaluation (PhD), human resource development (PhD), P-12 administration (PhD), post-secondary administration (PhD), sport administration (PhD); health professions education (Certificate); higher education administration (MA); human resources and organization development (MS), including health professions education, human resource leadership, workplace learning and performance; P-12 educational administration (Ed S), including principalship, supervisor of instruction. *Accreditation:* NCATE. *Program availability:* Part-time, evening/weekend, online learning. *Students:* 190 full-time (64 women), 516 part-time (298 women); includes 218 minority (131 Black or African American, non-Hispanic/Latino; 1 American Indian or Alaska Native, non-Hispanic/Latino; 16 Asian, non-Hispanic/Latino; 47 Hispanic/Latino; 2 Native Hawaiian or other Pacific Islander, non-Hispanic/Latino; 21 Two or more races, non-Hispanic/Latino), 3 international. Average age 36. 232 applicants, 84% accepted, 141 enrolled. In 2017, 68 master's, 2 doctorates, 17 other advanced degrees awarded. Application fee: $65. *Expenses:* Tuition, state resident: full-time $12,246; part-time $681 per credit hour. Tuition, nonresident: full-time $25,486; part-time $1417 per credit hour. *Required fees:* $196. Tuition and fees vary according to course load, program and reciprocity agreements. *Financial support:* Application deadline: 6/1; applicants required to submit FAFSA. *Faculty research:* Urban educational leadership and policy, human resource and organizational development, program evaluation, community and military partnerships, higher education, and economic education. *Total annual research expenditures:* $256,111. *Unit head:* Dr. Jeffrey Sun, Chair and Professor, 502-852-0618, E-mail: jeffrey.sun@louisville.edu. *Application contact:* Betty Hampton, Director of Graduate Student Services, 502-852-5597, Fax: 502-852-1465, E-mail: edadvise@louisville.edu. Website: http://louisville.edu/education/departments/eleod

University of Louisville, Graduate School, College of Education and Human Development, Departments of Early Childhood and Elementary Education, Middle and Secondary Education, and Special Education, Louisville, KY 40292-0001. Offers art education (MAT); autism and applied behavior analysis (Certificate); curriculum and instruction (PhD); early elementary education (MAT); exercise physiology (MS); health and physical education (MAT); health professions education (Certificate); higher education (MA); human resources and organization development (MS); instructional technology (M Ed); interdisciplinary early childhood education (MAT); middle school education (MAT); music education (MAT); secondary education (MAT); special education (MAT); sport administration (MS); teacher leadership (M Ed). *Program availability:* Part-time, evening/weekend. *Students:* 114 full-time (73 women), 173 part-time (114 women); includes 49 minority (19 Black or African American, non-Hispanic/Latino; 5 Asian, non-Hispanic/Latino; 13 Hispanic/Latino; 12 Two or more races, non-Hispanic/Latino), 7 international. Average age 29. 132 applicants, 73% accepted, 57 enrolled. In 2017, 70 master's, 2 doctorates, 2 other advanced degrees awarded. *Application deadline:* For spring admission, 1/1 priority date for international students. Application fee: $65. *Expenses:* Tuition, state resident: full-time $12,246; part-time $681 per credit hour. Tuition, nonresident: full-time $25,486; part-time $1417 per credit hour. *Required fees:* $196. Tuition and fees vary according to course load, program and reciprocity agreements. *Financial support:* Application deadline: 6/1; applicants required to submit FAFSA. *Faculty research:* STEM teaching and learning; content literacy for English language learners; social justice in teacher education; adolescent literacy; mathematics teacher development. *Total annual research expenditures:* $1.7 million. *Unit head:* Dr. Ann E. Larson, Dean, College of Education and Human Development, 502-852-6411, Fax: 502-852-1464, E-mail: ann@louisville.edu. *Application contact:* Betty Hampton, Director of Graduate Student Services, 502-852-5597, Fax: 502-852-1465, E-mail: edadvise@louisville.edu. Website: http://louisville.edu/delphi

University of Lynchburg, Graduate Studies, M Ed Program in Educational Leadership, Lynchburg, VA 24501-3199. Offers higher education (M Ed); PK-12 administrative and supervisory (M Ed). *Program availability:* Part-time, evening/weekend. *Faculty:* 17 full-time (10 women). *Students:* 10 full-time (4 women), 41 part-time (32 women); includes 6 minority (all Black or African American, non-Hispanic/Latino). Average age 34. 14 applicants, 100% accepted, 7 enrolled. In 2017, 43 master's awarded. *Degree requirements:* For master's, comprehensive exam (for some programs), internship; SLLC exam or comprehensive exam. *Entrance requirements:* For master's, GRE, minimum GPA of 3.0 (preferred), official transcripts (bachelor's, others as relevant), three letters of recommendation, career goals statement. Additional exam requirements/recommendations for international students: Required—TOEFL (minimum score 550 paper-based; 80 iBT), IELTS (minimum score 6). *Application deadline:* For fall admission, 7/31 for domestic students, 6/1 for international students; for spring admission, 11/30 for domestic students, 10/5 for international students. Applications are processed on a rolling basis. Application fee: $30. Electronic applications accepted. Application fee is waived when completed online. *Expenses:* $510 per credit tuition, $100 fees. *Financial support:* Career-related internships or fieldwork, Federal Work-Study, scholarships/grants, health care benefits, and unspecified assistantships available. Support available to part-time students. Financial award application deadline: 7/31; financial award applicants required to submit FAFSA. *Unit head:* Dr. John Walker, Professor/Director, Leadership Studies, 434-544-8032, E-mail: walker.jc@lynchburg.edu. *Application contact:* Ellen Thompson, Graduate Admissions Counselor, 434-544-8841, E-mail: thompson_e@lynchburg.edu. Website: http://www.lynchburg.edu/graduate/master-of-education-in-educational-leadership/

University of Maine, Graduate School, College of Education and Human Development, School of Educational Leadership, Higher Education, and Human Development, Orono, ME 04469. Offers educational leadership (M Ed, CAS); higher education (CAS); human development (MS). *Program availability:* Part-time. *Faculty:* 11 full-time (7 women), 10 part-time/adjunct (5 women). *Students:* 42 full-time (31 women), 67 part-time (49 women); includes 8 minority (1 Black or African American, non-Hispanic/Latino; 2 American Indian or Alaska Native, non-Hispanic/Latino; 3 Hispanic/Latino; 2 Two or more races, non-Hispanic/Latino). Average age 36. 73 applicants, 82% accepted, 25 enrolled. In 2017, 30 master's, 4 doctorates, 16 other advanced degrees awarded. *Degree requirements:* For master's, thesis (for some programs); for doctorate, comprehensive exam, thesis/dissertation. *Entrance requirements:* For master's, GRE General Test, MAT; for doctorate, GRE. Additional exam requirements/recommendations for international students: Required—TOEFL (minimum score 550 paper-based; 80 iBT), IELTS (minimum score 6.5). *Application deadline:* For fall admission, 2/1 priority date for domestic students. Applications are processed on a rolling basis. Application fee: $65. Electronic applications accepted. *Expenses:* Tuition, state resident: full-time $7722; part-time $429 per credit hour. Tuition, nonresident: full-time $25,146; part-time $1397 per credit hour. *Required fees:* $1162; $581 per credit hour. *Financial support:* In 2017–18, 30 students received support, including 5 teaching assistantships with full tuition reimbursements available (averaging $14,600 per year); career-related internships or fieldwork, Federal Work-Study, institutionally sponsored loans, tuition waivers (full and partial), and unspecified assistantships also available. Financial award application deadline: 3/1. *Faculty research:* Student hazing and hazing prevention, sexuality education, cross cultural perspectives on family, early childhood development, fatherhood/parenting, campus climate, social justice, rural higher education, gender in higher education, discourse, rural sociology, school-community relationships, instructional supervision, rural educational leadership. *Total annual research expenditures:* $130,000. *Unit head:* Dr. Jim Artesani, Associate Dean of Accreditation and Graduate Affairs, 207-581-4061, Fax: 207-581-3120. *Application contact:* Scott G. Delcourt, Senior Associate Dean of the Graduate School, 207-581-3291, Fax: 207-581-3232, E-mail: graduate@maine.edu. Website: http://www.umaine.edu/edhd

University of Manitoba, Faculty of Graduate Studies, Faculty of Education, Department of Educational Administration, Foundations and Psychology, Winnipeg, MB R3T 2N2, Canada. Offers adult and post-secondary education (M Ed); educational administration (M Ed); guidance and counseling (M Ed); inclusive special education (M Ed); social foundations of education (M Ed). *Degree requirements:* For master's, thesis or alternative.

University of Mary Hardin-Baylor, Graduate Studies in Education, Belton, TX 76513. Offers curriculum and instruction (M Ed); educational administration (M Ed, Ed D), including higher education (Ed D), leadership in nursing education (Ed D), P-12 (Ed D). *Program availability:* Part-time, evening/weekend. *Faculty:* 12 full-time (8 women), 5 part-time/adjunct (2 women). *Students:* 29 full-time (20 women), 79 part-time (55 women); includes 53 minority (35 Black or African American, non-Hispanic/Latino; 17 Hispanic/Latino; 1 Two or more races, non-Hispanic/Latino), 1 international. Average age 39. 15 applicants, 80% accepted, 10 enrolled. In 2017, 47 master's, 16 doctorates awarded. *Degree requirements:* For master's, comprehensive exam; for doctorate, thesis/dissertation. *Entrance requirements:* For master's, minimum GPA of 3.0, interview; for doctorate, minimum GPA of 3.5, interview, essay, resume, employment verification, 3 letters of recommendation. Additional exam requirements/recommendations for international students: Required—TOEFL (minimum score 60 iBT), IELTS (minimum score 4.5). *Application deadline:* For fall admission, 6/1 for domestic students, 4/30 priority date for international students; for spring admission, 11/1 for domestic students, 9/30 priority date for international students. Applications are processed on a rolling basis. Application fee: $35 ($135 for international students). Electronic applications accepted. *Expenses:* $920 per credit hour. *Financial support:* In 2017–18, 90 students received support. Federal Work-Study and scholarships for some active duty military personnel available. Support available to part-time students. Financial award application deadline: 6/1; financial award applicants required to submit FAFSA. *Faculty research:* Motivational orientation of preservice teachers. *Unit head:* Dr. Craig Hammonds, Director, Graduate Programs in Education, 254-295-4189, E-mail: rhammonds@umhb.edu. *Application contact:* Sharon Aguilera, Assistant Director, Graduate Admissions, 254-295-4835, E-mail: saguilera@umhb.edu. Website: https://go.umhb.edu/graduate/education/home

University of Massachusetts Amherst, Graduate School, College of Education, Program in Education, Amherst, MA 01003. Offers bilingual, English as a second language, and multicultural education (M Ed, Ed S); child study and early education (M Ed); children, families and schools (Ed D, Ed S); early childhood and elementary teacher education (M Ed); educational leadership (M Ed); educational policy and leadership (Ed D); higher education (M Ed); international education (M Ed); language, literacy and culture (Ed D); learning, media and technology (M Ed, Ed S); mathematics, science, and learning technologies (M Ed); reading and writing (M Ed); research, educational measurement and psychometrics (Ed D); school counselor education (M Ed, Ed S); school psychology (Ed S); science education (Ed S); secondary teacher education (M Ed); social justice education (M Ed, Ed D, Ed S); special education (M Ed, Ed D, Ed S); teacher education and school improvement (Ed D, Ed S). *Accreditation:* NCATE. *Program availability:* Part-time, online learning. Terminal master's awarded for partial completion of doctoral program. *Degree requirements:* For doctorate, comprehensive exam, thesis/dissertation. *Entrance requirements:* Additional exam requirements/recommendations for international students: Required—TOEFL (minimum score 550 paper-based; 80 iBT), IELTS (minimum score 6.5). Electronic applications accepted.

University of Massachusetts Amherst, Graduate School, Interdisciplinary Programs, Dual Degree Program in Education and Public Policy and Administration, Amherst, MA 01003. Offers MPPA/M Ed. *Entrance requirements:* Additional exam requirements/recommendations for international students: Required—TOEFL (minimum score 550 paper-based; 80 iBT), IELTS (minimum score 6.5). Electronic applications accepted.

University of Massachusetts Boston, College of Education and Human Development, Program in Higher Education, Boston, MA 02125-3393. Offers Ed D, PhD. *Students:* 5 full-time (3 women), 61 part-time (38 women); includes 29 minority (11 Black or African American, non-Hispanic/Latino; 7 Asian, non-Hispanic/Latino; 11 Hispanic/Latino). Average age 41. 35 applicants, 46% accepted, 13 enrolled. In 2017, 7 doctorates awarded. *Expenses:* Tuition, state resident: full-time $17,375. Tuition, nonresident: full-time $33,915. *Required fees:* $355. *Unit head:* Dr. Joseph Berger, Dean, 617-287-5000. *Application contact:* Graduate Admissions Coordinator, 617-287-6400, Fax: 617-287-6236, E-mail: bos.gadm@dpc.umassp.edu.

University of Memphis, Graduate School, College of Education, Department of Leadership, Memphis, TN 38152. Offers adult education (Ed D); community college teaching and leadership (Graduate Certificate); community education (Ed D); educational leadership (Ed D); higher education (Ed D); leadership (MS); policy studies (Ed D); school administration and supervision (MS); student personnel (MS). *Accreditation:* NCATE. *Program availability:* Part-time, evening/weekend, online learning. *Faculty:* 9 full-time (5 women), 6 part-time/adjunct (2 women). *Students:* 13 full-time (9 women), 154 part-time (96 women). Average age 35. 54 applicants, 93% accepted, 44 enrolled. In 2017, 19 master's, 26 doctorates, 4 other advanced degrees awarded. *Degree requirements:* For master's, comprehensive exam, thesis optional; for doctorate, comprehensive exam, thesis/dissertation. *Entrance requirements:* For master's, GRE, resume, letters of reference, statement of professional goals, current teacher certification, sample work, interview; for doctorate, GRE, resume, letters of reference, statement of professional goals, interview. Additional exam requirements/recommendations for international students: Required—TOEFL (minimum score 550 paper-based; 79 iBT). *Application deadline:* For fall admission, 6/15 for domestic students; for spring admission, 9/15 for domestic students; for summer admission, 2/15 for domestic students. Application fee: $35 ($60 for international students). Electronic applications accepted. *Expenses:* Contact institution. *Financial support:* In 2017–18, 70 students received support, including 4 research assistantships with full tuition reimbursements available (averaging $14,700 per year); teaching assistantships, Federal Work-Study, scholarships/grants, and unspecified assistantships also available. Financial award application deadline: 2/1; financial award applicants required to submit FAFSA. *Faculty research:* School improvement, social justice, online learning, adult learning, diversity. *Unit head:* Dr. Reginald Green, Interim Chair, 901-678-3445, E-mail: rlgreen1@memphis.edu.
Website: http://www.memphis.edu/lead

University of Miami, Graduate School, School of Education and Human Development, Department of Educational and Psychological Studies, Program in Higher Education Administration, Coral Gables, FL 33124. Offers enrollment management (MS Ed, Certificate); higher education leadership (Ed D); student life and development (MS Ed, Certificate). *Program availability:* Part-time, evening/weekend. Terminal master's awarded for partial completion of doctoral program. *Degree requirements:* For master's, comprehensive exam; for doctorate, thesis/dissertation, qualifying exam. *Entrance requirements:* For master's and doctorate, GRE General Test. Additional exam requirements/recommendations for international students: Required—TOEFL (minimum score 550 paper-based; 80 iBT); Recommended—IELTS (minimum score 6.5). Electronic applications accepted.

University of Minnesota, Twin Cities Campus, Graduate School, College of Education and Human Development, Department of Organizational Leadership, Policy and Development, Program in Higher Education, Minneapolis, MN 55455-0213. Offers higher education (MA, PhD); multicultural college teaching and learning (MA). *Students:* 44 full-time (33 women), 54 part-time (30 women); includes 27 minority (11 Black or African American, non-Hispanic/Latino; 1 American Indian or Alaska Native, non-Hispanic/Latino; 6 Asian, non-Hispanic/Latino; 7 Hispanic/Latino; 2 Two or more races, non-Hispanic/Latino), 5 international. Average age 37. 44 applicants, 43% accepted, 19 enrolled. In 2017, 16 master's, 16 doctorates awarded. Application fee: $75 ($95 for international students). *Unit head:* Dr. Heidi Barajas, Chair, 612-625-4823, E-mail: hbarajas@umn.edu. *Application contact:* Dr. Jeremy J. Hernandez, Director of Graduate Studies, 612-626-9377, E-mail: herna220@umn.edu.
Website: http://www.cehd.umn.edu/olpd/grad-programs/HiEd/

University of Mississippi, Graduate School, School of Education, University, MS 38677. Offers counselor education (M Ed, PhD); counselor education - play therapy (Ed S); early childhood (M Ed); educational leadership K-12 (M Ed, Ed D, PhD, Ed S); elementary education (M Ed, Ed D, Ed S); higher education/student personnel (Ed D, PhD); literacy education (M Ed); math education (Ed D); secondary education (M Ed, PhD, Ed S); special education (M Ed, PhD, Ed S); teacher corporations (MA); teacher education (MA). *Accreditation:* NCATE. *Faculty:* 65 full-time (40 women), 25 part-time/adjunct (5 women). *Students:* 185 full-time (148 women), 410 part-time (310 women); includes 193 minority (168 Black or African American, non-Hispanic/Latino; 7 Asian, non-Hispanic/Latino; 14 Hispanic/Latino; 4 Two or more races, non-Hispanic/Latino), 7 international. Average age 33. In 2017, 176 master's, 20 doctorates, 37 other advanced degrees awarded. *Entrance requirements:* For master's, GRE General Test, minimum GPA of 3.0; for doctorate, GRE General Test. Additional exam requirements/recommendations for international students: Required—TOEFL. *Application deadline:* For fall admission, 3/1 for domestic students; for spring admission, 10/1 for domestic students; for summer admission, 3/1 for domestic students. Applications are processed on a rolling basis. Application fee: $50. Electronic applications accepted. *Financial support:* Scholarships/grants available. Financial award application deadline: 3/1; financial award applicants required to submit FAFSA. *Unit head:* Dr. David Rock, Dean, 662-915-7063, Fax: 662-915-7249, E-mail: soe@olemiss.edu. *Application contact:* Dr. Joe Sumrall, Professor of Elementary Education, 662-915-7350, E-mail: soe@olemiss.edu.

University of Missouri, Office of Research and Graduate Studies, College of Education, Department of Educational Leadership and Policy Analysis, Columbia, MO 65211. Offers education administration (M Ed, MA, Ed D, PhD, Ed S); higher and adult education (M Ed, MA, Ed D, PhD, Ed S). *Program availability:* Part-time. *Degree requirements:* For doctorate, variable foreign language requirement, comprehensive exam (for some programs), thesis/dissertation. *Entrance requirements:* For master's, doctorate, and Ed S, minimum GPA of 3.0. Additional exam requirements/recommendations for international students: Required—TOEFL (minimum score 500 paper-based; 61 iBT), IELTS (minimum score 5.5). Electronic applications accepted.

University of Missouri–Kansas City, School of Education, Kansas City, MO 64110-2499. Offers administration (Ed D); counseling and guidance (MA, Ed S), including mental health counseling (Ed S), school counseling (Ed S); counseling psychology (PhD); curriculum and instruction (MA, Ed S), including language and literacy (Ed S); education (PhD), including higher education administration, PK-12 education administration; educational administration (MA, Ed S), including advanced principal (Ed S), beginning principal (Ed S), district-level administration (Ed S); reading education

(MA); special education (MA). PhD in education offered through the School of Graduate Studies. *Accreditation:* NCATE. *Program availability:* Part-time, evening/weekend. *Degree requirements:* For doctorate, thesis/dissertation, internship, practicum. *Entrance requirements:* For master's, GRE, minimum GPA of 2.75, 2 letters of reference, written statement of purpose; for doctorate, GRE, minimum GPA of 3.0; for Ed S, minimum GPA of 3.0. Additional exam requirements/recommendations for international students: Required—TOEFL (minimum score 550 paper-based; 80 iBT). *Faculty research:* Urban education, inquiry-based field study, theories of counseling and psychotherapy, school literacy, educational technology.

University of Missouri–St. Louis, College of Education, Department of Education Sciences and Professional Programs, St. Louis, MO 63121. Offers adult and higher education (M Ed); educational psychology (M Ed), including character and citizenship education, research and program evaluation; program evaluation (Certificate); school psychology (Ed S). *Students:* 19 full-time (17 women), 13 part-time (12 women); includes 4 minority (2 Black or African American, non-Hispanic/Latino; 2 Hispanic/Latino). 16 applicants, 56% accepted, 9 enrolled. *Degree requirements:* For other advanced degree, comprehensive exam, thesis or alternative, internship. *Entrance requirements:* For degree, GRE General Test, 2-4 letters of recommendation, personal interview. Additional exam requirements/recommendations for international students: Required—IELTS (minimum score 6.5); Recommended—TOEFL (minimum score 550 paper-based; 79 iBT). *Application deadline:* For fall admission, 2/15 priority date for domestic students, 2/15 for international students. Application fee: $50 ($40 for international students). Electronic applications accepted. *Expenses:* Tuition, state resident: part-time $476.50 per credit hour. Tuition, nonresident: part-time $1169.70 per credit hour. *Financial support:* Application deadline: 4/1; applicants required to submit FAFSA. *Faculty research:* Child/adolescent psychology, quantitative and qualitative methodology, evaluation processes, measurement and assessment. *Unit head:* Dr. Donald Gouwens, Chairperson, 314-516-4773, Fax: 314-516-5784, E-mail: gouwensd@umsl.edu. *Application contact:* 314-516-5458, Fax: 314-516-6996, E-mail: gradadm@umsl.edu.
Website: https://coe.umsl.edu/dept/espp.html

University of Nevada, Las Vegas, Graduate College, College of Education, Department of Educational Psychology and Higher Education, Las Vegas, NV 89154-3002. Offers chief diversity officer in higher education (Certificate); college sport leadership (Certificate); educational psychology (M Ed, MS, PhD, Ed S); higher education (M Ed, PhD, Certificate); psychology/learning and technology (PhD), including learning and technology; workforce development/educational leadership (PhD); PhD/JD. *Program availability:* Part-time, evening/weekend, 100% online, blended/hybrid learning. *Faculty:* 22 full-time (15 women), 12 part-time/adjunct (8 women). *Students:* 95 full-time (73 women), 108 part-time (75 women); includes 72 minority (19 Black or African American, non-Hispanic/Latino; 9 Asian, non-Hispanic/Latino; 32 Hispanic/Latino; 12 Two or more races, non-Hispanic/Latino), 5 international. Average age 36. 86 applicants, 65% accepted, 44 enrolled. In 2017, 33 master's, 6 doctorates, 8 other advanced degrees awarded. *Degree requirements:* For master's, comprehensive exam (for some programs), thesis (for some programs); for doctorate, comprehensive exam, thesis/dissertation. *Entrance requirements:* For master's, GRE General Test or GMAT (for some programs), letters of recommendation; writing sample; bachelor's degree; for doctorate, GMAT or GRE General Test, writing exam; for other advanced degree, GRE General Test (for some programs). Additional exam requirements/recommendations for international students: Required—TOEFL (minimum score 550 paper-based; 80 iBT), IELTS (minimum score 7). Application fee: $60 ($95 for international students). Electronic applications accepted. *Expenses:* $275 per credit, $850 per course, $7,969 per year resident, $22,157 per year non-resident, $7,094 non-resident fee (7 credits or more), $1,307 annual health insurance fee. *Financial support:* In 2017–18, 49 students received support, including 31 research assistantships with partial tuition reimbursements available (averaging $15,769 per year), 18 teaching assistantships with partial tuition reimbursements available (averaging $19,486 per year); institutionally sponsored loans, scholarships/grants, health care benefits, and unspecified assistantships also available. Financial award application deadline: 3/15; financial award applicants required to submit FAFSA. *Faculty research:* Innovation and change in educational settings; educational policy, finance, and marketing; psycho-educational assessment; student retention, persistence, development, language, and culture; statistical modeling, program evaluation, qualitative and quantitative research methods. *Total annual research expenditures:* $470,161. *Unit head:* Dr. Alice Corkill, Chair/Professor, 702-895-4164, E-mail: alice.corkill@unlv.edu. *Application contact:* Dr. Steve McCafferty, Graduate Coordinator, 702-895-3245, Fax: 702-895-1658, E-mail: mccaffes@unlv.nevada.edu.
Website: http://education.unlv.edu/ephe/

University of New Hampshire, Graduate School, Interdisciplinary Programs, Program in College Teaching, Durham, NH 03824. Offers Postbaccalaureate Certificate. *Program availability:* Part-time. *Entrance requirements:* Additional exam requirements/recommendations for international students: Required—TOEFL (minimum score 550 paper-based; 80 iBT). *Application deadline:* For fall admission, 7/1 for domestic students; for spring admission, 12/1 for domestic students; for summer admission, 4/1 for domestic students. Application fee: $25. Electronic applications accepted. *Financial support:* Fellowships, research assistantships, and teaching assistantships available. Financial award application deadline: 2/15. *Unit head:* Dr. Cari Moorhead, Interim Dean, 603-862-3007. *Application contact:* Dovev Levine, Assistant Dean, 603-862-2234, E-mail: college.teaching@unh.edu.

University of New Mexico, School of Medicine, Program in University Science Teaching, Albuquerque, NM 87131-2039. Offers Certificate.

The University of North Carolina at Greensboro, Graduate School, School of Education, Department of Teacher Education and Higher Education, Program in Curriculum and Teaching, Greensboro, NC 27412-5001. Offers higher education (PhD); teacher education and development (PhD). *Accreditation:* NCATE. *Degree requirements:* For doctorate, comprehensive exam, thesis/dissertation. *Entrance requirements:* For doctorate, GRE General Test. Additional exam requirements/recommendations for international students: Required—TOEFL. Electronic applications accepted.

The University of North Carolina Wilmington, Watson College of Education, Department of Educational Leadership, Wilmington, NC 28403-3297. Offers curriculum, instruction and supervision (M Ed); educational leadership and administration (Ed D), including curriculum and instruction; higher education (M Ed); school administration (MSA), including school administration. *Program availability:* Part-time, 100% online. *Faculty:* 14 full-time (11 women), 6 part-time/adjunct (4 women). *Students:* 39 full-time (24 women), 150 part-time (109 women); includes 56 minority (41 Black or African American, non-Hispanic/Latino; 7 American Indian or Alaska Native, non-Hispanic/Latino; 2 Asian, non-Hispanic/Latino; 4 Hispanic/Latino; 2 Native Hawaiian or other Pacific Islander, non-Hispanic/Latino), 1 international. Average age 36. 80 applicants, 74% accepted, 50 enrolled. In 2017, 53 master's, 20 doctorates awarded. *Degree requirements:* For master's, thesis or culminating project, e-Portfolio (for school administration); for doctorate, comprehensive exam, thesis/dissertation. *Entrance requirements:* For master's, GRE General Test, MAT, minimum B average in

undergraduate work, 3 letters of recommendation, education statement of interest essay, autobiographical statement, NC Class A teacher licensure in related field, minimum of 3 years' teaching experience; for doctorate, education statement of interest essay, master's degree in education field, 3 years of leadership experience. Additional exam requirements/recommendations for international students: Required—TOEFL (minimum score 550 paper-based; 79 iBT), IELTS (minimum score 6.5). *Application deadline:* For fall admission, 5/15 for domestic students; for spring admission, 10/15 for domestic students; for summer admission, 3/15 for domestic students. Applications are processed on a rolling basis. Application fee: $75. Electronic applications accepted. *Expenses:* Tuition, state resident: full-time $4626; part-time $226.76 per credit hour. Tuition, nonresident: full-time $17,834; part-time $874.22 per credit hour. *Required fees:* $2124. Tuition and fees vary according to program. *Financial support:* Scholarships/grants and unspecified assistantships available. Financial award application deadline: 1/1; financial award applicants required to submit FAFSA. Unit head: Dr. Marsha Carr, Interim Chair, 910-962-2913, Fax: 910-962-3609, E-mail: carrm@uncw.edu. *Application contact:* Dr. William Sterrett, Graduate Program Coordinator, 910-962-7995, E-mail: stewettw@uncw.edu.
Website: http://uncw.edu/ed/el/

University of Northern Colorado, Graduate School, College of Education and Behavioral Sciences, Department of Leadership, Policy and Development: Higher Education and P-12 Education, Program in Higher Education and Student Affairs Leadership, Greeley, CO 80639. Offers MA, PhD. *Program availability:* Part-time. *Entrance requirements:* For doctorate, GRE General Test, transcripts, 3 letters of recommendation. Electronic applications accepted.

University of Northern Iowa, Graduate College, College of Education, Department of Educational Leadership and Postsecondary Education, MA Program in Postsecondary Education: Student Affairs, Cedar Falls, IA 50614. Offers MA. *Degree requirements:* For master's, comprehensive exam, thesis or alternative. *Entrance requirements:* For master's, minimum GPA of 3.0. Additional exam requirements/recommendations for international students: Required—TOEFL (minimum score 500 paper-based; 61 iBT). Electronic applications accepted.

University of North Georgia, Doctor of Education Program in Higher Education Leadership and Practice, Dahlonega, GA 30597. Offers Ed D. *Program availability:* Part-time, evening/weekend, online only, 100% online. *Students:* 13 part-time (8 women); includes 2 minority (1 American Indian or Alaska Native, non-Hispanic/Latino; 1 Hispanic/Latino), 1 international. Average age 43. 35 applicants, 49% accepted, 13 enrolled. *Degree requirements:* For doctorate, thesis/dissertation. *Entrance requirements:* Additional exam requirements/recommendations for international students: Required—TOEFL (minimum score 550 paper-based; 79 iBT), IELTS (minimum score 6.5). *Application deadline:* For fall admission, 7/24 for domestic students. Application fee: $40. Electronic applications accepted. *Expenses:* Contact institution. *Financial support:* Application deadline: 3/17; applicants required to submit FAFSA. Unit head: Dr. Susan Brandenburg-Ayres, Dean, 706-864-1998, E-mail: susan.ayres@ung.edu. *Application contact:* Melinda Maxwell, Director of Graduate Admissions, 706-867-2077, E-mail: melinda.maxwell@ung.edu.
Website: https://ung.edu/teacher-education/graduate/doctor-of-education-with-a-major-in-higher-education-leadership-and-practice.php

University of North Texas, Robert B. Toulouse School of Graduate Studies, Denton, TX 76203-5459. Offers accounting (MS); applied anthropology (MA, MS); applied behavior analysis (Certificate); applied geography (MA); applied technology and performance improvement (M Ed, MS); art education (MA); art history (MA); art museum education (Certificate); arts leadership (Certificate); audiology (Au D); behavior analysis (MS); behavioral science (PhD); biochemistry and molecular biology (MS); biology (MA, MS); biomedical engineering (MS); business analysis (MS); chemistry (MS); clinical health psychology (PhD); communication studies (MA, MS); computer engineering (MS); computer science (MS); counseling (M Ed, MS), including clinical mental health counseling (MS), college and university counseling, elementary school counseling, secondary school counseling; creative writing (MA); criminal justice (MS); curriculum and instruction (M Ed); decision sciences (MBA); design (MA, MFA), including fashion design (MFA), innovation studies, interior design (MFA); early childhood studies (MS); economics (MS); educational leadership (M Ed, Ed D); educational psychology (MS, PhD), including family studies (MS), gifted and talented (MS), human development (MS), learning and cognition (MS), research, measurement and evaluation (MS); electrical engineering (MS); emergency management (MPA); engineering technology (MS); English (MA); English as a second language (MA); environmental science (MS); finance (MBA, MS); financial management (MPA); French (MA); health services management (MBA); higher education (M Ed, Ed D); history (MA, MS); hospitality management (MS); human resources management (MPA); information science (MS); information systems (PhD); information technologies (MBA); interdisciplinary studies (MA, MS); international studies (MA); international sustainable tourism (MS); jazz studies (MM); journalism (MA, MJ, Graduate Certificate), including interactive and virtual digital communication (Graduate Certificate), narrative journalism (Graduate Certificate), public relations (Graduate Certificate); kinesiology (MS); linguistics (MA); local government management (MPA); logistics (PhD); logistics and supply chain management (MBA); long-term care, senior housing, and aging services (MA); management (PhD); marketing (MBA); mathematics (MA, MS); mechanical and energy engineering (MS, PhD); music (MA), including ethnomusicology, music theory, musicology, performance; music composition (PhD); music education (MM Ed, PhD); nonprofit management (MPA); operations and supply chain management (MBA); performance (MM, DMA); philosophy (MA); political science (MA); professional and technical communication (MA); radio, television and film (MA, MFA); rehabilitation counseling (Certificate); sociology (MA); Spanish (MA); special education (M Ed); speech-language pathology (MS); strategic management (MBA); studio art (MFA); teaching (M Ed); MBA/MS. *Program availability:* Part-time, evening/weekend, online learning. Terminal master's awarded for partial completion of doctoral program. *Degree requirements:* For master's, variable foreign language requirement, comprehensive exam (for some programs), thesis (for some programs); for doctorate, variable foreign language requirement, comprehensive exam (for some programs), thesis/dissertation; for other advanced degree, variable foreign language requirement, comprehensive exam (for some programs). *Entrance requirements:* For master's and doctorate, GRE, GMAT. Additional exam requirements/recommendations for international students: Required—TOEFL (minimum score 550 paper-based; 79 iBT). Electronic applications accepted.

University of Oklahoma, Jeannine Rainbolt College of Education, Department of Educational Leadership and Policy Studies, Program in Adult and Higher Education, Norman, OK 73019. Offers adult and higher education (M Ed, PhD), including adult and workforce (M Ed), community college administration (M Ed), institutional research (M Ed), intercollegiate athletics administration (M Ed), student affairs (M Ed). *Accreditation:* NCATE. *Program availability:* Part-time, evening/weekend. *Students:* 110 full-time (69 women), 69 part-time (42 women); includes 66 minority (29 Black or African American, non-Hispanic/Latino; 10 American Indian or Alaska Native, non-Hispanic/Latino; 2 Asian, non-Hispanic/Latino; 13 Hispanic/Latino; 12 Two or more races, non-Hispanic/Latino), 5 international. Average age 29. 102 applicants, 60% accepted, 58 enrolled. In 2017, 70 master's, 1 doctorate awarded. Terminal master's awarded for

partial completion of doctoral program. *Degree requirements:* For master's, comprehensive exam, thesis optional; for doctorate, comprehensive exam, thesis/dissertation. *Entrance requirements:* For doctorate, GRE. Additional exam requirements/recommendations for international students: Required—TOEFL (minimum score 79 iBT) or IELTS (minimum score 6.5). *Application deadline:* For fall admission, 10/1 for domestic and international students; for spring admission, 4/1 for domestic and international students. Application fee: $50 ($100 for international students). Electronic applications accepted. *Expenses:* Tuition, state resident: full-time $5119; part-time $213.30 per credit hour. Tuition, nonresident: full-time $19,778; part-time $824.10 per credit hour. *Required fees:* $3458; $133.55 per credit hour. $126.50 per semester. *Financial support:* In 2017–18, 148 students received support. Fellowships, research assistantships, teaching assistantships, career-related internships or fieldwork, Federal Work-Study, institutionally sponsored loans, scholarships/grants, traineeships, health care benefits, tuition waivers, and unspecified assistantships available. Support available to part-time students. Financial award application deadline: 6/1; financial award applicants required to submit FAFSA. *Faculty research:* Education and social policy; gender and equity; collegiate athletics; higher education and student affairs; adult learning and workforce development. *Unit head:* Doo Hun Lim, Associate Professor, 405-325-7941, E-mail: dhlim@ou.edu.
Website: http://www.ou.edu/education/elps/graduate-programs/adult-and-higher-education-masters.html

University of Pennsylvania, Graduate School of Education, Division of Higher Education, Executive Doctorate Program in Higher Education Management, Philadelphia, PA 19104. Offers Ed D. *Program availability:* Evening/weekend. *Students:* Average age 44. 86 applicants, 31% accepted, 25 enrolled. In 2017, 21 doctorates awarded. *Entrance requirements:* For doctorate, bachelor's degree. Additional exam requirements/recommendations for international students: Required—TOEFL, IELTS. *Application deadline:* For summer admission, 3/1 priority date for domestic and international students. Application fee: $75. Electronic applications accepted. *Faculty research:* Access, choice, and equity in higher education, college finance and affordability, academic governance and leadership. *Unit head:* Eric Kaplan, Director, 215-573-9404. *Application contact:* Jessica Lundeen, Program Coordinator, 215-573-0588, E-mail: mlundeen@upenn.edu.
Website: http://www2.gse.upenn.edu/execdoc/

University of Pennsylvania, Graduate School of Education, Division of Higher Education, Program in Higher Education, Philadelphia, PA 19104. Offers MS Ed, Ed D, PhD. *Program availability:* Part-time. *Students:* Average age 31. 315 applicants, 50% accepted, 65 enrolled. In 2017, 45 master's, 8 doctorates awarded.

University of Phoenix–Bay Area Campus, College of Education, San Jose, CA 95134-1805. Offers administration and supervision (MA Ed); adult education and training (MA Ed); early childhood education (MA Ed); education (Ed S); educational leadership (Ed D); elementary teacher education (MA Ed); higher education administration (PhD); secondary teacher education (MA Ed); special education (MA Ed); teacher leadership (MA Ed). *Program availability:* Evening/weekend, online learning. *Degree requirements:* For master's, thesis (for some programs). *Entrance requirements:* For master's, minimum undergraduate GPA of 2.5, 3 years of work experience. Additional exam requirements/recommendations for international students: Required—TOEFL (minimum score 550 paper-based; 79 iBT). Electronic applications accepted.

University of Phoenix–Online Campus, School of Advanced Studies, Phoenix, AZ 85034-7209. Offers business administration (DBA); education (Ed S); educational leadership (Ed D), including curriculum and instruction, education technology, educational leadership; health administration (DHA); higher education administration (PhD); industrial/organizational psychology (PhD); nursing (PhD); organizational leadership (DM), including information systems and technology, organizational leadership. *Program availability:* Evening/weekend, online learning. *Degree requirements:* For doctorate, thesis/dissertation. *Entrance requirements:* Additional exam requirements/recommendations for international students: Required—TOEFL, TOEIC (Test of English as an International Communication), Berlitz Online English Proficiency Exam, PTE, or IELTS. Electronic applications accepted. *Expenses:* Contact institution.

University of Pittsburgh, School of Education, Department of Administrative and Policy Studies, Program in Higher Education Management, Pittsburgh, PA 15260. Offers M Ed, Ed D, PhD. *Program availability:* Part-time, evening/weekend. *Degree requirements:* For master's, thesis; for doctorate, thesis/dissertation. *Entrance requirements:* For doctorate, GRE General Test. Additional exam requirements/recommendations for international students: Required—TOEFL (minimum score 80 iBT). Electronic applications accepted.

University of Puerto Rico–Mayagüez, Graduate Studies, College of Arts and Sciences, Department of Mathematical Sciences, Mayagüez, PR 00681-9000. Offers applied mathematics (MS); pre-college math education (MS); pure mathematics (MS); scientific computing (MS); statistics (MS). *Program availability:* Part-time. *Degree requirements:* For master's, one foreign language, comprehensive exam, thesis. *Entrance requirements:* For master's, undergraduate degree in mathematics or its equivalent. Electronic applications accepted. *Faculty research:* Automata theory, linear algebra, logic.

University of Rochester, Margaret Warner Graduate School of Education and Human Development, Doctoral Programs in Education, Rochester, NY 14627. Offers counseling (Ed D); educational administration (Ed D); educational policy and theory (PhD); higher education (PhD); human development in educational context (PhD); teaching, curriculum, and change (PhD).

University of Rochester, Margaret Warner Graduate School of Education and Human Development, Master's Program in Higher Education, Rochester, NY 14627. Offers higher education (MS); higher education student affairs (MS).

University of St. Thomas, College of Arts and Sciences, Graduate Program in English, St. Paul, MN 55105. Offers creative writing and publishing (MA); English literature (MA); teaching college English (Certificate). *Program availability:* Part-time, evening/weekend. *Faculty:* 24 full-time (15 women). *Students:* 41 full-time (29 women); includes 4 minority (3 Black or African American, non-Hispanic/Latino; 1 Asian, non-Hispanic/Latino). Average age 30. 9 applicants, 89% accepted, 8 enrolled. In 2017, 16 master's awarded. *Degree requirements:* For master's, essay. *Entrance requirements:* For master's, minimum GPA of 3.0, minimum 5 upper-level undergraduate courses in literature, sample of written work, personal statement, BA from accredited university, transcripts. Additional exam requirements/recommendations for international students: Required—TOEFL (minimum score 80 iBT), IELTS (minimum score 6.5). *Application deadline:* For fall admission, 3/1 priority date for domestic and international students; for spring admission, 10/1 priority date for domestic and international students; for summer admission, 3/1 priority date for domestic and international students. Applications are processed on a rolling basis. Application fee: $0. Electronic applications accepted. *Expenses:* $2,572.50 per course, $857.50 per credit; $55 technology fee per semester part-time, $111 full-time. *Financial support:* In 2017–18, 23 students received support, including 18 fellowships with partial tuition reimbursements available (averaging $5,145 per year), 3 research assistantships (averaging $2,000 per year), 4 teaching

assistantships (averaging $750 per year); institutionally sponsored loans, scholarships/grants, traineeships, and unspecified assistantships also available. Support available to part-time students. Financial award application deadline: 3/1; financial award applicants required to submit FAFSA. *Faculty research:* Multicultural literature, literature and theory, regional writers, creative writing, 19th-century American literature. *Unit head:* Dr. Alexis Easley, Director, 651-962-5653, Fax: 651-962-5623, E-mail: maeasley@stthomas.edu. *Application contact:* Soren Hoeger-Lerdal, Coordinator, 651-962-5628, Fax: 651-962-5623, E-mail: gradenglish@stthomas.edu.
Website: http://www.stthomas.edu/english/graduate/

University of San Diego, School of Leadership and Education Sciences, Department of Leadership Studies, San Diego, CA 92110-2492. Offers higher education leadership (MA); leadership studies (MA, PhD, Certificate); nonprofit leadership and management (MA). *Program availability:* Part-time, evening/weekend. *Faculty:* 10 full-time (5 women), 18 part-time/adjunct (7 women). *Students:* 53 full-time (34 women), 202 part-time (140 women); includes 118 minority (24 Black or African American, non-Hispanic/Latino; 16 Asian, non-Hispanic/Latino; 64 Hispanic/Latino; 1 Native Hawaiian or other Pacific Islander, non-Hispanic/Latino; 13 Two or more races, non-Hispanic/Latino), 23 international. Average age 34. 243 applicants, 73% accepted, 77 enrolled. In 2017, 53 master's, 15 doctorates awarded. *Degree requirements:* For master's, thesis (for some programs), international experience; for doctorate, comprehensive exam, thesis/dissertation, international experience. *Entrance requirements:* For master's, GRE (recommended with GPA less than 3.25); for doctorate, GRE (less than 5 years old), master's degree, minimum GPA of 3.5 (recommended), resume. Additional exam requirements/recommendations for international students: Required—TOEFL (minimum score 580 paper-based; 83 iBT), TWE. Application fee: $45. Electronic applications accepted. *Financial support:* In 2017–18, 204 students received support. Career-related internships or fieldwork, Federal Work-Study, institutionally sponsored loans, unspecified assistantships, and stipends available. Support available to part-time students. Financial award application deadline: 4/1; financial award applicants required to submit FAFSA. *Faculty research:* Higher education administration policy and relations, organizational leadership, nonprofits and philanthropy, student affairs leadership. *Unit head:* Dr. Lea Hubbard, Graduate Program Director, 619-260-7818, E-mail: lhubbard@sandiego.edu. *Application contact:* Monica Mahon, Associate Director of Graduate Admissions, 619-260-4524, Fax: 619-260-4158, E-mail: grads@sandiego.edu.
Website: https://www.sandiego.edu/soles/leadership-studies/

University of South Carolina, The Graduate School, College of Education, Department of Educational Leadership and Policies, Program in Higher Education and Student Affairs, Columbia, SC 29208. Offers M Ed. *Accreditation:* NCATE. *Program availability:* Part-time. *Degree requirements:* For master's, comprehensive exam, thesis (for some programs). *Entrance requirements:* For master's, GRE General Test or MAT, letters of reference. Electronic applications accepted. *Faculty research:* Minorities in higher education, community college transfer problem, federal role in educational research.

University of South Dakota, Graduate School, School of Education, Division of Educational Leadership, Vermillion, SD 57069. Offers educational administration (MA, Ed D, Ed S), including adult and higher education (MA, Ed D); curriculum director, director of special education (Ed D, Ed S), preK-12 principal, school district superintendent (Ed D, Ed S). *Accreditation:* NCATE. *Program availability:* Part-time, evening/weekend, 100% online, blended/hybrid learning. *Degree requirements:* For master's and Ed S, comprehensive exam, thesis or alternative; for doctorate, comprehensive exam, thesis/dissertation. *Entrance requirements:* For master's, GRE General Test, MAT, minimum GPA of 2.7; for doctorate, minimum GPA of 2.7. Additional exam requirements/recommendations for international students: Required—TOEFL (minimum score 550 paper-based; 79 iBT). *Application deadline:* Applications are processed on a rolling basis. Application fee: $35. Electronic applications accepted. *Financial support:* Research assistantships with partial tuition reimbursements, teaching assistantships with partial tuition reimbursements, Federal Work-Study, traineeships, and unspecified assistantships available. Financial award applicants required to submit FAFSA. *Application contact:* Graduate School, 605-658-6140, Fax: 605-677-6118, E-mail: grad@usd.edu.
Website: http://www.usd.edu/education/educational-administration

University of Southern California, Graduate School, Rossier School of Education, Doctor of Education Programs, Los Angeles, CA 90089. Offers educational psychology (Ed D); higher education administration (Ed D); K-12 leadership in urban school settings (Ed D); teacher education in multicultural societies (Ed D). *Program availability:* Part-time, evening/weekend. *Degree requirements:* For doctorate, thesis/dissertation. *Entrance requirements:* For doctorate, GRE. Additional exam requirements/recommendations for international students: Required—TOEFL (minimum score 100 iBT). Electronic applications accepted. *Faculty research:* Data-driven decision-making in K-12 schools and districts; examination of college and university leadership and management in U. S. and Asia; studies in facilitating student learning; organizational change and the role of leaders; leadership, diversity, learning and accountability.

University of Southern California, Graduate School, Rossier School of Education, Doctor of Philosophy in Education Programs, Los Angeles, CA 90089. Offers educational psychology (PhD); higher education administration and policy (PhD); K-12 policy and practice (PhD). *Degree requirements:* For doctorate, thesis/dissertation, 63 units; qualifying exam; dissertation proposal and defense. *Entrance requirements:* For doctorate, GRE. Additional exam requirements/recommendations for international students: Required—TOEFL (minimum score 100 iBT). Electronic applications accepted. *Faculty research:* Diversity in higher education, organizational change, educational psychology, policy and politics of educational reform, economics of education and education policy.

University of Southern Maine, College of Management and Human Service, School of Education and Human Development, Program in Adult Education, Portland, ME 04103. Offers adult and higher education (MS); adult learning (CAS). *Accreditation:* TEAC. *Program availability:* Part-time, evening/weekend, online learning. *Degree requirements:* For master's and CAS, thesis or alternative. *Entrance requirements:* For master's, interview; for CAS, master's degree. Additional exam requirements/recommendations for international students: Required—TOEFL (minimum score 550 paper-based; 79 iBT). Electronic applications accepted. *Faculty research:* Older learners, lifelong learning institutes, teaching and learning in later age.

University of Southern Mississippi, College of Education and Psychology, Department of Educational Research and Administration, Hattiesburg, MS 39406-0001. Offers educational administration (M Ed, Ed D, PhD, Ed S); educational administration and supervision (M Ed); educational studies and research (MS); higher education (Ed D); higher education administration (PhD); higher education: student affairs (M Ed); research, evaluation, statistics, assessment (PhD). *Students:* 30 full-time (23 women), 3 part-time (all women). 44 applicants, 91% accepted, 33 enrolled. *Degree requirements:* For master's and Ed S, comprehensive exam, thesis (for some programs); for doctorate, comprehensive exam, thesis/dissertation. *Entrance requirements:* For master's and doctorate, GRE General Test, minimum GPA of 2.75. Additional exam requirements/recommendations for international students: Required—TOEFL. *Application deadline:* For fall admission, 2/1 for domestic students, 3/1 for international students. Applications

are processed on a rolling basis. Application fee: $60. *Expenses:* Tuition, state resident: full-time $3830. *Financial support:* Career-related internships or fieldwork, Federal Work-Study, and institutionally sponsored loans available. Financial award application deadline: 3/15; financial award applicants required to submit FAFSA. *Unit head:* Dr. Lilian Hill, Co-Chair, 601-266-4622.
Website: https://www.usm.edu/educational-research-administration

University of South Florida, College of Education, Department of Leadership, Counseling, Adult, Career and Higher Education, Tampa, FL 33620-9951. Offers adult education (MA, Ed D, PhD, Ed S); career and technical education (MA); career and workforce education (PhD); higher education/community college teaching (MA, Ed D, PhD); vocational education (Ed S). *Faculty:* 19 full-time (11 women). *Students:* 129 full-time (91 women), 274 part-time (187 women); includes 147 minority (71 Black or African American, non-Hispanic/Latino; 2 American Indian or Alaska Native, non-Hispanic/Latino; 9 Asian, non-Hispanic/Latino; 59 Hispanic/Latino; 6 Two or more races, non-Hispanic/Latino), 15 international. Average age 35. 158 applicants, 67% accepted, 83 enrolled. In 2017, 89 master's, 7 doctorates, 2 other advanced degrees awarded. Application fee: $30. *Total annual research expenditures:* $157,971. *Unit head:* Dr. Judith Ponticell, Chair, 813-974-4897, Fax: 813-974-5423, E-mail: jponticell@usf.edu.
Website: http://www.coedu.usf.edu/main/departments/ache/ache.html

University of South Florida, Innovative Education, Tampa, FL 33620-9951. Offers adult, career and higher education (Graduate Certificate), including college teaching, leadership in developing human resources, leadership in higher education; Africana studies (Graduate Certificate), including diasporas and health disparities, genocide and human rights; aging studies (Graduate Certificate), including gerontology; art research (Graduate Certificate), including museum studies; business foundations (Graduate Certificate); chemical and biomedical engineering (Graduate Certificate), including materials science and engineering, water, health and sustainability; child and family studies (Graduate Certificate), including positive behavior support; civil and industrial engineering (Graduate Certificate), including transportation systems analysis; community and family health (Graduate Certificate), including maternal and child health, social marketing and public health, violence and injury: prevention and intervention, women's health; criminology (Graduate Certificate), including criminal justice administration; data science for public administration (Graduate Certificate); digital humanities (Graduate Certificate); educational measurement and research (Graduate Certificate), including evaluation; English (Graduate Certificate), including comparative literary studies, creative writing, professional and technical communication; entrepreneurship (Graduate Certificate); environmental health (Graduate Certificate), including safety management; epidemiology and biostatistics (Graduate Certificate), including applied biostatistics, biostatistics, concepts and tools of epidemiology, epidemiology, epidemiology of infectious diseases; geography, environment and planning (Graduate Certificate), including community development, environmental policy and management, geographical information systems; geology (Graduate Certificate), including hydrogeology; global health (Graduate Certificate), including disaster management, global health and Latin American and Caribbean studies, global health practice, humanitarian assistance, infection control; government and international affairs (Graduate Certificate), including Cuban studies, globalization studies; health policy and management (Graduate Certificate), including health management and leadership, public health policy and programs; hearing specialist: early intervention (Graduate Certificate); industrial and management systems engineering (Graduate Certificate), including systems engineering, technology management; information studies (Graduate Certificate), including school library media specialist; information systems/decision sciences (Graduate Certificate), including analytics and business intelligence; instructional technology (Graduate Certificate), including distance education, Florida digital/virtual educator, instructional design, multimedia design, Web design; internal medicine, bioethics and medical humanities (Graduate Certificate), including biomedical ethics; Latin American and Caribbean studies (Graduate Certificate); leadership for coastal resiliency planning (Graduate Certificate); mass communications (Graduate Certificate), including multimedia journalism; mathematics and statistics (Graduate Certificate), including mathematics; medicine (Graduate Certificate), including aging and neuroscience, bioinformatics, biotechnology, brain fitness and memory management, clinical investigation, hand and upper limb rehabilitation, health informatics, health sciences, integrative weight management, intellectual property, medicine and gender, metabolic and nutritional medicine, metabolic cardiology, pharmacy sciences; national and competitive intelligence (Graduate Certificate); nursing (Graduate Certificate), including simulation based academic fellowship in advanced pain management; psychological and social foundations (Graduate Certificate), including career counseling, college teaching, diversity in education, mental health counseling, school counseling; public affairs (Graduate Certificate), including nonprofit management, public management, research administration; public health (Graduate Certificate), including assessing chemical toxicity and public health risks, health equity, pharmacoepidemiology, public health generalist, toxicology, translational research in adolescent behavioral health; public health practices (Graduate Certificate), including planning for healthy communities; rehabilitation and mental health counseling (Graduate Certificate), including integrative mental health care, marriage and family therapy, rehabilitation technology; secondary education (Graduate Certificate), including ESOL, foreign language education: culture and content, foreign language education: professional; social work (Graduate Certificate), including geriatric social work/clinical gerontology; special education (Graduate Certificate), including autism spectrum disorder, disabilities education: severe/profound; world languages (Graduate Certificate), including teaching English as a second language (TESL) or foreign language. *Unit head:* Dr. Cynthia DeLuca, Associate Vice President and Assistant Vice Provost, 813-974-3077, Fax: 813-974-7061, E-mail: deluca@usf.edu. *Application contact:* Owen Hooper, Director, Summer and Alternative Calendar Programs, 813-974-6917, E-mail: hooper@usf.edu.
Website: http://www.usf.edu/innovative-education/

The University of Texas at Arlington, Graduate School, College of Education, Department of Educational Leadership and Policy Studies, Arlington, TX 76019. Offers educational leadership (PhD); higher education (M Ed); principal certification (M Ed). *Program availability:* Part-time, evening/weekend, online learning. *Degree requirements:* For master's, 2 field-based practica; for doctorate, comprehensive exam, thesis/dissertation, 2 research-based practica. *Entrance requirements:* For master's, GRE, 3 references, minimum undergraduate GPA of 3.0 in last 60 hours of course work; for doctorate, GRE, resume, statement of intent, 3 reference forms, applicable master's degree. *Faculty research:* Lived realities of students of color in K-16 contexts, K-16 faculty, K-16 policy and law, K-16 student access, K-16 student success.

The University of Texas at San Antonio, College of Education and Human Development, Department of Educational Leadership and Policy Studies, San Antonio, TX 78249-0617. Offers educational leadership (Ed D); educational leadership and policy studies (M Ed), including educational leadership, higher education administration. *Program availability:* Part-time. *Faculty:* 22 full-time (10 women), 11 part-time/adjunct (6 women). *Students:* 40 full-time (27 women), 289 part-time (202 women); includes 230 minority (37 Black or African American, non-Hispanic/Latino; 3 Asian, non-Hispanic/Latino; 185 Hispanic/Latino; 5 Two or more races, non-Hispanic/Latino), 4 international. Average age 35. 107 applicants, 87% accepted, 70 enrolled. In 2017, 147 master's, 18

doctorates awarded. *Degree requirements:* For master's, comprehensive exam, thesis or alternative; for doctorate, comprehensive exam, thesis/dissertation. *Entrance requirements:* For master's, transcripts, statement of purpose, resume or curriculum vitae; for doctorate, GRE General Test, minimum GPA of 3.5 in a master's program, resume, three letters of recommendation, statement of purpose. Additional exam requirements/recommendations for international students: Required—TOEFL (minimum score 550 paper-based; 79 iBT), IELTS (minimum score 6.5). *Application deadline:* For fall admission, 6/15 for domestic students, 3/1 for international students; for spring admission, 10/15 for domestic students, 9/15 for international students. Application fee: $50 ($90 for international students). Electronic applications accepted. *Expenses:* Tuition, state resident: full-time $5495. Tuition, nonresident: full-time $21,938. *Required fees:* $1915. Tuition and fees vary according to program. *Financial support:* Fellowships available. Financial award application deadline: 2/1. *Faculty research:* Urban and international school leadership, student success, college access, higher education policy, multiculturalism, minority student achievement. *Total annual research expenditures:* $90,372. *Unit head:* Dr. Enrique Aleman, Department Chair, 210-458-5411, E-mail: enrique.aleman@utsa.edu. *Application contact:* Elisha Reynolds, Student Development Specialist, 210-458-6620, Fax: 210-458-5848, E-mail: elisha.reynolds@utsa.edu.
Website: http://education.utsa.edu/educational_leadership_and_policy_studies/

The University of Toledo, College of Graduate Studies, College of Social Justice and Human Service, Department of School Psychology, Higher Education and Counselor Education, Toledo, OH 43606-3390. Offers counselor education (MA, PhD); higher education (ME, PhD, Certificate); school psychology (MA, Ed S). *Program availability:* Part-time. *Degree requirements:* For master's, comprehensive exam, thesis or alternative; for doctorate, comprehensive exam, thesis/dissertation; for other advanced degree, thesis optional. *Entrance requirements:* For master's, doctorate, and other advanced degree, minimum cumulative GPA of 2.7 for all previous academic work, letters of recommendation. Additional exam requirements/recommendations for international students: Required—TOEFL (minimum score 550 paper-based; 80 iBT). Electronic applications accepted.

University of Utah, Graduate School, College of Education, Department of Educational Leadership and Policy, Salt Lake City, UT 84084. Offers educational leadership and policy (Ed D, PhD), including higher education administration (Ed D); K-12 (Ed D); K-12 school administration (M Ed); K-12 teacher instructional leadership (M Ed); student affairs (M Ed); MPA/PhD. *Program availability:* Part-time, evening/weekend. *Faculty:* 10 full-time (7 women), 2 part-time/adjunct (both women). *Students:* 60 full-time (40 women), 185 part-time (124 women); includes 54 minority (14 Black or African American, non-Hispanic/Latino; 5 American Indian or Alaska Native, non-Hispanic/Latino; 5 Asian, non-Hispanic/Latino; 24 Hispanic/Latino; 2 Native Hawaiian or other Pacific Islander, non-Hispanic/Latino; 4 Two or more races, non-Hispanic/Latino), 1 international. Average age 35. 181 applicants, 69% accepted, 90 enrolled. In 2017, 64 master's, 6 doctorates awarded. *Degree requirements:* For master's, comprehensive exam (for some programs), internship, capstone; for doctorate, thesis/dissertation, qualifying exam. *Entrance requirements:* For master's, minimum undergraduate GPA of 3.0, valid bachelor's degree, 3 years' teaching or leadership experience, Level 1 or 2 UT educator's license (for K-12 programs only); for doctorate, GRE General Test (taken with five years of applying), minimum undergraduate GPA of 3.0, valid master's degree. Additional exam requirements/recommendations for international students: Required—TOEFL (minimum score 550 paper-based). *Application deadline:* For fall admission, 1/15 priority date for domestic and international students; for winter admission, 2/1 for domestic and international students; for spring admission, 11/1 priority date for domestic and international students; for summer admission, 3/1 priority date for domestic and international students. Applications are processed on a rolling basis. Application fee: $55 ($65 for international students). Electronic applications accepted. *Expenses:* Contact institution. *Financial support:* In 2017–18, 12 students received support, including 1 fellowship with full tuition reimbursement available (averaging $15,000 per year), 2 research assistantships with full tuition reimbursements available (averaging $15,000 per year), 6 teaching assistantships with full tuition reimbursements available (averaging $15,000 per year); career-related internships or fieldwork, scholarships/grants, health care benefits, and unspecified assistantships also available. Support available to part-time students. Financial award application deadline: 3/1; financial award applicants required to submit FAFSA. *Faculty research:* Education accountability, college student diversity, K-12 educational administration and school leadership, student affairs, higher education. *Unit head:* Dr. Gerardo Lopez, Chair, 801-581-6971, Fax: 801-585-6756, E-mail: gerardo.lopez@utah.edu. *Application contact:* Marilynn S. Howard, Academic Coordinator, 801-581-6714, Fax: 801-585-6756, E-mail: marilynn.howard@utah.edu.
Website: http://elp.utah.edu/

University of Vermont, Graduate College, College of Education and Social Services, Program in Special Education, Grades K-12, Burlington, VT 05405. Offers M Ed. *Accreditation:* NCATE. *Degree requirements:* For master's, thesis or alternative. *Entrance requirements:* For master's, license (or eligible for licensure). Additional exam requirements/recommendations for international students: Required—TOEFL (minimum score 550 paper-based, 90 iBT) or IELTS (6.5). *Application deadline:* For fall admission, 2/15 for domestic and international students; for spring admission, 11/1 for domestic and international students. Application fee: $65. Electronic applications accepted. *Expenses:* Tuition, state resident: full-time $11,628; part-time $646 per credit. Tuition, nonresident: full-time $29,340; part-time $1630 per credit. *Required fees:* $1994; $10 per credit. Tuition and fees vary according to course load and program. *Financial support:* In 2017–18, 4 students received support. Research assistantships, teaching assistantships, career-related internships or fieldwork, and scholarships/grants available. Financial award application deadline: 3/1. *Unit head:* Dr. Michael Giangreco, Program Coordinator, 802-656-1144, E-mail: michael.giangreco@uvm.edu. *Application contact:* Roman Vogel, Graduate Program Support, 802-656-2936, E-mail: special.education@uvm.edu.
Website: https://www.uvm.edu/cess/doe/masters_education_special_education_k_12th_grade

University of Virginia, Curry School of Education, Department of Leadership, Foundations and Policy, Program in Higher Education, Charlottesville, VA 22903. Offers higher education (Ed S); student affairs practice (M Ed). *Students:* 38 full-time (21 women), 29 part-time (16 women); includes 18 minority (12 Black or African American, non-Hispanic/Latino; 1 Asian, non-Hispanic/Latino; 4 Hispanic/Latino; 1 Two or more races, non-Hispanic/Latino), 2 international. Average age 28. 22 applicants, 55% accepted, 11 enrolled. In 2017, 52 master's awarded. *Entrance requirements:* For master's, doctorate, and Ed S, GRE General Test, 2 letters of recommendation. Additional exam requirements/recommendations for international students: Required—TOEFL (minimum score 600 paper-based; 90 iBT), IELTS (minimum score 7). *Application deadline:* Applications are processed on a rolling basis. Application fee: $60. Electronic applications accepted. *Financial support:* Fellowships, research assistantships, and teaching assistantships available. Financial award applicants required to submit FAFSA. *Unit head:* Cristian Steinmetz, Program Coordinator, 434-924-3180, E-mail: highered@virginia.edu. *Application contact:* E-mail: curry-

admissions@virginia.edu.
Website: http://curry.virginia.edu/academics/areas-of-study/higher-education

University of Virginia, Curry School of Education, Program in Education, Charlottesville, VA 22903. Offers administration and supervision (PhD); applied developmental science (PhD); counselor education (PhD); curriculum and instruction (PhD); early childhood special education (MT); education evaluation (MT); educational psychology (PhD); educational research (PhD); elementary education (MT); English education (MT, PhD); foreign language education (MT); higher education (PhD); instructional technology (MT); kinesiology (MT, PhD); math education (PhD); reading education (PhD); research, statistics and evaluation (PhD); school psychology (PhD); science education (PhD); social studies education (MT, PhD); special education (PhD); world languages education (MT). *Students:* 431 full-time (353 women), 15 part-time (14 women); includes 100 minority (32 Black or African American, non-Hispanic/Latino; 33 Asian, non-Hispanic/Latino; 16 Hispanic/Latino; 19 Two or more races, non-Hispanic/Latino), 14 international. Average age 25. 264 applicants, 49% accepted, 83 enrolled. In 2017, 142 master's, 33 doctorates awarded. *Degree requirements:* For master's, comprehensive exam (for some programs); field project; for doctorate, comprehensive exam, thesis/dissertation. *Entrance requirements:* For doctorate, GRE General Test. Additional exam requirements/recommendations for international students: Required—TOEFL (minimum score 600 paper-based; 90 iBT), IELTS (minimum score 7). *Application deadline:* Applications are processed on a rolling basis. Application fee: $60. Electronic applications accepted. *Financial support:* Fellowships, research assistantships, and teaching assistantships available. Financial award application deadline: 1/5; financial award applicants required to submit FAFSA. *Unit head:* Robert C. Pianta, Dean, 434-924-3334, E-mail: pianta@virginia.edu. *Application contact:* E-mail: curry-admissions@virginia.edu.
Website: http://curry.virginia.edu/teacher-education

University of Washington, Graduate School, College of Education, Seattle, WA 98195. Offers curriculum and instruction (M Ed, Ed D, PhD), including educational technology, general curriculum (Ed D, PhD), language, literacy, and culture, mathematics education, multicultural education, reading and language arts education (Ed D), science education, social studies education, teaching and curriculum (M Ed); educational leadership and policy studies (M Ed, Ed D, PhD), including administration (Ed D), educational policy, organization, and leadership (M Ed, PhD), higher education, leadership for learning (Ed D), social and cultural foundations of education (M Ed, PhD); educational psychology (M Ed, PhD), including educational psychology (PhD), human development and cognition (M Ed), learning sciences, measurement, statistics and research design (M Ed), school psychology (M Ed); instructional leadership (M Ed); intercollegiate athletic leadership (M Ed); special education (M Ed, Ed D, PhD), including early childhood special education (M Ed), emotional and behavioral disabilities (M Ed), learning disabilities (M Ed), low-incidence disabilities (M Ed), severe disabilities (M Ed), special education (Ed D, PhD); teacher education (MIT). *Accreditation:* APA. *Program availability:* Part-time, evening/weekend. *Degree requirements:* For master's, thesis optional; for doctorate, thesis/dissertation. *Entrance requirements:* For master's and doctorate, GRE General Test, minimum GPA of 3.0. Additional exam requirements/recommendations for international students: Required—TOEFL. Electronic applications accepted. *Faculty research:* School restructuring/effective schools, special education interventions, literacy and writing, technology, school partnerships, teacher preparation.

The University of West Alabama, School of Graduate Studies, College of Education, Program in Student Affairs in Higher Education, Livingston, AL 35470. Offers M Ed. *Program availability:* Part-time, evening/weekend, 100% online. *Faculty:* 1 (woman) full-time, 3 part-time/adjunct (2 women). *Students:* 79 (53 women); includes 47 minority (45 Black or African American, non-Hispanic/Latino; 2 Hispanic/Latino). Average age 32. 34 applicants, 97% accepted, 29 enrolled. In 2017, 4 master's awarded. *Degree requirements:* For master's, comprehensive exam. *Entrance requirements:* For master's, GRE, minimum GPA of 2.75, criminal background check. Additional exam requirements/recommendations for international students: Required—TOEFL (minimum score 500 paper-based; 61 iBT). *Application deadline:* Applications are processed on a rolling basis. Application fee: $40. Electronic applications accepted. *Expenses:* Tuition, state resident: part-time $371 per credit hour. Tuition, nonresident: part-time $742 per credit hour. *Required fees:* $130 per semester. *Financial support:* Teaching assistantships, Federal Work-Study, scholarships/grants, and unspecified assistantships available. Support available to part-time students. Financial award application deadline: 3/1; financial award applicants required to submit FAFSA. *Unit head:* Dr. Reenay Rogers, Chair of Instructional Leadership and Support, 205-652-5423, E-mail: rrogers@uwa.edu. *Application contact:* Dr. B.J. Kimbrough, Dean of Graduate Studies, 205-652-3647, Fax: 205-652-3670, E-mail: bkimbrough@uwa.edu.

University of Wisconsin–La Crosse, College of Liberal Studies, Department of Student Affairs Administration, La Crosse, WI 54601-3742. Offers MS Ed, Ed D. *Program availability:* Part-time, evening/weekend, 100% online, blended/hybrid learning. *Students:* 31 full-time (25 women), 57 part-time (42 women); includes 14 minority (3 Black or African American, non-Hispanic/Latino; 1 American Indian or Alaska Native, non-Hispanic/Latino; 2 Asian, non-Hispanic/Latino; 4 Hispanic/Latino; 4 Two or more races, non-Hispanic/Latino), 1 international. Average age 27. 121 applicants, 51% accepted, 47 enrolled. In 2017, 45 master's awarded. *Degree requirements:* For master's, comprehensive exam (for some programs), thesis optional, electronic portfolio, applied research project. *Entrance requirements:* For master's, bachelor's degree from accredited institution, minimum GPA of 2.85, resume, essay, 2 references. Additional exam requirements/recommendations for international students: Required—TOEFL (minimum score 550 paper-based; 79 iBT). *Application deadline:* For fall admission, 2/1 priority date for domestic and international students. Electronic applications accepted. *Financial support:* Research assistantships with partial tuition reimbursements, Federal Work-Study, scholarships/grants, and health care benefits available. Support available to part-time students. Financial award application deadline: 3/15; financial award applicants required to submit FAFSA. *Faculty research:* Persistence; developing positive social justice behaviors in heterosexual white college men; equity; diversity; inclusion in higher education at both interpersonal and institutional levels; expanding student affairs administration research and practice beyond the traditional, majority, or dominant student experience; underrepresented students at historically white institutions; college men and masculinities; Latina/o college student leadership; ethnic cultural centers at HWIs. *Unit head:* Dr. Jodie Rindt, Department Chair, 608-785-6450, E-mail: jrindt@uwlax.edu. *Application contact:* Brandon Schaller, Senior Graduate Student Status Examiner, 608-785-8941, E-mail: admissions@uwlax.edu.
Website: http://www.uwlax.edu/saa/

University of Wisconsin–Madison, Graduate School, School of Education, Department of Educational Leadership and Policy Analysis, Madison, WI 53706-1380. Offers administration (Certificate); educational policy (MS, PhD); global higher education (MS). *Degree requirements:* For doctorate, thesis/dissertation. *Entrance requirements:* For master's and doctorate, GRE General Test. Electronic applications accepted.

University of Wisconsin–Milwaukee, Graduate School, School of Education, Department of Administrative Leadership, Milwaukee, WI 53201-0413. Offers administrative leadership (MS), including adult and continuing education leadership, educational administration and supervision, higher education administration; support

services for online students in higher education (Graduate Certificate); teaching and learning in higher education (Graduate Certificate). *Program availability:* Part-time. *Students:* 33 full-time (19 women), 195 part-time (132 women); includes 53 minority (22 Black or African American, non-Hispanic/Latino; 4 American Indian or Alaska Native, non-Hispanic/Latino; 4 Asian, non-Hispanic/Latino; 2 Hispanic/Latino; 21 Two or more races, non-Hispanic/Latino), 1 international. Average age 35. 117 applicants, 75% accepted, 53 enrolled. In 2017, 61 master's, 14 other advanced degrees awarded. *Degree requirements:* For master's, comprehensive exam, thesis or alternative. *Entrance requirements:* For master's, GRE General Test. Additional exam requirements/recommendations for international students: Required—TOEFL (minimum score 550 paper-based; 79 iBT), IELTS (minimum score 6.5). *Application deadline:* For fall admission, 1/1 priority date for domestic students; for spring admission, 9/1 for domestic students. Application fee: $56 ($96 for international students). Electronic applications accepted. *Financial support:* In 2017–18, 2 fellowships were awarded; research assistantships, teaching assistantships, career-related internships or fieldwork, health care benefits, unspecified assistantships, and project assistantships also available. Support available to part-time students. Financial award application deadline: 4/15; financial award applicants required to submit FAFSA. *Unit head:* Alan Shoho, Dean, 414-229-4181, E-mail: shoho@uwm.edu. *Application contact:* General Information Contact, 414-229-4721, E-mail: soeinfo@uwm.edu.
Website: http://uwm.edu/education/academics/administrative-leadership-department/

Upper Iowa University, Master of Education Program, Fayette, IA 52142-1857. Offers early childhood (M Ed); English as a second language (M Ed); higher education (M Ed); instructional strategist (M Ed); reading (M Ed); teacher leadership (M Ed).

Vanderbilt University, Peabody College, Department of Leadership, Policy, and Organizations, Nashville, TN 37240-1001. Offers education policy (MPP); educational leadership and policy (Ed D); higher education (M Ed); higher education leadership and policy (Ed D); independent school leadership (M Ed); international education policy and management (M Ed); leadership and learning in organizations (Ed D); leadership and organizational performance (M Ed). *Program availability:* Part-time, on-campus immersion once every semester. *Faculty:* 30 full-time (15 women), 19 part-time/adjunct (6 women). *Students:* 141 full-time (105 women), 139 part-time (84 women); includes 66 minority (32 Black or African American, non-Hispanic/Latino; 13 Asian, non-Hispanic/Latino; 14 Hispanic/Latino; 1 Native Hawaiian or other Pacific Islander, non-Hispanic/Latino; 6 Two or more races, non-Hispanic/Latino), 25 international. Average age 30. 525 applicants, 66% accepted, 139 enrolled. In 2017, 109 master's, 22 doctorates awarded. *Degree requirements:* For master's, comprehensive exam, thesis optional; for doctorate, thesis/dissertation, qualifying exams, residency. *Entrance requirements:* For master's and doctorate, GRE General Test. Additional exam requirements/recommendations for international students: Required—TOEFL (minimum score 550 paper-based; 80 iBT). *Application deadline:* For fall admission, 12/31 priority date for domestic and international students; for spring admission, 11/1 priority date for domestic and international students. Applications are processed on a rolling basis. Application fee: $0. Electronic applications accepted. *Financial support:* Fellowships with partial tuition reimbursements, research assistantships with partial tuition reimbursements, teaching assistantships with partial tuition reimbursements, Federal Work-Study, institutionally sponsored loans, scholarships/grants, tuition waivers (partial), and unspecified assistantships available. Support available to part-time students. Financial award application deadline: 1/15; financial award applicants required to submit FAFSA. *Faculty research:* Financial aid policies, teacher labor markets, school choice, educational leadership, higher education access and equity. *Unit head:* Dr. Ellen B. Goldring, Chair, 615-322-8000, Fax: 615-343-7094, E-mail: ellen.b.goldring@vanderbilt.edu. *Application contact:* Rosie Moody, Educational Coordinator, 615-322-8019, Fax: 615-343-7094, E-mail: rosie.moody@vanderbilt.edu.
Website: http://peabody.vanderbilt.edu/departments/lpo/index.php

Wagner College, Division of Graduate Studies, Education Department, Staten Island, NY 10301-4495. Offers childhood education/students with disabilities (MS Ed), including childhood education; early childhood education/students with disabilities (birth-grade 2) (MS Ed); higher education and learning organizations leadership (MA); secondary education/students with disabilities (MS Ed), including secondary education 7-12. *Accreditation:* NCATE. *Program availability:* Part-time, evening/weekend. *Faculty:* 5 full-time (4 women). *Students:* 41 full-time (29 women), 18 part-time (12 women); includes 14 minority (7 Black or African American, non-Hispanic/Latino; 3 Asian, non-Hispanic/Latino; 2 Hispanic/Latino; 2 Two or more races, non-Hispanic/Latino), 1 international. Average age 25. 47 applicants, 68% accepted, 25 enrolled. In 2017, 27 master's awarded. *Degree requirements:* For master's, thesis (for some programs). *Entrance requirements:* For master's, GRE, minimum GPA of 3.0. Additional exam requirements/recommendations for international students: Required—TOEFL (minimum score 550 paper-based; 79 iBT), IELTS (minimum score 6.5). *Application deadline:* For fall admission, 12/1 priority date for domestic and international students. Applications are processed on a rolling basis. Application fee: $60. Electronic applications accepted. *Financial support:* Unspecified assistantships and alumni fellowship available. Financial award application deadline: 4/15; financial award applicants required to submit FAFSA. *Faculty research:* School-community partnerships, civic engagement, educational accountability, micro-aggression and bullying, cross-cultural pedagogy with students and families. *Unit head:* Dr. Jason Fitzgerald, Department Chair, 718-420-4129, Fax: 718-390-3456, E-mail: jason.fitzgerald@wagner.edu. *Application contact:* Patricia Clancy, Assistant Director of Enrollment, 718-420-4464, Fax: 718-390-3105, E-mail: patricia.clancy@wagner.edu.
Website: http://www.wagner.edu/education/

Walden University, Graduate Programs, Richard W. Riley College of Education and Leadership, Minneapolis, MN 55401. Offers adult education (Post-Master's Certificate); adult learning (Graduate Certificate); college teaching and learning (Graduate Certificate); community college leadership (Ed D); curriculum, instruction and assessment (Ed D, Ed S, Graduate Certificate); developmental education (Graduate Certificate); early childhood administration, management, and leadership (Graduate Certificate); early childhood education (Ed D, Ed S); early childhood public policy and advocacy (Graduate Certificate); early childhood studies (MS), including administration, management and leadership, early childhood public policy and advocacy, teaching adults in the early childhood field, teaching and diversity in early childhood education; education (MS, PhD), including adolescent literacy and learning (MS); curriculum, instruction, and assessment (grades K-12) (MS); curriculum, instruction, assessment, and evaluation (PhD), early childhood leadership and advocacy (PhD), early childhood special education (PhD), educational leadership (MS), educational leadership and administration (principal preparation) (MS), educational technology and design (PhD), elementary reading and literacy (PreK-6) (MS), elementary reading and mathematics (grades K-6) (MS), global and comparative education (PhD), higher education leadership management and policy (PhD), integrating technology in the classroom (grades K-12) (MS), learning, instruction and innovation (PhD), mathematics (grades 5-8) (MS), mathematics (grades K-6) (MS), mathematics and science (grades K-8) (MS), organizational research, assessment, and evaluation (PhD), reading and literacy with a reading K-12 endorsement (MS), reading literacy assessment and evaluation (PhD), science (grades K-8) (MS), special education (non-licensure) (grades K-12) (MS), teacher leadership (grades K-12) (MS), teaching English language learners (grades K-

12) (MS); educational administration and leadership (Ed D); educational leadership and administration (principal preparation) (Ed S); educational technology (Ed D, Ed S, Post Master's Certificate); elementary reading and literacy (Graduate Certificate); engaging culturally diverse learners (Graduate Certificate); enrollment management and institutional marketing (Graduate Certificate); higher education (MS), including adult learning, college teaching and learning, enrollment management and institutional marketing, global higher education, leadership for student success, online and distance learning; higher education and adult learning (Ed D); higher education leadership and management (Ed D); higher education leadership for student success (Graduate Certificate); instructional design and technology (MS, Postbaccalaureate Certificate), including general program (MS), online learning (MS), training and performance improvement (MS); integrating technology in the classroom (Graduate Certificate); mathematics 5-8 (Graduate Certificate); mathematics K-6 (Graduate Certificate); online teaching for adult educators (Graduate Certificate); reading, literacy, and assessment (Ed D, Ed S); science K-8 (Graduate Certificate); special education (Ed D, Ed S, Graduate Certificate); special education (K-age 21) (MAT); teacher leadership (Graduate Certificate); teaching adults English as a second language (Graduate Certificate); teaching adults in the early childhood field (Graduate Certificate); teaching and diversity in early childhood education (Graduate Certificate); teaching English language learners (grades K-12) (Graduate Certificate); teaching K-12 students online (Graduate Certificate). *Accreditation:* NCATE. *Program availability:* Part-time, evening/weekend, online only, 100% online. *Degree requirements:* For doctorate, thesis/dissertation (for some programs), residency; for other advanced degree, residency for some programs. *Entrance requirements:* For master's, bachelor's degree or higher; minimum GPA of 2.5; official transcripts; goal statement (for some programs); access to computer and Internet; for doctorate, master's degree or higher; three years of related professional or academic experience (preferred); minimum GPA of 3.0; goal statement and current resume (for select programs); official transcripts; access to computer and Internet; for other advanced degree, relevant work experience; access to computer and Internet. Additional exam requirements/recommendations for international students: Required—TOEFL (minimum score 550 paper-based, 79 iBT), IELTS (minimum score 6.5), Michigan English Language Assessment Battery (minimum score 82), or PTE (minimum score 53). Electronic applications accepted.

Walden University, Graduate Programs, School of Social Work and Human Services, Minneapolis, MN 55401. Offers addictions and social work (DSW); advanced clinical practice (MSW); clinical expertise (DSW); criminal justice (DSW); disaster, crisis, and intervention (DSW); family studies and interventions (DSW); human and social services (PhD), including advanced research, community and social services, community intervention and leadership, conflict management, criminal justice, disaster crisis and intervention, family studies and intervention, gerontology, global social services, higher education, human services and nonprofit administration, mental health facilitation; medical social work (DSW); military social work (MSW); policy practice (DSW); social work (PhD), including addictions and social work, clinical expertise, criminal justice, disaster, crisis and intervention, family studies and interventions, medical social work, policy practice, social work administration; social work administration (DSW); social work in healthcare (MSW); social work with children and families (MSW). *Accreditation:* CSWE. *Program availability:* Part-time, evening/weekend, online only, 100% online. *Degree requirements:* For master's, residency (for some programs); for doctorate, thesis/dissertation, residency. *Entrance requirements:* For master's, bachelor's degree or higher; minimum GPA of 2.5; official transcripts; goal statement (for some programs); access to computer and Internet; for doctorate, master's degree or higher; three years of related professional or academic experience (preferred); minimum GPA of 3.0; goal statement and current resume (for select programs); official transcripts; access to computer and Internet. Additional exam requirements/recommendations for international students: Required—TOEFL (minimum score 550 paper-based, 79 iBT), IELTS (minimum score 6.5), Michigan English Language Assessment Battery (minimum score 82), or PTE (minimum score 53). Electronic applications accepted.

Walsh University, Graduate Programs, Program in Counseling and Human Development, North Canton, OH 44720-3396. Offers clinical mental health counseling (MA); school counseling (MA); student affairs in higher education (MA). *Accreditation:* ACA. *Program availability:* Part-time, evening/weekend. *Degree requirements:* For master's, comprehensive exam, internship, practicum. *Entrance requirements:* For master's, GRE (minimum score of 145 verbal and 146 quantitative) or MAT (minimum score of 397), interview, minimum GPA of 3.0, writing sample, reference forms, notarized affidavit of good moral conduct. Additional exam requirements/recommendations for international students: Required—TOEFL (minimum score 500 paper-based; 61 iBT). Electronic applications accepted. Application fee is waived when completed online. *Expenses:* Contact institution. *Faculty research:* Supervision of clinical mental health, clinical mental health practice/issues, clinical mental health skills development, advocacy, teaching and professional development, career development, refugee development in US, supervision in student affairs, offender treatment, domestic violence issues, alcohol and drug treatment issues, Professional identity and advocacy in school counseling, Efficacy in counseling clinic.

Wayland Baptist University, Graduate Programs, Program in Education, Plainview, TX 79072-6998. Offers education administration (M Ed); education diagnostics (M Ed); education literacy (M Ed); elementary certification (M Ed); English (M Ed); English as a second language (M Ed); higher education administration (M Ed); human resources (M Ed); instructional leadership (M Ed); instructional technology (M Ed); leadership training and development (M Ed); science education (M Ed); secondary certification (M Ed); social studies (M Ed); special education (M Ed); sports administration and management (M Ed). *Program availability:* Part-time, evening/weekend, 100% online. *Faculty:* 33 full-time (17 women), 28 part-time/adjunct (17 women). *Students:* 16 full-time (13 women), 221 part-time (143 women); includes 97 minority (26 Black or African American, non-Hispanic/Latino; 1 American Indian or Alaska Native, non-Hispanic/Latino; 5 Asian, non-Hispanic/Latino; 54 Hispanic/Latino; 11 Two or more races, non-Hispanic/Latino), 1 international. Average age 39. 32 applicants, 97% accepted, 23 enrolled. In 2017, 78 master's awarded. *Degree requirements:* For master's, comprehensive exam, capstone course. *Entrance requirements:* For master's, GRE, GMAT or MAT. Additional exam requirements/recommendations for international students: Required—TOEFL (minimum score 500 paper-based; 61 iBT). *Application deadline:* Applications are processed on a rolling basis. Application fee: $50. Electronic applications accepted. *Expenses:* Tuition: Full-time $11,250; part-time $625 per credit hour. *Required fees:* $1200. *Financial support:* Federal Work-Study, institutionally sponsored loans, and scholarships/grants available. Support available to part-time students. Financial award application deadline: 5/1; financial award applicants required to submit FAFSA. *Unit head:* Dr. Gene Whitfill, Dean, 806-291-1047, Fax: 806-291-1951, E-mail: whitfillg@wbu.edu. *Application contact:* Amanda Stanton, Coordinator of Graduate Studies, 806-291-3423, Fax: 806-291-1950, E-mail: stanton@wbu.edu.

West Chester University of Pennsylvania, College of Education and Social Work, Department of Counselor Education, West Chester, PA 19383. Offers clinical mental health counseling (MS); counseling (Certificate); higher education counseling (Post Master's Certificate); higher education counseling/student affairs (MS, Certificate); school counseling (M Ed). *Accreditation:* ACA; NCATE. *Program availability:* Part-time, evening/weekend. *Students:* 134 full-time (110 women), 40 part-time (32 women);

Higher Education

includes 38 minority (17 Black or African American, non-Hispanic/Latino; 2 Asian, non-Hispanic/Latino; 11 Hispanic/Latino; 8 Two or more races, non-Hispanic/Latino), 1 international. Average age 27. 177 applicants, 58% accepted, 58 enrolled. In 2017, 79 master's, 1 other advanced degree awarded. *Degree requirements:* For master's, comprehensive exam. *Entrance requirements:* For master's, minimum GPA of 3.0, three letters of reference. Additional exam requirements/recommendations for international students: Required—TOEFL or IELTS. *Application deadline:* For fall admission, 5/15 for international students; for spring admission, 10/15 for international students. Applications are processed on a rolling basis. Application fee: $50. Electronic applications accepted. *Expenses:* Tuition, state resident: full-time $9000; part-time $500 per credit. Tuition, nonresident: full-time $13,500; part-time $750 per credit. *Required fees:* $2959; $149.79 per credit. *Financial support:* Scholarships/grants and unspecified assistantships available. Financial award application deadline: 2/15; financial award applicants required to submit FAFSA. *Faculty research:* Bullying in the schools, adolescent cognitive development, counseling pedagogy, motivational interviewing. *Unit head:* Dr. Eric Owens, Chair, 610-436-2559, Fax: 610-425-7432, E-mail: eowens@wcupa.edu. *Application contact:* Dr. Cheryl Neale-McFall, Graduate Coordinator, 610-436-2559, Fax: 610-425-7432, E-mail: cneale-mcfall@wcupa.edu.
Website: http://www.wcupa.edu/education-socialWork/counselorEducation/

Western Governors University, Teachers College, Salt Lake City, UT 84107. Offers curriculum and instruction (MS); educational leadership (MS); educational studies (MA); educational studies (5-12) (MA), including mathematics; elementary education (K-8) (MAT, Postbaccalaureate Certificate); elementary education (PreK-8) (MAT); English language learning (K-12) (MA); instructional design (MAT); learning and technology (M Ed, MA); management and innovation (M Ed); mathematics (5-12) (MAT, Postbaccalaureate Certificate); mathematics (5-9) (MAT, Postbaccalaureate Certificate); mathematics education (5-12) (MA); mathematics education (5-9) (MA); mathematics education (K-6) (MA); measurement and evaluation (M Ed); science (5-12) (Postbaccalaureate Certificate); science (5-9) (MAT, Postbaccalaureate Certificate); science education (5-12) (MA), including biology, chemistry, geology, physics; science education (5-9) (MA); social science (5-12) (MAT, Postbaccalaureate Certificate); special education (MAT, MS). *Accreditation:* NCATE. *Program availability:* Evening/weekend, online learning. *Degree requirements:* For master's, capstone project. *Entrance requirements:* For master's and Postbaccalaureate Certificate, Readiness Assessment, transcripts. Additional exam requirements/recommendations for international students: Required—TOEFL (minimum score 450 paper-based; 80 iBT). Electronic applications accepted. *Expenses:* Contact institution.

Western Illinois University, School of Graduate Studies, College of Education and Human Services, Department of Educational Studies, Program in College Student Personnel, Macomb, IL 61455-1390. Offers college student personnel (MS), including higher education leadership, student affairs. *Accreditation:* NCATE. *Program availability:* Part-time. *Students:* 59 full-time (41 women), 9 part-time (5 women); includes 19 minority (4 Black or African American, non-Hispanic/Latino; 10 Hispanic/Latino; 5 Two or more races, non-Hispanic/Latino), 2 international. Average age 24. 79 applicants, 82% accepted, 32 enrolled. In 2017, 27 master's awarded. *Degree requirements:* For master's, thesis or alternative. *Entrance requirements:* For master's, interview. Additional exam requirements/recommendations for international students: Required—TOEFL (minimum score 550 paper-based; 80 iBT). *Application deadline:* For fall admission, 1/5 priority date for domestic students. Application fee: $30. Electronic applications accepted. *Financial support:* Unspecified assistantships available. Financial award applicants required to submit FAFSA. *Unit head:* Dr. Tracy Davis, Coordinator, 309-298-1183. *Application contact:* Dr. Nancy Parsons, Associate Provost and Director of Graduate Studies, 309-298-1806, Fax: 309-298-2345, E-mail: grad-office@wiu.edu.
Website: http://wiu.edu/csp/

Western Kentucky University, Graduate Studies, College of Education and Behavioral Sciences, Department of Counseling and Student Affairs, Bowling Green, KY 42101. Offers counseling (MA Ed), including marriage and family therapy, mental health counseling; school counseling (P-12) (MA Ed); student affairs in higher education (MA Ed). *Accreditation:* ACA; NCATE. *Program availability:* Part-time, evening/weekend. *Degree requirements:* For master's, comprehensive exam, thesis optional. *Entrance requirements:* For master's, GRE General Test. Additional exam requirements/recommendations for international students: Required—TOEFL (minimum score 555 paper-based; 79 iBT). *Faculty research:* Counselor education, research for residential workers.

Western Michigan University, Graduate College, College of Arts and Sciences, Department of Mathematics, Kalamazoo, MI 49008. Offers applied and computational mathematics (MS); mathematics education (MA, PhD), including collegiate mathematics education (PhD). *Degree requirements:* For doctorate, one foreign language, thesis/dissertation.

Western Washington University, Graduate School, Woodring College of Education, Department of Educational Leadership, Program in Continuing and College Education, Bellingham, WA 98225-5996. Offers M Ed. *Program availability:* Part-time, evening/weekend, online learning. *Degree requirements:* For master's, comprehensive exam, thesis optional. *Entrance requirements:* For master's, GRE General Test or MAT, minimum GPA of 3.0 in last 60 semester hours or last 90 quarter hours. Additional exam requirements/recommendations for international students: Required—TOEFL (minimum score 567 paper-based). Electronic applications accepted. *Faculty research:* Transfer of learning, postsecondary faculty development, action research as professional development, literacy education in community colleges, adult education in the Middle East, distance learning tools for graduate students.

West Virginia University, College of Education and Human Services, Morgantown, WV 26506. Offers audiology (Au D); autism spectrum disorder (MA); clinical rehabilitation and mental health counseling (MS); communication science and disorders (PhD); counseling (MA); counseling psychology (PhD); curriculum and instruction (Ed D); early childhood education (MA); early intervention (MA); education (PhD); educational leadership (MA, Ed D); educational leadership/public school administration (MA);

educational psychology (MA, Ed D); elementary education (MA); gifted education (MA); higher education administration (MA, Ed D); higher education curriculum and teaching (MA); institutional design and technology (MA); instructional design and technology (Ed D); literacy education (MA); secondary education (MA); secondary education/English (MA); special education (Ed D); speech pathology (MS). *Accreditation:* NCATE. *Program availability:* Part-time, evening/weekend, online learning. *Students:* 423 full-time (347 women), 367 part-time (316 women); includes 57 minority (14 Black or African American, non-Hispanic/Latino; 7 Asian, non-Hispanic/Latino; 20 Hispanic/Latino; 16 Two or more races, non-Hispanic/Latino), 13 international. *Degree requirements:* For master's, content exams; for doctorate, comprehensive exam, thesis/dissertation. *Entrance requirements:* Additional exam requirements/recommendations for international students: Required—TOEFL (minimum score 500 paper-based; 61 iBT). *Application deadline:* For fall admission, 8/1 for domestic students; for spring admission, 1/1 for domestic students; for summer admission, 5/1 for domestic students. Application fee: $60. Electronic applications accepted. *Expenses:* Tuition, state resident: full-time $9450. Tuition, nonresident: full-time $24,390. *Financial support:* Fellowships, research assistantships, teaching assistantships, career-related internships or fieldwork, Federal Work-Study, institutionally sponsored loans, health care benefits, tuition waivers (full and partial), and administrative assistantships available. Financial award applicants required to submit FAFSA. *Faculty research:* Internet training and integration for teachers, rural education, teacher preparation, organization of schools, evaluation of personnel. *Unit head:* Dr. Gypsy Denzine, Dean, 304-293-5703, Fax: 304-293-7565, E-mail: gypsy.denzine@mail.wvu.edu. *Application contact:* Dr. M. Cecil Smith, Associate Dean for Research and Graduate Education, 304-293-2174, Fax: 304-293-3802, E-mail: mcecil.smith@mail.wvu.edu.
Website: http://cehs.wvu.edu/

William Paterson University of New Jersey, College of Education, Wayne, NJ 07470-8420. Offers curriculum and learning (M Ed); early childhood education (Certificate); educational leadership (M Ed); educational media specialist (Certificate); elementary education (MAT, Certificate); elementary education subject area (Certificate); higher education administration (MA); learning disabilities consultant (Certificate); literacy (M Ed); middle level education (M Ed); middle school education subject area (Certificate); professional counseling (M Ed); reading specialist (Certificate); school library media specialist (Certificate); school principal (Certificate); school supervisor (Certificate); secondary education (MAT); special education (M Ed); teacher of students with disabilities (Certificate). *Accreditation:* NCATE. *Program availability:* Part-time, evening/weekend. *Faculty:* 37 full-time (25 women), 21 part-time/adjunct (16 women). *Students:* 73 full-time (54 women), 480 part-time (409 women); includes 153 minority (48 Black or African American, non-Hispanic/Latino; 13 Asian, non-Hispanic/Latino; 81 Hispanic/Latino; 11 Two or more races, non-Hispanic/Latino), 1 international. Average age 35. 347 applicants, 87% accepted, 226 enrolled. In 2017, 136 master's awarded. *Degree requirements:* For master's, comprehensive exam, thesis (for some programs), exit interview (for some programs); practicum/internship; minimum GPA of 3.0 (for some programs); exit portfolio (for some programs). *Entrance requirements:* For master's, GRE/MAT, minimum GPA of 2.75; teaching certificate; essay; interview; 2 letters of recommendation; personal statement. Additional exam requirements/recommendations for international students: Required—TOEFL (minimum score 550 paper-based; 79 iBT), IELTS (minimum score 6). *Application deadline:* For fall admission, 6/1 for domestic students, 3/1 for international students; for spring admission, 11/1 for domestic students, 10/1 for international students. Applications are processed on a rolling basis. Application fee: $50. Electronic applications accepted. *Expenses:* Tuition, state resident: full-time $13,920; part-time $6264 per year. Tuition, nonresident: full-time $21,700; part-time $9765 per year. *Required fees:* $80; $36 per year. Tuition and fees vary according to course load, degree level and program. *Financial support:* In 2017–18, 8,416 students received support. Career-related internships or fieldwork, Federal Work-Study, scholarships/grants, and unspecified assistantships available. Support available to part-time students. Financial award application deadline: 3/15; financial award applicants required to submit FAFSA. *Faculty research:* Code switching and creative writing, language instruction, teacher evaluation, preschools, history of educational theories. *Total annual research expenditures:* $311,226. *Unit head:* Dr. Dorothy Feola, Dean, 973-720-2138, Fax: 973-720-3647, E-mail: feolad@wpunj.edu. *Application contact:* Liana Fornarotto, Director of Education Enrollment and Certification, 973-720-2206, Fax: 973-720-2989, E-mail: fornarottol@wpunj.edu.
Website: http://www.wpunj.edu/coe

Wilmington University, College of Education, New Castle, DE 19720-6491. Offers applied technology in education (M Ed); career and technical education (M Ed); educational leadership (Ed D); elementary and secondary school counseling (M Ed); elementary studies (M Ed); ESOL literacy (M Ed); higher education leadership (Ed D); instruction: gifted and talented (M Ed); instruction: teacher of reading (M Ed); instruction: teaching and learning (M Ed); organizational leadership (Ed D); school leadership (M Ed); secondary education (MAT); special education (M Ed). *Accreditation:* NCATE. *Program availability:* Part-time, evening/weekend. *Faculty:* 23 full-time (13 women), 162 part-time/adjunct (99 women). *Students:* 546 full-time (394 women), 960 part-time (732 women); includes 320 minority (241 Black or African American, non-Hispanic/Latino; 12 American Indian or Alaska Native, non-Hispanic/Latino; 11 Asian, non-Hispanic/Latino; 28 Hispanic/Latino; 3 Native Hawaiian or other Pacific Islander, non-Hispanic/Latino; 25 Two or more races, non-Hispanic/Latino), 7 international. Average age 34. 1,068 applicants, 64% accepted, 582 enrolled. In 2017, 430 master's, 59 doctorates awarded. *Entrance requirements:* For master's, 2 letters of recommendation, interview. Additional exam requirements/recommendations for international students: Required—TOEFL (minimum score 500 paper-based). *Application deadline:* For fall admission, 4/30 for domestic students. Applications are processed on a rolling basis. Application fee: $35. Electronic applications accepted. *Expenses:* Tuition: Part-time $466 per credit. *Required fees:* $25 per semester. Tuition and fees vary according to degree level and campus/location. *Financial support:* Applicants required to submit FAFSA. *Unit head:* Dr. John C. Gray, Dean, 302-295-1139. *Application contact:* Laura Morris, Director of Admissions, 877-967-5464, E-mail: infocenter@wilmu.edu.
Website: http://www.wilmu.edu/education/

Middle School Education

Alaska Pacific University, Graduate Programs, Education Department, Program in Teaching, Anchorage, AK 99508-4672. Offers teaching (K-8) (MAT). *Degree requirements:* For master's, research project. *Entrance requirements:* For master's, GRE or MAT, PRAXIS, minimum GPA of 3.0.

Albany State University, College of Education, Albany, GA 31705-2717. Offers early childhood education (M Ed); educational leadership (Ed S); health and physical education (M Ed); middle grades education (M Ed); school counseling (M Ed); special education (M Ed). *Accreditation:* NCATE. *Program availability:* Part-time, evening/weekend, online learning. *Degree requirements:* For master's, comprehensive exam, internship, GACE Content Exam. *Entrance requirements:* For master's, GRE or MAT. Electronic applications accepted. *Faculty research:* GACE preparation, STEM (science, technology, engineering, and mathematics), technology education, special education, professional teacher development, health implications liberation philosophy, NET-Q, learning community, disabled or at-risk students.

American International College, School of Education, Springfield, MA 01109-3189. Offers early childhood education (M Ed, CAGS); education (MA, Ed D), including counseling psychology (MA), educational leadership and supervision (Ed D), professional counseling and supervision (Ed D); teaching and learning (Ed D); elementary education (M Ed, CAGS); middle education/secondary education (M Ed, CAGS); moderate disabilities (M Ed, CAGS); reading specialist (M Ed, CAGS); school adjustment counseling (MAEP, CAGS); school guidance counseling (MAEP, CAGS); school leadership (M Ed, CAGS). *Program availability:* Evening/weekend. *Faculty:* 1 (woman) full-time, 151 part-time/adjunct (95 women). *Students:* 1,082 full-time (910 women), 143 part-time (113 women); includes 109 minority (19 Black or African American, non-Hispanic/Latino; 2 American Indian or Alaska Native, non-Hispanic/Latino; 10 Asian, non-Hispanic/Latino; 58 Hispanic/Latino; 1 Native Hawaiian or other Pacific Islander, non-Hispanic/Latino; 19 Two or more races, non-Hispanic/Latino). Average age 34. 537 applicants, 77% accepted, 327 enrolled. In 2017, 486 master's, 112 other advanced degrees awarded. *Degree requirements:* For master's and CAGS, practicum/culminating experience. *Entrance requirements:* For master's, Communication and Literacy portion of the Massachusetts Tests for Education Licensure, graduate of accredited four-year college with minimum B- average in undergraduate course work; for CAGS, M Ed or master's degree in field related to licensure from accredited institution. *Application deadline:* Applications are processed on a rolling basis. Application fee: $50. Electronic applications accepted. *Expenses:* $439 per credit, $30 per term registration fee, $100 graduation fee, $110 technology fee. *Financial support:* Applicants required to submit FAFSA. *Unit head:* Sylvia Mason, Dean, 413-205-1743, Fax: 413-205-3943, E-mail: sylvia.mason@aic.edu. *Application contact:* Kerry Barnes, Dean of Graduate Admissions, 413-205-3703, Fax: 413-205-3051, E-mail: kerry.barnes@aic.edu.
Website: http://www.aic.edu/school-of-education/

Appalachian State University, Cratis D. Williams Graduate School, Department of Curriculum and Instruction, Boone, NC 28608. Offers curriculum specialist (MA); educational media (MA); elementary education (MA); middle grades education (MA), including language arts, mathematics, science, social studies. *Accreditation:* NCATE. *Program availability:* Part-time, evening/weekend, online learning. *Degree requirements:* For master's, comprehensive exam, thesis or alternative. *Entrance requirements:* For master's, GRE General Test or MAT, 3 letters of recommendation. Additional exam requirements/recommendations for international students: Required—TOEFL (minimum score 570 paper-based; 79 iBT), IELTS (minimum score 6.5). Electronic applications accepted. *Faculty research:* Media literacy, elementary teaching, curriculum development, online learning.

Arkansas State University, Graduate School, College of Education and Behavioral Science, School of Teacher Education and Leadership, State University, AR 72467. Offers community college administration (SCCT); curriculum and instruction (MSE); early childhood education (MSE); early childhood services (MS); educational leadership (MSE, Ed D, Ed S); educational theory and practice (MSE); middle level education (MAT, MSE); reading (MSE, Ed S); special education - gifted, talented, and creative (MSE); special education - instructional specialist grades 4-12 (MSE); special education - instructional specialist grades P-4 (MSE); special education, K-12 (MSE). *Accreditation:* NCATE. *Program availability:* Part-time, online learning. *Degree requirements:* For master's, comprehensive exam, thesis or alternative; for doctorate, comprehensive exam, thesis/dissertation; for other advanced degree, comprehensive exam. *Entrance requirements:* For master's, GRE General Test or MAT, appropriate bachelor's degree, official transcripts, immunization records, letters of reference, interview; for doctorate, GRE General Test or MAT, interview, master's degree, letters of reference, official transcript, personal statement, writing sample, immunization records; for other advanced degree, GRE General Test or MAT, interview, master's degree, official transcript, immunization records, letters of reference, 3 years of teaching experience, teaching license. Additional exam requirements/recommendations for international students: Required—TOEFL (minimum score 550 paper-based; 79 iBT), IELTS (minimum score 6), PTE (minimum score 56). Electronic applications accepted.

Augusta University, College of Education, Program in Curriculum and Instruction, Augusta, GA 30912. Offers curriculum and instruction (Ed S); elementary education (MAT); foreign language education (MAT); instruction (M Ed); middle grades education (MAT); music education (MAT); secondary education (MAT); special education (MAT). *Degree requirements:* For master's, thesis, portfolio. *Entrance requirements:* For master's, GRE, MAT, minimum GPA of 2.5.

Avila University, School of Education, Kansas City, MO 64145-1698. Offers advanced classroom management (MA); art K-12 (Teaching Certificate); educational technology (MA, Certificate); elementary education (Teaching Certificate); English as a second language (MA); English language learners (Advanced Certificate); middle school (Teaching Certificate); physical education K-12 (Teaching Certificate); secondary education (Teaching Certificate); special education (Teaching Certificate); special reading (Advanced Certificate); teaching and learning (MA). *Program availability:* Part-time, evening/weekend, online learning. *Faculty:* 6 full-time (5 women), 9 part-time/adjunct (8 women). *Students:* 81 full-time (63 women), 20 part-time (11 women); includes 14 minority (8 Black or African American, non-Hispanic/Latino; 2 Asian, non-Hispanic/Latino; 3 Hispanic/Latino; 1 Two or more races, non-Hispanic/Latino), 4 international. Average age 35. 92 applicants, 62% accepted, 40 enrolled. In 2017, 24 master's awarded. *Entrance requirements:* For master's, minimum GPA of 3.0, writing sample, recommendation, interview; for other advanced degree, foreign language. Additional exam requirements/recommendations for international students: Required—TOEFL (minimum score 580 paper-based; 92 iBT). *Application deadline:* Applications are processed on a rolling basis. Electronic applications accepted. *Expenses:* Contact institution. *Financial support:* In 2017–18, 14 students received support. Unspecified assistantships available. Financial

award applicants required to submit FAFSA. *Unit head:* Dr. Stacy Keith, Director of Graduate Education, 816-501-2446, Fax: 816-501-2915, E-mail: stacy.keith@avila.edu. *Application contact:* Cory Roup, Graduate Education Enrollment and Academic Advisor, 816-501-2464, E-mail: cory.roup@avila.edu.
Website: https://www.avila.edu/academics/graduate-studies/grad-education

Ball State University, Graduate School, College of Sciences and Humanities, Department of Mathematical Sciences, Muncie, IN 47306. Offers actuarial science (MA); elementary mathematics teacher leadership (Certificate); mathematics (MA, MS), including mathematics; mathematics education (MA), including mathematics education; middle school mathematics education (Certificate); post-secondary foundational mathematics teaching (MA, Certificate); statistical modeling (Certificate); statistics (MA, MS), including statistics. *Program availability:* Part-time, 100% online, blended/hybrid learning. *Faculty:* 13 full-time (5 women), 1 part-time/adjunct (0 women). *Students:* 26 full-time (7 women), 71 part-time (47 women); includes 11 minority (5 Black or African American, non-Hispanic/Latino; 4 Asian, non-Hispanic/Latino; 1 Hispanic/Latino; 1 Two or more races, non-Hispanic/Latino), 19 international. Average age 33. 106 applicants, 82% accepted, 35 enrolled. In 2017, 46 master's, 2 other advanced degrees awarded. *Entrance requirements:* For master's, minimum baccalaureate GPA of 2.75 or 3.0 in latter half of baccalaureate. Additional exam requirements/recommendations for international students: Required—TOEFL (minimum score 550 paper-based; 79 iBT), IELTS (minimum score 6.5). *Application deadline:* Applications are processed on a rolling basis. Application fee: $60. Electronic applications accepted. *Financial support:* In 2017–18, 23 students received support, including 23 teaching assistantships with partial tuition reimbursements available (averaging $13,022 per year); unspecified assistantships also available. Financial award application deadline: 3/1; financial award applicants required to submit FAFSA. *Faculty research:* Differential equations. *Unit head:* Dr. Michael Karls, Chairperson/Professor, 765-285-8640, Fax: 765-285-1721, E-mail: mkarls@bsu.edu.
Website: http://www.bsu.edu/math

Bellarmine University, Annsley Frazier Thornton School of Education, Louisville, KY 40205. Offers education and district leadership (Ed D); education and social change (PhD); elementary education (MA Ed, MAT); leadership in higher education (PhD); middle school education (MA Ed, MAT); principalship (Ed S); reading and writing (MA Ed); secondary education (MAT); teacher leadership (MA Ed). *Accreditation:* NCATE. *Program availability:* Part-time, evening/weekend. *Faculty:* 19 full-time (10 women), 36 part-time/adjunct (29 women). *Students:* 34 full-time (27 women), 204 part-time (158 women); includes 60 minority (43 Black or African American, non-Hispanic/Latino; 7 Asian, non-Hispanic/Latino; 7 Hispanic/Latino; 3 Two or more races, non-Hispanic/Latino). Average age 33. In 2017, 50 master's, 8 doctorates, 42 other advanced degrees awarded. *Degree requirements:* For master's, comprehensive exam (for some programs), thesis (for some programs); for doctorate, comprehensive exam (for some programs), thesis/dissertation; for Ed S, comprehensive exam (for some programs). *Entrance requirements:* For master's, GRE, baccalaureate degree from accredited institution; minimum cumulative GPA of 2.75; recommendations from employers, supervisors, or professors attesting to applicant's potential as graduate student; statement of intent to pursue graduate degree; for doctorate, GRE, minimum GPA of 3.5 in all graduate coursework; baccalaureate and master's degrees in education or fields directly relevant to education; three letters of recommendation; two essays (no more than 1,000 words each); resume or curriculum vitae; interview; for Ed S, master's degree in education; valid teaching certificate; three years of experience in teaching; three recommendations; minimum GPA of 3.0 in all graduate work; interview; essays; personal goal statement. Additional exam requirements/recommendations for international students: Required—TOEFL (minimum score 550 paper-based, 68 iBT), IELTS (minimum score 6), or Michigan English Language Assessment Battery. *Application deadline:* For fall admission, 8/1 priority date for domestic and international students; for spring admission, 12/1 priority date for domestic and international students; for summer admission, 4/10 priority date for domestic and international students. Applications are processed on a rolling basis. Application fee: $40. Electronic applications accepted. Tuition and fees vary according to program. *Financial support:* Scholarships/grants available. Financial award applicants required to submit FAFSA. *Faculty research:* Literacy, service-learning, dispositions, educational technology, special education. *Unit head:* Dr. Elizabeth Dinkins, Interim Dean, 502-272-7958, Fax: 502-272-8189, E-mail: edinkins@bellarmine.edu. *Application contact:* Sarah Schuble, Senior Graduate Admissions Recruiter, 502-272-8271, Fax: 502-272-8002, E-mail: sschuble@bellarmine.edu.
Website: http://www.bellarmine.edu/education/graduate

Berry College, Graduate Programs, Graduate Programs in Education, Program in Middle-Grades Education and Reading, Mount Berry, GA 30149-0159. Offers middle grades education (MAT); middle-grades education (M Ed); reading (M Ed). *Accreditation:* NCATE. *Program availability:* Part-time. In 2017, 1 master's awarded. *Degree requirements:* For master's, thesis, portfolio, oral exams. *Entrance requirements:* For master's, GRE General Test or MAT, minimum GPA of 2.5. Additional exam requirements/recommendations for international students: Required—TOEFL (minimum score 550 paper-based). *Application deadline:* For fall admission, 7/20 for domestic students, 5/1 for international students; for spring admission, 12/1 for domestic students, 10/1 for international students. Applications are processed on a rolling basis. Application fee: $25 ($30 for international students). Electronic applications accepted. *Expenses:* $8,370 full-time tuition plus $176 fees per year; $465 per credit hour part-time tuition. *Financial support:* Research assistantships with full tuition reimbursements, scholarships/grants, tuition waivers (partial), and unspecified assistantships available. Support available to part-time students. Financial award application deadline: 3/1; financial award applicants required to submit FAFSA. *Unit head:* Dr. Jacqueline McDowell, Dean, 706-236-1717, Fax: 706-238-5827, E-mail: jmcdowell@berry.edu. *Application contact:* Brett Kennedy, Assistant Vice President of Enrollment Management, 706-236-2215, Fax: 706-290-2178, E-mail: admissions@berry.edu.

Bloomsburg University of Pennsylvania, School of Graduate Studies, College of Education, Department of Teaching and Learning, Program in Middle Level Education Grades 4-8, Bloomsburg, PA 17815-1301. Offers language arts (M Ed); math (M Ed); science (M Ed); social studies (M Ed). *Accreditation:* NCATE. *Degree requirements:* For master's, thesis optional, practicum, student teaching. *Entrance requirements:* For master's, MAT, GRE, or PRAXIS, minimum QPA of 3.0, teaching certificate, U.S. citizenship, related undergraduate coursework, professional liability insurance, recent TB test. Additional exam requirements/recommendations for international students: Required—TOEFL (minimum score 550 paper-based), IELTS. Electronic applications accepted. *Expenses:* Tuition, state resident: full-time $10,000; part-time $500 per credit hour. Tuition, nonresident: full-time $15,000; part-time $750 per credit hour. *Required fees:* $2484; $110.75 per credit hour. $75 per term. Tuition and fees vary according to program.

Middle School Education

Brenau University, Sydney O. Smith Graduate School, College of Education, Gainesville, GA 30501. Offers early childhood (Ed S); early childhood education (M Ed, MAT); middle grades (Ed S); middle grades education (M Ed, MAT); secondary education (MAT); special education (M Ed, MAT). *Accreditation:* NCATE. *Program availability:* Part-time, evening/weekend, online learning. *Degree requirements:* For master's, thesis optional, comprehensive exam or applied research project, effective portfolio; for Ed S, thesis, applied research project. *Entrance requirements:* For master's, GRE, MAT, interview, minimum GPA of 3.0, 3 references, writing samples; for Ed S, GRE, MAT, master's degree, minimum GPA of 3.0, writing sample, letters of reference. Additional exam requirements/recommendations for international students: Required—TOEFL (minimum score 500 paper-based; 61 iBT); Recommended—IELTS (minimum score 5). Electronic applications accepted. *Expenses:* Contact institution.

Brooklyn College of the City University of New York, School of Education, Program in Middle Childhood Mathematics Education, Brooklyn, NY 11210-2889. Offers MS Ed. *Entrance requirements:* For master's, LAST, 2 letters of recommendation, essay, resume. Additional exam requirements/recommendations for international students: Required—TOEFL (minimum score 500 paper-based; 61 iBT). Electronic applications accepted.

Brooklyn College of the City University of New York, School of Education, Program in Middle Childhood Science Education, Brooklyn, NY 11210-2889. Offers biology (MA); chemistry (MA); earth science (MA); general science (MA); physics (MA). *Program availability:* Part-time, evening/weekend. *Entrance requirements:* For master's, LAST, interview, previous course work in education and mathematics, resume, 2 letters of recommendation, essay. Additional exam requirements/recommendations for international students: Required—TOEFL (minimum score 500 paper-based; 61 iBT). Electronic applications accepted. *Faculty research:* Geometric thinking, mastery of basic facts, problem-solving strategies, history of mathematics.

Brooklyn College of the City University of New York, School of Education, Program in Special Education, Brooklyn, NY 11210-2889. Offers autism spectrum disorders (AC); teacher of students with disabilities (MS Ed), including adolescence education, childhood education, early childhood education. *Program availability:* Part-time. *Entrance requirements:* For master's, LAST, interview; previous course work in education and psychology; minimum GPA of 3.0 in education, 2.8 overall; resume, 2 letters of recommendation; essay. Additional exam requirements/recommendations for international students: Required—TOEFL (minimum score 500 paper-based; 61 iBT). Electronic applications accepted. *Faculty research:* School reform, conflict resolution, curriculum for inclusive settings, urban issues in special education.

Cabrini University, Academic Affairs, Radnor, PA 19087. Offers accounting (M Acc); autism spectrum disorder (M Ed); biological sciences (MS), including civic leadership; criminology and criminal justice (MA); curriculum, instruction, and assessment (M Ed); educational leadership (M Ed, Ed D), including curriculum and instructional leadership (Ed D), preK-12 leadership (Ed D); English as a second language (M Ed); organizational leadership (DBA, PhD); preK to 4 (M Ed); reading specialist (M Ed); secondary education (M Ed), including biology, chemistry, English, English/communication, mathematics, social studies; special education grades 7-12 (M Ed); special education preK-8 (M Ed); teaching and learning (M Ed). *Program availability:* Part-time, evening/weekend. *Faculty:* 23 full-time (17 women), 46 part-time/adjunct (38 women). *Students:* 60 full-time (35 women), 559 part-time (435 women); includes 93 minority (66 Black or African American, non-Hispanic/Latino; 1 American Indian or Alaska Native, non-Hispanic/Latino; 8 Asian, non-Hispanic/Latino; 15 Hispanic/Latino; 3 Two or more races, non-Hispanic/Latino), 4 international. Average age 33. 290 applicants, 82% accepted, 154 enrolled. In 2017, 283 master's awarded. *Degree requirements:* For master's, comprehensive exam (for some programs), thesis (for some programs); for doctorate, comprehensive exam (for some programs), thesis/dissertation. *Entrance requirements:* For master's, professional resume, personal statement, two recommendations, official transcripts; for doctorate, official transcripts, minimum master's GPA of 3.0, two recommendations, interview with admissions committee. Additional exam requirements/recommendations for international students: Required—TOEFL (minimum score 80 iBT). *Application deadline:* For fall admission, 8/26 for domestic students, 8/1 for international students; for winter admission, 1/13 for domestic students, 12/20 for international students; for spring admission, 1/13 for domestic students, 12/20 for international students; for summer admission, 5/20 for domestic students, 4/30 for international students. Applications are processed on a rolling basis. Application fee: $50. Electronic applications accepted. Application fee is waived when completed online. *Expenses:* Contact institution. *Financial support:* In 2017–18, 1,459 students received support. Tuition waivers and unspecified assistantships available. Financial award application deadline: 5/1; financial award applicants required to submit FAFSA. *Unit head:* Dr. Maliha Zaman, 610-902-8502, Fax: 610-902-8797, E-mail: msz37@cabrini.edu. *Application contact:* Diane Greenwood, Director of Graduate Admissions, 610-902-8291, E-mail: diane.l.greenwood@cabrini.edu.
Website: http://cabrini.edu/graduate

California Lutheran University, Graduate Studies, Graduate School of Education, Thousand Oaks, CA 91360-2787. Offers counseling and guidance (MS), including college student personnel, counseling and guidance; educational leadership (MA, Ed D), including educational leadership (K-12) (Ed D), higher education leadership (Ed D); special education (MS); teacher leadership (M Ed); teaching (M Ed). *Accreditation:* NCATE. *Program availability:* Part-time, evening/weekend. *Faculty:* 21 full-time (18 women), 40 part-time/adjunct (27 women). *Students:* 390 full-time (303 women), 61 part-time (51 women); includes 228 minority (6 Black or African American, non-Hispanic/Latino; 2 American Indian or Alaska Native, non-Hispanic/Latino; 13 Asian, non-Hispanic/Latino; 186 Hispanic/Latino; 1 Native Hawaiian or other Pacific Islander, non-Hispanic/Latino; 20 Two or more races, non-Hispanic/Latino). Average age 31. 201 applicants, 76% accepted, 121 enrolled. In 2017, 129 master's, 19 doctorates awarded. *Degree requirements:* For master's, comprehensive exam or thesis; for doctorate, thesis/dissertation. *Entrance requirements:* For master's, GRE General Test, interview, minimum GPA of 3.0. *Application deadline:* For fall admission, 7/1 priority date for domestic students; for spring admission, 11/1 priority date for domestic students; for summer admission, 4/1 priority date for domestic students. Applications are processed on a rolling basis. Application fee: $50. Electronic applications accepted. *Expenses: Tuition:* Full-time $15,000. Full-time tuition and fees vary according to degree level and program. *Unit head:* Dr. Michael Hillis, Dean, 805-493-3421. *Application contact:* 805-493-3325, Fax: 805-493-3861, E-mail: clugrad@callutheran.edu.

California State University, Bakersfield, Division of Graduate Studies, School of Natural Sciences, Mathematics, and Engineering, Program in Teaching Mathematics, Bakersfield, CA 93311. Offers MA. *Entrance requirements:* For master's, minimum GPA of 2.5 for last 90 quarter units. *Expenses: Tuition,* state resident: full-time $7176; part-time $4164 per year. *Unit head:* Sophia Raczkowski, Chair, 661-654-3151, Fax: 661-664-2039. *Application contact:* Debbie Blowers, Assistant Director of Admissions and Evaluations, 661-654-3381, E-mail: dblowers@csub.edu.
Website: https://www.csub.edu/math/info/index.html

Cambridge College, School of Education, Boston, MA 02129. Offers autism specialist (M Ed); autism/behavior analyst (M Ed); behavior analyst (Post-Master's Certificate); behavioral management (M Ed); early childhood teacher (M Ed); education specialist in curriculum and instruction (CAGS); educational leadership (Ed D); elementary teacher (M Ed); English as a second language (M Ed, Certificate); general science (M Ed); health education (Post-Master's Certificate); health/family and consumer sciences (M Ed); history (M Ed); individualized (M Ed); information technology literacy (M Ed); instructional technology (M Ed); interdisciplinary studies (M Ed); library teacher (M Ed); literacy education (M Ed); mathematics (M Ed); mathematics specialist (Certificate); middle school mathematics and science (M Ed); school administration (M Ed, CAGS); school guidance counselor (M Ed); school nurse education (M Ed); school social worker/school adjustment counselor (M Ed); special education administrator (CAGS); special education/moderate disabilities (M Ed); teaching skills and methodologies (M Ed). *Program availability:* Part-time, evening/weekend, online learning. *Degree requirements:* For master's, thesis, internship/practicum (licensure program only); for doctorate, thesis/dissertation; for other advanced degree, thesis. *Entrance requirements:* For master's, interview, resume, documentation of licensure, 2 professional references; for doctorate, official transcripts, interview, resume, documentation of licensure (if any), written personal statement/essay, portfolio of scholarly and professional work, qualifying assessment, 2 professional references, health insurance, immunizations form; for other advanced degree, official transcripts, interview, resume, documentation of licensure (if any), written personal statement/essay, 2 professional references, health insurance, immunizations form. Additional exam requirements/recommendations for international students: Required—TOEFL (minimum score 550 paper-based; 79 iBT), Michigan English Language Assessment Battery (minimum score 85); Recommended—IELTS (minimum score 6). Electronic applications accepted. *Expenses:* Contact institution. *Faculty research:* Adult education, accelerated learning, mathematics education, brain compatible learning, special education and law.

Campbell University, Graduate and Professional Programs, School of Education, Buies Creek, NC 27506. Offers elementary education (M Ed); interdisciplinary studies (M Ed); middle grades education (M Ed); physical education (M Ed); school administration (MSA); school counseling (M Ed); secondary education (M Ed). *Accreditation:* NCATE. *Program availability:* Part-time, evening/weekend. *Degree requirements:* For master's, comprehensive exam. *Entrance requirements:* For master's, GRE General Test, minimum GPA of 2.7. *Faculty research:* Spiritual values and wellness issues in counseling, stress and professional burnout among counselors, thinking strategies, leadership, adaptive technology.

Canisius College, Graduate Division, School of Education and Human Services, Department of Teacher Education, Buffalo, NY 14208-1098. Offers adolescence education (MS Ed); childhood education (MS Ed); general education (MS Ed); special education (MS), including adolescence special education, advanced special education, childhood education grade 1-6, childhood special education. *Program availability:* Part-time, evening/weekend, 100% online, blended/hybrid learning. *Faculty:* 8 full-time (7 women), 9 part-time/adjunct (7 women). *Students:* 52 full-time (44 women), 32 part-time (24 women); includes 8 minority (5 Black or African American, non-Hispanic/Latino; 1 Hispanic/Latino; 2 Two or more races, non-Hispanic/Latino), 1 international. Average age 25. 59 applicants, 97% accepted, 47 enrolled. In 2017, 34 master's awarded. *Degree requirements:* For master's, research project or thesis, project internship. *Entrance requirements:* For master's, GRE (if cumulative GPA less than 2.7), transcripts, letters of recommendation. Additional exam requirements/recommendations for international students: Required—TOEFL (minimum score 550 paper-based, 79 iBT), IELTS (minimum score 6.5), or CAEL (minimum score 70). *Application deadline:* Applications are processed on a rolling basis. Application fee: $0. Electronic applications accepted. *Expenses: Tuition:* Full-time $22,860; part-time $820 per credit. *Required fees:* $720; $25 per credit. $65 per semester. One-time fee: $425. *Financial support:* Career-related internships or fieldwork, Federal Work-Study, scholarships/grants, tuition waivers (partial), and unspecified assistantships available. Support available to part-time students. Financial award application deadline: 4/30; financial award applicants required to submit FAFSA. *Unit head:* Dr. Michele A. Marable, Chair/Professor, 716-888-2317, E-mail: marablem@canisius.edu.
Website: http://www.canisius.edu/academics/graduate/

Capella University, School of Education, Doctoral Programs in Education, Minneapolis, MN 55402. Offers curriculum and instruction (PhD); educational leadership and management (Ed D); instructional design for online learning (PhD); K-12 studies in education (PhD); leadership for higher education (PhD); leadership in educational administration (PhD); postsecondary and adult education (PhD); professional studies in education (PhD); reading and literacy (Ed D); special education leadership (PhD); training and performance improvement (PhD).

Capella University, School of Education, Master's Programs in Education, Minneapolis, MN 55402. Offers adult education (MS); curriculum and instruction (MS); early childhood education (MS); enrollment management (MS); higher education leadership and management (MS); instructional design for online learning (MS); integrative studies (MS); K-12 studies in education (MS); leadership in educational administration (MS); reading and literacy (MS); special education teaching (MS).

Chestnut Hill College, School of Graduate Studies, Department of Education, Program in Elementary/Middle Education, Philadelphia, PA 19118-2693. Offers M Ed. *Program availability:* Part-time, evening/weekend. *Degree requirements:* For master's, thesis optional. *Entrance requirements:* For master's, PRAXIS I or proof of teaching certification, letters of recommendation, writing sample, 6 graduate credits with minimum B grade if undergraduate GPA less than 3.0. Additional exam requirements/recommendations for international students: Required—TOEFL (minimum score 500 paper-based), IELTS (minimum score 6.0), or TWE (minimum score 22). Electronic applications accepted. *Expenses:* Contact institution. *Faculty research:* Inclusive education, cultural issues in education.

Chestnut Hill College, School of Graduate Studies, Department of Education, Program in Reading, Philadelphia, PA 19118-2693. Offers reading specialist (M Ed), including K-12, special education 7-12, special education PreK-8. *Program availability:* Part-time, evening/weekend. *Degree requirements:* For master's, thesis optional. *Entrance requirements:* Additional exam requirements/recommendations for international students: Required—TOEFL (minimum score 500 paper-based) or IELTS (minimum score 6). Electronic applications accepted. *Expenses:* Contact institution. *Faculty research:* Inclusive education, cultural issues in education.

Chicago State University, School of Graduate and Professional Studies, College of Education, Department of Reading, Elementary Education, Library Information and Media Studies, Program in Middle School Education, Chicago, IL 60628. Offers MAT. *Unit head:* Mary Grace Bator, Chairperson. *Application contact:* Anika Miller, Graduate Studies Office, 773-995-2404, E-mail: g-studies1@csu.edu.

The Citadel, The Military College of South Carolina, Citadel Graduate College, Zucker Family School of Education, Charleston, SC 29409. Offers elementary/secondary school administration and supervision (M Ed); elementary/secondary school counseling (M Ed); interdisciplinary STEM education (M Ed); literacy education (M Ed, Graduate Certificate); middle grades (MAT), including English, mathematics, science, social studies; physical education (grades K-12) (MAT); school superintendency (Ed S); secondary education (MAT), including biology, English, mathematics, social studies; student affairs (Graduate Certificate); student affairs and college counseling (M Ed).

Accreditation: NCATE. *Program availability:* Part-time, evening/weekend, 100% online, blended/hybrid learning. *Degree requirements:* For master's, comprehensive exam (for some programs). *Entrance requirements:* For master's, GRE (minimum combined verbal and quantitative score of 290) or MAT (minimum score 396). Additional exam requirements/recommendations for international students: Required—TOEFL (minimum score 550 paper-based; 79 iBT). Electronic applications accepted. *Expenses:* Tuition, state resident: part-time $587 per credit hour. Tuition, nonresident: part-time $988 per credit hour. *Required fees:* $90 per term.

City College of the City University of New York, Graduate School, School of Education, Department of Secondary Education, New York, NY 10031-9198. Offers adolescent mathematics education (MA, AC); English education (MA); middle school mathematics education (MS); science education (MA); social studies education (AC). *Accreditation:* NCATE. *Entrance requirements:* For master's, Liberal Arts and Sciences Test (LAST), Content Specialty Test (CST). Additional exam requirements/recommendations for international students: Required—TOEFL.

Clarkson University, Program in Education, Schenectady, NY 12308. Offers adolescence education 7-12 (MAT); teaching of English to speakers of other languages (MAT); technology education K-12 (MAT). *Accreditation:* TEAC. *Faculty:* 3 full-time (all women), 23 part-time/adjunct (14 women). *Students:* 22 full-time (13 women), 12 part-time (8 women); includes 4 minority (1 Black or African American, non-Hispanic/Latino; 3 Asian, non-Hispanic/Latino), 6 international. 39 applicants, 72% accepted, 21 enrolled. In 2017, 28 master's awarded. *Degree requirements:* For master's, thesis (for some programs), thesis or project. *Entrance requirements:* For master's, GRE, minimum undergraduate GPA of 3.0. Additional exam requirements/recommendations for international students: Required—TOEFL (minimum score 550 paper-based, 80 iBT) or IELTS (6.5). *Application deadline:* Applications are processed on a rolling basis. Application fee: $50. Electronic applications accepted. *Expenses:* Contact institution. *Financial support:* Scholarships/grants available. *Unit head:* Dr. Catherine Snyder, Chair of Education, 518-631-9870, E-mail: csnyder@clarkson.edu. *Application contact:* Dan Capogna, Director of Graduate Admissions, 518-631-9910, E-mail: graduate@clarkson.edu.
Website: https://www.clarkson.edu/academics/graduate

Clemson University, Graduate School, College of Education, Department of Teaching and Learning, Clemson, SC 29634. Offers curriculum and instruction (PhD); middle level education (MAT); secondary math and science (MAT); STEAM education (Certificate); teaching and learning (M Ed). *Program availability:* Part-time, evening/weekend, 100% online. *Faculty:* 21 full-time (17 women). *Students:* 41 full-time (27 women), 94 part-time (78 women); includes 16 minority (8 Black or African American, non-Hispanic/Latino; 6 Hispanic/Latino; 1 Native Hawaiian or other Pacific Islander, non-Hispanic/Latino; 1 Two or more races, non-Hispanic/Latino), 3 international. Average age 29. 65 applicants, 62% accepted, 33 enrolled. In 2017, 74 master's awarded. *Degree requirements:* For master's, comprehensive exam; for doctorate, comprehensive exam, thesis/dissertation. *Entrance requirements:* For master's, doctorate, and Certificate, GRE General Test, unofficial transcripts, letters of recommendation. Additional exam requirements/recommendations for international students: Required—TOEFL (minimum score 540 paper-based; 80 iBT), IELTS (minimum score 7), PTE (minimum score 45). *Application deadline:* For fall admission, 4/15 for domestic and international students. Applications are processed on a rolling basis. Application fee: $80 ($90 for international students). Electronic applications accepted. *Expenses:* $5,767 per semester full-time resident, $10,918 per semester full-time non-resident, $656 per credit hour part-time resident, $1,310 per credit hour part-time non-resident, $915 per credit hour online; other fees may apply per session. *Financial support:* In 2017–18, 8 students received support, including 2 fellowships with partial tuition reimbursements available (averaging $3,500 per year), 1 research assistantship with partial tuition reimbursement available (averaging $18,000 per year), 5 teaching assistantships with partial tuition reimbursements available (averaging $18,000 per year); career-related internships or fieldwork also available. Financial award application deadline: 4/1. *Faculty research:* STEAM education, inquiry-based instruction, cultural hegemony and mathematics, equity and ethics, teacher effectiveness. *Total annual research expenditures:* $1.6 million. *Unit head:* Dr. Jeff Marshall, Department Chair, 864-656-2059, E-mail: marsha9@clemson.edu. *Application contact:* Alison Search, Student Services Coordinator, 864-250-8880, E-mail: alisonp@clemson.edu.
Website: http://www.clemson.edu/education/departments/teaching-learning/index.html

The College at Brockport, State University of New York, School of Education, Health, and Human Services, Department of Education and Human Development, Program in Adolescence Education, Brockport, NY 14420-2997. Offers adolescence biology education (MS Ed); adolescence chemistry education (MS Ed); adolescence English (MS Ed); adolescence mathematics (MS Ed); adolescence physics (MS Ed); adolescence social studies education (MS Ed). *Accreditation:* NCATE. *Program availability:* Part-time. *Students:* 50 part-time (28 women); includes 1 minority (Black or African American, non-Hispanic/Latino). 24 applicants, 79% accepted, 11 enrolled. In 2017, 18 master's awarded. *Degree requirements:* For master's, thesis or alternative. *Entrance requirements:* For master's, edTPA, GRE or MAT, minimum GPA of 3.0, letters of recommendation, statement of objectives, current resume. Additional exam requirements/recommendations for international students: Required—TOEFL (minimum score 550 paper-based; 79 iBT), IELTS (minimum score 6.5). *Application deadline:* For fall admission, 3/15 priority date for domestic and international students; for spring admission, 10/15 priority date for domestic and international students; for summer admission, 3/15 priority date for domestic students, 3/13 priority date for international students. Application fee: $80. Electronic applications accepted. *Expenses:* Tuition, state resident: full-time $10,870; part-time $453 per credit hour. Tuition, nonresident: full-time $22,210. *Required fees:* $988; $246 per semester. *Financial support:* Federal Work-Study, scholarships/grants, and unspecified assistantships available. Support available to part-time students. Financial award application deadline: 3/15; financial award applicants required to submit FAFSA. *Unit head:* Dr. Sue Robb, Chairperson, 585-395-5935, Fax: 585-395-2172, E-mail: srobb@brockport.edu. *Application contact:* Anne Walton, Coordinator of Certification and Graduate Advisement, 585-395-2326, Fax: 585-395-2172, E-mail: awalton@brockport.edu.
Website: https://www.brockport.edu/academics/education_human_development/department.html

College of Mount Saint Vincent, School of Professional and Graduate Studies, Department of Teacher Education, Riverdale, NY 10471-1093. Offers instructional technology and global perspectives (Certificate); middle level education (Certificate); multicultural studies (Certificate); teaching English to speakers of other languages (MS Ed); urban and multicultural education (MS Ed). *Accreditation:* TEAC. *Program availability:* Part-time. *Degree requirements:* For master's, comprehensive exam. *Entrance requirements:* For master's, interview, New York teaching certificate. Additional exam requirements/recommendations for international students: Required—TOEFL.

College of Saint Elizabeth, Program in Education, Morristown, NJ 07960-6989. Offers assistive technology (Certificate); education (MA); ESL (Certificate); Holocaust/genocide education (Certificate); middle school science (Certificate); online teaching in the 21st century (Certificate); teaching (Certificate), including K-12, K-6, teacher of students with

disabilities. *Program availability:* Part-time. *Faculty:* 3 full-time (2 women), 8 part-time/adjunct (6 women). *Students:* 1 (woman) full-time, 34 part-time (29 women); includes 1 minority (Hispanic/Latino). Average age 32. 25 applicants, 100% accepted, 24 enrolled. In 2017, 23 master's awarded. *Degree requirements:* For master's and Certificate, thesis. *Entrance requirements:* For master's, certification. Additional exam requirements/recommendations for international students: Required—TOEFL (minimum score 550 paper-based; 79 iBT), IELTS (minimum score 6.5). *Application deadline:* For fall admission, 5/1 for international students. Applications are processed on a rolling basis. Application fee: $35. Electronic applications accepted. Application fee is waived when completed online. *Financial support:* Career-related internships or fieldwork, scholarships/grants, and unspecified assistantships available. Financial award applicants required to submit FAFSA. *Unit head:* Dr. Joseph Ciccone, 973-290-4383, Fax: 973-290-4389, E-mail: jciccone@cse.edu. *Application contact:* Lori J. Fragoso, Director of Graduate and Continuing Studies Admissions, 973-290-4413, Fax: 973-290-4710, E-mail: apply@cse.edu.
Website: http://www.cse.edu/academics/prof-studies/education/

The College of Saint Rose, Graduate Studies, Thelma P. Lally School of Education, Teacher Education Programs, Albany, NY 12203-1419. Offers adolescence education (MS Ed, Advanced Certificate); adolescence education/special education (Advanced Certificate); childhood education (MS Ed); curriculum and instruction (MS Ed); early childhood education (MS Ed). *Students:* 69 full-time (60 women), 21 part-time (16 women); includes 7 minority (4 Black or African American, non-Hispanic/Latino; 2 Hispanic/Latino; 1 Two or more races, non-Hispanic/Latino), 1 international. Average age 27. 46 applicants, 52% accepted, 23 enrolled. In 2017, 43 master's awarded. *Entrance requirements:* For master's, minimum undergraduate GPA of 3.0. Additional exam requirements/recommendations for international students: Required—TOEFL (minimum score 550 paper-based; 80 iBT), IELTS (minimum score 6), PTE (minimum score 56). *Application deadline:* For fall admission, 4/1 priority date for domestic and international students; for spring admission, 10/15 priority date for domestic and international students; for summer admission, 3/15 priority date for domestic and international students. Applications are processed on a rolling basis. Application fee: $40. Electronic applications accepted. *Expenses:* Tuition: Full-time $7191; part-time $799 per credit hour. *Required fees:* $924; $462 per credit hour. Tuition and fees vary according to course load. *Financial support:* Career-related internships or fieldwork, scholarships/grants, tuition waivers (partial), and unspecified assistantships available. Support available to part-time students. Financial award application deadline: 4/15. *Unit head:* Dr. Drey Martone, Chair, 518-454-5262, E-mail: martoned@strose.edu. *Application contact:* Cris Murray, Assistant Vice President for Graduate Recruitment and Enrollment, 518-485-3390, Fax: 518-458-5479, E-mail: grad@strose.edu.
Website: https://www.strose.edu/academics/schools/school-of-education/

College of Staten Island of the City University of New York, Graduate Programs, School of Education, Program in Special Education, Staten Island, NY 10314-6600. Offers special education (MS Ed), including adolescence generalist: grades 7-12, grades 1-6. *Program availability:* Part-time, evening/weekend. *Faculty:* 3 full-time, 8 part-time/adjunct. *Students:* 144. 73 applicants, 73% accepted, 41 enrolled. In 2017, 39 master's awarded. *Degree requirements:* For master's, comprehensive exam, fieldwork; ten three-credit required courses and one elective for a total of 11 courses (33 credits) or 14 three-credit required courses and a three- to six-credit, field-based requirement for a total of 45-48 credits; research project. *Entrance requirements:* For master's, GRE General Test or an approved equivalent examination, BA/BS or 36 approved credits with minimum GPA of 3.0, 2 letters of recommendations, 1-2 page statement of experience. Additional exam requirements/recommendations for international students: Required—TOEFL (minimum score 550 paper-based; 79 iBT), IELTS (minimum score 6.5). *Application deadline:* For fall admission, 4/25 for domestic and international students; for spring admission, 11/25 for domestic and international students. Applications are processed on a rolling basis. Application fee: $125. Electronic applications accepted. *Expenses:* Tuition, state resident: full-time $10,450; part-time $440 per credit. Tuition, nonresident: full-time $19,320; part-time $440 per credit. *Required fees:* $181.10 per semester. Tuition and fees vary according to program. *Faculty research:* Disabilities studies, social justice, arts-based research on disabilities, assessment of students with disabilities, technological pedagogical and content knowledge (TPACK) in special education teachers, juvenile justice. *Unit head:* Diane Brescia, 718-982-3877, E-mail: diane.brescia@csi.cuny.edu. *Application contact:* Sasha Spence, Associate Director for Graduate Admissions, 718-982-2019, Fax: 718-982-2500, E-mail: sasha.spence@csi.cuny.edu.
Website: https://www.csi.cuny.edu/sites/default/files/pdf/admissions/grad/pdf/Education%20Fact%20Sheet.pdf

Columbus State University, Graduate Studies, College of Education and Health Professions, Department of Teacher Education, Columbus, GA 31907-5645. Offers curriculum and instruction in accomplished teaching (M Ed); early childhood education (M Ed, MAT, Ed S); middle grades education (M Ed, MAT, Ed S); secondary education (M Ed, MAT, Ed S), including biology (MAT), chemistry (MAT), earth and space science (MAT), English/language arts, general science (M Ed), history (MAT), mathematics, science (Ed S), social science (M Ed, Ed S); special education (M Ed, MAT, Ed S), including general curriculum (M Ed, MAT); teacher leadership (M Ed). *Accreditation:* NCATE. *Program availability:* Part-time, evening/weekend, 100% online, blended/hybrid learning. *Faculty:* 19 full-time (12 women), 24 part-time/adjunct (18 women). *Students:* 99 full-time (76 women), 181 part-time (143 women); includes 109 minority (94 Black or African American, non-Hispanic/Latino; 1 American Indian or Alaska Native, non-Hispanic/Latino; 1 Asian, non-Hispanic/Latino; 6 Hispanic/Latino; 7 Two or more races, non-Hispanic/Latino). Average age 34. 136 applicants, 63% accepted, 56 enrolled. In 2017, 119 master's, 8 other advanced degrees awarded. *Degree requirements:* For Ed S, thesis or alternative. *Entrance requirements:* For master's, GRE General Test, minimum undergraduate GPA of 2.75; for Ed S, GRE General Test, minimum undergraduate GPA of 2.75, graduate 3.0. Additional exam requirements/recommendations for international students: Required—TOEFL (minimum score 550 paper-based; 79 iBT). *Application deadline:* For fall admission, 6/30 for domestic students, 5/1 for international students; for spring admission, 11/1 for domestic and international students; for summer admission, 3/1 for domestic and international students. Applications are processed on a rolling basis. Application fee: $50. Electronic applications accepted. *Expenses:* Tuition, state resident: full-time $3708; part-time $2472 per year. Tuition, nonresident: full-time $14,418; part-time $9612 per year. *International tuition:* $19,218 full-time. *Required fees:* $1605. Tuition and fees vary according to program. *Financial support:* In 2017–18, 45 students received support, including 9 research assistantships with partial tuition reimbursements available (averaging $3,000 per year); career-related internships or fieldwork, Federal Work-Study, institutionally sponsored loans, scholarships/grants, tuition waivers (partial), and unspecified assistantships also available. Support available to part-time students. Financial award application deadline: 5/1; financial award applicants required to submit FAFSA. *Unit head:* Dr. Jan Burcham, Department Chair, 706-507-8519, Fax: 706-568-3134, E-mail: burcham_jan@columbusstate.edu. *Application contact:* Catrina Smith-Edmond, Assistant Director for Graduate and Global Admission, 706-507-8824, Fax: 706-568-5091, E-mail: smithedmond_catrina@columbusstate.edu.
Website: http://te.columbusstate.edu/

Middle School Education

Converse College, Program in Middle Level Education, Spartanburg, SC 29302. Offers language arts/English (MAT); mathematics (MAT); middle level education (M Ed); science (MAT); social studies (MAT). *Unit head:* Lienne Medford, Dean of Graduate Studies and Distance Education, 864-596-9082, E-mail: lienne.medford@converse.edu. *Application contact:* 864-596-9404, E-mail: graduate@converse.edu.

Daemen College, Education Department, Amherst, NY 14226-3592. Offers adolescence education (MS); childhood education (MS); childhood special education (MS); childhood special-alternative certification (MS); early childhood special-alternative certification (MS). *Accreditation:* TEAC. *Program availability:* Part-time. *Degree requirements:* For master's, thesis option, research thesis in lieu of comprehensive exam; completion of degree within 5 years. *Entrance requirements:* For master's, 2 letters of recommendation (professional and character), proof of initial certificate of license for professional programs, resume. Additional exam requirements/recommendations for international students: Required—TOEFL (minimum score 500 paper-based; 63 iBT), IELTS (minimum score 5.5). Electronic applications accepted. *Faculty research:* Transition for students with disabilities, early childhood special education, traumatic brain injury (TBI), reading assessment.

DePaul University, College of Education, Chicago, IL 60614. Offers bilingual-bicultural education (M Ed, MA); counseling (M Ed, MA), including clinical mental health counseling, college student development, school counseling; curriculum studies (M Ed, MA, Ed D); early childhood education (M Ed, MA, Ed D); educational leadership (M Ed, MA, Ed D), including Catholic leadership (M Ed, MA), general (M Ed, MA), higher education (M Ed, MA), physical education (M Ed, MA), principal preparation (M Ed); teacher preparation (M Ed); elementary education (M Ed, MA); middle grades education (M Ed); middle school mathematics education (MS); reading specialist (M Ed, MA); secondary education (M Ed, MA); social and cultural foundations in education (M Ed, MA); special education (MS); sport, fitness and recreation leadership (MS); value-creating education for global citizenship (M Ed); world languages education (M Ed, MA). *Program availability:* Part-time, evening/weekend, online learning. *Degree requirements:* For doctorate, thesis/dissertation. *Application deadline:* Applications are processed on a rolling basis. Application fee: $40. Electronic applications accepted. *Financial support:* Application deadline: 12/31; applicants required to submit FAFSA. *Unit head:* Dr. Paul Zionts, Dean, 773-325-7581, Fax: 773-325-7713, E-mail: pzionts@depaul.edu. *Application contact:* Dr. Paul Zionts, Dean, 773-325-7581, Fax: 773-325-7713, E-mail: pzionts@depaul.edu.
Website: http://education.depaul.edu

Drury University, Master in Education Program, Springfield, MO 5802. Offers curriculum and instruction (M Ed), including elementary, middle school, secondary; gifted education (M Ed); instructional leadership (M Ed); instructional technology (M Ed); integrated learning (M Ed); online teaching (M Ed); special education (M Ed); special reading (M Ed). *Accreditation:* NCATE. *Program availability:* Part-time, evening/weekend, 100% online, blended/hybrid learning. *Entrance requirements:* For master's, GRE, bachelor's degree with minimum GPA of 2.75. Additional exam requirements/recommendations for international students: Recommended—TOEFL (minimum score 80 iBT), IELTS (minimum score 6.5). Electronic applications accepted. *Expenses:* Contact institution. *Faculty research:* Gifted students, instructional technology, autism, diversity and social justice.

Duquesne University, School of Education, Department of Instruction and Leadership, Program in Middle Level (4-8) Education, Pittsburgh, PA 15282-0001. Offers MS Ed. *Program availability:* Part-time, evening/weekend. *Faculty:* 1 (woman) full-time. *Students:* 2 full-time (1 woman), 1 (woman) part-time. Average age 29. In 2017, 1 master's awarded. *Entrance requirements:* For master's, bachelor's degree. Additional exam requirements/recommendations for international students: Required—TOEFL (minimum score 550 paper-based). *Application deadline:* For fall admission, 9/1 for domestic students; for spring admission, 1/1 for domestic students. Applications are processed on a rolling basis. Application fee: $0. Electronic applications accepted. *Expenses:* $1,259 per credit. *Financial support:* Research assistantships available. *Faculty research:* Adolescent literacy; family engagement and community partnerships; factors that create highly effective teachers; notions and perceptions of being a well-educated person, models of teacher leadership. *Unit head:* Dr. Carla Meyer, Assistant Professor, 412-396-5838, Fax: 412-396-5388, E-mail: meyerc2@duq.edu. *Application contact:* Kelly McGinley, Graduate Admissions Assistant, 412-396-1559, Fax: 412-396-5585, E-mail: mcginleyk@duq.edu.
Website: http://www.duq.edu/academics/schools/education/graduate-programs-education/ms-middle-level-4-8

East Carolina University, Graduate School, College of Education, Department of Elementary and Middle Grades Education, Greenville, NC 27858-4353. Offers elementary education (MA Ed, MAT); middle grades education (MA Ed, MAT). *Accreditation:* NCATE. *Program availability:* Part-time, evening/weekend, online learning. *Students:* 13 full-time (12 women), 27 part-time (26 women); includes 9 minority (5 Black or African American, non-Hispanic/Latino; 1 Asian, non-Hispanic/Latino; 2 Hispanic/Latino; 1 Two or more races, non-Hispanic/Latino). Average age 29. 39 applicants, 97% accepted, 31 enrolled. In 2017, 11 master's awarded. *Degree requirements:* For master's, comprehensive exam, thesis optional. *Entrance requirements:* For master's, GRE or MAT, minimum GPA of 2.5, bachelor's degree in related field, teaching license (MA Ed). Additional exam requirements/recommendations for international students: Required—TOEFL. *Application deadline:* For fall admission, 6/1 priority date for domestic students. Applications are processed on a rolling basis. Application fee: $75. *Expenses:* Tuition, state resident: full-time $4749; part-time $297 per credit hour. Tuition, nonresident: full-time $17,898; part-time $1119 per credit hour. *Required fees:* $2691; $224 per credit hour. Part-time tuition and fees vary according to course load and program. *Financial support:* Federal Work-Study available. Support available to part-time students. Financial award application deadline: 3/1. *Unit head:* Dr. Ann Bullock, Chair, 252-328-1126, E-mail: bullockv@ecu.edu.
Website: http://www.ecu.edu/cs-educ/elmid/index.cfm

Eastern Illinois University, Graduate School, College of Education and Professional Studies, Department of Early Childhood, Elementary and Middle Level Education, Charleston, IL 61920. Offers curriculum and instruction (MS Ed). *Accreditation:* NCATE. *Program availability:* Part-time, evening/weekend. *Degree requirements:* For master's, comprehensive exam (for some programs), thesis (for some programs). *Entrance requirements:* For master's, GMAT or GRE. Additional exam requirements/recommendations for international students: Required—TOEFL (minimum score 500 paper-based; 61 iBT), IELTS (minimum score 6). *Application deadline:* For fall admission, 5/15 for domestic and international students; for spring admission, 10/15 for domestic and international students. Applications are processed on a rolling basis. Application fee: $30. Electronic applications accepted. *Financial support:* Research assistantships with full tuition reimbursements, teaching assistantships with full tuition reimbursements, career-related internships or fieldwork, Federal Work-Study, and unspecified assistantships available. Support available to part-time students. Financial award application deadline: 3/1; financial award applicants required to submit FAFSA. *Unit head:* Jeanne E. Okrasinski, Chair, 217-581-5728, Fax: 217-581-6300, E-mail: jeokrasinski@eiu.edu. *Application contact:* Jeanne E. Okrasinski, Chair, 217-581-5728, Fax: 217-581-6300, E-mail: jeokrasinski@eiu.edu.
Website: http://www.eiu.edu/elegrad/

Eastern Illinois University, Graduate School, College of Liberal Arts and Sciences, Department of Mathematics and Computer Science, Charleston, IL 61920. Offers elementary/middle school mathematics education (MA); mathematics (MA); secondary mathematics education (MA). *Program availability:* Part-time, evening/weekend. *Degree requirements:* For master's, comprehensive exam (for some programs), thesis (for some programs). *Entrance requirements:* For master's, GMAT or GRE. Additional exam requirements/recommendations for international students: Required—TOEFL (minimum score 500 paper-based; 61 iBT), IELTS (minimum score 6). *Application deadline:* For fall admission, 5/15 for domestic and international students; for spring admission, 10/15 for domestic and international students. Applications are processed on a rolling basis. Application fee: $30. Electronic applications accepted. *Financial support:* Teaching assistantships with full tuition reimbursements, career-related internships or fieldwork, Federal Work-Study, and unspecified assistantships available. Support available to part-time students. Financial award application deadline: 3/1; financial award applicants required to submit FAFSA. *Unit head:* Marshall B. Lassak, Chair, 217-581-6450, Fax: 217-581-6284, E-mail: mblassak@eiu.edu. *Application contact:* Peter S. Wiles, Graduate Coordinator, 217-581-6275, Fax: 217-581-6284, E-mail: pswiles@eiu.edu.
Website: http://www.eiu.edu/mathgrad

Eastern Michigan University, Graduate School, College of Education, Department of Teacher Education, Programs in K–12 Education, Ypsilanti, MI 48197. Offers middle school education (MA); secondary school education (MA). *Accreditation:* NCATE. *Program availability:* Part-time, evening/weekend, online learning. *Students:* 22 full-time (17 women), 34 part-time (27 women); includes 5 minority (3 Asian, non-Hispanic/Latino; 1 Hispanic/Latino; 1 Two or more races, non-Hispanic/Latino), 16 international. Average age 31. 50 applicants, 84% accepted, 23 enrolled. In 2017, 6 master's awarded. *Entrance requirements:* For master's, GRE. Additional exam requirements/recommendations for international students: Required—TOEFL. *Application deadline:* Applications are processed on a rolling basis. Application fee: $45. *Financial support:* Fellowships, research assistantships with full tuition reimbursements, teaching assistantships with full tuition reimbursements, career-related internships or fieldwork, Federal Work-Study, institutionally sponsored loans, scholarships/grants, tuition waivers (partial), and unspecified assistantships available. Support available to part-time students. Financial award applicants required to submit FAFSA. *Application contact:* Dr. Martha Kinney-Sedgwick, Department Head, 734-487-3260, Fax: 734-487-2101, E-mail: mkinneys@emich.edu.

Eastern Nazarene College, Adult and Graduate Studies, Division of Teacher Education, Quincy, MA 02170. Offers administration (M Ed); early childhood education (M Ed, Certificate); elementary education (M Ed, Certificate); English as a second language (Certificate); instructional enrichment and development (Certificate); middle school education (M Ed, Certificate); moderate special needs education (Certificate); principal (Certificate); program development and supervision (Certificate); secondary education (M Ed, Certificate); special education administrator (Certificate); special needs (M Ed); supervisor (Certificate); teacher of reading (M Ed, Certificate). M Ed also available through weekend program for administration, special needs, and teacher of reading only. *Program availability:* Part-time, evening/weekend. *Entrance requirements:* Additional exam requirements/recommendations for international students: Required—TOEFL (minimum score 550 paper-based).

Eastern University, Graduate Education Programs, St. Davids, PA 19087-3696. Offers ESL program specialist (K-12) (Certificate); general supervisor (PreK-12) (Certificate); health and physical education (K-12) (Certificate); middle level (4-8) (Certificate); multicultural education (M Ed) (Certificate); music (K-12) (Certificate); Pre K-4 (Certificate); Pre K-4 with special education (Certificate); reading (M Ed); reading specialist (K-12) (Certificate); reading supervisor (K-12) (Certificate); school counseling (MA, CAGS); school principalship (preK-12) (Certificate); school psychology (MS, CAGS); secondary biology education (7-12) (Certificate); secondary chemistry education (7-12) (Certificate); secondary communication education (7-12) (Certificate); secondary English education (7-12) (Certificate); secondary math education (7-12) (Certificate); secondary social studies education (7-12) (Certificate); special education (M Ed); special education (7-12) (Certificate); special education (Pre K-8) (Certificate); special education supervisor (K-12) (Certificate); TESOL (M Ed); world language (Certificate), including Spanish. *Program availability:* Part-time, evening/weekend, online learning. *Students:* 46 full-time (40 women), 115 part-time (93 women); includes 65 minority (42 Black or African American, non-Hispanic/Latino; 3 Asian, non-Hispanic/Latino; 14 Hispanic/Latino; 6 Two or more races, non-Hispanic/Latino), 1 international. Average age 32. In 2017, 72 master's awarded. *Entrance requirements:* Additional exam requirements/recommendations for international students: Required—TOEFL. *Application deadline:* Applications are processed on a rolling basis. Application fee: $35. Electronic applications accepted. Application fee is waived when completed online. *Expenses:* Contact institution. *Unit head:* Michael Dziedziak, Executive Director of Enrollment, 800-452-0996, E-mail: gpsadmissions@eastern.edu.
Website: https://www.eastern.edu/academics/programs/education-department-graduate-programs/graduate-programs

East Tennessee State University, School of Graduate Studies, College of Education, Department of Curriculum and Instruction, Johnson City, TN 37614. Offers advanced studies in teaching and learning (M Ed), including childhood literacy; educational technology (M Ed), including educational communications and technology, school library media; elementary education (M Ed); reading (M Ed, MA), including reading education (MA), storytelling (MA); response to intervention (Post-Master's Certificate); school library professional (Post-Master's Certificate); secondary education (M Ed); STEAM K-12 education (Postbaccalaureate Certificate); storytelling (Postbaccalaureate Certificate); teacher education (MAT), including elementary education K-5, middle grades education 4-8, middle grades education 6-8, secondary education 6-12 and preK-12, secondary education K-12. *Accreditation:* NCATE. *Program availability:* Part-time, evening/weekend, online learning. *Degree requirements:* For master's, comprehensive exam, thesis optional, student teaching, practicum; for other advanced degree, field work (school library); culminating experience (storytelling). *Entrance requirements:* For master's, GRE, SAT, ACT, PRAXIS, minimum GPA of 3.0, interview, 3 letters of recommendation, background check; for other advanced degree, master's degree, TN teaching license. Additional exam requirements/recommendations for international students: Required—TOEFL (minimum score 550 paper-based; 79 iBT). *Application deadline:* For fall admission, 6/1 for domestic students, 4/29 for international students; for spring admission, 11/1 for domestic students, 4/29 for international students. Application fee: $55 ($65 for international students). Electronic applications accepted. *Financial support:* Research assistantships with full tuition reimbursements, teaching assistantships with tuition reimbursements, career-related internships or fieldwork, institutionally sponsored loans, scholarships/grants, and unspecified assistantships available. Financial award application deadline: 7/1; financial award applicants required to submit FAFSA. *Faculty research:* Critical thinking; curriculum development in reading, math, and science education; cultural diversity; cognitive processes; effective teaching strategies. *Unit head:* Dr. Karin Keith, Chair, 423-439-7598, Fax: 423-439-8362, E-mail: keithkj@etsu.edu. *Application contact:* Dr. Aimee Govett, Graduate Coordinator, 423-439-7804, Fax: 423-439-5624, E-mail: govett@etsu.edu.
Website: http://www.etsu.edu/coe/cuai/

Edinboro University of Pennsylvania, Department of Middle and Secondary Education and Educational Leadership, Edinboro, PA 16444. Offers educational leadership (M Ed); middle and secondary instruction (M Ed). *Program availability:* Part-time, evening/weekend. *Degree requirements:* For master's, comprehensive exam, thesis or alternative, project. *Entrance requirements:* For master's, GRE or MAT, minimum QPA of 2.5. Electronic applications accepted.

Emory University, Laney Graduate School, Division of Educational Studies, Atlanta, GA 30322-1100. Offers educational studies (MA, PhD); middle grades teaching (MAT); secondary teaching (MAT). *Accreditation:* NCATE. Terminal master's awarded for partial completion of doctoral program. *Degree requirements:* For master's, thesis; for doctorate, comprehensive exam, thesis/dissertation. *Entrance requirements:* For master's and doctorate, GRE General Test, minimum GPA of 3.0. Additional exam requirements/recommendations for international students: Required—TOEFL. Electronic applications accepted. *Faculty research:* Educational policy, educational measurement, urban and multicultural education, mathematics and science education, comparative education.

Fayetteville State University, Graduate School, Programs in Middle Grades, Secondary, Special and Elementary Education, Fayetteville, NC 28301-4298. Offers middle grades (MA Ed); sociology (MA Ed); special education (MA Ed), including behavioral-emotional handicaps, mentally handicapped, specific training disability. *Accreditation:* NCATE. *Program availability:* Part-time, evening/weekend. *Faculty:* 8 full-time (5 women). *Students:* 14 full-time (7 women), 8 part-time (6 women); includes 16 minority (13 Black or African American, non-Hispanic/Latino; 1 Asian, non-Hispanic/Latino; 2 Hispanic/Latino). Average age 35. 10 applicants, 80% accepted, 7 enrolled. In 2017, 9 master's awarded. *Degree requirements:* For master's, comprehensive exam, internship. *Entrance requirements:* Additional exam requirements/recommendations for international students: Required—TOEFL. *Application deadline:* For fall admission, 4/15 for domestic students; for spring admission, 10/15 for domestic students. Applications are processed on a rolling basis. Application fee: $40. Electronic applications accepted. *Expenses:* Tuition, state resident: full-time $8604. Tuition, nonresident: full-time $19,669. *Financial support:* Application deadline: 3/1; applicants required to submit FAFSA. *Faculty research:* Students with disabilities and selected leadership behaviors, new vision for professional development, gifted and talented students, emotional and behavioral disabilities, professional development for high school biology teachers. *Unit head:* Dr. Cynthia Shamberger, Chair of Middle Grades, Secondary and Specialized Subjects, 910-672-1181, Fax: 910-672-1941, E-mail: cshamber@uncfsu.edu. *Application contact:* Debra D. Brown, Administrative Support Associate, 910-672-1181, Fax: 910-672-1596, E-mail: ddbrown@uncfsu.edu.

Fitchburg State University, Division of Graduate and Continuing Education, Program in Middle School Education, Fitchburg, MA 01420-2697. Offers English (M Ed); general science (M Ed); history (M Ed); math (M Ed). *Accreditation:* NCATE. *Program availability:* Part-time, evening/weekend. *Students:* 15 full-time (7 women), 5 part-time (2 women); includes 3 minority (2 Black or African American, non-Hispanic/Latino; 1 Two or more races, non-Hispanic/Latino). Average age 32. 11 applicants, 100% accepted, 10 enrolled. In 2017, 4 master's awarded. *Entrance requirements:* Additional exam requirements/recommendations for international students: Required—TOEFL (minimum score 550 paper-based; 79 iBT). *Application deadline:* For fall admission, 7/15 for international students; for spring admission, 12/1 for international students. Applications are processed on a rolling basis. Application fee: $50. Electronic applications accepted. *Expenses:* Contact institution. *Financial support:* In 2017–18, research assistantships with partial tuition reimbursements (averaging $5,500 per year) were awarded; Federal Work-Study, scholarships/grants, and unspecified assistantships also available. Support available to part-time students. Financial award application deadline: 3/1; financial award applicants required to submit FAFSA. *Unit head:* William Cortezia, Chair, 978-665-3193, Fax: 978-665-3658, E-mail: gce@fitchburgstate.edu. *Application contact:* Jinawa McNeil, Director of Admissions, 978-665-3140, Fax: 978-665-4540, E-mail: admissions@fitchburgstate.edu.
Website: http://www.fitchburgstate.edu

Florida Gulf Coast University, College of Education, Program in Curriculum and Instruction, Fort Myers, FL 33965-6565. Offers elementary education (M Ed); English education (M Ed); English speakers of other languages endorsement (M Ed); gifted education (M Ed); mathematics education (M Ed); middle school education (M Ed); reading education (M Ed); science education (M Ed); social science education (M Ed); special education (M Ed). *Program availability:* Part-time, evening/weekend, online learning. *Faculty:* 27 full-time (19 women), 44 part-time/adjunct (30 women). *Students:* 3 full-time (all women), 16 part-time (14 women); includes 4 minority (2 Black or African American, non-Hispanic/Latino; 2 Hispanic/Latino). Average age 30. 6 applicants, 100% accepted, 5 enrolled. In 2017, 4 master's awarded. *Degree requirements:* For master's, final project or portfolio. *Entrance requirements:* For master's, GRE General Test, MAT, minimum undergraduate GPA of 3.0 in last 2 years. Additional exam requirements/recommendations for international students: Required—TOEFL (minimum score 550 paper-based). *Application deadline:* For fall admission, 2/15 priority date for domestic students, 5/1 for international students; for spring admission, 12/1 for domestic students, 9/15 for international students. Applications are processed on a rolling basis. Application fee: $30. Electronic applications accepted. *Expenses:* Tuition, state resident: part-time $290 per credit hour. Tuition, nonresident: part-time $1173 per credit hour. *Required fees:* $127 per credit hour. Tuition and fees vary according to course load. *Financial support:* In 2017–18, 2 students received support. Application deadline: 6/30; applicants required to submit FAFSA. *Faculty research:* Internet in schools, technology in pre-service and in-service teacher training. *Unit head:* Dr. Vickie Johnston, Instructor, 239-590-7754, Fax: 239-590-7801, E-mail: vjohnston@fgcu.edu. *Application contact:* Keiana Desmore, Adviser/Counselor, 239-590-7759, Fax: 239-590-7801, E-mail: kdesmore@fgcu.edu.
Website: http://coe.fgcu.edu/c-imed/

Fontbonne University, Graduate Programs, St. Louis, MO 63105-3098. Offers accounting (MBA, MS); art (MA); art (K-12) (MAT); business (MBA); computer science (MS); deaf education (MA); early intervention in deaf education (MA); education (MA), including autism spectrum disorders, curriculum and instruction, diverse learners, early childhood education, reading, special education; elementary education (MAT); family and consumer sciences (MA), including multidisciplinary health communication studies; fine arts (MFA); instructional design and technology (MS); management and leadership (MM); middle school education (MAT); secondary education (MAT); special education (MAT); speech-language pathology (MS); supply chain management (MS); theatre (MA). *Program availability:* Part-time, evening/weekend, online learning. *Degree requirements:* For master's, comprehensive exam (for some programs), thesis (for some programs). *Entrance requirements:* Additional exam requirements/recommendations for international students: Required—TOEFL (minimum score 500 paper-based; 65 iBT). Electronic applications accepted.

Georgia College & State University, Graduate School, The John H. Lounsbury College of Education, Program in Middle Grades Education, Milledgeville, GA 31061. Offers M Ed, MAT. *Accreditation:* NCATE. *Program availability:* Part-time, evening/weekend. *Students:* 12 full-time (8 women), 24 part-time (20 women); includes 8 minority (6 Black or African American, non-Hispanic/Latino; 1 Hispanic/Latino; 1 Two or more races, non-Hispanic/Latino). Average age 32. 22 applicants, 100% accepted, 19 enrolled. In 2017, 1 master's awarded. *Degree requirements:* For master's, comprehensive exam, portfolio presentation, complete program within 6 years, minimum GPA of 3.0. *Entrance requirements:* For master's, 2 professional recommendations, transcripts, resume, verification of immunization, and minimum GPA of 2.75; Georgia T4 certification or evidence of qualification for one (for M Ed). *Application deadline:* For fall admission, 7/1 priority date for domestic students, 4/1 priority date for international students; for spring admission, 11/15 priority date for domestic students, 9/1 priority date for international students. Applications are processed on a rolling basis. Application fee: $40. Electronic applications accepted. *Expenses:* $288 per hour full-time, $2,592 per semester; $343 per semester fees. *Financial support:* Applicants required to submit FAFSA. *Unit head:* Dr. Joseph Peters, Dean, College of Education, 478-445-2518, Fax: 478-445-6582, E-mail: joseph.peters@gcsu.edu. *Application contact:* Shanda Brand, Graduate Admission Advisor, 478-445-1383, E-mail: shanda.brand@gcsu.edu.

Georgia Southern University, Jack N. Averitt College of Graduate Studies, College of Education, Department of Teaching and Learning, Program in Middle Grades Education, Statesboro, GA 30460. Offers middle grades (M Ed, MAT, Ed S). *Accreditation:* NCATE. *Program availability:* Part-time, evening/weekend, 100% online, blended/hybrid learning. *Students:* 9 full-time (8 women), 23 part-time (all women); includes 10 minority (9 Black or African American, non-Hispanic/Latino; 1 Two or more races, non-Hispanic/Latino). Average age 31. 9 applicants, 100% accepted, 9 enrolled. In 2017, 17 master's, 3 other advanced degrees awarded. *Degree requirements:* For master's, portfolio, transition point assessments, exit assessment; for Ed S, field-based research projects, assessments. *Entrance requirements:* For master's, GACE Basic Skills and Content Assessments (for MAT), minimum cumulative GPA of 2.5. Additional exam requirements/recommendations for international students: Required—TOEFL (minimum score 550 paper-based; 80 iBT), IELTS (minimum score 6). *Application deadline:* For fall admission, 3/15 priority date for domestic students, 3/14 priority date for international students; for spring admission, 10/1 priority date for domestic students, 10/1 for international students; for summer admission, 3/1 for domestic and international students. Applications are processed on a rolling basis. Application fee: $50. Electronic applications accepted. *Expenses:* Tuition, state resident: full-time $4986; part-time $3324 per year. Tuition, nonresident: full-time $21,982; part-time $15,352 per year. *Required fees:* $2092; $1802 per credit hour. $901 per semester. Tuition and fees vary according to course load, campus/location and program. *Financial support:* In 2017–18, 8 students received support. Career-related internships or fieldwork, Federal Work-Study, scholarships/grants, and unspecified assistantships available. Support available to part-time students. Financial award application deadline: 4/15; financial award applicants required to submit FAFSA. *Faculty research:* Gender, technology applications, early and young adolescent literature, content subjects and literacy, integrated curriculum, content subject learning. *Unit head:* Dr. Greg Chamblee, Program Coordinator, 912-478-5701, Fax: 912-478-0026, E-mail: gchamblee@georgiasouthern.edu. *Application contact:* Dr. Lydia Cross, Coordinator for Graduate Academic Services Center, 912-478-8664, E-mail: lcross@georgiasouthern.edu.
Website: http://coe.georgiasouthern.edu/ger/

Georgia Southwestern State University, School of Education, Americus, GA 31709-4693. Offers early childhood education (M Ed, Ed S); middle grades education (Ed S); middle grades language arts (M Ed); middle grades mathematics (M Ed); special education (M Ed). *Accreditation:* NCATE. *Faculty:* 17 full-time (7 women), 7 part-time/adjunct (all women). *Students:* 221 full-time (206 women), 5 part-time (all women); includes 70 minority (all Black or African American, non-Hispanic/Latino). Average age 35. In 2017, 89 master's, 94 Ed Ss awarded. *Degree requirements:* For master's, minimum cumulative GPA of 3.0; maximum of 6 credit hours with C grade; no courses with D grade; degree completed within 7 calendar years; for Ed S, minimum GPA of 3.25 in all courses with no grade less than a B; degree must be completed within 7 calendar years from date of initial enrollment in graduate work. *Entrance requirements:* For master's, undergraduate degree from accredited institution; professional Georgia Teaching Certificate or eligibility; minimum undergraduate GPA of 2.75 as reported on official final transcripts from all accredited institutions attended; 2 confidential Administrative Recommendation Forms; for Ed S, master's degree from accredited college or university; professional Georgia Teaching Certificate or eligibility; minimum graduate GPA of 3.0 as reported on official final graduate transcripts from all accredited institutions attended; 2 confidential Administrative Recommendation Forms. *Application deadline:* For summer admission, 4/15 for domestic students. Application fee: $25. Electronic applications accepted. *Expenses:* $257 per credit hour for online courses plus fees which vary according to number of enrolled credit hours. *Financial support:* Application deadline: 6/1; applicants required to submit FAFSA. *Unit head:* Dr. Rachel Abbott, Dean, 229-931-2145. *Application contact:* Whitney Ford, Admissions Specialist, Office of Graduate Admissions, 800-338-0082, Fax: 229-931-2983.
Website: https://gsw.edu/Academics/Schools-and-Departments/School-of-Education/index

Georgia State University, College of Education and Human Development, Department of Middle and Secondary Education, Atlanta, GA 30302-3083. Offers curriculum and instruction (Ed D); English education (MAT); mathematics education (M Ed, MAT); middle level education (MAT); reading, language and literacy education (M Ed, MAT), including reading instruction (M Ed); science education (M Ed, MAT), including biology (MAT), broad field science (MAT), chemistry (MAT), earth science (MAT), physics (MAT); social studies education (M Ed, MAT), including economics (MAT), geography (MAT), history (MAT), political science (MAT); teaching and learning (PhD), including language and literacy, mathematics education, music education, science education, social studies education, teaching and teacher education. *Accreditation:* NCATE. *Program availability:* Part-time, evening/weekend, online learning. *Faculty:* 24 full-time (18 women). *Students:* 179 full-time (110 women), 192 part-time (133 women); includes 193 minority (130 Black or African American, non-Hispanic/Latino; 1 American Indian or Alaska Native, non-Hispanic/Latino; 23 Asian, non-Hispanic/Latino; 25 Hispanic/Latino; 14 Two or more races, non-Hispanic/Latino), 6 international. Average age 33. 175 applicants, 58% accepted, 83 enrolled. In 2017, 81 master's, 17 doctorates awarded. *Entrance requirements:* For master's, GRE; GACE I (for initial teacher preparation programs), baccalaureate degree or equivalent, resume, goals statement, two letters of recommendation, minimum undergraduate GPA of 2.5; proof of initial teacher certification in the content area (for M Ed); for doctorate, GRE, resume, goals statement, writing sample, two letters of recommendation, minimum graduate GPA of 3.3, interview. *Application deadline:* For fall admission, 1/15 priority date for domestic and international students; for spring admission, 10/1 for domestic and international students. Application fee: $50. Electronic applications accepted. *Expenses:* Tuition, state resident: full-time $7020. Tuition, nonresident: full-time $22,518. *Required fees:* $2128. Tuition and fees vary according to degree level and program. *Financial support:* In 2017–18, fellowships with full tuition reimbursements (averaging $19,667 per year), research assistantships with full tuition reimbursements (averaging $5,436 per year), teaching assistantships with full tuition reimbursements (averaging $2,779 per year) were awarded; career-related internships or fieldwork, Federal Work-Study, scholarships/grants, health care benefits, tuition waivers (full and partial), and unspecified assistantships also available. Financial award application deadline: 3/15. *Faculty research:* Teacher education in language and literacy, mathematics, science, and social studies in urban middle and

Middle School Education

secondary school settings; learning technologies in school, community, and corporate settings; multicultural education and education for social justice; urban education; international education. *Unit head:* Dr. Dana L. Fox, Chair, 404-413-8060, Fax: 404-413-8063, E-mail: dfox@gsu.edu. *Application contact:* Bobbie Turner, Administrative Coordinator, 404-413-8405, Fax: 404-413-8063, E-mail: bnturner@gsu.edu. Website: http://mse.education.gsu.edu/

Gordon College, Graduate Education Program, Wenham, MA 01984-1899. Offers early childhood (M Ed); educational leadership (M Ed, Ed S); elementary education (M Ed); English as a second language (M Ed, Ed S); math specialist (M Ed); mathematics specialist (Ed S); middle school education (M Ed); moderate disabilities (M Ed); Montessori education (M Ed); reading (M Ed); secondary education (M Ed). *Program availability:* Part-time, evening/weekend. *Faculty:* 23 full-time (17 women), 32 part-time/adjunct (23 women). *Students:* 68 full-time (50 women), 114 part-time (99 women); includes 24 minority (2 Black or African American, non-Hispanic/Latino; 8 Asian, non-Hispanic/Latino; 13 Hispanic/Latino; 1 Two or more races, non-Hispanic/Latino), 10 international. Average age 34. 248 applicants, 100% accepted, 182 enrolled. In 2017, 99 master's, 16 Ed Ss awarded. *Degree requirements:* For master's, action research or clinical experience (for most programs); for Ed S, action research or clinical experience (for some programs). *Entrance requirements:* For master's, minimum undergraduate GPA of 3.0; 2 official undergraduate transcripts; professional resume; 3 recommendation letters (one professional reference, one academic reference, one personal reference); 500-700 word statement of purpose; for Ed S, minimum master's GPA of 3.3; 2 official transcripts from undergraduate and graduate schools; professional resume; 3 recommendation letters (one professional reference, one academic reference, one personal reference); 500-700 word statement of purpose. Additional exam requirements/recommendations for international students: Required—TOEFL (minimum score 550 paper-based, 80 iBT) or IELTS (minimum score 6.5). *Application deadline:* Applications are processed on a rolling basis. Application fee: $75. *Expenses:* $325 per credit tuition; $75 per semester administrative fee. *Financial support:* Applicants required to submit FAFSA. *Faculty research:* Reading, early childhood development, English language learners, universal design for learning. *Unit head:* Dr. Janet Arndt, Director of Graduate Studies, 978-867-4355, Fax: 978-867-4663. *Application contact:* Julie Lenocker, Program Administrator, 978-867-4322, Fax: 978-867-4663, E-mail: graduate-education@gordon.edu. Website: http://www.gordon.edu/graduate

Goucher College, Graduate Programs in Education, Baltimore, MD 21204-2794. Offers at-risk and diverse learners (M Ed, Certificate); athletic program leadership and administration (M Ed, Certificate); elementary education (MAT); literacy strategies for content learning (M Ed); middle school (M Ed, Certificate); Montessori studies (M Ed); reading instruction (M Ed, Certificate); reducing student, classroom, and school disruption (M Ed); school improvement leadership (M Ed); secondary education (MAT); special education (MAT), including elementary education; special education for certified elementary and secondary teachers (M Ed); teacher as leader in technology (M Ed). *Program availability:* Part-time, evening/weekend. *Degree requirements:* For master's, thesis (M Ed), final presentation (MAT). *Entrance requirements:* For master's, minimum GPA of 3.0. Additional exam requirements/recommendations for international students: Required—TOEFL (minimum score 550 paper-based; 80 iBT), IELTS (minimum score 7). *Application deadline:* For fall admission, 9/1 for domestic students; for spring admission, 1/15 for domestic students. Applications are processed on a rolling basis. Application fee: $75. Electronic applications accepted. *Expenses:* Contact institution. *Financial support:* Career-related internships or fieldwork and unspecified assistantships available. Support available to part-time students. Financial award application deadline: 4/15; financial award applicants required to submit FAFSA. *Faculty research:* Urban education, middle school, school improvement, teacher education, at-risk student achievement. *Unit head:* Dr. Phyllis Sunshine, Assistant Provost, 410-337-6047, Fax: 410-337-6394, E-mail: psunshin@goucher.edu. *Application contact:* Carlton E. Surbeck, III, Director of Admissions, 410-337-6100, Fax: 410-337-6085, E-mail: admissions@goucher.edu. Website: http://www.goucher.edu/graduate-programs/graduate-programs-in-education

Grand Valley State University, College of Education, Programs in General Education, Allendale, MI 49401-9403. Offers adult and higher education (M Ed); early childhood education (M Ed); educational differentiation (M Ed); educational leadership (M Ed); educational technology integration (M Ed); elementary education (M Ed); middle level education (M Ed); school library media services (M Ed); secondary level education (M Ed); teaching English to speakers of other languages (M Ed). *Program availability:* Part-time, evening/weekend, 100% online, blended/hybrid learning. *Students:* 24 part-time (16 women). Average age 41. In 2017, 5 master's awarded. *Degree requirements:* For master's, project or thesis. *Entrance requirements:* For master's, GRE General Test or minimum GPA of 3.0, last 60 credits from regionally-accredited college/university, 3 letters of recommendation. Additional exam requirements/recommendations for international students: Required—TOEFL (minimum iBT score of 80), IELTS (6.5), or Michigan English Language Assessment Battery (77). *Application deadline:* Applications are processed on a rolling basis. Application fee: $30. Electronic applications accepted. *Expenses:* $652 per credit hour. *Financial support:* In 2017–18, 2 students received support, including 2 fellowships; career-related internships or fieldwork, Federal Work-Study, scholarships/grants, and unspecified assistantships also available. *Faculty research:* Effectiveness of technology in education, parental involvement, effective teaching, effective schools research. *Unit head:* Dr. David Bair, Department Director, 616-331-6489, Fax: 616-331-6489, E-mail: baird@gvsu.edu. *Application contact:* Thomas Owens, Director, Student Information and Services Center, 616-331-6282, Fax: 616-331-6217, E-mail: owenst@gvsu.edu. Website: http://www.gvsu.edu/coe/

Hampton University, School of Liberal Arts and Education, Program in Teaching, Hampton, VA 23668. Offers biology education 6-12 (MT); English education 6-12 (MT); mathematics education 6-12 (MT); music education PreK-12 (MT). *Program availability:* Part-time. *Students:* 5 full-time (4 women); all minorities (all Black or African American, non-Hispanic/Latino). Average age 23. 6 applicants, 67% accepted, 1 enrolled. In 2017, 7 master's awarded. *Entrance requirements:* For master's, GRE General Test. Additional exam requirements/recommendations for international students: Required—TOEFL (minimum score 525 paper-based) or IELTS (6.5). *Application deadline:* For fall admission, 6/1 priority date for domestic students, 4/1 for international students; for spring admission, 11/1 priority date for domestic students, 9/1 for international students; for summer admission, 4/1 priority date for domestic students, 2/1 priority date for international students. Applications are processed on a rolling basis. Application fee: $35. Electronic applications accepted. *Expenses: Tuition:* Full-time $22,630; part-time $575 per semester hour. *Required fees:* $70. Tuition and fees vary according to program. *Financial support:* Application deadline: 6/30; applicants required to submit FAFSA. *Unit head:* Dr. Martha Jallim-Hall, Program Coordinator, 757-727-5793.

Hebrew College, Shoolman Graduate School of Jewish Education, Newton Centre, MA 02459. Offers early childhood Jewish education (Certificate); Jewish day school education (Certificate); Jewish education (MJ Ed); Jewish family education (Certificate); Jewish special education (Certificate); Jewish youth education, informal education and camping (Certificate). *Program availability:* Part-time, evening/weekend, online learning.

Degree requirements: For master's, one foreign language. *Entrance requirements:* For master's, GRE, interview. Additional exam requirements/recommendations for international students: Required—TOEFL.

Henderson State University, Graduate Studies, Teachers College, Department of Advanced Instructional Studies, Arkadelphia, AR 71999-0001. Offers developmental therapy (MSE); dyslexia therapy (Graduate Certificate); education (MAT); educational technology leadership (Graduate Certificate); English as a second language (MSE, Graduate Certificate); instructional facilitator (MSE, Graduate Certificate); middle level education (MAT); special education (K-12) (MAT, MSE); special education/early childhood (MAT). *Accreditation:* NCATE. *Program availability:* Part-time. *Entrance requirements:* For master's, GRE General Test or MAT, minimum GPA of 2.7, teacher certification. Additional exam requirements/recommendations for international students: Required—TOEFL (minimum score 600 paper-based); Recommended—IELTS (minimum score 6.5).

Hofstra University, School of Education, Programs in Teacher Education, Hempstead, NY 11549. Offers bilingual education (MA); bilingual extension (Advanced Certificate), including education/speech language pathology, intensive teacher institute; business education (MS Ed); curriculum studies (MS Ed); early childhood and childhood education (MS Ed); early childhood education (MA, MS Ed); educational technology (Advanced Certificate); elementary education (MA, MS Ed), including science, technology, engineering, and mathematics (STEM) (MA); English education (MS Ed); family and consumer science (MS Ed); fine arts and music education (Advanced Certificate); fine arts education (MS Ed); foreign language and TESOL (MS Ed); foreign language education (MA, MS Ed), including Arabic (MS Ed), biology, chemistry, Chinese (MS Ed), earth science, French, German, Italian (MS Ed), Mandarin (MS Ed), physics, Russian, Spanish; foundations of education (Advanced Certificate), including grades 5-6, grades 7-9; languages other than English and teaching English as a second language (MA); learning and teaching (Ed D), including applied linguistics, art education, arts and humanities, early childhood education, English education, human development, math education, math, science, and technology, multicultural education, physical education, science education, social studies education, special education; mathematics education (MA, MS Ed); music education (MA, MS Ed); science education (MA), including biology (MA, MS Ed), chemistry (MA, MS Ed), earth science (MA, MS Ed), physics (MA, MS Ed); secondary education (Advanced Certificate); social studies education (MA, MS Ed); teaching languages other than English and TESOL (MS Ed); technology for learning (MA); TESOL (MS Ed, Advanced Certificate); TESOL with specialization in STEM (MA); work based learning extension (Advanced Certificate). *Program availability:* Part-time, evening/weekend, blended/hybrid learning. *Students:* 119 full-time (83 women), 124 part-time (90 women); includes 54 minority (15 Black or African American, non-Hispanic/Latino; 9 Asian, non-Hispanic/Latino; 29 Hispanic/Latino; 1 Native Hawaiian or other Pacific Islander, non-Hispanic/Latino; 12 international. Average age 29. 205 applicants, 88% accepted, 93 enrolled. In 2017, 103 master's, 4 doctorates, 32 other advanced degrees awarded. *Degree requirements:* For master's, comprehensive exam, thesis (for some programs), exit project, student teaching, fieldwork, electronic portfolio, curriculum project, minimum GPA of 3.0; for doctorate, thesis/dissertation; for Advanced Certificate, 3 foreign languages, comprehensive exam (for some programs), thesis project. *Entrance requirements:* For master's, GRE, 2 letters of recommendation, portfolio, teacher certification (MA), interview, essay; for doctorate, GMAT, GRE, LSAT, or MAT; for Advanced Certificate, 2 letters of recommendation, essay, interview and/or portfolio, teaching certificate. Additional exam requirements/recommendations for international students: Required—TOEFL (minimum score 550 paper-based; 80 iBT). *Application deadline:* Applications are processed on a rolling basis. Application fee: $75. Electronic applications accepted. *Expenses: Tuition:* Full-time $1292. *Required fees:* $970. Tuition and fees vary according to program. *Financial support:* In 2017–18, 112 students received support, including 56 fellowships with full and partial tuition reimbursements available (averaging $4,998 per year), 2 research assistantships with full and partial tuition reimbursements available (averaging $8,753 per year); career-related internships or fieldwork, Federal Work-Study, institutionally sponsored loans, scholarships/grants, traineeships, tuition waivers (full and partial), and unspecified assistantships also available. Support available to part-time students. Financial award applicants required to submit FAFSA. *Faculty research:* Educational interventions that foster critical-thinking skills; teachers' attitudes about professional development; threats to teacher quality. *Unit head:* Dr. Eustace Thompson, Chairperson, 516-463-5749, Fax: 516-463-6275, E-mail: eustace.g.thompson@hofstra.edu. *Application contact:* Sunil Samuel, Assistant Vice President of Admissions, 516-463-4723, Fax: 516-463-4664, E-mail: graduateadmission@hofstra.edu. Website: http://www.hofstra.edu/education/

Hofstra University, School of Education, Specialized Programs in Education, Hempstead, NY 11549. Offers applied behavior analysis (Advanced Certificate); childhood special education (MS Ed); early childhood special education (MS Ed, Advanced Certificate); educational and policy leadership (Ed D); educational leadership (Advanced Certificate), including school building leader/school district business leader; educational leadership and policy studies (MS Ed), including K-12; elementary special education (MS Ed); gifted education (Advanced Certificate), including school building leader/school district business leader; health education (MS); health professions pedagogy and leadership (MS); higher education leadership and policy studies (MS Ed); inclusive early childhood special education (MS Ed); inclusive elementary special education (MS Ed); inclusive secondary special education (MS Ed); literacy studies (MA, MS Ed, Ed D, Advanced Certificate, including birth-grade 6 (MS Ed, Advanced Certificate), grades 5-12 (MS Ed, Advanced Certificate), literacy studies (Ed D)); pedagogy for health professions (Advanced Certificate); physical education (MS); school district business leader (Advanced Certificate); secondary education generalist - students with disabilities 7-12 (MS Ed), including students with disabilities 7-12; secondary special education generalist (MS Ed), including extension in secondary education; special education (MS Ed, Advanced Certificate); special education assessment and diagnosis (Advanced Certificate); special education early childhood intervention (MS Ed); special education: international perspectives (MS Ed); teaching students with severe or multiple disabilities (Advanced Certificate). *Program availability:* Part-time, evening/weekend, blended/hybrid learning. *Students:* 148 full-time (110 women), 249 part-time (188 women); includes 105 minority (54 Black or African American, non-Hispanic/Latino; 1 American Indian or Alaska Native, non-Hispanic/Latino; 13 Asian, non-Hispanic/Latino; 35 Hispanic/Latino; 1 Native Hawaiian or other Pacific Islander, non-Hispanic/Latino; 1 Two or more races, non-Hispanic/Latino), 1 international. Average age 32. 228 applicants, 93% accepted, 132 enrolled. In 2017, 97 master's, 22 doctorates, 31 other advanced degrees awarded. *Degree requirements:* For master's, one foreign language, comprehensive exam (for some programs), thesis (for some programs), electronic portfolio, capstone course, internship, practicum, student teaching, seminars, minimum GPA of 3.0; for doctorate, one foreign language, comprehensive exam, thesis/dissertation, qualifying hearing. *Entrance requirements:* For master's, GRE, interview, letters of recommendation, portfolio, essay, certification; for doctorate, GRE or MAT, interview, resume, essay, master's degree, 3 letters of recommendation, writing sample; for Advanced Certificate, GRE, interview, letters of recommendation, essay, professional experience, resume, master's degree. Additional exam requirements/recommendations for international students: Required—TOEFL

(minimum score 550 paper-based; 80 iBT). *Application deadline:* Applications are processed on a rolling basis. Application fee: $75. Electronic applications accepted. *Expenses: Tuition:* Full-time $1292. *Required fees:* $970. Tuition and fees vary according to program. *Financial support:* In 2017–18, 225 students received support, including 118 fellowships with full and partial tuition reimbursements available (averaging $3,887 per year), 12 research assistantships with full and partial tuition reimbursements available (averaging $7,215 per year); career-related internships or fieldwork, Federal Work-Study, institutionally sponsored loans, scholarships/grants, traineeships, tuition waivers (full and partial), and unspecified assistantships also available. Support available to part-time students. Financial award applicants required to submit FAFSA. *Faculty research:* Collaborative teaching and learning; language and culture; new media literacies; applied behavior analysis; K-12 leadership development. *Unit head:* Dr. Elfreda Blue, Chairperson, 516-463-5762, Fax: 516-463-6184, E-mail: elfreda.blue@hofstra.edu. *Application contact:* Sunil Samuel, Assistant Vice President of Admissions, 516-463-4723, Fax: 516-463-4664, E-mail: graduateadmission@hofstra.edu.
Website: http://www.hofstra.edu/education/

Hood College, Graduate School, Program in Secondary Mathematics Education, Frederick, MD 21701-8575. Offers high school (MS); middle school (MS); secondary mathematics education (Certificate). *Program availability:* Part-time, evening/weekend. *Faculty:* 2 full-time (1 woman), 3 part-time/adjunct (2 women). *Students:* 29 part-time (20 women); includes 2 minority (1 Black or African American, non-Hispanic/Latino; 1 Hispanic/Latino). Average age 32. 6 applicants, 100% accepted, 6 enrolled. In 2017, 8 master's awarded. *Degree requirements:* For master's, exitfolio, capstone/research project. *Entrance requirements:* For master's, minimum GPA of 2.75, initial teacher certification, essay. Additional exam requirements/recommendations for international students: Required—TOEFL (minimum score 575 paper-based; 89 iBT), IELTS (minimum score 6.5). *Application deadline:* For fall admission, 8/15 priority date for domestic students, 8/15 for international students; for spring admission, 12/1 priority date for domestic students, 12/1 for international students; for summer admission, 5/1 priority date for domestic students, 4/15 for international students. Applications are processed on a rolling basis. Application fee: $35. Electronic applications accepted. *Expenses:* $465 per credit hour plus $110 comprehensive fee per semseter. *Financial support:* Tuition waivers (partial) and unspecified assistantships available. Financial award applicants required to submit FAFSA. *Unit head:* Dr. April M. Boulton, Dean of the Graduate School, 301-696-3600, E-mail: gofurther@hood.edu. *Application contact:* Jan Marcus, Assistant Director of Graduate Admissions, 301-696-3600, E-mail: gofurther@hood.edu.
Website: http://www.hood.edu/graduate

Houston Baptist University, School of Humanities, Program in Liberal Arts, Houston, TX 77074-3298. Offers education (EC-12 art, music, physical education, or Spanish) (MLA); education (EC-6 generalist) (MLA); general liberal arts (MLA); specialization in education (4-8 or 7-12) (MLA). *Program availability:* Part-time, evening/weekend. *Students:* 11 full-time (7 women), 13 part-time (9 women); includes 12 minority (5 Black or African American, non-Hispanic/Latino; 2 Asian, non-Hispanic/Latino; 5 Hispanic/Latino). Average age 31. 26 applicants, 73% accepted, 12 enrolled. In 2017, 15 master's awarded. *Entrance requirements:* For master's, minimum GPA of 2.5, essay/personal statement, resume, bachelor's degree transcript. Additional exam requirements/recommendations for international students: Required—TOEFL (minimum score 80 iBT), IELTS (minimum score 6.5). *Application deadline:* For fall admission, 8/1 for domestic students, 6/1 for international students; for spring admission, 1/1 for domestic students, 11/1 for international students; for summer admission, 5/1 for domestic students, 3/1 for international students. Applications are processed on a rolling basis. Application fee: $0 ($100 for international students). Electronic applications accepted. Application fee is waived when completed online. *Expenses:* $18,000 tuition; $4,500 fees (general, technology and parking). *Financial support:* In 2017–18, 12 students received support. Federal Work-Study and scholarships/grants available. Support available to part-time students. Financial award application deadline: 4/1; financial award applicants required to submit FAFSA. *Unit head:* Dr. Collin Garbarino, Graduate Programs Director, 281-649-3679, E-mail: cgarbarino@hbu.edu. *Application contact:* Kathy Holston, Administrative Assistant to the Dean, 281-649-3404, E-mail: kholston@hbu.edu.
Website: http://www.hbu.edu/mla

Huntington University, Graduate School, Huntington, IN 46750-1299. Offers adolescent and young adult education (M Ed); business administration (MBA); counseling (MA), including licensed mental health counselor; early adolescent education (M Ed); elementary education (M Ed); global youth ministry (MA); occupational therapy (OTD); organizational leadership (MA); pastoral leadership (MA); TESOL education (M Ed). *Program availability:* Part-time, online learning. *Faculty:* 17 full-time (10 women), 14 part-time/adjunct (4 women). *Students:* 221 full-time (163 women), 22 part-time (13 women). *Degree requirements:* For master's, comprehensive exam (for some programs), thesis (for some programs). *Entrance requirements:* For master's, GRE (for counseling and education students only); for doctorate, GRE (for occupational therapy students). Additional exam requirements/recommendations for international students: Required—TOEFL (minimum score 85 iBT), IELTS (minimum score 6.5). *Application deadline:* For fall admission, 7/1 for domestic students, 5/1 for international students; for winter admission, 10/1 for domestic students, 9/1 for international students; for spring admission, 11/30 for domestic students, 10/30 for international students. Applications are processed on a rolling basis. Application fee: $30. Electronic applications accepted. *Expenses:* Contact institution. *Financial support:* Scholarships/grants and unspecified assistantships available. Support available to part-time students. Financial award application deadline: 8/1; financial award applicants required to submit FAFSA. *Faculty research:* Leadership, educational technology trends, evangelism, youth ministry, mental health. *Unit head:* Michael Wanous, Vice President for Academic Affairs, 260-359-4008, Fax: 260-359-4126, E-mail: mwanous@huntington.edu. *Application contact:* Evan Bennett, Assistant Director of Graduate Admissions, 260-359-4111, Fax: 260-359-4126, E-mail: graduate@huntington.edu.
Website: http://www.huntington.edu/graduate

James Madison University, The Graduate School, College of Education, Program in Education, Harrisonburg, VA 22807. Offers early childhood education (preK-3) (MAT); educational leadership (M Ed); educational technology (M Ed); elementary education (MAT); equity and cultural diversity (M Ed); inclusive early childhood education (MAT); K-8 mathematics specialist (M Ed); middle education (MAT); reading education (M Ed); secondary education (MAT); Spanish language and culture for educators (M Ed); TESOL (MAT). *Accreditation:* NCATE. *Program availability:* Part-time, evening/weekend. *Students:* 260 full-time (233 women), 158 part-time (100 women); includes 48 minority (10 Black or African American, non-Hispanic/Latino; 4 Asian, non-Hispanic/Latino; 26 Hispanic/Latino; 1 Native Hawaiian or other Pacific Islander, non-Hispanic/Latino; 7 Two or more races, non-Hispanic/Latino), 2 international. Average age 30. In 2017, 262 master's awarded. Application fee: $55. Electronic applications accepted. *Expenses:* Tuition, state resident: full-time $10,512; part-time $438 per credit hour. Tuition, nonresident: full-time $28,358; part-time $1162 per credit hour. *Required fees:* $1128. *Financial support:* In 2017–18, 23 students received support, including 1 teaching assistantship; career-related internships or fieldwork, Federal Work-Study, and

22 assistantships (averaging $7911) also available. Financial award application deadline: 3/1; financial award applicants required to submit FAFSA. *Unit head:* Dr. Phillip M. Wishon, Dean, 540-568-6572, E-mail: wishonpm@jmu.edu. *Application contact:* Lynette D. Michael, Director of Graduate Admissions, 540-568-6131 Ext. 6395, Fax: 540-568-7860, E-mail: michaeld@jmu.edu.
Website: http://www.jmu.edu/coe/index.shtml

James Madison University, The Graduate School, College of Education, Program in Middle Education, Harrisonburg, VA 22807. Offers MAT. *Accreditation:* NCATE. *Program availability:* Part-time, evening/weekend. *Students:* Average age 27. *Entrance requirements:* For master's, GRE General Test, minimum undergraduate GPA of 2.5. Additional exam requirements/recommendations for international students: Required—TOEFL. *Application deadline:* For fall admission, 5/1 priority date for domestic students; for spring admission, 9/1 priority date for domestic students. Applications are processed on a rolling basis. Application fee: $55. Electronic applications accepted. *Expenses:* Tuition, state resident: full-time $10,512; part-time $438 per credit hour. Tuition, nonresident: full-time $28,358; part-time $1162 per credit hour. *Required fees:* $1128. *Financial support:* Federal Work-Study and unspecified assistantships available. Financial award application deadline: 3/1; financial award applicants required to submit FAFSA. *Unit head:* Dr. Steven L. Purcell, Academic Unit Head, 540-568-6793. *Application contact:* Lynette M. Bible, Director of Graduate Admissions, 540-568-6395, Fax: 540-568-7860, E-mail: biblelm@jmu.edu.

Kansas State University, Graduate School, College of Education, Department of Curriculum and Instruction, Manhattan, KS 66506. Offers curriculum and instruction (Ed D, PhD); digital teaching and learning (MS); educational computing, design and online learning (MS); elementary/middle level curriculum and instruction (MS); online learning (Certificate); reading specialist endorsement (MS); reading/language arts (MS); teacher leader/school improvement (MS); teaching and learning (Certificate). *Accreditation:* NCATE. *Program availability:* Part-time, online learning. *Degree requirements:* For master's, comprehensive exam, portfolio, project, report or thesis; for doctorate, comprehensive exam, thesis/dissertation, preliminary exam; for Certificate, comprehensive exam, portfolio. *Entrance requirements:* For master's, minimum GPA of 3.0, 3 letters of recommendation; for doctorate, GRE, minimum GPA of 3.0, 3 letters of recommendation, evidence of scholarly writing; for Certificate, minimum GPA of 3.0, letters of recommendation. Additional exam requirements/recommendations for international students: Required—TOEFL (minimum score 550 paper-based; 80 iBT) or IELTS. Electronic applications accepted. *Faculty research:* Literacy and technology, critical race theory and diversity, achievement gaps, school improvement, teacher education.

Kennesaw State University, Leland and Clarice C. Bagwell College of Education, Program in Graduate Education, Kennesaw, GA 30144. Offers educational leadership (M Ed); educational leadership technology (M Ed); elementary and early childhood education (M Ed); instructional technology (M Ed); middle grades education (M Ed); reading (M Ed); secondary education (M Ed); special education (M Ed); teaching English to speakers of other languages (M Ed). *Accreditation:* NCATE. *Program availability:* Part-time. *Degree requirements:* For master's, thesis or alternative. *Entrance requirements:* For master's, GRE General Test, T-4 state certification, minimum GPA of 2.75. Additional exam requirements/recommendations for international students: Required—TOEFL (minimum score 550 paper-based; 80 iBT), IELTS (minimum score 6.5). Electronic applications accepted.

Kent State University, College of Education, Health and Human Services, School of Teaching, Learning and Curriculum Studies, Program in Junior High/Middle School, Kent, OH 44242-0001. Offers M Ed, MA. *Program availability:* Part-time. *Degree requirements:* For master's, thesis (for some programs). *Entrance requirements:* For master's, 2 letters of reference, goals statement. Additional exam requirements/recommendations for international students: Required—TOEFL (minimum score 550 paper-based; 80 iBT). Electronic applications accepted. *Expenses:* Tuition, state resident: full-time $11,310; part-time $515 per credit hour. Tuition, nonresident: full-time $20,396; part-time $928 per credit hour. *International tuition:* $18,544 full-time. *Faculty research:* Middle school reform, teacher action research.

Kutztown University of Pennsylvania, College of Education, Program in Secondary Education, Kutztown, PA 19530-0730. Offers biology (M Ed); curriculum and instruction (M Ed); English (M Ed); mathematics (M Ed); middle level (M Ed); social studies (M Ed); teaching (M Ed); transformational teaching and learning (Ed D). *Accreditation:* NCATE. *Program availability:* Part-time, evening/weekend, 100% online, blended/hybrid learning. *Faculty:* 4 full-time (3 women), 1 part-time/adjunct (0 women). *Students:* 33 full-time (21 women), 76 part-time (49 women); includes 6 minority (3 Black or African American, non-Hispanic/Latino; 3 Hispanic/Latino). Average age 32. 76 applicants, 91% accepted, 43 enrolled. In 2017, 31 master's awarded. *Degree requirements:* For master's, comprehensive exam, thesis optional; for doctorate, thesis/dissertation. *Entrance requirements:* For master's, GRE General Test, minimum undergraduate major GPA of 3.0, 3 letters of recommendation, copy of PRAXIS II or valid instructional I or II teaching certificate; for doctorate, master's or specialist degree in education or related field from regionally-accredited institution of higher learning with minimum graduate GPA of 3.25, significant educational experience, employment in an education setting (preferred). Additional exam requirements/recommendations for international students: Required—TOEFL (minimum score 550 paper-based, 79 iBT), IELTS (minimum score 6.5), or PTE (minimum score 53). *Application deadline:* For fall admission, 8/1 for domestic and international students; for spring admission, 12/1 for domestic and international students. Application fee: $35. Electronic applications accepted. *Expenses:* Tuition, state resident: part-time $500 per credit. Tuition, nonresident: part-time $750 per credit. *Required fees:* $115 per credit. One-time fee: $50 part-time. Tuition and fees vary according to degree level. *Financial support:* Career-related internships or fieldwork, Federal Work-Study, scholarships/grants, and unspecified assistantships available. Financial award application deadline: 3/1; financial award applicants required to submit FAFSA. *Unit head:* Dr. Theresa Stahler, Department Chair, 610-683-4259, Fax: 610-683-1338, E-mail: stahler@kutztown.edu. *Application contact:* Dr. Patricia Walsh Coates, Graduate Coordinator, 610-638-4289, Fax: 610-683-1338, E-mail: coates@kutztown.edu.
Website: https://www.kutztown.edu/academcs/graduate-programs/secondary-education.htm

LaGrange College, Graduate Programs, Department of Education, LaGrange, GA 30240-2999. Offers curriculum and instruction (M Ed, Ed S); middle grades (MAT); secondary education (MAT). *Program availability:* Part-time, evening/weekend. *Degree requirements:* For master's, comprehensive exam. *Entrance requirements:* For master's, GRE, MAT, minimum GPA of 2.5. Additional exam requirements/recommendations for international students: Required—TOEFL (minimum score 550 paper-based).

La Salle University, School of Arts and Sciences, Program in Education, Philadelphia, PA 19141-1199. Offers autism spectrum disorders (MA, Certificate); bilingual/bicultural studies (MA); classroom management (MA); dual early childhood and special education (MA); dual middle-level science and math and special education (MA); education (MA); English (MA); English as a second language (Certificate); history (MA); instructional coach (Certificate); instructional leadership (MA); reading specialist (MA, Certificate);

Middle School Education

secondary education (MA); special education (MA, Certificate). *Program availability:* Part-time, evening/weekend. *Faculty:* 5 full-time (4 women), 8 part-time/adjunct (5 women). *Students:* 2 full-time (1 woman), 110 part-time (81 women); includes 23 minority (11 Black or African American, non-Hispanic/Latino; 1 Asian, non-Hispanic/Latino; 7 Hispanic/Latino; 4 Two or more races, non-Hispanic/Latino). Average age 33. 137 applicants, 70% accepted, 63 enrolled. In 2017, 148 master's awarded. *Degree requirements:* For master's, comprehensive exam. *Entrance requirements:* For master's, MAT or GRE, 2 letters of recommendation; for Certificate, GMAT or GRE, 2 letters of recommendation. Additional exam requirements/recommendations for international students: Required—TOEFL. *Application deadline:* For fall admission, 8/15 priority date for domestic students, 7/15 for international students; for spring admission, 12/15 priority date for domestic students, 11/15 for international students; for summer admission, 4/15 priority date for domestic students, 3/15 for international students. Applications are processed on a rolling basis. Application fee: $35. Electronic applications accepted. Application fee is waived when completed online. *Expenses:* Contact institution. *Financial support:* In 2017–18, 19 students received support. Scholarships/grants available. Support available to part-time students. Financial award application deadline: 8/31; financial award applicants required to submit FAFSA. *Unit head:* Dr. Greer Richardson, Director, 215-951-1806, Fax: 215-951-1843, E-mail: graded@lasalle.edu. *Application contact:* Elizabeth Heenan, Director, Graduate and Adult Enrollment, 215-951-1100, Fax: 215-951-1462, E-mail: heenan@lasalle.edu. Website: http://www.lasalle.edu/grad-education-programs/

Lee University, Program in Education, Cleveland, TN 37320-3450. Offers art (MAT); curriculum and instruction (M Ed, Ed S); early childhood (MAT); educational leadership (M Ed, Ed S); elementary education (MAT); English and math (MAT); English and science (MAT); English and social studies (MAT); higher education administration (MS); history (MAT); history and economics (MAT); math and science (MAT); math and social studies (MAT); middle grades (MAT); science and social studies (MASW); secondary education (MAT); Spanish (MAT); special education (M Ed, MAT); TESOL (MAT). *Accreditation:* NCATE. *Program availability:* Part-time. *Faculty:* 15 full-time (7 women), 8 part-time/adjunct (3 women). *Students:* 28 full-time (21 women), 77 part-time (48 women); includes 12 minority (7 Black or African American, non-Hispanic/Latino; 2 Hispanic/Latino; 3 Two or more races, non-Hispanic/Latino), 1 international. Average age 31. 35 applicants, 83% accepted, 22 enrolled. In 2017, 54 master's, 4 other advanced degrees awarded. *Degree requirements:* For master's, variable foreign language requirement, thesis optional, internship. *Entrance requirements:* For master's, MAT or GRE General Test, minimum undergraduate GPA of 2.75, 3 letters of recommendation, interview, writing sample, official transcripts, background check; for Ed S, minimum undergraduate and master's GPA of 2.75, official transcripts for undergraduate and master's degrees. Additional exam requirements/recommendations for international students: Required—TOEFL (minimum score 61 iBT). *Application deadline:* For fall admission, 6/1 priority date for domestic and international students; for spring admission, 11/1 priority date for domestic and international students; for summer admission, 4/1 priority date for domestic and international students. Applications are processed on a rolling basis. Application fee: $25. Electronic applications accepted. *Expenses: Tuition:* Full-time $12,780; part-time $710 per credit hour. *Required fees:* $60; $60 per term. Tuition and fees vary according to program. *Financial support:* In 2017–18, 32 students received support. Career-related internships or fieldwork, Federal Work-Study, institutionally sponsored loans, scholarships/grants, and unspecified assistantships available. Financial award application deadline: 3/1; financial award applicants required to submit FAFSA. *Unit head:* Dr. William Kamm, Director, 423-614-8544, E-mail: wkamm@leeuniversity.edu. *Application contact:* Crystal Keeter, Graduate Education Secretary, 423-614-8544, E-mail: ckeeter@leeuniversity.edu. Website: http://www.leeuniversity.edu/academics/graduate/education

Le Moyne College, Department of Education, Syracuse, NY 13214. Offers adolescent education (MS Ed, MST); adolescent education/special education (MS Ed, MST); adolescent English (MST), including grades 7-12; adolescent English/special education (MST), including grades 7-12; adolescent foreign language (MST), including grades 7-12; adolescent history (MST), including grades 7-12; childhood education (MS Ed); childhood education/special education (MS Ed); elementary education (MS Ed); general education (MS Ed); inclusive childhood education (MST); literacy education (MS Ed), including birth to grade 6, grades 5-12; school building leader (MS Ed); school building leadership (CAS); school district business leader (MS Ed, CAS); school district leader (MS Ed); school district leadership (CAS); secondary education (MS Ed); special education (MS Ed); teaching English to speakers of other languages (MS Ed); urban studies (MS Ed). *Accreditation:* TEAC. *Program availability:* Part-time, evening/weekend. *Faculty:* 7 full-time (5 women), 20 part-time/adjunct (12 women). *Students:* 30 full-time (19 women), 126 part-time (93 women); includes 15 minority (7 Black or African American, non-Hispanic/Latino; 1 American Indian or Alaska Native, non-Hispanic/Latino; 1 Asian, non-Hispanic/Latino; 6 Hispanic/Latino), 4 international. Average age 29. 139 applicants, 65% accepted, 76 enrolled. In 2017, 82 master's, 43 CASs awarded. *Degree requirements:* For master's, thesis. *Entrance requirements:* For master's, bachelor's degree with minimum undergraduate GPA of 3.0, 2 letters of recommendation, transcripts. Additional exam requirements/recommendations for international students: Required—TOEFL (minimum score 550 paper-based; 79 iBT); Recommended—IELTS (minimum score 6.5). *Application deadline:* For fall admission, 4/1 priority date for domestic and international students; for spring admission, 10/1 priority date for domestic and international students; for summer admission, 3/1 priority date for domestic and international students. Applications are processed on a rolling basis. Application fee: $50. Electronic applications accepted. *Expenses:* $700 per credit hour. *Financial support:* In 2017–18, 30 students received support. Career-related internships or fieldwork, scholarships/grants, and health care benefits available. Support available to part-time students. Financial award applicants required to submit FAFSA. *Faculty research:* Minority teachers, special education, multiculturalism, literacy, technology, media literacy learning, autism, school district organization, service-learning, higher level problem solving, teacher leadership. *Unit head:* Dr. Stephen C. Fleury, Chair, Department of Education, 315-445-4376, Fax: 315-445-4744, E-mail: fleurysc@lemoyne.edu. *Application contact:* Kristen P. Richards, Senior Director of Enrollment Management, 315-445-5444, Fax: 315-445-6092, E-mail: trapaskp@lemoyne.edu. Website: http://www.lemoyne.edu/education

Lesley University, Graduate School of Education, Cambridge, MA 02138-2790. Offers arts, community, and education (M Ed); autism studies (Certificate); curriculum and instruction (M Ed, CAGS); early childhood education (M Ed); ecological teaching and learning (MS); educational studies (PhD), including adult learning, educational leadership, individually designed; elementary education (M Ed); emergent technologies for educators (Certificate); ESLArts: language learning through the arts (M Ed); high school education (M Ed); individually designed (M Ed); integrated teaching through the arts (M Ed); literacy for K-8 classroom teachers (M Ed); mathematics education (M Ed); middle school education (M Ed); moderate disabilities (M Ed); online learning (Certificate); reading (CAGS); science in education (M Ed); severe disabilities (M Ed); special needs (CAGS); specialist teacher of reading (M Ed); teacher of visual art (M Ed); technology in education (M Ed, CAGS). *Accreditation:* TEAC. *Program availability:* Part-time, evening/weekend, online learning. *Degree requirements:* For master's, practicum;

for doctorate, thesis/dissertation. *Entrance requirements:* For master's, Massachusetts Tests for Educator Licensure (MTEL), transcripts, statement of purpose, recommendations; interview (for special education); for doctorate, GRE General Test, transcripts, statement of purpose, recommendations, interview, master's degree, resume; for other advanced degree, interview, master's degree. Additional exam requirements/recommendations for international students: Required—TOEFL (minimum score 550 paper-based; 80 iBT). Electronic applications accepted. *Faculty research:* Assessment in literacy, mathematics and science; autism spectrum disorders; instructional technology and online learning; multicultural education and English language learners.

Lewis University, College of Education, Program in Middle Level Education, Romeoville, IL 60446. Offers MA. *Program availability:* Part-time. *Students:* 8 full-time (7 women), 2 part-time (both women); includes 3 minority (1 Black or African American, non-Hispanic/Latino; 1 Asian, non-Hispanic/Latino; 1 Hispanic/Latino). Average age 35. *Degree requirements:* For master's, comprehensive exam. *Entrance requirements:* For master's, writing exam, Test of Academic Proficiency/Basic Skills Test/ACT/SAT, bachelor's degree, minimum GPA of 2.75, 2 letters of recommendation. Additional exam requirements/recommendations for international students: Required—TOEFL (minimum score 550 paper-based; 79 iBT), IELTS (minimum score 6). *Application deadline:* For fall admission, 5/1 priority date for international students; for spring admission, 11/1 priority date for international students. Application fee: $40. Electronic applications accepted. Tuition and fees vary according to program. *Financial support:* Federal Work-Study, scholarships/grants, and unspecified assistantships available. Financial award application deadline: 5/1; financial award applicants required to submit FAFSA. *Unit head:* Dr. Pamela Jessee, Dean, 815-836-5316, E-mail: jesseepa@lewisu.edu. *Application contact:* Kathy Lisak, Graduate Admission Counselor, 815-836-5610, E-mail: grad@lewisu.edu. Website: http://www.lewisu.edu/academics/mastersmiddleleveleducation/index.htm

Liberty University, School of Education, Lynchburg, VA 24515. Offers curriculum and instruction (Ed D, Ed S), including elementary education, middle grades education, secondary education, special education; educational leadership (Ed D); gifted education (Certificate); math specialist (M Ed); middle grades (MAT, Certificate); reading specialist (M Ed); school leadership (Certificate); secondary education (MAT); sport management (MS), including coaching and athletic administration, outdoor adventure sport, sport administration, tourism. *Accreditation:* NCATE. *Program availability:* Part-time, online learning. *Students:* 1,966 full-time (1,428 women), 3,484 part-time (2,528 women); includes 1,323 minority (1,026 Black or African American, non-Hispanic/Latino; 29 American Indian or Alaska Native, non-Hispanic/Latino; 49 Asian, non-Hispanic/Latino; 100 Hispanic/Latino; 9 Native Hawaiian or other Pacific Islander, non-Hispanic/Latino; 110 Two or more races, non-Hispanic/Latino), 58 international. Average age 37. 3,748 applicants, 58% accepted, 1167 enrolled. In 2017, 656 master's, 110 doctorates, 316 other advanced degrees awarded. *Degree requirements:* For doctorate, comprehensive exam, thesis/dissertation. *Entrance requirements:* For master's, GRE General Test or MAT (if taken in or before 1999), 2 letters of recommendation, minimum undergraduate GPA of 3.0, curriculum vitae; for doctorate and other advanced degree, GRE General Test or MAT (if taken before 1999), minimum master's GPA of 3.0, 3 years of teaching experience. Additional exam requirements/recommendations for international students: Required—TOEFL (minimum score 600 paper-based; 100 iBT). *Application deadline:* For fall admission, 6/1 for domestic students; for spring admission, 11/1 for domestic students. Applications are processed on a rolling basis. Application fee: $50. Electronic applications accepted. *Expenses:* Contact institution. *Financial support:* Federal Work-Study and tuition waivers (partial) available. *Faculty research:* Self-determination, character education, bibliotherapy, learning styles, distance education. *Unit head:* Dr. Heather Schoffstall, Dean, 434-582-2445, Fax: 434-582-2468, E-mail: awgunter@liberty.edu. *Application contact:* Jay Bridge, Director of Graduate Admissions, 800-424-9595, Fax: 800-628-7977, E-mail: gradadmissions@liberty.edu. Website: http://www.liberty.edu/academics/education/graduate/

Lincoln University, Graduate Studies, Jefferson City, MO 65101. Offers business administration (MBA), including accounting, management, management information systems, public administration/policy; elementary teaching (M Ed); environmental science (MS); guidance and counseling (M Ed), including community/agency counseling, elementary school, secondary school; higher education (MA); history (MA); integrated agricultural systems (MS); middle school (M Ed); natural sciences (MS); secondary teaching (M Ed); sociology (MA); sociology/criminal justice (MA). *Program availability:* Part-time, evening/weekend, 100% online, blended/hybrid learning. *Students:* 40 full-time (23 women), 64 part-time (32 women); includes 33 minority (30 Black or African American, non-Hispanic/Latino; 2 Hispanic/Latino; 1 Two or more races, non-Hispanic/Latino), 12 international. Average age 33. 48 applicants, 81% accepted, 22 enrolled. In 2017, 46 master's awarded. *Degree requirements:* For master's, comprehensive exam, thesis optional. *Entrance requirements:* For master's, GRE, MAT, or GMAT, minimum GPA of 2.75 overall, 3.0 in courses related to specialization; 3 letters of recommendation; minimum C average in English composition; personal statement of purpose. Additional exam requirements/recommendations for international students: Required—TOEFL (minimum score 500 paper-based; 61 iBT), IELTS (minimum score 5.5), Michigan English Language Assessment Battery (minimum score 80). *Application deadline:* For fall admission, 7/1 priority date for domestic students, 5/1 priority date for international students; for spring admission, 11/1 priority date for domestic students, 10/1 priority date for international students; for summer admission, 6/1 priority date for domestic students. Applications are processed on a rolling basis. Application fee: $30. Electronic applications accepted. *Expenses:* Tuition, state resident: part-time $291 per credit hour. Tuition, nonresident: part-time $541.50 per credit hour. *Financial support:* In 2017–18, 2 fellowships with tuition reimbursements, 3 research assistantships with tuition reimbursements were awarded; Federal Work-Study, scholarships/grants, and unspecified assistantships also available. Support available to part-time students. Financial award application deadline: 3/1; financial award applicants required to submit FAFSA. *Unit head:* Dr. Debra F. Greene, Interim Provost, 573-681-5247, Fax: 573-681-5106, E-mail: gradschool@lincolnu.edu. *Application contact:* Irasema Steck, Administrative Assistant, 573-681-5247, Fax: 573-681-5106, E-mail: gradschool@lincolnu.edu. Website: http://www.lincolnu.edu/web/graduate-studies/graduate-studies

Long Island University–Hudson, Graduate School, Purchase, NY 10577. Offers autism (Advanced Certificate); bilingual education (Advanced Certificate); childhood education (MS Ed); crisis management (Advanced Certificate); early childhood education (MS Ed); educational leadership (MS Ed); health administration (MPA); literacy (MS Ed); marriage and family therapy (MS); mental health counseling (MS, Advanced Certificate), including credentialed alcoholism and substance abuse counselor (MS); middle childhood and adolescence education (MS Ed); pharmaceutics (MS), including cosmetic science, industrial pharmacy; public administration (MPA); school counseling (MS Ed, Advanced Certificate); school psychology (MS Ed); special education (MS Ed); TESOL (MS Ed); TESOL (all grades) (Advanced Certificate). *Program availability:* Part-time, evening/weekend. *Faculty:* 8 full-time (6 women), 41 part-time/adjunct (24 women). *Students:* 69 full-time (54 women), 249 part-time (200 women); includes 102 minority (29 Black or African American, non-Hispanic/Latino; 1 American Indian or Alaska Native, non-Hispanic/Latino; 9 Asian, non-Hispanic/Latino;

62 Hispanic/Latino; 1 Native Hawaiian or other Pacific Islander, non-Hispanic/Latino). Average age 33. 153 applicants, 96% accepted, 103 enrolled. In 2017, 138 master's, 36 other advanced degrees awarded. *Entrance requirements:* Additional exam requirements/recommendations for international students: Required—TOEFL. *Application deadline:* Applications are processed on a rolling basis. Application fee: $50. Electronic applications accepted. *Expenses:* Contact institution. *Financial support:* In 2017–18, 32 students received support. Scholarships/grants available. Support available to part-time students. Financial award application deadline: 2/15; financial award applicants required to submit FAFSA. *Unit head:* Dr. Sylvia Blake, Dean and Chief Operating Officer, 914-831-2700, E-mail: westchester@liu.edu. *Application contact:* Dr. Sylvia Blake, Dean and Chief Operating Officer, 914-831-2700, E-mail: westchester@liu.edu.

Long Island University–LIU Post, College of Education, Information and Technology, Brookville, NY 11548-1300. Offers adolescence education (MS); adolescence education 7-12 (MS); archives and records management (AC); art education (MS); childhood education (MS); childhood education/literacy B-6 (MS); childhood education/special education (MS); clinical mental health counseling (MS, AC); early childhood education (MS); early childhood education/childhood education (MS); educational leadership (AC); educational technology (MS); information studies (PhD); interdisciplinary educational studies (Ed D); middle childhood education (MS); music education (MS); public library administration (AC); school counselor (MS); special education (MS Ed); speech-language pathology (MA); students with disabilities, 7-12 generalist (AC); TESOL (MA). *Accreditation:* TEAC. *Program availability:* Part-time, 100% online, blended/hybrid learning. *Faculty:* 40 full-time (26 women), 73 part-time/adjunct (38 women). *Students:* 472 full-time (400 women), 696 part-time (543 women); includes 254 minority (93 Black or African American, non-Hispanic/Latino; 46 Asian, non-Hispanic/Latino; 105 Hispanic/Latino; 10 Two or more races, non-Hispanic/Latino), 33 international. Average age 33. 917 applicants, 82% accepted, 357 enrolled. In 2017, 408 master's, 31 other advanced degrees awarded. Terminal master's awarded for partial completion of doctoral program. *Degree requirements:* For master's, variable foreign language requirement, comprehensive exam (for some programs), thesis optional; for doctorate, comprehensive exam, thesis/dissertation. *Entrance requirements:* For master's and AC, GRE (for some programs). Additional exam requirements/recommendations for international students: Required—TOEFL (minimum score 550 paper-based, 75 iBT), IELTS, or PTE. *Application deadline:* Applications are processed on a rolling basis. Application fee: $50. Electronic applications accepted. *Expenses: Tuition:* Full-time $21,618; part-time $1201 per credit. *Required fees:* $1840; $920 per term. Tuition and fees vary according to course load. *Financial support:* In 2017–18, 376 students received support. Career-related internships or fieldwork, Federal Work-Study, institutionally sponsored loans, scholarships/grants, tuition waivers (partial), and unspecified assistantships available. Support available to part-time students. Financial award application deadline: 2/15; financial award applicants required to submit FAFSA. *Faculty research:* Sleep; use of technology to develop executive function by students with disabilities; early childhood literacy development through play; social justice through education; using a structured protocol to discuss Bad News. *Unit head:* Dr. Albert Inserra, Dean, 516-299-2210, E-mail: albert.inserra@liu.edu. *Application contact:* Rita Langdon, Graduate Admissions, 516-299-2900, Fax: 516-299-2137, E-mail: post-enroll@liu.edu.
Website: http://liu.edu/CWPost/Academics/College-of-Education-Information-and-Technology

Longwood University, College of Graduate and Professional Studies, College of Education and Human Services, Farmville, VA 23909. Offers education (MS), including algebra and middle school mathematics, counselor education, elementary and middle school mathematics, elementary education, elementary education initial licensure, health and physical education, special education general curriculum, special education initial licensure; reading, literacy and learning (M Ed); school librarianship (M Ed); social work and communication sciences and disorders (MS), including communication sciences and disorders. *Accreditation:* NCATE. *Program availability:* Part-time, evening/weekend. *Degree requirements:* For master's, comprehensive exam (for some programs), thesis optional, professional portfolio, internship, clinical experience, or practicum. *Entrance requirements:* For master's, PRAXIS I (for initial teaching licensure programs), GRE (for some programs), bachelor's degree from regionally-accredited institution, 2 recommendations (3 for some programs), minimum 500-word personal essay, official transcripts, minimum GPA of 2.75, valid teaching license (for some programs). Additional exam requirements/recommendations for international students: Required—TOEFL (minimum score 570 paper-based), IELTS (minimum score 6.5). Electronic applications accepted. *Expenses:* Contact institution.

Louisiana Tech University, Graduate School, College of Education, Ruston, LA 71272. Offers counseling and guidance (MA), including clinical mental health counseling, human services, orientation and mobility; counseling psychology (PhD); curriculum and instruction (M Ed); cyber education (Graduate Certificate); dynamics of domestic and family violence (Graduate Certificate); early childhood education - PreK-3 (MAT); educational leadership (M Ed, Ed D); elementary education and special education mild/moderate grades 1-5 (MAT); higher education administration (Graduate Certificate); industrial/organizational psychology (MA, PhD); kinesiology (MS); middle school education (MAT), including mathematics; orientation and mobility (Graduate Certificate); rehabilitation teaching for the blind (Graduate Certificate); secondary education (MAT), including agriculture, biology, business, chemistry, English; special education: visually impaired (MAT); teacher leader education (Graduate Certificate); visual impairments - blind education (Graduate Certificate). *Accreditation:* NCATE. *Program availability:* Part-time. *Faculty:* 28 full-time (16 women), 23 part-time/adjunct (22 women). *Students:* 269 full-time (192 women), 194 part-time (150 women); includes 127 minority (94 Black or African American, non-Hispanic/Latino; 2 American Indian or Alaska Native, non-Hispanic/Latino; 6 Asian, non-Hispanic/Latino; 16 Hispanic/Latino; 1 Native Hawaiian or other Pacific Islander, non-Hispanic/Latino; 8 Two or more races, non-Hispanic/Latino), 8 international. Average age 34. 226 applicants, 74% accepted, 60 enrolled. In 2017, 5 master's, 2 doctorates, 1 other advanced degree awarded. *Degree requirements:* For master's, thesis; for doctorate, thesis/dissertation. *Entrance requirements:* For master's and doctorate, GRE General Test. Additional exam requirements/recommendations for international students: Required—TOEFL (minimum score 550 paper-based; 80 iBT), IELTS (minimum score 6.5). *Application deadline:* For fall admission, 9/1 priority date for domestic students, 6/1 for international students; for winter admission, 11/1 priority date for domestic students, 9/1 for international students; for spring admission, 2/1 priority date for domestic students, 12/1 for international students; for summer admission, 5/1 priority date for domestic students, 3/1 for international students. Application fee: $40. Electronic applications accepted. *Expenses:* Tuition, state resident: full-time $5146. Tuition, nonresident: full-time $10,147. *International tuition:* $10,267 full-time. *Required fees:* $2273. *Financial support:* In 2017–18, 40 students received support, including 23 research assistantships (averaging $10,346 per year), 15 teaching assistantships (averaging $6,887 per year); fellowships and career-related internships or fieldwork also available. Financial award application deadline: 2/1. *Faculty research:* Blindness and the best methods for increasing independence for individuals who are blind or visually impaired; educating and investigating factors contributing to improvements in human performance across the lifespan and a reduction in injury rates during training. *Total*

annual research expenditures: $2.1 million. *Unit head:* Dr. Don Schillinger, Dean, 318-257-3712, E-mail: dschill@latech.edu. *Application contact:* Dr. Dawn Basinger, Associate Dean of Academic Affairs, 318-257-2977, Fax: 318-257-2379, E-mail: dbasing@latech.edu.
Website: http://education.latech.edu/

Lynn University, Donald E. and Helen L. Ross College of Education, Boca Raton, FL 33431-5598. Offers educational leadership (M Ed, Ed D), including K-12 (Ed D), school administration K-12 (M Ed); exceptional student education (M Ed), including school administration K-12. *Program availability:* Part-time, evening/weekend, online learning. *Faculty:* 6 full-time (4 women), 4 part-time/adjunct (3 women). *Students:* 31 full-time (23 women), 62 part-time (42 women); includes 32 minority (20 Black or African American, non-Hispanic/Latino; 1 American Indian or Alaska Native, non-Hispanic/Latino; 10 Hispanic/Latino; 1 Two or more races, non-Hispanic/Latino), 3 international. Average age 36. 46 applicants, 78% accepted, 30 enrolled. In 2017, 24 master's, 22 doctorates awarded. *Degree requirements:* For master's, comprehensive exam, thesis (for some programs), completion of degree in maximum of four calendar years; minimum cumulative GPA of 3.0 and B grade or higher in each course; orientation seminar (one credit); minimum of 40 credits; FTCE ESE K-12 Exam; for doctorate, thesis/dissertation, mid-program review; minimum cumulative GPA of 3.25 and B grade or higher in each course. *Entrance requirements:* For master's, bachelor's degree from accredited institution, minimum undergraduate GPA of 3.0, official undergraduate and graduate transcripts of all academic coursework attempted, current résumé, statement of professional goals, writing sample, two recent letters of recommendation; for doctorate, professional practice statement that identifies applicant's goals and explains how Lynn's program will help attain them, official transcript showing conferral of master's degree, two letters of recommendation from previous professors or employers, current resume, interview. Additional exam requirements/recommendations for international students: Required—TOEFL (minimum score 550 paper-based; 80 iBT), IELTS (minimum score 6.5). *Application deadline:* For fall admission, 8/18 for domestic students, 8/4 for international students; for spring admission, 12/15 for domestic students, 12/1 for international students; for summer admission, 4/17 for domestic students, 4/3 for international students. Applications are processed on a rolling basis. Application fee: $45. Electronic applications accepted. *Expenses:* $740 per credit (for master's degrees); $850 per credit (for EdD). *Financial support:* Career-related internships or fieldwork, Federal Work-Study, scholarships/grants, tuition waivers (partial), and unspecified assistantships available. Support available to part-time students. Financial award application deadline: 3/1; financial award applicants required to submit FAFSA. *Faculty research:* Student achievement, students with learning differences, teacher and student retention, student motivation and cognition, neuroscience leadership and learning. *Unit head:* Dr. Kathleen Weigel, Dean, College of Education, 561-237-7441, E-mail: kweigel@lynn.edu. *Application contact:* Steven Pruitt, Director of Graduate and Undergraduate Evening Admission, 561-237-7834, Fax: 561-237-7100, E-mail: spruitt@lynn.edu.
Website: http://www.lynn.edu/academics/colleges/education

Manhattanville College, School of Education, Jump Start Program, Purchase, NY 10577-2132. Offers childhood education and special education (grades 1-6) (MPS); early childhood education (birth-grade 2) (MAT); education (Advanced Certificate); English and special education (grades 5-12) (MPS); mathematics and special education (grades 5-12) (MPS); science and special education (grades 5-12) (MPS); social studies and special education (grades 5-12) (MPS); Spanish (grades 7-12) (MAT); TESOL (all grades) (MPS). *Program availability:* Part-time, evening/weekend. *Faculty:* 10 full-time (7 women), 39 part-time/adjunct (27 women). *Students:* 3 full-time (2 women), 40 part-time (24 women); includes 11 minority (3 Black or African American, non-Hispanic/Latino; 6 Hispanic/Latino; 1 Native Hawaiian or other Pacific Islander, non-Hispanic/Latino; 1 Two or more races, non-Hispanic/Latino). Average age 33. 25 applicants, 60% accepted, 7 enrolled. In 2017, 17 master's, 2 other advanced degrees awarded. *Degree requirements:* For master's, comprehensive exam (for some programs), thesis (for some programs), student teaching, research seminars, portfolios, internships, writing assessment; for Advanced Certificate, comprehensive exam (for some programs). *Entrance requirements:* For master's, GRE or MAT (for programs leading to certification), minimum GPA of 3.0, 2 letters of recommendation, interview, essay (2-3 page personal statement that describes reasons for choosing teaching or educational leadership as profession and philosophy of education), proof of immunization (for those born after 1957). Additional exam requirements/recommendations for international students: Required—TOEFL (minimum score 600 paper-based; 110 iBT); Recommended—IELTS (minimum score 8). *Application deadline:* Applications are processed on a rolling basis. Application fee: $75. Electronic applications accepted. *Expenses:* $915 per credit. *Financial support:* Teaching assistantships, career-related internships or fieldwork, Federal Work-Study, institutionally sponsored loans, scholarships/grants, and unspecified assistantships available. Financial award application deadline: 3/15; financial award applicants required to submit FAFSA. *Faculty research:* Early childhood and technology, professional development schools and community schools, students with emotional difficulties, literacy and adolescents, mindfulness, changing suburbs institute, and community schools, studying the effects of the environment on special populations, the most difficult cases, students who are presented with multiple challenges: learning, behavioral and ACE experiences who see criminal behavior as a way to cope; working on giving them the tools they need to succeed. *Unit head:* Dr. Shelly Wepner, Dean, 914-323-3153, E-mail: shelly.wepner@mville.edu. *Application contact:* Alissa Wilson, Director, Graduate Admissions, 914-323-3150, Fax: 914-694-1732, E-mail: edschool@mville.edu.
Website: http://www.mville.edu/programs/jump-start

Manhattanville College, School of Education, Program in Literacy Education, Purchase, NY 10577-2132. Offers literacy (birth-grade 6) and special education childhood (grades 1-6) (MPS); literacy 5-12 (MPS); literacy specialist (birth-grade 6) (MPS); literacy specialist (grades 5-12) (MPS); science of reading: multisensory instruction (Advanced Certificate). *Program availability:* Part-time, evening/weekend. *Faculty:* 4 full-time (all women), 8 part-time/adjunct (5 women). *Students:* 1 (woman) full-time, 21 part-time (20 women). Average age 31. 12 applicants, 92% accepted, 8 enrolled. In 2017, 7 master's, 3 Advanced Certificates awarded. *Degree requirements:* For master's, comprehensive exam (for some programs), thesis (for some programs), student teaching, research seminars, portfolios, internships, writing assessment; for Advanced Certificate, comprehensive exam (for some programs). *Entrance requirements:* For master's, GRE or MAT (for programs leading to certification), minimum GPA of 3.0, 2 letters of recommendation, interview, essay (2-3 page personal statement that describes reasons for choosing teaching or educational leadership as profession and philosophy of education), proof of immunization (for those born after 1957). Additional exam requirements/recommendations for international students: Required—TOEFL (minimum score 600 paper-based; 110 iBT); Recommended—IELTS (minimum score 8). *Application deadline:* Applications are processed on a rolling basis. Application fee: $75. Electronic applications accepted. *Expenses:* $915 per credit. *Financial support:* Teaching assistantships, career-related internships or fieldwork, Federal Work-Study, institutionally sponsored loans, scholarships/grants, and unspecified assistantships available. Financial award application deadline: 3/15; financial award applicants required to submit FAFSA. *Faculty research:* Power of story for literacy development, English learners. *Total annual research expenditures:* $800. *Unit head:* Dr. Shelly Wepner, Dean, 914-323-3153, Fax: 914-323-5493, E-mail: shelly.wepner@mville.edu. *Application contact:* Alissa Wilson, Director, Graduate Admissions, 914-323-3150, Fax: 914-694-1732, E-mail: edschool@mville.edu. Website: http://www.mville.edu/programs/literacy-education

Manhattanville College, School of Education, Program in Middle Childhood/Adolescence Education (Grades 5-12), Purchase, NY 10577-2132. Offers biology (MAT, Advanced Certificate); biology and special education (MPS); chemistry (MAT, Advanced Certificate); chemistry and special education (MPS); earth science (Advanced Certificate); education for sustainability (Advanced Certificate); English (MAT, Advanced Certificate); English and special education (MPS); literacy and special education (MPS); literacy specialist (MPS); math and special education (MPS); mathematics (MAT, Advanced Certificate); physics (MAT, Advanced Certificate); social studies (MAT); social studies and special education (MPS); special education generalist (MPS). *Program availability:* Part-time, evening/weekend. *Faculty:* 2 full-time (both women), 5 part-time/adjunct (1 woman). *Students:* 8 full-time (7 women), 28 part-time (16 women); includes 4 minority (1 Asian, non-Hispanic/Latino; 2 Hispanic/Latino; 1 Two or more races, non-Hispanic/Latino). Average age 31. 7 applicants, 86% accepted, 4 enrolled. In 2017, 13 master's, 1 other advanced degree awarded. *Degree requirements:* For master's, comprehensive exam (for some programs), thesis (for some programs), student teaching, research seminars, portfolios, internships, writing assessment; for Advanced Certificate, comprehensive exam (for some programs). *Entrance requirements:* For master's, GRE or MAT (for programs leading to certification), minimum GPA of 3.0, 2 letters of recommendation, interview, essay (2-3 page personal statement that describes reasons for choosing teaching or educational leadership as profession and philosophy of education), proof of immunization (for those born after 1957). Additional exam requirements/recommendations for international students: Required—TOEFL (minimum score 600 paper-based; 110 iBT); Recommended—IELTS (minimum score 8). *Application deadline:* Applications are processed on a rolling basis. Application fee: $75. Electronic applications accepted. *Expenses:* $915 per credit. *Financial support:* Teaching assistantships, career-related internships or fieldwork, Federal Work-Study, institutionally sponsored loans, scholarships/grants, and unspecified assistantships available. Financial award application deadline: 3/15; financial award applicants required to submit FAFSA. *Faculty research:* Education for sustainability. *Unit head:* Dr. Shelly Wepner, Dean, 914-323-3153, Fax: 914-323-5493, E-mail: shelly.wepner@mville.edu. *Application contact:* Alissa Wilson, Director, Graduate Admissions, 914-323-3150, Fax: 914-694-1732, E-mail: edschool@mville.edu. Website: http://www.mville.edu/programs#/search/19

Manhattanville College, School of Education, Program in Special Education, Purchase, NY 10577-2132. Offers childhood (grades 1-6) (MPS); childhood education (grades 1-6) and special education (MPS); early childhood (birth-grade 2) (MPS); early childhood (birth-grade 2) and special education (MPS); early childhood and childhood (birth-grade 6) (MPS); English (5-9 and 7-12) (MPS); grades 7-12 generalist (MPS); literacy (birth-grade 6) and special education childhood (grades 1-6) (MPS); literacy 5-12 (MPS); mathematics (5-9 and 7-12) (MPS); science (biology or chemistry 5-9 and 7-12) (MPS); social studies (5-9 and 7-12) (MPS); special education: childhood (grades 1-6) (Certificate); special education: early childhood (birth-grade 2) and childhood (grades 1-6) (Certificate); special education: early childhood (birth-grade 2) (Certificate); special education: grades 7-12 generalist (Certificate). *Program availability:* Part-time, evening/weekend. *Faculty:* 5 full-time (3 women), 24 part-time/adjunct (16 women). *Students:* 77 full-time (69 women), 154 part-time (132 women); includes 33 minority (9 Black or African American, non-Hispanic/Latino; 2 Asian, non-Hispanic/Latino; 22 Hispanic/Latino), 1 international. Average age 28. 87 applicants, 77% accepted, 57 enrolled. In 2017, 86 master's, 2 Certificates awarded. *Degree requirements:* For master's, comprehensive exam (for some programs), thesis (for some programs), student teaching, research seminars, portfolios, internships, writing assessment; for Certificate, comprehensive exam (for some programs). *Entrance requirements:* For master's, GRE or MAT (for programs leading to certification), minimum GPA of 3.0, 2 letters of recommendation, interview, essay (2-3 page personal statement that describes reasons for choosing teaching or educational leadership as profession and philosophy of education), proof of immunization (for those born after 1957). Additional exam requirements/recommendations for international students: Required—TOEFL (minimum score 600 paper-based; 110 iBT); Recommended—IELTS (minimum score 8). *Application deadline:* Applications are processed on a rolling basis. Application fee: $75. Electronic applications accepted. *Expenses:* $915 per credit. *Financial support:* Teaching assistantships, career-related internships or fieldwork, Federal Work-Study, institutionally sponsored loans, scholarships/grants, and unspecified assistantships available. Financial award application deadline: 3/15; financial award applicants required to submit FAFSA. *Faculty research:* Students with emotional difficulties, literacy and adolescents, mindfulness, studying the effects of the environment on special populations, the most difficult cases, students who are presented with multiple challenges: learning, behavioral and ACE experiences who see criminal behavior as a way to cope; working on giving them the tools they need to succeed emotionally and cognitively despite the odds stacked against them. *Unit head:* Dr. Shelly Wepner, Dean, 914-323-3153, Fax: 914-323-5493, E-mail: shelly.wepner@mville.edu. *Application contact:* Alissa Wilson, Director, Graduate Admissions, 914-323-3150, Fax: 914-694-1732, E-mail: edschool@mville.edu. Website: http://www.mville.edu/programs/special-education

Manhattanville College, School of Education, Program in Teaching of Languages Other than English, Purchase, NY 10577-2132. Offers adolescence education (grades 7-12) foreign language (MAT, Advanced Certificate), including French, Italian, Latin (Advanced Certificate), Latin (MAT), Spanish. *Program availability:* Part-time, evening/weekend. *Faculty:* 2 full-time (1 woman). *Students:* 3 part-time (2 women); includes 1 minority (Hispanic/Latino). Average age 31. In 2017, 4 master's, 1 other advanced degree awarded. *Degree requirements:* For master's, comprehensive exam (for some programs), thesis (for some programs), student teaching, research seminars, portfolios, internships, writing assessment; for Advanced Certificate, comprehensive exam (for some programs). *Entrance requirements:* For master's, GRE or MAT (for programs leading to certification), minimum GPA of 3.0, 2 letters of recommendation, interview, essay (2-3 page personal statement that describes reasons for choosing teaching or educational leadership as profession and philosophy of education), proof of immunization (for those born after 1957). Additional exam requirements/recommendations for international students: Required—TOEFL (minimum score 600 paper-based; 110 iBT); Recommended—IELTS (minimum score 8). *Application deadline:* Applications are processed on a rolling basis. Application fee: $75. Electronic applications accepted. *Expenses:* $915 per credit. *Financial support:* Teaching assistantships, career-related internships or fieldwork, Federal Work-Study, institutionally sponsored loans, scholarships/grants, and unspecified assistantships available. Financial award application deadline: 3/15; financial award applicants required to submit FAFSA. *Faculty research:* Changing suburbs institute and community schools. *Unit head:* Dr. Shelly Wepner, Dean, 914-323-3153, Fax: 914-323-5493. *Application contact:* Alissa Wilson, Director, Graduate Admissions, 914-323-3150, Fax: 914-694-1732, E-mail: edschool@mville.edu. Website: https://www.mville.edu/programs/teaching-languages-other-english

Mary Baldwin University, Graduate Studies, Program in Teaching, Staunton, VA 24401-3610. Offers elementary education (MAT); middle grades education (MAT). *Accreditation:* TEAC.

Marygrove College, Graduate Studies, Detroit, MI 48221-2599. Offers autism spectrum disorders (M Ed, Certificate); curriculum instruction and assessment (MAT); educational leadership (MA); educational technology (M Ed); effective teaching in the 21st century-classroom focus (MAT); effective teaching in the 21st century-technology focus (MAT); human resource management (MA, Certificate); mathematics 6-8 (MAT); mathematics K-5 (MAT); reading and literacy K-6 (MAT); reading specialist (M Ed); school administrator (Certificate); social justice (MA); special education (MAT); special education - learning disabilities (M Ed); teaching - pre-elementary education (M Ed); teaching - pre-secondary education (M Ed). *Program availability:* Part-time, evening/weekend, 100% online, blended/hybrid learning. *Students:* 163 full-time (123 women), 264 part-time (186 women). Average age 34. *Entrance requirements:* For master's, all official bachelor's transcripts. Additional exam requirements/recommendations for international students: Required—TOEFL (minimum score 550 paper-based; 80 iBT). *Application deadline:* Applications are processed on a rolling basis. Electronic applications accepted. *Expenses: Tuition:* Part-time $590 per credit hour. *Required fees:* $120 per semester. One-time fee: $25 part-time. *Financial support:* Applicants required to submit FAFSA. *Unit head:* Marygrove College Admissions, 313-927-1240, E-mail: info@marygrove.edu. *Application contact:* Marygrove College Admissions, 313-927-1240, E-mail: info@marygrove.edu.

Maryville University of Saint Louis, School of Education, St. Louis, MO 63141-7299. Offers early childhood education (MA Ed); educational leadership (Ed D); elementary education (MA Ed); higher education leadership (Ed D); literacy specialist (MA Ed); middle grades education (MA Ed); secondary teaching and inquiry (MA Ed); teacher as leader (MA Ed, Ed D). *Accreditation:* NCATE. *Program availability:* Part-time, 100% online, blended/hybrid learning. *Faculty:* 20 full-time (14 women), 19 part-time/adjunct (13 women). *Students:* 6 full-time (4 women), 337 part-time (250 women); includes 101 minority (85 Black or African American, non-Hispanic/Latino; 4 Asian, non-Hispanic/Latino; 8 Hispanic/Latino; 4 Two or more races, non-Hispanic/Latino), 3 international. Average age 38. In 2017, 34 master's, 67 doctorates awarded. *Degree requirements:* For master's, thesis, project. *Entrance requirements:* For master's, minimum cumulative GPA of 3.0, 3 professional recommendations, essays, interview with program faculty; for doctorate, minimum GPA of 3.0, 3 professional recommendations, essay, interview, on-site writing sample. Additional exam requirements/recommendations for international students: Required—TOEFL (minimum score 550 paper-based). *Application deadline:* Applications are processed on a rolling basis. Electronic applications accepted. *Expenses:* Contact institution. *Financial support:* Career-related internships or fieldwork, Federal Work-Study, tuition waivers (partial), and professional educator discounts available. Financial award application deadline: 4/1; financial award applicants required to submit FAFSA. *Faculty research:* Collaboration with public schools, pre-service program development, mathematics, diversity, literacy. *Unit head:* Dr. Cathy Bear, Dean, 314-529-9692, Fax: 314-529-9921, E-mail: cbear@maryville.edu. *Application contact:* Stacey Ruffin, Coordinator of Clinical Experiences and Graduate Programs, 314-529-9542, Fax: 314-529-9921, E-mail: teachered@maryville.edu. Website: http://www.maryville.edu/ed/graduate-programs/

McNeese State University, Doré School of Graduate Studies, Burton College of Education, Department of Education Professions, Program in Middle School Education Grades 4-8, Lake Charles, LA 70609. Offers middle school education grades 4-8 (Postbaccalaureate Certificate), including mathematics, science. *Entrance requirements:* For degree, PRAXIS, 2 letters of recommendation, autobiography. *Application deadline:* For fall admission, 5/15 priority date for domestic and international students; for spring admission, 10/15 priority date for domestic and international students. Applications are processed on a rolling basis. Application fee: $20 ($30 for international students). *Financial support:* Application deadline: 5/1. *Unit head:* Dr. Veronica Faye White, Head, 337-475-5400, Fax: 337-475-5272, E-mail: vfwhite@mcneese.edu. *Application contact:* Dr. Dustin M. Hebert, Director of Dore' School of Graduate Studies, 337-475-5396, Fax: 337-475-5397, E-mail: admissions@mcneese.edu.

Mercer University, Graduate Studies, Cecil B. Day Campus, Tift College of Education (Atlanta), Atlanta, GA 30341. Offers curriculum and instruction (PhD); early childhood education (M Ed, MAT, Ed S); educational leadership (PhD), including higher education leadership, P-12 school leadership; educational leadership P-12 (M Ed, Ed S); higher education leadership (M Ed); independent and charter school leadership (M Ed); middle grades education (M Ed, MAT); secondary education (M Ed, MAT); teacher leadership (Ed S). *Accreditation:* NCATE. *Program availability:* Part-time, evening/weekend. *Faculty:* 30 full-time (18 women), 34 part-time/adjunct (27 women). *Students:* 159 full-time (131 women), 284 part-time (229 women); includes 264 minority (232 Black or African American, non-Hispanic/Latino; 1 American Indian or Alaska Native, non-Hispanic/Latino; 9 Asian, non-Hispanic/Latino; 18 Hispanic/Latino; 4 Two or more races, non-Hispanic/Latino), 2 international. Average age 35. In 2017, 137 master's, 22 doctorates, 40 other advanced degrees awarded. *Degree requirements:* For master's and Ed S, research project; for doctorate, comprehensive exam, thesis/dissertation. *Entrance requirements:* For master's, GRE or MAT, minimum undergraduate GPA of 2.75; for doctorate, GRE; for Ed S, GRE or MAT, minimum GPA of 3.25; 3 years of certified teaching experience (for educational leadership and teacher leadership). Additional exam requirements/recommendations for international students: Required—TOEFL (minimum score 80 iBT). *Application deadline:* For fall admission, 8/1 for domestic and international students; for spring admission, 12/1 for domestic and international students; for summer admission, 5/1 for domestic and international students. Applications are processed on a rolling basis. Application fee: $25 ($50 for international students). Electronic applications accepted. *Expenses:* Contact institution. *Financial support:* Federal Work-Study and unspecified assistantships available. Support available to part-time students. Financial award application deadline: 5/1; financial award applicants required to submit FAFSA. *Faculty research:* Educational technology, multicultural and minority issues in education, educational leadership (P-12 and higher education), school discipline and school bullying, standards-based mathematics education. *Unit head:* Dr. Scott Davis, Dean, 478-301-2110, Fax: 478-301-5576. Website: http://education.mercer.edu/

Mercy College, School of Education, Program in Teaching Literacy, Dobbs Ferry, NY 10522-1189. Offers teaching literacy (Advanced Certificate); teaching literacy, birth-6 (MS); teaching literacy, grades 5-12 (MS). *Program availability:* Part-time, evening/weekend. *Students:* 3 full-time (all women), 36 part-time (33 women); includes 10 minority (3 Black or African American, non-Hispanic/Latino; 1 Asian, non-Hispanic/Latino; 6 Hispanic/Latino). Average age 32. 28 applicants, 43% accepted, 8 enrolled. In 2017, 17 master's awarded. *Degree requirements:* For master's, comprehensive exam (for some programs), thesis (for some programs). *Entrance requirements:* For master's, GRE, resume, undergraduate transcript. Additional exam requirements/recommendations for international students: Required—TOEFL (minimum score 600 paper-based; 100 iBT), IELTS (minimum score 8). *Application deadline:* For fall admission, 8/1 for international students. Applications are processed on a rolling basis.

Application fee: $40. Electronic applications accepted. *Expenses: Tuition:* Full-time $15,426; part-time $857 per credit hour. *Required fees:* $630; $158 per term. Tuition and fees vary according to course load, degree level and program. *Financial support:* Career-related internships or fieldwork, Federal Work-Study, scholarships/grants, and unspecified assistantships available. Support available to part-time students. Financial award applicants required to submit FAFSA. *Unit head:* Dr. Rose Rudnitski, Dean for the School of Education, 914-674-7447, Fax: 914-674-7352, E-mail: rrudnitski@mercy.edu. *Application contact:* Allison Gurdineer, Senior Director of Admissions, 877-637-2946, Fax: 914-674-7382, E-mail: admissions@mercy.edu. Website: https://www.mercy.edu/education/literacy-and-multilingual-studies

Merrimack College, School of Education and Social Policy, North Andover, MA 01845-5800. Offers community engagement (M Ed), including community organizations, higher education, PreK-12 education; criminology and criminal justice (MS); curriculum and instruction (M Ed); early childhood education (M Ed); educational leadership (CAGS), including instructional leadership; elementary education (M Ed); English as a second language (PreK-6) (M Ed); high school education (M Ed); higher education (M Ed), including leadership and organizational development, student affairs; middle school education (M Ed); moderate disabilities (PreK-8) (M Ed); school counseling (M Ed). *Program availability:* Part-time, evening/weekend, 100% online courses with immersion events and in-classroom practicum close to home. *Faculty:* 15 full-time, 36 part-time/adjunct. *Students:* 212 full-time (175 women), 121 part-time (101 women); includes 42 minority (6 Black or African American, non-Hispanic/Latino; 6 Asian, non-Hispanic/Latino; 27 Hispanic/Latino; 3 Two or more races, non-Hispanic/Latino), 3 international. Average age 27. 420 applicants, 84% accepted, 250 enrolled. In 2017, 177 master's awarded. *Degree requirements:* For master's, practicum, portfolio, and state test (for licensure track); capstone (for higher education, curriculum and instruction, and community engagement tracks); for CAGS, capstone. *Entrance requirements:* For master's, Massachusetts Teacher Education Licensure (MTEL), official transcripts from other colleges, resume, personal statement, 2 letters of recommendation. Additional exam requirements/recommendations for international students: Required—TOEFL (minimum score 84 iBT), IELTS (minimum score 6.5), PTE (minimum score 56). *Application deadline:* For fall admission, 8/24 for domestic students, 7/30 for international students; for spring admission, 1/10 for domestic students, 12/10 for international students; for summer admission, 5/10 for domestic students, 4/10 for international students. Applications are processed on a rolling basis. Application fee: $0. Electronic applications accepted. *Expenses:* Contact institution. *Financial support:* Fellowships with full tuition reimbursements, career-related internships or fieldwork, scholarships/grants, and health care benefits available. Support available to part-time students. Financial award application deadline: 5/1; financial award applicants required to submit FAFSA. *Application contact:* Alyssa Orlando, Graduate Admissions Counselor, 978-837-3563, E-mail: orlandoaf@merrimack.edu. Website: http://www.merrimack.edu/academics/graduate/education/

Middle Tennessee State University, College of Graduate Studies, College of Education, Department of Elementary and Special Education, Major in Curriculum and Instruction, Murfreesboro, TN 37132. Offers early childhood education (M Ed); elementary education (M Ed, Ed S); middle school education (M Ed). *Accreditation:* NCATE. *Program availability:* Part-time, evening/weekend, online learning. *Degree requirements:* For master's, comprehensive exam; for Ed S, comprehensive exam, thesis or alternative. *Entrance requirements:* For master's and Ed S, GRE, MAT or PRAXIS. Additional exam requirements/recommendations for international students: Required—TOEFL (minimum score 525 paper-based; 71 iBT) or IELTS (minimum score 6). Electronic applications accepted.

Milligan College, Area of Education, Milligan College, TN 37682. Offers combined preK-3/K-5 education (M Ed); educational leadership (Ed D, Ed S); K-5 education (M Ed); middle grades education (M Ed); preK-3 education (M Ed); preK-3 special education (M Ed); secondary education (M Ed). *Accreditation:* NCATE. *Program availability:* Part-time. *Faculty:* 6 full-time (4 women), 3 part-time/adjunct (2 women). *Students:* 27 full-time (20 women), 20 part-time (11 women); includes 2 minority (1 Hispanic/Latino; 1 Two or more races, non-Hispanic/Latino), 1 international. Average age 34. 17 applicants, 35% accepted, 6 enrolled. In 2017, 21 master's awarded. *Degree requirements:* For master's, thesis, portfolio, research project; for doctorate, thesis/dissertation, portfolio, research project. *Entrance requirements:* For master's, MAT, GRE General Test, ACT, SAT, or PRAXIS, undergraduate degree and supporting transcripts, professional recommendations, interview; for doctorate, MAT or GRE, master's degree and supporting transcripts, demonstrated scholastic ability, recognized leadership role within education, professional recommendations, essay/personal statement, portfolio (professional development plan, evidence of ability, knowledge and qualities), interview. Additional exam requirements/recommendations for international students: Required—TOEFL (minimum score 550 paper-based, 79 iBT) or IELTS (minimum score 6.5). *Application deadline:* For fall admission, 8/1 priority date for domestic students, 6/1 for international students; for spring admission, 11/15 priority date for domestic students, 12/1 for international students; for summer admission, 4/1 for domestic students. Applications are processed on a rolling basis. Application fee: $30. Electronic applications accepted. *Expenses:* $360 per hour tuition (M Ed); $475 per hour (Ed D and Ed S); $325 per semester tech/activity fees. *Financial support:* Scholarships/grants available. Financial award application deadline: 12/1; financial award applicants required to submit FAFSA. *Faculty research:* Assessment; school mental health; literacy; technology; educator preparation. *Unit head:* Dr. Angela Hilton-Prillhart, Area Chair of Education, 423-461-8769, Fax: 423-461-3103, E-mail: anhilton-prillhart@milligan.edu. *Application contact:* Melissa Dillow, Graduate Admissions Recruiter, Education, 423-461-8306, Fax: 423-461-8982, E-mail: msdillow@milligan.edu. Website: http://www.Milligan.edu/GPS

Minot State University, Graduate School, Teacher Education and Human Performance Department, Minot, ND 58707-0002. Offers elementary education (M Ed). *Accreditation:* NCATE. *Degree requirements:* For master's, thesis. *Entrance requirements:* For master's, 2 years of teaching experience, bachelor's degree in education, minimum GPA of 2.75. Additional exam requirements/recommendations for international students: Required—TOEFL (minimum score 79 iBT), IELTS (minimum score 6).

Mississippi State University, College of Education, Department of Curriculum, Instruction and Special Education, Mississippi State, MS 39762. Offers early childhood education (PhD); elementary education (MS, PhD, Ed S), including early childhood education (MS); general elementary education (MS); middle level education (MS); general curriculum and instruction (PhD); reading education (PhD); secondary education (MAT, MS, PhD, Ed S); special education (MAT, MS, PhD, Ed S). *Accreditation:* NCATE. *Program availability:* Part-time, evening/weekend. *Faculty:* 22 full-time (16 women), 1 (woman) part-time/adjunct. *Students:* 38 full-time (26 women), 170 part-time (131 women); includes 46 minority (37 Black or African American, non-Hispanic/Latino; 4 American Indian or Alaska Native, non-Hispanic/Latino; 2 Hispanic/Latino; 1 Native Hawaiian or other Pacific Islander, non-Hispanic/Latino; 2 Two or more races, non-Hispanic/Latino), 4 international. Average age 32. 88 applicants, 53% accepted, 39 enrolled. In 2017, 68 master's, 4 doctorates, 5 other advanced degrees awarded. *Degree requirements:* For master's, comprehensive exam; for doctorate, thesis/dissertation; for Ed S, comprehensive exam, thesis or alternative. *Entrance*

requirements: For master's, GRE, minimum GPA of 2.75 in junior and senior year, eligibility for initial teacher certification; for doctorate, GRE, minimum GPA of 3.4 on previous graduate work; for Ed S, GRE, minimum GPA of 3.2 on master's degree. Additional exam requirements/recommendations for international students: Required—TOEFL (minimum score 550 paper-based; 79 iBT); Recommended—IELTS (minimum score 6.5). *Application deadline:* For fall admission, 3/1 priority date for domestic students, 5/1 for international students; for spring admission, 9/1 priority date for domestic students, 9/1 for international students. Applications are processed on a rolling basis. Application fee: $60 ($80 for international students). Electronic applications accepted. *Expenses:* Tuition, state resident: full-time $8318; part-time $462.12 per credit hour. Tuition, nonresident: full-time $22,358; part-time $1242.12 per credit hour. *Required fees:* $110; $12.24 per credit hour. $6.12 per semester. *Financial support:* In 2017–18, 6 research assistantships with partial tuition reimbursements (averaging $11,307 per year) were awarded; Federal Work-Study, institutionally sponsored loans, scholarships/grants, and unspecified assistantships also available. Financial award application deadline: 4/1; financial award applicants required to submit FAFSA. *Faculty research:* Early childhood education, reading, rural schools, multicultural education, use of technology in instruction. *Unit head:* Dr. Linda Cornelious, Professor and Interim Head, 662-325-3747, Fax: 662-325-7857, E-mail: lcornelious@colled.msstate.edu. *Application contact:* Laken Drinker, Admissions and Enrollment Assistant, 662-325-8951, E-mail: ldrinker@grad.msstate.edu. Website: http://www.cise.msstate.edu/

Morehead State University, Graduate Programs, College of Education, Department of Curriculum and Instruction, Morehead, KY 40351. Offers curriculum and instruction (Ed S); elementary education (MA Ed), including elementary education, international education, middle school education, reading; secondary education (MA Ed); special education (MA Ed); teaching (MAT). *Program availability:* Part-time, evening/weekend. *Degree requirements:* For master's, comprehensive exam, thesis optional; for Ed S, thesis, oral exam. *Entrance requirements:* For master's, GRE General Test, minimum GPA of 2.75, teaching certificate; for Ed S, GRE General Test, interview, master's degree, minimum GPA of 3.5, work experience. Additional exam requirements/recommendations for international students: Required—TOEFL (minimum score 500 paper-based). Electronic applications accepted. *Faculty research:* Communicative competence of learning-disabled students, teaching social studies in elementary schools, ungraded primary school organization, study skills.

Morehead State University, Graduate Programs, College of Education, Department of Foundational and Graduate Studies in Education, Morehead, KY 40351. Offers adult and higher education (MA, Ed S); certified professional counselor (Ed S); counseling P-12 (MA); curriculum and instruction (Ed S); educational leadership (MA Ed); instructional leadership (Ed S); school administration (MA); school counseling (Ed S); teacher leader business and marketing content (MA Ed); teacher leader business and marketing technology (MA Ed); teacher leader educational technology (MA Ed); teacher leader English (MA Ed); teacher leader gifted education (MA Ed); teacher leader IECE certification (MA Ed); teacher leader interdisciplinary education P-5 (MA Ed); teacher leader middle grades (MA Ed); teacher leader non IECE certification (MA Ed); teacher leader reading/writing - non-certification (MA Ed); teacher leader reading/writing certification (MA Ed); teacher leader school communication - certification (MA Ed); teacher leader school communication - non-certification (MA Ed); teacher leader social studies (MA Ed); teacher leader special education (MA Ed). *Accreditation:* NCATE. *Program availability:* Part-time, evening/weekend. *Degree requirements:* For master's, thesis optional, oral and/or written comprehensive exams; for Ed S, thesis, oral exam. *Entrance requirements:* For master's, GRE General Test, minimum overall undergraduate GPA of 2.5; for Ed S, GRE General Test, interview, master's degree, minimum GPA of 3.5, work experience. Additional exam requirements/recommendations for international students: Required—TOEFL (minimum score 500 paper-based). Electronic applications accepted. *Faculty research:* Character education, school accountability, computer applications for school administrators.

Morehead State University, Graduate Programs, College of Education, Department of Middle Grades and Secondary Education, Morehead, KY 40351. Offers business and marketing education (MAT); English/language arts 5-9 (MAT); French (MAT); health P-12 (MAT); mathematics 5-9 (MAT); physical education P-12 (MAT); science 5-9 (MAT); secondary biology (MAT); secondary chemistry (MAT); secondary earth science (MAT); secondary English (MAT); secondary math (MAT); secondary physics (MAT); secondary social studies (MAT); social studies 5-9 (MAT); Spanish (MAT). *Program availability:* Part-time, evening/weekend. *Degree requirements:* For master's, portfolio. *Entrance requirements:* For master's, GRE or PRAXIS II content exam, minimum overall undergraduate GPA of 2.5. Additional exam requirements/recommendations for international students: Required—TOEFL (minimum score 500 paper-based). Electronic applications accepted.

Mount St. Joseph University, Graduate Education Program, Cincinnati, OH 45233-1670. Offers adolescent to young adult education (MA); dyslexia (Certificate); inclusive early childhood education (MA); middle childhood education (MA); multicultural special education (MA); reading science (MA). *Accreditation:* TEAC. *Program availability:* Part-time, evening/weekend, 100% online, blended/hybrid learning. *Faculty:* 6 full-time (5 women), 11 part-time/adjunct (8 women). *Students:* 37 full-time (30 women), 91 part-time (83 women); includes 13 minority (11 Black or African American, non-Hispanic/Latino; 1 Hispanic/Latino; 1 Two or more races, non-Hispanic/Latino). Average age 34. In 2017, 79 master's awarded. *Degree requirements:* For master's, comprehensive exam, thesis, research project, student teaching, clinical and field-based experiences. *Entrance requirements:* For master's, GRE (if GPA is below 3.0), letter of intent, 2 referrals, background check, interview, resume, minimum undergraduate GPA of 3.0. Additional exam requirements/recommendations for international students: Required—TOEFL (minimum score 560 paper-based; 83 iBT). *Application deadline:* Applications are processed on a rolling basis. Application fee: $50. Electronic applications accepted. *Expenses:* $600 per credit hour. *Financial support:* Applicants required to submit FAFSA. *Faculty research:* Foreign and second language learning problems/reading disabilities, multicultural/bilingual special education, science education, pedagogical content knowledge, early childhood, response to intervention. *Unit head:* Dr. Laura Saylor, Dean, 513-244-3263, E-mail: laura.saylor@msj.edu. *Application contact:* Mary Brigham, Assistant Director of Graduate Recruitment, 513-244-4233, Fax: 513-244-4629, E-mail: mary.brigham@msj.edu. Website: http://www.msj.edu/academics/graduate-programs/master-of-arts-initial-teacher-licensure-programs/

Mount Saint Mary College, Division of Education, Newburgh, NY 12550-3494. Offers adolescence and special education (MS Ed); childhood education (MS Ed); literacy education (MS Ed); middle school (7-9) (MS Ed). *Accreditation:* NCATE. *Program availability:* Part-time, evening/weekend. *Faculty:* 10 full-time (9 women), 3 part-time/adjunct (all women). *Students:* 11 full-time (9 women), 83 part-time (62 women); includes 9 minority (1 American Indian or Alaska Native, non-Hispanic/Latino; 6 Hispanic/Latino; 2 Two or more races, non-Hispanic/Latino). Average age 28. 20 applicants, 100% accepted, 16 enrolled. In 2017, 57 master's awarded. *Entrance requirements:* Additional exam requirements/recommendations for international students: Required—TOEFL (minimum score 80 iBT). *Application deadline:* Applications

Middle School Education

are processed on a rolling basis. Application fee: $45. Electronic applications accepted. Application fee is waived when completed online. *Expenses: Tuition:* Full-time $14,454; part-time $803 per credit. *Required fees:* $172; $86 per semester. *Financial support:* In 2017–18, 15 students received support. Unspecified assistantships available. Financial award application deadline: 4/15; financial award applicants required to submit FAFSA. *Faculty research:* Learning and teaching styles, computers in special education, language development. *Unit head:* Dr. Monica Merritt, Graduate Coordinator, 845-569-3430, Fax: 845-569-3535, E-mail: monica.merritt@msmc.edu. *Application contact:* Lisa Alvarez, Director of Admissions for Graduate Programs and Adult Degree Completion, 845-569-3166, Fax: 845-569-3450, E-mail: lisa.gallina@msmc.edu.
Website: http://www.msmc.edu/Academics/Graduate_Programs/Master_of_Science_in_Education

Mount Saint Vincent University, Graduate Programs, Faculty of Education, Program in Curriculum Studies, Halifax, NS B3M 2J6, Canada. Offers education of young adolescents (M Ed, MA Ed, MA-R); general studies (M Ed, MA Ed, MA-R); teaching English as a second language (M Ed, MA Ed, MA-R). *Program availability:* Part-time, evening/weekend, online learning. *Degree requirements:* For master's, thesis (for some programs). *Entrance requirements:* For master's, bachelor's degree in related field, minimum B average, 1 year of teaching experience. Electronic applications accepted. *Faculty research:* Science education, cultural studies, international education, curriculum development.

Murray State University, College of Education and Human Services, Department of Adolescent, Career, and Special Education, Murray, KY 42071. Offers career and technical education (MS); middle school teacher leader (MA Ed); secondary teacher leader (MA Ed); special education (MA Ed), including mild learning and behavior disorders, moderate to severe disabilities (P-12), teacher leader in special education learning and behavior disorders; teacher education and professional development (Ed S). *Accreditation:* NCATE. *Program availability:* Part-time. *Faculty:* 10 full-time (9 women). *Students:* 4 full-time (2 women), 78 part-time (56 women); includes 4 minority (2 Black or African American, non-Hispanic/Latino; 1 Asian, non-Hispanic/Latino; 1 Hispanic/Latino), 2 international. Average age 33. 13 applicants, 100% accepted, 8 enrolled. In 2017, 19 master's awarded. *Entrance requirements:* For master's and Ed S, GRE or GMAT, minimum university GPA of 2.75. Additional exam requirements/recommendations for international students: Required—TOEFL (minimum score 527 paper-based; 71 iBT). *Application deadline:* Applications are processed on a rolling basis. Application fee: $40 ($50 for international students). Electronic applications accepted. *Expenses:* Tuition, state resident: full-time $9504. Tuition, nonresident: full-time $26,811. *International tuition:* $14,400 full-time. Tuition and fees vary according to course load, degree level and reciprocity agreements. *Financial support:* Federal Work-Study and unspecified assistantships available. Financial award applicants required to submit FAFSA. *Unit head:* Dr. Barbara Washington, Chair, Department of Adolescent, Career and Special Education, 270-809-2262, Fax: 270-809-2540, E-mail: bwashington@murraystate.edu. *Application contact:* Kaitlyn Burzynski, Interim Assistant Director of Graduate Admission and Records, 270-809-5732, Fax: 270-809-3780, E-mail: msu.graduateadmissions@murraystate.edu.
Website: http://www.murraystate.edu/academics/CollegesDepartments/CollegeOfEducationandHumanServices/coehsacademicunits/AdolescentCareerSpecialEd/index.aspx

Murray State University, College of Education and Human Services, Department of Educational Studies, Leadership and Counseling, Murray, KY 42071. Offers college advising (Certificate); education administration (MA Ed); human development and leadership (MS, Certificate); library media (MA Ed); middle school teacher leader (MA Ed); P-20 and community leadership (Ed D); postsecondary education administration (MA Ed); school counseling (MA Ed); school guidance and counseling (Ed S); secondary teacher leader (MA Ed). *Program availability:* Part-time, evening/weekend, 100% online, blended/hybrid learning. *Faculty:* 38 full-time (16 women), 3 part-time/adjunct (1 woman). *Students:* 45 full-time (22 women), 190 part-time (140 women); includes 33 minority (25 Black or African American, non-Hispanic/Latino; 4 Asian, non-Hispanic/Latino; 3 Hispanic/Latino; 1 Two or more races, non-Hispanic/Latino), 6 international. Average age 35. 87 applicants, 77% accepted, 51 enrolled. In 2017, 21 master's, 16 doctorates, 12 other advanced degrees awarded. *Entrance requirements:* For master's and other advanced degree, GRE or GMAT, minimum university GPA of 2.75. Additional exam requirements/recommendations for international students: Required—TOEFL (minimum score 527 paper-based; 71 iBT). *Application deadline:* Applications are processed on a rolling basis. Application fee: $40 ($50 for international students). Electronic applications accepted. *Expenses:* Tuition, state resident: full-time $9504. Tuition, nonresident: full-time $26,811. *International tuition:* $14,400 full-time. Tuition and fees vary according to course load, degree level and reciprocity agreements. *Financial support:* Federal Work-Study and unspecified assistantships available. Financial award applicants required to submit FAFSA. *Unit head:* Dr. Susana Bloomdahl, Chair, Department of Educational Studies, Leadership and Counseling, 270-809-6471, Fax: 270-809-3799, E-mail: sbloomdahl@murraystate.edu. *Application contact:* Kaitlyn Burzynski, Interim Assistant Director for Graduate Admission and Records, 270-809-5732, Fax: 270-809-3780, E-mail: msu.graduateadmissions@murraystate.edu.
Website: http://www.murraystate.edu/academics/CollegesDepartments/CollegeOfEducationandHumanServices/coehsacademicunits/EducationalStudiesLeadershipandCounseli

National Louis University, National College of Education, Chicago, IL 60603. Offers administration and supervision (M Ed, Ed D, CAS, Ed S); curriculum and instruction (M Ed, MS Ed, CAS); early childhood administration (M Ed, CAS); early childhood education (M Ed, MAT, MS Ed, CAS); education (Ed D); educational psychology/human learning and development (M Ed, MS Ed, CAS, Ed S); elementary education (MAT); interdisciplinary curriculum and instruction (M Ed); mathematics education (M Ed, MS Ed, CAS); middle grades education (MAT); reading and language (M Ed, MS Ed, CAS); school psychology (M Ed, Ed S); science education (M Ed, MS Ed, CAS); secondary education (MAT); special education (M Ed, MAT, CAS); technology in education (M Ed, CAS). *Accreditation:* NCATE. *Program availability:* Part-time, evening/weekend. *Degree requirements:* For doctorate, comprehensive exam, thesis/dissertation. *Entrance requirements:* For master's, MAT or GRE, minimum GPA of 3.0; for doctorate, GRE General Test, minimum GPA of 3.25, interview, resume, writing sample, 4 recommendations. Additional exam requirements/recommendations for international students: Required—TOEFL (minimum score 550 paper-based; 79 iBT).

Nazareth College of Rochester, Graduate Studies, Department of Education, Program in Inclusive Adolescence Education, Rochester, NY 14618. Offers MS Ed. *Accreditation:* TEAC. *Entrance requirements:* For master's, minimum GPA of 3.0. Additional exam requirements/recommendations for international students: Required—TOEFL or IELTS.

New York Institute of Technology, School of Interdisciplinary Studies and Education, Department of Teacher Education, Old Westbury, NY 11568-8000. Offers adolescence education (MS), including math (MAT, MS), science; adolescent education (MAT), including biology, chemistry, English, math (MAT, MS), social studies; childhood education (MS); early childhood (MS). *Program availability:* Part-time, evening/weekend, 100% online, blended/hybrid learning. *Faculty:* 2 full-time (both women), 7 part-time/adjunct (3 women).

Students: 46 full-time (44 women), 30 part-time (22 women); includes 23 minority (8 Black or African American, non-Hispanic/Latino; 6 Asian, non-Hispanic/Latino; 8 Hispanic/Latino; 1 Two or more races, non-Hispanic/Latino), 2 international. Average age 29. 39 applicants, 72% accepted, 15 enrolled. In 2017, 14 master's awarded. *Entrance requirements:* For master's, GRE or MAT, BS or equivalent; minimum cumulative undergraduate GPA of 3.0; NY state provisional or initial certification (for MS in adolescence education); BS with major in biology, chemistry, economics, English, history, life sciences, math, physics, or psychology (for MS in childhood, early childhood education, and MAT); interview; personal statement. Additional exam requirements/recommendations for international students: Required—TOEFL (minimum score 79 iBT), IELTS (minimum score 6). *Application deadline:* Applications are processed on a rolling basis. Application fee: $50. Electronic applications accepted. *Expenses:* $1,285 per credit plus fees. *Financial support:* Career-related internships or fieldwork, Federal Work-Study, scholarships/grants, tuition waivers (full and partial), and unspecified assistantships available. Support available to part-time students. Financial award application deadline: 2/15; financial award applicants required to submit FAFSA. *Faculty research:* Evolving definition of new literacies and its impact on teaching and learning (twenty-first century skills), new literacies practices in teacher education, teachers' professional development, English language and literacy learning through mobile learning, teaching reading to culturally and linguistically diverse children. *Unit head:* Dr. Hui-Yin Hsu, Department Chair, 516-686-1322, Fax: 516-686-7655, E-mail: hhsu02@nyit.edu. *Application contact:* Alice Dolitsky, Director, Graduate Admissions, 516-686-7520, Fax: 516-686-1116, E-mail: nyitgrad@nyit.edu.
Website: http://www.nyit.edu/interdisciplinary/department_teacher_education

New York University, Steinhardt School of Culture, Education, and Human Development, Department of Teaching and Learning, New York, NY 10012. Offers clinically rich integrated science (MA), including clinically rich integrated science, teaching biology grades 7-12, teaching chemistry 7-12, teaching physics 7-12; early childhood and childhood education (MA), including childhood education, early childhood education, early childhood education/early childhood special education; English education (MA, PhD, Advanced Certificate), including clinically-based English education, grades 7-12 (MA), English education (PhD, Advanced Certificate), English education, grades 7-12 (MA); environmental conservation education (MA); literacy education (MA), including literacy 5-12, literacy B-6; mathematics education (MA), including teachers of mathematics 7-12; multilingual/multicultural studies (MA, PhD, Advanced Certificate), including bilingual education, foreign language education (MA), teaching English to speakers of other languages (MA, PhD), teaching foreign languages, 7-12 (MA), teaching French as a foreign language (MA), teaching Spanish as a foreign language (MA); social studies education (MA), including teaching art/social studies 7-12, teaching social studies 7-12; special education (MA), including childhood, early childhood; teaching and learning (Ed D, PhD). *Program availability:* Part-time. *Students:* Average age 25. 926 applicants, 68% accepted, 210 enrolled. In 2017, 290 master's, 10 doctorates, 27 other advanced degrees awarded. *Entrance requirements:* For doctorate, GRE General Test, interview; for Advanced Certificate, master's degree. Additional exam requirements/recommendations for international students: Required—TOEFL (minimum score 100 iBT). *Application deadline:* For fall admission, 12/1 priority date for domestic and international students; for spring admission, 10/1 for domestic and international students. Applications are processed on a rolling basis. Application fee: $75. Electronic applications accepted. *Expenses:* Tuition: Full-time $41,352; part-time $19,968 per year. *Required fees:* $2496; $1628 per unit. $814 per term. Tuition and fees vary according to course load and program. *Financial support:* Fellowships with full and partial tuition reimbursements, research assistantships with full and partial tuition reimbursements, teaching assistantships with full and partial tuition reimbursements, career-related internships or fieldwork, Federal Work-Study, institutionally sponsored loans, scholarships/grants, tuition waivers (partial), and unspecified assistantships available. Support available to part-time students. Financial award application deadline: 2/1; financial award applicants required to submit FAFSA. *Faculty research:* Cultural contexts for literacy learning, school restructuring, parenting and education, teacher learning, language assessment. *Unit head:* Dr. Susan Neuman, Chairperson, 212-998-5460, Fax: 212-995-4049. *Application contact:* 212-998-5030, Fax: 212-995-4328, E-mail: steinhardt.gradadmissions@nyu.edu.
Website: http://steinhardt.nyu.edu/teachlearn/

Niagara University, Graduate Division of Education, Concentration in Teacher Education, Niagara University, NY 14109. Offers early childhood and childhood education (MS Ed, Certificate); early childhood special education (MS); middle and adolescence education (MS Ed); special education (MS Ed), including 1-6, 7-12; special education (grades 1-12) (Certificate); teaching English to speakers of other languages (MS Ed, Certificate). *Accreditation:* NCATE. *Students:* 105 full-time (79 women), 109 part-time (88 women); includes 20 minority (9 Black or African American, non-Hispanic/Latino; 2 American Indian or Alaska Native, non-Hispanic/Latino; 1 Asian, non-Hispanic/Latino; 5 Hispanic/Latino; 3 Two or more races, non-Hispanic/Latino), 35 international. Average age 28. In 2017, 86 master's, 18 other advanced degrees awarded. *Entrance requirements:* For master's, GRE General Test or Academic Literacy Skills Test (ALST). Additional exam requirements/recommendations for international students: Required—TOEFL (minimum score 550 paper-based; 79 iBT), IELTS (minimum score 6). *Application deadline:* For fall admission, 8/1 for domestic students. Applications are processed on a rolling basis. Application fee: $30. *Expenses:* Contact institution. *Financial support:* Research assistantships with tuition reimbursements, teaching assistantships with tuition reimbursements, career-related internships or fieldwork, Federal Work-Study, scholarships/grants, and unspecified assistantships available. Financial award application deadline: 4/15; financial award applicants required to submit FAFSA. *Unit head:* Dr. Chandra Foote, Dean, College of Education, 716-286-8549, E-mail: cjf@niagara.edu. *Application contact:* Evan Pierce, Associate Director, Graduate Studies, 716-286-8327, E-mail: epierce@niagara.edu.
Website: http://www.niagara.edu/teacher-education

Nicholls State University, Graduate Studies, College of Education, Department of Teacher Education, Thibodaux, LA 70310. Offers curriculum and instruction (M Ed); educational leadership (M Ed); elementary education (MAT); human performance education (MAT); middle school education (MAT); secondary education (MAT). *Accreditation:* NCATE. *Program availability:* Part-time, evening/weekend, online learning. *Degree requirements:* For master's, comprehensive exam, portfolio. *Entrance requirements:* For master's, GRE General Test, teaching license. Electronic applications accepted.

North Carolina State University, Graduate School, College of Education, Department of Curriculum and Instruction, Program in Middle Grades Education, Raleigh, NC 27695. Offers M Ed, MS. *Accreditation:* NCATE. *Degree requirements:* For master's, thesis optional. *Entrance requirements:* For master's, GRE General Test or MAT, minimum GPA of 3.0 in major.

Northwestern State University of Louisiana, Graduate Studies and Research, College of Education and Human Development, Program in Middle School Education, Natchitoches, LA 71497. Offers MAT. *Degree requirements:* For master's, comprehensive exam, thesis or alternative. *Entrance requirements:* For master's, GRE General Test, minimum undergraduate GPA of 2.5. Additional exam requirements/recommendations for international students: Required—TOEFL. Electronic applications accepted.

Northwest Missouri State University, Graduate School, School of Education, Maryville, MO 64468-6001. Offers early childhood education (MS Ed); education leadership (MS Ed), including elementary, K-12, secondary; educational leadership (Ed S), including elementary school principalship, secondary school principalship, superintendency; educational leadership and policy analysis (Ed D); elementary education (MS Ed); elementary mathematics (MS Ed); higher education leadership (MS); middle school education (MS Ed); reading (MS Ed); special education (MS Ed); teacher leadership (MS Ed); teaching English language learners (MS Ed). *Accreditation:* NCATE. *Program availability:* Part-time. *Faculty:* 15 full-time (8 women). *Students:* 28 full-time (20 women), 170 part-time (114 women); includes 20 minority (7 Black or African American, non-Hispanic/Latino; 1 Asian, non-Hispanic/Latino; 8 Hispanic/Latino; 4 Two or more races, non-Hispanic/Latino). Average age 33. 168 applicants, 73% accepted, 114 enrolled. In 2017, 67 master's, 21 other advanced degrees awarded. *Degree requirements:* For master's, comprehensive exam; for Ed S, comprehensive exam, thesis. *Entrance requirements:* For master's, GRE General Test, writing sample; for Ed S, minimum graduate GPA of 3.25. Additional exam requirements/recommendations for international students: Required—TOEFL (minimum score 550 paper-based). *Application deadline:* For fall admission, 7/1 for domestic and international students; for spring admission, 11/15 for domestic and international students. Applications are processed on a rolling basis. Application fee: $0 ($50 for international students). Electronic applications accepted. *Expenses:* $389.11 per credit hour in-state tuition and fees, $641.97 out-of-state; $9,750 total cost (for online-based education program). *Financial support:* Research assistantships with full tuition reimbursements, teaching assistantships with full tuition reimbursements, and unspecified assistantships available. Financial award application deadline: 4/1; financial award applicants required to submit FAFSA. *Unit head:* Dr. Tim Wall, Director, 660-562-1179, E-mail: timwall@nwmissouri.edu.
Website: https://www.nwmissouri.edu/education/index.htm

Ohio University, Graduate College, Gladys W. and David H. Patton College of Education and Human Services, Department of Teacher Education, Athens, OH 45701-2979. Offers adolescent to young adult education (M Ed); curriculum and instruction (M Ed, PhD); early childhood/special education (M Ed); intervention specialist/mild-moderate needs (M Ed); intervention specialist/moderate-intensive needs (M Ed); middle childhood education (M Ed); reading education (M Ed). *Program availability:* Part-time, evening/weekend. *Degree requirements:* For master's, thesis or alternative; for doctorate, comprehensive exam, thesis/dissertation. *Entrance requirements:* For master's, GRE General Test or MAT (if GPA is below 2.9); for doctorate, GRE General Test, minimum GPA of 3.4, work experience. Additional exam requirements/recommendations for international students: Required—TOEFL (minimum score 550 paper-based; 80 iBT) or IELTS (minimum score 6.5). Electronic applications accepted. *Faculty research:* Cognition literacy, character education, teacher's education reform, disabilities.

Old Dominion University, Darden College of Education, Program in Elementary/Middle Education, Norfolk, VA 23529. Offers elementary education (Postbaccalaureate Certificate); instructional technology (MS Ed); library science (MS Ed). *Accreditation:* NCATE. *Program availability:* Part-time, evening/weekend, 100% online, blended/hybrid learning. *Faculty:* 21 full-time (19 women), 24 part-time/adjunct (22 women). *Students:* 134 full-time (127 women), 123 part-time (108 women); includes 60 minority (34 Black or African American, non-Hispanic/Latino; 1 American Indian or Alaska Native, non-Hispanic/Latino; 2 Asian, non-Hispanic/Latino; 15 Hispanic/Latino; 8 Two or more races, non-Hispanic/Latino). Average age 32. 213 applicants, 88% accepted, 172 enrolled. In 2017, 121 master's awarded. *Degree requirements:* For master's, comprehensive exam. *Entrance requirements:* For master's, GRE General Test or MAT; PRAXIS I, SAT or ACT, minimum GPA of 2.8. Additional exam requirements/recommendations for international students: Required—TOEFL (minimum score 600 paper-based). *Application deadline:* For fall admission, 6/1 priority date for domestic students; for winter admission, 11/1 priority date for domestic students; for spring admission, 3/1 priority date for domestic students. Applications are processed on a rolling basis. Application fee: $50. Electronic applications accepted. *Expenses:* Contact institution. *Financial support:* In 2017–18, 180 students received support. Unspecified assistantships available. Financial award application deadline: 2/15; financial award applicants required to submit FAFSA. *Faculty research:* Education pre-K to 6, school librarianship, reading, TESOL, literacy. *Unit head:* Dr. KaaVonia Hinton, Chair, Department of Teaching and Learning, 757-683-3284, Fax: 757-683-5862, E-mail: khintonj@odu.edu. *Application contact:* William Heffelfinger, Director of Graduate Admissions, 757-683-5554, Fax: 757-683-3255, E-mail: gradadmit@odu.edu.
Website: http://education.odu.edu/eci/

Pacific University, College of Education, Forest Grove, OR 97116-1797. Offers early childhood education (MAT); education (MAE); elementary education (MAT); ESOL (MAT); high school education (MAT); middle school education (MAT); special education (MAT); speech-language pathology (MS); STEM education (MAT); talented and gifted (M Ed); visual function in learning (M Ed). *Accreditation:* ASHA; NCATE. *Program availability:* Part-time, evening/weekend. *Degree requirements:* For master's, research project. *Entrance requirements:* For master's, California Basic Educational Skills Test, PRAXIS II, minimum undergraduate GPA of 2.75, 3.0 graduate. Additional exam requirements/recommendations for international students: Required—TOEFL. Electronic applications accepted. *Expenses:* Contact institution. *Faculty research:* Defining a culturally competent classroom, technology in the K-12 classroom, Socratic seminars, social studies education.

Piedmont College, School of Education, Demorest, GA 30535. Offers art education (MA, MAT); curriculum and instruction (Ed D, Ed S); early childhood education (MA, MAT); instructional technology (MA); middle grades education (MA, MAT); music education (MA, MAT); secondary education (MA, MAT); special education (MA, MAT). *Program availability:* Part-time, evening/weekend. *Students:* 341 full-time (268 women), 682 part-time (571 women); includes 182 minority (136 Black or African American, non-Hispanic/Latino; 2 American Indian or Alaska Native, non-Hispanic/Latino; 11 Asian, non-Hispanic/Latino; 32 Hispanic/Latino; 1 Two or more races, non-Hispanic/Latino). Average age 37. 333 applicants, 77% accepted, 103 enrolled. In 2017, 292 master's, 9 doctorates, 318 other advanced degrees awarded. *Degree requirements:* For master's, thesis, field experience in the classroom teaching; for doctorate, thesis/dissertation. *Entrance requirements:* For master's, GRE General Test, MAT; for Ed S, minimum graduate GPA of 3.5, valid teaching certificate. Additional exam requirements/recommendations for international students: Required—TOEFL (minimum score 550 paper-based). *Application deadline:* For fall admission, 7/15 for domestic students; for spring admission, 12/1 for domestic students. Applications are processed on a rolling basis. Electronic applications accepted. *Expenses:* Tuition: Full-time $9360; part-time $520 per credit hour. *Required fees:* $200; $200 per year. $100 per term. *Financial support:* Career-related internships or fieldwork, Federal Work-Study, and unspecified assistantships available. Support available to part-time students. Financial award applicants required to submit FAFSA. *Unit head:* Dr. Don Gnecco, Dean, 706-778-3000 Ext. 1201, Fax: 706-776-9608, E-mail: dgnecco@piedmont.edu. *Application contact:* Kathleen Carter, Director of Graduate Enrollment Management, 706-778-8500 Ext. 1181, Fax: 706-778-0150, E-mail: kanderson@piedmont.edu.

Point Park University, School of Arts and Sciences, Department of Education, Pittsburgh, PA 15222-1984. Offers adult learning and training (M Ed); athletic coaching (M Ed); curriculum and instruction (MA); educational administration (MA); leadership and administration (Ed D); secondary education (M Ed); special education grades 7-12 (M Ed); special education PreK-grade 8 (M Ed). *Program availability:* Part-time, evening/weekend, 100% online, blended/hybrid learning. *Degree requirements:* For master's, comprehensive exam (for some programs), thesis or alternative. *Entrance requirements:* For master's, minimum GPA of 3.0, resume, 2 letters of recommendation. Additional exam requirements/recommendations for international students: Required—TOEFL. Electronic applications accepted.

Portland State University, Graduate Studies, College of Liberal Arts and Sciences, Fariborz Maseeh Department of Mathematics and Statistics, Portland, OR 97207-0751. Offers applied statistics (Certificate); mathematical sciences (PhD); mathematics education (PhD); mathematics for middle school (Certificate); mathematics for teachers (MS); statistics (MS); MA/MS. *Faculty:* 35 full-time (10 women), 16 part-time/adjunct (5 women). *Students:* 82 full-time (30 women), 67 part-time (31 women); includes 37 minority (2 Black or African American, non-Hispanic/Latino; 1 American Indian or Alaska Native, non-Hispanic/Latino; 12 Asian, non-Hispanic/Latino; 18 Hispanic/Latino; 1 Native Hawaiian or other Pacific Islander, non-Hispanic/Latino; 3 Two or more races, non-Hispanic/Latino), 15 international. Average age 33. 108 applicants, 65% accepted, 46 enrolled. In 2017, 25 master's, 4 doctorates awarded. *Degree requirements:* For master's, comprehensive exam, thesis or alternative, 2 written examinations; for doctorate, thesis/dissertation, preliminary and comprehensive examinations. *Entrance requirements:* For master's, GRE General Test, GRE Subject Test, minimum GPA of 3.0 in upper-division course work or 2.75 cumulative undergraduate; for doctorate, GRE General Test. Additional exam requirements/recommendations for international students: Required—TOEFL (minimum score 550 paper-based; 80 iBT). *Application deadline:* For fall admission, 4/1 for domestic students, 3/1 for international students; for winter admission, 9/1 for domestic students, 7/1 for international students; for spring admission, 11/1 for domestic and international students; for summer admission, 2/1 for domestic and international students. Applications are processed on a rolling basis. Application fee: $65. *Expenses:* Tuition, state resident: full-time $14,436; part-time $401 per credit. Tuition, nonresident: full-time $21,780; part-time $605 per credit. *Required fees:* $1380; $22 per credit. $119 per quarter. One-time fee: $325. Tuition and fees vary according to program. *Financial support:* In 2017–18, 44 students received support, including 7 research assistantships with full and partial tuition reimbursements available (averaging $16,418 per year), 30 teaching assistantships with full and partial tuition reimbursements available (averaging $14,943 per year); Federal Work-Study, scholarships/grants, tuition waivers (full and partial), and unspecified assistantships also available. Support available to part-time students. Financial award application deadline: 3/1; financial award applicants required to submit FAFSA. *Faculty research:* Algebra, topology, statistical distribution theory, control theory, statistical robustness. *Total annual research expenditures:* $1.7 million. *Unit head:* Dr. John Caughman, Chair, 503-725-3634, E-mail: caughman@pdx.edu. *Application contact:* Kathie Leck, Graduate Program Administrator, 503-725-3604, Fax: 503-725-8244, E-mail: leck@pdx.edu.
Website: https://www.pdx.edu/math/

Queens College of the City University of New York, Division of Education, Department of Educational and Community Programs, Queens, NY 11367-1597. Offers bilingual pupil personnel (AC); counselor education (MS Ed); mental health counseling (MS); school building leader (AC); school district leader (AC); school psychologist (MS Ed); special education-childhood education (AC); special education-early childhood (MS Ed); teacher of special education 1-6 (MS Ed); teacher of special education birth-2 (MS Ed); teaching students with disabilities, grades 7-12 (MS Ed, AC). *Program availability:* Part-time. *Faculty:* 20 full-time (14 women), 63 part-time/adjunct (37 women). *Students:* 105 full-time (94 women), 423 part-time (350 women); includes 241 minority (40 Black or African American, non-Hispanic/Latino; 2 American Indian or Alaska Native, non-Hispanic/Latino; 50 Asian, non-Hispanic/Latino; 142 Hispanic/Latino; 1 Native Hawaiian or other Pacific Islander, non-Hispanic/Latino; 6 Two or more races, non-Hispanic/Latino), 5 international. Average age 28. 515 applicants, 57% accepted, 230 enrolled. In 2017, 163 master's, 74 other advanced degrees awarded. *Degree requirements:* For master's, research project; for AC, internship. *Entrance requirements:* For master's, minimum GPA of 3.0. Additional exam requirements/recommendations for international students: Required—TOEFL, IELTS. *Application deadline:* For fall admission, 3/1 for domestic students. Applications are processed on a rolling basis. Application fee: $125. Electronic applications accepted. *Financial support:* Career-related internships or fieldwork available. Financial award application deadline: 4/1; financial award applicants required to submit FAFSA. *Unit head:* Dr. Emilia Lopez, Chair, 718-997-5250, E-mail: emilia.lopez@qc.cuny.edu. *Application contact:* Elizabeth D'Amico-Ramirez, Assistant Director of Graduate Admissions, 718-997-5203, E-mail: elizabeth.damicoramirez@qc.cuny.edu.

Queens College of the City University of New York, Division of Education, Department of Elementary and Early Childhood Education, Queens, NY 11367-1597. Offers bilingual education (MAT, MS Ed, AC); childhood education (MAT, MS Ed); early childhood education birth-2 (MAT, MS Ed, AC); literacy education birth-grade 6 (MS Ed, AC). *Program availability:* Part-time, evening/weekend. *Students:* 112 full-time (98 women), 342 part-time (312 women); includes 243 minority (39 Black or African American, non-Hispanic/Latino; 87 Asian, non-Hispanic/Latino; 110 Hispanic/Latino; 7 Two or more races, non-Hispanic/Latino), 12 international. Average age 29. *Degree requirements:* For master's, research project. *Entrance requirements:* For master's, minimum GPA of 3.0. Additional exam requirements/recommendations for international students: Required—TOEFL, IELTS. *Application deadline:* For fall admission, 4/1 for domestic students. Applications are processed on a rolling basis. Application fee: $125. Electronic applications accepted. *Financial support:* Career-related internships or fieldwork available. Financial award application deadline: 4/1; financial award applicants required to submit FAFSA. *Unit head:* Daisuke Akiba, Chair, 718-997-5300, E-mail: daisuke.akiba@qc.cuny.edu. *Application contact:* Elizabeth D'Amico-Ramirez, Assistant Director of Graduate Admissions, 718-997-5203, E-mail: elizabeth.damicoramirez@qc.cuny.edu.

Roberts Wesleyan College, Graduate Teacher Education Programs, Rochester, NY 14624-1997. Offers adolescence and special education (M Ed); childhood and special education (M Ed); literacy education (M Ed); special education (M Ed). *Program availability:* Part-time, evening/weekend. *Degree requirements:* For master's, thesis. Electronic applications accepted.

Roger Williams University, Feinstein School of Humanities, Arts and Education, Bristol, RI 02809. Offers literacy education (MA); middle school certification (Certificate). *Program availability:* Part-time-only, evening/weekend. *Faculty:* 3 full-time (all women), 5 part-time/adjunct (4 women). *Students:* 14 part-time; includes 1 minority (Hispanic/Latino). Average age 33. 10 applicants, 100% accepted, 7 enrolled. In 2017, 10 master's awarded. *Entrance requirements:* For master's, resume, 2 letters of recommendation, college transcript, letter of intent, verification of active teaching license. Additional exam requirements/recommendations for international students: Required—TOEFL (minimum score 85 iBT), IELTS (minimum score 6.5). *Application deadline:* Applications are processed on a rolling basis. Application fee: $50. Electronic

Middle School Education

applications accepted. *Expenses:* $573 per credit hour, $258 graduation fee. *Financial support:* Application deadline: 4/1; applicants required to submit FAFSA. *Unit head:* Jeffrey Meriwether, Interim Dean, 401-254-3780, E-mail: jmeriwether@rwu.edu. *Application contact:* Marcus Hanscom, Director of Graduate Admissions, 401-254-3345, Fax: 401-254-3557, E-mail: gradadmit@rwu.edu.
Website: http://www.rwu.edu/academics/schools-and-colleges/fshae

Rowan University, Graduate School, College of Science and Mathematics, Department of Mathematics, Program in Middle Grades Math Education, Glassboro, NJ 08028-1701. Offers CGS. Electronic applications accepted. *Expenses:* Tuition, state resident: full-time $15,020; part-time $751 per semester hour. Tuition, nonresident: full-time $15,020; part-time $751 per semester hour. *Required fees:* $3158; $157.90 per semester hour. Tuition and fees vary according to course load, campus/location and program.

St. Bonaventure University, School of Graduate Studies, School of Education, Adolescence Education Program, St. Bonaventure, NY 14778-2284. Offers MS Ed. *Program availability:* Part-time. *Faculty:* 2 full-time (both women). *Students:* 6 full-time (3 women), 9 part-time (6 women). Average age 27. 1 applicant, 100% accepted, 1 enrolled. In 2017, 7 master's awarded. *Degree requirements:* For master's, comprehensive exam, minimum cumulative GPA of 3.0, electronic portfolio, student teaching. *Entrance requirements:* For master's, New York State Teacher Certification Exams, CST in subject area; SAT, ACT, GRE or MAT, bachelor's degree or thirty semester hours in an arts or sciences major in the subject area of teaching certification from an accredited college or university; official transcripts showing proof of degree and all college and university courses taken; at least six semester hours of university-level credit; letters of recommendation. Additional exam requirements/recommendations for international students: Required—TOEFL (minimum score 550 paper-based; 79 iBT). *Application deadline:* For fall admission, 6/15 priority date for domestic students, 2/1 priority date for international students; for spring admission, 10/1 for domestic students, 7/1 for international students. Applications are processed on a rolling basis. Application fee: $0. Electronic applications accepted. *Expenses:* $733 per credit hour, $100 graduation fee. *Financial support:* Federal Work-Study, scholarships/grants, health care benefits, and unspecified assistantships available. Support available to part-time students. Financial award application deadline: 4/15; financial award applicants required to submit FAFSA. *Faculty research:* Racial and gender diversity trends among teachers, brain compatible learning, critical and media literacy. *Unit head:* Dr. Amanda Winkelsas, Director, 716-375-2177, Fax: 716-375-2360, E-mail: awinkels@sbu.edu. *Application contact:* Bruce Campbell, Director of Graduate Admissions, 716-375-2429, Fax: 716-375-4015, E-mail: gradsch@sbu.edu.
Website: http://www.sbu.edu/academics/schools/education/graduate-degrees-certificates/msed-in-adolescence-education

St. Bonaventure University, School of Graduate Studies, School of Education, Literacy Programs, St. Bonaventure, NY 14778-2284. Offers adolescent literacy 5-12 (MS Ed); childhood literacy B-6 (MS Ed). *Accreditation:* NCATE. *Program availability:* Part-time, evening/weekend. *Faculty:* 2 part-time/adjunct (both women). *Students:* 7 full-time (all women), 3 part-time (1 woman); includes 2 minority (1 Black or African American, non-Hispanic/Latino; 1 Hispanic/Latino). Average age 23. 3 applicants, 100% accepted, 3 enrolled. In 2017, 13 master's awarded. *Degree requirements:* For master's, comprehensive exam, thesis optional, minimum cumulative GPA of 3.0, clinical practicum, literacy coaching internship, electronic portfolio. *Entrance requirements:* For master's, GRE or MAT, teaching certificate in matching area in-hand or pending, transcripts from all previous colleges, minimum GPA of 3.0, 2 references, interview, writing sample. Additional exam requirements/recommendations for international students: Required—TOEFL (minimum score 550 paper-based; 80 iBT). *Application deadline:* For fall admission, 6/15 priority date for domestic students, 2/1 for international students; for spring admission, 11/15 priority date for domestic students, 7/1 for international students. Applications are processed on a rolling basis. Application fee: $0. Electronic applications accepted. *Expenses:* $733 per credit hour, $100 graduation fee. *Financial support:* Federal Work-Study, scholarships/grants, health care benefits, and unspecified assistantships available. Support available to part-time students. Financial award application deadline: 4/15; financial award applicants required to submit FAFSA. *Unit head:* Dr. Lisa Buenaventura, Interim Program Director, 716-375-2394, Fax: 716-375-2360, E-mail: lbuenave@sbu.edu. *Application contact:* Bruce Campbell, Director of Graduate Admissions, 716-375-2429, Fax: 716-375-4015, E-mail: gradsch@sbu.edu.
Website: http://www.sbu.edu/academics/schools/education/graduate-degrees-certificates/msed-in-childhood-literacy

St. John Fisher College, Ralph C. Wilson Jr. School of Education, Program in Adolescence Education and Special Education, Rochester, NY 14618-3597. Offers adolescence education: biology with special education (MS Ed); adolescence education: chemistry with special education (MS Ed); adolescence education: English with special education (MS Ed); adolescence education: French with special education (MS Ed); adolescence education: math with special education (MS Ed); adolescence education: physics with special education (MS Ed); adolescence education: social studies with special education (MS Ed); adolescence education: Spanish with special education (MS Ed). *Program availability:* Part-time, evening/weekend. *Faculty:* 5 full-time (4 women), 7 part-time/adjunct (6 women). *Students:* 15 full-time (3 women), 4 part-time (all women); includes 4 minority (2 Black or African American, non-Hispanic/Latino; 1 Hispanic/Latino; 1 Two or more races, non-Hispanic/Latino). Average age 27. 34 applicants, 85% accepted, 12 enrolled. In 2017, 19 master's awarded. *Degree requirements:* For master's, field experiences, student teaching. *Entrance requirements:* For master's, LAST, 2 letters of recommendation, personal statement, current resume. Additional exam requirements/recommendations for international students: Required—TOEFL (minimum score 575 paper-based; 80 iBT). *Application deadline:* Applications are processed on a rolling basis. Application fee: $30. Electronic applications accepted. *Expenses:* Contact institution. *Financial support:* Scholarships/grants available. Financial award applicants required to submit FAFSA. *Faculty research:* Arts and humanities, urban schools, constructivist learning, at-risk students, mentoring. *Unit head:* Dr. Susan Hildenbrand, Program Director, 585-385-7297, E-mail: shildenbrand@sjfc.edu. *Application contact:* Michelle Gosier, Director of Transfer and Graduate Admissions, 585-385-8064, E-mail: mgosier@sjfc.edu.

Saint Joseph's University, College of Arts and Sciences, Graduate Programs in Education, Philadelphia, PA 19131-1395. Offers curriculum supervisor (Certificate); educational leadership (MS, Ed D); elementary education (MS, Certificate); elementary/middle school education (Certificate); organizational development and leadership (MS); principal (Certificate); professional education (MS); reading specialist (MS, Certificate); reading supervisor (Certificate); secondary education (MS, Certificate); special education (MS); special education 7-12 (Certificate); special education PK-8 (Certificate); superintendent's letter of eligibility (Certificate); supervisor of special education (Certificate); teacher of the deaf and hard of hearing (Certificate). *Program availability:* Part-time, evening/weekend, blended/hybrid learning. *Faculty:* 18 full-time (16 women), 63 part-time/adjunct (44 women). *Students:* 79 full-time (60 women), 793 part-time (604 women); includes 179 minority (125 Black or African American, non-Hispanic/Latino; 5 American Indian or Alaska Native, non-Hispanic/Latino; 15 Asian, non-Hispanic/Latino; 27 Hispanic/Latino; 1 Native Hawaiian or other Pacific Islander, non-Hispanic/Latino; 6 Two or more races, non-Hispanic/Latino), 12 international.

Average age 34. 375 applicants, 75% accepted, 189 enrolled. In 2017, 340 master's, 13 doctorates, 3 other advanced degrees awarded. *Degree requirements:* For master's, thesis or alternative; for doctorate, comprehensive exam, thesis/dissertation. *Entrance requirements:* For master's, 2 letters of recommendation, minimum GPA of 3.0, official transcripts, personal statement; for doctorate, GRE, master's degree from accredited institution, minimum graduate GPA of 3.5, computer competence, interview with program director. Additional exam requirements/recommendations for international students: Required—TOEFL (minimum score 550 paper-based; 80 iBT), IELTS (minimum score 6.5), PTE (minimum score 60). *Application deadline:* For fall admission, 7/15 for international students; for spring admission, 11/1 for international students. Applications are processed on a rolling basis. Application fee: $35. Electronic applications accepted. *Expenses:* Contact institution. *Financial support:* Scholarships/grants and unspecified assistantships available. Financial award application deadline: 5/1; financial award applicants required to submit FAFSA. *Faculty research:* Factors predicting early mathematics skills for low income children, early child care and development, preschool quality, parent communication and home-school collaboration issues, education of terminally ill children, preparing literacy teachers for urban schools. *Unit head:* Dr. John Vacca, Associate Dean, Education, 610-660-3131, E-mail: gradcas@sju.edu. *Application contact:* Graduate Admissions, College of Arts and Sciences, 610-660-3131, E-mail: gradcas@sju.edu.
Website: https://sites.sju.edu/education/graduate-programs/

Saint Peter's University, Graduate Programs in Education, Program in Teaching, Jersey City, NJ 07306-5997. Offers 6-8 middle school education (MA Ed, Certificate); K-12 secondary education (MA Ed, Certificate); K-5 elementary education (MA Ed, Certificate). *Program availability:* Part-time, evening/weekend. *Degree requirements:* For master's, comprehensive exam. *Entrance requirements:* For master's, GRE or MAT. Additional exam requirements/recommendations for international students: Required—TOEFL. Electronic applications accepted.

St. Thomas Aquinas College, Division of Teacher Education, Sparkill, NY 10976. Offers adolescence education (MST); childhood and special education (MST); childhood education (MST); educational leadership (MS Ed); reading (MS Ed, PMC); special education (MS Ed, PMC); teaching (MS Ed), including elementary education, middle school education, secondary education. *Accreditation:* NCATE. *Program availability:* Part-time, evening/weekend. *Degree requirements:* For master's, comprehensive exam, comprehensive professional portfolio; for PMC, action research project. *Entrance requirements:* For master's, New York State Qualifying Exam, GRE General Test or minimum GPA of 3.0, teaching certificate; for PMC, GRE General Test or minimum GPA of 3.0. Electronic applications accepted. *Faculty research:* Computer applications in education, adolescent special education students, literacy development, inclusive practices for special education students.

Salem College, Graduate Studies, Winston-Salem, NC 27101. Offers art education (MAT); elementary education (M Ed, MAT); language and literacy (M Ed); middle school education (MAT); organ (MM); piano (MM); school counseling (M Ed); second language studies (MAT); secondary education (MAT); special education (M Ed, MAT). *Accreditation:* NCATE. *Program availability:* Part-time, evening/weekend, online learning. *Faculty:* 8 full-time (all women), 11 part-time/adjunct (8 women). In 2017, 17 master's awarded. *Degree requirements:* For master's, practicum (MAT), action research project (M Ed). *Entrance requirements:* For master's, minimum GPA of 3.0, two academic/professional recommendations, acceptable criminal background check. Additional exam requirements/recommendations for international students: Recommended—TOEFL. *Application deadline:* For fall admission, 8/1 for domestic students, 7/15 for international students; for spring admission, 1/15 for domestic students; for summer admission, 5/1 for domestic students. Applications are processed on a rolling basis. Application fee: $30. Electronic applications accepted. *Expenses: Tuition:* Part-time $440 per semester hour. *Financial support:* Scholarships/grants available. Support available to part-time students. Financial award applicants required to submit FAFSA. *Faculty research:* Teacher professional development, adolescent literacy, instructional technology. *Application contact:* Sheryl Long, Director, 336-721-2658, Fax: 336-917-5384, E-mail: sheryl.long@salem.edu.
Website: http://www.salem.edu

Salem State University, School of Graduate Studies, Program in Middle School Education, Salem, MA 01970-5353. Offers humanities (M Ed); math/science (MAT). *Program availability:* Part-time, evening/weekend. *Entrance requirements:* For master's, GRE or MAT. Additional exam requirements/recommendations for international students: Required—TOEFL (minimum score 550 paper-based; 80 iBT) or IELTS (minimum score 5.5).

Salem State University, School of Graduate Studies, Program in Middle School General Science, Salem, MA 01970-5353. Offers MAT. *Program availability:* Part-time, evening/weekend. *Entrance requirements:* For master's, GRE or MAT. Additional exam requirements/recommendations for international students: Required—TOEFL (minimum score 550 paper-based; 80 iBT) or IELTS (minimum score 5.5).

Salem State University, School of Graduate Studies, Program in Middle School Math, Salem, MA 01970-5353. Offers MAT. *Program availability:* Part-time, evening/weekend. *Entrance requirements:* For master's, GRE or MAT. Additional exam requirements/recommendations for international students: Required—TOEFL (minimum score 550 paper-based; 80 iBT) or IELTS (minimum score 5.5).

Salisbury University, Program in Mathematics Education, Salisbury, MD 21801-6837. Offers mathematics (MSME), including high school, middle school. *Program availability:* Part-time. *Faculty:* 4 full-time (2 women), 2 part-time/adjunct (1 woman). *Students:* 1 (woman) full-time, 7 part-time (5 women). Average age 27. 5 applicants, 80% accepted, 4 enrolled. In 2017, 5 master's awarded. *Entrance requirements:* For master's, two letters of recommendation; transcripts from colleges and universities attended; personal statement. Additional exam requirements/recommendations for international students: Required—TOEFL (minimum score 550 paper-based; 79 iBT), IELTS (minimum score 6.5). *Application deadline:* For fall admission, 8/1 priority date for domestic and international students; for spring admission, 10/1 priority date for domestic and international students. Applications are processed on a rolling basis. Application fee: $65. Electronic applications accepted. *Expenses:* $392 per credit hour resident; $703 per credit hour non-resident; $92 per credit hour fees. *Financial support:* In 2017–18, 1 teaching assistantship with full tuition reimbursement (averaging $8,000 per year) was awarded; career-related internships or fieldwork and scholarships/grants also available. Support available to part-time students. Financial award application deadline: 3/1; financial award applicants required to submit FAFSA. *Faculty research:* Conceptual development of multiplicative reasoning; early childhood mathematics; teachers' attitudes towards mathematics. *Unit head:* Dr. Jennifer Bergner, Graduate Program Director, Mathematics Education, 410-677-5429, E-mail: jabergner@salisbury.edu.
Website: http://www.salisbury.edu/gsr/gradstudies/MSMEpage.html

Seton Hill University, Master of Arts Program in Elementary/Middle Level Education, Greensburg, PA 15601. Offers MA. *Program availability:* Part-time, evening/weekend, blended/hybrid learning. *Entrance requirements:* For master's, teacher's certification, 3 letters of recommendation, personal statement, transcripts, resume. Additional exam requirements/recommendations for international students: Required—TOEFL (minimum score 600 paper-based; 100 iBT), IELTS (minimum score 6.5). *Application deadline:* Applications are processed on a rolling basis. Application fee: $0. Electronic applications accepted. *Expenses: Tuition:* Part-time $734 per credit. Tuition and fees vary according to class time, course level, course load and program. *Financial support:* Federal Work-Study, scholarships/grants, and tuition discounts available. Financial award application deadline: 8/15; financial award applicants required to submit FAFSA. Website: https://www.setonhill.edu/academics/graduate-programs/elementary-middle-level-education-ma/

Shenandoah University, School of Education and Leadership, Winchester, VA 22601. Offers administration and supervision (Certificate); administrative leadership (D Ed); early childhood literacy (MS); educational administration (MSE); elementary school teacher education (Certificate); emphasis in teaching (MSE); health and physical education (Certificate); individualized focus (MS, MSE); literacy education (MS); middle school teacher education (Certificate); organizational leadership (MS, D Prof); reading licensure (MS, Certificate); reading non-licensure (MS); secondary school teacher education (Certificate); special education (MSE); writing (MS). *Accreditation:* TEAC. *Program availability:* Part-time, evening/weekend. *Faculty:* 8 full-time (7 women), 22 part-time/adjunct (16 women). *Students:* 16 full-time (14 women), 221 part-time (167 women); includes 32 minority (17 Black or African American, non-Hispanic/Latino; 1 American Indian or Alaska Native, non-Hispanic/Latino; 6 Asian, non-Hispanic/Latino; 5 Hispanic/Latino; 1 Native Hawaiian or other Pacific Islander, non-Hispanic/Latino; 2 Two or more races, non-Hispanic/Latino), 3 international. Average age 38. 81 applicants, 99% accepted, 63 enrolled. In 2017, 53 master's, 11 doctorates, 49 other advanced degrees awarded. *Degree requirements:* For master's, comprehensive exam (for some programs), thesis (for some programs); for doctorate, comprehensive exam, thesis/dissertation. *Entrance requirements:* For degree, PRAXIS Academic Core, SAT/ACT, PRAXIS Academic Core Math, or VCLA, three letters of recommendation, writing sample, undergraduate degree. Additional exam requirements/recommendations for international students: Required—TOEFL (minimum score 550 paper-based, 79 iBT) or IELTS (6.5). *Application deadline:* For fall admission, 5/1 priority date for domestic students, 5/1 for international students; for spring admission, 10/15 priority date for domestic students, 10/15 for international students; for summer admission, 3/15 priority date for domestic students, 3/15 for international students. Application fee: $30. Electronic applications accepted. *Expenses:* $15,600 tuition plus $1,296 fees (technology and student services). *Financial support:* In 2017–18, 26 students received support. Scholarships/grants and unspecified assistantships available. Financial award applicants required to submit FAFSA. *Faculty research:* Mentoring, behavior support for students, teacher change agency, educational technology in pedagogy, literacy education. *Unit head:* Jill Lindsey, PhD, Director, 540-535-7324, Fax: 540-665-4726, E-mail: jlindsey@su.edu. *Application contact:* Andrew Woodall, Executive Director of Recruitment and Admissions, 540-665-4581, Fax: 540-665-4627, E-mail: admit@su.edu.
Website: http://www.su.edu/education/

Shippensburg University of Pennsylvania, School of Graduate Studies, College of Education and Human Services, Department of Teacher Education, Shippensburg, PA 17257-2299. Offers curriculum and instruction (M Ed), including biology, early childhood education, elementary education, geography/earth science, history, mathematics, middle school education, modern languages; reading (M Ed). *Accreditation:* NCATE. *Program availability:* Part-time, evening/weekend, 100% online, blended/hybrid learning. *Faculty:* 13 full-time (8 women), 1 (woman) part-time/adjunct. *Students:* 10 full-time (7 women), 94 part-time (81 women); includes 10 minority (3 Black or African American, non-Hispanic/Latino; 2 Asian, non-Hispanic/Latino; 5 Hispanic/Latino), 1 international. Average age 34. 71 applicants, 86% accepted, 35 enrolled. In 2017, 23 master's awarded. *Degree requirements:* For master's, comprehensive exam (for some programs), thesis optional, practicum or internship; capstone seminar (for some programs). *Entrance requirements:* For master's, MAT or GRE (if GPA less than 2.75), interview, 3 letters of reference, questionnaire of teaching background and future goals, resume. Additional exam requirements/recommendations for international students: Required—TOEFL (minimum score 550 paper-based, 68 iBT) or IELTS (minimum score 6). *Application deadline:* For fall admission, 4/1 priority date for domestic students, 4/30 for international students; for spring admission, 9/1 priority date for domestic students, 9/30 for international students; for summer admission, 2/1 priority date for domestic students. Applications are processed on a rolling basis. Application fee: $45. Electronic applications accepted. *Expenses:* Tuition, state resident: part-time $500 per credit. Tuition, nonresident: part-time $750 per credit. *Required fees:* $145 per credit. *Financial support:* In 2017–18, 1 student received support. Career-related internships or fieldwork, scholarships/grants, unspecified assistantships, and resident hall director and student payroll positions available. Support available to part-time students. Financial award application deadline: 3/1; financial award applicants required to submit FAFSA. *Unit head:* Dr. Christine A. Royce, Chairperson, 717-477-1688, Fax: 717-477-4046, E-mail: caroyc@ship.edu. *Application contact:* Maya T. Mapp, Director of Admissions, 717-477-1231, Fax: 717-477-4016, E-mail: mtmapp@ship.edu.
Website: http://www.ship.edu/teacher/

Smith College, Graduate and Special Programs, Department of Education and Child Study, Program in Elementary Education, Northampton, MA 01063. Offers elementary education (MAT); middle school education (MAT). *Program availability:* Part-time. *Students:* 5 full-time (all women), 3 part-time (2 women). Average age 24. 15 applicants, 93% accepted, 8 enrolled. In 2017, 9 master's awarded. *Entrance requirements:* Additional exam requirements/recommendations for international students: Required—TOEFL (minimum score 595 paper-based; 97 iBT), IELTS. *Application deadline:* For fall admission, 4/15 for domestic students, 1/15 priority date for international students; for spring admission, 12/1 for domestic students. Applications are processed on a rolling basis. Application fee: $60. *Expenses:* Contact institution. *Financial support:* In 2017–18, 8 students received support, including 1 fellowship with full tuition reimbursement available; scholarships/grants and human resources employee benefit also available. Support available to part-time students. Financial award application deadline: 4/15; financial award applicants required to submit FAFSA. *Unit head:* Alan Rudnitsky, Graduate Student Adviser, 413-585-3261, E-mail: arudnits@smith.edu. *Application contact:* Ruth Morgan, Program Assistant, 413-585-3050, Fax: 413-585-3054, E-mail: gradstdy@smith.edu.
Website: http://www.smith.edu/educ/

Southeast Missouri State University, School of Graduate Studies, Department of Middle and Secondary Education, Cape Girardeau, MO 63701-4799. Offers MA. *Accreditation:* NCATE. *Program availability:* Part-time, online only, 100% online. *Faculty:* 5 full-time (3 women), 1 (woman) part-time/adjunct. *Students:* 4 full-time (3 women), 51 part-time (40 women); includes 5 minority (3 Black or African American, non-Hispanic/Latino; 2 Hispanic/Latino). Average age 31. 20 applicants, 100% accepted, 20 enrolled. In 2017, 19 master's awarded. *Degree requirements:* For master's, comprehensive exam, research paper. *Entrance requirements:* For master's, minimum undergraduate GPA of 2.75. Additional exam requirements/recommendations for international students: Required—TOEFL (minimum score 550 paper-based; 79 iBT), IELTS (minimum score 6), PTE (minimum score 53). *Application deadline:* For fall admission, 8/1 for domestic students, 6/1 for international students; for spring admission, 11/21 for domestic students, 10/1 for international students; for summer admission, 5/15 for domestic

students. Applications are processed on a rolling basis. Application fee: $30 ($40 for international students). Electronic applications accepted. *Expenses:* $270.35 per credit hour in-state tuition, $33.40 per credit hour fees. *Financial support:* In 2017–18, 2 students received support. Career-related internships or fieldwork, Federal Work-Study, scholarships/grants, traineeships, tuition waivers (full), and unspecified assistantships available. Financial award application deadline: 6/30; financial award applicants required to submit FAFSA. *Faculty research:* Assessment, technology, diversity. *Unit head:* Dr. Simin L. Cwick, Middle and Secondary Education Department Chair, 573-651-5965, E-mail: scwick@semo.edu. *Application contact:* Alisa Aleen McFerron, Assistant Director of Admissions for Operations, 573-651-5937, E-mail: amcferron@semo.edu.
Website: http://www.semo.edu/midsecondaryed/

Spalding University, Graduate Studies, College of Education, Programs in Education, Louisville, KY 40203-2188. Offers art teacher education (MAT); business teacher education (MAT); elementary school education (MAT); foreign language (MAT); high school education (MAT); middle school education (MAT); secondary education (MAT); special education (learning and behavioral disorders) (MAT); student guidance counselor (MA); teacher leader (M Ed). *Accreditation:* NCATE. *Program availability:* Part-time, evening/weekend. *Entrance requirements:* For master's, GRE General Test or MAT, interview, letters of recommendation, resume. Additional exam requirements/recommendations for international students: Required—TOEFL (minimum score 535 paper-based). Electronic applications accepted. *Faculty research:* Instructional technology, achievement gap, classroom management, assessment.

State University of New York at Fredonia, College of Education, Fredonia, NY 14063-1136. Offers curriculum and instruction (MS Ed); literacy education (MS Ed), including birth-grade 12, grades 5-12; TESOL (MS Ed). *Accreditation:* NCATE. *Program availability:* Part-time. *Faculty:* 11 full-time (9 women), 1 part-time/adjunct (0 women). *Students:* Average age 29. 60 applicants, 97% accepted, 39 enrolled. In 2017, 33 master's awarded. *Degree requirements:* For master's, thesis. *Entrance requirements:* For master's, GRE, minimum undergraduate GPA of 3.0. Additional exam requirements/recommendations for international students: Required—TOEFL (minimum score 79 iBT), IELTS (minimum score 6.5). *Application deadline:* For fall admission, 4/1 priority date for domestic and international students; for spring admission, 11/1 priority date for domestic students, 11/1 for international students. Applications are processed on a rolling basis. Application fee: $75. Electronic applications accepted. *Expenses:* Tuition, state resident: full-time $8154. Tuition, nonresident: full-time $16,650. *Required fees:* $1209. *Financial support:* In 2017–18, 4 teaching assistantships with full and partial tuition reimbursements (averaging $7,075 per year) were awarded. Financial award application deadline: 3/15; financial award applicants required to submit FAFSA. *Faculty research:* Positive behavioral intervention and support (PBIS), place-based science education, peer support for education, primary source material for social studies education, policies and practices in learning English language. *Unit head:* Dr. Christine Givner, Dean, 716-673-3311, E-mail: christine.givner@fredonia.edu. *Application contact:* Wendy S. Dunst, Interim Graduate Recruitment and Admissions Associate, 716-673-3808, Fax: 716-673-3712, E-mail: wendy.dunst@fredonia.edu.
Website: http://www.fredonia.edu/coe/

State University of New York at Fredonia, College of Liberal Arts and Sciences, Fredonia, NY 14063-1136. Offers biology (MS); English (MA); English education 7-12 (MA); interdisciplinary studies (MA, MS); math education (MS Ed); professional writing (CAS); speech pathology (MS); MA/MS. *Program availability:* Part-time, evening/weekend. *Students:* 73 full-time (62 women), 9 part-time (6 women); includes 7 minority (1 Black or African American, non-Hispanic/Latino; 1 Asian, non-Hispanic/Latino; 2 Hispanic/Latino; 1 Native Hawaiian or other Pacific Islander, non-Hispanic/Latino; 2 Two or more races, non-Hispanic/Latino). Average age 24. 200 applicants, 25% accepted, 43 enrolled. In 2017, 41 master's, 1 other advanced degree awarded. *Degree requirements:* For master's, comprehensive exam (for some programs), thesis (for some programs). *Entrance requirements:* For master's, GRE. Additional exam requirements/recommendations for international students: Required—TOEFL (minimum score 79 iBT), IELTS (minimum score 6.5). *Application deadline:* Applications are processed on a rolling basis. Application fee: $75. Electronic applications accepted. *Expenses:* Tuition, state resident: full-time $8154. Tuition, nonresident: full-time $16,650. *Required fees:* $1209. *Financial support:* In 2017–18, 5 students received support, including 14 teaching assistantships with full and partial tuition reimbursements available (averaging $5,957 per year); tuition waivers (full and partial) and unspecified assistantships also available. *Faculty research:* Immunology/microbiology, applied human physiology, ecology and evolution, invertebrate biology, molecular biology, biochemistry, physiology, animal behavior, science education, vertebrate physiology, cell biology, plant biology, developmental biology, aquatic ecology, bilingual language acquisition, bilingual language acquisition and disorders, augmentative and alternate communication with ALS, World War I, Zweig, environmental literature, editing, adolescent literature, pedagogy. *Unit head:* Dr. Andy Karafa, Dean, 716-673-3173, Fax: 716-673-3338, E-mail: andy.karafa@gmail.com. *Application contact:* Wendy S. Dunst, Interim Graduate Recruitment and Admissions Associate, 716-673-3808, Fax: 716-673-3712, E-mail: wendy.dunst@fredonia.edu.
Website: http://www.fredonia.edu/clas/

State University of New York at Oswego, Graduate Studies, School of Education, Department of Curriculum and Instruction, Oswego, NY 13126. Offers adolescence education (MST); art education (MAT); childhood education (MST); curriculum and instruction (MS Ed); literacy education (MS Ed); special education (MS Ed). *Program availability:* Part-time, evening/weekend. *Degree requirements:* For master's, comprehensive exam (for some programs), thesis optional. *Entrance requirements:* For master's, GRE General Test, minimum GPA of 2.7, provisional teaching certificate. Additional exam requirements/recommendations for international students: Required—TOEFL (minimum score 560 paper-based). *Faculty research:* Classroom applications for microcomputers; classroom questioning, wait-time, and achievement; values clarification and academic achievement.

State University of New York College at Potsdam, School of Education and Professional Studies, Program in Special Education, Potsdam, NY 13676. Offers adolescence (grades 7-12) (MS Ed); childhood (grades 1-6) (MS Ed); early childhood (birth-grade 2) (MS Ed). *Accreditation:* NCATE. *Program availability:* Part-time. *Degree requirements:* For master's, culminating experience. *Entrance requirements:* For master's, minimum GPA of 3.0 in last 60 hours of course work. Additional exam requirements/recommendations for international students: Required—TOEFL (minimum score 550 paper-based; 80 iBT), IELTS (minimum score 6). Electronic applications accepted.

Temple University, College of Education, Department of Teaching and Learning, Philadelphia, PA 19122-6096. Offers career and technical education (Ed M), including business, computing, and information technology, industrial education, marketing education; middle grades education (Ed M), including math and language arts, math and science, science and language arts; secondary education (Ed M), including English, math, social studies; teaching English to speakers of other languages (MS Ed); urban education (Ed M). *Program availability:* Part-time, evening/weekend. *Students:* 218 full-time (144 women), 296 part-time (183 women); includes 128 minority (74 Black or African American, non-Hispanic/Latino; 18 Asian, non-Hispanic/Latino; 25 Hispanic/

Middle School Education

Latino; 11 Two or more races, non-Hispanic/Latino), 13 international. 254 applicants, 54% accepted, 102 enrolled. In 2017, 128 master's awarded. Terminal master's awarded for partial completion of doctoral program. *Degree requirements:* For master's, thesis or alternative. *Entrance requirements:* Additional exam requirements/recommendations for international students: Required—TOEFL (minimum score 550 paper-based; 79 iBT). *Application deadline:* For fall admission, 4/1 for domestic students, 12/15 for international students; for spring admission, 10/1 for domestic students, 8/1 for international students. Application fee: $60. Electronic applications accepted. *Expenses:* Contact institution. *Financial support:* Fellowships, research assistantships, and teaching assistantships available. Financial award application deadline: 1/15; financial award applicants required to submit FAFSA. *Faculty research:* Workforce development, vocational education, technical education, industrial education, professional development, literacy, classroom management, school communities, curriculum development, instruction, applied linguistics, cross linguistic influence, bilingual education, oral proficiency, multilingualism. *Unit head:* Dr. Christine Woyshner, Chairperson, 215-204-6387, E-mail: christine.woyshner@temple.edu. *Application contact:* Sarah Stapleton, Assistant Director, Academic Operations, 215-204-8220, E-mail: sarah.stapleton@temple.edu.
Website: http://education.temple.edu/tl

Tennessee Technological University, College of Graduate Studies, College of Education, Department of Exercise Science, Physical Education and Wellness, Cookeville, TN 38505. Offers adapted physical education (MA); elementary/middle school physical education (MA); lifetime wellness (MA); sport management (MA). *Accreditation:* NCATE. *Program availability:* Part-time, online learning. *Faculty:* 7 full-time (0 women). *Students:* 17 full-time (8 women), 34 part-time (14 women); includes 10 minority (5 Black or African American, non-Hispanic/Latino; 1 Asian, non-Hispanic/Latino; 2 Hispanic/Latino; 2 Two or more races, non-Hispanic/Latino). 35 applicants, 71% accepted, 23 enrolled. In 2017, 28 master's awarded. *Degree requirements:* For master's, comprehensive exam, thesis or alternative. *Entrance requirements:* For master's, MAT or GRE. Additional exam requirements/recommendations for international students: Required—TOEFL (minimum score 527 paper-based; 71 iBT), IELTS (minimum score 5.5), PTE (minimum score 48), or TOEIC (Test of English as an International Communication). *Application deadline:* For fall admission, 8/1 for domestic students, 5/1 for international students; for spring admission, 12/1 for domestic students, 10/1 for international students; for summer admission, 5/1 for domestic students, 2/1 for international students. Applications are processed on a rolling basis. Application fee: $35 ($40 for international students). Electronic applications accepted. *Expenses:* Tuition, state resident: full-time $9925; part-time $565 per credit hour. Tuition, nonresident: full-time $22,993; part-time $1291 per credit hour. *Financial support:* Fellowships, research assistantships, teaching assistantships, and career-related internships or fieldwork available. Financial award application deadline: 4/1. *Unit head:* Dr. Christy Killman, Chairperson, 931-372-3467, Fax: 931-372-6319, E-mail: ckillman@tntech.edu. *Application contact:* Shelia K. Kendrick, Coordinator of Graduate Studies, 931-372-3808, Fax: 931-372-3497, E-mail: skendrick@tntech.edu.

Theological University of the Caribbean, Graduate Programs, Saint Just, PR 00978-0901. Offers childhood and adolescent education (MA); counseling and pastoral care (MA); ministry (D Min); missions (MA).

Tufts University, Graduate School of Arts and Sciences, Department of Education, Program in Education, Medford, MA 02155. Offers educational studies (MA); elementary education (MAT); middle and secondary education (MAT); museum education (MA); secondary education (MA); STEM education (MS, PhD). *Program availability:* Part-time. *Students:* 50 full-time (38 women), 9 part-time (8 women); includes 9 minority (2 Black or African American, non-Hispanic/Latino; 2 Asian, non-Hispanic/Latino; 4 Hispanic/Latino; 1 Two or more races, non-Hispanic/Latino), 4 international. Average age 28. 120 applicants, 71% accepted, 49 enrolled. In 2017, 51 master's awarded. *Degree requirements:* For master's, thesis optional. *Entrance requirements:* For master's, GRE General Test, portfolio (for art education only); for doctorate, GRE General Test, writing sample. Additional exam requirements/recommendations for international students: Required—TOEFL (minimum score 550 paper-based; 80 iBT), IELTS (minimum score 6.5). *Application deadline:* For fall admission, 1/2 for domestic and international students; for spring admission, 10/15 for domestic and international students. Applications are processed on a rolling basis. Application fee: $85. Electronic applications accepted. *Expenses:* Contact institution. *Financial support:* Research assistantships, teaching assistantships, Federal Work-Study, scholarships/grants, and tuition waivers (full and partial) available. Support available to part-time students. Financial award application deadline: 1/2. *Unit head:* Dr. David Hammer, Graduate Program Director, 617-627-2396. *Application contact:* Office of Graduate Admissions, 617-627-3395, E-mail: gradadmissions@tufts.edu.

Union College, Graduate Programs, Department of Education, Program in Middle Grades, Barbourville, KY 40906-1499. Offers MA. *Degree requirements:* For master's, thesis optional. *Entrance requirements:* For master's, GRE General Test, NTE.

University of Arkansas, Graduate School, College of Education and Health Professions, Department of Curriculum and Instruction, Fayetteville, AR 72701. Offers childhood education (MAT); curriculum and instruction (M Ed, PhD, Ed S); educational leadership (M Ed, Ed D, Ed S); educational technology (M Ed); middle-level education (MAT); secondary education (M Ed, MAT, Ed S); special education (M Ed, MAT). *Accreditation:* NCATE. In 2017, 230 master's, 16 doctorates awarded. *Degree requirements:* For doctorate, thesis/dissertation. *Entrance requirements:* For doctorate, GRE General Test or MAT. *Application deadline:* For fall admission, 8/1 for domestic students, 4/1 for international students; for spring admission, 12/1 for domestic students, 10/1 for international students; for summer admission, 4/15 for domestic students, 3/1 for international students. Applications are processed on a rolling basis. Application fee: $60. Electronic applications accepted. *Expenses:* Tuition, state resident: full-time $3782. Tuition, nonresident: full-time $10,238. *Financial support:* In 2017–18, 41 research assistantships, 2 teaching assistantships were awarded; fellowships with tuition reimbursements, career-related internships or fieldwork, and Federal Work-Study also available. Support available to part-time students. Financial award application deadline: 4/1; financial award applicants required to submit FAFSA. *Unit head:* Dr. Cheryl A. Murphy, Interim Department Head, 479-575-5111, Fax: 479-575-5119, E-mail: cmurphy@uark.edu. *Application contact:* Dr. Derrick Mears, Graduate Coordinator, 479-575-6195, Fax: 479-575-6676, E-mail: dmears@uark.edu.
Website: http://cied.uark.edu/

University of Arkansas at Little Rock, Graduate School, College of Education and Health Professions, Department of Teacher Education, Program in Middle Childhood Education, Little Rock, AR 72204-1099. Offers M Ed. *Degree requirements:* For master's, electronic portfolio. *Entrance requirements:* For master's, PRAXIS, minimum undergraduate GPA of 2.75 overall or 3.0 in the last 60 hours of undergraduate work; interview.

University of Bridgeport, School of Education, Department of Education, Bridgeport, CT 06604. Offers education (MS); educational management (Ed D, Diploma), including intermediate administrator or supervisor (Diploma), leadership (Ed D); elementary education (MS, Diploma), including early childhood education, elementary education; middle school education (MS); music education (MS); remedial reading and language

arts (Diploma); secondary education (MS, Diploma), including computer specialist (Diploma), international education (Diploma), reading specialist, secondary education. *Program availability:* Part-time, evening/weekend. *Degree requirements:* For master's, final exam, final project, or thesis; for doctorate, comprehensive exam, thesis/dissertation; for Diploma, thesis or alternative, final project. *Entrance requirements:* For master's, minimum undergraduate QPA of 2.67; for doctorate, GRE, MAT; for Diploma, GRE General Test or MAT, minimum graduate QPA of 3.0. Additional exam requirements/recommendations for international students: Recommended—TOEFL (minimum score 550 paper-based; 80 iBT), IELTS (minimum score 6.5). Electronic applications accepted. *Expenses:* Contact institution.

University of Central Florida, College of Community Innovation and Education, School of Teacher Education, Program in Teacher Education, Orlando, FL 32816. Offers art education (MAT); English language (MAT); mathematics education (MAT); middle school mathematics (MAT); middle school science (MAT); science education (MAT), including biology, chemistry, physics; social science education (MAT). *Accreditation:* NCATE. *Program availability:* Part-time, evening/weekend. *Students:* 11 full-time (9 women), 28 part-time (23 women); includes 15 minority (5 Black or African American, non-Hispanic/Latino; 2 Asian, non-Hispanic/Latino; 6 Hispanic/Latino; 2 Two or more races, non-Hispanic/Latino), 2 international. Average age 29. In 2017, 6 master's awarded. *Degree requirements:* For master's, thesis or alternative. *Entrance requirements:* For master's, Florida Teacher Certification Examination/General Knowledge Test or GRE General Test. Additional exam requirements/recommendations for international students: Required—TOEFL. *Application deadline:* For spring admission, 12/1 for domestic students; for summer admission, 4/15 for domestic students. Application fee: $30. Electronic applications accepted. *Expenses:* Tuition, state resident: part-time $288.16 per credit hour. Tuition, nonresident: part-time $1073.31 per credit hour. Tuition and fees vary according to program. *Financial support:* Fellowships, research assistantships, teaching assistantships, career-related internships or fieldwork, Federal Work-Study, institutionally sponsored loans, tuition waivers (partial), and unspecified assistantships available. Financial award application deadline: 3/1; financial award applicants required to submit FAFSA. *Unit head:* Dr. Michael Hynes, Director, 407-823-2005, E-mail: mychael.hynes@ucf.edu. *Application contact:* Associate Director, Graduate Admissions, 407-823-2766, Fax: 407-823-6442, E-mail: gradadmissions@ucf.edu.
Website: http://www.graduatecatalog.ucf.edu/programs/program.aspx?id=9727&program=Teacher%20Education%20MAT

University of Dayton, Department of Teacher Education, Dayton, OH 45469. Offers adolescence to young adult education (MS Ed); early childhood leadership and advocacy (MS Ed); interdisciplinary education (MS Ed), including visual arts; interdisciplinary education studies (MS Ed); leadership in educational systems (MS Ed); literacy (MS Ed); mathematics education (MS Ed); middle childhood education (MS Ed); multi-age education (MS Ed), including world languages; music education (MS Ed); teacher as leader (MS Ed); teacher education (MS Ed); technology-enhanced learning (MS Ed); trans-disciplinary early childhood education (MS Ed). *Program availability:* Part-time, 100% online. *Faculty:* 23 full-time (20 women), 41 part-time/adjunct (36 women). *Students:* 45 full-time (38 women), 68 part-time (57 women); includes 7 minority (3 Black or African American, non-Hispanic/Latino; 1 Hispanic/Latino; 3 Two or more races, non-Hispanic/Latino), 6 international. Average age 31. 106 applicants, 28% accepted. In 2017, 70 master's awarded. *Degree requirements:* For master's, variable foreign language requirement, thesis or alternative, internship (for teaching licensure or endorsement). *Entrance requirements:* For master's, GRE (minimum score of 149 verbal, 4 on writing) or MAT (minimum score of 396) if undergraduate GPA was under 2.75, minimum GPA of 2.75, 3 letters of recommendation, personal statement or resume, official transcripts. Additional exam requirements/recommendations for international students: Required—TOEFL (minimum score 550 paper-based; 80 iBT); Recommended—IELTS (minimum score 6.5). *Application deadline:* Applications are processed on a rolling basis. Application fee: $0 ($50 for international students). Electronic applications accepted. *Expenses:* Contact institution. *Financial support:* In 2017–18, 5 research assistantships with partial tuition reimbursements (averaging $9,640 per year) were awarded; teaching assistantships, career-related internships or fieldwork, institutionally sponsored loans, and unspecified assistantships also available. Financial award application deadline: 3/1; financial award applicants required to submit FAFSA. *Faculty research:* Social emotional learning, culturally responsive teaching, urban teaching, literacy, instructional strategies, pre-service teacher preparation. *Unit head:* Dr. Connie L. Bowman, Chair, 937-229-3348, E-mail: cbowman1@udayton.edu. *Application contact:* Gina Seiter, Coordinator of Graduate Programs and Licensing, 937-229-3103, E-mail: gseiter1@udayton.edu.
Website: https://www.udayton.edu/education/departments_and_programs/edt

University of Kentucky, Graduate School, College of Education, Program in Curriculum and Instruction, Lexington, KY 40506-0032. Offers curriculum and instruction (Ed D, PhD); elementary education (MA Ed); instructional system design (MS Ed); literacy (MA Ed); middle school education (MA Ed, MS Ed); secondary education (MA Ed, MS Ed). *Accreditation:* NCATE. *Degree requirements:* For master's, comprehensive exam, thesis optional; for doctorate, comprehensive exam, thesis/dissertation. *Entrance requirements:* For master's, GRE General Test, minimum undergraduate GPA of 2.75; for doctorate, GRE General Test, minimum graduate GPA of 3.0. Additional exam requirements/recommendations for international students: Required—TOEFL (minimum score 550 paper-based). Electronic applications accepted. *Faculty research:* Educational reform, multicultural education, classroom instructional practices, performance based assessment, primary school programs.

University of Louisville, Graduate School, College of Education and Human Development, Departments of Early Childhood and Elementary Education, Middle and Secondary Education, and Special Education, Louisville, KY 40292-0001. Offers art education (MAT); autism and applied behavior analysis (Certificate); curriculum and instruction (PhD); early elementary education (MAT); exercise physiology (MS); health and physical education (MAT); health professions education (Certificate); higher education (MA); human resources and organization development (MS); instructional technology (M Ed); interdisciplinary early childhood education (MAT); middle school education (MAT); music education (MAT); secondary education (MAT); special education (MAT); sport administration (MS); teacher leadership (M Ed). *Program availability:* Part-time, evening/weekend. *Students:* 114 full-time (73 women), 173 part-time (114 women); includes 49 minority (19 Black or African American, non-Hispanic/Latino; 5 Asian, non-Hispanic/Latino; 13 Hispanic/Latino; 12 Two or more races, non-Hispanic/Latino), 7 international. Average age 29. 132 applicants, 73% accepted, 57 enrolled. In 2017, 70 master's, 2 doctorates, 2 other advanced degrees awarded. *Application deadline:* For spring admission, 1/1 priority date for international students. Application fee: $65. *Expenses:* Tuition, state resident: full-time $12,246; part-time $681 per credit hour. Tuition, nonresident: full-time $25,486; part-time $1417 per credit hour. *Required fees:* $196. Tuition and fees vary according to course load, program and reciprocity agreements. *Financial support:* Application deadline: 6/1; applicants required to submit FAFSA. *Faculty research:* STEM teaching and learning; content literacy for English language learners; social justice in teacher education; adolescent literacy; mathematics teacher development. *Total annual research expenditures:* $1.7 million. *Unit head:* Dr. Ann E. Larson, Dean, College of Education and Human Development,

502-852-6411, Fax: 502-852-1464, E-mail: ann@louisville.edu. *Application contact:* Betty Hampton, Director of Graduate Student Services, 502-852-5597, Fax: 502-852-1465, E-mail: edadvise@louisville.edu.
Website: http://louisville.edu/delphi

University of Massachusetts Dartmouth, Graduate School, College of Arts and Sciences, School of Education, Department of STEM Education and Teacher Development, North Dartmouth, MA 02747-2300. Offers English as a second language (Postbaccalaureate Certificate); mathematics education (PhD); middle school education (MAT); secondary school education (MAT). *Program availability:* Part-time. *Faculty:* 9 full-time (6 women), 11 part-time/adjunct (7 women). *Students:* 26 full-time (15 women), 102 part-time (60 women); includes 16 minority (2 Black or African American, non-Hispanic/Latino; 2 Asian, non-Hispanic/Latino; 6 Hispanic/Latino; 6 Two or more races, non-Hispanic/Latino), 2 international. Average age 32. 60 applicants, 92% accepted, 51 enrolled. In 2017, 41 master's, 2 doctorates awarded. *Degree requirements:* For doctorate, thesis/dissertation. *Entrance requirements:* For master's, statement of purpose (minimum of 300 words), resume, 2 letters of recommendation, official transcripts; for doctorate, GRE, statement of purpose (minimum of 300 words), resume, official transcripts, 3 letters of recommendation. Additional exam requirements/recommendations for international students: Required—TOEFL (minimum score 533 paper-based; 72 iBT), IELTS (minimum score 6). *Application deadline:* For fall admission, 2/15 priority date for domestic students, 1/15 priority date for international students; for spring admission, 1/15 priority date for domestic students, 12/15 priority date for international students. Application fee: $60. Electronic applications accepted. *Expenses:* Tuition, state resident: full-time $15,449; part-time $643.71 per credit. Tuition, nonresident: full-time $27,880; part-time $1161.67 per credit. *Required fees:* $405; $25.88 per credit. Tuition and fees vary according to course load and reciprocity agreements. *Financial support:* In 2017–18, 2 fellowships (averaging $16,000 per year), 4 research assistantships (averaging $20,656 per year), 2 teaching assistantships (averaging $16,000 per year) were awarded; tuition waivers (full) and unspecified assistantships also available. Support available to part-time students. Financial award application deadline: 3/1; financial award applicants required to submit FAFSA. *Faculty research:* Mindfulness in education, literacies, assessment of teacher knowledge, curriculum tools for supporting mathematics learning. *Total annual research expenditures:* $1.6 million. *Unit head:* Traci Almeida, Coordinator of Graduate Admissions and Licensure, 508-999-8098, Fax: 508-910-8183, E-mail: talmeida@umassd.edu. *Application contact:* Steven Briggs, Director of Marketing and Recruitment for Graduate Studies, 508-999-8604, Fax: 508-999-8183, E-mail: graduate@umassd.edu.
Website: http://www.umassd.edu/cas/schoolofeducation/departments/stemeducationandteacherdevelopment/

University of Missouri–St. Louis, College of Education, Department of Educator Preparation, Innovation and Research, St. Louis, MO 63121. Offers elementary education (M Ed), including early childhood, general, reading; secondary education (M Ed), including curriculum and instruction, general, middle level education, reading, teaching English to speakers of other languages (TESOL); special education (M Ed), including autism and developmental disabilities, early childhood special education. *Program availability:* Part-time, evening/weekend. *Students:* 75 full-time (63 women), 462 part-time (363 women); includes 127 minority (85 Black or African American, non-Hispanic/Latino; 2 American Indian or Alaska Native, non-Hispanic/Latino; 8 Asian, non-Hispanic/Latino; 24 Hispanic/Latino; 8 Two or more races, non-Hispanic/Latino), 1 international. 247 applicants, 92% accepted, 153 enrolled. *Degree requirements:* For master's, comprehensive exam. *Entrance requirements:* Additional exam requirements/recommendations for international students: Recommended—TOEFL (minimum score 550 paper-based; 79 iBT), IELTS (minimum score 6.5). *Application deadline:* For fall admission, 7/1 priority date for domestic and international students; for spring admission, 12/1 priority date for domestic and international students. Application fee: $50 ($40 for international students). Electronic applications accepted. *Expenses:* Tuition, state resident: part-time $476.50 per credit hour. Tuition, nonresident: part-time $1169.70 per credit hour. *Financial support:* Application deadline: 4/1; applicants required to submit FAFSA. *Unit head:* Dr. Gayle Wilkinson, Chair, 314-516-5791. *Application contact:* 314-516-5458, Fax: 314-516-6996, E-mail: gadadm@umsl.edu.
Website: https://coe.umsl.edu/dept/epir.html

The University of North Carolina at Charlotte, Cato College of Education, Department of Middle, Secondary and K-12 Education, Charlotte, NC 28223-0001. Offers middle grades and secondary education (M Ed); teaching English as a second language (M Ed, Graduate Certificate). *Program availability:* Part-time. *Faculty:* 18 full-time (10 women), 5 part-time/adjunct (all women). *Students:* 3 full-time (all women), 93 part-time (85 women); includes 20 minority (18 Black or African American, non-Hispanic/Latino; 1 Asian, non-Hispanic/Latino; 1 Hispanic/Latino), 2 international. Average age 35. 71 applicants, 99% accepted, 61 enrolled. In 2017, 47 master's awarded. *Degree requirements:* For master's, thesis, comprehensive portfolio, or research project. *Entrance requirements:* For master's, GRE or MAT, bachelor's degree from accredited college or university; minimum GPA of 3.0 in undergraduate work; North Carolina Class A teaching license in appropriate middle grades or secondary education field; minimum of two years' teaching experience; written narrative providing statement of purpose for master's degree study; letters of recommendation; for Graduate Certificate, bachelor's degree from accredited institution; minimum undergraduate GPA of 2.5 overall or 3.0 in senior year, or 15 hours taken in the last 5 years; satisfactory recommendations from three persons knowledgeable of applicant's interactions with children or adolescents; statement of purpose. Additional exam requirements/recommendations for international students: Required—TOEFL (minimum score 523 paper-based, 70 iBT) or IELTS (6.5). *Application deadline:* For fall admission, 3/1 priority date for domestic and international students; for spring admission, 10/1 priority date for domestic and international students; for summer admission, 4/1 priority date for domestic and international students. Applications are processed on a rolling basis. Application fee: $75. Electronic applications accepted. *Expenses:* Tuition, state resident: full-time $4337. Tuition, nonresident: full-time $17,771. *Required fees:* $3211. Tuition and fees vary according to course load and program. *Financial support:* In 2017–18, 6 students received support, including 5 research assistantships (averaging $13,800 per year), 1 teaching assistantship (averaging $3,500 per year); career-related internships or fieldwork, institutionally sponsored loans, scholarships/grants, and unspecified assistantships also available. Support available to part-time students. Financial award application deadline: 3/1; financial award applicants required to submit FAFSA. *Total annual research expenditures:* $115,616. *Unit head:* Scott Kissau, Chair, 704-687-8875, E-mail: spkissau@uncc.edu. *Application contact:* Kathy B. Giddings, Director of Graduate Admissions, 704-687-5503, Fax: 704-687-1668, E-mail: gradadm@uncc.edu.
Website: http://mdsk.uncc.edu/

The University of North Carolina at Charlotte, Cato College of Education, Interdisciplinary Education Programs, Charlotte, NC 28223-0001. Offers art education (Graduate Certificate); child and family development: early childhood education (MAT); curriculum and instruction (PhD); elementary education (MAT); foreign language education (MAT); middle grades education (MAT); secondary education (MAT); special education (MAT); teaching (Graduate Certificate); teaching English as a second language (MAT); theatre education (Graduate Certificate). *Program availability:* Part-

time, 100% online, blended/hybrid learning. *Students:* 86 full-time (63 women), 533 part-time (423 women); includes 229 minority (169 Black or African American, non-Hispanic/Latino; 1 American Indian or Alaska Native, non-Hispanic/Latino; 7 Asian, non-Hispanic/Latino; 39 Hispanic/Latino; 13 Two or more races, non-Hispanic/Latino), 13 international. Average age 32. 382 applicants, 91% accepted, 253 enrolled. In 2017, 182 master's, 10 doctorates, 172 other advanced degrees awarded. *Degree requirements:* For master's, thesis or alternative, research project/portfolio. *Entrance requirements:* For master's, GRE or MAT, bachelor's degree, or its U.S. equivalent, from regionally-accredited college or university; minimum overall GPA of 3.0 on all previous work beyond high school; statement of purpose (essay); at least three recommendation forms; for doctorate, GRE or MAT, bachelor's degree (or its U.S. equivalent) from regionally-accredited college or university; minimum overall GPA of 3.5 in master's degree program; for Graduate Certificate, bachelor's degree from regionally-accredited university; minimum GPA of 2.75 on all post-secondary work attempted; transcripts; personal statement outlining why the applicant seeks admission to the program. Additional exam requirements/recommendations for international students: Required—TOEFL (minimum score 523 paper-based, 70 iBT) or IELTS (6.5). *Application deadline:* For fall admission, 3/1 priority date for domestic and international students; for spring admission, 10/1 priority date for domestic and international students; for summer admission, 4/1 priority date for domestic and international students. Applications are processed on a rolling basis. Application fee: $75. Electronic applications accepted. *Expenses:* Tuition, state resident: full-time $4337. Tuition, nonresident: full-time $17,771. *Required fees:* $3211. Tuition and fees vary according to course load and program. *Financial support:* Career-related internships or fieldwork, institutionally sponsored loans, scholarships/grants, and unspecified assistantships available. Support available to part-time students. Financial award application deadline: 3/1; financial award applicants required to submit FAFSA. *Unit head:* Dr. Ellen McIntyre, Dean, 704-687-8722, E-mail: ellen.mcintyre@uncc.edu. *Application contact:* Kathy B. Giddings, Director of Graduate Admissions, 704-687-5503, Fax: 704-687-1668, E-mail: gradadm@uncc.edu.
Website: http://education.uncc.edu/academic-programs

The University of North Carolina at Greensboro, Graduate School, School of Education, Department of Teacher Education and Higher Education, Greensboro, NC 27412-5001. Offers college teaching and adult learning (Certificate); curriculum and instruction (M Ed), including chemistry education, elementary education, English as a second language, French education, instructional technology, mathematics education, middle grades education, reading education, science education, social studies education, Spanish education; curriculum and teaching (PhD), including higher education, teacher education and development; English as a second language (Certificate); higher education (M Ed); supervision (M Ed). *Accreditation:* NCATE. *Program availability:* Part-time. *Degree requirements:* For doctorate, thesis/dissertation. *Entrance requirements:* For master's and doctorate, GRE General Test. Additional exam requirements/recommendations for international students: Required—TOEFL. Electronic applications accepted. *Faculty research:* Community college literacy program, middle school mathematics/computer mathematics.

The University of North Carolina Wilmington, Watson College of Education, Department of Early Childhood, Elementary, Middle, Literacy and Special Education, Wilmington, NC 28403-3297. Offers educational leadership, policy, and advocacy (M Ed); elementary education (M Ed, MAT); language and literacy (M Ed); middle grades education (MAT). *Accreditation:* NCATE. *Program availability:* Part-time, blended/hybrid learning. *Faculty:* 22 full-time (15 women), 2 part-time/adjunct (both women). *Students:* 82 full-time (70 women), 91 part-time (84 women); includes 51 minority (33 Black or African American, non-Hispanic/Latino; 3 American Indian or Alaska Native, non-Hispanic/Latino; 1 Asian, non-Hispanic/Latino; 8 Hispanic/Latino; 6 Two or more races, non-Hispanic/Latino). Average age 32. 68 applicants, 82% accepted, 45 enrolled. In 2017, 83 master's awarded. *Degree requirements:* For master's, thesis or alternative, exit portfolio, oral presentation, internship, research project (depending on specialization). *Entrance requirements:* For master's, 3 letters of recommendations, NC Class A teacher license in related field, education statement of interest essay. Additional exam requirements/recommendations for international students: Required—TOEFL (minimum score 550 paper-based; 79 iBT), IELTS (minimum score 6.5). *Application deadline:* For fall admission, 5/15 for domestic students; for spring admission, 10/15 for domestic students; for summer admission, 3/15 for domestic students. Applications are processed on a rolling basis. Application fee: $75. Electronic applications accepted. *Expenses:* Tuition, state resident: full-time $4626; part-time $226.76 per credit hour. Tuition, nonresident: full-time $17,834; part-time $874.22 per credit hour. *Required fees:* $2124. Tuition and fees vary according to program. *Financial support:* Scholarships/grants and unspecified assistantships available. Financial award application deadline: 1/1; financial award applicants required to submit FAFSA. *Unit head:* Dr. Kathy Fox, Chair, 910-962-3240, Fax: 910-962-3988, E-mail: foxk@uncw.edu. *Application contact:* Dr. Elizabeth Crawford, Graduate Program Coordinator, 910-962-2916, Fax: 910-962-3988, E-mail: crawforde@uncw.edu.
Website: http://www.uncw.edu/ed/eemls/index.html

University of Northern Iowa, Graduate College, College of Humanities, Arts and Sciences, Department of Mathematics, MA Program in Mathematics for the Middle Grades, Cedar Falls, IA 50614. Offers MA.

University of North Georgia, Master of Arts in Teaching Program, Dahlonega, GA 30597. Offers physical education (MAT); secondary education - English (MAT); secondary education - history (MAT); secondary education - mathematics (MAT); secondary education - middle grades (MAT). *Students:* 27 part-time (20 women). Average age 29. 12 applicants, 75% accepted, 7 enrolled. In 2017, 15 master's awarded. *Degree requirements:* For master's, internship, capstone. *Entrance requirements:* For master's, GRE or MAT, GACE I and II, GA pre-service application, lawful presence verification, official transcripts, GA Educator Ethics Program entry assessment. Additional exam requirements/recommendations for international students: Required—TOEFL (minimum score 550 paper-based; 79 iBT), IELTS (minimum score 6.5). *Application deadline:* For summer admission, 2/1 for domestic students. Application fee: $40. Electronic applications accepted. *Expenses:* Contact institution. *Financial support:* Application deadline: 3/17; applicants required to submit FAFSA. *Unit head:* Dr. Susan Brandenburg-Ayres, Dean, 706-864-1998, E-mail: susan.ayres@ung.edu. *Application contact:* Melinda Maxwell, Director of Graduate Admissions, 706-867-2077, E-mail: melinda.maxwell@ung.edu.
Website: https://ung.edu/teacher-education/graduate/master-of-arts-teaching.php

University of North Georgia, Program in Middle Grades Math and Science, Dahlonega, GA 30597. Offers M Ed. *Program availability:* Part-time, evening/weekend, online only, 100% online. *Students:* 6 full-time (all women), 12 part-time (8 women); includes 1 minority (Black or African American, non-Hispanic/Latino). Average age 29. 4 applicants, 75% accepted, 3 enrolled. In 2017, 8 master's awarded. *Degree requirements:* For master's, teaching practicum. *Entrance requirements:* For master's, baccalaureate degree from regionally-accredited, four-year institution with minimum cumulative GPA of 2.75; employment as teacher in middle grades classroom working with students at least 20 hours per week; clear/renewable teaching certificate in middle grades math or science in the state of Georgia or equivalent. Additional exam

Middle School Education

requirements/recommendations for international students: Required—TOEFL (minimum score 550 paper-based; 79 iBT), IELTS (minimum score 6.5). *Application deadline:* For fall admission, 7/24 for domestic students; for spring admission, 12/12 for domestic students; for summer admission, 4/26 for domestic students. Application fee: $40. Electronic applications accepted. *Expenses:* Contact institution. *Financial support:* Application deadline: 3/17; applicants required to submit FAFSA. *Unit head:* Dr. Susan Brandenburg-Ayres, Dean, 706-864-1998, E-mail: susan.ayres@ung.edu. *Application contact:* Melinda Maxwell, Director of Graduate Studies, 706-867-2077, E-mail: melinda.maxwell@ung.edu.
Website: https://ung.edu/teacher-education/graduate/master-education-middle-grades.php

University of Phoenix–Online Campus, College of Education, Phoenix, AZ 85034-7209. Offers administration and supervision (MAEd, Certificate); adult education and training (MAEd); curriculum and instruction (MAEd), including computer education, curriculum and instruction, English as a second language, language arts, mathematics, reading; early childhood education (MAEd); educational studies (MAEd); elementary teacher education (MAEd), including early childhood, elementary teacher education, high school middle level, middle level; principal licensure (Certificate); secondary teacher education (MAEd); special education (MAEd, Certificate); teacher education (MAEd), including middle level generalist; teacher education middle level mathematics (MAEd), including middle level mathematics; teacher education middle level science (MAEd), including middle level science; teacher education secondary mathematics (MAEd); teacher education secondary science (MAEd); teacher leadership (MAEd); teachers of English learners (Certificate); transition to teaching (Certificate), including elementary education, secondary education. *Program availability:* Evening/weekend, online learning. *Entrance requirements:* Additional exam requirements/recommendations for international students: Required—TOEFL, TOEIC (Test of English as an International Communication), Berlitz Online English Proficiency Exam, PTE, or IELTS. Electronic applications accepted. *Expenses:* Contact institution.

University of South Florida, St. Petersburg, College of Education, St. Petersburg, FL 33701. Offers educational leadership development (M Ed); elementary education (MA), including math/science; English education (MA); middle grades STEM education (MS); reading education (MA). *Program availability:* Part-time. *Degree requirements:* For master's, comprehensive exam, practicum, internship, comprehensive portfolio. *Entrance requirements:* For master's, State of Florida General Knowledge Test (GKT), Florida Teaching Certificate (for non-initial certification programs), letters of recommendation. Additional exam requirements/recommendations for international students: Required—TOEFL (minimum score 550 paper-based; 79 iBT); Recommended—IELTS. Electronic applications accepted.

University of the Cumberlands, Graduate Programs in Education, Williamsburg, KY 40769-1372. Offers all grades (P-12) (M Ed); business and marketing (MA Ed, MAT); counselor education and supervision (Ed D); director of pupil personnel (Certificate); director of special education (Certificate); educational administration and supervision (Ed S); educational leadership (Ed D); elementary education (MA Ed, MAT); instructional leadership - principalship (MA Ed); instructional leadership - school principal (Certificate); middle school education (MA Ed, MAT); reading and writing (MA Ed); school counseling (MA Ed); school superintendent (Certificate); secondary education (MA Ed, MAT); special education (MAT); supervisor of instruction (Certificate); teacher leader (MA Ed). *Program availability:* Part-time, evening/weekend, online learning. *Degree requirements:* For master's, comprehensive exam. Electronic applications accepted.

University of the District of Columbia, College of Arts and Sciences, Program in Teaching, Washington, DC 20008-1175. Offers elementary education (MAT); middle school mathematics (MAT); secondary English language arts (MAT); secondary social studies (MAT).

The University of Toledo, College of Graduate Studies, Judith Herb College of Education, Department of Curriculum and Instruction, Toledo, OH 43606-3390. Offers art education (ME); career and technical education (ME, Ed S); curriculum and instruction (ME, PhD, Ed S); early childhood education (Ed S); education and anthropology (MAE); education and biology (MES); education and chemistry (MES); education and classics (MAE); education and economics (MAE); education and English (MAE); education and French (MAE); education and geology (MES); education and German (MAE); education and history (MAE); education and mathematics (MAE, MES); education and physics (MES); education and political science (MAE); education and sociology (MAE); education and Spanish (MAE); educational media (PhD); educational technology (ME); educational technology: virtual educator (Certificate); elementary education (PhD); English as a second language (MAE); gifted and talented education (PhD); middle childhood education (ME); secondary education (ME, PhD); special education (PhD). *Accreditation:* NCATE. *Program availability:* Part-time, evening/weekend. *Degree requirements:* For master's, comprehensive exam, thesis or alternative; for doctorate, comprehensive exam, thesis/dissertation; for other advanced degree, thesis optional. *Entrance requirements:* For master's, doctorate, and other advanced degree, minimum cumulative GPA of 2.7 for all previous academic work, letters of recommendation. Additional exam requirements/recommendations for international students: Required—TOEFL (minimum score 550 paper-based; 80 iBT). Electronic applications accepted.

University of Vermont, Graduate College, College of Education and Social Services, Program in Middle Level Education, Burlington, VT 05405. Offers curriculum and instruction (MAT), including middle level education. *Program availability:* Part-time. *Entrance requirements:* For master's, resume, writing sample. Additional exam requirements/recommendations for international students: Required—TOEFL (minimum iBT score of 90) or IELTS (6.5). *Application deadline:* Applications are processed on a rolling basis. Application fee: $65. Electronic applications accepted. *Expenses:* Tuition, state resident: full-time $11,628; part-time $646 per credit. Tuition, nonresident: full-time $29,340; part-time $1630 per credit. *Required fees:* $1994; $10 per credit. Tuition and fees vary according to course load and program. *Financial support:* Career-related internships or fieldwork and scholarships/grants available. *Unit head:* Ken Reissig, Coordinator, 802-656-1411, E-mail: kenneth.reissig@uvm.edu.
Website: https://www.uvm.edu/cess/doe/mat_middlelevel

University of Vermont, Graduate College, College of Education and Social Services, Program in Special Education, Grades K-12, Burlington, VT 05405. Offers M Ed. *Accreditation:* NCATE. *Degree requirements:* For master's, thesis or alternative. *Entrance requirements:* For master's, license (or eligible for licensure). Additional exam requirements/recommendations for international students: Required—TOEFL (minimum score 550 paper-based, 90 iBT) or IELTS (6.5). *Application deadline:* For fall admission, 2/15 for domestic and international students; for spring admission, 11/1 for domestic and international students. Application fee: $65. Electronic applications accepted. *Expenses:* Tuition, state resident: full-time $11,628; part-time $646 per credit. Tuition, nonresident: full-time $29,340; part-time $1630 per credit. *Required fees:* $1994; $10 per credit. Tuition and fees vary according to course load and program. *Financial support:* In 2017–18, 4 students received support. Research assistantships, teaching assistantships, career-related internships or fieldwork, and scholarships/grants available. Financial award application deadline: 3/1. *Unit head:* Dr. Michael Giangreco,

Program Coordinator, 802-656-1144, E-mail: michael.giangreco@uvm.edu. *Application contact:* Roman Vogel, Graduate Program Support, 802-656-2936, E-mail: special.education@uvm.edu.
Website: https://www.uvm.edu/cess/doe/masters_education_special_education_k_12th_grade

University of Washington, Bothell, Program in Education, Bothell, WA 98011. Offers education (M Ed); leadership development for educators (M Ed); secondary/middle level endorsement (M Ed). *Program availability:* Part-time, evening/weekend. *Degree requirements:* For master's, thesis. *Entrance requirements:* Additional exam requirements/recommendations for international students: Required—TOEFL. Electronic applications accepted. *Faculty research:* Multicultural education in citizenship education, intercultural education, knowledge and practice in the principalship, educational public policy, national board certification for teachers, teacher learning in literacy, technology and its impact on teaching and learning of mathematics, reading assessments, professional development in literacy education and mobility, digital media, education and class.

University of West Florida, College of Education and Professional Studies, Department of Teacher Education and Educational Leadership, Program in Curriculum and Instruction, Pensacola, FL 32514-5750. Offers elementary education (M Ed); middle level education (M Ed); secondary education (M Ed). *Program availability:* Part-time, evening/weekend. *Entrance requirements:* For master's, GRE (minimum score 450 verbal) or MAT (minimum score 396) if bachelor's GPA less than 3.0, state teaching certification; letter of intent; two professional references. Additional exam requirements/recommendations for international students: Required—TOEFL (minimum score 550 paper-based).

University of Wisconsin–Milwaukee, Graduate School, School of Education, Department of Curriculum and Instruction, Milwaukee, WI 53201-0413. Offers curriculum and instruction (MS), including cross-curricular focus, early childhood education, English education, mathematics education, middle childhood/early adolescence education, reading education, science education, urban social studies education. *Program availability:* Part-time. *Students:* 17 full-time (13 women), 45 part-time (39 women); includes 13 minority (2 Black or African American, non-Hispanic/Latino; 3 Asian, non-Hispanic/Latino; 1 Hispanic/Latino; 7 Two or more races, non-Hispanic/Latino). Average age 33. 32 applicants, 66% accepted, 16 enrolled. In 2017, 26 master's awarded. *Entrance requirements:* Additional exam requirements/recommendations for international students: Required—TOEFL (minimum score 550 paper-based; 79 iBT), IELTS (minimum score 6.5). *Application deadline:* For fall admission, 1/1 priority date for domestic students; for spring admission, 9/1 for domestic students. Application fee: $56 ($96 for international students). Electronic applications accepted. *Financial support:* Fellowships, research assistantships, teaching assistantships, career-related internships or fieldwork, health care benefits, unspecified assistantships, and project assistantships available. Support available to part-time students. Financial award application deadline: 4/15; financial award applicants required to submit FAFSA. *Application contact:* General Information Contact, 414-229-4721, E-mail: soeinfo@uwm.edu.
Website: http://uwm.edu/education/academics/curriculum-instruction-department/

Ursuline College, School of Graduate and Professional Studies, Master Apprenticeship Program, Pepper Pike, OH 44124-4398. Offers adolescent to young adult education (MA); early childhood education (MA); middle childhood education (MA); special education (MA). *Accreditation:* NCATE. *Faculty:* 1 full-time (0 women), 6 part-time/adjunct (all women). *Students:* 19 full-time (16 women); includes 4 minority (all Black or African American, non-Hispanic/Latino). Average age 32. In 2017, 18 master's awarded. *Degree requirements:* For master's, comprehensive exam. *Entrance requirements:* For master's, minimum undergraduate GPA of 3.0. Additional exam requirements/recommendations for international students: Required—TOEFL (minimum score 500 paper-based). *Application deadline:* For fall admission, 8/1 priority date for domestic students. Applications are processed on a rolling basis. Application fee: $25. Electronic applications accepted. *Expenses:* Contact institution. *Financial support:* Application deadline: 3/1; applicants required to submit FAFSA. *Faculty research:* Longevity of female superintendents, expectations of student teacher mentors, qualities of successful student teachers, literacy preparation of K-12 student teachers. *Unit head:* Dr. Mary Jo Cherry, Director, 440-646-8147, Fax: 440-646-8328, E-mail: mcherry@ursuline.edu. *Application contact:* Melanie Steele, Director of Graduate Admission, 440-646-8146, Fax: 440-684-6138, E-mail: graduateadmissions@ursuline.edu.
Website: http://www.ursuline.edu/Academics/Graduate_Professional/Masters_Programs/MAP/index.html

Wagner College, Division of Graduate Studies, Education Department, Program in Secondary Education/Students with Disabilities, Staten Island, NY 10301-4495. Offers secondary education 7-12 (MS Ed), including language arts, languages other than English, mathematics and technology, science and technology, social studies. *Program availability:* Evening/weekend. *Faculty:* 2 full-time (1 woman), 7 part-time/adjunct (3 women). *Students:* 17 full-time (14 women), 6 part-time (4 women); includes 2 minority (1 Black or African American, non-Hispanic/Latino; 1 Asian, non-Hispanic/Latino). Average age 24. 15 applicants, 80% accepted, 11 enrolled. In 2017, 8 master's awarded. *Degree requirements:* For master's, thesis (for some programs), completion of state certification exams before student teaching. *Entrance requirements:* For master's, GRE, minimum GPA of 3.0, interview, recommendations. Additional exam requirements/recommendations for international students: Required—TOEFL (minimum score 550 paper-based; 79 iBT), IELTS (minimum score 6.5). *Application deadline:* For fall admission, 12/1 priority date for domestic and international students. Application fee: $60. Electronic applications accepted. *Expenses:* Contact institution. *Financial support:* Unspecified assistantships and alumni fellowship available. Financial award application deadline: 2/15; financial award applicants required to submit FAFSA. *Unit head:* Dr. Jason Fitzgerald, Department Chair, 718-420-4129, Fax: 718-390-3456, E-mail: jason.fitzgerald@wagner.edu. *Application contact:* Patricia Clancy, Assistant Director of Enrollment, 718-420-4464, Fax: 718-390-3105, E-mail: patricia.clancy@wagner.edu.
Website: http://www.wagner.edu/education

Webster University, School of Education, Department of Multidisciplinary Studies, St. Louis, MO 63119-3194. Offers applied educational psychology (MA, Ed S); communication arts (MA); early childhood education (MA, MAT); education and innovation (MA); educational technology (MET); elementary education (MAT); mathematics for educators (MA); middle school education (MAT); multidisciplinary studies (MAT); multimodal literacy for global impact (MA); reading (MA); secondary school education (MAT); special education (MA, MAT); teaching English as a second language (MA); transformative learning in the global community (Ed S). *Program availability:* Part-time. *Entrance requirements:* For master's, minimum GPA of 2.5. Additional exam requirements/recommendations for international students: Required—TOEFL.

Western Kentucky University, Graduate Studies, College of Education and Behavioral Sciences, School of Teacher Education, Bowling Green, KY 42101. Offers elementary education (MAE, Ed S); exceptional education: learning and behavioral disorders (MAE); exceptional education: moderate and severe disabilities (MAE); instructional design (MS); interdisciplinary early childhood education (MAE); library media education

(MS); literacy education (MAE); middle grades education (MAE); secondary education (MAE, Ed S). *Program availability:* Part-time, evening/weekend, online learning. *Degree requirements:* For master's, comprehensive exam. *Entrance requirements:* For master's, GRE General Test. Additional exam requirements/recommendations for international students: Required—TOEFL (minimum score 555 paper-based; 79 iBT). *Faculty research:* Teacher preparation in moderate/severe disabilities.

Wichita State University, Graduate School, College of Education, Department of Curriculum and Instruction, Wichita, KS 67260. Offers learning and instructional design (M Ed); special education (M Ed), including early childhood (M Ed, MAT), gifted, high incidence, low incidence; teaching (MAT), including early childhood (M Ed, MAT), middle level/secondary, transition to teaching. *Accreditation:* NCATE. *Program availability:* Part-time, evening/weekend, 100% online, blended/hybrid learning. *Entrance requirements:* For master's, MAT, minimum GPA of 2.75. *Unit head:* Dr. Kimberly McDowell, Department Head, 316-978-3322, E-mail: kim.mcdowell@wichita.edu. *Application contact:* Jordan Oleson, Admission Coordinator, 316-978-3095, Fax: 316-978-3253, E-mail: jordan.oleson@wichita.edu.

Widener University, School of Human Service Professions, Center for Education, Chester, PA 19013-5792. Offers adult education (M Ed); counseling in higher education (M Ed); counselor education (M Ed); early childhood education (M Ed); educational foundations (M Ed); educational leadership (M Ed); educational psychology (M Ed); elementary education (M Ed); English and language arts (M Ed); health education (M Ed); higher education leadership (Ed D); home and school visitor (M Ed); human sexuality (M Ed, PhD); mathematics education (M Ed); middle school education (M Ed); principalship (M Ed); reading and language arts (Ed D); reading education (M Ed); school administration (Ed D); science education (M Ed); social studies education (M Ed); special education (M Ed); technology education (M Ed). *Accreditation:* NCATE. *Program availability:* Part-time, evening/weekend. *Faculty:* 34 full-time (22 women), 37 part-time/adjunct (14 women). *Students:* 131 full-time (112 women), 244 part-time (179 women); includes 94 minority (58 Black or African American, non-Hispanic/Latino; 1 American Indian or Alaska Native, non-Hispanic/Latino; 1 Asian, non-Hispanic/Latino; 22 Hispanic/Latino; 12 Two or more races, non-Hispanic/Latino), 12 international. Average age 37. 140 applicants, 38% accepted, 26 enrolled. In 2017, 45 master's, 21 doctorates awarded. Terminal master's awarded for partial completion of doctoral program. *Degree requirements:* For doctorate, thesis/dissertation. *Entrance requirements:* For master's, minimum GPA of 2.5; for doctorate, GRE or MAT, minimum GPA of 2.0 (undergraduate), 3.5 (graduate). *Application deadline:* Applications are processed on a rolling basis. Application fee: $25 ($300 for international students). Electronic applications accepted. *Expenses:* Contact institution. *Financial support:* Career-related internships or fieldwork, tuition waivers (full and partial), and unspecified assistantships available. Support available to part-time students. Financial award application deadline: 5/1. *Faculty research:* Reading and cognition, adult education, technology education, educational leadership, special education. *Unit head:* Dr. Shawn Fitzgerald, Dean, 610-499-4294, Fax: 610-499-4623, E-mail: smfitzgerald@widener.edu. *Application contact:* Megan Kuft, Director of Graduate Admissions, 610-499-4124, E-mail: gradprograms@widener.edu.
Website: http://www.widener.edu/academics/schools/eics

Wilkes University, College of Graduate and Professional Studies, School of Education, Wilkes-Barre, PA 18766-0002. Offers educational development and strategies (MS Ed); educational leadership (MS Ed, Ed D); effective teaching (MS Ed); instructional media (MS Ed); instructional technology (MS Ed); international school leadership (MS Ed); international teaching and learning (MS Ed); literacy specialist (MS Ed); middle level education (MS Ed); online teaching (MS Ed); school business leadership (MS Ed); special education (MS Ed); teaching English to speakers of other languages (MS Ed). *Program availability:* Part-time, evening/weekend, 100% online, blended/hybrid learning. *Students:* 76 full-time (57 women), 1,586 part-time (1,204 women); includes 82 minority (10 Black or African American, non-Hispanic/Latino; 12 Asian, non-Hispanic/Latino; 41 Hispanic/Latino; 1 Native Hawaiian or other Pacific Islander, non-Hispanic/Latino; 18 Two or more races, non-Hispanic/Latino). Average age 34. In 2017, 619 master's, 23 doctorates awarded. *Entrance requirements:* Additional exam requirements/recommendations for international students: Required—TOEFL (minimum score 550 paper-based; 79 iBT). *Application deadline:* Applications are processed on a rolling basis. Application fee: $45 ($65 for international students). Electronic applications accepted. *Expenses:* Contact institution. *Financial support:* Unspecified assistantships available. Financial award application deadline: 3/1; financial award applicants required to submit FAFSA. *Unit head:* Dr. Rhonda Rabbitt, Dean, 570-408-4680, Fax: 570-408-7872, E-mail: rhonda.rabbitt@wilkes.edu. *Application contact:* Stephanie Wasmanski, Associate Director of Graduate Admissions, 570-408-5535, Fax: 570-408-7846, E-mail: stephanie.wasmanski@wilkes.edu.
Website: http://www.wilkes.edu/academics/graduate-programs/masters-programs/graduate-education/index.aspx

William Paterson University of New Jersey, College of Education, Wayne, NJ 07470-8420. Offers curriculum and learning (M Ed); early childhood education (Certificate); educational leadership (M Ed); educational media specialist (Certificate); elementary education (MAT, Certificate); elementary education subject area (Certificate); higher education administration (MA); learning disabilities consultant (Certificate); literacy (M Ed); middle level education (M Ed); middle school education subject area (Certificate); professional counseling (M Ed); reading specialist (Certificate); school library media specialist (Certificate); school principal (Certificate); school supervisor

(Certificate); secondary education (MAT); special education (M Ed); teacher of students with disabilities (Certificate). *Accreditation:* NCATE. *Program availability:* Part-time, evening/weekend. *Faculty:* 37 full-time (25 women), 21 part-time/adjunct (16 women). *Students:* 73 full-time (54 women), 480 part-time (409 women); includes 153 minority (48 Black or African American, non-Hispanic/Latino; 13 Asian, non-Hispanic/Latino; 81 Hispanic/Latino; 11 Two or more races, non-Hispanic/Latino), 1 international. Average age 35. 347 applicants, 87% accepted, 226 enrolled. In 2017, 136 master's awarded. *Degree requirements:* For master's, comprehensive exam, thesis (for some programs), exit interview (for some programs); practicum/internship; minimum GPA of 3.0 (for some programs); exit portfolio (for some programs). *Entrance requirements:* For master's, GRE/MAT, minimum GPA of 2.75; teaching certificate; essay; interview; 2 letters of recommendation; personal statement. Additional exam requirements/recommendations for international students: Required—TOEFL (minimum score 550 paper-based; 79 iBT), IELTS (minimum score 6). *Application deadline:* For fall admission, 6/1 for domestic students, 3/1 for international students; for spring admission, 11/1 for domestic students, 10/1 for international students. Applications are processed on a rolling basis. Application fee: $50. Electronic applications accepted. *Expenses:* Tuition, state resident: full-time $13,920; part-time $6264 per year. Tuition, nonresident: full-time $21,700; part-time $9765 per year. *Required fees:* $80; $36 per year. Tuition and fees vary according to course load, degree level and program. *Financial support:* In 2017–18, 8,416 students received support. Career-related internships or fieldwork, Federal Work-Study, scholarships/grants, and unspecified assistantships available. Support available to part-time students. Financial award application deadline: 3/15; financial award applicants required to submit FAFSA. *Faculty research:* Code switching and creative writing, language instruction, teacher evaluation, preschools, history of educational theories. *Total annual research expenditures:* $311,226. *Unit head:* Dr. Dorothy Feola, Dean, 973-720-2138, Fax: 973-720-3647, E-mail: feolad@wpunj.edu. *Application contact:* Liana Fornarotto, Director of Education Enrollment and Certification, 973-720-2206, Fax: 973-720-2989, E-mail: fornarottol@wpunj.edu.
Website: http://www.wpunj.edu/coe

Winston-Salem State University, MAT Program, Winston-Salem, NC 27110-0003. Offers middle grades education (MAT); special education (MAT). *Accreditation:* NCATE. *Program availability:* Part-time, evening/weekend, online learning. *Entrance requirements:* For master's, GRE, MAT, NC teacher licensure. Electronic applications accepted. *Faculty research:* Action research on issues in elementary classroom.

Worcester State University, Graduate School, Department of Education, Program in Middle School Education, Worcester, MA 01602-2597. Offers M Ed, Postbaccalaureate Certificate. *Program availability:* Part-time. *Students:* 1 (woman) full-time, 38 part-time (25 women); includes 2 minority (1 American Indian or Alaska Native, non-Hispanic/Latino; 1 Hispanic/Latino). Average age 35. 28 applicants, 86% accepted, 11 enrolled. In 2017, 4 master's awarded. *Degree requirements:* For master's, comprehensive exam (for some programs), thesis optional, portfolio. *Entrance requirements:* For master's, GRE General Test or MAT, initial license in middle school education from Commonwealth of Massachusetts; evidence of undergraduate or graduate course in adolescent/developmental psychology with minimum B grade or CLEP exam in human growth and development (minimum score of 50); for Postbaccalaureate Certificate, MTEL (content area, Communication and Literacy Skills). Additional exam requirements/recommendations for international students: Required—TOEFL (minimum score 550 paper-based; 79 iBT). *Application deadline:* For fall admission, 6/15 for domestic and international students; for spring admission, 11/1 for domestic and international students; for summer admission, 4/1 for domestic and international students. Applications are processed on a rolling basis. Application fee: $50. Electronic applications accepted. *Expenses:* Tuition, state resident: full-time $3042; part-time $169 per credit hour. Tuition, nonresident: full-time $3042; part-time $169 per credit hour. *Required fees:* $2754; $153 per credit hour. *Financial support:* Career-related internships or fieldwork, scholarships/grants, and unspecified assistantships available. Financial award application deadline: 3/1; financial award applicants required to submit FAFSA. *Unit head:* Dr. Sara Young, Program Coordinator, 508-929-8246, E-mail: syoung3@worcester.edu. *Application contact:* Sara Grady, Associate Dean for Graduate Studies and Professional Development, 508-929-8130, E-mail: sara.grady@worcester.edu.

Youngstown State University, Graduate School, Beeghly College of Education, Department of Teacher Education, Program in Early Childhood Education, Youngstown, OH 44555-0001. Offers MS Ed. *Accreditation:* NCATE. *Program availability:* Part-time, evening/weekend. *Degree requirements:* For master's, comprehensive exam. *Entrance requirements:* For master's, GRE, MAT, or teaching certificate; minimum GPA of 2.7. Additional exam requirements/recommendations for international students: Required—TOEFL.

Youngstown State University, Graduate School, Beeghly College of Education, Department of Teacher Education, Program in Middle Childhood Education, Youngstown, OH 44555-0001. Offers MS Ed. *Accreditation:* NCATE. *Program availability:* Part-time, evening/weekend, thesis optional. *Degree requirements:* For master's, comprehensive exam, thesis optional. *Entrance requirements:* For master's, GRE, MAT, or teaching certificate; minimum GPA of 2.7. Additional exam requirements/recommendations for international students: Required—TOEFL. *Faculty research:* Critical reflectivity, gender issues in classroom instruction, collaborative research and analysis, literacy methodology.

Secondary Education

Acacia University, American Graduate School of Education, Tempe, AZ 85284. Offers educational administration (M Ed); elementary education (MA); English as a second language (M Ed); secondary education (MA); special education (M Ed).

Adelphi University, Ruth S. Ammon School of Education, Program in Adolescent Education, Garden City, NY 11530-0701. Offers MA. *Program availability:* Part-time, evening/weekend. *Students:* 47 full-time (35 women), 10 part-time (4 women); includes 15 minority (6 Black or African American, non-Hispanic/Latino; 1 American Indian or Alaska Native, non-Hispanic/Latino; 1 Asian, non-Hispanic/Latino; 5 Hispanic/Latino; 2 Two or more races, non-Hispanic/Latino). Average age 24. 43 applicants, 72% accepted, 14 enrolled. In 2017, 44 master's awarded. *Entrance requirements:* For master's, 2 letters of recommendation, resume. Additional exam requirements/recommendations for international students: Required—TOEFL (minimum score 550 paper-based; 80 iBT), IELTS (minimum score 6.5). *Application deadline:* For fall admission, 4/1 for international students; for spring admission, 11/1 for international students. Applications are processed on a rolling basis. Application fee: $50. Electronic

applications accepted. *Expenses:* Contact institution. *Financial support:* Research assistantships with partial tuition reimbursements, teaching assistantships, career-related internships or fieldwork, institutionally sponsored loans, scholarships/grants, traineeships, and unspecified assistantships available. Support available to part-time students. Financial award application deadline: 2/15; financial award applicants required to submit FAFSA. *Faculty research:* Methods to enhance the development of teaching dispositions, ethical and moral issues in education. *Unit head:* Dr. Robert Linne, Director, 516-877-4411, E-mail: linne@adelphi.edu. *Application contact:* Christine Murphy, Director of Admissions, 516-877-3050, Fax: 516-877-3039, E-mail: graduateadmissions@adelphi.edu.

Alabama Agricultural and Mechanical University, School of Graduate Studies, College of Education, Humanities, and Behavioral Sciences, Department of Educational Leadership and Secondary Education, Huntsville, AL 35811. Offers biology (M Ed); business/marketing education (M Ed, Ed S); chemistry (M Ed); collaborative teacher secondary education (M Ed, Ed S); education (M Ed, Ed S); English language arts

Secondary Education

(M Ed); family/consumer science education (M Ed, Ed S); general science (M Ed); general social science (M Ed); mathematics (M Ed, Ed S); physics (M Ed, Ed S); technology education (M Ed). *Accreditation:* NCATE. *Program availability:* Evening/weekend. *Degree requirements:* For master's, comprehensive exam; for Ed S, thesis. *Entrance requirements:* For master's, GRE General Test. Additional exam requirements/recommendations for international students: Required—TOEFL (minimum score 500 paper-based; 61 iBT). Electronic applications accepted. *Faculty research:* World peace through education, computer-assisted instruction.

Alabama State University, College of Education, Department of Curriculum and Instruction, Montgomery, AL 36101-0271. Offers early childhood education (M Ed, Ed S); elementary education (M Ed, Ed S); secondary education (M Ed, Ed S), including biology education, English language arts education (M Ed), history education, math education, music education (M Ed), reading education (M Ed), social science education; special education (M Ed). *Program availability:* Part-time. *Faculty:* 7 full-time (4 women), 7 part-time/adjunct (4 women). *Students:* 43 full-time (35 women), 71 part-time (62 women); includes 112 minority (111 Black or African American, non-Hispanic/Latino; 1 Two or more races, non-Hispanic/Latino). Average age 22. 47 applicants, 66% accepted, 19 enrolled. In 2017, 21 master's, 13 Ed Ss awarded. *Degree requirements:* For master's, comprehensive exam, thesis optional; for Ed S, comprehensive exam, thesis. *Entrance requirements:* For master's, GRE General Test, MAT, writing competency test; for Ed S, writing competency test, GRE, MAT. Additional exam requirements/recommendations for international students: Required—TOEFL (minimum score 500 paper-based). *Application deadline:* For fall admission, 4/15 for domestic and international students; for spring admission, 11/15 for domestic and international students; for summer admission, 3/15 for domestic and international students. Applications are processed on a rolling basis. Application fee: $25. Electronic applications accepted. *Expenses:* Tuition, state resident: part-time $412 per credit hour. Tuition, nonresident: part-time $824 per credit hour. *Required fees:* $685 per semester. *Financial support:* Research assistantships available. Financial award application deadline: 6/30; financial award applicants required to submit FAFSA. *Unit head:* Dr. Joyce Johnson, Acting Chairperson, 334-229-4485, Fax: 334-229-5603, E-mail: jjohnson@alasu.edu. *Application contact:* Dr. William Person, Dean of Graduate Studies, 334-229-4274, Fax: 334-229-4928, E-mail: wperson@alasu.edu. Website: http://www.alasu.edu/academics/colleges—departments/college-of-education/curriculum—instruction/index.aspx

Alcorn State University, School of Graduate Studies, School of Psychology and Education, Lorman, MS 39096-7500. Offers agricultural education (MS Ed); elementary education (MS Ed, Ed S); guidance and counseling (MS Ed); industrial education (MS Ed); secondary education (MS Ed), including health and physical education; special education (MS Ed). *Accreditation:* NCATE. *Degree requirements:* For master's, thesis optional.

American International College, School of Education, Springfield, MA 01109-3189. Offers early childhood education (M Ed, CAGS); education (MA, Ed D), including counseling psychology (MA), educational leadership and supervision (Ed D), professional counseling and supervision (Ed D), teaching and learning (Ed D); elementary education (M Ed, CAGS); middle education/secondary education (M Ed, CAGS); moderate disabilities (M Ed, CAGS); reading specialist (M Ed, CAGS); school adjustment counseling (MAEP, CAGS); school guidance counseling (MAEP, CAGS); school leadership (M Ed, CAGS). *Program availability:* Evening/weekend. *Faculty:* 1 (woman) full-time, 151 part-time/adjunct (95 women). *Students:* 1,082 full-time (910 women), 143 part-time (113 women); includes 109 minority (19 Black or African American, non-Hispanic/Latino; 2 American Indian or Alaska Native, non-Hispanic/Latino; 10 Asian, non-Hispanic/Latino; 58 Hispanic/Latino; 1 Native Hawaiian or other Pacific Islander, non-Hispanic/Latino; 19 Two or more races, non-Hispanic/Latino). Average age 34. 537 applicants, 77% accepted, 327 enrolled. In 2017, 486 master's, 112 other advanced degrees awarded. *Degree requirements:* For master's and CAGS, practicum/culminating experience. *Entrance requirements:* For master's, Communication and Literacy portion of the Massachusetts Tests for Education Licensure, graduate of accredited four-year college with minimum B- average in undergraduate course work; for CAGS, M Ed or master's degree in field related to licensure from accredited institution. *Application deadline:* Applications are processed on a rolling basis. Application fee: $50. Electronic applications accepted. *Expenses:* $439 per credit, $30 per term registration fee, $100 graduation fee, $110 technology fee. *Financial support:* Applicants required to submit FAFSA. *Unit head:* Sylvia Mason, Dean, 413-205-1743, Fax: 413-205-3943, E-mail: sylvia.mason@aic.edu. *Application contact:* Kerry Barnes, Dean of Graduate Admissions, 413-205-3703, Fax: 413-205-3051, E-mail: kerry.barnes@aic.edu.
Website: http://www.aic.edu/school-of-education/

American Public University System, AMU/APU Graduate Programs, Charles Town, WV 25414. Offers accounting (MS); applied business analytics (MS); business administration (MBA); criminal justice (MA); cybersecurity studies (MS); educational leadership (M Ed); environmental policy and management (MS); global security (DGS); health information management (MS); history (MA), including American military history, American Revolution, civil war, war since 1945, World War II; information technology (MS); international relations and conflict resolution (MA), including American politics and government, comparative government and development, general, international relations, public policy; national security studies (MA); nursing (MSN); political science (MA); public policy (MPP); reverse logistics management (MA), including comparative and security issues, conflict resolution, international and transnational security issues, peacekeeping; space studies (MS); sports management (MS); strategic intelligence (DSI); teaching (M Ed), including secondary social studies; transportation and logistics management (MA). *Program availability:* Part-time, evening/weekend, online only, 100% online. *Students:* 455 full-time (274 women), 7,939 part-time (3,353 women); includes 2,793 minority (1,429 Black or African American, non-Hispanic/Latino; 48 American Indian or Alaska Native, non-Hispanic/Latino; 205 Asian, non-Hispanic/Latino; 766 Hispanic/Latino; 62 Native Hawaiian or other Pacific Islander, non-Hispanic/Latino; 283 Two or more races, non-Hispanic/Latino), 101 international. Average age 37. In 2017, 2,977 master's awarded. *Degree requirements:* For master's, comprehensive exam or practicum. *Entrance requirements:* For master's, official transcript showing earned bachelor's degree from institution accredited by recognized accrediting body. Additional exam requirements/recommendations for international students: Required—TOEFL (minimum score 550 paper-based), IELTS (minimum score 6.5). *Application deadline:* Applications are processed on a rolling basis. Application fee: $0. Electronic applications accepted. *Expenses:* Tuition: Full-time $6300; part-time $350 per credit. *Required fees:* $300; $50 per course. *Financial support:* Scholarships/grants available. Financial award applicants required to submit FAFSA. *Unit head:* Dr. Wallace Boston, President, 877-468-6268, Fax: 304-728-2348, E-mail: president@apus.edu. *Application contact:* Yoci Deal, Associate Vice President, Graduate and International Admissions, 877-468-6268, Fax: 304-724-3764, E-mail: info@apus.edu.
Website: http://www.apus.edu

Andrews University, School of Graduate Studies, School of Education, Department of Teaching, Learning, and Curriculum, Berrien Springs, MI 49104. Offers curriculum and instruction (MA, Ed D, PhD, Ed S); elementary education (MAT); secondary education

(MAT), including biology, education, English, English as a second language, French, history, physics; teacher education (MAT). *Faculty:* 7 full-time (5 women). *Students:* 14 full-time (8 women), 7 part-time (6 women); includes 5 minority (all Black or African American, non-Hispanic/Latino), 9 international. Average age 39. 29 applicants, 31% accepted, 4 enrolled. In 2017, 5 master's, 3 doctorates awarded. *Entrance requirements:* For master's, GRE Subject Test. Additional exam requirements/recommendations for international students: Required—TOEFL (minimum score 550 paper-based). *Application deadline:* For fall admission, 8/15 for domestic students. Applications are processed on a rolling basis. Application fee: $40. *Unit head:* Dr. Lee C. Davidson, Chair, 269-471-6364. *Application contact:* Justina Clayburn, Supervisor of Graduate Admission, 800-253-2874, Fax: 269-471-6321, E-mail: graduate@andrews.edu.

Aquinas College, School of Education, Nashville, TN 37205-2005. Offers elementary education (MAT); secondary education (MAT); teaching and learning (M Ed).

Arcadia University, School of Education, Glenside, PA 19038-3295. Offers art education (M Ed); computer education (CAS); curriculum (CAS); curriculum studies (M Ed); early childhood education (M Ed), including individualized, master teacher, research in child development; educational leadership (M Ed, Ed D, CAS); elementary education (M Ed); English education (MA Ed); environmental education (MA Ed); instructional technology (M Ed); language arts (M Ed); library science (M Ed); mathematics education (M Ed, MA Ed); music education (MA Ed); psychology (MA Ed); reading (M Ed, CAS); science education (M Ed, CAS); secondary education (M Ed, CAS); special education (M Ed, Ed D, CAS); theater arts (MA Ed); written communication (MA Ed). *Accreditation:* NASAD. *Program availability:* Part-time, evening/weekend, online learning. Electronic applications accepted. *Expenses:* Contact institution.

Argosy University, Atlanta, College of Education, Atlanta, GA 30328. Offers educational leadership (MAEd, Ed D, Ed S), including higher education administration (Ed D), K-12 education (Ed D); teaching and learning (MAEd, Ed D, Ed S), including education technology (Ed D), higher education (Ed D), K-12 education (Ed D).

Argosy University, Chicago, College of Education, Chicago, IL 60601. Offers adult education and training (MA Ed); community college executive leadership (Ed D); educational leadership (MA Ed, Ed D, Ed S), including district leadership (Ed D), higher education administration (Ed D), K-12 education (Ed D); instructional leadership (Ed D, Ed S), including higher education (Ed D), K-12 education (Ed D). *Program availability:* Online learning.

Argosy University, Hawai`i, College of Education, Honolulu, HI 96813. Offers adult education and training (MAEd); educational leadership (Ed D), including higher education administration, K-12 education; instructional leadership (Ed D), including higher education, K-12 education; school psychology (MA).

Argosy University, Los Angeles, College of Education, Los Angeles, CA 90045. Offers community college executive leadership (Ed D); educational leadership (MA Ed, Ed D), including higher education administration (Ed D), K-12 education (Ed D); instructional leadership (MA Ed, Ed D), including higher education (Ed D), K-12 education (Ed D), multiple subject teacher preparation (MA Ed), single subject teacher preparation (MA Ed).

Argosy University, Northern Virginia, College of Education, Arlington, VA 22209. Offers community college executive leadership (Ed D); educational leadership (MA Ed, Ed D, Ed S), including higher education administration (Ed D), K-12 education (Ed D); instructional leadership (MA Ed, Ed D, Ed S), including higher education (Ed D), K-12 education (Ed D).

Argosy University, Orange County, College of Education, Orange, CA 92868. Offers community college executive leadership (Ed D); educational leadership (MA Ed, Ed D), including higher education administration (Ed D), K-12 education (Ed D); instructional leadership (MA Ed, Ed D), including education technology (Ed D), higher education (Ed D), K-12 education (Ed D), multiple subject teacher preparation (MA Ed), single subject teacher preparation (MA Ed).

Argosy University, Phoenix, College of Education, Phoenix, AZ 85021. Offers adult education and training (MA Ed); advanced educational administration (Ed D, Ed S); community college executive leadership (Ed D); educational administration (MA Ed); educational leadership (MA Ed, Ed D, Ed S), including education technology (Ed D), higher education administration (Ed D), K-12 education (Ed D); higher and postsecondary education (MA Ed); initial educational administration (Ed D); school psychology (MA); teaching and learning (MA Ed, Ed D, Ed S), including education technology (Ed D), higher education (Ed D), K-12 education (Ed D).

Argosy University, Seattle, College of Education, Seattle, WA 98121. Offers adult education and training (MA Ed); community college executive leadership (Ed D); educational leadership (MA Ed, Ed D), including higher education administration (Ed D), K-12 education (Ed D); higher and postsecondary education (MA Ed); instructional leadership (MA Ed, Ed D), including education technology (Ed D), higher education (Ed D), K-12 education (Ed D).

Argosy University, Tampa, College of Education, Tampa, FL 33607. Offers community college executive leadership (Ed D); educational leadership (MA Ed, Ed D, Ed S), including higher education administration (Ed D), K-12 education (Ed D); school counseling (MA); teaching and learning (MA Ed, Ed D, Ed S), including higher education (Ed D), K-12 education (Ed D).

Argosy University, Twin Cities, College of Education, Eagan, MN 55121. Offers advanced educational administration (Ed D, Ed S); educational leadership (MA Ed, Ed D, Ed S), including higher education administration (Ed D), K-12 education (Ed D); higher and postsecondary education (MA Ed); initial educational administration (Ed D, Ed S); instructional leadership (MA Ed, Ed D, Ed S), including education technology (Ed D), higher education (Ed D), K-12 education (Ed D).

Arizona State University at the Tempe campus, Mary Lou Fulton Teachers College, Program in Curriculum and Instruction, Phoenix, AZ 85069. Offers curriculum and instruction (M Ed, MA); elementary education (M Ed); physical education (MPE); secondary education (M Ed). *Program availability:* Part-time, evening/weekend, online learning. Terminal master's awarded for partial completion of doctoral program. *Degree requirements:* For master's, thesis or alternative, applied project, interactive Program of Study (iPOS) submitted before completing 50 percent of required credit hours. *Entrance requirements:* For master's, GRE or GMAT (for some programs), minimum GPA of 3.0 or equivalent in last 2 years of work leading to bachelor's degree, 3 letters of recommendation, personal statement describing research and career goals, curriculum vitae or resume, IVP fingerprint clearance card (for those seeking Arizona certification). Additional exam requirements/recommendations for international students: Required—TOEFL, IELTS, or PTE. Electronic applications accepted. *Expenses:* Contact institution. *Faculty research:* Early childhood, media and computers, elementary education, secondary education, English education, bilingual education, language and literacy, science education, engineering education, exercise and wellness education.

Auburn University at Montgomery, College of Education, Department of Curriculum, Instruction, and Technology, Montgomery, AL 36124-4023. Offers elementary education

(M Ed, Ed S); instructional technology (Ed S); secondary education (M Ed). *Faculty:* 12 full-time (8 women), 8 part-time/adjunct (all women). *Students:* 43 full-time (34 women), 81 part-time (65 women); includes 39 minority (38 Black or African American, non-Hispanic/Latino; 1 Hispanic/Latino), 2 international. Average age 33. 99 applicants, 70% accepted, 37 enrolled. In 2017, 47 master's awarded. *Degree requirements:* For master's, comprehensive exam, thesis (for some programs). *Entrance requirements:* For master's, GRE or MAT. Additional exam requirements/recommendations for international students: Recommended—TOEFL (minimum score 500 paper-based; 61 iBT), IELTS (minimum score 5.5), TSE (minimum score 44). *Application deadline:* For fall admission, 7/15 for international students; for spring admission, 11/15 for international students; for summer admission, 4/15 for international students. Applications are processed on a rolling basis. Application fee: $25. Electronic applications accepted. *Expenses:* Tuition, state resident: full-time $6930; part-time $385 per credit hour. Tuition, nonresident: full-time $15,588; part-time $866 per credit hour. *Required fees:* $640. *Financial support:* Application deadline: 3/1; applicants required to submit FAFSA. *Unit head:* Dr. Kellie Shumack, Head, 334-244-3737, Fax: 334-244-3835, E-mail: kshumack@aum.edu. *Application contact:* Dr. Rhonda Morton, Associate Dean/Graduate Coordinator, 334-224-3287, Fax: 334-244-3978, E-mail: rmorton@aum.edu.
Website: http://education.aum.edu/academic-departments/curriculum-instruction-technology

Augusta University, College of Education, Program in Curriculum and Instruction, Augusta, GA 30912. Offers curriculum and instruction (Ed S); elementary education (MAT); foreign language education (MAT); instruction (M Ed); middle grades education (MAT); music education (MAT); secondary education (MAT); special education (MAT). *Degree requirements:* For master's, thesis, portfolio. *Entrance requirements:* For master's, GRE, MAT, minimum GPA of 2.5.

Austin Peay State University, College of Graduate Studies, College of Education, Department of Educational Specialties, Clarksville, TN 37044. Offers administration and supervision (Ed S); counseling and guidance (Ed S); curriculum and instruction (MA Ed); education leadership (MA Ed); elementary education (Ed S); reading (MA Ed); secondary education (Ed S). *Program availability:* Part-time, evening/weekend, online learning. *Faculty:* 15 full-time (9 women), 5 part-time/adjunct (4 women). *Students:* 73 full-time (54 women), 139 part-time (106 women); includes 49 minority (23 Black or African American, non-Hispanic/Latino; 4 Asian, non-Hispanic/Latino; 12 Hispanic/Latino; 10 Two or more races, non-Hispanic/Latino), 1 international. Average age 35. 72 applicants, 96% accepted, 42 enrolled. In 2017, 94 master's, 12 Ed Ss awarded. *Degree requirements:* For master's, comprehensive exam, thesis optional. *Entrance requirements:* For master's, GRE General Test, MAT, minimum undergraduate GPA of 2.75. Additional exam requirements/recommendations for international students: Required—TOEFL (minimum score 500 paper-based). *Application deadline:* For fall admission, 8/8 priority date for domestic students. Applications are processed on a rolling basis. Application fee: $45 ($50 for international students). Electronic applications accepted. *Expenses:* Tuition, state resident: full-time $7686; part-time $427 per credit hour. Tuition, nonresident: full-time $20,268; part-time $1126 per credit hour. *Required fees:* $1529; $76.45 per credit hour. *Financial support:* Research assistantships with full tuition reimbursements, career-related internships or fieldwork, Federal Work-Study, institutionally sponsored loans, scholarships/grants, and unspecified assistantships available. Support available to part-time students. Financial award application deadline: 4/1; financial award applicants required to submit FAFSA. *Unit head:* Dr. Moniqueka Gold, Chair, 931-221-7696, Fax: 931-221-1292, E-mail: goldm@apsu.edu. *Application contact:* Megan Mitchell, Coordinator of Graduate Admissions, 800-859-4723, Fax: 931-221-7641, E-mail: gradadmissions@apsu.edu.

Avila University, School of Education, Kansas City, MO 64145-1698. Offers advanced classroom management (MA); art K-12 (Teaching Certificate); educational technology (MA, Certificate); elementary education (Teaching Certificate); English as a second language (MA); English language learners (Advanced Certificate); middle school (Teaching Certificate); physical education K-12 (Teaching Certificate); secondary education (Teaching Certificate); special education (Teaching Certificate); special reading (Advanced Certificate); teaching and learning (MA). *Program availability:* Part-time, evening/weekend, online learning. *Faculty:* 6 full-time (5 women), 9 part-time/adjunct (8 women). *Students:* 81 full-time (63 women), 20 part-time (11 women); includes 14 minority (8 Black or African American, non-Hispanic/Latino; 2 Asian, non-Hispanic/Latino; 3 Hispanic/Latino; 1 Two or more races, non-Hispanic/Latino), 4 international. Average age 35. 92 applicants, 62% accepted, 40 enrolled. In 2017, 24 master's awarded. *Entrance requirements:* For master's, minimum GPA of 3.0, writing sample, recommendation, interview; for other advanced degree, foreign language. Additional exam requirements/recommendations for international students: Required—TOEFL (minimum score 580 paper-based; 92 iBT). *Application deadline:* Applications are processed on a rolling basis. Electronic applications accepted. *Expenses:* Contact institution. *Financial support:* In 2017–18, 14 students received support. Unspecified assistantships available. Financial award applicants required to submit FAFSA. *Unit head:* Dr. Stacy Keith, Director of Graduate Education, 816-501-2446, Fax: 816-501-2915, E-mail: stacy.keith@avila.edu. *Application contact:* Cory Roup, Graduate Education Enrollment and Academic Advisor, 816-501-2464, E-mail: cory.roup@avila.edu.
Website: https://www.avila.edu/academics/graduate-studies/grad-education

Ball State University, Graduate School, Teachers College, Department of Educational Studies, Program in Secondary Education, Muncie, IN 47306. Offers MA. *Accreditation:* NCATE. *Program availability:* Part-time, online only, 100% online. *Students:* 4 full-time (2 women), 20 part-time (15 women); includes 4 minority (1 Black or African American, non-Hispanic/Latino; 3 Hispanic/Latino). Average age 29. 16 applicants, 75% accepted, 8 enrolled. In 2017, 11 master's awarded. *Entrance requirements:* For master's, minimum baccalaureate GPA of 2.75 or 3.0 in latter half of baccalaureate. Additional exam requirements/recommendations for international students: Required—TOEFL (minimum score 550 paper-based; 79 iBT), IELTS (minimum score 6.5). *Application deadline:* For fall admission, 7/1 for domestic students; for spring admission, 12/1 for domestic students; for summer admission, 3/1 for domestic students. Applications are processed on a rolling basis. Application fee: $60. Electronic applications accepted. *Financial support:* Teaching assistantships with partial tuition reimbursements and unspecified assistantships available. Financial award application deadline: 3/1; financial award applicants required to submit FAFSA. *Unit head:* Dr. Theresa Kruczek, Interim Chair, 765-285-8049, E-mail: tkruczek@bsu.edu.
Website: http://www.bsu.edu/edstudies

Bard College, Master of Arts in Teaching Program, Annandale-on-Hudson, NY 12504. Offers secondary education (MAT), including biology, history, literature, mathematics, Spanish; MS/MAT. *Program availability:* Part-time. *Degree requirements:* For master's, year-long teaching residencies in area middle and high schools. *Entrance requirements:* For master's, GRE General Test, resume, 3 letters of recommendation, personal statement, official transcripts. Additional exam requirements/recommendations for international students: Required—TOEFL. Electronic applications accepted. Application fee is waived when completed online.

Bellarmine University, Annsley Frazier Thornton School of Education, Louisville, KY 40205. Offers education and district leadership (Ed D); education and social change (PhD); elementary education (MA Ed, MAT); leadership in higher education (PhD); middle school education (MA Ed, MAT); principalship (Ed S); reading and writing (MA Ed); secondary education (MAT); teacher leadership (MA Ed). *Accreditation:* NCATE. *Program availability:* Part-time, evening/weekend. *Faculty:* 19 full-time (10 women), 36 part-time/adjunct (29 women). *Students:* 34 full-time (27 women), 204 part-time (158 women); includes 60 minority (43 Black or African American, non-Hispanic/Latino; 7 Asian, non-Hispanic/Latino; 7 Hispanic/Latino; 3 Two or more races, non-Hispanic/Latino). Average age 33. In 2017, 50 master's, 8 doctorates, 42 other advanced degrees awarded. *Degree requirements:* For master's, comprehensive exam (for some programs), thesis (for some programs); for doctorate, comprehensive exam (for some programs), thesis/dissertation; for Ed S, comprehensive exam (for some programs). *Entrance requirements:* For master's, GRE, baccalaureate degree from accredited institution; minimum cumulative GPA of 2.75; recommendations from employers, supervisors, or professors attesting to applicant's potential as graduate student; statement of intent to pursue graduate degree; for doctorate, GRE, minimum GPA of 3.5 in all graduate coursework; baccalaureate and master's degrees in education or fields directly relevant to education; three letters of recommendation; two essays (no more than 1,000 words each); resume or curriculum vitae; interview; for Ed S, master's degree in education; valid teaching certificate; three years of experience in teaching; three recommendations; minimum GPA of 3.0 in all graduate work; interview; essays; personal goal statement. Additional exam requirements/recommendations for international students: Required—TOEFL (minimum score 550 paper-based, 68 iBT), IELTS (minimum score 6), or Michigan English Language Assessment Battery. *Application deadline:* For fall admission, 8/1 priority date for domestic and international students; for spring admission, 12/1 priority date for domestic and international students; for summer admission, 4/10 priority date for domestic and international students. Applications are processed on a rolling basis. Application fee: $40. Electronic applications accepted. Tuition and fees vary according to program. *Financial support:* Scholarships/grants available. Financial award applicants required to submit FAFSA. *Faculty research:* Literacy, service-learning, dispositions, educational technology, special education. *Unit head:* Dr. Elizabeth Dinkins, Interim Dean, 502-272-7958, Fax: 502-272-8189, E-mail: edinkins@bellarmine.edu. *Application contact:* Sarah Schuble, Senior Graduate Admissions Recruiter, 502-272-8271, Fax: 502-272-8002, E-mail: sschuble@bellarmine.edu.
Website: http://www.bellarmine.edu/education/graduate

Benedictine University, Graduate Programs, Program in Education, Lisle, IL 60532. Offers curriculum and instruction and collaborative teaching (M Ed); elementary education (MA Ed); leadership and administration (M Ed); reading and literacy (M Ed); secondary education (MA Ed); special education (MA Ed). *Program availability:* Part-time, evening/weekend. *Degree requirements:* For master's, comprehensive exam, thesis (for some programs). *Entrance requirements:* For master's, GRE or MAT. Additional exam requirements/recommendations for international students: Required—TOEFL (minimum score 550 paper-based). Electronic applications accepted. *Expenses:* Contact institution.

Berry College, Graduate Programs, Graduate Programs in Education, Program in Secondary Education, Mount Berry, GA 30149-0159. Offers MAT. In 2017, 3 master's awarded. *Degree requirements:* For master's, thesis, portfolio, oral exams. *Entrance requirements:* For master's, GRE General Test or MAT, minimum GPA of 2.5. Additional exam requirements/recommendations for international students: Required—TOEFL (minimum score 550 paper-based). *Application deadline:* For fall admission, 7/20 for domestic students, 5/1 for international students; for spring admission, 12/1 for domestic students, 10/1 for international students. Applications are processed on a rolling basis. Application fee: $25 ($30 for international students). Electronic applications accepted. *Expenses:* $8,370 full-time tuition plus $176 fees per year; $465 per credit hour part-time tuition. *Financial support:* Research assistantships with full tuition reimbursements, scholarships/grants, tuition waivers (partial), and unspecified assistantships available. Support available to part-time students. Financial award application deadline: 3/1; financial award applicants required to submit FAFSA. *Unit head:* Dr. Jacqueline McDowell, Dean, Charter School of Education and Human Sciences, 706-236-1717, Fax: 706-238-5827, E-mail: jmcdowell@berry.edu. *Application contact:* Brett Kennedy, Assistant Vice President of Enrollment Management, 706-236-2215, Fax: 706-290-2178, E-mail: admissions@berry.edu.
Website: http://www.berry.edu/academics/education/graduate/

Bethel University, Graduate School, St. Paul, MN 55112-6999. Offers business administration (MBA); classroom management (Certificate); counseling (MA); K-12 education (MA); leadership (Ed D); leadership foundations (Certificate); nurse educator (MS, Certificate); nurse-midwifery (MS); physician assistant (MS); special education (MA); strategic leadership (MA); teaching (MA); teaching and learning (Certificate). *Program availability:* Part-time, evening/weekend, 100% online, blended/hybrid learning. *Faculty:* 22 full-time (16 women), 70 part-time/adjunct (44 women). *Students:* 611 full-time (431 women), 393 part-time (249 women); includes 176 minority (82 Black or African American, non-Hispanic/Latino; 4 American Indian or Alaska Native, non-Hispanic/Latino; 31 Asian, non-Hispanic/Latino; 39 Hispanic/Latino; 2 Native Hawaiian or other Pacific Islander, non-Hispanic/Latino; 18 Two or more races, non-Hispanic/Latino), 9 international. Average age 36. 668 applicants, 42% accepted, 223 enrolled. In 2017, 287 master's, 30 doctorates, 172 other advanced degrees awarded. *Degree requirements:* For master's, comprehensive exam (for some programs), thesis (for some programs); for doctorate, comprehensive exam, thesis/dissertation. *Entrance requirements:* Additional exam requirements/recommendations for international students: Required—TOEFL (minimum score 550 paper-based, 80 iBT) or IELTS. *Application deadline:* Applications are processed on a rolling basis. Application fee: $0. Electronic applications accepted. *Expenses:* Contact institution. *Financial support:* Teaching assistantships, career-related internships or fieldwork, and scholarships/grants available. Support available to part-time students. Financial award applicants required to submit FAFSA. *Unit head:* Dr. Randy Bergen, Associate Provost, 651-635-8000, Fax: 651-635-8004, E-mail: r-bergen@bethel.edu. *Application contact:* Director of Admissions, 651-635-8000, Fax: 651-635-8004, E-mail: gs@bethel.edu.
Website: https://www.bethel.edu/graduate/

Binghamton University, State University of New York, Graduate School, College of Community and Public Affairs, Department of Teaching, Learning and Educational Leadership, Program in Adolescence Education, Binghamton, NY 13902-6000. Offers biology education (MAT, MS Ed); chemistry education (MAT, MS Ed); earth science education (MAT, MS Ed); English education (MAT, MS Ed); French education (MAT, MS Ed); mathematical sciences education (MAT, MS Ed); physics (MAT, MS Ed); social studies (MAT, MS Ed); Spanish education (MAT, MS Ed). *Accreditation:* TEAC. *Program availability:* Part-time, evening/weekend. *Students:* 53 full-time (32 women), 9 part-time (3 women); includes 10 minority (2 Black or African American, non-Hispanic/Latino; 1 Asian, non-Hispanic/Latino; 5 Hispanic/Latino; 2 Two or more races, non-Hispanic/Latino). Average age 27. 51 applicants, 88% accepted, 31 enrolled. In 2017, 36 master's awarded. *Degree requirements:* For master's, portfolio. *Entrance requirements:* For master's, GRE General Test, teaching certification. Additional exam requirements/recommendations for international students: Required—TOEFL (minimum score 550 paper-based; 80 iBT). *Application deadline:* For fall admission, 2/1 priority date for domestic and international

Secondary Education

students; for spring admission, 10/15 priority date for domestic and international students. Application fee: $75. Electronic applications accepted. *Financial support:* In 2017–18, 4 students received support. Research assistantships, teaching assistantships, career-related internships or fieldwork, Federal Work-Study, institutionally sponsored loans, scholarships/grants, health care benefits, tuition waivers (full and partial), and unspecified assistantships available. Financial award applicants required to submit FAFSA. *Unit head:* Dr. Susan Strehle, Dean, 607-777-7329, E-mail: sstrehle@binghamton.edu. *Application contact:* Ben Balkaya, Assistant Dean and Director, 607-777-2151, Fax: 607-777-2501, E-mail: balkaya@binghamton.edu.

Blue Mountain College, Program in Secondary Education - Biology, Blue Mountain, MS 38610. Offers M Ed. *Program availability:* Part-time, evening/weekend. *Faculty:* 1 part-time/adjunct (0 women). *Students:* 1 (woman) part-time. Average age 31. *Degree requirements:* For master's, comprehensive exam. *Entrance requirements:* For master's, PRAXIS, GRE, or MAT, official transcripts; bachelor's degree in a field of education from an accredited college or university; teaching certificate; three recommendations. Additional exam requirements/recommendations for international students: Required—TOEFL (minimum score 550 paper-based). *Application deadline:* For fall admission, 7/15 priority date for domestic students; for spring admission, 12/1 priority date for domestic students; for summer admission, 5/1 priority date for domestic students. Applications are processed on a rolling basis. Electronic applications accepted. *Expenses: Tuition:* Full-time $6030; part-time $335 per semester hour. *Required fees:* $790; $790 per semester hour. *Financial support:* Scholarships/grants available. Financial award application deadline: 6/30; financial award applicants required to submit FAFSA. *Unit head:* Dr. Jenetta R. Waddell, Dean of Graduate Studies, 662-685-4771 Ext. 118, Fax: 662-815-2919, E-mail: jwaddell@bmc.edu. *Application contact:* Jean Harrington, Administrative Assistant in Department of Education, 662-685-4771 Ext. 238, Fax: 662-815-2919, E-mail: jharrington@bmc.edu. Website: http://www.bmc.edu/master_of_education.asp

Bob Jones University, Graduate Programs, Greenville, SC 29614. Offers accountancy (MS); Bible (MA); Bible translation (MA); Biblical studies (Certificate); broadcast management (MS); business administration (MBA); church history (MA, PhD); church ministries (MA); church music (MM); cinema and video production (MA); counseling (MS); curriculum and instruction (Ed D); divinity (M Div); dramatic production (MA); educational leadership (MS, Ed D, Ed S); elementary education (M Ed, MAT); English (M Ed, MA, MAT); fine arts (MA); graphic design (MA); history (M Ed, MA); illustration (MA); interpretative speech (MA); mathematics (M Ed, MAT); medical missions (Certificate); ministry (MM, D Min); multi-categorical special education (M Ed, MAT); music (M Ed); New Testament interpretation (PhD); Old Testament interpretation (PhD); orchestral instrument performance (MM); organ performance (MM); pastoral studies (MA); personnel services (MS, Ed S); piano pedagogy (MM); piano performance (MM); platform arts (MA); radio and television broadcasting (MS); rhetoric and public address (MA); secondary education (M Ed); studio art (MA); teaching Bible (MA); theology (MA, PhD); voice performance (MM); youth ministries (MA); M Div/MM.

Boston College, Lynch School of Education, Program in Secondary Education, Chestnut Hill, MA 02467-3800. Offers M Ed, MAT, MST. *Accreditation:* TEAC. *Program availability:* Part-time, evening/weekend. *Students:* 34 full-time (23 women), 11 part-time (6 women); includes 12 minority (3 Black or African American, non-Hispanic/Latino; 2 Asian, non-Hispanic/Latino; 6 Hispanic/Latino; 1 Two or more races, non-Hispanic/Latino), 1 international. Average age 25. 90 applicants, 81% accepted, 34 enrolled. In 2017, 28 master's awarded. *Degree requirements:* For master's, comprehensive exam. *Entrance requirements:* For master's, GRE General Test or MAT. Additional exam requirements/recommendations for international students: Required—TOEFL (minimum score 100 iBT). *Application deadline:* For fall admission, 12/1 priority date for domestic students, 12/1 for international students; for spring admission, 11/1 priority date for domestic and international students. Application fee: $65. Electronic applications accepted. *Financial support:* Fellowships with tuition reimbursements, research assistantships with tuition reimbursements, teaching assistantships with tuition reimbursements, Federal Work-Study, scholarships/grants, and tuition waivers (full and partial) available. Support available to part-time students. Financial award applicants required to submit FAFSA. *Unit head:* Dr. Susan Bruce, Chairperson, 617-552-4214, Fax: 617-552-0398. *Application contact:* Kimberly Rose, Graduate Admission Assistant, 617-552-4214, Fax: 617-552-0398, E-mail: roseki@bc.edu.

Bowie State University, Graduate Programs, Program in Secondary Education, Bowie, MD 20715-9465. Offers M Ed. *Accreditation:* NCATE. *Program availability:* Part-time, evening/weekend. *Degree requirements:* For master's, comprehensive exam, thesis optional, research paper. *Entrance requirements:* For master's, minimum undergraduate GPA of 3.0, bachelor's degree in education, teaching certificate, teaching experience. Electronic applications accepted.

Brandeis University, Graduate School of Arts and Sciences, Program in Education, Waltham, MA 02454-9110. Offers Jewish day schools (MAT); public elementary education (MAT); secondary education (MAT), including Bible, biology, chemistry, Chinese, English, history, Jewish day schools, math, physics; teacher leadership (Ed M, AGC). *Faculty:* 4 full-time (2 women), 11 part-time/adjunct (10 women). *Students:* 21 full-time (19 women), 38 part-time (33 women); includes 5 minority (1 Black or African American, non-Hispanic/Latino; 3 Asian, non-Hispanic/Latino; 1 Hispanic/Latino), 8 international. Average age 34. 93 applicants, 78% accepted, 55 enrolled. In 2017, 43 master's, 10 other advanced degrees awarded. *Degree requirements:* For master's, thesis or alternative, internship; research project. *Entrance requirements:* For master's, GRE General Test or MAT, transcripts, letters of recommendation, resume, statement of purpose. Additional exam requirements/recommendations for international students: Required—PTE (minimum score 68), TOEFL (minimum score 600 paper-based, 100 iBT) or IELTS (7). *Application deadline:* For fall admission, 12/1 priority date for domestic students. Applications are processed on a rolling basis. Application fee: $75. Electronic applications accepted. *Expenses:* $32,440 (MAT), $17,520 (M Ed), $23,360 (AGS); $88 fees. *Financial support:* In 2017–18, 61 students received support. Scholarships/grants available. Financial award application deadline: 4/15; financial award applicants required to submit FAFSA. *Faculty research:* Teacher education, education, teaching, elementary education, secondary education, Jewish education, English, history, biology, chemistry, physics, math, Chinese, Bible/Tanakh. *Unit head:* Marya Levenson, Director, 781-736-2002, E-mail: mlevenso@brandeis.edu. *Application contact:* Manuel Tuan, Department Coordinator, 781-736-2002, E-mail: tuan@brandeis.edu. Website: http://www.brandeis.edu/gsas/programs/education.html

Brandman University, School of Education, Irvine, CA 92618. Offers curriculum and instruction (MAE); educational administration (MAE); educational leadership (MAE); educational leadership and administration (MAE); elementary education (MAT); instructional technology: teaching the 21st century learner (MAE); leadership in early childhood education (MAE); organizational leadership (Ed D); school counseling (MA); secondary education (MAT); special education (MA); teaching and learning (MAE). *Expenses: Tuition:* Part-time $640 per credit hour. Tuition and fees vary according to degree level and program. *Unit head:* Dr. Christine G. Zeppos, Dean, 949-341-9948, E-mail: zeppos@brandman.edu. *Application contact:* Dr. Christine G. Zeppos, Dean, 949-341-9948, E-mail: zeppos@brandman.edu. Website: https://www.brandman.edu/academic-programs/education

Brenau University, Sydney O. Smith Graduate School, College of Education, Gainesville, GA 30501. Offers early childhood (Ed S); early childhood education (M Ed, MAT); middle grades (Ed S); middle grades education (M Ed, MAT); secondary education (MAT); special education (M Ed, MAT). *Accreditation:* NCATE. *Program availability:* Part-time, evening/weekend, online learning. *Degree requirements:* For master's, thesis optional, comprehensive exam or applied research project, effective portfolio; for Ed S, thesis, applied research project. *Entrance requirements:* For master's, GRE, MAT, interview, minimum GPA of 3.0, 3 references, writing samples; for Ed S, GRE, MAT, master's degree, minimum GPA of 3.0, writing sample, letters of reference. Additional exam requirements/recommendations for international students: Required—TOEFL (minimum score 500 paper-based; 61 iBT); Recommended—IELTS (minimum score 5). Electronic applications accepted. *Expenses:* Contact institution.

Bridgewater State University, College of Graduate Studies, College of Education and Allied Studies, Department of Secondary Education and Professional Programs, Program in Secondary Education, Bridgewater, MA 02325. Offers MAT. *Accreditation:* NCATE. *Program availability:* Part-time, evening/weekend. *Entrance requirements:* For master's, GRE General Test.

Brooklyn College of the City University of New York, School of Education, Program in Adolescence Science Education and Special Subjects, Brooklyn, NY 11210-2889. Offers adolescence science education (MAT); biology teacher (7-12) (MA); chemistry teacher (7-12) (MA); earth science teacher (7-12) (MAT); English teacher (7-12) (MA); French teacher (7-12) (MA); mathematics teacher (7-12) (MA); music teacher (MA); physics teacher (7-12) (MA); social studies teacher (7-12) (MA); Spanish teacher (7-12) (MA). *Program availability:* Part-time, evening/weekend. *Degree requirements:* For master's, comprehensive exam (for some programs), thesis (for some programs). *Entrance requirements:* For master's, LAST, previous course work in education, resume, 2 letters of recommendation, essay. Additional exam requirements/recommendations for international students: Required—TOEFL (minimum score 500 paper-based; 61 iBT). Electronic applications accepted. *Faculty research:* Interdisciplinary education, semiotics, discourse analysis, autobiography, teacher identity.

Brown University, Graduate School, Department of Education, Program in Teaching, Providence, RI 02912. Offers elementary education (MAT); English (MAT); history/social studies (MAT); science (MAT); secondary education (MAT). *Degree requirements:* For master's, student teaching, portfolio. *Entrance requirements:* For master's, GRE General Test, transcript, personal statement, 3 letters of recommendation, interview, writing sample (English applicants only). Additional exam requirements/recommendations for international students: Required—TOEFL (minimum score 577 paper-based). Electronic applications accepted. *Faculty research:* Literacy, English language learners, diversity, special education, biodiversity.

Cabrini University, Academic Affairs, Radnor, PA 19087. Offers accounting (M Acc); autism spectrum disorder (M Ed); biological sciences (MS), including civic leadership; criminology and criminal justice (MA); curriculum, instruction, and assessment (M Ed); educational leadership (M Ed, Ed D), including curriculum and instructional leadership (Ed D), preK-12 leadership (Ed D); English as a second language (M Ed); organizational leadership (DBA, PhD); preK to 4 (M Ed); reading specialist (M Ed); secondary education (M Ed), including biology, chemistry, English, English/communication, mathematics, social studies; special education grades 7-12 (M Ed); special education preK-8 (M Ed); teaching and learning (M Ed). *Program availability:* Part-time, evening/weekend. *Faculty:* 23 full-time (17 women), 46 part-time/adjunct (38 women). *Students:* 60 full-time (35 women), 559 part-time (435 women); includes 93 minority (66 Black or African American, non-Hispanic/Latino; 1 American Indian or Alaska Native, non-Hispanic/Latino; 8 Asian, non-Hispanic/Latino; 15 Hispanic/Latino; 3 Two or more races, non-Hispanic/Latino), 4 international. Average age 33. 290 applicants, 82% accepted, 154 enrolled. In 2017, 283 master's awarded. *Degree requirements:* For master's, comprehensive exam (for some programs), thesis (for some programs); for doctorate, comprehensive exam (for some programs), thesis/dissertation. *Entrance requirements:* For master's, professional resume, personal statement, two recommendations, official transcripts; for doctorate, official transcripts, minimum master's GPA of 3.0, two recommendations, interview with admissions committee. Additional exam requirements/recommendations for international students: Required—TOEFL (minimum score 80 iBT). *Application deadline:* For fall admission, 8/26 for domestic students, 8/1 for international students; for winter admission, 1/13 for domestic students, 12/20 for international students; for spring admission, 1/13 for domestic students, 12/20 for international students; for summer admission, 5/20 for domestic students, 4/30 for international students. Applications are processed on a rolling basis. Application fee: $50. Electronic applications accepted. Application fee is waived when completed online. *Expenses:* Contact institution. *Financial support:* In 2017–18, 1,459 students received support. Tuition waivers and unspecified assistantships available. Financial award application deadline: 5/1; financial award applicants required to submit FAFSA. *Unit head:* Dr. Maliha Zaman, 610-902-8502, Fax: 610-902-8797, E-mail: msz37@cabrini.edu. *Application contact:* Diane Greenwood, Director of Graduate Admissions, 610-902-8291, E-mail: diane.l.greenwood@cabrini.edu. Website: http://cabrini.edu/graduate

California State University, Bakersfield, Division of Graduate Studies, School of Natural Sciences, Mathematics, and Engineering, Program in Teaching Mathematics, Bakersfield, CA 93311. Offers MA. *Entrance requirements:* For master's, minimum GPA of 2.5 for last 90 quarter units. *Expenses:* Tuition, state resident: full-time $7176; part-time $4164 per year. *Unit head:* Sophia Raczkowski, Chair, 661-654-3151, Fax: 661-664-2039. *Application contact:* Debbie Blowers, Assistant Director of Admissions and Evaluations, 661-654-3381, E-mail: dblowers@csub.edu. Website: https://www.csub.edu/math/info/index.html

California State University, Fullerton, Graduate Studies, College of Education, Department of Secondary Education, Fullerton, CA 92831-3599. Offers teacher instruction (MS); teaching foundational mathematics (MS). *Program availability:* Part-time. *Faculty:* 4 full-time (3 women), 1 (woman) part-time/adjunct. *Students:* 38 part-time (24 women); includes 15 minority (1 Black or African American, non-Hispanic/Latino; 3 Asian, non-Hispanic/Latino; 9 Hispanic/Latino; 2 Two or more races, non-Hispanic/Latino). Average age 29. 29 applicants, 76% accepted, 21 enrolled. Application fee: $55. *Financial support:* Career-related internships or fieldwork, Federal Work-Study, institutionally sponsored loans, and scholarships/grants available. Support available to part-time students. Financial award application deadline: 3/1; financial award applicants required to submit FAFSA. *Unit head:* Dr. Grace Cho, Chair, 657-278-3283, E-mail: gcho@fullerton.edu. *Application contact:* Admissions/Applications, 657-278-2371.

California State University, Long Beach, Graduate Studies, College of Education, Department of Teacher Education, Long Beach, CA 90840. Offers elementary education (MA); secondary education (MA). *Program availability:* Part-time, evening/weekend. *Degree requirements:* For master's, comprehensive exam or thesis. *Entrance requirements:* For master's, GRE General Test, minimum GPA of 2.75. Electronic applications accepted. *Faculty research:* Teacher stress and burnout, new teacher induction.

California State University, Long Beach, Graduate Studies, College of Natural Sciences and Mathematics, Department of Mathematics and Statistics, Long Beach, CA 90840. Offers mathematics (MS), including applied mathematics, applied statistics, mathematics education for secondary school teachers. *Program availability:* Part-time. *Degree requirements:* For master's, comprehensive exam or thesis. Electronic applications accepted. *Faculty research:* Algebra, functional analysis, partial differential equations, operator theory, numerical analysis.

California State University, Northridge, Graduate Studies, Michael D. Eisner College of Education, Department of Secondary Education, Northridge, CA 91330. Offers educational technology (MA); English education (MA); mathematics education (MA); secondary science education (MA); teaching and learning (MA). *Accreditation:* NCATE. *Program availability:* Part-time. *Students:* 9 full-time (5 women), 85 part-time (57 women); includes 37 minority (2 Black or African American, non-Hispanic/Latino; 12 Asian, non-Hispanic/Latino; 20 Hispanic/Latino; 1 Native Hawaiian or other Pacific Islander, non-Hispanic/Latino; 2 Two or more races, non-Hispanic/Latino; 1 international. Average age 37. 63 applicants, 78% accepted, 45 enrolled. *Degree requirements:* For master's, thesis optional. *Entrance requirements:* For master's, GRE General Test or minimum GPA of 3.0. Additional exam requirements/recommendations for international students: Required—TOEFL. *Application deadline:* For fall admission, 11/30 for domestic students. Application fee: $55. *Financial support:* Application deadline: 3/1. *Unit head:* Dr. Julie Gainsburg, Chair, 818-677-2580. *Application contact:* Dr. Michael Rivas, Graduate Advisor, 818-677-6792, E-mail: michael.rivas@csun.edu. Website: http://www.csun.edu/eisner-education/secondary-education

California State University, Stanislaus, College of Education, Kinesiology and Social Work, MA Program in Education, Turlock, CA 95382. Offers curriculum and instruction (MA), including education technology, elementary education, multilingual education, physical education, reading, secondary education, special education; school administration (MA); school counseling (MA). *Program availability:* Part-time, evening/weekend. *Degree requirements:* For master's, comprehensive exam (for some programs), thesis (for some programs). *Entrance requirements:* For master's, MAT, GRE, or CBEST (varies by concentration), 3 letters of recommendation, personal statement. Additional exam requirements/recommendations for international students: Required—TOEFL (minimum score 550 paper-based). Electronic applications accepted. *Faculty research:* Children's perspectives on historical events, method elementary schools dual language education, K-12 reading programs.

California University of Pennsylvania, School of Graduate Studies and Research, College of Education and Human Services, Program in Secondary Education, California, PA 15419-1394. Offers advanced studies in secondary education and teacher leadership (M Ed); secondary education (MAT). *Program availability:* Part-time, evening/weekend, online learning. *Degree requirements:* For master's, comprehensive exam, thesis. *Entrance requirements:* For master's, PRAXIS, minimum GPA of 3.0. Additional exam requirements/recommendations for international students: Required—TOEFL (minimum score 550 paper-based; 80 iBT). *Application deadline:* For fall admission, 8/1 priority date for domestic and international students; for winter admission, 12/1 priority date for domestic and international students; for spring admission, 5/1 priority date for domestic and international students. Applications are processed on a rolling basis. Application fee: $25. Electronic applications accepted. *Financial support:* Applicants required to submit FAFSA. *Faculty research:* The effectiveness of online instruction, student-centered instruction strategies in secondary education, computer technology in education, environmental education, multi-media in education. *Unit head:* Dr. Michael Perrotti, Graduate Coordinator, 724-938-5678, E-mail: perrotti@calu.edu. *Application contact:* Suzanne C. Powers, Director of Graduate Admissions and Recruitment, 724-938-4029, Fax: 724-938-5712, E-mail: powers_s@cup.edu. Website: http://www.calu.edu/academics/colleges/education/secondary-ed-administrative-leadership/

Campbell University, Graduate and Professional Programs, School of Education, Buies Creek, NC 27506. Offers elementary education (M Ed); interdisciplinary studies (M Ed); middle grades education (M Ed); physical education (M Ed); school administration (MSA); school counseling (M Ed); secondary education (M Ed). *Accreditation:* NCATE. *Program availability:* Part-time, evening/weekend. *Degree requirements:* For master's, comprehensive exam. *Entrance requirements:* For master's, GRE General Test, minimum GPA of 2.7. *Faculty research:* Spiritual values and wellness issues in counseling, stress and professional burnout among counselors, thinking strategies, leadership, adaptive technology.

Canisius College, Graduate Division, School of Education and Human Services, Department of Graduate Education and Leadership, Buffalo, NY 14208-1098. Offers business and marketing education (MS Ed); college student personnel (MS Ed); deaf education (MS Ed); deaf/adolescent education, grades 7-12 (MS Ed); deaf/childhood education, grades 1-6 (MS Ed); differentiated instruction (MS Ed); education administration (MS); educational administration (MS Ed); educational technologies (Certificate); gifted education extension (Certificate); literacy (MS Ed); reading (Certificate); school building leadership (MS Ed, Certificate); school district leadership (Certificate); teacher leader (Certificate); TESOL (MS Ed). *Accreditation:* NCATE. *Program availability:* Part-time, evening/weekend, 100% online, blended/hybrid learning. *Faculty:* 5 full-time (all women), 21 part-time/adjunct (16 women). *Students:* 85 full-time (67 women), 189 part-time (151 women); includes 31 minority (18 Black or African American, non-Hispanic/Latino; 3 American Indian or Alaska Native, non-Hispanic/Latino; 3 Asian, non-Hispanic/Latino; 4 Hispanic/Latino; 3 Two or more races, non-Hispanic/Latino), 1 international. Average age 31. 83 applicants, 96% accepted, 74 enrolled. In 2017, 94 master's, 47 other advanced degrees awarded. *Entrance requirements:* For master's, GRE (if cumulative GPA less than 2.7), transcripts, two letters of recommendation. Additional exam requirements/recommendations for international students: Required—TOEFL (minimum score 550 paper-based, 79 iBT), IELTS (minimum score 6.5), or CAEL (minimum score 70). *Application deadline:* Applications are processed on a rolling basis. Application fee: $0. Electronic applications accepted. *Expenses: Tuition:* Full-time $22,860; part-time $820 per credit. *Required fees:* $720; $25 per credit. $65 per semester. One-time fee: $425. *Financial support:* Career-related internships or fieldwork, Federal Work-Study, scholarships/grants, tuition waivers (partial), and unspecified assistantships available. Support available to part-time students. Financial award application deadline: 4/30; financial award applicants required to submit FAFSA. *Faculty research:* Asperger's disease, autism, private higher education, reading strategies. *Unit head:* Dr. Anne Marie Tryjankowski, Chair/Associate Professor of Graduate Education and Leadership, 716-888-3715, Fax: 716-888-3142, E-mail: tryjanka@canisius.edu.

Carroll University, Graduate Programs in Education, Waukesha, WI 53186-5593. Offers adult and continuing education (M Ed); educational leadership (MS); PK-12 (M Ed). *Program availability:* Part-time, evening/weekend. *Degree requirements:* For master's, thesis. *Entrance requirements:* For master's, minimum undergraduate GPA of 2.5 in related field. Additional exam requirements/recommendations for international students: Required—TOEFL. Electronic applications accepted. *Faculty research:* Qualitative research methods, whole language approaches to teaching, the writing process, multicultural education, gifted/talented learners.

Carson-Newman University, Graduate Program in Education, Jefferson City, TN 37760. Offers curriculum and instruction (M Ed); educational leadership (M Ed); elementary education (MAT); school counseling (MS); secondary education (MAT); teaching English as a second language (MATESL). *Accreditation:* NCATE. *Program availability:* Part-time, evening/weekend, 100% online, blended/hybrid learning. *Faculty:* 20 full-time (11 women), 16 part-time/adjunct (13 women). *Students:* 63 full-time (37 women), 488 part-time (362 women); includes 60 minority (46 Black or African American, non-Hispanic/Latino; 2 American Indian or Alaska Native, non-Hispanic/Latino; 1 Asian, non-Hispanic/Latino; 5 Hispanic/Latino; 1 Native Hawaiian or other Pacific Islander, non-Hispanic/Latino; 5 Two or more races, non-Hispanic/Latino), 29 international. Average age 35. 204 applicants, 100% accepted, 188 enrolled. In 2017, 211 master's awarded. *Degree requirements:* For master's, thesis or alternative. *Entrance requirements:* For master's, PRAXIS II or GRE with minimum score of 290 on the verbal and quantitative components (for MAT), minimum GPA of 3.0 in major, 2.5 overall. Additional exam requirements/recommendations for international students: Recommended—TOEFL (minimum score 79 iBT), IELTS (minimum score 6.5), TSE (minimum score 53). *Application deadline:* For fall admission, 7/15 priority date for domestic students. Applications are processed on a rolling basis. Application fee: $50. *Expenses: Tuition:* Full-time $10,516; part-time $478 per credit hour. *Required fees:* $240; $120 per semester. One-time fee: $150. *Financial support:* Federal Work-Study and unspecified assistantships available. Financial award applicants required to submit FAFSA. *Unit head:* Dr. Kim Hawkins, Chair, 865-471-3314, E-mail: khawkins@cn.edu. *Application contact:* Nilma Stewart, Graduate Admissions and Services Adviser, 865-471-3230, Fax: 865-471-3875, E-mail: adults@cn.edu. Website: http://www.cn.edu/adult-graduate-studies

The Catholic University of America, School of Arts and Sciences, Department of Education, Washington, DC 20064. Offers Catholic school leadership (MA); education (Certificate); secondary education (MA); special education (MA), including early childhood, non-categorical. *Accreditation:* NCATE. *Program availability:* Part-time. *Faculty:* 8 full-time (7 women), 3 part-time/adjunct (all women). *Students:* 9 full-time (all women), 25 part-time (14 women); includes 2 minority (both Hispanic/Latino), 4 international. Average age 39. 24 applicants, 63% accepted, 9 enrolled. In 2017, 9 master's awarded. *Degree requirements:* For master's, comprehensive exam, thesis or alternative; for Certificate, action research project. *Entrance requirements:* For master's, GRE General Test or MAT, statement of purpose, official copies of academic transcripts, three letters of recommendation, interview; for Certificate, PRAXIS I, statement of purpose, official copies of academic transcripts, three letters of recommendation, interview. Additional exam requirements/recommendations for international students: Required—TOEFL (minimum score 550 paper-based; 80 iBT). *Application deadline:* For fall admission, 7/15 priority date for domestic students, 7/1 for international students; for spring admission, 11/15 priority date for domestic students, 11/1 for international students. Applications are processed on a rolling basis. Application fee: $55. Electronic applications accepted. *Expenses:* Contact institution. *Financial support:* Fellowships, research assistantships, teaching assistantships, Federal Work-Study, scholarships/grants, tuition waivers (full and partial), and unspecified assistantships available. Financial award application deadline: 2/1; financial award applicants required to submit FAFSA. *Faculty research:* Special education, early childhood education, educational psychology, Catholic school administration, leadership and policy studies, counseling, curriculum and instruction. *Unit head:* Dr. Agnes Cave, Chair, 202-319-5805, Fax: 202-319-5815, E-mail: cave@cua.edu. *Application contact:* Dr. Steven Brown, Director of Graduate Admissions, 202-319-5057, Fax: 202-319-6533, E-mail: cua-admissions@cua.edu. Website: http://education.cua.edu/

Centenary College of Louisiana, Graduate Programs, Department of Education, Shreveport, LA 71104. Offers elementary education (MAT); secondary education (MAT). *Program availability:* Part-time, evening/weekend. *Degree requirements:* For master's, comprehensive exam. *Entrance requirements:* For master's, PRAXIS I and II (for MAT), undergraduate degree, minimum GPA of 2.5. *Expenses:* Contact institution. *Faculty research:* Teachers as advocates for teachers, portfolio assessment, disabled readers.

Central Connecticut State University, School of Graduate Studies, School of Engineering, Science and Technology, Department of Mathematical Sciences, New Britain, CT 06050-4010. Offers data mining (MS, Certificate); mathematics (MA, MS), including actuarial science (MA), computer science (MA), statistics (MA); mathematics education leadership (Sixth Year Certificate); mathematics for secondary education (Certificate). *Program availability:* Part-time, evening/weekend, 100% online. *Faculty:* 15 full-time (4 women). *Students:* 17 full-time (10 women), 65 part-time (36 women); includes 17 minority (8 Black or African American, non-Hispanic/Latino; 5 Asian, non-Hispanic/Latino; 3 Hispanic/Latino; 1 Two or more races, non-Hispanic/Latino), 2 international. Average age 35. 68 applicants, 81% accepted, 31 enrolled. In 2017, 21 master's, 5 other advanced degrees awarded. *Degree requirements:* For master's, comprehensive exam, thesis or alternative, special project; for other advanced degree, qualifying exam. *Entrance requirements:* For master's, minimum undergraduate GPA of 2.7; for other advanced degree, minimum undergraduate GPA of 3.0, essay, letters of recommendation. Additional exam requirements/recommendations for international students: Required—TOEFL (minimum score 550 paper-based; 79 iBT); Recommended—IELTS (minimum score 6.5). *Application deadline:* For fall admission, 8/1 for domestic students, 5/1 for international students; for spring admission, 11/1 for domestic and international students. Applications are processed on a rolling basis. Application fee: $50. Electronic applications accepted. *Expenses: Tuition, area resident:* Full-time $6757. Tuition, state resident: full-time $9750; part-time $374 per credit. Tuition, nonresident: full-time $18,102; part-time $374 per credit. *Required fees:* $4635; $255 per credit. *Financial support:* In 2017–18, 25 students received support. Career-related internships or fieldwork, Federal Work-Study, scholarships/grants, and unspecified assistantships available. Support available to part-time students. Financial award application deadline: 3/1; financial award applicants required to submit FAFSA. *Faculty research:* Statistics, actuarial mathematics, computer systems and engineering, computer programming techniques, operations research. *Unit head:* Dr. Philip Halloran, Chair, 860-832-2835, E-mail: halloranp@ccsu.edu. *Application contact:* Patricia Gardner, Associate Director of Graduate Studies, 860-832-2350, Fax: 860-832-2362. Website: http://www.ccsu.edu/mathematics/

Central Michigan University, Central Michigan University Global Campus, Program in Educational Leadership, Mount Pleasant, MI 48859. Offers K-12 leadership (Ed D). *Program availability:* Part-time, evening/weekend. *Entrance requirements:* Additional exam requirements/recommendations for international students: Required—TOEFL. Electronic applications accepted.

Central Michigan University, College of Graduate Studies, College of Education and Human Services, Department of Teacher Education and Professional Development, Mount Pleasant, MI 48859. Offers educational technology (MA, Graduate Certificate); elementary education (MA), including classroom teaching, early childhood; reading and literacy K-12 (MA); secondary education (MA). *Program availability:* Part-time, evening/weekend. *Degree requirements:* For master's, thesis or alternative. Electronic applications accepted. *Faculty research:* Integrating literacy across the curriculum, science teaching and aesthetic learning in science, diversity education, educational technology, educational psychology and child development.

Secondary Education

Central Michigan University, College of Graduate Studies, College of Science and Technology, Department of Chemistry, Mount Pleasant, MI 48859. Offers chemistry (MS); teaching chemistry (MA), including teaching college chemistry, teaching high school chemistry. *Program availability:* Part-time. *Degree requirements:* For master's, comprehensive exam, thesis or alternative. *Entrance requirements:* For master's, GRE. Electronic applications accepted. *Faculty research:* Analytical and organic-inorganic chemistry, biochemistry, catalysis, dendrimer and polymer studies, nanotechnology.

Chadron State College, School of Professional and Graduate Studies, Department of Education, Chadron, NE 69337. Offers business (MA Ed); community counseling (MA Ed); educational administration (MS Ed, Sp Ed); elementary education (MS Ed); history (MA Ed); language and literature (MA Ed); secondary administration (MS Ed); secondary education (MS Ed). *Accreditation:* NCATE. *Program availability:* Part-time, evening/weekend, online learning. *Degree requirements:* For master's, thesis optional. *Entrance requirements:* For master's, GRE General Test, GRE Writing Test, minimum GPA of 2.75 or 12 graduate hours at CSC with minimum GPA of 3.25. Additional exam requirements/recommendations for international students: Required—TOEFL. Electronic applications accepted. *Faculty research:* Rural education, technology, mental health.

Chaminade University of Honolulu, Office of Professional and Continuing Education, Program in Education, Honolulu, HI 96816-1578. Offers child development (M Ed); early childhood education (Montessori) (MAT); early childhood education (PK-3) (MAT); educational leadership (M Ed); elementary education (MAT); instructional leadership (M Ed); Montessori (M Ed); secondary education (MAT); special education (MAT); teacher leader (M Ed). *Program availability:* Part-time, evening/weekend, 100% online, blended/hybrid learning. *Faculty:* 7 full-time (3 women), 8 part-time/adjunct (6 women). *Students:* 86 full-time (68 women), 88 part-time (64 women); includes 113 minority (7 Black or African American, non-Hispanic/Latino; 2 American Indian or Alaska Native, non-Hispanic/Latino; 46 Asian, non-Hispanic/Latino; 7 Hispanic/Latino; 51 Native Hawaiian or other Pacific Islander, non-Hispanic/Latino), 6 international. Average age 34. 61 applicants, 98% accepted, 49 enrolled. In 2017, 91 master's awarded. *Degree requirements:* For master's, thesis or alternative. *Entrance requirements:* For master's, PRAXIS (for MAT), minimum GPA of 2.75 (for M Ed), 3.0 (for MAT); 2 letters of recommendation, resume, writing sample (for MAT). Additional exam requirements/recommendations for international students: Required—TOEFL (minimum score 550 paper-based; 79 iBT). *Application deadline:* Applications are processed on a rolling basis. Application fee: $40. Electronic applications accepted. *Expenses:* $780 per credit hour plus $93 fee per online class. *Financial support:* Applicants required to submit FAFSA. *Unit head:* Dr. Dale Fryxell, Dean, 808-739-4652, Fax: 808-739-4607, E-mail: edu-office@chaminade.edu. *Application contact:* 808-735-4755, E-mail: gradserv@chaminade.edu.
Website: https://education.chaminade.edu/

Chapman University, Donna Ford Attallah College of Educational Studies, Orange, CA 92866. Offers counseling (MA), including school counseling (MA, Credential); curriculum and instruction (MA), including elementary education, secondary education; education (PhD), including cultural and curricular studies, disability studies, leadership studies, school psychology (PhD, Credential); educational psychology (MA); leadership development (MA); multiple subjects (Credential), including Spanish/English bilingual; pupil personnel services (Credential), including school counseling (MA, Credential), school psychology (PhD, Credential); school psychology (Ed S); single subject (Credential); special education (MA, Credential), including mild/moderate (Credential), moderate/severe (Credential); teaching (MA), including elementary education, secondary education, secondary music education. *Accreditation:* TEAC. *Program availability:* Part-time, evening/weekend. *Faculty:* 32 full-time (18 women), 37 part-time/adjunct (26 women). *Students:* 170 full-time (140 women), 180 part-time (129 women); includes 164 minority (6 Black or African American, non-Hispanic/Latino; 38 Asian, non-Hispanic/Latino; 101 Hispanic/Latino; 1 Native Hawaiian or other Pacific Islander, non-Hispanic/Latino; 18 Two or more races, non-Hispanic/Latino), 10 international. Average age 28. 143 applicants, 63% accepted, 64 enrolled. In 2017, 126 master's, 18 doctorates awarded. *Application deadline:* Applications are processed on a rolling basis. Application fee: $60. Electronic applications accepted. *Expenses:* Contact institution. *Financial support:* Fellowships and scholarships/grants available. Financial award application deadline: 3/2; financial award applicants required to submit FAFSA. *Unit head:* Dr. Margaret Grogan, Dean, 714-516-5968, E-mail: grogan@chapman.edu. *Application contact:* Shannon McCance, Graduate Admission Counselor, 714-516-5236, E-mail: smccance@chapman.edu.
Website: http://www.chapman.edu/CES/

Chatham University, Program in Education, Pittsburgh, PA 15232-2826. Offers early childhood education (MAT); elementary education (MAT); environmental education (K-12) (MAT); secondary art (MAT); secondary biology education (MAT); secondary chemistry education (MAT); secondary English education (MAT); secondary math education (MAT); secondary physics education (MAT); secondary social studies education (MAT); special education (MAT). *Faculty:* 1 (woman) full-time, 15 part-time/adjunct (13 women). *Students:* 31 full-time (23 women), 3 part-time (1 woman); includes 9 minority (8 Black or African American, non-Hispanic/Latino; 1 Hispanic/Latino). Average age 30. 25 applicants, 60% accepted, 9 enrolled. In 2017, 23 master's awarded. *Degree requirements:* For master's, thesis, teaching experience. *Entrance requirements:* For master's, minimum GPA of 3.0, sample of written work, recommendation letters. Additional exam requirements/recommendations for international students: Required—TOEFL (minimum score 600 paper-based; 100 iBT), IELTS (minimum score 7), TWE. *Application deadline:* For fall admission, 4/1 priority date for domestic and international students; for spring admission, 11/1 priority date for domestic students, 10/1 priority date for international students. Applications are processed on a rolling basis. Application fee: $45. Electronic applications accepted. Application fee is waived when completed online. *Expenses:* Tuition: Full-time $16,740; part-time $930 per credit. *Required fees:* $486; $27 per credit. $243 per semester. *Financial support:* Career-related internships or fieldwork available. Financial award applicants required to submit FAFSA. *Faculty research:* Gifted education, environmental education, technology in education, writing as learning, class size and achievement. *Application contact:* Katie Noel, Assistant Director of Graduate Admission, 412-365-2758, Fax: 412-365-1609, E-mail: gradadmissions@chatham.edu.
Website: http://www.chatham.edu/mat

Chestnut Hill College, School of Graduate Studies, Department of Education, Program in Secondary Education, Philadelphia, PA 19118-2693. Offers M Ed. *Program availability:* Part-time, evening/weekend. *Degree requirements:* For master's, thesis optional. *Entrance requirements:* For master's, PRAXIS I or proof of teaching certification, letters of recommendation; writing sample; 6 graduate credits with minimum B grade if undergraduate GPA less than 3.0. Additional exam requirements/recommendations for international students: Required—TOEFL (minimum score 500 paper-based), IELTS (minimum score 6.0), or TWE (minimum score 22). Electronic applications accepted. *Expenses:* Contact institution. *Faculty research:* Science teaching.

Chicago State University, School of Graduate and Professional Studies, College of Education, Department of Educational Leadership, Curriculum and Foundations, Program in Curriculum and Instruction, Chicago, IL 60628. Offers instructional foundations (MS Ed), including adult education, elementary education, secondary education. *Degree requirements:* For master's, comprehensive exam, thesis optional. *Entrance requirements:* For master's, minimum GPA of 2.75. *Application deadline:* For fall admission, 7/1 for domestic students; for spring admission, 11/10 for domestic students. Application fee: $25. *Unit head:* Dr. Cathryn Busch, Chairperson. *Application contact:* Anika Miller, Graduate Studies Office, 773-995-2404, E-mail: g-studies1@csu.edu.

The Citadel, The Military College of South Carolina, Citadel Graduate College, Zucker Family School of Education, Charleston, SC 29409. Offers elementary/secondary school administration and supervision (M Ed); elementary/secondary school counseling (M Ed); interdisciplinary STEM education (M Ed); literacy education (M Ed, Graduate Certificate); middle grades (MAT), including English, mathematics, science, social studies; physical education (grades K-12) (MAT); school superintendency (Ed S); secondary education (MAT), including biology, English, mathematics, social studies; student affairs (Graduate Certificate); student affairs and college counseling (M Ed). *Accreditation:* NCATE. *Program availability:* Part-time, evening/weekend, 100% online, blended/hybrid learning. *Degree requirements:* For master's, comprehensive exam (for some programs). *Entrance requirements:* For master's, GRE (minimum combined verbal and quantitative score of 290) or MAT (minimum score 396). Additional exam requirements/recommendations for international students: Required—TOEFL (minimum score 550 paper-based; 79 iBT). Electronic applications accepted. *Expenses:* Tuition, state resident: part-time $587 per credit hour. Tuition, nonresident: part-time $988 per credit hour. *Required fees:* $90 per term.

City College of the City University of New York, Graduate School, School of Education, Department of Secondary Education, New York, NY 10031-9198. Offers adolescent mathematics education (MA, AC); English education (MA); middle school mathematics education (MS); science education (MA); social studies education (AC). *Accreditation:* NCATE. *Entrance requirements:* For master's, Liberal Arts and Sciences Test (LAST), Content Specialty Test (CST). Additional exam requirements/recommendations for international students: Required—TOEFL.

Clarkson University, Program in Education, Schenectady, NY 12308. Offers adolescence education 7-12 (MAT); teaching of English to speakers of other languages (MAT); technology education K-12 (MAT). *Accreditation:* TEAC. *Faculty:* 3 full-time (all women), 23 part-time/adjunct (14 women). *Students:* 22 full-time (13 women), 12 part-time (8 women); includes 4 minority (1 Black or African American, non-Hispanic/Latino; 3 Asian, non-Hispanic/Latino), 6 international. 39 applicants, 72% accepted, 21 enrolled. In 2017, 28 master's awarded. *Degree requirements:* For master's, thesis (for some programs), thesis or project. *Entrance requirements:* For master's, GRE, minimum undergraduate GPA of 3.0. Additional exam requirements/recommendations for international students: Required—TOEFL (minimum score 550 paper-based, 80 iBT) or IELTS (6.5). *Application deadline:* Applications are processed on a rolling basis. Application fee: $50. Electronic applications accepted. *Expenses:* Contact institution. *Financial support:* Scholarships/grants available. *Unit head:* Dr. Catherine Snyder, Chair of Education, 518-631-9870, E-mail: csnyder@clarkson.edu. *Application contact:* Dan Capogna, Director of Graduate Admissions, 518-631-9910, E-mail: graduate@clarkson.edu.
Website: https://www.clarkson.edu/academics/graduate

Clemson University, Graduate School, College of Education, Department of Teaching and Learning, Clemson, SC 29634. Offers curriculum and instruction (PhD); middle level education (MAT); secondary math and science (MAT); STEAM education (Certificate); teaching and learning (M Ed). *Program availability:* Part-time, evening/weekend, 100% online. *Faculty:* 21 full-time (17 women). *Students:* 41 full-time (27 women), 94 part-time (78 women); includes 16 minority (8 Black or African American, non-Hispanic/Latino; 6 Hispanic/Latino; 1 Native Hawaiian or other Pacific Islander, non-Hispanic/Latino; 1 Two or more races, non-Hispanic/Latino), 3 international. Average age 29. 65 applicants, 62% accepted, 33 enrolled. In 2017, 74 master's awarded. *Degree requirements:* For master's, comprehensive exam; for doctorate, comprehensive exam, thesis/dissertation. *Entrance requirements:* For master's, doctorate, and Certificate, GRE General Test, unofficial transcripts, letters of recommendation. Additional exam requirements/recommendations for international students: Required—TOEFL (minimum score 540 paper-based; 80 iBT), IELTS (minimum score 7), PTE (minimum score 45). *Application deadline:* For fall admission, 4/15 for domestic and international students. Applications are processed on a rolling basis. Application fee: $80 ($90 for international students). Electronic applications accepted. *Expenses:* $5,767 per semester full-time resident, $10,918 per semester full-time non-resident, $656 per credit hour part-time resident, $1,310 per credit hour part-time non-resident, $915 per credit hour online; other fees may apply per session. *Financial support:* In 2017–18, 8 students received support, including 2 fellowships with partial tuition reimbursements available (averaging $3,500 per year), 1 research assistantship with partial tuition reimbursement available (averaging $18,000 per year), 5 teaching assistantships with partial tuition reimbursements available (averaging $18,000 per year); career-related internships or fieldwork also available. Financial award application deadline: 4/1. *Faculty research:* STEAM education, inquiry-based instruction, cultural hegemony and mathematics, equity and ethics, teacher effectiveness. *Total annual research expenditures:* $1.6 million. *Unit head:* Dr. Jeff Marshall, Department Chair, 864-656-2059, E-mail: marsha9@clemson.edu. *Application contact:* Alison Search, Student Services Coordinator, 864-250-8880, E-mail: alisonp@clemson.edu.
Website: http://www.clemson.edu/education/departments/teaching-learning/index.html

Colgate University, Master of Arts in Teaching Program, Hamilton, NY 13346-1386. Offers MAT. *Accreditation:* TEAC. *Degree requirements:* For master's, special project or thesis. *Entrance requirements:* For master's, GRE General Test, interview. *Faculty research:* Culturally-responsive teaching, comparative education, moral development in education, politics in education, educational psychology.

The College of New Jersey, Office of Graduate and Advancing Education, School of Education, Department of Educational Administration and Secondary Education, Program in Secondary Education, Ewing, NJ 08628. Offers MAT. *Degree requirements:* For master's, comprehensive exam. *Entrance requirements:* For master's, GRE, minimum GPA of 3.0 in field or 2.75 overall. Additional exam requirements/recommendations for international students: Required—TOEFL. Electronic applications accepted.

College of St. Joseph, Graduate Programs, Division of Education, Program in Secondary Education, Rutland, VT 05701-3899. Offers English (M Ed); social studies (M Ed). *Program availability:* Part-time, evening/weekend. *Degree requirements:* For master's, comprehensive exam. *Entrance requirements:* For master's, PRAXIS I, official college transcripts; 2 letters of reference; minimum GPA of 3.0 (initial licensure) or 2.7 (nonlicensure); interview. Additional exam requirements/recommendations for international students: Required—TOEFL (minimum score 550 paper-based). Electronic applications accepted.

The College of Saint Rose, Graduate Studies, Thelma P. Lally School of Education, Programs in Special Education, Albany, NY 12203-1419. Offers adolescence education/special education (MS Ed); childhood education/special education (MS Ed); childhood special education (MS Ed); early childhood special education (MS Ed); special education (Certificate); special education professional (MS Ed). *Accreditation:* NCATE. *Students:* 8 full-time (5 women), 13 part-time (11 women), 1 international. Average age 27. 11 applicants, 82% accepted, 5 enrolled. In 2017, 15 master's awarded. *Degree requirements:* For master's, comprehensive exam (for some programs), thesis or alternative, research project. *Entrance requirements:* For master's, minimum undergraduate GPA of 3.0. Additional exam requirements/recommendations for international students: Required—TOEFL (minimum score 550 paper-based; 80 iBT), IELTS (minimum score 6), PTE (minimum score 56). *Application deadline:* For fall admission, 4/1 priority date for domestic and international students; for spring admission, 10/15 priority date for domestic and international students; for summer admission, 3/15 priority date for domestic and international students. Applications are processed on a rolling basis. Application fee: $40. Electronic applications accepted. *Expenses: Tuition:* Full-time $7191; part-time $799 per credit hour. *Required fees:* $924; $462 per credit hour. Tuition and fees vary according to course load. *Financial support:* Career-related internships or fieldwork, scholarships/grants, tuition waivers (partial), and unspecified assistantships available. Support available to part-time students. Financial award application deadline: 4/15. *Unit head:* Franics Ihle, Chair, 518-337-4885, E-mail: ihlef@strose.edu. *Application contact:* Cris Murray, Assistant Vice President for Graduate Recruitment and Enrollment, 518-485-3390, E-mail: grad@strose.edu. Website: https://www.strose.edu/special-education/

The College of Saint Rose, Graduate Studies, Thelma P. Lally School of Education, Teacher Education Programs, Albany, NY 12203-1419. Offers adolescence education (MS Ed, Advanced Certificate); adolescence education/special education (Advanced Certificate); childhood education (MS Ed); curriculum and instruction (MS Ed); early childhood education (MS Ed). *Students:* 69 full-time (60 women), 21 part-time (16 women); includes 7 minority (4 Black or African American, non-Hispanic/Latino; 2 Hispanic/Latino; 1 Two or more races, non-Hispanic/Latino), 1 international. Average age 27. 46 applicants, 52% accepted, 23 enrolled. In 2017, 43 master's awarded. *Entrance requirements:* For master's, minimum undergraduate GPA of 3.0. Additional exam requirements/recommendations for international students: Required—TOEFL (minimum score 550 paper-based; 80 iBT), IELTS (minimum score 6), PTE (minimum score 56). *Application deadline:* For fall admission, 4/1 priority date for domestic and international students; for spring admission, 10/15 priority date for domestic and international students; for summer admission, 3/15 priority date for domestic and international students. Applications are processed on a rolling basis. Application fee: $40. Electronic applications accepted. *Expenses: Tuition:* Full-time $7191; part-time $799 per credit hour. *Required fees:* $924; $462 per credit hour. Tuition and fees vary according to course load. *Financial support:* Career-related internships or fieldwork, scholarships/grants, tuition waivers (partial), and unspecified assistantships available. Support available to part-time students. Financial award application deadline: 4/15. *Unit head:* Dr. Drey Martone, Chair, 518-454-5262, E-mail: martoned@strose.edu. *Application contact:* Cris Murray, Assistant Vice President for Graduate Recruitment and Enrollment, 518-485-3390, Fax: 518-458-5479, E-mail: grad@strose.edu. Website: https://www.strose.edu/academics/schools/school-of-education/

College of Staten Island of the City University of New York, Graduate Programs, School of Education, Program in Adolescence Education, Staten Island, NY 10314-6600. Offers adolescence education (MS Ed), including biology, English, mathematics, social studies. *Program availability:* Part-time, evening/weekend. *Faculty:* 23 full-time, 6 part-time/adjunct. *Students:* 87. 45 applicants, 67% accepted, 23 enrolled. In 2017, 21 master's awarded. *Degree requirements:* For master's, thesis, educational research project supervised by faculty. *Entrance requirements:* For master's, GRE General Test or an approved equivalent examination, relevant bachelor's degree, minimum overall GPA of 3.0, two letters of recommendation, one- or two-page personal statement. Additional exam requirements/recommendations for international students: Required—TOEFL (minimum score 550 paper-based; 79 iBT), IELTS (minimum score 6.5). *Application deadline:* For fall admission, 4/25 for domestic and international students; for spring admission, 11/25 for domestic and international students. Applications are processed on a rolling basis. Application fee: $125. Electronic applications accepted. *Expenses:* Tuition, state resident: full-time $10,450; part-time $440 per credit. Tuition, nonresident: full-time $19,320; part-time $440 per credit. *Required fees:* $181.10 per semester. Tuition and fees vary according to program. *Faculty research:* Development and assessment of TPACK (technological pedagogical content knowledge), technology and differentiation in stem classrooms, teacher effectiveness and student achievement, teacher knowledge, knowledge transfer from college to classroom. *Unit head:* Diane Brescia, 718-982-3877, E-mail: diane.brescia@csi.cuny.edu. *Application contact:* Sasha Spence, Associate Director for Graduate Admissions, 718-982-2019, Fax: 718-982-2500, E-mail: sasha.spence@csi.cuny.edu. Website: http://www.csi.cuny.edu/catalog/graduate/graduate-programs-in-education.htm#o2608

College of Staten Island of the City University of New York, Graduate Programs, School of Education, Program in Special Education, Staten Island, NY 10314-6600. Offers special education (MS Ed), including adolescence generalist: grades 7-12, grades 1-6. *Program availability:* Part-time, evening/weekend. *Faculty:* 3 full-time, 8 part-time/adjunct. *Students:* 144. 73 applicants, 73% accepted, 41 enrolled. In 2017, 39 master's awarded. *Degree requirements:* For master's, comprehensive exam, fieldwork; ten three-credit required courses and one elective for a total of 11 courses (33 credits) or 14 three-credit required courses and a three- to six-credit, field-based requirement for a total of 45-48 credits; research project. *Entrance requirements:* For master's, GRE General Test or an approved equivalent examination, BA/BS or 36 approved credits with minimum GPA of 3.0, 2 letters of recommendations, 1-2 page statement of experience. Additional exam requirements/recommendations for international students: Required—TOEFL (minimum score 550 paper-based; 79 iBT), IELTS (minimum score 6.5). *Application deadline:* For fall admission, 4/25 for domestic and international students; for spring admission, 11/25 for domestic and international students. Applications are processed on a rolling basis. Application fee: $125. Electronic applications accepted. *Expenses:* Tuition, state resident: full-time $10,450; part-time $440 per credit. Tuition, nonresident: full-time $19,320; part-time $440 per credit. *Required fees:* $181.10 per semester. Tuition and fees vary according to program. *Faculty research:* Disabilities studies, social justice, arts-based research on disabilities, assessment of students with disabilities, technological pedagogical and content knowledge (TPACK) in special education teachers, juvenile justice. *Unit head:* Diane Brescia, 718-982-3877, E-mail: diane.brescia@csi.cuny.edu. *Application contact:* Sasha Spence, Associate Director for Graduate Admissions, 718-982-2019, Fax: 718-982-2500, E-mail: sasha.spence@csi.cuny.edu. Website: https://www.csi.cuny.edu/sites/default/files/pdf/admissions/grad/pdf/Education%20Fact%20Sheet.pdf

The College of William and Mary, School of Education, Program in Curriculum and Instruction, Williamsburg, VA 23187-8795. Offers elementary education (MA Ed); English as a second language/bilingual education (MA Ed); gifted education (MA Ed); literacy leadership (MA Ed); math specialist (MA Ed); secondary education (MA Ed), including English, foreign language, math, science, social studies; special education (MA Ed). *Accreditation:* NCATE. *Program availability:* Part-time. *Faculty:* 23 full-time (16 women), 40 part-time/adjunct (32 women). *Students:* 85 full-time (63 women), 16 part-

time (15 women); includes 18 minority (5 Black or African American, non-Hispanic/Latino; 4 Asian, non-Hispanic/Latino; 7 Hispanic/Latino; 2 Two or more races, non-Hispanic/Latino), 1 international. Average age 27. 152 applicants, 83% accepted, 90 enrolled. In 2017, 67 master's awarded. *Degree requirements:* For master's, project. *Entrance requirements:* For master's, GRE, MAT, PRAXIS Core Academic Skills for Educators, minimum GPA of 2.5. Additional exam requirements/recommendations for international students: Required—TOEFL (minimum score 100 iBT), IELTS (minimum score 7). *Application deadline:* For fall admission, 1/15 for domestic and international students; for spring admission, 10/1 for domestic and international students. Application fee: $50. Electronic applications accepted. *Expenses:* $9,630 resident full-time, $535 resident part-time per credit hour; $25,920 nonresident full-time, $1,265 nonresident part-time per credit hour; $5,944 full-time fees. *Financial support:* In 2017–18, 35 students received support, including 7 research assistantships (averaging $6,678 per year); scholarships/grants and unspecified assistantships also available. Financial award application deadline: 1/15; financial award applicants required to submit FAFSA. *Faculty research:* Educational technology, professional development and evaluation, inclusive education, rural education, education policy. *Unit head:* Dr. Jeremy D. Stoddard, Department Chair, 757-221-2348, E-mail: jdstod@wm.edu. *Application contact:* Dorothy Smith Osborne, Assistant Dean for Academic Programs and Student Services, 757-221-2317, E-mail: dsosbo@wm.edu. Website: http://education.wm.edu

The Colorado College, Education Department, Program in Secondary Education, Colorado Springs, CO 80903-3294. Offers art teaching (K-12) (MAT); English teaching (MAT); foreign language teaching (MAT); mathematics teaching (MAT); music teaching (MAT); science teaching (MAT); social studies teaching (MAT). *Degree requirements:* For master's, thesis, internship. Electronic applications accepted.

Columbus State University, Graduate Studies, College of Education and Health Professions, Department of Teacher Education, Columbus, GA 31907-5645. Offers curriculum and instruction in accomplished teaching (M Ed); early childhood education (M Ed, MAT, Ed S); middle grades education (M Ed, MAT, Ed S); secondary education (M Ed, MAT, Ed S), including biology (MAT), chemistry (MAT), earth and space science (MAT), English/language arts, general science (M Ed), history (MAT), mathematics, science (Ed S), social science (M Ed, Ed S); special education (M Ed, MAT, Ed S), including general curriculum (M Ed, MAT); teacher leadership (M Ed). *Accreditation:* NCATE. *Program availability:* Part-time, evening/weekend, 100% online, blended/hybrid learning. *Faculty:* 19 full-time (12 women), 24 part-time/adjunct (18 women). *Students:* 99 full-time (76 women), 181 part-time (143 women); includes 109 minority (94 Black or African American, non-Hispanic/Latino; 1 American Indian or Alaska Native, non-Hispanic/Latino; 1 Asian, non-Hispanic/Latino; 6 Hispanic/Latino; 7 Two or more races, non-Hispanic/Latino). Average age 34. 136 applicants, 63% accepted, 56 enrolled. In 2017, 119 master's, 8 other advanced degrees awarded. *Degree requirements:* For Ed S, thesis or alternative. *Entrance requirements:* For master's, GRE General Test, minimum undergraduate GPA of 2.75; for Ed S, GRE General Test, minimum undergraduate GPA of 2.75, graduate 3.0. Additional exam requirements/recommendations for international students: Required—TOEFL (minimum score 550 paper-based; 79 iBT). *Application deadline:* For fall admission, 6/30 for domestic students, 5/1 for international students; for spring admission, 11/1 for domestic and international students; for summer admission, 3/1 for domestic and international students. Applications are processed on a rolling basis. Application fee: $50. Electronic applications accepted. *Expenses:* Tuition, state resident: full-time $3708; part-time $2472 per year. Tuition, nonresident: full-time $14,418; part-time $9612 per year. *International tuition:* $19,218 full-time. *Required fees:* $1605. Tuition and fees vary according to program. *Financial support:* In 2017–18, 45 students received support, including 9 research assistantships with partial tuition reimbursements available (averaging $3,000 per year); career-related internships or fieldwork, Federal Work-Study, institutionally sponsored loans, scholarships/grants, tuition waivers (partial), and unspecified assistantships also available. Support available to part-time students. Financial award application deadline: 5/1; financial award applicants required to submit FAFSA. *Unit head:* Dr. Jan Burcham, Department Chair, 706-507-8519, Fax: 706-568-3134, E-mail: burcham_jan@columbusstate.edu. *Application contact:* Catrina Smith-Edmond, Assistant Director for Graduate and Global Admission, 706-507-8824, Fax: 706-568-5091, E-mail: smithedmond_catrina@columbusstate.edu. Website: http://te.columbusstate.edu/

Concordia University, College of Education, Portland, OR 97211-6099. Offers career and technical education (M Ed); curriculum and instruction (M Ed), including adolescent literacy, career and technical education, e-learning/technology education, early childhood education, English for speakers of other languages, English language development, environmental education, mathematics, methods and curriculum, reading, science, teacher leadership, the inclusive classroom; early childhood (MAT); education leadership (Ed D); educational administration (M Ed); elementary education (MAT); secondary education (MAT); special education (M Ed); teacher leadership (Ed D). *Program availability:* Part-time, online learning. *Degree requirements:* For master's, comprehensive exam, work samples/portfolio. *Entrance requirements:* For master's, California Basic Educational Skills Test or PRAXIS I, minimum undergraduate GPA of 2.8, graduate 3.0; 2 letters of recommendation. Additional exam requirements/recommendations for international students: Required—TOEFL (minimum score 525 paper-based). Electronic applications accepted. *Faculty research:* Learner-centered classroom, brain-based learning, future of online learning.

Concordia University Chicago, College of Education, Program in Teaching, River Forest, IL 60305-1499. Offers early childhood education (MAT); elementary education (MAT); secondary education (MAT). *Degree requirements:* For master's, thesis or alternative. *Entrance requirements:* For master's, minimum GPA of 2.9. Additional exam requirements/recommendations for international students: Required—TOEFL (minimum score 550 paper-based). Electronic applications accepted.

Concordia University, Nebraska, Graduate Programs in Education, Program in Educational Administration, Seward, NE 68434. Offers elementary and secondary education (M Ed); elementary education (M Ed); secondary education (M Ed). *Accreditation:* NCATE. *Program availability:* Part-time. *Degree requirements:* For master's, thesis or alternative. *Entrance requirements:* For master's, GRE, MAT, or NTE, BS in education or equivalent, minimum GPA of 3.0.

Converse College, Program in Secondary Education, Spartanburg, SC 29302. Offers biology (MAT); chemistry (MAT); English (M Ed, MAT); mathematics (M Ed, MAT); natural sciences (M Ed); social sciences (M Ed, MAT). *Program availability:* Part-time. *Degree requirements:* For master's, capstone paper. *Entrance requirements:* For master's, NTE or PRAXIS II (M Ed), minimum GPA of 2.75, 2 recommendations. *Application deadline:* For fall admission, 8/1 for domestic and international students; for winter admission, 11/15 for domestic and international students; for spring admission, 1/15 for domestic and international students. Applications are processed on a rolling basis. Application fee: $40. Electronic applications accepted. *Financial support:* Available to part-time students. Applicants required to submit FAFSA. *Unit head:* Lienne Medford, Dean of Graduate Studies and Distance Education, 864-596-9082, E-mail: lienne.medford@converse.edu. *Application contact:* 864-596-9404, E-mail: graduate@converse.edu.

Secondary Education

Cornell University, Graduate School, Graduate Fields of Agriculture and Life Sciences, Field of Education, Ithaca, NY 14853. Offers adult and extension education (MPS, MS, PhD); learning, teaching, and social policy (MPS, MS, PhD); mathematics 7-12 (MS). Terminal master's awarded for partial completion of doctoral program. *Degree requirements:* For master's, thesis (MS); for doctorate, comprehensive exam, thesis/dissertation. *Entrance requirements:* For master's and doctorate, GRE General Test, sample of written work (recommended), 2 letters of recommendation. Additional exam requirements/recommendations for international students: Required—TOEFL (minimum score 550 paper-based; 77 iBT). Electronic applications accepted. *Faculty research:* Moral development and professional ethics, public issues education and community development, socio/political issues in public education, teacher education and curriculum in agricultural science and mathematics, extension research.

Creighton University, Graduate School, College of Arts and Sciences, Department of Education, Program in Teaching, Omaha, NE 68178-0001. Offers elementary teaching (M Ed); secondary teaching (M Ed). *Program availability:* Part-time. *Faculty:* 10 full-time (5 women). *Students:* 8 full-time (6 women), 22 part-time (17 women); includes 1 minority (Asian, non-Hispanic/Latino). Average age 26. In 2017, 23 master's awarded. *Degree requirements:* For master's, portfolio. *Entrance requirements:* For master's, 3 letters of recommendation, 2 writing samples. Additional exam requirements/recommendations for international students: Required—TOEFL (minimum score 90 iBT). *Application deadline:* For fall admission, 7/1 priority date for domestic students, 3/1 priority date for international students; for winter admission, 12/1 priority date for domestic students, 6/1 priority date for international students; for spring admission, 3/1 priority date for domestic and international students; for summer admission, 3/1 for domestic and international students. Application fee: $50. Electronic applications accepted. Part-time tuition and fees vary according to course load, degree level, campus/location and program. *Financial support:* Scholarships/grants and tuition waivers (partial) available. Support available to part-time students. Financial award applicants required to submit FAFSA. *Unit head:* Dr. Debra Ponec, Director, 402-280-2557, E-mail: dlponec@creighton.edu. *Application contact:* Lindsay Johnson, Director of Graduate and Adult Recruitment, 402-280-2703, Fax: 402-280-2423, E-mail: gradschool@creighton.edu.

Dakota Wesleyan University, Program in Education, Mitchell, SD 57301-4398. Offers curriculum and instruction (MA Ed); educational policy and administration (MA Ed); preK-12 principal certification (MA Ed); secondary certification (MA Ed). *Program availability:* Part-time, evening/weekend. *Degree requirements:* For master's, comprehensive exam, thesis optional, electronic portfolio. *Entrance requirements:* For master's, minimum GPA of 2.7, elementary statistics course, statement of purpose, official transcripts, resume, three letters of recommendation. Additional exam requirements/recommendations for international students: Required—TOEFL (minimum score 500 paper-based), IELTS (minimum score 6.5). Electronic applications accepted. *Faculty research:* Math, political policy, technology in the classroom.

Dallas Baptist University, Dorothy M. Bush College of Education, Teaching Program, Dallas, TX 75211-9299. Offers distance learning (MAT); early childhood through grade 6 certification (MAT); early childhood-12 (MAT); elementary (MAT); English as a second language (MAT); Montessori (MAT); multisensory (MAT); secondary (MAT). *Program availability:* Part-time, evening/weekend. *Application deadline:* Applications are processed on a rolling basis. Application fee: $25. Electronic applications accepted. Application fee is waived when completed online. *Expenses: Tuition:* Full-time $16,308; part-time $906 per credit hour. *Required fees:* $900; $450 per semester. Tuition and fees vary according to course load and degree level. *Unit head:* Dr. Neil Dugger, Dean, 214-333-5202, E-mail: neil@dbu.edu. *Application contact:* Dr. DeAnna Jenkins, Program Director, 214-333-5402, E-mail: deannaj@dbu.edu.
Website: http://www3.dbu.edu/graduate/mat.asp

Delta State University, Graduate Programs, College of Arts and Sciences, Division of Languages and Literature, Cleveland, MS 38733-0001. Offers secondary education (M Ed), including English. *Program availability:* Part-time. *Degree requirements:* For master's, thesis or alternative.

Delta State University, Graduate Programs, College of Arts and Sciences, Division of Social Sciences and History, Cleveland, MS 38733-0001. Offers community development (MS); social justice and criminology (MSJC); social science secondary education (M Ed), including history, social sciences. *Program availability:* Part-time, online learning. *Degree requirements:* For master's, thesis or alternative.

Delta State University, Graduate Programs, College of Education, Division of Teacher Education, Leadership, and Research, Cleveland, MS 38733-0001. Offers educational administration and supervision (M Ed, Ed S); elementary education (M Ed, MAT, Ed S); professional studies (Ed D), including counselor education, elementary education, higher education; secondary education (MAT); special education (M Ed). *Accreditation:* NCATE. *Program availability:* Part-time, evening/weekend. *Degree requirements:* For master's, thesis optional. *Entrance requirements:* For master's, GRE General Test; for Ed S, master's degree, teaching certificate. Electronic applications accepted. *Faculty research:* Thinking skills, writing across the curriculum, mathematics/science education.

DePaul University, College of Education, Chicago, IL 60614. Offers bilingual-bicultural education (M Ed, MA); counseling (M Ed, MA), including clinical mental health counseling, college student development, school counseling; curriculum studies (M Ed, MA, Ed D); early childhood education (M Ed, MA, Ed D); educational leadership (M Ed, MA, Ed D), including Catholic leadership (M Ed, MA), general (M Ed, MA), higher education (M Ed, MA), physical education (M Ed, MA), principal preparation (M Ed), teacher preparation (M Ed); elementary education (M Ed, MA); middle grades education (M Ed); middle school mathematics education (MS); reading specialist (M Ed, MA); secondary education (M Ed, MA); social and cultural foundations in education (M Ed, MA); special education (M Ed); sport, fitness and recreation leadership (MS); value-creating education for global citizenship (M Ed); world languages education (M Ed, MA). *Program availability:* Part-time, evening/weekend, online learning. *Degree requirements:* For doctorate, thesis/dissertation. *Application deadline:* Applications are processed on a rolling basis. Application fee: $40. Electronic applications accepted. *Financial support:* Application deadline: 12/31; applicants required to submit FAFSA. *Unit head:* Dr. Paul Zionts, Dean, 773-325-7581, Fax: 773-325-7713, E-mail: pzionts@depaul.edu. *Application contact:* Dr. Paul Zionts, Dean, 773-325-7581, Fax: 773-325-7713, E-mail: pzionts@depaul.edu.
Website: http://education.depaul.edu

DeSales University, Division of Liberal Arts and Social Sciences, Center Valley, PA 18034-9568. Offers criminal justice (MCJ); digital forensics (MCJ, Postbaccalaureate Certificate); education (M Ed), including instructional technology, secondary education, special education, teaching English to speakers of other languages; investigative forensics (MCJ, Postbaccalaureate Certificate). *Program availability:* Part-time, 100% online, blended/hybrid learning. *Faculty:* 5 full-time (3 women), 15 part-time/adjunct (9 women). *Students:* 54 full-time (36 women), 112 part-time (68 women); includes 23 minority (3 Black or African American, non-Hispanic/Latino; 1 Asian, non-Hispanic/Latino; 17 Hispanic/Latino; 2 Two or more races, non-Hispanic/Latino), 1 international. Average age 33. 114 applicants, 64% accepted, 41 enrolled. In 2017, 41 master's awarded. *Entrance requirements:* For master's, bachelor's degree from accredited institution, minimum undergraduate GPA of 3.0, personal statement showing potential of graduate work, three letters of recommendation, professional goal statement. Additional exam requirements/recommendations for international students: Required—TOEFL. *Application deadline:* Applications are processed on a rolling basis. Application fee: $50. Electronic applications accepted. *Expenses: Tuition:* Part-time $840 per credit. Full-time tuition and fees vary according to course load, degree level and program. *Financial support:* Applicants required to submit FAFSA. *Unit head:* Ronald Nordone, Dean of Graduate Education, 610-282-1100 Ext. 1289, E-mail: ronald.nordone@desales.edu. *Application contact:* Julia Ferraro, Director of Graduate Admissions, 610-282-1100 Ext. 1768, E-mail: gradadmissions@desales.edu.

Dominican University, School of Education, River Forest, IL 60305-1099. Offers child life studies (MS); early childhood education (MS); education (MAT); elementary education (MA Ed); English as a second language (MA Ed); reading (MA Ed); secondary education (MAT); special education (MS). *Accreditation:* NCATE. *Program availability:* Part-time, evening/weekend, 100% online, blended/hybrid learning. *Faculty:* 8 full-time (6 women), 42 part-time/adjunct (38 women). *Students:* 5 full-time (all women), 261 part-time (206 women); includes 45 minority (16 Black or African American, non-Hispanic/Latino; 1 American Indian or Alaska Native, non-Hispanic/Latino; 5 Asian, non-Hispanic/Latino; 18 Hispanic/Latino; 5 Two or more races, non-Hispanic/Latino), 1 international. Average age 32. 95 applicants, 98% accepted, 72 enrolled. In 2017, 206 master's awarded. *Entrance requirements:* For master's, Illinois Test of Basic Skills. Additional exam requirements/recommendations for international students: Required—TOEFL (minimum score 550 paper-based; 79 iBT). *Application deadline:* Applications are processed on a rolling basis. Application fee: $25. *Expenses:* Contact institution. *Financial support:* Career-related internships or fieldwork, scholarships/grants, tuition waivers (partial), and unspecified assistantships available. Support available to part-time students. Financial award application deadline: 8/15; financial award applicants required to submit FAFSA. *Faculty research:* Governance of private education institutions, reading and language arts, inclusion, organizational planning, leadership and vision. *Unit head:* Dr. Colleen Reardon, Interim Executive Director, School of Education, 708-524-6643, Fax: 708-524-6665, E-mail: creardon@dom.edu. *Application contact:* Benjamin Mueller, Senior Graduate Marketing and Recruitment Coordinator, 708-524-6456, Fax: 708-524-6665, E-mail: bmueller@dom.edu.
Website: http://educate.dom.edu/

Drew University, Caspersen School of Graduate Studies, Madison, NJ 07940-1493. Offers conflict resolution and leadership (Certificate), including community leadership, moderation, peace building; education (M Ed); finance (MA); history and culture (MA, PhD), including American history, book history, British history, European history, Holocaust and genocide (M Litt, MA, D Litt, PhD), intellectual history, Irish history, print culture, public history; K-12 education (MAT), including art, biology, chemistry, elementary education, English, French, Italian, math, secondary education, special education, teacher of students with disabilities; liberal studies (M Litt, D Litt), including history, Holocaust and genocide (M Litt, MA, D Litt, PhD), Irish/Irish-American studies, literature (M Litt, MMH, D Litt, DMH, CMH), religion, spirituality, teaching in the two-year college, writing; medical humanities (MMH, DMH, CMH), including arts, health, healthcare, literature (M Litt, MMH, D Litt, DMH, CMH); scientific research; poetry (MFA). *Program availability:* Part-time, evening/weekend. *Faculty:* 4 full-time (2 women), 29 part-time/adjunct (15 women). *Students:* 77 full-time (42 women), 175 part-time (114 women); includes 39 minority (12 Black or African American, non-Hispanic/Latino; 6 Asian, non-Hispanic/Latino; 16 Hispanic/Latino; 5 Two or more races, non-Hispanic/Latino), 11 international. Average age 41. 126 applicants, 75% accepted, 52 enrolled. In 2017, 38 master's, 23 doctorates, 35 other advanced degrees awarded. Terminal master's awarded for partial completion of doctoral program. *Degree requirements:* For master's and other advanced degree, thesis (for some programs); for doctorate, one foreign language, comprehensive exam (for some programs), thesis/dissertation. *Entrance requirements:* For master's, PRAXIS Core and Subject Area tests (for MAT), GRE/GMAT (for M Fin), resume, transcripts, writing sample, personal statement, letters of recommendation; for doctorate, GRE (PhD in history and culture), resume, transcripts, writing sample, personal statement, letters of recommendation; for other advanced degree, resume, transcripts, personal statement. Additional exam requirements/recommendations for international students: Required—TOEFL (minimum score 587 paper-based; 80 iBT), IELTS (minimum score 6), TWE (minimum score 4). *Application deadline:* For fall admission, 8/1 for domestic students, 6/1 for international students; for spring admission, 12/1 for domestic students, 10/1 for international students. Applications are processed on a rolling basis. Application fee: $35. Electronic applications accepted. *Financial support:* Fellowships, research assistantships, teaching assistantships, career-related internships or fieldwork, Federal Work-Study, scholarships/grants, and unspecified assistantships available. Support available to part-time students. Financial award applicants required to submit FAFSA. *Faculty research:* Irish history and culture, conflict resolution and leadership. *Application contact:* Leanne Horinko, Director of Caspersen Admissions, 973-408-3280, E-mail: gradm@drew.edu.
Website: http://www.drew.edu/caspersen

Drury University, Master in Education Program, Springfield, MO 5802. Offers curriculum and instruction (M Ed), including elementary, middle school, secondary; gifted education (M Ed); instructional leadership (M Ed); instructional technology (M Ed); integrated learning (M Ed); online teaching (M Ed); special education (M Ed); special reading (M Ed). *Accreditation:* NCATE. *Program availability:* Part-time, evening/weekend, 100% online, blended/hybrid learning. *Entrance requirements:* For master's, GRE, bachelor's degree with minimum GPA of 2.75. Additional exam requirements/recommendations for international students: Recommended—TOEFL (minimum score 80 iBT), IELTS (minimum score 6.5). Electronic applications accepted. *Expenses:* Contact institution. *Faculty research:* Gifted students, instructional technology, autism, diversity and social justice.

Duquesne University, School of Education, Department of Instruction and Leadership, Program in Secondary Education, Pittsburgh, PA 15282-0001. Offers biology (MS Ed); chemistry (MS Ed); English (MS Ed); K-12 education (MS Ed), including Latin; mathematics (MS Ed); physics (MS Ed); social studies (MS Ed). *Program availability:* Part-time, evening/weekend. *Faculty:* 5 full-time (4 women). *Students:* 22 full-time (10 women); includes 3 minority (2 Black or African American, non-Hispanic/Latino; 1 Two or more races, non-Hispanic/Latino). Average age 26. 8 applicants, 100% accepted, 5 enrolled. In 2017, 9 master's awarded. *Entrance requirements:* For master's, two letters of recommendation, letter of intent, interview, bachelor's degree. Additional exam requirements/recommendations for international students: Required—TOEFL (minimum score 550 paper-based), IELTS (minimum score 7). *Application deadline:* For fall admission, 9/1 for domestic students; for spring admission, 1/2 for domestic students. Applications are processed on a rolling basis. Application fee: $0. Electronic applications accepted. *Expenses:* $1,259 per credit. *Financial support:* Research assistantships and Federal Work-Study available. Support available to part-time students. *Faculty research:* Factors that create highly effective teachers; how to best support teachers to support students in reform-oriented environments; urban education; models of teacher leadership; improving instruction in mathematics/science/social studies/English. *Unit head:* Dr. Melissa Boston, Associate Dean for Teacher Education/Professor, 412-396.6109, Fax: 412-396-5585, E-mail: bostonm@duq.edu. *Application contact:* Kelly

McGinley, Graduate Admissions Assistant, 412-396-1559, Fax: 412-396-5585, E-mail: mcginleyk@duq.edu. Website: http://www.duq.edu/academics/schools/education/graduate-programs-education/ms-ed-secondary-education

D'Youville College, Department of Education, Buffalo, NY 14201-1084. Offers educational leadership (Ed D); elementary education (MS Ed); secondary education (MS Ed); special education (MS Ed). *Program availability:* Part-time, evening/weekend. *Degree requirements:* For master's, one foreign language, comprehensive exam, project or thesis. *Entrance requirements:* For master's, GRE (if GPA less than 2.75), minimum GPA of 3.0. Additional exam requirements/recommendations for international students: Required—TOEFL (minimum score 500 paper-based). Electronic applications accepted. *Faculty research:* Developmental disabilities, multiculturalism, early childhood education.

Eastern Connecticut State University, School of Education and Professional Studies/ Graduate Division, Program in Secondary Education, Willimantic, CT 06226-2295. Offers MS. *Accreditation:* NCATE. *Program availability:* Part-time, evening/weekend. *Faculty:* 9 full-time (5 women), 12 part-time/adjunct (9 women). *Students:* 25 full-time (11 women), 13 part-time (8 women); includes 5 minority (1 Black or African American, non-Hispanic/Latino; 2 Asian, non-Hispanic/Latino; 2 Hispanic/Latino). Average age 28. 17 applicants, 76% accepted, 11 enrolled. In 2017, 20 master's awarded. *Degree requirements:* For master's, thesis optional. *Entrance requirements:* For master's, PRAXIS I, PRAXIS II, minimum GPA of 3.0, bachelor's degree from accredited institution. Additional exam requirements/recommendations for international students: Required—TOEFL (minimum score 550 paper-based; 79 iBT); Recommended—IELTS (minimum score 6). *Application deadline:* For fall admission, 7/6 priority date for domestic and international students; for spring admission, 11/3 priority date for domestic and international students. Applications are processed on a rolling basis. Application fee: $50. Electronic applications accepted. *Expenses: Tuition, area resident:* Full-time $12,252. Tuition, state resident: full-time $15,245; part-time $582 per credit hour. Tuition, nonresident: full-time $24,828; part-time $582 per credit hour. *Required fees:* $40 per semester. Full-time tuition and fees vary according to reciprocity agreements. *Financial support:* Research assistantships, teaching assistantships, career-related internships or fieldwork, institutionally sponsored loans, and unspecified assistantships available. Financial award application deadline: 3/1; financial award applicants required to submit FAFSA. *Unit head:* Dr. Jeanelle Day, Advisor, 860-465-4532, Fax: 860-465-5099, E-mail: dayj@easternct.edu. *Application contact:* Paula Goyette, Graduate Division, School of Education and Professional Studies, 860-465-5292, Fax: 860-465-4538, E-mail: graduateadmissions@easternct.edu.

Eastern Illinois University, Graduate School, College of Liberal Arts and Sciences, Department of Mathematics and Computer Science, Charleston, IL 61920. Offers elementary/middle school mathematics education (MA); mathematics (MA); secondary mathematics education (MA). *Program availability:* Part-time, evening/weekend. *Degree requirements:* For master's, comprehensive exam (for some programs), thesis (for some programs). *Entrance requirements:* For master's, GMAT or GRE. Additional exam requirements/recommendations for international students: Required—TOEFL (minimum score 500 paper-based; 61 iBT), IELTS (minimum score 6). *Application deadline:* For fall admission, 5/15 for domestic and international students; for spring admission, 10/15 for domestic and international students. Applications are processed on a rolling basis. Application fee: $30. Electronic applications accepted. *Financial support:* Teaching assistantships with full tuition reimbursements, career-related internships or fieldwork, Federal Work-Study, and unspecified assistantships available. Support available to part-time students. Financial award application deadline: 3/1; financial award applicants required to submit FAFSA. *Unit head:* Marshall B. Lassak, Chair, 217-581-6450, Fax: 217-581-6284, E-mail: mblassak@eiu.edu. *Application contact:* Peter S. Wiles, Graduate Coordinator, 217-581-6275, Fax: 217-581-6284, E-mail: pswiles@eiu.edu. Website: http://www.eiu.edu/mathgrad/

Eastern Kentucky University, The Graduate School, College of Education, Department of Curriculum and Instruction, Program in Secondary and Higher Education, Richmond, KY 40475-3102. Offers secondary education (MA Ed), including agricultural education, art education, biological sciences education, business education, English education, geography education, history education, home economics education, industrial education, mathematical sciences education, physical education, school health education. *Accreditation:* NCATE. *Program availability:* Part-time. *Entrance requirements:* For master's, GRE General Test, minimum GPA of 2.5.

Eastern Michigan University, Graduate School, College of Education, Department of Teacher Education, Programs in K–12 Education, Ypsilanti, MI 48197. Offers middle school education (MA); secondary school education (MA). *Accreditation:* NCATE. *Program availability:* Part-time, evening/weekend, online learning. *Students:* 22 full-time (17 women), 34 part-time (27 women); includes 5 minority (3 Asian, non-Hispanic/ Latino; 1 Hispanic/Latino; 1 Two or more races, non-Hispanic/Latino), 16 international. Average age 31. 50 applicants, 84% accepted, 23 enrolled. In 2017, 6 master's awarded. *Entrance requirements:* For master's, GRE. Additional exam requirements/ recommendations for international students: Required—TOEFL. *Application deadline:* Applications are processed on a rolling basis. Application fee: $45. *Financial support:* Fellowships, research assistantships with full tuition reimbursements, teaching assistantships with full tuition reimbursements, career-related internships or fieldwork, Federal Work-Study, institutionally sponsored loans, scholarships/grants, tuition waivers (partial), and unspecified assistantships available. Support available to part-time students. Financial award applicants required to submit FAFSA. *Application contact:* Dr. Martha Kinney-Sedgwick, Department Head, 734-487-3260, Fax: 734-487-2101, E-mail: mkinneys@emich.edu.

Eastern Nazarene College, Adult and Graduate Studies, Division of Teacher Education, Quincy, MA 02170. Offers administration (M Ed); early childhood education (M Ed, Certificate); elementary education (M Ed, Certificate); English as a second language (Certificate); instructional enrichment and development (Certificate); middle school education (M Ed, Certificate); moderate special needs education (Certificate); principal (Certificate); program development and supervision (Certificate); secondary education (M Ed, Certificate); special education administrator (Certificate); special needs (M Ed); supervisor (Certificate); teacher of reading (M Ed, Certificate). M Ed also available through weekend program for administration, special needs, and teacher of reading only. *Program availability:* Part-time, evening/weekend. *Entrance requirements:* Additional exam requirements/recommendations for international students: Required— TOEFL (minimum score 550 paper-based).

Eastern New Mexico University, Graduate School, College of Education and Technology, Department of Educational Studies, Portales, NM 88130. Offers counseling (MA); education (M Ed), including educational administration, secondary education; school counseling (M Ed); special education (M Ed, M Sp Ed), including early childhood special education (M Sp Ed), general special education (M Sp Ed), gifted education pedagogy (M Ed), special education pedagogy (M Ed). *Accreditation:* NCATE. *Program availability:* Part-time, evening/weekend, online learning. *Degree requirements:* For master's, comprehensive exam, thesis optional. *Entrance requirements:* For master's, writing assessment, minimum GPA of 3.0, letter of recommendation, photocopy of teaching license; Level II teaching license (for M Ed in educational administration).

Additional exam requirements/recommendations for international students: Required— TOEFL (minimum score 550 paper-based; 79 iBT), IELTS (minimum score 6). *Application deadline:* For fall admission, 7/20 priority date for domestic students, 6/20 priority date for international students; for spring admission, 12/15 priority date for domestic students, 11/15 priority date for international students. Applications are processed on a rolling basis. Application fee: $10. Electronic applications accepted. *Financial support:* Applicants required to submit FAFSA. *Unit head:* Dr. Rebecca Davis, Educational Administration/Special Education Graduate Coordinator, 575-562-2526, Fax: 575-562-2559, E-mail: rebecca.davis@enmu.edu. *Application contact:* Cheryl Reeves, Senior Secretary, 575-562-2443, Fax: 575-562-2559, E-mail: cheryl.reeves@ enmu.edu. Website: http://education.enmu.edu

Eastern Oregon University, Master of Arts in Teaching Program, La Grande, OR 97850. Offers elementary education (MAT); secondary education (MAT). *Faculty:* 12 full-time (9 women), 4 part-time/adjunct (1 woman). *Students:* 53 full-time (41 women), 2 part-time (both women); includes 6 minority (5 Hispanic/Latino; 1 Two or more races, non-Hispanic/Latino), 1 international. Average age 29. In 2017, 32 master's awarded. *Degree requirements:* For master's, thesis. *Entrance requirements:* For master's, NTE. *Application deadline:* For fall admission, 3/1 for domestic students. Applications are processed on a rolling basis. Electronic applications accepted. *Expenses:* $404.50 per credit. *Financial support:* In 2017–18, 24 students received support. Federal Work-Study, scholarships/grants, and tuition waivers (full and partial) available. Support available to part-time students. *Unit head:* Dr. Danny Ray Mielke, Dean of College of Business and Education, 541-962-3399, Fax: 541-962-3701, E-mail: dmeilke@eou.edu. *Application contact:* Janet Frye, Administrative Support, MAT/MS Graduate Admission, 541-962-3772, Fax: 541-962-3701, E-mail: jfrye@eou.edu. Website: https://www.eou.edu/cobe/ed/mat/

Eastern University, Graduate Education Programs, St. Davids, PA 19087-3696. Offers ESL program specialist (K-12) (Certificate); general supervisor (PreK-12) (Certificate); health and physical education (K-12) (Certificate); middle level (4-8) (Certificate); multicultural education (M Ed); music (K-12) (Certificate); Pre K-4 (Certificate); Pre K-4 with special education (Certificate); reading (M Ed); reading specialist (K-12) (Certificate); reading supervisor (K-12) (Certificate); school counseling (MA, CAGS); school principalship (preK-12) (Certificate); school psychology (MS, CAGS); secondary biology education (7-12) (Certificate); secondary chemistry education (7-12) (Certificate); secondary communication education (7-12) (Certificate); secondary English education (7-12) (Certificate); secondary math education (7-12) (Certificate); secondary social studies education (7-12) (Certificate); special education (M Ed); special education (7-12) (Certificate); special education (Pre K-8) (Certificate); special education supervisor (K-12) (Certificate); TESOL (M Ed); world language (Certificate), including Spanish. *Program availability:* Part-time, evening/weekend, online learning. *Students:* 46 full-time (40 women), 115 part-time (93 women); includes 65 minority (42 Black or African American, non-Hispanic/Latino; 3 Asian, non-Hispanic/Latino; 14 Hispanic/Latino; 6 Two or more races, non-Hispanic/Latino), 1 international. Average age 32. In 2017, 72 master's awarded. *Entrance requirements:* Additional exam requirements/recommendations for international students: Required—TOEFL. *Application deadline:* Applications are processed on a rolling basis. Application fee: $35. Electronic applications accepted. Application fee is waived when completed online. *Expenses:* Contact institution. *Unit head:* Michael Dziedziak, Executive Director of Enrollment, 800-452-0996, E-mail: gpsadmissions@eastern.edu. Website: https://www.eastern.edu/academics/programs/education-department-graduate-programs/graduate-programs

East Stroudsburg University of Pennsylvania, Graduate and Extended Studies, College of Education, Department of Professional and Secondary Education, East Stroudsburg, PA 18301-2999. Offers professional and secondary education (Ed D); secondary education (M Ed). *Accreditation:* NCATE. *Program availability:* Part-time, evening/weekend, online learning. *Faculty:* 5 full-time (4 women), 8 part-time/adjunct (5 women). *Students:* 21 full-time (12 women), 125 part-time (84 women); includes 30 minority (10 Black or African American, non-Hispanic/Latino; 2 Asian, non-Hispanic/ Latino; 15 Hispanic/Latino; 3 Two or more races, non-Hispanic/Latino), 2 international. Average age 38. 37 applicants, 86% accepted, 26 enrolled. In 2017, 12 master's, 2 doctorates awarded. *Degree requirements:* For master's, independent research problem or comprehensive assessment portfolio. *Entrance requirements:* For master's, PRAXIS/ teacher certification, letter of recommendation, Pennsylvania Department of Education requirements. Additional exam requirements/recommendations for international students: Recommended—TOEFL (minimum score 560 paper-based; 83 iBT), IELTS. *Application deadline:* For fall admission, 7/31 priority date for domestic students, 5/30 priority date for international students; for spring admission, 11/30 for domestic students, 10/31 for international students. Applications are processed on a rolling basis. Application fee: $50. Electronic applications accepted. *Expenses:* Tuition, state resident: full-time $4500; part-time $3000 per credit. Tuition, nonresident: full-time $6750; part-time $4500 per credit. *Required fees:* $2642; $1756 per credit. $878 per semester. Tuition and fees vary according to course load, campus/location and program. *Financial support:* Research assistantships with tuition reimbursements, career-related internships or fieldwork, Federal Work-Study, and unspecified assistantships available. Support available to part-time students. Financial award application deadline: 3/1; financial award applicants required to submit FAFSA. *Unit head:* Dr. Beth Sockman, Chair, 570-422-3374, Fax: 570-422-3942, E-mail: bsockman@esu.edu. *Application contact:* Kevin Quintero, Associate Director, Graduate and Extended Studies, 570-422-3890, Fax: 570-422-2711, E-mail: kquintero@esu.edu.

East Tennessee State University, School of Graduate Studies, College of Education, Department of Curriculum and Instruction, Johnson City, TN 37614. Offers advanced studies in teaching and learning (M Ed), including childhood literacy; educational technology (M Ed), including educational communications and technology, school library media; elementary education (M Ed); reading (M Ed, MA), including reading education (MA), storytelling (MA); response to intervention (Post-Master's Certificate); school library professional (Post-Master's Certificate); secondary education (M Ed); STEAM K-12 education (Postbaccalaureate Certificate); storytelling (Postbaccalaureate Certificate); teacher education (MAT), including elementary education K-5, middle grades education 4-8, middle grades education 6-8, secondary education 6-12 and preK-12, secondary education K-12. *Accreditation:* NCATE. *Program availability:* Part-time, evening/weekend, online learning. *Degree requirements:* For master's, comprehensive exam, thesis optional, student teaching, practicum; for other advanced degree, field work (school library); culminating experience (storytelling). *Entrance requirements:* For master's, GRE, SAT, ACT, PRAXIS, minimum GPA of 3.0, interview, 3 letters of recommendation, background check; for other advanced degree, master's degree, TN teaching license. Additional exam requirements/recommendations for international students: Required—TOEFL (minimum score 550 paper-based; 79 iBT). *Application deadline:* For fall admission, 6/1 for domestic students, 4/29 for international students; for spring admission, 11/1 for domestic students, 4/29 for international students. Application fee: $55 ($65 for international students). Electronic applications accepted. *Financial support:* Research assistantships with full tuition reimbursements, teaching assistantships with tuition reimbursements, career-related internships or fieldwork, institutionally sponsored loans, scholarships/grants, and unspecified

assistantships available. Financial award application deadline: 7/1; financial award applicants required to submit FAFSA. *Faculty research:* Critical thinking; curriculum development in reading, math, and science education; cultural diversity; cognitive processes; effective teaching strategies. *Unit head:* Dr. Karin Keith, Chair, 423-439-7598, Fax: 423-439-8362, E-mail: keithkj@etsu.edu. *Application contact:* Dr. Aimee Govett, Graduate Coordinator, 423-439-7804, Fax: 423-439-5624, E-mail: govett@etsu.edu.
Website: http://www.etsu.edu/coe/cuai/

Edinboro University of Pennsylvania, Department of Middle and Secondary Education and Educational Leadership, Edinboro, PA 16444. Offers educational leadership (M Ed); middle and secondary instruction (M Ed). *Program availability:* Part-time, evening/weekend. *Degree requirements:* For master's, comprehensive exam, thesis or alternative, project. *Entrance requirements:* For master's, GRE or MAT, minimum QPA of 2.5. Electronic applications accepted.

Elms College, Division of Education, Chicopee, MA 01013-2839. Offers early childhood education (MAT); education (M Ed, CAGS); elementary education (MAT); English as a second language (MAT); reading (MAT); secondary education (MAT), including biology education, English education, Spanish education; special education (MAT). *Program availability:* Part-time, evening/weekend. *Faculty:* 4 full-time (all women), 8 part-time/adjunct (7 women). *Students:* 6 full-time (4 women), 127 part-time (107 women); includes 8 minority (2 Asian, non-Hispanic/Latino; 6 Hispanic/Latino). Average age 33. 42 applicants, 88% accepted, 36 enrolled. In 2017, 50 master's, 6 other advanced degrees awarded. *Degree requirements:* For master's, thesis (for some programs). *Entrance requirements:* For master's, Massachusetts Educators Certification Test, minimum GPA of 3.0; for CAGS, master's degree in education. Additional exam requirements/recommendations for international students: Required—TOEFL. *Application deadline:* For fall admission, 7/1 priority date for domestic students; for spring admission, 11/1 priority date for domestic students. Applications are processed on a rolling basis. Application fee: $30. *Expenses: Tuition:* Full-time $13,860; part-time $770 per credit hour. *Required fees:* $200. Tuition and fees vary according to degree level and program. *Financial support:* In 2017–18, 2 teaching assistantships with partial tuition reimbursements were awarded. Financial award applicants required to submit FAFSA. *Unit head:* Dr. Mary Janeczek, Chair, Division of Education, 413-594-2761, Fax: 413-592-4871, E-mail: janeczke@elms.edu. *Application contact:* School of Graduate and Professional Studies, 413-265-2445, E-mail: graduateeducation@elms.edu.

Emory University, Laney Graduate School, Division of Educational Studies, Atlanta, GA 30322-1100. Offers educational studies (MA, PhD); middle grades teaching (MAT); secondary teaching (MAT). *Accreditation:* NCATE. Terminal master's awarded for partial completion of doctoral program. *Degree requirements:* For master's, thesis; for doctorate, comprehensive exam, thesis/dissertation. *Entrance requirements:* For master's and doctorate, GRE General Test, minimum GPA of 3.0. Additional exam requirements/recommendations for international students: Required—TOEFL. Electronic applications accepted. *Faculty research:* Educational policy, educational measurement, urban and multicultural education, mathematics and science education, comparative education.

Endicott College, Van Loan School of Graduate and Professional Studies, Program in Secondary Education, Beverly, MA 01915-2096. Offers M Ed. *Program availability:* Part-time, evening/weekend, 100% online, blended/hybrid learning. *Faculty:* 4 full-time (3 women), 10 part-time/adjunct (5 women). *Students:* 14 full-time (6 women), 14 part-time (7 women); includes 1 minority (Two or more races, non-Hispanic/Latino). Average age 32. 7 applicants, 100% accepted, 7 enrolled. In 2017, 29 master's awarded. *Degree requirements:* For master's, thesis, practicum, seminar. *Entrance requirements:* For master's, Massachusetts Tests for Educator Licensure (MTEL) Communication and Literacy Test and Subject Matter Test, MAT or GRE, bachelor's degree from accredited college, transcript, two recommendations, essay. Additional exam requirements/recommendations for international students: Required—TOEFL. *Application deadline:* Applications are processed on a rolling basis. Application fee: $50. Electronic applications accepted. *Expenses:* Contact institution. *Financial support:* Applicants required to submit FAFSA. *Unit head:* Dr. Aubry Threlkeld, Director of Graduate Licensure Programs, 978-232-2408, Fax: 978-232-3000, E-mail: athrelke@endicott.edu. *Application contact:* Ian Menchini, Director, Graduate Enrollment and Advising, 978-232-5292, Fax: 978-232-3000, E-mail: imenchin@endicott.edu.
Website: https://vanloan.endicott.edu/programs-of-study/masters-programs/educator-preparation-program/secondary-education-program

Evangel University, Department of Education, Springfield, MO 65802. Offers curriculum and instruction (M Ed); educational leadership (M Ed); literacy (M Ed); secondary teaching (M Ed). *Accreditation:* NCATE. *Program availability:* Part-time, evening/weekend, 100% online, blended/hybrid learning. *Faculty:* 8 full-time (5 women), 8 part-time/adjunct (5 women). *Students:* 1 (woman) full-time, 47 part-time (41 women); includes 2 minority (both Hispanic/Latino). Average age 37. 16 applicants, 100% accepted, 14 enrolled. In 2017, 14 master's awarded. *Entrance requirements:* For master's, PRAXIS II (preferred) or GRE, minimum undergraduate GPA of 3.0. Additional exam requirements/recommendations for international students: Required—TOEFL (minimum score 550 paper-based). *Application deadline:* For fall admission, 7/15 priority date for domestic students, 8/1 for international students; for spring admission, 11/15 priority date for domestic students, 12/1 for international students. Applications are processed on a rolling basis. Application fee: $25. Electronic applications accepted. Application fee is waived when completed online. *Expenses: Tuition:* Full-time $7200; part-time $4800 per credit hour. *Required fees:* $210; $155 per semester. *Financial support:* In 2017–18, 23 students received support. Scholarships/grants and unspecified assistantships available. Financial award application deadline: 4/1; financial award applicants required to submit FAFSA. *Unit head:* Dr. Susan Langston, Program Coordinator, 417-865-2815 Ext. 8552, E-mail: langstons@evangel.edu. *Application contact:* Michael Mann, Enrollment Coordinator, Graduate Studies, 417-865-2815 Ext. 8276, Fax: 417-575-5484, E-mail: mannm@evangel.edu.
Website: http://www.evangel.edu/academics/graduate-studies/graduate-programs

Fairfield University, Graduate School of Education and Allied Professions, Fairfield, CT 06824. Offers applied behavior analysis (ATC); applied psychology (MA); clinical mental health counseling (MA, CAS); educational technology (MA); elementary education (MA, CAS); family studies (MA); integration of spirituality and religion in counseling (ATC); marriage and family therapy (MA); reading and language development (Sixth Year Certificate); school counseling (MA, CAS); school psychology (MA, CAS); school-based marriage and family therapy (ATC); secondary education (MA); special education (MA, CAS); substance abuse counseling (ATC); teaching (Certificate); teaching and foundations (MA, CAS); TESOL, world languages, and bilingual education (MA, CAS). *Accreditation:* NCATE. *Program availability:* Part-time, evening/weekend. *Faculty:* 23 full-time (17 women), 39 part-time/adjunct (28 women). *Students:* 199 full-time (168 women), 251 part-time (206 women); includes 85 minority (21 Black or African American, non-Hispanic/Latino; 9 Asian, non-Hispanic/Latino; 49 Hispanic/Latino; 6 Two or more races, non-Hispanic/Latino), 4 international. Average age 32. 370 applicants, 56% accepted, 125 enrolled. In 2017, 136 master's, 28 other advanced degrees awarded. *Degree requirements:* For master's, comprehensive exam. *Entrance requirements:* For master's, minimum GPA of 3.0, 2 recommendations, resume.

Additional exam requirements/recommendations for international students: Required—TOEFL (minimum score 550 paper-based; 84 iBT) or IELTS (minimum score 7.5). *Application deadline:* For fall admission, 2/15 for international students; for spring admission, 10/1 for international students. Application fee: $60. Electronic applications accepted. *Expenses:* $750 per credit hour. *Financial support:* In 2017–18, 34 students received support. Career-related internships or fieldwork and unspecified assistantships available. Support available to part-time students. Financial award applicants required to submit FAFSA. *Faculty research:* Reading and literacy, writing, social justice and inequality in education, addictions and mental health issues, therapeutic relationships and clinical supervision. *Unit head:* Dr. Robert D. Hannafin, Dean, 203-254-4250, Fax: 203-254-4241, E-mail: rhannafin@fairfield.edu. *Application contact:* Marianne Gumpper, Director of Graduate Admission, 203-254-4184, Fax: 203-254-4073, E-mail: gradadmis@fairfield.edu.
Website: http://www.fairfield.edu/gseap

Fayetteville State University, Graduate School, Programs in Middle Grades, Secondary, Special and Elementary Education, Fayetteville, NC 28301-4298. Offers middle grades (MA Ed); sociology (MA Ed); special education (MA Ed), including behavioral-emotional handicaps, mentally handicapped, specific training disability. *Accreditation:* NCATE. *Program availability:* Part-time, evening/weekend. *Faculty:* 8 full-time (5 women). *Students:* 14 full-time (7 women), 8 part-time (6 women); includes 16 minority (13 Black or African American, non-Hispanic/Latino; 1 Asian, non-Hispanic/Latino; 2 Hispanic/Latino). Average age 35. 10 applicants, 80% accepted, 7 enrolled. In 2017, 9 master's awarded. *Degree requirements:* For master's, comprehensive exam, internship. *Entrance requirements:* Additional exam requirements/recommendations for international students: Required—TOEFL. *Application deadline:* For fall admission, 4/15 for domestic students; for spring admission, 10/15 for domestic students. Applications are processed on a rolling basis. Application fee: $40. Electronic applications accepted. *Expenses:* Tuition, state resident: full-time $8604. Tuition, nonresident: full-time $19,669. *Financial support:* Application deadline: 3/1; applicants required to submit FAFSA. *Faculty research:* Students with disabilities and selected leadership behaviors, new vision for professional development, gifted and talented students, emotional and behavioral disabilities, professional development for high school biology teachers. *Unit head:* Dr. Cynthia Shamberger, Chair of Middle Grades, Secondary and Specialized Subjects, 910-672-1181, Fax: 910-672-1941, E-mail: cshamber@uncfsu.edu. *Application contact:* Debra D. Brown, Administrative Support Associate, 910-672-1181, Fax: 910-672-1596, E-mail: ddbrown@uncfsu.edu.

Florida Agricultural and Mechanical University, Division of Graduate Studies, Research, and Continuing Education, College of Education, Program in Secondary Education and Foundation, Tallahassee, FL 32307-3200. Offers biology (M Ed); chemistry (MS Ed); English (MS Ed); history (MS Ed); math (MS Ed); physics (MS Ed). *Accreditation:* NCATE. *Degree requirements:* For master's, thesis (for some programs). *Entrance requirements:* For master's, GRE General Test, minimum GPA of 3.0. Additional exam requirements/recommendations for international students: Required—TOEFL.

Fontbonne University, Graduate Programs, St. Louis, MO 63105-3098. Offers accounting (MBA, MS); art (MA); art (K-12) (MAT); business (MBA); computer science (MS); deaf education (MA); early intervention in deaf education (MA); education (MA), including autism spectrum disorders, curriculum and instruction, diverse learners, early childhood education, reading, special education; elementary education (MAT); family and consumer sciences (MA), including multidisciplinary health communication studies; fine arts (MFA); instructional design and technology (MS); management and leadership (MM); middle school education (MAT); secondary education (MAT); special education (MAT); speech-language pathology (MS); supply chain management (MS); theatre (MA). *Program availability:* Part-time, evening/weekend, online learning. *Degree requirements:* For master's, comprehensive exam (for some programs), thesis (for some programs). *Entrance requirements:* Additional exam requirements/recommendations for international students: Required—TOEFL (minimum score 500 paper-based; 65 iBT). Electronic applications accepted.

Frostburg State University, College of Education, Department of Educational Professions, Program in Curriculum and Instruction, Frostburg, MD 21532. Offers curriculum and instruction (Ed D); educational technology (M Ed); elementary education (M Ed); secondary education (M Ed). *Program availability:* Part-time, evening/weekend. *Faculty:* 2. *Students:* 45 part-time (33 women); includes 1 minority (Two or more races, non-Hispanic/Latino). Average age 34. 15 applicants, 93% accepted, 11 enrolled. In 2017, 5 master's, 1 doctorate awarded. *Degree requirements:* For master's, thesis or alternative. *Entrance requirements:* For master's, teaching certificate. Additional exam requirements/recommendations for international students: Required—TOEFL. *Application deadline:* For fall admission, 7/15 priority date for domestic students. Applications are processed on a rolling basis. Application fee: $45. Electronic applications accepted. *Expenses:* Tuition, state resident: part-time $433 per credit hour. Tuition, nonresident: part-time $557 per credit hour. *Required fees:* $121 per credit hour. $27 per term. *Financial support:* In 2017–18, 2 research assistantships with full tuition reimbursements (averaging $5,000 per year) were awarded. Financial award application deadline: 4/1; financial award applicants required to submit FAFSA. *Unit head:* Dr. Jennifer Rankin, Coordinator, 301-687-7010, E-mail: jerankin@frostburg.edu. *Application contact:* Vickie Mazer, Director, Graduate Services, 301-687-7053, Fax: 301-687-4597, E-mail: vmmazer@frostburg.edu.

Frostburg State University, College of Education, Department of Educational Professions, Program in Secondary Teaching, Frostburg, MD 21532. Offers MAT. *Students:* 10 full-time (6 women). Average age 27. 29 applicants, 52% accepted, 9 enrolled. In 2017, 13 master's awarded. *Entrance requirements:* For master's, PRAXIS I, entry portfolio. Additional exam requirements/recommendations for international students: Required—TOEFL. Application fee: $45. *Expenses:* Tuition, state resident: part-time $433 per credit hour. Tuition, nonresident: part-time $557 per credit hour. *Required fees:* $121 per credit hour. $27 per term. *Financial support:* In 2017–18, 1 research assistantship was awarded. *Unit head:* Dr. Jennifer Bishoff, Coordinator, 301-687-3169, E-mail: jlbishoff@frostburg.edu. *Application contact:* Vickie Mazer, Director, Graduate Services, 301-687-7053, Fax: 301-687-4597, E-mail: vmmazer@frostburg.edu.

Gallaudet University, The Graduate School, Washington, DC 20002-3625. Offers American Sign Language/English bilingual early childhood deaf education: birth to 5 (Certificate); audiology (Au D); clinical psychology (PhD); deaf and hard of hearing infants, toddlers, and their families (Certificate); deaf education (MA, Ed S); deaf history (Certificate); deaf studies (Certificate); educating deaf students with disabilities (Certificate); education: teacher preparation (MA), including deaf education, early childhood education and deaf education, elementary education and deaf education, secondary education and deaf education; educational neuroscience (PhD); hearing, speech and language sciences (MS, PhD); international development (MA); interpretation (MA, PhD), including combined interpreting practice and research (MA), interpreting research (MA); linguistics (MA, PhD); mental health counseling (MA); peer mentoring (Certificate); public administration (MPA); school counseling (MA); school psychology (Psy S); sign language teaching (MA); social work (MSW); speech-language pathology (MS). *Program availability:* Part-time. Terminal master's awarded for partial completion of doctoral program. *Degree requirements:* For master's, comprehensive exam (for some programs), thesis optional; for doctorate, comprehensive exam, thesis/dissertation. *Entrance requirements:* For master's and doctorate, GRE General Test or MAT, letters of recommendation, interviews, goals statement, American Sign Language proficiency interview, written English competency. Additional exam requirements/recommendations for international students: Required—TOEFL. Electronic applications accepted. *Faculty research:* Signing math dictionaries, telecommunications access, cancer genetics, linguistics, visual language and visual learning, integrated quantum materials, deaf legal discourse, advance recruitment and retention in geosciences.

George Mason University, College of Education and Human Development, Programs in Curriculum and Instruction, Fairfax, VA 22030. Offers advanced international baccalaureate (M Ed); assistive technology (M Ed); designing digital learning in schools (M Ed); early childhood education (M Ed); early childhood education for diverse learners (M Ed); elementary education (M Ed); English as a second language (M Ed); gifted child education (M Ed); history (M Ed); literacy (M Ed), including PK-12 classroom teachers, reading specialist; literacy leadership for diverse schools (M Ed), including K-12 reading; physical education (M Ed); science K-12 (M Ed); secondary education (M Ed), including biology, chemistry, earth science, English, history/social science, math, physics; special education (M Ed); teacher leadership (M Ed); teaching culturally, linguistically diverse and exceptional learners (M Ed); transformative teaching (M Ed). *Program availability:* Part-time, evening/weekend, 100% online, blended/hybrid learning. *Faculty:* 41 full-time (36 women), 45 part-time/adjunct (37 women). *Students:* 173 full-time (151 women), 729 part-time (611 women); includes 271 minority (65 Black or African American, non-Hispanic/Latino; 5 American Indian or Alaska Native, non-Hispanic/Latino; 88 Asian, non-Hispanic/Latino; 94 Hispanic/Latino; 1 Native Hawaiian or other Pacific Islander, non-Hispanic/Latino; 18 Two or more races, non-Hispanic/Latino), 28 international. Average age 32. 426 applicants, 91% accepted, 289 enrolled. In 2017, 349 master's awarded. *Degree requirements:* For master's, thesis. *Entrance requirements:* For master's, PRAXIS Core (for some programs), 2 letters of recommendation, interview, program goals statement; 9 hours of complete licensure endorsement requirements (for elementary education); minimum GPA of 3.0 in applicant's last 60 hours of undergraduate coursework (for secondary education); at least 1 year of teaching experience (for literacy). Additional exam requirements/recommendations for international students: Required—TOEFL (minimum score 575 paper-based; 88 iBT), IELTS (minimum score 6.5), PTE (minimum score 59). *Application deadline:* For fall admission, 4/2 priority date for domestic and international students; for spring admission, 11/1 for domestic and international students. Application fee: $75 ($80 for international students). Electronic applications accepted. *Expenses:* Tuition, state resident: full-time $11,228; part-time $459.50 per credit. Tuition, nonresident: full-time $30,932; part-time $1280.50 per credit. *Required fees:* $3252; $135.50 per credit. Part-time tuition and fees vary according to course load and program. *Financial support:* In 2017–18, 2 students received support, including 2 teaching assistantships; career-related internships or fieldwork, Federal Work-Study, scholarships/grants, unspecified assistantships, and health care benefits (for full-time research or teaching assistantship recipients) also available. Support available to part-time students. Financial award application deadline: 3/1; financial award applicants required to submit FAFSA. *Faculty research:* Teacher preparation and professional development; adaptive teaching; wonder in science teacher preparation; literacy (digital, adolescent); site based course instruction. *Unit head:* Rebecca Fox, Professor and Academic Program Coordinator, 703-993-4123, E-mail: rfox@gmu.edu.
Website: http://gse.gmu.edu/programs/gsemasters

The George Washington University, Graduate School of Education and Human Development, Department of Curriculum and Pedagogy, Program in Secondary Education, Washington, DC 20052. Offers Arabic (M Ed); Italian (M Ed); math (M Ed); physics (M Ed); Russian (M Ed). Programs also offered in Arlington and Ashburn, VA. *Accreditation:* NCATE. *Students:* 10 full-time (7 women), 26 part-time (16 women); includes 10 minority (5 Black or African American, non-Hispanic/Latino; 2 American Indian or Alaska Native, non-Hispanic/Latino; 1 Asian, non-Hispanic/Latino; 2 Two or more races, non-Hispanic/Latino), 1 international. Average age 31. 66 applicants, 62% accepted, 22 enrolled. In 2017, 17 master's awarded. *Entrance requirements:* For master's, GRE General Test or MAT, interview, minimum GPA of 2.75. *Application deadline:* For fall admission, 1/15 priority date for domestic students; for spring admission, 10/1 for domestic students. Applications are processed on a rolling basis. Application fee: $75. *Expenses:* Tuition: Full-time $28,800; part-time $1655 per credit hour. *Required fees:* $45; $2.75 per credit hour. *Financial support:* Fellowships, career-related internships or fieldwork, Federal Work-Study, tuition waivers (full and partial), and stipends available. Financial award application deadline: 1/15; financial award applicants required to submit FAFSA. *Unit head:* Prof. Curtis Pyke, Chair, 202-994-4516, E-mail: cpyke@gwu.edu. *Application contact:* Sarah Lang, Director of Graduate Admissions, 202-994-1447, Fax: 202-994-7207, E-mail: slang@gwu.edu.

Georgia College & State University, Graduate School, The John H. Lounsbury College of Education, Program in Secondary Education, Milledgeville, GA 31061. Offers MAT. *Program availability:* Part-time, evening/weekend, online learning. *Students:* 28 full-time (19 women), 40 part-time (24 women); includes 21 minority (18 Black or African American, non-Hispanic/Latino; 1 Asian, non-Hispanic/Latino; 1 Hispanic/Latino; 1 Two or more races, non-Hispanic/Latino). Average age 28. 20 applicants, 100% accepted, 17 enrolled. In 2017, 35 master's awarded. *Degree requirements:* For master's, comprehensive exam, minimum GPA of 3.0, complete program within 6 years. *Entrance requirements:* For master's, GACE, 2 recommendations, transcripts, proof of immunization, resume, minimum GPA of 2.75. *Application deadline:* For fall admission, 7/1 priority date for domestic students; for spring admission, 11/1 priority date for domestic students; for summer admission, 4/1 priority date for domestic students. Applications are processed on a rolling basis. Application fee: $40. Electronic applications accepted. *Expenses:* $288 per semester hour full-time, $2,592 per semester; $343 per semester fees. *Financial support:* In 2017–18, 7 students received support. Unspecified assistantships available. Financial award application deadline: 3/1; financial award applicants required to submit FAFSA. *Unit head:* Dr. Joseph Peters, Dean, College of Education, 478-445-2518, Fax: 478-445-6582, E-mail: joseph.peters@gcsu.edu. *Application contact:* Shanda Brand, Graduate Admission Advisor, 478-445-1383, Fax: 478-445-6582, E-mail: shanda.brand@gcsu.edu.

Georgia Southern University, Jack N. Averitt College of Graduate Studies, College of Education, Department of Teaching and Learning, Program in Secondary Education, Statesboro, GA 30460. Offers M Ed, MAT, Ed S. *Program availability:* Part-time, evening/weekend, 100% online, blended/hybrid learning. *Students:* 32 full-time (18 women), 45 part-time (24 women); includes 9 minority (5 Black or African American, non-Hispanic/Latino; 1 Asian, non-Hispanic/Latino; 1 Hispanic/Latino; 2 Two or more races, non-Hispanic/Latino), 1 international. Average age 31. 22 applicants, 95% accepted, 20 enrolled. In 2017, 25 master's, 7 other advanced degrees awarded. *Degree requirements:* For master's, portfolio, transition point assessments, exit assessment; for Ed S, field based research project, assessments. *Entrance requirements:* For master's, GACE (for MAT), minimum cumulative GPA of 2.5. Additional exam requirements/recommendations for international students: Required—TOEFL (minimum score 550 paper-based; 80 iBT), IELTS (minimum score 6). *Application deadline:* For fall admission, 3/15 priority date for domestic and international

students; for spring admission, 10/1 priority date for domestic students, 10/1 for international students; for summer admission, 3/1 for domestic and international students. Applications are processed on a rolling basis. Application fee: $50. Electronic applications accepted. *Expenses:* Tuition, state resident: full-time $4986; part-time $3324 per year. Tuition, nonresident: full-time $21,982; part-time $15,352 per year. *Required fees:* $2092; $1802 per credit hour. $901 per semester. Tuition and fees vary according to course load, campus/location and program. *Financial support:* In 2017–18, 12 students received support, including 4 fellowships with full tuition reimbursements available (averaging $7,750 per year); career-related internships or fieldwork, Federal Work-Study, and tuition waivers (full) also available. Support available to part-time students. Financial award application deadline: 4/15; financial award applicants required to submit FAFSA. *Faculty research:* Social studies education, mathematics education, science education, language arts education, dispositions. *Unit head:* Dr. Heather Scott, Program Director, 912-478-0356, Fax: 912-478-0026, E-mail: hscott@georgiasouthern.edu. *Application contact:* Dr. Lydia Cross, Director for Graduate Academic Services Center, 912-478-8664, E-mail: lcross@georgiasouthern.edu.

Georgia Southern University–Armstrong Campus, College of Graduate Studies, Department of Secondary, Adult, and Physical Education, Savannah, GA 31419-1997. Offers adolescent and adult education (Certificate); adult education and community leadership (M Ed); curriculum and instruction (M Ed); secondary education (MAT). *Program availability:* Part-time, evening/weekend, online learning. *Faculty:* 8 full-time (all women), 4 part-time/adjunct (3 women). *Students:* 19 full-time (16 women), 106 part-time (60 women); includes 41 minority (31 Black or African American, non-Hispanic/Latino; 1 Asian, non-Hispanic/Latino; 3 Hispanic/Latino; 6 Two or more races, non-Hispanic/Latino), 1 international. Average age 33. 83 applicants, 48% accepted, 40 enrolled. In 2017, 43 master's, 1 other advanced degree awarded. *Degree requirements:* For master's, comprehensive exam (for some programs), thesis (for some programs), capstone project (for M Ed). *Entrance requirements:* For master's, edTPA (for MAT). Additional exam requirements/recommendations for international students: Required—TOEFL (minimum score 523 paper-based). *Application deadline:* For fall admission, 6/30 priority date for domestic students, 5/1 priority date for international students; for spring admission, 11/15 priority date for domestic students, 9/15 priority date for international students; for summer admission, 4/15 priority date for domestic students, 9/15 for international students. Applications are processed on a rolling basis. Application fee: $30. Electronic applications accepted. *Expenses:* Tuition, state resident: part-time $211 per credit hour. Tuition, nonresident: part-time $782 per credit hour. *Required fees:* $737 per semester. Tuition and fees vary according to course load, degree level, campus/location and program. *Financial support:* In 2017–18, research assistantships with full tuition reimbursements (averaging $5,000 per year) were awarded; career-related internships or fieldwork, Federal Work-Study, scholarships/grants, and unspecified assistantships also available. Support available to part-time students. Financial award application deadline: 3/15; financial award applicants required to submit FAFSA. *Faculty research:* Quality of teacher leadership, classroom management and first year teachers; edTPA preparation and success of candidates; social justice issues related to educational preparation; recruitment of STEM teachers. *Unit head:* Dr. Amelia Adkins, Department Head, 912-344-2562, E-mail: amee.adkins@armstrong.edu. *Application contact:* McKenzie Peterman, Graduate Admissions Specialist, 912-478-5678, Fax: 912-478-0740, E-mail: mpeterman@georgiasouthern.edu.
Website: http://www.armstrong.edu/Education/adolescent_adult_education2/aaed_welcome

Georgia State University, College of Education and Human Development, Department of Middle and Secondary Education, Atlanta, GA 30302-3083. Offers curriculum and instruction (Ed D); English education (MAT); mathematics education (M Ed, MAT); middle level education (MAT); reading, language and literacy education (M Ed, MAT), including reading instruction (M Ed); science education (M Ed, MAT), including biology (MAT), broad field science (MAT), chemistry (MAT), earth science (MAT), physics (MAT); social studies education (M Ed, MAT), including economics (MAT), geography (MAT), history (MAT), political science (MAT); teaching and learning (PhD), including language and literacy, mathematics education, music education, science education, social studies education, teaching and teacher education. *Accreditation:* NCATE. *Program availability:* Part-time, evening/weekend, online learning. *Faculty:* 24 full-time (18 women). *Students:* 179 full-time (110 women), 192 part-time (133 women); includes 193 minority (130 Black or African American, non-Hispanic/Latino; 1 American Indian or Alaska Native, non-Hispanic/Latino; 23 Asian, non-Hispanic/Latino; 25 Hispanic/Latino; 14 Two or more races, non-Hispanic/Latino), 6 international. Average age 33. 175 applicants, 58% accepted, 83 enrolled. In 2017, 81 master's, 17 doctorates awarded. *Entrance requirements:* For master's, GRE; GACE I (for initial teacher preparation programs), baccalaureate degree or equivalent, resume, goals statement, two letters of recommendation, minimum undergraduate GPA of 2.5; proof of initial teacher certification in the content area (for M Ed); for doctorate, GRE, resume, goals statement, writing sample, two letters of recommendation, minimum graduate GPA of 3.3, interview. *Application deadline:* For fall admission, 1/15 priority date for domestic and international students; for spring admission, 10/1 for domestic and international students. Application fee: $50. Electronic applications accepted. *Expenses:* Tuition, state resident: full-time $7020. Tuition, nonresident: full-time $22,518. *Required fees:* $2128. Tuition and fees vary according to degree level and program. *Financial support:* In 2017–18, fellowships with full tuition reimbursements (averaging $19,667 per year), research assistantships with full tuition reimbursements (averaging $5,436 per year), teaching assistantships with full tuition reimbursements (averaging $2,779 per year) were awarded; career-related internships or fieldwork, Federal Work-Study, scholarships/grants, health care benefits, tuition waivers (full and partial), and unspecified assistantships also available. Financial award application deadline: 3/15. *Faculty research:* Teacher education in language and literacy, mathematics, science, and social studies in urban middle and secondary school settings; learning technologies in school, community, and corporate settings; multicultural education and education for social justice; urban education; international education. *Unit head:* Dr. Dana L. Fox, Chair, 404-413-8060, Fax: 404-413-8063, E-mail: dfox@gsu.edu. *Application contact:* Bobbie Turner, Administrative Coordinator, 404-413-8405, Fax: 404-413-8063, E-mail: bnturner@gsu.edu.
Website: http://mse.education.gsu.edu/

Gonzaga University, School of Education, Spokane, WA 99258. Offers clinical mental health counseling (MA); educational leadership (M Ed, Ed D); elementary education (MIT); marriage and family counseling (MA); school counseling (MA); secondary education (MIT); special education (M Ed, MIT); sport and athletic administration (MA). *Accreditation:* NCATE. *Program availability:* Part-time, evening/weekend, 100% online, blended/hybrid learning. *Faculty:* 16 full-time (11 women), 31 part-time/adjunct (19 women). *Students:* 108 full-time (90 women), 225 part-time (140 women); includes 34 minority (4 Black or African American, non-Hispanic/Latino; 2 American Indian or Alaska Native, non-Hispanic/Latino; 5 Asian, non-Hispanic/Latino; 18 Hispanic/Latino; 5 Two or more races, non-Hispanic/Latino), 114 international. Average age 31. 367 applicants, 74% accepted, 160 enrolled. In 2017, 175 master's awarded. *Degree requirements:* For master's, comprehensive exam. *Entrance requirements:* For master's, GRE, MAT, and/or Washington Educator Skills Test-Basic (WEST-B), Washington Educator Skills Test-Endorsements (WEST-E), official transcripts from all colleges or universities attended,

interview, two letters of recommendation, resume, essay, minimum GPA of 3.0. Additional exam requirements/recommendations for international students: Required—TOEFL (minimum score 580 paper-based, 88 iBT) or IELTS (minimum score 6.5). *Application deadline:* Applications are processed on a rolling basis. Application fee: $50. Electronic applications accepted. *Expenses:* $990 per credit. *Financial support:* In 2017–18, 51 students received support. Scholarships/grants and unspecified assistantships available. Support available to part-time students. Financial award applicants required to submit FAFSA. *Unit head:* Dr. Vincent Alfonso, Dean, 509-313-3594, Fax: 509-313-5821, E-mail: alfonso@gonzaga.edu. *Application contact:* Meg Martens, Graduate Admissions Program Specialist, 509-313-4314, E-mail: martens@gonzaga.edu.
Website: https://www.gonzaga.edu/school-of-education

Gordon College, Graduate Education Program, Wenham, MA 01984-1899. Offers early childhood (M Ed); educational leadership (M Ed, Ed S); elementary education (M Ed); English as a second language (M Ed, Ed S); math specialist (M Ed); mathematics specialist (Ed S); middle school education (M Ed); moderate disabilities (M Ed); Montessori education (M Ed); reading (M Ed, Ed S); secondary education (M Ed). *Program availability:* Part-time, evening/weekend. *Faculty:* 23 full-time (17 women), 32 part-time/adjunct (23 women). *Students:* 68 full-time (50 women), 114 part-time (99 women); includes 24 minority (2 Black or African American, non-Hispanic/Latino; 8 Asian, non-Hispanic/Latino; 1 Two or more races, non-Hispanic/Latino; 13 Hispanic/Latino), 10 international. Average age 34. 248 applicants, 100% accepted, 182 enrolled. In 2017, 99 master's, 16 Ed Ss awarded. *Degree requirements:* For master's, action research or clinical experience (for most programs); for Ed S, action research or clinical experience (for some programs). *Entrance requirements:* For master's, minimum undergraduate GPA of 3.0; 2 official undergraduate transcripts; professional resume; 3 recommendation letters (one professional reference, one academic reference, one personal reference); 500-700 word statement of purpose; for Ed S, minimum master's GPA of 3.3; 2 official transcripts from undergraduate and graduate schools; professional resume; 3 recommendation letters (one professional reference, one academic reference, one personal reference); 500-700 word statement of purpose. Additional exam requirements/recommendations for international students: Required—TOEFL (minimum score 550 paper-based, 80 iBT) or IELTS (minimum score 6.5). *Application deadline:* Applications are processed on a rolling basis. Application fee: $75. *Expenses:* $325 per credit tuition; $75 per semester administrative fee. *Financial support:* Applicants required to submit FAFSA. *Faculty research:* Reading, early childhood development, English language learners, universal design for learning. *Unit head:* Dr. Janet Arndt, Director of Graduate Studies, 978-867-4355, Fax: 978-867-4663. *Application contact:* Julie Lenocker, Program Administrator, 978-867-4322, Fax: 978-867-4663, E-mail: graduate-education@gordon.edu.
Website: http://www.gordon.edu/graduate

Goucher College, Graduate Programs in Education, Baltimore, MD 21204-2794. Offers at-risk and diverse learners (M Ed, Certificate); athletic program leadership and administration (M Ed, Certificate); elementary education (MAT); literacy strategies for content learning (M Ed); middle school (M Ed, Certificate); Montessori studies (M Ed); reading instruction (M Ed, Certificate); reducing student, classroom, and school disruption (M Ed); school improvement leadership (M Ed); secondary education (MAT); special education (MAT), including elementary education; special education for certified elementary and secondary teachers (M Ed); teacher as leader in technology (M Ed). *Program availability:* Part-time, evening/weekend. *Degree requirements:* For master's, thesis (M Ed), final presentation (MAT). *Entrance requirements:* For master's, minimum GPA of 3.0. Additional exam requirements/recommendations for international students: Required—TOEFL (minimum score 550 paper-based; 80 iBT), IELTS (minimum score 7). *Application deadline:* For fall admission, 9/1 for domestic students; for spring admission, 1/15 for domestic students. Applications are processed on a rolling basis. Application fee: $75. Electronic applications accepted. *Expenses:* Contact institution. *Financial support:* Career-related internships or fieldwork and unspecified assistantships available. Support available to part-time students. Financial award application deadline: 4/15; financial award applicants required to submit FAFSA. *Faculty research:* Urban education, middle school, school improvement, teacher education, at-risk student achievement. *Unit head:* Dr. Phyllis Sunshine, Assistant Provost, 410-337-6047, Fax: 410-337-6394, E-mail: psunshin@goucher.edu. *Application contact:* Carlton E. Surbeck, III, Director of Admissions, 410-337-6100, Fax: 410-337-6085, E-mail: admissions@goucher.edu.
Website: http://www.goucher.edu/graduate-programs/graduate-programs-in-education

Grand Canyon University, College of Education, Phoenix, AZ 85017-1097. Offers autism spectrum disorders (MA); curriculum and instruction (MA); early childhood education (M Ed); educational administration (M Ed); educational leadership (M Ed); elementary education (M Ed); gifted education (MA); instructional technology (MS); K-12 leadership (Ed S); reading (MA); secondary education (M Ed); secondary humanities education (M Ed); secondary STEM education (M Ed); special education (M Ed); teaching and learning (Ed D); teaching English to speakers of other languages (MA). *Program availability:* Part-time, evening/weekend, online learning. *Degree requirements:* For master's, publishable research paper (M Ed), e-portfolio. *Entrance requirements:* For master's, undergraduate degree from accredited, GCU-approved college, university, or program with minimum GPA 2.8. Additional exam requirements/recommendations for international students: Required—TOEFL (minimum score 550 paper-based; 79 iBT), IELTS (minimum score 6). Electronic applications accepted.

Grand Valley State University, College of Education, Programs in General Education, Allendale, MI 49401-9403. Offers adult and higher education (M Ed); early childhood education (M Ed); educational differentiation (M Ed); educational leadership (M Ed); educational technology integration (M Ed); elementary education (M Ed); middle level education (M Ed); school library media services (M Ed); secondary level education (M Ed); teaching English to speakers of other languages (M Ed). *Program availability:* Part-time, evening/weekend, 100% online, blended/hybrid learning. *Students:* 24 part-time (16 women). Average age 41. In 2017, 5 master's awarded. *Degree requirements:* For master's, project or thesis. *Entrance requirements:* For master's, GRE General Test or minimum GPA of 3.0, last 60 credits from regionally-accredited college/university, 3 letters of recommendation. Additional exam requirements/recommendations for international students: Required—TOEFL (minimum iBT score of 80), IELTS (6.5), or Michigan English Language Assessment Battery (77). *Application deadline:* Applications are processed on a rolling basis. Application fee: $30. Electronic applications accepted. *Expenses:* $652 per credit hour. *Financial support:* In 2017-18, 2 students received support, including 2 fellowships; career-related internships or fieldwork, Federal Work-Study, scholarships/grants, and unspecified assistantships also available. *Faculty research:* Effectiveness of technology in education, parental involvement, effective teaching, effective schools research. *Unit head:* Dr. David Bair, Department Director, 616-331-6489, Fax: 616-331-6489, E-mail: baird@gvsu.edu. *Application contact:* Thomas Owens, Director, Student Information and Services Center, 616-331-6282, Fax: 616-331-6217, E-mail: owenst@gvsu.edu.
Website: http://www.gvsu.edu/coe

Greenville University, Program in Education, Greenville, IL 62246-0159. Offers education (MAT); elementary education (MAE); secondary education (MAE). *Degree*

requirements: For master's, thesis (for some programs). *Entrance requirements:* For master's, GRE, Illinois Basic Skills Test, teacher certification. Electronic applications accepted.

Harding University, Cannon-Clary College of Education, Searcy, AR 72149-0001. Offers advanced studies in teaching and learning (M Ed); art (MSE); behavioral science (MSE); counseling (MS, Ed S); early childhood education (M Ed, MSE); education (MSE); educational leadership (M Ed, Ed S); elementary education (M Ed); English (MSE); French (MSE); history/social science (MSE); kinesiology (MSE); math (MSE); reading (M Ed); secondary education (M Ed); Spanish (MSE); teaching (MAT); teaching English as a second language (MSE). *Accreditation:* NCATE. *Program availability:* Part-time, evening/weekend. *Faculty:* 22 full-time (9 women), 51 part-time/adjunct (37 women). *Students:* 135 full-time (95 women), 316 part-time (231 women); includes 77 minority (46 Black or African American, non-Hispanic/Latino; 7 American Indian or Alaska Native, non-Hispanic/Latino; 4 Asian, non-Hispanic/Latino; 9 Hispanic/Latino; 11 Two or more races, non-Hispanic/Latino), 11 international. Average age 34. 128 applicants, 87% accepted, 111 enrolled. In 2017, 153 master's, 24 other advanced degrees awarded. *Degree requirements:* For master's, comprehensive exam (for some programs), thesis optional, portfolio(s); for Ed S, comprehensive exam, portfolio, project. *Entrance requirements:* For master's, GRE, MAT, PRAXIS; for Ed S, MAT or GRE. Additional exam requirements/recommendations for international students: Required—TOEFL (minimum score 550 paper-based; 79 iBT). *Application deadline:* For fall admission, 8/1 for domestic and international students; for spring admission, 1/1 for domestic and international students. Applications are processed on a rolling basis. Application fee: $35. Tuition and fees vary according to course load, degree level, campus/location and program. *Financial support:* In 2017–18, 33 students received support. Unspecified assistantships available. *Faculty research:* Reading, comprehension, school violence, educational technology, behavior, college choice, differentiated instruction, brain-based teaching. *Unit head:* Dr. Clara Carroll, Chair, 501-279-4501, Fax: 501-279-4083, E-mail: ccarroll@harding.edu. *Application contact:* Information Contact, 501-279-4315, E-mail: gradstudiesedu@harding.edu.
Website: http://www.harding.edu/education

Hawai'i Pacific University, College of Professional Studies, Program in Secondary Education, Honolulu, HI 96813. Offers M Ed. *Accreditation:* TEAC. *Program availability:* Part-time, evening/weekend. *Faculty:* 4 full-time (3 women), 6 part-time/adjunct (3 women). *Students:* 15 full-time (9 women), 4 part-time (2 women); includes 14 minority (2 Black or African American, non-Hispanic/Latino; 5 Asian, non-Hispanic/Latino; 2 Hispanic/Latino; 5 Two or more races, non-Hispanic/Latino). Average age 34. 16 applicants, 69% accepted, 7 enrolled. In 2017, 19 master's awarded. *Entrance requirements:* For master's, minimum undergraduate GPA of 3.0, background check. Additional exam requirements/recommendations for international students: Recommended—TOEFL (minimum score 550 paper-based; 80 iBT), IELTS (minimum score 6), TWE (minimum score 5). *Application deadline:* For fall admission, 1/15 priority date for domestic students; for spring admission, 10/15 priority date for domestic students. Applications are processed on a rolling basis. Application fee: $50. Electronic applications accepted. *Expenses:* Tuition: Full-time $18,000; part-time $1000 per credit. *Required fees:* $200; $26 per credit. Tuition and fees vary according to course load and program. *Financial support:* In 2017–18, 3 students received support. Career-related internships or fieldwork, Federal Work-Study, scholarships/grants, tuition waivers (partial), and unspecified assistantships available. Financial award application deadline: 3/1; financial award applicants required to submit FAFSA. *Unit head:* Dr. Linda Wheeler, Field Director, 808-356-5229, E-mail: lwheeler@hpu.edu. *Application contact:* Danny Lam, Assistant Director of Graduate Admissions, 808-544-1135, E-mail: graduate@hpu.edu.
Website: https://www.hpu.edu/cps/education/me-secondary.html

High Point University, Norcross Graduate School, High Point, NC 27268. Offers athletic training (MSAT); business administration (MBA); educational leadership (M Ed, Ed D); elementary education (M Ed, MAT); pharmacy (Pharm D); physical therapy (DPT); physician assistant studies (MPAS); secondary mathematics (M Ed, MAT); special education (M Ed); strategic communication (MA). *Accreditation:* NCATE. *Program availability:* Part-time, evening/weekend. *Degree requirements:* For master's, comprehensive exam (for some programs), thesis (for some programs). *Entrance requirements:* For master's, GMAT (MBA), GRE, MAT, minimum GPA of 3.0. Additional exam requirements/recommendations for international students: Required—TOEFL (minimum score 550 paper-based). Electronic applications accepted.

Hofstra University, School of Education, Programs in Teacher Education, Hempstead, NY 11549. Offers bilingual education (MA); bilingual extension (Advanced Certificate), including education/speech language pathology, intensive teacher institute; business education (MS Ed); curriculum studies (MS Ed); early childhood and childhood education (MS Ed); early childhood education (MA, MS Ed); educational technology (Advanced Certificate); elementary education (MA, MS Ed), including science, technology, engineering, and mathematics (STEM) (MA); English education (MS Ed); family and consumer science (MS Ed); fine arts and music education (Advanced Certificate); fine arts education (MS Ed); foreign language and TESOL (MS Ed); foreign language education (MA, MS Ed), including Arabic (MS Ed), biology, chemistry, Chinese (MS Ed), earth science, French, German, Italian (MS Ed), Mandarin (MS Ed), physics, Russian, Spanish; foundations of education (Advanced Certificate), including grades 5-6, grades 7-9; languages other than English and teaching English as a second language (MA); learning and teaching (Ed D), including applied linguistics, art education, arts and humanities, early childhood education, English education, human development, math education, math, science, and technology, multicultural education, physical education, science education, social studies education, special education; mathematics education (MA, MS Ed); music education (MA, MS Ed); science education (MA), including biology (MA, MS Ed), chemistry (MA, MS Ed), earth science (MA, MS Ed), physics (MA, MS Ed); secondary education (Advanced Certificate); social studies education (MA, MS Ed); teaching languages other than English and TESOL (MS Ed); technology for learning (MA); TESOL (MS Ed, Advanced Certificate); TESOL with specialization in STEM (MA); work based learning extension (Advanced Certificate). *Program availability:* Part-time, evening/weekend, blended/hybrid learning. *Students:* 119 full-time (83 women), 124 part-time (90 women); includes 54 minority (15 Black or African American, non-Hispanic/Latino; 9 Asian, non-Hispanic/Latino; 29 Hispanic/Latino; 1 Native Hawaiian or other Pacific Islander, non-Hispanic/Latino), 12 international. Average age 29. 205 applicants, 88% accepted, 93 enrolled. In 2017, 103 master's, 4 doctorates, 32 other advanced degrees awarded. *Degree requirements:* For master's, comprehensive exam, thesis (for some programs), exit project, student teaching, fieldwork, electronic portfolio, curriculum project, minimum GPA of 3.0; for doctorate, thesis/dissertation; for Advanced Certificate, 3 foreign languages, comprehensive exam (for some programs), thesis project. *Entrance requirements:* For master's, GRE, 2 letters of recommendation, portfolio, teacher certification (MA), interview, essay; for doctorate, GMAT, GRE, LSAT, or MAT; for Advanced Certificate, 2 letters of recommendation, essay, interview and/or portfolio, teaching certificate. Additional exam requirements/recommendations for international students: Required—TOEFL (minimum score 550 paper-based; 80 iBT). *Application deadline:* Applications are processed on a rolling basis. Application fee: $75. Electronic applications accepted. *Expenses:* Tuition: Full-time $1292. *Required fees:* $970. Tuition and fees vary according to program. *Financial support:* In 2017-18, 112

students received support, including 56 fellowships with full and partial tuition reimbursements available (averaging $4,998 per year), 2 research assistantships with full and partial tuition reimbursements available (averaging $8,753 per year); career-related internships or fieldwork, Federal Work-Study, institutionally sponsored loans, scholarships/grants, traineeships, tuition waivers (full and partial), and unspecified assistantships also available. Support available to part-time students. Financial award applicants required to submit FAFSA. *Faculty research:* Educational interventions that foster critical-thinking skills; teachers' attitudes about professional development; threats to teacher quality. *Unit head:* Dr. Eustace Thompson, Chairperson, 516-463-5749, Fax: 516-463-6275, E-mail: eustace.g.thompson@hofstra.edu. *Application contact:* Sunil Samuel, Assistant Vice President of Admissions, 516-463-4723, Fax: 516-463-4664, E-mail: graduateadmission@hofstra.edu.
Website: http://www.hofstra.edu/education/

Hofstra University, School of Education, Specialized Programs in Education, Hempstead, NY 11549. Offers applied behavior analysis (Advanced Certificate); childhood special education (MS Ed); early childhood special education (MS Ed, Advanced Certificate); educational and policy leadership (Ed D); educational leadership (Advanced Certificate), including school building leader/school district business leader; educational leadership and policy studies (MS Ed), including K-12; elementary special education (MS Ed); gifted education (Advanced Certificate), including school building leader/school district business leader; health education (MS); health professions pedagogy and leadership (MS); higher education leadership and policy studies (MS Ed); inclusive early childhood special education (MS Ed); inclusive elementary special education (MS Ed); inclusive secondary special education (MS Ed); literacy studies (MA, MS Ed, Ed D, Advanced Certificate), including birth-grade 6 (MS Ed, Advanced Certificate), grades 5-12 (MS Ed, Advanced Certificate), literacy studies (Ed D); pedagogy for health professions (Advanced Certificate); physical education (MS); school district business leader (Advanced Certificate); secondary education generalist - students with disabilities 7-12 (MS Ed), including students with disabilities 7-12; secondary special education generalist (MS Ed), including extension in secondary education; special education (MS Ed, Advanced Certificate); special education assessment and diagnosis (Advanced Certificate); special education early childhood intervention (MS Ed); special education: international perspectives (MS Ed); teaching students with severe or multiple disabilities (Advanced Certificate). *Program availability:* Part-time, evening/weekend, blended/hybrid learning. *Students:* 148 full-time (110 women), 249 part-time (188 women); includes 105 minority (54 Black or African American, non-Hispanic/Latino; 1 American Indian or Alaska Native, non-Hispanic/Latino; 13 Asian, non-Hispanic/Latino; 35 Hispanic/Latino; 1 Native Hawaiian or other Pacific Islander, non-Hispanic/Latino; 1 Two or more races, non-Hispanic/Latino), 1 international. Average age 32. 228 applicants, 93% accepted, 132 enrolled. In 2017, 97 master's, 22 doctorates, 31 other advanced degrees awarded. *Degree requirements:* For master's, one foreign language, comprehensive exam (for some programs), thesis (for some programs), electronic portfolio, capstone course, internship, practicum, student teaching, seminars, minimum GPA of 3.0; for doctorate, one foreign language, comprehensive exam, thesis/dissertation, qualifying hearing. *Entrance requirements:* For master's, GRE, interview, letters of recommendation, portfolio, essay, certification; for doctorate, GRE or MAT, interview, resume, essay, master's degree, 3 letters of recommendation, writing sample; for Advanced Certificate, GRE, interview, letters of recommendation, essay, professional experience, resume, master's degree. Additional exam requirements/recommendations for international students: Required—TOEFL (minimum score 550 paper-based; 80 iBT). *Application deadline:* Applications are processed on a rolling basis. Application fee: $75. Electronic applications accepted. *Expenses:* Tuition: Full-time $1292. *Required fees:* $970. Tuition and fees vary according to program. *Financial support:* In 2017–18, 225 students received support, including 118 fellowships with full and partial tuition reimbursements available (averaging $3,887 per year), 12 research assistantships with full and partial tuition reimbursements available (averaging $7,215 per year); career-related internships or fieldwork, Federal Work-Study, institutionally sponsored loans, scholarships/grants, traineeships, tuition waivers (full and partial), and unspecified assistantships also available. Support available to part-time students. Financial award applicants required to submit FAFSA. *Faculty research:* Collaborative teaching and learning; language and culture; new media literacies; applied behavior analysis; K-12 leadership development. *Unit head:* Dr. Elfreda Blue, Chairperson, 516-463-5762, Fax: 516-463-6184, E-mail: elfreda.blue@hofstra.edu. *Application contact:* Sunil Samuel, Assistant Vice President of Admissions, 516-463-4723, Fax: 516-463-4664, E-mail: graduateadmission@hofstra.edu.
Website: http://www.hofstra.edu/education/

Hood College, Graduate School, Department of Education, Frederick, MD 21701-8575. Offers curriculum and instruction (MS), including elementary education, elementary science and mathematics education, secondary education, special education; education, multidisciplinary studies (MS); educational leadership (MS, Certificate); reading specialization (MS); STEM education (Certificate). *Accreditation:* NCATE. *Program availability:* Part-time-only, evening/weekend. *Faculty:* 6 full-time (4 women), 35 part-time/adjunct (27 women). *Students:* 3 full-time (all women), 329 part-time (265 women); includes 62 minority (35 Black or African American, non-Hispanic/Latino; 4 Asian, non-Hispanic/Latino; 14 Hispanic/Latino; 9 Two or more races, non-Hispanic/Latino), 3 international. Average age 33. 76 applicants, 100% accepted, 63 enrolled. In 2017, 53 master's, 58 other advanced degrees awarded. *Degree requirements:* For master's, action research project, portfolio (for reading specialization); for Certificate, STEM capstone activity. *Entrance requirements:* For master's, minimum GPA of 2.75, teaching certification, writing sample during interview, letter of recommendation from principal (for educational leadership program only). Additional exam requirements/recommendations for international students: Required—TOEFL (minimum score 575 paper-based; 89 iBT), IELTS (minimum score 6.5). *Application deadline:* For fall admission, 8/15 priority date for domestic students, 8/5 for international students; for spring admission, 12/1 priority date for domestic students, 12/1 for international students; for summer admission, 5/1 priority date for domestic students, 4/15 for international students. Applications are processed on a rolling basis. Application fee: $35. Electronic applications accepted. *Expenses:* $465 per credit plus $110 comprehensive fee per semester. *Financial support:* Tuition waivers (partial) and unspecified assistantships available. Financial award applicants required to submit FAFSA. *Faculty research:* Leadership, action research, brain research, learning styles. *Unit head:* Dr. April M. Boulton, Dean of the Graduate School, 301-696-3612, E-mail: gofurther@hood.edu. *Application contact:* Jan Marcus, Assistant Director of Graduate Admissions, 301-696-3600, E-mail: gofurther@hood.edu.
Website: http://www.hood.edu/academics/education/index.html

Hood College, Graduate School, Program in Secondary Mathematics Education, Frederick, MD 21701-8575. Offers high school (MS); middle school (MS); secondary mathematics education (Certificate). *Program availability:* Part-time, evening/weekend. *Faculty:* 2 full-time (1 woman), 3 part-time/adjunct (2 women). *Students:* 29 part-time (20 women); includes 2 minority (1 Black or African American, non-Hispanic/Latino; 1 Hispanic/Latino). Average age 32. 6 applicants, 100% accepted, 6 enrolled. In 2017, 8 master's awarded. *Degree requirements:* For master's, exitfolio, capstone/research project. *Entrance requirements:* For master's, minimum GPA of 2.75, initial teacher certification, essay. Additional exam requirements/recommendations for international students: Required—TOEFL (minimum score 575 paper-based; 89 iBT), IELTS (minimum

score 6.5). *Application deadline:* For fall admission, 8/15 priority date for domestic students, 8/15 for international students; for spring admission, 12/1 priority date for domestic students, 12/1 for international students; for summer admission, 5/1 priority date for domestic students, 4/15 for international students. Applications are processed on a rolling basis. Application fee: $35. Electronic applications accepted. *Expenses:* $465 per credit hour plus $110 comprehensive fee per semester. *Financial support:* Tuition waivers (partial) and unspecified assistantships available. Financial award applicants required to submit FAFSA. *Unit head:* Dr. April M. Boulton, Dean of the Graduate School, 301-696-3600, E-mail: gofurther@hood.edu. *Application contact:* Jan Marcus, Assistant Director of Graduate Admissions, 301-696-3600, E-mail: gofurther@hood.edu.
Website: http://www.hood.edu/graduate

Hope International University, School of Graduate and Professional Studies, Program in Education, Fullerton, CA 92831-3138. Offers education administration (MA); elementary education (ME); secondary education (ME). *Program availability:* Part-time, evening/weekend. *Degree requirements:* For master's, comprehensive exam (for some programs), thesis. *Entrance requirements:* For master's, minimum GPA of 3.0, 2 references. Additional exam requirements/recommendations for international students: Required—TOEFL (minimum score 550 paper-based; 86 iBT); Recommended—IELTS (minimum score 6.5). Electronic applications accepted. *Expenses:* Contact institution. *Faculty research:* Distance education.

Howard University, School of Education, Department of Curriculum and Instruction, Program in Secondary Education, Washington, DC 20059-0002. Offers M Ed. *Accreditation:* NCATE. *Degree requirements:* For master's, comprehensive exam, thesis (for some programs), expository writing exam, internships, practicum. *Entrance requirements:* For master's, PRAXIS I, GRE, minimum GPA of 2.7. Additional exam requirements/recommendations for international students: Required—TOEFL (minimum score 550 paper-based; 79 iBT). Electronic applications accepted.

Hunter College of the City University of New York, Graduate School, School of Arts and Sciences, Department of Mathematics and Statistics, New York, NY 10065-5085. Offers adolescent mathematics education (MA); applied mathematics (MA); bioinformatics (MA); pure mathematics (MA); statistics (MA). *Program availability:* Part-time, evening/weekend. *Degree requirements:* For master's, one foreign language, comprehensive exam, thesis (for some programs). *Entrance requirements:* For master's, GRE General Test, 24 credits in mathematics. Additional exam requirements/recommendations for international students: Required—TOEFL. *Faculty research:* Data analysis, dynamical systems, computer graphics, topology, statistical decision theory.

Hunter College of the City University of New York, Graduate School, School of Education, Programs in Secondary Education, New York, NY 10065-5085. Offers biology education (MA); chemistry education (MA); earth science (MA); English education (MA); French education (MA); Italian education (MA); mathematics education (MA); physics education (MA); social studies education (MA); Spanish education (MA). *Accreditation:* NCATE. *Degree requirements:* For master's, thesis. *Entrance requirements:* Additional exam requirements/recommendations for international students: Required—TOEFL.

Idaho State University, Office of Graduate Studies, College of Education, Department of Teaching and Educational Studies, Pocatello, ID 83209-8059. Offers deaf education (M Ed); elementary education (M Ed); human exceptionality (M Ed); literacy (M Ed); music education (M Ed); secondary education (M Ed). *Program availability:* Part-time. *Degree requirements:* For master's, comprehensive exam, thesis (for some programs), oral thesis defense or written comprehensive exam and oral exam. *Entrance requirements:* For master's, GRE or MAT, minimum undergraduate GPA of 3.0, bachelor's degree, professional experience in an educational context. Additional exam requirements/recommendations for international students: Required—TOEFL (minimum score 550 paper-based; 80 iBT). Electronic applications accepted. *Faculty research:* Literacy, school psychology, special education.

Immaculata University, College of Graduate Studies, Program in Educational Leadership, Immaculata, PA 19345. Offers educational leadership (MA, Ed D); principal (Certificate); secondary education (Certificate); supervisor of special education (Certificate). *Program availability:* Part-time, evening/weekend. *Degree requirements:* For master's, comprehensive exam, thesis optional; for doctorate, comprehensive exam, thesis/dissertation. *Entrance requirements:* For master's, GRE or MAT, minimum GPA of 3.0; for doctorate, GRE General Test or MAT, minimum GPA of 3.5. Additional exam requirements/recommendations for international students: Required—TOEFL. Electronic applications accepted. *Faculty research:* Cooperative learning, school-based management, whole language, performance assessment.

Indiana University Bloomington, School of Education, Department of Curriculum and Instruction, Bloomington, IN 47405-7000. Offers art education (MS, Ed D, PhD); curriculum studies (Ed D, PhD); elementary education (MS, Ed D, PhD, Ed S); mathematics education (MS, Ed D, PhD); science education (MS, Ed D, PhD); secondary education (MS, Ed D, PhD); social studies education (MS, PhD); special education (PhD, Ed S). *Accreditation:* NCATE. *Program availability:* Part-time, evening/weekend. Terminal master's awarded for partial completion of doctoral program. *Degree requirements:* For doctorate, thesis/dissertation; for Ed S, comprehensive exam or project. *Entrance requirements:* For master's, doctorate, and Ed S, GRE General Test. Electronic applications accepted.

Indiana University Northwest, School of Education, Gary, IN 46408. Offers educational leadership (MS Ed); elementary education (MS Ed); K-12 online teaching (Graduate Certificate); secondary education (MS Ed). *Accreditation:* NCATE. *Program availability:* Part-time, evening/weekend. *Entrance requirements:* For master's, GRE General Test or MAT, minimum GPA of 3.0. Electronic applications accepted. *Expenses:* Contact institution.

Indiana University–Purdue University Fort Wayne, College of Education and Public Policy, Department of Educational Studies, Fort Wayne, IN 46805-1499. Offers elementary education (MS Ed); secondary education (MS Ed). *Accreditation:* NCATE. *Program availability:* Part-time. *Entrance requirements:* For master's, minimum GPA of 2.5, three professional letters of recommendation. Additional exam requirements/recommendations for international students: Required—TOEFL (minimum score 550 paper-based; 79 iBT). *Faculty research:* International faculty, gender in Burmese refugee narratives, planning effective instruction.

Indiana University South Bend, School of Education, South Bend, IN 46615. Offers addiction counseling (MS Ed); alcohol and drug counseling (Graduate Certificate); clinical mental health counseling (MS Ed); educational leadership (MS Ed); elementary education (MS Ed); marriage, couple, and family counseling (MS Ed); school counseling (MS Ed); secondary education (MS Ed); special education (MAT, MS Ed), including intense intervention (MS Ed), mild intervention (MS Ed). *Accreditation:* NCATE. *Program availability:* Part-time, evening/weekend. *Degree requirements:* For master's, thesis or alternative, exit project. *Entrance requirements:* For master's, letters of recommendation, GRE or minimum GPA of 3.0. Additional exam requirements/recommendations for international students: Required—TOEFL. Electronic applications accepted. *Expenses:* Contact institution. *Faculty research:* Professional dispositions, early childhood literacy, online learning, program assessments, problem-based learning.

Secondary Education

Indiana University Southeast, School of Education, New Albany, IN 47150. Offers counselor education (MS Ed); elementary education (MS Ed); secondary education (MS Ed). *Accreditation:* NCATE. *Program availability:* Part-time, evening/weekend. *Entrance requirements:* For master's, minimum undergraduate GPA of 2.5, graduate 3.0. Electronic applications accepted. *Faculty research:* Learning styles, technology, constructivism, group process, innovative math strategies.

Instituto Tecnologico de Santo Domingo, Graduate School, Area of Humanities and Social Sciences, Santo Domingo, Dominican Republic. Offers accounting (Certificate); adult education (Certificate); applied linguistics (MA); economics (MA); education (M Ed); educational psychology (MA, Certificate); gender and development (MA, Certificate); humanistic studies (MA); international marketing management (Certificate); international relations in the Caribbean basin (Certificate); intervention systems in family therapy (MA); linguistic and literary communication (Certificate); pedagogical support (MA); social science education (M Ed); sustainable human development (MA); terminal illness and death psychology (Certificate); youth and adult education (M Ed).

Ithaca College, School of Humanities and Sciences, Program in Adolescence Education, Ithaca, NY 14850. Offers English (MAT). *Program availability:* Part-time. *Faculty:* 11 full-time (7 women), 1 part-time/adjunct (0 women). *Students:* 12 full-time (7 women); includes 1 minority (Hispanic/Latino), 1 international. Average age 24. 18 applicants, 72% accepted, 11 enrolled. In 2017, 19 master's awarded. *Degree requirements:* For master's, thesis or alternative, student teaching. *Entrance requirements:* Additional exam requirements/recommendations for international students: Required—TOEFL (minimum score 550 paper-based; 80 iBT). *Application deadline:* For fall admission, 3/19 for domestic and international students. Applications are processed on a rolling basis. Application fee: $40. Electronic applications accepted. *Expenses:* Contact institution. *Financial support:* In 2017–18, 11 students received support, including 11 research assistantships (averaging $8,056 per year); career-related internships or fieldwork, Federal Work-Study, scholarships/grants, and unspecified assistantships also available. Support available to part-time students. Financial award application deadline: 3/1; financial award applicants required to submit FAFSA. *Unit head:* Dr. Peter Martin, Chair, 607-274-1076, E-mail: pmartin@ithaca.edu. *Application contact:* Nicole Eversley Bradwell, Director, Office of Admission, 607-274-3124, Fax: 607-274-1263, E-mail: admission@ithaca.edu. Website: http://www.ithaca.edu/gradprograms/education/programs/aded

Jacksonville State University, College of Graduate Studies and Continuing Education, College of Education and Professional Studies, Program in Secondary Education, Jacksonville, AL 36265-1602. Offers MS Ed. *Accreditation:* NCATE. *Program availability:* Part-time, evening/weekend. *Degree requirements:* For master's, comprehensive exam, thesis (for some programs). *Entrance requirements:* For master's, GRE General Test or MAT. Additional exam requirements/recommendations for international students: Required—TOEFL (minimum score 500 paper-based; 61 iBT). Electronic applications accepted.

James Madison University, The Graduate School, College of Education, Program in Education, Harrisonburg, VA 22807. Offers early childhood education (preK-3) (MAT); educational leadership (M Ed); educational technology (M Ed); elementary education (MAT); equity and cultural diversity (M Ed); inclusive early childhood education (MAT); K-8 mathematics specialist (M Ed); middle education (MAT); reading education (M Ed); secondary education (MAT); Spanish language and culture for educators (M Ed); TESOL (MAT). *Accreditation:* NCATE. *Program availability:* Part-time, evening/weekend. *Students:* 260 full-time (233 women), 158 part-time (100 women); includes 48 minority (10 Black or African American, non-Hispanic/Latino; 4 Asian, non-Hispanic/Latino; 26 Hispanic/Latino; 1 Native Hawaiian or other Pacific Islander, non-Hispanic/Latino; 7 Two or more races, non-Hispanic/Latino), 2 international. Average age 30. In 2017, 262 master's awarded. Application fee: $55. Electronic applications accepted. *Expenses:* Tuition, state resident: full-time $10,512; part-time $438 per credit hour. Tuition, nonresident: full-time $28,358; part-time $1162 per credit hour. *Required fees:* $1128. *Financial support:* In 2017–18, 23 students received support, including 1 teaching assistantship; career-related internships or fieldwork, Federal Work-Study, and 22 assistantships (averaging $7911) also available. Financial award application deadline: 3/1; financial award applicants required to submit FAFSA. *Unit head:* Dr. Phillip M. Wishon, Dean, 540-568-6572, E-mail: wishonpm@jmu.edu. *Application contact:* Lynette D. Michael, Director of Graduate Admissions, 540-568-6131 Ext. 6395, Fax: 540-568-7860, E-mail: michaeld@jmu.edu. Website: http://www.jmu.edu/coe/index.shtml

James Madison University, The Graduate School, College of Education, Program in Secondary Education, Harrisonburg, VA 22807. Offers MAT. *Accreditation:* NCATE. *Program availability:* Part-time, evening/weekend. *Students:* Average age 27. *Entrance requirements:* For master's, GRE General Test. Additional exam requirements/recommendations for international students: Required—TOEFL. *Application deadline:* For fall admission, 5/1 priority date for domestic students; for spring admission, 9/1 priority date for domestic students. Applications are processed on a rolling basis. Application fee: $55. Electronic applications accepted. *Expenses:* Tuition, state resident: full-time $10,512; part-time $438 per credit hour. Tuition, nonresident: full-time $28,358; part-time $1162 per credit hour. *Required fees:* $1128. *Financial support:* Federal Work-Study and unspecified assistantships available. Financial award application deadline: 3/1; financial award applicants required to submit FAFSA. *Unit head:* Dr. Steven L. Purcell, Academic Unit Head, 540-568-6793. *Application contact:* Lynette M. Bible, Director of Graduate Admissions, 540-568-6395, Fax: 540-568-7860, E-mail: biblelm@jmu.edu.

John Brown University, Graduate Education Programs, Siloam Springs, AR 72761-2121. Offers curriculum and instruction (M Ed); secondary education (MAT). *Program availability:* Part-time, evening/weekend. *Entrance requirements:* For master's, GRE (minimum score of 300). Additional exam requirements/recommendations for international students: Required—TOEFL (minimum score 550 paper-based; 79 iBT). Electronic applications accepted.

Johns Hopkins University, School of Education, Master's Programs in Education, Baltimore, MD 21218. Offers counseling (MS), including clinical mental health counseling, school counseling; education (MS), including educational studies, gifted education, reading, school administration and supervision, technology for educators; elementary education (MAT); health professions (M Ed); intelligence analysis (MS); organizational leadership (MS); secondary education (MAT), including biology, chemistry, earth/space science, English, physics, social studies; special education (MS), including early childhood special education, general special education studies, mild to moderate disabilities, severe disabilities. *Program availability:* Part-time, evening/weekend, 100% online, blended/hybrid learning. *Degree requirements:* For master's, comprehensive exam (for some programs), portfolio, capstone project and/or internship; PRAXIS II (subject area assessments) for initial teacher preparation programs that lead to licensure. *Entrance requirements:* For master's, GRE (for full-time programs only); PRAXIS I/core or state-approved alternative (for initial teacher preparation programs that lead to licensure), minimum of bachelor's degree from regionally- or nationally-accredited institution; minimum GPA of 3.0 in all previous programs of study; official transcripts from all post-secondary institutions attended; essay; curriculum vitae/resume; letters of recommendation (3 for full-time programs, 2 for part-time programs);

dispositions survey. Additional exam requirements/recommendations for international students: Required—TOEFL (minimum score 600 paper-based; 100 iBT), IELTS (minimum score 7). Electronic applications accepted. *Expenses:* Contact institution.

Johnson & Wales University, Graduate Studies, MAT Program in Teacher Education, Providence, RI 02903-3703. Offers business education and secondary special education (MAT); culinary arts education (MAT); elementary education and elementary special education (MAT). *Program availability:* Part-time, evening/weekend. *Entrance requirements:* For master's, MAT, minimum GPA of 2.75. Additional exam requirements/recommendations for international students: Required—TOEFL (minimum score 550 paper-based) or IELTS (recommended). *Application deadline:* For fall admission, 8/21 priority date for domestic students, 6/15 priority date for international students; for winter admission, 11/15 priority date for domestic students, 10/1 priority date for international students. Applications are processed on a rolling basis. Application fee: $0. *Expenses:* Tuition: Full-time $12,636; part-time $702 per credit hour. *Financial support:* Unspecified assistantships available. Financial award application deadline: 5/1. *Faculty research:* Secondary education, student teaching, educational reform, evaluation procedures. *Unit head:* Karen Swoboda, Director, 401-598-1922, Fax: 401-598-1125. *Application contact:* Graduate School Admissions, 401-598-1015, Fax: 401-598-1286, E-mail: gradadm@jwu.edu.

Kennesaw State University, Leland and Clarice C. Bagwell College of Education, Program in Graduate Education, Kennesaw, GA 30144. Offers educational leadership (M Ed); educational leadership technology (M Ed); elementary and early childhood education (M Ed); instructional technology (M Ed); middle grades education (M Ed); reading (M Ed); secondary education (M Ed); special education (M Ed); teaching English to speakers of other languages (M Ed). *Accreditation:* NCATE. *Program availability:* Part-time. *Degree requirements:* For master's, thesis or alternative. *Entrance requirements:* For master's, GRE General Test, T-4 state certification, minimum GPA of 2.75. Additional exam requirements/recommendations for international students: Required—TOEFL (minimum score 550 paper-based; 80 iBT), IELTS (minimum score 6.5). Electronic applications accepted.

Kennesaw State University, Leland and Clarice C. Bagwell College of Education, Program in Teaching, Kennesaw, GA 30144. Offers art education (MAT); biology (MAT); chemistry (MAT); foreign language education (Chinese and Spanish) (MAT); physics (MAT); secondary English (MAT); secondary mathematics (MAT); special education (MAT); teaching English to speakers of other languages (MAT). *Program availability:* Part-time, evening/weekend. *Entrance requirements:* For master's, GRE, GACE I (state certificate exam), minimum GPA of 2.75, 2 recommendations, resume. Additional exam requirements/recommendations for international students: Required—TOEFL (minimum score 550 paper-based; 80 iBT), IELTS (minimum score 6.5). Electronic applications accepted.

Kent State University, College of Arts and Sciences, Department of Mathematical Sciences, Kent, OH 44242-0001. Offers applied mathematics (MA, MS, PhD); mathematics for secondary teachers (MA, MS, PhD). *Program availability:* Part-time. *Faculty:* 24 full-time (7 women). *Students:* 71 full-time (27 women), 33 part-time (12 women); includes 7 minority (1 Black or African American, non-Hispanic/Latino; 5 Asian, non-Hispanic/Latino; 1 Hispanic/Latino), 45 international. Average age 29. 77 applicants, 75% accepted, 22 enrolled. In 2017, 13 master's, 7 doctorates awarded. *Degree requirements:* For master's, comprehensive exam (for some programs), thesis (for some programs); for doctorate, comprehensive exam, thesis/dissertation. *Entrance requirements:* For master's, bachelor's degree with proficiency in numerical analysis and statistics, goal statement, resume or vita, 3 letters of recommendation; for doctorate, official transcript(s), goal statement, three letters of recommendation, resume or vita, passage of the departmental qualifying examination at the master's level. Additional exam requirements/recommendations for international students: Required—TOEFL (minimum score 525 paper-based, 71 iBT), Michigan English Language Assessment Battery (minimum score 74), IELTS (minimum score 6.0) or PTE (minimum score 50). *Application deadline:* For fall admission, 5/1 for domestic and international students; for spring admission, 10/1 for domestic and international students; for summer admission, 2/1 for domestic and international students. Applications are processed on a rolling basis. Application fee: $45 ($70 for international students). Electronic applications accepted. *Expenses:* Tuition, state resident: full-time $11,310; part-time $515 per credit hour. Tuition, nonresident: full-time $20,396; part-time $928 per credit hour. *International tuition:* $18,544 full-time. *Financial support:* Fellowships with full tuition reimbursements, research assistantships with full tuition reimbursements, teaching assistantships with full tuition reimbursements, scholarships/grants, and unspecified assistantships available. Financial award application deadline: 1/31. *Unit head:* Dr. Brian Hayashi, Professor and Chair, 330-672-8914, E-mail: bhayashi@kent.edu. *Application contact:* Artem Zvavitch, Professor and Graduate Coordinator, 330-672-3316, E-mail: zvavitch@math.kent.edu. Website: http://www.kent.edu/math/

Kent State University, College of Education, Health and Human Services, School of Teaching, Learning and Curriculum Studies, Program in Secondary Education, Kent, OH 44242-0001. Offers MAT. *Accreditation:* NCATE. *Entrance requirements:* For master's, GRE General Test, 2 letters of reference, moral character form. Additional exam requirements/recommendations for international students: Required—TOEFL (minimum score 550 paper-based; 80 iBT). Electronic applications accepted. *Expenses:* Tuition, state resident: full-time $11,310; part-time $515 per credit hour. Tuition, nonresident: full-time $20,396; part-time $928 per credit hour. *International tuition:* $18,544 full-time. *Faculty research:* Creativity in science, women in science, teaching of writing, curriculum theory, mathematical reasoning.

Keuka College, Program in Childhood Education/Literacy, Keuka Park, NY 14478. Offers literacy 5-12 (MS); literacy B-6 (MS). *Degree requirements:* For master's, thesis, capstone project/student-led research project. *Entrance requirements:* For master's, GRE, minimum GPA of 3.0; 3 letters of recommendation (2 academic and one from cooperating teacher from student teaching or other professional). Additional exam requirements/recommendations for international students: Required—TOEFL (minimum score 550 paper-based). Electronic applications accepted. *Expenses:* Contact institution. *Faculty research:* Marginalized populations, international literacy, teacher assessment.

Kutztown University of Pennsylvania, College of Education, Program in Secondary Education, Kutztown, PA 19530-0730. Offers biology (M Ed); curriculum and instruction (M Ed); English (M Ed); mathematics (M Ed); middle level (M Ed); social studies (M Ed); teaching (M Ed); transformational teaching and learning (Ed D). *Accreditation:* NCATE. *Program availability:* Part-time, evening/weekend, 100% online, blended/hybrid learning. *Faculty:* 4 full-time (3 women), 1 part-time/adjunct (0 women). *Students:* 33 full-time (21 women), 76 part-time (49 women); includes 6 minority (3 Black or African American, non-Hispanic/Latino; 3 Hispanic/Latino). Average age 32. 76 applicants, 91% accepted, 43 enrolled. In 2017, 31 master's awarded. *Degree requirements:* For master's, comprehensive exam, thesis optional; for doctorate, thesis/dissertation. *Entrance requirements:* For master's, GRE General Test, minimum undergraduate major GPA of 3.0, 3 letters of recommendation, copy of PRAXIS II or valid instructional I or II teaching certificate; for doctorate, master's or specialist degree in education or related field from regionally-accredited institution of higher learning with minimum graduate GPA of 3.25,

significant educational experience, employment in an education setting (preferred). Additional exam requirements/recommendations for international students: Required—TOEFL (minimum score 550 paper-based, 79 iBT), IELTS (minimum score 6.5), or PTE (minimum score 53). *Application deadline:* For fall admission, 8/1 for domestic and international students; for spring admission, 12/1 for domestic and international students. Application fee: $35. Electronic applications accepted. *Expenses:* Tuition, state resident: part-time $500 per credit. Tuition, nonresident: part-time $750 per credit. *Required fees:* $115 per credit. One-time fee: $50 part-time. Tuition and fees vary according to degree level. *Financial support:* Career-related internships or fieldwork, Federal Work-Study, scholarships/grants, and unspecified assistantships available. Financial award application deadline: 3/1; financial award applicants required to submit FAFSA. *Unit head:* Dr. Theresa Stahler, Department Chair, 610-683-4259, Fax: 610-683-1338, E-mail: stahler@kutztown.edu. *Application contact:* Dr. Patricia Walsh Coates, Graduate Coordinator, 610-638-4289, Fax: 610-683-1338, E-mail: coates@kutztown.edu.
Website: https://www.kutztown.edu/academcs/graduate-programs/secondary-education.htm

LaGrange College, Graduate Programs, Department of Education, LaGrange, GA 30240-2999. Offers curriculum and instruction (M Ed, Ed S); middle grades (MAT); secondary education (MAT). *Program availability:* Part-time, evening/weekend. *Degree requirements:* For master's, comprehensive exam. *Entrance requirements:* For master's, GRE, MAT, minimum GPA of 2.5. Additional exam requirements/recommendations for international students: Required—TOEFL (minimum score 550 paper-based).

Lake Forest College, Master of Arts in Teaching Program, Lake Forest, IL 60045. Offers elementary education (MAT); K-12 French (MAT); K-12 music (MAT); K-12 Spanish (MAT); K-12 visual art (MAT); secondary biology (MAT); secondary chemistry (MAT); secondary English (MAT); secondary history (MAT); secondary mathematics (MAT). *Degree requirements:* For master's, comprehensive exam, portfolio. *Entrance requirements:* For master's, GRE.

Lancaster Bible College, Graduate School, Lancaster, PA 17601-5036. Offers adult ministries (MA); Bible (MA); children and family ministry (MA); church planting (MA); consulting resource teacher (M Ed); elementary school counseling (M Ed); leadership (PhD); leadership studies (MA); marriage and family counseling (MA); mental health counseling (MA); pastoral studies (MA); secondary school counseling (M Ed); sports ministry (MA); student ministry (MA); town and country ministry (MA). *Program availability:* Part-time, evening/weekend. *Degree requirements:* For master's, comprehensive exam (for some programs), thesis (for some programs). *Entrance requirements:* For master's, bachelor's degree with a minimum of 30 credits of course work in Bible, minimum undergraduate GPA of 3.0, interview. Additional exam requirements/recommendations for international students: Required—TOEFL.

La Salle University, School of Arts and Sciences, Program in Education, Philadelphia, PA 19141-1199. Offers autism spectrum disorders (MA, Certificate); bilingual/bicultural studies (MA); classroom management (MA); dual early childhood and special education (MA); dual middle-level science and math and special education (MA); education (MA); English (MA); English as a second language (Certificate); history (MA); instructional coach (Certificate); instructional leadership (MA); reading specialist (MA, Certificate); secondary education (MA); special education (MA, Certificate). *Program availability:* Part-time, evening/weekend. *Faculty:* 5 full-time (4 women), 8 part-time/adjunct (5 women). *Students:* 2 full-time (1 woman), 110 part-time (81 women); includes 23 minority (11 Black or African American, non-Hispanic/Latino; 1 Asian, non-Hispanic/Latino; 7 Hispanic/Latino; 4 Two or more races, non-Hispanic/Latino). Average age 33. 137 applicants, 70% accepted, 63 enrolled. In 2017, 148 master's awarded. *Degree requirements:* For master's, comprehensive exam. *Entrance requirements:* For master's, MAT or GRE, 2 letters of recommendation; for Certificate, GMAT or GRE, 2 letters of recommendation. Additional exam requirements/recommendations for international students: Required—TOEFL. *Application deadline:* For fall admission, 8/15 priority date for domestic students, 7/15 for international students; for spring admission, 12/15 priority date for domestic students, 11/15 for international students; for summer admission, 4/15 priority date for domestic students, 3/15 for international students. Applications are processed on a rolling basis. Application fee: $35. Electronic applications accepted. Application fee is waived when completed online. *Expenses:* Contact institution. *Financial support:* In 2017–18, 19 students received support. Scholarships/grants available. Support available to part-time students. Financial award application deadline: 8/31; financial award applicants required to submit FAFSA. *Unit head:* Dr. Greer Richardson, Director, 215-951-1806, Fax: 215-951-1843, E-mail: graded@lasalle.edu. *Application contact:* Elizabeth Heenan, Director, Graduate and Adult Enrollment, 215-951-1100, Fax: 215-951-1462, E-mail: heenan@lasalle.edu.
Website: http://www.lasalle.edu/grad-education-programs/

Lee University, Program in Education, Cleveland, TN 37320-3450. Offers art (MAT); curriculum and instruction (M Ed, Ed S); early childhood (MAT); educational leadership (M Ed, Ed S); elementary education (MAT); English and math (MAT); English and science (MAT); English and social studies (MAT); higher education administration (MS); history (MAT); history and economics (MAT); math and science (MAT); math and social studies (MAT); middle grades (MAT); science and social studies (MASW); secondary education (MAT); Spanish (MAT); special education (M Ed, MAT); TESOL (MAT). *Accreditation:* NCATE. *Program availability:* Part-time. *Faculty:* 15 full-time (7 women), 8 part-time/adjunct (3 women). *Students:* 28 full-time (21 women), 77 part-time (48 women); includes 12 minority (7 Black or African American, non-Hispanic/Latino; 2 Hispanic/Latino; 3 Two or more races, non-Hispanic/Latino), 1 international. Average age 31. 35 applicants, 83% accepted, 22 enrolled. In 2017, 54 master's, 4 other advanced degrees awarded. *Degree requirements:* For master's, variable foreign language requirement, thesis optional, internship. *Entrance requirements:* For master's, MAT or GRE General Test, minimum undergraduate GPA of 2.75, 3 letters of recommendation, interview, writing sample, official transcripts, background check; for Ed S, minimum undergraduate and master's GPA of 2.75, official transcripts for undergraduate and master's degrees. Additional exam requirements/recommendations for international students: Required—TOEFL (minimum score 61 iBT). *Application deadline:* For fall admission, 6/1 priority date for domestic and international students; for spring admission, 11/1 priority date for domestic and international students; for summer admission, 4/1 priority date for domestic and international students. Applications are processed on a rolling basis. Application fee: $25. Electronic applications accepted. *Expenses: Tuition:* Full-time $12,780; part-time $710 per credit hour. *Required fees:* $60; $60 per term. Tuition and fees vary according to program. *Financial support:* In 2017–18, 32 students received support. Career-related internships or fieldwork, Federal Work-Study, institutionally sponsored loans, scholarships/grants, and unspecified assistantships available. Financial award application deadline: 3/1; financial award applicants required to submit FAFSA. *Unit head:* Dr. William Kamm, Director, 423-614-8544, E-mail: wkamm@leeuniversity.edu. *Application contact:* Crystal Keeter, Graduate Education Secretary, 423-614-8544, E-mail: ckeeter@leeuniversity.edu.
Website: http://www.leeuniversity.edu/academics/graduate/education

Le Moyne College, Department of Education, Syracuse, NY 13214. Offers adolescent education (MS Ed, MST); adolescent education/special education (MS Ed, MST);

adolescent English (MST), including grades 7-12; adolescent English/special education (MST), including grades 7-12; adolescent foreign language (MST), including grades 7-12; adolescent history (MST), including grades 7-12; childhood education (MS Ed); childhood education/special education (MS Ed); elementary education (MS Ed); general education (MS Ed); inclusive childhood education (MST); literacy education (MS Ed), including birth to grade 6, grades 5-12; school building leader (MS Ed); school building leadership (CAS); school district business leader (MS Ed, CAS); school district leader (MS Ed); school district leadership (CAS); secondary education (MS Ed); special education (MS Ed); teaching English to speakers of other languages (MS Ed); urban studies (MS Ed). *Accreditation:* TEAC. *Program availability:* Part-time, evening/weekend. *Faculty:* 7 full-time (5 women), 20 part-time/adjunct (12 women). *Students:* 30 full-time (19 women), 126 part-time (93 women); includes 15 minority (7 Black or African American, non-Hispanic/Latino; 1 American Indian or Alaska Native, non-Hispanic/Latino; 1 Asian, non-Hispanic/Latino; 6 Hispanic/Latino), 4 international. Average age 29. 139 applicants, 65% accepted, 76 enrolled. In 2017, 82 master's, 43 CASs awarded. *Degree requirements:* For master's, thesis. *Entrance requirements:* For master's, bachelor's degree with minimum undergraduate GPA of 3.0, 2 letters of recommendation, transcripts. Additional exam requirements/recommendations for international students: Required—TOEFL (minimum score 550 paper-based; 79 iBT); Recommended—IELTS (minimum score 6.5). *Application deadline:* For fall admission, 4/1 priority date for domestic and international students; for spring admission, 10/1 priority date for domestic and international students; for summer admission, 3/1 priority date for domestic and international students. Applications are processed on a rolling basis. Application fee: $50. Electronic applications accepted. *Expenses:* $700 per credit hour. *Financial support:* In 2017–18, 30 students received support. Career-related internships or fieldwork, scholarships/grants, and health care benefits available. Support available to part-time students. Financial award applicants required to submit FAFSA. *Faculty research:* Minority teachers, special education, multiculturalism, literacy, technology, media literacy learning, autism, school district organization, service-learning, higher level problem solving, teacher leadership. *Unit head:* Dr. Stephen C. Fleury, Chair, Department of Education, 315-445-4376, Fax: 315-445-4744, E-mail: fleurysc@lemoyne.edu. *Application contact:* Kristen P. Richards, Senior Director of Enrollment Management, 315-445-5444, Fax: 315-445-6092, E-mail: trapaskp@lemoyne.edu.
Website: http://www.lemoyne.edu/education

Lenoir-Rhyne University, Graduate Programs, School of Education, Master of Arts in Teaching Secondary Education Program, Hickory, NC 28601. Offers MAT. *Entrance requirements:* For master's, GRE (minimum score of 147 on each of the verbal and quantitative sections and 3.5 on the analytical) or MAT (minimum score of 390); or PRAXIS I (minimum scores of Reading 176, Writing 173, and Math 173), official transcripts from all undergraduate and graduate institutions attended, resume, essay, criminal background check. *Expenses:* Contact institution.

Lesley University, Graduate School of Education, Cambridge, MA 02138-2790. Offers arts, community, and education (M Ed); autism studies (Certificate); curriculum and instruction (M Ed, CAGS); early childhood education (M Ed); ecological teaching and learning (MS); educational studies (PhD), including adult learning, educational leadership, individually designed; elementary education (M Ed); emergent technologies for educators (Certificate); ESLArts: language learning through the arts (M Ed); high school education (M Ed); individually designed (M Ed); integrated teaching through the arts (M Ed); literacy for K-8 classroom teachers (M Ed); mathematics education (M Ed); middle school education (M Ed); moderate disabilities (M Ed); online learning (Certificate); reading (CAGS); science in education (M Ed); severe disabilities (M Ed); special needs (CAGS); specialist teacher of reading (M Ed); teacher of visual art (M Ed); technology in education (M Ed, CAGS). *Accreditation:* TEAC. *Program availability:* Part-time, evening/weekend, online learning. *Degree requirements:* For master's, practicum; for doctorate, thesis/dissertation. *Entrance requirements:* For master's, Massachusetts Tests for Educator Licensure (MTEL), transcripts, statement of purpose, recommendations; interview (for special education); for doctorate, GRE General Test, transcripts, statement of purpose, recommendations, interview, master's degree, resume; for other advanced degree, interview, master's degree. Additional exam requirements/recommendations for international students: Required—TOEFL (minimum score 550 paper-based; 80 iBT). Electronic applications accepted. *Faculty research:* Assessment in literacy, mathematics and science; autism spectrum disorders; instructional technology and online learning; multicultural education and English language learners.

Lewis & Clark College, Graduate School of Education and Counseling, Department of Teacher Education, Program in Secondary Education, Portland, OR 97219-7899. Offers MAT. *Accreditation:* NCATE. *Entrance requirements:* For master's, prior experience working with children and/or youth; minimum undergraduate GPA of 2.75. Additional exam requirements/recommendations for international students: Required—TOEFL (minimum score 575 paper-based). Electronic applications accepted. *Faculty research:* Classroom management, classroom assessment, science education, classroom ethnography, moral development.

Lewis University, College of Education, Program in Secondary Education, Romeoville, IL 60446. Offers biology (MA); chemistry (MA); English (MA); history (MA); math (MA); physics (MA); psychology and social science (MA). *Program availability:* Part-time. *Students:* 19 full-time (9 women), 22 part-time (12 women); includes 10 minority (3 Black or African American, non-Hispanic/Latino; 1 Asian, non-Hispanic/Latino; 5 Hispanic/Latino; 2 Two or more races, non-Hispanic/Latino). Average age 27. *Degree requirements:* For master's, comprehensive exam, departmental qualifying exam. *Entrance requirements:* For master's, writing exam, Test of Academic Proficiency/Basic Skills Test/ACT/SAT, bachelor's degree, minimum GPA of 2.75, 2 letters of recommendation. Additional exam requirements/recommendations for international students: Required—TOEFL (minimum score 550 paper-based; 79 iBT), IELTS (minimum score 6). *Application deadline:* For fall admission, 5/1 priority date for international students; for spring admission, 11/15 priority date for international students. Applications are processed on a rolling basis. Application fee: $40. Electronic applications accepted. Tuition and fees vary according to program. *Financial support:* Federal Work-Study, scholarships/grants, and unspecified assistantships available. Financial award application deadline: 5/1; financial award applicants required to submit FAFSA. *Unit head:* Dr. Lauren Rentfro, Program Director, 815-836-5026, E-mail: rentfrla@lewisu.edu. *Application contact:* Kathy Lisak, Graduate Admissions Counselor, 815-836-5610, E-mail: grad@lewisu.edu.

Liberty University, School of Education, Lynchburg, VA 24515. Offers curriculum and instruction (Ed D, Ed S), including elementary education, middle grades education, secondary education, special education; educational leadership (Ed D); gifted education (Certificate); math specialist (M Ed); middle grades (MAT, Certificate); reading specialist (M Ed); school leadership (Certificate); secondary education (MAT); sport management (MS), including coaching and athletic administration, outdoor adventure sport, sport administration, tourism. *Accreditation:* NCATE. *Program availability:* Part-time, online learning. *Students:* 1,966 full-time (1,428 women), 3,484 part-time (2,528 women); includes 1,323 minority (1,026 Black or African American, non-Hispanic/Latino; 29 American Indian or Alaska Native, non-Hispanic/Latino; 49 Asian, non-Hispanic/Latino;

Secondary Education

100 Hispanic/Latino; 9 Native Hawaiian or other Pacific Islander, non-Hispanic/Latino; 110 Two or more races, non-Hispanic/Latino; 58 international. Average age 37. 3,748 applicants, 58% accepted, 1167 enrolled. In 2017, 656 master's, 110 doctorates, 316 other advanced degrees awarded. *Degree requirements:* For doctorate, comprehensive exam, thesis/dissertation. *Entrance requirements:* For master's, GRE General Test or MAT (if taken in or before 1999), 2 letters of recommendation, minimum undergraduate GPA of 3.0, curriculum vitae; for doctorate and other advanced degree, GRE General Test or MAT (if taken before 1999), minimum master's GPA of 3.0, 3 years of teaching experience. Additional exam requirements/recommendations for international students: Required—TOEFL (minimum score 600 paper-based; 100 iBT). *Application deadline:* For fall admission, 6/1 for domestic students; for spring admission, 11/1 for domestic students. Applications are processed on a rolling basis. Application fee: $50. Electronic applications accepted. *Expenses:* Contact institution. *Financial support:* Federal Work-Study and tuition waivers (partial) available. *Faculty research:* Self-determination, character education, bibliotherapy, learning styles, distance education. *Unit head:* Dr. Heather Schoffstall, Dean, 434-582-2445, Fax: 434-582-2468, E-mail: awgunter@liberty.edu. *Application contact:* Jay Bridge, Director of Graduate Admissions, 800-424-9595, Fax: 800-628-7977, E-mail: gradadmissions@liberty.edu.
Website: http://www.liberty.edu/academics/education/graduate/

Lincoln University, Graduate Studies, Jefferson City, MO 65101. Offers business administration (MBA), including accounting, management, management information systems, public administration/policy; elementary teaching (M Ed); environmental science (MS); guidance and counseling (M Ed), including community/agency counseling, elementary school, secondary school; higher education (MA); history (MA); integrated agricultural systems (MS); middle school (M Ed); natural sciences (MS); secondary teaching (M Ed); sociology (MA); sociology/criminal justice (MA). *Program availability:* Part-time, evening/weekend, 100% online, blended/hybrid learning. *Students:* 40 full-time (23 women), 64 part-time (32 women); includes 33 minority (30 Black or African American, non-Hispanic/Latino; 2 Hispanic/Latino; 1 Two or more races, non-Hispanic/Latino), 12 international. Average age 33. 48 applicants, 81% accepted, 22 enrolled. In 2017, 46 master's awarded. *Degree requirements:* For master's, comprehensive exam, thesis optional. *Entrance requirements:* For master's, GRE, MAT, or GMAT, minimum GPA of 2.75 overall, 3.0 in courses related to specialization; 3 letters of recommendation; minimum C average in English composition; personal statement of purpose. Additional exam requirements/recommendations for international students: Required—TOEFL (minimum score 500 paper-based; 61 iBT), IELTS (minimum score 5.5), Michigan English Language Assessment Battery (minimum score 80). *Application deadline:* For fall admission, 7/1 priority date for domestic students, 5/1 priority date for international students; for spring admission, 11/1 priority date for domestic students, 10/1 priority date for international students; for summer admission, 6/1 priority date for domestic students. Applications are processed on a rolling basis. Application fee: $30. Electronic applications accepted. *Expenses:* Tuition, state resident: part-time $291 per credit hour. Tuition, nonresident: part-time $541.50 per credit hour. *Financial support:* In 2017–18, 2 fellowships with tuition reimbursements, 3 research assistantships with tuition reimbursements were awarded; Federal Work-Study, scholarships/grants, and unspecified assistantships also available. Support available to part-time students. Financial award application deadline: 3/1; financial award applicants required to submit FAFSA. *Unit head:* Dr. Debra F. Greene, Interim Provost, 573-681-5247, Fax: 573-681-5106, E-mail: gradschool@lincolnu.edu. *Application contact:* Irasema Steck, Administrative Assistant, 573-681-5247, Fax: 573-681-5106, E-mail: gradschool@lincolnu.edu.
Website: http://www.lincolnu.edu/web/graduate-studies/graduate-studies

Long Island University–LIU Post, College of Education, Information and Technology, Brookville, NY 11548-1300. Offers adolescence education (MS); adolescence education 7-12 (MS); archives and records management (AC); art education (MS); childhood education (MS); childhood education/literacy B-6 (MS); childhood education/special education (MS); clinical mental health counseling (MS, AC); early childhood education (MS); early childhood education/childhood education (MS); educational leadership (AC); educational technology (MS); information studies (PhD); interdisciplinary educational studies (Ed D); middle childhood education (MS); music education (MS); public library administration (AC); school counselor (MS); special education (MS Ed); speech-language pathology (MA); students with disabilities, 7-12 generalist (AC); TESOL (MA). *Accreditation:* TEAC. *Program availability:* Part-time, 100% online, blended/hybrid learning. *Faculty:* 40 full-time (26 women), 73 part-time/adjunct (38 women). *Students:* 472 full-time (400 women), 696 part-time (543 women); includes 254 minority (93 Black or African American, non-Hispanic/Latino; 46 Asian, non-Hispanic/Latino; 105 Hispanic/Latino; 10 Two or more races, non-Hispanic/Latino), 33 international. Average age 33. 917 applicants, 82% accepted, 357 enrolled. In 2017, 408 master's, 31 other advanced degrees awarded. Terminal master's awarded for partial completion of doctoral program. *Degree requirements:* For master's, variable foreign language requirement, comprehensive exam (for some programs), thesis optional; for doctorate, comprehensive exam, thesis/dissertation. *Entrance requirements:* For master's and AC, GRE (for some programs). Additional exam requirements/recommendations for international students: Required—TOEFL (minimum score 550 paper-based, 75 iBT), IELTS, or PTE. *Application deadline:* Applications are processed on a rolling basis. Application fee: $50. Electronic applications accepted. *Expenses: Tuition:* Full-time $21,618; part-time $1201 per credit. *Required fees:* $1840; $920 per term. Tuition and fees vary according to course load. *Financial support:* In 2017–18, 376 students received support. Career-related internships or fieldwork, Federal Work-Study, institutionally sponsored loans, scholarships/grants, tuition waivers (partial), and unspecified assistantships available. Support available to part-time students. Financial award application deadline: 2/15; financial award applicants required to submit FAFSA. *Faculty research:* Sleep; use of technology to develop executive function by students with disabilities; early childhood literacy development through play; social justice through education; using a structured protocol to discuss Bad News. *Unit head:* Dr. Albert Inserra, Dean, 516-299-2210, E-mail: albert.inserra@liu.edu. *Application contact:* Rita Langdon, Graduate Admissions, 516-299-2900, Fax: 516-299-2137, E-mail: post-enroll@liu.edu.
Website: http://liu.edu/CWPost/Academics/College-of-Education-Information-and-Technology

Louisiana State University and Agricultural & Mechanical College, Graduate School, College of Human Sciences and Education, Department of Educational Theory, Policy and Practice, Baton Rouge, LA 70803. Offers counseling (M Ed, MA, Ed S); educational administration (M Ed, MA, PhD, Ed S); educational technology (MA); elementary education (M Ed, MAT); higher education (PhD); research methodology (PhD); secondary education (M Ed, MAT). *Accreditation:* ACA (one or more programs are accredited); NCATE. *Faculty:* 34 full-time (22 women). *Students:* 213 full-time (159 women), 228 part-time (178 women); includes 164 minority (123 Black or African American, non-Hispanic/Latino; 7 Asian, non-Hispanic/Latino; 27 Hispanic/Latino; 1 Native Hawaiian or other Pacific Islander, non-Hispanic/Latino; 6 Two or more races, non-Hispanic/Latino), 13 international. Average age 32. 231 applicants, 61% accepted, 82 enrolled. In 2017, 125 master's, 26 doctorates, 28 other advanced degrees awarded. *Financial support:* In 2017–18, 3 fellowships (averaging $12,129 per year), 2 research

assistantships (averaging $16,019 per year), 96 teaching assistantships (averaging $16,061 per year) were awarded. *Total annual research expenditures:* $356,867.

Louisiana Tech University, Graduate School, College of Education, Ruston, LA 71272. Offers counseling and guidance (MA), including clinical mental health counseling, human services, orientation and mobility; counseling psychology (PhD); curriculum and instruction (M Ed); cyber education (Graduate Certificate); dynamics of domestic and family violence (Graduate Certificate); early childhood education - PreK-3 (MAT); educational leadership (M Ed, Ed D); elementary education and special education mild/moderate grades 1-5 (MAT); higher education administration (Graduate Certificate); industrial/organizational psychology (MA, PhD); kinesiology (MS); middle school education (MAT), including mathematics; orientation and mobility (Graduate Certificate); rehabilitation teaching for the blind (Graduate Certificate); secondary education (MAT), including agriculture, biology, business, chemistry, English; special education: visually impaired (MAT); teacher leader education (Graduate Certificate); visual impairments - blind education (Graduate Certificate). *Accreditation:* NCATE. *Program availability:* Part-time. *Faculty:* 28 full-time (16 women), 23 part-time/adjunct (22 women). *Students:* 269 full-time (192 women), 194 part-time (150 women); includes 127 minority (94 Black or African American, non-Hispanic/Latino; 2 American Indian or Alaska Native, non-Hispanic/Latino; 6 Asian, non-Hispanic/Latino; 16 Hispanic/Latino; 1 Native Hawaiian or other Pacific Islander, non-Hispanic/Latino; 8 Two or more races, non-Hispanic/Latino), 8 international. Average age 34. 226 applicants, 74% accepted, 60 enrolled. In 2017, 5 master's, 2 doctorates, 1 other advanced degree awarded. *Degree requirements:* For master's, thesis; for doctorate, thesis/dissertation. *Entrance requirements:* For master's and doctorate, GRE General Test. Additional exam requirements/recommendations for international students: Required—TOEFL (minimum score 550 paper-based; 80 iBT), IELTS (minimum score 6.5). *Application deadline:* For fall admission, 9/1 priority date for domestic students, 6/1 for international students; for winter admission, 11/1 priority date for domestic students, 9/1 for international students; for spring admission, 2/1 priority date for domestic students, 12/1 for international students; for summer admission, 5/1 priority date for domestic students, 3/1 for international students. Application fee: $40. Electronic applications accepted. *Expenses:* Tuition, state resident: full-time $5146. Tuition, nonresident: full-time $10,147. *International tuition:* $10,267 full-time. *Required fees:* $2273. *Financial support:* In 2017–18, 40 students received support, including 23 research assistantships (averaging $10,346 per year), 15 teaching assistantships (averaging $6,887 per year); fellowships and career-related internships or fieldwork also available. Financial award application deadline: 2/1. *Faculty research:* Blindness and the best methods for increasing independence for individuals who are blind or visually impaired; educating and investigating factors contributing to improvements in human performance across the lifespan and a reduction in injury rates during training. *Total annual research expenditures:* $2.1 million. *Unit head:* Dr. Don Schillinger, Dean, 318-257-3712, E-mail: dschill@latech.edu. *Application contact:* Dr. Dawn Basinger, Associate Dean of Academic Affairs, 318-257-2977, Fax: 318-257-2379, E-mail: dbasing@latech.edu.
Website: http://education.latech.edu/

Loyola Marymount University, School of Education, Program in Secondary Education, Los Angeles, CA 90045-2659. Offers MA. *Unit head:* Dr. Liza Mastrippolito, Assistant Director, Department of Elementary and Secondary Education, 310-568-6697, E-mail: smastrip@lmu.edu. *Application contact:* Chake H. Kouyoumjian, Associate Dean of Graduate Studies, 310-338-2721, Fax: 310-338-6086, E-mail: graduateinfo@lmu.edu.
Website: http://soe.lmu.edu/academics/secondaryeducation

Loyola University Chicago, School of Education, Program in Teaching and Learning, Chicago, IL 60660. Offers elementary education (M Ed); English language teaching and learning (M Ed); secondary education (M Ed); special education (M Ed). *Accreditation:* NCATE. *Faculty:* 18 full-time (12 women), 33 part-time/adjunct (29 women). *Students:* 19 full-time (13 women), 20 part-time (17 women); includes 7 minority (1 Black or African American, non-Hispanic/Latino; 2 Asian, non-Hispanic/Latino; 4 Hispanic/Latino). Average age 27. 129 applicants, 48% accepted, 28 enrolled. In 2017, 38 master's awarded. *Degree requirements:* For master's, comprehensive exam. *Entrance requirements:* For master's, Illinois Basic Skills Test, 3 letters of recommendation, minimum GPA of 3.0, resume. Additional exam requirements/recommendations for international students: Required—TOEFL (minimum score 550 paper-based; 79 iBT). *Application deadline:* For summer admission, 3/1 priority date for domestic and international students. Application fee: $50. Electronic applications accepted. Application fee is waived when completed online. *Expenses:* $949 per semester hour, $2,847 per course, $8,541-$11,388 full-time semester tuition; $432 per semester fees; $225 additional fees (first semester only). *Financial support:* In 2017–18, 12 fellowships with partial tuition reimbursements were awarded; institutionally sponsored loans, scholarships/grants, and unspecified assistantships also available. Support available to part-time students. Financial award application deadline: 2/1; financial award applicants required to submit FAFSA. *Faculty research:* Positive behavior support, school reform, school improvement. *Unit head:* Dr. Hank Bohanon, Program Chair, 312-915-7009, E-mail: hbohano@luc.edu. *Application contact:* Mirtza Campbell, Information Contact, 312-915-8907, E-mail: mcampbell11@luc.edu.

Loyola University Maryland, Graduate Programs, School of Education, Master of Arts in Teaching Program, Baltimore, MD 21210-2699. Offers elementary education (MAT); secondary education (MAT). *Program availability:* Part-time. *Faculty:* 36 full-time (27 women), 23 part-time/adjunct (15 women). *Students:* 11 full-time (8 women), 149 part-time (133 women); includes 58 minority (43 Black or African American, non-Hispanic/Latino; 4 Asian, non-Hispanic/Latino; 7 Hispanic/Latino; 1 Native Hawaiian or other Pacific Islander, non-Hispanic/Latino; 3 Two or more races, non-Hispanic/Latino). Average age 32. *Entrance requirements:* For master's, essay, 2 letters of recommendation, resume, transcript. Additional exam requirements/recommendations for international students: Required—TOEFL (minimum score 550 paper-based), IELTS (minimum score 7). *Application deadline:* For spring admission, 11/1 for domestic students. Applications are processed on a rolling basis. Application fee: $60. Electronic applications accepted. *Expenses:* Contact institution. *Financial support:* Scholarships/grants available. Financial award application deadline: 4/15; financial award applicants required to submit FAFSA. *Application contact:* Brandon Gumabon, 410-617-2559, E-mail: bggumabon@loyola.edu.
Website: http://www.loyola.edu/soe/academics/graduate/mat.aspx

Loyola University New Orleans, College of Arts and Sciences, Master of Arts in Teaching Program, New Orleans, LA 70118-6195. Offers MAT. *Program availability:* Part-time. *Faculty:* 1 (woman) full-time, 1 (woman) part-time/adjunct. *Students:* 8 full-time (4 women), 12 part-time (8 women); includes 7 minority (3 Black or African American, non-Hispanic/Latino; 2 American Indian or Alaska Native, non-Hispanic/Latino; 1 Asian, non-Hispanic/Latino; 1 Hispanic/Latino). Average age 32. 10 applicants, 100% accepted, 10 enrolled. *Application deadline:* Applications are processed on a rolling basis. Electronic applications accepted. *Expenses:* $409 per credit hour. *Financial support:* Applicants required to submit FAFSA. *Unit head:* Dr. Glenda Hembree, Office of Teacher Education, 504-865-3081, E-mail: gghembre@loyno.edu. *Application contact:* 800-4LOYOLA, Fax: 504-865-3383, E-mail: admit@loyno.edu.
Website: http://cas.loyno.edu/teacher-education/mat

Manhattanville College, School of Education, Program in Middle Childhood/Adolescence Education (Grades 5-12), Purchase, NY 10577-2132. Offers biology (MAT, Advanced Certificate); biology and special education (MPS); chemistry (MAT, Advanced Certificate); chemistry and special education (MPS); earth science (Advanced Certificate); education for sustainability (Advanced Certificate); English (MAT, Advanced Certificate); English and special education (MPS); literacy and special education (MPS); literacy specialist (MPS); math and special education (MPS); mathematics (MAT, Advanced Certificate); physics (MAT, Advanced Certificate); social studies (MAT); social studies and special education (MPS); special education generalist (MPS). *Program availability:* Part-time, evening/weekend. *Faculty:* 2 full-time (both women), 5 part-time/adjunct (1 woman). *Students:* 8 full-time (7 women), 28 part-time (16 women); includes 4 minority (1 Asian, non-Hispanic/Latino; 2 Hispanic/Latino; 1 Two or more races, non-Hispanic/Latino). Average age 31. 7 applicants, 86% accepted, 4 enrolled. In 2017, 13 master's, 1 other advanced degree awarded. *Degree requirements:* For master's, comprehensive exam (for some programs), thesis (for some programs), student teaching, research seminars, portfolios, internships, writing assessment; for Advanced Certificate, comprehensive exam (for some programs). *Entrance requirements:* For master's, GRE or MAT (for programs leading to certification), minimum GPA of 3.0, 2 letters of recommendation, interview, essay (2-3 page personal statement that describes reasons for choosing teaching or educational leadership as profession and philosophy of education), proof of immunization (for those born after 1957). Additional exam requirements/recommendations for international students: Required—TOEFL (minimum score 600 paper-based; 110 iBT); Recommended—IELTS (minimum score 8). *Application deadline:* Applications are processed on a rolling basis. Application fee: $75. Electronic applications accepted. *Expenses:* $915 per credit. *Financial support:* Teaching assistantships, career-related internships or fieldwork, Federal Work-Study, institutionally sponsored loans, scholarships/grants, and unspecified assistantships available. Financial award application deadline: 3/15; financial award applicants required to submit FAFSA. *Faculty research:* Education for sustainability. *Unit head:* Dr. Shelly Wepner, Dean, 914-323-3153, Fax: 914-323-5493, E-mail: shelly.wepner@mville.edu. *Application contact:* Alissa Wilson, Director, Graduate Admissions, 914-323-3150, Fax: 914-694-1732, E-mail: edschool@mville.edu.
Website: http://www.mville.edu/programs#/search/19

Manhattanville College, School of Education, Program in Special Education, Purchase, NY 10577-2132. Offers childhood (grades 1-6) (MPS); childhood education (grades 1-6) and special education (MPS); early childhood (birth-grade 2) (MPS); early childhood (birth-grade 2) and special education (MPS); early childhood and childhood (birth-grade 2) (MPS); English (5-9 and 7-12) (MPS); grades 7-12 generalist (MPS); literacy (birth-grade 6) and special education childhood (grades 1-6) (MPS); literacy 5-12 (MPS); mathematics (5-9 and 7-12) (MPS); science (biology or chemistry 5-9 and 7-12) (MPS); social studies (5-9 and 7-12) (MPS); special education: childhood (grades 1-6) (Certificate); special education: early childhood (birth-grade 2) and childhood (grades 1-6) (Certificate); special education: early childhood (birth-grade 2) (Certificate); special education: grades 7-12 generalist (Certificate). *Program availability:* Part-time, evening/weekend. *Faculty:* 5 full-time (3 women), 24 part-time/adjunct (16 women). *Students:* 77 full-time (69 women), 154 part-time (132 women); includes 33 minority (9 Black or African American, non-Hispanic/Latino; 2 Asian, non-Hispanic/Latino; 22 Hispanic/Latino), 1 international. Average age 28. 87 applicants, 77% accepted, 57 enrolled. In 2017, 86 master's, 2 Certificates awarded. *Degree requirements:* For master's, comprehensive exam (for some programs), thesis (for some programs), student teaching, research seminars, portfolios, internships, writing assessment; for Certificate, comprehensive exam (for some programs). *Entrance requirements:* For master's, GRE or MAT (for programs leading to certification), minimum GPA of 3.0, 2 letters of recommendation, interview, essay (2-3 page personal statement that describes reasons for choosing teaching or educational leadership as profession and philosophy of education), proof of immunization (for those born after 1957). Additional exam requirements/recommendations for international students: Required—TOEFL (minimum score 600 paper-based; 110 iBT); Recommended—IELTS (minimum score 8). *Application deadline:* Applications are processed on a rolling basis. Application fee: $915 per credit. *Financial support:* Teaching assistantships, career-related internships or fieldwork, Federal Work-Study, institutionally sponsored loans, scholarships/grants, and unspecified assistantships available. Financial award application deadline: 3/15; financial award applicants required to submit FAFSA. *Faculty research:* Students with emotional difficulties, literacy and adolescents, mindfulness, studying the effects of the environment on special populations, the most difficult cases, students who are presented with multiple challenges: learning, behavioral and ACE experiences who see criminal behavior as a way to cope; working on giving them the tools they need to succeed emotionally and cognitively despite the odds stacked against them. *Unit head:* Dr. Shelly Wepner, Dean, 914-323-3153, Fax: 914-323-5493, E-mail: shelly.wepner@mville.edu. *Application contact:* Alissa Wilson, Director, Graduate Admissions, 914-323-3150, Fax: 914-694-1732, E-mail: edschool@mville.edu.
Website: http://www.mville.edu/programs/special-education

Mansfield University of Pennsylvania, Graduate Studies, Department of Education and Special Education, Mansfield, PA 16933. Offers elementary education (M Ed); secondary education (MS); special education (M Ed). *Accreditation:* NCATE (one or more programs are accredited). *Program availability:* Part-time, evening/weekend, online learning. *Degree requirements:* For master's, comprehensive exam, thesis optional. *Entrance requirements:* For master's, minimum GPA of 3.0. Additional exam requirements/recommendations for international students: Required—TOEFL (minimum score 550 paper-based). Electronic applications accepted.

Marquette University, Graduate School, College of Education, Department of Educational Policy and Leadership, Milwaukee, WI 53201-1881. Offers college student personnel administration (M Ed); curriculum and instruction (MA); education (MA); educational administration (M Ed); educational policy and foundations (MA); elementary education (Certificate); literacy (MA); principal (Certificate); reading specialist (Certificate); reading teacher (Certificate); secondary education (Certificate); superintendent (Certificate). *Program availability:* Part-time, evening/weekend. Terminal master's awarded for partial completion of doctoral program. *Degree requirements:* For master's, comprehensive exam, thesis (for some programs); for doctorate, thesis/dissertation, qualifying exam. *Entrance requirements:* For master's, GRE General Test or MAT, official transcripts from all current and previous colleges/universities except Marquette, three letters of recommendation, statement of purpose; for doctorate, GRE General Test, MAT, sample of written work, official transcripts from all current and previous colleges/universities except Marquette, three letters of recommendation, statement of purpose, resume/curriculum vitae; for Certificate, GRE General Test or MAT, master's degree. Additional exam requirements/recommendations for international students: Required—TOEFL (minimum score 530 paper-based). *Expenses:* Contact institution. *Faculty research:* Leadership; social justice in education; development of lifelong learners; race, class, and schooling in historical perspective; urban teacher education.

Marymount University, School of Education and Human Services, Program in Education, Arlington, VA 22207-4299. Offers curriculum and instruction (M Ed); elementary education (M Ed); professional studies (M Ed); secondary education (M Ed); special education: general curriculum (M Ed). *Accreditation:* NCATE. *Program availability:* Part-time, evening/weekend. *Faculty:* 7 full-time (all women), 10 part-time/adjunct (7 women). *Students:* 51 full-time (40 women), 92 part-time (61 women); includes 33 minority (9 Black or African American, non-Hispanic/Latino; 9 Asian, non-Hispanic/Latino; 10 Hispanic/Latino; 5 Two or more races, non-Hispanic/Latino), 11 international. Average age 34. 39 applicants, 97% accepted, 30 enrolled. In 2017, 72 master's awarded. *Degree requirements:* For master's, thesis or alternative, capstone/internship. *Entrance requirements:* For master's, GRE or MAT and PRAXIS I or SAT/ACT and Virginia Communication and Literacy Assessment (VCLA), 2 letters of recommendation, resume, interview, minimum undergraduate GPA of 2.75 or 3.25 in the last 60 hours. Additional exam requirements/recommendations for international students: Required—TOEFL (minimum score 600 paper-based; 96 iBT), IELTS (minimum score 6.5). *Application deadline:* Applications are processed on a rolling basis. Application fee: $40. Electronic applications accepted. *Expenses:* $715 per credit. *Financial support:* In 2017–18, 7 students received support, including 2 teaching assistantships with full and partial tuition reimbursements available (averaging $14,520 per year); career-related internships or fieldwork, Federal Work-Study, scholarships/grants, and unspecified assistantships also available. Support available to part-time students. Financial award application deadline: 3/1; financial award applicants required to submit FAFSA. *Unit head:* Dr. Lisa Turissini, Chair, Education, 703-526-1668, Fax: 703-284-1631, E-mail: lisa.turissini@marymount.edu. *Application contact:* Francesca Reed, Director, Graduate Admissions, 703-284-5901, Fax: 703-527-3815, E-mail: grad.admissions@marymount.edu.
Website: http://www.marymount.edu/Academics/School-of-Education-Human-Services/Graduate-Programs/Education-(M-Ed-)

Maryville University of Saint Louis, School of Education, St. Louis, MO 63141-7299. Offers early childhood education (MA Ed); educational leadership (Ed D); elementary education (MA Ed); higher education leadership (Ed D); literacy specialist (MA Ed); middle grades education (MA Ed); secondary teaching and inquiry (MA Ed); teacher as leader (MA Ed, Ed D). *Accreditation:* NCATE. *Program availability:* Part-time, 100% online, blended/hybrid learning. *Faculty:* 20 full-time (14 women), 19 part-time/adjunct (13 women). *Students:* 6 full-time (4 women), 337 part-time (290 women); includes 101 minority (85 Black or African American, non-Hispanic/Latino; 4 Asian, non-Hispanic/Latino; 8 Hispanic/Latino; 4 Two or more races, non-Hispanic/Latino), 3 international. Average age 38. In 2017, 34 master's, 67 doctorates awarded. *Degree requirements:* For master's, thesis, project. *Entrance requirements:* For master's, minimum cumulative GPA of 3.0, 3 professional recommendations, essays, interview with program faculty; for doctorate, minimum GPA of 3.0, 3 professional recommendations, essay, interview, on-site writing sample. Additional exam requirements/recommendations for international students: Required—TOEFL (minimum score 550 paper-based). *Application deadline:* Applications are processed on a rolling basis. Electronic applications accepted. *Expenses:* Contact institution. *Financial support:* Career-related internships or fieldwork, Federal Work-Study, tuition waivers (partial), and professional educator discounts available. Financial award application deadline: 4/1; financial award applicants required to submit FAFSA. *Faculty research:* Collaboration with public schools, pre-service program development, mathematics, diversity, literacy. *Unit head:* Dr. Cathy Bear, Dean, 314-529-9692, Fax: 314-529-9921, E-mail: cbear@maryville.edu. *Application contact:* Stacey Ruffin, Coordinator of Clinical Experiences and Graduate Programs, 314-529-9542, Fax: 314-529-9921, E-mail: teachered@maryville.edu.
Website: http://www.maryville.edu/ed/graduate-programs/

Marywood University, Academic Affairs, Reap College of Education and Human Development, Department of Education, Program in Secondary/K-12 Education, Scranton, PA 18509-1598. Offers MAT. *Program availability:* Part-time. Electronic applications accepted.

McDaniel College, Graduate and Professional Studies, Program in Elementary and Secondary Education, Westminster, MD 21157-4390. Offers elementary education (MS); elementary STEM instructional leader (Postbaccalaureate Certificate); equity and excellence in education (Postbaccalaureate Certificate); learning technology specialist (Postbaccalaureate Certificate); secondary education (MS). *Accreditation:* NCATE. *Program availability:* Part-time, evening/weekend. *Faculty:* 3 full-time (2 women), 27 part-time/adjunct (22 women). *Students:* 16 full-time (8 women), 148 part-time (114 women); includes 30 minority (17 Black or African American, non-Hispanic/Latino; 5 Asian, non-Hispanic/Latino; 7 Hispanic/Latino; 1 Two or more races, non-Hispanic/Latino), 1 international. Average age 34. 34 applicants, 97% accepted, 18 enrolled. In 2017, 24 master's, 47 other advanced degrees awarded. *Degree requirements:* For master's, comprehensive exam (for some programs), thesis optional. *Entrance requirements:* For master's, PRAXIS, 2 references. Additional exam requirements/recommendations for international students: Required—TOEFL (minimum score 79 iBT), IELTS (minimum score 6). *Application deadline:* For fall admission, 6/1 priority date for domestic students; for spring admission, 11/1 priority date for domestic students; for summer admission, 3/1 priority date for domestic students. Applications are processed on a rolling basis. Application fee: $75. Electronic applications accepted. *Expenses: Tuition:* Full-time $11,760; part-time $490 per credit hour. Tuition and fees vary according to course load and program. *Financial support:* Application deadline: 3/1; applicants required to submit FAFSA. *Unit head:* Fax: 410-857-2515, E-mail: gradadms@mcdaniel.edu. *Application contact:* Penny Pfeiffer, Senior Graduate Enrollment Management Specialist, 410-857-2513, Fax: 410-857-2515, E-mail: ppfeiffer@mcdaniel.edu.

McNeese State University, Doré School of Graduate Studies, Burton College of Education, Department of Education Professions, Program in Curriculum and Instruction, Lake Charles, LA 70609. Offers academically gifted education (M Ed); elementary education (M Ed); reading (M Ed); secondary education (M Ed); special education (M Ed). *Program availability:* Evening/weekend. *Entrance requirements:* For master's, GRE, teaching certificate. *Application deadline:* For fall admission, 5/15 priority date for domestic and international students; for spring admission, 10/15 priority date for domestic and international students. Applications are processed on a rolling basis. Application fee: $20 ($30 for international students). *Financial support:* Application deadline: 5/1. *Unit head:* Dr. Brett C. Welch, Director, 337-475-5405, Fax: 337-475-5272, E-mail: bwelch@mcneese.edu. *Application contact:* Dr. Dustin M. Hebert, Director of Dore' School of Graduate Studies, 337-475-5396, Fax: 337-475-5397, E-mail: admissions@mcneese.edu.

McNeese State University, Doré School of Graduate Studies, Burton College of Education, Department of Education Professions, Program in Secondary Education, Lake Charles, LA 70609. Offers MAT. *Program availability:* Evening/weekend. *Degree requirements:* For master's, comprehensive exam, field experiences. *Entrance requirements:* For master's, GRE General Test, PRAXIS I and II, autobiography, two letters of recommendation. *Application deadline:* For fall admission, 5/15 priority date for domestic and international students; for spring admission, 10/15 priority date for domestic and international students. Applications are processed on a rolling basis. Application fee: $20 ($30 for international students). *Financial support:* Application deadline: 5/1. *Unit head:* Dr. Brett C Welch, Director, 337-475-5405, Fax: 337-475-5272, E-mail: bwelch@mcneese.edu. *Application contact:* Dr. Dustin M Hebert, Director of Dore' School of Graduate Studies, 337-475-5396, Fax: 337-475-5397, E-mail: admissions@mcneese.edu.
Website: http://www.mcneese.edu/gep/master-of-arts-in-teaching-in-secondary-educatio

Secondary Education

McNeese State University, Doré School of Graduate Studies, Burton College of Education, Department of Education Professions, Program in Secondary Education Grades 6-12, Lake Charles, LA 70609. Offers Postbaccalaureate Certificate. *Entrance requirements:* For degree, PRAXIS, 2 letters of recommendation, autobiography. *Application deadline:* For fall admission, 5/15 priority date for domestic and international students; for spring admission, 10/15 priority date for domestic and international students. Applications are processed on a rolling basis. Application fee: $20 ($30 for international students). *Financial support:* Application deadline: 5/1. *Unit head:* Dr. Veronica Faye White, Head, 337-475-5400, Fax: 337-475-5272, E-mail: vfwhite@mcneese.edu. *Application contact:* Dr. Dustin M. Hebert, Director of Dore' School of Graduate Studies, 337-475-5396, Fax: 337-475-5397, E-mail: admissions@mcneese.edu.

Medaille College, Program in Education, Buffalo, NY 14214-2695. Offers adolescent education (MS Ed); curriculum and instruction (MS Ed); education preparation (MS Ed); literacy (MS Ed); special education (MS). *Accreditation:* TEAC. *Program availability:* Part-time, evening/weekend. *Degree requirements:* For master's, comprehensive exam (for some programs), thesis or alternative. *Entrance requirements:* For master's, minimum undergraduate GPA of 2.7. Additional exam requirements/recommendations for international students: Required—TOEFL (minimum score 550 paper-based). Electronic applications accepted. *Faculty research:* Curriculum planning, truancy, tracking minority students, curriculum design, mentoring students.

Mercer University, Graduate Studies, Cecil B. Day Campus, Tift College of Education (Atlanta), Atlanta, GA 30341. Offers curriculum and instruction (PhD); early childhood education (M Ed, MAT, Ed S); educational leadership (PhD), including higher education leadership, P-12 school leadership; educational leadership P-12 (M Ed, Ed S); higher education leadership (M Ed); independent and charter school leadership (M Ed); middle grades education (M Ed, MAT); secondary education (M Ed, MAT); teacher leadership (Ed S). *Accreditation:* NCATE. *Program availability:* Part-time, evening/weekend. *Faculty:* 30 full-time (18 women), 34 part-time/adjunct (27 women). *Students:* 159 full-time (131 women), 284 part-time (229 women); includes 264 minority (232 Black or African American, non-Hispanic/Latino; 1 American Indian or Alaska Native, non-Hispanic/Latino; 9 Asian, non-Hispanic/Latino; 18 Hispanic/Latino; 4 Two or more races, non-Hispanic/Latino), 2 international. Average age 35. In 2017, 137 master's, 22 doctorates, 40 other advanced degrees awarded. *Degree requirements:* For master's and Ed S, research project; for doctorate, comprehensive exam, thesis/dissertation. *Entrance requirements:* For master's, GRE or MAT, minimum undergraduate GPA of 2.75; for doctorate, GRE; for Ed S, GRE or MAT, minimum GPA of 3.25; 3 years of certified teaching experience (for educational leadership and teacher leadership). Additional exam requirements/recommendations for international students: Required—TOEFL (minimum score 80 iBT). *Application deadline:* For fall admission, 8/1 for domestic and international students; for spring admission, 12/1 for domestic and international students; for summer admission, 5/1 for domestic and international students. Applications are processed on a rolling basis. Application fee: $25 ($50 for international students). Electronic applications accepted. *Expenses:* Contact institution. *Financial support:* Federal Work-Study and unspecified assistantships available. Support available to part-time students. Financial award application deadline: 5/1; financial award applicants required to submit FAFSA. *Faculty research:* Educational technology, multicultural and minority issues in education, educational leadership (P-12 and higher education), school discipline and school bullying, standards-based mathematics education. *Unit head:* Dr. Scott Davis, Dean, 478-301-2110, Fax: 478-301-5576.
Website: http://education.mercer.edu/

Mercer University, Graduate Studies, Macon Campus, Tift College of Education (Macon), Macon, GA 31207. Offers curriculum and instruction (PhD); early childhood education (M Ed, Ed S); educational leadership (M Ed, PhD, Ed S), including higher education (PhD), P-12; higher education leadership (M Ed); independent and charter school leadership (M Ed); secondary education (MAT); teacher leadership (Ed S). *Accreditation:* NCATE. *Program availability:* Part-time, evening/weekend, 100% online, blended/hybrid learning. *Faculty:* 13 full-time (8 women), 1 part-time/adjunct (0 women). *Students:* 33 full-time (18 women), 51 part-time (37 women); includes 49 minority (44 Black or African American, non-Hispanic/Latino; 2 Asian, non-Hispanic/Latino; 2 Hispanic/Latino; 1 Two or more races, non-Hispanic/Latino), 1 international. Average age 32. In 2017, 22 master's, 17 doctorates awarded. *Degree requirements:* For master's, research project report; for doctorate, comprehensive exam, thesis/dissertation. *Entrance requirements:* For master's, GRE or MAT, minimum GPA of 2.75; for doctorate, GRE, minimum GPA of 3.5; interview; writing sample; 3 recommendations; for Ed S, GRE or MAT, minimum GPA of 3.5 (for teacher leadership), 3.0 (for educational leadership). Additional exam requirements/recommendations for international students: Required—TOEFL (minimum score 80 iBT). *Application deadline:* For fall admission, 8/1 for domestic and international students; for spring admission, 12/1 for domestic and international students. Applications are processed on a rolling basis. Application fee: $35. Electronic applications accepted. *Expenses:* Contact institution. *Financial support:* Federal Work-Study, institutionally sponsored loans, and unspecified assistantships available. Support available to part-time students. Financial award application deadline: 5/1; financial award applicants required to submit FAFSA. *Faculty research:* Teacher effectiveness, specific learning disabilities, inclusion. *Unit head:* Dr. Scott Davis, Dean, 478-301-2110, Fax: 478-301-5576, E-mail: davis_ds@mercer.edu.
Website: http://education.mercer.edu/

Mercy College, School of Education, Program in Adolescence Education, Dobbs Ferry, NY 10522-1189. Offers MS. *Program availability:* Part-time, evening/weekend, blended/hybrid learning. *Students:* 43 full-time (27 women), 44 part-time (27 women); includes 44 minority (16 Black or African American, non-Hispanic/Latino; 3 Asian, non-Hispanic/Latino; 23 Hispanic/Latino; 2 Two or more races, non-Hispanic/Latino). Average age 32. 64 applicants, 50% accepted, 16 enrolled. In 2017, 34 master's awarded. *Degree requirements:* For master's, comprehensive exam (for some programs), thesis (for some programs). *Entrance requirements:* For master's, GRE, resume, undergraduate transcript. Additional exam requirements/recommendations for international students: Required—TOEFL (minimum score 600 paper-based; 100 iBT), IELTS (minimum score 8). *Application deadline:* For fall admission, 8/1 for international students. Applications are processed on a rolling basis. Application fee: $40. Electronic applications accepted. *Expenses:* Tuition: Full-time $15,426; part-time $857 per credit hour. Required fees: $630; $158 per term. Tuition and fees vary according to course load, degree level and program. *Financial support:* Career-related internships or fieldwork, Federal Work-Study, scholarships/grants, and unspecified assistantships available. Support available to part-time students. Financial award applicants required to submit FAFSA. *Unit head:* Dr. Rose Rudnitski, Dean for the School of Education, 914-674-7447, Fax: 914-674-7352, E-mail: rrudnitski@mercy.edu. *Application contact:* Allison Gurdineer, Senior Director of Admissions, 877-637-2946, Fax: 914-674-7382, E-mail: admissions@mercy.edu.
Website: https://www.mercy.edu/education/secondary-education

Mercy College, School of Education, Program in Teaching Literacy, Dobbs Ferry, NY 10522-1189. Offers teaching literacy (Advanced Certificate); teaching literacy, birth-6 (MS); teaching literacy, grades 5-12 (MS). *Program availability:* Part-time, evening/weekend. *Students:* 3 full-time (all women), 36 part-time (33 women); includes 10 minority (3 Black or African American, non-Hispanic/Latino; 1 Asian, non-Hispanic/Latino; 6 Hispanic/Latino). Average age 32. 28 applicants, 43% accepted, 8 enrolled. In

2017, 17 master's awarded. *Degree requirements:* For master's, comprehensive exam (for some programs), thesis (for some programs). *Entrance requirements:* For master's, GRE, resume, undergraduate transcript. Additional exam requirements/recommendations for international students: Required—TOEFL (minimum score 600 paper-based; 100 iBT), IELTS (minimum score 8). *Application deadline:* For fall admission, 8/1 for international students. Applications are processed on a rolling basis. Application fee: $40. Electronic applications accepted. *Expenses: Tuition:* Full-time $15,426; part-time $857 per credit hour. *Required fees:* $630; $158 per term. Tuition and fees vary according to course load, degree level and program. *Financial support:* Career-related internships or fieldwork, Federal Work-Study, scholarships/grants, and unspecified assistantships available. Support available to part-time students. Financial award applicants required to submit FAFSA. *Unit head:* Dr. Rose Rudnitski, Dean for the School of Education, 914-674-7447, Fax: 914-674-7352, E-mail: rrudnitski@mercy.edu. *Application contact:* Allison Gurdineer, Senior Director of Admissions, 877-637-2946, Fax: 914-674-7382, E-mail: admissions@mercy.edu.
Website: https://www.mercy.edu/education/literacy-and-multilingual-studies

Mercyhurst University, Graduate Studies, Program in Secondary Education: Pedagogy and Practice, Erie, PA 16546. Offers MS. *Program availability:* Part-time, evening/weekend. *Entrance requirements:* For master's, GRE or PRAXIS I, resume, essay, three professional references, transcripts. Additional exam requirements/recommendations for international students: Required—TOEFL.

Merrimack College, School of Education and Social Policy, North Andover, MA 01845-5800. Offers community engagement (M Ed), including community organizations, higher education, PreK-12 education; criminology and criminal justice (MS); curriculum and instruction (M Ed); early childhood education (M Ed); educational leadership (CAGS), including instructional leadership; elementary education (M Ed); English as a second language (PreK-6) (M Ed); high school education (M Ed); higher education (M Ed), including leadership and organizational development, student affairs; middle school education (M Ed); moderate disabilities (PreK-8) (M Ed); school counseling (M Ed). *Program availability:* Part-time, evening/weekend, 100% online courses with immersion events and in-classroom practicum close to home. *Faculty:* 15 full-time, 36 part-time/adjunct. *Students:* 212 full-time (175 women), 121 part-time (101 women); includes 42 minority (6 Black or African American, non-Hispanic/Latino; 6 Asian, non-Hispanic/Latino; 27 Hispanic/Latino; 3 Two or more races, non-Hispanic/Latino), 3 international. Average age 27. 420 applicants, 84% accepted, 250 enrolled. In 2017, 177 master's awarded. *Degree requirements:* For master's, practicum, portfolio, and state test (for licensure track); capstone (for higher education, curriculum and instruction, and community engagement tracks); for CAGS, capstone. *Entrance requirements:* For master's, Massachusetts Teacher Education Licensure (MTEL), official transcripts from other colleges, resume, personal statement, 2 letters of recommendation. Additional exam requirements/recommendations for international students: Required—TOEFL (minimum score 84 iBT), IELTS (minimum score 6.5), PTE (minimum score 56). *Application deadline:* For fall admission, 8/24 for domestic students, 7/30 for international students; for spring admission, 1/10 for domestic students, 12/10 for international students; for summer admission, 5/10 for domestic students, 4/10 for international students. Applications are processed on a rolling basis. Application fee: $0. Electronic applications accepted. *Expenses:* Contact institution. *Financial support:* Fellowships with full tuition reimbursements, career-related internships or fieldwork, scholarships/grants, and health care benefits available. Support available to part-time students. Financial award application deadline: 5/1; financial award applicants required to submit FAFSA. *Application contact:* Alyssa Orlando, Graduate Admissions Counselor, 978-837-3563, E-mail: orlandoaf@merrimack.edu.
Website: http://www.merrimack.edu/academics/graduate/

Middle Tennessee State University, College of Graduate Studies, College of Education, Department of Educational Leadership, Program in Curriculum and Instruction, Murfreesboro, TN 37132. Offers curriculum and instruction (M Ed, Ed S); English as a second language (M Ed); secondary education (M Ed); technology and curriculum design (Ed S). *Accreditation:* NCATE. *Program availability:* Part-time, evening/weekend, online learning. *Degree requirements:* For master's, comprehensive exam; for Ed S, comprehensive exam, thesis or alternative. *Entrance requirements:* For master's and Ed S, GRE, MAT or PRAXIS. Additional exam requirements/recommendations for international students: Required—TOEFL (minimum score 525 paper-based; 71 iBT) or IELTS (minimum score 6). Electronic applications accepted.

Milligan College, Area of Education, Milligan College, TN 37682. Offers combined preK-3/K-5 education (M Ed); educational leadership (Ed D, Ed S); K-5 education (M Ed); middle grades education (M Ed); preK-3 education (M Ed); preK-3 special education (M Ed); secondary education (M Ed). *Accreditation:* NCATE. *Program availability:* Part-time. *Faculty:* 6 full-time (4 women), 3 part-time/adjunct (2 women). *Students:* 27 full-time (20 women), 20 part-time (11 women); includes 2 minority (1 Hispanic/Latino; 1 Two or more races, non-Hispanic/Latino), 1 international. Average age 34. 17 applicants, 35% accepted, 6 enrolled. In 2017, 21 master's awarded. *Degree requirements:* For master's, MAT, thesis, portfolio, research project; for doctorate, thesis/dissertation, portfolio, research project. *Entrance requirements:* For master's, MAT, GRE General Test, ACT, SAT, or PRAXIS, undergraduate degree and supporting transcripts, professional recommendations, interview; for doctorate, MAT or GRE, master's degree and supporting transcripts, demonstrated scholastic ability, recognized leadership role within education, professional recommendations, essay/personal statement, portfolio (professional development plan, evidence of ability, knowledge and qualities), interview. Additional exam requirements/recommendations for international students: Required—TOEFL (minimum score 550 paper-based, 79 iBT) or IELTS (6.5). *Application deadline:* For fall admission, 8/1 priority date for domestic students, 6/1 for international students; for spring admission, 11/15 priority date for domestic students, 12/1 for international students; for summer admission, 4/1 for domestic students. Applications are processed on a rolling basis. Application fee: $30. Electronic applications accepted. *Expenses:* $360 per hour tuition (M Ed), $475 per hour (Ed D and Ed S); $325 per semester tech/activity fees. *Financial support:* Scholarships/grants available. Financial award application deadline: 12/1; financial award applicants required to submit FAFSA. *Faculty research:* Assessment; school mental health; literacy; technology; educator preparation. *Unit head:* Dr. Angela Hilton-Prillhart, Area Chair of Education, 423-461-8769, Fax: 423-461-3103, E-mail: anhilton-prillhart@milligan.edu. *Application contact:* Melissa Dillow, Graduate Admissions Recruiter, Education, 423-461-8306, Fax: 423-461-8982, E-mail: msdillow@milligan.edu.
Website: http://www.Milligan.edu/GPS

Mississippi College, Graduate School, School of Education, Department of Teacher Education and Leadership, Clinton, MS 39058. Offers art (M Ed); biological science (M Ed); business education (M Ed); computer science (M Ed); dyslexia therapy (M Ed); educational leadership (M Ed, Ed D, Ed S); elementary education (M Ed, Ed S); English (M Ed); higher education administration (MS); mathematics (M Ed); secondary education (M Ed); social studies (history) (M Ed); teaching arts (M Ed). *Program availability:* Part-time, online learning. *Degree requirements:* For master's, comprehensive exam, thesis optional. *Entrance requirements:* For master's, NTE. Additional exam requirements/recommendations for international students: Recommended—TOEFL, IELTS. Electronic applications accepted.

Mississippi State University, College of Education, Department of Curriculum, Instruction and Special Education, Mississippi State, MS 39762. Offers early childhood education (PhD); elementary education (MS, PhD, Ed S), including early childhood education (MS); general elementary education (MS); middle level education (MS); general curriculum and instruction (PhD); reading education (PhD); secondary education (MAT, MS, PhD, and Ed S); special education (MAT, MS, PhD, Ed S). *Accreditation:* NCATE. *Program availability:* Part-time, evening/weekend. *Faculty:* 22 full-time (16 women), 1 (woman) part-time/adjunct. *Students:* 38 full-time (26 women), 170 part-time (131 women); includes 46 minority (37 Black or African American, non-Hispanic/Latino; 4 American Indian or Alaska Native, non-Hispanic/Latino; 2 Hispanic/Latino; 1 Native Hawaiian or other Pacific Islander, non-Hispanic/Latino; 2 Two or more races, non-Hispanic/Latino), 4 international. Average age 32. 88 applicants, 53% accepted, 39 enrolled. In 2017, 68 master's, 4 doctorates, 5 other advanced degrees awarded. *Degree requirements:* For master's, comprehensive exam; for doctorate, thesis/dissertation; for Ed S, comprehensive exam, thesis or alternative. *Entrance requirements:* For master's, GRE, minimum GPA of 2.75 in junior and senior year, eligibility for initial teacher certification; for doctorate, GRE, minimum GPA of 3.4 on previous graduate work; for Ed S, GRE, minimum GPA of 3.2 on master's degree. Additional exam requirements/recommendations for international students: Required—TOEFL (minimum score 550 paper-based; 79 iBT); Recommended—IELTS (minimum score 6.5). *Application deadline:* For fall admission, 3/1 priority date for domestic students, 5/1 for international students; for spring admission, 9/1 priority date for domestic students, 9/1 for international students. Applications are processed on a rolling basis. Application fee: $60 ($80 for international students). Electronic applications accepted. *Expenses:* Tuition, state resident: full-time $8318; part-time $462.12 per credit hour. Tuition, nonresident: full-time $22,358; part-time $1242.12 per credit hour. *Required fees:* $110; $12.24 per credit hour. $6.12 per semester. *Financial support:* In 2017–18, 6 research assistantships with partial tuition reimbursements (averaging $11,307 per year) were awarded; Federal Work-Study, institutionally sponsored loans, scholarships/grants, and unspecified assistantships also available. Financial award application deadline: 4/1; financial award applicants required to submit FAFSA. *Faculty research:* Early childhood education, reading, rural schools, multicultural education, use of technology in instruction. *Unit head:* Dr. Linda Cornelious, Professor and Interim Head, 662-325-3747, Fax: 662-325-7857, E-mail: lcornelious@colled.msstate.edu. *Application contact:* Laken Drinker, Admissions and Enrollment Assistant, 662-325-8951, E-mail: ldrinker@grad.msstate.edu.
Website: http://www.cise.msstate.edu/

Missouri State University, Graduate College, College of Education, Department of Counseling, Leadership, and Special Education, Program in Educational Administration, Springfield, MO 65897. Offers elementary principal (MS Ed, Ed S); secondary principal (MS Ed, Ed S); superintendent (Ed S). *Program availability:* Part-time, evening/weekend. *Faculty:* 5 full-time (2 women), 1 part-time/adjunct (0 women). *Students:* 8 full-time (4 women), 60 part-time (42 women); includes 7 minority (1 American Indian or Alaska Native, non-Hispanic/Latino; 4 Hispanic/Latino; 2 Two or more races, non-Hispanic/Latino). Average age 26. 46 applicants, 98% accepted, 31 enrolled. In 2017, 18 master's, 8 Ed Ss awarded. *Degree requirements:* For master's and Ed S, comprehensive exam, thesis or alternative. *Entrance requirements:* For master's, minimum GPA of 2.75; for Ed S, GRE General Test, MAT, minimum GPA of 2.75. Additional exam requirements/recommendations for international students: Required—TOEFL (minimum score 550 paper-based; 79 iBT), IELTS (minimum score 6). *Application deadline:* For fall admission, 7/20 priority date for domestic students, 5/1 for international students; for spring admission, 12/20 priority date for domestic students, 9/1 for international students; for summer admission, 5/20 priority date for domestic students. Applications are processed on a rolling basis. Application fee: $35 ($50 for international students). Electronic applications accepted. *Expenses:* Tuition, state resident: full-time $2915; part-time $2021 per credit hour. Tuition, nonresident: full-time $5354; part-time $3647 per credit hour. *International tuition:* $11,992 full-time. *Required fees:* $173; $173 per credit hour. Tuition and fees vary according to class time, course level, course load, degree level, campus/location and program. *Financial support:* Career-related internships or fieldwork, Federal Work-Study, institutionally sponsored loans, scholarships/grants, and unspecified assistantships available. Financial award application deadline: 3/31; financial award applicants required to submit FAFSA. *Unit head:* Dr. James Satterfield, Department Head, 417-836-5392, Fax: 417-836-4918, E-mail: clse@missouristate.edu. *Application contact:* Stephanie Praschan, Director, Graduate Enrollment Management, 417-836-5330, Fax: 417-836-6200, E-mail: stephaniepraschan@missouristate.edu.
Website: http://education.missouristate.edu/edadmin/

Missouri State University, Graduate College, College of Education, Department of Reading, Foundations, and Technology, Master of Arts in Teaching Program, Springfield, MO 65897. Offers MAT. *Program availability:* Part-time. *Faculty:* 17 full-time (11 women), 14 part-time/adjunct (13 women). *Students:* 10 full-time (8 women), 63 part-time (50 women); includes 7 minority (6 Hispanic/Latino; 1 Two or more races, non-Hispanic/Latino). Average age 33. 26 applicants, 77% accepted, 9 enrolled. In 2017, 21 master's awarded. *Degree requirements:* For master's, comprehensive exam, project. *Entrance requirements:* For master's, PRAXIS II. Additional exam requirements/recommendations for international students: Required—TOEFL (minimum score 550 paper-based; 79 iBT), IELTS (minimum score 6). *Application deadline:* For fall admission, 2/15 priority date for domestic and international students; for summer admission, 2/15 priority date for domestic students. Application fee: $35 ($50 for international students). Electronic applications accepted. *Expenses:* Tuition, state resident: full-time $2915; part-time $2021 per credit hour. Tuition, nonresident: full-time $5354; part-time $3647 per credit hour. *International tuition:* $11,992 full-time. *Required fees:* $173; $173 per credit hour. Tuition and fees vary according to class time, course level, course load, degree level, campus/location and program. *Financial support:* Federal Work-Study, institutionally sponsored loans, scholarships/grants, tuition waivers (full), and unspecified assistantships available. Financial award application deadline: 3/31; financial award applicants required to submit FAFSA. *Unit head:* Dr. Emmett Sawyer, Interim Department Head, 417-836-6769, E-mail: rft@missouristate.edu. *Application contact:* Stephanie Praschan, Coordinator of Graduate Admissions, 417-836-5330, Fax: 417-836-6200, E-mail: stephaniepraschan@missouristate.edu.

Missouri State University, Graduate College, College of Health and Human Services, Department of Kinesiology, Springfield, MO 65897. Offers health promotion and wellness management (MS); secondary education (MS Ed), including physical education. *Program availability:* Part-time. *Faculty:* 14 full-time (6 women). *Students:* 21 full-time (11 women), 11 part-time (4 women); includes 4 minority (1 Black or African American, non-Hispanic/Latino; 1 Asian, non-Hispanic/Latino; 1 Hispanic/Latino; 1 Two or more races, non-Hispanic/Latino), 2 international. Average age 24. 23 applicants, 48% accepted, 11 enrolled. In 2017, 8 master's awarded. *Degree requirements:* For master's, comprehensive exam, thesis or alternative. *Entrance requirements:* For master's, GRE (for MS), minimum GPA of 2.8 (MS); 9-12 teaching certification (MS Ed). Additional exam requirements/recommendations for international students: Required—TOEFL (minimum score 550 paper-based; 79 iBT), IELTS (minimum score 6). *Application deadline:* For fall admission, 7/20 priority date for domestic students, 5/1 for international students; for spring admission, 12/20 priority date for domestic students, 9/

1 for international students. Applications are processed on a rolling basis. Application fee: $35 ($50 for international students). Electronic applications accepted. *Expenses:* Tuition, state resident: full-time $2915; part-time $2021 per credit hour. Tuition, nonresident: full-time $5354; part-time $3647 per credit hour. *International tuition:* $11,992 full-time. *Required fees:* $173; $173 per credit hour. Tuition and fees vary according to class time, course level, course load, degree level, campus/location and program. *Financial support:* In 2017–18, 7 teaching assistantships with partial tuition reimbursements (averaging $8,772 per year) were awarded; Federal Work-Study, institutionally sponsored loans, scholarships/grants, and unspecified assistantships also available. Financial award application deadline: 3/31; financial award applicants required to submit FAFSA. *Unit head:* Dr. Sarah McCallister, Head, 417-836-6582, Fax: 417-836-5371, E-mail: sarahmccallister@missouristate.edu. *Application contact:* Stephanie Praschan, Director, Graduate Enrollment Management, 417-836-5330, Fax: 417-836-6200, E-mail: stephaniepraschan@missouristate.edu.
Website: http://www.missouristate.edu/kinesiology/

Missouri State University, Graduate College, College of Natural and Applied Sciences, Department of Biology, Springfield, MO 65897. Offers biology (MS); natural and applied science (MNAS), including biology (MNAS, MS Ed); secondary education (MS Ed), including biology (MNAS, MS Ed). *Faculty:* 18 full-time (3 women), 7 part-time/adjunct (2 women). *Students:* 21 full-time (12 women), 26 part-time (16 women); includes 5 minority (1 Asian, non-Hispanic/Latino; 3 Hispanic/Latino; 1 Two or more races, non-Hispanic/Latino), 5 international. Average age 26. 28 applicants, 46% accepted, 13 enrolled. In 2017, 20 master's awarded. *Degree requirements:* For master's, comprehensive exam, thesis or alternative. *Entrance requirements:* For master's, GRE (MS, MNAS), 24 hours of course work in biology (MS); minimum GPA of 3.0 (MS, MNAS); 9-12 teacher certification (MS Ed). Additional exam requirements/recommendations for international students: Required—TOEFL (minimum score 550 paper-based; 79 iBT), IELTS (minimum score 6). *Application deadline:* For fall admission, 7/20 priority date for domestic students, 5/1 for international students; for spring admission, 12/20 priority date for domestic students, 9/1 for international students; for summer admission, 5/20 priority date for domestic students. Applications are processed on a rolling basis. Application fee: $35 ($50 for international students). Electronic applications accepted. *Expenses:* Tuition, state resident: full-time $2915; part-time $2021 per credit hour. Tuition, nonresident: full-time $5354; part-time $3647 per credit hour. *International tuition:* $11,992 full-time. *Required fees:* $173; $173 per credit hour. Tuition and fees vary according to class time, course level, course load, degree level, campus/location and program. *Financial support:* In 2017–18, 2 research assistantships with full tuition reimbursements (averaging $10,672 per year), 26 teaching assistantships with full tuition reimbursements (averaging $9,746 per year) were awarded; Federal Work-Study, institutionally sponsored loans, scholarships/grants, and unspecified assistantships also available. Financial award application deadline: 3/31; financial award applicants required to submit FAFSA. *Faculty research:* Hibernation physiology of bats, behavioral ecology of salamanders, mussel conservation, plant evolution and systematics, cellular/molecular mechanisms involved in migraine pathology. *Unit head:* Dr. S. Alicia Mathis, Department Head, 417-836-5126, Fax: 417-836-6934, E-mail: biology@missouristate.edu. *Application contact:* Stephanie Praschan, Director, Graduate Enrollment Management, 417-836-5330, Fax: 417-836-6200, E-mail: stephaniepraschan@missouristate.edu.
Website: http://biology.missouristate.edu/

Missouri State University, Graduate College, College of Natural and Applied Sciences, Department of Chemistry, Springfield, MO 65897. Offers chemistry (MS); natural and applied science (MNAS), including chemistry (MNAS, MS Ed); secondary education (MS Ed), including chemistry (MNAS, MS Ed). *Program availability:* Part-time. *Faculty:* 15 full-time (2 women). *Students:* 12 full-time (6 women), 7 part-time (2 women); includes 3 minority (1 Hispanic/Latino; 2 Two or more races, non-Hispanic/Latino), 3 international. Average age 27. 11 applicants, 45% accepted, 5 enrolled. In 2017, 10 master's awarded. *Degree requirements:* For master's, comprehensive exam, thesis. *Entrance requirements:* For master's, GRE General Test (MS, MNAS), minimum undergraduate GPA of 3.0 (MS and MNAS), 9-12 teacher certification (MS Ed). Additional exam requirements/recommendations for international students: Required—TOEFL (minimum score 550 paper-based; 79 iBT), IELTS (minimum score 6). *Application deadline:* For fall admission, 7/20 priority date for domestic students, 5/1 for international students; for spring admission, 12/20 priority date for domestic students, 9/1 for international students; for summer admission, 5/20 priority date for domestic students. Applications are processed on a rolling basis. Application fee: $35 ($50 for international students). Electronic applications accepted. *Expenses:* Tuition, state resident: full-time $2915; part-time $2021 per credit hour. Tuition, nonresident: full-time $5354; part-time $3647 per credit hour. *International tuition:* $11,992 full-time. *Required fees:* $173; $173 per credit hour. Tuition and fees vary according to class time, course level, course load, degree level, campus/location and program. *Financial support:* In 2017–18, 17 teaching assistantships with full tuition reimbursements (averaging $8,772 per year) were awarded; Federal Work-Study, institutionally sponsored loans, scholarships/grants, and unspecified assistantships also available. Financial award application deadline: 3/31; financial award applicants required to submit FAFSA. *Faculty research:* Polyethylene glycol derivatives, electrochemiluminescence of environmental systems, enzymology, environmental organic pollutants, DNA repair via nuclear magnetic resonance (NMR). *Unit head:* Dr. Bryan Breyfogle, Department Head, 417-836-5601, Fax: 417-836-5507, E-mail: chemistry@missouristate.edu. *Application contact:* Stephanie Praschan, Director, Graduate Enrollment Management, 417-836-5330, Fax: 417-836-6200, E-mail: stephaniepraschan@missouristate.edu.
Website: http://chemistry.missouristate.edu/

Missouri State University, Graduate College, College of Natural and Applied Sciences, Department of Geography, Geology, and Planning, Springfield, MO 65897. Offers geography, geology, and planning (Certificate); natural and applied science (MNAS), including geography, geology and planning; secondary education (MS Ed), including earth science, physical geography. *Program availability:* Part-time, evening/weekend. *Faculty:* 18 full-time (4 women), 1 part-time/adjunct (0 women). *Students:* 27 full-time (10 women), 7 part-time (6 women); includes 2 minority (both Two or more races, non-Hispanic/Latino), 3 international. Average age 29. 27 applicants, 48% accepted, 13 enrolled. In 2017, 32 master's awarded. *Degree requirements:* For master's, comprehensive exam, thesis (for some programs). *Entrance requirements:* For master's, GRE General Test (MS, MNAS), minimum undergraduate GPA of 3.0 (MS, MNAS), 9-12 teacher certification (MS Ed). Additional exam requirements/recommendations for international students: Required—TOEFL (minimum score 550 paper-based; 79 iBT), IELTS (minimum score 6). *Application deadline:* For fall admission, 7/20 priority date for domestic students, 5/1 for international students; for spring admission, 12/20 priority date for domestic students, 9/1 for international students. Applications are processed on a rolling basis. Application fee: $35 ($50 for international students). Electronic applications accepted. *Expenses:* Tuition, state resident: full-time $2915; part-time $2021 per credit hour. Tuition, nonresident: full-time $5354; part-time $3647 per credit hour. *International tuition:* $11,992 full-time. *Required fees:* $173; $173 per credit hour. Tuition and fees vary according to class time, course level, course load, degree level, campus/location and program. *Financial support:* In 2017–18, 3 research assistantships with full tuition reimbursements (averaging $11,574 per year), 15 teaching

assistantships with full tuition reimbursements (averaging $9,365 per year) were awarded; career-related internships or fieldwork, Federal Work-Study, institutionally sponsored loans, scholarships/grants, and unspecified assistantships also available. Financial award application deadline: 3/31; financial award applicants required to submit FAFSA. *Faculty research:* Stratigraphy and ancient meteorite impacts, environmental geochemistry of karst, hyperspectral image processing, water quality, small town planning. *Unit head:* Dr. Toby Dogwiler, Department Head, 417-836-5800, Fax: 417-836-6934, E-mail: tobydogwiler@missouristate.edu. *Application contact:* Stephanie Praschan, Director, Graduate Enrollment Management, 417-836-5330, Fax: 417-836-6200, E-mail: stephaniepraschan@missouristate.edu.
Website: http://geosciences.missouristate.edu/

Missouri State University, Graduate College, College of Natural and Applied Sciences, Department of Mathematics, Springfield, MO 65897. Offers mathematics (MS); natural and applied science (MNAS), including mathematics (MNAS, MS Ed); secondary education (MS Ed), including mathematics (MNAS, MS Ed). *Program availability:* Part-time. *Faculty:* 21 full-time (4 women). *Students:* 12 full-time (3 women), 19 part-time (8 women); includes 1 minority (Black or African American, non-Hispanic/Latino), 7 international. Average age 29. 18 applicants, 72% accepted, 8 enrolled. In 2017, 7 master's awarded. *Degree requirements:* For master's, comprehensive exam, thesis or alternative. *Entrance requirements:* For master's, GRE (MS, MNAS), minimum undergraduate GPA of 3.0 (MS, MNAS), 9-12 teacher certification (MS Ed). Additional exam requirements/recommendations for international students: Required—TOEFL (minimum score 550 paper-based; 79 iBT), IELTS (minimum score 6). *Application deadline:* For fall admission, 7/20 priority date for domestic students, 5/1 for international students; for spring admission, 12/20 priority date for domestic students, 9/1 for international students. Applications are processed on a rolling basis. Application fee: $35 ($50 for international students). Electronic applications accepted. *Expenses:* Tuition, state resident: full-time $2915; part-time $2021 per credit hour. Tuition, nonresident: full-time $5354; part-time $3647 per credit hour. *International tuition:* $11,992 full-time. *Required fees:* $173; $173 per credit hour. Tuition and fees vary according to class time, course level, course load, degree level, campus/location and program. *Financial support:* In 2017–18, 11 teaching assistantships with full tuition reimbursements (averaging $10,672 per year) were awarded; Federal Work-Study, institutionally sponsored loans, scholarships/grants, and unspecified assistantships also available. Financial award application deadline: 3/31; financial award applicants required to submit FAFSA. *Faculty research:* Harmonic analysis, commutative algebra, number theory, K-theory, probability. *Unit head:* Dr. William Bray, Department Head, 417-836-5112, Fax: 417-836-6966, E-mail: mathematics@missouristate.edu. *Application contact:* Stephanie Praschan, Director, Graduate Enrollment Management, 417-836-5330, Fax: 417-836-6200, E-mail: stephaniepraschan@missouristate.edu.
Website: http://math.missouristate.edu/

Missouri State University, Graduate College, College of Natural and Applied Sciences, Department of Physics, Astronomy, and Materials Science, Springfield, MO 65897. Offers materials science (MS); natural and applied science (MNAS), including physics (MNAS, MS Ed); secondary education (MS Ed), including physics (MNAS, MS Ed). *Program availability:* Part-time. *Faculty:* 9 full-time (0 women). *Students:* 10 full-time (1 woman), 5 part-time (0 women), 10 international. Average age 26. 12 applicants, 92% accepted, 5 enrolled. In 2017, 14 master's awarded. *Degree requirements:* For master's, comprehensive exam, thesis. *Entrance requirements:* For master's, GRE (MS, MNAS), minimum undergraduate GPA of 3.0 (MS and MNAS), 9-12 teaching certification (MS Ed). Additional exam requirements/recommendations for international students: Required—TOEFL (minimum score 550 paper-based; 79 iBT), IELTS (minimum score 6). *Application deadline:* For fall admission, 7/20 priority date for domestic students, 5/1 for international students; for spring admission, 12/20 priority date for domestic students, 9/1 for international students. Applications are processed on a rolling basis. Application fee: $35 ($50 for international students). Electronic applications accepted. *Expenses:* Tuition, state resident: full-time $2915; part-time $2021 per credit hour. Tuition, nonresident: full-time $5354; part-time $3647 per credit hour. *International tuition:* $11,992 full-time. *Required fees:* $173; $173 per credit hour. Tuition and fees vary according to class time, course level, course load, degree level, campus/location and program. *Financial support:* In 2017–18, 6 research assistantships with full tuition reimbursements (averaging $10,672 per year), 11 teaching assistantships with full tuition reimbursements (averaging $10,672 per year) were awarded; Federal Work-Study, institutionally sponsored loans, scholarships/grants, and unspecified assistantships also available. Financial award application deadline: 3/31; financial award applicants required to submit FAFSA. *Faculty research:* Nanocomposites, ferroelectricity, infrared focal plane array sensors, biosensors, pulsating stars. *Unit head:* Dr. David Cornelison, Department Head, 417-836-4467, Fax: 417-836-6226, E-mail: physics@missouristate.edu. *Application contact:* Stephanie Praschan, Director, Graduate Enrollment Management, 417-836-5330, Fax: 417-836-6200, E-mail: stephaniepraschan@missouristate.edu.
Website: http://physics.missouristate.edu/

Missouri State University, Graduate College, Darr College of Agriculture, Springfield, MO 65897. Offers plant science (MS); secondary education (MS Ed), including agriculture. *Program availability:* Part-time. *Faculty:* 16 full-time (5 women), 1 part-time/adjunct (0 women). *Students:* 23 full-time (10 women), 31 part-time (15 women); includes 3 minority (1 Black or African American, non-Hispanic/Latino; 2 Two or more races, non-Hispanic/Latino), 2 international. Average age 23. 24 applicants, 42% accepted, 10 enrolled. In 2017, 23 master's awarded. *Degree requirements:* For master's, comprehensive exam, thesis or alternative. *Entrance requirements:* For master's, GRE (MS in plant science, MNAS), 9-12 teacher certification (MS Ed), minimum GPA of 3.0 (MS plant science, MNAS). Additional exam requirements/recommendations for international students: Required—TOEFL (minimum score 550 paper-based; 79 iBT), IELTS (minimum score 6). *Application deadline:* For fall admission, 7/20 priority date for domestic students, 5/1 for international students; for spring admission, 12/20 priority date for domestic students, 9/1 for international students; for summer admission, 5/20 priority date for domestic students. Applications are processed on a rolling basis. Application fee: $35 ($50 for international students). Electronic applications accepted. *Expenses:* Tuition, state resident: full-time $2915; part-time $2021 per credit hour. Tuition, nonresident: full-time $5354; part-time $3647 per credit hour. *International tuition:* $11,992 full-time. *Required fees:* $173; $173 per credit hour. Tuition and fees vary according to class time, course level, course load, degree level, campus/location and program. *Financial support:* In 2017–18, 7 research assistantships with full tuition reimbursements (averaging $9,365 per year), 6 teaching assistantships with full tuition reimbursements (averaging $8,450 per year) were awarded; Federal Work-Study, institutionally sponsored loans, scholarships/grants, and unspecified assistantships also available. Financial award application deadline: 3/31; financial award applicants required to submit FAFSA. *Faculty research:* Grapevine biotechnology, agricultural marketing, Asian elephant reproduction, poultry science, integrated pest management. *Unit head:* Dr. Ronald Del Vecchio, Dean, 417-836-5050, E-mail: darr@missouristate.edu. *Application contact:* Stephanie Praschan, Director, Graduate Enrollment Management, 417-836-5330, Fax: 417-836-6200, E-mail: stephaniepraschan@missouristate.edu.
Website: http://ag.missouristate.edu/

Monmouth University, Graduate Studies, School of Education, West Long Branch, NJ 07764-1898. Offers applied behavior analysis (Certificate); autism (Certificate); director of school counseling services (Post-Master's Certificate); early childhood (M Ed); educational leadership (Ed D); elementary education (MAT), including elementary level, secondary level; English as a second language (M Ed); learning disabilities teacher-consultant (Post-Master's Certificate); literacy (MS Ed); school counseling (MS Ed); special education (MS Ed), including autism, learning disabilities teacher-consultant, teacher of students with disabilities, teaching in inclusive settings; speech-language pathology (MS Ed); student affairs and college counseling (MS Ed); supervisor (Post-Master's Certificate); teaching English to speakers of other languages (Certificate). *Accreditation:* NCATE. *Program availability:* Part-time, evening/weekend, 100% online, blended/hybrid learning. *Faculty:* 23 full-time (19 women), 33 part-time/adjunct (25 women). *Students:* 175 full-time (163 women), 168 part-time (142 women); includes 54 minority (10 Black or African American, non-Hispanic/Latino; 4 Asian, non-Hispanic/Latino; 32 Hispanic/Latino; 8 Two or more races, non-Hispanic/Latino). Average age 27. In 2017, 160 master's, 3 other advanced degrees awarded. *Entrance requirements:* For master's, GRE taken within last 5 years (for MS Ed in speech-language pathology); SAT (minimum combined score of 1660 in 3 sections), ACT (23), GRE (minimum score of 4.0 on analytical writing section and minimum combined score of 310 on quantitative and verbal sections), or passing scores on 3 parts of Core Academic Skills Educators, minimum GPA of 3.0 in major; 2 letters of recommendation (for some programs); resume, personal statement or essay (depending on program). Additional exam requirements/recommendations for international students: Required—TOEFL (minimum score 550 paper-based; 79 iBT), IELTS (minimum score 6), Michigan English Language Assessment Battery (minimum score 77) or Certificate of Advanced English (minimum score 160). *Application deadline:* For fall admission, 7/15 priority date for domestic students, 7/1 for international students; for spring admission, 12/1 priority date for domestic students, 11/1 for international students; for summer admission, 5/1 for domestic students. Applications are processed on a rolling basis. Application fee: $50. Electronic applications accepted. *Expenses: Tuition:* Full-time $21,366; part-time $7122 per credit. *Required fees:* $700; $175 per term. *Financial support:* In 2017–18, 125 students received support. Institutionally sponsored loans, scholarships/grants, and unspecified assistantships available. Support available to part-time students. Financial award applicants required to submit FAFSA. *Faculty research:* Multicultural literacy, science and mathematics teaching strategies, teacher as reflective practitioner, children with disabilities. *Unit head:* Dr. John E. Henning, Dean, 732-263-5513, Fax: 732-263-5277. *Application contact:* Laurie Kuhn, Associate Director of Graduate Admission, 732-571-3452, Fax: 732-263-5123, E-mail: gradadm@monmouth.edu.
Website: http://www.monmouth.edu/academics/schools/education/default.asp

Montana State University Billings, College of Education, Department of Educational Theory and Practice, Option in Curriculum and Instruction, Billings, MT 59101. Offers K-8 elementary education (M Ed); secondary education (M Ed). *Accreditation:* NCATE. *Program availability:* Part-time. *Degree requirements:* For master's, thesis or professional paper and/or field experience. *Entrance requirements:* For master's, GRE General Test or MAT, minimum GPA of 3.0. Additional exam requirements/recommendations for international students: Required—TOEFL (minimum score 79 iBT), IELTS (minimum score 6.5). *Application deadline:* Applications are processed on a rolling basis. Application fee: $40. Electronic applications accepted. *Expenses:* Tuition, state resident: full-time $11,740; part-time $7880 per year. Tuition, nonresident: full-time $32,200; part-time $24,140 per year. *Financial support:* Teaching assistantships with partial tuition reimbursements, career-related internships or fieldwork, Federal Work-Study, institutionally sponsored loans, scholarships/grants, tuition waivers (partial), and unspecified assistantships available. Support available to part-time students. Financial award application deadline: 5/1; financial award applicants required to submit FAFSA. *Faculty research:* Social studies education, science education. *Unit head:* Dr. Cindy Dell, Chair, Educational Theory and Practice, 406-657-1614, Fax: 406-657-2807, E-mail: cdell@msubillings.edu. *Application contact:* Dr. Cindy Dell, Chair, Educational Theory and Practice, 406-657-1614, Fax: 406-657-2807, E-mail: cdell@msubillings.edu.
Website: http://www.msubillings.edu/grad/program-med_curric_and_instruct.htm

Morehead State University, Graduate Programs, College of Education, Department of Curriculum and Instruction, Morehead, KY 40351. Offers curriculum and instruction (Ed S); elementary education (MA Ed), including elementary education, international education, middle school education, reading; secondary education (MA Ed); special education (MA Ed); teaching (MAT). *Program availability:* Part-time, evening/weekend. *Degree requirements:* For master's, comprehensive exam, thesis optional; for Ed S, thesis, oral exam. *Entrance requirements:* For master's, GRE General Test, minimum GPA of 2.75, teaching certificate; for Ed S, GRE General Test, interview, master's degree, minimum GPA of 3.5, work experience. Additional exam requirements/recommendations for international students: Required—TOEFL (minimum score 500 paper-based). Electronic applications accepted. *Faculty research:* Communicative competence of learning-disabled students, teaching social studies in elementary schools, ungraded primary school organization, study skills.

Morehead State University, Graduate Programs, College of Education, Department of Middle Grades and Secondary Education, Morehead, KY 40351. Offers business and marketing education (MAT); English/language arts 5-9 (MAT); French (MAT); health P-12 (MAT); mathematics 5-9 (MAT); physical education P-12 (MAT); science 5-9 (MAT); secondary biology (MAT); secondary chemistry (MAT); secondary earth science (MAT); secondary English (MAT); secondary math (MAT); secondary physics (MAT); secondary social studies (MAT); social studies 5-9 (MAT); Spanish (MAT). *Program availability:* Part-time, evening/weekend. *Degree requirements:* For master's, portfolio. *Entrance requirements:* For master's, GRE or PRAXIS II content exam, minimum overall undergraduate GPA of 2.5. Additional exam requirements/recommendations for international students: Required—TOEFL (minimum score 500 paper-based). Electronic applications accepted.

Mount St. Joseph University, Graduate Education Program, Cincinnati, OH 45233-1670. Offers adolescent to young adult education (MA); dyslexia (Certificate); inclusive early childhood education (MA); middle childhood education (MA); multicultural special education (MA); reading science (MA). *Accreditation:* TEAC. *Program availability:* Part-time, evening/weekend, 100% online, blended/hybrid learning. *Faculty:* 6 full-time (5 women), 11 part-time/adjunct (8 women). *Students:* 37 full-time (30 women), 91 part-time (83 women); includes 13 minority (11 Black or African American, non-Hispanic/Latino; 1 Hispanic/Latino; 1 Two or more races, non-Hispanic/Latino). Average age 34. In 2017, 79 master's awarded. *Degree requirements:* For master's, comprehensive exam, thesis, research project, student teaching, clinical and field-based experiences. *Entrance requirements:* For master's, GRE (if GPA is below 3.0), letter of intent, 2 referrals, background check, interview, resume, minimum undergraduate GPA of 3.0. Additional exam requirements/recommendations for international students: Required—TOEFL (minimum score 560 paper-based; 83 iBT). *Application deadline:* Applications are processed on a rolling basis. Application fee: $50. Electronic applications accepted. *Expenses:* $600 per credit hour. *Financial support:* Applicants required to submit FAFSA. *Faculty research:* Foreign and second language learning problems/reading disabilities, multicultural/bilingual special education, science education, pedagogical content knowledge, early childhood, response to intervention. *Unit head:* Dr. Laura Saylor, Dean, 513-244-3263, E-mail: laura.saylor@msj.edu. *Application contact:* Mary

Brigham, Assistant Director of Graduate Recruitment, 513-244-4233, Fax: 513-244-4629, E-mail: mary.brigham@msj.edu. Website: http://www.msj.edu/academics/graduate-programs/master-of-arts-initial-teacher-licensure-programs/

Murray State University, College of Education and Human Services, Department of Adolescent, Career, and Special Education, Murray, KY 42071. Offers career and technical education (MS); middle school teacher leader (MA Ed); secondary teacher leader (MA Ed); special education (MA Ed), including mild learning and behavior disorders, moderate to severe disabilities (P-12), teacher leader in special education learning and behavior disorders; teacher education and professional development (Ed S). *Accreditation:* NCATE. *Program availability:* Part-time. *Faculty:* 10 full-time (9 women). *Students:* 4 full-time (2 women), 78 part-time (56 women); includes 4 minority (2 Black or African American, non-Hispanic/Latino; 1 Asian, non-Hispanic/Latino; 1 Hispanic/Latino), 2 international. Average age 33. 13 applicants, 100% accepted, 8 enrolled. In 2017, 19 master's awarded. *Entrance requirements:* For master's and Ed S, GRE or GMAT, minimum university GPA of 2.75. Additional exam requirements/recommendations for international students: Required—TOEFL (minimum score 527 paper-based; 71 iBT). *Application deadline:* Applications are processed on a rolling basis. Application fee: $40 ($50 for international students). Electronic applications accepted. *Expenses:* Tuition, state resident: full-time $9504. Tuition, nonresident: full-time $26,811. *International tuition:* $14,400 full-time. Tuition and fees vary according to course load, degree level and reciprocity agreements. *Financial support:* Federal Work-Study and unspecified assistantships available. Financial award applicants required to submit FAFSA. *Unit head:* Dr. Barbara Washington, Chair, Department of Adolescent, Career and Special Education, 270-809-2262, Fax: 270-809-2540, E-mail: bwashington@murraystate.edu. *Application contact:* Kaitlyn Burzynski, Interim Assistant Director of Graduate Admission and Records, 270-809-5732, Fax: 270-809-3780, E-mail: msu.graduateadmissions@murraystate.edu.
Website: http://www.murraystate.edu/academics/CollegesDepartments/CollegeOfEducationandHumanServices/coehsacademicunits/AdolescentCareerSpecialEd/index.aspx

Murray State University, College of Education and Human Services, Department of Educational Studies, Leadership and Counseling, Murray, KY 42071. Offers college advising (Certificate); education administration (MA Ed); human development and leadership (MS, Certificate); library media (MA Ed); middle school teacher leader (MA Ed); P-20 and community leadership (Ed D); postsecondary education administration (MA Ed); school counseling (MA Ed); school guidance and counseling (Ed S); secondary teacher leader (MA Ed). *Program availability:* Part-time, evening/weekend, 100% online, blended/hybrid learning. *Faculty:* 38 full-time (16 women), 3 part-time/adjunct (1 woman). *Students:* 45 full-time (22 women), 190 part-time (140 women); includes 33 minority (25 Black or African American, non-Hispanic/Latino; 4 Asian, non-Hispanic/Latino; 3 Hispanic/Latino; 1 Two or more races, non-Hispanic/Latino), 6 international. Average age 35. 87 applicants, 77% accepted, 51 enrolled. In 2017, 21 master's, 16 doctorates, 12 other advanced degrees awarded. *Entrance requirements:* For master's and other advanced degree, GRE or GMAT, minimum university GPA of 2.75. Additional exam requirements/recommendations for international students: Required—TOEFL (minimum score 527 paper-based; 71 iBT). *Application deadline:* Applications are processed on a rolling basis. Application fee: $40 ($50 for international students). Electronic applications accepted. *Expenses:* Tuition, state resident: full-time $9504. Tuition, nonresident: full-time $26,811. *International tuition:* $14,400 full-time. Tuition and fees vary according to course load, degree level and reciprocity agreements. *Financial support:* Federal Work-Study and unspecified assistantships available. Financial award applicants required to submit FAFSA. *Unit head:* Dr. Susana Bloomdahl, Chair, Department of Educational Studies, Leadership and Counseling, 270-809-6471, Fax: 270-809-3799, E-mail: sbloomdahl@murraystate.edu. *Application contact:* Kaitlyn Burzynski, Interim Assistant Director for Graduate Admission and Records, 270-809-5732, Fax: 270-809-3780, E-mail: msu.graduateadmissions@murraystate.edu.
Website: http://www.murraystate.edu/academics/CollegesDepartments/CollegeOfEducationandHumanServices/coehsacademicunits/EducationalStudiesLeadershipandCounseli

National Louis University, National College of Education, Chicago, IL 60603. Offers administration and supervision (M Ed, Ed D, CAS, Ed S); curriculum and instruction (M Ed, MS Ed, CAS); early childhood administration (M Ed, CAS); early childhood education (M Ed, MAT, MS Ed, CAS); education (Ed D); educational psychology/human learning and development (M Ed, MS Ed, CAS, Ed S); elementary education (MAT); interdisciplinary curriculum and instruction (M Ed); mathematics education (M Ed, MS Ed, CAS); middle grades education (MAT); reading and language (M Ed, MS Ed, CAS); school psychology (M Ed, Ed S); science education (M Ed, MS Ed, CAS); secondary education (MAT); special education (M Ed, MAT, CAS); technology in education (M Ed, CAS). *Accreditation:* NCATE. *Program availability:* Part-time, evening/weekend. *Degree requirements:* For doctorate, comprehensive exam, thesis/dissertation. *Entrance requirements:* For master's, MAT or GRE, minimum GPA of 3.0; for doctorate, GRE General Test, minimum GPA of 3.25, interview, resume, writing sample, 4 recommendations. Additional exam requirements/recommendations for international students: Required—TOEFL (minimum score 550 paper-based; 79 iBT).

Neumann University, Graduate Program in Education, Aston, PA 19014-1298. Offers education (MS), including administrative certification (school principal PK-12), autism, early elementary education, secondary education, special education. *Program availability:* Part-time, evening/weekend, 100% online, blended/hybrid learning. *Faculty:* 6 full-time (5 women), 16 part-time/adjunct (7 women). *Students:* 68 full-time (56 women), 108 part-time (93 women); includes 36 minority (28 Black or African American, non-Hispanic/Latino; 3 Hispanic/Latino; 5 Two or more races, non-Hispanic/Latino). Average age 33. 83 applicants, 69% accepted, 36 enrolled. In 2017, 114 master's awarded. *Entrance requirements:* For master's, official transcripts from all institutions attended, letter of intent, three professional references, copy of any teaching certifications. Additional exam requirements/recommendations for international students: Required—TOEFL (minimum score 70 iBT). *Application deadline:* Applications are processed on a rolling basis. Application fee: $0. Electronic applications accepted. *Expenses:* $700 per credit hour (for on-campus master's-level education courses); $480 per credit hour (for online or off-campus master's-level education courses). *Financial support:* Scholarships/grants and health care benefits available. Support available to part-time students. Financial award application deadline: 3/15; financial award applicants required to submit FAFSA. *Unit head:* Dr. Stephanie Smith-Budhai, Director of Graduate Education, 610-358-4249, E-mail: budhais@neumann.edu. *Application contact:* Dr. Erika K. Davis, Director of Adult and Graduate Admissions, 800-9-NEUMANN Ext. 5208, Fax: 610-361-2548, E-mail: gradadultadmiss@neumann.edu.
Website: https://www.neumann.edu/academics/grad/education/index.asp

New Jersey City University, Debra Cannon Partridge Wolfe College of Education, Department of Elementary and Secondary Education, Jersey City, NJ 07305-1597. Offers elementary education (MAT); secondary education (MAT). *Program availability:* Part-time, evening/weekend. *Entrance requirements:* Additional exam requirements/recommendations for international students: Required—TOEFL (minimum score 79 iBT).

New York Institute of Technology, School of Interdisciplinary Studies and Education, Department of Teacher Education, Old Westbury, NY 11568-8000. Offers adolescence education (MS), including math (MAT, MS); science; adolescent education (MAT), including biology, chemistry, English, math (MAT, MS), social studies; childhood education (MS). *Program availability:* Part-time, evening/weekend, 100% online, blended/hybrid learning. *Faculty:* 2 full-time (both women), 7 part-time/adjunct (3 women). *Students:* 46 full-time (44 women), 30 part-time (22 women); includes 23 minority (8 Black or African American, non-Hispanic/Latino; 6 Asian, non-Hispanic/Latino; 8 Hispanic/Latino; 1 Two or more races, non-Hispanic/Latino), 2 international. Average age 29. 39 applicants, 72% accepted, 14 enrolled. In 2017, 14 master's awarded. *Entrance requirements:* For master's, GRE or MAT, BS or equivalent; minimum cumulative undergraduate GPA of 3.0; NY state provisional or initial certification (for MS in adolescence education); BS with major in biology, chemistry, economics, English, history, life sciences, math, physics, or psychology (for MS in childhood, early childhood education, and MAT); interview; personal statement. Additional exam requirements/recommendations for international students: Required—TOEFL (minimum score 79 iBT), IELTS (minimum score 6). *Application deadline:* Applications are processed on a rolling basis. Application fee: $50. Electronic applications accepted. *Expenses:* $1,285 per credit plus fees. *Financial support:* Career-related internships or fieldwork, Federal Work-Study, scholarships/grants, tuition waivers (full and partial), and unspecified assistantships available. Support available to part-time students. Financial award application deadline: 2/15; financial award applicants required to submit FAFSA. *Faculty research:* Evolving definition of new literacies and its impact on teaching and learning (twenty-first century skills), new literacies practices in teacher education, teachers' professional development, English language and literacy learning through mobile learning, teaching reading to culturally and linguistically diverse children. *Unit head:* Dr. Hui-Yin Hsu, Department Chair, 516-686-1322, Fax: 516-686-7655, E-mail: hhsu02@nyit.edu. *Application contact:* Alice Dolitsky, Director, Graduate Admissions, 516-686-7520, Fax: 516-686-1116, E-mail: nyitgrad@nyit.edu.
Website: http://www.nyit.edu/interdisciplinary/department_teacher_education

New York University, Steinhardt School of Culture, Education, and Human Development, Department of Art and Art Professions, Program in Art Education, New York, NY 10003-5799. Offers art, education, and community practice (MA); teachers of art, all grades (MA); teaching art/social studies 7-12 (MA), including 5-6 extension. *Accreditation:* TEAC. *Program availability:* Part-time. *Students:* Average age 35. 57 applicants, 63% accepted, 22 enrolled. In 2017, 13 master's awarded. *Entrance requirements:* For master's, portfolio. Additional exam requirements/recommendations for international students: Required—TOEFL (minimum score 100 iBT). *Application deadline:* For fall admission, 12/1 priority date for domestic and international students. Applications are processed on a rolling basis. Application fee: $75. Electronic applications accepted. *Expenses:* Tuition: Full-time $41,352; part-time $19,968 per year. *Required fees:* $2496; $1628 per unit. $814 per term. Tuition and fees vary according to course load and program. *Financial support:* Career-related internships or fieldwork, Federal Work-Study, and tuition waivers (partial) available. Support available to part-time students. Financial award application deadline: 2/1; financial award applicants required to submit FAFSA. *Faculty research:* Multicultural aesthetic inquiry, urban art education, feminism, equity and social justice. *Unit head:* Prof. Dipti Desai, Director, 212-998-5700, Fax: 212-995-4320, E-mail: dd25@nyu.edu. *Application contact:* 212-998-5030, Fax: 212-995-4328, E-mail: steinhardt.gradadmissions@nyu.edu.
Website: http://steinhardt.nyu.edu/art/education

New York University, Steinhardt School of Culture, Education, and Human Development, Department of Music and Performing Arts Professions, Program in Educational Theatre, New York, NY 10012. Offers educational theatre and English 7-12 (MA); educational theatre and social studies 7-12 (MA); educational theatre in colleges and communities (MA, Ed D, PhD); educational theatre, all grades (MA). *Program availability:* Part-time. *Students:* Average age 28. 90 applicants, 76% accepted, 37 enrolled. In 2017, 47 master's, 5 doctorates awarded. *Entrance requirements:* For master's, audition; for doctorate, GRE General Test, interview. Additional exam requirements/recommendations for international students: Required—TOEFL (minimum score 100 iBT). *Application deadline:* For fall admission, 12/1 priority date for domestic and international students; for spring admission, 10/1 for domestic and international students. Applications are processed on a rolling basis. Application fee: $75. Electronic applications accepted. *Expenses:* Tuition: Full-time $41,352; part-time $19,968 per year. *Required fees:* $2496; $1628 per unit. $814 per term. Tuition and fees vary according to course load and program. *Financial support:* Teaching assistantships with partial tuition reimbursements, career-related internships or fieldwork, Federal Work-Study, institutionally sponsored loans, and scholarships/grants available. Support available to part-time students. Financial award application deadline: 2/1; financial award applicants required to submit FAFSA. *Faculty research:* Theatre for young audiences, drama in education, applied theatre, arts education assessment, reflective praxis. *Unit head:* Prof. David Montgomery, Director, 212-998-5869, Fax: 212-995-4043, E-mail: dm635@nyu.edu. *Application contact:* 212-998-5030, Fax: 212-995-4328, E-mail: steinhardt.gradadmissions@nyu.edu.
Website: http://steinhardt.nyu.edu/music/edtheatre

New York University, Steinhardt School of Culture, Education, and Human Development, Department of Teaching and Learning, Program in English Education, New York, NY 10012-1019. Offers clinically-based English education, grades 7-12 (MA); English education (PhD, Advanced Certificate); English education, grades 7-12 (MA). *Accreditation:* TEAC. *Program availability:* Part-time. *Students:* Average age 33. 81 applicants, 78% accepted, 21 enrolled. In 2017, 27 master's, 6 doctorates awarded. *Entrance requirements:* For doctorate, GRE General Test, interview; for Advanced Certificate, master's degree. Additional exam requirements/recommendations for international students: Required—TOEFL (minimum score 100 iBT). *Application deadline:* For fall admission, 12/1 priority date for domestic and international students; for spring admission, 10/1 for domestic and international students. Applications are processed on a rolling basis. Application fee: $75. Electronic applications accepted. *Expenses:* Tuition: Full-time $41,352; part-time $19,968 per year. *Required fees:* $2496; $1628 per unit. $814 per term. Tuition and fees vary according to course load and program. *Financial support:* Fellowships with full and partial tuition reimbursements, teaching assistantships with full and partial tuition reimbursements, career-related internships or fieldwork, Federal Work-Study, institutionally sponsored loans, scholarships/grants, tuition waivers (partial), and unspecified assistantships available. Support available to part-time students. Financial award application deadline: 2/1; financial award applicants required to submit FAFSA. *Faculty research:* Making meaning of literature, teaching of literature, urban adolescent literacy and equity, literacy development and globalization, digital media and literacy. *Unit head:* Prof. Sarah W. Beck, Chairperson, 212-998-5473, Fax: 212-995-4049, E-mail: sarah.beck@nyu.edu. *Application contact:* 212-998-5030, Fax: 212-995-4328, E-mail: steinhardt.gradadmissions@nyu.edu.
Website: http://steinhardt.nyu.edu/teachlearn/english

New York University, Steinhardt School of Culture, Education, and Human Development, Department of Teaching and Learning, Program in Multilingual/Multicultural Studies, New York, NY 10012. Offers bilingual education (MA, PhD,

Secondary Education

Advanced Certificate); foreign language education (MA); teaching English to speakers of other languages (MA, PhD); teaching foreign languages, 7-12 (MA), including Chinese, French, Italian, Japanese, Spanish; teaching French as a foreign language (MA), including teaching English to speakers of other languages; teaching Spanish as a foreign language (MA), including teaching English to speakers of other languages. MA in teaching English to speakers of other languages also offered in collaboration with NYU Shanghai. *Accreditation:* TEAC. *Program availability:* Part-time, evening/weekend. *Students:* Average age 29. 431 applicants, 61% accepted, 92 enrolled. In 2017, 121 master's, 1 doctorate, 2 other advanced degrees awarded. *Entrance requirements:* For doctorate, GRE General Test, interview; for Advanced Certificate, master's degree. Additional exam requirements/recommendations for international students: Required—TOEFL (minimum score 100 iBT). *Application deadline:* For fall admission, 12/1 priority date for domestic and international students; for spring admission, 10/1 for domestic and international students. Applications are processed on a rolling basis. Application fee: $75. Electronic applications accepted. *Expenses: Tuition:* Full-time $41,352; part-time $19,968 per year. *Required fees:* $2496; $1628 per unit. $814 per term. Tuition and fees vary according to course load and program. *Financial support:* Fellowships with full and partial tuition reimbursements, career-related internships or fieldwork, Federal Work-Study, institutionally sponsored loans, scholarships/grants, and tuition waivers (partial) available. Support available to part-time students. Financial award application deadline: 2/1; financial award applicants required to submit FAFSA. *Faculty research:* Second language acquisition, cross-cultural communication, technology-enhanced language learning, language variation, action learning. *Unit head:* Prof. Shondel Nero, Director, 212-998-5757, E-mail: shondel.nero@nyu.edu. *Application contact:* 212-998-5030, Fax: 212-995-4328, E-mail: steinhardt.gradadmissions@nyu.edu.
Website: http://steinhardt.nyu.edu/teachlearn/mms

New York University, Steinhardt School of Culture, Education, and Human Development, Department of Teaching and Learning, Program in Social Studies Education, New York, NY 10012. Offers teaching art/social studies 7-12 (MA), including 5-6 extension; teaching social studies 7-12 (MA). *Accreditation:* TEAC. *Program availability:* Part-time, evening/weekend. *Students:* Average age 24. 47 applicants, 81% accepted, 11 enrolled. In 2017, 8 master's awarded. *Entrance requirements:* Additional exam requirements/recommendations for international students: Required—TOEFL (minimum score 100 iBT). *Application deadline:* For fall admission, 12/1 priority date for domestic and international students; for spring admission, 10/1 for domestic and international students. Applications are processed on a rolling basis. Application fee: $75. Electronic applications accepted. *Expenses: Tuition:* Full-time $41,352; part-time $19,968 per year. *Required fees:* $2496; $1628 per unit. $814 per term. Tuition and fees vary according to course load and program. *Financial support:* Career-related internships or fieldwork, Federal Work-Study, institutionally sponsored loans, scholarships/grants, and tuition waivers (partial) available. Support available to part-time students. Financial award application deadline: 2/1; financial award applicants required to submit FAFSA. *Faculty research:* Social studies education reform, ethnography and oral history, civic education, labor history and social studies curriculum, material culture. *Unit head:* Dr. Diana Turk, Chairperson, 212-998-5492, Fax: 212-995-4049, E-mail: dt23@nyu.edu. *Application contact:* 212-998-5030, Fax: 212-995-4328, E-mail: steinhardt.gradadmissions@nyu.edu.
Website: http://steinhardt.nyu.edu/teachlearn/social_studies

Niagara University, Graduate Division of Education, Concentration in Teacher Education, Niagara University, NY 14109. Offers early childhood and childhood education (MS Ed, Certificate); early childhood special education (MS); middle and adolescence education (MS Ed); special education (MS Ed), including 1-6, 7-12; special education (grades 1-12) (Certificate); teaching English to speakers of other languages (MS Ed, Certificate). *Accreditation:* NCATE. *Students:* 105 full-time (79 women), 109 part-time (88 women); includes 20 minority (9 Black or African American, non-Hispanic/Latino; 2 American Indian or Alaska Native, non-Hispanic/Latino; 1 Asian, non-Hispanic/Latino; 5 Hispanic/Latino; 3 Two or more races, non-Hispanic/Latino), 35 international. Average age 28. In 2017, 86 master's, 18 other advanced degrees awarded. *Entrance requirements:* For master's, GRE General Test or Academic Literacy Skills Test (ALST). Additional exam requirements/recommendations for international students: Required—TOEFL (minimum score 550 paper-based; 79 iBT), IELTS (minimum score 6). *Application deadline:* For fall admission, 8/1 for domestic students. Applications are processed on a rolling basis. Application fee: $30. *Expenses:* Contact institution. *Financial support:* Research assistantships with tuition reimbursements, teaching assistantships with tuition reimbursements, career-related internships or fieldwork, Federal Work-Study, scholarships/grants, and unspecified assistantships available. Financial award application deadline: 4/15; financial award applicants required to submit FAFSA. *Unit head:* Dr. Chandra Foote, Dean, College of Education, 716-286-8549, E-mail: cjf@niagara.edu. *Application contact:* Evan Pierce, Associate Director, Graduate Studies, 716-286-8327, E-mail: epierce@niagara.edu.
Website: http://www.niagara.edu/teacher-education

Nicholls State University, Graduate Studies, College of Education, Department of Teacher Education, Thibodaux, LA 70310. Offers curriculum and instruction (M Ed); educational leadership (M Ed); elementary education (MAT); human performance education (MAT); middle school education (MAT); secondary education (MAT). *Accreditation:* NCATE. *Program availability:* Part-time, evening/weekend, online learning. *Degree requirements:* For master's, comprehensive exam, portfolio. *Entrance requirements:* For master's, GRE General Test, teaching license. Electronic applications accepted.

Norfolk State University, School of Graduate Studies, School of Education, Department of Secondary Education and School Leadership, Norfolk, VA 23504. Offers principal preparation (MA); secondary education (MAT); urban education/administration (MA), including teaching. *Accreditation:* NCATE. *Program availability:* Part-time. *Entrance requirements:* For master's, GRE General Test, PRAXIS I, minimum GPA of 3.0 in major, 2.5 overall. Additional exam requirements/recommendations for international students: Required—TOEFL (minimum score 500 paper-based).

North Carolina Agricultural and Technical State University, School of Graduate Studies, College of Arts and Sciences, Department of Mathematics, Greensboro, NC 27411. Offers applied mathematics (MS), including secondary education. *Accreditation:* NCATE. *Program availability:* Part-time, evening/weekend. *Degree requirements:* For master's, comprehensive exam, thesis or alternative, qualifying exam. *Entrance requirements:* For master's, GRE General Test, minimum GPA of 3.0.

North Carolina State University, Graduate School, College of Education, Department of Curriculum and Instruction, Program in Secondary English Education, Raleigh, NC 27695. Offers M Ed, MS Ed. *Degree requirements:* For master's, thesis optional.

Northeastern Illinois University, College of Graduate Studies and Research, Daniel L. Goodwin College of Education, MAT Program in Secondary Education, Chicago, IL 60625. Offers language arts (MAT); mathematics (MAT); science (MAT); social science (MAT). *Expenses:* Tuition, state resident: full-time $7274; part-time $404.11 per credit hour. Tuition, nonresident: full-time $14,548; part-time $808.23 per credit hour. *Required fees:* $1284. *Unit head:* Dr. Brian Schultz, Department Chair, 773-442-5327, E-mail: b-schultz@neiu.edu. *Application contact:* Martha Narvaez, Graduate Admission Representative, 773-442-6006, E-mail: m-narvaez@neiu.edu.

Northeastern Illinois University, College of Graduate Studies and Research, Daniel L. Goodwin College of Education, MSI Program in Language Arts - Secondary Education, Chicago, IL 60625-4699. Offers MSI. *Expenses:* Tuition, state resident: full-time $7274; part-time $404.11 per credit hour. Tuition, nonresident: full-time $14,548; part-time $808.23 per credit hour. *Required fees:* $1284. *Unit head:* Dr. Maureen D. Smith, Dean, 773-442-5500. *Application contact:* Ada Umeh, Admission Director, Graduate College, 773-442-6008, Fax: 773-442-6040, E-mail: a-umeh@neiu.edu.

Northern Arizona University, College of Arts and Letters, Department of English, Flagstaff, AZ 86011. Offers applied linguistics (PhD); creative writing (MFA), including creative writing; English (MA), including literature, professional writing, rhetoric, writing, and digital media studies, secondary education; professional writing (Graduate Certificate); rhetoric, writing and digital media studies (Graduate Certificate); teaching English as a second language (MA, Graduate Certificate). *Program availability:* Part-time, 100% online, blended/hybrid learning. *Faculty:* 62 full-time (43 women), 3 part-time/adjunct (2 women). *Students:* 115 full-time (78 women), 115 part-time (89 women); includes 57 minority (11 Black or African American, non-Hispanic/Latino; 3 American Indian or Alaska Native, non-Hispanic/Latino; 4 Asian, non-Hispanic/Latino; 26 Hispanic/Latino; 13 Two or more races, non-Hispanic/Latino), 19 international. Average age 35. 189 applicants, 56% accepted, 92 enrolled. In 2017, 82 master's, 5 doctorates, 15 other advanced degrees awarded. *Degree requirements:* For master's, variable foreign language requirement, comprehensive exam (for some programs), thesis (for some programs); for doctorate, variable foreign language requirement, comprehensive exam (for some programs), thesis/dissertation (for some programs); for Graduate Certificate, comprehensive exam (for some programs). *Entrance requirements:* Additional exam requirements/recommendations for international students: Required—TOEFL (minimum score 80 iBT), IELTS (minimum score 6.5). *Application deadline:* For fall admission, 1/30 for domestic and international students; for spring admission, 10/1 for domestic and international students. Application fee: $65. Electronic applications accepted. *Expenses:* Tuition, state resident: full-time $9240; part-time $458 per credit hour. Tuition, nonresident: full-time $21,588; part-time $1199 per credit hour. *Required fees:* $1021; $14 per credit hour. $646 per semester. Tuition and fees vary according to course load, campus/location and program. *Financial support:* In 2017–18, 69 students received support, including 4 fellowships with full and partial tuition reimbursements available (averaging $16,250 per year), 2 research assistantships with full and partial tuition reimbursements available (averaging $16,250 per year), 65 teaching assistantships with full and partial tuition reimbursements available (averaging $16,250 per year); institutionally sponsored loans, health care benefits, tuition waivers (full and partial), and unspecified assistantships also available. Financial award application deadline: 2/1; financial award applicants required to submit FAFSA. *Unit head:* Dr. Steven Rosendale, Chair, 928-523-4911, Fax: 928-523-7074, E-mail: steven.rosendale@nau.edu. *Application contact:* Tina Sutton, Coordinator, Graduate College, 928-523-4348, Fax: 928-523-8950, E-mail: graduate@nau.edu.
Website: https://nau.edu/cal/english/

Northern Arizona University, College of Education, Department of Teaching and Learning, Flagstaff, AZ 86011. Offers curriculum and instruction (Ed D); early childhood education (M Ed); elementary education (M Ed); secondary education (M Ed). *Program availability:* Part-time, 100% online, blended/hybrid learning. *Faculty:* 28 full-time (24 women), 1 (woman) part-time/adjunct. *Students:* 82 full-time (71 women), 181 part-time (167 women); includes 87 minority (19 Black or African American, non-Hispanic/Latino; 11 American Indian or Alaska Native, non-Hispanic/Latino; 4 Asian, non-Hispanic/Latino; 47 Hispanic/Latino; 1 Native Hawaiian or other Pacific Islander, non-Hispanic/Latino; 5 Two or more races, non-Hispanic/Latino), 7 international. Average age 36. 106 applicants, 95% accepted, 99 enrolled. In 2017, 79 master's, 5 doctorates awarded. *Degree requirements:* For master's, variable foreign language requirement, comprehensive exam (for some programs), thesis (for some programs); for doctorate, variable foreign language requirement, comprehensive exam (for some programs), thesis/dissertation (for some programs). *Entrance requirements:* Additional exam requirements/recommendations for international students: Required—TOEFL (minimum score 80 iBT), IELTS (minimum score 6.5). *Application deadline:* For fall admission, 2/15 for domestic and international students; for spring admission, 9/15 for domestic and international students. Applications are processed on a rolling basis. Application fee: $65. Electronic applications accepted. *Expenses:* Tuition, state resident: full-time $9240; part-time $458 per credit hour. Tuition, nonresident: full-time $21,588; part-time $1199 per credit hour. *Required fees:* $1021; $14 per credit hour. $646 per semester. Tuition and fees vary according to course load, campus/location and program. *Financial support:* In 2017–18, 5 students received support, including 1 research assistantship with full and partial tuition reimbursement available (averaging $13,500 per year), 4 teaching assistantships with full and partial tuition reimbursements available (averaging $13,500 per year); institutionally sponsored loans, health care benefits, tuition waivers (full and partial), and unspecified assistantships also available. Financial award application deadline: 2/1; financial award applicants required to submit FAFSA. *Unit head:* Dr. Pamela Powell, Chair, 928-523-5644, Fax: 928-523-1929, E-mail: pamela.powell@nau.edu. *Application contact:* Tina Sutton, Coordinator, Graduate College, 928-523-4348, Fax: 928-523-8950, E-mail: graduate@nau.edu.
Website: https://nau.edu/coe/Teaching-and-Learning/

Northwest Christian University, School of Education and Counseling, Eugene, OR 97401-3745. Offers clinical mental health counseling (MA); elementary teaching (MAT); English for speakers of other languages (MAT); physical education (MAT); school counseling (MA); secondary teaching (MAT); special education (MAT). *Program availability:* Part-time, evening/weekend, online learning. *Faculty:* 9 full-time (4 women), 14 part-time/adjunct (10 women). *Students:* 77 full-time (60 women), 44 part-time (30 women); includes 19 minority (4 Black or African American, non-Hispanic/Latino; 1 American Indian or Alaska Native, non-Hispanic/Latino; 3 Asian, non-Hispanic/Latino; 2 Hispanic/Latino; 1 Native Hawaiian or other Pacific Islander, non-Hispanic/Latino; 8 Two or more races, non-Hispanic/Latino). Average age 34. In 2017, 58 master's awarded. *Degree requirements:* For master's, thesis (for some programs). *Entrance requirements:* For master's, GRE or MAT, minimum undergraduate GPA of 3.0, interview, 2-3 page statement of purpose, two letters of recommendation, resume, background check. Additional exam requirements/recommendations for international students: Required—TOEFL (minimum score 550 paper-based; 80 iBT). *Application deadline:* Applications are processed on a rolling basis. Electronic applications accepted. *Expenses:* $640 to $660 per credit tuition, $90 per semester technology fee. *Financial support:* Applicants required to submit FAFSA. *Unit head:* Elizabeth Wosley-George, Director, 541-349-7465, Fax: 541-684-7310, E-mail: ewosleygeorge@nwcu.edu. *Application contact:* Billy Dorsch, Admission Counselor for Graduate Studies, 541-684-7279, Fax: 541-349-5281, E-mail: wdorsch@nwcu.edu.

Northwestern Oklahoma State University, School of Professional Studies, Program in Secondary Education, Alva, OK 73717-2799. Offers M Ed. *Accreditation:* NCATE. *Program availability:* Part-time. *Degree requirements:* For master's, thesis optional, portfolio. *Entrance requirements:* For master's, GRE General Test or MAT, minimum GPA of 2.75. *Faculty research:* Teacher education, professional school models of pedagogy, competency exams for teachers, teacher accreditation/certification.

Northwestern State University of Louisiana, Graduate Studies and Research, College of Education and Human Development, Program in Secondary Education, Natchitoches, LA 71497. Offers MAT. *Degree requirements:* For master's, comprehensive exam, thesis or alternative. *Entrance requirements:* For master's, GRE General Test, minimum undergraduate GPA of 2.5. Additional exam requirements/recommendations for international students: Required—TOEFL. Electronic applications accepted.

Northwestern State University of Louisiana, Graduate Studies and Research, College of Education and Human Development, Programs in Educational Leadership and Instruction, Natchitoches, LA 71497. Offers counseling (Ed S); educational leadership (M Ed, Ed S); educational technology (Ed S); elementary teaching (Ed S); reading (Ed S); secondary teaching (Ed S); special education (Ed S). *Accreditation:* NASAD. *Degree requirements:* For master's, comprehensive exam, thesis (for some programs). *Entrance requirements:* For master's and Ed S, GRE General Test. Additional exam requirements/recommendations for international students: Required—TOEFL. Electronic applications accepted.

Northwestern University, The Graduate School, School of Education and Social Policy, Education and Social Policy Program, Evanston, IL 60035. Offers elementary teaching (MS); secondary teaching (MS); teacher leadership (MS). *Program availability:* Part-time, evening/weekend. *Degree requirements:* For master's, research project. *Entrance requirements:* For master's, GRE General Test, Illinois State Board of Education Basic Skills Exam (secondary and elementary), bachelor's degree. Additional exam requirements/recommendations for international students: Recommended—TOEFL. Electronic applications accepted. *Faculty research:* Cultural context and literacy, philosophy of education and interpretive discussion, productivity, enhancing research and teaching, motivation, new and junior faculty issues, professional development for K-12 teachers to improve math and science teaching, female/underrepresented students/faculty in STEM disciplines.

Oakland University, Graduate Study and Lifelong Learning, School of Education and Human Services, Department of Teacher Development and Educational Studies, Rochester, MI 48309-4401. Offers educational studies (M Ed); elementary education (MAT); secondary education (MAT); teaching and learning (Graduate Certificate). *Entrance requirements:* For master's, minimum GPA of 3.0. Electronic applications accepted. *Expenses:* Tuition, state resident: full-time $16,950; part-time $706.25 per credit. Tuition, nonresident: full-time $24,648; part-time $1027 per credit.

Ohio University, Graduate College, Gladys W. and David H. Patton College of Education and Human Services, Department of Teacher Education, Athens, OH 45701-2979. Offers adolescent to young adult education (M Ed); curriculum and instruction (M Ed, PhD); early childhood/special education (M Ed); intervention specialist/mild-moderate needs (M Ed); intervention specialist/moderate-intensive needs (M Ed); middle childhood education (M Ed); reading education (M Ed). *Program availability:* Part-time, evening/weekend. *Degree requirements:* For master's, thesis or alternative; for doctorate, comprehensive exam, thesis/dissertation. *Entrance requirements:* For master's, GRE General Test or MAT (if GPA is below 2.9); for doctorate, GRE General Test, minimum GPA of 3.4, work experience. Additional exam requirements/recommendations for international students: Required—TOEFL (minimum score 550 paper-based; 80 iBT) or IELTS (minimum score 6.5). Electronic applications accepted. *Faculty research:* Cognition literacy, character education, teacher's education reform, disabilities.

Old Dominion University, Darden College of Education, Programs in Secondary Education, Norfolk, VA 23529. Offers chemistry (MS Ed); English (MS Ed); secondary education (MS Ed). *Accreditation:* NCATE. *Program availability:* Part-time, evening/weekend, online learning. *Faculty:* 13 full-time (7 women), 10 part-time/adjunct (7 women). *Students:* 52 full-time (35 women), 88 part-time (71 women); includes 31 minority (13 Black or African American, non-Hispanic/Latino; 1 American Indian or Alaska Native, non-Hispanic/Latino; 3 Asian, non-Hispanic/Latino; 6 Hispanic/Latino; 2 Native Hawaiian or other Pacific Islander, non-Hispanic/Latino; 6 Two or more races, non-Hispanic/Latino). Average age 34. 75 applicants, 71% accepted, 53 enrolled. In 2017, 56 master's awarded. *Degree requirements:* For master's, comprehensive exam, thesis. *Entrance requirements:* For master's, GRE General Test or MAT, PRAXIS I (for licensure), minimum GPA of 2.8, teaching certificate. Additional exam requirements/recommendations for international students: Required—TOEFL. *Application deadline:* For fall admission, 6/1 for domestic and international students; for winter admission, 11/1 for domestic and international students; for spring admission, 3/1 for domestic and international students. Applications are processed on a rolling basis. Application fee: $50. Electronic applications accepted. *Expenses:* Tuition, state resident: full-time $8928; part-time $496 per credit. Tuition, nonresident: full-time $22,482; part-time $1249 per credit. *Required fees:* $66 per semester. *Financial support:* In 2017–18, 56 students received support, including fellowships (averaging $15,000 per year), research assistantships with tuition reimbursements available (averaging $9,000 per year), teaching assistantships with tuition reimbursements available (averaging $15,000 per year). Financial award application deadline: 2/15; financial award applicants required to submit FAFSA. *Faculty research:* Use of technology, writing project for teachers, geography teaching, reading. *Unit head:* Dr. KaaVonia Hinton, Department Chair, 757-683-5958, Fax: 757-683-5862, E-mail: khintonj@odu.edu. *Application contact:* William Heffelfinger, Director of Graduate Admissions, 757-683-5554, Fax: 757-683-3255, E-mail: gradadmit@odu.edu.
Website: http://education.odu.edu/eci/secondary/

Olivet Nazarene University, Graduate School, Division of Education, Program in Secondary Education, Bourbonnais, IL 60914. Offers MAT. *Accreditation:* NCATE. *Program availability:* Evening/weekend. *Degree requirements:* For master's, thesis or alternative.

Pacific Union College, Education Department, Angwin, CA 94508-9707. Offers education (M Ed); elementary teaching (MAT); secondary teaching (MAT). *Program availability:* Part-time. *Faculty:* 3 full-time (1 woman), 1 (woman) part-time/adjunct. *Students:* 3 full-time (2 women), 4 part-time (2 women); includes 1 minority (Black or African American, non-Hispanic/Latino). Average age 45. 4 applicants, 100% accepted, 4 enrolled. In 2017, 1 master's awarded. *Degree requirements:* For master's, thesis, action research project, field experiences. *Entrance requirements:* For master's, GRE General Test, two interviews, teaching credential, letters of recommendation, essay. *Application deadline:* For fall admission, 8/30 for domestic and international students; for summer admission, 6/1 for domestic and international students. Applications are processed on a rolling basis. Application fee: $0. *Expenses:* $29,469 per year, $9,823 per quarter. *Financial support:* Scholarships/grants available. Support available to part-time students. Financial award application deadline: 9/25. *Unit head:* Prof. Thomas Lee, Department Chair, 707-965-6646, Fax: 707-965-6645, E-mail: tdlee@puc.edu. *Application contact:* Cherith Mundy, Credential Analyst, 707-965-6643, Fax: 707-965-6645, E-mail: teachingcredentials@puc.edu.
Website: http://www.puc.edu/academics/departments/education/

Pacific University, College of Education, Forest Grove, OR 97116-1797. Offers early childhood education (MAT); education (MAE); elementary education (MAT); ESOL (MAT); high school education (MAT); middle school education (MAT); special education

(MAT); speech-language pathology (MS); STEM education (MAT); talented and gifted (M Ed); visual function in learning (M Ed). *Accreditation:* ASHA; NCATE. *Program availability:* Part-time, evening/weekend. *Degree requirements:* For master's, research project. *Entrance requirements:* For master's, California Basic Educational Skills Test, PRAXIS II, minimum undergraduate GPA of 2.75, 3.0 graduate. Additional exam requirements/recommendations for international students: Required—TOEFL. Electronic applications accepted. *Expenses:* Contact institution. *Faculty research:* Defining a culturally competent classroom, technology in the K-12 classroom, Socratic seminars, social studies education.

Piedmont College, School of Education, Demorest, GA 30535. Offers art education (MA, MAT); curriculum and instruction (Ed D, Ed S); early childhood education (MA, MAT); instructional technology (MA); middle grades education (MA, MAT); music education (MA, MAT); secondary education (MA, MAT); special education (MA, MAT). *Program availability:* Part-time, evening/weekend. *Students:* 341 full-time (268 women), 682 part-time (571 women); includes 182 minority (136 Black or African American, non-Hispanic/Latino; 2 American Indian or Alaska Native, non-Hispanic/Latino; 11 Asian, non-Hispanic/Latino; 32 Hispanic/Latino; 1 Two or more races, non-Hispanic/Latino). Average age 37. 333 applicants, 77% accepted, 103 enrolled. In 2017, 292 master's, 9 doctorates, 318 other advanced degrees awarded. *Degree requirements:* For master's, thesis, field experience in the classroom teaching; for doctorate, thesis/dissertation. *Entrance requirements:* For master's, GRE General Test, MAT; for Ed S, minimum graduate GPA of 3.5, valid teaching certificate. Additional exam requirements/recommendations for international students: Required—TOEFL (minimum score 550 paper-based). *Application deadline:* For fall admission, 7/15 for domestic students; for spring admission, 12/1 for domestic students. Applications are processed on a rolling basis. Electronic applications accepted. *Expenses: Tuition:* Full-time $9360; part-time $520 per credit hour. *Required fees:* $200; $200 per year. $100 per term. *Financial support:* Career-related internships or fieldwork, Federal Work-Study, and unspecified assistantships available. Support available to part-time students. Financial award applicants required to submit FAFSA. *Unit head:* Dr. Don Gnecco, Dean, 706-778-3000 Ext. 1201, Fax: 706-776-9608, E-mail: dgnecco@piedmont.edu. *Application contact:* Kathleen Carter, Director of Graduate Enrollment Management, 706-778-8500 Ext. 1181, Fax: 706-778-0150, E-mail: kanderson@piedmont.edu.

Pittsburg State University, Graduate School, College of Education, Department of Teaching and Leadership, Pittsburg, KS 66762. Offers autism spectrum disorder (Certificate); district level (Certificate); education (MS), including school health; educational leadership (MS); educational technology (MS); general school administration (Ed S), including advanced studies in leadership; secondary education (MAT); special education (MAT, MS), including special education teaching (MS); teaching (MS); TESOL (Certificate). *Program availability:* Part-time, online only, 100% online, blended/hybrid learning. *Students:* 475 (345 women); includes 57 minority (12 Black or African American, non-Hispanic/Latino; 9 American Indian or Alaska Native, non-Hispanic/Latino; 3 Asian, non-Hispanic/Latino; 17 Hispanic/Latino; 16 Two or more races, non-Hispanic/Latino), 1 international. In 2017, 195 master's, 11 other advanced degrees awarded. Terminal master's awarded for partial completion of doctoral program. *Degree requirements:* For master's and other advanced degree, thesis or alternative. *Entrance requirements:* For master's, PPST. Additional exam requirements/recommendations for international students: Required—TOEFL (minimum score 520 paper-based; 68 iBT), IELTS (minimum score 6), PTE (minimum score 47). *Application deadline:* For fall admission, 6/1 for international students; for spring admission, 10/15 for international students; for summer admission, 4/1 for international students. Applications are processed on a rolling basis. Application fee: $35 ($60 for international students). Electronic applications accepted. *Expenses:* Contact institution. *Financial support:* In 2017–18, 3 teaching assistantships with full tuition reimbursements (averaging $5,500 per year) were awarded; career-related internships or fieldwork, Federal Work-Study, and unspecified assistantships also available. Financial award application deadline: 2/1; financial award applicants required to submit FAFSA. *Faculty research:* Special education, autism spectrum disorder, reading, educational technology, leadership. *Unit head:* Dr. Alice Sagehorn, Chairperson, 620-235-4508, Fax: 620-235-4520, E-mail: asagehorn@pittstate.edu. *Application contact:* Lisa Allen, Assistant Director of Graduate and Continuing Studies, 620-235-4223, Fax: 620-235-4219, E-mail: lallen@pittstate.edu.

Plymouth State University, College of Graduate Studies, Graduate Studies in Education, Program in Secondary Education, Plymouth, NH 03264-1595. Offers curriculum and instruction (M Ed); language education (M Ed); library media (M Ed); physical education (M Ed); social studies education (M Ed); special education (M Ed). *Program availability:* Part-time, evening/weekend. *Entrance requirements:* For master's, MAT.

Point Park University, School of Arts and Sciences, Department of Education, Pittsburgh, PA 15222-1984. Offers adult learning and training (MA); athletic coaching (M Ed); curriculum and instruction (MA); educational administration (MA); leadership and administration (Ed D); secondary education (MA); special education grades 7-12 (M Ed); special education PreK-grade 8 (M Ed). *Program availability:* Part-time, evening/weekend, 100% online, blended/hybrid learning. *Degree requirements:* For master's, comprehensive exam (for some programs), thesis or alternative. *Entrance requirements:* For master's, minimum GPA of 3.0, resume, 2 letters of recommendation. Additional exam requirements/recommendations for international students: Required—TOEFL. Electronic applications accepted.

Prescott College, Graduate Programs, Program in Education, Prescott, AZ 86301. Offers early childhood education (MA); early childhood special education (MA); education (MA); elementary education (MA); environmental education leadership and administration (MA); equine-assisted learning (MA); school guidance counseling (MA); secondary education (MA); special education: learning disabilities (MA); special education: mental retardation (MA); special education: serious emotional disabilities (MA); student-directed independent study (MA); sustainability education (PhD). *Program availability:* Part-time, online learning. *Degree requirements:* For master's, thesis, fieldwork or internship, practicum; for doctorate, thesis/dissertation. *Entrance requirements:* For master's, 2 letters of recommendation, resume; for doctorate, 3 letters of recommendation, resume, official transcripts, personal statement, program proposal. Additional exam requirements/recommendations for international students: Required—TOEFL (minimum score 500 paper-based). Electronic applications accepted.

Providence College, Program in Special Education, Providence, RI 02918. Offers special education (M Ed), including elementary teaching, secondary teaching. *Program availability:* Part-time, evening/weekend. *Degree requirements:* For master's, comprehensive exam, portfolio. *Entrance requirements:* Additional exam requirements/recommendations for international students: Required—TOEFL (minimum score 577 paper-based; 90 iBT).

Providence College, Programs in Administration, Providence, RI 02918. Offers elementary administration (M Ed); secondary administration (M Ed). *Program availability:* Part-time, evening/weekend. *Degree requirements:* For master's, comprehensive exam, portfolio. *Entrance requirements:* Additional exam requirements/recommendations for international students: Required—TOEFL (minimum score 577 paper-based; 90 iBT).

Secondary Education

Providence College, Providence Alliance for Catholic Teachers (PACT) Program, Providence, RI 02918. Offers secondary education (M Ed). *Entrance requirements:* For master's, GRE/MAT/PRAXIS. Additional exam requirements/recommendations for international students: Required—TOEFL (minimum score 550 paper-based; 90 iBT).

Purdue University Global, School of Teacher Education, Davenport, IA 52807. Offers education (M Ed); secondary education (M Ed); teaching and learning (MA); teaching literacy and language: grades 6-12 (MA); teaching literacy and language: grades K-6 (MA); teaching mathematics: grades 6-8 (MA); teaching mathematics: grades 9-12 (MA); teaching mathematics: grades K-5 (MA); teaching science: grades 6-12 (MA); teaching science: grades K-6 (MA); teaching students with special needs (MA); teaching with technology (MA). *Program availability:* Part-time, evening/weekend, online learning. *Entrance requirements:* Additional exam requirements/recommendations for international students: Required—TOEFL (minimum score 550 paper-based; 80 iBT).

Queens College of the City University of New York, Division of Education, Department of Secondary Education and Youth Services, Queens, NY 11367-1597. Offers adolescent biology (MAT); art (MS Ed); biology (MS Ed, AC); chemistry (MS Ed, AC); earth sciences (MS Ed, AC); English (MS Ed, AC); French (MS Ed); Italian (MS Ed, AC); literacy education (MS Ed); mathematics (MS Ed, AC); music (MS Ed, AC); physics (MS Ed, AC); social studies (MS Ed, AC); Spanish (MS Ed, AC). *Program availability:* Part-time, evening/weekend. *Students:* 28 full-time (16 women), 349 part-time (202 women); includes 165 minority (18 Black or African American, non-Hispanic/Latino; 56 Asian, non-Hispanic/Latino; 83 Hispanic/Latino; 8 Two or more races, non-Hispanic/Latino), 14 international. Average age 29. *Degree requirements:* For master's, research project. *Entrance requirements:* For master's, minimum GPA of 3.0. Additional exam requirements/recommendations for international students: Required—TOEFL, IELTS. *Application deadline:* For fall admission, 4/1 for domestic students; for spring admission, 11/1 for domestic students. Applications are processed on a rolling basis. Application fee: $125. Electronic applications accepted. *Financial support:* Career-related internships or fieldwork available. Financial award application deadline: 4/1; financial award applicants required to submit FAFSA. *Unit head:* Dr. Eleanor Armour-Thomas, Chairperson, 718-997-5150, E-mail: eleanor.armour-thomas@qc.cuny.edu. *Application contact:* Elizabeth D'Amico-Ramirez, Assistant Director of Graduate Admissions, 718-997-5203, E-mail: elizabeth.damicoramirez@qc.cuny.edu.

Quinnipiac University, School of Education, Program in Secondary Education, Hamden, CT 06518-1940. Offers biology (MAT); English (MAT); history (MAT); mathematics (MAT); Spanish (MAT). *Accreditation:* NCATE. *Faculty:* 8 full-time (5 women), 27 part-time/adjunct (19 women). *Students:* 27 full-time (20 women); includes 5 minority (1 Black or African American, non-Hispanic/Latino; 3 Hispanic/Latino; 1 Two or more races, non-Hispanic/Latino). 43 applicants, 98% accepted, 36 enrolled. In 2017, 34 master's awarded. *Entrance requirements:* For master's, PRAXIS I or PRAXIS Core Academic Skills Exam, minimum GPA of 3.0, interview. *Application deadline:* For fall admission, 5/1 priority date for domestic students. Applications are processed on a rolling basis. Application fee: $45. Electronic applications accepted. *Financial support:* Career-related internships or fieldwork, Federal Work-Study, and unspecified assistantships available. Financial award application deadline: 6/1; financial award applicants required to submit FAFSA. *Faculty research:* Multicultural and urban education/leadership, challenges of teaching diverse learners, scholarship of teaching and learning, technology and teaching, humor and education. *Unit head:* Mordechai Gordon, Program Director, 203-582-8442, E-mail: mordechai.gordon@qu.edu. *Application contact:* Office of Graduate Admissions, 203-582-8672, Fax: 203-582-3443, E-mail: graduate@qu.edu.
Website: http://www.qu.edu/gradeducation

Regis University, College of Contemporary Liberal Studies, Denver, CO 80221-1099. Offers creative writing (MFA); criminology (M Sc); curriculum, instruction and assessment (M Ed); education - teacher leadership (M Ed); educational leadership (M Ed); elementary education (M Ed); literacy (Certificate); reading (M Ed); secondary education (M Ed); special education (M Ed); teacher academic leadership (Certificate); teacher leadership (MA); teacher/educational leadership (M Ed); teaching the linguistically diverse (M Ed). *Program availability:* Part-time, evening/weekend, 100% online, blended/hybrid learning. *Degree requirements:* For master's, thesis (for some programs). *Entrance requirements:* For master's, official transcript reflecting baccalaureate degree awarded from regionally-accredited college or university, work experience, resume, letters of recommendation. Additional exam requirements/recommendations for international students: Required—TOEFL (minimum score 550 paper-based; 82 iBT). Electronic applications accepted. *Expenses:* Contact institution.

Rhode Island College, School of Graduate Studies, Feinstein School of Education and Human Development, Department of Educational Studies, Providence, RI 02908-1991. Offers advanced studies in teaching and learning (M Ed); English (MAT); French (MAT); history (MAT); math (MAT); secondary education (MAT); Spanish (MAT); teaching English as a second language (M Ed). *Accreditation:* NCATE. *Program availability:* Part-time, evening/weekend. *Faculty:* 2. *Students:* 1 (woman) full-time, 62 part-time (58 women); includes 10 minority (1 Black or African American, non-Hispanic/Latino; 2 Asian, non-Hispanic/Latino; 6 Hispanic/Latino; 1 Two or more races, non-Hispanic/Latino). Average age 37. In 2017, 31 master's awarded. *Degree requirements:* For master's, capstone or comprehensive assessment. *Entrance requirements:* For master's, GRE or MAT (for most programs), minimum undergraduate GPA of 3.0; baccalaureate degree in English, French, history, math or Spanish; 3 letters of recommendation; interview. Additional exam requirements/recommendations for international students: Recommended—TOEFL (minimum score 550 paper-based; 79 iBT). *Application deadline:* For fall admission, 3/1 for domestic students; for spring admission, 11/1 for domestic students. Applications are processed on a rolling basis. Application fee: $50. Electronic applications accepted. *Expenses:* Tuition, state resident: full-time $9768; part-time $407 per credit. Tuition, nonresident: full-time $19,008; part-time $792 per credit. *Required fees:* $696; $29 per credit. One-time fee: $200 full-time; $100 part-time. Tuition and fees vary according to course load. *Financial support:* In 2017–18, 3 teaching assistantships with full tuition reimbursements (averaging $2,500 per year) were awarded; career-related internships or fieldwork, Federal Work-Study, scholarships/grants, health care benefits, and unspecified assistantships also available. Support available to part-time students. Financial award application deadline: 5/15; financial award applicants required to submit FAFSA. *Unit head:* Dr. Leslie Bogad, Chair, 401-456-8170. *Application contact:* Graduate Studies, 401-456-8700.
Website: http://www.ric.edu/educationalStudies/

Rider University, College of Education and Human Services, Teacher Certification Program, Lawrenceville, NJ 08648-3001. Offers bilingual education (Certificate); business education (Certificate); early childhood education (Certificate); elementary education (Certificate); English as a second language (Certificate); English education (Certificate); mathematics education (Certificate); science education (Certificate); secondary education (Certificate); social studies education (Certificate); world languages (Certificate), including French, German, Spanish. *Program availability:* Part-time, online learning. *Degree requirements:* For Certificate, internship, professional portfolio. *Entrance requirements:* For degree, PRAXIS, resume. Additional exam requirements/recommendations for international students: Required—TOEFL (minimum

score 550 paper-based). Electronic applications accepted. *Faculty research:* Conceptual foundations for optimal development of creativity; creative theory, cognitive processes in mathematics learning, teacher collaboration.

Roberts Wesleyan College, Graduate Teacher Education Programs, Rochester, NY 14624-1997. Offers adolescence and special education (M Ed); childhood and special education (M Ed); literacy education (M Ed); special education (M Ed). *Program availability:* Part-time, evening/weekend. *Degree requirements:* For master's, thesis. Electronic applications accepted.

Rochester Institute of Technology, Graduate Enrollment Services, National Technical Institute for the Deaf, Research and Teacher Education Department, MS Program in Secondary Education for the Deaf and Hard of Hearing, Rochester, NY 14623. Offers MS. *Program availability:* Part-time, evening/weekend, blended/hybrid learning. *Students:* 18 full-time (13 women), 1 (woman) part-time; includes 3 minority (1 Black or African American, non-Hispanic/Latino; 2 Hispanic/Latino), 6 international. Average age 28. 24 applicants, 33% accepted, 5 enrolled. In 2017, 11 master's awarded. *Entrance requirements:* For master's, GRE, minimum cumulative GPA of 3.0. *Application deadline:* For fall admission, 6/1 priority date for domestic and international students. Applications are processed on a rolling basis. Application fee: $65. Electronic applications accepted. *Expenses:* $1,815 per credit hour. *Financial support:* Fellowships with partial tuition reimbursements, research assistantships with partial tuition reimbursements, teaching assistantships with partial tuition reimbursements, career-related internships or fieldwork, scholarships/grants, and unspecified assistantships available. Support available to part-time students. Financial award applicants required to submit FAFSA. *Faculty research:* Effective use of technology and online learning in teaching deaf students; strategies for inclusive instruction/deaf students with other disabilities; effective literacy instruction strategies for DHH readers; single case experimental design methods; STEM language, literacy and learning; deaf studies; international deaf education; stereotype threat effects on mathematical performance. *Unit head:* Dr. Gerald C. Bateman, Director, 585-475-6480, E-mail: gcbnmp@rit.edu. *Application contact:* Diane Ellison, Senior Associate Vice President, Graduate Enrollment Services, 585-475-2229, Fax: 585-475-7164, E-mail: gradinfo@rit.edu.
Website: http://www.ntid.rit.edu/msse/

Rockford University, Graduate Studies, Department of Education, Program in Secondary Education, Rockford, IL 61108-2393. Offers MAT. *Program availability:* Part-time, evening/weekend. *Degree requirements:* For master's, thesis optional. *Entrance requirements:* For master's, GRE General Test, basic skills test (for students seeking certification), 3 letters of recommendation. Additional exam requirements/recommendations for international students: Required—TOEFL (minimum score 550 paper-based; 79 iBT). Electronic applications accepted.

Roosevelt University, Graduate Division, College of Education, Program in Secondary Education, Chicago, IL 60605. Offers MA. *Students:* 8 full-time (6 women), 15 part-time (8 women); includes 5 minority (1 Black or African American, non-Hispanic/Latino; 3 Hispanic/Latino; 1 Native Hawaiian or other Pacific Islander, non-Hispanic/Latino). Average age 28. 27 applicants, 100% accepted, 10 enrolled. In 2017, 12 master's awarded. *Application deadline:* Applications are processed on a rolling basis. Application fee: $40. Electronic applications accepted. *Financial support:* Scholarships/grants and unspecified assistantships available. *Application contact:* Laura Lag, Associate Dean for Graduate Admission, 312-853-4753, E-mail: llag@roosevelt.edu.
Website: https://www.roosevelt.edu/academics/programs/masters-in-secondary-education-ma

St. Bonaventure University, School of Graduate Studies, School of Education, Literacy Programs, St. Bonaventure, NY 14778-2284. Offers adolescent literacy 5-12 (MS Ed); childhood literacy B-6 (MS Ed). *Accreditation:* NCATE. *Program availability:* Part-time, evening/weekend. *Faculty:* 2 part-time/adjunct (both women). *Students:* 7 full-time (all women), 3 part-time (1 woman); includes 2 minority (1 Black or African American, non-Hispanic/Latino; 1 Hispanic/Latino). Average age 23. 3 applicants, 100% accepted, 3 enrolled. In 2017, 13 master's awarded. *Degree requirements:* For master's, comprehensive exam, thesis optional, minimum cumulative GPA of 3.0, clinical practicum, literacy coaching internship, electronic portfolio. *Entrance requirements:* For master's, GRE or MAT, teaching certificate in matching area in-hand or pending, transcripts from all previous colleges, minimum GPA of 3.0, 2 references, interview, writing sample. Additional exam requirements/recommendations for international students: Required—TOEFL (minimum score 550 paper-based; 80 iBT). *Application deadline:* For fall admission, 6/15 priority date for domestic students, 2/1 for international students; for spring admission, 11/15 priority date for domestic students, 7/1 for international students. Applications are processed on a rolling basis. Application fee: $0. Electronic applications accepted. *Expenses:* $733 per credit hour, $100 graduation fee. *Financial support:* Federal Work-Study, scholarships/grants, health care benefits, and unspecified assistantships available. Support available to part-time students. Financial award application deadline: 4/15; financial award applicants required to submit FAFSA. *Unit head:* Dr. Lisa Buenaventura, Interim Program Director, 716-375-2394, Fax: 716-375-2360, E-mail: lbuenave@sbu.edu. *Application contact:* Bruce Campbell, Director of Graduate Admissions, 716-375-2429, Fax: 716-375-4015, E-mail: gradsch@sbu.edu.
Website: http://www.sbu.edu/academics/schools/education/graduate-degrees-certificates/msed-in-childhood-literacy

St. John's University, The School of Education, Department of Curriculum and Instruction, Program in Adolescent Education, Queens, NY 11439. Offers MS Ed. *Program availability:* Part-time, online learning. *Students:* 20 full-time (9 women), 226 part-time (129 women); includes 145 minority (54 Black or African American, non-Hispanic/Latino; 1 American Indian or Alaska Native, non-Hispanic/Latino; 33 Asian, non-Hispanic/Latino; 48 Hispanic/Latino; 9 Two or more races, non-Hispanic/Latino), 2 international. Average age 30. In 2017, 94 master's awarded. *Degree requirements:* For master's, thesis. *Entrance requirements:* For master's, GRE, MAT, or PRAXIS, statement of goals (personal essay), official undergraduate transcripts, initial teaching certification. Additional exam requirements/recommendations for international students: Required—TOEFL, IELTS. *Application deadline:* For fall admission, 8/17 for domestic and international students; for summer admission, 5/15 for domestic and international students. Application fee: $70. Electronic applications accepted. *Expenses: Tuition:* Full-time $44,280; part-time $1230 per credit. *Required fees:* $340; $340 per credit. Tuition and fees vary according to course load, degree level and program. *Financial support:* Fellowships, research assistantships, scholarships/grants, and unspecified assistantships available. Support available to part-time students. Financial award application deadline: 2/1; financial award applicants required to submit FAFSA. *Faculty research:* Digital and nondigital literacies; youth participatory action research; young adolescents' learning; self-efficacy in literacy learning; using problem solving as an approach for math learning. *Unit head:* Dr. Daniel Ness, Chair, 718-990-2717, E-mail: nessd@stjohns.edu. *Application contact:* Dr. Daniel Ness, Chair, 718-990-2717, E-mail: nessd@stjohns.edu.
Website: https://www.stjohns.edu/academics/schools-and-colleges/school-education/programs-and-majors/adolescent-education-master-science-education

Saint Joseph's University, College of Arts and Sciences, Graduate Programs in Education, Philadelphia, PA 19131-1395. Offers curriculum supervisor (Certificate);

educational leadership (MS, Ed D); elementary education (MS, Certificate); elementary/middle school education (Certificate); organizational development and leadership (MS); principal (Certificate); professional education (MS); reading specialist (MS, Certificate); reading supervisor (Certificate); secondary education (MS, Certificate); special education (MS); special education 7-12 (Certificate); special education PK-8 (Certificate); superintendent's letter of eligibility (Certificate); supervisor of special education (Certificate); teacher of the deaf and hard of hearing (Certificate). *Program availability:* Part-time, evening/weekend, blended/hybrid learning. *Faculty:* 18 full-time (16 women), 63 part-time/adjunct (44 women). *Students:* 79 full-time (60 women), 793 part-time (604 women); includes 179 minority (125 Black or African American, non-Hispanic/Latino; 5 American Indian or Alaska Native, non-Hispanic/Latino; 15 Asian, non-Hispanic/Latino; 27 Hispanic/Latino; 1 Native Hawaiian or other Pacific Islander, non-Hispanic/Latino; 6 Two or more races, non-Hispanic/Latino), 12 international. Average age 34. 375 applicants, 75% accepted, 189 enrolled. In 2017, 340 master's, 13 doctorates, 3 other advanced degrees awarded. *Degree requirements:* For master's, thesis or alternative; for doctorate, comprehensive exam, thesis/dissertation. *Entrance requirements:* For master's, 2 letters of recommendation, minimum GPA of 3.0, official transcripts, personal statement; for doctorate, GRE, master's degree from accredited institution, minimum graduate GPA of 3.5, computer competence, interview with program director. Additional exam requirements/recommendations for international students: Required—TOEFL (minimum score 550 paper-based; 80 iBT), IELTS (minimum score 6.5), PTE (minimum score 60). *Application deadline:* For fall admission, 7/15 for international students; for spring admission, 11/1 for international students. Applications are processed on a rolling basis. Application fee: $35. Electronic applications accepted. *Expenses:* Contact institution. *Financial support:* Scholarships/grants and unspecified assistantships available. Financial award application deadline: 5/1; financial award applicants required to submit FAFSA. *Faculty research:* Factors predicting early mathematics skills for low income children, early child care and development, preschool quality, parent communication and home-school collaboration issues, education of terminally ill children, preparing literacy teachers for urban schools. *Unit head:* Dr. John Vacca, Associate Dean, Education, 610-660-3131, E-mail: gradcas@sju.edu. *Application contact:* Graduate Admissions, College of Arts and Sciences, 610-660-3131, E-mail: gradcas@sju.edu.
Website: https://sites.sju.edu/education/graduate-programs/

Saint Mary's University of Minnesota, Schools of Graduate and Professional Programs, Graduate School of Education, Instruction Program, Winona, MN 55987-1399. Offers MA. *Unit head:* Delores Roethke, Director, 612-238-4511, E-mail: droethke@smumn.edu. *Application contact:* James Callinan, Director of Admissions for Graduate and Professional Programs, 612-728-5158, Fax: 612-728-5121, E-mail: jcallina@smumn.edu.
Website: http://www.smumn.edu/graduate-home/areas-of-study/graduate-school-of-education/ma-in-instruction

Saint Peter's University, Graduate Programs in Education, Program in Teaching, Jersey City, NJ 07306-5997. Offers 6-8 middle school education (MA Ed, Certificate); K-12 secondary education (MA Ed, Certificate); K-5 elementary education (MA Ed, Certificate). *Program availability:* Part-time, evening/weekend. *Degree requirements:* For master's, comprehensive exam. *Entrance requirements:* For master's, GRE or MAT. Additional exam requirements/recommendations for international students: Required—TOEFL. Electronic applications accepted.

St. Thomas Aquinas College, Division of Teacher Education, Sparkill, NY 10976. Offers adolescence education (MST); childhood and special education (MST); childhood education (MST); educational leadership (MS Ed); reading (MS Ed, PMC); special education (MS Ed, PMC); teaching (MS Ed), including elementary education, middle school education, special education. *Accreditation:* NCATE. *Program availability:* Part-time, evening/weekend. *Degree requirements:* For master's, comprehensive exam, comprehensive professional portfolio; for PMC, action research project. *Entrance requirements:* For master's, New York State Qualifying Exam, GRE General Test or minimum GPA of 3.0, teaching certificate; for PMC, GRE General Test or minimum GPA of 3.0. Electronic applications accepted. *Faculty research:* Computer applications in education, adolescent special education students, literacy development, inclusive practices for special education students.

Saint Xavier University, Graduate Studies, School of Education, Chicago, IL 60655-3105. Offers counseling (MA); curriculum and instruction (MA); early childhood education (MA); educational administration (MA); elementary education (MA); individualized studies (MA), including educational technology, English as a second language (ESL), ISTEM (integrative science, technology, engineering, and math), science education; music education (MA); reading (MA); secondary education (MA); Spanish education (MA); special education (MA); teaching and leadership (MA). *Accreditation:* NCATE. *Program availability:* Part-time, evening/weekend. *Degree requirements:* For master's, thesis or project. *Entrance requirements:* For master's, minimum GPA of 3.0. *Expenses:* Contact institution.

Salem College, Graduate Studies, Winston-Salem, NC 27101. Offers art education (MAT); elementary education (M Ed, MAT); language and literacy (M Ed); middle school education (MAT); organ (MM); piano (MM); school counseling (M Ed); second language studies (MAT); secondary education (MAT); special education (M Ed, MAT). *Accreditation:* NCATE. *Program availability:* Part-time, evening/weekend, online learning. *Faculty:* 8 full-time (all women), 11 part-time/adjunct (8 women). In 2017, 17 master's awarded. *Degree requirements:* For master's, practicum (MAT), action research project (M Ed). *Entrance requirements:* For master's, minimum GPA of 3.0, two academic/professional recommendations, acceptable criminal background check. Additional exam requirements/recommendations for international students: Recommended—TOEFL. *Application deadline:* For fall admission, 8/1 for domestic students, 7/15 for international students; for spring admission, 1/15 for domestic students; for summer admission, 5/1 for domestic students. Applications are processed on a rolling basis. Application fee: $30. Electronic applications accepted. *Expenses:* Tuition: Part-time $440 per semester hour. *Financial support:* Scholarships/grants available. Support available to part-time students. Financial award applicants required to submit FAFSA. *Faculty research:* Teacher professional development, adolescent literacy, instructional technology. *Application contact:* Sheryl Long, Director, 336-721-2658, Fax: 336-917-5384, E-mail: sheryl.long@salem.edu.
Website: http://www.salem.edu

Salem State University, School of Graduate Studies, Program in Secondary Education, Salem, MA 01970-5353. Offers M Ed. *Program availability:* Part-time, evening/weekend. *Entrance requirements:* For master's, GRE or MAT. Additional exam requirements/recommendations for international students: Required—TOEFL (minimum score 550 paper-based; 80 iBT) or IELTS (minimum score 5.5).

Salem State University, School of Graduate Studies, Program in Spanish, Salem, MA 01970-5353. Offers MAT. *Program availability:* Part-time, evening/weekend. *Entrance requirements:* For master's, GRE or MAT. Additional exam requirements/recommendations for international students: Required—TOEFL (minimum score 550 paper-based; 80 iBT) or IELTS (minimum score 5.5).

Salisbury University, Program in Mathematics Education, Salisbury, MD 21801-6837. Offers mathematics education (MSME), including high school, middle school. *Program availability:* Part-time. *Faculty:* 4 full-time (2 women), 2 part-time/adjunct (1 woman). *Students:* 1 (woman) full-time, 7 part-time (5 women). Average age 27. 5 applicants, 80% accepted, 4 enrolled. In 2017, 5 master's awarded. *Entrance requirements:* For master's, two letters of recommendation; transcripts from colleges and universities attended; personal statement. Additional exam requirements/recommendations for international students: Required—TOEFL (minimum score 550 paper-based; 79 iBT), IELTS (minimum score 6.5). *Application deadline:* For fall admission, 8/1 priority date for domestic and international students; for spring admission, 10/1 priority date for domestic and international students. Applications are processed on a rolling basis. Application fee: $65. Electronic applications accepted. *Expenses:* $392 per credit hour resident; $703 per credit hour non-resident; $92 per credit hour fees. *Financial support:* In 2017–18, 1 teaching assistantship with full tuition reimbursement (averaging $8,000 per year) was awarded; career-related internships or fieldwork and scholarships/grants also available. Support available to part-time students. Financial award application deadline: 3/1; financial award applicants required to submit FAFSA. *Faculty research:* Conceptual development of multiplicative reasoning; early childhood mathematics; teachers' attitudes towards mathematics. *Unit head:* Dr. Jennifer Bergner, Graduate Program Director, Mathematics Education, 410-677-5429, E-mail: jabergner@salisbury.edu.
Website: http://www.salisbury.edu/gsr/gradstudies/MSMEpage.html

Salisbury University, Program in Teaching, Salisbury, MD 21801-6837. Offers secondary education (MAT). *Faculty:* 4 full-time (3 women). *Students:* 8 full-time (2 women), 1 (woman) part-time; includes 1 minority (Hispanic/Latino). Average age 29. In 2017, 7 master's awarded. *Degree requirements:* For master's, comprehensive exam. *Entrance requirements:* For master's, three letters of recommendation; transcripts from all institutions attended; undergraduate degree in one of specified areas; structured interview; minimum cumulative GPA of 3.0 in undergraduate program or prior graduate degree. Additional exam requirements/recommendations for international students: Required—TOEFL (minimum score 550 paper-based; 79 iBT), IELTS (minimum score 6.5). *Application deadline:* For winter admission, 12/15 priority date for domestic and international students. Application fee: $65. Electronic applications accepted. *Expenses:* $392 per credit hour resident; $703 per credit hour non-resident; $92 per credit hour fees. *Financial support:* In 2017–18, 2 students received support. Career-related internships or fieldwork and scholarships/grants available. Support available to part-time students. Financial award application deadline: 3/1; financial award applicants required to submit FAFSA. *Faculty research:* Technology; standards; classroom management. *Unit head:* Dr. Starlin Weaver, Graduate Program Director, Teaching, 410-548-5787, E-mail: sdweaver@salisbury.edu.
Website: http://www.salisbury.edu/gsr/gradstudies/MATpage.html

Samford University, Orlean Beeson School of Education, Birmingham, AL 35229. Offers educational leadership (MSE, Ed D); elementary education (MS Ed, MSE); gifted (MSE); instructional design and technology (MSE); instructional leadership (MSE, Ed S); secondary education (MSE); special education (MSE). *Accreditation:* NCATE. *Program availability:* Part-time, evening/weekend, 100% online, blended/hybrid learning. *Faculty:* 11 full-time (7 women), 22 part-time/adjunct (12 women). *Students:* 206 full-time (144 women), 102 part-time (75 women); includes 124 minority (113 Black or African American, non-Hispanic/Latino; 3 American Indian or Alaska Native, non-Hispanic/Latino; 3 Asian, non-Hispanic/Latino; 2 Hispanic/Latino; 3 Two or more races, non-Hispanic/Latino), 1 international. Average age 37. 134 applicants, 84% accepted, 76 enrolled. In 2017, 79 master's, 34 doctorates, 21 other advanced degrees awarded. *Degree requirements:* For master's and Ed S, comprehensive exam; for doctorate, comprehensive exam, thesis/dissertation. *Entrance requirements:* For master's, GRE, MAT, PRAXIS II, interview, transcripts, essay, recommendations, teaching certification; for doctorate, resume, transcripts, interview, essay; for Ed S, teaching certification, transcripts, essay, interview. Additional exam requirements/recommendations for international students: Required—TOEFL (minimum score 90 iBT), IELTS (minimum score 6.5). *Application deadline:* For fall admission, 7/15 for domestic and international students; for winter admission, 11/15 for domestic and international students; for spring admission, 11/15 for domestic and international students; for summer admission, 4/15 for domestic and international students. Application fee: $35. Electronic applications accepted. *Expenses:* $813 per credit hour, $100 School of Education fee, $175 technology fee. *Financial support:* In 2017–18, 220 students received support. Scholarships/grants and unspecified assistantships available. Financial award application deadline: 2/15; financial award applicants required to submit FAFSA. *Faculty research:* Principal leadership's and teacher organizational commitment mentoring, professional development, and middle grades leadership coaching and administrator effectiveness character development programs in schools teacher efficacy related STEM and professional growth. *Unit head:* Dr. Bonnie Rabe, Interim Dean, 205-726-2565, E-mail: brabe@samford.edu. *Application contact:* Brooke Karr, Graduate Admissions Office Coordinator, 205-729-2783, Fax: 205-726-4233, E-mail: kbgilrea@samford.edu.
Website: http://www.samford.edu/education/

San Diego State University, Graduate and Research Affairs, College of Education, School of Teacher Education, Program in Secondary Curriculum and Instruction, San Diego, CA 92182. Offers MA. *Accreditation:* NCATE. *Entrance requirements:* For master's, GRE General Test, letters of reference. Additional exam requirements/recommendations for international students: Required—TOEFL. Electronic applications accepted.

San Francisco State University, Division of Graduate Studies, College of Education, Department of Secondary Education, San Francisco, CA 94132-1722. Offers mathematics education (MA); secondary education (MA, Credential). *Accreditation:* NCATE. *Unit head:* Dr. Maika Watanabe, Chair, 415-338-1622, Fax: 415-338-0914, E-mail: watanabe@sfsu.edu. *Application contact:* Administrative Office Coordinator, 415-338-7649, Fax: 415-338-0914, E-mail: seced@sfsu.edu.
Website: http://secondaryed.sfsu.edu/

Seattle Pacific University, Master of Arts in Teaching Program, Seattle, WA 98119-1997. Offers MAT. *Accreditation:* NCATE. *Program availability:* Part-time, evening/weekend. *Students:* 51 full-time (45 women), 81 part-time (53 women); includes 21 minority (4 Black or African American, non-Hispanic/Latino; 1 American Indian or Alaska Native, non-Hispanic/Latino; 7 Asian, non-Hispanic/Latino; 5 Hispanic/Latino; 4 Two or more races, non-Hispanic/Latino). Average age 32. 47 applicants, 62% accepted, 23 enrolled. In 2017, 70 master's awarded. *Degree requirements:* For master's, field experience, internship. *Entrance requirements:* For master's, GRE or MAT, WEST-B, WEST-E, official transcript(s) from each college/university attended, resume, personal statement (one to two pages), two to four letters of recommendation, endorsement verification form, moral character and personal fitness policy form. *Application deadline:* For fall admission, 3/15 for domestic students. Application fee: $50. Electronic applications accepted. *Expenses:* Contact institution. *Financial support:* Scholarships/grants available. Financial award applicants required to submit FAFSA. *Application contact:* The Graduate Center, 206-281-2091.
Website: http://spu.edu/academics/school-of-education/graduate-programs/masters-programs/masters-of-arts-in-teaching

Secondary Education

Shenandoah University, School of Education and Leadership, Winchester, VA 22601. Offers administration and supervision (Certificate); administrative leadership (D Ed); early childhood literacy (MS); educational administration (MSE); elementary school teacher education (Certificate); emphasis in teaching (MSE); health and physical education (Certificate); individualized focus (MS, MSE); literacy education (MS); middle school teacher education (Certificate); organizational leadership (MS, D Prof); reading licensure (MS, Certificate); reading non-licensure (MS); secondary school teacher education (Certificate); special education (MSE); writing (MS). *Accreditation:* TEAC. *Program availability:* Part-time, evening/weekend. *Faculty:* 8 full-time (7 women), 22 part-time/adjunct (16 women). *Students:* 16 full-time (14 women), 221 part-time (167 women); includes 32 minority (17 Black or African American, non-Hispanic/Latino; 1 American Indian or Alaska Native, non-Hispanic/Latino; 6 Asian, non-Hispanic/Latino; 5 Hispanic/Latino; 1 Native Hawaiian or other Pacific Islander, non-Hispanic/Latino; 2 Two or more races, non-Hispanic/Latino), 3 international. Average age 38. 81 applicants, 99% accepted, 63 enrolled. In 2017, 53 master's, 11 doctorates, 49 other advanced degrees awarded. *Degree requirements:* For master's, comprehensive exam (for some programs), thesis (for some programs); for doctorate, comprehensive exam, thesis/dissertation. *Entrance requirements:* For degree, PRAXIS Academic Core, SAT/ACT, PRAXIS Academic Core Math, or VCLA, three letters of recommendation, writing sample, undergraduate degree. Additional exam requirements/recommendations for international students: Required—TOEFL (minimum score 550 paper-based, 79 iBT) or IELTS (6.5). *Application deadline:* For fall admission, 5/1 priority date for domestic students, 5/1 for international students; for spring admission, 10/15 priority date for domestic students, 10/15 for international students; for summer admission, 3/15 priority date for domestic students, 3/15 for international students. Application fee: $30. Electronic applications accepted. *Expenses:* $15,600 tuition plus $1,296 fees (technology and student services). *Financial support:* In 2017–18, 26 students received support. Scholarships/grants and unspecified assistantships available. Financial award applicants required to submit FAFSA. *Faculty research:* Mentoring, behavior support for students, teacher change agency, educational technology in pedagogy, literacy education. *Unit head:* Jill Lindsey, PhD, Director, 540-535-7324, Fax: 540-665-4726, E-mail: jlindsey@su.edu. *Application contact:* Andrew Woodall, Executive Director of Recruitment and Admissions, 540-665-4581, Fax: 540-665-4627, E-mail: admit@su.edu.
Website: http://www.su.edu/education/

Siena Heights University, Graduate College, Adrian, MI 49221-1796. Offers clinical mental health counseling (MA); educational leadership (Specialist); leadership (MA), including health care leadership, organizational leadership; teacher education (MA), including early childhood education, early childhood education: Montessori, education leadership: principal, elementary education: reading K-12, leadership: higher education, secondary education: reading K-12, special education: cognitive impairment, special education: learning disabilities. *Program availability:* Part-time, evening/weekend. *Degree requirements:* For master's, thesis, presentation. *Entrance requirements:* For master's, minimum GPA of 3.0, current resume, essay, all post-secondary transcripts, 3 letters of reference, conviction disclosure form; copy of teaching certificate (for some education programs); for Specialist, master's degree, minimum GPA of 3.0, current resume, essay, all post-secondary transcripts, 3 letters of reference, conviction disclosure form; copy of teaching certificate (for some education programs). Electronic applications accepted.

Sierra Nevada College, Teacher Education Program, Incline Village, NV 89451. Offers advanced teaching and leadership (M Ed); elementary education (MAT); secondary education (MAT). *Program availability:* Part-time, evening/weekend, online learning. *Degree requirements:* For master's, comprehensive exam, thesis, PRAXIS I and II. *Entrance requirements:* For master's, 2 letters of recommendation, minimum GPA of 3.0. Electronic applications accepted.

Simpson College, Department of Education, Indianola, IA 50125-1297. Offers secondary education (MAT). *Degree requirements:* For master's, PRAXIS II, electronic portfolio. *Entrance requirements:* For master's, bachelor's degree; minimum cumulative GPA of 2.75, 3.0 in major; 3 letters of recommendation.

Slippery Rock University of Pennsylvania, Graduate Studies (Recruitment), College of Education, Department of Secondary Education/Foundations of Education, Slippery Rock, PA 16057-1383. Offers secondary education (M Ed), including English, math/science, social studies. *Accreditation:* NCATE. *Program availability:* Part-time, evening/weekend, 100% online. *Degree requirements:* For master's, comprehensive exam, thesis (for some programs). *Entrance requirements:* For master's, copy of teaching certification and two letters of recommendation (for some programs). Additional exam requirements/recommendations for international students: Required—TOEFL (minimum score 550 paper-based; 80 iBT). Electronic applications accepted. *Expenses:* Contact institution.

Smith College, Graduate and Special Programs, Department of Chemistry, Northampton, MA 01063. Offers secondary education (MAT), including chemistry. *Program availability:* Part-time. *Entrance requirements:* Additional exam requirements/recommendations for international students: Required—TOEFL (minimum score 595 paper-based; 97 iBT), IELTS. *Application deadline:* For fall admission, 4/15 for domestic students, 1/15 for international students; for spring admission, 12/1 for domestic students. Applications are processed on a rolling basis. Application fee: $60. *Expenses:* Contact institution. *Financial support:* Scholarships/grants available. Support available to part-time students. Financial award application deadline: 4/15; financial award applicants required to submit CSS PROFILE or FAFSA. *Unit head:* Kevin Shea, Chair, 413-585-4687, E-mail: kshea@smith.edu. *Application contact:* Ruth Morgan, Program Assistant, 413-585-3050, Fax: 413-585-3054, E-mail: gradstdy@smith.edu.
Website: http://www.science.smith.edu/departments/chem/

Smith College, Graduate and Special Programs, Department of Education and Child Study, Program in Secondary Education, Northampton, MA 01063. Offers secondary education (MAT), including biological sciences education, chemistry education, English education, geology education, government education, history education, mathematics education, physics education. *Program availability:* Part-time. *Students:* 5 full-time (all women), 2 part-time (0 women); includes 3 minority (1 Asian, non-Hispanic/Latino; 2 Hispanic/Latino). Average age 29. 13 applicants, 92% accepted, 5 enrolled. In 2017, 5 master's awarded. *Entrance requirements:* Additional exam requirements/recommendations for international students: Required—TOEFL (minimum score 595 paper-based; 97 iBT), IELTS. *Application deadline:* For fall admission, 4/15 for domestic students, 1/15 priority date for international students; for spring admission, 12/1 for domestic students. Applications are processed on a rolling basis. Application fee: $60. *Expenses:* Contact institution. *Financial support:* In 2017–18, 5 students received support, including 3 fellowships with full tuition reimbursements available; scholarships/grants and human resources employee benefit also available. Support available to part-time students. Financial award application deadline: 4/15; financial award applicants required to submit CSS PROFILE or FAFSA. *Unit head:* Rosetta Cohen, Graduate Student Advisor, 413-585-3266, E-mail: rcohen@smith.edu. *Application contact:* Ruth Morgan, Program Assistant, 413-585-3050, Fax: 413-585-3054, E-mail: gradstdy@smith.edu.
Website: http://www.smith.edu/educ/

Smith College, Graduate and Special Programs, Department of English Language and Literature, Northampton, MA 01063. Offers secondary education (MAT), including English education. *Program availability:* Part-time. *Students:* 1 (woman) full-time; minority (Asian, non-Hispanic/Latino). Average age 22. 4 applicants, 75% accepted, 1 enrolled. In 2017, 1 master's awarded. *Entrance requirements:* Additional exam requirements/recommendations for international students: Required—TOEFL (minimum score 595 paper-based; 97 iBT), IELTS. *Application deadline:* For fall admission, 4/15 for domestic students, 1/15 for international students; for spring admission, 12/1 for domestic students. Applications are processed on a rolling basis. Application fee: $60. *Expenses:* Contact institution. *Financial support:* In 2017–18, 1 student received support, including 1 fellowship with full tuition reimbursement available; scholarships/grants also available. Support available to part-time students. Financial award application deadline: 4/15; financial award applicants required to submit CSS PROFILE or FAFSA. *Unit head:* Craig Davis, Graduate Adviser, 413-585-3327, E-mail: crdavis@smith.edu. *Application contact:* Ruth Morgan, Program Assistant, 413-585-3050, Fax: 413-585-3054, E-mail: gradstdy@smith.edu.
Website: http://www.smith.edu/english/

Smith College, Graduate and Special Programs, Department of Government, Northampton, MA 01063. Offers secondary education (MAT), including government education. *Program availability:* Part-time. *Students:* 1 (woman) full-time; minority (Hispanic/Latino). Average age 23. 1 applicant, 100% accepted, 1 enrolled. *Entrance requirements:* Additional exam requirements/recommendations for international students: Required—TOEFL (minimum score 595 paper-based; 97 iBT), IELTS. *Application deadline:* For fall admission, 4/15 for domestic students, 1/15 for international students; for spring admission, 12/1 for domestic students. Applications are processed on a rolling basis. Application fee: $60. *Expenses:* Contact institution. *Financial support:* In 2017–18, 1 student received support, including 1 fellowship with full tuition reimbursement available; scholarships/grants also available. Support available to part-time students. Financial award application deadline: 4/15; financial award applicants required to submit CSS PROFILE or FAFSA. *Unit head:* Gregory White, Department Chair, 413-585-3542, E-mail: gwhite@smith.edu. *Application contact:* Ruth Morgan, Program Assistant, 413-585-3050, Fax: 413-585-3054, E-mail: gradstdy@smith.edu.
Website: http://www.smith.edu/gov/

Smith College, Graduate and Special Programs, Department of History, Northampton, MA 01063. Offers secondary education (MAT), including history education. *Program availability:* Part-time. *Students:* 2 full-time (both women), 1 part-time (0 women); includes 1 minority (Hispanic/Latino). Average age 30. 3 applicants, 100% accepted, 1 enrolled. In 2017, 2 master's awarded. *Entrance requirements:* Additional exam requirements/recommendations for international students: Required—TOEFL (minimum score 595 paper-based; 97 iBT), IELTS. *Application deadline:* For fall admission, 4/15 for domestic students, 1/15 for international students; for spring admission, 12/1 for domestic students. Applications are processed on a rolling basis. Application fee: $60. *Expenses:* Contact institution. *Financial support:* In 2017–18, 3 students received support, including 1 fellowship with full tuition reimbursement available; scholarships/grants also available. Support available to part-time students. Financial award application deadline: 4/15; financial award applicants required to submit CSS PROFILE or FAFSA. *Unit head:* Joshua Birk, Graduate Student Adviser, 413-585-3740, E-mail: jbirk@smith.edu. *Application contact:* Ruth Morgan, Program Assistant, 413-585-3050, Fax: 413-585-3054, E-mail: gradstdy@smith.edu.
Website: http://www.smith.edu/history/

Smith College, Graduate and Special Programs, Department of Mathematics, Northampton, MA 01063. Offers secondary education (MAT), including mathematics education. *Program availability:* Part-time. *Students:* 1 applicant, 100% accepted. In 2017, 1 master's awarded. *Entrance requirements:* Additional exam requirements/recommendations for international students: Required—TOEFL (minimum score 595 paper-based; 97 iBT), IELTS. *Application deadline:* For fall admission, 4/15 for domestic students, 1/15 for international students; for spring admission, 12/1 for domestic students. Applications are processed on a rolling basis. Application fee: $60. *Expenses:* Contact institution. *Financial support:* Scholarships/grants available. Support available to part-time students. Financial award application deadline: 4/15; financial award applicants required to submit CSS PROFILE or FAFSA. *Unit head:* Julianna Tymoczko, Department Chair, 413-585-3775, E-mail: jtymoczko@smith.edu. *Application contact:* Ruth Morgan, Program Assistant, 413-585-3050, Fax: 413-585-3054, E-mail: gradstdy@smith.edu.
Website: http://www.math.smith.edu/

Smith College, Graduate and Special Programs, Department of Physics, Northampton, MA 01063. Offers secondary education (MAT), including physics education. *Program availability:* Part-time. *Students:* 1 part-time (0 women). Average age 37. 1 applicant, 100% accepted, 1 enrolled. In 2017, 1 master's awarded. *Entrance requirements:* Additional exam requirements/recommendations for international students: Required—TOEFL (minimum score 595 paper-based; 97 iBT), IELTS. *Application deadline:* For fall admission, 4/15 for domestic students, 1/15 for international students; for spring admission, 12/1 for domestic students. Applications are processed on a rolling basis. Application fee: $60. *Expenses:* Contact institution. *Financial support:* In 2017–18, 1 student received support. Scholarships/grants available. Support available to part-time students. Financial award application deadline: 4/15; financial award applicants required to submit CSS PROFILE or FAFSA. *Unit head:* Gary Felder, Chair, 413-585-4489, E-mail: gfelder@smith.edu. *Application contact:* Ruth Morgan, Program Assistant, 413-585-3050, Fax: 413-585-3054, E-mail: gradstdy@smith.edu.

South Carolina State University, College of Graduate and Professional Studies, Department of Education, Orangeburg, SC 29117-0001. Offers early childhood education (MAT); education (M Ed); elementary education (M Ed, MAT); English (MAT); general science/biology (MAT); mathematics (MAT); secondary education (M Ed), including biology education, business education, counselor education, English education, home economics education, industrial education, mathematics education, science education, social studies education; special education (M Ed), including emotionally handicapped, learning disabilities, mentally handicapped. *Accreditation:* NCATE. *Program availability:* Part-time, evening/weekend. *Faculty:* 11 full-time (6 women), 4 part-time/adjunct (2 women). *Students:* 26 full-time (18 women), 22 part-time (17 women); includes 41 minority (all Black or African American, non-Hispanic/Latino), 1 international. Average age 33. 25 applicants, 100% accepted, 19 enrolled. In 2017, 6 master's awarded. *Degree requirements:* For master's, thesis optional, departmental qualifying exam. *Entrance requirements:* For master's, GRE General Test, NTE, interview, teaching certificate. *Application deadline:* For fall admission, 6/15 priority date for domestic students, 6/15 for international students; for spring admission, 11/1 for domestic and international students. Application fee: $25. Electronic applications accepted. *Expenses:* Tuition, state resident: full-time $9388; part-time $607 per credit hour. Tuition, nonresident: full-time $19,968; part-time $1194 per credit hour. *Required fees:* $766; $766 per credit hour. *Financial support:* Fellowships, career-related internships or fieldwork, Federal Work-Study, and scholarships/grants available. Financial award application deadline: 6/1. *Unit head:* Dr. Charlie Spell, Interim Chair, Department of Education, 803-536-8963, Fax: 803-516-4568, E-mail: cspell@scsu.edu. *Application contact:* Curtis Foskey, Coordinator of Graduate Studies, 803-536-8419, Fax: 803-536-8812, E-mail: cfoskey@scsu.edu.

Southeast Missouri State University, School of Graduate Studies, Department of Educational Leadership and Counseling, Program in Educational Administration, Cape Girardeau, MO 63701-4799. Offers educational leadership (Ed D); higher education administration (MA); secondary administration (MA); teacher leadership (MA, Ed S). *Accreditation:* NCATE. *Program availability:* Part-time, evening/weekend, online only, 100% online. *Faculty:* 7 full-time (4 women), 4 part-time/adjunct (1 woman). *Students:* 45 full-time (31 women), 203 part-time (133 women); includes 24 minority (18 Black or African American, non-Hispanic/Latino; 1 American Indian or Alaska Native, non-Hispanic/Latino; 4 Asian, non-Hispanic/Latino; 1 Two or more races, non-Hispanic/Latino), 13 international. Average age 32. 105 applicants, 100% accepted, 105 enrolled. In 2017, 29 master's, 31 other advanced degrees awarded. *Degree requirements:* For master's and Ed S, comprehensive exam, thesis or alternative, paper; for doctorate, comprehensive exam, thesis/dissertation. *Entrance requirements:* For master's, minimum GPA of 3.5; for doctorate, GRE, interview; for Ed S, minimum GPA of 3.7. Additional exam requirements/recommendations for international students: Required—TOEFL (minimum score 550 paper-based; 79 iBT), IELTS (minimum score 6), PTE (minimum score 53). *Application deadline:* For fall admission, 8/1 for domestic students, 6/1 for international students; for spring admission, 11/21 for domestic students, 10/1 for international students; for summer admission, 5/15 for domestic students. Applications are processed on a rolling basis. Application fee: $30 ($40 for international students). Electronic applications accepted. *Expenses:* $270.35 per credit hour in-state tuition, $33.40 per credit hour fees. *Financial support:* In 2017–18, 22 students received support. Career-related internships or fieldwork, Federal Work-Study, scholarships/grants, traineeships, tuition waivers (full), and unspecified assistantships available. Financial award application deadline: 6/30; financial award applicants required to submit FAFSA. *Faculty research:* Learning and technology; leadership, equity and social justice in P-12 schools and higher education; school culture; leadership and academic achievement; school leadership and student success. *Unit head:* Dr. C. P. Gause, Professor/Chair, 573-651-2137, Fax: 573-986-6512, E-mail: cgause@semo.edu. *Application contact:* Dr. Lisa Bertrand, Professor/Coordinator, 573-651-5080, Fax: 573-986-6512, E-mail: lbertrand@semo.edu.
Website: http://www.semo.edu/eduleadcounsel/

Southeast Missouri State University, School of Graduate Studies, Department of Middle and Secondary Education, Cape Girardeau, MO 63701-4799. Offers MA. *Accreditation:* NCATE. *Program availability:* Part-time, online only, 100% online. *Faculty:* 5 full-time (3 women), 1 (woman) part-time/adjunct, *Students:* 4 full-time (3 women), 51 part-time (40 women); includes 5 minority (3 Black or African American, non-Hispanic/Latino; 2 Hispanic/Latino). Average age 31. 20 applicants, 100% accepted, 20 enrolled. In 2017, 19 master's awarded. *Degree requirements:* For master's, comprehensive exam, research paper. *Entrance requirements:* For master's, minimum undergraduate GPA of 2.75. Additional exam requirements/recommendations for international students: Required—TOEFL (minimum score 550 paper-based; 79 iBT), IELTS (minimum score 6), PTE (minimum score 53). *Application deadline:* For fall admission, 8/1 for domestic students, 6/1 for international students; for spring admission, 11/21 for domestic students, 10/1 for international students; for summer admission, 5/15 for domestic students. Applications are processed on a rolling basis. Application fee: $30 ($40 for international students). Electronic applications accepted. *Expenses:* $270.35 per credit hour in-state tuition, $33.40 per credit hour fees. *Financial support:* In 2017–18, 2 students received support. Career-related internships or fieldwork, Federal Work-Study, scholarships/grants, traineeships, tuition waivers (full), and unspecified assistantships available. Financial award application deadline: 6/30; financial award applicants required to submit FAFSA. *Faculty research:* Assessment, technology, diversity. *Unit head:* Dr. Simin L. Cwick, Middle and Secondary Education Department Chair, 573-651-5965, E-mail: scwick@semo.edu. *Application contact:* Alisa Aleen McFerron, Assistant Director of Admissions for Operations, 573-651-5937, E-mail: amcferron@semo.edu.
Website: http://www.semo.edu/midsecondaryed/

Southern Oregon University, Graduate Studies, School of Education, Ashland, OR 97520. Offers elementary education (MA Ed, MS Ed), including classroom teacher, early childhood, handicapped learner, reading, supervision; secondary education (MA Ed, MS Ed), including classroom teacher, handicapped learner, reading, supervision; teaching (MAT). *Program availability:* Online learning. *Degree requirements:* For master's, thesis optional. *Entrance requirements:* For master's, GRE General Test, minimum cumulative GPA of 3.0 in the last 90 quarter credits (60 semester credits) of undergraduate coursework. Additional exam requirements/recommendations for international students: Required—TOEFL (minimum score 540 paper-based; 76 iBT), IELTS (minimum score 6), ELPT (minimum score 964) or ELS (minimum score 112). Electronic applications accepted.

Southern University and Agricultural and Mechanical College, Graduate School, College of Education, Department of Curriculum and Instruction, Baton Rouge, LA 70813. Offers elementary education (M Ed); media (M Ed); secondary education (M Ed). *Degree requirements:* For master's, comprehensive exam, thesis optional. *Entrance requirements:* For master's, GMAT or GRE General Test. Additional exam requirements/recommendations for international students: Required—TOEFL (minimum score 525 paper-based).

Southwestern Assemblies of God University, Thomas F. Harrison School of Graduate Studies, Program in Education, Waxahachie, TX 75165-5735. Offers Christian school administration (MS); curriculum development (MS); early education administration (M Ed); middle and secondary education (M Ed). *Degree requirements:* For master's, comprehensive written and oral exams. *Entrance requirements:* For master's, GRE General Test, minimum GPA of 2.5. Electronic applications accepted.

Southwestern Oklahoma State University, College of Professional and Graduate Studies, School of Behavioral Sciences and Education, Weatherford, OK 73096-3098. Offers community counseling (M Ed); early childhood education (M Ed); educational administration (M Ed); elementary education (M Ed); health sciences and microbiology (M Ed); kinesiology (M Ed); parks and recreation management (M Ed); school counseling (M Ed); school psychology (MS); school psychometry (M Ed); secondary education (M Ed); special education (M Ed). *Accreditation:* NCATE. *Program availability:* Part-time, evening/weekend, online learning. *Degree requirements:* For master's, exam. *Entrance requirements:* For master's, GRE General Test or minimum undergraduate GPA of 3.0. Additional exam requirements/recommendations for international students: Required—TOEFL.

Spalding University, Graduate Studies, College of Education, Programs in Education, Louisville, KY 40203-2188. Offers art teacher education (MAT); business teacher education (MAT); elementary school education (MAT); foreign language (MAT); high school education (MAT); middle school education (MAT); secondary education (MAT); special education (learning and behavioral disorders) (MAT); student guidance counselor (MA); teacher leader (M Ed). *Accreditation:* NCATE. *Program availability:* Part-time, evening/weekend. *Entrance requirements:* For master's, GRE General Test or MAT, interview, letters of recommendation, resume. Additional exam requirements/recommendations for international students: Required—TOEFL (minimum score 535 paper-based). Electronic applications accepted. *Faculty research:* Instructional technology, achievement gap, classroom management, assessment.

Springfield College, Graduate Programs, Programs in Education, Springfield, MA 01109-3797. Offers early childhood education (M Ed); educational studies (M Ed); elementary education (M Ed); secondary education (M Ed); special education (M Ed, CAGS). *Program availability:* Part-time, evening/weekend. *Students:* 18 applicants, 72% accepted, 12 enrolled. In 2017, 22 master's awarded. *Entrance requirements:* For master's, Massachusetts Tests for Educator Licensure (MTEL). Additional exam requirements/recommendations for international students: Required—TOEFL (minimum score 550 paper-based); Recommended—IELTS (minimum score 7). *Application deadline:* For fall admission, 1/15 for domestic and international students; for winter admission, 11/1 for domestic and international students; for spring admission, 11/1 for domestic and international students. Applications are processed on a rolling basis. Application fee: $50. Electronic applications accepted. *Expenses:* Contact institution. *Financial support:* Fellowships with partial tuition reimbursements, teaching assistantships with partial tuition reimbursements, career-related internships or fieldwork, Federal Work-Study, institutionally sponsored loans, scholarships/grants, and unspecified assistantships available. Financial award application deadline: 3/1; financial award applicants required to submit FAFSA. *Unit head:* Linda Davis-Delano, Director of Education Preparation and Licensure, 413-748-3295, E-mail: ldelano@springfield.edu. *Application contact:* Anne Griffin, Director of Graduate Admissions, 413-748-3225, Fax: 413-748-3694, E-mail: agriffin2@springfield.edu.
Website: http://springfield.edu/wtp

Spring Hill College, Graduate Programs, Program in Education, Mobile, AL 36608-1791. Offers early childhood education (MAT, MS Ed); educational theory (MS Ed); elementary education (MAT, MS Ed); secondary education (MAT, MS Ed). *Program availability:* Part-time. *Faculty:* 2 full-time (both women). *Students:* 15 part-time (14 women); includes 6 minority (5 Black or African American, non-Hispanic/Latino; 1 Hispanic/Latino). Average age 30. In 2017, 5 master's awarded. *Degree requirements:* For master's, comprehensive exam, completion of program within 6 calendar years of entrance into graduate studies at Spring Hill; documentation of course field assignments (MS) or completion of internship (MAT). *Entrance requirements:* For master's, GRE, MAT, or PRAXIS (varies by program), bachelor's degree with minimum undergraduate GPA of 3.0; class B certificate (for MS); minimum number of hours in specific fields (for MAT). Additional exam requirements/recommendations for international students: Required—TOEFL (minimum score 550 paper-based; 80 iBT), IELTS (minimum score 6.5), CPE or CAE (minimum score C), Michigan English Language Assessment Battery (minimum score 90). *Application deadline:* For fall admission, 8/1 priority date for domestic and international students; for spring admission, 12/1 priority date for domestic and international students. Applications are processed on a rolling basis. Application fee: $25 ($35 for international students). Electronic applications accepted. *Expenses:* Contact institution. *Financial support:* Applicants required to submit FAFSA. *Unit head:* Dr. Lori P. Aultman, Chair of Education, 251-380-3473, Fax: 251-460-2184, E-mail: laultman@shc.edu. *Application contact:* Robert Stewart, Vice President of Enrollment, 251-380-3030, Fax: 251-460-2186, E-mail: rstewart@shc.edu.
Website: http://ug.shc.edu/graduate-degrees/master-science-education/

Stanford University, Graduate School of Education, Teacher Education Program, Stanford, CA 94305-2004. Offers elementary education (MAE); secondary education (MAE). *Degree requirements:* For master's, thesis. *Entrance requirements:* For master's, GRE General Test. Electronic applications accepted. *Expenses: Tuition:* Full-time $48,987; part-time $10,620 per quarter. One-time fee: $400. Tuition and fees vary according to program.

State University of New York at Fredonia, College of Education, Fredonia, NY 14063-1136. Offers curriculum and instruction (MS Ed); literacy education (MS Ed), including birth-grade 12, grades 5-12; TESOL (MS Ed). *Accreditation:* NCATE. *Program availability:* Part-time. *Faculty:* 11 full-time (9 women), 1 part-time/adjunct (0 women). *Students:* Average age 29. 60 applicants, 97% accepted, 39 enrolled. In 2017, 33 master's awarded. *Degree requirements:* For master's, thesis. *Entrance requirements:* For master's, GRE, minimum undergraduate GPA of 3.0. Additional exam requirements/recommendations for international students: Required—TOEFL (minimum score 79 iBT), IELTS (minimum score 6.5). *Application deadline:* For fall admission, 4/1 priority date for domestic and international students; for spring admission, 11/1 priority date for domestic students, 11/1 for international students. Applications are processed on a rolling basis. Application fee: $75. Electronic applications accepted. *Expenses:* Tuition, state resident: full-time $8154. Tuition, nonresident: full-time $16,650. *Required fees:* $1209. *Financial support:* In 2017–18, 4 teaching assistantships with full and partial tuition reimbursements (averaging $7,075 per year) were awarded. Financial award application deadline: 3/15; financial award applicants required to submit FAFSA. *Faculty research:* Positive behavioral intervention and support (PBIS), place-based science education, peer support for education, primary source material for social studies education, policies and practices in learning English language. *Unit head:* Dr. Christine Givner, Dean, 716-673-3311, E-mail: christine.givner@fredonia.edu. *Application contact:* Wendy S. Dunst, Interim Graduate Recruitment and Admissions Associate, 716-673-3808, Fax: 716-673-3712, E-mail: wendy.dunst@fredonia.edu.
Website: http://www.fredonia.edu/coe/

State University of New York at New Paltz, Graduate and Extended Learning School, School of Education, Department of Educational Studies and Leadership, Program in Special Education, New Paltz, NY 12561. Offers adolescence special education (7-12) (MS Ed); adolescence special education and literacy (MS Ed); childhood special education (1-6) (MS Ed); childhood special education and literacy (MS Ed); early childhood special education (B-2) (MS Ed). *Accreditation:* NCATE. *Program availability:* Part-time, evening/weekend. *Faculty:* 3 full-time (2 women). *Students:* 11 full-time (7 women), 37 part-time (31 women); includes 4 minority (1 Asian, non-Hispanic/Latino; 3 Hispanic/Latino). 29 applicants, 93% accepted, 24 enrolled. In 2017, 28 master's awarded. *Entrance requirements:* For master's, minimum GPA of 3.0 (3.2 for special education and literacy programs), New York state teaching certificate. Additional exam requirements/recommendations for international students: Required—TOEFL (minimum score 550 paper-based; 80 iBT), IELTS (minimum score 6.5). *Application deadline:* For fall admission, 3/15 priority date for domestic students, 3/15 for international students; for spring admission, 11/1 for domestic and international students. Application fee: $50. Electronic applications accepted. *Financial support:* Application deadline: 8/1. *Unit head:* Dr. Jane Sileo, Coordinator, 845-257-2835, E-mail: sileoj@newpaltz.edu. *Application contact:* Vika Shock, Director of Graduate Admissions, 845-257-3286, E-mail: gradschool@newpaltz.edu.
Website: http://www.newpaltz.edu/schoolofed/department-of-teaching—learning/special_ed.html

State University of New York at Oswego, Graduate Studies, School of Education, Department of Curriculum and Instruction, Oswego, NY 13126. Offers adolescence education (MST); art education (MAT); childhood education (MST); curriculum and instruction (MS Ed); literacy education (MS Ed); special education (MS Ed). *Program availability:* Part-time, evening/weekend. *Degree requirements:* For master's, comprehensive exam (for some programs), thesis optional. *Entrance requirements:* For master's, GRE General Test, minimum GPA of 2.7, provisional teaching certificate. Additional exam requirements/recommendations for international students: Required—TOEFL (minimum score 560 paper-based). *Faculty research:* Classroom applications for microcomputers; classroom questioning, wait-time, and achievement; values clarification and academic achievement.

Secondary Education

State University of New York at Plattsburgh, School of Education, Health, and Human Services, Program in Teacher Education: Adolescence Education, Plattsburgh, NY 12901-2681. Offers adolescence education (MST); biology 7-12 (MST); chemistry 7-12 (MST); earth science 7-12 (MST); English 7-12 (MST); French 7-12 (MST); mathematics 7-12 (MST); physics 7-12 (MST); social studies 7-12 (MST); Spanish 7-12 (MST). *Accreditation:* TEAC. *Program .availability:* Part-time, evening/weekend. *Entrance requirements:* For master's, minimum GPA of 2.75. Additional exam requirements/recommendations for international students: Required—TOEFL.

State University of New York College at Cortland, Graduate Studies, School of Arts and Sciences, Programs in Adolescence Education, Cortland, NY 13045. Offers biology (MAT); chemistry (MAT); English (MAT, MS Ed); mathematics (MAT); mathematics and physics (MS Ed); physics (MAT, MS Ed). *Accreditation:* NCATE. *Program availability:* Part-time, evening/weekend. *Degree requirements:* For master's, one foreign language, comprehensive exam (for some programs), thesis (for some programs). *Entrance requirements:* For master's, GRE General Test.

State University of New York College at Geneseo, Graduate Studies, School of Education, Program in Adolescence Education, Geneseo, NY 14454-1401. Offers English 7-12 (MS Ed); French 7-12 (MS Ed); social studies 7-12 (MS Ed); Spanish 7-12 (MS Ed). *Program availability:* Part-time, evening/weekend. *Faculty:* 8 full-time (6 women), 1 (woman) part-time/adjunct. *Students:* 3 full-time (2 women), 2 part-time (1 woman). Average age 27. 9 applicants, 56% accepted, 3 enrolled. In 2017, 6 master's awarded. *Degree requirements:* For master's, 2 foreign languages, comprehensive examination, thesis or research project. *Entrance requirements:* For master's, GRE, MAT, EAS, edTPA, PRAXIS, or another substantially equivalent test, proof of New York State initial certification or equivalent certification from another state. Additional exam requirements/recommendations for international students: Required—TOEFL (minimum score 525 paper-based; 71 iBT), IELTS (minimum score 6.5), PTE, iTEP. *Application deadline:* For fall admission, 4/1 priority date for domestic students; for spring admission, 11/1 priority date for domestic students; for summer admission, 4/1 priority date for domestic students. Applications are processed on a rolling basis. Application fee: $50. Electronic applications accepted. *Expenses:* Contact institution. *Financial support:* In 2017–18, 3 students received support. Fellowships, research assistantships, scholarships/grants, health care benefits, tuition waivers (full and partial), and unspecified assistantships available. Support available to part-time students. Financial award application deadline: 4/1; financial award applicants required to submit FAFSA. *Unit head:* Dr. Anjoo Sikka, Dean of School of Education, 585-245-5151, Fax: 585-245-5220, E-mail: sikka@geneseo.edu. *Application contact:* Michael R. George, Director of Graduate Admissions, 585-245-5148, Fax: 585-245-5550, E-mail: georgem@geneseo.edu.

State University of New York College at Potsdam, School of Education and Professional Studies, Program in Secondary Education, Potsdam, NY 13676. Offers English education (MST); mathematics education (MST); science education (MST), including biology, chemistry, earth science, physics; social studies education (MST). *Accreditation:* NCATE. *Degree requirements:* For master's, culminating experience. *Entrance requirements:* For master's, minimum GPA of 2.75 in last 60 hours of course work (3.0 for English program). Additional exam requirements/recommendations for international students: Required—TOEFL (minimum score 550 paper-based; 80 iBT), IELTS (minimum score 6.5). Electronic applications accepted.

Stephen F. Austin State University, Graduate School, College of Education, Department of Secondary Education and Educational Leadership, Nacogdoches, TX 75962. Offers educational leadership (Ed D); secondary education (M Ed). *Accreditation:* NCATE. *Degree requirements:* For master's, comprehensive exam; for doctorate, thesis/dissertation. *Entrance requirements:* For master's, GRE General Test; for doctorate, GRE General Test, interview, writing sample. Additional exam requirements/recommendations for international students: Required—TOEFL. Electronic applications accepted.

Sul Ross State University, Rio Grande College of Sul Ross State University, Alpine, TX 79832. Offers business administration (MBA); teacher education (M Ed), including bilingual education, counseling, educational diagnostics, elementary education, general education, reading, school administration, secondary education. *Program availability:* Part-time, evening/weekend, online learning. *Degree requirements:* For master's, comprehensive exam, thesis optional, minimum GPA of 3.0. *Entrance requirements:* For master's, GMAT or GRE General Test, minimum GPA of 2.5 in last 60 hours of undergraduate work. Additional exam requirements/recommendations for international students: Required—TOEFL.

Tarleton State University, College of Graduate Studies, College of Education, Department of Curriculum and Instruction, Stephenville, TX 76402. Offers curriculum and instruction (M Ed); educational diagnostician (M Ed); elementary education (M Ed); instructional design and technology (M Ed); instructional leadership (M Ed); secondary education (M Ed); special education (M Ed); technology applications (M Ed); technology director (M Ed). *Program availability:* Part-time, evening/weekend. *Faculty:* 7 full-time (5 women), 4 part-time/adjunct (2 women). *Students:* 7 full-time (6 women), 156 part-time (137 women), includes 40 minority (11 Black or African American, non-Hispanic/Latino; 25 Hispanic/Latino; 4 Two or more races, non-Hispanic/Latino). Average age 38. 55 applicants, 96% accepted, 46 enrolled. In 2017, 33 master's awarded. *Degree requirements:* For master's, comprehensive exam, thesis (for some programs). *Entrance requirements:* For master's, GRE General Test, minimum GPA of 3.0. Additional exam requirements/recommendations for international students: Required—TOEFL (minimum score 550 paper-based; 80 iBT), IELTS (minimum score 6). *Application deadline:* For fall admission, 8/15 priority date for domestic students; for spring admission, 1/7 for domestic students. Applications are processed on a rolling basis. Application fee: $45 ($145 for international students). Electronic applications accepted. *Expenses:* Contact institution. *Financial support:* Research assistantships, teaching assistantships, career-related internships or fieldwork, Federal Work-Study, and institutionally sponsored loans available. Support available to part-time students. Financial award application deadline: 5/1; financial award applicants required to submit FAFSA. *Unit head:* Dr. Jordan Barkley, Dean, 254-968-9089, E-mail: jbarkley@tarleton.edu. *Application contact:* Information Contact, 254-968-9104, Fax: 254-968-9670, E-mail: gradoffice@tarleton.edu. Website: http://www.tarleton.edu/cimasters/

Teachers College, Columbia University, Department of Curriculum and Teaching, New York, NY 10027-6696. Offers curriculum and teaching (Ed M, MA, Ed D); curriculum and teaching: elementary education (MA); curriculum and teaching: secondary education (MA); early childhood education (MA, Ed D); early childhood education: special education (MA); elementary education-gifted extension (MA); elementary inclusive education (MA); gifted education (MA); literacy specialist (MA); secondary inclusive education (MA); special inclusive elementary education (MA). *Program availability:* Part-time, evening/weekend. *Students:* 196 full-time (181 women), 181 part-time (161 women); includes 141 minority (45 Black or African American, non-Hispanic/Latino; 2 American Indian or Alaska Native, non-Hispanic/Latino; 45 Asian, non-Hispanic/Latino; 35 Hispanic/Latino; 14 Two or more races, non-Hispanic/Latino), 37 international. Average age 30. 509 applicants, 72% accepted, 155 enrolled. Terminal master's awarded for partial completion of doctoral program. *Degree requirements:* For doctorate, thesis/dissertation. *Unit head:* Prof. Daniel Friedrich, Chair, E-mail: friedrich@

exchange.tc.columbia.edu. *Application contact:* David Estrella, Director of Admission, 212-678-3305, Fax: 212-678-4171, E-mail: estrella@tc.columbia.edu.

Temple University, College of Education, Department of Teaching and Learning, Philadelphia, PA 19122-6096. Offers career and technical education (Ed M), including business, computing, and information technology, industrial education, marketing education; middle grades education (Ed M), including math and language arts, math and science, science and language arts; secondary education (Ed M), including English, math, social studies; teaching English to speakers of other languages (MS Ed); urban education (Ed M). *Program availability:* Part-time, evening/weekend. *Students:* 218 full-time (144 women), 296 part-time (183 women); includes 128 minority (74 Black or African American, non-Hispanic/Latino; 18 Asian, non-Hispanic/Latino; 25 Hispanic/Latino; 11 Two or more races, non-Hispanic/Latino), 13 international. 254 applicants, 54% accepted, 102 enrolled. In 2017, 128 master's awarded. Terminal master's awarded for partial completion of doctoral program. *Degree requirements:* For master's, thesis or alternative. *Entrance requirements:* Additional exam requirements/recommendations for international students: Required—TOEFL (minimum score 550 paper-based; 79 iBT). *Application deadline:* For fall admission, 4/1 for domestic students, 12/15 for international students; for spring admission, 10/1 for domestic students, 8/1 for international students. Application fee: $60. Electronic applications accepted. *Expenses:* Contact institution. *Financial support:* Fellowships, research assistantships, and teaching assistantships available. Financial award application deadline: 1/15; financial award applicants required to submit FAFSA. *Faculty research:* Workforce development, vocational education, technical education, industrial education, professional development, literacy, classroom management, school communities, curriculum development, instruction, applied linguistics, cross linguistic influence, bilingual education, oral proficiency, multilingualism. *Unit head:* Dr. Christine Woyshner, Chairperson, 215-204-6387, E-mail: christine.woyshner@temple.edu. *Application contact:* Sarah Stapleton, Assistant Director, Academic Operations, 215-204-8220, E-mail: sarah.stapleton@temple.edu. Website: http://education.temple.edu/tl

Tennessee Technological University, College of Graduate Studies, College of Education, Department of Curriculum and Instruction, Program in Secondary Education, Cookeville, TN 38505. Offers MA, Ed S. *Accreditation:* NCATE. *Program availability:* Part-time, evening/weekend. *Faculty:* 7 full-time (0 women). *Students:* 9 full-time (4 women), 24 part-time (14 women); includes 2 minority (1 Black or African American, non-Hispanic/Latino; 1 Two or more races, non-Hispanic/Latino). 17 applicants, 76% accepted, 12 enrolled. In 2017, 25 master's, 1 other advanced degree awarded. *Degree requirements:* For master's and Ed S, comprehensive exam, thesis or alternative. *Entrance requirements:* For master's and Ed S, MAT or GRE. Additional exam requirements/recommendations for international students: Required—TOEFL (minimum score 527 paper-based; 71 iBT), IELTS (minimum score 5.5), PTE (minimum score 48), or TOEIC (Test of English as an International Communication). *Application deadline:* For fall admission, 8/1 for domestic students, 5/1 for international students; for spring admission, 12/1 for domestic students, 10/1 for international students; for summer admission, 5/1 for domestic students, 2/1 for international students. Applications are processed on a rolling basis. Application fee: $35 ($40 for international students). Electronic applications accepted. *Expenses:* Tuition, state resident: full-time $9925; part-time $565 per credit hour. Tuition, nonresident: full-time $22,993; part-time $1291 per credit hour. *Financial support:* Fellowships, research assistantships, teaching assistantships, and career-related internships or fieldwork available. Financial award application deadline: 4/1. *Unit head:* Dr. Jeremy Wendt, Interim Chairperson, 931-372-3181, Fax: 931-372-6270, E-mail: jwendt@tntech.edu. *Application contact:* Shelia K. Kendrick, Coordinator of Graduate Studies, 931-372-3808, Fax: 931-372-3497, E-mail: skendrick@tntech.edu.

Texas A&M University–Commerce, College of Education and Human Services, Commerce, TX 75429. Offers counseling (M Ed, MS, PhD); early childhood education (M Ed, MS); educational administration (M Ed, MS, Ed D); educational psychology (PhD); educational technology leadership (M Ed, MS); educational technology library science (M Ed, MS); elementary education (M Ed); health, kinesiology and sports studies (MS); higher education (MS, Ed D); psychology (MS); reading (M Ed, MS); secondary education (M Ed, MS); social work (MSW); special education (M Ed, MS); supervision, curriculum and instruction-elementary education (Ed D); training and development (MS). *Program availability:* Part-time, evening/weekend, 100% online, blended/hybrid learning. *Faculty:* 91 full-time (51 women), 38 part-time/adjunct (31 women). *Students:* 400 full-time (310 women), 1,400 part-time (1,117 women); includes 724 minority (412 Black or African American, non-Hispanic/Latino; 8 American Indian or Alaska Native, non-Hispanic/Latino; 24 Asian, non-Hispanic/Latino; 220 Hispanic/Latino; 60 Two or more races, non-Hispanic/Latino), 18 international. Average age 37. 951 applicants, 46% accepted, 331 enrolled. In 2017, 564 master's, 24 doctorates awarded. *Degree requirements:* For master's, comprehensive exam, thesis optional, departmental qualifying exams (for some programs); for doctorate, comprehensive exam, thesis/dissertation, departmental qualifying exam; for SSP, comprehensive exam, thesis optional. *Entrance requirements:* For master's and doctorate, GRE General Test. Additional exam requirements/recommendations for international students: Required—TOEFL (minimum score 550 paper-based; 79 iBT), IELTS (minimum score 6). *Application deadline:* For fall admission, 6/1 priority date for international students; for spring admission, 10/15 priority date for international students; for summer admission, 3/15 priority date for international students. Applications are processed on a rolling basis. Application fee: $50. Electronic applications accepted. *Expenses:* Tuition, state resident: full-time $3630. Tuition, nonresident: full-time $11,100. *Required fees:* $2564. Tuition and fees vary according to course load, degree level and program. *Financial support:* In 2017–18, 84 students received support, including 40 research assistantships with partial tuition reimbursements available (averaging $10,800 per year), 12 teaching assistantships with partial tuition reimbursements available (averaging $13,000 per year); career-related internships or fieldwork, Federal Work-Study, institutionally sponsored loans, scholarships/grants, health care benefits, and unspecified assistantships also available. Financial award application deadline: 6/15; financial award applicants required to submit FAFSA. *Faculty research:* Cognitive and bilingual education, positive behavioral intervention, literacy, math readiness. *Total annual research expenditures:* $1.1 million. *Unit head:* Dr. Timothy Letzring, Dean, 903-886-5181, Fax: 903-886-5905, E-mail: tim.letzring@tamuc.edu. *Application contact:* Vicky Turner, Doctoral Degree and Special Programs Coordinator, 903-886-5167, E-mail: vicky.turner@tamuc.edu. Website: http://www.tamuc.edu/academics/graduateSchool/programs/education/default.aspx

Texas A&M University–Corpus Christi, College of Graduate Studies, College of Education and Human Development, Program in Secondary Education, Corpus Christi, TX 78412. Offers MS. *Program availability:* Part-time, evening/weekend, online learning. *Students:* 5 full-time (3 women), 23 part-time (17 women); includes 13 minority (all Hispanic/Latino). Average age 31. 25 applicants, 64% accepted, 11 enrolled. In 2017, 9 master's awarded. *Degree requirements:* For master's, comprehensive exam, capstone experience. *Entrance requirements:* For master's, minimum GPA of 3.0 in last 60 hours. Additional exam requirements/recommendations for international students: Required—TOEFL (minimum score 550 paper-based; 79 iBT), IELTS (minimum score 6.5). *Application deadline:* For fall admission, 8/19 priority date for domestic students, 7/26 priority date for international students; for spring admission, 1/13 priority date for domestic students, 12/20 priority date for international students; for summer admission, 5/25 priority date for domestic students, 5/1 priority date for international students. Applications are processed on a rolling basis. Application fee: $50 ($70 for international students). Electronic applications accepted. *Expenses:* Tuition, state resident: full-time $3568; part-time $198.24 per credit hour. Tuition, nonresident: full-time $11,038; part-time $613.24 per credit hour. *Required fees:* $2129; $1422.58 per semester. Tuition and fees vary according to program. *Financial support:* Research assistantships, teaching assistantships, career-related internships or fieldwork, Federal Work-Study, institutionally sponsored loans, scholarships/grants, health care benefits, and unspecified assistantships available. Support available to part-time students. Financial award application deadline: 3/15; financial award applicants required to submit FAFSA. *Unit head:* Dr. Carmen Tejeda-Delgado, Associate Professor/Chair, 361-825-2860, E-mail: carmen.tejeda-delgado@tamucc.edu. *Application contact:* Graduate Admissions Coordinator, 361-825-2177, Fax: 361-825-2755, E-mail: gradweb@tamucc.edu. Website: http://macprogram.tamucc.edu/

Texas Southern University, College of Education, Area of Curriculum and Instruction, Houston, TX 77004-4584. Offers bilingual education (M Ed); curriculum and instruction (Ed D); secondary education (M Ed). *Program availability:* Part-time, evening/weekend. *Degree requirements:* For master's, comprehensive exam; for doctorate, comprehensive exam, thesis/dissertation. *Entrance requirements:* For master's, GRE General Test, minimum GPA of 2.5; for doctorate, GRE General Test or MAT, master's degree, minimum B+ average. Additional exam requirements/recommendations for international students: Required—TOEFL. Electronic applications accepted.

Texas State University, The Graduate College, College of Education, Program in Secondary Education, San Marcos, TX 78666. Offers M Ed, MA. *Program availability:* Part-time, evening/weekend. *Faculty:* 14 full-time (9 women), 7 part-time/adjunct (5 women). *Students:* 42 full-time (27 women), 28 part-time (20 women); includes 25 minority (4 Black or African American, non-Hispanic/Latino; 3 Asian, non-Hispanic/Latino; 17 Hispanic/Latino; 1 Two or more races, non-Hispanic/Latino). Average age 30. 46 applicants, 74% accepted, 14 enrolled. In 2017, 35 master's awarded. *Degree requirements:* For master's, comprehensive exam, thesis (for some programs). *Entrance requirements:* For master's, baccalaureate degree from regionally-accredited institution with minimum GPA of 2.75 in last 60 hours of course work (for M Ed), 3.4 (for MA); statement of purpose identifying research interest (for MA). Additional exam requirements/recommendations for international students: Required—TOEFL (minimum iBT scores: 22 listening, 22 reading, 24 speaking, 21 writing). *Application deadline:* For fall admission, 2/15 priority date for domestic and international students; for spring admission, 10/15 for domestic students, 10/1 for international students; for summer admission, 4/15 for domestic students, 3/15 for international students. Applications are processed on a rolling basis. Application fee: $40 ($90 for international students). Electronic applications accepted. *Expenses:* Tuition, state resident: full-time $7868; part-time $3934 per semester. Tuition, nonresident: full-time $17,828; part-time $8914 per semester. *Required fees:* $2092; $1435 per semester. Tuition and fees vary according to course load. *Financial support:* In 2017–18, 40 students received support, including 2 teaching assistantships (averaging $12,308 per year); research assistantships, career-related internships or fieldwork, Federal Work-Study, institutionally sponsored loans, scholarships/grants, and unspecified assistantships also available. Support available to part-time students. Financial award application deadline: 3/1; financial award applicants required to submit FAFSA. *Faculty research:* Positive behavioral intervention and support, guidance and consultation, Impact of developmental integrated reading and writing, research and evaluation of teacher preparation in Texas. *Total annual research expenditures:* $993,129. *Unit head:* Dr. Nathan Bond, Graduate Advisor, 512-245-3098, Fax: 512-245-7911, E-mail: jb50@txstate.edu. *Application contact:* Dr. Andrea Golato, Dean of Graduate School, 512-245-2581, Fax: 512-245-8365, E-mail: gradcollege@txstate.edu. Website: http://www.education.txstate.edu/ci/degrees-programs/graduate/secondary-education.html

Texas Tech University, Graduate School, College of Education, Department of Curriculum and Instruction, Lubbock, TX 79409. Offers bilingual education (M Ed); curriculum and instruction (M Ed); elementary education (M Ed); language/literacy education (M Ed); multidisciplinary science (MS); secondary education (M Ed). *Accreditation:* NCATE. *Program availability:* Part-time, evening/weekend, online learning. *Faculty:* 22 full-time (14 women), 2 part-time/adjunct (1 woman). *Students:* 64 full-time (50 women), 247 part-time (205 women); includes 100 minority (26 Black or African American, non-Hispanic/Latino; 1 American Indian or Alaska Native, non-Hispanic/Latino; 11 Asian, non-Hispanic/Latino; 54 Hispanic/Latino; 8 Two or more races, non-Hispanic/Latino), 39 international. Average age 39. 157 applicants, 56% accepted, 71 enrolled. In 2017, 20 master's, 21 doctorates awarded. Terminal master's awarded for partial completion of doctoral program. *Degree requirements:* For master's, comprehensive exam (for some programs), thesis optional; for doctorate, comprehensive exam, thesis/dissertation. *Entrance requirements:* For master's, bachelor's degree; resume; letter of intent; academic writing sample; 2 letters of recommendation; for doctorate, GRE, master's degree; resume; letter of intent; academic writing sample; 3 letters of recommendation. Additional exam requirements/recommendations for international students: Required—TOEFL (minimum score 550 paper-based; 79 iBT). *Application deadline:* For fall admission, 6/1 priority date for domestic students, 1/15 priority date for international students; for spring admission, 9/1 priority date for domestic students, 6/15 priority date for international students. Applications are processed on a rolling basis. Application fee: $60. Electronic applications accepted. *Expenses:* Contact institution. *Financial support:* In 2017–18, 96 students received support, including 92 fellowships (averaging $3,321 per year), 37 research assistantships (averaging $12,336 per year); teaching assistantships, Federal Work-Study, institutionally sponsored loans, scholarships/grants, health care benefits, and unspecified assistantships also available. Support available to part-time students. Financial award application deadline: 2/1; financial award applicants required to submit FAFSA. *Faculty research:* Teacher education, curriculum studies, bilingual education, science and math education, language and literacy education. *Total annual research expenditures:* $107,999. *Unit head:* Dr. Fanni Liu Coward, Interim Chairperson, 806-834-4475, Fax: 806-742-2179, E-mail: fanni.coward@ttu.edu. *Application contact:* Brianna Sanchez, Coordinator, 806-834-2353, Fax: 806-742-2179, E-mail: brianna.sanchez@ttu.edu. Website: http://www.educ.ttu.edu

Towson University, College of Education, Program in Secondary Education, Towson, MD 21252-0001. Offers M Ed. *Accreditation:* NCATE. *Program availability:* Part-time, evening/weekend. *Students:* 4 full-time (3 women), 25 part-time (18 women); includes 2 minority (1 Black or African American, non-Hispanic/Latino; 1 Two or more races, non-Hispanic/Latino), 1 international. *Degree requirements:* For master's, thesis optional. *Entrance requirements:* For master's, Maryland teaching certification or permission of program director, minimum GPA of 3.0. *Application deadline:* For fall admission, 1/17 for domestic students, 5/15 for international students; for spring admission, 10/15 for domestic students, 12/1 for international students. Applications are processed on a rolling basis. Application fee: $45. Electronic applications accepted. *Expenses:* Tuition, state resident: full-time $7960; part-time $398 per unit. Tuition, nonresident: full-time $16,480; part-time $824 per unit. *Required fees:* $2600; $130 per year. $390 per term.

Financial support: Application deadline: 4/1. *Unit head:* Dr. Todd Kenreich, Graduate Program Director, 410-704-4956, E-mail: scedmed@towson.edu. *Application contact:* Coverley Beidleman, Assistant Director of Graduate Admissions, 410-704-5630, Fax: 410-704-3030, E-mail: cbeidleman@towson.edu. Website: http://www.towson.edu/coe/departments/secondary/gradsecondary/

Towson University, College of Education, Program in Teaching, Towson, MD 21252-0001. Offers early childhood education (MAT); elementary education (MAT); secondary education (MAT); special education (MAT). *Students:* 64 full-time (44 women), 48 part-time (34 women); includes 16 minority (5 Black or African American, non-Hispanic/Latino; 5 Asian, non-Hispanic/Latino; 5 Hispanic/Latino; 1 Two or more races, non-Hispanic/Latino). *Entrance requirements:* For master's, ACT, GRE, PRAXIS I or SAT, 2 letters of reference, resume, minimum GPA of 3.0, essay. *Application deadline:* For fall admission, 1/17 for domestic students, 5/15 for international students; for spring admission, 10/15 for domestic students, 12/1 for international students. Applications are processed on a rolling basis. Application fee: $45. Electronic applications accepted. *Expenses:* Tuition, state resident: full-time $7960; part-time $398 per unit. Tuition, nonresident: full-time $16,480; part-time $824 per unit. *Required fees:* $2600; $130 per year. $390 per term. *Financial support:* Application deadline: 4/1. *Unit head:* Dr. Pamela Wruble, Graduate Program Director, 410-704-4935, E-mail: pwruble@towson.edu. *Application contact:* Coverley Beidleman, Assistant Director of Graduate Admissions, 410-704-5630, Fax: 410-704-3030, E-mail: grads@towson.edu. Website: https://www.towson.edu/coe/departments/teaching/

Trevecca Nazarene University, Graduate Education Program, Nashville, TN 37210-2877. Offers accountability and instructional leadership (Ed S); curriculum and instruction for Christian school educators (M Ed); curriculum and instruction K-12 (M Ed); educational leadership (M Ed); English second language (M Ed); library and information science (MLI Sc); special education: visual impairments (M Ed); teaching (MAT), including teaching 6-12, teaching K-5. *Accreditation:* NCATE. *Program availability:* Part-time, evening/weekend, online learning. *Faculty:* 8 full-time (6 women), 22 part-time/adjunct (18 women). *Students:* 150 full-time (114 women), 3 part-time (1 woman); includes 54 minority (49 Black or African American, non-Hispanic/Latino; 4 Hispanic/Latino; 1 Two or more races, non-Hispanic/Latino). Average age 36. In 2017, 57 master's, 4 other advanced degrees awarded. *Degree requirements:* For master's, comprehensive exam, exit assessment/e-portfolio. *Entrance requirements:* For master's, GRE or MAT, PRAXIS (for MAT), minimum GPA of 3.0, official transcript from regionally-accredited institution, references, interview, writing sample, at least 3 years' successful teaching experience (for M Ed in educational leadership); for Ed S, GRE or MAT, master's degree with minimum GPA of 3.0, official transcript from regionally accredited institution, at least 3 years' successful teaching experience, interview, writing sample, background and fingerprinting check, recommendations. Additional exam requirements/recommendations for international students: Required—TOEFL (minimum score 550 paper-based). *Application deadline:* Applications are processed on a rolling basis. Electronic applications accepted. *Expenses:* Contact institution. *Financial support:* Applicants required to submit FAFSA. *Unit head:* Dr. Suzie Harris, Dean, School of Education, 615-248-1201, Fax: 615-248-1597, E-mail: admissions_ged@trevecca.edu. *Application contact:* 844-TNU-GRAD, E-mail: sgcsadmissions@trevecca.edu. Website: http://www.trevecca.edu/soe

Trinity Washington University, School of Education, Washington, DC 20017-1094. Offers clinical mental health counseling (MA); early childhood education (MAT); educating for change (M Ed); educational administration (MSA); elementary education (MAT); reading (M Ed); school counseling (MA); secondary education (MAT), including English, social studies; special education (MAT). *Accreditation:* NCATE. *Program availability:* Part-time, evening/weekend. *Degree requirements:* For master's, thesis (for some programs), capstone project(s). *Entrance requirements:* For master's, PRAXIS I, minimum GPA of 2.8. Additional exam requirements/recommendations for international students: Required—TOEFL (minimum score 550 paper-based). *Faculty research:* Technology, literacy, special education, organizations, inclusion models.

Troy University, Graduate School, College of Education, Program in Secondary Education, Troy, AL 36082. Offers MS. *Accreditation:* NCATE. *Program availability:* Part-time, evening/weekend. *Faculty:* 3 full-time (2 women). *Students:* 10 full-time (5 women), 7 part-time (6 women); includes 1 minority (Black or African American, non-Hispanic/Latino). Average age 27. 6 applicants, 67% accepted, 3 enrolled. In 2017, 13 master's awarded. *Degree requirements:* For master's, comprehensive exam, thesis. *Entrance requirements:* For master's, GRE (minimum score of 850 on old exam or 290 on new exam), GMAT (minimum score of 380), or MAT (minimum score of 385), bachelor's degree; minimum undergraduate GPA of 2.5 or 3.0 on last 30 semester hours, letter of recommendation. Additional exam requirements/recommendations for international students: Required—TOEFL (minimum score 523 paper-based; 70 iBT), IELTS (minimum score 6). *Application deadline:* Applications are processed on a rolling basis. Application fee: $50. Electronic applications accepted. *Expenses:* Tuition, state resident: part-time $417 per credit hour. Tuition, nonresident: part-time $834 per credit hour. *Required fees:* $42 per credit hour. $50 per semester. Tuition and fees vary according to campus/location. *Financial support:* Fellowships, career-related internships or fieldwork, and scholarships/grants available. Support available to part-time students. Financial award applicants required to submit FAFSA. *Unit head:* Dr. Ruth Busby, Chair, Teacher Education, 334-670-3546, Fax: 334-808-6666, E-mail: rsbusby@troy.edu. *Application contact:* Jessica A. Kimbro, Director of Graduate Admissions, 334-670-3178, E-mail: bcamp@troy.edu.

Tufts University, Graduate School of Arts and Sciences, Department of Education, Program in Education, Medford, MA 02155. Offers educational studies (MA); elementary education (MAT); middle and secondary education (MAT); museum education (MA); secondary education (MA); STEM education (MS, PhD). *Program availability:* Part-time. *Students:* 50 full-time (38 women), 9 part-time (8 women); includes 9 minority (2 Black or African American, non-Hispanic/Latino; 2 Asian, non-Hispanic/Latino; 4 Hispanic/Latino; 1 Two or more races, non-Hispanic/Latino), 4 international. Average age 28. 120 applicants, 71% accepted, 49 enrolled. In 2017, 51 master's awarded. *Degree requirements:* For master's, thesis optional. *Entrance requirements:* For master's, GRE General Test, portfolio (for art education only); for doctorate, GRE General Test, writing sample. Additional exam requirements/recommendations for international students: Required—TOEFL (minimum score 550 paper-based; 80 iBT), IELTS (minimum score 6.5). *Application deadline:* For fall admission, 1/2 for domestic and international students; for spring admission, 10/15 for domestic and international students. Applications are processed on a rolling basis. Application fee: $85. Electronic applications accepted. *Expenses:* Contact institution. *Financial support:* Research assistantships, teaching assistantships, Federal Work-Study, scholarships/grants, and tuition waivers (full and partial) available. Support available to part-time students. Financial award application deadline: 1/2. *Unit head:* Dr. David Hammer, Graduate Program Director, 617-627-2396. *Application contact:* Office of Graduate Admissions, 617-627-3395, E-mail: gradadmissions@tufts.edu.

Union College, Graduate Programs, Department of Education, Program in Secondary Education, Barbourville, KY 40906-1499. Offers MA. *Degree requirements:* For master's, thesis optional. *Entrance requirements:* For master's, GRE General Test, NTE.

Secondary Education

Universidad Metropolitana, School of Education, Program in Teaching of Physical Education, San Juan, PR 00928-1150. Offers teaching of adult physical education (M Ed); teaching of elementary physical education (M Ed); teaching of secondary physical education (M Ed). *Degree requirements:* For master's, thesis or alternative. *Entrance requirements:* For master's, EXADEP, interview. Electronic applications accepted.

The University of Akron, Graduate School, College of Education, Department of Curricular and Instructional Studies, Program in Adolescent to Young Adult Education, Akron, OH 44325. Offers chemistry (MS); chemistry and physics (MS); earth science (MS); earth science and chemistry (MS); earth science and physics (MS); integrated language arts (MS); integrated mathematics (MS); integrated social studies (MS); life science (MS); life science and chemistry (MS); life science and earth science (MS); life science and physics (MS); physics (MS). *Accreditation:* NCATE. *Students:* 16 full-time (6 women), 6 part-time (3 women); includes 6 minority (2 Black or African American, non-Hispanic/Latino; 1 Asian, non-Hispanic/Latino; 3 Two or more races, non-Hispanic/Latino). Average age 30. 8 applicants, 100% accepted, 8 enrolled. In 2017, 8 master's awarded. *Degree requirements:* For master's, comprehensive exam. *Entrance requirements:* For master's, minimum GPA of 3.0. Additional exam requirements/recommendations for international students: Required—TOEFL (minimum score 79 iBT), IELTS (minimum score 6.5). *Application deadline:* For fall admission, 3/1 for domestic and international students; for spring admission, 10/1 for domestic and international students. Applications are processed on a rolling basis. Application fee: $45 ($70 for international students). Electronic applications accepted. *Unit head:* Dr. Evonn Welton, Interim Department Chair, 330-972-6742, E-mail: ewelton@uakron.edu. *Application contact:* Kelly Chaff, College Program Specialist, 330-972-7028, E-mail: klchaff@uakron.edu.
Website: http://www.uakron.edu/academic-programs/graduate-programs.dot

The University of Alabama, Graduate School, College of Education, Department of Curriculum and Instruction, Tuscaloosa, AL 35487. Offers elementary education (MA, Ed D, PhD, Ed S); secondary education (MA, Ed D, PhD, Ed S). *Program availability:* Part-time, evening/weekend, 100% online, blended/hybrid learning. *Faculty:* 22 full-time (13 women), 6 part-time/adjunct (4 women). *Students:* 62 full-time (42 women), 94 part-time (67 women); includes 19 minority (9 Black or African American, non-Hispanic/Latino; 1 American Indian or Alaska Native, non-Hispanic/Latino; 3 Asian, non-Hispanic/Latino; 3 Hispanic/Latino; 3 Two or more races, non-Hispanic/Latino), 21 international. Average age 34. 85 applicants, 64% accepted, 44 enrolled. In 2017, 55 master's, 9 doctorates, 13 other advanced degrees awarded. *Degree requirements:* For master's, comprehensive exam, thesis (for some programs); for doctorate, comprehensive exam, thesis/dissertation; for Ed S, comprehensive exam, thesis. *Entrance requirements:* For master's and Ed S, MAT and/or GRE; for doctorate, GRE. Additional exam requirements/recommendations for international students: Recommended—TOEFL (minimum score 550 paper-based), IELTS (minimum score 6.5). *Application deadline:* For fall admission, 7/15 priority date for domestic students, 1/15 priority date for international students; for spring admission, 11/15 priority date for domestic students, 6/1 priority date for international students; for summer admission, 5/1 priority date for domestic students, 3/1 priority date for international students. Applications are processed on a rolling basis. Application fee: $50 ($60 for international students). Electronic applications accepted. *Financial support:* In 2017–18, 18 students received support, including research assistantships with tuition reimbursements available (averaging $13,140 per year), teaching assistantships with tuition reimbursements available (averaging $13,140 per year); institutionally sponsored loans, traineeships, and unspecified assistantships also available. Financial award application deadline: 12/31; financial award applicants required to submit FAFSA. *Faculty research:* Teacher education, diversity, integration of curriculum, technology, pedagogical content knowledge. *Total annual research expenditures:* $145,886. *Unit head:* Dr. Cynthia Camille Sunal, Chair, 205-348-8264, Fax: 205-348-9863, E-mail: cvsunal@ua.edu. *Application contact:* Dr. Kathy S. Wetzel, Assistant Dean for Student Services, 205-348-1154, Fax: 205-348-0080, E-mail: kwetzel@bamaed.ua.edu.
Website: http://courseleaf.ua.edu/education/curriculumandinstruction/

The University of Alabama at Birmingham, School of Education, Program in High School Education, Birmingham, AL 35294. Offers MA Ed. *Accreditation:* NCATE. *Degree requirements:* For master's, thesis optional. *Entrance requirements:* For master's, GRE General Test, MAT, or NTE, minimum GPA of 3.0. Electronic applications accepted.

The University of Alabama in Huntsville, School of Graduate Studies, College of Education, Huntsville, AL 35899. Offers autism spectrum disorders (M Ed, Graduate Certificate); biology (MAT); chemistry (MAT); differentiated instruction in elementary education (M Ed); English language arts (MAT); English speakers of other languages (M Ed, MAT); history (MAT); mathematics (MAT); physics (MAT); reading education (M Ed); secondary education (M Ed).

University of Alaska Southeast, Graduate Programs, Program in Education, Juneau, AK 99801. Offers educational leadership (M Ed); elementary education (MAT); learning design and technology (M Ed); mathematics education (M Ed); reading specialist (M Ed); secondary education (MAT); special education (M Ed, MAT). *Accreditation:* NCATE. *Program availability:* Part-time, evening/weekend, online learning. *Degree requirements:* For master's, comprehensive exam or project, portfolio. *Entrance requirements:* For master's, PRAXIS, minimum GPA of 3.0, writing sample, letters of recommendation. Electronic applications accepted. *Faculty research:* Applied classroom research, culturally responsive practices, action research, teaching effectiveness.

University of Alberta, Faculty of Graduate Studies and Research, Department of Secondary Education, Edmonton, AB T6G 2E1, Canada. Offers M Ed, Ed D, PhD. *Program availability:* Part-time. *Degree requirements:* For master's, thesis or alternative, 1 year of residency; for doctorate, thesis/dissertation, 2 years of residency (PhD), 1 year of residency (Ed D). *Entrance requirements:* For master's, teaching certificate, 2 years of teaching experience; for doctorate, master's degree. *Faculty research:* Curriculum studies, teacher education, subject area specializations.

The University of Arizona, College of Education, Department of Teaching, Learning and Sociocultural Studies, Program in Teaching and Teacher Education, Tucson, AZ 85721. Offers M Ed, MA, PhD. *Program availability:* Part-time, evening/weekend. *Degree requirements:* For master's, thesis optional; for doctorate, comprehensive exam, thesis/dissertation. *Entrance requirements:* For master's, writing sample, 1 year of teaching experience, 3 letters of recommendation; for doctorate, GRE General Test (minimum score 1000), minimum GPA of 3.5, 2 years of teaching experience, 3 letters of recommendation, writing sample. Additional exam requirements/recommendations for international students: Required—TOEFL (minimum score 550 paper-based; 79 iBT). Electronic applications accepted. *Faculty research:* Staff development, science education, environmental education, math education.

The University of Arizona, College of Science, Department of Mathematics, Program in Secondary Mathematics Education, Tucson, AZ 85721. Offers MA. *Program availability:* Part-time. *Degree requirements:* For master's, thesis, internships, colloquium, business courses. *Entrance requirements:* For master's, GRE, minimum GPA of 3.0, statement of purpose. Additional exam requirements/recommendations for

international students: Required—TOEFL (minimum score 550 paper-based). *Faculty research:* Algebra, coding theory, graph theory, combinatorics, probability.

University of Arkansas, Graduate School, College of Education and Health Professions, Department of Curriculum and Instruction, Program in Secondary Education, Fayetteville, AR 72701. Offers M Ed, MAT, Ed S. *Accreditation:* NCATE. In 2017, 40 master's awarded. *Application deadline:* For fall admission, 8/1 for domestic students, 4/1 for international students; for spring admission, 12/1 for domestic students, 10/1 for international students; for summer admission, 4/15 for domestic students, 3/1 for international students. Applications are processed on a rolling basis. Application fee: $60. Electronic applications accepted. *Expenses:* Tuition, state resident: full-time $3782. Tuition, nonresident: full-time $10,238. *Financial support:* Fellowships with tuition reimbursements, research assistantships, teaching assistantships, career-related internships or fieldwork, and Federal Work-Study available. Support available to part-time students. Financial award application deadline: 4/1; financial award applicants required to submit FAFSA. *Faculty research:* Mathematics. *Unit head:* Dr. Freddie Bowles, Program Coordinator, 479-575-3035, E-mail: fbowles@uark.edu. *Application contact:* Dr. Freddie Bowles, Graduate Coordinator, 479-575-3035, Fax: 479-575-6676, E-mail: fbowles@uark.edu.
Website: https://seed.uark.edu

University of Arkansas at Little Rock, Graduate School, College of Education and Health Professions, Department of Teacher Education, Program in Secondary Education, Little Rock, AR 72204-1099. Offers M Ed. *Accreditation:* NCATE. *Program availability:* Part-time. *Degree requirements:* For master's, comprehensive exam. *Entrance requirements:* For master's, interview, minimum GPA of 2.75, GRE General Test or teaching certificate.

University of Arkansas at Pine Bluff, School of Education, Pine Bluff, AR 71601-2799. Offers elementary education (M Ed); secondary education (M Ed), including English education, mathematics education, science education, social studies education; teaching (MAT). *Accreditation:* NCATE. *Program availability:* Part-time, evening/weekend. *Degree requirements:* For master's, comprehensive exam. *Entrance requirements:* For master's, GRE, minimum GPA of 2.75, NTE or Standard Arkansas Teaching Certificate. *Faculty research:* Teacher certification, accreditation, assessment, standards, portfolio development, rehabilitation, technology.

University of Bridgeport, School of Education, Department of Education, Bridgeport, CT 06604. Offers education (MS); educational management (Ed D, Diploma), including intermediate administrator or supervisor (Diploma), leadership (Ed D); elementary education (MS, Diploma), including early childhood education, elementary education; middle school education (MS); music education (MS); remedial reading and language arts (Diploma); secondary education (MS, Diploma), including computer specialist (Diploma), international education (Diploma), reading specialist, secondary education. *Program availability:* Part-time, evening/weekend. *Degree requirements:* For master's, final exam, final project, or thesis; for doctorate, comprehensive exam, thesis/dissertation; for Diploma, thesis or alternative, final project. *Entrance requirements:* For master's, minimum undergraduate QPA of 2.67; for doctorate, GRE, MAT; for Diploma, GRE General Test or MAT, minimum graduate QPA of 3.0. Additional exam requirements/recommendations for international students: Recommended—TOEFL (minimum score 550 paper-based; 80 iBT), IELTS (minimum score 6.5). Electronic applications accepted. *Expenses:* Contact institution.

University of California, Irvine, School of Education, Irvine, CA 92697. Offers educational administration (Ed D); educational administration and leadership (Ed D); elementary and secondary education (MAT). *Program availability:* Part-time, evening/weekend. *Students:* 210 full-time (157 women), 1 (woman) part-time; includes 104 minority (1 Black or African American, non-Hispanic/Latino; 46 Asian, non-Hispanic/Latino; 39 Hispanic/Latino; 1 Native Hawaiian or other Pacific Islander, non-Hispanic/Latino; 17 Two or more races, non-Hispanic/Latino), 20 international. Average age 27. 451 applicants, 46% accepted, 147 enrolled. In 2017, 130 master's, 7 doctorates awarded. *Entrance requirements:* For master's, GRE, minimum GPA of 3.0; for doctorate, GRE General Test, minimum GPA of 3.0. Additional exam requirements/recommendations for international students: Required—TOEFL (minimum score 550 paper-based). *Application deadline:* For fall admission, 1/2 priority date for domestic students, 1/2 for international students. Application fee: $105 ($125 for international students). Electronic applications accepted. *Financial support:* Fellowships, research assistantships with full tuition reimbursements, institutionally sponsored loans, traineeships, health care benefits, and unspecified assistantships available. Financial award application deadline: 3/1; financial award applicants required to submit FAFSA. *Faculty research:* Education technology, learning theory, social theory, cultural diversity, postmodernism. *Unit head:* Richard Arum, Dean, 949-824-2534, E-mail: richard.arum@uci.edu. *Application contact:* Denise Earley, Assistant Director of Student Affairs, 949-824-4022, E-mail: denise.earley@uci.edu.
Website: http://education.uci.edu/

University of Central Oklahoma, The Jackson College of Graduate Studies, College of Education and Professional Studies, Department of Educational Sciences, Foundations and Research, Edmond, OK 73034-5209. Offers secondary education (M Ed). *Program availability:* Part-time. *Faculty:* 8 full-time (5 women). *Students:* 6 full-time (3 women), 45 part-time (32 women); includes 16 minority (2 Black or African American, non-Hispanic/Latino; 4 American Indian or Alaska Native, non-Hispanic/Latino; 1 Asian, non-Hispanic/Latino; 2 Hispanic/Latino; 7 Two or more races, non-Hispanic/Latino). Average age 34. 28 applicants, 89% accepted, 15 enrolled. In 2017, 23 master's awarded. *Degree requirements:* For master's, comprehensive exam (for some programs). *Entrance requirements:* Additional exam requirements/recommendations for international students: Required—TOEFL (minimum score 550 paper-based; 79 iBT), IELTS (minimum score 6.5). *Application deadline:* For fall admission, 7/15 for international students; for spring admission, 11/15 for international students. Applications are processed on a rolling basis. Application fee: $60. Electronic applications accepted. *Expenses:* Tuition, state resident: full-time $5375; part-time $268.75 per credit hour. Tuition, nonresident: full-time $13,295; part-time $664.75 per credit hour. *Required fees:* $626; $31.30 per credit hour. One-time fee: $50. Tuition and fees vary according to program. *Financial support:* In 2017–18, 10 students received support, including 1 research assistantship with partial tuition reimbursement available (averaging $2,958 per year); teaching assistantships, career-related internships or fieldwork, scholarships/grants, tuition waivers (partial), and unspecified assistantships also available. Financial award application deadline: 3/31; financial award applicants required to submit FAFSA. *Unit head:* Dr. Mike Nelson, Chair, 405-974-5431, Fax: 405-974-3830. *Application contact:* Carlie Wellington, Assistant Director, CEPS Graduate Enrollment, 405-974-5105, Fax: 405-974-3851, E-mail: gradcoll@uco.edu.
Website: http://sites.uco.edu/ceps/dept/Education-Programs/esfr/index.asp

University of Colorado Denver, School of Education and Human Development, Information and Learning Technologies Program, Denver, CO 80217. Offers e-learning design and implementation (MA); instructional design and adult learning (MA); K-12 teaching (MA). *Program availability:* Part-time, evening/weekend, online learning. *Degree requirements:* For master's, comprehensive exam (for some programs), comprehensive exam or online portfolio; 30 credit hours. *Entrance requirements:* For master's, GRE or MAT (if GPA is below 2.75), resume, statement of intent, three letters of recommendation, transcripts from all colleges/universities previously attended. Additional exam requirements/recommendations for international students: Required—TOEFL (minimum score 537 paper-based; 75 iBT); Recommended—IELTS (minimum score 6.5). Electronic applications accepted. *Expenses:* Contact institution. *Faculty research:* Technology for educational management, instructional design foundations, e-learning, educational design.

University of Colorado Denver, School of Education and Human Development, Teacher Education Programs, Denver, CO 80217. Offers elementary linguistically diverse education (MA); elementary math and science education (MA); elementary math education (MA); elementary reading and writing (MA); elementary science education (MA); secondary English education (MA); secondary linguistically diverse education (MA); secondary math education (MA); secondary reading and writing (MA); secondary science education (MA); special education (MA). *Accreditation:* NCATE. *Program availability:* Part-time, evening/weekend. *Degree requirements:* For master's, comprehensive exam. *Entrance requirements:* For master's, GRE or MAT (for those with GPA below 2.75), transcripts, resume, letters of recommendation. Additional exam requirements/recommendations for international students: Required—TOEFL (minimum score 537 paper-based; 75 iBT); Recommended—IELTS (minimum score 6.5). Electronic applications accepted. *Expenses:* Contact institution. *Faculty research:* Linguistically diverse education/ESL, elementary reading and writing, elementary teacher education, secondary teacher education, special education.

University of Connecticut, Graduate School, Neag School of Education, Department of Curriculum and Instruction, Program in Secondary Education, Storrs, CT 06269. Offers MA, PhD. *Accreditation:* NCATE. Terminal master's awarded for partial completion of doctoral program. *Degree requirements:* For master's, comprehensive exam, thesis or alternative; for doctorate, thesis/dissertation. *Entrance requirements:* For doctorate, GRE General Test. Additional exam requirements/recommendations for international students: Required—TOEFL (minimum score 550 paper-based). Electronic applications accepted.

University of Dayton, Department of Teacher Education, Dayton, OH 45469. Offers adolescence to young adult education (MS Ed); early childhood leadership and advocacy (MS Ed); interdisciplinary education (MS Ed), including visual arts; interdisciplinary education studies (MS Ed); leadership in educational systems (MS Ed); literacy (MS Ed); mathematics education (MS Ed); middle childhood education (MS Ed); multi-age education (MS Ed), including world languages; music education (MS Ed); teacher as leader (MS Ed); teacher education (MS Ed); technology-enhanced learning (MS Ed); trans-disciplinary early childhood education (MS Ed). *Program availability:* Part-time, 100% online. *Faculty:* 23 full-time (38 women), 41 part-time/adjunct (36 women). *Students:* 45 full-time (38 women), 68 part-time (57 women); includes 7 minority (3 Black or African American, non-Hispanic/Latino; 1 Hispanic/Latino; 3 Two or more races, non-Hispanic/Latino), 6 international. Average age 31. 106 applicants, 28% accepted. In 2017, 70 master's awarded. *Degree requirements:* For master's, variable foreign language requirement, thesis or alternative, internship (for teaching licensure or endorsement). *Entrance requirements:* For master's, GRE (minimum score of 149 verbal, 4 on writing) or MAT (minimum score of 396) if undergraduate GPA was under 2.75, minimum GPA of 2.75, 3 letters of recommendation, personal statement or resume, official transcripts. Additional exam requirements/recommendations for international students: Required—TOEFL (minimum score 550 paper-based; 80 iBT); Recommended—IELTS (minimum score 6.5). *Application deadline:* Applications are processed on a rolling basis. Application fee: $0 ($50 for international students). Electronic applications accepted. *Expenses:* Contact institution. *Financial support:* In 2017–18, 5 research assistantships with partial tuition reimbursements (averaging $9,640 per year) were awarded; teaching assistantships, career-related internships or fieldwork, institutionally sponsored loans, and unspecified assistantships also available. Financial award application deadline: 3/1; financial award applicants required to submit FAFSA. *Faculty research:* Social emotional learning, culturally responsive teaching, urban teaching, literacy, instructional strategies, pre-service teacher education preparation. *Unit head:* Dr. Connie L. Bowman, Chair, 937-229-3348, E-mail: cbowman1@udayton.edu. *Application contact:* Gina Seiter, Coordinator of Graduate Programs and Licensing, 937-229-3103, E-mail: gseiter1@udayton.edu. Website: https://www.udayton.edu/education/departments_and_programs/edt

University of Guam, Office of Graduate Studies, School of Education, Program in Secondary Education, Mangilao, GU 96923. Offers M Ed. *Degree requirements:* For master's, thesis, comprehensive oral and written exams. *Entrance requirements:* For master's, GRE General Test. Additional exam requirements/recommendations for international students: Required—TOEFL.

University of Illinois at Chicago, College of Education, Department of Curriculum and Instruction, Chicago, IL 60607-7128. Offers curriculum studies (PhD); elementary education (M Ed); secondary education (M Ed). *Program availability:* Part-time, evening/weekend. *Degree requirements:* For doctorate, thesis/dissertation. *Entrance requirements:* For master's, minimum GPA of 2.75; for doctorate, GRE General Test, minimum GPA of 2.75. Additional exam requirements/recommendations for international students: Required—TOEFL. Electronic applications accepted. *Faculty research:* Curriculum theory, curriculum development, research on teaching, curriculum and context, reading/literacy.

University of Indianapolis, Graduate Programs, School of Education, Indianapolis, IN 46227-3697. Offers art education (MAT); biology (MAT); chemistry (MAT); curriculum and instruction (MA); earth sciences (MAT); education (MA, MAT); educational leadership (MA); elementary education (MA); English (MAT); French (MAT); math (MAT); physical education (MAT); physics (MAT); secondary education (MA), including art education, education, English education, social studies education; social studies (MAT); Spanish (MAT). *Accreditation:* NCATE. *Program availability:* Part-time, evening/weekend. *Entrance requirements:* For master's, GRE Subject Test, PRAXIS I, minimum GPA of 2.5, 3 letters of recommendation, interview. Additional exam requirements/recommendations for international students: Required—TOEFL (minimum score 550 paper-based). *Faculty research:* Assessment of teacher education, perceptions of prospective teachers by parents.

The University of Iowa, Graduate College, College of Education, Department of Teaching and Learning, Program in Education, Iowa City, IA 52242-1316. Offers art education (MA); developmental reading (MA); elementary education (MA); English education (MA, MAT); foreign and second language education (MAT); foreign language education (MA); foreign language/ESL education (PhD); language, literacy and culture (PhD); mathematics education (MA, MAT, PhD); music education (MM, PhD); science education (MA); secondary education (MA); social studies (MA, PhD). *Degree requirements:* For master's, thesis optional, exam; for doctorate, comprehensive exam, thesis/dissertation. *Entrance requirements:* For master's and doctorate, GRE General Test, minimum GPA of 3.0. Additional exam requirements/recommendations for international students: Required—TOEFL (minimum score 550 paper-based; 81 iBT). Electronic applications accepted.

University of Kentucky, Graduate School, College of Education, Program in Curriculum and Instruction, Lexington, KY 40506-0032. Offers curriculum and instruction (Ed D, PhD); elementary education (MA Ed); instructional system design (MS Ed);

literacy (MA Ed); middle school education (MA Ed, MS Ed); secondary education (MA Ed, MS Ed). *Accreditation:* NCATE. *Degree requirements:* For master's, comprehensive exam, thesis optional; for doctorate, comprehensive exam, thesis/dissertation. *Entrance requirements:* For master's, GRE General Test, minimum undergraduate GPA of 2.75; for doctorate, GRE General Test, minimum graduate GPA of 3.0. Additional exam requirements/recommendations for international students: Required—TOEFL (minimum score 550 paper-based). Electronic applications accepted. *Faculty research:* Educational reform, multicultural education, classroom instructional practices, performance based assessment, primary school programs.

University of La Verne, Regional and Online Campuses, Graduate Programs, High Desert Campus, Victorville, CA 92392. Offers business administration for experienced professionals (MBA); educational (special emphasis) (M Ed); educational counseling (MS); leadership and management (MS); multiple subject (elementary) (Credential); preliminary administrative services (Credential); pupil personnel services (Credential); single subject (secondary) (Credential). *Students:* 7 full-time (3 women), 16 part-time (12 women); includes 14 minority (3 Black or African American, non-Hispanic/Latino; 1 American Indian or Alaska Native, non-Hispanic/Latino; 1 Asian, non-Hispanic/Latino; 9 Hispanic/Latino). Average age 41. In 2017, 9 master's awarded. *Application deadline:* Applications are processed on a rolling basis. Application fee: $50. *Expenses:* Contact institution. *Financial support:* Application deadline: 3/2; applicants required to submit FAFSA. *Unit head:* Juli Roberts, Regional Campus Director, 760-955-6448, Fax: 760-843-9505, E-mail: jroberts@laverne.edu. *Application contact:* Admissions, 760-955-6440, Fax: 760-955-6443, E-mail: hdcv@laverne.edu. Website: https://laverne.edu/locations/

University of La Verne, Regional and Online Campuses, Graduate Programs, Kern County Campus, Bakersfield, CA 93301. Offers business administration for experienced professionals (MBA-EP); education (special emphasis) (M Ed); educational counseling (MS); educational leadership (M Ed); health administration (MHA); leadership and management (MS); mild/moderate education specialist (Credential); multiple subject (elementary) (Credential); organizational leadership (Ed D); preliminary administrative services (Credential); single subject (secondary) (Credential); special education studies (MS). *Program availability:* Part-time, evening/weekend. *Students:* Average age 36. In 2017, 3 master's awarded. *Application deadline:* Applications are processed on a rolling basis. Application fee: $50. *Expenses:* Contact institution. *Financial support:* Institutionally sponsored loans available. Financial award application deadline: 3/2; financial award applicants required to submit FAFSA. *Unit head:* Nora Dominguez, Regional Campus Director, 661-861-6802, E-mail: ndominguez@laverne.edu. *Application contact:* Rebecca Murillo, Associate Director of Admissions, 661-861-6807, E-mail: rmurillo@laverne.edu. Website: https://laverne.edu/locations/

University of La Verne, Regional and Online Campuses, Graduate Programs, Ventura County/Point Mugu Naval Air Station Campuses, Oxnard, CA 93036. Offers business administration for experienced professionals (MS); educational counseling (MS); educational leadership (M Ed); leadership and management (MS); multiple subject (elementary) (Credential); pupil personnel services (Credential); single subject (secondary) (Credential). *Program availability:* Part-time, evening/weekend. *Students:* Average age 38. In 2017, 19 master's awarded. Application fee: $50. *Expenses:* Contact institution. *Financial support:* Institutionally sponsored loans available. Financial award application deadline: 3/2; financial award applicants required to submit FAFSA. *Unit head:* Kitt Vincent, Senior Executive Director, 805-788-6202, E-mail: kvincent@laverne.edu. *Application contact:* Mike Stadler, Assistant Director/Academic Advisor, 805-986-6909, E-mail: mstadler3@laverne.edu. Website: https://laverne.edu/locations/

University of Louisiana at Monroe, Graduate School, College of Arts, Education, and Sciences, School of Education, Program in Secondary Education, Monroe, LA 71209-0001. Offers MAT. *Accreditation:* NCATE. *Program availability:* Part-time, evening/weekend. *Faculty:* 11 full-time (7 women). *Students:* 3 full-time (1 woman), 11 part-time (5 women); includes 4 minority (2 Black or African American, non-Hispanic/Latino; 1 Hispanic/Latino; 1 Two or more races, non-Hispanic/Latino). Average age 30. 16 applicants, 19% accepted, 2 enrolled. In 2017, 14 master's awarded. *Entrance requirements:* For master's, GRE General Test, PRAXIS, minimum GPA of 2.5. Additional exam requirements/recommendations for international students: Required—TOEFL (minimum score 500 paper-based; 61 iBT). *Application deadline:* For fall admission, 8/24 priority date for domestic students, 7/1 for international students; for winter admission, 12/14 priority date for domestic students; for spring admission, 1/19 for domestic students, 11/1 for international students. Applications are processed on a rolling basis. Application fee: $20 ($30 for international students). Electronic applications accepted. *Expenses:* Tuition, state resident: full-time $6489; part-time $479 per hour. Tuition, nonresident: full-time $12,100; part-time $479 per hour. *Required fees:* $8860; $802 per hour. $3273 per semester. *Financial support:* Career-related internships or fieldwork, Federal Work-Study, and unspecified assistantships available. Financial award application deadline: 4/1; financial award applicants required to submit FAFSA.

University of Louisville, Graduate School, College of Education and Human Development, Departments of Early Childhood and Elementary Education, Middle and Secondary Education, and Special Education, Louisville, KY 40292-0001. Offers art education (MAT); autism and applied behavior analysis (Certificate); curriculum and instruction (PhD); early elementary education (MAT); exercise physiology (MS); health and physical education (MAT); health professions education (Certificate); higher education (MA); human resources and organization development (MS); instructional technology (M Ed); interdisciplinary early childhood education (MAT); middle school education (MAT); music education (MAT); secondary education (MAT); special education (MAT); sport administration (MS); teacher leadership (M Ed). *Program availability:* Part-time, evening/weekend. *Students:* 114 full-time (73 women), 173 part-time (114 women); includes 49 minority (19 Black or African American, non-Hispanic/Latino; 5 Asian, non-Hispanic/Latino; 13 Hispanic/Latino; 12 Two or more races, non-Hispanic/Latino), 7 international. Average age 29. 132 applicants, 73% accepted, 57 enrolled. In 2017, 70 master's, 2 doctorates, 2 other advanced degrees awarded. *Application deadline:* For spring admission, 1/1 priority date for international students. Application fee: $65. *Expenses:* Tuition, state resident: full-time $12,246; part-time $681 per credit hour. Tuition, nonresident: full-time $25,486; part-time $1417 per credit hour. *Required fees:* $196. Tuition and fees vary according to course load, program and reciprocity agreements. *Financial support:* Application deadline: 6/1; applicants required to submit FAFSA. *Faculty research:* STEM teaching and learning; content literacy for English language learners; social justice in teacher education; adolescent literacy; mathematics teacher development. *Total annual research expenditures:* $1.7 million. *Unit head:* Dr. Ann E. Larson, Dean, College of Education and Human Development, 502-852-6411, Fax: 502-852-1464, E-mail: ann@louisville.edu. *Application contact:* Betty Hampton, Director of Graduate Student Services, 502-852-5597, Fax: 502-852-1465, E-mail: edadvise@louisville.edu. Website: http://louisville.edu/delphi

University of Mary Hardin-Baylor, Graduate Studies in Education, Belton, TX 76513. Offers curriculum and instruction (M Ed); educational administration (M Ed, Ed D), including higher education (Ed D), leadership in nursing education (Ed D), P-12 (Ed D).

Secondary Education

Program availability: Part-time, evening/weekend. *Faculty:* 12 full-time (8 women), 5 part-time/adjunct (2 women). *Students:* 29 full-time (20 women), 79 part-time (55 women); includes 53 minority (35 Black or African American, non-Hispanic/Latino; 17 Hispanic/Latino; 1 Two or more races, non-Hispanic/Latino), 1 international. Average age 39. 15 applicants, 80% accepted, 10 enrolled. In 2017, 47 master's, 16 doctorates awarded. *Degree requirements:* For master's, comprehensive exam; for doctorate, thesis/dissertation. *Entrance requirements:* For master's, minimum GPA of 3.0, interview; for doctorate, minimum GPA of 3.5, interview, essay, resume, employment verification, 3 letters of recommendation. Additional exam requirements/recommendations for international students: Required—TOEFL (minimum score 60 iBT), IELTS (minimum score 4.5). *Application deadline:* For fall admission, 6/1 for domestic students, 4/30 priority date for international students; for spring admission, 11/1 for domestic students, 9/30 priority date for international students. Applications are processed on a rolling basis. Application fee: $35 ($135 for international students). Electronic applications accepted. *Expenses:* $920 per credit hour. *Financial support:* In 2017–18, 90 students received support. Federal Work-Study and scholarships for some active duty military personnel available. Support available to part-time students. Financial award application deadline: 6/1; financial award applicants required to submit FAFSA. *Faculty research:* Motivational orientation of preservice teachers. *Unit head:* Dr. Craig Hammonds, Director, Graduate Programs in Education, 254-295-4189, E-mail: rhammonds@umhb.edu. *Application contact:* Sharon Aguilera, Assistant Director, Graduate Admissions, 254-295-4835, E-mail: saguilera@umhb.edu. Website: https://go.umhb.edu/graduate/education/home

University of Maryland, College Park, Academic Affairs, College of Education, Department of Teaching, Learning, Policy and Leadership, College Park, MD 20742. Offers reading (M Ed, MA, PhD, CAGS); secondary education (M Ed, MA, Ed D, PhD, CAGS); teaching English to speakers of other languages (M Ed). *Accreditation:* NCATE. *Program availability:* Part-time, evening/weekend, online learning. *Degree requirements:* For master's, comprehensive exam, seminar paper; for doctorate, comprehensive exam, thesis/dissertation, published paper, oral exam. *Entrance requirements:* For master's, GRE General Test or MAT, minimum GPA of 3.0, 3 letters of recommendation; for doctorate, GRE General Test or MAT, minimum undergraduate GPA of 3.0, graduate 3.5; 3 letters of recommendation. Electronic applications accepted. *Faculty research:* Teacher preparation, curriculum study, in-service education.

University of Massachusetts Amherst, Graduate School, College of Education, Program in Education, Amherst, MA 01003. Offers bilingual, English as a second language, and multicultural education (M Ed, Ed S); child study and early education (M Ed); children, families and schools (Ed D, Ed S); early childhood and elementary teacher education (M Ed); educational leadership (M Ed); educational policy and leadership (Ed D); higher education (M Ed); international education (M Ed); language, literacy and culture (Ed D); learning, media and technology (M Ed, Ed S); mathematics, science, and learning technologies (Ed D); reading and writing (M Ed); research, educational measurement and psychometrics (Ed D); school counselor education (M Ed, Ed S); school psychology (Ed S); science education (Ed S); secondary teacher education (M Ed); social justice education (M Ed, Ed D, Ed S); special education (M Ed, Ed D, Ed S); teacher education and school improvement (Ed D, Ed S). *Accreditation:* NCATE. *Program availability:* Part-time, online learning. Terminal master's awarded for partial completion of doctoral program. *Degree requirements:* For doctorate, comprehensive exam, thesis/dissertation. *Entrance requirements:* Additional exam requirements/recommendations for international students: Required—TOEFL (minimum score 550 paper-based; 80 iBT), IELTS (minimum score 6.5). Electronic applications accepted.

University of Massachusetts Dartmouth, Graduate School, College of Arts and Sciences, School of Education, Department of STEM Education and Teacher Development, North Dartmouth, MA 02747-2300. Offers English as a second language (Postbaccalaureate Certificate); mathematics education (PhD); middle school education (MAT); secondary school education (MAT). *Program availability:* Part-time. *Faculty:* 9 full-time (6 women), 11 part-time/adjunct (7 women). *Students:* 26 full-time (15 women), 102 part-time (60 women); includes 16 minority (2 Black or African American, non-Hispanic/Latino; 2 Asian, non-Hispanic/Latino; 6 Hispanic/Latino; 6 Two or more races, non-Hispanic/Latino), 2 international. Average age 32. 60 applicants, 92% accepted, 51 enrolled. In 2017, 41 master's, 2 doctorates awarded. *Degree requirements:* For doctorate, thesis/dissertation. *Entrance requirements:* For master's, statement of purpose (minimum of 300 words), resume, 2 letters of recommendation, official transcripts; for doctorate, GRE, statement of purpose (minimum of 300 words), resume, official transcripts, 3 letters of recommendation. Additional exam requirements/recommendations for international students: Required—TOEFL (minimum score 533 paper-based; 72 iBT), IELTS (minimum score 6). *Application deadline:* For fall admission, 2/15 priority date for domestic students, 1/15 priority date for international students; for spring admission, 1/15 priority date for domestic students, 12/15 priority date for international students. Application fee: $60. Electronic applications accepted. *Expenses:* Tuition, state resident: full-time $15,449; part-time $643.71 per credit. Tuition, nonresident: full-time $27,880; part-time $1161.67 per credit. *Required fees:* $405; $25.88 per credit. Tuition and fees vary according to course load and reciprocity agreements. *Financial support:* In 2017–18, 2 fellowships (averaging $16,000 per year), 4 research assistantships (averaging $20,656 per year), 2 teaching assistantships (averaging $16,000 per year) were awarded; tuition waivers (full) and unspecified assistantships also available. Support available to part-time students. Financial award application deadline: 3/1; financial award applicants required to submit FAFSA. *Faculty research:* Mindfulness in education, literacies, assessment of teacher knowledge, curriculum tools for supporting mathematics learning. *Total annual research expenditures:* $1.6 million. *Unit head:* Traci Almeida, Coordinator of Graduate Admissions and Licensure, 508-999-8098, Fax: 508-910-8183, E-mail: talmeida@umassd.edu. *Application contact:* Steven Briggs, Director of Marketing and Recruitment for Graduate Studies, 508-999-8604, Fax: 508-999-8183, E-mail: graduate@umassd.edu.
Website: http://www.umassd.edu/cas/schoolofeducation/departments/stemeducationandteacherdevelopment/

University of Memphis, Graduate School, College of Education, Department of Instruction and Curriculum Leadership, Memphis, TN 38152. Offers advanced studies in teaching and learning (M Ed); applied behavior analysis (Graduate Certificate); autism studies (Graduate Certificate); early childhood education (MAT, MS, Ed D); elementary education (MAT); instruction and curriculum (MS, Ed D); instruction design and technology (MS, Ed D); instructional design and technology (Graduate Certificate); literacy, leadership, and coaching (Graduate Certificate); reading (MS, Ed D); school library information specialist (Graduate Certificate); secondary education (MAT); special education (MAT, MS, Ed D); STEM teacher leadership (Graduate Certificate); urban education (Graduate Certificate). *Accreditation:* NCATE (one or more programs are accredited). *Program availability:* Part-time. *Faculty:* 22 full-time (14 women), 14 part-time/adjunct (10 women). *Students:* 36 full-time (27 women), 351 part-time (271 women); includes 159 minority (132 Black or African American, non-Hispanic/Latino; 1 American Indian or Alaska Native, non-Hispanic/Latino; 7 Asian, non-Hispanic/Latino; 10 Hispanic/Latino; 9 Two or more races, non-Hispanic/Latino), 4 international. Average age 35. 170 applicants, 85% accepted, 111 enrolled. In 2017, 84 master's, 14

doctorates, 32 other advanced degrees awarded. Terminal master's awarded for partial completion of doctoral program. *Degree requirements:* For master's, comprehensive exam, thesis or alternative; for doctorate, comprehensive exam, thesis/dissertation. *Entrance requirements:* For master's, GRE General Test, PRAXIS, minimum GPA of 2.5, letters of reference; for doctorate, GRE General Test, GRE Subject Test, 2 years of teaching experience, letters of reference, statement of purpose, interview. Additional exam requirements/recommendations for international students: Required—TOEFL (minimum score 550 paper-based; 79 iBT). *Application deadline:* For fall admission, 4/1 priority date for domestic students; for spring admission, 10/1 priority date for domestic students; for summer admission, 2/1 priority date for domestic students. Applications are processed on a rolling basis. Application fee: $35 ($60 for international students). Electronic applications accepted. *Expenses:* Contact institution. *Financial support:* In 2017–18, 2 research assistantships with full tuition reimbursements (averaging $10,000 per year), 3 teaching assistantships with full tuition reimbursements (averaging $10,666 per year) were awarded; career-related internships or fieldwork, Federal Work-Study, institutionally sponsored loans, scholarships/grants, traineeships, and unspecified assistantships also available. Support available to part-time students. Financial award application deadline: 2/1; financial award applicants required to submit FAFSA. *Faculty research:* Effective urban teachers, preparation and retention of urban teachers, technology utilization in schools, field-based teacher preparation programs, effective use of online instruction. *Unit head:* Dr. Angiline Powell, Interim Chair, 901-678-3310, E-mail: apowell3@memphis.edu. *Application contact:* Dr. James Meindl, Coordinator of Graduate Studies, 901-678-3310, E-mail: jnmeindl@memphis.edu.
Website: http://www.memphis.edu/icl/

University of Michigan–Flint, School of Education and Human Services, Department of Education, Flint, MI 48502-1950. Offers curriculum and instruction (Ed S); early childhood education (MA); education (Ed D); educational leadership (Ed S); educational technology (MA), including curriculum and instruction, developer; literacy education (MA); secondary education with certification (MA). *Program availability:* Part-time, evening/weekend, 100% online, mixed mode format (for some programs). *Faculty:* 18 full-time (11 women), 26 part-time/adjunct (13 women). *Students:* 34 full-time (23 women), 192 part-time (137 women); includes 61 minority (46 Black or African American, non-Hispanic/Latino; 2 Asian, non-Hispanic/Latino; 5 Hispanic/Latino; 2 Native Hawaiian or other Pacific Islander, non-Hispanic/Latino; 6 Two or more races, non-Hispanic/Latino), 2 international. Average age 39. 124 applicants, 87% accepted, 81 enrolled. In 2017, 89 master's, 3 doctorates awarded. *Degree requirements:* For master's, thesis optional; for doctorate, thesis/dissertation. *Entrance requirements:* For master's, bachelor's degree from regionally-accredited institution, minimum overall undergraduate GPA of 3.0; for doctorate, Ed S; minimum overall graduate GPA of 3.3 (6.0 on a 9.0 scale) or equivalent; at least 3 years of work experience in a P-16 educational institution or in an education-related position; for Ed S, MA or MS in education-related field from accredited institution; minimum overall graduate GPA of 3.0 (6.0 on a 9.0 scale) or equivalent; at least 3 years of work experience in an educational setting. Additional exam requirements/recommendations for international students: Required—TOEFL (minimum score 84 iBT), IELTS (minimum score 6.5). *Application deadline:* For fall admission, 8/1 for domestic students, 5/1 for international students; for winter admission, 11/15 for domestic students, 9/15 for international students; for spring admission, 3/15 for domestic students, 1/15 for international students; for summer admission, 5/15 for domestic students. Applications are processed on a rolling basis. Application fee: $55. Electronic applications accepted. *Expenses:* Contact institution. *Financial support:* Federal Work-Study, scholarships/grants, and unspecified assistantships available. Financial award application deadline: 3/1; financial award applicants required to submit FAFSA. *Unit head:* Dr. Mary Jo Finney, Department Chair/Associate Professor, 810-766-6617, E-mail: mjfinney@umflint.edu. *Application contact:* Bradley T. Maki, Director of Graduate Admissions, 810-762-3171, Fax: 810-766-6789, E-mail: bmaki@umflint.edu.
Website: https://www.umflint.edu/education/graduate-programs

University of Mississippi, Graduate School, School of Education, University, MS 38677. Offers counselor education (M Ed, PhD); counselor education - play therapy (Ed S); early childhood (M Ed); educational leadership K-12 (M Ed, Ed D, PhD, Ed S); elementary education (M Ed, Ed D, Ed S); higher education/student personnel (Ed D, PhD); literacy education (M Ed); math education (Ed D); secondary education (M Ed, PhD, Ed S); special education (M Ed, PhD, Ed S); teacher corporations (MA); teacher education (MA). *Accreditation:* NCATE. *Faculty:* 65 full-time (40 women), 25 part-time/adjunct (5 women). *Students:* 185 full-time (148 women), 410 part-time (310 women); includes 193 minority (168 Black or African American, non-Hispanic/Latino; 7 Asian, non-Hispanic/Latino; 14 Hispanic/Latino; 4 Two or more races, non-Hispanic/Latino), 7 international. Average age 33. In 2017, 176 master's, 20 doctorates, 37 other advanced degrees awarded. *Entrance requirements:* For master's, GRE General Test, minimum GPA of 3.0; for doctorate, GRE General Test. Additional exam requirements/recommendations for international students: Required—TOEFL. *Application deadline:* For fall admission, 3/1 for domestic students; for spring admission, 10/1 for domestic students; for summer admission, 3/1 for domestic students. Applications are processed on a rolling basis. Application fee: $50. Electronic applications accepted. *Financial support:* Scholarships/grants available. Financial award application deadline: 3/1; financial award applicants required to submit FAFSA. *Unit head:* Dr. David Rock, Dean, 662-915-7063, Fax: 662-915-7249, E-mail: soe@olemiss.edu. *Application contact:* Dr. Joe Sumrall, Professor of Elementary Education, 662-915-7350, E-mail: soe@olemiss.edu.

University of Missouri–St. Louis, College of Education, Department of Educator Preparation, Innovation and Research, St. Louis, MO 63121. Offers elementary education (M Ed), including early childhood, general, reading; secondary education (M Ed), including curriculum and instruction, general, middle level education, reading, teaching English to speakers of other languages (TESOL); special education (M Ed), including autism and developmental disabilities, early childhood special education. *Program availability:* Part-time, evening/weekend. *Students:* 75 full-time (63 women), 462 part-time (363 women); includes 127 minority (85 Black or African American, non-Hispanic/Latino; 2 American Indian or Alaska Native, non-Hispanic/Latino; 8 Asian, non-Hispanic/Latino; 24 Hispanic/Latino; 8 Two or more races, non-Hispanic/Latino), 1 international. 247 applicants, 92% accepted, 153 enrolled. *Degree requirements:* For master's, comprehensive exam. *Entrance requirements:* Additional exam requirements/recommendations for international students: Recommended—TOEFL (minimum score 550 paper-based; 79 iBT), IELTS (minimum score 6.5). *Application deadline:* For fall admission, 7/1 priority date for domestic and international students; for spring admission, 12/1 priority date for domestic and international students. Application fee: $50 ($40 for international students). Electronic applications accepted. *Expenses:* Tuition, state resident: part-time $476.50 per credit hour. Tuition, nonresident: part-time $1169.70 per credit hour. *Financial support:* Application deadline: 4/1; applicants required to submit FAFSA. *Unit head:* Dr. Gayle Wilkinson, Chair, 314-516-5791. *Application contact:* 314-516-5458, Fax: 314-516-6996, E-mail: gadadm@umsl.edu.
Website: https://coe.umsl.edu/dept/epir.html

University of Montevallo, College of Education, Program in Secondary/High School Education, Montevallo, AL 35115. Offers M Ed. *Accreditation:* NCATE. *Students:* 32 full-time (20 women), 46 part-time (28 women); includes 16 minority (14 Black or African American, non-Hispanic/Latino; 1 Hispanic/Latino; 1 Two or more races, non-Hispanic/

Latino). *Entrance requirements:* For master's, GRE General Test, MAT, minimum undergraduate GPA of 2.5. Additional exam requirements/recommendations for international students: Required—TOEFL (minimum score 550 paper-based). *Application deadline:* For fall admission, 7/15 for domestic students; for spring admission, 11/15 for domestic students. Application fee: $30. *Expenses:* Tuition, state resident: full-time $9888. Tuition, nonresident: full-time $21,144. *Required fees:* $1920. *Financial support:* Federal Work-Study, scholarships/grants, and unspecified assistantships available. *Unit head:* Dr. Charlotte Daughhetee, Interim Dean, 205-665-6360, E-mail: daughc@montevallo.edu. *Application contact:* Colleen Kennedy, Graduate Program Assistant, 205-665-6350, E-mail: ckennedy@montevallo.edu.

University of Nebraska at Kearney, College of Education, Department of Teacher Education, Kearney, NE 68849-0001. Offers curriculum and instruction (MA Ed), including early childhood education, elementary education, English as a second language, instructional effectiveness, reading/special education, secondary education; instructional technology (MS Ed), including information technology, instructional technology, school librarian; reading PK-12 (MA Ed); special education (MA Ed), including advanced practitioner: assistive technology specialist, advanced practitioner: behavioral interventionist, advanced practitioner: inclusive collaboration specialist, gifted, teacher education. *Program availability:* Part-time, evening/weekend, online only, 100% online. *Degree requirements:* For master's, comprehensive exam, thesis optional. *Entrance requirements:* For master's, portfolio or GRE. Additional exam requirements/recommendations for international students: Recommended—TOEFL (minimum score 550 paper-based; 79 iBT), IELTS (minimum score 6.5). Electronic applications accepted. *Expenses:* Contact institution.

University of Nebraska at Omaha, Graduate Studies, College of Education, Department of Teacher Education, Program in Secondary Education, Omaha, NE 68182. Offers instruction in urban schools (Certificate); secondary education (MS). *Accreditation:* NCATE. *Program availability:* Part-time, evening/weekend. *Degree requirements:* For master's, comprehensive exam, thesis (for some programs). *Entrance requirements:* For master's, minimum GPA of 3.0, transcripts. Additional exam requirements/recommendations for international students: Required—TOEFL, IELTS, PTE. Electronic applications accepted.

University of Nevada, Las Vegas, Graduate College, College of Education, Department of Teaching and Learning, Las Vegas, NV 89154-3005. Offers curriculum and instruction (M Ed, MS, Ed D, PhD, Ed S), including teacher education (PhD); elementary teaching (Certificate); online teaching and training (Certificate); secondary teaching (Certificate); social justice studies (Certificate); teaching and learning (PhD). *Program availability:* Part-time, evening/weekend. *Faculty:* 27 full-time (13 women), 10 part-time/adjunct (8 women). *Students:* 315 full-time (222 women), 244 part-time (161 women); includes 226 minority (58 Black or African American, non-Hispanic/Latino; 2 American Indian or Alaska Native, non-Hispanic/Latino; 24 Asian, non-Hispanic/Latino; 104 Hispanic/Latino; 2 Native Hawaiian or other Pacific Islander, non-Hispanic/Latino; 36 Two or more races, non-Hispanic/Latino), 10 international. Average age 35. 234 applicants, 89% accepted, 174 enrolled. In 2017, 153 master's, 16 doctorates, 3 other advanced degrees awarded. *Degree requirements:* For master's, comprehensive exam (for some programs), thesis (for some programs); for doctorate, comprehensive exam, thesis/dissertation, defense of dissertation; for other advanced degree, comprehensive exam (for some programs), oral presentation of special project or professional paper. *Entrance requirements:* For master's, bachelor's degree with minimum GPA 2.75; for doctorate, GRE General Test, master's degree with minimum GPA of 3.0; statement of purpose; demonstration of oral communication skills; 3 letters of recommendation; for other advanced degree, PRAXIS Core (for some programs); PRAXIS II (for some programs), bachelor's degree (for some programs). Additional exam requirements/recommendations for international students: Required—TOEFL (minimum score 550 paper-based; 80 iBT), IELTS (minimum score 7). *Application deadline:* For fall admission, 6/1 for domestic students, 5/1 for international students; for spring admission, 11/1 for domestic students, 10/1 for international students; for summer admission, 3/15 for domestic students. Application fee: $60 ($95 for international students). Electronic applications accepted. *Expenses:* $275 per credit, $850 per course, $7,969 per year resident, $22,157 per year non-resident, $7,094 non-resident fee (7 credits or more), $1,307 annual health insurance fee. *Financial support:* In 2017–18, 36 students received support, including 13 research assistantships with full tuition reimbursements available (averaging $18,065 per year), 23 teaching assistantships with full tuition reimbursements available (averaging $19,564 per year); institutionally sponsored loans, scholarships/grants, health care benefits, and unspecified assistantships also available. Financial award application deadline: 3/15; financial award applicants required to submit FAFSA. *Faculty research:* Content area and critical literacy, education in content areas, teacher education, STEM education, immersive environments/simulations/games. *Total annual research expenditures:* $1.1 million. *Unit head:* Dr. Emily Lin, Chair/Professor, 702-895-6407, Fax: 702-895-4898, E-mail: emily.lin@unlv.edu. *Application contact:* Dr. Travis Olson, Graduate Coordinator, 702-895-0471, Fax: 702-895-4898, E-mail: travis.olson@unlv.edu. Website: http://tl.unlv.edu/

University of Nevada, Reno, Graduate School, College of Education, Department of Curriculum, Teaching and Learning, Program in Secondary Education, Reno, NV 89557. Offers M Ed, MA, MS. *Degree requirements:* For master's, thesis optional. *Entrance requirements:* For master's, GRE General Test, minimum GPA of 2.75. Additional exam requirements/recommendations for international students: Required—TOEFL (minimum score 500 paper-based; 61 iBT), IELTS (minimum score 6). Electronic applications accepted. *Faculty research:* Educational trends, pedagogy.

University of New Hampshire, Graduate School, College of Liberal Arts, Department of Education, Program in Secondary Education, Durham, NH 03824. Offers M Ed, MAT. *Program availability:* Part-time. *Students:* 16 full-time (11 women), 34 part-time (25 women); includes 2 minority (1 Hispanic/Latino; 1 Two or more races, non-Hispanic/Latino). Average age 25. 24 applicants, 88% accepted, 17 enrolled. In 2017, 67 master's awarded. *Entrance requirements:* For master's, PRAXIS, Department of Education background check. Additional exam requirements/recommendations for international students: Required—TOEFL (minimum score 550 paper-based; 80 iBT). *Application deadline:* For fall admission, 4/15 for domestic and international students; for spring admission, 11/1 for domestic students; for summer admission, 4/15 for domestic students. Application fee: $65. Electronic applications accepted. *Financial support:* In 2017–18, 4 students received support. Fellowships, research assistantships, teaching assistantships, career-related internships or fieldwork, Federal Work-Study, scholarships/grants, and tuition waivers (full and partial) available. Support available to part-time students. Financial award application deadline: 2/15. *Unit head:* Paula Salvio, Chair, 603-862-0024, E-mail: education.department@unh.edu. *Application contact:* Cindy Glidden, Department Coordinator, 603-862-2311, E-mail: education.department@unh.edu. Website: http://cola.unh.edu/education

University of New Hampshire, Graduate School Manchester Campus, Manchester, NH 03101. Offers business administration (MBA); cybersecurity policy and risk management (MS); educational administration and supervision (Ed S); educational studies (M Ed); elementary education (M Ed); information technology (MS); public administration (MPA); public health (MPH, Certificate); secondary education (M Ed,

MAT); social work (MSW); substance use disorders (Certificate). *Program availability:* Part-time, evening/weekend. *Students:* 13 full-time (6 women), 17 part-time (0 women); includes 7 minority (1 Black or African American, non-Hispanic/Latino; 4 Asian, non-Hispanic/Latino; 1 Hispanic/Latino; 1 Two or more races, non-Hispanic/Latino), 10 international. Average age 33. 42 applicants, 71% accepted, 8 enrolled. In 2017, 4 master's awarded. *Entrance requirements:* Additional exam requirements/recommendations for international students: Required—TOEFL (minimum score 550 paper-based; 80 iBT). *Application deadline:* For fall admission, 6/1 for domestic students, 4/1 for international students; for spring admission, 12/1 for domestic students. Application fee: $65. Electronic applications accepted. *Financial support:* Fellowships, research assistantships, teaching assistantships, Federal Work-Study, scholarships/grants, health care benefits, and unspecified assistantships available. Support available to part-time students. Financial award application deadline: 2/15; financial award applicants required to submit FAFSA. *Unit head:* Candice Morey, Educational Programs Coordinator, 603-641-4313, E-mail: unhm.gradcenter@unh.edu. Website: http://www.gradschool.unh.edu/manchester/

University of New Mexico, Graduate Studies, College of Education, Program in Secondary Education, Albuquerque, NM 87131-2039. Offers math, science, and educational technology (MA). *Program availability:* Part-time. *Students:* Average age 33. 35 applicants, 80% accepted, 22 enrolled. In 2017, 42 master's awarded. *Degree requirements:* For master's, comprehensive exam, thesis optional. *Entrance requirements:* For master's, minimum overall GPA of 3.0, some experience working with students, NMTA or teacher's licensure, 3 letters of reference, letter of intent. Additional exam requirements/recommendations for international students: Required—TOEFL (minimum score 500 paper-based). *Application deadline:* For fall admission, 2/1 for domestic students; for spring admission, 10/1 for domestic students. Application fee: $50. Electronic applications accepted. *Financial support:* Teaching assistantships with partial tuition reimbursements, career-related internships or fieldwork, scholarships/grants, and unspecified assistantships available. Financial award application deadline: 4/15. *Faculty research:* Secondary education, teacher education, reflective practice, teacher leadership, student learning. *Unit head:* Dr. Cheryl Torrez, Chair, 505-277-0911, Fax: 505-277-0455, E-mail: ted@unm.edu. *Application contact:* Robert Romero, Administrative Assistant, 505-277-0513, Fax: 505-277-0455, E-mail: ted@unm.edu. Website: http://coe.unm.edu/departments-programs/teelp/secondary-education/index.html

University of North Alabama, College of Education, Department of Secondary Education, Program in Secondary Education, Florence, AL 35632-0001. Offers secondary education (MA Ed); special education (MA Ed). *Accreditation:* NCATE. *Program availability:* Part-time, 100% online, blended/hybrid learning. *Faculty:* 7 full-time (3 women), 2 part-time/adjunct (1 woman). *Students:* 44 full-time (26 women), 30 part-time (19 women); includes 9 minority (4 Black or African American, non-Hispanic/Latino; 2 American Indian or Alaska Native, non-Hispanic/Latino; 1 Hispanic/Latino; 2 Two or more races, non-Hispanic/Latino). Average age 31. 49 applicants, 86% accepted, 21 enrolled. In 2017, 27 master's awarded. *Degree requirements:* For master's, comprehensive exam. *Entrance requirements:* For master's, GRE, MAT, or NTE, minimum GPA of 2.5, Alabama Class B Certificate or equivalent, teaching experience. Additional exam requirements/recommendations for international students: Required—TOEFL (minimum score 79 iBT), IELTS (minimum score 6), PTE (minimum score 54). *Application deadline:* Applications are processed on a rolling basis. Application fee: $50 ($100 for international students). Electronic applications accepted. *Expenses:* Tuition, state resident: full-time $7824; part-time $5943 per year. Tuition, nonresident: full-time $15,648; part-time $11,736 per year. *Required fees:* $3064; $2298 per unit. Tuition and fees vary according to course load and reciprocity agreements. *Financial support:* In 2017–18, 19 students received support. Federal Work-Study, scholarships/grants, and unspecified assistantships available. Financial award application deadline: 2/1; financial award applicants required to submit FAFSA. *Unit head:* Dr. Jessica Mitchell, Interim Chair, 256-765-4575, E-mail: jmitchell12@una.edu. *Application contact:* Hillary N. Coats, Graduate Admissions Coordinator, 256-765-4447, E-mail: graduate@una.edu. Website: https://www.una.edu/education/departments/secondary-education.html

The University of North Carolina at Chapel Hill, Graduate School, School of Education, Program in Secondary Education, Chapel Hill, NC 27599. Offers English (Grades 9-12) (MAT); English as a second language (MAT); French (Grades K-12) (MAT); German (Grades K-12) (MAT); Japanese (Grades K-12) (MAT); Latin (Grades 9-12) (MAT); mathematics (Grades 9-12) (MAT); music (Grades K-12) (MAT); science (Grades 9-12) (MAT); social studies (Grades 9-12) (MAT); Spanish (Grades K-12) (MAT). *Accreditation:* NCATE. *Degree requirements:* For master's, comprehensive exam. *Entrance requirements:* For master's, GRE General Test, minimum GPA of 3.0 during last 2 years of undergraduate course work. Additional exam requirements/recommendations for international students: Required—TOEFL (minimum score 550 paper-based). Electronic applications accepted.

The University of North Carolina at Charlotte, Cato College of Education, Department of Middle, Secondary and K-12 Education, Charlotte, NC 28223-0001. Offers middle grades and secondary education (M Ed); teaching English as a second language (M Ed, Graduate Certificate). *Program availability:* Part-time. *Faculty:* 18 full-time (10 women), 5 part-time/adjunct (all women). *Students:* 3 full-time (all women), 93 part-time (85 women); includes 20 minority (18 Black or African American, non-Hispanic/Latino; 1 Asian, non-Hispanic/Latino; 1 Hispanic/Latino), 2 international. Average age 35. 71 applicants, 99% accepted, 61 enrolled. In 2017, 47 master's awarded. *Degree requirements:* For master's, thesis, comprehensive portfolio, or research project. *Entrance requirements:* For master's, GRE or MAT, bachelor's degree from accredited college or university; minimum GPA of 3.0 in undergraduate work; North Carolina Class A teaching license in appropriate middle grades or secondary education field; minimum of two years' teaching experience; written narrative providing statement of purpose for master's degree study; letters of recommendation; for Graduate Certificate, bachelor's degree from accredited institution; minimum undergraduate GPA of 2.5 overall or 3.0 in senior year, or 15 hours taken in the last 5 years; satisfactory recommendations from three persons knowledgeable of applicant's interactions with children or adolescents; statement of purpose. Additional exam requirements/recommendations for international students: Required—TOEFL (minimum score 523 paper-based, 70 iBT) or IELTS (6.5). *Application deadline:* For fall admission, 3/1 priority date for domestic and international students; for spring admission, 10/1 priority date for domestic and international students; for summer admission, 4/1 priority date for domestic and international students. Applications are processed on a rolling basis. Application fee: $75. Electronic applications accepted. *Expenses:* Tuition, state resident: full-time $4337. Tuition, nonresident: full-time $17,771. *Required fees:* $3211. Tuition and fees vary according to course load and program. *Financial support:* In 2017–18, 6 students received support, including 5 research assistantships (averaging $13,800 per year), 1 teaching assistantship (averaging $3,500 per year); career-related internships or fieldwork, institutionally sponsored loans, scholarships/grants, and unspecified assistantships also available. Support available to part-time students. Financial award application deadline: 3/1; financial award applicants required to submit FAFSA. *Total annual research expenditures:* $115,616. *Unit head:* Scott Kissau, Chair, 704-687-8875, E-mail: spkissau@uncc.edu. *Application contact:* Kathy B. Giddings, Director of Graduate Admissions, 704-687-5503, Fax: 704-687-1668, E-mail: gradadm@uncc.edu. Website: http://mdsk.uncc.edu/

SECTION 24: INSTRUCTIONAL LEVELS

Secondary Education

The University of North Carolina at Charlotte, Cato College of Education, Interdisciplinary Education Programs, Charlotte, NC 28223-0001. Offers art education (Graduate Certificate); child and family development: early childhood education (MAT); curriculum and instruction (PhD); elementary education (MAT); foreign language education (MAT); middle grades education (MAT); secondary education (MAT); special education (MAT); teaching (Graduate Certificate); teaching English as a second language (MAT); theatre education (Graduate Certificate). *Program availability:* Part-time, 100% online, blended/hybrid learning. *Students:* 86 full-time (63 women), 533 part-time (423 women); includes 229 minority (169 Black or African American, non-Hispanic/Latino; 1 American Indian or Alaska Native, non-Hispanic/Latino; 7 Asian, non-Hispanic/Latino; 39 Hispanic/Latino; 13 Two or more races, non-Hispanic/Latino), 13 international. Average age 32. 382 applicants, 91% accepted, 253 enrolled. In 2017, 182 master's, 10 doctorates, 172 other advanced degrees awarded. *Degree requirements:* For master's, thesis or alternative, research project/portfolio. *Entrance requirements:* For master's, GRE or MAT, bachelor's degree, or its U.S. equivalent, from regionally-accredited college or university; minimum overall GPA of 3.0 on all previous work beyond high school; statement of purpose (essay); at least three recommendation forms; for doctorate, GRE or MAT, bachelor's degree (or its U.S. equivalent) from regionally-accredited college or university; minimum overall GPA of 3.5 in master's degree program; for Graduate Certificate, bachelor's degree from regionally-accredited university; minimum GPA of 2.75 on all post-secondary work attempted; transcripts; personal statement outlining why the applicant seeks admission to the program. Additional exam requirements/recommendations for international students: Required— TOEFL (minimum score 523 paper-based, 70 iBT) or IELTS (6.5). *Application deadline:* For fall admission, 3/1 priority date for domestic and international students; for spring admission, 10/1 priority date for domestic and international students; for summer admission, 4/1 priority date for domestic and international students. Applications are processed on a rolling basis. Application fee: $75. Electronic applications accepted. *Expenses:* Tuition, state resident: full-time $4337. Tuition, nonresident: full-time $17,771. *Required fees:* $3211. Tuition and fees vary according to course load and program. *Financial support:* Career-related internships or fieldwork, institutionally sponsored loans, scholarships/grants, and unspecified assistantships available. Support available to part-time students. Financial award application deadline: 3/1; financial award applicants required to submit FAFSA. *Unit head:* Dr. Ellen McIntyre, Dean, 704-687-8722, E-mail: ellen.mcintyre@uncc.edu. *Application contact:* Kathy B. Giddings, Director of Graduate Admissions, 704-687-5503, Fax: 704-687-1668, E-mail: gradadm@uncc.edu.
Website: http://education.uncc.edu/academic-programs

The University of North Carolina Wilmington, Watson College of Education, Department of Instructional Technology, Foundations and Secondary Education, Wilmington, NC 28403-3297. Offers English as a second language (M Ed, MAT); instructional technology (MS); secondary education (M Ed, MAT). *Program availability:* Part-time, blended/hybrid learning. *Faculty:* 15 full-time (9 women). *Students:* 38 full-time (24 women), 90 part-time (63 women); includes 29 minority (12 Black or African American, non-Hispanic/Latino; 2 Asian, non-Hispanic/Latino; 10 Hispanic/Latino; 5 Two or more races, non-Hispanic/Latino). Average age 34. 51 applicants, 84% accepted, 39 enrolled. In 2017, 44 master's awarded. *Degree requirements:* For master's, thesis or research project/portfolio. *Entrance requirements:* For master's, GRE or MAT, education statement of interest essay, 3 letters of recommendation. Additional exam requirements/recommendations for international students: Required—TOEFL (minimum score 550 paper-based; 79 iBT), IELTS (minimum score 6.5). *Application deadline:* For fall admission, 5/15 for domestic students; for spring admission, 10/15 for domestic students; for summer admission, 3/15 for domestic students. Applications are processed on a rolling basis. Application fee: $75. Electronic applications accepted. *Expenses:* Tuition, state resident: full-time $4626; part-time $226.76 per credit hour. Tuition, nonresident: full-time $17,834; part-time $874.22 per credit hour. *Required fees:* $2124. Tuition and fees vary according to program. *Financial support:* Scholarships/grants and unspecified assistantships available. Financial award application deadline: 1/1; financial award applicants required to submit FAFSA. *Unit head:* Dr. Eleni Pappamihiel, Chair, 910-962-2746, Fax: 910-962-3609, E-mail: pappamihieln@uncw.edu. *Application contact:* Dr. Mahnaz Moallem, Graduate Coordinator, 910-962-4183, E-mail: moallemm@uncw.edu.
Website: http://www.uncw.edu/ed/itfse/

University of Northern Iowa, Graduate College, College of Humanities, Arts and Sciences, Department of Languages and Literatures, MA Program in Teaching English in Secondary Schools, Cedar Falls, IA 50614. Offers MA.

University of Northern Iowa, Graduate College, College of Humanities, Arts and Sciences, Department of Mathematics, MA Program in Mathematics, Cedar Falls, IA 50614. Offers community college teaching (MA); mathematics (MA); secondary teaching (MA).

University of North Florida, College of Education and Human Services, Department of Foundations and Secondary Education, Jacksonville, FL 32224. Offers adult learning (M Ed); professional education (M Ed). *Accreditation:* NCATE. *Program availability:* Part-time, evening/weekend. *Entrance requirements:* For master's, GRE General Test, minimum GPA of 3.0 in last 60 hours, interview, 3 letters of recommendation. Additional exam requirements/recommendations for international students: Required—TOEFL (minimum score 500 paper-based; 61 iBT). Electronic applications accepted. *Faculty research:* Using children's literature to enhance metalinguistic awareness, education, oral language diagnosis of middle-schoolers, science inquiry teaching and learning.

University of North Georgia, Master of Arts in Teaching Program, Dahlonega, GA 30597. Offers physical education (MAT); secondary education - English (MAT); secondary education - history (MAT); secondary education - mathematics (MAT); secondary education - middle grades (MAT). *Students:* 27 part-time (20 women). Average age 29. 12 applicants, 75% accepted, 7 enrolled. In 2017, 15 master's awarded. *Degree requirements:* For master's, internship, capstone. *Entrance requirements:* For master's, GRE or MAT, GACE I and II, GA pre-service application, lawful presence verification, official transcripts, GA Educator Ethics Program entry assessment. Additional exam requirements/recommendations for international students: Required—TOEFL (minimum score 550 paper-based; 79 iBT), IELTS (minimum score 6.5). *Application deadline:* For summer admission, 2/1 for domestic students. Application fee: $40. Electronic applications accepted. *Expenses:* Contact institution. *Financial support:* Application deadline: 3/17; applicants required to submit FAFSA. *Unit head:* Dr. Susan Brandenburg-Ayres, Dean, 706-864-1998, E-mail: susan.ayres@ung.edu. *Application contact:* Melinda Maxwell, Director of Graduate Admissions, 706-867-2077, E-mail: melinda.maxwell@ung.edu.
Website: https://ung.edu/teacher-education/graduate/master-of-arts-teaching.php

University of Pennsylvania, Graduate School of Education, Division of Teaching, Learning, and Leadership, Teacher Education Program, Philadelphia, PA 19104. Offers elementary education (MS Ed); secondary education (MS Ed). *Students:* Average age 25. 123 applicants, 81% accepted. In 2017, 60 master's awarded. *Degree requirements:* For master's, thesis or alternative, student teaching, portfolio. *Entrance requirements:* For master's, GRE, bachelor's degree. Additional exam requirements/recommendations for international students: Required—TOEFL, IELTS. *Application deadline:* For summer admission, 6/1 priority date for domestic students, 6/1 for international students. Applications are processed on a rolling basis. Application fee: $75. Electronic applications accepted. *Financial support:* In 2017–18, 53 students received support. Federal Work-Study and scholarships/grants available. Financial award applicants required to submit FAFSA. *Faculty research:* Teacher competencies, social justice teaching, teacher practitioner inquiry. *Unit head:* Maureen Cotterill, Program Manager, 215-898-7364.
Website: http://www2.gse.upenn.edu/tep/

University of Phoenix–Bay Area Campus, College of Education, San Jose, CA 95134-1805. Offers administration and supervision (MA Ed); adult education and training (MA Ed); early childhood education (MA Ed); education (Ed S); educational leadership (Ed D); elementary teacher education (MA Ed); higher education administration (PhD); secondary teacher education (MA Ed); special education (MA Ed); teacher leadership (MA Ed). *Program availability:* Evening/weekend, online learning. *Degree requirements:* For master's, thesis (for some programs). *Entrance requirements:* For master's, minimum undergraduate GPA of 2.5, 3 years of work experience. Additional exam requirements/recommendations for international students: Required—TOEFL (minimum score 550 paper-based; 79 iBT). Electronic applications accepted.

University of Phoenix–Central Valley Campus, College of Education, Fresno, CA 93720-1552. Offers curriculum and instruction (MA Ed); curriculum and instruction-computer education (MA Ed); elementary teacher education (MA Ed); secondary teacher education (MA Ed).

University of Phoenix–Hawaii Campus, College of Education, Honolulu, HI 96813-3800. Offers administration and supervision (MA Ed); curriculum and instruction (MA Ed); elementary education (MA Ed); secondary education (MA Ed); special education (MA Ed); teacher education for elementary licensure (MA Ed). *Program availability:* Evening/weekend. *Degree requirements:* For master's, thesis (for some programs). *Entrance requirements:* For master's, minimum undergraduate GPA of 2.5, 3 years of work experience. Additional exam requirements/recommendations for international students: Required—TOEFL (minimum score 550 paper-based; 79 iBT). Electronic applications accepted.

University of Phoenix–Online Campus, College of Education, Phoenix, AZ 85034-7209. Offers administration and supervision (MAEd, Certificate); adult education and training (MAEd); curriculum and instruction (MAEd), including computer education, curriculum and instruction, English as a second language, language arts, mathematics, reading; early childhood education (MAEd); educational studies (MAEd); elementary teacher education (MAEd), including early childhood, elementary teacher education, high school middle level, middle level; principal licensure (Certificate); secondary teacher education (MAEd); special education (MAEd, Certificate); teacher education (MAEd), including middle level generalist; teacher education middle level mathematics (MAEd), including middle level mathematics; teacher education middle level science (MAEd), including middle level science; teacher education secondary mathematics (MAEd); teacher education secondary science (MAEd); teacher leadership (MAEd); teachers of English learners (Certificate); transition to teaching (Certificate), including elementary education, secondary education. *Program availability:* Evening/weekend, online learning. *Entrance requirements:* Additional exam requirements/recommendations for international students: Required—TOEFL, TOEIC (Test of English as an International Communication), Berlitz Online English Proficiency Exam, PTE, or IELTS. Electronic applications accepted. *Expenses:* Contact institution.

University of Phoenix–Phoenix Campus, College of Education, Tempe, AZ 85282-2371. Offers administration and supervision (MA Ed); adult education and training (MA Ed); curriculum and instruction reading (MA Ed); early childhood education (MA Ed); education studies (MA Ed); elementary teacher education (MA Ed); secondary teacher education (MA Ed); special education (MA Ed); teacher leadership (MA Ed). *Program availability:* Evening/weekend, online learning. *Entrance requirements:* Additional exam requirements/recommendations for international students: Required—TOEFL, TOEIC (Test of English as an International Communication), Berlitz Online English Proficiency Exam, PTE, or IELTS. Electronic applications accepted. *Expenses:* Contact institution.

University of Phoenix–Sacramento Valley Campus, College of Education, Sacramento, CA 95833-4334. Offers adult education (MA Ed); curriculum instruction (MA Ed); elementary teacher education (MA Ed); secondary teacher education (MA Ed); teacher education (Certificate). *Program availability:* Evening/weekend. *Degree requirements:* For master's, thesis (for some programs). *Entrance requirements:* For master's, 3 years of work experience, minimum undergraduate GPA of 2.5. Additional exam requirements/recommendations for international students: Required—TOEFL (minimum score 550 paper-based; 79 iBT). Electronic applications accepted.

University of Phoenix–San Diego Campus, College of Education, San Diego, CA 92123. Offers curriculum and instruction (MA Ed), including computer education, curriculum and instruction, English as a second language; elementary teacher education (MA Ed); secondary teacher education (MA Ed). *Program availability:* Evening/weekend. *Degree requirements:* For master's, thesis (for some programs). *Entrance requirements:* For master's, 3 years of work experience, minimum undergraduate GPA of 3.0. Additional exam requirements/recommendations for international students: Required—TOEFL (minimum score 550 paper-based; 79 iBT). Electronic applications accepted.

University of Pittsburgh, School of Education, Department of Instruction and Learning, Program in Secondary Education, Pittsburgh, PA 15260. Offers English and communications education (M Ed, MAT); foreign language education (M Ed, MAT); language, literacy and culture education (Ed D, PhD); mathematics education (M Ed, MAT, Ed D, PhD); science education (M Ed, MAT, Ed D, PhD); secondary education (PhD); social studies education (M Ed, MAT); STEM education (Ed D). *Program availability:* Part-time, evening/weekend. *Degree requirements:* For master's, thesis; for doctorate, thesis/dissertation. *Entrance requirements:* For master's, PRAXIS I; for doctorate, GRE General Test. Additional exam requirements/recommendations for international students: Required—TOEFL. Electronic applications accepted.

University of Puget Sound, School of Education, Program in Teaching, Tacoma, WA 98416. Offers elementary education (MAT); secondary education (MAT). *Accreditation:* NASM. *Degree requirements:* For master's, project. *Entrance requirements:* For master's, WEST-E or NES, WEST-B or ACT/SAT, two education foundation prerequisite courses; minor in content area (for secondary education). Additional exam requirements/recommendations for international students: Required—TOEFL (minimum score 550 paper-based; 90 iBT). Electronic applications accepted. *Expenses:* Contact institution. *Faculty research:* Pre-service teacher learning, public school partnerships and professional development, creating equitable classrooms, literacy development, teaching social studies.

University of St. Francis, College of Education, Joliet, IL 60435-6169. Offers educational leadership (MS, Ed D); elementary education (M Ed); reading (MS); secondary education (M Ed), including English education, math education, science education, social studies education, visual arts education; special education (M Ed); teaching and learning (MS); TESOL (Certificate). *Accreditation:* NCATE. *Program availability:* Part-time, evening/weekend, 100% online, blended/hybrid learning. *Faculty:* 11 full-time (8 women), 52 part-time/adjunct (36 women). *Students:* 39 full-time (32

women), 411 part-time (318 women); includes 106 minority (57 Black or African American, non-Hispanic/Latino; 8 Asian, non-Hispanic/Latino; 37 Hispanic/Latino; 4 Two or more races, non-Hispanic/Latino), 4 international. Average age 37. 277 applicants, 55% accepted, 137 enrolled. In 2017, 199 master's, 28 doctorates awarded. *Degree requirements:* For master's, comprehensive exam; for doctorate, thesis/dissertation. *Entrance requirements:* Additional exam requirements/recommendations for international students: Required—TOEFL (minimum score 550 paper-based; 79 iBT), IELTS (minimum score 6). *Application deadline:* Applications are processed on a rolling basis. Application fee: $30. Electronic applications accepted. Application fee is waived when completed online. *Expenses:* $365 to $748 per credit hour. *Financial support:* In 2017–18, 40 students received support. Scholarships/grants and unspecified assistantships available. Support available to part-time students. Financial award applicants required to submit FAFSA. *Unit head:* Dr. John Gambro, Dean, 815-740-3829, Fax: 815-740-2264, E-mail: jgambro@stfrancis.edu. *Application contact:* Sandra Sloka, Director of Admissions for Graduate and Degree Completion Programs, 800-735-7500, Fax: 815-740-3431, E-mail: ssloka@stfrancis.edu.
Website: http://www.stfrancis.edu/academics/college-of-education/

University of Saint Francis, Graduate School, Department of Education, Fort Wayne, IN 46808-3994. Offers secondary education (MAT); special education (MS Ed), including intense intervention, mild intervention. *Accreditation:* NCATE. *Program availability:* Part-time, evening/weekend, online only, 100% online. *Faculty:* 4 full-time (3 women), 3 part-time/adjunct (all women). *Students:* 6 full-time (5 women), 19 part-time (15 women); includes 1 minority (Hispanic/Latino). Average age 33. 17 applicants, 100% accepted, 14 enrolled. In 2017, 8 master's awarded. *Entrance requirements:* For master's, GRE (minimum composite score of 280 verbal and quantitative subtests) or MAT (minimum score of 389) if undergraduate GPA is below a 2.8 or prior graduate level GPA is below 3.0; GRE, ACT, SAT, or CASA exam if no license, minimum undergraduate GPA of 2.8; resume (if GPA is below 3.0); standard teaching license and/or bachelor's degree from regionally-accredited institution; background check; two professional recommendations. Additional exam requirements/recommendations for international students: Required—TOEFL (minimum score 550 paper-based) or IELTS (minimum score 6.5). *Application deadline:* For fall admission, 7/1 for international students; for spring admission, 11/1 for international students; for summer admission, 3/1 for international students. Applications are processed on a rolling basis. Application fee: $0. Electronic applications accepted. *Expenses:* $475 per hour (for MAT); $905 per hour (for MS Ed). *Financial support:* Federal Work-Study, scholarships/grants, and unspecified assistantships available. Financial award application deadline: 4/15; financial award applicants required to submit FAFSA. *Unit head:* Mary Riepenhoff, Assistant Professor/Department Chair, 260-399-7700 Ext. 8409, Fax: 260-399-8170, E-mail: mriepenhoff@sf.edu. *Application contact:* Kyle Richardson, Associate Director of Enrollment Services for Adult Learning, 260-399-7700 Ext. 6310, Fax: 260-399-8152, E-mail: krichardson@sf.edu.
Website: https://education.sf.edu/

University of Saint Joseph, Department of Education, West Hartford, CT 06117-2700. Offers curriculum and instruction (MA); elementary education (MAT); instructional technology (MA); literacy (MA); secondary education (MAT); TESOL (MA). *Program availability:* Part-time, evening/weekend. *Degree requirements:* For master's, comprehensive exam, thesis or alternative. *Entrance requirements:* For master's, 2 letters of recommendation. *Application deadline:* Applications are processed on a rolling basis. Application fee: $50. Electronic applications accepted. Application fee is waived when completed online. *Financial support:* Career-related internships or fieldwork and unspecified assistantships available. Support available to part-time students. Financial award applicants required to submit FAFSA.
Website: https://www.usj.edu/academics/schools/sasbe/education/

University of St. Thomas, School of Education and Human Services, Houston, TX 77006-4696. Offers all level education (M Ed); bilingual/dual language (M Ed); Catholic school teaching (M Ed); Catholic/private school leadership (M Ed); counselor education (M Ed); curriculum and instruction (M Ed); education (Ed D); educational leadership (M Ed); elementary teaching (M Ed); English as a second language (M Ed); exceptionality/educational diagnostician (M Ed); exceptionality/special education (M Ed); generalist (M Ed); reading (M Ed); secondary teaching (M Ed); teaching (MAT). *Accreditation:* TEAC. *Program availability:* Part-time, evening/weekend, online learning. *Faculty:* 33 full-time (22 women), 43 part-time/adjunct (26 women). *Students:* 119 full-time (97 women), 597 part-time (529 women); includes 478 minority (166 Black or African American, non-Hispanic/Latino; 29 Asian, non-Hispanic/Latino; 277 Hispanic/Latino; 2 Native Hawaiian or other Pacific Islander, non-Hispanic/Latino; 4 Two or more races, non-Hispanic/Latino), 19 international. Average age 36. 306 applicants, 91% accepted, 181 enrolled. In 2017, 328 master's awarded. *Degree requirements:* For master's, thesis, field experience. *Entrance requirements:* For master's, GRE or MAT if GPA is below 3.0, bachelor's degree; minimum GPA of 2.75 in bachelor's degree or last 60 credit hours; official transcripts from all institutions; goal statement of 250-300 words; 1 reference. Additional exam requirements/recommendations for international students: Required—TOEFL (minimum score 94 iBT), IELTS (minimum score 7), PTE (minimum score 53). *Application deadline:* Applications are processed on a rolling basis. Application fee: $35. Electronic applications accepted. *Expenses:* Contact institution. *Financial support:* In 2017–18, 27 students received support. Federal Work-Study, scholarships/grants, and state work-study, institutional employment available. Support available to part-time students. Financial award application deadline: 4/15; financial award applicants required to submit FAFSA. *Faculty research:* Leadership, diversity, personality traits, second language acquisition. *Unit head:* Dr. Paul C. Paese, Dean, 713-942-5999, Fax: 713-525-3871, E-mail: paesep@stthom.edu. *Application contact:* 713-525-3540, E-mail: education@stthom.edu.
Website: http://www.stthom.edu/Academics/School_of_Education_and_Human_Services/Index.aqf

The University of Scranton, Panuska College of Professional Studies, Department of Education, Program in Secondary Education, Scranton, PA 18510. Offers MS. *Accreditation:* NCATE. *Program availability:* Part-time, evening/weekend. *Degree requirements:* For master's, comprehensive exam (for some programs), thesis (for some programs), capstone experience. *Entrance requirements:* For master's, minimum GPA of 3.0, three letters of reference. Additional exam requirements/recommendations for international students: Required—TOEFL (minimum score 500 paper-based; 80 iBT), IELTS (minimum score 6.5). Electronic applications accepted.

University of South Alabama, College of Education and Professional Studies, Department of Leadership and Teacher Education, Mobile, AL 36688. Offers art education (M Ed); early childhood education (M Ed); educational leadership (M Ed, Ed D); elementary education (M Ed); reading education (M Ed); science education (M Ed); secondary education (M Ed); special education (M Ed). *Accreditation:* NCATE. *Program availability:* Part-time. *Faculty:* 15 full-time (11 women), 10 part-time/adjunct (6 women). *Students:* 203 full-time (154 women), 90 part-time (68 women); includes 73 minority (54 Black or African American, non-Hispanic/Latino; 3 American Indian or Alaska Native, non-Hispanic/Latino; 4 Asian, non-Hispanic/Latino; 10 Hispanic/Latino; 2 Two or more races, non-Hispanic/Latino). Average age 34. 134 applicants, 55% accepted, 57 enrolled. In 2017, 73 master's, 8 doctorates awarded. *Degree*

requirements: For master's, comprehensive exam, thesis (for some programs); for doctorate, comprehensive exam, thesis/dissertation. *Entrance requirements:* For master's, GRE General Test or MAT, minimum GPA of 3.0; for doctorate, GRE, minimum graduate GPA of 3.25, 3 years of experience in field, 3 letters of recommendation, interview, official transcripts. Additional exam requirements/recommendations for international students: Required—TOEFL. *Application deadline:* For fall admission, 7/15 for domestic students, 6/15 for international students; for spring admission, 11/15 for domestic students, 11/1 for international students; for summer admission, 4/15 for domestic students, 4/1 for international students. Applications are processed on a rolling basis. Application fee: $35. Electronic applications accepted. *Expenses:* Tuition, state resident: full-time $10,104; part-time $421 per semester hour. Tuition, nonresident: full-time $20,208; part-time $842 per semester hour. *Financial support:* Fellowships, research assistantships, teaching assistantships, career-related internships or fieldwork, Federal Work-Study, institutionally sponsored loans, scholarships/grants, and unspecified assistantships available. Support available to part-time students. Financial award application deadline: 3/31; financial award applicants required to submit FAFSA. *Unit head:* Dr. Susan Santoli, Chair/Director of Graduate Studies, 251-380-2836, Fax: 251-380-2748, E-mail: ssantoli@southalabama.edu.
Website: http://www.southalabama.edu/colleges/ceps/lte/index.html

University of South Carolina, The Graduate School, College of Education, Department of Instruction and Teacher Education, Program in Secondary Education, Columbia, SC 29208. Offers art education (IMA, MAT); business education (IMA, MAT); English (MAT); foreign language (MAT); health education (MAT); mathematics (MAT); science (IMA, MAT); secondary (Ed D); secondary education (MT, PhD); social studies (MAT); theatre and speech (MAT). IMA and MT offered jointly with the subject areas. *Accreditation:* NCATE. *Degree requirements:* For master's, comprehensive exam, thesis (for some programs), foreign language (MA); for doctorate, one foreign language, comprehensive exam, thesis/dissertation. *Entrance requirements:* For master's, GRE General Test or MAT, teaching certificate (IMA, M Ed), interview; for doctorate, GRE General Test or MAT, interview. *Faculty research:* Middle school programs, professional development, school collaboration.

University of South Dakota, Graduate School, School of Education, Division of Curriculum and Instruction, Program in Secondary Education, Vermillion, SD 57069. Offers secondary education (MA), including English language learning, science, technology and math (STEM), secondary education plus certification. *Accreditation:* NCATE. *Program availability:* Part-time, online learning. *Degree requirements:* For master's, comprehensive exam, thesis or alternative. *Entrance requirements:* For master's, GRE General Test, MAT, minimum GPA of 2.7. Additional exam requirements/recommendations for international students: Required—TOEFL (minimum score 550 paper-based; 79 iBT). *Application deadline:* Applications are processed on a rolling basis. Application fee: $35. Electronic applications accepted. *Financial support:* Research assistantships with partial tuition reimbursements, teaching assistantships with partial tuition reimbursements, career-related internships or fieldwork, Federal Work-Study, and unspecified assistantships available. Financial award applicants required to submit FAFSA. *Application contact:* Graduate School, 605-658-6140, Fax: 605-677-6118.
Website: http://www.usd.edu/ci

University of Southern Indiana, Graduate Studies, Pott College of Science, Engineering, and Education, Department of Teacher Education, Program in Secondary Education, Evansville, IN 47712-3590. Offers secondary education (MSE), including mathematics teaching. *Accreditation:* NCATE. *Program availability:* Part-time, evening/weekend. *Faculty:* 4 full-time (3 women), 2 part-time/adjunct (1 woman). *Students:* 1 (woman) full-time. Average age 30. In 2017, 3 master's awarded. *Entrance requirements:* For master's, PRAXIS II, bachelor's degree with minimum cumulative GPA of 2.75 from college or university accredited by NCATE or comparable association; minimum GPA of 3.0 in all courses taken at graduate level at all schools attended; teaching license. Additional exam requirements/recommendations for international students: Required—TOEFL (minimum score 550 paper-based; 79 iBT), IELTS (minimum score 6). *Application deadline:* For fall admission, 7/1 priority date for domestic students, 1/1 priority date for international students. Applications are processed on a rolling basis. Application fee: $40. Electronic applications accepted. *Expenses:* Tuition, state resident: full-time $9394. Tuition, nonresident: full-time $17,917. *Required fees:* $510. *Financial support:* In 2017–18, 6 students received support. Federal Work-Study, institutionally sponsored loans, scholarships/grants, tuition waivers (full and partial), and unspecified assistantships available. Financial award application deadline: 3/1; financial award applicants required to submit FAFSA. *Unit head:* Dr. Bonnie Beach, Associate Dean, 812-465-1620, E-mail: blbeach@usi.edu. *Application contact:* Dr. Mayola Rowser, Director, Graduate Studies, 812-465-7015, Fax: 812-464-1956, E-mail: mrowser@usi.edu.
Website: http://www.usi.edu/science/teacher-education/programs/mse

University of Southern Mississippi, College of Education and Psychology, Department of Curriculum, Instruction and Special Education, Hattiesburg, MS 39406-0001. Offers elementary education (M Ed, PhD); instructional technology (MS); instructional technology and design (PhD); secondary education (MAT); special education (M Ed, PhD). *Program availability:* Part-time, online learning. *Students:* 25 full-time (18 women), 5 part-time (3 women). 41 applicants, 59% accepted, 22 enrolled. *Degree requirements:* For master's, comprehensive exam, thesis (for some programs); for doctorate, comprehensive exam, thesis/dissertation. *Entrance requirements:* For master's, GRE General Test, MAT, minimum GPA of 3.0; for doctorate, GRE General Test, minimum GPA of 3.5. Additional exam requirements/recommendations for international students: Required—TOEFL, IELTS. *Application deadline:* For fall admission, 3/1 priority date for domestic students, 3/1 for international students; for spring admission, 1/10 priority date for domestic and international students. Applications are processed on a rolling basis. Application fee: $60. *Expenses:* Tuition, state resident: full-time $3830. *Financial support:* Research assistantships with tuition reimbursements, teaching assistantships with full tuition reimbursements, Federal Work-Study, institutionally sponsored loans, scholarships/grants, health care benefits, tuition waivers (partial), and unspecified assistantships available. Financial award application deadline: 3/15; financial award applicants required to submit FAFSA. *Faculty research:* Mathematical problem solving, integrative curriculum, writing process, teacher education models. *Unit head:* Dr. Jeff Hinton, Chair.
Website: https://www.usm.edu/elementary-special-technology-education

University of South Florida, Innovative Education, Tampa, FL 33620-9951. Offers adult, career and higher education (Graduate Certificate), including college teaching, leadership in developing human resources, leadership in higher education; Africana studies (Graduate Certificate), including diasporas and health disparities, genocide and human rights; aging studies (Graduate Certificate), including gerontology; art research (Graduate Certificate), including museum studies; business foundations (Graduate Certificate); chemical and biomedical engineering (Graduate Certificate), including materials science and engineering, water, health and sustainability; child and family studies (Graduate Certificate), including positive behavior support; civil and industrial engineering (Graduate Certificate), including transportation systems analysis; community and family health (Graduate Certificate), including maternal and child health,

social marketing and public health, violence and injury: prevention and intervention, women's health; criminology (Graduate Certificate), including criminal justice administration; data science for public administration (Graduate Certificate); digital humanities (Graduate Certificate); educational measurement and research (Graduate Certificate), including evaluation; English (Graduate Certificate), including comparative literary studies, creative writing, professional and technical communication; entrepreneurship (Graduate Certificate); environmental health (Graduate Certificate), including safety management; epidemiology and biostatistics (Graduate Certificate), including applied biostatistics, biostatistics, concepts and tools of epidemiology, epidemiology, epidemiology of infectious diseases; geography, environment and planning (Graduate Certificate), including community development, environmental policy and management, geographical information systems; geology (Graduate Certificate), including hydrogeology; global health (Graduate Certificate), including disaster management, global health and Latin American and Caribbean studies, global health practice, humanitarian assistance, infection control; government and international affairs (Graduate Certificate), including Cuban studies, globalization studies; health policy and management (Graduate Certificate), including health management and leadership, public health policy and programs; hearing specialist: early intervention (Graduate Certificate); industrial and management systems engineering (Graduate Certificate), including systems engineering, technology management; information studies (Graduate Certificate), including school library media specialist; information systems/decision sciences (Graduate Certificate), including analytics and business intelligence; instructional technology (Graduate Certificate), including distance education, Florida digital/virtual educator, instructional design, multimedia design, Web design; internal medicine, bioethics and medical humanities (Graduate Certificate), including biomedical ethics; Latin American and Caribbean studies (Graduate Certificate); leadership for coastal resiliency planning (Graduate Certificate); mass communications (Graduate Certificate), including multimedia journalism; mathematics and statistics (Graduate Certificate), including mathematics; medicine (Graduate Certificate), including aging and neuroscience, bioinformatics, biotechnology, brain fitness and memory management, clinical investigation, hand and upper limb rehabilitation, health informatics, health sciences, integrative weight management, intellectual property, medicine and gender, metabolic and nutritional medicine, metabolic cardiology, pharmacy sciences; national and competitive intelligence (Graduate Certificate); nursing (Graduate Certificate), including simulation based academic fellowship in advanced pain management; psychological and social foundations (Graduate Certificate), including career counseling, college teaching, diversity in education, mental health counseling, school counseling; public affairs (Graduate Certificate), including nonprofit management, public management, research administration; public health (Graduate Certificate), including assessing chemical toxicity and public health risks, health equity, pharmacoepidemiology, public health generalist, toxicology, translational research in adolescent behavioral health; public health practices (Graduate Certificate), including planning for healthy communities; rehabilitation and mental health counseling (Graduate Certificate), including integrative mental health care, marriage and family therapy, rehabilitation technology; secondary education (Graduate Certificate), including ESOL, foreign language education: culture and content, foreign language education: professional; social work (Graduate Certificate), including geriatric social work/clinical gerontology; special education (Graduate Certificate), including autism spectrum disorder, disabilities education: severe/profound; world languages (Graduate Certificate), including teaching English as a second language (TESL) or foreign language. *Unit head:* Dr. Cynthia DeLuca, Associate Vice President and Assistant Vice Provost, 813-974-3077, Fax: 813-974-7061, E-mail: deluca@usf.edu. *Application contact:* Owen Hooper, Director, Summer and Alternative Calendar Programs, 813-974-6917, E-mail: hooper@usf.edu.
Website: http://www.usf.edu/innovative-education/

The University of Tennessee, Graduate School, College of Education, Health and Human Sciences, Program in Education, Knoxville, TN 37996. Offers art education (MS); counseling education (PhD); cultural studies in education (PhD); curriculum (MS, Ed S); curriculum, educational research and evaluation (Ed D, PhD); early childhood education (PhD); early childhood special education (MS); education of deaf and hard of hearing (MS); educational administration and policy studies (Ed D, PhD); educational administration and supervision (Ed S); educational psychology (Ed D, PhD); elementary education (MS, Ed S); elementary teaching (MS); English education (MS, Ed S); exercise science (PhD); foreign language/ESL education (MS, Ed S); instructional technology (MS, Ed D, PhD, Ed S); literacy, language and ESL education (PhD); literacy, language education, and ESL education (Ed D); mathematics education (MS, Ed S); modified and comprehensive special education (MS); reading education (MS, Ed S); school counseling (Ed S); school psychology (PhD, Ed S); science education (MS, Ed S); secondary teaching (MS); social foundations (MS); social science education (MS, Ed S); socio-cultural foundations of sports and education (PhD); special education (Ed S); teacher education (Ed D, PhD). *Accreditation:* NCATE. *Program availability:* Part-time, evening/weekend. *Degree requirements:* For master's and Ed S, thesis optional; for doctorate, variable foreign language requirement, thesis/dissertation. *Entrance requirements:* For master's, minimum GPA of 2.7; for doctorate and Ed S, GRE General Test, minimum GPA of 2.7. Additional exam requirements/recommendations for international students: Required—TOEFL. Electronic applications accepted.

The University of Tennessee at Chattanooga, School of Education, Chattanooga, TN 37403. Offers counseling (M Ed), including community counseling, school counseling; education (M Ed, Post-Master's Certificate), including elementary education (M Ed), school leadership (Post-Master's Certificate); elementary education (M Ed); learning and leadership (Ed D), including educational leadership; school leadership (Post-Master's Certificate); school leadership: principal licensure (Ed S); secondary education (M Ed); special education (M Ed). *Accreditation:* ACA; NCATE. *Program availability:* Part-time. *Students:* 43 full-time (30 women), 58 part-time (47 women); includes 18 minority (9 Black or African American, non-Hispanic/Latino; 1 Asian, non-Hispanic/Latino; 1 Hispanic/Latino; 7 Two or more races, non-Hispanic/Latino). Average age 31. 118 applicants, 75% accepted, 33 enrolled. In 2017, 59 master's, 7 other advanced degrees awarded. *Degree requirements:* For master's, comprehensive exam, thesis optional, culminating experience; for other advanced degree, internship. *Entrance requirements:* For master's, GRE General Test, PPST 1, teaching certificate; for other advanced degree, two letters of recommendation, graduate degree in education, teaching certificate with three years of experience. Additional exam requirements/recommendations for international students: Required—TOEFL (minimum score 550 paper-based; 79 iBT), IELTS (minimum score 6). *Application deadline:* For fall admission, 6/15 for domestic students, 7/1 for international students; for spring admission, 11/1 for domestic and international students. Applications are processed on a rolling basis. Application fee: $35 ($40 for international students). Electronic applications accepted. *Expenses:* Contact institution. *Financial support:* Research assistantships, teaching assistantships, career-related internships or fieldwork, institutionally sponsored loans, scholarships/grants, and unspecified assistantships available. Support available to part-time students. Financial award application deadline: 7/1; financial award applicants required to submit FAFSA. *Faculty research:* School counseling, community counseling, elementary and secondary education, school

leadership and administration. *Total annual research expenditures:* $576,495. *Unit head:* Dr. Renee Murley, Director, 423-425-4684, Fax: 423-425-5380, E-mail: renee-murley@utc.edu. *Application contact:* Dr. Joanne Romagni, Dean of the Graduate School, 423-425-4478, Fax: 423-425-5223, E-mail: joanne-romagni@utc.edu.
Website: https://www.utc.edu/school-education/

The University of Tennessee at Martin, Graduate Programs, College of Education, Health and Behavioral Sciences, Program in Teaching, Martin, TN 38238. Offers curriculum and instruction (MS Ed), including 7-12, K-6; initial licensure (MS Ed), including elementary education, secondary education; initial licensure K-12 (MS Ed), including physical education, special education; interdisciplinary (MS Ed). *Program availability:* Part-time, online only, 100% online. *Students:* 20 full-time (17 women), 92 part-time (66 women); includes 20 minority (14 Black or African American, non-Hispanic/Latino; 2 Hispanic/Latino; 4 Two or more races, non-Hispanic/Latino). Average age 32. 79 applicants, 70% accepted, 38 enrolled. In 2017, 14 master's awarded. *Entrance requirements:* Additional exam requirements/recommendations for international students: Required—TOEFL (minimum score 525 paper-based; 71 iBT). *Application deadline:* For fall admission, 7/27 for domestic and international students; for spring admission, 12/17 for domestic and international students; for summer admission, 5/10 for domestic and international students. Applications are processed on a rolling basis. Electronic applications accepted. *Expenses:* Tuition, state resident: full-time $8658; part-time $481 per credit hour. Tuition, nonresident: full-time $14,418; part-time $801 per credit hour. *International tuition:* $22,602 full-time. *Required fees:* $1404; $79 per credit hour. Part-time tuition and fees vary according to course load. *Financial support:* In 2017–18, 26 students received support, including 1 research assistantship with full tuition reimbursement available (averaging $6,283 per year), 5 teaching assistantships with full tuition reimbursements available (averaging $7,001 per year); scholarships/grants and tuition waivers also available. Financial award applicants required to submit FAFSA. *Faculty research:* Special education, science/math/technology, school reform, reading. *Unit head:* Cynthia West, Dean, 731-881-7125, Fax: 731-881-7975, E-mail: cwest@utm.edu. *Application contact:* Jolene L. Cunningham, Student Services Specialist, 731-881-7012, Fax: 731-881-7499, E-mail: jcunningham@utm.edu.

The University of Texas Rio Grande Valley, College of Education and P-16 Integration, Department of Teaching and Learning, Edinburg, TX 78539. Offers curriculum and instruction (M Ed, Ed D); educational technology (M Ed). *Program availability:* Part-time, evening/weekend. *Faculty:* 24. *Students:* 199. In 2017, 54 master's, 2 doctorates awarded. *Degree requirements:* For master's, comprehensive exam, thesis optional; for doctorate, comprehensive exam, thesis/dissertation. *Entrance requirements:* For master's, minimum GPA of 3.0. Additional exam requirements/recommendations for international students: Required—TOEFL (minimum score 550 paper-based; 79 iBT), IELTS (minimum score 6.5). *Application deadline:* For fall admission, 4/15 for domestic students; for spring admission, 11/1 for domestic students; for summer admission, 3/1 for domestic students. Applications are processed on a rolling basis. Application fee: $50 ($75 for international students). Electronic applications accepted. *Expenses:* Tuition, state resident: full-time $5550; part-time $417 per credit hour. Tuition, nonresident: full-time $13,020; part-time $832 per credit hour. *Required fees:* $1169. *Financial support:* Research assistantships, institutionally sponsored loans, scholarships/grants, and unspecified assistantships available. Financial award application deadline: 4/15; financial award applicants required to submit FAFSA. *Faculty research:* Teacher education, mathematics education, science education, educational technology, pedagogy. *Unit head:* Dr. James Jupp, Chair, 956-665-3401, E-mail: james.jupp@utrgv.edu. *Application contact:* Stephanie Ozuna, Graduate Student Recruiter, 956-665-3558, E-mail: stephanie.ozuna@utrgv.edu.

University of the Cumberlands, Graduate Programs in Education, Williamsburg, KY 40769-1372. Offers all grades (P-12) (M Ed); business and marketing (MA Ed, MAT); counselor education and supervision (Ed D); director of pupil personnel (Certificate); director of special education (Certificate); educational administration and supervision (Ed S); educational leadership (Ed D); elementary education (MA Ed, MAT); instructional leadership - principalship (MA Ed); instructional leadership - school principal (Certificate); middle school education (MA Ed, MAT); reading and writing (MA Ed); school counseling (MA Ed); school superintendent (Certificate); secondary education (MA Ed, MAT); special education (MAT); supervisor of instruction (Certificate); teacher leader (MA Ed). *Program availability:* Part-time, evening/weekend, online learning. *Degree requirements:* For master's, comprehensive exam. Electronic applications accepted.

University of the District of Columbia, College of Arts and Sciences, Program in Teaching, Washington, DC 20008-1175. Offers elementary education (MAT); middle school mathematics (MAT); secondary English language arts (MAT); secondary social studies (MAT).

University of the Virgin Islands, College of Science and Mathematics, St. Thomas, VI 00802. Offers marine and environmental science (MS); mathematics for secondary teachers (MA). *Program availability:* Part-time, online learning. *Degree requirements:* For master's, comprehensive exam, thesis. *Entrance requirements:* For master's, GRE, minimum GPA of 2.5. Additional exam requirements/recommendations for international students: Required—TOEFL (minimum score 550 paper-based). Electronic applications accepted.

The University of Toledo, College of Graduate Studies, Judith Herb College of Education, Department of Curriculum and Instruction, Toledo, OH 43606-3390. Offers art education (ME); career and technical education (ME, Ed S); curriculum and instruction (ME, PhD, Ed S); early childhood education (Ed S); education and anthropology (MAE); education and biology (MES); education and chemistry (MES); education and classics (MAE); education and economics (MAE); education and English (MAE); education and French (MAE); education and geology (MES); education and German (MAE); education and history (MAE); education and mathematics (MAE, MES); education and physics (MES); education and political science (MAE); education and sociology (MAE); education and Spanish (MAE); educational media (PhD); educational technology (ME); educational technology: virtual educator (Certificate); elementary education (PhD); English as a second language (MAE); gifted and talented education (PhD); middle childhood education (ME); secondary education (ME, PhD); special education (PhD). *Accreditation:* NCATE. *Program availability:* Part-time, evening/weekend. *Degree requirements:* For master's, comprehensive exam, thesis or alternative; for doctorate, comprehensive exam, thesis/dissertation; for other advanced degree, thesis optional. *Entrance requirements:* For master's, doctorate, and other advanced degree, minimum cumulative GPA of 2.7 for all previous academic work, letters of recommendation. Additional exam requirements/recommendations for international students: Required—TOEFL (minimum score 550 paper-based; 80 iBT). Electronic applications accepted.

University of Utah, Graduate School, College of Education, Department of Educational Leadership and Policy, Salt Lake City, UT 84084. Offers educational leadership and policy (Ed D, PhD), including higher education administration (Ed D), K-12 (Ed D); K-12 school administration (M Ed); K-12 teacher instructional leadership (M Ed); student affairs (M Ed); MPA/PhD. *Program availability:* Part-time, evening/weekend. *Faculty:* 10 full-time (7 women), 2 part-time/adjunct (both women). *Students:* 60 full-time (40 women), 185 part-time (124 women); includes 54 minority (14 Black or African

American, non-Hispanic/Latino; 5 American Indian or Alaska Native, non-Hispanic/Latino; 5 Asian, non-Hispanic/Latino; 24 Hispanic/Latino; 2 Native Hawaiian or other Pacific Islander, non-Hispanic/Latino; 4 Two or more races, non-Hispanic/Latino; 1 international. Average age 35. 181 applicants, 69% accepted, 90 enrolled. In 2017, 64 master's, 6 doctorates awarded. *Degree requirements:* For master's, comprehensive exam (for some programs), internship, capstone; for doctorate, thesis/dissertation, qualifying exam. *Entrance requirements:* For master's, minimum undergraduate GPA of 3.0, valid bachelor's degree, 3 years' teaching or leadership experience, Level 1 or 2 UT educator's license (for K-12 programs only); for doctorate, GRE General Test (taken with five years of applying), minimum undergraduate GPA of 3.0, valid master's degree. Additional exam requirements/recommendations for international students: Required—TOEFL (minimum score 550 paper-based). *Application deadline:* For fall admission, 1/15 priority date for domestic and international students; for winter admission, 2/1 for domestic and international students; for spring admission, 11/1 priority date for domestic and international students; for summer admission, 3/1 priority date for domestic and international students. Applications are processed on a rolling basis. Application fee: $55 ($65 for international students). Electronic applications accepted. *Expenses:* Contact institution. *Financial support:* In 2017–18, 12 students received support, including 1 fellowship with full tuition reimbursement available (averaging $15,000 per year), 2 research assistantships with full tuition reimbursements available (averaging $15,000 per year), 6 teaching assistantships with full tuition reimbursements available (averaging $15,000 per year); career-related internships or fieldwork, scholarships/grants, health care benefits, and unspecified assistantships also available. Support available to part-time students. Financial award application deadline: 3/1; financial award applicants required to submit FAFSA. *Faculty research:* Education accountability, college student diversity, K-12 educational administration and school leadership, student affairs, higher education. *Unit head:* Dr. Gerardo Lopez, Chair, 801-581-6971, Fax: 801-585-6756, E-mail: gerardo.lopez@utah.edu. *Application contact:* Marilynn S. Howard, Academic Coordinator, 801-581-6714, Fax: 801-585-6756, E-mail: marilynn.howard@utah.edu.
Website: http://elp.utah.edu/

University of Vermont, Graduate College, College of Education and Social Services, Program in Secondary Education, Burlington, VT 05405. Offers curriculum and instruction (MAT), including secondary education. *Entrance requirements:* For master's, major or its equivalent in a state-approved licensing area. Additional exam requirements/recommendations for international students: Required—TOEFL (minimum iBT score of 90) or IELTS (6.5). *Application deadline:* For fall admission, 2/1 for domestic and international students. Application fee: $65. Electronic applications accepted. *Expenses:* Tuition, state resident: full-time $11,628; part-time $646 per credit. Tuition, nonresident: full-time $29,340; part-time $1630 per credit. *Required fees:* $1994; $10 per credit. Tuition and fees vary according to course load and program. *Financial support:* In 2017–18, 2 students received support. Career-related internships or fieldwork and scholarships/grants available. Financial award application deadline: 3/1. *Unit head:* Regina Toolin, Coordinator, 802-656-1411, E-mail: regina.toolin@uvm.edu.
Website: https://www.uvm.edu/cess/doe/mat_secondary

University of Washington, Bothell, Program in Education, Bothell, WA 98011. Offers education (M Ed); leadership development for educators (M Ed); secondary/middle level endorsement (M Ed). *Program availability:* Part-time, evening/weekend. *Degree requirements:* For master's, thesis. *Entrance requirements:* Additional exam requirements/recommendations for international students: Required—TOEFL. Electronic applications accepted. *Faculty research:* Multicultural education in citizenship education, intercultural education, knowledge and practice in the principalship, educational public policy, national board certification for teachers, teacher learning in literacy, technology and its impact on teaching and learning of mathematics, reading assessments, professional development in literacy education and mobility, digital media, education and class.

The University of West Alabama, School of Graduate Studies, College of Education, Program in Secondary Education, Livingston, AL 35470. Offers biology (MAT); English language arts (MAT); high school 6-12 (M Ed); history (MAT); mathematics (MAT); science (MAT); social science (MAT). *Program availability:* Part-time, evening/weekend, 100% online. *Faculty:* 21 full-time (7 women), 5 part-time/adjunct (1 woman). *Students:* 259 (183 women); includes 61 minority (51 Black or African American, non-Hispanic/Latino; 2 American Indian or Alaska Native, non-Hispanic/Latino; 3 Asian, non-Hispanic/Latino; 2 Hispanic/Latino; 3 Two or more races, non-Hispanic/Latino). Average age 32. 58 applicants, 93% accepted, 45 enrolled. In 2017, 80 master's awarded. *Degree requirements:* For master's, comprehensive exam, thesis optional. *Entrance requirements:* For master's, GRE, minimum GPA of 2.75, verification of background clearance/fingerprints, valid bachelor's-level Professional Educator Certificate in same teaching field. Additional exam requirements/recommendations for international students: Required—TOEFL (minimum score 500 paper-based; 61 iBT). *Application deadline:* Applications are processed on a rolling basis. Application fee: $40. Electronic applications accepted. *Expenses:* Tuition, state resident: part-time $371 per credit hour. Tuition, nonresident: part-time $742 per credit hour. *Required fees:* $130 per semester. *Financial support:* Teaching assistantships, Federal Work-Study, scholarships/grants, and unspecified assistantships available. Support available to part-time students. Financial award application deadline: 3/1; financial award applicants required to submit FAFSA. *Unit head:* Dr. Jodie Winship, Chair of Teaching and Learning, 205-652-5415, Fax: 205-652-3706, E-mail: jwinship@uwa.edu. *Application contact:* Dr. B. J. Kimbrough, Dean of Graduate Studies, 205-652-3647, Fax: 205-652-3670, E-mail: bkimbrough@uwa.edu.

University of West Florida, College of Education and Professional Studies, Department of Teacher Education and Educational Leadership, Program in Curriculum and Instruction, Pensacola, FL 32514-5750. Offers elementary education (M Ed); middle level education (M Ed); secondary education (M Ed). *Program availability:* Part-time, evening/weekend. *Entrance requirements:* For master's, GRE (minimum score 450 verbal) or MAT (minimum score 396) if bachelor's GPA less than 3.0, state teaching certification; letter of intent; two professional references. Additional exam requirements/recommendations for international students: Required—TOEFL (minimum score 550 paper-based).

University of West Georgia, College of Education, Carrollton, GA 30118. Offers business education (M Ed); early childhood education (M Ed, Ed S); educational leadership (M Ed, Ed S); media (M Ed, Ed S); professional counseling (M Ed, Ed S); professional counseling and supervision (Ed D); reading instruction (M Ed); school improvement (Ed D); secondary education (M Ed); special education (M Ed, Ed S), including teaching (M Ed); speech language pathology (M Ed); teaching (MAT). *Accreditation:* NCATE. *Program availability:* Part-time, evening/weekend, 100% online, blended/hybrid learning. *Faculty:* 45 full-time (28 women), 1,243 part-time (1,039 women); includes 538 minority (456 Black or African American, non-Hispanic/Latino; 19 Asian, non-Hispanic/Latino; 46 Hispanic/Latino; 1 Native Hawaiian or other Pacific Islander, non-Hispanic/Latino; 16 Two or more races, non-Hispanic/Latino), 7 international. Average age 36. 685 applicants, 78% accepted, 429 enrolled. In 2017, 299 master's, 30 doctorates, 218 other advanced degrees awarded. *Entrance requirements:* Additional exam requirements/recommendations for

international students: Required—TOEFL (minimum score 523 paper-based; 69 iBT); Recommended—IELTS (minimum score 6.5). *Application deadline:* For fall admission, 7/21 for domestic students, 6/1 for international students; for spring admission, 11/30 for domestic students, 10/15 for international students; for summer admission, 4/15 for domestic students, 3/30 for international students. Applications are processed on a rolling basis. Application fee: $40. Electronic applications accepted. Tuition and fees vary according to degree level and program. *Financial support:* Fellowships, research assistantships, teaching assistantships, career-related internships or fieldwork, Federal Work-Study, institutionally sponsored loans, scholarships/grants, and unspecified assistantships available. Support available to part-time students. Financial award application deadline: 4/1; financial award applicants required to submit FAFSA. *Unit head:* Dr. Diane Hoff, Dean, College of Education, 678-839-6570, Fax: 678-839-6098, E-mail: dhoff@westga.edu. *Application contact:* Dr. Toby Ziglar, Assistant Dean of the Graduate School, 678-839-1394, Fax: 678-839-1395, E-mail: graduate@westga.edu.
Website: http://www.westga.edu/education/

University of Wisconsin–Eau Claire, College of Education and Human Sciences, Program in Secondary Education, Eau Claire, WI 54702-4004. Offers professional development (ME-PD), including library science, professional development. *Program availability:* Part-time, online learning. *Degree requirements:* For master's, comprehensive exam, thesis, research paper, portfolio or written exam; oral exam. *Entrance requirements:* For master's, certification to teach, minimum GPA of 2.75. Additional exam requirements/recommendations for international students: Required—TOEFL (minimum score 79 iBT).

University of Wisconsin–Milwaukee, Graduate School, College of Letters and Science, Department of English, Milwaukee, WI 53201-0413. Offers English (MA, PhD), including creative writing, English language and linguistics, English secondary education, literary and critical studies, literature and cultural theory (PhD), literature and language studies, literature, culture, and media, media, cinema and digital studies, professional and technical communication (MA), professional and technical writing, professional writing (PhD), rhetoric and composition (PhD), rhetoric and writing. *Students:* 90 full-time (54 women), 42 part-time (17 women); includes 12 minority (2 Black or African American, non-Hispanic/Latino; 1 American Indian or Alaska Native, non-Hispanic/Latino; 4 Asian, non-Hispanic/Latino; 1 Hispanic/Latino; 4 Two or more races, non-Hispanic/Latino), 9 international. Average age 34. 166 applicants, 21% accepted, 27 enrolled. In 2017, 10 master's, 12 doctorates awarded. *Degree requirements:* For master's, thesis or alternative; for doctorate, one foreign language, thesis/dissertation. *Entrance requirements:* For master's, GRE General Test, GRE Subject Test; for doctorate, GRE. Additional exam requirements/recommendations for international students: Required—TOEFL (minimum score 550 paper-based; 79 iBT), IELTS (minimum score 6.5). *Application deadline:* For fall admission, 1/1 priority date for domestic students; for spring admission, 9/1 for domestic students. Application fee: $56 ($96 for international students). Electronic applications accepted. *Financial support:* Fellowships, research assistantships, teaching assistantships, career-related internships or fieldwork, unspecified assistantships, and project assistantships available. Support available to part-time students. Financial award application deadline: 4/15; financial award applicants required to submit FAFSA. *Unit head:* Mark Netzloff, Department Chair, 414-229-4511, E-mail: netzloff@uwm.edu. *Application contact:* General Information Contact, 414-229-4982, Fax: 414-229-6967, E-mail: gradschool@uwm.edu.
Website: https://uwm.edu/english/

University of Wisconsin–Stevens Point, College of Fine Arts and Communication, Department of Music, Stevens Point, WI 54481-3897. Offers elementary/secondary (MM Ed); studio pedagogy (MM Ed); Suzuki talent education (MM Ed). *Accreditation:* NASM. *Program availability:* Part-time. *Degree requirements:* For master's, thesis or alternative. *Entrance requirements:* For master's, teaching certificate. *Faculty research:* Music education, music composition, music performance.

Ursuline College, School of Graduate and Professional Studies, Master Apprenticeship Program, Pepper Pike, OH 44124-4398. Offers adolescent to young adult education (MA); early childhood education (MA); middle childhood education (MA); special education (MA). *Accreditation:* NCATE. *Faculty:* 1 full-time (0 women), 6 part-time/adjunct (all women). *Students:* 19 full-time (16 women); includes 4 minority (all Black or African American, non-Hispanic/Latino). Average age 32. In 2017, 18 master's awarded. *Degree requirements:* For master's, comprehensive exam. *Entrance requirements:* For master's, minimum undergraduate GPA of 3.0. Additional exam requirements/recommendations for international students: Required—TOEFL (minimum score 500 paper-based). *Application deadline:* For fall admission, 8/1 priority date for domestic students. Applications are processed on a rolling basis. Application fee: $25. Electronic applications accepted. *Expenses:* Contact institution. *Financial support:* Application deadline: 3/1; applicants required to submit FAFSA. *Faculty research:* Longevity of female superintendents, expectations of student teacher mentors, qualities of successful student teachers, literacy preparation of K-12 student teachers. *Unit head:* Dr. Mary Jo Cherry, Director, 440-646-8147, Fax: 440-646-8328, E-mail: mcherry@ursuline.edu. *Application contact:* Melanie Steele, Director of Graduate Admission, 440-646-8146, Fax: 440-684-6138, E-mail: graduateadmissions@ursuline.edu.
Website: http://www.ursuline.edu/Academics/Graduate_Professional/Masters_Programs/MAP/index.html

Utah State University, School of Graduate Studies, Emma Eccles Jones College of Education and Human Services, Program in Secondary Education, Logan, UT 84322. Offers M Ed, MA, MS. *Program availability:* Part-time, evening/weekend. *Degree requirements:* For master's, thesis (for some programs). *Entrance requirements:* For master's, GRE General Test or MAT, minimum GPA of 3.0, 1 year teaching, teaching license, letters of recommendation. Additional exam requirements/recommendations for international students: Required—TOEFL. Electronic applications accepted. *Faculty research:* Character education, science education, reading/writing skills, mathematics education, pre-service teacher education.

Valparaiso University, Graduate School and Continuing Education, Programs in Education, Valparaiso, IN 46383. Offers initial licensure (M Ed), including Chinese teaching, elementary education, secondary education; instructional leadership (M Ed); school psychology (Ed S); secondary education (M Ed); M Ed/Ed S. *Accreditation:* NCATE. *Program availability:* Part-time, evening/weekend, online learning. *Entrance requirements:* For master's, GRE General Test, minimum GPA of 3.0. Additional exam requirements/recommendations for international students: Required—TOEFL (minimum score 550 paper-based; 80 iBT), IELTS (minimum score 6). Electronic applications accepted. *Expenses: Tuition:* Full-time $11,340; part-time $630 per credit hour. *Required fees:* $520; $250 per year. $125 per semester. Tuition and fees vary according to program and reciprocity agreements.

Vanderbilt University, Peabody College, Department of Teaching and Learning, Nashville, TN 37240-1001. Offers elementary education (M Ed); English language learners (M Ed); learning and design (M Ed); learning, diversity, and urban studies (M Ed); reading education (M Ed); secondary education (M Ed). *Accreditation:* NCATE. *Program availability:* Part-time. *Faculty:* 43 full-time (32 women), 28 part-time/adjunct (25 women). *Students:* 139 full-time (110 women), 35 part-time (23 women); includes 31 minority (18 Black or African American, non-Hispanic/Latino; 1 American Indian or

Secondary Education

Alaska Native, non-Hispanic/Latino; 6 Asian, non-Hispanic/Latino; 4 Hispanic/Latino; 2 Two or more races, non-Hispanic/Latino), 44 international. Average age 26. 510 applicants, 69% accepted, 113 enrolled. In 2017, 87 master's awarded. *Degree requirements:* For master's, comprehensive exam, thesis optional. *Entrance requirements:* For master's, GRE General Test, MAT. Additional exam requirements/recommendations for international students: Required—TOEFL (minimum score 550 paper-based; 80 iBT). *Application deadline:* For fall admission, 12/31 priority date for domestic and international students; for spring admission, 11/1 priority date for domestic and international students. Applications are processed on a rolling basis. Application fee: $0. Electronic applications accepted. *Financial support:* Fellowships with partial tuition reimbursements, research assistantships with partial tuition reimbursements, teaching assistantships with partial tuition reimbursements, Federal Work-Study, institutionally sponsored loans, scholarships/grants, tuition waivers (partial), and unspecified assistantships available. Support available to part-time students. Financial award application deadline: 1/15; financial award applicants required to submit FAFSA. *Faculty research:* Children's learning and development in core conceptual domains (STEM, English language arts, social studies); classroom discourse structures that teachers can learn and use to support students' learning and development K-6; intervention and design-based research on educational improvement at classroom, school, and district levels; design-based and learning sciences research on relations between learning in schools and other settings. *Unit head:* Dr. Deborah Rowe, Chair, 615-322-8100, Fax: 615-322-8999, E-mail: deborah.w.rowe@vanderbilt.edu. *Application contact:* Angela Saylor, Educational Coordinator, 615-322-8092, Fax: 615-322-8999, E-mail: angela.saylor@vanderbilt.edu.

Virginia Wesleyan University, Graduate Studies, Virginia Beach, VA 23455. Offers business administration (MBA); secondary and PreK-12 education (MA Ed). *Program availability:* Online learning.

Wagner College, Division of Graduate Studies, Education Department, Program in Secondary Education/Students with Disabilities, Staten Island, NY 10301-4495. Offers secondary education 7-12 (MS Ed), including language arts, languages other than English, mathematics and technology, science and technology, social studies. *Program availability:* Evening/weekend. *Faculty:* 2 full-time (1 woman), 7 part-time/adjunct (3 women). *Students:* 17 full-time (14 women), 6 part-time (4 women); includes 2 minority (1 Black or African American, non-Hispanic/Latino; 1 Asian, non-Hispanic/Latino). Average age 24. 15 applicants, 80% accepted, 11 enrolled. In 2017, 8 master's awarded. *Degree requirements:* For master's, thesis (for some programs), completion of state certification exams before student teaching. *Entrance requirements:* For master's, GRE, minimum GPA of 3.0, interview, recommendations. Additional exam requirements/recommendations for international students: Required—TOEFL (minimum score 550 paper-based; 79 iBT), IELTS (minimum score 6.5). *Application deadline:* For fall admission, 12/1 priority date for domestic and international students. Application fee: $60. Electronic applications accepted. *Expenses:* Contact institution. *Financial support:* Unspecified assistantships and alumni fellowship available. Financial award application deadline: 2/15; financial award applicants required to submit FAFSA. *Unit head:* Dr. Jason Fitzgerald, Department Chair, 718-420-4129, Fax: 718-390-3456, E-mail: jason.fitzgerald@wagner.edu. *Application contact:* Patricia Clancy, Assistant Director of Enrollment, 718-420-4464, Fax: 718-390-3105, E-mail: patricia.clancy@wagner.edu. Website: http://www.wagner.edu/education

Wake Forest University, Graduate School of Arts and Sciences, Department of Education, Winston-Salem, NC 27109. Offers secondary education (MA Ed). *Accreditation:* ACA; NCATE. *Faculty:* 6 full-time (3 women). *Students:* 12 full-time (8 women); includes 2 minority (1 Black or African American, non-Hispanic/Latino; 1 Hispanic/Latino). Average age 24. 20 applicants, 75% accepted, 12 enrolled. In 2017, 10 master's awarded. *Degree requirements:* For master's, thesis optional. *Entrance requirements:* For master's, GRE General Test. Additional exam requirements/recommendations for international students: Required—TOEFL (minimum score 550 paper-based). *Application deadline:* For fall admission, 1/15 for domestic students, 1/15 priority date for international students. Application fee: $75. Electronic applications accepted. *Expenses:* Contact institution. *Financial support:* In 2017–18, 13 students received support, including 10 fellowships with full tuition reimbursements available (averaging $49,000 per year), 3 teaching assistantships with full tuition reimbursements available (averaging $49,000 per year); scholarships/grants and tuition waivers (full and partial) also available. Financial award application deadline: 2/15. *Faculty research:* Teaching and learning. *Unit head:* Dr. Adam Friedman, Chair, 336-758-5507, Fax: 336-758-4591, E-mail: amfriedman@wfu.edu. *Application contact:* Dr. Leah McCoy, Program Director, 336-758-5498, Fax: 336-758-4591, E-mail: mccoy@wfu.edu. Website: http://college.wfu.edu/education/graduate-program/overview-of-graduate-programs/

Washington State University, College of Education, Department of Teaching and Learning, Pullman, WA 99164-2132. Offers cultural studies and social thought in education (PhD); curriculum and instruction (Ed M, MA); English language learners (Ed M, MA); language, literacy and technology (PhD); literacy education (Ed M, MA); mathematics education (PhD); special education (Ed M, MA, PhD); teacher leadership (Ed D); teaching (MIT), including elementary education, secondary education. Programs offered at the Pullman, Spokane, Tri-cities, Vancouver and Global (online) campuses. *Program availability:* Part-time, online learning. *Degree requirements:* For master's, comprehensive exam, thesis, oral or written exam; for doctorate, comprehensive exam, thesis/dissertation, oral and written exam. *Entrance requirements:* For master's, GRE General Test, minimum GPA of 3.0, 3 letters of recommendation, letter of intent, transcripts, resume/curriculum vitae; for doctorate, GRE General Test, minimum GPA of 3.0, 3 letters of recommendation, letter of intent, transcripts, writing sample, resume/curriculum vitae. Additional exam requirements/recommendations for international students: Required—TOEFL (minimum score 550 paper-based; 80 iBT). Electronic applications accepted. *Faculty research:* Intersection of gender, youth cultures and schooling; examination of ideology of power in children's literature; early childhood special education; analyzing pre-service and in-service teacher development; second language acquisition.

Washington University in St. Louis, The Graduate School, Department of Education, Program in Secondary Education, St. Louis, MO 63130-4899. Offers MAT. *Degree requirements:* For master's, thesis or alternative. *Entrance requirements:* For master's, GRE General Test or MAT. Additional exam requirements/recommendations for international students: Required—TOEFL. Electronic applications accepted.

Wayland Baptist University, Graduate Programs, Program in Education, Plainview, TX 79072-6998. Offers education administration (M Ed); education diagnostics (M Ed); education literacy (M Ed); elementary certification (M Ed); English (M Ed); English as a second language (M Ed); higher education administration (M Ed); human resources (M Ed); instructional leadership (M Ed); instructional technology (M Ed); leadership training and development (M Ed); science education (M Ed); secondary certification (M Ed); social studies (M Ed); special education (M Ed); sports administration and management (M Ed). *Program availability:* Part-time, evening/weekend, 100% online. *Faculty:* 33 full-time (17 women), 28 part-time/adjunct (17 women). *Students:* 16 full-time (13 women), 221 part-time (143 women); includes 97 minority (26 Black or African American, non-Hispanic/Latino; 1 American Indian or Alaska Native, non-Hispanic/

Latino; 5 Asian, non-Hispanic/Latino; 54 Hispanic/Latino; 11 Two or more races, non-Hispanic/Latino), 1 international. Average age 39. 32 applicants, 97% accepted, 23 enrolled. In 2017, 78 master's awarded. *Degree requirements:* For master's, comprehensive exam, capstone course. *Entrance requirements:* For master's, GRE, GMAT or MAT. Additional exam requirements/recommendations for international students: Required—TOEFL (minimum score 500 paper-based; 61 iBT). *Application deadline:* Applications are processed on a rolling basis. Application fee: $50. Electronic applications accepted. *Expenses:* Tuition: Full-time $11,250; part-time $625 per credit hour. *Required fees:* $1200. *Financial support:* Federal Work-Study, institutionally sponsored loans, and scholarships/grants available. Support available to part-time students. Financial award application deadline: 5/1; financial award applicants required to submit FAFSA. *Unit head:* Dr. Gene Whitfill, Dean, 806-291-1047, Fax: 806-291-1951, E-mail: whitfillg@wbu.edu. *Application contact:* Amanda Stanton, Coordinator of Graduate Studies, 806-291-3423, Fax: 806-291-1950, E-mail: stanton@wbu.edu.

Wayne State University, College of Education, Division of Teacher Education, Detroit, MI 48202. Offers art education (M Ed); bilingual/bicultural education (Certificate); curriculum and instruction (Ed D, PhD, Ed S), including English as a second language (MAT, Ed D, Ed S), K-12 curriculum (PhD); elementary education (MAT), including bilingual/bicultural education (M Ed, MAT), early childhood education (M Ed, MAT), English as a second language (MAT, Ed D, Ed S), foreign language education, science education (M Ed, MAT), special education (M Ed, MAT); elementary mathematics specialist (Certificate); English as a second language (Certificate); reading (M Ed, Ed S); reading, language and literature (Ed D); secondary education (MAT), including bilingual/bicultural education (M Ed, MAT), early childhood education (M Ed, MAT), English as a second language (MAT, Ed D, Ed S), English education, foreign language education, mathematics education (M Ed, MAT), science education (M Ed, MAT), social studies education (M Ed, MAT), special education (MAT), including career and technical education; teaching and learning (M Ed), including bilingual/bicultural education (M Ed, MAT), early childhood education (M Ed, MAT), elementary education, foreign language, mathematics education (M Ed, MAT), science education (M Ed, MAT), social studies education (M Ed, MAT), special education (M Ed, MAT). *Program availability:* Part-time, blended/hybrid learning. *Faculty:* 22. *Students:* 126 full-time (96 women), 317 part-time (258 women); includes 134 minority (95 Black or African American, non-Hispanic/Latino; 1 American Indian or Alaska Native, non-Hispanic/Latino; 8 Asian, non-Hispanic/Latino; 17 Hispanic/Latino; 1 Native Hawaiian or other Pacific Islander, non-Hispanic/Latino; 12 Two or more races, non-Hispanic/Latino), 13 international. Average age 37. 260 applicants, 33% accepted, 57 enrolled. In 2017, 111 master's, 13 doctorates, 7 other advanced degrees awarded. *Degree requirements:* For master's, essay or project (for some M Ed programs), professional field experience (for MAT programs); for doctorate, thesis/dissertation. *Entrance requirements:* For master's, Michigan Test for Teacher Certification (for most programs), verification of participation in group work with children (for MAT programs), Michigan State Police criminal background check; for doctorate, minimum undergraduate GPA of 3.0, graduate 3.5; interview; curriculum vitae; references; master's degree (for most programs). Additional exam requirements/recommendations for international students: Required—TOEFL (minimum score 550 paper-based; 79 iBT), TWE (minimum score 5.5); Recommended—IELTS (minimum score 6.5). *Application deadline:* For fall admission, 6/1 priority date for domestic students, 5/1 priority date for international students; for winter admission, 10/1 priority date for domestic students, 9/1 priority date for international students; for spring admission, 2/1 priority date for domestic students, 1/1 priority date for international students. Applications are processed on a rolling basis. Application fee: $50. Electronic applications accepted. *Expenses:* Tuition, state resident: full-time $10,224; part-time $638.98 per credit hour. Tuition, nonresident: full-time $22,145; part-time $1384.04 per credit hour. Tuition and fees vary according to course load and program. *Financial support:* In 2017–18, 78 students received support, including 4 fellowships (averaging $13,500 per year), 1 research assistantship with tuition reimbursement available (averaging $16,000 per year); Federal Work-Study, scholarships/grants, and unspecified assistantships also available. Support available to part-time students. Financial award applicants required to submit FAFSA. *Faculty research:* Improving students' skill achievement in mathematics, improving elementary children's understanding of informational text, teachers' use of their pedagogical and mathematical knowledge in the interactive work of teaching, the intersection of identity construction in teaching and learning, identifying effective methods of literacy instruction and assessments for bilingual students in elementary language arts classrooms. *Unit head:* Dr. Thomas Edwards, Interim Associate Dean for Teacher Education, 313-577-3886, E-mail: t.g.edwards@wayne.edu. *Application contact:* 313-577-0902, E-mail: askcoe@wayne.edu. Website: http://coe.wayne.edu/ted/index.php

Webster University, School of Education, Department of Multidisciplinary Studies, St. Louis, MO 63119-3194. Offers applied educational psychology (MA, Ed S); communication arts (MA); early childhood education (MA, MAT); education and innovation (MA); educational technology (MET); elementary education (MAT); mathematics for educators (MA); middle school education (MAT); multidisciplinary studies (MAT); multimodal literacy for global impact (MA); reading (MA); secondary school education (MAT); special education (MA, MAT); teaching English as a second language (MA); transformative learning in the global community (Ed S). *Program availability:* Part-time. *Entrance requirements:* For master's, minimum GPA of 2.5. Additional exam requirements/recommendations for international students: Required—TOEFL.

Western Kentucky University, Graduate Studies, College of Education and Behavioral Sciences, School of Teacher Education, Bowling Green, KY 42101. Offers elementary education (MAE, Ed S); exceptional education: learning and behavioral disorders (MAE); exceptional education: moderate and severe disabilities (MAE); instructional design (MS); interdisciplinary early childhood education (MAE); library media education (MS); literacy education (MAE); middle grades education (MAE); secondary education (MAE, Ed S). *Program availability:* Part-time, evening/weekend, online learning. *Degree requirements:* For master's, comprehensive exam. *Entrance requirements:* For master's, GRE General Test. Additional exam requirements/recommendations for international students: Required—TOEFL (minimum score 555 paper-based; 79 iBT). *Faculty research:* Teacher preparation in moderate/severe disabilities.

Western New Mexico University, Graduate Division, School of Education, Silver City, NM 88062-0680. Offers bilingual education (MAT); educational leadership (MA); elementary education (MAT); reading (MAT); secondary education (MAT); special education (MAT); TESOL (teaching English to speakers of other languages) (MAT). *Accreditation:* NCATE. *Program availability:* Part-time, online learning. *Degree requirements:* For master's, comprehensive exam. *Entrance requirements:* For master's, minimum GPA of 3.0 in last 64 hours of undergraduate study. Additional exam requirements/recommendations for international students: Required—TOEFL (minimum score 550 paper-based; 79 iBT). Electronic applications accepted. *Faculty research:* International education, electronic reading assessment, developing STEM teachers.

Western Oregon University, Graduate Programs, College of Education, Division of Teacher Education, Program in Secondary Education, Monmouth, OR 97361. Offers bilingual education (MS Ed); health (MS Ed); humanities (MAT, MS Ed); initial licensure

(MAT); mathematics (MAT, MS Ed); science (MAT, MS Ed); social science (MAT, MS Ed). *Accreditation:* NCATE. *Program availability:* Part-time, evening/weekend. *Degree requirements:* For master's, thesis optional, written exam. *Entrance requirements:* For master's, minimum GPA of 3.0, teaching license. Additional exam requirements/recommendations for international students: Required—TOEFL (minimum score 550 paper-based; 79 iBT), IELTS (minimum score 6.5). *Faculty research:* Literacy, science in primary grades, geography education, retention, teacher burnout.

Western Washington University, Graduate School, Woodring College of Education, Department of Secondary Education, Bellingham, WA 98225-5996. Offers MIT. *Accreditation:* NCATE. *Program availability:* Part-time. *Degree requirements:* For master's, comprehensive exam, thesis optional. *Entrance requirements:* For master's, GRE General Test or MAT, minimum GPA of 3.0 in last 60 semester hours or last 90 quarter hours, secondary teaching certification. Additional exam requirements/recommendations for international students: Required—TOEFL (minimum score 567 paper-based). Electronic applications accepted. *Faculty research:* Service learning, controversial issues in classroom, trauma-sensitive teaching-learning, measuring a teacher's "withitness".

Westfield State University, College of Graduate and Continuing Education, Department of Education, Programs in Secondary Education, Westfield, MA 01086. Offers biology teacher education (M Ed), including secondary education-biology; history teacher education (M Ed), including secondary education-history; mathematics teacher education (M Ed), including secondary education-mathematics; physical education teacher education (M Ed), including secondary education-physical education. *Accreditation:* NCATE. *Program availability:* Part-time, evening/weekend. *Students:* 4 full-time (0 women), 36 part-time (22 women); includes 3 minority (2 Black or African American, non-Hispanic/Latino; 1 Two or more races, non-Hispanic/Latino). Average age 34. 12 applicants, 92% accepted, 9 enrolled. In 2017, 17 master's awarded. *Degree requirements:* For master's, comprehensive exam, practicum. *Entrance requirements:* For master's, GRE General Test or MAT, minimum undergraduate GPA of 2.8. Additional exam requirements/recommendations for international students: Recommended—TOEFL (minimum score 550 paper-based; 79 iBT). *Application deadline:* For fall admission, 7/1 for domestic students; for spring admission, 11/1 for domestic students; for summer admission, 4/1 for domestic students. Applications are processed on a rolling basis. Application fee: $50. *Expenses:* Tuition, state resident: part-time $332 per credit. Tuition, nonresident: part-time $332 per credit. *Required fees:* $75 per semester. Tuition and fees vary according to program. *Financial support:* Unspecified assistantships and SOS scholarships (for education majors only) available. Financial award application deadline: 3/1; financial award applicants required to submit FAFSA. *Unit head:* Dr. Laura Baker, Department Chair, 413-572-5324, E-mail: lbaker@westfield.ma.edu. *Application contact:* Shelly Henrichon, Coordinator of College of Graduate and Continuing Education Admissions, 413-572-8022, Fax: 413-572-5227, E-mail: mhenrichon@westfield.ma.edu.

West Virginia University, College of Education and Human Services, Morgantown, WV 26506. Offers audiology (Au D); autism spectrum disorder (MA); clinical rehabilitation and mental health counseling (MS); communication science and disorders (PhD); counseling (MA); counseling psychology (PhD); curriculum and instruction (Ed D); early childhood education (MA); early intervention (MA); education (PhD); educational leadership (MA, Ed D); educational leadership/public school administration (MA); educational psychology (MA, Ed D); elementary education (MA); gifted education (MA); higher education administration (MA, Ed D); higher education curriculum and teaching (MA); institutional design and technology (MA); instructional design and technology (Ed D); literacy education (MA); secondary education (MA); secondary education/English (MA); special education (Ed D); speech pathology (MS). *Accreditation:* NCATE. *Program availability:* Part-time, evening/weekend, online learning. *Students:* 423 full-time (347 women), 367 part-time (316 women); includes 57 minority (14 Black or African American, non-Hispanic/Latino; 7 Asian, non-Hispanic/Latino; 20 Hispanic/Latino; 16 Two or more races, non-Hispanic/Latino), 13 international. *Degree requirements:* For master's, content exams; for doctorate, comprehensive exam, thesis/dissertation. *Entrance requirements:* Additional exam requirements/recommendations for international students: Required—TOEFL (minimum score 500 paper-based; 61 iBT). *Application deadline:* For fall admission, 8/1 for domestic students; for spring admission, 1/1 for domestic students; for summer admission, 5/1 for domestic students. Application fee: $60. Electronic applications accepted. *Expenses:* Tuition, state resident: full-time $9450. Tuition, nonresident: full-time $24,390. *Financial support:* Fellowships, research assistantships, teaching assistantships, career-related internships or fieldwork, Federal Work-Study, institutionally sponsored loans, health care benefits, tuition waivers (full and partial), and administrative assistantships available. Financial award applicants required to submit FAFSA. *Faculty research:* Internet training and integration for teachers, rural education, teacher preparation, organization of schools, evaluation of personnel. *Unit head:* Dr. Gypsy Denzine, Dean, 304-293-5703, Fax: 304-293-7565, E-mail: gypsy.denzine@mail.wvu.edu. *Application contact:* Dr. M. Cecil Smith, Associate Dean for Research and Graduate Education, 304-293-2174, Fax: 304-293-3802, E-mail: mcecil.smith@mail.wvu.edu.
Website: http://cehs.wvu.edu/

Wheaton College, Graduate School, Department of Education, Wheaton, IL 60187-5593. Offers elementary education (MAT); secondary education (MAT). *Accreditation:* NCATE. *Faculty:* 1 full-time (0 women), 1 part-time/adjunct (0 women). *Students:* 24 full-time (13 women); includes 4 minority (3 Asian, non-Hispanic/Latino; 1 Hispanic/Latino), 1 international. Average age 24. 18 applicants, 100% accepted, 17 enrolled. In 2017, 11 master's awarded. *Degree requirements:* For master's, thesis or alternative. *Entrance requirements:* For master's, GRE General Test or MAT. Additional exam requirements/recommendations for international students: Required—TOEFL (minimum score 550 paper-based; 80 iBT), IELTS (minimum score 6.5). *Application deadline:* For fall admission, 5/1 for domestic students, 1/1 for international students; for spring admission, 11/1 for domestic students. Applications are processed on a rolling basis. Application fee: $30. Electronic applications accepted. *Expenses: Tuition:* Full-time $19,800; part-time $825 per credit hour. Tuition and fees vary according to degree level and program. *Financial support:* Career-related internships or fieldwork and Federal Work-Study available. Financial award application deadline: 3/1; financial award applicants required to submit FAFSA. *Unit head:* Dr. Paul Egeland, Chair, 630-752-5041, E-mail: education.dept@wheaton.edu. *Application contact:* Director of Graduate Admissions, 630-752-5195, Fax: 630-752-7047, E-mail: graduate.admissions@wheaton.edu.
Website: https://www.wheaton.edu/academics/programs/education/master-of-arts-in-teaching/

Whittier College, Graduate Programs, Department of Education and Child Development, Program in Secondary Education, Whittier, CA 90608-0634. Offers MA Ed. *Program availability:* Part-time, evening/weekend. *Degree requirements:* For master's, thesis. *Entrance requirements:* For master's, GRE General Test, MAT.

Whitworth University, School of Education, Graduate Studies in Education, Spokane, WA 99251-0001. Offers administration (M Ed); counseling (M Ed), including school counselors, social agency/church setting; elementary education (M Ed); gifted and talented (MAT); secondary education (M Ed); special education (MAT); teaching (MIT).

Accreditation: NCATE. *Program availability:* Part-time, evening/weekend. *Degree requirements:* For master's, comprehensive exam, thesis (for some programs). *Entrance requirements:* For master's, GRE General Test, MAT. Additional exam requirements/recommendations for international students: Required—TOEFL. *Faculty research:* Rural program development, mainstreaming, special needs learners.

Wichita State University, Graduate School, College of Education, Department of Curriculum and Instruction, Wichita, KS 67260. Offers learning and instructional design (M Ed); special education (M Ed), including early childhood (M Ed, MAT), gifted, high incidence, low incidence; teaching (MAT), including early childhood (M Ed, MAT), middle level/secondary, transition to teaching. *Accreditation:* NCATE. *Program availability:* Part-time, evening/weekend, 100% online, blended/hybrid learning. *Entrance requirements:* For master's, MAT, minimum GPA of 2.75. *Unit head:* Dr. Kimberly McDowell, Department Head, 316-978-3322, E-mail: kim.mcdowell@wichita.edu. *Application contact:* Jordan Oleson, Admission Coordinator, 316-978-3095, Fax: 316-978-3253, E-mail: jordan.oleson@wichita.edu.

William Carey University, School of Education, Hattiesburg, MS 39401. Offers art education (M Ed); art of teaching (M Ed); elementary education (M Ed, Ed S); English education (M Ed); gifted education (M Ed); history and social science (M Ed); mild/moderate disabilities (M Ed); secondary education (M Ed). *Accreditation:* NCATE. *Program availability:* Part-time. *Degree requirements:* For master's, comprehensive exam. *Entrance requirements:* For master's, GRE, MAT, minimum GPA of 2.5, Class A teacher's license. Additional exam requirements/recommendations for international students: Required—TOEFL (minimum score 550 paper-based).

William Paterson University of New Jersey, College of Education, Wayne, NJ 07470-8420. Offers curriculum and learning (M Ed); early childhood education (Certificate); educational leadership (M Ed); educational media specialist (Certificate); elementary education (MAT, Certificate); elementary education subject area (Certificate); higher education administration (MA); learning disabilities consultant (Certificate); literacy (M Ed); middle level education (M Ed); middle school education subject area (Certificate); professional counseling (M Ed); reading specialist (Certificate); school library media specialist (Certificate); school principal (Certificate); school supervisor (Certificate); secondary education (MAT); special education (M Ed); teacher of students with disabilities (Certificate). *Accreditation:* NCATE. *Program availability:* Part-time, evening/weekend. *Faculty:* 37 full-time (25 women), 21 part-time/adjunct (16 women). *Students:* 73 full-time (54 women), 480 part-time (409 women); includes 153 minority (48 Black or African American, non-Hispanic/Latino; 13 Asian, non-Hispanic/Latino; 81 Hispanic/Latino; 11 Two or more races, non-Hispanic/Latino), 1 international. Average age 35. 347 applicants, 87% accepted, 226 enrolled. In 2017, 136 master's awarded. *Degree requirements:* For master's, comprehensive exam, thesis (for some programs), exit interview (for some programs); practicum/internship; minimum GPA of 3.0 (for some programs); exit portfolio (for some programs). *Entrance requirements:* For master's, GRE/MAT, minimum GPA of 2.75; teaching certificate; essay; interview; 2 letters of recommendation; personal statement. Additional exam requirements/recommendations for international students: Required—TOEFL (minimum score 550 paper-based; 79 iBT), IELTS (minimum score 6). *Application deadline:* For fall admission, 6/1 for domestic students, 3/1 for international students; for spring admission, 11/1 for domestic students, 10/1 for international students. Applications are processed on a rolling basis. Application fee: $50. Electronic applications accepted. *Expenses:* Tuition, state resident: full-time $13,920; part-time $6264 per year. Tuition, nonresident: full-time $21,700; part-time $9765 per year. *Required fees:* $80; $36 per year. Tuition and fees vary according to course load, degree level and program. *Financial support:* In 2017–18, 8,416 students received support. Career-related internships or fieldwork, Federal Work-Study, scholarships/grants, and unspecified assistantships available. Support available to part-time students. Financial award application deadline: 3/15; financial award applicants required to submit FAFSA. *Faculty research:* Code switching and creative writing, language instruction, teacher evaluation, preschools, history of educational theories. *Total annual research expenditures:* $311,226. *Unit head:* Dr. Dorothy Feola, Dean, 973-720-2138, Fax: 973-720-3647, E-mail: feolad@wpunj.edu. *Application contact:* Liana Fornarotto, Director of Education Enrollment and Certification, 973-720-2206, Fax: 973-720-2989, E-mail: fornarottol@wpunj.edu.
Website: http://www.wpunj.edu/coe

Wilmington University, College of Education, New Castle, DE 19720-6491. Offers applied technology in education (M Ed); career and technical education (M Ed); educational leadership (Ed D); elementary and secondary school counseling (M Ed); elementary studies (M Ed); ESOL literacy (M Ed); higher education leadership (Ed D); instruction: gifted and talented (M Ed); instruction: teacher of reading (M Ed); instruction: teaching and learning (M Ed); organizational leadership (Ed D); school leadership (M Ed); secondary education (MAT); special education (M Ed). *Accreditation:* NCATE. *Program availability:* Part-time, evening/weekend. *Faculty:* 23 full-time (13 women), 162 part-time/adjunct (99 women). *Students:* 546 full-time (394 women), 960 part-time (732 women); includes 320 minority (241 Black or African American, non-Hispanic/Latino; 12 American Indian or Alaska Native, non-Hispanic/Latino; 11 Asian, non-Hispanic/Latino; 28 Hispanic/Latino; 3 Native Hawaiian or other Pacific Islander, non-Hispanic/Latino; 25 Two or more races, non-Hispanic/Latino), 7 international. Average age 34. 1,068 applicants, 64% accepted, 582 enrolled. In 2017, 430 master's, 59 doctorates awarded. *Entrance requirements:* For master's, 2 letters of recommendation, interview. Additional exam requirements/recommendations for international students: Required—TOEFL (minimum score 500 paper-based). *Application deadline:* For fall admission, 4/30 for domestic students. Applications are processed on a rolling basis. Application fee: $35. Electronic applications accepted. *Expenses: Tuition:* Part-time $466 per credit. *Required fees:* $25 per semester. Tuition and fees vary according to degree level and campus/location. *Financial support:* Applicants required to submit FAFSA. *Unit head:* Dr. John C. Gray, Dean, 302-295-1139. *Application contact:* Laura Morris, Director of Admissions, 877-967-5464, E-mail: infocenter@wilmu.edu.
Website: http://www.wilmu.edu/education/

Wilson College, Graduate Programs, Chambersburg, PA 17201-1285. Offers accounting (M Acc); choreography and visual art (MFA); education (M Ed); educational technology (MET); healthcare administration (MHA); humanities (MA), including art and culture, critical/cultural theory, English language and literature, women's studies; management (MSM); nursing (MSN), including nursing education, nursing leadership and management; special education (MSE). *Program availability:* Evening/weekend. *Degree requirements:* For master's, project. *Entrance requirements:* For master's, PRAXIS, minimum undergraduate cumulative GPA of 3.0, 2 letters of recommendation, current certification for eligibility to teach in grades K-12, resume, personal interview. Electronic applications accepted.

Winthrop University, College of Education, Program in Secondary Education, Rock Hill, SC 29733. Offers M Ed. *Accreditation:* NCATE. *Program availability:* Part-time. *Students:* 14 full-time (13 women), 28 part-time (27 women); includes 7 minority (6 Black or African American, non-Hispanic/Latino; 1 Two or more races, non-Hispanic/Latino). Average age 31. In 2017, 18 master's awarded. *Entrance requirements:* For master's, PRAXIS, minimum GPA of 3.0, South Carolina Class III Teaching Certificate. Additional exam requirements/recommendations for international students: Required—TOEFL (minimum score 550 paper-based; 79 iBT), IELTS (minimum score 6). *Application*

Secondary Education

deadline: For fall admission, 7/15 priority date for domestic students; for spring admission, 12/1 for domestic students. Applications are processed on a rolling basis. Application fee: $50. Electronic applications accepted. *Financial support:* Career-related internships or fieldwork, Federal Work-Study, scholarships/grants, and unspecified assistantships available. Support available to part-time students. Financial award application deadline: 2/1; financial award applicants required to submit FAFSA. *Unit head:* Marshall Jones, Graduate Program Advisor, 803-323-4937, E-mail: jonesmg@winthrop.edu. *Application contact:* 800-411-7041, Fax: 803-323-2292, E-mail: gradschool@winthrop.edu. Website: http://www.winthrop.edu/graduateschool

Worcester State University, Graduate School, Department of Education, Program in Secondary Education, Worcester, MA 01602-2597. Offers M Ed, Ed S, Postbaccalaureate Certificate. *Program availability:* Part-time. *Students:* 3 full-time (2 women), 75 part-time (42 women); includes 8 minority (1 Black or African American, non-Hispanic/Latino; 1 American Indian or Alaska Native, non-Hispanic/Latino; 1 Asian, non-Hispanic/Latino; 3 Hispanic/Latino; 2 Two or more races, non-Hispanic/Latino), 1 international. Average age 32. 64 applicants, 72% accepted, 26 enrolled. In 2017, 7 master's, 28 Ed Ss awarded. *Degree requirements:* For master's, comprehensive exam, thesis, portfolio. *Entrance requirements:* For master's, GRE General Test or MAT, secondary school license (grades 8-12) from Commonwealth of Massachusetts in relevant field of licensure; evidence of undergraduate or graduate course in adolescent/developmental psychology with minimum B grade or CLEP exam in human growth and development (minimum score of 50); for other advanced degree, MTEL in content area (for Postbaccalaureate Certificate), M Ed or master's degree in related field with minimum GPA of 3.0 (for CAGS); evidence of an undergraduate or graduate course in adolescent/developmental psychology with minimum B grade or CLEP exam in human growth and development with minimum score of 50 (for Post-Baccalaureate Certificate). Additional exam requirements/recommendations for international students: Required—TOEFL (minimum score 550 paper-based; 79 iBT). *Application deadline:* For fall admission, 6/15 for domestic and international students; for spring admission, 11/1 for domestic and international students; for summer admission, 4/1 for domestic and international students. Applications are processed on a rolling basis. Application fee: $50. Electronic applications accepted. *Expenses:* Tuition, state resident: full-time $3042; part-time $169 per credit hour. Tuition, nonresident: full-time $3042; part-time $169 per credit hour. *Required fees:* $2754; $153 per credit hour. *Financial support:* Career-related internships or fieldwork, scholarships/grants, and unspecified assistantships available. Financial award application deadline: 3/1; financial award applicants required to submit FAFSA. *Unit head:* Dr. Sara Young, Coordinator, 508-929-8246, E-mail: syoung3@worcester.edu. *Application contact:* Sara Grady, Associate Dean for Graduate Studies and Professional Development, 508-929-8130, E-mail: sara.grady@worcester.edu.

Wright State University, Graduate School, College of Education and Human Services, Department of Teacher Education, Programs in Classroom Teacher Education, Dayton, OH 45435. Offers M Ed, MA. *Accreditation:* NCATE. *Degree requirements:* For master's, thesis (for some programs). *Entrance requirements:* For master's, GRE General Test, MAT, PRAXIS II. Additional exam requirements/recommendations for international students: Required—TOEFL.

Xavier University, College of Social Sciences, Health and Education, School of Education, Department of Secondary and Special Education, Cincinnati, OH 45207. Offers secondary education (M Ed); special education (M Ed). *Entrance requirements:* Additional exam requirements/recommendations for international students: Required—TOEFL (minimum score 550 paper-based; 79 iBT). Application fee is waived when completed online. *Expenses:* Contact institution.

Youngstown State University, Graduate School, Beeghly College of Education, Department of Teacher Education, Program in Middle Childhood Education, Youngstown, OH 44555-0001. Offers MS Ed. *Accreditation:* NCATE. *Program availability:* Part-time, evening/weekend. *Degree requirements:* For master's, comprehensive exam, thesis optional. *Entrance requirements:* For master's, GRE, MAT, or teaching certificate; minimum GPA of 2.7. Additional exam requirements/recommendations for international students: Required—TOEFL. *Faculty research:* Critical reflectivity, gender issues in classroom instruction, collaborative research and analysis, literacy methodology.

Section 25
Special Focus

This section contains a directory of institutions offering graduate work in special focus. Additional information about programs listed in the directory may be obtained by writing directly to the dean of a graduate school or chair of a department at the address given in the directory.

For programs offering related work, see also in this book *Administration, Instruction, and Theory; Education; Instructional Levels; Leisure Studies and Recreation; Physical Education and Kinesiology;* and *Subject Areas.* In other guides in this series:

Graduate Programs in the Humanities, Arts & Social Sciences

See *Psychology and Counseling (School Psychology)* and *Public, Regional, and Industrial Affairs (Urban Studies)*

Graduate Programs in the Biological/Biomedical Sciences and Health-Related Medical Professions

See *Health-Related Professions*

CONTENTS

Program Directories

Featured School: Display and Close-Up

See:

Education of Students with Severe/Multiple Disabilities

Cleveland State University, College of Graduate Studies, College of Education and Human Services, Department of Teacher Education, Cleveland, OH 44115. Offers art education (M Ed); early childhood education (M Ed); foreign language education (M Ed); middle childhood mathematics and science education (M Ed); special education (M Ed), including mild/moderate disabilities, moderate/intensive disabilities; teaching English to speakers of other languages (M Ed). *Program availability:* Part-time, evening/weekend. *Faculty:* 19 full-time (14 women), 32 part-time/adjunct (27 women). *Students:* 80 full-time (60 women), 361 part-time (277 women); includes 119 minority (86 Black or African American, non-Hispanic/Latino; 5 Asian, non-Hispanic/Latino; 16 Hispanic/Latino; 12 Two or more races, non-Hispanic/Latino), 20 international. Average age 34. 177 applicants, 55% accepted, 68 enrolled. In 2017, 137 master's awarded. *Degree requirements:* For master's, comprehensive exam (for some programs), thesis or alternative. *Entrance requirements:* For master's, GRE General Test or MAT, minimum GPA of 2.75. Additional exam requirements/recommendations for international students: Required—TOEFL (minimum score 550 paper-based; 78 iBT), IELTS (minimum score 6). *Application deadline:* For fall admission, 7/1 priority date for domestic students, 5/15 for international students; for spring admission, 11/15 for domestic students, 11/1 for international students; for summer admission, 4/1 for domestic students, 3/15 for international students. Applications are processed on a rolling basis. Application fee: $30. *Financial support:* In 2017–18, 13 research assistantships with full tuition reimbursements (averaging $15,845 per year) were awarded; tuition waivers (partial) and unspecified assistantships also available. Financial award application deadline: 2/15; financial award applicants required to submit FAFSA. *Faculty research:* Early childhood education, literacy education, special education: mild/moderate, moderate/intensive, early childhood intervention specialist; teaching English to speakers of other languages (TESOL). *Total annual research expenditures:* $275,907. *Unit head:* Dr. Tachelle Banks, Department Chairperson, 216-687-4600, Fax: 216-687-5379, E-mail: t.i.banks@csuohio.edu. *Application contact:* Rosalyn Adams, Administrative Coordinator, 216-523-7139, Fax: 216-687-5491, E-mail: r.m.adams@csuohio.edu. Website: http://www.csuohio.edu/cehs/te/te

Georgia State University, College of Education and Human Development, Department of Educational Psychology, Special Education, and Communication Disorders, Program in Multiple and Severe Disabilities, Atlanta, GA 30302-3083. Offers early childhood special education (M Ed); special education adapted curriculum (intellectual disabilities) (M Ed); special education deaf education (M Ed); special education general and adapted curriculum (autism spectrum disorders) (M Ed); special education physical and health disabilities (orthopedic impairments) (M Ed). *Accreditation:* NCATE. *Program availability:* Part-time. *Entrance requirements:* For master's, GRE. Application fee: $50. Electronic applications accepted. *Expenses:* Tuition, state resident: full-time $7020. Tuition, nonresident: full-time $22,518. *Required fees:* $2128. Tuition and fees vary according to degree level and program. *Financial support:* Fellowships, research assistantships, teaching assistantships, scholarships/grants, health care benefits, and unspecified assistantships available. *Faculty research:* Literacy, language, behavioral supports. *Unit head:* Dr. Kathryn Wolff Heller, Professor, 404-413-8040, E-mail: kheller@gsu.edu. *Application contact:* Sandy Vaughn, Senior Administrative Coordinator, 404-413-8318, Fax: 404-413-8043, E-mail: svaughn@gsu.edu.

Hunter College of the City University of New York, Graduate School, School of Education, Department of Special Education, New York, NY 10065-5085. Offers blind and visually impaired (MS Ed); severe/multiple disabilities (MS Ed). *Accreditation:* NCATE. *Degree requirements:* For master's, comprehensive exam, thesis, student teaching practica, clinical teaching lab courses, New York State Teacher Certification Exams. *Entrance requirements:* For master's, minimum GPA of 2.8. Additional exam requirements/recommendations for international students: Required—TOEFL, TWE. *Faculty research:* Mathematics learning disabilities; street behavior; assessment; bilingual special education; families, diversity, and disabilities.

Norfolk State University, School of Graduate Studies, School of Education, Department of Special Education, Program in Severe Disabilities, Norfolk, VA 23504. Offers MA. *Accreditation:* NCATE. *Program availability:* Part-time. *Degree requirements:* For master's, thesis or alternative. *Entrance requirements:* For master's, GRE, minimum GPA of 3.0 in major, 2.5 overall.

Syracuse University, School of Education, MS Program in Inclusive Special Education: Severe/Multiple Disabilities, Syracuse, NY 13244. Offers MS. *Program availability:* Part-time. *Students:* Average age 27. *Entrance requirements:* For master's, GRE, baccalaureate degree from regionally-accredited college/university, New York State initial certification in students with disabilities, strong professor and/or employer recommendations, personal statement, interview. Additional exam requirements/recommendations for international students: Required—TOEFL (minimum score 100 iBT). *Application deadline:* For fall admission, 1/15 priority date for domestic and international students; for spring admission, 10/15 priority date for domestic and international students. Applications are processed on a rolling basis. Application fee: $75. Electronic applications accepted. *Financial support:* Fellowships with full tuition reimbursements, research assistantships, teaching assistantships, career-related internships or fieldwork, and scholarships/grants available. Financial award application deadline: 1/15. *Faculty research:* Teaching children and adolescents with autism, augmentation of communication in the inclusive classroom, families of students with disabilities, positive approaches to challenging behaviors, creating safe and peaceful schools. *Unit head:* Dr. Gail Ensher, Program Coordinator, 315-443-9650, E-mail: glensher@syr.edu. *Application contact:* Speranza Migliore, Graduate Admissions Recruiter, 315-443-2505, E-mail: gradrcrt@syr.edu.
Website: http://soe.syr.edu/academic/teaching_and_leadership/graduate/masters/inclusive_special_education_grades_1_6/admissions.aspx

Teachers College, Columbia University, Department of Health and Behavior Studies, New York, NY 10027-6696. Offers applied behavior analysis (MA, PhD); applied educational psychology: school psychology (Ed M, PhD); behavioral nutrition (PhD), including nutrition (Ed D, PhD); community health education (MS); community nutrition education (Ed M), including community nutrition education; education of deaf and hard of hearing (MA, PhD); health education (MA, Ed D); hearing impairment (Ed D); intellectual disability/autism (MA, Ed D, PhD); nursing education (Ed D, Advanced Certificate); nutrition and education (MS); nutrition and exercise physiology (MS); nutrition and public health (MS); nutrition education (Ed D), including nutrition (Ed D, PhD); physical disabilities (Ed D); reading specialist (MA); severe or multiple disabilities (MA); special education (Ed M, MA, Ed D); teaching of sign language (MA). *Program availability:* Part-time, evening/weekend. *Students:* 245 full-time (226 women), 242 part-time (219 women); includes 167 minority (52 Black or African American, non-Hispanic/Latino; 2 American Indian or Alaska Native, non-Hispanic/Latino; 55 Asian, non-Hispanic/Latino; 48 Hispanic/Latino; 1 Native Hawaiian or other Pacific Islander, non-Hispanic/Latino; 9 Two or more races, non-Hispanic/Latino), 60 international. Average age 30. 480 applicants, 59% accepted, 157 enrolled. Terminal master's awarded for partial completion of doctoral program. *Unit head:* Prof. Dolores Perin, Chair, E-mail: dp111@tc.columbia.edu. *Application contact:* David Estrella, Director of Admission, 212-678-3305, E-mail: estrella@tc.columbia.edu.
Website: http://www.tc.columbia.edu/health-and-behavior-studies/

University of Illinois at Urbana–Champaign, Graduate College, College of Education, Department of Special Education, Champaign, IL 61820. Offers Ed M, MS, Ed D, PhD, CAS. *Program availability:* Part-time, online learning.

West Liberty University, College of Education and Human Performance, West Liberty, WV 26074. Offers community education research and leadership (MA Ed); innovative instruction (MA Ed); leadership in disability services (MA Ed); leadership studies (MA Ed); multi-categorical special education (MA Ed); reading specialist (MA Ed); sports leadership and coaching (MA Ed). *Accreditation:* NCATE. *Program availability:* Part-time, evening/weekend. *Students:* 18 full-time (12 women), 74 part-time (60 women); includes 2 minority (1 Black or African American, non-Hispanic/Latino; 1 Native Hawaiian or other Pacific Islander, non-Hispanic/Latino). Average age 32. *Degree requirements:* For master's, capstone experience. *Entrance requirements:* For master's, minimum GPA of 2.5 or 3.0 (depending on track). Additional exam requirements/recommendations for international students: Required—TOEFL. *Application deadline:* Applications are processed on a rolling basis. Application fee: $0. Electronic applications accepted. Tuition and fees vary according to course load and program. *Financial support:* Teaching assistantships and unspecified assistantships available. *Unit head:* Dr. Catherine Monteroso, Interim Dean, 304-336-8247, E-mail: cmonteroso@westliberty.edu. *Application contact:* Sara Sweeney, Director, Office of Graduate Studies, 304-336-8545, E-mail: sara.sweeney@westliberty.edu.
Website: http://westliberty.edu/education/

Education of the Gifted

Arkansas State University, Graduate School, College of Education and Behavioral Science, School of Teacher Education and Leadership, State University, AR 72467. Offers community college administration (SCCT); curriculum and instruction (MSE); early childhood education (MSE); early childhood services (MS); educational leadership (MSE, Ed D, Ed S); educational theory and practice (MSE); middle level education (MAT, MSE); reading (MSE, Ed S); special education - gifted, talented, and creative (MSE); special education - instructional specialist grades 4-12 (MSE); special education - instructional specialist grades P-4 (MSE); special education, K-12 (MSE). *Accreditation:* NCATE. *Program availability:* Part-time, online learning. *Degree requirements:* For master's, comprehensive exam, thesis or alternative; for doctorate, comprehensive exam, thesis/dissertation; for other advanced degree, comprehensive exam. *Entrance requirements:* For master's, GRE General Test or MAT, appropriate bachelor's degree, official transcripts, immunization records, letters of reference, interview; for doctorate, GRE General Test or MAT, interview, master's degree, letters of reference, official transcript, personal statement, writing sample, immunization records; for other advanced degree, GRE General Test or MAT, interview, master's degree, official transcript, immunization records, letters of reference, 3 years of teaching experience, teaching license. Additional exam requirements/recommendations for international students: Required—TOEFL (minimum score 550 paper-based; 79 iBT), IELTS (minimum score 6), PTE (minimum score 56). Electronic applications accepted.

Ball State University, Graduate School, Teachers College, Department of Educational Psychology, Muncie, IN 47306. Offers educational psychology (MA, MS), including educational psychology (MA, MS, PhD); educational psychology (PhD), including educational psychology (MA, MS, PhD); gifted and talented education (Certificate); human development and learning (Certificate); instructional design and assessment (Certificate); neuropsychology (Certificate); quantitative psychology (MS); response to intervention (Certificate); school psychology (MA, PhD), including school psychology (MA, PhD, Ed S); school psychology (Ed S), including school psychology (MA, PhD, Ed S). *Program availability:* 100% online. *Faculty:* 24 full-time (15 women), 3 part-time/adjunct (all women). *Students:* 68 full-time (49 women), 122 part-time (106 women); includes 33 minority (16 Black or African American, non-Hispanic/Latino; 4 Asian, non-Hispanic/Latino; 7 Hispanic/Latino; 6 Two or more races, non-Hispanic/Latino), 3 international. Average age 32. 146 applicants, 42% accepted, 47 enrolled. In 2017, 49 master's, 8 doctorates, 20 other advanced degrees awarded. *Degree requirements:* For doctorate, thesis/dissertation; for other advanced degree, thesis. *Entrance requirements:* For master's, GRE General Test, minimum baccalaureate GPA of 2.75 or 3.0 in latter half of baccalaureate, professional goals and self-assessment; for doctorate, GRE General Test, minimum graduate GPA of 3.2; for other advanced degree, GRE General Test. Additional exam requirements/recommendations for international students: Required—TOEFL (minimum score 550 paper-based; 79 iBT), IELTS (minimum score 6.5). *Application deadline:* Applications are processed on a rolling basis. Application fee: $60. Electronic applications accepted. *Financial support:* In 2017–18, 40 students received support, including 29 research assistantships with partial tuition reimbursements available (averaging $12,276 per year), 3 teaching assistantships with partial tuition reimbursements available (averaging $11,167 per year); unspecified assistantships also available. Financial award application deadline: 3/1; financial award applicants required to submit FAFSA. *Unit head:* Dr. Jerell Cassady, Chairperson, 765-285-8503, E-mail: jccassady@bsu.edu. *Application contact:* Dr. Jerrell Cassady, Chairperson, 765-285-8503, Fax: 765-285-5455, E-mail: jccassady@bsu.edu. Website: http://www.bsu.edu/edpsych

Barry University, School of Education, Program in Curriculum and Instruction, Miami Shores, FL 33161-6695. Offers accomplished teacher (Ed S); culture, language and literacy (TESOL) (PhD); curriculum evaluation and research (PhD); early childhood (Ed S); early childhood education (PhD); elementary (Ed S); elementary education (PhD); ESOL (Ed S); gifted (Ed S); Montessori (Ed S); PKP/elementary (Ed S); reading (Ed S); reading, language and cognition (PhD). *Entrance requirements:* For doctorate, GRE, minimum GPA of 3.25.

Barry University, School of Education, Program in Exceptional Student Education, Miami Shores, FL 33161-6695. Offers MS, Ed S. *Program availability:* Part-time, evening/weekend. *Degree requirements:* For master's, comprehensive exam; for Ed S, practicum. *Entrance requirements:* For master's, GRE General Test or MAT, minimum GPA of 3.0; for Ed S, GRE General Test, minimum GPA of 3.0. Electronic applications accepted.

Barry University, School of Education, Program in Leadership and Education, Miami Shores, FL 33161-6695. Offers educational technology (PhD); exceptional student education (PhD); higher education administration (PhD); human resource development (PhD); leadership (PhD). *Program availability:* Part-time, evening/weekend. *Degree requirements:* For doctorate, thesis/dissertation. *Entrance requirements:* For doctorate, GRE General Test, minimum GPA of 3.25. Electronic applications accepted.

Canisius College, Graduate Division, School of Education and Human Services, Department of Graduate Education and Leadership, Buffalo, NY 14208-1098. Offers business and marketing education (MS Ed); college student personnel (MS Ed); deaf education (MS Ed); deaf/adolescent education, grades 7-12 (MS Ed); deaf/childhood education, grades 1-6 (MS Ed); differentiated instruction (MS Ed); education administration (MS); educational administration (MS Ed); educational technologies (Certificate); gifted education extension (Certificate); literacy (MS Ed); reading (Certificate); school building leadership (MS Ed, Certificate); school district leadership (Certificate); teacher leader (Certificate); TESOL (MS Ed). *Accreditation:* NCATE. *Program availability:* Part-time, evening/weekend, 100% online, blended/hybrid learning. *Faculty:* 5 full-time (all women), 21 part-time/adjunct (16 women). *Students:* 85 full-time (67 women), 189 part-time (151 women); includes 31 minority (18 Black or African American, non-Hispanic/Latino; 3 American Indian or Alaska Native, non-Hispanic/Latino; 3 Asian, non-Hispanic/Latino; 4 Hispanic/Latino; 3 Two or more races, non-Hispanic/Latino), 1 international. Average age 31. 83 applicants, 96% accepted, 74 enrolled. In 2017, 94 master's, 47 other advanced degrees awarded. *Entrance requirements:* For master's, GRE (if cumulative GPA less than 2.7), transcripts, two letters of recommendation. Additional exam requirements/recommendations for international students: Required—TOEFL (minimum score 550 paper-based, 79 iBT), IELTS (minimum score 6.5), or CAEL (minimum score 70). *Application deadline:* Applications are processed on a rolling basis. Application fee: $0. Electronic applications accepted. *Expenses: Tuition:* Full-time $22,860; part-time $820 per credit. *Required fees:* $720; $25 per credit. $65 per semester. One-time fee: $425. *Financial support:* Career-related internships or fieldwork, Federal Work-Study, scholarships/grants, tuition waivers (partial), and unspecified assistantships available. Support available to part-time students. Financial award application deadline: 4/30; financial award applicants required to submit FAFSA. *Faculty research:* Asperger's disease, autism, private higher education, reading strategies. *Unit head:* Dr. Anne Marie Tryjankowski, Chair/Associate Professor of Graduate Education and Leadership, 716-888-3715, Fax: 716-888-3142, E-mail: tryjanka@canisius.edu.

Carlos Albizu University, Miami Campus, Graduate Programs, Miami, FL 33172-2209. Offers clinical psychology (PhD, Psy D); entrepreneurship (MBA); exceptional student education (MS); human services (PhD); industrial/organizational psychology (MS); marriage and family therapy (MS); mental health counseling (MS); nonprofit management (MBA); organizational management (MBA); psychology (MS); speech and language pathology (MS); teaching English for speakers of other languages (MS). *Accreditation:* APA. *Program availability:* Part-time, evening/weekend, 100% online, blended/hybrid learning. *Faculty:* 32 full-time (24 women), 27 part-time/adjunct (15 women). *Students:* 411 full-time (345 women), 248 part-time (215 women); includes 562 minority (53 Black or African American, non-Hispanic/Latino; 4 Asian, non-Hispanic/Latino; 498 Hispanic/Latino; 7 Two or more races, non-Hispanic/Latino), 23 international. Average age 34. 391 applicants, 42% accepted, 154 enrolled. In 2017, 96 master's, 54 doctorates awarded. Terminal master's awarded for partial completion of doctoral program. *Degree requirements:* For master's, comprehensive exam (for some programs), integrative project (for MBA); research project (for exceptional student education, teaching English as a second language); for doctorate, comprehensive examinations, internship, project/dissertation. *Entrance requirements:* For master's, GRE/EXADEP, bachelor's degree from accredited institution, minimum GPA of 3.0, 3 letters of recommendation, interview, resume, statement of purpose, official transcripts; for doctorate, GRE (for Psy D), 3 letters of recommendation, resume, interview, statement of purpose, official transcripts; bachelor's degree and minimum GPA of 3.25 (for Psy D); master's degree and minimum GPA of 3.0 (for PhD). Additional exam requirements/recommendations for international students: Required—Michigan Test of English Language Proficiency. *Application deadline:* For fall admission, 4/1 priority date for domestic students, 5/1 priority date for international students; for spring admission, 11/1 priority date for domestic students, 9/1 priority date for international students. Applications are processed on a rolling basis. Application fee: $50. Electronic applications accepted. Application fee is waived when completed online. *Expenses:* Contact institution. *Financial support:* In 2017–18, 145 students received support. Federal Work-Study, scholarships/grants, unspecified assistantships, and tuition discounts available. Financial award application deadline: 6/1; financial award applicants required to submit FAFSA. *Faculty research:* Psychotherapy, forensic psychology, neuropsychology, special education, speech-language pathology, criminal justice. *Unit head:* Dr. Etiony Aldorondo, Provost, 305-593-1223 Ext. 3138, Fax: 305-592-7930, E-mail: ealdorondo@albizu.edu. *Application contact:* Sonia Feliciano, Institutional Director of Student Recruitment, 305-593-1223 Ext. 3108, Fax: 305-477-8983, E-mail: sfeliciano@albizu.edu.

Carthage College, Division of Teacher Education, Kenosha, WI 53140. Offers classroom guidance and counseling (M Ed); creative arts (M Ed); gifted and talented children (M Ed); language arts (M Ed); modern language (M Ed); natural sciences (M Ed); reading (M Ed, Certificate); social sciences (M Ed); teacher leadership (M Ed). *Program availability:* Part-time, evening/weekend. *Degree requirements:* For master's, thesis optional. *Entrance requirements:* For master's, MAT, minimum B average, letters of reference.

The College of New Rochelle, Graduate School, Division of Education, Program in Gifted Education, New Rochelle, NY 10805-2308. Offers Certificate. *Program*

availability: Part-time. *Degree requirements:* For Certificate, practicum. *Expenses: Tuition:* Full-time $17,406. *Required fees:* $1120.

The College of William and Mary, School of Education, Program in Curriculum and Instruction, Williamsburg, VA 23187-8795. Offers elementary education (MA Ed); English as a second language/bilingual education (MA Ed); gifted education (MA Ed); literacy leadership (MA Ed); math specialist (MA Ed); secondary education (MA Ed), including English, foreign language, math, science, social studies; special education (MA Ed). *Accreditation:* NCATE. *Program availability:* Part-time. *Faculty:* 23 full-time (16 women), 40 part-time/adjunct (32 women). *Students:* 85 full-time (63 women), 16 part-time (15 women); includes 18 minority (5 Black or African American, non-Hispanic/Latino; 4 Asian, non-Hispanic/Latino; 7 Hispanic/Latino; 2 Two or more races, non-Hispanic/Latino), 1 international. Average age 27. 152 applicants, 83% accepted, 90 enrolled. In 2017, 67 master's awarded. *Degree requirements:* For master's, project. *Entrance requirements:* For master's, GRE, MAT, PRAXIS Core Academic Skills for Educators, minimum GPA of 2.5. Additional exam requirements/recommendations for international students: Required—TOEFL (minimum score 100 iBT), IELTS (minimum score 7). *Application deadline:* For fall admission, 1/15 for domestic and international students; for spring admission, 10/1 for domestic and international students. Application fee: $50. Electronic applications accepted. *Expenses:* $9,630 resident full-time, $535 resident part-time per credit hour; $25,920 nonresident full-time, $1,265 nonresident part-time per credit hour; $5,944 full-time fees. *Financial support:* In 2017–18, 35 students received support, including 7 research assistantships (averaging $6,678 per year); scholarships/grants and unspecified assistantships also available. Financial award application deadline: 1/15; financial award applicants required to submit FAFSA. *Faculty research:* Educational technology, professional development and evaluation, inclusive education, rural education, education policy. *Unit head:* Dr. Jeremy D. Stoddard, Department Chair, 757-221-2348, E-mail: jdstod@wm.edu. *Application contact:* Dorothy Smith Osborne, Assistant Dean for Academic Programs and Student Services, 757-221-2317, E-mail: dsosbo@wm.edu.
Website: http://education.wm.edu

Colorado Mesa University, Center for Teacher Education, Grand Junction, CO 81501-3122. Offers educational leadership (MAEd); English for speakers of other languages (MAEd); exceptional learner/special education (MAEd); teacher education (Graduate Certificate); teacher leader (MAEd). *Accreditation:* NCATE. *Program availability:* Part-time. *Degree requirements:* For master's, comprehensive exam (for some programs), capstone presentation. *Entrance requirements:* For master's, 3 professional letters of recommendation, Colorado teaching license, minimum baccalaureate GPA of 3.0; for Graduate Certificate, minimum baccalaureate GPA of 3.0. Additional exam requirements/recommendations for international students: Required—TOEFL (minimum score 550 paper-based). Electronic applications accepted. *Expenses:* Contact institution. *Faculty research:* K-8 STEM instruction, special education inclusion, elementary math literacy, secondary literacy, elementary/early childhood education literacy.

Converse College, Program in Gifted Education, Spartanburg, SC 29302. Offers M Ed. *Program availability:* Part-time. *Degree requirements:* For master's, capstone paper. *Entrance requirements:* For master's, NTE or PRAXIS II, minimum GPA of 2.75, teaching certificate, 2 recommendations. *Application deadline:* For fall admission, 8/1 for domestic and international students; for winter admission, 11/15 for domestic and international students; for spring admission, 1/15 for domestic and international students. Applications are processed on a rolling basis. Application fee: $40. Electronic applications accepted. *Financial support:* Career-related internships or fieldwork available. Support available to part-time students. Financial award applicants required to submit FAFSA. *Faculty research:* Identification of gifted minorities, arts in gifted education. *Unit head:* Lee Givens, Department Chair, 864-596-9476, E-mail: lee.givens@converse.edu. *Application contact:* E-mail: graduate@converse.edu.

Drury University, Master in Education Program, Springfield, MO 5802. Offers curriculum and instruction (M Ed), including elementary, middle school, secondary; gifted education (M Ed); instructional leadership (M Ed); instructional technology (M Ed); integrated learning (M Ed); online teaching (M Ed); special education (M Ed); special reading (M Ed). *Accreditation:* NCATE. *Program availability:* Part-time, evening/weekend, 100% online, blended/hybrid learning. *Entrance requirements:* For master's, GRE, bachelor's degree with minimum GPA of 2.75. Additional exam requirements/recommendations for international students: Recommended—TOEFL (minimum score 80 iBT), IELTS (minimum score 6.5). Electronic applications accepted. *Expenses:* Contact institution. *Faculty research:* Gifted students, instructional technology, autism, diversity and social justice.

Eastern New Mexico University, Graduate School, College of Education and Technology, Department of Educational Studies, Program in Special Education, Portales, NM 88130. Offers early childhood special education (M Sp Ed); general special education (M Sp Ed); gifted education pedagogy (M Ed); special education pedagogy (M Ed). *Program availability:* Part-time. *Degree requirements:* For master's, comprehensive exam, thesis optional. *Entrance requirements:* For master's, writing assessment, minimum GPA of 3.0, letter of recommendation, photocopy of teaching license or confirmation of entrance into alternative licensure program, special education license or minimum 30 hours of undergraduate course work. Additional exam requirements/recommendations for international students: Required—TOEFL (minimum score 550 paper-based; 79 iBT), IELTS (minimum score 6). *Application deadline:* For fall admission, 7/20 priority date for domestic students, 6/20 priority date for international students; for spring admission, 12/15 priority date for domestic students, 11/15 priority date for international students. Applications are processed on a rolling basis. Application fee: $10. Electronic applications accepted. *Financial support:* Applicants required to submit FAFSA. *Unit head:* Dr. Rebecca Davis, Graduate Coordinator, 575-392-6840, E-mail: rebecca.davis@enmu.edu. *Application contact:* Cheryl Reeves, Senior Secretary, 575-562-2443, Fax: 575-562-2559, E-mail: cheryl.reeves@enmu.edu.

Elon University, Program in Education, Elon, NC 27244-2010. Offers elementary education (M Ed); gifted education (M Ed); special education (M Ed). *Accreditation:* NCATE. *Program availability:* Part-time. *Faculty:* 8 full-time (6 women), 2 part-time/adjunct (both women). *Students:* 24 part-time (22 women); includes 13 minority (2 Black or African American, non-Hispanic/Latino; 2 Asian, non-Hispanic/Latino; 8 Hispanic/Latino; 1 Two or more races, non-Hispanic/Latino). Average age 23. 29 applicants, 69% accepted, 16 enrolled. In 2017, 10 master's awarded. *Entrance requirements:* For master's, GRE, MAT. Additional exam requirements/recommendations for international students: Required—TOEFL (minimum score 550 paper-based; 79 iBT). *Application deadline:* For fall admission, 5/1 for domestic students. Applications are processed on a rolling basis. Application fee: $50. Electronic applications accepted. *Financial support:* Federal Work-Study and scholarships/grants available. Support available to part-time students. Financial award application deadline: 6/1; financial award applicants required to submit FAFSA. *Faculty research:* Teaching reading to low-achieving second and third graders, pre- and post-student teaching attitudes, children's writing, whole language methodology, critical creative thinking. *Unit head:* Dr. Ann Bullock, Dean of the School of Education/Professor, 336-278-5900, E-mail: abullock9@elon.edu. *Application contact:* Art Fadde, Director of Graduate Admissions, 800-334-8448 Ext. 3, Fax: 336-278-7699, E-mail: afadde@elon.edu.
Website: http://www.elon.edu/med

Education of the Gifted

Emporia State University, Program in Special Education, Emporia, KS 66801-5415. Offers behavior disorders (MS); gifted, talented, and creative (MS); interrelated special education (MS). *Accreditation:* NCATE. *Program availability:* Part-time. *Faculty:* 30 full-time (24 women), 1 part-time/adjunct (0 women). *Students:* 4 full-time (2 women), 160 part-time (119 women); includes 9 minority (3 Black or African American, non-Hispanic/Latino; 1 Asian, non-Hispanic/Latino; 3 Hispanic/Latino; 2 Two or more races, non-Hispanic/Latino). 29 applicants, 72% accepted, 21 enrolled. In 2017, 55 master's awarded. *Degree requirements:* For master's, comprehensive exam or thesis, practicum. *Entrance requirements:* For master's, GRE General Test or MAT, essay exam, appropriate bachelor's degree, teacher certification, letters of recommendation. Additional exam requirements/recommendations for international students: Required—TOEFL (minimum score 520 paper-based; 68 iBT). *Application deadline:* For fall admission, 8/15 priority date for domestic students. Applications are processed on a rolling basis. Application fee: $30 ($75 for international students). Electronic applications accepted. *Expenses:* Tuition, state resident: full-time $6084; part-time $253.50 per credit hour. Tuition, nonresident: full-time $18,924; part-time $788.50 per credit hour. *Required fees:* $1943; $80.95 per credit hour. Tuition and fees vary according to campus/location. *Financial support:* In 2017–18, 4 teaching assistantships with full tuition reimbursements (averaging $7,344 per year) were awarded; Federal Work-Study, institutionally sponsored loans, health care benefits, and unspecified assistantships also available. Financial award application deadline: 3/15; financial award applicants required to submit FAFSA. *Unit head:* Dr. Matt Siemears, Chair, 620-341-6057, E-mail: msiemear@emporia.edu. *Application contact:* Mary Sewell, Admissions Coordinator, 800-950-GRAD, Fax: 620-341-5909, E-mail: msewell@emporia.edu. Website: http://www.emporia.edu/elecse/sped/

Florida Gulf Coast University, College of Education, Program in Curriculum and Instruction, Fort Myers, FL 33965-6565. Offers elementary education (M Ed); English education (M Ed); English speakers of other languages endorsement (M Ed); gifted education (M Ed); mathematics education (M Ed); middle school education (M Ed); reading education (M Ed); science education (M Ed); social science education (M Ed); special education (M Ed). *Program availability:* Part-time, evening/weekend, online learning. *Faculty:* 27 full-time (19 women), 44 part-time/adjunct (30 women). *Students:* 3 full-time (all women), 16 part-time (14 women); includes 4 minority (2 Black or African American, non-Hispanic/Latino; 2 Hispanic/Latino). Average age 30. 6 applicants, 100% accepted, 5 enrolled. In 2017, 4 master's awarded. *Degree requirements:* For master's, final project or portfolio. *Entrance requirements:* For master's, GRE General Test, MAT, minimum undergraduate GPA of 3.0 in last 2 years. Additional exam requirements/recommendations for international students: Required—TOEFL (minimum score 550 paper-based). *Application deadline:* For fall admission, 2/15 priority date for domestic students, 5/1 for international students; for spring admission, 12/1 for domestic students, 9/15 for international students. Applications are processed on a rolling basis. Application fee: $30. Electronic applications accepted. *Expenses:* Tuition, state resident: part-time $290 per credit hour. Tuition, nonresident: part-time $1173 per credit hour. *Required fees:* $127 per credit hour. Tuition and fees vary according to course load. *Financial support:* In 2017–18, 2 students received support. Application deadline: 6/30; applicants required to submit FAFSA. *Faculty research:* Internet in schools, technology in pre-service and in-service teacher training. *Unit head:* Dr. Vickie Johnston, Instructor, 239-590-7754, Fax: 239-590-7801, E-mail: vjohnston@fgcu.edu. *Application contact:* Keiana Desmore, Adviser/Counselor, 239-590-7759, Fax: 239-590-7801, E-mail: kdesmore@fgcu.edu.
Website: http://coe.fgcu.edu/c-imed/

George Mason University, College of Education and Human Development, Programs in Curriculum and Instruction, Fairfax, VA 22030. Offers advanced international baccalaureate (M Ed); assistive technology (M Ed); designing digital learning in schools (M Ed); early childhood education (M Ed); early childhood education for diverse learners (M Ed); elementary education (M Ed); English as a second language (M Ed); gifted child education (M Ed); history (M Ed); literacy (M Ed), including PK-12 classroom teachers, reading specialist; literacy leadership for diverse schools (M Ed), including K-12 reading; physical education (M Ed); science K-12 (M Ed); secondary education (M Ed), including biology, chemistry, earth science, English, history/social science, math, physics; special education (M Ed); teacher leadership (M Ed); teaching culturally, linguistically diverse and exceptional learners (M Ed); transformative teaching (M Ed). *Program availability:* Part-time, evening/weekend, 100% online, blended/hybrid learning. *Faculty:* 41 full-time (36 women), 45 part-time/adjunct (37 women). *Students:* 173 full-time (151 women), 729 part-time (611 women); includes 271 minority (65 Black or African American, non-Hispanic/Latino; 5 American Indian or Alaska Native, non-Hispanic/Latino; 88 Asian, non-Hispanic/Latino; 94 Hispanic/Latino; 1 Native Hawaiian or other Pacific Islander, non-Hispanic/Latino; 18 Two or more races, non-Hispanic/Latino), 28 international. Average age 32. 426 applicants, 91% accepted, 289 enrolled. In 2017, 349 master's awarded. *Degree requirements:* For master's, thesis. *Entrance requirements:* For master's, PRAXIS Core (for some programs), 2 letters of recommendation, interview, program goals statement; 9 hours of complete licensure endorsement requirements (for elementary education); minimum GPA of 3.0 in applicant's last 60 hours of undergraduate coursework (for secondary education); at least 1 year of teaching experience (for literacy). Additional exam requirements/recommendations for international students: Required—TOEFL (minimum score 575 paper-based; 88 iBT), IELTS (minimum score 6.5), PTE (minimum score 59). *Application deadline:* For fall admission, 4/2 priority date for domestic and international students; for spring admission, 11/1 for domestic and international students. Application fee: $75 ($80 for international students). Electronic applications accepted. *Expenses:* Tuition, state resident: full-time $11,228; part-time $459.50 per credit. Tuition, nonresident: full-time $30,932; part-time $1280.50 per credit. *Required fees:* $3252; $135.50 per credit. Part-time tuition and fees vary according to course load and program. *Financial support:* In 2017–18, 2 students received support, including 2 teaching assistantships; career-related internships or fieldwork, Federal Work-Study, scholarships/grants, unspecified assistantships, and health care benefits (for full-time research or teaching assistantship recipients) also available. Support available to part-time students. Financial award application deadline: 3/1; financial award applicants required to submit FAFSA. *Faculty research:* Teacher preparation and professional development; adaptive teaching; wonder in science teacher preparation; literacy (digital, adolescent); site based course instruction. *Unit head:* Rebecca Fox, Professor and Academic Program Coordinator, 703-993-4123, E-mail: rfox@gmu.edu.
Website: http://gse.gmu.edu/programs/gsemasters

Grand Canyon University, College of Education, Phoenix, AZ 85017-1097. Offers autism spectrum disorders (MA); curriculum and instruction (MA); early childhood education (M Ed); educational administration (M Ed); educational leadership (M Ed); elementary education (M Ed); gifted education (M Ed); instructional technology (MS); K-12 leadership (Ed S); reading (MA); secondary education (M Ed); secondary humanities education (M Ed); secondary STEM education (M Ed); special education (M Ed); teaching and learning (Ed D); teaching English to speakers of other languages (MA). *Program availability:* Part-time, evening/weekend, online learning. *Degree requirements:* For master's, publishable research paper (M Ed), e-portfolio. *Entrance requirements:* For master's, undergraduate degree from accredited, GCU-approved college, university, or program with minimum GPA 2.8. Additional exam requirements/recommendations for

international students: Required—TOEFL (minimum score 550 paper-based; 79 iBT), IELTS (minimum score 6). Electronic applications accepted.

Hardin-Simmons University, Graduate School, Irvin School of Education, Department of Educational Studies, Program in Gifted Education, Abilene, TX 79698-0001. Offers M Ed. *Program availability:* Part-time. *Faculty:* 2 full-time (both women), 1 (woman) part-time/adjunct. *Students:* 31 part-time (28 women); includes 5 minority (2 Black or African American, non-Hispanic/Latino; 3 Hispanic/Latino). Average age 38. 11 applicants, 100% accepted, 9 enrolled. In 2017, 6 master's awarded. *Degree requirements:* For master's, comprehensive exam. *Entrance requirements:* For master's, minimum undergraduate GPA of 3.0 in major, 2.7 overall. Additional exam requirements/recommendations for international students: Required—TOEFL (minimum score 550 paper-based; 79 iBT). *Application deadline:* For fall admission, 8/15 priority date for domestic students, 4/1 for international students; for spring admission, 1/5 priority date for domestic students, 9/1 for international students. Applications are processed on a rolling basis. Application fee: $50 ($150 for international students). Electronic applications accepted. *Expenses:* Tuition: Full-time $13,500; part-time $750 per semester hour. *Required fees:* $220 per term. One-time fee: $50. Tuition and fees vary according to course load, campus/location and program. *Financial support:* In 2017–18, 8 students received support. Fellowships and scholarships/grants available. Support available to part-time students. Financial award application deadline: 6/30; financial award applicants required to submit FAFSA. *Faculty research:* Experiences of gifted learners in college, use of authentic assessment, brain research and how it works in learning, theories of multiple intelligence beyond Howard Gardner. *Unit head:* Dr. Mary Christopher, Program Director, 325-670-1510, Fax: 325-670-1397, E-mail: mchris@hsutx.edu. *Application contact:* Dr. Nancy Kucinski, Dean of Graduate Studies, 325-670-1298, Fax: 325-670-1564, E-mail: gradoff@hsutx.edu.

Hofstra University, School of Education, Specialized Programs in Education, Hempstead, NY 11549. Offers applied behavior analysis (Advanced Certificate); childhood special education (MS Ed); early childhood special education (MS Ed, Advanced Certificate); educational and policy leadership (Ed D); educational leadership (Advanced Certificate), including school building leader/school district business leader; educational leadership and policy studies (MS Ed), including K-12; elementary special education (MS Ed); gifted education (Advanced Certificate), including school building leader/school district business leader; health education (MS); health professions pedagogy and leadership (MS); higher education leadership and policy studies (MS Ed); inclusive early childhood special education (MS Ed); inclusive elementary special education (MS Ed); inclusive secondary special education (MS Ed); literacy studies (MA, MS Ed, Ed D, Advanced Certificate), including birth-grade 6 (MS Ed, Advanced Certificate), grades 5-12 (MS Ed, Advanced Certificate), literacy studies (Ed D); pedagogy for health professions (Advanced Certificate); physical education (MS); school district business leader (Advanced Certificate); secondary education generalist - students with disabilities 7-12 (MS Ed), including students with disabilities 7-12; secondary special education generalist (MS Ed), including extension in secondary education; special education (MS Ed, Advanced Certificate); special education assessment and diagnosis (Advanced Certificate); special education early childhood intervention (MS Ed); special education: international perspectives (MS Ed); teaching students with severe or multiple disabilities (Advanced Certificate). *Program availability:* Part-time, evening/weekend, blended/hybrid learning. *Students:* 148 full-time (110 women), 249 part-time (188 women); includes 105 minority (54 Black or African American, non-Hispanic/Latino; 1 American Indian or Alaska Native, non-Hispanic/Latino; 13 Asian, non-Hispanic/Latino; 35 Hispanic/Latino; 1 Native Hawaiian or other Pacific Islander, non-Hispanic/Latino; 1 Two or more races, non-Hispanic/Latino), 1 international. Average age 32. 228 applicants, 93% accepted, 132 enrolled. In 2017, 97 master's, 22 doctorates, 31 other advanced degrees awarded. *Degree requirements:* For master's, one foreign language, comprehensive exam (for some programs), thesis (for some programs), electronic portfolio, capstone course, internship, practicum, student teaching, seminars, minimum GPA 3.0; for doctorate, one foreign language, comprehensive exam, thesis/dissertation, qualifying hearing. *Entrance requirements:* For master's, GRE, interview, letters of recommendation, portfolio, essay, certification; for doctorate, GRE or MAT, interview, resume, essay, master's degree, 3 letters of recommendation, writing sample; for Advanced Certificate, GRE, interview, letters of recommendation, essay, professional experience, resume, master's degree. Additional exam requirements/recommendations for international students: Required—TOEFL (minimum score 550 paper-based; 80 iBT). *Application deadline:* Applications are processed on a rolling basis. Application fee: $75. Electronic applications accepted. *Expenses: Tuition:* Full-time $1292. *Required fees:* $970. Tuition and fees vary according to program. *Financial support:* In 2017–18, 225 students received support, including 118 fellowships with full and partial tuition reimbursements available (averaging $3,887 per year), 12 research assistantships with full and partial tuition reimbursements available (averaging $7,215 per year); career-related internships or fieldwork, Federal Work-Study, institutionally sponsored loans, scholarships/grants, traineeships, tuition waivers (full and partial), and unspecified assistantships also available. Support available to part-time students. Financial award applicants required to submit FAFSA. *Faculty research:* Collaborative teaching and learning; language and culture; new media literacies; applied behavior analysis; K-12 leadership development. *Unit head:* Dr. Elfreda Blue, Chairperson, 516-463-5762, Fax: 516-463-6184, E-mail: elfreda.blue@hofstra.edu. *Application contact:* Sunil Samuel, Assistant Vice President of Admissions, 516-463-4723, Fax: 516-463-4664, E-mail: graduateadmission@hofstra.edu.
Website: http://www.hofstra.edu/education/

James Madison University, The Graduate School, College of Education, Program in Special Education, Harrisonburg, VA 22801. Offers adapted curriculum (MAT); autism (M Ed); behavior specialist (M Ed); early childhood special education (MAT); general curriculum K-12 special education (MAT); gifted education (M Ed); inclusive early childhood special education (MAT); instructional specialist (M Ed); K-12 special education (MAT); visual impairments (M Ed). *Accreditation:* NCATE. *Program availability:* Part-time. *Students:* 27 full-time (26 women), 11 part-time (5 women); includes 2 minority (1 Black or African American, non-Hispanic/Latino; 1 Two or more races, non-Hispanic/Latino). Average age 30. In 2017, 27 master's awarded. Application fee: $55. Electronic applications accepted. *Expenses:* Tuition, state resident: full-time $10,512; part-time $438 per credit hour. Tuition, nonresident: full-time $28,358; part-time $1162 per credit hour. *Required fees:* $1128. *Financial support:* In 2017–18, 6 students received support. Fellowships, Federal Work-Study, and 6 assistantships (averaging $7911) available. Financial award application deadline: 3/1; financial award applicants required to submit FAFSA. *Unit head:* Dr. David A. Slykhuis, Interim Department Head, 540-568-4314, E-mail: slykhuda@jmu.edu. *Application contact:* Lynette D. Michael, Director of Graduate Admissions, 540-568-6131 Ext. 6395, Fax: 540-568-7860, E-mail: michaeld@jmu.edu.
Website: http://www.jmu.edu/coe/efex/index.shtml

Johns Hopkins University, School of Education, Certificate Programs in Education, Baltimore, MD 21218. Offers advanced methods for differentiated instruction and inclusive education (Graduate Certificate); applied behavior analysis (Post-Master's Certificate); clinical mental health counseling (Post-Master's Certificate); counseling (Advanced Certificate); data-based decision making and organizational improvement

(Graduate Certificate); early intervention/preschool special education specialist (Graduate Certificate); education of students with autism and other pervasive developmental disorders (Graduate Certificate); educational leadership for independent schools (Graduate Certificate); evidence-based teaching in the health professions (Post-Master's Certificate); gifted education (Graduate Certificate); leadership in technology integration (Graduate Certificate); mind, brain and teaching (Graduate Certificate); school administration and supervision (Graduate Certificate); urban education (Graduate Certificate). *Program availability:* Part-time-only, evening/weekend, 100% online, blended/hybrid learning. *Entrance requirements:* For degree, minimum of bachelor's degree from regionally- or nationally-accredited institution (master's degree for some programs); minimum GPA of 3.0 in all previous programs of study; official transcripts from all post-secondary institutions attended; essay; curriculum vitae/resume; two letters of recommendation; dispositions survey. Electronic applications accepted. *Expenses:* Contact institution.

Johns Hopkins University, School of Education, Master's Programs in Education, Baltimore, MD 21218. Offers counseling (MS), including clinical mental health counseling, school counseling; education (MS), including educational studies, gifted education, reading, school administration and supervision, technology for educators; elementary education (MAT); health professions (M Ed); intelligence analysis (MS); organizational leadership (MS); secondary education (MAT), including biology, chemistry, earth/space science, English, physics, social studies; special education (MS), including early childhood special education, general special education studies, mild to moderate disabilities, severe disabilities. *Program availability:* Part-time, evening/weekend, 100% online, blended/hybrid learning. *Degree requirements:* For master's, comprehensive exam (for some programs), portfolio, capstone project and/or internship; PRAXIS II (subject area assessments) for initial teacher preparation programs that lead to licensure. *Entrance requirements:* For master's, GRE (for full-time programs only); PRAXIS I/core or state-approved alternative (for initial teacher preparation programs that lead to licensure), minimum of bachelor's degree from regionally- or nationally-accredited institution; minimum GPA of 3.0 in all previous programs of study; official transcripts from all post-secondary institutions attended; essay; curriculum vitae/resume; letters of recommendation (3 for full-time programs, 2 for part-time programs); dispositions survey. Additional exam requirements/recommendations for international students: Required—TOEFL (minimum score 600 paper-based; 100 iBT), IELTS (minimum score 7). Electronic applications accepted. *Expenses:* Contact institution.

Kent State University, College of Education, Health and Human Services, School of Lifespan Development and Educational Sciences, Kent, OH 44242-0001. Offers clinical mental health counseling (M Ed); counseling (Ed S); counseling and human development services (PhD); educational psychology (M Ed, MA); human development and family studies (MA); instructional technology (M Ed, PhD), including computer technology (M Ed), educational psychology (PhD), general instructional technology (M Ed); rehabilitation counseling (M Ed); school counseling (M Ed); school psychology (PhD, Ed S), special education (M Ed, PhD, Ed S), including deaf education (M Ed), early childhood education (M Ed), educational interpreter K-12 (M Ed), general special education (M Ed), gifted education (M Ed), mild/moderate intervention (M Ed), moderate/intensive intervention (M Ed), special education (PhD, Ed S), transition to work (M Ed). *Program availability:* Part-time, evening/weekend. *Degree requirements:* For master's, thesis optional; for doctorate, comprehensive exam, thesis/dissertation. *Entrance requirements:* For master's, doctorate, and Ed S, GRE General Test. Additional exam requirements/recommendations for international students: Required—TOEFL (minimum score 550 paper-based; 80 iBT). Electronic applications accepted. *Expenses:* Tuition, state resident: full-time $11,310; part-time $515 per credit hour. Tuition, nonresident: full-time $20,396; part-time $928 per credit hour. *International tuition:* $18,544 full-time.

Liberty University, School of Education, Lynchburg, VA 24515. Offers curriculum and instruction (Ed D, Ed S), including elementary education, middle grades education, secondary education, special education; educational leadership (Ed D); gifted education (Certificate); math specialist (M Ed); middle grades (MAT, Certificate); reading specialist (M Ed); school leadership (Certificate); secondary education (MAT); sport management (MS), including coaching and athletic administration, outdoor adventure sport, sport administration, tourism. *Accreditation:* NCATE. *Program availability:* Part-time, online learning. *Students:* 1,966 full-time (1,428 women), 3,484 part-time (2,528 women); includes 1,323 minority (1,026 Black or African American, non-Hispanic/Latino; 29 American Indian or Alaska Native, non-Hispanic/Latino; 49 Asian, non-Hispanic/Latino; 100 Hispanic/Latino; 9 Native Hawaiian or other Pacific Islander, non-Hispanic/Latino; 110 Two or more races, non-Hispanic/Latino), 58 international. Average age 37. 3,748 applicants, 58% accepted, 1167 enrolled. In 2017, 656 master's, 110 doctorates, 316 other advanced degrees awarded. *Degree requirements:* For doctorate, comprehensive exam, thesis/dissertation. *Entrance requirements:* For master's, GRE General Test or MAT (if taken in or before 1999), 2 letters of recommendation, minimum undergraduate GPA of 3.0, curriculum vitae; for doctorate and other advanced degree, GRE General Test or MAT (if taken before 1999), minimum master's GPA of 3.0, 3 years of teaching experience. Additional exam requirements/recommendations for international students: Required—TOEFL (minimum score 600 paper-based; 100 iBT). *Application deadline:* For fall admission, 6/1 for domestic students; for spring admission, 11/1 for domestic students. Applications are processed on a rolling basis. Application fee: $50. Electronic applications accepted. *Expenses:* Contact institution. *Financial support:* Federal Work-Study and tuition waivers (partial) available. *Faculty research:* Self-determination, character education, bibliotherapy, learning styles, distance education. *Unit head:* Dr. Heather Schoffstall, Dean, 434-582-2445, Fax: 434-582-2468, E-mail: awgunter@liberty.edu. *Application contact:* Jay Bridge, Director of Graduate Admissions, 800-424-9595, Fax: 800-628-7977, E-mail: gradadmissions@liberty.edu.
Website: http://www.liberty.edu/academics/education/graduate/

Lindenwood University, Graduate Programs, School of Education, St. Charles, MO 63301-1695. Offers behavioral analysis (MA); education (MA), including autism spectrum disorders, character education, early intervention in autism and sensory impairment, gifted, technology; educational administration (MA, Ed D, Ed S); English to speakers of other languages (MA); instructional leadership (Ed D, Ed S); library media (MA); professional counseling (MA); school administration (MA, Ed S); school counseling (MA); teaching (MA). *Program availability:* Part-time, evening/weekend, 100% online, blended/hybrid learning. *Faculty:* 47 full-time (31 women), 213 part-time/adjunct (135 women). *Students:* 434 full-time (319 women), 1,292 part-time (989 women); includes 387 minority (313 Black or African American, non-Hispanic/Latino; 9 American Indian or Alaska Native, non-Hispanic/Latino; 13 Asian, non-Hispanic/Latino; 37 Hispanic/Latino; 1 Native Hawaiian or other Pacific Islander, non-Hispanic/Latino; 14 Two or more races, non-Hispanic/Latino), 20 international. Average age 36. 828 applicants, 61% accepted, 378 enrolled. In 2017, 431 master's, 63 doctorates, 94 other advanced degrees awarded. *Degree requirements:* For master's, thesis (for some programs), minimum GPA of 3.0; for doctorate, thesis/dissertation, minimum GPA of 3.0; for Ed S, comprehensive exam, project, minimum GPA of 3.0. *Entrance requirements:* For master's, interview, minimum undergraduate cumulative GPA of 3.0, writing sample, letter of recommendation; for doctorate, GRE, minimum graduate GPA of 3.4, resume, interview, writing sample, 4 letters of recommendation; for Ed S, master's degree in education, relevant work experience. Additional exam requirements/recommendations

for international students: Required—TOEFL (minimum score 550 paper-based; 80 iBT); Recommended—IELTS (minimum score 6.5). *Application deadline:* For fall admission, 8/27 priority date for domestic and international students; for spring admission, 1/14 priority date for domestic and international students; for summer admission, 6/4 priority date for domestic and international students. Applications are processed on a rolling basis. Application fee: $30 ($100 for international students). Electronic applications accepted. *Expenses: Tuition:* Full-time $16,300; part-time $460 per credit. *Required fees:* $660; $330 per credit. Tuition and fees vary according to degree level and program. *Financial support:* In 2017–18, 1,615 students received support. Career-related internships or fieldwork, Federal Work-Study, institutionally sponsored loans, scholarships/grants, tuition waivers (partial), and unspecified assistantships available. Financial award application deadline: 6/30; financial award applicants required to submit FAFSA. *Unit head:* Dr. Anthony Scheffler, Dean, School of Education, 636-949-4618, Fax: 636-949-4197, E-mail: ascheffler@lindenwood.edu. *Application contact:* Kara Schilli, Director, Evening and Graduate Admissions, 636-949-4349, Fax: 636-949-4109, E-mail: adultadmissions@lindenwood.edu.
Website: http://www.lindenwood.edu/academics/academic-schools/school-of-education/

Lynn University, Donald E. and Helen L. Ross College of Education, Boca Raton, FL 33431-5598. Offers educational leadership (M Ed, Ed D), including K-12 (Ed D); school administration K-12 (M Ed); exceptional student education (M Ed), including school administration K-12. *Program availability:* Part-time, evening/weekend, online learning. *Faculty:* 6 full-time (4 women), 4 part-time/adjunct (3 women). *Students:* 31 full-time (23 women), 62 part-time (42 women); includes 32 minority (20 Black or African American, non-Hispanic/Latino; 1 American Indian or Alaska Native, non-Hispanic/Latino; 10 Hispanic/Latino; 1 Two or more races, non-Hispanic/Latino), 3 international. Average age 36. 46 applicants, 78% accepted, 30 enrolled. In 2017, 24 master's, 22 doctorates awarded. *Degree requirements:* For master's, comprehensive exam, thesis (for some programs), completion of degree in maximum of four calendar years; minimum cumulative GPA of 3.0 and B grade or higher in each course; orientation seminar (one credit); minimum of 40 credits; FTCE ESE K-12 Exam; for doctorate, thesis/dissertation, mid-program review; minimum cumulative GPA of 3.25 and B grade or higher in each course. *Entrance requirements:* For master's, bachelor's degree from accredited institution, minimum undergraduate GPA of 3.0, official undergraduate and graduate transcripts of all academic coursework attempted, current résumé, statement of professional goals, writing sample, two recent letters of recommendation; for doctorate, professional practice statement that identifies applicant's goals and explains how Lynn's program will help attain them, official transcript showing conferral of master's degree, two letters of recommendation from previous professors or employers, current resume, interview. Additional exam requirements/recommendations for international students: Required—TOEFL (minimum score 550 paper-based; 80 iBT), IELTS (minimum score 6.5). *Application deadline:* For fall admission, 8/18 for domestic students, 8/4 for international students; for spring admission, 12/15 for domestic students, 12/1 for international students; for summer admission, 4/17 for domestic students, 4/3 for international students. Applications are processed on a rolling basis. Application fee: $45. Electronic applications accepted. *Expenses:* $740 per credit (for master's degrees); $850 per credit (for EdD). *Financial support:* Career-related internships or fieldwork, Federal Work-Study, scholarships/grants, tuition waivers (partial), and unspecified assistantships available. Support available to part-time students. Financial award application deadline: 3/1; financial award applicants required to submit FAFSA. *Faculty research:* Student achievement, students with learning differences, teacher and student retention, student motivation and cognition, neuroscience leadership and learning. *Unit head:* Dr. Kathleen Weigel, Dean, College of Education, 561-237-7441, E-mail: kweigel@lynn.edu. *Application contact:* Steven Pruitt, Director of Graduate and Undergraduate Evening Admission, 561-237-7834, Fax: 561-237-7100, E-mail: spruitt@lynn.edu.
Website: http://www.lynn.edu/academics/colleges/education

McNeese State University, Doré School of Graduate Studies, Burton College of Education, Department of Education Professions, Program in Curriculum and Instruction, Lake Charles, LA 70609. Offers academically gifted education (M Ed); elementary education (M Ed); reading (M Ed); secondary education (M Ed); special education (M Ed). *Program availability:* Evening/weekend. *Entrance requirements:* For master's, GRE, teaching certificate. *Application deadline:* For fall admission, 5/15 priority date for domestic and international students; for spring admission, 10/15 priority date for domestic and international students. Applications are processed on a rolling basis. Application fee: $20 ($30 for international students). *Financial support:* Application deadline: 5/1. *Unit head:* Dr. Brett C. Welch, Director, 337-475-5405, Fax: 337-475-5272, E-mail: bwelch@mcneese.edu. *Application contact:* Dr. Dustin M. Hebert, Director of Dore' School of Graduate Studies, 337-475-5396, Fax: 337-475-5397, E-mail: admissions@mcneese.edu.

Meredith College, School of Education, Health and Human Sciences, Raleigh, NC 27607-5298. Offers academically and intellectually gifted (M Ed); elementary education (M Ed, MAT); English as a second language (M Ed, MAT); health and physical education (MAT); nutrition, health and human performance (MS, Postbaccalaureate Certificate), including dietetic internship (Postbaccalaureate Certificate), nutrition (MS); psychology (MA), including industrial/organizational psychology; reading (M Ed); special education (MAT); special education (general curriculum) (M Ed). *Accreditation:* NCATE. *Program availability:* Part-time, evening/weekend. *Students:* 25 full-time (24 women), 22 part-time (all women); includes 13 minority (8 Black or African American, non-Hispanic/Latino; 1 American Indian or Alaska Native, non-Hispanic/Latino; 1 Asian, non-Hispanic/Latino; 3 Hispanic/Latino). Average age 31. 57 applicants, 54% accepted, 31 enrolled. In 2017, 14 master's awarded. *Degree requirements:* For master's, thesis optional. *Entrance requirements:* For master's, GRE General Test or MAT, minimum GPA of 2.5, teaching license, recommendations. Additional exam requirements/recommendations for international students: Required—TOEFL. *Application deadline:* For fall admission, 7/1 priority date for domestic students; for spring admission, 11/1 priority date for domestic students. Applications are processed on a rolling basis. Application fee: $50. Electronic applications accepted. *Expenses:* Contact institution. *Financial support:* Career-related internships or fieldwork, institutionally sponsored loans, and tuition waivers (partial) available. Support available to part-time students. Financial award application deadline: 2/15; financial award applicants required to submit FAFSA. *Unit head:* Dr. Monica McKinney, Graduate Program Manager, 919-760-8056, Fax: 919-760-2303, E-mail: mckinneym@meredith.edu.
Website: https://www.meredith.edu/school-of-education-health-and-human-sciences

Millersville University of Pennsylvania, College of Graduate Studies and Adult Learning, College of Education and Human Services, Department of Early, Middle, and Exceptional Education, Program in Gifted Education, Millersville, PA 17551-0302. Offers M Ed. *Program availability:* Part-time, evening/weekend, blended/hybrid learning. *Faculty:* 9 full-time (4 women), 11 part-time/adjunct (8 women). *Students:* 3 full-time (2 women), 25 part-time (19 women). Average age 32. 19 applicants, 95% accepted, 9 enrolled. In 2017, 6 master's awarded. *Degree requirements:* For master's, thesis optional, clinical practicum, evaluation of coursework. *Entrance requirements:* For master's, GRE or MAT (if GPA is lower than 3.0), teaching certificate. Additional exam requirements/recommendations for international students: Required—TOEFL (minimum score 80 iBT), IELTS (minimum score 6.5), PTE (minimum score 60). *Application*

Education of the Gifted

deadline: Applications are processed on a rolling basis. Application fee: $40. Electronic applications accepted. *Expenses:* $500 per credit resident tuition and fees; $750 per credit non-resident tuition and fees; $114.75 per credit general fee (maximum of 12 credits); technology fee $27 per credit (resident), $39 per credit (non-resident). *Financial support:* Unspecified assistantships available. Financial award application deadline: 3/15; financial award applicants required to submit FAFSA. *Faculty research:* Online education, STEM education, gifted education. *Unit head:* Dr. Marcia Nell, Department Chair, 717-871-7344, E-mail: marcia.nell@millersville.edu. *Application contact:* Dr. Victor S. DeSantis, Dean of College of Graduate Studies and Adult Learning/Associate Provost for Civic and Community Engagement, 717-871-7619, Fax: 717-871-7954, E-mail: victor.desantis@millersville.edu.
Website: http://www.millersville.edu/academics/educ/eled/graduate-programs/gifted-education.php#MasterofEducationDegreeinGiftedEducation

Mississippi University for Women, Graduate School, College of Education and Human Sciences, Columbus, MS 39701-9998. Offers differentiated instruction (M Ed); educational leadership (M Ed); gifted studies (M Ed); reading/literacy (M Ed); teaching (MAT). *Accreditation:* ASHA; NCATE. *Program availability:* Part-time. *Degree requirements:* For master's, comprehensive exam, thesis optional. *Entrance requirements:* For master's, GRE General Test or NTE (M Ed in gifted education or MS in speech/language pathology), MAT (M Ed in instructional management), minimum QPA of 3.0.

Morehead State University, Graduate Programs, College of Education, Department of Foundational and Graduate Studies in Education, Morehead, KY 40351. Offers adult and higher education (MA, Ed S); certified professional counselor (Ed S); counseling P-12 (MA); curriculum and instruction (Ed S); educational technology (MA Ed); instructional leadership (Ed S); school administration (MA); school counseling (Ed S); teacher leader business and marketing content (MA Ed); teacher leader business and marketing technology (MA Ed); teacher leader educational technology (MA Ed); teacher leader English (MA Ed); teacher leader gifted education (MA Ed); teacher leader IECE certification (MA Ed); teacher leader interdisciplinary education P-5 (MA Ed); teacher leader middle grades (MA Ed); teacher leader non IECE certification (MA Ed); teacher leader reading/writing - non-certification (MA Ed); teacher leader reading/writing certification (MA Ed); teacher leader school communication - certification (MA Ed); teacher leader school communication - non-certification (MA Ed); teacher leader social studies (MA Ed); teacher leader special education (MA Ed). *Accreditation:* NCATE. *Program availability:* Part-time, evening/weekend. *Degree requirements:* For master's, thesis optional, oral and/or written comprehensive exams; for Ed S, thesis, oral exam. *Entrance requirements:* For master's, GRE General Test, minimum overall undergraduate GPA of 2.5; for Ed S, GRE General Test, interview, master's degree, minimum GPA of 3.5, work experience. Additional exam requirements/recommendations for international students: Required—TOEFL (minimum score 500 paper-based). Electronic applications accepted. *Faculty research:* Character education, school accountability, computer applications for school administrators.

Northeastern Illinois University, College of Graduate Studies and Research, Daniel L. Goodwin College of Education, Program in Gifted Education, Chicago, IL 60625. Offers MA. *Program availability:* Part-time, evening/weekend. *Degree requirements:* For master's, comprehensive exam, thesis or alternative. *Entrance requirements:* For master's, teaching certificate or previous course work in history or philosophy of education, minimum GPA of 2.75. Additional exam requirements/recommendations for international students: Required—TOEFL (minimum score 550 paper-based; 79 iBT). *Application deadline:* For fall admission, 4/1 priority date for domestic students; for spring admission, 8/15 for domestic students. Applications are processed on a rolling basis. Application fee: $30. Electronic applications accepted. *Expenses:* Tuition, state resident: full-time $7274; part-time $404.11 per credit hour. Tuition, nonresident: full-time $14,548; part-time $808.23 per credit hour. *Required fees:* $1284. *Faculty research:* Effect of inclusion in public school gifted programs, social and emotional needs of gifted children, problem-based learning strategies. *Unit head:* Dr. Michele Kane, Professor and Program Director, 773-442-5594, E-mail: m-kane1@neiu.edu. *Application contact:* Martha Narvaez, Graduate Admission Representative, 773-442-6006, E-mail: m-narvaez@neiu.edu.

Pacific University, College of Education, Forest Grove, OR 97116-1797. Offers early childhood education (MAT); education (MAE); elementary education (MAT); ESOL (MAT); high school education (MAT); middle school education (MAT); special education (MAT); speech-language pathology (MS); STEM education (MAT); talented and gifted (M Ed); visual function in learning (M Ed). *Accreditation:* ASHA; NCATE. *Program availability:* Part-time, evening/weekend. *Degree requirements:* For master's, research project. *Entrance requirements:* For master's, California Basic Educational Skills Test, PRAXIS II, minimum undergraduate GPA of 2.75, 3.0 graduate. Additional exam requirements/recommendations for international students: Required—TOEFL. Electronic applications accepted. *Expenses:* Contact institution. *Faculty research:* Defining a culturally competent classroom, technology in the K-12 classroom, Socratic seminars, social studies education.

Purdue University, Graduate School, College of Education, Department of Educational Studies, West Lafayette, IN 47907. Offers administration (MS Ed, PhD, Ed S); counseling and development (MS Ed, PhD); education of the gifted (MS Ed); educational psychology (MS Ed, PhD); foundations of education (MS Ed, PhD); higher education administration (MS Ed, PhD); special education (MS Ed, PhD). *Accreditation:* ACA (one or more programs are accredited); NCATE (one or more programs are accredited). *Program availability:* Part-time, evening/weekend. *Faculty:* 29 full-time (22 women), 1 part-time/adjunct (0 women). *Students:* 78 full-time (60 women), 226 part-time (162 women); includes 45 minority (16 Black or African American, non-Hispanic/Latino; 8 Asian, non-Hispanic/Latino; 15 Hispanic/Latino; 6 Two or more races, non-Hispanic/Latino), 45 international. Average age 32. 214 applicants, 53% accepted, 70 enrolled. In 2017, 38 master's, 20 doctorates, 4 other advanced degrees awarded. *Degree requirements:* For master's, thesis optional; for doctorate, thesis/dissertation, oral and written exams; for Ed S, oral presentation, project. *Entrance requirements:* For master's, GRE General Test (except for special education if undergraduate GPA is higher than a 3.0), minimum undergraduate GPA of 3.0; for doctorate and Ed S, GRE General Test (minimum combined score of 1000, 300 for new scoring), minimum undergraduate GPA of 3.0. Additional exam requirements/recommendations for international students: Required—TOEFL (minimum score 550 paper-based; 77 iBT), TWE (minimum score 5). *Application deadline:* Applications are processed on a rolling basis. Application fee: $60 ($75 for international students). Electronic applications accepted. *Financial support:* Fellowships with full tuition reimbursements, research assistantships with full tuition reimbursements, teaching assistantships with full tuition reimbursements, career-related internships or fieldwork, and tuition waivers (full) available. Support available to part-time students. Financial award application deadline: 3/1; financial award applicants required to submit FAFSA. *Faculty research:* Motivation, learning disabilities, school learning, group processes, cognitive development. *Unit head:* F. Richard Olenchak, Head, 765-494-9170, E-mail: olenchak@purdue.edu. *Application contact:* Heather Brinkman, Graduate Contact, 765-494-2345, Fax: 765-494-5832, E-mail: hbrinkma@purdue.edu.
Website: http://www.edst.purdue.edu/

Regent University, Graduate School, School of Education, Virginia Beach, VA 23464-9800. Offers education (M Ed, Ed D, PhD), including adult education (Ed D, PhD, Ed S), advanced educational leadership (Ed D, PhD, Ed S), character education (Ed D, PhD, Ed S), Christian education leadership (Ed D, PhD, Ed S), Christian school administration (M Ed), curriculum and instruction (Ed D, PhD, Ed S), curriculum and instruction - adult education (M Ed), curriculum and instruction - Christian school (M Ed), curriculum and instruction - gifted and talented (M Ed), curriculum and instruction - STEM education (M Ed), curriculum and instruction - teacher leader (M Ed), discipleship for ministry (M Ed), educational leadership (M Ed), educational psychology (Ed D, PhD, Ed S), educational technology and online learning (Ed D, PhD, Ed S), elementary education (M Ed), exceptional education executive leadership (Ed D, PhD, Ed S), higher education (Ed D, PhD, Ed S), higher education leadership and management (Ed D, PhD, Ed S), instructional design and technology (M Ed), K-12 school leadership (Ed D, PhD, Ed S), K-12 special education (M Ed), leadership in mathematics education (M Ed), reading specialist (M Ed), special education (Ed D, PhD, Ed S), student affairs (M Ed), TESOL - adult education (M Ed), TESOL - K-12 (M Ed); educational specialist (Ed S), including adult education (Ed D, PhD, Ed S), advanced educational leadership (Ed D, PhD, Ed S), character education (Ed D, PhD, Ed S), Christian education leadership (Ed D, PhD, Ed S), curriculum and instruction (Ed D, PhD, Ed S), educational psychology (Ed D, PhD, Ed S), educational technology and online learning (Ed D, PhD, Ed S), exceptional education executive leadership (Ed D, PhD, Ed S), higher education (Ed D, PhD, Ed S), higher education leadership and management (Ed D, PhD, Ed S), K-12 school leadership (Ed D, PhD, Ed S), special education (Ed D, PhD, Ed S). *Accreditation:* TEAC. *Program availability:* Part-time, evening/weekend, 100% online, blended/hybrid learning. *Faculty:* 22 full-time (10 women), 44 part-time/adjunct (32 women). *Students:* 80 full-time (59 women), 945 part-time (750 women); includes 432 minority (352 Black or African American, non-Hispanic/Latino; 4 American Indian or Alaska Native, non-Hispanic/Latino; 14 Asian, non-Hispanic/Latino; 43 Hispanic/Latino; 19 Two or more races, non-Hispanic/Latino), 12 international. Average age 40. 1,125 applicants, 49% accepted, 436 enrolled. In 2017, 316 master's, 24 doctorates awarded. *Degree requirements:* For master's, thesis or alternative; for doctorate, comprehensive exam, thesis/dissertation. *Entrance requirements:* For master's, Virginia Communication and Literacy Assessment (VCLA), PRAXIS, college transcripts, writing sample, interview; for doctorate, GRE, writing sample, resume, transcripts, interview. Additional exam requirements/recommendations for international students: Required—TOEFL (minimum score 577 paper-based). *Application deadline:* For fall admission, 4/1 priority date for domestic students; for spring admission, 10/15 priority date for domestic students. Applications are processed on a rolling basis. Application fee: $50. Electronic applications accepted. *Expenses:* Contact institution. *Financial support:* In 2017–18, 669 students received support, including 1 fellowship (averaging $10,000 per year); career-related internships or fieldwork, scholarships/grants, and unspecified assistantships also available. Support available to part-time students. *Faculty research:* Christian school administration, curriculum and instruction, educational technology and online learning, higher education, special education. *Unit head:* Dr. Donald Finn, Dean, 757-352-4278, Fax: 757-352-4318, E-mail: dfinn@regent.edu. *Application contact:* Heidi Cece, Assistant Vice President of Enrollment Management, 800-373-5504, Fax: 757-352-4381, E-mail: admissions@regent.edu.
Website: https://www.regent.edu/school-of-education/

St. Bonaventure University, School of Graduate Studies, School of Education, Differentiated Instruction Program, St. Bonaventure, NY 14778-2284. Offers gifted education (MS Ed, Adv C); gifted education and students with disabilities (MS Ed). *Program availability:* Part-time, evening/weekend. *Faculty:* 2 full-time (both women), 1 (woman) part-time/adjunct. *Students:* 18 full-time (17 women), 9 part-time (7 women), 1 international. Average age 26. 6 applicants, 83% accepted, 4 enrolled. In 2017, 17 master's awarded. *Degree requirements:* For master's, comprehensive exam, internship, portfolio; for Adv C, practicum, portfolio. *Entrance requirements:* For master's, GRE or MAT, disabilities or special education teaching certification (or letter of eligibility); interview; transcripts from all colleges previously attended; 2 letters of recommendation; writing sample; for Adv C, teaching certification (or letter of eligibility); interview; transcripts from all colleges previously attended; 2 references; master's degree; writing sample. Additional exam requirements/recommendations for international students: Required—TOEFL (minimum score 550 paper-based; 79 iBT). *Application deadline:* For fall admission, 6/1 priority date for domestic students, 2/1 priority date for international students; for spring admission, 11/15 priority date for domestic students, 7/1 priority date for international students. Applications are processed on a rolling basis. Application fee: $0. Electronic applications accepted. *Expenses:* $733 per credit hour, $100 graduation fee. *Financial support:* Federal Work-Study, scholarships/grants, health care benefits, and unspecified assistantships available. Support available to part-time students. Financial award application deadline: 4/15; financial award applicants required to submit FAFSA. *Faculty research:* Disproportionality in special education, gifted education, teacher education and curriculum, specializing in authentic and responsive pedagogy for diverse learners. *Unit head:* Dr. Rene' Hauser, Director, 716-375-4078, Fax: 716-375-2360, E-mail: rhauser@sbu.edu. *Application contact:* Bruce Campbell, Director of Graduate Admissions, 716-375-2429, Fax: 716-375-4015, E-mail: gradsch@sbu.edu.
Website: http://www.sbu.edu/academics/post-master's-in-differentiated-instruction

St. John's University, The School of Education, Department of Administrative and Instructional Leadership, Program in Instructional Leadership, Queens, NY 11439. Offers gifted education (Adv C); instructional leadership (Ed D, Adv C). *Program availability:* Part-time, blended/hybrid learning. *Students:* 9 full-time (7 women), 128 part-time (83 women); includes 48 minority (27 Black or African American, non-Hispanic/Latino; 1 American Indian or Alaska Native, non-Hispanic/Latino; 8 Asian, non-Hispanic/Latino; 11 Hispanic/Latino; 1 Two or more races, non-Hispanic/Latino), 3 international. Average age 41. 51 applicants, 96% accepted, 30 enrolled. In 2017, 24 doctorates, 3 Adv Cs awarded. *Degree requirements:* For doctorate, comprehensive exam, thesis/dissertation. *Entrance requirements:* For doctorate, GRE, official master's transcript, statement of purpose; for Adv C, statement of purpose, official master's transcripts, teaching certification. Additional exam requirements/recommendations for international students: Required—TOEFL, IELTS. *Application deadline:* For fall admission, 8/17 for domestic and international students; for summer admission, 5/15 for domestic and international students. Application fee: $70. Electronic applications accepted. *Expenses: Tuition:* Full-time $44,280; part-time $1230 per credit. *Required fees:* $340; $340 per credit. Tuition and fees vary according to course load, degree level and program. *Financial support:* Fellowships, research assistantships, scholarships/grants, and unspecified assistantships available. Support available to part-time students. Financial award application deadline: 2/1; financial award applicants required to submit FAFSA. *Faculty research:* Mathematics learning disabilities and difficulties with students identified as learning disabled or students who are English language learners, identification of mathematical giftedness in students who are English language learners, effects of parental participation and parenting behaviors on the science and mathematics academic achievement of school-age students, analysis of major theoretical perspectives in curriculum design and implementation. *Unit head:* Dr. Rene Parmar, Chair, 718-990-2503, E-mail: parmarr@stjohns.edu. *Application contact:* Dr. Rene Parmar, Chair, 718-990-2503, E-mail: parmarr@stjohns.edu.
Website: https://www.stjohns.edu/academics/schools-and-colleges/school-education/programs-and-majors/instructional-leadership-doctor-education

Saint Leo University, Graduate Studies in Education, Saint Leo, FL 33574-6665. Offers educational leadership (M Ed), including Catholic school administration; exceptional student education (M Ed); instructional design (MS, Certificate); instructional leadership (M Ed); reading (M Ed, Certificate); school leadership (Ed S). *Program availability:* Part-time, evening/weekend, online only, 100% online. *Faculty:* 8 full-time (all women), 18 part-time/adjunct (11 women). *Students:* 1 (woman) full-time, 360 part-time (282 women); includes 95 minority (56 Black or African American, non-Hispanic/Latino; 1 American Indian or Alaska Native, non-Hispanic/Latino; 1 Asian, non-Hispanic/Latino; 31 Hispanic/Latino; 6 Two or more races, non-Hispanic/Latino), 1 international. Average age 37. 214 applicants, 69% accepted, 125 enrolled. In 2017, 158 master's, 5 other advanced degrees awarded. *Degree requirements:* For master's, appropriate State of Florida certification tests, internship. *Entrance requirements:* For master's, GRE (minimum score of 1000), MAT (minimum score of 410), or minimum undergraduate GPA of 3.0 in final 2 years, official transcripts, current resumé, 2 professional recommendations, personal statement, bachelor's degree from regionally-accredited university, valid professional teaching certificate; for other advanced degree, valid professional teaching certificate (for Ed S). Additional exam requirements/recommendations for international students: Required—TOEFL (minimum score 550 paper-based; 78 iBT). *Application deadline:* For fall admission, 7/1 priority date for domestic students, 7/1 for international students; for winter admission, 7/1 for international students; for spring admission, 11/1 priority date for domestic students. Applications are processed on a rolling basis. Application fee: $80. Electronic applications accepted. *Expenses:* $480 per credit (for M Ed), $670 per credit (for Ed S). *Financial support:* In 2017–18, 17 students received support. Career-related internships or fieldwork, scholarships/grants, health care benefits, and tuition remission for Saint Leo employees and their dependents available. Financial award application deadline: 3/1; financial award applicants required to submit FAFSA. *Faculty research:* Impact of partnerships with K-12 school and university programs. *Unit head:* Dr. Fern Aefsky, Director of Graduate Studies in Education, 352-588-8309, Fax: 352-588-8861, E-mail: kara.winkler@saintleo.edu. *Application contact:* Mark Russum, Assistant Vice President, Enrollment, 800-707-8846, Fax: 352-588-7873, E-mail: grad.admissions@saintleo.edu. Website: http://www.saintleo.edu/education-master-degree

Saint Mary's University of Minnesota, Schools of Graduate and Professional Programs, Graduate School of Education, Education Program, Winona, MN 55987-1399. Offers culturally responsive teaching (Certificate); education (MA); gifted inclusive education (Certificate). *Unit head:* Lynn Albee, Director, 612-728-5128, Fax: 612-728-5121, E-mail: lalbee@smumn.edu. *Application contact:* James Callinan, Director of Admissions for Graduate and Professional Programs, 612-728-5158, Fax: 612-728-5121, E-mail: jcallina@smumn.edu. Website: http://www.smumn.edu/graduate-home/areas-of-study/graduate-school-of-education/ma-in-education

St. Thomas University, School of Leadership Studies, Institute for Education, Miami Gardens, FL 33054-6459. Offers earth/space science (Certificate); educational administration (MS, Certificate); educational leadership (Ed D); elementary education (MS); ESOL (Certificate); gifted education (Certificate); instructional technology (MS, Certificate); professional/studies (Certificate); reading (MS, Certificate); special education (MS). *Program availability:* Part-time, evening/weekend. *Degree requirements:* For master's, comprehensive exam; for doctorate, comprehensive exam, thesis/dissertation. *Entrance requirements:* For master's, interview, minimum GPA of 3.0 or GRE; for doctorate, GRE or MAT. Additional exam requirements/recommendations for international students: Required—TOEFL (minimum score 550 paper-based; 79 iBT). Electronic applications accepted.

Samford University, Orlean Beeson School of Education, Birmingham, AL 35229. Offers educational leadership (MSE, Ed D); elementary education (MS Ed, MSE); gifted (MSE); instructional design and technology (MSE); instructional leadership (MSE, Ed S); secondary education (MSE); special education (MSE). *Accreditation:* NCATE. *Program availability:* Part-time, evening/weekend, 100% online, blended/hybrid learning. *Faculty:* 11 full-time (7 women), 22 part-time/adjunct (12 women). *Students:* 206 full-time (144 women), 102 part-time (75 women); includes 124 minority (113 Black or African American, non-Hispanic/Latino; 3 American Indian or Alaska Native, non-Hispanic/Latino; 3 Asian, non-Hispanic/Latino; 2 Hispanic/Latino; 3 Two or more races, non-Hispanic/Latino), 1 international. Average age 37. 134 applicants, 84% accepted, 76 enrolled. In 2017, 79 master's, 34 doctorates, 21 other advanced degrees awarded. *Degree requirements:* For master's and Ed S, comprehensive exam; for doctorate, comprehensive exam, thesis/dissertation. *Entrance requirements:* For master's, GRE, MAT, PRAXIS II, interview, transcripts, essay, recommendations, teaching certification; for doctorate, resume, transcripts, interview, essay; for Ed S, teaching certification, transcripts, essay, interview. Additional exam requirements/recommendations for international students: Required—TOEFL (minimum score 90 iBT), IELTS (minimum score 6.5). *Application deadline:* For fall admission, 7/15 for domestic and international students; for winter admission, 11/15 for domestic and international students; for spring admission, 11/15 for domestic and international students; for summer admission, 4/15 for domestic and international students. Application fee: $35. Electronic applications accepted. *Expenses:* $813 per credit hour, $100 School of Education fee, $175 technology fee. *Financial support:* In 2017–18, 220 students received support. Scholarships/grants and unspecified assistantships available. Financial award application deadline: 2/15; financial award applicants required to submit FAFSA. *Faculty research:* Principal leadership's and teacher organizational commitment mentoring, professional development, and middle grades leadership coaching and administrator effectiveness character development programs in schools teacher efficacy related STEM and professional growth. *Unit head:* Dr. Bonnie Rabe, Interim Dean, 205-726-2565, E-mail: brabe@samford.edu. *Application contact:* Brooke Karr, Graduate Admissions Office Coordinator, 205-729-2783, Fax: 205-726-4233, E-mail: kbgilrea@samford.edu. Website: http://www.samford.edu/education/

Southeastern University, College of Education, Lakeland, FL 33801-6099. Offers curriculum and instruction (Ed D); educational leadership (M Ed); elementary education (M Ed); exceptional student education (M Ed); exceptional student education/educational therapy (M Ed); kinesiology (M Ed); organizational leadership (Ed D); reading education (M Ed); teaching English to speakers of other languages (M Ed). *Faculty:* 8 full-time (5 women), 12 part-time/adjunct (7 women). *Students:* 139 full-time (109 women), 225 part-time (172 women); includes 107 minority (57 Black or African American, non-Hispanic/Latino; 2 Asian, non-Hispanic/Latino; 48 Hispanic/Latino), 4 international. Average age 40. Application fee: $50. Electronic applications accepted. *Unit head:* James A. Anderson, Dean, 863-667-5366, E-mail: jaanderson2@seu.edu. Website: http://www.seu.edu/education/

Southern Arkansas University–Magnolia, School of Graduate Studies, Magnolia, AR 71753. Offers agriculture (MS); business administration (MBA), including agribusiness, social entrepreneurship, supply chain management; clinical and mental health counseling (MS); computer and information sciences (MS), including cyber security and privacy, data science, information technology; gifted and talented (M Ed), including curriculum and instruction, educational administration and supervision, gifted and talented P-8/7-12, instructional specialist P-4; higher, adult and lifelong education

(M Ed); kinesiology (M Ed), including coaching; library media and information specialist (M Ed); public administration (MPA); school counseling K-12 (M Ed); student affairs and college counseling (M Ed); teaching (MAT). *Accreditation:* NCATE. *Program availability:* Part-time, 100% online, blended/hybrid learning. *Faculty:* 36 full-time (20 women), 31 part-time/adjunct (12 women). *Students:* 242 full-time (89 women), 889 part-time (459 women); includes 167 minority (143 Black or African American, non-Hispanic/Latino; 7 American Indian or Alaska Native, non-Hispanic/Latino; 7 Asian, non-Hispanic/Latino; 3 Hispanic/Latino; 7 Two or more races, non-Hispanic/Latino), 562 international. Average age 28. 400 applicants, 100% accepted, 239 enrolled. In 2017, 875 master's awarded. *Degree requirements:* For master's, comprehensive exam (for some programs), thesis optional. *Entrance requirements:* For master's, GRE, MAT or GMAT, minimum GPA of 2.5. Additional exam requirements/recommendations for international students: Required—TOEFL (minimum score 550 paper-based), IELTS (minimum score 6). *Application deadline:* For fall admission, 7/20 for domestic students, 7/10 for international students; for spring admission, 12/1 for domestic students, 11/15 for international students; for summer admission, 4/1 for domestic students, 5/1 for international students. Applications are processed on a rolling basis. Application fee: $25 ($50 for international students). Electronic applications accepted. *Expenses:* Tuition, state resident: full-time $6038. Tuition, nonresident: full-time $8558. *Required fees:* $804. One-time fee: $110 full-time. Tuition and fees vary according to course load. *Financial support:* Career-related internships or fieldwork, Federal Work-Study, scholarships/grants, tuition waivers (full), and unspecified assistantships available. Financial award applicants required to submit FAFSA. *Faculty research:* Alternative certification for teachers, supervision of instruction, instructional leadership, counseling. *Unit head:* Dr. Kim Bloss, Dean, School of Graduate Studies, 870-235-4150, Fax: 870-235-5227, E-mail: kkbloss@saumag.edu. *Application contact:* Shrijana Malakar, Admissions Specialist, 870-235-4150, Fax: 870-235-5227, E-mail: smalakar@saumag.edu. Website: http://www.saumag.edu/graduate

Southern Methodist University, Annette Caldwell Simmons School of Education and Human Development, Department of Teaching and Learning, Dallas, TX 75275. Offers bilingual/ESL education (MBE); education (M Ed, PhD); gifted education (MBE); reading and writing (M Ed); special education (M Ed). *Program availability:* Part-time, evening/weekend. Terminal master's awarded for partial completion of doctoral program. *Degree requirements:* For master's, comprehensive exam, minimum GPA of 3.0; for doctorate, thesis/dissertation, qualifying exams, major area paper, evidence of teaching competency, dissemination of research (e.g., conference presentation), professional portfolio. *Entrance requirements:* For master's, minimum GPA of 3.0 or GRE, 3 letters of recommendation; for doctorate, GRE, minimum GPA of 3.3, 3 years of full-time teaching, 3 letters of recommendation, interview. Additional exam requirements/recommendations for international students: Required—TOEFL. Electronic applications accepted. *Faculty research:* Reading intervention, mathematics intervention, bilingual education, new literacies.

Teachers College, Columbia University, Department of Curriculum and Teaching, New York, NY 10027-6696. Offers curriculum and teaching (Ed M, MA, Ed D); curriculum and teaching: elementary education (MA); curriculum and teaching: secondary education (MA); early childhood education (MA, Ed D); early childhood education: special education (MA); elementary education-gifted extension (MA); elementary inclusive education (MA); gifted education (MA); literacy specialist (MA); secondary inclusive education (MA); special inclusive elementary education (MA). *Program availability:* Part-time, evening/weekend. *Students:* 196 full-time (181 women), 181 part-time (161 women); includes 141 minority (45 Black or African American, non-Hispanic/Latino; 2 American Indian or Alaska Native, non-Hispanic/Latino; 45 Asian, non-Hispanic/Latino; 35 Hispanic/Latino; 14 Two or more races, non-Hispanic/Latino), 37 international. Average age 30. 509 applicants, 72% accepted, 155 enrolled. Terminal master's awarded for partial completion of doctoral program. *Degree requirements:* For doctorate, thesis/dissertation. *Unit head:* Prof. Daniel Friedrich, Chair, E-mail: friedrich@exchange.tc.columbia.edu. *Application contact:* David Estrella, Director of Admission, 212-678-3305, Fax: 212-678-4171, E-mail: estrella@tc.columbia.edu.

Tennessee Technological University, College of Graduate Studies, College of Education, Department of Curriculum and Instruction, Program in Exceptional Learning, Cookeville, TN 38505. Offers applied behavior analysis (PhD); literacy (PhD); program planning and evaluation (PhD); STEM education (PhD). *Program availability:* Part-time, evening/weekend. *Students:* 9 full-time (4 women), 32 part-time (24 women); includes 2 minority (1 Black or African American, non-Hispanic/Latino; 1 Two or more races, non-Hispanic/Latino), 4 international. 24 applicants, 54% accepted, 11 enrolled. In 2017, 10 doctorates awarded. *Degree requirements:* For doctorate, comprehensive exam, thesis/dissertation. *Entrance requirements:* For doctorate, GRE, minimum GPA of 3.0. Additional exam requirements/recommendations for international students: Required—TOEFL (minimum score 550 paper-based; 79 iBT), IELTS (minimum score 5.5), PTE (minimum score 53), or TOEIC (Test of English as an International Communication). *Application deadline:* For fall admission, 8/1 for domestic students, 5/1 for international students; for spring admission, 12/1 for domestic students, 10/1 for international students; for summer admission, 5/1 for domestic students, 2/1 for international students. Applications are processed on a rolling basis. Application fee: $35 ($40 for international students). Electronic applications accepted. *Expenses:* Tuition, state resident: full-time $9925; part-time $565 per credit hour. Tuition, nonresident: full-time $22,993; part-time $1291 per credit hour. *Financial support:* Fellowships, research assistantships, and teaching assistantships available. Financial award application deadline: 4/1. *Unit head:* Dr. Lisa Zagumny, Director, 931-372-3078, Fax: 931-372-3517, E-mail: lzagumny@tntech.edu. *Application contact:* Shelia K. Kendrick, Coordinator of Graduate Studies, 931-372-3808, Fax: 931-372-3497, E-mail: skendrick@tntech.edu. Website: https://www.tntech.edu/education/elphd/

University at Buffalo, the State University of New York, Graduate School, Graduate School of Education, Department of Learning and Instruction, Buffalo, NY 14260. Offers biology education (Ed M, Certificate); chemistry education (Ed M, Certificate); childhood education (Ed M); childhood education with bilingual extension (Ed M); college teaching (Advanced Certificate); curriculum, instruction and the science of learning (PhD); early childhood education (Ed M); early childhood education with bilingual extension (Ed M); earth science education (Ed M, Certificate); education and technology (Ed M); education studies (Ed M); educational technology and new literacies (Certificate); educational technology and new literacies (Advanced Certificate); elementary education (Ed D); English education (Ed M, Certificate); English education studies (Ed M); English for speakers of other languages (Ed M); foreign and second language education (PhD); French education (Ed M, Certificate); German education (Ed M, Certificate); gifted education (Certificate); Latin education (Ed M, Certificate); literacy education studies (Ed M); literacy specialist (Ed M); literacy teaching and learning (Certificate); mathematics education (Ed M, Certificate); music education (Ed M, Certificate); music education studies (Ed M); music learning theory (Advanced Certificate); online education (Advanced Certificate); physics education (Ed M, Certificate); science and the public (Ed M); social studies education (Ed M, Certificate); Spanish education (Ed M, Certificate); special education (PhD); teaching English to speakers of other languages (Ed M). *Program availability:* Part-time, evening/weekend, 100% online. *Faculty:* 26 full-

Education of the Gifted

time (19 women), 74 part-time/adjunct (52 women). *Students:* 172 full-time (122 women), 325 part-time (226 women); includes 44 minority (25 Black or African American, non-Hispanic/Latino; 5 American Indian or Alaska Native, non-Hispanic/Latino; 14 Asian, non-Hispanic/Latino; 57 international. Average age 33. 316 applicants, 78% accepted, 174 enrolled. In 2017, 109 master's, 34 doctorates, 15 other advanced degrees awarded. *Degree requirements:* For master's, comprehensive exam; for doctorate, thesis/dissertation, research analysis exam, research experience. *Entrance requirements:* For master's, letters of reference; for doctorate, GRE General Test or MAT, interview, writing sample, letters of recommendation. Additional exam requirements/recommendations for international students: Required—TOEFL (minimum score 600 paper-based; 96 iBT). *Application deadline:* For fall admission, 2/1 priority date for domestic and international students; for spring admission, 11/15 priority date for domestic students, 10/1 for international students. Applications are processed on a rolling basis. Application fee: $50. Electronic applications accepted. *Financial support:* In 2017–18, 42 fellowships (averaging $5,181 per year), 44 research assistantships with tuition reimbursements (averaging $10,908 per year) were awarded; teaching assistantships, career-related internships or fieldwork, Federal Work-Study, institutionally sponsored loans, scholarships/grants, tuition waivers (full and partial), and unspecified assistantships also available. Financial award application deadline: 2/28; financial award applicants required to submit FAFSA. *Faculty research:* Science assessment, foreign language teaching and learning, early learning, new literacies, gender and education. *Total annual research expenditures:* $413,233. *Unit head:* Dr. David Bruce, Chair, 716-645-4069, Fax: 716-645-3161, E-mail: gse-info@buffalo.edu. *Application contact:* Luann Zak, Admissions Assistant, 716-645-2110, Fax: 716-645-7937, E-mail: luannzak@buffalo.edu.
Website: http://gse.buffalo.edu/lai

The University of Alabama, Graduate School, College of Education, Department of Special Education and Multiple Abilities, Tuscaloosa, AL 35487. Offers collaborative special education (M Ed, Ed S); early intervention (M Ed, Ed S); gifted and talented education (M Ed, Ed S); multiple abilities (M Ed); special education (Ed D, PhD). *Program availability:* Part-time, evening/weekend. *Faculty:* 9 full-time (7 women). *Students:* 31 full-time (29 women), 30 part-time (all women); includes 12 minority (7 Black or African American, non-Hispanic/Latino; 1 Asian, non-Hispanic/Latino; 1 Hispanic/Latino; 3 Two or more races, non-Hispanic/Latino). Average age 32. 45 applicants, 58% accepted, 21 enrolled. In 2017, 16 master's, 1 doctorate awarded. Terminal master's awarded for partial completion of doctoral program. *Degree requirements:* For master's, comprehensive exam, thesis optional; for doctorate, one foreign language, comprehensive exam, thesis/dissertation. *Entrance requirements:* For master's, GRE, minimum undergraduate GPA of 3.0, teaching certificate, 3 letters of recommendation; for doctorate, GRE, 3 years of teaching experience, minimum undergraduate GPA of 3.25. Additional exam requirements/recommendations for international students: Required—TOEFL. *Application deadline:* Applications are processed on a rolling basis. Application fee: $50 ($60 for international students). Electronic applications accepted. *Financial support:* In 2017–18, 18 students received support, including research assistantships with tuition reimbursements available (averaging $9,000 per year), teaching assistantships with tuition reimbursements available (averaging $9,000 per year); health care benefits and unspecified assistantships also available. Financial award application deadline: 7/1; financial award applicants required to submit FAFSA. *Faculty research:* Gifted education, mild disabilities, early intervention, severe disabilities, behavior disorders. *Total annual research expenditures:* $39,904. *Unit head:* Dr. Robert Alexander McWilliam, Professor and Department Head, 205-348-6527, Fax: 205-348-6782, E-mail: ramcwilliam@ua.edu. *Application contact:* Bernice Ofori-Parku, Office Associate II, 205-348-6093, Fax: 205-348-6782, E-mail: bsoforiparku@ua.edu.
Website: http://education.ua.edu/departments/spema/

University of Arkansas at Little Rock, Graduate School, College of Education and Health Professions, Department of Educational Leadership, Program in Gifted and Talented Education, Little Rock, AR 72204-1099. Offers M Ed, Graduate Certificate. *Degree requirements:* For Graduate Certificate, comprehensive exam. *Entrance requirements:* For degree, teacher license.

University of Central Arkansas, Graduate School, College of Education, Department of Early Childhood and Special Education, Conway, AR 72035-0001. Offers gifted and talented education (Graduate Certificate); instructional facilitator (Graduate Certificate); reading education (MSE); special education (MSE, Graduate Certificate), including collaborative instructional specialist (ages 0-8) (MSE), collaborative instructional specialist (grades 4-12) (MSE), special education instructional specialist grades 4-12 (Graduate Certificate), special education instructional specialist P-4 (Graduate Certificate). *Program availability:* Part-time, evening/weekend, online learning. *Degree requirements:* For master's, comprehensive exam, thesis optional. *Entrance requirements:* For master's, GRE General Test, minimum GPA of 2.7. Additional exam requirements/recommendations for international students: Required—TOEFL (minimum score 550 paper-based; 80 iBT). Electronic applications accepted.

University of Central Arkansas, Graduate School, College of Education, Department of Leadership Studies, Conway, AR 72035-0001. Offers college student personnel (MS); district-level administration (PMC); educational leadership - district level (Ed S); instructional technology (MS); library media and information technology (MS); school counseling (MS); school leadership (MS); school-based leadership adult education program administration (PMC); school-based leadership building administration (PMC); school-based leadership curriculum administration (PMC); school-based leadership gifted and talented program administration (PMC); school-based leadership special education program administration (PMC). *Accreditation:* NCATE. *Program availability:* Part-time, evening/weekend, online learning. *Degree requirements:* For master's and other advanced degree, comprehensive exam. *Entrance requirements:* For master's, GRE. Additional exam requirements/recommendations for international students: Required—TOEFL (minimum score 80 iBT). Electronic applications accepted. *Expenses:* Contact institution.

University of Connecticut, Graduate School, Neag School of Education, Department of Educational Psychology, Program in Gifted and Talented Education, Storrs, CT 06269. Offers Graduate Certificate. *Accreditation:* NCATE. Terminal master's awarded for partial completion of doctoral program. *Entrance requirements:* Additional exam requirements/recommendations for international students: Required—TOEFL (minimum score 550 paper-based). Electronic applications accepted.

University of Louisiana at Lafayette, College of Education, Graduate Studies and Research in Education, Program in Education of the Gifted, Lafayette, LA 70504. Offers M Ed. *Accreditation:* NCATE. *Degree requirements:* For master's, thesis or alternative. *Entrance requirements:* For master's, GRE General Test, teaching certificate. Additional exam requirements/recommendations for international students: Required—TOEFL (minimum score 550 paper-based). Electronic applications accepted.

University of Minnesota, Twin Cities Campus, Graduate School, College of Education and Human Development, Department of Educational Psychology, Minneapolis, MN 55455-0213. Offers autism spectrum disorder (Certificate); counseling and student personnel psychology (MA); early childhood special education (M Ed); psychological foundations of education (MA, PhD); quantitative methods in education (MA, PhD); school psychology (MA, PhD, Ed S); special education (M Ed, MA, PhD); talent development and gifted education (Certificate). *Accreditation:* APA (one or more programs are accredited). *Faculty:* 30 full-time (15 women). *Students:* 250 full-time (185 women), 63 part-time (49 women); includes 49 minority (6 Black or African American, non-Hispanic/Latino; 19 Asian, non-Hispanic/Latino; 14 Hispanic/Latino; 10 Two or more races, non-Hispanic/Latino), 36 international. Average age 29. 264 applicants, 45% accepted, 110 enrolled. In 2017, 94 master's, 18 doctorates, 10 other advanced degrees awarded. Application fee: $75 ($95 for international students). *Financial support:* In 2017–18, 22 fellowships, 63 research assistantships (averaging $14,194 per year), 37 teaching assistantships (averaging $10,351 per year) were awarded. *Faculty research:* Achievement gap; autism; behavioral and social-emotional development; improving skills in mathematics, reading, and comprehension; measuring and analyzing student change. *Total annual research expenditures:* $6 million. *Unit head:* Dr. Geoffrey Maruyama, Chair, 612-624-1003, Fax: 612-625-5861, E-mail: geoff@umn.edu. *Application contact:* Dr. Ernest Davenport, Director of Graduate Studies, 612-624-1040, E-mail: lqr6576@umn.edu.
Website: http://www.cehd.umn.edu/EdPsych

University of Missouri, Office of Research and Graduate Studies, College of Education, Department of Special Education, Columbia, MO 65211. Offers administration and supervision of special education (PhD); behavior disorders (M Ed, PhD); curriculum development of exceptional students (M Ed, PhD); early childhood special education (M Ed, PhD); general special education (M Ed, MA, PhD); learning and instruction (M Ed); learning disabilities (M Ed, PhD); mental retardation (M Ed, PhD). *Accreditation:* TEAC. *Program availability:* Part-time, evening/weekend, online learning. *Degree requirements:* For master's, comprehensive exam, thesis or alternative; for doctorate, comprehensive exam, thesis/dissertation. *Entrance requirements:* For master's and doctorate, GRE General Test, letters of recommendation. Additional exam requirements/recommendations for international students: Required—TOEFL (minimum score 500 paper-based; 61 iBT). Electronic applications accepted.

University of Nebraska at Kearney, College of Education, Department of Teacher Education, Kearney, NE 68849-0001. Offers curriculum and instruction (MA Ed), including early childhood education, elementary education, English as a second language, instructional effectiveness, reading/special education, secondary education; instructional technology (MS Ed), including information technology, instructional technology, school librarian; reading PK-12 (MA Ed); special education (MA Ed), including advanced practitioner: assistive technology specialist, advanced practitioner: behavioral interventionist, advanced practitioner: inclusive collaboration specialist, gifted, teacher education. *Program availability:* Part-time, evening/weekend, online only, 100% online. *Degree requirements:* For master's, comprehensive exam, thesis optional. *Entrance requirements:* For master's, portfolio or GRE. Additional exam requirements/recommendations for international students: Recommended—TOEFL (minimum score 550 paper-based; 79 iBT), IELTS (minimum score 6.5). Electronic applications accepted. *Expenses:* Contact institution.

The University of North Carolina at Charlotte, Cato College of Education, Department of Special Education and Child Development, Charlotte, NC 28223-0001. Offers academically or intellectually gifted (Graduate Certificate); autism spectrum disorders (Graduate Certificate); child and family development: birth through kindergarten (Graduate Certificate); child and family studies: early education (M Ed); special education (M Ed, PhD, Graduate Certificate), including academically or intellectually gifted (M Ed). *Program availability:* Part-time, 100% online, blended/hybrid learning. *Faculty:* 22 full-time (16 women), 9 part-time/adjunct (6 women). *Students:* 19 full-time (16 women), 108 part-time (102 women); includes 16 minority (10 Black or African American, non-Hispanic/Latino; 2 Hispanic/Latino; 4 Two or more races, non-Hispanic/Latino), 5 international. Average age 38. 72 applicants, 94% accepted, 52 enrolled. In 2017, 23 master's, 2 doctorates, 43 other advanced degrees awarded. *Degree requirements:* For master's, thesis or alternative, research project; for doctorate, thesis/dissertation, portfolio; for Graduate Certificate, internship. *Entrance requirements:* For master's, GRE or MAT, personal statement, letters of recommendation; for doctorate, GRE or MAT, 2 official transcripts of all academic work attempted since high school indicating minimum GPA of 3.5 in graduate degree program; at least 3 references of someone who knows applicant's current work and/or academic achievements in previous degree work; two-page essay; current resume or curriculum vitae; writing sample; documentation of teaching; for Graduate Certificate, undergraduate degree from regionally-accredited four-year institution; minimum cumulative undergraduate GPA of 3.0; three recommendations from persons knowledgeable of applicant's interaction with children and families; statement of purpose; clear criminal background check. Additional exam requirements/recommendations for international students: Required—TOEFL (minimum score 523 paper-based, 70 iBT) or IELTS (6.5). *Application deadline:* For fall admission, 12/1 for domestic and international students; for spring admission, 10/1 priority date for domestic and international students; for summer admission, 4/1 priority date for domestic and international students. Applications are processed on a rolling basis. Application fee: $75. Electronic applications accepted. *Expenses:* Tuition, state resident: full-time $4337. Tuition, nonresident: full-time $17,771. *Required fees:* $3211. Tuition and fees vary according to course load and program. *Financial support:* In 2017–18, 8 students received support, including 7 research assistantships (averaging $10,112 per year), 1 teaching assistantship (averaging $3,500 per year); career-related internships or fieldwork, institutionally sponsored loans, scholarships/grants, and unspecified assistantships also available. Support available to part-time students. Financial award application deadline: 3/1; financial award applicants required to submit FAFSA. *Total annual research expenditures:* $3.9 million. *Unit head:* Dr. Belva Collins, Chair, 704-687-8828, E-mail: belva.collins@uncc.edu. *Application contact:* Kathy B. Giddings, Director of Graduate Admissions, 704-687-5503, Fax: 704-687-1668, E-mail: gradadm@uncc.edu.
Website: http://spcd.uncc.edu/

University of Northern Colorado, Graduate School, College of Education and Behavioral Sciences, School of Special Education, Greeley, CO 80639. Offers deaf/hard of hearing (MA); early childhood special education (MA); gifted and talented (MA); special education (MA, PhD); visual impairment (MA). *Program availability:* Part-time, evening/weekend, online learning. *Degree requirements:* For master's, comprehensive exam, thesis or alternative; for doctorate, comprehensive exam, thesis/dissertation. *Entrance requirements:* For master's, letters of recommendation, interview; for doctorate, GRE General Test, resume. Electronic applications accepted.

University of North Texas, Robert B. Toulouse School of Graduate Studies, Denton, TX 76203-5459. Offers accounting (MS); applied anthropology (MA, MS); applied behavior analysis (Certificate); applied geography (MA); applied technology and performance improvement (M Ed, MS); art education (MA); art history (MA); art museum education (Certificate); arts leadership (Certificate); audiology (Au D); behavior analysis (MS); behavioral science (PhD); biochemistry and molecular biology (MS); biology (MA, MS); biomedical engineering (MS); business analysis (MS); chemistry (MS); clinical health psychology (PhD); communication studies (MA, MS); computer engineering (MS); computer science (MS); counseling (M Ed, MS), including clinical mental health counseling (MS), college and university counseling, elementary school counseling, secondary school counseling; creative writing (MA); criminal justice (MS); curriculum and instruction (M Ed); decision sciences (MBA); design (MA, MFA), including fashion design (MFA), innovation studies, interior design (MFA); early childhood studies (MS); economics (MS); educational leadership (M Ed, Ed D); educational psychology (MS, PhD), including family studies (MS), gifted and talented (MS), human development (MS), learning and cognition (MS), research, measurement and evaluation (MS); electrical engineering (MS); emergency management (MPA); engineering technology (MS); English (MA); English as a second language (MA); environmental science (MS); finance (MBA, MS); financial management (MPA); French (MA); health services management (MBA); higher education (M Ed, Ed D); history (MA, MS); hospitality management (MS); human resources management (MPA); information science (MS); information systems (PhD); information technologies (MBA); interdisciplinary studies (MA, MS); international studies (MA); international sustainable tourism (MS); jazz studies (MM); journalism (MA, MJ, Graduate Certificate), including interactive and virtual digital communication (Graduate Certificate), narrative journalism (Graduate Certificate), public relations (Graduate Certificate); kinesiology (MS); linguistics (MA); local government management (MPA); logistics (PhD); logistics and supply chain management (MBA); long-term care, senior housing, and aging services (MA); management (PhD); marketing (MBA); mathematics (MA, MS); mechanical and energy engineering (MS, PhD); music (MA), including ethnomusicology, music theory, musicology, performance; music composition (PhD); music education (MM Ed, PhD); nonprofit management (MPA); operations and supply chain management (MBA); performance (MM, DMA); philosophy (MA); political science (MA); professional and technical communication (MA); radio, television and film (MA, MFA); rehabilitation counseling (Certificate); sociology (MA); Spanish (MA); special education (M Ed); speech-language pathology (MA); strategic management (MBA); studio art (MFA); teaching (M Ed); MBA/MS. *Program availability:* Part-time, evening/weekend, online learning. Terminal master's awarded for partial completion of doctoral program. *Degree requirements:* For master's, variable foreign language requirement, comprehensive exam (for some programs), thesis (for some programs); for doctorate, variable foreign language requirement, comprehensive exam (for some programs), thesis/dissertation; for other advanced degree, variable foreign language requirement, comprehensive exam (for some programs). *Entrance requirements:* For master's and doctorate, GRE, GMAT. Additional exam requirements/recommendations for international students: Required—TOEFL (minimum score 550 paper-based; 79 iBT). Electronic applications accepted.

University of Southern Maine, College of Management and Human Service, School of Education and Human Development, Program in Special Education, Portland, ME 04103. Offers gifted and talented education (CGS); special education (MS); teaching all students (CGS); youth with moderate to severe disabilities (CGS). *Accreditation:* TEAC. *Program availability:* Part-time, evening/weekend. *Degree requirements:* For master's, thesis or alternative, portfolio. *Entrance requirements:* For master's, proof of teacher certification. Additional exam requirements/recommendations for international students: Required—TOEFL (minimum score 550 paper-based; 79 iBT). Electronic applications accepted. *Faculty research:* Special education, gifted and talented education, diversity education, positive behavioral interventions and supports.

The University of Toledo, College of Graduate Studies, Judith Herb College of Education, Department of Curriculum and Instruction, Toledo, OH 43606-3390. Offers art education (ME); career and technical education (ME, Ed S); curriculum and instruction (ME, PhD, Ed S); early childhood education (Ed S); education and anthropology (MAE); education and biology (MES); education and chemistry (MES); education and classics (MAE); education and economics (MAE); education and English (MAE); education and French (MAE); education and geology (MES); education and German (MAE); education and history (MAE); education and mathematics (MAE, MES); education and physics (MES); education and political science (MAE); education and sociology (MAE); education and Spanish (MAE); educational media (PhD); educational technology (ME); educational technology: virtual educator (Certificate); elementary education (PhD); English as a second language (MAE); gifted and talented education (PhD); middle childhood education (ME); secondary education (ME, PhD); special education (PhD). *Accreditation:* NCATE. *Program availability:* Part-time, evening/weekend. *Degree requirements:* For master's, comprehensive exam, thesis or alternative; for doctorate, comprehensive exam, thesis/dissertation; for other advanced degree, thesis optional. *Entrance requirements:* For master's, doctorate, and other advanced degree, minimum cumulative GPA of 2.7 for all previous academic work, letters of recommendation. Additional exam requirements/recommendations for international students: Required—TOEFL (minimum score 550 paper-based; 80 iBT). Electronic applications accepted.

University of Virginia, Curry School of Education, Department of Leadership, Foundations and Policy, Program in Educational Psychology, Charlottesville, VA 22903. Offers applied developmental science (M Ed); educational evaluation (M Ed); educational psychology (M Ed, Ed D, Ed S); educational research (Ed D); gifted education (M Ed); instructional technology (M Ed, Ed S); research statistics and evaluation (Ed D); school psychology (Ed D). *Students:* 36 full-time (29 women), 3 part-time (2 women); includes 14 minority (5 Black or African American, non-Hispanic/Latino; 4 Asian, non-Hispanic/Latino; 3 Hispanic/Latino; 2 Two or more races, non-Hispanic/Latino), 7 international. Average age 24. 85 applicants, 80% accepted, 37 enrolled. In 2017, 35 master's, 1 doctorate awarded. *Degree requirements:* For master's, comprehensive exam. *Entrance requirements:* For master's and doctorate, GRE General Test, 2 letters of recommendation. Additional exam requirements/recommendations for international students: Required—TOEFL (minimum score 600 paper-based; 90 iBT), IELTS (minimum score 7). *Application deadline:* Applications are processed on a rolling basis. Application fee: $60. Electronic applications accepted. *Financial support:* Fellowships, research assistantships, and teaching assistantships available. Financial award application deadline: 1/5; financial award applicants required to submit FAFSA. *Unit head:* Sara Rimm-Kaufman, Program Director, 434-982-2863, E-mail: serk@virginia.edu. *Application contact:* E-mail: curry-admissions@virginia.edu. Website: http://curry.virginia.edu/academics/areas-of-study/educational-psychology

Viterbo University, Graduate Programs in Education, La Crosse, WI 54601-4797. Offers cross-categorical special education (Certificate); director of instruction (Certificate); director of special education and pupil services (Certificate); early childhood (Certificate); education (MAE); literacy coaching (Certificate); PreK-12 principal/supervisor of special education (Certificate); principal (Certificate); reading specialist endorsement (Certificate); reading teacher (Certificate); reading teacher 5-12 endorsement (Certificate); reading teacher K-8 endorsement (Certificate); superintendent (Certificate); talented and gifted endorsement (Certificate); Wisconsin school business administrator (Certificate). Weekend courses available in summer. *Accreditation:* NCATE. *Program availability:* Part-time, evening/weekend. *Degree requirements:* For master's, comprehensive exam, thesis, 30 credits of course work. *Entrance requirements:* For master's, BS, transcripts, teaching license, written narrative. Electronic applications accepted. *Expenses:* Contact institution.

Western Washington University, Graduate School, Woodring College of Education, Department of Special Education, Bellingham, WA 98225-5996. Offers M Ed. *Accreditation:* NCATE. *Program availability:* Part-time. *Degree requirements:* For master's, comprehensive exam, thesis optional. *Entrance requirements:* For master's, GRE General Test or MAT, minimum GPA of 3.0 in last 60 semester hours or last 90 quarter hours. Additional exam requirements/recommendations for international students: Required—TOEFL (minimum score 567 paper-based). Electronic applications accepted. *Faculty research:* Applied behavioral analysis, controversial practices, infant/toddler social-emotional interventions, reflective practices in teacher education.

West Virginia University, College of Education and Human Services, Morgantown, WV 26506. Offers audiology (Au D); autism spectrum disorder (MA); clinical rehabilitation and mental health counseling (MS); communication science and disorders (PhD); counseling (MA); counseling psychology (PhD); curriculum and instruction (Ed D); early childhood education (MA); early intervention (MA); education (PhD); educational leadership (MA, Ed D); educational leadership/public school administration (MA); educational psychology (MA, Ed D); elementary education (MA); gifted education (MA); higher education administration (MA, Ed D); higher education curriculum and teaching (MA); institutional design and technology (MA); instructional design and technology (Ed D); literacy education (MA); secondary education (MA); secondary education/English (MA); special education (Ed D); speech pathology (MS). *Accreditation:* NCATE. *Program availability:* Part-time, evening/weekend, online learning. *Students:* 423 full-time (347 women), 367 part-time (316 women); includes 57 minority (14 Black or African American, non-Hispanic/Latino; 7 Asian, non-Hispanic/Latino; 20 Hispanic/Latino; 16 Two or more races, non-Hispanic/Latino), 13 international. *Degree requirements:* For master's, content exams; for doctorate, comprehensive exam, thesis/dissertation. *Entrance requirements:* Additional exam requirements/recommendations for international students: Required—TOEFL (minimum score 500 paper-based; 61 iBT). *Application deadline:* For fall admission, 8/1 for domestic students; for spring admission, 1/1 for domestic students; for summer admission, 5/1 for domestic students. Application fee: $60. Electronic applications accepted. *Expenses:* Tuition, state resident: full-time $9450. Tuition, nonresident: full-time $24,390. *Financial support:* Fellowships, research assistantships, teaching assistantships, career-related internships or fieldwork, Federal Work-Study, institutionally sponsored loans, health care benefits, tuition waivers (full and partial), and administrative assistantships available. Financial award applicants required to submit FAFSA. *Faculty research:* Internet training and integration for teachers, rural education, teacher preparation, organization of schools, evaluation of personnel. *Unit head:* Dr. Gypsy Denzine, Dean, 304-293-5703, Fax: 304-293-7565, E-mail: gypsy.denzine@mail.wvu.edu. *Application contact:* Dr. M. Cecil Smith, Associate Dean for Research and Graduate Education, 304-293-2174, Fax: 304-293-3802, E-mail: mcecil.smith@mail.wvu.edu. Website: http://cehs.wvu.edu/

Whitworth University, School of Education, Graduate Studies in Education, Program in Gifted and Talented, Spokane, WA 99251-0001. Offers MAT. *Accreditation:* NCATE. *Program availability:* Part-time, evening/weekend. *Degree requirements:* For master's, comprehensive exam, thesis (for some programs). *Entrance requirements:* For master's, GRE General Test, MAT.

Wichita State University, Graduate School, College of Education, Department of Curriculum and Instruction, Wichita, KS 67260. Offers learning and instructional design (M Ed); special education (M Ed), including early childhood (M Ed, MAT), gifted, high incidence, low incidence; teaching (MAT), including early childhood (M Ed, MAT), middle level/secondary, transition to teaching. *Accreditation:* NCATE. *Program availability:* Part-time, evening/weekend, 100% online, blended/hybrid learning. *Entrance requirements:* For master's, MAT, minimum GPA of 2.75. *Unit head:* Dr. Kimberly McDowell, Department Head, 316-978-3322, E-mail: kim.mcdowell@wichita.edu. *Application contact:* Jordan Oleson, Admission Coordinator, 316-978-3095, Fax: 316-978-3253, E-mail: jordan.oleson@wichita.edu.

William Carey University, School of Education, Hattiesburg, MS 39401. Offers art education (M Ed); art of teaching (M Ed); elementary education (M Ed, Ed S); English education (M Ed); gifted education (M Ed); history and social science (M Ed); mild/moderate disabilities (M Ed); secondary education (M Ed). *Accreditation:* NCATE. *Program availability:* Part-time. *Degree requirements:* For master's, comprehensive exam. *Entrance requirements:* For master's, GRE, MAT, minimum GPA of 2.5, Class A teacher's license. Additional exam requirements/recommendations for international students: Required—TOEFL (minimum score 550 paper-based).

Wilmington University, College of Education, New Castle, DE 19720-6491. Offers applied technology in education (M Ed); career and technical education (M Ed); educational leadership (Ed D); elementary and secondary school counseling (M Ed); elementary studies (M Ed); ESOL literacy (M Ed); higher education leadership (Ed D); instruction: gifted and talented (M Ed); instruction: teacher of reading (M Ed); instruction: teaching and learning (M Ed); organizational leadership (Ed D); school leadership (M Ed); secondary education (MAT); special education (M Ed). *Accreditation:* NCATE. *Program availability:* Part-time, evening/weekend. *Faculty:* 23 full-time (13 women), 162 part-time/adjunct (99 women). *Students:* 546 full-time (394 women), 960 part-time (732 women); includes 320 minority (241 Black or African American, non-Hispanic/Latino; 12 American Indian or Alaska Native, non-Hispanic/Latino; 11 Asian, non-Hispanic/Latino; 28 Hispanic/Latino; 3 Native Hawaiian or other Pacific Islander, non-Hispanic/Latino; 25 Two or more races, non-Hispanic/Latino), 7 international. Average age 34. 1,068 applicants, 64% accepted, 582 enrolled. In 2017, 430 master's, 59 doctorates awarded. *Entrance requirements:* For master's, 2 letters of recommendation, interview. Additional exam requirements/recommendations for international students: Required—TOEFL (minimum score 500 paper-based). *Application deadline:* For fall admission, 4/30 for domestic students. Applications are processed on a rolling basis. Application fee: $35. Electronic applications accepted. *Expenses: Tuition:* Part-time $466 per credit. *Required fees:* $25 per semester. Tuition and fees vary according to degree level and campus/location. *Financial support:* Applicants required to submit FAFSA. *Unit head:* Dr. John C. Gray, Dean, 302-295-1139. *Application contact:* Laura Morris, Director of Admissions, 877-967-5464, E-mail: infocenter@wilmu.edu. Website: http://www.wilmu.edu/education/

Youngstown State University, Graduate School, Beeghly College of Education, Department of Teacher Education, Program in Special Education, Youngstown, OH 44555-0001. Offers gifted and talented education (MS Ed); special education (MS Ed). *Accreditation:* NCATE. *Program availability:* Part-time, evening/weekend. *Degree requirements:* For master's, comprehensive exam. *Entrance requirements:* For master's, GRE, MAT, or teaching certificate; interview; minimum GPA of 2.7. Additional exam requirements/recommendations for international students: Required—TOEFL. *Faculty research:* Learning disabilities, learning styles, developing self-esteem and social skills of severe behaviorally handicapped students, inclusion.

English as a Second Language

Acacia University, American Graduate School of Education, Tempe, AZ 85284. Offers educational administration (M Ed); elementary education (MA); English as a second language (M Ed); secondary education (MA); special education (M Ed).

Adelphi University, Ruth S. Ammon School of Education, Program in Teaching English to Speakers of Other Languages, Garden City, NY 11530-0701. Offers MA, Certificate. *Program availability:* Part-time, evening/weekend. *Students:* 21 full-time (19 women), 23 part-time (20 women); includes 24 minority (4 Black or African American, non-Hispanic/Latino; 2 Asian, non-Hispanic/Latino; 17 Hispanic/Latino; 1 Two or more races, non-Hispanic/Latino), 7 international. Average age 29. 74 applicants, 58% accepted, 21 enrolled. In 2017, 36 master's, 11 other advanced degrees awarded. *Entrance requirements:* For master's, 2 letters of recommendation, resume. Additional exam requirements/recommendations for international students: Required—TOEFL (minimum score 550 paper-based; 80 iBT), IELTS (minimum score 6.5). *Application deadline:* For fall admission, 4/1 priority date for domestic students; for spring admission, 11/1 priority date for domestic students. Applications are processed on a rolling basis. Application fee: $50. Electronic applications accepted. *Expenses:* Contact institution. *Financial support:* Research assistantships with partial tuition reimbursements, teaching assistantships, career-related internships or fieldwork, institutionally sponsored loans, scholarships/grants, traineeships, and unspecified assistantships available. Support available to part-time students. Financial award application deadline: 2/15; financial award applicants required to submit FAFSA. *Faculty research:* Theories of language acquisition, English as a second language in the content areas, apprenticeship in English as a second language instruction. *Unit head:* Eva Roca, Director, 516-877-4072, E-mail: rocaz@adelphi.edu. *Application contact:* E-mail: graduateadmissions@adelphi.edu.

Albright College, Graduate Division, Reading, PA 19612-5234. Offers early childhood education (MS); elementary education (MS); English as a second language (MA); general education (MA); special education (MS). *Program availability:* Part-time, evening/weekend. *Degree requirements:* For master's, thesis. *Entrance requirements:* For master's, GRE General Test or MAT, minimum undergraduate GPA of 3.0, 2 letters of recommendation, interview. Additional exam requirements/recommendations for international students: Recommended—TOEFL (minimum score 525 paper-based). Electronic applications accepted.

Alliant International University–San Diego, Shirley M. Hufstedler School of Education, Program in Teaching English to Speakers of Other Languages, San Diego, CA 92131. Offers MA, Ed D, Certificate. *Program availability:* Part-time. *Degree requirements:* For doctorate, thesis/dissertation. *Entrance requirements:* For master's, minimum GPA of 2.5, letters of recommendation; for doctorate, minimum GPA of 3.0, letters of recommendation. Additional exam requirements/recommendations for international students: Required—TOEFL (minimum score 575 paper-based; 83 iBT), TWE (minimum score 5). Electronic applications accepted. *Faculty research:* Global education, psycho-linguistics, bilingualism and education, curriculum and instruction.

Alliant International University–San Francisco, Shirley M. Hufstedler School of Education, Teacher Education Programs, San Francisco, CA 94133. Offers auditory oral education (Certificate); CLAD (Certificate); education specialist: mild/moderate disabilities (Credential); preliminary multiple subject (Credential); preliminary single subject (Credential); professional clear multiple subject (Credential); professional clear single subject (Credential); special education (MA); teaching (MA); TESOL (Certificate). *Program availability:* Part-time, evening/weekend. *Degree requirements:* For master's, thesis. *Entrance requirements:* For degree, California Basic Educational Skills Test, minimum GPA of 2.5. Additional exam requirements/recommendations for international students: Required—TOEFL (minimum score 550 paper-based), TWE (minimum score 5). Electronic applications accepted. *Faculty research:* Curriculum development, first year teachers, cross-cultural issues in teaching, biliteracy.

American College of Education, Graduate Programs, Indianapolis, IN 46204. Offers curriculum and instruction (M Ed), including bilingual, ESL; educational leadership (M Ed); educational technology (M Ed).

American University, College of Arts and Sciences, Department of World Languages and Cultures, Washington, DC 20016-8045. Offers Spanish: Latin American studies (MA); teaching English as a foreign language (MA); teaching English to speakers of other languages (MA, Certificate); translation: French (Certificate); translation: Russian (Certificate); translation: Spanish (Certificate). *Program availability:* Part-time, evening/weekend. *Faculty:* 43 full-time (33 women), 23 part-time/adjunct (17 women). *Students:* 17 full-time (14 women), 19 part-time (15 women); includes 10 minority (2 Black or African American, non-Hispanic/Latino; 6 Hispanic/Latino; 2 Two or more races, non-Hispanic/Latino), 5 international. Average age 32. 39 applicants, 97% accepted, 9 enrolled. In 2017, 16 master's, 11 other advanced degrees awarded. *Degree requirements:* For master's, one foreign language, comprehensive exam, thesis or alternative. *Entrance requirements:* For master's, GRE, writing sample, statement of purpose, transcripts, 2 letters of recommendation, resume; for Certificate, bachelor's degree, statement of purpose, transcripts, resume. Additional exam requirements/recommendations for international students: Required—TOEFL (minimum score 600 paper-based; 100 iBT). *Application deadline:* For fall admission, 2/1 priority date for domestic students; for spring admission, 11/1 priority date for domestic students. Application fee: $55. *Expenses:* Contact institution. *Financial support:* Institutionally sponsored loans, scholarships/grants, and unspecified assistantships available. Financial award application deadline: 2/1; financial award applicants required to submit FAFSA. *Unit head:* Henry Gerfen, Chair, 202-885-2385, Fax: 202-885-1076, E-mail: gerfen@american.edu. *Application contact:* Jonathan Harper, Director of Graduate Recruitment, 202-885-3622, E-mail: jharper@american.edu. Website: http://www.american.edu/cas/wlc/

The American University in Cairo, School of Humanities and Social Sciences, Cairo, Egypt. Offers Arab and Islamic civilizations (Graduate Diploma); Arabic studies (MA); comparative literary studies (Graduate Diploma); Egyptology and Coptology (MA); English and comparative literature (MA); humanities and social sciences (Graduate Diploma); philosophy (MA); psychology (MA); sociology and anthropology (MA); teaching Arabic as a foreign language (MA); teaching English to speakers of other languages (MA). *Program availability:* Part-time, evening/weekend. *Faculty:* 52 full-time (27 women), 7 part-time/adjunct (3 women). *Students:* 52 full-time (41 women), 159 part-time (119 women), 38 international. Average age 31. 209 applicants, 36% accepted, 39 enrolled. In 2017, 73 master's awarded. *Degree requirements:* For master's, comprehensive exam (for some programs), thesis (for some programs). *Entrance requirements:* Additional exam requirements/recommendations for international students: Required—TOEFL (minimum score 450 paper-based; 45 iBT), IELTS (minimum score 5). *Application deadline:* For fall admission, 2/1 priority date for domestic and international students; for spring admission, 10/15 priority date for

domestic and international students. Applications are processed on a rolling basis. Application fee: $85. Electronic applications accepted. *Financial support:* Fellowships with partial tuition reimbursements, scholarships/grants, tuition waivers (partial), and unspecified assistantships available. Financial award application deadline: 3/10. *Faculty research:* English literature, political science, psychology, sociology, anthropology and Egyptology, philosophy, Arabic studies, history, teaching Arabic as a foreign language, teaching English to speakers of other languages. *Unit head:* Dr. Robert Switzer, Interim Dean, 20-2-2615-1068, E-mail: nbowditch@aucegypt.edu. *Application contact:* Maha Hegazi, Director for Graduate Admissions, 20-2-2615-1462, E-mail: mahahegazi@aucegypt.edu.
Website: http://www.aucegypt.edu/huss/Pages/default.aspx

American University of Armenia, Graduate Programs, Yerevan, Armenia. Offers business administration (MBA); computer and information science (MS), including business management, design and manufacturing, energy (ME, MS), industrial engineering and systems management; economics (MS); industrial engineering and systems management (ME), including business, computer aided design/manufacturing, energy (ME, MS), information technology; law (LL M); political science and international affairs (MPSIA); public health (MPH); teaching English as a foreign language (MA). *Program availability:* Part-time, evening/weekend. *Degree requirements:* For master's, thesis (for some programs), capstone/project. *Entrance requirements:* For master's, GRE, GMAT, or LSAT. Additional exam requirements/recommendations for international students: Recommended—TOEFL (minimum score 79 iBT), IELTS (minimum score 6.5). *Faculty research:* Microfinance, finance (rural/development, international, corporate), firm life cycle theory, TESOL, language proficiency testing, public policy, administrative law, economic development, cryptography, artificial intelligence, energy efficiency/renewable energy, computer-aided design/manufacturing, health financing, tuberculosis control, mother/child health, preventive ophthalmology, post-earthquake psychopathological investigations, tobacco control, environmental health risk assessments.

American University of Beirut, Graduate Programs, Faculty of Arts and Sciences, 1107 2020, Lebanon. Offers anthropology (MA); Arab and Middle Eastern history (PhD); Arabic language and literature (MA, PhD); archaeology (MA); art history and curating (MA); biology (MS); cell and molecular biology (PhD); chemistry (MS); clinical psychology (MA); computational sciences (MS); computer science (MS); economics (MA); education (MA), including administration and policy studies, elementary education, mathematics education, psychology school guidance, psychology test and measurements, science education, teaching English as a foreign language; English language (MA); English literature (MA); environmental policy planning (MS); financial economics (MAFE); general psychology (MA); geology (MS); history (MA); Islamic studies (MA); mathematics (MS); media studies (MA); Middle East studies (MA); philosophy (MA); physics (MS); political studies (MA); public administration (MA); public policy and international affairs (MA); sociology (MA); theoretical physics (PhD). *Program availability:* Part-time. *Faculty:* 108 full-time (36 women), 5 part-time/adjunct (4 women). *Students:* 251 full-time (180 women), 233 part-time (172 women). Average age 26. 425 applicants, 65% accepted, 121 enrolled. In 2017, 47 master's, 2 doctorates awarded. *Degree requirements:* For master's, one foreign language, comprehensive exam, thesis (for some programs), project; for doctorate, one foreign language, comprehensive exam, thesis/dissertation. *Entrance requirements:* For master's, GRE General Test (for some programs); for doctorate, GRE General Test (GRE Subject Test for theoretical physics). Additional exam requirements/recommendations for international students: Required—TOEFL (minimum score 583 paper-based; 97 iBT), IELTS (minimum score 7). *Application deadline:* For fall admission, 2/8 for domestic students; for spring admission, 11/3 for domestic students. Application fee: $50. Electronic applications accepted. *Expenses:* Contact institution. *Financial support:* In 2017–18, 29 fellowships, 40 research assistantships were awarded; teaching assistantships, scholarships/grants, tuition waivers (full and partial), and unspecified assistantships also available. Financial award application deadline: 4/4. *Unit head:* Dr. Nadia Maria El Cheikh, Dean, Faculty of Arts and Sciences, 961-1-374374 Ext. 3800, Fax: 961-1-744461, E-mail: nmcheikh@aub.edu.lb. *Application contact:* Rima Rassi, Graduate Studies Officer, 961-1-350000 Ext. 3833, Fax: 961-1-744461, E-mail: rr46@aub.edu.lb.
Website: http://www.aub.edu.lb/fas/pages/default.aspx

American University of Sharjah, Graduate Programs, 26666, United Arab Emirates. Offers accounting (MS); biomedical engineering (MSBME); business administration (MBA); chemical engineering (MS Ch E); civil engineering (MSCE); computer engineering (MS); electrical engineering (MSEE); engineering systems management (MS, PhD); mathematics (MS); mechanical engineering (MSME); mechatronics engineering (MS); teaching English to speakers of other languages (MA); translation and interpreting (MA); urban planning (MUP). *Program availability:* Part-time, evening/weekend. *Students:* 108 full-time (73 women), 287 part-time (207 women). Average age 27. 203 applicants, 83% accepted, 121 enrolled. In 2017, 114 master's awarded. *Degree requirements:* For master's, thesis (for some programs). *Entrance requirements:* For master's, GMAT (for MBA). Additional exam requirements/recommendations for international students: Required—TOEFL (minimum score 550 paper-based; 80 iBT), TWE (minimum score 5); Recommended—IELTS (minimum score 6.5). *Application deadline:* For fall admission, 8/5 priority date for domestic students, 7/1 priority date for international students; for spring admission, 12/30 priority date for domestic students, 12/9 for international students; for summer admission, 5/21 for domestic and international students. Applications are processed on a rolling basis. Application fee: $110. Electronic applications accepted. *Expenses: Tuition:* Full-time $20,000; part-time $1350 per credit. Tuition and fees vary according to degree level and program. *Financial support:* In 2017–18, 82 students received support, including 54 research assistantships, 54 teaching assistantships; scholarships/grants also available. Financial award application deadline: 6/3. *Faculty research:* Water pollution, management and waste water treatment, energy and sustainability, air pollution, Islamic finance, family business and small and medium enterprises. *Unit head:* Salwa Mohammed, Office of Graduate Studies, 971-65515-2934, E-mail: ogs@aus.edu. *Application contact:* Salwa H. Mohammed, Office of Graduate Studies, 971-65152934, E-mail: ogs@aus.edu.
Website: https://www.aus.edu/masters-degrees

Anaheim University, Program in Teaching English to Speakers of Other Languages, Anaheim, CA 92806-5150. Offers MA, Ed D, Certificate, Diploma. *Program availability:* Part-time, evening/weekend, online only, 100% online.

Andrews University, School of Graduate Studies, School of Education, Department of Teaching, Learning, and Curriculum, Berrien Springs, MI 49104. Offers curriculum and instruction (MA, Ed D, PhD, Ed S); elementary education (MAT); secondary education (MAT), including biology, education, English, English as a second language, French, history, physics; teacher education (MAT). *Faculty:* 7 full-time (5 women). *Students:* 14 full-time (8 women), 7 part-time (6 women); includes 5 minority (all Black or African

American, non-Hispanic/Latino), 9 international. Average age 39. 29 applicants, 31% accepted, 4 enrolled. In 2017, 5 master's, 3 doctorates awarded. *Entrance requirements:* For master's, GRE Subject Test. Additional exam requirements/recommendations for international students: Required—TOEFL (minimum score 550 paper-based). *Application deadline:* For fall admission, 8/15 for domestic students. Applications are processed on a rolling basis. Application fee: $40. *Unit head:* Dr. Lee C. Davidson, Chair, 269-471-6364. *Application contact:* Justina Clayburn, Supervisor of Graduate Admission, 800-253-2874, Fax: 269-471-6321, E-mail: graduate@andrews.edu.

Angelo State University, College of Graduate Studies and Research, College of Arts and Humanities, Department of English and Modern Languages, San Angelo, TX 76909. Offers English (MA); TESOL (MA). *Program availability:* Part-time, evening/weekend. *Students:* 8 full-time (7 women), 11 part-time (9 women); includes 5 minority (1 Asian, non-Hispanic/Latino; 4 Hispanic/Latino), 2 international. Average age 29. *Degree requirements:* For master's, comprehensive exam. *Entrance requirements:* For master's, essay. Additional exam requirements/recommendations for international students: Required—TOEFL or IELTS. *Application deadline:* For fall admission, 7/15 priority date for domestic students, 6/10 for international students; for spring admission, 12/1 priority date for domestic students, 11/1 for international students. Applications are processed on a rolling basis. Application fee: $40 ($50 for international students). Electronic applications accepted. *Expenses:* Tuition, state resident: full-time $3856. Tuition, nonresident: full-time $11,324. *Required fees:* $2650. *Financial support:* Teaching assistantships, Federal Work-Study, scholarships/grants, and unspecified assistantships available. Support available to part-time students. Financial award application deadline: 3/1; financial award applicants required to submit FAFSA. *Unit head:* Dr. Laurence E. Musgrove, Chair, 325-486-6138, Fax: 325-942-2208, E-mail: laurence.musgrove@angelo.edu.
Website: http://www.angelo.edu/dept/english_modern_languages/

Arizona State University at the Tempe campus, College of Liberal Arts and Sciences, Department of English, Tempe, AZ 85287-0302. Offers applied linguistics (PhD); creative writing (MFA); English (MA, PhD), including comparative literature (MA), linguistics (MA), literature, rhetoric and composition (MA), rhetoric, composition, and linguistics (PhD); film and media studies (MAS), including American media and popular culture; linguistics (Graduate Certificate); teaching English to speakers of other languages (MTESOL); translation studies (Graduate Certificate). Terminal master's awarded for partial completion of doctoral program. *Degree requirements:* For master's, variable foreign language requirement, comprehensive exam (for some programs), thesis (for some programs), interactive Program of Study (iPOS) submitted before completing 50 percent of required credit hours; for doctorate, variable foreign language requirement, comprehensive exam, thesis/dissertation, interactive Program of Study (iPOS) submitted before completing 50 percent of required credit hours. *Entrance requirements:* For master's and doctorate, GRE, minimum GPA of 3.0 or equivalent in last 2 years of work leading to bachelor's degree. Additional exam requirements/recommendations for international students: Required—TOEFL, IELTS, or PTE. Electronic applications accepted.

Arkansas Tech University, College of Arts and Humanities, Russellville, AR 72801. Offers applied sociology (MS); English (M Ed, MA); history (MA); liberal arts (MLA); multi-media journalism (MA); psychology (MS); teaching English as a second language (MA). *Program availability:* Part-time, 100% online, blended/hybrid learning. *Students:* 35 full-time (22 women), 122 part-time (94 women); includes 34 minority (11 Black or African American, non-Hispanic/Latino; 2 Asian, non-Hispanic/Latino; 19 Hispanic/Latino; 2 Two or more races, non-Hispanic/Latino), 19 international. Average age 34. In 2017, 85 master's awarded. *Degree requirements:* For master's, comprehensive exam (for some programs), thesis (for some programs), project. *Entrance requirements:* Additional exam requirements/recommendations for international students: Required—TOEFL (minimum score 550 paper-based; 79 iBT), IELTS (minimum score 6.5), PTE (minimum score 58). *Application deadline:* For fall admission, 3/1 priority date for domestic students, 5/1 priority date for international students; for spring admission, 10/1 priority date for domestic and international students. Applications are processed on a rolling basis. Application fee: $40 ($90 for international students). Electronic applications accepted. *Expenses:* Tuition, state resident: full-time $6816; part-time $284 per credit hour. Tuition, nonresident: full-time $13,632; part-time $568 per credit hour. *Required fees:* $420 per semester. Tuition and fees vary according to course load. *Financial support:* In 2017–18, research assistantships with full and partial tuition reimbursements (averaging $4,800 per year), teaching assistantships with full and partial tuition reimbursements (averaging $4,800 per year) were awarded; career-related internships or fieldwork, Federal Work-Study, scholarships/grants, health care benefits, and unspecified assistantships also available. Support available to part-time students. Financial award application deadline: 4/15; financial award applicants required to submit FAFSA. *Unit head:* Dr. Jeffrey Woods, Dean, 479-968-0274, Fax: 479-964-0812, E-mail: jwoods@atu.edu. *Application contact:* Dr. Mary B. Gunter, Dean of Graduate College, 479-968-0398, Fax: 479-964-0542, E-mail: gradcollege@atu.edu.
Website: http://www.atu.edu/humanities/

Asbury University, School of Graduate and Professional Studies, Wilmore, KY 40390-1198. Offers biology: alternative certificate (MA Ed); chemistry: alternative certificate (MA Ed); English (MA Ed); English as a second language (MA Ed); ESL (MA Ed); French (MA Ed); Latin: alternative certificate (MA Ed); mathematics: alternative certificate (MA Ed); reading/writing endorsement (MA Ed); social studies (MA Ed); social work (MSW), including child and family services; Spanish (MA Ed); special education (MA Ed); special education: alternative certificate (MA Ed); teacher as leader endorsement (MA Ed). *Accreditation:* NCATE. *Program availability:* Part-time. *Degree requirements:* For master's, action research project, portfolio. *Entrance requirements:* For master's, PRAXIS/NTE, minimum GPA of 2.75, letters of recommendation. Additional exam requirements/recommendations for international students: Required—TOEFL (minimum score 550 paper-based). Electronic applications accepted.

Aurora University, School of Education and Human Performance, Aurora, IL 60506-4892. Offers applied behavioral analysis (MS); bilingual-ESL education (MA); educational leadership with principal endorsement (MA); educational technology (MA); leadership in adult learning higher education (Ed D); leadership in curriculum and instruction (Ed D); leadership in educational administration (Ed D); reading instruction (MA); special education (MA). *Accreditation:* NCATE. *Program availability:* Part-time, evening/weekend. *Faculty:* 15 full-time (8 women), 39 part-time/adjunct (20 women). *Students:* 421 full-time (299 women), 142 part-time (89 women); includes 90 minority (25 Black or African American, non-Hispanic/Latino; 7 Asian, non-Hispanic/Latino; 50 Hispanic/Latino; 2 Native Hawaiian or other Pacific Islander, non-Hispanic/Latino; 6 Two or more races, non-Hispanic/Latino). Average age 37. 169 applicants, 95% accepted, 59 enrolled. In 2017, 175 master's, 36 doctorates awarded. *Degree requirements:* For master's, student teaching; for doctorate, comprehensive exam, thesis/dissertation. *Entrance requirements:* For master's, 2 years of teaching experience, valid teaching certificate, resume; for doctorate, appropriate master's degree, two references, curriculum vitae, personal statement, professional project, reflective essay. Additional exam requirements/recommendations for international students: Required—TOEFL (minimum score 550 paper-based; 79 iBT). *Application deadline:* For fall admission, 6/1

for international students; for spring admission, 10/1 for international students. Applications are processed on a rolling basis. Application fee: $0. Electronic applications accepted. *Expenses:* Contact institution. *Financial support:* In 2017–18, 34 students received support. Federal Work-Study, scholarships/grants, and unspecified assistantships available. Support available to part-time students. Financial award applicants required to submit FAFSA. *Unit head:* Dr. Jen Buckley, Dean, School of Education and Human Performance, 630-844-1542, Fax: 630-844-6155, E-mail: jbuckley@aurora.edu. *Application contact:* Elizabeth Botica, Graduate Education Recruiter, 630-947-8918, E-mail: ebotica@aurora.edu.
Website: http://aurora.edu/education

Avila University, School of Education, Kansas City, MO 64145-1698. Offers advanced classroom management (MA); art K-12 (Teaching Certificate); educational technology (MA, Certificate); elementary education (Teaching Certificate); English as a second language (MA); English language learners (Advanced Certificate); middle school (Teaching Certificate); physical education K-12 (Teaching Certificate); secondary education (Teaching Certificate); special education (Teaching Certificate); special reading (Advanced Certificate); teaching and learning (MA). *Program availability:* Part-time, evening/weekend, online learning. *Faculty:* 6 full-time (5 women), 9 part-time/adjunct (8 women). *Students:* 81 full-time (63 women), 20 part-time (11 women); includes 14 minority (8 Black or African American, non-Hispanic/Latino; 2 Asian, non-Hispanic/Latino; 3 Hispanic/Latino; 1 Two or more races, non-Hispanic/Latino), 4 international. Average age 35. 92 applicants, 62% accepted, 40 enrolled. In 2017, 24 master's awarded. *Entrance requirements:* For master's, minimum GPA of 3.0, writing sample, recommendation, interview; for other advanced degree, foreign language. Additional exam requirements/recommendations for international students: Required—TOEFL (minimum score 580 paper-based; 92 iBT). *Application deadline:* Applications are processed on a rolling basis. Electronic applications accepted. *Expenses:* Contact institution. *Financial support:* In 2017–18, 14 students received support. Unspecified assistantships available. Financial award applicants required to submit FAFSA. *Unit head:* Dr. Stacy Keith, Director of Graduate Education, 816-501-2446, Fax: 816-501-2915, E-mail: stacy.keith@avila.edu. *Application contact:* Cory Roup, Graduate Education Enrollment and Academic Advisor, 816-501-2464, E-mail: cory.roup@avila.edu.
Website: https://www.avila.edu/academics/graduate-studies/grad-education

Azusa Pacific University, College of Liberal Arts and Sciences, Program in Teaching English to Speakers of Other Languages, Azusa, CA 91702-7000. Offers MA. *Program availability:* 100% online.

Ball State University, Graduate School, College of Sciences and Humanities, Department of English, Program in Linguistics, Muncie, IN 47306. Offers linguistics (MA); teaching English to speakers of other languages (TESOL) and linguistics (MA). *Program availability:* Part-time. *Students:* 8 full-time (3 women), 1 (woman) part-time; includes 1 minority (Asian, non-Hispanic/Latino), 7 international. Average age 28. 6 applicants, 67% accepted, 2 enrolled. In 2017, 2 master's awarded. *Entrance requirements:* For master's, GRE General Test, minimum baccalaureate GPA of 2.75 or 3.0 in latter half of baccalaureate, statement of purpose, writing sample, three letters of recommendation. Additional exam requirements/recommendations for international students: Required—TOEFL (minimum score 550 paper-based; 79 iBT), IELTS (minimum score 6.5). *Application deadline:* Applications are processed on a rolling basis. Application fee: $60. Electronic applications accepted. *Financial support:* Research assistantships with partial tuition reimbursements and teaching assistantships with partial tuition reimbursements available. Financial award application deadline: 3/1; financial award applicants required to submit FAFSA. *Faculty research:* Descriptive and theoretical linguistics. *Unit head:* Dr. Deborah Mix, Assistant Chair of Programs, 765-285-8401, Fax: 765-285-3765, E-mail: dmmix@bsu.edu. *Application contact:* Dr. Deborah Mix, Assistant Chair of Programs, 765-285-8401, Fax: 765-285-3765, E-mail: dmmix@bsu.edu.
Website: http://www.bsu.edu/english/

Barry University, School of Education, Program in Curriculum and Instruction, Miami Shores, FL 33161-6695. Offers accomplished teacher (Ed S); culture, language and literacy (TESOL) (PhD); curriculum evaluation and research (PhD); early childhood (Ed S); early childhood education (PhD); elementary (Ed S); elementary education (PhD); ESOL (Ed S); gifted (Ed S); Montessori (Ed S); PKP/elementary (Ed S); reading (Ed S); reading, language and cognition (PhD). *Entrance requirements:* For doctorate, GRE, minimum GPA of 3.25.

Barry University, School of Education, Program in Technology and TESOL, Miami Shores, FL 33161-6695. Offers MS, Ed S.

Barry University, School of Education, Program in TESOL, Miami Shores, FL 33161-6695. Offers TESOL (MS); TESOL international (MS). *Entrance requirements:* For master's, GRE or MAT.

Binghamton University, State University of New York, Graduate School, College of Community and Public Affairs, Department of Teaching, Learning and Educational Leadership, Program in TESOL Education, Binghamton, NY 13902-6000. Offers MA, MS Ed. *Students:* 13 full-time (9 women), 13 part-time (12 women); includes 4 minority (all Hispanic/Latino), 4 international. Average age 36. 34 applicants, 71% accepted, 14 enrolled. *Degree requirements:* For master's, capstone project or thesis, practicum. *Application deadline:* Applications are processed on a rolling basis. *Financial support:* In 2017–18, 1 student received support. *Unit head:* Tami Mann, Senior Staff Assistant, 607-777-5322, E-mail: tmann@binghamton.edu. *Application contact:* Ben Balkaya, Assistant Dean and Director, 607-777-2151, Fax: 607-777-2501, E-mail: balkaya@binghamton.edu.

Biola University, Cook School of Intercultural Studies, La Mirada, CA 90639-0001. Offers anthropology (MA); applied linguistics (MA); intercultural education (PhD); intercultural studies (PhD); linguistics (Certificate); linguistics and Biblical languages (MA); missiology (D Miss); missions (MA); teaching English to speakers of other languages (MA, Certificate). *Program availability:* Part-time, 100% online. *Faculty:* 19. *Students:* 127 full-time (64 women), 123 part-time (70 women); includes 72 minority (9 Black or African American, non-Hispanic/Latino; 2 American Indian or Alaska Native, non-Hispanic/Latino; 41 Asian, non-Hispanic/Latino; 17 Hispanic/Latino; 3 Two or more races, non-Hispanic/Latino), 26 international. In 2017, 28 master's, 16 doctorates awarded. *Entrance requirements:* For master's, minimum undergraduate GPA of 3.0; for doctorate, master's degree or equivalent, 3 years of cross-cultural experience, minimum graduate GPA of 3.3. Additional exam requirements/recommendations for international students: Required—TOEFL. *Application deadline:* For fall admission, 7/1 for domestic students, 6/1 for international students; for spring admission, 12/1 for domestic students; for summer admission, 5/1 for domestic students. Applications are processed on a rolling basis. Application fee: $65. Electronic applications accepted. *Financial support:* Scholarships/grants available. Support available to part-time students. Financial award applicants required to submit FAFSA. *Faculty research:* Linguistics, anthropology, intercultural studies, teaching English to speakers of other languages, missions, missiology. *Unit head:* Dr. Bulus Y. Galadima, Dean, 562-903-4844. *Application contact:* Graduate Admissions Office, 562-903-4752, E-mail: graduate.admissions@biola.edu.
Website: http://cook.biola.edu

English as a Second Language

Bishop's University, School of Education, Sherbrooke, QC J1M 1Z7, Canada. Offers advanced studies in education (Diploma); education (M Ed, MA); teaching English as a second language (Certificate). *Program availability:* Part-time, online learning. *Degree requirements:* For master's, thesis (for some programs). *Entrance requirements:* For master's, teaching license, 2 years of teaching experience. *Faculty research:* Integration of special needs students, multigrade classes/small schools, leadership in organizational development, second language acquisition.

Boise State University, College of Arts and Sciences, Department of English, Boise, ID 83725-0399. Offers English literature (MA); English, rhetoric and composition (MA); teaching English language (MA); technical communication (MA). *Program availability:* Part-time. *Faculty:* 26. *Students:* 44 full-time (28 women), 38 part-time (29 women); includes 6 minority (2 American Indian or Alaska Native, non-Hispanic/Latino; 2 Asian, non-Hispanic/Latino; 1 Hispanic/Latino; 1 Two or more races, non-Hispanic/Latino), 3 international. Average age 33. 242 applicants, 15% accepted, 28 enrolled. In 2017, 29 master's awarded. *Degree requirements:* For master's, thesis (for some programs). *Entrance requirements:* For master's, GRE General Test, minimum GPA of 3.0. Additional exam requirements/recommendations for international students: Required—TOEFL (minimum score 550 paper-based; 80 iBT), IELTS (minimum score 6). *Application deadline:* For fall admission, 4/15 for domestic and international students; for spring admission, 10/15 for domestic and international students. Application fee: $65 ($95 for international students). Electronic applications accepted. *Expenses:* Tuition, state resident: full-time $6471; part-time $390 per credit. Tuition, nonresident: full-time $21,787; part-time $685 per credit. *Required fees:* $2283; $100 per term. Part-time tuition and fees vary according to course load and program. *Financial support:* Teaching assistantships, scholarships/grants, and unspecified assistantships available. Financial award application deadline: 1/15; financial award applicants required to submit FAFSA. *Unit head:* Dr. Michelle Payne, Chair, 208-426-3426, Fax: 208-426-4373, E-mail: mpayne@boisestate.edu. *Application contact:* Dr. Tom Hillard, Director, 208-426-2991, E-mail: thomashillard@boisestate.edu.
Website: http://english.boisestate.edu/graduate-programs/

Boise State University, College of Education, Department of Literacy, Language and Culture, Boise, ID 83725-0399. Offers bilingual education (M Ed); English as a new language (M Ed); literacy (MA). *Accreditation:* NCATE. *Program availability:* Part-time, evening/weekend. *Faculty:* 11 full-time (6 women). *Students:* 10 full-time (9 women), 53 part-time (46 women); includes 9 minority (1 Black or African American, non-Hispanic/Latino; 2 Asian, non-Hispanic/Latino; 5 Hispanic/Latino; 1 Native Hawaiian or other Pacific Islander, non-Hispanic/Latino), 6 international. Average age 36. 20 applicants, 75% accepted, 12 enrolled. In 2017, 26 master's awarded. *Degree requirements:* For master's, thesis optional. *Entrance requirements:* For master's, minimum GPA of 3.0. Additional exam requirements/recommendations for international students: Required—TOEFL (minimum score 550 paper-based; 80 iBT), IELTS (minimum score 6). Application fee: $65 ($95 for international students). Electronic applications accepted. *Expenses:* Tuition, state resident: full-time $6471; part-time $390 per credit. Tuition, nonresident: full-time $21,787; part-time $685 per credit. *Required fees:* $2283; $100 per term. Part-time tuition and fees vary according to course load and program. *Financial support:* Scholarships/grants and unspecified assistantships available. Financial award applicants required to submit FAFSA. *Unit head:* Dr. Maggie Chase, Department Chair, 208-426-3206, E-mail: maggiechase@boisestate.edu. *Application contact:* Dr. Arturo Rodriguez, Program Coordinator, 208-426-2243, E-mail: arturorodriguez@boisestate.edu.
Website: https://education.boisestate.edu/literacy/master-of-arts/

Boricua College, Program in TESOL Education (K-12), New York, NY 10032-1560. Offers MS. *Program availability:* Evening/weekend. *Degree requirements:* For master's, thesis. *Entrance requirements:* For master's, interview by the faculty.

Brigham Young University, Graduate Studies, College of Humanities, Department of Linguistics, Provo, UT 84602. Offers linguistics (MA); teaching English as a second language (MA). *Program availability:* Part-time. *Faculty:* 23 full-time (4 women), 8 part-time/adjunct (6 women). *Students:* 38 full-time (29 women), 24 part-time (18 women); includes 11 minority (1 American Indian or Alaska Native, non-Hispanic/Latino; 5 Asian, non-Hispanic/Latino; 4 Hispanic/Latino; 1 Native Hawaiian or other Pacific Islander, non-Hispanic/Latino), 12 international. Average age 31. 31 applicants, 87% accepted, 24 enrolled. In 2017, 18 master's awarded. *Degree requirements:* For master's, 2 foreign languages, thesis. *Entrance requirements:* For master's, GRE General Test, minimum GPA of 3.0 in last 60 hours of course work. Additional exam requirements/recommendations for international students: Required—TOEFL (minimum score 580 paper-based; 90 iBT), TWE. *Application deadline:* 1/15 for domestic and international students. Application fee: $50. Electronic applications accepted. *Expenses:* Contact institution. *Financial support:* In 2017–18, 62 students received support, including 8 research assistantships with partial tuition reimbursements available (averaging $7,200 per year), 8 teaching assistantships with partial tuition reimbursements available (averaging $2,079 per year); fellowships with partial tuition reimbursements available, career-related internships or fieldwork, scholarships/grants, unspecified assistantships, and travel to conference presentations also available. Financial award application deadline: 7/1. *Faculty research:* Teaching English to speakers of other languages, second language acquisition, computational linguistics, semiotics and semantics, computer-assisted language instruction, forensic linguistics, endangered language documentation. *Unit head:* Dr. Norman Evans, Chair, 801-422-8472, E-mail: norm_evans@byu.edu. *Application contact:* Mary Beth Wald, Graduate Program Manager, 801-422-9010, Fax: 801-422-9010, E-mail: marybeth_wald@byu.edu.
Website: http://linguistics.byu.edu/

Brock University, Faculty of Graduate Studies, Faculty of Humanities, Program in Applied Linguistics, St. Catharines, ON L2S 3A1, Canada. Offers MA. *Program availability:* Part-time. *Degree requirements:* For master's, thesis optional. *Entrance requirements:* For master's, honours degree with a background in English, English linguistics, teaching English as a second language, or a comparable field. Additional exam requirements/recommendations for international students: Required—TOEFL (minimum score 630 paper-based; 109 iBT), IELTS (minimum score 8), TWE (minimum score 5.5). Electronic applications accepted. *Expenses:* Contact institution. *Faculty research:* Metalinguistic ability in subsequent language learning, language teaching methodology, forensic linguistics, philosophy of education, culturally appropriate pedagogy.

Brown University, Graduate School, Department of Portuguese and Brazilian Studies, Providence, RI 02912. Offers Brazilian studies (AM); English as a second language and cross-cultural studies (AM); Portuguese and Brazilian studies (AM, PhD); Portuguese bilingual education and cross-cultural studies (AM). *Degree requirements:* For doctorate, thesis/dissertation.

Buena Vista University, School of Education, Storm Lake, IA 50588. Offers curriculum and instruction (M Ed), including effective teaching, TESL; school guidance and counseling (MS Ed). Program offered in summer only. *Program availability:* Part-time, evening/weekend, online learning. *Degree requirements:* For master's, thesis, fieldwork/practicum, capstone portfolio. *Entrance requirements:* For master's, Analytical Writing Assessment (in-house), minimum undergraduate GPA of 2.75. Electronic applications accepted. *Faculty research:* Reading, curriculum, educational psychology, special education.

Cabrini University, Academic Affairs, Radnor, PA 19087. Offers accounting (M Acc); autism spectrum disorder (M Ed); biological sciences (MS), including civic leadership; criminology and criminal justice (MA); curriculum, instruction, and assessment (M Ed); educational leadership (M Ed, Ed D), including curriculum and instructional leadership (Ed D), preK-12 leadership (Ed D); English as a second language (M Ed); organizational leadership (DBA, PhD); preK to 4 (M Ed); reading specialist (M Ed); secondary education (M Ed), including biology, chemistry, English, English/communication, mathematics, social studies; special education grades 7-12 (M Ed); special education preK-8 (M Ed); teaching and learning (M Ed). *Program availability:* Part-time, evening/weekend. *Faculty:* 23 full-time (17 women), 46 part-time/adjunct (38 women). *Students:* 60 full-time (35 women), 559 part-time (435 women); includes 93 minority (66 Black or African American, non-Hispanic/Latino; 1 American Indian or Alaska Native, non-Hispanic/Latino; 8 Asian, non-Hispanic/Latino; 15 Hispanic/Latino; 3 Two or more races, non-Hispanic/Latino), 4 international. Average age 33. 290 applicants, 82% accepted, 154 enrolled. In 2017, 283 master's awarded. *Degree requirements:* For master's, comprehensive exam (for some programs), thesis (for some programs); for doctorate, comprehensive exam (for some programs), thesis/dissertation. *Entrance requirements:* For master's, professional resume, personal statement, two recommendations, official transcripts; for doctorate, official transcripts, minimum master's GPA of 3.0, two recommendations, interview with admissions committee. Additional exam requirements/recommendations for international students: Required—TOEFL (minimum score 80 iBT). *Application deadline:* For fall admission, 8/26 for domestic students, 8/1 for international students; for winter admission, 1/13 for domestic students, 12/20 for international students; for spring admission, 1/13 for domestic students, 12/20 for international students; for summer admission, 5/20 for domestic students, 4/30 for international students. Applications are processed on a rolling basis. Application fee: $50. Electronic applications accepted. Application fee is waived when completed online. *Expenses:* Contact institution. *Financial support:* In 2017–18, 1,459 students received support. Tuition waivers and unspecified assistantships available. Financial award application deadline: 5/1; financial award applicants required to submit FAFSA. *Unit head:* Dr. Maliha Zaman, 610-902-8502, Fax: 610-902-8797, E-mail: msz37@cabrini.edu. *Application contact:* Diane Greenwood, Director of Graduate Admissions, 610-902-8291, E-mail: diane.l.greenwood@cabrini.edu.
Website: http://cabrini.edu/graduate

California Baptist University, Program in English, Riverside, CA 92504-3206. Offers English pedagogy (MA); literature (MA); teaching English to speakers of other languages (TESOL) (MA). *Program availability:* Part-time, evening/weekend. *Faculty:* 13 full-time (8 women), 1 (woman) part-time/adjunct. *Students:* 3 full-time (2 women), 26 part-time (19 women); includes 14 minority (4 Black or African American, non-Hispanic/Latino; 1 Asian, non-Hispanic/Latino; 9 Hispanic/Latino), 3 international. Average age 28. 11 applicants, 45% accepted, 4 enrolled. In 2017, 8 master's awarded. *Degree requirements:* For master's, comprehensive exam, project, or thesis. *Entrance requirements:* For master's, GRE (for applicants with a GPA below 2.75) or CSET, minimum undergraduate GPA of 2.75; 18 semester hours of course work in English beyond freshman level; three recommendations; essay; demonstration of writing; interview. Additional exam requirements/recommendations for international students: Required—TOEFL (minimum score 80 iBT). *Application deadline:* For fall admission, 8/1 priority date for domestic students, 7/1 for international students; for spring admission, 12/1 priority date for domestic students, 11/1 for international students. Applications are processed on a rolling basis. Application fee: $45. Electronic applications accepted. *Expenses:* Contact institution. *Financial support:* In 2017–18, 5 students received support. Federal Work-Study and scholarships/grants available. Financial award applicants required to submit CSS PROFILE or FAFSA. *Faculty research:* Classical mythology and folklore, multicultural literature, genre studies, science fiction and fantasy literature, intercultural rhetoric. *Unit head:* Dr. Gayne Anacker, Dean, College of Arts and Sciences, 951-343-4682, E-mail: ganacker@calbaptist.edu. *Application contact:* Dr. Laura Veltman, Director, Master of Arts Program in English, 951-343-4276, Fax: 951-343-4661, E-mail: lveltman@calbaptist.edu.
Website: http://www.calbaptist.edu/maenglish/

California State University, Dominguez Hills, College of Arts and Humanities, Department of English, Carson, CA 90747-0001. Offers English literature (MA); rhetoric and composition (Certificate); teaching English as a second language (MA, Certificate). *Program availability:* Part-time, evening/weekend. *Degree requirements:* For master's, comprehensive exam (for some programs), thesis or alternative. *Entrance requirements:* For master's, minimum GPA of 3.0 in last 60 units. Additional exam requirements/recommendations for international students: Required—TOEFL (minimum score 550 paper-based). Electronic applications accepted. *Faculty research:* Gender studies, transnationalism, discourse analysis, visual culture, Shakespeare.

California State University, East Bay, Office of Graduate Studies, College of Letters, Arts, and Social Sciences, Department of English, Hayward, CA 94542-3000. Offers English (MA); teaching English to speaker of other languages (MA). *Program availability:* Part-time. *Faculty:* 20 full-time (10 women), 26 part-time/adjunct (18 women). *Students:* 14 full-time (8 women), 30 part-time (20 women); includes 19 minority (3 Black or African American, non-Hispanic/Latino; 4 Asian, non-Hispanic/Latino; 10 Hispanic/Latino; 2 Two or more races, non-Hispanic/Latino), 8 international. Average age 34. 34 applicants, 74% accepted, 17 enrolled. In 2017, 19 master's awarded. *Degree requirements:* For master's, one foreign language, comprehensive exam, thesis optional. *Entrance requirements:* For master's, minimum GPA of 3.0 in field; 2 letters of recommendation; academic or professional writing sample; teaching experience and some degree of bilingualism (preferred for TESOL). Additional exam requirements/recommendations for international students: Required—TOEFL (minimum score 550 paper-based); Recommended—IELTS (minimum score 6.5). *Application deadline:* For fall admission, 6/1 for domestic and international students. Applications are processed on a rolling basis. Application fee: $55. Electronic applications accepted. *Financial support:* Fellowships, teaching assistantships, career-related internships or fieldwork, Federal Work-Study, institutionally sponsored loans, and scholarships/grants available. Support available to part-time students. Financial award application deadline: 3/2; financial award applicants required to submit FAFSA. *Unit head:* Dr. Sarah Nielsen, Acting Chair, 510-885-3151, Fax: 510-885-4797. *Application contact:* Philip Cole-Regis, Administrative Support Coordinator, 510-885-3286, E-mail: philip.coleregis@csueastbay.edu.
Website: http://www20.csueastbay.edu/class/departments/english/index.html

California State University, Fresno, Division of Research and Graduate Studies, College of Arts and Humanities, Department of Linguistics, Fresno, CA 93740-8027. Offers linguistics (MA), including teaching English as a second language. *Program availability:* Part-time, evening/weekend. *Degree requirements:* For master's, comprehensive exam. *Entrance requirements:* For master's, GRE General Test, minimum GPA of 3.0. Additional exam requirements/recommendations for international students: Required—TOEFL. Electronic applications accepted. *Faculty research:* Communication systems, bilingual education, animal communication, conflict resolution, literacy programs.

California State University, Long Beach, Graduate Studies, College of Liberal Arts, Department of Linguistics, Long Beach, CA 90840. Offers general linguistics (MA);

language and culture (MA); special concentration (MA); teaching English to speakers of other languages (MA, Graduate Certificate). *Program availability:* Part-time, evening/weekend. *Degree requirements:* For master's, one foreign language, comprehensive exam, thesis optional. Electronic applications accepted. *Faculty research:* Pedagogy of language instruction, role of language in society, Khmer language instruction.

California State University, Sacramento, College of Arts and Letters, Department of English, Sacramento, CA 95819. Offers composition (MA); creative writing (MA); literature (MA); teaching English to speakers of other languages (MA). *Program availability:* Part-time. *Students:* 25 full-time (15 women), 36 part-time (27 women); includes 18 minority (4 Black or African American, non-Hispanic/Latino; 3 Asian, non-Hispanic/Latino; 11 Hispanic/Latino). Average age 30. 47 applicants, 81% accepted, 31 enrolled. In 2017, 19 master's awarded. *Degree requirements:* For master's, thesis, project, or comprehensive exam; TESOL exam; writing proficiency exam. *Entrance requirements:* For master's, portfolio (creative writing); minimum GPA of 3.0 in English and overall during previous 2 years. Additional exam requirements/recommendations for international students: Required—TOEFL (minimum score 600 paper-based; 100 iBT). *Application deadline:* For fall admission, 2/15 for domestic students, 3/1 for international students; for spring admission, 9/30 for international students. Applications are processed on a rolling basis. Application fee: $55. Electronic applications accepted. *Expenses:* Contact institution. *Financial support:* Teaching assistantships, career-related internships or fieldwork, Federal Work-Study, and scholarships/grants available. Support available to part-time students. Financial award application deadline: 3/1; financial award applicants required to submit FAFSA. *Faculty research:* Teaching composition, remedial writing. *Unit head:* Dr. David Toise, Chair, 916-278-6586, E-mail: dwtoise@csus.edu. *Application contact:* Jose Martinez, Graduate Admissions Supervisor, 916-278-7871, E-mail: martinj@skymail.csus.edu. Website: http://www.csus.edu/engl

California State University, Stanislaus, College of the Arts, Humanities and Social Sciences, MA Program in English, Turlock, CA 95382. Offers literature (Certificate); rhetoric and teaching writing (MA); teaching English to speakers of other languages (MA). *Program availability:* Part-time. *Degree requirements:* For master's, comprehensive exam, thesis or alternative. *Entrance requirements:* For master's, GRE, minimum GPA of 3.0, 2 letters of reference, personal statement. Additional exam requirements/recommendations for international students: Required—TOEFL (minimum score 575 paper-based), TWE (minimum score 4). Electronic applications accepted. *Faculty research:* Transnational literacies, Renaissance and medieval literature, abolition writings and slave narratives, qualitative writing.

Cambridge College, School of Education, Boston, MA 02129. Offers autism specialist (M Ed); autism/behavior analyst (M Ed); behavior analyst (Post-Master's Certificate); behavioral management (M Ed); early childhood teacher (M Ed); education specialist in curriculum and instruction (CAGS); educational leadership (Ed D); elementary teacher (M Ed); English as a second language (M Ed, Certificate); general science (M Ed); health education (Post-Master's Certificate); health/family and consumer sciences (M Ed); history (M Ed); individualized (M Ed); information technology literacy (M Ed); instructional technology (M Ed); interdisciplinary studies (M Ed); library teacher (M Ed); literacy education (M Ed); mathematics (M Ed); mathematics specialist (Certificate); middle school mathematics and science (M Ed); school administration (M Ed, CAGS); school guidance counselor (M Ed); school nurse education (M Ed); school social worker/school adjustment counselor (M Ed); special education administrator (CAGS); special education/moderate disabilities (M Ed); teaching skills and methodologies (M Ed). *Program availability:* Part-time, evening/weekend, online learning. *Degree requirements:* For master's, thesis, internship/practicum (licensure program only); for doctorate, thesis/dissertation; for other advanced degree, thesis. *Entrance requirements:* For master's, interview, resume, documentation of licensure, 2 professional references; for doctorate, official transcripts, interview, resume, documentation of licensure (if any), written personal statement/essay, portfolio of scholarly and professional work, qualifying assessment, 2 professional references, health insurance, immunizations form; for other advanced degree, official transcripts, interview, resume, documentation of licensure (if any), written personal statement/essay, 2 professional references, health insurance, immunizations form. Additional exam requirements/recommendations for international students: Required—TOEFL (minimum score 550 paper-based; 79 iBT), Michigan English Language Assessment Battery (minimum score 85); Recommended—IELTS (minimum score 6). Electronic applications accepted. *Expenses:* Contact institution. *Faculty research:* Adult education, accelerated learning, mathematics education, brain compatible learning, special education and law.

Canisius College, Graduate Division, School of Education and Human Services, Department of Graduate Education and Leadership, Buffalo, NY 14208-1098. Offers business and marketing education (MS Ed); college student personnel (MS Ed); deaf education (MS Ed); deaf/adolescent education, grades 7-12 (MS Ed); deaf/childhood education, grades 1-6 (MS Ed); differentiated instruction (MS Ed); education administration (MS); educational administration (MS Ed); educational technologies (Certificate); gifted education extension (Certificate); literacy (MS Ed); reading (Certificate); school building leadership (MS Ed, Certificate); school district leadership (Certificate); teacher leader (Certificate); TESOL (MS Ed). *Accreditation:* NCATE. *Program availability:* Part-time, evening/weekend, 100% online, blended/hybrid learning. *Faculty:* 5 full-time (all women), 21 part-time/adjunct (16 women). *Students:* 85 full-time (67 women), 189 part-time (151 women); includes 31 minority (18 Black or African American, non-Hispanic/Latino; 3 American Indian or Alaska Native, non-Hispanic/Latino; 3 Asian, non-Hispanic/Latino; 4 Hispanic/Latino; 3 Two or more races, non-Hispanic/Latino), 1 international. Average age 31. 83 applicants, 96% accepted, 74 enrolled. In 2017, 94 master's, 47 other advanced degrees awarded. *Entrance requirements:* For master's, GRE (if cumulative GPA less than 2.7), transcripts, two letters of recommendation. Additional exam requirements/recommendations for international students: Required—TOEFL (minimum score 550 paper-based, 79 iBT), IELTS (minimum score 6.5), or CAEL (minimum score 70). *Application deadline:* Applications are processed on a rolling basis. Application fee: $0. Electronic applications accepted. *Expenses: Tuition:* Full-time $22,860; part-time $820 per credit. *Required fees:* $720; $25 per credit. $65 per semester. One-time fee: $425. *Financial support:* Career-related internships or fieldwork, Federal Work-Study, scholarships/grants, tuition waivers (partial), and unspecified assistantships available. Support available to part-time students. Financial award application deadline: 4/30; financial award applicants required to submit FAFSA. *Faculty research:* Asperger's disease, autism, private higher education, reading strategies. *Unit head:* Dr. Anne Marie Tryjankowski, Chair/Associate Professor of Graduate Education and Leadership, 716-888-3715, Fax: 716-888-3142, E-mail: tryjanka@canisius.edu.

Carlos Albizu University, Miami Campus, Graduate Programs, Miami, FL 33172-2209. Offers clinical psychology (PhD, Psy D); entrepreneurship (MBA); exceptional student education (MS); human services (PhD); industrial/organizational psychology (MS); marriage and family therapy (MS); mental health counseling (MS); nonprofit management (MBA); organizational management (MBA); psychology (MS); speech and language pathology (MS); teaching English for speakers of other languages (MS). *Accreditation:* APA. *Program availability:* Part-time, evening/weekend, 100% online, blended/hybrid learning. *Faculty:* 32 full-time (24 women), 27 part-time/adjunct (15 women). *Students:* 411 full-time (345 women), 248 part-time (215 women); includes 562 minority (53 Black or African American, non-Hispanic/Latino; 4 Asian, non-Hispanic/Latino; 498 Hispanic/Latino; 7 Two or more races, non-Hispanic/Latino), 23 international. Average age 34. 391 applicants, 42% accepted, 154 enrolled. In 2017, 96 master's, 54 doctorates awarded. Terminal master's awarded for partial completion of doctoral program. *Degree requirements:* For master's, comprehensive exam (for some programs), integrative project (for MBA); research project (for exceptional student education, teaching English as a second language); for doctorate, comprehensive examinations, internship, project/dissertation. *Entrance requirements:* For master's, GRE/EXADEP, bachelor's degree from accredited institution, minimum GPA of 3.0, 3 letters of recommendation, interview, resume, statement of purpose, official transcripts; for doctorate, GRE (for Psy D), 3 letters of recommendation, resume, interview, statement of purpose, official transcripts; bachelor's degree and minimum GPA of 3.25 (for Psy D); master's degree and minimum GPA of 3.0 (for PhD). Additional exam requirements/recommendations for international students: Required—Michigan Test of English Language Proficiency. *Application deadline:* For fall admission, 4/1 priority date for domestic students, 5/1 priority date for international students; for spring admission, 11/1 priority date for domestic students, 9/1 priority date for international students. Applications are processed on a rolling basis. Application fee: $50. Electronic applications accepted. Application fee is waived when completed online. *Expenses:* Contact institution. *Financial support:* In 2017–18, 145 students received support. Federal Work-Study, scholarships/grants, unspecified assistantships, and tuition discounts available. Financial award application deadline: 6/1; financial award applicants required to submit FAFSA. *Faculty research:* Psychotherapy, forensic psychology, neuropsychology, special education, speech-language pathology, criminal justice. *Unit head:* Dr. Etiony Aldarondo, Provost, 305-593-1223 Ext. 3138, Fax: 305-592-7930, E-mail: ealdarondo@albizu.edu. *Application contact:* Sonia Feliciano, Institutional Director of Student Recruitment, 305-593-1223 Ext. 3108, Fax: 305-477-8983, E-mail: sfeliciano@albizu.edu.

Carson-Newman University, Graduate Program in Education, Jefferson City, TN 37760. Offers curriculum and instruction (M Ed); educational leadership (M Ed); elementary education (MAT); school counseling (MS); secondary education (MAT); teaching English as a second language (MATESL). *Accreditation:* NCATE. *Program availability:* Part-time, evening/weekend, 100% online, blended/hybrid learning. *Faculty:* 20 full-time (11 women), 16 part-time/adjunct (13 women). *Students:* 63 full-time (37 women), 488 part-time (362 women); includes 60 minority (46 Black or African American, non-Hispanic/Latino; 2 American Indian or Alaska Native, non-Hispanic/Latino; 1 Asian, non-Hispanic/Latino; 5 Hispanic/Latino; 1 Native Hawaiian or other Pacific Islander, non-Hispanic/Latino; 5 Two or more races, non-Hispanic/Latino), 29 international. Average age 35. 204 applicants, 100% accepted, 188 enrolled. In 2017, 211 master's awarded. *Degree requirements:* For master's, thesis or alternative. *Entrance requirements:* For master's, PRAXIS II or GRE with minimum score of 290 on the verbal and quantitative components (for MAT), minimum GPA of 3.0 in major, 2.5 overall. Additional exam requirements/recommendations for international students: Recommended—TOEFL (minimum score 79 iBT), IELTS (minimum score 6.5), TSE (minimum score 53). *Application deadline:* For fall admission, 7/15 priority date for domestic students. Applications are processed on a rolling basis. Application fee: $50. *Expenses:* Tuition: Full-time $10,516; part-time $478 per credit hour. *Required fees:* $240; $120 per semester. One-time fee: $150. *Financial support:* Federal Work-Study and unspecified assistantships available. Financial award applicants required to submit FAFSA. *Unit head:* Dr. Kim Hawkins, Chair, 865-471-3314, E-mail: khawkins@cn.edu. *Application contact:* Nilma Stewart, Graduate Admissions and Services Adviser, 865-471-3230, Fax: 865-471-3875, E-mail: adults@cn.edu. Website: http://www.cn.edu/adult-graduate-studies

Central Connecticut State University, School of Graduate Studies, College of Liberal Arts and Social Sciences, Department of English, New Britain, CT 06050-4010. Offers English (MA); English education (MAT); teaching English to speakers of other languages (MS, Certificate). *Program availability:* Part-time, evening/weekend. *Faculty:* 6 full-time (4 women), 1 part-time/adjunct (0 women). *Students:* 17 full-time (12 women), 43 part-time (37 women); includes 16 minority (5 Black or African American, non-Hispanic/Latino; 1 Asian, non-Hispanic/Latino; 8 Hispanic/Latino; 2 Two or more races, non-Hispanic/Latino), 2 international. Average age 33. 35 applicants, 77% accepted, 16 enrolled. In 2017, 17 master's, 3 other advanced degrees awarded. *Degree requirements:* For master's, comprehensive exam, thesis or alternative; for Certificate, qualifying exam. *Entrance requirements:* For master's, minimum undergraduate GPA of 3.0, writing sample, letters of recommendation, essay. Additional exam requirements/recommendations for international students: Required—TOEFL (minimum score 550 paper-based; 79 iBT); Recommended—IELTS (minimum score 6.5). *Application deadline:* For fall admission, 8/1 for domestic students, 5/1 for international students; for spring admission, 11/1 for domestic and international students. Applications are processed on a rolling basis. Application fee: $50. Electronic applications accepted. *Expenses:* Tuition, area resident: Full-time $6757. Tuition, state resident: full-time $9750; part-time $374 per credit. Tuition, nonresident: full-time $18,102; part-time $374 per credit. *Required fees:* $4635; $255 per credit. *Financial support:* In 2017–18, 9 students received support. Career-related internships or fieldwork, Federal Work-Study, scholarships/grants, and unspecified assistantships available. Support available to part-time students. Financial award application deadline: 3/1; financial award applicants required to submit FAFSA. *Unit head:* Dr. Stephen Cohen, Chair, 860-832-2795, E-mail: cohens@ccsu.edu. *Application contact:* Patricia Gardner, Associate Director of Graduate Studies, 860-832-2350, Fax: 860-832-2362. Website: http://www.ccsu.edu/english

Central Michigan University, College of Graduate Studies, College of Humanities and Social and Behavioral Sciences, Department of English Language and Literature, Mount Pleasant, MI 48859. Offers English composition and communication (MA); English language and literature (MA), including children's and young adult literature, creative writing, English language and literature; TESOL: teaching English to speakers of other languages (MA). *Program availability:* Part-time, evening/weekend. *Degree requirements:* For master's, thesis or alternative. Electronic applications accepted. *Faculty research:* Composition theory, science fiction history and bibliography, children's and young adult literature, nineteenth century American literature, applied linguistics.

Central Washington University, School of Graduate Studies and Research, College of Arts and Humanities, Department of English, Ellensburg, WA 98926. Offers literature (MA); professional and creative writing (MA); teaching English to speakers of other languages (MA). *Program availability:* Part-time. *Entrance requirements:* For master's, GRE General Test, minimum GPA of 3.0, writing sample. Additional exam requirements/recommendations for international students: Required—TOEFL (minimum score 550 paper-based; 79 iBT) or IELTS (minimum score 6.5). *Application deadline:* For fall admission, 2/1 priority date for domestic students; for winter admission, 10/1 for domestic students; for spring admission, 1/1 for domestic students. Applications are processed on a rolling basis. Application fee: $50. Electronic applications accepted. *Financial support:* Application deadline: 3/1; applicants required to submit FAFSA. *Unit head:* Dr. Bobby Cummings, Graduate Coordinator, 509-963-1075, E-mail: bobby.cummings@cwu.edu. *Application contact:* Justine Eason, Admissions Program Coordinator, 509-963-3103, Fax: 509-963-1799, E-mail: masters@cwu.edu. Website: http://www.cwu.edu/~english/

English as a Second Language

City College of the City University of New York, Graduate School, School of Education, Department of Teaching, Learning and Culture, New York, NY 10031-9198. Offers bilingual education (MS); childhood education (MS); early childhood education (MS); educational theatre (MS); literacy (MS); TESOL (MS). *Accreditation:* NCATE. *Degree requirements:* For master's, thesis. *Entrance requirements:* For master's, Liberal Arts and Sciences Test (LAST), Content Specialty Test (CST). Additional exam requirements/recommendations for international students: Required—TOEFL.

Clarkson University, Program in Education, Schenectady, NY 12308. Offers adolescence education 7-12 (MAT); teaching of English to speakers of other languages (MAT); technology education K-12 (MAT). *Accreditation:* TEAC. *Faculty:* 3 full-time (all women), 23 part-time/adjunct (14 women). *Students:* 22 full-time (13 women), 12 part-time (8 women); includes 4 minority (1 Black or African American, non-Hispanic/Latino; 3 Asian, non-Hispanic/Latino), 6 international. 39 applicants, 72% accepted, 21 enrolled. In 2017, 28 master's awarded. *Degree requirements:* For master's, thesis (for some programs), thesis or project. *Entrance requirements:* For master's, GRE, minimum undergraduate GPA of 3.0. Additional exam requirements/recommendations for international students: Required—TOEFL (minimum score 550 paper-based, 80 iBT) or IELTS (6.5). *Application deadline:* Applications are processed on a rolling basis. Application fee: $50. Electronic applications accepted. *Expenses:* Contact institution. *Financial support:* Scholarships/grants available. *Unit head:* Dr. Catherine Snyder, Chair of Education, 518-631-9870, E-mail: csnyder@clarkson.edu. *Application contact:* Dan Capogna, Director of Graduate Admissions, 518-631-9910, E-mail: graduate@clarkson.edu.
Website: https://www.clarkson.edu/academics/graduate

Cleveland State University, College of Graduate Studies, College of Education and Human Services, Department of Teacher Education, Cleveland, OH 44115. Offers art education (M Ed); early childhood education (M Ed); foreign language education (M Ed); middle childhood mathematics and science education (M Ed); special education (M Ed), including mild/moderate disabilities, moderate/intensive disabilities; teaching English to speakers of other languages (M Ed). *Program availability:* Part-time, evening/weekend. *Faculty:* 19 full-time (14 women), 32 part-time/adjunct (27 women). *Students:* 80 full-time (60 women), 361 part-time (277 women); includes 119 minority (86 Black or African American, non-Hispanic/Latino; 5 Asian, non-Hispanic/Latino; 16 Hispanic/Latino; 12 Two or more races, non-Hispanic/Latino), 20 international. Average age 34. 177 applicants, 55% accepted, 68 enrolled. In 2017, 137 master's awarded. *Degree requirements:* For master's, comprehensive exam (for some programs), thesis or alternative. *Entrance requirements:* For master's, GRE General Test or MAT, minimum GPA of 2.75. Additional exam requirements/recommendations for international students: Required—TOEFL (minimum score 550 paper-based; 78 iBT), IELTS (minimum score 6). *Application deadline:* For fall admission, 7/1 priority date for domestic students, 5/15 for international students; for spring admission, 11/15 for domestic students, 11/1 for international students; for summer admission, 4/1 for domestic students, 3/15 for international students. Applications are processed on a rolling basis. Application fee: $30. *Financial support:* In 2017–18, 13 research assistantships with full tuition reimbursements (averaging $15,845 per year) were awarded; tuition waivers (partial) and unspecified assistantships also available. Financial award application deadline: 2/15; financial award applicants required to submit FAFSA. *Faculty research:* Early childhood education, literacy education, special education: mild/moderate, moderate/intensive, early childhood intervention specialist), teaching English to speakers of other languages (TESOL). *Total annual research expenditures:* $275,907. *Unit head:* Dr. Tachelle Banks, Department Chairperson, 216-687-4600, Fax: 216-687-5379, E-mail: t.i.banks@csuohio.edu. *Application contact:* Rosalyn Adams, Administrative Coordinator, 216-523-7139, Fax: 216-687-5491, E-mail: r.m.adams@csuohio.edu.
Website: http://www.csuohio.edu/cehs/te/te

Coastal Carolina University, Spadoni College of Education, Conway, SC 29528-6054. Offers education (MAT); educational leadership (M Ed, Ed S); English for speakers of other languages (Certificate); instructional technology (M Ed, Ed S); language, literacy and culture (M Ed); learning and teaching (M Ed); online teaching and training (Certificate); special education (M Ed). *Accreditation:* NCATE. *Program availability:* Part-time, evening/weekend, 100% online, blended/hybrid learning. *Faculty:* 16 full-time (9 women), 22 part-time/adjunct (15 women). *Students:* 43 full-time (22 women), 345 part-time (290 women); includes 70 minority (51 Black or African American, non-Hispanic/Latino; 3 American Indian or Alaska Native, non-Hispanic/Latino; 3 Asian, non-Hispanic/Latino; 8 Hispanic/Latino; 1 Native Hawaiian or other Pacific Islander, non-Hispanic/Latino; 4 Two or more races, non-Hispanic/Latino). Average age 33. 288 applicants, 77% accepted, 157 enrolled. In 2017, 151 master's, 28 other advanced degrees awarded. *Degree requirements:* For master's and other advanced degree, comprehensive exam. *Entrance requirements:* For master's, GRE, GMAT, 2 letters of recommendation, evidence of teacher certification, official transcripts; for other advanced degree, official transcripts, 3 letters of reference, master's degree in related field with minimum overall cumulative GPA of 3.0. Additional exam requirements/recommendations for international students: Required—TOEFL (minimum score 550 paper-based; 79 iBT), IELTS (minimum score 6.5). *Application deadline:* For fall admission, 5/1 priority date for domestic and international students; for spring admission, 11/1 priority date for domestic and international students; for summer admission, 3/1 priority date for domestic and international students. Applications are processed on a rolling basis. Application fee: $45. Electronic applications accepted. *Expenses:* Tuition, state resident: full-time $576, part-time $576 per credit hour. Tuition, nonresident: full-time $9369; part-time $1041 per credit hour. *Required fees:* $90; $5 per credit hour. *Financial support:* Fellowships, research assistantships, teaching assistantships, and tuition waivers available. Financial award application deadline: 3/1; financial award applicants required to submit FAFSA. *Unit head:* Dr. Edward Jadallah, Dean/Vice President for Online Education and Teaching Excellence, 843-349-2773, Fax: 843-349-2106, E-mail: ejadalla@coastal.edu. *Application contact:* Dr. James O. Luken, Associate Provost for Graduate Program/Vice-Dean of the Coastal Environment, 843-349-2235, Fax: 843-349-6444, E-mail: joluken@coastal.edu.
Website: https://www.coastal.edu/education/

College of Charleston, Graduate School, School of Education, Health, and Human Performance, Program in English to Speakers of Other Languages, Charleston, SC 29424-0001. Offers Certificate. *Program availability:* Part-time, online learning. *Entrance requirements:* Additional exam requirements/recommendations for international students: Required—TOEFL (minimum score 81 iBT). Electronic applications accepted.

College of Mount Saint Vincent, School of Professional and Graduate Studies, Department of Teacher Education, Riverdale, NY 10471-1093. Offers instructional technology and global perspectives (Certificate); middle level education (Certificate); multicultural studies (Certificate); teaching English to speakers of other languages (MS Ed); urban and multicultural education (MS Ed). *Accreditation:* TEAC. *Program availability:* Part-time. *Degree requirements:* For master's, comprehensive exam. *Entrance requirements:* For master's, interview, New York teaching certificate. Additional exam requirements/recommendations for international students: Required—TOEFL.

The College of New Jersey, Office of Graduate and Advancing Education, School of Education, Department of Special Education, Language and Literacy, Program in Teaching English as a Second Language, Ewing, NJ 08628. Offers English as a second language (M Ed); teaching English as a second language (Certificate). *Accreditation:* NCATE. *Program availability:* Part-time. *Degree requirements:* For master's, comprehensive exam. *Entrance requirements:* For master's, GRE General Test, minimum GPA of 3.0 in field or 2.75 overall. Additional exam requirements/recommendations for international students: Required—TOEFL. Electronic applications accepted.

The College of New Rochelle, Graduate School, Division of Education, Program in Multilingual/Multicultural Education, New Rochelle, NY 10805-2308. Offers bilingual education (Certificate); multilingual/multicultural education (Certificate); teaching English to speakers of other languages (MS Ed, Certificate). *Program availability:* Part-time, evening/weekend. *Degree requirements:* For master's, student teaching or practicum. *Entrance requirements:* For master's, interview, minimum GPA of 3.0 in field, 2.7 overall. *Expenses: Tuition:* Full-time $17,406. *Required fees:* $1120.

College of Saint Elizabeth, Program in Education, Morristown, NJ 07960-6989. Offers assistive technology (Certificate); education (MA); ESL (Certificate); Holocaust/genocide education (Certificate); middle school science (Certificate); online teaching in the 21st century (Certificate); teaching (Certificate), including K-12, K-6, teacher of students with disabilities. *Program availability:* Part-time. *Faculty:* 3 full-time (2 women), 8 part-time/adjunct (6 women). *Students:* 1 (woman) full-time, 34 part-time (29 women); includes 1 minority (Hispanic/Latino). Average age 32. 25 applicants, 100% accepted, 24 enrolled. In 2017, 23 master's awarded. *Degree requirements:* For master's and Certificate, thesis. *Entrance requirements:* For master's, certification. Additional exam requirements/recommendations for international students: Required—TOEFL (minimum score 550 paper-based; 79 iBT), IELTS (minimum score 6.5). *Application deadline:* For fall admission, 5/1 for international students. Applications are processed on a rolling basis. Application fee: $35. Electronic applications accepted. Application fee is waived when completed online. *Financial support:* Career-related internships or fieldwork, scholarships/grants, and unspecified assistantships available. Financial award applicants required to submit FAFSA. *Unit head:* Dr. Joseph Ciccone, 973-290-4383, Fax: 973-290-4389, E-mail: jciccone@cse.edu. *Application contact:* Lori J. Fragoso, Director of Graduate and Continuing Studies Admissions, 973-290-4413, Fax: 973-290-4710, E-mail: apply@cse.edu.
Website: http://www.cse.edu/academics/prof-studies/education/

College of Saint Mary, Program in Education, Omaha, NE 68106. Offers assessment leadership (MSE); English as a second language (MSE). *Program availability:* Part-time. *Entrance requirements:* For master's, technology competency test or equivalent, minimum cumulative GPA of 3.0, teaching certificate, 2 letters of reference, resume.

College of Staten Island of the City University of New York, Graduate Programs, School of Education, Program in Teaching of English to Speakers of Other Languages, Staten Island, NY 10314-6600. Offers MS Ed, Advanced Certificate. *Program availability:* Part-time, evening/weekend. *Faculty:* 2 full-time, 7 part-time/adjunct. *Students:* 78. 42 applicants, 55% accepted, 21 enrolled. In 2017, 7 master's awarded. *Degree requirements:* For master's, comprehensive exam, fieldwork; twelve three-credit courses (36 credits); research project under faculty supervision; for Advanced Certificate, seven three-credit courses (21 credits). *Entrance requirements:* For master's, baccalaureate degree in liberal arts and sciences major or 36 approved credits in liberal arts and sciences, one year of college level foreign language, minimum overall GPA of 3.0, two letters of recommendation, one- or two-page personal statement; for Advanced Certificate, courses required for New York State initial certificate in early childhood, childhood or adolescence education or its equivalent from another state; baccalaureate degree in a liberal arts and sciences major, or 36 credits in a liberal arts and sciences concentration, with minimum overall GPA of 3.0. Additional exam requirements/recommendations for international students: Required—TOEFL (minimum score 550 paper-based; 79 iBT), IELTS (minimum score 6.5). *Application deadline:* For fall admission, 4/25 for domestic and international students; for spring admission, 11/25 for domestic and international students. Applications are processed on a rolling basis. Application fee: $125. Electronic applications accepted. *Expenses:* Tuition, state resident: full-time $10,450; part-time $440 per credit. Tuition, nonresident: full-time $19,320; part-time $440 per credit. *Required fees:* $181.10 per semester. Tuition and fees vary according to program. *Faculty research:* Application of critical pedagogies focusing on intersections of race, class, culture, and gender in first and second language literacies; urban education; second language acquisition in secondary education; cross-linguistic predictors in reading comprehension; students with interrupted or inconsistent formal education (SIFE). *Unit head:* Dr. Rachel Grant, Graduate Faculty Advisor, 718-982-3740, E-mail: rachel.grant@csi.cuny.edu. *Application contact:* Sasha Spence, Associate Director for Graduate Admissions, 718-982-2019, Fax: 718-982-2500, E-mail: sasha.spence@csi.cuny.edu.
Website: https://www.csi.cuny.edu/sites/default/files/pdf/admissions/grad/pdf/TESOL%20Advanced%20Certificate%20Fact%20Sheet.pdf

The College of William and Mary, School of Education, Program in Curriculum and Instruction, Williamsburg, VA 23187-8795. Offers elementary education (MA Ed); English as a second language/bilingual education (MA Ed); gifted education (MA Ed); literacy leadership (MA Ed); math specialist (MA Ed); secondary education (MA Ed), including English, foreign language, math, science, social studies; special education (MA Ed). *Accreditation:* NCATE. *Program availability:* Part-time. *Faculty:* 23 full-time (16 women), 40 part-time/adjunct (32 women). *Students:* 85 full-time (63 women), 16 part-time (15 women); includes 18 minority (5 Black or African American, non-Hispanic/Latino; 4 Asian, non-Hispanic/Latino; 7 Hispanic/Latino; 2 Two or more races, non-Hispanic/Latino), 1 international. Average age 27. 152 applicants, 83% accepted, 90 enrolled. In 2017, 67 master's awarded. *Degree requirements:* For master's, project. *Entrance requirements:* For master's, GRE, MAT, PRAXIS Core Academic Skills for Educators, minimum GPA of 2.5. Additional exam requirements/recommendations for international students: Required—TOEFL (minimum score 100 iBT), IELTS (minimum score 7). *Application deadline:* For fall admission, 1/15 for domestic and international students; for spring admission, 10/1 for domestic and international students. Application fee: $50. Electronic applications accepted. *Expenses:* $9,630 resident full-time, $535 resident part-time per credit hour; $25,920 nonresident full-time, $1,265 nonresident part-time per credit hour; $5,944 full-time fees. *Financial support:* In 2017–18, 35 students received support, including 7 research assistantships (averaging $6,678 per year); scholarships/grants and unspecified assistantships also available. Financial award application deadline: 1/15; financial award applicants required to submit FAFSA. *Faculty research:* Educational technology, professional development and evaluation, inclusive education, rural education, education policy. *Unit head:* Dr. Jeremy D. Stoddard, Department Chair, 757-221-2348, E-mail: jdstod@wm.edu. *Application contact:* Dorothy Smith Osborne, Assistant Dean for Academic Programs and Student Services, 757-221-2317, E-mail: dsosbo@wm.edu.
Website: http://education.wm.edu

Colorado Mesa University, Center for Teacher Education, Grand Junction, CO 81501-3122. Offers educational leadership (MAEd); English for speakers of other languages (MAEd); exceptional learner/special education (MAEd); teacher education (Graduate Certificate); teacher leader (MAEd). *Accreditation:* NCATE. *Program availability:* Part-time. *Degree requirements:* For master's, comprehensive exam (for some programs), capstone presentation. *Entrance requirements:* For master's, 3 professional letters of recommendation, Colorado teaching license, minimum baccalaureate GPA of 3.0; for Graduate Certificate, minimum baccalaureate GPA of 3.0. Additional exam requirements/recommendations for international students: Required—TOEFL (minimum score 550 paper-based). Electronic applications accepted. *Expenses:* Contact institution. *Faculty research:* K-8 STEM instruction, special education inclusion, elementary math literacy, secondary literacy, elementary/early childhood education literacy.

Columbia International University, Columbia Graduate School, Columbia, SC 29203. Offers Bible teaching (MABT); counseling (MACN); early childhood and elementary education (MAT); educational administration (M Ed); educational leadership (PhD); instruction and learning (M Ed); teaching English as a foreign language (Certificate); teaching English as a foreign language and intercultural studies (MATF). *Program availability:* Part-time, evening/weekend, online learning. *Degree requirements:* For master's, internships, professional project. *Entrance requirements:* For master's, MAT; GRE (for some programs), minimum GPA of 2.7. Additional exam requirements/recommendations for international students: Required—TOEFL. Electronic applications accepted.

Columbus State University, Graduate Studies, College of Letters and Sciences, Program in Teaching English to Speakers of Other Languages, Columbus, GA 31907-5645. Offers teaching English to speakers of other languages (Certificate). *Program availability:* Part-time, evening/weekend, blended/hybrid learning. *Faculty:* 3 full-time (0 women). *Students:* 1 full-time (0 women). Average age 31. 1 applicant. In 2017, 1 Certificate awarded. *Entrance requirements:* Additional exam requirements/recommendations for international students: Required—TOEFL (minimum score 550 paper-based; 79 iBT). *Application deadline:* For fall admission, 6/30 for domestic and international students; for spring admission, 11/1 for domestic and international students; for summer admission, 5/1 for domestic and international students. Applications are processed on a rolling basis. Application fee: $50. Electronic applications accepted. *Expenses:* Tuition, state resident: full-time $3708; part-time $2472 per year. Tuition, nonresident: full-time $14,418; part-time $9612 per year. *International tuition:* $19,218 full-time. *Required fees:* $1605. Tuition and fees vary according to program. *Financial support:* In 2017–18, 1 student received support. Application deadline: 5/1; applicants required to submit FAFSA. *Unit head:* Dr. Dennis Rome, Dean, 706-568-2056, E-mail: rome_dennis@columbusstate.edu. *Application contact:* Catrina Smith-Edmond, Assistant Director for Graduate and Global Admission, 706-507-8824, Fax: 706-568-5091, E-mail: smithedmond_catrina@columbusstate.edu.

Concordia University, College of Education, Portland, OR 97211-6099. Offers career and technical education (M Ed); curriculum and instruction (M Ed), including adolescent literacy, career and technical education, e-learning/technology education, early childhood education, English for speakers of other languages, English language development, environmental education, mathematics, methods and curriculum, reading, science, teacher leadership, the inclusive classroom; early childhood (MAT); education leadership (Ed D); educational administration (M Ed); elementary education (MAT); secondary education (MAT); special education (M Ed); teacher leadership (Ed D). *Program availability:* Part-time, online learning. *Degree requirements:* For master's, comprehensive exam, work samples/portfolio. *Entrance requirements:* For master's, California Basic Educational Skills Test or PRAXIS I, minimum undergraduate GPA of 2.8, graduate 3.0; 2 letters of recommendation. Additional exam requirements/recommendations for international students: Required—TOEFL (minimum score 525 paper-based). Electronic applications accepted. *Faculty research:* Learner-centered classroom, brain-based learning, future of online learning.

Concordia University, School of Graduate Studies, Faculty of Arts and Science, Department of Education, Program in Applied Linguistics, Montréal, QC H3G 1M8, Canada. Offers applied linguistics (MA); teaching English as a second language (Certificate).

Cornerstone University, Graduate Programs, Grand Rapids, MI 49525-5897. Offers business administration (MBA); education (MA Ed); management (MSM); teaching English to speakers of other languages (MA, Graduate Certificate). Programs also offered at Holland, Kalamazoo, and Troy, MI campuses. *Program availability:* Part-time, online learning. *Degree requirements:* For master's, comprehensive exam (for some programs), thesis (for some programs). *Entrance requirements:* For master's, minimum GPA of 2.5, 2 letters of reference. Additional exam requirements/recommendations for international students: Required—TOEFL (minimum score 575 paper-based). Electronic applications accepted.

Dallas Baptist University, Dorothy M. Bush College of Education, Program in Bilingual Education, Dallas, TX 75211-9299. Offers bilingual education (M Ed), including dual language, English as a second language/multilingual. *Program availability:* Part-time, evening/weekend. *Application deadline:* Applications are processed on a rolling basis. Application fee: $25. Electronic applications accepted. Application fee is waived when completed online. *Expenses: Tuition:* Full-time $16,308; part-time $906 per credit hour. *Required fees:* $900; $450 per semester. Tuition and fees vary according to course load and degree level. *Unit head:* Dr. Neil Dugger, Dean, 214-333-5202, E-mail: neil@dbu.edu. *Application contact:* Dr. Adelita Baker, Program Director, 214-333-5515, E-mail: adelita@dbu.edu.
Website: http://www3.dbu.edu/graduate/bilingual_education.asp

Dallas Baptist University, Dorothy M. Bush College of Education, Program in Curriculum and Instruction, Dallas, TX 75211-9299. Offers Christian school administration (M Ed); distance learning (M Ed); English as a second language (M Ed); instructional technology (M Ed); professional life coaching (M Ed); special education (M Ed); supervision (M Ed). *Program availability:* Part-time, evening/weekend, online learning. *Application deadline:* Applications are processed on a rolling basis. Application fee: $25. Electronic applications accepted. Application fee is waived when completed online. *Expenses: Tuition:* Full-time $16,308; part-time $906 per credit hour. *Required fees:* $900; $450 per semester. Tuition and fees vary according to course load and degree level. *Unit head:* Dr. Neil Dugger, Dean, 214-333-5202, E-mail: neil@dbu.edu. *Application contact:* Dr. Deborah Tribble, Program Director, 214-333-5831, E-mail: debbiet@dbu.edu.
Website: http://www3.dbu.edu/graduate/curriculum_instruction.asp

Dallas Baptist University, Dorothy M. Bush College of Education, Program in Reading and English as a Second Language, Dallas, TX 75211-9299. Offers bilingual education (M Ed); reading and English as a second language (M Ed). *Program availability:* Part-time, evening/weekend. *Application deadline:* Applications are processed on a rolling basis. Application fee: $25. Electronic applications accepted. Application fee is waived when completed online. *Expenses: Tuition:* Full-time $16,308; part-time $906 per credit hour. *Required fees:* $900; $450 per semester. Tuition and fees vary according to course load and degree level. *Unit head:* Dr. Neil Dugger, Dean, 214-333-5202, E-mail: neil@dbu.edu. *Application contact:* Dr. Adelita Baker, Program Director, 214-333-5515, E-mail: adelita@dbu.edu.
Website: http://www3.dbu.edu/graduate/english_reading.asp

Dallas Baptist University, Dorothy M. Bush College of Education, Teaching Program, Dallas, TX 75211-9299. Offers distance learning (MAT); early childhood through grade 6

certification (MAT); early childhood-12 (MAT); elementary (MAT); English as a second language (MAT); Montessori (MAT); multisensory (MAT); secondary (MAT). *Program availability:* Part-time, evening/weekend. *Application deadline:* Applications are processed on a rolling basis. Application fee: $25. Electronic applications accepted. Application fee is waived when completed online. *Expenses: Tuition:* Full-time $16,308; part-time $906 per credit hour. *Required fees:* $900; $450 per semester. Tuition and fees vary according to course load and degree level. *Unit head:* Dr. Neil Dugger, Dean, 214-333-5202, E-mail: neil@dbu.edu. *Application contact:* Dr. DeAnna Jenkins, Program Director, 214-333-5402, E-mail: deannaj@dbu.edu.
Website: http://www3.dbu.edu/graduate/mat.asp

Dallas Baptist University, Graduate School of Ministry, Program in Global Leadership, Dallas, TX 75211-9299. Offers church planting (MA); East Asian Studies (MA); English as a second language (MA); general studies (MA); global communication (MA); global studies (MA); international business (MA); leading the nonprofit organization (MA); missions (MA); small group ministry (MA); urban ministry (MA). *Program availability:* Part-time, evening/weekend. *Application deadline:* Applications are processed on a rolling basis. Application fee: $25. Electronic applications accepted. Application fee is waived when completed online. *Expenses: Tuition:* Full-time $16,308; part-time $906 per credit hour. *Required fees:* $900; $450 per semester. Tuition and fees vary according to course load and degree level. *Unit head:* Dr. Robert R. Brooks, Dean, 214-333-5494, Fax: 214-333-5673, E-mail: bobb@dbu.edu. *Application contact:* Dr. Brent Thomason, Program Director, 214-333-5236, E-mail: brentt@dbu.edu.
Website: http://www.dbu.edu/ministry/degree-programs/m-a-in-global-leadership

Dallas Baptist University, Liberal Arts Program, Dallas, TX 75211-9299. Offers art (MLA); Christian studies (MLA); commercial art (MLA); East Asian studies (MLA); English (MLA); English as a second language (MLA); fine arts (MLA); history (MLA); missions (MLA); political science (MLA). *Program availability:* Part-time, evening/weekend. *Application deadline:* Applications are processed on a rolling basis. Application fee: $25. Electronic applications accepted. Application fee is waived when completed online. *Expenses: Tuition:* Full-time $16,308; part-time $906 per credit hour. *Required fees:* $900; $450 per semester. Tuition and fees vary according to course load and degree level. *Unit head:* Jared Ingram, Director, 214-333-5584, E-mail: jaredi@dbu.edu. *Application contact:* Bobby Soto, Director of Admissions, 214-333-5242, E-mail: bobby@dbu.edu.
Website: http://www3.dbu.edu/graduate/mla.asp

Dallas Baptist University, Professional Development Program, Dallas, TX 75211-9299. Offers accounting (MA); church leadership (MA); communication (MA); counseling (MA); criminal justice (MA); English as a second language (MA); finance (MA); higher education (MA); leadership studies (MA); management (MA). *Program availability:* Part-time, evening/weekend. *Application deadline:* Applications are processed on a rolling basis. Application fee: $25. Electronic applications accepted. Application fee is waived when completed online. *Expenses: Tuition:* Full-time $16,308; part-time $906 per credit hour. *Required fees:* $900; $450 per semester. Tuition and fees vary according to course load and degree level. *Unit head:* Jared Ingram, Program Director, 214-333-5584, E-mail: jaredi@dbu.edu. *Application contact:* Bobby Soto, Director of Admissions, 214-333-5242, E-mail: bobby@dbu.edu.
Website: http://www3.dbu.edu/graduate/mapd.asp

DeSales University, Division of Liberal Arts and Social Sciences, Center Valley, PA 18034-9568. Offers criminal justice (MCJ); digital forensics (MCJ, Postbaccalaureate Certificate); education (M Ed), including instructional technology, secondary education, special education, teaching English to speakers of other languages; investigative forensics (MCJ, Postbaccalaureate Certificate). *Program availability:* Part-time, 100% online, blended/hybrid learning. *Faculty:* 5 full-time (3 women), 15 part-time/adjunct (9 women). *Students:* 54 full-time (36 women), 112 part-time (68 women); includes 23 minority (3 Black or African American, non-Hispanic/Latino; 1 Asian, non-Hispanic/Latino; 17 Hispanic/Latino; 2 Two or more races, non-Hispanic/Latino), 1 international. Average age 33. 114 applicants, 64% accepted, 41 enrolled. In 2017, 41 master's awarded. *Entrance requirements:* For master's, bachelor's degree from accredited institution, minimum undergraduate GPA of 3.0, personal statement showing potential of graduate work, three letters of recommendation, professional goal statement. Additional exam requirements/recommendations for international students: Required—TOEFL. *Application deadline:* Applications are processed on a rolling basis. Application fee: $50. Electronic applications accepted. *Expenses: Tuition:* Part-time $840 per credit. Full-time tuition and fees vary according to course load, degree level and program. *Financial support:* Applicants required to submit FAFSA. *Unit head:* Ronald Nordone, Dean of Graduate Education, 610-282-1100 Ext. 1289, E-mail: ronald.nordone@desales.edu. *Application contact:* Julia Ferraro, Director of Graduate Admissions, 610-282-1100 Ext. 1768, E-mail: gradadmissions@desales.edu.

Dominican University, School of Education, River Forest, IL 60305-1099. Offers child life studies (MS); early childhood education (MS); education (MAT); elementary education (MA Ed); English as a second language (MA Ed); reading (MA Ed); secondary education (MAT); special education (MS). *Accreditation:* NCATE. *Program availability:* Part-time, evening/weekend, 100% online, blended/hybrid learning. *Faculty:* 8 full-time (6 women), 42 part-time/adjunct (38 women). *Students:* 5 full-time (all women), 261 part-time (206 women); includes 45 minority (16 Black or African American, non-Hispanic/Latino; 1 American Indian or Alaska Native, non-Hispanic/Latino; 5 Asian, non-Hispanic/Latino; 18 Hispanic/Latino; 5 Two or more races, non-Hispanic/Latino), 1 international. Average age 32. 95 applicants, 98% accepted, 72 enrolled. In 2017, 206 master's awarded. *Entrance requirements:* For master's, Illinois Test of Basic Skills. Additional exam requirements/recommendations for international students: Required—TOEFL (minimum score 550 paper-based; 79 iBT). *Application deadline:* Applications are processed on a rolling basis. Application fee: $25. *Expenses:* Contact institution. *Financial support:* Career-related internships or fieldwork, scholarships/grants, tuition waivers (partial), and unspecified assistantships available. Support available to part-time students. Financial award application deadline: 8/15; financial award applicants required to submit FAFSA. *Faculty research:* Governance of private education institutions, reading and language arts, inclusion, organizational planning, leadership and vision. *Unit head:* Dr. Colleen Reardon, Interim Executive Director, School of Education, 708-524-6643, Fax: 708-524-6665, E-mail: creardon@dom.edu. *Application contact:* Benjamin Mueller, Senior Graduate Marketing and Recruitment Coordinator, 708-524-6456, Fax: 708-524-6665, E-mail: bmueller@dom.edu.
Website: http://educate.dom.edu/

Duquesne University, School of Education, Department of Instruction and Leadership, Program in English as a Second Language, Pittsburgh, PA 15282-0001. Offers MS Ed. *Program availability:* Part-time, evening/weekend. *Faculty:* 3 full-time (2 women). *Students:* 17 full-time (12 women), 1 (woman) part-time; includes 5 minority (1 Black or African American, non-Hispanic/Latino; 2 Asian, non-Hispanic/Latino; 2 Hispanic/Latino), 6 international. Average age 30. 30 applicants, 100% accepted, 6 enrolled. In 2017, 7 master's awarded. *Degree requirements:* For master's, thesis optional. *Entrance requirements:* For master's, bachelor's degree. Additional exam requirements/recommendations for international students: Required—TOEFL (minimum score 550 paper-based), IELTS (minimum score 7). *Application deadline:* For fall admission, 9/1 for

English as a Second Language

domestic students; for spring admission, 1/1 for domestic students. Applications are processed on a rolling basis. Application fee: $0. Electronic applications accepted. *Expenses:* $1,259 per credit. *Faculty research:* Bilingual language acquisition; social factors that affect language acquisition; teaching and interaction with English language learners in electronic classrooms; identity and motivation in second language acquisition; second-language teacher education with focus on teacher identity, beliefs, and dispositions. *Unit head:* Dr. Laura Mahalingappa, Associate Professor and Director, 412-396-6111, Fax: 412-396-1997, E-mail: mahalingappa1@duq.edu. *Application contact:* Kelly McGinley, Graduate Admissions Assistant, 412-396-1559, Fax: 412-396-5585, E-mail: mcginleyk@duq.edu.
Website: http://wwwtest.duq.edu/academics/schools/education/graduate-programs-education/english-second-language

East Carolina University, Graduate School, Thomas Harriot College of Arts and Sciences, Department of English, Greenville, NC 27858-4353. Offers creative writing (MA); English studies (MA); linguistics (MA); literature (MA); multicultural and transnational literatures (MA, Certificate); professional communication (Certificate); rhetoric and composition (MA); rhetoric, writing, and professional communication (PhD); teaching English in the two-year college (Certificate); teaching English to speakers of other languages (MA, Certificate); technical and professional communication (MA). *Program availability:* Part-time, evening/weekend, online learning. *Students:* 40 full-time (27 women), 74 part-time (57 women); includes 33 minority (23 Black or African American, non-Hispanic/Latino; 2 Asian, non-Hispanic/Latino; 4 Hispanic/Latino; 4 Two or more races, non-Hispanic/Latino). Average age 35. 36 applicants, 94% accepted, 25 enrolled. In 2017, 23 master's, 4 doctorates, 24 other advanced degrees awarded. *Degree requirements:* For master's, comprehensive exam, thesis optional; for doctorate, comprehensive exam, thesis/dissertation. *Entrance requirements:* For master's, GRE General Test or MAT; for doctorate, GRE General Test or MAT, writing samples. Additional exam requirements/recommendations for international students: Recommended—TOEFL (minimum score 78 iBT), IELTS (minimum score 6.5), TWE. *Application deadline:* For fall admission, 7/31 priority date for domestic students, 2/1 priority date for international students; for spring admission, 11/30 priority date for domestic students, 10/1 priority date for international students. Applications are processed on a rolling basis. Application fee: $75. Electronic applications accepted. *Expenses:* Tuition, state resident: full-time $4749; part-time $297 per credit hour. Tuition, nonresident: full-time $17,898; part-time $1119 per credit hour. *Required fees:* $2691; $224 per credit hour. Part-time tuition and fees vary according to course load and program. *Financial support:* Research assistantships with partial tuition reimbursements, teaching assistantships with partial tuition reimbursements, and Federal Work-Study available. Support available to part-time students. Financial award application deadline: 3/1. *Faculty research:* Technical and professional communication, rhetoric/composition, multicultural and transnational literature, creative writing, film studies. *Unit head:* Dr. Marianne Montgomery, Chair, 252-328-6687, E-mail: montgomerym@ecu.edu. *Application contact:* Dean of Graduate School, 252-328-6012, Fax: 252-328-6071, E-mail: gradschool@ecu.edu.
Website: http://www.ecu.edu/cs-cas/engl/

Eastern Michigan University, Graduate School, College of Arts and Sciences, Department of World Languages, Program in Teaching English to Speakers of Other Languages, Ypsilanti, MI 48197. Offers MA, Graduate Certificate. *Program availability:* Part-time, evening/weekend, online learning. *Students:* 2 full-time (both women), 55 part-time (49 women); includes 12 minority (1 Black or African American, non-Hispanic/Latino; 5 Asian, non-Hispanic/Latino; 4 Hispanic/Latino; 2 Two or more races, non-Hispanic/Latino), 9 international. Average age 35. 31 applicants, 81% accepted, 13 enrolled. In 2017, 11 master's awarded. *Degree requirements:* For master's, one foreign language. *Entrance requirements:* Additional exam requirements/recommendations for international students: Required—TOEFL. *Application deadline:* Applications are processed on a rolling basis. Application fee: $45. *Financial support:* Fellowships, research assistantships with full tuition reimbursements, teaching assistantships with full tuition reimbursements, career-related internships or fieldwork, Federal Work-Study, institutionally sponsored loans, scholarships/grants, tuition waivers (partial), and unspecified assistantships available. Support available to part-time students. Financial award applicants required to submit FAFSA. *Application contact:* Dr. Ildiko Porter-Szucs, Program Advisor, 734-487-6487, Fax: 734-487-3411, E-mail: jporters@emich.edu.

Eastern Nazarene College, Adult and Graduate Studies, Division of Teacher Education, Quincy, MA 02170. Offers administration (M Ed); early childhood education (M Ed, Certificate); elementary education (M Ed, Certificate); English as a second language (Certificate); instructional enrichment and development (Certificate); middle school education (M Ed, Certificate); moderate special needs education (Certificate); principal (Certificate); program development and supervision (Certificate); secondary education (M Ed, Certificate); special education administrator (Certificate); special needs (M Ed); supervisor (Certificate); teacher of reading (M Ed, Certificate). M Ed also available through weekend program for administration, special needs, and teacher of reading only. *Program availability:* Part-time, evening/weekend. *Entrance requirements:* Additional exam requirements/recommendations for international students: Required—TOEFL (minimum score 550 paper-based).

Eastern New Mexico University, Graduate School, College of Education and Technology, Department of Curriculum and Instruction, Portales, NM 88130. Offers alternative licensure in elementary education (M Ed); bilingual education (M Ed); career and technical education (M Ed); educational technology (M Ed); elementary education (M Ed); English as a second language (M Ed); pedagogy and learning (M Ed); reading/literacy (M Ed). *Program availability:* Part-time, online learning. *Degree requirements:* For master's, comprehensive exam, thesis optional. *Entrance requirements:* For master's, writing assessment, minimum GPA of 3.0, photocopy of teaching license, letter of recommendation. Additional exam requirements/recommendations for international students: Required—TOEFL (minimum score 550 paper-based; 79 iBT), IELTS (minimum score 6). *Application deadline:* For fall admission, 7/20 priority date for domestic students, 6/20 priority date for international students; for spring admission, 12/15 priority date for domestic students, 11/15 priority date for international students. Applications are processed on a rolling basis. Application fee: $10. Electronic applications accepted. *Financial support:* Applicants required to submit FAFSA. *Unit head:* Dr. Mary Daughrity, Graduate Coordinator, 575-562-2481, Fax: 575-562-2559, E-mail: mary.daughrity@enmu.edu. *Application contact:* Cheryl Reeves, Senior Secretary, 575-562-2443, E-mail: cheryl.reeves@enmu.edu.
Website: http://education.enmu.edu

Eastern University, Graduate Education Programs, St. Davids, PA 19087-3696. Offers ESL program specialist (K-12) (Certificate); general supervisor (PreK-12) (Certificate); health and physical education (K-12) (Certificate); middle level (4-8) (Certificate); multicultural education (M Ed) (Certificate); music (K-12) (Certificate); Pre K-4 (Certificate); Pre K-4 with special education (Certificate); reading (M Ed) (Certificate); reading specialist (K-12) (Certificate); reading supervisor (K-12) (Certificate); school counseling (MA, CAGS); school principalship (preK-12) (Certificate); school psychology (MS, CAGS); secondary biology education (7-12) (Certificate); secondary chemistry education (7-12) (Certificate); secondary communication education (7-12) (Certificate); secondary English education (7-12) (Certificate); secondary math education (7-12) (Certificate);

secondary social studies education (7-12) (Certificate); special education (M Ed); special education (7-12) (Certificate); special education (Pre K-8) (Certificate); special education supervisor (K-12) (Certificate); TESOL (M Ed); world language (Certificate), including Spanish. *Program availability:* Part-time, evening/weekend, online learning. *Students:* 46 full-time (40 women), 115 part-time (93 women); includes 65 minority (42 Black or African American, non-Hispanic/Latino; 3 Asian, non-Hispanic/Latino; 14 Hispanic/Latino; 6 Two or more races, non-Hispanic/Latino), 1 international. Average age 32. In 2017, 72 master's awarded. *Entrance requirements:* Additional exam requirements/recommendations for international students: Required—TOEFL. *Application deadline:* Applications are processed on a rolling basis. Application fee: $35. Electronic applications accepted. Application fee is waived when completed online. *Expenses:* Contact institution. *Unit head:* Michael Dziedziak, Executive Director of Enrollment, 800-452-0996, E-mail: gpsadmissions@eastern.edu.
Website: https://www.eastern.edu/academics/programs/education-department-graduate-programs/graduate-programs

Eastern Washington University, Graduate Studies, College of Arts, Letters and Education, Department of English, Cheney, WA 99004-2431. Offers literature (MA); rhetoric, composition, and technical communication (MA); teaching English as a second language (MA). *Faculty:* 14. *Students:* 61 full-time (40 women), 11 part-time (9 women); includes 3 minority (1 Asian, non-Hispanic/Latino; 2 Hispanic/Latino), 7 international. Average age 34. 91 applicants, 52% accepted, 33 enrolled. In 2017, 32 master's awarded. *Degree requirements:* For master's, comprehensive exam, thesis or alternative. *Entrance requirements:* For master's, GRE General Test, minimum GPA of 3.0. Additional exam requirements/recommendations for international students: Required—TOEFL (minimum score 580 paper-based; 92 iBT), IELTS (minimum score 7), PTE (minimum score 6). *Application deadline:* For fall admission, 4/1 priority date for domestic students; for spring admission, 1/15 for domestic students. Applications are processed on a rolling basis. Application fee: $50. *Expenses:* Tuition, state resident: full-time $11,191; part-time $373.06 per credit. Tuition, nonresident: full-time $25,995; part-time $866.52 per credit. *Financial support:* Teaching assistantships with partial tuition reimbursements, career-related internships or fieldwork, Federal Work-Study, institutionally sponsored loans, scholarships/grants, health care benefits, tuition waivers (partial), and unspecified assistantships available. Support available to part-time students. Financial award application deadline: 2/1; financial award applicants required to submit FAFSA. *Application contact:* Kathy White, Advisor/Recruiter for Graduate Studies, 509-359-2491, E-mail: gradprograms@ewu.edu.
Website: http://www.ewu.edu/CALE/Programs/English.xml

East Tennessee State University, School of Graduate Studies, College of Arts and Sciences, Department of Literature and Language, Johnson City, TN 37614. Offers healthcare translation and interpreting (Postbaccalaureate Certificate); literature (MA); teaching English to speakers of other languages (Postbaccalaureate Certificate). *Program availability:* Part-time, evening/weekend. *Degree requirements:* For master's, comprehensive exam, thesis optional; for Postbaccalaureate Certificate, one foreign language. *Entrance requirements:* For master's, GRE General Test, minimum undergraduate GPA of 3.0 in English, writing sample, three letters of recommendation; for Postbaccalaureate Certificate, GRE General Test, speaking and listening assessment, resume, three letters of recommendation, two years of coursework or basic proficiency in a foreign language. Additional exam requirements/recommendations for international students: Required—TOEFL (minimum score 550 paper-based; 79 iBT). *Application deadline:* For fall admission, 6/1 for domestic students, 4/29 for international students; for spring admission, 11/1 for domestic students, 9/29 for international students. Application fee: $55 ($65 for international students). Electronic applications accepted. *Financial support:* Research assistantships with full tuition reimbursements, teaching assistantships with full tuition reimbursements, career-related internships or fieldwork, institutionally sponsored loans, scholarships/grants, and unspecified assistantships available. Financial award application deadline: 7/1; financial award applicants required to submit FAFSA. *Faculty research:* Linguistics and dialectology, English education, critical literary theory, literary biography, environmental literature, modern and ancient languages. *Unit head:* Dr. Katherine Weiss, Chair, 423-439-4347, Fax: 423-439-7193, E-mail: weisk01@etsu.edu. *Application contact:* Dr. Michael A. Cody, Assistant Chair for Graduate Studies, 423-439-6676, Fax: 423-439-5624, E-mail: codym@etsu.edu.
Website: http://www.etsu.edu/cas/litlang/

Elms College, Division of Education, Chicopee, MA 01013-2839. Offers early childhood education (MAT); education (M Ed, CAGS); elementary education (MAT); English as a second language (MAT); reading (MAT); secondary education (MAT), including biology education, English education, Spanish education; special education (MAT). *Program availability:* Part-time, evening/weekend. *Faculty:* 4 full-time (all women), 8 part-time/adjunct (7 women). *Students:* 6 full-time (4 women), 127 part-time (107 women); includes 8 minority (2 Asian, non-Hispanic/Latino; 6 Hispanic/Latino). Average age 33. 42 applicants, 88% accepted, 36 enrolled. In 2017, 50 master's, 6 other advanced degrees awarded. *Degree requirements:* For master's, thesis (for some programs). *Entrance requirements:* For master's, Massachusetts Educators Certification Test, minimum GPA of 3.0; for CAGS, master's degree in education. Additional exam requirements/recommendations for international students: Required—TOEFL. *Application deadline:* For fall admission, 7/1 priority date for domestic students; for spring admission, 11/1 priority date for domestic students. Applications are processed on a rolling basis. Application fee: $30. *Expenses: Tuition:* Full-time $13,860; part-time $770 per credit hour. *Required fees:* $200. Tuition and fees vary according to degree level and program. *Financial support:* In 2017–18, 2 teaching assistantships with partial tuition reimbursements were awarded. Financial award applicants required to submit FAFSA. *Unit head:* Dr. Mary Janeczek, Chair, Division of Education, 413-594-2761, Fax: 413-592-4871, E-mail: janeczeke@elms.edu. *Application contact:* School of Graduate and Professional Studies, 413-265-2445, E-mail: graduateeducation@elms.edu.

Emporia State University, Program in Teaching English to Speakers of Other Languages, Emporia, KS 66801-5415. Offers TESOL (Certificate). *Program availability:* Part-time. *Faculty:* 7 full-time (3 women). *Students:* 15 part-time (13 women); includes 4 minority (1 Asian, non-Hispanic/Latino; 1 Hispanic/Latino; 2 Two or more races, non-Hispanic/Latino), 1 international. 10 applicants, 40% accepted, 4 enrolled. In 2017, 17 master's, 2 other advanced degrees awarded. *Degree requirements:* For master's, comprehensive exam, thesis optional. *Entrance requirements:* For master's, minimum undergraduate GPA of 2.75 over last 60 hours. Additional exam requirements/recommendations for international students: Required—TOEFL (minimum score 520 paper-based; 68 iBT). *Application deadline:* For fall admission, 8/15 priority date for domestic students. Applications are processed on a rolling basis. Application fee: $30 ($75 for international students). Electronic applications accepted. *Expenses:* Tuition, state resident: full-time $6084; part-time $253.50 per credit hour. Tuition, nonresident: full-time $18,924; part-time $788.50 per credit hour. *Required fees:* $1943; $80.95 per credit hour. Tuition and fees vary according to campus/location. *Financial support:* Federal Work-Study, institutionally sponsored loans, health care benefits, and unspecified assistantships available. Financial award application deadline: 2/15. *Unit head:* Dr. Abdellah Salim Sehlaoui, Professor, 620-341-5237, E-mail: asehlaou@emporia.edu. *Application contact:* Mary Sewell, Admissions Coordinator, 800-950-GRAD, Fax: 620-341-5909, E-mail: msewell@emporia.edu.

Erikson Institute, Academic Programs, Chicago, IL 60654. Offers administration (Certificate); bilingual/ESL (Certificate); child development (MS); early childhood education (MS); infant mental health (Certificate); infant studies (Certificate); MS/MSW. MS/MSW offered jointly with Loyola University Chicago. *Program availability:* Part-time, evening/weekend. *Degree requirements:* For master's, comprehensive exam, internship; for Certificate, internship. *Entrance requirements:* For master's and Certificate, minimum GPA of 2.75. Additional exam requirements/recommendations for international students: Required—TOEFL. *Faculty research:* Assessment strategies from early childhood through elementary years; language, literacy, and the arts in children's development; inclusive special education; parent-child relationships; cognitive development.

Fairfield University, Graduate School of Education and Allied Professions, Fairfield, CT 06824. Offers applied behavior analysis (ATC); applied psychology (MA); clinical mental health counseling (MA, CAS); educational technology (MA); elementary education (MA, CAS); family studies (MA); integration of spirituality and religion in counseling (ATC); marriage and family therapy (MA); reading and language development (Sixth Year Certificate); school counseling (MA, CAS); school psychology (MA, CAS); school-based marriage and family therapy (ATC); secondary education (MA); special education (MA, CAS); substance abuse counseling (ATC); teaching (Certificate); teaching and foundations (MA, CAS); TESOL, world languages, and bilingual education (MA, CAS). *Accreditation:* NCATE. *Program availability:* Part-time, evening/weekend. *Faculty:* 23 full-time (17 women), 39 part-time/adjunct (28 women). *Students:* 199 full-time (168 women), 251 part-time (206 women); includes 85 minority (21 Black or African American, non-Hispanic/Latino; 9 Asian, non-Hispanic/Latino; 49 Hispanic/Latino; 6 Two or more races, non-Hispanic/Latino), 4 international. Average age 32. 370 applicants, 56% accepted, 125 enrolled. In 2017, 136 master's, 28 other advanced degrees awarded. *Degree requirements:* For master's, comprehensive exam. *Entrance requirements:* For master's, minimum GPA of 3.0, 2 recommendations, resume. Additional exam requirements/recommendations for international students: Required—TOEFL (minimum score 550 paper-based; 84 iBT) or IELTS (minimum score 7.5). *Application deadline:* For fall admission, 2/15 for international students; for spring admission, 10/1 for international students. Application fee: $60. Electronic applications accepted. *Expenses:* $750 per credit hour. *Financial support:* In 2017–18, 34 students received support. Career-related internships or fieldwork and unspecified assistantships available. Support available to part-time students. Financial award applicants required to submit FAFSA. *Faculty research:* Reading and literacy, writing, social justice and inequality in education, addictions and mental health issues, therapeutic relationships and clinical supervision. *Unit head:* Dr. Robert D. Hannafin, Dean, 203-254-4250, Fax: 203-254-4241, E-mail: rhannafin@fairfield.edu. *Application contact:* Marianne Gumpper, Director of Graduate Admission, 203-254-4184, Fax: 203-254-4073, E-mail: gradadmis@fairfield.edu.
Website: http://www.fairfield.edu/gseap

Florida Atlantic University, College of Education, Department of Curriculum, Culture, and Educational Inquiry, Boca Raton, FL 33431-0991. Offers curriculum and instruction (M Ed, PhD, Ed S); early childhood education (M Ed); multicultural education (M Ed); TESOL and bilingual education (MA). *Program availability:* Part-time, evening/weekend. *Faculty:* 10 full-time (8 women), 2 part-time/adjunct (both women). *Students:* 15 full-time (13 women), 81 part-time (65 women); includes 28 minority (11 Black or African American, non-Hispanic/Latino; 3 Asian, non-Hispanic/Latino; 12 Hispanic/Latino; 2 Two or more races, non-Hispanic/Latino), 3 international. Average age 36. 54 applicants, 37% accepted, 14 enrolled. In 2017, 23 master's, 5 doctorates, 4 other advanced degrees awarded. *Entrance requirements:* Additional exam requirements/recommendations for international students: Required—TOEFL (minimum score 500 paper-based; 61 iBT), IELTS (minimum score 6). *Application deadline:* For fall admission, 7/1 for domestic students, 2/15 for international students; for spring admission, 11/1 for domestic students, 7/15 for international students. Application fee: $30. *Expenses:* Tuition, state resident: full-time $7400; part-time $369.82 per credit. Tuition, nonresident: full-time $20,496; part-time $1042.81 per credit. *Faculty research:* Multicultural education, early intervention strategies, family literacy, religious diversity in schools, early childhood curriculum. *Unit head:* Dr. Dilys Schoorman, Chair, 561-297-3965, E-mail: dschoorm@fau.edu. *Application contact:* Dr. Eliah Watlington, Associate Dean, 561-296-8520, Fax: 261-297-2991, E-mail: ewatling@fau.edu.
Website: http://www.coe.fau.edu/academicdepartments/ccei

Florida Gulf Coast University, College of Education, Program in Curriculum and Instruction, Fort Myers, FL 33965-6565. Offers elementary education (M Ed); English education (M Ed); English speakers of other languages endorsement (M Ed); gifted education (M Ed); mathematics education (M Ed); middle school education (M Ed); reading education (M Ed); science education (M Ed); social science education (M Ed); special education (M Ed). *Program availability:* Part-time, evening/weekend, online learning. *Faculty:* 27 full-time (19 women), 44 part-time/adjunct (30 women). *Students:* 3 full-time (all women), 16 part-time (14 women); includes 4 minority (2 Black or African American, non-Hispanic/Latino; 2 Hispanic/Latino). Average age 30. 6 applicants, 100% accepted, 5 enrolled. In 2017, 4 master's awarded. *Degree requirements:* For master's, final project or portfolio. *Entrance requirements:* For master's, GRE General Test, MAT, minimum undergraduate GPA of 3.0 in last 2 years. Additional exam requirements/recommendations for international students: Required—TOEFL (minimum score 550 paper-based). *Application deadline:* For fall admission, 2/15 priority date for domestic students, 5/1 for international students; for spring admission, 12/1 for domestic students, 9/15 for international students. Applications are processed on a rolling basis. Application fee: $30. Electronic applications accepted. *Expenses:* Tuition, state resident: part-time $290 per credit hour. Tuition, nonresident: part-time $1173 per credit hour. *Required fees:* $127 per credit hour. Tuition and fees vary according to course load. *Financial support:* In 2017–18, 2 students received support. Application deadline: 6/30; applicants required to submit FAFSA. *Faculty research:* Internet in schools, technology in pre-service and in-service teacher training. *Unit head:* Dr. Vickie Johnston, Instructor, 239-590-7754, Fax: 239-590-7801, E-mail: vjohnston@fgcu.edu. *Application contact:* Keiana Desmore, Adviser/Counselor, 239-590-7759, Fax: 239-590-7801, E-mail: kdesmore@fgcu.edu.
Website: http://coe.fgcu.edu/c-imed/

Florida International University, College of Arts, Sciences, and Education, Department of Leadership and Professional Studies, Miami, FL 33199. Offers adult education and human resource development (MS, Ed D); counseling (MS), including rehabilitation counseling, school counseling; counselor education (MS), including clinical mental health counseling; educational administration and supervision (Ed D); educational leadership (MS, Certificate, Ed S); higher education (Ed D); higher education administration (MS); international and comparative education (MS); recreation and sport management (MS), including recreation and sport management, recreational therapy; school psychology (Ed S); urban education (MS), including instruction in urban settings, learning technologies, multicultural/bilingual, multicultural/TESOL, urban education. *Program availability:* Part-time, evening/weekend. *Faculty:* 60 full-time (41 women), 112 part-time/adjunct (77 women). *Students:* 221 full-time (162 women), 301 part-time (239 women); includes 418 minority (127 Black or African American, non-Hispanic/Latino; 9 Asian, non-Hispanic/Latino; 271 Hispanic/Latino; 11 Two or more races, non-Hispanic/Latino), 10 international. Average age 31. 330 applicants, 55%

accepted, 100 enrolled. In 2017, 181 master's, 6 doctorates awarded. *Degree requirements:* For doctorate, thesis/dissertation. *Entrance requirements:* For master's, minimum GPA of 3.0; for doctorate and other advanced degree, GRE General Test. Additional exam requirements/recommendations for international students: Required—TOEFL (minimum score 550 paper-based; 80 iBT), IELTS (minimum score 6.3). *Application deadline:* For fall admission, 6/1 priority date for domestic students, 4/1 for international students; for winter admission, 10/1 priority date for domestic students, 9/1 for international students; for spring admission, 3/1 priority date for domestic students, 2/1 for international students. Applications are processed on a rolling basis. Application fee: $30. Electronic applications accepted. *Expenses:* Tuition, state resident: full-time $8912; part-time $446 per credit hour. Tuition, nonresident: full-time $21,393; part-time $992 per credit hour. *Required fees:* $390; $195 per semester. *Financial support:* Fellowships, research assistantships with tuition reimbursements, teaching assistantships with tuition reimbursements, Federal Work-Study, and tuition waivers (full and partial) available. Support available to part-time students. Financial award applicants required to submit FAFSA. *Unit head:* Dr. Benjamin Baez, Chair, 305-348-3214, Fax: 305-348-1515, E-mail: benjamin.baez@fiu.edu. *Application contact:* Nanett Rojas, Assistant Director, Graduate Admissions, 305-348-7464, Fax: 305-348-7441, E-mail: gradadm@fiu.edu.
Website: http://education.fiu.edu

Florida International University, College of Arts, Sciences, and Education, Department of Teaching and Learning, Miami, FL 33199. Offers art education (MA, MS); curriculum and instruction (MS, Ed D, PhD, Ed S), including curriculum development (MS), elementary education (MS), English education (MS), learning technologies (MS), mathematics education (MS), modern language education (MS), physical education (MS), science education (MS), social studies education (MS), special education (MS); early childhood education (MS); exceptional student education (Ed D); foreign language education (MS), including foreign language education, teaching English to speakers of other languages (TESOL); language, literacy and culture (PhD); mathematics, science, and learning technologies (PhD); physical education (MS), including sport and fitness; reading education (MS). *Program availability:* Part-time, evening/weekend. *Faculty:* 60 full-time (41 women), 112 part-time/adjunct (77 women). *Students:* 165 full-time (139 women), 191 part-time (148 women); includes 270 minority (56 Black or African American, non-Hispanic/Latino; 12 Asian, non-Hispanic/Latino; 191 Hispanic/Latino; 11 Two or more races, non-Hispanic/Latino), 13 international. Average age 34. 238 applicants, 68% accepted, 107 enrolled. In 2017, 184 master's, 15 doctorates awarded. *Degree requirements:* For doctorate, comprehensive exam, thesis/dissertation. *Entrance requirements:* For master's, GRE General Test, Florida General Knowledge Test or Florida College Level Academic Skills Test; for doctorate and Ed S, GRE General Test. Additional exam requirements/recommendations for international students: Required—TOEFL (minimum score 550 paper-based; 80 iBT), IELTS (minimum score 6.3). *Application deadline:* For fall admission, 6/1 priority date for domestic students, 4/1 for international students; for winter admission, 10/1 priority date for domestic students, 9/1 for international students; for spring admission, 3/1 priority date for domestic students, 2/1 for international students. Applications are processed on a rolling basis. Application fee: $30. Electronic applications accepted. *Expenses:* Tuition, state resident: full-time $8912; part-time $446 per credit hour. Tuition, nonresident: full-time $21,393; part-time $992 per credit hour. *Required fees:* $390; $195 per semester. *Financial support:* Research assistantships with tuition reimbursements and teaching assistantships with tuition reimbursements available. *Unit head:* Dr. Lynn Miller, Chair, 305-348-2005, Fax: 305-348-2086, E-mail: lynne.miller@fiu.edu. *Application contact:* Nanett Rojas, Assistant Director, Graduate Admissions, 305-348-7464, Fax: 305-348-7441, E-mail: gradadm@fiu.edu.
Website: https://tl.fiu.edu/

Florida State University, The Graduate School, College of Education, School of Teacher Education, Tallahassee, FL 32306-4450. Offers curriculum and instruction (MS, PhD, Ed S), including early childhood education, elementary education, English education, foreign and second language education, mathematics education, reading and language arts, science education, social science education, special education, visual disabilities education (MS); teaching English to speakers of other languages (Certificate). *Program availability:* Part-time, evening/weekend, 100% online, blended/hybrid learning, asynchronous, minimal on-campus study. *Faculty:* 41 full-time (33 women), 21 part-time/adjunct (18 women). *Students:* 133 full-time (93 women), 84 part-time (69 women); includes 48 minority (20 Black or African American, non-Hispanic/Latino; 2 Asian, non-Hispanic/Latino; 19 Hispanic/Latino; 7 Two or more races, non-Hispanic/Latino), 52 international. Average age 31. 146 applicants, 56% accepted, 52 enrolled. In 2017, 91 master's, 7 doctorates, 1 other advanced degree awarded. Terminal master's awarded for partial completion of doctoral program. *Degree requirements:* For master's and other advanced degree, comprehensive exam, thesis optional; for doctorate, comprehensive exam, thesis/dissertation, diagnostic exam, preliminary exam, prospectus defense, dissertation defense. *Entrance requirements:* For master's, doctorate, and other advanced degree, GRE General Test, minimum upper-division GPA of 3.0. Additional exam requirements/recommendations for international students: Required—TOEFL (minimum score 550 paper-based, 80 iBT), Michigan English Language Assessment Battery (minimum score 77), IELTS (minimum score 6.5) or PTE (minimum score 55). Application fee: $30. Electronic applications accepted. *Financial support:* Fellowships, research assistantships, teaching assistantships, scholarships/grants, tuition waivers (full and partial), and unspecified assistantships available. Financial award application deadline: 1/15; financial award applicants required to submit FAFSA. *Faculty research:* Identifying effective intervention strategies to improve reading skills; improving literacy teaching and learning through technology; understanding of student sense making, problem solving, the history and structure of STEM disciplines, and teacher education to support the development of ambitious instruction that supports the STEM learning of all students; examining practices of international education; identifying ways to support the professional development of teachers. *Unit head:* Dr. Sherry Southerland, Professor/Department Chair, 850-644-6885, Fax: 850-644-2725, E-mail: ssoutherland@admin.fsu.edu. *Application contact:* Britni DeZerga, Academic Program Specialist, 850-644-2122, Fax: 850-644-7736, E-mail: bpurvis@fsu.edu.
Website: http://education.fsu.edu

Fordham University, Graduate School of Education, Division of Curriculum and Teaching, New York, NY 10023. Offers curriculum and teaching (MSE); early childhood education (MSE); elementary education (MST); special education (MSE, Adv C); teaching English as a second language (MSE). *Accreditation:* NCATE. *Program availability:* Part-time, evening/weekend. *Degree requirements:* For Adv C, thesis. *Entrance requirements:* Additional exam requirements/recommendations for international students: Required—TOEFL (minimum score 577 paper-based; 90 iBT), IELTS (minimum score 7). Electronic applications accepted.

Framingham State University, Graduate Studies, Program in the Teaching of English as a Second Language, Framingham, MA 01701-9101. Offers M Ed, Graduate Certificate. *Unit head:* Mary-Ann Stadtler-Chester, Program Coordinator, E-mail: mstadtlerchester@framingham.edu. *Application contact:* 508-626-4550, Fax: 508-626-4030, E-mail: dgce@frc.mass.edu.

English as a Second Language

Fresno Pacific University, Graduate Programs, School of Education, Program in Reading and Language Arts, Fresno, CA 93702-4709. Offers reading (Certificate); reading/English as a second language (MA Ed); reading/language arts (MA Ed). *Program availability:* Part-time, evening/weekend. *Degree requirements:* For master's, thesis or alternative. *Entrance requirements:* For master's, three references. Additional exam requirements/recommendations for international students: Required—TOEFL (minimum score 550 paper-based). Electronic applications accepted. *Expenses:* Contact institution.

Furman University, Graduate Division, Department of Education, Greenville, SC 29613. Offers curriculum and instruction (MA); early childhood education (MA); educational leadership (Ed S); English as a second language (MA); literacy (MA); school leadership (MA); special education (MA). *Accreditation:* NCATE. *Program availability:* Part-time, online learning. *Degree requirements:* For master's, comprehensive exam (for some programs), thesis or alternative. *Entrance requirements:* For master's, PRAXIS II. *Faculty research:* Literacy, pedagogy and practice, social justice, advanced leadership, achievement in high poverty schools.

Gannon University, School of Graduate Studies, College of Humanities, Education, and Social Sciences, School of Education, Program in English as a Second Language, Erie, PA 16541-0001. Offers Certificate. *Program availability:* Part-time, evening/ weekend, 100% online. *Degree requirements:* For Certificate, comprehensive exam, practicum. *Entrance requirements:* For degree, 3 letters of recommendation, bachelor's degree from regionally-accredited college or university with minimum GPA of 3.0, valid Pennsylvania Instructional I or II teaching certificate. Additional exam requirements/ recommendations for international students: Required—TOEFL (minimum score 79 iBT). Electronic applications accepted. Application fee is waived when completed online. *Expenses:* Contact institution.

George Fox University, College of Education, Graduate Teaching and Leading Program, Newberg, OR 97132-2697. Offers administrative leadership (Ed S); continuing administrator license (Certificate); educational leadership (M Ed); educational technology (M Ed); English for speakers of other languages (M Ed); ESOL (Certificate); initial administrator license (Certificate); reading (M Ed, Certificate); special education (M Ed); teaching (MAT). *Accreditation:* NCATE. *Program availability:* Part-time, evening/ weekend, online learning. *Degree requirements:* For master's, thesis (for some programs). *Entrance requirements:* For master's, minimum undergraduate GPA of 3.0 during previous 2 years of course work, resume, 3 professional recommendations on university forms, official transcripts. Additional exam requirements/recommendations for international students: Required—TOEFL (minimum score 577 paper-based; 90 iBT). Electronic applications accepted. *Expenses:* Contact institution.

George Mason University, College of Education and Human Development, Programs in Curriculum and Instruction, Fairfax, VA 22030. Offers advanced international baccalaureate (M Ed); assistive technology (M Ed); designing digital learning in schools (M Ed); early childhood education (M Ed); early childhood education for diverse learners (M Ed); elementary education (M Ed); English as a second language (M Ed); gifted child education (M Ed); history (M Ed); literacy (M Ed), including PK-12 classroom teachers, reading specialist; literacy leadership for diverse schools (M Ed), including K-12 reading; physical education (M Ed); science K-12 (M Ed); secondary education (M Ed), including biology, chemistry, earth science, English, history/social science, math, physics; special education (M Ed); teacher leadership (M Ed); teaching culturally, linguistically diverse and exceptional learners (M Ed); transformative teaching (M Ed). *Program availability:* Part-time, evening/weekend, 100% online, blended/hybrid learning. *Faculty:* 41 full-time (36 women), 45 part-time/adjunct (37 women). *Students:* 173 full-time (151 women), 729 part-time (611 women); includes 271 minority (65 Black or African American, non-Hispanic/Latino; 5 American Indian or Alaska Native, non-Hispanic/Latino; 88 Asian, non-Hispanic/Latino; 94 Hispanic/Latino; 1 Native Hawaiian or other Pacific Islander, non-Hispanic/Latino; 18 Two or more races, non-Hispanic/Latino), 28 international. Average age 32. 426 applicants, 91% accepted, 289 enrolled. In 2017, 349 master's awarded. *Degree requirements:* For master's, thesis. *Entrance requirements:* For master's, PRAXIS Core (for some programs), 2 letters of recommendation, interview, program goals statement; 9 hours of complete licensure endorsement requirements (for elementary education); minimum GPA of 3.0 in applicant's last 60 hours of undergraduate coursework (for secondary education); at least 1 year of teaching experience (for literacy). Additional exam requirements/recommendations for international students: Required—TOEFL (minimum score 575 paper-based; 88 iBT), IELTS (minimum score 6.5), PTE (minimum score 59). *Application deadline:* For fall admission, 4/2 priority date for domestic and international students; for spring admission, 11/1 for domestic and international students. Application fee: $75 ($80 for international students). Electronic applications accepted. *Expenses:* Tuition, state resident: full-time $11,228; part-time $459.50 per credit. Tuition, nonresident: full-time $30,932; part-time $1280.50 per credit. *Required fees:* $3252; $135.50 per credit. Part-time tuition and fees vary according to course load and program. *Financial support:* In 2017–18, 2 students received support, including 2 teaching assistantships; career-related internships or fieldwork, Federal Work-Study, scholarships/grants, unspecified assistantships, and health care benefits (for full-time research or teaching assistantship recipients) also available. Support available to part-time students. Financial award application deadline: 3/1; financial award applicants required to submit FAFSA. *Faculty research:* Teacher preparation and professional development; adaptive teaching; wonder in science teacher preparation; literacy (digital, adolescent); site based course instruction. *Unit head:* Dr. Rebecca Fox, Professor and Academic Program Coordinator, 703-993-4123, E-mail: rfox@gmu.edu.
Website: http://gse.gmu.edu/programs/gsemasters

Gonzaga University, English Language Center, Spokane, WA 99258. Offers teaching English as a second language (MA). *Program availability:* Part-time. *Faculty:* 9 full-time (8 women), 3 part-time/adjunct (all women). *Students:* 3 part-time (2 women); includes 1 minority (Hispanic/Latino). Average age 29. In 2017, 15 master's awarded. *Degree requirements:* For master's, research thesis or research project. *Entrance requirements:* For master's, two letters of recommendation, written statement of purpose, two official transcripts from each college or university attended. Additional exam requirements/ recommendations for international students: Required—TOEFL (minimum score of 580 paper-based, 88 iBT) or IELTS (minimum score of 6.5). *Application deadline:* Applications are processed on a rolling basis. Application fee: $50. Electronic applications accepted. *Expenses:* Contact institution. *Financial support:* In 2017–18, 5 students received support. Scholarships/grants available. Support available to part-time students. Financial award applicants required to submit FAFSA. *Unit head:* Melissa Heid, Manager, Center for Global Engagement, 509-313-6560, E-mail: heid@gonzaga.edu.
Website: https://www.gonzaga.edu/academics/global-engagement/departments/english-language-center

Gordon College, Graduate Education Program, Wenham, MA 01984-1899. Offers early childhood (M Ed); educational leadership (M Ed, Ed S); elementary education (M Ed); English as a second language (M Ed, Ed S); math specialist (M Ed); mathematics specialist (Ed S); middle school education (M Ed); moderate disabilities (M Ed); Montessori education (M Ed); reading (M Ed, Ed S); secondary education (M Ed). *Program availability:* Part-time, evening/weekend. *Faculty:* 23 full-time (17 women), 32 part-time/adjunct (23 women). *Students:* 68 full-time (50 women), 114 part-time (99 women); includes 24 minority (2 Black or African American, non-Hispanic/Latino; 8 Asian, non-Hispanic/Latino; 13 Hispanic/Latino; 1 Two or more races, non-Hispanic/ Latino), 10 international. Average age 34. 248 applicants, 100% accepted, 182 enrolled. In 2017, 99 master's, 16 Ed Ss awarded. *Degree requirements:* For master's, action research or clinical experience (for most programs); for Ed S, action research or clinical experience (for some programs). *Entrance requirements:* For master's, minimum undergraduate GPA of 3.0; 2 official undergraduate transcripts; professional resume; 3 recommendation letters (one professional reference, one academic reference, one personal reference); 500-700 word statement of purpose; for Ed S, minimum master's GPA of 3.3; 2 official transcripts from undergraduate and graduate schools; professional resume; 3 recommendation letters (one professional reference, one academic reference, one personal reference); 500-700 word statement of purpose. Additional exam requirements/recommendations for international students: Required—TOEFL (minimum score 550 paper-based, 80 iBT) or IELTS (minimum score 6.5). *Application deadline:* Applications are processed on a rolling basis. Application fee: $75. *Expenses:* $325 per credit tuition; $75 per semester administrative fee. *Financial support:* Applicants required to submit FAFSA. *Faculty research:* Reading, early childhood development, English language learners, universal design for learning. *Unit head:* Dr. Janet Arndt, Director of Graduate Studies, 978-867-4355, Fax: 978-867-4663. *Application contact:* Julie Lenocker, Program Administrator, 978-867-4322, Fax: 978-867-4663, E-mail: graduate-education@gordon.edu.
Website: http://www.gordon.edu/graduate

Grand Canyon University, College of Education, Phoenix, AZ 85017-1097. Offers autism spectrum disorders (MA); curriculum and instruction (MA); early childhood education (M Ed); educational administration (M Ed); educational leadership (M Ed); elementary education (M Ed); gifted education (MA); instructional technology (MS); K-12 leadership (Ed S); reading (MA); secondary education (M Ed); secondary humanities education (M Ed); secondary STEM education (M Ed); special education (M Ed); teaching and learning (Ed D); teaching English to speakers of other languages (MA). *Program availability:* Part-time, evening/weekend, online learning. *Degree requirements:* For master's, publishable research paper (M Ed), e-portfolio. *Entrance requirements:* For master's, undergraduate degree from accredited, GCU-approved college, university, or program with minimum GPA 2.8. Additional exam requirements/recommendations for international students: Required—TOEFL (minimum score 550 paper-based; 79 iBT), IELTS (minimum score 6). Electronic applications accepted.

Grand Valley State University, College of Education, Programs in General Education, Allendale, MI 49401-9403. Offers adult and higher education (M Ed); early childhood education (M Ed); educational differentiation (M Ed); educational leadership (M Ed); educational technology integration (M Ed); elementary education (M Ed); middle level education (M Ed); school library media services (M Ed); secondary level education (M Ed); teaching English to speakers of other languages (M Ed). *Program availability:* Part-time, evening/weekend, 100% online, blended/hybrid learning. *Students:* 24 part-time (16 women). Average age 41. In 2017, 5 master's awarded. *Degree requirements:* For master's, project or thesis. *Entrance requirements:* For master's, GRE General Test or minimum GPA of 3.0, last 60 credits from regionally-accredited college/university, 3 letters of recommendation. Additional exam requirements/recommendations for international students: Required—TOEFL (minimum iBT score of 80), IELTS (6.5), or Michigan English Language Assessment Battery (77). *Application deadline:* Applications are processed on a rolling basis. Application fee: $30. Electronic applications accepted. *Expenses:* $652 per credit hour. *Financial support:* In 2017–18, 2 students received support, including 2 fellowships; career-related internships or fieldwork, Federal Work-Study, scholarships/grants, and unspecified assistantships also available. *Faculty research:* Effectiveness of technology in education, parental involvement, effective teaching, effective schools research. *Unit head:* Dr. David Bair, Department Director, 616-331-6489, Fax: 616-331-6489, E-mail: baird@gvsu.edu. *Application contact:* Thomas Owens, Director, Student Information and Services Center, 616-331-6282, Fax: 616-331-6217, E-mail: owenst@gvsu.edu.
Website: http://www.gvsu.edu/coe/

Greensboro College, Program in Teaching English to Speakers of Other Languages, Greensboro, NC 27401-1875. Offers MA. *Accreditation:* NCATE. *Program availability:* Part-time, evening/weekend. *Degree requirements:* For master's, thesis, portfolio, project. *Entrance requirements:* For master's, GRE or MAT, 2 letters of recommendation, writing sample. Additional exam requirements/recommendations for international students: Required—TOEFL (minimum score 550 paper-based). Electronic applications accepted.

Hamline University, School of Education, St. Paul, MN 55104-1284. Offers education (MA Ed, Ed D); English as a second language (MA); literacy education (MA); natural science and environmental education (MA Ed); teaching (MAT); teaching English to speakers of other languages (MA). *Accreditation:* NCATE (one or more programs are accredited). *Program availability:* Part-time, evening/weekend, 100% online, blended/ hybrid learning. *Faculty:* 23 full-time (15 women), 43 part-time/adjunct (30 women). *Students:* 79 full-time (60 women), 898 part-time (692 women); includes 139 minority (31 Black or African American, non-Hispanic/Latino; 1 American Indian or Alaska Native, non-Hispanic/Latino; 58 Asian, non-Hispanic/Latino; 33 Hispanic/Latino; 16 Two or more races, non-Hispanic/Latino), 8 international. Average age 35. 366 applicants, 78% accepted, 193 enrolled. In 2017, 236 master's, 7 doctorates awarded. *Degree requirements:* For master's, thesis (for some programs), thesis or capstone project; for doctorate, comprehensive exam, thesis/dissertation. *Entrance requirements:* For master's, official transcripts, essay, letters of recommendation, minimum GPA of 3.0 from bachelor's work; resume and/or writing samples (for some programs); for doctorate, personal statement, master's degree with minimum GPA of 3.0, letters of recommendation, writing sample. Additional exam requirements/recommendations for international students: Required—TOEFL (minimum score 550 paper-based; 80 iBT), IELTS (minimum score 6.5). *Application deadline:* For fall admission, 6/1 for domestic and international students; for spring admission, 11/1 for domestic and international students; for summer admission, 3/1 for domestic and international students. Applications are processed on a rolling basis. Application fee: $0 ($100 for international students). Electronic applications accepted. *Expenses:* $466 per credit (for MA Ed), $625 per credit (for MATESOL), $569 per credit (for MAT), $721 per credit plus fees (for EdD). *Financial support:* Career-related internships or fieldwork, Federal Work-Study, and scholarships/grants available. Support available to part-time students. Financial award application deadline: 4/20; financial award applicants required to submit FAFSA. *Faculty research:* Adult basic education, service-learning, teacher dispositions, diversity, technology. *Unit head:* Dr. Marcela Kostihova, Dean, 651-523-2206, Fax: 651-523-2489, E-mail: cladean@hamline.edu. *Application contact:* Shawn Skoog, Director of Graduate Recruitment and Admission, 651-523-2900, Fax: 651-523-3058, E-mail: gradprog@hamline.edu.
Website: http://www.hamline.edu/education

Harding University, Cannon-Clary College of Education, Searcy, AR 72149-0001. Offers advanced studies in teaching and learning (M Ed); art (MSE); behavioral science (MSE); counseling (MS, Ed S); early childhood special education (M Ed, MSE); education (MSE); educational leadership (M Ed, Ed S); elementary education (M Ed);

English (MSE); French (MSE); history/social science (MSE); kinesiology (MSE); math (MSE); reading (M Ed); secondary education (M Ed); Spanish (MSE); teaching (MAT); teaching English as a second language (MSE). *Accreditation:* NCATE. *Program availability:* Part-time, evening/weekend. *Faculty:* 22 full-time (9 women), 51 part-time/adjunct (37 women). *Students:* 135 full-time (95 women), 316 part-time (231 women); includes 77 minority (46 Black or African American, non-Hispanic/Latino; 7 American Indian or Alaska Native, non-Hispanic/Latino; 4 Asian, non-Hispanic/Latino; 9 Hispanic/Latino; 11 Two or more races, non-Hispanic/Latino), 11 international. Average age 34. 128 applicants, 87% accepted, 111 enrolled. In 2017, 153 master's, 24 other advanced degrees awarded. *Degree requirements:* For master's, comprehensive exam (for some programs), thesis optional, portfolio(s); for Ed S, comprehensive exam, portfolio, project. *Entrance requirements:* For master's, GRE, MAT, PRAXIS; for Ed S, MAT or GRE. Additional exam requirements/recommendations for international students: Required—TOEFL (minimum score 550 paper-based; 79 iBT). *Application deadline:* For fall admission, 8/1 for domestic and international students; for spring admission, 1/1 for domestic and international students. Applications are processed on a rolling basis. Application fee: $35. Tuition and fees vary according to course load, degree level, campus/location and program. *Financial support:* In 2017–18, 33 students received support. Unspecified assistantships available. *Faculty research:* Reading, comprehension, school violence, educational technology, behavior, college choice, differentiated instruction, brain-based teaching. *Unit head:* Dr. Clara Carroll, Chair, 501-279-4501, Fax: 501-279-4083, E-mail: ccarroll@harding.edu. *Application contact:* Information Contact, 501-279-4315, E-mail: gradstudiesedu@harding.edu. Website: http://www.harding.edu/education

Hawai`i Pacific University, College of Liberal Arts, Program in Teaching English to Speakers of Other Languages, Honolulu, HI 96813. Offers MA. *Program availability:* Part-time. *Faculty:* 3 full-time (2 women), 1 part-time/adjunct (0 women). *Students:* 14 full-time (8 women), 9 part-time (5 women); includes 10 minority (2 Black or African American, non-Hispanic/Latino; 2 Asian, non-Hispanic/Latino; 2 Hispanic/Latino; 4 Two or more races, non-Hispanic/Latino), 5 international. Average age 33. 20 applicants, 90% accepted, 10 enrolled. In 2017, 7 master's awarded. *Entrance requirements:* For master's, two letters of recommendation, statement of purpose, transcripts, second language requirement. Additional exam requirements/recommendations for international students: Required—TOEFL (minimum score 550 paper-based; 80 iBT), IELTS (minimum score 6), TWE (minimum score 5). *Application deadline:* For fall admission, 1/15 priority date for domestic students; for spring admission, 10/15 priority date for domestic students. Applications are processed on a rolling basis. Application fee: $50. Electronic applications accepted. *Expenses: Tuition:* Full-time $18,000; part-time $1000 per credit. *Required fees:* $200; $26 per credit. Tuition and fees vary according to course load and program. *Financial support:* In 2017–18, 6 students received support. Career-related internships or fieldwork, Federal Work-Study, scholarships/grants, tuition waivers (partial), and unspecified assistantships available. Financial award application deadline: 3/1; financial award applicants required to submit FAFSA. *Unit head:* Dr. Mark Tjarks, Department Chair, 808-566-2445, E-mail: mtjarks@hpu.edu. *Application contact:* Danny Lam, Assistant Director of Graduate Admissions, 808-544-1135, E-mail: graduate@hpu.edu.
Website: https://www.hpu.edu/cla/english-linguistics/ma-tesol.html

Henderson State University, Graduate Studies, Teachers College, Department of Advanced Instructional Studies, Arkadelphia, AR 71999-0001. Offers developmental therapy (MSE); dyslexia therapy (Graduate Certificate); education (MAT); educational technology leadership (Graduate Certificate); English as a second language (MSE, Graduate Certificate); instructional facilitator (MSE, Graduate Certificate); middle level education (MAT); special education (K-12) (MAT, MSE); special education/early childhood (MAT). *Accreditation:* NCATE. *Program availability:* Part-time. *Entrance requirements:* For master's, GRE General Test or MAT, minimum GPA of 2.7, teacher certification. Additional exam requirements/recommendations for international students: Required—TOEFL (minimum score 600 paper-based); Recommended—IELTS (minimum score 6.5).

Heritage University, Graduate Programs in Education, Program in Professional Studies, Toppenish, WA 98948-9599. Offers bilingual education/ESL (M Ed); biology (M Ed); English and literature (M Ed); reading/literacy (M Ed); special education (M Ed). *Program availability:* Part-time, evening/weekend. *Degree requirements:* For master's, comprehensive exam (for some programs), thesis (for some programs).

Hofstra University, College of Liberal Arts and Sciences, Programs in Forensic Linguistics and Applied Linguistics, Hempstead, NY 11549. Offers applied linguistics (TESOL) (MA); linguistics (MA), including forensic linguistics. *Program availability:* Part-time. *Students:* 28 full-time (21 women), 7 part-time (5 women); includes 15 minority (4 Black or African American, non-Hispanic/Latino; 3 Asian, non-Hispanic/Latino; 8 Hispanic/Latino), 2 international. Average age 27. 41 applicants, 90% accepted, 23 enrolled. In 2017, 22 master's awarded. *Degree requirements:* For master's, thesis, 36 credits, capstone, minimum GPA of 3.0. *Entrance requirements:* For master's, bachelor's degree in related area, interview, 2 letters of recommendation. Additional exam requirements/recommendations for international students: Required—TOEFL (minimum score 550 paper-based; 80 iBT). *Application deadline:* Applications are processed on a rolling basis. Application fee: $75. Electronic applications accepted. *Expenses: Tuition:* Full-time $1292. *Required fees:* $970. Tuition and fees vary according to program. *Financial support:* In 2017–18, 31 students received support, including 9 fellowships with full and partial tuition reimbursements available (averaging $4,731 per year), 1 research assistantship with full and partial tuition reimbursement available (averaging $1,698 per year); career-related internships or fieldwork, Federal Work-Study, institutionally sponsored loans, scholarships/grants, tuition waivers (full and partial), and unspecified assistantships also available. Support available to part-time students. Financial award applicants required to submit FAFSA. *Faculty research:* Threatening language, legal interpretation, cross-examination strategies in assault trials. *Unit head:* Dr. Patricia Welch, Chairperson, 516-463-6453, E-mail: patricia.m.welch@hofstra.edu. *Application contact:* Sunil Samuel, Assistant Vice President of Admissions, 516-463-4723, Fax: 516-463-4664, E-mail: graduateadmission@hofstra.edu.
Website: http://www.hofstra.edu/hclas

Hofstra University, School of Education, Programs in Teacher Education, Hempstead, NY 11549. Offers bilingual education (MA); bilingual extension (Advanced Certificate), including education/speech language pathology, intensive teacher institute; business education (MS Ed); curriculum studies (MS Ed); early childhood and childhood education (MS Ed); early childhood education (MA, MS Ed); educational technology (Advanced Certificate); elementary education (MA, MS Ed), including science, technology, engineering, and mathematics (STEM) (MA); English education (MS Ed); family and consumer science (MS Ed); fine arts and music education (Advanced Certificate); fine arts education (MS Ed); foreign language and TESOL (MS Ed); foreign language education (MA, MS Ed), including Arabic (MS Ed), biology, chemistry, Chinese (MS Ed), earth science, French, German, Italian (MS Ed), Mandarin (MS Ed), physics, Russian, Spanish; foundations of education (Advanced Certificate), including grades 5-6, grades 7-9; languages other than English and teaching English as a second language (MA); learning and teaching (Ed D), including applied linguistics, art education, arts and humanities, early childhood education, English education, human development, math

education, math, science, and technology, multicultural education, physical education, science education, social studies education, special education; mathematics education (MA, MS Ed); music education (MA, MS Ed); science education (MA), including biology (MA, MS Ed), chemistry (MA, MS Ed), earth science (MA, MS Ed), physics (MA, MS Ed); secondary education (Advanced Certificate); social studies education (MA, MS Ed); teaching languages other than English and TESOL (MS Ed); technology for learning (MA); TESOL (MS Ed, Advanced Certificate); TESOL with specialization in STEM (MA); work based learning extension (Advanced Certificate). *Program availability:* Part-time, evening/weekend, blended/hybrid learning. *Students:* 119 full-time (83 women), 124 part-time (90 women); includes 54 minority (15 Black or African American, non-Hispanic/Latino; 9 Asian, non-Hispanic/Latino; 29 Hispanic/Latino; 1 Native Hawaiian or other Pacific Islander, non-Hispanic/Latino), 12 international. Average age 29. 205 applicants, 88% accepted, 93 enrolled. In 2017, 103 master's, 4 doctorates, 32 other advanced degrees awarded. *Degree requirements:* For master's, comprehensive exam, thesis (for some programs), exit project, student teaching, fieldwork, electronic portfolio, curriculum project, minimum GPA of 3.0; for doctorate, thesis/dissertation; for Advanced Certificate, 3 foreign languages, comprehensive exam (for some programs), thesis project. *Entrance requirements:* For master's, GRE, 2 letters of recommendation, portfolio, teacher certification (MA), interview, essay; for doctorate, GMAT, GRE, LSAT, or MAT; for Advanced Certificate, 2 letters of recommendation, essay, interview and/or portfolio, teaching certificate. Additional exam requirements/recommendations for international students: Required—TOEFL (minimum score 550 paper-based; 80 iBT). *Application deadline:* Applications are processed on a rolling basis. Application fee: $75. Electronic applications accepted. *Expenses: Tuition:* Full-time $1292. *Required fees:* $970. Tuition and fees vary according to program. *Financial support:* In 2017–18, 112 students received support, including 56 fellowships with full and partial tuition reimbursements available (averaging $4,998 per year), 2 research assistantships with full and partial tuition reimbursements available (averaging $8,753 per year); career-related internships or fieldwork, Federal Work-Study, institutionally sponsored loans, scholarships/grants, traineeships, tuition waivers (full and partial), and unspecified assistantships also available. Support available to part-time students. Financial award applicants required to submit FAFSA. *Faculty research:* Educational interventions that foster critical-thinking skills; teachers' attitudes about professional development; threats to teacher quality. *Unit head:* Dr. Eustace Thompson, Chairperson, 516-463-5749, Fax: 516-463-6275, E-mail: eustace.g.thompson@hofstra.edu. *Application contact:* Sunil Samuel, Assistant Vice President of Admissions, 516-463-4723, Fax: 516-463-4664, E-mail: graduateadmission@hofstra.edu.
Website: http://www.hofstra.edu/education/

Holy Family University, Graduate and Professional Programs, School of Education, Master of Education Programs, Philadelphia, PA 19114. Offers early elementary education (PreK-Grade 4) (M Ed); education leadership (M Ed); general education (M Ed); reading specialist (M Ed); special education (M Ed); TESOL and literacy (M Ed). *Program availability:* Part-time. *Degree requirements:* For master's, thesis optional. Electronic applications accepted. *Expenses: Tuition:* Full-time $13,518; part-time $9012 per credit hour. Tuition and fees vary according to degree level and program.

Houston Baptist University, College of Education and Behavioral Sciences, Programs in Education, Houston, TX 77074-3298. Offers bilingual education (M Ed); counselor education (M Ed); curriculum and instruction (M Ed); curriculum and instruction (EC-6 bilingual) (M Ed); curriculum and instruction in all-level art, Spanish, music, or physical education (M Ed); curriculum and instruction in EC-6 and special education (EC-12) (M Ed); curriculum and instruction in instructional technology (M Ed); curriculum and instruction in mathematics, science, or social studies (4-8) (M Ed); curriculum and instruction with EC-6 generalist (M Ed); curriculum and instruction with English language arts and reading (4-8) (M Ed); educational administration (M Ed); educational diagnostician (M Ed); executive educational leadership (Ed D); higher education in business management (M Ed); higher education in Christian studies (M Ed); higher education in counseling (M Ed); higher education in educational technology (M Ed); reading (M Ed); special educational leadership (Ed D). *Program availability:* Part-time, evening/weekend, 100% online, blended/hybrid learning. *Students:* 83 full-time (65 women), 187 part-time (156 women); includes 189 minority (114 Black or African American, non-Hispanic/Latino; 2 American Indian or Alaska Native, non-Hispanic/Latino; 9 Asian, non-Hispanic/Latino; 58 Hispanic/Latino; 6 Two or more races, non-Hispanic/Latino), 7 international. Average age 36. 309 applicants, 31% accepted, 70 enrolled. In 2017, 92 master's awarded. *Degree requirements:* For master's, comprehensive exam; for doctorate, thesis/dissertation. *Entrance requirements:* For master's, minimum GPA of 2.75, two recommendations, resume, bachelor's degree conferred transcript; interview (for non-certified teachers); for doctorate, GRE, 5 letters of recommendation. Additional exam requirements/recommendations for international students: Required—TOEFL (minimum score 80 iBT), IELTS (minimum score 6.5). *Application deadline:* For fall admission, 8/1 for domestic students, 6/1 for international students; for spring admission, 1/1 for domestic students, 11/1 for international students; for summer admission, 5/1 for domestic students, 3/1 for international students. Applications are processed on a rolling basis. Application fee: $0 ($100 for international students). Electronic applications accepted. Application fee is waived when completed online. *Expenses:* $22,000 tuition; $4,500 fees (general, technology and parking). *Financial support:* In 2017–18, 59 students received support. Research assistantships, teaching assistantships, Federal Work-Study, and scholarships/grants available. Support available to part-time students. Financial award application deadline: 4/1; financial award applicants required to submit FAFSA. *Faculty research:* Autism and inclusion, integrating technology into instruction, school change and leadership trust. *Unit head:* Dr. Charlotte Fontenot, Director, Graduate Programs, 281-649-3078, Fax: 281-649-3361, E-mail: cfontenot@hbu.edu. *Application contact:* Kristy Wright, Administrative Assistant for Graduate Programs, 281-649-3094, Fax: 281-649-3361, E-mail: kwright@hbu.edu.
Website: http://www.hbu.edu/MED

Humboldt State University, Academic Programs, College of Arts, Humanities, and Social Sciences, Department of English, Arcata, CA 95521-8299. Offers English (MA), including composition studies and pedagogy, literary and cultural studies, teaching English as a second language. *Degree requirements:* For master's, variable foreign language requirement, thesis or alternative, qualifying exam. *Entrance requirements:* For master's, GRE, minimum GPA of 3.0, 3 letters of recommendation, sample of writing. Additional exam requirements/recommendations for international students: Required—TOEFL (minimum score 500 paper-based). *Faculty research:* Teaching of writing, literature.

Hunter College of the City University of New York, Graduate School, School of Education, Department of Curriculum and Teaching, Program in Teaching English as a Second Language, New York, NY 10065-5085. Offers MA. *Accreditation:* NCATE. *Degree requirements:* For master's, one foreign language, thesis, comprehensive exam or essay, New York state teacher certification exams. *Entrance requirements:* For master's, minimum GPA of 2.8, 2 letters of recommendation, interview. Additional exam requirements/recommendations for international students: Required—TOEFL (minimum score 600 paper-based), TWE (minimum score 5).

English as a Second Language

Huntington University, Graduate School, Huntington, IN 46750-1299. Offers adolescent and young adult education (M Ed); business administration (MBA); counseling (MA), including licensed mental health counselor; early adolescent education (M Ed); elementary education (M Ed); global youth ministry (MA); occupational therapy (OTD); organizational leadership (MA); pastoral leadership (MA); TESOL education (M Ed). *Program availability:* Part-time, online learning. *Faculty:* 17 full-time (10 women), 14 part-time/adjunct (4 women). *Students:* 221 full-time (163 women), 22 part-time (13 women). *Degree requirements:* For master's, comprehensive exam (for some programs), thesis (for some programs). *Entrance requirements:* For master's, GRE (for counseling and education students only); for doctorate, GRE (for occupational therapy students). Additional exam requirements/recommendations for international students: Required—TOEFL (minimum score 85 iBT), IELTS (minimum score 6.5). *Application deadline:* For fall admission, 7/1 for domestic students, 5/1 for international students; for winter admission, 10/1 for domestic students, 9/1 for international students; for spring admission, 11/30 for domestic students, 10/30 for international students. Applications are processed on a rolling basis. Application fee: $30. Electronic applications accepted. *Expenses:* Contact institution. *Financial support:* Scholarships/grants and unspecified assistantships available. Support available to part-time students. Financial award application deadline: 8/1; financial award applicants required to submit FAFSA. *Faculty research:* Leadership, educational technology trends, evangelism, youth ministry, mental health. *Unit head:* Michael Wanous, Vice President for Academic Affairs, 260-359-4008, Fax: 260-359-4126, E-mail: mwanous@huntington.edu. *Application contact:* Evan Bennett, Assistant Director of Graduate Admissions, 260-359-4111, Fax: 260-359-4126, E-mail: graduate@huntington.edu.
Website: http://www.huntington.edu/graduate

Idaho State University, Office of Graduate Studies, College of Arts and Letters, Department of English and Philosophy, Pocatello, ID 83209-8056. Offers English (MA); English and the teaching of English (PhD); TESOL (Post-Master's Certificate). *Program availability:* Part-time. *Degree requirements:* For master's, one foreign language, comprehensive exam, thesis optional; for doctorate, one foreign language, comprehensive exam, thesis/dissertation, 2 papers, 2 teaching internships; for Post-Master's Certificate, 6 credits of elective linguistics, practicum. *Entrance requirements:* For master's, GRE General Test (minimum 50th percentile ranking), general literature exam, minimum GPA of 3.0, 3 letters of recommendation, 5-page writing sample; for doctorate, GRE General Test, GRE Subject Test, minimum GPA of 3.5, writing examples, 3 letters of recommendation, master's degree in English; for Post-Master's Certificate, GRE (minimum 35th percentile on verbal section), bachelor's degree, minimum undergraduate GPA of 3.0 in last 2 years, 3 letters of recommendation, knowledge of second language. Additional exam requirements/recommendations for international students: Required—TOEFL (minimum score 550 paper-based; 80 iBT). Electronic applications accepted. *Faculty research:* American literature, Renaissance literature, composition and rhetoric, Intermountain West studies, ethics.

Immaculata University, College of Graduate Studies, Program in Cultural and Linguistic Diversity, Immaculata, PA 19345. Offers bilingual studies (MA); TESOL (MA). *Program availability:* Part-time, evening/weekend. *Degree requirements:* For master's, one foreign language, comprehensive exam, thesis optional, professional experience. *Entrance requirements:* For master's, GRE or MAT, proficiency in Spanish or Asian language, minimum GPA of 3.0. Additional exam requirements/recommendations for international students: Required—TOEFL, IELTS. Electronic applications accepted. *Faculty research:* Cognitive learning, Caribbean literature and culture, English as a second language, teaching English to speakers of other languages.

Indiana State University, College of Graduate and Professional Studies, College of Arts and Sciences, Department of Languages, Literatures, and Linguistics, Terre Haute, IN 47809. Offers applied linguistics/teaching English as a second language (MA); language education (PhD); Spanish/teaching english as a second language (MA); TESL/TEFL (CAS). *Degree requirements:* For master's, comprehensive exam. Electronic applications accepted.

Indiana University Bloomington, University Graduate School, College of Arts and Sciences, Department of Second Language Studies, Bloomington, IN 47405-7000. Offers second language studies (MA, PhD); TESOL and applied linguistics (MA). *Entrance requirements:* Additional exam requirements/recommendations for international students: Required—TOEFL (minimum score 100 iBT). Electronic applications accepted.

Indiana University of Pennsylvania, School of Graduate Studies and Research, College of Humanities and Social Sciences, Department of English, PhD Program in Composition and Teaching English to Speakers of Other Languages, Indiana, PA 15705. Offers PhD. *Program availability:* Part-time. *Faculty:* 22 full-time (10 women). *Students:* 18 full-time (11 women), 79 part-time (48 women); includes 9 minority (2 Black or African American, non-Hispanic/Latino; 4 Asian, non-Hispanic/Latino; 2 Hispanic/Latino; 1 Two or more races, non-Hispanic/Latino), 38 international. Average age 38. 108 applicants, 57% accepted, 7 enrolled. In 2017, 22 doctorates awarded. *Degree requirements:* For doctorate, one foreign language, comprehensive exam, thesis/dissertation. *Entrance requirements:* For doctorate, 2 letters of recommendation. Additional exam requirements/recommendations for international students: Required—TOEFL (minimum score 600 paper-based). *Application deadline:* For fall admission, 2/1 priority date for domestic students; for summer admission, 11/1 priority date for domestic students. Applications are processed on a rolling basis. Application fee: $50. Electronic applications accepted. *Expenses:* Contact institution. *Financial support:* In 2017–18, 18 research assistantships with tuition reimbursements (averaging $6,398 per year), 5 teaching assistantships with partial tuition reimbursements (averaging $11,652 per year) were awarded; fellowships with full tuition reimbursements, career-related internships or fieldwork, Federal Work-Study, scholarships/grants, and unspecified assistantships also available. Support available to part-time students. Financial award application deadline: 4/15; financial award applicants required to submit FAFSA. *Unit head:* Dr. Sharon Deckert, Graduate Coordinator, 724-357-2261, E-mail: sharon.deckert@iup.edu. Website: http://www.iup.edu/english/grad/composition-tesol-phd/default.aspx

Indiana University of Pennsylvania, School of Graduate Studies and Research, College of Humanities and Social Sciences, Department of English, Program in English: TESOL, Indiana, PA 15705. Offers MA. *Program availability:* Part-time. *Faculty:* 22 full-time (10 women). *Students:* 19 full-time (11 women), 3 part-time (1 woman); includes 2 minority (1 Black or African American, non-Hispanic/Latino; 1 Two or more races, non-Hispanic/Latino), 13 international. Average age 28. 32 applicants, 75% accepted, 8 enrolled. In 2017, 10 master's awarded. *Degree requirements:* For master's, thesis optional. *Entrance requirements:* For master's, two letters of recommendation. Additional exam requirements/recommendations for international students: Required—TOEFL (minimum score 580 paper-based). *Application deadline:* Applications are processed on a rolling basis. Application fee: $50. Electronic applications accepted. *Expenses:* Contact institution. *Financial support:* In 2017–18, 4 research assistantships with tuition reimbursements (averaging $2,628 per year) were awarded; fellowships with full tuition reimbursements, Federal Work-Study, scholarships/grants, and unspecified assistantships also available. Financial award application deadline: 4/15; financial award applicants required to submit FAFSA. *Unit head:* Dr. Gloria Park, Director, 724-357-

3095, E-mail: gloria.park@iup.edu.
Website: http://www.iup.edu/english/grad/tesol-ma/default.aspx

Indiana University–Purdue University Fort Wayne, College of Arts and Sciences, Department of English and Linguistics, Fort Wayne, IN 46805-1499. Offers English (MA, MAT); TENL (teaching English as a new language) (Certificate). *Program availability:* Part-time. *Degree requirements:* For master's, one foreign language, thesis (for some programs), teaching certificate (for MAT). *Entrance requirements:* For master's, GRE General Test, minimum GPA of 3.0, major or minor in English, 3 letters of recommendation; for Certificate, bachelor's degree with minimum GPA of 2.5. Additional exam requirements/recommendations for international students: Required—TOEFL (minimum score 600 paper-based; 79 iBT). *Faculty research:* Hebrew names and the vernacular Savior in Anglo-Saxon England.

Indiana University–Purdue University Indianapolis, School of Education, Indianapolis, IN 46202-5155. Offers curriculum and instruction (MS); early childhood (MS); educational leadership (MS, Certificate); English as a second language (Certificate); kindergarten (Certificate); language education (MS); reading (Certificate); school counseling (MS); special education (MS, Certificate). *Program availability:* Part-time, evening/weekend. Terminal master's awarded for partial completion of doctoral program. *Degree requirements:* For master's, thesis optional. *Entrance requirements:* For master's, GRE General Test, minimum GPA of 2.5; for Certificate, official transcripts. Additional exam requirements/recommendations for international students: Required—TOEFL (minimum score 60 iBT), IELTS (minimum score 5.5). Electronic applications accepted. *Expenses:* Contact institution. *Faculty research:* Educational policies and school leaders' responses to these; issues of intersectionality in the experiences of African American lesbian, gay, and bisexual students attending historically black colleges and universities and those who belong to black Greek-letter organizations; students' experiential knowledge and their evolving disciplinary-specific literacy and understanding; innovative program development; urban ESL teacher preparation; target-based instructional coaching.

Indiana University–Purdue University Indianapolis, School of Liberal Arts, Department of English, Indianapolis, IN 46202. Offers English (MA); teaching English to speakers of other languages (TESOL) (MA, Certificate); teaching literature (Certificate); teaching writing (Certificate). *Entrance requirements:* For master's, GRE. Additional exam requirements/recommendations for international students: Required—TOEFL.

Inter American University of Puerto Rico, Arecibo Campus, Programs in Education, Arecibo, PR 00614-4050. Offers administration and educational supervision (MA Ed); counseling and guidance (MA Ed); curriculum and teaching (MA Ed), including biology education, English as a second language, history education, math education, Spanish; elementary education (MA Ed). *Accreditation:* TEAC. *Degree requirements:* For master's, comprehensive exam, thesis optional. *Entrance requirements:* For master's, GRE, EXADEP, bachelor's degree in education or teaching license (administration and supervision) or courses in education and psychology (counseling and guidance), minimum GPA of 2.5 in last 60 credits.

Inter American University of Puerto Rico, Barranquitas Campus, Program in Education, Barranquitas, PR 00794. Offers curriculum and teaching (M Ed), including biology, English as a second language, history, Spanish; educational leadership and management (MA); elementary education (M Ed); information and library service technology (M Ed); special education (MA). *Accreditation:* TEAC. *Program availability:* Part-time, evening/weekend. *Faculty:* 1 full-time (0 women), 3 part-time/adjunct (2 women). *Students:* 17 full-time (16 women), 2 part-time (both women); all minorities (all Hispanic/Latino). Average age 34. 9 applicants, 89% accepted, 8 enrolled. In 2017, 5 master's awarded. *Degree requirements:* For master's, 2 foreign languages, comprehensive exam, thesis (for some programs). *Entrance requirements:* For master's, GRE or EXADEP, bachelor's degree or its equivalent from accredited institution, official academic transcript from institution that conferred bachelor's degree, minimum GPA of 2.5, two recommendation letters, interview (for some programs), essay (for some programs). *Application deadline:* Applications are processed on a rolling basis. Application fee: $31. Electronic applications accepted. *Expenses:* $3,392 full-time tuition plus $652 fees. *Financial support:* Applicants required to submit FAFSA. *Unit head:* Juan A. Negron-Berrios, PhD, Chancellor, 787-857-3600 Ext. 2002, Fax: 787-857-2125, E-mail: janegron@br.inter.edu. *Application contact:* Aramilda Cartagena-Santiago, Dean of Students, 787-857-3600 Ext. 2009, Fax: 787-857-2125, E-mail: aramildacartagena@br.inter.edu.

Inter American University of Puerto Rico, Metropolitan Campus, Graduate Programs, Program in Teaching English as a Second Language, San Juan, PR 00919-1293. Offers MA. *Program availability:* Part-time, evening/weekend. *Degree requirements:* For master's, comprehensive exam, thesis or alternative. *Entrance requirements:* For master's, GRE General Test or EXADEP, interview, minimum GPA of 2.5. Electronic applications accepted.

Inter American University of Puerto Rico, Ponce Campus, Graduate School, Mercedita, PR 00715-1602. Offers accounting (MBA); biology (M Ed); chemistry (M Ed); criminal justice (MA); elementary education (M Ed); English as a Second Language (M Ed); finance (MBA); history (M Ed); human resources (MBA); marketing (MBA); mathematics (M Ed); Spanish (M Ed). *Entrance requirements:* For master's, minimum GPA of 2.5.

Inter American University of Puerto Rico, San Germán Campus, Graduate Studies Center, Program in Teaching English as a Second Language, San Germán, PR 00683-5008. Offers MA. *Accreditation:* TEAC. *Program availability:* Part-time, evening/weekend. *Degree requirements:* For master's, comprehensive exam. *Entrance requirements:* For master's, GRE General Test or EXADEP, minimum GPA of 3.0.

Iowa State University of Science and Technology, Program in Teaching English as a Second Language/Applied Linguistics, Ames, IA 50011. Offers MA. *Entrance requirements:* For master's, GRE, official academic transcripts, resume, three letters of recommendation, statement of personal goals, writing sample. Additional exam requirements/recommendations for international students: Required—TOEFL (minimum score 600 paper-based; 100 iBT), IELTS (minimum score 7). Electronic applications accepted.

James Madison University, The Graduate School, College of Education, Program in Education, Harrisonburg, VA 22807. Offers early childhood education (preK-3) (MAT); educational leadership (M Ed); educational technology (M Ed); elementary education (MAT); equity and cultural diversity (M Ed); inclusive early childhood education (MAT); K-8 mathematics specialist (M Ed); middle education (MAT); reading education (M Ed); secondary education (MAT); Spanish language and culture for educators (M Ed); TESOL (MAT). *Accreditation:* NCATE. *Program availability:* Part-time, evening/weekend. *Students:* 260 full-time (233 women), 158 part-time (100 women); includes 48 minority (10 Black or African American, non-Hispanic/Latino; 4 Asian, non-Hispanic/Latino; 26 Hispanic/Latino; 1 Native Hawaiian or other Pacific Islander, non-Hispanic/Latino; 7 Two or more races, non-Hispanic/Latino), 2 international. Average age 30. In 2017, 262 master's awarded. Application fee: $55. Electronic applications accepted. *Expenses:* Tuition, state resident: full-time $10,512; part-time $438 per credit hour. Tuition, nonresident: full-time $28,358; part-time $1162 per credit hour. *Required fees:* $1128. *Financial support:* In 2017–18, 23 students received support, including 1

teaching assistantship; career-related internships or fieldwork, Federal Work-Study, and 22 assistantships (averaging $7911) also available. Financial award application deadline: 3/1; financial award applicants required to submit FAFSA. *Unit head:* Dr. Phillip M. Wishon, Dean, 540-568-6572, E-mail: wishonpm@jmu.edu. *Application contact:* Lynette D. Michael, Director of Graduate Admissions, 540-568-6131 Ext. 6395, Fax: 540-568-7860, E-mail: michaeld@jmu.edu.
Website: http://www.jmu.edu/coe/index.shtml

Kansas State University, Graduate School, College of Arts and Sciences, Department of Modern Languages, Manhattan, KS 66506. Offers literature (MA), including French, German, Spanish; second language acquisition (MA), including French, German, Spanish, teaching English as a foreign language. *Program availability:* Part-time, evening/weekend, blended/hybrid learning. *Degree requirements:* For master's, thesis optional. *Entrance requirements:* For master's, teaching certificate. Additional exam requirements/recommendations for international students: Required—TOEFL (minimum score 550 paper-based; 83 iBT), TOEFL (minimum speaking-portion score of 26). Electronic applications accepted. *Faculty research:* Second language acquisitions; U.S. Latino literature; Francophone literature; German, French, Spanish, and Spanish-American literature from the Middle Ages to the modern era; teaching English as a foreign language; linguistics.

Kansas State University, Graduate School, College of Education, Department of Educational Leadership, Manhattan, KS 66506. Offers adult learning (Certificate); educational leadership (MS, Ed D, PhD); leadership dynamics for adult learners (Certificate); qualitative research (Certificate); social justice education (Certificate); teaching English as a second language for adult learners (Certificate). *Accreditation:* NCATE. *Program availability:* Online learning. *Degree requirements:* For master's, comprehensive exam; for doctorate, comprehensive exam, thesis/dissertation. *Entrance requirements:* For master's, minimum undergraduate GPA of 3.0; for doctorate, MAT (for educational administration); GRE General Test (for adult education), minimum GPA of 3.0 in last 60 hours. Additional exam requirements/recommendations for international students: Required—TOEFL. Electronic applications accepted. *Faculty research:* Educational law, school finance, school facilities, organizational leadership, adult learning, distance learning/education.

Kean University, College of Education, Program in Instruction and Curriculum, Union, NJ 07083. Offers bilingual/bicultural education (MA); teaching English as a second language (MA). *Accreditation:* NCATE. *Program availability:* Part-time. *Faculty:* 13 full-time (7 women). *Students:* 3 full-time (2 women), 26 part-time (23 women); includes 19 minority (1 Black or African American, non-Hispanic/Latino; 18 Hispanic/Latino), 2 international. Average age 35. 10 applicants, 100% accepted, 8 enrolled. In 2017, 10 master's awarded. *Degree requirements:* For master's, comprehensive exam (for some programs), thesis optional, two-semester advanced seminar. *Entrance requirements:* For master's, GRE General Test or MAT; PRAXIS (for some programs), minimum GPA of 3.0, personal statement, professional resume/curriculum vitae, commitment to working with children, certification (for some programs), two letters of recommendation. Additional exam requirements/recommendations for international students: Required—TOEFL (minimum score 550 paper-based; 79 iBT), IELTS (minimum score 6.5). *Application deadline:* For fall admission, 6/30 for domestic and international students; for spring admission, 12/1 for domestic and international students. Applications are processed on a rolling basis. Application fee: $75. Electronic applications accepted. *Expenses:* Tuition, state resident: full-time $13,419; part-time $653 per credit. Tuition, nonresident: full-time $18,188; part-time $801 per credit. *Required fees:* $3382; $154 per credit. Tuition and fees vary according to course level, course load, degree level and program. *Financial support:* Scholarships/grants and unspecified assistantships available. Financial award applicants required to submit FAFSA. *Unit head:* Dr. Gail Verdi, Program Coordinator, 908-737-3908, E-mail: gverdi@kean.edu. *Application contact:* Brittany Gerstenhaber, Admissions Counselor, 908-737-7100, E-mail: grad-adm@kean.edu.
Website: http://grad.kean.edu/masters-programs/bilingualbicultural-education-instruction-and-curriculum

Kennesaw State University, Leland and Clarice C. Bagwell College of Education, Program in Graduate Education, Kennesaw, GA 30144. Offers educational leadership (M Ed); educational leadership technology (M Ed); elementary and early childhood education (M Ed); instructional technology (M Ed); middle grades education (M Ed); reading (M Ed); secondary education (M Ed); special education (M Ed); teaching English to speakers of other languages (M Ed). *Accreditation:* NCATE. *Program availability:* Part-time. *Degree requirements:* For master's, thesis or alternative. *Entrance requirements:* For master's, GRE General Test, T-4 state certification, minimum GPA of 2.75. Additional exam requirements/recommendations for international students: Required—TOEFL (minimum score 550 paper-based; 80 iBT), IELTS (minimum score 6.5). Electronic applications accepted.

Kennesaw State University, Leland and Clarice C. Bagwell College of Education, Program in Teaching, Kennesaw, GA 30144. Offers art education (MAT); biology (MAT); chemistry (MAT); foreign language education (Chinese and Spanish) (MAT); physics (MAT); secondary English (MAT); secondary mathematics (MAT); special education (MAT); teaching English to speakers of other languages (MAT). *Program availability:* Part-time, evening/weekend. *Entrance requirements:* For master's, GRE, GACE I (state certificate exam), minimum GPA of 2.75, 2 recommendations, resume. Additional exam requirements/recommendations for international students: Required—TOEFL (minimum score 550 paper-based; 80 iBT), IELTS (minimum score 6.5). Electronic applications accepted.

Kent State University, College of Arts and Sciences, Department of English, Kent, OH 44240-0001. Offers creative writing (MFA); English (MA, PhD); English for teachers (MA); literature and writing (MA); rhetoric and composition (PhD); teaching English as a second language (MA). MFA program offered jointly with Cleveland State University, The University of Akron, and Youngstown State University. *Program availability:* Part-time. *Faculty:* 25 full-time (13 women), 2 part-time/adjunct (1 woman). *Students:* 101 full-time (69 women), 19 part-time (11 women); includes 10 minority (4 Black or African American, non-Hispanic/Latino; 1 Asian, non-Hispanic/Latino; 2 Hispanic/Latino; 3 Two or more races, non-Hispanic/Latino), 20 international. Average age 34. 63 applicants, 76% accepted, 18 enrolled. In 2017, 37 master's, 6 doctorates awarded. *Degree requirements:* For master's, one foreign language, thesis (for some programs), final portfolio, final exam, or thesis (for MA in teaching English as a second language); for doctorate, one foreign language, comprehensive exam, thesis/dissertation. *Entrance requirements:* For master's, GRE General Test, goal statement, 3 letters of recommendation, 8-15 page writing sample relevant to the field of study (waived for MA in English for teachers concentration), transcripts; for doctorate, GRE General Test, statement of purpose, 3 letters of recommendation, 8-15 page writing sample relevant to field of study, transcripts. Additional exam requirements/recommendations for international students: Required—TOEFL (minimum score 587 paper-based, 94 iBT), Michigan English Language Assessment Battery (minimum score 82), IELTS (minimum score 7.0) or PTE (minimum score 65). *Application deadline:* For fall admission, 1/15 for domestic and international students. Applications are processed on a rolling basis. Application fee: $45 ($70 for international students). Electronic applications accepted. *Expenses:* Tuition, state resident: full-time $11,310; part-time $515 per credit hour. Tuition, nonresident: full-time $20,396; part-time $928 per credit hour. *International*

tuition: $18,544 full-time. *Financial support:* Fellowships with full tuition reimbursements, teaching assistantships with full tuition reimbursements, and unspecified assistantships available. Financial award application deadline: 1/15. *Unit head:* Dr. Robert Trogdon, Chair, 330-672-2676, E-mail: rtrogdon@kent.edu. *Application contact:* Wesley Raabe, Graduate Studies Coordinator, E-mail: wraabe@kent.edu.
Website: http://www.kent.edu/english/

Langston University, School of Education and Behavioral Sciences, Langston, OK 73050. Offers bilingual/multicultural (M Ed); elementary education (M Ed); English as a second language (M Ed); rehabilitation counseling (M Sc); urban education (M Ed). *Accreditation:* CORE; NCATE (one or more programs are accredited). *Program availability:* Part-time. *Degree requirements:* For master's, comprehensive exam, thesis optional. *Entrance requirements:* For master's, GRE, writing skills test, minimum GPA of 2.5, 3 letters of recommendation. Additional exam requirements/recommendations for international students: Required—TOEFL, TWE. *Faculty research:* Bilingual/multicultural education, financing post-secondary education.

La Salle University, School of Arts and Sciences, Hispanic Institute, Philadelphia, PA 19141-1199. Offers bilingual/bicultural studies (MA); ESL program specialist (Certificate); interpretation: English/Spanish-Spanish/English (Certificate); teaching English to speakers of other languages (MA); translation and interpretation (MA); translation: English/Spanish-Spanish/English (Certificate). *Program availability:* Part-time, evening/weekend. *Faculty:* 2 full-time (1 woman), 5 part-time/adjunct (1 woman). *Students:* 1 (woman) full-time, 37 part-time (26 women); includes 21 minority (7 Black or African American, non-Hispanic/Latino; 1 American Indian or Alaska Native, non-Hispanic/Latino; 1 Asian, non-Hispanic/Latino; 10 Hispanic/Latino; 2 Two or more races, non-Hispanic/Latino), 2 international. Average age 33. 24 applicants, 79% accepted, 11 enrolled. In 2017, 4 master's, 1 other advanced degree awarded. *Degree requirements:* For master's, one foreign language, project or thesis. *Entrance requirements:* For master's, GRE, MAT, or GMAT, professional resume; two letters of recommendation; for Certificate, GRE, MAT, or GMAT, professional resume; two letters of recommendation; evidence of an advanced level in Spanish. Additional exam requirements/recommendations for international students: Required—TOEFL. *Application deadline:* For fall admission, 8/15 priority date for domestic students, 7/15 for international students; for spring admission, 12/15 priority date for domestic students, 11/15 for international students; for summer admission, 4/15 priority date for domestic students, 3/15 for international students. Applications are processed on a rolling basis. Application fee: $35. Electronic applications accepted. Application fee is waived when completed online. *Expenses:* Contact institution. *Financial support:* In 2017–18, 10 students received support. Scholarships/grants available. Support available to part-time students. Financial award application deadline: 8/31; financial award applicants required to submit FAFSA. *Faculty research:* Puerto Rican literature, cross-cultural communication, English as a second language methodology, Spanish language. *Unit head:* Guadalupe Da Costa Montesinos, Director, 215-951-1209, Fax: 215-991-3506, E-mail: montesin@lasalle.edu. *Application contact:* Elizabeth Heenan, Director, Graduate and Adult Enrollment, 215-951-1100, Fax: 215-951-1462, E-mail: heenan@lasalle.edu.
Website: http://www.lasalle.edu/hispanic-institute/

La Salle University, School of Arts and Sciences, Program in Education, Philadelphia, PA 19141-1199. Offers autism spectrum disorders (MA, Certificate); bilingual/bicultural studies (MA); classroom management (MA); dual early childhood and special education (MA); dual middle-level science and math and special education (MA); education (MA); English (MA); English as a second language (Certificate); history (MA); instructional coach (Certificate); instructional leadership (MA); reading specialist (MA, Certificate); secondary education (MA); special education (MA, Certificate). *Program availability:* Part-time, evening/weekend. *Faculty:* 5 full-time (4 women), 8 part-time/adjunct (5 women). *Students:* 2 full-time (1 woman), 110 part-time (81 women); includes 23 minority (11 Black or African American, non-Hispanic/Latino; 1 Asian, non-Hispanic/Latino; 7 Hispanic/Latino; 4 Two or more races, non-Hispanic/Latino). Average age 33. 137 applicants, 70% accepted, 63 enrolled. In 2017, 148 master's awarded. *Degree requirements:* For master's, comprehensive exam. *Entrance requirements:* For master's, MAT or GRE, 2 letters of recommendation; for Certificate, GMAT or GRE, 2 letters of recommendation. Additional exam requirements/recommendations for international students: Required—TOEFL. *Application deadline:* For fall admission, 8/15 priority date for domestic students, 7/15 for international students; for spring admission, 12/15 priority date for domestic students, 11/15 for international students; for summer admission, 4/15 priority date for domestic students, 3/15 for international students. Applications are processed on a rolling basis. Application fee: $35. Electronic applications accepted. Application fee is waived when completed online. *Expenses:* Contact institution. *Financial support:* In 2017–18, 19 students received support. Scholarships/grants available. Support available to part-time students. Financial award application deadline: 8/31; financial award applicants required to submit FAFSA. *Unit head:* Dr. Greer Richardson, Director, 215-951-1806, Fax: 215-951-1843, E-mail: graded@lasalle.edu. *Application contact:* Elizabeth Heenan, Director, Graduate and Adult Enrollment, 215-951-1100, Fax: 215-951-1462, E-mail: heenan@lasalle.edu.
Website: http://www.lasalle.edu/grad-education-programs/

Lasell College, Graduate and Professional Studies in Education, Newton, MA 02466-2709. Offers curriculum, leadership, and inclusion (M Ed); elementary education (M Ed); special education (M Ed), including moderate disabilities; teaching bilingual/English learners with disabilities (Graduate Certificate). *Program availability:* Part-time-only, evening/weekend, blended/hybrid learning. *Faculty:* 3 full-time (all women), 5 part-time/adjunct (4 women). *Students:* 8 full-time (7 women), 43 part-time (38 women); includes 4 minority (2 Asian, non-Hispanic/Latino; 1 Hispanic/Latino; 1 Two or more races, non-Hispanic/Latino), 1 international. Average age 28. 23 applicants, 74% accepted, 10 enrolled. In 2017, 15 master's awarded. *Degree requirements:* For master's, minimum GPA of 3.0; practicum. *Entrance requirements:* For master's, Massachusetts Tests for Educator Licensure (MTEL) Curriculum and Literacy foundations of reading and writing subtest, one-page personal statement, 2 letters of recommendation, resume, bachelor's degree transcript. Additional exam requirements/recommendations for international students: Required—TOEFL (minimum score 550 paper-based, 79 iBT) or IELTS (minimum score 6). *Application deadline:* For fall admission, 8/31 priority date for domestic students, 6/30 priority date for international students; for spring admission, 12/31 priority date for domestic students, 10/31 priority date for international students. Applications are processed on a rolling basis. Electronic applications accepted. *Expenses:* $600 per credit. *Financial support:* Federal Work-Study, scholarships/grants, and tuition discounts available. Support available to part-time students. Financial award application deadline: 8/31; financial award applicants required to submit FAFSA. *Faculty research:* Inclusion, English language learners, literacy, and urban education; teacher inquiry; universal design for learning, deaf-blindness, and visual impairments; social and emotional learning; educational law, applied behavior analysis, and classroom management. *Unit head:* Eric Turner, Vice President of Graduate and Professional Studies, 617-243-2071, Fax: 617-243-2450, E-mail: gradinfo@lasell.edu. *Application contact:* Adrienne Franciosi, Director of Graduate Enrollment, 617-243-2214, Fax: 617-243-2450, E-mail: gradinfo@lasell.edu.
Website: http://www.lasell.edu/academics/graduate-and-professional-studies/programs-of-study/master-of-education.html

English as a Second Language

Lee University, Program in Education, Cleveland, TN 37320-3450. Offers art (MAT); curriculum and instruction (M Ed, Ed S); early childhood (MAT); educational leadership (M Ed, Ed S); elementary education (MAT); English and math (MAT); English and science (MAT); English and social studies (MAT); higher education administration (MS); history (MAT); history and economics (MAT); math and science (MAT); math and social studies (MAT); middle grades (MAT); science and social studies (MASW); secondary education (MAT); Spanish (MAT); special education (M Ed, MAT); TESOL (MAT). *Accreditation:* NCATE. *Program availability:* Part-time. *Faculty:* 15 full-time (7 women), 8 part-time/adjunct (3 women). *Students:* 28 full-time (21 women), 77 part-time (48 women); includes 12 minority (7 Black or African American, non-Hispanic/Latino; 2 Hispanic/Latino; 3 Two or more races, non-Hispanic/Latino), 1 international. Average age 31. 35 applicants, 83% accepted, 22 enrolled. In 2017, 54 master's, 4 other advanced degrees awarded. *Degree requirements:* For master's, variable foreign language requirement, thesis optional, internship. *Entrance requirements:* For master's, MAT or GRE General Test, minimum undergraduate GPA of 2.75, 3 letters of recommendation, interview, writing sample, official transcripts, background check; for Ed S, minimum undergraduate and master's GPA of 2.75, official transcripts for undergraduate and master's degrees. Additional exam requirements/recommendations for international students: Required—TOEFL (minimum score 61 iBT). *Application deadline:* For fall admission, 6/1 priority date for domestic and international students; for spring admission, 11/1 priority date for domestic and international students; for summer admission, 4/1 priority date for domestic and international students. Applications are processed on a rolling basis. Application fee: $25. Electronic applications accepted. *Expenses: Tuition:* Full-time $12,780; part-time $710 per credit hour. *Required fees:* $60; $60 per term. Tuition and fees vary according to program. *Financial support:* In 2017–18, 32 students received support. Career-related internships or fieldwork, Federal Work-Study, institutionally sponsored loans, scholarships/grants, and unspecified assistantships available. Financial award application deadline: 3/1; financial award applicants required to submit FAFSA. *Unit head:* Dr. William Kamm, Director, 423-614-8544, E-mail: wkamm@leeuniversity.edu. *Application contact:* Crystal Keeter, Graduate Education Secretary, 423-614-8544, E-mail: ckeeter@leeuniversity.edu.
Website: http://www.leeuniversity.edu/academics/graduate/education

Lehman College of the City University of New York, School of Education, Department of Middle and High School Education, Program in Teaching English to Speakers of Other Languages, Bronx, NY 10468-1589. Offers MS Ed. *Accreditation:* NCATE. *Degree requirements:* For master's, thesis. *Entrance requirements:* For master's, minimum GPA of 3.0.

Le Moyne College, Department of Education, Syracuse, NY 13214. Offers adolescent education (MS Ed, MST); adolescent education/special education (MS Ed, MST); adolescent English (MST), including grades 7-12; adolescent English/special education (MST), including grades 7-12; adolescent foreign language (MST), including grades 7-12; adolescent history (MST), including grades 7-12; childhood education (MS Ed); childhood education/special education (MS Ed); elementary education (MS Ed); general education (MS Ed); inclusive childhood education (MST); literacy education (MS Ed), including birth to grade 6, grades 5-12; school building leader (MS Ed); school building leadership (CAS); school district business leader (MS Ed, CAS); school district leader (MS Ed); school district leadership (CAS); secondary education (MS Ed); special education (MS Ed); teaching English to speakers of other languages (MS Ed); urban studies (MS Ed). *Accreditation:* TEAC. *Program availability:* Part-time, evening/weekend. *Faculty:* 7 full-time (5 women), 20 part-time/adjunct (12 women). *Students:* 30 full-time (19 women), 126 part-time (93 women); includes 15 minority (7 Black or African American, non-Hispanic/Latino; 1 American Indian or Alaska Native, non-Hispanic/Latino; 1 Asian, non-Hispanic/Latino; 6 Hispanic/Latino), 4 international. Average age 29. 139 applicants, 65% accepted, 76 enrolled. In 2017, 82 master's, 43 CASs awarded. *Degree requirements:* For master's, thesis. *Entrance requirements:* For master's, bachelor's degree with minimum undergraduate GPA of 3.0, 2 letters of recommendation, transcripts. Additional exam requirements/recommendations for international students: Required—TOEFL (minimum score 550 paper-based; 79 iBT); Recommended—IELTS (minimum score 6.5). *Application deadline:* For fall admission, 4/1 priority date for domestic and international students; for spring admission, 10/1 priority date for domestic and international students; for summer admission, 3/1 priority date for domestic and international students. Applications are processed on a rolling basis. Application fee: $50. Electronic applications accepted. *Expenses:* $700 per credit hour. *Financial support:* In 2017–18, 30 students received support. Career-related internships or fieldwork, scholarships/grants, and health care benefits available. Support available to part-time students. Financial award applicants required to submit FAFSA. *Faculty research:* Minority teachers, special education, multiculturalism, literacy, technology, media literacy learning, autism, school district organization, service-learning, higher level problem solving, teacher leadership. *Unit head:* Dr. Stephen C. Fleury, Chair, Department of Education, 315-445-4376, Fax: 315-445-4744, E-mail: fleurysc@lemoyne.edu. *Application contact:* Kristen P. Richards, Senior Director of Enrollment Management, 315-445-5444, Fax: 315-445-6092, E-mail: trapaskp@lemoyne.edu.
Website: http://www.lemoyne.edu/education

Lesley University, Graduate School of Education, Cambridge, MA 02138-2790. Offers arts, community, and education (M Ed); autism studies (Certificate); curriculum and instruction (M Ed, CAGS); early childhood education (M Ed); ecological teaching and learning (MS); educational studies (PhD), including adult learning, educational leadership, individually designed; elementary education (M Ed); emergent technologies for educators (Certificate); ESLArts: language learning through the arts (M Ed); high school education (M Ed); individually designed (M Ed); integrated teaching through the arts (M Ed); literacy for K-8 classroom teachers (M Ed); mathematics education (M Ed); middle school education (M Ed); moderate disabilities (M Ed); online learning (Certificate); reading (CAGS); science in education (M Ed); severe disabilities (M Ed); special needs (CAGS); specialist teacher of reading (M Ed); teacher of visual art (M Ed); technology in education (M Ed, CAGS). *Accreditation:* TEAC. *Program availability:* Part-time, evening/weekend, online learning. *Degree requirements:* For master's, practicum; for doctorate, thesis/dissertation. *Entrance requirements:* For master's, Massachusetts Tests for Educator Licensure (MTEL), transcripts, statement of purpose, recommendations; interview (for special education); for doctorate, GRE General Test, transcripts, statement of purpose, recommendations, interview, master's degree, resume; for other advanced degree, interview, master's degree. Additional exam requirements/recommendations for international students: Required—TOEFL (minimum score 550 paper-based; 80 iBT). Electronic applications accepted. *Faculty research:* Assessment in literacy, mathematics and science; autism spectrum disorders; instructional technology and online learning; multicultural education and English language learners.

Lewis University, College of Education, Program in Curriculum and Instruction: Literacy and English Language Learning, Romeoville, IL 60446. Offers M Ed. *Program availability:* Part-time. *Degree requirements:* For master's, comprehensive exam. *Entrance requirements:* For master's, Test of Academic Proficiency/Basic Skills Test/ACT/SAT, bachelor's degree, minimum undergraduate GPA of 2.75, state licensure with teaching endorsement. Additional exam requirements/recommendations for international students: Required—TOEFL (minimum score 550 paper-based; 79 iBT),

IELTS (minimum score 6). *Application deadline:* For fall admission, 5/1 priority date for international students; for spring admission, 11/1 for international students. Application fee: $40. Electronic applications accepted. Tuition and fees vary according to program. *Financial support:* Federal Work-Study and unspecified assistantships available. Financial award application deadline: 5/1; financial award applicants required to submit FAFSA. *Unit head:* Dr. Pamela Jessee, Dean, 815-836-5316, E-mail: jesseepa@lewisu.edu. *Application contact:* Kathy Lisak, Graduate Admission Counselor, 815-836-5610, E-mail: grad@lewisu.edu.
Website: http://www.lewisu.edu/academics/literacy-ELL/index.htm

Lewis University, College of Education, Program in English as a Second Language, Romeoville, IL 60446. Offers M Ed. *Program availability:* Part-time, evening/weekend. *Students:* 4 full-time (2 women), 9 part-time (7 women); includes 1 minority (Hispanic/Latino), 5 international. Average age 33. *Degree requirements:* For master's, comprehensive exam, departmental qualifying exam. *Entrance requirements:* For master's, writing exam, Test of Academic Proficiency/Basic Skills Test/ACT/SAT, bachelor's degree, minimum GPA of 2.75, 2 letters of recommendation, writing sample, professional educator license. Additional exam requirements/recommendations for international students: Required—TOEFL (minimum score 550 paper-based; 79 iBT), IELTS (minimum score 6). *Application deadline:* For fall admission, 5/1 priority date for international students; for spring admission, 11/15 priority date for international students. Application fee: $40. Electronic applications accepted. Tuition and fees vary according to program. *Financial support:* Federal Work-Study, scholarships/grants, and unspecified assistantships available. Financial award application deadline: 5/1; financial award applicants required to submit FAFSA. *Unit head:* Dr. Deb Augsburger, Program Director, 815-838-0500, E-mail: augsbude@lewisu.edu. *Application contact:* Kathy Lisak, Graduate Admission Counselor, 815-836-5610, E-mail: grad@lewisu.edu.

Lindenwood University, Graduate Programs, School of Education, St. Charles, MO 63301-1695. Offers behavioral analysis (MA); education (MA), including autism spectrum disorders, character education, early intervention in autism and sensory impairment, gifted, technology; educational administration (MA, Ed D, Ed S); English to speakers of other languages (MA); instructional leadership (Ed D, Ed S); library media (MA); professional counseling (MA); school administration (MA, Ed S); school counseling (MA); teaching (MA). *Program availability:* Part-time, evening/weekend, 100% online, blended/hybrid learning. *Faculty:* 47 full-time (31 women), 213 part-time/adjunct (135 women). *Students:* 434 full-time (319 women), 1,292 part-time (989 women); includes 387 minority (313 Black or African American, non-Hispanic/Latino; 9 American Indian or Alaska Native, non-Hispanic/Latino; 13 Asian, non-Hispanic/Latino; 37 Hispanic/Latino; 1 Native Hawaiian or other Pacific Islander, non-Hispanic/Latino; 14 Two or more races, non-Hispanic/Latino), 20 international. Average age 36. 828 applicants, 61% accepted, 378 enrolled. In 2017, 431 master's, 63 doctorates, 94 other advanced degrees awarded. *Degree requirements:* For master's, thesis (for some programs), minimum GPA of 3.0; for doctorate, thesis/dissertation, minimum GPA of 3.0; for Ed S, comprehensive exam, project, minimum GPA of 3.0. *Entrance requirements:* For master's, interview, minimum undergraduate cumulative GPA of 3.0, writing sample, letter of recommendation; for doctorate, GRE, minimum graduate GPA of 3.4, resume, interview, writing sample, 4 letters of recommendation; for Ed S, master's degree in education, relevant work experience. Additional exam requirements/recommendations for international students: Required—TOEFL (minimum score 550 paper-based; 80 iBT); Recommended—IELTS (minimum score 6.5). *Application deadline:* For fall admission, 8/27 priority date for domestic and international students; for spring admission, 1/14 priority date for domestic and international students; for summer admission, 6/4 priority date for domestic and international students. Applications are processed on a rolling basis. Application fee: $30 ($100 for international students). Electronic applications accepted. *Expenses: Tuition:* Full-time $16,300; part-time $460 per credit. *Required fees:* $660; $330 per credit. Tuition and fees vary according to degree level and program. *Financial support:* In 2017–18, 1,615 students received support. Career-related internships or fieldwork, Federal Work-Study, institutionally sponsored loans, scholarships/grants, tuition waivers (partial), and unspecified assistantships available. Financial award application deadline: 6/30; financial award applicants required to submit FAFSA. *Unit head:* Dr. Anthony Scheffler, Dean, School of Education, 636-949-4618, Fax: 636-949-4197, E-mail: ascheffler@lindenwood.edu. *Application contact:* Kara Schilli, Director, Evening and Graduate Admissions, 636-949-4349, Fax: 636-949-4109, E-mail: adultadmissions@lindenwood.edu.
Website: http://www.lindenwood.edu/academics/academic-schools/school-of-education/

Long Island University–Hudson, Graduate School, Purchase, NY 10577. Offers autism (Advanced Certificate); bilingual education (Advanced Certificate); childhood education (MS Ed); crisis management (Advanced Certificate); early childhood education (MS Ed); educational leadership (MS Ed); health administration (MPA); literacy (MS Ed); marriage and family therapy (MS); mental health counseling (MS, Advanced Certificate), including credentialed alcoholism and substance abuse counselor (MS); middle childhood and adolescence education (MS Ed); pharmaceutics (MS), including cosmetic science, industrial pharmacy; public administration (MPA); school counseling (MS Ed, Advanced Certificate); school psychology (MS Ed); special education (MS Ed); TESOL (MS Ed); TESOL (all grades) (Advanced Certificate). *Program availability:* Part-time, evening/weekend. *Faculty:* 8 full-time (6 women), 41 part-time/adjunct (24 women). *Students:* 69 full-time (54 women), 249 part-time (200 women); includes 102 minority (29 Black or African American, non-Hispanic/Latino; 1 American Indian or Alaska Native, non-Hispanic/Latino; 9 Asian, non-Hispanic/Latino; 62 Hispanic/Latino; 1 Native Hawaiian or other Pacific Islander, non-Hispanic/Latino). Average age 33. 153 applicants, 96% accepted, 103 enrolled. In 2017, 138 master's, 36 other advanced degrees awarded. *Entrance requirements:* Additional exam requirements/recommendations for international students: Required—TOEFL. *Application deadline:* Applications are processed on a rolling basis. Application fee: $50. Electronic applications accepted. *Expenses:* Contact institution. *Financial support:* In 2017–18, 32 students received support. Scholarships/grants available. Support available to part-time students. Financial award application deadline: 2/15; financial award applicants required to submit FAFSA. *Unit head:* Dr. Sylvia Blake, Dean and Chief Operating Officer, 914-831-2700, E-mail: westchester@liu.edu. *Application contact:* Dr. Sylvia Blake, Dean and Chief Operating Officer, 914-831-2700, E-mail: westchester@liu.edu.

Long Island University–LIU Brooklyn, School of Education, Brooklyn, NY 11201-8423. Offers adolescence urban education (MS Ed); applied behavior analysis (Advanced Certificate); bilingual education (Advanced Certificate); bilingual education in urban setting (MS Ed); bilingual school counselor (MS Ed, Advanced Certificate); childhood urban education (MS Ed); childhood/early childhood education (MS Ed); childhood/early childhood urban education (MS Ed); early childhood urban education (MS Ed, Advanced Certificate); educational leadership (Advanced Certificate); marriage and family therapy (MS, Advanced Certificate); mental health counseling (MS, Advanced Certificate); school building district leader (Advanced Certificate); school counselor (MS Ed, Advanced Certificate); school psychologist (MS Ed); teaching students with disabilities (MS Ed); teaching urban children with disabilities (MS Ed); TESOL (MS Ed, Advanced Certificate). *Accreditation:* TEAC. *Program availability:* Part-time, evening/weekend, 100% online. *Faculty:* 14 full-time (12 women), 42 part-time/adjunct (32 women). *Students:* 140 full-time (130 women), 563 part-time (414 women);

includes 417 minority (183 Black or African American, non-Hispanic/Latino; 1 American Indian or Alaska Native, non-Hispanic/Latino; 32 Asian, non-Hispanic/Latino; 187 Hispanic/Latino; 14 Two or more races, non-Hispanic/Latino), 10 international. Average age 31. 449 applicants, 82% accepted, 264 enrolled. In 2017, 408 master's, 31 other advanced degrees awarded. *Entrance requirements:* For master's, GRE. Additional exam requirements/recommendations for international students: Required—TOEFL (minimum score 527 paper-based, 75 iBT), IELTS, or PTE. *Application deadline:* Applications are processed on a rolling basis. Application fee: $50. Electronic applications accepted. *Expenses: Tuition:* Full-time $21,618; part-time $1201 per credit. *Required fees:* $1840; $920 per term. Tuition and fees vary according to course load. *Financial support:* In 2017–18, 58 students received support. Career-related internships or fieldwork, Federal Work-Study, scholarships/grants, and unspecified assistantships available. Support available to part-time students. Financial award application deadline: 2/15; financial award applicants required to submit FAFSA. *Faculty research:* Diversity issues in education and mental health care, inclusion - disability studies, sustainability, teacher professional development. *Unit head:* Dean, 718-488-1055, E-mail: bkln-admissions@liu.edu. *Application contact:* Bayu Sutrisno, Graduate Admissions Counselor, 718-488-1011, Fax: 718-780-6110, E-mail: bkln-admissions@liu.edu.
Website: http://www.liu.edu/Brooklyn/Academics/School-of-Education

Long Island University–LIU Post, College of Education, Information and Technology, Brookville, NY 11548-1300. Offers adolescence education (MS); adolescence education 7-12 (MS); archives and records management (AC); art education (MS); childhood education (MS); childhood education/literacy B-6 (MS); childhood education/special education (MS); clinical mental health counseling (MS, AC); early childhood education (MS); early childhood education/childhood education (MS); educational leadership (AC); educational technology (MS); information studies (PhD); interdisciplinary educational studies (Ed D); middle childhood education (MS); music education (MS); public library administration (AC); school counselor (MS); special education (MS Ed); speech-language pathology (MA); students with disabilities, 7-12 generalist (AC); TESOL (MA). *Accreditation:* TEAC. *Program availability:* Part-time, 100% online, blended/hybrid learning. *Faculty:* 40 full-time (26 women), 73 part-time/adjunct (38 women). *Students:* 472 full-time (400 women), 696 part-time (543 women); includes 254 minority (93 Black or African American, non-Hispanic/Latino; 46 Asian, non-Hispanic/Latino; 105 Hispanic/Latino; 10 Two or more races, non-Hispanic/Latino), 33 international. Average age 33. 917 applicants, 82% accepted, 357 enrolled. In 2017, 408 master's, 31 other advanced degrees awarded. Terminal master's awarded for partial completion of doctoral program. *Degree requirements:* For master's, variable foreign language requirement, comprehensive exam (for some programs), thesis optional; for doctorate, comprehensive exam, thesis/dissertation. *Entrance requirements:* For master's and AC, GRE (for some programs). Additional exam requirements/recommendations for international students: Required—TOEFL (minimum score 550 paper-based, 75 iBT), IELTS, or PTE. *Application deadline:* Applications are processed on a rolling basis. Application fee: $50. Electronic applications accepted. *Expenses: Tuition:* Full-time $21,618; part-time $1201 per credit. *Required fees:* $1840; $920 per term. Tuition and fees vary according to course load. *Financial support:* In 2017–18, 376 students received support. Career-related internships or fieldwork, Federal Work-Study, institutionally sponsored loans, scholarships/grants, tuition waivers (partial), and unspecified assistantships available. Support available to part-time students. Financial award application deadline: 2/15; financial award applicants required to submit FAFSA. *Faculty research:* Sleep; use of technology to develop executive function by students with disabilities; early childhood literacy development through play; social justice through education; using a structured protocol to discuss Bad News. *Unit head:* Dr. Albert Inserra, Dean, 516-299-2210, E-mail: albert.inserra@liu.edu. *Application contact:* Rita Langdon, Graduate Admissions, 516-299-2900, Fax: 516-299-2137, E-mail: post-enroll@liu.edu.
Website: http://liu.edu/CWPost/Academics/College-of-Education-Information-and-Technology

Long Island University–Riverhead, Graduate Programs, Riverhead, NY 11901. Offers applied behavior analysis (Advanced Certificate); childhood education (MS), including grades 1-6; cybersecurity policy (Advanced Certificate); homeland security management (MS, Advanced Certificate); literacy education (MS); literacy education B-6 (MS); teaching students with disabilities (MS), including grades 1-6; TESOL (Advanced Certificate). *Accreditation:* TEAC. *Program availability:* Part-time. *Faculty:* 4 full-time (1 woman), 11 part-time/adjunct (5 women). *Students:* 17 full-time (14 women), 58 part-time (36 women); includes 14 minority (4 Black or African American, non-Hispanic/Latino; 1 American Indian or Alaska Native, non-Hispanic/Latino; 1 Asian, non-Hispanic/Latino; 6 Hispanic/Latino; 2 Two or more races, non-Hispanic/Latino). Average age 32. 68 applicants, 79% accepted, 26 enrolled. In 2017, 30 master's, 7 other advanced degrees awarded. *Entrance requirements:* Additional exam requirements/recommendations for international students: Required—TOEFL or IELTS. *Application deadline:* Applications are processed on a rolling basis. Application fee: $50. Electronic applications accepted. *Expenses:* Contact institution. *Financial support:* In 2017–18, 53 students received support. Scholarships/grants available. Support available to part-time students. Financial award application deadline: 2/15; financial award applicants required to submit FAFSA. *Unit head:* Dr. Abagail VanVlerah, Dean and Chief Operating Officer, 631-299-3831, E-mail: abagail.vanvlerah@liu.edu. *Application contact:* Jean Conroy, Associate Dean, 631-287-8301, E-mail: jean.conroy@liu.edu.

Madonna University, Program in Teaching English to Speakers of Other Languages, Livonia, MI 48150-1173. Offers MATESOL. *Program availability:* Part-time, evening/weekend. *Degree requirements:* For master's, one foreign language, thesis or alternative. Electronic applications accepted.

Manhattanville College, School of Education, Jump Start Program, Purchase, NY 10577-2132. Offers childhood education and special education (grades 1-6) (MPS); early childhood education (birth-grade 2) (MAT); education (Advanced Certificate); English and special education (grades 5-12) (MPS); mathematics and special education (grades 5-12) (MPS); science and special education (grades 5-12) (MPS); social studies and special education (grades 5-12) (MPS); Spanish (grades 7-12) (MAT); TESOL (all grades) (MPS). *Program availability:* Part-time, evening/weekend. *Faculty:* 10 full-time (7 women), 39 part-time/adjunct (27 women). *Students:* 3 full-time (2 women), 40 part-time (24 women); includes 11 minority (3 Black or African American, non-Hispanic/Latino; 6 Hispanic/Latino; 1 Native Hawaiian or other Pacific Islander, non-Hispanic/Latino; 1 Two or more races, non-Hispanic/Latino). Average age 33. 25 applicants, 60% accepted, 7 enrolled. In 2017, 17 master's, 2 other advanced degrees awarded. *Degree requirements:* For master's, comprehensive exam (for some programs), thesis (for some programs), student teaching, research seminars, portfolios, internships, writing assessment; for Advanced Certificate, comprehensive exam (for some programs). *Entrance requirements:* For master's, GRE or MAT (for programs leading to certification), minimum GPA of 3.0, 2 letters of recommendation, interview, essay (2-3 page personal statement that describes reasons for choosing teaching or educational leadership as profession and philosophy of education), proof of immunization (for those born after 1957). Additional exam requirements/recommendations for international students: Required—TOEFL (minimum score 600 paper-based; 110 iBT); Recommended—IELTS (minimum score 8). *Application deadline:* Applications are processed on a rolling basis. Application fee: $75. Electronic applications accepted.

Expenses: $915 per credit. *Financial support:* Teaching assistantships, career-related internships or fieldwork, Federal Work-Study, institutionally sponsored loans, scholarships/grants, and unspecified assistantships available. Financial award application deadline: 3/15; financial award applicants required to submit FAFSA. *Faculty research:* Early childhood and technology, professional development schools and community schools, students with emotional difficulties, literacy and adolescents, mindfulness, changing suburbs institute, and community schools, studying the effects of the environment on special populations, the most difficult cases, students who are presented with multiple challenges: learning, behavioral and ACE experiences who see criminal behavior as a way to cope; working on giving them the tools they need to succeed. *Unit head:* Dr. Shelly Wepner, Dean, 914-323-3153, E-mail: shelly.wepner@mville.edu. *Application contact:* Alissa Wilson, Director, Graduate Admissions, 914-323-3150, Fax: 914-694-1732, E-mail: edschool@mville.edu.
Website: http://www.mville.edu/programs/jump-start

Manhattanville College, School of Education, Program in Teaching English to Speakers of Other Languages, Purchase, NY 10577-2132. Offers adult and international settings (MPS); bilingual education (childhood/Spanish) (Advanced Certificate); teaching English as a second language (all grades) (MPS, Certificate). *Program availability:* Part-time, evening/weekend. *Faculty:* 2 full-time (1 woman), 6 part-time/adjunct (4 women). *Students:* 5 full-time (all women), 22 part-time (17 women); includes 8 minority (1 Black or African American, non-Hispanic/Latino; 7 Hispanic/Latino). Average age 31. 9 applicants, 100% accepted, 8 enrolled. In 2017, 13 master's, 3 Advanced Certificates awarded. *Degree requirements:* For master's, comprehensive exam (for some programs), thesis (for some programs), student teaching, research seminars, portfolios, internships, writing assessment; for other advanced degree, comprehensive exam (for some programs). *Entrance requirements:* For master's, GRE or MAT (for programs leading to certification), minimum GPA of 3.0, 2 letters of recommendation, interview, essay (2-3 page personal statement that describes reasons for choosing teaching or educational leadership as profession and philosophy of education), proof of immunization (for those born after 1957). Additional exam requirements/recommendations for international students: Required—TOEFL (minimum score 600 paper-based; 110 iBT); Recommended—IELTS (minimum score 8). *Application deadline:* Applications are processed on a rolling basis. Application fee: $75. Electronic applications accepted. *Expenses:* $915 per credit. *Financial support:* Teaching assistantships, career-related internships or fieldwork, Federal Work-Study, institutionally sponsored loans, scholarships/grants, and unspecified assistantships available. Financial award application deadline: 3/15; financial award applicants required to submit FAFSA. *Faculty research:* Changing suburbs institute and community schools. *Unit head:* Dr. Shelly Wepner, Dean, 914-323-3153, Fax: 914-323-5493, E-mail: shelly.wepner@mville.edu. *Application contact:* Alissa Wilson, Director, Graduate Admissions, 914-323-3150, Fax: 914-694-1732, E-mail: edschool@mville.edu.
Website: http://www.mville.edu/programs/tesol-teaching-english-speakers-other-languages

Marlboro College, Graduate and Professional Studies, Program in Teaching English to Speakers of Other Languages, Marlboro, VT 05344. Offers MAT. *Degree requirements:* For master's, 36 credits, final learning portfolio. *Entrance requirements:* For master's, 2 letters of recommendation, letter of intent, transcripts, interview. Additional exam requirements/recommendations for international students: Required—TOEFL (minimum score of 577 paper-based, 90 iBT) or IELTS (minimum score of 7). *Application deadline:* For spring admission, 4/5 priority date for domestic students, 3/1 for international students. Applications are processed on a rolling basis. Application fee: $0. Electronic applications accepted. *Expenses:* Contact institution. *Financial support:* Scholarships/grants available. Financial award application deadline: 4/5; financial award applicants required to submit FAFSA. *Unit head:* Beverley Burkett, Chair, 802-451-7514, Fax: 802-258-9201, E-mail: bburkett@gradschool.marlboro.edu. *Application contact:* Amanda Mehegan, Assistant Director of Graduate Admissions, 802-451-7506, Fax: 802-258-9201, E-mail: graduateadmissions@marlboro.edu.
Website: https://www.marlboro.edu/academics/graduate/tesol

McDaniel College, Graduate and Professional Studies, Program in TESOL, Westminster, MD 21157-4390. Offers MS. *Program availability:* Part-time, evening/weekend, online only, 100% online. *Faculty:* 5 part-time/adjunct (3 women). *Students:* 4 full-time (2 women), 20 part-time (18 women); includes 6 minority (1 Black or African American, non-Hispanic/Latino; 1 Asian, non-Hispanic/Latino; 4 Hispanic/Latino). Average age 30. 11 applicants, 100% accepted, 8 enrolled. In 2017, 6 master's awarded. *Degree requirements:* For master's, thesis optional, portfolio. *Entrance requirements:* For master's, PRAXIS I, bachelor's degree from accredited institution with minimum cumulative GPA of 2.75; statement of intent; three references. Additional exam requirements/recommendations for international students: Required—TOEFL (minimum score 79 iBT), IELTS (minimum score 6). *Application deadline:* For fall admission, 6/1 priority date for domestic students; for spring admission, 11/1 priority date for domestic students; for summer admission, 3/1 priority date for domestic students. Applications are processed on a rolling basis. Application fee: $75. Electronic applications accepted. *Expenses: Tuition:* Full-time $11,760; part-time $490 per credit hour. Tuition and fees vary according to course load and program. *Financial support:* Application deadline: 3/1; applicants required to submit FAFSA. *Unit head:* E-mail: gradadms@mcdaniel.edu. *Application contact:* Crystal L. Perry, Assistant Director, Graduate Enrollment Management, 410-857-2516, Fax: 410-857-2515, E-mail: cperry@mcdaniel.edu.

Mercy College, School of Education, Program in Teaching English to Speakers of Other Languages (TESOL), Dobbs Ferry, NY 10522-1189. Offers MS, Advanced Certificate. *Program availability:* Part-time, evening/weekend, blended/hybrid learning. *Students:* 7 full-time (all women), 34 part-time (32 women); includes 24 minority (2 Black or African American, non-Hispanic/Latino; 22 Hispanic/Latino). Average age 32. 31 applicants, 29% accepted, 4 enrolled. In 2017, 27 master's awarded. *Degree requirements:* For master's, comprehensive exam (for some programs). *Entrance requirements:* For master's, GRE, resume, interview, undergraduate transcript. Additional exam requirements/recommendations for international students: Required—TOEFL (minimum score 600 paper-based; 100 iBT), IELTS (minimum score 8). *Application deadline:* For fall admission, 8/1 for international students. Applications are processed on a rolling basis. Application fee: $40. Electronic applications accepted. *Expenses: Tuition:* Full-time $15,426; part-time $857 per credit hour. *Required fees:* $630; $158 per term. Tuition and fees vary according to course load, degree level and program. *Financial support:* Career-related internships or fieldwork, Federal Work-Study, scholarships/grants, and unspecified assistantships available. Support available to part-time students. Financial award applicants required to submit FAFSA. *Unit head:* Dr. Rose Rudnitski, Dean for the School of Education, 914-674-7447, Fax: 914-674-7352, E-mail: rrudnitski@mercy.edu. *Application contact:* Allison Gurdineer, Senior Director of Admissions, 877-637-2946, Fax: 914-674-7382, E-mail: admissions@mercy.edu.
Website: https://www.mercy.edu/degrees-programs/ms-teaching-english-speakers-other-languages-tesol

Meredith College, School of Education, Health and Human Sciences, Raleigh, NC 27607-5298. Offers academically and intellectually gifted (M Ed); elementary education (M Ed, MAT); English as a second language (M Ed, MAT); health and physical education (MAT); nutrition, health and human performance (MS, Postbaccalaureate

English as a Second Language

Certificate), including dietetic internship (Postbaccalaureate Certificate), nutrition (MS); psychology (MA), including industrial/organizational psychology; reading (M Ed); special education (MAT); special education (general certification) (M Ed). *Accreditation:* NCATE. *Program availability:* Part-time, evening/weekend. *Students:* 25 full-time (24 women), 22 part-time (all women); includes 13 minority (8 Black or African American, non-Hispanic/Latino; 1 American Indian or Alaska Native, non-Hispanic/Latino; 1 Asian, non-Hispanic/Latino; 3 Hispanic/Latino). Average age 31. 57 applicants, 54% accepted, 31 enrolled. In 2017, 14 master's awarded. *Degree requirements:* For master's, thesis optional. *Entrance requirements:* For master's, GRE General Test or MAT, minimum GPA of 2.5, teaching license, recommendations. Additional exam requirements/recommendations for international students: Required—TOEFL. *Application deadline:* For fall admission, 7/1 priority date for domestic students; for spring admission, 11/1 priority date for domestic students. Applications are processed on a rolling basis. Application fee: $50. Electronic applications accepted. *Expenses:* Contact institution. *Financial support:* Career-related internships or fieldwork, institutionally sponsored loans, and tuition waivers (partial) available. Support available to part-time students. Financial award application deadline: 2/15; financial award applicants required to submit FAFSA. *Unit head:* Dr. Monica McKinney, Graduate Program Manager, 919-760-8056, Fax: 919-760-2303, E-mail: mckinneym@meredith.edu.
Website: https://www.meredith.edu/school-of-education-health-and-human-sciences

Merrimack College, School of Education and Social Policy, North Andover, MA 01845-5800. Offers community engagement (M Ed), including community organizations, higher education, PreK-12 education; criminology and criminal justice (MS); curriculum and instruction (M Ed); early childhood education (M Ed); educational leadership (CAGS), including instructional leadership; elementary education (M Ed); English as a second language (PreK-6) (M Ed); high school education (M Ed); higher education (M Ed), including leadership and organizational development, student affairs; middle school education (M Ed); moderate disabilities (PreK-8) (M Ed); school counseling (M Ed). *Program availability:* Part-time, evening/weekend, 100% online courses with immersion events and in-classroom practicum close to home. *Faculty:* 15 full-time, 36 part-time/adjunct. *Students:* 212 full-time (175 women), 121 part-time (101 women); includes 42 minority (6 Black or African American, non-Hispanic/Latino; 6 Asian, non-Hispanic/Latino; 27 Hispanic/Latino; 3 Two or more races, non-Hispanic/Latino), 3 international. Average age 27. 420 applicants, 84% accepted, 250 enrolled. In 2017, 177 master's awarded. *Degree requirements:* For master's, practicum, portfolio, and state test (for licensure track); capstone (for higher education, curriculum and instruction, and community engagement tracks); for CAGS, capstone. *Entrance requirements:* For master's, Massachusetts Teacher Education Licensure (MTEL), official transcripts from other colleges, resume, personal statement, 2 letters of recommendation. Additional exam requirements/recommendations for international students: Required—TOEFL (minimum score 84 iBT), IELTS (minimum score 6.5), PTE (minimum score 56). *Application deadline:* For fall admission, 8/24 for domestic students, 7/30 for international students; for spring admission, 1/10 for domestic students, 12/10 for international students; for summer admission, 5/10 for domestic students, 4/10 for international students. Applications are processed on a rolling basis. Application fee: $0. Electronic applications accepted. *Expenses:* Contact institution. *Financial support:* Fellowships with full tuition reimbursements, career-related internships or fieldwork, scholarships/grants, and health care benefits available. Support available to part-time students. Financial award application deadline: 5/1; financial award applicants required to submit FAFSA. *Application contact:* Alyssa Orlando, Graduate Admissions Counselor, 978-837-3563, E-mail: orlandoaf@merrimack.edu.
Website: http://www.merrimack.edu/academics/graduate/education/

Messiah College, Program in Education, Mechanicsburg, PA 17055. Offers curriculum and instruction (M Ed); special education (M Ed); teaching English to speakers of other languages (M Ed). *Program availability:* Part-time, online learning. Electronic applications accepted. *Faculty research:* Socio-cultural perspectives on education, TESOL, autism, special education.

Michigan State University, The Graduate School, College of Arts and Letters, Department of Linguistics and Germanic, Slavic, Asian, and African Languages, East Lansing, MI 48824. Offers German studies (MA, PhD); linguistics (MA, PhD); teaching English to speakers of other languages (MA). *Program availability:* Part-time, evening/weekend. *Entrance requirements:* For master's, GRE General Test, minimum GPA of 3.2 in last 2 undergraduate years, 2 years of college-level foreign language, 3 letters of recommendation, portfolio (German studies); for doctorate, GRE General Test, minimum graduate GPA of 3.5, 3 letters of recommendation, master's degree or sufficient graduate course work in linguistics or language of study, master's thesis or major research paper. Additional exam requirements/recommendations for international students: Required—TOEFL. Electronic applications accepted.

MidAmerica Nazarene University, Professional and Graduate Studies in Education, Olathe, KS 66062-1899. Offers ESOL (M Ed); reading specialist (M Ed); technology enhanced teaching (M Ed). *Accreditation:* NCATE. *Program availability:* Part-time, evening/weekend, online only, 100% online. *Entrance requirements:* For master's, bachelor's degree from an accredited college or university, minimum undergraduate GPA of 3.0, valid teaching license. Additional exam requirements/recommendations for international students: Required—TOEFL (minimum score 81 iBT), IELTS (minimum score 6). Electronic applications accepted. *Expenses:* Contact institution.

Middlebury Institute of International Studies at Monterey, Graduate School of Translation, Interpretation and Language Education, Program in Teaching English to Speakers of Other Languages, Monterey, CA 93940-2691. Offers MATESOL. *Degree requirements:* For master's, portfolio, oral defense. *Entrance requirements:* For master's, minimum GPA of 3.0. Additional exam requirements/recommendations for international students: Required—TOEFL (minimum score 600 paper-based; 100 iBT). Electronic applications accepted.

Middle Tennessee State University, College of Graduate Studies, College of Education, Department of Educational Leadership, Program in Curriculum and Instruction, Murfreesboro, TN 37132. Offers curriculum and instruction (M Ed, Ed S); English as a second language (M Ed, Ed S); secondary education (M Ed); technology and curriculum design (Ed S). *Accreditation:* NCATE. *Program availability:* Part-time, evening/weekend, online learning. *Degree requirements:* For master's, comprehensive exam; for Ed S, comprehensive exam, thesis or alternative. *Entrance requirements:* For master's and Ed S, GRE, MAT or PRAXIS. Additional exam requirements/recommendations for international students: Required—TOEFL (minimum score 525 paper-based; 71 iBT) or IELTS (minimum score 6). Electronic applications accepted.

Millersville University of Pennsylvania, College of Graduate Studies and Adult Learning, College of Education and Human Services, Department of Early, Middle, and Exceptional Education, Program in Language and Literacy: ESL, Millersville, PA 17551-0302. Offers language and literacy education (M Ed), including English as a second language. *Program availability:* Part-time, evening/weekend. *Faculty:* 9 full-time (4 women), 11 part-time/adjunct (8 women). *Students:* 11 part-time (9 women); includes 2 minority (both Hispanic/Latino). Average age 29. 5 applicants, 100% accepted, 2 enrolled. In 2017, 8 master's awarded. *Degree requirements:* For master's, thesis optional. *Entrance requirements:* For master's, GRE or MAT if undergraduate cumulative GPA is lower than 3.0, teaching certificate. Additional exam requirements/

recommendations for international students: Required—TOEFL (minimum score 80 iBT), IELTS (minimum score 6.5), PTE (minimum score 60). *Application deadline:* Applications are processed on a rolling basis. Application fee: $40. Electronic applications accepted. *Expenses:* $500 per credit resident tuition and fees; $750 per credit non-resident tuition and fees; $114.75 per credit general fee (maximum of 12 credits); technology fee $27 per credit (resident); $39 per credit (non-resident). *Financial support:* In 2017–18, 1 student received support. Unspecified assistantships available. Financial award application deadline: 3/15; financial award applicants required to submit FAFSA. *Faculty research:* Student engagement, English language learners, literacy pedagogy, assessment and diagnosis. *Unit head:* Dr. Marcia Nell, Department Chair, 717-871-7344, E-mail: marcia.nell@millersville.edu. *Application contact:* Dr. Victor S. DeSantis, Dean of College of Graduate Studies and Adult Learning/Associate Provost for Civic and Community Engagement, 717-871-7619, Fax: 717-871-7954, E-mail: victor.desantis@millersville.edu.
Website: http://www.millersville.edu/academics/educ/eled/graduate-programs/language-and-literacy.php

Minnesota State University Mankato, College of Graduate Studies and Research, College of Arts and Humanities, Department of English, Mankato, MN 56001. Offers communication and composition (MA); creative writing (MFA); English studies (MA); teaching English as a second language (MA, Certificate); technical communication (MA, Certificate). *Program availability:* Part-time. *Degree requirements:* For master's, one foreign language, comprehensive exam, thesis or alternative. *Entrance requirements:* For master's, minimum GPA of 3.0 during previous 2 years, writing sample (MFA). Additional exam requirements/recommendations for international students: Required—TOEFL (minimum score 500 paper-based; 61 iBT). Electronic applications accepted.

Minnesota State University Moorhead, Graduate Studies, College of Humanities and Social Sciences, Moorhead, MN 56563. Offers teaching English as a second language (MA). *Program availability:* Part-time, evening/weekend. *Faculty:* 7. *Students:* 9 part-time (8 women). Average age 33. 2 applicants, 50% accepted. In 2017, 1 master's awarded. *Degree requirements:* For master's, comprehensive exam (for some programs), thesis, final oral defense. *Entrance requirements:* For master's, essay, writing sample, minimum GPA of 3.0. Additional exam requirements/recommendations for international students: Required—TOEFL (minimum score 550 paper-based). *Application deadline:* For fall admission, 4/15 for domestic students; for spring admission, 11/15 for domestic students. Applications are processed on a rolling basis. Application fee: $20. Electronic applications accepted. *Expenses:* Tuition, state resident: full-time $9000; part-time $374 per credit. Tuition, nonresident: full-time $18,000; part-time $748 per credit. *Required fees:* $1055; $43.96 per credit. Tuition and fees vary according to degree level, program and reciprocity agreements. *Financial support:* Federal Work-Study and unspecified assistantships available. Financial award application deadline: 10/1; financial award applicants required to submit FAFSA. *Unit head:* Dr. Randy Cagle, Dean, 218-477-2477, E-mail: caglera@mnstate.edu. *Application contact:* Karla Wenger, Graduate Studies Office Manager, 218-477-2344, Fax: 218-477-2482, E-mail: wengerk@mnstate.edu.
Website: http://www.mnstate.edu/chss/

Mississippi College, Graduate School, College of Arts and Sciences, School of Humanities and Social Sciences, Department of Modern Languages, Clinton, MS 39058. Offers teaching English to speakers of other languages (MA, MS). *Program availability:* Part-time. *Degree requirements:* For master's, thesis (for some programs). *Entrance requirements:* For master's, GRE or NTE. Additional exam requirements/recommendations for international students: Recommended—TOEFL, IELTS. Electronic applications accepted.

Missouri State University, Graduate College, College of Arts and Letters, Department of English, Springfield, MO 65897. Offers applied second language acquisition (MASLA); English (MA); English education (MS Ed); teaching English to speakers of other languages (Certificate); writing (MA). MASLA offered with the Department of Modern and Classical Languages. *Program availability:* Part-time, evening/weekend. *Faculty:* 25 full-time (18 women), 5 part-time/adjunct (2 women). *Students:* 34 full-time (26 women), 85 part-time (73 women); includes 9 minority (1 Black or African American, non-Hispanic/Latino; 1 Asian, non-Hispanic/Latino; 3 Hispanic/Latino; 1 Native Hawaiian or other Pacific Islander, non-Hispanic/Latino; 3 Two or more races, non-Hispanic/Latino), 14 international. Average age 26. 97 applicants, 65% accepted, 56 enrolled. In 2017, 57 master's awarded. *Degree requirements:* For master's, one foreign language, comprehensive exam, thesis or alternative. *Entrance requirements:* For master's, GRE (for MA), 9-12 teacher certification (MS Ed); minimum GPA of 3.0 (MA); personal statement (200- to 250-word description of reasons and goals behind interest in English graduate studies); at least two letters of recommendation from individuals able to speak of the applicant's academic achievements and potential; writing sample. Additional exam requirements/recommendations for international students: Required—TOEFL (minimum score 550 paper-based; 79 iBT), IELTS (minimum score 6). *Application deadline:* For fall admission, 3/1 priority date for domestic students, 3/1 for international students; for spring admission, 10/1 priority date for domestic students, 10/1 for international students. Applications are processed on a rolling basis. Application fee: $35 ($50 for international students). Electronic applications accepted. *Expenses:* Tuition, state resident: full-time $2915; part-time $2021 per credit hour. Tuition, nonresident: full-time $5354; part-time $3647 per credit hour. *International tuition:* $11,992 full-time. *Required fees:* $173; $173 per credit hour. Tuition and fees vary according to class time, course level, course load, degree level, campus/location and program. *Financial support:* In 2017–18, 23 teaching assistantships with full tuition reimbursements (averaging $8,772 per year) were awarded; Federal Work-Study, institutionally sponsored loans, scholarships/grants, and unspecified assistantships also available. Financial award application deadline: 3/31; financial award applicants required to submit FAFSA. *Faculty research:* History of rhetoric, modern poetry, African-American literature, digital writing, teaching English to speakers of other languages. *Unit head:* Dr. W. D. Blackmon, Department Head, 417-836-5107, Fax: 417-836-6940, E-mail: english@missouristate.edu. *Application contact:* Stephanie Praschan, Director, Graduate Enrollment Management, 417-836-5330, Fax: 417-836-6200, E-mail: stephaniepraschan@missouristate.edu.
Website: http://english.missouristate.edu/

Missouri Western State University, Program in Assessment, St. Joseph, MO 64507-2294. Offers K-12 cross-categorical special education (MAS); TESOL (MAS, Graduate Certificate); writing (MAS). *Program availability:* Part-time. *Students:* 29 part-time (25 women); includes 1 minority (Black or African American, non-Hispanic/Latino). Average age 38. 8 applicants, 100% accepted, 4 enrolled. In 2017, 9 master's, 3 other advanced degrees awarded. *Entrance requirements:* For master's, minimum GPA of 2.75. Additional exam requirements/recommendations for international students: Recommended—TOEFL (minimum score 79 iBT), IELTS (minimum score 6). *Application deadline:* For fall admission, 7/15 for domestic and international students; for spring admission, 10/1 for domestic and international students; for summer admission, 3/15 for domestic students. Applications are processed on a rolling basis. Application fee: $45 ($50 for international students). Electronic applications accepted. *Expenses:* Tuition, state resident: full-time $6391; part-time $336 per credit hour. Tuition, nonresident: full-time $11,483; part-time $604 per credit hour. *Required fees:* $542; $99

per credit hour. $176 per semester. One-time fee: $45. Tuition and fees vary according to course load and program. *Financial support:* Scholarships/grants and unspecified assistantships available. Support available to part-time students. *Unit head:* Dr. Susan Bashinski, Director of Graduate Programs in Education, 816-271-5629, E-mail: sbashinski@missouriwestern.edu. *Application contact:* Dr. Benjamin D. Caldwell, Dean of the Graduate School, 816-271-4394, Fax: 816-271-4525, E-mail: graduate@missouriwestern.edu.
Website: https://www.missouriwestern.edu/masa/

Molloy College, Graduate Education Program, Rockville Centre, NY 11571-5002. Offers adolescent education in biology (MS); adolescent special education (Advanced Certificate); bilingual extension (Advanced Certificate); childhood education (MS); childhood special education (Advanced Certificate); early childhood education (MS); educational technology (MS); English (MS); mathematics (MS); social studies (MS); Spanish (MS); special education on both childhood and adolescent levels (MS); teaching English to speakers of other languages (TESOL) in grades pre-K to 12 (MS); TESOL (Advanced Certificate). *Accreditation:* NCATE. *Program availability:* Part-time, evening/weekend. *Faculty:* 18 full-time (17 women), 11 part-time/adjunct (9 women). *Students:* 102 full-time (80 women), 217 part-time (167 women); includes 65 minority (16 Black or African American, non-Hispanic/Latino; 7 Asian, non-Hispanic/Latino; 38 Hispanic/Latino; 4 Two or more races, non-Hispanic/Latino), 1 international. Average age 41. 153 applicants, 68% accepted, 85 enrolled. In 2017, 95 master's, 3 other advanced degrees awarded. *Entrance requirements:* Additional exam requirements/recommendations for international students: Required—TOEFL (minimum score 550 paper-based; 79 iBT). *Application deadline:* Applications are processed on a rolling basis. Application fee: $60. Electronic applications accepted. *Expenses: Tuition:* Full-time $19,980; part-time $1110 per credit. *Required fees:* $1040. Tuition and fees vary according to course load and degree level. *Financial support:* Application deadline: 3/1; applicants required to submit FAFSA. *Faculty research:* English Language Learners; social emotional needs of students; gifted education; cultural diversity; collaborative teaching methods. *Unit head:* Joanne O'Brien, Associate Dean and Director of Graduate Education Programs, 516-323-3116, E-mail: jobrien@molloy.edu. *Application contact:* Jaclyn Machowicz, Assistant Director for Admissions, 516-323-4010, E-mail: jmachowicz@molloy.edu.

Monmouth University, Graduate Studies, School of Education, West Long Branch, NJ 07764-1898. Offers applied behavior analysis (Certificate); autism (Certificate); director of school counseling services (Post-Master's Certificate); early childhood (M Ed); educational leadership (Ed D); elementary education (MAT), including elementary level, secondary level; English as a second language (M Ed); learning disabilities teacher-consultant (Post-Master's Certificate); literacy (MS Ed); school counseling (MS Ed); special education (MS Ed), including autism, learning disabilities teacher-consultant, teacher of students with disabilities, teaching in inclusive settings; speech-language pathology (MS Ed); student affairs and college counseling (MS Ed); supervisor (Post-Master's Certificate); teaching English to speakers of other languages (Certificate). *Accreditation:* NCATE. *Program availability:* Part-time, evening/weekend, 100% online, blended/hybrid learning. *Faculty:* 23 full-time (19 women), 33 part-time/adjunct (25 women). *Students:* 175 full-time (163 women), 168 part-time (142 women); includes 54 minority (10 Black or African American, non-Hispanic/Latino; 4 Asian, non-Hispanic/Latino; 32 Hispanic/Latino; 8 Two or more races, non-Hispanic/Latino). Average age 27. In 2017, 160 master's, 3 other advanced degrees awarded. *Entrance requirements:* For master's, GRE taken within last 5 years (for MS Ed in speech-language pathology); SAT (minimum combined score of 1660 in 3 sections), ACT (23), GRE (minimum score of 4.0 on analytical writing section and minimum combined score of 310 on quantitative and verbal sections), or passing scores on 3 parts of Core Academic Skills Educators, minimum GPA of 3.0 in major; 2 letters of recommendation (for some programs); resume, personal statement or essay (depending on program). Additional exam requirements/recommendations for international students: Required—TOEFL (minimum score 550 paper-based; 79 iBT), IELTS (minimum score 6), Michigan English Language Assessment Battery (minimum score 77) or Certificate of Advanced English (minimum score 160). *Application deadline:* For fall admission, 7/15 priority date for domestic students, 7/1 for international students; for spring admission, 12/1 priority date for domestic students, 11/1 for international students; for summer admission, 5/1 for domestic students. Applications are processed on a rolling basis. Application fee: $50. Electronic applications accepted. *Expenses: Tuition:* Full-time $21,366; part-time $7122 per credit. *Required fees:* $700; $175 per term. *Financial support:* In 2017–18, 125 students received support. Institutionally sponsored loans, scholarships/grants, and unspecified assistantships available. Support available to part-time students. Financial award applicants required to submit FAFSA. *Faculty research:* Multicultural literacy, science and mathematics teaching strategies, teacher as reflective practitioner, children with disabilities. *Unit head:* Dr. John E. Henning, Dean, 732-263-5513, Fax: 732-263-5277. *Application contact:* Laurie Kuhn, Associate Director of Graduate Admission, 732-571-3452, Fax: 732-263-5123, E-mail: gradadm@monmouth.edu.
Website: http://www.monmouth.edu/academics/schools/education/default.asp

Montclair State University, The Graduate School, College of Education and Human Services, MAT Program in Teaching, Montclair, NJ 07043-1624. Offers art (MAT); biology (MAT); chemistry (MAT); earth science (MAT); English (MAT); French (MAT); health and physical education (MAT); health education (MAT); mathematics (MAT); music (MAT); physical education (MAT); physical science (MAT); social studies (MAT); Spanish (MAT); teacher of English as a second language (MAT). *Degree requirements:* For master's, comprehensive exam, thesis or alternative. *Entrance requirements:* For master's, interview, 2 letters of recommendation. Additional exam requirements/recommendations for international students: Required—TOEFL (minimum score 83 iBT), IELTS (minimum score 6.5). Electronic applications accepted.

Montclair State University, The Graduate School, College of Humanities and Social Sciences, Teaching English to Speakers of Other Languages Certificate Program, Montclair, NJ 07043-1624. Offers Certificate. *Program availability:* Part-time, evening/weekend. *Degree requirements:* For Certificate, comprehensive exam. *Entrance requirements:* For degree, 2 letters of recommendation, essay. Additional exam requirements/recommendations for international students: Required—TOEFL (minimum score 83 iBT), IELTS (minimum score 6.5). Electronic applications accepted. *Faculty research:* Language learning and technology research, interlanguage, bilingual pragmatics.

Mount Saint Vincent University, Graduate Programs, Faculty of Education, Program in Curriculum Studies, Halifax, NS B3M 2J6, Canada. Offers education of young adolescents (M Ed, MA Ed, MA-R); general studies (M Ed, MA Ed, MA-R); teaching English as a second language (M Ed, MA Ed, MA-R). *Program availability:* Part-time, evening/weekend, online learning. *Degree requirements:* For master's, thesis (for some programs). *Entrance requirements:* For master's, bachelor's degree in related field, minimum B average, 1 year of teaching experience. Electronic applications accepted. *Faculty research:* Science education, cultural studies, international education, curriculum development.

Multnomah University, Graduate Programs, Portland, OR 97220-5898. Offers counseling (MA); global development and justice (MA); teaching (MA); TESOL (MA). *Program availability:* Part-time, evening/weekend. *Faculty:* 6 full-time (5 women), 12 part-time/adjunct (7 women). *Students:* 69 full-time (53 women), 18 part-time (13 women); includes 22 minority (5 Black or African American, non-Hispanic/Latino; 3 Asian, non-Hispanic/Latino; 9 Hispanic/Latino; 5 Two or more races, non-Hispanic/Latino). Average age 30. 71 applicants, 58% accepted, 30 enrolled. In 2017, 57 master's awarded. *Degree requirements:* For master's, variable foreign language requirement, comprehensive exam (for some programs), thesis (for some programs). *Entrance requirements:* For master's, interview; references; writing sample (for counseling). Additional exam requirements/recommendations for international students: Required—TOEFL (minimum score 550 paper-based). *Application deadline:* For fall admission, 8/1 for domestic students, 12/1 for international students; for spring admission, 12/1 for domestic and international students. Application fee: $40. Electronic applications accepted. *Expenses: Tuition:* Full-time $8720; part-time $5450 per credit hour. *Required fees:* $110; $55 per credit hour. Tuition and fees vary according to course load, degree level and program. *Financial support:* Career-related internships or fieldwork and scholarships/grants available. Support available to part-time students. Financial award application deadline: 7/1; financial award applicants required to submit FAFSA. *Unit head:* Dr. Daniel Scalberg, Academic Dean, 503-251-6441, E-mail: dscalberg@multnomah.edu. *Application contact:* Mindy Kate Hasenkamp, Director of Admissions, 503-251-6483, Fax: 503-254-1268, E-mail: admiss@multnomah.edu.

Murray State University, College of Humanities and Fine Arts, Department of English and Philosophy, Murray, KY 42071. Offers creative writing (MFA); English (MA); English pedagogy and technology (DA); gender studies (Certificate); teaching English to speakers of other languages (TESOL) (MA). *Program availability:* Part-time, 100% online, blended/hybrid learning. *Faculty:* 26 full-time (14 women), 1 part-time/adjunct (0 women). *Students:* 31 full-time (12 women), 91 part-time (61 women); includes 11 minority (5 Black or African American, non-Hispanic/Latino; 2 American Indian or Alaska Native, non-Hispanic/Latino; 2 Asian, non-Hispanic/Latino; 2 Two or more races, non-Hispanic/Latino), 23 international. Average age 36. 55 applicants, 95% accepted, 30 enrolled. In 2017, 21 master's awarded. *Entrance requirements:* For master's, doctorate, and Certificate, GRE or GMAT, minimum university GPA of 2.75. Additional exam requirements/recommendations for international students: Required—TOEFL (minimum score 527 paper-based; 71 iBT). *Application deadline:* Applications are processed on a rolling basis. Application fee: $40 ($50 for international students). Electronic applications accepted. *Expenses:* Tuition, state resident: full-time $9504. Tuition, nonresident: full-time $26,811. *International tuition:* $14,400 full-time. Tuition and fees vary according to course load, degree level and reciprocity agreements. *Financial support:* In 2017–18, 3 teaching assistantships were awarded; Federal Work-Study and unspecified assistantships also available. Financial award applicants required to submit FAFSA. *Unit head:* Dr. Sue Sroda, Chair, Department of English and Philosophy, 270-809-4715, Fax: 270-809-4545, E-mail: msroda@murraystate.edu. *Application contact:* Kaitlyn Burzynski, Interim Assistant Director for Graduate Admission and Records, 270-809-5732, Fax: 270-809-3780, E-mail: msu.graduateadmissions@murraystate.edu.
Website: https://www.murraystate.edu/academics/CollegesDepartments/CollegeOfHumanitiesAndFineArts/EnglishAndPhilosophy/index.aspx

Nazareth College of Rochester, Graduate Studies, Department of Education, Program in Teaching English to Speakers of Other Languages, Rochester, NY 14618. Offers MS Ed. *Accreditation:* TEAC. *Entrance requirements:* For master's, minimum GPA of 3.0. Additional exam requirements/recommendations for international students: Required—TOEFL or IELTS.

New Jersey City University, Debra Cannon Partridge Wolfe College of Education, Department of Multicultural Education, Jersey City, NJ 07305-1597. Offers bilingual/bicultural education (MA); English as a second language (MA). *Program availability:* Part-time, evening/weekend. *Entrance requirements:* For master's, GRE General Test or MAT. Additional exam requirements/recommendations for international students: Required—TOEFL.

Newman University, Master of Science in Education Program, Wichita, KS 67213-2097. Offers building leadership (MS Ed); curriculum and instruction (MS Ed), including English as a second language, reading specialist; organizational leadership (MS Ed). *Accreditation:* NCATE. *Program availability:* Part-time, evening/weekend, online learning. *Degree requirements:* For master's, thesis optional. *Entrance requirements:* For master's, 3 years' full-time teaching experience, minimum GPA of 3.0, writing sample, 2 letters of recommendation, evidence of teaching certification. Additional exam requirements/recommendations for international students: Required—TOEFL (minimum score 600 paper-based; 100 iBT). Electronic applications accepted. *Expenses:* Contact institution. *Faculty research:* Online course design and deliver, staff engagement, classroom action.

New Mexico State University, College of Education, Department of Curriculum and Instruction, Las Cruces, NM 88003. Offers bilingual education (MA); curriculum and instruction (MA, Ed D, PhD); early childhood education (MA); educational diagnostics (Ed S); language, literacy and culture (MA); learning design and technologies (MA); teaching (MAT), including dance, Spanish; teaching English to speakers of other languages (MA). *Accreditation:* NCATE. *Program availability:* Part-time, evening/weekend, 100% online. *Faculty:* 22 full-time (17 women), 7 part-time/adjunct (2 women). *Students:* 113 full-time (79 women), 194 part-time (138 women); includes 171 minority (15 Black or African American, non-Hispanic/Latino; 3 American Indian or Alaska Native, non-Hispanic/Latino; 4 Asian, non-Hispanic/Latino; 142 Hispanic/Latino; 7 Two or more races, non-Hispanic/Latino), 37 international. Average age 36. 106 applicants, 80% accepted, 56 enrolled. In 2017, 82 master's, 15 doctorates, 1 other advanced degree awarded. *Entrance requirements:* For master's, minimum cumulative GPA of 3.0; for doctorate, portfolio, minimum cumulative GPA of 3.0. Additional exam requirements/recommendations for international students: Required—TOEFL (minimum score 550 paper-based; 79 iBT), IELTS (minimum score 6.5). *Application deadline:* For fall admission, 12/15 priority date for domestic and international students; for spring admission, 11/1 for domestic students. Applications are processed on a rolling basis. Application fee: $40 ($50 for international students). Electronic applications accepted. *Expenses:* Tuition, state resident: full-time $4390. Tuition, nonresident: full-time $15,309. *Required fees:* $853. *Financial support:* In 2017–18, 97 students received support, including 2 fellowships (averaging $4,390 per year), 1 research assistantship (averaging $17,368 per year), 10 teaching assistantships (averaging $17,489 per year); career-related internships or fieldwork, Federal Work-Study, scholarships/grants, traineeships, health care benefits, and unspecified assistantships also available. Support available to part-time students. Financial award application deadline: 3/1. *Faculty research:* STEM education, bilingual and English as a second language education, critical pedagogy/multicultural education, learning design and technology, early childhood education. *Total annual research expenditures:* $13,518. *Unit head:* Dr. David Rutledge, Department Head, 575-646-5411, Fax: 575-646-5436, E-mail: rutledge@nmsu.edu. *Application contact:* Dr. David Rutledge, Associate Department Head for Graduate Programs, 575-646-5411, Fax: 575-646-5436, E-mail: rutledge@nmsu.edu.
Website: http://tpal.nmsu.edu/

The New School, Schools of Public Engagement, Program in Teaching English to Speakers of Other Languages, New York, NY 10011. Offers teaching English to speakers of other languages (MA). *Program availability:* Part-time, evening/weekend,

English as a Second Language

100% online. *Faculty:* 5 part-time/adjunct (3 women). *Students:* 11 full-time (10 women), 33 part-time (22 women); includes 8 minority (1 Black or African American, non-Hispanic/Latino; 7 Hispanic/Latino), 6 international. Average age 41. 33 applicants, 85% accepted, 16 enrolled. In 2017, 21 master's awarded. *Degree requirements:* For master's, thesis optional. *Entrance requirements:* For master's, two letters of recommendation, statement of purpose, resume, transcripts, interview. Additional exam requirements/recommendations for international students: Required—TOEFL (minimum score 92 iBT), IELTS (minimum score 7), PTE (minimum score 68). *Application deadline:* For fall admission, 1/15 priority date for domestic and international students; for spring admission, 10/15 priority date for domestic and international students; for summer admission, 1/15 priority date for domestic and international students. Applications are processed on a rolling basis. Application fee: $50. Electronic applications accepted. *Expenses:* $1,557 per credit. *Financial support:* In 2017–18, 27 students received support. Career-related internships or fieldwork, Federal Work-Study, scholarships/grants, and unspecified assistantships available. Support available to part-time students. Financial award application deadline: 2/1; financial award applicants required to submit FAFSA. *Application contact:* Merida Gasbarro, Director, 212-229-5600 Ext. 1108, E-mail: escandom@newschool.edu.
Website: https://www.newschool.edu/public-engagement/ma-teaching-english-to-speakers-of-other-languages/

New York University, Steinhardt School of Culture, Education, and Human Development, Department of Teaching and Learning, Program in Multilingual/Multicultural Studies, New York, NY 10012. Offers bilingual education (MA, PhD, Advanced Certificate); foreign language education (MA); teaching English to speakers of other languages (MA, PhD); teaching foreign languages, 7-12 (MA), including Chinese, French, Italian, Japanese, Spanish; teaching French as a foreign language (MA), including teaching English to speakers of other languages; teaching Spanish as a foreign language (MA), including teaching English to speakers of other languages. MA in teaching English to speakers of other languages also offered in collaboration with NYU Shanghai. *Accreditation:* TEAC. *Program availability:* Part-time, evening/weekend. *Students:* Average age 29. 431 applicants, 61% accepted, 92 enrolled. In 2017, 121 master's, 1 doctorate, 2 other advanced degrees awarded. *Entrance requirements:* For doctorate, GRE General Test, interview; for Advanced Certificate, master's degree. Additional exam requirements/recommendations for international students: Required—TOEFL (minimum score 100 iBT). *Application deadline:* For fall admission, 12/1 priority date for domestic and international students; for spring admission, 10/1 for domestic and international students. Applications are processed on a rolling basis. Application fee: $75. Electronic applications accepted. *Expenses: Tuition:* Full-time $41,352; part-time $19,968 per year. *Required fees:* $2496; $1628 per unit. $814 per term. Tuition and fees vary according to course load and program. *Financial support:* Fellowships with full and partial tuition reimbursements, career-related internships or fieldwork, Federal Work-Study, institutionally sponsored loans, scholarships/grants, and tuition waivers (partial) available. Support available to part-time students. Financial award application deadline: 2/1; financial award applicants required to submit FAFSA. *Faculty research:* Second language acquisition, cross-cultural communication, technology-enhanced language learning, language variation, action learning. *Unit head:* Prof. Shondel Nero, Director, 212-998-5757, E-mail: shondel.nero@nyu.edu. *Application contact:* 212-998-5030, Fax: 212-995-4328, E-mail: steinhardt.gradadmissions@nyu.edu.
Website: http://steinhardt.nyu.edu/teachlearn/mms

Niagara University, Graduate Division of Education, Concentration in Teacher Education, Niagara University, NY 14109. Offers early childhood and childhood education (MS Ed, Certificate); early childhood special education (MS); middle and adolescence education (MS Ed); special education (MS Ed), including 1-6, 7-12; special education (grades 1-12) (Certificate); teaching English to speakers of other languages (MS Ed, Certificate). *Accreditation:* NCATE. *Students:* 105 full-time (79 women), 109 part-time (88 women); includes 20 minority (9 Black or African American, non-Hispanic/Latino; 2 American Indian or Alaska Native, non-Hispanic/Latino; 1 Asian, non-Hispanic/Latino; 5 Hispanic/Latino; 3 Two or more races, non-Hispanic/Latino), 35 international. Average age 28. In 2017, 86 master's, 18 other advanced degrees awarded. *Entrance requirements:* For master's, GRE General Test or Academic Literacy Skills Test (ALST). Additional exam requirements/recommendations for international students: Required—TOEFL (minimum score 550 paper-based; 79 iBT), IELTS (minimum score 6). *Application deadline:* For fall admission, 8/1 for domestic students. Applications are processed on a rolling basis. Application fee: $30. *Expenses:* Contact institution. *Financial support:* Research assistantships with tuition reimbursements, teaching assistantships with tuition reimbursements, career-related internships or fieldwork, Federal Work-Study, scholarships/grants, and unspecified assistantships available. Financial award application deadline: 4/15; financial award applicants required to submit FAFSA. *Unit head:* Dr. Chandra Foote, Dean, College of Education, 716-286-8549, E-mail: cjf@niagara.edu. *Application contact:* Evan Pierce, Associate Director, Graduate Studies, 716-286-8327, E-mail: epierce@niagara.edu.
Website: http://www.niagara.edu/teacher-education

Northeastern Illinois University, College of Graduate Studies and Research, College of Arts and Sciences, Program in Teaching English to Speakers of Other Languages, Chicago, IL 60625. Offers MA. *Expenses:* Tuition, state resident: full-time $7,874; part-time $404.11 per credit hour. Tuition, nonresident: full-time $14,548; part-time $808.23 per credit hour. *Required fees:* $1284. *Unit head:* Dr. Jeanine Ntihirageza, Department Chair, 773-442-5873, E-mail: j-ntihirageza@neiu.edu. *Application contact:* Martha Narvaez, Graduate Admission Representative, 773-442-6006, E-mail: m-narvaez@neiu.edu.

Northern Arizona University, College of Arts and Letters, Department of English, Flagstaff, AZ 86011. Offers applied linguistics (PhD); creative writing (MFA), including creative writing; English (MA), including literature, professional writing, rhetoric, writing, and digital media studies, secondary education; professional writing (Graduate Certificate); rhetoric, writing and digital media studies (Graduate Certificate); teaching English as a second language (MA, Graduate Certificate). *Program availability:* Part-time, 100% online, blended/hybrid learning. *Faculty:* 62 full-time (43 women), 3 part-time/adjunct (2 women). *Students:* 115 full-time (78 women), 115 part-time (89 women); includes 57 minority (11 Black or African American, non-Hispanic/Latino; 3 American Indian or Alaska Native, non-Hispanic/Latino; 4 Asian, non-Hispanic/Latino; 26 Hispanic/Latino; 13 Two or more races, non-Hispanic/Latino), 19 international. Average age 35. 189 applicants, 56% accepted, 92 enrolled. In 2017, 82 master's, 5 doctorates, 15 other advanced degrees awarded. *Degree requirements:* For master's, variable foreign language requirement, comprehensive exam (for some programs), thesis (for some programs); for doctorate, variable foreign language requirement, comprehensive exam (for some programs), thesis/dissertation (for some programs); for Graduate Certificate, comprehensive exam (for some programs). *Entrance requirements:* Additional exam requirements/recommendations for international students: Required—TOEFL (minimum score 80 iBT), IELTS (minimum score 6.5). *Application deadline:* For fall admission, 1/30 for domestic and international students; for spring admission, 10/1 for domestic and international students. Application fee: $65. Electronic applications accepted. *Expenses:* Tuition, state resident: full-time $9240; part-time $458 per credit hour. Tuition, nonresident: full-time $21,588; part-time $1199 per credit hour. *Required fees:* $1021; $14 per credit hour. $646 per semester. Tuition and fees vary according to course load,

campus/location and program. *Financial support:* In 2017–18, 69 students received support, including 4 fellowships with full and partial tuition reimbursements available (averaging $16,250 per year), 2 research assistantships with full and partial tuition reimbursements available (averaging $16,250 per year), 65 teaching assistantships with full and partial tuition reimbursements available (averaging $16,250 per year); institutionally sponsored loans, health care benefits, tuition waivers (full and partial), and unspecified assistantships also available. Financial award application deadline: 2/1; financial award applicants required to submit FAFSA. *Unit head:* Dr. Steven Rosendale, Chair, 928-523-4911, Fax: 928-523-7074, E-mail: steven.rosendale@nau.edu. *Application contact:* Tina Sutton, Coordinator, Graduate College, 928-523-4348, Fax: 928-523-8950, E-mail: graduate@nau.edu.
Website: https://nau.edu/cal/english/

Northern Arizona University, College of Education, Department of Educational Specialties, Flagstaff, AZ 86011. Offers autism spectrum disorders (Certificate); bilingual/multicultural education (M Ed), including bilingual, ESL; career and technical education (M Ed, Certificate); educational technology (M Ed, Certificate); English as a second language (Certificate); positive behavior support (Certificate); special education (M Ed), including early childhood special education, mild/moderate disabilities. *Program availability:* Part-time, 100% online, blended/hybrid learning. *Faculty:* 31 full-time (19 women), 2 part-time/adjunct (1 woman). *Students:* 66 full-time (52 women), 203 part-time (147 women); includes 83 minority (20 Black or African American, non-Hispanic/Latino; 12 American Indian or Alaska Native, non-Hispanic/Latino; 5 Asian, non-Hispanic/Latino; 38 Hispanic/Latino; 3 Native Hawaiian or other Pacific Islander, non-Hispanic/Latino; 5 Two or more races, non-Hispanic/Latino), 6 international. Average age 37. 157 applicants, 94% accepted, 148 enrolled. In 2017, 119 master's, 26 Certificates awarded. *Degree requirements:* For master's, variable foreign language requirement, comprehensive exam (for some programs), thesis (for some programs); for Certificate, comprehensive exam (for some programs). *Entrance requirements:* Additional exam requirements/recommendations for international students: Required—TOEFL (minimum score 80 iBT), IELTS (minimum score 6.5). *Application deadline:* For fall admission, 3/1 for domestic and international students; for spring admission, 10/1 for domestic and international students. Applications are processed on a rolling basis. Application fee: $65. Electronic applications accepted. *Expenses:* Tuition, state resident: full-time $9240; part-time $458 per credit hour. Tuition, nonresident: full-time $21,588; part-time $1199 per credit hour. *Required fees:* $1021; $14 per credit hour. $646 per semester. Tuition and fees vary according to course load, campus/location and program. *Financial support:* In 2017–18, 11 students received support, including 1 fellowship with full and partial tuition reimbursement available (averaging $12,000 per year), 10 teaching assistantships with full and partial tuition reimbursements available (averaging $12,000 per year); Federal Work-Study, institutionally sponsored loans, health care benefits, tuition waivers (full and partial), and unspecified assistantships also available. Financial award application deadline: 2/1; financial award applicants required to submit FAFSA. *Unit head:* Dr. Shadow Armfield, Chair, 928-523-7651, Fax: 928-523-1929, E-mail: laura.sujo-montes@nau.edu. *Application contact:* Tina Sutton, Coordinator, Graduate College, 928-523-4348, Fax: 928-523-8950, E-mail: graduate@nau.edu.
Website: https://nau.edu/coe/Ed-Specialties/

Northern Michigan University, Office of Graduate Education and Research, College of Arts and Sciences, Department of English, Marquette, MI 49855-5301. Offers creative writing (MFA); literature (MA); pedagogy (MA); teaching English to speakers of other languages (Graduate Certificate); theater (MA); writing (MA). *Program availability:* Part-time, evening/weekend. Terminal master's awarded for partial completion of doctoral program. *Degree requirements:* For master's, capstone project: thesis, practicum or portfolio (for MA); thesis (for MFA); for Graduate Certificate, one foreign language. *Entrance requirements:* For master's, minimum GPA of 3.0; bachelor's degree in English or minimum of 30 credit hours in undergraduate English; statement of purpose; resume; critical essay; 3 letters of recommendation; for Graduate Certificate, bachelor's degree. Additional exam requirements/recommendations for international students: Required—TOEFL (minimum score 550 paper-based; 79 iBT), IELTS (minimum score 6.5). *Application deadline:* For fall admission, 2/1 for domestic students; for winter admission, 2/1 for domestic students; for spring admission, 3/17 for domestic students. Applications are processed on a rolling basis. Application fee: $50. Electronic applications accepted. *Expenses:* Tuition, state resident: full-time $9417; part-time $542 per credit hour. Tuition, nonresident: full-time $12,873; part-time $758 per credit hour. Tuition and fees vary according to course load, degree level and program. *Financial support:* Research assistantships with full tuition reimbursements, teaching assistantships with full tuition reimbursements, Federal Work-Study, institutionally sponsored loans, and unspecified assistantships available. Support available to part-time students. Financial award application deadline: 3/1; financial award applicants required to submit FAFSA. *Faculty research:* Modern Arabic literature, British literature (medieval to contemporary), postcolonial literature, Native and African-American literature, creative writing, critical theory, pedagogy. *Unit head:* Lynn Domina, Head, 906-227-2711, E-mail: ldomina@nmu.edu. *Application contact:* Dr. Russell Prather, Director of MA Program/Professor, 906-227-2857, E-mail: rprather@nmu.edu.
Website: http://www.nmu.edu/english/

Northwest Christian University, School of Education and Counseling, Eugene, OR 97401-3745. Offers clinical mental health counseling (MA); elementary teaching (MAT); English for speakers of other languages (MAT); physical education (MAT); school counseling (MA); secondary teaching (MAT); special education (MAT). *Program availability:* Part-time, evening/weekend, online learning. *Faculty:* 9 full-time (4 women), 14 part-time/adjunct (10 women). *Students:* 77 full-time (60 women), 44 part-time (30 women); includes 19 minority (4 Black or African American, non-Hispanic/Latino; 1 American Indian or Alaska Native, non-Hispanic/Latino; 3 Asian, non-Hispanic/Latino; 2 Hispanic/Latino; 1 Native Hawaiian or other Pacific Islander, non-Hispanic/Latino; 8 Two or more races, non-Hispanic/Latino). Average age 34. In 2017, 58 master's awarded. *Degree requirements:* For master's, thesis (for some programs). *Entrance requirements:* For master's, GRE or MAT, minimum undergraduate GPA of 3.0, interview, 2-3 page statement of purpose, two letters of recommendation, resume, background check. Additional exam requirements/recommendations for international students: Required—TOEFL (minimum score 550 paper-based; 80 iBT). *Application deadline:* Applications are processed on a rolling basis. Electronic applications accepted. *Expenses:* $640 to $660 per credit tuition, $90 per semester technology fee. *Financial support:* Applicants required to submit FAFSA. *Unit head:* Elizabeth Wosley-George, Director, 541-349-7465, Fax: 541-684-7310, E-mail: ewosleygeorge@nwcu.edu. *Application contact:* Billy Dorsch, Admission Counselor for Graduate Studies, 541-684-7279, Fax: 541-349-5281, E-mail: wdorsch@nwcu.edu.

Northwest Missouri State University, Graduate School, School of Education, Maryville, MO 64468-6001. Offers early childhood education (MS Ed); education leadership (MS Ed), including elementary, K-12, secondary; educational leadership (Ed S), including elementary school principalship, secondary school principalship, superintendency; educational leadership and policy analysis (Ed D); elementary education (MS Ed); elementary mathematics (MS Ed); higher education leadership (MS); middle school education (MS Ed); reading (MS Ed); special education (MS Ed); teacher leadership (MS Ed); teaching English language learners (MS Ed). *Accreditation:*

NCATE. *Program availability:* Part-time. *Faculty:* 15 full-time (8 women). *Students:* 28 full-time (20 women), 170 part-time (114 women); includes 20 minority (7 Black or African American, non-Hispanic/Latino; 1 Asian, non-Hispanic/Latino; 8 Hispanic/Latino; 4 Two or more races, non-Hispanic/Latino). Average age 33. 168 applicants, 73% accepted, 114 enrolled. In 2017, 67 master's, 21 other advanced degrees awarded. *Degree requirements:* For master's, comprehensive exam; for Ed S, comprehensive exam, thesis. *Entrance requirements:* For master's, GRE General Test, writing sample; for Ed S, minimum graduate GPA of 3.25. Additional exam requirements/recommendations for international students: Required—TOEFL (minimum score 550 paper-based). *Application deadline:* For fall admission, 7/1 for domestic and international students; for spring admission, 11/15 for domestic and international students. Applications are processed on a rolling basis. Application fee: $0 ($50 for international students). Electronic applications accepted. *Expenses:* $389.11 per credit hour in-state tuition and fees, $641.97 out-of-state; $9,750 total cost (for online-based education program). *Financial support:* Research assistantships with full tuition reimbursements, teaching assistantships with full tuition reimbursements, and unspecified assistantships available. Financial award application deadline: 4/1; financial award applicants required to submit FAFSA. *Unit head:* Dr. Tim Wall, Director, 660-562-1179, E-mail: timwall@nwmissouri.edu.
Website: https://www.nwmissouri.edu/education/index.htm

Notre Dame of Maryland University, Graduate Studies, Program in Teaching English to Speakers of Other Languages, Baltimore, MD 21210-2476. Offers MA. *Accreditation:* NCATE. *Program availability:* Part-time, evening/weekend. *Entrance requirements:* Additional exam requirements/recommendations for international students: Required—TOEFL (minimum score 500 paper-based; 68 iBT). Electronic applications accepted.

Nyack College, School of Education, Nyack, NY 10960. Offers childhood education (MS); childhood special education (MS); TESOL (MAT, MS). *Program availability:* Part-time, evening/weekend, 100% online, blended/hybrid learning. *Students:* 22 full-time (20 women), 27 part-time (23 women); includes 23 minority (10 Black or African American, non-Hispanic/Latino; 1 American Indian or Alaska Native, non-Hispanic/Latino; 1 Asian, non-Hispanic/Latino; 10 Hispanic/Latino; 1 Two or more races, non-Hispanic/Latino), 2 international. Average age 34. In 2017, 25 master's awarded. *Degree requirements:* For master's, comprehensive exam, clinical experience. *Entrance requirements:* For master's, GRE, transcripts, autobiography and statement on reasons for pursuing graduate study in education, recommendations, 6 credits of language, evidence of computer literacy, introductory course in psychology. Additional exam requirements/recommendations for international students: Required—TOEFL (minimum score 550 paper-based; 80 iBT), GRE. *Application deadline:* Applications are processed on a rolling basis. Application fee: $30. Electronic applications accepted. *Expenses:* $725 per credit. *Financial support:* Scholarships/grants available. Financial award applicants required to submit FAFSA. *Unit head:* Dr. JoAnn Looney, Dean, 845-675-4538. *Application contact:* Emma Chery, Admissions Associate, 845-770-5708, E-mail: admissions.grad@nyack.edu.
Website: http://www.nyack.edu/edu

Oakland University, Graduate Study and Lifelong Learning, College of Arts and Sciences, Department of Linguistics, Rochester, MI 48309-4401. Offers linguistics (MA); teaching English as a second language (Certificate). *Program availability:* Part-time, evening/weekend. *Entrance requirements:* For master's, minimum GPA of 3.0. Additional exam requirements/recommendations for international students: Required—TOEFL (minimum score 550 paper-based). *Expenses:* Tuition, state resident: full-time $16,950; part-time $706.25 per credit. Tuition, nonresident: full-time $24,648; part-time $1027 per credit.

Ohio Dominican University, Division of Education, Program in Teaching English to Speakers of Other Languages, Columbus, OH 43219-2099. Offers MA. *Program availability:* Part-time, evening/weekend, 100% online, blended/hybrid learning. *Faculty:* 1 full-time (0 women), 1 (woman) part-time/adjunct. *Students:* 2 full-time (both women), 13 part-time (11 women); includes 1 minority (Asian, non-Hispanic/Latino), 3 international. Average age 33. 10 applicants, 50% accepted, 4 enrolled. In 2017, 11 master's awarded. *Degree requirements:* For master's, thesis. *Entrance requirements:* For master's, bachelor's degree with minimum cumulative GPA of 3.0, 3 letters of recommendation. Additional exam requirements/recommendations for international students: Required—TOEFL (minimum score 550 paper-based), IELTS (minimum score 6.5). *Application deadline:* For fall admission, 9/15 for domestic students, 6/10 for international students; for spring admission, 1/4 for domestic students, 11/2 for international students; for summer admission, 5/30 for domestic students. Applications are processed on a rolling basis. Application fee: $25. Electronic applications accepted. *Expenses:* $600 per credit hour, $175 per semester technology fee, $50 per semester activity fee. *Financial support:* Applicants required to submit FAFSA. *Unit head:* Dr. Timothy A. Micek, Director, 614-251-4675, E-mail: micekt@ohiodominican.edu. *Application contact:* John W. Naughton, Associate Vice President for Enrollment Management, 614-251-4721, Fax: 614-251-6654, E-mail: grad@ohiodominican.edu.
Website: http://www.ohiodominican.edu/academics/graduate/ma-tesol

Oklahoma City University, Petree College of Arts and Sciences, Oklahoma City, OK 73106-1402. Offers applied behavioral studies (M Ed); applied sociology: nonprofit leadership (MA); creative writing (MFA); criminology (MS); early childhood education (M Ed); elementary education (M Ed); general studies (MLA); leadership/management (MLA); moving image arts (MFA); professional counseling (M Ed); teaching (MA); teaching English to speakers of other languages (MA). *Program availability:* Part-time, evening/weekend. *Faculty:* 6 full-time (2 women), 16 part-time/adjunct (10 women). *Students:* 84 full-time (61 women), 32 part-time (23 women); includes 31 minority (13 Black or African American, non-Hispanic/Latino; 3 American Indian or Alaska Native, non-Hispanic/Latino; 1 Asian, non-Hispanic/Latino; 9 Hispanic/Latino; 5 Two or more races, non-Hispanic/Latino), 30 international. Average age 34. 192 applicants, 67% accepted, 57 enrolled. In 2017, 65 master's awarded. *Degree requirements:* For master's, capstone/practicum. *Entrance requirements:* For master's, bachelor's degree from accredited institution with minimum GPA of 3.0, essay, recommendation letters. Additional exam requirements/recommendations for international students: Required—TOEFL (minimum score 550 paper-based; 80 iBT). *Application deadline:* Applications are processed on a rolling basis. Application fee: $50. Electronic applications accepted. *Expenses:* $8,580. *Financial support:* In 2017–18, 19 students received support. Federal Work-Study, institutionally sponsored loans, scholarships/grants, and tuition waivers (full and partial) available. Support available to part-time students. Financial award application deadline: 6/1; financial award applicants required to submit FAFSA. *Unit head:* Dr. Amy Cataldi, Dean, 405-208-5446, Fax: 405-208-5447, E-mail: acataldi@okcu.edu. *Application contact:* Michael Harrington, Director of Graduate Admissions, 800-633-7242, Fax: 405-208-5356, E-mail: gadmissions@okcu.edu.
Website: https://www.okcu.edu/artsci/home

Old Dominion University, College of Arts and Letters, Program in Applied Linguistics, Norfolk, VA 23529. Offers sociolinguistics (MA); TESOL (MA). *Program availability:* Part-time. *Faculty:* 4 full-time (all women). *Students:* 7 full-time (4 women), 7 part-time (5 women); includes 6 minority (1 Black or African American, non-Hispanic/Latino; 1 Asian, non-Hispanic/Latino; 1 Hispanic/Latino; 3 Two or more races, non-Hispanic/Latino), 3 international. Average age 32. 23 applicants, 91% accepted, 11 enrolled. In 2017, 9 master's awarded. *Degree requirements:* For master's, one foreign language, comprehensive exam, thesis optional, program portfolio. *Entrance requirements:* For master's, GRE General Test, sample of written work; 12 hours in English, 9 on the upper-level; minimum B average; letters of recommendation; resume; essay. Additional exam requirements/recommendations for international students: Required—TOEFL (minimum score 570 paper-based; 88 iBT). *Application deadline:* For fall admission, 3/15 priority date for domestic and international students; for spring admission, 10/1 priority date for domestic and international students. Applications are processed on a rolling basis. Application fee: $50. Electronic applications accepted. *Expenses:* Tuition, state resident: full-time $8928; part-time $496 per credit. Tuition, nonresident: full-time $22,482; part-time $1249 per credit. *Required fees:* $66 per semester. *Financial support:* In 2017–18, 6 students received support. Career-related internships or fieldwork, institutionally sponsored loans, and unspecified assistantships available. Financial award application deadline: 2/15. *Faculty research:* Discourse analysis, phonology, syntax, second language acquisition, gender, sociolinguistics. *Unit head:* Dr. Bridget Anderson, Graduate Program Director, 757-683-4020, Fax: 757-683-3241, E-mail: linggpd@odu.edu. *Application contact:* Dr. David C. Earnest, Associate Dean, 757-683-6077, Fax: 757-683-5746, E-mail: dearnest@odu.edu.
Website: https://www.odu.edu/academics/programs/masters/applied-linguistics

Pacific University, College of Education, Forest Grove, OR 97116-1797. Offers early childhood education (MAT); education (MAE); elementary education (MAT); ESOL (MAT); high school education (MAT); middle school education (MAT); special education (MAT); speech-language pathology (MS); STEM education (MAT); talented and gifted (M Ed); visual function in learning (M Ed). *Accreditation:* ASHA; NCATE. *Program availability:* Part-time, evening/weekend. *Degree requirements:* For master's, research project. *Entrance requirements:* For master's, California Basic Educational Skills Test, PRAXIS II, minimum undergraduate GPA of 2.75, 3.0 graduate. Additional exam requirements/recommendations for international students: Required—TOEFL. Electronic applications accepted. *Expenses:* Contact institution. *Faculty research:* Defining a culturally competent classroom, technology in the K-12 classroom, Socratic seminars, social studies education.

Penn State Harrisburg, Graduate School, School of Behavioral Sciences and Education, Middletown, PA 17057. Offers adult education in the health and medical professions (Certificate); applied behavior analysis (MA); applied clinical psychology (MA); applied psychological research (MA); community psychology and social change (MA); English as a second language (ESL) program specialist and leadership (Certificate); health education (M Ed); lifelong learning and adult education (M Ed, D Ed); literacy education (M Ed); literacy leadership (Certificate); psychology: applications in clinical psychology (Certificate); psychology: health psychology (Certificate); teaching and curriculum (M Ed); training and development (M Ed, Certificate). *Program availability:* Part-time, evening/weekend. *Unit head:* Dr. Mukund S. Kulkarni, Chancellor, 717-948-6105, Fax: 717-948-6452. *Application contact:* Robert W. Coffman, Jr., Director of Enrollment Management, Recruitment and Admissions, 717-948-6250, Fax: 717-948-6325, E-mail: hbgadmit@psu.edu.
Website: https://harrisburg.psu.edu/behavioral-sciences-and-education/

Penn State University Park, Graduate School, College of the Liberal Arts, Department of Applied Linguistics, University Park, PA 16802. Offers applied linguistics (PhD); teaching English as a second language (MA). *Unit head:* Dr. Susan Welch, Dean, 814-865-7691, Fax: 814-863-2085. *Application contact:* Lori Hawn, Director, Graduate Student Services, 814-865-1795, Fax: 814-863-4627, E-mail: l-gswww@lists.psu.edu.
Website: http://aplng.la.psu.edu/

Penn State York, Graduate School, York, PA 17403. Offers ESL specialist (Certificate); teaching and curriculum (M Ed). *Students:* 16 part-time (13 women); includes 2 minority (1 Black or African American, non-Hispanic/Latino; 1 Two or more races, non-Hispanic/Latino). Average age 35. 3 applicants, 67% accepted, 2 enrolled. In 2017, 2 master's awarded. Application fee: $65. *Expenses:* Contact institution. *Unit head:* Dr. Regina Vasilatos-Younken, Vice Provost for Graduate Education/Dean, Graduate School, 814-865-2516, Fax: 814-863-4627. *Application contact:* Lori Hawn, Director, Graduate Student Services, 814-865-1795, Fax: 814-863-4627, E-mail: l-gswww@lists.psu.edu.
Website: http://www.gradschool.psu.edu/

Pittsburg State University, Graduate School, College of Education, Department of Teaching and Leadership, Pittsburg, KS 66762. Offers autism spectrum disorder (Certificate); district level (Certificate); education (MS), including school health; educational leadership (MS); educational technology (MS); general school administration (Ed S), including advanced studies in leadership; secondary education (MAT); special education (MAT, MS), including special education teaching (MS); teaching (MS); TESOL (Certificate). *Program availability:* Part-time, online only, 100% online, blended/hybrid learning. *Students:* 475 (345 women); includes 57 minority (12 Black or African American, non-Hispanic/Latino; 9 American Indian or Alaska Native, non-Hispanic/Latino; 3 Asian, non-Hispanic/Latino; 17 Hispanic/Latino; 16 Two or more races, non-Hispanic/Latino), 1 international. In 2017, 195 master's, 11 other advanced degrees awarded. Terminal master's awarded for partial completion of doctoral program. *Degree requirements:* For master's and other advanced degree, thesis or alternative. *Entrance requirements:* For master's, PPST. Additional exam requirements/recommendations for international students: Required—TOEFL (minimum score 520 paper-based; 68 iBT), IELTS (minimum score 6), PTE (minimum score 47). *Application deadline:* For fall admission, 6/1 for international students; for spring admission, 10/15 for international students; for summer admission, 4/1 for international students. Applications are processed on a rolling basis. Application fee: $35 ($60 for international students). Electronic applications accepted. *Expenses:* Contact institution. *Financial support:* In 2017–18, 3 teaching assistantships with full tuition reimbursements (averaging $5,500 per year) were awarded; career-related internships or fieldwork, Federal Work-Study, and unspecified assistantships also available. Financial award application deadline: 2/1; financial award applicants required to submit FAFSA. *Faculty research:* Special education, autism spectrum disorder, reading, educational technology, leadership. *Unit head:* Dr. Alice Sagehorn, Chairperson, 620-235-4508, Fax: 620-235-4520, E-mail: asagehorn@pittstate.edu. *Application contact:* Lisa Allen, Assistant Director of Graduate and Continuing Studies, 620-235-4223, Fax: 620-235-4219, E-mail: lallen@pittstate.edu.

Pontifical Catholic University of Puerto Rico, College of Education, Program in English as a Second Language, Ponce, PR 00717-0777. Offers M Ed. *Degree requirements:* For master's, comprehensive exam, thesis (for some programs). *Entrance requirements:* For master's, GRE, 2 letters of recommendation, interview, minimum GPA of 2.75.

Portland State University, Graduate Studies, College of Liberal Arts and Sciences, Department of Applied Linguistics, Portland, OR 97207-0751. Offers teaching English as a second language (Certificate); teaching English to speakers of other languages (MA). *Program availability:* Part-time. *Faculty:* 11 full-time (8 women), 1 (woman) part-time/adjunct. *Students:* 23 full-time (15 women), 18 part-time (11 women); includes 5 minority (2 Asian, non-Hispanic/Latino; 2 Hispanic/Latino; 1 Two or more races, non-Hispanic/Latino), 5 international. Average age 35. 41 applicants, 83% accepted, 14 enrolled. In 2017, 32 master's awarded. *Degree requirements:* For master's, one foreign language, comprehensive exam, thesis, portfolio, culminating experience. *Entrance requirements:*

English as a Second Language

For master's, bachelor's degree with minimum undergraduate GPA of 3.0, 2 letters of recommendation, personal statement, resume. Additional exam requirements/recommendations for international students: Required—TOEFL (minimum score 600 paper-based; 100 iBT), IELTS (minimum score 7). *Application deadline:* For fall admission, 2/1 priority date for domestic students, 2/1 for international students. Application fee: $65. Electronic applications accepted. *Expenses:* Tuition, state resident: full-time $14,436; part-time $401 per credit. Tuition, nonresident: full-time $21,780; part-time $605 per credit. *Required fees:* $1380; $22 per credit. $119 per quarter. One-time fee: $325. Tuition and fees vary according to program. *Financial support:* In 2017–18, 11 students received support, including 1 research assistantship with partial tuition reimbursement available (averaging $6,390 per year), 1 teaching assistantship with partial tuition reimbursement available (averaging $7,056 per year); career-related internships or fieldwork, Federal Work-Study, scholarships/grants, tuition waivers (partial), and unspecified assistantships also available. Support available to part-time students. Financial award application deadline: 3/1; financial award applicants required to submit FAFSA. *Faculty research:* Sociolinguistics, linguistics and cognitive science, language proficiency testing, lexical phrases and language teaching, teaching English as a second language methodology. *Total annual research expenditures:* $402,997. *Unit head:* Dr. Tucker Childs, Chair, 503-725-4099, Fax: 503-725-4139, E-mail: childst@pdx.edu. *Application contact:* 503-725-2040, Fax: 503-725-4139, E-mail: linginfo@pdx.edu. Website: http://www.pdx.edu/linguistics/

Post University, Program in Education, Waterbury, CT 06723-2540. Offers curriculum and instruction (M Ed); education (M Ed); educational technology (M Ed); higher education administration (MS); learning design and technology (M Ed); online teaching (M Ed); teaching English to speakers of other languages (TESOL) (M Ed). *Program availability:* Online learning. *Entrance requirements:* For master's, resume. *Expenses:* Tuition: Part-time $730 per credit hour. Part-time tuition and fees vary according to degree level and program. *Application contact:* Veronica Montalvo, Vice President, Online Education Enrollment Management and Admissions, 203-596-6164, E-mail: vmontalvo@post.edu.

Providence University College & Theological Seminary, Theological Seminary, Otterburne, MB R0A 1G0, Canada. Offers children's ministry (Certificate); Christian studies (MA, Certificate); counseling (MA); cross-cultural discipleship (Certificate); divinity (M Div); educational studies (MA), including counseling psychology, educational ministries, student development, teaching English to speakers of other languages, training teachers of English to speakers of other languages; global studies (MA); lay counseling (Diploma); ministry (D Min); teaching English to speakers of other languages (Certificate); theological studies (MA); training teacher of English to speakers of other languages (Certificate); youth ministry (Certificate). *Accreditation:* ATS. *Program availability:* Part-time. *Degree requirements:* For master's, variable foreign language requirement, thesis (for some programs); for doctorate, thesis/dissertation. *Entrance requirements:* Additional exam requirements/recommendations for international students: Recommended—TOEFL (minimum score 550 paper-based). *Faculty research:* Studies in Isaiah, theology of sin.

Queens College of the City University of New York, Arts and Humanities Division, Department of Linguistics and Communication Disorders, Queens, NY 11367-1597. Offers applied linguistics (MA); speech-language pathology (MA); TESOL (MS Ed, Post-Master's Certificate); TESOL and bilingual education (Post-Master's Certificate). *Accreditation:* ASHA. *Program availability:* Part-time. *Faculty:* 22 full-time (16 women), 19 part-time/adjunct (13 women). *Students:* 37 full-time (34 women), 123 part-time (112 women); includes 62 minority (10 Black or African American, non-Hispanic/Latino; 17 Asian, non-Hispanic/Latino; 32 Hispanic/Latino; 3 Two or more races, non-Hispanic/Latino), 3 international. Average age 27. 390 applicants, 25% accepted, 81 enrolled. In 2017, 59 master's, 24 other advanced degrees awarded. *Degree requirements:* For master's, 400 hours of supervised clinical teaching (for MA in speech-language pathology); 50-100 hours of student teaching (for MS Ed). *Entrance requirements:* For master's, minimum GPA of 3.0. Additional exam requirements/recommendations for international students: Required—TOEFL, IELTS. *Application deadline:* For fall admission, 4/1 for domestic students. Applications are processed on a rolling basis. Application fee: $125. Electronic applications accepted. *Expenses:* Contact institution. *Financial support:* Career-related internships or fieldwork available. Financial award application deadline: 4/1; financial award applicants required to submit FAFSA. *Unit head:* Arlene Kraat, Chair, 718-997-2940, E-mail: arlene.kraat@qc.cuny.edu. *Application contact:* Elizabeth D'Amico-Ramirez, Assistant Director of Graduate Admissions, 718-997-5203, E-mail: elizabeth.damicoramirez@qc.cuny.edu.

Quincy University, Master of Science in Education Programs, Quincy, IL 62301-2699. Offers curriculum and instruction (MS Ed), including bilingual/English as a second language; education studies (MS Ed); leadership (MS Ed); reading education (MS Ed); teacher leader (MS Ed). *Program availability:* Part-time, evening/weekend, online learning. *Degree requirements:* For master's, comprehensive exam (for some programs), thesis optional. *Entrance requirements:* For master's, MAT or GRE, personal resume. Additional exam requirements/recommendations for international students: Required—TOEFL (minimum score 550 paper-based; 79 iBT). *Application deadline:* Applications are processed on a rolling basis. Application fee: $25. Electronic applications accepted. Application fee is waived when completed online. *Expenses:* Tuition: Part-time $450 per credit hour. *Financial support:* Applicants required to submit FAFSA. *Unit head:* Dr. Bruce Alan Spitzer, Director, 217-228-5432 Ext. 3106, E-mail: spitzbr@quincy.edu. *Application contact:* Office of Admissions, 217-228-5210, Fax: 217-228-5479, E-mail: admissions@quincy.edu. Website: http://www.quincy.edu/academics/graduate-programs/education

Regent University, Graduate School, School of Education, Virginia Beach, VA 23464-9800. Offers education (M Ed, Ed D, PhD), including adult education (Ed D, PhD, Ed S), advanced educational leadership (Ed D, PhD, Ed S), character education (Ed D, PhD, Ed S), Christian education leadership (Ed D, PhD, Ed S), Christian school administration (M Ed), curriculum and instruction (Ed D, PhD, Ed S), curriculum and instruction - adult education (M Ed), curriculum and instruction - Christian school (M Ed), curriculum and instruction - gifted and talented (M Ed), curriculum and instruction - STEM education (M Ed), curriculum and instruction - teacher leader (M Ed), discipleship for ministry (M Ed), educational leadership (M Ed), educational psychology (Ed D, PhD, Ed S), educational technology and online learning (Ed D, PhD, Ed S), elementary education (M Ed), exceptional education executive leadership (Ed D, PhD, Ed S), higher education (Ed D, PhD, Ed S), higher education leadership and management (Ed D, PhD, Ed S), instructional design and technology (M Ed), K-12 school leadership (Ed D, PhD, Ed S), K-12 special education (M Ed), leadership in mathematics education (M Ed), reading specialist (M Ed), special education (Ed D, PhD, Ed S), student affairs (M Ed), TESOL - adult education (M Ed), TESOL - K-12 (M Ed); educational specialist (Ed S), including adult education (Ed D, PhD, Ed S), advanced educational leadership (Ed D, PhD, Ed S), character education (Ed D, PhD, Ed S), Christian education leadership (Ed D, PhD, Ed S), curriculum and instruction (Ed D, PhD, Ed S), educational psychology (Ed D, PhD, Ed S), educational technology and online learning (Ed D, PhD, Ed S), exceptional education executive leadership (Ed D, PhD, Ed S), higher education (Ed D, PhD, Ed S), higher education leadership and management (Ed D, PhD, Ed S), K-12 school

leadership (Ed D, PhD, Ed S), special education (Ed D, PhD, Ed S). *Accreditation:* TEAC. *Program availability:* Part-time, evening/weekend, 100% online, blended/hybrid learning. *Faculty:* 22 full-time (10 women), 44 part-time/adjunct (32 women). *Students:* 80 full-time (59 women), 945 part-time (750 women); includes 432 minority (352 Black or African American, non-Hispanic/Latino; 4 American Indian or Alaska Native, non-Hispanic/Latino; 14 Asian, non-Hispanic/Latino; 43 Hispanic/Latino; 19 Two or more races, non-Hispanic/Latino), 12 international. Average age 40. 1,125 applicants, 49% accepted, 436 enrolled. In 2017, 316 master's, 24 doctorates awarded. *Degree requirements:* For master's, thesis or alternative; for doctorate, comprehensive exam, thesis/dissertation. *Entrance requirements:* For master's, Virginia Communication and Literacy Assessment (VCLA), PRAXIS, college transcripts, writing sample, interview; for doctorate, GRE, writing sample, resume, transcripts, interview. Additional exam requirements/recommendations for international students: Required—TOEFL (minimum score 577 paper-based). *Application deadline:* For fall admission, 4/1 priority date for domestic students; for spring admission, 10/15 priority date for domestic students. Applications are processed on a rolling basis. Application fee: $50. Electronic applications accepted. *Expenses:* Contact institution. *Financial support:* In 2017–18, 669 students received support, including 1 fellowship (averaging $10,000 per year); career-related internships or fieldwork, scholarships/grants, and unspecified assistantships also available. Support available to part-time students. *Faculty research:* Christian school administration, curriculum and instruction, educational technology and online learning, higher education, special education. *Unit head:* Dr. Donald Finn, Dean, 757-352-4278, Fax: 757-352-4318, E-mail: dfinn@regent.edu. *Application contact:* Heidi Cece, Assistant Vice President of Enrollment Management, 800-373-5504, Fax: 757-352-4381, E-mail: admissions@regent.edu. Website: https://www.regent.edu/school-of-education/

Rhode Island College, School of Graduate Studies, Feinstein School of Education and Human Development, Department of Educational Studies, Providence, RI 02908-1991. Offers advanced studies in teaching and learning (M Ed); English (MAT); French (MAT); history (MAT); math (MAT); secondary education (MAT); Spanish (MAT); teaching English as a second language (M Ed). *Accreditation:* NCATE. *Program availability:* Part-time, evening/weekend. *Faculty:* 2. *Students:* 1 (woman) full-time, 62 part-time (58 women); includes 10 minority (1 Black or African American, non-Hispanic/Latino; 2 Asian, non-Hispanic/Latino; 6 Hispanic/Latino; 1 Two or more races, non-Hispanic/Latino). Average age 37. In 2017, 31 master's awarded. *Degree requirements:* For master's, capstone or comprehensive assessment. *Entrance requirements:* For master's, GRE or MAT (for most programs), minimum undergraduate GPA of 3.0; baccalaureate degree in English, French, history, math or Spanish; 3 letters of recommendation; interview. Additional exam requirements/recommendations for international students: Recommended—TOEFL (minimum score 550 paper-based; 79 iBT). *Application deadline:* For fall admission, 3/1 for domestic students; for spring admission, 11/1 for domestic students. Applications are processed on a rolling basis. Application fee: $50. Electronic applications accepted. *Expenses:* Tuition, state resident: full-time $9768; part-time $407 per credit. Tuition, nonresident: full-time $19,008; part-time $792 per credit. *Required fees:* $696; $29 per credit. One-time fee: $200 full-time; $100 part-time. Tuition and fees vary according to course load. *Financial support:* In 2017–18, 3 teaching assistantships with full tuition reimbursements (averaging $2,500 per year) were awarded; career-related internships or fieldwork, Federal Work-Study, scholarships/grants, health care benefits, and unspecified assistantships also available. Support available to part-time students. Financial award application deadline: 5/15; financial award applicants required to submit FAFSA. *Unit head:* Dr. Leslie Bogad, Chair, 401-456-8170. *Application contact:* Graduate Studies, 401-456-8700. Website: http://www.ric.edu/educationalStudies/

Rider University, College of Education and Human Services, Teacher Certification Program, Lawrenceville, NJ 08648-3001. Offers bilingual education (Certificate); business education (Certificate); early childhood education (Certificate); elementary education (Certificate); English as a second language (Certificate); English education (Certificate); mathematics education (Certificate); science education (Certificate); secondary education (Certificate); social studies education (Certificate); world languages (Certificate), including French, German, Spanish. *Program availability:* Part-time, online learning. *Degree requirements:* For Certificate, internship, professional portfolio. *Entrance requirements:* For degree, PRAXIS, resume. Additional exam requirements/recommendations for international students: Required—TOEFL (minimum score 550 paper-based). Electronic applications accepted. *Faculty research:* Conceptual foundations for optimal development of creativity; creative theory, cognitive processes in mathematics learning, teacher collaboration.

Rowan University, Graduate School, College of Education, Department of Language, Literacy, and Sociocultural Education, Program in ESL Education, Glassboro, NJ 08028-1701. Offers CGS. Electronic applications accepted. *Expenses:* Tuition, state resident: full-time $15,020; part-time $751 per semester hour. Tuition, nonresident: full-time $15,020; part-time $751 per semester hour. *Required fees:* $3158; $157.90 per semester hour. Tuition and fees vary according to course load, campus/location and program.

Rutgers University–New Brunswick, Graduate School of Education, Department of Learning and Teaching, Program in Language Education, Piscataway, NJ 08854-8097. Offers English as a second language education (Ed M); language education (Ed M, Ed D). *Program availability:* Part-time. Terminal master's awarded for partial completion of doctoral program. *Degree requirements:* For master's, comprehensive exam; for doctorate, thesis/dissertation, concept paper, qualifying exam. *Entrance requirements:* For master's, GRE General Test, minimum GPA of 3.0; for doctorate, GRE General Test, minimum GPA of 3.5. Additional exam requirements/recommendations for international students: Required—TOEFL. Electronic applications accepted. *Faculty research:* Linguistics, sociolinguistics, cross-cultural/international communication.

St. Cloud State University, School of Graduate Studies, College of Liberal Arts, Department of English, St. Cloud, MN 56301-4498. Offers English (MA, MS); teaching English as a second language (MA). *Program availability:* Part-time. *Degree requirements:* For master's, thesis or alternative. *Entrance requirements:* For master's, GRE General Test, minimum GPA of 2.75. Additional exam requirements/recommendations for international students: Required—Michigan English Language Assessment Battery; Recommended—TOEFL (minimum score 550 paper-based), IELTS (minimum score 6.5). Electronic applications accepted.

St. John's University, The School of Education, Department of Education Specialties, Program in Teaching English to Speakers of Other Languages and Bilingual Education, Queens, NY 11439. Offers bilingual education (Adv C); childhood education and teaching English to speakers of other languages (MS Ed); teaching English to speakers of other languages (MS Ed, Adv C). *Students:* 21 full-time (19 women), 83 part-time (73 women); includes 39 minority (4 Black or African American, non-Hispanic/Latino; 9 Asian, non-Hispanic/Latino; 24 Hispanic/Latino; 2 Two or more races, non-Hispanic/Latino), 8 international. Average age 32. 54 applicants, 91% accepted, 35 enrolled. In 2017, 47 master's, 71 Adv Cs awarded. *Degree requirements:* For Adv C, one foreign language. *Entrance requirements:* For master's, GRE, MAT, or PRAXIS, statement of goals (personal essay), official undergraduate transcripts, initial teaching certification; for

Adv C, initial teaching certification, first master's transcripts, statement of purpose. Additional exam requirements/recommendations for international students: Required—TOEFL, IELTS. *Application deadline:* For fall admission, 8/17 for domestic and international students; for summer admission, 5/15 for domestic and international students. Application fee: $70. Electronic applications accepted. *Expenses: Tuition:* Full-time $44,280; part-time $1230 per credit. *Required fees:* $340; $340 per credit. Tuition and fees vary according to course load, degree level and program. *Financial support:* Fellowships, research assistantships, scholarships/grants, and unspecified assistantships available. Support available to part-time students. Financial award application deadline: 2/1; financial award applicants required to submit FAFSA. *Faculty research:* Second language learning and academic achievement, heritage language education, assessing the progress of English language learners toward English acquisition, dual language acquisition, study of English Creoles and dialects of other English's, literacy development for ESL learners; investigating Caribbean and Creole language and culture, education law. *Unit head:* Dr. John Spiridakis, Chair, 718-990-5591, E-mail: spiridaj@stjohns.edu. *Application contact:* Dr. John Spiridakis, Chair, 718-990-5591, E-mail: spiridaj@stjohns.edu.
Website: https://www.stjohns.edu/academics/schools-and-colleges/school-education/programs-and-majors/tesol-master-science-education

Saint Michael's College, Graduate Programs, Program in Teaching English to Speakers of Other Languages, Colchester, VT 05439. Offers MATESOL, Certificate. *Program availability:* Part-time, evening/weekend. *Faculty:* 6 full-time (3 women), 2 part-time/adjunct (1 woman). *Students:* 14 full-time (6 women), 22 part-time (15 women); includes 4 minority (2 Black or African American, non-Hispanic/Latino; 2 Hispanic/Latino), 11 international. Average age 33. 17 applicants, 94% accepted, 8 enrolled. In 2017, 17 master's awarded. *Degree requirements:* For master's, one foreign language, comprehensive exam (for some programs), thesis or alternative, capstone paper or portfolio. *Entrance requirements:* For master's, minimum GPA of 3.0, resume, essay. Additional exam requirements/recommendations for international students: Required—TOEFL (minimum score 550 paper-based; 79 iBT); Recommended—IELTS. *Application deadline:* For fall admission, 7/1 for domestic students, 6/1 for international students; for spring admission, 12/1 for domestic students, 10/1 for international students; for summer admission, 4/1 for domestic students, 2/1 for international students. Applications are processed on a rolling basis. Application fee: $50. *Expenses: Tuition:* Part-time $590 per credit. *Financial support:* Research assistantships, career-related internships or fieldwork, Federal Work-Study, institutionally sponsored loans, and scholarships/grants available. Financial award applicants required to submit FAFSA. *Faculty research:* Language teaching methodology, discourse analysis, second language acquisition, language assessment, sociolinguistics, K-12 English as a second language for children. *Unit head:* Dr. Elizabeth O'Dowd, Director, 802-654-2276, Fax: 802-654-2595, E-mail: eodowd@smcvt.edu. *Application contact:* Kirstin Van Luling, Administrative Assistant, 802-654-2684, Fax: 802-654-2595, E-mail: tesol@smcvt.edu.
Website: http://www.smcvt.edu/graduate-programs/academic-programs/teaching-english-to-speakers-of-other-languages.aspx

St. Thomas University, School of Leadership Studies, Institute for Education, Miami Gardens, FL 33054-6459. Offers earth/space science (Certificate); educational administration (MS, Certificate); educational leadership (Ed D); elementary education (MS); ESOL (Certificate); gifted education (Certificate); instructional technology (MS, Certificate); professional/studies (Certificate); reading (MS, Certificate); special education (MS). *Program availability:* Part-time, evening/weekend. *Degree requirements:* For master's, comprehensive exam; for doctorate, comprehensive exam, thesis/dissertation. *Entrance requirements:* For master's, interview, minimum GPA of 3.0 or GRE; for doctorate, GRE or MAT. Additional exam requirements/recommendations for international students: Required—TOEFL (minimum score 550 paper-based; 79 iBT). Electronic applications accepted.

Saint Xavier University, Graduate Studies, School of Education, Chicago, IL 60655-3105. Offers counseling (MA); curriculum and instruction (MA); early childhood education (MA); educational administration (MA); elementary education (MA); individualized studies (MA), including educational technology, English as a second language (ESL), ISTEM (integrative science, technology, engineering, and math), science education (MA); music education (MA); reading (MA); secondary education (MA); Spanish education (MA); special education (MA); teaching and leadership (MA). *Accreditation:* NCATE. *Program availability:* Part-time, evening/weekend. *Degree requirements:* For master's, thesis or project. *Entrance requirements:* For master's, minimum GPA of 3.0. *Expenses:* Contact institution.

Salem College, Graduate Studies, Winston-Salem, NC 27101. Offers art education (MAT); elementary education (M Ed, MAT); language and literacy (M Ed); middle school education (MAT); organ (MM); piano (MM); school counseling (M Ed); second language studies (MAT); secondary education (MAT); special education (M Ed, MAT). *Accreditation:* NCATE. *Program availability:* Part-time, evening/weekend, online learning. *Faculty:* 8 full-time (all women), 11 part-time/adjunct (8 women). In 2017, 17 master's awarded. *Degree requirements:* For master's, practicum (MAT), action research project (M Ed). *Entrance requirements:* For master's, minimum GPA of 3.0, two academic/professional recommendations, acceptable criminal background check. Additional exam requirements/recommendations for international students: Recommended—TOEFL. *Application deadline:* For fall admission, 8/1 for domestic students, 7/15 for international students; for spring admission, 1/15 for domestic students; for summer admission, 5/1 for domestic students. Applications are processed on a rolling basis. Application fee: $30. Electronic applications accepted. *Expenses: Tuition:* Part-time $440 per semester hour. *Financial support:* Scholarships/grants available. Support available to part-time students. Financial award applicants required to submit FAFSA. *Faculty research:* Teacher professional development, adolescent literacy, instructional technology. *Application contact:* Sheryl Long, Director, 336-721-2658, Fax: 336-917-5384, E-mail: sheryl.long@salem.edu.
Website: http://www.salem.edu

Salem State University, School of Graduate Studies, Program in Teaching English as a Second Language, Salem, MA 01970-5353. Offers MAT. *Program availability:* Part-time, evening/weekend. *Entrance requirements:* Additional exam requirements/recommendations for international students: Required—TOEFL (minimum score 550 paper-based; 80 iBT) or IELTS (minimum score 5.5).

Salisbury University, Department of English, Salisbury, MD 21801-6837. Offers English (MA), including TESOL. *Program availability:* Part-time. *Faculty:* 10 full-time (6 women). *Students:* 15 full-time (12 women), 14 part-time (11 women); includes 1 minority (Black or African American, non-Hispanic/Latino), 2 international. Average age 34. 27 applicants, 37% accepted, 10 enrolled. In 2017, 26 master's awarded. *Degree requirements:* For master's, comprehensive exam, thesis optional. *Entrance requirements:* For master's, GRE/MAT/PRAXIS I, two letters of recommendation; transcripts from all colleges and universities attended; bachelor's degree in English or related field; personal statement; minimum GPA of 3.0. Additional exam requirements/recommendations for international students: Required—TOEFL (minimum score 550 paper-based; 79 iBT), IELTS (minimum score 6.5). *Application deadline:* For fall admission, 8/1 for domestic and international students; for spring admission, 1/1 for domestic and international students. Application fee: $65. Electronic applications

accepted. *Expenses:* $392 per credit hour resident; $703 per credit hour non-resident; $92 per credit hour fees. *Financial support:* In 2017–18, 8 students received support, including 11 teaching assistantships with full tuition reimbursements available (averaging $11,275 per year); career-related internships or fieldwork and scholarships/grants also available. Support available to part-time students. Financial award application deadline: 3/1; financial award applicants required to submit FAFSA. *Faculty research:* Literature; linguistics; film studies; rhetoric and composition; TESOL. *Unit head:* Dr. Christopher Vilmar, Graduate Program Director, English, 410-677-6511, E-mail: csvilmar@salisbury.edu.
Website: http://www.salisbury.edu/gsr/gradstudies/ENGpage.html

San Diego State University, Graduate and Research Affairs, College of Arts and Letters, Department of Linguistics and Oriental Languages, San Diego, CA 92182. Offers applied linguistics and English as a second language (CAL); computational linguistics (MA); English as a second language/applied linguistics (MA); general linguistics (MA). *Degree requirements:* For master's, one foreign language, comprehensive exam, thesis optional. *Entrance requirements:* For master's, GRE General Test, 2 letters of recommendation. Additional exam requirements/recommendations for international students: Required—TOEFL (minimum score 570 paper-based). Electronic applications accepted. *Faculty research:* Cross-cultural linguistic studies of semantics.

San Francisco State University, Division of Graduate Studies, College of Liberal and Creative Arts, Department of English Language and Literature, Program in Teaching English to Speakers of Other Languages, San Francisco, CA 94132-1722. Offers MA. *Program availability:* Part-time. *Degree requirements:* For master's, comprehensive exam (for some programs), thesis (for some programs). *Application deadline:* Applications are processed on a rolling basis. Electronic applications accepted. *Unit head:* Dr. Sugie Goen-Salter, Chair, 415-338-7582, Fax: 415-338-6159, E-mail: sgoen@sfsu.edu. *Application contact:* Dr. David Olsher, Coordinator, 415-338-2827, Fax: 415-338-6159, E-mail: olsher@sfsu.edu.
Website: http://english.sfsu.edu/graduate-matesol/

San Jose State University, Graduate Studies and Research, College of Humanities and the Arts, San Jose, CA 95192-0088. Offers art (MA, MFA), including digital media art (MFA), history and visual culture (MA), photography (MFA), pictorial art (MFA), spatial art (MFA); English (MA, MFA), including creative writing (MFA); linguistics (MA); music (MM); music education (MA); philosophy (MA); Spanish (MA); teaching English to speakers of other languages (MA). *Program availability:* Part-time. *Faculty:* 35 full-time (17 women), 19 part-time/adjunct (11 women). *Students:* 129 full-time (79 women), 106 part-time (71 women); includes 117 minority (5 Black or African American, non-Hispanic/Latino; 29 Asian, non-Hispanic/Latino; 44 Hispanic/Latino; 39 Two or more races, non-Hispanic/Latino), 28 international. Average age 35. 204 applicants, 65% accepted, 79 enrolled. In 2017, 85 master's awarded. *Degree requirements:* For master's, one foreign language, comprehensive exam (for some programs), thesis (for some programs), graduate writing assessment, special study/project, recital. *Entrance requirements:* Additional exam requirements/recommendations for international students: Required—TOEFL (minimum score 550 paper-based; 80 iBT), IELTS (minimum score 6.5), PTE (minimum score 53). *Application deadline:* For fall admission, 2/1 for domestic and international students. Applications are processed on a rolling basis. Application fee: $55. Electronic applications accepted. *Expenses:* Tuition, state resident: full-time $7176. Tuition, nonresident: full-time $16,680. Tuition and fees vary according to course load and program. *Financial support:* Fellowships, research assistantships, Federal Work-Study, scholarships/grants, traineeships, tuition waivers (full and partial), and unspecified assistantships available. Support available to part-time students. Financial award application deadline: 4/28; financial award applicants required to submit FAFSA. *Unit head:* Dr. Shannon Miller, Dean, 408-924-4300, Fax: 408-924-4365, E-mail: shannon.miller@sjsu.edu.
Website: http://www.sjsu.edu/humanitiesandarts/

Seattle Pacific University, MA in Teaching English to Speakers of Other Languages Program, Seattle, WA 98119-1997. Offers K-12 (MA). *Program availability:* Part-time. *Students:* 2 full-time (both women), 11 part-time (10 women); includes 1 minority (Hispanic/Latino), 3 international. Average age 38. 5 applicants. In 2017, 6 master's awarded. *Degree requirements:* For master's, one foreign language, practicum. *Entrance requirements:* For master's, GRE (minimum score of 155 verbal/500 old scoring, 3.5 analytical writing) or MAT (minimum score of 400), bachelor's degree; letters of recommendation; official copies of transcripts; minimum GPA of 3.0; personal statement; essay; resume. Additional exam requirements/recommendations for international students: Required—TOEFL (minimum score 600 paper-based). *Application deadline:* For fall admission, 8/1 priority date for domestic students; for winter admission, 12/1 for domestic students; for spring admission, 3/1 for domestic students; for summer admission, 5/1 for domestic students. Applications are processed on a rolling basis. Application fee: $50. Electronic applications accepted. *Expenses:* Contact institution. *Financial support:* Career-related internships or fieldwork available. Financial award applicants required to submit FAFSA. *Faculty research:* Second language acquisition. *Unit head:* Dr. Kathryn Bartholomew, Program Director, 206-281-3533, Fax: 206-281-2500, E-mail: kbarthol@spu.edu. *Application contact:* 206-281-2091.
Website: http://www.spu.edu/depts/tesol/

Seattle University, College of Education, Program in Teaching English to Speakers of Other Languages, Seattle, WA 98122-1090. Offers M Ed, MA, Certificate. *Accreditation:* NCATE. *Program availability:* Part-time. *Faculty:* 1 full-time (0 women). *Students:* 6 full-time (4 women), 29 part-time (17 women); includes 9 minority (6 Asian, non-Hispanic/Latino; 3 Hispanic/Latino), 3 international. Average age 31. 19 applicants, 63% accepted, 10 enrolled. In 2017, 14 master's awarded. *Degree requirements:* For master's, comprehensive exam, thesis, internship. *Entrance requirements:* For master's, GRE, MAT, or minimum GPA of 3.0. Additional exam requirements/recommendations for international students: Required—TOEFL. *Application deadline:* For fall admission, 8/20 priority date for domestic students; for winter admission, 11/20 for domestic students; for spring admission, 2/20 for domestic students. Applications are processed on a rolling basis. Application fee: $55. *Expenses: Tuition:* Full-time $12,960. *Required fees:* $570. Tuition and fees vary according to program. *Financial support:* In 2017–18, 1 student received support. Career-related internships or fieldwork and Federal Work-Study available. Support available to part-time students. Financial award applicants required to submit FAFSA. *Unit head:* Dr. Jian Yang, Coordinator, 209-296-5908, E-mail: tesol@seattleu.edu. *Application contact:* Janet Shandley, Associate Dean of Graduate Admissions, 206-296-5900, Fax: 206-298-5656, E-mail: grad_admissions@seattleu.edu.
Website: https://www.seattleu.edu/education/tesol/

Simon Fraser University, Office of Graduate Studies and Postdoctoral Fellows, Faculty of Education, Program in Teaching English as a Second/Foreign Language, Burnaby, BC V5A 1S6, Canada. Offers M Ed. *Program availability:* Part-time, evening/weekend. *Degree requirements:* For master's, comprehensive exam. *Entrance requirements:* For master's, minimum GPA of 3.0 (on scale of 4.33) or 3.33 based on last 60 credits of undergraduate courses. Additional exam requirements/recommendations for international students: Recommended—TOEFL (minimum score 580 paper-based; 93

iBT), IELTS (minimum score 7), TWE (minimum score 5). Electronic applications accepted. *Faculty research:* Internationalization of higher education, international student experiences, language practices and language ideology in the globalized political economy, integration of immigrants, minorities and international students in educational settings, critical and psychoanalytical perspectives on second language learning, pedagogy, and curriculum.

SIT Graduate Institute, Graduate Programs, Master's Program in Teaching English as a Second Language, Brattleboro, VT 05302-0676. Offers MAT. *Degree requirements:* For master's, one foreign language, thesis, teaching practice. *Entrance requirements:* For master's, 3 letters of reference. Additional exam requirements/recommendations for international students: Required—TOEFL. *Faculty research:* Teaching English to speakers of other languages (TESOL).

Slippery Rock University of Pennsylvania, Graduate Studies (Recruitment), College of Liberal Arts, Department of Modern Languages and Cultures, Slippery Rock, PA 16057-1383. Offers teaching English to speakers of other languages (MA). *Program availability:* Part-time, evening/weekend, blended/hybrid learning, 1 evening class per week on campus. *Degree requirements:* For master's, thesis (for some programs), practicum or end project. *Entrance requirements:* For master's, two letters of recommendation, statement of intent, official transcripts, minimum GPA of 2.75. Additional exam requirements/recommendations for international students: Required—TOEFL (minimum score 550 paper-based; 80 iBT). Electronic applications accepted. *Expenses:* Contact institution.

Southeastern University, College of Education, Lakeland, FL 33801-6099. Offers curriculum and instruction (Ed D); educational leadership (M Ed); elementary education (M Ed); exceptional student education (M Ed); exceptional student education/ educational therapy (M Ed); kinesiology (M Ed); organizational leadership (Ed D); reading education (M Ed); teaching English to speakers of other languages (M Ed). *Faculty:* 8 full-time (5 women), 12 part-time/adjunct (7 women). *Students:* 139 full-time (109 women), 225 part-time (172 women); includes 107 minority (57 Black or African American, non-Hispanic/Latino; 2 Asian, non-Hispanic/Latino; 48 Hispanic/Latino), 4 international. Average age 40. Application fee: $50. Electronic applications accepted. *Unit head:* James A. Anderson, Dean, 863-667-5366, E-mail: jaanderson2@seu.edu. Website: http://www.seu.edu/

Southeast Missouri State University, School of Graduate Studies, Department of English, Cape Girardeau, MO 63701-4799. Offers teaching English to speakers of other languages (MA). *Program availability:* Part-time, evening/weekend, online learning. *Faculty:* 17 full-time (8 women). *Students:* 44 full-time (33 women), 36 part-time (27 women); includes 1 minority (Hispanic/Latino), 28 international. Average age 31. 35 applicants, 94% accepted, 28 enrolled. In 2017, 42 master's awarded. *Degree requirements:* For master's, comprehensive exam (for some programs), thesis optional. *Entrance requirements:* Additional exam requirements/recommendations for international students: Required—TOEFL (minimum score 550 paper-based; 79 iBT), IELTS (minimum score 6), PTE (minimum score 53). *Application deadline:* For fall admission, 8/1 for domestic students, 6/1 for international students; for spring admission, 11/21 for domestic students, 10/1 for international students; for summer admission, 5/15 for domestic students. Applications are processed on a rolling basis. Application fee: $30 ($40 for international students). Electronic applications accepted. *Expenses:* $270.35 per credit hour in-state tuition, $33.40 per credit hour fees. *Financial support:* In 2017–18, 17 students received support, including 25 teaching assistantships with full tuition reimbursements available; career-related internships or fieldwork, Federal Work-Study, scholarships/grants, traineeships, tuition waivers (full), and unspecified assistantships also available. Financial award application deadline: 6/30; financial award applicants required to submit FAFSA. *Faculty research:* Literature, creative writing, technical writing, secondary English education, teaching English as a second language. *Unit head:* Dr. Susan Kendrick, Department of English Chair, 573-651-2156, Fax: 573-651-5188, E-mail: skendrick@semo.edu. *Application contact:* 573-651-2590, E-mail: admissions@semo.edu. Website: http://www.semo.edu/english/

Southern Connecticut State University, School of Graduate Studies, School of Arts and Sciences, Department of World Languages and Literatures, New Haven, CT 06515-1355. Offers multicultural-bilingual education/teaching English to speakers of other languages (MS); romance languages (MA). *Program availability:* Part-time, evening/ weekend. *Degree requirements:* For master's, one foreign language, thesis or alternative. *Entrance requirements:* For master's, interview, minimum undergraduate GPA of 2.7. Electronic applications accepted.

Southern Illinois University Carbondale, Graduate School, College of Liberal Arts, Department of Linguistics, Program in Teaching English to Speakers of Other Languages, Carbondale, IL 62901-4701. Offers MA. *Entrance requirements:* Additional exam requirements/recommendations for international students: Required—TOEFL (minimum score 90 iBT).

Southern Illinois University Edwardsville, Graduate School, College of Arts and Sciences, Department of English Language and Literature, Program in Teaching English as a Second Language, Edwardsville, IL 62026. Offers MA, Postbaccalaureate Certificate. *Program availability:* Part-time, evening/weekend. *Degree requirements:* For master's, one foreign language, thesis (for some programs), final exam. *Entrance requirements:* Additional exam requirements/recommendations for international students: Required—TOEFL (minimum score 550 paper-based, 79 iBT), IELTS (minimum score 6.5), Michigan Test of English Language Proficiency or PTE. Electronic applications accepted.

Southern New Hampshire University, School of Education, Manchester, NH 03106-1045. Offers curriculum and instruction (M Ed), including dyslexia studies and language-based learning disabilities, educational leadership, reading, special education, technology integration; dyslexia studies and language-based learning disabilities (Certificate); early childhood and special education (M Ed); educational leadership (M Ed, Ed D); educational studies (M Ed); elementary and special education (M Ed); field based education (M Ed); higher education administration (MS); teaching English as a foreign language (MS). *Program availability:* Part-time, evening/weekend, online learning. *Degree requirements:* For master's, comprehensive exam (for some programs), thesis or alternative. *Entrance requirements:* For master's, PRAXIS I, minimum GPA of 2.75. Additional exam requirements/recommendations for international students: Required—TOEFL (minimum score 550 paper-based). *Application deadline:* Applications are processed on a rolling basis. Application fee: $40. Electronic applications accepted. *Expenses:* Contact institution. *Financial support:* Institutionally sponsored loans available. Financial award applicants required to submit FAFSA. *Unit head:* Raymond McNulty, Dean, 603-668-2211, Fax: 603-629-4673. *Application contact:* Office of Graduate Admission, 888-327-SNHU, Fax: 603-644-3144, E-mail: enroll@ snhu.edu.

Southwest Minnesota State University, Department of Education, Marshall, MN 56258. Offers ESL (MS); math (MS); reading (MS); special education (MS), including developmental disabilities, early childhood education, emotional behavioral disorders, learning disabilities; teaching, learning and leadership (MS). *Program availability:* Part-time, evening/weekend, online learning. *Entrance requirements:* Additional exam

requirements/recommendations for international students: Required—TOEFL or IELTS; Recommended—TOEFL (minimum score 550 paper-based; 80 iBT), IELTS.

State University of New York at Fredonia, College of Education, Fredonia, NY 14063-1136. Offers curriculum and instruction (MS Ed); literacy education (MS Ed), including birth-grade 12, grades 5-12; TESOL (MS Ed). *Accreditation:* NCATE. *Program availability:* Part-time. *Faculty:* 11 full-time (9 women), 1 part-time/adjunct (0 women). *Students:* Average age 29. 60 applicants, 97% accepted, 39 enrolled. In 2017, 33 master's awarded. *Degree requirements:* For master's, thesis. *Entrance requirements:* For master's, GRE, minimum undergraduate GPA of 3.0. Additional exam requirements/ recommendations for international students: Required—TOEFL (minimum score 79 iBT), IELTS (minimum score 6.5). *Application deadline:* For fall admission, 4/1 priority date for domestic and international students; for spring admission, 11/1 priority date for domestic students, 11/1 for international students. Applications are processed on a rolling basis. Application fee: $75. Electronic applications accepted. *Expenses:* Tuition, state resident: full-time $8154. Tuition, nonresident: full-time $16,650. *Required fees:* $1209. *Financial support:* In 2017–18, 4 teaching assistantships with full and partial tuition reimbursements (averaging $7,075 per year) were awarded. Financial award application deadline: 3/15; financial award applicants required to submit FAFSA. *Faculty research:* Positive behavioral intervention and support (PBIS), place-based science education, peer support for education, primary source material for social studies education, policies and practices in learning English language. *Unit head:* Dr. Christine Givner, Dean, 716-673-3311, E-mail: christine.givner@fredonia.edu. *Application contact:* Wendy S. Dunst, Interim Graduate Recruitment and Admissions Associate, 716-673-3808, Fax: 716-673-3712, E-mail: wendy.dunst@fredonia.edu. Website: http://www.fredonia.edu/coe/

State University of New York at New Paltz, Graduate and Extended Learning School, School of Education, Department of Teaching and Learning, Program in Second Language Education, New Paltz, NY 12561. Offers second language education (MS Ed); teaching English language learners (AC). *Accreditation:* NCATE. *Program availability:* Part-time, evening/weekend. *Students:* 10 full-time (9 women), 39 part-time (35 women); includes 13 minority (2 Asian, non-Hispanic/Latino; 9 Hispanic/Latino; 2 Two or more races, non-Hispanic/Latino). 45 applicants, 78% accepted, 25 enrolled. In 2017, 34 master's awarded. *Degree requirements:* For master's, practicum. *Entrance requirements:* For master's, minimum GPA of 3.0, 12 credits of a foreign language. Additional exam requirements/recommendations for international students: Required— TOEFL (minimum score 575 paper-based; 90 iBT), IELTS (minimum score 7). *Application deadline:* For fall admission, 4/15 priority date for domestic and international students. Application fee: $50. Electronic applications accepted. *Financial support:* Application deadline: 8/1. *Unit head:* Prof. Devon Duhaney, Coordinator, 845-257-2853, E-mail: duhaneyd@newpaltz.edu. *Application contact:* Vika Shock, Director of Graduate Admissions, 845-257-3286, Fax: 845-257-3284, E-mail: gradschool@newpaltz.edu. Website: http://www.newpaltz.edu/secondaryed/sec_ed_msed_2nd_lang_ed.html

State University of New York College at Cortland, Graduate Studies, School of Arts and Sciences, Department of Modern Languages, Cortland, NY 13045. Offers second language education (MS Ed). *Accreditation:* NCATE.

Stony Brook University, State University of New York, Graduate School, College of Arts and Sciences, Department of Linguistics, Program in Teaching English to Speakers of Other Languages, Stony Brook, NY 11794. Offers MA. *Accreditation:* NCATE. *Students:* 28 full-time (22 women), 21 part-time (20 women); includes 10 minority (3 Black or African American, non-Hispanic/Latino; 1 Asian, non-Hispanic/Latino; 5 Hispanic/Latino; 1 Two or more races, non-Hispanic/Latino), 1 international. Average age 26. 101 applicants, 51% accepted, 28 enrolled. In 2017, 22 master's awarded. *Degree requirements:* For master's, minimum GPA of 3.0. *Entrance requirements:* For master's, GRE, statement of purpose, curriculum vitae, 3 letters of recommendation, official transcripts. Additional exam requirements/recommendations for international students: Required—TOEFL (minimum score 85 iBT). *Application deadline:* For fall admission, 6/20 for domestic students, 4/15 for international students; for spring admission, 10/1 for domestic students. Application fee: $100. Electronic applications accepted. *Expenses:* Contact institution. *Financial support:* Fellowships, research assistantships, and teaching assistantships available. *Unit head:* Dr. Richard Larson, Chair, 631-632-7776, E-mail: richard.larson@stonybrook.edu. *Application contact:* Michelle Carbone, Coordinator, 631-632-7774, Fax: 631-632-9789, E-mail: michelle.carbone@stonybrook.edu. Website: https://linguistics.stonybrook.edu/programs/graduate/ma/tesol.html

Syracuse University, College of Arts and Sciences, CAS Program in Language Teaching: TESOL/TLOTE, Syracuse, NY 13244. Offers CAS. *Program availability:* Part-time. In 2017, 12 CASs awarded. *Entrance requirements:* Additional exam requirements/recommendations for international students: Required—TOEFL (minimum score 600 paper-based; 100 iBT), IELTS (minimum score 7). *Application deadline:* For fall admission, 1/10 priority date for domestic and international students. Applications are processed on a rolling basis. Application fee: $75. Electronic applications accepted. *Faculty research:* Linguistic analysis, methods for language teaching, teaching English. *Unit head:* Dr. Amanda Brown, Coordinator, 315-443-2244, E-mail: abrown08@syr.edu. Website: http://lll.syr.edu/tesol/certificate.html

Syracuse University, College of Arts and Sciences, MA Program in Linguistic Studies, Syracuse, NY 13244. Offers linguistic studies (MA), including information representation and retrieval, language acquisition, language, culture, and society, linguistic theory, logic and language, teaching language (TESOL/TLOTE). *Program availability:* Part-time. *Students:* Average age 25. *Degree requirements:* For master's, comprehensive exam, thesis or alternative. *Entrance requirements:* For master's, GRE General Test, personal statement detailing interest in field of linguistics and possible concentration areas, transcripts, three recommendation letters. Additional exam requirements/ recommendations for international students: Required—TOEFL (minimum score 100 iBT). *Application deadline:* For fall admission, 1/15 priority date for domestic and international students. Application fee: $75. Electronic applications accepted. *Financial support:* Teaching assistantships with tuition reimbursements available. Financial award application deadline: 1/15. *Faculty research:* Information representation and retrieval, language acquisition, linguistic theory, logic and language, teaching languages. *Unit head:* Dr. Gerald R. Greenberg, Director, 315-443-1414, E-mail: ggreenbe@syr.edu. *Application contact:* Jaklin Kornfilt, Professor of Linguistics and Director of the Linguistic Studies Program, 315-443-5375, E-mail: kornfilt@syr.edu. Website: http://lll.syr.edu/linguistics/graduate.html

Syracuse University, School of Education, MS Program in Teaching English Language Learners (Pre-K-12), Syracuse, NY 13244. Offers MS. *Program availability:* Part-time. *Students:* Average age 22. *Entrance requirements:* For master's, GRE or MAT, baccalaureate degree from regionally-accredited college/university, strong teacher and/ or employer recommendations, 12 credits in a language other than English, personal statement. Additional exam requirements/recommendations for international students: Required—TOEFL (minimum score 100 iBT). *Application deadline:* For fall admission, 1/ 15 priority date for domestic and international students. Application fee: $75. Electronic applications accepted. *Financial support:* Fellowships with full tuition reimbursements, teaching assistantships, career-related internships or fieldwork, scholarships/grants, and tuition waivers available. Financial award application deadline: 1/15; financial award applicants required to submit FAFSA. *Unit head:* Dr. Zaline Roy-Campbell, Program Coordinator, 315-443-8194, E-mail: zmroycam@syr.edu. *Application contact:* Speranza Migliore, Graduate Admissions Recruiter, 315-443-2505, E-mail: gradrcrt@syr.edu. Website: http://soe.syr.edu/academic/reading_language_arts/graduate/masters/teaching_english_language_learners/default.aspx

Taylor College and Seminary, Graduate and Professional Programs, Edmonton, AB T6J 4T3, Canada. Offers Christian studies (Diploma); intercultural studies (MA, Diploma), including intercultural studies (Diploma), TESOL; theology (M Div, MTS). *Accreditation:* ATS. *Program availability:* Part-time, online learning. *Degree requirements:* For master's, thesis optional. *Entrance requirements:* Additional exam requirements/recommendations for international students: Required—TOEFL (minimum score 550 paper-based; 80 iBT), IELTS (minimum score 6.5). *Faculty research:* Biblical studies, administration and organization, world religions, ethics, missiology.

Teachers College, Columbia University, Department of Arts and Humanities, New York, NY 10027. Offers applied linguistics (MA, Ed D); art and art education (Ed M, MA, Ed D, Ed DCT); arts administration (MA); bilingual and bicultural education (MA); global competence (Certificate); history and education (Ed D, PhD); music and music education (Ed DCT); philosophy and education (MA, Ed D, PhD); social studies education (Ed M, PhD); teaching English to speakers of other languages (Ed M); teaching of English and English education (Ed M, MA, Ed D, PhD), including English education (Ed M, Ed D, PhD), teaching of English (MA); teaching of social studies (MA); TESOL (MA, Ed D). *Program availability:* Part-time, evening/weekend. *Students:* 391 full-time (305 women), 418 part-time (283 women); includes 246 minority (62 Black or African American, non-Hispanic/Latino; 3 American Indian or Alaska Native, non-Hispanic/Latino; 94 Asian, non-Hispanic/Latino; 75 Hispanic/Latino; 12 Two or more races, non-Hispanic/Latino), 209 international. Average age 30. 1,053 applicants, 60% accepted, 334 enrolled. Terminal master's awarded for partial completion of doctoral program. *Financial support:* Fellowships, research assistantships, teaching assistantships, career-related internships or fieldwork, Federal Work-Study, institutionally sponsored loans, tuition waivers (full and partial), and unspecified assistantships available. Support available to part-time students. *Unit head:* Prof. William Gaudelli, Department Chair, E-mail: gaudelli@tc.columbia.edu. *Application contact:* David Estrella, Director of Admissions, 212-678-3305, Fax: 212-678-4171, E-mail: estrella@tc.columbia.edu.

Temple University, College of Education, Department of Teaching and Learning, Philadelphia, PA 19122-6096. Offers career and technical education (Ed M), including business, computing, and information technology, industrial education, marketing education; middle grades education (Ed M), including math and language arts, math and science, science and language arts; secondary education (Ed M), including English, math, social studies; teaching English to speakers of other languages (MS Ed); urban education (Ed M). *Program availability:* Part-time, evening/weekend. *Students:* 218 full-time (144 women), 296 part-time (183 women); includes 128 minority (74 Black or African American, non-Hispanic/Latino; 18 Asian, non-Hispanic/Latino; 25 Hispanic/Latino; 11 Two or more races, non-Hispanic/Latino), 13 international. 254 applicants, 54% accepted, 102 enrolled. In 2017, 128 master's awarded. Terminal master's awarded for partial completion of doctoral program. *Degree requirements:* For master's, thesis or alternative. *Entrance requirements:* Additional exam requirements/recommendations for international students: Required—TOEFL (minimum score 550 paper-based; 79 iBT). *Application deadline:* For fall admission, 4/1 for domestic students, 12/15 for international students; for spring admission, 10/1 for domestic students, 8/1 for international students. Application fee: $60. Electronic applications accepted. *Expenses:* Contact institution. *Financial support:* Fellowships, research assistantships, and teaching assistantships available. Financial award application deadline: 1/15; financial award applicants required to submit FAFSA. *Faculty research:* Workforce development, vocational education, technical education, industrial education, professional development, literacy, classroom management, school communities, curriculum development, instruction, applied linguistics, cross linguistic influence, bilingual education, oral proficiency, multilingualism. *Unit head:* Dr. Christine Woyshner, Chairperson, 215-204-6387, E-mail: christine.woyshner@temple.edu. *Application contact:* Sarah Stapleton, Assistant Director, Academic Operations, 215-204-8220, E-mail: sarah.stapleton@temple.edu.
Website: http://education.temple.edu/tl

Tennessee Technological University, College of Graduate Studies, College of Interdisciplinary Studies, School of Professional Studies, Cookeville, TN 38505. Offers health care administration (MPS); human resources leadership (MPS); public safety (MPS); strategic leadership (MPS); teaching English to speakers of other languages (MPS); training and development (MPS). *Program availability:* Part-time, evening/weekend, online learning. *Students:* 20 full-time (11 women), 74 part-time (46 women); includes 18 minority (11 Black or African American, non-Hispanic/Latino; 1 Hispanic/Latino; 1 Native Hawaiian or other Pacific Islander, non-Hispanic/Latino; 5 Two or more races, non-Hispanic/Latino), 1 international. 50 applicants, 82% accepted, 29 enrolled. In 2017, 23 master's awarded. *Degree requirements:* For master's, comprehensive exam, thesis or alternative. *Entrance requirements:* For master's, GRE. Additional exam requirements/recommendations for international students: Required—TOEFL (minimum score 527 paper-based; 71 iBT), IELTS (minimum score 5.5), PTE (minimum score 48), or TOEIC (Test of English as an International Communication). *Application deadline:* For fall admission, 7/1 for domestic students, 5/1 for international students; for spring admission, 11/1 for domestic students, 10/1 for international students; for summer admission, 5/1 for domestic students, 2/1 for international students. Applications are processed on a rolling basis. Application fee: $35 ($40 for international students). Electronic applications accepted. *Expenses:* Tuition, state resident: full-time $9925; part-time $565 per credit hour. Tuition, nonresident: full-time $22,993; part-time $1291 per credit hour. *Financial support:* Application deadline: 4/1. *Unit head:* Dr. Joseph Roberts, Interim Director, School of Professional Studies, 931-372-6223, E-mail: jmroberts@tntech.edu. *Application contact:* Shelia K. Kendrick, Coordinator of Graduate Studies, 931-372-3808, Fax: 931-372-3497, E-mail: skendrick@tntech.edu.
Website: https://www.tntech.edu/is/sps/

Texas A&M University–Commerce, College of Humanities, Social Sciences and Arts, Commerce, TX 75429. Offers applied criminology (MS); applied linguistics (MA, MS); art (MA, MFA); computational linguistics (Graduate Certificate); creative writing (Graduate Certificate); criminal justice management (Graduate Certificate); criminal justice studies (Graduate Certificate); English (MA, MS, PhD); film studies (Graduate Certificate); history (MA, MS); history of Christianity (Graduate Certificate); Holocaust studies (Graduate Certificate); homeland security (Graduate Certificate); music education (MM); music performance (MM); political science (MS, MA); public history (Graduate Certificate); sociology (MS); Spanish (MA); studies in children's and adolescent literature and culture (Graduate Certificate); teaching English to speakers of other languages (Graduate Certificate); theater (MA, MS); world history (Graduate Certificate). *Program availability:* Part-time. *Faculty:* 56 full-time (26 women), 10 part-time/adjunct (5 women). *Students:* 133 full-time (85 women), 439 part-time (311 women); includes 204 minority (79 Black or African American, non-Hispanic/Latino; 4 American Indian or Alaska Native, non-Hispanic/Latino; 9 Asian, non-Hispanic/Latino; 98 Hispanic/Latino; 14 Two or more races, non-Hispanic/Latino), 26 international. Average age 36. 261 applicants, 50% accepted, 113

enrolled. In 2017, 105 master's, 5 doctorates awarded. *Degree requirements:* For master's, one foreign language, comprehensive exam, thesis (for some programs); for doctorate, one foreign language, comprehensive exam, thesis/dissertation, departmental qualifying exam. *Entrance requirements:* For master's and doctorate, GRE General Test. Additional exam requirements/recommendations for international students: Required—TOEFL (minimum score 550 paper-based; 79 iBT), IELTS (minimum score 6). *Application deadline:* Applications are processed on a rolling basis. Application fee: $50. Electronic applications accepted. *Expenses:* Contact institution. *Financial support:* In 2017–18, 43 students received support, with 9 research assistantships with partial tuition reimbursements available (averaging $9,000 per year), 68 teaching assistantships with partial tuition reimbursements available (averaging $9,000 per year); Federal Work-Study, institutionally sponsored loans, scholarships/grants, health care benefits, and unspecified assistantships also available. Financial award application deadline: 5/1; financial award applicants required to submit FAFSA. *Unit head:* Dr. William F. Kuracina, Interim Dean, 903-886-5166, Fax: 903-886-5774, E-mail: william.kuracina@tamuc.edu. *Application contact:* Vicky Turner, Doctoral Degree and Special Programs Coordinator, 903-886-5167, E-mail: vicky.turner@tamuc.edu.
Website: http://www.tamuc.edu/academics/graduateSchool/programs/humanitiesSocialScienceArts/default.aspx

Texas A&M University–Kingsville, College of Graduate Studies, College of Education and Human Performance, Department of Teacher and Bilingual Education, Program in Bilingual Education, Kingsville, TX 78363. Offers M Ed, Ed D. *Degree requirements:* For master's, comprehensive exam. *Entrance requirements:* For master's, GRE General Test, MAT, minimum GPA of 3.0.

Touro College, Graduate School of Education, New York, NY 10010. Offers education and special education (MS); instructional technology (MS); mathematics education (MS); school leadership (MS); teaching English to speakers of other languages (MS); teaching literacy (MS). *Accreditation:* TEAC. *Program availability:* Part-time, evening/weekend, online learning. *Faculty:* 52 full-time (34 women), 199 part-time/adjunct (136 women). *Students:* 756 full-time (686 women), 3,833 part-time (3,492 women). Average age 33. 1,422 applicants, 50% accepted, 675 enrolled. In 2017, 6 master's awarded. *Entrance requirements:* Additional exam requirements/recommendations for international students: Required—TOEFL (minimum score 83 iBT), IELTS (minimum score 6.5). *Application deadline:* For fall admission, 8/26 for domestic students, 7/15 for international students; for spring admission, 12/31 for domestic students, 12/15 for international students. Applications are processed on a rolling basis. Application fee: $50. *Financial support:* Federal Work-Study available. Financial award applicants required to submit FAFSA. *Faculty research:* Equity assistance, language development, scholarly communications, Latin American studies and cultural sensitivity, behavior management techniques and strategies in special education. *Unit head:* Dr. Jacob Easley, III, Dean, 212-463-0400 Ext. 5561, Fax: 212-462-4889, E-mail: jeasley@touro.edu. *Application contact:* Sharmilee Hoopnarine, Admissions, 212-463-0400.

Trevecca Nazarene University, Graduate Education Program, Nashville, TN 37210-2877. Offers accountability and instructional leadership (Ed S); curriculum and instruction for Christian school educators (M Ed); curriculum and instruction K-12 (M Ed); educational leadership (M Ed); English second language (M Ed); library and information science (MLI Sc); special education: visual impairments (M Ed); teaching (MAT), including teaching 6-12, teaching K-5. *Accreditation:* NCATE. *Program availability:* Part-time, evening/weekend, online learning. *Faculty:* 8 full-time (6 women), 22 part-time/adjunct (18 women). *Students:* 150 full-time (114 women), 3 part-time (1 woman); includes 54 minority (49 Black or African American, non-Hispanic/Latino; 4 Hispanic/Latino; 1 Two or more races, non-Hispanic/Latino). Average age 36. In 2017, 57 master's, 4 other advanced degrees awarded. *Degree requirements:* For master's, comprehensive exam, exit assessment/e-portfolio. *Entrance requirements:* For master's, GRE or MAT; PRAXIS (for MAT), minimum GPA of 3.0, official transcript from regionally-accredited institution, references, interview, writing sample, at least 3 years' successful teaching experience (for M Ed in educational leadership); for Ed S, GRE or MAT, master's degree with minimum GPA of 3.0, official transcript from regionally accredited institution, at least 3 years' successful teaching experience, interview, writing sample, background and fingerprinting check, recommendations. Additional exam requirements/recommendations for international students: Required—TOEFL (minimum score 550 paper-based). *Application deadline:* Applications are processed on a rolling basis. Electronic applications accepted. *Expenses:* Contact institution. *Financial support:* Applicants required to submit FAFSA. *Unit head:* Dr. Suzie Harris, Dean, School of Education, 615-248-1201, Fax: 615-248-1597, E-mail: admissions_ged@trevecca.edu. *Application contact:* 844-TNU-GRAD, E-mail: sgcsadmissions@trevecca.edu.
Website: http://www.trevecca.edu/soe

Trinity Western University, School of Graduate Studies, Program in Teaching English to Speakers of Other Languages (TESOL), Langley, BC V2Y 1Y1, Canada. Offers MA. *Program availability:* Part-time, online learning. *Degree requirements:* For master's, project. *Entrance requirements:* For master's, minimum GPA of 3.0. Additional exam requirements/recommendations for international students: Required—TOEFL (minimum score 600 paper-based). *Faculty research:* ESL methodology, second language acquisition, computer assisted language learning.

Troy University, Graduate School, College of Education, Program in Second Language Instruction, Troy, AL 36082. Offers MS. *Program availability:* Part-time, evening/weekend. *Faculty:* 2 full-time (both women), 1 (woman) part-time/adjunct. *Students:* 9 full-time (8 women), 5 part-time (all women); includes 2 minority (1 Black or African American, non-Hispanic/Latino; 1 Asian, non-Hispanic/Latino). Average age 28. 6 applicants, 83% accepted. In 2017, 15 master's awarded. *Degree requirements:* For master's, thesis or capstone. *Entrance requirements:* For master's, GRE (minimum score of 850 on old exam or 290 on new exam), GMAT (minimum score of 380), or MAT (minimum score of 385), bachelor's degree; minimum undergraduate GPA of 2.5 or 3.0 on last 30 semester hours; letters of recommendation. Additional exam requirements/recommendations for international students: Required—TOEFL (minimum score 523 paper-based; 70 iBT), IELTS (minimum score 6). *Application deadline:* Applications are processed on a rolling basis. Application fee: $50. Electronic applications accepted. *Expenses:* Tuition, state resident: part-time $417 per credit hour. Tuition, nonresident: part-time $834 per credit hour. *Required fees:* $42 per credit hour. $50 per semester. Tuition and fees vary according to campus/location. *Financial support:* Fellowships, career-related internships or fieldwork, and scholarships/grants available. Support available to part-time students. Financial award applicants required to submit FAFSA. *Unit head:* Dr. Jan Oliver, Chair, Leadership Development and Professional Studies, 334-670-3546, Fax: 334-808-6666, E-mail: oliverj@troy.edu. *Application contact:* Jessica A. Kimbro, Director of Graduate Admissions, 334-670-3178, E-mail: jacord@troy.edu.

Universidad del Este, Graduate School, Carolina, PR 00984. Offers accounting (MBA); adult education (M Ed); agribusiness (MBA); criminal justice and criminology (MA); curriculum and instruction - early education (M Ed); curriculum and instruction - elementary (M Ed); curriculum and instruction - English (M Ed); curriculum and instruction - Spanish (M Ed); human resources (MBA); information security management (MBA); information technology and Web business development (MBA); management (MBA); public policy (MPA); social work (MA), including clinical social work; special education (M Ed); strategic leadership (MBA).

English as a Second Language

Universidad del Turabo, Graduate Programs, Programs in Education, Program in Teaching English as a Second Language, Gurabo, PR 00778-3030. Offers M Ed. *Entrance requirements:* For master's, GRE, EXADEP, GMAT, interview, official transcript, essay, recommendation letters. Electronic applications accepted.

University at Buffalo, the State University of New York, Graduate School, Graduate School of Education, Department of Learning and Instruction, Buffalo, NY 14260. Offers biology education (Ed M, Certificate); chemistry education (Ed M, Certificate); childhood education (Ed M); childhood education with bilingual extension (Ed M); college teaching (Advanced Certificate); curriculum, instruction and the science of learning (PhD); early childhood education (Ed M); early childhood education with bilingual extension (Ed M); earth science education (Ed M, Certificate); education and technology (Ed M); education studies (Ed M); educational technology and new literacies (Certificate); educational technology and new literacies (Advanced Certificate); elementary education (Ed D); English education (Ed M, Certificate); English education studies (Ed M); English for speakers of other languages (Ed M); foreign and second language education (PhD); French education (Ed M, Certificate); German education (Ed M, Certificate); gifted education (Certificate); Latin education (Ed M, Certificate); literacy education studies (Ed M); literacy specialist (Ed M); literacy teaching and learning (Certificate); mathematics education (Ed M, Certificate); music education (Ed M, Certificate); music education studies (Ed M); music learning theory (Advanced Certificate); online education (Advanced Certificate); physics education (Ed M, Certificate); science and the public (Ed M); social studies education (Ed M, Certificate); Spanish education (Ed M, Certificate); special education (PhD); teaching English to speakers of other languages (Ed M). *Program availability:* Part-time, evening/weekend, 100% online. *Faculty:* 26 full-time (19 women), 74 part-time/adjunct (52 women). *Students:* 172 full-time (122 women), 325 part-time (226 women); includes 44 minority (25 Black or African American, non-Hispanic/Latino; 5 American Indian or Alaska Native, non-Hispanic/Latino; 14 Asian, non-Hispanic/Latino; 57 international. Average age 33. 316 applicants, 78% accepted, 174 enrolled. In 2017, 109 master's, 34 doctorates, 15 other advanced degrees awarded. *Degree requirements:* For master's, comprehensive exam; for doctorate, thesis/dissertation, research analysis exam, research experience. *Entrance requirements:* For master's, letters of reference; for doctorate, GRE General Test or MAT, interview, writing sample, letters of recommendation. Additional exam requirements/recommendations for international students: Required—TOEFL (minimum score 600 paper-based; 96 iBT). *Application deadline:* For fall admission, 2/1 priority date for domestic and international students; for spring admission, 11/15 priority date for domestic students, 10/1 for international students. Applications are processed on a rolling basis. Application fee: $50. Electronic applications accepted. *Financial support:* In 2017–18, 42 fellowships (averaging $5,181 per year), 44 research assistantships with tuition reimbursements (averaging $10,908 per year) were awarded; teaching assistantships, career-related internships or fieldwork, Federal Work-Study, institutionally sponsored loans, scholarships/grants, tuition waivers (full and partial), and unspecified assistantships also available. Financial award application deadline: 2/28; financial award applicants required to submit FAFSA. *Faculty research:* Science assessment, foreign language teaching and learning, early learning, new literacies, gender and education. *Total annual research expenditures:* $413,233. *Unit head:* Dr. David Bruce, Chair, 716-645-4069, Fax: 716-645-3161, E-mail: gse-info@buffalo.edu. *Application contact:* Luann Zak, Admissions Assistant, 716-645-2110, Fax: 716-645-7937, E-mail: luannzak@buffalo.edu.
Website: http://gse.buffalo.edu/lai

The University of Alabama, Graduate School, College of Arts and Sciences, Department of English, Tuscaloosa, AL 35487. Offers composition and rhetoric (PhD); creative writing (MFA), including fiction, poetry; literature (MA, PhD); rhetoric and composition (MA); teaching English as a second language (MATESOL). *Faculty:* 37 full-time (21 women). *Students:* 123 full-time (71 women), 11 part-time (8 women); includes 22 minority (10 Black or African American, non-Hispanic/Latino; 1 Asian, non-Hispanic/Latino; 6 Hispanic/Latino; 5 Two or more races, non-Hispanic/Latino; 2 international. Average age 29. 378 applicants, 17% accepted, 44 enrolled. In 2017, 32 master's, 7 doctorates awarded. *Degree requirements:* For master's, one foreign language, comprehensive exam, thesis; for doctorate, 2 foreign languages, comprehensive exam, thesis/dissertation. *Entrance requirements:* For master's, GRE (minimum score of 300, except for MFA), minimum GPA of 3.0, critical writing sample; for doctorate, GRE (minimum score of 300), minimum GPA of 3.5 on master's or equivalent graduate work, critical writing sample. Additional exam requirements/recommendations for international students: Recommended—TOEFL (minimum score 550 paper-based; 79 iBT). *Application deadline:* For fall admission, 12/20 for domestic and international students. Application fee: $50 ($60 for international students). Electronic applications accepted. *Financial support:* In 2017–18, 113 students received support, including fellowships with full tuition reimbursements available (averaging $15,000 per year), research assistantships with full tuition reimbursements available (averaging $13,500 per year), teaching assistantships with full tuition reimbursements available (averaging $13,500 per year); career-related internships or fieldwork, scholarships/grants, health care benefits, and unspecified assistantships also available. Financial award application deadline: 12/20. *Faculty research:* American literature, British literature, composition/rhetoric, applied linguistics, creative writing. *Unit head:* Prof. Joel Brouwer, Department Chair, 205-348-5065, Fax: 205-348-1388, E-mail: joel.brouwer@ua.edu. *Application contact:* Jennifer Fuqua, Graduate Coordinator, 205-348-0766, Fax: 205-348-1388, E-mail: jfuqua@ua.edu.

The University of Alabama at Birmingham, School of Education, Program in English as a Second Language, Birmingham, AL 35294-1250. Offers MA Ed, Ed S. *Program availability:* Part-time, evening/weekend. *Degree requirements:* For master's, variable foreign language requirement, comprehensive exam. *Entrance requirements:* For master's, MAT (minimum score of 388 scaled, 35 raw) or GRE (minimum 290 on current test). Additional exam requirements/recommendations for international students: Required—TOEFL, IELTS. Electronic applications accepted. *Expenses:* Contact institution. *Faculty research:* How mainstream teachers learn to implement ESL best practices and how they help their colleagues through collaborative mentoring; language use, identity, and the relationship between school and community empowering K-12 administrators to become EL advocates; oral English proficiency of non-native English speakers pursuing graduate degrees in education and factors related to their identity and perceptions of self-efficacy as teachers.

The University of Alabama in Huntsville, School of Graduate Studies, College of Arts, Humanities, and Social Sciences, Department of English, Huntsville, AL 35899. Offers education (MA); English (MA); technical writing (Certificate); TESOL (Certificate). *Program availability:* Part-time, evening/weekend. *Degree requirements:* For master's, one foreign language, comprehensive exam, thesis or alternative, oral and written exams. *Entrance requirements:* For master's and Certificate, GRE General Test, minimum GPA of 3.0. Additional exam requirements/recommendations for international students: Required—TOEFL (minimum score 500 paper-based; 80 iBT), IELTS (minimum score 6.5). Electronic applications accepted. *Faculty research:* Fiction and identity, Shakespeare, science fiction, eighteenth-century literature, technical writing.

The University of Alabama in Huntsville, School of Graduate Studies, College of Education, Huntsville, AL 35899. Offers autism spectrum disorders (M Ed, Graduate Certificate); biology (MAT); chemistry (MAT); differentiated instruction in elementary education (M Ed); English language arts (MAT); English speakers of other languages (M Ed, MAT); history (MAT); mathematics (MAT); physics (MAT); reading education (M Ed); secondary education (M Ed).

University of Alberta, Faculty of Graduate Studies and Research, Department of Educational Psychology, Edmonton, AB T6G 2E1, Canada. Offers counseling psychology (M Ed, PhD); educational psychology (M Ed, PhD); instructional technology (M Ed); school counseling (M Ed); school psychology (M Ed, PhD); special education (M Ed, PhD); special education-deafness studies (M Ed); teaching English as a second language (M Ed). *Program availability:* Part-time. *Degree requirements:* For master's, thesis optional; for doctorate, comprehensive exam, thesis/dissertation. *Entrance requirements:* For master's and doctorate, minimum GPA of 3.0. Additional exam requirements/recommendations for international students: Required—TOEFL. *Faculty research:* Human learning, development and assessment.

The University of Arizona, College of Humanities, Department of English, English Language/Linguistics Program, Tucson, AZ 85721. Offers English (MA, PhD); ESL (MA). *Entrance requirements:* Additional exam requirements/recommendations for international students: Required—TOEFL (minimum score 550 paper-based; 79 iBT); Recommended—IELTS (minimum score 7). Electronic applications accepted.

The University of Arizona, Graduate Interdisciplinary Programs, Graduate Interdisciplinary Program in Second Language Acquisition and Teaching, Tucson, AZ 85721. Offers PhD. *Degree requirements:* For doctorate, one foreign language, comprehensive exam, thesis/dissertation. *Entrance requirements:* For doctorate, GRE, 3 letters of recommendation, writing sample. Additional exam requirements/recommendations for international students: Required—TOEFL (minimum score 550 paper-based; 79 iBT); Recommended—TWE. Electronic applications accepted.

University of Arkansas at Little Rock, Graduate School, College of Arts, Letters, and Sciences, Department of International and Second Language Studies, Little Rock, AR 72204-1099. Offers second languages (MA). *Degree requirements:* For master's, comprehensive exam, thesis. *Entrance requirements:* For master's, GRE or MAT, bachelor's degree; 3 letters of reference; personal interview; minimum overall undergraduate GPA of 2.75, 3.0 in last 60 hours.

The University of British Columbia, Faculty of Education, Department of Language and Literacy Education, Vancouver, BC V6T 1Z2, Canada. Offers literacy education (M Ed, MA, PhD); modern languages education (M Ed, MA); teaching English as a second language (M Ed, MA, PhD). *Program availability:* Part-time, evening/weekend. *Degree requirements:* For master's, thesis (MA); for doctorate, thesis/dissertation. *Entrance requirements:* For master's and doctorate, minimum B+ average in last 2 years with minimum 2 courses at A standing. Additional exam requirements/recommendations for international students: Required—TOEFL, TWE. Electronic applications accepted. *Expenses:* Contact institution. *Faculty research:* Language and literacy development, second language acquisition, Asia Pacific language curriculum, children's literature, whole language instruction.

University of California, Berkeley, UC Berkeley Extension, Certificate Programs in Education, Berkeley, CA 94720-1500. Offers college admissions and career planning (Certificate); teaching English as a second language (Certificate).

University of California, Los Angeles, Graduate Division, College of Letters and Science, Department of Applied Linguistics and Teaching English as a Second Language, Los Angeles, CA 90095. Offers applied linguistics (PhD); applied linguistics and teaching English as a second language (MA); teaching English as a second language (Certificate). *Degree requirements:* For master's, one foreign language, thesis; for doctorate, one foreign language, thesis/dissertation, oral and written qualifying exams. *Entrance requirements:* For master's and doctorate, bachelor's degree; minimum undergraduate GPA of 3.0 (or its equivalent if letter grade system not used). Additional exam requirements/recommendations for international students: Required—TOEFL. Electronic applications accepted.

University of California, Riverside, Graduate Division, Graduate School of Education, Riverside, CA 92521. Offers applied behavior analysis (M Ed); diversity and equity (M Ed); education policy analysis and leadership (PhD); education specialist (Credential); education, society, and culture (MA, PhD); educational psychology (MA, PhD); general education (M Ed); higher education administration and policy (M Ed, PhD); multiple subject (Credential); research, evaluation, measurement and statistics (MA); school psychology (PhD); single subject (Credential); special education (M Ed, PhD); special education and autism (MA); TESOL (M Ed). *Faculty:* 29 full-time (16 women), 2 part-time/adjunct (1 woman). *Students:* 241 full-time (188 women). 396 applicants, 42% accepted, 166 enrolled. In 2017, 130 master's, 15 doctorates, 14 other advanced degrees awarded. Terminal master's awarded for partial completion of doctoral program. *Degree requirements:* For master's, comprehensive exams or thesis (MA), case study or analytical report (M Ed); for doctorate, comprehensive exam, thesis/dissertation, written and oral qualifying exams, college teaching practicum. *Entrance requirements:* For master's, GRE General Test (for MA); CBEST and CSET (for M Ed in general education only), UCR Extension TESOL certificate (for M Ed with TESOL emphasis only); for doctorate, GRE General Test, writing sample; for Credential, CBEST, CSET. Additional exam requirements/recommendations for international students: Required—TOEFL (minimum score 550 paper-based; 80 iBT), IELTS (minimum score 7). *Application deadline:* For fall admission, 9/1 for domestic students, 6/1 for international students; for winter admission, 11/15 for domestic students, 9/1 for international students; for spring admission, 3/1 for domestic students, 12/1 for international students. Applications are processed on a rolling basis. Application fee: $80 ($100 for international students). Electronic applications accepted. *Expenses:* Tuition, state resident: full-time $5746. Tuition, nonresident: full-time $10,780. Tuition and fees vary according to campus/location and program. *Financial support:* In 2017–18, 105 students received support, including 16 fellowships with full tuition reimbursements available (averaging $31,000 per year), 25 research assistantships with full tuition reimbursements available (averaging $31,000 per year), 10 teaching assistantships with full tuition reimbursements available (averaging $31,000 per year); career-related internships or fieldwork, Federal Work-Study, institutionally sponsored loans, scholarships/grants, and unspecified assistantships also available. Financial award application deadline: 12/15. *Faculty research:* Responsiveness to intervention, faculty core, response to intervention of English language learners, advanced modeling techniques, study on social capital, trust, and motivation. *Total annual research expenditures:* $1.7 million. *Unit head:* Thomas Smith, Dean, 951-827-4633, E-mail: thomas.smith@ucr.edu. *Application contact:* Heather Killeen, Graduate Program Coordinator, 951-827-6362, E-mail: heather.killeen@ucr.edu.
Website: http://www.education.ucr.edu/

University of Central Florida, College of Arts and Humanities, Department of Modern Languages and Literatures, Program in Teaching English to Speakers of Other Languages, Orlando, FL 32816. Offers teaching English as a foreign language (Certificate); teaching English to speakers of other languages (MA). *Accreditation:* NCATE. *Program availability:* Part-time, evening/weekend. *Students:* 14 full-time (7 women), 21 part-time (13 women); includes 11 minority (1 Black or African American, non-Hispanic/Latino; 10 Hispanic/Latino), 5 international. Average age 35. 45

applicants, 91% accepted, 22 enrolled. In 2017, 24 master's, 22 other advanced degrees awarded. *Degree requirements:* For master's, comprehensive exam, thesis or alternative. *Entrance requirements:* For master's, GRE General Test, minimum GPA of 3.0 in last 60 hours, letters of recommendation. Additional exam requirements/recommendations for international students: Required—TOEFL. *Application deadline:* For fall admission, 7/1 for domestic students; for spring admission, 12/1 for domestic students; for summer admission, 4/1 for domestic students. Application fee: $30. Electronic applications accepted. *Expenses:* Tuition, state resident: part-time $288.16 per credit hour. Tuition, nonresident: part-time $1073.31 per credit hour. Tuition and fees vary according to program. *Financial support:* In 2017–18, 5 students received support, including 1 fellowship (averaging $5,000 per year), 1 research assistantship with partial tuition reimbursement available (averaging $1,764 per year), 5 teaching assistantships with partial tuition reimbursements available (averaging $9,088 per year); career-related internships or fieldwork, Federal Work-Study, institutionally sponsored loans, health care benefits, tuition waivers (partial), and unspecified assistantships also available. Financial award application deadline: 3/1; financial award applicants required to submit FAFSA. *Unit head:* Dr. Gergana Vitanova, Director, 407-823-2472, E-mail: gergana.vitanova@ucf.edu. *Application contact:* Associate Director, Graduate Admissions, 407-823-2766, Fax: 407-823-6442, E-mail: gradadmissions@ucf.edu. Website: http://mll.cah.ucf.edu/graduate/index.php#TESOL

University of Central Florida, College of Community Innovation and Education, Education Doctoral Programs, Orlando, FL 32816. Offers curriculum and instruction (Ed D); education (PhD), including communication sciences and disorders, counselor education, early childhood education, elementary education, exceptional education, exercise physiology, higher education, instructional design and technology, mathematics education, methodology, measurement and analysis, reading education, science education, social science education, TESOL; educational leadership (Ed D). *Students:* 122 full-time (86 women), 129 part-time (88 women); includes 64 minority (24 Black or African American, non-Hispanic/Latino; 1 American Indian or Alaska Native, non-Hispanic/Latino; 9 Asian, non-Hispanic/Latino; 24 Hispanic/Latino; 6 Two or more races, non-Hispanic/Latino), 26 international. Average age 38. 195 applicants, 47% accepted, 72 enrolled. In 2017, 89 doctorates awarded. *Entrance requirements:* For doctorate, GRE, letters of recommendation, goal statement, resume, writing sample. Application fee: $30. Electronic applications accepted. *Expenses:* Tuition, state resident: part-time $288.16 per credit hour. Tuition, nonresident: part-time $1073.31 per credit hour. Tuition and fees vary according to program. *Financial support:* In 2017–18, 77 students received support, including 28 fellowships with partial tuition reimbursements available (averaging $5,733 per year), 29 research assistantships with partial tuition reimbursements available (averaging $10,230 per year), 54 teaching assistantships with partial tuition reimbursements available (averaging $11,614 per year); health care benefits also available. Financial award application deadline: 3/1; financial award applicants required to submit FAFSA. *Unit head:* Dr. Edward Robinson, Director of Doctoral Programs, 407-823-6106, E-mail: edward.robinson@ucf.edu. *Application contact:* Associate Director, Graduate Admissions, 407-823-2766, Fax: 407-823-6442, E-mail: gradadmissions@ucf.edu. Website: https://edcollege.ucf.edu/academic-programs/graduate/

University of Central Florida, College of Community Innovation and Education, School of Teacher Education, Orlando, FL 32816. Offers applied learning and instruction (MA); curriculum and instruction (M Ed); elementary education (M Ed, MA); exceptional student education (M Ed, MA, Certificate), including autism spectrum disorders (Certificate), exceptional student education (M Ed), exceptional student education K-12 (MA), intervention specialist (Certificate), pre-kindergarten disabilities (Certificate), severe or profound disabilities (Certificate), special education (Certificate); K-8 mathematics and science education (M Ed, Certificate); reading education (M Ed, Certificate); teacher education (MAT), including art education, English language, mathematics education, middle school mathematics, middle school science, science education, social science education; world languages education - English for speakers of other languages (ESOL) (Certificate); world languages education - languages other than English (LOTE) (Certificate). *Program availability:* Part-time, evening/weekend. *Students:* 63 full-time (59 women), 218 part-time (190 women); includes 104 minority (34 Black or African American, non-Hispanic/Latino; 1 American Indian or Alaska Native, non-Hispanic/Latino; 13 Asian, non-Hispanic/Latino; 52 Hispanic/Latino; 4 Two or more races, non-Hispanic/Latino), 5 international. Average age 31. 189 applicants, 78% accepted, 98 enrolled. In 2017, 124 master's, 16 other advanced degrees awarded. *Degree requirements:* For Certificate, thesis or alternative. *Entrance requirements:* For degree, GRE General Test, minimum GPA of 3.0. Additional exam requirements/recommendations for international students: Required—TOEFL. *Application deadline:* For fall admission, 7/15 for domestic students; for spring admission, 12/15 for domestic students. Application fee: $30. Electronic applications accepted. *Expenses:* Tuition, state resident: part-time $288.16 per credit hour. Tuition, nonresident: part-time $1073.31 per credit hour. Tuition and fees vary according to program. *Financial support:* In 2017–18, 5 students received support, including 1 fellowship with partial tuition reimbursement available (averaging $1,000 per year), 4 research assistantships with partial tuition reimbursements available (averaging $5,617 per year), 1 teaching assistantship with partial tuition reimbursement available (averaging $9,086 per year); career-related internships or fieldwork, Federal Work-Study, institutionally sponsored loans, health care benefits, tuition waivers (partial), and unspecified assistantships also available. Financial award application deadline: 3/1; financial award applicants required to submit FAFSA. *Unit head:* Dr. Michael Hynes, Director, 407-823-1768, E-mail: michael.hynes@ucf.edu. *Application contact:* Associate Director, Graduate Admissions, 407-823-2766, Fax: 407-823-6442, E-mail: gradadmissions@ucf.edu. Website: https://ccie.ucf.edu/teachered/

University of Central Missouri, The Graduate School, Warrensburg, MO 64093. Offers accountancy (MA); accounting (MBA); applied mathematics (MS); aviation safety (MA); biology (MS); business administration (MBA); career and technical education leadership (MS); college student personnel administration (MS); communication (MA); computer science (MS); counseling (MS); criminal justice (MS); educational leadership (Ed D); educational technology (MS); elementary and early childhood education (MSE); English (MA); environmental studies (MA); finance (MBA); history (MA); human services/educational technology (Ed S); human services/learning resources (Ed S); human services/professional counseling (Ed S); industrial hygiene (MS); industrial management (MS); information systems (MBA); information technology (MS); kinesiology (MS); library science and information services (MS); literacy education (MSE); marketing (MBA); mathematics (MS); music (MA); occupational safety management (MS); psychology (MS); rural family nursing (MS); school administration (MSE); social gerontology (MS); sociology (MA); special education (MSE); speech language pathology (MS); superintendency (Ed S); teaching (MAT); teaching English as a second language (MA); technology (MS); technology management (PhD); theatre (MA). *Program availability:* Part-time, 100% online, blended/hybrid learning. *Faculty:* 337 full-time (145 women), 41 part-time/adjunct (28 women). *Students:* 785 full-time (398 women), 1,633 part-time (1,063 women); includes 231 minority (102 Black or African American, non-Hispanic/Latino; 4 American Indian or Alaska Native, non-Hispanic/Latino; 16 Asian, non-Hispanic/Latino; 52 Hispanic/Latino; 57 Two or more races, non-Hispanic/Latino), 692 international. Average age 30. In 2017, 2,605 master's, 122 other advanced degrees

awarded. *Degree requirements:* For master's and Ed S, comprehensive exam (for some programs), thesis (for some programs). *Entrance requirements:* Additional exam requirements/recommendations for international students: Required—TOEFL (minimum score 550 paper-based; 79 iBT). *Application deadline:* For fall admission, 6/1 priority date for domestic and international students; for spring admission, 10/1 priority date for domestic and international students; for summer admission, 4/1 priority date for domestic and international students. Applications are processed on a rolling basis. Application fee: $30 ($75 for international students). Electronic applications accepted. *Expenses:* Tuition, state resident: full-time $8771; part-time $292.35 per credit hour. Tuition, nonresident: full-time $17,541; part-time $584.70 per credit hour. *Required fees:* $372; $24.78 per credit hour. *Financial support:* In 2017–18, 99 students received support. Research assistantships, teaching assistantships, career-related internships or fieldwork, Federal Work-Study, scholarships/grants, and administrative and laboratory assistantships available. Support available to part-time students. Financial award application deadline: 3/1; financial award applicants required to submit FAFSA. *Unit head:* Shellie Hewitt, Director of Graduate and International Student Services, 660-543-4621, Fax: 660-543-4778, E-mail: hewitt@ucmo.edu. *Application contact:* 660-543-4621, E-mail: admit_intl@ucmo.edu. Website: http://www.ucmo.edu/graduate/

University of Central Oklahoma, The Jackson College of Graduate Studies, College of Education and Professional Studies, Department of Curriculum and Instruction, Edmond, OK 73034-5209. Offers bilingual education/teaching English as a second language (M Ed); early childhood education (M Ed); elementary education (M Ed). *Program availability:* Part-time. *Faculty:* 14 full-time (12 women), 4 part-time/adjunct (3 women). *Students:* 25 full-time (21 women), 67 part-time (60 women); includes 33 minority (8 Black or African American, non-Hispanic/Latino; 3 American Indian or Alaska Native, non-Hispanic/Latino; 2 Asian, non-Hispanic/Latino; 16 Hispanic/Latino; 4 Two or more races, non-Hispanic/Latino), 14 international. Average age 33. 44 applicants, 93% accepted, 31 enrolled. In 2017, 27 master's awarded. *Degree requirements:* For master's, comprehensive exam (for some programs), thesis optional. *Entrance requirements:* Additional exam requirements/recommendations for international students: Required—TOEFL (minimum score 550 paper-based; 79 iBT), IELTS (minimum score 6.5). *Application deadline:* For fall admission, 7/15 for international students; for spring admission, 11/15 for international students. Applications are processed on a rolling basis. Application fee: $60. Electronic applications accepted. *Expenses:* Tuition, state resident: full-time $5375; part-time $268.75 per credit hour. Tuition, nonresident: full-time $13,295; part-time $664.75 per credit hour. *Required fees:* $626; $31.30 per credit hour. One-time fee: $50. Tuition and fees vary according to program. *Financial support:* In 2017–18, 13 students received support. Research assistantships, teaching assistantships, career-related internships or fieldwork, Federal Work-Study, scholarships/grants, tuition waivers (partial), and unspecified assistantships available. Financial award application deadline: 3/31; financial award applicants required to submit FAFSA. *Unit head:* Dr. Paulette Shreck, Chair, 405-974-5721, Fax: 405-974-3858. *Application contact:* Carlie Wellington, Assistant Director, CEPS Graduate Enrollment, 405-974-5105, Fax: 405-974-3851, E-mail: gradcoll@uco.edu.

University of Central Oklahoma, The Jackson College of Graduate Studies, College of Liberal Arts, Department of English, Edmond, OK 73034-5209. Offers composition and rhetoric (MA); creative writing (MA); literature (MA); teaching English as a second language (MA). *Program availability:* Part-time. *Faculty:* 21 full-time (14 women). *Students:* 30 full-time (17 women), 45 part-time (23 women); includes 19 minority (3 Black or African American, non-Hispanic/Latino; 3 American Indian or Alaska Native, non-Hispanic/Latino; 2 Asian, non-Hispanic/Latino; 3 Hispanic/Latino; 2 Native Hawaiian or other Pacific Islander, non-Hispanic/Latino; 4 Two or more races, non-Hispanic/Latino), 13 international. Average age 32. 34 applicants, 76% accepted, 18 enrolled. In 2017, 30 master's awarded. *Degree requirements:* For master's, variable foreign language requirement, comprehensive exam (for some programs), thesis (for some programs), portfolio. *Entrance requirements:* For master's, 18-24 hours of course work in English language and literature; writing sample; essay. Additional exam requirements/recommendations for international students: Required—TOEFL (minimum score 550 paper-based; 79 iBT), IELTS (minimum score 6.5). *Application deadline:* For fall admission, 7/15 for international students; for spring admission, 11/15 for international students. Applications are processed on a rolling basis. Application fee: $60. Electronic applications accepted. *Expenses:* Tuition, state resident: full-time $5375; part-time $268.75 per credit hour. Tuition, nonresident: full-time $13,295; part-time $664.75 per credit hour. *Required fees:* $626; $31.30 per credit hour. One-time fee: $50. Tuition and fees vary according to program. *Financial support:* In 2017–18, 22 students received support, including 4 research assistantships with partial tuition reimbursements available (averaging $11,830 per year), 8 teaching assistantships with partial tuition reimbursements available (averaging $11,830 per year); career-related internships or fieldwork, Federal Work-Study, scholarships/grants, tuition waivers (partial), and unspecified assistantships also available. Financial award application deadline: 3/31; financial award applicants required to submit FAFSA. *Unit head:* Dr. Matt Hollrah, Chairperson, 405-974-5540, Fax: 405-974-3823, E-mail: gradcoll@uco.edu. Website: http://www.uco.edu/la/english/

University of Cincinnati, Graduate School, College of Education, Criminal Justice, and Human Services, School of Education, Program in Literacy and Second Language Studies, Cincinnati, OH 45221. Offers M Ed, Ed D. *Accreditation:* NCATE. *Program availability:* Part-time. *Degree requirements:* For master's, thesis or alternative; for doctorate, thesis/dissertation. *Entrance requirements:* For master's, GRE General Test. Additional exam requirements/recommendations for international students: Required—TOEFL (minimum score 550 paper-based), TWE (minimum score 4.5), OEPT. Electronic applications accepted. *Expenses: Tuition, area resident:* Full-time $14,468. Tuition, state resident: full-time $14,968; part-time $754 per credit hour. Tuition, nonresident: full-time $24,210; part-time $1311 per credit hour. *International tuition:* $26,460 full-time. *Required fees:* $3958; $84 per credit hour. One-time fee: $85 full-time. Tuition and fees vary according to course load, degree level and program.

University of Colorado Colorado Springs, College of Education, Colorado Springs, CO 80918. Offers counseling and human services (MA); curriculum and instruction (MA); educational leadership (MA); educational leadership, research and policy (PhD); special education (MA); teaching English to speakers of other languages (MA). *Accreditation:* ACA; NCATE. *Program availability:* Part-time, evening/weekend, 100% online, blended/hybrid learning. *Faculty:* 30 full-time (21 women), 61 part-time/adjunct (38 women). *Students:* 190 full-time (132 women), 286 part-time (202 women); includes 117 minority (20 Black or African American, non-Hispanic/Latino; 2 American Indian or Alaska Native, non-Hispanic/Latino; 12 Asian, non-Hispanic/Latino; 59 Hispanic/Latino; 24 Two or more races, non-Hispanic/Latino), 6 international. Average age 36. 169 applicants, 85% accepted, 113 enrolled. In 2017, 160 master's, 16 doctorates awarded. *Degree requirements:* For master's, comprehensive exam, thesis or alternative, microcomputer proficiency; for doctorate, comprehensive exam, thesis/dissertation, research lab. *Entrance requirements:* For master's and doctorate, GRE General Test. Additional exam requirements/recommendations for international students: Recommended—TOEFL (minimum score 550 paper-based; 80 iBT), IELTS (minimum score 6). *Application deadline:* For fall admission, 1/28 priority date for domestic and

international students; for spring admission, 11/1 priority date for domestic and international students. Applications are processed on a rolling basis. Application fee: $60 ($100 for international students). Electronic applications accepted. *Expenses:* $10,350 per year resident tuition, $20,935 nonresident, $11,961 nonresidential online; annual costs vary depending on program, course-load, and residency status. *Financial support:* In 2017–18, 81 students received support. Career-related internships or fieldwork, Federal Work-Study, scholarships/grants, and unspecified assistantships available. Support available to part-time students. Financial award application deadline: 3/1; financial award applicants required to submit FAFSA. *Faculty research:* Linguistically diverse education (LDE), educational policy, evidence-based reading and writing instruction, relational and social aggression, positive behavior supports, inclusive schooling, K-12 education policy. *Total annual research expenditures:* $607,967. *Unit head:* Dr. Valerie Martin Conley, Dean, 719-255-4133, E-mail: vmconley@uccs.edu. *Application contact:* The College of Education Student Resource Office, 719-255-4996, E-mail: education@uccs.edu.
Website: http://www.uccs.edu/coe

University of Dayton, Department of English, Dayton, OH 45469. Offers literary and cultural studies (MA); teaching English to speakers of other languages (TESOL) (MA); writing and rhetoric (MA). *Program availability:* Part-time. *Faculty:* 22 full-time (11 women). *Students:* 20 full-time (14 women), 1 (woman) part-time; includes 2 minority (both Black or African American, non-Hispanic/Latino), 7 international. Average age 26. 35 applicants, 34% accepted. In 2017, 9 master's awarded. *Degree requirements:* For master's, thesis optional. *Entrance requirements:* For master's, 24 undergraduate-level semester hours in literature and/or writing; minimum GPA of 3.0; transcripts; personal statement; 8-10 page writing sample; three professional letters of recommendation. Additional exam requirements/recommendations for international students: Required—TOEFL (minimum score 550 paper-based, 80 iBT) or IELTS. *Application deadline:* For fall admission, 6/15 priority date for domestic and international students; for spring admission, 12/15 priority date for domestic and international students. Applications are processed on a rolling basis. Application fee: $0 ($50 for international students). Electronic applications accepted. Tuition and fees vary according to degree level and program. *Financial support:* In 2017–18, 9 teaching assistantships with full tuition reimbursements (averaging $11,105 per year) were awarded; institutionally sponsored loans also available. Financial award application deadline: 3/1; financial award applicants required to submit FAFSA. *Faculty research:* Gender and Victorian periodicals; literature and human rights; Paul Lawrence Dunbar; the archetype of the Indian princess; Amish country. *Unit head:* Dr. Andrew Slade, Chair, 937-229-3434, Fax: 937-229-3563, E-mail: aslade1@udayton.edu. *Application contact:* Dr. Tereza Szeghi, Director of Graduate Studies, 937-229-3443, E-mail: tszeghi@udayton.edu.
Website: https://www.udayton.edu/artssciences/academics/english/welcome/index.php

University of Delaware, College of Education and Human Development, School of Education, Newark, DE 19716. Offers education (PhD); educational leadership (Ed D); higher education (M Ed); instruction (MI); reading (M Ed); school leadership (M Ed); school psychology (MA, Ed S); teaching English as a second language (TESL) (MA). *Accreditation:* NCATE. *Program availability:* Part-time, evening/weekend. Terminal master's awarded for partial completion of doctoral program. *Degree requirements:* For master's, comprehensive exam (for some programs), thesis (for some programs); for doctorate, comprehensive exam (for some programs), thesis/dissertation. *Entrance requirements:* For master's and doctorate, GRE, 3 letters of recommendation. Additional exam requirements/recommendations for international students: Required—TOEFL (minimum score 600 paper-based). Electronic applications accepted. *Faculty research:* Teacher education; curriculum theory and development; community based education models, educational leadership.

The University of Findlay, Office of Graduate Admissions, Findlay, OH 45840. Offers applied security and analytics (MSAS); athletic training (MAT); business (MBA), including certified management accountant, certified public accountant, health care management, hospitality management; education (MA Ed, Ed D), including children's literature (MA Ed), curriculum and teaching (MA Ed), education (MA Ed), educational administration (MA Ed), human resource development (MA Ed), mathematics (MA Ed), reading (MA Ed), science education (MA Ed), superintendent (Ed D), teaching (Ed D), technology (MA Ed); environmental, safety, and health management (MSEM); health informatics (MS); occupational therapy (MOT); pharmacy (Pharm D); physical therapy (DPT); physician assistant (MPA); rhetoric and writing (MA); teaching English to speakers of other languages (TESOL) and applied linguistics (MA). *Program availability:* Part-time, evening/weekend, 100% online, blended/hybrid learning. *Students:* 688 full-time (430 women), 553 part-time (308 women), 170 international. Average age 28. In 2017, 366 master's, 137 doctorates awarded. *Degree requirements:* For master's, comprehensive exam (for some programs), thesis (for some programs), cumulative project, capstone project; for doctorate, thesis/dissertation (for some programs). *Entrance requirements:* For master's, GRE/GMAT, bachelor's degree from accredited institution, minimum undergraduate GPA of 2.5 in last 64 hours of course work; for doctorate, GRE, MAT, minimum cumulative GPA of 3.0. Additional exam requirements/recommendations for international students: Required—TOEFL (minimum score 79 iBT), IELTS (minimum score 7), PTE (minimum score 61). *Application deadline:* Applications are processed on a rolling basis. Electronic applications accepted. *Financial support:* In 2017–18, 10 research assistantships with partial tuition reimbursements (averaging $7,200 per year), 35 teaching assistantships with partial tuition reimbursements (averaging $7,200 per year) were awarded; Federal Work-Study, institutionally sponsored loans, and unspecified assistantships also available. Financial award applicants required to submit FAFSA. *Unit head:* Christopher M. Harris, Director of Admissions, 419-434-4347, E-mail: harrisc1@findlay.edu. *Application contact:* Madeline Fauser Brennan, Graduate Admissions Counselor, 419-434-4636, Fax: 419-434-4898, E-mail: fauserbrennan@findlay.edu.
Website: http://www.findlay.edu/admissions/graduate/Pages/default.aspx

University of Florida, Graduate School, College of Liberal Arts and Sciences, Department of Linguistics, Gainesville, FL 32611. Offers linguistics (MA, PhD); teaching English as a second language (Certificate). *Program availability:* Part-time. Terminal master's awarded for partial completion of doctoral program. *Degree requirements:* For master's, one foreign language, comprehensive exam, thesis (for some programs); for doctorate, 2 foreign languages, comprehensive exam, thesis/dissertation. *Entrance requirements:* For master's and doctorate, GRE General Test, minimum GPA of 3.0. Additional exam requirements/recommendations for international students: Required—TOEFL (minimum score 550 paper-based; 80 iBT), IELTS (minimum score 6). Electronic applications accepted. *Faculty research:* Language documentation, psycholinguistics and neuro-linguistics, theoretical linguistics, sociolinguistics second language acquisition.

University of Guam, Office of Graduate Studies, School of Education, Program in Teaching English to Speakers of Other Languages, Mangilao, GU 96923. Offers M Ed. *Degree requirements:* For master's, comprehensive oral and written exams, special project or thesis. *Entrance requirements:* For master's, GRE General Test. Additional exam requirements/recommendations for international students: Required—TOEFL.

University of Hawaii at Manoa, Office of Graduate Education, College of Languages, Linguistics and Literature, Department of Second Language Studies, Honolulu, HI

96822. Offers English as a second language (MA, Graduate Certificate); second language acquisition (PhD). *Program availability:* Part-time. *Degree requirements:* For master's, 2 foreign languages, thesis optional; for doctorate, 2 foreign languages, comprehensive exam, thesis/dissertation. *Entrance requirements:* For master's, GRE General Test, minimum GPA of 3.0; for doctorate, GRE General Test, MA, scholarly publications. Additional exam requirements/recommendations for international students: Required—TOEFL (minimum score 600 paper-based; 100 iBT), IELTS (minimum score 7). *Faculty research:* Second language use, second language analysis, second language pedagogy and testing, second language learning, qualitative and quantitative research methods for second languages.

University of Illinois at Chicago, College of Liberal Arts and Sciences, School of Literatures, Cultural Studies and Linguistics, Chicago, IL 60607-7128. Offers French and Francophone studies (MA); Germanic studies (MA); Hispanic and Italian studies (MAT, PhD), including Hispanic linguistics (PhD), Hispanic literary and cultural studies (PhD), teaching of Spanish (MAT); linguistics (MA), including teaching English to speakers of other languages/applied linguistics; Slavic and Baltic languages and literatures (MA), including Slavic studies (MA, PhD); Slavic and Baltic languages and literatures (PhD), including Slavic studies (MA, PhD). *Program availability:* Part-time. Terminal master's awarded for partial completion of doctoral program. *Degree requirements:* For master's, one foreign language, exam. *Entrance requirements:* For master's, minimum GPA of 2.75. Additional exam requirements/recommendations for international students: Required—TOEFL. Electronic applications accepted. *Faculty research:* International studies, religious (Catholic, Jewish) studies, moving image arts.

University of Illinois at Springfield, Graduate Programs, College of Education and Human Services, Department of Educational Leadership, Springfield, IL 62703-5407. Offers chief school business official (CAS); educational leadership (MA, CAS); educational technology (Graduate Certificate); English as a second language (Graduate Certificate); higher education online pedagogy (Graduate Certificate); leadership and learning (Graduate Certificate); legal aspects of education (Graduate Certificate). *Program availability:* Part-time, evening/weekend, 100% online, blended/hybrid learning. *Faculty:* 4 full-time (1 woman), 14 part-time/adjunct (11 women). *Students:* 2 full-time (1 woman), 109 part-time (70 women); includes 15 minority (10 Black or African American, non-Hispanic/Latino; 1 American Indian or Alaska Native, non-Hispanic/Latino; 1 Asian, non-Hispanic/Latino; 3 Hispanic/Latino). Average age 35. 46 applicants, 57% accepted, 23 enrolled. In 2017, 30 master's, 5 other advanced degrees awarded. *Degree requirements:* For master's, capstone course. *Entrance requirements:* For master's, minimum undergraduate GPA of 3.0, valid Illinois Teaching License, minimum of two years of successful teaching experience, portfolio that includes letters of recommendation, interview. Additional exam requirements/recommendations for international students: Required—TOEFL (minimum score 500 paper-based; 61 iBT). *Application deadline:* Applications are processed on a rolling basis. Application fee: $60 ($75 for international students). Electronic applications accepted. *Expenses:* Tuition, state resident: full-time $7896; part-time $329 per credit hour. Tuition, nonresident: full-time $16,200; part-time $675 per credit hour. Tuition and fees vary according to program. *Financial support:* In 2017–18, research assistantships with full tuition reimbursements (averaging $10,249 per year), teaching assistantships with full tuition reimbursements (averaging $10,303 per year) were awarded; fellowships, career-related internships or fieldwork, Federal Work-Study, scholarships/grants, health care benefits, and unspecified assistantships also available. Support available to part-time students. Financial award application deadline: 11/15; financial award applicants required to submit FAFSA. *Unit head:* Dr. Scott Day, Program Administrator, 217-206-7520, Fax: 217-206-6775, E-mail: day.scott@uis.edu.
Website: http://www.uis.edu/edl/

University of Illinois at Urbana–Champaign, Graduate College, College of Liberal Arts and Sciences, School of Literatures, Cultures and Linguistics, Department of Linguistics, Champaign, IL 61820. Offers linguistics (MA, PhD); teaching of English as a second language (MA).

University of Illinois at Urbana–Champaign, Graduate College, College of Liberal Arts and Sciences, School of Literatures, Cultures and Linguistics, Program in Second Language Acquisition and Teacher Education, Champaign, IL 61820. Offers PhD.

The University of Iowa, Graduate College, College of Education, Department of Teaching and Learning, Program in Education, Iowa City, IA 52242-1316. Offers art education (MA); developmental reading (MA); elementary education (MA); English education (MA, MAT); foreign and second language education (MAT); foreign language education (MA); foreign language/ESL education (PhD); language, literacy and culture (PhD); mathematics education (MA, MAT, PhD); music education (MM, PhD); science education (MA); secondary education (MA); social studies (MA, PhD). *Degree requirements:* For master's, thesis optional, exam; for doctorate, comprehensive exam, thesis/dissertation. *Entrance requirements:* For master's and doctorate, GRE General Test, minimum GPA of 3.0. Additional exam requirements/recommendations for international students: Required—TOEFL (minimum score 550 paper-based; 81 iBT). Electronic applications accepted.

The University of Manchester, School of Languages, Linguistics and Cultures, Manchester, United Kingdom. Offers Arab world studies (PhD); Chinese studies (M Phil, PhD); East Asian studies (M Phil, PhD); English language (PhD); French studies (M Phil, PhD); German studies (M Phil, PhD); interpreting studies (PhD); Italian studies (M Phil, PhD); Japanese studies (M Phil, PhD); Latin American cultural studies (M Phil, PhD); linguistics (M Phil, PhD); Middle Eastern studies (M Phil, PhD); Polish studies (M Phil, PhD); Portuguese studies (M Phil, PhD); Russian studies (M Phil, PhD); Spanish studies (M Phil, PhD); translation and intercultural studies (M Phil, PhD).

University of Manitoba, Faculty of Graduate Studies, Faculty of Education, Department of Curriculum, Teaching and Learning, Winnipeg, MB R3T 2N2, Canada. Offers language and literacy (M Ed); second language education (M Ed); studies in curriculum, teaching and learning (M Ed). *Degree requirements:* For master's, thesis or alternative.

University of Maryland, Baltimore County, The Graduate School, College of Arts, Humanities and Social Sciences, Department of Education, Program in Teaching English to Speakers of Other Languages, Baltimore, MD 21250. Offers MA, Postbaccalaureate Certificate. *Program availability:* Part-time, evening/weekend, 100% online, blended/hybrid learning. *Faculty:* 4 full-time (all women), 15 part-time/adjunct (10 women). *Students:* 27 full-time (20 women), 97 part-time (81 women); includes 28 minority (8 Black or African American, non-Hispanic/Latino; 14 Asian, non-Hispanic/Latino; 6 Hispanic/Latino). Average age 35. 34 applicants, 97% accepted, 32 enrolled. In 2017, 32 master's, 22 other advanced degrees awarded. *Degree requirements:* For master's, thesis optional; for Postbaccalaureate Certificate, internship. *Entrance requirements:* For master's, GRE (minimum score 500 verbal, 150 on the new version, or 297 composite), 3 letters of reference, statement of purpose. Additional exam requirements/recommendations for international students: Required—TOEFL (minimum score 550 paper-based; 80 iBT). *Application deadline:* For fall admission, 8/1 priority date for domestic students, 4/1 priority date for international students; for spring admission, 1/1 priority date for domestic students, 11/1 priority date for international students. Applications are processed on a rolling basis. Application fee: $50. Electronic applications accepted. *Expenses: Required fees:* $132. *Financial support:* In 2017–18,

34 students received support, including 1 research assistantship with full tuition reimbursement available (averaging $13,000 per year); career-related internships or fieldwork, Federal Work-Study, scholarships/grants, and unspecified assistantships also available. *Faculty research:* Adult education, bilingual language learning, online instruction, English grammar, cross-culture communication, ESL teacher professional identity. *Unit head:* Doaa Rashed, Director, 410-455-6773, E-mail: doaa1@umbc.edu. *Application contact:* Keneisha Murrell, Graduate Assistant, 410-455-3061, E-mail: esol@umbc.edu.
Website: http://www.umbc.edu/education/

University of Maryland, College Park, Academic Affairs, College of Education, Department of Teaching, Learning, Policy and Leadership, College Park, MD 20742. Offers (M Ed, MA, PhD, CAGS); secondary education (M Ed, MA, Ed D, PhD, CAGS); teaching English to speakers of other languages (M Ed). *Accreditation:* NCATE. *Program availability:* Part-time, evening/weekend, online learning. *Degree requirements:* For master's, comprehensive exam, seminar paper; for doctorate, comprehensive exam, thesis/dissertation, published paper, oral exam. *Entrance requirements:* For master's, GRE General Test or MAT, minimum GPA of 3.0, 3 letters of recommendation; for doctorate, GRE General Test or MAT, minimum undergraduate GPA of 3.0, graduate 3.5; 3 letters of recommendation. Electronic applications accepted. *Faculty research:* Teacher preparation, curriculum study, in-service education.

University of Massachusetts Amherst, Graduate School, College of Education, Program in Education, Amherst, MA 01003. Offers bilingual, English as a second language, and multicultural education (M Ed, Ed S); child study and early education (M Ed); children, families and schools (Ed D, Ed S); early childhood and elementary teacher education (M Ed); educational leadership (M Ed); educational policy and leadership (Ed D); higher education (M Ed); international education (M Ed); language, literacy and culture (Ed D); learning, media and technology (M Ed, Ed S); mathematics, science, and learning technologies (M Ed); reading and writing (M Ed); research, educational measurement and psychometrics (Ed D); school counselor education (M Ed, Ed S); school psychology (Ed S); science education (Ed S); secondary teacher education (M Ed); social justice education (M Ed, Ed D, Ed S); special education (M Ed, Ed D, Ed S); teacher education and school improvement (Ed D, Ed S). *Accreditation:* NCATE. *Program availability:* Part-time, online learning. Terminal master's awarded for partial completion of doctoral program. *Degree requirements:* For doctorate, comprehensive exam, thesis/dissertation. *Entrance requirements:* Additional exam requirements/recommendations for international students: Required—TOEFL (minimum score 550 paper-based; 80 iBT), IELTS (minimum score 6.5). Electronic applications accepted.

University of Massachusetts Dartmouth, Graduate School, College of Arts and Sciences, School of Education, Department of STEM Education and Teacher Development, North Dartmouth, MA 02747-2300. Offers English as a second language (Postbaccalaureate Certificate); mathematics education (PhD); middle school education (MAT); secondary school education (MAT). *Program availability:* Part-time. *Faculty:* 9 full-time (6 women), 11 part-time/adjunct (7 women). *Students:* 26 full-time (15 women), 102 part-time (60 women); includes 16 minority (2 Black or African American, non-Hispanic/Latino; 2 Asian, non-Hispanic/Latino; 6 Hispanic/Latino; 6 Two or more races, non-Hispanic/Latino), 2 international. Average age 32. 60 applicants, 92% accepted, 51 enrolled. In 2017, 41 master's, 2 doctorates awarded. *Degree requirements:* For doctorate, thesis/dissertation. *Entrance requirements:* For master's, statement of purpose (minimum of 300 words), resume, 2 letters of recommendation, official transcripts; for doctorate, GRE, statement of purpose (minimum of 300 words), resume, official transcripts, 3 letters of recommendation. Additional exam requirements/recommendations for international students: Required—TOEFL (minimum score 533 paper-based; 72 iBT), IELTS (minimum score 6). *Application deadline:* For fall admission, 2/15 priority date for domestic students, 1/15 priority date for international students; for spring admission, 1/15 priority date for domestic students, 12/15 priority date for international students. Application fee: $60. Electronic applications accepted. *Expenses:* Tuition, state resident: full-time $15,449; part-time $643.71 per credit. Tuition, nonresident: full-time $27,880; part-time $1161.67 per credit. *Required fees:* $405; $25.88 per credit. Tuition and fees vary according to course load and reciprocity agreements. *Financial support:* In 2017–18, 2 fellowships (averaging $16,000 per year), 4 research assistantships (averaging $20,656 per year), 2 teaching assistantships (averaging $16,000 per year) were awarded; tuition waivers (full) and unspecified assistantships also available. Support available to part-time students. Financial award application deadline: 3/1; financial award applicants required to submit FAFSA. *Faculty research:* Mindfulness in education, literacies, assessment of teacher knowledge, curriculum tools for supporting mathematics learning. *Total annual research expenditures:* $1.6 million. *Unit head:* Traci Almeida, Coordinator of Graduate Admissions and Licensure, 508-999-8098, Fax: 508-910-8183, E-mail: talmeida@umassd.edu. *Application contact:* Steven Briggs, Director of Marketing and Recruitment for Graduate Studies, 508-999-8604, Fax: 508-999-8183, E-mail: graduate@umassd.edu.
Website: http://www.umassd.edu/cas/schoolofeducation/departments/stemeducationandteacherdevelopment/

University of Memphis, Graduate School, College of Arts and Sciences, Department of English, Memphis, TN 38152. Offers African-American literature (Graduate Certificate); applied linguistics (PhD); composition studies (PhD); creative writing (MFA); English as a second language (MA); linguistics (MA); literary and cultural studies (PhD), including African-American literature; literature (MA); professional writing (MA, PhD); teaching English as a second/foreign language (Graduate Certificate). *Program availability:* Part-time, evening/weekend, 100% online. *Faculty:* 30 full-time (15 women). *Students:* 73 full-time (34 women), 80 part-time (52 women); includes 35 minority (20 Black or African American, non-Hispanic/Latino; 3 Asian, non-Hispanic/Latino; 9 Hispanic/Latino; 3 Two or more races, non-Hispanic/Latino), 36 international. Average age 35. 78 applicants, 88% accepted, 35 enrolled. In 2017, 27 master's, 15 doctorates, 10 other advanced degrees awarded. Terminal master's awarded for partial completion of doctoral program. *Degree requirements:* For master's, one foreign language, comprehensive exam, thesis optional; for doctorate, 2 foreign languages, comprehensive exam, thesis/dissertation, qualifying exam. *Entrance requirements:* For master's, GRE, minimum undergraduate GPA of 3.0, statement of purpose, two letters of recommendation; for doctorate, GRE, minimum undergraduate and graduate GPA of 3.25, statement of purpose, writing sample, three letters of recommendation. Additional exam requirements/recommendations for international students: Required—TOEFL. *Application deadline:* For fall admission, 1/15 for domestic students; for spring admission, 10/15 for domestic students. Applications are processed on a rolling basis. Application fee: $35 ($60 for international students). Electronic applications accepted. *Expenses:* Contact institution. *Financial support:* In 2017–18, 123 students received support, including 16 research assistantships with full tuition reimbursements available (averaging $15,704 per year), 23 teaching assistantships with full tuition reimbursements available (averaging $22,076 per year); Federal Work-Study, scholarships/grants, and unspecified assistantships also available. Financial award application deadline: 2/1; financial award applicants required to submit FAFSA. *Faculty research:* Applied linguistics, British and American literature, professional writing, composition studies. *Unit head:* Dr. Joshua Phillips, Chair, 901-678-2651, Fax: 901-678-2226, E-mail: jsphllps@memphis.edu. *Application contact:* Dr. Jeffrey Scraba, Coordinator of Graduate Studies, 901-678-4768, Fax: 901-678-2226, E-mail: jscraba@memphis.edu.
Website: http://www.memphis.edu/english

University of Minnesota, Twin Cities Campus, Graduate School, College of Education and Human Development, Department of Curriculum and Instruction, Minneapolis, MN 55455-0213. Offers art education (M Ed, MA, PhD); curriculum and instruction (M Ed, MA, PhD); elementary education (MA, PhD); English education (PhD); language and immersion education (Certificate); learning technologies (MA, PhD); literacy education (MA, PhD); second language education (MA, PhD); social studies education (MA, PhD); STEM education (MA, PhD); teaching (M Ed), including mathematics, science, social studies, teaching; teaching English to speakers of other languages (MA); technology enhanced learning (Certificate). *Faculty:* 37 full-time (21 women). *Students:* 401 full-time (282 women), 303 part-time (212 women); includes 139 minority (26 Black or African American, non-Hispanic/Latino; 4 American Indian or Alaska Native, non-Hispanic/Latino; 34 Asian, non-Hispanic/Latino; 45 Hispanic/Latino; 1 Native Hawaiian or other Pacific Islander, non-Hispanic/Latino; 29 Two or more races, non-Hispanic/Latino), 43 international. Average age 32. 596 applicants, 61% accepted, 330 enrolled. In 2017, 316 master's, 30 doctorates, 19 other advanced degrees awarded. Application fee: $75 ($95 for international students). *Financial support:* In 2017–18, 3 fellowships, 56 research assistantships with full tuition reimbursements (averaging $11,118 per year), 67 teaching assistantships with full tuition reimbursements (averaging $11,975 per year) were awarded. *Faculty research:* Teaching and learning; influence of cultural, linguistic, social, political, and technological factors on teaching, learning and educational research; relationship between educational practice and a democratic and just society; urban education; immigrant education, racial justice and education. *Total annual research expenditures:* $2.2 million. *Unit head:* Dr. Cynthia Lewis, Chair, 612-625-6313, E-mail: lewis@umn.edu. *Application contact:* Dr. Gillian Roehrig, Director of Graduate Studies, 612-625-0561, E-mail: roehr013@umn.edu.
Website: http://www.cehd.umn.edu/ci

University of Minnesota, Twin Cities Campus, Graduate School, College of Liberal Arts, Institute of Linguistics, English as a Second Language, and Slavic Languages and Literatures (ILES), English as a Second Language Program, Minneapolis, MN 55455-0213. Offers MA. *Degree requirements:* For master's, one foreign language, comprehensive exam, thesis. *Entrance requirements:* For master's, GRE, 3 letters of recommendation. Additional exam requirements/recommendations for international students: Required—TOEFL (minimum score 600 paper-based). Electronic applications accepted. *Faculty research:* Second language acquisitions, communication strategies, English for specific purposes, literacy, speech act, proymatics in general, language assessment, discourse analysis, research methods.

University of Missouri–St. Louis, College of Education, Department of Educator Preparation, Innovation and Research, St. Louis, MO 63121. Offers elementary education (M Ed), including early childhood, general, reading; secondary education (M Ed), including curriculum and instruction, general, middle level education, reading, teaching English to speakers of other languages (TESOL); special education (M Ed), including autism and developmental disabilities, early childhood special education. *Program availability:* Part-time, evening/weekend. *Students:* 75 full-time (63 women), 462 part-time (363 women); includes 127 minority (85 Black or African American, non-Hispanic/Latino; 2 American Indian or Alaska Native, non-Hispanic/Latino; 8 Asian, non-Hispanic/Latino; 24 Hispanic/Latino; 8 Two or more races, non-Hispanic/Latino), 1 international. 247 applicants, 92% accepted, 153 enrolled. *Degree requirements:* For master's, comprehensive exam. *Entrance requirements:* Additional exam requirements/recommendations for international students: Recommended—TOEFL (minimum score 550 paper-based; 79 iBT), IELTS (minimum score 6.5). *Application deadline:* For fall admission, 7/1 priority date for domestic and international students; for spring admission, 12/1 priority date for domestic and international students. Application fee: $50 ($40 for international students). Electronic applications accepted. *Expenses:* Tuition, state resident: part-time $476.50 per credit hour. Tuition, nonresident: part-time $1169.70 per credit hour. *Financial support:* Application deadline: 4/1; applicants required to submit FAFSA. *Unit head:* Dr. Gayle Wilkinson, Chair, 314-516-5791. *Application contact:* 314-516-5458, Fax: 314-516-6996, E-mail: gadadm@umsl.edu.
Website: https://coe.umsl.edu/dept/epir.html

University of Nebraska at Kearney, College of Education, Department of Teacher Education, Kearney, NE 68849-0001. Offers curriculum and instruction (MA Ed), including early childhood education, elementary education, English as a second language, instructional effectiveness, reading/special education, secondary education; instructional technology (MS Ed), including information technology, instructional technology, school librarian; reading PK-12 (MA Ed); special education (MA Ed), including advanced practitioner: assistive technology specialist, advanced practitioner: behavioral interventionist, advanced practitioner: inclusive collaboration specialist, gifted, teacher education. *Program availability:* Part-time, evening/weekend, online only, 100% online. *Degree requirements:* For master's, comprehensive exam, thesis optional. *Entrance requirements:* For master's, portfolio or GRE. Additional exam requirements/recommendations for international students: Recommended—TOEFL (minimum score 550 paper-based; 79 iBT), IELTS (minimum score 6.5). Electronic applications accepted. *Expenses:* Contact institution.

University of Nebraska at Omaha, Graduate Studies, College of Arts and Sciences, Department of English, Omaha, NE 68182. Offers advanced writing (Certificate); English (MA); teaching English to speakers of other languages (Certificate); technical communication (Certificate). *Program availability:* Part-time, evening/weekend. *Degree requirements:* For master's, comprehensive exam, thesis (for some programs). *Entrance requirements:* For master's, GRE or MAT, minimum GPA of 3.0, transcripts, 3 letters of recommendation, statement of purpose, writing sample; for Certificate, minimum GPA of 3.0, transcripts, statement of purpose. Additional exam requirements/recommendations for international students: Required—TOEFL, IELTS, PTE. Electronic applications accepted.

University of Nevada, Las Vegas, Graduate College, College of Education, Department of Educational and Clinical Studies, Las Vegas, NV 89154-3066. Offers addiction studies (Advanced Certificate); counselor education (M Ed, MS), including clinical mental health (MS), school counseling (M Ed); early childhood education (M Ed); early childhood special education (Certificate), including infancy, preschool; English language learning (M Ed); mental health counseling (Advanced Certificate); special education (M Ed, PhD); PhD/JD. *Program availability:* Part-time. *Faculty:* 18 full-time (9 women), 28 part-time/adjunct (22 women). *Students:* 281 full-time (230 women), 193 part-time (148 women); includes 211 minority (54 Black or African American, non-Hispanic/Latino; 2 American Indian or Alaska Native, non-Hispanic/Latino; 28 Asian, non-Hispanic/Latino; 95 Hispanic/Latino; 4 Native Hawaiian or other Pacific Islander, non-Hispanic/Latino; 28 Two or more races, non-Hispanic/Latino), 13 international. Average age 34. 262 applicants, 76% accepted, 161 enrolled. In 2017, 204 master's, 8 doctorates, 1 other advanced degree awarded. *Degree requirements:* For master's, comprehensive exam (for some programs); for doctorate, comprehensive exam, thesis/dissertation; for other advanced degree, final project. *Entrance requirements:* For

English as a Second Language

master's, bachelor's degree; letter of recommendation; statement of purpose; for doctorate, GRE General Test, statement of purpose; writing sample; 3 letters of recommendation. Additional exam requirements/recommendations for international students: Required—TOEFL (minimum score 550 paper-based; 80 iBT), IELTS (minimum score 7). Application fee: $60 ($95 for international students). Electronic applications accepted. *Expenses:* $275 per credit, $850 per course, $7,969 per year resident, $22,157 per year non-resident, $7,094 non-resident fee (7 credits or more), $1,307 annual health insurance fee. *Financial support:* In 2017–18, 35 students received support, including 10 research assistantships with full tuition reimbursements available (averaging $13,775 per year), 25 teaching assistantships with full tuition reimbursements available (averaging $17,140 per year); institutionally sponsored loans, scholarships/grants, health care benefits, and unspecified assistantships also available. Financial award application deadline: 3/15; financial award applicants required to submit FAFSA. *Faculty research:* Multicultural issues in counseling, academic interventions for students with disabilities, establishment of pro-social skills in young children with severe disabilities, inclusive strategies for students with disabilities, language and literacy for English language learners. *Total annual research expenditures:* $1.1 million. *Unit head:* Dr. Monica Brown, Interim Department Chair/Professor, 702-895-3167, Fax: 702-895-3205, E-mail: monica.brown@unlv.edu. *Application contact:* Dr. Joseph Morgan, Graduate Coordinator, 702-895-3329, Fax: 702-895-3205, E-mail: joseph.morgan@unlv.edu.
Website: http://education.unlv.edu/ecs/

University of Nevada, Reno, Graduate School, College of Education, Department of Educational Specialties, Program in Teaching English to Speakers of Other Languages, Reno, NV 89557. Offers MA. Terminal master's awarded for partial completion of doctoral program. *Degree requirements:* For master's, thesis optional. *Entrance requirements:* For master's, minimum GPA of 2.75. Additional exam requirements/recommendations for international students: Required—TOEFL (minimum score 500 paper-based; 61 iBT), IELTS (minimum score 6). Electronic applications accepted. *Faculty research:* Bilingualism, multicultural education.

University of New Mexico, Graduate Studies, College of Education, Program in Language, Literacy and Sociocultural Studies, Albuquerque, NM 87131. Offers American Indian education (MA); bilingual education (MA, PhD); educational linguistics (PhD); educational thought and sociocultural studies (MA, PhD); literacy/language arts (MA, PhD); social studies (MA); TESOL (MA, PhD). *Faculty:* 16 full-time (10 women), 4 part-time/adjunct (all women). *Students:* 56 full-time (34 women), 129 part-time (97 women); includes 93 minority (7 Black or African American, non-Hispanic/Latino; 15 American Indian or Alaska Native, non-Hispanic/Latino; 9 Asian, non-Hispanic/Latino; 56 Hispanic/Latino; 6 Two or more races, non-Hispanic/Latino), 44 international. Average age 40. 61 applicants, 38% accepted, 23 enrolled. In 2017, 36 master's, 4 doctorates awarded. *Degree requirements:* For master's, comprehensive exam, thesis optional; for doctorate, comprehensive exam, thesis/dissertation, research skills. *Entrance requirements:* For master's, letter of intent, 3 letters of recommendation, resume, BA/BS, department demographic form, transcripts; for doctorate, writing sample, letter of intent, 3 letters of recommendation, resume, BA/BS, MA, department demographic form, transcripts. Additional exam requirements/recommendations for international students: Required—TOEFL. *Application deadline:* For fall admission, 12/1 for domestic and international students; for spring admission, 9/15 for domestic and international students. Application fee: $50. Electronic applications accepted. *Financial support:* Fellowships, research assistantships, teaching assistantships, career-related internships or fieldwork, institutionally sponsored loans, scholarships/grants, and unspecified assistantships available. Support available to part-time students. Financial award application deadline: 3/1; financial award applicants required to submit FAFSA. *Faculty research:* School reform, professional development, history of education, Native American education, politics of education, feminism and issues of sexual identity, critical race theory, bilingualism, literacy reading, adolescent literature, second language acquisition, critical theory and schooling, indigenous languages. *Unit head:* Dr. Lois M. Meyer, Chair, 505-277-7244, Fax: 505-277-8362, E-mail: lsmeyer@unm.edu. *Application contact:* Debra Schaffer, Administrative Assistant, 505-277-0437, Fax: 505-277-8362, E-mail: schaffer@unm.edu.
Website: http://coe.unm.edu/departments-programs/llss/index.html

The University of North Carolina at Chapel Hill, Graduate School, School of Education, Program in Secondary Education, Chapel Hill, NC 27599. Offers English (Grades 9-12) (MAT); English as a second language (MAT); French (Grades K-12) (MAT); German (Grades K-12) (MAT); Japanese (Grades K-12) (MAT); Latin (Grades 9-12) (MAT); mathematics (Grades 9-12) (MAT); music (Grades K-12) (MAT); science (Grades 9-12) (MAT); social studies (Grades 9-12) (MAT); Spanish (Grades K-12) (MAT). *Accreditation:* NCATE. *Degree requirements:* For master's, comprehensive exam. *Entrance requirements:* For master's, GRE General Test, minimum GPA of 3.0 during last 2 years of undergraduate course work. Additional exam requirements/recommendations for international students: Required—TOEFL (minimum score 550 paper-based). Electronic applications accepted.

The University of North Carolina at Charlotte, Cato College of Education, Department of Middle, Secondary and K-12 Education, Charlotte, NC 28223-0001. Offers middle grades and secondary education (M Ed); teaching English as a second language (M Ed, Graduate Certificate). *Program availability:* Part-time. *Faculty:* 18 full-time (10 women), 5 part-time/adjunct (all women). *Students:* 3 full-time (all women), 93 part-time (85 women); includes 20 minority (18 Black or African American, non-Hispanic/Latino; 1 Asian, non-Hispanic/Latino; 1 Hispanic/Latino), 2 international. Average age 35. 71 applicants, 99% accepted, 61 enrolled. In 2017, 47 master's awarded. *Degree requirements:* For master's, thesis, comprehensive portfolio, or research project. *Entrance requirements:* For master's, GRE or MAT, bachelor's degree from accredited college or university; minimum GPA of 3.0 in undergraduate work; North Carolina Class A teaching license in appropriate middle grades or secondary education field; minimum of two years' teaching experience; written narrative providing statement of purpose for master's degree study; letters of recommendation; for Graduate Certificate, bachelor's degree from accredited institution; minimum undergraduate GPA of 2.5 overall or 3.0 in senior year, or 15 hours taken in the last 5 years; satisfactory recommendations from three persons knowledgeable of applicant's interactions with children or adolescents; statement of purpose. Additional exam requirements/recommendations for international students: Required—TOEFL (minimum score 523 paper-based, 70 iBT) or IELTS (6.5). *Application deadline:* For fall admission, 3/1 priority date for domestic and international students; for spring admission, 10/1 priority date for domestic and international students; for summer admission, 4/1 priority date for domestic and international students. Applications are processed on a rolling basis. Application fee: $75. Electronic applications accepted. *Expenses:* Tuition, state resident: full-time $4337. Tuition, nonresident: full-time $17,771. *Required fees:* $3211. Tuition and fees vary according to course load and program. *Financial support:* In 2017–18, 6 students received support, including 5 research assistantships (averaging $13,800 per year), 1 teaching assistantship (averaging $3,500 per year); career-related internships or fieldwork, institutionally sponsored loans, scholarships/grants, and unspecified assistantships also available. Support available to part-time students. Financial award application deadline: 3/1; financial award applicants required to submit FAFSA. *Total annual research expenditures:* $115,616. *Unit head:* Scott Kissau, Chair, 704-687-8875, E-mail: spkissau@uncc.edu. *Application contact:* Kathy B. Giddings, Director of Graduate Admissions, 704-687-5503, Fax: 704-687-1668, E-mail: gradadm@uncc.edu.
Website: http://mdsk.uncc.edu

The University of North Carolina at Charlotte, Cato College of Education, Interdisciplinary Education Programs, Charlotte, NC 28223-0001. Offers art education (Graduate Certificate); child and family development: early childhood education (MAT); curriculum and instruction (PhD); elementary education (MAT); foreign language education (MAT); middle grades education (MAT); secondary education (MAT); special education (MAT); teaching (Graduate Certificate); teaching English as a second language (MAT); theatre education (Graduate Certificate). *Program availability:* Part-time, 100% online, blended/hybrid learning. *Students:* 86 full-time (63 women), 533 part-time (423 women); includes 229 minority (169 Black or African American, non-Hispanic/Latino; 1 American Indian or Alaska Native, non-Hispanic/Latino; 7 Asian, non-Hispanic/Latino; 39 Hispanic/Latino; 13 Two or more races, non-Hispanic/Latino), 13 international. Average age 32. 382 applicants, 91% accepted, 253 enrolled. In 2017, 182 master's, 10 doctorates, 172 other advanced degrees awarded. *Degree requirements:* For master's, thesis or alternative, research project/portfolio. *Entrance requirements:* For master's, GRE or MAT, bachelor's degree, or its U.S. equivalent, from regionally-accredited college or university; minimum overall GPA of 3.0 on all previous work beyond high school; statement of purpose (essay); at least three recommendation forms; for doctorate, GRE or MAT, bachelor's degree (or its U.S. equivalent) from regionally-accredited college or university; minimum overall GPA of 3.5 in master's degree program; for Graduate Certificate, bachelor's degree from regionally-accredited university; minimum GPA of 2.75 on all post-secondary work attempted; transcripts; personal statement outlining why the applicant seeks admission to the program. Additional exam requirements/recommendations for international students: Required—TOEFL (minimum score 523 paper-based, 70 iBT) or IELTS (6.5). *Application deadline:* For fall admission, 3/1 priority date for domestic and international students; for spring admission, 10/1 priority date for domestic and international students; for summer admission, 4/1 priority date for domestic and international students. Applications are processed on a rolling basis. Application fee: $75. Electronic applications accepted. *Expenses:* Tuition, state resident: full-time $4337. Tuition, nonresident: full-time $17,771. *Required fees:* $3211. Tuition and fees vary according to course load and program. *Financial support:* Career-related internships or fieldwork, institutionally sponsored loans, scholarships/grants, and unspecified assistantships available. Support available to part-time students. Financial award application deadline: 3/1; financial award applicants required to submit FAFSA. *Unit head:* Dr. Ellen McIntyre, Dean, 704-687-8722, E-mail: ellen.mcintyre@uncc.edu. *Application contact:* Kathy B. Giddings, Director of Graduate Admissions, 704-687-5503, Fax: 704-687-1668, E-mail: gradadm@uncc.edu.
Website: http://education.uncc.edu/academic-programs

The University of North Carolina at Greensboro, Graduate School, School of Education, Department of Teacher Education and Higher Education, Greensboro, NC 27412-5001. Offers college teaching and adult learning (Certificate); curriculum and instruction (M Ed), including chemistry education, elementary education, English as a second language, French education, instructional technology, mathematics education, middle grades education, reading education, science education, social studies education, Spanish education; curriculum and teaching (PhD), including higher education, teacher education and development; English as a second language (Certificate); higher education (M Ed); supervision (M Ed). *Accreditation:* NCATE. *Program availability:* Part-time. *Degree requirements:* For doctorate, thesis/dissertation. *Entrance requirements:* For master's and doctorate, GRE General Test. Additional exam requirements/recommendations for international students: Required—TOEFL. Electronic applications accepted. *Faculty research:* Community college literacy program, middle school mathematics/computer mathematics.

The University of North Carolina Wilmington, Watson College of Education, Department of Instructional Technology, Foundations and Secondary Education, Wilmington, NC 28403-3297. Offers English as a second language (M Ed, MAT); instructional technology (MS); secondary education (M Ed, MAT). *Program availability:* Part-time, blended/hybrid learning. *Faculty:* 15 full-time (9 women). *Students:* 38 full-time (24 women), 90 part-time (63 women); includes 29 minority (12 Black or African American, non-Hispanic/Latino; 2 Asian, non-Hispanic/Latino; 10 Hispanic/Latino; 5 Two or more races, non-Hispanic/Latino). Average age 34. 51 applicants, 84% accepted, 30 enrolled. In 2017, 44 master's awarded. *Degree requirements:* For master's, thesis or research project/portfolio. *Entrance requirements:* For master's, GRE or MAT, education statement of interest essay, 3 letters of recommendation. Additional exam requirements/recommendations for international students: Required—TOEFL (minimum score 550 paper-based; 79 iBT), IELTS (minimum score 6.5). *Application deadline:* For fall admission, 5/15 for domestic students; for spring admission, 10/15 for domestic students; for summer admission, 3/15 for domestic students. Applications are processed on a rolling basis. Application fee: $75. Electronic applications accepted. *Expenses:* Tuition, state resident: full-time $4626; part-time $226.76 per credit hour. Tuition, nonresident: full-time $17,834; part-time $874.22 per credit hour. *Required fees:* $2124. Tuition and fees vary according to program. *Financial support:* Scholarships/grants and unspecified assistantships available. Financial award application deadline: 1/1; financial award applicants required to submit FAFSA. *Unit head:* Dr. Eleni Pappamihiel, Chair, 910-962-2746, Fax: 910-962-3609, E-mail: pappamihieln@uncw.edu. *Application contact:* Dr. Mahnaz Moallem, Graduate Coordinator, 910-962-4183, E-mail: moallemm@uncw.edu.
Website: http://www.uncw.edu/ed/itfse/

University of Northern Colorado, Graduate School, College of Education and Behavioral Sciences, School of Teacher Education, Greeley, CO 80639. Offers curriculum studies (MAT); educational studies (Ed D); elementary education (MAT); English education (MAT); literacy (MA); multilingual education (MA), including TESOL, world languages; teaching diverse learners (MA). *Accreditation:* NCATE. *Program availability:* Part-time, evening/weekend. *Degree requirements:* For master's, comprehensive exam, thesis or alternative; for doctorate, comprehensive exam, thesis/dissertation. *Entrance requirements:* For master's and doctorate, GRE General Test, 3 letters of recommendation. Electronic applications accepted.

University of Northern Iowa, Graduate College, College of Humanities, Arts and Sciences, Department of Languages and Literatures, MA Program in Teaching English to Speakers of Other Languages, Cedar Falls, IA 50614. Offers MA. *Degree requirements:* For master's, comprehensive exam, thesis or research paper.

University of North Florida, College of Education and Human Services, Department of Childhood Education, Literacy, and TESOL, Jacksonville, FL 32224. Offers literacy (M Ed); professional education (M Ed); TESOL (M Ed). *Accreditation:* NCATE. *Program availability:* Part-time, evening/weekend. *Entrance requirements:* For master's, GRE General Test, minimum GPA of 3.0 in last 60 hours, 3 letters of recommendation, interview. Additional exam requirements/recommendations for international students: Required—TOEFL (minimum score 500 paper-based). Electronic applications accepted. *Faculty research:* Social context of and processes in learning, inter-disciplinary instruction, cross-cultural conflict resolution, the Vygotskian perspective on literacy diagnosis and instruction, performance poetry and teaching the language arts through drama.

University of North Texas, Robert B. Toulouse School of Graduate Studies, Denton, TX 76203-5459. Offers accounting (MS); applied anthropology (MA, MS); applied behavior analysis (Certificate); applied geography (MA); applied technology and performance improvement (M Ed, MS); art education (MA); art history (MA); art museum education (Certificate); arts leadership (Certificate); audiology (Au D); behavior analysis (MS); behavioral science (PhD); biochemistry and molecular biology (MS); biology (MA, MS); biomedical engineering (MS); business analysis (MS); chemistry (MS); clinical health psychology (PhD); communication studies (MA, MS); computer engineering (MS); computer science (MS); counseling (M Ed, MS), including clinical mental health counseling (MS), college and university counseling, elementary school counseling, secondary school counseling; creative writing (MA); criminal justice (MS); curriculum and instruction (M Ed); decision sciences (MBA); design (MA, MFA), including fashion design (MFA), innovation studies, interior design (MFA); early childhood studies (MS); economics (MS); educational leadership (M Ed, Ed D); educational psychology (MS, PhD), including family studies (MS), gifted and talented (MS), human development (MS), learning and cognition (MS), research, measurement and evaluation (MS); electrical engineering (MS); emergency management (MPA); engineering technology (MS); English (MA); English as a second language (MA); environmental science (MS); finance (MBA, MS); financial management (MPA); French (MA); health services management (MBA); higher education (M Ed, Ed D); history (MA, MS); hospitality management (MS); human resources management (MPA); information science (MS); information systems (PhD); information technologies (MBA); interdisciplinary studies (MA, MS); international studies (MA); international sustainable tourism (MS); jazz studies (MM); journalism (MA, MJ, Graduate Certificate), including interactive and virtual digital communication (Graduate Certificate), narrative journalism (Graduate Certificate), public relations (Graduate Certificate); kinesiology (MS); linguistics (MA); local government management (MPA); logistics (PhD); logistics and supply chain management (MBA); long-term care, senior housing, and aging services (MA); management (PhD); marketing (MBA); mathematics (MA, MS); mechanical and energy engineering (MS, PhD); music (MA), including ethnomusicology, music theory, musicology, performance; music composition (PhD); music education (MM Ed, PhD); nonprofit management (MPA); operations and supply chain management (MBA); performance (MM, DMA); philosophy (MA); political science (MA); professional and technical communication (MA); radio, television and film (MA, MFA); rehabilitation counseling (Certificate); sociology (MA); Spanish (MA); special education (M Ed); speech-language pathology (MS); strategic management (MBA); studio art (MFA); teaching (M Ed); MBA/MS. *Program availability:* Part-time, evening/weekend, online learning. Terminal master's awarded for partial completion of doctoral program. *Degree requirements:* For master's, variable foreign language requirement, comprehensive exam (for some programs), thesis (for some programs); for doctorate, variable foreign language requirement, comprehensive exam (for some programs), thesis/dissertation; for other advanced degree, variable foreign language requirement, comprehensive exam (for some programs). *Entrance requirements:* For master's and doctorate, GRE, GMAT. Additional exam requirements/recommendations for international students: Required—TOEFL (minimum score 550 paper-based; 79 iBT). Electronic applications accepted.

University of Pennsylvania, Graduate School of Education, Division of Educational Linguistics, Program in Teaching English to Speakers of Other Languages, Philadelphia, PA 19104. Offers MS Ed. *Program availability:* Part-time, online learning. *Students:* Average age 25. 348 applicants, 39% accepted, 76 enrolled. In 2017, 69 master's awarded.

University of Phoenix–Online Campus, College of Education, Phoenix, AZ 85034-7209. Offers administration and supervision (MAEd, Certificate); adult education and training (MAEd); curriculum and instruction (MAEd), including computer education, curriculum and instruction, English as a second language, language arts, mathematics, reading; early childhood education (MAEd); educational studies (MAEd); elementary teacher education (MAEd), including early childhood, elementary teacher education, high school middle level, middle level; principal licensure (Certificate); secondary teacher education (MAEd); special education (MAEd, Certificate); teacher education (MAEd), including middle level generalist; teacher education middle level mathematics (MAEd), including middle level mathematics; teacher education middle level science (MAEd), including middle level science; teacher education secondary mathematics (MAEd); teacher education secondary science (MAEd); teacher leadership (MAEd); teachers of English learners (Certificate); transition to teaching (Certificate), including elementary education, secondary education. *Program availability:* Evening/weekend, online learning. *Entrance requirements:* Additional exam requirements/recommendations for international students: Required—TOEFL, TOEIC (Test of English as an International Communication), Berlitz Online English Proficiency Exam, PTE, or IELTS. Electronic applications accepted. *Expenses:* Contact institution.

University of Phoenix–San Diego Campus, College of Education, San Diego, CA 92123. Offers curriculum and instruction (MA Ed), including computer education, curriculum and instruction, English as a second language; elementary teacher education (MA Ed); secondary teacher education (MA Ed). *Program availability:* Evening/weekend. *Degree requirements:* For master's, thesis (for some programs). *Entrance requirements:* For master's, 3 years of work experience, minimum undergraduate GPA of 3.0. Additional exam requirements/recommendations for international students: Required—TOEFL (minimum score 550 paper-based; 79 iBT). Electronic applications accepted.

University of Pittsburgh, Kenneth P. Dietrich School of Arts and Sciences, Program in Hispanic Linguistics, Pittsburgh, PA 15260. Offers TESOL (PhD). *Faculty:* 2 full-time (1 woman). *Students:* 4 full-time (all women); includes 3 minority (all Hispanic/Latino). Average age 32. In 2017, 2 doctorates awarded. Terminal master's awarded for partial completion of doctoral program. *Degree requirements:* For doctorate, 2 foreign languages, comprehensive exam, thesis/dissertation. *Entrance requirements:* For doctorate, GRE General Test, proficiency in Spanish. Additional exam requirements/recommendations for international students: Required—TOEFL (minimum score 600 paper-based; 100 iBT). *Application deadline:* For fall admission, 12/15 priority date for domestic and international students. Application fee: $50. Electronic applications accepted. *Financial support:* In 2017–18, 6 students received support, including 2 fellowships with full tuition reimbursements available (averaging $18,620 per year), 3 teaching assistantships with full tuition reimbursements available (averaging $17,190 per year). Financial award application deadline: 12/15; financial award applicants required to submit FAFSA. *Faculty research:* Hispanic linguistics, second language acquisition, phonetics, prosody, language variation and change. *Unit head:* Dr. Shelome Gooden, Chair, 412-624-5922, Fax: 412-624-5520, E-mail: sgooden@pitt.edu. *Application contact:* Margaret Bupp, Graduate Student Services Administrator, 412-624-6568, Fax: 412-624-5520, E-mail: maggiebupp@pitt.edu.
Website: http://www.linguistics.pitt.edu

University of Pittsburgh, Kenneth P. Dietrich School of Arts and Sciences, TESOL Certificate Program, Pittsburgh, PA 15260. Offers Certificate. *Program availability:* Part-time. *Faculty:* 7 full-time (4 women). *Students:* 12 full-time (10 women), 7 part-time (3 women); includes 1 minority (Black or African American, non-Hispanic/Latino), 4 international. Average age 28. 21 applicants, 81% accepted, 8 enrolled. *Entrance requirements:* Additional exam requirements/recommendations for international students: Required—TOEFL (minimum score 600 paper-based; 100 iBT), IELTS

(minimum score 7.5). *Application deadline:* For spring admission, 3/15 for domestic and international students. Application fee: $50. *Faculty research:* Second language acquisition, applied linguistics, sociolinguistics, second language pedagogy, linguistic theory. *Unit head:* Dr. Shelome Gooden, 412-624-5520, E-mail: sgooden@pitt.edu. *Application contact:* Dr. Dawn E. McCormick, Senior Lecturer/TESOL Advisor, 412-624-5902, Fax: 412-624-6130, E-mail: mccormic@pitt.edu.
Website: http://www.linguistics.pitt.edu/esl-tesol/tesol-certificate

University of Portland, School of Education, Portland, OR 97203-5798. Offers education (MA, MAT); educational leadership (M Ed); English for speakers of other languages (M Ed); initial administrator licensure (M Ed); neuroeducation (M Ed, Ed D); organizational leadership and development (Ed D); reading (M Ed); school leadership and development (Ed D); special education (M Ed). M Ed also available through the Graduate Outreach Program for teachers residing in the Oregon and Washington state areas. *Accreditation:* NCATE. *Program availability:* Part-time, evening/weekend. *Entrance requirements:* For master's, minimum GPA of 3.0, teaching certificate, letters of recommendation, resume, statement of goals, official transcripts. Additional exam requirements/recommendations for international students: Required—TOEFL (minimum score 550 paper-based; 80 iBT), IELTS (minimum score 7). *Faculty research:* Multicultural education, supervision/leadership.

University of Puerto Rico–Río Piedras, College of Education, Program in Teaching English as a Second Language, San Juan, PR 00931-3300. Offers M Ed. *Program availability:* Part-time. *Degree requirements:* For master's, thesis. *Entrance requirements:* For master's, PAEG or GRE, minimum GPA of 3.0, letter of recommendation. *Faculty research:* Second language acquisition, bilingual education.

University of St. Francis, College of Education, Joliet, IL 60435-6169. Offers educational leadership (MS, Ed D); elementary education (M Ed); reading (MS); secondary education (M Ed), including English education, math education, science education, social studies education, visual arts education; special education (M Ed); teaching and learning (MS); TESOL (Certificate). *Accreditation:* NCATE. *Program availability:* Part-time, evening/weekend, 100% online, blended/hybrid learning. *Faculty:* 11 full-time (8 women), 52 part-time/adjunct (36 women). *Students:* 39 full-time (32 women), 411 part-time (318 women); includes 106 minority (57 Black or African American, non-Hispanic/Latino; 8 Asian, non-Hispanic/Latino; 37 Hispanic/Latino; 4 Two or more races, non-Hispanic/Latino), 4 international. Average age 37. 277 applicants, 55% accepted, 137 enrolled. In 2017, 199 master's, 28 doctorates awarded. *Degree requirements:* For master's, comprehensive exam; for doctorate, thesis/dissertation. *Entrance requirements:* Additional exam requirements/recommendations for international students: Required—TOEFL (minimum score 550 paper-based; 79 iBT), IELTS (minimum score 6). *Application deadline:* Applications are processed on a rolling basis. Application fee: $30. Electronic applications accepted. Application fee is waived when completed online. *Expenses:* $365 to $748 per credit hour. *Financial support:* In 2017–18, 40 students received support. Scholarships/grants and unspecified assistantships available. Support available to part-time students. Financial award applicants required to submit FAFSA. *Unit head:* Dr. John Gambro, Dean, 815-740-3829, Fax: 815-740-2264, E-mail: jgambro@stfrancis.edu. *Application contact:* Sandra Sloka, Director of Admissions for Graduate and Degree Completion Programs, 800-735-7500, Fax: 815-740-3431, E-mail: ssloka@stfrancis.edu.
Website: http://www.stfrancis.edu/academics/college-of-education/

University of Saint Joseph, Department of Education, West Hartford, CT 06117-2700. Offers curriculum and instruction (MA); elementary education (MAT); instructional technology (MA); literacy (MA); secondary education (MAT); TESOL (MA). *Program availability:* Part-time, evening/weekend. *Degree requirements:* For master's, comprehensive exam, thesis or alternative. *Entrance requirements:* For master's, 2 letters of recommendation. *Application deadline:* Applications are processed on a rolling basis. Application fee: $50. Electronic applications accepted. Application fee is waived when completed online. *Financial support:* Career-related internships or fieldwork and unspecified assistantships available. Support available to part-time students. Financial award applicants required to submit FAFSA.
Website: https://www.usj.edu/academics/schools/sasbe/education/

University of St. Thomas, School of Education and Human Services, Houston, TX 77006-4696. Offers all level education (M Ed); bilingual/dual language (M Ed); Catholic school teaching (M Ed); Catholic/private school leadership (M Ed); counselor education (M Ed); curriculum and instruction (M Ed); education (Ed D); educational leadership (M Ed); elementary teaching (M Ed); English as a second language (M Ed); exceptionality/educational diagnostician (M Ed); exceptionality/special education (M Ed); generalist (M Ed); reading (M Ed); secondary teaching (M Ed); teaching (MAT). *Accreditation:* TEAC. *Program availability:* Part-time, evening/weekend, online learning. *Faculty:* 33 full-time (22 women), 43 part-time/adjunct (26 women). *Students:* 119 full-time (97 women), 597 part-time (529 women); includes 478 minority (166 Black or African American, non-Hispanic/Latino; 29 Asian, non-Hispanic/Latino; 277 Hispanic/Latino; 2 Native Hawaiian or other Pacific Islander, non-Hispanic/Latino; 4 Two or more races, non-Hispanic/Latino), 19 international. Average age 36. 306 applicants, 91% accepted, 181 enrolled. In 2017, 328 master's awarded. *Degree requirements:* For master's, thesis, field experience. *Entrance requirements:* For master's, GRE or MAT if GPA is below 3.0, bachelor's degree; minimum GPA of 2.75 in bachelor's degree or last 60 credit hours; official transcripts from all institutions; goal statement of 250-300 words; 1 reference. Additional exam requirements/recommendations for international students: Required—TOEFL (minimum score 94 iBT), IELTS (minimum score 7), PTE (minimum score 53). *Application deadline:* Applications are processed on a rolling basis. Application fee: $35. Electronic applications accepted. *Expenses:* Contact institution. *Financial support:* In 2017–18, 27 students received support. Federal Work-Study, scholarships/grants, and state work-study, institutional employment available. Support available to part-time students. Financial award application deadline: 4/15; financial award applicants required to submit FAFSA. *Faculty research:* Leadership, diversity, personality traits, second language acquisition. *Unit head:* Dr. Paul C. Paese, Dean, 713-942-5999, Fax: 713-525-3871, E-mail: paesep@stthom.edu. *Application contact:* 713-525-3540, E-mail: education@stthom.edu.
Website: http://www.stthom.edu/Academics/
School_of_Education_and_Human_Services/Index.aqf

University of San Diego, School of Leadership and Education Sciences, Department of Learning and Teaching, San Diego, CA 92110-2492. Offers curriculum and instruction (M Ed); inclusive learning (M Ed); literacy and digital learning (M Ed); school leadership (M Ed); special education (M Ed); STEAM (science, technology, engineering, arts, and mathematics) (M Ed); TESOL, literacy and culture (M Ed). *Program availability:* Part-time, evening/weekend. *Faculty:* 9 full-time (7 women), 30 part-time/adjunct (24 women). *Students:* 160 full-time (128 women), 221 part-time (176 women); includes 131 minority (10 Black or African American, non-Hispanic/Latino; 24 Asian, non-Hispanic/Latino; 83 Hispanic/Latino; 1 Native Hawaiian or other Pacific Islander, non-Hispanic/Latino; 13 Two or more races, non-Hispanic/Latino), 20 international. Average age 33. 398 applicants, 84% accepted, 196 enrolled. In 2017, 151 master's awarded. *Degree requirements:* For master's, thesis (for some programs), international experience. *Entrance requirements:* For master's, California Basic Educational Skills Test, California Subject Examination for Teachers. Additional exam requirements/recommendations for

English as a Second Language

international students: Required—TOEFL (minimum score 580 paper-based; 83 iBT), TWE. *Application deadline:* Applications are processed on a rolling basis. Application fee: $45. Electronic applications accepted. *Financial support:* In 2017–18, 65 students received support. Career-related internships or fieldwork, Federal Work-Study, institutionally sponsored loans, and stipends available. Financial award application deadline: 4/1; financial award applicants required to submit FAFSA. *Faculty research:* Action research methodology, cultural studies, instructional theories and practices, second language acquisition, school reform. *Unit head:* Dr. Maya Kalyanpur, Chair, 619-260-7655, E-mail: mkalyanpur@sandiego.edu. *Application contact:* Monica Mahon, Associate Director of Graduate Admissions, 619-260-4524, Fax: 619-260-4158, E-mail: grads@sandiego.edu.
Website: http://www.sandiego.edu/soles/learning-and-teaching/

University of South Africa, College of Human Sciences, Pretoria, South Africa. Offers adult education (M Ed); African languages (MA, PhD); African politics (MA, PhD); Afrikaans (MA, PhD); ancient history (MA, PhD); ancient Near Eastern studies (MA, PhD); anthropology (MA, PhD); applied linguistics (MA); Arabic (MA, PhD); archaeology (MA); art history (MA); Biblical archaeology (MA); Biblical studies (M Th, D Th, PhD); Christian spirituality (M Th, D Th); church history (M Th, D Th); classical studies (MA, PhD); clinical psychology (MA, PhD); communication (MA, PhD); comparative education (M Ed, Ed D); consulting psychology (D Admin, D Com, PhD); curriculum studies (M Ed, Ed D); development studies (M Admin, MA, D Admin, PhD); didactics (M Ed, Ed D); education (M Tech); education management (M Ed, Ed D); educational psychology (M Ed); English (MA); environmental education (M Ed); French (MA, PhD); German (MA, PhD); Greek (MA); guidance and counseling (M Ed); health studies (MA, PhD), including health sciences education (MA), health services management (MA), medical and surgical nursing science (critical care general) (MA), midwifery and neonatal nursing science (MA), trauma and emergency care (MA); history (MA, PhD); history of education (Ed D); inclusive education (M Ed, Ed D); information and communications technology policy and regulation (MA); information science (MA, MIS, PhD); international politics (MA, PhD); Islamic studies (MA, PhD); Italian (MA, PhD); Judaica (MA, PhD); linguistics (MA, PhD); mathematical education (M Ed); mathematics education (MA); missiology (M Th, D Th); modern Hebrew (MA, PhD); musicology (MA, MMus, D Mus, PhD); natural science education (M Ed); New Testament (M Th, D Th); Old Testament (D Th); pastoral therapy (M Th, D Th); philosophy (MA); philosophy of education (M Ed, Ed D); politics (MA, PhD); Portuguese (MA, PhD); practical theology (M Th, D Th); psychology (MA, MS, PhD); psychology of education (M Ed, Ed D); public health (MA); religious studies (MA, D Th, PhD); Romance languages (MA); Russian (MA, PhD); Semitic languages (MA, PhD); social behavior studies in HIV/AIDS (MA); social science (mental health) (MA); social science in development studies (MA); social science in psychology (MA); social science in social work (MA); social science in sociology (MA); social work (MSW, DSW, PhD); socio-education (M Ed, Ed D); sociolinguistics (MA); sociology (MA, PhD); Spanish (MA, PhD); systematic theology (M Th, D Th); TESOL (teaching English to speakers of other languages) (MA); theological ethics (M Th, D Th); theory of literature (MA, PhD); urban ministries (D Th); urban ministry (M Th).

University of South Carolina, The Graduate School, College of Arts and Sciences, Linguistics Program, Columbia, SC 29208. Offers linguistics (MA, PhD); teaching English to speakers of other languages (Certificate). *Program availability:* Part-time. Terminal master's awarded for partial completion of doctoral program. *Degree requirements:* For master's, one foreign language, comprehensive exam, thesis optional; for doctorate, 3 foreign languages, comprehensive exam, thesis/dissertation. *Entrance requirements:* For master's and Certificate, GRE General Test, minimum GPA of 3.0; for doctorate, GRE General Test, minimum GPA of 3.5. Additional exam requirements/recommendations for international students: Required—TOEFL. Electronic applications accepted. *Faculty research:* Second language acquisition, sociolinguistics, syntax, historical linguistics and phonology.

University of South Dakota, Graduate School, School of Education, Division of Curriculum and Instruction, Program in Elementary Education, Vermillion, SD 57069. Offers elementary education (MA), including early childhood education, English language learning, reading specialist/literacy coach, science, technology and math (STEM). *Accreditation:* NCATE. *Program availability:* Part-time, 100% online, blended/hybrid learning. *Degree requirements:* For master's, comprehensive exam, thesis or alternative. *Entrance requirements:* For master's, GRE General Test, MAT, minimum GPA of 2.7. Additional exam requirements/recommendations for international students: Required—TOEFL (minimum score 550 paper-based; 79 iBT). *Application deadline:* Applications are processed on a rolling basis. Application fee: $35. Electronic applications accepted. *Financial support:* Research assistantships with partial tuition reimbursements, teaching assistantships with partial tuition reimbursements, career-related internships or fieldwork, Federal Work-Study, and unspecified assistantships available. Financial award applicants required to submit FAFSA. *Application contact:* Graduate School, 605-658-6140, Fax: 605-677-6118, E-mail: grad@usd.edu.
Website: http://www.usd.edu/ci

University of South Dakota, Graduate School, School of Education, Division of Curriculum and Instruction, Program in Secondary Education, Vermillion, SD 57069. Offers secondary education (MA), including English language learning, science, technology and math (STEM), secondary education plus certification. *Accreditation:* NCATE. *Program availability:* Part-time, online learning. *Degree requirements:* For master's, comprehensive exam, thesis or alternative. *Entrance requirements:* For master's, GRE General Test, MAT, minimum GPA of 2.7. Additional exam requirements/recommendations for international students: Required—TOEFL (minimum score 550 paper-based; 79 iBT). *Application deadline:* Applications are processed on a rolling basis. Application fee: $35. Electronic applications accepted. *Financial support:* Research assistantships with partial tuition reimbursements, teaching assistantships with partial tuition reimbursements, career-related internships or fieldwork, Federal Work-Study, and unspecified assistantships available. Financial award applicants required to submit FAFSA. *Application contact:* Graduate School, 605-658-6140, Fax: 605-677-6118.
Website: http://www.usd.edu/ci

University of Southern California, Graduate School, Rossier School of Education, Master's Programs in Education, Los Angeles, CA 90089-4038. Offers educational counseling (ME); marriage, family and child counseling (MMFT); postsecondary administration and student affairs [PASA] (ME); school counseling (ME); teaching (online) (MAT); teaching and teaching credential (MAT); teaching English to speakers of other languages (MAT). *Program availability:* Part-time, evening/weekend, online learning. *Degree requirements:* For master's, thesis optional. *Entrance requirements:* For master's, GRE (for all programs except MAT). Additional exam requirements/recommendations for international students: Required—TOEFL (minimum score 100 iBT). Electronic applications accepted. *Faculty research:* College access and equity, preparing teachers for culturally diverse populations, sociocultural basis of learning as mediated by instruction with focus on reading and literacy in English learners, social and political aspects of teaching and learning English, school counselor development and training.

University of Southern Indiana, Graduate Studies, College of Liberal Arts, Program in Second Language Acquisition, Policy, and Culture, Evansville, IN 47712-3590. Offers

MA. *Program availability:* Part-time. *Faculty:* 2 full-time (0 women). *Students:* 16 full-time (9 women), 3 part-time (all women); includes 4 minority (3 Asian, non-Hispanic/Latino; 1 Hispanic/Latino), 6 international. Average age 35. In 2017, 5 master's awarded. *Entrance requirements:* For master's, minimum GPA of 3.0, letter of intent, 3 letters of recommendation. Additional exam requirements/recommendations for international students: Required—TOEFL (minimum score 550 paper-based; 79 iBT), IELTS (minimum score 6). Application fee: $40. *Expenses:* Tuition, state resident: full-time $9394. Tuition, nonresident: full-time $17,917. *Required fees:* $510. *Financial support:* In 2017–18, 3 students received support. Federal Work-Study, scholarships/grants, tuition waivers (full and partial), and unspecified assistantships available. Financial award application deadline: 3/1; financial award applicants required to submit FAFSA. *Unit head:* Dr. Jessica Jensen, Program Director, 812-465-1292, E-mail: jgjensen@usi.edu. *Application contact:* Dr. Mayola Rowser, Director, Graduate Studies, 812-465-7015, E-mail: mrowser@usi.edu.
Website: http://www.usi.edu/liberal-arts/ma-language/

University of Southern Maine, College of Management and Human Service, School of Education and Human Development, Program in Literacy Education, Portland, ME 04103. Offers applied literacy (MS Ed); English as a second language (MS Ed, CAS, CGS); literacy education (MS Ed, CAS, CGS). *Accreditation:* TEAC. *Program availability:* Part-time, evening/weekend. *Degree requirements:* For master's, comprehensive exam, thesis or alternative; for other advanced degree, thesis or alternative. *Entrance requirements:* For master's, teacher certification; for other advanced degree, master's degree. Additional exam requirements/recommendations for international students: Required—TOEFL (minimum score 550 paper-based; 79 iBT). Electronic applications accepted. *Faculty research:* Teacher research in literacy, multiliteracies, learning to teach culturally and linguistically diverse students, motivation to read.

University of South Florida, College of Arts and Sciences, Department of World Languages, Tampa, FL 33620-9951. Offers French (MA); linguistics (MA); linguistics and applied linguistics studies (PhD); linguistics: English as a second language (MA); Spanish (MA). *Program availability:* Part-time, evening/weekend. *Faculty:* 18 full-time (14 women). *Students:* 40 full-time (34 women), 9 part-time (7 women); includes 20 minority (1 Black or African American, non-Hispanic/Latino; 1 Asian, non-Hispanic/Latino; 16 Hispanic/Latino; 2 Two or more races, non-Hispanic/Latino), 16 international. Average age 33. 65 applicants, 62% accepted, 18 enrolled. In 2017, 30 master's awarded. *Degree requirements:* For master's, one foreign language, comprehensive exam, thesis optional; for doctorate, one foreign language, comprehensive exam, thesis/dissertation. *Entrance requirements:* For master's, GRE General Test, minimum undergraduate GPA of 3.0 and 2-3 letters of recommendation; two-page statement of purpose written in Spanish (for Spanish program); oral interview (for Spanish and French programs); writing sample (for French program); for doctorate, GRE General Test, minimum GPA of 3.5 or international equivalent; master's degree or equivalent academic level; statement of purpose; current curriculum vitae; three letters of recommendation; personal interview with faculty; evidence of research experience or scholarly promise. Additional exam requirements/recommendations for international students: Required—TOEFL minimum score 600 paper-based; 80 iBT or IELTS minimum score 6.5 (for MA); TOEFL minimum score 550 paper-based; 80 iBT or IELTS minimum score 6.5 (for PhD). *Application deadline:* For fall admission, 1/15 for domestic and international students; for spring admission, 10/15 for domestic students, 9/15 for international students. Application fee: $30. Electronic applications accepted. *Financial support:* In 2017–18, 10 students received support, including 43 teaching assistantships with tuition reimbursements available (averaging $10,152 per year); tuition waivers (partial) and unspecified assistantships also available. Financial award application deadline: 6/30. *Faculty research:* Second language acquisition, instructional technology, foreign language education, English for speakers of other languages, distance learning. Total annual research expenditures: $7,706. *Unit head:* Dr. Stephan Schindler, Chair and Professor, 813-974-2548, Fax: 813-905-9937, E-mail: skschindler@usf.edu. *Application contact:* Patricia Garcia, Academic Program Specialist, 813-974-2548, Fax: 813-905-9937, E-mail: pgarcia@usf.edu.
Website: http://languages.usf.edu/

University of South Florida, Innovative Education, Tampa, FL 33620-9951. Offers adult, career and higher education (Graduate Certificate), including college teaching, leadership in developing human resources, leadership in higher education; Africana studies (Graduate Certificate), including diasporas and health disparities, genocide and human rights; aging studies (Graduate Certificate), including gerontology; art research (Graduate Certificate), including museum studies; business foundations (Graduate Certificate); chemical and biomedical engineering (Graduate Certificate), including materials science and engineering, water, health and sustainability; child and family studies (Graduate Certificate), including positive behavior support; civil and industrial engineering (Graduate Certificate), including transportation systems analysis; community and family health (Graduate Certificate), including maternal and child health, social marketing and public health, violence and injury: prevention and intervention, women's health; criminology (Graduate Certificate), including criminal justice administration; data science for public administration (Graduate Certificate); digital humanities (Graduate Certificate); educational measurement and research (Graduate Certificate), including evaluation; English (Graduate Certificate), including comparative literary studies, creative writing, professional and technical communication; entrepreneurship (Graduate Certificate); environmental health (Graduate Certificate), including safety management; epidemiology and biostatistics (Graduate Certificate), including applied biostatistics, biostatistics, concepts and tools of epidemiology, epidemiology, epidemiology of infectious diseases; geography, environment and planning (Graduate Certificate), including community development, environmental policy and management, geographical information systems; geology (Graduate Certificate), including hydrogeology; global health (Graduate Certificate), including disaster management, global health and Latin American and Caribbean studies, global health practice, humanitarian assistance, infection control; government and international affairs (Graduate Certificate), including Cuban studies, globalization studies; health policy and management (Graduate Certificate), including health management and leadership, public health policy and programs; hearing specialist: early intervention (Graduate Certificate); industrial and management systems engineering (Graduate Certificate), including systems engineering, technology management; information studies (Graduate Certificate), including school library media specialist; information systems/decision sciences (Graduate Certificate), including analytics and business intelligence; instructional technology (Graduate Certificate), including distance education, Florida digital/virtual educator, instructional design, multimedia design, Web design; internal medicine, bioethics and medical humanities (Graduate Certificate), including biomedical ethics; Latin American and Caribbean studies (Graduate Certificate); leadership for coastal resiliency planning (Graduate Certificate); mass communications (Graduate Certificate), including multimedia journalism; mathematics and statistics (Graduate Certificate), including mathematics; medicine (Graduate Certificate), including aging and neuroscience, bioinformatics, biotechnology, brain fitness and memory management, clinical investigation, hand and upper limb rehabilitation, health informatics, health sciences, integrative weight management, intellectual property, medicine and gender, metabolic and nutritional medicine, metabolic cardiology, pharmacy sciences; national

and competitive intelligence (Graduate Certificate); nursing (Graduate Certificate), including simulation based academic fellowship in advanced pain management; psychological and social foundations (Graduate Certificate), including career counseling, college teaching, diversity in education, mental health counseling, school counseling; public affairs (Graduate Certificate), including nonprofit management, public management, research administration; public health (Graduate Certificate), including assessing chemical toxicity and public health risks, health equity, pharmacoepidemiology, public health generalist, toxicology, translational research in adolescent behavioral health; public health practices (Graduate Certificate), including planning for healthy communities; rehabilitation and mental health counseling (Graduate Certificate), including integrative mental health care, marriage and family therapy, rehabilitation technology; secondary education (Graduate Certificate), including ESOL, foreign language education: culture and content, foreign language education: professional; social work (Graduate Certificate), including geriatric social work/clinical gerontology; special education (Graduate Certificate), including autism spectrum disorder, disabilities education: severe/profound; world languages (Graduate Certificate), including teaching English as a second language (TESL) or foreign language. *Unit head:* Dr. Cynthia DeLuca, Associate Vice President and Assistant Vice Provost, 813-974-3077, Fax: 813-974-7061, E-mail: deluca@usf.edu. *Application contact:* Owen Hooper, Director, Summer and Alternative Calendar Programs, 813-974-6917, E-mail: hooper@usf.edu.
Website: http://www.usf.edu/innovative-education/

The University of Tennessee, Graduate School, College of Education, Health and Human Sciences, Program in Education, Knoxville, TN 37996. Offers art education (MS); counseling education (PhD); cultural studies in education (PhD); curriculum (MS, Ed S); curriculum, educational research and evaluation (Ed D, PhD); early childhood education (PhD); early childhood special education (MS); education of deaf and hard of hearing (MS); educational administration and policy studies (Ed D, PhD); educational administration and supervision (Ed S); educational psychology (Ed D, PhD); elementary education (MS, Ed S); elementary teaching (MS); English education (MS, Ed S); exercise science (PhD); foreign language/ESL education (MS, Ed S); instructional technology (MS, Ed D, PhD, Ed S); literacy, language and ESL education (PhD); literacy, language education, and ESL education (Ed D); mathematics education (MS, Ed S); modified and comprehensive special education (MS); reading education (MS, Ed S); school counseling (Ed S); school psychology (PhD, Ed S); science education (MS, Ed S); secondary teaching (MS); social foundations (MS); social science education (MS, Ed S); socio-cultural foundations of sports and education (PhD); special education (Ed S); teacher education (Ed D, PhD). *Accreditation:* NCATE. *Program availability:* Part-time, evening/weekend. *Degree requirements:* For master's and Ed S, thesis optional; for doctorate, variable foreign language requirement, thesis/dissertation. *Entrance requirements:* For master's, minimum GPA of 2.7; for doctorate and Ed S, GRE General Test, minimum GPA of 2.7. Additional exam requirements/recommendations for international students: Required—TOEFL. Electronic applications accepted.

The University of Texas at Arlington, Graduate School, College of Liberal Arts, Department of Linguistics and TESOL, Program in Teaching English to Speakers of Other Languages, Arlington, TX 76019. Offers MA. *Accreditation:* NCATE. *Program availability:* Part-time, evening/weekend. *Degree requirements:* For master's, comprehensive exam (for some programs), thesis optional. *Entrance requirements:* For master's, GRE General Test, minimum undergraduate GPA of 3.0, 6 credits of undergraduate foundation courses, equivalent of 2 years of university-level foreign language study. Additional exam requirements/recommendations for international students: Required—TOEFL (minimum score 550 paper-based). Electronic applications accepted.

The University of Texas at El Paso, Graduate School, College of Liberal Arts, Department of Languages and Linguistics, El Paso, TX 79968-0001. Offers linguistics (MA); Spanish (MA); teaching English to speakers of other languages (Certificate). *Program availability:* Part-time, evening/weekend. *Degree requirements:* For master's, thesis optional. *Entrance requirements:* For master's, GRE General Test, departmental exam, minimum GPA of 3.0, letters of recommendation. Additional exam requirements/recommendations for international students: Required—TOEFL; Recommended—IELTS. Electronic applications accepted.

The University of Texas at San Antonio, College of Education and Human Development, Department of Bicultural and Bilingual Studies, San Antonio, TX 78249-0617. Offers bicultural and bilingual studies (MA), including bicultural and bilingual education, bicultural studies; culture, literacy, and language (PhD); teaching English as a second language (MA). *Program availability:* Part-time, evening/weekend. *Faculty:* 18 full-time (16 women). *Students:* 40 full-time (29 women), 82 part-time (68 women); includes 77 minority (2 Black or African American, non-Hispanic/Latino; 2 Asian, non-Hispanic/Latino; 72 Hispanic/Latino; 1 Two or more races, non-Hispanic/Latino) 3 international. Average age 35. 64 applicants, 80% accepted, 28 enrolled. In 2017, 34 master's, 13 doctorates awarded. *Degree requirements:* For master's, one language, comprehensive exam, thesis optional; for doctorate, one foreign language, comprehensive exam, thesis/dissertation. *Entrance requirements:* For master's, bachelor's degree with 18 credit hours in field of study or in another appropriate field of study; for doctorate, GRE General Test, resume or curriculum vitae, 3 letters of recommendation, statement of purpose, master's degree. Additional exam requirements/recommendations for international students: Required—TOEFL (minimum score 550 paper-based; 79 iBT), IELTS (minimum score 6.5). *Application deadline:* For fall admission, 6/15 for domestic students, 3/15 for international students; for spring admission, 10/15 for domestic students, 9/15 for international students. Applications are processed on a rolling basis. Application fee: $50 ($90 for international students). Electronic applications accepted. *Expenses:* Contact institution. *Financial support:* Fellowships, research assistantships, teaching assistantships, scholarships/grants, and unspecified assistantships available. Financial award application deadline: 4/15. *Faculty research:* Bilingual and ESL teacher preparation; transnational communities; applied linguistics; cultural studies; bilingualism, biliteracy and second language acquisition. *Total annual research expenditures:* $2,246. *Unit head:* Dr. Patricia Sanchez, Chair, 210-458-4426, Fax: 210-458-5962, E-mail: patricia.sanchez@utsa.edu. *Application contact:* Rahnuma Islam, Student Development Specialist, 210-458-6619, Fax: 210-458-5576, E-mail: rahnuma.islam@utsa.edu.
Website: http://education.utsa.edu/bicultural-bilingual_studies

The University of Texas at San Antonio, College of Education and Human Development, Department of Educational Psychology, San Antonio, TX 78207. Offers applied behavior analysis (Certificate); educational psychology (MA), including applied educational psychology, behavior assessment and intervention, general educational psychology, program evaluation; language acquisition and bilingual psychoeducational assessment (Certificate); school psychology (MA). *Program availability:* Part-time. *Faculty:* 9 full-time (5 women), 1 (woman) part-time/adjunct. *Students:* 34 full-time (27 women), 40 part-time (35 women); includes 52 minority (5 Black or African American, non-Hispanic/Latino; 1 Asian, non-Hispanic/Latino; 43 Hispanic/Latino; 3 Two or more races, non-Hispanic/Latino). Average age 28. 46 applicants, 72% accepted, 23 enrolled. In 2017, 16 master's, 23 other advanced degrees awarded. *Degree requirements:* For master's, comprehensive exam, thesis (for some programs). *Entrance requirements:* For master's, GRE, bachelor's degree with 18 credit hours in field of study or in another appropriate field of study, two letters of recommendation, statement of purpose; for Certificate, 18 hours in psychology, sociology, education, or anything related (for applied behavioral analysis); minimum GPA of 2.7 in last 30 hours (for language acquisition and bilingual psychoeducational assessment). Additional exam requirements/recommendations for international students: Required—TOEFL (minimum score 550 paper-based; 79 iBT), IELTS (minimum score 6.5). *Application deadline:* For fall admission, 6/15 for domestic students, 3/1 for international students; for spring admission, 10/15 for domestic students, 9/15 for international students; for summer admission, 3/1 for international students. Applications are processed on a rolling basis. Application fee: $50 ($90 for international students). Electronic applications accepted. *Expenses:* Tuition, state resident: full-time $5495. Tuition, nonresident: full-time $21,938. *Required fees:* $1915. Tuition and fees vary according to program. *Financial support:* Research assistantships available. Financial award applicants required to submit FAFSA. *Faculty research:* Teacher consultation and culturally responsive school psychology practices, youth mentoring, cross-age peer mentoring, adolescent connectedness, pair counseling. *Total annual research expenditures:* $168,976. *Unit head:* Dr. Jeremy Sullivan, Department Chair, 210-458-2650, Fax: 210-458-2019, E-mail: jeremy.sullivan@utsa.edu.
Website: http://education.utsa.edu/educational_psychology

The University of Texas of the Permian Basin, Office of Graduate Studies, School of Education, Program in Bilingual/English as a Second Language Education, Odessa, TX 79762-0001. Offers MA. *Degree requirements:* For master's, comprehensive exam (for some programs), thesis (for some programs). *Entrance requirements:* For master's, GRE General Test. Additional exam requirements/recommendations for international students: Required—TOEFL (minimum score 550 paper-based).

The University of Texas Rio Grande Valley, College of Education and P-16 Integration, Department of Bilingual and Literacy Studies, Edinburg, TX 78539. Offers bilingual education (M Ed), including dual language, ESL; reading and literacy (M Ed), including adolescent literacy, biliteracy, digital literacy, reading specialist. *Program availability:* Part-time, evening/weekend. *Faculty:* 17 full-time (13 women). *Students:* 29. In 2017, 11 master's awarded. *Degree requirements:* For master's, comprehensive exam (for some programs), thesis optional. *Entrance requirements:* For master's, minimum GPA of 3.0 in undergraduate coursework. Additional exam requirements/recommendations for international students: Required—TOEFL (minimum score 550 paper-based; 79 iBT), IELTS (minimum score 6.5). *Application deadline:* For fall admission, 4/15 for domestic students; for spring admission, 11/1 for domestic students; for summer admission, 3/1 for domestic students. Application fee: $50 ($75 for international students). Electronic applications accepted. *Expenses:* Tuition, state resident: full-time $5550; part-time $417 per credit hour. Tuition, nonresident: full-time $13,020; part-time $832 per credit hour. *Required fees:* $1169. *Financial support:* Research assistantships, institutionally sponsored loans, scholarships/grants, and unspecified assistantships available. Financial award application deadline: 4/15; financial award applicants required to submit FAFSA. *Faculty research:* Bilingual education, reading instruction, multicultural education, English as a second language. *Unit head:* Dr. Janine M. Schall, Chair, 956-665-5106, E-mail: janine.schall@utrgv.edu. *Application contact:* Stephanie Ozuna, Graduate Student Recruiter, 956-665-3558, E-mail: stephanie.ozuna@utrgv.edu.

The University of Texas Rio Grande Valley, College of Liberal Arts, Department of Writing and Language Studies, Edinburg, TX 78539. Offers English as a second language (MA). *Program availability:* Part-time. *Faculty:* 17 full-time (9 women). *Students:* 2 full-time (1 woman), 8 part-time (6 women); includes 8 minority (all Hispanic/Latino). Average age 30. 2 applicants, 100% accepted, 2 enrolled. *Degree requirements:* For master's, comprehensive exam, thesis or alternative. *Entrance requirements:* For master's, GRE General Test, minimum GPA of 3.0. Additional exam requirements/recommendations for international students: Required—TOEFL or IELTS. Application fee: $50 ($100 for international students). *Expenses:* Tuition, state resident: full-time $5550; part-time $417 per credit hour. Tuition, nonresident: full-time $13,020; part-time $832 per credit hour. *Required fees:* $1169. *Financial support:* Application deadline: 6/1. *Faculty research:* Latin American literature, women's literature, Caribbean literature, Latina/o studies, sociolinguistics, applied linguistics, creative writing. *Unit head:* Colin Charlton, Chair, E-mail: colin.charlton@utrgv.edu.

University of the Southwest, Graduate Programs, Hobbs, NM 88240-9129. Offers business administration (MBA); curriculum and instruction (MSE); curriculum and instruction: bilingual (MSE); curriculum and instruction: TESOL (MSE); early childhood education (MSE); educational administration (MSE); mental health counseling (MSE); school counseling (MSE); special education (MSE); sports management (MBA). *Program availability:* Part-time, evening/weekend, online learning. *Degree requirements:* For master's, comprehensive exam, thesis (for some programs). *Entrance requirements:* Additional exam requirements/recommendations for international students: Recommended—TOEFL. Electronic applications accepted.

The University of Toledo, College of Graduate Studies, College of Languages, Literature and Social Sciences, Department of English Language and Literature, Toledo, OH 43606-3390. Offers English as a second language (MA); teaching of writing (Certificate). *Program availability:* Part-time. *Degree requirements:* For master's, thesis. *Entrance requirements:* For master's, GRE if GPA is less than 3.0, minimum cumulative point-hour ratio of 2.7 for all previous academic work, three letters of recommendation, transcripts from all prior institutions attended, critical essay; for Certificate, statement of purpose, transcripts from all prior institutions attended, 2 letters of recommendation. Additional exam requirements/recommendations for international students: Required—TOEFL (minimum score 550 paper-based; 80 iBT). Electronic applications accepted. *Faculty research:* Literary criticism, linguistics, creative writing, folklore and cultural studies.

The University of Toledo, College of Graduate Studies, Judith Herb College of Education, Department of Curriculum and Instruction, Toledo, OH 43606-3390. Offers art education (ME); career and technical education (ME, Ed S); curriculum and instruction (ME, PhD, Ed S); early childhood education (Ed S); education and anthropology (MAE); education and biology (MES); education and chemistry (MES); education and classics (MAE); education and economics (MAE); education and English (MAE); education and French (MAE); education and geology (MES); education and German (MAE); education and history (MAE); education and mathematics (MAE, MES); education and physics (MES); education and political science (MAE); education and sociology (MAE); education and Spanish (MAE); educational media (PhD); educational technology (ME); educational technology: virtual educator (Certificate); elementary education (PhD); English as a second language (MAE); gifted and talented education (PhD); middle childhood education (ME); secondary education (ME, PhD); special education (PhD). *Accreditation:* NCATE. *Program availability:* Part-time, evening/weekend. *Degree requirements:* For master's, comprehensive exam, thesis or alternative; for doctorate, comprehensive exam, thesis/dissertation; for other advanced degree, thesis optional. *Entrance requirements:* For master's, doctorate, and other advanced degree, minimum cumulative GPA of 2.7 for all previous academic work, letters of recommendation. Additional exam requirements/recommendations for international students: Required—TOEFL (minimum score 550 paper-based; 80 iBT). Electronic applications accepted.

English as a Second Language

University of Washington, Graduate School, College of Arts and Sciences, Department of English, Seattle, WA 98195. Offers creative writing (MFA); English as a second language (MAT); English literature and language (MA, MAT, PhD). *Program availability:* Part-time. Terminal master's awarded for partial completion of doctoral program. *Degree requirements:* For master's, one foreign language, thesis (for some programs); for doctorate, one foreign language, thesis/dissertation. *Entrance requirements:* For master's, GRE General Test, GRE Subject Test (MA and MAT in English), minimum GPA of 3.0; for doctorate, GRE General Test, GRE Subject Test. Additional exam requirements/recommendations for international students: Required—TOEFL. Electronic applications accepted. *Faculty research:* English and American literature, critical theory, creative writing, language theory.

University of Wisconsin–Madison, Graduate School, School of Education, Department of Curriculum and Instruction, Madison, WI 53706-1380. Offers curriculum and instruction (MS, PhD); English as a second language (MS). *Accreditation:* NASM (one or more programs are accredited). *Degree requirements:* For doctorate, thesis/dissertation.

University of Wisconsin–Milwaukee, Graduate School, College of Letters and Science, Department of Linguistics, Milwaukee, WI 53201-0413. Offers linguistics (MA, PhD), including teaching English to speakers of other languages (MA); teaching English to speakers of other languages, adult- and university-level (Graduate Certificate). *Students:* 19 full-time (5 women), 12 part-time (11 women); includes 1 minority (Two or more races, non-Hispanic/Latino), 18 international. Average age 33. 47 applicants, 34% accepted, 12 enrolled. In 2017, 4 master's, 2 other advanced degrees awarded. Electronic applications accepted. *Unit head:* Hamid Ouali, Department Chair, 414-229-1113, E-mail: ouali@uwm.edu. *Application contact:* General Information Contact, 414-229-4982, Fax: 414-229-6967, E-mail: gradschool@uwm.edu. Website: http://www4.uwm.edu/letsci/linguistics/

University of Wisconsin–River Falls, Outreach and Graduate Studies, College of Arts and Science, Program in Teaching English to Speakers of Other Languages, River Falls, WI 54022. Offers MA.

Upper Iowa University, Master of Education Program, Fayette, IA 52142-1857. Offers early childhood (M Ed); English as a second language (M Ed); higher education (M Ed); instructional strategist (M Ed); reading (M Ed); teacher leadership (M Ed).

Utah Valley University, Program in Education, Orem, UT 84058-5999. Offers educational technology (M Ed); elementary mathematics (M Ed); elementary STEM (M Ed); English as a second language (M Ed); reading (M Ed); teachers as leaders (M Ed). *Accreditation:* TEAC. *Program availability:* Part-time. *Degree requirements:* For master's, project. *Entrance requirements:* For master's, GRE, 3 letters of recommendation, interview, essay. Additional exam requirements/recommendations for international students: Required—TOEFL (minimum score 83 iBT). Electronic applications accepted. *Expenses:* Contact institution.

Valley City State University, Online Graduate Programs, Valley City, ND 58072. Offers elementary education (M Ed); English education (M Ed); library and information technologies (M Ed); teaching (MAT); teaching and technology (M Ed); teaching English language learners (M Ed); technology education (M Ed). *Accreditation:* NCATE. *Program availability:* Part-time, evening/weekend, online only, 100% online. *Faculty:* 21 full-time (12 women), 15 part-time/adjunct (11 women). *Students:* 12 full-time (9 women), 138 part-time (99 women); includes 5 minority (3 Hispanic/Latino; 2 Two or more races, non-Hispanic/Latino). Average age 36. 13 applicants, 92% accepted, 12 enrolled. In 2017, 45 master's awarded. *Degree requirements:* For master's, action research report, comprehensive portfolio. *Entrance requirements:* For master's, GRE, MAT, PRAXIS II or National Teaching Board for Professional Standards (if GPA is less than 3.0). Additional exam requirements/recommendations for international students: Required—TOEFL (minimum score 525 paper-based; 71 iBT); Recommended—IELTS (minimum score 5.5). *Application deadline:* For fall admission, 7/21 for domestic and international students; for spring admission, 12/8 for domestic and international students; for summer admission, 5/5 for domestic and international students. Applications are processed on a rolling basis. Application fee: $35. Electronic applications accepted. *Expenses:* $384.21 per credit. *Financial support:* In 2017–18, 16 students received support. Scholarships/grants, tuition waivers (full and partial), and unspecified assistantships available. Financial award applicants required to submit FAFSA. *Faculty research:* Universal accessibility, instructional design and technology, gender communication, STEM education in K-12, English language learners. *Unit head:* Dr. Sheri Okland, Dean, 701-845-7184, E-mail: sheri.l.okland@vcsu.edu. *Application contact:* Misty Lindgren, Graduate Studies, 701-845-7303, Fax: 701-845-7190, E-mail: misty.lindgren@vcsu.edu. Website: http://www.vcsu.edu/graduate

Valparaiso University, Graduate School and Continuing Education, TESOL Program, Valparaiso, IN 46383. Offers MA, Certificate. *Program availability:* Part-time, evening/weekend. *Entrance requirements:* For master's, minimum GPA of 3.0. Additional exam requirements/recommendations for international students: Required—TOEFL (minimum score 550 paper-based; 80 iBT), IELTS (minimum score 6). Electronic applications accepted. *Expenses: Tuition:* Full-time $11,340; part-time $630 per credit hour. *Required fees:* $520; $250 per year. $125 per semester. Tuition and fees vary according to program and reciprocity agreements.

Virginia International University, School of Education, Fairfax, VA 22030. Offers applied linguistics (MS); education (M Ed); teaching English to speakers of other languages (MA). *Program availability:* Part-time, online learning. *Entrance requirements:* For master's, bachelor's degree. Additional exam requirements/recommendations for international students: Required—TOEFL (minimum score 550 paper-based; 80 iBT), IELTS (minimum score 6). Electronic applications accepted.

Walden University, Graduate Programs, Richard W. Riley College of Education and Leadership, Minneapolis, MN 55401. Offers adult education (Post-Master's Certificate); adult learning (Graduate Certificate); college teaching and learning (Graduate Certificate); community college leadership (Ed D); curriculum, instruction and assessment (Ed D, Ed S, Graduate Certificate); developmental education (Graduate Certificate); early childhood administration, management, and leadership (Graduate Certificate); early childhood education (Ed D, Ed S); early childhood public policy and advocacy (Graduate Certificate); early childhood studies (MS), including administration, management and leadership, early childhood public policy and advocacy, teaching adults in the early childhood field, teaching and diversity in early childhood education; education (MS, PhD), including adolescent literacy and learning (MS), curriculum, instruction, and assessment (grades K-12) (MS), curriculum, instruction, assessment, and evaluation (PhD), early childhood leadership and advocacy (PhD), early childhood special education (PhD), educational leadership (MS), educational leadership and administration (principal preparation) (MS), educational technology and design (PhD), elementary reading and literacy (PreK-6) (MS), elementary reading and mathematics (grades K-6) (MS), global and comparative education (PhD), higher education leadership management and policy (PhD), integrating technology in the classroom (grades K-12) (MS), learning, instruction and innovation (PhD), mathematics (grades 5-8) (MS), mathematics (grades K-6) (MS), mathematics and science (grades K-8) (MS), organizational research, assessment, and evaluation (PhD), reading and literacy with a

reading K-12 endorsement (MS), reading literacy assessment and evaluation (PhD), science (grades K-8) (MS), special education (non-licensure) (grades K-12) (MS), teacher leadership (grades K-12) (MS), teaching English language learners (grades K-12) (MS); educational administration and leadership (Ed D); educational leadership and administration (principal preparation) (Ed S); educational technology (Ed D, Ed S, Post Master's Certificate); elementary reading and literacy (Graduate Certificate); engaging culturally diverse learners (Graduate Certificate); enrollment management and institutional marketing (Graduate Certificate); higher education (MS), including adult learning, college teaching and learning, enrollment management and institutional marketing, global higher education, leadership for student success, online and distance learning; higher education and adult learning (Ed D); higher education leadership and management (Ed D); higher education leadership for student success (Graduate Certificate); instructional design and technology (MS, Postbaccalaureate Certificate), including general program (MS), online learning (MS), training and performance improvement (MS); integrating technology in the classroom (Graduate Certificate); mathematics 5-8 (Graduate Certificate); mathematics K-6 (Graduate Certificate); online teaching for adult educators (Graduate Certificate); reading, literacy, and assessment (Ed D, Ed S); science K-8 (Graduate Certificate); special education (Ed D, Ed S, Graduate Certificate); special education (K-age 21) (MAT); teacher leadership (Graduate Certificate); teaching adults English as a second language (Graduate Certificate); teaching adults in the early childhood field (Graduate Certificate); teaching and diversity in early childhood education (Graduate Certificate); teaching English language learners (grades K-12) (Graduate Certificate); teaching K-12 students online (Graduate Certificate). *Accreditation:* NCATE. *Program availability:* Part-time, evening/weekend, online only, 100% online. *Degree requirements:* For doctorate, thesis/dissertation (for some programs), residency; for other advanced degree, residency (for some programs). *Entrance requirements:* For master's, bachelor's degree or higher; minimum GPA of 2.5; official transcripts; goal statement (for some programs); access to computer and Internet; for doctorate, master's degree or higher; three years of related professional or academic experience (preferred); minimum GPA of 3.0; goal statement and current resume (for select programs); official transcripts; access to computer and Internet; for other advanced degree, relevant work experience; access to computer and Internet. Additional exam requirements/recommendations for international students: Required—TOEFL (minimum score 550 paper-based, 79 iBT), IELTS (minimum score 6.5), Michigan English Language Assessment Battery (minimum score 82), or PTE (minimum score 53). Electronic applications accepted.

Washington State University, College of Education, Department of Teaching and Learning, Pullman, WA 99164-2132. Offers cultural studies and social thought in education (PhD); curriculum and instruction (Ed M, MA); English language learners (Ed M, MA); language, literacy and technology (PhD); literacy education (Ed M, MA); mathematics education (PhD); special education (Ed M, MA, PhD); teacher leadership (Ed D); teaching (MIT), including elementary education, secondary education. Programs offered at the Pullman, Spokane, Tri-cities, Vancouver and Global (online) campuses. *Program availability:* Part-time, online learning. *Degree requirements:* For master's, comprehensive exam, thesis, oral or written exam; for doctorate, comprehensive exam, thesis/dissertation, oral and written exam. *Entrance requirements:* For master's, GRE General Test, minimum GPA of 3.0, 3 letters of recommendation, letter of intent, transcripts, resume/curriculum vitae; for doctorate, GRE General Test, minimum GPA of 3.0, 3 letters of recommendation, letter of intent, transcripts, writing sample, resume/curriculum vitae. Additional exam requirements/recommendations for international students: Required—TOEFL (minimum score 550 paper-based; 80 iBT). Electronic applications accepted. *Faculty research:* Intersection of gender, youth cultures and schooling; examination of ideology of power in children's literature; early childhood special education; analyzing pre-service and in-service teacher development; second language acquisition.

Wayland Baptist University, Graduate Programs, Program in Education, Plainview, TX 79072-6998. Offers education administration (M Ed); education diagnostics (M Ed); education literacy (M Ed); elementary certification (M Ed); English (M Ed); English as a second language (M Ed); higher education administration (M Ed); human resources (M Ed); instructional leadership (M Ed); instructional technology (M Ed); leadership training and development (M Ed); science education (M Ed); secondary certification (M Ed); social studies (M Ed); special education (M Ed); sports administration and management (M Ed). *Program availability:* Part-time, evening/weekend, 100% online. *Faculty:* 33 full-time (17 women), 28 part-time/adjunct (17 women). *Students:* 16 full-time (13 women), 221 part-time (143 women); includes 97 minority (26 Black or African American, non-Hispanic/Latino; 1 American Indian or Alaska Native, non-Hispanic/Latino; 5 Asian, non-Hispanic/Latino; 54 Hispanic/Latino; 11 Two or more races, non-Hispanic/Latino), 1 international. Average age 39. 32 applicants, 97% accepted, 23 enrolled. In 2017, 78 master's awarded. *Degree requirements:* For master's, comprehensive exam, capstone course. *Entrance requirements:* For master's, GRE, GMAT or MAT. Additional exam requirements/recommendations for international students: Required—TOEFL (minimum score 500 paper-based; 61 iBT). *Application deadline:* Applications are processed on a rolling basis. Application fee: $50. Electronic applications accepted. *Expenses: Tuition:* Full-time $11,250; part-time $625 per credit hour. *Required fees:* $1200. *Financial support:* Federal Work-Study, institutionally sponsored loans, and scholarships/grants available. Support available to part-time students. Financial award application deadline: 5/1; financial award applicants required to submit FAFSA. *Unit head:* Dr. Gene Whitfill, Dean, 806-291-1047, Fax: 806-291-1951, E-mail: whitfillg@wbu.edu. *Application contact:* Amanda Stanton, Coordinator of Graduate Studies, 806-291-3423, Fax: 806-291-1950, E-mail: stanton@wbu.edu.

Wayne State College, School of Education and Counseling, Department of Educational Foundations and Leadership, Program in Curriculum and Instruction, Wayne, NE 68787. Offers alternative education (MSE); business and information technology education (MSE); communication arts education (MSE); early childhood education (MSE); elementary education (MSE); English as a second language (MSE); English education (MSE); family and consumer sciences education (MSE); industrial technology and vocational education (MSE); learning communities (MSE); mathematics education (MSE); music education (MSE); science education (MSE); social science education (MSE). *Accreditation:* NCATE. *Program availability:* Part-time, evening/weekend. *Degree requirements:* For master's, comprehensive exam, thesis optional. *Entrance requirements:* For master's, GRE General Test. Additional exam requirements/recommendations for international students: Required—TOEFL (minimum score 550 paper-based).

Wayne State University, College of Education, Division of Teacher Education, Detroit, MI 48202. Offers art education (M Ed); bilingual/bicultural education (Certificate); curriculum and instruction (Ed D, PhD, Ed S), including English as a second language (MAT, Ed D, Ed S), K-12 curriculum (PhD); elementary education (MAT), including bilingual/bicultural education (M Ed, MAT), early childhood education (M Ed, MAT), English as a second language (MAT, Ed D, Ed S), foreign language education, science education (M Ed, MAT), special education (M Ed, MAT); elementary mathematics specialist (Certificate); English as a second language (Certificate); reading (M Ed, Ed S); reading, language and literature (Ed D); secondary education (MAT), including bilingual/bicultural education (M Ed, MAT), early childhood education (M Ed, MAT), English as a second language (MAT, Ed D, Ed S), English education, foreign language education,

mathematics education (M Ed, MAT), science education (M Ed, MAT), social studies education (M Ed, MAT); special education (MAT), including career and technical education; teaching and learning (M Ed), including bilingual/bicultural education (M Ed, MAT), early childhood education (M Ed, MAT), elementary education, foreign language, mathematics education (M Ed, MAT), science education (M Ed, MAT), social studies education (M Ed, MAT), special education (M Ed, MAT). *Program availability:* Part-time, blended/hybrid learning. *Faculty:* 22. *Students:* 126 full-time (96 women), 317 part-time (258 women); includes 134 minority (95 Black or African American, non-Hispanic/Latino; 1 American Indian or Alaska Native, non-Hispanic/Latino; 8 Asian, non-Hispanic/Latino; 17 Hispanic/Latino; 1 Native Hawaiian or other Pacific Islander, non-Hispanic/Latino; 12 Two or more races, non-Hispanic/Latino), 13 international. Average age 37. 260 applicants, 33% accepted, 57 enrolled. In 2017, 111 master's, 13 doctorates, 7 other advanced degrees awarded. *Degree requirements:* For master's, essay or project (for some M Ed programs), professional field experience (for MAT programs); for doctorate, thesis/dissertation. *Entrance requirements:* For master's, Michigan Test for Teacher Certification (for most programs), verification of participation in group work with children (for MAT programs), Michigan State Police criminal background check; for doctorate, minimum undergraduate GPA of 3.0, graduate 3.5; interview; curriculum vitae; references; master's degree (for most programs). Additional exam requirements/recommendations for international students: Required—TOEFL (minimum score 550 paper-based; 79 iBT), TWE (minimum score 5.5); Recommended—IELTS (minimum score 6.5). *Application deadline:* For fall admission, 6/1 priority date for domestic students, 5/1 priority date for international students; for winter admission, 10/1 priority date for domestic students, 9/1 priority date for international students; for spring admission, 2/1 priority date for domestic students, 1/1 priority date for international students. Applications are processed on a rolling basis. Application fee: $50. Electronic applications accepted. *Expenses:* Tuition, state resident: full-time $10,224; part-time $638.98 per credit hour. Tuition, nonresident: full-time $22,145; part-time $1384.04 per credit hour. Tuition and fees vary according to course load and program. *Financial support:* In 2017–18, 78 students received support, including 4 fellowships (averaging $13,500 per year), 1 research assistantship with tuition reimbursement available (averaging $16,000 per year); Federal Work-Study, scholarships/grants, and unspecified assistantships also available. Support available to part-time students. Financial award applicants required to submit FAFSA. *Faculty research:* Improving students' skill achievement in mathematics, improving elementary children's understanding of informational text, teachers' use of their pedagogical and mathematical knowledge in the interactive work of teaching, the intersection of identity construction in teaching and learning, identifying effective methods of literacy instruction and assessments for bilingual students in elementary language arts classrooms. *Unit head:* Dr. Thomas Edwards, Interim Associate Dean for Teacher Education, 313-577-3886, E-mail: t.g.edwards@wayne.edu. *Application contact:* 313-577-0902, E-mail: askcoe@wayne.edu.
Website: http://coe.wayne.edu/ted/index.php

Webster University, School of Education, Department of Multidisciplinary Studies, St. Louis, MO 63119-3194. Offers applied educational psychology (MA, Ed S); communication arts (MA); early childhood education (MA, MAT); education and innovation (MA); educational technology (MET); elementary education (MAT); mathematics for educators (MA); middle school education (MAT); multidisciplinary studies (MAT); multimodal literacy for global impact (MA); reading (MA); secondary school education (MAT); special education (MA, MAT); teaching English as a second language (MA); transformative learning in the global community (Ed S). *Program availability:* Part-time. *Entrance requirements:* For master's, minimum GPA of 2.5. Additional exam requirements/recommendations for international students: Required—TOEFL.

West Chester University of Pennsylvania, College of Arts and Humanities, Program in Teaching English as a Second Language, West Chester, PA 19383. Offers MA, Certificate. *Program availability:* Part-time, evening/weekend, 100% online. *Students:* 7 full-time (6 women), 23 part-time (19 women); includes 3 minority (2 Hispanic/Latino; 1 Two or more races, non-Hispanic/Latino), 1 international. Average age 32. 17 applicants, 88% accepted, 10 enrolled. In 2017, 6 master's, 3 other advanced degrees awarded. *Degree requirements:* For master's, comprehensive exam, capstone review and teaching philosophy. *Entrance requirements:* For master's, minimum GPA of 2.8, two letters of recommendation, prior introduction to linguistics coursework, goals statement, experience in learning a second language (recommended); for Certificate, prior PA teaching certification. Additional exam requirements/recommendations for international students: Required—TOEFL or IELTS. *Application deadline:* For fall admission, 5/15 for international students; for spring admission, 10/15 for international students. Applications are processed on a rolling basis. Application fee: $50. Electronic applications accepted. *Expenses:* Tuition, state resident: full-time $9000; part-time $500 per credit. Tuition, nonresident: full-time $13,500; part-time $750 per credit. *Required fees:* $2959; $149.79 per credit. *Financial support:* Scholarships/grants and unspecified assistantships available. Financial award application deadline: 2/15; financial award applicants required to submit FAFSA. *Faculty research:* Second language acquisition, language teaching methods, discourse analysis, computer-assisted language learning, language teacher development. *Unit head:* Dr. Esther Smidt, Director of TESOL Program, 610-738-0410, E-mail: csmidt@wcupa.edu. *Application contact:* Office of Graduate Studies and Extended Education, 610-436-2943, Fax: 610-436-2763, E-mail: gradstudy@wcupa.edu.
Website: http://www.wcupa.edu/_admissions/sch_dgr/tesl.aspx

Western Carolina University, Graduate School, College of Arts and Sciences, Department of English, Cullowhee, NC 28723. Offers literature (MA); professional writing (MA); rhetoric and composition (MA); teaching English to speakers of other languages (Certificate); technical and professional writing (Certificate). *Program availability:* Part-time, evening/weekend. *Students:* 31. *Degree requirements:* For master's, one foreign language, comprehensive exam, thesis (for some programs). *Entrance requirements:* For master's, appropriate undergraduate degree, writing sample, 3 letters of recommendation. Additional exam requirements/recommendations for international students: Required—TOEFL (minimum score 550 paper-based, 79 iBT) or IELTS (6.5). *Application deadline:* For fall admission, 2/15 priority date for domestic and international students; for spring admission, 11/15 priority date for domestic students, 10/15 priority date for international students. Applications are processed on a rolling basis. Application fee: $65. Electronic applications accepted. *Expenses:* $10,000 per year in-state full-time; $20,308 per year out-of-state full-time. *Financial support:* In 2017–18, 1 research assistantship with full and partial tuition reimbursement (averaging $9,000 per year), 16 teaching assistantships with full and partial tuition reimbursements (averaging $9,500 per year) were awarded; career-related internships or fieldwork, institutionally sponsored loans, scholarships/grants, and unspecified assistantships also available. Financial award application deadline: 2/15; financial award applicants required to submit FAFSA. *Faculty research:* Teaching English to speakers of other languages (TESOL), language assessment, applied linguistics, poetry, folk and fairy tales, post World War II British literature, Appalachian and Southern literature. *Unit head:* Dr. Brent Kinser, Department Head, E-mail: bkinser@wcu.edu. *Application contact:* Bobbi Smith, Graduate Admissions Coordinator, E-mail: bobbismith@email.wcu.edu.

Website: https://www.wcu.edu/learn/departments-schools-colleges/cas/humanities/english/enggrad/index.aspx

Western Illinois University, School of Graduate Studies, College of Education and Human Services, Department of Educational Studies, Program in Educational and Interdisciplinary Studies, Macomb, IL 61455-1390. Offers educational and interdisciplinary studies (MS Ed); teaching English to speakers of other languages (Certificate). *Accreditation:* NCATE. *Program availability:* Part-time. *Students:* 6 full-time (all women), 29 part-time (25 women); includes 4 minority (1 Asian, non-Hispanic/Latino; 2 Hispanic/Latino; 1 Two or more races, non-Hispanic/Latino), 2 international. Average age 42. 15 applicants, 73% accepted, 10 enrolled. In 2017, 15 master's, 10 Certificates awarded. *Degree requirements:* For master's, thesis or alternative. *Entrance requirements:* For master's, minimum GPA of 2.75, interview. Additional exam requirements/recommendations for international students: Required—TOEFL (minimum score 550 paper-based; 80 iBT). *Application deadline:* Applications are processed on a rolling basis. Application fee: $30. Electronic applications accepted. *Financial support:* In 2017–18, 1 research assistantship with full tuition reimbursement (averaging $7,544 per year) was awarded; unspecified assistantships also available. Financial award applicants required to submit FAFSA. *Unit head:* Dr. Greg Montalvo, Interim Chairperson, 309-298-1183. *Application contact:* Dr. Nancy Parsons, Associate Provost and Director of Graduate Studies, 309-298-1806, Fax: 309-298-2345, E-mail: grad-office@wiu.edu.
Website: http://www.wiu.edu/coehs/es/programs/eis/eis.php

Western Kentucky University, Graduate Studies, Potter College of Arts and Letters, Department of English, Bowling Green, KY 42101. Offers education (MA); English (MA Ed); literature (MA), including American literature, British literature, literary theory, women writers, world literature; teaching English as a second language (MA); writing (MA). *Program availability:* Part-time, evening/weekend. *Degree requirements:* For master's, comprehensive exam, thesis optional, final exam. *Entrance requirements:* For master's, GRE General Test, minimum GPA of 2.75. Additional exam requirements/recommendations for international students: Required—TOEFL (minimum score 555 paper-based; 79 iBT). *Faculty research:* Improving writing, linking teacher knowledge and performance, Victorian women writers, Kentucky women writers, Kentucky poets.

Western New Mexico University, Graduate Division, School of Education, Silver City, NM 88062-0680. Offers bilingual education (MAT); educational leadership (MA); elementary education (MAT); reading (MAT); secondary education (MAT); special education (MAT); TESOL (teaching English to speakers of other languages) (MAT). *Accreditation:* NCATE. *Program availability:* Part-time, online learning. *Degree requirements:* For master's, comprehensive exam. *Entrance requirements:* For master's, minimum GPA of 3.0 in last 64 hours of undergraduate study. Additional exam requirements/recommendations for international students: Required—TOEFL (minimum score 550 paper-based; 79 iBT). Electronic applications accepted. *Faculty research:* International education, electronic reading assessment, developing STEM teachers.

Wheaton College, Graduate School, Department of Intercultural Studies, Wheaton, IL 60187-5593. Offers global engagement (Certificate); intercultural studies (MA); intercultural studies/teaching English as a second language (MA); teaching English as a second language (Certificate). *Program availability:* Part-time. *Faculty:* 1 full-time (0 women), 6 part-time/adjunct (all women). *Students:* 18 full-time (13 women), 32 part-time (23 women); includes 8 minority (2 Black or African American, non-Hispanic/Latino; 3 Asian, non-Hispanic/Latino; 2 Hispanic/Latino; 1 Two or more races, non-Hispanic/Latino), 11 international. Average age 33. 32 applicants, 97% accepted, 12 enrolled. In 2017, 20 master's awarded. *Degree requirements:* For master's, comprehensive exam, thesis or alternative. *Entrance requirements:* For master's, GRE General Test, MAT. Additional exam requirements/recommendations for international students: Required—TOEFL (minimum score 550 paper-based; 80 iBT), IELTS (minimum score 6.5). *Application deadline:* For fall admission, 5/1 for domestic students, 1/1 for international students; for spring admission, 11/1 for domestic students. Applications are processed on a rolling basis. Application fee: $30. Electronic applications accepted. *Expenses:* Tuition: Full-time $19,800; part-time $825 per credit hour. Tuition and fees vary according to degree level and program. *Financial support:* Career-related internships or fieldwork, scholarships/grants, and unspecified assistantships available. Financial award application deadline: 3/1; financial award applicants required to submit FAFSA. *Unit head:* Dr. Robert Gallagher, Chair, 630-752-5948, E-mail: intercultural.studies@wheaton.edu. *Application contact:* Director of Graduate Admissions, 630-752-5195, Fax: 630-752-5047, E-mail: graduate.admissions@wheaton.edu.
Website: https://www.wheaton.edu/graduate-school/degrees/ma-in-intercultural-studies/

Wilkes University, College of Graduate and Professional Studies, School of Education, Wilkes-Barre, PA 18766-0002. Offers educational development and strategies (MS Ed); educational leadership (MS Ed, Ed D); effective teaching (MS Ed); instructional media (MS Ed); instructional technology (MS Ed); international school leadership (MS Ed); international teaching and learning (MS Ed); literacy specialist (MS Ed); middle level education (MS Ed); online teaching (MS Ed); school business leadership (MS Ed); special education (MS Ed); teaching English to speakers of other languages (MS Ed). *Program availability:* Part-time, evening/weekend, 100% online, blended/hybrid learning. *Students:* 76 full-time (57 women), 1,586 part-time (1,204 women); includes 82 minority (10 Black or African American, non-Hispanic/Latino; 12 Asian, non-Hispanic/Latino; 41 Hispanic/Latino; 1 Native Hawaiian or other Pacific Islander, non-Hispanic/Latino; 18 Two or more races, non-Hispanic/Latino). Average age 34. In 2017, 619 master's, 23 doctorates awarded. *Entrance requirements:* Additional exam requirements/recommendations for international students: Required—TOEFL (minimum score 550 paper-based; 79 iBT). *Application deadline:* Applications are processed on a rolling basis. Application fee: $45 ($65 for international students). Electronic applications accepted. *Expenses:* Contact institution. *Financial support:* Unspecified assistantships available. Financial award application deadline: 3/1; financial award applicants required to submit FAFSA. *Unit head:* Dr. Rhonda Rabbitt, Dean, 570-408-4680, Fax: 570-408-7872, E-mail: rhonda.rabbitt@wilkes.edu. *Application contact:* Stephanie Wasmanski, Associate Director of Graduate Admissions, 570-408-5535, Fax: 570-408-7846, E-mail: stephanie.wasmanski@wilkes.edu.
Website: http://www.wilkes.edu/academics/graduate-programs/masters-programs/graduate-education/index.aspx

William Paterson University of New Jersey, College of Humanities and Social Sciences, Wayne, NJ 07470-8420. Offers applied sociology (MA); assessment and evaluation research (Certificate); bilingual education (Certificate); clinical and counseling psychology (MA); clinical psychology (Psy D); creative and professional writing (MFA); English (MA); history (MA); public policy and international affairs (MA); teaching English as a second language (Certificate). *Program availability:* Part-time. *Faculty:* 36 full-time (21 women), 10 part-time/adjunct (5 women). *Students:* 62 full-time (44 women), 102 part-time (71 women); includes 76 minority (12 Black or African American, non-Hispanic/Latino; 8 Asian, non-Hispanic/Latino; 50 Hispanic/Latino; 6 Two or more races, non-Hispanic/Latino), 6 international. Average age 33. 156 applicants, 51% accepted, 52 enrolled. In 2017, 39 master's awarded. *Degree requirements:* For master's, thesis (for some programs), internship (for some programs). *Entrance requirements:* For master's, GRE/MAT, minimum GPA of 3.0; 2 letters of recommendation; writing sample/personal statement. Additional exam requirements/recommendations for international students:

Required—TOEFL (minimum score 550 paper-based; 79 iBT), IELTS (minimum score 6). *Application deadline:* For fall admission, 6/1 for domestic students, 3/1 for international students; for spring admission, 11/1 for domestic students, 10/1 for international students. Applications are processed on a rolling basis. Application fee: $50. Electronic applications accepted. *Expenses:* Tuition, state resident: full-time $13,920; part-time $6264 per year. Tuition, nonresident: full-time $21,700; part-time $9765 per year. *Required fees:* $80; $36 per year. Tuition and fees vary according to course load, degree level and program. *Financial support:* In 2017–18, 3,480 students received support. Career-related internships or fieldwork, Federal Work-Study, scholarships/grants, and unspecified assistantships available. Support available to part-time students. Financial award application deadline: 3/15; financial award applicants required to submit FAFSA. *Faculty research:* Relationship violence, work-family balance, social development of Japan, theories justifying war, reactions to trauma. *Total annual research expenditures:* $32,300. *Unit head:* Dr. Kara Rabbitt, Dean, 973-720-2180, Fax: 973-720-2955, E-mail: rabbittk@wpunj.edu. *Application contact:* Tinu Adeniran, Associate Director, Graduate Admissions, 973-720-2764, Fax: 973-720-2035, E-mail: adenirant@wpunj.edu.
Website: http://www.wpunj.edu/cohss

Wilmington University, College of Education, New Castle, DE 19720-6491. Offers applied technology in education (M Ed); career and technical education (M Ed); educational leadership (Ed D); elementary and secondary school counseling (M Ed); elementary studies (M Ed); ESOL literacy (M Ed); higher education leadership (Ed D); instruction: gifted and talented (M Ed); instruction: teacher of reading (M Ed); instruction: teaching and learning (M Ed); organizational leadership (Ed D); school leadership (M Ed); secondary education (MAT); special education (M Ed). *Accreditation:* NCATE. *Program availability:* Part-time, evening/weekend. *Faculty:* 23 full-time (13 women), 162 part-time/adjunct (99 women). *Students:* 546 full-time (394 women), 960 part-time (732 women); includes 320 minority (241 Black or African American, non-Hispanic/Latino; 12 American Indian or Alaska Native, non-Hispanic/Latino; 11 Asian, non-Hispanic/Latino; 28 Hispanic/Latino; 3 Native Hawaiian or other Pacific Islander, non-Hispanic/Latino; 25 Two or more races, non-Hispanic/Latino), 7 international. Average age 34. 1,068 applicants, 64% accepted, 582 enrolled. In 2017, 430 master's, 59 doctorates awarded. *Entrance requirements:* For master's, 2 letters of recommendation, interview. Additional exam requirements/recommendations for international students: Required—TOEFL

(minimum score 500 paper-based). *Application deadline:* For fall admission, 4/30 for domestic students. Applications are processed on a rolling basis. Application fee: $35. Electronic applications accepted. *Expenses: Tuition:* Part-time $466 per credit. *Required fees:* $25 per semester. Tuition and fees vary according to degree level and campus/location. *Financial support:* Applicants required to submit FAFSA. *Unit head:* Dr. John C. Gray, Dean, 302-295-1139. *Application contact:* Laura Morris, Director of Admissions, 877-967-5464, E-mail: infocenter@wilmu.edu.
Website: http://www.wilmu.edu/education/

Winona State University, College of Liberal Arts, Department of English, Winona, MN 55987. Offers English (MS); literature and language (MA); TESOL (MA). *Program availability:* Part-time. *Degree requirements:* For master's, thesis or alternative.

Worcester State University, Graduate School, Department of Education, Program in English as a Second Language, Worcester, MA 01602-2597. Offers M Ed, Postbaccalaureate Certificate. *Program availability:* Part-time, evening/weekend. *Students:* 3 full-time (1 woman), 16 part-time (15 women); includes 3 minority (all Hispanic/Latino). Average age 38. 10 applicants, 90% accepted, 9 enrolled. In 2017, 3 other advanced degrees awarded. *Degree requirements:* For master's, one foreign language. *Entrance requirements:* For master's, GRE or MAT, bachelor's degree from accredited institution with minimum cumulative GPA of 2.75, current teaching license in ESL at initial or professional level, essay, official transcripts, two letters of recommendation. Additional exam requirements/recommendations for international students: Required—TOEFL (minimum score 550 paper-based; 79 iBT). *Application deadline:* For fall admission, 6/15 for domestic and international students; for spring admission, 11/1 for domestic and international students; for summer admission, 4/1 for domestic and international students. Applications are processed on a rolling basis. Application fee: $50. Electronic applications accepted. *Expenses:* Tuition, state resident: full-time $3042; part-time $169 per credit hour. Tuition, nonresident: full-time $3042; part-time $169 per credit hour. *Required fees:* $2754; $153 per credit hour. *Financial support:* Career-related internships or fieldwork, scholarships/grants, and unspecified assistantships available. Financial award applicants required to submit FAFSA. *Unit head:* Dr. Margarita Perez, Coordinator, 508-929-8609, E-mail: mperez@worcester.edu. *Application contact:* Sara Grady, Associate Dean of Graduate Studies and Professional Development, 508-929-8130, E-mail: sara.grady@worcester.edu.

Multilingual and Multicultural Education

Alliant International University–San Francisco, Shirley M. Hufstedler School of Education, Teacher Education Programs, San Francisco, CA 94133. Offers auditory oral education (Certificate); CLAD (Certificate); education specialist: mild/moderate disabilities (Credential); preliminary multiple subject (Credential); preliminary single subject (Credential); professional clear multiple subject (Credential); professional clear single subject (Credential); special education (MA); teaching (MA); TESOL (Certificate). *Program availability:* Part-time, evening/weekend. *Degree requirements:* For master's, thesis. *Entrance requirements:* For degree, California Basic Educational Skills Test, minimum GPA of 2.5. Additional exam requirements/recommendations for international students: Required—TOEFL (minimum score 550 paper-based), TWE (minimum score 5). Electronic applications accepted. *Faculty research:* Curriculum development, first year teachers, cross-cultural issues in teaching, biliteracy.

American College of Education, Graduate Programs, Indianapolis, IN 46204. Offers curriculum and instruction (M Ed), including bilingual, ESL; educational leadership (M Ed); educational technology (M Ed).

Bank Street College of Education, Graduate School, Program in Bilingual Education, New York, NY 10025. Offers bilingual childhood special education (Ed M); bilingual early childhood general education (MS Ed); bilingual early childhood special and general education (MS Ed); bilingual early childhood special education (Ed M, MS Ed); bilingual elementary/childhood general education (MS Ed); bilingual elementary/childhood special and general education (MS Ed); bilingual elementary/childhood special education (MS Ed). *Degree requirements:* For master's, thesis. *Entrance requirements:* For master's, interview, fluency in Spanish and English, essays. Additional exam requirements/recommendations for international students: Required—TOEFL (minimum score 600 paper-based; 100 iBT), IELTS (minimum score 7). Electronic applications accepted. *Faculty research:* Dual language education, language immersion, bilingual education in the urban classroom, community and school partnerships.

Boise State University, College of Education, Department of Literacy, Language and Culture, Boise, ID 83725-0399. Offers bilingual education (M Ed); English as a new language (M Ed); literacy (MA). *Accreditation:* NCATE. *Program availability:* Part-time, evening/weekend. *Faculty:* 11 full-time (6 women). *Students:* 10 full-time (9 women), 53 part-time (46 women); includes 9 minority (1 Black or African American, non-Hispanic/Latino; 2 Asian, non-Hispanic/Latino; 5 Hispanic/Latino; 1 Native Hawaiian or other Pacific Islander, non-Hispanic/Latino), 6 international. Average age 36. 20 applicants, 75% accepted, 12 enrolled. In 2017, 26 master's awarded. *Degree requirements:* For master's, thesis optional. *Entrance requirements:* For master's, minimum GPA of 3.0. Additional exam requirements/recommendations for international students: Required—TOEFL (minimum score 550 paper-based; 80 iBT), IELTS (minimum score 6). Application fee: $65 ($95 for international students). Electronic applications accepted. *Expenses:* Tuition, state resident: full-time $6471; part-time $390 per credit. Tuition, nonresident: full-time $21,787; part-time $685 per credit. *Required fees:* $2283; $100 per term. Part-time tuition and fees vary according to course load and program. *Financial support:* Scholarships/grants and unspecified assistantships available. Financial award applicants required to submit FAFSA. *Unit head:* Dr. Maggie Chase, Department Chair, 208-426-3206, E-mail: maggiechase@boisestate.edu. *Application contact:* Dr. Arturo Rodriguez, Program Coordinator, 208-426-2243, E-mail: arturorodriguez@boisestate.edu.
Website: https://education.boisestate.edu/literacy/master-of-arts/

Brooklyn College of the City University of New York, School of Education, Program in Childhood Education, Brooklyn, NY 11210-2889. Offers bilingual education (MS Ed); liberal arts (MS Ed); mathematics (MS Ed); science and environmental education (MS Ed). *Program availability:* Part-time, evening/weekend. *Entrance requirements:* For master's, LAST, interview, previous course work in education, writing sample, resume, 2 letters of recommendation. Additional exam requirements/recommendations for international students: Required—TOEFL (minimum score 500 paper-based; 61 iBT). Electronic applications accepted. *Faculty research:* Emotional intelligence, multiculturalism, arts immersion, the Holocaust.

Brown University, Graduate School, Department of Portuguese and Brazilian Studies, Providence, RI 02912. Offers Brazilian studies (AM); English as a second language and cross-cultural studies (AM); Portuguese and Brazilian studies (AM, PhD); Portuguese bilingual education and cross-cultural studies (AM). *Degree requirements:* For doctorate, thesis/dissertation.

Buffalo State College, State University of New York, The Graduate School, Faculty of Applied Science and Education, Department of Exceptional Education, Program in Teaching Bilingual Exceptional Individuals, Buffalo, NY 14222-1095. Offers MS Ed. *Accreditation:* NCATE. *Program availability:* Part-time, evening/weekend. *Degree requirements:* For master's, project. *Entrance requirements:* For master's, minimum GPA of 2.5. Additional exam requirements/recommendations for international students: Required—TOEFL (minimum score 550 paper-based).

California State University, Fullerton, Graduate Studies, College of Education, Department of Elementary and Bilingual Education, Fullerton, CA 92831-3599. Offers bilingual/bicultural education (MS); educational technology (MS); elementary curriculum and instruction (MS). *Accreditation:* NCATE. *Program availability:* Part-time. *Faculty:* 10 full-time (7 women), 10 part-time/adjunct (8 women). *Students:* 224 full-time (194 women), 191 part-time (162 women); includes 218 minority (6 Black or African American, non-Hispanic/Latino; 1 American Indian or Alaska Native, non-Hispanic/Latino; 65 Asian, non-Hispanic/Latino; 127 Hispanic/Latino; 1 Native Hawaiian or other Pacific Islander, non-Hispanic/Latino; 18 Two or more races, non-Hispanic/Latino), 3 international. Average age 32. 272 applicants, 69% accepted, 170 enrolled. *Degree requirements:* For master's, comprehensive exam, project or thesis. *Entrance requirements:* For master's, minimum GPA of 2.5, teaching certificate. Application fee: $55. *Financial support:* Career-related internships or fieldwork, Federal Work-Study, institutionally sponsored loans, and scholarships/grants available. Support available to part-time students. Financial award application deadline: 3/1; financial award applicants required to submit FAFSA. *Faculty research:* Teacher training and tracking, model for improvement of teaching. *Unit head:* Lisa Kirtman, Chair, 657-278-4731. *Application contact:* Admissions/Applications, 657-278-2371.
Website: http://ed.fullerton.edu/EDEL/

California State University, Northridge, Graduate Studies, Michael D. Eisner College of Education, Department of Elementary Education, Northridge, CA 91330. Offers curriculum and instruction (MA); language and literacy (MA); multilingual/multicultural education (MA). *Accreditation:* NCATE. *Program availability:* Part-time, evening/weekend. *Students:* 3 full-time (all women), 62 part-time (56 women); includes 37 minority (7 Asian, non-Hispanic/Latino; 26 Hispanic/Latino; 4 Two or more races, non-Hispanic/Latino). Average age 30. 42 applicants, 50% accepted, 19 enrolled. In 2017, 103 master's awarded. *Degree requirements:* For master's, comprehensive exam. *Entrance requirements:* For master's, GRE General Test or minimum GPA of 3.0. Additional exam requirements/recommendations for international students: Required—TOEFL. *Application deadline:* For fall admission, 11/30 for domestic students. Application fee: $55. *Financial support:* Federal Work-Study available. Financial award application deadline: 3/1. *Unit head:* Dr. Joyce Burstein, Chair, 818-677-2621.
Website: http://www.csun.edu/eisner-education/elementary-education

California State University, Sacramento, College of Education, Graduate and Professional Studies in Education, Sacramento, CA 95819. Offers behavioral science and gender equity (MA); child development (MA); counseling (MS); curriculum and instruction (MA); education (Ed D), including K-12 and community college; education leadership and policy studies (MA), including higher education, PreK-12; education specialist (Ed S), including school psychology; educational technology (MA); language and literacy (MA); multicultural education (MA); school psychology (MA); special education (MA); workforce development advocacy (MA). *Program availability:* Part-time, evening/weekend, blended/hybrid learning. *Students:* 381 full-time (294 women), 135 part-time (101 women); includes 296 minority (44 Black or African American, non-Hispanic/Latino; 1 American Indian or Alaska Native, non-Hispanic/Latino; 94 Asian, non-Hispanic/Latino; 153 Hispanic/Latino; 4 Native Hawaiian or other Pacific Islander, non-Hispanic/Latino), 3 international. Average age 32. 553 applicants, 53% accepted, 292 enrolled. In 2017, 147 master's, 13 doctorates, 10 other advanced degrees awarded. *Degree requirements:* For master's, thesis or project; writing proficiency exam; for doctorate, thesis/dissertation. *Entrance requirements:* For master's and doctorate,

GRE. Additional exam requirements/recommendations for international students: Required—TOEFL (minimum score 550 paper-based; 80 iBT); Recommended—IELTS (minimum score 7), TSE. *Application deadline:* For fall admission, 2/15 for domestic students, 1/15 for international students. Applications are processed on a rolling basis. Application fee: $55. Electronic applications accepted. *Expenses:* Contact institution. *Financial support:* Career-related internships or fieldwork, Federal Work-Study, and scholarships/grants available. Support available to part-time students. Financial award application deadline: 3/1; financial award applicants required to submit FAFSA. *Unit head:* Dr. Elizabeth Liles, Chair, 916-278-5942, E-mail: coe@csus.edu. *Application contact:* Jose Martinez, Graduate Admissions Supervisor, 916-278-7871, E-mail: martinj@skymail.csus.edu.
Website: http://www.csus.edu/coe/academics/graduate/index.html

California State University, Stanislaus, College of Education, Kinesiology and Social Work, MA Program in Education, Turlock, CA 95382. Offers curriculum and instruction (MA), including education technology, elementary education, multilingual education, physical education, reading, secondary education, special education; school administration (MA); school counseling (MA). *Program availability:* Part-time, evening/weekend. *Degree requirements:* For master's, comprehensive exam (for some programs), thesis (for some programs). *Entrance requirements:* For master's, MAT, GRE, or CBEST (varies by concentration), 3 letters of recommendation, personal statement. Additional exam requirements/recommendations for international students: Required—TOEFL (minimum score 550 paper-based). Electronic applications accepted. *Faculty research:* Children's perspectives on historical events, method elementary schools dual language education, K-12 reading programs.

Chicago State University, School of Graduate and Professional Studies, College of Education, Department of Special Education, Early Childhood Education and Bilingual Education, Program in Bilingual Education, Chicago, IL 60628. Offers MS Ed. *Accreditation:* NCATE. *Degree requirements:* For master's, comprehensive exam, thesis optional. *Entrance requirements:* For master's, minimum GPA of 2.75. *Application deadline:* For fall admission, 7/1 for domestic students; for spring admission, 11/10 for domestic students. Application fee: $25. *Unit head:* Dr. Maria Teresa Garreton, Director, 773-995-3932, Fax: 773-995-4532, E-mail: m-garreton@csu.edu. *Application contact:* Anika Miller, Graduate Studies Office, 773-995-2404, E-mail: g-studies1@csu.edu.

City College of the City University of New York, Graduate School, School of Education, Department of Teaching, Learning and Culture, Program in Bilingual Education, New York, NY 10031-9198. Offers MS. *Accreditation:* NCATE. *Program availability:* Part-time. *Degree requirements:* For master's, thesis. *Entrance requirements:* For master's, Liberal Arts and Sciences Test (LAST), Content Specialty Test (CST). Additional exam requirements/recommendations for international students: Required—TOEFL.

The College at Brockport, State University of New York, School of Education, Health, and Human Services, Department of Education and Human Development, Program in Bilingual Education, Brockport, NY 14420-2997. Offers MS Ed, AGC. *Accreditation:* NCATE. *Program availability:* Part-time. *Students:* 10 part-time (8 women); includes 3 minority (all Hispanic/Latino). 4 applicants, 100% accepted, 2 enrolled. In 2017, 2 master's, 5 AGCs awarded. *Degree requirements:* For master's, thesis or alternative. *Entrance requirements:* For master's, edTPA, GRE or MAT, minimum GPA of 3.0, letters of recommendation, statement of objectives, demonstrated proficiency in Spanish at the advanced level, appropriate provisional or initial teaching certificate; for AGC, minimum GPA of 3.0, appropriate New York state teaching certification, demonstrated proficiency in Spanish at the advanced level. Additional exam requirements/recommendations for international students: Required—TOEFL (minimum score 550 paper-based; 79 iBT), IELTS (minimum score 6.5). *Application deadline:* For fall admission, 3/15 priority date for domestic and international students; for spring admission, 10/15 priority date for domestic and international students. Application fee: $80. Electronic applications accepted. *Expenses:* Tuition, state resident: full-time $10,870; part-time $453 per credit hour. Tuition, nonresident: full-time $22,210. *Required fees:* $988; $246 per semester. *Financial support:* Federal Work-Study, scholarships/grants, and unspecified assistantships available. Support available to part-time students. Financial award application deadline: 3/15; financial award applicants required to submit FAFSA. *Unit head:* Dr. Sue Robb, Chairperson, 585-395-5935, Fax: 585-395-2172, E-mail: srobb@brockport.edu. *Application contact:* Anne Walton, Coordinator of Certification and Graduate Advisement, 585-395-2326, Fax: 585-395-2172, E-mail: awalton@brockport.edu.
Website: https://www.brockport.edu/academics/education_human_development/department.html

College of Mount Saint Vincent, School of Professional and Graduate Studies, Department of Teacher Education, Riverdale, NY 10471-1093. Offers instructional technology and global perspectives (Certificate); middle level education (Certificate); multicultural studies (Certificate); teaching English to speakers of other languages (MS Ed); urban and multicultural education (MS Ed). *Accreditation:* TEAC. *Program availability:* Part-time. *Degree requirements:* For master's, comprehensive exam. *Entrance requirements:* For master's, interview, New York teaching certificate. Additional exam requirements/recommendations for international students: Required—TOEFL.

The College of New Rochelle, Graduate School, Division of Education, Program in Multilingual/Multicultural Education, New Rochelle, NY 10805-2308. Offers bilingual education (Certificate); multilingual/multicultural education (Certificate); teaching to speakers of other languages (MS Ed, Certificate). *Program availability:* Part-time, evening/weekend. *Degree requirements:* For master's, student teaching or practicum. *Entrance requirements:* For master's, interview, minimum GPA of 3.0 in field, 2.7 overall. *Expenses: Tuition:* Full-time $17,406. *Required fees:* $1120.

College of Staten Island of the City University of New York, Graduate Programs, School of Education, Program in Bilingual Education, Staten Island, NY 10314-6600. Offers Advanced Certificate. *Program availability:* Part-time, evening/weekend. *Entrance requirements:* For degree, New York State Initial Teaching Certification (certification in TESOL and World Languages not acceptable); BA with minimum GPA of 3.0; proficiency in language other than English. Additional exam requirements/recommendations for international students: Required—TOEFL (minimum score 550 paper-based; 79 iBT), IELTS (minimum score 6.5). *Application deadline:* For fall admission, 4/25 priority date for domestic and international students; for spring admission, 11/25 priority date for domestic and international students. Applications are processed on a rolling basis. Application fee: $125. Electronic applications accepted. *Expenses:* Tuition, state resident: full-time $10,450; part-time $440 per credit. Tuition, nonresident: full-time $19,320; part-time $440 per credit. *Required fees:* $181.10 per semester. Tuition and fees vary according to program. *Unit head:* Dr. Rachel Grant, Program Coordinator, 719-982-3740, E-mail: rachel.grant@csi.cuny.edu. *Application contact:* Sasha Spence, Associate Director for Graduate Admissions, 718-982-2019, Fax: 718-982-2500, E-mail: sasha.spence@csi.cuny.edu.
Website: https://www.csi.cuny.edu/sites/default/files/pdf/admissions/grad/pdf/Bilingual_Advanced_Certificate.pdf

The College of William and Mary, School of Education, Program in Curriculum and Instruction, Williamsburg, VA 23187-8795. Offers elementary education (MA Ed); English as a second language/bilingual education (MA Ed); gifted education (MA Ed); literacy leadership (MA Ed); math specialist (MA Ed); secondary education (MA Ed), including English, foreign language, math, science, social studies; special education (MA Ed). *Accreditation:* NCATE. *Program availability:* Part-time. *Faculty:* 23 full-time (16 women), 40 part-time/adjunct (32 women). *Students:* 85 full-time (63 women), 16 part-time (15 women); includes 18 minority (5 Black or African American, non-Hispanic/Latino; 4 Asian, non-Hispanic/Latino; 7 Hispanic/Latino; 2 Two or more races, non-Hispanic/Latino), 1 international. Average age 27. 152 applicants, 83% accepted, 90 enrolled. In 2017, 67 master's awarded. *Degree requirements:* For master's, project. *Entrance requirements:* For master's, GRE, MAT, PRAXIS Core Academic Skills for Educators, minimum GPA of 2.5. Additional exam requirements/recommendations for international students: Required—TOEFL (minimum score 100 iBT), IELTS (minimum score 7). *Application deadline:* For fall admission, 1/15 for domestic and international students; for spring admission, 10/1 for domestic and international students. Application fee: $50. Electronic applications accepted. *Expenses:* $9,630 resident full-time, $535 resident part-time per credit hour; $25,920 nonresident full-time, $1,265 nonresident part-time per credit hour; $5,944 full-time fees. *Financial support:* In 2017–18, 35 students received support, including 7 research assistantships (averaging $6,678 per year); scholarships/grants and unspecified assistantships also available. Financial award application deadline: 1/15; financial award applicants required to submit FAFSA. *Faculty research:* Educational technology, professional development and evaluation, inclusive education, rural education, education policy. *Unit head:* Dr. Jeremy D. Stoddard, Department Chair, 757-221-2348, E-mail: jdstod@wm.edu. *Application contact:* Dorothy Smith Osborne, Assistant Dean for Academic Programs and Student Services, 757-221-2317, E-mail: dsosbo@wm.edu.
Website: http://education.wm.edu

Columbia International University, Columbia Graduate School, Columbia, SC 29203. Offers Bible teaching (MABT); counseling (MACN); early childhood and elementary education (MAT); educational administration (M Ed); educational leadership (PhD); instruction and learning (M Ed); teaching English as a foreign language (Certificate); teaching English as a foreign language and intercultural studies (MATF). *Program availability:* Part-time, evening/weekend, online learning. *Degree requirements:* For master's, internships, professional project. *Entrance requirements:* For master's, MAT; GRE (for some programs), minimum GPA of 2.7. Additional exam requirements/recommendations for international students: Required—TOEFL. Electronic applications accepted.

Dallas Baptist University, Dorothy M. Bush College of Education, Program in Bilingual Education, Dallas, TX 75211-9299. Offers bilingual education (M Ed), including dual language, English as a second language/multilingual. *Program availability:* Part-time, evening/weekend. *Application deadline:* Applications are processed on a rolling basis. Application fee: $25. Electronic applications accepted. Application fee is waived when completed online. *Expenses: Tuition:* Full-time $16,308; part-time $906 per credit hour. *Required fees:* $900; $450 per semester. Tuition and fees vary according to course load and degree level. *Unit head:* Dr. Neil Dugger, Dean, 214-333-5202, E-mail: neil@dbu.edu. *Application contact:* Dr. Adelita Baker, Program Director, 214-333-5515, E-mail: adelita@dbu.edu.
Website: http://www3.dbu.edu/graduate/bilingual_education.asp

Dallas Baptist University, Dorothy M. Bush College of Education, Program in Reading and English as a Second Language, Dallas, TX 75211-9299. Offers bilingual education (M Ed); reading and English as a second language (M Ed). *Program availability:* Part-time, evening/weekend. *Application deadline:* Applications are processed on a rolling basis. Application fee: $25. Electronic applications accepted. Application fee is waived when completed online. *Expenses: Tuition:* Full-time $16,308; part-time $906 per credit hour. *Required fees:* $900; $450 per semester. Tuition and fees vary according to course load and degree level. *Unit head:* Dr. Neil Dugger, Dean, 214-333-5202, E-mail: neil@dbu.edu. *Application contact:* Dr. Adelita Baker, Program Director, 214-333-5515, E-mail: adelita@dbu.edu.
Website: http://www3.dbu.edu/graduate/english_reading.asp

DePaul University, College of Education, Chicago, IL 60614. Offers bilingual-bicultural education (M Ed, MA); counseling (M Ed, MA), including clinical mental health counseling, college student development, school counseling; curriculum studies (M Ed, MA, Ed D); early childhood education (M Ed, MA, Ed D); educational leadership (M Ed, MA, Ed D), including Catholic leadership (M Ed, MA), general (M Ed, MA), higher education (M Ed, MA), physical education (M Ed, MA), principal preparation (M Ed), teacher preparation (M Ed); elementary education (M Ed, MA); middle grades education (M Ed); middle school mathematics education (MS); reading specialist (M Ed, MA); secondary education (M Ed, MA); social and cultural foundations in education (M Ed, MA); special education (M Ed); sport, fitness and recreation leadership (MS); value-creating education for global citizenship (M Ed); world languages education (M Ed, MA). *Program availability:* Part-time, evening/weekend, online learning. *Degree requirements:* For doctorate, thesis/dissertation. *Application deadline:* Applications are processed on a rolling basis. Application fee: $40. Electronic applications accepted. *Financial support:* Application deadline: 12/31; applicants required to submit FAFSA. *Unit head:* Dr. Paul Zionts, Dean, 773-325-7581, Fax: 773-325-7713, E-mail: pzionts@depaul.edu. *Application contact:* Dr. Paul Zionts, Dean, 773-325-7581, Fax: 773-325-7713, E-mail: pzionts@depaul.edu.
Website: http://education.depaul.edu

Eastern New Mexico University, Graduate School, College of Education and Technology, Department of Curriculum and Instruction, Portales, NM 88130. Offers alternative licensure in elementary education (M Ed); bilingual education (M Ed); career and technical education (M Ed); educational technology (M Ed); elementary education (M Ed); English as a second language (M Ed); pedagogy and learning (M Ed); reading/literacy (M Ed). *Program availability:* Part-time, online learning. *Degree requirements:* For master's, comprehensive exam, thesis optional. *Entrance requirements:* For master's, writing assessment, minimum GPA of 3.0, photocopy of teaching license, letter of recommendation. Additional exam requirements/recommendations for international students: Required—TOEFL (minimum score 550 paper-based; 79 iBT), IELTS (minimum score 6). *Application deadline:* For fall admission, 7/20 priority date for domestic students, 6/20 priority date for international students; for spring admission, 12/15 priority date for domestic students, 11/15 priority date for international students. Applications are processed on a rolling basis. Application fee: $10. Electronic applications accepted. *Financial support:* Applicants required to submit FAFSA. *Unit head:* Dr. Mary Daughrity, Graduate Coordinator, 575-562-2481, Fax: 575-562-2559, E-mail: mary.daughrity@enmu.edu. *Application contact:* Cheryl Reeves, Senior Secretary, 575-562-2443, E-mail: cheryl.reeves@enmu.edu.
Website: http://education.enmu.edu

Eastern University, Graduate Education Programs, St. Davids, PA 19087-3696. Offers ESL program specialist (K-12) (Certificate); general supervisor (PreK-12) (Certificate); health and physical education (K-12) (Certificate); middle level (4-8) (Certificate); multicultural education (M Ed); music (K-12) (Certificate); Pre K-4 (Certificate); Pre K-4 with special education (Certificate); reading (M Ed); reading specialist (K-12)

Multilingual and Multicultural Education

(Certificate); reading supervisor (K-12) (Certificate); school counseling (MA, CAGS); school principalship (preK-12) (Certificate); school psychology (MS, CAGS); secondary biology education (7-12) (Certificate); secondary chemistry education (7-12) (Certificate); secondary communication education (7-12) (Certificate); secondary English education (7-12) (Certificate); secondary math education (7-12) (Certificate); secondary social studies education (7-12) (Certificate); special education (M Ed); special education (7-12) (Certificate); special education (Pre K-8) (Certificate); special education supervisor (K-12) (Certificate); TESOL (M Ed); world language (Certificate), including Spanish. *Program availability:* Part-time, evening/weekend, online learning. *Students:* 46 full-time (40 women), 115 part-time (93 women); includes 65 minority (42 Black or African American, non-Hispanic/Latino; 3 Asian, non-Hispanic/Latino; 14 Hispanic/Latino; 6 Two or more races, non-Hispanic/Latino), 1 international. Average age 32. In 2017, 72 master's awarded. *Entrance requirements:* Additional exam requirements/recommendations for international students: Required—TOEFL. *Application deadline:* Applications are processed on a rolling basis. Application fee: $35. Electronic applications accepted. Application fee is waived when completed online. *Expenses:* Contact institution. *Unit head:* Michael Dziedziak, Executive Director of Enrollment, 800-452-0996, E-mail: gpsadmissions@eastern.edu.
Website: https://www.eastern.edu/academics/programs/education-department-graduate-programs/graduate-programs

Fairfield University, Graduate School of Education and Allied Professions, Fairfield, CT 06824. Offers applied behavior analysis (ATC); applied psychology (MA); clinical mental health counseling (MA, CAS); educational technology (MA); elementary education (MA, CAS); family studies (MA); integration of spirituality and religion in counseling (ATC); marriage and family therapy (MA); reading and language development (Sixth Year Certificate); school counseling (MA, CAS); school psychology (MA, CAS); school-based marriage and family therapy (ATC); secondary education (MA); special education (MA, CAS); substance abuse counseling (ATC); teaching (Certificate); teaching and foundations (MA, CAS); TESOL, world languages, and bilingual education (MA, CAS). *Accreditation:* NCATE. *Program availability:* Part-time, evening/weekend. *Faculty:* 23 full-time (17 women), 39 part-time/adjunct (28 women). *Students:* 199 full-time (168 women), 251 part-time (206 women); includes 85 minority (21 Black or African American, non-Hispanic/Latino; 9 Asian, non-Hispanic/Latino; 49 Hispanic/Latino; 6 Two or more races, non-Hispanic/Latino), 4 international. Average age 32. 370 applicants, 56% accepted, 125 enrolled. In 2017, 136 master's, 28 other advanced degrees awarded. *Degree requirements:* For master's, comprehensive exam. *Entrance requirements:* For master's, minimum GPA of 3.0, 2 recommendations, resume. Additional exam requirements/recommendations for international students: Required—TOEFL (minimum score 550 paper-based; 84 iBT) or IELTS (minimum score 7.5). *Application deadline:* For fall admission, 2/15 for international students; for spring admission, 10/1 for international students. Application fee: $60. Electronic applications accepted. *Expenses:* $750 per credit hour. *Financial support:* In 2017–18, 34 students received support. Career-related internships or fieldwork and unspecified assistantships available. Support available to part-time students. Financial award applicants required to submit FAFSA. *Faculty research:* Reading and literacy, writing, social justice and inequality in education, addictions and mental health issues, therapeutic relationships and clinical supervision. *Unit head:* Dr. Robert D. Hannafin, Dean, 203-254-4250, Fax: 203-254-4241, E-mail: rhannafin@fairfield.edu. *Application contact:* Marianne Gumpper, Director of Graduate Admission, 203-254-4184, Fax: 203-254-4073, E-mail: gradadmis@fairfield.edu.
Website: http://www.fairfield.edu/gseap

Fairleigh Dickinson University, Metropolitan Campus, University College: Arts, Sciences, and Professional Studies, Peter Sammartino School of Education, Program in Multilingual Education, Teaneck, NJ 07666-1914. Offers MA. *Accreditation:* TEAC.

Florida Atlantic University, College of Education, Department of Curriculum, Culture, and Educational Inquiry, Boca Raton, FL 33431-0991. Offers curriculum and instruction (M Ed, PhD, Ed S); early childhood education (M Ed); multicultural education (M Ed); TESOL and bilingual education (MA). *Program availability:* Part-time, evening/weekend. *Faculty:* 10 full-time (8 women), 2 part-time/adjunct (both women). *Students:* 15 full-time (13 women), 81 part-time (65 women); includes 28 minority (11 Black or African American, non-Hispanic/Latino; 3 Asian, non-Hispanic/Latino; 12 Hispanic/Latino; 2 Two or more races, non-Hispanic/Latino), 3 international. Average age 36. 54 applicants, 37% accepted, 14 enrolled. In 2017, 23 master's, 5 doctorates, 4 other advanced degrees awarded. *Entrance requirements:* Additional exam requirements/recommendations for international students: Required—TOEFL (minimum score 500 paper-based; 61 iBT), IELTS (minimum score 6). *Application deadline:* For fall admission, 7/1 for domestic students, 2/15 for international students; for spring admission, 11/1 for domestic students, 7/15 for international students. Application fee: $30. *Expenses:* Tuition, state resident: full-time $7400; part-time $369.82 per credit. Tuition, nonresident: full-time $20,496; part-time $1042.81 per credit. *Faculty research:* Multicultural education, early intervention strategies, family literacy, religious diversity in schools, early childhood curriculum. *Unit head:* Dr. Dilys Schoorman, Chair, 561-297-3965, E-mail: dschoorm@fau.edu. *Application contact:* Dr. Eliah Watlington, Associate Dean, 561-296-8520, Fax: 261-297-2991, E-mail: ewatling@fau.edu.
Website: http://www.coe.fau.edu/academicdepartments/ccei/

Florida Atlantic University, College of Education, Department of Teaching and Learning, Boca Raton, FL 33431-0991. Offers curriculum and instruction (M Ed), including art, biology, chemistry, English, French, German, mathematics, music, physics, Pre-K and primary education, reading, social sciences, Spanish; elementary education (M Ed); environmental education (M Ed); reading education (M Ed); social foundations of education (M Ed), including educational psychology, educational technology, multilingual education. *Accreditation:* NCATE. *Program availability:* Part-time, evening/weekend. *Faculty:* 13 full-time (10 women), 1 part-time/adjunct (0 women). *Students:* 26 full-time (22 women), 43 part-time (39 women); includes 19 minority (9 Black or African American, non-Hispanic/Latino; 1 Asian, non-Hispanic/Latino; 8 Hispanic/Latino; 1 Two or more races, non-Hispanic/Latino), 3 international. Average age 30. 91 applicants, 57% accepted, 33 enrolled. In 2017, 25 master's awarded. *Entrance requirements:* For master's, GRE General Test, minimum GPA of 3.0 in last 2 years of undergraduate course work. Additional exam requirements/recommendations for international students: Required—TOEFL (minimum score 500 paper-based; 61 iBT), IELTS (minimum score 6). *Application deadline:* For fall admission, 7/1 for domestic students, 2/15 for international students; for spring admission, 11/1 for domestic students, 7/15 for international students. Applications are processed on a rolling basis. Application fee: $30. *Expenses:* Tuition, state resident: full-time $7400; part-time $369.82 per credit. Tuition, nonresident: full-time $20,496; part-time $1042.81 per credit. *Financial support:* Fellowships with partial tuition reimbursements, research assistantships with partial tuition reimbursements, teaching assistantships with partial tuition reimbursements, career-related internships or fieldwork, scholarships/grants, and unspecified assistantships available. *Faculty research:* Technology, teaching English to speakers of other languages, math teaching, electronic portfolio assessment, global perspectives through social studies. *Unit head:* Dr. Barbara Ridener, Chairperson, 561-297-3588, E-mail: bridener@fau.edu. *Application contact:* Dr. Eliah Watlington, Associate Dean, 561-296-8520, Fax: 261-297-

Florida International University, College of Arts, Sciences, and Education, Department of Leadership and Professional Studies, Miami, FL 33199. Offers adult education and human resource development (MS, Ed D); counseling (MS), including rehabilitation counseling, school counseling; counselor education (MS), including clinical mental health counseling; educational administration and supervision (Ed D); educational leadership (MS, Certificate, Ed S); higher education (Ed D); higher education administration (MS); international and comparative education (MS); recreation and sport management (MS), including recreation and sport management, recreational therapy; school psychology (Ed S); urban education (MS), including instruction in urban settings, learning technologies, multicultural/bilingual, multicultural/TESOL, urban education. *Program availability:* Part-time, evening/weekend. *Faculty:* 60 full-time (41 women), 112 part-time/adjunct (77 women). *Students:* 221 full-time (162 women), 301 part-time (239 women); includes 418 minority (127 Black or African American, non-Hispanic/Latino; 9 Asian, non-Hispanic/Latino; 271 Hispanic/Latino; 11 Two or more races, non-Hispanic/Latino), 10 international. Average age 31. 330 applicants, 55% accepted, 100 enrolled. In 2017, 181 master's, 6 doctorates awarded. *Degree requirements:* For master's, thesis/dissertation. *Entrance requirements:* For master's, minimum GPA of 3.0; for doctorate and other advanced degree, GRE General Test. Additional exam requirements/recommendations for international students: Required—TOEFL (minimum score 550 paper-based; 80 iBT), IELTS (minimum score 6.3). *Application deadline:* For fall admission, 6/1 priority date for domestic students, 4/1 for international students; for winter admission, 10/1 priority date for domestic students, 9/1 for international students; for spring admission, 3/1 priority date for domestic students, 2/1 for international students. Applications are processed on a rolling basis. Application fee: $30. Electronic applications accepted. *Expenses:* Tuition, state resident: full-time $8912; part-time $446 per credit hour. Tuition, nonresident: full-time $21,393; part-time $992 per credit hour. *Required fees:* $390; $195 per semester. *Financial support:* Fellowships, research assistantships with tuition reimbursements, teaching assistantships with tuition reimbursements, Federal Work-Study, and tuition waivers (full and partial) available. Support available to part-time students. Financial award applicants required to submit FAFSA. *Unit head:* Dr. Benjamin Baez, Chair, 305-348-3214, Fax: 305-348-1515, E-mail: benjamin.baez@fiu.edu. *Application contact:* Nanett Rojas, Assistant Director, Graduate Admissions, 305-348-7464, Fax: 305-348-7441, E-mail: gradadm@fiu.edu.
Website: http://education.fiu.edu

Gallaudet University, The Graduate School, Washington, DC 20002-3625. Offers American Sign Language/English bilingual early childhood deaf education: birth to 5 (Certificate); audiology (Au D); clinical psychology (PhD); deaf and hard of hearing infants, toddlers, and their families (Certificate); deaf education (MA, Ed S); deaf history (Certificate); deaf studies (Certificate); educating deaf students with disabilities (Certificate); education: teacher preparation (MA), including deaf education, early childhood education and deaf education, elementary education and deaf education, secondary education and deaf education; educational neuroscience (PhD); hearing, speech and language sciences (MS, PhD); international development (MA); interpretation (MA, PhD), including combined interpreting practice and research (MA), interpreting research (MA); linguistics (MA, PhD); mental health counseling (MA); peer mentoring (Certificate); public administration (MPA); school counseling (MA); school psychology (Psy S); sign language teaching (MA); social work (MSW); speech-language pathology (MS). *Program availability:* Part-time. Terminal master's awarded for partial completion of doctoral program. *Degree requirements:* For master's, comprehensive exam (for some programs), thesis optional; for doctorate, comprehensive exam, thesis/dissertation. *Entrance requirements:* For master's and doctorate, GRE General Test or MAT, letters of recommendation, interviews, goals statement, American Sign Language proficiency interview, written English competency. Additional exam requirements/recommendations for international students: Required—TOEFL. Electronic applications accepted. *Faculty research:* Signing math dictionaries, telecommunications access, cancer genetics, linguistics, visual language and visual learning, integrated quantum materials, deaf legal discourse, advance recruitment and retention in geosciences.

George Mason University, College of Education and Human Development, Programs in Curriculum and Instruction, Fairfax, VA 22030. Offers advanced international baccalaureate (M Ed); assistive technology (M Ed); designing digital learning in schools (M Ed); early childhood education (M Ed); early childhood education for diverse learners (M Ed); elementary education (M Ed); English as a second language (M Ed); gifted child education (M Ed); history (M Ed); literacy (M Ed), including PK-12 classroom teachers, reading specialist; literacy leadership for diverse schools (M Ed), including K-12 reading; physical education (M Ed); science K-12 (M Ed); secondary education (M Ed), including biology, chemistry, earth science, English, history/social science, math, physics; special education (M Ed); teacher leadership (M Ed); teaching culturally, linguistically diverse and exceptional learners (M Ed); transformative teaching (M Ed). *Program availability:* Part-time, evening/weekend, 100% online, blended/hybrid learning. *Faculty:* 41 full-time (36 women), 45 part-time/adjunct (37 women). *Students:* 173 full-time (151 women), 729 part-time (611 women); includes 271 minority (65 Black or African American, non-Hispanic/Latino; 5 American Indian or Alaska Native, non-Hispanic/Latino; 88 Asian, non-Hispanic/Latino; 94 Hispanic/Latino; 1 Native Hawaiian or other Pacific Islander, non-Hispanic/Latino; 18 Two or more races, non-Hispanic/Latino), 28 international. Average age 32. 426 applicants, 91% accepted, 289 enrolled. In 2017, 349 master's awarded. *Degree requirements:* For master's, thesis. *Entrance requirements:* For master's, PRAXIS Core (for some programs), 2 letters of recommendation, interview, program goals statement; 9 hours of complete licensure endorsement requirements (for elementary education); minimum GPA of 3.0 in applicant's last 60 hours of undergraduate coursework (for secondary education); at least 1 year of teaching experience (for literacy). Additional exam requirements/recommendations for international students: Required—TOEFL (minimum score 575 paper-based; 88 iBT), IELTS (minimum score 6.5), PTE (minimum score 59). *Application deadline:* For fall admission, 4/2 priority date for domestic and international students; for spring admission, 11/1 for domestic and international students. Application fee: $75 ($80 for international students). Electronic applications accepted. *Expenses:* Tuition, state resident: full-time $11,228; part-time $459.50 per credit. Tuition, nonresident: full-time $30,932; part-time $1280.50 per credit. *Required fees:* $3252; $135.50 per credit. Part-time tuition and fees vary according to course load and program. *Financial support:* In 2017–18, 2 students received support, including 2 teaching assistantships; career-related internships or fieldwork, Federal Work-Study, scholarships/grants, unspecified assistantships, and health care benefits (for full-time research or teaching assistantship recipients) also available. Support available to part-time students. Financial award application deadline: 3/1; financial award applicants required to submit FAFSA. *Faculty research:* Teacher preparation and professional development; adaptive teaching; wonder in science teacher preparation; literacy (digital, adolescent); site based course instruction. *Unit head:* Rebecca Fox, Professor and Academic Program Coordinator, 703-993-4123, E-mail: rfox@gmu.edu.
Website: http://gse.gmu.edu/programs/gsemasters

The George Washington University, Graduate School of Education and Human Development, Department of Counseling and Human Development, Washington, DC

20052. Offers clinical mental health counseling (MA); counseling (PhD, Ed S); counseling culturally and linguistically diverse persons (MA Ed/HD, Certificate); forensic rehabilitation counseling (Graduate Certificate); job development and placement (Graduate Certificate); rehabilitation counseling (MA Ed/HD), including autism spectrum disorder, substance abuse and psychiatric disabilities, traumatic brain injury; school counseling (MA Ed, Graduate Certificate). *Accreditation:* ACA (one or more programs are accredited). *Program availability:* Part-time, evening/weekend. *Faculty:* 14 full-time (9 women). *Students:* 119 full-time (91 women), 71 part-time (60 women); includes 72 minority (27 Black or African American, non-Hispanic/Latino; 3 American Indian or Alaska Native, non-Hispanic/Latino; 16 Asian, non-Hispanic/Latino; 21 Hispanic/Latino; 5 Two or more races, non-Hispanic/Latino), 15 international. Average age 32. 343 applicants, 50% accepted, 74 enrolled. In 2017, 57 master's, 5 doctorates, 11 other advanced degrees awarded. *Degree requirements:* For master's and other advanced degree, comprehensive exam; for doctorate, comprehensive exam, thesis/dissertation. *Entrance requirements:* For master's, GRE General Test or MAT, minimum GPA of 2.75; for doctorate, GRE General Test or MAT, interview, minimum GPA of 3.3; for other advanced degree, GRE General Test or MAT, minimum GPA of 3.3. *Application deadline:* For fall admission, 1/15 priority date for domestic students; for spring admission, 10/1 for domestic students. Applications are processed on a rolling basis. Application fee: $75. *Expenses: Tuition:* Full-time $28,800; part-time $1655 per credit hour. *Required fees:* $45; $2.75 per credit hour. *Financial support:* In 2017–18, 58 students received support. Fellowships with tuition reimbursements available, research assistantships, teaching assistantships with tuition reimbursements available, career-related internships or fieldwork, Federal Work-Study, and tuition waivers (full and partial) available. Financial award application deadline: 1/15. *Faculty research:* Multiculturalism and counseling, models of adult development. *Unit head:* Dr. Kenneth C. Hergenrather, Chair, 202-994-1334, E-mail: hergenkc@gwu.edu. *Application contact:* Sarah Lang, Director of Graduate Admissions, 202-994-1447, Fax: 202-994-7207, E-mail: slang@gwu.edu.

The George Washington University, Graduate School of Education and Human Development, Department of Special Education and Disability Studies, Program in Bilingual Special Education, Washington, DC 20052. Offers MA Ed, Certificate. *Expenses: Tuition:* Full-time $28,800; part-time $1655 per credit hour. *Required fees:* $45; $2.75 per credit hour. *Unit head:* Michael Feuer, Dean, 202-994-6161, E-mail: mjfeuer@gwu.edu. *Application contact:* Sarah Lang, Director of Graduate Admissions, 202-994-1447, Fax: 202-994-7207, E-mail: slang@gwu.edu.

The George Washington University, Graduate School of Education and Human Development, Department of Special Education and Disability Studies, Program in Special Education for Culturally and Linguistically Diverse Persons, Washington, DC 20052. Offers MA Ed, Certificate. *Students:* 7 full-time (all women), 33 part-time (28 women); includes 15 minority (3 Black or African American, non-Hispanic/Latino; 4 Asian, non-Hispanic/Latino; 7 Hispanic/Latino; 1 Two or more races, non-Hispanic/Latino), 2 international. Average age 33. 50 applicants, 64% accepted, 17 enrolled. In 2017, 17 master's, 20 Certificates awarded. *Expenses: Tuition:* Full-time $28,800; part-time $1655 per credit hour. *Required fees:* $45; $2.75 per credit hour. *Unit head:* Doran Gresham, 202-994-2780, E-mail: dgresham@gwu.edu.

Georgia Southern University, Jack N. Averitt College of Graduate Studies, College of Education, Department of Curriculum, Foundations, and Reading, Program in Curriculum Studies, Statesboro, GA 30460. Offers curriculum studies (Ed D), including cultural curriculum, instructional improvement, multicultural studies, teaching and learning. *Program availability:* Part-time. *Students:* 24 full-time (19 women), 119 part-time (93 women); includes 39 minority (28 Black or African American, non-Hispanic/Latino; 2 Asian, non-Hispanic/Latino; 5 Hispanic/Latino; 4 Two or more races, non-Hispanic/Latino), 2 international. Average age 41. In 2017, 26 doctorates awarded. *Degree requirements:* For doctorate, comprehensive exam, thesis/dissertation, exams; assessments. *Entrance requirements:* For doctorate, GRE or MAT, letters of reference, minimum GPA of 3.5, writing sample. Additional exam requirements/recommendations for international students: Required—TOEFL (minimum score 550 paper-based; 80 iBT), IELTS (minimum score 6). *Application deadline:* For summer admission, 1/30 for domestic students. Application fee: $50. Electronic applications accepted. *Expenses:* Tuition, state resident: full-time $4986; part-time $3324 per year. Tuition, nonresident: full-time $21,982; part-time $15,352 per year. *Required fees:* $2092; $1802 per credit hour. $901 per semester. Tuition and fees vary according to course load, campus/location and program. *Financial support:* In 2017–18, 7 students received support, including 1 research assistantship with full tuition reimbursement available (averaging $7,750 per year); teaching assistantships, career-related internships or fieldwork, Federal Work-Study, scholarships/grants, and unspecified assistantships also available. Financial award application deadline: 4/15; financial award applicants required to submit FAFSA. *Faculty research:* Curriculum theory, cultural studies, narrative research, postmodern theory, critical race theory, international education, feminism, media literacy, documentary studies, post human condition, social and cultural foundations of education, democracy and education. *Unit head:* Dr. Daniel Chapman, Program Coordinator, 912-478-5715, E-mail: dechapman@georgiasouthern.edu. *Application contact:* Dr. Lydia Cross, Coordinator for Graduate Student Recruitment, 912-478-8664, E-mail: lcross@georgiasouthern.edu. Website: http://coe.georgiasouthern.edu/cs/

Graduate Institute of Applied Linguistics, Graduate Programs, Dallas, TX 75236. Offers applied linguistics (MA, Certificate); language development (MA). *Program availability:* Part-time. *Degree requirements:* For master's, one foreign language, comprehensive exam (for some programs), thesis (for some programs). *Entrance requirements:* For master's, GRE. Additional exam requirements/recommendations for international students: Required—TOEFL (minimum score 577 paper-based; 90 iBT). Electronic applications accepted. *Faculty research:* Minority languages, endangered languages, language documentation.

Heritage University, Graduate Programs in Education, Program in Professional Studies, Toppenish, WA 98948-9599. Offers bilingual education/ESL (M Ed); biology (M Ed); English and literature (M Ed); reading/literacy (M Ed); special education (M Ed). *Program availability:* Part-time, evening/weekend. *Degree requirements:* For master's, comprehensive exam (for some programs), thesis (for some programs).

Hofstra University, School of Education, Programs in Teacher Education, Hempstead, NY 11549. Offers bilingual education (MA); bilingual extension (Advanced Certificate), including education/speech language pathology, intensive teacher institute; business education (MS Ed); curriculum studies (MS Ed); early childhood and childhood education (MS Ed); early childhood education (MA, MS Ed); educational technology (Advanced Certificate); elementary education (MA, MS Ed), including science, technology, engineering, and mathematics (STEM) (MA); English education (MS Ed); family and consumer science (MS Ed); fine arts and music education (Advanced Certificate); fine arts education (MS Ed); foreign language and TESOL (MS Ed); foreign language education (MA, MS Ed), including Arabic (MS Ed), biology, chemistry, Chinese (MS Ed), earth science, French, German, Italian (MS Ed), Mandarin (MS Ed), physics, Russian, Spanish; foundations of education (Advanced Certificate), including grades 5-6, grades 7-9; languages other than English and teaching English as a second language (MA); learning and teaching (Ed D), including applied linguistics, art education, arts and humanities, early childhood education, English education, human development, math education, math, science, and technology, multicultural education, physical education, science education, social studies education, special education; mathematics education (MA, MS Ed); music education (MA, MS Ed); science education (MA), including biology (MA, MS Ed), chemistry (MA, MS Ed), earth science (MA, MS Ed), physics (MA, MS Ed); secondary education (Advanced Certificate); social studies education (MA, MS Ed); teaching languages other than English and TESOL (MS Ed); technology for learning (MA); TESOL (MS Ed, Advanced Certificate); TESOL with specialization in STEM (MA); work based learning extension (Advanced Certificate). *Program availability:* Part-time, evening/weekend, blended/hybrid learning. *Students:* 119 full-time (83 women), 124 part-time (90 women); includes 54 minority (15 Black or African American, non-Hispanic/Latino; 9 Asian, non-Hispanic/Latino; 29 Hispanic/Latino; 1 Native Hawaiian or other Pacific Islander, non-Hispanic/Latino), 12 international. Average age 29. 205 applicants, 88% accepted, 93 enrolled. In 2017, 103 master's, 4 doctorates, 32 other advanced degrees awarded. *Degree requirements:* For master's, comprehensive exam, thesis (for some programs), exit project, student teaching, fieldwork, electronic portfolio, curriculum project, minimum GPA of 3.0; for doctorate, thesis/dissertation; for Advanced Certificate, 3 foreign languages, comprehensive exam (for some programs), thesis project. *Entrance requirements:* For master's, GRE, 2 letters of recommendation, portfolio, teacher certification (MA), interview, essay; for doctorate, GMAT, GRE, LSAT, or MAT; for Advanced Certificate, 2 letters of recommendation, essay, interview and/or portfolio, teaching certificate. Additional exam requirements/recommendations for international students: Required—TOEFL (minimum score 550 paper-based; 80 iBT). *Application deadline:* Applications are processed on a rolling basis. Application fee: $75. Electronic applications accepted. *Expenses: Tuition:* Full-time $1292. *Required fees:* $970. Tuition and fees vary according to program. *Financial support:* In 2017–18, 112 students received support, including 56 fellowships with full and partial tuition reimbursements available (averaging $4,998 per year), 2 research assistantships with full and partial tuition reimbursements available (averaging $8,753 per year); career-related internships or fieldwork, Federal Work-Study, institutionally sponsored loans, scholarships/grants, traineeships, tuition waivers (full and partial), and unspecified assistantships also available. Support available to part-time students. Financial award applicants required to submit FAFSA. *Faculty research:* Educational interventions that foster critical-thinking skills; teachers' attitudes about professional development; threats to teacher quality. *Unit head:* Dr. Eustace Thompson, Chairperson, 516-463-5749, Fax: 516-463-6275, E-mail: eustace.g.thompson@hofstra.edu. *Application contact:* Sunil Samuel, Assistant Vice President of Admissions, 516-463-4723, Fax: 516-463-4664, E-mail: graduateadmission@hofstra.edu. Website: http://www.hofstra.edu/education/

Houston Baptist University, College of Education and Behavioral Sciences, Programs in Education, Houston, TX 77074-3298. Offers bilingual education (M Ed); counselor education (M Ed); curriculum and instruction (M Ed); curriculum and instruction (EC-6 bilingual) (M Ed); curriculum and instruction in all-level art, Spanish, music, or physical education (M Ed); curriculum and instruction in EC-6 and special education (EC-12) (M Ed); curriculum and instruction in instructional technology (M Ed); curriculum and instruction in mathematics, science, or social studies (4-8) (M Ed); curriculum and instruction with EC-6 generalist (M Ed); curriculum and instruction with English language arts and reading (4-8) (M Ed); educational administration (M Ed); educational diagnostician (M Ed); executive educational leadership (Ed D); higher education in business management (M Ed); higher education in Christian studies (M Ed); higher education in counseling (M Ed); higher education in educational technology (M Ed); reading (M Ed); special educational leadership (Ed D). *Program availability:* Part-time, evening/weekend, 100% online, blended/hybrid learning. *Students:* 83 full-time (65 women), 187 part-time (156 women); includes 189 minority (114 Black or African American, non-Hispanic/Latino; 2 American Indian or Alaska Native, non-Hispanic/Latino; 9 Asian, non-Hispanic/Latino; 58 Hispanic/Latino; 6 Two or more races, non-Hispanic/Latino), 7 international. Average age 36. 309 applicants, 31% accepted, 70 enrolled. In 2017, 92 master's awarded. *Degree requirements:* For master's, comprehensive exam; for doctorate, thesis/dissertation. *Entrance requirements:* For master's, minimum GPA of 2.75, two recommendations, resume, bachelor's degree conferred transcript; interview (for non-certified teachers); for doctorate, GRE, 5 letters of recommendation. Additional exam requirements/recommendations for international students: Required—TOEFL (minimum score 80 iBT), IELTS (minimum score 6.5). *Application deadline:* For fall admission, 8/1 for domestic students, 6/1 for international students; for spring admission, 1/1 for domestic students, 11/1 for international students; for summer admission, 5/1 for domestic students, 3/1 for international students. Applications are processed on a rolling basis. Application fee: $0 ($100 for international students). Electronic applications accepted. Application fee is waived when completed online. *Expenses:* $22,000 tuition; $4,500 fees (general, technology and parking). *Financial support:* In 2017–18, 59 students received support. Research assistantships, teaching assistantships, Federal Work-Study, and scholarships/grants available. Support available to part-time students. Financial award application deadline: 4/1; financial award applicants required to submit FAFSA. *Faculty research:* Autism and inclusion, integrating technology into instruction, school change and leadership trust. *Unit head:* Dr. Charlotte Fontenot, Director, Graduate Programs, 281-649-3078, Fax: 281-649-3361, E-mail: cfontenot@hbu.edu. *Application contact:* Kristy Wright, Administrative Assistant for Graduate Programs, 281-649-3094, Fax: 281-649-3361, E-mail: kwright@hbu.edu. Website: http://www.hbu.edu/MED

Howard University, Cathy Hughes School of Communications, Department of Strategic, Legal and Management Communication, Washington, DC 20059-0002. Offers intercultural communication (MA, PhD); organizational communication (MA, PhD). Offered through the Graduate School of Arts and Sciences. *Program availability:* Part-time. Terminal master's awarded for partial completion of doctoral program. *Degree requirements:* For master's, comprehensive or thesis; for doctorate, one foreign language, comprehensive exam, thesis/dissertation. *Entrance requirements:* For master's, English proficiency exam, GRE General Test, minimum GPA of 3.0; for doctorate, English proficiency exam, GRE General Test, master's degree in related field, minimum GPA of 3.5. Additional exam requirements/recommendations for international students: Required—TOEFL. *Faculty research:* Media effects, black discourse, development communication, African-American organizations.

Hunter College of the City University of New York, Graduate School, School of Education, Department of Curriculum and Teaching, Program in Bilingual Education, New York, NY 10065-5085. Offers MS. *Accreditation:* NCATE. *Degree requirements:* For master's, one foreign language, thesis, research seminar, student teaching experience or practicum, New York State Teacher Certification Exams. *Entrance requirements:* For master's, interview, minimum GPA of 2.8, writing sample in English and Spanish. Additional exam requirements/recommendations for international students: Required—TOEFL, TWE. *Faculty research:* Teacher effectiveness, language development, Spanish language and linguistics and multicultural education.

Immaculata University, College of Graduate Studies, Program in Cultural and Linguistic Diversity, Immaculata, PA 19345. Offers bilingual studies (MA); TESOL (MA). *Program availability:* Part-time, evening/weekend. *Degree requirements:* For master's, one foreign language, comprehensive exam, thesis optional, professional experience.

Multilingual and Multicultural Education

Entrance requirements: For master's, GRE or MAT, proficiency in Spanish or Asian language, minimum GPA of 3.0. Additional exam requirements/recommendations for international students: Required—TOEFL, IELTS. Electronic applications accepted. *Faculty research:* Cognitive learning, Caribbean literature and culture, English as a second language, teaching English to speakers of other languages.

Indiana State University, College of Graduate and Professional Studies, College of Arts and Sciences, Department of Languages, Literatures, and Linguistics, Terre Haute, IN 47809. Offers applied linguistics/teaching English as a second language (MA); language education (PhD); Spanish/teaching english as a second language (MA); TESL/TEFL (CAS). *Degree requirements:* For master's, comprehensive exam. Electronic applications accepted.

Indiana University Bloomington, University Graduate School, College of Arts and Sciences, Department of Second Language Studies, Bloomington, IN 47405-7000. Offers second language studies (MA, PhD); TESOL and applied linguistics (MA). *Entrance requirements:* Additional exam requirements/recommendations for international students: Required—TOEFL (minimum score 100 iBT). Electronic applications accepted.

James Madison University, The Graduate School, College of Education, Program in Education, Harrisonburg, VA 22807. Offers early childhood education (preK-3) (MAT); educational leadership (M Ed); educational technology (M Ed); elementary education (MAT); equity and cultural diversity (M Ed); inclusive early childhood education (MAT); K-8 mathematics specialist (M Ed); middle education (MAT); reading education (M Ed); secondary education (MAT); Spanish language and culture for educators (M Ed); TESOL (MAT). *Accreditation:* NCATE. *Program availability:* Part-time, evening/weekend. *Students:* 260 full-time (233 women), 158 part-time (100 women); includes 48 minority (10 Black or African American, non-Hispanic/Latino; 4 Asian, non-Hispanic/Latino; 26 Hispanic/Latino; 1 Native Hawaiian or other Pacific Islander, non-Hispanic/Latino; 7 Two or more races, non-Hispanic/Latino), 2 international. Average age 30. In 2017, 262 master's awarded. Application fee: $55. Electronic applications accepted. *Expenses:* Tuition, state resident: full-time $10,512; part-time $438 per credit hour. Tuition, nonresident: full-time $28,358; part-time $1162 per credit hour. *Required fees:* $1128. *Financial support:* In 2017–18, 23 students received support, including 1 teaching assistantship; career-related internships or fieldwork, Federal Work-Study, and 22 assistantships (averaging $7911) also available. Financial award application deadline: 3/1; financial award applicants required to submit FAFSA. *Unit head:* Dr. Phillip M. Wishon, Dean, 540-568-6572, E-mail: wishonpm@jmu.edu. *Application contact:* Lynette D. Michael, Director of Graduate Admissions, 540-568-6131 Ext. 6395, Fax: 540-568-7860, E-mail: michaeld@jmu.edu.
Website: http://www.jmu.edu/coe/index.shtml

Kean University, College of Education, Program in Instruction and Curriculum, Union, NJ 07083. Offers bilingual/bicultural education (MA); teaching English as a second language (MA). *Accreditation:* NCATE. *Program availability:* Part-time. *Faculty:* 13 full-time (7 women). *Students:* 3 full-time (2 women), 26 part-time (23 women); includes 19 minority (1 Black or African American, non-Hispanic/Latino; 18 Hispanic/Latino), 2 international. Average age 35. 10 applicants, 100% accepted, 8 enrolled. In 2017, 10 master's awarded. *Degree requirements:* For master's, comprehensive exam (for some programs), thesis optional. *Entrance requirements:* For master's, GRE General Test or MAT; PRAXIS (for some programs), minimum GPA of 3.0, personal statement, professional resume/curriculum vitae, commitment to working with children, certification (for some programs), two letters of recommendation. Additional exam requirements/recommendations for international students: Required—TOEFL (minimum score 550 paper-based; 79 iBT), IELTS (minimum score 6.5). *Application deadline:* For fall admission, 6/30 for domestic and international students; for spring admission, 12/1 for domestic and international students. Applications are processed on a rolling basis. Application fee: $75. Electronic applications accepted. *Expenses:* Tuition, state resident: full-time $13,419; part-time $653 per credit. Tuition, nonresident: full-time $18,188; part-time $801 per credit. *Required fees:* $3382; $154 per credit. Tuition and fees vary according to course level, course load, degree level and program. *Financial support:* Scholarships/grants and unspecified assistantships available. Financial award applicants required to submit FAFSA. *Unit head:* Dr. Gail Verdi, Program Coordinator, 908-737-3908, E-mail: gverdi@kean.edu. *Application contact:* Brittany Gerstenhaber, Admissions Counselor, 908-737-7100, E-mail: grad-adm@kean.edu.
Website: http://grad.kean.edu/masters-programs/bilingualbicultural-education-instruction-and-curriculum

Langston University, School of Education and Behavioral Sciences, Langston, OK 73050. Offers bilingual/multicultural (M Ed); elementary education (M Ed); English as a second language (M Ed); rehabilitation counseling (M Sc); urban education (M Ed). *Accreditation:* CORE; NCATE (one or more programs are accredited). *Program availability:* Part-time. *Degree requirements:* For master's, comprehensive exam, thesis optional. *Entrance requirements:* For master's, GRE, writing skills test, minimum GPA of 2.5, 3 letters of recommendation. Additional exam requirements/recommendations for international students: Required—TOEFL, TWE. *Faculty research:* Bilingual/multicultural education, financing post-secondary education.

La Salle University, School of Arts and Sciences, Hispanic Institute, Philadelphia, PA 19141-1199. Offers bilingual/bicultural studies (MA); ESL program specialist (Certificate); interpretation: English/Spanish-Spanish/English (Certificate); teaching English to speakers of other languages (MA); translation and interpretation (MA); translation: English/Spanish-Spanish/English (Certificate). *Program availability:* Part-time, evening/weekend. *Faculty:* 2 full-time (1 woman), 5 part-time/adjunct (1 woman). *Students:* 1 (woman) full-time, 37 part-time (26 women); includes 21 minority (7 Black or African American, non-Hispanic/Latino; 1 American Indian or Alaska Native, non-Hispanic/Latino; 1 Asian, non-Hispanic/Latino; 10 Hispanic/Latino; 2 Two or more races, non-Hispanic/Latino), 2 international. Average age 33. 24 applicants, 79% accepted, 11 enrolled. In 2017, 4 master's, 1 other advanced degree awarded. *Degree requirements:* For master's, one foreign language, project or thesis. *Entrance requirements:* For master's, GRE, MAT, or GMAT, professional resume; two letters of recommendation; for Certificate, GRE, MAT, or GMAT, professional resume; two letters of recommendation; evidence of an advanced level in Spanish. Additional exam requirements/recommendations for international students: Required—TOEFL. *Application deadline:* For fall admission, 8/15 priority date for domestic students, 7/15 for international students; for spring admission, 12/15 priority date for domestic students, 11/15 for international students; for summer admission, 4/15 priority date for domestic students, 3/15 for international students. Applications are processed on a rolling basis. Application fee: $35. Electronic applications accepted. Application fee is waived when completed online. *Expenses:* Contact institution. *Financial support:* In 2017–18, 10 students received support. Scholarships/grants available. Support available to part-time students. Financial award application deadline: 8/31; financial award applicants required to submit FAFSA. *Faculty research:* Puerto Rican literature, cross-cultural communication, English as a second language methodology, Spanish language. *Unit head:* Guadalupe Da Costa Montesinos, Director, 215-951-1209, Fax: 215-991-3506, E-mail: montesin@lasalle.edu. *Application contact:* Elizabeth Heenan, Director, Graduate and Adult Enrollment, 215-951-1100, Fax: 215-951-1462, E-mail: heenan@lasalle.edu.
Website: http://www.lasalle.edu/hispanic-institute/

La Salle University, School of Arts and Sciences, Program in Education, Philadelphia, PA 19141-1199. Offers autism spectrum disorders (MA, Certificate); bilingual/bicultural studies (MA); classroom management (MA); dual early childhood and special education (MA); dual middle-level science and math and special education (MA); education (MA); English (MA); English as a second language (Certificate); history (MA); instructional coach (Certificate); instructional leadership (MA); reading specialist (MA, Certificate); secondary education (MA); special education (MA, Certificate). *Program availability:* Part-time, evening/weekend. *Faculty:* 5 full-time (4 women), 8 part-time/adjunct (5 women). *Students:* 2 full-time (1 woman), 110 part-time (81 women); includes 23 minority (11 Black or African American, non-Hispanic/Latino; 1 Asian, non-Hispanic/Latino; 7 Hispanic/Latino; 4 Two or more races, non-Hispanic/Latino). Average age 33. 137 applicants, 70% accepted, 63 enrolled. In 2017, 148 master's awarded. *Degree requirements:* For master's, comprehensive exam. *Entrance requirements:* For master's, MAT or GRE, 2 letters of recommendation; for Certificate, GMAT or GRE, 2 letters of recommendation. Additional exam requirements/recommendations for international students: Required—TOEFL. *Application deadline:* For fall admission, 8/15 priority date for domestic students, 7/15 for international students; for spring admission, 12/15 priority date for domestic students, 11/15 for international students; for summer admission, 4/15 priority date for domestic students, 3/15 for international students. Applications are processed on a rolling basis. Application fee: $35. Electronic applications accepted. Application fee is waived when completed online. *Expenses:* Contact institution. *Financial support:* In 2017–18, 19 students received support. Scholarships/grants available. Support available to part-time students. Financial award application deadline: 8/31; financial award applicants required to submit FAFSA. *Unit head:* Dr. Greer Richardson, Director, 215-951-1806, Fax: 215-951-1843, E-mail: graded@lasalle.edu. *Application contact:* Elizabeth Heenan, Director, Graduate and Adult Enrollment, 215-951-1100, Fax: 215-951-1462, E-mail: heenan@lasalle.edu.
Website: http://www.lasalle.edu/grad-education-programs/

Lehman College of the City University of New York, School of Education, Department of Specialized Services in Education, Bronx, NY 10468-1589. Offers guidance and counseling (MS Ed); reading teacher (MS Ed); teachers of special education (MS Ed), including bilingual special education, early special education, emotional handicaps, learning disabilities, mental retardation. *Program availability:* Part-time, evening/weekend. *Faculty research:* Battered women, whole language classrooms, parent education, mainstreaming.

Lehman College of the City University of New York, School of Education, Department of Specialized Services in Education, Teachers of Special Education Program, Option in Bilingual Special Education, Bronx, NY 10468-1589. Offers MS Ed. *Accreditation:* NCATE. *Entrance requirements:* For master's, minimum GPA of 3.0.

Long Island University–Hudson, Graduate School, Purchase, NY 10577. Offers autism (Advanced Certificate); bilingual education (Advanced Certificate); childhood education (MS Ed); crisis management (Advanced Certificate); early childhood education (MS Ed); educational leadership (MS Ed); health administration (MPA); literacy (MS Ed); marriage and family therapy (MS); mental health counseling (MS, Advanced Certificate), including credentialed alcoholism and substance abuse counselor (MS); middle childhood and adolescence education (MS Ed); pharmaceutics (MS), including cosmetic science, industrial pharmacy; public administration (MPA); school counseling (MS Ed, Advanced Certificate); school psychology (MS Ed); special education (MS Ed); TESOL (MS Ed); TESOL (all grades) (Advanced Certificate). *Program availability:* Part-time, evening/weekend. *Faculty:* 8 full-time (6 women), 41 part-time/adjunct (24 women). *Students:* 69 full-time (54 women), 249 part-time (200 women); includes 102 minority (29 Black or African American, non-Hispanic/Latino; 1 American Indian or Alaska Native, non-Hispanic/Latino; 9 Asian, non-Hispanic/Latino; 62 Hispanic/Latino; 1 Native Hawaiian or other Pacific Islander, non-Hispanic/Latino). Average age 33. 153 applicants, 96% accepted, 103 enrolled. In 2017, 138 master's, 36 other advanced degrees awarded. *Entrance requirements:* Additional exam requirements/recommendations for international students: Required—TOEFL. *Application deadline:* Applications are processed on a rolling basis. Application fee: $50. Electronic applications accepted. *Expenses:* Contact institution. *Financial support:* In 2017–18, 32 students received support. Scholarships/grants available. Support available to part-time students. Financial award application deadline: 2/15; financial award applicants required to submit FAFSA. *Unit head:* Dr. Sylvia Blake, Dean and Chief Operating Officer, 914-831-2700, E-mail: westchester@liu.edu. *Application contact:* Dr. Sylvia Blake, Dean and Chief Operating Officer, 914-831-2700, E-mail: westchester@liu.edu.

Long Island University–LIU Brooklyn, School of Education, Brooklyn, NY 11201-8423. Offers adolescence urban education (MS Ed); applied behavior analysis (Advanced Certificate); bilingual education (Advanced Certificate); bilingual education in urban setting (MS Ed); bilingual school counselor (MS Ed, Advanced Certificate); childhood urban education (MS Ed); childhood/early childhood education (MS Ed); childhood/early childhood urban education (MS Ed); early childhood urban education (MS Ed, Advanced Certificate); educational leadership (Advanced Certificate); marriage and family therapy (MS, Advanced Certificate); mental health counseling (MS, Advanced Certificate); school building district leader (Advanced Certificate); school counselor (MS Ed, Advanced Certificate); school psychologist (MS Ed); teaching students with disabilities (MS Ed); teaching urban children with disabilities (MS Ed); TESOL (MS Ed, Advanced Certificate). *Accreditation:* TEAC. *Program availability:* Part-time, evening/weekend, 100% online. *Faculty:* 14 full-time (12 women), 42 part-time/adjunct (32 women). *Students:* 140 full-time (130 women), 563 part-time (414 women); includes 417 minority (183 Black or African American, non-Hispanic/Latino; 1 American Indian or Alaska Native, non-Hispanic/Latino; 32 Asian, non-Hispanic/Latino; 187 Hispanic/Latino; 14 Two or more races, non-Hispanic/Latino), 10 international. Average age 31. 449 applicants, 82% accepted, 264 enrolled. In 2017, 408 master's, 31 other advanced degrees awarded. *Entrance requirements:* For master's, GRE. Additional exam requirements/recommendations for international students: Required—TOEFL (minimum score 527 paper-based, 75 iBT), IELTS, or PTE. *Application deadline:* Applications are processed on a rolling basis. Application fee: $50. Electronic applications accepted. *Expenses: Tuition:* Full-time $21,618; part-time $1201 per credit. *Required fees:* $1840; $920 per term. Tuition and fees vary according to course load. *Financial support:* In 2017–18, 58 students received support. Career-related internships or fieldwork, Federal Work-Study, scholarships/grants, and unspecified assistantships available. Support available to part-time students. Financial award application deadline: 2/15; financial award applicants required to submit FAFSA. *Faculty research:* Diversity issues in education and mental health care, inclusion - disability studies, sustainability, teacher professional development. *Unit head:* Dean, 718-488-1055, E-mail: bkln-admissions@liu.edu. *Application contact:* Bayu Sutrisno, Graduate Admissions Counselor, 718-488-1011, Fax: 718-780-6110, E-mail: bkln-admissions@liu.edu.
Website: http://www.liu.edu/Brooklyn/Academics/School-of-Education

Loyola Marymount University, School of Education, Program in Bilingual Elementary Education, Los Angeles, CA 90045-2659. Offers MA. *Unit head:* Dr. Francisco Ramos, Program Director, Bilingual Education, 310-338-4515, E-mail: framos@lmu.edu. *Application contact:* Chake H. Kouyoumjian, Associate Dean of Graduate Studies, 310-338-2721, Fax: 310-338-6086, E-mail: graduateinfo@lmu.edu.
Website: http://soe.lmu.edu/academics/bilingualeducation

Loyola Marymount University, School of Education, Program in Bilingual Secondary Education, Los Angeles, CA 90045-2659. Offers MA. *Unit head:* Dr. Francisco Ramos, Program Director, Bilingual Education, 310-338-4515, E-mail: framos@lmu.edu. *Application contact:* Chake H. Kouyoumjian, Associate Dean of Graduate Studies, 310-338-2721, Fax: 310-388-6086, E-mail: graduateinfo@lmu.edu. Website: http://soe.lmu.edu/academics/bilingualeducation

Manhattan College, Graduate Programs, School of Education and Health, Program in Special Education, Riverdale, NY 10471. Offers adolescence education students with disabilities generalist extension in English or math or social studies - grades 7-12 (MS Ed); bilingual education (Advanced Certificate); dual childhood/students with disabilities - grades 1-6 (MS Ed); students with disabilities - grades 1-6 (MS Ed). *Program availability:* Part-time, evening/weekend. *Degree requirements:* For master's, thesis, internship (if not certified). *Entrance requirements:* For master's, GRE, minimum GPA of 3.0. Additional exam requirements/recommendations for international students: Required—TOEFL (minimum score 550 paper-based; 80 iBT), IELTS (minimum score 6). Electronic applications accepted. Application fee is waived when completed online. *Expenses:* Contact institution.

Manhattanville College, School of Education, Program in Teaching English to Speakers of Other Languages, Purchase, NY 10577-2132. Offers adult and international settings (MPS); bilingual education (childhood/Spanish) (Advanced Certificate); teaching English as a second language (all grades) (MPS, Certificate). *Program availability:* Part-time, evening/weekend. *Faculty:* 2 full-time (1 woman), 6 part-time/adjunct (4 women). *Students:* 5 full-time (all women), 22 part-time (17 women); includes 8 minority (1 Black or African American, non-Hispanic/Latino; 7 Hispanic/Latino). Average age 31. 9 applicants, 100% accepted, 8 enrolled. In 2017, 13 master's, 3 Advanced Certificates awarded. *Degree requirements:* For master's, comprehensive exam (for some programs), thesis (for some programs), student teaching, research seminars, portfolios, internships, writing assessment; for other advanced degree, comprehensive exam (for some programs). *Entrance requirements:* For master's, GRE or MAT (for programs leading to certification), minimum GPA of 3.0, 2 letters of recommendation, interview, essay (2-3 page personal statement that describes reasons for choosing teaching or educational leadership as profession and philosophy of education), proof of immunization (for those born after 1957). Additional exam requirements/recommendations for international students: Required—TOEFL (minimum score 600 paper-based; 110 iBT); Recommended—IELTS (minimum score 8). *Application deadline:* Applications are processed on a rolling basis. Application fee: $75. Electronic applications accepted. *Expenses:* $915 per credit. *Financial support:* Teaching assistantships, career-related internships or fieldwork, Federal Work-Study, institutionally sponsored loans, scholarships/grants, and unspecified assistantships available. Financial award application deadline: 3/15; financial award applicants required to submit FAFSA. *Faculty research:* Changing suburbs institute and community schools. *Unit head:* Dr. Shelly Wepner, Dean, 914-323-3153, Fax: 914-323-5493, E-mail: shelly.wepner@mville.edu. *Application contact:* Alissa Wilson, Director, Graduate Admissions, 914-323-3150, Fax: 914-694-1732, E-mail: edschool@mville.edu. Website: http://www.mville.edu/programs/tesol-teaching-english-speakers-other-languages

Molloy College, Graduate Education Program, Rockville Centre, NY 11571-5002. Offers adolescent education in biology (MS); adolescent special education (Advanced Certificate); bilingual extension (Advanced Certificate); childhood education (MS); childhood special education (Advanced Certificate); early childhood education (MS); educational technology (MS); English (MS); mathematics (MS); social studies (MS); Spanish (MS); special education on both childhood and adolescent levels (MS); teaching English to speakers of other languages (TESOL) in grades pre-K to 12 (MS); TESOL (Advanced Certificate). *Accreditation:* NCATE. *Program availability:* Part-time, evening/weekend. *Faculty:* 18 full-time (17 women), 11 part-time/adjunct (9 women). *Students:* 102 full-time (80 women), 217 part-time (167 women); includes 65 minority (16 Black or African American, non-Hispanic/Latino; 7 Asian, non-Hispanic/Latino; 38 Hispanic/Latino; 4 Two or more races, non-Hispanic/Latino), 1 international. Average age 41. 153 applicants, 68% accepted, 85 enrolled. In 2017, 95 master's, 3 other advanced degrees awarded. *Entrance requirements:* Additional exam requirements/recommendations for international students: Required—TOEFL (minimum score 550 paper-based; 79 iBT). *Application deadline:* Applications are processed on a rolling basis. Application fee: $60. Electronic applications accepted. *Expenses: Tuition:* Full-time $19,980; part-time $1110 per credit. *Required fees:* $1040. Tuition and fees vary according to course load and degree level. *Financial support:* Application deadline: 3/1; applicants required to submit FAFSA. *Faculty research:* English Language Learners; social emotional needs of students; gifted education; cultural diversity; collaborative teaching methods. *Unit head:* Joanne O'Brien, Associate Dean and Director of Graduate Education Programs, 516-323-3116, E-mail: jobrien@molloy.edu. *Application contact:* Jaclyn Machowicz, Assistant Director for Admissions, 516-323-4010, E-mail: jmachowicz@molloy.edu.

Mount St. Joseph University, Graduate Education Program, Cincinnati, OH 45233-1670. Offers adolescent to young adult education (MA); dyslexia (Certificate); inclusive early childhood education (MA); middle childhood education (MA); multicultural special education (MA); reading science (MA). *Accreditation:* TEAC. *Program availability:* Part-time, evening/weekend, 100% online, blended/hybrid learning. *Faculty:* 6 full-time (5 women), 11 part-time/adjunct (8 women). *Students:* 37 full-time (30 women), 91 part-time (83 women); includes 13 minority (11 Black or African American, non-Hispanic/Latino; 1 Hispanic/Latino; 1 Two or more races, non-Hispanic/Latino). Average age 34. In 2017, 79 master's awarded. *Degree requirements:* For master's, comprehensive exam, thesis, research project, student teaching, clinical and field-based experiences. *Entrance requirements:* For master's, GRE (if GPA is below 3.0), letter of intent, 2 referrals, background check, interview, resume, minimum undergraduate GPA of 3.0. Additional exam requirements/recommendations for international students: Required—TOEFL (minimum score 560 paper-based; 83 iBT). *Application deadline:* Applications are processed on a rolling basis. Application fee: $50. Electronic applications accepted. *Expenses:* $600 per credit hour. *Financial support:* Applicants required to submit FAFSA. *Faculty research:* Foreign and second language learning problems/reading disabilities, multicultural/bilingual special education, science education, pedagogical content knowledge, early childhood, response to intervention. *Unit head:* Dr. Laura Saylor, Dean, 513-244-3263, E-mail: laura.saylor@msj.edu. *Application contact:* Mary Brigham, Assistant Director of Graduate Recruitment, 513-244-4233, Fax: 513-244-4629, E-mail: mary.brigham@msj.edu. Website: http://www.msj.edu/academics/graduate-programs/master-of-arts-initial-teacher-licensure-programs/

New Jersey City University, Debra Cannon Partridge Wolfe College of Education, Department of Multicultural Education, Jersey City, NJ 07305-1597. Offers bilingual/bicultural education (MA); English as a second language (MA). *Program availability:* Part-time, evening/weekend. *Entrance requirements:* For master's, GRE General Test or MAT. Additional exam requirements/recommendations for international students: Required—TOEFL.

New Mexico State University, College of Education, Department of Communication Disorders, Las Cruces, NM 88003. Offers communication disorders (MA); curriculum and instruction (Ed S), including special education (MA, Ed S), special education/deaf-hard of hearing (MA, Ed S); education (MA), including autism spectrum disorders (MA, Ed D, PhD), special education (MA, Ed S), special education/deaf-hard of hearing (MA, Ed S), speech-language pathology; special education (Ed D, PhD), including autism spectrum disorders (MA, Ed D, PhD), bilingual/multicultural special education. *Accreditation:* ASHA (one or more programs are accredited); NCATE. *Program availability:* Part-time, evening/weekend, online learning. *Faculty:* 13 full-time (10 women), 4 part-time/adjunct (3 women). *Students:* 45 full-time (41 women), 56 part-time (45 women); includes 64 minority (1 Black or African American, non-Hispanic/Latino; 2 American Indian or Alaska Native, non-Hispanic/Latino; 4 Asian, non-Hispanic/Latino; 56 Hispanic/Latino; 1 Two or more races, non-Hispanic/Latino), 6 international. Average age 33. 164 applicants, 36% accepted, 32 enrolled. In 2017, 41 master's, 3 doctorates, 7 other advanced degrees awarded. *Degree requirements:* For master's, comprehensive exam, thesis optional; for doctorate, comprehensive exam, thesis/dissertation. *Entrance requirements:* For master's, GRE General Test or MAT. Additional exam requirements/recommendations for international students: Required—TOEFL (minimum score 550 paper-based; 79 iBT), IELTS (minimum score 6.5). *Application deadline:* For fall admission, 2/1 priority date for domestic students. Applications are processed on a rolling basis. Application fee: $40 ($50 for international students). Electronic applications accepted. *Expenses:* Tuition, state resident: full-time $4390. Tuition, nonresident: full-time $15,309. *Required fees:* $853. *Financial support:* In 2017–18, 33 students received support, including 1 fellowship (averaging $4,390 per year), 1 research assistantship (averaging $8,482 per year), 14 teaching assistantships (averaging $10,386 per year); career-related internships or fieldwork, Federal Work-Study, scholarships/grants, traineeships, health care benefits, and unspecified assistantships also available. Support available to part-time students. Financial award application deadline: 3/1. *Faculty research:* Multicultural special education, multicultural communication disorders, mild disability, multicultural assessment, deaf education, early childhood, bilingual special education. *Total annual research expenditures:* $182,251. *Unit head:* Dr. Victoria White, Interim Department Head, 575-646-5973, Fax: 575-646-7712, E-mail: vwhite@nmsu.edu. *Application contact:* Dr. Victoria White, Interim Department Head, 575-646-5973, Fax: 575-646-7712, E-mail: vwhite@nmsu.edu. Website: https://cd.nmsu.edu/

New Mexico State University, College of Education, Department of Curriculum and Instruction, Las Cruces, NM 88003. Offers bilingual education (MA); curriculum and instruction (MA, Ed D, PhD); early childhood education (MA); educational diagnostics (Ed S); language, literacy and culture (MA); learning design and technologies (MA); teaching (MAT), including dance, Spanish; teaching English to speakers of other languages (MA). *Accreditation:* NCATE. *Program availability:* Part-time, evening/weekend, 100% online. *Faculty:* 22 full-time (11 women), 7 part-time/adjunct (2 women). *Students:* 113 full-time (79 women), 194 part-time (138 women); includes 171 minority (15 Black or African American, non-Hispanic/Latino; 3 American Indian or Alaska Native, non-Hispanic/Latino; 4 Asian, non-Hispanic/Latino; 142 Hispanic/Latino; 7 Two or more races, non-Hispanic/Latino), 37 international. Average age 36. 106 applicants, 80% accepted, 56 enrolled. In 2017, 82 master's, 15 doctorates, 1 other advanced degree awarded. *Entrance requirements:* For master's, minimum cumulative GPA of 3.0; for doctorate, portfolio, minimum cumulative GPA of 3.0. Additional exam requirements/recommendations for international students: Required—TOEFL (minimum score 550 paper-based; 79 iBT), IELTS (minimum score 6.5). *Application deadline:* For fall admission, 12/15 priority date for domestic and international students; for spring admission, 11/1 for domestic students. Applications are processed on a rolling basis. Application fee: $40 ($50 for international students). Electronic applications accepted. *Expenses:* Tuition, state resident: full-time $4390. Tuition, nonresident: full-time $15,309. *Required fees:* $853. *Financial support:* In 2017–18, 97 students received support, including 2 fellowships (averaging $4,390 per year), 1 research assistantship (averaging $17,368 per year), 10 teaching assistantships (averaging $17,489 per year); career-related internships or fieldwork, Federal Work-Study, scholarships/grants, traineeships, health care benefits, and unspecified assistantships also available. Support available to part-time students. Financial award application deadline: 3/1. *Faculty research:* STEM education, bilingual and English as a second language education, critical pedagogy/multicultural education, learning design and technology, early childhood education. *Total annual research expenditures:* $13,518. *Unit head:* Dr. David Rutledge, Department Head, 575-646-5411, Fax: 575-646-5436, E-mail: rutledge@nmsu.edu. *Application contact:* Dr. David Rutledge, Associate Department Head for Graduate Programs, 575-646-5411, Fax: 575-646-5436, E-mail: rutledge@nmsu.edu. Website: http://tpal.nmsu.edu/

New York University, Steinhardt School of Culture, Education, and Human Development, Department of Humanities and Social Sciences in the Professions, Program in Sociology of Education, New York, NY 10012. Offers education policy (MA); social and cultural studies of education (MA); sociology of education (PhD). *Program availability:* Part-time. *Students:* Average age 26. 96 applicants, 45% accepted, 8 enrolled. In 2017, 24 master's, 2 doctorates awarded. *Entrance requirements:* For master's, letters of recommendation; for doctorate, GRE General Test, interview. Additional exam requirements/recommendations for international students: Required—TOEFL (minimum score 100 iBT). *Application deadline:* For fall admission, 12/1 priority date for domestic and international students; for spring admission, 10/1 for domestic and international students. Applications are processed on a rolling basis. Application fee: $75. Electronic applications accepted. *Expenses: Tuition:* Full-time $41,352; part-time $19,968 per year. *Required fees:* $2496; $1628 per unit. $814 per term. Tuition and fees vary according to course load and program. *Financial support:* Fellowships with full and partial tuition reimbursements, Federal Work-Study, institutionally sponsored loans, scholarships/grants, and tuition waivers (partial) available. Support available to part-time students. Financial award application deadline: 2/1; financial award applicants required to submit FAFSA. *Faculty research:* Legal and institutional environments of schools; social inequality; high school reform and achievement; urban schooling, economics and education, educational policy. *Unit head:* Prof. Lisa Stulberg, Program Director, 212-992-9373, Fax: 212-995-4832, E-mail: lisa.stulberg@nyu.edu. *Application contact:* 212-998-5030, Fax: 212-995-4328, E-mail: steinhardt.gradadmissions@nyu.edu. Website: http://steinhardt.nyu.edu/humsocsci/sociology

New York University, Steinhardt School of Culture, Education, and Human Development, Department of Teaching and Learning, Program in Multilingual/Multicultural Studies, New York, NY 10012. Offers bilingual education (MA, PhD, Advanced Certificate); foreign language education (MA); teaching English to speakers of other languages (MA, PhD); teaching foreign languages, 7-12 (MA), including Chinese, French, Italian, Japanese, Spanish; teaching French as a foreign language (MA), including teaching English to speakers of other languages; teaching Spanish as a foreign language (MA), including teaching English to speakers of other languages. MA in teaching English to speakers of other languages also offered in collaboration with NYU Shanghai. *Accreditation:* TEAC. *Program availability:* Part-time, evening/weekend. *Students:* Average age 29. 431 applicants, 61% accepted, 92 enrolled. In 2017, 121 master's, 1 doctorate, 2 other advanced degrees awarded. *Entrance requirements:* For doctorate, GRE General Test, interview; for Advanced Certificate, master's degree. Additional exam requirements/recommendations for international students: Required—

Multilingual and Multicultural Education

TOEFL (minimum score 100 iBT). *Application deadline:* For fall admission, 12/1 priority date for domestic and international students; for spring admission, 10/1 for domestic and international students. Applications are processed on a rolling basis. Application fee: $75. Electronic applications accepted. *Expenses:* Tuition: Full-time $41,352; part-time $19,968 per year. *Required fees:* $2496; $1628 per unit. $814 per term. Tuition and fees vary according to course load and program. *Financial support:* Fellowships with full and partial tuition reimbursements, career-related internships or fieldwork, Federal Work-Study, institutionally sponsored loans, scholarships/grants, and tuition waivers (partial) available. Support available to part-time students. Financial award application deadline: 2/1; financial award applicants required to submit FAFSA. *Faculty research:* Second language acquisition, cross-cultural communication, technology-enhanced language learning, language variation, action learning. *Unit head:* Prof. Shondel Nero, Director, 212-998-5757, E-mail: shondel.nero@nyu.edu. *Application contact:* 212-998-5030, Fax: 212-995-4328, E-mail: steinhardt.gradadmissions@nyu.edu.
Website: http://steinhardt.nyu.edu/teachlearn/mms

Northern Arizona University, College of Education, Department of Educational Specialties, Flagstaff, AZ 86011. Offers autism spectrum disorders (Certificate); bilingual/multicultural education (M Ed), including bilingual, ESL; career and technical education (M Ed, Certificate); educational technology (M Ed, Certificate); English as a second language (Certificate); positive behavior support (Certificate); special education (M Ed), including early childhood special education, mild/moderate disabilities. *Program availability:* Part-time, 100% online, blended/hybrid learning. *Faculty:* 31 full-time (19 women), 2 part-time/adjunct (1 woman). *Students:* 66 full-time (52 women), 203 part-time (147 women); includes 83 minority (20 Black or African American, non-Hispanic/Latino; 12 American Indian or Alaska Native, non-Hispanic/Latino; 5 Asian, non-Hispanic/Latino; 38 Hispanic/Latino; 3 Native Hawaiian or other Pacific Islander, non-Hispanic/Latino; 5 Two or more races, non-Hispanic/Latino), 6 international. Average age 37. 157 applicants, 94% accepted, 148 enrolled. In 2017, 119 master's, 26 Certificates awarded. *Degree requirements:* For master's, variable foreign language requirement, comprehensive exam (for some programs), thesis (for some programs); for Certificate, comprehensive exam (for some programs). *Entrance requirements:* Additional exam requirements/recommendations for international students: Required—TOEFL (minimum score 80 iBT), IELTS (minimum score 6.5). *Application deadline:* For fall admission, 3/1 for domestic and international students; for spring admission, 10/1 for domestic and international students. Applications are processed on a rolling basis. Application fee: $65. Electronic applications accepted. *Expenses:* Tuition, state resident: full-time $9240; part-time $458 per credit hour. Tuition, nonresident: full-time $21,588; part-time $1199 per credit hour. *Required fees:* $1021; $14 per credit hour. $646 per semester. Tuition and fees vary according to course load, campus/location and program. *Financial support:* In 2017–18, 11 students received support, including 1 fellowship with full and partial tuition reimbursement available (averaging $12,000 per year), 10 teaching assistantships with full and partial tuition reimbursements available (averaging $12,000 per year); Federal Work-Study, institutionally sponsored loans, health care benefits, tuition waivers (full and partial), and unspecified assistantships also available. Financial award application deadline: 2/1; financial award applicants required to submit FAFSA. *Unit head:* Dr. Shadow Armfield, Chair, 928-523-7651, Fax: 928-523-1929, E-mail: laura.sujo-montes@nau.edu. *Application contact:* Tina Sutton, Coordinator, Graduate College, 928-523-4348, Fax: 928-523-8950, E-mail: graduate@nau.edu.
Website: https://nau.edu/coe/Ed-Specialties/

Queens College of the City University of New York, Arts and Humanities Division, Department of Linguistics and Communication Disorders, Queens, NY 11367-1597. Offers applied linguistics (MA); speech-language pathology (MA); TESOL (MS Ed, Post-Master's Certificate); TESOL and bilingual education (Post-Master's Certificate). *Accreditation:* ASHA. *Program availability:* Part-time. *Faculty:* 22 full-time (16 women), 19 part-time/adjunct (13 women). *Students:* 37 full-time (34 women), 123 part-time (112 women); includes 62 minority (10 Black or African American, non-Hispanic/Latino; 17 Asian, non-Hispanic/Latino; 32 Hispanic/Latino; 3 Two or more races, non-Hispanic/Latino), 3 international. Average age 27. 390 applicants, 25% accepted, 81 enrolled. In 2017, 59 master's, 24 other advanced degrees awarded. *Degree requirements:* For master's, 400 hours of supervised clinical teaching (for MA in speech-language pathology); 50-100 hours of student teaching (for MS Ed). *Entrance requirements:* For master's, minimum GPA of 3.0. Additional exam requirements/recommendations for international students: Required—TOEFL, IELTS. *Application deadline:* For fall admission, 4/1 for domestic students. Applications are processed on a rolling basis. Application fee: $125. Electronic applications accepted. *Expenses:* Contact institution. *Financial support:* Career-related internships or fieldwork available. Financial award application deadline: 4/1; financial award applicants required to submit FAFSA. *Unit head:* Arlene Kraat, Chair, 718-997-2940, E-mail: arlene.kraat@qc.cuny.edu. *Application contact:* Elizabeth D'Amico-Ramirez, Assistant Director of Graduate Admissions, 718-997-5203, E-mail: elizabeth.damicoramirez@qc.cuny.edu.

Queens College of the City University of New York, Division of Education, Department of Elementary and Early Childhood Education, Queens, NY 11367-1597. Offers bilingual education (MAT, MS Ed, AC); childhood education (MAT, MS Ed); early childhood education birth-2 (MAT, MS Ed, AC); literacy education birth-grade 6 (MS Ed, AC). *Program availability:* Part-time, evening/weekend. *Students:* 112 full-time (98 women), 342 part-time (312 women); includes 243 minority (39 Black or African American, non-Hispanic/Latino; 87 Asian, non-Hispanic/Latino; 110 Hispanic/Latino; 7 Two or more races, non-Hispanic/Latino), 12 international. Average age 29. *Degree requirements:* For master's, research project. *Entrance requirements:* For master's, minimum GPA of 3.0. Additional exam requirements/recommendations for international students: Required—TOEFL, IELTS. *Application deadline:* For fall admission, 4/1 for domestic students. Applications are processed on a rolling basis. Application fee: $125. Electronic applications accepted. *Financial support:* Career-related internships or fieldwork available. Financial award application deadline: 4/1; financial award applicants required to submit FAFSA. *Unit head:* Daisuke Akiba, Chair, 718-997-5300, E-mail: daisuke.akiba@qc.cuny.edu. *Application contact:* Elizabeth D'Amico-Ramirez, Assistant Director of Graduate Admissions, 718-997-5203, E-mail: elizabeth.damicoramirez@qc.cuny.edu.

Quincy University, Master of Science in Education Programs, Quincy, IL 62301-2699. Offers curriculum and instruction (MS Ed), including bilingual/English as a second language; education studies (MS Ed); leadership (MS Ed); reading education (MS Ed); teacher leader (MS Ed). *Program availability:* Part-time, evening/weekend, online learning. *Degree requirements:* For master's, comprehensive exam (for some programs), thesis optional. *Entrance requirements:* For master's, MAT or GRE, personal resume. Additional exam requirements/recommendations for international students: Required—TOEFL (minimum score 550 paper-based; 79 iBT). *Application deadline:* Applications are processed on a rolling basis. Application fee: $25. Electronic applications accepted. Application fee is waived when completed online. *Expenses:* Tuition: Part-time $450 per credit hour. *Financial support:* Applicants required to submit FAFSA. *Unit head:* Dr. Bruce Alan Spitzer, Director, 217-228-5432 Ext. 3106, E-mail: spitzbr@quincy.edu. *Application contact:* Office of Admissions, 217-228-5210, Fax: 217-228-5479, E-mail: admissions@quincy.edu.
Website: http://www.quincy.edu/academics/graduate-programs/education

Rider University, College of Education and Human Services, Teacher Certification Program, Lawrenceville, NJ 08648-3001. Offers bilingual education (Certificate); business education (Certificate); early childhood education (Certificate); elementary education (Certificate); English as a second language (Certificate); English education (Certificate); mathematics education (Certificate); science education (Certificate); secondary education (Certificate); social studies education (Certificate); world languages (Certificate), including French, German, Spanish. *Program availability:* Part-time, online learning. *Degree requirements:* For Certificate, internship, professional portfolio. *Entrance requirements:* For degree, PRAXIS, resume. Additional exam requirements/recommendations for international students: Required—TOEFL (minimum score 550 paper-based). Electronic applications accepted. *Faculty research:* Conceptual foundations for optimal development of creativity; creative theory, cognitive processes in mathematics learning, teacher collaboration.

Rutgers University–New Brunswick, Graduate School-New Brunswick, Program in Spanish, Piscataway, NJ 08854-8097. Offers bilingualism and second language acquisition (MA, PhD); Spanish (MA, MAT, PhD); Spanish literature (MA, PhD); translation (MA). *Program availability:* Part-time. *Degree requirements:* For master's, comprehensive exam (for some programs), thesis (for some programs); for doctorate, 2 foreign languages, comprehensive exam, thesis/dissertation. *Entrance requirements:* For master's and doctorate, GRE General Test. Additional exam requirements/recommendations for international students: Required—TOEFL. Electronic applications accepted. *Faculty research:* Hispanic literature, Luso-Brazilian literature, Spanish linguistics, Spanish translation.

St. John's University, The School of Education, Department of Education Specialties, Program in Teaching English to Speakers of Other Languages and Bilingual Education, Queens, NY 11439. Offers bilingual education (Adv C); childhood education and teaching English to speakers of other languages (MS Ed); teaching English to speakers of other languages (MS Ed, Adv C). *Students:* 21 full-time (19 women), 83 part-time (73 women); includes 39 minority (4 Black or African American, non-Hispanic/Latino; 9 Asian, non-Hispanic/Latino; 24 Hispanic/Latino; 2 Two or more races, non-Hispanic/Latino), 8 international. Average age 32. 54 applicants, 91% accepted, 35 enrolled. In 2017, 47 master's, 71 Adv Cs awarded. *Degree requirements:* For Adv C, one foreign language. *Entrance requirements:* For master's, GRE, MAT, or PRAXIS, statement of goals (personal essay), official undergraduate transcripts, initial teaching certification; for Adv C, initial teaching certification, first master's transcripts, statement of purpose. Additional exam requirements/recommendations for international students: Required—TOEFL, IELTS. *Application deadline:* For fall admission, 8/17 for domestic and international students; for summer admission, 5/15 for domestic and international students. Application fee: $70. Electronic applications accepted. *Expenses: Tuition:* Full-time $44,280; part-time $1230 per credit. *Required fees:* $340; $340 per credit. Tuition and fees vary according to course load, degree level and program. *Financial support:* Fellowships, research assistantships, scholarships/grants, and unspecified assistantships available. Support available to part-time students. Financial award application deadline: 2/1; financial award applicants required to submit FAFSA. *Faculty research:* Second language learning and academic achievement, heritage language education, assessing the progress of English language learners toward English acquisition, dual language acquisition, study of English Creoles and dialects of other English's, literacy development for ESL learners; investigating Caribbean and Creole language and culture, education law. *Unit head:* Dr. John Spiridaj, Chair, 718-990-5591, E-mail: spiridaj@stjohns.edu. *Application contact:* Dr. John Spiridakis, Chair, 718-990-5591, E-mail: spiridaj@stjohns.edu.
Website: https://www.stjohns.edu/academics/schools-and-colleges/school-education/programs-and-majors/tesol-master-science-education

Saint Mary's University of Minnesota, Schools of Graduate and Professional Programs, Graduate School of Education, Education Program, Winona, MN 55987-1399. Offers culturally responsive teaching (Certificate); education (MA); gifted inclusive education (Certificate). *Unit head:* Lynn Albee, Director, 612-728-5128, Fax: 612-728-5121, E-mail: lalbee@smumn.edu. *Application contact:* James Callinan, Director of Admissions for Graduate and Professional Programs, 612-728-5158, Fax: 612-728-5121, E-mail: jcallina@smumn.edu.
Website: http://www.smumn.edu/graduate-home/areas-of-study/graduate-school-of-education/ma-in-education

San Diego State University, Graduate and Research Affairs, College of Education, Department of Policy Studies in Language and Cross Cultural Education, San Diego, CA 92182. Offers multi-cultural emphasis (PhD); policy studies in language and cross cultural education (MA). *Accreditation:* NCATE. *Entrance requirements:* For master's, GRE General Test, letters of reference; for doctorate, GRE General Test, 3 letters of reference, resumé. Additional exam requirements/recommendations for international students: Required—TOEFL. Electronic applications accepted.

Southern Connecticut State University, School of Graduate Studies, School of Arts and Sciences, Department of World Languages and Literatures, New Haven, CT 06515-1355. Offers multicultural-bilingual education/teaching English to speakers of other languages (MS); romance languages (MA). *Program availability:* Part-time, evening/weekend. *Degree requirements:* For master's, one foreign language, thesis or alternative. *Entrance requirements:* For master's, interview, minimum undergraduate GPA of 2.7. Electronic applications accepted.

Southern Methodist University, Annette Caldwell Simmons School of Education and Human Development, Department of Teaching and Learning, Dallas, TX 75275. Offers bilingual/ESL education (MBE); education (M Ed, PhD); gifted education (MBE); reading and writing (M Ed); special education (M Ed). *Program availability:* Part-time, evening/weekend. Terminal master's awarded for partial completion of doctoral program. *Degree requirements:* For master's, comprehensive exam, minimum GPA of 3.0; for doctorate, thesis/dissertation, qualifying exams, major area paper, evidence of teaching competency, dissemination of research (e.g., conference presentation), professional portfolio. *Entrance requirements:* For master's, minimum GPA of 3.0 or GRE, 3 letters of recommendation; for doctorate, GRE, minimum GPA of 3.3, 3 years of full-time teaching, 3 letters of recommendation, interview. Additional exam requirements/recommendations for international students: Required—TOEFL. Electronic applications accepted. *Faculty research:* Reading intervention, mathematics intervention, bilingual education, new literacies.

State University of New York at New Paltz, Graduate and Extended Learning School, School of Education, Department of Educational Studies and Leadership, Program in Humanistic/Multicultural Education, New Paltz, NY 12561. Offers humanistic/multicultural education (MPS); multicultural education (AC). *Accreditation:* NCATE. *Program availability:* Part-time, evening/weekend. *Faculty:* 4 full-time (all women). *Students:* 7 full-time (6 women), 26 part-time (18 women); includes 9 minority (3 Black or African American, non-Hispanic/Latino; 6 Hispanic/Latino), 1 international. 8 applicants, 75% accepted, 5 enrolled. In 2017, 14 master's awarded. *Entrance requirements:* For master's, minimum GPA of 3.0. Additional exam requirements/recommendations for international students: Required—TOEFL (minimum score 550 paper-based; 80 iBT), IELTS (minimum score 6.5). *Application deadline:* For fall admission, 4/15 priority date for domestic students, 4/15 for international students; for spring admission, 10/15 for domestic and international students. Application fee: $50. Electronic applications

accepted. *Financial support:* Application deadline: 8/1. *Unit head:* Dr. Nancy Schniedewind, Coordinator, 845-257-2827, E-mail: schniedn@newpaltz.edu. *Application contact:* Vika Shock, Director of Graduate Admissions, 845-257-3286, E-mail: gradschool@newpaltz.edu.
Website: http://www.newpaltz.edu/edstudies/humanistic.html

State University of New York College at Geneseo, Graduate Studies, School of Education, Program in Childhood Multicultural Education, Geneseo, NY 14454-1401. Offers MS Ed. *Program availability:* Part-time, evening/weekend. *Students:* 5 applicants. In 2017, 1 master's awarded. *Degree requirements:* For master's, culminating experience: thesis or research project. *Entrance requirements:* For master's, GRE, MAT, EAS, edTPA, PRAXIS, or another substantially equivalent test, proof of New York State initial certification or equivalent certification from another state. Additional exam requirements/recommendations for international students: Required—TOEFL (minimum score 525 paper-based; 71 iBT), IELTS (minimum score 6.5), PTE, iTEP. *Application deadline:* For fall admission, 4/1 priority date for domestic students; for spring admission, 11/1 priority date for domestic students; for summer admission, 4/1 priority date for domestic students. Applications are processed on a rolling basis. Application fee: $50. Electronic applications accepted. *Expenses:* Contact institution. *Financial support:* Fellowships, scholarships/grants, health care benefits, tuition waivers (full and partial), and unspecified assistantships available. Support available to part-time students. Financial award application deadline: 4/1; financial award applicants required to submit FAFSA. *Unit head:* Dr. Anjoo Sikka, Dean of the School of Education, 585-245-5151, Fax: 585-245-5220, E-mail: sikka@geneseo.edu. *Application contact:* Michael R. George, Director of Graduate Admissions, 585-245-5040, Fax: 585-245-5550, E-mail: georgem@geneseo.edu.

Sul Ross State University, Rio Grande College of Sul Ross State University, Alpine, TX 79832. Offers business administration (MBA); teacher education (M Ed), including bilingual education, counseling, educational diagnostics, elementary education, general education, reading, school administration, secondary education. *Program availability:* Part-time, evening/weekend, online learning. *Degree requirements:* For master's, comprehensive exam, thesis optional, minimum GPA of 3.0. *Entrance requirements:* For master's, GMAT or GRE General Test, minimum GPA of 2.5 in last 60 hours of undergraduate work. Additional exam requirements/recommendations for international students: Required—TOEFL.

Teachers College, Columbia University, Department of Arts and Humanities, New York, NY 10027. Offers applied linguistics (MA, Ed D); art and art education (Ed M, MA, Ed D, Ed DCT); arts administration (MA); bilingual and bicultural education (MA); global competence (Certificate); history and education (Ed D, PhD); music and music education (Ed DCT); philosophy and education (MA, Ed D, PhD); social studies education (Ed M, PhD); teaching English to speakers of other languages (Ed M); teaching of English and English education (Ed M, MA, Ed D, PhD), including English education (Ed M, Ed D, PhD), teaching of English (MA); teaching of social studies (MA); TESOL (MA, Ed D). *Program availability:* Part-time, evening/weekend. *Students:* 391 full-time (305 women), 418 part-time (283 women); includes 246 minority (62 Black or African American, non-Hispanic/Latino; 3 American Indian or Alaska Native, non-Hispanic/Latino; 94 Asian, non-Hispanic/Latino; 75 Hispanic/Latino; 12 Two or more races, non-Hispanic/Latino), 209 international. Average age 30. 1,053 applicants, 60% accepted, 334 enrolled. Terminal master's awarded for partial completion of doctoral program. *Financial support:* Fellowships, research assistantships, teaching assistantships, career-related internships or fieldwork, Federal Work-Study, institutionally sponsored loans, tuition waivers (full and partial), and unspecified assistantships available. Support available to part-time students. *Unit head:* Prof. William Gaudelli, Department Chair, E-mail: gaudelli@tc.columbia.edu. *Application contact:* David Estrella, Director of Admissions, 212-678-3305, Fax: 212-678-4171, E-mail: estrella@tc.columbia.edu.

Texas A&M University, College of Education and Human Development, Department of Educational Psychology, College Station, TX 77843. Offers bilingual education (M Ed, MS); counseling psychology (PhD); educational psychology (M Ed, MS, PhD); educational technology (M Ed); school psychology (PhD); special education (M Ed, MS). *Accreditation:* APA (one or more programs are accredited). *Program availability:* Part-time, evening/weekend, blended/hybrid learning. *Faculty:* 45. *Students:* 165 full-time (131 women), 248 part-time (210 women); includes 144 minority (24 Black or African American, non-Hispanic/Latino; 3 American Indian or Alaska Native, non-Hispanic/Latino; 21 Asian, non-Hispanic/Latino; 84 Hispanic/Latino; 2 Native Hawaiian or other Pacific Islander, non-Hispanic/Latino; 10 Two or more races, non-Hispanic/Latino), 45 international. Average age 33. 171 applicants, 44% accepted, 47 enrolled. In 2017, 141 master's, 28 doctorates awarded. *Degree requirements:* For master's, thesis optional; for doctorate, thesis/dissertation. *Entrance requirements:* For master's and doctorate, GRE General Test. Additional exam requirements/recommendations for international students: Required—TOEFL (minimum score 550 paper-based; 80 iBT), IELTS (minimum score 6), PTE (minimum score 53). *Application deadline:* For fall admission, 12/1 for domestic students; for spring admission, 10/15 for domestic students. Application fee: $50 ($90 for international students). Electronic applications accepted. *Expenses:* Contact institution. *Financial support:* In 2017–18, 210 students received support, including 4 fellowships with tuition reimbursements available (averaging $24,775 per year), 102 research assistantships with tuition reimbursements available (averaging $10,698 per year), 19 teaching assistantships with tuition reimbursements available (averaging $7,177 per year); career-related internships or fieldwork, institutionally sponsored loans, scholarships/grants, traineeships, health care benefits, tuition waivers (full and partial), and unspecified assistantships also available. Support available to part-time students. Financial award application deadline: 3/15; financial award applicants required to submit FAFSA. *Unit head:* Dr. Victor Willson, Department Head, 979-845-1394, E-mail: v-willson@tamu.edu. *Application contact:* Kristie Stramaski, Senior Academic Advisor, 979-845-1833, E-mail: epsyadvisor@tamu.edu. Website: http://epsy.tamu.edu

Texas A&M University–Kingsville, College of Graduate Studies, College of Education and Human Performance, Department of Teacher and Bilingual Education, Program in Bilingual Education, Kingsville, TX 78363. Offers M Ed, Ed D. *Degree requirements:* For master's, comprehensive exam. *Entrance requirements:* For master's, GRE General Test, MAT, minimum GPA of 3.0.

Texas A&M University–San Antonio, Department of Educator and Leadership Preparation, San Antonio, TX 78224. Offers bilingual education (MS); early childhood education (M Ed); educational administration (MA); reading specialization (MS); special education (M Ed), including educational diagnostician. *Program availability:* Part-time, evening/weekend, online learning. *Faculty:* 19 full-time (14 women), 8 part-time/adjunct (2 women). *Students:* 24 full-time (21 women), 188 part-time (143 women); includes 163 minority (7 Black or African American, non-Hispanic/Latino; 1 Asian, non-Hispanic/Latino; 149 Hispanic/Latino; 6 Two or more races, non-Hispanic/Latino), 1 international. Average age 36. 191 applicants, 62% accepted, 67 enrolled. In 2017, 70 master's awarded. *Degree requirements:* For master's, comprehensive exam, thesis or alternative. *Entrance requirements:* For master's, GRE (Quantitative and Verbal) or MAT. Additional exam requirements/recommendations for international students: Required—TOEFL (minimum score 550 paper-based; 79 iBT), IELTS (minimum score

6). *Application deadline:* For fall admission, 3/15 priority date for domestic and international students; for spring admission, 11/1 priority date for domestic and international students; for summer admission, 4/1 priority date for domestic and international students. Applications are processed on a rolling basis. Application fee: $35 ($50 for international students). Electronic applications accepted. *Expenses:* Tuition, state resident: full-time $3475; part-time $1930 per semester. Tuition, nonresident: full-time $10,945; part-time $6080 per semester. *Required fees:* $2148; $1412 per year. $706 per semester. Tuition and fees vary according to course load. *Financial support:* In 2017–18, 16 students received support. Research assistantships, Federal Work-Study, scholarships/grants, and tuition waivers available. Financial award application deadline: 3/15; financial award applicants required to submit FAFSA. *Faculty research:* Equity in education, biliteracy practices among Latina and immigrants, academic achievement of low socio-economic students, equity practices in instruction and educational leadership in diverse settings, racial identity development and multicultural education. *Unit head:* Dr. Debbie Vera, Department Chair. *Application contact:* Caitie Garza, Graduate Admissions Coordinator, 210-784-1300, E-mail: beajaguar@tamusa.edu.
Website: http://www.tamusa.edu/collegeofeducationandhumandevelopment/educatorleadershippreparation/index.html

Texas Southern University, College of Education, Area of Curriculum and Instruction, Houston, TX 77004-4584. Offers bilingual education (M Ed); curriculum and instruction (Ed D); secondary education (M Ed). *Program availability:* Part-time, evening/weekend. *Degree requirements:* For master's, comprehensive exam; for doctorate, comprehensive exam, thesis/dissertation. *Entrance requirements:* For master's, GRE General Test, minimum GPA of 2.5; for doctorate, GRE General Test or MAT, master's degree, minimum B+ average. Additional exam requirements/recommendations for international students: Required—TOEFL. Electronic applications accepted.

Texas State University, The Graduate College, College of Education, Program in Elementary Education - Bilingual/Bicultural, San Marcos, TX 78666. Offers M Ed, MA. *Program availability:* Part-time. *Faculty:* 4 full-time (2 women), 2 part-time/adjunct (both women). *Students:* 3 full-time (2 women), 3 part-time (all women); includes 5 minority (all Hispanic/Latino), 1 international. Average age 36. 6 applicants, 67% accepted, 2 enrolled. In 2017, 7 master's awarded. *Degree requirements:* For master's, comprehensive exam, thesis (for some programs). *Entrance requirements:* For master's, baccalaureate degree from regionally-accredited institution with minimum GPA of 2.75 in last 60 hours of course work; meeting with bilingual coordinator to ensure proficiency in written and spoken Spanish; statement of purpose; three letters of recommendation. Additional exam requirements/recommendations for international students: Required—TOEFL (minimum score 550 paper-based; 78 iBT), IELTS (minimum score 6.5). *Application deadline:* For fall admission, 2/15 priority date for domestic and international students; for spring admission, 10/15 for domestic students, 10/1 for international students; for summer admission, 4/15 for domestic students, 3/15 for international students. Applications are processed on a rolling basis. Application fee: $40 ($90 for international students). Electronic applications accepted. *Expenses:* Tuition, state resident: full-time $7868; part-time $3934 per semester. Tuition, nonresident: full-time $17,828; part-time $8914 per semester. *Required fees:* $2092; $1435 per semester. Tuition and fees vary according to course load. *Financial support:* In 2017–18, 5 students received support. Research assistantships, teaching assistantships, career-related internships or fieldwork, Federal Work-Study, institutionally sponsored loans, scholarships/grants, and unspecified assistantships available. Support available to part-time students. Financial award application deadline: 3/1; financial award applicants required to submit FAFSA. *Unit head:* Dr. Mary Esther Huerta, Graduate Advisor, 512-245-3099, Fax: 512-245-7911, E-mail: mh75@txstate.edu. *Application contact:* Dr. Andrea Golato, Dean of Graduate School, 512-245-2581, Fax: 512-245-8365, E-mail: gradcollege@txstate.edu.
Website: http://www.gradcollege.txstate.edu/programs/bilingual-bicultural.html

Texas Tech University, Graduate School, College of Education, Department of Curriculum and Instruction, Lubbock, TX 79409. Offers bilingual education (M Ed); curriculum and instruction (M Ed); elementary education (M Ed); language/literacy education (M Ed); multidisciplinary science (MS); secondary education (M Ed). *Accreditation:* NCATE. *Program availability:* Part-time, evening/weekend, online learning. *Faculty:* 22 full-time (14 women), 2 part-time/adjunct (1 woman). *Students:* 64 full-time (50 women), 247 part-time (205 women); includes 100 minority (26 Black or African American, non-Hispanic/Latino; 1 American Indian or Alaska Native, non-Hispanic/Latino; 11 Asian, non-Hispanic/Latino; 54 Hispanic/Latino; 8 Two or more races, non-Hispanic/Latino), 39 international. Average age 39. 157 applicants, 56% accepted, 71 enrolled. In 2017, 20 master's, 21 doctorates awarded. Terminal master's awarded for partial completion of doctoral program. *Degree requirements:* For master's, comprehensive exam (some programs), thesis optional; for doctorate, comprehensive exam, thesis/dissertation. *Entrance requirements:* For master's, bachelor's degree; resume; letter of intent; academic writing sample; 2 letters of recommendation; for doctorate, GRE, master's degree; resume; letter of intent; academic writing sample; 3 letters of recommendation. Additional exam requirements/recommendations for international students: Required—TOEFL (minimum score 550 paper-based; 79 iBT). *Application deadline:* For fall admission, 6/1 priority date for domestic students, 1/15 priority date for international students; for spring admission, 9/1 priority date for domestic students, 6/15 priority date for international students. Applications are processed on a rolling basis. Application fee: $60. Electronic applications accepted. *Expenses:* Contact institution. *Financial support:* In 2017–18, 96 students received support, including 92 fellowships (averaging $3,321 per year), 37 research assistantships (averaging $12,336 per year); teaching assistantships, Federal Work-Study, institutionally sponsored loans, scholarships/grants, health care benefits, and unspecified assistantships also available. Support available to part-time students. Financial award application deadline: 2/1; financial award applicants required to submit FAFSA. *Faculty research:* Teacher education, curriculum studies, bilingual education, science and math education, language and literacy education. *Total annual research expenditures:* $107,999. *Unit head:* Dr. Fanni Liu Coward, Interim Chairperson, 806-834-4475, Fax: 806-742-2179, E-mail: fanni.coward@ttu.edu. *Application contact:* Brianna Sanchez, Coordinator, 806-834-2353, Fax: 806-742-2179, E-mail: brianna.sanchez@ttu.edu.
Website: http://www.educ.ttu.edu

University at Buffalo, the State University of New York, Graduate School, Graduate School of Education, Department of Learning and Instruction, Buffalo, NY 14260. Offers biology education (Ed M, Certificate); chemistry education (Ed M, Certificate); childhood education (Ed M); childhood education with bilingual extension (Ed M); college teaching (Advanced Certificate); curriculum, instruction and the science of learning (PhD); early childhood education (Ed M); early childhood education with bilingual extension (Ed M); earth science education (Ed M, Certificate); education and technology (Ed M); education studies (Ed M); educational technology and new literacies (Certificate); educational technology and new literacies (Advanced Certificate); elementary education (Ed D); English education (Ed M, Certificate); English education studies (Ed M); English for speakers of other languages (Ed M); foreign and second language education (PhD); French education (Ed M, Certificate); German education (Ed M, Certificate); gifted education (Certificate); Latin education (Ed M, Certificate); literacy education studies

Multilingual and Multicultural Education

(Ed M); literacy specialist (Ed M); literacy teaching and learning (Certificate); mathematics education (Ed M, Certificate); music education (Ed M, Certificate); music education studies (Ed M); music learning theory (Advanced Certificate); online education (Advanced Certificate); physics education (Ed M, Certificate); science and the public (Ed M); social studies education (Ed M, Certificate); Spanish education (Ed M, Certificate); special education (PhD); teaching English to speakers of other languages (Ed M). *Program availability:* Part-time, evening/weekend, 100% online. *Faculty:* 26 full-time (19 women), 74 part-time/adjunct (52 women). *Students:* 172 full-time (122 women), 325 part-time (226 women); includes 44 minority (25 Black or African American, non-Hispanic/Latino; 5 American Indian or Alaska Native, non-Hispanic/Latino; 14 Asian, non-Hispanic/Latino); 57 international. Average age 33. 316 applicants, 78% accepted, 174 enrolled. In 2017, 109 master's, 34 doctorates, 15 other advanced degrees awarded. *Degree requirements:* For master's, comprehensive exam; for doctorate, thesis/dissertation, research analysis exam, research experience. *Entrance requirements:* For master's, letters of reference; for doctorate, GRE General Test or MAT, interview, writing sample, letters of recommendation. Additional exam requirements/recommendations for international students: Required—TOEFL (minimum score 600 paper-based; 96 iBT). *Application deadline:* For fall admission, 2/1 priority date for domestic and international students; for spring admission, 11/15 priority date for domestic students, 10/1 for international students. Applications are processed on a rolling basis. Application fee: $50. Electronic applications accepted. *Financial support:* In 2017–18, 42 fellowships (averaging $5,181 per year), 44 research assistantships with tuition reimbursements (averaging $10,908 per year) were awarded; teaching assistantships, career-related internships or fieldwork, Federal Work-Study, institutionally sponsored loans, scholarships/grants, tuition waivers (full and partial), and unspecified assistantships also available. Financial award application deadline: 2/28; financial award applicants required to submit FAFSA. *Faculty research:* Science assessment, foreign language teaching and learning, early learning, new literacies, gender and education. *Total annual research expenditures:* $413,233. *Unit head:* Dr. David Bruce, Chair, 716-645-4069, Fax: 716-645-3161, E-mail: gse-info@buffalo.edu. *Application contact:* Luann Zak, Admissions Assistant, 716-645-2110, Fax: 716-645-7937, E-mail: luannzak@buffalo.edu.
Website: http://gse.buffalo.edu/lai

University of Alaska Fairbanks, College of Liberal Arts, Department of Cross-Cultural Studies, Fairbanks, AK 99775-6300. Offers MA. *Program availability:* Part-time. *Degree requirements:* For master's, comprehensive exam, project, oral defense of project. *Entrance requirements:* For master's, bachelor's degree from accredited institution with minimum cumulative undergraduate and major GPA of 3.0. Additional exam requirements/recommendations for international students: Required—TOEFL (minimum score 550 paper-based; 79 iBT), IELTS (minimum score 8.5). Electronic applications accepted. *Faculty research:* Alaska native literature, oral traditions, history, law and policy, cultures, art; Native American religion and philosophy.

University of Alaska Fairbanks, College of Liberal Arts, Program in Linguistics, Fairbanks, AK 99775-6280. Offers applied linguistics (MA), including language documentation, second language acquisition teacher education. *Program availability:* Part-time. *Degree requirements:* For master's, one foreign language, comprehensive exam, oral defense of project or thesis. *Entrance requirements:* For master's, bachelor's degree from accredited institution with minimum cumulative undergraduate and major GPA of 3.0. Additional exam requirements/recommendations for international students: Required—TOEFL (minimum score 550 paper-based; 79 iBT), IELTS (minimum score 6.5). Electronic applications accepted. *Faculty research:* Second language acquisition/teaching, Inupiaq, Athabaskan languages, language maintenance and shift, phonology, morphology.

University of Alberta, Faculty of Graduate Studies and Research, Facultè Saint Jean, Edmonton, AB T6G 2E1, Canada. Offers M Ed. *Program availability:* Part-time, evening/weekend, online learning. *Degree requirements:* For master's, thesis (for some programs). *Entrance requirements:* For master's, proficiency in French, 2 years of teaching experience. *Faculty research:* First and second language acquisition, first and second language learning through subject matter, cultural transmission.

University of Calgary, Faculty of Graduate Studies, Werklund School of Education, Graduate Division of Educational Research, Calgary, AB T2N 1N4, Canada. Offers adult learning (M Ed, MA, Ed D, PhD); curriculum and learning (M Ed, MA, Ed D, PhD); educational leadership (M Ed, MA, Ed D, PhD); languages and diversity (M Ed, MA, Ed D, PhD); learning sciences (M Ed, MA, Ed D, PhD). Ed D in educational leadership offered via distance delivery. *Program availability:* Part-time, evening/weekend, online learning. *Degree requirements:* For master's, thesis (for some programs); for doctorate, thesis/dissertation, candidacy exam. *Entrance requirements:* For master's, minimum GPA of 3.0, 3 letters of reference; for doctorate, minimum GPA of 3.5, 3 letters of reference. Additional exam requirements/recommendations for international students: Required—TOEFL, IELTS. Electronic applications accepted. *Faculty research:* Curriculum, leadership, technology, contexts, gifted, second language teaching, work place and adult learning.

University of California, Riverside, Graduate Division, Graduate School of Education, Riverside, CA 92521. Offers applied behavior analysis (M Ed); diversity and equity (M Ed); education policy analysis and leadership (PhD); education specialist (Credential); education, society, and culture (MA, PhD); educational psychology (MA, PhD); general education (M Ed); higher education administration and policy (M Ed, PhD); multiple subject (Credential); research, evaluation, measurement and statistics (MA); school psychology (PhD); single subject (Credential); special education (M Ed, PhD); special education and autism (MA); TESOL (M Ed). *Faculty:* 29 full-time (16 women), 2 part-time/adjunct (1 woman). *Students:* 241 full-time (188 women). 396 applicants, 42% accepted, 166 enrolled. In 2017, 130 master's, 15 doctorates, 14 other advanced degrees awarded. Terminal master's awarded for partial completion of doctoral program. *Degree requirements:* For master's, comprehensive exams or thesis (MA), case study or analytical report (M Ed); for doctorate, comprehensive exam, thesis/dissertation, written and oral qualifying exams, college teaching practicum. *Entrance requirements:* For master's, GRE General Test (for MA); CBEST and CSET (for M Ed in general education only), UCR Extension TESOL certificate (for M Ed with TESOL emphasis only); for doctorate, GRE General Test, writing sample; for Credential, CBEST, CSET. Additional exam requirements/recommendations for international students: Required—TOEFL (minimum score 550 paper-based; 80 iBT), IELTS (minimum score 7). *Application deadline:* For fall admission, 9/1 for domestic students, 6/1 for international students; for winter admission, 11/15 for domestic students, 9/1 for international students; for spring admission, 3/1 for domestic students, 12/1 for international students. Applications are processed on a rolling basis. Application fee: $80 ($100 for international students). Electronic applications accepted. *Expenses:* Tuition, state resident: full-time $5746. Tuition, nonresident: full-time $10,780. Tuition and fees vary according to campus/location and program. *Financial support:* In 2017–18, 105 students received support, including 18 fellowships with full tuition reimbursements available (averaging $31,000 per year), 25 research assistantships with full tuition reimbursements available (averaging $31,000 per year), 10 teaching assistantships with full tuition reimbursements available (averaging $31,000 per year); career-related internships or fieldwork, Federal Work-Study, institutionally sponsored

loans, scholarships/grants, and unspecified assistantships also available. Financial award application deadline: 12/15. *Faculty research:* Responsiveness to intervention, faculty core, response to intervention of English language learners, advanced modeling techniques, study on social capital, trust, and motivation. *Total annual research expenditures:* $1.7 million. *Unit head:* Thomas Smith, Dean, 951-827-4633, E-mail: thomas.smith@ucr.edu. *Application contact:* Heather Killeen, Graduate Program Coordinator, 951-827-6362, E-mail: heather.killeen@ucr.edu.
Website: http://www.education.ucr.edu/

University of California, San Diego, Graduate Division, Program in Education Studies, La Jolla, CA 92093. Offers education (M Ed, PhD); educational leadership (Ed D); teaching and learning (MA, Ed D), including bilingual education (MA), curriculum design (MA). Ed D offered jointly with California State University, San Marcos. *Students:* 88 full-time (64 women), 54 part-time (36 women). 261 applicants, 57% accepted, 77 enrolled. In 2017, 68 master's, 13 doctorates awarded. *Degree requirements:* For master's, thesis (for some programs), student teaching; for doctorate, comprehensive exam, thesis/dissertation. *Entrance requirements:* For master's, GRE General Test; CBEST and appropriate CSET exam (for select tracks), current teaching or educational assignment (for select tracks); for doctorate, GRE General Test, current teaching or educational assignment (for select tracks). Additional exam requirements/recommendations for international students: Required—TOEFL (minimum score 550 paper-based; 80 iBT), IELTS (minimum score 7). *Application deadline:* For fall admission, 2/2 for domestic students. Application fee: $105 ($125 for international students). Electronic applications accepted. *Financial support:* Fellowships, career-related internships or fieldwork, and scholarships/grants available. Financial award applicants required to submit FAFSA. *Faculty research:* Language, culture and literacy development of deaf/hard of hearing children; equity issues in education; educational reform; evaluation, assessment, and research methodologies; distributed learning. *Unit head:* Carolyn Hofstetter, Chair, 858-822-6688, E-mail: ajdaly@ucsd.edu. *Application contact:* Giselle Van Luit, Graduate Coordinator, 858-534-2958, E-mail: edsinfo@ucsd.edu.

University of Colorado Boulder, Graduate School, School of Education, Division of Social Multicultural and Bilingual Foundations, Boulder, CO 80309. Offers educational equity and cultural diversity (PhD); multicultural education (MA). *Accreditation:* NCATE. *Students:* 44 full-time (42 women), 95 part-time (83 women); includes 40 minority (1 American Indian or Alaska Native, non-Hispanic/Latino; 37 Hispanic/Latino; 2 Two or more races, non-Hispanic/Latino), 3 international. Average age 36. 79 applicants, 78% accepted, 29 enrolled. In 2017, 90 master's, 4 doctorates awarded. Terminal master's awarded for partial completion of doctoral program. *Degree requirements:* For master's, comprehensive exam, thesis or alternative; for doctorate, one foreign language, comprehensive exam, thesis/dissertation. *Entrance requirements:* For master's, GRE General Test or MAT, minimum undergraduate GPA of 2.75; for doctorate, GRE General Test. *Application deadline:* For fall admission, 12/1 for domestic and international students; for spring admission, 9/1 for domestic and international students. Application fee: $60 ($80 for international students). Electronic applications accepted. Application fee is waived when completed online. *Financial support:* In 2017–18, 91 students received support, including 14 fellowships (averaging $4,259 per year), 14 research assistantships with full and partial tuition reimbursements available (averaging $34,281 per year), 8 teaching assistantships with full and partial tuition reimbursements available (averaging $8,993 per year); institutionally sponsored loans, scholarships/grants, health care benefits, and unspecified assistantships also available. Financial award application deadline: 2/15; financial award applicants required to submit FAFSA. *Application contact:* E-mail: edadvise@colorado.edu.
Website: http://www.colorado.edu/education/

University of Colorado Denver, School of Education and Human Development, Teacher Education Programs, Denver, CO 80217. Offers elementary linguistically diverse education (MA); elementary math and science education (MA); elementary math education (MA); elementary reading and writing (MA); elementary science education (MA); secondary English education (MA); secondary linguistically diverse education (MA); secondary math education (MA); secondary reading and writing (MA); secondary science education (MA); special education (MA). *Accreditation:* NCATE. *Program availability:* Part-time, evening/weekend. *Degree requirements:* For master's, comprehensive exam. *Entrance requirements:* For master's, GRE or MAT (for those with GPA below 2.75), transcripts, resume, letters of recommendation. Additional exam requirements/recommendations for international students: Required—TOEFL (minimum score 537 paper-based; 75 iBT); Recommended—IELTS (minimum score 6.5). Electronic applications accepted. *Expenses:* Contact institution. *Faculty research:* Linguistically diverse education/ESL, elementary reading and writing, elementary teacher education, secondary teacher education, special education.

University of Connecticut, Graduate School, Neag School of Education, Department of Curriculum and Instruction, Program in Bilingual and Bicultural Education, Storrs, CT 06269. Offers MA, PhD. *Accreditation:* NCATE. Terminal master's awarded for partial completion of doctoral program. *Degree requirements:* For master's, comprehensive exam; for doctorate, thesis/dissertation. *Entrance requirements:* For doctorate, GRE General Test. Additional exam requirements/recommendations for international students: Required—TOEFL (minimum score 550 paper-based). Electronic applications accepted.

University of Delaware, College of Education and Human Development, School of Education, Newark, DE 19716. Offers education (PhD); educational leadership (Ed D); higher education (M Ed); instruction (MI); reading (M Ed); school leadership (M Ed); school psychology (MA, Ed S); teaching English as a second language (TESL) (MA). *Accreditation:* NCATE. *Program availability:* Part-time, evening/weekend. Terminal master's awarded for partial completion of doctoral program. *Degree requirements:* For master's, comprehensive exam (for some programs), thesis (for some programs); for doctorate, comprehensive exam (for some programs), thesis/dissertation. *Entrance requirements:* For master's and doctorate, GRE, 3 letters of recommendation. Additional exam requirements/recommendations for international students: Required—TOEFL (minimum score 600 paper-based). Electronic applications accepted. *Faculty research:* Teacher education; curriculum theory and development; community based education models, educational leadership.

University of Houston–Clear Lake, School of Education, Program in Foundations and Professional Studies, Houston, TX 77058-1002. Offers counseling (MS); instructional technology (MS); multicultural studies (MS). *Program availability:* Part-time, evening/weekend. *Degree requirements:* For master's, thesis optional. *Entrance requirements:* For master's, GRE or minimum GPA of 3.0 in last 60 hours. Additional exam requirements/recommendations for international students: Required—TOEFL (minimum score 550 paper-based). Electronic applications accepted.

University of Maryland, Baltimore County, The Graduate School, College of Arts, Humanities and Social Sciences, Department of Modern Languages and Linguistics, Program in Intercultural Communication, Baltimore, MD 21250. Offers MA. *Program availability:* Part-time, evening/weekend. *Faculty:* 16 full-time (9 women). *Students:* 10 full-time (6 women), 2 part-time (1 woman); includes 2 minority (both Hispanic/Latino), 3 international. Average age 29. 10 applicants, 70% accepted, 4 enrolled. In 2017, 4 master's awarded. *Degree requirements:* For master's, one foreign language, comprehensive exam (for some programs), thesis (for some programs). *Entrance*

requirements: For master's, GRE General Test, minimum GPA of 3.0, 3 letters of recommendation, self-evaluation and statement of support, resume, writing sample in modern language. Additional exam requirements/recommendations for international students: Required—TOEFL (minimum score 550 paper-based, 80 iBT) or IELTS. *Application deadline:* For fall admission, 1/31 for domestic and international students. Application fee: $50. Electronic applications accepted. *Expenses:* Contact institution. *Financial support:* In 2017–18, 7 students received support, including 5 teaching assistantships with full tuition reimbursements available (averaging $12,874 per year); Federal Work-Study, scholarships/grants, health care benefits, and tuition waivers (full) also available. Financial award application deadline: 1/31; financial award applicants required to submit FAFSA. *Faculty research:* Comparative television research-cross-cultural; cultural studies; social developments in Latin America; intercultural communication; French civilization and cultural studies; language, gender and sexuality; sociolinguistics; African linguistics; immigrants in U.S. and Latin American societies. *Unit head:* Dr. Edward Larkey, Interim Director, 410-455-2104, Fax: 410-455-1025, E-mail: larkey@umbc.edu.
Website: http://www.umbc.edu/mll/incc/

University of Maryland, Baltimore County, The Graduate School, College of Arts, Humanities and Social Sciences, Program in Language, Literacy, and Culture, Baltimore, MD 21250. Offers PhD. *Program availability:* Part-time, evening/weekend. *Faculty:* 4 full-time (2 women), 1 (woman) part-time/adjunct. *Students:* 22 full-time (16 women), 38 part-time (26 women); includes 24 minority (20 Black or African American, non-Hispanic/Latino; 2 Asian, non-Hispanic/Latino; 1 Hispanic/Latino; 1 Two or more races, non-Hispanic/Latino), 6 international. Average age 40. 23 applicants, 52% accepted, 11 enrolled. In 2017, 1 doctorate awarded. *Degree requirements:* For doctorate, comprehensive exam, thesis/dissertation. *Entrance requirements:* For doctorate, research writing sample; resume or curriculum vitae; master's degree; 3 letters of recommendation. Additional exam requirements/recommendations for international students: Required—TOEFL (minimum score 80 iBT). *Application deadline:* For fall admission, 12/1 for domestic and international students. Application fee: $50. Electronic applications accepted. *Expenses: Required fees:* $132. *Financial support:* In 2017–18, 12 research assistantships with full and partial tuition reimbursements, 3 teaching assistantships with full and partial tuition reimbursements were awarded; scholarships/grants, health care benefits, tuition waivers (full and partial), and unspecified assistantships also available. Support available to part-time students. Financial award application deadline: 12/1. *Faculty research:* Educational equity, identity, intercultural communication, technology and communication, workplace diversity. *Unit head:* Dr. Cedric Herring, Director, 410-455-2313, Fax: 410-455-8947, E-mail: cherring@umbc.edu. *Application contact:* Liz Steenrod, Program Management Specialist, 410-455-2376, Fax: 410-455-8947, E-mail: llc@umbc.edu.
Website: http://llc.umbc.edu

University of Massachusetts Amherst, Graduate School, College of Education, Program in Education, Amherst, MA 01003. Offers bilingual, English as a second language, and multicultural education (M Ed, Ed S); child study and early education (M Ed); children, families and schools (Ed D, Ed S); early childhood and elementary teacher education (M Ed); educational leadership (M Ed); educational policy and leadership (Ed D); higher education (M Ed); international education (M Ed); language, literacy and culture (Ed D); learning, media and technology (M Ed, Ed S); mathematics, science, and learning technologies (Ed D); reading and writing (M Ed); research, educational measurement and psychometrics (Ed D); school counselor education (M Ed, Ed S); school psychology (Ed S); science education (Ed S); secondary teacher education (M Ed); social justice education (M Ed, Ed D, Ed S); special education (M Ed, Ed D, Ed S); teacher education and school improvement (Ed D, Ed S). *Accreditation:* NCATE. *Program availability:* Part-time, online learning. Terminal master's awarded for partial completion of doctoral program. *Degree requirements:* For doctorate, comprehensive exam, thesis/dissertation. *Entrance requirements:* Additional exam requirements/recommendations for international students: Required—TOEFL (minimum score 550 paper-based; 80 iBT), IELTS (minimum score 6.5). Electronic applications accepted.

University of Miami, Graduate School, School of Education and Human Development, Department of Teaching and Learning, Program in Teaching and Learning, Coral Gables, FL 33124. Offers language and literacy learning in multilingual settings (PhD); science, technology, engineering and mathematics (PhD); special education (PhD). *Degree requirements:* For doctorate, thesis/dissertation, qualifying exam, electronic portfolio. *Entrance requirements:* For doctorate, GRE General Test. Additional exam requirements/recommendations for international students: Required—TOEFL (minimum score 550 paper-based; 80 iBT); Recommended—IELTS (minimum score 6.5). Electronic applications accepted. *Faculty research:* Teacher education, multicultural education, special education, second language acquisition, math and science education.

University of Minnesota, Twin Cities Campus, Graduate School, College of Education and Human Development, Department of Curriculum and Instruction, Minneapolis, MN 55455-0213. Offers art education (M Ed, MA, PhD); curriculum and instruction (M Ed, MA, PhD); elementary education (MA, PhD); English education (PhD); language and immersion education (Certificate); learning technologies (MA, PhD); literacy education (MA, PhD); second language education (MA, PhD); social studies education (MA, PhD); STEM education (MA, PhD); teaching (M Ed), including mathematics, science, social studies, teaching; teaching English to speakers of other languages (MA); technology enhanced learning (Certificate). *Faculty:* 37 full-time (21 women). *Students:* 401 full-time (282 women), 303 part-time (212 women); includes 139 minority (26 Black or African American, non-Hispanic/Latino; 4 American Indian or Alaska Native, non-Hispanic/Latino; 34 Asian, non-Hispanic/Latino; 45 Hispanic/Latino; 1 Native Hawaiian or other Pacific Islander, non-Hispanic/Latino; 29 Two or more races, non-Hispanic/Latino), 43 international. Average age 32. 596 applicants, 61% accepted, 330 enrolled. In 2017, 316 master's, 30 doctorates, 19 other advanced degrees awarded. Application fee: $75 ($95 for international students). *Financial support:* In 2017–18, 3 fellowships, 56 research assistantships with full tuition reimbursements (averaging $11,118 per year), 67 teaching assistantships with full tuition reimbursements (averaging $11,975 per year) were awarded. *Faculty research:* Teaching and learning; influence of cultural, linguistic, social, political, and technological factors on teaching, learning and educational research; relationship between educational practice and a democratic and just society; urban education; immigrant education, racial justice and education. *Total annual research expenditures:* $2.2 million. *Unit head:* Dr. Cynthia Lewis, Chair, 612-625-6313, E-mail: lewis@umn.edu. *Application contact:* Dr. Gillian Roehrig, Director of Graduate Studies, 612-625-0561, E-mail: roehr013@umn.edu.
Website: http://www.cehd.umn.edu/ci

University of New Mexico, Graduate Studies, College of Education, Program in Language, Literacy and Sociocultural Studies, Albuquerque, NM 87131. Offers American Indian education (MA); bilingual education (MA, PhD); educational linguistics (PhD); educational thought and sociocultural studies (MA, PhD); literacy/language arts (MA, PhD); social studies (MA); TESOL (MA, PhD). *Faculty:* 16 full-time (10 women), 4 part-time/adjunct (all women). *Students:* 56 full-time (34 women), 129 part-time (97 women); includes 93 minority (7 Black or African American, non-Hispanic/Latino; 15

American Indian or Alaska Native, non-Hispanic/Latino; 9 Asian, non-Hispanic/Latino; 56 Hispanic/Latino; 6 Two or more races, non-Hispanic/Latino), 44 international. Average age 40. 61 applicants, 38% accepted, 23 enrolled. In 2017, 36 master's, 4 doctorates awarded. *Degree requirements:* For master's, comprehensive exam, thesis optional; for doctorate, comprehensive exam, thesis/dissertation, research skills. *Entrance requirements:* For master's, letter of intent, 3 letters of recommendation, resume, BA/BS, department demographic form, transcripts; for doctorate, writing sample, letter of intent, 3 letters of recommendation, resume, BA/BS, MA, department demographic form, transcripts. Additional exam requirements/recommendations for international students: Required—TOEFL. *Application deadline:* For fall admission, 12/1 for domestic and international students; for spring admission, 9/15 for domestic and international students. Application fee: $50. Electronic applications accepted. *Financial support:* Fellowships, research assistantships, teaching assistantships, career-related internships or fieldwork, institutionally sponsored loans, scholarships/grants, and unspecified assistantships available. Support available to part-time students. Financial award application deadline: 3/1; financial award applicants required to submit FAFSA. *Faculty research:* School reform, professional development, history of education, Native American education, politics of education, feminism and issues of sexual identity, critical race theory, bilingualism, literacy reading, adolescent literature, second language acquisition, critical theory and schooling, indigenous languages. *Unit head:* Dr. Lois M. Meyer, Chair, 505-277-7244, Fax: 505-277-8362, E-mail: lsmeyer@unm.edu. *Application contact:* Debra Schaffer, Administrative Assistant, 505-277-0437, Fax: 505-277-8362, E-mail: schaffer@unm.edu.
Website: http://coe.unm.edu/departments-programs/llss/index.html

University of New Mexico, Graduate Studies, College of Education, Program in Multicultural Teacher and Childhood Education, Albuquerque, NM 87131-2039. Offers Ed D, PhD. *Accreditation:* NCATE. *Program availability:* Part-time. *Faculty:* 1 part-time/adjunct (0 women). *Students:* 2 full-time (0 women), 10 part-time (7 women); includes 5 minority (4 Hispanic/Latino; 1 Two or more races, non-Hispanic/Latino). Average age 47. 5 applicants, 20% accepted. In 2017, 1 doctorate awarded. *Degree requirements:* For doctorate, comprehensive exam, thesis/dissertation. *Entrance requirements:* For doctorate, GRE, master's degree, minimum GPA of 3.0, 3 years of teaching experience, 3-5 letters of reference, letter of intent, professional writing sample. Additional exam requirements/recommendations for international students: Required—TOEFL (minimum score 550 paper-based). *Application deadline:* For fall admission, 1/15 priority date for domestic students, 1/15 for international students; for spring admission, 10/30 for domestic and international students. Application fee: $50. Electronic applications accepted. *Financial support:* Fellowships, research assistantships, teaching assistantships with partial tuition reimbursements, scholarships/grants, and unspecified assistantships available. Financial award application deadline: 3/1; financial award applicants required to submit FAFSA. *Faculty research:* Teacher education, clinical preparation, reflective practice, science education, mathematics education, social justice, technology education, media literacy. *Unit head:* Dr. Cheryl Torrez, Department Chair, 505-277-9611, Fax: 505-277-0455, E-mail: ted@unm.edu. *Application contact:* Robert Romero, Program Coordinator, 505-277-0513, Fax: 505-277-0455, E-mail: ted@unm.edu.
Website: https://coe.unm.edu/departments-programs/ifce/ecme/

The University of North Carolina at Greensboro, Graduate School, School of Education, Department of Educational Leadership and Cultural Foundations, Greensboro, NC 27412-5001. Offers curriculum and teaching (PhD), including cultural studies; educational leadership (Ed D, Ed S); school administration (MSA). *Accreditation:* NCATE. *Degree requirements:* For doctorate, thesis/dissertation. *Entrance requirements:* For master's, doctorate, and Ed S, GRE General Test. Additional exam requirements/recommendations for international students: Required—TOEFL. Electronic applications accepted.

University of Northern Colorado, Graduate School, College of Education and Behavioral Sciences, School of Teacher Education, Greeley, CO 80639. Offers curriculum studies (MAT); educational studies (Ed D); elementary education (MAT); English education (MAT); literacy (MA); multilingual education (MA), including TESOL, world languages; teaching diverse learners (MA). *Accreditation:* NCATE. *Program availability:* Part-time, evening/weekend. *Degree requirements:* For master's, comprehensive exam, thesis or alternative; for doctorate, comprehensive exam, thesis/dissertation. *Entrance requirements:* For master's and doctorate, GRE General Test, 3 letters of recommendation. Electronic applications accepted.

University of Pennsylvania, Graduate School of Education, Division of Educational Linguistics, Program in Intercultural Communication, Philadelphia, PA 19104. Offers MS Ed. *Program availability:* Part-time. *Students:* Average age 25. 110 applicants, 46% accepted, 20 enrolled. In 2017, 22 master's awarded.

University of St. Thomas, School of Education and Human Services, Houston, TX 77006-4696. Offers all level education (M Ed); bilingual/dual language (M Ed); Catholic school teaching (M Ed); Catholic/private school leadership (M Ed); counselor education (M Ed); curriculum and instruction (M Ed); education (Ed D); educational leadership (M Ed); elementary teaching (M Ed); English as a second language (M Ed); exceptionality/educational diagnostician (M Ed); exceptionality/special education (M Ed); generalist (M Ed); reading (M Ed); secondary teaching (M Ed); teaching (MAT). *Accreditation:* TEAC. *Program availability:* Part-time, evening/weekend, online learning. *Faculty:* 33 full-time (22 women), 43 part-time/adjunct (26 women). *Students:* 119 full-time (97 women), 597 part-time (529 women); includes 478 minority (166 Black or African American, non-Hispanic/Latino; 29 Asian, non-Hispanic/Latino; 277 Hispanic/Latino; 2 Native Hawaiian or other Pacific Islander, non-Hispanic/Latino; 4 Two or more races, non-Hispanic/Latino), 19 international. Average age 36. 306 applicants, 91% accepted, 181 enrolled. In 2017, 328 master's awarded. *Degree requirements:* For master's, thesis, field experience. *Entrance requirements:* For master's, GRE or MAT if GPA is below 3.0, bachelor's degree; minimum GPA of 2.75 in bachelor's degree or last 60 credit hours; official transcripts from all institutions; goal statement of 250-300 words; 1 reference. Additional exam requirements/recommendations for international students: Required—TOEFL (minimum score 94 iBT), IELTS (minimum score 7), PTE (minimum score 53). *Application deadline:* Applications are processed on a rolling basis. Application fee: $35. Electronic applications accepted. *Expenses:* Contact institution. *Financial support:* In 2017–18, 27 students received support. Federal Work-Study, scholarships/grants, and state work-study, institutional employment available. Support available to part-time students. Financial award application deadline: 4/15; financial award applicants required to submit FAFSA. *Faculty research:* Leadership, diversity, personality traits, second language acquisition. *Unit head:* Dr. Paul C. Paese, Dean, 713-942-5999, Fax: 713-525-3871, E-mail: paesep@stthom.edu. *Application contact:* 713-525-3540, E-mail: education@stthom.edu.
Website: http://www.stthom.edu/Academics/School_of_Education_and_Human_Services/Index.aqf

University of San Francisco, School of Education, Department of International and Multicultural Education, San Francisco, CA 94117-1080. Offers MA, Ed D. *Program availability:* Part-time, evening/weekend. *Degree requirements:* For doctorate, thesis/dissertation. *Entrance requirements:* Additional exam requirements/recommendations for international students: Required—TOEFL, IELTS, PTE. Electronic applications accepted.

Multilingual and Multicultural Education

University of Southern California, Graduate School, Rossier School of Education, Doctor of Education Programs, Los Angeles, CA 90089. Offers educational psychology (Ed D); higher education administration (Ed D); K-12 leadership in urban school settings (Ed D); teacher education in multicultural societies (Ed D). *Program availability:* Part-time, evening/weekend. *Degree requirements:* For doctorate, thesis/dissertation. *Entrance requirements:* For doctorate, GRE. Additional exam requirements/recommendations for international students: Required—TOEFL (minimum score 100 iBT). Electronic applications accepted. *Faculty research:* Data-driven decision-making in K-12 schools and districts; examination of college and university leadership and management in U. S. and Asia; studies in facilitating student learning; organizational change and the role of leaders; leadership, diversity, learning and accountability.

The University of Tennessee, Graduate School, College of Education, Health and Human Sciences, Program in Education, Knoxville, TN 37996. Offers art education (MS); counseling education (PhD); cultural studies in education (PhD); curriculum (MS, Ed S); curriculum, educational research and evaluation (Ed D, PhD); early childhood education (PhD); early childhood special education (MS); education of deaf and hard of hearing (MS); educational administration and policy studies (Ed D, PhD); educational administration and supervision (Ed S); educational psychology (Ed D, PhD); elementary education (MS, Ed S); elementary teaching (MS); English education (MS, Ed S); exercise science (PhD); foreign language/ESL education (MS, Ed S); instructional technology (MS, Ed D, PhD, Ed S); literacy, language and ESL education (PhD); literacy, language education, and ESL education (Ed D); mathematics education (MS, Ed S); modified and comprehensive special education (MS); reading education (MS, Ed S); school counseling (Ed S); school psychology (PhD, Ed S); science education (MS, Ed S); secondary teaching (MS); social foundations (MS); social science education (MS, Ed S); socio-cultural foundations of sports and education (PhD); special education (Ed S); teacher education (Ed D, PhD). *Accreditation:* NCATE. *Program availability:* Part-time, evening/weekend. *Degree requirements:* For master's and Ed S, thesis optional; for doctorate, variable foreign language requirement, thesis/dissertation. *Entrance requirements:* For master's, minimum GPA of 2.7; for doctorate and Ed S, GRE General Test, minimum GPA of 2.7. Additional exam requirements/recommendations for international students: Required—TOEFL. Electronic applications accepted.

The University of Texas at Austin, Graduate School, College of Education, Department of Curriculum and Instruction, Austin, TX 78712-1111. Offers bilingual/bicultural education (M Ed, MA, PhD); cultural studies in education (M Ed, MA, PhD); early childhood education (M Ed, MA, PhD); language and literacy studies (M Ed, PhD); learning technologies (M Ed, MA, PhD); physical education (M Ed, MA, PhD). Terminal master's awarded for partial completion of doctoral program. *Degree requirements:* For doctorate, thesis/dissertation. *Entrance requirements:* For master's and doctorate, GRE General Test. Electronic applications accepted.

The University of Texas at Austin, Graduate School, College of Education, Department of Special Education, Austin, TX 78712-1111. Offers autism and developmental disabilities (Ed D, PhD); autism and developmental disability (M Ed, MA); early childhood special education (M Ed, MA, Ed D, PhD); learning disabilities (Ed D, PhD); learning disabilities/behavior disorders (M Ed, MA); multicultural special education (M Ed, MA, Ed D, PhD); rehabilitation counselor (M Ed); rehabilitation counselor education (Ed D, PhD); special education administration (Ed D, PhD). *Accreditation:* CORE. *Program availability:* Part-time, evening/weekend, online learning. *Degree requirements:* For master's, thesis or alternative; for doctorate, thesis/dissertation. *Entrance requirements:* For master's and doctorate, GRE General Test. *Faculty research:* Anchored instruction, reading disabilities, multicultural/bilingual.

The University of Texas at El Paso, Graduate School, College of Liberal Arts, Department of English, El Paso, TX 79968-0001. Offers bilingual professional writing (Certificate); English and American literature (MA); rhetoric and composition (PhD); rhetoric and writing studies (MA); teaching English (MAT). *Program availability:* Part-time, evening/weekend. *Degree requirements:* For master's, thesis optional. *Entrance requirements:* For master's, GRE General Test, minimum GPA of 3.0. Additional exam requirements/recommendations for international students: Required—TOEFL. Electronic applications accepted. *Faculty research:* Literature, creative writing, literary theory.

The University of Texas at San Antonio, College of Education and Human Development, Department of Bicultural and Bilingual Studies, San Antonio, TX 78249-0617. Offers bicultural and bilingual studies (MA), including bicultural and bilingual education, bicultural studies; culture, literacy, and language (PhD); teaching English as a second language (MA). *Program availability:* Part-time, evening/weekend. *Faculty:* 18 full-time (16 women). *Students:* 40 full-time (29 women), 82 part-time (68 women); includes 77 minority (2 Black or African American, non-Hispanic/Latino; 2 Asian, non-Hispanic/Latino; 72 Hispanic/Latino; 1 Two or more races, non-Hispanic/Latino), 3 international. Average age 35. 64 applicants, 80% accepted, 28 enrolled. In 2017, 34 master's, 13 doctorates awarded. *Degree requirements:* For master's, one foreign language, comprehensive exam, thesis optional; for doctorate, one foreign language, comprehensive exam, thesis/dissertation. *Entrance requirements:* For master's, bachelor's degree with 18 credit hours in field of study or in another appropriate field of study; for doctorate, GRE General Test, resume or curriculum vitae, 3 letters of recommendation, statement of purpose, master's degree. Additional exam requirements/recommendations for international students: Required—TOEFL (minimum score 550 paper-based; 79 iBT), IELTS (minimum score 6.5). *Application deadline:* For fall admission, 6/15 for domestic students, 3/15 for international students; for spring admission, 10/15 for domestic students, 9/15 for international students. Applications are processed on a rolling basis. Application fee: $50 ($90 for international students). Electronic applications accepted. *Expenses:* Contact institution. *Financial support:* Fellowships, research assistantships, teaching assistantships, scholarships/grants, and unspecified assistantships available. Financial award application deadline: 4/15. *Faculty research:* Bilingual and ESL teacher preparation; transnational communities; applied linguistics; cultural studies; bilingualism, biliteracy and second language acquisition. Total annual research expenditures: $2,246. *Unit head:* Dr. Patricia Sanchez, Chair, 210-458-4426, Fax: 210-458-5962, E-mail: patricia.sanchez@utsa.edu. *Application contact:* Rahnuma Islam, Student Development Specialist, 210-458-6619, Fax: 210-458-5576, E-mail: rahnuma.islam@utsa.edu.
Website: http://education.utsa.edu/bicultural-bilingual_studies

The University of Texas Rio Grande Valley, College of Education and P-16 Integration, Department of Bilingual and Literacy Studies, Edinburg, TX 78539. Offers bilingual education (M Ed), including dual language, ESL; reading and literacy (M Ed), including adolescent literacy, biliteracy, digital literacy, reading specialist. *Program availability:* Part-time, evening/weekend. *Faculty:* 17 full-time (13 women). *Students:* 29. In 2017, 11 master's awarded. *Degree requirements:* For master's, comprehensive exam (for some programs), thesis optional. *Entrance requirements:* For master's, minimum GPA of 3.0 in undergraduate coursework. Additional exam requirements/recommendations for international students: Required—TOEFL (minimum score 550 paper-based; 79 iBT), IELTS (minimum score 6.5). *Application deadline:* For fall admission, 4/15 for domestic students; for spring admission, 11/1 for domestic students; for summer admission, 3/1 for domestic students. Application fee: $50 ($75 for

international students). Electronic applications accepted. *Expenses:* Tuition, state resident: full-time $5550; part-time $417 per credit hour. Tuition, nonresident: full-time $13,020; part-time $832 per credit hour. *Required fees:* $1169. *Financial support:* Research assistantships, institutionally sponsored loans, scholarships/grants, and unspecified assistantships available. Financial award application deadline: 4/15; financial award applicants required to submit FAFSA. *Faculty research:* Bilingual education, reading instruction, multicultural education, English as a second language. *Unit head:* Dr. Janine M. Schall, Chair, 956-665-5106, E-mail: janine.schall@utrgv.edu. *Application contact:* Stephanie Ozuna, Graduate Student Recruiter, 956-665-3558, E-mail: stephanie.ozuna@utrgv.edu.

University of the Southwest, Graduate Programs, Hobbs, NM 88240-9129. Offers business administration (MBA); curriculum and instruction (MSE); curriculum and instruction: bilingual (MSE); curriculum and instruction: TESOL (MSE); early childhood education (MSE); educational administration (MSE); mental health counseling (MSE); school counseling (MSE); special education (MSE); sports management (MBA). *Program availability:* Part-time, evening/weekend, online learning. *Degree requirements:* For master's, comprehensive exam, thesis (for some programs). *Entrance requirements:* Additional exam requirements/recommendations for international students: Recommended—TOEFL. Electronic applications accepted.

University of Washington, Graduate School, College of Education, Seattle, WA 98195. Offers curriculum and instruction (M Ed, Ed D, PhD), including educational technology, general curriculum (Ed D, PhD), language, literacy, and culture, mathematics education, multicultural education, reading and language arts education (Ed D), science education, social studies education, teaching and curriculum (M Ed); educational leadership and policy studies (M Ed, Ed D, PhD), including administration (Ed D), educational policy, organization, and leadership (M Ed, PhD), higher education, leadership for learning (Ed D), social and cultural foundations of education (M Ed, PhD); educational psychology (M Ed, PhD), including educational psychology (PhD), human development and cognition (M Ed), learning sciences, measurement, statistics and research design (M Ed), school psychology (M Ed); instructional leadership (M Ed); intercollegiate athletic leadership (M Ed); special education (M Ed, Ed D, PhD), including early childhood special education (M Ed), emotional and behavioral disabilities (M Ed), learning disabilities (M Ed), low-incidence disabilities (M Ed), severe disabilities (M Ed), special education (Ed D, PhD); teacher education (MIT). *Accreditation:* APA. *Program availability:* Part-time, evening/weekend. *Degree requirements:* For master's, thesis optional; for doctorate, thesis/dissertation. *Entrance requirements:* For master's and doctorate, GRE General Test, minimum GPA of 3.0. Additional exam requirements/recommendations for international students: Required—TOEFL. Electronic applications accepted. *Faculty research:* School restructuring/effective schools, special education interventions, literacy and writing, technology, school partnerships, teacher preparation.

University of Wisconsin–Milwaukee, Graduate School, School of Education, Department of Exceptional Education, Milwaukee, WI 53201-0413. Offers autism spectrum disorders (Graduate Certificate); exceptional education (MS); transition for students with disabilities (Graduate Certificate); urban education (PhD), including adult, continuing and higher education leadership, art education, curriculum and instruction, exceptional education, mathematics education, multicultural studies, social foundations of education. *Program availability:* Part-time. *Students:* 45 full-time (34 women), 68 part-time (54 women); includes 46 minority (27 Black or African American, non-Hispanic/Latino; 7 Asian, non-Hispanic/Latino; 1 Hispanic/Latino; 11 Two or more races, non-Hispanic/Latino), 4 international. Average age 39. 43 applicants, 53% accepted, 19 enrolled. In 2017, 12 master's, 13 doctorates, 8 other advanced degrees awarded. *Entrance requirements:* Additional exam requirements/recommendations for international students: Required—TOEFL (minimum score 550 paper-based; 79 iBT), IELTS (minimum score 6.5). *Application deadline:* For fall admission, 1/1 priority date for domestic students; for spring admission, 9/1 for domestic students. Application fee: $56 ($96 for international students). Electronic applications accepted. *Financial support:* Fellowships, research assistantships, teaching assistantships, career-related internships or fieldwork, health care benefits, and unspecified assistantships available. Support available to part-time students. Financial award application deadline: 4/15; financial award applicants required to submit FAFSA. *Faculty research:* Emotional disturbance, hearing impairment, learning disabilities, mental retardation. *Application contact:* General Information Contact, 414-229-4721, E-mail: soeinfo@uwm.edu. Website: http://uwm.edu/education/academics/exceptional-edu-department/

Utah State University, School of Graduate Studies, College of Humanities and Social Sciences, Department of Languages, Philosophy, and Communication Studies, Logan, UT 84322. Offers second language teaching (MSLT). *Entrance requirements:* For master's, GRE General Test or MAT, minimum GPA of 3.0. Additional exam requirements/recommendations for international students: Required—TOEFL.

Vanderbilt University, Peabody College, Department of Teaching and Learning, Nashville, TN 37240-1001. Offers elementary education (M Ed); English language learners (M Ed); learning and design (M Ed); learning, diversity, and urban studies (M Ed); reading education (M Ed); secondary education (M Ed). *Accreditation:* NCATE. *Program availability:* Part-time. *Faculty:* 43 full-time (32 women), 28 part-time/adjunct (25 women). *Students:* 139 full-time (110 women), 35 part-time (23 women); includes 31 minority (18 Black or African American, non-Hispanic/Latino; 1 American Indian or Alaska Native, non-Hispanic/Latino; 6 Asian, non-Hispanic/Latino; 4 Hispanic/Latino; 2 Two or more races, non-Hispanic/Latino), 44 international. Average age 26. 510 applicants, 69% accepted, 113 enrolled. In 2017, 87 master's awarded. *Degree requirements:* For master's, comprehensive exam, thesis optional. *Entrance requirements:* For master's, GRE General Test, MAT. Additional exam requirements/recommendations for international students: Required—TOEFL (minimum score 550 paper-based; 80 iBT). *Application deadline:* For fall admission, 12/31 priority date for domestic and international students; for spring admission, 11/1 priority date for domestic and international students. Applications are processed on a rolling basis. Application fee: $0. Electronic applications accepted. *Financial support:* Fellowships with partial tuition reimbursements, research assistantships with partial tuition reimbursements, teaching assistantships with partial tuition reimbursements, Federal Work-Study, institutionally sponsored loans, scholarships/grants, tuition waivers (partial), and unspecified assistantships available. Support available to part-time students. Financial award application deadline: 1/15; financial award applicants required to submit FAFSA. *Faculty research:* Children's learning and development in core conceptual domains (STEM, English language arts, social studies); classroom discourse structures that teachers can learn and use to support students' learning and development K-6; intervention and design-based research on educational improvement at classroom, school, and district levels; design-based and learning sciences research on relations between learning in schools and other settings. *Unit head:* Dr. Deborah Rowe, Chair, 615-322-8100, Fax: 615-322-8999, E-mail: deborah.w.rowe@vanderbilt.edu. *Application contact:* Angela Saylor, Educational Coordinator, 615-322-8092, Fax: 615-322-8999, E-mail: angela.saylor@vanderbilt.edu.

Vanderbilt University, Program in Learning, Teaching and Diversity, Nashville, TN 37240-1001. Offers PhD. *Faculty:* 18 full-time (10 women), 1 (woman) part-time/adjunct. *Students:* 36 full-time (29 women); includes 11 minority (2 Black or African American, non-Hispanic/Latino; 5 Asian, non-Hispanic/Latino; 4 Two or more races, non-Hispanic/

Latino), 2 international. Average age 32. 126 applicants, 7% accepted, 7 enrolled. In 2017, 9 doctorates awarded. *Degree requirements:* For doctorate, comprehensive exam, thesis/dissertation, qualifying examinations. *Entrance requirements:* For doctorate, GRE General Test. Additional exam requirements/recommendations for international students: Required—TOEFL (minimum score 570 paper-based; 88 iBT). *Application deadline:* For fall admission, 12/1 for domestic and international students. Application fee: $0. Electronic applications accepted. *Expenses:* Contact institution. *Financial support:* Fellowships with partial tuition reimbursements, research assistantships with full tuition reimbursements, teaching assistantships with full tuition reimbursements, Federal Work-Study, institutionally sponsored loans, scholarships/grants, traineeships, and health care benefits available. Financial award application deadline: 1/15; financial award applicants required to submit CSS PROFILE or FAFSA. *Faculty research:* New pedagogies for math, science, and language; the support of English language learners; the uses of new technology and media in the classroom; middle school mathematics and the institutional setting of teaching. *Unit head:* Dr. Melissa Gresalfi, Director of Graduate Studies, 615-322-8227, Fax: 615-322-8014, E-mail: melissa.gresalfi@vanderbilt.edu. *Application contact:* Angela Saylor, Educational Coordinator, 615-322-8092, Fax: 615-322-8014, E-mail: angela.saylor@vanderbilt.edu.
Website: http://peabody.vanderbilt.edu/departments/tl/index.php

Walden University, Graduate Programs, Richard W. Riley College of Education and Leadership, Minneapolis, MN 55401. Offers adult education (Post-Master's Certificate); adult learning (Graduate Certificate); college teaching and learning (Graduate Certificate); community college leadership (Ed D); curriculum, instruction and assessment (Ed D, Ed S, Graduate Certificate); developmental education (Graduate Certificate); early childhood administration, management, and leadership (Graduate Certificate); early childhood education (Ed D, Ed S); early childhood public policy and advocacy (Graduate Certificate); early childhood studies (MS), including administration, management and leadership, early childhood public policy and advocacy, teaching adults in the early childhood field, teaching and diversity in early childhood education; education (MS, PhD), including adolescent literacy and learning (MS), curriculum, instruction, and assessment (grades K-12) (MS), curriculum, instruction, assessment, and evaluation (PhD), early childhood leadership and advocacy (PhD), early childhood special education (PhD), educational leadership (MS), educational leadership and administration (principal preparation) (MS), educational technology and design (PhD), elementary reading and literacy (PreK-6) (MS), elementary reading and mathematics (grades K-6) (MS), global and comparative education (PhD), higher education leadership management and policy (PhD), integrating technology in the classroom (grades K-12) (MS), learning, instruction and innovation (PhD), mathematics (grades 5-8) (MS), mathematics (grades K-6) (MS), mathematics and science (grades K-8) (MS), organizational research, assessment, and evaluation (PhD), reading and literacy with a reading K-12 endorsement (MS), reading literacy assessment and evaluation (PhD), science (grades K-8) (MS), special education (non-licensure) (grades K-12) (MS), teacher leadership (grades K-12) (MS), teaching English language learners (grades K-12) (MS); educational administration and leadership (Ed D); educational leadership and administration (principal preparation) (Ed S); educational technology (Ed D, Ed S, Post Master's Certificate); elementary reading and literacy (Graduate Certificate); engaging culturally diverse learners (Graduate Certificate); enrollment management and institutional marketing (Graduate Certificate); higher education (MS), including adult learning, college teaching and learning, enrollment management and institutional marketing, global higher education, leadership for student success, online and distance learning; higher education and adult learning (Ed D); higher education leadership and management (Ed D); higher education leadership for student success (Graduate Certificate); instructional design and technology (MS, Postbaccalaureate Certificate), including general program (MS), online learning (MS), training and performance improvement (MS); integrating technology in the classroom (Graduate Certificate); mathematics 5-8 (Graduate Certificate); mathematics K-6 (Graduate Certificate); online teaching for adult educators (Graduate Certificate); reading, literacy, and assessment (Ed D, Ed S); science K-8 (Graduate Certificate); special education (Ed D, Ed S, Graduate Certificate); special education (K-age 21) (MAT); teacher leadership (Graduate Certificate); teaching adults English as a second language (Graduate Certificate); teaching adults in the early childhood field (Graduate Certificate); teaching and diversity in early childhood education (Graduate Certificate); teaching English language learners (grades K-12) (Graduate Certificate); teaching K-12 students online (Graduate Certificate). *Accreditation:* NCATE. *Program availability:* Part-time, evening/weekend, online only, 100% online. *Degree requirements:* For doctorate, thesis/dissertation, residency; for other advanced degree, residency (for some programs). *Entrance requirements:* For master's, bachelor's degree or higher; minimum GPA of 2.5; official transcripts; goal statement (for some programs); access to computer and Internet; for doctorate, master's degree or higher; three years of related professional or academic experience (preferred); minimum GPA of 3.0; goal statement and current resume (for select programs); official transcripts; access to computer and Internet; for other advanced degree, relevant work experience; access to computer and Internet. Additional exam requirements/recommendations for international students: Required—TOEFL (minimum score 550 paper-based, 79 iBT), IELTS (minimum score 6.5), Michigan English Language Assessment Battery (minimum score 82), or PTE (minimum score 53). Electronic applications accepted.

Wayne State University, College of Education, Division of Teacher Education, Detroit, MI 48202. Offers art education (M Ed); bilingual/bicultural education (Certificate); curriculum and instruction (Ed D, PhD, Ed S), including English as a second language (MAT, Ed D, Ed S), K-12 curriculum (PhD); elementary education (MAT), including bilingual/bicultural education (M Ed, MAT), early childhood education (M Ed, MAT), English as a second language (MAT, Ed D, Ed S), foreign language education, science education (M Ed, MAT), special education (M Ed, MAT); elementary mathematics specialist (Certificate); English as a second language (Certificate); reading (M Ed, Ed S); reading, language and literature (Ed D); secondary education (MAT), including bilingual/bicultural education (M Ed, MAT), early childhood education (M Ed, MAT), English as a second language (MAT, Ed D, Ed S), English education, foreign language education, mathematics education (M Ed, MAT), science education (M Ed, MAT), social studies education (M Ed, MAT); special education (MAT), including career and technical education; teaching and learning (M Ed), including bilingual/bicultural education (M Ed, MAT), early childhood education (M Ed, MAT), elementary education, foreign language, mathematics education (M Ed, MAT), science education (M Ed, MAT), social studies education (M Ed, MAT), special education (M Ed, MAT). *Program availability:* Part-time, blended/hybrid learning. *Students:* 22. *Students:* 126 full-time (96 women), 317 part-time (258 women); includes 134 minority (95 Black or African American, non-Hispanic/Latino; 1 American Indian or Alaska Native, non-Hispanic/Latino; 8 Asian, non-Hispanic/Latino; 17 Hispanic/Latino; 1 Native Hawaiian or other Pacific Islander, non-Hispanic/Latino; 12 Two or more races, non-Hispanic/Latino), 13 international. Average age 37. 260 applicants, 33% accepted, 57 enrolled. In 2017, 111 master's, 13 doctorates, 7 other

advanced degrees awarded. *Degree requirements:* For master's, essay or project (for some M Ed programs), professional field experience (for MAT programs); for doctorate, thesis/dissertation. *Entrance requirements:* For master's, Michigan Test for Teacher Certification (for most programs), verification of participation in group work with children (for MAT programs), Michigan State Police criminal background check; for doctorate, minimum undergraduate GPA of 3.0, graduate 3.5; interview; curriculum vitae; references; master's degree (for most programs). Additional exam requirements/recommendations for international students: Required—TOEFL (minimum score 550 paper-based; 79 iBT), TWE (minimum score 5.5); Recommended—IELTS (minimum score 6.5). *Application deadline:* For fall admission, 6/1 priority date for domestic students, 5/1 priority date for international students; for winter admission, 10/1 priority date for domestic students, 9/1 priority date for international students; for spring admission, 2/1 priority date for domestic students, 1/1 priority date for international students. Applications are processed on a rolling basis. Application fee: $50. Electronic applications accepted. *Expenses:* Tuition, state resident: full-time $10,224; part-time $638.98 per credit hour. Tuition, nonresident: full-time $22,145; part-time $1384.04 per credit hour. Tuition and fees vary according to course load and program. *Financial support:* In 2017–18, 78 students received support, including 4 fellowships (averaging $13,500 per year), 1 research assistantship with tuition reimbursement available (averaging $16,000 per year); Federal Work-Study, scholarships/grants, and unspecified assistantships also available. Support available to part-time students. Financial award applicants required to submit FAFSA. *Faculty research:* Improving students' skill achievement in mathematics, improving elementary children's understanding of informational text, teachers' use of their pedagogical and mathematical knowledge in the interactive work of teaching, the intersection of identity construction in teaching and learning, identifying effective methods of literacy instruction and assessments for bilingual students in elementary language arts classrooms. *Unit head:* Dr. Thomas Edwards, Interim Associate Dean for Teacher Education, 313-577-3886, E-mail: t.g.edwards@wayne.edu. *Application contact:* E-mail: askcoe@wayne.edu.
Website: http://coe.wayne.edu/ted/index.php

Western New Mexico University, Graduate Division, School of Education, Silver City, NM 88062-0680. Offers bilingual education (MAT); educational leadership (MA); elementary education (MAT); reading (MAT); secondary education (MAT); special education (MAT); TESOL (teaching English to speakers of other languages) (MAT). *Accreditation:* NCATE. *Program availability:* Part-time, online learning. *Degree requirements:* For master's, comprehensive exam. *Entrance requirements:* For master's, minimum GPA of 3.0 in last 64 hours of undergraduate study. Additional exam requirements/recommendations for international students: Required—TOEFL (minimum score 550 paper-based; 79 iBT). Electronic applications accepted. *Faculty research:* International education, electronic reading assessment, developing STEM teachers.

Western Oregon University, Graduate Programs, College of Education, Division of Teacher Education, Program in Secondary Education, Monmouth, OR 97361. Offers bilingual education (MS Ed); health (MS Ed); humanities (MAT, MS Ed); initial licensure (MAT); mathematics (MAT, MS Ed); science (MAT, MS Ed); social science (MAT, MS Ed). *Accreditation:* NCATE. *Program availability:* Part-time, evening/weekend. *Degree requirements:* For master's, thesis optional, written exam. *Entrance requirements:* For master's, minimum GPA of 3.0, teaching license. Additional exam requirements/recommendations for international students: Required—TOEFL (minimum score 550 paper-based; 79 iBT), IELTS (minimum score 6.5). *Faculty research:* Literacy, science in primary grades, geography education, retention, teacher burnout.

William Paterson University of New Jersey, College of Humanities and Social Sciences, Wayne, NJ 07470-8420. Offers applied sociology (MA); assessment and evaluation research (Certificate); bilingual education (Certificate); clinical and counseling psychology (MA); clinical psychology (Psy D); creative and professional writing (MFA); English (MA); history (MA); public policy and international affairs (MA); teaching English as a second language (Certificate). *Program availability:* Part-time. *Faculty:* 36 full-time (21 women), 10 part-time/adjunct (5 women). *Students:* 62 full-time (44 women), 102 part-time (71 women); includes 76 minority (12 Black or African American, non-Hispanic/Latino; 8 Asian, non-Hispanic/Latino; 50 Hispanic/Latino; 6 Two or more races, non-Hispanic/Latino), 6 international. Average age 33. 156 applicants, 51% accepted, 52 enrolled. In 2017, 39 master's awarded. *Degree requirements:* For master's, thesis (for some programs), internship (for some programs). *Entrance requirements:* For master's, GRE/MAT, minimum GPA of 3.0; 2 letters of recommendation; writing sample/personal statement. Additional exam requirements/recommendations for international students: Required—TOEFL (minimum score 550 paper-based; 79 iBT), IELTS (minimum score 6). *Application deadline:* For fall admission, 6/1 for domestic students, 3/1 for international students; for spring admission, 11/1 for domestic students, 10/1 for international students. Applications are processed on a rolling basis. Application fee: $50. Electronic applications accepted. *Expenses:* Tuition, state resident: full-time $13,920; part-time $6264 per year. Tuition, nonresident: full-time $21,700; part-time $9765 per year. *Required fees:* $80; $36 per year. Tuition and fees vary according to course load, degree level and program. *Financial support:* In 2017–18, 3,480 students received support. Career-related internships or fieldwork, Federal Work-Study, scholarships/grants, and unspecified assistantships available. Support available to part-time students. Financial award application deadline: 3/15; financial award applicants required to submit FAFSA. *Faculty research:* Relationship violence, work-family balance, social development of Japan, theories justifying war, reactions to trauma. *Total annual research expenditures:* $32,300. *Unit head:* Dr. Kara Rabbitt, Dean, 973-720-2180, Fax: 973-720-2955, E-mail: rabbittk@wpunj.edu. *Application contact:* Tinu Adeniran, Associate Director, Graduate Admissions, 973-720-2764, Fax: 973-720-2035, E-mail: adenirant@wpunj.edu.
Website: http://www.wpunj.edu/cohss

Winona State University, College of Education, Department of Education Studies, Winona, MN 55987. Offers multicultural education (Certificate). *Accreditation:* NCATE. *Program availability:* Part-time, evening/weekend.

Xavier University, College of Social Sciences, Health and Education, School of Education, Department of Childhood Education and Literacy, Cincinnati, OH 45207. Offers children's multicultural literature (M Ed); elementary education (M Ed); Montessori education (M Ed); reading (M Ed). *Program availability:* Part-time. *Degree requirements:* For master's, comprehensive exam, thesis, 30 semester hours. *Entrance requirements:* For master's, GRE, MAT, official transcript; 3 letters of recommendation (for Montessori education); resume; statement of purpose. Additional exam requirements/recommendations for international students: Required—TOEFL (minimum score 550 paper-based; 79 iBT). Electronic applications accepted. Application fee is waived when completed online. *Expenses:* Contact institution. *Faculty research:* Multicultural literacy/fluency, early literacy development, writing/creative and across curriculum, assessment of reading abilities.

Special Education

Acacia University, American Graduate School of Education, Tempe, AZ 85284. Offers educational administration (M Ed); elementary education (MA); English as a second language (M Ed); secondary education (MA); special education (M Ed).

Acadia University, Faculty of Professional Studies, School of Education, Program in Inclusive Education, Wolfville, NS B4P 2R6, Canada. Offers M Ed. *Program availability:* Part-time. *Entrance requirements:* For master's, bachelor's degree in education, minimum B average in undergraduate course work, course work in special education. Additional exam requirements/recommendations for international students: Required—TOEFL (minimum score 580 paper-based; 93 iBT), IELTS (minimum score 6.5). *Application deadline:* For fall admission, 3/15 priority date for domestic and international students. Applications are processed on a rolling basis. Application fee: $50. *Financial support:* Application deadline: 3/15. *Faculty research:* Technology and human interaction, inclusive education and community, accommodating diversity, program evaluation. *Unit head:* Dr. Ann Vibert, Director, 902-585-1229, E-mail: ann.vibert@acadiau.ca. *Application contact:* Sheila Langille, Secretary, 902-585-1229, Fax: 902-585-1071, E-mail: sheila.langille@acadiau.ca.
Website: http://education.acadiau.ca/

Adelphi University, Ruth S. Ammon School of Education, Program in Special Education, Garden City, NY 11530-0701. Offers MS, Certificate. *Program availability:* Part-time, evening/weekend. *Students:* 37 full-time (31 women), 39 part-time (35 women); includes 20 minority (5 Black or African American, non-Hispanic/Latino; 3 Asian, non-Hispanic/Latino; 12 Hispanic/Latino), 2 international. Average age 28. 89 applicants, 54% accepted, 25 enrolled. In 2017, 22 master's, 36 other advanced degrees awarded. *Entrance requirements:* For master's, 2 letters of recommendation, resume detailing paid/volunteer experience and organizational membership. Additional exam requirements/recommendations for international students: Required—TOEFL (minimum score 550 paper-based; 80 iBT), IELTS (minimum score 6.5). *Application deadline:* For fall admission, 4/1 for international students; for spring admission, 11/1 for international students. Application fee: $50. Electronic applications accepted. *Expenses:* Contact institution. *Financial support:* Research assistantships with partial tuition reimbursements, teaching assistantships, career-related internships or fieldwork, institutionally sponsored loans, scholarships/grants, traineeships, and unspecified assistantships available. Support available to part-time students. Financial award application deadline: 2/15; financial award applicants required to submit FAFSA. *Unit head:* Dr. Anne Mungai, Director, 516-877-4096, E-mail: mungai@adelphi.edu. *Application contact:* E-mail: graduateadmissions@adelphi.edu.

Alabama Agricultural and Mechanical University, School of Graduate Studies, College of Education, Humanities, and Behavioral Sciences, Department of Reading, Elementary, Early Childhood and Special Education, Huntsville, AL 35811. Offers early childhood education (MS Ed, Ed S); elementary education (MS Ed, Ed S); reading/literacy (PhD); special education collaborative teacher training (MS Ed, Ed S). *Accreditation:* NCATE. *Program availability:* Evening/weekend. *Degree requirements:* For master's, comprehensive exam; for Ed S, thesis. *Entrance requirements:* For master's, GRE General Test. Additional exam requirements/recommendations for international students: Required—TOEFL (minimum score 500 paper-based; 61 iBT). Electronic applications accepted. *Faculty research:* Multicultural education, learning styles, diagnostic-prescriptive instruction.

Alabama State University, College of Education, Department of Curriculum and Instruction, Montgomery, AL 36101-0271. Offers early childhood education (M Ed, Ed S); elementary education (M Ed, Ed S); secondary education (M Ed, Ed S), including biology education, English language arts education (M Ed), history education, math education, music education (M Ed), reading education (M Ed), social science education; special education (M Ed). *Program availability:* Part-time. *Faculty:* 7 full-time (4 women), 7 part-time/adjunct (4 women). *Students:* 43 full-time (35 women), 71 part-time (62 women); includes 112 minority (111 Black or African American, non-Hispanic/Latino; 1 Two or more races, non-Hispanic/Latino). Average age 22. 47 applicants, 66% accepted, 19 enrolled. In 2017, 21 master's, 13 Ed Ss awarded. *Degree requirements:* For master's, comprehensive exam, thesis optional; for Ed S, comprehensive exam, thesis. *Entrance requirements:* For master's, GRE General Test, MAT, writing competency test; for Ed S, writing competency test, GRE, MAT. Additional exam requirements/recommendations for international students: Required—TOEFL (minimum score 500 paper-based). *Application deadline:* For fall admission, 4/15 for domestic and international students; for spring admission, 11/15 for domestic and international students; for summer admission, 3/15 for domestic and international students. Applications are processed on a rolling basis. Application fee: $25. *Expenses:* Tuition, state resident: part-time $412 per credit hour. Tuition, nonresident: part-time $824 per credit hour. *Required fees:* $685 per semester. *Financial support:* Research assistantships available. Financial award application deadline: 6/30; financial award applicants required to submit FAFSA. *Unit head:* Dr. Joyce Johnson, Acting Chairperson, 334-229-4485, Fax: 334-229-5603, E-mail: jjohnson@alasu.edu. *Application contact:* Dr. William Person, Dean of Graduate Studies, 334-229-4274, Fax: 334-229-4928, E-mail: wperson@alasu.edu.
Website: http://www.alasu.edu/academics/colleges—departments/college-of-education/curriculum—instruction/index.aspx

Albany State University, College of Education, Albany, GA 31705-2717. Offers early childhood education (M Ed); educational leadership (Ed S); health and physical education (M Ed); middle grades education (M Ed); school counseling (M Ed); special education (M Ed). *Accreditation:* NCATE. *Program availability:* Part-time, evening/weekend, online learning. *Degree requirements:* For master's, comprehensive exam, internship, GACE Content Exam. *Entrance requirements:* For master's, GRE or MAT. Electronic applications accepted. *Faculty research:* GACE preparation, STEM (science, technology, engineering, and mathematics), technology education, special education, professional teacher development, health implications liberation philosophy, NET-Q, learning community, disabled or at-risk students.

Albright College, Graduate Division, Reading, PA 19612-5234. Offers early childhood education (MS); elementary education (MS); English as a second language (MA); general education (MA); special education (MS). *Program availability:* Part-time, evening/weekend. *Degree requirements:* For master's, thesis. *Entrance requirements:* For master's, GRE General Test or MAT, minimum undergraduate GPA of 3.0, 2 letters of recommendation, interview. Additional exam requirements/recommendations for international students: Recommended—TOEFL (minimum score 525 paper-based). Electronic applications accepted.

Alcorn State University, School of Graduate Studies, School of Psychology and Education, Lorman, MS 39096-7500. Offers agricultural education (MS Ed); elementary education (MS Ed, Ed S); guidance and counseling (MS Ed); industrial education (MS Ed); secondary education (MS Ed), including health and physical education; special education (MS Ed). *Accreditation:* NCATE. *Degree requirements:* For master's, thesis optional.

Alliant International University–San Francisco, Shirley M. Hufstedler School of Education, Teacher Education Programs, San Francisco, CA 94133. Offers auditory oral education (Certificate); CLAD (Certificate); education specialist: mild/moderate disabilities (Credential); preliminary multiple subject (Credential); preliminary single subject (Credential); professional clear multiple subject (Credential); professional clear single subject (Credential); special education (MA); teaching (MA); TESOL (Certificate). *Program availability:* Part-time, evening/weekend. *Degree requirements:* For master's, thesis. *Entrance requirements:* For degree, California Basic Educational Skills Test, minimum GPA of 2.5. Additional exam requirements/recommendations for international students: Required—TOEFL (minimum score 550 paper-based), TWE (minimum score 5). Electronic applications accepted. *Faculty research:* Curriculum development, first year teachers, cross-cultural issues in teaching, biliteracy.

Alverno College, School of Professional Studies - Education Division, Milwaukee, WI 53234-3922. Offers adaptive education (MA); administrative leadership (MA); adult education and organizational development (MA); adult educational and instructional design (MA); adult educational and instructional technology (MA); global connections in the humanities (MA); instructional leadership (MA); instructional technology for K-12 settings (MA); professional development (MA); reading education (MA); reading education with adaptive education (MA); science education (MA); special education (MA); teaching in alternative schools (MA). *Accreditation:* NCATE. *Program availability:* Part-time, evening/weekend. *Faculty:* 3 full-time (2 women), 23 part-time/adjunct (17 women). *Students:* 37 full-time (34 women), 68 part-time (65 women); includes 27 minority (16 Black or African American, non-Hispanic/Latino; 1 American Indian or Alaska Native, non-Hispanic/Latino; 1 Asian, non-Hispanic/Latino; 7 Hispanic/Latino; 2 Two or more races, non-Hispanic/Latino). Average age 35. 67 applicants, 100% accepted, 51 enrolled. In 2017, 68 master's awarded. *Degree requirements:* For master's, presentation/defense of proposal, conference presentation of inquiry projects. *Entrance requirements:* For master's, bachelor's degree in related field, communication samples from work setting, 3 letters of recommendation. Additional exam requirements/recommendations for international students: Required—TOEFL. *Application deadline:* For fall admission, 7/15 priority date for domestic and international students; for spring admission, 12/15 priority date for domestic and international students. Applications are processed on a rolling basis. Application fee: $0. Electronic applications accepted. *Expenses:* Contact institution. *Financial support:* Federal Work-Study and scholarships/grants available. Support available to part-time students. Financial award applicants required to submit FAFSA. *Faculty research:* Student self-assessment, self-reflection, integration of curriculum, identifying needs of students in strategic situations and designing appropriate classroom strategies. *Unit head:* Dr. Patricia Luebke, Dean, School of Professional Studies, 414-382-6368, Fax: 414-382-6354, E-mail: patricia.luebke@alverno.edu. *Application contact:* Katie Kipp, Graduate Admissions Counselor, 414-382-6045, Fax: 414-382-6354, E-mail: katie.kipp@alverno.edu.

American International College, School of Education, Springfield, MA 01109-3189. Offers early childhood education (M Ed, CAGS); education (MA, Ed D), including counseling psychology (MA), educational leadership and supervision (Ed D), professional counseling and supervision (Ed D), teaching and learning (Ed D); elementary education (M Ed, CAGS); middle education/secondary education (M Ed, CAGS); moderate disabilities (M Ed, CAGS); reading specialist (M Ed, CAGS); school adjustment counseling (MAEP, CAGS); school guidance counseling (MAEP, CAGS); school leadership (M Ed, CAGS). *Program availability:* Evening/weekend. *Faculty:* 1 (woman) full-time, 151 part-time/adjunct (95 women). *Students:* 1,082 full-time (910 women), 143 part-time (113 women); includes 109 minority (19 Black or African American, non-Hispanic/Latino; 2 American Indian or Alaska Native, non-Hispanic/Latino; 10 Asian, non-Hispanic/Latino; 58 Hispanic/Latino; 1 Native Hawaiian or other Pacific Islander, non-Hispanic/Latino; 19 Two or more races, non-Hispanic/Latino). Average age 34. 537 applicants, 77% accepted, 327 enrolled. In 2017, 486 master's, 112 other advanced degrees awarded. *Degree requirements:* For master's and CAGS, practicum/culminating experience. *Entrance requirements:* For master's, Communication and Literacy portion of the Massachusetts Tests for Education Licensure, graduate of accredited four-year college with minimum B- average in undergraduate course work; for CAGS, M Ed or master's degree in field related to licensure from accredited institution. *Application deadline:* Applications are processed on a rolling basis. Application fee: $50. Electronic applications accepted. *Expenses:* $439 per credit, $30 per term registration fee, $100 graduation fee, $110 technology fee. *Financial support:* Applicants required to submit FAFSA. *Unit head:* Sylvia Mason, Dean, 413-205-1743, Fax: 413-205-3943, E-mail: sylvia.mason@aic.edu. *Application contact:* Kerry Barnes, Dean of Graduate Admissions, 413-205-3703, Fax: 413-205-3051, E-mail: kerry.barnes@aic.edu.
Website: http://www.aic.edu/school-of-education/

American University of Puerto Rico, Program in Education, Bayamon, PR 00960-2037. Offers art education (M Ed); elementary education 4-6 (M Ed); elementary education K-3 (M Ed); general science education (M Ed); physical education (M Ed); special education (M Ed). *Program availability:* Part-time, evening/weekend. *Faculty:* 17 part-time/adjunct (7 women). *Students:* 22 full-time (18 women), 54 part-time (42 women); all minorities (all Hispanic/Latino). Average age 33. 22 applicants, 86% accepted, 19 enrolled. In 2017, 53 master's awarded. *Entrance requirements:* For master's, EXADEP, GRE, or MAT, 2 letters of recommendation, minimum GPA of 2.5. *Application deadline:* For fall admission, 8/1 for domestic students; for winter admission, 10/18 for domestic students; for spring admission, 3/15 for domestic students. Applications are processed on a rolling basis. Application fee: $25. Tuition and fees vary according to course load and degree level. *Financial support:* In 2017–18, 79 students received support, including 76 fellowships (averaging $400 per year), 55 teaching assistantships (averaging $1,741 per year). Financial award applicants required to submit FAFSA. *Unit head:* Prof. Bolivar Ramirez-Carlo, III, Dean of Faculty, 787-620-2040 Ext. 2010, Fax: 787-620-2958, E-mail: bramirez@aupr.edu. *Application contact:* Keren I. Llanos-Figueroa, Information Contact, 787-620-2040 Ext. 2021, Fax: 787-785-7377, E-mail: oficnaadmisiones@aupr.edu.

Andrews University, School of Graduate Studies, School of Education, Department of Graduate Psychology and Counseling, Program in Special Education, Berrien Springs, MI 49104. Offers MS. *Students:* 4 applicants, 25% accepted. In 2017, 1 master's awarded. *Entrance requirements:* Additional exam requirements/recommendations for international students: Required—TOEFL (minimum score 550 paper-based). Application fee: $40. *Unit head:* Dr. Nona Elmendorf-Steele, Dean, 269-471-6468. *Application contact:* Justina Clayburn, Supervisor of Graduate Admission, 800-253-2874, Fax: 269-471-6321, E-mail: graduate@andrews.edu.

Antioch University New England, Graduate School, Department of Applied Psychology, Program in Autism Spectrum Disorders, Keene, NH 03431-3552. Offers applied behavior analysis (Certificate); applied behavior analysis internship (Certificate); autism spectrum disorders (Certificate). *Entrance requirements:* Additional exam requirements/recommendations for international students: Required—TOEFL (minimum score 550 paper-based).

Antioch University New England, Graduate School, Department of Education, Experienced Educators Program, Keene, NH 03431-3552. Offers foundations of education (M Ed), including applied behavioral analysis, autism spectrum disorders, educating for sustainability, next-generation learning using technology, problem-based learning using critical skills, teacher leadership; principal certification (PMC). *Degree requirements:* For master's, thesis, practicum. *Entrance requirements:* For master's, previous course work and work experience in education. Additional exam requirements/recommendations for international students: Required—TOEFL (minimum score 550 paper-based). Electronic applications accepted. *Expenses:* Contact institution. *Faculty research:* Classroom action research, school restructuring, problem-based learning, brain-based learning.

Antioch University New England, Graduate School, Department of Education, Integrated Learning Program, Keene, NH 03431-3552. Offers early childhood education (M Ed); elementary education (M Ed), including arts and humanities, science and environmental education; special education (M Ed). *Degree requirements:* For master's, internship. *Entrance requirements:* For master's, previous course work or work experience in education. Additional exam requirements/recommendations for international students: Required—TOEFL (minimum score 550 paper-based). Electronic applications accepted. *Expenses:* Contact institution. *Faculty research:* Problem-based learning, place-based education, mathematics education, democratic classrooms, art education.

Appalachian State University, Cratis D. Williams Graduate School, Department of Reading Education and Special Education, Boone, NC 28608. Offers reading education (MA); special education (MA). *Accreditation:* ASHA. *Program availability:* Part-time, evening/weekend, online learning. *Degree requirements:* For master's, comprehensive exam, thesis optional. *Entrance requirements:* For master's, GRE General Test or MAT, 3 letters of recommendation. Additional exam requirements/recommendations for international students: Required—TOEFL (minimum score 570 paper-based; 79 iBT), IELTS (minimum score 6.5). Electronic applications accepted. *Faculty research:* Special education, language arts, reading.

Arcadia University, College of Arts and Sciences, Department of Psychology, Glenside, PA 19038-3295. Offers applied behavior analysis (MAC); autism (MAC); child/family therapy (MAC); community public health (MAC); counseling/international peace and conflict resolution dual degree (MAC); mental health counseling (MAC); trauma (MAC). *Program availability:* Part-time. *Degree requirements:* For master's, practicum. *Entrance requirements:* For master's, GRE General Test or MAT. *Expenses:* Contact institution.

Arcadia University, School of Education, Glenside, PA 19038-3295. Offers art education (M Ed); computer education (CAS); curriculum (CAS); curriculum studies (M Ed); early childhood education (M Ed), including individualized, master teacher, research in child development; educational leadership (M Ed, Ed D, CAS); elementary education (M Ed); English education (MA Ed); environmental education (MA Ed); instructional technology (M Ed); language arts (M Ed); library science (M Ed); mathematics education (M Ed, MA Ed); music education (MA Ed); psychology (MA Ed); reading (M Ed, CAS); science education (M Ed, CAS); secondary education (M Ed, CAS); special education (M Ed, Ed D, CAS); theater arts (MA Ed); written communication (MA Ed). *Accreditation:* NASAD. *Program availability:* Part-time, evening/weekend, online learning. Electronic applications accepted. *Expenses:* Contact institution.

Arizona State University at the Tempe campus, Mary Lou Fulton Teachers College, Program in Special Education, Phoenix, AZ 85069. Offers autism spectrum disorder (Graduate Certificate); special education (M Ed). *Program availability:* Online learning. *Degree requirements:* For master's, thesis or alternative, applied project, student teaching, interactive Program of Study (iPOS) submitted before completing 50 percent of required credit hours. *Entrance requirements:* For master's, Arizona Educator Proficiency Assessments (AEPA), minimum GPA of 3.0 or equivalent in last 2 years of work leading to bachelor's degree, 3 letters of recommendation, personal statement, resume, IVP fingerprint clearance card (for those seeking Arizona certification). Additional exam requirements/recommendations for international students: Required—TOEFL, IELTS, or PTE. Electronic applications accepted.

Arkansas State University, Graduate School, College of Education and Behavioral Science, Department of Psychology and Counseling, State University, AR 72467. Offers clinical mental health counseling (Graduate Certificate); college student personnel services (MS); dyslexia therapy (Graduate Certificate); psychological science (MS); psychology and counseling (Ed S); rehabilitation counseling (MRC); school counseling (MSE); student affairs (Graduate Certificate). *Accreditation:* ACA (one or more programs are accredited); CORE (one or more programs are accredited); NCATE. *Program availability:* Part-time. *Degree requirements:* For master's and other advanced degree, comprehensive exam, thesis or alternative. *Entrance requirements:* For master's, GRE General Test or MAT (for MSE), appropriate bachelor's degree, interview, letters of reference, official transcripts, immunization records, written statement, 2-3 page autobiography; for other advanced degree, GRE General Test, interview, master's degree, letters of reference, official transcript, personal statement, immunization records. Additional exam requirements/recommendations for international students: Required—TOEFL (minimum score 550 paper-based; 79 iBT), IELTS (minimum score 6), PTE (minimum score 56). Electronic applications accepted.

Arkansas State University, Graduate School, College of Education and Behavioral Science, School of Teacher Education and Leadership, State University, AR 72467. Offers community college administration (SCCT); curriculum and instruction (MSE); early childhood education (MSE); early childhood services (MS); educational leadership (MSE, Ed D, Ed S); educational theory and practice (MSE); middle level education (MAT, MSE); reading (MSE, Ed S); special education - gifted, talented, and creative (MSE); special education - instructional specialist grades 4-12 (MSE); special education - instructional specialist grades P-4 (MSE); special education, K-12 (MSE). *Accreditation:* NCATE. *Program availability:* Part-time, online learning. *Degree requirements:* For master's, comprehensive exam, thesis or alternative; for doctorate, comprehensive exam, thesis/dissertation; for other advanced degree, comprehensive exam. *Entrance requirements:* For master's, GRE General Test or MAT, appropriate bachelor's degree, official transcripts, immunization records, letters of reference, interview; for doctorate, GRE General Test or MAT, interview, master's degree, letters of reference, official transcript, personal statement, writing sample, immunization records; for other advanced degree, GRE General Test or MAT, interview, master's degree, official transcript, immunization records, letters of reference, 3 years of teaching experience, teaching license. Additional exam requirements/recommendations for international students: Required—TOEFL (minimum score 550 paper-based; 79 iBT), IELTS (minimum score 6), PTE (minimum score 56). Electronic applications accepted.

Arkansas State University, Graduate School, College of Nursing and Health Professions, Department of Communication Disorders, State University, AR 72467. Offers communication disorders (MCD); dyslexia therapy (Graduate Certificate). *Accreditation:* ASHA. *Program availability:* Part-time. *Degree requirements:* For master's, comprehensive exam, thesis or alternative. *Entrance requirements:* For master's, GRE General Test, appropriate bachelor's degree, letters of recommendation, official transcripts, immunization records. Additional exam requirements/recommendations for international students: Required—TOEFL (minimum score 550 paper-based; 79 iBT), IELTS (minimum score 6), PTE (minimum score 56). Electronic applications accepted. *Expenses:* Contact institution.

Arkansas Tech University, College of Education, Russellville, AR 72801. Offers college student personnel (MS); educational leadership (M Ed, Ed S); instructional technology (M Ed); school counseling and leadership (M Ed); school leadership (Ed D); special education K-12 (M Ed); strength and conditioning studies (MS); teaching (MAT); teaching, learning, and leadership (M Ed). *Accreditation:* NCATE. *Program availability:* Part-time, evening/weekend, 100% online, blended/hybrid learning. *Students:* 80 full-time (45 women), 433 part-time (328 women); includes 114 minority (81 Black or African American, non-Hispanic/Latino; 4 American Indian or Alaska Native, non-Hispanic/Latino; 1 Asian, non-Hispanic/Latino; 13 Hispanic/Latino; 15 Two or more races, non-Hispanic/Latino), 2 international. Average age 34. In 2017, 132 master's, 8 doctorates, 3 other advanced degrees awarded. *Degree requirements:* For master's, comprehensive exam, thesis optional, action research project; for doctorate, thesis/dissertation. *Entrance requirements:* Additional exam requirements/recommendations for international students: Required—TOEFL (minimum score 550 paper-based; 79 iBT), IELTS (minimum score 6.5), PTE (minimum score 58). *Application deadline:* For fall admission, 3/1 priority date for domestic students, 5/1 priority date for international students; for spring admission, 10/1 priority date for domestic and international students. Applications are processed on a rolling basis. Application fee: $40 ($90 for international students). Electronic applications accepted. *Expenses:* Tuition, state resident: full-time $6816; part-time $284 per credit hour. Tuition, nonresident: full-time $13,632; part-time $568 per credit hour. *Required fees:* $420 per semester. Tuition and fees vary according to course load. *Financial support:* In 2017–18, research assistantships with full and partial tuition reimbursements (averaging $4,800 per year), teaching assistantships with full and partial tuition reimbursements (averaging $4,800 per year) were awarded; career-related internships or fieldwork, Federal Work-Study, scholarships/grants, health care benefits, and unspecified assistantships also available. Support available to part-time students. Financial award application deadline: 4/15; financial award applicants required to submit FAFSA. *Unit head:* Dr. Mary Gunter, Dean, 479-964-3217, E-mail: mgunter@atu.edu.
Website: http://www.atu.edu/education/

Asbury University, School of Graduate and Professional Studies, Wilmore, KY 40390-1198. Offers biology: alternative certificate (MA Ed); chemistry: alternative certificate (MA Ed); English (MA Ed); English as a second language (MA Ed); ESL (MA Ed); French (MA Ed); Latin: alternative certificate (MA Ed); mathematics: alternative certificate (MA Ed); reading/writing endorsement (MA Ed); social studies (MA Ed); social work (MSW), including child and family services; Spanish (MA Ed); special education (MA Ed); special education: alternative certificate (MA Ed); teacher as leader endorsement (MA Ed). *Accreditation:* NCATE. *Program availability:* Part-time. *Degree requirements:* For master's, action research project, portfolio. *Entrance requirements:* For master's, PRAXIS/NTE, minimum GPA of 2.75, letters of recommendation. Additional exam requirements/recommendations for international students: Required—TOEFL (minimum score 550 paper-based). Electronic applications accepted.

Assumption College, Special Education Program, Worcester, MA 01609-1296. Offers positive behavior support (CAGS); special education (MA). *Program availability:* Part-time, evening/weekend. *Faculty:* 2 full-time (both women), 3 part-time/adjunct (all women). *Students:* 32 full-time (26 women), 45 part-time (39 women); includes 11 minority (4 Black or African American, non-Hispanic/Latino; 6 Hispanic/Latino; 1 Two or more races, non-Hispanic/Latino). Average age 28. 8 applicants, 88% accepted, 6 enrolled. In 2017, 9 master's, 12 other advanced degrees awarded. *Degree requirements:* For master's, comprehensive exam, internship, practicum. *Entrance requirements:* For master's, bachelor's degree with minimum GPA of 3.0, three letters of recommendation, official transcripts, personal statement, current resume, teacher certification documents (if certified or licensed); for CAGS, MA or M Ed, minimum one year of full-time employment in educational setting, three letters of recommendation, official transcripts, personal statement, current resume, interview. Additional exam requirements/recommendations for international students: Required—TOEFL (minimum score 540 paper-based; 76 iBT), IELTS (minimum score 6). *Application deadline:* Applications are processed on a rolling basis. Application fee: $30. Electronic applications accepted. *Expenses:* Full-time $11,952; part-time $664 per credit. *Required fees:* $70 per term. *Financial support:* In 2017–18, 4 students received support. Tuition waivers (full and partial), unspecified assistantships, and institutional discounts available. Financial award applicants required to submit FAFSA. *Unit head:* Dr. Nanho Vander Hart, Director, 508-767-7380, Fax: 508-767-7263, E-mail: nvanderh@assumption.edu. *Application contact:* Karen Stoyanoff, Director of Recruitment for Graduate Enrollment, 508-767-7442, Fax: 508-799-4915, E-mail: graduate@assumption.edu.
Website: http://graduate.assumption.edu/special-education/graduate-programs

Auburn University, Graduate School, College of Education, Department of Special Education, Rehabilitation, Counseling and School Psychology, Auburn University, AL 36849. Offers M Ed, MS, PhD. *Accreditation:* CORE; NCATE. *Program availability:* Part-time. *Faculty:* 19 full-time (15 women), 5 part-time/adjunct (4 women). *Students:* 162 full-time (137 women), 70 part-time (61 women); includes 62 minority (44 Black or African American, non-Hispanic/Latino; 1 Asian, non-Hispanic/Latino; 12 Hispanic/Latino; 1 Native Hawaiian or other Pacific Islander, non-Hispanic/Latino; 4 Two or more races, non-Hispanic/Latino), 4 international. Average age 29. 227 applicants, 48% accepted, 88 enrolled. In 2017, 61 master's, 16 doctorates awarded. *Degree requirements:* For master's, thesis (for some programs); for doctorate, thesis/dissertation. *Entrance requirements:* For master's, GRE General Test; for doctorate, GRE General Test, interview. *Application deadline:* Applications are processed on a rolling basis. Application fee: $50 ($60 for international students). Electronic applications accepted. *Expenses:* Tuition, state resident: full-time $10,974; part-time $519 per credit hour. Tuition, nonresident: full-time $29,658; part-time $1557 per credit hour. *Required fees:* $816 per semester. Tuition and fees vary according to degree level and program. *Financial support:* Research assistantships, teaching assistantships, and Federal Work-Study available. Support available to part-time students. Financial award application deadline: 3/15; financial award applicants required to submit FAFSA. *Faculty research:* Emotional conflict/behavior disorders, gifted and talented, learning disabilities, mental retardation, multi-handicapped. *Unit head:* Dr. Jamie Carney, Head, 334-844-2885. *Application contact:* Dr. George Flowers, Dean of the Graduate School, 334-844-2125.

Auburn University at Montgomery, College of Education, Department of Counselor, Leadership, and Special Education, Montgomery, AL 36124-4023. Offers counselor education (M Ed, Ed S), including clinical mental health counseling, school counseling; early childhood special education (M Ed); instructional leadership (M Ed, Ed S); special

Special Education

education/collaborative teacher (M Ed, Ed S). *Accreditation:* ACA; NCATE. *Program availability:* Part-time, evening/weekend. *Faculty:* 7 full-time (4 women), 2 part-time/adjunct (both women). *Students:* 27 full-time (23 women), 57 part-time (51 women); includes 40 minority (38 Black or African American, non-Hispanic/Latino; 2 Hispanic/Latino). Average age 34. 76 applicants, 72% accepted, 26 enrolled. In 2017, 37 master's awarded. *Degree requirements:* For master's and Ed S, comprehensive exam. *Entrance requirements:* For master's, GRE General Test or MAT, certification, BS in teaching; for Ed S, GRE General Test or MAT, certification. Additional exam requirements/recommendations for international students: Recommended—TOEFL (minimum score 500 paper-based; 61 iBT), IELTS (minimum score 5.5), TSE (minimum score 44). *Application deadline:* For fall admission, 7/15 for international students; for spring admission, 11/15 for international students; for summer admission, 4/15 for international students. Applications are processed on a rolling basis. Electronic applications accepted. *Expenses:* Tuition, state resident: full-time $6930; part-time $385 per credit hour. Tuition, nonresident: full-time $15,588; part-time $866 per credit hour. *Required fees:* $640. *Financial support:* Career-related internships or fieldwork and scholarships/grants available. Support available to part-time students. Financial award application deadline: 3/1; financial award applicants required to submit FAFSA. *Unit head:* Dr. Samuel Flynt, Head, 334-244-3835, Fax: 334-244-3101, E-mail: sflynt@aum.edu. *Application contact:* Dr. Rhonda Morton, Associate Dean/Graduate Coordinator, 334-244-3287, Fax: 334-244-3978, E-mail: rmorton@aum.edu.
Website: http://education.aum.edu/academic-departments/counselor-leadership-and-special-education

Augustana University, MA in Education Program, Sioux Falls, SD 57197. Offers instructional strategies (MA); reading (MA); special populations (MA); STEM (MA); technology (MA). *Accreditation:* NCATE. *Program availability:* Part-time-only, evening/weekend, online only, 100% online. *Faculty:* 7 full-time (5 women), 6 part-time/adjunct (5 women). *Students:* 288 part-time (250 women); includes 20 minority (2 Black or African American, non-Hispanic/Latino; 2 American Indian or Alaska Native, non-Hispanic/Latino; 1 Asian, non-Hispanic/Latino; 11 Hispanic/Latino; 1 Native Hawaiian or other Pacific Islander, non-Hispanic/Latino; 3 Two or more races, non-Hispanic/Latino), 3 international. Average age 32. 47 applicants, 77% accepted, 35 enrolled. In 2017, 84 master's awarded. *Degree requirements:* For master's, thesis. *Entrance requirements:* For master's, appropriate bachelor's degree, minimum GPA of 3.0, teaching certificate. Additional exam requirements/recommendations for international students: Required—TOEFL (minimum score 550 paper-based). *Application deadline:* For fall admission, 8/1 for domestic and international students; for spring admission, 11/1 for domestic and international students; for summer admission, 4/1 for domestic and international students. Applications are processed on a rolling basis. Application fee: $60. Electronic applications accepted. *Expenses:* Contact institution. *Financial support:* Multicultural education, education of students with autism, well-being in school settings, factors that predict academic hopefulness. *Unit head:* Dr. Laurie Daily, Chair, 605-274-5211, E-mail: laurie.daily@augie.edu. *Application contact:* Julia Paulich, Graduate Coordinator, 605-274-4043, Fax: 605-274-4450, E-mail: graduate@augie.edu.
Website: http://www.augie.edu/master-arts-education

Augusta University, College of Education, Program in Curriculum and Instruction, Augusta, GA 30912. Offers curriculum and instruction (Ed S); elementary education (MAT); foreign language education (MAT); instruction (M Ed); middle grades education (MAT); music education (MAT); secondary education (MAT); special education (MAT). *Degree requirements:* For master's, thesis, portfolio. *Entrance requirements:* For master's, GRE, MAT, minimum GPA of 2.5.

Aurora University, School of Education and Human Performance, Aurora, IL 60506-4892. Offers applied behavioral analysis (MS); bilingual-ESL education (MA); educational leadership with principal endorsement (MA); educational technology (MA); leadership in adult learning higher education (MA); leadership in curriculum and instruction (Ed D); leadership in educational administration (Ed D); reading instruction (MA); special education (MA). *Accreditation:* NCATE. *Program availability:* Part-time, evening/weekend. *Faculty:* 15 full-time (8 women), 39 part-time/adjunct (20 women). *Students:* 421 full-time (299 women), 142 part-time (89 women); includes 90 minority (25 Black or African American, non-Hispanic/Latino; 7 Asian, non-Hispanic/Latino; 50 Hispanic/Latino; 2 Native Hawaiian or other Pacific Islander, non-Hispanic/Latino; 6 Two or more races, non-Hispanic/Latino). Average age 37. 169 applicants, 95% accepted, 59 enrolled. In 2017, 175 master's, 36 doctorates awarded. *Degree requirements:* For master's, student teaching; for doctorate, comprehensive exam, thesis/dissertation. *Entrance requirements:* For master's, 2 years of teaching experience, valid teaching certificate, resume; for doctorate, appropriate master's degree, two references, curriculum vitae, personal statement, professional project, reflective essay. Additional exam requirements/recommendations for international students: Required—TOEFL (minimum score 550 paper-based; 79 iBT). *Application deadline:* For fall admission, 6/1 for international students; for spring admission, 10/1 for international students. Applications are processed on a rolling basis. Application fee: $0. Electronic applications accepted. *Expenses:* Contact institution. *Financial support:* In 2017–18, 34 students received support. Federal Work-Study, scholarships/grants, and unspecified assistantships available. Support available to part-time students. Financial award applicants required to submit FAFSA. *Unit head:* Dr. Jen Buckley, Dean, School of Education and Human Performance, 630-844-1542, Fax: 630-844-6155, E-mail: jbuckley@aurora.edu. *Application contact:* Elizabeth Botica, Graduate Education Recruiter, 630-947-8918, E-mail: ebotica@aurora.edu.
Website: http://aurora.edu/education

Averett University, Master in Education Program, Danville, VA 24541-3692. Offers administration and supervision (M Ed); curriculum and instruction (M Ed); special education with endorsement (M Ed); special education with licensure (M Ed). *Program availability:* Part-time, online only, 100% online. *Faculty:* 2 full-time (1 woman), 14 part-time/adjunct (11 women). *Students:* 38 full-time (32 women), 46 part-time (28 women); includes 33 minority (29 Black or African American, non-Hispanic/Latino; 1 Hispanic/Latino; 3 Two or more races, non-Hispanic/Latino). Average age 38. 155 applicants, 52% accepted, 59 enrolled. In 2017, 50 master's awarded. *Degree requirements:* For master's, 30-credit core curriculum, minimum GPA of 3.0 throughout program, completion of degree requirements within six years from start of program. *Entrance requirements:* For master's, PRAXIS I, GRE, or MAT; writing proficiency test, minimum cumulative GPA of 3.0 over the last 60 hours of undergraduate study toward a baccalaureate degree, three letters of recommendation, Virginia teaching license (or eligibility). Additional exam requirements/recommendations for international students: Required—TOEFL (minimum score 600 paper-based; 100 iBT). *Application deadline:* Applications are processed on a rolling basis. Electronic applications accepted. *Expenses:* Contact institution. *Financial support:* Application deadline: 3/1; applicants required to submit FAFSA. *Faculty research:* Digital story telling for instruction and assessment; online collaborative tools; digital field trips with Google Earth; teacher preparation in special education in Kenya, Malawi, Zambia, and Zimbabwe; self-efficacy of regular education teachers regarding inclusion of special education students in their classrooms. *Total annual research expenditures:* $5,000. *Unit head:* Dr. Sue Davis, Education Chair, 434-791-5741, Fax: 434-791-5020, E-mail: suedavis@averett.edu.
Website: http://gps.averett.edu/online/education/

Avila University, School of Education, Kansas City, MO 64145-1698. Offers advanced classroom management (MA); art K-12 (Teaching Certificate); educational technology (MA, Certificate); elementary education (Teaching Certificate); English as a second language (MA); English language learners (Advanced Certificate); middle school (Teaching Certificate); physical education K-12 (Teaching Certificate); secondary education (Teaching Certificate); special education (Teaching Certificate); special reading (Advanced Certificate); teaching and learning (MA). *Program availability:* Part-time, evening/weekend, online learning. *Faculty:* 6 full-time (5 women), 9 part-time/adjunct (8 women). *Students:* 81 full-time (63 women), 20 part-time (11 women); includes 14 minority (8 Black or African American, non-Hispanic/Latino; 2 Asian, non-Hispanic/Latino; 3 Hispanic/Latino; 1 Two or more races, non-Hispanic/Latino), 4 international. Average age 35. 92 applicants, 62% accepted, 40 enrolled. In 2017, 24 master's awarded. *Entrance requirements:* For master's, minimum GPA of 3.0, writing sample, recommendation, interview; for other advanced degree, foreign language. Additional exam requirements/recommendations for international students: Required—TOEFL (minimum score 580 paper-based; 92 iBT). *Application deadline:* Applications are processed on a rolling basis. Electronic applications accepted. *Expenses:* Contact institution. *Financial support:* In 2017–18, 14 students received support. Unspecified assistantships available. Financial award applicants required to submit FAFSA. *Unit head:* Dr. Stacy Keith, Director of Graduate Education, 816-501-2446, Fax: 816-501-2915, E-mail: stacy.keith@avila.edu. *Application contact:* Cory Roup, Graduate Education Enrollment and Academic Advisor, 816-501-2464, E-mail: cory.roup@avila.edu.
Website: https://www.avila.edu/academics/graduate-studies/grad-education

Azusa Pacific University, School of Education, Department of Teacher Education, Program in Special Education, Azusa, CA 91702-7000. Offers MA Ed. *Accreditation:* NCATE. *Program availability:* Part-time, evening/weekend. *Degree requirements:* For master's, core exams, oral presentations. *Entrance requirements:* For master's, 12 units of course work in education, minimum GPA of 3.0.

Baldwin Wallace University, Graduate Programs, School of Education, Specialization in Mild/Moderate Educational Needs, Berea, OH 44017-2088. Offers MA Ed. *Accreditation:* NCATE. *Program availability:* Part-time, evening/weekend, 100% online. *Students:* 11 full-time (all women), 23 part-time (20 women); includes 3 minority (2 Black or African American, non-Hispanic/Latino; 1 Two or more races, non-Hispanic/Latino). Average age 35. 13 applicants, 54% accepted, 4 enrolled. In 2017, 15 master's awarded. *Degree requirements:* For master's, capstone practicum. *Entrance requirements:* For master's, bachelor's degree in field, MAT or minimum GPA of 3.0. Additional exam requirements/recommendations for international students: Required—TOEFL (minimum score 550 paper-based; 79 iBT). *Application deadline:* For fall admission, 8/15 priority date for domestic students; for spring admission, 12/15 priority date for domestic students. Applications are processed on a rolling basis. Application fee: $25. Electronic applications accepted. Application fee is waived when completed online. *Expenses:* $721 per credit hour. *Financial support:* Career-related internships or fieldwork available. Financial award applicants required to submit FAFSA. *Faculty research:* Adult adjustment of individuals formerly identified as having mild/moderate special education needs, professional development of special educators, teacher beliefs and special education, classroom assessment practices. *Unit head:* Dr. Debra Janas, Coordinator, 440-826-8177, Fax: 440-826-3779, E-mail: djanas@bw.edu. *Application contact:* Winnie W. Gerhardt, Director of Transfer, Adult and Graduate Admission, 440-826-2222, Fax: 440-826-3830, E-mail: admission@bw.edu.
Website: http://www.bw.edu/academics/master-of-arts-in-education/maed-mild-moderate/

Ball State University, Graduate School, Teachers College, Department of Educational Studies, Muncie, IN 47306. Offers adult education (MA, Ed D, Certificate), including adult and community education (MA), adult, higher and community education (Ed D); college and university teaching (Certificate); community college leadership (Certificate); community education (Certificate); computer education (Certificate); curriculum and educational technology (MA); diversity studies (Certificate); educational studies (PhD), including educational studies; executive development for public service (MA); middle-level education (Certificate); qualitative research in education (Certificate); secondary education (MA); student affairs administration in higher education (MA), including student affairs administration in higher education. *Accreditation:* NCATE. *Program availability:* Part-time, 100% online, blended/hybrid learning. *Faculty:* 17 full-time (13 women), 8 part-time/adjunct (6 women). *Students:* 94 full-time (60 women), 221 part-time (167 women); includes 62 minority (42 Black or African American, non-Hispanic/Latino; 2 Asian, non-Hispanic/Latino; 14 Hispanic/Latino; 4 Two or more races, non-Hispanic/Latino), 6 international. Average age 36. 272 applicants, 46% accepted, 105 enrolled. In 2017, 108 master's, 7 doctorates, 13 other advanced degrees awarded. *Entrance requirements:* For master's, minimum baccalaureate GPA of 2.75 or 3.0 in latter half of baccalaureate; for doctorate, minimum graduate GPA of 3.2. Additional exam requirements/recommendations for international students: Required—TOEFL (minimum score 550 paper-based; 79 iBT), IELTS (minimum score 6.5). *Application deadline:* Applications are processed on a rolling basis. Application fee: $60. Electronic applications accepted. *Financial support:* In 2017–18, 17 students received support, including 14 research assistantships with partial tuition reimbursements available (averaging $10,663 per year), 2 teaching assistantships with partial tuition reimbursements available (averaging $12,000 per year); unspecified assistantships also available. Financial award application deadline: 3/1; financial award applicants required to submit FAFSA. *Unit head:* Dr. Theresa Kruczek, Interim Chair, 765-285-8049, E-mail: tkruczek@bsu.edu.
Website: http://www.bsu.edu/edstudies

Ball State University, Graduate School, Teachers College, Department of Special Education, Program in Applied Behavior Analysis, Muncie, IN 47306. Offers applied behavior analysis (MA), including autism. *Program availability:* Part-time, online only, 100% online. *Students:* 158 full-time (144 women), 1,911 part-time (1,762 women); includes 454 minority (144 Black or African American, non-Hispanic/Latino; 72 Asian, non-Hispanic/Latino; 197 Hispanic/Latino; 3 Native Hawaiian or other Pacific Islander, non-Hispanic/Latino; 38 Two or more races, non-Hispanic/Latino), 18 international. Average age 29. 858 applicants, 76% accepted, 485 enrolled. In 2017, 615 master's awarded. *Entrance requirements:* For master's, minimum baccalaureate GPA of 2.75 or 3.0 in latter half of baccalaureate. Additional exam requirements/recommendations for international students: Required—TOEFL (minimum score 550 paper-based; 79 iBT), IELTS (minimum score 6.5). *Application deadline:* For fall admission, 7/10 for domestic students; for spring admission, 11/15 for domestic students; for summer admission, 4/15 for domestic students. Applications are processed on a rolling basis. Application fee: $60. Electronic applications accepted. *Financial support:* Research assistantships with partial tuition reimbursements available. Financial award application deadline: 3/1; financial award applicants required to submit FAFSA. *Unit head:* Dr. David McIntosh, Chairperson, 765-285-5700, Fax: 765-285-4280, E-mail: demcintosh@bsu.edu.
Website: http://www.bsu.edu/specialeducation

Ball State University, Graduate School, Teachers College, Department of Special Education, Program in Special Education, Muncie, IN 47306. Offers special education (MA, Ed D). *Program availability:* Part-time, 100% online, blended/hybrid learning.

Students: 24 full-time (22 women), 220 part-time (197 women); includes 31 minority (15 Black or African American, non-Hispanic/Latino; 5 Asian, non-Hispanic/Latino; 7 Hispanic/Latino; 4 Two or more races, non-Hispanic/Latino), 7 international. Average age 33. 112 applicants, 75% accepted, 65 enrolled. In 2017, 91 master's, 2 doctorates awarded. *Degree requirements:* For doctorate, thesis/dissertation. *Entrance requirements:* For master's, minimum baccalaureate GPA of 2.75 or 3.0 in latter half of baccalaureate; for doctorate, GRE General Test, minimum graduate GPA of 3.2. Additional exam requirements/recommendations for international students: Required—TOEFL (minimum score 550 paper-based; 79 iBT), IELTS (minimum score 6.5). *Application deadline:* For fall admission, 7/10 for domestic students; for spring admission, 11/15 for domestic students; for summer admission, 4/15 for domestic students. Applications are processed on a rolling basis. Application fee: $60. Electronic applications accepted. *Financial support:* Research assistantships with partial tuition reimbursements available. Financial award application deadline: 3/1; financial award applicants required to submit FAFSA. *Unit head:* Dr. David McIntosh, Chairperson, 765-285-5700, Fax: 765-285-4280, E-mail: demcintosh@bsu.edu.
Website: http://www.bsu.edu/specialeducation

Bank Street College of Education, Graduate School, Program in Infant and Family Development and Early Intervention, New York, NY 10025. Offers infant and family development (MS Ed); infant and family early childhood special and general education (MS Ed); infant and family/early childhood special education (Ed M). *Degree requirements:* For master's, thesis. *Entrance requirements:* For master's, interview, essays. Additional exam requirements/recommendations for international students: Required—TOEFL (minimum score 600 paper-based; 100 iBT), IELTS (minimum score 7). Electronic applications accepted. *Faculty research:* Early intervention, early attachment practice in infant and toddler childcare, parenting skills in adolescents.

Bank Street College of Education, Graduate School, Program in Special Education, New York, NY 10025. Offers early childhood special and general education (MS Ed); early childhood special education (Ed M, MS Ed); elementary/childhood special and general education (MS Ed); elementary/childhood special education (MS Ed); elementary/childhood special education certification (Ed M). *Degree requirements:* For master's, thesis. *Entrance requirements:* For master's, interview, essays. Additional exam requirements/recommendations for international students: Required—TOEFL (minimum score 600 paper-based; 100 iBT), IELTS (minimum score 7). Electronic applications accepted. *Faculty research:* Teaching students with disabilities, inclusion, observation and assessment, early intervention, neurodevelopmental assessment, equity and social justice in education.

Barry University, School of Education, Program in Education for Teachers of Students with Hearing Impairments, Miami Shores, FL 33161-6695. Offers MS.

Barry University, School of Education, Program in Exceptional Student Education, Miami Shores, FL 33161-6695. Offers MS, Ed S. *Program availability:* Part-time, evening/weekend. *Degree requirements:* For master's, comprehensive exam; for Ed S, practicum. *Entrance requirements:* For master's, GRE General Test or MAT, minimum GPA of 3.0; for Ed S, GRE General Test, minimum GPA of 3.0. Electronic applications accepted.

Barry University, School of Education, Program in Leadership and Education, Miami Shores, FL 33161-6695. Offers educational technology (PhD); exceptional student education (PhD); higher education administration (PhD); human resource development (PhD); leadership (PhD). *Program availability:* Part-time, evening/weekend. *Degree requirements:* For doctorate, thesis/dissertation. *Entrance requirements:* For doctorate, GRE General Test, minimum GPA of 3.25. Electronic applications accepted.

Bayamón Central University, Graduate Programs, Program in Education, Bayamón, PR 00960-1725. Offers administration and supervision (MA Ed); commercial education (MA Ed); elementary education (K–3) (MA Ed); family counseling (Graduate Certificate); guidance and counseling (MA Ed); pre-elementary teacher (MA Ed); rehabilitation counseling (MA Ed); special education (MA Ed), including attention deficit disorder, education of the autistic, learning disabilities. *Program availability:* Part-time, evening/weekend. *Degree requirements:* For master's, comprehensive exam. *Entrance requirements:* For master's, EXADEP, bachelor's degree in education or related field.

Baylor University, Graduate School, School of Education, Department of Educational Psychology, Waco, TX 76798. Offers applied behavior analysis (MS Ed); educational psychology (MA, MS Ed, PhD); exceptionalities (PhD); gifted and talented studies (MS Ed); learning and development (PhD); quantitative methods (MA); school psychology (Ed S). *Accreditation:* NCATE. *Faculty:* 11 full-time (6 women). *Students:* 45 full-time (41 women), 11 part-time (10 women); includes 16 minority (1 Black or African American, non-Hispanic/Latino; 3 Asian, non-Hispanic/Latino; 10 Hispanic/Latino; 2 Two or more races, non-Hispanic/Latino), 4 international. Average age 29. 90 applicants, 33% accepted, 30 enrolled. In 2017, 24 master's, 1 doctorate, 7 other advanced degrees awarded. Terminal master's awarded for partial completion of doctoral program. *Degree requirements:* For master's, thesis optional; for doctorate, comprehensive exam, thesis/dissertation; for Ed S, comprehensive exam, thesis or alternative. *Entrance requirements:* For master's, GRE, minimum GPA of 3.0; for doctorate, GRE General Test, master's degree; for Ed S, GRE General Test. Additional exam requirements/recommendations for international students: Required—TOEFL (minimum score 550 paper-based; 80 iBT), IELTS (minimum score 6.5). *Application deadline:* For fall admission, 2/1 priority date for domestic and international students. Application fee: $80. Electronic applications accepted. *Financial support:* In 2017–18, 42 students received support, including 20 fellowships with full and partial tuition reimbursements available, 22 research assistantships with full and partial tuition reimbursements available; career-related internships or fieldwork, Federal Work-Study, institutionally sponsored loans, scholarships/grants, health care benefits, tuition waivers (full and partial), unspecified assistantships, and stipends also available. Financial award application deadline: 2/1; financial award applicants required to submit FAFSA. *Faculty research:* Individual differences, quantitative methods, gifted and talented, special education, school psychology, autism, applied behavior analysis, learning, human development. *Total annual research expenditures:* $300,000. *Unit head:* Dr. Susan K. Johnsen, Professor and Interim Chair, 254-710-6116, E-mail: susan_johnsen@baylor.edu. *Application contact:* Heather Tindle, Office Manager, 254-710-3112, E-mail: heather_tindle@baylor.edu.
Website: http://www.baylor.edu/soe/EDP/

Bay Path University, Program in Clinical Mental Health Counseling, Longmeadow, MA 01106-2292. Offers clinical mental health counseling (MS), including alcohol and drug abuse counseling, early intervention. Program also offered in Sturbridge and Burlington, MA. *Program availability:* Part-time, blended/hybrid learning. *Students:* 68 full-time (59 women), 82 part-time (75 women); includes 42 minority (21 Black or African American, non-Hispanic/Latino; 19 Hispanic/Latino; 2 Two or more races, non-Hispanic/Latino), 11 international. Average age 32. In 2017, 21 master's awarded. *Degree requirements:* For master's, 48 course credits plus 12 credit practicum, internship. *Application deadline:* Applications are processed on a rolling basis. Application fee: $45. Electronic applications accepted. Application fee is waived when completed online. *Expenses:* $815 per credit. *Financial support:* Unspecified assistantships available. Financial award applicants required to submit FAFSA. *Unit head:* Dr. Mark Benander, Director,

413-565-1332, E-mail: mbenander@baypath.edu. *Application contact:* Diane Ranaldi, Dean of Graduate Admissions, 413-565-1332, Fax: 413-565-1250, E-mail: dranaldi@baypath.edu.
Website: http://graduate.baypath.edu/graduate-programs/programs-on-campus/ms-programs/clinical-mental-health

Bay Path University, Program in Education, Longmeadow, MA 01106-2292. Offers MS Ed/Ed S. *Program availability:* Part-time, 100% online. *Students:* 37 full-time (34 women), 100 part-time (84 women); includes 14 minority (7 Black or African American, non-Hispanic/Latino; 1 Asian, non-Hispanic/Latino; 5 Hispanic/Latino; 1 Two or more races, non-Hispanic/Latino). Average age 32. *Application deadline:* Applications are processed on a rolling basis. Application fee: $45. Electronic applications accepted. Application fee is waived when completed online. *Expenses:* $505 per credit. *Financial support:* Unspecified assistantships available. Financial award applicants required to submit FAFSA. *Unit head:* Dr. Karen DeAngelis, Program Coordinator, E-mail: kdeangelis@baypath.edu. *Application contact:* Diane Ranaldi, Dean of Graduate Admissions, 413-565-1332, Fax: 413-565-1250, E-mail: dranaldi@baypath.edu.
Website: http://graduate.baypath.edu/Graduate-Programs/Programs-On-Campus/MS-Programs/Education-Special-Education

Bemidji State University, School of Graduate Studies, Bemidji, MN 56601. Offers biology (MS); education (MS); English (MA, MS); environmental studies (MS); mathematics (MS); mathematics (elementary and middle level education) (MS); special education (M Sp Ed). *Program availability:* Part-time, online learning. *Degree requirements:* For master's, comprehensive exam, thesis (for some programs). *Entrance requirements:* For master's, GRE; GMAT, letters of recommendation, letters of interest. Additional exam requirements/recommendations for international students: Required—TOEFL (minimum score 550 paper-based; 80 iBT). Electronic applications accepted. *Expenses:* Contact institution. *Faculty research:* Human performance, sport, and health: physical education teacher education, continuum models, spiritual health, intellectual health, resiliency, health priorities; psychology: health psychology, college student drinking behavior, micro-aggressions, infant cognition, false memories, leadership assessment; biology: structure and dynamics of forest communities, aquatic and riverine ecology, interaction between animal populations and aquatic environments, cellular motility.

Benedictine University, Graduate Programs, Program in Education, Lisle, IL 60532. Offers curriculum and instruction and collaborative teaching (M Ed); elementary education (MA Ed); leadership and administration (M Ed); reading and literacy (M Ed); secondary education (MA Ed); special education (MA Ed). *Program availability:* Part-time, evening/weekend. *Degree requirements:* For master's, comprehensive exam, thesis (for some programs). *Entrance requirements:* For master's, GRE or MAT. Additional exam requirements/recommendations for international students: Required—TOEFL (minimum score 550 paper-based). Electronic applications accepted. *Expenses:* Contact institution.

Bethel University, Graduate School, St. Paul, MN 55112-6999. Offers business administration (MBA); classroom management (Certificate); counseling (MA); K-12 education (MA); leadership (Ed D); leadership foundations (Certificate); nurse educator (MS, Certificate); nurse-midwifery (MS); physician assistant (MS); special education (MA); strategic leadership (MA); teaching (MA); teaching and learning (Certificate). *Program availability:* Part-time, evening/weekend, 100% online, blended/hybrid learning. *Faculty:* 22 full-time (16 women), 70 part-time/adjunct (44 women). *Students:* 611 full-time (431 women), 393 part-time (249 women); includes 176 minority (82 Black or African American, non-Hispanic/Latino; 4 American Indian or Alaska Native, non-Hispanic/Latino; 31 Asian, non-Hispanic/Latino; 39 Hispanic/Latino; 2 Native Hawaiian or other Pacific Islander, non-Hispanic/Latino; 18 Two or more races, non-Hispanic/Latino), 9 international. Average age 36. 668 applicants, 42% accepted, 223 enrolled. In 2017, 287 master's, 30 doctorates, 172 other advanced degrees awarded. *Degree requirements:* For master's, comprehensive exam (for some programs), thesis (for some programs); for doctorate, comprehensive exam, thesis/dissertation. *Entrance requirements:* Additional exam requirements/recommendations for international students: Required—TOEFL (minimum score 550 paper-based, 80 iBT) or IELTS. *Application deadline:* Applications are processed on a rolling basis. Application fee: $0. Electronic applications accepted. *Expenses:* Contact institution. *Financial support:* Teaching assistantships, career-related internships or fieldwork, and scholarships/grants available. Support available to part-time students. Financial award applicants required to submit FAFSA. *Unit head:* Dr. Randy Bergen, Associate Provost, 651-635-8000, Fax: 651-635-8004, E-mail: r-bergen@bethel.edu. *Application contact:* Director of Admissions, 651-635-8000, Fax: 651-635-8004, E-mail: gs@bethel.edu.
Website: https://www.bethel.edu/graduate/

Binghamton University, State University of New York, Graduate School, College of Community and Public Affairs, Department of Teaching, Learning and Educational Leadership, Program in Special Education, Binghamton, NY 13902-6000. Offers MS Ed. *Accreditation:* TEAC. *Program availability:* Part-time, evening/weekend. *Students:* 25 full-time (23 women), 14 part-time (12 women); includes 4 minority (3 Hispanic/Latino; 1 Two or more races, non-Hispanic/Latino). Average age 26. 31 applicants, 77% accepted, 16 enrolled. In 2017, 26 master's awarded. *Degree requirements:* For master's, portfolio. *Entrance requirements:* For master's, GRE General Test, teaching certification. Additional exam requirements/recommendations for international students: Required—TOEFL (minimum score 550 paper-based; 80 iBT). *Application deadline:* For fall admission, 2/1 priority date for domestic and international students; for spring admission, 10/15 priority date for domestic and international students. Application fee: $75. Electronic applications accepted. *Financial support:* In 2017–18, 2 students received support, including 1 fellowship with full tuition reimbursement available (averaging $4,500 per year); career-related internships or fieldwork, Federal Work-Study, institutionally sponsored loans, and unspecified assistantships also available. Support available to part-time students. Financial award applicants required to submit FAFSA. *Unit head:* Dr. Susan Strehle, Dean, 607-777-7329, E-mail: sstrehle@binghamton.edu. *Application contact:* Ben Balkaya, Assistant Dean and Director, 607-777-2151, Fax: 607-777-2501, E-mail: balkaya@binghamton.edu.

Biola University, School of Education, La Mirada, CA 90639-0001. Offers curriculum and instruction (Certificate); early childhood (MA Ed, MAT); multiple subject (MAT); single subject (MAT); special education (MA Ed, MAT, Certificate). *Program availability:* Part-time, evening/weekend, online learning. *Faculty:* 16. *Students:* 67 full-time (52 women), 164 part-time (142 women); includes 97 minority (8 Black or African American, non-Hispanic/Latino; 1 American Indian or Alaska Native, non-Hispanic/Latino; 51 Asian, non-Hispanic/Latino; 30 Hispanic/Latino; 7 Two or more races, non-Hispanic/Latino), 4 international. 164 applicants, 87% accepted, 116 enrolled. In 2017, 25 master's awarded. *Entrance requirements:* For master's, CBEST, CSET, GRE (waived if cumulative GPA is 3.5 or above or if CBEST and all CSET subtests are passed). Additional exam requirements/recommendations for international students: Required—TOEFL (minimum score 100 iBT). *Application deadline:* For fall admission, 7/1 for domestic students, 6/1 for international students; for spring admission, 12/1 for domestic students; for summer admission, 5/1 for domestic students. Applications are processed on a rolling basis. Application fee: $65. Electronic applications accepted. *Financial support:* Scholarships/grants available. Support available to part-time students.

Special Education

Financial award applicants required to submit FAFSA. *Faculty research:* Early childhood education, elementary education, special education, curriculum development, teacher preparation. *Unit head:* Dr. June Hetzel, Dean, 562-903-4715. *Application contact:* Graduate Admissions Office, 562-903-4752, E-mail: graduate.admissions@biola.edu. Website: http://education.biola.edu/

Bloomsburg University of Pennsylvania, School of Graduate Studies, College of Education, Department of Exceptionality Programs, Program in Special Education, Bloomsburg, PA 17815-1301. Offers M Ed, MS, Certificate. *Accreditation:* NCATE. *Degree requirements:* For master's, thesis, minimum QPA of 3.0, practicum. *Entrance requirements:* For master's, teaching certificate, minimum QPA of 2.8, letter of intent, 2 letters of recommendation, interview, professional liability insurance, recent TB screening. Additional exam requirements/recommendations for international students: Required—TOEFL (minimum score 550 paper-based), IELTS. Electronic applications accepted. *Expenses:* Tuition, state resident: full-time $10,000; part-time $500 per credit hour. Tuition, nonresident: full-time $15,000; part-time $750 per credit hour. *Required fees:* $2484; $110.75 per credit hour. $75 per term. Tuition and fees vary according to program.

Bluffton University, Programs in Education, Bluffton, OH 45817. Offers intervention specialist (MA Ed); leadership (MA Ed); reading (MA Ed). *Accreditation:* NCATE. *Program availability:* Part-time, 100% online, blended/hybrid learning, videoconference. *Faculty:* 2 full-time (1 woman), 1 part-time/adjunct (0 women). *Students:* 7 full-time (4 women), 11 part-time (10 women); includes 1 minority (Black or African American, non-Hispanic/Latino). Average age 29. 14 applicants, 64% accepted, 9 enrolled. In 2017, 7 master's awarded. *Degree requirements:* For master's, action research project, public presentation. *Entrance requirements:* For master's, PRAXIS I, bachelor's degree, minimum GPA of 3.0. Additional exam requirements/recommendations for international students: Required—TOEFL. *Application deadline:* For fall admission, 8/15 priority date for domestic students, 6/15 priority date for international students; for spring admission, 12/15 priority date for domestic students, 9/15 priority date for international students. Applications are processed on a rolling basis. Electronic applications accepted. *Expenses:* $456 per credit hour tuition, $50 per semester technology fee ($100 for more than 6 hours). *Financial support:* In 2017–18, 2 students received support. Unspecified assistantships available. Financial award application deadline: 6/15; financial award applicants required to submit FAFSA. *Unit head:* Dr. Amy K. Mullins, Director of Graduate Programs in Education, 419-358-3457, E-mail: mullinsa@bluffton.edu. *Application contact:* Nancey Schortgen, Program Representative, 419-358-3202, Fax: 419-358-3399, E-mail: schortgenn@bluffton.edu. Website: http://www.bluffton.edu/grad/

Bob Jones University, Graduate Programs, Greenville, SC 29614. Offers accountancy (MS); Bible (MA); Bible translation (MA); Biblical studies (Certificate); broadcast management (MS); business administration (MBA); church history (MA, PhD); church ministries (MA); church music (MM); cinema and video production (MA); counseling (MS); curriculum and instruction (Ed D); divinity (M Div); dramatic production (MA); educational leadership (MS, Ed D, Ed S); elementary education (M Ed, MAT); English (M Ed, MA, MAT); fine arts (MA); graphic design (MA); history (M Ed, MA); illustration (MA); interpretative speech (MA); mathematics (M Ed, MAT); medical missions (Certificate); ministry (MM, D Min); multi-categorical special education (M Ed, MAT); music (M Ed); New Testament interpretation (PhD); Old Testament interpretation (PhD); orchestral instrument performance (MM); organ performance (MM); pastoral studies (MA); personnel services (MS, Ed S); piano pedagogy (MM); piano performance (MM); platform arts (MA); radio and television broadcasting (MS); rhetoric and public address (MA); secondary education (M Ed); studio art (MA); teaching Bible (MA); theology (MA, PhD); voice performance (MM); youth ministries (MA); M Div/MM.

Boise State University, College of Education, Department of Early and Special Education, Boise, ID 83725-0399. Offers early and special education (M Ed). *Accreditation:* NCATE. *Program availability:* Part-time. *Faculty:* 14. *Students:* 29 full-time (27 women), 13 part-time (10 women); includes 4 minority (2 Asian, non-Hispanic/Latino; 1 Hispanic/Latino; 1 Native Hawaiian or other Pacific Islander, non-Hispanic/Latino). Average age 38. 18 applicants, 33% accepted, 3 enrolled. In 2017, 10 master's awarded. *Degree requirements:* For master's, thesis optional. *Entrance requirements:* For master's, minimum GPA of 3.0. Additional exam requirements/recommendations for international students: Required—TOEFL (minimum score 587 paper-based; 95 iBT), IELTS (minimum score 6.5). *Application deadline:* For fall admission, 3/31 for domestic and international students. Application fee: $65 ($95 for international students). Electronic applications accepted. *Expenses:* Tuition, state resident: full-time $6471; part-time $390 per credit. Tuition, nonresident: full-time $21,787; part-time $685 per credit. *Required fees:* $2283; $100 per term. Part-time tuition and fees vary according to course load and program. *Financial support:* Scholarships/grants and unspecified assistantships available. Financial award application deadline: 3/31; financial award applicants required to submit FAFSA. *Unit head:* Dr. Deb Carter, Department Chair, 208-426-2804, E-mail: debcarter@boisestate.edu. *Application contact:* Dr. Carrie Semmelroth, Graduate Coordinator, 208-426-2818, E-mail: carriesemmelroth@boisestate.edu. Website: http://education.boisestate.edu/spedecs/

Boston College, Lynch School of Education, Program in Moderate Special Needs, Chestnut Hill, MA 02467-3800. Offers M Ed, CAES. *Accreditation:* TEAC. *Program availability:* Part-time, evening/weekend. *Students:* 20 full-time (19 women), 9 part-time (8 women); includes 4 minority (2 Black or African American, non-Hispanic/Latino; 1 Asian, non-Hispanic/Latino; 1 Hispanic/Latino). Average age 23. 38 applicants, 92% accepted, 22 enrolled. In 2017, 25 master's awarded. *Degree requirements:* For master's and CAES, comprehensive exam. *Entrance requirements:* For master's, GRE General Test or MAT, general licensure at the elementary or secondary level; for CAES, GRE General Test or MAT. Additional exam requirements/recommendations for international students: Required—TOEFL (minimum score 100 iBT). *Application deadline:* For fall admission, 12/1 priority date for domestic and international students; for spring admission, 11/1 priority date for domestic and international students. Application fee: $65. Electronic applications accepted. *Financial support:* Fellowships with tuition reimbursements, research assistantships with tuition reimbursements, teaching assistantships with tuition reimbursements, Federal Work-Study, scholarships/grants, and tuition waivers available. Financial award applicants required to submit FAFSA. *Unit head:* Dr. Susan Bruce, Chairperson, 617-552-4214, Fax: 617-552-0398. *Application contact:* Kimberly Rose, Graduate Admission Assistant, 617-552-4214, Fax: 617-552-0398, E-mail: roseki@bc.edu.

Boston College, Lynch School of Education, Program in Severe Special Needs, Chestnut Hill, MA 02467-3800. Offers M Ed, CAES. *Accreditation:* TEAC. *Program availability:* Part-time, evening/weekend. *Students:* 4 full-time (3 women), 14 part-time (12 women); includes 4 minority (2 Asian, non-Hispanic/Latino; 2 Hispanic/Latino), 1 international. Average age 24. 12 applicants, 83% accepted, 7 enrolled. In 2017, 13 master's awarded. *Degree requirements:* For master's, comprehensive exam. *Entrance requirements:* For master's, GRE General Test or MAT. Additional exam requirements/recommendations for international students: Required—TOEFL (minimum score 100 iBT). *Application deadline:* For fall admission, 12/1 priority date for domestic and international students; for spring admission, 11/1 priority date for domestic and international students. Application fee: $65. Electronic applications accepted. *Financial support:* Fellowships with tuition reimbursements, research assistantships with tuition

reimbursements, teaching assistantships with tuition reimbursements, Federal Work-Study, scholarships/grants, and tuition waivers (full and partial) available. Financial award applicants required to submit FAFSA. *Unit head:* Dr. Susan Bruce, Chairperson, 617-552-4214, Fax: 617-552-0398. *Application contact:* Kimberly Rose, Graduate Admission Assistant, 617-552-4214, Fax: 617-552-0398, E-mail: roseki@bc.edu.

Bowie State University, Graduate Programs, Program in Special Education, Bowie, MD 20715-9465. Offers M Ed. *Accreditation:* NCATE. *Program availability:* Part-time, evening/weekend. *Degree requirements:* For master's, comprehensive exam, thesis optional, research paper. *Entrance requirements:* For master's, teaching experience, 3 professional letters of recommendation. Electronic applications accepted.

Bowling Green State University, Graduate College, College of Education and Human Development, School of Intervention Services, Program in Special Education, Bowling Green, OH 43403. Offers assistive technology (M Ed); autism spectrum disorders (M Ed); general special education (M Ed); intervention specialist: mild/moderate disabilities (M Ed); intervention specialist: moderate/intensive disabilities (M Ed); secondary transition/transition-to-work (M Ed). *Accreditation:* NCATE. *Program availability:* Part-time. *Degree requirements:* For master's, thesis or alternative. *Entrance requirements:* For master's, GRE General Test. Additional exam requirements/recommendations for international students: Required—TOEFL. Electronic applications accepted. *Faculty research:* Reading and special populations, deafness, early childhood, gifted and talented, behavior disorders.

Brandman University, School of Education, Irvine, CA 92618. Offers curriculum and instruction (MAE); educational administration (MAE); educational leadership (MAE); educational leadership and administration (MA); elementary education (MAT); instructional technology: teaching the 21st century learner (MAE); leadership in early childhood education (MAE); organizational leadership (Ed D); school counseling (MA); secondary education (MAT); special education (MA); teaching and learning (MAE). *Expenses:* Tuition: Part-time $640 per credit hour. Tuition and fees vary according to degree level and program. *Unit head:* Dr. Christine G. Zeppos, Dean, 949-341-9948, E-mail: zeppos@brandman.edu. *Application contact:* Dr. Christine G. Zeppos, Dean, 949-341-9948, E-mail: zeppos@brandman.edu. Website: https://www.brandman.edu/academic-programs/education

Brandon University, Faculty of Education, Brandon, MB R7A 6A9, Canada. Offers curriculum and instruction (M Ed, Diploma); educational administration (M Ed, Diploma); guidance and counseling (M Ed, Diploma); special education (M Ed, Diploma). *Degree requirements:* For master's, thesis. *Entrance requirements:* For master's, minimum GPA of 3.0, teaching certificate or equivalent. Additional exam requirements/recommendations for international students: Required—TOEFL. *Faculty research:* Comparative education, environmental studies, parent/school council.

Brenau University, Sydney O. Smith Graduate School, College of Education, Gainesville, GA 30501. Offers early childhood (Ed S); early childhood education (M Ed, MAT); middle grades (Ed S); middle grades education (M Ed, MAT); secondary education (MAT); special education (M Ed, MAT). *Accreditation:* NCATE. *Program availability:* Part-time, evening/weekend, online learning. *Degree requirements:* For master's, thesis optional, comprehensive exam or applied research project, effective portfolio; for Ed S, thesis, applied research project. *Entrance requirements:* For master's, GRE, MAT, interview, minimum GPA of 3.0, 3 references, writing samples; for Ed S, GRE, MAT, master's degree, minimum GPA of 3.0, writing sample, letters of reference. Additional exam requirements/recommendations for international students: Required—TOEFL (minimum score 500 paper-based; 61 iBT); Recommended—IELTS (minimum score 5). Electronic applications accepted. *Expenses:* Contact institution.

Bridgewater State University, College of Graduate Studies, College of Education and Allied Studies, Department of Special Education, Bridgewater, MA 02325. Offers M Ed. *Accreditation:* NCATE. *Program availability:* Part-time, evening/weekend. *Entrance requirements:* For master's, GRE General Test or Massachusetts Test for Educator Licensure.

Brigham Young University, Graduate Studies, David O. McKay School of Education, Department of Counseling Psychology and Special Education, Provo, UT 84602. Offers counseling psychology (PhD); school psychology (Ed S); special education (MS). *Program availability:* Part-time. *Faculty:* 14 full-time (4 women), 9 part-time/adjunct (4 women). *Students:* 70 full-time (47 women), 20 part-time (18 women); includes 11 minority (1 Black or African American, non-Hispanic/Latino; 2 American Indian or Alaska Native, non-Hispanic/Latino; 1 Asian, non-Hispanic/Latino; 4 Hispanic/Latino; 3 Native Hawaiian or other Pacific Islander, non-Hispanic/Latino), 4 international. Average age 29. 76 applicants, 38% accepted, 28 enrolled. In 2017, 1 master's, 6 doctorates, 10 other advanced degrees awarded. *Degree requirements:* For master's and Ed S, comprehensive exam, thesis; for doctorate, comprehensive exam, thesis/dissertation. *Entrance requirements:* For master's, GRE General Test, minimum cumulative GPA of 3.0 in undergraduate coursework; for doctorate and Ed S, GRE General Test, minimum cumulative GPA of 3.0 in undergraduate coursework. Additional exam requirements/recommendations for international students: Required—TOEFL (minimum score 580 paper-based; 85 iBT), IELTS (minimum score 7). *Application deadline:* For fall admission, 1/15 for domestic and international students. Application fee: $50. Electronic applications accepted. *Expenses:* Tuition: Full-time $6880; part-time $405 per credit hour. Tuition and fees vary according to course load, program and student's religious affiliation. *Financial support:* In 2017–18, 64 students received support, including 64 research assistantships (averaging $9,270 per year); institutionally sponsored loans and tuition waivers (partial) also available. Financial award application deadline: 3/31. *Faculty research:* Autism, religious and spiritual values in counseling, school-based crisis intervention, behavior interventions in MTSS framework, counseling and psychotherapy process and outcomes. *Unit head:* Dr. Lane Fischer, Department Chair, 801-422-3857, E-mail: lane_fischer@byu.edu. *Application contact:* Diane E. Hancock, Executive Secretary, 801-422-3859, E-mail: diane_hancock@byu.edu. Website: http://education.byu.edu/cpse/

Brooklyn College of the City University of New York, School of Education, Program in Special Education, Brooklyn, NY 11210-2889. Offers autism spectrum disorders (AC); teacher of students with disabilities (MS Ed), including adolescence education, childhood education, early childhood education. *Program availability:* Part-time. *Entrance requirements:* For master's, LAST, interview; previous course work in education and psychology; minimum GPA of 3.0 in education, 2.8 overall; resume, 2 letters of recommendation; essay. Additional exam requirements/recommendations for international students: Required—TOEFL (minimum score 500 paper-based; 61 iBT). Electronic applications accepted. *Faculty research:* School reform, conflict resolution, curriculum for inclusive settings, urban issues in special education.

Buffalo State College, State University of New York, The Graduate School, Faculty of Applied Science and Education, Department of Exceptional Education, Programs in Special Education, Buffalo, NY 14222-1095. Offers special education (MS Ed); special education: adolescents (MS Ed); special education: childhood (MS Ed); special education: early childhood (MS Ed). *Accreditation:* NCATE. *Program availability:* Part-time, evening/weekend. *Degree requirements:* For master's, thesis or project. *Entrance requirements:* For master's, minimum GPA of 2.5. Additional exam requirements/recommendations for international students: Required—TOEFL (minimum score 550 paper-based).

Cabrini University, Academic Affairs, Radnor, PA 19087. Offers accounting (M Acc); autism spectrum disorder (M Ed); biological sciences (MS), including civic leadership; criminology and criminal justice (MA); curriculum, instruction, and assessment (M Ed); educational leadership (M Ed, Ed D), including curriculum and instructional leadership (Ed D), preK-12 leadership (Ed D); English as a second language (M Ed); organizational leadership (DBA, PhD); preK to 4 (M Ed); reading specialist (M Ed); secondary education (M Ed), including biology, chemistry, English, English/communication, mathematics, social studies; special education grades 7-12 (M Ed); special education preK-8 (M Ed); teaching and learning (M Ed). *Program availability:* Part-time, evening/weekend. *Faculty:* 23 full-time (17 women), 46 part-time/adjunct (38 women). *Students:* 60 full-time (35 women), 559 part-time (435 women); includes 93 minority (66 Black or African American, non-Hispanic/Latino; 1 American Indian or Alaska Native, non-Hispanic/Latino; 8 Asian, non-Hispanic/Latino; 15 Hispanic/Latino; 3 Two or more races, non-Hispanic/Latino), 4 international. Average age 33. 290 applicants, 82% accepted, 154 enrolled. In 2017, 283 master's awarded. *Degree requirements:* For master's, comprehensive exam (for some programs), thesis (for some programs); for doctorate, comprehensive exam (for some programs), thesis/dissertation. *Entrance requirements:* For master's, professional resume, personal statement, two recommendations, official transcripts; for doctorate, official transcripts, minimum master's GPA of 3.0, two recommendations, interview with admissions committee. Additional exam requirements/recommendations for international students: Required—TOEFL (minimum score 80 iBT). *Application deadline:* For fall admission, 8/26 for domestic students, 8/1 for international students; for winter admission, 1/13 for domestic students, 12/20 for international students; for spring admission, 1/13 for domestic students, 12/20 for international students; for summer admission, 5/20 for domestic students, 4/30 for international students. Applications are processed on a rolling basis. Application fee: $50. Electronic applications accepted. Application fee is waived when completed online. *Expenses:* Contact institution. *Financial support:* In 2017–18, 1,459 students received support. Tuition waivers and unspecified assistantships available. Financial award application deadline: 5/1; financial award applicants required to submit FAFSA. *Unit head:* Dr. Maliha Zaman, 610-902-8502, Fax: 610-902-8797, E-mail: msz37@cabrini.edu. *Application contact:* Diane Greenwood, Director of Graduate Admissions, 610-902-8291, E-mail: diane.l.greenwood@cabrini.edu.
Website: http://cabrini.edu/graduate

Caldwell University, School of Education, Caldwell, NJ 07006-6195. Offers curriculum and instruction (MA); education leadership (Ed D); educational administration (MA); elementary, secondary or preschool endorsement, special ed, ESL (Postbaccalaureate Certificate); learning disabilities teacher-consultant (Post-Master's Certificate); literacy instruction (MA); principal (Post-Master's Certificate); reading specialist (Post-Master's Certificate); special education (MA), including special education, teaching of students with disabilities, teaching of students with disabilities and learning disabilities teacher-consultant; superintendent (Post-Master's Certificate); supervisor (Post-Master's Certificate). *Program availability:* Part-time, evening/weekend. *Faculty:* 10 full-time (6 women), 21 part-time/adjunct (12 women). *Students:* 37 full-time (30 women), 225 part-time (177 women); includes 47 minority (19 Black or African American, non-Hispanic/Latino; 3 Asian, non-Hispanic/Latino; 23 Hispanic/Latino; 2 Two or more races, non-Hispanic/Latino). Average age 35. 189 applicants, 57% accepted, 85 enrolled. In 2017, 47 master's awarded. *Degree requirements:* For master's, comprehensive exam (for some programs), thesis (for some programs); for doctorate, thesis/dissertation. *Entrance requirements:* For master's, PRAXIS, 3 years of work experience, prior teaching certification; for doctorate, GRE or MAT; for other advanced degree, two letters of recommendation; interview (for some programs). Additional exam requirements/recommendations for international students: Required—TOEFL (minimum score 580 paper-based, 70 iBT), IELTS (6), or ELS Level 112 Certification of Completion. *Application deadline:* For fall admission, 6/1 for domestic students; for spring admission, 12/1 for domestic students; for summer admission, 4/1 for domestic students. Applications are processed on a rolling basis. Application fee: $50. Electronic applications accepted. *Expenses:* $950 per credit (for master's and certificate programs); $1,125 per credit (for doctoral programs). *Financial support:* Unspecified assistantships available. Financial award applicants required to submit FAFSA. *Faculty research:* Curriculum and instruction, secondary education, special education, education and technology, literacy instruction, higher education administration, education leadership. *Unit head:* Dr. Joan Moriarity, Associate Dean, 973-618-3626, E-mail: jmoriarity@caldwell.edu. *Application contact:* Tom Disch, Senior Admissions Counselor, 973-618-3544, E-mail: graduate@caldwell.edu.

California Baptist University, Program in Education, Riverside, CA 92504-3206. Offers educational leadership (MS); educational leadership for faith-based institutions (MS); educational leadership for public institutions (MS); educational technology (MS); instructional computer applications (MS); international education (MS); leadership and adult learning (MS); leadership and organizational studies (MS); online teaching and learning (MS); reading (MS); science education (MA); special education in mild/moderate disabilities (MS); special education in moderate/severe disabilities (MS); teacher leadership (MS); teaching (MS); teaching and learning (MS). *Program availability:* Part-time, evening/weekend, 100% online, blended/hybrid learning. *Faculty:* 19 full-time (11 women), 36 part-time/adjunct (22 women). *Students:* 232 full-time (182 women), 315 part-time (247 women); includes 264 minority (33 Black or African American, non-Hispanic/Latino; 4 American Indian or Alaska Native, non-Hispanic/Latino; 11 Asian, non-Hispanic/Latino; 186 Hispanic/Latino; 7 Native Hawaiian or other Pacific Islander, non-Hispanic/Latino; 23 Two or more races, non-Hispanic/Latino). Average age 34. 217 applicants, 64% accepted, 129 enrolled. In 2017, 196 master's awarded. *Degree requirements:* For master's, comprehensive exam, project, or thesis. *Entrance requirements:* For master's, minimum undergraduate GPA of 2.75; 500-word essay; three letters of recommendation; two prerequisite courses completed with minimum C grade. Additional exam requirements/recommendations for international students: Required—TOEFL (minimum score 80 iBT). *Application deadline:* For fall admission, 8/1 priority date for domestic students, 7/1 for international students; for spring admission, 12/1 priority date for domestic students, 11/1 for international students. Applications are processed on a rolling basis. Application fee: $45. Electronic applications accepted. *Expenses:* Contact institution. *Financial support:* In 2017–18, 162 students received support. Federal Work-Study and scholarships/grants available. Financial award applicants required to submit CSS PROFILE or FAFSA. *Faculty research:* Leadership development, complexity theory, faith and learning, special education, social and philosophical contexts of education. *Unit head:* Dr. John Shoup, Dean, School of Education, 951-343-4516, E-mail: jshoup@calbaptist.edu. *Application contact:* Gavin Andrew, Graduate Admissions Counselor, 951-552-8437, E-mail: gandrew@calbaptist.edu.
Website: http://www.calbaptist.edu/mastersined/

California Lutheran University, Graduate Studies, Graduate School of Education, Thousand Oaks, CA 91360-2787. Offers counseling and guidance (MS), including college student personnel, counseling and guidance; educational leadership (MA, Ed D); including educational leadership (K-12) (Ed D); higher education leadership (Ed D); special education (MS); teacher leadership (M Ed); teaching (M Ed). *Accreditation:* NCATE. *Program availability:* Part-time, evening/weekend. *Faculty:* 21 full-time (18 women), 40 part-time/adjunct (27 women). *Students:* 390 full-time (303 women), 61 part-time (51 women); includes 228 minority (6 Black or African American, non-Hispanic/Latino; 2 American Indian or Alaska Native, non-Hispanic/Latino; 13 Asian, non-Hispanic/Latino; 186 Hispanic/Latino; 1 Native Hawaiian or other Pacific Islander, non-Hispanic/Latino; 20 Two or more races, non-Hispanic/Latino). Average age 31. 201 applicants, 76% accepted, 121 enrolled. In 2017, 129 master's, 19 doctorates awarded. *Degree requirements:* For master's, comprehensive exam or thesis; for doctorate, thesis/dissertation. *Entrance requirements:* For master's, GRE General Test, interview, minimum GPA of 3.0. *Application deadline:* For fall admission, 7/1 priority date for domestic students; for spring admission, 11/1 priority date for domestic students; for summer admission, 4/1 priority date for domestic students. Applications are processed on a rolling basis. Application fee: $50. Electronic applications accepted. *Expenses: Tuition:* Full-time $15,000. Full-time tuition and fees vary according to degree level and program. *Unit head:* Dr. Michael Hillis, Dean, 805-493-3421. *Application contact:* 805-493-3325, Fax: 805-493-3861, E-mail: clugrad@callutheran.edu.

California State University, Bakersfield, Division of Graduate Studies, School of Social Sciences and Education, Program in Special Education, Bakersfield, CA 93311. Offers MA. *Accreditation:* NCATE. *Faculty:* 4 full-time (all women), 10 part-time/adjunct (7 women). *Students:* 19 full-time (16 women), 27 part-time (18 women); includes 27 minority (1 Black or African American, non-Hispanic/Latino; 3 Asian, non-Hispanic/Latino; 22 Hispanic/Latino; 1 Two or more races, non-Hispanic/Latino). Average age 33. *Degree requirements:* For master's, thesis or alternative, project or culminating exam. *Entrance requirements:* For master's, 3 letters of recommendation, minimum GPA of 2.67, interview. *Application deadline:* Applications are processed on a rolling basis. Application fee: $55. *Expenses:* Tuition, state resident: full-time $7176; part-time $4164 per year. *Unit head:* Dr. Callie Lewis-Chiu, Director, 661-654-3055, Fax: 661-654-2479, E-mail: clewis19@csub.edu. *Application contact:* Julia Bavier, Admissions and Graduation Advisor, 661-654-3193, Fax: 661-654-2479, E-mail: jbavier@csub.edu. Website: https://www.csub.edu/specialed/index.html

California State University, Chico, Office of Graduate Studies, College of Communication and Education, School of Education, Chico, CA 95929-0722. Offers curriculum and instruction (MA); teaching English learners and special education advising patterns (MA), including special education, teaching English learners. *Program availability:* Part-time. *Degree requirements:* For master's, thesis or project and comprehensive exam. *Entrance requirements:* For master's, writing assessment, two letters of recommendation, statement of purpose. Additional exam requirements/recommendations for international students: Required—TOEFL (minimum score 550 paper-based; 80 iBT), IELTS (minimum score 6.5), PTE (minimum score 59). Electronic applications accepted.

California State University, Dominguez Hills, College of Education, Division of Teacher Education, Program in Special Education, Carson, CA 90747-0001. Offers early childhood special education (MA). *Program availability:* Part-time, evening/weekend. *Degree requirements:* For master's, comprehensive exam, thesis or alternative. *Entrance requirements:* For master's, minimum GPA of 2.75 in last 60 units, 3 letters of recommendation. Additional exam requirements/recommendations for international students: Required—TOEFL.

California State University, East Bay, Office of Graduate Studies, College of Education and Allied Studies, Department of Educational Psychology, Special Education Program, Hayward, CA 94542-3000. Offers mild-moderate disabilities (MS); moderate-severe disabilities (MS). *Accreditation:* NCATE. *Faculty:* 8 full-time (5 women), 21 part-time/adjunct (16 women). *Students:* 23 full-time (18 women), 13 part-time (11 women); includes 9 minority (1 Black or African American, non-Hispanic/Latino; 2 Asian, non-Hispanic/Latino; 5 Hispanic/Latino; 1 Two or more races, non-Hispanic/Latino). Average age 35. 27 applicants, 67% accepted, 18 enrolled. In 2017, 9 master's awarded. *Degree requirements:* For master's, project or thesis. *Entrance requirements:* For master's, GRE or MAT, interview, minimum GPA of 2.5 during previous 2 years of course work. Additional exam requirements/recommendations for international students: Required—TOEFL (minimum score 550 paper-based). *Application deadline:* For fall admission, 6/1 for domestic and international students. Application fee: $55. Electronic applications accepted. *Financial support:* Career-related internships or fieldwork, Federal Work-Study, and institutionally sponsored loans available. Support available to part-time students. Financial award application deadline: 3/2; financial award applicants required to submit FAFSA. *Unit head:* Dr. Jack Davis, Chair, Educational Psychology, 510-885-3052, E-mail: jack.davis@csueastbay.edu. *Application contact:* Prof. Linda Smetana, Graduate Coordinator, 510-885-4489, Fax: 510-885-4642, E-mail: linda.smetana@csueastbay.edu.
Website: http://www20.csueastbay.edu/ceas/departments/epsy/

California State University, Fresno, Division of Research and Graduate Studies, Kremen School of Education and Human Development, Department of Literacy, Early, Bilingual, and Special Education, Fresno, CA 93740-8027. Offers education (MA), including early childhood education, reading/language arts; special education (MA). *Accreditation:* NCATE. *Program availability:* Part-time, evening/weekend. *Degree requirements:* For master's, thesis or alternative. *Entrance requirements:* For master's, GRE General Test, MAT, minimum GPA of 2.75. Additional exam requirements/recommendations for international students: Required—TOEFL. Electronic applications accepted. *Faculty research:* Reading recovery, monitoring/tutoring programs, character and academics, professional ethics, low-performing partnership schools.

California State University, Fullerton, Graduate Studies, College of Education, Department of Special Education, Fullerton, CA 92831-3599. Offers MS. *Accreditation:* NCATE. *Program availability:* Part-time. *Faculty:* 7 full-time (6 women), 3 part-time/adjunct (all women). *Students:* 21 full-time (20 women), 113 part-time (105 women); includes 67 minority (1 Black or African American, non-Hispanic/Latino; 11 Asian, non-Hispanic/Latino; 49 Hispanic/Latino; 6 Two or more races, non-Hispanic/Latino). Average age 33. 69 applicants, 71% accepted, 45 enrolled. *Degree requirements:* For master's, comprehensive exam, project or thesis. *Entrance requirements:* For master's, minimum GPA of 2.75. Application fee: $55. *Financial support:* Career-related internships or fieldwork, Federal Work-Study, institutionally sponsored loans, and scholarships/grants available. Support available to part-time students. Financial award application deadline: 3/1; financial award applicants required to submit FAFSA. *Unit head:* Dr. Melinda Pierson, Chair, 657-278-4711. *Application contact:* Admissions/Applications, 657-278-2371.

California State University, Long Beach, Graduate Studies, College of Education, Department of Advanced Studies in Education and Counseling, Long Beach, CA 90840. Offers counseling (MS), including marriage and family therapy, school counseling, student development in higher education; education (MA, Ed D); educational administration (MA, Ed D); educational psychology (MA); special education (MS). *Program availability:* Part-time, evening/weekend. *Entrance requirements:* For master's, GRE General Test, minimum GPA of 2.75. Electronic applications accepted.

California State University, Los Angeles, Graduate Studies, Charter College of Education, Division of Special Education and Counseling, Los Angeles, CA 90032-8530. Offers counseling (MS), including applied behavior analysis, community college counseling, rehabilitation counseling, school counseling, school psychology; special education (MA, PhD). *Accreditation:* ACA. *Program availability:* Part-time, evening/

Special Education

weekend. *Entrance requirements:* For master's, minimum GPA of 2.75 in last 90 units of course work, teaching certificate. Additional exam requirements/recommendations for international students: Required—TOEFL (minimum score 500 paper-based). Electronic applications accepted.

California State University, Northridge, Graduate Studies, Michael D. Eisner College of Education, Department of Special Education, Northridge, CA 91330. Offers early childhood special education (MA); education of the deaf and hard of hearing (MA); educational therapy (MA); mild/moderate disabilities (MA); moderate/severe disabilities (MA). *Accreditation:* NCATE. *Students:* 33 full-time (31 women), 83 part-time (72 women); includes 51 minority (3 Black or African American, non-Hispanic/Latino; 5 Asian, non-Hispanic/Latino; 40 Hispanic/Latino; 3 Two or more races, non-Hispanic/Latino), 7 international. Average age 35. 73 applicants, 48% accepted, 30 enrolled. In 2017, 103 master's awarded. *Entrance requirements:* For master's, GRE General Test (if cumulative undergraduate GPA less than 3.0). Additional exam requirements/recommendations for international students: Required—TOEFL. *Application deadline:* For fall admission, 11/30 for domestic students. Application fee: $55. *Financial support:* Application deadline: 3/1. *Faculty research:* Teacher training, classroom aide training. *Unit head:* Dr. Kathryn Peckham-Hardin, Chair, 818-677-2596. *Application contact:* Dr. Ellen Schneiderman, Graduate Studies Coordinator, 818-677-2649.
Website: http://www.csun.edu/eisner-education/special-education

California State University, Sacramento, College of Education, Graduate and Professional Studies in Education, Sacramento, CA 95819. Offers behavioral science and gender equity (MA); child development (MA); counseling (MS); curriculum and instruction (MA); education (Ed D), including K-12 and community college; education leadership and policy studies (MA), including higher education, PreK-12; education specialist (Ed S), including school psychology; educational technology (MA); language and literacy (MA); multicultural education (MA); school psychology (MA); special education (MA); workforce development advocacy (MA). *Program availability:* Part-time, evening/weekend, blended/hybrid learning. *Students:* 381 full-time (294 women), 135 part-time (101 women); includes 296 minority (44 Black or African American, non-Hispanic/Latino; 1 American Indian or Alaska Native, non-Hispanic/Latino; 94 Asian, non-Hispanic/Latino; 153 Hispanic/Latino; 4 Native Hawaiian or other Pacific Islander, non-Hispanic/Latino), 3 international. Average age 32. 553 applicants, 53% accepted, 292 enrolled. In 2017, 147 master's, 13 doctorates, 10 other advanced degrees awarded. *Degree requirements:* For master's, thesis or project; writing proficiency exam; for doctorate, thesis/dissertation. *Entrance requirements:* For master's and doctorate, GRE. Additional exam requirements/recommendations for international students: Required—TOEFL (minimum score 550 paper-based; 80 iBT); Recommended—IELTS (minimum score 7), TSE. *Application deadline:* For fall admission, 2/15 for domestic students, 1/15 for international students. Applications are processed on a rolling basis. Application fee: $55. Electronic applications accepted. *Expenses:* Contact institution. *Financial support:* Career-related internships or fieldwork, Federal Work-Study, and scholarships/grants available. Support available to part-time students. Financial award application deadline: 3/1; financial award applicants required to submit FAFSA. *Unit head:* Dr. Elizabeth Liles, Chair, 916-278-5942, E-mail: coe@csus.edu. *Application contact:* Jose Martinez, Graduate Admissions Supervisor, 916-278-7871, E-mail: martinj@skymail.csus.edu.
Website: http://www.csus.edu/coe/academics/graduate/index.html

California State University, San Marcos, College of Education, Health and Human Services, School of Education, San Marcos, CA 92096-0001. Offers education (MA); educational administration (MA); educational leadership (Ed D); literacy education (MA); special education (MA). *Accreditation:* NCATE (one or more programs are accredited). *Program availability:* Part-time, evening/weekend. *Entrance requirements:* For master's, minimum GPA of 3.0, teaching credentials, 1 year of teaching experience. *Application deadline:* For fall admission, 2/1 priority date for domestic students. Applications are processed on a rolling basis. Application fee: $55. *Expenses:* Tuition, state resident: full-time $7176. Tuition, nonresident: full-time $9504. *Financial support:* Applicants required to submit FAFSA. *Faculty research:* Multicultural literature, art as knowledge, poetry and second language acquisition, restructuring K–12 education and improving the training of K–8 science teachers. *Unit head:* Pat Stall, Director, 760-750-4386, E-mail: pstall@csusm.edu.
Website: http://www.csusm.edu/education/

California State University, Stanislaus, College of Education, Kinesiology and Social Work, MA Program in Education, Turlock, CA 95382. Offers curriculum and instruction (MA), including education technology, elementary education, multilingual education, physical education, reading, secondary education, special education; school administration (MA); school counseling (MA). *Program availability:* Part-time, evening/weekend. *Degree requirements:* For master's, comprehensive exam (for some programs), thesis (for some programs). *Entrance requirements:* For master's, MAT, GRE, or CBEST (varies by concentration), 3 letters of recommendation, personal statement. Additional exam requirements/recommendations for international students: Required—TOEFL (minimum score 550 paper-based). Electronic applications accepted. *Faculty research:* Children's perspectives on historical events, method elementary schools dual language education, K-12 reading programs.

California University of Pennsylvania, School of Graduate Studies and Research, College of Education and Human Services, Department of Special Education, California, PA 15419-1394. Offers autism (M Ed); general special education (M Ed). *Accreditation:* NCATE. *Program availability:* Part-time, evening/weekend. *Degree requirements:* For master's, comprehensive exam, thesis optional. *Entrance requirements:* For master's, MAT, PRAXIS. Additional exam requirements/recommendations for international students: Required—TOEFL (minimum score 550 paper-based; 80 iBT). *Application deadline:* For fall admission, 8/1 priority date for domestic and international students; for winter admission, 12/1 priority date for domestic and international students; for spring admission, 5/1 priority date for domestic and international students. Applications are processed on a rolling basis. Application fee: $25. Electronic applications accepted. *Financial support:* Applicants required to submit FAFSA. *Faculty research:* Case-based instruction, electronic performance support tools, students with disabilities, teacher preparation, No Child Left Behind. *Unit head:* James Burton, Interim Associate Dean, 724-938-4142, E-mail: burton@calu.edu. *Application contact:* Suzanne C. Powers, Director of Graduate Admissions and Recruitment, 724-938-4029, Fax: 724-938-5712, E-mail: powers_s@cup.edu.

Cambridge College, School of Education, Boston, MA 02129. Offers autism specialist (M Ed); autism/behavior analyst (M Ed); behavior analyst (Post-Master's Certificate); behavioral management (M Ed); early childhood teacher (M Ed); education specialist in curriculum and instruction (CAGS); educational leadership (Ed D); elementary teacher (M Ed); English as a second language (M Ed, Certificate); general science (M Ed); health education (Post-Master's Certificate); health/family and consumer sciences (M Ed); history (M Ed); individualized (M Ed); information technology literacy (M Ed); instructional technology (M Ed); interdisciplinary studies (M Ed); library teacher (M Ed); literacy education (M Ed); mathematics (M Ed); mathematics specialist (Certificate); middle school mathematics and science (M Ed); school administration (M Ed, CAGS); school guidance counselor (M Ed); school nurse education (M Ed); school social worker (M Ed); school adjustment counselor (M Ed); special education administrator (CAGS); special

education/moderate disabilities (M Ed); teaching skills and methodologies (M Ed). *Program availability:* Part-time, evening/weekend, online learning. *Degree requirements:* For master's, thesis, internship/practicum (licensure program only); for doctorate, thesis/dissertation; for other advanced degree, thesis. *Entrance requirements:* For master's, interview, resume, documentation of licensure, 2 professional references; for doctorate, official transcripts, interview, resume, documentation of licensure (if any), written personal statement/essay, portfolio of scholarly and professional work, qualifying assessment, 2 professional references, health insurance, immunizations form; for other advanced degree, official transcripts, interview, resume, documentation of licensure (if any), written personal statement/essay, 2 professional references, health insurance, immunizations form. Additional exam requirements/recommendations for international students: Required—TOEFL (minimum score 550 paper-based; 79 iBT), Michigan English Language Assessment Battery (minimum score 85); Recommended—IELTS (minimum score 6). Electronic applications accepted. *Expenses:* Contact institution. *Faculty research:* Adult education, accelerated learning, mathematics education, brain compatible learning, special education and law.

Campbellsville University, School of Education, Campbellsville, KY 42718-2799. Offers education (MA); school counseling (MA); school improvement (MA); special education (MASE); special education-teacher leader (MA); teacher leader (MA); teaching (MAT), including middle grades biology, middle grades chemistry, middle grades English. *Accreditation:* NCATE. *Program availability:* Part-time, evening/weekend, 100% online, blended/hybrid learning. *Faculty:* 15 full-time (10 women), 14 part-time/adjunct (9 women). *Students:* 26 full-time (20 women), 155 part-time (122 women); includes 14 minority (13 Black or African American, non-Hispanic/Latino; 1 Hispanic/Latino). Average age 35. 199 applicants, 34% accepted, 57 enrolled. In 2017, 96 master's awarded. *Degree requirements:* For master's, comprehensive exam (for some programs), thesis, research paper. *Entrance requirements:* For master's, GRE or PRAXIS, minimum undergraduate GPA of 2.75, teaching certificate, professional growth plan, letters of recommendation, interview. Additional exam requirements/recommendations for international students: Recommended—TOEFL (minimum score 550 paper-based; 79 iBT), IELTS (minimum score 6). *Application deadline:* Applications are processed on a rolling basis. Application fee: $25. Electronic applications accepted. Application fee is waived when completed online. *Expenses:* $399 per credit hour. *Financial support:* Unspecified assistantships and employee tuition waivers available. Financial award applicants required to submit FAFSA. *Faculty research:* Professional development, curriculum development, school governance, assessment, special education. *Unit head:* Dr. Beverly Ennis, Dean, 270-789-5344, Fax: 270-789-5206, E-mail: bcennis@campbellsville.edu. *Application contact:* Monica Bamwine, Assistant Director of Graduate Admissions, 270-789-5221, Fax: 270-789-5071, E-mail: mkbamwine@campbellsville.edu.

Canisius College, Graduate Division, School of Education and Human Services, Department of Graduate Education and Leadership, Buffalo, NY 14208-1098. Offers business and marketing education (MS Ed); college student personnel (MS Ed); deaf education (MS Ed); deaf/adolescent education, grades 7-12 (MS Ed); deaf/childhood education, grades 1-6 (MS Ed); differentiated instruction (MS Ed); education administration (MS); educational administration (MS Ed); educational technologies (Certificate); gifted education extension (Certificate); literacy (MS Ed); reading (Certificate); school building leadership (MS Ed, Certificate); school district leadership (Certificate); teacher leader (Certificate); TESOL (MS Ed). *Accreditation:* NCATE. *Program availability:* Part-time, evening/weekend, 100% online, blended/hybrid learning. *Faculty:* 5 full-time (all women), 21 part-time/adjunct (16 women). *Students:* 85 full-time (67 women), 189 part-time (151 women); includes 31 minority (18 Black or African American, non-Hispanic/Latino; 3 American Indian or Alaska Native, non-Hispanic/Latino; 3 Asian, non-Hispanic/Latino; 4 Hispanic/Latino; 3 Two or more races, non-Hispanic/Latino), 1 international. Average age 31. 83 applicants, 96% accepted, 74 enrolled. In 2017, 94 master's, 47 other advanced degrees awarded. *Entrance requirements:* For master's, GRE (if cumulative GPA less than 2.7), transcripts, two letters of recommendation. Additional exam requirements/recommendations for international students: Required—TOEFL (minimum score 550 paper-based, 79 iBT), IELTS (minimum score 6.5), or CAEL (minimum score 70). *Application deadline:* Applications are processed on a rolling basis. Application fee: $0. Electronic applications accepted. *Expenses:* Tuition: Full-time $22,860; part-time $820 per credit. *Required fees:* $720; $25 per credit. $65 per semester. One-time fee: $425. *Financial support:* Career-related internships or fieldwork, Federal Work-Study, scholarships/grants, tuition waivers (partial), and unspecified assistantships available. Support available to part-time students. Financial award application deadline: 4/30; financial award applicants required to submit FAFSA. *Faculty research:* Asperger's disease, autism, private higher education, reading strategies. *Unit head:* Dr. Anne Marie Tryjankowski, Chair/Associate Professor of Graduate Education and Leadership, 716-888-3715, Fax: 716-888-3142, E-mail: tryjanka@canisius.edu.

Canisius College, Graduate Division, School of Education and Human Services, Department of Teacher Education, Buffalo, NY 14208-1098. Offers adolescence education (MS Ed); childhood education (MS Ed); general education (MS Ed); special education (MS), including adolescence special education, advanced special education, childhood education grade 1-6, childhood special education. *Program availability:* Part-time, evening/weekend, 100% online, blended/hybrid learning. *Faculty:* 8 full-time (7 women), 9 part-time/adjunct (7 women). *Students:* 52 full-time (44 women), 32 part-time (24 women); includes 8 minority (5 Black or African American, non-Hispanic/Latino; 2 Hispanic/Latino; 2 Two or more races, non-Hispanic/Latino), 1 international. Average age 25. 59 applicants, 97% accepted, 47 enrolled. In 2017, 34 master's awarded. *Degree requirements:* For master's, research project or thesis, project internship. *Entrance requirements:* For master's, GRE (if cumulative GPA less than 2.7), transcripts, letters of recommendation. Additional exam requirements/recommendations for international students: Required—TOEFL (minimum score 550 paper-based, 79 iBT), IELTS (minimum score 6.5), or CAEL (minimum score 70). *Application deadline:* Applications are processed on a rolling basis. Application fee: $0. Electronic applications accepted. *Expenses:* Tuition: Full-time $22,860; part-time $820 per credit. *Required fees:* $720; $25 per credit. $65 per semester. One-time fee: $425. *Financial support:* Career-related internships or fieldwork, Federal Work-Study, scholarships/grants, tuition waivers (partial), and unspecified assistantships available. Support available to part-time students. Financial award application deadline: 4/30; financial award applicants required to submit FAFSA. *Unit head:* Dr. Michele A. Marable, Chair/Professor, 716-888-2317, E-mail: marablem@canisius.edu.
Website: http://www.canisius.edu/academics/graduate/

Capella University, School of Education, Doctoral Programs in Education, Minneapolis, MN 55402. Offers curriculum and instruction (PhD); educational leadership and management (Ed D); instructional design for online learning (PhD); K-12 studies in education (PhD); leadership for higher education (PhD); leadership in educational administration (PhD); postsecondary and adult education (PhD); professional studies in education (PhD); reading and literacy (Ed D); special education leadership (PhD); training and performance improvement (PhD).

Capella University, School of Education, Master's Programs in Education, Minneapolis, MN 55402. Offers adult education (MS); curriculum and instruction (MS); early childhood education (MS); enrollment management (MS); higher education leadership and management (MS); instructional design for online learning (MS); integrative studies (MS); K-12 studies in education (MS); leadership in educational administration (MS); reading and literacy (MS); special education teaching (MS).

Cardinal Stritch University, College of Education and Leadership, Department of Special Education, Milwaukee, WI 53217-3985. Offers special education (PhD); urban special education (MA). *Accreditation:* NCATE. *Program availability:* Part-time, evening/weekend. *Students:* 15 full-time (13 women), 16 part-time (13 women); includes 1 minority (Black or African American, non-Hispanic/Latino). Average age 35. 50 applicants, 100% accepted, 49 enrolled. In 2017, 13 master's awarded. *Degree requirements:* For master's, comprehensive exam, thesis, practica; for doctorate, thesis/dissertation. *Entrance requirements:* For master's, 2 letters of recommendation, minimum GPA of 2.75; for doctorate, 3 letters of recommendation, minimum GPA of 3.5. Additional exam requirements/recommendations for international students: Required—TOEFL (minimum score 550 paper-based; 79 iBT), IELTS (minimum score 6.5). *Application deadline:* For fall admission, 7/15 priority date for domestic students; for spring admission, 12/15 priority date for domestic students. Applications are processed on a rolling basis. Electronic applications accepted. *Expenses:* Tuition varies by program. *Financial support:* Research assistantships with partial tuition reimbursements, Federal Work-Study, and scholarships/grants available. Financial award applicants required to submit FAFSA. *Unit head:* 414-410-4000. *Application contact:* 800-347-8822 Ext. 4042, E-mail: admissions@stritch.edu.

Caribbean University, Graduate School, Bayamón, PR 00960-0493. Offers administration and supervision (MA Ed); criminal justice (MA); curriculum and instruction (MA Ed, PhD), including elementary education (MA Ed), English education (MA Ed), history education (MA Ed), mathematics education (MA Ed), primary education (MA Ed), science education (MA Ed), Spanish education (MA Ed); educational technology in instructional systems (MA Ed); gerontology (MSN); human resources (MBA); museology, archiving and art history (MA Ed); neonatal pediatrics (MSN); physical education (MA Ed); special education (MA Ed). *Entrance requirements:* For master's, interview, minimum GPA of 2.5.

Carlos Albizu University, Miami Campus, Graduate Programs, Miami, FL 33172-2209. Offers clinical psychology (PhD, Psy D); entrepreneurship (MBA); exceptional student education (MS); human services (PhD); industrial/organizational psychology (MS); marriage and family therapy (MS); mental health counseling (MS); nonprofit management (MBA); organizational management (MBA); psychology (MS); speech and language pathology (MS); teaching English for speakers of other languages (MS). *Accreditation:* APA. *Program availability:* Part-time, evening/weekend, 100% online, blended/hybrid learning. *Faculty:* 32 full-time (24 women), 27 part-time/adjunct (15 women). *Students:* 411 full-time (345 women), 248 part-time (215 women); includes 562 minority (53 Black or African American, non-Hispanic/Latino; 4 Asian, non-Hispanic/Latino; 498 Hispanic/Latino; 7 Two or more races, non-Hispanic/Latino), 23 international. Average age 34. 391 applicants, 42% accepted, 154 enrolled. In 2017, 96 master's, 54 doctorates awarded. Terminal master's awarded for partial completion of doctoral program. *Degree requirements:* For master's, comprehensive exam (for some programs), integrative project (for MBA); research project (for exceptional student education, teaching English as a second language); for doctorate, comprehensive examinations, internship, project/dissertation. *Entrance requirements:* For master's, GRE/EXADEP, bachelor's degree from accredited institution, minimum GPA of 3.0, 3 letters of recommendation, interview, resume, statement of purpose, official transcripts; for doctorate, GRE (for Psy D), 3 letters of recommendation, resume, interview, statement of purpose, official transcripts; bachelor's degree and minimum GPA of 3.25 (for Psy D); master's degree and minimum GPA of 3.0 (for PhD). Additional exam requirements/recommendations for international students: Required—Michigan Test of English Language Proficiency. *Application deadline:* For fall admission, 4/1 priority date for domestic students, 5/1 priority date for international students; for spring admission, 11/1 priority date for domestic students, 9/1 priority date for international students. Applications are processed on a rolling basis. Application fee: $50. Electronic applications accepted. Application fee is waived when completed online. *Expenses:* Contact institution. *Financial support:* In 2017–18, 145 students received support. Federal Work-Study, scholarships/grants, unspecified assistantships, and tuition discounts available. Financial award application deadline: 6/1; financial award applicants required to submit FAFSA. *Faculty research:* Psychotherapy, forensic psychology, neuropsychology, special education, speech-language pathology, criminal justice. *Unit head:* Dr. Etiony Aldarondo, Provost, 305-593-1223 Ext. 3138, Fax: 305-592-7930, E-mail: ealdarondo@albizu.edu. *Application contact:* Sonia Feliciano, Institutional Director of Student Recruitment, 305-593-1223 Ext. 3108, Fax: 305-477-8983, E-mail: sfeliciano@albizu.edu.

Carlow University, College of Learning and Innovation, Program in Education, Pittsburgh, PA 15213-3165. Offers early childhood education (M Ed); education (M Ed); online instructional design and technology (Certificate); special education (M Ed), including early childhood. *Program availability:* Part-time, evening/weekend, 100% online, blended/hybrid learning. *Students:* 44 full-time (41 women), 14 part-time (13 women); includes 12 minority (8 Black or African American, non-Hispanic/Latino; 1 Asian, non-Hispanic/Latino; 3 Two or more races, non-Hispanic/Latino). Average age 31. 16 applicants, 100% accepted, 12 enrolled. In 2017, 22 master's, 1 Certificate awarded. *Entrance requirements:* For master's, personal essay; resume or curriculum vitae; two recommendations; official transcripts; interview; minimum undergraduate GPA of 3.0. Additional exam requirements/recommendations for international students: Required—TOEFL (minimum score 550 paper-based). *Application deadline:* Applications are processed on a rolling basis. Electronic applications accepted. *Expenses:* Tuition: Full-time $12,103; part-time $825 per credit hour. Tuition and fees vary according to program. *Financial support:* Application deadline: 4/1; applicants required to submit FAFSA. *Unit head:* Dr. Keeley Baronak, Chair, Department of Education, 412-578-6135, Fax: 412-578-8816, E-mail: kobaronak@carlow.edu. *Application contact:* 412-578-6059, E-mail: gradstudies@carlow.edu.
Website: http://www.carlow.edu/education.aspx

Castleton University, Division of Graduate Studies, Department of Education, Program in Special Education, Castleton, VT 05735. Offers MA Ed, CAGS. *Program availability:* Part-time, evening/weekend. *Degree requirements:* For master's, thesis or alternative; for CAGS, publishable paper. *Entrance requirements:* For master's, GRE General Test, MAT, interview, minimum undergraduate GPA of 3.0; for CAGS, educational research, master's degree, minimum undergraduate GPA of 3.0.

The Catholic University of America, School of Arts and Sciences, Department of Education, Washington, DC 20064. Offers Catholic school leadership (MA); education (Certificate); secondary education (MA); special education (MA), including early childhood, non-categorical. *Accreditation:* NCATE. *Program availability:* Part-time. *Faculty:* 8 full-time (7 women), 3 part-time/adjunct (all women). *Students:* 9 full-time (all women), 25 part-time (14 women); includes 2 minority (both Hispanic/Latino), 4 international. Average age 39. 24 applicants, 63% accepted, 9 enrolled. In 2017, 9 master's awarded. *Degree requirements:* For master's, comprehensive exam, thesis or alternative; for Certificate, action research project. *Entrance requirements:* For master's, GRE General Test or MAT, statement of purpose, official copies of academic transcripts, three letters of recommendation, interview; for Certificate, PRAXIS I, statement of purpose, official copies of academic transcripts, three letters of recommendation, interview. Additional exam requirements/recommendations for international students: Required—TOEFL (minimum score 550 paper-based; 80 iBT). *Application deadline:* For fall admission, 7/15 priority date for domestic students, 7/1 for international students; for spring admission, 11/15 priority date for domestic students, 11/1 for international students. Applications are processed on a rolling basis. Application fee: $55. Electronic applications accepted. *Expenses:* Contact institution. *Financial support:* Fellowships, research assistantships, teaching assistantships, Federal Work-Study, scholarships/grants, tuition waivers (full and partial), and unspecified assistantships available. Financial award application deadline: 2/1; financial award applicants required to submit FAFSA. *Faculty research:* Special education, early childhood education, educational psychology, Catholic school administration, leadership and policy studies, counseling, curriculum and instruction. *Unit head:* Dr. Agnes Cave, Chair, 202-319-5805, Fax: 202-319-5815, E-mail: cave@cua.edu. *Application contact:* Dr. Steven Brown, Director of Graduate Admissions, 202-319-5057, Fax: 202-319-6533, E-mail: cua-admissions@cua.edu.
Website: http://education.cua.edu/

Centenary University, Program in Education, Hackettstown, NJ 07840-2100. Offers education practice (M Ed); educational leadership (MA, Ed D); instructional leadership (MA); reading (M Ed); special education (MA). *Accreditation:* TEAC. *Program availability:* Part-time, evening/weekend, online learning. *Degree requirements:* For master's, thesis. *Entrance requirements:* For master's, interview, minimum undergraduate GPA of 2.8.

Central Connecticut State University, School of Graduate Studies, School of Education and Professional Studies, Department of Special Education and Interventions, New Britain, CT 06050-4010. Offers MS, Certificate. *Program availability:* Part-time, evening/weekend. *Faculty:* 9 full-time (5 women), 11 part-time/adjunct (9 women). *Students:* 69 full-time (51 women), 115 part-time (94 women); includes 33 minority (10 Black or African American, non-Hispanic/Latino; 1 American Indian or Alaska Native, non-Hispanic/Latino; 1 Asian, non-Hispanic/Latino; 14 Hispanic/Latino; 7 Two or more races, non-Hispanic/Latino). Average age 30. 96 applicants, 86% accepted, 58 enrolled. In 2017, 67 master's, 14 other advanced degrees awarded. *Degree requirements:* For master's, thesis or alternative; for Certificate, qualifying exam. *Entrance requirements:* For master's, minimum undergraduate GPA of 2.7, teacher certification. Additional exam requirements/recommendations for international students: Required—TOEFL (minimum score 550 paper-based; 79 iBT); Recommended—IELTS (minimum score 6.5). *Application deadline:* For fall admission, 8/1 for domestic students, 5/1 for international students; for spring admission, 11/1 for domestic and international students. Applications are processed on a rolling basis. Application fee: $50. Electronic applications accepted. *Expenses:* Tuition, area resident: Full-time $6757. Tuition, state resident: full-time $9750; part-time $374 per credit. Tuition, nonresident: full-time $18,102; part-time $374 per credit. *Required fees:* $4635; $255 per credit. *Financial support:* In 2017–18, 17 students received support. Career-related internships or fieldwork, Federal Work-Study, scholarships/grants, and unspecified assistantships available. Support available to part-time students. Financial award application deadline: 3/1; financial award applicants required to submit FAFSA. *Faculty research:* Learning disabilities and language development, consulting teacher practice, occupational and special education, teaching emotionally disturbed students. *Unit head:* Dr. Joan Nicoll-Senft, Chair, 860-832-2400, E-mail: nicoll-senftj@ccsu.edu. *Application contact:* Patricia Gardner, Associate Director of Graduate Studies, 860-832-2350, Fax: 860-832-2362.
Website: http://www.ccsu.edu/sped/

Central Michigan University, College of Graduate Studies, College of Education and Human Services, Department of Counseling and Special Education, Program in Special Education, Mount Pleasant, MI 48859. Offers autism (Graduate Certificate); special education (MA), including the master teacher. *Accreditation:* TEAC. *Program availability:* Part-time. *Degree requirements:* For master's, comprehensive exam (for some programs), thesis or alternative. *Entrance requirements:* For master's, Michigan elementary or secondary provisional, permanent, or life certificate or special education endorsement. Electronic applications accepted. *Faculty research:* Mainstreaming, learning disabled, attention and organization disorders.

Chaminade University of Honolulu, Office of Professional and Continuing Education, Program in Education, Honolulu, HI 96816-1578. Offers child development (M Ed); early childhood education (Montessori) (MAT); early childhood education (PK-3) (MAT); educational leadership (M Ed); elementary education (MAT); instructional leadership (M Ed); Montessori (M Ed); secondary education (MAT); special education (MAT); teacher leader (M Ed). *Program availability:* Part-time, evening/weekend, 100% online, blended/hybrid learning. *Faculty:* 7 full-time (3 women), 8 part-time/adjunct (6 women). *Students:* 86 full-time (68 women), 88 part-time (64 women); includes 113 minority (7 Black or African American, non-Hispanic/Latino; 2 American Indian or Alaska Native, non-Hispanic/Latino; 46 Asian, non-Hispanic/Latino; 7 Hispanic/Latino; 51 Native Hawaiian or other Pacific Islander, non-Hispanic/Latino), 6 international. Average age 34. 61 applicants, 98% accepted, 49 enrolled. In 2017, 91 master's awarded. *Degree requirements:* For master's, thesis or alternative. *Entrance requirements:* For master's, PRAXIS (for MAT), minimum GPA of 2.75 (for M Ed), 3.0 (for MAT); 2 letters of recommendation, resume, writing sample (for MAT). Additional exam requirements/recommendations for international students: Required—TOEFL (minimum score 550 paper-based; 79 iBT). *Application deadline:* Applications are processed on a rolling basis. Application fee: $40. Electronic applications accepted. *Expenses:* $780 per credit hour plus $93 fee per online class. *Financial support:* Applicants required to submit FAFSA. *Unit head:* Dr. Dale Fryxell, Dean, 808-739-4652, Fax: 808-739-4607, E-mail: edu-office@chaminade.edu. *Application contact:* 808-735-4755, E-mail: gradserv@chaminade.edu.
Website: https://education.chaminade.edu/

Chapman University, Donna Ford Attallah College of Educational Studies, Orange, CA 92866. Offers counseling (MA), including school counseling (MA, Credential); curriculum and instruction (MA), including elementary education, secondary education; education (PhD), including cultural and curricular studies, disability studies, leadership studies, school psychology (PhD, Credential); educational psychology (MA); leadership development (MA); multiple subjects (Credential), including Spanish/English bilingual; pupil personnel services (Credential), including school counseling (MA, Credential), school psychology (PhD, Credential); school psychology (Ed S); single subject (Credential); special education (MA, Credential), including mild/moderate (Credential), moderate/severe (Credential); teaching (MA), including elementary education, secondary education, secondary music education. *Accreditation:* TEAC. *Program availability:* Part-time, evening/weekend. *Faculty:* 32 full-time (18 women), 37 part-time/adjunct (26 women). *Students:* 170 full-time (140 women), 180 part-time (129 women); includes 164 minority (6 Black or African American, non-Hispanic/Latino; 38 Asian, non-Hispanic/Latino; 101 Hispanic/Latino; 1 Native Hawaiian or other Pacific Islander, non-Hispanic/Latino; 18 Two or more races, non-Hispanic/Latino), 10 international. Average age 28. 143 applicants, 63% accepted, 64 enrolled. In 2017, 126 master's, 18 doctorates awarded. *Application deadline:* Applications are processed on a rolling basis. Application fee: $60. Electronic applications accepted. *Expenses:* Contact institution.

Special Education

Financial support: Fellowships and scholarships/grants available. Financial award application deadline: 3/2; financial award applicants required to submit FAFSA. *Unit head:* Dr. Margaret Grogan, Dean, 714-516-5968, E-mail: grogan@chapman.edu. *Application contact:* Shannon McCance, Graduate Admission Counselor, 714-516-5236, E-mail: smccance@chapman.edu.
Website: http://www.chapman.edu/CES/

Chatham University, Program in Education, Pittsburgh, PA 15232-2826. Offers early childhood education (MAT); elementary education (MAT); environmental education (K-12) (MAT); secondary art (MAT); secondary biology education (MAT); secondary chemistry education (MAT); secondary English education (MAT); secondary math education (MAT); secondary physics education (MAT); secondary social studies education (MAT); special education (MAT). *Faculty:* 1 (woman) full-time, 15 part-time/adjunct (13 women). *Students:* 31 full-time (23 women), 3 part-time (1 woman); includes 9 minority (8 Black or African American, non-Hispanic/Latino; 1 Hispanic/Latino). Average age 30. 25 applicants, 60% accepted, 9 enrolled. In 2017, 23 master's awarded. *Degree requirements:* For master's, thesis, teaching experience. *Entrance requirements:* For master's, minimum GPA of 3.0, sample of written work, recommendation letters. Additional exam requirements/recommendations for international students: Required—TOEFL (minimum score 600 paper-based; 100 iBT), IELTS (minimum score 7), TWE. *Application deadline:* For fall admission, 4/1 priority date for domestic and international students; for spring admission, 11/1 priority date for domestic students, 10/1 priority date for international students. Applications are processed on a rolling basis. Application fee: $45. Electronic applications accepted. Application fee is waived when completed online. *Expenses: Tuition:* Full-time $16,740; part-time $930 per credit. *Required fees:* $486; $27 per credit. $243 per semester. *Financial support:* Career-related internships or fieldwork available. Financial award applicants required to submit FAFSA. *Faculty research:* Gifted education, environmental education, technology in education, writing as learning, class size and achievement. *Application contact:* Katie Noel, Assistant Director of Graduate Admission, 412-365-2758, Fax: 412-365-1609, E-mail: gradadmission@chatham.edu.
Website: http://www.chatham.edu/mat

Chestnut Hill College, School of Graduate Studies, Department of Education, Program in Early Education, Philadelphia, PA 19118-2693. Offers early education (M Ed), including Montessori certificate preparation, preK-4 education, preK-4 education and special education preK-8. *Program availability:* Part-time, evening/weekend. *Degree requirements:* For master's, thesis optional. *Entrance requirements:* For master's, PRAXIS I or proof of teaching certification, writing sample, letters of recommendation, 6 graduate credits with minimum B grade or minimum undergraduate GPA of 3.0. Additional exam requirements/recommendations for international students: Required—TOEFL (minimum score 500 paper-based), IELTS (minimum score 6.0), or TWE (minimum score 22). Electronic applications accepted. *Expenses:* Contact institution. *Faculty research:* Gender issues, early childhood education standardized testing.

Chestnut Hill College, School of Graduate Studies, Department of Education, Program in Reading, Philadelphia, PA 19118-2693. Offers reading specialist (M Ed), including K-12, special education 7-12, special education PreK-8. *Program availability:* Part-time, evening/weekend. *Degree requirements:* For master's, thesis optional. *Entrance requirements:* Additional exam requirements/recommendations for international students: Required—TOEFL (minimum score 500 paper-based) or IELTS (minimum score 6). Electronic applications accepted. *Expenses:* Contact institution. *Faculty research:* Inclusive education, cultural issues in education.

Chestnut Hill College, School of Graduate Studies, Department of Education, Program in Special Education, Philadelphia, PA 19118-2693. Offers special education (M Ed), including 7-12, PreK-8. *Program availability:* Part-time, evening/weekend. *Degree requirements:* For master's, thesis optional. *Entrance requirements:* For master's, PRAXIS I or proof of teaching certification, letters of recommendation, writing sample, 6 graduate credits with minimum B grade if undergraduate GPA less than 3.0. Additional exam requirements/recommendations for international students: Required—TOEFL (minimum score 500 paper-based), IELTS (minimum score 6), or TWE (minimum score 22). Electronic applications accepted. *Expenses:* Contact institution. *Faculty research:* Inclusive education, cultural issues in education.

Chestnut Hill College, School of Graduate Studies, Division of Psychology, Program in Clinical and Counseling Psychology, Philadelphia, PA 19118-2693. Offers clinical and counseling psychology (MS, CAS), including child and adolescent therapy, child and adolescent therapy with autism spectrum disorders, co-occurring disorders, couple and family therapy, diverse and underserved communities, generalist (MS), trauma studies. *Program availability:* Part-time, evening/weekend. *Degree requirements:* For master's, thesis optional, practica. *Entrance requirements:* For master's, GRE General Test, writing sample, letters of recommendation. Additional exam requirements/recommendations for international students: Required—TOEFL (minimum score 500 paper-based), IELTS (minimum score 6.0), or TWE (minimum score 22). Electronic applications accepted. *Expenses:* Contact institution. *Faculty research:* Play therapy, eating disorders, addictions, group psychology and group therapy, health psychology.

Cheyney University of Pennsylvania, Graduate Programs, Program in Special Education, Cheyney, PA 19319. Offers M Ed. *Program availability:* Part-time, evening/weekend. *Degree requirements:* For master's, thesis. *Entrance requirements:* For master's, GRE General Test, MAT, minimum GPA of 2.75. Electronic applications accepted.

Chicago State University, School of Graduate and Professional Studies, College of Education, Department of Special Education, Early Childhood Education and Bilingual Education, Program in Special Education, Chicago, IL 60628. Offers MS Ed. *Accreditation:* NCATE. *Entrance requirements:* For master's, minimum GPA of 2.75. *Application deadline:* For fall admission, 7/1 for domestic students; for spring admission, 11/10 for domestic students. Application fee: $25. *Faculty research:* Assistive technology, teacher efficiency. *Unit head:* Dr. Florah Luseno, Chairperson, 773-995-2086, E-mail: fluseno@csu.edu. *Application contact:* Daphne G. Townsend, Admissions and Records Officer II, 773-995-2404, Fax: 773-995-3671, E-mail: g-studies1@csu.edu.

City College of the City University of New York, Graduate School, School of Education, Department of Leadership and Special Education, New York, NY 10031-9198. Offers educational leadership (MS, AC); teacher of students with disabilities in adolescent education (MS Ed); teacher of students with disabilities in childhood education (MS Ed). *Degree requirements:* For master's, thesis, research paper. *Entrance requirements:* For master's, Liberal Arts and Sciences Test (LAST), Content Specialty Test (CST), interview; minimum GPA of 3.0 in major, 2.5 overall. Additional exam requirements/recommendations for international students: Required—TOEFL. *Faculty research:* Dynamics of organizational change, impact of laws on educational policy, leadership development in schools.

City University of Seattle, Graduate Division, Albright School of Education, Seattle, WA 98121. Offers administrator certification (Certificate); curriculum and instruction (M Ed); elementary education (MIT); guidance and counseling (M Ed); leadership (M Ed); reading and literacy (M Ed); school counseling (M Ed); special education (MIT); superintendent certification (Certificate). *Program availability:* Part-time, evening/weekend, online learning. *Degree requirements:* For master's, comprehensive exam (for

some programs), thesis (for some programs). *Entrance requirements:* For master's, baccalaureate degree or equivalent from an accredited or otherwise recognized institution. Additional exam requirements/recommendations for international students: Required—TOEFL (minimum score 567 paper-based; 87 iBT); Recommended—IELTS. Electronic applications accepted. *Expenses:* Contact institution.

Claremont Graduate University, Graduate Programs, School of Educational Studies, Claremont, CA 91711-6160. Offers Africana education (Certificate); education and policy (MA, PhD); higher education/student affairs (MA, PhD); human development (MA, PhD); public school administration (MA, PhD); quantitative evaluation (MA, PhD); special education (MA, PhD); teacher education (MA); teaching and learning (MA, PhD); urban leadership (PhD); MBA/PhD. PhD program offered jointly with San Diego State University. *Program availability:* Part-time. Terminal master's awarded for partial completion of doctoral program. *Entrance requirements:* For master's and doctorate, GRE General Test. Additional exam requirements/recommendations for international students: Required—TOEFL (minimum score 75 iBT). Electronic applications accepted. *Faculty research:* Education administration, K-12 and higher education, multicultural education, education policy, diversity in higher education, faculty issues.

Clarion University of Pennsylvania, College of Arts, Education and Sciences, Master of Education Program, Clarion, PA 16214. Offers curriculum and instruction (M Ed); early childhood (M Ed); math education (M Ed); reading (M Ed); science education (M Ed); special education (M Ed); technology (M Ed). *Accreditation:* NCATE. *Program availability:* Part-time, evening/weekend, online only, 100% online, blended/hybrid learning. *Faculty:* 6 full-time (3 women). *Students:* 11 full-time (all women), 101 part-time (82 women); includes 4 minority (2 Black or African American, non-Hispanic/Latino; 1 Hispanic/Latino; 1 Two or more races, non-Hispanic/Latino). Average age 30. 80 applicants, 98% accepted, 33 enrolled. In 2017, 52 master's awarded. *Degree requirements:* For master's, comprehensive exam, thesis, or portfolio. *Entrance requirements:* For master's, minimum QPA of 3.0. Additional exam requirements/recommendations for international students: Required—TOEFL (minimum score 550 paper-based; 80 iBT) or IELTS (7). *Application deadline:* For fall admission, 8/15 priority date for domestic students, 7/15 priority date for international students; for winter admission, 11/1 priority date for domestic students; for spring admission, 1/7 priority date for domestic students, 11/15 priority date for international students; for summer admission, 4/1 priority date for domestic students. Applications are processed on a rolling basis. Application fee: $40. Electronic applications accepted. *Expenses:* $655.05 per credit. *Financial support:* Career-related internships or fieldwork and scholarships/grants available. Support available to part-time students. Financial award application deadline: 3/1; financial award applicants required to submit FAFSA. *Unit head:* Dr. John McCullough, Chair, Department of Education, 814-393-2404, Fax: 814-393-2446, E-mail: gradstudies@clarion.edu. *Application contact:* Dana Bearer, Associate Director for Transfer, Adult, and Graduate Programs, 814-393-2337, Fax: 814-393-2722, E-mail: gradstudies@clarion.edu.

Clarion University of Pennsylvania, College of Arts, Education and Sciences, Master's Program in Special Education, Clarion, PA 16214. Offers MS. *Accreditation:* NCATE. *Program availability:* Part-time. *Faculty:* 6 full-time (5 women), 3 part-time/adjunct (all women). *Students:* 11 full-time (all women), 3 part-time (all women). Average age 25. 14 applicants, 79% accepted, 5 enrolled. In 2017, 8 master's awarded. *Degree requirements:* For master's, thesis or alternative. *Entrance requirements:* For master's, minimum QPA of 3.0. Additional exam requirements/recommendations for international students: Required—TOEFL (minimum score 550 paper-based, 80 iBT) or IELTS (7). *Application deadline:* For fall admission, 8/15 priority date for domestic students, 7/15 priority date for international students; for winter admission, 11/1 priority date for domestic students; for spring admission, 1/7 priority date for domestic students, 11/15 priority date for international students; for summer admission, 4/1 priority date for domestic students. Applications are processed on a rolling basis. Application fee: $40. Electronic applications accepted. *Expenses:* $655.05 per credit. *Financial support:* Career-related internships or fieldwork, scholarships/grants, and health care benefits available. Support available to part-time students. Financial award application deadline: 3/1; financial award applicants required to submit FAFSA. *Unit head:* Dr. Rick Sabousky, Chair, 814-393-2294, Fax: 814-393-1951, E-mail: sabousky@clarion.edu. *Application contact:* Dana Bearer, Associate Director Transfer, Adult and Graduate Admissions, 814-393-2337, E-mail: gradstudies@clarion.edu.

Clark Atlanta University, School of Education, Department of Curriculum and Instruction, Atlanta, GA 30314. Offers special education general curriculum (MA); teaching math and science (MAT). *Program availability:* Part-time. *Faculty:* 5 full-time (4 women), 6 part-time/adjunct (2 women). *Students:* 8 full-time (2 women), 4 part-time (1 woman); includes 6 minority (all Black or African American, non-Hispanic/Latino), 5 international. Average age 34. 10 applicants, 90% accepted, 3 enrolled. In 2017, 1 master's awarded. *Degree requirements:* For master's, one foreign language, comprehensive exam. *Entrance requirements:* For master's, GRE General Test, minimum undergraduate GPA of 2.6. Additional exam requirements/recommendations for international students: Required—TOEFL (minimum score 500 paper-based; 61 iBT). *Application deadline:* For fall admission, 4/1 for domestic and international students; for spring admission, 11/1 for domestic and international students. Applications are processed on a rolling basis. Application fee: $40 ($55 for international students). *Financial support:* Career-related internships or fieldwork, Federal Work-Study, scholarships/grants, and unspecified assistantships available. Support available to part-time students. Financial award application deadline: 4/30; financial award applicants required to submit FAFSA. *Unit head:* Dr. James Young, Chairperson, 404-880-6079, E-mail: jyoung@cau.edu.
Website: http://www.cau.edu/school-of-education/Dept-of-Curriculum-and-Instruction/index.html

Clemson University, Graduate School, College of Education, Department of Education and Human Development, Clemson, SC 29634. Offers counselor education (M Ed, Ed S), including mental health counseling, school counseling, student affairs (M Ed); learning sciences (PhD); literacy (M Ed); literacy, language and culture (PhD); special education (M Ed, MAT, PhD). *Program availability:* Part-time, evening/weekend, 100% online. *Faculty:* 32 full-time (22 women). *Students:* 445 full-time (355 women), 169 part-time (159 women); includes 126 minority (52 Black or African American, non-Hispanic/Latino; 16 Asian, non-Hispanic/Latino; 34 Hispanic/Latino; 24 Two or more races, non-Hispanic/Latino), 5 international. Average age 28. 401 applicants, 60% accepted, 135 enrolled. In 2017, 212 master's, 1 doctorate, 117 other advanced degrees awarded. *Degree requirements:* For master's, thesis (for some programs); for doctorate, comprehensive exam (for some programs), thesis/dissertation. *Entrance requirements:* For master's and doctorate, GRE General Test, unofficial transcripts, letters of recommendation. Additional exam requirements/recommendations for international students: Required—TOEFL (minimum score 80 iBT), IELTS (minimum score 7), PTE (minimum score 54). *Application deadline:* For fall admission, 3/1 priority date for domestic and international students; for spring admission, 10/1 priority date for domestic and international students. Applications are processed on a rolling basis. Application fee: $80 ($90 for international students). Electronic applications accepted. *Expenses:* $5,174 per semester full-time resident, $9,714 per semester full-time non-resident, $511 per credit hour part-time resident, $1,017 per credit hour part-time non-resident; $741

per credit hour online; other fees may apply per session. *Financial support:* In 2017–18, 84 students received support, including 9 fellowships with partial tuition reimbursements available (averaging $8,148 per year), 18 teaching assistantships with partial tuition reimbursements available (averaging $13,707 per year); career-related internships or fieldwork and unspecified assistantships also available. Financial award application deadline: 3/1. *Total annual research expenditures:* $1.2 million. *Unit head:* Dr. Debi Switzer, Department Chair, 864-656-5098, E-mail: debi@clemson.edu. *Application contact:* Julie Jones, Student Services Program Coordinator, 864-656-5096, E-mail: jgambre@clemson.edu.
Website: http://www.clemson.edu/education/departments/education-human-development/index.html

Cleveland State University, College of Graduate Studies, College of Education and Human Services, Department of Teacher Education, Cleveland, OH 44115. Offers art education (M Ed); early childhood education (M Ed); foreign language education (M Ed); middle childhood mathematics and science education (M Ed); special education (M Ed), including mild/moderate disabilities, moderate/intensive disabilities; teaching English to speakers of other languages (M Ed). *Program availability:* Part-time, evening/weekend. *Faculty:* 19 full-time (14 women), 32 part-time/adjunct (27 women). *Students:* 80 full-time (60 women), 361 part-time (277 women); includes 119 minority (86 Black or African American, non-Hispanic/Latino; 5 Asian, non-Hispanic/Latino; 16 Hispanic/Latino; 12 Two or more races, non-Hispanic/Latino), 20 international. Average age 34. 177 applicants, 55% accepted, 68 enrolled. In 2017, 137 master's awarded. *Degree requirements:* For master's, comprehensive exam (for some programs), thesis or alternative. *Entrance requirements:* For master's, GRE General Test or MAT, minimum GPA of 2.75. Additional exam requirements/recommendations for international students: Required—TOEFL (minimum score 550 paper-based; 78 iBT), IELTS (minimum score 6). *Application deadline:* For fall admission, 7/1 priority date for domestic students, 5/15 for international students; for spring admission, 11/15 for domestic students, 11/1 for international students; for summer admission, 4/1 for domestic students, 3/15 for international students. Applications are processed on a rolling basis. Application fee: $30. *Financial support:* In 2017–18, 13 research assistantships with full tuition reimbursements (averaging $15,845 per year) were awarded; tuition waivers (partial) and unspecified assistantships also available. Financial award application deadline: 2/15; financial award applicants required to submit FAFSA. *Faculty research:* Early childhood education, literacy education, special education: mild/moderate, moderate/intensive, early childhood intervention specialist), teaching English to speakers of other languages (TESOL). *Total annual research expenditures:* $275,907. *Unit head:* Dr. Tachelle Banks, Department Chairperson, 216-687-4600, Fax: 216-687-5379, E-mail: t.i.banks@csuohio.edu. *Application contact:* Rosalyn Adams, Administrative Coordinator, 216-523-7139, Fax: 216-687-5491, E-mail: r.m.adams@csuohio.edu.
Website: http://www.csuohio.edu/cehs/te/te

Coastal Carolina University, Spadoni College of Education, Conway, SC 29528-6054. Offers education (MAT); educational leadership (M Ed, Ed S); English for speakers of other languages (Certificate); instructional technology (M Ed, Ed S); language, literacy and culture (M Ed); learning and teaching (M Ed); online teaching and training (Certificate); special education (M Ed). *Accreditation:* NCATE. *Program availability:* Part-time, evening/weekend, 100% online, blended/hybrid learning. *Faculty:* 16 full-time (9 women), 22 part-time/adjunct (15 women). *Students:* 43 full-time (22 women), 345 part-time (290 women); includes 70 minority (51 Black or African American, non-Hispanic/Latino; 3 American Indian or Alaska Native, non-Hispanic/Latino; 3 Asian, non-Hispanic/Latino; 8 Hispanic/Latino; 1 Native Hawaiian or other Pacific Islander, non-Hispanic/Latino; 4 Two or more races, non-Hispanic/Latino). Average age 33. 288 applicants, 77% accepted, 157 enrolled. In 2017, 151 master's, 28 other advanced degrees awarded. *Degree requirements:* For master's and other advanced degree, comprehensive exam. *Entrance requirements:* For master's, GRE, GMAT, 2 letters of recommendation, evidence of teacher certification, official transcripts; for other advanced degree, official transcripts, 3 letters of reference, master's degree in related field with minimum overall cumulative GPA of 3.0. Additional exam requirements/recommendations for international students: Required—TOEFL (minimum score 550 paper-based; 79 iBT), IELTS (minimum score 6.5). *Application deadline:* For fall admission, 5/1 priority date for domestic and international students; for spring admission, 11/1 priority date for domestic and international students; for summer admission, 3/1 priority date for domestic and international students. Applications are processed on a rolling basis. Application fee: $45. Electronic applications accepted. *Expenses:* Tuition, state resident: full-time $5184; part-time $576 per credit hour. Tuition, nonresident: full-time $9369; part-time $1041 per credit hour. *Required fees:* $90; $5 per credit hour. *Financial support:* Fellowships, research assistantships, teaching assistantships, and tuition waivers available. Financial award application deadline: 3/1; financial award applicants required to submit FAFSA. *Unit head:* Dr. Edward Jadallah, Dean/Vice President for Online Education and Teaching Excellence, 843-349-2773, Fax: 843-349-2106, E-mail: ejadalla@coastal.edu. *Application contact:* Dr. James O. Luken, Associate Provost for Graduate Program/Vice-Dean of the Coastal Environment, 843-349-2235, Fax: 843-349-6444, E-mail: joluken@coastal.edu.
Website: https://www.coastal.edu/education/

College of Charleston, Graduate School, School of Education, Health, and Human Performance, Department of Foundations, Secondary, and Special Education, Program in Special Education, Charleston, SC 29424-0001. Offers MAT. *Program availability:* Part-time, evening/weekend. *Entrance requirements:* For master's, GRE, minimum GPA of 2.5, 2 letters of recommendation. Additional exam requirements/recommendations for international students: Required—TOEFL (minimum score 81 iBT). Electronic applications accepted.

The College of New Jersey, Office of Graduate and Advancing Education, School of Education, Department of Special Education, Language and Literacy, Program in Special Education, Ewing, NJ 08628. Offers M Ed, MAT. *Accreditation:* NCATE. *Program availability:* Part-time. *Degree requirements:* For master's, comprehensive exam. *Entrance requirements:* For master's, GRE General Test, minimum GPA of 3.0 in field or 2.75 overall. Additional exam requirements/recommendations for international students: Required—TOEFL. Electronic applications accepted.

The College of New Jersey, Office of Graduate and Advancing Education, School of Education, Department of Special Education, Language and Literacy, Program in Special Education with Learning Disabilities, Ewing, NJ 08628. Offers Certificate. *Accreditation:* NCATE. *Program availability:* Part-time. *Entrance requirements:* Additional exam requirements/recommendations for international students: Required—TOEFL. Electronic applications accepted.

The College of New Rochelle, Graduate School, Division of Education, Program in Special Education, New Rochelle, NY 10805-2308. Offers MS Ed. *Program availability:* Part-time. *Degree requirements:* For master's, practicum. *Entrance requirements:* For master's, interview, minimum GPA of 3.0 in field, 2.7 overall. *Expenses:* Tuition: Full-time $17,406. *Required fees:* $1120.

College of Saint Elizabeth, Program in Education, Morristown, NJ 07960-6989. Offers assistive technology (Certificate); education (MA); ESL (Certificate); Holocaust/genocide education (Certificate); middle school science (Certificate); online teaching in the 21st century (Certificate); teaching (Certificate), including K-12, K-6, teacher of students with

disabilities. *Program availability:* Part-time. *Faculty:* 3 full-time (2 women), 8 part-time/adjunct (6 women). *Students:* 1 (woman) full-time, 34 part-time (29 women); includes 1 minority (Hispanic/Latino). Average age 32. 25 applicants, 100% accepted, 24 enrolled. In 2017, 23 master's awarded. *Degree requirements:* For master's and Certificate, thesis. *Entrance requirements:* For master's, certification. Additional exam requirements/recommendations for international students: Required—TOEFL (minimum score 550 paper-based; 79 iBT), IELTS (minimum score 6.5). *Application deadline:* For fall admission, 5/1 for international students. Applications are processed on a rolling basis. Application fee: $35. Electronic applications accepted. Application fee is waived when completed online. *Financial support:* Career-related internships or fieldwork, scholarships/grants, and unspecified assistantships available. Financial award applicants required to submit FAFSA. *Unit head:* Dr. Joseph Ciccone, 973-290-4383, Fax: 973-290-4389, E-mail: jciccone@cse.edu. *Application contact:* Lori J. Fragoso, Director of Graduate and Continuing Studies Admissions, 973-290-4413, Fax: 973-290-4710, E-mail: apply@cse.edu.
Website: http://www.cse.edu/academics/prof-studies/education/

College of St. Joseph, Graduate Programs, Division of Education, Program in Special Education, Rutland, VT 05701-3899. Offers M Ed. *Program availability:* Part-time, evening/weekend. *Degree requirements:* For master's, comprehensive exam. *Entrance requirements:* For master's, PRAXIS I (for initial licensure), official college transcripts; 2 letters of reference; minimum GPA of 3.0 (initial licensure) or 2.7 (nonlicensure); interview. Additional exam requirements/recommendations for international students: Required—TOEFL (minimum score 550 paper-based). Electronic applications accepted. *Faculty research:* Co-teaching, Response to Intervention (RTI).

The College of Saint Rose, Graduate Studies, Thelma P. Lally School of Education, Programs in Special Education, Albany, NY 12203-1419. Offers adolescence education/special education (MS Ed); childhood education/special education (MS Ed); childhood special education (MS Ed); early childhood special education (MS Ed); special education (Certificate); special education professional (MS Ed). *Accreditation:* NCATE. *Students:* 8 full-time (5 women), 13 part-time (11 women), 1 international. Average age 27. 11 applicants, 82% accepted, 5 enrolled. In 2017, 15 master's awarded. *Degree requirements:* For master's, comprehensive exam (for some programs), thesis or alternative, research project. *Entrance requirements:* For master's, minimum undergraduate GPA of 3.0. Additional exam requirements/recommendations for international students: Required—TOEFL (minimum score 550 paper-based; 80 iBT), IELTS (minimum score 6), PTE (minimum score 56). *Application deadline:* For fall admission, 4/1 priority date for domestic and international students; for spring admission, 10/15 priority date for domestic and international students; for summer admission, 3/15 priority date for domestic and international students. Applications are processed on a rolling basis. Application fee: $40. Electronic applications accepted. *Expenses:* Tuition: Full-time $7191; part-time $799 per credit hour. *Required fees:* $924; $462 per credit hour. Tuition and fees vary according to course load. *Financial support:* Career-related internships or fieldwork, scholarships/grants, tuition waivers (partial), and unspecified assistantships available. Support available to part-time students. Financial award application deadline: 4/15. *Unit head:* Dr. Francis Ihle, Chair, 518-337-4885, E-mail: ihlef@strose.edu. *Application contact:* Cris Murray, Assistant Vice President for Graduate Recruitment and Enrollment, 518-485-3390, E-mail: grad@strose.edu.
Website: https://www.strose.edu/special-education/

The College of Saint Rose, Graduate Studies, Thelma P. Lally School of Education, Teacher Education Programs, Albany, NY 12203-1419. Offers adolescence education (MS Ed, Advanced Certificate); adolescence education/special education (Advanced Certificate); childhood education (MS Ed); curriculum and instruction (MS Ed); early childhood education (MS Ed). *Students:* 69 full-time (60 women), 21 part-time (16 women); includes 7 minority (4 Black or African American, non-Hispanic/Latino; 2 Hispanic/Latino; 1 Two or more races, non-Hispanic/Latino), 1 international. Average age 27. 46 applicants, 52% accepted, 23 enrolled. In 2017, 43 master's awarded. *Entrance requirements:* For master's, minimum undergraduate GPA of 3.0. Additional exam requirements/recommendations for international students: Required—TOEFL (minimum score 550 paper-based; 80 iBT), IELTS (minimum score 6), PTE (minimum score 56). *Application deadline:* For fall admission, 4/1 priority date for domestic and international students; for spring admission, 10/15 priority date for domestic and international students; for summer admission, 3/15 priority date for domestic and international students. Applications are processed on a rolling basis. Application fee: $40. Electronic applications accepted. *Expenses:* Tuition: Full-time $7191; part-time $799 per credit hour. *Required fees:* $924; $462 per credit hour. Tuition and fees vary according to course load. *Financial support:* Career-related internships or fieldwork, scholarships/grants, tuition waivers (partial), and unspecified assistantships available. Support available to part-time students. Financial award application deadline: 4/15. *Unit head:* Dr. Drey Martone, Chair, 518-454-5262, E-mail: martoned@strose.edu. *Application contact:* Cris Murray, Assistant Vice President for Graduate Recruitment and Enrollment, 518-485-3390, Fax: 518-458-5479, E-mail: grad@strose.edu.
Website: https://www.strose.edu/academics/schools/school-of-education/

College of Staten Island of the City University of New York, Graduate Programs, Division of Humanities and Social Sciences, Program in Autism Spectrum Disorders, Staten Island, NY 10314-6600. Offers Advanced Certificate. *Program availability:* Part-time, evening/weekend. *Faculty:* 2 part-time/adjunct (0 women). *Students:* 5. 7 applicants, 71% accepted, 2 enrolled. In 2017, 3 Advanced Certificates awarded. *Degree requirements:* For Advanced Certificate, 12 credits. *Entrance requirements:* For degree, bachelor's degree with minimum GPA of 3.0 in psychology/education/speech-language pathology/science/letters/society or a related field or enrolled in graduate program; 2 letters of recommendation; résumé. Additional exam requirements/recommendations for international students: Required—TOEFL (minimum score 550 paper-based; 79 iBT), IELTS (minimum score 6.5). *Application deadline:* For fall admission, 5/16 priority date for domestic and international students; for spring admission, 11/25 priority date for domestic and international students. Applications are processed on a rolling basis. Application fee: $125. Electronic applications accepted. *Expenses:* Tuition, state resident: full-time $10,450; part-time $440 per credit. Tuition, nonresident: full-time $19,320; part-time $440 per credit. *Required fees:* $181.10 per semester. Tuition and fees vary according to program. *Faculty research:* Autism spectrum disorder, nonverbal communication, applied behavior analysis, computer-mediated interventions. *Unit head:* Dr. Kristen Gillespie-Lynch, Graduate Program Coordinator, 718-982-4121, Fax: 718-982-4114, E-mail: kristen.gillespie@csi.cuny.edu. *Application contact:* Sasha Spence, Associate Director for Graduate Admissions, 718-982-2019, Fax: 718-982-2500, E-mail: sasha.spence@csi.cuny.edu.
Website: http://www.csi.cuny.edu/catalog/graduate/autism-spectrum-disorders-advanced-certificate.htm

College of Staten Island of the City University of New York, Graduate Programs, School of Education, Program in Special Education, Staten Island, NY 10314-6600. Offers special education (MS Ed), including adolescence generalist: grades 7-12, grades 1-6. *Program availability:* Part-time, evening/weekend. *Faculty:* 3 full-time, 8 part-time/adjunct. *Students:* 144. 73 applicants, 73% accepted, 41 enrolled. In 2017, 39 master's awarded. *Degree requirements:* For master's, comprehensive exam, fieldwork; ten three-credit required courses and one elective for a total of 11 courses (33 credits) or

Special Education

14 three-credit required courses and a three- to six-credit, field-based requirement for a total of 45-48 credits; research project. *Entrance requirements:* For master's, GRE General Test or an approved equivalent examination, BA/BS or 36 approved credits with minimum GPA of 3.0, 2 letters of recommendations, 1-2 page statement of experience. Additional exam requirements/recommendations for international students: Required—TOEFL (minimum score 550 paper-based; 79 iBT), IELTS (minimum score 6.5). *Application deadline:* For fall admission, 4/25 for domestic and international students; for spring admission, 11/25 for domestic and international students. Applications are processed on a rolling basis. Application fee: $125. Electronic applications accepted. *Expenses:* Tuition, state resident: full-time $10,450; part-time $440 per credit. Tuition, nonresident: full-time $19,320; part-time $440 per credit. *Required fees:* $181.10 per semester. Tuition and fees vary according to program. *Faculty research:* Disabilities studies, social justice, arts-based research on disabilities, assessment of students with disabilities, technological pedagogical and content knowledge (TPACK) in special education teachers, juvenile justice. *Unit head:* Diane Brescia, 718-982-3877, E-mail: diane.brescia@csi.cuny.edu. *Application contact:* Sasha Spence, Associate Director for Graduate Admissions, 718-982-2019, Fax: 718-982-2500, E-mail: sasha.spence@csi.cuny.edu.
Website: https://www.csi.cuny.edu/sites/default/files/pdf/admissions/grad/pdf/Education%20Fact%20Sheet.pdf

The College of William and Mary, School of Education, Program in Curriculum and Instruction, Williamsburg, VA 23187-8795. Offers elementary education (MA Ed); English as a second language/bilingual education (MA Ed); gifted education (MA Ed); literacy leadership (MA Ed); math specialist (MA Ed); secondary education (MA Ed), including English, foreign language, math, science, social studies; special education (MA Ed). *Accreditation:* NCATE. *Program availability:* Part-time. *Faculty:* 23 full-time (16 women), 40 part-time/adjunct (32 women). *Students:* 85 full-time (63 women), 16 part-time (15 women); includes 18 minority (5 Black or African American, non-Hispanic/Latino; 4 Asian, non-Hispanic/Latino; 7 Hispanic/Latino; 2 Two or more races, non-Hispanic/Latino), 1 international. Average age 27. 152 applicants, 83% accepted, 90 enrolled. In 2017, 67 master's awarded. *Degree requirements:* For master's, project. *Entrance requirements:* For master's, GRE, MAT, PRAXIS Core Academic Skills for Educators, minimum GPA of 2.5. Additional exam requirements/recommendations for international students: Required—TOEFL (minimum score 100 iBT), IELTS (minimum score 7). *Application deadline:* For fall admission, 1/15 for domestic and international students; for spring admission, 10/1 for domestic and international students. Application fee: $50. Electronic applications accepted. *Expenses:* $9,630 resident full-time, $535 resident part-time per credit hour; $25,920 nonresident full-time, $1,265 nonresident part-time per credit hour; $5,944 full-time fees. *Financial support:* In 2017-18, 35 students received support, including 7 research assistantships (averaging $6,678 per year); scholarships/grants and unspecified assistantships also available. Financial award application deadline: 1/15; financial award applicants required to submit FAFSA. *Faculty research:* Educational technology, professional development and evaluation, inclusive education, rural education, education policy. *Unit head:* Dr. Jeremy D. Stoddard, Department Chair, 757-221-2348, E-mail: jdstod@wm.edu. *Application contact:* Dorothy Smith Osborne, Assistant Dean for Academic Programs and Student Services, 757-221-2317, E-mail: dsosbo@wm.edu.
Website: http://education.wm.edu

Colorado Christian University, Program in Curriculum and Instruction, Lakewood, CO 80226. Offers corporate education (MACI); early childhood educator (MACI); elementary educator (MACI); instructional technology (MACI); master educator (MACI); online course developer (MACI); online teaching and learning (MACI); special education generalist (MACI). *Program availability:* Part-time, evening/weekend. *Degree requirements:* For master's, thesis optional, practicum. *Entrance requirements:* For master's, interviews, letters of recommendation. Additional exam requirements/recommendations for international students: Required—TOEFL. Electronic applications accepted. *Expenses:* Contact institution.

Colorado Mesa University, Center for Teacher Education, Grand Junction, CO 81501-3122. Offers educational leadership (MAEd); English for speakers of other languages (MAEd); exceptional learner/special education (MAEd); teacher education (Graduate Certificate); teacher leader (MAEd). *Accreditation:* NCATE. *Program availability:* Part-time. *Degree requirements:* For master's, comprehensive exam (for some programs), capstone presentation. *Entrance requirements:* For master's, 3 professional letters of recommendation, Colorado teaching license, minimum baccalaureate GPA of 3.0; for Graduate Certificate, minimum baccalaureate GPA of 3.0. Additional exam requirements/recommendations for international students: Required—TOEFL (minimum score 550 paper-based). Electronic applications accepted. *Expenses:* Contact institution. *Faculty research:* K-8 STEM instruction, special education inclusion, elementary math literacy, secondary literacy, elementary/early childhood education literacy.

Colorado State University–Pueblo, College of Education, Engineering and Professional Studies, Education Program, Pueblo, CO 81001-4901. Offers art education (M Ed); foreign language education (M Ed); health and physical education (M Ed); instructional technology (M Ed); linguistically diverse education (M Ed); music education (M Ed); special education (M Ed). *Accreditation:* TEAC. *Program availability:* Part-time. *Degree requirements:* For master's, portfolio. *Entrance requirements:* For master's, 3 recommendations, teaching license. Additional exam requirements/recommendations for international students: Required—TOEFL (minimum score 500 paper-based). Electronic applications accepted. *Faculty research:* Portfolio assessment, math education, science education.

Columbus State University, Graduate Studies, College of Education and Health Professions, Department of Teacher Education, Columbus, GA 31907-5645. Offers curriculum and instruction in accomplished teaching (M Ed); early childhood education (M Ed, MAT, Ed S); middle grades education (M Ed, MAT, Ed S); secondary education (M Ed, MAT, Ed S), including biology (MAT), chemistry (MAT), earth and space science (MAT), English/language arts, general science (M Ed), history (MAT), mathematics, science (Ed S), social science (M Ed, Ed S); special education (M Ed, MAT, Ed S), including general curriculum (M Ed, MAT); teacher leadership (M Ed). *Accreditation:* NCATE. *Program availability:* Part-time, evening/weekend, 100% online, blended/hybrid learning. *Faculty:* 19 full-time (12 women), 24 part-time/adjunct (18 women). *Students:* 99 full-time (76 women), 181 part-time (143 women); includes 109 minority (94 Black or African American, non-Hispanic/Latino; 1 American Indian or Alaska Native, non-Hispanic/Latino; 1 Asian, non-Hispanic/Latino; 6 Hispanic/Latino; 7 Two or more races, non-Hispanic/Latino). Average age 34. 136 applicants, 63% accepted, 56 enrolled. In 2017, 119 master's, 8 other advanced degrees awarded. *Degree requirements:* For Ed S, thesis or alternative. *Entrance requirements:* For master's, GRE General Test, minimum undergraduate GPA of 2.75; for Ed S, GRE General Test, minimum undergraduate GPA of 2.75, graduate 3.0. Additional exam requirements/recommendations for international students: Required—TOEFL (minimum score 550 paper-based; 79 iBT). *Application deadline:* For fall admission, 6/30 for domestic students, 5/1 for international students; for spring admission, 11/1 for domestic and international students; for summer admission, 3/1 for domestic and international students. Applications are processed on a rolling basis. Application fee: $50. Electronic

applications accepted. *Expenses:* Tuition, state resident: full-time $3708; part-time $2472 per year. Tuition, nonresident: full-time $14,418; part-time $9612 per year. *International tuition:* $19,218 full-time. *Required fees:* $1605. Tuition and fees vary according to program. *Financial support:* In 2017–18, 45 students received support, including 9 research assistantships with partial tuition reimbursements available (averaging $3,000 per year); career-related internships or fieldwork, Federal Work-Study, institutionally sponsored loans, scholarships/grants, tuition waivers (partial), and unspecified assistantships also available. Support available to part-time students. Financial award application deadline: 5/1; financial award applicants required to submit FAFSA. *Unit head:* Dr. Jan Burcham, Department Chair, 706-507-8519, Fax: 706-568-3134, E-mail: burcham_jan@columbusstate.edu. *Application contact:* Catrina Smith-Edmond, Assistant Director for Graduate and Global Admission, 706-507-8824, Fax: 706-568-5091, E-mail: smithedmond_catrina@columbusstate.edu.
Website: http://te.columbusstate.edu/

Concordia College–New York, Program in Childhood Special Education, Bronxville, NY 10708-1998. Offers MS Ed.

Concordia University, College of Education, Portland, OR 97211-6099. Offers career and technical education (M Ed); curriculum and instruction (M Ed), including adolescent literacy, career and technical education, e-learning/technology education, early childhood education, English for speakers of other languages, English language development, environmental education, mathematics, methods and curriculum, reading, science, teacher leadership, the inclusive classroom; early childhood (MAT); education leadership (Ed D); educational administration (M Ed); elementary education (MAT); secondary education (MAT); special education (M Ed); teacher leadership (Ed D). *Program availability:* Part-time, online learning. *Degree requirements:* For master's, comprehensive exam, work samples/portfolio. *Entrance requirements:* For master's, California Basic Educational Skills Test or PRAXIS I, minimum undergraduate GPA of 2.8, graduate 3.0; 2 letters of recommendation. Additional exam requirements/recommendations for international students: Required—TOEFL (minimum score 525 paper-based). Electronic applications accepted. *Faculty research:* Learner-centered classroom, brain-based learning, future of online learning.

Concordia University, St. Paul, College of Education, St. Paul, MN 55104-5494. Offers classroom instruction (MA Ed), including K-12 reading; differentiated instruction (MA Ed); early childhood education (MA Ed); education (Ed D); educational leadership (MA Ed); educational technology (MA Ed, Certificate); K-12 principal licensure (Ed S); special education (MA Ed), including autism spectrum disorder, emotional and behavioral disorders, learning disabilities; superintendent (Ed S); teaching (MAT). *Accreditation:* NCATE. *Program availability:* Part-time, evening/weekend, 100% online, blended/hybrid learning. *Faculty:* 15 full-time (8 women), 86 part-time/adjunct (56 women). *Students:* 955 full-time (731 women), 42 part-time (28 women); includes 105 minority (35 Black or African American, non-Hispanic/Latino; 5 American Indian or Alaska Native, non-Hispanic/Latino; 31 Asian, non-Hispanic/Latino; 19 Hispanic/Latino; 15 Two or more races, non-Hispanic/Latino), 9 international. Average age 34. 409 applicants, 87% accepted, 347 enrolled. In 2017, 386 master's, 104 other advanced degrees awarded. *Degree requirements:* For master's, thesis (for some programs); for doctorate, thesis/dissertation, capstone projects; for other advanced degree, e-folio review of competencies. *Entrance requirements:* For master's, official transcripts from regionally-accredited institution stating the conferral of a bachelor's degree with minimum cumulative GPA of 3.0; personal statement; professional resume; practitioner in field through work or volunteerism; resume; for doctorate, minimum master's or specialist degree GPA of 3.25; transcript; writing sample; three letters of recommendation; current resume; on-campus interview; for other advanced degree, minimum master's or specialist degree GPA of 3.25; transcript; statement covering employment history and long-term academic and professional goals; two letters of recommendation; interview with program director. Additional exam requirements/recommendations for international students: Recommended—TOEFL (minimum score 547 paper-based; 78 iBT), IELTS (minimum score 6). *Application deadline:* For fall admission, 8/1 for domestic and international students; for spring admission, 12/1 for domestic and international students; for summer admission, 5/1 for domestic and international students. Applications are processed on a rolling basis. Application fee: $0. Electronic applications accepted. *Expenses:* $395 per credit (for MA in education); $440 per credit (for MAT); $615 per credit (for EdD). *Financial support:* In 2017–18, 105 students received support. Scholarships/grants and unspecified assistantships available. Financial award applicants required to submit FAFSA. *Faculty research:* Differentiated instruction in K-12 educational settings; educational leadership; effective online pedagogy in higher education; equine-assisted learning; faculty development in higher education. *Unit head:* Lonn Maly, Dean, 651-641-8203, E-mail: maly@csp.edu. *Application contact:* Amber Faletti, Director of Enrollment Management, 651-641-8838, Fax: 651-603-6320, E-mail: faletti@csp.edu.

Concordia University Wisconsin, Graduate Programs, Department of Education, Mequon, WI 53097-2402. Offers art education (MS Ed); early childhood (MS Ed); educational administration (MS Ed); environmental education (MS Ed); family studies (MS Ed); literacy (MS Ed); school counseling (MS Ed); special education (MS Ed). *Program availability:* Part-time, evening/weekend, online learning. *Degree requirements:* For master's, comprehensive exam, thesis or alternative. *Entrance requirements:* For master's, minimum GPA of 3.0, teaching license. Additional exam requirements/recommendations for international students: Required—TOEFL. *Faculty research:* Motivation, developmental learning, learning styles.

Concord University, Graduate Studies, Athens, WV 24712-1000. Offers educational leadership and supervision (M Ed); health promotion (MA); reading specialist (M Ed); social work (MSW); special education (M Ed); teaching (MAT). *Program availability:* Part-time, evening/weekend, 100% online. *Faculty:* 16 full-time (10 women), 7 part-time/adjunct (4 women). *Students:* 146 full-time (117 women), 195 part-time (161 women); includes 26 minority (15 Black or African American, non-Hispanic/Latino; 1 American Indian or Alaska Native, non-Hispanic/Latino; 4 Asian, non-Hispanic/Latino; 1 Hispanic/Latino; 5 Two or more races, non-Hispanic/Latino). Average age 34. 591 applicants, 99% accepted, 144 enrolled. In 2017, 114 master's awarded. *Degree requirements:* For master's, thesis (for some programs). *Entrance requirements:* For master's, GRE or MAT, baccalaureate degree with minimum GPA of 2.5 from regionally-accredited institution; teaching license; 2 letters of recommendation; completed disposition assessment form. *Application deadline:* Applications are processed on a rolling basis. Application fee: $30. Electronic applications accepted. *Expenses:* Tuition, state resident: full-time $8132; part-time $453 per semester hour. Tuition, nonresident: full-time $14,180; part-time $788 per semester hour. *Financial support:* Tuition waivers and unspecified assistantships available. Financial award applicants required to submit FAFSA. *Unit head:* Dr. Cheryl Barnes, Director, 304-384-6306, E-mail: cbarnes@concord.edu. *Application contact:* Debra Moore, Special Events Assistant, 304-384-5113, E-mail: dlm@concord.edu.
Website: http://www.concord.edu/graduate

Converse College, Program in Special Education, Spartanburg, SC 29302. Offers intellectual disabilities (MAT); learning disabilities (MAT); special education (M Ed). *Program availability:* Part-time. *Degree requirements:* For master's, capstone paper. *Entrance requirements:* For master's, NTE or PRAXIS II (M Ed), minimum GPA of 2.75,

2 recommendations. *Application deadline:* For fall admission, 8/1 for domestic and international students; for winter admission, 11/15 for domestic and international students; for spring admission, 1/15 for domestic and international students. Applications are processed on a rolling basis. Application fee: $40. Electronic applications accepted. *Financial support:* Available to part-time students. Applicants required to submit FAFSA. *Unit head:* Lienne Medford, Dean of Graduate Studies and Distance Education, 864-596-9082, E-mail: lienne.medford@converse.edu. *Application contact:* 864-596-9404, E-mail: graduate@converse.edu.

Coppin State University, Division of Graduate Studies, Division of Education, Department of Special Education, Baltimore, MD 21216-3698. Offers M Ed. *Program availability:* Part-time, evening/weekend. *Degree requirements:* For master's, exit portfolio. *Entrance requirements:* For master's, PRAXIS I, minimum GPA of 3.0, interview, writing sample, resume, references. *Faculty research:* Survey of colleges and universities in Maryland with programs for the learning disabled.

Curry College, Graduate Studies, Program in Education, Milton, MA 02186-9984. Offers elementary education (M Ed); foundations (non-license) (M Ed); reading (M Ed, Certificate); special education (M Ed). *Program availability:* Part-time, evening/weekend. *Degree requirements:* For master's, project or thesis. *Entrance requirements:* For master's, interview, recommendations, resume, written statement. Additional exam requirements/recommendations for international students: Required—TOEFL (minimum score 550 paper-based; 80 iBT). *Expenses:* Contact institution. *Faculty research:* Classroom trauma, therapeutic writing, inclusionary practices.

Daemen College, Education Department, Amherst, NY 14226-3592. Offers adolescence education (MS); childhood education (MS); childhood special education (MS); childhood special-alternative certification (MS); early childhood special-alternative certification (MS). *Accreditation:* TEAC. *Program availability:* Part-time. *Degree requirements:* For master's, thesis optional, research thesis in lieu of comprehensive exam; completion of degree within 5 years. *Entrance requirements:* For master's, 2 letters of recommendation (professional and character), proof of initial certificate of license for professional programs, resume. Additional exam requirements/recommendations for international students: Required—TOEFL (minimum score 500 paper-based; 63 iBT), IELTS (minimum score 5.5). Electronic applications accepted. *Faculty research:* Transition for students with disabilities, early childhood special education, traumatic brain injury (TBI), reading assessment.

Dallas Baptist University, Dorothy M. Bush College of Education, Program in Curriculum and Instruction, Dallas, TX 75211-9299. Offers Christian school administration (M Ed); distance learning (M Ed); English as a second language (M Ed); instructional technology (M Ed); professional life coaching (M Ed); special education (M Ed); supervision (M Ed). *Program availability:* Part-time, evening/weekend, online learning. *Application deadline:* Applications are processed on a rolling basis. Application fee: $25. Electronic applications accepted. Application fee is waived when completed online. *Expenses: Tuition:* Full-time $16,308; part-time $906 per credit hour. *Required fees:* $900; $450 per semester. Tuition and fees vary according to course load and degree level. *Unit head:* Dr. Neil Dugger, Dean, 214-333-5202, E-mail: neil@dbu.edu. *Application contact:* Dr. Deborah Tribble, Program Director, 214-333-5831, E-mail: debbiet@dbu.edu.
Website: http://www3.dbu.edu/graduate/curriculum_instruction.asp

Dallas Baptist University, Dorothy M. Bush College of Education, Program in Special Education, Dallas, TX 75211-9299. Offers diagnostician (M Ed). *Program availability:* Part-time, evening/weekend. *Application deadline:* Applications are processed on a rolling basis. Application fee: $25. Electronic applications accepted. Application fee is waived when completed online. *Expenses: Tuition:* Full-time $16,308; part-time $906 per credit hour. *Required fees:* $900; $450 per semester. Tuition and fees vary according to course load and degree level. *Unit head:* Dr. Neil Dugger, Dean, 214-333-5202, E-mail: neil@dbu.edu. *Application contact:* Dr. Mary Beth Sanders, Program Director, 214-333-5547, E-mail: marys@dbu.edu.
Website: http://www3.dbu.edu/graduate/special_education.asp

Delaware State University, Graduate Programs, College of Education, Health and Public Policy, Program in Special Education, Dover, DE 19901-2277. Offers MA. *Program availability:* Part-time, evening/weekend. *Degree requirements:* For master's, comprehensive exam, thesis optional. *Entrance requirements:* For master's, GRE General Test, minimum GPA of 3.0 in field, 2.75 overall. Additional exam requirements/recommendations for international students: Required—TOEFL (minimum score 550 paper-based). Electronic applications accepted. *Faculty research:* Curriculum and instruction, distributive education.

Delta State University, Graduate Programs, College of Education, Division of Teacher Education, Leadership, and Research, Program in Special Education, Cleveland, MS 38733-0001. Offers M Ed. *Accreditation:* NCATE. *Program availability:* Part-time, evening/weekend. *Degree requirements:* For master's, thesis optional, practicum.

DePaul University, College of Education, Chicago, IL 60614. Offers bilingual-bicultural education (M Ed, MA); counseling (M Ed, MA), including clinical mental health counseling, college student development, school counseling; curriculum studies (M Ed, MA, Ed D); early childhood education (M Ed, MA, Ed D); educational leadership (M Ed, MA, Ed D), including Catholic leadership (M Ed, MA), general (M Ed, MA), higher education (M Ed, MA), physical education (M Ed, MA), principal preparation (M Ed); teacher preparation (M Ed); elementary education (M Ed, MA); middle grades education (M Ed); middle school mathematics education (MS); reading specialist (M Ed, MA); secondary education (M Ed, MA); social and cultural foundations in education (M Ed, MA); special education (M Ed); sport, fitness and recreation leadership (MS); value-creating education for global citizenship (M Ed); world languages education (M Ed, MA). *Program availability:* Part-time, evening/weekend, online learning. *Degree requirements:* For doctorate, thesis/dissertation. *Application deadline:* Applications are processed on a rolling basis. Application fee: $40. Electronic applications accepted. *Financial support:* Application deadline: 12/31; applicants required to submit FAFSA. *Unit head:* Dr. Paul Zionts, Dean, 773-325-7713, Fax: 773-325-7713, E-mail: pzionts@depaul.edu. *Application contact:* Dr. Paul Zionts, Dean, 773-325-7581, Fax: 773-325-7713, E-mail: pzionts@depaul.edu.
Website: http://education.depaul.edu

DeSales University, Division of Liberal Arts and Social Sciences, Center Valley, PA 18034-9568. Offers criminal justice (MCJ); digital forensics (MCJ, Postbaccalaureate Certificate); education (M Ed), including instructional technology, secondary education, special education, teaching English to speakers of other languages; investigative forensics (MCJ, Postbaccalaureate Certificate). *Program availability:* Part-time, 100% online, blended/hybrid learning. *Faculty:* 5 full-time (3 women), 15 part-time/adjunct (9 women). *Students:* 54 full-time (36 women), 112 part-time (68 women); includes 23 minority (3 Black or African American, non-Hispanic/Latino; 1 Asian, non-Hispanic/Latino; 17 Hispanic/Latino; 2 Two or more races, non-Hispanic/Latino), 1 international. Average age 33. 114 applicants, 64% accepted, 41 enrolled. In 2017, 41 master's awarded. *Entrance requirements:* For master's, bachelor's degree from accredited institution, minimum undergraduate GPA of 3.0, personal statement showing potential of graduate work, three letters of recommendation, professional goal statement. Additional exam requirements/recommendations for international students: Required—TOEFL.

Application deadline: Applications are processed on a rolling basis. Application fee: $50. Electronic applications accepted. *Expenses: Tuition:* Part-time $840 per credit. Full-time tuition and fees vary according to course load, degree level and program. *Financial support:* Applicants required to submit FAFSA. *Unit head:* Ronald Nordone, Dean of Graduate Education, 610-282-1100 Ext. 1289, E-mail: ronald.nordone@desales.edu. *Application contact:* Julia Ferraro, Director of Graduate Admissions, 610-282-1100 Ext. 1768, E-mail: gradadmissions@desales.edu.

Dominican College, Division of Teacher Education, Orangeburg, NY 10962-1210. Offers education/teaching of individuals with multiple disabilities (MS Ed). *Program availability:* Part-time, evening/weekend, online learning. *Faculty:* 2 full-time (1 woman), 7 part-time/adjunct (all women). *Students:* 3 full-time (all women), 48 part-time (30 women); includes 9 minority (1 Black or African American, non-Hispanic/Latino; 1 Asian, non-Hispanic/Latino; 7 Hispanic/Latino). In 2017, 18 master's awarded. *Degree requirements:* For master's, comprehensive exam (for some programs), thesis. *Entrance requirements:* For master's, 3 letters of recommendation (written by former or current work supervisors or instructors), interview. Additional exam requirements/recommendations for international students: Required—TOEFL (minimum score 90 iBT). *Application deadline:* Applications are processed on a rolling basis. *Expenses: Tuition:* Part-time $900 per credit. One-time fee: $200. Tuition and fees vary according to degree level and program. *Financial support:* Application deadline: 2/1; applicants required to submit FAFSA. *Unit head:* Dr. Mike Kelly, Director, 845-848-4090, Fax: 845-359-7802, E-mail: mike.kelly@dc.edu. *Application contact:* Christina Lifshey, Assistant Director of Graduate Admissions, 845-848-7908 Ext. 15, Fax: 845-365-3150, E-mail: admissions@dc.edu.

Dominican University, School of Education, River Forest, IL 60305-1099. Offers child life studies (MS); early childhood education (MS); education (MAT); elementary education (MA Ed); English as a second language (MA Ed); reading (MA Ed); secondary education (MAT); special education (MS). *Accreditation:* NCATE. *Program availability:* Part-time, evening/weekend, 100% online, blended/hybrid learning. *Faculty:* 8 full-time (6 women), 42 part-time/adjunct (38 women). *Students:* 5 full-time (all women), 261 part-time (206 women); includes 45 minority (16 Black or African American, non-Hispanic/Latino; 1 American Indian or Alaska Native, non-Hispanic/Latino; 5 Asian, non-Hispanic/Latino; 18 Hispanic/Latino; 5 Two or more races, non-Hispanic/Latino), 1 international. Average age 32. 95 applicants, 98% accepted, 72 enrolled. In 2017, 206 master's awarded. *Entrance requirements:* For master's, Illinois Test of Basic Skills. Additional exam requirements/recommendations for international students: Required—TOEFL (minimum score 550 paper-based; 79 iBT). *Application deadline:* Applications are processed on a rolling basis. Application fee: $25. *Expenses:* Contact institution. *Financial support:* Career-related internships or fieldwork, scholarships/grants, tuition waivers (partial), and unspecified assistantships available. Support available to part-time students. Financial award application deadline: 8/15; financial award applicants required to submit FAFSA. *Faculty research:* Governance of private education institutions, reading and language arts, inclusion, organizational planning, leadership and vision. *Unit head:* Dr. Colleen Reardon, Interim Executive Director, School of Education, 708-524-6643, Fax: 708-524-6665, E-mail: creardon@dom.edu. *Application contact:* Benjamin Mueller, Senior Graduate Marketing and Recruitment Coordinator, 708-524-6456, Fax: 708-524-6665, E-mail: bmueller@dom.edu.
Website: http://educate.dom.edu/

Dominican University of California, Programs in Education plus Teacher Preparation, San Rafael, CA 94901-2298. Offers multiple subject (MS); single subject (MS). *Program availability:* Part-time, evening/weekend. *Faculty:* 9 full-time (7 women), 10 part-time/adjunct (9 women). *Students:* 51 full-time (38 women), 79 part-time (59 women); includes 29 minority (1 Black or African American, non-Hispanic/Latino; 1 American Indian or Alaska Native, non-Hispanic/Latino; 4 Asian, non-Hispanic/Latino; 16 Hispanic/Latino; 2 Native Hawaiian or other Pacific Islander, non-Hispanic/Latino; 5 Two or more races, non-Hispanic/Latino). Average age 35. 44 applicants, 98% accepted, 35 enrolled. In 2017, 37 master's awarded. *Degree requirements:* For master's, thesis. *Entrance requirements:* Additional exam requirements/recommendations for international students: Required—TOEFL (minimum score 550 paper-based; 80 iBT), IELTS (minimum score 6.5). *Application deadline:* For fall admission, 5/15 priority date for domestic and international students; for spring admission, 11/15 priority date for domestic and international students. Applications are processed on a rolling basis. Application fee: $0. Electronic applications accepted. *Expenses:* $810 per unit. *Financial support:* In 2017–18, 61 students received support. Scholarships/grants available. Support available to part-time students. Financial award application deadline: 3/2; financial award applicants required to submit FAFSA. *Unit head:* Pauline Camp, Director of Operations, 415-458-3779, E-mail: pauline.camp@dominican.edu. *Application contact:* Michael Lavigna, Assistant Director, Graduate Admissions, 415-485-3246, Fax: 415-485-3253, E-mail: gradmissions@dominican.edu.
Website: https://www.dominican.edu/academics/lae/department-of-education/teaching-credentials

Drake University, School of Education, Des Moines, IA 50311-4516. Offers applied behavior analysis (MS); counseling (MS); education (PhD); education administration (Ed D); educational leadership (MSE, Ed D); effective teaching (MSE); leadership development (MS); literacy (Ed S); literacy education (MSE); rehabilitation administration (MS); rehabilitation placement (MS); special education (MSE); STEM education (MSE); teacher education (5-12) (MAT); teacher education (K-8) (MST); teacher effectiveness and professional development (MSE). *Program availability:* Part-time, evening/weekend. *Degree requirements:* For master's and Ed S, comprehensive exam, internships (for some programs); for doctorate, comprehensive exam, thesis/dissertation, internships (for some programs). *Entrance requirements:* For master's, GRE General Test, MAT, or Drake Writing Assessment, resume, 2 letters of recommendation; for doctorate, GRE General Test or MAT, master's degree, 3 letters of recommendation; for Ed S, GRE General Test or MAT. Additional exam requirements/recommendations for international students: Required—TOEFL (minimum score 550 paper-based). *Application deadline:* For fall admission, 7/1 priority date for domestic students, 6/1 priority date for international students; for spring admission, 11/1 priority date for domestic students, 10/1 priority date for international students. Applications are processed on a rolling basis. Application fee: $25. Electronic applications accepted. *Expenses:* Contact institution. *Financial support:* Research assistantships, career-related internships or fieldwork, and unspecified assistantships available. Support available to part-time students. *Faculty research:* Counseling and rehabilitation, behavioral supports, inquiry-based science methods, teacher quality enhancement. *Unit head:* Dr. Janet McMahill, Dean, 515-271-3829, E-mail: janet.mcmahill@drake.edu.
Website: http://www.drake.edu/soe/

Drew University, Caspersen School of Graduate Studies, Madison, NJ 07940-1493. Offers conflict resolution and leadership (Certificate), including community leadership, moderation, peace building; education (M Ed); finance (MA); history and culture (MA, PhD), including American history, book history, British history, European history, Holocaust and genocide (M Litt, MA, D Litt, PhD), intellectual history, Irish history, print culture, public history; K-12 education (MAT), including art, biology, chemistry, elementary education, English, French, Italian, math, secondary education, special

Special Education

education, teacher of students with disabilities; liberal studies (M Litt, D Litt), including history, Holocaust and genocide (M Litt, MA, D Litt, PhD), Irish/Irish-American studies, literature (M Litt, MMH, D Litt, DMH, CMH), religion, spirituality, teaching in the two-year college, writing; medical humanities (MMH, DMH, CMH), including arts, health, healthcare, literature (M Litt, MMH, D Litt, DMH, CMH), scientific research; poetry (MFA). *Program availability:* Part-time, evening/weekend. *Faculty:* 4 full-time (2 women), 29 part-time/adjunct (15 women). *Students:* 77 full-time (42 women), 175 part-time (114 women); includes 39 minority (12 Black or African American, non-Hispanic/Latino; 6 Asian, non-Hispanic/Latino; 16 Hispanic/Latino; 5 Two or more races, non-Hispanic/Latino), 11 international. Average age 41. 126 applicants, 75% accepted, 52 enrolled. In 2017, 38 master's, 23 doctorates, 35 other advanced degrees awarded. Terminal master's awarded for partial completion of doctoral program. *Degree requirements:* For master's and other advanced degree, thesis (for some programs); for doctorate, one foreign language, comprehensive exam (for some programs), thesis/dissertation. *Entrance requirements:* For master's, PRAXIS Core and Subject Area tests (for MAT), GRE/GMAT (for M Fin), resume, transcripts, writing sample, personal statement, letters of recommendation; for doctorate, GRE (PhD in history and culture), resume, transcripts, writing sample, personal statement, letters of recommendation; for other advanced degree, resume, transcripts, personal statement. Additional exam requirements/recommendations for international students: Required—TOEFL (minimum score 587 paper-based; 80 iBT), IELTS (minimum score 6), TWE (minimum score 4). *Application deadline:* For fall admission, 8/1 for domestic students, 6/1 for international students; for spring admission, 12/1 for domestic students, 10/1 for international students. Applications are processed on a rolling basis. Application fee: $35. Electronic applications accepted. *Financial support:* Fellowships, research assistantships, teaching assistantships, career-related internships or fieldwork, Federal Work-Study, scholarships/grants, and unspecified assistantships available. Support available to part-time students. Financial award applicants required to submit FAFSA. *Faculty research:* Irish history and culture, conflict resolution and leadership. *Application contact:* Leanne Horinko, Director of Caspersen Admissions, 973-408-3280, E-mail: gradm@drew.edu. Website: http://www.drew.edu/caspersen

Drexel University, Goodwin College of Professional Studies, School of Education, Philadelphia, PA 19104-2875. Offers applied behavior analysis (MS); creativity and innovation (MS); education improvement and transformation (MS); educational administration (MS); educational leadership and management (Ed D); educational leadership development and learning technologies (PhD); global and international education (MS); higher education (MS); human resources development (MS); learning technologies (MS); mathematics, learning and teaching (MS); special education (MS); teaching, learning and curriculum (MS). *Program availability:* Part-time, evening/weekend, online learning. *Degree requirements:* For doctorate, thesis/dissertation. *Entrance requirements:* For doctorate, GRE or GMAT. Additional exam requirements/recommendations for international students: Required—TOEFL, IELTS. Electronic applications accepted. Application fee is waived when completed online. *Expenses:* Contact institution. *Faculty research:* Leadership development, mathematics education, literacy, autism, educational technology.

See Display on page 654 and Close-Up on page 719.

Drury University, Master in Education Program, Springfield, MO 5802. Offers curriculum and instruction (M Ed), including elementary, middle school, secondary; gifted education (M Ed); instructional leadership (M Ed); instructional technology (M Ed); integrated learning (M Ed); online teaching (M Ed); special education (M Ed); special reading (M Ed). *Accreditation:* NCATE. *Program availability:* Part-time, evening/weekend, 100% online, blended/hybrid learning. *Entrance requirements:* For master's, GRE, bachelor's degree with minimum GPA of 2.75. Additional exam requirements/recommendations for international students: Recommended—TOEFL (minimum score 80 iBT), IELTS (minimum score 6.5). Electronic applications accepted. *Expenses:* Contact institution. *Faculty research:* Gifted students, instructional technology, autism, diversity and social justice.

Duquesne University, School of Education, Department of Counseling, Psychology, and Special Education, Program in Special Education, Pittsburgh, PA 15282-0001. Offers cognitive, behavior, physical/health disabilities (MS Ed); community and special education support (MS Ed); special education (PhD); special education 7-12 (MS Ed); special education PreK-8 (MS Ed). *Program availability:* Part-time, evening/weekend. *Students:* 35 full-time (23 women); includes 4 minority (1 Black or African American, non-Hispanic/Latino; 2 Hispanic/Latino; 1 Two or more races, non-Hispanic/Latino), 16 international. Average age 30. 43 applicants, 74% accepted, 17 enrolled. In 2017, 6 master's awarded. *Entrance requirements:* For master's, bachelor's degree; for doctorate, GRE, interview, three reference letters. Additional exam requirements/recommendations for international students: Required—TOEFL (minimum score 550 paper-based), IELTS (minimum score 6.5). *Application deadline:* For fall admission, 8/15 for domestic students; for spring admission, 1/2 for domestic students; for summer admission, 5/15 for domestic students. Applications are processed on a rolling basis. Application fee: $0. Electronic applications accepted. *Expenses:* $1,259 per credit. *Financial support:* Research assistantships available. Support available to part-time students. *Unit head:* Dr. Temple Lovelace, Associate Professor/Program Director, 412-396.4159, Fax: 412-396-1340, E-mail: lovelacet@duq.edu. *Application contact:* Kelly McGinley, Graduate Admissions Assistant, 412-396-1559, Fax: 412-396-5585, E-mail: mcginleyk@duq.edu.

D'Youville College, Department of Education, Buffalo, NY 14201-1084. Offers educational leadership (Ed D); elementary education (MS Ed); secondary education (MS Ed); special education (MS Ed). *Program availability:* Part-time, evening/weekend. *Degree requirements:* For master's, one foreign language, comprehensive exam, project or thesis. *Entrance requirements:* For master's, GRE (if GPA less than 2.75), minimum GPA of 3.0. Additional exam requirements/recommendations for international students: Required—TOEFL (minimum score 500 paper-based). Electronic applications accepted. *Faculty research:* Developmental disabilities, multiculturalism, early childhood education.

East Carolina University, Graduate School, College of Education, Department of Special Education, Foundations, and Research, Greenville, NC 27858-4353. Offers assistive technology (Certificate); autism (Certificate); special education (MA Ed, MAT), including behavioral-emotional disabilities (MA Ed), intellectual disabilities (MA Ed), learning disabilities (MA Ed), low-incidence disabilities (MA Ed). *Program availability:* Part-time, evening/weekend, online learning. *Students:* 1 (woman) full-time, 61 part-time (56 women); includes 15 minority (8 Black or African American, non-Hispanic/Latino; 2 American Indian or Alaska Native, non-Hispanic/Latino; 1 Asian, non-Hispanic/Latino; 2 Hispanic/Latino; 2 Two or more races, non-Hispanic/Latino). Average age 31. 26 applicants, 92% accepted, 22 enrolled. In 2017, 10 master's, 6 other advanced degrees awarded. *Degree requirements:* For master's, comprehensive exam, thesis optional. *Entrance requirements:* For master's, GRE General Test or MAT, interview, bachelor's degree in related field, minimum GPA of 2.5, teaching license. Additional exam requirements/recommendations for international students: Required—TOEFL. *Application deadline:* For fall admission, 6/1 priority date for domestic students. Applications are processed on a rolling basis. Application fee: $75. *Expenses:* Tuition, state resident: full-time $4749; part-time $297 per credit hour. Tuition, nonresident: full-

time $17,898; part-time $1119 per credit hour. *Required fees:* $2691; $224 per credit hour. Part-time tuition and fees vary according to course load and program. *Financial support:* Research assistantships, teaching assistantships, and Federal Work-Study available. Support available to part-time students. Financial award application deadline: 6/1; financial award applicants required to submit FAFSA. *Unit head:* Dr. Guili Zhang, Interim Chair, 252-328-4989, E-mail: zhangg@ecu.edu. Website: http://www.ecu.edu/cs-educ/sefr/index.cfm

Eastern Illinois University, Graduate School, College of Education and Professional Studies, Department of Special Education, Charleston, IL 61920. Offers MS Ed. *Accreditation:* NCATE. *Program availability:* Part-time, evening/weekend. *Degree requirements:* For master's, comprehensive exam (for some programs), thesis (for some programs). *Entrance requirements:* For master's, GMAT or GRE. Additional exam requirements/recommendations for international students: Required—TOEFL (minimum score 500 paper-based; 61 iBT), IELTS (minimum score 6). *Application deadline:* For fall admission, 5/15 for domestic and international students; for spring admission, 10/15 for domestic and international students. Applications are processed on a rolling basis. Application fee: $30. Electronic applications accepted. *Financial support:* Teaching assistantships with full tuition reimbursements, career-related internships or fieldwork, Federal Work-Study, and unspecified assistantships available. Support available to part-time students. Financial award application deadline: 3/1; financial award applicants required to submit FAFSA. *Unit head:* Kathlene Shank, Chair, 217-581-5315, Fax: 217-581-7004, E-mail: ksshank@eiu.edu. *Application contact:* Kathlene Shank, Chair, 217-581-5315, Fax: 217-581-7004, E-mail: ksshank@eiu.edu. Website: http://www.eiu.edu/specedgrad

Eastern Kentucky University, The Graduate School, College of Education, Department of Special Education, Richmond, KY 40475-3102. Offers communication disorders (MA Ed). *Accreditation:* NCATE. *Program availability:* Part-time. *Degree requirements:* For master's, comprehensive exam. *Entrance requirements:* For master's, GRE General Test, MAT, minimum GPA of 2.5. *Faculty research:* Personnel needs in communication disorders, education needs of people who stutter, attention of special ed teacher.

Eastern Mennonite University, Program in Teacher Education, Harrisonburg, VA 22802-2462. Offers curriculum and instruction (MA Ed); diverse needs (MA Ed); literacy (MA Ed); restorative justice in education (MA Ed). *Accreditation:* NCATE. *Program availability:* Part-time. *Degree requirements:* For master's, portfolio, research projects. *Entrance requirements:* For master's, 1 year of teaching experience, interview, minimum undergraduate GPA of 2.75. Additional exam requirements/recommendations for international students: Required—TOEFL (minimum score 550 paper-based). *Application deadline:* Applications are processed on a rolling basis. Application fee: $50. Electronic applications accepted. *Expenses:* Contact institution. *Financial support:* Federal Work-Study and scholarships/grants available. Financial award application deadline: 6/30; financial award applicants required to submit FAFSA. *Faculty research:* Effective literacy instruction for middle school English language learners, beginning teacher's emotional experiences, constructivist learning environments, restorative discipline. *Unit head:* Cathy Smeltzer Erb, Chair, 540-432-4638. *Application contact:* Yvonne Martin, Office Assistant, 540-432-4350, Fax: 540-432-4071, E-mail: yvonne.martin@emu.edu. Website: http://www.emu.edu/maed/

Eastern Michigan University, Graduate School, College of Education, Department of Special Education, Program in Autism Spectrum Disorders, Ypsilanti, MI 48197. Offers MA. *Students:* 5 full-time (all women), 34 part-time (27 women); includes 3 minority (2 Black or African American, non-Hispanic/Latino; 1 Two or more races, non-Hispanic/Latino). Average age 35. 7 applicants, 100% accepted, 4 enrolled. In 2017, 5 master's awarded. Application fee: $45. *Application contact:* Dr. Sally Burton-Hoyle, Program Coordinator, 734-487-3300, Fax: 734-487-2473, E-mail: sburtonh@emich.edu.

Eastern Michigan University, Graduate School, College of Education, Department of Special Education, Program in Cognitive Impairment, Ypsilanti, MI 48197. Offers M Ed. *Students:* 10 full-time (7 women), 16 part-time (10 women); includes 4 minority (3 Black or African American, non-Hispanic/Latino; 1 Hispanic/Latino). Average age 34. 6 applicants, 100% accepted, 3 enrolled. In 2017, 7 master's awarded. Application fee: $45. *Application contact:* Dr. Phil Smith, Advisor, 734-487-2788, Fax: 734-487-2473, E-mail: psmith16@emich.edu.

Eastern Michigan University, Graduate School, College of Education, Department of Special Education, Program in Emotional Impairment, Ypsilanti, MI 48197. Offers M Ed. *Students:* 3 full-time (1 woman), 9 part-time (4 women); includes 4 minority (all Black or African American, non-Hispanic/Latino). Average age 43. 4 applicants, 100% accepted, 1 enrolled. In 2017, 7 master's awarded. Application fee: $45. *Application contact:* Dr. David Winters, Department Head, 734-487-3300, Fax: 734-487-2473, E-mail: david.winters@emich.edu.

Eastern Michigan University, Graduate School, College of Education, Department of Special Education, Program in Learning Disabilities, Ypsilanti, MI 48197. Offers MA. *Students:* 16 part-time (13 women); includes 2 minority (both Hispanic/Latino). Average age 31. 8 applicants, 75% accepted, 4 enrolled. In 2017, 11 master's awarded. Application fee: $45. *Application contact:* Dr. Loreena Parks, Coordinator, 734-487-2769, Fax: 734-487-2473, E-mail: lparks1@emich.edu.

Eastern Michigan University, Graduate School, College of Education, Department of Special Education, Program in Physical/Other Health Impairment, Ypsilanti, MI 48197. Offers M Ed. *Students:* 4 part-time (all women). Average age 41. 1 applicant, 100% accepted. In 2017, 2 master's awarded. Application fee: $45. *Application contact:* Dr. Jacquelyn McGinnis, Advisor, 734-487-3300, Fax: 734-487-2473, E-mail: jmcginnis@emich.edu.

Eastern Michigan University, Graduate School, College of Education, Department of Special Education, Program in Visual Impairment, Ypsilanti, MI 48197. Offers M Ed. Application fee: $45. *Application contact:* Dr. Alicia Li, Advisor, 734-487-3300, Fax: 734-487-2473, E-mail: tli@emich.edu.

Eastern Michigan University, Graduate School, College of Education, Department of Special Education, Programs in Special Education, Ypsilanti, MI 48197. Offers MA, SPA. *Accreditation:* NCATE. *Program availability:* Part-time, evening/weekend, online learning. *Students:* 3 full-time (2 women), 35 part-time (31 women); includes 6 minority (4 Black or African American, non-Hispanic/Latino; 1 Hispanic/Latino; 1 Two or more races, non-Hispanic/Latino), 3 international. Average age 39. 15 applicants, 80% accepted, 7 enrolled. In 2017, 4 master's, 3 other advanced degrees awarded. *Entrance requirements:* For master's, GRE General Test. Additional exam requirements/recommendations for international students: Required—TOEFL. *Application deadline:* Applications are processed on a rolling basis. Application fee: $45. *Financial support:* Fellowships, research assistantships with full tuition reimbursements, teaching assistantships with full tuition reimbursements, career-related internships or fieldwork, Federal Work-Study, institutionally sponsored loans, scholarships/grants, tuition waivers (partial), and unspecified assistantships available. Support available to part-time students. Financial award applicants required to submit FAFSA. *Application contact:* Dr. Derrick Fries, Advisor, 734-487-3300, Fax: 734-487-2473, E-mail: dfries@emich.edu.

Eastern Michigan University, Graduate School, College of Education, Department of Teacher Education, Program in Urban/Diversity Education, Ypsilanti, MI 48197. Offers MA. In 2017, 1 master's awarded. Application fee: $45. *Application contact:* Dr. Patricia Williams-Boyd, Advisor, 734-487-3260, Fax: 734-487-2101, E-mail: pwilliams1@emich.edu.

Eastern Nazarene College, Adult and Graduate Studies, Division of Teacher Education, Quincy, MA 02170. Offers administration (M Ed); early childhood education (M Ed, Certificate); elementary education (M Ed, Certificate); English as a second language (Certificate); instructional enrichment and development (Certificate); middle school education (M Ed, Certificate); moderate special needs education (Certificate); principal (Certificate); program development and supervision (Certificate); secondary education (M Ed, Certificate); special education administrator (Certificate); special needs (M Ed); supervisor (Certificate); teacher of reading (M Ed, Certificate). M Ed also available through weekend program for administration, special needs, and teacher of reading only. *Program availability:* Part-time, evening/weekend. *Entrance requirements:* Additional exam requirements/recommendations for international students: Required—TOEFL (minimum score 550 paper-based).

Eastern New Mexico University, Graduate School, College of Education and Technology, Department of Educational Studies, Program in Special Education, Portales, NM 88130. Offers early childhood special education (M Sp Ed); general special education (M Sp Ed); gifted education pedagogy (M Ed); special education pedagogy (M Ed). *Program availability:* Part-time. *Degree requirements:* For master's, comprehensive exam, thesis optional. *Entrance requirements:* For master's, writing assessment, minimum GPA of 3.0, letter of recommendation, photocopy of teaching license or confirmation of entrance into alternative licensure program, special education license or minimum 30 hours of undergraduate course work. Additional exam requirements/recommendations for international students: Required—TOEFL (minimum score 550 paper-based; 79 iBT), IELTS (minimum score 6). *Application deadline:* For fall admission, 7/20 priority date for domestic students, 6/20 priority date for international students; for spring admission, 12/15 priority date for domestic students, 11/15 priority date for international students. Applications are processed on a rolling basis. Application fee: $10. Electronic applications accepted. *Financial support:* Applicants required to submit FAFSA. *Unit head:* Dr. Rebecca Davis, Graduate Coordinator, 575-392-6840, E-mail: rebecca.davis@enmu.edu. *Application contact:* Cheryl Reeves, Senior Secretary, 575-562-2443, Fax: 575-562-2559, E-mail: cheryl.reeves@enmu.edu.

Eastern University, Graduate Education Programs, St. Davids, PA 19087-3696. Offers ESL program specialist (K-12) (Certificate); general supervisor (PreK-12) (Certificate); health and physical education (K-12) (Certificate); middle level (4-8) (Certificate); multicultural education (M Ed); music (K-12) (Certificate); Pre K-4 (Certificate); Pre K-4 with special education (Certificate); reading (M Ed); reading specialist (K-12) (Certificate); reading supervisor (K-12) (Certificate); school counseling (MA, CAGS); school principalship (preK-12) (Certificate); school psychology (MS, CAGS); secondary biology education (7-12) (Certificate); secondary chemistry education (7-12) (Certificate); secondary communication education (7-12) (Certificate); secondary English education (7-12) (Certificate); secondary math education (7-12) (Certificate); secondary social studies education (7-12) (Certificate); special education (M Ed); special education (7-12) (Certificate); special education (Pre K-8) (Certificate); special education supervisor (K-12) (Certificate); TESOL (M Ed); world language (Certificate), including Spanish. *Program availability:* Part-time, evening/weekend, online learning. *Students:* 46 full-time (40 women), 115 part-time (93 women); includes 65 minority (42 Black or African American, non-Hispanic/Latino; 3 Asian, non-Hispanic/Latino; 14 Hispanic/Latino; 6 Two or more races, non-Hispanic/Latino), 1 international. Average age 32. In 2017, 72 master's awarded. *Entrance requirements:* Additional exam requirements/recommendations for international students: Required—TOEFL. *Application deadline:* Applications are processed on a rolling basis. Application fee: $35. Electronic applications accepted. Application fee is waived when completed online. *Expenses:* Contact institution. *Unit head:* Michael Dziedziak, Executive Director of Enrollment, 800-452-0996, E-mail: gpsadmissions@eastern.edu.
Website: https://www.eastern.edu/academics/programs/education-department-graduate-programs/graduate-programs

East Stroudsburg University of Pennsylvania, Graduate and Extended Studies, College of Education, Department of Special Education and Rehabilitation, East Stroudsburg, PA 18301-2999. Offers special education (M Ed). *Program availability:* Part-time, evening/weekend, online learning. *Faculty:* 4 full-time (3 women), 1 (woman) part-time/adjunct. *Students:* 11 full-time (8 women), 49 part-time (46 women); includes 4 minority (2 Black or African American, non-Hispanic/Latino; 1 American Indian or Alaska Native, non-Hispanic/Latino; 1 Hispanic/Latino). Average age 31. 32 applicants, 78% accepted, 19 enrolled. In 2017, 15 master's awarded. *Degree requirements:* For master's, comprehensive exam. *Entrance requirements:* For master's, PRAXIS/teacher certification, letter of recommendation, Pennsylvania Department of Education requirements. Additional exam requirements/recommendations for international students: Recommended—TOEFL (minimum score 560 paper-based; 83 iBT), IELTS. *Application deadline:* For fall admission, 7/31 priority date for domestic students, 6/30 priority date for international students; for spring admission, 11/30 for domestic students, 10/31 for international students. Applications are processed on a rolling basis. Application fee: $50. Electronic applications accepted. *Expenses:* Tuition, state resident: full-time $4500; part-time $3000 per credit. Tuition, nonresident: full-time $6750; part-time $4500 per credit. *Required fees:* $2642; $1756 per credit. $878 per semester. Tuition and fees vary according to course load, campus/location and program. *Financial support:* Research assistantships with tuition reimbursements, career-related internships or fieldwork, Federal Work-Study, and unspecified assistantships available. Support available to part-time students. Financial award application deadline: 3/1; financial award applicants required to submit FAFSA. *Unit head:* Dr. Gina Scala, Chair, 570-422-3781, Fax: 570-422-3198, E-mail: gscala@esu.edu. *Application contact:* Kevin Quintero, Associate Director, Graduate and Extended Studies, 570-422-3890, Fax: 570-422-2711, E-mail: kquintero@esu.edu.

East Tennessee State University, School of Graduate Studies, College of Education, Department of Educational Foundations and Special Education, Johnson City, TN 37614. Offers community leadership (Post-Master's Certificate), including early childhood special education (M Ed, Post-Master's Certificate), high incidence disabilities (M Ed, Post-Master's Certificate), low incidence disabilities (M Ed, Post-Master's Certificate); special education (M Ed, Post-Master's Certificate), including advanced studies in special education (M Ed), early childhood special education, high incidence disabilities, low incidence disabilities. *Program availability:* Part-time. *Degree requirements:* For master's, thesis (for some programs), practicum, residency, or thesis. *Entrance requirements:* For master's, PRAXIS I or Tennessee teaching license (for special education only), minimum GPA of 3.0 (or complete probationary period with no grade lower than B for first 9 graduate hours for early childhood education), 2-page essay outlining past experience with individuals with disabilities and goals for acquiring an advanced degree in special education; for Post-Master's Certificate, bachelor's or master's degree in early childhood or related field; two years of experience working with young children (preferred). Additional exam requirements/recommendations for international students: Required—TOEFL (minimum score 550 paper-based; 79 iBT).

Application deadline: For fall admission, 3/15 for domestic and international students. Application fee: $65 ($65 for international students). *Financial support:* Fellowships with full tuition reimbursements, research assistantships with full tuition reimbursements, teaching assistantships with full tuition reimbursements, career-related internships or fieldwork, institutionally sponsored loans, scholarships/grants, and unspecified assistantships available. Financial award application deadline: 7/1; financial award applicants required to submit FAFSA. *Faculty research:* Teaching students with significant disabilities, problem-solving in toddlers, children and their development and learning, connecting classroom environment to student engagement in PreK-3, bilingual education in Ecuador, positive discipline/behavior support programs, early childhood relationships, international and comparative special education. *Unit head:* Dr. Cathy Galyon-Keramidas, Chair, 423-439-7688, E-mail: galyonkerami@etsu.edu. *Application contact:* Dr. Cynthia Chambers, Graduate Program Coordinator, 423-439-7586, Fax: 423-439-5624, E-mail: chamberc@etsu.edu.
Website: http://www.etsu.edu/coe/efse/

Edgewood College, School of Education, Madison, WI 53711-1997. Offers adult learning (MA Ed); director of special education and pupil services (Certificate); education (MA Ed); teaching and learning (MA Ed). *Accreditation:* NCATE (one or more programs are accredited). *Program availability:* Part-time, evening/weekend. *Faculty:* 13 full-time (9 women), 15 part-time/adjunct (10 women). *Students:* 157 full-time (106 women), 188 part-time (133 women); includes 65 minority (26 Black or African American, non-Hispanic/Latino; 1 American Indian or Alaska Native, non-Hispanic/Latino; 8 Asian, non-Hispanic/Latino; 23 Hispanic/Latino; 7 Two or more races, non-Hispanic/Latino), 14 international. Average age 37. In 2017, 68 master's, 34 doctorates awarded. *Degree requirements:* For master's, practicum, research project; for doctorate, comprehensive exam, thesis/dissertation. *Entrance requirements:* For master's, minimum GPA of 2.75, 2 letters of recommendation, personal statement; for doctorate, resume, letter of intent, 2 letters of recommendation, interview, writing sample. Additional exam requirements/recommendations for international students: Required—TOEFL (minimum score 525 paper-based; 72 iBT). *Application deadline:* For fall admission, 8/15 for domestic students, 5/1 for international students; for spring admission, 1/8 for domestic students, 11/1 for international students. Applications are processed on a rolling basis. Application fee: $30. Electronic applications accepted. *Expenses:* Tuition: Part-time $930 per credit. *Financial support:* Applicants required to submit FAFSA. *Faculty research:* Urban high schools, transgender students, literacy pedagogy, funds of knowledge, English language learners. *Unit head:* Dr. Timothy D. Slekar, Dean, 608-663-2293, E-mail: tslekar@edgewood.edu. *Application contact:* Joann Eastman, Admissions Counselor, 608-663-3250, Fax: 608-663-2214, E-mail: gps@edgewood.edu.
Website: https://www.edgewood.edu/academics/schools/school-of-education

Edinboro University of Pennsylvania, Department of Counseling, School Psychology and Special Education, Edinboro, PA 16444. Offers counseling (MA), including art therapy, clinical mental health counseling, college counseling, rehabilitation counseling, school counseling; educational psychology (M Ed); school psychology (Ed S); special education (M Ed), including autism, behavior management. *Accreditation:* ACA. *Program availability:* Part-time, evening/weekend. *Degree requirements:* For master's, thesis or alternative, competency exam; for Ed S, thesis or alternative. *Entrance requirements:* For master's and Ed S, GRE or MAT, minimum QPA of 2.5. Electronic applications accepted.

Elmhurst College, Graduate Programs, Program in Early Childhood Special Education, Elmhurst, IL 60126-3296. Offers M Ed. *Program availability:* Part-time, evening/weekend. *Faculty:* 2 full-time (both women), 1 (woman) part-time/adjunct. *Students:* 9 full-time (all women), 5 part-time (all women); includes 4 minority (2 Black or African American, non-Hispanic/Latino; 1 Asian, non-Hispanic/Latino; 1 Hispanic/Latino). Average age 28. 16 applicants, 63% accepted, 10 enrolled. In 2017, 13 master's awarded. *Entrance requirements:* For master's, 3 recommendations, resume, statement of purpose. Additional exam requirements/recommendations for international students: Required—TOEFL (minimum score 550 paper-based; 79 iBT). *Application deadline:* Applications are processed on a rolling basis. Application fee: $0. Electronic applications accepted. *Expenses:* Contact institution. *Financial support:* In 2017-18, 11 students received support. Scholarships/grants and unspecified assistantships available. Support available to part-time students. Financial award application deadline: 3/1; financial award applicants required to submit FAFSA. *Unit head:* Dr. Therese Wehman, Director, 630-617-3231, E-mail: theresew@elmhurst.edu. *Application contact:* Timothy J. Panfil, Director of Enrollment Management, 630-617-3300 Ext. 3256, Fax: 630-617-6471, E-mail: panfilt@elmhurst.edu.
Website: http://www.elmhurst.edu/ecse

Elmhurst College, Graduate Programs, Program in Special Education, Elmhurst, IL 60126-3296. Offers MS Ed. *Program availability:* Part-time, evening/weekend. *Faculty:* 3 full-time (all women), 1 (woman) part-time/adjunct. *Students:* 6 part-time (all women); includes 1 minority (Hispanic/Latino). Average age 29. *Entrance requirements:* For master's, 3 recommendations, resume, statement of purpose. Additional exam requirements/recommendations for international students: Required—TOEFL (minimum score 550 paper-based; 79 iBT). *Application deadline:* Applications are processed on a rolling basis. Application fee: $0. Electronic applications accepted. *Expenses:* Contact institution. *Financial support:* In 2017-18, 3 students received support. Scholarships/grants available. Support available to part-time students. Financial award application deadline: 3/1; financial award applicants required to submit FAFSA. *Unit head:* Lisa Burke, Department Chair of Education, 630-617-5197, E-mail: lisab@elmhurst.edu. *Application contact:* Timothy J. Panfil, Director of Enrollment Management, 630-617-3300 Ext. 3256, Fax: 630-617-6471, E-mail: panfilt@elmhurst.edu.
Website: http://www.elmhurst.edu/admission/graduate/se

Elms College, Division of Education, Chicopee, MA 01013-2839. Offers early childhood education (MAT); education (M Ed, CAGS); elementary education (MAT); English as a second language (MAT); reading (MAT); secondary education (MAT), including biology education, English education, Spanish education; special education (MAT). *Program availability:* Part-time, evening/weekend. *Faculty:* 4 full-time (all women), 8 part-time/adjunct (7 women). *Students:* 6 full-time (4 women), 127 part-time (107 women); includes 8 minority (2 Asian, non-Hispanic/Latino; 6 Hispanic/Latino). Average age 33. 42 applicants, 88% accepted, 36 enrolled. In 2017, 50 master's, 6 other advanced degrees awarded. *Degree requirements:* For master's, thesis (for some programs). *Entrance requirements:* For master's, Massachusetts Educators Certification Test, minimum GPA of 3.0; for CAGS, master's degree in education. Additional exam requirements/recommendations for international students: Required—TOEFL. *Application deadline:* For fall admission, 7/1 priority date for domestic students; for spring admission, 11/1 priority date for domestic students. Applications are processed on a rolling basis. Application fee: $30. *Expenses:* Tuition: Full-time $13,860; part-time $770 per credit hour. *Required fees:* $200. Tuition and fees vary according to degree level and program. *Financial support:* In 2017-18, 2 teaching assistantships with partial tuition reimbursements were awarded. Financial award applicants required to submit FAFSA. *Unit head:* Dr. Mary Janeczek, Chair, Division of Education, 413-594-2761, Fax: 413-592-4871, E-mail: janeczeke@elms.edu. *Application contact:* School of Graduate and Professional Studies, 413-265-2445, E-mail: graduateeducation@elms.edu.

Elon University, Program in Education, Elon, NC 27244-2010. Offers elementary education (M Ed); gifted education (M Ed); special education (M Ed). *Accreditation:* NCATE. *Program availability:* Part-time. *Faculty:* 8 full-time (6 women), 2 part-time/adjunct (both women). *Students:* 24 part-time (22 women); includes 13 minority (2 Black or African American, non-Hispanic/Latino; 2 Asian, non-Hispanic/Latino; 8 Hispanic/Latino; 1 Two or more races, non-Hispanic/Latino). Average age 23. 29 applicants, 69% accepted, 16 enrolled. In 2017, 10 master's awarded. *Entrance requirements:* For master's, GRE, MAT. Additional exam requirements/recommendations for international students: Required—TOEFL (minimum score 550 paper-based; 79 iBT). *Application deadline:* For fall admission, 5/1 for domestic students. Applications are processed on a rolling basis. Application fee: $50. Electronic applications accepted. *Financial support:* Federal Work-Study and scholarships/grants available. Support available to part-time students. Financial award application deadline: 6/1; financial award applicants required to submit FAFSA. *Faculty research:* Teaching reading to low-achieving second and third graders, pre- and post-student teaching attitudes, children's writing, whole language methodology, critical creative thinking. *Unit head:* Dr. Ann Bullock, Dean of the School of Education/Professor, 336-278-5900, E-mail: abullock9@elon.edu. *Application contact:* Art Fadde, Director of Graduate Admissions, 800-334-8448 Ext. 3, Fax: 336-278-7699, E-mail: afadde@elon.edu.
Website: http://www.elon.edu/med

Emmanuel College, Graduate and Professional Programs, Graduate Programs in Education, Boston, MA 02115. Offers moderate learning disabilities (Certificate); urban education (M Ed). *Program availability:* Part-time, evening/weekend. *Faculty:* 1 (woman) full-time, 7 part-time/adjunct (all women). *Students:* 5 full-time (all women), 11 part-time (7 women); includes 6 minority (1 Black or African American, non-Hispanic/Latino; 1 Asian, non-Hispanic/Latino; 4 Hispanic/Latino). Average age 28. 21 applicants, 38% accepted, 4 enrolled. In 2017, 13 master's awarded. *Degree requirements:* For master's, 36 credits, including 6-credit practicum. *Entrance requirements:* For master's, transcripts from all regionally-accredited institutions attended (showing proof of bachelor's degree completion), 2 letters of recommendation, essay, resume. Additional exam requirements/recommendations for international students: Required—TOEFL. *Application deadline:* Applications are processed on a rolling basis. Electronic applications accepted. *Expenses:* $24,112 (for M Ed); $6,576 (for Certificate in moderate disabilities). *Financial support:* Application deadline: 2/15; applicants required to submit FAFSA. *Unit head:* Cindy O'Callaghan, Dean of Academic Administration and Graduate and Professional Programs, 617-735-9700, E-mail: gpp@emmanuel.edu. *Application contact:* Helen Muterperl, Director of Graduate and Professional Programs, 617-735-9700, Fax: 617-507-0434, E-mail: gpp@emmanuel.edu.
Website: http://www.emmanuel.edu/graduate-professional-programs/academics/education.html

Emporia State University, Program in Special Education, Emporia, KS 66801-5415. Offers behavior disorders (MS); gifted, talented, and creative (MS); interrelated special education (MS). *Accreditation:* NCATE. *Program availability:* Part-time. *Faculty:* 30 full-time (24 women), 1 part-time/adjunct (0 women). *Students:* 4 full-time (2 women), 160 part-time (119 women); includes 9 minority (3 Black or African American, non-Hispanic/Latino; 1 Asian, non-Hispanic/Latino; 3 Hispanic/Latino; 2 Two or more races, non-Hispanic/Latino). 29 applicants, 72% accepted, 21 enrolled. In 2017, 55 master's awarded. *Degree requirements:* For master's, comprehensive exam or thesis, practicum. *Entrance requirements:* For master's, GRE General Test or MAT, essay exam, appropriate bachelor's degree, teacher certification, letters of recommendation. Additional exam requirements/recommendations for international students: Required—TOEFL (minimum score 520 paper-based; 68 iBT). *Application deadline:* For fall admission, 8/15 priority date for domestic students. Applications are processed on a rolling basis. Application fee: $30 ($75 for international students). Electronic applications accepted. *Expenses:* Tuition, state resident: full-time $6084; part-time $253.50 per credit hour. Tuition, nonresident: full-time $18,924; part-time $788.50 per credit hour. *Required fees:* $1943; $80.95 per credit hour. Tuition and fees vary according to campus/location. *Financial support:* In 2017–18, 4 teaching assistantships with full tuition reimbursements (averaging $7,344 per year) were awarded; Federal Work-Study, institutionally sponsored loans, health care benefits, and unspecified assistantships also available. Financial award application deadline: 3/15; financial award applicants required to submit FAFSA. *Unit head:* Dr. Matt Siemears, Chair, 620-341-6057, E-mail: msiemear@emporia.edu. *Application contact:* Mary Sewell, Admissions Coordinator, 800-950-GRAD, Fax: 620-341-5909, E-mail: msewell@emporia.edu.
Website: http://www.emporia.edu/elecse/sped/

Endicott College, Van Loan School of Graduate and Professional Studies, Program in Autism and Applied Behavior Analysis, Beverly, MA 01915-2096. Offers applied behavior analysis (M Ed, PhD); autism (Certificate); autism and applied behavior analysis (M Ed). *Program availability:* Part-time, evening/weekend, 100% online, blended/hybrid learning. *Faculty:* 5 full-time (3 women), 23 part-time/adjunct (18 women). *Students:* 21 full-time (19 women), 178 part-time (149 women); includes 39 minority (12 Black or African American, non-Hispanic/Latino; 9 Asian, non-Hispanic/Latino; 17 Hispanic/Latino; 1 Two or more races, non-Hispanic/Latino), 1 international. Average age 31. 66 applicants, 95% accepted, 54 enrolled. In 2017, 59 master's awarded. *Degree requirements:* For master's, thesis; for doctorate, thesis/dissertation, qualifying examination. *Entrance requirements:* For master's, MAT or GRE, undergraduate transcript, two recommendations, personal statement. Additional exam requirements/recommendations for international students: Required—TOEFL. *Application deadline:* Applications are processed on a rolling basis. Application fee: $50. Electronic applications accepted. *Expenses:* Contact institution. *Financial support:* Applicants required to submit FAFSA. *Faculty research:* ABA intervention for autism, behavioral assessment, evidence-based treatments. *Unit head:* Dr. Mary Jane Weiss, Director of Autism and Applied Behavior Analysis, 978-232-2199, E-mail: mweiss@endicott.edu. *Application contact:* Ian Menchini, Director, Graduate Enrollment and Advising, 978-232-5292, Fax: 978-232-3000, E-mail: imenchin@endicott.edu.
Website: http://www.endicott.edu/VanLoan/Institute-Behavioral-Studies/Degree-Programs/Master-Ed-Autism-ABA.aspx

Endicott College, Van Loan School of Graduate and Professional Studies, Special Education and Applied Behavior Analysis Program, Beverly, MA 01915-2096. Offers applied behavior analysis (M Ed, Post-Master's Certificate); special education (M Ed). *Program availability:* Part-time, evening/weekend, 100% online, blended/hybrid learning. *Faculty:* 5 full-time (3 women), 23 part-time/adjunct (18 women). *Students:* 50 full-time (41 women), 90 part-time (79 women); includes 9 minority (4 Black or African American, non-Hispanic/Latino; 2 Asian, non-Hispanic/Latino; 3 Hispanic/Latino). Average age 29. 26 applicants, 100% accepted, 21 enrolled. In 2017, 101 master's, 9 other advanced degrees awarded. *Degree requirements:* For master's, comprehensive exam, thesis, practicum. *Entrance requirements:* For master's, MAT or GRE, Massachusetts teaching certificate, letters of recommendation, undergraduate transcript, essay. Additional exam requirements/recommendations for international students: Required—TOEFL. *Application deadline:* Applications are processed on a rolling basis. Application fee: $50. Electronic applications accepted. *Expenses:* Contact institution. *Financial support:* Career-related internships or fieldwork, Federal Work-Study, and institutionally sponsored loans available. Financial award applicants required to submit FAFSA. *Faculty research:* Evidence-based treatments, developmental disabilities, challenging

behaviors, staff training/management, behavioral assessments. *Unit head:* Allyson Penaloza, Assistant Director and Recruiter, 978-816-7642, Fax: 978-232-3000, E-mail: apenaloz@endicott.edu. *Application contact:* Ian Menchini, Director, Graduate Enrollment and Advising, 978-232-5292, E-mail: imenchin@endicott.edu.
Website: https://vanloan.endicott.edu/programs-of-study/masters-programs/educator-preparation-program/special-education-moderate-disabilities-program

Fairfield University, Graduate School of Education and Allied Professions, Fairfield, CT 06824. Offers applied behavior analysis (ATC); applied psychology (MA); clinical mental health counseling (MA, CAS); educational technology (MA); elementary education (MA, CAS); family studies (MA); integration of spirituality and religion in counseling (ATC); marriage and family therapy (MA); reading and language development (Sixth Year Certificate); school counseling (MA, CAS); school psychology (MA, CAS); school-based marriage and family therapy (ATC); secondary education (MA); special education (MA, CAS); substance abuse counseling (ATC); teaching (Certificate); teaching and foundations (MA, CAS); TESOL, world languages, and bilingual education (MA, CAS). *Accreditation:* NCATE. *Program availability:* Part-time, evening/weekend. *Faculty:* 23 full-time (17 women), 39 part-time/adjunct (28 women). *Students:* 199 full-time (168 women), 251 part-time (206 women); includes 85 minority (21 Black or African American, non-Hispanic/Latino; 9 Asian, non-Hispanic/Latino; 49 Hispanic/Latino; 6 Two or more races, non-Hispanic/Latino), 4 international. Average age 32. 370 applicants, 56% accepted, 125 enrolled. In 2017, 136 master's, 28 other advanced degrees awarded. *Degree requirements:* For master's, comprehensive exam. *Entrance requirements:* For master's, minimum GPA of 3.0, 2 recommendations, resume. Additional exam requirements/recommendations for international students: Required—TOEFL (minimum score 550 paper-based; 84 iBT) or IELTS (minimum score 7.5). *Application deadline:* For fall admission, 2/15 for international students; for spring admission, 10/1 for international students. Application fee: $60. Electronic applications accepted. *Expenses:* $750 per credit hour. *Financial support:* In 2017–18, 34 students received support. Career-related internships or fieldwork and unspecified assistantships available. Support available to part-time students. Financial award applicants required to submit FAFSA. *Faculty research:* Reading and literacy, writing, social justice and inequality in education, addictions and mental health issues, therapeutic relationships and clinical supervision. *Unit head:* Dr. Robert D. Hannafin, Dean, 203-254-4250, Fax: 203-254-4241, E-mail: rhannafin@fairfield.edu. *Application contact:* Marianne Gumpper, Director of Graduate Admission, 203-254-4184, Fax: 203-254-4073, E-mail: gradadmis@fairfield.edu.
Website: http://www.fairfield.edu/gseap

Fairleigh Dickinson University, Metropolitan Campus, University College: Arts, Sciences, and Professional Studies, Peter Sammartino School of Education, Program in Learning Disabilities, Teaneck, NJ 07666-1914. Offers MA. *Accreditation:* TEAC.

Fairmont State University, Programs in Education, Fairmont, WV 26554. Offers digital media, new literacies and learning (M Ed); education (MAT); exercise science, fitness and wellness (M Ed); professional studies (M Ed); reading (M Ed); special education (M Ed). *Accreditation:* NCATE. *Program availability:* Part-time, evening/weekend, 100% online. *Entrance requirements:* For master's, GRE. Additional exam requirements/recommendations for international students: Required—TOEFL (minimum score 80 iBT), IELTS (minimum score 6.5). Electronic applications accepted.

Ferris State University, College of Education and Human Services, School of Education, Big Rapids, MI 49307. Offers curriculum and instruction (M Ed), including special education, subject area; educational leadership (MS); instructor (MSCTE); post-secondary administration (MSCTE); training and development (MSCTE). *Program availability:* Part-time, evening/weekend, blended/hybrid learning. *Faculty:* 7 full-time (4 women), 9 part-time/adjunct (6 women). *Students:* 4 full-time (1 woman), 40 part-time (23 women); includes 7 minority (3 Black or African American, non-Hispanic/Latino; 2 Hispanic/Latino; 2 Two or more races, non-Hispanic/Latino), 4 international. Average age 37. 13 applicants, 92% accepted, 7 enrolled. In 2017, 36 master's awarded. *Degree requirements:* For master's, thesis, research paper or project. *Entrance requirements:* For master's, minimum undergraduate GPA of 3.0. Additional exam requirements/recommendations for international students: Required—TOEFL (minimum score 500 paper-based, 79 iBT) or IELTS. *Application deadline:* For fall admission, 7/1 priority date for domestic and international students; for spring admission, 11/1 priority date for domestic and international students; for summer admission, 3/1 priority date for domestic and international students. Applications are processed on a rolling basis. Application fee: $30. Electronic applications accepted. Application fee is waived when completed online. *Financial support:* Career-related internships or fieldwork and scholarships/grants available. Support available to part-time students. Financial award applicants required to submit FAFSA. *Faculty research:* Suicide prevention, reading, women in education, special needs, administration. *Unit head:* Arrick L. Jackson, Dean, 231-591-2702, Fax: 231-591-2043, E-mail: arrickjackson@ferris.edu. *Application contact:* Liza Ing, Graduate Program Coordinator, 231-591-5362, Fax: 231-591-2043, E-mail: lizaIng@ferris.edu.
Website: http://www.ferris.edu/education/education/

Fitchburg State University, Division of Graduate and Continuing Education, Program in Special Education, Fitchburg, MA 01420-2697. Offers guided studies: dyslexia specialist (M Ed); guided studies: individualized (M Ed); guided studies: professional (M Ed); moderate disabilities: initial licensure (5-12) (M Ed); moderate disabilities: initial licensure (PK-8) (M Ed); teacher of students with severe disabilities (M Ed). *Accreditation:* NCATE. *Program availability:* Part-time, evening/weekend. *Faculty:* 8 full-time (5 women), 24 part-time/adjunct (21 women). *Students:* 192 full-time (170 women), 118 part-time (102 women); includes 19 minority (6 Black or African American, non-Hispanic/Latino; 2 American Indian or Alaska Native, non-Hispanic/Latino; 1 Asian, non-Hispanic/Latino; 4 Hispanic/Latino; 6 Two or more races, non-Hispanic/Latino). Average age 33. 71 applicants, 100% accepted, 58 enrolled. In 2017, 70 master's awarded. *Degree requirements:* For master's, internship. *Entrance requirements:* Additional exam requirements/recommendations for international students: Required—TOEFL (minimum score 550 paper-based; 79 iBT). *Application deadline:* For fall admission, 7/15 for international students; for spring admission, 12/1 for international students. Applications are processed on a rolling basis. Application fee: $50. Electronic applications accepted. *Expenses:* Contact institution. *Financial support:* In 2017–18, research assistantships with partial tuition reimbursements (averaging $5,500 per year) were awarded; Federal Work-Study, scholarships/grants, and unspecified assistantships also available. Support available to part-time students. Financial award application deadline: 3/1; financial award applicants required to submit FAFSA. *Unit head:* Dr. Anne Howard, Chair, 978-665-3309, Fax: 978-665-3658, E-mail: gce@fitchburgstate.edu. *Application contact:* Jinawa McNeil, Director of Admissions, 978-665-3140, Fax: 978-665-4540, E-mail: admissions@fitchburgstate.edu.

Flagler College, Program in Deaf Education, St. Augustine, FL 32085-1027. Offers MA.

Florida Atlantic University, College of Education, Department of Exceptional Student Education, Boca Raton, FL 33431-0991. Offers M Ed, Ed D. *Accreditation:* NCATE. *Program availability:* Part-time, evening/weekend. *Faculty:* 13 full-time (6 women). *Students:* 19 full-time (18 women), 39 part-time (36 women); includes 20 minority (8 Black or African American, non-Hispanic/Latino; 2 Asian, non-Hispanic/Latino; 8 Hispanic/Latino; 2 Two or more races, non-Hispanic/Latino). Average age 32. 34

applicants, 62% accepted, 15 enrolled. In 2017, 12 master's, 2 doctorates awarded. *Degree requirements:* For master's, thesis optional, internship; for doctorate, comprehensive exam, thesis/dissertation, internship. *Entrance requirements:* For master's, GRE General Test, minimum GPA of 3.0 during previous 2 years; for doctorate, GRE General Test, 3 years of teaching experience, interview. Additional exam requirements/recommendations for international students: Required—TOEFL (minimum score 500 paper-based; 61 iBT), IELTS (minimum score 6). *Application deadline:* For fall admission, 7/1 for domestic students, 2/15 for international students; for spring admission, 11/1 for domestic students, 7/15 for international students. Applications are processed on a rolling basis. Application fee: $30. Electronic applications accepted. *Expenses:* Tuition, state resident: full-time $7400; part-time $369.82 per credit. Tuition, nonresident: full-time $20,496; part-time $1042.81 per credit. *Financial support:* Fellowships with tuition reimbursements, research assistantships with tuition reimbursements, teaching assistantships with partial tuition reimbursements, career-related internships or fieldwork, Federal Work-Study, scholarships/grants, tuition waivers (partial), and unspecified assistantships available. Support available to part-time students. Financial award applicants required to submit FAFSA. *Faculty research:* Instructional design, assessment, educational reform, behavioral research, social integration. *Unit head:* Ellen Ismalom, 561-297-3284, E-mail: eismalon@fau.edu.
Website: http://www.coe.fau.edu/academicdepartments/ese/

Florida Gulf Coast University, College of Education, Program in Curriculum and Instruction, Fort Myers, FL 33965-6565. Offers elementary education (M Ed); English education (M Ed); English speakers of other languages endorsement (M Ed); gifted education (M Ed); mathematics education (M Ed); middle school education (M Ed); reading education (M Ed); science education (M Ed); social science education (M Ed); special education (M Ed). *Program availability:* Part-time, evening/weekend, online learning. *Faculty:* 27 full-time (19 women), 44 part-time/adjunct (30 women). *Students:* 3 full-time (all women), 16 part-time (14 women); includes 4 minority (2 Black or African American, non-Hispanic/Latino; 2 Hispanic/Latino). Average age 30. 6 applicants, 100% accepted, 5 enrolled. In 2017, 4 master's awarded. *Degree requirements:* For master's, final project or portfolio. *Entrance requirements:* For master's, GRE General Test, MAT, minimum undergraduate GPA of 3.0 in last 2 years. Additional exam requirements/recommendations for international students: Required—TOEFL (minimum score 550 paper-based). *Application deadline:* For fall admission, 2/15 priority date for domestic students, 5/1 for international students; for spring admission, 12/1 for domestic students, 9/15 for international students. Applications are processed on a rolling basis. Application fee: $30. Electronic applications accepted. *Expenses:* Tuition, state resident: part-time $290 per credit hour. Tuition, nonresident: part-time $1173 per credit hour. *Required fees:* $127 per credit hour. Tuition and fees vary according to course load. *Financial support:* In 2017–18, 2 students received support. Application deadline: 6/30; applicants required to submit FAFSA. *Faculty research:* Internet in schools, technology in pre-service and in-service teacher training. *Unit head:* Dr. Vickie Johnston, Instructor, 239-590-7754, Fax: 239-590-7801, E-mail: vjohnston@fgcu.edu. *Application contact:* Keiana Desmore, Adviser/Counselor, 239-590-7759, Fax: 239-590-7801, E-mail: kdesmore@fgcu.edu.
Website: http://coe.fgcu.edu/c-imed/

Florida Gulf Coast University, College of Education, Program in Special Education, Fort Myers, FL 33965-6565. Offers behavior disorders (M Ed); mental retardation (M Ed); specific learning disabilities (M Ed); varying exceptionalities (M Ed). *Program availability:* Part-time, evening/weekend. *Faculty:* 27 full-time (19 women), 44 part-time/adjunct (30 women). *Students:* 7 part-time (all women); includes 2 minority (1 Black or African American, non-Hispanic/Latino; 1 Hispanic/Latino). Average age 33. 7 applicants, 86% accepted, 3 enrolled. In 2017, 5 master's awarded. *Degree requirements:* For master's, thesis or alternative. *Entrance requirements:* For master's, GRE General Test, MAT, minimum GPA of 3.0. Additional exam requirements/recommendations for international students: Required—TOEFL (minimum score 550 paper-based). *Application deadline:* For fall admission, 7/1 priority date for domestic students, 7/1 for international students; for spring admission, 10/15 priority date for domestic students, 10/15 for international students. Applications are processed on a rolling basis. Application fee: $30. Electronic applications accepted. *Expenses:* Tuition, state resident: part-time $290 per credit hour. Tuition, nonresident: part-time $1173 per credit hour. *Required fees:* $127 per credit hour. Tuition and fees vary according to course load. *Financial support:* Application deadline: 6/30; applicants required to submit FAFSA. *Faculty research:* Inclusion, interacting with families, alternative certification. *Unit head:* Dr. Douglas Carothers, Associate Professor, 239-590-7822, E-mail: dcarothe@fgcu.edu. *Application contact:* Andrew Wilson, Office Manager, 239-590-7747, Fax: 239-590-7801, E-mail: awillson@fgcu.edu.

Florida International University, College of Arts, Sciences, and Education, Department of Teaching and Learning, Miami, FL 33199. Offers art education (MA, MS); curriculum and instruction (MS, Ed D, PhD, Ed S), including curriculum development (MS), elementary education (MS), English education (MS), learning technologies (MS), mathematics education (MS), modern language education (MS), physical education (MS), science education (MS), social studies education (MS), special education (MS); early childhood education (MS); exceptional student education (Ed D); foreign language education (MS), including foreign language education, teaching English to speakers of other languages (TESOL); language, literacy and culture (PhD); mathematics, science, and learning technologies (PhD); physical education (MS), including sport and fitness; reading education (MS). *Program availability:* Part-time, evening/weekend. *Faculty:* 60 full-time (41 women), 112 part-time/adjunct (77 women). *Students:* 165 full-time (139 women), 191 part-time (148 women); includes 270 minority (56 Black or African American, non-Hispanic/Latino; 12 Asian, non-Hispanic/Latino; 191 Hispanic/Latino; 11 Two or more races, non-Hispanic/Latino), 13 international. Average age 34. 238 applicants, 68% accepted, 107 enrolled. In 2017, 184 master's, 15 doctorates awarded. *Degree requirements:* For doctorate, comprehensive exam, thesis/dissertation. *Entrance requirements:* For master's, GRE General Test, Florida General Knowledge Test or Florida College Level Academic Skills Test; for doctorate and Ed S, GRE General Test. Additional exam requirements/recommendations for international students: Required—TOEFL (minimum score 550 paper-based; 80 iBT), IELTS (minimum score 6.3). *Application deadline:* For fall admission, 6/1 priority date for domestic students, 4/1 for international students; for winter admission, 10/1 priority date for domestic students, 9/1 for international students; for spring admission, 3/1 priority date for domestic students, 2/1 for international students. Applications are processed on a rolling basis. Application fee: $30. Electronic applications accepted. *Expenses:* Tuition, state resident: full-time $8912; part-time $446 per credit hour. Tuition, nonresident: full-time $21,393; part-time $992 per credit hour. *Required fees:* $390; $195 per semester. *Financial support:* Research assistantships with tuition reimbursements and teaching assistantships with tuition reimbursements available. *Unit head:* Dr. Lynn Miller, Chair, 305-348-2005, Fax: 305-348-2086, E-mail: lynne.miller@fiu.edu. *Application contact:* Nanett Rojas, Assistant Director, Graduate Admissions, 305-348-7464, Fax: 305-348-7441, E-mail: gradadm@fiu.edu.
Website: https://tl.fiu.edu/

Florida Memorial University, School of Education, Miami-Dade, FL 33054. Offers elementary education (MS); exceptional student education (MS); reading (MS). *Degree*

requirements: For master's, comprehensive exam or thesis, field and clinical experiences, exit exam. *Entrance requirements:* For master's, GRE, CLAST, PRAXIS I, baccalaureate or graduate degree with minimum GPA of 3.0 in last 60 hours, 3 recommendations. Additional exam requirements/recommendations for international students: Recommended—TOEFL.

Florida State University, The Graduate School, College of Education, School of Teacher Education, Tallahassee, FL 32306-4450. Offers curriculum and instruction (MS, PhD, Ed S), including early childhood education, elementary education, English education, foreign and second language education, mathematics education, reading and language arts, science education, social science education, special education, visual disabilities education (MS); teaching English to speakers of other languages (Certificate). *Program availability:* Part-time, evening/weekend, 100% online, blended/hybrid learning, asynchronous, minimal on-campus study. *Faculty:* 41 full-time (33 women), 21 part-time/adjunct (18 women). *Students:* 133 full-time (93 women), 84 part-time (69 women); includes 48 minority (20 Black or African American, non-Hispanic/Latino; 2 Asian, non-Hispanic/Latino; 19 Hispanic/Latino; 7 Two or more races, non-Hispanic/Latino), 52 international. Average age 31. 146 applicants, 56% accepted, 52 enrolled. In 2017, 91 master's, 7 doctorates, 1 other advanced degree awarded. Terminal master's awarded for partial completion of doctoral program. *Degree requirements:* For master's and other advanced degree, comprehensive exam, thesis optional; for doctorate, comprehensive exam, thesis/dissertation, diagnostic exam, preliminary exam, prospectus defense, dissertation defense. *Entrance requirements:* For master's, doctorate, and other advanced degree, GRE General Test, minimum upper-division GPA of 3.0. Additional exam requirements/recommendations for international students: Required—TOEFL (minimum score 550 paper-based, 80 iBT), Michigan English Language Assessment Battery (minimum score 77), IELTS (minimum score 6.5) or PTE (minimum score 55). Application fee: $30. Electronic applications accepted. *Financial support:* Fellowships, research assistantships, teaching assistantships, scholarships/grants, tuition waivers (full and partial), and unspecified assistantships available. Financial award application deadline: 1/15; financial award applicants required to submit FAFSA. *Faculty research:* Identifying effective intervention strategies to improve reading skills; improving literacy teaching and learning through technology; understanding of student sense making, problem solving, the history and structure of STEM disciplines, and teacher education to support the development of ambitious instruction that supports the STEM learning of all students; examining practices of international education; identifying ways to support the professional development of teachers. *Unit head:* Dr. Sherry Southerland, Professor/Department Chair, 850-644-6885, Fax: 850-644-2725, E-mail: ssoutherland@admin.fsu.edu. *Application contact:* Britni DeZerga, Academic Program Specialist, 850-644-2122, Fax: 850-644-7736, E-mail: bpurvis@fsu.edu.
Website: http://education.fsu.edu

Fontbonne University, Graduate Programs, St. Louis, MO 63105-3098. Offers accounting (MBA, MS); art (MA); art (K-12) (MAT); business (MBA); computer science (MS); deaf education (MA); early intervention in deaf education (MA); education (MA), including autism spectrum disorders, curriculum and instruction, diverse learners, early childhood education, reading, special education; elementary education (MAT); family and consumer sciences (MA), including multidisciplinary health communication studies; fine arts (MFA); instructional design and technology (MS); management and leadership (MM); middle school education (MAT); secondary education (MAT); special education (MAT); speech-language pathology (MS); supply chain management (MS); theatre (MA). *Program availability:* Part-time, evening/weekend, online learning. *Degree requirements:* For master's, comprehensive exam (for some programs), thesis (for some programs). *Entrance requirements:* Additional exam requirements/recommendations for international students: Required—TOEFL (minimum score 500 paper-based; 65 iBT). Electronic applications accepted.

Fordham University, Graduate School of Education, Division of Curriculum and Teaching, New York, NY 10023. Offers curriculum and teaching (MSE); early childhood education (MSE); elementary education (MST); special education (MSE, Adv C); teaching English as a second language (MSE). *Accreditation:* NCATE. *Program availability:* Part-time, evening/weekend. *Degree requirements:* For Adv C, thesis. *Entrance requirements:* Additional exam requirements/recommendations for international students: Required—TOEFL (minimum score 577 paper-based; 90 iBT), IELTS (minimum score 7). Electronic applications accepted.

Fort Hays State University, Graduate School, College of Education, Department of Special Education, Hays, KS 67601-4099. Offers MS. *Accreditation:* NCATE. *Degree requirements:* For master's, comprehensive exam, thesis optional. *Entrance requirements:* Additional exam requirements/recommendations for international students: Required—TOEFL (minimum score 550 paper-based). Electronic applications accepted. *Faculty research:* Severe behavior disorders, early childhood language, multicultural speech.

Framingham State University, Graduate Studies, Program in Special Education, Framingham, MA 01701-9101. Offers M Ed. *Program availability:* Part-time, evening/weekend. *Entrance requirements:* For master's, MAT, interview. *Unit head:* Dr. Robert Freyermuth, Program Coordinator. *Application contact:* Graduate Office, 508-626-4550, Fax: 508-626-4030, E-mail: dgce@frc.mass.edu.

Francis Marion University, Graduate Programs, School of Education, Florence, SC 29502-0547. Offers learning disabilities (M Ed, MAT). *Accreditation:* NCATE. *Program availability:* Part-time. *Degree requirements:* For master's, comprehensive exam (for some programs), thesis (for some programs), supervised internship (for MAT). *Entrance requirements:* For master's, GRE General Test, MAT, NTE, or PRAXIS II, official transcripts; two letters of recommendation. Additional exam requirements/recommendations for international students: Required—TOEFL (minimum score 550 paper-based; 79 iBT). *Faculty research:* Identification and alternate assessment of at-risk students.

Franklin Pierce University, Graduate and Professional Studies, Rindge, NH 03461-0060. Offers curriculum and instruction (M Ed); elementary education (MS Ed); emerging network technologies (Graduate Certificate); energy and sustainability studies (MBA, Graduate Certificate); health administration (MBA, Graduate Certificate); human resource management (MBA, Graduate Certificate); information technology (MBA); leadership (MBA); nursing education (MS); nursing leadership (MS); physical therapy (DPT); physician assistant studies (MPAS); special education (M Ed); sports management (MBA). *Accreditation:* APTA. *Program availability:* Part-time, 100% online, blended/hybrid learning. *Degree requirements:* For master's, concentrated original research projects; student teaching; fieldwork and/or internship; leadership project; PRAXIS I and II (for M Ed); for doctorate, concentrated original research projects, clinical fieldwork and/or internship, leadership project. *Entrance requirements:* For master's, minimum GPA of 2.5, 3 letters of recommendation; competencies in accounting, economics, statistics, and computer skills through life experience or undergraduate coursework (for MBA); certification/e-portfolio, minimum C grade in all education courses (for M Ed); license to practice as RN (for MS); for doctorate, GRE, 80 hours of observation/work in PT settings; completion of anatomy, chemistry, physics, and statistics; minimum GPA of 3.0. Additional exam requirements/recommendations for international students: Required—TOEFL (minimum score 550 paper-based; 61 iBT).

Special Education

Electronic applications accepted. *Faculty research:* Evidence-based practice in sports physical therapy, human resource management in economic crisis, leadership in nursing, innovation in sports facility management, differentiated learning and understanding by design.

Freed-Hardeman University, Program in Education, Henderson, TN 38340-2399. Offers curriculum and instruction (M Ed); school counseling (M Ed), including administration and supervision, special education; school leadership (Ed S). *Accreditation:* NCATE. *Program availability:* Part-time, evening/weekend. *Degree requirements:* For master's, comprehensive exam, thesis optional; for Ed S, thesis. *Entrance requirements:* For master's, GRE General Test or NTE; for Ed S, 3 years of teaching experience. Additional exam requirements/recommendations for international students: Required—TOEFL (minimum score 500 paper-based).

Fresno Pacific University, Graduate Programs, School of Education, Division of Special Education, Fresno, CA 93702-4709. Offers MA. *Program availability:* Part-time, evening/weekend. *Degree requirements:* For master's, thesis or alternative. *Entrance requirements:* Additional exam requirements/recommendations for international students: Required—TOEFL (minimum score 550 paper-based).

Frostburg State University, College of Education, Department of Educational Professions, Program in Special Education, Frostburg, MD 21532. Offers M Ed. *Accreditation:* NCATE. *Program availability:* Part-time, evening/weekend. *Faculty:* 3. *Students:* 5 full-time (4 women), 42 part-time (31 women); includes 5 minority (2 Black or African American, non-Hispanic/Latino; 1 Asian, non-Hispanic/Latino; 1 Hispanic/Latino; 1 Two or more races, non-Hispanic/Latino). Average age 32. 17 applicants, 94% accepted, 9 enrolled. In 2017, 15 master's awarded. *Degree requirements:* For master's, thesis or alternative, PRAXIS II (special education section). *Entrance requirements:* For master's, teaching certificate. Additional exam requirements/recommendations for international students: Required—TOEFL. *Application deadline:* For fall admission, 7/15 priority date for domestic students. Applications are processed on a rolling basis. Application fee: $45. Electronic applications accepted. *Expenses:* Tuition, state resident: part-time $433 per credit hour. Tuition, nonresident: part-time $557 per credit hour. *Required fees:* $121 per credit hour. $27 per term. *Financial support:* In 2017–18, 1 research assistantship with full tuition reimbursement (averaging $5,000 per year) was awarded. Financial award application deadline: 4/1; financial award applicants required to submit FAFSA. *Unit head:* Jamey Tobery-Nystrom, Coordinator, 240-527-2735, E-mail: jctoberynystrom@frostburg.edu. *Application contact:* Vickie Mazer, Director, Graduate Services, 301-687-7053, Fax: 301-687-4597, E-mail: vmmazer@frostburg.edu.

Furman University, Graduate Division, Department of Education, Greenville, SC 29613. Offers curriculum and instruction (MA); early childhood education (MA); educational leadership (Ed S); English as a second language (MA); literacy (MA); school leadership (MA); special education (MA). *Accreditation:* NCATE. *Program availability:* Part-time, online learning. *Degree requirements:* For master's, comprehensive exam (for some programs), thesis or alternative. *Entrance requirements:* For master's, PRAXIS II. *Faculty research:* Literacy, pedagogy and practice, social justice, advanced leadership, achievement in high poverty schools.

Gallaudet University, The Graduate School, Washington, DC 20002-3625. Offers American Sign Language/English bilingual early childhood deaf education: birth to 5 (Certificate); audiology (Au D); clinical psychology (PhD); deaf and hard of hearing infants, toddlers, and their families (Certificate); deaf education (MA, Ed S); deaf history (Certificate); deaf studies (Certificate); educating deaf students with disabilities (Certificate); education: teacher preparation (MA), including deaf education, early childhood education and deaf education, elementary education and deaf education, secondary education and deaf education; educational neuroscience (PhD); hearing, speech and language sciences (MS, PhD); international development (MA); interpretation (MA, PhD), including combined interpreting practice and research (MA); interpreting research (MA); linguistics (MA, PhD); mental health counseling (MA); peer mentoring (Certificate); public administration (MPA); school counseling (MA); school psychology (Psy S); sign language teaching (MA); social work (MSW); speech-language pathology (MS). *Program availability:* Part-time. Terminal master's awarded for partial completion of doctoral program. *Degree requirements:* For master's, comprehensive exam (for some programs), thesis optional; for doctorate, comprehensive exam, thesis/dissertation. *Entrance requirements:* For master's and doctorate, GRE General Test or MAT, letters of recommendation, interviews, goals statement, American Sign Language proficiency interview, written English competency. Additional exam requirements/recommendations for international students: Required—TOEFL. Electronic applications accepted. *Faculty research:* Signing math dictionaries, telecommunications access, cancer genetics, linguistics, visual language and visual learning, integrated quantum materials, deaf legal discourse, advance recruitment and retention in geosciences.

George Fox University, College of Education, Graduate Teaching and Leading Program, Newberg, OR 97132-2697. Offers administrative leadership (Ed S); continuing administrator license (Certificate); educational leadership (M Ed); educational technology (M Ed); English for speakers of other languages (M Ed); ESOL (Certificate); initial administrator license (Certificate); reading (M Ed, Certificate); special education (M Ed); teaching (MAT). *Accreditation:* NCATE. *Program availability:* Part-time, evening/weekend, online learning. *Degree requirements:* For master's, thesis (for some programs). *Entrance requirements:* For master's, minimum undergraduate GPA of 3.0 during previous 2 years of course work, resume, 3 professional recommendations on university forms, official transcripts. Additional exam requirements/recommendations for international students: Required—TOEFL (minimum score 577 paper-based; 90 iBT). Electronic applications accepted. *Expenses:* Contact institution.

George Mason University, College of Education and Human Development, Program in Special Education, Fairfax, VA 22030. Offers M Ed, Certificate. *Program availability:* Part-time, evening/weekend, 100% online. *Faculty:* 23 full-time (19 women), 40 part-time/adjunct (37 women). *Students:* 71 full-time (64 women), 560 part-time (464 women); includes 196 minority (78 Black or African American, non-Hispanic/Latino; 1 American Indian or Alaska Native, non-Hispanic/Latino; 52 Asian, non-Hispanic/Latino; 52 Hispanic/Latino; 13 Two or more races, non-Hispanic/Latino), 11 international. Average age 34. 263 applicants, 91% accepted, 185 enrolled. In 2017, 224 master's awarded. *Degree requirements:* For master's, professional portfolio. *Entrance requirements:* For master's, bachelor's degree from regionally-accredited institution with minimum GPA of 3.0 cumulative or in last 60 credits of undergraduate study (or PRAXIS I, SAT, ACT or VCLA); 2 official transcripts; 2 letters of recommendation; goals statement. Additional exam requirements/recommendations for international students: Required—TOEFL (minimum score 575 paper-based; 88 iBT), IELTS (minimum score 6.5), PTE (minimum score 59). *Application deadline:* For fall admission, 4/2 priority date for domestic and international students; for spring admission, 11/1 for domestic and international students. Application fee: $75 ($80 for international students). Electronic applications accepted. *Expenses:* $775 per credit. *Financial support:* In 2017–18, 1 student received support, including 1 research assistantship; career-related internships or fieldwork, Federal Work-Study, and scholarships/grants also available. Financial award application deadline: 3/1; financial award applicants required to submit FAFSA. *Faculty research:* Adapted captions through interactive video, DEVISE Project (multisensory virtual learning environment), KIHd System Project (teachers utilizing Kellar Institute handheld data system and Literary Online). *Unit head:* Pam Baker, Director, 703-993-1787, Fax: 703-993-3681, E-mail: pbaker5@gmu.edu. *Application contact:* Jancy Templeton, Advisor, 703-993-2387, Fax: 703-993-3681, E-mail: jtemple1@gmu.edu.
Website: http://gse.gmu.edu/programs/sped/

George Mason University, College of Education and Human Development, Programs in Curriculum and Instruction, Fairfax, VA 22030. Offers advanced international baccalaureate (M Ed); assistive technology (M Ed); designing digital learning in schools (M Ed); early childhood education (M Ed); early childhood education for diverse learners (M Ed); elementary education (M Ed); English as a second language (M Ed); gifted child education (M Ed); history (M Ed); literacy (M Ed), including PK-12 classroom teachers, reading specialist; literacy leadership for diverse schools (M Ed), including K-12 reading; physical education (M Ed); science K-12 (M Ed); secondary education (M Ed), including biology, chemistry, earth science, English, history/social science, math, physics; special education (M Ed); teacher leadership (M Ed); teaching culturally, linguistically diverse and exceptional learners (M Ed); transformative teaching (M Ed). *Program availability:* Part-time, evening/weekend, 100% online, blended/hybrid learning. *Faculty:* 41 full-time (36 women), 45 part-time/adjunct (37 women). *Students:* 173 full-time (151 women), 729 part-time (611 women); includes 271 minority (65 Black or African American, non-Hispanic/Latino; 5 American Indian or Alaska Native, non-Hispanic/Latino; 88 Asian, non-Hispanic/Latino; 94 Hispanic/Latino; 1 Native Hawaiian or other Pacific Islander, non-Hispanic/Latino; 18 Two or more races, non-Hispanic/Latino), 28 international. Average age 32. 426 applicants, 91% accepted, 289 enrolled. In 2017, 349 master's awarded. *Degree requirements:* For master's, thesis. *Entrance requirements:* For master's, PRAXIS Core (for some programs), 2 letters of recommendation, interview, program goals statement; 9 hours of complete licensure endorsement requirements (for elementary education); minimum GPA of 3.0 in applicant's last 60 hours of undergraduate coursework (for secondary education); at least 1 year of teaching experience (for literacy). Additional exam requirements/recommendations for international students: Required—TOEFL (minimum score 575 paper-based; 88 iBT), IELTS (minimum score 6.5), PTE (minimum score 59). *Application deadline:* For fall admission, 4/2 priority date for domestic and international students; for spring admission, 11/1 for domestic and international students. Application fee: $75 ($80 for international students). Electronic applications accepted. *Expenses:* Tuition, state resident: full-time $11,228; part-time $459.50 per credit. Tuition, nonresident: full-time $30,932; part-time $1280.50 per credit. *Required fees:* $3252; $135.50 per credit. Part-time tuition and fees vary according to course load and program. *Financial support:* In 2017–18, 2 students received support, including 2 teaching assistantships; career-related internships or fieldwork, Federal Work-Study, scholarships/grants, unspecified assistantships, and health care benefits (for full-time research or teaching assistantship recipients) also available. Support available to part-time students. Financial award application deadline: 3/1; financial award applicants required to submit FAFSA. *Faculty research:* Teacher preparation and professional development; adaptive teaching; wonder in science teacher preparation; literacy (digital, adolescent); site based course instruction. *Unit head:* Rebecca Fox, Professor and Academic Program Coordinator, 703-993-4123, E-mail: rfox@gmu.edu.
Website: http://gse.gmu.edu/programs/gsemasters

Georgetown College, Department of Education, Georgetown, KY 40324-1696. Offers reading and writing (MA Ed); special education (MA Ed); teaching (MA Ed). *Accreditation:* NCATE. *Program availability:* Part-time. *Degree requirements:* For master's, portfolio. *Entrance requirements:* For master's, teaching certificate, minimum GPA of 2.7 or GRE General Test.

The George Washington University, Graduate School of Education and Human Development, Department of Counseling and Human Development, Washington, DC 20052. Offers clinical mental health counseling (MA); counseling (PhD, Ed S); counseling culturally and linguistically diverse persons (MA Ed/HD, Certificate); forensic rehabilitation counseling (Graduate Certificate); job development and placement (Graduate Certificate); rehabilitation counseling (MA Ed/HD), including autism spectrum disorder, substance abuse and psychiatric disabilities, traumatic brain injury; school counseling (MA Ed, Graduate Certificate). *Accreditation:* ACA (one or more programs are accredited). *Program availability:* Part-time, evening/weekend. *Faculty:* 14 full-time (9 women). *Students:* 119 full-time (91 women), 71 part-time (60 women); includes 72 minority (27 Black or African American, non-Hispanic/Latino; 3 American Indian or Alaska Native, non-Hispanic/Latino; 16 Asian, non-Hispanic/Latino; 21 Hispanic/Latino; 5 Two or more races, non-Hispanic/Latino), 15 international. Average age 32. 343 applicants, 50% accepted, 74 enrolled. In 2017, 57 master's, 5 doctorates, 11 other advanced degrees awarded. *Degree requirements:* For master's and other advanced degree, comprehensive exam; for doctorate, comprehensive exam, thesis/dissertation. *Entrance requirements:* For master's, GRE General Test or MAT, minimum GPA of 2.75; for doctorate, GRE General Test or MAT, interview, minimum GPA of 3.3; for other advanced degree, GRE General Test or MAT, minimum GPA of 3.3. *Application deadline:* For fall admission, 1/15 priority date for domestic students; for spring admission, 10/1 for domestic students. Applications are processed on a rolling basis. Application fee: $75. *Expenses:* Tuition: Full-time $28,800; part-time $1655 per credit hour. *Required fees:* $45; $2.75 per credit hour. *Financial support:* In 2017–18, 58 students received support. Fellowships with tuition reimbursements available, research assistantships, teaching assistantships with tuition reimbursements available, career-related internships or fieldwork, Federal Work-Study, and tuition waivers (full and partial) available. Financial award application deadline: 1/15. *Faculty research:* Multiculturalism and counseling, models of adult development. *Unit head:* Dr. Kenneth C. Hergenrather, Chair, 202-994-1334, E-mail: hergenkc@gwu.edu. *Application contact:* Sarah Lang, Director of Graduate Admissions, 202-994-1447, Fax: 202-994-7207, E-mail: slang@gwu.edu.

The George Washington University, Graduate School of Education and Human Development, Department of Special Education and Disability Studies, Program in Bilingual Special Education, Washington, DC 20052. Offers MA Ed, Certificate. *Expenses:* Tuition: Full-time $28,800; part-time $1655 per credit hour. *Required fees:* $45; $2.75 per credit hour. *Unit head:* Michael Feuer, Dean, 202-994-6161, E-mail: mjfeuer@gwu.edu. *Application contact:* Sarah Lang, Director of Graduate Admissions, 202-994-1447, Fax: 202-994-7207, E-mail: slang@gwu.edu.

The George Washington University, Graduate School of Education and Human Development, Department of Special Education and Disability Studies, Program in Early Childhood Special Education, Washington, DC 20052. Offers infant special education (MA Ed/HD). *Accreditation:* NCATE. *Students:* 16 full-time (all women), 5 part-time (all women); includes 3 minority (1 Black or African American, non-Hispanic/Latino; 1 Asian, non-Hispanic/Latino; 1 Two or more races, non-Hispanic/Latino), 13 international. Average age 27. 33 applicants, 73% accepted, 11 enrolled. In 2017, 16 master's awarded. *Entrance requirements:* For master's, GRE General Test or MAT, minimum GPA of 2.75. *Application deadline:* For fall admission, 1/15 priority date for domestic students; for spring admission, 10/1 for domestic students. Applications are processed on a rolling basis. Application fee: $75. *Expenses:* Tuition: Full-time $28,800; part-time $1655 per credit hour. *Required fees:* $45; $2.75 per credit hour. *Financial support:* In 2017–18, 19 students received support. Fellowships, career-related internships or fieldwork, Federal Work-Study, and tuition waivers (full) available. Financial award application deadline: 1/15; financial award applicants required to submit FAFSA. *Faculty research:* Computer-assisted instruction and learning, disabled learner assessment of preschool, handicapped children. *Unit head:* Dr. Marian H. Jarrett, Faculty Coordinator, 202-994-1509, E-mail: mjarrett@gwu.edu. *Application contact:* Sarah Lang, Director of Graduate Admissions, 202-994-1447, Fax: 202-994-7207, E-mail: slang@gwu.edu.

The George Washington University, Graduate School of Education and Human Development, Department of Special Education and Disability Studies, Program in Secondary Special Education and Transition Services, Washington, DC 20052. Offers adolescents with emotional and behavioral disabilities (MA Ed/HD); adolescents with learning disabilities (MA Ed/HD); brain injury special education (MA Ed/HD); brain injury specialist (MA Ed/HD); interdisciplinary transition services (MA Ed/HD). *Expenses: Tuition:* Full-time $28,800; part-time $1655 per credit hour. *Unit head:* Michael Feuer, Dean, 202-994-6161, E-mail: mjfeuer@gwu.edu. *Application contact:* Sarah Lang, Director of Graduate Admissions, 202-994-1447, Fax: 202-994-7207, E-mail: slang@gwu.edu.
Website: http://gsehd.gwu.edu/

The George Washington University, Graduate School of Education and Human Development, Department of Special Education and Disability Studies, Program in Special Education, Washington, DC 20052. Offers Ed D, Ed S. *Accreditation:* NCATE. *Students:* 8 full-time (all women), 46 part-time (36 women); includes 23 minority (12 Black or African American, non-Hispanic/Latino; 3 Asian, non-Hispanic/Latino; 6 Hispanic/Latino; 2 Two or more races, non-Hispanic/Latino), 6 international. Average age 40. 17 applicants, 59% accepted, 4 enrolled. In 2017, 3 doctorates, 10 other advanced degrees awarded. *Degree requirements:* For doctorate, comprehensive exam, thesis/dissertation; for Ed S, comprehensive exam. *Entrance requirements:* For doctorate and Ed S, GRE General Test or MAT, interview, minimum GPA of 3.3. *Application deadline:* For fall admission, 1/15 priority date for domestic students; for spring admission, 10/1 for domestic students. Applications are processed on a rolling basis. Application fee: $75. *Expenses: Tuition:* Full-time $28,800; part-time $1655 per credit hour. *Required fees:* $45; $2.75 per credit hour. *Financial support:* In 2017–18, 46 students received support. Fellowships, research assistantships, career-related internships or fieldwork, Federal Work-Study, and tuition waivers (partial) available. Financial award application deadline: 1/15; financial award applicants required to submit FAFSA. *Unit head:* Dr. Carol Kochhar, Faculty Coordinator, 202-994-1536, E-mail: kochhar@gwu.edu. *Application contact:* Sarah Lang, Director of Graduate Admissions, 202-994-1447, Fax: 202-994-7207, E-mail: slang@gwu.edu.

The George Washington University, Graduate School of Education and Human Development, Department of Special Education and Disability Studies, Program in Special Education for Children with Emotional and Behavioral Disabilities, Washington, DC 20052. Offers MA Ed/HD. *Accreditation:* NCATE. *Students:* 7 full-time (5 women), 4 part-time (3 women); includes 7 minority (5 Black or African American, non-Hispanic/Latino; 2 Asian, non-Hispanic/Latino). Average age 31. 25 applicants, 60% accepted, 11 enrolled. In 2017, 13 master's awarded. *Entrance requirements:* For master's, PRAXIS, interview, minimum GPA of 2.75, two recommendations. *Application deadline:* For fall admission, 1/15 priority date for domestic students. Applications are processed on a rolling basis. Application fee: $75. *Expenses: Tuition:* Full-time $28,800; part-time $1655 per credit hour. *Required fees:* $45; $2.75 per credit hour. *Financial support:* Fellowships, career-related internships or fieldwork, and Federal Work-Study available. Financial award application deadline: 1/15; financial award applicants required to submit FAFSA. *Faculty research:* Action research on the act of teaching emotionally disturbed students, teacher training. *Unit head:* Elisabeth Rice, Program Coordinator, 202-994-1535, E-mail: ehess@gwu.edu. *Application contact:* Sarah Lang, Director of Admission, 202-994-1447, Fax: 202-994-7207, E-mail: slang@gwu.edu.

The George Washington University, Graduate School of Education and Human Development, Department of Special Education and Disability Studies, Program in Special Education for Culturally and Linguistically Diverse Persons, Washington, DC 20052. Offers MA Ed/HD, Certificate. *Students:* 7 full-time (all women), 33 part-time (28 women); includes 15 minority (3 Black or African American, non-Hispanic/Latino; 4 Asian, non-Hispanic/Latino; 7 Hispanic/Latino; 1 Two or more races, non-Hispanic/Latino), 2 international. Average age 33. 50 applicants, 64% accepted, 17 enrolled. In 2017, 17 master's, 20 Certificates awarded. *Expenses: Tuition:* Full-time $28,800; part-time $1655 per credit hour. *Required fees:* $45; $2.75 per credit hour. *Unit head:* Doran Gresham, 202-994-2780, E-mail: dgresham@gwu.edu.

The George Washington University, Graduate School of Education and Human Development, Department of Special Education and Disability Studies, Program in Transition Special Education, Washington, DC 20052. Offers Teaching Certificate. *Accreditation:* NCATE. *Program availability:* Evening/weekend. *Students:* 10 part-time (all women). Average age 40. 7 applicants, 71% accepted, 5 enrolled. In 2017, 6 Teaching Certificates awarded. *Entrance requirements:* For degree, GRE General Test or MAT, interview, minimum GPA of 2.75. *Application deadline:* For fall admission, 1/15 priority date for domestic students; for spring admission, 10/1 for domestic students. Applications are processed on a rolling basis. Application fee: $75. *Expenses: Tuition:* Full-time $28,800; part-time $1655 per credit hour. *Required fees:* $45; $2.75 per credit hour. *Financial support:* Fellowships, research assistantships, career-related internships or fieldwork, Federal Work-Study, tuition waivers (full and partial), and stipends available. Financial award application deadline: 1/15. *Faculty research:* Computer applications for transition, transition follow-up research, curriculum-based vocational assessment, traumatic brain injury. *Unit head:* Dr. Lynda West, Coordinator, 202-994-1533, E-mail: lwest@gwu.edu. *Application contact:* Sarah Lang, Director of Graduate Admissions, 202-994-1447, Fax: 202-994-7207, E-mail: slang@gwu.edu.

Georgia College & State University, Graduate School, The John H. Lounsbury College of Education, Program in Special Education, Milledgeville, GA 31061. Offers M Ed, MAT, Ed S. *Accreditation:* NCATE. *Program availability:* Part-time, evening/weekend, blended/hybrid learning. *Students:* 28 full-time (21 women), 14 part-time (13 women); includes 10 minority (9 Black or African American, non-Hispanic/Latino; 1 American Indian or Alaska Native, non-Hispanic/Latino), 1 international. Average age 34. 1 applicant, 100% accepted, 1 enrolled. In 2017, 20 master's, 13 other advanced degrees awarded. *Degree requirements:* For master's, comprehensive exam, complete program within 6 years, minimum GPA of 3.0; for Ed S, comprehensive exam, complete program within 4 years, electronic portfolio presentation, minimum GPA of 3.0. *Entrance requirements:* For master's, GACE (for MAT), 2 professional recommendations, transcript, immunization verification, resume; minimum undergraduate GPA of 2.75 or 3 years' teaching experience (for M Ed); for Ed S, certification in special education, transcript, 2 letters of recommendation from professional references, resume, statement of purpose. *Application deadline:* For fall admission, 7/1 priority date for domestic students; for spring admission, 11/1 priority date for domestic students; for summer admission, 4/1 priority date for domestic students. Applications are processed on a rolling basis. Electronic applications accepted. *Expenses:* $288 per credit hour full-time, $2,592 per semester; fees $343. *Financial support:* Application deadline: 3/1; applicants required to submit FAFSA. *Unit head:* Dr. Joseph Peters, Dean, College of Education, 478-445-2518, Fax: 478-445-6582, E-mail: joseph.peters@gcsu.edu. *Application*

contact: Shanda Brand, Graduate Admissions Advisor, 478-445-1383, E-mail: shanda.brand@gcsu.edu.

Georgian Court University, School of Arts and Sciences, Lakewood, NJ 08701-2697. Offers applied behavior analysis (MA); autism spectrum disorders (Certificate); clinical mental health counseling (MA); criminal justice and human rights (MS); holistic health studies (MA, Certificate); homeland security (Certificate); instructional technology (CPC); mercy spirituality (Certificate); parish business management (Certificate); professional counselor (Certificate); school psychology (MA, Certificate); theology (MA, Certificate). *Program availability:* Part-time, evening/weekend. *Faculty:* 18 full-time (11 women), 8 part-time/adjunct (4 women). *Students:* 100 full-time (86 women), 92 part-time (67 women); includes 34 minority (9 Black or African American, non-Hispanic/Latino; 1 Asian, non-Hispanic/Latino; 20 Hispanic/Latino; 4 Two or more races, non-Hispanic/Latino), 2 international. Average age 34. 187 applicants, 56% accepted, 78 enrolled. In 2017, 58 master's, 20 other advanced degrees awarded. *Degree requirements:* For master's, comprehensive exam (for some programs), thesis (for some programs). *Entrance requirements:* For master's, GRE, GMAT, or NTE/PRAXIS, 3 letters of recommendation. Additional exam requirements/recommendations for international students: Required—TOEFL (minimum score 500 paper-based). *Application deadline:* For fall admission, 8/15 for domestic students, 5/1 for international students; for spring admission, 1/15 for domestic students, 10/1 for international students. Applications are processed on a rolling basis. Application fee: $40. Electronic applications accepted. *Expenses: Tuition:* Part-time $839 per credit. *Required fees:* $248 per semester. Tuition and fees vary according to campus/location and program. *Financial support:* Scholarships/grants, health care benefits, and unspecified assistantships available. Financial award application deadline: 4/15; financial award applicants required to submit FAFSA. *Unit head:* Dr. Mary Chinery, Dean, 732-987-2493, Fax: 732-987-2007, E-mail: mchinery@georgian.edu. *Application contact:* Patrick Givens, Director of Graduate and Professional Studies Admissions, 732-987-2736, Fax: 732-987-2000, E-mail: gps@georgian.edu.
Website: https://georgian.edu/academics/school-of-arts-sciences/

Georgian Court University, School of Education, Lakewood, NJ 08701-2697. Offers administration and leadership (MA); autism spectrum disorders (Certificate); education (M Ed, MA, MAT); instructional technology (M Mat SE, Certificate). *Accreditation:* TEAC. *Program availability:* Part-time, evening/weekend. *Faculty:* 11 full-time (7 women), 40 part-time/adjunct (22 women). *Students:* 49 full-time (42 women), 472 part-time (388 women); includes 101 minority (42 Black or African American, non-Hispanic/Latino; 12 Asian, non-Hispanic/Latino; 44 Hispanic/Latino; 3 Two or more races, non-Hispanic/Latino). Average age 34. 412 applicants, 56% accepted, 153 enrolled. In 2017, 81 master's awarded. *Degree requirements:* For master's, comprehensive exam (for some programs), thesis (for some programs). *Entrance requirements:* For master's, GRE, GMAT or NTE/PRAXIS, 3 letters of recommendation. Additional exam requirements/recommendations for international students: Required—TOEFL (minimum score 550 paper-based). *Application deadline:* For fall admission, 8/15 priority date for domestic students, 5/1 for international students; for spring admission, 1/15 priority date for domestic students, 10/1 for international students. Applications are processed on a rolling basis. Application fee: $40. Electronic applications accepted. *Expenses: Tuition:* Part-time $839 per credit. *Required fees:* $248 per semester. Tuition and fees vary according to campus/location and program. *Financial support:* Scholarships/grants, health care benefits, and unspecified assistantships available. Financial award application deadline: 4/15; financial award applicants required to submit FAFSA. *Unit head:* Dr. Lynn DeCapua, Dean, 732-987-2729, E-mail: ldecapua@georgian.edu. *Application contact:* Patrick Givens, Director of Graduate and Professional Studies Admissions, 732-987-2736, Fax: 732-987-2000, E-mail: gps@georgian.edu.
Website: http://georgian.edu/academics/school-of-education/

Georgia Southern University, Jack N. Averitt College of Graduate Studies, College of Education, Department of Teaching and Learning, Program in Special Education, Statesboro, GA 30460. Offers M Ed, MAT, Ed S. *Accreditation:* NCATE. *Program availability:* Part-time, evening/weekend, online only, 100% online. *Students:* 52 full-time (47 women), 54 part-time (45 women); includes 14 minority (11 Black or African American, non-Hispanic/Latino; 1 Hispanic/Latino; 2 Two or more races, non-Hispanic/Latino). Average age 32. 3 applicants, 100% accepted, 2 enrolled. In 2017, 37 master's, 9 other advanced degrees awarded. *Degree requirements:* For master's, portfolio, transition point assessments, exit assessment; for Ed S, field based research projects, assessments. *Entrance requirements:* For master's, GACE Basic Skills and Content Assessments (for MAT), minimum cumulative GPA of 2.5. Additional exam requirements/recommendations for international students: Required—TOEFL (minimum score 550 paper-based; 80 iBT), IELTS (minimum score 6). *Application deadline:* For fall admission, 3/15 priority date for domestic and international students; for spring admission, 10/1 priority date for domestic students, 10/1 for international students; for summer admission, 3/1 for domestic and international students. Applications are processed on a rolling basis. Application fee: $50. Electronic applications accepted. *Expenses:* Tuition, state resident: full-time $4986; part-time $3324 per year. Tuition, nonresident: full-time $21,982; part-time $15,352 per year. *Required fees:* $2092; $1802 per credit hour. $901 per semester. Tuition and fees vary according to course load, campus/location and program. *Financial support:* In 2017–18, 32 students received support. Career-related internships or fieldwork, Federal Work-Study, and scholarships/grants available. Support available to part-time students. Financial award application deadline: 4/15; financial award applicants required to submit FAFSA. *Faculty research:* Learning disorders, behavior disorders, education of the mentally retarded, PBIS, STEM education. *Unit head:* Dr. Bruce Field, Department Chair, 912-478-5203, Fax: 912-478-0026, E-mail: bfield@georgiasouthern.edu. *Application contact:* Dr. Lydia Cross, Coordinator for Graduate Academic Services Center, 912-478-8664, E-mail: lcross@georgiasouthern.edu.

Georgia Southern University–Armstrong Campus, College of Graduate Studies, Department of Childhood and Exceptional Student Education, Savannah, GA 31419-1997. Offers early childhood education (M Ed, MAT); reading (Certificate); special education (M Ed, MAT); special education transition specialist (Certificate). *Accreditation:* NCATE. *Program availability:* Part-time, evening/weekend. *Faculty:* 14 full-time (11 women), 1 (woman) part-time/adjunct. *Students:* 7 full-time (6 women), 214 part-time (195 women); includes 79 minority (63 Black or African American, non-Hispanic/Latino; 3 Asian, non-Hispanic/Latino; 6 Hispanic/Latino; 7 Two or more races, non-Hispanic/Latino). Average age 34. 159 applicants, 50% accepted, 69 enrolled. In 2017, 72 master's, 3 other advanced degrees awarded. *Degree requirements:* For master's, portfolio. *Entrance requirements:* For master's, MAT, Georgia Assessment for the Certification of Educators. Additional exam requirements/recommendations for international students: Required—TOEFL (minimum score 523 paper-based; 70 iBT). *Application deadline:* For fall admission, 7/1 priority date for domestic students, 5/1 priority date for international students; for spring admission, 11/15 priority date for domestic students, 9/15 priority date for international students; for summer admission, 4/15 priority date for domestic students, 9/15 for international students. Applications are processed on a rolling basis. Application fee: $30. Electronic applications accepted. *Expenses:* Tuition, state resident: part-time $211 per credit hour. Tuition, nonresident: part-time $782 per credit hour. *Required fees:* $737 per semester. Tuition and fees vary according to course load, degree level, campus/location and program. *Financial support:*

Special Education

In 2017–18, research assistantships with full tuition reimbursements (averaging $5,000 per year) were awarded; career-related internships or fieldwork, Federal Work-Study, and scholarships/grants also available. Support available to part-time students. Financial award application deadline: 3/15; financial award applicants required to submit FAFSA. *Faculty research:* Literacy, instructional design, poetry, working with local schools. *Unit head:* Dr. John Hobe, Department Head, 912-344-2619, Fax: 912-344-3443, E-mail: john.hobe@armstrong.edu. *Application contact:* McKenzie Peterman, Assistant Director of Graduate Admissions, 912-344-2503, Fax: 912-344-3417, E-mail: graduate@armstrong.edu.
Website: https://www.armstrong.edu/academic-departments/education-ceed

Georgia Southwestern State University, School of Education, Americus, GA 31709-4693. Offers early childhood education (M Ed, Ed S); middle grades education (Ed S); middle grades language arts (M Ed); middle grades mathematics (M Ed); special education (M Ed). *Accreditation:* NCATE. *Faculty:* 17 full-time (7 women), 7 part-time/adjunct (all women). *Students:* 221 full-time (206 women), 5 part-time (all women); includes 70 minority (all Black or African American, non-Hispanic/Latino). Average age 35. In 2017, 89 master's, 94 Ed Ss awarded. *Degree requirements:* For master's, minimum cumulative GPA of 3.0; maximum of 6 credit hours with C grade; no courses with D grade; degree completed within 7 calendar years; for Ed S, minimum GPA of 3.25 in all courses with no grade less than a B; degree must be completed within 7 calendar years from date of initial enrollment in graduate work. *Entrance requirements:* For master's, undergraduate degree from accredited institution; professional Georgia Teaching Certificate or eligibility; minimum undergraduate GPA of 2.75 as reported on official final transcripts from all accredited institutions attended; 2 confidential Administrative Recommendation Forms; for Ed S, master's degree from accredited college or university; professional Georgia Teaching Certificate or eligibility; minimum graduate GPA of 3.0 as reported on official final graduate transcripts from all accredited institutions attended; 2 confidential Administrative Recommendation Forms. *Application deadline:* For summer admission, 4/15 for domestic students. Application fee: $25. Electronic applications accepted. *Expenses:* $257 per credit hour for online courses plus fees which vary according to number of enrolled credit hours. *Financial support:* Application deadline: 6/1; applicants required to submit FAFSA. *Unit head:* Dr. Rachel Abbott, Dean, 229-931-2145. *Application contact:* Whitney Ford, Admissions Specialist, Office of Graduate Admissions, 800-338-0082, Fax: 229-931-2983.
Website: https://gsw.edu/Academics/Schools-and-Departments/School-of-Education/index

Georgia State University, College of Education and Human Development, Department of Educational Psychology, Special Education, and Communication Disorders, Program in Behavior and Learning Disabilities, Atlanta, GA 30302-3083. Offers M Ed. *Accreditation:* NCATE. *Program availability:* Part-time, evening/weekend. *Entrance requirements:* For master's, GRE (minimum scores at or above the 50th percentile), GACE Basics Skills Assessment, two official transcripts, minimum GPA of 3.0, certification in special education/T4 certificate, written statement of goals, resume, two letters of recommendation. Application fee: $50. Electronic applications accepted. *Expenses:* Tuition, state resident: full-time $7020. Tuition, nonresident: full-time $22,518. *Required fees:* $2128. Tuition and fees vary according to degree level and program. *Financial support:* Fellowships, research assistantships, teaching assistantships, scholarships/grants, health care benefits, and unspecified assistantships available. *Faculty research:* Academic and behavioral supports for students with emotional/behavior disorders; academic interventions for learning disabilities; cultural, socioeconomic, and linguistic diversity; language and literacy development, disorders, and instruction; positive behavior supports. *Unit head:* Dr. Kristine Jolivette, Associate Professor, 404-413-8040, Fax: 404-413-8043, E-mail: kjolivette@gsu.edu. *Application contact:* Sandy Vaughn, Senior Administrative Coordinator, 404-413-8318, Fax: 404-413-8043, E-mail: svaughn@gsu.edu.
Website: http://esc.education.gsu.edu/academics-and-admissions/special-education/behavior-learning-disabilities-bld/

Georgia State University, College of Education and Human Development, Department of Educational Psychology, Special Education, and Communication Disorders, Program in Education of Students with Exceptionalities, Atlanta, GA 30302-3083. Offers autism spectrum disorders (PhD); behavior disorders (PhD); communication disorders (PhD); early childhood special education (PhD); learning disabilities (PhD); mental retardation (PhD); orthopedic impairments (PhD); sensory impairments (PhD). *Accreditation:* NCATE. *Program availability:* Part-time, evening/weekend. Application fee: $50. Electronic applications accepted. *Expenses:* Tuition, state resident: full-time $7020. Tuition, nonresident: full-time $22,518. *Required fees:* $2128. Tuition and fees vary according to degree level and program. *Financial support:* Fellowships, research assistantships, scholarships/grants, health care benefits, and unspecified assistantships available. *Faculty research:* Academic and behavioral supports for students with emotional/behavior disorders; academic interventions for learning disabilities; cultural, socioeconomic, and linguistic diversity; language and literacy development, disorders, and instruction. *Unit head:* Dr. Kristine Jolivette, Associate Professor, 404-413-8040, Fax: 404-413-8043, E-mail: kjolivette@gsu.edu. *Application contact:* Sandy Vaughn, Senior Administrative Coordinator, 404-413-8318, Fax: 404-413-8043, E-mail: svaughn@gsu.edu.
Website: http://esc.education.gsu.edu/academics-and-admissions/special-education/education-of-students-with-exceptionalities-ph-d/

Georgia State University, College of Education and Human Development, Department of Educational Psychology, Special Education, and Communication Disorders, Program in Multiple and Severe Disabilities, Atlanta, GA 30302-3083. Offers early childhood special education (M Ed); special education adapted curriculum (intellectual disabilities) (M Ed); special education deaf education (M Ed); special education general and adapted curriculum (autism spectrum disorders) (M Ed); special education physical and health disabilities (orthopedic impairments) (M Ed). *Accreditation:* NCATE. *Program availability:* Part-time. *Entrance requirements:* For master's, GRE. Application fee: $50. Electronic applications accepted. *Expenses:* Tuition, state resident: full-time $7020. Tuition, nonresident: full-time $22,518. *Required fees:* $2128. Tuition and fees vary according to degree level and program. *Financial support:* Fellowships, research assistantships, teaching assistantships, scholarships/grants, health care benefits, and unspecified assistantships available. *Faculty research:* Literacy, language, behavioral supports. *Unit head:* Dr. Kathryn Wolff Heller, Professor, 404-413-8040, E-mail: kheller@gsu.edu. *Application contact:* Sandy Vaughn, Senior Administrative Coordinator, 404-413-8318, Fax: 404-413-8043, E-mail: svaughn@gsu.edu.

Gonzaga University, School of Education, Spokane, WA 99258. Offers clinical mental health counseling (MA); educational leadership (M Ed, Ed D); elementary education (MIT); marriage and family counseling (MA); school counseling (MA); secondary education (MIT); special education (M Ed, MIT); sport and athletic administration (MA). *Accreditation:* NCATE. *Program availability:* Part-time, evening/weekend, 100% online, blended/hybrid learning. *Faculty:* 16 full-time (11 women), 31 part-time/adjunct (19 women). *Students:* 108 full-time (90 women), 225 part-time (140 women); includes 34 minority (4 Black or African American, non-Hispanic/Latino; 2 American Indian or Alaska Native, non-Hispanic/Latino; 5 Asian, non-Hispanic/Latino; 18 Hispanic/Latino; 5 Two or more races, non-Hispanic/Latino), 114 international. Average age 31. 367 applicants,

74% accepted, 160 enrolled. In 2017, 175 master's awarded. *Degree requirements:* For master's, comprehensive exam. *Entrance requirements:* For master's, GRE, MAT, and/or Washington Educator Skills Test-Basic (WEST-B), Washington Educator Skills Test-Endorsements (WEST-E), official transcripts from all colleges or universities attended, interview, two letters of recommendation, resume, essay, minimum GPA of 3.0. Additional exam requirements/recommendations for international students: Required—TOEFL (minimum score 580 paper-based, 88 iBT) or IELTS (minimum score 6.5). *Application deadline:* Applications are processed on a rolling basis. Application fee: $50. Electronic applications accepted. *Expenses:* $990 per credit. *Financial support:* In 2017–18, 51 students received support. Scholarships/grants and unspecified assistantships available. Support available to part-time students. Financial award applicants required to submit FAFSA. *Unit head:* Dr. Vincent Alfonso, Dean, 509-313-3594, Fax: 509-313-5821, E-mail: alfonso@gonzaga.edu. *Application contact:* Meg Martens, Graduate Admissions Program Specialist, 509-313-4314, E-mail: martens@gonzaga.edu.
Website: https://www.gonzaga.edu/school-of-education

Gordon College, Graduate Education Program, Wenham, MA 01984-1899. Offers early childhood (M Ed); educational leadership (M Ed, Ed S); elementary education (M Ed); English as a second language (M Ed, Ed S); math specialist (M Ed); mathematics specialist (Ed S); middle school education (M Ed); moderate disabilities (M Ed); Montessori education (M Ed); reading (M Ed, Ed S); secondary education (M Ed). *Program availability:* Part-time, evening/weekend. *Faculty:* 23 full-time (17 women), 32 part-time/adjunct (23 women). *Students:* 68 full-time (50 women), 114 part-time (99 women); includes 24 minority (2 Black or African American, non-Hispanic/Latino; 8 Asian, non-Hispanic/Latino; 13 Hispanic/Latino; 1 Two or more races, non-Hispanic/Latino), 10 international. Average age 34. 248 applicants, 100% accepted, 182 enrolled. In 2017, 99 master's, 16 Ed Ss awarded. *Degree requirements:* For master's, action research or clinical experience (for most programs); for Ed S, action research or clinical experience (for some programs). *Entrance requirements:* For master's, minimum undergraduate GPA of 3.0; 2 official undergraduate transcripts; professional resume; 3 recommendation letters (one professional reference, one academic reference, one personal reference); 500-700 word statement of purpose; for Ed S, minimum master's GPA of 3.3; 2 official transcripts from undergraduate and graduate schools; professional resume; 3 recommendation letters (one professional reference, one academic reference, one personal reference); 500-700 word statement of purpose. Additional exam requirements/recommendations for international students: Required—TOEFL (minimum score 550 paper-based, 80 iBT) or IELTS (minimum score 6.5). *Application deadline:* Applications are processed on a rolling basis. Application fee: $75. *Expenses:* $325 per credit tuition; $75 per semester administrative fee. *Financial support:* Applicants required to submit FAFSA. *Faculty research:* Reading, early childhood development, English language learners, universal design for learning. *Unit head:* Dr. Janet Arndt, Director of Graduate Studies, 978-867-4355, Fax: 978-867-4663. *Application contact:* Julie Lenocker, Program Administrator, 978-867-4322, Fax: 978-867-4663, E-mail: graduate-education@gordon.edu.
Website: http://www.gordon.edu/graduate

Goucher College, Graduate Programs in Education, Baltimore, MD 21204-2794. Offers at-risk and diverse learners (M Ed, Certificate); athletic program leadership and administration (M Ed, Certificate); elementary education (MAT); literacy strategies for content learning (M Ed); middle school (M Ed, Certificate); Montessori studies (M Ed); reading instruction (M Ed, Certificate); reducing student, classroom, and school disruption (M Ed); school improvement leadership (M Ed); secondary education (MAT); special education (MAT), including elementary education; special education for certified elementary and secondary teachers (M Ed); teacher as leader in technology (M Ed). *Program availability:* Part-time, evening/weekend. *Degree requirements:* For master's, thesis (M Ed), final presentation (MAT). *Entrance requirements:* For master's, minimum GPA of 3.0. Additional exam requirements/recommendations for international students: Required—TOEFL (minimum score 550 paper-based; 80 iBT), IELTS (minimum score 7). *Application deadline:* For fall admission, 9/1 for domestic students; for spring admission, 1/15 for domestic students. Applications are processed on a rolling basis. Application fee: $75. Electronic applications accepted. *Expenses:* Contact institution. *Financial support:* Career-related internships or fieldwork and unspecified assistantships available. Support available to part-time students. Financial award application deadline: 4/15; financial award applicants required to submit FAFSA. *Faculty research:* Urban education, middle school, school improvement, teacher education, at-risk student achievement. *Unit head:* Dr. Phyllis Sunshine, Assistant Provost, 410-337-6047, Fax: 410-337-6394, E-mail: psunshin@goucher.edu. *Application contact:* Carlton E. Surbeck, III, Director of Admissions, 410-337-6100, Fax: 410-337-6085, E-mail: admissions@goucher.edu.
Website: http://www.goucher.edu/graduate-programs/graduate-programs-in-education

Governors State University, College of Education, Program in Multi-Categorical Special Education, University Park, IL 60484. Offers MA. *Accreditation:* NCATE. *Program availability:* Part-time. *Faculty:* 20 full-time (12 women), 40 part-time/adjunct (28 women). *Students:* 5 full-time (4 women), 12 part-time (10 women); includes 9 minority (7 Black or African American, non-Hispanic/Latino; 1 Asian, non-Hispanic/Latino; 1 Hispanic/Latino). Average age 34. 5 applicants, 40% accepted. In 2017, 16 master's awarded. *Application deadline:* For fall admission, 4/1 for domestic students. Applications are processed on a rolling basis. Application fee: $50. Electronic applications accepted. *Expenses:* Tuition, state resident: full-time $8472; part-time $353 per credit hour. Tuition, nonresident: full-time $16,944; part-time $706 per credit hour. *Required fees:* $1824; $76 per credit hour. $38 per term. Tuition and fees vary according to course load, degree level and program. *Financial support:* Application deadline: 5/1; applicants required to submit FAFSA. *Unit head:* Timothy Harrington, Chair, Division of Education, 708-534-5000 Ext. 4361, E-mail: tharrington2@govst.edu.

Graceland University, Gleazer School of Education, Independence, MO 64050. Offers curriculum and instruction: collaborative learning and teaching (M Ed); differentiated instruction (M Ed); instructional leadership (M Ed); literacy instruction (M Ed); management in a quality classroom (M Ed); special education (M Ed); technology integration (M Ed). *Accreditation:* NCATE. *Program availability:* Part-time, 100% online. *Faculty:* 2 full-time (both women), 13 part-time/adjunct (10 women). *Students:* 117 full-time (102 women), 62 part-time (54 women); includes 8 minority (3 Black or African American, non-Hispanic/Latino; 1 Asian, non-Hispanic/Latino; 2 Hispanic/Latino; 1 Native Hawaiian or other Pacific Islander, non-Hispanic/Latino; 1 Two or more races, non-Hispanic/Latino), 1 international. Average age 35. 28 applicants, 100% accepted, 19 enrolled. In 2017, 64 master's awarded. *Degree requirements:* For master's, action research capstone. *Entrance requirements:* For master's, minimum GPA of 3.0, teaching certificate, current teaching contract and license, two letters of reference, statement of professional goals, verification of ongoing access to computer technology, including email and Internet. Additional exam requirements/recommendations for international students: Required—TOEFL (minimum score 550 paper-based; 79 iBT). *Application deadline:* For fall admission, 10/1 for domestic students; for winter admission, 11/15 for domestic students; for spring admission, 2/15 priority date for domestic students; for summer admission, 6/1 for domestic students. Application fee: $50. Electronic applications accepted. *Expenses:* Contact institution. *Financial support:* In 2017–18, 3 students received support. Tuition waivers available. Financial award

applicants required to submit FAFSA. *Faculty research:* Literacy, technology, faculty mentoring, adult literacy, e-learning, online teaching. *Unit head:* Dr. Lee Bash, Interim Dean, 641-784-5072, E-mail: bash@graceland.edu. *Application contact:* Jeanette Calipetro, Admissions Representative, 816-423-4716, Fax: 816-833-2990, E-mail: jcali1@graceland.edu.
Website: http://www.graceland.edu/education

Grambling State University, School of Graduate Studies and Research, College of Education, Department of Curriculum and Instruction, Grambling, LA 71245. Offers curriculum and instruction (MS); special education (M Ed). *Program availability:* Part-time. *Degree requirements:* For master's, comprehensive exam, thesis (for some programs). *Entrance requirements:* Additional exam requirements/recommendations for international students: Required—TOEFL (minimum score 500 paper-based; 62 iBT).

Grand Canyon University, College of Education, Phoenix, AZ 85017-1097. Offers autism spectrum disorders (MA); curriculum and instruction (MA); early childhood education (M Ed); educational administration (M Ed); educational leadership (M Ed); elementary education (M Ed); gifted education (MA); instructional technology (MS); K-12 leadership (Ed S); reading (MA); secondary education (M Ed); secondary humanities education (M Ed); secondary STEM education (M Ed); special education (M Ed); teaching and learning (Ed D); teaching English to speakers of other languages (MA). *Program availability:* Part-time, evening/weekend, online learning. *Degree requirements:* For master's, publishable research paper (M Ed), e-portfolio. *Entrance requirements:* For master's, undergraduate degree from accredited, GCU-approved college, university, or program with minimum GPA 2.8. Additional exam requirements/recommendations for international students: Required—TOEFL (minimum score 550 paper-based; 79 iBT), IELTS (minimum score 6). Electronic applications accepted.

Grand Valley State University, College of Education, Program in Special Education, Allendale, MI 49401-9403. Offers cognitive impairment (M Ed); early childhood developmental delay (M Ed); emotional impairment (M Ed); learning disabilities (M Ed); special education (M Ed). *Accreditation:* NCATE. *Program availability:* Part-time, evening/weekend. *Students:* 3 full-time (1 woman), 68 part-time (54 women); includes 4 minority (2 Hispanic/Latino; 2 Two or more races, non-Hispanic/Latino), 4 international. Average age 33. 8 applicants, 100% accepted, 3 enrolled. In 2017, 32 master's awarded. *Degree requirements:* For master's, project or thesis. *Entrance requirements:* For master's, GRE General Test or minimum GPA of 3.0, last 60 credits from regionally-accredited college/university, 3 letters of recommendation. Additional exam requirements/recommendations for international students: Required—TOEFL (minimum iBT score of 80), IELTS (6.5), or Michigan English Language Assessment Battery (77). *Application deadline:* Applications are processed on a rolling basis. Application fee: $30. Electronic applications accepted. *Expenses:* $652 per credit hour. *Financial support:* In 2017–18, 10 students received support, including 10 fellowships; career-related internships or fieldwork, Federal Work-Study, scholarships/grants, and unspecified assistantships also available. *Faculty research:* Evaluation of special education program effects, adaptive behavior assessment, language development, writing disorders, comparative effects of presentation methods. *Unit head:* Dr. Amy Schelling, Director of Special Education, 616-331-6243, Fax: 616-331-6294, E-mail: schellia@gvsu.edu. *Application contact:* Thomas Owens, Director, Student Information and Services Center, 616-331-6282, Fax: 616-331-6217, E-mail: owenst@gvsu.edu.

Greensboro College, Program in Education, Greensboro, NC 27401-1875. Offers elementary education (M Ed); special education (M Ed). *Program availability:* Part-time, evening/weekend. *Degree requirements:* For master's, thesis. *Entrance requirements:* For master's, GRE, teacher license, 2 years of teaching experience, 2 letters of recommendation. Additional exam requirements/recommendations for international students: Required—TOEFL (minimum score 550 paper-based). Electronic applications accepted.

Gwynedd Mercy University, School of Education, Gwynedd Valley, PA 19437-0901. Offers education (Ed D); educational administration (MS); master teacher (MS); school counseling (MS); special education (MS). *Program availability:* Part-time, evening/weekend, 100% online. *Faculty:* 8 full-time (5 women), 38 part-time/adjunct (24 women). *Students:* 579 full-time (430 women); includes 130 minority (90 Black or African American, non-Hispanic/Latino; 11 Asian, non-Hispanic/Latino; 26 Hispanic/Latino; 3 Two or more races, non-Hispanic/Latino). Average age 36. 127 applicants, 18% accepted, 9 enrolled. In 2017, 106 master's awarded. *Degree requirements:* For master's, thesis, internship, practicum. *Entrance requirements:* For master's, GRE or MAT; PRAXIS I, minimum GPA of 3.0. *Application deadline:* Applications are processed on a rolling basis. *Expenses:* $550 per credit (master's degrees); $965 per credit (doctoral); $17 part-time fee, $165 graduation fee. *Financial support:* In 2017–18, 2 research assistantships were awarded; career-related internships or fieldwork, Federal Work-Study, institutionally sponsored loans, tuition waivers (full and partial), and unspecified assistantships also available. Financial award applicants required to submit FAFSA. *Faculty research:* Learning and the brain, reading literacy, ethics and moral judgment, leadership, teaching and multicultural education. *Unit head:* Dr. Heather Pfleger, Dean, 215-646-7300 Ext. 21581, E-mail: pfleger.h@gmercyu.edu. *Application contact:* Graduate Program Coordinator, 877-499-6333, E-mail: graduate@gmercyu.edu.
Website: https://www.gmercyu.edu/academics/graduate-education-programs

Harding University, Cannon-Clary College of Education, Searcy, AR 72149-0001. Offers advanced studies in teaching and learning (M Ed); art (MSE); behavioral science (MSE); counseling (MS, Ed S); early childhood special education (M Ed, MSE); education (MSE); educational leadership (M Ed, Ed S); elementary education (M Ed); English (MSE); French (MSE); history/social science (MSE); kinesiology (MSE); math (MSE); reading (M Ed); secondary education (M Ed); Spanish (MSE); teaching (MAT); teaching English as a second language (MSE). *Accreditation:* NCATE. *Program availability:* Part-time, evening/weekend. *Faculty:* 22 full-time (9 women), 51 part-time/adjunct (37 women). *Students:* 135 full-time (95 women), 316 part-time (231 women); includes 77 minority (46 Black or African American, non-Hispanic/Latino; 7 American Indian or Alaska Native, non-Hispanic/Latino; 4 Asian, non-Hispanic/Latino; 9 Hispanic/Latino; 11 Two or more races, non-Hispanic/Latino), 11 international. Average age 34. 128 applicants, 87% accepted, 111 enrolled. In 2017, 153 master's, 24 other advanced degrees awarded. *Degree requirements:* For master's, comprehensive exam (for some programs), thesis optional, portfolio(s); for Ed S, comprehensive exam, portfolio, project. *Entrance requirements:* For master's, GRE, MAT, PRAXIS; for Ed S, MAT or GRE. Additional exam requirements/recommendations for international students: Required—TOEFL (minimum score 550 paper-based; 79 iBT). *Application deadline:* For fall admission, 8/1 for domestic and international students; for spring admission, 1/1 for domestic and international students. Applications are processed on a rolling basis. Application fee: $35. Tuition and fees vary according to course load, degree level, campus/location and program. *Financial support:* In 2017–18, 33 students received support. Unspecified assistantships available. *Faculty research:* Reading, comprehension, school violence, educational technology, behavior, college choice, differentiated instruction, brain-based teaching. *Unit head:* Dr. Clara Carroll, Chair, 501-279-4501, Fax: 501-279-4083, E-mail: ccarroll@harding.edu. *Application contact:* Information Contact, 501-279-4315, E-mail: gradstudiesedu@harding.edu.
Website: http://www.harding.edu/education

Hebrew College, Shoolman Graduate School of Jewish Education, Newton Centre, MA 02459. Offers early childhood Jewish education (Certificate); Jewish day school education (Certificate); Jewish education (MJ Ed); Jewish family education (Certificate); Jewish special education (Certificate); Jewish youth education, informal education and camping (Certificate). *Program availability:* Part-time, evening/weekend, online learning. *Degree requirements:* For master's, one foreign language. *Entrance requirements:* For master's, GRE, interview. Additional exam requirements/recommendations for international students: Required—TOEFL.

Henderson State University, Graduate Studies, Teachers College, Department of Advanced Instructional Studies, Arkadelphia, AR 71999-0001. Offers developmental therapy (MSE); dyslexia therapy (Graduate Certificate); education (MAT); educational technology leadership (Graduate Certificate); English as a second language (MSE, Graduate Certificate); instructional facilitator (MSE, Graduate Certificate); middle level education (MAT); special education (K-12) (MAT, MSE); special education/early childhood (MAT). *Accreditation:* NCATE. *Program availability:* Part-time. *Entrance requirements:* For master's, GRE General Test or MAT, minimum GPA of 2.7, teacher certification. Additional exam requirements/recommendations for international students: Required—TOEFL (minimum score 600 paper-based); Recommended—IELTS (minimum score 6.5).

Heritage University, Graduate Programs in Education, Program in Professional Studies, Toppenish, WA 98948-9599. Offers bilingual education/ESL (M Ed); biology (M Ed); English and literature (M Ed); reading/literacy (M Ed); special education (M Ed). *Program availability:* Part-time, evening/weekend. *Degree requirements:* For master's, comprehensive exam (for some programs), thesis (for some programs).

High Point University, Norcross Graduate School, High Point, NC 27268. Offers athletic training (MSAT); business administration (MBA); educational leadership (M Ed, Ed D); elementary education (M Ed, MAT); pharmacy (Pharm D); physical therapy (DPT); physician assistant studies (MPAS); secondary mathematics (M Ed, MAT); special education (M Ed); strategic communication (MA). *Accreditation:* NCATE. *Program availability:* Part-time, evening/weekend. *Degree requirements:* For master's, comprehensive exam (for some programs), thesis (for some programs). *Entrance requirements:* For master's, GMAT (MBA), GRE, MAT, minimum GPA of 3.0. Additional exam requirements/recommendations for international students: Required—TOEFL (minimum score 550 paper-based). Electronic applications accepted.

Hofstra University, School of Education, Programs in Teacher Education, Hempstead, NY 11549. Offers bilingual education (MA); bilingual extension (Advanced Certificate), including education/speech language pathology, intensive teacher institute; business education (MS Ed); curriculum studies (MS Ed); early childhood and childhood education (MS Ed); early childhood education (MA, MS Ed); educational technology (Advanced Certificate); elementary education (MA, MS Ed), including science, technology, engineering, and mathematics (STEM) (MA); English education (MS Ed); family and consumer science (MS Ed); fine arts and music education (Advanced Certificate); fine arts education (MS Ed); foreign language and TESOL (MS Ed); foreign language education (MA, MS Ed), including Arabic (MS Ed), biology, chemistry, Chinese (MS Ed), earth science, French, German, Italian (MS Ed), Mandarin (MS Ed), physics, Russian, Spanish; foundations of education (Advanced Certificate), including grades 5-6, grades 7-9; languages other than English and teaching English as a second language (MA); learning and teaching (Ed D), including applied linguistics, art education, arts and humanities, early childhood education, English education, human development, math education, math, science, and technology, multicultural education, physical education, science education, social studies education, special education; mathematics education (MA, MS Ed); music education (MA, MS Ed); science education (MA), including biology (MA, MS Ed), chemistry (MA, MS Ed), earth science (MA, MS Ed), physics (MA, MS Ed); secondary education (Advanced Certificate); social studies education (MA, MS Ed); teaching languages other than English and TESOL (MS Ed); technology for learning (MA); TESOL (MS Ed, Advanced Certificate); TESOL with specialization in STEM (MA); work based learning extension (Advanced Certificate). *Program availability:* Part-time, evening/weekend, blended/hybrid learning. *Students:* 119 full-time (83 women), 124 part-time (90 women); includes 54 minority (15 Black or African American, non-Hispanic/Latino; 9 Asian, non-Hispanic/Latino; 29 Hispanic/Latino; 1 Native Hawaiian or other Pacific Islander, non-Hispanic/Latino), 12 international. Average age 29. 205 applicants, 88% accepted, 93 enrolled. In 2017, 103 master's, 4 doctorates, 32 other advanced degrees awarded. *Degree requirements:* For master's, comprehensive exam, thesis (for some programs), exit project, student teaching, fieldwork, electronic portfolio, curriculum project, minimum GPA of 3.0; for doctorate, thesis/dissertation; for Advanced Certificate, 3 foreign languages, comprehensive exam (for some programs), thesis project. *Entrance requirements:* For master's, GRE, 2 letters of recommendation, portfolio, teacher certification (MA), interview, essay; for doctorate, GMAT, GRE, LSAT, or MAT; for Advanced Certificate, 2 letters of recommendation, essay, interview and/or portfolio, teaching certificate. Additional exam requirements/recommendations for international students: Required—TOEFL (minimum score 550 paper-based; 80 iBT). *Application deadline:* Applications are processed on a rolling basis. Application fee: $75. Electronic applications accepted. *Expenses:* Tuition: Full-time $1292. *Required fees:* $970. Tuition and fees vary according to program. *Financial support:* In 2017–18, 112 students received support, including 56 fellowships with full and partial tuition reimbursements available (averaging $4,998 per year), 2 research assistantships with full and partial tuition reimbursements available (averaging $8,753 per year); career-related internships or fieldwork, Federal Work-Study, institutionally sponsored loans, scholarships/grants, traineeships, tuition waivers (full and partial), and unspecified assistantships also available. Support available to part-time students. Financial award applicants required to submit FAFSA. *Faculty research:* Educational interventions that foster critical-thinking skills; teachers' attitudes about professional development; threats to teacher quality. *Unit head:* Dr. Eustace Thompson, Chairperson, 516-463-5749, Fax: 516-463-6275, E-mail: eustace.g.thompson@hofstra.edu. *Application contact:* Sunil Samuel, Assistant Vice President of Admissions, 516-463-4723, Fax: 516-463-4664, E-mail: graduateadmission@hofstra.edu.
Website: http://www.hofstra.edu/education/

Hofstra University, School of Education, Specialized Programs in Education, Hempstead, NY 11549. Offers applied behavior analysis (Advanced Certificate); childhood special education (MS Ed); early childhood special education (MS Ed, Advanced Certificate); educational and policy leadership (Ed D); educational leadership (Advanced Certificate), including school building leader/school district business leader; educational leadership and policy studies (MS Ed), including K-12; elementary special education (MS Ed); gifted education (Advanced Certificate), including school building leader/school district business leader; health education (MS); health professions pedagogy and leadership (MS); higher education leadership and policy studies (MS Ed); inclusive early childhood special education (MS Ed); inclusive elementary special education (MS Ed); inclusive secondary special education (MS Ed); literacy studies (MA, MS Ed, Ed D, Advanced Certificate), including birth-grade 6 (MS Ed, Advanced Certificate), grades 5-12 (MS Ed, Advanced Certificate), literacy studies (Ed D); pedagogy for health professions (Advanced Certificate); physical education (MS); school district business leader (Advanced Certificate); secondary education generalist - students with disabilities 7-12 (MS Ed), including students with disabilities 7-12;

secondary special education generalist (MS Ed), including extension in secondary education; special education (MS Ed, Advanced Certificate); special education assessment and diagnosis (Advanced Certificate); special education early childhood intervention (MS Ed); special education: international perspectives (MS Ed); teaching students with severe or multiple disabilities (Advanced Certificate). *Program availability:* Part-time, evening/weekend, blended/hybrid learning. *Students:* 148 full-time (110 women), 249 part-time (188 women); includes 105 minority (54 Black or African American, non-Hispanic/Latino; 1 American Indian or Alaska Native, non-Hispanic/Latino; 13 Asian, non-Hispanic/Latino; 35 Hispanic/Latino; 1 Native Hawaiian or other Pacific Islander, non-Hispanic/Latino; 1 Two or more races, non-Hispanic/Latino), 1 international. Average age 32. 228 applicants, 93% accepted, 132 enrolled. In 2017, 97 master's, 22 doctorates, 31 other advanced degrees awarded. *Degree requirements:* For master's, one foreign language, comprehensive exam (for some programs), thesis (for some programs), electronic portfolio, capstone course, internship, practicum, student teaching, seminars, minimum GPA of 3.0; for doctorate, one foreign language, comprehensive exam, thesis/dissertation, qualifying hearing. *Entrance requirements:* For master's, GRE, interview, letters of recommendation, portfolio, essay, certification; for doctorate, GRE or MAT, interview, resume, essay, master's degree, 3 letters of recommendation, writing sample; for Advanced Certificate, GRE, interview, letters of recommendation, essay, professional experience, resume, master's degree. Additional exam requirements/recommendations for international students: Required—TOEFL (minimum score 550 paper-based; 80 iBT). *Application deadline:* Applications are processed on a rolling basis. Application fee: $75. Electronic applications accepted. *Expenses:* Tuition: Full-time $1292. *Required fees:* $970. Tuition and fees vary according to program. *Financial support:* In 2017–18, 225 students received support, including 118 fellowships with full and partial tuition reimbursements available (averaging $3,887 per year), 12 research assistantships with full and partial tuition reimbursements available (averaging $7,215 per year); career-related internships or fieldwork, Federal Work-Study, institutionally sponsored loans, scholarships/grants, traineeships, tuition waivers (full and partial), and unspecified assistantships also available. Support available to part-time students. Financial award applicants required to submit FAFSA. *Faculty research:* Collaborative teaching and learning; language and culture; new media literacies; applied behavior analysis; K-12 leadership development. *Unit head:* Dr. Elfreda Blue, Chairperson, 516-463-5762, Fax: 516-463-6184, E-mail: elfreda.blue@hofstra.edu. *Application contact:* Sunil Samuel, Assistant Vice President of Admissions, 516-463-4723, Fax: 516-463-4664, E-mail: graduateadmission@hofstra.edu.
Website: http://www.hofstra.edu/education/

Holy Family University, Graduate and Professional Programs, School of Education, Master of Education Programs, Philadelphia, PA 19114. Offers early elementary education (PreK-Grade 4) (M Ed); education leadership (M Ed); general education (M Ed); reading specialist (M Ed); special education (M Ed); TESOL and literacy (M Ed). *Program availability:* Part-time. *Degree requirements:* For master's, thesis optional. Electronic applications accepted. *Expenses:* Tuition: Full-time $13,518; part-time $9012 per credit hour. Tuition and fees vary according to degree level and program.

Holy Names University, Graduate Division, Department of Education, Oakland, CA 94619-1699. Offers educational therapy (Certificate); mild/moderate disabilities (Ed S); multiple subject teaching (Credential); single subject teaching (Credential); urban education: educational therapy (M Ed); urban education: K-12 education (M Ed); urban education: special education (M Ed). *Program availability:* Part-time. *Degree requirements:* For master's, comprehensive exam, research paper, thesis or project. *Entrance requirements:* For master's, minimum undergraduate GPA of 2.6 overall, 3.0 in major; personal statement; two recommendations; interview. Additional exam requirements/recommendations for international students: Required—TOEFL (minimum score 550 paper-based; 79 iBT). Electronic applications accepted. Application fee is waived when completed online. *Faculty research:* Cognitive development, language development, learning handicaps.

Hood College, Graduate School, Department of Education, Frederick, MD 21701-8575. Offers curriculum and instruction (MS), including elementary education, elementary science and mathematics education, secondary education, special education; education, multidisciplinary studies (MS); educational leadership (MS, Certificate); reading specialization (MS); STEM education (Certificate). *Accreditation:* NCATE. *Program availability:* Part-time-only, evening/weekend. *Faculty:* 6 full-time (4 women), 35 part-time/adjunct (27 women). *Students:* 3 full-time (all women), 329 part-time (265 women); includes 62 minority (35 Black or African American, non-Hispanic/Latino; 4 Asian, non-Hispanic/Latino; 14 Hispanic/Latino; 9 Two or more races, non-Hispanic/Latino), 3 international. Average age 33. 76 applicants, 100% accepted, 63 enrolled. In 2017, 53 master's, 58 other advanced degrees awarded. *Degree requirements:* For master's, action research project, portfolio (for reading specialization); for Certificate, STEM capstone activity. *Entrance requirements:* For master's, minimum GPA of 2.75, teaching certification, writing sample during interview, letter of recommendation from principal (for educational leadership program only). Additional exam requirements/recommendations for international students: Required—TOEFL (minimum score 575 paper-based; 89 iBT), IELTS (minimum score 6.5). *Application deadline:* For fall admission, 8/15 priority date for domestic students, 8/5 for international students; for spring admission, 12/1 priority date for domestic students, 12/1 for international students; for summer admission, 5/1 priority date for domestic students, 4/15 for international students. Applications are processed on a rolling basis. Application fee: $35. Electronic applications accepted. *Expenses:* $465 per credit plus $110 comprehensive fee per semester. *Financial support:* Tuition waivers (partial) and unspecified assistantships available. Financial award applicants required to submit FAFSA. *Faculty research:* Leadership, action research, brain research, learning styles. *Unit head:* Dr. April M. Boulton, Dean of the Graduate School, 301-696-3612, E-mail: gofurther@hood.edu. *Application contact:* Jan Marcus, Assistant Director of Graduate Admissions, 301-696-3600, E-mail: gofurther@hood.edu.
Website: http://www.hood.edu/academics/education/index.html

Houston Baptist University, College of Education and Behavioral Sciences, Programs in Education, Houston, TX 77074-3298. Offers bilingual education (M Ed); counselor education (M Ed); curriculum and instruction (M Ed); curriculum and instruction (EC-6 bilingual) (M Ed); curriculum and instruction in all-level art, Spanish, music, or physical education (M Ed); curriculum and instruction in EC-6 and special education (EC-12) (M Ed); curriculum and instruction in instructional technology (M Ed); curriculum and instruction in mathematics, science, or social studies (4-8) (M Ed); curriculum and instruction with EC-6 generalist (M Ed); curriculum and instruction with English language arts and reading (4-8) (M Ed); educational administration (M Ed); educational diagnostician (M Ed); executive educational leadership (Ed D); higher education in business management (M Ed); higher education in Christian studies (M Ed); higher education in counseling (M Ed); higher education in educational technology (M Ed); reading (M Ed); special educational leadership (Ed D). *Program availability:* Part-time, evening/weekend, 100% online, blended/hybrid learning. *Students:* 83 full-time (65 women), 187 part-time (156 women); includes 189 minority (114 Black or African American, non-Hispanic/Latino; 2 American Indian or Alaska Native, non-Hispanic/Latino; 9 Asian, non-Hispanic/Latino; 58 Hispanic/Latino; 6 Two or more races, non-Hispanic/Latino), 7 international. Average age 36. 309 applicants, 31% accepted, 70

enrolled. In 2017, 92 master's awarded. *Degree requirements:* For master's, comprehensive exam; for doctorate, thesis/dissertation. *Entrance requirements:* For master's, minimum GPA of 2.75, two recommendations, resume, bachelor's degree conferred transcript; interview (for non-certified teachers); for doctorate, GRE, 5 letters of recommendation. Additional exam requirements/recommendations for international students: Required—TOEFL (minimum score 80 iBT), IELTS (minimum score 6.5). *Application deadline:* For fall admission, 8/1 for domestic students, 6/1 for international students; for spring admission, 1/1 for domestic students, 11/1 for international students; for summer admission, 5/1 for domestic students, 3/1 for international students. Applications are processed on a rolling basis. Application fee: $0 ($100 for international students). Electronic applications accepted. Application fee is waived when completed online. *Expenses:* $22,000 tuition; $4,500 fees (general, technology and parking). *Financial support:* In 2017–18, 59 students received support. Research assistantships, teaching assistantships, Federal Work-Study, and scholarships/grants available. Support available to part-time students. Financial award application deadline: 4/1; financial award applicants required to submit FAFSA. *Faculty research:* Autism and inclusion, integrating technology into instruction, school change and leadership trust. *Unit head:* Dr. Charlotte Fontenot, Director, Graduate Programs, 281-649-3078, Fax: 281-649-3361, E-mail: cfontenot@hbu.edu. *Application contact:* Kristy Wright, Administrative Assistant for Graduate Programs, 281-649-3094, Fax: 281-649-3361, E-mail: kwright@hbu.edu.
Website: http://www.hbu.edu/MED

Howard University, School of Education, Department of Curriculum and Instruction, Program in Special Education, Washington, DC 20059-0002. Offers M Ed. *Accreditation:* NCATE. *Program availability:* Part-time. *Degree requirements:* For master's, comprehensive exam, thesis (for some programs), expository writing exam, internships, practicum. *Entrance requirements:* For master's, minimum GPA of 2.7. Additional exam requirements/recommendations for international students: Required—TOEFL (minimum score 550 paper-based; 79 iBT). Electronic applications accepted.

Hunter College of the City University of New York, Graduate School, School of Education, Department of Special Education, New York, NY 10065-5085. Offers blind and visually impaired (MS Ed); severe/multiple disabilities (MS Ed). *Accreditation:* NCATE. *Degree requirements:* For master's, comprehensive exam, thesis, student teaching practica, clinical teaching lab courses, New York State Teacher Certification Exams. *Entrance requirements:* For master's, minimum GPA of 2.8. Additional exam requirements/recommendations for international students: Required—TOEFL, TWE. *Faculty research:* Mathematics learning disabilities; street behavior; assessment; bilingual special education; families, diversity, and disabilities.

Idaho State University, Office of Graduate Studies, College of Education, Department of Teaching and Educational Studies, Pocatello, ID 83209-8059. Offers deaf education (M Ed); elementary education (M Ed); human exceptionality (M Ed); literacy (M Ed); music education (M Ed); secondary education (M Ed). *Program availability:* Part-time. *Degree requirements:* For master's, comprehensive exam, thesis (for some programs), oral thesis defense or written comprehensive exam and oral exam. *Entrance requirements:* For master's, GRE or MAT, minimum undergraduate GPA of 3.0, bachelor's degree, professional experience in an educational context. Additional exam requirements/recommendations for international students: Required—TOEFL (minimum score 550 paper-based; 80 iBT). Electronic applications accepted. *Faculty research:* Literacy, school psychology, special education.

Illinois State University, Graduate School, College of Education, Department of Special Education, Normal, IL 61790. Offers MS, MS Ed, Ed D, Certificate. *Accreditation:* NCATE. *Degree requirements:* For doctorate, thesis/dissertation, 2 terms of residency. *Entrance requirements:* For master's, GRE General Test, minimum GPA of 3.0 in last 60 hours; for doctorate, GRE General Test. *Faculty research:* Center for adult learning leadership, promoting a learning community, autism spectrum professional development and technical assistance project, preparing qualified personnel to provide early intervention for children who are deaf.

Immaculata University, College of Graduate Studies, Program in Educational Leadership, Immaculata, PA 19345. Offers educational leadership (MA, Ed D); principal (Certificate); secondary education (Certificate); supervisor of special education (Certificate). *Program availability:* Part-time, evening/weekend. *Degree requirements:* For master's, comprehensive exam, thesis optional; for doctorate, comprehensive exam, thesis/dissertation. *Entrance requirements:* For master's, GRE or MAT, minimum GPA of 3.0; for doctorate, GRE General Test or MAT, minimum GPA of 3.5. Additional exam requirements/recommendations for international students: Required—TOEFL. Electronic applications accepted. *Faculty research:* Cooperative learning, school-based management, whole language, performance assessment.

Indiana University Bloomington, School of Education, Department of Curriculum and Instruction, Bloomington, IN 47405-7000. Offers art education (MS, Ed D, PhD); curriculum studies (Ed D, PhD); elementary education (MS, Ed D, PhD, Ed S); mathematics education (MS, Ed D, PhD); science education (MS, Ed D, PhD); secondary education (MS, Ed D, PhD); social studies education (MS, PhD); special education (PhD, Ed S). *Accreditation:* NCATE. *Program availability:* Part-time, evening/weekend. Terminal master's awarded for partial completion of doctoral program. *Degree requirements:* For doctorate, thesis/dissertation; for Ed S, comprehensive exam or project. *Entrance requirements:* For master's, doctorate, and Ed S, GRE General Test. Electronic applications accepted.

Indiana University of Pennsylvania, School of Graduate Studies and Research, College of Education and Communications, Department of Communication Disorders, Special Education, and Disability Services, Program in Special Education, Indiana, PA 15705. Offers M Ed. *Accreditation:* NCATE. *Program availability:* Part-time. *Faculty:* 10 full-time (8 women), 3 part-time/adjunct (2 women). *Students:* 2 full-time (both women), 15 part-time (12 women); includes 1 minority (Hispanic/Latino). Average age 30. 23 applicants, 96% accepted, 5 enrolled. In 2017, 7 master's awarded. *Degree requirements:* For master's, comprehensive exam, thesis optional. *Entrance requirements:* For master's, 2 letters of recommendation. Additional exam requirements/recommendations for international students: Required—TOEFL (minimum score 540 paper-based). *Application deadline:* For fall admission, 3/1 for domestic students; for spring admission, 7/1 for domestic students. Applications are processed on a rolling basis. Application fee: $50. Electronic applications accepted. *Expenses:* Tuition, state resident: full-time $12,000; part-time $500 per credit. Tuition, nonresident: full-time $18,000; part-time $750 per credit. *Required fees:* $4073; $165.55 per credit. $64 per term. *Financial support:* In 2017–18, 2 research assistantships with tuition reimbursements (averaging $5,440 per year) were awarded; career-related internships or fieldwork, Federal Work-Study, scholarships/grants, and unspecified assistantships also available. Support available to part-time students. Financial award application deadline: 4/15; financial award applicants required to submit FAFSA. *Unit head:* Dr. Alexandria Kappel, Graduate Coordinator, 724-357-2454, E-mail: alexandria.kappel@iup.edu.
Website: http://www.iup.edu/grad/edex/default.aspx

Indiana University–Purdue University Fort Wayne, College of Education and Public Policy, Department of Professional Studies, Fort Wayne, IN 46805-1499. Offers couple and family counseling (MS Ed); educational leadership (MS Ed); school counseling (MS Ed); special education (MS Ed, Certificate). *Program availability:* Part-time. *Degree requirements:* For master's, comprehensive exam, practicum, internship, portfolio. *Entrance requirements:* For master's, minimum GPA of 2.5, three professional letters of recommendation. Additional exam requirements/recommendations for international students: Required—TOEFL (minimum score 550 paper-based; 79 iBT). *Faculty research:* Learning opportunities with deafness and the hearing impaired, adolescent emotion, student evaluation of teaching.

Indiana University–Purdue University Indianapolis, School of Education, Indianapolis, IN 46202-5155. Offers curriculum and instruction (MS); early childhood (MS); educational leadership (MS, Certificate); English as a second language (Certificate); kindergarten (Certificate); language education (MS); reading (Certificate); school counseling (MS); special education (MS, Certificate). *Program availability:* Part-time, evening/weekend. Terminal master's awarded for partial completion of doctoral program. *Degree requirements:* For master's, thesis optional. *Entrance requirements:* For master's, GRE General Test, minimum GPA of 2.5; for Certificate, official transcripts. Additional exam requirements/recommendations for international students: Required—TOEFL (minimum score 60 iBT), IELTS (minimum score 5.5). Electronic applications accepted. *Expenses:* Contact institution. *Faculty research:* Educational policies and school leaders' responses to these; issues of intersectionality in the experiences of African American lesbian, gay, and bisexual students attending historically black colleges and universities and those who belong to black Greek-letter organizations; students' experiential knowledge and their evolving disciplinary-specific literacy and understanding; innovative program development; urban ESL teacher preparation; target-based instructional coaching.

Indiana University South Bend, School of Education, South Bend, IN 46615. Offers addiction counseling (MS Ed); alcohol and drug counseling (Graduate Certificate); clinical mental health counseling (MS Ed); educational leadership (MS Ed); elementary education (MS Ed); marriage, couple, and family counseling (MS Ed); school counseling (MS Ed); secondary education (MS Ed); special education (MAT, MS Ed), including intense intervention (MS Ed), mild intervention (MS Ed). *Accreditation:* NCATE. *Program availability:* Part-time, evening/weekend. *Degree requirements:* For master's, thesis or alternative, exit project. *Entrance requirements:* For master's, letters of recommendation, GRE or minimum GPA of 3.0. Additional exam requirements/recommendations for international students: Required—TOEFL. Electronic applications accepted. *Expenses:* Contact institution. *Faculty research:* Professional dispositions, early childhood literacy, online learning, program assessments, problem-based learning.

Inter American University of Puerto Rico, Barranquitas Campus, Program in Education, Barranquitas, PR 00794. Offers curriculum and teaching (M Ed), including biology, English as a second language, history, Spanish; educational leadership and management (MA); elementary education (M Ed); information and library service technology (M Ed); special education (MA). *Accreditation:* TEAC. *Program availability:* Part-time, evening/weekend. *Faculty:* 1 full-time (0 women), 3 part-time/adjunct (2 women). *Students:* 17 full-time (16 women), 2 part-time (both women); all minorities (all Hispanic/Latino). Average age 34. 9 applicants, 89% accepted, 8 enrolled. In 2017, 5 master's awarded. *Degree requirements:* For master's, 2 foreign languages, comprehensive exam, thesis (for some programs). *Entrance requirements:* For master's, GRE or EXADEP, bachelor's degree or its equivalent from accredited institution, official academic transcript from institution that conferred bachelor's degree, minimum GPA of 2.5, two recommendation letters, interview (for some programs), essay (for some programs). *Application deadline:* Applications are processed on a rolling basis. Application fee: $31. Electronic applications accepted. *Expenses:* $3,392 full-time tuition plus $652 fees. *Financial support:* Applicants required to submit FAFSA. *Unit head:* Juan A. Negron-Berrios, PhD, Chancellor, 787-857-3600 Ext. 2002, Fax: 787-857-2125, E-mail: janegron@br.inter.edu. *Application contact:* Aramilda Cartagena-Santiago, Dean of Students, 787-857-3600 Ext. 2009, Fax: 787-857-2125, E-mail: aramildacartagena@br.inter.edu.

Inter American University of Puerto Rico, Fajardo Campus, Graduate Programs, Fajardo, PR 00738-7003. Offers computer science (MS); educational management and leadership (MA Ed); general business (MBA); human resources (MBA); management information systems (MBA); marketing (MBA); special education (MA Ed). *Program availability:* Online learning. *Faculty:* 1 full-time (0 women), 25 part-time/adjunct (13 women). *Students:* 1 (woman) full-time, 126 part-time (81 women).

Inter American University of Puerto Rico, Metropolitan Campus, Graduate Programs, Program in Special Education, San Juan, PR 00919-1293. Offers MA. *Degree requirements:* For master's, comprehensive exam. *Entrance requirements:* For master's, GRE or EXADEP, interview. Electronic applications accepted.

Inter American University of Puerto Rico, San Germán Campus, Graduate Studies Center, Program in Special Education, San Germán, PR 00683-5008. Offers MA. *Accreditation:* TEAC. *Program availability:* Part-time, evening/weekend. *Degree requirements:* For master's, comprehensive exam. *Entrance requirements:* For master's, GRE General Test or EXADEP, minimum GPA of 3.0.

Iona College, School of Arts and Science, Department of Education, New Rochelle, NY 10801-1890. Offers adolescence education: biology (MS Ed, MST); adolescence education: English (MS Ed); adolescence education: mathematics (MST); adolescence education: social studies (MS Ed, MST); adolescence education: Spanish (MS Ed); adolescence special education 5-12 (MST); childhood and special education (MST); early childhood and childhood (MST); educational leadership (MS Ed). *Accreditation:* NCATE. *Program availability:* Part-time, evening/weekend. *Faculty:* 7 full-time (5 women), 2 part-time/adjunct (1 woman). *Students:* 23 full-time (18 women), 26 part-time (19 women); includes 12 minority (4 Black or African American, non-Hispanic/Latino; 8 Hispanic/Latino). Average age 26. 33 applicants, 97% accepted, 20 enrolled. In 2017, 31 master's awarded. *Degree requirements:* For master's, thesis or alternative. *Entrance requirements:* For master's, minimum GPA of 3.0, NY State teaching certificate and bachelor's degree (for MS Ed). Additional exam requirements/recommendations for international students: Required—TOEFL (minimum score 550 paper-based; 80 iBT), IELTS (minimum score 6.5). *Application deadline:* For fall admission, 8/1 priority date for domestic students, 5/1 priority date for international students; for spring admission, 1/1 priority date for domestic students, 9/1 priority date for international students. Applications are processed on a rolling basis. Electronic applications accepted. Tuition and fees vary according to program. *Financial support:* In 2017–18, 16 students received support. Unspecified assistantships available. Support available to part-time students. Financial award application deadline: 4/15; financial award applicants required to submit FAFSA. *Faculty research:* Engaging teacher educators in scientific process, cross-national comparisons of mathematics teaching, questioning strategies in the classroom, research methods, literacy development. *Unit head:* Margaret Smith, PhD, Chair, 914-633-2210, Fax: 914-633-2608, E-mail: msmith@iona.edu. *Application contact:* Richard McMahon, Coordinator, Graduate School of Education, 914-633-2552, E-mail: rmcmahon@iona.edu.
Website: http://www.iona.edu/Academics/School-of-Arts-Science/Departments/Education/Graduate-Programs.aspx

Iowa State University of Science and Technology, Department of Education, Ames, IA 50011. Offers curriculum and instructional technology (M Ed, MS, PhD); elementary education (M Ed, MS); historical, philosophical, and comparative studies in education (M Ed, MS); special education (M Ed, MS, PhD). *Degree requirements:* For master's, thesis or alternative; for doctorate, thesis/dissertation. *Entrance requirements:* For master's and doctorate, GRE General Test. Additional exam requirements/recommendations for international students: Required—TOEFL (minimum score 560 paper-based; 83 iBT), IELTS (minimum score 6.5). Electronic applications accepted.

Jackson State University, Graduate School, College of Education and Human Development, Department of Special Education, Jackson, MS 39217. Offers special education (MS Ed, Ed S). *Accreditation:* NCATE. *Program availability:* Part-time, evening/weekend, online only, 100% online, blended/hybrid learning. *Degree requirements:* For master's, comprehensive exam, thesis or alternative. *Entrance requirements:* For master's, GRE General Test. Additional exam requirements/recommendations for international students: Required—TOEFL (minimum score 520 paper-based; 67 iBT). Electronic applications accepted. *Expenses:* Contact institution.

Jacksonville State University, College of Graduate Studies and Continuing Education, College of Education and Professional Studies, Program in Special Education, Jacksonville, AL 36265-1602. Offers MS Ed. *Accreditation:* NCATE. *Degree requirements:* For master's, comprehensive exam, thesis (for some programs). *Entrance requirements:* For master's, GRE General Test or MAT. Additional exam requirements/recommendations for international students: Required—TOEFL (minimum score 500 paper-based; 61 iBT). Electronic applications accepted.

James Madison University, The Graduate School, College of Education, Program in Special Education, Harrisonburg, VA 22801. Offers adapted curriculum (MAT); autism (M Ed); behavior specialist (M Ed); early childhood special education (MAT); general curriculum K-12 special education (MAT); gifted education (M Ed); inclusive early childhood special education (MAT); instructional specialist (M Ed); K-12 special education (MAT); visual impairments (MAT). *Accreditation:* NCATE. *Program availability:* Part-time. *Students:* 27 full-time (26 women), 11 part-time (5 women); includes 2 minority (1 Black or African American, non-Hispanic/Latino; 1 Two or more races, non-Hispanic/Latino). Average age 30. In 2017, 27 master's awarded. Application fee: $55. *Expenses:* Tuition, state resident: full-time $10,512; part-time $438 per credit hour. Tuition, nonresident: full-time $28,358; part-time $1162 per credit hour. *Required fees:* $1128. *Financial support:* In 2017–18, 6 students received support. Fellowships, Federal Work-Study, and 6 assistantships (averaging $7911) available. Financial award application deadline: 3/1; financial award applicants required to submit FAFSA. *Unit head:* Dr. David A. Slykhuis, Interim Department Head, 540-568-4314, E-mail: slykhuda@jmu.edu. *Application contact:* Lynette D. Michael, Director of Graduate Admissions, 540-568-6131 Ext. 6395, Fax: 540-568-7860, E-mail: michaeld@jmu.edu.
Website: http://www.jmu.edu/coe/efex/index.shtml

Johns Hopkins University, School of Education, Certificate Programs in Education, Baltimore, MD 21218. Offers advanced methods for differentiated instruction and inclusive education (Graduate Certificate); applied behavior analysis (Post-Master's Certificate); clinical mental health counseling (Post-Master's Certificate); counseling (Advanced Certificate); data-based decision making and organizational improvement (Graduate Certificate); early intervention/preschool special education specialist (Graduate Certificate); education of students with autism and other pervasive developmental disorders (Graduate Certificate); educational leadership for independent schools (Graduate Certificate); evidence-based teaching in the health professions (Post-Master's Certificate); gifted education (Graduate Certificate); leadership in technology integration (Graduate Certificate); mind, brain and teaching (Graduate Certificate); school administration and supervision (Graduate Certificate); urban education (Graduate Certificate). *Program availability:* Part-time-only, evening/weekend, 100% online, blended/hybrid learning. *Entrance requirements:* For degree, minimum of bachelor's degree from regionally- or nationally-accredited institution (master's degree for some programs); minimum GPA of 3.0 in all previous programs of study; official transcripts from all post-secondary institutions attended; essay; curriculum vitae/resume; two letters of recommendation; dispositions survey. Electronic applications accepted. *Expenses:* Contact institution.

Johns Hopkins University, School of Education, Master's Programs in Education, Baltimore, MD 21218. Offers counseling (MS), including clinical mental health counseling, school counseling; education (MS), including educational studies, gifted education, reading, school administration and supervision, technology for educators; elementary education (MAT); health professions (M Ed); intelligence analysis (MS); organizational leadership (MS); secondary education (MAT), including biology, chemistry, earth/space science, English, physics, social studies; special education (MS), including early childhood special education, general special education studies, mild to moderate disabilities, severe disabilities. *Program availability:* Part-time, evening/weekend, 100% online, blended/hybrid learning. *Degree requirements:* For master's, comprehensive exam (for some programs), portfolio, capstone project and/or internship; PRAXIS II (subject area assessments) for initial teacher preparation programs that lead to licensure. *Entrance requirements:* For master's, GRE (for full-time programs only); PRAXIS I/core or state-approved alternative (for initial teacher preparation programs that lead to licensure), minimum of bachelor's degree from regionally- or nationally-accredited institution; minimum GPA of 3.0 in all previous programs of study; official transcripts from all post-secondary institutions attended; essay; curriculum vitae/resume; letters of recommendation (3 for full-time programs, 2 for part-time programs); dispositions survey. Additional exam requirements/recommendations for international students: Required—TOEFL (minimum score 600 paper-based; 100 iBT), IELTS (minimum score 7). Electronic applications accepted. *Expenses:* Contact institution.

Johnson & Wales University, Graduate Studies, MAT Program in Teacher Education, Providence, RI 02903-3703. Offers business education and secondary special education (MAT); culinary arts education (MAT); elementary education and elementary special education (MAT). *Program availability:* Part-time, evening/weekend. *Entrance requirements:* For master's, MAT, minimum GPA of 2.75. Additional exam requirements/recommendations for international students: Required—TOEFL (minimum score 550 paper-based) or IELTS (recommended). *Application deadline:* For fall admission, 8/21 priority date for domestic students, 6/15 priority date for international students; for winter admission, 11/15 priority date for domestic students, 10/1 priority date for international students. Applications are processed on a rolling basis. Application fee: $0. *Expenses:* Tuition: Full-time $12,636; part-time $702 per credit hour. *Financial support:* Unspecified assistantships available. Financial award application deadline: 5/1. *Faculty research:* Secondary education, student teaching, educational reform, evaluation procedures. *Unit head:* Karen Swoboda, Director, 401-598-1922, Fax: 401-598-1125. *Application contact:* Graduate School Admissions, 401-598-1015, Fax: 401-598-1286, E-mail: gradadm@jwu.edu.

Kansas State University, Graduate School, College of Education, Department of Special Education, Counseling and Student Affairs, Manhattan, KS 66506. Offers academic advising (MS, Certificate); counseling and student development (MS), including college student development, school counseling; special education (MS, Ed D); special education, counseling, and student affairs (PhD). *Accreditation:* ACA;

Special Education

NCATE. *Program availability:* Part-time, online learning. *Degree requirements:* For master's, comprehensive exam; for doctorate, comprehensive exam, thesis/dissertation. *Entrance requirements:* For master's, minimum undergraduate GPA of 3.0; for doctorate, GRE General Test, minimum GPA of 3.0 in last 60 hours. Additional exam requirements/recommendations for international students: Required—TOEFL. Electronic applications accepted. *Faculty research:* Counseling supervision, academic advising, career development, student development, universal design for learning, autism, learning disabilities.

Kean University, College of Education, Program in Special Education, Union, NJ 07083. Offers autism and developmental disabilities (MA); learning and behavioral disabilities (MA). *Accreditation:* NCATE. *Program availability:* Part-time. *Faculty:* 11 full-time (10 women). *Students:* 6 full-time (5 women), 63 part-time (48 women); includes 18 minority (9 Black or African American, non-Hispanic/Latino; 3 Asian, non-Hispanic/Latino; 6 Hispanic/Latino). Average age 33. 25 applicants, 100% accepted, 21 enrolled. In 2017, 40 master's awarded. *Degree requirements:* For master's, comprehensive exam, thesis, portfolio, two semesters of advanced seminar. *Entrance requirements:* For master's, GRE General Test or MAT, minimum GPA of 3.0, New Jersey Standard Instructional Certificate or Certificate of Eligibility with Advanced Standing, 2 letters of recommendation, transcripts. Additional exam requirements/recommendations for international students: Required—TOEFL (minimum score 550 paper-based; 79 iBT), IELTS (minimum score 6.5). *Application deadline:* For fall admission, 6/30 for domestic and international students; for spring admission, 12/1 for domestic and international students. Applications are processed on a rolling basis. Application fee: $75. Electronic applications accepted. *Expenses:* Tuition, state resident: full-time $13,419; part-time $653 per credit. Tuition, nonresident: full-time $18,188; part-time $801 per credit. *Required fees:* $3382; $154 per credit. Tuition and fees vary according to course level, course load, degree level and program. *Financial support:* Scholarships/grants and unspecified assistantships available. Financial award applicants required to submit FAFSA. *Unit head:* Dr. Beverly Kling, Program Coordinator, 908-737-3845, E-mail: bkling@kean.edu. *Application contact:* Brittany Gerstenhaber, Admissions Counselor, 908-737-7100, E-mail: gradadmissions@kean.edu.
Website: http://grad.kean.edu/masters-programs/special-education-autism-and-developmental-disabilities

Keene State College, School of Professional and Graduate Studies, Keene, NH 03435. Offers curriculum and instruction (M Ed); education leadership (PMC); educational leadership (M Ed); school counselor (M Ed, PMC); special education (M Ed). *Accreditation:* NCATE. *Program availability:* Part-time, evening/weekend. *Faculty:* 6 full-time (3 women), 7 part-time/adjunct (2 women). *Students:* 20 full-time (14 women), 42 part-time (20 women); includes 2 minority (1 Black or African American, non-Hispanic/Latino; 1 Asian, non-Hispanic/Latino), 1 international. Average age 31. 33 applicants, 58% accepted, 17 enrolled. In 2017, 39 master's awarded. *Degree requirements:* For master's, thesis (for some programs). *Entrance requirements:* For master's, PRAXIS I, 3 references; official transcripts; minimum GPA of 2.5; interview; essay; teacher/educator certificate; work/internship experience. Additional exam requirements/recommendations for international students: Required—TOEFL (minimum score 550 paper-based; 61 iBT). *Application deadline:* For fall admission, 4/1 for domestic and international students; for spring admission, 11/1 for domestic and international students; for summer admission, 3/1 for domestic and international students. Applications are processed on a rolling basis. Application fee: $50. Electronic applications accepted. *Expenses:* Tuition, state resident: full-time $9360; part-time $520 per credit. Tuition, nonresident: full-time $10,260; part-time $570 per credit. *Required fees:* $1908; $106 per credit. Tuition and fees vary according to course load. *Financial support:* In 2017–18, 19 students received support. Career-related internships or fieldwork, Federal Work-Study, institutionally sponsored loans, scholarships/grants, and unspecified assistantships available. Support available to part-time students. Financial award application deadline: 3/1; financial award applicants required to submit FAFSA. *Unit head:* Dr. Marie Kalich, Dean of Professional and Graduate Studies, 603-358-2885, E-mail: kkalich@keene.edu. *Application contact:* Carl Ditkoff, Graduate Program Assistant, 603-358-2497, E-mail: kscgraduatestudies@keene.edu.
Website: http://www.keene.edu/academics/graduate/

Kennesaw State University, Leland and Clarice C. Bagwell College of Education, Program in Graduate Education, Kennesaw, GA 30144. Offers educational leadership (M Ed); educational leadership technology (M Ed); elementary and early childhood education (M Ed); instructional technology (M Ed); middle grades education (M Ed); reading (M Ed); secondary education (M Ed); special education (M Ed); teaching English to speakers of other languages (M Ed). *Accreditation:* NCATE. *Program availability:* Part-time. *Degree requirements:* For master's, thesis or alternative. *Entrance requirements:* For master's, GRE General Test, T-4 state certification, minimum GPA of 2.75. Additional exam requirements/recommendations for international students: Required—TOEFL (minimum score 550 paper-based; 80 iBT), IELTS (minimum score 6.5). Electronic applications accepted.

Kennesaw State University, Leland and Clarice C. Bagwell College of Education, Program in Teaching, Kennesaw, GA 30144. Offers art education (MAT); biology (MAT); chemistry (MAT); foreign language education (Chinese and Spanish) (MAT); physics (MAT); secondary English (MAT); secondary mathematics (MAT); special education (MAT); teaching English to speakers of other languages (MAT). *Program availability:* Part-time, evening/weekend. *Entrance requirements:* For master's, GRE, GACE I (state certificate exam), minimum GPA of 2.75, 2 recommendations, resume. Additional exam requirements/recommendations for international students: Required—TOEFL (minimum score 550 paper-based; 80 iBT), IELTS (minimum score 6.5). Electronic applications accepted.

Kent State University, College of Education, Health and Human Services, School of Lifespan Development and Educational Sciences, Program in Special Education, Kent, OH 44242-0001. Offers deaf education (M Ed); early childhood education (M Ed); educational interpreter K-12 (M Ed); general special education (M Ed); mild/moderate intervention (M Ed); special education (PhD, Ed S); transition to work (M Ed). *Accreditation:* NCATE. *Degree requirements:* For doctorate, comprehensive exam, thesis/dissertation. *Entrance requirements:* For master's, minimum undergraduate GPA of 2.75, moral character form, 2 letters of reference, goals statement; for doctorate and Ed S, GRE General Test, goals statement, 2 letters of reference, interview, resume. Additional exam requirements/recommendations for international students: Required—TOEFL (minimum score 550 paper-based; 80 iBT). Electronic applications accepted. *Expenses:* Tuition, state resident: full-time $11,310; part-time $515 per credit hour. Tuition, nonresident: full-time $20,396; part-time $928 per credit hour. *International tuition:* $18,544 full-time. *Faculty research:* Social/emotional needs of gifted, inclusion transition services, early intervention/ecobehavioral assessments, applied behavioral analysis.

Kentucky State University, College of Professional Studies, Frankfort, KY 40601. Offers nursing (DNP); public administration (MPA), including human resource management; special education (MA). *Program availability:* Part-time, evening/weekend, 100% online, blended/hybrid learning. *Faculty:* 9 full-time (7 women), 3 part-time/adjunct (all women). *Students:* 29 full-time (18 women), 29 part-time (24 women); includes 42 minority (40 Black or African American, non-Hispanic/Latino; 1 Asian, non-

Hispanic/Latino; 1 Two or more races, non-Hispanic/Latino). Average age 35. 17 applicants, 53% accepted, 7 enrolled. In 2017, 11 master's, 4 doctorates awarded. *Degree requirements:* For master's, comprehensive exam, thesis optional; for doctorate, comprehensive exam, thesis/dissertation optional, 180 clinical hours. *Entrance requirements:* For master's, GMAT, GRE, transcript, essay, letters of recommendation; for doctorate, RN license; resume; graduate research and statistics courses (strongly recommended). Additional exam requirements/recommendations for international students: Required—TOEFL (minimum score 525 paper-based, 41 iBT) or IELTS (minimum score 4). *Application deadline:* For fall admission, 7/1 for domestic students, 4/1 for international students; for spring admission, 11/15 for domestic students, 8/15 for international students; for summer admission, 5/1 for domestic students, 2/1 for international students. Applications are processed on a rolling basis. Application fee: $30 ($100 for international students). Electronic applications accepted. *Expenses:* Contact institution. *Financial support:* In 2017–18, 54 students received support, including 1 research assistantship (averaging $1,350 per year); scholarships/grants, tuition waivers (partial), and unspecified assistantships also available. Financial award application deadline: 4/15; financial award applicants required to submit FAFSA. *Faculty research:* Risk assessment and failure modeling for the public sector implication of property rights on economic development, the social stability of communities, civil peace of nations. *Total annual research expenditures:* $414,831. *Unit head:* Dr. Kristen Broady, Assistant Vice President and Dean of Graduate Programs, 502-597-6386, E-mail: kristen.broady@kysu.edu. *Application contact:* Dr. James Obielodan, Director of Graduate Studies, 502-597-4723, E-mail: james.obielodan@kysu.edu.
Website: http://kysu.edu/academics/college-of-professional-studies/

Lamar University, College of Graduate Studies, College of Education and Human Development, Department of Counseling and Special Populations, Beaumont, TX 77701. Offers clinical mental health counseling (M Ed); school counseling (M Ed); special education (M Ed), including special education. *Accreditation:* ACA. *Faculty:* 15 full-time (12 women), 22 part-time/adjunct (18 women). *Students:* 27 full-time (22 women), 1,362 part-time (1,200 women); includes 700 minority (359 Black or African American, non-Hispanic/Latino; 6 American Indian or Alaska Native, non-Hispanic/Latino; 18 Asian, non-Hispanic/Latino; 305 Hispanic/Latino; 1 Native Hawaiian or other Pacific Islander, non-Hispanic/Latino; 11 Two or more races, non-Hispanic/Latino), 2 international. Average age 37. 1,317 applicants, 66% accepted, 234 enrolled. In 2017, 645 master's awarded. *Entrance requirements:* Additional exam requirements/recommendations for international students: Required—TOEFL (minimum score 550 paper-based; 79 iBT), IELTS (minimum score 6.5). *Application deadline:* For fall admission, 8/10 for domestic students, 7/1 for international students; for spring admission, 1/5 for domestic students, 12/1 for international students. Applications are processed on a rolling basis. Application fee: $25 ($50 for international students). Electronic applications accepted. *Expenses:* Contact institution. *Financial support:* Applicants required to submit FAFSA. *Unit head:* Dr. Rebecca Weinbaum, Interim Chair, 409-880-8978, Fax: 409-880-2263. *Application contact:* Deidre Mayer, Interim Director, Admissions and Academic Services, 409-880-8888, Fax: 409-880-7419, E-mail: gradmissions@lamar.edu.
Website: http://education.lamar.edu/counseling-and-special-populations

Lamar University, College of Graduate Studies, College of Fine Arts and Communication, Department of Deaf Studies and Deaf Education, Beaumont, TX 77701. Offers MS, Ed D. *Accreditation:* ASHA. *Program availability:* Part-time, evening/weekend. *Faculty:* 12 full-time (8 women), 1 (woman) part-time/adjunct. *Students:* 16 full-time (11 women), 11 part-time (7 women); includes 8 minority (4 Black or African American, non-Hispanic/Latino; 4 Hispanic/Latino), 5 international. Average age 40. 21 applicants, 86% accepted, 12 enrolled. In 2017, 2 master's, 3 doctorates awarded. *Degree requirements:* For master's, thesis optional; for doctorate, thesis/dissertation. *Entrance requirements:* For master's, GRE General Test, performance IQ score of 115 (for deaf students), minimum GPA of 2.5; for doctorate, GRE General Test, performance IQ score of 115 (for deaf students). Additional exam requirements/recommendations for international students: Required—TOEFL (minimum score 550 paper-based; 79 iBT), IELTS (minimum score 6.5). *Application deadline:* For fall admission, 8/10 for domestic students, 7/1 for international students; for spring admission, 1/5 for domestic students, 12/1 for international students. Applications are processed on a rolling basis. Application fee: $25 ($50 for international students). Electronic applications accepted. *Expenses:* Contact institution. *Financial support:* In 2017–18, 27 fellowships were awarded; research assistantships also available. Financial award application deadline: 4/1; financial award applicants required to submit FAFSA. *Faculty research:* Multicultural and deaf teacher training, central auditory processing, voice sign language. *Unit head:* Dr. Diane Clark, Chair, 409-880-8170, Fax: 409-880-2265. *Application contact:* Deidre Mayer, Interim Director, Admissions and Academic Services, 409-880-8888, Fax: 409-880-7419, E-mail: gradmissions@lamar.edu.
Website: http://fineartscomm.lamar.edu/deaf-studies-deaf-education

Lancaster Bible College, Graduate School, Lancaster, PA 17601-5036. Offers adult ministries (MA); Bible (MA); children and family ministry (MA); church planting (MA); consulting resource teacher (M Ed); elementary school counseling (M Ed); leadership (PhD); leadership studies (MA); marriage and family counseling (MA); mental health counseling (MA); pastoral studies (MA); secondary school counseling (M Ed); sports ministry (MA); student ministry (MA); town and country ministry (MA). *Program availability:* Part-time, evening/weekend. *Degree requirements:* For master's, comprehensive exam (for some programs), thesis (for some programs). *Entrance requirements:* For master's, bachelor's degree with a minimum of 30 credits of course work in Bible, minimum undergraduate GPA of 3.0, interview. Additional exam requirements/recommendations for international students: Required—TOEFL.

La Salle University, School of Arts and Sciences, Program in Education, Philadelphia, PA 19141-1199. Offers autism spectrum disorders (MA, Certificate); bilingual/bicultural studies (MA); classroom management (MA); dual early childhood and special education (MA); dual middle-level science and math and special education (MA); education (MA); English (MA); English as a second language (Certificate); history (MA); instructional coach (Certificate); instructional leadership (MA); reading specialist (MA, Certificate); secondary education (MA); special education (MA, Certificate). *Program availability:* Part-time, evening/weekend. *Faculty:* 5 full-time (4 women), 8 part-time/adjunct (5 women). *Students:* 2 full-time (1 woman), 110 part-time (81 women); includes 23 minority (11 Black or African American, non-Hispanic/Latino; 1 Asian, non-Hispanic/Latino; 7 Hispanic/Latino; 4 Two or more races, non-Hispanic/Latino). Average age 33. 137 applicants, 70% accepted, 63 enrolled. In 2017, 148 master's awarded. *Degree requirements:* For master's, comprehensive exam. *Entrance requirements:* For master's, MAT or GRE, 2 letters of recommendation; for Certificate, GMAT or GRE, 2 letters of recommendation. Additional exam requirements/recommendations for international students: Required—TOEFL. *Application deadline:* For fall admission, 8/15 priority date for domestic students, 7/15 for international students; for spring admission, 12/15 priority date for domestic students, 11/15 for international students; for summer admission, 4/15 priority date for domestic students, 3/15 for international students. Applications are processed on a rolling basis. Application fee: $35. Electronic applications accepted. Application fee is waived when completed online. *Expenses:* Contact institution. *Financial support:* In 2017–18, 19 students received support. Scholarships/grants available. Support available to part-time students. Financial award application deadline: 8/31; financial award applicants required to submit FAFSA. *Unit head:* Dr. Greer Richardson, Director, 215-951-1806, Fax: 215-951-1843, E-mail: graded@lasalle.edu. *Application contact:* Elizabeth Heenan, Director, Graduate and Adult Enrollment, 215-951-1100, Fax: 215-951-1462, E-mail: heenan@lasalle.edu. Website: http://www.lasalle.edu/grad-education-programs/

Lasell College, Graduate and Professional Studies in Education, Newton, MA 02466-2709. Offers curriculum, leadership, and inclusion (M Ed); elementary education (M Ed); special education (M Ed), including moderate disabilities; teaching bilingual/English learners with disabilities (Graduate Certificate). *Program availability:* Part-time-only, evening/weekend, blended/hybrid learning. *Faculty:* 3 full-time (all women), 5 part-time/ adjunct (4 women). *Students:* 8 full-time (7 women), 43 part-time (38 women); includes 4 minority (2 Asian, non-Hispanic/Latino; 1 Hispanic/Latino; 1 Two or more races, non-Hispanic/Latino), 1 international. Average age 28. 23 applicants, 74% accepted, 10 enrolled. In 2017, 15 master's awarded. *Degree requirements:* For master's, minimum GPA of 3.0; practicum. *Entrance requirements:* For master's, Massachusetts Tests for Educator Licensure (MTEL) Curriculum and Literacy foundations of reading and writing subtest, one-page personal statement, 2 letters of recommendation, resume, bachelor's degree transcript. Additional exam requirements/recommendations for international students: Required—TOEFL (minimum score 550 paper-based, 79 iBT) or IELTS (minimum score 6). *Application deadline:* For fall admission, 8/31 priority date for domestic students, 6/30 priority date for international students; for spring admission, 12/ 31 priority date for domestic students, 10/31 priority date for international students. Applications are processed on a rolling basis. Electronic applications accepted. *Expenses:* $600 per credit. *Financial support:* Federal Work-Study, scholarships/grants, and tuition discounts available. Support available to part-time students. Financial award application deadline: 8/31; financial award applicants required to submit FAFSA. *Faculty research:* Inclusion, English language learners, literacy, and urban education; teacher inquiry; universal design for learning, deaf-blindness, and visual impairments; social and emotional learning; educational law, applied behavior analysis, and classroom management. *Unit head:* Eric Turner, Vice President of Graduate and Professional Studies, 617-243-2071, Fax: 617-243-2450, E-mail: gradinfo@lasell.edu. *Application contact:* Adrienne Franciosi, Director of Graduate Enrollment, 617-243-2214, Fax: 617-243-2450, E-mail: gradinfo@lasell.edu. Website: http://www.lasell.edu/academics/graduate-and-professional-studies/programs-of-study/master-of-education.html

Lee University, Program in Education, Cleveland, TN 37320-3450. Offers art (MAT); curriculum and instruction (M Ed, Ed S); early childhood (MAT); educational leadership (M Ed, Ed S); elementary education (MAT); English and math (MAT); English and science (MAT); English and social studies (MAT); higher education administration (MS); history (MAT); history and economics (MAT); math and science (MAT); math and social studies (MAT); middle grades (MAT); science and social studies (MASW); secondary education (MAT); Spanish (MAT); special education (M Ed, MAT); TESOL (MAT). *Accreditation:* NCATE. *Program availability:* Part-time. *Faculty:* 15 full-time (7 women), 8 part-time/adjunct (3 women). *Students:* 28 full-time (21 women), 77 part-time (48 women); includes 12 minority (7 Black or African American, non-Hispanic/Latino; 2 Hispanic/Latino; 3 Two or more races, non-Hispanic/Latino), 1 international. Average age 31. 35 applicants, 83% accepted, 22 enrolled. In 2017, 54 master's, 4 other advanced degrees awarded. *Degree requirements:* For master's, variable foreign language requirement, thesis optional, internship. *Entrance requirements:* For master's, MAT or GRE General Test, minimum undergraduate GPA of 2.75, 3 letters of recommendation, interview, writing sample, official transcripts, background check; for Ed S, minimum undergraduate and master's GPA of 2.75, official transcripts for undergraduate and master's degrees. Additional exam requirements/recommendations for international students: Required—TOEFL (minimum score 61 iBT). *Application deadline:* For fall admission, 6/1 priority date for domestic and international students; for spring admission, 11/1 priority date for domestic and international students; for summer admission, 4/1 priority date for domestic and international students. Applications are processed on a rolling basis. Application fee: $25. Electronic applications accepted. *Expenses:* Tuition: Full-time $12,780; part-time $710 per credit hour. *Required fees:* $60; $60 per term. Tuition and fees vary according to program. *Financial support:* In 2017–18, 32 students received support. Career-related internships or fieldwork, Federal Work-Study, institutionally sponsored loans, scholarships/grants, and unspecified assistantships available. Financial award application deadline: 3/1; financial award applicants required to submit FAFSA. *Unit head:* Dr. William Kamm, Director, 423-614-8544, E-mail: wkamm@leeuniversity.edu. *Application contact:* Crystal Keeter, Graduate Education Secretary, 423-614-8544, E-mail: ckeeter@leeuniversity.edu. Website: http://www.leeuniversity.edu/academics/graduate/education

Lehigh University, College of Education, Program in Special Education, Bethlehem, PA 18015. Offers M Ed, PhD. *Program availability:* Part-time. *Faculty:* 5 full-time (all women), 4 part-time/adjunct (all women). *Students:* 17 full-time (13 women), 37 part-time (31 women); includes 4 minority (1 Black or African American, non-Hispanic/Latino; 1 Asian, non-Hispanic/Latino; 1 Hispanic/Latino; 1 Two or more races, non-Hispanic/ Latino), 5 international. Average age 29. 31 applicants, 71% accepted, 13 enrolled. In 2017, 13 master's, 1 doctorate awarded. *Degree requirements:* For doctorate, comprehensive exam, thesis/dissertation, qualifying exam. *Entrance requirements:* For master's, minimum GPA of 3.0, 2 academic letters of recommendation, essay, transcripts; for doctorate, GRE General Test, minimum GPA of 3.0, 2 academic letters of recommendation, essay, transcripts. Additional exam requirements/recommendations for international students: Required—TOEFL (minimum iBT score of 93) or IELTS (6.5). *Application deadline:* For fall admission, 1/15 for domestic and international students; for summer admission, 1/15 for domestic and international students. Applications are processed on a rolling basis. Application fee: $65. Electronic applications accepted. *Expenses:* Contact institution. *Financial support:* In 2017–18, 20 students received support, including 13 research assistantships with full and partial tuition reimbursements available (averaging $15,283 per year); fellowships and unspecified assistantships also available. Financial award application deadline: 1/31. *Faculty research:* Special education, autism spectrum disorder, emotional and behavioral disorders, positive behavior support, early childhood special education, ADHD, intellectual disability, intensive instruction, language development, learning disabilities. *Total annual research expenditures:* $334,803. *Unit head:* Dr. Linda Bambara, Director, 610-758-3271, Fax: 610-758-6223, E-mail: lmb1@lehigh.edu. *Application contact:* Donna Toothman, Coordinator, 610-758-3230, Fax: 610-758-3243, E-mail: djt2@lehigh.edu. Website: https://ed.lehigh.edu/academics/programs/special-education

Lehman College of the City University of New York, School of Education, Department of Specialized Services in Education, Bronx, NY 10468-1589. Offers guidance and counseling (MS Ed); reading teacher (MS Ed); teachers of special education (MS Ed), including bilingual special education, early special education, emotional handicaps, learning disabilities, mental retardation. *Program availability:* Part-time, evening/weekend. *Faculty research:* Battered women, whole language classrooms, parent education, mainstreaming.

Lehman College of the City University of New York, School of Education, Department of Specialized Services in Education, Teachers of Special Education

Program, Option in Bilingual Special Education, Bronx, NY 10468-1589. Offers MS Ed. *Accreditation:* NCATE. *Entrance requirements:* For master's, minimum GPA of 3.0.

Lehman College of the City University of New York, School of Education, Department of Specialized Services in Education, Teachers of Special Education Program, Option in Early Special Education, Bronx, NY 10468-1589. Offers MS Ed. *Accreditation:* NCATE. *Entrance requirements:* For master's, minimum GPA of 3.0.

Lehman College of the City University of New York, School of Education, Department of Specialized Services in Education, Teachers of Special Education Program, Option in Emotional Handicaps, Bronx, NY 10468-1589. Offers MS Ed. *Accreditation:* NCATE. *Program availability:* Part-time, evening/weekend. *Entrance requirements:* For master's, minimum GPA of 2.7. *Faculty research:* Behavioral disorders, self-evaluation, applied behavior analysis.

Lehman College of the City University of New York, School of Education, Department of Specialized Services in Education, Teachers of Special Education Program, Option in Learning Disabilities, Bronx, NY 10468-1589. Offers MS Ed. *Accreditation:* NCATE. *Program availability:* Part-time, evening/weekend. *Entrance requirements:* For master's, interview, minimum GPA of 2.7. *Faculty research:* Emergent literacy, language-based classrooms, primary and secondary social contexts of language and literacy, innovative in-service education models, adult literacy.

Lehman College of the City University of New York, School of Education, Department of Specialized Services in Education, Teachers of Special Education Program, Option in Mental Retardation, Bronx, NY 10468-1589. Offers MS Ed. *Accreditation:* NCATE. *Program availability:* Part-time, evening/weekend. *Entrance requirements:* For master's, minimum GPA of 2.7. *Faculty research:* Conductive education, homeless infants and their families, infant stimulation, hospitalizing infants with AIDS, legislation PL99-457.

Le Moyne College, Department of Education, Syracuse, NY 13214. Offers adolescent education (MS Ed, MST); adolescent education/special education (MS Ed, MST); adolescent English (MST), including grades 7-12; adolescent English/special education (MST), including grades 7-12; adolescent foreign language (MST), including grades 7-12; adolescent history (MST), including grades 7-12; childhood education (MS Ed); childhood education/special education (MS Ed); elementary education (MS Ed); general education (MS Ed); inclusive childhood education (MST); literacy education (MS Ed), including birth to grade 6, grades 5-12; school building leader (MS Ed); school building leadership (CAS); school district business leader (MS Ed, CAS); school district leader (MS Ed); school district leadership (CAS); secondary education (MS Ed); special education (MS Ed); teaching English to speakers of other languages (MS Ed); urban studies (MS Ed). *Accreditation:* TEAC. *Program availability:* Part-time, evening/ weekend. *Faculty:* 7 full-time (5 women), 20 part-time/adjunct (12 women). *Students:* 30 full-time (19 women), 126 part-time (93 women); includes 15 minority (7 Black or African American, non-Hispanic/Latino; 1 American Indian or Alaska Native, non-Hispanic/ Latino; 1 Asian, non-Hispanic/Latino; 6 Hispanic/Latino), 4 international. Average age 29. 139 applicants, 65% accepted, 76 enrolled. In 2017, 82 master's, 43 CASs awarded. *Degree requirements:* For master's, thesis. *Entrance requirements:* For master's, bachelor's degree with minimum undergraduate GPA of 3.0, 2 letters of recommendation, transcripts. Additional exam requirements/recommendations for international students: Required—TOEFL (minimum score 550 paper-based; 79 iBT); Recommended—IELTS (minimum score 6.5). *Application deadline:* For fall admission, 4/1 priority date for domestic and international students; for spring admission, 10/1 priority date for domestic and international students; for summer admission, 3/1 priority date for domestic and international students. Applications are processed on a rolling basis. Application fee: $50. Electronic applications accepted. *Expenses:* $700 per credit hour. *Financial support:* In 2017–18, 30 students received support. Career-related internships or fieldwork, scholarships/grants, and health care benefits available. Support available to part-time students. Financial award applicants required to submit FAFSA. *Faculty research:* Minority teachers, special education, multiculturalism, literacy, technology, media literacy learning, autism, school district organization, service-learning, higher level problem solving, teacher leadership. *Unit head:* Dr. Stephen C. Fleury, Chair, Department of Education, 315-445-4376, Fax: 315-445-4744, E-mail: fleurysc@lemoyne.edu. *Application contact:* Kristen P. Richards, Senior Director of Enrollment Management, 315-445-5444, Fax: 315-445-6092, E-mail: trapaskp@ lemoyne.edu. Website: http://www.lemoyne.edu/education

Lesley University, Graduate School of Education, Cambridge, MA 02138-2790. Offers arts, community, and education (M Ed); autism studies (Certificate); curriculum and instruction (M Ed, CAGS); early childhood education (M Ed); ecological teaching and learning (MS); educational studies (PhD), including adult learning, educational leadership, individually designed; elementary education (M Ed); emergent technologies for educators (Certificate); ESLArts: language learning through the arts (M Ed); high school education (M Ed); individually designed (M Ed); integrated teaching through the arts (M Ed); literacy for K-8 classroom teachers (M Ed); mathematics education (M Ed); middle school education (M Ed); moderate disabilities (M Ed); online learning (Certificate); reading (CAGS); science in education (M Ed); severe disabilities (M Ed); special needs (CAGS); specialist teacher of reading (M Ed); teacher of visual art (M Ed); technology in education (M Ed, CAGS). *Accreditation:* TEAC. *Program availability:* Part-time, evening/weekend, online learning. *Degree requirements:* For master's, practicum; for doctorate, thesis/dissertation. *Entrance requirements:* For master's, Massachusetts Tests for Educator Licensure (MTEL), transcripts, statement of purpose, recommendations; interview (for special education); for doctorate, GRE General Test, transcripts, statement of purpose, recommendations, interview, master's degree, resume; for other advanced degree, interview, master's degree. Additional exam requirements/recommendations for international students: Required—TOEFL (minimum score 550 paper-based; 80 iBT). Electronic applications accepted. *Faculty research:* Assessment in literacy, mathematics and science; autism spectrum disorders; instructional technology and online learning; multicultural education and English language learners.

Lewis & Clark College, Graduate School of Education and Counseling, Department of Teacher Education, Program in Special Education, Portland, OR 97219-7899. Offers M Ed. *Accreditation:* NCATE. *Program availability:* Part-time, evening/weekend. *Entrance requirements:* For master's, minimum GPA of 2.75. Additional exam requirements/recommendations for international students: Required—TOEFL (minimum score 575 paper-based). Electronic applications accepted.

Lewis University, College of Education, Program in Early Childhood Special Education, Romeoville, IL 60446. Offers MA. *Program availability:* Part-time. *Students:* 9 full-time (8 women), 7 part-time (all women); includes 5 minority (all Hispanic/Latino). Average age 32. *Degree requirements:* For master's, comprehensive exam. *Entrance requirements:* For master's, writing exam, Test of Academic Proficiency/Basic Skills Test/ACT/SAT, bachelor's degree, minimum undergraduate GPA of 2.75, two letters of recommendation, professional educator license, interview. Additional exam requirements/recommendations for international students: Required—TOEFL (minimum score 550 paper-based; 79 iBT), IELTS (minimum score 6). *Application deadline:* For fall admission, 5/1 priority date for international students; for spring admission, 11/1 priority

date for international students. Application fee: $40. Electronic applications accepted. Tuition and fees vary according to program. *Financial support:* Federal Work-Study and unspecified assistantships available. Financial award application deadline: 5/1; financial award applicants required to submit FAFSA. *Unit head:* Dr. Pamela Jessee, Dean, 815-836-5316, E-mail: jesseepa@lewisu.edu. *Application contact:* Linda Campbell, Graduate Admission Counselor, 815-836-5704, Fax: 815-836-5578, E-mail: campbeli@lewisu.edu.
Website: http://www.lewisu.edu/academics/grad-education/earlychildhood/index.htm

Lewis University, College of Education, Program in Special Education, Romeoville, IL 60446. Offers MA. *Program availability:* Part-time. *Students:* 37 part-time (27 women); includes 3 minority (2 Black or African American, non-Hispanic/Latino; 1 Hispanic/Latino), 1 international. Average age 31. *Degree requirements:* For master's, comprehensive exam, departmental qualifying exam. *Entrance requirements:* For master's, writing exam, Test of Academic Proficiency/Basic Skills Test/ACT/SAT, bachelor's degree, minimum GPA of 2.75, 2 letters of recommendation. Additional exam requirements/recommendations for international students: Required—TOEFL (minimum score 550 paper-based; 80 iBT), IELTS (minimum score 6). *Application deadline:* For fall admission, 5/1 priority date for international students; for spring admission, 11/15 priority date for international students. Applications are processed on a rolling basis. Application fee: $40. Electronic applications accepted. Tuition and fees vary according to program. *Financial support:* Federal Work-Study, scholarships/grants, and unspecified assistantships available. Financial award application deadline: 5/1; financial award applicants required to submit FAFSA. *Unit head:* Dr. Mary Fisher, Program Director, 815-838-0500, E-mail: fisherma@lewisu.edu. *Application contact:* Kathy Lisak, Graduate Admission Counselor, 815-836-5610, E-mail: grad@lewisu.edu.

Liberty University, School of Education, Lynchburg, VA 24515. Offers curriculum and instruction (Ed D, Ed S), including elementary education, middle grades education, secondary education, special education; educational leadership (Ed D); gifted education (Certificate); math specialist (M Ed); middle grades (MAT, Certificate); reading specialist (M Ed); school leadership (Certificate); secondary education (MAT); sport management (MS), including coaching and athletic administration, outdoor adventure sport, sport administration, tourism. *Accreditation:* NCATE. *Program availability:* Part-time, online learning. *Students:* 1,966 full-time (1,428 women), 3,484 part-time (2,528 women); includes 1,323 minority (1,026 Black or African American, non-Hispanic/Latino; 29 American Indian or Alaska Native, non-Hispanic/Latino; 49 Asian, non-Hispanic/Latino; 100 Hispanic/Latino; 9 Native Hawaiian or other Pacific Islander, non-Hispanic/Latino; 110 Two or more races, non-Hispanic/Latino), 58 international. Average age 37. 3,748 applicants, 58% accepted, 1167 enrolled. In 2017, 656 master's, 110 doctorates, 316 other advanced degrees awarded. *Degree requirements:* For doctorate, comprehensive exam, thesis/dissertation. *Entrance requirements:* For master's, GRE General Test or MAT (if taken in or before 1999), 2 letters of recommendation, minimum undergraduate GPA of 3.0, curriculum vitae; for doctorate and other advanced degree, GRE General Test or MAT (if taken before 1999), minimum master's GPA of 3.0, 3 years of teaching experience. Additional exam requirements/recommendations for international students: Required—TOEFL (minimum score 600 paper-based; 100 iBT). *Application deadline:* For fall admission, 6/1 for domestic students; for spring admission, 11/1 for domestic students. Applications are processed on a rolling basis. Application fee: $50. Electronic applications accepted. *Expenses:* Contact institution. *Financial support:* Federal Work-Study and tuition waivers (partial) available. *Faculty research:* Self-determination, character education, bibliotherapy, learning styles, distance education. *Unit head:* Dr. Heather Schoffstall, Dean, 434-582-2445, Fax: 434-582-2468, E-mail: awgunter@liberty.edu. *Application contact:* Jay Bridge, Director of Graduate Admissions, 800-424-9595, Fax: 800-628-7977, E-mail: gradadmissions@liberty.edu.
Website: http://www.liberty.edu/academics/education/graduate/

Lincoln University, Graduate Programs, Philadelphia, PA 19104. Offers counseling (MSC); early childhood education (M Ed), including PreK-4; early childhood education and special education (M Ed); educational leadership (M Ed), including principal certification; finance (MBA); human resources management (MBA); human services delivery (MAHS). *Program availability:* Part-time, evening/weekend. *Faculty:* 9 full-time (3 women), 25 part-time/adjunct (15 women). *Students:* 196 full-time (138 women), 68 part-time (46 women); includes 236 minority (227 Black or African American, non-Hispanic/Latino; 1 American Indian or Alaska Native, non-Hispanic/Latino; 7 Hispanic/Latino; 1 Two or more races, non-Hispanic/Latino), 3 international. Average age 34. 120 applicants, 100% accepted, 95 enrolled. In 2017, 126 master's awarded. *Degree requirements:* For master's, comprehensive exam, thesis or alternative, capstone, grant proposal. *Entrance requirements:* For master's, official academic transcript(s), letters of recommendation, personal statement, resume, supervisor's evaluation form. Additional exam requirements/recommendations for international students: Recommended—TOEFL (minimum score 500 paper-based; 71 iBT), IELTS. *Application deadline:* For fall admission, 8/1 priority date for domestic students, 7/1 priority date for international students; for spring admission, 12/1 priority date for domestic students, 10/1 for international students. Applications are processed on a rolling basis. Application fee: $50. Electronic applications accepted. *Expenses:* Contact institution. *Financial support:* Scholarships/grants available. Financial award application deadline: 6/30; financial award applicants required to submit FAFSA. *Unit head:* Dr. Patricia Pierce Ramsey, Provost, 484-365-7437, Fax: 484-365-8108, E-mail: provost@lincoln.edu. *Application contact:* Jernice Lea, Director, University City Student Services and Admissions, 215-590-8231, Fax: 215-387-3859, E-mail: jlea@lincoln.edu.
Website: http://www.lincoln.edu/admissions/graduate-admissions

Lipscomb University, College of Education, Nashville, TN 37204-3951. Offers applied behavior analysis (MS, Certificate); coaching for learning (M Ed, Certificate, Ed S); educational leadership (M Ed, Ed S); English language learning (M Ed, Ed S); instructional coaching (M Ed, Certificate, Ed S); instructional practice (M Ed); learning organizations and strategic change (Ed D); literacy coaching (Certificate, Ed S); reading specialty (M Ed, Ed S); school counseling (M Ed, Ed S); special education (M Ed); teaching, learning, and leading (M Ed); technology integration (M Ed, Ed S); technology integration specialist (Certificate). *Accreditation:* NCATE. *Program availability:* Part-time, evening/weekend, 100% online. *Faculty:* 21 full-time (14 women), 42 part-time/adjunct (29 women). *Students:* 565 full-time (452 women), 59 part-time (45 women); includes 154 minority (102 Black or African American, non-Hispanic/Latino; 2 American Indian or Alaska Native, non-Hispanic/Latino; 8 Asian, non-Hispanic/Latino; 26 Hispanic/Latino; 16 Two or more races, non-Hispanic/Latino). Average age 32. 395 applicants, 54% accepted, 196 enrolled. In 2017, 162 master's, 30 doctorates, 54 other advanced degrees awarded. *Degree requirements:* For master's, comprehensive exam, portfolio, research project and presentation; for doctorate, practical capstone project in experiential setting. *Entrance requirements:* For master's, MAT (minimum score 31) or GRE General Test (minimum score 294), 2 reference letters, goals statement, writing sample, interview; for doctorate, MAT or GRE General Test, 3 reference letters, artifact of demonstrated academic excellence, written personal statements, interview. Additional exam requirements/recommendations for international students: Required—TOEFL (minimum score 570 paper-based; 80 iBT). *Application deadline:* For fall admission, 8/29 priority date for domestic students; for spring admission, 1/15 priority date for domestic students. Applications are processed on a rolling basis. Application fee: $50 ($75 for international students). Electronic applications accepted. *Expenses:* Contact institution.

Financial support: Scholarships/grants, unspecified assistantships, and partnerships with local school districts available. Financial award applicants required to submit FAFSA. *Faculty research:* Facilitative learning styles, leadership, student assessment, interactive multimedia inclusion, learning organizations and strategic change. *Unit head:* Dr. Deborah Boyd, Director of Graduate Studies, 615-966-6263, E-mail: deborah.boyd@lipscomb.edu. *Application contact:* Amanda Logsdon, Director of Enrollment and Outreach, 615-966-7199, E-mail: amanda.logsdon@lipscomb.edu.
Website: http://www.lipscomb.edu/education/graduate-programs

London Metropolitan University, Graduate Programs, London, United Kingdom. Offers applied psychology (M Sc); architecture (MA); biomedical science (M Sc); blood science (M Sc); cancer pharmacology (M Sc); computer networking and cyber security (M Sc); computing and information systems (M Sc); conference interpreting (MA); counter-terrorism studies (M Sc); creative, digital and professional writing (MA); crime, violence and prevention (M Sc); criminology (M Sc); curating contemporary art (MA); data analytics (M Sc); digital media (MA); early childhood studies (MA); education (MA, Ed D); financial services law, regulation and compliance (LL M); food science (M Sc); forensic psychology (M Sc); health and social care management and policy (M Sc); human nutrition (M Sc); human resource management (MA); human rights and international conflict (MA); information technology (M Sc); intelligence and security studies (M Sc); international oil, gas and energy law (LL M); international relations (MA); interpreting (MA); learning and teaching in higher education (MA); legal practice (LL M); media and entertainment law (LL M); organizational and consumer psychology (M Sc); psychological therapy (M Sc); psychology of mental health (M Sc); public health (M Sc); public policy and management (MPA); security studies (M Sc); social work (M Sc); spatial planning and urban design (MA); sports therapy (M Sc); supporting older children and young people with dyslexia (MA); teaching languages (MA), including Arabic, English; translation (MA); woman and child abuse (MA).

Long Island University–Brentwood Campus, Graduate Programs, Brentwood, NY 11717. Offers childhood education (MS), including grades 1-6; childhood education/literacy B-6 (MS); childhood education/special education (grades 1-6) (MS); clinical mental health counseling (MS, Advanced Certificate); criminal justice (MS); early childhood education (MS); educational leadership (MS Ed); family nurse practitioner (MS, Advanced Certificate); health administration (MPA); library and information science (MS); literacy (B-6) (MS Ed); school counselor (MS, Advanced Certificate); social work (MSW); special education (MS Ed); students with disabilities generalist (grades 7-12) (Advanced Certificate). *Program availability:* Part-time. *Faculty:* 14 full-time (9 women), 22 part-time/adjunct (11 women). *Students:* 111 full-time (89 women), 47 part-time (34 women); includes 35 minority (8 Black or African American, non-Hispanic/Latino; 1 American Indian or Alaska Native, non-Hispanic/Latino; 3 Asian, non-Hispanic/Latino; 22 Hispanic/Latino; 1 Two or more races, non-Hispanic/Latino), 1 international. Average age 30. 110 applicants, 82% accepted, 63 enrolled. In 2017, 58 master's, 5 other advanced degrees awarded. *Entrance requirements:* For master's and Advanced Certificate, GRE. Additional exam requirements/recommendations for international students: Required—TOEFL or IELTS. *Application deadline:* Applications are processed on a rolling basis. Application fee: $50. Electronic applications accepted. *Expenses:* Tuition: Full-time $21,168; part-time $1201 per credit. *Required fees:* $1840; $920 per term. Tuition and fees vary according to course load. *Financial support:* In 2017–18, 121 students received support. Scholarships/grants available. Support available to part-time students. Financial award application deadline: 2/15; financial award applicants required to submit FAFSA. *Unit head:* Dr. Abby Van Vlerah, Dean and Chief Operating Officer, 631-299-3831, E-mail: abagail.vanvlerah@liu.edu. *Application contact:* Scott Aug, Associate Director of Enrollment Management, 631-287-8506, E-mail: scott.aug@liu.edu.
Website: http://liu.edu/brentwood

Long Island University–Hudson, Graduate School, Purchase, NY 10577. Offers autism (Advanced Certificate); bilingual education (Advanced Certificate); childhood education (MS Ed); crisis management (Advanced Certificate); early childhood education (MS Ed); educational leadership (MS Ed); health administration (MPA); literacy (MS Ed); marriage and family therapy (MS); mental health counseling (MS, Advanced Certificate, including credentialed alcoholism and substance abuse counselor (MS); middle childhood and adolescence education (MS Ed); pharmaceutics (MS), including cosmetic science, industrial pharmacy; public administration (MPA); school counseling (MS Ed, Advanced Certificate); school psychology (MS Ed); special education (MS Ed); TESOL (MS Ed); TESOL (all grades) (Advanced Certificate). *Program availability:* Part-time, evening/weekend. *Faculty:* 8 full-time (6 women), 41 part-time/adjunct (24 women). *Students:* 69 full-time (54 women), 249 part-time (200 women); includes 102 minority (29 Black or African American, non-Hispanic/Latino; 1 American Indian or Alaska Native, non-Hispanic/Latino; 9 Asian, non-Hispanic/Latino; 62 Hispanic/Latino; 1 Native Hawaiian or other Pacific Islander, non-Hispanic/Latino). Average age 33. 153 applicants, 96% accepted, 103 enrolled. In 2017, 138 master's, 36 other advanced degrees awarded. *Entrance requirements:* Additional exam requirements/recommendations for international students: Required—TOEFL. *Application deadline:* Applications are processed on a rolling basis. Application fee: $50. Electronic applications accepted. *Expenses:* Contact institution. *Financial support:* In 2017–18, 32 students received support. Scholarships/grants available. Support available to part-time students. Financial award application deadline: 2/15; financial award applicants required to submit FAFSA. *Unit head:* Dr. Sylvia Blake, Dean and Chief Operating Officer, 914-831-2700, E-mail: westchester@liu.edu. *Application contact:* Dr. Sylvia Blake, Dean and Chief Operating Officer, 914-831-2700, E-mail: westchester@liu.edu.

Long Island University–LIU Brooklyn, School of Education, Brooklyn, NY 11201-8423. Offers adolescence urban education (MS Ed); applied behavior analysis (Advanced Certificate); bilingual education (Advanced Certificate); bilingual education in urban setting (MS Ed); bilingual school counselor (MS Ed, Advanced Certificate); childhood urban education (MS Ed); childhood/early childhood education (MS Ed); childhood/early childhood urban education (MS Ed); early childhood urban education (MS Ed, Advanced Certificate); educational leadership (Advanced Certificate); marriage and family therapy (MS, Advanced Certificate); mental health counseling (MS, Advanced Certificate); school building district leader (Advanced Certificate); school counselor (MS Ed, Advanced Certificate); school psychologist (MS Ed); teaching students with disabilities (MS Ed); teaching urban children with disabilities (MS Ed); TESOL (MS Ed, Advanced Certificate). *Accreditation:* TEAC. *Program availability:* Part-time, evening/weekend, 100% online. *Faculty:* 14 full-time (12 women), 42 part-time/adjunct (32 women). *Students:* 140 full-time (130 women), 563 part-time (414 women); includes 417 minority (183 Black or African American, non-Hispanic/Latino; 1 American Indian or Alaska Native, non-Hispanic/Latino; 32 Asian, non-Hispanic/Latino; 187 Hispanic/Latino; 14 Two or more races, non-Hispanic/Latino), 10 international. Average age 31. 449 applicants, 82% accepted, 264 enrolled. In 2017, 408 master's, 31 other advanced degrees awarded. *Entrance requirements:* For master's, GRE. Additional exam requirements/recommendations for international students: Required—TOEFL (minimum score 527 paper-based, 75 iBT), IELTS, or PTE. *Application deadline:* Applications are processed on a rolling basis. Application fee: $50. Electronic applications accepted. *Expenses:* Tuition: Full-time $21,618; part-time $1201 per credit. *Required fees:* $1840; $920 per term. Tuition and fees vary according to course load.

Financial support: In 2017–18, 58 students received support. Career-related internships or fieldwork, Federal Work-Study, scholarships/grants, and unspecified assistantships available. Support available to part-time students. Financial award application deadline: 2/15; financial award applicants required to submit FAFSA. *Faculty research:* Diversity issues in education and mental health care, inclusion - disability studies, sustainability, teacher professional development. *Unit head:* Dean, 718-488-1055, E-mail: bkln-admissions@liu.edu. *Application contact:* Bayu Sutrisno, Graduate Admissions Counselor, 718-488-1011, Fax: 718-780-6110, E-mail: bkln-admissions@liu.edu. Website: http://www.liu.edu/Brooklyn/Academics/School-of-Education

Long Island University–LIU Post, College of Education, Information and Technology, Brookville, NY 11548-1300. Offers adolescence education (MS); adolescence education 7-12 (MS); archives and records management (AC); art education (MS); childhood education (MS); childhood education/literacy B-6 (MS); childhood education/special education (MS); clinical mental health counseling (MS, AC); early childhood education (MS); early childhood education/childhood education (MS); educational leadership (AC); educational technology (MS); information studies (PhD); interdisciplinary educational studies (Ed D); middle childhood education (MS); music education (MS); public library administration (AC); school counselor (MS); special education (MS Ed); speech-language pathology (MA); students with disabilities, 7-12 generalist (AC); TESOL (MA). *Accreditation:* TEAC. *Program availability:* Part-time, 100% online, blended/hybrid learning. *Faculty:* 40 full-time (26 women), 73 part-time/adjunct (38 women). *Students:* 472 full-time (400 women), 696 part-time (543 women); includes 254 minority (93 Black or African American, non-Hispanic/Latino; 46 Asian, non-Hispanic/Latino; 105 Hispanic/Latino; 10 Two or more races, non-Hispanic/Latino), 33 international. Average age 33. 917 applicants, 82% accepted, 357 enrolled. In 2017, 408 master's, 31 other advanced degrees awarded. Terminal master's awarded for partial completion of doctoral program. *Degree requirements:* For master's, variable foreign language requirement, comprehensive exam (for some programs), thesis optional; for doctorate, comprehensive exam, thesis/dissertation. *Entrance requirements:* For master's and AC, GRE (for some programs). Additional exam requirements/recommendations for international students: Required—TOEFL (minimum score 550 paper-based, 75 iBT), IELTS, or PTE. *Application deadline:* Applications are processed on a rolling basis. Application fee: $50. Electronic applications accepted. *Expenses:* Tuition: Full-time $21,618; part-time $1201 per credit. *Required fees:* $1840; $920 per term. Tuition and fees vary according to course load. *Financial support:* In 2017–18, 376 students received support. Career-related internships or fieldwork, Federal Work-Study, institutionally sponsored loans, scholarships/grants, tuition waivers (partial), and unspecified assistantships available. Support available to part-time students. Financial award application deadline: 2/15; financial award applicants required to submit FAFSA. *Faculty research:* Sleep; use of technology to develop executive function by students with disabilities; early childhood literacy development through play; social justice through education; using a structured protocol to discuss Bad News. *Unit head:* Dr. Albert Inserra, Dean, 516-299-2210, E-mail: albert.inserra@liu.edu. *Application contact:* Rita Langdon, Graduate Admissions, 516-299-2900, Fax: 516-299-2137, E-mail: post-enroll@liu.edu. Website: http://liu.edu/CWPost/Academics/College-of-Education-Information-and-Technology

Long Island University–Riverhead, Graduate Programs, Riverhead, NY 11901. Offers applied behavior analysis (Advanced Certificate); childhood education (MS), including grades 1-6; cybersecurity policy (Advanced Certificate); homeland security management (MS, Advanced Certificate); literacy education (MS); literacy education B-6 (MS); teaching students with disabilities (MS), including grades 1-6; TESOL (Advanced Certificate). *Accreditation:* TEAC. *Program availability:* Part-time. *Faculty:* 4 full-time (1 woman), 11 part-time/adjunct (5 women). *Students:* 17 full-time (14 women), 58 part-time (36 women); includes 14 minority (4 Black or African American, non-Hispanic/Latino; 1 American Indian or Alaska Native, non-Hispanic/Latino; 1 Asian, non-Hispanic/Latino; 6 Hispanic/Latino; 2 Two or more races, non-Hispanic/Latino). Average age 32. 68 applicants, 79% accepted, 26 enrolled. In 2017, 30 master's, 7 other advanced degrees awarded. *Entrance requirements:* Additional exam requirements/recommendations for international students: Required—TOEFL or IELTS. *Application deadline:* Applications are processed on a rolling basis. Application fee: $50. Electronic applications accepted. *Expenses:* Contact institution. *Financial support:* In 2017–18, 53 students received support. Scholarships/grants available. Support available to part-time students. Financial award application deadline: 2/15; financial award applicants required to submit FAFSA. *Unit head:* Dr. Abagail VanVlerah, Dean and Chief Operating Officer, 631-299-3831, E-mail: abagail.vanvlerah@liu.edu. *Application contact:* Jean Conroy, Associate Dean, 631-287-8301, E-mail: jean.conroy@liu.edu.

Longwood University, College of Graduate and Professional Studies, College of Education and Human Services, Farmville, VA 23909. Offers education (MS), including algebra and middle school mathematics, counselor education, elementary and middle school mathematics, elementary education, elementary education initial licensure, health and physical education, special education general curriculum, special education initial licensure; reading, literacy and learning (M Ed); school librarianship (M Ed); social work and communication sciences and disorders (MS), including communication sciences and disorders. *Accreditation:* NCATE. *Program availability:* Part-time, evening/weekend. *Degree requirements:* For master's, comprehensive exam (for some programs), thesis optional, professional portfolio, internship, clinical experience, or practicum. *Entrance requirements:* For master's, PRAXIS I (for initial teaching licensure programs); GRE (for some programs), bachelor's degree from regionally-accredited institution, 2 recommendations (3 for some programs), minimum 500-word personal essay, official transcripts, minimum GPA of 2.75, valid teaching license (for some programs). Additional exam requirements/recommendations for international students: Required—TOEFL (minimum score 570 paper-based), IELTS (minimum score 6.5). Electronic applications accepted. *Expenses:* Contact institution.

Loras College, Graduate Division, Program in Education with an Emphasis in Special Education, Dubuque, IA 52004-0178. Offers instructional strategist I K-6 and 7-12 (MA). *Program availability:* Part-time, evening/weekend. *Degree requirements:* For master's, comprehensive exam, thesis optional. *Entrance requirements:* For master's, minimum cumulative undergraduate GPA of 3.0.

Louisiana Tech University, Graduate School, College of Education, Ruston, LA 71272. Offers counseling and guidance (MA), including clinical mental health counseling, human services, orientation and mobility; counseling psychology (PhD); curriculum and instruction (M Ed); cyber education (Graduate Certificate); dynamics of domestic and family violence (Graduate Certificate); early childhood education - PreK-3 (MAT); educational leadership (M Ed, Ed D); elementary education and special education mild/moderate grades 1-5 (MAT); higher education administration (Graduate Certificate); industrial/organizational psychology (MA, PhD); kinesiology (MS); middle school education (MAT), including mathematics; orientation and mobility (Graduate Certificate); rehabilitation teaching for the blind (Graduate Certificate); secondary education (MAT), including agriculture, biology, business, chemistry, English; special education: visually impaired (MAT); teacher leader education (Graduate Certificate); visual impairments - blind education (Graduate Certificate). *Accreditation:* NCATE. *Program availability:* Part-time. *Faculty:* 28 full-time (16 women), 23 part-time/adjunct (22 women). *Students:* 269

full-time (192 women), 194 part-time (150 women); includes 127 minority (94 Black or African American, non-Hispanic/Latino; 2 American Indian or Alaska Native, non-Hispanic/Latino; 6 Asian, non-Hispanic/Latino; 16 Hispanic/Latino; 1 Native Hawaiian or other Pacific Islander, non-Hispanic/Latino; 8 Two or more races, non-Hispanic/Latino), 8 international. Average age 34. 226 applicants, 74% accepted, 60 enrolled. In 2017, 5 master's, 2 doctorates, 1 other advanced degree awarded. *Degree requirements:* For master's, thesis; for doctorate, thesis/dissertation. *Entrance requirements:* For master's and doctorate, GRE General Test. Additional exam requirements/recommendations for international students: Required—TOEFL (minimum score 550 paper-based; 80 iBT), IELTS (minimum score 6.5). *Application deadline:* For fall admission, 9/1 priority date for domestic students, 6/1 for international students; for winter admission, 11/1 priority date for domestic students, 9/1 for international students; for spring admission, 2/1 priority date for domestic students, 12/1 for international students; for summer admission, 5/1 priority date for domestic students, 3/1 for international students. Application fee: $40. Electronic applications accepted. *Expenses:* Tuition, state resident: full-time $5146. Tuition, nonresident: full-time $10,147. *International tuition:* $10,267 full-time. *Required fees:* $2273. *Financial support:* In 2017–18, 40 students received support, including 23 research assistantships (averaging $10,346 per year), 15 teaching assistantships (averaging $6,887 per year); fellowships and career-related internships or fieldwork also available. Financial award application deadline: 2/1. *Faculty research:* Blindness and the best methods for increasing independence for individuals who are blind or visually impaired; educating and investigating factors contributing to improvements in human performance across the lifespan and a reduction in injury rates during training. *Total annual research expenditures:* $2.1 million. *Unit head:* Dr. Don Schillinger, Dean, 318-257-3712, E-mail: dschill@latech.edu. *Application contact:* Dr. Dawn Basinger, Associate Dean of Academic Affairs, 318-257-2977, Fax: 318-257-2379, E-mail: dbasing@latech.edu. Website: http://education.latech.edu/

Loyola Marymount University, School of Education, Program in Special Education, Los Angeles, CA 90045-2659. Offers MA. *Unit head:* Dr. Diana Limon, Acting Director, Special Education, 310-338-4262, E-mail: dlimon@lmu.edu. *Application contact:* Chake H. Kouyoumjian, Associate Dean of Graduate Studies, 310-338-2721, Fax: 310-338-6086, E-mail: graduateinfo@lmu.edu. Website: http://soe.lmu.edu/academics/specialeducation

Loyola University Chicago, School of Education, Program in Teaching and Learning, Chicago, IL 60660. Offers elementary education (M Ed); English language teaching and learning (M Ed); secondary education (M Ed); special education (M Ed). *Accreditation:* NCATE. *Faculty:* 18 full-time (12 women), 33 part-time/adjunct (29 women). *Students:* 19 full-time (13 women), 20 part-time (17 women); includes 7 minority (1 Black or African American, non-Hispanic/Latino; 2 Asian, non-Hispanic/Latino; 4 Hispanic/Latino). Average age 27. 129 applicants, 48% accepted, 28 enrolled. In 2017, 38 master's awarded. *Degree requirements:* For master's, comprehensive exam. *Entrance requirements:* For master's, Illinois Basic Skills Test, 3 letters of recommendation, minimum GPA of 3.0, resume. Additional exam requirements/recommendations for international students: Required—TOEFL (minimum score 550 paper-based; 79 iBT). *Application deadline:* For summer admission, 3/1 priority date for domestic and international students. Application fee: $50. Electronic applications accepted. Application fee is waived when completed online. *Expenses:* $949 per semester hour, $2,847 per course, $8,541-$11,388 full-time semester tuition; $432 per semester fees, $225 additional fees (first semester only). *Financial support:* In 2017–18, 12 fellowships with partial tuition reimbursements were awarded; institutionally sponsored loans, scholarships/grants, and unspecified assistantships also available. Support available to part-time students. Financial award application deadline: 2/1; financial award applicants required to submit FAFSA. *Faculty research:* Positive behavior support, school reform, school improvement. *Unit head:* Dr. Hank Bohanon, Program Chair, 312-915-7009, E-mail: hbohano@luc.edu. *Application contact:* Mirtza Campbell, Information Contact, 312-915-8907, E-mail: mcampbell11@luc.edu.

Lynn University, Donald E. and Helen L. Ross College of Education, Boca Raton, FL 33431-5598. Offers educational leadership (M Ed, Ed D), including K-12 (Ed D); school administration K-12 (M Ed); exceptional student education (M Ed), including school administration K-12. *Program availability:* Part-time, evening/weekend, online learning. *Faculty:* 6 full-time (4 women), 4 part-time/adjunct (3 women). *Students:* 31 full-time (23 women), 62 part-time (42 women); includes 32 minority (20 Black or African American, non-Hispanic/Latino; 1 American Indian or Alaska Native, non-Hispanic/Latino; 10 Hispanic/Latino; 1 Two or more races, non-Hispanic/Latino), 3 international. Average age 36. 46 applicants, 78% accepted, 30 enrolled. In 2017, 24 master's, 22 doctorates awarded. *Degree requirements:* For master's, comprehensive exam, thesis (for some programs), completion of degree in maximum of four calendar years; minimum cumulative GPA of 3.0 and B grade or higher in each course; orientation seminar (one credit); minimum of 40 credits; FTCE ESE K-12 Exam; for doctorate, thesis/dissertation, mid-program review; minimum cumulative GPA of 3.25 and B grade or higher in each course. *Entrance requirements:* For master's, bachelor's degree from accredited institution, minimum undergraduate GPA of 3.0, official undergraduate and graduate transcripts of all academic coursework attempted, current résumé, statement of professional goals, writing sample, two recent letters of recommendation; for doctorate, professional practice statement that identifies applicant's goals and explains how Lynn's program will help attain them, official transcript showing conferral of master's degree, two letters of recommendation from previous professors or employers, current resume, interview. Additional exam requirements/recommendations for international students: Required—TOEFL (minimum score 550 paper-based; 80 iBT), IELTS (minimum score 6.5). *Application deadline:* For fall admission, 8/18 for domestic students, 8/4 for international students; for spring admission, 12/15 for domestic students, 12/1 for international students; for summer admission, 4/17 for domestic students, 4/3 for international students. Applications are processed on a rolling basis. Application fee: $45. Electronic applications accepted. *Expenses:* $740 per credit (for master's degrees); $850 per credit (for EdD). *Financial support:* Career-related internships or fieldwork, Federal Work-Study, scholarships/grants, tuition waivers (partial), and unspecified assistantships available. Support available to part-time students. Financial award application deadline: 3/1; financial award applicants required to submit FAFSA. *Faculty research:* Student achievement, students with learning differences, teacher and student retention, student motivation and cognition, neuroscience leadership and learning. *Unit head:* Dr. Kathleen Weigel, Dean, College of Education, 561-237-7441, E-mail: kweigel@lynn.edu. *Application contact:* Steven Pruitt, Director of Graduate and Undergraduate Evening Admission, 561-237-7834, Fax: 561-237-7100, E-mail: spruitt@lynn.edu. Website: http://www.lynn.edu/academics/colleges/education

Madonna University, Programs in Education, Livonia, MI 48150-1173. Offers Catholic school leadership (MSA); educational leadership (MSA); learning disabilities (MAT); literacy education (MAT); teaching and learning (MAT). *Accreditation:* NCATE. *Program availability:* Part-time, evening/weekend. *Degree requirements:* For master's, thesis or alternative. Electronic applications accepted.

Malone University, Graduate Program in Education, Canton, OH 44709. Offers curriculum and instruction (MA); curriculum, instruction, and professional development

Special Education

(MA); educational leadership (principal license) (MA); intervention specialist (MA). *Accreditation:* NCATE. *Program availability:* Part-time, evening/weekend. *Degree requirements:* For master's, research project. *Entrance requirements:* For master's, minimum GPA of 3.0, teaching license. Additional exam requirements/recommendations for international students: Required—TOEFL (minimum score 550 paper-based; 79 iBT). *Faculty research:* Educational leadership styles: Jesus as master teacher, assessment accommodations for English language learners, preparing culturally proficient teachers, using naturally occurring text in the classroom to meet the syntactic needs of students with learning disabilities, using tablet instructional technology to meet the needs of students with disabilities.

Manhattan College, Graduate Programs, School of Education and Health, Program in Special Education, Riverdale, NY 10471. Offers adolescence education students with disabilities generalist extension in English or math or social studies - grades 7-12 (MS Ed); bilingual education (Advanced Certificate); dual childhood/students with disabilities - grades 1-6 (MS Ed); students with disabilities - grades 1-6 (MS Ed). *Program availability:* Part-time, evening/weekend. *Degree requirements:* For master's, thesis, internship (if not certified). *Entrance requirements:* For master's, GRE, minimum GPA of 3.0. Additional exam requirements/recommendations for international students: Required—TOEFL (minimum score 550 paper-based; 80 iBT), IELTS (minimum score 6). Electronic applications accepted. Application fee is waived when completed online. *Expenses:* Contact institution.

Manhattanville College, School of Education, Jump Start Program, Purchase, NY 10577-2132. Offers childhood education and special education (grades 1-6) (MPS); early childhood education (birth-grade 2) (MAT); education (Advanced Certificate); English and special education (grades 5-12) (MPS); mathematics and special education (grades 5-12) (MPS); science and special education (grades 5-12) (MPS); social studies and special education (grades 5-12) (MPS); Spanish (grades 7-12) (MAT); TESOL (all grades) (MPS). *Program availability:* Part-time, evening/weekend. *Faculty:* 10 full-time (7 women), 39 part-time/adjunct (27 women). *Students:* 3 full-time (2 women), 40 part-time (24 women); includes 11 minority (3 Black or African American, non-Hispanic/Latino; 6 Hispanic/Latino; 1 Native Hawaiian or other Pacific Islander, non-Hispanic/Latino; 1 Two or more races, non-Hispanic/Latino). Average age 33. 25 applicants, 60% accepted, 7 enrolled. In 2017, 17 master's, 2 other advanced degrees awarded. *Degree requirements:* For master's, comprehensive exam (for some programs), thesis (for some programs), student teaching, research seminars, portfolios, internships, writing assessment; for Advanced Certificate, comprehensive exam (for some programs). *Entrance requirements:* For master's, GRE or MAT (for programs leading to certification), minimum GPA of 3.0, 2 letters of recommendation, interview, essay (2-3 page personal statement that describes reasons for choosing teaching or educational leadership as profession and philosophy of education), proof of immunization (for those born after 1957). Additional exam requirements/recommendations for international students: Required—TOEFL (minimum score 600 paper-based; 110 iBT); Recommended—IELTS (minimum score 8). *Application deadline:* Applications are processed on a rolling basis. Application fee: $75. Electronic applications accepted. *Expenses:* $915 per credit. *Financial support:* Teaching assistantships, career-related internships or fieldwork, Federal Work-Study, institutionally sponsored loans, scholarships/grants, and unspecified assistantships available. Financial award application deadline: 3/15; financial award applicants required to submit FAFSA. *Faculty research:* Early childhood and technology, professional development schools and community schools, students with emotional difficulties, literacy and adolescents, mindfulness, changing suburbs institute, and community schools, studying the effects of the environment on special populations, the most difficult cases, students who are presented with multiple challenges: learning, behavioral and ACE experiences who see criminal behavior as a way to cope; working on giving them the tools they need to succeed. *Unit head:* Dr. Shelly Wepner, Dean, 914-323-3153, E-mail: shelly.wepner@mville.edu. *Application contact:* Alissa Wilson, Director, Graduate Admissions, 914-323-3150, Fax: 914-694-1732, E-mail: edschool@mville.edu. Website: http://www.mville.edu/programs/jump-start

Manhattanville College, School of Education, Program in Childhood Education, Purchase, NY 10577-2132. Offers childhood education (grades 1-6) (MAT, MPS); early childhood (birth - grade 2) (MAT); special education (grades 1-6) (MPS, Certificate); special education: early childhood (birth - grade 2) and childhood (grades 1-6) (Certificate); special education: early childhood and childhood (birth - grade 6) (MPS). *Program availability:* Part-time, evening/weekend. *Faculty:* 3 full-time (all women), 7 part-time/adjunct (5 women). *Students:* 7 full-time (all women), 28 part-time (23 women); includes 8 minority (2 Black or African American, non-Hispanic/Latino; 6 Hispanic/Latino). Average age 29. 27 applicants, 93% accepted, 22 enrolled. In 2017, 13 master's awarded. *Degree requirements:* For master's, comprehensive exam (for some programs), thesis (for some programs), student teaching, research seminars, portfolios, internships, writing assessment; for Certificate, comprehensive exam (for some programs). *Entrance requirements:* For master's, GRE or MAT (for programs leading to certification), minimum GPA of 3.0, 2 letters of recommendation, interview, essay (2-3 page personal statement that describes reasons for choosing teaching or educational leadership as profession and philosophy of education), proof of immunization (for those born after 1957). Additional exam requirements/recommendations for international students: Required—TOEFL (minimum score 600 paper-based; 110 iBT); Recommended—IELTS (minimum score 8). *Application deadline:* Applications are processed on a rolling basis. Application fee: $75. Electronic applications accepted. *Expenses:* $915 per credit. *Financial support:* Teaching assistantships, career-related internships or fieldwork, Federal Work-Study, institutionally sponsored loans, scholarships/grants, and unspecified assistantships available. Financial award application deadline: 3/15; financial award applicants required to submit FAFSA. *Faculty research:* Early childhood and technology, professional development schools and community schools. *Unit head:* Dr. Shelly Wepner, Dean, 914-323-3153, Fax: 914-323-5493, E-mail: shelly.wepner@mville.edu. *Application contact:* Alissa Wilson, Director, Graduate Admissions, 914-323-3150, Fax: 914-694-1732, E-mail: edschool@mville.edu. Website: http://www.mville.edu/programs/childhood-education

Manhattanville College, School of Education, Program in Early Childhood Education, Purchase, NY 10577-2132. Offers childhood education (grades 1-6) (MAT); early childhood and special education (birth-grade 2) (MPS); early childhood education (birth-grade 2) (MAT); special education (birth-grade 2) (MPS); special education (birth-grade 6) (MPS); special education: early childhood (birth - grade 2) and childhood (grades 1-6) (Certificate); special education: early childhood (birth-grade 2) (Certificate). *Program availability:* Part-time, evening/weekend. *Faculty:* 2 full-time (both women), 3 part-time/adjunct (all women). *Students:* 7 full-time (all women), 22 part-time (21 women); includes 1 minority (Hispanic/Latino). Average age 29. 21 applicants, 81% accepted, 12 enrolled. In 2017, 10 master's awarded. *Degree requirements:* For master's, comprehensive exam (for some programs), thesis (for some programs), student teaching, research seminars, portfolios, internships, writing assessment; for Certificate, comprehensive exam (for some programs). *Entrance requirements:* For master's, GRE or MAT (for programs leading to certification), minimum GPA of 3.0, 2 letters of recommendation, interview, essay (2-3 page personal statement that describes reasons for choosing teaching or educational leadership as profession and philosophy of

education), proof of immunization (for those born after 1957). Additional exam requirements/recommendations for international students: Required—TOEFL (minimum score 600 paper-based; 110 iBT); Recommended—IELTS (minimum score 8). *Application deadline:* Applications are processed on a rolling basis. Application fee: $75. Electronic applications accepted. *Expenses:* $915 per credit. *Financial support:* Teaching assistantships, career-related internships or fieldwork, Federal Work-Study, institutionally sponsored loans, scholarships/grants, and unspecified assistantships available. Financial award application deadline: 3/15; financial award applicants required to submit FAFSA. *Faculty research:* Early childhood and technology. *Unit head:* Dr. Shelly Wepner, Dean, 914-323-3153, Fax: 914-323-5493, E-mail: shelly.wepner@mville.edu. *Application contact:* Alissa Wilson, Director, Graduate Admissions, 914-323-3150, Fax: 914-694-1732, E-mail: edschool@mville.edu. Website: http://www.mville.edu/programs/early-childhood-education

Manhattanville College, School of Education, Program in Literacy Education, Purchase, NY 10577-2132. Offers literacy (birth-grade 6) and special education childhood (grades 1-6) (MPS); literacy 5-12 (MPS); literacy specialist (birth-grade 6) (MPS); literacy specialist (grades 5-12) (MPS); science of reading: multisensory instruction (Advanced Certificate). *Program availability:* Part-time, evening/weekend. *Faculty:* 4 full-time (all women), 8 part-time/adjunct (5 women). *Students:* 1 (woman) full-time, 21 part-time (20 women). Average age 31. 12 applicants, 92% accepted, 8 enrolled. In 2017, 7 master's, 3 Advanced Certificates awarded. *Degree requirements:* For master's, comprehensive exam (for some programs), thesis (for some programs), student teaching, research seminars, portfolios, internships, writing assessment; for Advanced Certificate, comprehensive exam (for some programs). *Entrance requirements:* For master's, GRE or MAT (for programs leading to certification), minimum GPA of 3.0, 2 letters of recommendation, interview, essay (2-3 page personal statement that describes reasons for choosing teaching or educational leadership as profession and philosophy of education), proof of immunization (for those born after 1957). Additional exam requirements/recommendations for international students: Required—TOEFL (minimum score 600 paper-based; 110 iBT); Recommended—IELTS (minimum score 8). *Application deadline:* Applications are processed on a rolling basis. Application fee: $75. Electronic applications accepted. *Expenses:* $915 per credit. *Financial support:* Teaching assistantships, career-related internships or fieldwork, Federal Work-Study, institutionally sponsored loans, scholarships/grants, and unspecified assistantships available. Financial award application deadline: 3/15; financial award applicants required to submit FAFSA. *Faculty research:* Power of story for literacy development, English learners. *Total annual research expenditures:* $800. *Unit head:* Dr. Shelly Wepner, Dean, 914-323-3153, Fax: 914-323-5493, E-mail: shelly.wepner@mville.edu. *Application contact:* Alissa Wilson, Director, Graduate Admissions, 914-323-3150, Fax: 914-694-1732, E-mail: edschool@mville.edu. Website: http://www.mville.edu/programs/literacy-education

Manhattanville College, School of Education, Program in Middle Childhood/Adolescence Education (Grades 5-12), Purchase, NY 10577-2132. Offers biology (MAT, Advanced Certificate); biology and special education (MPS); chemistry (MAT, Advanced Certificate); chemistry and special education (MPS); earth science (Advanced Certificate); education for sustainability (Advanced Certificate); English (MAT, Advanced Certificate); English and special education (MPS); literacy and special education (MPS); literacy specialist (MPS); math and special education (MPS); mathematics (MAT, Advanced Certificate); physics (MAT, Advanced Certificate); social studies (MAT); social studies and special education (MPS); special education generalist (MPS). *Program availability:* Part-time, evening/weekend. *Faculty:* 2 full-time (both women), 5 part-time/adjunct (1 woman). *Students:* 8 full-time (7 women), 28 part-time (16 women); includes 4 minority (1 Asian, non-Hispanic/Latino; 2 Hispanic/Latino; 1 Two or more races, non-Hispanic/Latino). Average age 31. 7 applicants, 86% accepted, 4 enrolled. In 2017, 13 master's, 1 other advanced degree awarded. *Degree requirements:* For master's, comprehensive exam (for some programs), thesis (for some programs), student teaching, research seminars, portfolios, internships, writing assessment; for Advanced Certificate, comprehensive exam (for some programs). *Entrance requirements:* For master's, GRE or MAT (for programs leading to certification), minimum GPA of 3.0, 2 letters of recommendation, interview, essay (2-3 page personal statement that describes reasons for choosing teaching or educational leadership as profession and philosophy of education), proof of immunization (for those born after 1957). Additional exam requirements/recommendations for international students: Required—TOEFL (minimum score 600 paper-based; 110 iBT); Recommended—IELTS (minimum score 8). *Application deadline:* Applications are processed on a rolling basis. Application fee: $75. Electronic applications accepted. *Expenses:* $915 per credit. *Financial support:* Teaching assistantships, career-related internships or fieldwork, Federal Work-Study, institutionally sponsored loans, scholarships/grants, and unspecified assistantships available. Financial award application deadline: 3/15; financial award applicants required to submit FAFSA. *Faculty research:* Education for sustainability. *Unit head:* Dr. Shelly Wepner, Dean, 914-323-3153, Fax: 914-323-5493, E-mail: shelly.wepner@mville.edu. *Application contact:* Alissa Wilson, Director, Graduate Admissions, 914-323-3150, Fax: 914-694-1732, E-mail: edschool@mville.edu. Website: http://www.mville.edu/programs#/search/19

Manhattanville College, School of Education, Program in Special Education, Purchase, NY 10577-2132. Offers childhood (grades 1-6) (MPS); childhood education (grades 1-6) and special education (MPS); early childhood (birth-grade 2) (MPS); early childhood (birth-grade 2) and special education (MPS); early childhood and childhood (birth-grade 6) (MPS); English (5-9 and 7-12) (MPS); grades 7-12 generalist (MPS); literacy (birth-grade 6) and special education childhood (grades 1-6) (MPS); literacy 5-12 (MPS); mathematics (5-9 and 7-12) (MPS); science (biology or chemistry 5-9 and 7-12) (MPS); social studies (5-9 and 7-12) (MPS); special education: childhood (grades 1-6) (Certificate); special education: early childhood (birth-grade 2) and childhood (grades 1-6) (Certificate); special education: early childhood (birth-grade 2) (Certificate); special education: grades 7-12 generalist (Certificate). *Program availability:* Part-time, evening/weekend. *Faculty:* 5 full-time (3 women), 24 part-time/adjunct (16 women). *Students:* 77 full-time (69 women), 154 part-time (132 women); includes 33 minority (9 Black or African American, non-Hispanic/Latino; 2 Asian, non-Hispanic/Latino; 22 Hispanic/Latino), 1 international. Average age 28. 87 applicants, 77% accepted, 57 enrolled. In 2017, 86 master's, 2 Certificates awarded. *Degree requirements:* For master's, comprehensive exam (for some programs), thesis (for some programs), student teaching, research seminars, portfolios, internships, writing assessment; for Certificate, comprehensive exam (for some programs). *Entrance requirements:* For master's, GRE or MAT (for programs leading to certification), minimum GPA of 3.0, 2 letters of recommendation, interview, essay (2-3 page personal statement that describes reasons for choosing teaching or educational leadership as profession and philosophy of education), proof of immunization (for those born after 1957). Additional exam requirements/recommendations for international students: Required—TOEFL (minimum score 600 paper-based; 110 iBT); Recommended—IELTS (minimum score 8). *Application deadline:* Applications are processed on a rolling basis. Application fee: $75. Electronic applications accepted. *Expenses:* $915 per credit. *Financial support:* Teaching assistantships, career-related internships or fieldwork, Federal Work-Study, institutionally sponsored loans, scholarships/grants, and unspecified assistantships available. Financial award application deadline: 3/15; financial award applicants required

to submit FAFSA. *Faculty research:* Students with emotional difficulties, literacy and adolescents, mindfulness, studying the effects of the environment on special populations, the most difficult cases, students who are presented with multiple challenges: learning, behavioral and ACE experiences who see criminal behavior as a way to cope; working on giving them the tools they need to succeed emotionally and cognitively despite the odds stacked against them. *Unit head:* Dr. Shelly Wepner, Dean, 914-323-3153, Fax: 914-323-5493, E-mail: shelly.wepner@mville.edu. *Application contact:* Alissa Wilson, Director, Graduate Admissions, 914-323-3150, Fax: 914-694-1732, E-mail: edschool@mville.edu.
Website: http://www.mville.edu/programs/special-education

Mansfield University of Pennsylvania, Graduate Studies, Department of Education and Special Education, Mansfield, PA 16933. Offers elementary education (M Ed); secondary education (MS); special education (M Ed). *Accreditation:* NCATE (one or more programs are accredited). *Program availability:* Part-time, evening/weekend, online learning. *Degree requirements:* For master's, comprehensive exam, thesis optional. *Entrance requirements:* For master's, minimum GPA of 3.0. Additional exam requirements/recommendations for international students: Required—TOEFL (minimum score 550 paper-based). Electronic applications accepted.

Marian University, School of Education, Fond du Lac, WI 54935-4699. Offers curriculum and instruction leadership (PhD); educational administration (PhD); educational leadership (MAE); educational technology (MAE); leadership studies (PhD); special education (MAE); teacher education (MAE). *Accreditation:* NCATE. *Program availability:* Part-time, evening/weekend, online learning. *Degree requirements:* For master's, exam, field-based experience project, portfolio; for doctorate, comprehensive exam, thesis/dissertation, field-based experience. *Entrance requirements:* For master's, minimum GPA of 3.0, BA in education or related field, teaching license; for doctorate, GRE, MAT, resume, 2 writing samples, interview. Additional exam requirements/recommendations for international students: Required—TOEFL (minimum score 525 paper-based; 70 iBT). *Faculty research:* At-risk youth, multicultural issues, values in education, teaching/learning strategies.

Marshall University, Academic Affairs Division, College of Education and Professional Development, Program in Special Education, Huntington, WV 25755. Offers MA. *Accreditation:* NCATE. *Program availability:* Part-time, evening/weekend. *Students:* 38 full-time (33 women), 85 part-time (67 women); includes 5 minority (3 Black or African American, non-Hispanic/Latino; 1 Hispanic/Latino; 1 Two or more races, non-Hispanic/Latino). Average age 34. In 2017, 44 master's awarded. *Degree requirements:* For master's, thesis optional, comprehensive or oral assessment, research project. *Entrance requirements:* For master's, GRE General Test or MAT, minimum GPA of 3.0. Application fee: $40. *Financial support:* Federal Work-Study, tuition waivers (full), and unspecified assistantships available. Support available to part-time students. Financial award applicants required to submit FAFSA. *Faculty research:* Teaching the severely handicapped, career/vocational education, education of the gifted. *Unit head:* Dr. Joyce Meikamp, Director, 304-746-1983, E-mail: jmeikamp@marshall.edu. *Application contact:* Information Contact, 304-746-1900, Fax: 304-746-1902, E-mail: services@marshall.edu.

Martin Luther College, Graduate Studies, New Ulm, MN 56073. Offers early childhood director (MS Ed Admin); educational technology (MS Ed); instruction (MS Ed); leadership (MS Ed); principal (MS Ed Admin); special education (MS Ed). *Program availability:* Part-time, evening/weekend, online learning. *Faculty:* 8 full-time (1 woman), 21 part-time/adjunct (10 women). *Students:* 1 (woman) full-time, 81 part-time (28 women); includes 2 minority (1 Asian, non-Hispanic/Latino; 1 Two or more races, non-Hispanic/Latino), 2 international. Average age 37. 23 applicants, 100% accepted, 23 enrolled. In 2017, 25 master's awarded. *Degree requirements:* For master's, capstone project or comprehensive exam. *Entrance requirements:* For master's, undergraduate degree in education from an accredited college or university, minimum undergraduate GPA of 3.0. Additional exam requirements/recommendations for international students: Required—TOEFL (minimum score 550 paper-based; 80 iBT); Recommended—IELTS (minimum score 6.5). *Application deadline:* Applications are processed on a rolling basis. Application fee: $35. Electronic applications accepted. *Expenses:* $315 per credit. *Financial support:* In 2017–18, 4 students received support. Scholarships/grants available. Financial award application deadline: 9/1. *Faculty research:* Principal effectiveness, principal support, cognitive load in math instruction, reading strategies in multigrade classrooms, mentor provided professional development for new teachers. *Unit head:* John E. Meyer, Director of Graduate Studies, 507-354-8221 Ext. 398, E-mail: meyerjd@mlc-wels.edu.
Website: https://mlc-wels.edu/graduate-studies/

Marygrove College, Graduate Studies, Detroit, MI 48221-2599. Offers autism spectrum disorders (M Ed, Certificate); curriculum instruction and assessment (MAT); educational leadership (MA); educational technology (M Ed); effective teaching in the 21st century-classroom focus (MAT); effective teaching in the 21st century-technology focus (MAT); human resource management (MA, Certificate); mathematics 6-8 (MAT); mathematics K-5 (MAT); reading and literacy K-6 (MAT); reading specialist (M Ed); school administrator (Certificate); social justice (MA); special education (MAT); special education - learning disabilities (M Ed); teaching - pre-elementary education (M Ed); teaching - pre-secondary education (M Ed). *Program availability:* Part-time, evening/weekend, 100% online, blended/hybrid learning. *Students:* 163 full-time (123 women), 264 part-time (186 women). Average age 34. *Entrance requirements:* For master's, all official bachelor's transcripts. Additional exam requirements/recommendations for international students: Required—TOEFL (minimum score 550 paper-based; 80 iBT). *Application deadline:* Applications are processed on a rolling basis. Electronic applications accepted. *Expenses: Tuition:* Part-time $590 per credit hour. *Required fees:* $120 per semester. One-time fee: $25 part-time. *Financial support:* Applicants required to submit FAFSA. *Unit head:* Marygrove College Admissions, 313-927-1240, E-mail: info@marygrove.edu. *Application contact:* Marygrove College Admissions, 313-927-1240, E-mail: info@marygrove.edu.

Marymount University, School of Education and Human Services, Program in Education, Arlington, VA 22207-4299. Offers curriculum and instruction (M Ed); elementary education (M Ed); professional studies (M Ed); secondary education (M Ed); special education: general curriculum (M Ed). *Accreditation:* NCATE. *Program availability:* Part-time, evening/weekend. *Faculty:* 7 full-time (all women), 10 part-time/adjunct (7 women). *Students:* 51 full-time (40 women), 92 part-time (61 women); includes 33 minority (9 Black or African American, non-Hispanic/Latino; 9 Asian, non-Hispanic/Latino; 10 Hispanic/Latino; 5 Two or more races, non-Hispanic/Latino), 11 international. Average age 34. 39 applicants, 97% accepted, 30 enrolled. In 2017, 72 master's awarded. *Degree requirements:* For master's, thesis or alternative, capstone/internship. *Entrance requirements:* For master's, GRE or MAT and PRAXIS I or SAT/ACT and Virginia Communication and Literacy Assessment (VCLA), 2 letters of recommendation, resume, interview, minimum undergraduate GPA of 2.75 or 3.25 in the last 60 hours. Additional exam requirements/recommendations for international students: Required—TOEFL (minimum score 600 paper-based; 96 iBT), IELTS (minimum score 6.5). *Application deadline:* Applications are processed on a rolling basis. Application fee: $40. Electronic applications accepted. *Expenses:* $715 per credit. *Financial support:* In 2017–18, 7 students received support, including 2 teaching

assistantships with full and partial tuition reimbursements available (averaging $14,520 per year); career-related internships or fieldwork, Federal Work-Study, scholarships/grants, and unspecified assistantships also available. Support available to part-time students. Financial award application deadline: 3/1; financial award applicants required to submit FAFSA. *Unit head:* Dr. Lisa Turissini, Chair, Education, 703-526-1668, Fax: 703-284-1631, E-mail: lisa.turissini@marymount.edu. *Application contact:* Francesca Reed, Director, Graduate Admissions, 703-284-5901, Fax: 703-527-3815, E-mail: grad.admissions@marymount.edu.
Website: http://www.marymount.edu/Academics/School-of-Education-Human-Services/Graduate-Programs/Education-(M-Ed-)

Marywood University, Academic Affairs, Reap College of Education and Human Development, Department of Education, Program in Special Education, Scranton, PA 18509-1598. Offers MS. *Accreditation:* NCATE. *Program availability:* Part-time. Electronic applications accepted.

Marywood University, Academic Affairs, Reap College of Education and Human Development, Department of Education, Program in Special Education Administration and Supervision, Scranton, PA 18509-1598. Offers MS. *Accreditation:* NCATE. *Program availability:* Part-time. Electronic applications accepted.

Massachusetts College of Liberal Arts, Graduate Programs, North Adams, MA 01247-4100. Offers business (MBA); educational administration (M Ed); educational leadership (CAGS); instruction and curriculum (M Ed); instructional technology (M Ed); physical education and health (M Ed); reading (M Ed); special education (M Ed). *Program availability:* Part-time, evening/weekend. *Degree requirements:* For master's, thesis. *Entrance requirements:* For master's, writing sample.

McDaniel College, Graduate and Professional Studies, Program in Deaf Education, Westminster, MD 21157-4390. Offers MS. *Accreditation:* NCATE. *Program availability:* Part-time. *Faculty:* 3 full-time (1 woman), 2 part-time/adjunct (both women). *Students:* 5 full-time (4 women), 18 part-time (9 women); includes 2 minority (both Hispanic/Latino), 4 international. Average age 31. 4 applicants, 75% accepted, 2 enrolled. In 2017, 7 master's awarded. *Degree requirements:* For master's, comprehensive exam, thesis optional. *Entrance requirements:* For master's, American Sign Language Proficiency Interview (ASLPI); English Proficiency Essay (EPE). Additional exam requirements/recommendations for international students: Required—TOEFL (minimum score 79 iBT), IELTS (minimum score 6). *Application deadline:* For fall admission, 6/1 priority date for domestic students; for spring admission, 11/1 priority date for domestic students; for summer admission, 3/1 priority date for domestic students. Applications are processed on a rolling basis. Application fee: $75. Electronic applications accepted. *Expenses: Tuition:* Full-time $11,760; part-time $490 per credit hour. Tuition and fees vary according to course load and program. *Financial support:* Career-related internships or fieldwork, institutionally sponsored loans, and scholarships/grants available. Financial award application deadline: 3/1; financial award applicants required to submit FAFSA. *Faculty research:* Mainstreaming of multi-handicapped children. *Unit head:* Fax: 410-857-2516, E-mail: gradadms@mcdaniel.edu. *Application contact:* Anna Collins, Program Assistant, 410-857-2506, Fax: 410-857-2515, E-mail: deafedoffice@mcdaniel.edu.

McDaniel College, Graduate and Professional Studies, Program in Special Education, Westminster, MD 21157-4390. Offers MS. *Accreditation:* NCATE. *Program availability:* Part-time, evening/weekend. *Faculty:* 2 full-time (1 woman), 4 part-time/adjunct (2 women). *Students:* 3 full-time (all women), 28 part-time (25 women); includes 2 minority (1 Black or African American, non-Hispanic/Latino; 1 Two or more races, non-Hispanic/Latino), 1 international. Average age 31. 8 applicants, 100% accepted, 6 enrolled. In 2017, 12 master's awarded. *Degree requirements:* For master's, comprehensive exam, thesis optional. *Entrance requirements:* For master's, PRAXIS, 3 recommendations. Additional exam requirements/recommendations for international students: Required—TOEFL (minimum score 79 iBT), IELTS (minimum score 6). *Application deadline:* For fall admission, 6/1 priority date for domestic students; for spring admission, 11/1 priority date for domestic students; for summer admission, 3/1 priority date for domestic students. Applications are processed on a rolling basis. Application fee: $75. Electronic applications accepted. *Expenses: Tuition:* Full-time $11,760; part-time $490 per credit hour. Tuition and fees vary according to course load and program. *Financial support:* Application deadline: 3/1; applicants required to submit FAFSA. *Unit head:* E-mail: gradadms@mcdaniel.edu. *Application contact:* Crystal L. Perry, Assistant Director, Graduate Enrollment Management, 410-857-2516, Fax: 410-857-2515, E-mail: cperry@mcdaniel.edu.

McKendree University, Graduate Programs, Programs in Education, Lebanon, IL 62254-1299. Offers curriculum design and instruction (Ed D, Ed S); educational administration and leadership (MA Ed); educational studies (MA Ed); higher education administrative services (MA Ed); music education (MA Ed); reading (MA Ed); special education (MA Ed); teacher leadership (MA Ed); teaching certification (MA Ed). *Accreditation:* NCATE. *Program availability:* Part-time, evening/weekend, online learning. *Entrance requirements:* For master's, official transcripts from all institutions previously attended, minimum GPA of 3.0, resume, references; for doctorate, GRE (within the past 5 years), master's degree in education and Ed S, or the equivalent, from regionally-accredited institution; official transcripts from all institutions previously attended; curriculum vitae/resume; essay/personal statement; two years of teaching/professional experience; for Ed S, GRE (within the past 5 years), master's degree in education from regionally-accredited institution of higher education; official transcripts from all institutions previously attended; curriculum vitae/resume; essay/personal statement; two years of teaching/professional experience. Additional exam requirements/recommendations for international students: Required—TOEFL. Electronic applications accepted.

McNeese State University, Doré School of Graduate Studies, Burton College of Education, Department of Education Professions, Program in Curriculum and Instruction, Lake Charles, LA 70609. Offers academically gifted education (M Ed); elementary education (M Ed); reading (M Ed); secondary education (M Ed); special education (M Ed). *Program availability:* Evening/weekend. *Entrance requirements:* For master's, GRE, teaching certificate. *Application deadline:* For fall admission, 5/15 priority date for domestic and international students; for spring admission, 10/15 priority date for domestic and international students. Applications are processed on a rolling basis. Application fee: $20 ($30 for international students). *Financial support:* Application deadline: 5/1. *Unit head:* Dr. Brett C. Welch, Director, 337-475-5405, Fax: 337-475-5272, E-mail: bwelch@mcneese.edu. *Application contact:* Dr. Dustin M. Hebert, Director of Dore' School of Graduate Studies, 337-475-5396, Fax: 337-475-5397, E-mail: admissions@mcneese.edu.

McNeese State University, Doré School of Graduate Studies, Burton College of Education, Department of Education Professions, Program in Special Education, Mild/Moderate for Elementary Education Grades 1-5, Lake Charles, LA 70609. Offers Postbaccalaureate Certificate. *Entrance requirements:* For degree, PRAXIS, 2 letters of recommendation, autobiography. *Application deadline:* For fall admission, 5/15 priority date for domestic and international students; for spring admission, 10/15 priority date for domestic and international students. Applications are processed on a rolling basis. Application fee: $20 ($30 for international students). *Financial support:* Application

Special Education

deadline: 5/1. *Unit head:* Dr. Veronica Faye White, Head, 337-475-5400, Fax: 337-475-5272, E-mail: vfwhite@mcneese.edu. *Application contact:* Dr. Dustin M. Hebert, Director of Dore' School of Graduate Studies, 337-475-5396, Fax: 337-475-5397, E-mail: admissions@mcneese.edu.

Medaille College, Program in Education, Buffalo, NY 14214-2695. Offers adolescent education (MS Ed); curriculum and instruction (MS Ed); education preparation (MS Ed); literacy (MS Ed); special education (MS). *Accreditation:* TEAC. *Program availability:* Part-time, evening/weekend. *Degree requirements:* For master's, comprehensive exam (for some programs), thesis or alternative. *Entrance requirements:* For master's, minimum undergraduate GPA of 2.7. Additional exam requirements/recommendations for international students: Required—TOEFL (minimum score 550 paper-based). Electronic applications accepted. *Faculty research:* Curriculum planning, truancy, tracking minority students, curriculum design, mentoring students.

Mercyhurst University, Graduate Studies, Program in Special Education, Erie, PA 16546. Offers applied behavior analysis (MS); autism (MS); generalist (MS); higher education leadership and disabilities (MS). *Program availability:* Part-time, evening/weekend. *Degree requirements:* For master's, thesis optional. *Entrance requirements:* For master's, GRE or PRAXIS I, interview, resume, essay, three professional references, transcripts. Additional exam requirements/recommendations for international students: Required—TOEFL. Electronic applications accepted. *Faculty research:* College-age learning disabled program, teacher preparation/collaboration, applied behavior analysis, special education policy issues.

Meredith College, School of Education, Health and Human Sciences, Raleigh, NC 27607-5298. Offers academically and intellectually gifted (M Ed); elementary education (M Ed, MAT); English as a second language (M Ed, MAT); health and physical education (MAT); nutrition, health and human performance (MS, Postbaccalaureate Certificate), including dietetic internship (Postbaccalaureate Certificate), nutrition (MS); psychology (MA), including industrial/organizational psychology; reading (M Ed); special education (MAT); special education (general curriculum) (M Ed). *Accreditation:* NCATE. *Program availability:* Part-time, evening/weekend. *Students:* 25 full-time (24 women), 22 part-time (all women); includes 13 minority (8 Black or African American, non-Hispanic/Latino; 1 American Indian or Alaska Native, non-Hispanic/Latino; 1 Asian, non-Hispanic/Latino; 3 Hispanic/Latino). Average age 31. 57 applicants, 54% accepted, 31 enrolled. In 2017, 14 master's awarded. *Degree requirements:* For master's, thesis optional. *Entrance requirements:* For master's, GRE General Test or MAT, minimum GPA of 2.5, teaching license, recommendations. Additional exam requirements/recommendations for international students: Required—TOEFL. *Application deadline:* For fall admission, 7/1 priority date for domestic students; for spring admission, 11/1 priority date for domestic students. Applications are processed on a rolling basis. Application fee: $50. Electronic applications accepted. *Expenses:* Contact institution. *Financial support:* Career-related internships or fieldwork, institutionally sponsored loans, and tuition waivers (partial) available. Support available to part-time students. Financial award application deadline: 2/15; financial award applicants required to submit FAFSA. *Unit head:* Dr. Monica McKinney, Graduate Program Manager, 919-760-8056, Fax: 919-760-2303, E-mail: mckinneym@meredith.edu.
Website: https://www.meredith.edu/school-of-education-health-and-human-sciences

Merrimack College, School of Education and Social Policy, North Andover, MA 01845-5800. Offers community engagement (M Ed), including community organizations, higher education, PreK-12 education; criminology and criminal justice (MS); curriculum and instruction (M Ed); early childhood education (M Ed); educational leadership (CAGS), including instructional leadership; elementary education (M Ed); English as a second language (PreK-6) (M Ed); high school education (M Ed); higher education (M Ed), including leadership and organizational development, student affairs; middle school education (M Ed); moderate disabilities (PreK-8) (M Ed); school counseling (M Ed). *Program availability:* Part-time, evening/weekend, 100% online courses with immersion events and in-classroom practicum close to home. *Faculty:* 15 full-time, 36 part-time/adjunct. *Students:* 212 full-time (175 women), 121 part-time (101 women); includes 42 minority (6 Black or African American, non-Hispanic/Latino; 6 Asian, non-Hispanic/Latino; 27 Hispanic/Latino; 3 Two or more races, non-Hispanic/Latino), 3 international. Average age 27. 420 applicants, 84% accepted, 250 enrolled. In 2017, 177 master's awarded. *Degree requirements:* For master's, practicum, portfolio, and state test (for licensure track); capstone (for higher education, curriculum and instruction, and community engagement tracks); for CAGS, capstone. *Entrance requirements:* For master's, Massachusetts Teacher Education Licensure (MTEL), official transcripts from other colleges, resume, personal statement, 2 letters of recommendation. Additional exam requirements/recommendations for international students: Required—TOEFL (minimum score 84 iBT), IELTS (minimum score 6.5), PTE (minimum score 56). *Application deadline:* For fall admission, 8/24 for domestic students, 7/30 for international students; for spring admission, 1/10 for domestic students, 12/10 for international students; for summer admission, 5/10 for domestic students, 4/10 for international students. Applications are processed on a rolling basis. Application fee: $0. Electronic applications accepted. *Expenses:* Contact institution. *Financial support:* Fellowships with full tuition reimbursements, career-related internships or fieldwork, scholarships/grants, and health care benefits available. Support available to part-time students. Financial award application deadline: 5/1; financial award applicants required to submit FAFSA. *Application contact:* Alyssa Orlando, Graduate Admissions Counselor, 978-837-3563, E-mail: orlandoaf@merrimack.edu.
Website: http://www.merrimack.edu/academics/graduate/education/

Messiah College, Program in Education, Mechanicsburg, PA 17055. Offers curriculum and instruction (M Ed); special education (M Ed); teaching English to speakers of other languages (M Ed). *Program availability:* Part-time, online learning. Electronic applications accepted. *Faculty research:* Socio-cultural perspectives on education, TESOL, autism, special education.

Metropolitan College of New York, Program in Childhood/Special Education, New York, NY 10006. Offers dual childhood 1-6 special education (MS). *Accreditation:* NCATE. *Students:* 22 full-time (16 women), 1 (woman) part-time; includes 21 minority (15 Black or African American, non-Hispanic/Latino; 6 Hispanic/Latino). Average age 36. 44 applicants, 30% accepted, 10 enrolled. In 2017, 16 master's awarded. *Entrance requirements:* For master's, GRE or MAT, minimum GPA of 3.0, 2 letters of reference, interview, resume. Additional exam requirements/recommendations for international students: Required—TOEFL (minimum score 550 paper-based; 80 iBT), IELTS (minimum score 6.5). *Application deadline:* Applications are processed on a rolling basis. Application fee: $45. Electronic applications accepted. *Expenses:* $807 per semester credit, $395 fee per semester. *Financial support:* Career-related internships or fieldwork, Federal Work-Study, institutionally sponsored loans, and scholarships/grants available. Financial award application deadline: 8/15; financial award applicants required to submit FAFSA. *Faculty research:* Classroom management, learner autonomy, teacher research, math and gender, intelligence. *Unit head:* Dr. Patrick Ianniello, Director, 212-343-1234 Ext. 2424, E-mail: pianniello@metropolitan.edu. *Application contact:* Steebo Varghese, Associate Director of Admissions, 212-343-1234 Ext. 2708, E-mail: svarghese@mcny.edu.
Website: https://www.mcny.edu/academics/audrey-cohen-school-human-services-education/master-science-education-dual-childhood-grades-1-6special-education/

Metropolitan State University of Denver, School of Education, Denver, CO 80204. Offers elementary education (MAT); special education (MAT). *Expenses:* Contact institution.

Michigan State University, The Graduate School, College of Education, Department of Counseling, Educational Psychology and Special Education, East Lansing, MI 48824. Offers counseling (MA); educational psychology and educational technology (PhD); educational technology (MA); measurement and quantitative methods (PhD); rehabilitation counseling (MA); rehabilitation counselor education (PhD); school psychology (MA, PhD, Ed S); special education (MA, PhD). *Accreditation:* APA (one or more programs are accredited); CORE (one or more programs are accredited). *Program availability:* Part-time. *Entrance requirements:* Additional exam requirements/recommendations for international students: Required—TOEFL. Electronic applications accepted.

Middle Tennessee State University, College of Graduate Studies, College of Education, Department of Elementary and Special Education, Major in Special Education, Murfreesboro, TN 37132. Offers M Ed. *Accreditation:* NCATE. *Program availability:* Part-time, evening/weekend, online learning. *Degree requirements:* For master's, comprehensive exam. *Entrance requirements:* For master's, GRE, MAT or PRAXIS. Additional exam requirements/recommendations for international students: Required—TOEFL (minimum score 525 paper-based; 71 iBT) or IELTS (minimum score 6). Electronic applications accepted.

Midwestern State University, Billie Doris McAda Graduate School, West College of Education, Program in Special Education, Wichita Falls, TX 76308. Offers M Ed. *Program availability:* Part-time, evening/weekend. *Degree requirements:* For master's, comprehensive exam. *Entrance requirements:* For master's, GRE General Test, MAT, or GMAT, Texas teacher certificate or equivalent minimum GPA of 3.0 in previous education courses. Additional exam requirements/recommendations for international students: Required—TOEFL (minimum score 550 paper-based). Electronic applications accepted. *Faculty research:* Fragile-X syndrome, phenylketonuria and other causes of handicapping conditions, autism, social development of students with disabilities.

Millersville University of Pennsylvania, College of Graduate Studies and Adult Learning, College of Education and Human Services, Department of Early, Middle, and Exceptional Education, Program in Special Education, Millersville, PA 17551-0302. Offers M Ed. *Accreditation:* NCATE. *Program availability:* Part-time, evening/weekend, blended/hybrid learning. *Faculty:* 9 full-time (4 women), 11 part-time/adjunct (8 women). *Students:* 9 part-time (8 women). Average age 32. 4 applicants, 100% accepted, 3 enrolled. In 2017, 3 master's awarded. *Degree requirements:* For master's, comprehensive exam, thesis (for some programs), clinical practicum. *Entrance requirements:* For master's, GRE or MAT, teaching certificate, interview, three current professional letters of recommendation. Additional exam requirements/recommendations for international students: Required—TOEFL (minimum score 80 iBT), IELTS (minimum score 6.5), PTE (minimum score 60). *Application deadline:* Applications are processed on a rolling basis. Application fee: $40. Electronic applications accepted. *Expenses:* $500 per credit resident tuition and fees; $750 per credit non-resident tuition and fees; $114.75 per credit general fee (maximum of 12 credits); technology fee $27 per credit (resident), $39 per credit (non-resident). *Financial support:* Unspecified assistantships available. Financial award application deadline: 3/15; financial award applicants required to submit FAFSA. *Faculty research:* Interventions, assistive technology, communication methods, identification of students with exceptionalities. *Unit head:* Dr. Marcia Nell, Department Chair, 717-871-7344, E-mail: marcia.nell@millersville.edu. *Application contact:* Dr. Victor S. DeSantis, Dean of College of Graduate Studies and Adult Learning/Associate Provost for Civic and Community Engagement, 717-871-7619, Fax: 717-871-7954, E-mail: victor.desantis@millersville.edu.
Website: https://www.millersville.edu/edfoundations/m_ed_sped.php

Millersville University of Pennsylvania, College of Graduate Studies and Adult Learning, College of Education and Human Services, Department of Early, Middle, and Exceptional Education, Program in Special Education: 7-12 Option, Millersville, PA 17551-0302. Offers M Ed. *Program availability:* Part-time, evening/weekend, blended/hybrid learning. *Faculty:* 9 full-time (4 women), 11 part-time/adjunct (8 women). *Students:* 1 (woman) full-time. Average age 26. 2 applicants, 100% accepted, 1 enrolled. *Degree requirements:* For master's, thesis (for some programs), clinical practicum. *Entrance requirements:* For master's, GRE or MAT, teaching certificate; interview; 3 current professional letters of recommendation. Additional exam requirements/recommendations for international students: Required—TOEFL (minimum score 80 iBT), IELTS (minimum score 6.5), PTE (minimum score 60). *Application deadline:* Applications are processed on a rolling basis. Application fee: $40. Electronic applications accepted. *Expenses:* $500 per credit resident tuition and fees; $750 per credit non-resident tuition and fees; $114.75 per credit general fee (maximum of 12 credits); technology fee $27 per credit (resident), $39 per credit (non-resident). *Financial support:* Unspecified assistantships available. Financial award application deadline: 3/15; financial award applicants required to submit FAFSA. *Faculty research:* Interventions, assistive technology, communication methods, identification of students with exceptionalities. *Unit head:* Dr. Marcia Nell, Department Chair, 717-871-7344, E-mail: marcia.nell@millersville.edu. *Application contact:* Dr. Victor S. DeSantis, Dean of College of Graduate Studies and Adult Learning/Associate Provost for Civic and Community Engagement, 717-871-7619, Fax: 717-871-7954, E-mail: victor.desantis@millersville.edu.
Website: https://www.millersville.edu/edfoundations/m_ed_sped.php

Millersville University of Pennsylvania, College of Graduate Studies and Adult Learning, College of Education and Human Services, Department of Early, Middle, and Exceptional Education, Program in Special Education: PreK-8 Option, Millersville, PA 17551-0302. Offers M Ed. *Program availability:* Part-time, evening/weekend, blended/hybrid learning. *Faculty:* 9 full-time (4 women), 11 part-time/adjunct (8 women). *Students:* 1 full-time (0 women), 7 part-time (6 women). Average age 31. 2 applicants, 100% accepted, 2 enrolled. *Degree requirements:* For master's, thesis (for some programs), clinical practicum. *Entrance requirements:* For master's, GRE or MAT, teaching certificate; interview; 3 current professional letters of recommendation. Additional exam requirements/recommendations for international students: Required—TOEFL (minimum score 80 iBT), IELTS (minimum score 6.5), PTE (minimum score 60). *Application deadline:* Applications are processed on a rolling basis. Application fee: $40. Electronic applications accepted. *Expenses:* $500 per credit resident tuition and fees; $750 per credit non-resident tuition and fees; $114.75 per credit general fee (maximum of 12 credits); technology fee $27 per credit (resident), $39 per credit (non-resident). *Financial support:* Unspecified assistantships available. Financial award application deadline: 3/15; financial award applicants required to submit FAFSA. *Faculty research:* Interventions, assistive technology, communication methods, identification of students with exceptionalities. *Unit head:* Dr. Marcia Nell, Department Chair, 717-871-7344, E-mail: marcia.nell@millersville.edu. *Application contact:* Dr. Victor S. DeSantis, Dean of College of Graduate Studies and Adult Learning/Associate Provost for Civic and Community Engagement, 717-871-7619, Fax: 717-871-7954, E-mail: victor.desantis@millersville.edu.
Website: https://www.millersville.edu/edfoundations/m_ed_sped.php

Milligan College, Area of Education, Milligan College, TN 37682. Offers combined preK-3/K-5 education (M Ed); educational leadership (Ed D, Ed S); K-5 education (M Ed); middle grades education (M Ed); preK-3 education (M Ed); preK-3 special education (M Ed); secondary education (M Ed). *Accreditation:* NCATE. *Program availability:* Part-time. *Faculty:* 6 full-time (4 women), 3 part-time/adjunct (2 women). *Students:* 27 full-time (20 women), 20 part-time (11 women); includes 2 minority (1 Hispanic/Latino; 1 Two or more races, non-Hispanic/Latino), 1 international. Average age 34. 17 applicants, 35% accepted, 6 enrolled. In 2017, 21 master's awarded. *Degree requirements:* For master's, thesis, portfolio, research project; for doctorate, thesis/dissertation, portfolio, research project. *Entrance requirements:* For master's, MAT, GRE General Test, ACT, SAT, or PRAXIS, undergraduate degree and supporting transcripts, professional recommendations, interview; for doctorate, MAT or GRE, master's degree and supporting transcripts, demonstrated scholastic ability, recognized leadership role within education, professional recommendations, essay/personal statement, portfolio (professional development plan, evidence of ability, knowledge and qualities), interview. Additional exam requirements/recommendations for international students: Required—TOEFL (minimum score 550 paper-based, 79 iBT) or IELTS (6.5). *Application deadline:* For fall admission, 8/1 priority date for domestic students, 6/1 for international students; for spring admission, 11/15 priority date for domestic students, 12/1 for international students; for summer admission, 4/1 for domestic students. Applications are processed on a rolling basis. Application fee: $30. Electronic applications accepted. *Expenses:* $360 per hour tuition (M Ed), $475 per hour (Ed D and Ed S); $325 per semester tech/activity fees. *Financial support:* Scholarships/grants available. Financial award application deadline: 12/1; financial award applicants required to submit FAFSA. *Faculty research:* Assessment; school mental health; literacy; technology; educator preparation. *Unit head:* Dr. Angela Hilton-Prillhart, Area Chair of Education, 423-461-8769, Fax: 423-461-3103, E-mail: anhilton-prillhart@milligan.edu. *Application contact:* Melissa Dillow, Graduate Admissions Recruiter, Education, 423-461-8306, Fax: 423-461-8982, E-mail: msdillow@milligan.edu.
Website: http://www.Milligan.edu/GPS

Minnesota State University Mankato, College of Graduate Studies and Research, College of Education, Department of Special Education, Mankato, MN 56001. Offers emotional and behavioral disorders (MS, Certificate); learning disabilities (MS, Certificate). *Accreditation:* NCATE. *Program availability:* Part-time, online learning. *Degree requirements:* For master's, comprehensive exam, thesis or alternative. *Entrance requirements:* For master's, Council for Exceptional Children pre-program assessment, minimum GPA of 3.2 during previous 2 years. Additional exam requirements/recommendations for international students: Required—TOEFL. Electronic applications accepted.

Minnesota State University Moorhead, Graduate Studies, College of Education and Human Services, Moorhead, MN 56563. Offers counseling and student affairs (MS); curriculum and instruction (MS); educational leadership (MS, Ed D, Ed S); special education (MS); speech-language pathology (MS). *Accreditation:* NCATE. *Program availability:* Part-time, 100% online, blended/hybrid learning. *Faculty:* 22. *Students:* 117 full-time (101 women), 337 part-time (253 women). Average age 32. 248 applicants, 49% accepted. In 2017, 149 master's, 16 other advanced degrees awarded. *Degree requirements:* For master's, comprehensive exam (for some programs), thesis, final oral defense; for doctorate, comprehensive exam (for some programs), thesis/dissertation, final oral defense. *Entrance requirements:* For master's, GRE, essay, letter of intent, letters of reference, teaching license, teaching verification, minimum cumulative GPA of 3.0; for doctorate, official transcripts; letter of intent; resume or curriculum vitae; master's degree; personal essay. Additional exam requirements/recommendations for international students: Required—TOEFL (minimum score 550 paper-based); Recommended—IELTS (minimum score 6.5). *Application deadline:* Applications are processed on a rolling basis. Application fee: $20. Electronic applications accepted. *Expenses:* Tuition, state resident: full-time $9000; part-time $374 per credit. Tuition, nonresident: full-time $18,000; part-time $748 per credit. *Required fees:* $1055; $43.96 per credit. Tuition and fees vary according to degree level, program and reciprocity agreements. *Financial support:* Federal Work-Study and unspecified assistantships available. Financial award application deadline: 10/1; financial award applicants required to submit FAFSA. *Unit head:* Dr. Ok-Hee Lee, Dean, 218-477-2095, E-mail: okheelee@mnstate.edu. *Application contact:* Karla Wenger, Office Manager, 218-477-2344, Fax: 218-477-2482, E-mail: wengerk@mnstate.edu.
Website: http://www.mnstate.edu/cehs/

Minot State University, Graduate School, Program in Special Education, Minot, ND 58707-0002. Offers deaf/hard of hearing education (MS); specific learning disabilities (MS). *Accreditation:* NCATE. *Degree requirements:* For master's, comprehensive exam (for some programs), thesis (for some programs). *Entrance requirements:* For master's, minimum GPA of 2.75, bachelor's degree in education or related field, teacher licensure (for some concentrations). Additional exam requirements/recommendations for international students: Required—TOEFL (minimum score 79 iBT), IELTS (minimum score 6).

Misericordia University, College of Health Sciences and Education, Program in Education, Dallas, PA 18612-1098. Offers instructional technology (MS); reading specialist (MS); special education (MS). *Program availability:* Part-time, evening/weekend. *Entrance requirements:* For master's, minimum undergraduate GPA of 3.0. Additional exam requirements/recommendations for international students: Required—TOEFL. Electronic applications accepted.

Mississippi College, Graduate School, School of Education, Department of Teacher Education and Leadership, Clinton, MS 39058. Offers art (M Ed); biological science (M Ed); business education (M Ed); computer science (M Ed); dyslexia therapy (M Ed); educational leadership (M Ed, Ed D, Ed S); elementary education (M Ed, Ed S); English (M Ed); higher education administration (MS); mathematics (M Ed); secondary education (M Ed); social studies (history) (M Ed); teaching arts (M Ed). *Program availability:* Part-time, online learning. *Degree requirements:* For master's, comprehensive exam, thesis optional. *Entrance requirements:* For master's, NTE. Additional exam requirements/recommendations for international students: Recommended—TOEFL, IELTS. Electronic applications accepted.

Mississippi State University, College of Education, Department of Curriculum, Instruction and Special Education, Mississippi State, MS 39762. Offers early childhood education (PhD); elementary education (MS, PhD, Ed S), including early childhood education (MS), general elementary education (MS), middle level education (MS); general curriculum and instruction (PhD); reading education (PhD); secondary education (MAT, MS, PhD, Ed S); special education (MAT, MS, PhD, Ed S). *Accreditation:* NCATE. *Program availability:* Part-time, evening/weekend. *Faculty:* 22 full-time (16 women), 1 (woman) part-time/adjunct. *Students:* 38 full-time (26 women), 170 part-time (131 women); includes 46 minority (37 Black or African American, non-Hispanic/Latino; 4 American Indian or Alaska Native, non-Hispanic/Latino; 2 Hispanic/Latino; 1 Native Hawaiian or other Pacific Islander, non-Hispanic/Latino; 2 Two or more races, non-Hispanic/Latino), 4 international. Average age 32. 88 applicants, 53% accepted, 39 enrolled. In 2017, 68 master's, 4 doctorates, 5 other advanced degrees awarded. *Degree requirements:* For master's, comprehensive exam; for doctorate, thesis/dissertation; for Ed S, comprehensive exam, thesis or alternative. *Entrance*

requirements: For master's, GRE, minimum GPA of 2.75 in junior and senior year, eligibility for initial teacher certification; for doctorate, GRE, minimum GPA of 3.4 on previous graduate work; for Ed S, GRE, minimum GPA of 3.2 on master's degree. Additional exam requirements/recommendations for international students: Required—TOEFL (minimum score 550 paper-based; 79 iBT); Recommended—IELTS (minimum score 6.5). *Application deadline:* For fall admission, 3/1 priority date for domestic students, 5/1 for international students; for spring admission, 9/1 priority date for domestic students, 9/1 for international students. Applications are processed on a rolling basis. Application fee: $60 ($80 for international students). Electronic applications accepted. *Expenses:* Tuition, state resident: full-time $8318; part-time $462.12 per credit hour. Tuition, nonresident: full-time $22,358; part-time $1242.12 per credit hour. *Required fees:* $110; $12.24 per credit hour. $6.12 per semester. *Financial support:* In 2017–18, 6 research assistantships with partial tuition reimbursements (averaging $11,307 per year) were awarded; Federal Work-Study, institutionally sponsored loans, scholarships/grants, and unspecified assistantships also available. Financial award application deadline: 4/1; financial award applicants required to submit FAFSA. *Faculty research:* Early childhood education, reading, rural schools, multicultural education, use of technology in instruction. *Unit head:* Dr. Linda Cornelious, Professor and Interim Head, 662-325-3747, Fax: 662-325-7857, E-mail: lcornelious@colled.msstate.edu. *Application contact:* Laken Drinker, Admissions and Enrollment Assistant, 662-325-8951, E-mail: ldrinker@grad.msstate.edu.
Website: http://www.cise.msstate.edu/

Missouri State University, Graduate College, College of Education, Department of Counseling, Leadership, and Special Education, Program in Special Education, Springfield, MO 65897. Offers MS Ed. *Program availability:* Part-time, evening/weekend, 100% online, blended/hybrid learning. *Faculty:* 7 full-time (6 women), 3 part-time/adjunct (2 women). *Students:* 8 full-time (6 women), 67 part-time (56 women); includes 7 minority (3 Black or African American, non-Hispanic/Latino; 3 Hispanic/Latino; 1 Two or more races, non-Hispanic/Latino), 2 international. Average age 30. 21 applicants, 67% accepted, 11 enrolled. In 2017, 28 master's awarded. *Degree requirements:* For master's, comprehensive exam, thesis or alternative. *Entrance requirements:* For master's, GRE or minimum GPA of 3.0, teaching certificate. Additional exam requirements/recommendations for international students: Required—TOEFL (minimum score 550 paper-based; 79 iBT), IELTS (minimum score 6). *Application deadline:* For fall admission, 7/20 priority date for domestic students, 5/1 for international students; for spring admission, 12/20 priority date for domestic students, 9/1 for international students; for summer admission, 5/20 priority date for domestic students. Applications are processed on a rolling basis. Application fee: $35 ($50 for international students). Electronic applications accepted. *Expenses:* Tuition, state resident: full-time $2915; part-time $2021 per credit hour. Tuition, nonresident: full-time $5354; part-time $3647 per credit hour. *International tuition:* $11,992 full-time. *Required fees:* $173; $173 per credit hour. Tuition and fees vary according to class time, course level, course load, degree level, campus/location and program. *Financial support:* Federal Work-Study, institutionally sponsored loans, scholarships/grants, and unspecified assistantships available. Financial award application deadline: 3/31; financial award applicants required to submit FAFSA. *Unit head:* Dr. James Satterfield, Department Head, 417-836-5392, Fax: 417-836-4918, E-mail: spe@missouristate.edu. *Application contact:* Stephanie Praschan, Director, Graduate Enrollment Management, 417-836-5300, Fax: 417-836-6200, E-mail: stephaniepraschan@missouristate.edu.
Website: http://education.missouristate.edu/sped/

Missouri Western State University, Program in Assessment, St. Joseph, MO 64507-2294. Offers K-12 cross-categorical special education (MAS); TESOL (MAS, Graduate Certificate); writing (MAS). *Program availability:* Part-time. *Students:* 29 part-time (25 women); includes 1 minority (Black or African American, non-Hispanic/Latino). Average age 38. 8 applicants, 100% accepted, 4 enrolled. In 2017, 9 master's, 3 other advanced degrees awarded. *Entrance requirements:* For master's, minimum GPA of 2.75. Additional exam requirements/recommendations for international students: Recommended—TOEFL (minimum score 79 iBT), IELTS (minimum score 6). *Application deadline:* For fall admission, 7/15 for domestic and international students; for spring admission, 10/1 for domestic and international students; for summer admission, 3/15 for domestic students. Applications are processed on a rolling basis. Application fee: $45 ($50 for international students). Electronic applications accepted. *Expenses:* Tuition, state resident: full-time $6391; part-time $336 per credit hour. Tuition, nonresident: full-time $11,483; part-time $604 per credit hour. *Required fees:* $542; $99 per credit hour. $176 per semester. One-time fee: $45. Tuition and fees vary according to course load and program. *Financial support:* Scholarships/grants and unspecified assistantships available. Support available to part-time students. *Unit head:* Dr. Susan Bashinski, Director of Graduate Programs in Education, 816-271-5629, E-mail: sbashinski@missouriwestern.edu. *Application contact:* Dr. Benjamin D. Caldwell, Dean of the Graduate School, 816-271-4394, Fax: 816-271-4525, E-mail: graduate@missouriwestern.edu.
Website: https://www.missouriwestern.edu/masa/

Molloy College, Graduate Education Program, Rockville Centre, NY 11571-5002. Offers adolescent education in biology (MS); adolescent special education (Advanced Certificate); bilingual extension (Advanced Certificate); childhood education (MS); childhood special education (Advanced Certificate); early childhood education (MS); educational technology (MS); English (MS); mathematics (MS); social studies (MS); Spanish (MS); special education on both childhood and adolescent levels (MS); teaching English to speakers of other languages (TESOL) in grades pre-K to 12 (MS); TESOL (Advanced Certificate). *Accreditation:* NCATE. *Program availability:* Part-time, evening/weekend. *Faculty:* 18 full-time (17 women), 11 part-time/adjunct (9 women). *Students:* 102 full-time (80 women), 217 part-time (167 women); includes 65 minority (16 Black or African American, non-Hispanic/Latino; 7 Asian, non-Hispanic/Latino; 38 Hispanic/Latino; 4 Two or more races, non-Hispanic/Latino), 1 international. Average age 41. 153 applicants, 68% accepted, 85 enrolled. In 2017, 95 master's, 3 other advanced degrees awarded. *Entrance requirements:* Additional exam requirements/recommendations for international students: Required—TOEFL (minimum score 550 paper-based; 79 iBT). *Application deadline:* Applications are processed on a rolling basis. Application fee: $60. Electronic applications accepted. *Expenses: Tuition:* Full-time $19,980; part-time $1110 per credit. *Required fees:* $1040. Tuition and fees vary according to course load and degree level. *Financial support:* Application deadline: 3/1; applicants required to submit FAFSA. *Faculty research:* English Language Learners; social emotional needs of students; gifted education; cultural diversity; collaborative teaching methods. *Unit head:* Joanne O'Brien, Associate Dean and Director of Graduate Education Programs, 516-323-3116, E-mail: jobrien@molloy.edu. *Application contact:* Jaclyn Machowicz, Assistant Director for Admissions, 516-323-4010, E-mail: jmachowicz@molloy.edu.

Monmouth University, Graduate Studies, School of Education, West Long Branch, NJ 07764-1898. Offers applied behavior analysis (Certificate); autism (Certificate); director of school counseling services (Post-Master's Certificate); early childhood (M Ed); educational leadership (Ed D); elementary education (MAT), including elementary level, secondary level; English as a second language (M Ed); learning disabilities teacher-consultant (Post-Master's Certificate); literacy (MS Ed); school counseling (MS Ed); special education (MS Ed), including autism, learning disabilities teacher-consultant,

Special Education

teacher of students with disabilities, teaching in inclusive settings; speech-language pathology (MS Ed); student affairs and college counseling (MS Ed); supervisor (Post-Master's Certificate); teaching English to speakers of other languages (Certificate). *Accreditation:* NCATE. *Program availability:* Part-time, evening/weekend, 100% online, blended/hybrid learning. *Faculty:* 23 full-time (19 women), 33 part-time/adjunct (25 women). *Students:* 175 full-time (163 women), 168 part-time (142 women); includes 54 minority (10 Black or African American, non-Hispanic/Latino; 4 Asian, non-Hispanic/Latino; 32 Hispanic/Latino; 8 Two or more races, non-Hispanic/Latino). Average age 27. In 2017, 160 master's, 3 other advanced degrees awarded. *Entrance requirements:* For master's, GRE taken within last 5 years (for MS Ed in speech-language pathology); SAT (minimum combined score of 1660 in 3 sections), ACT (23), GRE (minimum score of 4.0 on analytical writing section and minimum combined score of 310 on quantitative and verbal sections), or passing scores on 3 parts of Core Academic Skills Educators, minimum GPA of 3.0 in major; 2 letters of recommendation (for some programs); resume, personal statement or essay (depending on program). Additional exam requirements/recommendations for international students: Required—TOEFL (minimum score 550 paper-based; 79 iBT), IELTS (minimum score 6), Michigan English Language Assessment Battery (minimum score 77) or Certificate of Advanced English (minimum score 160). *Application deadline:* For fall admission, 7/15 priority date for domestic students, 7/1 for international students; for spring admission, 12/1 priority date for domestic students, 11/1 for international students; for summer admission, 5/1 for domestic students. Applications are processed on a rolling basis. Application fee: $50. Electronic applications accepted. *Expenses: Tuition:* Full-time $21,366; part-time $7122 per credit. *Required fees:* $700; $175 per term. *Financial support:* In 2017–18, 125 students received support. Institutionally sponsored loans, scholarships/grants, and unspecified assistantships available. Support available to part-time students. Financial award applicants required to submit FAFSA. *Faculty research:* Multicultural literacy, science and mathematics teaching strategies, teacher as reflective practitioner, children with disabilities. *Unit head:* Dr. John E. Henning, Dean, 732-263-5513, Fax: 732-263-5277. *Application contact:* Laurie Kuhn, Associate Director of Graduate Admission, 732-571-3452, Fax: 732-263-5123, E-mail: gradadm@monmouth.edu.
Website: http://www.monmouth.edu/academics/schools/education/default.asp

Montana State University Billings, College of Education, Department of Educational Theory and Practice, Program in Special Education, Billings, MT 59101. Offers advanced studies (MS Sp Ed); applied behavior analysis (MS Sp Ed); generalist (MS Sp Ed). *Accreditation:* NCATE. *Program availability:* Part-time. *Degree requirements:* For master's, thesis or professional paper and/or field experience. *Entrance requirements:* For master's, GRE General Test or MAT, minimum GPA of 3.0. Additional exam requirements/recommendations for international students: Required—TOEFL (minimum score 79 iBT), IELTS (minimum score 6.5). *Application deadline:* Applications are processed on a rolling basis. Application fee: $40. Electronic applications accepted. *Expenses:* Tuition, state resident: full-time $11,740; part-time $7880 per year. Tuition, nonresident: full-time $32,200; part-time $24,140 per year. *Financial support:* Research assistantships with partial tuition reimbursements, teaching assistantships with partial tuition reimbursements, career-related internships or fieldwork, Federal Work-Study, institutionally sponsored loans, scholarships/grants, tuition waivers (partial), and unspecified assistantships available. Support available to part-time students. Financial award application deadline: 5/1; financial award applicants required to submit FAFSA. *Unit head:* Dr. Cindy Dell, Chair, Educational Theory and Practice, 406-657-1614, E-mail: cdell@msubillings.edu. *Application contact:* Dr. Cindy Dell, Chair, Educational Theory and Practice, 406-657-1614, E-mail: cdell@msubillings.edu.

Montclair State University, The Graduate School, College of Education and Human Services, Program in Inclusive Early Childhood Education, Montclair, NJ 07043-1624. Offers M Ed. *Degree requirements:* For master's, comprehensive exam, thesis or alternative. *Entrance requirements:* For master's, GRE General Test, interview, 2 letters of recommendation. Additional exam requirements/recommendations for international students: Required—TOEFL (minimum score 83 iBT), IELTS (minimum score 6.5). Electronic applications accepted.

Morehead State University, Graduate Programs, College of Education, Department of Curriculum and Instruction, Morehead, KY 40351. Offers curriculum and instruction (Ed S); elementary education (MA Ed), including elementary education, international education, middle school education, reading; secondary education (MA Ed); special education (MA Ed); teaching (MAT). *Program availability:* Part-time, evening/weekend. *Degree requirements:* For master's, comprehensive exam, thesis optional; for Ed S, thesis, oral exam. *Entrance requirements:* For master's, GRE General Test, minimum GPA of 2.75, teaching certificate; for Ed S, GRE General Test, interview, master's degree, minimum GPA of 3.5, work experience. Additional exam requirements/recommendations for international students: Required—TOEFL (minimum score 500 paper-based). Electronic applications accepted. *Faculty research:* Communicative competence of learning-disabled students, teaching social studies in elementary schools, ungraded primary school organization, study skills.

Morehead State University, Graduate Programs, College of Education, Department of Early Childhood, Elementary and Special Education, Morehead, KY 40351. Offers learning and behavioral disorders P-12 (MAT); moderate and severe disabilities P-12 (MAT). *Program availability:* Part-time, evening/weekend. *Degree requirements:* For master's, thesis. *Entrance requirements:* For master's, GRE or PRAXIS II content exam, minimum overall undergraduate GPA of 2.5. Additional exam requirements/recommendations for international students: Required—TOEFL (minimum score 500 paper-based). Electronic applications accepted.

Morehead State University, Graduate Programs, College of Education, Department of Foundational and Graduate Studies in Education, Morehead, KY 40351. Offers adult and higher education (MA, Ed S); certified professional counselor (Ed S); counseling P-12 (MA); curriculum and instruction (Ed S); educational technology (MA Ed); instructional leadership (Ed S); school administration (MA); school counseling (Ed S); teacher leader business and marketing content (MA Ed); teacher leader business and marketing technology (MA Ed); teacher leader educational technology (MA Ed); teacher leader English (MA Ed); teacher leader gifted education (MA Ed); teacher leader IECE certification (MA Ed); teacher leader interdisciplinary education P-5 (MA Ed); teacher leader middle grades (MA Ed); teacher leader non IECE certification (MA Ed); teacher leader reading/writing - non-certification (MA Ed); teacher leader reading/writing certification (MA Ed); teacher leader school communication - certification (MA Ed); teacher leader school communication - non-certification (MA Ed); teacher leader social studies (MA Ed); teacher leader special education (MA Ed). *Accreditation:* NCATE. *Program availability:* Part-time, evening/weekend. *Degree requirements:* For master's, thesis optional, oral and/or written comprehensive exams; for Ed S, thesis, oral exam. *Entrance requirements:* For master's, GRE General Test, minimum overall undergraduate GPA of 2.5; for Ed S, GRE General Test, interview, master's degree, minimum GPA of 3.5, work experience. Additional exam requirements/recommendations for international students: Required—TOEFL (minimum score 500 paper-based). Electronic applications accepted. *Faculty research:* Character education, school accountability, computer applications for school administrators.

Morningside College, Graduate Programs, Sharon Walker School of Education, Sioux City, IA 51106. Offers professional educator (MAT); special education (MAT), including instructional strategist: mild/moderate (7-12), instructional strategist: mild/moderate (K-6), K-12 instructional strategist: behavior disorders/learning disabilities, K-12 instructional strategist: mental disabilities. *Program availability:* Part-time, online only, 100% online. *Faculty:* 4 full-time (1 woman), 83 part-time/adjunct (62 women). *Students:* 18 full-time (15 women), 864 part-time (721 women); includes 29 minority (4 Black or African American, non-Hispanic/Latino; 3 American Indian or Alaska Native, non-Hispanic/Latino; 1 Asian, non-Hispanic/Latino; 18 Hispanic/Latino; 1 Native Hawaiian or other Pacific Islander, non-Hispanic/Latino; 2 Two or more races, non-Hispanic/Latino), 1 international. Average age 33. 314 applicants, 73% accepted, 162 enrolled. In 2017, 375 master's awarded. *Entrance requirements:* For master's, writing sample. *Application deadline:* Applications are processed on a rolling basis. Electronic applications accepted. *Expenses:* Contact institution. *Financial support:* In 2017–18, 266 students received support. Institutionally sponsored loans and tuition waivers (partial) available. Support available to part-time students. Financial award applicants required to submit FAFSA. *Unit head:* Barbara Chambers, Director, 712-274-5465, Fax: 712-274-5488, E-mail: chambersb@morningside.edu. *Application contact:* Tracy Sursely, Student Records Enrollment Coordinator, 712-274-5576, Fax: 712-274-5101, E-mail: surselyt@morningside.edu.

Mount Mercy University, Program in Education, Cedar Rapids, IA 52402-4797. Offers reading (MA Ed); special education (MA Ed); teacher leadership (MA Ed). *Entrance requirements:* For master's, minimum cumulative GPA of 3.0, 2 letters of recommendation, resume, valid teaching license. Additional exam requirements/recommendations for international students: Required—TOEFL (minimum score 570 paper-based; 88 iBT). Electronic applications accepted.

Mount St. Joseph University, Graduate Education Program, Cincinnati, OH 45233-1670. Offers adolescent to young adult education (MA); dyslexia (Certificate); inclusive early childhood education (MA); middle childhood education (MA); multicultural special education (MA); reading science (MA). *Accreditation:* TEAC. *Program availability:* Part-time, evening/weekend, 100% online, blended/hybrid learning. *Faculty:* 6 full-time (5 women), 11 part-time/adjunct (8 women). *Students:* 37 full-time (30 women), 91 part-time (83 women); includes 13 minority (11 Black or African American, non-Hispanic/Latino; 1 Hispanic/Latino; 1 Two or more races, non-Hispanic/Latino). Average age 34. In 2017, 79 master's awarded. *Degree requirements:* For master's, comprehensive exam, thesis, research project, student teaching, clinical and field-based experiences. *Entrance requirements:* For master's, GRE (if GPA is below 3.0), letter of intent, 2 referrals, background check, interview, resume, minimum undergraduate GPA of 3.0. Additional exam requirements/recommendations for international students: Required—TOEFL (minimum score 560 paper-based; 83 iBT). *Application deadline:* Applications are processed on a rolling basis. Application fee: $50. Electronic applications accepted. *Expenses:* $600 per credit hour. *Financial support:* Applicants required to submit FAFSA. *Faculty research:* Foreign and second language learning problems/reading disabilities, multicultural/bilingual special education, science education, pedagogical content knowledge, early childhood, response to intervention. *Unit head:* Dr. Laura Saylor, Dean, 513-244-3263, E-mail: laura.saylor@msj.edu. *Application contact:* Mary Brigham, Assistant Director of Graduate Recruitment, 513-244-4233, Fax: 513-244-4629, E-mail: mary.brigham@msj.edu.
Website: http://www.msj.edu/academics/graduate-programs/master-of-arts-initial-teacher-licensure-programs/

Mount Saint Mary College, Division of Education, Newburgh, NY 12550-3494. Offers adolescence and special education (MS Ed); childhood education (MS Ed); literacy education (MS Ed); middle school (7-9) (MS Ed). *Accreditation:* NCATE. *Program availability:* Part-time, evening/weekend. *Faculty:* 10 full-time (9 women), 3 part-time/adjunct (all women). *Students:* 11 full-time (9 women), 83 part-time (62 women); includes 9 minority (1 American Indian or Alaska Native, non-Hispanic/Latino; 6 Hispanic/Latino; 2 Two or more races, non-Hispanic/Latino). Average age 28. 20 applicants, 100% accepted, 16 enrolled. In 2017, 57 master's awarded. *Entrance requirements:* Additional exam requirements/recommendations for international students: Required—TOEFL (minimum score 80 iBT). *Application deadline:* Applications are processed on a rolling basis. Application fee: $45. Electronic applications accepted. Application fee is waived when completed online. *Expenses: Tuition:* Full-time $14,454; part-time $803 per credit. *Required fees:* $172; $86 per semester. *Financial support:* In 2017–18, 15 students received support. Unspecified assistantships available. Financial award application deadline: 4/15; financial award applicants required to submit FAFSA. *Faculty research:* Learning and teaching styles, computers in special education, language development. *Unit head:* Dr. Monica Merritt, Graduate Coordinator, 845-569-3430, Fax: 845-569-3535, E-mail: monica.merritt@msmc.edu. *Application contact:* Lisa Alvarez, Director of Admissions for Graduate Programs and Adult Degree Completion, 845-569-3166, Fax: 845-569-3450, E-mail: lisa.gallina@msmc.edu.
Website: http://www.msmc.edu/Academics/Graduate_Programs/Master_of_Science_in_Education

Mount Saint Vincent University, Graduate Programs, Faculty of Education, Program in Educational Psychology, Halifax, NS B3M 2J6, Canada. Offers education of the blind or visually impaired (M Ed, MA Ed); education of the deaf or hard of hearing (M Ed, MA Ed); educational psychology (MA-R); human relations (M Ed, MA Ed). *Program availability:* Part-time, evening/weekend, online learning. *Degree requirements:* For master's, thesis (for some programs). *Entrance requirements:* For master's, bachelor's degree in related field, 1 year of teaching experience. Electronic applications accepted. *Faculty research:* Personality measurement, values reasoning, aggression and sexuality, power and control, quantitative and qualitative research methodologies.

Murray State University, College of Education and Human Services, Department of Adolescent, Career, and Special Education, Murray, KY 42071. Offers career and technical education (MS); middle school teacher leader (MA Ed); secondary teacher leader (MA Ed); special education (MA Ed), including mild learning and behavior disorders, moderate to severe disabilities (P-12), teacher leader in special education learning and behavior disorders; teacher education and professional development (Ed S). *Accreditation:* NCATE. *Program availability:* Part-time. *Faculty:* 10 full-time (9 women). *Students:* 4 full-time (2 women), 78 part-time (56 women); includes 4 minority (2 Black or African American, non-Hispanic/Latino; 1 Asian, non-Hispanic/Latino; 1 Hispanic/Latino), 2 international. Average age 33. 13 applicants, 100% accepted, 8 enrolled. In 2017, 19 master's awarded. *Entrance requirements:* For master's and Ed S, GRE or GMAT, minimum university GPA of 2.75. Additional exam requirements/recommendations for international students: Required—TOEFL (minimum score 527 paper-based; 71 iBT). *Application deadline:* Applications are processed on a rolling basis. Application fee: $40 ($50 for international students). Electronic applications accepted. *Expenses:* Tuition, state resident: full-time $9504. Tuition, nonresident: full-time $26,811. *International tuition:* $14,400 full-time. Tuition and fees vary according to course load, degree level and reciprocity agreements. *Financial support:* Federal Work-Study and unspecified assistantships available. Financial award applicants required to submit FAFSA. *Unit head:* Dr. Barbara Washington, Chair, Department of Adolescent, Career and Special Education, 270-809-2262, Fax: 270-809-2540, E-mail: bwashington@murraystate.edu. *Application contact:* Kaitlyn Burzynski, Interim Assistant

Director of Graduate Admission and Records, 270-809-5732, Fax: 270-809-3780, E-mail: msu.graduateadmissions@murraystate.edu. Website: http://www.murraystate.edu/academics/CollegesDepartments/CollegeOfEducationandHumanServices/coehsacademicunits/AdolescentCareerSpecialEd/index.aspx

National Louis University, National College of Education, Chicago, IL 60603. Offers administration and supervision (M Ed, Ed D, CAS, Ed S); curriculum and instruction (M Ed, MS Ed, CAS); early childhood administration (M Ed, CAS); early childhood education (M Ed, MAT, MS Ed, CAS); education (Ed D); educational psychology/human learning and development (M Ed, MS Ed, CAS, Ed S); elementary education (MAT); interdisciplinary curriculum and instruction (M Ed); mathematics education (M Ed, MS Ed, CAS); middle grades education (MAT); reading and language (M Ed, MS Ed, CAS); school psychology (M Ed, Ed S); science education (M Ed, MS Ed, CAS); secondary education (MAT); special education (M Ed, MAT, CAS); technology in education (M Ed, CAS). *Accreditation:* NCATE. *Program availability:* Part-time, evening/weekend. *Degree requirements:* For doctorate, comprehensive exam, thesis/dissertation. *Entrance requirements:* For master's, MAT or GRE, minimum GPA of 3.0; for doctorate, GRE General Test, minimum GPA of 3.25, interview, resume, writing sample, 4 recommendations. Additional exam requirements/recommendations for international students: Required—TOEFL (minimum score 550 paper-based; 79 iBT).

National University, Academic Affairs, Sanford College of Education, La Jolla, CA 92037-1011. Offers advanced teaching practices (MS); applied behavior analysis (MS); applied school leadership (MS); e-teaching and learning (Certificate); education (MA); educational administration (MS); educational and instructional technology (MS); educational counseling (MS); higher education administration (MS); inspired teaching and learning (M Ed); school psychology (MS); special education (MA, MS). *Program availability:* Part-time, evening/weekend, 100% online, blended/hybrid learning. *Degree requirements:* For master's, thesis (for some programs). *Entrance requirements:* For master's, interview, minimum GPA of 2.5. Additional exam requirements/recommendations for international students: Required—TOEFL (minimum score 550 paper-based; 79 iBT), IELTS (minimum score 6). *Application deadline:* Applications are processed on a rolling basis. Application fee: $60 ($65 for international students). Electronic applications accepted. *Expenses: Tuition:* Part-time $430 per quarter hour. *Financial support:* Career-related internships or fieldwork, institutionally sponsored loans, scholarships/grants, and tuition waivers (partial) available. Support available to part-time students. Financial award application deadline: 6/30. *Faculty research:* Teacher education, special education, educational effectiveness, teaching abroad, school counseling. *Unit head:* Dr. Judy Mantle, Dean, 858-642-8320, E-mail: soe@nu.edu. *Application contact:* Brandon Jouganatos, Vice President for Enrollment Services, 800-628-8648, E-mail: advisor@nu.edu. Website: http://www.nu.edu/OurPrograms/SchoolOfEducation.html

National University College, Graduate Programs, Bayamón, PR 00960. Offers digital marketing (MBA); general business (MBA); special education (M Ed).

Neumann University, Graduate Program in Education, Aston, PA 19014-1298. Offers education (MS), including administrative certification (school principal PK-12), autism, early elementary education, secondary education, special education. *Program availability:* Part-time, evening/weekend, 100% online, blended/hybrid learning. *Faculty:* 6 full-time (5 women), 16 part-time/adjunct (7 women). *Students:* 68 full-time (56 women), 108 part-time (93 women); includes 36 minority (28 Black or African American, non-Hispanic/Latino; 3 Hispanic/Latino; 5 Two or more races, non-Hispanic/Latino). Average age 33. 83 applicants, 69% accepted, 36 enrolled. In 2017, 114 master's awarded. *Entrance requirements:* For master's, official transcripts from all institutions attended, letter of intent, three professional references, copy of any teaching certifications. Additional exam requirements/recommendations for international students: Required—TOEFL (minimum score 70 iBT). *Application deadline:* Applications are processed on a rolling basis. Application fee: $0. Electronic applications accepted. *Expenses:* $700 per credit hour (for on-campus master's-level education courses); $480 per credit hour (for online or off-campus master's-level education courses). *Financial support:* Scholarships/grants and health care benefits available. Support available to part-time students. Financial award application deadline: 3/15; financial award applicants required to submit FAFSA. *Unit head:* Dr. Stephanie Smith-Budhai, Director of Graduate Education, 610-358-4249, E-mail: budhais@neumann.edu. *Application contact:* Dr. Erika K. Davis, Director of Adult and Graduate Admissions, 800-9-NEUMANN Ext. 5208, Fax: 610-361-2548, E-mail: gradadultadmiss@neumann.edu. Website: https://www.neumann.edu/academics/grad/education/index.asp

New England College, Program in Education, Henniker, NH 03242-3293. Offers higher education administration (MS, Ed D); K-12 leadership (Ed D); literacy and language arts (M Ed); meeting the needs of all learners/special education (M Ed); teacher leadership/school reform (M Ed). *Program availability:* Part-time, evening/weekend.

New Jersey City University, Debra Cannon Partridge Wolfe College of Education, Department of Special Education, Jersey City, NJ 07305-1597. Offers MA. *Accreditation:* TEAC. *Program availability:* Part-time, evening/weekend. *Entrance requirements:* Additional exam requirements/recommendations for international students: Required—TOEFL (minimum score 79 iBT). *Faculty research:* Mainstreaming the handicapped child and the autistic child.

New Mexico Highlands University, Graduate Studies, School of Education, Las Vegas, NM 87701. Offers curriculum and instruction (MA); educational leadership (MA); professional counseling (MA); special education (MA). *Accreditation:* NCATE. *Program availability:* Part-time. *Degree requirements:* For master's, comprehensive exam, thesis or alternative. *Entrance requirements:* For master's, minimum undergraduate GPA of 3.0. Additional exam requirements/recommendations for international students: Required—TOEFL (minimum score 540 paper-based). *Faculty research:* Middle school curriculum, integrated computer applications for pre-service classroom teachers, adolescent literacy, narrative cognitive modes in New Mexico multicultural setting, math and math education.

New Mexico State University, College of Education, Department of Communication Disorders, Las Cruces, NM 88003. Offers communication disorders (MA); curriculum and instruction (Ed S), including special education (MA, Ed S), special education/deaf-hard of hearing (MA, Ed S); education (MA), including autism spectrum disorders (MA, Ed D, PhD), special education (MA, Ed S), special education/deaf-hard of hearing (MA, Ed S); speech-language pathology (MA); special education (Ed D, PhD), including autism spectrum disorders (MA, Ed D, PhD), bilingual/multicultural special education. *Accreditation:* ASHA (one or more programs are accredited); NCATE. *Program availability:* Part-time, evening/weekend, online learning. *Faculty:* 13 full-time (10 women), 4 part-time/adjunct (3 women). *Students:* 45 full-time (41 women), 56 part-time (45 women); includes 64 minority (1 Black or African American, non-Hispanic/Latino; 2 American Indian or Alaska Native, non-Hispanic/Latino; 4 Asian, non-Hispanic/Latino; 56 Hispanic/Latino; 1 Two or more races, non-Hispanic/Latino), 6 international. Average age 33. 164 applicants, 36% accepted, 32 enrolled. In 2017, 41 master's, 3 doctorates, 7 other advanced degrees awarded. *Degree requirements:* For master's, comprehensive exam, thesis optional; for doctorate, comprehensive exam, thesis/dissertation. *Entrance requirements:* For master's, GRE General Test or MAT.

Additional exam requirements/recommendations for international students: Required—TOEFL (minimum score 550 paper-based; 79 iBT), IELTS (minimum score 6.5). *Application deadline:* For fall admission, 2/1 priority date for domestic students. Applications are processed on a rolling basis. Application fee: $40 ($50 for international students). Electronic applications accepted. *Expenses: Tuition,* state resident: full-time $4390. Tuition, nonresident: full-time $15,309. *Required fees:* $853. *Financial support:* In 2017–18, 33 students received support, including 1 fellowship (averaging $4,390 per year), 1 research assistantship (averaging $8,482 per year), 14 teaching assistantships (averaging $10,386 per year); career-related internships or fieldwork, Federal Work-Study, scholarships/grants, traineeships, health care benefits, and unspecified assistantships also available. Support available to part-time students. Financial award application deadline: 3/1. *Faculty research:* Multicultural special education, multicultural communication disorders, mild disability, multicultural assessment, deaf education, early childhood, bilingual special education. *Total annual research expenditures:* $182,251. *Unit head:* Dr. Victoria White, Interim Department Head, 575-646-5973, Fax: 575-646-7712, E-mail: vwhite@nmsu.edu. *Application contact:* Dr. Victoria White, Interim Department Head, 575-646-5973, Fax: 575-646-7712, E-mail: vwhite@nmsu.edu. Website: https://cd.nmsu.edu/

New York University, Steinhardt School of Culture, Education, and Human Development, Department of Teaching and Learning, Program in Early Childhood and Childhood Education, New York, NY 10012. Offers childhood education (MA); early childhood education (MA); early childhood education/early childhood special education (MA). *Accreditation:* TEAC. *Program availability:* Part-time. *Faculty:* 9 full-time (all women). *Students:* 59 full-time (55 women), 24 part-time (22 women); includes 25 minority (3 Black or African American, non-Hispanic/Latino; 15 Asian, non-Hispanic/Latino; 5 Hispanic/Latino; 2 Two or more races, non-Hispanic/Latino), 8 international. Average age 28. 91 applicants, 68% accepted, 15 enrolled. In 2017, 57 master's awarded. *Degree requirements:* For master's, thesis (for some programs). *Entrance requirements:* Additional exam requirements/recommendations for international students: Required—TOEFL (minimum score 100 iBT). *Application deadline:* For fall admission, 12/1 priority date for domestic and international students; for spring admission, 10/1 for domestic and international students. Applications are processed on a rolling basis. Application fee: $75. Electronic applications accepted. *Expenses: Tuition:* Full-time $41,352; part-time $19,968 per year. *Required fees:* $2496; $1628 per unit. $814 per term. Tuition and fees vary according to course load and program. *Financial support:* Fellowships with full and partial tuition reimbursements, career-related internships or fieldwork, Federal Work-Study, institutionally sponsored loans, scholarships/grants, tuition waivers (partial), and unspecified assistantships available. Support available to part-time students. Financial award application deadline: 2/1; financial award applicants required to submit FAFSA. *Faculty research:* Teacher evaluation and beliefs about teaching, early literacy development, language arts, child development and education, cultural differences. *Unit head:* Dr. 212-998-5460, Fax: 212-995-4049. *Application contact:* 212-998-5030, Fax: 212-995-4328, E-mail: steinhardt.gradadmissions@nyu.edu. Website: http://steinhardt.nyu.edu/teachlearn/childhood

New York University, Steinhardt School of Culture, Education, and Human Development, Department of Teaching and Learning, Program in Special Education, New York, NY 10012-1019. Offers childhood (MA); early childhood (MA). *Accreditation:* TEAC. *Program availability:* Part-time. *Students:* Average age 25. 101 applicants, 81% accepted, 12 enrolled. In 2017, 8 master's awarded. *Entrance requirements:* Additional exam requirements/recommendations for international students: Required—TOEFL (minimum score 100 iBT). *Application deadline:* For fall admission, 12/1 priority date for domestic and international students. Applications are processed on a rolling basis. Application fee: $75. Electronic applications accepted. *Expenses: Tuition:* Full-time $41,352; part-time $19,968 per year. *Required fees:* $2496; $1628 per unit. $814 per term. Tuition and fees vary according to course load and program. *Financial support:* Career-related internships or fieldwork, Federal Work-Study, institutionally sponsored loans, scholarships/grants, and tuition waivers (partial) available. Support available to part-time students. Financial award application deadline: 2/1; financial award applicants required to submit FAFSA. *Faculty research:* Special education referrals, attention deficit disorders in children, mainstreaming, curriculum-based assessment and program implementation, special education policy. *Unit head:* Prof. Joan Rosenberg, Director, 212-998-5554, Fax: 212-995-4049, E-mail: joanrosenberg@nyu.edu. *Application contact:* 212-998-5030, Fax: 212-995-4328, E-mail: steinhardt.gradadmissions@nyu.edu. Website: http://steinhardt.nyu.edu/teachlearn/special/ma

Niagara University, Graduate Division of Education, Concentration in Teacher Education, Niagara University, NY 14109. Offers early childhood and childhood education (MS Ed, Certificate); early childhood special education (MS); middle and adolescence education (MS Ed); special education (MS Ed), including 1-6, 7-12; special education (grades 1-12) (Certificate); teaching English to speakers of other languages (MS Ed, Certificate). *Accreditation:* NCATE. *Students:* 105 full-time (79 women), 109 part-time (88 women); includes 20 minority (9 Black or African American, non-Hispanic/Latino; 2 American Indian or Alaska Native, non-Hispanic/Latino; 1 Asian, non-Hispanic/Latino; 5 Hispanic/Latino; 3 Two or more races, non-Hispanic/Latino), 35 international. Average age 28. In 2017, 86 master's, 18 other advanced degrees awarded. *Entrance requirements:* For master's, GRE General Test or Academic Literacy Skills Test (ALST). Additional exam requirements/recommendations for international students: Required—TOEFL (minimum score 550 paper-based; 79 iBT), IELTS (minimum score 6). *Application deadline:* For fall admission, 8/1 for domestic students. Applications are processed on a rolling basis. Application fee: $30. *Expenses:* Contact institution. *Financial support:* Research assistantships with tuition reimbursements, teaching assistantships with tuition reimbursements, career-related internships or fieldwork, Federal Work-Study, scholarships/grants, and unspecified assistantships available. Financial award application deadline: 4/15; financial award applicants required to submit FAFSA. *Unit head:* Dr. Chandra Foote, Dean, College of Education, 716-286-8549, E-mail: cjf@niagara.edu. *Application contact:* Evan Pierce, Associate Director, Graduate Studies, 716-286-8327, E-mail: epierce@niagara.edu. Website: http://www.niagara.edu/teacher-education

Norfolk State University, School of Graduate Studies, School of Education, Department of Special Education, Norfolk, VA 23504. Offers severe disabilities (MA). *Accreditation:* NCATE. *Program availability:* Part-time. *Degree requirements:* For master's, thesis or alternative. *Entrance requirements:* For master's, minimum GPA of 3.0 in major, 2.5 overall.

North Carolina Central University, School of Education, Special Education Program, Durham, NC 27707-3129. Offers emotional disabilities (M Ed, MAT); learning disabilities (M Ed, MAT); visual impairment (M Ed, MAT). *Accreditation:* NCATE. *Program availability:* Part-time, evening/weekend. *Degree requirements:* For master's, comprehensive exam, thesis or alternative. *Entrance requirements:* For master's, GRE, minimum GPA of 3.0 in major, 2.5 overall. Additional exam requirements/recommendations for international students: Required—TOEFL. *Application deadline:* For fall admission, 8/1 for domestic students. Application fee: $30. *Expenses:* Tuition, state resident: full-time $2770; part-time $692.50 per credit hour. Tuition, nonresident: full-time $9247; part-time $2311.75 per credit hour. *Financial support:* Application deadline: 5/1; applicants required to submit FAFSA.

Special Education

North Carolina State University, Graduate School, College of Education, Department of Curriculum and Instruction, Program in Special Education, Raleigh, NC 27695. Offers M Ed, MS. *Accreditation:* NCATE. *Degree requirements:* For master's, thesis optional. *Entrance requirements:* For master's, GRE General Test and MAT, minimum GPA of 3.0 in major. Electronic applications accepted. *Faculty research:* Nature of disabilities, intervention research.

Northeastern Illinois University, College of Graduate Studies and Research, Daniel L. Goodwin College of Education, Program in Learning Behavior Specialist I, Chicago, IL 60625. Offers MA. *Entrance requirements:* For master's, bachelor's degree, minimum GPA of 2.75, two professional letters of recommendation. Electronic applications accepted. *Expenses:* Tuition, state resident: full-time $7274; part-time $404.11 per credit hour. Tuition, nonresident: full-time $14,548; part-time $808.23 per credit hour. *Required fees:* $1284. *Unit head:* Dr. Sandra Beyda-Lorie, Department Chair, 773-442-5583, E-mail: s-beyda@neiu.edu.

Northeastern Illinois University, College of Graduate Studies and Research, Daniel L. Goodwin College of Education, Program in Learning Behavior Specialist II, Chicago, IL 60625. Offers MS. *Entrance requirements:* For master's, Illinois Test of Basic Skills (or equivalent), bachelor's degree; minimum GPA of 2.75 undergraduate, 3.0 graduate; writing sample; interview. Electronic applications accepted. *Expenses:* Tuition, state resident: full-time $7274; part-time $404.11 per credit hour. Tuition, nonresident: full-time $14,548; part-time $808.23 per credit hour. *Required fees:* $1284. *Unit head:* Dr. Sandra Beyda-Lorie, Department Chair, 773-442-5583, E-mail: s-beyda@neiu.edu. *Application contact:* Martha Narvaez, Graduate Admission Representative, 773-442-6006, E-mail: m-narvaez@neiu.edu.

Northeastern State University, College of Education, Department of Curriculum and Instruction, Program in Special Education-Autism Spectrum Disorders, Tahlequah, OK 74464-2399. Offers M Ed. *Program availability:* Part-time. *Faculty:* 2 full-time (both women). *Students:* 6 full-time (5 women), 37 part-time (33 women); includes 16 minority (4 Black or African American, non-Hispanic/Latino; 6 American Indian or Alaska Native, non-Hispanic/Latino; 2 Asian, non-Hispanic/Latino; 1 Hispanic/Latino; 3 Two or more races, non-Hispanic/Latino), 1 international. Average age 37. In 2017, 8 master's awarded. *Degree requirements:* For master's, thesis. *Entrance requirements:* For master's, MAT or GRE. Additional exam requirements/recommendations for international students: Required—TOEFL. *Application deadline:* For fall admission, 6/1 priority date for domestic students. Applications are processed on a rolling basis. Application fee: $0 ($25 for international students). Electronic applications accepted. *Expenses:* Tuition, state resident: part-time $222 per credit hour. Tuition, nonresident: part-time $501.75 per credit hour. *Required fees:* $37.40 per credit hour. Tuition and fees vary according to degree level. *Financial support:* Teaching assistantships available. Financial award application deadline: 3/1. *Unit head:* Jarilyn Haney, Program Chair, 918-449-3786, E-mail: haneyjw@nsuok.edu. *Application contact:* Josh McCollum, Graduate Coordinator, 918-444-2093, E-mail: mccolluj@nsuok.edu.

Northeastern University, College of Professional Studies, Boston, MA 02115-5096. Offers applied nutrition (MS); college athletics administration (MSL); commerce and economic development (MS); corporate and organizational communication (MS); criminal justice (MS); digital media (MPS); elearning and instructional design (M Ed); elementary education (MAT); geographic information technology (MPS); global studies and international relations (MS); higher education administration (M Ed); homeland security (MA); human services (MS); informatics (MS); leadership (MS); learning analytics (M Ed); learning and instruction (M Ed); nonprofit management (MS); professional sports administration (MSL); project management (MS); regulatory affairs for drugs, biologics, and medical devices (MS); respiratory care leadership (MS); special education (M Ed); technical communication (MS). *Program availability:* Part-time, evening/weekend, 100% online, blended/hybrid learning. *Faculty:* 82 full-time (51 women), 853 part-time/adjunct (366 women). *Students:* 5,278 full-time (3,230 women). In 2017, 1,586 master's awarded. *Application deadline:* Applications are processed on a rolling basis. Application fee: $0. Electronic applications accepted. *Expenses:* Contact institution. *Financial support:* Applicants required to submit FAFSA. *Unit head:* Dr. Mary Loeffelholz, Dean of the College of Professional Studies. *Application contact:* E-mail: cpsadmissions@northeastern.edu.
Website: https://cps.northeastern.edu/

Northern Arizona University, College of Education, Department of Educational Specialties, Flagstaff, AZ 86011. Offers autism spectrum disorders (Certificate); bilingual/multicultural education (M Ed), including bilingual, ESL; career and technical education (M Ed, Certificate); educational technology (M Ed, Certificate); English as a second language (Certificate); positive behavior support (Certificate); special education (M Ed), including early childhood special education, mild/moderate disabilities. *Program availability:* Part-time, 100% online, blended/hybrid learning. *Faculty:* 31 full-time (19 women), 2 part-time/adjunct (1 woman). *Students:* 66 full-time (52 women), 203 part-time (147 women); includes 83 minority (20 Black or African American, non-Hispanic/Latino; 12 American Indian or Alaska Native, non-Hispanic/Latino; 5 Asian, non-Hispanic/Latino; 38 Hispanic/Latino; 3 Native Hawaiian or other Pacific Islander, non-Hispanic/Latino; 5 Two or more races, non-Hispanic/Latino), 6 international. Average age 37. 157 applicants, 94% accepted, 148 enrolled. In 2017, 119 master's, 26 Certificates awarded. *Degree requirements:* For master's, variable foreign language requirement, comprehensive exam (for some programs), thesis (for some programs); for Certificate, comprehensive exam (for some programs). *Entrance requirements:* Additional exam requirements/recommendations for international students: Required—TOEFL (minimum score 80 iBT), IELTS (minimum score 6.5). *Application deadline:* For fall admission, 3/1 for domestic and international students; for spring admission, 10/1 for domestic and international students. Applications are processed on a rolling basis. Application fee: $65. Electronic applications accepted. *Expenses:* Tuition, state resident: full-time $9240; part-time $458 per credit hour. Tuition, nonresident: full-time $21,588; part-time $1199 per credit hour. *Required fees:* $1021; $14 per credit hour. $646 per semester. Tuition and fees vary according to course load, campus/location and program. *Financial support:* In 2017–18, 11 students received support, including 1 fellowship with full and partial tuition reimbursement available (averaging $12,000 per year), 10 teaching assistantships with full and partial tuition reimbursements available (averaging $12,000 per year); Federal Work-Study, institutionally sponsored loans, health care benefits, tuition waivers (full and partial), and unspecified assistantships also available. Financial award application deadline: 2/1; financial award applicants required to submit FAFSA. *Unit head:* Dr. Shadow Armfield, Chair, 928-523-7651, Fax: 928-523-1929, E-mail: laura.sujo-montes@nau.edu. *Application contact:* Tina Sutton, Coordinator, Graduate College, 928-523-4348, Fax: 928-523-8950, E-mail: graduate@nau.edu.
Website: https://nau.edu/coe/Ed-Specialties/

Northern Illinois University, Graduate School, College of Education, Department of Special and Early Education, De Kalb, IL 60115-2854. Offers curriculum and instruction (MS Ed); early childhood education (MS Ed); elementary education (MS Ed); special education (MS Ed). *Program availability:* Part-time, evening/weekend. *Faculty:* 22 full-time (14 women), 2 part-time/adjunct (both women). *Students:* 40 full-time (33 women), 79 part-time (65 women); includes 16 minority (5 Black or African American, non-Hispanic/Latino; 3 Asian, non-Hispanic/Latino; 6 Hispanic/Latino; 2 Two or more races, non-Hispanic/Latino). Average age 32. 48 applicants, 83% accepted, 25 enrolled. In

2017, 58 master's awarded. *Degree requirements:* For master's, comprehensive exam, thesis optional. *Entrance requirements:* For master's, GRE General Test or MAT, minimum undergraduate GPA of 2.75. Additional exam requirements/recommendations for international students: Required—TOEFL (minimum score 550 paper-based). *Application deadline:* For fall admission, 6/1 for domestic students, 5/1 for international students; for spring admission, 11/1 for domestic students, 10/1 for international students. Applications are processed on a rolling basis. Application fee: $40. Electronic applications accepted. *Financial support:* In 2017–18, 17 research assistantships with full tuition reimbursements were awarded; fellowships with full tuition reimbursements, teaching assistantships with full tuition reimbursements, career-related internships or fieldwork, Federal Work-Study, scholarships/grants, tuition waivers (full), and unspecified assistantships also available. Support available to part-time students. Financial award applicants required to submit FAFSA. *Faculty research:* Teacher certification, stress reduction during student teaching, teaching history, portfolios in student teaching. *Unit head:* Gregory Conderman, Chair, 815-753-1619, E-mail: seed@niu.edu. *Application contact:* Gail Myers, Clerk, Graduate Advising, 815-753-0381, E-mail: gmyers@niu.edu.
Website: http://www.cedu.niu.edu/seed/

Northern Kentucky University, Office of Graduate Programs, College of Education and Human Services, Program in Teaching, Highland Heights, KY 41099. Offers education (Certificate); special education (Certificate); teaching (MAT). *Degree requirements:* For master's, comprehensive exam, thesis optional. *Entrance requirements:* For master's, GRE. Additional exam requirements/recommendations for international students: Required—TOEFL (minimum score 79 iBT); Recommended—IELTS (minimum score 6.5). Electronic applications accepted. *Faculty research:* Teacher education, classroom management.

Northern Michigan University, Office of Graduate Education and Research, College of Health Sciences and Professional Studies, School of Education, Leadership and Public Service, Marquette, MI 49855-5301. Offers administration and supervision (MAE); instruction (MAE); learning disabilities (MAE); postsecondary biology education (MS); reading education (MAE), including reading, reading specialist. *Accreditation:* TEAC. *Program availability:* Part-time, online learning. *Degree requirements:* For master's, thesis (for some programs). *Entrance requirements:* For master's, minimum GPA of 3.0. Additional exam requirements/recommendations for international students: Required—TOEFL (minimum score 550 paper-based; 79 iBT), IELTS (minimum score 6.5). *Application deadline:* For fall admission, 7/1 priority date for domestic students; for winter admission, 11/15 for domestic students; for spring admission, 3/17 for domestic students. Applications are processed on a rolling basis. Application fee: $50. Electronic applications accepted. *Expenses:* Tuition, state resident: full-time $9417; part-time $542 per credit hour. Tuition, nonresident: full-time $12,873; part-time $758 per credit hour. Tuition and fees vary according to course load, degree level and program. *Financial support:* Research assistantships with full tuition reimbursements, career-related internships or fieldwork, Federal Work-Study, institutionally sponsored loans, and unspecified assistantships available. Support available to part-time students. Financial award application deadline: 3/1; financial award applicants required to submit FAFSA. *Unit head:* Dr. Joseph Lubig, Associate Dean for Teacher Education, 906-227-1880, Fax: 906-227-2764, E-mail: jlubig@nmu.edu. *Application contact:* Dr. Joseph Lubig, Associate Dean for Teacher Education, 906-227-1880, Fax: 906-227-2764, E-mail: jlubig@nmu.edu.
Website: http://www.nmu.edu/education/

Northern Vermont University–Johnson, Program in Education, Johnson, VT 05656. Offers applied behavior analysis (MA Ed); curriculum and instruction (MA Ed); foundations of education (MA Ed); special education (MA Ed). *Program availability:* Part-time. *Faculty:* 5 full-time (3 women), 4 part-time/adjunct (3 women). *Students:* 3 full-time (all women), 36 part-time (30 women). In 2017, 23 master's awarded. *Degree requirements:* For master's, thesis or alternative, exit interview. *Entrance requirements:* For master's, interview. Additional exam requirements/recommendations for international students: Required—TOEFL. *Application deadline:* For fall admission, 5/1 for domestic students, 2/1 for international students. Applications are processed on a rolling basis. Electronic applications accepted. *Expenses:* Tuition, state resident: part-time $572 per credit hour. Tuition, nonresident: part-time $832 per credit hour. *Financial support:* Scholarships/grants and unspecified assistantships available. Financial award application deadline: 3/1; financial award applicants required to submit FAFSA. *Unit head:* Dr. Kathleen Brinegar, Chair, Department of Education, 802-635-1472, Fax: 802-635-1465, E-mail: kathleen.brinegar@jsc.edu. *Application contact:* Catherine H. Higley, Administrative Assistant, 800-635-2356 Ext. 1244, Fax: 802-635-1248, E-mail: catherine.higley@jsc.edu.
Website: http://www.jsc.edu/academics/education/majors-and-minors/master-of-arts-in-education/

Northern Vermont University–Lyndon, Graduate Programs in Education, Department of Education, Lyndonville, VT 05851. Offers curriculum and instruction (M Ed); reading specialist (M Ed); special education (M Ed); teaching and counseling (M Ed). *Program availability:* Part-time, evening/weekend. *Degree requirements:* For master's, exam or major field project. *Entrance requirements:* Additional exam requirements/recommendations for international students: Recommended—TOEFL (minimum score 500 paper-based).

Northwest Christian University, School of Education and Counseling, Eugene, OR 97401-3745. Offers clinical mental health counseling (MA); elementary teaching (MAT); English for speakers of other languages (MAT); physical education (MAT); school counseling (MA); secondary teaching (MAT); special education (MAT). *Program availability:* Part-time, evening/weekend, online learning. *Faculty:* 9 full-time (4 women), 14 part-time/adjunct (10 women). *Students:* 77 full-time (60 women), 44 part-time (30 women); includes 19 minority (4 Black or African American, non-Hispanic/Latino; 1 American Indian or Alaska Native, non-Hispanic/Latino; 3 Asian, non-Hispanic/Latino; 2 Hispanic/Latino; 1 Native Hawaiian or other Pacific Islander, non-Hispanic/Latino; 8 Two or more races, non-Hispanic/Latino). Average age 34. In 2017, 58 master's awarded. *Degree requirements:* For master's, thesis (for some programs). *Entrance requirements:* For master's, GRE or MAT, minimum undergraduate GPA of 3.0, interview, 2-3 page statement of purpose, two letters of recommendation, resume, background check. Additional exam requirements/recommendations for international students: Required—TOEFL (minimum score 550 paper-based; 80 iBT). *Application deadline:* Applications are processed on a rolling basis. Electronic applications accepted. *Expenses:* $640 to $660 per credit tuition, $90 per semester technology fee. *Financial support:* Applicants required to submit FAFSA. *Unit head:* Elizabeth Wosley-George, Director, 541-349-7465, Fax: 541-684-7310, E-mail: ewosleygeorge@nwcu.edu. *Application contact:* Billy Dorsch, Admission Counselor for Graduate Studies, 541-684-7279, Fax: 541-349-5281, E-mail: wdorsch@nwcu.edu.

Northwestern State University of Louisiana, Graduate Studies and Research, College of Education and Human Development, Program in Special Education, Natchitoches, LA 71497. Offers M Ed, MAT. *Degree requirements:* For master's, comprehensive exam, thesis (for some programs). *Entrance requirements:* For master's, GRE General Test. Additional exam requirements/recommendations for international students: Required—TOEFL. Electronic applications accepted.

Northwestern State University of Louisiana, Graduate Studies and Research, College of Education and Human Development, Programs in Educational Leadership and Instruction, Natchitoches, LA 71497. Offers counseling (Ed S); educational leadership (M Ed, Ed S); educational technology (Ed S); elementary teaching (Ed S); reading (Ed S); secondary teaching (Ed S); special education (Ed S). *Accreditation:* NASAD. *Degree requirements:* For master's, comprehensive exam, thesis (for some programs). *Entrance requirements:* For master's and Ed S, GRE General Test. Additional exam requirements/recommendations for international students: Required—TOEFL. Electronic applications accepted.

Northwest Missouri State University, Graduate School, School of Education, Maryville, MO 64468-6001. Offers early childhood education (MS Ed); education leadership (MS Ed), including elementary, K-12, secondary; educational leadership (Ed S), including elementary school principalship, secondary school principalship, superintendency; educational leadership and policy analysis (Ed D); elementary education (MS Ed); elementary mathematics (MS Ed); higher education leadership (MS); middle school education (MS Ed); reading (MS Ed); special education (MS Ed); teacher leadership (MS Ed); teaching English language learners (MS Ed). *Accreditation:* NCATE. *Program availability:* Part-time. *Faculty:* 15 full-time (8 women). *Students:* 28 full-time (20 women), 170 part-time (114 women); includes 20 minority (7 Black or African American, non-Hispanic/Latino; 1 Asian, non-Hispanic/Latino; 8 Hispanic/Latino; 4 Two or more races, non-Hispanic/Latino). Average age 33. 168 applicants, 73% accepted, 114 enrolled. In 2017, 67 master's, 21 other advanced degrees awarded. *Degree requirements:* For master's, comprehensive exam; for Ed S, comprehensive exam, thesis. *Entrance requirements:* For master's, GRE General Test, writing sample; for Ed S, minimum graduate GPA of 3.25. Additional exam requirements/recommendations for international students: Required—TOEFL (minimum score 550 paper-based). *Application deadline:* For fall admission, 7/1 for domestic and international students; for spring admission, 11/15 for domestic and international students. Applications are processed on a rolling basis. Application fee: $0 ($50 for international students). Electronic applications accepted. *Expenses:* $389.11 per credit hour in-state tuition and fees, $641.97 out-of-state; $9,750 total cost (for online-based education program). *Financial support:* Research assistantships with full tuition reimbursements, teaching assistantships with full tuition reimbursements, and unspecified assistantships available. Financial award application deadline: 4/1; financial award applicants required to submit FAFSA. *Unit head:* Dr. Tim Wall, Director, 660-562-1179, E-mail: timwall@nwmissouri.edu.
Website: https://www.nwmissouri.edu/education/index.htm

Northwest Nazarene University, Graduate Education Program, Nampa, ID 83686-5897. Offers curriculum and instruction (M Ed); educational leadership (M Ed, Ed D, PhD, Ed S), including building administrator (M Ed, Ed S), director of special education (Ed S), leadership and organizational development (Ed S), superintendent (Ed S). *Accreditation:* ACA (one or more programs are accredited); NCATE. *Program availability:* Part-time, online only, 100% online, 2-week face-to-face residency (for doctoral programs). *Students:* Average age 39. 96 applicants, 72% accepted, 67 enrolled. In 2017, 59 master's, 13 doctorates, 33 other advanced degrees awarded. *Degree requirements:* For master's, comprehensive exam (for some programs), action research project; for doctorate, thesis/dissertation; for Ed S, comprehensive exam, research project. *Entrance requirements:* For master's, minimum undergraduate GPA of 3.0 overall or during final 30 semester credits, undergraduate degree, valid teaching certificate; for doctorate, Ed S or equivalent, minimum GPA of 3.5; for Ed S, undergraduate degree, valid teaching certificate. Additional exam requirements/recommendations for international students: Recommended—TOEFL. *Application deadline:* Applications are processed on a rolling basis. Application fee: $50. Electronic applications accepted. *Expenses:* Contact institution. *Financial support:* Research assistantships available. Financial award application deadline: 1/15; financial award applicants required to submit FAFSA. *Faculty research:* Action research, cooperative learning, accountability, institutional accreditation. *Unit head:* Dr. Heidi Curtis, Chair, 208-467-8250, E-mail: hlcurtis@nnu.edu. *Application contact:* Charlene Brown, Admissions Counselor, 208-467-8492, Fax: 208-467-8384, E-mail: gradeducationinfo@nnu.edu.
Website: http://www.nnu.edu/graded/

Notre Dame College, Graduate Programs, South Euclid, OH 44121-4293. Offers mild/moderate needs (M Ed); reading (M Ed); security policy studies (MA, Graduate Certificate); technology (M Ed). *Program availability:* Part-time, evening/weekend. *Degree requirements:* For master's, thesis. *Entrance requirements:* For master's, GRE General Test, MAT, minimum undergraduate GPA of 2.75, valid teaching certificate, bachelor's degree in an education-related field from accredited college or university, official transcripts of most recent college work. *Faculty research:* Cognitive psychology, teaching critical thinking in the classroom.

Notre Dame de Namur University, Division of Academic Affairs, School of Education and Psychology, Program in Special Education, Belmont, CA 94002-1908. Offers MA. *Program availability:* Part-time, evening/weekend. *Students:* 15 full-time (all women), 18 part-time (9 women). Average age 32. *Degree requirements:* For master's, thesis optional, capstone course. *Entrance requirements:* For master's, interview, minimum GPA of 2.5. Additional exam requirements/recommendations for international students: Required—TOEFL (minimum score 550 paper-based; 79 iBT). *Application deadline:* For fall admission, 8/1 priority date for domestic students; for spring admission, 12/1 priority date for domestic students. Applications are processed on a rolling basis. Application fee: $60. Electronic applications accepted. *Expenses:* Tuition: Full-time $16,128; part-time $8064 per credit hour. *Required fees:* $80; $80 per credit hour. $40 per semester. *Financial support:* Career-related internships or fieldwork available. Support available to part-time students. Financial award applicants required to submit FAFSA. *Unit head:* Sungho Park, Program Director, Special Education, 650-508-3762, E-mail: spark1@ndnu.edu.

Nyack College, School of Education, Nyack, NY 10960. Offers childhood education (MS); childhood special education (MS); TESOL (MAT, MS). *Program availability:* Part-time, evening/weekend, 100% online, blended/hybrid learning. *Students:* 22 full-time (20 women), 27 part-time (23 women); includes 23 minority (10 Black or African American, non-Hispanic/Latino; 1 American Indian or Alaska Native, non-Hispanic/Latino; 1 Asian, non-Hispanic/Latino; 10 Hispanic/Latino; 1 Two or more races, non-Hispanic/Latino), 2 international. Average age 34. In 2017, 25 master's awarded. *Degree requirements:* For master's, comprehensive exam, clinical experience. *Entrance requirements:* For master's, GRE, transcripts, autobiography and statement on reasons for pursuing graduate study in education, recommendations, 6 credits of language, evidence of computer literacy, introductory course in psychology. Additional exam requirements/recommendations for international students: Required—TOEFL (minimum score 550 paper-based; 80 iBT), GRE. *Application deadline:* Applications are processed on a rolling basis. Application fee: $30. Electronic applications accepted. *Expenses:* $725 per credit. *Financial support:* Scholarships/grants available. Financial award applicants required to submit FAFSA. *Unit head:* Dr. JoAnn Looney, Dean, 845-675-4538. *Application contact:* Emma Chery, Admissions Associate, 845-770-5708, E-mail: admissions.grad@nyack.edu.
Website: http://www.nyack.edu/edu

Oakland University, Graduate Study and Lifelong Learning, School of Education and Human Services, Department of Human Development and Child Studies, Program in Special Education, Rochester, MI 48309-4401. Offers applied behavior analysis (Graduate Certificate); autism spectrum disorder (Graduate Certificate); emotional impairment (Graduate Certificate); special education (M Ed), including applied behavior analysis, autism spectrum disorder, emotional impairment, specific learning disabilities; specific learning disabilities (Graduate Certificate). *Accreditation:* TEAC. *Entrance requirements:* For master's, minimum GPA of 3.0, interview. Additional exam requirements/recommendations for international students: Required—TOEFL (minimum score 550 paper-based). Electronic applications accepted. *Expenses:* Tuition, state resident: full-time $16,950; part-time $706.25 per credit. Tuition, nonresident: full-time $24,648; part-time $1027 per credit.

The Ohio State University, Graduate School, College of Arts and Sciences, Division of Social and Behavioral Sciences, Department of Psychology, Columbus, OH 43210. Offers behavioral neuroscience (PhD); clinical psychology (PhD); cognitive psychology (PhD); developmental psychology (PhD); intellectual and developmental disabilities psychology (PhD); quantitative psychology (PhD); social psychology (PhD). *Accreditation:* APA. *Faculty:* 52. *Students:* 144 full-time (86 women); includes 18 minority (8 Asian, non-Hispanic/Latino; 10 Hispanic/Latino), 28 international. Average age 26. In 2017, 21 doctorates awarded. *Entrance requirements:* For doctorate, GRE General Test. Additional exam requirements/recommendations for international students: Required—TOEFL (minimum score 600 paper-based; 100 iBT); Recommended—IELTS (minimum score 8). *Application deadline:* For fall admission, 12/1 for domestic and international students. Applications are processed on a rolling basis. Application fee: $60 ($70 for international students). Electronic applications accepted. *Financial support:* Fellowships, research assistantships, and teaching assistantships available. *Unit head:* Dr. John Bruno, Chair, 614-292-3038, E-mail: bruno.1@osu.edu. *Application contact:* Graduate and Professional Admissions, 614-292-9444, Fax: 614-292-3895, E-mail: gpadmissions@osu.edu.
Website: http://psychology.osu.edu/

Ohio University, Graduate College, Gladys W. and David H. Patton College of Education and Human Services, Department of Teacher Education, Athens, OH 45701-2979. Offers adolescent to young adult education (M Ed); curriculum and instruction (M Ed, PhD); early childhood/special education (M Ed); intervention specialist/mild-moderate needs (M Ed); intervention specialist/moderate-intensive needs (M Ed); middle childhood education (M Ed); reading education (M Ed). *Program availability:* Part-time, evening/weekend. *Degree requirements:* For master's, thesis or alternative; for doctorate, comprehensive exam, thesis/dissertation. *Entrance requirements:* For master's, GRE General Test or MAT (if GPA is below 2.9); for doctorate, GRE General Test, minimum GPA of 3.4, work experience. Additional exam requirements/recommendations for international students: Required—TOEFL (minimum score 550 paper-based; 80 iBT) or IELTS (minimum score 6.5). Electronic applications accepted. *Faculty research:* Cognition literacy, character education, teacher's education reform, disabilities.

Old Dominion University, Darden College of Education, Program in Special Education, Norfolk, VA 23529. Offers adapted curriculum K-12 (MS Ed); early childhood special education (MS Ed); general curriculum K-12 (MS Ed); special education (PhD). *Accreditation:* NCATE. *Program availability:* Part-time, evening/weekend, 100% online, blended/hybrid learning. *Faculty:* 13 full-time (10 women), 10 part-time/adjunct (7 women). *Students:* 39 full-time (35 women), 67 part-time (57 women); includes 30 minority (17 Black or African American, non-Hispanic/Latino; 4 Asian, non-Hispanic/Latino; 4 Hispanic/Latino; 5 Two or more races, non-Hispanic/Latino), 7 international. Average age 33. 65 applicants, 40% accepted, 26 enrolled. In 2017, 24 master's, 1 doctorate awarded. *Degree requirements:* For master's, comprehensive exam, thesis or alternative, VCLA; for doctorate, comprehensive exam, thesis/dissertation. *Entrance requirements:* For master's, GRE General Test or MAT, PRAXIS Core Academic Skills for Educator Tests, minimum GPA of 2.8; for doctorate, GRE General Test or MAT. Additional exam requirements/recommendations for international students: Recommended—TOEFL (minimum score 550 paper-based). *Application deadline:* For fall admission, 6/1 priority date for domestic and international students; for winter admission, 11/1 priority date for domestic and international students; for spring admission, 3/1 priority date for domestic and international students. Applications are processed on a rolling basis. Application fee: $55. Electronic applications accepted. Application fee is waived when completed online. *Expenses:* $45,000 (for MS Ed); $90,000 (for PhD). *Financial support:* In 2017–18, 50 students received support, including 1 research assistantship (averaging $5,000 per year), 3 teaching assistantships with full tuition reimbursements available (averaging $15,000 per year); fellowships, scholarships/grants, and unspecified assistantships also available. Support available to part-time students. Financial award application deadline: 2/15; financial award applicants required to submit FAFSA. *Faculty research:* Inclusion, autism spectrum disorder, functional behavioral assessment, infant, preschool, and school-age children and youth with disabilities, distance learning. *Total annual research expenditures:* $3.6 million. *Unit head:* Dr. Sabra Gear, Graduate Program Director, 757-683-4383, Fax: 757-683-4129, E-mail: sgear@odu.edu. *Application contact:* William Heffelfinger, Director of Graduate Admissions, 757-683-5554, Fax: 757-683-3255, E-mail: gradadmit@odu.edu.
Website: https://www.odu.edu/cdse/academics/sped

Ottawa University, Graduate Studies-Arizona, Program in Education, Ottawa, KS 66067-3399. Offers community college counseling (MA); curriculum and instruction (MA); early childhood (MA); education intervention (MA); education leadership (MA); education technology (MA); Montessori early childhood education (MA); Montessori elementary education (MA); professional development (MA); school guidance counseling (MA); special education - cross categorical (MA). Programs offered in Mesa, Phoenix, Tempe and West Valley, AZ. *Accreditation:* NCATE. *Program availability:* Part-time. *Degree requirements:* For master's, thesis or alternative. *Entrance requirements:* For master's, minimum undergraduate GPA of 3.0, copy of current state certification or teaching license. Additional exam requirements/recommendations for international students: Required—TOEFL (minimum score 550 paper-based). Electronic applications accepted. *Expenses:* Contact institution.

Pace University, School of Education, New York, NY 10038. Offers adolescent education (MST), including biology, chemistry, earth science, English, foreign languages, mathematics, physics, social studies; childhood education (MST); early childhood development, learning and intervention (MST); educational technology studies (MS); inclusive adolescent education (MST), including biology, chemistry, earth science, English, foreign languages, mathematics, physics, social studies; integrated instruction for educational technology (Certificate); integrated instruction for literacy and technology (Certificate); literacy (MS Ed); special education (MS Ed). *Accreditation:* NCATE. *Program availability:* Part-time, evening/weekend, 100% online, blended/hybrid learning. *Faculty:* 19 full-time (13 women), 86 part-time/adjunct (49 women). *Students:* 91 full-time (76 women), 548 part-time (401 women); includes 247 minority (112 Black or African American, non-Hispanic/Latino; 2 American Indian or Alaska Native, non-Hispanic/Latino; 31 Asian, non-Hispanic/Latino; 93 Hispanic/Latino; 1 Native Hawaiian or other Pacific Islander, non-Hispanic/Latino; 8 Two or more races, non-Hispanic/

Special Education

Latino), 6 international. Average age 30. 188 applicants, 86% accepted, 114 enrolled. In 2017, 213 master's, 8 other advanced degrees awarded. *Degree requirements:* For master's and Certificate, certification exams. *Entrance requirements:* For master's, GRE (for initial certification programs only), teaching certificate (for MS Ed in literacy and special education programs only). Additional exam requirements/recommendations for international students: Required—TOEFL (minimum score 88 iBT), IELTS or PTE. *Application deadline:* For fall admission, 8/1 priority date for domestic students, 6/1 for international students; for spring admission, 12/1 priority date for domestic students, 10/1 for international students. Applications are processed on a rolling basis. Application fee: $70. Electronic applications accepted. *Expenses:* Contact institution. *Financial support:* In 2017–18, 17 students received support, including 17 research assistantships with partial tuition reimbursements available (averaging $6,020 per year); career-related internships or fieldwork, Federal Work-Study, scholarships/grants, and unspecified assistantships also available. Financial award application deadline: 9/1; financial award applicants required to submit FAFSA. *Faculty research:* STEM education, TESOL, teacher education, special education, language and literary development. *Total annual research expenditures:* $29,706. *Unit head:* Dr. Xiao-Lei Wang, Dean, School of Education, 914-773-3876, E-mail: xwang@pace.edu. *Application contact:* Susan Ford-Goldschein, Director of Graduate Admissions, 212-346-1531, Fax: 212-346-1585, E-mail: graduateadmission@pace.edu. Website: http://www.pace.edu/school-of-education

Pacific Oaks College, Graduate School, Program in Education, Pasadena, CA 91103. Offers preliminary education specialist (MA); preliminary multiple subject (MA). *Program availability:* Online learning. *Degree requirements:* For master's, practicum. *Entrance requirements:* For master's, bachelor's degree from accredited college or university.

Pacific University, College of Education, Forest Grove, OR 97116-1797. Offers early childhood education (MAT); education (MAE); elementary education (MAT); ESOL (MAT); high school education (MAT); middle school education (MAT); special education (MAT); speech-language pathology (MS); STEM education (MAT); talented and gifted (M Ed); visual function in learning (M Ed). *Accreditation:* ASHA; NCATE. *Program availability:* Part-time, evening/weekend. *Degree requirements:* For master's, research project. *Entrance requirements:* For master's, California Basic Educational Skills Test, PRAXIS II, minimum undergraduate GPA of 2.75, 3.0 graduate. Additional exam requirements/recommendations for international students: Required—TOEFL. Electronic applications accepted. *Expenses:* Contact institution. *Faculty research:* Defining a culturally competent classroom, technology in the K-12 classroom, Socratic seminars, social studies education.

Penn State University Park, Graduate School, College of Education, Department of Educational Psychology, Counseling, and Special Education, University Park, PA 16802. Offers counselor education (M Ed, D Ed, PhD, Certificate); educational psychology (MS, PhD, Certificate); school psychology (M Ed, MS, PhD, Certificate); special education (M Ed, MS, PhD). *Unit head:* Dr. David H. Monk, Dean, 814-865-2523, Fax: 814-865-0555. *Application contact:* Lori Hawn, Director, Graduate Student Services, 814-865-1795, Fax: 814-863-4627, E-mail: l-gswww@lists.psu.edu. Website: http://ed.psu.edu/epcse

Piedmont College, School of Education, Demorest, GA 30535. Offers art education (MA, MAT); curriculum and instruction (Ed D, Ed S); early childhood education (MA, MAT); instructional technology (MA); middle grades education (MA, MAT); music education (MA, MAT); secondary education (MA, MAT); special education (MA, MAT). *Program availability:* Part-time, evening/weekend. *Students:* 341 full-time (268 women), 682 part-time (571 women); includes 182 minority (136 Black or African American, non-Hispanic/Latino; 2 American Indian or Alaska Native, non-Hispanic/Latino; 11 Asian, non-Hispanic/Latino; 32 Hispanic/Latino; 1 Two or more races, non-Hispanic/Latino). Average age 37. 333 applicants, 77% accepted, 103 enrolled. In 2017, 292 master's, 9 doctorates, 318 other advanced degrees awarded. *Degree requirements:* For master's, thesis, field experience in the classroom teaching; for doctorate, thesis/dissertation. *Entrance requirements:* For master's, GRE General Test, MAT; for Ed S, minimum graduate GPA of 3.5, valid teaching certificate. Additional exam requirements/recommendations for international students: Required—TOEFL (minimum score 550 paper-based). *Application deadline:* For fall admission, 7/15 for domestic students; for spring admission, 12/1 for domestic students. Applications are processed on a rolling basis. Electronic applications accepted. *Expenses:* Tuition: Full-time $9360; part-time $520 per credit hour. *Required fees:* $200; $200 per year. $100 per term. *Financial support:* Career-related internships or fieldwork, Federal Work-Study, and unspecified assistantships available. Support available to part-time students. Financial award applicants required to submit FAFSA. *Unit head:* Dr. Don Gnecco, Dean, 706-778-3000 Ext. 1201, Fax: 706-776-9608, E-mail: dgnecco@piedmont.edu. *Application contact:* Kathleen Carter, Director of Graduate Enrollment Management, 706-778-8500 Ext. 1181, Fax: 706-778-0150, E-mail: kanderson@piedmont.edu.

Pittsburg State University, Graduate School, College of Education, Department of Teaching and Leadership, Advanced Studies in Leadership Program, Pittsburg, KS 66762. Offers advanced studies in leadership (Ed S), including general school administration, special education. *Program availability:* Part-time, online only, 100% online. *Students:* 87. In 2017, 11 Ed Ss awarded. *Degree requirements:* For Ed S, thesis optional. *Entrance requirements:* Additional exam requirements/recommendations for international students: Required—TOEFL (minimum score 520 paper-based; 68 iBT), IELTS (minimum score 6), PTE (minimum score 47). *Application deadline:* For fall admission, 6/1 for international students; for spring admission, 10/15 for international students; for summer admission, 4/1 for international students. Applications are processed on a rolling basis. Application fee: $35 ($65 for international students). Electronic applications accepted. *Expenses:* Contact institution. *Financial support:* Application deadline: 2/1; applicants required to submit FAFSA. *Unit head:* Dr. Brenda Roberts, Program Coordinator, 620-235-4498, Fax: 620-235-4520, E-mail: broberts@pittstate.edu. *Application contact:* Lisa Allen, Assistant Director of Graduate and Continuing Studies, 620-235-4218, Fax: 620-235-4219, E-mail: lallen@pittstate.edu.

Pittsburg State University, Graduate School, College of Education, Department of Teaching and Leadership, Program in Special Education, Pittsburg, KS 66762. Offers MAT, MS. *Accreditation:* NCATE. *Program availability:* Part-time, online only, 100% online. *Students:* 95. In 2017, 32 master's awarded. Terminal master's awarded for partial completion of doctoral program. *Degree requirements:* For master's, thesis or alternative. *Entrance requirements:* For master's, PPST. Additional exam requirements/recommendations for international students: Required—TOEFL (minimum score 520 paper-based; 68 iBT), IELTS (minimum score 6), PTE (minimum score 47). *Application deadline:* For fall admission, 7/15 for domestic students, 6/1 for international students; for spring admission, 12/15 for domestic students, 10/15 for international students; for summer admission, 5/15 for domestic students, 4/1 for international students. Applications are processed on a rolling basis. Application fee: $35 ($60 for international students). Electronic applications accepted. *Expenses:* Contact institution. *Financial support:* In 2017–18, teaching assistantships (averaging $5,000 per year) were awarded; career-related internships or fieldwork, Federal Work-Study, and unspecified assistantships also available. Financial award application deadline: 2/1; financial award applicants required to submit FAFSA. *Unit head:* Dr. Brian Sims, Program Coordinator, 620-235-6090, Fax: 620-235-4498, E-mail: bsims@pittstate.edu. *Application contact:*

Lisa Allen, Assistant Director of Graduate and Continuing Studies, 620-235-4218, Fax: 620-235-4219, E-mail: lallen@pittstate.edu.

Plymouth State University, College of Graduate Studies, Graduate Studies in Education, Program in Secondary Education, Plymouth, NH 03264-1595. Offers curriculum and instruction (M Ed); language education (M Ed); library media (M Ed); physical education (M Ed); social studies education (M Ed); special education (M Ed). *Program availability:* Part-time, evening/weekend. *Entrance requirements:* For master's, MAT.

Point Loma Nazarene University, School of Education, Program in Special Education, San Diego, CA 92106-2899. Offers MA. *Program availability:* Part-time, evening/weekend. *Students:* 8 full-time (all women), 38 part-time (30 women); includes 19 minority (1 Black or African American, non-Hispanic/Latino; 2 Asian, non-Hispanic/Latino; 15 Hispanic/Latino; 1 Two or more races, non-Hispanic/Latino). Average age 35. 3 applicants, 100% accepted. In 2017, 30 master's awarded. *Entrance requirements:* For master's, letters of recommendation, essay, interview. Additional exam requirements/recommendations for international students: Required—TOEFL. *Application deadline:* For fall admission, 8/4 priority date for domestic students; for spring admission, 12/8 priority date for domestic students; for summer admission, 4/13 priority date for domestic students. Applications are processed on a rolling basis. Application fee: $50. Electronic applications accepted. *Expenses:* Contact institution. *Financial support:* Career-related internships or fieldwork and scholarships/grants available. Support available to part-time students. Financial award applicants required to submit FAFSA. *Faculty research:* Co-teaching, inclusion, teacher preparation, intern teacher support. *Unit head:* Dr. Shirlee Gibbs, Special Education Coordinator, 619-849-2852, E-mail: shirleegibbs@pointloma.edu. *Application contact:* Joanie Joy, Senior Director of Enrollment Management, 619-329-6785, E-mail: gradinfo@pointloma.edu. Website: https://www.pointloma.edu/schools-departments-colleges/school-education

Point Park University, School of Arts and Sciences, Department of Education, Pittsburgh, PA 15222-1984. Offers adult learning and training (MA); athletic coaching (M Ed); curriculum and instruction (MA); educational administration (MA); leadership and administration (Ed D); secondary education (M Ed); special education grades 7-12 (M Ed); special education PreK-grade 8 (M Ed). *Program availability:* Part-time, evening/weekend, 100% online, blended/hybrid learning. *Degree requirements:* For master's, comprehensive exam (for some programs), thesis or alternative. *Entrance requirements:* For master's, minimum GPA of 3.0, resume, 2 letters of recommendation. Additional exam requirements/recommendations for international students: Required—TOEFL. Electronic applications accepted.

Prescott College, Graduate Programs, Program in Education, Prescott, AZ 86301. Offers early childhood education (MA); early childhood special education (MA); education (MA); elementary education (MA); environmental education leadership and administration (MA); equine-assisted learning (MA); school guidance counseling (MA); secondary education (MA); special education: learning disabilities (MA); special education: mental retardation (MA); special education: serious emotional disabilities (MA); student-directed independent study (MA); sustainability education (PhD). *Program availability:* Part-time, online learning. *Degree requirements:* For master's, thesis, fieldwork or internship, practicum; for doctorate, thesis/dissertation. *Entrance requirements:* For master's, 2 letters of recommendation, resume; for doctorate, 3 letters of recommendation, resume, official transcripts, personal statement, program proposal. Additional exam requirements/recommendations for international students: Required—TOEFL (minimum score 500 paper-based). Electronic applications accepted.

Providence College, Program in Special Education, Providence, RI 02918. Offers special education (M Ed), including elementary teaching, secondary teaching. *Program availability:* Part-time, evening/weekend. *Degree requirements:* For master's, comprehensive exam, portfolio. *Entrance requirements:* Additional exam requirements/recommendations for international students: Required—TOEFL (minimum score 577 paper-based; 90 iBT).

Purdue University, Graduate School, College of Education, Department of Educational Studies, West Lafayette, IN 47907. Offers administration (MS Ed, PhD, Ed S); counseling and development (MS Ed, PhD); education of the gifted (MS Ed); educational psychology (MS Ed, PhD); foundations of education (MS Ed, PhD); higher education administration (MS Ed, PhD); special education (MS Ed, PhD). *Accreditation:* ACA (one or more programs are accredited); NCATE (one or more programs are accredited). *Program availability:* Part-time, evening/weekend. *Faculty:* 29 full-time (22 women), 1 part-time/adjunct (0 women). *Students:* 78 full-time (60 women), 226 part-time (162 women); includes 45 minority (16 Black or African American, non-Hispanic/Latino; 8 Asian, non-Hispanic/Latino; 15 Hispanic/Latino; 6 Two or more races, non-Hispanic/Latino), 45 international. Average age 32. 214 applicants, 53% accepted, 70 enrolled. In 2017, 38 master's, 20 doctorates, 4 other advanced degrees awarded. *Degree requirements:* For master's, thesis optional; for doctorate, thesis/dissertation, oral and written exams; for Ed S, oral presentation, project. *Entrance requirements:* For master's, GRE General Test (except for special education if undergraduate GPA is higher than a 3.0), minimum undergraduate GPA of 3.0; for doctorate and Ed S, GRE General Test (minimum combined score of 1000, 300 for new scoring), minimum undergraduate GPA of 3.0. Additional exam requirements/recommendations for international students: Required—TOEFL (minimum score 550 paper-based; 77 iBT), TWE (minimum score 5). *Application deadline:* Applications are processed on a rolling basis. Application fee: $60 ($75 for international students). Electronic applications accepted. *Financial support:* Fellowships with full tuition reimbursements, research assistantships with full tuition reimbursements, teaching assistantships with full tuition reimbursements, career-related internships or fieldwork, and tuition waivers (full) available. Support available to part-time students. Financial award application deadline: 3/1; financial award applicants required to submit FAFSA. *Faculty research:* Motivation, learning disabilities, school learning, group processes, cognitive development. *Unit head:* F. Richard Olenchak, Head, 765-494-9170, E-mail: olenchak@purdue.edu. *Application contact:* Heather Brinkman, Graduate Contact, 765-494-2345, Fax: 765-494-5832, E-mail: hbrinkma@purdue.edu. Website: http://www.edst.purdue.edu/

Purdue University Global, School of Teacher Education, Davenport, IA 52807. Offers education (M Ed); secondary education (M Ed); teaching and learning (MA); teaching literacy and language: grades 6-12 (MA); teaching literacy and language: grades K-6 (MA); teaching mathematics: grades 6-8 (MA); teaching mathematics: grades 9-12 (MA); teaching mathematics: grades K-5 (MA); teaching science: grades 6-12 (MA); teaching science: grades K-6 (MA); teaching students with special needs (MA); teaching with technology (MA). *Program availability:* Part-time, evening/weekend, online learning. *Entrance requirements:* Additional exam requirements/recommendations for international students: Required—TOEFL (minimum score 500 paper-based; 80 iBT).

Purdue University Northwest, Graduate Studies Office, School of Education, Program in Special Education, Hammond, IN 46323-2094. Offers MS Ed.

Queens College of the City University of New York, Division of Education, Department of Educational and Community Programs, Queens, NY 11367-1597. Offers bilingual pupil personnel (AC); counselor education (MS Ed); mental health counseling (MS); school building leader (AC); school district leader (AC); school psychologist

(MS Ed); special education-childhood education (AC); special education-early childhood (MS Ed); teacher of special education 1-6 (MS Ed); teacher of special education birth-2 (MS Ed); teaching students with disabilities, grades 7-12 (MS Ed, AC). *Program availability:* Part-time. *Faculty:* 20 full-time (14 women), 63 part-time/adjunct (37 women). *Students:* 105 full-time (94 women), 423 part-time (350 women); includes 241 minority (40 Black or African American, non-Hispanic/Latino; 2 American Indian or Alaska Native, non-Hispanic/Latino; 50 Asian, non-Hispanic/Latino; 142 Hispanic/Latino; 1 Native Hawaiian or other Pacific Islander, non-Hispanic/Latino; 6 Two or more races, non-Hispanic/Latino), 5 international. Average age 28. 515 applicants, 57% accepted, 230 enrolled. In 2017, 163 master's, 74 other advanced degrees awarded. *Degree requirements:* For master's, research project; for AC, internship. *Entrance requirements:* For master's, minimum GPA of 3.0. Additional exam requirements/recommendations for international students: Required—TOEFL, IELTS. *Application deadline:* For fall admission, 3/1 for domestic students. Applications are processed on a rolling basis. Application fee: $125. Electronic applications accepted. *Financial support:* Career-related internships or fieldwork available. Financial award application deadline: 4/1; financial award applicants required to submit FAFSA. *Unit head:* Dr. Emilia Lopez, Chair, 718-997-5250, E-mail: emilia.lopez@qc.cuny.edu. *Application contact:* Elizabeth D'Amico-Ramirez, Assistant Director of Graduate Admissions, 718-997-5203, E-mail: elizabeth.damicoramirez@qc.cuny.edu.

Radford University, College of Graduate Studies and Research, Program in Special Education, Radford, VA 24142. Offers MS, Certificate. *Accreditation:* NCATE. *Program availability:* Part-time, evening/weekend. *Faculty:* 9 full-time (7 women), 10 part-time/adjunct (9 women). *Students:* 26 full-time (20 women), 74 part-time (67 women); includes 17 minority (8 Black or African American, non-Hispanic/Latino; 5 Hispanic/Latino; 4 Two or more races, non-Hispanic/Latino). Average age 33. 48 applicants, 100% accepted, 41 enrolled. In 2017, 41 master's awarded. *Degree requirements:* For master's, comprehensive exam. *Entrance requirements:* For master's, minimum GPA of 2.75, 3 letters of reference, resume, personal essay, official transcripts. Additional exam requirements/recommendations for international students: Required—TOEFL (minimum score 550 paper-based; 79 iBT), IELTS (minimum score 6.5). *Application deadline:* For fall admission, 4/1 priority date for domestic students, 12/1 for international students; for spring admission, 11/1 priority date for domestic students, 7/1 for international students. Applications are processed on a rolling basis. Application fee: $50. Electronic applications accepted. *Expenses:* Tuition, state resident: full-time $8336; part-time $347 per credit hour. Tuition, nonresident: full-time $16,862; part-time $702 per credit hour. *Required fees:* $3220; $135 per credit hour. Tuition and fees vary according to course load and program. *Financial support:* In 2017–18, 4 students received support, including 1 research assistantship (averaging $5,000 per year), 3 teaching assistantships (averaging $7,000 per year); career-related internships or fieldwork, scholarships/grants, and unspecified assistantships also available. Support available to part-time students. Financial award application deadline: 3/1; financial award applicants required to submit FAFSA. *Unit head:* Dr. Elizabeth Altieri, Special Education Graduate Program Coordinator, 540-831-5590, E-mail: ealtieri@radford.edu. Website: http://www.radford.edu/content/cehd/home/teacher-ed/programs/special-educationms.html

Ramapo College of New Jersey, Master of Arts in Special Education Program, Mahwah, NJ 07430-1680. Offers MA. *Program availability:* Part-time, evening/weekend. *Faculty:* 2 full-time (both women), 3 part-time/adjunct (1 woman). *Students:* 44 part-time (40 women); includes 4 minority (3 Hispanic/Latino; 1 Two or more races, non-Hispanic/Latino). Average age 28. 43 applicants, 70% accepted, 25 enrolled. In 2017, 18 master's awarded. *Degree requirements:* For master's, thesis, field internship, applied capstone research component. *Entrance requirements:* For master's, official transcript of baccalaureate degree from accredited institution with minimum recommended GPA of 3.0; personal statement; 2 letters of recommendation; resume; state-issued teaching certificate. Additional exam requirements/recommendations for international students: Required—TOEFL (minimum score 550 paper-based; 79 iBT); Recommended—IELTS (minimum score 6). *Application deadline:* For fall admission, 5/1 for domestic and international students. Applications are processed on a rolling basis. Application fee: $65. Electronic applications accepted. *Expenses:* $690.60 per credit tuition, $56.95 per credit fees. *Financial support:* Career-related internships or fieldwork available. Financial award application deadline: 3/1; financial award applicants required to submit FAFSA. *Faculty research:* Differentiated instruction, inclusion, charter schools, technology integration in content areas, infusing literacy strategies in education, undergraduate and graduate students working with school based kids with autism. *Unit head:* Dr. Julie Norflus-Good, Director, 201-684-7246, E-mail: jgood@ramapo.edu. *Application contact:* M. Joyce Wilson, Secretarial Assistant, 201-684-7721, Fax: 201-684-6699, E-mail: jwilson@ramapo.edu. Website: http://www.ramapo.edu/mase/

Randolph College, Programs in Education, Lynchburg, VA 24503. Offers curriculum and instruction (MAT); special education-learning disabilities (M Ed, MAT). *Accreditation:* TEAC. *Entrance requirements:* For master's, minimum GPA of 3.0 in prerequisite education coursework, 2.7 in major or field of interest (MAT); teaching license (M Ed); 2 recommendations; interview.

Regent University, Graduate School, School of Education, Virginia Beach, VA 23464-9800. Offers education (M Ed, Ed D, PhD), including adult education (Ed D, PhD, Ed S), advanced educational leadership (Ed D, PhD, Ed S), character education (Ed D, PhD, Ed S), Christian education leadership (Ed D, PhD, Ed S), Christian school administration (M Ed), curriculum and instruction (Ed D, PhD, Ed S), curriculum and instruction - adult education (M Ed), curriculum and instruction - Christian school (M Ed), curriculum and instruction - gifted and talented (M Ed), curriculum and instruction - STEM education (M Ed), curriculum and instruction - teacher leader (M Ed), discipleship for ministry (M Ed), educational leadership (M Ed), educational psychology (Ed D, PhD, Ed S), educational technology and online learning (Ed D, PhD, Ed S), elementary education (M Ed), exceptional education executive leadership (Ed D, PhD, Ed S), higher education (Ed D, PhD, Ed S), higher education leadership and management (Ed D, PhD, Ed S), instructional design and technology (M Ed), K-12 school leadership (Ed D, PhD, Ed S), K-12 special education (M Ed), leadership in mathematics education (M Ed), reading specialist (M Ed), special education (Ed D, PhD, Ed S), student affairs (M Ed), TESOL - adult education (M Ed), TESOL - K-12 (M Ed); educational specialist (Ed S), including adult education (Ed D, PhD, Ed S), advanced educational leadership (Ed D, PhD, Ed S), character education (Ed D, PhD, Ed S), Christian education leadership (Ed D, PhD, Ed S), curriculum and instruction (Ed D, PhD, Ed S), educational psychology (Ed D, PhD, Ed S), educational technology and online learning (Ed D, PhD, Ed S), exceptional education executive leadership (Ed D, PhD, Ed S), higher education (Ed D, PhD, Ed S), higher education leadership and management (Ed D, PhD, Ed S), K-12 school leadership (Ed D, PhD, Ed S), special education (Ed D, PhD, Ed S). *Accreditation:* TEAC. *Program availability:* Part-time, evening/weekend, 100% online, blended/hybrid learning. *Faculty:* 22 full-time (10 women), 44 part-time/adjunct (32 women). *Students:* 80 full-time (59 women), 945 part-time (750 women); includes 432 minority (352 Black or African American, non-Hispanic/Latino; 4 American Indian or Alaska Native, non-Hispanic/Latino; 14 Asian, non-Hispanic/Latino; 43 Hispanic/Latino; 19 Two or more races, non-Hispanic/Latino), 12 international. Average age 40. 1,125 applicants, 49% accepted, 436 enrolled. In 2017, 316 master's, 24 doctorates awarded. *Degree*

requirements: For master's, thesis or alternative; for doctorate, comprehensive exam, thesis/dissertation. *Entrance requirements:* For master's, Virginia Communication and Literacy Assessment (VCLA), PRAXIS, college transcripts, writing sample, interview; for doctorate, GRE, writing sample, resume, transcripts, interview. Additional exam requirements/recommendations for international students: Required—TOEFL (minimum score 577 paper-based). *Application deadline:* For fall admission, 4/1 priority date for domestic students; for spring admission, 10/15 priority date for domestic students. Applications are processed on a rolling basis. Application fee: $50. Electronic applications accepted. *Expenses:* Contact institution. *Financial support:* In 2017–18, 669 students received support, including 1 fellowship (averaging $10,000 per year); career-related internships or fieldwork, scholarships/grants, and unspecified assistantships also available. Support available to part-time students. *Faculty research:* Christian school administration, curriculum and instruction, educational technology and online learning, higher education, special education. *Unit head:* Dr. Donald Finn, Dean, 757-352-4278, Fax: 757-352-4318, E-mail: dfinn@regent.edu. *Application contact:* Heidi Cece, Assistant Vice President of Enrollment Management, 800-373-5504, Fax: 757-352-4381, E-mail: admissions@regent.edu. Website: https://www.regent.edu/school-of-education/

Regis College, Department of Education, Weston, MA 02493. Offers elementary teacher (M Ed); higher education leadership (Ed D); special education (M Ed). *Program availability:* Part-time, evening/weekend. *Degree requirements:* For doctorate, thesis/dissertation, capstone project. *Entrance requirements:* For master's, GRE or MAT, personal statement, recommendations, resume/curriculum vitae, official transcripts, interview; for doctorate, personal statement, recommendations, resume/curriculum vitae, official transcripts, presentation/interview. Additional exam requirements/recommendations for international students: Required—TOEFL (minimum score 560 paper-based; 79 iBT); Recommended—IELTS (minimum score 6.5). *Application deadline:* Applications are processed on a rolling basis. Application fee: $65. Electronic applications accepted. *Financial support:* Federal Work-Study, scholarships/grants, and unspecified assistantships available. Financial award applicants required to submit FAFSA. *Unit head:* Dr. Priscilla Boerger, Department Chair/Graduate Program Director, 781-768-7422, E-mail: priscilla.boerger@regiscollege.edu.

Regis University, College of Contemporary Liberal Studies, Denver, CO 80221-1099. Offers creative writing (MFA); criminology (M Sc); curriculum, instruction and assessment (M Ed); education - teacher leadership (M Ed); educational leadership (M Ed); elementary education (M Ed); literacy (Certificate); reading (M Ed); secondary education (M Ed); special education (M Ed); teacher academic leadership (Certificate); teacher leadership (MA); teacher/educational leadership (M Ed); teaching the linguistically diverse (M Ed). *Program availability:* Part-time, evening/weekend, 100% online, blended/hybrid learning. *Degree requirements:* For master's, thesis (for some programs). *Entrance requirements:* For master's, official transcript reflecting baccalaureate degree awarded from regionally-accredited college or university, work experience, resume, letters of recommendation. Additional exam requirements/recommendations for international students: Required—TOEFL (minimum score 550 paper-based; 82 iBT). Electronic applications accepted. *Expenses:* Contact institution.

Rhode Island College, School of Graduate Studies, Feinstein School of Education and Human Development, Department of Special Education, Providence, RI 02908-1991. Offers autism education (CGS); severe intellectual disabilities (CGS); special education (M Ed). *Accreditation:* NCATE. *Program availability:* Part-time, evening/weekend. *Faculty:* 2. *Students:* 4 full-time (all women), 42 part-time (41 women); includes 5 minority (2 Black or African American, non-Hispanic/Latino; 3 Hispanic/Latino). Average age 31. In 2017, 30 master's awarded. *Degree requirements:* For master's, comprehensive assessment/assignment. *Entrance requirements:* For master's, GRE General Test or MAT, undergraduate transcripts; minimum undergraduate GPA of 3.0; 3 letters of recommendation; for CGS, GRE or MAT, master's degree or equivalent, teaching certificate, 3 letters of recommendation, interview. Additional exam requirements/recommendations for international students: Recommended—TOEFL (minimum score 550 paper-based; 79 iBT). *Application deadline:* For fall admission, 3/1 for domestic students; for spring admission, 11/1 for domestic students. Applications are processed on a rolling basis. Application fee: $50. Electronic applications accepted. *Expenses:* Tuition, state resident: full-time $9768; part-time $407 per credit. Tuition, nonresident: full-time $19,008; part-time $792 per credit. *Required fees:* $696; $29 per credit. One-time fee: $200 full-time; $100 part-time. Tuition and fees vary according to course load. *Financial support:* Teaching assistantships with full tuition reimbursements, career-related internships or fieldwork, Federal Work-Study, scholarships/grants, health care benefits, and unspecified assistantships available. Support available to part-time students. Financial award application deadline: 5/15; financial award applicants required to submit FAFSA. *Unit head:* Dr. Ying Hui-Michael, Chair, 401-456-8024, E-mail: yhui@ric.edu. *Application contact:* Graduate Studies, 401-456-8700. Website: http://www.ric.edu/specialEducation/

Rider University, College of Education and Human Services, Program in Special Education, Lawrenceville, NJ 08648-3001. Offers special education (MA); teacher of students with disabilities (Certificate). *Program availability:* Part-time, evening/weekend. *Degree requirements:* For master's, comprehensive exam. *Entrance requirements:* For master's, letters of reference, resume, NJ teaching license, interview. Additional exam requirements/recommendations for international students: Required—TOEFL (minimum score 550 paper-based). Electronic applications accepted. *Faculty research:* Collaboration/inclusive, practice, service learning, transition.

Rivier University, School of Graduate Studies, Department of Education, Nashua, NH 03060. Offers curriculum and instruction (M Ed); early childhood education (M Ed); educational administration (M Ed); educational studies (M Ed); elementary education (M Ed); elementary education and general special education (M Ed); emotional and behavioral disorders (M Ed); general social education (M Ed); leadership and learning (Ed D, CAGS); learning disabilities (M Ed); learning disabilities and reading (M Ed); mental health counseling (MA); reading (M Ed); school counseling (M Ed). *Program availability:* Part-time, evening/weekend. *Degree requirements:* For master's, comprehensive exam (for some programs), internships. *Entrance requirements:* For master's, GRE General Test or MAT.

Robert Morris University, School of Education and Social Sciences, Moon Township, PA 15108-1189. Offers business education (MS); counseling psychology (MS); education (Postbaccalaureate Certificate); higher education (MS); instructional leadership (MS), including education; instructional management and leadership (PhD); literacy (MS); special education (MS). *Accreditation:* TEAC. *Program availability:* Part-time, evening/weekend, online learning. *Faculty:* 18 full-time (10 women), 5 part-time/adjunct (2 women). *Students:* 151 part-time (90 women); includes 23 minority (12 Black or African American, non-Hispanic/Latino; 2 Asian, non-Hispanic/Latino; 2 Hispanic/Latino; 7 Two or more races, non-Hispanic/Latino), 4 international. Average age 34. 51 applicants, 39% accepted, 10 enrolled. In 2017, 31 master's, 16 doctorates awarded. *Degree requirements:* For doctorate, thesis/dissertation. *Entrance requirements:* Additional exam requirements/recommendations for international students: Required—TOEFL (minimum score 550 paper-based; 79 iBT). *Application deadline:* For fall admission, 7/1 priority date for domestic and international students; for spring

Special Education

admission, 11/1 priority date for domestic and international students. Applications are processed on a rolling basis. Application fee: $35. Electronic applications accepted. *Expenses:* $890 per credit tuition, $80 per credit university fee. *Unit head:* Dr. George Semich, Acting Dean, 412-397-6032, Fax: 412-397-6044, E-mail: semich@rmu.edu. *Application contact:* E-mail: graduateadmissions@rmu.edu. Website: http://www.rmu.edu/web/cms/schools/sess/

Roberts Wesleyan College, Graduate Teacher Education Programs, Rochester, NY 14624-1997. Offers adolescence and special education (M Ed); childhood and special education (M Ed); literacy education (M Ed); special education (M Ed). *Program availability:* Part-time, evening/weekend. *Degree requirements:* For master's, thesis. Electronic applications accepted.

Rochester Institute of Technology, Graduate Enrollment Services, National Technical Institute for the Deaf, Research and Teacher Education Department, MS Program in Secondary Education for the Deaf and Hard of Hearing, Rochester, NY 14623. Offers MS. *Program availability:* Part-time, evening/weekend, blended/hybrid learning. *Students:* 18 full-time (13 women), 1 (woman) part-time; includes 3 minority (1 Black or African American, non-Hispanic/Latino; 2 Hispanic/Latino), 6 international. Average age 28. 24 applicants, 33% accepted, 5 enrolled. In 2017, 11 master's awarded. *Entrance requirements:* For master's, GRE, minimum cumulative GPA of 3.0. *Application deadline:* For fall admission, 6/1 priority date for domestic and international students. Applications are processed on a rolling basis. Application fee: $65. Electronic applications accepted. *Expenses:* $1,815 per credit hour. *Financial support:* Fellowships with partial tuition reimbursements, research assistantships with partial tuition reimbursements, teaching assistantships with partial tuition reimbursements, career-related internships or fieldwork, scholarships/grants, and unspecified assistantships available. Support available to part-time students. Financial award applicants required to submit FAFSA. *Faculty research:* Effective use of technology and online learning in teaching deaf students; strategies for inclusive instruction/deaf students with other disabilities; effective literacy instruction strategies for DHH readers; single case experimental design methods; STEM language, literacy and learning; deaf studies; international deaf education; stereotype threat effects on mathematical performance. *Unit head:* Dr. Gerald C. Bateman, Director, 585-475-6480, E-mail: gcbnmp@rit.edu. *Application contact:* Diane Ellison, Senior Associate Vice President, Graduate Enrollment Services, 585-475-2229, Fax: 585-475-7164, E-mail: gradinfo@rit.edu.
Website: http://www.ntid.rit.edu/msse/

Rockford University, Graduate Studies, Department of Education, Program in Special Education, Rockford, IL 61108-2393. Offers MAT. *Program availability:* Part-time, evening/weekend. *Degree requirements:* For master's, thesis optional. *Entrance requirements:* For master's, GRE General Test, 3 letters of recommendation. Additional exam requirements/recommendations for international students: Required—TOEFL (minimum score 550 paper-based; 79 iBT). Electronic applications accepted.

Roosevelt University, Graduate Division, College of Education, Program in Special Education, Chicago, IL 60605. Offers MA. *Students:* 2 full-time (1 woman), 2 part-time (0 women); includes 1 minority (Hispanic/Latino). Average age 26. 6 applicants, 100% accepted, 1 enrolled. In 2017, 3 master's awarded. *Application deadline:* Applications are processed on a rolling basis. Application fee: $40. Electronic applications accepted. *Financial support:* Scholarships/grants and unspecified assistantships available. *Application contact:* Laura Lag, Associate Dean for Graduate Admission, 312-853-4753, E-mail: llag@roosevelt.edu.
Website: https://www.roosevelt.edu/

Rowan University, Graduate School, College of Education, Department of Interdisciplinary and Inclusive Education, Autism Spectrum Disorders Certificate of Graduate Study Program, Glassboro, NJ 08028-1701. Offers CGS. Electronic applications accepted. *Expenses:* Tuition, state resident: full-time $15,020; part-time $751 per semester hour. Tuition, nonresident: full-time $15,020; part-time $751 per semester hour. *Required fees:* $3158; $157.90 per semester hour. Tuition and fees vary according to course load, campus/location and program.

Rowan University, Graduate School, College of Education, Department of Interdisciplinary and Inclusive Education, Program in Learning Disabilities, Glassboro, NJ 08028-1701. Offers MA, CGS. *Accreditation:* NCATE. *Program availability:* Part-time, evening/weekend. *Degree requirements:* For master's, comprehensive exam, thesis. *Entrance requirements:* For master's, GRE General Test, minimum GPA of 2.8, 1 year of teaching experience. Additional exam requirements/recommendations for international students: Required—TOEFL. Electronic applications accepted. *Expenses:* Tuition, state resident: full-time $15,020; part-time $751 per semester hour. Tuition, nonresident: full-time $15,020; part-time $751 per semester hour. *Required fees:* $3158; $157.90 per semester hour. Tuition and fees vary according to course load, campus/location and program.

Rowan University, Graduate School, College of Education, Department of Interdisciplinary and Inclusive Education, Program in Special Education, Glassboro, NJ 08028-1701. Offers MA, CGS. *Accreditation:* NCATE. *Program availability:* Part-time, evening/weekend. *Degree requirements:* For master's, comprehensive exam, thesis. *Entrance requirements:* For master's, GRE General Test, minimum GPA of 2.8. Additional exam requirements/recommendations for international students: Required—TOEFL. Electronic applications accepted. *Expenses:* Tuition, state resident: full-time $15,020; part-time $751 per semester hour. Tuition, nonresident: full-time $15,020; part-time $751 per semester hour. *Required fees:* $3158; $157.90 per semester hour. Tuition and fees vary according to course load, campus/location and program.

Rowan University, Graduate School, College of Education, Department of Interdisciplinary and Inclusive Education, Teacher of Students with Disabilities Post-Baccalaureate Certification Program, Glassboro, NJ 08028-1701. Offers Postbaccalaureate Certificate. *Program availability:* Part-time, online learning. *Entrance requirements:* For degree, official transcripts from all colleges attended; current professional resume; two letters of recommendation; minimum cumulative undergraduate GPA of 2.75; essay; BA or BS. Electronic applications accepted. *Expenses:* Tuition, state resident: full-time $15,020; part-time $751 per semester hour. Tuition, nonresident: full-time $15,020; part-time $751 per semester hour. *Required fees:* $3158; $157.90 per semester hour. Tuition and fees vary according to course load, campus/location and program.

Rutgers University–New Brunswick, Graduate School of Education, Department of Educational Psychology, Program in Special Education, Piscataway, NJ 08854-8097. Offers Ed M, Ed D. *Program availability:* Part-time, evening/weekend. *Degree requirements:* For doctorate, thesis/dissertation, residency. *Entrance requirements:* For master's, GRE General Test, 3 letters of recommendation; for doctorate, GRE General Test, 3 letters of recommendation, master's degree. Additional exam requirements/recommendations for international students: Required—TOEFL (minimum score 550 paper-based; 83 iBT). Electronic applications accepted. *Faculty research:* Pre- and in-service teacher education, teacher development, inclusion, early identification and intervention of reading disabilities, special education law and social policy.

Sage Graduate School, Esteves School of Education, Program in Childhood Special Education, Troy, NY 12180-4115. Offers MS Ed. *Accreditation:* NCATE. *Program* *availability:* Part-time, evening/weekend. *Faculty:* 2 full-time (both women), 8 part-time/adjunct (4 women). *Students:* 3 full-time (2 women), 8 part-time (all women); includes 2 minority (1 Black or African American, non-Hispanic/Latino; 1 Asian, non-Hispanic/Latino). Average age 25. 12 applicants, 33% accepted, 3 enrolled. In 2017, 2 master's awarded. *Degree requirements:* For master's, thesis optional. *Entrance requirements:* For master's, bachelor's degree in a liberal arts or sciences area or the equivalent. Additional exam requirements/recommendations for international students: Required—TOEFL (minimum score 550 paper-based). *Application deadline:* Applications are processed on a rolling basis. Application fee: $30. Electronic applications accepted. Tuition and fees vary according to degree level and program. *Financial support:* Fellowships, research assistantships, scholarships/grants, and unspecified assistantships available. Financial award application deadline: 3/1; financial award applicants required to submit FAFSA. *Faculty research:* Effective behavioral strategies for classroom instruction. *Unit head:* Dr. John Pelizza, Interim Dean, Esteves School of Education, 518-244-2051, Fax: 518-244-2334, E-mail: pelizj@sage.edu. *Application contact:* Tracey McLeod, Chair and Assistant Professor, 518-244-3132, Fax: 518-244-2334, E-mail: mcleot@sage.edu.

Sage Graduate School, Esteves School of Education, Program in Literacy/Childhood Special Education, Troy, NY 12180-4115. Offers MS Ed. *Accreditation:* NCATE. *Program availability:* Part-time, evening/weekend. *Faculty:* 2 full-time (both women), 8 part-time/adjunct (4 women). *Students:* 1 (woman) full-time, 7 part-time (6 women). Average age 28. 6 applicants. In 2017, 3 master's awarded. *Entrance requirements:* For master's, current teacher certification, interview with appropriate advisor, assessment of writing. Additional exam requirements/recommendations for international students: Required—TOEFL (minimum score 550 paper-based). *Application deadline:* Applications are processed on a rolling basis. Application fee: $30. Electronic applications accepted. Tuition and fees vary according to degree level and program. *Financial support:* Fellowships, research assistantships, scholarships/grants, and unspecified assistantships available. Financial award application deadline: 3/1; financial award applicants required to submit FAFSA. *Faculty research:* Commonalities in the roles of reading specialists and resource/consultant teachers. *Unit head:* Dr. John Pelizza, Interim Dean, Esteves School of Education, 518-244-2051, Fax: 518-244-2334, E-mail: pelizj@sage.edu. *Application contact:* Dr. Kathleen Gormley, Chair and Professor of Education, 518-244-2403, Fax: 518-244-2334, E-mail: gormlk@sage.edu.

Sage Graduate School, Esteves School of Education, Program in Special Education, Troy, NY 12180-4115. Offers MS Ed. *Program availability:* Part-time, evening/weekend. *Faculty:* 2 full-time (both women), 8 part-time/adjunct (4 women). *Students:* 3 part-time (all women). Average age 25. 3 applicants. In 2017, 5 master's awarded. *Entrance requirements:* For master's, interview with advisor, assessment of writing skills, New York state initial certification in childhood education or closely-related field. Additional exam requirements/recommendations for international students: Required—TOEFL (minimum score 550 paper-based). *Application deadline:* Applications are processed on a rolling basis. Application fee: $30. Electronic applications accepted. Tuition and fees vary according to degree level and program. *Financial support:* Fellowships, research assistantships, scholarships/grants, and unspecified assistantships available. Financial award application deadline: 3/1; financial award applicants required to submit FAFSA. *Unit head:* Dr. John Pelizza, Interim Dean, Esteves School of Education, 518-244-2051, Fax: 518-244-2334, E-mail: pelizj@sage.edu. *Application contact:* Tracey McLeod, Assistant Professor, 518-244-3132, Fax: 518-244-2334, E-mail: mcleot@sage.edu.

Saginaw Valley State University, College of Education, Program in Special Education, University Center, MI 48710. Offers MAT. *Program availability:* Part-time, evening/weekend. *Students:* 6 full-time (all women), 57 part-time (50 women). Average age 34. 22 applicants, 86% accepted, 12 enrolled. In 2017, 25 master's awarded. *Degree requirements:* For master's, capstone course and practicum or thesis. *Entrance requirements:* For master's, minimum GPA of 3.0, teacher certification. Additional exam requirements/recommendations for international students: Required—TOEFL (minimum score 550 paper-based; 79 iBT). *Application deadline:* For fall admission, 7/15 for international students; for winter admission, 11/15 for international students; for spring admission, 4/15 for international students. Applications are processed on a rolling basis. Application fee: $30 ($90 for international students). Electronic applications accepted. *Expenses:* Tuition, state resident: full-time $10,156; part-time $564.20 per credit hour. Tuition, nonresident: full-time $19,336; part-time $1074.20 per credit hour. *Required fees:* $263; $14.60 per credit hour. Tuition and fees vary according to degree level and program. *Financial support:* Federal Work-Study and scholarships/grants available. Support available to part-time students. Financial award applicants required to submit FAFSA. *Unit head:* Dr. Dottie Millar, Professor, Teacher Education, 989-964-4958, Fax: 989-964-4563, E-mail: coeconnect@svsu.edu. *Application contact:* Jenna Briggs, Director, Graduate and International Admissions, 989-964-6096, Fax: 989-964-2788, E-mail: gradadm@svsu.edu.

St. Bonaventure University, School of Graduate Studies, School of Education, Differentiated Instruction Program, St. Bonaventure, NY 14778-2284. Offers gifted education (MS Ed, Adv C); gifted education and students with disabilities (MS Ed). *Program availability:* Part-time, evening/weekend. *Faculty:* 2 full-time (both women), 1 (woman) part-time/adjunct. *Students:* 18 full-time (17 women), 9 part-time (7 women), 1 international. Average age 26. 6 applicants, 83% accepted, 4 enrolled. In 2017, 17 master's awarded. *Degree requirements:* For master's, comprehensive exam, internship, portfolio; for Adv C, practicum, portfolio. *Entrance requirements:* For master's, GRE or MAT, disabilities or special education teaching certification (or letter of eligibility); interview; transcripts from all colleges previously attended; 2 letters of recommendation; writing sample; for Adv C, teaching certification (or letter of eligibility); interview; transcripts from all colleges previously attended; 2 references; master's degree; writing sample. Additional exam requirements/recommendations for international students: Required—TOEFL (minimum score 550 paper-based; 79 iBT). *Application deadline:* For fall admission, 6/15 priority date for domestic students, 2/1 priority date for international students; for spring admission, 11/15 priority date for domestic students, 7/1 priority date for international students. Applications are processed on a rolling basis. Application fee: $0. Electronic applications accepted. *Expenses:* $733 per credit hour, $100 graduation fee. *Financial support:* Federal Work-Study, scholarships/grants, health care benefits, and unspecified assistantships available. Support available to part-time students. Financial award application deadline: 4/15; financial award applicants required to submit FAFSA. *Faculty research:* Disproportionality in special education, gifted education, teacher education and curriculum, specializing in authentic and responsive pedagogy for diverse learners. *Unit head:* Dr. Rene' Hauser, Director, 716-375-4078, Fax: 716-375-2360, E-mail: rhauser@sbu.edu. *Application contact:* Bruce Campbell, Director of Graduate Admissions, 716-375-2429, Fax: 716-375-4015, E-mail: gradsch@sbu.edu.
Website: http://www.sbu.edu/academics/post-master's-in-differentiated-instruction

St. Cloud State University, School of Graduate Studies, School of Education, Department of Special Education, St. Cloud, MN 56301-4498. Offers developmental/cognitive disabilities (MS); emotional/behavioral disorders (MS); gifted and talented (MS); learning disabilities (MS); special education (MS). *Accreditation:* NCATE. *Degree requirements:* For master's, thesis or alternative. *Entrance requirements:* For master's, GRE General Test, minimum GPA of 2.75. Additional exam requirements/

recommendations for international students: Required—Michigan English Language Assessment Battery; Recommended—TOEFL (minimum score 550 paper-based), IELTS (minimum score 6.5). Electronic applications accepted.

St. John Fisher College, Ralph C. Wilson Jr. School of Education, Program in Adolescence Education and Special Education, Rochester, NY 14618-3597. Offers adolescence education: biology with special education (MS Ed); adolescence education: chemistry with special education (MS Ed); adolescence education: English with special education (MS Ed); adolescence education: French with special education (MS Ed); adolescence education: math with special education (MS Ed); adolescence education: physics with special education (MS Ed); adolescence education: social studies with special education (MS Ed); adolescence education: Spanish with special education (MS Ed). *Program availability:* Part-time, evening/weekend. *Faculty:* 5 full-time (4 women), 7 part-time/adjunct (6 women). *Students:* 15 full-time (3 women), 4 part-time (all women); includes 4 minority (2 Black or African American, non-Hispanic/Latino; 1 Hispanic/Latino; 1 Two or more races, non-Hispanic/Latino). Average age 27. 34 applicants, 85% accepted, 12 enrolled. In 2017, 19 master's awarded. *Degree requirements:* For master's, field experiences, student teaching. *Entrance requirements:* For master's, LAST, 2 letters of recommendation, personal statement, current resume. Additional exam requirements/recommendations for international students: Required—TOEFL (minimum score 575 paper-based; 80 iBT). *Application deadline:* Applications are processed on a rolling basis. Application fee: $30. Electronic applications accepted. *Expenses:* Contact institution. *Financial support:* Scholarships/grants available. Financial award applicants required to submit FAFSA. *Faculty research:* Arts and humanities, urban schools, constructivist learning, at-risk students, mentoring. *Unit head:* Dr. Susan Hildenbrand, Program Director, 585-385-7297, E-mail: shildenbrand@sjfc.edu. *Application contact:* Michelle Gosier, Director of Transfer and Graduate Admissions, 585-385-8064, E-mail: mgosier@sjfc.edu.

St. John Fisher College, Ralph C. Wilson Jr. School of Education, Program in Childhood Education/Special Education, Rochester, NY 14618-3597. Offers childhood education (MS); childhood education/special education (Certificate). *Program availability:* Part-time, evening/weekend. *Faculty:* 5 full-time (3 women), 6 part-time/adjunct (5 women). *Students:* 22 full-time (19 women), 8 part-time (all women); includes 4 minority (1 Black or African American, non-Hispanic/Latino; 1 Asian, non-Hispanic/Latino; 1 Hispanic/Latino; 1 Two or more races, non-Hispanic/Latino). Average age 26. 33 applicants, 70% accepted, 14 enrolled. In 2017, 17 master's awarded. *Degree requirements:* For master's, field experience, student teaching. *Entrance requirements:* For master's, LAST, 2 letters of recommendation, personal statement, current resume. Additional exam requirements/recommendations for international students: Required—TOEFL (minimum score 575 paper-based; 80 iBT). *Application deadline:* Applications are processed on a rolling basis. Application fee: $30. Electronic applications accepted. *Expenses:* Contact institution. *Financial support:* Scholarships/grants available. Financial award applicants required to submit FAFSA. *Faculty research:* Professional development, science assessment, multi-cultural, educational technology. *Unit head:* Dr. Susan Hildenbrand, Program Director, 585-385-7297, E-mail: shildenbrand@sjfc.edu. *Application contact:* Michelle Gosier, Associate Director of Transfer and Graduate Admissions, 585-385-8064, E-mail: mgosier@sjfc.edu.
Website: https://www.sjfc.edu/graduate-programs/ms-in-childhood-special-education/

St. John's University, The School of Education, Department of Education Specialties, Program in Special Education, Queens, NY 11439. Offers childhood and childhood special education (MS Ed); teaching children with disabilities in adolescent education (Adv C); teaching children with disabilities in adolescent education (7-12) (MS Ed); teaching children with disabilities in childhood education (Adv C); teaching children with disabilities in childhood education (1-6) (MS Ed); teaching students with disabilities and early childhood education (B-2) (MS Ed). *Program availability:* Part-time, evening/weekend, 100% online. *Students:* 44 full-time (40 women), 196 part-time (137 women); includes 117 minority (53 Black or African American, non-Hispanic/Latino; 16 Asian, non-Hispanic/Latino; 40 Hispanic/Latino; 1 Native Hawaiian or other Pacific Islander, non-Hispanic/Latino; 7 Two or more races, non-Hispanic/Latino), 3 international. Average age 30. In 2017, 132 master's, 2 Adv Cs awarded. *Degree requirements:* For master's and Adv C, comprehensive exam, minimum overall GPA of 3.0 at time of graduation, 150 hours of practicum in-field experience in a special needs setting, teaching portfolio. *Entrance requirements:* For master's, GRE, MAT, or PRAXIS, statement of goals (personal essay), official undergraduate transcripts, initial teaching certification; for Adv C, initial teaching certification, first master's transcripts, statement of purpose. Additional exam requirements/recommendations for international students: Required—TOEFL, IELTS. *Application deadline:* For fall admission, 8/17 for domestic and international students; for summer admission, 5/15 for domestic and international students. Application fee: $70. Electronic applications accepted. *Expenses:* Tuition: Full-time $44,280; part-time $1230 per credit. *Required fees:* $340; $340 per credit. Tuition and fees vary according to course load, degree level and program. *Financial support:* Fellowships, research assistantships, scholarships/grants, and unspecified assistantships available. Support available to part-time students. Financial award application deadline: 2/1; financial award applicants required to submit FAFSA. *Faculty research:* Evidence-based practices for prevention of peer victimization/abuse; autism and intellectual disabilities; interpersonal decision making, empowerment and self-determination skills; academic motivation, literacy skill development, language and communication skills among adolescents with learning disabilities. *Unit head:* Dr. John Spiridakis, Chair, 718-990-5591, E-mail: spiridaj@stjohns.edu. *Application contact:* Dr. John Spiridakis, Chair, 718-990-5591, E-mail: spiridaj@stjohns.edu.

St. Joseph's College, Long Island Campus, Programs in Education, Field in Special Education, Patchogue, NY 11772-2399. Offers MA. *Program availability:* Part-time, evening/weekend. *Faculty:* 9 full-time (7 women), 11 part-time/adjunct (5 women). *Students:* 13 full-time (12 women), 113 part-time (93 women); includes 11 minority (1 Asian, non-Hispanic/Latino; 7 Hispanic/Latino; 3 Two or more races, non-Hispanic/Latino). Average age 25. 87 applicants, 89% accepted, 56 enrolled. In 2017, 63 master's awarded. *Entrance requirements:* For master's, GRE, PRAXIS Core Academic Skills, or MAT, resume, two completed letter of reference forms, copies of certificates granted by the New York State Education Department, official transcripts, completed medical form. Application fee: $25. *Expenses:* Tuition: Full-time $17,550; part-time $975 per credit. *Required fees:* $362. *Financial support:* In 2017–18, 41 students received support. Federal Work-Study available. *Unit head:* Joan Silver, Associate Professor/Director of MA in Childhood and Adolescence Education with an annotation in Severe and Multiple Disabilities, 631-687-1219, E-mail: jsilver@sjcny.edu.

St. Joseph's College, Long Island Campus, Programs in Education, Field of Infant/Toddler Early Childhood Special Education, Patchogue, NY 11772-2399. Offers MA. *Program availability:* Part-time, evening/weekend. *Faculty:* 6 full-time (5 women), 5 part-time/adjunct (all women). *Students:* 31 full-time (30 women), 95 part-time (87 women); includes 19 minority (1 Black or African American, non-Hispanic/Latino; 1 Asian, non-Hispanic/Latino; 17 Hispanic/Latino). Average age 27. 83 applicants, 77% accepted, 53 enrolled. In 2017, 7 master's awarded. *Entrance requirements:* For master's, official transcripts, two letters of recommendation, resume, copies of all teaching certificates, completed medical form. Additional exam requirements/recommendations for international students: Recommended—TOEFL (minimum score 550 paper-based; 79

iBT), IELTS (minimum score 7). *Application deadline:* Applications are processed on a rolling basis. Application fee: $25. Electronic applications accepted. *Expenses:* Tuition: Full-time $17,550; part-time $975 per credit. *Required fees:* $362. *Financial support:* In 2017–18, 32 students received support. Applicants required to submit FAFSA. *Unit head:* Katherine Granelli, Director of MA in Infant/Toddler Early Childhood Special Education, 631-687-1217, E-mail: kgranelli@sjcny.edu.

St. Joseph's College, Long Island Campus, Programs in Education, Field of Literacy and Cognition, Patchogue, NY 11772-2399. Offers literacy 5-12 (MA); literacy and cognition birth-6 (MA); literacy birth-12 (MA); literacy/cognition and special education (MA). *Program availability:* Part-time, evening/weekend. *Faculty:* 8 full-time (6 women), 7 part-time/adjunct (3 women). *Students:* 5 full-time (all women), 110 part-time (106 women); includes 10 minority (1 Black or African American, non-Hispanic/Latino; 1 American Indian or Alaska Native, non-Hispanic/Latino; 1 Asian, non-Hispanic/Latino; 5 Hispanic/Latino; 2 Two or more races, non-Hispanic/Latino). Average age 24. 71 applicants, 85% accepted, 54 enrolled. In 2017, 47 master's awarded. *Entrance requirements:* For master's, GRE, PRAXIS Core Academic Skills, or MAT, resume, two completed letter of reference forms, copies of certificates granted by the New York State Education Department, official transcripts. Additional exam requirements/recommendations for international students: Recommended—TOEFL (minimum score 550 paper-based; 79 iBT), IELTS (minimum score 7). *Application deadline:* Applications are processed on a rolling basis. Application fee: $25. Electronic applications accepted. *Expenses:* Tuition: Full-time $17,550; part-time $975 per credit. *Required fees:* $362. *Financial support:* In 2017–18, 53 students received support. Federal Work-Study available. *Unit head:* Karen Megay-Nespoli, Associate Professor/Director of MA in Literacy and Cognition, 631-687-1212, E-mail: kmegay-nespoli@sjcny.edu.

St. Joseph's College, New York, Programs in Education, Field of Special Education, Brooklyn, NY 11205-3688. Offers severe and multiple disabilities (MA). *Program availability:* Part-time, evening/weekend. *Faculty:* 3 full-time (all women), 1 (woman) part-time/adjunct. *Students:* 16 part-time (10 women); includes 3 minority (1 Black or African American, non-Hispanic/Latino; 2 Hispanic/Latino). Average age 23. 14 applicants, 100% accepted, 8 enrolled. In 2017, 21 master's awarded. *Entrance requirements:* For master's, GRE, PRAXIS or MAT, official transcripts, two letters of recommendation, resume, copy of teaching certification. Additional exam requirements/recommendations for international students: Required—TOEFL (minimum score 80 iBT). *Application deadline:* Applications are processed on a rolling basis. Application fee: $25. Electronic applications accepted. *Expenses:* Tuition: Full-time $17,550; part-time $975 per credit. *Required fees:* $362. *Financial support:* In 2017–18, 13 students received support. *Unit head:* Susan Straut-Collard, Professor/Associate Chair/Director of the MA in Childhood and Adolescence Special Education, 718-940-5689, E-mail: sstrautcollard@sjcny.edu.
Website: http://www.sjcny.edu

Saint Joseph's University, College of Arts and Sciences, Graduate Programs in Education, Philadelphia, PA 19131-1395. Offers curriculum supervisor (Certificate); educational leadership (MS, Ed D); elementary education (MS, Certificate); elementary/middle school education (Certificate); organizational development and leadership (MS); principal (Certificate); professional education (MS); reading specialist (MS, Certificate); reading supervisor (Certificate); secondary education (MS, Certificate); special education (MS); special education 7-12 (Certificate); special education PK-8 (Certificate); superintendent's letter of eligibility (Certificate); supervisor of special education (Certificate); teacher of the deaf and hard of hearing (Certificate). *Program availability:* Part-time, evening/weekend, blended/hybrid learning. *Faculty:* 18 full-time (16 women), 63 part-time/adjunct (44 women). *Students:* 79 full-time (60 women), 793 part-time (604 women); includes 179 minority (125 Black or African American, non-Hispanic/Latino; 5 American Indian or Alaska Native, non-Hispanic/Latino; 15 Asian, non-Hispanic/Latino; 27 Hispanic/Latino; 1 Native Hawaiian or other Pacific Islander, non-Hispanic/Latino; 6 Two or more races, non-Hispanic/Latino), 12 international. Average age 34. 375 applicants, 75% accepted, 189 enrolled. In 2017, 340 master's, 13 doctorates, 3 other advanced degrees awarded. *Degree requirements:* For master's, thesis or alternative; for doctorate, comprehensive exam, thesis/dissertation. *Entrance requirements:* For master's, 2 letters of recommendation, minimum GPA of 3.0, official transcripts, personal statement; for doctorate, GRE, master's degree from accredited institution, minimum graduate GPA of 3.5, computer competence, interview with program director. Additional exam requirements/recommendations for international students: Required—TOEFL (minimum score 550 paper-based; 80 iBT), IELTS (minimum score 6.5), PTE (minimum score 60). *Application deadline:* For fall admission, 7/15 for international students; for spring admission, 11/1 for international students. Applications are processed on a rolling basis. Application fee: $35. Electronic applications accepted. *Expenses:* Contact institution. *Financial support:* Scholarships/grants and unspecified assistantships available. Financial award application deadline: 5/1; financial award applicants required to submit FAFSA. *Faculty research:* Factors predicting early mathematics skills for low income children, early child care and development, preschool quality, parent communication and home-school collaboration issues, education of terminally ill children, preparing literacy teachers for urban schools. *Unit head:* Dr. John Vacca, Associate Dean, Education, 610-660-3131, E-mail: gradcas@sju.edu. *Application contact:* Graduate Admissions, College of Arts and Sciences, 610-660-3131, E-mail: gradcas@sju.edu.
Website: https://sites.sju.edu/education/graduate-programs/

Saint Louis University, Graduate Programs, School of Education, Department of Educational Studies, St. Louis, MO 63103. Offers curriculum and instruction (MA, Ed D, PhD); educational foundations (MA, Ed D, PhD); special education (MA); teaching (MAT). *Accreditation:* NCATE. *Program availability:* Part-time. *Degree requirements:* For master's, comprehensive exam; for doctorate, comprehensive exam, thesis/dissertation, preliminary oral and written exams. *Entrance requirements:* For master's, GRE General Test or MAT, letters of recommendation, resume; for doctorate, GRE General Test, letters of recommendation, resumé, goal statement, transcripts. Additional exam requirements/recommendations for international students: Required—TOEFL (minimum score 525 paper-based). Electronic applications accepted. *Faculty research:* Teacher preparation, multicultural issues, children with special needs, qualitative research in education, inclusion.

Saint Mary's College of California, Kalmanovitz School of Education, Program in Special Education, Moraga, CA 94575. Offers M Ed. *Program availability:* Part-time. *Degree requirements:* For master's, thesis or project. *Entrance requirements:* For master's, writing proficiency exam, interview, minimum GPA of 3.0, teaching experience. *Faculty research:* Consultation model, impact of gifted model on special education.

Saint Mary's University of Minnesota, Schools of Graduate and Professional Programs, Graduate School of Education, Educational Administration Program, Winona, MN 55987-1399. Offers educational administration (Certificate, Ed S), including director of special education, K-12 principal, superintendent. *Unit head:* Dr. William Bjorum, Director, 612-728-5126, Fax: 612-728-5121, E-mail: wbjorum@smumn.edu. *Application contact:* James Callinan, Director of Admissions for Graduate and Professional Programs, 612-728-5158, Fax: 612-728-5121, E-mail: jcallina@smumn.edu.
Website: https://www.smumn.edu/academics/graduate/education/programs/ed.s.-in-educational-administration

Special Education

Saint Mary's University of Minnesota, Schools of Graduate and Professional Programs, Graduate School of Education, Special Education Program, Winona, MN 55987-1399. Offers behavioral disorders (Certificate); learning disabilities (Certificate); special education (MA). *Program availability:* Part-time, evening/weekend, online learning. *Unit head:* Dr. Judith Nagel Lam, Director, 612-238-4565, E-mail: jnagel@smumn.edu. *Application contact:* James Callinan, Director of Admission, 612-728-5158, Fax: 612-728-5121, E-mail: jcallina@smumn.edu.
Website: http://www.smumn.edu/graduate-home/areas-of-study/graduate-school-of-education/ma-in-special-education

Saint Michael's College, Graduate Programs, Program in Education, Colchester, VT 05439. Offers arts in education (CAGS); literacy (M Ed); school leadership (CAGS); special education (M Ed). *Program availability:* Part-time, evening/weekend. *Students:* 7 full-time (3 women), 204 part-time (173 women); includes 8 minority (1 Black or African American, non-Hispanic/Latino; 1 American Indian or Alaska Native, non-Hispanic/Latino; 3 Hispanic/Latino; 3 Two or more races, non-Hispanic/Latino). Average age 38. 23 applicants, 65% accepted, 10 enrolled. In 2017, 32 master's awarded. *Degree requirements:* For master's, thesis. *Entrance requirements:* For master's, minimum GPA of 3.0, official transcripts, essay, interview. *Application deadline:* Applications are processed on a rolling basis. Application fee: $50. Electronic applications accepted. *Expenses: Tuition:* Part-time $590 per credit. *Financial support:* Fellowships with partial tuition reimbursements and scholarships/grants available. Support available to part-time students. Financial award applicants required to submit FAFSA. *Faculty research:* Integrative curriculum, moral and spiritual dimensions of education, learning styles, multiple intelligences, integrating technology into the curriculum. *Unit head:* Jonathan Silverman, Department Chair, 802-654-2306, Fax: 802-654-2664, E-mail: jsilverman@smcvt.edu. *Application contact:* Lindsay A. Damici, Marketing Communications Manager, 802-654-2556, Fax: 802-654-2732.
Website: http://www.smcvt.edu/graduate-programs/academic-programs/education.aspx

Saint Peter's University, Graduate Programs in Education, Program in Special Education, Jersey City, NJ 07306-5997. Offers literacy (MA Ed). *Program availability:* Part-time, evening/weekend. *Degree requirements:* For master's, comprehensive exam. *Entrance requirements:* For master's, GRE or MAT. Additional exam requirements/recommendations for international students: Required—TOEFL. Electronic applications accepted.

St. Thomas Aquinas College, Division of Teacher Education, Sparkill, NY 10976. Offers adolescence education (MST); childhood and special education (MST); childhood education (MST); educational leadership (MS Ed); reading (MS Ed, PMC); special education (MS Ed, PMC); teaching (MS Ed), including elementary education, middle school education, secondary education. *Accreditation:* NCATE. *Program availability:* Part-time, evening/weekend. *Degree requirements:* For master's, comprehensive exam, comprehensive professional portfolio; for PMC, action research project. *Entrance requirements:* For master's, New York State Qualifying Exam, GRE General Test or minimum GPA of 3.0, teaching certificate; for PMC, GRE General Test or minimum GPA of 3.0. Electronic applications accepted. *Faculty research:* Computer applications in education, adolescent special education students, literacy development, inclusive practices for special education students.

St. Thomas University, School of Leadership Studies, Institute for Education, Miami Gardens, FL 33054-6459. Offers earth/space science (Certificate); educational administration (MS, Certificate); educational leadership (Ed D); elementary education (MS); ESOL (Certificate); gifted education (Certificate); instructional technology (MS, Certificate); professional/studies (Certificate); reading (MS, Certificate); special education (MS). *Program availability:* Part-time, evening/weekend. *Degree requirements:* For master's, comprehensive exam; for doctorate, comprehensive exam, thesis/dissertation. *Entrance requirements:* For master's, interview, minimum GPA of 3.0 or GRE; for doctorate, GRE or MAT. Additional exam requirements/recommendations for international students: Required—TOEFL (minimum score 550 paper-based; 79 iBT). Electronic applications accepted.

Saint Vincent College, Program in Education, Latrobe, PA 15650-2690. Offers curriculum and instruction (MS); instructional design and technology (MS); school administration and supervision (MS); special education (MS). *Program availability:* Part-time, evening/weekend. *Degree requirements:* For master's, comprehensive exam. *Entrance requirements:* For master's, GRE (if undergraduate GPA less than 3.0). Additional exam requirements/recommendations for international students: Required—TOEFL (minimum score 550 paper-based). *Faculty research:* Assessment and instructional technology.

Saint Xavier University, Graduate Studies, School of Education, Chicago, IL 60655-3105. Offers counseling (MA); curriculum and instruction (MA); early childhood education (MA); educational administration (MA); elementary education (MA); individualized studies (MA), including educational technology, English as a second language (ESL), ISTEM (integrative science, technology, engineering, and math), science education; music education (MA); reading (MA); secondary education (MA); Spanish education (MA); special education (MA); teaching and leadership (MA). *Accreditation:* NCATE. *Program availability:* Part-time, evening/weekend. *Degree requirements:* For master's, thesis or project. *Entrance requirements:* For master's, minimum GPA of 3.0. *Expenses:* Contact institution.

Salem College, Graduate Studies, Winston-Salem, NC 27101. Offers art education (MAT); elementary education (M Ed, MAT); language and literacy (M Ed); middle school education (MAT); organ (MM); piano (MM); school counseling (M Ed); second language studies (MAT); secondary education (MAT); special education (M Ed, MAT). *Accreditation:* NCATE. *Program availability:* Part-time, evening/weekend, online learning. *Faculty:* 8 full-time (all women), 11 part-time/adjunct (8 women). In 2017, 17 master's awarded. *Degree requirements:* For master's, practicum (MAT), action research project (M Ed). *Entrance requirements:* For master's, minimum GPA of 3.0, two academic/professional recommendations, acceptable criminal background check. Additional exam requirements/recommendations for international students: Recommended—TOEFL. *Application deadline:* For fall admission, 8/1 for domestic students, 7/15 for international students; for spring admission, 1/15 for domestic students; for summer admission, 5/1 for domestic students. Applications are processed on a rolling basis. Application fee: $30. Electronic applications accepted. *Expenses: Tuition:* Part-time $440 per semester hour. *Financial support:* Scholarships/grants available. Support available to part-time students. Financial award applicants required to submit FAFSA. *Faculty research:* Teacher professional development, adolescent literacy, instructional technology. *Application contact:* Sheryl Long, Director, 336-721-2658, Fax: 336-917-5384, E-mail: sheryl.long@salem.edu.
Website: http://www.salem.edu

Salem State University, School of Graduate Studies, Program in Special Education, Salem, MA 01970-5353. Offers M Ed. *Accreditation:* NCATE. *Program availability:* Part-time, evening/weekend. *Entrance requirements:* For master's, GRE, MAT. Additional exam requirements/recommendations for international students: Required—TOEFL (minimum score 550 paper-based; 80 iBT) or IELTS (minimum score 5.5).

Salus University, College of Education and Rehabilitation, Elkins Park, PA 19027-1598. Offers education of children and youth with visual and multiple impairments (M Ed, Certificate); low vision rehabilitation (MS, Certificate); occupational therapy (MS); orientation and mobility therapy (MS, Certificate); speech-language pathology (MS); vision rehabilitation therapy (MS, Certificate); OD/MS. *Accreditation:* AOTA. *Program availability:* Part-time, online learning. *Entrance requirements:* For master's, GRE or MAT, letters of reference (3), interviews (2). Additional exam requirements/recommendations for international students: Required—TOEFL, TWE. *Expenses:* Contact institution. *Faculty research:* Knowledge utilization, technology transfer.

Samford University, Orlean Beeson School of Education, Birmingham, AL 35229. Offers educational leadership (MSE, Ed D); elementary education (MS Ed, MSE); gifted (MSE); instructional design and technology (MSE); instructional leadership (MSE, Ed S); secondary education (MSE); special education (MSE). *Accreditation:* NCATE. *Program availability:* Part-time, evening/weekend, 100% online, blended/hybrid learning. *Faculty:* 11 full-time (7 women), 22 part-time/adjunct (12 women). *Students:* 206 full-time (144 women), 102 part-time (75 women); includes 124 minority (113 Black or African American, non-Hispanic/Latino; 3 American Indian or Alaska Native, non-Hispanic/Latino; 3 Asian, non-Hispanic/Latino; 2 Hispanic/Latino; 3 Two or more races, non-Hispanic/Latino), 1 international. Average age 37. 134 applicants, 84% accepted, 76 enrolled. In 2017, 79 master's, 34 doctorates, 21 other advanced degrees awarded. *Degree requirements:* For master's and Ed S, comprehensive exam; for doctorate, comprehensive exam, thesis/dissertation. *Entrance requirements:* For master's, GRE, MAT, PRAXIS II, interview, transcripts, essay, recommendations, teaching certification; for doctorate, resume, transcripts, interview, essay; for Ed S, teaching certification, transcripts, essay, interview. Additional exam requirements/recommendations for international students: Required—TOEFL (minimum score 90 iBT), IELTS (minimum score 6.5). *Application deadline:* For fall admission, 7/15 for domestic and international students; for winter admission, 11/15 for domestic and international students; for spring admission, 11/15 for domestic and international students; for summer admission, 4/15 for domestic and international students. Application fee: $35. Electronic applications accepted. *Expenses:* $813 per credit hour, $100 School of Education fee, $175 technology fee. *Financial support:* In 2017–18, 220 students received support. Scholarships/grants and unspecified assistantships available. Financial award application deadline: 2/15; financial award applicants required to submit FAFSA. *Faculty research:* Principal leadership's and teacher organizational commitment mentoring, professional development, and middle grades leadership coaching and administrator effectiveness character development programs in schools teacher efficacy related STEM and professional growth. *Unit head:* Dr. Bonnie Rabe, Interim Dean, 205-726-2565, E-mail: brabe@samford.edu. *Application contact:* Brooke Karr, Graduate Admissions Office Coordinator, 205-729-2783, Fax: 205-726-4233, E-mail: kbgilrea@samford.edu.
Website: http://www.samford.edu/education/

Sam Houston State University, College of Education, Department of Language, Literacy, and Special Populations, Huntsville, TX 77341. Offers international literacy (M Ed); reading (M Ed); special education (M Ed, MA), including low incidence disabilities and autism. *Program availability:* Part-time, evening/weekend, online learning. *Degree requirements:* For master's, comprehensive exam (for some programs), thesis optional, comprehensive portfolio; for doctorate, comprehensive exam, thesis/dissertation. *Entrance requirements:* For master's, GRE General Test, MAT, writing sample, recommendations; for doctorate, GRE General Test, MAT, master's degree, personal statement, recommendations. Additional exam requirements/recommendations for international students: Required—TOEFL (minimum score 550 paper-based; 79 iBT), IELTS (minimum score 6.5). Electronic applications accepted.

San Diego State University, Graduate and Research Affairs, College of Education, Department of Administration, Rehabilitation and Post-Secondary Education, San Diego, CA 92182. Offers educational leadership in post-secondary education (MA); rehabilitation counseling (MS), including deafness. *Program availability:* Evening/weekend, online learning. *Degree requirements:* For master's, comprehensive exam (for some programs), thesis (for some programs). *Entrance requirements:* For master's, GRE General Test, letters of reference. Additional exam requirements/recommendations for international students: Required—TOEFL. Electronic applications accepted. *Faculty research:* Rehabilitation in cultural diversity, distance learning technology.

San Diego State University, Graduate and Research Affairs, College of Education, Department of Special Education, San Diego, CA 92182. Offers MA. *Accreditation:* NCATE. *Program availability:* Evening/weekend. *Entrance requirements:* For master's, GRE General Test, letters of reference. Additional exam requirements/recommendations for international students: Required—TOEFL. Electronic applications accepted.

San Francisco State University, Division of Graduate Studies, College of Education, Department of Special Education, San Francisco, CA 94132-1722. Offers augmentative and alternative communication (AC); autism spectrum (AC); early childhood special education (AC); education specialist (Credential); orientation and mobility (Credential); special education (MA, PhD), including early childhood special education (MA), mild to moderate disabilities (MA), moderate to severe disabilities (MA), orientation and mobility (MA), visual impairments (MA). PhD offered jointly with University of California, Berkeley. *Accreditation:* NCATE. *Unit head:* Dr. Yvonne Bui, Chair, 415-338-2503, Fax: 415-338-0566, E-mail: ybui@sfsu.edu. *Application contact:* Jeanne Oh, Academic Office Coordinator, 415-338-2501, Fax: 415-338-0566, E-mail: joh2@sfsu.edu.
Website: http://sped.sfsu.edu/home

San Ignacio University, Graduate Programs, Doral, FL 33178. Offers business administration (MBA), including human resources management, international business, marketing management; education (M Ed), including early childhood education, educational leadership, special education; hospitality management (MA), including gastronomy and restaurant management, tourism management.

Seattle University, College of Education, Program in Special Education, Seattle, WA 98122-1090. Offers M Ed, MA, Certificate. *Faculty:* 1 (woman) full-time, 1 (woman) part-time/adjunct. *Students:* 11 part-time (8 women); includes 4 minority (2 Hispanic/Latino; 2 Two or more races, non-Hispanic/Latino). Average age 40. 7 applicants, 71% accepted, 4 enrolled. In 2017, 2 master's awarded. *Entrance requirements:* For master's, GRE, MAT or minimum GPA of 3.0, 1 year of K-12 teaching experience; for Certificate, master's degree, minimum GPA of 3.0, 1 year of K-12 teaching experience. *Application deadline:* For fall admission, 8/20 priority date for domestic students; for winter admission, 11/20 priority date for domestic students; for spring admission, 2/20 priority date for domestic students. *Expenses: Tuition:* Full-time $12,960. *Required fees:* $570. Tuition and fees vary according to program. *Financial support:* In 2017–18, 5 students received support. *Unit head:* Dr. Katherine Schlick Noe, Director, 206-296-5768, E-mail: kschlnoe@seattleu.edu. *Application contact:* Janet Shandley, Associate Dean of Graduate Admissions, 206-296-5900, Fax: 206-298-5656, E-mail: grad_admissions@seattleu.edu.
Website: https://www.seattleu.edu/education/specialed/

Seton Hall University, College of Education and Human Services, Department of Educational Studies, South Orange, NJ 07079-2697. Offers instructional design and technology (MA); special education (MA). *Program availability:* Part-time, evening/

weekend, blended/hybrid learning. *Degree requirements:* For master's, comprehensive exam, capstone project. *Entrance requirements:* For master's, GRE or MAT, PRAXIS (for certification candidates), minimum GPA of 2.75. Electronic applications accepted. *Expenses:* Contact institution. *Faculty research:* Special education, applied behavioral analysis, educational technology.

Seton Hill University, Master of Arts Program in Special Education, Greensburg, PA 15601. Offers MA. *Program availability:* Part-time, evening/weekend, blended/hybrid learning. *Entrance requirements:* For master's, 3 letters of recommendation, copy of teacher's certification, transcripts, resume, letter of intent. Additional exam requirements/recommendations for international students: Required—TOEFL (minimum score 600 paper-based; 100 iBT), IELTS (minimum score 6.5). *Application deadline:* Applications are processed on a rolling basis. Application fee: $0. Electronic applications accepted. *Expenses: Tuition:* Part-time $734 per credit. Tuition and fees vary according to class time, course level, course load and program. *Financial support:* Scholarships/grants and tuition discounts available. Financial award application deadline: 8/15; financial award applicants required to submit FAFSA. Website: http://www.setonhill.edu/academics/graduate_programs/special_education

Seton Hill University, Program in Special Education: Autism Specialization, Greensburg, PA 15601. Offers MA. *Program availability:* Part-time, evening/weekend, online only, 100% online, blended/hybrid learning. *Faculty:* 4 full-time (all women), 6 part-time/adjunct (4 women). *Students:* 2 full-time (1 woman), 7 part-time (all women). Average age 27. 7 applicants, 29% accepted, 1 enrolled. In 2017, 1 master's awarded. *Entrance requirements:* For master's, 3 letters of recommendation, transcripts, letter of intent, resume. Additional exam requirements/recommendations for international students: Required—TOEFL (minimum score 600 paper-based; 100 iBT), IELTS (minimum score 6.5). *Application deadline:* Applications are processed on a rolling basis. Application fee: $0. Electronic applications accepted. *Expenses: Tuition:* Part-time $734 per credit. Tuition and fees vary according to class time, course level, course load and program. *Financial support:* Scholarships/grants and tuition discounts available. Financial award applicants required to submit FAFSA. *Faculty research:* Autism, integrating technology into instruction. *Unit head:* Jennifer Suppo, Director, 724-552-4377, E-mail: jsuppo@setonhill.edu. *Application contact:* E-mail: gadmit@setonhill.edu. Website: https://www.setonhill.edu/academics/graduate-programs/special-education-autism-specialization-ma/

Shenandoah University, School of Education and Leadership, Winchester, VA 22601. Offers administration and supervision (Certificate); administrative leadership (D Ed); early childhood literacy (MS); educational administration (MSE); elementary school teacher education (Certificate); emphasis in teaching (MSE); health and physical education (Certificate); individualized focus (MS, MSE); literacy education (MS); middle school teacher education (Certificate); organizational leadership (MS, D Prof); reading licensure (MS, Certificate); reading non-licensure (MS); secondary school teacher education (Certificate); special education (MSE); writing (MS). *Accreditation:* TEAC. *Program availability:* Part-time, evening/weekend. *Faculty:* 8 full-time (7 women), 22 part-time/adjunct (16 women). *Students:* 16 full-time (14 women), 221 part-time (167 women); includes 32 minority (17 Black or African American, non-Hispanic/Latino; 1 American Indian or Alaska Native, non-Hispanic/Latino; 6 Asian, non-Hispanic/Latino; 5 Hispanic/Latino; 1 Native Hawaiian or other Pacific Islander, non-Hispanic/Latino; 2 Two or more races, non-Hispanic/Latino), 3 international. Average age 38. 81 applicants, 99% accepted, 63 enrolled. In 2017, 53 master's, 11 doctorates, 49 other advanced degrees awarded. *Degree requirements:* For master's, comprehensive exam (for some programs), thesis (for some programs); for doctorate, comprehensive exam, thesis/dissertation. *Entrance requirements:* For degree, PRAXIS Academic Core, SAT/ACT, PRAXIS Academic Core Math, or VCLA, three letters of recommendation, writing sample, undergraduate degree. Additional exam requirements/recommendations for international students: Required—TOEFL (minimum score 550 paper-based, 79 iBT) or IELTS (6.5). *Application deadline:* For fall admission, 5/1 priority date for domestic students, 5/1 for international students; for spring admission, 10/15 priority date for domestic students, 10/15 for international students; for summer admission, 3/15 priority date for domestic students, 3/15 for international students. Application fee: $30. Electronic applications accepted. *Expenses:* $15,600 tuition plus $1,296 fees (technology and student services). *Financial support:* In 2017–18, 26 students received support. Scholarships/grants and unspecified assistantships available. Financial award applicants required to submit FAFSA. *Faculty research:* Mentoring, behavior support for students, teacher change agency, educational technology in pedagogy, literacy education. *Unit head:* Jill Lindsey, PhD, Director, 540-535-7324, Fax: 540-665-4726, E-mail: jlindsey@su.edu. *Application contact:* Andrew Woodall, Executive Director of Recruitment and Admissions, 540-665-4581, Fax: 540-665-4627, E-mail: admit@su.edu. Website: http://www.su.edu/education/

Shippensburg University of Pennsylvania, School of Graduate Studies, College of Education and Human Services, Department of Educational Leadership and Special Education, Shippensburg, PA 17257-2299. Offers educational leadership (M Ed, Ed D); special education (M Ed), including behavior disorders, intellectual disabilities, learning disabilities. *Accreditation:* NCATE. *Program availability:* Part-time, evening/weekend, blended/hybrid learning. *Faculty:* 6 full-time (2 women), 8 part-time/adjunct (5 women). *Students:* 13 full-time (7 women), 106 part-time (60 women); includes 5 minority (3 Black or African American, non-Hispanic/Latino; 1 Asian, non-Hispanic/Latino; 1 Two or more races, non-Hispanic/Latino), 16 international. Average age 34. 80 applicants, 69% accepted, 44 enrolled. In 2017, 22 master's awarded. *Degree requirements:* For master's, candidacy, thesis, or practicum; for doctorate, comprehensive exam, thesis/dissertation, candidacy exam; 24 credits (six 4-credit residencies) of field-based courses leading to the superintendent's letter of eligibility. *Entrance requirements:* For master's, GRE or MAT (if GPA is less than 2.75), 2 years of successful teaching experience; 3 letters of reference; 2 years of successful teaching experience; interview; statement of purpose; writing sample; personal goals statement; resume; for doctorate, resume; three letters of recommendation; 500-1000 word goals statement; teaching certifications and endorsements currently held; experience as public school administrator or supervisor that requires an administrative/supervisory certificate. Additional exam requirements/recommendations for international students: Required—TOEFL (minimum score 550 paper-based, 68 iBT) or IELTS (minimum score 6). *Application deadline:* For fall admission, 2/1 for domestic students, 4/30 for international students; for spring admission, 7/1 for domestic students, 9/30 for international students. Applications are processed on a rolling basis. Application fee: $45. Electronic applications accepted. *Expenses:* Tuition, state resident: part-time $500 per credit. Tuition, nonresident: part-time $750 per credit. *Required fees:* $145 per credit. *Financial support:* In 2017–18, 2 students received support. Career-related internships or fieldwork, scholarships/grants, unspecified assistantships, and resident hall director and student payroll positions available. Support available to part-time students. Financial award application deadline: 3/1; financial award applicants required to submit FAFSA. *Unit head:* Dr. Thomas C. Gibbon, Departmental Chair, 717-477-1498, Fax: 717-477-4036, E-mail: tcgibb@ship.edu. *Application contact:* Maya T. Mapp, Director of Admissions, 717-477-1231, Fax: 717-477-4016, E-mail: mtmap@ship.edu. Website: http://www.ship.edu/else/

Siena Heights University, Graduate College, Adrian, MI 49221-1796. Offers clinical mental health counseling (MA); educational leadership (Specialist); leadership (MA), including health care leadership, organizational leadership; teacher education (MA), including early childhood education, early childhood education: Montessori, education leadership: principal, elementary education: reading K-12, leadership: higher education, secondary education: reading K-12, special education: cognitive impairment, special education: learning disabilities. *Program availability:* Part-time, evening/weekend. *Degree requirements:* For master's, thesis, presentation. *Entrance requirements:* For master's, minimum GPA of 3.0, current resume, essay, all post-secondary transcripts, 3 letters of reference, conviction disclosure form; copy of teaching certificate (for some education programs); for Specialist, master's degree, minimum GPA of 3.0, current resume, essay, all post-secondary transcripts, 3 letters of reference, conviction disclosure form; copy of teaching certificate (for some education programs). Electronic applications accepted.

Simmons College, School of Social Work, Boston, MA 02115. Offers behavior analysis (MS, PhD, Ed S); education (MS Ed); social work (MSW, PhD); special education (MS Ed), including moderate and severe disabilities; teaching (MAT), including elementary education; MSW/MBA. *Accreditation:* CSWE (one or more programs are accredited). *Program availability:* Part-time, 100% online, blended/hybrid learning. *Faculty:* 57 full-time (47 women), 48 part-time/adjunct (36 women). *Students:* 878 full-time (757 women), 979 part-time (869 women); includes 468 minority (213 Black or African American, non-Hispanic/Latino; 1 American Indian or Alaska Native, non-Hispanic/Latino; 45 Asian, non-Hispanic/Latino; 152 Hispanic/Latino; 3 Native Hawaiian or other Pacific Islander, non-Hispanic/Latino; 54 Two or more races, non-Hispanic/Latino), 12 international. Average age 30. 1,521 applicants, 74% accepted, 545 enrolled. In 2017, 611 master's, 7 doctorates, 1 other advanced degree awarded. Terminal master's awarded for partial completion of doctoral program. *Degree requirements:* For master's, thesis (for some programs); for doctorate, comprehensive exam (for some programs), thesis/dissertation (for some programs). *Entrance requirements:* For master's, GRE, MAT, Massachusetts Tests for Education Licensure (for different programs), minimum grade of B in introductory statistics course within five years prior to entering program, resume, transcripts, three letters of recommendation, personal statement; for doctorate, GRE, BCBA Analyst Exam. Additional exam requirements/recommendations for international students: Required—TOEFL (minimum score 600 paper-based; 100 iBT). *Application deadline:* For fall admission, 8/1 for domestic students; for spring admission, 12/15 for domestic students; for summer admission, 5/1 for domestic students. Applications are processed on a rolling basis. Application fee: $35. Electronic applications accepted. *Expenses:* $1,001 per credit hour, $3,003 per course, $55 activity fee per semester. *Financial support:* In 2017–18, 12 fellowships with partial tuition reimbursements were awarded; scholarships/grants and unspecified assistantships also available. Support available to part-time students. Financial award applicants required to submit FAFSA. *Unit head:* Dr. Cheryl Parks, Dean, 617-521-3293, E-mail: cheryl.parks@simmons.edu. *Application contact:* Carlos D. Frontado, Director of Admissions, 617-521-3920, Fax: 617-521-3980, E-mail: ssw@simmons.edu. Website: http://www.simmons.edu/ssw/

Slippery Rock University of Pennsylvania, Graduate Studies (Recruitment), College of Education, Department of Special Education, Slippery Rock, PA 16057-1383. Offers autism (M Ed); master teacher (M Ed), including birth to grade 8, grades 7 to 12; special education (Ed D); supervision (M Ed); technology for online instruction (M Ed). *Accreditation:* NCATE. *Program availability:* Part-time, evening/weekend, 100% online. *Degree requirements:* For master's, thesis optional. *Entrance requirements:* For master's, minimum GPA of 3.0, official transcripts, teaching certification. Additional exam requirements/recommendations for international students: Required—TOEFL (minimum score 550 paper-based; 80 iBT). Electronic applications accepted. *Expenses:* Contact institution.

Sonoma State University, School of Education, Rohnert Park, CA 94928. Offers administrative services (Credential); curriculum, teaching, and learning (MA); early childhood education (MA); education specialist (Credential); educational leadership (MA); multiple subject (Credential); reading and literacy (MA, Credential); single subject (Credential); special education (MA). *Accreditation:* NCATE. *Program availability:* Part-time, evening/weekend. *Entrance requirements:* For master's, minimum GPA of 2.5. Additional exam requirements/recommendations for international students: Required—TOEFL (minimum score 500 paper-based). Application fee: $55. *Financial support:* Fellowships, research assistantships, career-related internships or fieldwork, and Federal Work-Study available. Support available to part-time students. Financial award application deadline: 3/2; financial award applicants required to submit FAFSA. *Unit head:* Dr. Carlos Ayala, Dean, 707-664-4412, E-mail: carlos.ayala@sonoma.edu. *Application contact:* Dr. Karen Grady, Coordinator of Graduate Studies, 707-664-3328, E-mail: karen.grady@sonoma.edu. Website: http://www.sonoma.edu/education/

South Carolina State University, College of Graduate and Professional Studies, Department of Education, Orangeburg, SC 29117-0001. Offers early childhood education (MAT); education (M Ed); elementary education (M Ed, MAT); English (MAT); general science/biology (MAT); mathematics (MAT); secondary education (M Ed), including biology education, business education, counselor education, English education, home economics education, industrial education, mathematics education, science education, social studies education; special education (M Ed), including emotionally handicapped, learning disabilities, mentally handicapped. *Accreditation:* NCATE. *Program availability:* Part-time, evening/weekend. *Faculty:* 11 full-time (6 women), 4 part-time/adjunct (2 women). *Students:* 26 full-time (18 women), 22 part-time (17 women); includes 41 minority (all Black or African American, non-Hispanic/Latino), 1 international. Average age 33. 25 applicants, 100% accepted, 19 enrolled. In 2017, 23 master's awarded. *Degree requirements:* For master's, thesis optional, departmental qualifying exam. *Entrance requirements:* For master's, GRE General Test, NTE, interview, teaching certificate. *Application deadline:* For fall admission, 6/15 priority date for domestic students, 6/15 for international students; for spring admission, 11/1 for domestic and international students. Application fee: $25. Electronic applications accepted. *Expenses:* Tuition, state resident: full-time $9388; part-time $607 per credit hour. Tuition, nonresident: full-time $19,968; part-time $1194 per credit hour. *Required fees:* $766; $766 per credit hour. *Financial support:* Fellowships, career-related internships or fieldwork, Federal Work-Study, and scholarships/grants available. Financial award application deadline: 6/1. *Unit head:* Dr. Charlie Spell, Interim Chair, Department of Education, 803-536-8963, Fax: 803-516-4568, E-mail: cspell@scsu.edu. *Application contact:* Curtis Foskey, Coordinator of Graduate Studies, 803-536-8419, Fax: 803-536-8812, E-mail: cfoskey@scsu.edu.

Southeastern Louisiana University, College of Education, Department of Teaching and Learning, Hammond, LA 70402. Offers curriculum and instruction (M Ed); elementary education (MAT); special education (M Ed); special education: early interventionist (MAT). *Accreditation:* NCATE. *Program availability:* Part-time, evening/weekend. *Faculty:* 14 full-time (all women), 2 part-time/adjunct (1 woman). *Students:* 19 full-time (16 women), 115 part-time (104 women); includes 13 minority (3 Black or African American, non-Hispanic/Latino; 5 Hispanic/Latino; 5 Two or more races, non-Hispanic/Latino), 1 international. Average age 37. 55 applicants, 45% accepted, 18

Special Education

enrolled. In 2017, 29 master's awarded. *Degree requirements:* For master's, comprehensive exam (for some programs), thesis (for some programs), action research project, oral defense of research project, portfolio, teaching certificate, minimum cumulative GPA of 3.0. *Entrance requirements:* For master's, GRE (verbal and quantitative), PRAXIS (for MAT), Prospective Education Candidate (PEC) self-assessment survey; competency on a technology performance assessment in education or three-hour graduate-level technology course; orientation seminar. Additional exam requirements/recommendations for international students: Required—TOEFL (minimum score 500 paper-based; 61 iBT). *Application deadline:* For fall admission, 7/15 priority date for domestic students, 6/1 priority date for international students; for spring admission, 12/1 priority date for domestic students, 10/1 priority date for international students. Applications are processed on a rolling basis. Application fee: $20 ($30 for international students). Electronic applications accepted. *Expenses:* Tuition, state resident: full-time $6684. Tuition, nonresident: full-time $19,162. *Required fees:* $2088. *Financial support:* In 2017–18, 5 students received support. Research assistantships, teaching assistantships, career-related internships or fieldwork, Federal Work-Study, institutionally sponsored loans, scholarships/grants, and unspecified assistantships available. Support available to part-time students. Financial award application deadline: 5/1; financial award applicants required to submit FAFSA. *Faculty research:* Teacher in services, STEM, educational technology, pre-service teacher education. *Unit head:* Dr. Colleen Klein-Ezell, Department Head, 985-549-2221, Fax: 985-549-5009, E-mail: colleen.klein-ezell@southeastern.edu. *Application contact:* Amanda Harper, Graduate Admissions Analyst, 985-549-5620, Fax: 985-549-5632, E-mail: admissions@southeastern.edu.
Website: http://www.southeastern.edu/acad_research/depts/teach_lrn/index.html

Southeast Missouri State University, School of Graduate Studies, Department of Elementary, Early and Special Education, Program in Exceptional Child Education, Cape Girardeau, MO 63701-4799. Offers MA. *Accreditation:* NCATE. *Program availability:* Part-time, evening/weekend, 100% online. *Faculty:* 11 full-time (9 women), 1 (woman) part-time/adjunct. *Students:* 4 full-time (all women), 45 part-time (41 women); includes 1 minority (Black or African American, non-Hispanic/Latino). Average age 33. 13 applicants, 100% accepted, 13 enrolled. In 2017, 12 master's awarded. *Degree requirements:* For master's, action research project and presentation. *Entrance requirements:* For master's, state licensure exam or GRE, minimum GPA of 2.75; teaching certificate. Additional exam requirements/recommendations for international students: Required—TOEFL (minimum score 95 iBT), IELTS (minimum score 7), PTE. *Application deadline:* For fall admission, 8/1 for domestic students, 6/1 for international students; for spring admission, 11/21 for domestic students, 10/1 for international students; for summer admission, 5/15 for domestic students. Applications are processed on a rolling basis. Application fee: $40 ($40 for international students). Electronic applications accepted. *Expenses:* $270.35 in-state tuition per credit hour, $33.40 fees per credit hour. *Financial support:* In 2017–18, 3 students received support. Career-related internships or fieldwork, Federal Work-Study, scholarships/grants, traineeships, tuition waivers (full), and unspecified assistantships available. Financial award application deadline: 6/30; financial award applicants required to submit FAFSA. *Faculty research:* Instructional and assistive technology, teacher candidate professional dispositions, autism spectrum disorder, grow your own programs. *Unit head:* Dr. Julie Ray, Department of Elementary, Early, and Special Education Chair/Professor, 573-651-2444, E-mail: jaray@semo.edu. *Application contact:* Dr. Nancy Aguinaga, 573-651-2122, E-mail: naguinaga@semo.edu.
Website: http://www.semo.edu/eese/

Southern Connecticut State University, School of Graduate Studies, School of Education, Program in Special Education, New Haven, CT 06515-1355. Offers MS Ed. *Program availability:* Part-time, evening/weekend. *Degree requirements:* For master's, thesis or alternative. *Entrance requirements:* For master's, interview. Electronic applications accepted.

Southern Illinois University Carbondale, Graduate School, College of Education and Human Services, Department of Educational Psychology and Special Education, Program in Special Education, Carbondale, IL 62901-4701. Offers special education (MS Ed, PhD), including behavior (MS Ed), curriculum (MS Ed), early childhood special education (MS Ed), special education supervision (MS Ed). *Accreditation:* NCATE. *Program availability:* Part-time. *Degree requirements:* For master's, thesis. *Entrance requirements:* For master's, GRE General Test, minimum GPA of 2.7. Additional exam requirements/recommendations for international students: Required—TOEFL. *Faculty research:* Applied and action research; scientific methods used to evaluate effectiveness of products and programs for the handicapped; scientific methods used to develop generalizations about instructional, motivational, and learning processes of the handicapped.

Southern Illinois University Edwardsville, Graduate School, School of Education, Health, and Human Behavior, Department of Special Education and Communication Disorders, Program in Special Education, Edwardsville, IL 62026. Offers MS Ed, Post-Master's Certificate. *Program availability:* Part-time, evening/weekend. *Degree requirements:* For master's, thesis or alternative, final project. *Entrance requirements:* Additional exam requirements/recommendations for international students: Required—TOEFL (minimum score 550 paper-based; 79 iBT), IELTS (minimum score 6.5). Electronic applications accepted.

Southern Methodist University, Annette Caldwell Simmons School of Education and Human Development, Department of Teaching and Learning, Dallas, TX 75275. Offers bilingual/ESL education (MBE); education (M Ed, PhD); gifted education (MBE); reading and writing (M Ed); special education (M Ed). *Program availability:* Part-time, evening/weekend. Terminal master's awarded for partial completion of doctoral program. *Degree requirements:* For master's, comprehensive exam, minimum GPA of 3.0; for doctorate, thesis/dissertation, qualifying exams, major area paper, evidence of teaching competency, dissemination of research (e.g., conference presentation), professional portfolio. *Entrance requirements:* For master's, minimum GPA of 3.0 or GRE, 3 letters of recommendation; for doctorate, GRE, minimum GPA of 3.3, 3 years of full-time teaching, 3 letters of recommendation, interview. Additional exam requirements/recommendations for international students: Required—TOEFL. Electronic applications accepted. *Faculty research:* Reading intervention, mathematics intervention, bilingual education, new literacies.

Southern New Hampshire University, School of Education, Manchester, NH 03106-1045. Offers curriculum and instruction (M Ed), including dyslexia studies and language-based learning disabilities, educational leadership, reading, special education, technology integration; dyslexia studies and language-based learning disabilities (Certificate); early childhood and special education (M Ed); educational leadership (M Ed, Ed D); educational studies (M Ed); elementary and special education (M Ed); field based education (M Ed); higher education administration (MS); teaching English as a foreign language (MS). *Program availability:* Part-time, evening/weekend, online learning. *Degree requirements:* For master's, comprehensive exam (for some programs), thesis or alternative. *Entrance requirements:* For master's, PRAXIS I, minimum GPA of 2.75. Additional exam requirements/recommendations for international students: Required—TOEFL (minimum score 550 paper-based). *Application deadline:* Applications are processed on a rolling basis. Application fee: $40. Electronic

applications accepted. *Expenses:* Contact institution. *Financial support:* Institutionally sponsored loans available. Financial award applicants required to submit FAFSA. *Unit head:* Raymond McNulty, Dean, 603-668-2211, Fax: 603-629-4673. *Application contact:* Office of Graduate Admission, 888-327-SNHU, Fax: 603-644-3144, E-mail: enroll@snhu.edu.

Southern Oregon University, Graduate Studies, School of Education, Ashland, OR 97520. Offers elementary education (MA Ed, MS Ed), including classroom teacher, early childhood, handicapped learner, reading, supervision; secondary education (MA Ed, MS Ed), including classroom teacher, handicapped learner, reading, supervision; teaching (MAT). *Program availability:* Online learning. *Degree requirements:* For master's, thesis optional. *Entrance requirements:* For master's, GRE General Test, minimum cumulative GPA of 3.0 in the last 90 quarter credits (60 semester credits) of undergraduate coursework. Additional exam requirements/recommendations for international students: Required—TOEFL (minimum score 540 paper-based; 76 iBT), IELTS (minimum score 6), ELPT (minimum score 964) or ELS (minimum score 112). Electronic applications accepted.

Southern University and Agricultural and Mechanical College, Graduate School and College of Education, Department of Special Education, Baton Rouge, LA 70813. Offers M Ed, PhD. *Accreditation:* NCATE. *Program availability:* Part-time, evening/weekend. *Degree requirements:* For master's, comprehensive exam, thesis optional; for doctorate, thesis/dissertation, comprehensive qualifying exam, oral defense of dissertation. *Entrance requirements:* For master's, GMAT or GRE General Test, PRAXIS; for doctorate, GRE General Test, PRAXIS, letters of recommendation, 2 years experience (individuals with disabilities). Additional exam requirements/recommendations for international students: Required—TOEFL. *Faculty research:* Classroom discipline/management, minority students in gifted/special education, learning styles/brain hemisphericity, school violence and prevention, certifications for special education teachers.

Southwestern College, Education Programs, Winfield, KS 67156-2499. Offers curriculum and instruction (M Ed); early childhood education (M Ed); educational leadership (Ed D), including higher education leadership, PK-12 education leadership; special education (M Ed), including high-incidence disabilities, low-incidence disabilities; teaching (MA). *Accreditation:* NCATE. *Program availability:* Part-time, evening/weekend, 100% online, blended/hybrid learning. *Faculty:* 6 full-time (5 women), 12 part-time/adjunct (10 women). *Students:* 12 full-time (10 women), 77 part-time (51 women); includes 12 minority (5 Black or African American, non-Hispanic/Latino; 2 American Indian or Alaska Native, non-Hispanic/Latino; 1 Asian, non-Hispanic/Latino; 3 Hispanic/Latino; 1 Native Hawaiian or other Pacific Islander, non-Hispanic/Latino), 10 international. Average age 39. 29 applicants, 86% accepted, 18 enrolled. In 2017, 52 master's, 11 doctorates awarded. *Degree requirements:* For master's, practicum, portfolio; for doctorate, thesis/dissertation, professional portfolio. *Entrance requirements:* For master's, baccalaureate degree, minimum GPA of 3.0, valid teaching certificate (for special education); for doctorate, GRE if no master's degree, baccalaureate degree with minimum GPA of 3.25 and current teaching experience, or master's degree with minimum GPA of 3.5. Additional exam requirements/recommendations for international students: Required—TOEFL (minimum score 550 paper-based; 80 iBT). *Application deadline:* Applications are processed on a rolling basis. Application fee: $40. Electronic applications accepted. *Expenses:* $577 per credit hour, $509 online (for master's programs); $609 per credit hour (for doctorate program). *Financial support:* In 2017–18, 9 students received support. Unspecified assistantships and employee tuition waivers available. Financial award applicants required to submit FAFSA. *Unit head:* Dana Pentz, Director of Education Operations, 620-229-6253, E-mail: dana.pentz@sckans.edu. *Application contact:* Dennis Russell, Director of Admissions and Student Services, 888-684-5335 Ext. 3372, Fax: 888-684-5218, E-mail: dennis.russell@sckans.edu.
Website: http://www.sckans.edu/graduate/education-med/

Southwestern Oklahoma State University, College of Professional and Graduate Studies, School of Behavioral Sciences and Education, Specialization in Special Education, Weatherford, OK 73096-3098. Offers M Ed. M Ed distance learning degree program offered to Oklahoma residents only. *Accreditation:* NCATE. *Program availability:* Part-time, evening/weekend. *Degree requirements:* For master's, exam. *Entrance requirements:* For master's, GRE General Test or minimum undergraduate GPA of 3.0. Additional exam requirements/recommendations for international students: Required—TOEFL.

Southwest Minnesota State University, Department of Education, Marshall, MN 56258. Offers ESL (MS); math (MS); reading (MS); special education (MS), including developmental disabilities, early childhood education, emotional behavioral disorders, learning disabilities; teaching, learning and leadership (MS). *Program availability:* Part-time, evening/weekend, online learning. *Entrance requirements:* Additional exam requirements/recommendations for international students: Required—TOEFL or IELTS; Recommended—TOEFL (minimum score 550 paper-based; 80 iBT), IELTS.

Spalding University, Graduate Studies, College of Education, Programs in Education, Louisville, KY 40203-2188. Offers art teacher education (MAT); business teacher education (MAT); elementary school education (MAT); foreign language (MAT); high school education (MAT); middle school education (MAT); secondary education (MAT); special education (learning and behavioral disorders) (MAT); student guidance counselor (MA); teacher leader (M Ed). *Accreditation:* NCATE. *Program availability:* Part-time, evening/weekend. *Entrance requirements:* For master's, GRE General Test or MAT, interview, letters of recommendation, resume. Additional exam requirements/recommendations for international students: Required—TOEFL (minimum score 535 paper-based). Electronic applications accepted. *Faculty research:* Instructional technology, achievement gap, classroom management, assessment.

Spring Arbor University, School of Education, Spring Arbor, MI 49283-9799. Offers education (MAE); reading (MAR); special education (MSE). *Accreditation:* TEAC. *Program availability:* Part-time, evening/weekend, online learning. *Degree requirements:* For master's, thesis. *Entrance requirements:* For master's, official transcripts from all institutions attended, including evidence of an earned bachelor's degree from regionally-accredited college or university with minimum cumulative GPA of 3.0 for the last two years of the bachelor's degree; two professional letters of recommendation. Additional exam requirements/recommendations for international students: Required—TOEFL (minimum score 600 paper-based). Electronic applications accepted.

Springfield College, Graduate Programs, Programs in Education, Springfield, MA 01109-3797. Offers early childhood education (M Ed); educational studies (M Ed); elementary education (M Ed); secondary education (M Ed); special education (M Ed, CAGS). *Program availability:* Part-time, evening/weekend. *Students:* 18 applicants, 72% accepted, 12 enrolled. In 2017, 22 master's awarded. *Entrance requirements:* For master's, Massachusetts Tests for Educator Licensure (MTEL). Additional exam requirements/recommendations for international students: Required—TOEFL (minimum score 550 paper-based); Recommended—IELTS (minimum score 7). *Application deadline:* For fall admission, 1/15 for domestic and international students; for winter admission, 11/1 for domestic and international students; for spring admission, 11/1 for domestic and international students. Applications are processed on a rolling basis. Application fee: $50. Electronic applications accepted. *Expenses:* Contact institution.

Financial support: Fellowships with partial tuition reimbursements, teaching assistantships with partial tuition reimbursements, career-related internships or fieldwork, Federal Work-Study, institutionally sponsored loans, scholarships/grants, and unspecified assistantships available. Financial award application deadline: 3/1; financial award applicants required to submit FAFSA. *Unit head:* Linda Davis-Delano, Director of Education Preparation and Licensure, 413-748-3295, E-mail: ldelano@springfield.edu. *Application contact:* Anne Griffin, Director of Graduate Admissions, 413-748-3225, Fax: 413-748-3694, E-mail: agriffin2@springfield.edu.
Website: http://springfield.edu/wtp

State University of New York at New Paltz, Graduate and Extended Learning School, School of Education, Department of Educational Studies and Leadership, Program in Special Education, New Paltz, NY 12561. Offers adolescence special education (7-12) (MS Ed); adolescence special education and literacy (MS Ed); childhood special education (1-6) (MS Ed); childhood special education and literacy (MS Ed); early childhood special education (B-2) (MS Ed). *Accreditation:* NCATE. *Program availability:* Part-time, evening/weekend. *Faculty:* 3 full-time (2 women). *Students:* 11 full-time (7 women), 37 part-time (31 women); includes 4 minority (1 Asian, non-Hispanic/Latino; 3 Hispanic/Latino). 29 applicants, 93% accepted, 24 enrolled. In 2017, 28 master's awarded. *Entrance requirements:* For master's, minimum GPA of 3.0 (3.2 for special education and literacy programs), New York state teaching certificate. Additional exam requirements/recommendations for international students: Required—TOEFL (minimum score 550 paper-based; 80 iBT), IELTS (minimum score 6.5). *Application deadline:* For fall admission, 3/15 priority date for domestic students, 3/15 for international students; for spring admission, 11/1 for domestic and international students. Application fee: $50. Electronic applications accepted. *Financial support:* Application deadline: 8/1. *Unit head:* Dr. Jane Sileo, Coordinator, 845-257-2835, E-mail: sileoj@newpaltz.edu. *Application contact:* Vika Shock, Director of Graduate Admissions, 845-257-3286, E-mail: gradschool@newpaltz.edu.
Website: http://www.newpaltz.edu/schoolofed/department-of-teaching—learning/special_ed.html

State University of New York at Oswego, Graduate Studies, School of Education, Department of Curriculum and Instruction, Oswego, NY 13126. Offers adolescence education (MST); art education (MAT); childhood education (MST); curriculum and instruction (MS Ed); literacy education (MS Ed); special education (MS Ed). *Program availability:* Part-time, evening/weekend. *Degree requirements:* For master's, comprehensive exam (for some programs), thesis optional. *Entrance requirements:* For master's, GRE General Test, minimum GPA of 2.7, provisional teaching certificate. Additional exam requirements/recommendations for international students: Required—TOEFL (minimum score 560 paper-based). *Faculty research:* Classroom applications for microcomputers; classroom questioning, wait-time, and achievement; values clarification and academic achievement.

State University of New York at Plattsburgh, School of Education, Health, and Human Services, Program in Teacher Education: Special Education, Plattsburgh, NY 12901-2681. Offers birth to grade 2 (MS Ed); birth to grade 6 (MS Ed); grades 1 to 6 (MS Ed); grades 7 to 12 (MS Ed). *Accreditation:* TEAC. *Program availability:* Part-time, evening/weekend. *Entrance requirements:* For master's, minimum GPA of 2.75. Additional exam requirements/recommendations for international students: Required—TOEFL. *Faculty research:* Inclusion behavior management technology, applied behavior analysis.

State University of New York College at Cortland, Graduate Studies, School of Education, Programs in Teaching Students with Disabilities, Cortland, NY 13045. Offers MS Ed. *Accreditation:* NCATE. *Program availability:* Part-time, evening/weekend. *Degree requirements:* For master's, one foreign language, comprehensive exam, thesis (for some programs). *Entrance requirements:* For master's, provisional certification. Additional exam requirements/recommendations for international students: Required—TOEFL.

State University of New York College at Oneonta, Graduate Programs, Division of Education, Department of Educational Psychology, Counseling and Special Education, Oneonta, NY 13820-4015. Offers school counselor K-12 (MS Ed, CAS); special education (MS Ed). *Accreditation:* NCATE. *Program availability:* Part-time, evening/weekend. *Degree requirements:* For master's, comprehensive exam. *Entrance requirements:* For master's, GRE General Test.

State University of New York College at Potsdam, School of Education and Professional Studies, Program in Special Education, Potsdam, NY 13676. Offers adolescence (grades 7-12) (MS Ed); childhood (grades 1-6) (MS Ed); early childhood (birth-grade 2) (MS Ed). *Accreditation:* NCATE. *Program availability:* Part-time. *Degree requirements:* For master's, culminating experience. *Entrance requirements:* For master's, minimum GPA of 3.0 in last 60 hours of course work. Additional exam requirements/recommendations for international students: Required—TOEFL (minimum score 550 paper-based; 80 iBT), IELTS (minimum score 6). Electronic applications accepted.

Stephen F. Austin State University, Graduate School, College of Education, Department of Human Services, Nacogdoches, TX 75962. Offers counseling (MA); school psychology (MA); special education (M Ed); speech-language pathology (MS). *Accreditation:* ACA (one or more programs are accredited); ASHA (one or more programs are accredited); CORE; NCATE. *Degree requirements:* For master's, comprehensive exam, thesis (for some programs). *Entrance requirements:* For master's, GRE General Test, minimum GPA of 2.8. Additional exam requirements/recommendations for international students: Required—TOEFL.

Syracuse University, School of Education, MS Program in Early Childhood Special Education, Syracuse, NY 13244. Offers MS. *Program availability:* Part-time. *Entrance requirements:* For master's, GRE, baccalaureate degree from regionally-accredited college/university, strong teacher and/or employer recommendations, personal statement, experience working with children. Additional exam requirements/recommendations for international students: Required—TOEFL (minimum score 100 iBT). *Application deadline:* For fall admission, 1/15 priority date for domestic and international students; for spring admission, 10/15 priority date for domestic and international students; for summer admission, 1/15 priority date for domestic and international students. Applications are processed on a rolling basis. Application fee: $75. Electronic applications accepted. *Financial support:* Fellowships with full tuition reimbursements, research assistantships, teaching assistantships, career-related internships or fieldwork, and scholarships/grants available. Financial award application deadline: 1/15; financial award applicants required to submit FAFSA. *Faculty research:* Teaching children with diverse backgrounds and abilities, home-based itinerant teaching, early childhood special education, general preschool teaching, teacher consulting. *Unit head:* Dr. Benjamin Dotger, Department Chair, 315-443-2685, E-mail: bdotger@syr.edu. *Application contact:* Speranza Migliore, Graduate Admissions Recruiter, 315-443-2505, E-mail: gradrcrt@syr.edu.
Website: http://soe.syr.edu/academic/teaching_and_leadership/graduate/masters/early_childhood_special_education/default.aspx

Syracuse University, School of Education, MS Program in Inclusive Special Education (Grades 1-6), Syracuse, NY 13244. Offers MS. *Program availability:* Part-time. In 2017, 6 master's awarded. *Entrance requirements:* For master's, GRE, baccalaureate degree from regionally-accredited college/university, initial New York State certification in childhood education, three letters of recommendation, personal statement, transcripts. Additional exam requirements/recommendations for international students: Required—TOEFL (minimum score 100 iBT). *Application deadline:* For fall admission, 1/15 priority date for domestic and international students; for spring admission, 10/15 priority date for domestic and international students. Applications are processed on a rolling basis. Application fee: $75. Electronic applications accepted. *Financial support:* Fellowships with full tuition reimbursements, research assistantships, teaching assistantships, career-related internships or fieldwork, and scholarships/grants available. Financial award application deadline: 1/15; financial award applicants required to submit FAFSA. *Faculty research:* Creating safe and peaceful schools, adapting instruction for diverse student needs, early intervention for children's reading problems, teaching children with autism, augmentative and alternative communication in inclusive classrooms. *Unit head:* Dr. Christine Ashby, Assistant Professor/Inclusive Master's Program Coordinator, 315-443-8689, E-mail: ceashby@syr.edu. *Application contact:* Speranza Migliore, Graduate Admissions Recruiter, 315-443-2505, E-mail: gradrcrt@syr.edu.
Website: http://soe.syr.edu/academic/teaching_and_leadership/graduate/masters/inclusive_special_education_grades_1_6/default.aspx

Syracuse University, School of Education, MS Program in Inclusive Special Education (Grades 7-12), Syracuse, NY 13244. Offers MS. *Program availability:* Part-time. *Students:* Average age 29. In 2017, 2 master's awarded. *Entrance requirements:* For master's, GRE, baccalaureate degree from regionally-accredited college/university, recommendation letters, personal statement, experience working with youth. Additional exam requirements/recommendations for international students: Required—TOEFL (minimum score 100 iBT). *Application deadline:* For fall admission, 1/15 priority date for domestic and international students; for spring admission, 10/15 priority date for domestic and international students. Applications are processed on a rolling basis. Application fee: $75. Electronic applications accepted. *Financial support:* Fellowships with full tuition reimbursements, research assistantships, teaching assistantships, career-related internships or fieldwork, and scholarships/grants available. Financial award application deadline: 1/15; financial award applicants required to submit FAFSA. *Faculty research:* Students with disabilities, inclusive education and disability studies, extensive placements in schools, adapting instruction for diverse student needs, assistive technologies. *Unit head:* Dr. Christine Ashby, Assistant Professor, 315-443-8689, E-mail: ceashby@syr.edu. *Application contact:* Speranza Migliore, Graduate Admissions Recruiter, 315-443-2505, E-mail: gradrcrt@syr.edu.
Website: http://soe.syr.edu/academic/teaching_and_leadership/graduate/masters/inclusive_special_education_grades_7_12/default.aspx

Syracuse University, School of Education, MS Program in Inclusive Special Education: Severe/Multiple Disabilities, Syracuse, NY 13244. Offers MS. *Program availability:* Part-time. *Students:* Average age 27. *Entrance requirements:* For master's, GRE, baccalaureate degree from regionally-accredited college/university, New York State initial certification in students with disabilities, strong professor and/or employer recommendations, personal statement, interview. Additional exam requirements/recommendations for international students: Required—TOEFL (minimum score 100 iBT). *Application deadline:* For fall admission, 1/15 priority date for domestic and international students; for spring admission, 10/15 priority date for domestic and international students. Applications are processed on a rolling basis. Application fee: $75. Electronic applications accepted. *Financial support:* Fellowships with full tuition reimbursements, research assistantships, teaching assistantships, career-related internships or fieldwork, and scholarships/grants available. Financial award application deadline: 1/15. *Faculty research:* Teaching children and adolescents with autism, augmentation of communication in the inclusive classroom, families of students with disabilities, positive approaches to challenging behaviors, creating safe and peaceful schools. *Unit head:* Dr. Gail Ensher, Program Coordinator, 315-443-9650, E-mail: glensher@syr.edu. *Application contact:* Speranza Migliore, Graduate Admissions Recruiter, 315-443-2505, E-mail: gradrcrt@syr.edu.
Website: http://soe.syr.edu/academic/teaching_and_leadership/graduate/masters/inclusive_special_education_grades_1_6/admissions.aspx

Syracuse University, School of Education, PhD Program in Special Education, Syracuse, NY 13244. Offers PhD. *Program availability:* Part-time. *Degree requirements:* For doctorate, comprehensive exam, thesis/dissertation. *Entrance requirements:* For doctorate, GRE General Test, master's degree, interview, writing sample, disability experience (preferred), three letters of recommendation. Additional exam requirements/recommendations for international students: Required—TOEFL (minimum score 100 iBT). *Application deadline:* For fall admission, 10/15 priority date for domestic and international students. Applications are processed on a rolling basis. Application fee: $75. Electronic applications accepted. *Financial support:* Fellowships with full tuition reimbursements, research assistantships, teaching assistantships, career-related internships or fieldwork, and institutionally sponsored loans available. Support available to part-time students. Financial award application deadline: 1/15. *Faculty research:* Curriculum development and field-based projects, psychoeducational evaluation and planning, perspectives on learning disabilities, teaching children and adolescents with autism, positive approaches to challenging behavior. *Unit head:* Dr. Beth Ferri, Program Director, 315-443-1465, E-mail: baferri@syr.edu. *Application contact:* Speranza Migliore, Graduate Admissions Recruiter, 315-443-2505, E-mail: gradrcrt@syr.edu.
Website: http://soe.syr.edu/academic/teaching_and_leadership/graduate/PhD/special_education/default.aspx

Tarleton State University, College of Graduate Studies, College of Education, Department of Curriculum and Instruction, Stephenville, TX 76402. Offers curriculum and instruction (M Ed); educational diagnostician (M Ed); elementary education (M Ed); instructional design and technology (M Ed); instructional leadership (M Ed); secondary education (M Ed); special education (M Ed); technology applications (M Ed); technology director (M Ed). *Program availability:* Part-time, evening/weekend. *Faculty:* 7 full-time (5 women), 4 part-time/adjunct (2 women). *Students:* 7 full-time (6 women), 156 part-time (137 women); includes 40 minority (11 Black or African American, non-Hispanic/Latino; 25 Hispanic/Latino; 4 Two or more races, non-Hispanic/Latino). Average age 38. 55 applicants, 96% accepted, 46 enrolled. In 2017, 33 master's awarded. *Degree requirements:* For master's, comprehensive exam, thesis (for some programs). *Entrance requirements:* For master's, GRE General Test, minimum GPA of 3.0. Additional exam requirements/recommendations for international students: Required—TOEFL (minimum score 550 paper-based; 80 iBT), IELTS (minimum score 6). *Application deadline:* For fall admission, 8/15 priority date for domestic students; for spring admission, 1/7 for domestic students. Applications are processed on a rolling basis. Application fee: $45 ($145 for international students). Electronic applications accepted. *Expenses:* Contact institution. *Financial support:* Research assistantships, teaching assistantships, career-related internships or fieldwork, Federal Work-Study, and institutionally sponsored loans available. Support available to part-time students. Financial award application deadline: 5/1; financial award applicants required to submit FAFSA. *Unit head:* Dr. Jordan Barkley, Dean, 254-968-9089, E-mail: jbarkley@tarleton.edu. *Application contact:* Information Contact, 254-968-9104, Fax: 254-968-9670, E-mail: gradoffice@tarleton.edu.
Website: http://www.tarleton.edu/cimasters/

Special Education

Teachers College, Columbia University, Department of Curriculum and Teaching, New York, NY 10027-6696. Offers curriculum and teaching (Ed M, MA, Ed D); curriculum and teaching: elementary education (MA); curriculum and teaching: secondary education (MA); early childhood education (MA, Ed D); early childhood education: special education (MA); elementary education-gifted extension (MA); elementary inclusive education (MA); gifted education (MA); literacy specialist (MA); secondary inclusive education (MA); special inclusive elementary education (MA). *Program availability:* Part-time, evening/weekend. *Students:* 196 full-time (181 women), 181 part-time (161 women); includes 141 minority (45 Black or African American, non-Hispanic/Latino; 2 American Indian or Alaska Native, non-Hispanic/Latino; 45 Asian, non-Hispanic/Latino; 35 Hispanic/Latino; 14 Two or more races, non-Hispanic/Latino), 37 international. Average age 30. 509 applicants, 72% accepted, 155 enrolled. Terminal master's awarded for partial completion of doctoral program. *Degree requirements:* For doctorate, thesis/dissertation. *Unit head:* Prof. Daniel Friedrich, Chair, E-mail: friedrich@exchange.tc.columbia.edu. *Application contact:* David Estrella, Director of Admission, 212-678-3305, Fax: 212-678-4171, E-mail: estrella@tc.columbia.edu.

Teachers College, Columbia University, Department of Health and Behavior Studies, New York, NY 10027-6696. Offers applied behavior analysis (MA, PhD); applied educational psychology: school psychology (Ed M, PhD); behavioral nutrition (PhD), including nutrition (Ed D, PhD); community health education (MS); community nutrition education (Ed M), including community nutrition education; education of deaf and hard of hearing (MA, PhD); health education (MA, Ed D); hearing impairment (Ed D); intellectual disability/autism (MA, Ed D, PhD); nursing education (Ed D, Advanced Certificate); nutrition and education (MS); nutrition and exercise physiology (MS); nutrition and public health (MS); nutrition education (Ed D), including nutrition (Ed D, PhD); physical disabilities (Ed D); reading specialist (MA); severe or multiple disabilities (MA); special education (Ed M, MA, Ed D); teaching of sign language (MA). *Program availability:* Part-time, evening/weekend. *Students:* 245 full-time (226 women), 242 part-time (219 women); includes 167 minority (52 Black or African American, non-Hispanic/Latino; 2 American Indian or Alaska Native, non-Hispanic/Latino; 55 Asian, non-Hispanic/Latino; 48 Hispanic/Latino; 1 Native Hawaiian or other Pacific Islander, non-Hispanic/Latino; 9 Two or more races, non-Hispanic/Latino), 60 international. Average age 30. 480 applicants, 59% accepted, 157 enrolled. Terminal master's awarded for partial completion of doctoral program. *Unit head:* Prof. Dolores Perin, Chair, E-mail: dp111@tc.columbia.edu. *Application contact:* David Estrella, Director of Admission, 212-678-3305, E-mail: estrella@tc.columbia.edu.
Website: http://www.tc.columbia.edu/health-and-behavior-studies/

Teachers College of San Joaquin, Master's Program in Education, Stockton, CA 95206. Offers early education (M Ed); educational inquiry (M Ed); educational leadership and school development (M Ed); science, technology, engineering, and mathematics (M Ed); special education (M Ed).

Tennessee State University, The School of Graduate Studies and Research, College of Education, Department of Teaching and Learning, Nashville, TN 37209-1561. Offers curriculum and instruction (M Ed, Ed D); elementary education (M Ed); special education (M Ed). *Accreditation:* NCATE. *Degree requirements:* For doctorate, thesis/dissertation. *Entrance requirements:* For master's, GRE General Test, GRE Subject Test, or MAT, minimum GPA of 2.5; for doctorate, GRE General Test, GRE Subject Test, or MAT, minimum GPA of 3.25. Electronic applications accepted. *Faculty research:* Multicultural education, teacher education reform, whole language, interactive video teaching, English as a second language.

Tennessee Technological University, College of Graduate Studies, College of Education, Department of Curriculum and Instruction, Program in Special Education, Cookeville, TN 38505. Offers MA, Ed S. *Accreditation:* NCATE. *Program availability:* Part-time. *Faculty:* 6 full-time (3 women). *Students:* 3 full-time (all women), 13 part-time (9 women). 11 applicants, 55% accepted, 5 enrolled. In 2017, 7 master's, 1 other advanced degree awarded. *Degree requirements:* For master's and Ed S, comprehensive exam, thesis or alternative. *Entrance requirements:* For master's and Ed S, MAT or GRE. Additional exam requirements/recommendations for international students: Required—TOEFL (minimum score 527 paper-based; 71 iBT), IELTS (minimum score 5.5), PTE (minimum score 48), or TOEIC (Test of English as an International Communication). *Application deadline:* For fall admission, 8/1 for domestic students, 5/1 for international students; for spring admission, 12/1 for domestic students, 10/1 for international students; for summer admission, 5/1 for domestic students, 2/1 for international students. Applications are processed on a rolling basis. Application fee: $35 ($40 for international students). Electronic applications accepted. *Expenses:* Tuition, state resident: full-time $9925; part-time $565 per credit hour. Tuition, nonresident: full-time $22,993; part-time $1291 per credit hour. *Financial support:* Fellowships, research assistantships, teaching assistantships, and career-related internships or fieldwork available. Financial award application deadline: 4/1. *Unit head:* Dr. Jeremy Wendt, Interim Chairperson, 931-372-3181, Fax: 931-372-6270, E-mail: jwendt@tntech.edu. *Application contact:* Shelia K. Kendrick, Coordinator of Graduate Studies, 931-372-3808, Fax: 931-372-3497, E-mail: skendrick@tntech.edu.

Texas A&M International University, Office of Graduate Studies and Research, College of Education, Department of Professional Programs, Laredo, TX 78041. Offers educational administration (MS Ed); generic special education (MS Ed); school counseling (MS). *Entrance requirements:* Additional exam requirements/recommendations for international students: Required—TOEFL (minimum score 550 paper-based; 79 iBT).

Texas A&M University, College of Education and Human Development, Department of Educational Psychology, College Station, TX 77843. Offers bilingual education (M Ed, MS); counseling psychology (PhD); educational psychology (M Ed, MS, PhD); educational technology (M Ed); school psychology (PhD); special education (M Ed, MS). *Accreditation:* APA (one or more programs are accredited). *Program availability:* Part-time, evening/weekend, blended/hybrid learning. *Faculty:* 45. *Students:* 165 full-time (131 women), 248 part-time (210 women); includes 144 minority (24 Black or African American, non-Hispanic/Latino; 3 American Indian or Alaska Native, non-Hispanic/Latino; 21 Asian, non-Hispanic/Latino; 84 Hispanic/Latino; 2 Native Hawaiian or other Pacific Islander, non-Hispanic/Latino; 10 Two or more races, non-Hispanic/Latino), 45 international. Average age 33. 171 applicants, 44% accepted, 47 enrolled. In 2017, 141 master's, 28 doctorates awarded. *Degree requirements:* For master's, thesis optional; for doctorate, thesis/dissertation. *Entrance requirements:* For master's and doctorate, GRE General Test. Additional exam requirements/recommendations for international students: Required—TOEFL (minimum score 550 paper-based; 80 iBT), IELTS (minimum score 6), PTE (minimum score 53). *Application deadline:* For fall admission, 12/1 for domestic students; for spring admission, 10/15 for domestic students. Application fee: $50 ($90 for international students). Electronic applications accepted. *Expenses:* Contact institution. *Financial support:* In 2017–18, 210 students received support, including 4 fellowships with tuition reimbursements available (averaging $24,775 per year), 102 research assistantships with tuition reimbursements available (averaging $10,698 per year), 19 teaching assistantships with tuition reimbursements available (averaging $7,177 per year); career-related internships or fieldwork, institutionally sponsored loans, scholarships/grants, traineeships, health care benefits, tuition waivers (full and partial), and unspecified assistantships also available. Support available to part-time students. Financial award application deadline: 3/15; financial award applicants required to submit FAFSA. *Unit head:* Dr. Victor Willson, Department Head, 979-845-1394, E-mail: v-willson@tamu.edu. *Application contact:* Kristie Stramaski, Senior Academic Advisor, 979-845-1833, E-mail: epsyadvisor@tamu.edu. Website: http://epsy.tamu.edu

Texas A&M University–Commerce, College of Education and Human Services, Commerce, TX 75429. Offers counseling (M Ed, MS, PhD); early childhood education (M Ed, MS); educational administration (M Ed, MS, Ed D); educational psychology (PhD); educational technology leadership (M Ed, MS); educational technology library science (M Ed, MS); elementary education (M Ed); health, kinesiology and sports studies (MS); higher education (MS, Ed D); psychology (MS); reading (M Ed, MS); secondary education (M Ed, MS); social work (MSW); special education (M Ed, MS); supervision, curriculum and instruction-elementary education (Ed D); training and development (MS). *Program availability:* Part-time, evening/weekend, 100% online, blended/hybrid learning. *Faculty:* 91 full-time (51 women), 38 part-time/adjunct (31 women). *Students:* 400 full-time (310 women), 1,400 part-time (1,117 women); includes 724 minority (412 Black or African American, non-Hispanic/Latino; 8 American Indian or Alaska Native, non-Hispanic/Latino; 24 Asian, non-Hispanic/Latino; 220 Hispanic/Latino; 60 Two or more races, non-Hispanic/Latino), 18 international. Average age 37. 951 applicants, 46% accepted, 331 enrolled. In 2017, 564 master's, 24 doctorates awarded. *Degree requirements:* For master's, comprehensive exam, thesis optional, departmental qualifying exams (for some programs); for doctorate, comprehensive exam, thesis/dissertation, departmental qualifying exam; for SSP, comprehensive exam, thesis optional. *Entrance requirements:* For master's and doctorate, GRE General Test. Additional exam requirements/recommendations for international students: Required—TOEFL (minimum score 550 paper-based; 79 iBT), IELTS (minimum score 6). *Application deadline:* For fall admission, 6/1 priority date for international students; for spring admission, 10/15 priority date for international students; for summer admission, 3/15 priority date for international students. Applications are processed on a rolling basis. Application fee: $50. Electronic applications accepted. *Expenses:* Tuition, state resident: full-time $3630. Tuition, nonresident: full-time $11,100. *Required fees:* $2564. Tuition and fees vary according to course load, degree level and program. *Financial support:* In 2017–18, 84 students received support, including 40 research assistantships with partial tuition reimbursements available (averaging $10,800 per year), 12 teaching assistantships with partial tuition reimbursements available (averaging $13,000 per year); career-related internships or fieldwork, Federal Work-Study, institutionally sponsored loans, scholarships/grants, health care benefits, and unspecified assistantships also available. Financial award application deadline: 6/15; financial award applicants required to submit FAFSA. *Faculty research:* Cognitive and bilingual education, positive behavioral intervention, literacy, math readiness. *Total annual research expenditures:* $1.1 million. *Unit head:* Dr. Timothy Letzring, Dean, 903-886-5181, Fax: 903-886-5905, E-mail: tim.letzring@tamuc.edu. *Application contact:* Vicky Turner, Doctoral Degree and Special Programs Coordinator, 903-886-5167, E-mail: vicky.turner@tamuc.edu.
Website: http://www.tamuc.edu/academics/graduateSchool/programs/education/default.aspx

Texas A&M University–Corpus Christi, College of Graduate Studies, College of Education and Human Development, Program in Special Education, Corpus Christi, TX 78412. Offers MS. *Program availability:* Part-time, evening/weekend. *Students:* 29 part-time (28 women); includes 15 minority (3 Black or African American, non-Hispanic/Latino; 12 Hispanic/Latino). Average age 40. 15 applicants, 73% accepted, 9 enrolled. In 2017, 8 master's awarded. *Degree requirements:* For master's, comprehensive exam. *Entrance requirements:* For master's, minimum GPA of 3.0 in last 60 hours; essay (approximately 300-400 words in length). Additional exam requirements/recommendations for international students: Required—TOEFL (minimum score 550 paper-based; 79 iBT), IELTS (minimum score 6.5). *Application deadline:* For fall admission, 7/15 priority date for domestic students, 5/1 priority date for international students; for spring admission, 11/15 priority date for domestic students, 9/1 priority date for international students; for summer admission, 4/15 priority date for domestic students, 2/1 priority date for international students. Applications are processed on a rolling basis. Application fee: $50 ($70 for international students). Electronic applications accepted. *Expenses:* Tuition, state resident: full-time $3568; part-time $198.24 per credit hour. Tuition, nonresident: full-time $11,038; part-time $613.24 per credit hour. *Required fees:* $2129; $1422.58 per semester. Tuition and fees vary according to program. *Financial support:* In 2017–18, 5 students received support. Research assistantships, teaching assistantships, career-related internships or fieldwork, Federal Work-Study, institutionally sponsored loans, scholarships/grants, health care benefits, and unspecified assistantships available. Support available to part-time students. Financial award application deadline: 3/15. *Unit head:* Dr. Karen McCaleb, Chair, 361-825-2449, E-mail: karen.mccaleb@tamucc.edu. *Application contact:* Graduate Admissions Coordinator, 361-825-2177, Fax: 361-825-2755, E-mail: gradweb@tamucc.edu.
Website: http://gradschool.tamucc.edu/degrees/education/special_ed.html

Texas A&M University–Kingsville, College of Graduate Studies, College of Education and Human Performance, Department of Teacher and Bilingual Education, Program in Special Education, Kingsville, TX 78363. Offers M Ed. *Program availability:* Part-time, evening/weekend. *Degree requirements:* For master's, variable foreign language requirement, comprehensive exam, thesis (for some programs). *Entrance requirements:* For master's, GRE, MAT, GMAT. Additional exam requirements/recommendations for international students: Required—TOEFL (minimum score 550 paper-based; 79 iBT). Electronic applications accepted.

Texas A&M University–San Antonio, Department of Educator and Leadership Preparation, San Antonio, TX 78224. Offers bilingual education (MS); early childhood education (M Ed); educational administration (MA); reading specialization (MS); special education (M Ed), including educational diagnostician. *Program availability:* Part-time, evening/weekend, online learning. *Faculty:* 19 full-time (14 women), 8 part-time/adjunct (2 women). *Students:* 24 full-time (21 women), 188 part-time (143 women); includes 163 minority (7 Black or African American, non-Hispanic/Latino; 1 Asian, non-Hispanic/Latino; 149 Hispanic/Latino; 6 Two or more races, non-Hispanic/Latino), 1 international. Average age 36. 191 applicants, 62% accepted, 67 enrolled. In 2017, 70 master's awarded. *Degree requirements:* For master's, comprehensive exam, thesis or alternative. *Entrance requirements:* For master's, GRE (Quantitative and Verbal) or MAT. Additional exam requirements/recommendations for international students: Required—TOEFL (minimum score 550 paper-based; 79 iBT), IELTS (minimum score 6). *Application deadline:* For fall admission, 3/15 priority date for domestic and international students; for spring admission, 11/1 priority date for domestic and international students; for summer admission, 4/1 priority date for domestic and international students. Applications are processed on a rolling basis. Application fee: $35 ($50 for international students). Electronic applications accepted. *Expenses:* Tuition, state resident: full-time $3475; part-time $1930 per semester. Tuition, nonresident: full-time $10,945; part-time $6080 per semester. *Required fees:* $2148; $1412 per year. $706 per semester. Tuition and fees vary according to course load. *Financial support:* In 2017–18, 16 students received support. Research assistantships, Federal Work-Study, scholarships/grants, and tuition waivers available. Financial award

application deadline: 3/15; financial award applicants required to submit FAFSA. *Faculty research:* Equity in education, biliteracy practices among Latina and immigrants, academic achievement of low socio-economic students, equity practices in instruction and educational leadership in diverse settings, racial identity development and multicultural education. *Unit head:* Dr. Debbie Vera, Department Chair. *Application contact:* Caitie Garza, Graduate Admissions Coordinator, 210-784-1300, E-mail: beajaguar@tamusa.edu.
Website: http://www.tamusa.edu/collegeofeducationandhumandevelopment/educatorleadershippreparation/index.html

Texas A&M University–Texarkana, Graduate Studies and Research, College of Education and Liberal Arts, Texarkana, TX 75503. Offers adult education (MS); curriculum and instruction (M Ed); education (MS); educational administration (M Ed); English (MA); instructional technology (MS); interdisciplinary studies (MA, MS); special education (MS). *Program availability:* Part-time, evening/weekend. *Degree requirements:* For master's, comprehensive exam (for some programs), thesis optional. *Entrance requirements:* For master's, minimum GPA of 2.5 on last 60 hours of bachelor's degree. Additional exam requirements/recommendations for international students: Required—TOEFL. Electronic applications accepted.

Texas Christian University, College of Education, Master's Programs in Education, Fort Worth, TX 76129. Offers counseling (M Ed); curriculum and instruction (M Ed), including curriculum studies, language and literacy, math education, science education; education (MAT); educational leadership (M Ed); special education (M Ed). *Program availability:* Part-time, evening/weekend. *Faculty:* 29 full-time (21 women), 3 part-time/adjunct (1 woman). *Students:* 124 full-time (94 women), 14 part-time (12 women); includes 52 minority (14 Black or African American, non-Hispanic/Latino; 2 American Indian or Alaska Native, non-Hispanic/Latino; 3 Asian, non-Hispanic/Latino; 28 Hispanic/Latino; 5 Two or more races, non-Hispanic/Latino), 1 international. Average age 28. 172 applicants, 69% accepted, 86 enrolled. In 2017, 62 master's awarded. *Degree requirements:* For master's, comprehensive exam (for some programs), thesis (for some programs). *Entrance requirements:* For master's, GRE General Test; Pre-Admission Content Test (for MAT). Additional exam requirements/recommendations for international students: Required—TOEFL (minimum score 550 paper-based; 80 iBT). *Application deadline:* For fall admission, 3/1 for domestic and international students; for spring admission, 11/16 for domestic and international students; for summer admission, 3/1 for domestic and international students. Application fee: $60. Electronic applications accepted. *Financial support:* In 2017–18, 124 students received support, including 1 research assistantship with full tuition reimbursement available (averaging $15,000 per year), 29 teaching assistantships with full tuition reimbursements available (averaging $15,000 per year); career-related internships or fieldwork, scholarships/grants, and unspecified assistantships also available. Support available to part-time students. Financial award application deadline: 3/1. *Unit head:* Dr. Jan Lacina, Associate Dean, 817-257-6786, Fax: 817-257-7466, E-mail: j.lacina@tcu.edu. *Application contact:* Lori Kimball, Administrative Program Specialist, 817-257-7661, Fax: 817-257-7466, E-mail: l.kimball@tcu.edu.
Website: http://coe.tcu.edu/graduate-overview/

Texas State University, The Graduate College, College of Education, Program in Special Education, San Marcos, TX 78666. Offers M Ed. *Program availability:* Part-time. *Faculty:* 11 full-time (9 women), 6 part-time/adjunct (all women). *Students:* 42 full-time (27 women), 28 part-time (20 women); includes 25 minority (4 Black or African American, non-Hispanic/Latino; 3 Asian, non-Hispanic/Latino; 17 Hispanic/Latino; 1 Two or more races, non-Hispanic/Latino). Average age 30. 43 applicants, 77% accepted, 14 enrolled. In 2017, 18 master's awarded. *Degree requirements:* For master's, comprehensive exam. *Entrance requirements:* For master's, baccalaureate degree from regionally-accredited institution with minimum GPA of 2.75 in last 60 hours of course work, statement of purpose, resume (include license, certificates, teaching experience), 2 letters of recommendation from those familiar with professional work (at least one supervisor). Additional exam requirements/recommendations for international students: Required—IELTS, TOEFL (minimum iBT scores: 22 listening, 22 reading, 24 speaking, 21 writing). *Application deadline:* For fall admission, 2/15 priority date for domestic and international students; for spring admission, 10/15 for domestic students, 10/1 for international students; for summer admission, 4/15 for domestic students, 3/15 for international students. Applications are processed on a rolling basis. Application fee: $40 ($90 for international students). Electronic applications accepted. *Expenses:* Tuition, state resident: full-time $7868; part-time $3934 per semester. Tuition, nonresident: full-time $17,828; part-time $8914 per semester. *Required fees:* $2092; $1435 per semester. Tuition and fees vary according to course load. *Financial support:* In 2017–18, 25 students received support, including 3 research assistantships (averaging $14,079 per year), 2 teaching assistantships (averaging $12,152 per year); fellowships, career-related internships or fieldwork, Federal Work-Study, institutionally sponsored loans, scholarships/grants, and unspecified assistantships also available. Support available to part-time students. Financial award application deadline: 3/1; financial award applicants required to submit FAFSA. *Faculty research:* Research and technical assistance for Texas juvenile justice department, autism, first responders online trial, interaction parent training. *Total annual research expenditures:* $131,636. *Unit head:* Dr. Brenda Scheuermann, Graduate Adviser, 512-245-2157, Fax: 512-245-7911, E-mail: bs10@txstate.edu. *Application contact:* Dr. Andrea Golato, Dean of Graduate School, 512-245-2581, Fax: 512-245-8365, E-mail: gradcollege@txstate.edu.
Website: http://www.education.txstate.edu/ci/degrees-certifications/graduate/special-education.html

Texas Tech University, Graduate School, College of Education, Department of Educational Psychology and Leadership, Lubbock, TX 79409. Offers counselor education (M Ed, PhD); educational leadership (M Ed, Ed D, PhD); educational psychology (M Ed, PhD); higher education (M Ed); higher education administration (Ed D); higher education research (PhD); instructional technology (M Ed, Ed D); special education (M Ed, Ed D, PhD). *Accreditation:* ACA; NCATE. *Program availability:* Part-time, evening/weekend. *Faculty:* 64 full-time (30 women), 6 part-time/adjunct (all women). *Students:* 263 full-time (193 women), 637 part-time (490 women); includes 307 minority (84 Black or African American, non-Hispanic/Latino; 3 American Indian or Alaska Native, non-Hispanic/Latino; 4 Asian, non-Hispanic/Latino; 193 Hispanic/Latino; 23 Two or more races, non-Hispanic/Latino), 48 international. Average age 36. 510 applicants, 47% accepted, 185 enrolled. In 2017, 209 master's, 64 doctorates awarded. Terminal master's awarded for partial completion of doctoral program. *Degree requirements:* For master's, comprehensive exam, thesis optional; for doctorate, comprehensive exam, thesis/dissertation. *Entrance requirements:* For master's, GRE (for some programs); for doctorate, GRE. Additional exam requirements/recommendations for international students: Required—TOEFL (minimum score 550 paper-based; 79 iBT). *Application deadline:* For fall admission, 6/1 priority date for domestic students, 1/15 priority date for international students; for spring admission, 9/1 priority date for domestic students, 6/15 priority date for international students. Applications are processed on a rolling basis. Application fee: $60. Electronic applications accepted. *Expenses:* Contact institution. *Financial support:* In 2017–18, 366 students received support, including 360 fellowships (averaging $3,231 per year), 63 research assistantships (averaging $11,899 per year); teaching assistantships, scholarships/grants, and unspecified assistantships also available. Support available to

part-time students. Financial award application deadline: 1/3; financial award applicants required to submit FAFSA. *Faculty research:* Cognitive, motivational, and developmental processes in learning; counseling education; instructional technology; generic special education and sensory impairment; community college administration; K-12 school administration. *Total annual research expenditures:* $127,956. *Unit head:* Dr. Hansel Burley, Chair, 806-834-5135, Fax: 806-742-2179, E-mail: hansel.burley@ttu.edu. *Application contact:* Pam Smith, Admissions Advisor, 806-834-2969, Fax: 806-742-2179, E-mail: pam.smith@ttu.edu.
Website: http://www.educ.ttu.edu/

Texas Woman's University, Graduate School, College of Professional Education, Department of Teacher Education, Denton, TX 76204. Offers educational administration (M Ed, MA); special education (M Ed, PhD), including educational diagnostician (M Ed), intervention specialist (M Ed); teaching, learning, and curriculum (M Ed, MA). *Program availability:* Part-time. *Faculty:* 9 full-time (7 women), 1 (woman) part-time/adjunct. *Students:* 20 full-time (17 women), 92 part-time (79 women); includes 41 minority (11 Black or African American, non-Hispanic/Latino; 1 American Indian or Alaska Native, non-Hispanic/Latino; 3 Asian, non-Hispanic/Latino; 24 Hispanic/Latino; 2 Two or more races, non-Hispanic/Latino), 1 international. Average age 38. 48 applicants, 71% accepted, 29 enrolled. In 2017, 36 master's, 4 doctorates awarded. Terminal master's awarded for partial completion of doctoral program. *Degree requirements:* For master's, comprehensive exam, thesis, professional paper (M Ed); for doctorate, comprehensive exam, thesis/dissertation, residency. *Entrance requirements:* For master's, minimum GPA of 3.0 on last 60 undergraduate hours, 2 letters of reference, resume, copy of certifications, teacher service record, statement of intent, interview (for MAT); for doctorate, GRE General Test, minimum GPA of 3.0, 3 letters of reference, resume, copy of certifications, teacher service record, statement of intent. Additional exam requirements/recommendations for international students: Required—TOEFL (minimum score 550 paper-based; 79 iBT); Recommended—IELTS (minimum score 6.5), TSE (minimum score 53). *Application deadline:* For fall admission, 7/1 priority date for domestic students, 3/1 priority date for international students; for spring admission, 11/1 priority date for domestic students, 7/1 priority date for international students. Applications are processed on a rolling basis. Application fee: $50 ($75 for international students). Electronic applications accepted. *Expenses:* $7,520 per year full-time in-state; $16,820 per year full-time out-of-state. *Financial support:* In 2017–18, 21 students received support, including 5 research assistantships (averaging $32,980 per year); career-related internships or fieldwork, Federal Work-Study, institutionally sponsored loans, scholarships/grants, traineeships, health care benefits, and unspecified assistantships also available. Support available to part-time students. Financial award application deadline: 3/1; financial award applicants required to submit FAFSA. *Faculty research:* Experiential learning, classroom management, learning disabilities, staff and professional development, technology in the classroom. *Total annual research expenditures:* $272,198. *Unit head:* Dr. Diane Myers, Chair, 940-898-2271, Fax: 940-898-2270, E-mail: teachereducation@twu.edu. *Application contact:* Korie Hawkins, Associate Director of Admissions, Graduate Recruitment, 940-898-3188, Fax: 940-898-3081, E-mail: admissions@twu.edu.
Website: http://www.twu.edu/teacher-education/

Touro College, Graduate School of Education, New York, NY 10010. Offers education and special education (MS); instructional technology (MS); mathematics education (MS); school leadership (MS); teaching English to speakers of other languages (MS); teaching literacy (MS). *Accreditation:* TEAC. *Program availability:* Part-time, evening/weekend, online learning. *Faculty:* 52 full-time (34 women), 199 part-time/adjunct (136 women). *Students:* 756 full-time (686 women), 3,833 part-time (3,492 women). Average age 33. 1,422 applicants, 50% accepted, 675 enrolled. In 2017, 6 master's awarded. *Entrance requirements:* Additional exam requirements/recommendations for international students: Required—TOEFL (minimum score 83 iBT), IELTS (minimum score 6.5). *Application deadline:* For fall admission, 8/26 for domestic students, 7/15 for international students; for spring admission, 12/31 for domestic students, 12/15 for international students. Applications are processed on a rolling basis. Application fee: $50. *Financial support:* Federal Work-Study available. Financial award applicants required to submit FAFSA. *Faculty research:* Equity assistance, language development, scholarly communications, Latin American studies and cultural sensitivity, behavior management techniques and strategies in special education. *Unit head:* Dr. Jacob Easley, III, Dean, 212-463-0400 Ext. 5561, Fax: 212-462-4889, E-mail: jeasley@touro.edu. *Application contact:* Sharmilee Hoopnarine, Admissions, 212-463-0400.

Towson University, College of Education, Program in Special Education, Towson, MD 21252-0001. Offers special education (M Ed); teacher as leader in autism spectrum disorder (M Ed). *Accreditation:* NCATE. *Program availability:* Part-time, evening/weekend. *Students:* 3 full-time (all women), 156 part-time (145 women); includes 19 minority (6 Black or African American, non-Hispanic/Latino; 2 Asian, non-Hispanic/Latino; 10 Hispanic/Latino; 1 Two or more races, non-Hispanic/Latino). *Degree requirements:* For master's, thesis optional. *Entrance requirements:* For master's, letter of recommendation, bachelor's degree, professional teacher certification, minimum GPA of 3.0. *Application deadline:* For fall admission, 1/17 for domestic students, 5/15 for international students; for spring admission, 10/15 for domestic students, 12/1 for international students. Applications are processed on a rolling basis. Application fee: $45. Electronic applications accepted. *Expenses:* Tuition, state resident: full-time $7960; part-time $398 per unit. Tuition, nonresident: full-time $16,480; part-time $824 per unit. *Required fees:* $2600; $130 per year. $390 per term. *Unit head:* Dr. Andrea Parrish, Graduate Program Director, 410-704-3835, E-mail: aparrish@towson.edu. *Application contact:* Coverley Beidleman, Assistant Director of Graduate Admissions, 410-704-5630, Fax: 410-704-3030, E-mail: cbeidleman@towson.edu.
Website: http://www.towson.edu/coe/departments/specialed/gradspecialed/

Towson University, College of Education, Program in Teaching, Towson, MD 21252-0001. Offers early childhood education (MAT); elementary education (MAT); secondary education (MAT); special education (MAT). *Students:* 64 full-time (44 women), 48 part-time (34 women); includes 16 minority (5 Black or African American, non-Hispanic/Latino; 5 Asian, non-Hispanic/Latino; 5 Hispanic/Latino; 1 Two or more races, non-Hispanic/Latino). *Entrance requirements:* For master's, ACT, GRE, PRAXIS I or SAT, 2 letters of reference, resume, minimum GPA of 3.0, essay. *Application deadline:* For fall admission, 1/17 for domestic students, 5/15 for international students; for spring admission, 10/15 for domestic students, 12/1 for international students. Applications are processed on a rolling basis. Application fee: $45. Electronic applications accepted. *Expenses:* Tuition, state resident: full-time $7960; part-time $398 per unit. Tuition, nonresident: full-time $16,480; part-time $824 per unit. *Required fees:* $2600; $130 per year. $390 per term. *Financial support:* Application deadline: 4/1. *Unit head:* Dr. Pamela Wruble, Graduate Program Director, 410-704-4935, E-mail: pwruble@towson.edu. *Application contact:* Coverley Beidleman, Assistant Director of Graduate Admissions, 410-704-5630, Fax: 410-704-3030, E-mail: grads@towson.edu.
Website: https://www.towson.edu/coe/departments/teaching/

Towson University, College of Health Professions, Program in Autism Studies, Towson, MD 21252-0001. Offers Postbaccalaureate Certificate. *Students:* 13 full-time (all women), 36 part-time (33 women); includes 8 minority (4 Black or African American, non-Hispanic/Latino; 2 Hispanic/Latino; 2 Two or more races, non-Hispanic/Latino).

Special Education

Entrance requirements: For degree, bachelor's degree with minimum GPA of 3.0, 30 hours of human service activity as part of field experience, volunteer or paid work in the last five years. *Application deadline:* For fall admission, 1/17 for domestic students, 5/15 for international students; for spring admission, 10/15 for domestic students, 12/1 for international students. Applications are processed on a rolling basis. *Application fee:* $45. Electronic applications accepted. *Expenses:* Tuition, state resident: full-time $7960; part-time $398 per unit. Tuition, nonresident: full-time $16,480; part-time $824 per unit. *Required fees:* $2600; $130 per year. $390 per term. *Unit head:* Dr. Connie Anderson, Graduate Program Director, 410-704-4640, E-mail: connieanderson@towson.edu. *Application contact:* Coverley Beidleman, Assistant Director of Graduate Admissions, 410-704-5630, Fax: 410-704-3030, E-mail: cbeidleman@towson.edu. Website: http://www.towson.edu/chp/departments/interprofessional/grad/autismpbc/

Trevecca Nazarene University, Graduate Education Program, Nashville, TN 37210-2877. Offers accountability and instructional leadership (Ed S); curriculum and instruction for Christian school educators (M Ed); curriculum and instruction K-12 (M Ed); educational leadership (M Ed); English second language (M Ed); library and information science (MLI Sc); special education: visual impairments (M Ed); teaching (MAT), including teaching 6-12, teaching K-5. *Accreditation:* NCATE. *Program availability:* Part-time, evening/weekend, online learning. *Faculty:* 8 full-time (6 women), 22 part-time/adjunct (18 women). *Students:* 150 full-time (114 women), 3 part-time (1 woman); includes 54 minority (49 Black or African American, non-Hispanic/Latino; 4 Hispanic/Latino; 1 Two or more races, non-Hispanic/Latino). Average age 36. In 2017, 57 master's, 4 other advanced degrees awarded. *Degree requirements:* For master's, comprehensive exam, exit assessment/e-portfolio. *Entrance requirements:* For master's, GRE or MAT; PRAXIS (for MAT), minimum GPA of 3.0, official transcript from regionally-accredited institution, references, interview, writing sample, at least 3 years' successful teaching experience (for M Ed in educational leadership); for Ed S, GRE or MAT, master's degree with minimum GPA of 3.0, official transcript from regionally accredited institution, at least 3 years' successful teaching experience, interview, writing sample, background and fingerprinting check, recommendations. Additional exam requirements/recommendations for international students: Required—TOEFL (minimum score 550 paper-based). *Application deadline:* Applications are processed on a rolling basis. Electronic applications accepted. *Expenses:* Contact institution. *Financial support:* Applicants required to submit FAFSA. *Unit head:* Dr. Suzie Harris, Dean, School of Education, 615-248-1201, Fax: 615-248-1597, E-mail: admissions_ged@trevecca.edu. *Application contact:* 844-TNU-GRAD, E-mail: sgcsadmissions@trevecca.edu. Website: http://www.trevecca.edu/soe

Trinity Baptist College, Graduate Programs, Jacksonville, FL 32221. Offers Bible (MA); curriculum and instruction (M Ed); educational leadership (M Ed); special education (M Ed). *Program availability:* Online learning. *Faculty:* 6 full-time (1 woman), 5 part-time/adjunct (1 woman). *Students:* 13 part-time (5 women). *Entrance requirements:* For master's, GRE (for M Ed), 2 letters of recommendation; minimum GPA of 2.5 (for M Min), 3.0 (for M Ed); goals essay; official transcripts. *Application fee:* $45. *Expenses:* *Tuition:* Part-time $295 per hour. *Required fees:* $50 per term. One-time fee: $45 part-time. *Unit head:* Dr. Matthew Beemer, Senior Vice President, 904-596-2400, Fax: 904-596-2531, E-mail: mbeemer@tbc.edu.

Trinity Christian College, Program in Special Education, Palos Heights, IL 60463-0929. Offers MA. *Program availability:* Evening/weekend. *Degree requirements:* For master's, project. *Entrance requirements:* For master's, valid teaching license, official transcripts, two letters of recommendation. Electronic applications accepted.

Trinity Washington University, School of Education, Washington, DC 20017-1094. Offers clinical mental health counseling (MA); early childhood education (MAT); educating for change (M Ed); educational administration (MSA); elementary education (MAT); reading (M Ed); school counseling (MA); secondary education (MAT), including English, social studies; special education (MAT). *Accreditation:* NCATE. *Program availability:* Part-time, evening/weekend. *Degree requirements:* For master's, thesis (for some programs), capstone project(s). *Entrance requirements:* For master's, PRAXIS I, minimum GPA of 2.8. Additional exam requirements/recommendations for international students: Required—TOEFL (minimum score 550 paper-based). *Faculty research:* Technology, literacy, special education, organizations, inclusion models.

Tusculum College, Program in Curriculum and Instruction, Greeneville, TN 37743-9997. Offers special education (MA Ed). *Program availability:* Evening/weekend. *Degree requirements:* For master's, thesis or alternative. *Entrance requirements:* For master's, NTE, PRAXIS II, GRE, MAT, 3 years of work experience, minimum GPA of 3.0, bachelor's degree. Additional exam requirements/recommendations for international students: Required—TOEFL (minimum score 540 paper-based; 73 iBT). *Application deadline:* Applications are processed on a rolling basis. *Application fee:* $0. *Unit head:* Dr. Tricia Hunsader, Dean, School of Education, 423-636-7300 Ext. 5693, E-mail: thunsader@tusculum.edu. *Application contact:* Lindsey Seal, Director of Enrollment, 423-636-7300 Ext. 5006, E-mail: lseal@tusculum.edu. Website: http://home.tusculum.edu/gps/graduate-degrees/master-arts-education-curriculum-instruction/

Union College, Graduate Programs, Department of Education, Program in Special Education, Barbourville, KY 40906-1499. Offers MA. *Degree requirements:* For master's, thesis optional. *Entrance requirements:* For master's, GRE General Test, NTE.

Universidad del Este, Graduate School, Carolina, PR 00984. Offers accounting (MBA); adult education (M Ed); agribusiness (MBA); criminal justice and criminology (MA); curriculum and instruction - early education (M Ed); curriculum and instruction - elementary (M Ed); curriculum and instruction - English (M Ed); curriculum and instruction - Spanish (M Ed); human resources (MBA); information security management (MBA); information technology and Web business development (MBA); management (MBA); public policy (MPA); social work (MA), including clinical social work; special education (M Ed); strategic leadership (MBA).

Universidad del Turabo, Graduate Programs, Programs in Education, Program in Special Education, Gurabo, PR 00778-3030. Offers M Ed. *Program availability:* Part-time, evening/weekend. *Entrance requirements:* For master's, GRE, EXADEP, GMAT, interview, official transcript, essay, recommendation letters. Electronic applications accepted.

Universidad Iberoamericana, Graduate School, Santo Domingo D.N., Dominican Republic. Offers business administration (MBA, PMBA); constitutional law (LL M); dentistry (DMD); educational management (MA); integrated marketing communication (MA); psychopedagogical intervention (M Ed); real estate law (LL M); strategic management of human talent (MM).

Universidad Metropolitana, School of Education, Program in Special Education, San Juan, PR 00928-1150. Offers M Ed. *Degree requirements:* For master's, thesis or alternative. Electronic applications accepted.

Université de Sherbrooke, Faculty of Education, Program in Special Education, Sherbrooke, QC J1K 2R1, Canada. Offers M Ed, Diploma. *Program availability:* Part-time, evening/weekend. *Degree requirements:* For master's, thesis.

University at Buffalo, the State University of New York, Graduate School, Graduate School of Education, Department of Learning and Instruction, Buffalo, NY 14260. Offers biology education (Ed M, Certificate); chemistry education (Ed M, Certificate); childhood education (Ed M); childhood education with bilingual extension (Ed M); college teaching (Advanced Certificate); curriculum, instruction and the science of learning (PhD); early childhood education (Ed M); early childhood education with bilingual extension (Ed M); earth science education (Ed M, Certificate); education and technology (Ed M); education studies (Ed M); educational technology and new literacies (Certificate); educational technology and new literacies (Advanced Certificate); elementary education (Ed D); English education (Ed M, Certificate); English education studies (Ed M); English for speakers of other languages (Ed M); foreign and second language education (PhD); French education (Ed M, Certificate); German education (Ed M, Certificate); gifted education (Certificate); Latin education (Ed M, Certificate); literacy education studies (Ed M); literacy specialist (Ed M); literacy teaching and learning (Certificate); mathematics education (Ed M, Certificate); music education (Ed M, Certificate); music education studies (Ed M); music learning theory (Advanced Certificate); online education (Advanced Certificate); physics education (Ed M, Certificate); science and the public (Ed M); social studies education (Ed M, Certificate); Spanish education (Ed M, Certificate); special education (PhD); teaching English to speakers of other languages (Ed M). *Program availability:* Part-time, evening/weekend, 100% online. *Faculty:* 26 full-time (19 women), 74 part-time/adjunct (52 women). *Students:* 172 full-time (122 women), 325 part-time (226 women); includes 44 minority (25 Black or African American, non-Hispanic/Latino; 5 American Indian or Alaska Native, non-Hispanic/Latino; 14 Asian, non-Hispanic/Latino), 57 international. Average age 33. 316 applicants, 78% accepted, 174 enrolled. In 2017, 109 master's, 34 doctorates, 15 other advanced degrees awarded. *Degree requirements:* For master's, comprehensive exam; for doctorate, thesis/dissertation, research analysis exam, research experience. *Entrance requirements:* For master's, letters of reference; for doctorate, GRE General Test or MAT, interview, writing sample, letters of recommendation. Additional exam requirements/recommendations for international students: Required—TOEFL (minimum score 600 paper-based; 96 iBT). *Application deadline:* For fall admission, 2/1 priority date for domestic and international students; for spring admission, 11/15 priority date for domestic students, 10/1 for international students. Applications are processed on a rolling basis. *Application fee:* $50. Electronic applications accepted. *Financial support:* In 2017–18, 42 fellowships (averaging $5,181 per year), 44 research assistantships with tuition reimbursements (averaging $10,908 per year) were awarded; teaching assistantships, career-related internships or fieldwork, Federal Work-Study, institutionally sponsored loans, scholarships/grants, tuition waivers (full and partial), and unspecified assistantships also available. Financial award application deadline: 2/28; financial award applicants required to submit FAFSA. *Faculty research:* Science assessment, foreign language teaching and learning, early learning, new literacies, gender and education. *Total annual research expenditures:* $413,233. *Unit head:* Dr. David Bruce, Chair, 716-645-4069, Fax: 716-645-3161, E-mail: gse-info@buffalo.edu. *Application contact:* Luann Zak, Admissions Assistant, 716-645-2110, Fax: 716-645-7937, E-mail: luannzak@buffalo.edu. Website: http://gse.buffalo.edu/lai

The University of Akron, Graduate School, College of Education, Department of Curricular and Instructional Studies, Program in Special Education, Akron, OH 44325. Offers MA. *Accreditation:* NCATE. *Students:* 19 full-time (15 women), 22 part-time (16 women); includes 8 minority (all Black or African American, non-Hispanic/Latino), 3 international. Average age 31. 10 applicants, 80% accepted, 5 enrolled. In 2017, 17 master's awarded. *Degree requirements:* For master's, comprehensive exam. *Entrance requirements:* For master's, valid teaching license. Additional exam requirements/recommendations for international students: Required—TOEFL (minimum score 79 iBT), IELTS (minimum score 6.5). *Application deadline:* Applications are processed on a rolling basis. *Application fee:* $45 ($70 for international students). Electronic applications accepted. *Unit head:* Dr. Evonn Welton, Interim Department Chair, 330-972-6742, E-mail: ewelton@uakron.edu. *Application contact:* Kelly Chaff, College Program Specialist, 330-972-7028, E-mail: klchaff@uakron.edu. Website: http://www.uakron.edu/education/academic-programs/graduate-programs.dot

The University of Alabama, Graduate School, College of Education, Department of Special Education and Multiple Abilities, Tuscaloosa, AL 35487. Offers collaborative special education (M Ed, Ed S); early intervention (M Ed, Ed S); gifted and talented education (M Ed, Ed S); multiple abilities (M Ed); special education (Ed D, PhD). *Program availability:* Part-time, evening/weekend. *Faculty:* 9 full-time (7 women). *Students:* 31 full-time (29 women), 30 part-time (all women); includes 12 minority (7 Black or African American, non-Hispanic/Latino; 1 Asian, non-Hispanic/Latino; 1 Hispanic/Latino; 3 Two or more races, non-Hispanic/Latino). Average age 32. 45 applicants, 58% accepted, 21 enrolled. In 2017, 16 master's, 1 doctorate awarded. Terminal master's awarded for partial completion of doctoral program. *Degree requirements:* For master's, comprehensive exam, thesis optional; for doctorate, one foreign language, comprehensive exam, thesis/dissertation. *Entrance requirements:* For master's, GRE, minimum undergraduate GPA of 3.0, teaching certificate, 3 letters of recommendation; for doctorate, GRE, 3 years of teaching experience, minimum undergraduate GPA of 3.25. Additional exam requirements/recommendations for international students: Required—TOEFL. *Application deadline:* Applications are processed on a rolling basis. *Application fee:* $50 ($60 for international students). Electronic applications accepted. *Financial support:* In 2017–18, 18 students received support, including research assistantships with tuition reimbursements available (averaging $9,000 per year), teaching assistantships with tuition reimbursements available (averaging $9,000 per year); health care benefits and unspecified assistantships also available. Financial award application deadline: 7/1; financial award applicants required to submit FAFSA. *Faculty research:* Gifted education, mild disabilities, early intervention, severe disabilities, behavior disorders. *Total annual research expenditures:* $39,904. *Unit head:* Dr. Robert Alexander McWilliam, Professor and Department Head, 205-348-6527, Fax: 205-348-6782, E-mail: ramcwilliam@ua.edu. *Application contact:* Bernice Ofori-Parku, Office Associate II, 205-348-6093, Fax: 205-348-6782, E-mail: bsoforiparku@ua.edu. Website: http://education.ua.edu/departments/spema/

The University of Alabama at Birmingham, School of Education, Program in Special Education, Birmingham, AL 35294. Offers MA Ed. *Accreditation:* NCATE. *Degree requirements:* For master's, thesis optional. *Entrance requirements:* For master's, GRE General Test or NTE, minimum GPA of 3.0. Electronic applications accepted.

The University of Alabama in Huntsville, School of Graduate Studies, College of Education, Huntsville, AL 35899. Offers autism spectrum disorders (M Ed, Graduate Certificate); biology (MAT); chemistry (MAT); differentiated instruction in elementary education (M Ed); English language arts (MAT); English speakers of other languages (M Ed, MAT); history (MAT); mathematics (MAT); physics (MAT); reading education (M Ed); secondary education (M Ed).

University of Alaska Anchorage, College of Education, Program in Special Education, Anchorage, AK 99508. Offers early childhood special education (M Ed); special education (M Ed, Certificate). *Program availability:* Part-time. *Degree requirements:* For master's, comprehensive exam (for some programs), thesis or alternative. *Entrance* *requirements:* For master's, GRE or MAT, interview, minimum GPA of 2.75. Additional exam requirements/recommendations for international students: Required—TOEFL (minimum score 550 paper-based). *Faculty research:* Mild disabilities, substance abuse issues for educators, partnerships to improve at-risk youth, analysis of planning models for teachers in special education.

University of Alaska Fairbanks, School of Education, Program in Education, Fairbanks, AK 99775-6480. Offers special education (M Ed). *Program availability:* 100% online, blended/hybrid learning. *Degree requirements:* For master's, comprehensive exam, oral defense of project or thesis. *Entrance requirements:* For master's, GRE General Test, PRAXIS I, PRAXIS II, bachelor's degree from accredited institution with minimum cumulative undergraduate and major GPA of 3.0, writing sample, evidence of technology competence, criminal background check. Additional exam requirements/ recommendations for international students: Required—TOEFL (minimum score 550 paper-based; 79 iBT), IELTS (minimum score 6.5). Electronic applications accepted.

University of Alaska Southeast, Graduate Programs, Program in Education, Juneau, AK 99801. Offers educational leadership (M Ed); elementary education (MAT); learning design and technology (M Ed); mathematics education (M Ed); reading specialist (M Ed); secondary education (MAT); special education (M Ed, MAT). *Accreditation:* NCATE. *Program availability:* Part-time, evening/weekend, online learning. *Degree requirements:* For master's, comprehensive exam or project, portfolio. *Entrance requirements:* For master's, PRAXIS, minimum GPA of 3.0, writing sample, letters of recommendation. Electronic applications accepted. *Faculty research:* Applied classroom research, culturally responsive practices, action research, teaching effectiveness.

University of Alberta, Faculty of Graduate Studies and Research, Department of Educational Psychology, Edmonton, AB T6G 2E1, Canada. Offers counseling psychology (M Ed, PhD); educational psychology (M Ed, PhD); instructional technology (M Ed); school counseling (M Ed); school psychology (M Ed, PhD); special education (M Ed, PhD); special education-deafness studies (M Ed); teaching English as a second language (M Ed). *Program availability:* Part-time. *Degree requirements:* For master's, thesis optional; for doctorate, comprehensive exam, thesis/dissertation. *Entrance requirements:* For master's and doctorate, minimum GPA of 3.0. Additional exam requirements/recommendations for international students: Required—TOEFL. *Faculty research:* Human learning, development and assessment.

The University of Arizona, College of Education, Department of Disability and Psychoeducational Studies, Program in Special Education, Tucson, AZ 85721. Offers cross-categorical special education (MA); deaf and hard of hearing (MA); learning disabilities (MA); severe and multiple disabilities (MA); special education (PhD); visual impairment (MA). *Program availability:* Part-time. *Entrance requirements:* Additional exam requirements/recommendations for international students: Required—TOEFL (minimum score 550 paper-based; 79 iBT). Electronic applications accepted.

University of Arkansas, Graduate School, College of Education and Health Professions, Department of Curriculum and Instruction, Program in Special Education, Fayetteville, AR 72701. Offers M Ed, MAT. *Accreditation:* NCATE. *Program availability:* Part-time, evening/weekend, online learning. In 2017, 12 master's awarded. *Entrance requirements:* For master's, GRE General Test or MAT. *Application deadline:* For fall admission, 8/1 for domestic students, 4/1 for international students; for spring admission, 12/1 for domestic students, 10/1 for international students; for summer admission, 4/15 for domestic students, 3/1 for international students. Applications are processed on a rolling basis. Application fee: $60. Electronic applications accepted. *Expenses:* Tuition, state resident: full-time $3782. Tuition, nonresident: full-time $10,238. *Financial support:* Fellowships, research assistantships, teaching assistantships, career-related internships or fieldwork, and Federal Work-Study available. Support available to part-time students. Financial award application deadline: 4/1; financial award applicants required to submit FAFSA. *Unit head:* Dr. Peggy Schaefer-Whitby, Program Coordinator, 479-575-3302, E-mail: pschaefe@uark.edu. *Application contact:* Dr. Peggy Schaefer-Whitby, Graduate Coordinator, 479-575-3302, Fax: 479-575-6676, E-mail: pschaefe@uark.edu.
Website: https://sped.uark.edu

University of Arkansas at Little Rock, Graduate School, College of Education and Health Professions, Department of Counseling, Adult and Rehabilitation Education, Little Rock, AR 72204-1099. Offers adult education (M Ed); counselor education (M Ed); rehabilitation counseling (MA, Graduate Certificate); rehabilitation for the blind: orientation and mobility (MA). *Accreditation:* CORE; NCATE. *Program availability:* Part-time. *Entrance requirements:* For master's, interview, minimum GPA of 2.75. *Faculty research:* Low vision, orientation and mobility instruction.

University of Arkansas at Little Rock, Graduate School, College of Education and Health Professions, Department of Teacher Education, Program in Special Education, Little Rock, AR 72204-1099. Offers M Ed. *Accreditation:* NCATE. *Program availability:* Part-time, evening/weekend. *Degree requirements:* For master's, comprehensive exam, portfolio or thesis. *Entrance requirements:* For master's, interview, minimum GPA of 2.75, GRE General Test or teaching certificate.

The University of British Columbia, Faculty of Education, Department of Educational and Counseling Psychology, and Special Education, Vancouver, BC V6T 1Z4, Canada. Offers counseling psychology (M Ed, MA, PhD); guidance studies (Diploma); human development, learning and culture (M Ed, MA, PhD); measurement, evaluation, and research methodology (M Ed, MA, PhD); school psychology (M Ed, MA, PhD); special education (M Ed, MA, PhD, Diploma). *Program availability:* Part-time. *Degree requirements:* For master's, thesis (for some programs); for doctorate, comprehensive exam, thesis/dissertation. *Entrance requirements:* For master's, GRE General Test (for MA in counseling psychology); for doctorate, GRE General Test. Additional exam requirements/recommendations for international students: Required—TOEFL. Electronic applications accepted. *Expenses:* Contact institution. *Faculty research:* Women, family, social problems, career transition, stress and coping problems.

University of California, Berkeley, Graduate Division, School of Education, Program in Special Education, Berkeley, CA 94720-1500. Offers PhD. Program held jointly with San Francisco State University. *Degree requirements:* For doctorate, thesis/dissertation, oral qualifying exam. *Entrance requirements:* For doctorate, GRE General Test, minimum undergraduate GPA of 3.0 during last 2 years, 3 letters of recommendation. Electronic applications accepted.

University of California, Berkeley, Graduate Division, School of Education, Programs in Education, Berkeley, CA 94720-1500. Offers development in mathematics and science (MA); education in mathematics, science, and technology (MA, PhD); human development and education (MA, PhD); leadership education (MA); special education (PhD); teacher education (MA); MA/Credential; PhD/Credential; PhD/MA. Terminal master's awarded for partial completion of doctoral program. *Degree requirements:* For master's, exam or thesis; for doctorate, thesis/dissertation, oral qualifying exam. *Entrance requirements:* For master's and doctorate, GRE General Test, minimum GPA of 3.0 during last 2 years of undergraduate course work. Electronic applications accepted. *Faculty research:* Human development, social and moral educational psychology, developmental teacher preparation.

University of California, Los Angeles, Graduate Division, Graduate School of Education and Information Studies, Program in Special Education, Los Angeles, CA 90095. Offers PhD. Program offered jointly with California State University, Los Angeles. *Degree requirements:* For doctorate, thesis/dissertation, oral and written qualifying exams. *Entrance requirements:* For doctorate, GRE General Test, minimum undergraduate GPA of 3.0. Additional exam requirements/recommendations for international students: Required—TOEFL (minimum score 560 paper-based; 87 iBT). Electronic applications accepted.

University of California, Riverside, Graduate Division, Graduate School of Education, Riverside, CA 92521. Offers applied behavior analysis (M Ed); diversity and equity (M Ed); education policy analysis and leadership (PhD); education specialist (Credential); education, society, and culture (MA, PhD); educational psychology (MA, PhD); general education (M Ed); higher education administration and policy (M Ed, PhD); multiple subject (Credential); research, evaluation, measurement and statistics (MA); school psychology (PhD); single subject (Credential); special education (M Ed, PhD); special education and autism (MA); TESOL (M Ed). *Faculty:* 29 full-time (16 women), 2 part-time/adjunct (1 woman). *Students:* 241 full-time (188 women). 396 applicants, 42% accepted, 166 enrolled. In 2017, 130 master's, 15 doctorates, 14 other advanced degrees awarded. Terminal master's awarded for partial completion of doctoral program. *Degree requirements:* For master's, comprehensive exams or thesis (MA), case study or analytical report (M Ed); for doctorate, comprehensive exam, thesis/ dissertation, written and oral qualifying exams, college teaching practicum. *Entrance requirements:* For master's, GRE General Test (for MA); CBEST and CSET (for M Ed in general education only), UCR Extension TESOL certificate (for M Ed with TESOL emphasis only); for doctorate, GRE General Test, writing sample; for Credential, CBEST, CSET. Additional exam requirements/recommendations for international students: Required—TOEFL (minimum score 550 paper-based; 80 iBT), IELTS (minimum score 7). *Application deadline:* For fall admission, 9/1 for domestic students, 6/1 for international students; for winter admission, 11/15 for domestic students, 9/1 for international students; for spring admission, 3/1 for domestic students, 12/1 for international students. Applications are processed on a rolling basis. Application fee: $80 ($100 for international students). Electronic applications accepted. *Expenses:* Tuition, state resident: full-time $5746. Tuition, nonresident: full-time $10,780. Tuition and fees vary according to campus/location and program. *Financial support:* In 2017–18, 105 students received support, including 16 fellowships with full tuition reimbursements available (averaging $31,000 per year), 25 research assistantships with full tuition reimbursements available (averaging $31,000 per year), 10 teaching assistantships with full tuition reimbursements available (averaging $31,000 per year); career-related internships or fieldwork, Federal Work-Study, institutionally sponsored loans, scholarships/grants, and unspecified assistantships also available. Financial award application deadline: 12/15. *Faculty research:* Responsiveness to intervention, faculty core, response to intervention of English language learners, advanced modeling techniques, study on social capital, trust, and motivation. *Total annual research expenditures:* $1.7 million. *Unit head:* Thomas Smith, Dean, 951-827-4633, E-mail: thomas.smith@ucr.edu. *Application contact:* Heather Killeen, Graduate Program Coordinator, 951-827-6362, E-mail: heather.killeen@ucr.edu.
Website: http://www.education.ucr.edu/

University of Central Arkansas, Graduate School, College of Education, Department of Early Childhood and Special Education, Program in Special Education, Conway, AR 72035-0001. Offers collaborative instructional specialist (ages 0-8) (MSE); collaborative instructional specialist (grades 4-12) (MSE); special education instructional specialist grades 4-12 (Graduate Certificate); special education instructional specialist P-4 (Graduate Certificate). *Accreditation:* NCATE. *Program availability:* Part-time, evening/ weekend, online learning. *Degree requirements:* For master's, comprehensive exam, thesis optional. *Entrance requirements:* For master's, GRE General Test, minimum GPA of 2.7. Additional exam requirements/recommendations for international students: Required—TOEFL (minimum score 550 paper-based; 80 iBT).

University of Central Arkansas, Graduate School, College of Education, Department of Leadership Studies, Conway, AR 72035-0001. Offers college student personnel (MS); district-level administration (PMC); educational leadership - district level (Ed S); instructional technology (MS); library media and information technology (MS); school counseling (MS); school leadership (MS); school-based leadership adult education program administration (PMC); school-based leadership building administration (PMC); school-based leadership curriculum administration (PMC); school-based leadership gifted and talented program administration (PMC); school-based leadership special education program administration (PMC). *Accreditation:* NCATE. *Program availability:* Part-time, evening/weekend, online learning. *Degree requirements:* For master's and other advanced degree, comprehensive exam. *Entrance requirements:* For master's, GRE. Additional exam requirements/recommendations for international students: Required—TOEFL (minimum score 80 iBT). Electronic applications accepted. *Expenses:* Contact institution.

University of Central Florida, College of Community Innovation and Education, School of Teacher Education, Program in Exceptional Student Education, Orlando, FL 32816. Offers autism spectrum disorders (Certificate); exceptional student education (M Ed); exceptional student education K-12 (MA); intervention specialist (Certificate); pre-kindergarten disabilities (Certificate); severe or profound disabilities (Certificate); special education (Certificate). *Accreditation:* NCATE. *Program availability:* Part-time, evening/ weekend. *Students:* 15 full-time (13 women), 181 part-time (162 women); includes 76 minority (38 Black or African American, non-Hispanic/Latino; 1 American Indian or Alaska Native, non-Hispanic/Latino; 34 Hispanic/Latino; 3 Two or more races, non-Hispanic/Latino), 1 international. Average age 37. 119 applicants, 91% accepted, 80 enrolled. In 2017, 58 master's, 70 other advanced degrees awarded. *Degree requirements:* For master's, comprehensive exam, thesis or alternative. *Entrance requirements:* For master's, GRE General Test. Additional exam requirements/ recommendations for international students: Required—TOEFL. *Application deadline:* For fall admission, 7/15 for domestic students; for spring admission, 11/15 for domestic students; for summer admission, 4/1 for domestic students. Application fee: $30. Electronic applications accepted. *Expenses:* Tuition, state resident: part-time $288.16 per credit hour. Tuition, nonresident: part-time $1073.31 per credit hour. Tuition and fees vary according to program. *Financial support:* Career-related internships or fieldwork, Federal Work-Study, institutionally sponsored loans, and unspecified assistantships available. Financial award application deadline: 3/1; financial award applicants required to submit FAFSA. *Unit head:* Dr. Mary Little, Program Coordinator, 407-823-3275, E-mail: mary.little@ucf.edu. *Application contact:* Associate Director, Graduate Admissions, 407-823-2766, Fax: 407-823-6442, E-mail: gradadmissions@ucf.edu.
Website: http://education.ucf.edu/exed/

University of Central Missouri, The Graduate School, Warrensburg, MO 64093. Offers accountancy (MA); accounting (MBA); applied mathematics (MS); aviation safety (MA); biology (MS); business administration (MBA); career and technical education leadership (MS); college student personnel administration (MS); communication (MA); computer science (MS); counseling (MS); criminal justice (MS); educational leadership (Ed D); educational technology (MS); elementary and early childhood education (MSE); English

(MA); environmental studies (MA); finance (MBA); history (MA); human services/educational technology (Ed S); human services/learning resources (Ed S); human services/professional counseling (Ed S); industrial hygiene (MS); industrial management (MS); information systems (MBA); information technology (MS); kinesiology (MS); library science and information services (MS); literacy education (MSE); marketing (MBA); mathematics (MS); music (MA); occupational safety management (MS); psychology (MS); rural family nursing (MS); school administration (MSE); social gerontology (MS); sociology (MA); special education (MSE); speech language pathology (MS); superintendency (Ed S); teaching (MAT); teaching English as a second language (MA); technology (MS); technology management (PhD); theatre (MA). *Program availability:* Part-time, 100% online, blended/hybrid learning. *Faculty:* 337 full-time (145 women), 41 part-time/adjunct (28 women). *Students:* 785 full-time (398 women), 1,633 part-time (1,063 women); includes 231 minority (102 Black or African American, non-Hispanic/Latino; 4 American Indian or Alaska Native, non-Hispanic/Latino; 16 Asian, non-Hispanic/Latino; 52 Hispanic/Latino; 57 Two or more races, non-Hispanic/Latino), 692 international. Average age 30. In 2017, 2,605 master's, 122 other advanced degrees awarded. *Degree requirements:* For master's and Ed S, comprehensive exam (for some programs), thesis (for some programs). *Entrance requirements:* Additional exam requirements/recommendations for international students: Required—TOEFL (minimum score 550 paper-based; 79 iBT). *Application deadline:* For fall admission, 6/1 priority date for domestic and international students; for spring admission, 10/1 priority date for domestic and international students; for summer admission, 4/1 priority date for domestic and international students. Applications are processed on a rolling basis. Application fee: $30 ($75 for international students). Electronic applications accepted. *Expenses:* Tuition, state resident: full-time $8771; part-time $292.35 per credit hour. Tuition, nonresident: full-time $17,541; part-time $584.70 per credit hour. *Required fees:* $372; $24.78 per credit hour. *Financial support:* In 2017–18, 99 students received support. Research assistantships, teaching assistantships, career-related internships or fieldwork, Federal Work-Study, scholarships/grants, and administrative and laboratory assistantships available. Support available to part-time students. Financial award application deadline: 3/1; financial award applicants required to submit FAFSA. *Unit head:* Shellie Hewitt, Director of Graduate and International Student Services, 660-543-4621, Fax: 660-543-4778, E-mail: hewitt@ucmo.edu. *Application contact:* 660-543-4621, E-mail: admit_intl@ucmo.edu.
Website: http://www.ucmo.edu/graduate/

University of Central Oklahoma, The Jackson College of Graduate Studies, College of Education and Professional Studies, Donna Nigh Department of Advanced Professional and Special Services, Edmond, OK 73034-5209. Offers educational leadership (M Ed); library media education (M Ed); reading (M Ed); school counseling (M Ed); special education (M Ed), including mild/moderate disabilities, severe-profound/multiple disabilities; speech-language pathology (MS). *Accreditation:* ASHA. *Program availability:* Part-time. *Faculty:* 17 full-time (12 women), 8 part-time/adjunct (4 women). *Students:* 73 full-time (65 women), 286 part-time (239 women); includes 91 minority (41 Black or African American, non-Hispanic/Latino; 8 American Indian or Alaska Native, non-Hispanic/Latino; 5 Asian, non-Hispanic/Latino; 20 Hispanic/Latino; 17 Two or more races, non-Hispanic/Latino), 3 international. Average age 35. 146 applicants, 83% accepted, 91 enrolled. In 2017, 128 master's awarded. *Degree requirements:* For master's, comprehensive exam (for some programs), thesis (for some programs). *Entrance requirements:* Additional exam requirements/recommendations for international students: Required—TOEFL (minimum score 550 paper-based; 79 iBT), IELTS (minimum score 6.5). *Application deadline:* For fall admission, 7/15 for international students; for spring admission, 11/15 for international students; for summer admission, 1/31 for domestic students. Applications are processed on a rolling basis. Application fee: $60. Electronic applications accepted. *Expenses:* Tuition, state resident: full-time $5375; part-time $268.75 per credit hour. Tuition, nonresident: full-time $13,295; part-time $664.75 per credit hour. *Required fees:* $626; $31.30 per credit hour. One-time fee: $50. Tuition and fees vary according to program. *Financial support:* In 2017–18, 74 students received support, including 1 research assistantship with partial tuition reimbursement available (averaging $2,958 per year), 1 teaching assistantship with partial tuition reimbursement available (averaging $5,915 per year); career-related internships or fieldwork, scholarships/grants, tuition waivers (partial), and unspecified assistantships also available. Financial award application deadline: 3/31; financial award applicants required to submit FAFSA. *Unit head:* Dr. Cheryl Evans, Chair, 405-974-5437, Fax: 405-974-3857. *Application contact:* Carlie Wellington, Assistant Director, CEPS Graduate Enrollment, 405-974-5105, Fax: 405-974-3851, E-mail: gradcoll@uco.edu.
Website: http://sites.uco.edu/ceps/dept/Education-Programs/apss/index.asp

University of Cincinnati, Graduate School, College of Education, Criminal Justice, and Human Services, School of Education, Program in Special Education, Cincinnati, OH 45221. Offers M Ed, Ed D. *Accreditation:* NCATE. *Program availability:* Part-time. *Degree requirements:* For master's, thesis or alternative; for doctorate, thesis/dissertation. *Entrance requirements:* For master's, GRE General Test; for doctorate, GRE General Test, GRE Subject Test. Additional exam requirements/recommendations for international students: Required—TOEFL (minimum score 550 paper-based), TWE (minimum score 4.5), OEPT. Electronic applications accepted. *Expenses: Tuition, area resident:* Full-time $14,468. Tuition, state resident: full-time $14,968; part-time $754 per credit hour. Tuition, nonresident: full-time $24,210; part-time $1311 per credit hour. *International tuition:* $26,460 full-time. *Required fees:* $3958; $84 per credit hour. One-time fee: $85 full-time. Tuition and fees vary according to course load, degree level and program.

University of Colorado Colorado Springs, College of Education, Colorado Springs, CO 80918. Offers counseling and human services (MA); curriculum and instruction (MA); educational leadership (MA); educational leadership, research and policy (PhD); special education (MA); teaching English to speakers of other languages (MA). *Accreditation:* ACA; NCATE. *Program availability:* Part-time, evening/weekend, 100% online, blended/hybrid learning. *Faculty:* 30 full-time (21 women), 61 part-time/adjunct (38 women). *Students:* 190 full-time (132 women), 286 part-time (202 women); includes 117 minority (20 Black or African American, non-Hispanic/Latino; 2 American Indian or Alaska Native, non-Hispanic/Latino; 12 Asian, non-Hispanic/Latino; 59 Hispanic/Latino; 24 Two or more races, non-Hispanic/Latino), 6 international. Average age 36. 169 applicants, 85% accepted, 113 enrolled. In 2017, 160 master's, 16 doctorates awarded. *Degree requirements:* For master's, comprehensive exam, thesis or alternative, microcomputer proficiency; for doctorate, comprehensive exam, thesis/dissertation, research lab. *Entrance requirements:* For master's and doctorate, GRE General Test. Additional exam requirements/recommendations for international students: Recommended—TOEFL (minimum score 550 paper-based; 80 iBT), IELTS (minimum score 6). *Application deadline:* For fall admission, 1/28 priority date for domestic and international students; for spring admission, 11/1 priority date for domestic and international students. Applications are processed on a rolling basis. Application fee: $60 ($100 for international students). Electronic applications accepted. *Expenses:* $10,350 per year resident tuition, $20,935 nonresident, $11,961 nonresidential online; annual costs vary depending on program, course-load, and residency status. *Financial support:* In 2017–18, 81 students received support. Career-related internships or fieldwork, Federal Work-Study, scholarships/grants, and unspecified assistantships available. Support available to part-time students. Financial award application deadline: 3/1; financial award applicants required to submit FAFSA. *Faculty research:* Linguistically diverse education (LDE), educational policy, evidence-based reading and writing instruction, relational and social aggression, positive behavior supports, inclusive schooling, K-12 education policy. *Total annual research expenditures:* $607,967. *Unit head:* Dr. Valerie Martin Conley, Dean, 719-255-4133, E-mail: vmconley@uccs.edu. *Application contact:* The College of Education Student Resource Office, 719-255-4996, E-mail: education@uccs.edu.
Website: http://www.uccs.edu/coe

University of Colorado Denver, School of Education and Human Development, Early Childhood Education Program, Denver, CO 80217. Offers early childhood education (MA); special education (MA). *Accreditation:* NCATE. *Program availability:* Part-time, evening/weekend, online learning. *Degree requirements:* For master's, comprehensive exam, fieldwork, practica, 40 credit hours. *Entrance requirements:* For master's, GRE or MAT (if GPA is below 2.75), minimum GPA of 2.75, resume, three letters of recommendation, documented experience with young children, transcripts from all previous colleges/universities attended. Additional exam requirements/recommendations for international students: Required—TOEFL (minimum score 537 paper-based; 75 iBT); Recommended—IELTS (minimum score 6.5). Electronic applications accepted. *Expenses:* Contact institution. *Faculty research:* Early childhood growth and development, faculty development, adult learning, gender and equity issues, research methodology.

University of Colorado Denver, School of Education and Human Development, Program in Educational Leadership and Innovation, Denver, CO 80217. Offers educational studies and research (PhD), including administrative leadership and policy, early childhood special education, math education, research, assessment and evaluation, science education, urban ecologies. *Program availability:* Part-time, evening/weekend. *Degree requirements:* For doctorate, comprehensive exam, thesis/dissertation, 75 credit hours (for PhD). *Entrance requirements:* For doctorate, GRE or equivalent, resume or curriculum vitae, letters of recommendation, master's degree or equivalent, completion of basic or advanced statistics course with minimum B grade. Additional exam requirements/recommendations for international students: Required—TOEFL (minimum score 537 paper-based; 75 iBT); Recommended—IELTS (minimum score 6.5). Electronic applications accepted. *Expenses:* Contact institution. *Faculty research:* Administrative leadership and policy studies, early childhood education, research in diversity, paraprofessionals in education, urban schools lab.

University of Colorado Denver, School of Education and Human Development, Teacher Education Programs, Denver, CO 80217. Offers elementary linguistically diverse education (MA); elementary math and science education (MA); elementary math education (MA); elementary reading and writing (MA); elementary science education (MA); secondary English education (MA); secondary linguistically diverse education (MA); secondary math education (MA); secondary reading and writing (MA); secondary science education (MA); special education (MA). *Accreditation:* NCATE. *Program availability:* Part-time, evening/weekend. *Degree requirements:* For master's, comprehensive exam. *Entrance requirements:* For master's, GRE or MAT (for those with GPA below 2.75), transcripts, resume, letters of recommendation. Additional exam requirements/recommendations for international students: Required—TOEFL (minimum score 537 paper-based; 75 iBT); Recommended—IELTS (minimum score 6.5). Electronic applications accepted. *Expenses:* Contact institution. *Faculty research:* Linguistically diverse education/ESL, elementary reading and writing, elementary teacher education, secondary teacher education, special education.

University of Denver, Morgridge College of Education, Denver, CO 80208. Offers child, family and school psychology (MA, PhD, Ed S); counseling psychology (MA, PhD); curriculum and instruction (MA, Ed D, PhD); curriculum instruction and teaching (Certificate); early childhood special education (MA, Certificate); educational leadership and policy studies (MA, Ed D, PhD, Certificate); higher education (Ed D, PhD); library and information science (MLIS); research methods and statistics (MA, PhD). *Accreditation:* ALA; APA (one or more programs are accredited). *Program availability:* Part-time, evening/weekend, online learning. *Faculty:* 39 full-time (29 women), 60 part-time/adjunct (42 women). *Students:* 502 full-time (406 women), 361 part-time (267 women); includes 233 minority (54 Black or African American, non-Hispanic/Latino; 6 American Indian or Alaska Native, non-Hispanic/Latino; 25 Asian, non-Hispanic/Latino; 113 Hispanic/Latino; 35 Two or more races, non-Hispanic/Latino), 52 international. Average age 31. 1,167 applicants, 64% accepted, 415 enrolled. In 2017, 285 master's, 51 doctorates, 157 other advanced degrees awarded. Terminal master's awarded for partial completion of doctoral program. *Degree requirements:* For master's, comprehensive exam; for doctorate, 2 foreign languages, comprehensive exam, thesis/dissertation. *Entrance requirements:* For master's and doctorate, GRE General Test or GMAT. Additional exam requirements/recommendations for international students: Required—TOEFL (minimum score 550 paper-based; 80 iBT). *Application deadline:* Applications are processed on a rolling basis. Application fee: $65. Electronic applications accepted. *Expenses:* $31,935 per year full-time. *Financial support:* In 2017–18, 765 students received support, including 26 research assistantships with tuition reimbursements available (averaging $10,957 per year), 38 teaching assistantships with tuition reimbursements available (averaging $3,391 per year); career-related internships or fieldwork, Federal Work-Study, institutionally sponsored loans, scholarships/grants, and unspecified assistantships also available. Support available to part-time students. Financial award application deadline: 2/15; financial award applicants required to submit FAFSA. *Faculty research:* Early childhood education, educational leadership, access and opportunity to postsecondary education, marriage and family therapy, data management and archival research. *Unit head:* Dr. Karen Riley, Dean, 303-871-3665, Fax: 303-871-4456, E-mail: karen.riley@du.edu. *Application contact:* Jodi Dye, Director of Admissions, 303-871-2510, Fax: 303-871-4456, E-mail: jodi.dye@du.edu.
Website: http://morgridge.du.edu

University of Detroit Mercy, College of Liberal Arts and Education, Detroit, MI 48221. Offers addiction counseling (MA); addiction studies (Certificate); clinical mental health counseling (MA); clinical psychology (MA, PhD); computer and information systems (MS); criminal justice (MA); curriculum and instruction (MA); economics (MA); educational administration (MA); financial economics (MA); industrial/organizational psychology (MA); information assurance (MS); intelligence analysis (MA); liberal studies (MALS); religious studies (MA); school counseling (MA, Certificate); school psychology (Spec); security administration (MS); special education: emotionally impaired/behaviorally disordered (MA); special education: learning disabilities (MA). *Program availability:* Part-time, evening/weekend. *Degree requirements:* For doctorate, departmental qualifying exam. *Faculty research:* Psychology of aging, history of technology, Renaissance humanism, U.S. and Japanese economic relations.

University of Florida, Graduate School, College of Education, School of Special Education, School Psychology and Early Childhood Studies, Gainesville, FL 32611. Offers early childhood education (M Ed, MAE); school psychology (M Ed, MAE, Ed D, PhD, Ed S); special education (M Ed, MAE, Ed D, PhD, Ed S). *Accreditation:* NCATE. *Program availability:* Part-time, evening/weekend, online learning. *Degree requirements:* For master's, comprehensive exam (for some programs), thesis (MAE); for doctorate, comprehensive exam, thesis/dissertation. *Entrance requirements:* For master's and doctorate, GRE General Test, minimum GPA of 3.0; for Ed S, GRE General Test. Additional exam requirements/recommendations for international students: Required—TOEFL (minimum score 550 paper-based; 80 iBT), IELTS (minimum score 6). Electronic applications accepted. *Faculty research:* Teacher quality/teacher education, early childhood, autism, academic and behavioral assessment and interventions.

University of Georgia, College of Education, Department of Communication Sciences and Special Education, Athens, GA 30602. Offers communication science and disorders (M Ed, MA, PhD, Ed S); special education (Ed D). *Accreditation:* ASHA (one or more programs are accredited). Terminal master's awarded for partial completion of doctoral program. *Degree requirements:* For master's, comprehensive exam (for some programs), thesis (for some programs); for doctorate, thesis/dissertation. *Entrance requirements:* For master's, doctorate, and Ed S, GRE General Test. Additional exam requirements/recommendations for international students: Required—TOEFL. Electronic applications accepted.

University of Guam, Office of Graduate Studies, School of Education, Program in Special Education, Mangilao, GU 96923. Offers M Ed. *Degree requirements:* For master's, comprehensive oral and written exams, special project or thesis. *Entrance requirements:* For master's, GRE General Test. Additional exam requirements/recommendations for international students: Required—TOEFL. *Faculty research:* Mainstreaming, multiculturalism.

University of Hawaii at Manoa, Office of Graduate Education, College of Education, Department of Special Education, Honolulu, HI 96822. Offers M Ed. *Accreditation:* NCATE. *Program availability:* Part-time. *Degree requirements:* For master's, thesis optional. *Entrance requirements:* For master's, GRE General Test, interview, minimum GPA of 3.0. Additional exam requirements/recommendations for international students: Required—TOEFL (minimum score 580 paper-based; 92 iBT), IELTS (minimum score 5). *Faculty research:* Mild/moderate/severe disabilities, early childhood interventions, inclusion, transition.

University of Hawaii at Manoa, Office of Graduate Education, College of Education, PhD in Education Program, Honolulu, HI 96822. Offers curriculum and instruction (PhD); educational administration (PhD); educational foundations (PhD); educational policy studies (PhD); educational psychology (PhD); exceptionalities (PhD); kinesiology (PhD); learning design and technology (PhD). *Program availability:* Part-time, evening/weekend. *Degree requirements:* For doctorate, thesis/dissertation. *Entrance requirements:* For doctorate, GRE General Test, sample of written work. Additional exam requirements/recommendations for international students: Required—TOEFL (minimum score 600 paper-based; 100 iBT), IELTS (minimum score 7).

University of Houston, College of Education, Department of Educational Psychology, Houston, TX 77204. Offers administration and supervision - higher education (M Ed); counseling (M Ed); counseling psychology (PhD); educational psychology (M Ed); school psychology (PhD); school psychology and individual differences (PhD); special education (M Ed). *Accreditation:* NCATE. *Program availability:* Part-time, evening/weekend, online learning. *Degree requirements:* For master's, comprehensive exam or thesis; for doctorate, comprehensive exam, thesis/dissertation. *Entrance requirements:* For master's, GRE, transcripts, 3 letters of recommendation, curriculum vita, goal statement; for doctorate, GRE, transcripts, 3 letters of recommendation, curriculum vita, goal statement, writing sample, interview. Additional exam requirements/recommendations for international students: Required—TOEFL (minimum score 550 paper-based; 79 iBT), IELTS (minimum score 6.5). Electronic applications accepted. *Faculty research:* Evidence-based assessment and intervention, multicultural issues in psychology, social and cultural context of learning, systemic barriers to college, motivational aspects of self-regulated learning.

University of Houston–Victoria, School of Education, Health Professions and Human Development, Victoria, TX 77901-4450. Offers administration and supervision (M Ed); adult and higher education (M Ed); counselor education (M Ed); curriculum and instruction (M Ed); dyslexia education (Certificate); educational technology (M Ed); special education (M Ed). *Program availability:* Part-time, evening/weekend, online learning. *Degree requirements:* For master's, comprehensive exam, project or thesis. *Entrance requirements:* For master's, GRE General Test. Additional exam requirements/recommendations for international students: Required—TOEFL. Electronic applications accepted. *Faculty research:* Reading and language arts education, evaluation and diagnosis of special children's abilities.

University of Idaho, College of Graduate Studies, College of Education, Health and Human Sciences, Department of Curriculum and Instruction, Moscow, ID 83844. Offers career and technology education (M Ed); curriculum and instruction (M Ed, Ed S); special education (M Ed). *Faculty:* 29. *Students:* 25 full-time (19 women), 39 part-time (34 women). Average age 37. In 2017, 33 master's, 2 Ed Ss awarded. *Entrance requirements:* For master's, minimum GPA of 3.0. Additional exam requirements/recommendations for international students: Required—TOEFL (minimum score 79 iBT). *Application deadline:* For fall admission, 8/1 for domestic students; for spring admission, 12/15 for domestic students. Applications are processed on a rolling basis. Application fee: $60. Electronic applications accepted. *Expenses:* Tuition, state resident: full-time $6722; part-time $430 per credit hour. Tuition, nonresident: full-time $23,046; part-time $1337 per credit hour. *Required fees:* $2142; $63 per credit hour. *Financial support:* Research assistantships and teaching assistantships available. Financial award applicants required to submit FAFSA. *Unit head:* Dr. Allen Kitchel, Interim Chair, 208-885-6587, E-mail: teached@uidaho.edu. *Application contact:* Sean Scoggin, Graduate Recruitment Coordinator, 208-885-4001, Fax: 208-885-4406, E-mail: graduateadmissions@uidaho.edu.
Website: http://www.uidaho.edu/ed/ci

University of Illinois at Chicago, College of Education, Department of Special Education, Chicago, IL 60607-7128. Offers M Ed, PhD. *Program availability:* Part-time. Terminal master's awarded for partial completion of doctoral program. *Degree requirements:* For doctorate, thesis/dissertation. *Entrance requirements:* For master's, minimum GPA of 2.75; for doctorate, GRE General Test, minimum GPA of 2.75. Additional exam requirements/recommendations for international students: Required—TOEFL. Electronic applications accepted. *Faculty research:* Teaching and learning for special learners, individual differences.

University of Illinois at Urbana–Champaign, Graduate College, College of Education, Department of Special Education, Champaign, IL 61820. Offers Ed M, MS, Ed D, PhD, CAS. *Program availability:* Part-time, online learning.

The University of Iowa, Graduate College, College of Education, Department of Teaching and Learning, Program in Special Education, Iowa City, IA 52242-1316. Offers MA, PhD. *Degree requirements:* For master's, thesis optional, exam; for doctorate, comprehensive exam, thesis/dissertation. *Entrance requirements:* For master's and doctorate, GRE General Test, minimum GPA of 3.0. Additional exam requirements/recommendations for international students: Required—TOEFL (minimum score 550 paper-based; 81 iBT). Electronic applications accepted.

The University of Kansas, Graduate Studies, School of Education, Department of Special Education, Lawrence, KS 66045. Offers autism spectrum disorder (Certificate);

early childhood unified (MS Ed); special and inclusive education leadership (Certificate); special education (PhD). *Accreditation:* NCATE. *Program availability:* Part-time, online learning. *Students:* 68 full-time (57 women), 333 part-time (296 women); includes 59 minority (20 Black or African American, non-Hispanic/Latino; 2 American Indian or Alaska Native, non-Hispanic/Latino; 14 Asian, non-Hispanic/Latino; 7 Hispanic/Latino; 1 Native Hawaiian or other Pacific Islander, non-Hispanic/Latino; 15 Two or more races, non-Hispanic/Latino), 23 international. Average age 34. 261 applicants, 70% accepted, 150 enrolled. In 2017, 140 master's, 4 doctorates, 28 other advanced degrees awarded. *Entrance requirements:* For master's, minimum GPA of 3.0, official transcripts, 3 letters of reference, professional resume; for doctorate, GRE General Test, official transcripts, 3 letters of reference, professional resume, professional writing sample. Application fee: $65 ($85 for international students). Electronic applications accepted. *Financial support:* Fellowships, research assistantships, teaching assistantships, Federal Work-Study, scholarships/grants, and unspecified assistantships available. Support available to part-time students. Financial award application deadline: 2/21; financial award applicants required to submit FAFSA. *Faculty research:* Autism spectrum disorders, learning disabilities research, leadership development, qualitative research and evaluation. *Unit head:* Elizabeth B. Kozleski, Chair, 785-864-0556, E-mail: elizabeth.kozleski@ku.edu. *Application contact:* Graduate Admission Contact, 785-864-4342, E-mail: specialeduadm@ku.edu.
Website: http://specialedu.ku.edu/

University of Kentucky, Graduate School, College of Education, Program in Special Education, Lexington, KY 40506-0032. Offers early childhood (MS Ed); rehabilitation counseling (MRC, PhD); special education (MS Ed, PhD). *Accreditation:* CORE; NCATE. Terminal master's awarded for partial completion of doctoral program. *Degree requirements:* For master's, comprehensive exam, thesis optional; for doctorate, comprehensive exam, thesis/dissertation. *Entrance requirements:* For master's, GRE General Test, minimum undergraduate GPA of 2.75; for doctorate, GRE General Test, minimum graduate GPA of 3.0. Additional exam requirements/recommendations for international students: Required—TOEFL (minimum score 550 paper-based). Electronic applications accepted. *Faculty research:* Applied behavior analysis applications in special education, single subject research design in classroom settings, transition research across life span, rural special education personnel.

University of La Verne, LaFetra College of Education, Program in Special Education, La Verne, CA 91750-4443. Offers mild/moderate education specialist (Credential); special education studies (MS). *Students:* 22 full-time (19 women), 69 part-time (51 women); includes 49 minority (5 Black or African American, non-Hispanic/Latino; 5 Asian, non-Hispanic/Latino; 38 Hispanic/Latino; 1 Two or more races, non-Hispanic/Latino). Average age 35. *Entrance requirements:* For master's, bachelor's degree, minimum undergraduate GPA of 3.0. Application fee: $50. *Expenses:* Contact institution. *Financial support:* Scholarships/grants and traineeships available. *Unit head:* Dr. Patricia Taylor, Program Chairperson, 909-448-4637, E-mail: ptaylor@laverne.edu. *Application contact:* Kristen Ahn, Assistant Director of Graduate Admissions, 909-448-4480, Fax: 909-971-2295, E-mail: sahn@laverne.edu.
Website: https://education.laverne.edu/special-education/

University of La Verne, Regional and Online Campuses, Graduate Credential Program in Education, California Statewide Campus, La Verne, CA 91750-4443. Offers administration services (preliminary) (Credential); education specialist: mild/moderate (Credential); English (Certificate); multiple subject teaching (Credential); pupil personnel services: school counseling (Credential); single subject teaching (Credential); special education (MS); special emphasis (M Ed). *Accreditation:* NCATE. *Program availability:* Part-time. *Faculty:* 3 full-time (2 women), 25 part-time/adjunct (19 women). *Students:* 120 full-time (95 women), 62 part-time (47 women); includes 47 minority (3 Black or African American, non-Hispanic/Latino; 2 American Indian or Alaska Native, non-Hispanic/Latino; 2 Asian, non-Hispanic/Latino; 40 Hispanic/Latino). Average age 31. In 2017, 25 master's, 61 other advanced degrees awarded. *Entrance requirements:* For degree, California Basic Educational Skills Test, minimum undergraduate GPA of 2.75, 3 letters of recommendation, interview. *Application deadline:* Applications are processed on a rolling basis. Application fee: $50. *Expenses:* Contact institution. *Financial support:* Application deadline: 3/2; applicants required to submit FAFSA. *Unit head:* Pam Bergovoy, Assistant Dean, Regional and Online Campuses/Director, Center for Educators, 909-448-4953, E-mail: pbergovoy@laverne.edu. *Application contact:* 877-468-6858, E-mail: gradadmission@laverne.edu.
Website: https://laverne.edu/locations/

University of La Verne, Regional and Online Campuses, Graduate Programs, High Desert Campus, Victorville, CA 92392. Offers business administration for experienced professionals (MBA); educational (special emphasis) (M Ed); educational counseling (MS); leadership and management (MS); multiple subject (elementary) (Credential); preliminary administrative services (Credential); pupil personnel services (Credential); single subject (secondary) (Credential). *Students:* 7 full-time (3 women), 16 part-time (12 women); includes 14 minority (3 Black or African American, non-Hispanic/Latino; 1 American Indian or Alaska Native, non-Hispanic/Latino; 1 Asian, non-Hispanic/Latino; 9 Hispanic/Latino). Average age 41. In 2017, 9 master's awarded. *Application deadline:* Applications are processed on a rolling basis. Application fee: $50. *Expenses:* Contact institution. *Financial support:* Application deadline: 3/2; applicants required to submit FAFSA. *Unit head:* Juli Roberts, Regional Campus Director, 760-955-6448, Fax: 760-843-9505, E-mail: jroberts@laverne.edu. *Application contact:* Admissions, 760-955-6440, Fax: 760-955-6443, E-mail: hdcv@laverne.edu.
Website: https://laverne.edu/locations/

University of La Verne, Regional and Online Campuses, Graduate Programs, Kern County Campus, Bakersfield, CA 93301. Offers business administration for experienced professionals (MBA-EP); education (special emphasis) (M Ed); educational counseling (MS); educational leadership (M Ed); health administration (MHA); leadership and management (MS); mild/moderate education specialist (Credential); multiple subject (elementary) (Credential); organizational leadership (Ed D); preliminary administrative services (Credential); single subject (secondary) (Credential); special education studies (MS). *Program availability:* Part-time, evening/weekend. *Students:* Average age 36. In 2017, 3 master's awarded. *Application deadline:* Applications are processed on a rolling basis. Application fee: $50. *Expenses:* Contact institution. *Financial support:* Institutionally sponsored loans available. Financial award application deadline: 3/2; financial award applicants required to submit FAFSA. *Unit head:* Nora Dominguez, Regional Campus Director, 661-861-6802, E-mail: ndominguez@laverne.edu. *Application contact:* Rebecca Murillo, Associate Director of Admissions, 661-861-6807, E-mail: rmurillo@laverne.edu.
Website: https://laverne.edu/locations/

University of La Verne, Regional and Online Campuses, Master's Programs in Education, California Statewide Campus, La Verne, CA 91750-4443. Offers administration services (preliminary) (Credential); education specialist: mild/moderate (Credential); educational counseling (MS); educational leadership (M Ed); multiple subject teaching (Credential); pupil personnel services: school counseling (Credential); single subject teaching (Credential); special education studies (MS); special emphasis (M Ed). *Accreditation:* NCATE. *Students:* 106 full-time (88 women), 75 part-time (55 women); includes 112 minority (4 Black or African American, non-Hispanic/Latino; 5

Special Education

Asian, non-Hispanic/Latino; 102 Hispanic/Latino; 1 Two or more races, non-Hispanic/Latino). Average age 35. In 2017, 76 master's, 82 other advanced degrees awarded. *Entrance requirements:* For master's, California Basic Educational Skills Test, 3 letters of recommendation, teaching credential. *Application deadline:* Applications are processed on a rolling basis. Application fee: $50. *Expenses:* Contact institution. *Financial support:* Application deadline: 3/2; applicants required to submit FAFSA. *Unit head:* Pam Bergovoy, Assistant Dean, Regional and Online Campuses/Director, Center for Educators, 909-448-4953, E-mail: pbergovoy@laverne.edu. *Application contact:* 877-468-6858, E-mail: gradadmission@laverne.edu.
Website: http://www.laverne.edu/locations

University of Louisiana at Monroe, Graduate School, College of Arts, Education, and Sciences, School of Education, Program in Special Education, Monroe, LA 71209-0001. Offers MAT. *Accreditation:* NCATE. *Program availability:* Part-time, evening/weekend. *Faculty:* 11 full-time (7 women). *Students:* 2 full-time (both women), 15 part-time (12 women); includes 4 minority (3 Black or African American, non-Hispanic/Latino; 1 Hispanic/Latino). Average age 30. 18 applicants, 28% accepted, 4 enrolled. In 2017, 14 master's awarded. *Entrance requirements:* For master's, GRE General Test, minimum GPA of 2.5. Additional exam requirements/recommendations for international students: Required—TOEFL (minimum score 500 paper-based; 61 iBT). *Application deadline:* For fall admission, 8/22 priority date for domestic students, 7/1 for international students; for winter admission, 12/12 priority date for domestic students; for spring admission, 1/17 for domestic students, 11/1 for international students. Applications are processed on a rolling basis. Application fee: $20 ($30 for international students). Electronic applications accepted. *Expenses:* Tuition, state resident: full-time $6489; part-time $479 per hour. Tuition, nonresident: full-time $12,100; part-time $479 per hour. *Required fees:* $8860; $802 per hour. $3273 per semester. *Financial support:* In 2017–18, 5 students received support. Research assistantships, career-related internships or fieldwork, Federal Work-Study, and unspecified assistantships available. Financial award application deadline: 4/1; financial award applicants required to submit FAFSA.

University of Louisville, Graduate School, College of Education and Human Development, Departments of Early Childhood and Elementary Education, Middle and Secondary Education, and Special Education, Louisville, KY 40292-0001. Offers art education (MAT); autism and applied behavior analysis (Certificate); curriculum and instruction (PhD); early elementary education (MAT); exercise physiology (MS); health and physical education (MAT); health professions education (Certificate); higher education (MA); human resources and organization development (MS); instructional technology (M Ed); interdisciplinary early childhood education (MAT); middle school education (MAT); music education (MAT); secondary education (MAT); special education (MAT); sport administration (MS); teacher leadership (M Ed). *Program availability:* Part-time, evening/weekend. *Students:* 114 full-time (73 women), 173 part-time (114 women); includes 49 minority (19 Black or African American, non-Hispanic/Latino; 5 Asian, non-Hispanic/Latino; 13 Hispanic/Latino; 12 Two or more races, non-Hispanic/Latino), 7 international. Average age 29. 132 applicants, 73% accepted, 57 enrolled. In 2017, 70 master's, 2 doctorates, 2 other advanced degrees awarded. *Application deadline:* For spring admission, 1/1 priority date for international students. Application fee: $65. *Expenses:* Tuition, state resident: full-time $12,246; part-time $681 per credit hour. Tuition, nonresident: full-time $25,486; part-time $1417 per credit hour. *Required fees:* $196. Tuition and fees vary according to course load, program and reciprocity agreements. *Financial support:* Application deadline: 6/1; applicants required to submit FAFSA. *Faculty research:* STEM teaching and learning; content literacy for English language learners; social justice in teacher education; adolescent literacy; mathematics teacher development. *Total annual research expenditures:* $1.7 million. *Unit head:* Dr. Ann E. Larson, Dean, College of Education and Human Development, 502-852-6411, Fax: 502-852-1464, E-mail: ann@louisville.edu. *Application contact:* Betty Hampton, Director of Graduate Student Services, 502-852-5597, Fax: 502-852-1465, E-mail: edadvise@louisville.edu.
Website: http://louisville.edu/delphi

University of Lynchburg, Graduate Studies, M Ed Program in Special Education, Lynchburg, VA 24501-3199. Offers M Ed. *Program availability:* Part-time, evening/weekend. *Faculty:* 17 full-time (10 women). *Students:* 3 full-time (1 woman), 24 part-time (21 women); includes 5 minority (4 Black or African American, non-Hispanic/Latino; 1 Hispanic/Latino), 1 international. Average age 35. 14 applicants, 100% accepted, 7 enrolled. In 2017, 15 master's awarded. *Degree requirements:* For master's, comprehensive exam, internship; practicum. *Entrance requirements:* For master's, GRE, minimum GPA of 3.0 (preferred), official transcripts (bachelor's, others as relevant), three letters of recommendation, career goals statement. Additional exam requirements/recommendations for international students: Required—TOEFL (minimum score 550 paper-based; 80 iBT), IELTS (minimum score 6). *Application deadline:* For fall admission, 7/31 for domestic students, 6/1 for international students; for spring admission, 11/30 for domestic students, 10/15 for international students. Applications are processed on a rolling basis. Application fee: $30. Electronic applications accepted. Application fee is waived when completed online. *Expenses:* $510 per credit tuition, $100 fees. *Financial support:* Federal Work-Study, scholarships/grants, health care benefits, and unspecified assistantships available. Support available to part-time students. Financial award application deadline: 7/31; financial award applicants required to submit FAFSA. *Unit head:* Dr. Deanna Cash, Program Director, Special Education Program, 434-544.8635, E-mail: cash.d@lynchburg.edu. *Application contact:* Ellen Thompson, Graduate Admissions Counselor, 434-544-8841, E-mail: thompson_e@lynchburg.edu.
Website: http://www.lynchburg.edu/graduate/master-of-education-in-special-education/

University of Maine, Graduate School, College of Education and Human Development, School of Learning and Teaching, Orono, ME 04469. Offers counselor education (M Ed, MA, MS, CAS); early childhood teacher (CGS); education (PhD), including counselor education, literacy education, prevention and intervention studies; elementary education (M Ed, CAS); individualized education (M Ed); literacy education (CAS); response to intervention for behavior (CGS); secondary education (M Ed, CAS); social studies education (M Ed); special education (M Ed, CAS). *Program availability:* Part-time. *Faculty:* 21 full-time (12 women), 37 part-time/adjunct (29 women). *Students:* 84 full-time (73 women), 190 part-time (165 women); includes 19 minority (1 Black or African American, non-Hispanic/Latino; 9 American Indian or Alaska Native, non-Hispanic/Latino; 2 Asian, non-Hispanic/Latino; 4 Hispanic/Latino; 3 Two or more races, non-Hispanic/Latino), 4 international. Average age 38. 141 applicants, 94% accepted, 91 enrolled. In 2017, 74 master's, 3 doctorates, 36 other advanced degrees awarded. *Degree requirements:* For master's, thesis (for some programs), for doctorate, comprehensive exam, thesis/dissertation. *Entrance requirements:* For master's, GRE General Test, MAT. Additional exam requirements/recommendations for international students: Required—TOEFL (minimum score 550 paper-based; 80 iBT), IELTS (minimum score 6.5). *Application deadline:* For fall admission, 2/1 priority date for domestic students. Applications are processed on a rolling basis. Application fee: $65. Electronic applications accepted. *Expenses:* Tuition, state resident: full-time $7722; part-time $429 per credit hour. Tuition, nonresident: full-time $25,146; part-time $1397 per credit hour. *Required fees:* $1162; $581 per credit hour. *Financial support:* In 2017–18, 14 students received support, including 11 teaching assistantships (averaging $15,200 per year); Federal Work-Study, scholarships/grants, and unspecified

assistantships also available. Financial award application deadline: 3/1. *Faculty research:* Gender and leadership, virtual reality, using writing to improve performance in athletics, digital citizenship, professional development for special and general education. *Total annual research expenditures:* $5 million. *Unit head:* Dr. Jim Artesani, Associate Dean of Accreditation and Graduate Affairs, 207-581-4061. *Application contact:* Scott G. Delcourt, Assistant Vice President for Graduate Studies and Senior Associate Dean, 207-581-3291, Fax: 207-581-3232, E-mail: graduate@maine.edu.
Website: http://umaine.edu/edhd/

University of Manitoba, Faculty of Graduate Studies, Faculty of Education, Department of Educational Administration, Foundations and Psychology, Winnipeg, MB R3T 2N2, Canada. Offers adult and post-secondary education (M Ed); educational administration (M Ed); guidance and counseling (M Ed); inclusive special education (M Ed); social foundations of education (M Ed). *Degree requirements:* For master's, thesis or alternative.

University of Mary, Liffrig Family School of Education and Behavioral Sciences, Department of Education, Bismarck, ND 58504-9652. Offers curriculum, instruction and assessment (M Ed); education (Ed D); elementary administration (M Ed); reading (M Ed); secondary administration (M Ed); special education strategist (M Ed). *Program availability:* Part-time. *Degree requirements:* For master's, portfolio or thesis. *Entrance requirements:* For master's, interview, letters of reference, minimum GPA of 2.5. Additional exam requirements/recommendations for international students: Required—TOEFL (minimum score 500 paper-based; 71 iBT). Electronic applications accepted.

University of Maryland Eastern Shore, Graduate Programs, Department of Education, Program in Special Education, Princess Anne, MD 21853. Offers M Ed. *Accreditation:* NCATE. *Degree requirements:* For master's, comprehensive exam, seminar paper, internship. *Entrance requirements:* For master's, PRAXIS I, interview, minimum GPA of 3.0. Additional exam requirements/recommendations for international students: Required—TOEFL (minimum score 80 iBT). Electronic applications accepted.

University of Massachusetts Amherst, Graduate School, College of Education, Program in Education, Amherst, MA 01003. Offers bilingual, English as a second language, and multicultural education (M Ed, Ed S); child study and early education (M Ed); children, families and schools (Ed D, Ed S); early childhood and elementary teacher education (M Ed); educational leadership (M Ed); educational policy and leadership (Ed D); higher education (M Ed); international education (M Ed); language, literacy and culture (Ed D); learning, media and technology (M Ed, Ed S); mathematics, science, and learning technologies (Ed D); reading and writing (M Ed); research, educational measurement and psychometrics (Ed D); school counselor education (M Ed, Ed S); school psychology (Ed S); science education (Ed S); secondary teacher education (M Ed); social justice education (M Ed, Ed D, Ed S); special education (M Ed, Ed D, Ed S); teacher education and school improvement (Ed D, Ed S). *Accreditation:* NCATE. *Program availability:* Part-time, online learning. Terminal master's awarded for partial completion of doctoral program. *Degree requirements:* For doctorate, comprehensive exam, thesis/dissertation. *Entrance requirements:* Additional exam requirements/recommendations for international students: Required—TOEFL (minimum score 550 paper-based; 80 iBT), IELTS (minimum score 6.5). Electronic applications accepted.

University of Massachusetts Boston, College of Education and Human Development, Program in Special Education, Boston, MA 02125-3393. Offers M Ed. *Program availability:* Part-time, evening/weekend. *Students:* 3 full-time (2 women), 42 part-time (33 women); includes 6 minority (3 Black or African American, non-Hispanic/Latino; 3 Hispanic/Latino), 1 international. Average age 28. 20 applicants, 70% accepted, 11 enrolled. In 2017, 35 master's awarded. *Entrance requirements:* For master's, GRE General Test or MAT, minimum GPA of 2.75. *Application deadline:* For fall admission, 3/1 for domestic students; for spring admission, 11/1 for domestic students. *Expenses:* Tuition, state resident: full-time $17,375. Tuition, nonresident: full-time $33,915. *Required fees:* $355. *Financial support:* Research assistantships, teaching assistantships, career-related internships or fieldwork, Federal Work-Study, and unspecified assistantships available. Support available to part-time students. Financial award application deadline: 3/1; financial award applicants required to submit FAFSA. *Faculty research:* Inclusionary learning, cross-cultural special needs, special education restructuring. *Application contact:* Graduate Admissions Coordinator, 617-287-6400, Fax: 617-287-6236, E-mail: bos.gadm@dpc.umassp.edu.

University of Massachusetts Dartmouth, Graduate School, College of Arts and Sciences, Department of Psychology, North Dartmouth, MA 02747-2300. Offers autism studies (Graduate Certificate); psychology - applied behavioral analysis (MA, Post-Master's Certificate); psychology - clinical (MA); psychology - research (MA). *Program availability:* Part-time. *Faculty:* 20 full-time (12 women), 8 part-time/adjunct (2 women). *Students:* 40 full-time (31 women), 57 part-time (52 women); includes 19 minority (4 Black or African American, non-Hispanic/Latino; 3 Asian, non-Hispanic/Latino; 7 Hispanic/Latino; 5 Two or more races, non-Hispanic/Latino), 1 international. Average age 29. 96 applicants, 54% accepted, 39 enrolled. In 2017, 21 master's awarded. *Degree requirements:* For master's, comprehensive exam (for some programs), thesis or comprehensive exam (for psychology - clinical); thesis (for psychology - research). *Entrance requirements:* For master's and other advanced degree, statement of purpose (minimum of 300 words), resume, 3 letters of recommendation, official transcripts. Additional exam requirements/recommendations for international students: Required—TOEFL (minimum score 533 paper-based; 72 iBT), IELTS (minimum score 6). *Application deadline:* For fall admission, 3/1 priority date for domestic students, 2/1 priority date for international students. Application fee: $60. Electronic applications accepted. *Expenses:* Tuition, state resident: full-time $15,449; part-time $643.71 per credit. Tuition, nonresident: full-time $27,880; part-time $1161.67 per credit. *Required fees:* $405; $25.88 per credit. Tuition and fees vary according to course load and reciprocity agreements. *Financial support:* In 2017–18, 1 research assistantship (averaging $12,000 per year), 2 teaching assistantships (averaging $14,000 per year) were awarded; tuition waivers (full and partial) and unspecified assistantships also available. Support available to part-time students. Financial award application deadline: 3/1; financial award applicants required to submit FAFSA. *Faculty research:* Health inequities, language and cognitive development, interethnic dating and marriage, executive function and implicit learning in deaf children, behavioral medicine. *Total annual research expenditures:* $344,000. *Unit head:* Mahzad Hojjat, Graduate Program Director, Research Psychology, 508-999-8951, E-mail: mhojjat@umassd.edu. *Application contact:* Steven Briggs, Director of Marketing and Recruitment for Graduate Studies, 508-999-8604, Fax: 508-999-8183, E-mail: graduate@umassd.edu.
Website: http://www.umassd.edu/cas/psychology

University of Memphis, Graduate School, College of Education, Department of Instruction and Curriculum Leadership, Memphis, TN 38152. Offers advanced studies in teaching and learning (M Ed); applied behavior analysis (Graduate Certificate); autism studies (Graduate Certificate); early childhood education (MAT, MS, Ed D); elementary education (MAT); instruction and curriculum (MS, Ed D); instruction design and technology (MS, Ed D); instructional design and technology (Graduate Certificate); literacy, leadership, and coaching (Graduate Certificate); reading (MS, Ed D); school library information specialist (Graduate Certificate); secondary education (MAT); special education (MAT, MS, Ed D); STEM teacher leadership (Graduate Certificate); urban

education (Graduate Certificate). *Accreditation:* NCATE (one or more programs are accredited). *Program availability:* Part-time. *Faculty:* 22 full-time (14 women), 14 part-time/adjunct (10 women). *Students:* 36 full-time (27 women), 351 part-time (271 women); includes 159 minority (132 Black or African American, non-Hispanic/Latino; 1 American Indian or Alaska Native, non-Hispanic/Latino; 7 Asian, non-Hispanic/Latino; 10 Hispanic/Latino; 9 Two or more races, non-Hispanic/Latino), 4 international. Average age 35. 170 applicants, 85% accepted, 111 enrolled. In 2017, 84 master's, 14 doctorates, 32 other advanced degrees awarded. Terminal master's awarded for partial completion of doctoral program. *Degree requirements:* For master's, comprehensive exam, thesis or alternative; for doctorate, comprehensive exam, thesis/dissertation. *Entrance requirements:* For master's, GRE General Test, PRAXIS, minimum GPA of 2.5, letters of reference; for doctorate, GRE General Test, GRE Subject Test, 2 years of teaching experience, letters of reference, statement of purpose, interview. Additional exam requirements/recommendations for international students: Required—TOEFL (minimum score 550 paper-based; 79 iBT). *Application deadline:* For fall admission, 4/1 priority date for domestic students; for spring admission, 10/1 priority date for domestic students; for summer admission, 2/1 priority date for domestic students. Applications are processed on a rolling basis. Application fee: $35 ($60 for international students). Electronic applications accepted. *Expenses:* Contact institution. *Financial support:* In 2017–18, 2 research assistantships with full tuition reimbursements (averaging $10,000 per year), 3 teaching assistantships with full tuition reimbursements (averaging $10,666 per year) were awarded; career-related internships or fieldwork, Federal Work-Study, institutionally sponsored loans, scholarships/grants, traineeships, and unspecified assistantships also available. Support available to part-time students. Financial award application deadline: 2/1; financial award applicants required to submit FAFSA. *Faculty research:* Effective urban teachers, preparation and retention of urban teachers, technology utilization in schools, field-based teacher preparation programs, effective use of online instruction. *Unit head:* Dr. Angiline Powell, Interim Chair, 901-678-3310, E-mail: apowell3@memphis.edu. *Application contact:* Dr. James Meindl, Coordinator of Graduate Studies, 901-678-3310, E-mail: jnmeindl@memphis.edu.
Website: http://www.memphis.edu/icl/

University of Miami, Graduate School, School of Education and Human Development, Department of Teaching and Learning, Program in Early Childhood Special Education, Coral Gables, FL 33124. Offers MS Ed, Ed S. *Program availability:* Part-time, evening/weekend. *Degree requirements:* For master's, electronic portfolio. *Entrance requirements:* For master's, GRE General Test. Additional exam requirements/recommendations for international students: Required—TOEFL (minimum score 550 paper-based; 80 iBT); Recommended—IELTS (minimum score 6.5). Electronic applications accepted.

University of Miami, Graduate School, School of Education and Human Development, Department of Teaching and Learning, Program in Teaching and Learning, Coral Gables, FL 33124. Offers language and literacy learning in multilingual settings (PhD); science, technology, engineering and mathematics (PhD); special education (PhD). *Degree requirements:* For doctorate, thesis/dissertation, qualifying exam, electronic portfolio. *Entrance requirements:* For doctorate, GRE General Test. Additional exam requirements/recommendations for international students: Required—TOEFL (minimum score 550 paper-based; 80 iBT); Recommended—IELTS (minimum score 6.5). Electronic applications accepted. *Faculty research:* Teacher education, multicultural education, special education, second language acquisition, math and science education.

University of Michigan–Dearborn, College of Education, Health, and Human Services, Master of Education Program in Special Education, Dearborn, MI 48126. Offers M Ed. *Accreditation:* TEAC. *Program availability:* Part-time, evening/weekend, 100% online. *Faculty:* 2 full-time (1 woman), 1 part-time/adjunct (0 women). *Students:* 9 part-time (8 women); includes 1 minority (Black or African American, non-Hispanic/Latino). Average age 34. 4 applicants, 75% accepted. In 2017, 10 master's awarded. *Entrance requirements:* For master's, minimum GPA of 3.0; statement of purpose; 3 letters of recommendation. Additional exam requirements/recommendations for international students: Required—TOEFL (minimum score 560 paper-based; 84 iBT), IELTS (minimum score 6.5). *Application deadline:* For fall admission, 8/1 priority date for domestic students, 5/1 priority date for international students; for winter admission, 12/1 priority date for domestic students, 9/1 priority date for international students; for spring admission, 4/1 priority date for domestic students, 1/1 priority date for international students. Applications are processed on a rolling basis. Application fee: $60. Electronic applications accepted. *Expenses:* $683 per credit hour in-state; $1,176 per credit hour out-state. *Financial support:* Career-related internships or fieldwork and scholarships/grants available. Financial award application deadline: 3/1; financial award applicants required to submit FAFSA. *Faculty research:* Technology and teaching, pedagogy and interventions, education policy, learning disabilities, literacy. *Unit head:* Dr. Stein Brunvand, Director, Master's Programs, 313-583-6415, E-mail: sbrunvan@umich.edu. *Application contact:* Office of Graduate Studies, 313-583-6321, E-mail: umd-graduatestudies@umich.edu.
Website: http://umdearborn.edu/cehhs/cehhs_medsped/

University of Minnesota, Twin Cities Campus, Graduate School, College of Education and Human Development, Department of Educational Psychology, Program in Special Education, Minneapolis, MN 55455-0213. Offers M Ed, MA, PhD. *Students:* 101 full-time (79 women), 22 part-time (18 women); includes 19 minority (2 Black or African American, non-Hispanic/Latino; 9 Asian, non-Hispanic/Latino; 5 Hispanic/Latino; 3 Two or more races, non-Hispanic/Latino), 8 international. Average age 29. 101 applicants, 59% accepted, 53 enrolled. In 2017, 33 master's, 2 doctorates awarded. Application fee: $75 ($95 for international students). *Unit head:* Dr. Geoffrey Maruyama, Chair, 612-625-5861, Fax: 612-624-8241, E-mail: geoff@umn.edu. *Application contact:* Dr. Ernest Davenport, Director of Graduate Studies, 612-624-1040, E-mail: lqr6576@umn.edu.
Website: http://www.cehd.umn.edu/EdPsych/Programs/SpecialEd/

University of Mississippi, Graduate School, School of Education, University, MS 38677. Offers counselor education (M Ed, PhD); counselor education - play therapy (Ed S); early childhood (M Ed); educational leadership K-12 (M Ed, Ed D, PhD, Ed S); elementary education (M Ed, Ed D, Ed S); higher education/student personnel (Ed D, PhD); literacy education (M Ed); math education (Ed D); secondary education (M Ed, PhD, Ed S); special education (M Ed, PhD, Ed S); teacher corporations (MA); teacher education (MA). *Accreditation:* NCATE. *Faculty:* 65 full-time (40 women), 25 part-time/adjunct (5 women). *Students:* 185 full-time (148 women), 410 part-time (310 women); includes 193 minority (168 Black or African American, non-Hispanic/Latino; 7 Asian, non-Hispanic/Latino; 14 Hispanic/Latino; 4 Two or more races, non-Hispanic/Latino), 7 international. Average age 33. In 2017, 176 master's, 20 doctorates, 37 other advanced degrees awarded. *Entrance requirements:* For master's, GRE General Test, minimum GPA of 3.0; for doctorate, GRE General Test. Additional exam requirements/recommendations for international students: Required—TOEFL. *Application deadline:* For fall admission, 3/1 for domestic students; for spring admission, 10/1 for domestic students; for summer admission, 3/1 for domestic students. Applications are processed on a rolling basis. Application fee: $50. Electronic applications accepted. *Financial support:* Scholarships/grants available. Financial award application deadline: 3/1; financial award applicants required to submit FAFSA. *Unit head:* Dr. David Rock, Dean,

662-915-7063, Fax: 662-915-7249, E-mail: soe@olemiss.edu. *Application contact:* Dr. Joe Sumrall, Professor of Elementary Education, 662-915-7350, E-mail: soe@olemiss.edu.

University of Missouri, Office of Research and Graduate Studies, College of Education, Department of Special Education, Columbia, MO 65211. Offers administration and supervision of special education (PhD); behavior disorders (M Ed, PhD); curriculum development of exceptional students (M Ed, PhD); early childhood special education (M Ed, PhD); general special education (M Ed, MA, PhD); learning and instruction (M Ed); learning disabilities (M Ed, PhD); mental retardation (M Ed, PhD). *Accreditation:* TEAC. *Program availability:* Part-time, evening/weekend, online learning. *Degree requirements:* For master's, comprehensive exam, thesis or alternative; for doctorate, comprehensive exam, thesis/dissertation. *Entrance requirements:* For master's and doctorate, GRE General Test, letters of recommendation. Additional exam requirements/recommendations for international students: Required—TOEFL (minimum score 500 paper-based; 61 iBT). Electronic applications accepted.

University of Missouri–Kansas City, School of Education, Kansas City, MO 64110-2499. Offers administration (Ed D); counseling and guidance (MA, Ed S), including mental health counseling (Ed S), school counseling (Ed S); counseling psychology (PhD); curriculum and instruction (MA, Ed S), including language and literacy (Ed S); education (PhD), including higher education administration, PK-12 education administration; educational administration (MA, Ed S), including advanced principal (Ed S), beginning principal (Ed S), district-level administration (Ed S); reading education (MA); special education (MA). PhD in education offered through the School of Graduate Studies. *Accreditation:* NCATE. *Program availability:* Part-time, evening/weekend. *Degree requirements:* For doctorate, thesis/dissertation, internship, practicum. *Entrance requirements:* For master's, GRE, minimum GPA of 2.75, 2 letters of reference, written statement of purpose; for doctorate, GRE, minimum GPA of 3.0; for Ed S, minimum GPA of 3.0. Additional exam requirements/recommendations for international students: Required—TOEFL (minimum score 550 paper-based; 80 iBT). *Faculty research:* Urban education, inquiry-based field study, theories of counseling and psychotherapy, school literacy, educational technology.

University of Missouri–St. Louis, College of Education, Department of Educator Preparation, Innovation and Research, St. Louis, MO 63121. Offers elementary education (M Ed), including early childhood, general, reading; secondary education (M Ed), including curriculum and instruction, general, middle level education, reading, teaching English to speakers of other languages (TESOL); special education (M Ed), including autism and developmental disabilities, early childhood special education. *Program availability:* Part-time, evening/weekend. *Students:* 75 full-time (63 women), 462 part-time (363 women); includes 127 minority (85 Black or African American, non-Hispanic/Latino; 2 American Indian or Alaska Native, non-Hispanic/Latino; 8 Asian, non-Hispanic/Latino; 24 Hispanic/Latino; 8 Two or more races, non-Hispanic/Latino), 1 international. 247 applicants, 92% accepted, 153 enrolled. *Degree requirements:* For master's, comprehensive exam. *Entrance requirements:* Additional exam requirements/recommendations for international students: Recommended—TOEFL (minimum score 550 paper-based; 79 iBT), IELTS (minimum score 6.5). *Application deadline:* For fall admission, 7/1 priority date for domestic and international students; for spring admission, 12/1 priority date for domestic and international students. Application fee: $50 ($40 for international students). Electronic applications accepted. *Expenses:* Tuition, state resident: part-time $476.50 per credit hour. Tuition, nonresident: part-time $1169.70 per credit hour. *Financial support:* Application deadline: 4/1; applicants required to submit FAFSA. *Unit head:* Dr. Gayle Wilkinson, Chair, 314-516-5791. *Application contact:* 314-516-5458, Fax: 314-516-6996, E-mail: gadadm@umsl.edu.
Website: https://www.umsl.edu/dept/epir.html

University of Nebraska at Kearney, College of Education, Department of Educational Administration, Kearney, NE 68849-0001. Offers curriculum supervisor of academic area (MA Ed); school principalship 7-12 (MA Ed); school principalship PK-8 (MA Ed); school superintendent (Ed S); supervisor of special education (MA Ed). *Accreditation:* NCATE. *Program availability:* Part-time, evening/weekend, online only, 100% online. *Degree requirements:* For master's and Ed S, comprehensive exam, thesis optional. *Entrance requirements:* For master's, letters of recommendation, resume, letter of interest; for Ed S, letters of recommendation, resume, essay. Additional exam requirements/recommendations for international students: Recommended—TOEFL (minimum score 550 paper-based; 79 iBT), IELTS (minimum score 6.5). Electronic applications accepted. *Faculty research:* Leadership and organizational behavior.

University of Nebraska at Kearney, College of Education, Department of Teacher Education, Kearney, NE 68849-0001. Offers curriculum and instruction (MA Ed), including early childhood education, elementary education, English as a second language, instructional effectiveness, reading/special education, secondary education; instructional technology (MS Ed), including information technology, instructional technology, school librarian; reading PK-12 (MA Ed); special education (MA Ed), including advanced practitioner: assistive technology specialist, advanced practitioner: behavioral interventionist, advanced practitioner: inclusive collaboration specialist, gifted, teacher education. *Program availability:* Part-time, evening/weekend, online only, 100% online. *Degree requirements:* For master's, comprehensive exam, thesis optional. *Entrance requirements:* For master's, portfolio or GRE. Additional exam requirements/recommendations for international students: Recommended—TOEFL (minimum score 550 paper-based; 79 iBT), IELTS (minimum score 6.5). Electronic applications accepted. *Expenses:* Contact institution.

University of Nebraska at Kearney, College of Education, Kinesiology and Sport Sciences Department, Kearney, NE 68849-0001. Offers general physical education (MA Ed), including recreation and leisure, sports administration; physical education exercise science (MA Ed); physical education master teacher (MA Ed), including pedagogy, special populations. *Program availability:* Part-time, evening/weekend, 100% online. *Degree requirements:* For master's, comprehensive exam, thesis optional. *Entrance requirements:* For master's, GRE General Test (for some programs), personal statement. Additional exam requirements/recommendations for international students: Recommended—TOEFL (minimum score 550 paper-based; 79 iBT), IELTS (minimum score 6.5). Electronic applications accepted. *Faculty research:* Ergonomic aids, nutrition, motor development, sports pedagogy, applied behavior analysis, physical activity and wellness, athletic training, therapeutic interventions, exercise physiology, endocrinology and metabolism.

University of Nebraska at Omaha, Graduate Studies, College of Education, Department of Special Education and Communication Disorders, Omaha, NE 68182. Offers special education (MS); speech-language pathology (MS). *Accreditation:* ASHA; NCATE. *Program availability:* Part-time, evening/weekend. *Degree requirements:* For master's, comprehensive exam, thesis (for some programs). *Entrance requirements:* For master's, minimum GPA of 3.0, statement of purpose, 2 letters of recommendation, copy of teaching certificate. Additional exam requirements/recommendations for international students: Required—TOEFL, IELTS, PTE. Electronic applications accepted.

University of Nebraska–Lincoln, Graduate College, College of Education and Human Sciences, Department of Special Education and Communication Disorders, Program in

Special Education

Special Education, Lincoln, NE 68588. Offers M Ed, MA, Ed S. *Accreditation:* NCATE; TEAC. *Degree requirements:* For master's, thesis required. *Entrance requirements:* For master's, GRE. Additional exam requirements/recommendations for international students: Required—TOEFL (minimum score 500 paper-based). Electronic applications accepted.

University of Nebraska–Lincoln, Graduate College, College of Education and Human Sciences, Department of Teaching, Learning and Teacher Education, Lincoln, NE 68588. Offers adult and continuing education (MA); educational studies (Ed D, PhD), including special education (Ed D); teaching, learning and teacher education (M Ed, MA, MST, Ed D, PhD); vocational and adult education (M Ed, MA). *Accreditation:* NCATE. *Degree requirements:* For master's, thesis optional. *Entrance requirements:* Additional exam requirements/recommendations for international students: Required—TOEFL (minimum score 550 paper-based). Electronic applications accepted. *Faculty research:* Teacher education, instructional leadership, literacy education, technology, improvement of school curriculum.

University of Nevada, Las Vegas, Graduate College, College of Education, Department of Educational and Clinical Studies, Las Vegas, NV 89154-3066. Offers addiction studies (Advanced Certificate); counselor education (M Ed, MS), including clinical mental health (MS); school counseling (M Ed); early childhood education (M Ed); early childhood special education (Certificate), including infancy, preschool; English language learning (M Ed); mental health counseling (Advanced Certificate); special education (M Ed, PhD); PhD/JD. *Program availability:* Part-time. *Faculty:* 18 full-time (9 women), 28 part-time/adjunct (22 women). *Students:* 281 full-time (230 women), 193 part-time (148 women); includes 211 minority (54 Black or African American, non-Hispanic/Latino; 2 American Indian or Alaska Native, non-Hispanic/Latino; 28 Asian, non-Hispanic/Latino; 95 Hispanic/Latino; 4 Native Hawaiian or other Pacific Islander, non-Hispanic/Latino; 28 Two or more races, non-Hispanic/Latino), 13 international. Average age 34. 262 applicants, 76% accepted, 161 enrolled. In 2017, 204 master's, 8 doctorates, 1 other advanced degree awarded. *Degree requirements:* For master's, comprehensive exam (for some programs); for doctorate, comprehensive exam, thesis/dissertation; for other advanced degree, final project. *Entrance requirements:* For master's, bachelor's degree; letter of recommendation; statement of purpose; for doctorate, GRE General Test, statement of purpose; writing sample; 3 letters of recommendation. Additional exam requirements/recommendations for international students: Required—TOEFL (minimum score 550 paper-based; 80 iBT), IELTS (minimum score 7). Application fee: $60 ($95 for international students). Electronic applications accepted. *Expenses:* $275 per credit, $850 per course, $7,969 per year resident, $22,157 per year non-resident, $7,094 non-resident fee (7 credits or more), $1,307 annual health insurance fee. *Financial support:* In 2017–18, 35 students received support, including 10 research assistantships with full tuition reimbursements available (averaging $13,775 per year), 25 teaching assistantships with full tuition reimbursements available (averaging $17,140 per year); institutionally sponsored loans, scholarships/grants, health care benefits, and unspecified assistantships also available. Financial award application deadline: 3/15; financial award applicants required to submit FAFSA. *Faculty research:* Multicultural issues in counseling, academic interventions for students with disabilities, establishment of pro-social skills in young children with severe disabilities, inclusive strategies for students with disabilities, language and literacy for English language learners. *Total annual research expenditures:* $1.1 million. *Unit head:* Dr. Monica Brown, Interim Department Chair/Professor, 702-895-3167, Fax: 702-895-3205, E-mail: monica.brown@unlv.edu. *Application contact:* Dr. Joseph Morgan, Graduate Coordinator, 702-895-3329, Fax: 702-895-3205, E-mail: joseph.morgan@unlv.edu. Website: http://education.unlv.edu/ecs/

University of Nevada, Reno, Graduate School, College of Education, Department of Curriculum, Teaching and Learning, Reno, NV 89557. Offers curriculum and instruction (PhD); curriculum, teaching and learning (Ed D, PhD); elementary education (M Ed, MA, MS); secondary education (M Ed, MA, MS); special education and disability studies (PhD). *Degree requirements:* For master's, thesis optional; for doctorate, thesis/dissertation. *Entrance requirements:* For master's, GRE General Test, minimum GPA of 2.75; for doctorate, GRE General Test, minimum GPA of 3.0. Additional exam requirements/recommendations for international students: Required—TOEFL (minimum score 500 paper-based; 61 iBT), IELTS (minimum score 6). Electronic applications accepted. *Faculty research:* Education, curricula, pedagogy.

University of Nevada, Reno, Graduate School, College of Education, Department of Educational Specialties, Program in Special Education, Reno, NV 89557. Offers M Ed, MA, MS, Ed D, PhD. Terminal master's awarded for partial completion of doctoral program. *Degree requirements:* For master's, thesis optional; for doctorate, thesis/dissertation. *Entrance requirements:* For master's, minimum GPA of 2.75; for doctorate, GRE General Test, minimum GPA of 3.0. Additional exam requirements/recommendations for international students: Required—TOEFL (minimum score 500 paper-based; 61 iBT), IELTS (minimum score 6). Electronic applications accepted. *Faculty research:* Learning disabilities, equity and diversity in educational settings.

University of New Hampshire, Graduate School, College of Liberal Arts, Department of Education, Program in Early Childhood Education, Durham, NH 03824. Offers early childhood education (M Ed); early childhood education: special needs (M Ed). *Program availability:* Part-time. *Students:* 4 full-time (3 women), 6 part-time (all women). Average age 32. 9 applicants, 78% accepted, 4 enrolled. In 2017, 13 master's awarded. *Entrance requirements:* For master's, PRAXIS, Department of Education background check. Additional exam requirements/recommendations for international students: Required—TOEFL (minimum score 550 paper-based; 80 iBT). *Application deadline:* For fall admission, 3/1 priority date for domestic students, 3/1 for international students; for spring admission, 11/1 for domestic students. Application fee: $65. Electronic applications accepted. *Financial support:* In 2017–18, 4 students received support. Fellowships, research assistantships, teaching assistantships, career-related internships or fieldwork, Federal Work-Study, scholarships/grants, and tuition waivers (full and partial) available. Support available to part-time students. Financial award application deadline: 2/15. *Unit head:* Leslie Couse, Chair, 603-862-0638, E-mail: education.department@unh.edu. *Application contact:* Cindy Glidden, Department Coordinator, 603-862-2381, E-mail: education.department@unh.edu. Website: http://cola.unh.edu/education

University of New Hampshire, Graduate School, College of Liberal Arts, Department of Education, Program in Special Education, Durham, NH 03824. Offers special education (M Ed); special education administration (Postbaccalaureate Certificate). *Program availability:* Part-time. *Students:* 6 full-time (all women), 1 part-time (0 women). Average age 24. 8 applicants, 88% accepted, 5 enrolled. In 2017, 9 master's awarded. *Entrance requirements:* For master's, PRAXIS, Department of Education background check. Additional exam requirements/recommendations for international students: Required—TOEFL (minimum score 550 paper-based; 80 iBT). *Application deadline:* For fall admission, 4/15 for domestic and international students; for spring admission, 11/1 for domestic students; for summer admission, 4/1 for domestic students. Application fee: $65. Electronic applications accepted. *Financial support:* In 2017–18, 1 student received support. Fellowships, research assistantships, teaching assistantships, career-related internships or fieldwork, Federal Work-Study, scholarships/grants, and tuition waivers (full and partial) available. Support available to part-time students. Financial award application deadline: 2/15. *Unit head:* Paula Salvio, Chair, 603-862-0024, E-mail:

education.department@unh.edu. *Application contact:* Cindy Glidden, Department Coordinator, 603-862-2311, E-mail: education.department@unh.edu. Website: http://cola.unh.edu/education

University of New Mexico, Graduate Studies, College of Education, Program in Intensive Social, Language and Behavioral Needs, Albuquerque, NM 87131-2039. Offers Graduate Certificate. *Program availability:* Part-time, evening/weekend. *Faculty:* 2 full-time (both women). *Students:* 6 part-time (all women). Average age 44. 5 applicants, 80% accepted, 3 enrolled. In 2017, 1 Graduate Certificate awarded. *Entrance requirements:* Additional exam requirements/recommendations for international students: Required—TOEFL (minimum score 550 paper-based). *Application deadline:* For fall admission, 3/31 priority date for domestic students, 3/1 for international students; for spring admission, 9/30 priority date for domestic students, 8/1 for international students. Applications are processed on a rolling basis. Application fee: $50. Electronic applications accepted. *Financial support:* Fellowships available. Financial award application deadline: 3/1; financial award applicants required to submit FAFSA. *Unit head:* Prof. Ruth Luckasson, Chair, 505-266-6510, Fax: 505-277-6929, E-mail: ruthl@unm.edu. *Application contact:* Jo Sanchez, Information Contact, 505-277-5018, Fax: 505-277-8679, E-mail: jsanchez@unm.edu. Website: http://coe.unm.edu

University of New Mexico, Graduate Studies, College of Education, Program in Special Education, Albuquerque, NM 87131. Offers learning and behavioral exceptionalities (MA); mental retardation and severe disabilities (MA); special education (Ed D, PhD, Ed S). *Accreditation:* NCATE. *Program availability:* Part-time, evening/weekend. *Faculty:* 8 full-time (7 women). *Students:* 36 full-time (30 women), 62 part-time (52 women); includes 38 minority (2 Black or African American, non-Hispanic/Latino; 1 American Indian or Alaska Native, non-Hispanic/Latino; 3 Asian, non-Hispanic/Latino; 32 Hispanic/Latino), 11 international. Average age 37. 24 applicants, 50% accepted, 12 enrolled. In 2017, 37 master's, 6 doctorates, 4 other advanced degrees awarded. *Degree requirements:* For master's, comprehensive exam, thesis optional; for doctorate, comprehensive exam, thesis/dissertation, screening, proposal hearing. *Entrance requirements:* For master's, minimum GPA of 3.2; for doctorate, minimum GPA of 3.2, 2 years of relevant experience; for Ed S, special education degree, 2 years of teaching experience with people with disabilities, writing sample, minimum GPA of 3.2. *Application deadline:* For fall admission, 3/31 priority date for domestic students; for spring admission, 9/30 priority date for domestic students. Applications are processed on a rolling basis. Application fee: $50. Electronic applications accepted. *Financial support:* Fellowships, research assistantships, teaching assistantships, career-related internships or fieldwork, Federal Work-Study, scholarships/grants, traineeships, health care benefits, unspecified assistantships, and stipends available. Support available to part-time students. Financial award application deadline: 3/1; financial award applicants required to submit FAFSA. *Faculty research:* Mathematics instruction, bilingual special education, inclusive education, autism, reading instruction for students with cognitive disabilities, alternative assessment, human rights and disability, applied behavior analysis, bilingualism, language and literacy, mathematics, science instruction, special education. *Unit head:* Prof. Ruth Luckasson, Chair, 505-277-6510, Fax: 505-277-6929, E-mail: luckasson@unm.edu. *Application contact:* Della Gallegos, Information Contact, 505-277-5018, Fax: 505-277-8679, E-mail: dgalle06@unm.edu. Website: http://coe.unm.edu/departments-programs/es/special-education-program/index.html

University of New Orleans, Graduate School, College of Education and Human Development, Department of Special Education and Habilitative Services, New Orleans, LA 70148. Offers M Ed, PhD. *Accreditation:* NCATE. *Program availability:* Evening/weekend. *Degree requirements:* For doctorate, variable foreign language requirement, thesis/dissertation. *Entrance requirements:* For master's, GRE General Test; for doctorate, GRE General Test, GRE Subject Test. Additional exam requirements/recommendations for international students: Required—TOEFL (minimum score 550 paper-based; 79 iBT). Electronic applications accepted. *Faculty research:* Inclusion, transition, early childhood, mild/moderate, severe/profound.

University of North Alabama, College of Education, Department of Elementary Education, Collaborative Teacher Special Education Program, Florence, AL 35632-0001. Offers MA Ed. *Accreditation:* NCATE. *Program availability:* Part-time, 100% online. *Faculty:* 5 full-time (all women), 3 part-time/adjunct (1 woman). *Students:* 3 full-time (all women), 15 part-time (13 women). Average age 33. 5 applicants, 100% accepted, 4 enrolled. In 2017, 4 master's awarded. *Degree requirements:* For master's, comprehensive exam. *Entrance requirements:* For master's, GRE, MAT, or NTE, minimum GPA of 2.5, Alabama Class B Certificate or equivalent, teaching experience. Additional exam requirements/recommendations for international students: Required—TOEFL (minimum score 79 iBT), IELTS (minimum score 6), PTE (minimum score 54). *Application deadline:* Applications are processed on a rolling basis. Application fee: $50 ($100 for international students). Electronic applications accepted. *Expenses:* Tuition, state resident: full-time $7824; part-time $5943 per year. Tuition, nonresident: full-time $15,648; part-time $11,736 per year. *Required fees:* $3064; $2298 per unit. Tuition and fees vary according to course load and reciprocity agreements. *Financial support:* Federal Work-Study, scholarships/grants, and unspecified assistantships available. Financial award application deadline: 2/1; financial award applicants required to submit FAFSA. *Unit head:* Dr. Donna Lefort, Dean, College of Education and Human Sciences, 256-765-4252, E-mail: dpjacobs@una.edu. *Application contact:* Hillary N. Coats, Graduate Admissions Coordinator, 256-765-4447, E-mail: graduate@una.edu. Website: https://www.una.edu/education/departments/elementary-education.html

University of North Alabama, College of Education, Department of Secondary Education, Program in Secondary Education, Florence, AL 35632-0001. Offers secondary education (MA Ed); special education (MA Ed). *Accreditation:* NCATE. *Program availability:* Part-time, 100% online, blended/hybrid learning. *Faculty:* 7 full-time (3 women), 2 part-time/adjunct (1 woman). *Students:* 44 full-time (26 women), 30 part-time (19 women); includes 9 minority (4 Black or African American, non-Hispanic/Latino; 2 American Indian or Alaska Native, non-Hispanic/Latino; 1 Hispanic/Latino; 2 Two or more races, non-Hispanic/Latino). Average age 31. 49 applicants, 86% accepted, 21 enrolled. In 2017, 27 master's awarded. *Degree requirements:* For master's, comprehensive exam. *Entrance requirements:* For master's, GRE, MAT, or NTE, minimum GPA of 2.5, Alabama Class B Certificate or equivalent, teaching experience. Additional exam requirements/recommendations for international students: Required—TOEFL (minimum score 79 iBT), IELTS (minimum score 6), PTE (minimum score 54). *Application deadline:* Applications are processed on a rolling basis. Application fee: $50 ($100 for international students). Electronic applications accepted. *Expenses:* Tuition, state resident: full-time $7824; part-time $5943 per year. Tuition, nonresident: full-time $15,648; part-time $11,736 per year. *Required fees:* $3064; $2298 per unit. Tuition and fees vary according to course load and reciprocity agreements. *Financial support:* In 2017–18, 19 students received support. Federal Work-Study, scholarships/grants, and unspecified assistantships available. Financial award application deadline: 2/1; financial award applicants required to submit FAFSA. *Unit head:* Dr. Jessica Mitchell, Interim Chair, 256-765-4575, E-mail: jmitchell12@una.edu. *Application contact:* Hillary N. Coats, Graduate Admissions Coordinator, 256-765-4447, E-mail: graduate@una.edu. Website: https://www.una.edu/education/departments/secondary-education.html

The University of North Carolina at Charlotte, Cato College of Education, Department of Special Education and Child Development, Charlotte, NC 28223-0001. Offers academically or intellectually gifted (Graduate Certificate); autism spectrum disorders (Graduate Certificate); child and family development: birth through kindergarten (Graduate Certificate); child and family studies: early education (M Ed); special education (M Ed, PhD, Graduate Certificate), including academically or intellectually gifted (M Ed). *Program availability:* Part-time, 100% online, blended/hybrid learning. *Faculty:* 22 full-time (16 women), 9 part-time/adjunct (6 women). *Students:* 19 full-time (16 women), 108 part-time (102 women); includes 16 minority (10 Black or African American, non-Hispanic/Latino; 2 Hispanic/Latino; 4 Two or more races, non-Hispanic/Latino), 5 international. Average age 38. 72 applicants, 94% accepted, 52 enrolled. In 2017, 23 master's, 2 doctorates, 43 other advanced degrees awarded. *Degree requirements:* For master's, thesis or alternative, research project; for doctorate, thesis/dissertation, portfolio; for Graduate Certificate, internship. *Entrance requirements:* For master's, GRE or MAT, personal statement, letters of recommendation; for doctorate, GRE or MAT, 2 official transcripts of all academic work attempted since high school indicating minimum GPA of 3.5 in graduate degree program; at least 3 references of someone who knows applicant's current work and/or academic achievements in previous degree work; two-page essay; current resume or curriculum vitae; writing sample; documentation of teaching; for Graduate Certificate, undergraduate degree from regionally-accredited four-year institution; minimum cumulative undergraduate GPA of 3.0; three recommendations from persons knowledgeable of applicant's interaction with children and families; statement of purpose; clear criminal background check. Additional exam requirements/recommendations for international students: Required—TOEFL (minimum score 523 paper-based, 70 iBT) or IELTS (6.5). *Application deadline:* For fall admission, 12/1 for domestic and international students; for spring admission, 10/1 priority date for domestic and international students; for summer admission, 4/1 priority date for domestic and international students. Applications are processed on a rolling basis. Application fee: $75. Electronic applications accepted. *Expenses:* Tuition, state resident: full-time $4337. Tuition, nonresident: full-time $17,771. *Required fees:* $3211. Tuition and fees vary according to course load and program. *Financial support:* In 2017–18, 8 students received support, including 7 research assistantships (averaging $10,112 per year), 1 teaching assistantship (averaging $3,500 per year); career-related internships or fieldwork, institutionally sponsored loans, scholarships/grants, and unspecified assistantships also available. Support available to part-time students. Financial award application deadline: 3/1; financial award applicants required to submit FAFSA. *Total annual research expenditures:* $3.9 million. *Unit head:* Dr. Belva Collins, Chair, 704-687-8828, E-mail: belva.collins@uncc.edu. *Application contact:* Kathy B. Giddings, Director of Graduate Admissions, 704-687-5503, Fax: 704-687-1668, E-mail: gradadm@uncc.edu. Website: http://spcd.uncc.edu/

The University of North Carolina at Charlotte, Cato College of Education, Interdisciplinary Education Programs, Charlotte, NC 28223-0001. Offers art education (Graduate Certificate); child and family development: early childhood education (MAT); curriculum and instruction (PhD); elementary education (MAT); foreign language education (MAT); middle grades education (MAT); secondary education (MAT); special education (MAT); teaching (Graduate Certificate); teaching English as a second language (MAT); theatre education (Graduate Certificate). *Program availability:* Part-time, 100% online, blended/hybrid learning. *Students:* 86 full-time (63 women), 533 part-time (423 women); includes 229 minority (169 Black or African American, non-Hispanic/Latino; 1 American Indian or Alaska Native, non-Hispanic/Latino; 7 Asian, non-Hispanic/Latino; 39 Hispanic/Latino; 13 Two or more races, non-Hispanic/Latino), 13 international. Average age 32. 382 applicants, 91% accepted, 253 enrolled. In 2017, 182 master's, 10 doctorates, 172 other advanced degrees awarded. *Degree requirements:* For master's, thesis or alternative, research project/portfolio. *Entrance requirements:* For master's, GRE or MAT, bachelor's degree, or its U.S. equivalent, from regionally-accredited college or university; minimum overall GPA of 3.0 on all previous work beyond high school; statement of purpose (essay); at least three recommendation forms; for doctorate, GRE or MAT, bachelor's degree (or its U.S. equivalent) from regionally-accredited college or university; minimum overall GPA of 3.5 in master's degree program; for Graduate Certificate, bachelor's degree from regionally-accredited university; minimum GPA of 2.75 on all post-secondary work attempted; transcripts; personal statement outlining why the applicant seeks admission to the program. Additional exam requirements/recommendations for international students: Required—TOEFL (minimum score 523 paper-based, 70 iBT) or IELTS (6.5). *Application deadline:* For fall admission, 3/1 priority date for domestic and international students; for spring admission, 10/1 priority date for domestic and international students; for summer admission, 4/1 priority date for domestic and international students. Applications are processed on a rolling basis. Application fee: $75. Electronic applications accepted. *Expenses:* Tuition, state resident: full-time $4337. Tuition, nonresident: full-time $17,771. *Required fees:* $3211. Tuition and fees vary according to course load and program. *Financial support:* Career-related internships or fieldwork, institutionally sponsored loans, scholarships/grants, and unspecified assistantships available. Support available to part-time students. Financial award application deadline: 3/1; financial award applicants required to submit FAFSA. *Unit head:* Dr. Ellen McIntyre, Dean, 704-687-8722, E-mail: ellen.mcintyre@uncc.edu. *Application contact:* Kathy B. Giddings, Director of Graduate Admissions, 704-687-5503, Fax: 704-687-1668, E-mail: gradadm@uncc.edu. Website: http://education.uncc.edu/academic-programs

The University of North Carolina at Greensboro, Graduate School, School of Education, Department of Specialized Education Services, Greensboro, NC 27412-5001. Offers cross-categorical special education (M Ed); interdisciplinary studies in special education (M Ed); leadership early care and education (Certificate); special education (M Ed, PhD). *Degree requirements:* For master's, thesis or alternative. *Entrance requirements:* For master's, GRE General Test. Additional exam requirements/recommendations for international students: Required—TOEFL. Electronic applications accepted.

The University of North Carolina Wilmington, Watson College of Education, Department of Early Childhood, Elementary, Middle, Literacy and Special Education, Wilmington, NC 28403-3297. Offers educational leadership, policy, and advocacy (M Ed); elementary education (M Ed, MAT); language and literacy (M Ed); middle grades education (MAT). *Accreditation:* NCATE. *Program availability:* Part-time, blended/hybrid learning. *Faculty:* 22 full-time (15 women), 2 part-time/adjunct (both women). *Students:* 82 full-time (70 women), 91 part-time (84 women); includes 51 minority (33 Black or African American, non-Hispanic/Latino; 3 American Indian or Alaska Native, non-Hispanic/Latino; 1 Asian, non-Hispanic/Latino; 8 Hispanic/Latino; 6 Two or more races, non-Hispanic/Latino). Average age 32. 68 applicants, 82% accepted, 45 enrolled. In 2017, 83 master's awarded. *Degree requirements:* For master's, thesis or alternative, exit portfolio, oral presentation, internship, research project (depending on specialization). *Entrance requirements:* For master's, 3 letters of recommendations, NC Class A teacher license in related field, education statement of interest essay. Additional exam requirements/recommendations for international students: Required—TOEFL (minimum score 550 paper-based; 79 iBT), IELTS (minimum score 6.5). *Application deadline:* For fall admission, 5/15 for domestic students; for spring admission, 10/15 for domestic students; for summer admission, 3/15 for domestic students. Applications are processed on a rolling basis. Application fee: $75. Electronic applications accepted. *Expenses:* Tuition, state resident: full-time $4626; part-time $226.76 per credit hour. Tuition, nonresident: full-time $17,834; part-time $874.22 per credit hour. *Required fees:* $2124. Tuition and fees vary according to program. *Financial support:* Scholarships/grants and unspecified assistantships available. Financial award application deadline: 1/1; financial award applicants required to submit FAFSA. *Unit head:* Dr. Kathy Fox, Chair, 910-962-3240, Fax: 910-962-3988, E-mail: foxk@uncw.edu. *Application contact:* Dr. Elizabeth Crawford, Graduate Program Coordinator, 910-962-2916, Fax: 910-962-3988, E-mail: crawforde@uncw.edu. Website: http://www.uncw.edu/ed/eemls/index.html

University of North Dakota, Graduate School, College of Education and Human Development, Program in Special Education, Grand Forks, ND 58202. Offers M Ed, MS. *Accreditation:* NCATE. *Program availability:* Part-time, online learning. *Degree requirements:* For master's, comprehensive exam, thesis or alternative. *Entrance requirements:* For master's, minimum GPA of 3.0. Additional exam requirements/recommendations for international students: Required—TOEFL (minimum score 550 paper-based; 79 iBT), IELTS (minimum score 6.5). Electronic applications accepted. *Faculty research:* Visual, emotional, and mental disabilities; early childhood.

University of Northern Colorado, Graduate School, College of Education and Behavioral Sciences, Department of American Sign Language and Interpreting Studies, Greeley, CO 80639. Offers teaching American Sign Language (MA).

University of Northern Colorado, Graduate School, College of Education and Behavioral Sciences, School of Special Education, Greeley, CO 80639. Offers deaf/hard of hearing (MA); early childhood special education (MA); gifted and talented (MA); special education (MA, PhD); visual impairment (MA). *Program availability:* Part-time, evening/weekend, online learning. *Degree requirements:* For master's, comprehensive exam, thesis or alternative; for doctorate, comprehensive exam, thesis/dissertation. *Entrance requirements:* For master's, letters of recommendation, interview; for doctorate, GRE General Test, resume. Electronic applications accepted.

University of Northern Colorado, Graduate School, College of Education and Behavioral Sciences, School of Teacher Education, Program in Teaching Diverse Learners, Greeley, CO 80639. Offers MA. *Program availability:* Online learning.

University of Northern Iowa, Graduate College, College of Education, Department of Special Education, MAE Program in Special Education, Cedar Falls, IA 50614. Offers career/vocational programming and transition (MAE); consultant (MAE); field specialization (MAE).

University of North Florida, College of Education and Human Services, Department of Exceptional, Deaf, and Interpreter Education, Jacksonville, FL 32224. Offers American Sign Language (MS); American Sign Language/English interpreting (M Ed); applied behavior analysis (M Ed); autism (M Ed); deaf education (M Ed); disability services (M Ed); exceptional student education (M Ed). *Accreditation:* NCATE. *Program availability:* Part-time, evening/weekend. *Entrance requirements:* For master's, GRE General Test, minimum GPA of 3.0 in last 60 hours, interview, 3 letters of recommendation. Additional exam requirements/recommendations for international students: Required—TOEFL (minimum score 500 paper-based). Electronic applications accepted. *Faculty research:* Transportation, energy, communications, healthcare, nano-science and engineering, unmanned aircraft systems, biomedical applications.

University of North Texas, Robert B. Toulouse School of Graduate Studies, Denton, TX 76203-5459. Offers accounting (MS); applied anthropology (MA, MS); applied behavior analysis (Certificate); applied geography (MA); applied technology and performance improvement (M Ed, MS); art education (MA); art history (MA); art museum education (Certificate); arts leadership (Certificate); audiology (Au D); behavior analysis (MS); behavioral science (PhD); biochemistry and molecular biology (MS); biology (MA, MS); biomedical engineering (MS); business analysis (MS); chemistry (MS); clinical health psychology (PhD); communication studies (MA, MS); computer engineering (MS); computer science (MS); counseling (M Ed, MS), including clinical mental health counseling (MS), college and university counseling, elementary school counseling, secondary school counseling; creative writing (MA); criminal justice (MS); curriculum and instruction (M Ed); decision sciences (MBA); design (MA, MFA), including fashion design (MFA), innovation studies, interior design (MFA); early childhood studies (MS); economics (MS); educational leadership (M Ed, Ed D); educational psychology (MS, PhD), including family studies (MS), gifted and talented (MS), human development (MS), learning and cognition (MS), research, measurement and evaluation (MS); electrical engineering (MS); emergency management (MPA); engineering technology (MS); English (MA); English as a second language (MA); environmental science (MS); finance (MBA, MS); financial management (MPA); French (MA); health services management (MBA); higher education (M Ed, Ed D); history (MA, MS); hospitality management (MS); human resources management (MPA); information science (MS); information systems (PhD); information technologies (MBA); interdisciplinary studies (MA, MS); international studies (MA); international sustainable tourism (MS); jazz studies (MM); journalism (MA, MJ, Graduate Certificate), including interactive and virtual digital communication (Graduate Certificate), narrative journalism (Graduate Certificate), public relations (Graduate Certificate); kinesiology (MS); linguistics (MA); local government management (MPA); logistics (PhD); logistics and supply chain management (MBA); long-term care, senior housing, and aging services (MA); management (PhD); marketing (MBA); mathematics (MA, MS); mechanical and energy engineering (MS, PhD); music (MA), including ethnomusicology, music theory, musicology, performance; music composition (PhD); music education (MM Ed, PhD); nonprofit management (MPA); operations and supply chain management (MBA); performance (MM, DMA); philosophy (MA); political science (MA); professional and technical communication (MA); radio, television and film (MA, MFA); rehabilitation counseling (Certificate); sociology (MS); Spanish (MA); special education (M Ed); speech-language pathology (MA); strategic management (MBA); studio art (MFA); teaching (M Ed); MBA/MS. *Program availability:* Part-time, evening/weekend, online learning. Terminal master's awarded for partial completion of doctoral program. *Degree requirements:* For master's, variable foreign language requirement, comprehensive exam (for some programs), thesis (for some programs); for doctorate, variable foreign language requirement, comprehensive exam (for some programs), thesis/dissertation; for other advanced degree, variable foreign language requirement, comprehensive exam (for some programs). *Entrance requirements:* For master's and doctorate, GRE, GMAT. Additional exam requirements/recommendations for international students: Required—TOEFL (minimum score 550 paper-based; 79 iBT). Electronic applications accepted.

University of Oklahoma, Jeannine Rainbolt College of Education, Department of Educational Psychology, Program in Special Education, Norman, OK 73019. Offers applied behavior analysis (M Ed); higher education and community support (PhD); higher education professor (PhD); school instruction and leadership (PhD); secondary transition education (M Ed). *Accreditation:* NCATE. *Program availability:* Part-time, 100% online, blended/hybrid learning. *Students:* 25 full-time (21 women), 81 part-time (72 women); includes 20 minority (4 Black or African American, non-Hispanic/Latino; 5 American Indian or Alaska Native, non-Hispanic/Latino; 1 Asian, non-Hispanic/Latino; 5 Hispanic/Latino; 5 Two or more races, non-Hispanic/Latino), 4 international. Average

Special Education

age 36. 49 applicants, 59% accepted, 23 enrolled. In 2017, 11 master's, 1 doctorate awarded. Terminal master's awarded for partial completion of doctoral program. *Degree requirements:* For master's, thesis optional; for doctorate, comprehensive exam, thesis/dissertation. *Entrance requirements:* For doctorate, GRE. Additional exam requirements/recommendations for international students: Required—TOEFL (minimum score 79 iBT) or IELTS (minimum score 6.5). *Application deadline:* For fall admission, 2/1 for domestic and international students. Application fee: $50 ($100 for international students). Electronic applications accepted. *Expenses:* Tuition, state resident: full-time $5119; part-time $213.30 per credit hour. Tuition, nonresident: full-time $19,778; part-time $824.10 per credit hour. *Required fees:* $3458; $133.55 per credit hour. $126.50 per semester. *Financial support:* In 2017–18, 60 students received support. Research assistantships with full and partial tuition reimbursements available, teaching assistantships with full and partial tuition reimbursements available, and scholarships/grants available. Financial award application deadline: 6/1; financial award applicants required to submit FAFSA. *Faculty research:* K-12 literacy instruction for struggling readers; reading, writing, spelling, and mathematics interventions; applied behavioral analysis; secondary transition; self-determination and post-secondary outcomes. *Unit head:* Dr. Nancy E. Marchand-Martella, Chair, Department of Educational Psychology, 405-325-0624, Fax: 405-325-6655, E-mail: nmarchand-martella@ou.edu. *Application contact:* Anna Steele, Graduate Programs Specialist, 405-325-4525, Fax: 405-325-7390, E-mail: jrcoe_gps@ou.edu.
Website: http://www.ou.edu/education/edpy.html

University of Oklahoma Health Sciences Center, Graduate College, College of Allied Health, Department of Communication Sciences and Disorders, Oklahoma City, OK 73190. Offers audiology (MS, Au D, PhD); communication sciences and disorders (Certificate), including reading, speech-language pathology; education of the deaf (MS); speech-language pathology (MS, PhD). *Accreditation:* ASHA (one or more programs are accredited). *Program availability:* Part-time. Terminal master's awarded for partial completion of doctoral program. *Degree requirements:* For master's, comprehensive exam, thesis optional; for doctorate, one foreign language, comprehensive exam, thesis/dissertation. *Entrance requirements:* For master's and doctorate, GRE General Test, 3 letters of recommendation. Additional exam requirements/recommendations for international students: Required—TOEFL (minimum score 550 paper-based). *Faculty research:* Event-related potentials, cleft palate, fluency disorders, language disorders, hearing and speech science.

University of Oregon, Graduate School, College of Education, Eugene, OR 97403. Offers communication disorders and sciences (MA, MS, PhD); counseling psychology (PhD); couples and family therapy (MS); critical and sociocultural studies in education (PhD); curriculum and teacher education (MA, MS); educational leadership (MS, D Ed, PhD); prevention science (M Ed, MS, PhD); school psychology (MS, PhD); special education (M Ed, MA, MS, PhD). *Program availability:* Part-time. Terminal master's awarded for partial completion of doctoral program. *Degree requirements:* For master's, exam, paper, or project; for doctorate, comprehensive exam, thesis/dissertation. *Entrance requirements:* Additional exam requirements/recommendations for international students: Required—TOEFL. *Faculty research:* Basic and applied research in teaching, learning and habilitation in all settings, schooling effectiveness.

University of Phoenix–Bay Area Campus, College of Education, San Jose, CA 95134-1805. Offers administration and supervision (MA Ed); adult education and training (MA Ed); early childhood education (MA Ed); education (Ed S); educational leadership (Ed D); elementary teacher education (MA Ed); higher education administration (PhD); secondary teacher education (MA Ed); special education (MA Ed); teacher leadership (MA Ed). *Program availability:* Evening/weekend, online learning. *Degree requirements:* For master's, thesis (for some programs). *Entrance requirements:* For master's, minimum undergraduate GPA of 2.5, 3 years of work experience. Additional exam requirements/recommendations for international students: Required—TOEFL (minimum score 550 paper-based; 79 iBT). Electronic applications accepted.

University of Phoenix–Hawaii Campus, College of Education, Honolulu, HI 96813-3800. Offers administration and supervision (MA Ed); curriculum and instruction (MA Ed); elementary education (MA Ed); secondary education (MA Ed); special education (MA Ed); teacher education for elementary licensure (MA Ed). *Program availability:* Evening/weekend. *Degree requirements:* For master's, thesis (for some programs). *Entrance requirements:* For master's, minimum undergraduate GPA of 2.5, 3 years of work experience. Additional exam requirements/recommendations for international students: Required—TOEFL (minimum score 550 paper-based; 79 iBT). Electronic applications accepted.

University of Phoenix–Online Campus, College of Education, Phoenix, AZ 85034-7209. Offers administration and supervision (MAEd, Certificate); adult education and training (MAEd); curriculum and instruction (MAEd), including computer education, curriculum and instruction, English as a second language, language arts, mathematics, reading; early childhood education (MAEd); educational studies (MAEd); elementary teacher education (MAEd), including early childhood, elementary teacher education, high school middle level, middle level; principal licensure (Certificate); secondary teacher education (MAEd); special education (MAEd, Certificate); teacher education (MAEd), including middle level generalist; teacher education middle level mathematics (MAEd), including middle level mathematics; teacher education middle level science (MAEd), including middle level science; teacher education secondary mathematics (MAEd); teacher education secondary science (MAEd); teacher leadership (MAEd); teachers of English learners (Certificate); transition to teaching (Certificate), including elementary education, secondary education. *Program availability:* Evening/weekend, online learning. *Entrance requirements:* Additional exam requirements/recommendations for international students: Required—TOEFL, TOEIC (Test of English as an International Communication), Berlitz Online English Proficiency Exam, PTE, or IELTS. Electronic applications accepted. *Expenses:* Contact institution.

University of Phoenix–Phoenix Campus, College of Education, Tempe, AZ 85282-2371. Offers administration and supervision (MA Ed); adult education and training (MA Ed); curriculum and instruction reading (MA Ed); early childhood education (MA Ed); education studies (MA Ed); elementary teacher education (MA Ed); secondary teacher education (MA Ed); special education (MA Ed); teacher leadership (MA Ed). *Program availability:* Evening/weekend, online learning. *Entrance requirements:* Additional exam requirements/recommendations for international students: Required—TOEFL, TOEIC (Test of English as an International Communication), Berlitz Online English Proficiency Exam, PTE, or IELTS. Electronic applications accepted. *Expenses:* Contact institution.

University of Pittsburgh, School of Education, Department of Instruction and Learning, Program in Special Education, Pittsburgh, PA 15260. Offers applied behavior analysis (M Ed); early intervention (M Ed, PhD); general special education (M Ed, Ed D); special education teacher preparation (M Ed); vision studies (M Ed, PhD). *Program availability:* Part-time, evening/weekend. *Degree requirements:* For master's; for doctorate, thesis/dissertation. *Entrance requirements:* For master's, PRAXIS I; for doctorate, GRE General Test. Additional exam requirements/recommendations for international students: Required—TOEFL.

University of Portland, School of Education, Portland, OR 97203-5798. Offers education (MA, MAT); educational leadership (M Ed); English for speakers of other languages (M Ed); initial administrator licensure (M Ed); neuroeducation (M Ed, Ed D); organizational leadership and development (Ed D); reading (M Ed); school leadership and development (Ed D); special education (M Ed). M Ed also available through the Graduate Outreach Program for teachers residing in the Oregon and Washington state areas. *Accreditation:* NCATE. *Program availability:* Part-time, evening/weekend. *Entrance requirements:* For master's, minimum GPA of 3.0, teaching certificate, letters of recommendation, resume, statement of goals, official transcripts. Additional exam requirements/recommendations for international students: Required—TOEFL (minimum score 550 paper-based; 80 iBT), IELTS (minimum score 7). *Faculty research:* Multicultural education, supervision/leadership.

University of Puerto Rico–Medical Sciences Campus, Graduate School of Public Health, Department of Human Development, Program in Developmental Disabilities-Early Intervention, San Juan, PR 00936-5067. Offers Certificate. *Program availability:* Part-time, evening/weekend.

University of Puerto Rico–Río Piedras, College of Education, Program in Special and Differentiated Education, San Juan, PR 00931-3300. Offers M Ed. *Degree requirements:* For master's, GRE or PAEG, interview, minimum GPA of 3.0, letter of recommendation.

University of Rhode Island, Graduate School, Alan Shawn Feinstein College of Education and Professional Studies, School of Education, Kingston, RI 02881. Offers education (PhD); reading (MA); special education (MA). *Accreditation:* NCATE. *Program availability:* Part-time, evening/weekend. *Faculty:* 18 full-time (12 women). *Students:* 59 full-time (44 women), 145 part-time (114 women); includes 24 minority (6 Black or African American, non-Hispanic/Latino; 6 American Indian or Alaska Native, non-Hispanic/Latino; 7 Asian, non-Hispanic/Latino; 3 Hispanic/Latino; 2 Two or more races, non-Hispanic/Latino), 6 international. 91 applicants, 65% accepted, 53 enrolled. In 2017, 50 master's, 9 doctorates awarded. *Entrance requirements:* For master's, 2 letters of recommendation; personal statement; two official transcripts; interview and minimum undergraduate GPA of 3.0 (for special education applicants); for doctorate, GRE, 3 letters of recommendation, resume, personal statement, two copies of official transcripts. Additional exam requirements/recommendations for international students: Required—TOEFL. Application fee: $65. Electronic applications accepted. *Expenses:* Tuition, state resident: full-time $12,706; part-time $786 per credit. Tuition, nonresident: full-time $25,216; part-time $1401 per credit. *Required fees:* $1598; $45 per credit. One-time fee: $30 part-time. *Financial support:* In 2017–18, 1 research assistantship with tuition reimbursement (averaging $8,862 per year), 5 teaching assistantships with tuition reimbursements (averaging $17,795 per year) were awarded. Financial award applicants required to submit FAFSA. *Unit head:* Dr. David Byrd, Director, School of Education, 401-874-5484, Fax: 401-874-5471, E-mail: dbyrd@uri.edu. *Application contact:* Graduate Admissions, 401-874-2262, E-mail: gradadm@etal.uri.edu.
Website: http://www.uri.edu/hss/education/

University of Rio Grande, Graduate School, Rio Grande, OH 45674. Offers athletic coaching leadership (M Ed); educational leadership (M Ed); integrated arts (M Ed); intervention specialist in early childhood (M Ed); intervention specialist in mild/moderate (M Ed). *Accreditation:* NCATE. *Program availability:* Part-time. *Degree requirements:* For master's, final research project, portfolio. *Entrance requirements:* For master's, minimum GPA of 2.7 in major, 2.5 overall. Additional exam requirements/recommendations for international students: Required—TOEFL. *Faculty research:* Interagency collaboration, reading and mathematics, learning styles, college access, literacy.

University of St. Francis, College of Education, Joliet, IL 60435-6169. Offers educational leadership (MS, Ed D); elementary education (M Ed); reading (MS); secondary education (M Ed), including English education, math education, science education, social studies education, visual arts education; special education (M Ed); teaching and learning (MS); TESOL (Certificate). *Accreditation:* NCATE. *Program availability:* Part-time, evening/weekend, 100% online, blended/hybrid learning. *Faculty:* 11 full-time (8 women), 52 part-time/adjunct (36 women). *Students:* 39 full-time (32 women), 411 part-time (318 women); includes 106 minority (57 Black or African American, non-Hispanic/Latino; 8 Asian, non-Hispanic/Latino; 37 Hispanic/Latino; 4 Two or more races, non-Hispanic/Latino), 4 international. Average age 37. 277 applicants, 55% accepted, 137 enrolled. In 2017, 199 master's, 28 doctorates awarded. *Degree requirements:* For master's, comprehensive exam; for doctorate, thesis/dissertation. *Entrance requirements:* Additional exam requirements/recommendations for international students: Required—TOEFL (minimum score 550 paper-based; 79 iBT), IELTS (minimum score 6). *Application deadline:* Applications are processed on a rolling basis. Application fee: $30. Electronic applications accepted. Application fee is waived when completed online. *Expenses:* $365 to $748 per credit hour. *Financial support:* In 2017–18, 40 students received support. Scholarships/grants and unspecified assistantships available. Support available to part-time students. Financial award applicants required to submit FAFSA. *Unit head:* Dr. John Gambro, Dean, 815-740-3829, Fax: 815-740-2264, E-mail: jgambro@stfrancis.edu. *Application contact:* Sandra Sloka, Director of Admissions for Graduate and Degree Completion Programs, 800-735-7500, Fax: 815-740-3431, E-mail: ssloka@stfrancis.edu.
Website: http://www.stfrancis.edu/academics/college-of-education/

University of Saint Francis, Graduate School, Department of Education, Fort Wayne, IN 46808-3994. Offers secondary education (MAT); special education (MS Ed), including intense intervention, mild intervention. *Accreditation:* NCATE. *Program availability:* Part-time, evening/weekend, online only, 100% online. *Faculty:* 4 full-time (3 women), 3 part-time/adjunct (all women). *Students:* 6 full-time (5 women), 19 part-time (15 women); includes 1 minority (Hispanic/Latino). Average age 33. 17 applicants, 100% accepted, 14 enrolled. In 2017, 8 master's awarded. *Entrance requirements:* For master's, GRE (minimum composite score of 280 verbal and quantitative subtests) or MAT (minimum score of 389) if undergraduate GPA is below a 2.8 or prior graduate level GPA is below 3.0; GRE, ACT, SAT, or CASA exam if no license, minimum undergraduate GPA of 2.8; resume (if GPA is below 3.0); standard teaching license and/or bachelor's degree from regionally-accredited institution; background check; two professional recommendations. Additional exam requirements/recommendations for international students: Required—TOEFL (minimum score 550 paper-based) or IELTS (minimum score 6.5). *Application deadline:* For fall admission, 7/1 for international students; for spring admission, 11/1 for international students; for summer admission, 3/1 for international students. Applications are processed on a rolling basis. Application fee: $0. Electronic applications accepted. *Expenses:* $475 per hour (for MAT); $905 per hour (for MS Ed). *Financial support:* Federal Work-Study, scholarships/grants, and unspecified assistantships available. Financial award application deadline: 4/15; financial award applicants required to submit FAFSA. *Unit head:* Mary Riepenhoff, Assistant Professor/Department Chair, 260-399-7700 Ext. 8409, Fax: 260-399-8170, E-mail: mriepenhoff@sf.edu. *Application contact:* Kyle Richardson, Associate Director of Enrollment Services for Adult Learning, 260-399-7700 Ext. 6310, Fax: 260-399-8152, E-mail: krichardson@sf.edu.
Website: https://education.sf.edu/

University of Saint Joseph, Program in Special Education, West Hartford, CT 06117-2700. Offers autism spectrum disorders (Graduate Certificate); special education (MA). *Program availability:* Part-time, evening/weekend. *Degree requirements:* For master's, thesis. *Application deadline:* Applications are processed on a rolling basis. Application fee: $50. Electronic applications accepted. Application fee is waived when completed online. *Financial support:* Career-related internships or fieldwork and unspecified assistantships available. Support available to part-time students. Financial award applicants required to submit FAFSA.

University of Saint Mary, Graduate Programs, Program in Special Education, Leavenworth, KS 66048-5082. Offers MA. *Program availability:* Part-time, evening/weekend. *Entrance requirements:* For master's, bachelor's degree, minimum undergraduate GPA of 2.75, two letters of recommendation, teaching certification. Electronic applications accepted. *Expenses:* Contact institution.

University of St. Thomas, College of Education, Leadership and Counseling, Department of Special Education, St. Paul, MN 55105-1096. Offers MA, Certificate, Ed S. *Accreditation:* NCATE. *Program availability:* Part-time-only, evening/weekend, online only, 100% online, blended/hybrid learning. *Degree requirements:* For master's, thesis; for other advanced degree, professional portfolio. *Entrance requirements:* For master's, minimum GPA of 3.0 or MAT; for other advanced degree, MAT or minimum GPA of 2.75. Additional exam requirements/recommendations for international students: Required—TOEFL (minimum score 550 paper-based; 80 iBT). *Application deadline:* For fall admission, 7/15 priority date for domestic and international students; for spring admission, 12/9 priority date for domestic and international students; for summer admission, 4/3 priority date for domestic and international students. Applications are processed on a rolling basis. Electronic applications accepted. *Expenses:* Contact institution. *Financial support:* Fellowships, research assistantships, institutionally sponsored loans, and scholarships/grants available. Support available to part-time students. Financial award application deadline: 8/1; financial award applicants required to submit FAFSA. *Faculty research:* Reading and math fluency, inclusion curriculum for developmental disorders, parent involvement in positive behavior supports, children's friendships, preschool inclusion. *Unit head:* Stephanie O'Brien, Coordinator, 651-962-4980, Fax: 651-962-4169, E-mail: stephanie.obrien@stthomas.edu.

University of St. Thomas, School of Education and Human Services, Houston, TX 77006-4696. Offers all level education (M Ed); bilingual/dual language (M Ed); Catholic school teaching (M Ed); Catholic/private school leadership (M Ed); counselor education (M Ed); curriculum and instruction (M Ed); education (Ed D); educational leadership (M Ed); elementary teaching (M Ed); English as a second language (M Ed); exceptionality/educational diagnostician (M Ed); exceptionality/special education (M Ed); generalist (M Ed); reading (M Ed); secondary teaching (M Ed); teaching (MAT). *Accreditation:* TEAC. *Program availability:* Part-time, evening/weekend, online learning. *Faculty:* 33 full-time (22 women), 43 part-time/adjunct (26 women). *Students:* 119 full-time (97 women), 597 part-time (529 women); includes 478 minority (166 Black or African American, non-Hispanic/Latino; 29 Asian, non-Hispanic/Latino; 277 Hispanic/Latino; 2 Native Hawaiian or other Pacific Islander, non-Hispanic/Latino; 4 Two or more races, non-Hispanic/Latino), 19 international. Average age 36. 306 applicants, 91% accepted, 181 enrolled. In 2017, 328 master's awarded. *Degree requirements:* For master's, thesis, field experience. *Entrance requirements:* For master's, GRE or MAT if GPA is below 3.0, bachelor's degree; minimum GPA of 2.75 in bachelor's degree or last 60 credit hours; official transcripts from all institutions; goal statement of 250-300 words; 1 reference. Additional exam requirements/recommendations for international students: Required—TOEFL (minimum score 94 iBT), IELTS (minimum score 7), PTE (minimum score 53). *Application deadline:* Applications are processed on a rolling basis. Application fee: $35. Electronic applications accepted. *Expenses:* Contact institution. *Financial support:* In 2017–18, 27 students received support. Federal Work-Study, scholarships/grants, and state work-study, institutional employment available. Support available to part-time students. Financial award application deadline: 4/15; financial award applicants required to submit FAFSA. *Faculty research:* Leadership, diversity, personality traits, second language acquisition. *Unit head:* Dr. Paul C. Paese, Dean, 713-942-5999, Fax: 713-525-3871, E-mail: paesep@stthom.edu. *Application contact:* 713-525-3540, E-mail: education@stthom.edu.
Website: http://www.stthom.edu/Academics/
School_of_Education_and_Human_Services/Index.aqf

University of San Diego, School of Leadership and Education Sciences, Department of Learning and Teaching, San Diego, CA 92110-2492. Offers curriculum and instruction (M Ed); inclusive learning (M Ed); literacy and digital learning (M Ed); school leadership (M Ed); special education (M Ed); STEAM (science, technology, engineering, arts, and mathematics) (M Ed); TESOL, literacy and culture (M Ed). *Program availability:* Part-time, evening/weekend. *Faculty:* 9 full-time (7 women), 30 part-time/adjunct (24 women). *Students:* 160 full-time (128 women), 221 part-time (176 women); includes 131 minority (10 Black or African American, non-Hispanic/Latino; 24 Asian, non-Hispanic/Latino; 83 Hispanic/Latino; 1 Native Hawaiian or other Pacific Islander, non-Hispanic/Latino; 13 Two or more races, non-Hispanic/Latino), 20 international. Average age 33. 398 applicants, 84% accepted, 196 enrolled. In 2017, 151 master's awarded. *Degree requirements:* For master's, thesis (for some programs), international experience. *Entrance requirements:* For master's, California Basic Educational Skills Test, California Subject Examination for Teachers. Additional exam requirements/recommendations for international students: Required—TOEFL (minimum score 580 paper-based; 83 iBT), TWE. *Application deadline:* Applications are processed on a rolling basis. Application fee: $45. Electronic applications accepted. *Financial support:* In 2017–18, 65 students received support. Career-related internships or fieldwork, Federal Work-Study, institutionally sponsored loans, and stipends available. Financial award application deadline: 4/1; financial award applicants required to submit FAFSA. *Faculty research:* Action research methodology, cultural studies, instructional theories and practices, second language acquisition, school reform. *Unit head:* Dr. Maya Kalyanpur, Chair, 619-260-7655, E-mail: mkalyanpur@sandiego.edu. *Application contact:* Monica Mahon, Associate Director of Graduate Admissions, 619-260-4524, Fax: 619-260-4158, E-mail: grads@sandiego.edu.
Website: http://www.sandiego.edu/soles/learning-and-teaching/

University of San Francisco, School of Education, Department of Learning and Instruction, San Francisco, CA 94117-1080. Offers digital technologies for teaching and learning (MA); learning and instruction (MA, Ed D); special education (MA, Ed D); teaching reading (MA). *Program availability:* Part-time, evening/weekend. *Degree requirements:* For doctorate, thesis/dissertation. *Entrance requirements:* Additional exam requirements/recommendations for international students: Required—TOEFL, IELTS, PTE. Electronic applications accepted.

University of Saskatchewan, College of Graduate Studies and Research, College of Education, Department of Educational Psychology and Special Education, Saskatoon, SK S7N 5A2, Canada. Offers M Ed, PhD, Diploma. *Degree requirements:* For master's, thesis (for some programs); for doctorate, comprehensive exam (for some programs), thesis/dissertation. *Entrance requirements:* Additional exam requirements/recommendations for international students: Required—TOEFL (minimum score 80 iBT); Recommended—IELTS (minimum score 6.5). Electronic applications accepted.

The University of Scranton, Panuska College of Professional Studies, Department of Education, Program in Special Education, Scranton, PA 18510. Offers MS. *Program availability:* Part-time. *Degree requirements:* For master's, comprehensive exam (for some programs), thesis (for some programs), capstone experience. *Entrance requirements:* For master's, GRE General Test accepted but not required, minimum GPA of 3.0, three letters of reference. Additional exam requirements/recommendations for international students: Required—TOEFL (minimum score 500 paper-based; 80 iBT), IELTS (minimum score 6.5). Electronic applications accepted. Application fee is waived when completed online.

University of South Alabama, College of Education and Professional Studies, Department of Leadership and Teacher Education, Mobile, AL 36688. Offers art education (M Ed); early childhood education (M Ed); educational leadership (M Ed, Ed D); elementary education (M Ed); reading education (M Ed); science education (M Ed); secondary education (M Ed); special education (M Ed). *Accreditation:* NCATE. *Program availability:* Part-time. *Faculty:* 15 full-time (11 women), 10 part-time/adjunct (6 women). *Students:* 203 full-time (154 women), 90 part-time (68 women); includes 73 minority (54 Black or African American, non-Hispanic/Latino; 3 American Indian or Alaska Native, non-Hispanic/Latino; 4 Asian, non-Hispanic/Latino; 10 Hispanic/Latino; 2 Two or more races, non-Hispanic/Latino). Average age 34. 134 applicants, 55% accepted, 57 enrolled. In 2017, 73 master's, 8 doctorates awarded. *Degree requirements:* For master's, comprehensive exam, thesis (for some programs); for doctorate, comprehensive exam, thesis/dissertation. *Entrance requirements:* For master's, GRE General Test or MAT, minimum GPA of 3.0; for doctorate, GRE, minimum graduate GPA of 3.25, 3 years of experience in field, 3 letters of recommendation, interview, official transcripts. Additional exam requirements/recommendations for international students: Required—TOEFL. *Application deadline:* For fall admission, 7/15 for domestic students, 6/15 for international students; for spring admission, 11/15 for domestic students, 11/1 for international students; for summer admission, 4/15 for domestic students, 4/1 for international students. Applications are processed on a rolling basis. Application fee: $35. Electronic applications accepted. *Expenses:* Tuition, state resident: full-time $10,104; part-time $421 per semester hour. Tuition, nonresident: full-time $20,208; part-time $842 per semester hour. *Financial support:* Fellowships, research assistantships, teaching assistantships, career-related internships or fieldwork, Federal Work-Study, institutionally sponsored loans, scholarships/grants, and unspecified assistantships available. Support available to part-time students. Financial award application deadline: 3/31; financial award applicants required to submit FAFSA. *Unit head:* Dr. Susan Santoli, Chair/Director of Graduate Studies, 251-380-2836, Fax: 251-380-2748, E-mail: ssantoli@southalabama.edu.
Website: http://www.southalabama.edu/colleges/ceps/lte/index.html

University of South Carolina, The Graduate School, College of Education, Department of Educational Studies, Program in Special Education, Columbia, SC 29208. Offers M Ed, MAT, PhD. *Accreditation:* NCATE. *Program availability:* Part-time. *Degree requirements:* For master's, comprehensive exam; for doctorate, one foreign language, comprehensive exam, thesis/dissertation. *Entrance requirements:* For master's, GRE General Test, MAT, interview, sample of written work; for doctorate, GRE General Test or MAT, interview, sample of written work. *Faculty research:* Strategy training, transition, technology, rural special education, behavior management.

University of South Carolina Upstate, Graduate Programs, Spartanburg, SC 29303-4999. Offers early childhood education (M Ed); elementary education (M Ed); informatics (MS); special education: visual impairment (M Ed). *Accreditation:* NCATE. *Program availability:* Part-time, evening/weekend. *Degree requirements:* For master's, professional portfolio. *Entrance requirements:* For master's, GRE General Test or MAT, interview, minimum undergraduate GPA of 2.5, teaching certificate, 2 letters of recommendation. *Faculty research:* Promoting university diversity awareness, rough and tumble play, social justice education, American Indian literatures and cultures, diversity and multicultural education, science teaching strategy.

University of South Dakota, Graduate School, School of Education, Division of Curriculum and Instruction, Program in Special Education, Vermillion, SD 57069. Offers special education (MA), including advanced specialist in disabilities, early childhood special education, multicategorical special education K-12. *Accreditation:* NCATE. *Program availability:* Part-time, online learning. *Degree requirements:* For master's, comprehensive exam, thesis or alternative. *Entrance requirements:* For master's, GRE General Test, MAT, minimum GPA of 2.7. Additional exam requirements/recommendations for international students: Required—TOEFL (minimum score 550 paper-based; 79 iBT). *Application deadline:* Applications are processed on a rolling basis. Application fee: $35. Electronic applications accepted. *Financial support:* Research assistantships with partial tuition reimbursements, teaching assistantships with partial tuition reimbursements, career-related internships or fieldwork, Federal Work-Study, and unspecified assistantships available. Financial award applicants required to submit FAFSA. *Application contact:* Graduate School, 605-658-6140, Fax: 605-677-6118, E-mail: grad@usd.edu.
Website: http://www.usd.edu/ci

University of South Dakota, Graduate School, School of Education, Division of Educational Leadership, Vermillion, SD 57069. Offers educational administration (MA, Ed D, Ed S), including adult and higher education (MA, Ed D), curriculum director, director of special education (Ed D, Ed S), preK-12 principal, school district superintendent (Ed D, Ed S). *Accreditation:* NCATE. *Program availability:* Part-time, evening/weekend, 100% online, blended/hybrid learning. *Degree requirements:* For master's and Ed S, comprehensive exam, thesis or alternative; for doctorate, comprehensive exam, thesis/dissertation. *Entrance requirements:* For master's, GRE General Test, MAT, minimum GPA of 2.7; for doctorate, minimum GPA of 2.7. Additional exam requirements/recommendations for international students: Required—TOEFL (minimum score 550 paper-based; 79 iBT). *Application deadline:* Applications are processed on a rolling basis. Application fee: $35. Electronic applications accepted. *Financial support:* Research assistantships with partial tuition reimbursements, teaching assistantships with partial tuition reimbursements, Federal Work-Study, traineeships, and unspecified assistantships available. Financial award applicants required to submit FAFSA. *Application contact:* Graduate School, 605-658-6140, Fax: 605-677-6118, E-mail: grad@usd.edu.
Website: http://www.usd.edu/education/educational-administration

University of Southern Maine, College of Management and Human Service, School of Education and Human Development, Program in Special Education, Portland, ME 04103. Offers gifted and talented education (CGS); special education (MS); teaching all students (CGS); youth with moderate to severe disabilities (CGS). *Accreditation:* TEAC. *Program availability:* Part-time, evening/weekend. *Degree requirements:* For master's, thesis or alternative, portfolio. *Entrance requirements:* For master's, proof of teacher certification. Additional exam requirements/recommendations for international students: Required—TOEFL (minimum score 550 paper-based; 79 iBT). Electronic applications accepted. *Faculty research:* Special education, gifted and talented education, diversity education, positive behavioral interventions and supports.

University of Southern Mississippi, College of Education and Psychology, Department of Curriculum, Instruction and Special Education, Hattiesburg, MS 39406-0001. Offers elementary education (M Ed, PhD); instructional technology (MS);

Special Education

instructional technology and design (PhD); secondary education (MAT); special education (M Ed, PhD). *Program availability:* Part-time, online learning. *Students:* 25 full-time (18 women), 5 part-time (3 women). 41 applicants, 59% accepted, 22 enrolled. *Degree requirements:* For master's, comprehensive exam, thesis (for some programs); for doctorate, comprehensive exam, thesis/dissertation. *Entrance requirements:* For master's, GRE General Test, MAT, minimum GPA of 3.0; for doctorate, GRE General Test, minimum GPA of 3.5. Additional exam requirements/recommendations for international students: Required—TOEFL, IELTS. *Application deadline:* For fall admission, 3/1 priority date for domestic students, 3/1 for international students; for spring admission, 1/10 priority date for domestic and international students. Applications are processed on a rolling basis. Application fee: $60. *Expenses:* Tuition, state resident: full-time $3830. *Financial support:* Research assistantships with tuition reimbursements, teaching assistantships with full tuition reimbursements, Federal Work-Study, institutionally sponsored loans, scholarships/grants, health care benefits, tuition waivers (partial), and unspecified assistantships available. Financial award application deadline: 3/15; financial award applicants required to submit FAFSA. *Faculty research:* Mathematical problem solving, integrative curriculum, writing process, teacher education models. *Unit head:* Dr. Jeff Hinton, Chair.
Website: https://www.usm.edu/elementary-special-technology-education

University of South Florida, Innovative Education, Tampa, FL 33620-9951. Offers adult, career and higher education (Graduate Certificate), including college teaching, leadership in developing human resources, leadership in higher education; Africana studies (Graduate Certificate), including diasporas and health disparities, genocide and human rights; aging studies (Graduate Certificate), including gerontology; art research (Graduate Certificate), including museum studies; business foundations (Graduate Certificate); chemical and biomedical engineering (Graduate Certificate), including materials science and engineering, water, health and sustainability; child and family studies (Graduate Certificate), including positive behavior support; civil and industrial engineering (Graduate Certificate), including transportation systems analysis; community and family health (Graduate Certificate), including maternal and child health, social marketing and public health, violence and injury: prevention and intervention, women's health; criminology (Graduate Certificate), including criminal justice administration; data science for public administration (Graduate Certificate); digital humanities (Graduate Certificate); educational measurement and research (Graduate Certificate), including evaluation; English (Graduate Certificate), including comparative literary studies, creative writing, professional and technical communication; entrepreneurship (Graduate Certificate); environmental health (Graduate Certificate), including safety management; epidemiology and biostatistics (Graduate Certificate), including applied biostatistics, biostatistics, concepts and tools of epidemiology, epidemiology, epidemiology of infectious diseases; geography, environment and planning (Graduate Certificate), including community development, environmental policy and management, geographical information systems; geology (Graduate Certificate), including hydrogeology; global health (Graduate Certificate), including disaster management, global health and Latin American and Caribbean studies, global health practice, humanitarian assistance, infection control; government and international affairs (Graduate Certificate), including Cuban studies, globalization studies; health policy and management (Graduate Certificate), including health management and leadership, public health policy and programs; hearing specialist: early intervention (Graduate Certificate); industrial and management systems engineering (Graduate Certificate), including systems engineering, technology management; information studies (Graduate Certificate), including school library media specialist; information systems/decision sciences (Graduate Certificate), including analytics and business intelligence; instructional technology (Graduate Certificate), including distance education, Florida digital/virtual educator, instructional design, multimedia design, Web design; internal medicine, bioethics and medical humanities (Graduate Certificate), including biomedical ethics; Latin American and Caribbean studies (Graduate Certificate); leadership for coastal resiliency planning (Graduate Certificate); mass communications (Graduate Certificate), including multimedia journalism; mathematics and statistics (Graduate Certificate), including mathematics; medicine (Graduate Certificate), including aging and neuroscience, bioinformatics, biotechnology, brain fitness and memory management, clinical investigation, hand and upper limb rehabilitation, health informatics, health sciences, integrative weight management, intellectual property, medicine and gender, metabolic and nutritional medicine, metabolic cardiology, pharmacy sciences; national and competitive intelligence (Graduate Certificate); nursing (Graduate Certificate), including simulation based academic fellowship in advanced pain management; psychological and social foundations (Graduate Certificate), including career counseling, college teaching, diversity in education, mental health counseling, school counseling; public affairs (Graduate Certificate), including nonprofit management, public management, research administration; public health (Graduate Certificate), including assessing chemical toxicity and public health risks, health equity, pharmacoepidemiology, public health generalist, toxicology, translational research in adolescent behavioral health; public health practices (Graduate Certificate), including planning for healthy communities; rehabilitation and mental health counseling (Graduate Certificate), including integrative mental health care, marriage and family therapy, rehabilitation technology; secondary education (Graduate Certificate), including ESOL, foreign language education: culture and content, foreign language education: professional; social work (Graduate Certificate), including geriatric social work/clinical gerontology; special education (Graduate Certificate), including autism spectrum disorder, disabilities education: severe/profound; world languages (Graduate Certificate), including teaching English as a second language (TESL) or foreign language. *Unit head:* Dr. Cynthia DeLuca, Associate Vice President and Assistant Vice Provost, 813-974-3077, Fax: 813-974-7061, E-mail: deluca@usf.edu. *Application contact:* Owen Hooper, Director, Summer and Alternative Calendar Programs, 813-974-6917, E-mail: hooper@usf.edu.
Website: http://www.usf.edu/innovative-education/

The University of Tennessee, Graduate School, College of Education, Health and Human Sciences, Program in Education, Knoxville, TN 37996. Offers art education (MS); counseling education (PhD); cultural studies in education (PhD); curriculum (MS, Ed S); curriculum, educational research and evaluation (Ed D, PhD); early childhood education (PhD); early childhood special education (MS); education of deaf and hard of hearing (MS); educational administration and policy studies (Ed D, PhD); educational administration and supervision (Ed S); educational psychology (Ed D, PhD); elementary education (MS, Ed S); elementary teaching (MS, Ed S); English education (MS, Ed S); exercise science (PhD); foreign language/ESL education (MS, Ed S); instructional technology (MS, Ed D, PhD, Ed S); literacy, language and ESL education (PhD); literacy, language education, and ESL education (Ed D); mathematics education (MS, Ed S); modified and comprehensive special education (MS); reading education (MS, Ed S); school counseling (Ed S); school psychology (PhD, Ed S); science education (MS, Ed S); secondary teaching (MS); social foundations (MS); social science education (MS, Ed S); socio-cultural foundations of sports and education (PhD); special education (Ed S); teacher education (Ed D, PhD). *Accreditation:* NCATE. *Program availability:* Part-time, evening/weekend. *Degree requirements:* For master's and Ed S, thesis optional; for doctorate, variable foreign language requirement, thesis/dissertation. *Entrance requirements:* For master's, minimum GPA of 2.7; for doctorate and Ed S,

GRE General Test, minimum GPA of 2.7. Additional exam requirements/recommendations for international students: Required—TOEFL. Electronic applications accepted.

The University of Tennessee at Chattanooga, School of Education, Chattanooga, TN 37403. Offers counseling (M Ed), including community counseling, school counseling; education (M Ed, Post-Master's Certificate), including elementary education (M Ed); school leadership (Post-Master's Certificate); elementary education (M Ed); learning and leadership (Ed D), including educational leadership; school leadership (Post-Master's Certificate); school leadership: principal licensure (Ed S); secondary education (M Ed); special education (M Ed). *Accreditation:* ACA; NCATE. *Program availability:* Part-time. *Students:* 43 full-time (30 women), 58 part-time (47 women); includes 18 minority (9 Black or African American, non-Hispanic/Latino; 1 Asian, non-Hispanic/Latino; 1 Hispanic/Latino; 7 Two or more races, non-Hispanic/Latino). Average age 31. 118 applicants, 75% accepted, 33 enrolled. In 2017, 59 master's, 7 other advanced degrees awarded. *Degree requirements:* For master's, comprehensive exam, thesis optional, culminating experience; for other advanced degree, internship. *Entrance requirements:* For master's, GRE General Test, PPST 1, teaching certificate; for other advanced degree, two letters of recommendation, graduate degree in education, teaching certificate with three years of experience. Additional exam requirements/recommendations for international students: Required—TOEFL (minimum score 550 paper-based; 79 iBT), IELTS (minimum score 6). *Application deadline:* For fall admission, 6/15 for domestic students, 7/1 for international students; for spring admission, 11/1 for domestic and international students. Applications are processed on a rolling basis. Application fee: $35 ($40 for international students). Electronic applications accepted. *Expenses:* Contact institution. *Financial support:* Research assistantships, teaching assistantships, career-related internships or fieldwork, institutionally sponsored loans, scholarships/grants, and unspecified assistantships available. Support available to part-time students. Financial award application deadline: 7/1; financial award applicants required to submit FAFSA. *Faculty research:* School counseling, community counseling, elementary and secondary education, school leadership and administration. *Total annual research expenditures:* $576,495. *Unit head:* Dr. Renee Murley, Director, 423-425-4684, Fax: 423-425-5380, E-mail: renee-murley@utc.edu. *Application contact:* Dr. Joanne Romagni, Dean of the Graduate School, 423-425-4478, Fax: 423-425-5223, E-mail: joanne-romagni@utc.edu.
Website: https://www.utc.edu/school-education/

The University of Tennessee at Martin, Graduate Programs, College of Education, Health and Behavioral Sciences, Program in Teaching, Martin, TN 38238. Offers curriculum and instruction (MS Ed), including 7-12, K-6; initial licensure (MS Ed), including elementary education, secondary education; initial licensure K-12 (MS Ed), including physical education, special education; interdisciplinary (MS Ed). *Program availability:* Part-time, online only, 100% online. *Students:* 20 full-time (17 women), 92 part-time (66 women); includes 20 minority (14 Black or African American, non-Hispanic/Latino; 2 Hispanic/Latino; 4 Two or more races, non-Hispanic/Latino). Average age 32. 79 applicants, 70% accepted, 38 enrolled. In 2017, 14 master's awarded. *Entrance requirements:* Additional exam requirements/recommendations for international students: Required—TOEFL (minimum score 525 paper-based; 71 iBT). *Application deadline:* For fall admission, 7/27 for domestic and international students; for spring admission, 12/17 for domestic and international students; for summer admission, 5/10 for domestic and international students. Applications are processed on a rolling basis. Electronic applications accepted. *Expenses:* Tuition, state resident: full-time $8658; part-time $481 per credit hour. Tuition, nonresident: full-time $14,418; part-time $801 per credit hour. *International tuition:* $22,602 full-time. *Required fees:* $1404; $79 per credit hour. Part-time tuition and fees vary according to course load. *Financial support:* In 2017–18, 26 students received support, including 1 research assistantship with full tuition reimbursement available (averaging $6,283 per year), 5 teaching assistantships with full tuition reimbursements available (averaging $7,001 per year); scholarships/grants and tuition waivers also available. Financial award applicants required to submit FAFSA. *Faculty research:* Special education, science/math/technology, school reform, reading. *Unit head:* Cynthia West, Dean, 731-881-7125, Fax: 731-881-7975, E-mail: cwest@utm.edu. *Application contact:* Jolene L. Cunningham, Student Services Specialist, 731-881-7012, Fax: 731-881-7499, E-mail: jcunningham@utm.edu.

The University of Texas at Austin, Graduate School, College of Education, Department of Special Education, Austin, TX 78712-1111. Offers autism and developmental disabilities (Ed D, PhD); autism and developmental disability (M Ed, MA); early childhood special education (M Ed, MA, Ed D, PhD); learning disabilities (Ed D, PhD); learning disabilities/behavior disorders (M Ed, MA); multicultural special education (M Ed, MA, Ed D, PhD); rehabilitation counselor (M Ed); rehabilitation counselor education (Ed D, PhD); special education administration (Ed D, PhD). *Accreditation:* CORE. *Program availability:* Part-time, evening/weekend, online learning. *Degree requirements:* For master's, thesis or alternative; for doctorate, thesis/dissertation. *Entrance requirements:* For master's and doctorate, GRE General Test. *Faculty research:* Anchored instruction, reading disabilities, multicultural/bilingual.

The University of Texas at El Paso, Graduate School, College of Education, Department of Educational Psychology and Special Services, El Paso, TX 79968-0001. Offers educational diagnostics (M Ed); guidance and counseling (M Ed); special education (M Ed). *Program availability:* Part-time, evening/weekend. *Degree requirements:* For master's, thesis optional. *Entrance requirements:* For master's, minimum GPA of 3.0. Additional exam requirements/recommendations for international students: Required—TOEFL. Electronic applications accepted.

The University of Texas at San Antonio, College of Education and Human Development, Department of Interdisciplinary Learning and Teaching, San Antonio, TX 78249-0617. Offers education (MA), including curriculum and instruction, early childhood and elementary education, instructional technology, reading and literacy, special education; interdisciplinary learning and teaching (PhD). *Program availability:* Part-time, evening/weekend. *Faculty:* 24 full-time (16 women), 5 part-time/adjunct (3 women). *Students:* 73 full-time (57 women), 227 part-time (206 women); includes 179 minority (25 Black or African American, non-Hispanic/Latino; 10 Asian, non-Hispanic/Latino; 140 Hispanic/Latino; 1 Native Hawaiian or other Pacific Islander, non-Hispanic/Latino; 3 Two or more races, non-Hispanic/Latino), 7 international. Average age 34. 107 applicants, 88% accepted, 70 enrolled. In 2017, 103 master's, 5 doctorates awarded. *Degree requirements:* For master's, comprehensive exam, thesis optional, 36 hours of course work without thesis (33 with thesis); for doctorate, comprehensive exam, thesis/dissertation, minimum of 60 semester credit hours. *Entrance requirements:* For master's, bachelor's degree with minimum GPA of 3.0 in last 60 hours of coursework; 18 hours of undergraduate coursework in education or related field; for doctorate, GRE, transcripts from all colleges and universities attended, professional vitae demonstrating experience in work environment where education was primary professional emphasis, 3 letters of recommendation, statement of purpose, minimum GPA of 3.5. Additional exam requirements/recommendations for international students: Required—TOEFL (minimum score 550 paper-based; 79 iBT), IELTS (minimum score 6.5). *Application deadline:* For fall admission, 6/15 for domestic students, 3/1 for international students; for spring admission, 10/15 for domestic students, 9/15 for international students. Applications are processed on a rolling basis. Application fee: $50 ($90 for international students).

Electronic applications accepted. *Expenses:* Tuition, state resident: full-time $5495. Tuition, nonresident: full-time $21,938. *Required fees:* $1915. Tuition and fees vary according to program. *Financial support:* Career-related internships or fieldwork, Federal Work-Study, and scholarships/grants available. Support available to part-time students. *Faculty research:* Explorations of science, learning and teaching, family involvement in early childhood, culturally-responsive literacy instruction in diverse settings, STEM education, autism spectrum disorder. *Total annual research expenditures:* $511,331. *Unit head:* Dr. Mari R. Cortez, Department Chair, 210-458-4414, Fax: 210-458-7281, E-mail: mari.cortez@utsa.edu. *Application contact:* Elizabeth Narvaez, Student Development Specialist, 210-458-7443, E-mail: elizabeth.narvaez@utsa.edu.
Website: http://education.utsa.edu/interdisciplinary_learning_and_teaching/

The University of Texas at Tyler, College of Education and Psychology, School of Education, Tyler, TX 75799-0001. Offers early childhood education (M Ed, MA); reading (M Ed, MA); special education (M Ed, MA). *Program availability:* Part-time, evening/weekend. *Degree requirements:* For master's, comprehensive exam, thesis (for some programs), research project. *Entrance requirements:* For master's, GRE General Test. Additional exam requirements/recommendations for international students: Required—TOEFL. Electronic applications accepted. *Faculty research:* Improving quality in childcare settings, play and creativity, teacher interactions, effects of modeling on early childhood teachers, biofeedback, literacy instruction.

The University of Texas Health Science Center at San Antonio, Joe R. and Teresa Lozano Long School of Medicine, San Antonio, TX 78229-3900. Offers deaf education and hearing (MS); medicine (MD); MPH/MD. *Accreditation:* LCME/AMA. *Degree requirements:* For master's, comprehensive exam, practicum assignments. *Entrance requirements:* For master's, minimum GPA of 3.0, interview, 3 professional letters of recommendation; for doctorate, MCAT. Electronic applications accepted. *Expenses:* Contact institution. *Faculty research:* Geriatrics, diabetes, cancer, AIDS, obesity.

The University of Texas of the Permian Basin, Office of Graduate Studies, School of Education, Program in Special Education, Odessa, TX 79762-0001. Offers MA. *Degree requirements:* For master's, comprehensive exam (for some programs), thesis (for some programs). *Entrance requirements:* For master's, GRE General Test. Additional exam requirements/recommendations for international students: Required—TOEFL (minimum score 550 paper-based).

The University of Texas Rio Grande Valley, College of Education and P-16 Integration, Department of Human Development and School Services, Edinburg, TX 78539. Offers early childhood education (M Ed); early childhood special education (M Ed); school psychology (MA); special education (M Ed). *Program availability:* Part-time, evening/weekend. *Faculty:* 14. *Students:* 131. In 2017, 164 master's awarded. *Degree requirements:* For master's, comprehensive exam (for some programs). *Entrance requirements:* For master's, minimum GPA of 3.0. Additional exam requirements/recommendations for international students: Required—TOEFL (minimum score 550 paper-based; 79 iBT), IELTS (minimum score 6.5). *Application deadline:* For fall admission, 4/15 for domestic students; for spring admission, 11/1 for domestic students; for summer admission, 3/1 for domestic students. Applications are processed on a rolling basis. Application fee: $50 ($75 for international students). Electronic applications accepted. *Expenses:* Tuition, state resident: full-time $5550; part-time $417 per credit hour. Tuition, nonresident: full-time $13,020; part-time $832 per credit hour. *Required fees:* $1169. *Financial support:* Research assistantships, career-related internships or fieldwork, institutionally sponsored loans, and scholarships/grants available. Financial award application deadline: 4/15; financial award applicants required to submit FAFSA. *Faculty research:* Special education, assessment practice, behavior interventions, mental retardation, early childhood. *Unit head:* Dr. John Lowdermilk, Chair, 956-665-3466, E-mail: john.lowdermilk@utrgv.edu. *Application contact:* Stephanie Ozuna, Graduate Student Recruiter, 956-665-3661, E-mail: stephanie.ozuna@utrgv.edu.

University of the Cumberlands, Graduate Programs in Education, Williamsburg, KY 40769-1372. Offers all grades (P-12) (M Ed); business and marketing (MA Ed, MAT); counselor education and supervision (Ed D); director of pupil personnel (Certificate); director of special education (Certificate); educational administration and supervision (Ed S); educational leadership (Ed D); elementary education (MA Ed, MAT); instructional leadership - principalship (MA Ed); instructional leadership - school principal (Certificate); middle school education (MA Ed, MAT); reading and writing (MA Ed); school counseling (MA Ed); school superintendent (Certificate); secondary education (MA Ed, MAT); special education (MAT); supervisor of instruction (Certificate); teacher leader (MA Ed). *Program availability:* Part-time, evening/weekend, online learning. *Degree requirements:* For master's, comprehensive exam. Electronic applications accepted.

University of the Pacific, Gladys L. Benerd School of Education, Stockton, CA 95211-0197. Offers curriculum and instruction (MA, Ed D); education (M Ed); educational administration and leadership (MA, Ed D); educational and school psychology (MA, Ed D); school psychology (Ed S); special education (MA); teacher education (MA). *Accreditation:* NCATE. *Faculty:* 19 full-time (12 women), 48 part-time/adjunct (39 women). *Students:* 141 full-time (115 women), 305 part-time (236 women); includes 219 minority (41 Black or African American, non-Hispanic/Latino; 44 Asian, non-Hispanic/Latino; 105 Hispanic/Latino; 2 Native Hawaiian or other Pacific Islander, non-Hispanic/Latino; 27 Two or more races, non-Hispanic/Latino), 7 international. Average age 33. 144 applicants, 83% accepted, 94 enrolled. In 2017, 231 master's, 8 doctorates awarded. *Degree requirements:* For doctorate, thesis/dissertation. *Entrance requirements:* For master's, GRE General Test; for doctorate, GRE General Test, GRE Subject Test. Additional exam requirements/recommendations for international students: Required—TOEFL. *Application deadline:* For fall admission, 3/1 priority date for domestic students; for spring admission, 10/15 for domestic students. Applications are processed on a rolling basis. Application fee: $75. *Financial support:* Teaching assistantships and institutionally sponsored loans available. Support available to part-time students. Financial award application deadline: 3/1; financial award applicants required to submit FAFSA. *Unit head:* Dr. Vanessa Sheared, Dean, 209-946-2683, E-mail: lwebster@pacific.edu. *Application contact:* Office of Graduate Admissions, 209-946-2344.

University of the Southwest, Graduate Programs, Hobbs, NM 88240-9129. Offers business administration (MBA); curriculum and instruction (MSE); curriculum and instruction: bilingual (MSE); curriculum and instruction: TESOL (MSE); early childhood education (MSE); educational administration (MSE); mental health counseling (MSE); school counseling (MSE); special education (MSE); sports management (MBA). *Program availability:* Part-time, evening/weekend, online learning. *Degree requirements:* For master's, comprehensive exam, thesis (for some programs). *Entrance requirements:* Additional exam requirements/recommendations for international students: Recommended—TOEFL. Electronic applications accepted.

The University of Toledo, College of Graduate Studies, Judith Herb College of Education, Department of Curriculum and Instruction, Toledo, OH 43606-3390. Offers art education (ME); career and technical education (ME, Ed S); curriculum and instruction (ME, PhD, Ed S); early childhood education (Ed S); education and

anthropology (MAE); education and biology (MES); education and chemistry (MES); education and classics (MAE); education and economics (MAE); education and English (MAE); education and French (MAE); education and geology (MES); education and German (MAE); education and history (MAE); education and mathematics (MAE, MES); education and physics (MES); education and political science (MAE); education and sociology (MAE); education and Spanish (MAE); educational media (PhD); educational technology (ME); educational technology: virtual educator (Certificate); elementary education (PhD); English as a second language (MAE); gifted and talented education (PhD); middle childhood education (ME); secondary education (ME, PhD); special education (PhD). *Accreditation:* NCATE. *Program availability:* Part-time, evening/weekend. *Degree requirements:* For master's, comprehensive exam, thesis or alternative; for doctorate, comprehensive exam, thesis/dissertation; for other advanced degree, thesis optional. *Entrance requirements:* For master's, doctorate, and other advanced degree, minimum cumulative GPA of 2.7 for all previous academic work, letters of recommendation. Additional exam requirements/recommendations for international students: Required—TOEFL (minimum score 550 paper-based; 80 iBT). Electronic applications accepted.

The University of Toledo, College of Graduate Studies, Judith Herb College of Education, Department of Early Childhood, Physical and Special Education, Toledo, OH 43606-3390. Offers early childhood education (ME); physical education (ME); special education (ME). *Program availability:* Part-time. *Degree requirements:* For master's, thesis. *Entrance requirements:* For master's, minimum cumulative GPA of 2.7 for all previous academic work, letters of recommendation. Additional exam requirements/recommendations for international students: Required—TOEFL (minimum score 550 paper-based; 80 iBT). Electronic applications accepted.

University of Utah, Graduate School, College of Education, Department of Special Education, Salt Lake City, UT 84112. Offers board certified behavior analyst (M Ed, MS, PhD); deaf and hard of hearing (M Ed); deaf/blind (M Ed, MS); early childhood deaf and hard of hearing (MS); early childhood special education (M Ed, MS, PhD); early childhood vision impairments (M Ed); mild/moderate disabilities (M Ed, MS, PhD); severe disabilities (M Ed, MS, PhD); visual impairment (M Ed, MS). *Program availability:* Part-time, evening/weekend, 100% online, blended/hybrid learning. *Faculty:* 9 full-time (6 women), 8 part-time/adjunct (7 women). *Students:* 45 full-time (41 women), 26 part-time (24 women); includes 6 minority (4 Asian, non-Hispanic/Latino; 2 Hispanic/Latino). Average age 31. 30 applicants, 97% accepted, 28 enrolled. In 2017, 29 master's awarded. Terminal master's awarded for partial completion of doctoral program. *Degree requirements:* For master's, comprehensive, thesis (for some programs), qualifying exam; for doctorate, thesis/dissertation, qualifying exam. *Entrance requirements:* For master's, GRE, minimum GPA of 3.0; for doctorate, GRE General Test, minimum GPA of 3.5. Additional exam requirements/recommendations for international students: Required—TOEFL (minimum score 600 paper-based; 100 iBT); Recommended—IELTS (minimum score 7). *Application deadline:* For fall admission, 3/1 for domestic and international students; for spring admission, 11/1 for domestic and international students; for summer admission, 5/16 for domestic and international students. Application fee: $55 ($65 for international students). Electronic applications accepted. *Financial support:* In 2017–18, 22 students received support, including 33 fellowships with partial tuition reimbursements available (averaging $4,350 per year), 3 teaching assistantships with tuition reimbursements available (averaging $10,000 per year); career-related internships or fieldwork and health care benefits also available. Support available to part-time students. Financial award application deadline: 3/1; financial award applicants required to submit FAFSA. *Faculty research:* Inclusive education, positive behavior support, reading, instruction and intervention strategies. *Total annual research expenditures:* $139,750. *Unit head:* Dr. Robert E. O'Neill, Chair, 801-581-8121, Fax: 801-585-6476, E-mail: rob.oneill@utah.edu. *Application contact:* Patty Davis, Academic Advisor, 801-581-4764, Fax: 801-585-6476, E-mail: patty.davis@utah.edu.
Website: http://special-ed.utah.edu/

University of Vermont, Graduate College, College of Education and Social Services, Program in Early Childhood Special Education, Burlington, VT 05405. Offers M Ed. *Program availability:* Part-time, evening/weekend. *Entrance requirements:* Additional exam requirements/recommendations for international students: Required—TOEFL (minimum iBT score of 90) or IELTS (6.5). *Application deadline:* For fall admission, 2/15 for domestic and international students; for spring admission, 11/1 for domestic and international students. Application fee: $65. Electronic applications accepted. *Expenses:* Tuition, state resident: full-time $11,628; part-time $646 per credit. Tuition, nonresident: full-time $29,340; part-time $1630 per credit. *Required fees:* $1994; $10 per credit. Tuition and fees vary according to course load and program. *Financial support:* Scholarships/grants available. *Unit head:* Dr. Michael Giancreco, Coordinator, 802-656-2936, E-mail: ecse_grad@uvm.edu.
Website: https://www.uvm.edu/cess/doe/med_earlychild_specialed

University of Vermont, Graduate College, College of Education and Social Services, Program in Special Education, Grades K-12, Burlington, VT 05405. Offers M Ed. *Accreditation:* NCATE. *Degree requirements:* For master's, thesis or alternative. *Entrance requirements:* For master's, license (or eligible for licensure). Additional exam requirements/recommendations for international students: Required—TOEFL (minimum score 550 paper-based, 90 iBT) or IELTS (6.5). *Application deadline:* For fall admission, 2/15 for domestic and international students; for spring admission, 11/1 for domestic and international students. Application fee: $65. Electronic applications accepted. *Expenses:* Tuition, state resident: full-time $11,628; part-time $646 per credit. Tuition, nonresident: full-time $29,340; part-time $1630 per credit. *Required fees:* $1994; $10 per credit. Tuition and fees vary according to course load and program. *Financial support:* In 2017–18, 4 students received support. Research assistantships, teaching assistantships, career-related internships or fieldwork, and scholarships/grants available. Financial award application deadline: 3/1. *Unit head:* Dr. Michael Giangreco, Program Coordinator, 802-656-1144, E-mail: michael.giangreco@uvm.edu. *Application contact:* Roman Vogel, Graduate Program Support, 802-656-2936, E-mail: special.education@uvm.edu.
Website: https://www.uvm.edu/cess/doe/masters_education_special_education_k_12th_grade

University of Victoria, Faculty of Graduate Studies, Faculty of Education, Department of Educational Psychology and Leadership Studies, Victoria, BC V8W 2Y2, Canada. Offers aboriginal communities counseling (M Ed); counseling (M Ed, MA); educational psychology (M Ed, MA, PhD), including counseling psychology (M Ed, MA), leadership studies (PhD), learning and development (MA, PhD), measurement and evaluation, special education (M Ed, MA); leadership studies (M Ed, MA). *Program availability:* Part-time. *Degree requirements:* For master's, thesis (for some programs), comprehensive exam (M Ed); for doctorate, comprehensive exam, thesis/dissertation, candidacy exam. *Entrance requirements:* For master's, 2 years of work experience in a relevant field; for doctorate, GRE, 2 years of work experience in a relevant field, minimum B average. Additional exam requirements/recommendations for international students: Required—TOEFL (minimum score 575 paper-based), IELTS (minimum score 7). *Faculty research:* Learning and development (child, adolescent and adult), special education and exceptional children.

Special Education

University of Virginia, Curry School of Education, Department of Curriculum, Instruction, and Special Education, Program in Special Education, Charlottesville, VA 22903. Offers M Ed, Ed D, Ed S. *Accreditation:* TEAC. In 2017, 1 master's awarded. *Entrance requirements:* For master's, doctorate, and Ed S, GRE General Test, 2 letters of recommendation. Additional exam requirements/recommendations for international students: Required—TOEFL (minimum score 600 paper-based; 90 iBT), IELTS (minimum score 7). *Application deadline:* Applications are processed on a rolling basis. Application fee: $60. Electronic applications accepted. *Financial support:* Applicants required to submit FAFSA. *Unit head:* William Therrien, Program Area Director, 434-246-2962, E-mail: wjt2c@virginia.edu. *Application contact:* E-mail: curry-admissions@virginia.edu.
Website: http://curry.virginia.edu/academics/areas-of-study/special-education

University of Virginia, Curry School of Education, Program in Education, Charlottesville, VA 22903. Offers administration and supervision (PhD); applied developmental science (PhD); counselor education (PhD); curriculum and instruction (PhD); early childhood special education (MT); education evaluation (PhD); educational psychology (PhD); educational research (PhD); elementary education (MT); English education (MT, PhD); foreign language education (MT); higher education (PhD); instructional technology (PhD); kinesiology (MT, PhD); math education (PhD); reading education (PhD); research, statistics and evaluation (PhD); school psychology (PhD); science education (PhD); social studies education (MT, PhD); special education (PhD); world languages education (MT). *Students:* 431 full-time (353 women), 15 part-time (14 women); includes 100 minority (32 Black or African American, non-Hispanic/Latino; 33 Asian, non-Hispanic/Latino; 16 Hispanic/Latino; 19 Two or more races, non-Hispanic/Latino), 14 international. Average age 25. 264 applicants, 49% accepted, 83 enrolled. In 2017, 142 master's, 33 doctorates awarded. *Degree requirements:* For master's, comprehensive exam (for some programs), field project; for doctorate, comprehensive exam, thesis/dissertation. *Entrance requirements:* For doctorate, GRE General Test. Additional exam requirements/recommendations for international students: Required—TOEFL (minimum score 600 paper-based; 90 iBT), IELTS (minimum score 7). *Application deadline:* Applications are processed on a rolling basis. Application fee: $60. Electronic applications accepted. *Financial support:* Fellowships, research assistantships, and teaching assistantships available. Financial award application deadline: 1/5; financial award applicants required to submit FAFSA. *Unit head:* Robert C. Pianta, Dean, 434-924-3334, E-mail: pianta@virginia.edu. *Application contact:* E-mail: curry-admissions@virginia.edu.
Website: http://curry.virginia.edu/teacher-education

University of Washington, Graduate School, College of Education, Program in Special Education, Seattle, WA 98195. Offers early childhood special education (M Ed); emotional and behavioral disabilities (M Ed); learning disabilities (M Ed); low-incidence disabilities (M Ed); severe disabilities (M Ed); special education (Ed D, PhD). *Degree requirements:* For master's, thesis optional; for doctorate, thesis/dissertation. *Entrance requirements:* For master's and doctorate, GRE General Test, minimum GPA of 3.0. Additional exam requirements/recommendations for international students: Required—TOEFL.

University of Washington, Tacoma, Graduate Programs, Program in Education, Tacoma, WA 98402-3100. Offers education (M Ed); educational administration (principal or program administrator certification) (M Ed); elementary education teacher certification (M Ed); elementary education/special education teacher certification (M Ed); secondary science or math teacher certification (M Ed). *Program availability:* Part-time, evening/weekend. *Degree requirements:* For master's, culminating project. *Entrance requirements:* For master's, WEST-B, WEST-E (teacher certification programs only), official sealed transcript from every college/university attended, personal goal statement, letters of recommendation, copy of valid teaching certificate. Additional exam requirements/recommendations for international students: Required—TOEFL (minimum score 580 paper-based; 92 iBT). Electronic applications accepted. *Faculty research:* Global learning communities for English/Chinese languages, evaluation of mathematics and reading intervention programs, response to intervention, school-wide behavioral and emotional support, mathematics education and culturally responsive mathematics education.

The University of West Alabama, School of Graduate Studies, College of Education, Program in Special Education, Livingston, AL 35470. Offers collaborative special education 6-12 (Ed S); collaborative special education K-6 (Ed S); special education collaborative teacher 6-12 (M Ed); special education collaborative teacher K-6 (M Ed). *Accreditation:* NCATE. *Program availability:* Part-time, evening/weekend, 100% online. *Faculty:* 7 full-time (all women), 28 part-time/adjunct (21 women). *Students:* 221 (190 women); includes 61 minority (52 Black or African American, non-Hispanic/Latino; 1 Asian, non-Hispanic/Latino; 2 Hispanic/Latino; 6 Two or more races, non-Hispanic/Latino). Average age 34. 56 applicants, 93% accepted, 37 enrolled. In 2017, 48 master's, 25 Ed Ss awarded. *Degree requirements:* For master's, comprehensive exam, thesis optional; for Ed S, comprehensive exam. *Entrance requirements:* For master's, GRE, minimum GPA of 2.75, verification of background clearance/fingerprints, valid bachelor's-level Professional Educator Certificate in any teaching area. Additional exam requirements/recommendations for international students: Required—TOEFL (minimum score 500 paper-based; 61 iBT). *Application deadline:* Applications are processed on a rolling basis. Application fee: $40. Electronic applications accepted. *Expenses:* Tuition, state resident: part-time $371 per credit hour. Tuition, nonresident: part-time $742 per credit hour. *Required fees:* $130 per semester. *Financial support:* Teaching assistantships, Federal Work-Study, scholarships/grants, and unspecified assistantships available. Support available to part-time students. Financial award application deadline: 3/1; financial award applicants required to submit FAFSA. *Unit head:* Dr. Jodie Winship, Chair of Teaching and Learning, 205-652-5415, Fax: 205-652-3706, E-mail: jwinship@uwa.edu. *Application contact:* Dr. B. J. Kimbrough, Dean of Graduate Studies, 205-652-3647, Fax: 205-652-3670, E-mail: bkimbrough@uwa.edu.

The University of Western Ontario, Faculty of Graduate Studies, Social Sciences Division, Faculty of Education, Program in Educational Studies, London, ON N6A 5B8, Canada. Offers curriculum studies (M Ed); educational policy studies (M Ed); educational psychology/special education (M Ed). *Program availability:* Part-time. *Faculty research:* Reflective practice, gender and schooling, feminist pedagogy, narrative inquiry, second language, multiculturalism in Canada, education and law.

University of West Florida, College of Education and Professional Studies, Department of Teacher Education and Educational Leadership, Program in Exceptional Student Education, Pensacola, FL 32514-5750. Offers applied behavior analysis (MA); special and alternative education (MA). *Accreditation:* NCATE. *Program availability:* Part-time, evening/weekend, online learning. *Entrance requirements:* For master's, GRE (minimum score 450 verbal) or MAT (minimum score 396) if bachelor's GPA less than 3.0, state teaching certification; letter of intent; two professional references. Additional exam requirements/recommendations for international students: Required—TOEFL (minimum score 550 paper-based). *Faculty research:* Memory, semantic structure, remedial programming.

University of West Georgia, College of Education, Carrollton, GA 30118. Offers business education (M Ed); early childhood education (M Ed, Ed S); educational leadership (M Ed, Ed S); media (M Ed, Ed S); professional counseling (M Ed, Ed S); professional counseling and supervision (Ed D); reading instruction (M Ed); school improvement (Ed D); secondary education (M Ed); special education (M Ed, Ed S), including teaching (M Ed); speech language pathology (M Ed); teaching (MAT). *Accreditation:* NCATE. *Program availability:* Part-time, evening/weekend, 100% online, blended/hybrid learning. *Faculty:* 45 full-time (28 women). *Students:* 344 full-time (286 women), 1,243 part-time (1,039 women); includes 538 minority (456 Black or African American, non-Hispanic/Latino; 19 Asian, non-Hispanic/Latino; 46 Hispanic/Latino; 1 Native Hawaiian or other Pacific Islander, non-Hispanic/Latino; 16 Two or more races, non-Hispanic/Latino), 7 international. Average age 36. 685 applicants, 78% accepted, 429 enrolled. In 2017, 299 master's, 30 doctorates, 218 other advanced degrees awarded. *Entrance requirements:* Additional exam requirements/recommendations for international students: Required—TOEFL (minimum score 523 paper-based; 69 iBT); Recommended—IELTS (minimum score 6.5). *Application deadline:* For fall admission, 7/21 for domestic students, 6/1 for international students; for spring admission, 11/30 for domestic students, 10/15 for international students; for summer admission, 4/15 for domestic students, 3/30 for international students. Applications are processed on a rolling basis. Application fee: $40. Electronic applications accepted. Tuition and fees vary according to degree level and program. *Financial support:* Fellowships, research assistantships, teaching assistantships, career-related internships or fieldwork, Federal Work-Study, institutionally sponsored loans, scholarships/grants, and unspecified assistantships available. Support available to part-time students. Financial award application deadline: 4/1; financial award applicants required to submit FAFSA. *Unit head:* Dr. Diane Hoff, Dean, College of Education, 678-839-6570, Fax: 678-839-6098, E-mail: dhoff@westga.edu. *Application contact:* Dr. Toby Ziglar, Assistant Dean of the Graduate School, 678-839-1394, Fax: 678-839-1395, E-mail: graduate@westga.edu.
Website: http://www.westga.edu/education/

University of Wisconsin–Eau Claire, College of Education and Human Sciences, Program in Special Education, Eau Claire, WI 54702-4004. Offers MSE. *Program availability:* Part-time. *Degree requirements:* For master's, comprehensive exam, thesis, research paper, or written exam; oral exam. *Entrance requirements:* For master's, minimum GPA of 2.75. Additional exam requirements/recommendations for international students: Required—TOEFL (minimum score 79 iBT).

University of Wisconsin–La Crosse, School of Education, La Crosse, WI 54601-3742. Offers English language arts elementary (Graduate Certificate); professional development in education (ME-PD); reading (MS Ed); special education (MS Ed). *Program availability:* Part-time, evening/weekend. *Faculty:* 6 full-time (4 women), 8 part-time/adjunct (6 women). *Students:* 70 part-time (51 women); includes 2 minority (1 Asian, non-Hispanic/Latino; 1 Two or more races, non-Hispanic/Latino). Average age 30. 59 applicants, 100% accepted, 34 enrolled. In 2017, 69 master's, 1 other advanced degree awarded. *Entrance requirements:* For master's, GRE. Additional exam requirements/recommendations for international students: Required—TOEFL (minimum score 550 paper-based; 79 iBT). *Application deadline:* Applications are processed on a rolling basis. Electronic applications accepted. *Financial support:* Research assistantships, Federal Work-Study, scholarships/grants, health care benefits, and tuition waivers (partial) available. Support available to part-time students. Financial award application deadline: 3/15; financial award applicants required to submit FAFSA. *Unit head:* Marcie Wycoff-Horn, Dean, School of Education, 608-785-6786, E-mail: mwycoff-horn@uwlax.edu. *Application contact:* Brandon Schaller, Senior Graduate Student Status Examiner, 608-785-8941, E-mail: admissions@uwlax.edu.
Website: https://www.uwlax.edu/soe/

University of Wisconsin–Madison, Graduate School, School of Education, Department of Rehabilitation Psychology and Special Education, Program in Special Education, Madison, WI 53706-1380. Offers MA, MS, PhD. *Degree requirements:* For doctorate, thesis/dissertation. Electronic applications accepted.

University of Wisconsin–Milwaukee, Graduate School, School of Education, Department of Exceptional Education, Milwaukee, WI 53201-0413. Offers autism spectrum disorders (Graduate Certificate); exceptional education (MS); transition for students with disabilities (Graduate Certificate); urban education (PhD), including adult, continuing and higher education leadership, art education, curriculum and instruction, exceptional education, mathematics education, multicultural studies, social foundations of education. *Program availability:* Part-time. *Students:* 45 full-time (34 women), 68 part-time (54 women); includes 46 minority (27 Black or African American, non-Hispanic/Latino; 7 Asian, non-Hispanic/Latino; 1 Hispanic/Latino; 11 Two or more races, non-Hispanic/Latino), 4 international. Average age 39. 43 applicants, 53% accepted, 19 enrolled. In 2017, 12 master's, 13 doctorates, 8 other advanced degrees awarded. *Entrance requirements:* Additional exam requirements/recommendations for international students: Required—TOEFL (minimum score 550 paper-based; 79 iBT), IELTS (minimum score 6.5). *Application deadline:* For fall admission, 1/1 priority date for domestic students; for spring admission, 9/1 for domestic students. Application fee: $56 ($96 for international students). Electronic applications accepted. *Financial support:* Fellowships, research assistantships, teaching assistantships, career-related internships or fieldwork, health care benefits, and unspecified assistantships available. Support available to part-time students. Financial award application deadline: 4/15; financial award applicants required to submit FAFSA. *Faculty research:* Emotional disturbance, hearing impairment, learning disabilities, mental retardation. *Application contact:* General Information Contact, 414-229-4721, E-mail: soeinfo@uwm.edu.
Website: http://uwm.edu/education/academics/exceptional-edu-department/

University of Wisconsin–Oshkosh, Graduate Studies, College of Education and Human Services, Department of Special Education, Oshkosh, WI 54901. Offers cross-categorical (MSE); early childhood: exceptional education needs (MSE); non-licensure (MSE). *Program availability:* Part-time, evening/weekend. *Degree requirements:* For master's, comprehensive exam (for some programs), thesis or alternative, field report. *Entrance requirements:* For master's, interview, minimum GPA of 3.0, teaching license, letters of recommendation. Additional exam requirements/recommendations for international students: Required—TOEFL (minimum score 550 paper-based; 79 iBT). Electronic applications accepted. *Faculty research:* Private agency contributions to the disabled, graduation requirements for exceptional education needs students, direct instruction in spelling for learning disabled, effects of behavioral parent training, secondary education programming issues.

University of Wisconsin–Stevens Point, College of Professional Studies, School of Education, Program in Education—General/Special, Stevens Point, WI 54481-3897. Offers MSE. *Program availability:* Part-time. *Degree requirements:* For master's, comprehensive exam, thesis or alternative. *Entrance requirements:* For master's, minimum undergraduate GPA of 3.0, 2 years teaching experience, letters of recommendation, teacher certification. *Faculty research:* Curriculum and instruction, early childhood special education, standards-based education.

University of Wisconsin–Superior, Graduate Division, Department of Teacher Education, Program in Special Education, Superior, WI 54880-4500. Offers emotional/behavior disabilities (MSE); learning disabilities (MSE). *Program availability:* Part-time, evening/weekend, online learning. *Degree requirements:* For master's, research project. *Entrance requirements:* For master's, minimum GPA of 2.75, teaching certificate. Electronic applications accepted.

University of Wisconsin–Whitewater, School of Graduate Studies, College of Education and Professional Studies, Department of Special Education, Whitewater, WI 53190-1790. Offers cross categorical licensure (MSE); professional development (MSE); special education (Postbaccalaureate Certificate). *Accreditation:* NCATE. *Program availability:* Part-time, evening/weekend, online learning. *Degree requirements:* For master's, thesis or alternative. *Entrance requirements:* Additional exam requirements/recommendations for international students: Required—TOEFL (minimum score 550 paper-based; 80 iBT), IELTS (minimum score 6). Electronic applications accepted.

University of Wyoming, College of Education, Program in Special Education, Laramie, WY 82071. Offers MA, PhD, Ed S. *Degree requirements:* For master's, comprehensive exam, thesis. *Entrance requirements:* For master's, GRE, 2 years teaching experience, 3 letters of recommendation, writing sample. *Faculty research:* Self-determination; transition; digital learning; severe disabilities; response to intervention.

Ursuline College, School of Graduate and Professional Studies, Master Apprenticeship Program, Pepper Pike, OH 44124-4398. Offers adolescent to young adult education (MA); early childhood education (MA); middle childhood education (MA); special education (MA). *Accreditation:* NCATE. *Faculty:* 1 full-time (0 women), 6 part-time/adjunct (all women). *Students:* 19 full-time (16 women); includes 4 minority (all Black or African American, non-Hispanic/Latino). Average age 32. In 2017, 18 master's awarded. *Degree requirements:* For master's, comprehensive exam. *Entrance requirements:* For master's, minimum undergraduate GPA of 3.0. Additional exam requirements/recommendations for international students: Required—TOEFL (minimum score 500 paper-based). *Application deadline:* For fall admission, 8/1 priority date for domestic students. Applications are processed on a rolling basis. Application fee: $25. Electronic applications accepted. *Expenses:* Contact institution. *Financial support:* Application deadline: 3/1; applicants required to submit FAFSA. *Faculty research:* Longevity of female superintendents, expectations of student teacher mentors, qualities of successful student teachers, literacy preparation of K-12 student teachers. *Unit head:* Dr. Mary Jo Cherry, Director, 440-646-8147, Fax: 440-646-8328, E-mail: mcherry@ursuline.edu. *Application contact:* Melanie Steele, Director of Graduate Admission, 440-646-8146, Fax: 440-684-6138, E-mail: graduateadmissions@ursuline.edu.
Website: http://www.ursuline.edu/Academics/Graduate_Professional/Masters_Programs/MAP/index.html

Utah State University, School of Graduate Studies, Emma Eccles Jones College of Education and Human Services, Department of Special Education and Rehabilitation, Logan, UT 84322. Offers disability disciplines (PhD); rehabilitation counseling (MRC); special education (M Ed, MS, Ed S). *Program availability:* Part-time, online learning. *Degree requirements:* For master's, thesis (for some programs), internships (for some programs); for doctorate, comprehensive exam, thesis/dissertation. *Entrance requirements:* For master's and doctorate, GRE General Test, minimum GPA of 3.0. Additional exam requirements/recommendations for international students: Required—TOEFL (minimum score 550 paper-based). Electronic applications accepted. *Faculty research:* Applied behavior analysis, effective instructional practices, early childhood teacher training research, distance education, multicultural rehabilitation.

Valdosta State University, Department of Communication Sciences and Disorders, Valdosta, GA 31698. Offers communication disorders (M Ed); communication sciences and disorders (SLPD); special education (MAT, Ed S). *Accreditation:* ASHA. *Degree requirements:* For master's, comprehensive exam. *Entrance requirements:* For master's, GRE or MAT. Additional exam requirements/recommendations for international students: Required—TOEFL. *Application deadline:* For fall admission, 3/1 for domestic and international students; for spring admission, 7/1 for domestic and international students. Application fee: $45. Electronic applications accepted. *Financial support:* Research assistantships, Federal Work-Study, scholarships/grants, and unspecified assistantships available. *Unit head:* Dr. Corine Myers-Jennings, Head, 229-219-1327, Fax: 229-219-1335, E-mail: cmjennin@valdosta.edu. *Application contact:* Tonya R. Crawford, Administrative Secretary, 229-219-1327, Fax: 229-245-3853, E-mail: tocrawford@valdosta.edu.
Website: https://www.valdosta.edu/colleges/education/communication-sciences-and-disorders/

Vanderbilt University, Peabody College, Department of Special Education, Nashville, TN 37240-1001. Offers M Ed. *Accreditation:* NCATE. *Program availability:* Part-time. *Faculty:* 26 full-time (18 women), 12 part-time/adjunct (10 women). *Students:* 96 full-time (87 women), 10 part-time (all women); includes 20 minority (4 Black or African American, non-Hispanic/Latino; 5 Asian, non-Hispanic/Latino; 3 Hispanic/Latino; 8 Two or more races, non-Hispanic/Latino), 2 international. Average age 24. 127 applicants, 58% accepted, 51 enrolled. In 2017, 43 master's awarded. *Degree requirements:* For master's, comprehensive exam, thesis optional. *Entrance requirements:* For master's, GRE General Test. Additional exam requirements/recommendations for international students: Required—TOEFL (minimum score 550 paper-based; 80 iBT). *Application deadline:* For fall admission, 12/31 priority date for domestic and international students; for spring admission, 11/1 priority date for domestic and international students. Applications are processed on a rolling basis. Application fee: $0. Electronic applications accepted. *Financial support:* Fellowships with partial tuition reimbursements, research assistantships with partial tuition reimbursements, teaching assistantships with partial tuition reimbursements, Federal Work-Study, institutionally sponsored loans, scholarships/grants, traineeships, health care benefits, tuition waivers (partial), and unspecified assistantships available. Support available to part-time students. Financial award application deadline: 1/15; financial award applicants required to submit CSS PROFILE or FAFSA. *Faculty research:* Early language and social skills development, learning and behavior disorders, autism and developmental/intellectual disabilities, low vision and blindness, giftedness and diversity. *Unit head:* Dr. Joseph Wehby, Chair, 615-322-8150, Fax: 615-343-1570, E-mail: joseph.wehby@vanderbilt.edu. *Application contact:* Alfred Brady, Admissions Coordinator, 615-322-8195, Fax: 615-343-1570, E-mail: alfred.l.brady@vanderbilt.edu.

Vanderbilt University, PhD Program in Special Education, Nashville, TN 37240-1001. Offers PhD. *Faculty:* 17 full-time (11 women). *Students:* 45 full-time (41 women); includes 7 minority (2 Asian, non-Hispanic/Latino; 2 Hispanic/Latino; 3 Two or more races, non-Hispanic/Latino), 1 international. Average age 31. 45 applicants, 13% accepted, 5 enrolled. In 2017, 8 doctorates awarded. *Degree requirements:* For doctorate, thesis/dissertation, qualifying examinations. *Entrance requirements:* For doctorate, GRE. Additional exam requirements/recommendations for international students: Required—TOEFL (minimum score 570 paper-based; 88 iBT). *Application deadline:* For fall admission, 12/1 for domestic and international students. Application fee: $0. Electronic applications accepted. *Expenses:* Contact institution. *Financial support:* Fellowships with full tuition reimbursements, research assistantships with full tuition reimbursements, teaching assistantships with full tuition reimbursements, Federal Work-Study, institutionally sponsored loans, traineeships, and health care benefits available. Financial award application deadline: 1/15; financial award applicants required to submit CSS PROFILE or FAFSA. *Faculty research:* Early language and social skills development, learning and behavior disorders, autism and developmental/intellectual disabilities, low vision and blindness, giftedness and diversity. *Unit head:* Dr. Joseph Wehby, Chair, 615-322-8150, Fax: 615-343-1570, E-mail: joseph.wehby@

vanderbilt.edu. *Application contact:* Dr. Robert Hodapp, Director of Graduate Studies, 615-322-8150, Fax: 615-343-1570, E-mail: robert.hodapp@vanderbilt.edu.

Vanderbilt University, School of Medicine, Department of Hearing and Speech Sciences, Nashville, TN 37240-1001. Offers audiology (Au D, PhD); education of the deaf (MDE); speech-language pathology (MS, PhD). *Accreditation:* ASHA. *Faculty:* 21 full-time (7 women). *Students:* 31 full-time (21 women); includes 2 minority (1 Hispanic/Latino; 1 Two or more races, non-Hispanic/Latino), 4 international. Average age 28. 21 applicants, 33% accepted, 4 enrolled. In 2017, 7 doctorates awarded. *Degree requirements:* For master's, thesis optional; for doctorate, thesis/dissertation, final and qualifying exams. *Entrance requirements:* For master's and doctorate, GRE General Test. Additional exam requirements/recommendations for international students: Required—TOEFL. *Application deadline:* For fall admission, 1/15 for domestic and international students. Application fee: $0. Electronic applications accepted. *Financial support:* Fellowships with full tuition reimbursements, research assistantships with full tuition reimbursements, career-related internships or fieldwork, institutionally sponsored loans, traineeships, and tuition waivers (full and partial) available. Financial award application deadline: 1/15; financial award applicants required to submit FAFSA. *Faculty research:* Child language. *Total annual research expenditures:* $3.6 million. *Unit head:* Dr. Anne Marie Tharpe, Chair, 615-936-5103, Fax: 615-936-5014, E-mail: anne.m.tharpe@vanderbilt.edu. *Application contact:* Todd Ricketts, Director of Graduate Studies, 615-936-5103, Fax: 615-936-6114, E-mail: todd.a.ricketts@vanderbilt.edu.
Website: https://ww2.mc.vanderbilt.edu/ghss/

Virginia Commonwealth University, Graduate School, School of Education, Doctoral Program in Education, Richmond, VA 23284-9005. Offers art education (PhD); counselor education and supervision (PhD); curriculum, culture and change (PhD); educational leadership (PhD); educational psychology (PhD); leadership (Ed D); research and evaluation (PhD); special education and disability leadership (PhD); sport leadership (PhD); urban services leadership (PhD). *Accreditation:* NCATE. *Program availability:* Part-time. *Degree requirements:* For doctorate, thesis/dissertation. *Entrance requirements:* For doctorate, GRE (for PhD), MAT (for Ed D), interview, master's degree, writing sample. Additional exam requirements/recommendations for international students: Required—TOEFL (minimum score 600 paper-based; 100 iBT). Electronic applications accepted.

Virginia Commonwealth University, Graduate School, School of Education, Program in Special Education, Richmond, VA 23284-9005. Offers early childhood (M Ed); general education (M Ed); severe disabilities (M Ed). *Accreditation:* NCATE. *Degree requirements:* For master's, comprehensive exam. *Entrance requirements:* For master's, GRE General Test or MAT. Additional exam requirements/recommendations for international students: Required—TOEFL (minimum score 600 paper-based; 100 iBT). Electronic applications accepted.

Viterbo University, Graduate Programs in Education, La Crosse, WI 54601-4797. Offers cross-categorical special education (Certificate); director of instruction (Certificate); director of special education and pupil services (Certificate); early childhood (Certificate); education (MAE); literacy coaching (Certificate); PreK-12 principal/supervisor of special education (Certificate); principal (Certificate); reading specialist endorsement (Certificate); reading teacher (Certificate); reading teacher 5-12 endorsement (Certificate); reading teacher K-8 endorsement (Certificate); superintendent (Certificate); talented and gifted endorsement (Certificate); Wisconsin school business administrator (Certificate). Weekend courses available in summer. *Accreditation:* NCATE. *Program availability:* Part-time, evening/weekend. *Degree requirements:* For master's, comprehensive exam, thesis, 30 credits of course work. *Entrance requirements:* For master's, BS, transcripts, teaching license, written narrative. Electronic applications accepted. *Expenses:* Contact institution.

Wagner College, Division of Graduate Studies, Education Department, Program in Childhood Education/Students with Disabilities, Staten Island, NY 10301-4495. Offers childhood education (MS Ed). *Program availability:* Part-time, evening/weekend. *Faculty:* 4 full-time (all women), 1 part-time/adjunct (0 women). *Students:* 3 full-time (all women), 5 part-time (4 women); includes 3 minority (1 Black or African American, non-Hispanic/Latino; 1 Asian, non-Hispanic/Latino; 1 Hispanic/Latino). Average age 27. 11 applicants, 45% accepted, 2 enrolled. In 2017, 8 master's awarded. *Degree requirements:* For master's, thesis (for some programs), passage of New York State certification exams before student teaching. *Entrance requirements:* For master's, GRE, minimum GPA of 3.0, interview, recommendations. Additional exam requirements/recommendations for international students: Required—TOEFL (minimum score 550 paper-based; 79 iBT), IELTS (minimum score 6.5). *Application deadline:* For fall admission, 2/15 priority date for domestic and international students. Applications are processed on a rolling basis. Application fee: $60. Electronic applications accepted. *Expenses:* $1,140 per credit. *Financial support:* Unspecified assistantships available. Financial award applicants required to submit FAFSA. *Unit head:* Dr. Jason Fitzgerald, Department Chair, 718-420-4129, Fax: 718-390-3456, E-mail: jason.fitzgerald@wagner.edu. *Application contact:* Patricia Clancy, Assistant Director of Enrollment, 718-420-4464, Fax: 718-390-3105, E-mail: patricia.clancy@wagner.edu.
Website: http://www.wagner.edu/education

Wagner College, Division of Graduate Studies, Education Department, Program in Early Childhood Education/Students with Disabilities (Birth-Grade 2), Staten Island, NY 10301-4495. Offers MS Ed. *Program availability:* Part-time, evening/weekend. *Faculty:* 4 full-time (3 women), 1 (woman) part-time/adjunct. *Students:* 7 full-time (all women), 1 (woman) part-time; includes 2 minority (1 Asian, non-Hispanic/Latino; 1 Two or more races, non-Hispanic/Latino). Average age 23. 2 applicants, 50% accepted, 1 enrolled. In 2017, 4 master's awarded. *Degree requirements:* For master's, thesis. *Entrance requirements:* For master's, minimum GPA of 3.0, valid initial NY State Certificate or equivalent, interview, recommendations. Additional exam requirements/recommendations for international students: Recommended—TOEFL (minimum score 550 paper-based; 79 iBT), IELTS (minimum score 6.5). *Application deadline:* For fall admission, 4/15 priority date for domestic and international students; for spring admission, 10/15 priority date for domestic and international students. Applications are processed on a rolling basis. Application fee: $60. Electronic applications accepted. *Expenses:* $1,140 per credit. *Financial support:* Unspecified assistantships and alumni fellowship available. Financial award application deadline: 4/15; financial award applicants required to submit FAFSA. *Unit head:* Dr. Jason Fitzgerald, Department Chair, 718-420-4129, Fax: 718-390-3456, E-mail: jason.fitzgerald@wagner.edu. *Application contact:* Patricia Clancy, Assistant Director of Enrollment, 718-420-4464, Fax: 718-390-3105, E-mail: patricia.clancy@wagner.edu.
Website: http://www.wagner.edu/education

Wagner College, Division of Graduate Studies, Education Department, Program in Secondary Education/Students with Disabilities, Staten Island, NY 10301-4495. Offers secondary education 7-12 (MS Ed), including language arts, languages other than English, mathematics and technology, science and technology, social studies. *Program availability:* Evening/weekend. *Faculty:* 2 full-time (1 woman), 7 part-time/adjunct (3 women). *Students:* 17 full-time (14 women), 6 part-time (4 women); includes 2 minority (1 Black or African American, non-Hispanic/Latino; 1 Asian, non-Hispanic/Latino). Average age 24. 15 applicants, 80% accepted, 11 enrolled. In 2017, 8 master's awarded. *Degree requirements:* For master's, thesis (for some programs), completion of

Special Education

state certification exams before student teaching. *Entrance requirements:* For master's, GRE, minimum GPA of 3.0, interview, recommendations. Additional exam requirements/recommendations for international students: Required—TOEFL (minimum score 550 paper-based; 79 iBT), IELTS (minimum score 6.5). *Application deadline:* For fall admission, 12/1 priority date for domestic and international students. Application fee: $60. Electronic applications accepted. *Expenses:* Contact institution. *Financial support:* Unspecified assistantships and alumni fellowship available. Financial award application deadline: 2/15; financial award applicants required to submit FAFSA. *Unit head:* Dr. Jason Fitzgerald, Department Chair, 718-420-4129, Fax: 718-390-3456, E-mail: jason.fitzgerald@wagner.edu. *Application contact:* Patricia Clancy, Assistant Director of Enrollment, 718-420-4464, Fax: 718-390-3105, E-mail: patricia.clancy@wagner.edu. Website: http://www.wagner.edu/education

Walden University, Graduate Programs, Richard W. Riley College of Education and Leadership, Minneapolis, MN 55401. Offers adult education (Post-Master's Certificate); adult learning (Graduate Certificate); college teaching and learning (Graduate Certificate); community college leadership (Ed D); curriculum, instruction and assessment (Ed D, Ed S, Graduate Certificate); developmental education (Graduate Certificate); early childhood administration, management, and leadership (Graduate Certificate); early childhood education (Ed D, Ed S); early childhood public policy and advocacy (Graduate Certificate); early childhood studies (MS), including administration, management and leadership, early childhood public policy and advocacy, teaching adults in the early childhood field, teaching and diversity in early childhood education; education (MS, PhD), including adolescent literacy and learning (MS), curriculum, instruction, and assessment (grades K-12) (MS), curriculum, instruction, assessment, and evaluation (PhD), early childhood leadership and advocacy (PhD), early childhood special education (PhD), educational leadership (MS), educational leadership and administration (principal preparation) (MS), educational technology and design (PhD), elementary reading and literacy (PreK-6) (MS), elementary reading and mathematics (grades K-6) (MS), global and comparative education (PhD), higher education leadership management and policy (PhD), integrating technology in the classroom (grades K-12) (MS), learning, instruction and innovation (PhD), mathematics (grades 5-8) (MS), mathematics (grades K-6) (MS), mathematics and science (grades K-8) (MS), organizational research, assessment, and evaluation (PhD), reading and literacy with a reading K-12 endorsement (MS), reading literacy assessment and evaluation (PhD), science (grades K-8) (MS), special education (non-licensure) (grades K-12) (MS), teacher leadership (grades K-12) (MS), teaching English language learners (grades K-12) (MS); educational administration and leadership (Ed D); educational leadership and administration (principal preparation) (Ed S); educational technology (Ed D, Ed S, Post Master's Certificate); elementary reading and literacy (Graduate Certificate); engaging culturally diverse learners (Graduate Certificate); enrollment management and institutional marketing (Graduate Certificate); higher education (MS), including adult learning, college teaching and learning, enrollment management and institutional marketing, global higher education, leadership for student success, online and distance learning; higher education and adult learning (Ed D); higher education leadership and management (Ed D); higher education leadership for student success (Graduate Certificate); instructional design and technology (MS, Postbaccalaureate Certificate), including general program (MS), online learning (MS), training and performance improvement (MS); integrating technology in the classroom (Graduate Certificate); mathematics 5-8 (Graduate Certificate); mathematics K-6 (Graduate Certificate); online teaching for adult educators (Graduate Certificate); reading, literacy, and assessment (Ed D, Ed S); science K-8 (Graduate Certificate); special education (Ed D, Ed S, Graduate Certificate); special education (K-age 21) (MAT); teacher leadership (Graduate Certificate); teaching adults English as a second language (Graduate Certificate); teaching adults in the early childhood field (Graduate Certificate); teaching and diversity in early childhood education (Graduate Certificate); teaching English language learners (grades K-12) (Graduate Certificate); teaching K-12 students online (Graduate Certificate). *Accreditation:* NCATE. *Program availability:* Part-time, evening/weekend, online only, 100% online. *Degree requirements:* For doctorate, thesis/dissertation (for some programs), residency; for other advanced degree, residency (for some programs). *Entrance requirements:* For master's, bachelor's degree or higher; minimum GPA of 2.5; official transcripts; goal statement (for some programs); access to computer and Internet; for doctorate, master's degree or higher; three years of related professional or academic experience (preferred); minimum GPA of 3.0; goal statement and current resume (for select programs); official transcripts; access to computer and Internet; for other advanced degree, relevant work experience; access to computer and Internet. Additional exam requirements/recommendations for international students: Required—TOEFL (minimum score 550 paper-based, 79 iBT), IELTS (minimum score 6.5), Michigan English Language Assessment Battery (minimum score 82), or PTE (minimum score 53). Electronic applications accepted.

Walla Walla University, Graduate Studies, School of Education and Psychology, College Place, WA 99324. Offers curriculum and instruction (M Ed, MAT); educational leadership (M Ed, MAT); literacy instruction (M Ed, MAT); special education (M Ed, MAT). *Program availability:* Part-time. *Entrance requirements:* For master's, GRE General Test, minimum GPA of 2.75. Additional exam requirements/recommendations for international students: Required—TOEFL (minimum score 550 paper-based; 79 iBT). *Application deadline:* For fall admission, 4/1 priority date for domestic students. Applications are processed on a rolling basis. Application fee: $50. Electronic applications accepted. *Financial support:* Research assistantships, teaching assistantships, Federal Work-Study, and tuition waivers (partial) available. Support available to part-time students. Financial award application deadline: 4/30; financial award applicants required to submit FAFSA. *Faculty research:* Admissions/retention, instructional psychology, moral development, teaching of reading. *Unit head:* Dr. Debbie Muthersbaugh, Dean, 509-527-2212, Fax: 509-527-2248, E-mail: debbie.muthersbaugh@wallawalla.edu. *Application contact:* Dr. Joe G. Galusha, Dean of Graduate Studies, 509-527-2421, Fax: 509-527-2237, E-mail: joe.galusha@wallawalla.edu.
Website: https://wallawalla.edu/academics/areas-of-study/undergraduate-programs/education-and-psychology/

Washburn University, College of Arts and Sciences, Department of Education, Topeka, KS 66621. Offers curriculum and instruction (M Ed); educational leadership (M Ed); reading (M Ed); special education (M Ed). *Accreditation:* NCATE. *Program availability:* Part-time. *Degree requirements:* For master's, comprehensive exam, thesis or alternative, portfolio, comprehensive paper, or action research project. *Entrance requirements:* For master's, department exam, GRE General Test, or MAT, minimum GPA of 3.0 in graduate coursework or last 60 hours of undergraduate coursework. Additional exam requirements/recommendations for international students: Required—TOEFL (minimum score 80 iBT). *Faculty research:* Reading/literature/literacy, foundations, special education, diversity, teaching and technology.

Washington State University, College of Education, Department of Teaching and Learning, Pullman, WA 99164-2132. Offers cultural studies and social thought in education (PhD); curriculum and instruction (Ed M, MA); English language learners (Ed M, MA); language, literacy and technology (PhD); literacy education (Ed M, MA); mathematics education (PhD); special education (Ed M, MA, PhD); teacher leadership (Ed D); teaching (MIT), including elementary education, secondary education. Programs

offered at the Pullman, Spokane, Tri-cities, Vancouver and Global (online) campuses. *Program availability:* Part-time, online learning. *Degree requirements:* For master's, comprehensive exam, thesis, oral or written exam; for doctorate, comprehensive exam, thesis/dissertation, oral and written exam. *Entrance requirements:* For master's, GRE General Test, minimum GPA of 3.0, 3 letters of recommendation, letter of intent, transcripts, resume/curriculum vitae; for doctorate, GRE General Test, minimum GPA of 3.0, 3 letters of recommendation, letter of intent, transcripts, writing sample, resume/curriculum vitae. Additional exam requirements/recommendations for international students: Required—TOEFL (minimum score 550 paper-based; 80 iBT). Electronic applications accepted. *Faculty research:* Intersection of gender, youth cultures and schooling; examination of ideology of power in children's literature; early childhood special education; analyzing pre-service and in-service teacher development; second language acquisition.

Washington University in St. Louis, School of Medicine, Program in Audiology and Communication Sciences, St. Louis, MO 63110. Offers audiology (Au D); deaf education (MS); speech and hearing sciences (PhD). *Accreditation:* ASHA (one or more programs are accredited). *Faculty:* 22 full-time (12 women), 18 part-time/adjunct (12 women). *Students:* 67 full-time (61 women). Average age 24. 129 applicants, 34% accepted, 20 enrolled. In 2017, 8 master's, 14 doctorates awarded. *Degree requirements:* For master's, comprehensive exam, thesis, independent study project, oral exam; for doctorate, comprehensive exam, thesis/dissertation, capstone project. *Entrance requirements:* For master's and doctorate, GRE General Test, minimum B average in previous college/university coursework (recommended). Additional exam requirements/recommendations for international students: Required—TOEFL (minimum score 100 iBT). *Application deadline:* For fall admission, 2/15 for domestic and international students. Application fee: $25. Electronic applications accepted. *Expenses:* $38,000 per academic year (all-inclusive). *Financial support:* In 2017–18, 67 students received support, including 67 fellowships with full and partial tuition reimbursements available (averaging $17,879 per year), 6 teaching assistantships with partial tuition reimbursements available (averaging $1,500 per year); Federal Work-Study, scholarships/grants, traineeships, health care benefits, tuition waivers (partial), and unspecified assistantships also available. Financial award application deadline: 2/15; financial award applicants required to submit FAFSA. *Faculty research:* Audiology, deaf education, speech and hearing sciences, sensory neuroscience. *Unit head:* Dr. William W. Clark, Program Director, 314-747-0104, Fax: 314-747-0105. *Application contact:* Beth Elliott, Director, Finance and Student/Academic Affairs, 314-747-0104, Fax: 314-747-0105, E-mail: elliottb@wustl.edu.
Website: http://pacs.wustl.edu/

Wayland Baptist University, Graduate Programs, Program in Education, Plainview, TX 79072-6998. Offers education administration (M Ed); education diagnostics (M Ed); education literacy (M Ed); elementary certification (M Ed); English (M Ed); English as a second language (M Ed); higher education administration (M Ed); human resources (M Ed); instructional leadership (M Ed); instructional technology (M Ed); leadership training and development (M Ed); science education (M Ed); secondary certification (M Ed); social studies (M Ed); special education (M Ed); sports administration and management (M Ed). *Program availability:* Part-time, evening/weekend, 100% online. *Faculty:* 33 full-time (17 women), 28 part-time/adjunct (17 women). *Students:* 16 full-time (13 women), 221 part-time (143 women); includes 97 minority (26 Black or African American, non-Hispanic/Latino; 1 American Indian or Alaska Native, non-Hispanic/Latino; 5 Asian, non-Hispanic/Latino; 54 Hispanic/Latino; 11 Two or more races, non-Hispanic/Latino), 1 international. Average age 39. 32 applicants, 97% accepted, 23 enrolled. In 2017, 78 master's awarded. *Degree requirements:* For master's, comprehensive exam, capstone course. *Entrance requirements:* For master's, GRE, GMAT or MAT. Additional exam requirements/recommendations for international students: Required—TOEFL (minimum score 500 paper-based; 61 iBT). *Application deadline:* Applications are processed on a rolling basis. Application fee: $50. Electronic applications accepted. *Expenses:* Tuition: Full-time $11,250; part-time $625 per credit hour. *Required fees:* $1200. *Financial support:* Federal Work-Study, institutionally sponsored loans, and scholarships/grants available. Support available to part-time students. Financial award application deadline: 5/1; financial award applicants required to submit FAFSA. *Unit head:* Dr. Gene Whitfill, Dean, 806-291-1047, Fax: 806-291-1951, E-mail: whitfillg@wbu.edu. *Application contact:* Amanda Stanton, Coordinator of Graduate Studies, 806-291-3423, Fax: 806-291-1950, E-mail: stanton@wbu.edu.

Waynesburg University, Graduate and Professional Studies, Canonsburg, PA 15370. Offers business (MBA), including energy management, finance, health systems, human resources, leadership, market development; counseling (MA), including addictions counseling, clinical mental health; counselor education and supervision (PhD); criminal investigation (MA); education (M Ed), including autism, curriculum and instruction, educational leadership, online teaching; nursing (MSN), including administration, education, informatics; nursing practice (DNP); special education (M Ed); technology (M Ed); MSN/MBA. *Accreditation:* AACN. *Program availability:* Part-time, evening/weekend. *Degree requirements:* For doctorate, thesis/dissertation. *Entrance requirements:* Additional exam requirements/recommendations for international students: Required—TOEFL. Electronic applications accepted.

Wayne State College, School of Education and Counseling, Department of Counseling and Special Education, Program in Special Education, Wayne, NE 68787. Offers MSE. *Accreditation:* NCATE. *Program availability:* Part-time, evening/weekend. *Degree requirements:* For master's, comprehensive exam, thesis. *Entrance requirements:* For master's, GRE General Test, minimum GPA of 3.0. Additional exam requirements/recommendations for international students: Required—TOEFL (minimum score 550 paper-based). Electronic applications accepted.

Wayne State University, College of Education, Division of Teacher Education, Detroit, MI 48202. Offers art education (M Ed); bilingual/bicultural education (Certificate); curriculum and instruction (Ed D, PhD, Ed S), including English as a second language (MAT, Ed D, Ed S), K-12 curriculum (PhD); elementary education (MAT), including bilingual/bicultural education (M Ed, MAT), early childhood education (M Ed, MAT), English as a second language (MAT, Ed D, Ed S), foreign language education, science education (M Ed, MAT), special education (M Ed, MAT); elementary mathematics specialist (Certificate); English as a second language (Certificate); reading (M Ed, Ed S); reading, language and literature (Ed D); secondary education (MAT), including bilingual/bicultural education (M Ed, MAT), early childhood education (M Ed, MAT), English as a second language (MAT, Ed D, Ed S), English education, foreign language education, mathematics education (M Ed, MAT), science education (M Ed, MAT), social studies education (M Ed, MAT); special education (MAT), including career and technical education; teaching and learning (M Ed, MAT), including bilingual/bicultural education (M Ed, MAT), early childhood education (M Ed, MAT), elementary education, foreign language, mathematics education (M Ed, MAT), science education (M Ed, MAT), social studies education (M Ed, MAT), special education (M Ed, MAT). *Program availability:* Part-time, blended/hybrid learning. *Faculty:* 22. *Students:* 126 full-time (96 women), 317 part-time (258 women); includes 134 minority (95 Black or African American, non-Hispanic/Latino; 1 American Indian or Alaska Native, non-Hispanic/Latino; 8 Asian, non-Hispanic/Latino; 17 Hispanic/Latino; 1 Native Hawaiian or other Pacific Islander, non-Hispanic/Latino; 12 Two or more races, non-Hispanic/Latino), 13 international. Average age 37. 260

applicants, 33% accepted, 57 enrolled. In 2017, 111 master's, 13 doctorates, 7 other advanced degrees awarded. *Degree requirements:* For master's, essay or project (for some M Ed programs), professional field experience (for MAT programs); for doctorate, thesis/dissertation. *Entrance requirements:* For master's, Michigan Test for Teacher Certification (for most programs), verification of participation in group work with children (for MAT programs), Michigan State Police criminal background check; for doctorate, minimum undergraduate GPA of 3.0, graduate 3.5; interview; curriculum vitae; references; master's degree (for most programs). Additional exam requirements/recommendations for international students: Required—TOEFL (minimum score 550 paper-based; 79 iBT), TWE (minimum score 5.5); Recommended—IELTS (minimum score 6.5). *Application deadline:* For fall admission, 6/1 priority date for domestic students, 5/1 priority date for international students; for winter admission, 10/1 priority date for domestic students, 9/1 priority date for international students; for spring admission, 2/1 priority date for domestic students, 1/1 priority date for international students. Applications are processed on a rolling basis. Application fee: $50. Electronic applications accepted. *Expenses:* Tuition, state resident: full-time $10,224; part-time $638.98 per credit hour. Tuition, nonresident: full-time $22,145; part-time $1384.04 per credit hour. Tuition and fees vary according to course load and program. *Financial support:* In 2017–18, 78 students received support, including 4 fellowships (averaging $13,500 per year), 1 research assistantship with tuition reimbursement available (averaging $16,000 per year); Federal Work-Study, scholarships/grants, and unspecified assistantships also available. Support available to part-time students. Financial award applicants required to submit FAFSA. *Faculty research:* Improving students' skill achievement in mathematics, improving elementary children's understanding of informational text, teachers' use of their pedagogical and mathematical knowledge in the interactive work of teaching, the intersection of identity construction in teaching and learning, identifying effective methods of literacy instruction and assessments for bilingual students in elementary language arts classrooms. *Unit head:* Dr. Thomas Edwards, Interim Associate Dean for Teacher Education, 313-577-3886, E-mail: t.g.edwards@wayne.edu. *Application contact:* 313-577-0902, E-mail: askcoe@wayne.edu.
Website: http://coe.wayne.edu/ted/index.php

Webster University, School of Education, Department of Multidisciplinary Studies, St. Louis, MO 63119-3194. Offers applied educational psychology (MA, Ed S); communication arts (MA); early childhood education (MA, MAT); education and innovation (MA); educational technology (MET); elementary education (MAT); mathematics for educators (MA); middle school education (MAT); multidisciplinary studies (MAT); multimodal literacy for global impact (MA); reading (MA); secondary school education (MAT); special education (MA, MAT); teaching English as a second language (MA); transformative learning in the global community (Ed S). *Program availability:* Part-time. *Entrance requirements:* For master's, minimum GPA of 2.5. Additional exam requirements/recommendations for international students: Required—TOEFL.

West Chester University of Pennsylvania, College of Education and Social Work, Department of Special Education, West Chester, PA 19383. Offers autism (Certificate); special education (Teaching Certificate); special education (M Ed); universal design for learning and assistive technology (Certificate). *Accreditation:* NCATE. *Program availability:* Part-time, 100% online. *Students:* 13 full-time (11 women), 182 part-time (163 women); includes 13 minority (5 Black or African American, non-Hispanic/Latino; 4 Asian, non-Hispanic/Latino; 4 Two or more races, non-Hispanic/Latino). Average age 30. 101 applicants, 85% accepted, 61 enrolled. In 2017, 43 master's, 27 Certificates awarded. *Degree requirements:* For master's, minimum GPA of 3.0, action research; for other advanced degree, minimum GPA of 3.0; modified student teaching. *Entrance requirements:* For master's, GRE if GPA is below 3.0, two letters of recommendation; for other advanced degree, GRE if GPA is below 3.0. Additional exam requirements/recommendations for international students: Required—TOEFL or IELTS. *Application deadline:* For fall admission, 5/15 for international students; for spring admission, 10/15 for international students. Applications are processed on a rolling basis. Application fee: $50. Electronic applications accepted. *Expenses:* Tuition, state resident: full-time $9000; part-time $500 per credit. Tuition, nonresident: full-time $13,500; part-time $750 per credit. *Required fees:* $2959; $149.79 per credit. *Financial support:* Scholarships/grants and unspecified assistantships available. Financial award application deadline: 2/15; financial award applicants required to submit FAFSA. *Faculty research:* Instructional strategies for students with moderate to severe disabilities; family involvement for families of students with disabilities; instructional strategies for students with autism; math instruction for students with learning disabilities; transitions for students with disabilities; behavior management for students with behavior disorders. *Unit head:* Dr. Beatrice Adera, Interim Chairperson, 610-436-0040, Fax: 610-436-3102, E-mail: badera@wcupa.edu. *Application contact:* Dr. S. Christy Hicks, Graduate Coordinator, 610-436-3067, E-mail: shicks@wcupa.edu.
Website: http://www.wcupa.edu/education-socialWork/specialEducation/

Western Connecticut State University, Division of Graduate Studies, School of Professional Studies, Department of Education and Educational Psychology, Special Education Option, Danbury, CT 06810-6885. Offers MS. *Program availability:* Part-time. *Degree requirements:* For master's, thesis or research project. *Entrance requirements:* For master's, minimum GPA of 2.8, teaching certificate. Additional exam requirements/recommendations for international students: Recommended—TOEFL (minimum score 550 paper-based; 79 iBT), IELTS (minimum score 6). *Expenses:* Tuition, state resident: full-time $6757; part-time $374 per credit hour. Tuition, nonresident: full-time $18,102; part-time $374 per credit hour. *Required fees:* $4994; $190 per credit hour. $60 per term. Tuition and fees vary according to degree level and program. *Faculty research:* Education and development of exceptional, gifted, talented, and disabled students in a regular (mainstream) classroom.

Western Governors University, Teachers College, Salt Lake City, UT 84107. Offers curriculum and instruction (MS); educational leadership (MS); educational studies (MA); educational studies (5-12) (MA), including mathematics; elementary education (K-8) (MAT, Postbaccalaureate Certificate); elementary education (PreK-8) (MAT); English language learning (K-12) (MA); instructional design (MAT); learning and technology (M Ed, MA); management and innovation (M Ed); mathematics (5-12) (MAT, Postbaccalaureate Certificate); mathematics (5-9) (MAT, Postbaccalaureate Certificate); mathematics education (5-12) (MA); mathematics education (5-9) (MA); mathematics education (K-6) (MA); measurement and evaluation (M Ed); science (5-12) (Postbaccalaureate Certificate); science (5-9) (MAT, Postbaccalaureate Certificate); science education (5-12) (MA), including biology, chemistry, geology, physics; science education (5-9) (MA); social science (5-12) (MAT, Postbaccalaureate Certificate); special education (MAT, MS). *Accreditation:* NCATE. *Program availability:* Evening/weekend, online learning. *Degree requirements:* For master's, capstone project. *Entrance requirements:* For master's and Postbaccalaureate Certificate, Readiness Assessment, transcripts. Additional exam requirements/recommendations for international students: Required—TOEFL (minimum score 450 paper-based; 80 iBT). Electronic applications accepted. *Expenses:* Contact institution.

Western Illinois University, School of Graduate Studies, College of Education and Human Services, Department of Curriculum and Instruction, Program in Special

Education, Macomb, IL 61455-1390. Offers MS Ed. *Accreditation:* NCATE. *Program availability:* Part-time. *Students:* 18 part-time (17 women). Average age 34. 3 applicants, 100% accepted, 2 enrolled. In 2017, 5 master's awarded. *Degree requirements:* For master's, comprehensive exam, thesis or alternative. *Entrance requirements:* For master's, teacher certification. Additional exam requirements/recommendations for international students: Required—TOEFL (minimum score 550 paper-based; 80 iBT). *Application deadline:* Applications are processed on a rolling basis. Application fee: $30. Electronic applications accepted. *Financial support:* Applicants required to submit FAFSA. *Unit head:* Dr. Barry Witten, Interim Chairperson, 309-298-1961. *Application contact:* Dr. Nancy Parsons, Associate Provost and Director of Graduate Studies, 309-298-1806, Fax: 309-298-2345, E-mail: grad-office@wiu.edu.
Website: http://www.wiu.edu/coehs/curriculum_and_instruction/prospective_students/spedgrad.php

Western Kentucky University, Graduate Studies, College of Education and Behavioral Sciences, School of Teacher Education, Bowling Green, KY 42101. Offers elementary education (MAE, Ed S); exceptional education: learning and behavioral disorders (MAE); exceptional education: moderate and severe disabilities (MAE); instructional design (MS); interdisciplinary early childhood education (MAE); library media education (MS); literacy education (MAE); middle grades education (MAE); secondary education (MAE, Ed S). *Program availability:* Part-time, evening/weekend, online learning. *Degree requirements:* For master's, comprehensive exam. *Entrance requirements:* For master's, GRE General Test. Additional exam requirements/recommendations for international students: Required—TOEFL (minimum score 555 paper-based; 79 iBT). *Faculty research:* Teacher preparation in moderate/severe disabilities.

Western Michigan University, Graduate College, College of Education and Human Development, Department of Special Education and Literacy Studies, Kalamazoo, MI 49008. Offers literacy studies (MA); special education (MA, Ed D), including clinical teacher (MA); teaching children with visual impairments (MA).

Western New Mexico University, Graduate Division, School of Education, Silver City, NM 88062-0680. Offers bilingual education (MAT); educational leadership (MA); elementary education (MAT); reading (MAT); secondary education (MAT); special education (MAT); TESOL (teaching English to speakers of other languages) (MAT). *Accreditation:* NCATE. *Program availability:* Part-time, online learning. *Degree requirements:* For master's, comprehensive exam. *Entrance requirements:* For master's, minimum GPA of 3.0 in last 64 hours of undergraduate study. Additional exam requirements/recommendations for international students: Required—TOEFL (minimum score 550 paper-based; 79 iBT). Electronic applications accepted. *Faculty research:* International education, electronic reading assessment, developing STEM teachers.

Western Oregon University, Graduate Programs, College of Education, Division of Special Education, Program in Deaf Education, Monmouth, OR 97361. Offers MS Ed. *Accreditation:* NCATE. *Program availability:* Part-time, evening/weekend. *Degree requirements:* For master's, thesis, portfolio. *Entrance requirements:* For master's, California Basic Educational Skills Test or PRAXIS, GRE General Test or MAT, interview, minimum GPA of 3.0, teaching license. Additional exam requirements/recommendations for international students: Required—TOEFL (minimum score 550 paper-based; 79 iBT), IELTS (minimum score 6.5). *Faculty research:* Effects of infant massage on the interactions between high-risk infants and their caregivers, work sample methodology.

Western Oregon University, Graduate Programs, College of Education, Division of Special Education, Special Education Program, Monmouth, OR 97361. Offers MS Ed. *Program availability:* Part-time, evening/weekend. *Degree requirements:* For master's, comprehensive exam (for some programs), thesis optional, oral exam, portfolio, written exam. *Entrance requirements:* For master's, California Basic Educational Skills Test or PRAXIS, GRE General Test or MAT, interview, minimum GPA of 3.0, teaching license. Additional exam requirements/recommendations for international students: Required—TOEFL (minimum score 550 paper-based; 79 iBT), IELTS (minimum score 6.5). *Faculty research:* Interpreter teacher training, hearing disabilities, mental retardation.

Westfield State University, College of Graduate and Continuing Education, Department of Education, Program in Special Education, Westfield, MA 01086. Offers moderate disabilities, 5-12 (M Ed); moderate disabilities, preK-8 (M Ed). *Accreditation:* NCATE. *Program availability:* Part-time, evening/weekend. *Students:* 1 (woman) full-time, 24 part-time (20 women); includes 2 minority (1 Hispanic/Latino; 1 Two or more races, non-Hispanic/Latino). Average age 31. 9 applicants, 100% accepted, 8 enrolled. In 2017, 12 master's awarded. *Degree requirements:* For master's, comprehensive exam, practicum. *Entrance requirements:* For master's, GRE General Test or MAT, minimum undergraduate GPA of 2.8. Additional exam requirements/recommendations for international students: Recommended—TOEFL (minimum score 550 paper-based; 79 iBT). *Application deadline:* For fall admission, 7/1 for domestic students; for spring admission, 11/1 for domestic students; for summer admission, 4/1 for domestic students. Applications are processed on a rolling basis. Application fee: $50. *Expenses:* Tuition, state resident: part-time $332 per credit. Tuition, nonresident: part-time $332 per credit. *Required fees:* $75 per semester. Tuition and fees vary according to program. *Financial support:* Unspecified assistantships and SOS scholarships (for education majors only) available. Financial award application deadline: 3/1; financial award applicants required to submit FAFSA. *Unit head:* Dr. Laura Baker, Department Chair, 413-572-5324, E-mail: lbaker@westfield.ma.edu. *Application contact:* Shelly Henrichon, Coordinator of College of Graduate and Continuing Education Admissions, 413-572-8022, Fax: 413-572-5227, E-mail: mhenrichon@westfield.ma.edu.

West Liberty University, College of Education and Human Performance, West Liberty, WV 26074. Offers community education research and leadership (MA Ed); innovative instruction (MA Ed); leadership in disability services (MA Ed); leadership studies (MA Ed); multi-categorical special education (MA Ed); reading specialist (MA Ed); sports leadership and coaching (MA Ed). *Accreditation:* NCATE. *Program availability:* Part-time, evening/weekend. *Students:* 18 full-time (12 women), 74 part-time (60 women); includes 2 minority (1 Black or African American, non-Hispanic/Latino; 1 Native Hawaiian or other Pacific Islander, non-Hispanic/Latino). Average age 32. *Degree requirements:* For master's, capstone experience. *Entrance requirements:* For master's, minimum GPA of 2.5 or 3.0 (depending on track). Additional exam requirements/recommendations for international students: Required—TOEFL. *Application deadline:* Applications are processed on a rolling basis. Application fee: $0. Electronic applications accepted. Tuition and fees vary according to course load and program. *Financial support:* Teaching assistantships and unspecified assistantships available. *Unit head:* Dr. Catherine Monteroso, Interim Dean, 304-336-8247, E-mail: cmonteroso@westliberty.edu. *Application contact:* Sara Sweeney, Director, Office of Graduate Studies, 304-336-8545, E-mail: sara.sweeney@westliberty.edu.
Website: http://westliberty.edu/education/

Westminster College, Graduate School, Program in Special Education and Reading Specialist, New Wilmington, PA 16172-0001. Offers M Ed. *Program availability:* Part-time, evening/weekend. *Degree requirements:* For master's, comprehensive exam, portfolio. *Entrance requirements:* For master's, minimum GPA of 3.0. *Application deadline:* For fall admission, 8/15 priority date for domestic students; for spring admission, 1/8 priority date for domestic students. Applications are processed on a

Special Education

rolling basis. Application fee: $35. *Expenses: Tuition:* Part-time $454 per semester hour. *Required fees:* $235.50 per course. Tuition and fees vary according to course load. *Financial support:* Career-related internships or fieldwork and scholarships/grants available. *Unit head:* Dr. Amy Camardese, Chair, 724-946-7183. *Application contact:* Dr. Amy Camardese, Chair, 724-946-7183.

West Virginia University, College of Education and Human Services, Morgantown, WV 26506. Offers audiology (Au D); autism spectrum disorder (MA); clinical rehabilitation and mental health counseling (MS); communication science and disorders (PhD); counseling (MA); counseling psychology (PhD); curriculum and instruction (Ed D); early childhood education (MA); early intervention (MA); education (PhD); educational leadership (MA, Ed D); educational leadership/public school administration (MA); educational psychology (MA, Ed D); elementary education (MA); gifted education (MA); higher education administration (MA, Ed D); higher education curriculum and teaching (MA); institutional design and technology (MA); instructional design and technology (Ed D); literacy education (MA); secondary education (MA); secondary education/ English (MA); special education (MA); speech pathology (MS). *Accreditation:* NCATE. *Program availability:* Part-time, evening/weekend, online learning. *Students:* 423 full-time (347 women), 367 part-time (339 women); includes 57 minority (14 Black or African American, non-Hispanic/Latino; 7 Asian, non-Hispanic/Latino; 20 Hispanic/Latino; 16 Two or more races, non-Hispanic/Latino), 13 international. *Degree requirements:* For master's, content exams; for doctorate, comprehensive exam, thesis/dissertation. *Entrance requirements:* Additional exam requirements/recommendations for international students: Required—TOEFL (minimum score 500 paper-based; 61 iBT). *Application deadline:* For fall admission, 8/1 for domestic students; for spring admission, 1/1 for domestic students; for summer admission, 5/1 for domestic students. Application fee: $60. Electronic applications accepted. *Expenses:* Tuition, state resident: full-time $9450. Tuition, nonresident: full-time $24,390. *Financial support:* Fellowships, research assistantships, teaching assistantships, career-related internships or fieldwork, Federal Work-Study, institutionally sponsored loans, health care benefits, tuition waivers (full and partial), and administrative assistantships available. Financial award applicants required to submit FAFSA. *Faculty research:* Internet training and integration for teachers, rural education, teacher preparation, organization of schools, evaluation of personnel. *Unit head:* Dr. Gypsy Denzine, Dean, 304-293-5703, Fax: 304-293-7565, E-mail: gypsy.denzine@mail.wvu.edu. *Application contact:* Dr. M. Cecil Smith, Associate Dean for Research and Graduate Education, 304-293-2174, Fax: 304-293-3802, E-mail: mcecil.smith@mail.wvu.edu.
Website: http://cehs.wvu.edu/

Whitworth University, School of Education, Graduate Studies in Education, Program in Special Education, Spokane, WA 99251-0001. Offers MAT. *Accreditation:* NCATE. *Program availability:* Part-time, evening/weekend. *Degree requirements:* For master's, comprehensive exam, internship, practicum, research project, or thesis. *Entrance requirements:* For master's, GRE General Test, MAT. Additional exam requirements/recommendations for international students: Required—TOEFL.

Wichita State University, Graduate School, College of Education, Department of Curriculum and Instruction, Wichita, KS 67260. Offers learning and instructional design (M Ed); special education (M Ed), including early childhood (M Ed, MAT), gifted, high incidence, low incidence; teaching (MAT), including early childhood (M Ed, MAT), middle level/secondary, transition to teaching. *Accreditation:* NCATE. *Program availability:* Part-time, evening/weekend, 100% online, blended/hybrid learning. *Entrance requirements:* For master's, MAT, minimum GPA of 2.75. *Unit head:* Dr. Kimberly McDowell, Department Head, 316-978-3322, E-mail: kim.mcdowell@wichita.edu. *Application contact:* Jordan Oleson, Admission Coordinator, 316-978-3095, Fax: 316-978-3253, E-mail: jordan.oleson@wichita.edu.

Widener University, School of Human Service Professions, Center for Education, Chester, PA 19013-5792. Offers adult education (M Ed); counseling in higher education (M Ed); counselor education (M Ed); early childhood education (M Ed); educational foundations (M Ed); educational leadership (M Ed); educational psychology (M Ed); elementary education (M Ed); English and language arts (M Ed); health education (M Ed); higher education leadership (Ed D); home and school visitor (M Ed); human sexuality (M Ed, PhD); mathematics education (M Ed); middle school education (M Ed); principalship (M Ed); reading and language arts (Ed D); reading education (M Ed); school administration (Ed D); science education (M Ed); social studies education (M Ed); special education (M Ed); technology education (M Ed). *Accreditation:* NCATE. *Program availability:* Part-time, evening/weekend. *Faculty:* 34 full-time (22 women), 37 part-time/adjunct (14 women). *Students:* 131 full-time (112 women), 244 part-time (179 women); includes 94 minority (58 Black or African American, non-Hispanic/Latino; 1 American Indian or Alaska Native, non-Hispanic/Latino; 1 Asian, non-Hispanic/Latino; 22 Hispanic/Latino; 12 Two or more races, non-Hispanic/Latino), 12 international. Average age 37. 140 applicants, 38% accepted, 26 enrolled. In 2017, 45 master's, 21 doctorates awarded. Terminal master's awarded for partial completion of doctoral program. *Degree requirements:* For doctorate, thesis/dissertation. *Entrance requirements:* For master's, minimum GPA of 2.5; for doctorate, GRE or MAT, minimum GPA of 2.0 (undergraduate), 3.5 (graduate). *Application deadline:* Applications are processed on a rolling basis. Application fee: $25 ($300 for international students). Electronic applications accepted. *Expenses:* Contact institution. *Financial support:* Career-related internships or fieldwork, tuition waivers (full and partial), and unspecified assistantships available. Support available to part-time students. Financial award application deadline: 5/1. *Faculty research:* Reading and cognition, adult education, technology education, educational leadership, special education. *Unit head:* Dr. Shawn Fitzgerald, Dean, 610-499-4294, Fax: 610-499-4623, E-mail: smfitzgerald@widener.edu. *Application contact:* Megan Kuft, Director of Graduate Admissions, 610-499-4124, E-mail: gradprograms@widener.edu.
Website: http://www.widener.edu/academics/schools/eics

Wilkes University, College of Graduate and Professional Studies, School of Education, Wilkes-Barre, PA 18766-0002. Offers educational development and strategies (MS Ed); educational leadership (MS Ed, Ed D); effective teaching (MS Ed); instructional media (MS Ed); instructional technology (MS Ed); international school leadership (MS Ed); international teaching and learning (MS Ed); literacy specialist (MS Ed); middle level education (MS Ed); online teaching (MS Ed); school business leadership (MS Ed); special education (MS Ed); teaching English to speakers of other languages (MS Ed). *Program availability:* Part-time, evening/weekend, 100% online, blended/hybrid learning. *Students:* 76 full-time (57 women), 1,586 part-time (1,204 women); includes 82 minority (10 Black or African American, non-Hispanic/Latino; 12 Asian, non-Hispanic/Latino; 41 Hispanic/Latino; 1 Native Hawaiian or other Pacific Islander, non-Hispanic/Latino; 18 Two or more races, non-Hispanic/Latino). Average age 34. In 2017, 619 master's, 23 doctorates awarded. *Entrance requirements:* Additional exam requirements/recommendations for international students: Required—TOEFL (minimum score 550 paper-based; 79 iBT). *Application deadline:* Applications are processed on a rolling basis. Application fee: $45 ($65 for international students). Electronic applications accepted. *Expenses:* Contact institution. *Financial support:* Unspecified assistantships available. Financial award application deadline: 3/1; financial award applicants required to submit FAFSA. *Unit head:* Dr. Rhonda Rabbitt, Dean, 570-408-4680, Fax: 570-408-7872, E-mail: rhonda.rabbitt@wilkes.edu. *Application contact:* Stephanie Wasmanski,

Associate Director of Graduate Admissions, 570-408-5535, Fax: 570-408-7846, E-mail: stephanie.wasmanski@wilkes.edu.
Website: http://www.wilkes.edu/academics/graduate-programs/masters-programs/graduate-education/index.aspx

William Carey University, School of Education, Hattiesburg, MS 39401. Offers art education (M Ed); art of teaching (M Ed); elementary education (M Ed and E S); English education (M Ed); gifted education (M Ed); history and social science (M Ed); mild/moderate disabilities (M Ed); secondary education (M Ed). *Accreditation:* NCATE. *Program availability:* Part-time. *Degree requirements:* For master's, comprehensive exam. *Entrance requirements:* For master's, GRE, MAT, minimum GPA of 2.5, Class A teacher's license. Additional exam requirements/recommendations for international students: Required—TOEFL (minimum score 550 paper-based).

William Paterson University of New Jersey, College of Education, Wayne, NJ 07470-8420. Offers curriculum and learning (M Ed); early childhood education (Certificate); educational leadership (M Ed); educational media specialist (Certificate); elementary education (MAT, Certificate); elementary education subject area (Certificate); higher education administration (MA); learning disabilities consultant (Certificate); literacy (M Ed); middle level education (M Ed); middle school education subject area (Certificate); professional counseling (M Ed); reading specialist (Certificate); school library media specialist (Certificate); school principal (Certificate); school supervisor (Certificate); secondary education (MAT); special education (M Ed); teacher of students with disabilities (Certificate). *Accreditation:* NCATE. *Program availability:* Part-time, evening/weekend. *Faculty:* 37 full-time (25 women), 21 part-time/adjunct (16 women). *Students:* 73 full-time (54 women), 480 part-time (409 women); includes 153 minority (48 Black or African American, non-Hispanic/Latino; 13 Asian, non-Hispanic/Latino; 81 Hispanic/Latino; 11 Two or more races, non-Hispanic/Latino), 1 international. Average age 35. 347 applicants, 87% accepted, 226 enrolled. In 2017, 136 master's awarded. *Degree requirements:* For master's, comprehensive exam, thesis (for some programs), exit interview (for some programs); practicum/internship; minimum GPA of 3.0 (for some programs); exit portfolio (for some programs). *Entrance requirements:* For master's, GRE/MAT, minimum GPA of 2.75; teaching certificate; essay; interview; 2 letters of recommendation; personal statement. Additional exam requirements/recommendations for international students: Required—TOEFL (minimum score 550 paper-based; 79 iBT), IELTS (minimum score 6). *Application deadline:* For fall admission, 6/1 for domestic students, 3/1 for international students; for spring admission, 11/1 for domestic students, 10/1 for international students. Applications are processed on a rolling basis. Application fee: $50. Electronic applications accepted. *Expenses:* Tuition, state resident: full-time $13,920; part-time $6264 per year. Tuition, nonresident: full-time $21,700; part-time $9765 per year. *Required fees:* $80; $36 per year. Tuition and fees vary according to course load, degree level and program. *Financial support:* In 2017–18, 8,416 students received support. Career-related internships or fieldwork, Federal Work-Study, scholarships/grants, and unspecified assistantships available. Support available to part-time students. Financial award application deadline: 3/15; financial award applicants required to submit FAFSA. *Faculty research:* Code switching and creative writing, language instruction, teacher evaluation, preschools, history of educational theories. *Total annual research expenditures:* $311,226. *Unit head:* Dr. Dorothy Feola, Dean, 973-720-2138, Fax: 973-720-3647, E-mail: feolad@wpunj.edu. *Application contact:* Liana Fornarotto, Director of Education Enrollment and Certification, 973-720-2206, Fax: 973-720-2989, E-mail: fornarottol@wpunj.edu.
Website: http://www.wpunj.edu/coe

Wilmington College, Department of Education, Wilmington, OH 45177. Offers reading (M Ed); special education (M Ed). *Accreditation:* TEAC. *Program availability:* Part-time. *Degree requirements:* For master's, comprehensive exam. *Entrance requirements:* For master's, GRE or MAT, minimum GPA of 3.0, 2 letters of recommendation. Additional exam requirements/recommendations for international students: Required—TOEFL. *Faculty research:* Reading instruction, special education practices, conflict resolution in the schools, models of higher education for teachers.

Wilmington University, College of Education, New Castle, DE 19720-6491. Offers applied technology in education (M Ed); career and technical education (M Ed); educational leadership (Ed D); elementary and secondary school counseling (M Ed); elementary studies (M Ed); ESOL literacy (M Ed); higher education leadership (Ed D); instruction: gifted and talented (M Ed); instruction: teacher of reading (M Ed); instruction: teaching and learning (M Ed); organizational leadership (Ed D); school leadership (M Ed); secondary education (MAT); special education (M Ed). *Accreditation:* NCATE. *Program availability:* Part-time, evening/weekend. *Faculty:* 23 full-time (13 women), 162 part-time/adjunct (99 women). *Students:* 546 full-time (394 women), 960 part-time (732 women); includes 320 minority (241 Black or African American, non-Hispanic/Latino; 12 American Indian or Alaska Native, non-Hispanic/Latino; 11 Asian, non-Hispanic/Latino; 28 Hispanic/Latino; 3 Native Hawaiian or other Pacific Islander, non-Hispanic/Latino; 25 Two or more races, non-Hispanic/Latino), 7 international. Average age 34. 1,068 applicants, 64% accepted, 582 enrolled. In 2017, 430 master's, 59 doctorates awarded. *Entrance requirements:* For master's, 2 letters of recommendation, interview. Additional exam requirements/recommendations for international students: Required—TOEFL (minimum score 500 paper-based). *Application deadline:* For fall admission, 4/30 for domestic students. Applications are processed on a rolling basis. Application fee: $35. Electronic applications accepted. *Expenses: Tuition:* Part-time $466 per credit. *Required fees:* $25 per semester. Tuition and fees vary according to degree level and campus/location. *Financial support:* Applicants required to submit FAFSA. *Unit head:* Dr. John C. Gray, Dean, 302-295-1139. *Application contact:* Laura Morris, Director of Admissions, 877-967-5464, E-mail: infocenter@wilmu.edu.
Website: http://www.wilmu.edu/education/

Wilson College, Graduate Programs, Chambersburg, PA 17201-1285. Offers accounting (M Acc); choreography and visual art (MFA); education (M Ed); educational technology (MET); healthcare administration (MHA); humanities (MA), including art and culture, critical/cultural theory, English language and literature, women's studies; management (MSM); nursing (MSN), including nursing education, nursing leadership and management; special education (MSE). *Program availability:* Evening/weekend. *Degree requirements:* For master's, project. *Entrance requirements:* For master's, PRAXIS, minimum undergraduate cumulative GPA of 3.0, 2 letters of recommendation, current certification for eligibility to teach in grades K-12, resume, personal interview. Electronic applications accepted.

Winona State University, College of Education, Department of Special Education, Winona, MN 55987. Offers special education (MS), including developmental disabilities, learning disabilities. *Program availability:* Part-time, evening/weekend. *Degree requirements:* For master's, comprehensive exam, thesis.

Winston-Salem State University, MAT Program, Winston-Salem, NC 27110-0003. Offers middle grades education (MAT); special education (MAT). *Accreditation:* NCATE. *Program availability:* Part-time, evening/weekend, online learning. *Entrance requirements:* For master's, GRE, MAT, NC teacher licensure. Electronic applications accepted. *Faculty research:* Action research on issues in elementary classroom.

Winthrop University, College of Education, Program in Special Education, Rock Hill, SC 29733. Offers M Ed. *Accreditation:* NCATE. *Program availability:* Part-time.

Students: 30 part-time (15 women); includes 4 minority (all Black or African American, non-Hispanic/Latino). Average age 33. In 2017, 7 master's awarded. *Entrance requirements:* For master's, PRAXIS, South Carolina Class III Teaching Certificate, sample of written work. Additional exam requirements/recommendations for international students: Required—TOEFL (minimum score 550 paper-based; 79 iBT), IELTS (minimum score 6). *Application deadline:* For fall admission, 7/15 priority date for domestic students; for spring admission, 12/1 for domestic students. Applications are processed on a rolling basis. Application fee: $50. Electronic applications accepted. *Financial support:* Career-related internships or fieldwork, Federal Work-Study, scholarships/grants, and unspecified assistantships available. Support available to part-time students. Financial award application deadline: 2/1; financial award applicants required to submit FAFSA. *Unit head:* Dr. Lisa Harris, Graduate Program Advisor, 803-323-2453, E-mail: harrisl@winthrop.edu. *Application contact:* 800-411-7041, Fax: 803-323-2292, E-mail: gradschool@winthrop.edu.
Website: http://www.winthrop.edu/graduateschool

Worcester State University, Graduate School, Department of Education, Program in Moderate Disabilities, Worcester, MA 01602-2597. Offers M Ed, Postbaccalaureate Certificate. *Program availability:* Part-time, evening/weekend. *Students:* 1 (woman) full-time, 23 part-time (17 women); includes 2 minority (both Two or more races, non-Hispanic/Latino). Average age 35. 29 applicants, 55% accepted, 8 enrolled. In 2017, 8 master's, 8 other advanced degrees awarded. *Degree requirements:* For master's, comprehensive exam (for some programs), thesis optional. *Entrance requirements:* For master's, GRE General Test or MAT, initial license as a teacher of students with moderate disabilities from the Commonwealth of Massachusetts; for Postbaccalaureate Certificate, MTEL (Communication and Literacy, Foundations of Reading, and General Curriculum), bachelor's degree with minimum GPA of 2.7. Additional exam requirements/recommendations for international students: Required—TOEFL (minimum score 550 paper-based; 79 iBT). *Application deadline:* For fall admission, 6/15 for domestic and international students; for spring admission, 11/1 for domestic and international students; for summer admission, 4/1 for domestic and international students. Applications are processed on a rolling basis. Application fee: $50. Electronic

applications accepted. *Expenses:* Tuition, state resident: full-time $3042; part-time $169 per credit hour. Tuition, nonresident: full-time $3042; part-time $169 per credit hour. *Required fees:* $2754; $153 per credit hour. *Financial support:* Career-related internships or fieldwork, scholarships/grants, and unspecified assistantships available. Financial award application deadline: 3/1; financial award applicants required to submit FAFSA. *Unit head:* Dr. Sue Foo, Coordinator, 508-929-8071, E-mail: sfoo@worcester.edu. *Application contact:* Sara Grady, Associate Dean for Graduate Studies and Professional Development, 508-929-8130, E-mail: sara.grady@worcester.edu.

Wright State University, Graduate School, College of Education and Human Services, Department of Teacher Education, Programs in Intervention Specialist, Dayton, OH 45435. Offers intervention specialist (M Ed). *Accreditation:* NCATE. *Degree requirements:* For master's, thesis (for some programs). *Entrance requirements:* For master's, GRE General Test, MAT. Additional exam requirements/recommendations for international students: Required—TOEFL.

Xavier University, College of Social Sciences, Health and Education, School of Education, Department of Secondary and Special Education, Cincinnati, OH 45207. Offers secondary education (M Ed); special education (M Ed). *Entrance requirements:* Additional exam requirements/recommendations for international students: Required—TOEFL (minimum score 550 paper-based; 79 iBT). Application fee is waived when completed online. *Expenses:* Contact institution.

Youngstown State University, Graduate School, Beeghly College of Education, Department of Teacher Education, Program in Special Education, Youngstown, OH 44555-0001. Offers gifted and talented education (MS Ed); special education (MS Ed). *Accreditation:* NCATE. *Program availability:* Part-time, evening/weekend. *Degree requirements:* For master's, comprehensive exam. *Entrance requirements:* For master's, GRE, MAT, or teaching certificate; interview; minimum GPA of 2.7. Additional exam requirements/recommendations for international students: Required—TOEFL. *Faculty research:* Learning disabilities, learning styles, developing self-esteem and social skills of severe behaviorally handicapped students, inclusion.

Urban Education

Alvernia University, School of Graduate Studies, Program in Education, Reading, PA 19607-1799. Offers urban education (M Ed). *Program availability:* Part-time, evening/weekend. *Degree requirements:* For master's, thesis optional. *Entrance requirements:* For master's, GRE or MAT (alumni excluded). Electronic applications accepted.

Bakke Graduate University, Programs in Pastoral Ministry and Business, Dallas, TX 75243-7039. Offers business administration (MBA); church and ministry multiplication (D Min); global urban leadership (MA); leadership (D Min); ministry in complex contexts (D Min); social and civic entrepreneurship (MA); theology of work (D Min); theology reflection (D Min); transformational leadership (DTL); urban youth ministry (D Min). *Program availability:* Part-time, online learning. *Faculty:* 5 full-time (3 women), 27 part-time/adjunct (12 women). *Students:* 120 full-time (48 women), 54 part-time (24 women). *Degree requirements:* For master's, thesis; for doctorate, thesis/dissertation. *Entrance requirements:* For master's, 2 years of ministry experience, BA in Biblical studies or theology; for doctorate, 3 years of ministry experience, M Div. Additional exam requirements/recommendations for international students: Required—TOEFL. *Application deadline:* For fall admission, 7/1 priority date for domestic students; for winter admission, 12/1 for domestic students; for spring admission, 3/15 for domestic students. Applications are processed on a rolling basis. Application fee: $50. Electronic applications accepted. *Expenses:* Tuition: Full-time $6120; part-time $3000 per credit. *Required fees:* $50 per course. $50 per quarter. *Financial support:* Scholarships/grants and tuition waivers (partial) available. Financial award applicants required to submit FAFSA. *Faculty research:* Theological systems, church management, worship. *Unit head:* Dr. Gwen Dewey, Senior Vice President of International Partnerships, 214-329-4447 Ext. 119, E-mail: gwen.dewey@bgu.edu. *Application contact:* Traci Tucker, Director of Admissions, 214-329-4447 Ext. 122, Fax: 214-347-9367, E-mail: traci.tucker@bgu.edu.
Website: http://www.bgu.edu/

Brown University, Graduate School, Department of Education, Program in Urban Education Policy, Providence, RI 02912. Offers AM. *Entrance requirements:* For master's, GRE General Test, official transcripts, 3 letters of recommendation, personal statement. Additional exam requirements/recommendations for international students: Required—TOEFL. Electronic applications accepted. *Faculty research:* Mayoral control of school systems.

Cardinal Stritch University, College of Education and Leadership, Department of Education, Milwaukee, WI 53217-3985. Offers educational leadership (MS); higher education student affairs leadership (MS); leadership for the advancement of learning and service (Ed D, PhD); leadership for the advancement of learning and service in higher education (Ed D, PhD); teaching (MAT); urban education (MA). *Accreditation:* NCATE. *Program availability:* Part-time, evening/weekend, 100% online, blended/hybrid learning. *Students:* 73 full-time (57 women), 332 part-time (220 women); includes 113 minority (59 Black or African American, non-Hispanic/Latino; 2 American Indian or Alaska Native, non-Hispanic/Latino; 10 Asian, non-Hispanic/Latino; 38 Hispanic/Latino; 1 Native Hawaiian or other Pacific Islander, non-Hispanic/Latino; 3 Two or more races, non-Hispanic/Latino), 7 international. Average age 35. 137 applicants, 97% accepted, 104 enrolled. In 2017, 135 master's, 28 doctorates awarded. *Degree requirements:* For master's, comprehensive exam, thesis (for some programs), research project, faculty recommendation; for doctorate, thesis/dissertation, practica, field experience. *Entrance requirements:* For master's, 2 letters of recommendation, minimum GPA of 3.0; for doctorate, minimum GPA of 3.5 in master's coursework, 3 letters of recommendation. Additional exam requirements/recommendations for international students: Required—TOEFL (minimum score 550 paper-based; 79 iBT), IELTS (minimum score 6.5). *Application deadline:* For fall admission, 7/15 priority date for domestic students; for spring admission, 12/15 priority date for domestic students. Applications are processed on a rolling basis. Application fee: $0. Electronic applications accepted. *Expenses:* Tuition varies by program. *Financial support:* Fellowships, research assistantships with partial tuition reimbursements, career-related internships or fieldwork, Federal Work-Study, and scholarships/grants available. Financial award applicants required to submit FAFSA. *Application contact:* 800-347-8822 Ext. 4042, E-mail: admissions@stritch.edu.

Cheyney University of Pennsylvania, Graduate Programs, Program in Urban Education, Cheyney, PA 19319. Offers M Ed. *Program availability:* Part-time, evening/weekend. *Degree requirements:* For master's, thesis or alternative. Electronic applications accepted.

Claremont Graduate University, Graduate Programs, School of Educational Studies, Claremont, CA 91711-6160. Offers Africana education (Certificate); education and policy (MA, PhD); higher education/student affairs (MA, PhD); human development (MA, PhD); public school administration (MA, PhD); quantitative evaluation (MA, PhD); special education (MA, PhD); teacher education (MA); teaching and learning (MA, PhD); urban leadership (PhD); MBA/PhD. PhD program offered jointly with San Diego State University. *Program availability:* Part-time. Terminal master's awarded for partial completion of doctoral program. *Entrance requirements:* For master's and doctorate, GRE General Test. Additional exam requirements/recommendations for international students: Required—TOEFL (minimum score 75 iBT). Electronic applications accepted. *Faculty research:* Education administration, K-12 and higher education, multicultural education, education policy, diversity in higher education, faculty issues.

Cleveland State University, College of Graduate Studies, College of Education and Human Services, Program in Urban Education, Cleveland, OH 44115. Offers PhD. *Program availability:* Part-time. *Faculty:* 19 full-time (10 women), 12 part-time/adjunct (7 women). *Students:* 35 full-time (25 women), 50 part-time (34 women); includes 30 minority (22 Black or African American, non-Hispanic/Latino; 2 Asian, non-Hispanic/Latino; 5 Hispanic/Latino; 1 Two or more races, non-Hispanic/Latino), 3 international. Average age 40. In 2017, 14 doctorates awarded. *Degree requirements:* For doctorate, one foreign language, comprehensive exam, thesis/dissertation. *Entrance requirements:* For doctorate, GRE General Test, minimum graduate GPA of 3.25. Additional exam requirements/recommendations for international students: Required—TOEFL (minimum score 550 paper-based; 78 iBT), IELTS (minimum score 6). *Application deadline:* For fall admission, 2/1 for domestic and international students. Application fee: $30. *Financial support:* In 2017–18, 16 students received support, including 12 research assistantships with tuition reimbursements available (averaging $10,325 per year), 4 teaching assistantships with tuition reimbursements available (averaging $10,325 per year); tuition waivers (full and partial) and tuition grants with hourly work assignments also available. Financial award application deadline: 4/30; financial award applicants required to submit FAFSA. *Faculty research:* Equity issues (race, ethnicity, and gender), education development consequences for special needs of urban populations, urban education programming, counseling the violent or aggressive adolescent. *Unit head:* Dr. Graham Stead, Director, 216-875-9869, Fax: 216-875-9697, E-mail: g.b.stead@csuohio.edu. *Application contact:* Rita M. Grabowski, Administrative Coordinator, 216-687-4697, Fax: 216-875-9697, E-mail: r.grabowski@csuohio.edu.
Website: http://www.csuohio.edu/cehs/doc/doc

College of Mount Saint Vincent, School of Professional and Graduate Studies, Department of Teacher Education, Riverdale, NY 10471-1093. Offers instructional technology and global perspectives (Certificate); middle level education (Certificate); multicultural studies (Certificate); teaching English to speakers of other languages (MS Ed); urban and multicultural education (MS Ed). *Accreditation:* TEAC. *Program availability:* Part-time. *Degree requirements:* For master's, comprehensive exam. *Entrance requirements:* For master's, interview, New York teaching certificate. Additional exam requirements/recommendations for international students: Required—TOEFL.

Eastern Michigan University, Graduate School, College of Education, Department of Teacher Education, Program in Urban/Diversity Education, Ypsilanti, MI 48197. Offers MA. In 2017, 1 master's awarded. Application fee: $45. *Application contact:* Dr. Patricia Williams-Boyd, Advisor, 734-487-3260, Fax: 734-487-2101, E-mail: pwilliams1@emich.edu.

Eastern Michigan University, Graduate School, College of Education, Department of Teacher Education, Programs in Curriculum and Instruction, Ypsilanti, MI 48197. Offers advanced teaching and learning (MA); early literacy instruction (Graduate Certificate); instructional leadership (MA); learning, motivation and creativity (Graduate Certificate); literacy coaching (Graduate Certificate); online teaching (Certificate); secondary literacy instruction (Graduate Certificate); urban and diversity education (MA). *Students:* 1 full-time (0 women), 22 part-time (19 women); includes 6 minority (2 Black or African American, non-Hispanic/Latino; 1 Hispanic/Latino; 3 Two or more races, non-Hispanic/Latino). Average age 31. 15 applicants, 67% accepted, 7 enrolled. In 2017, 15 master's, 1 other advanced degree awarded. Application fee: $45. *Application contact:* Dr. Virginia Harder, Graduate Coordinator/Advisor, 734-487-2729, Fax: 734-487-2101, E-mail: vharder1@emich.edu.

Emmanuel College, Graduate and Professional Programs, Graduate Programs in Education, Boston, MA 02115. Offers moderate learning disabilities (Certificate); urban education (M Ed). *Program availability:* Part-time, evening/weekend. *Faculty:* 1 (woman) full-time, 7 part-time/adjunct (all women). *Students:* 5 full-time (all women), 11 part-time (7 women); includes 6 minority (1 Black or African American, non-Hispanic/Latino; 1 Asian, non-Hispanic/Latino; 4 Hispanic/Latino). Average age 28. 21 applicants, 38% accepted, 4 enrolled. In 2017, 13 master's awarded. *Degree requirements:* For master's, 36 credits, including 6-credit practicum. *Entrance requirements:* For master's, transcripts from all regionally-accredited institutions attended (showing proof of bachelor's degree completion), 2 letters of recommendation, essay, resume. Additional exam requirements/recommendations for international students: Required—TOEFL. *Application deadline:* Applications are processed on a rolling basis. Electronic applications accepted. *Expenses:* $24,112 (for M Ed); $6,576 (for Certificate in moderate disabilities). *Financial support:* Application deadline: 2/15; applicants required to submit FAFSA. *Unit head:* Cindy O'Callaghan, Dean of Academic Administration and Graduate and Professional Programs, 617-735-9700, E-mail: gpp@emmanuel.edu. *Application contact:* Helen Muterperl, Director of Graduate and Professional Programs, 617-735-9700, Fax: 617-507-0434, E-mail: gpp@emmanuel.edu. Website: http://www.emmanuel.edu/graduate-professional-programs/academics/education.html

Florida International University, College of Arts, Sciences, and Education, Department of Leadership and Professional Studies, Miami, FL 33199. Offers adult education and human resource development (MS, Ed D); counseling (MS), including rehabilitation counseling, school counseling; counselor education (MS), including clinical mental health counseling; educational administration and supervision (Ed D); educational leadership (MS, Certificate, Ed S); higher education (Ed D); higher education administration (MS); international and comparative education (MS); recreation and sport management (MS), including recreation and sport management, recreational therapy; school psychology (Ed S); urban education (MS), including instruction in urban settings, learning technologies, multicultural/bilingual, multicultural/TESOL, urban education. *Program availability:* Part-time, evening/weekend. *Faculty:* 60 full-time (41 women), 112 part-time/adjunct (77 women). *Students:* 221 full-time (162 women), 301 part-time (239 women); includes 418 minority (127 Black or African American, non-Hispanic/Latino; 9 Asian, non-Hispanic/Latino; 271 Hispanic/Latino; 11 Two or more races, non-Hispanic/Latino), 10 international. Average age 31. 330 applicants, 55% accepted, 100 enrolled. In 2017, 181 master's, 6 doctorates awarded. *Degree requirements:* For doctorate, thesis/dissertation. *Entrance requirements:* For master's, minimum GPA of 3.0; for doctorate and other advanced degree, GRE General Test. Additional exam requirements/recommendations for international students: Required—TOEFL (minimum score 550 paper-based; 80 iBT), IELTS (minimum score 6.3). *Application deadline:* For fall admission, 6/1 priority date for domestic students, 4/1 for international students; for winter admission, 10/1 priority date for domestic students, 9/1 for international students; for spring admission, 3/1 priority date for domestic students, 2/1 for international students. Applications are processed on a rolling basis. Application fee: $30. Electronic applications accepted. *Expenses:* Tuition, state resident: full-time $8912; part-time $446 per credit hour. Tuition, nonresident: full-time $21,393; part-time $992 per credit hour. *Required fees:* $390; $195 per semester. *Financial support:* Fellowships, research assistantships with tuition reimbursements, teaching assistantships with tuition reimbursements, Federal Work-Study, and tuition waivers (full and partial) available. Support available to part-time students. Financial award applicants required to submit FAFSA. *Unit head:* Dr. Benjamin Baez, Chair, 305-348-3214, Fax: 305-348-1515, E-mail: benjamin.baez@fiu.edu. *Application contact:* Nanett Rojas, Assistant Director, Graduate Admissions, 305-348-7464, Fax: 305-348-7441, E-mail: gradadm@fiu.edu. Website: http://education.fiu.edu

Georgia State University, College of Education and Human Development, Department of Early Childhood Education, Atlanta, GA 30302-3083. Offers early childhood and elementary education (PhD); early childhood education (M Ed, Ed S); mathematics education (M Ed); urban education (M Ed). *Accreditation:* NCATE. *Program availability:* Part-time, evening/weekend. *Faculty:* 27 full-time (22 women). *Students:* 74 full-time (68 women), 22 part-time (21 women); includes 49 minority (41 Black or African American, non-Hispanic/Latino; 4 Asian, non-Hispanic/Latino; 2 Hispanic/Latino; 2 Two or more races, non-Hispanic/Latino), 3 international. Average age 30. 49 applicants, 65% accepted, 25 enrolled. In 2017, 27 master's, 3 doctorates awarded. *Entrance requirements:* For master's, GRE, undergraduate diploma; for doctorate and Ed S, GRE, master's degree. *Application deadline:* Applications are processed on a rolling basis. Application fee: $50. Electronic applications accepted. *Expenses:* Tuition, state resident: full-time $7020. Tuition, nonresident: full-time $22,518. *Required fees:* $2128. Tuition and fees vary according to degree level and program. *Financial support:* In 2017-18, fellowships with full tuition reimbursements (averaging $24,000 per year), research assistantships with full tuition reimbursements (averaging $4,000 per year), teaching assistantships with full tuition reimbursements (averaging $2,000 per year) were awarded; career-related internships or fieldwork, Federal Work-Study, institutionally sponsored loans, scholarships/grants, traineeships, health care benefits, tuition waivers (partial), and unspecified assistantships also available. Support available to part-time students. Financial award applicants required to submit FAFSA. *Faculty research:* Teacher development; language arts/literacy education; mathematics education; intersection of science, urban, and multicultural education; diversity in education. *Unit head:* Dr. Barbara Meyers, Department Chair, 404-413-8021, Fax: 404-413-8023, E-mail: barbara@gsu.edu. *Application contact:* Elaine King Jones, Administrative Curriculum Specialist, 404-413-8234, Fax: 404-413-8023, E-mail: ekjones@gsu.edu. Website: http://ecee.education.gsu.edu/

Georgia State University, College of Education and Human Development, Department of Educational Policy Studies, Program in Educational Leadership, Atlanta, GA 30302-3083. Offers educational leadership (M Ed, Ed D, Ed S); urban teacher leadership (M Ed). *Accreditation:* NCATE. *Program availability:* Part-time. *Entrance requirements:* For master's, GRE; for doctorate and Ed S, GRE, MAT. *Application deadline:* Applications are processed on a rolling basis. Application fee: $50. Electronic applications accepted. *Expenses:* Tuition, state resident: full-time $7020. Tuition, nonresident: full-time $22,518. *Required fees:* $2128. Tuition and fees vary according to degree level and program. *Financial support:* Fellowships, research assistantships, teaching assistantships, career-related internships or fieldwork, scholarships/grants, health care benefits, tuition waivers, and unspecified assistantships available. Support available to part-time students. Financial award application deadline: 3/15. *Faculty research:* Practices with diverse populations, leadership and success, the cohort model of instruction, technology in the schools, instructional supervision and academic coaching. *Unit head:* Dr. Jami Berry, Clinical Assistant Professor, 404-413-8030, Fax: 404-413-8003, E-mail: jberry2@gsu.edu. *Application contact:* Aishah Cowan, Administrative Academic Specialist, 404-413-8273, Fax: 404-413-8033, E-mail: acowan@gsu.edu. Website: http://eps.education.gsu.edu/programs-courses/educational-leadership/

The Graduate Center, City University of New York, Graduate Studies, Program in Urban Education, New York, NY 10016-4039. Offers PhD. *Students:* 98 full-time (71 women), 14 part-time (13 women); includes 56 minority (19 Black or African American, non-Hispanic/Latino; 5 Asian, non-Hispanic/Latino; 26 Hispanic/Latino; 6 Two or more races, non-Hispanic/Latino), 4 international. Average age 40. 104 applicants, 18% accepted, 16 enrolled. In 2017, 21 doctorates awarded. *Entrance requirements:* For doctorate, GRE General Test. Additional exam requirements/recommendations for international students: Required—TOEFL. *Application deadline:* For fall admission, 1/15 for domestic students. Application fee: $125. Electronic applications accepted. *Financial support:* In 2017-18, 75 students received support, including 72 fellowships, 1 teaching assistantship. *Unit head:* Prof. Wendy Luttrell, Executive Officer, 212-817-8281, Fax: 212-817-1515, E-mail: wluttrell@gc.cuny.edu. *Application contact:* Les Gribben, Director of Admissions, 212-817-7470, Fax: 212-817-1624, E-mail: lgribben@gc.cuny.edu.

Grand View University, Graduate Studies, Des Moines, IA 50316-1599. Offers athletic training (MS); clinical nurse leader (MSN, Post Master's Certificate); nursing education (MSN, Post Master's Certificate); organizational leadership (MS); sport management (MS); teacher leadership (M Ed); urban education (M Ed). *Program availability:* Part-time, evening/weekend. *Degree requirements:* For master's, completion of all required coursework in common core and selected track with minimum cumulative GPA of 3.0 and no more than two grades of C. *Entrance requirements:* For master's, GRE, GMAT, or essay, minimum undergraduate GPA of 3.0, professional resume, 3 letters of recommendation, interview. Additional exam requirements/recommendations for international students: Required—TOEFL (minimum score 550 paper-based). Electronic applications accepted.

Holy Names University, Graduate Division, Department of Education, Oakland, CA 94619-1699. Offers educational therapy (Certificate); mild/moderate disabilities (Ed S); multiple subject teaching (Credential); single subject teaching (Credential); urban education: educational therapy (M Ed); urban education: K-12 education (M Ed); urban education: special education (M Ed). *Program availability:* Part-time. *Degree requirements:* For master's, comprehensive exam, research paper, thesis or project. *Entrance requirements:* For master's, minimum undergraduate GPA of 2.6 overall, 3.0 in major; personal statement; two recommendations; interview. Additional exam requirements/recommendations for international students: Required—TOEFL (minimum score 550 paper-based; 79 iBT). Electronic applications accepted. Application fee is waived when completed online. *Faculty research:* Cognitive development, language development, learning handicaps.

Johns Hopkins University, School of Education, Certificate Programs in Education, Baltimore, MD 21218. Offers advanced methods for differentiated instruction and inclusive education (Graduate Certificate); applied behavior analysis (Post-Master's Certificate); clinical mental health counseling (Post-Master's Certificate); counseling (Advanced Certificate); data-based decision making and organizational improvement (Graduate Certificate); early intervention/preschool special education specialist (Graduate Certificate); education of students with autism and other pervasive developmental disorders (Graduate Certificate); educational leadership for independent schools (Graduate Certificate); evidence-based teaching in the health professions (Post-Master's Certificate); gifted education (Graduate Certificate); leadership in technology integration (Graduate Certificate); mind, brain and teaching (Graduate Certificate); school administration and supervision (Graduate Certificate); urban education (Graduate Certificate). *Program availability:* Part-time-only, evening/weekend, 100% online, blended/hybrid learning. *Entrance requirements:* For degree, minimum of bachelor's degree from regionally- or nationally-accredited institution (master's degree for some programs); minimum GPA of 3.0 in all previous programs of study; official transcripts from all post-secondary institutions attended; essay; curriculum vitae/resume; two letters of recommendation; dispositions survey. Electronic applications accepted. *Expenses:* Contact institution.

Langston University, School of Education and Behavioral Sciences, Langston, OK 73050. Offers bilingual/multicultural (M Ed); elementary education (M Ed); English as a second language (M Ed); rehabilitation counseling (M Sc); urban education (M Ed). *Accreditation:* CORE, NCATE (one or more programs are accredited). *Program availability:* Part-time. *Degree requirements:* For master's, comprehensive exam, thesis optional. *Entrance requirements:* For master's, GRE, writing skills test, minimum GPA of 2.5, 3 letters of recommendation. Additional exam requirements/recommendations for international students: Required—TOEFL, TWE. *Faculty research:* Bilingual/multicultural education, financing post-secondary education.

Long Island University–LIU Brooklyn, School of Education, Brooklyn, NY 11201-8423. Offers adolescence urban education (MS Ed); applied behavior analysis (Advanced Certificate); bilingual education (Advanced Certificate); bilingual education in urban setting (MS Ed); bilingual school counselor (MS Ed, Advanced Certificate); childhood urban education (MS Ed); childhood/early childhood education (MS Ed); childhood/early childhood urban education (MS Ed); early childhood urban education (MS Ed, Advanced Certificate); educational leadership (Advanced Certificate); marriage and family therapy (MS, Advanced Certificate); mental health counseling (MS, Advanced Certificate); school building district leader (Advanced Certificate); school counselor (MS Ed, Advanced Certificate); school psychologist (MS Ed); teaching students with disabilities (MS Ed); teaching urban children with disabilities (MS Ed); TESOL (MS Ed, Advanced Certificate). *Accreditation:* TEAC. *Program availability:* Part-time, evening/weekend, 100% online. *Faculty:* 14 full-time (12 women), 42 part-time/adjunct (32 women). *Students:* 140 full-time (130 women), 563 part-time (414 women); includes 417 minority (183 Black or African American, non-Hispanic/Latino; 1 American Indian or Alaska Native, non-Hispanic/Latino; 32 Asian, non-Hispanic/Latino; 187 Hispanic/Latino; 14 Two or more races, non-Hispanic/Latino), 10 international. Average age 31. 449 applicants, 82% accepted, 264 enrolled. In 2017, 408 master's, 31 other advanced degrees awarded. *Entrance requirements:* For master's, GRE. Additional exam requirements/recommendations for international students: Required—TOEFL (minimum score 527 paper-based, 75 iBT), IELTS, or PTE. *Application deadline:* Applications are processed on a rolling basis. Application fee: $50. Electronic applications accepted. *Expenses:* Tuition: Full-time $21,618; part-time $1201 per credit. *Required fees:* $1840; $920 per term. Tuition and fees vary according to course load. *Financial support:* In 2017-18, 58 students received support. Career-related internships or fieldwork, Federal Work-Study, scholarships/grants, and unspecified assistantships available. Support available to part-time students. Financial award application deadline: 2/15; financial award applicants required to submit FAFSA. *Faculty research:* Diversity issues in education and mental health care, inclusion - disability studies, sustainability, teacher professional development. *Unit head:* Dean, 718-488-1055, E-mail: bkln-admissions@liu.edu. *Application contact:* Bayu Sutrisno, Graduate Admissions Counselor, 718-488-1011, Fax: 718-780-6110, E-mail: bkln-admissions@liu.edu. Website: http://www.liu.edu/Brooklyn/Academics/School-of-Education

Loyola Marymount University, School of Education, JD/MA Program in Urban Education, Los Angeles, CA 90045-2659. Offers JD/MA. *Unit head:* Dr. Edmundo Litton, Chair, Department of Specialized Programs in Urban Education, 310-338-1859, E-mail: elitton@lmu.edu. *Application contact:* Chake H. Kouyoumjian, Associate Dean of Graduate Studies, 310-338-2721, Fax: 310-338-6086, E-mail: graduateinfo@lmu.edu. Website: http://lls.edu/admissionsaid/degreeprograms/jdprograms/majdprogram

Loyola Marymount University, School of Education, Program in Literacy Instruction for Urban Environments, Los Angeles, CA 90045-2659. Offers MA. *Unit head:* Dr. Candace

Poindexter, Director, Literacy and Educational Studies, 310-338-7314, E-mail: cpoindex@lmu.edu. *Application contact:* Chake H. Kouyoumjian, Associate Dean of Graduate Studies, 310-338-2721, Fax: 310-338-6086, E-mail: graduateinfo@lmu.edu. Website: http://soe.lmu.edu/academics/literacyinstructionforurbanenvironmentsonline

Loyola Marymount University, School of Education, Program in Urban Education, Los Angeles, CA 90045-2659. Offers MA. *Unit head:* Dr. Edmundo Litton, Chair, Department of Specialized Programs in Urban Education, 310-338-1859, E-mail: elitton@lmu.edu. *Application contact:* Chake H. Kouyoumjian, Associate Dean of Graduate Studies, 310-338-2721, Fax: 310-338-6086, E-mail: graduateinfo@lmu.edu. Website: http://soe.lmu.edu

Manhattanville College, School of Education, Jump Start Program, Purchase, NY 10577-2132. Offers childhood education and special education (grades 1-6) (MPS); early childhood education (birth-grade 2) (MAT); education (Advanced Certificate); English and special education (grades 5-12) (MPS); mathematics and special education (grades 5-12) (MPS); science and special education (grades 5-12) (MPS); social studies and special education (grades 5-12) (MPS); Spanish (grades 7-12) (MAT); TESOL (all grades) (MPS). *Program availability:* Part-time, evening/weekend. *Faculty:* 10 full-time (7 women), 39 part-time/adjunct (27 women). *Students:* 3 full-time (2 women), 40 part-time (24 women); includes 11 minority (3 Black or African American, non-Hispanic/Latino; 6 Hispanic/Latino; 1 Native Hawaiian or other Pacific Islander, non-Hispanic/Latino; 1 Two or more races, non-Hispanic/Latino). Average age 33. 25 applicants, 60% accepted, 7 enrolled. In 2017, 17 master's, 2 other advanced degrees awarded. *Degree requirements:* For master's, comprehensive exam (for some programs), thesis (for some programs), student teaching, research seminars, portfolios, internships, writing assessment; for Advanced Certificate, comprehensive exam (for some programs). *Entrance requirements:* For master's, GRE or MAT (for programs leading to certification), minimum GPA of 3.0, 2 letters of recommendation, interview, essay (2-3 page personal statement that describes reasons for choosing teaching or educational leadership as profession and philosophy of education), proof of immunization (for those born after 1957). Additional exam requirements/recommendations for international students: Required—TOEFL (minimum score 600 paper-based; 110 iBT); Recommended—IELTS (minimum score 8). *Application deadline:* Applications are processed on a rolling basis. Application fee: $75. Electronic applications accepted. *Expenses:* $915 per credit. *Financial support:* Teaching assistantships, career-related internships or fieldwork, Federal Work-Study, institutionally sponsored loans, scholarships/grants, and unspecified assistantships available. Financial award application deadline: 3/15; financial award applicants required to submit FAFSA. *Faculty research:* Early childhood and technology, professional development schools and community schools, students with emotional difficulties, literacy and adolescents, mindfulness, changing suburbs institute, and community schools, studying the effects of the environment on special populations, the most difficult cases, students who are presented with multiple challenges: learning, behavioral and ACE experiences who see criminal behavior as a way to cope; working on giving them the tools they need to succeed. *Unit head:* Dr. Shelly Wepner, Dean, 914-323-3153, E-mail: shelly.wepner@mville.edu. *Application contact:* Alissa Wilson, Director, Graduate Admissions, 914-323-3150, Fax: 914-694-1732, E-mail: edschool@mville.edu. Website: http://www.mville.edu/programs/jump-start

Morgan State University, School of Graduate Studies, School of Education and Urban Studies, Department of Advanced Studies, Leadership and Policy, Program in Urban Educational Leadership, Baltimore, MD 21251. Offers Ed D. *Accreditation:* NCATE. *Program availability:* Part-time, evening/weekend. *Application deadline:* For fall admission, 2/1 for domestic students; for spring admission, 10/1 for domestic students. Applications are processed on a rolling basis. Application fee: $0. *Expenses:* Tuition, state resident: part-time $433 per credit. Tuition, nonresident: part-time $851 per credit. *Required fees:* $81.50 per credit. *Financial support:* Application deadline: 4/1. *Faculty research:* Multicultural education, cooperative learning, psychology of cognition. *Unit head:* Dr. Warren C. Hayman, Graduate Coordinator, 443-885-3215, E-mail: warren.hayman@morgan.edu. *Application contact:* Dr. Dean Campbell, Graduate Recruitment Specialist, 443-885-3185, Fax: 443-885-8226, E-mail: dean.campbell@morgan.edu.

New Jersey City University, Debra Cannon Partridge Wolfe College of Education, Department of Educational Leadership and Counseling, Jersey City, NJ 07305-1597. Offers counselor education (MA); educational administration and supervision (MA); urban education (MA). *Accreditation:* TEAC. *Program availability:* Part-time, evening/weekend. *Entrance requirements:* Additional exam requirements/recommendations for international students: Required—TOEFL (minimum score 79 iBT).

New Jersey City University, Debra Cannon Partridge Wolfe College of Education, Department of Modern Languages, Jersey City, NJ 07305-1597. Offers urban education world language (MA).

Norfolk State University, School of Graduate Studies, School of Education, Department of Secondary Education and School Leadership, Program in Urban Education/Administration, Norfolk, VA 23504. Offers teaching (MA). *Accreditation:* NCATE. *Program availability:* Part-time. *Entrance requirements:* For master's, GRE General Test, PRAXIS I, minimum GPA of 3.0 in major, 2.5 overall.

Northeastern Illinois University, College of Graduate Studies and Research, Daniel L. Goodwin College of Education, Program in Inner City Studies, Chicago, IL 60625. Offers MA. *Program availability:* Part-time, evening/weekend. *Degree requirements:* For master's, comprehensive exam, thesis or alternative. *Entrance requirements:* For master's, minimum GPA of 2.75. Additional exam requirements/recommendations for international students: Required—TOEFL (minimum score 550 paper-based; 79 iBT). *Application deadline:* For fall admission, 4/1 priority date for domestic students; for spring admission, 8/15 for domestic students. Applications are processed on a rolling basis. Application fee: $30. Electronic applications accepted. *Expenses:* Tuition, state resident: full-time $7274; part-time $404.11 per credit hour. Tuition, nonresident: full-time $14,548; part-time $808.23 per credit hour. *Required fees:* $1284. *Unit head:* Dr. Brian Schultz, Department Chair, 773-442-5327, E-mail: b-schultz@neiu.edu. *Application contact:* Martha Narvaez, Graduate Admission Representative, 773-442-6006, E-mail: m-narvaez@neiu.edu.

Providence College, Program in Urban Teaching, Providence, RI 02918. Offers M Ed. *Program availability:* Part-time, evening/weekend. *Entrance requirements:* Additional exam requirements/recommendations for international students: Required—TOEFL (minimum score 577 paper-based; 90 iBT).

Teachers College, Columbia University, Department of Organization and Leadership, New York, NY 10027-6696. Offers adult education guided intensive study (Ed D); adult learning and leadership (Ed M, MA, Ed D); educational leadership (Ed D); higher and postsecondary education (MA, Ed D); leadership, policy and politics (Ed D); nurse executive (MA, Ed D), including administration studies (MA); professorial studies (MA); private school leadership (Ed M, MA); public school building leadership (Ed M, MA); social and organizational psychology (MA); urban education leaders (Ed D); MA/MBA. *Program availability:* Part-time, evening/weekend. *Students:* 342 full-time (244 women), 378 part-time (256 women); includes 288 minority (106 Black or African American, non-Hispanic/Latino; 69 Asian, non-Hispanic/Latino; 92 Hispanic/Latino; 21 Two or more races, non-Hispanic/Latino), 86 international. Average age 33. 1,063 applicants, 59% accepted, 405 enrolled. *Degree requirements:* For doctorate, thesis/dissertation. *Unit head:* Prof. Bill Baldwin, Chair, E-mail: wjb12@tc.columbia.edu. *Application contact:* David Estrella, Director of Admission, 212-678-3305, E-mail: estrella@tc.columbia.edu.

Temple University, College of Education, Department of Teaching and Learning, Philadelphia, PA 19122-6096. Offers career and technical education (Ed M), including business, computing, and information technology, industrial education, marketing education; middle grades education (Ed M), including math and language arts, math and science, science and language arts; secondary education (Ed M), including English, math, social studies; teaching English to speakers of other languages (MS Ed); urban education (Ed M). *Program availability:* Part-time, evening/weekend. *Students:* 218 full-time (144 women), 296 part-time (183 women); includes 128 minority (74 Black or African American, non-Hispanic/Latino; 18 Asian, non-Hispanic/Latino; 25 Hispanic/Latino; 11 Two or more races, non-Hispanic/Latino), 13 international. 254 applicants, 54% accepted, 102 enrolled. In 2017, 128 master's awarded. Terminal master's awarded for partial completion of doctoral program. *Degree requirements:* For master's, thesis or alternative. *Entrance requirements:* Additional exam requirements/recommendations for international students: Required—TOEFL (minimum score 550 paper-based; 79 iBT). *Application deadline:* For fall admission, 4/1 for domestic students, 12/15 for international students; for spring admission, 10/1 for domestic students, 8/1 for international students. Application fee: $60. Electronic applications accepted. *Expenses:* Contact institution. *Financial support:* Fellowships, research assistantships, and teaching assistantships available. Financial award application deadline: 1/15; financial award applicants required to submit FAFSA. *Faculty research:* Workforce development, vocational education, technical education, industrial education, professional development, literacy, classroom management, school communities, curriculum development, instruction, applied linguistics, cross linguistic influence, bilingual education, oral proficiency, multilingualism. *Unit head:* Dr. Christine Woyshner, Chairperson, 215-204-6387, E-mail: christine.woyshner@temple.edu. *Application contact:* Sarah Stapleton, Assistant Director, Academic Operations, 215-204-8220, E-mail: sarah.stapleton@temple.edu. Website: http://education.temple.edu/tl

University of Chicago, Graham School of Continuing Liberal and Professional Studies, Urban Teacher Education Program, Chicago, IL 60637. Offers MAT. *Faculty:* 8. *Students:* 58 full-time (47 women); includes 25 minority (10 Black or African American, non-Hispanic/Latino; 5 Asian, non-Hispanic/Latino; 8 Hispanic/Latino; 2 Two or more races, non-Hispanic/Latino). Average age 26. 54 applicants, 69% accepted, 31 enrolled. In 2017, 27 master's awarded. *Degree requirements:* For master's, exams; student teaching. *Entrance requirements:* For master's, ACT or TAP, 3 letters of recommendation, statement of purpose, transcripts, resume or curriculum vitae. *Application deadline:* For fall admission, 7/1 for domestic students. Applications are processed on a rolling basis. Application fee: $50. Electronic applications accepted. *Expenses:* Contact institution. *Financial support:* Federal Work-Study, institutionally sponsored loans, and tuition waivers (partial) available. Financial award application deadline: 7/1; financial award applicants required to submit FAFSA. *Unit head:* Jeanette Bartley, Co-Director, 773-702-2797, E-mail: jrbartley@uchicago.edu. *Application contact:* Diane New-Hardy, Student Services Administrator/Assistant Recruiter/Admissions Coordinator, E-mail: dianenew@uchicago.edu. Website: http://utep.uchicago.edu/

University of Houston–Downtown, College of Public Service, Department of Urban Education, Houston, TX 77002. Offers curriculum and instruction (MAT). *Program availability:* Part-time, evening/weekend. *Faculty:* 12 full-time (6 women), 2 part-time/adjunct (0 women). *Students:* 10 full-time (7 women), 45 part-time (44 women); includes 44 minority (19 Black or African American, non-Hispanic/Latino; 1 American Indian or Alaska Native, non-Hispanic/Latino; 1 Asian, non-Hispanic/Latino; 23 Hispanic/Latino). Average age 36. 29 applicants, 93% accepted, 14 enrolled. In 2017, 7 master's awarded. *Degree requirements:* For master's, capstone course with completed project, position paper, grant proposal, empirical study, curriculum development/revision, or advanced technology project presented at annual Graduate Project Exhibition. *Entrance requirements:* For master's, GRE, personal statement, 3 recommendation forms. Additional exam requirements/recommendations for international students: Required—TOEFL (minimum score 550 paper-based; 80 iBT). *Application deadline:* For fall admission, 7/15 for domestic and international students; for spring admission, 11/15 for domestic and international students. Application fee: $35 ($60 for international students). Electronic applications accepted. *Expenses:* $335 per credit resident; $700 per credit non-resident. *Financial support:* Federal Work-Study and scholarships/grants available. Financial award application deadline: 4/1; financial award applicants required to submit FAFSA. *Unit head:* Dr. Christal Burnett, Department Chair, 713-226-5521, Fax: 713-226-5294, E-mail: burnettc@uhd.edu. *Application contact:* Ceshia Love, Director of Admissions, 713-221-8093, Fax: 713-223-7408, E-mail: gradadmissions@uhd.edu. Website: https://www.uhd.edu/academics/public-service/urban-education/Pages/default.aspx

University of Illinois at Chicago, College of Education, Department of Educational Policy Studies, Chicago, IL 60607-7128. Offers policy studies (M Ed); policy studies in urban education (PhD); urban education leadership (Ed D). *Faculty research:* Social foundations of education, educational organizations and leadership, education policy analysis, understanding and addressing educational problems in urban contexts.

University of Massachusetts Boston, College of Education and Human Development, Program in Urban Education, Leadership, and Policy Studies, Boston, MA 02125-3393. Offers Ed D, PhD. *Program availability:* Part-time, evening/weekend. *Faculty:* 13 full-time (8 women), 21 part-time/adjunct (12 women). *Students:* 7 full-time (all women), 32 part-time (22 women); includes 17 minority (6 Black or African American, non-Hispanic/Latino; 1 American Indian or Alaska Native, non-Hispanic/Latino; 8 Hispanic/Latino; 2 Two or more races, non-Hispanic/Latino), 3 international. Average age 36. 31 applicants, 45% accepted, 9 enrolled. In 2017, 3 doctorates awarded. *Entrance requirements:* For doctorate, GRE General Test or MAT, minimum GPA of 2.75. *Application deadline:* For fall admission, 3/15 for domestic students. Application fee: $25 ($40 for international students). *Expenses:* Tuition, state resident: full-time $17,375. Tuition, nonresident: full-time $33,915. *Required fees:* $355. *Financial support:* Research assistantships, teaching assistantships, career-related internships or fieldwork, Federal Work-Study, and unspecified assistantships available. Support available to part-time students. Financial award application deadline: 3/1; financial award applicants required to submit FAFSA. *Faculty research:* School reform, race and culture in schools, race and higher education, language, literacy and writing. *Unit head:* Dr. Tricia Kress, Director, 617-287-7646, E-mail: tricia.kress@umb.edu. *Application contact:* Graduate Admissions Coordinator, 617-287-6400, Fax: 617-287-6236, E-mail: bos.gadm@dpc.umassp.edu.

University of Memphis, Graduate School, College of Education, Department of Instruction and Curriculum Leadership, Memphis, TN 38152. Offers advanced studies in teaching and learning (M Ed); applied behavior analysis (Graduate Certificate); autism studies (Graduate Certificate); early childhood education (MAT, MS, Ed D); elementary education (MAT); instruction and curriculum (MS, Ed D); instruction design and

technology (MS, Ed D); instructional design and technology (Graduate Certificate); literacy, leadership, and coaching (Graduate Certificate); reading (MS, Ed D); school library information specialist (Graduate Certificate); secondary education (MAT); special education (MAT, MS, Ed D); STEM teacher leadership (Graduate Certificate); urban education (Graduate Certificate). *Accreditation:* NCATE (one or more programs are accredited). *Program availability:* Part-time. *Faculty:* 22 full-time (14 women), 14 part-time/adjunct (10 women). *Students:* 36 full-time (27 women), 351 part-time (271 women); includes 159 minority (132 Black or African American, non-Hispanic/Latino; 1 American Indian or Alaska Native, non-Hispanic/Latino; 7 Asian, non-Hispanic/Latino; 10 Hispanic/Latino; 9 Two or more races, non-Hispanic/Latino), 4 international. Average age 35. 170 applicants, 85% accepted, 111 enrolled. In 2017, 84 master's, 14 doctorates, 32 other advanced degrees awarded. Terminal master's awarded for partial completion of doctoral program. *Degree requirements:* For master's, comprehensive exam, thesis or alternative; for doctorate, comprehensive exam, thesis/dissertation. *Entrance requirements:* For master's, GRE General Test, PRAXIS, minimum GPA of 2.5, letters of reference; for doctorate, GRE General Test, GRE Subject Test, 2 years of teaching experience, letters of reference, statement of purpose, interview. Additional exam requirements/recommendations for international students: Required—TOEFL (minimum 550 paper-based; 79 iBT). *Application deadline:* For fall admission, 4/1 priority date for domestic students; for spring admission, 10/1 priority date for domestic students; for summer admission, 2/1 priority date for domestic students. Applications are processed on a rolling basis. Application fee: $35 ($60 for international students). Electronic applications accepted. *Expenses:* Contact institution. *Financial support:* In 2017–18, 2 research assistantships with full tuition reimbursements (averaging $10,000 per year), 3 teaching assistantships with full tuition reimbursements (averaging $10,666 per year) were awarded; career-related internships or fieldwork, Federal Work-Study, institutionally sponsored loans, scholarships/grants, traineeships, and unspecified assistantships also available. Support available to part-time students. Financial award application deadline: 2/1; financial award applicants required to submit FAFSA. *Faculty research:* Effective urban teachers, preparation and retention of urban teachers, technology utilization in schools, field-based teacher preparation programs, effective use of online instruction. *Unit head:* Dr. Angiline Powell, Interim Chair, 901-678-3310, E-mail: apowell3@memphis.edu. *Application contact:* Dr. James Meindl, Coordinator of Graduate Studies, 901-678-3310, E-mail: jnmeindl@memphis.edu.
Website: http://www.memphis.edu/icl/

University of Michigan–Dearborn, College of Education, Health, and Human Services, Doctoral Program in Education, Dearborn, MI 48126. Offers curriculum and practice (Ed D); educational leadership (Ed D); metropolitan education (Ed D). *Program availability:* Part-time, evening/weekend. *Faculty:* 5 full-time (3 women), 1 part-time/adjunct (0 women). *Students:* 2 full-time (1 woman), 13 part-time (9 women); includes 8 minority (7 Black or African American, non-Hispanic/Latino; 1 Hispanic/Latino). Average age 45. 15 applicants, 27% accepted, 3 enrolled. In 2017, 9 doctorates awarded. *Degree requirements:* For doctorate, comprehensive exam, thesis/dissertation. *Entrance requirements:* For doctorate, GRE (taken within the last 5 years), master's degree with minimum GPA of 3.3, 3 letters of recommendation (1 from faculty), 3 years' professional and/or teaching experience. Additional exam requirements/recommendations for international students: Required—TOEFL (minimum score 560 paper-based; 84 iBT), IELTS (minimum score 6.5). *Application deadline:* For fall admission, 3/1 for domestic and international students. Application fee: $60. Electronic applications accepted. *Expenses:* $683 per credit hour in-state; $1,176 per credit hour out-state. *Financial support:* In 2017–18, 2 students received support. Scholarships/grants available. Financial award application deadline: 3/1; financial award applicants required to submit FAFSA. *Faculty research:* Urban education, educational leadership, assessment and evaluation, research methods, science education. *Unit head:* Dr. Chris Burke, Director, 313-593-5319, E-mail: cjfburke@umich.edu. *Application contact:* Office of Graduate Studies, 313-583-6321, E-mail: umd-graduatestudies@umich.edu.
Website: http://umdearborn.edu/cehhs/cehhs_edd/

University of Michigan–Dearborn, College of Education, Health, and Human Services, Master of Arts Program in Community Based Education, Dearborn, MI 48126. Offers MA. *Program availability:* Part-time, evening/weekend. *Faculty:* 1 full-time (0 women), 1 part-time/adjunct (0 women). *Students:* 8 part-time (5 women); includes 5 minority (4 Black or African American, non-Hispanic/Latino; 1 Two or more races, non-Hispanic/Latino). Average age 35. 6 applicants, 50% accepted, 3 enrolled. *Degree requirements:* For master's, essay. *Entrance requirements:* Additional exam requirements/recommendations for international students: Required—TOEFL (minimum score 560 paper-based; 84 iBT), IELTS (minimum score 6.5). *Application deadline:* For fall admission, 8/1 for domestic students, 5/1 for international students; for winter admission, 12/1 for domestic students, 9/1 for international students; for spring admission, 4/1 for domestic students, 1/1 for international students. Applications are processed on a rolling basis. Application fee: $60. Electronic applications accepted. *Expenses:* $683 per credit hour in-state; $1,176 per credit hour out-state. *Financial support:* In 2017–18, 8 students received support. Scholarships/grants available. Financial award application deadline: 3/1; financial award applicants required to submit FAFSA. *Faculty research:* Community based education, ecojustice education, multicultural education, place based education, urban education. *Unit head:* Dr. Chris Burke, 313-593-5319, E-mail: cjfburke@umich.edu. *Application contact:* Dr. Stein Brunvand, Director, Master's Programs, 313-583-6415, E-mail: sbrunvan@umich.edu.
Website: https://umdearborn.edu/cehhs/graduate-programs/areas-study/ma-community-based-education

University of Nebraska at Omaha, Graduate Studies, College of Education, Department of Teacher Education, Program in Secondary Education, Omaha, NE 68182. Offers instruction in urban schools (Certificate); secondary education (MS). *Accreditation:* NCATE. *Program availability:* Part-time, evening/weekend. *Degree requirements:* For master's, comprehensive exam, thesis (for some programs). *Entrance requirements:* For master's, minimum GPA of 3.0, transcripts. Additional exam requirements/recommendations for international students: Required—TOEFL, IELTS, PTE. Electronic applications accepted.

University of Pennsylvania, Graduate School of Education, Teach for America Program, Philadelphia, PA 19104. Offers MS Ed. Program designed for Teach For America corps members teaching in Philadelphia public and charter schools. *Program availability:* Evening/weekend. *Students:* Average age 25. 70 applicants, 96% accepted, 58 enrolled. In 2017, 55 master's awarded. *Entrance requirements:* For master's, bachelor's degree; Teach for America placement. Additional exam requirements/recommendations for international students: Required—TOEFL, IELTS. *Application deadline:* Applications are processed on a rolling basis. Application fee: $75. Electronic applications accepted. *Unit head:* Mary DelSavio, Program Director, 215-746-4855, E-mail: mary1@upenn.edu.
Website: http://www.gse.upenn.edu/exec-ed/tfa

University of San Francisco, School of Education, Department of Teacher Education, San Francisco, CA 94117-1080. Offers digital media and learning (MA); teaching (MA); teaching reading (MA); teaching urban education and social justice (MA). *Program*

availability: Part-time. *Entrance requirements:* Additional exam requirements/recommendations for international students: Required—TOEFL, IELTS, PTE. Electronic applications accepted.

University of Southern California, Graduate School, Rossier School of Education, Doctor of Education Programs, Los Angeles, CA 90089. Offers educational psychology (Ed D); higher education administration (Ed D); K-12 leadership in urban school settings (Ed D); teacher education in multicultural societies (Ed D). *Program availability:* Part-time, evening/weekend. *Degree requirements:* For doctorate, thesis/dissertation. *Entrance requirements:* For doctorate, GRE. Additional exam requirements/recommendations for international students: Required—TOEFL (minimum score 100 iBT). Electronic applications accepted. *Faculty research:* Data-driven decision-making in K-12 schools and districts; examination of college and university leadership and management in U. S. and Asia; studies in facilitating student learning; organizational change and the role of leaders; leadership, diversity, learning and accountability.

University of Wisconsin–Milwaukee, Graduate School, School of Education, Department of Curriculum and Instruction, Milwaukee, WI 53201-0413. Offers curriculum and instruction (MS), including cross-curricular focus, early childhood education, English education, mathematics education, middle childhood/early adolescence education, reading education, science education, urban social studies education. *Program availability:* Part-time. *Students:* 17 full-time (13 women), 45 part-time (39 women); includes 13 minority (2 Black or African American, non-Hispanic/Latino; 3 Asian, non-Hispanic/Latino; 1 Hispanic/Latino; 7 Two or more races, non-Hispanic/Latino). Average age 33. 32 applicants, 66% accepted, 16 enrolled. In 2017, 26 master's awarded. *Entrance requirements:* Additional exam requirements/recommendations for international students: Required—TOEFL (minimum score 550 paper-based; 79 iBT), IELTS (minimum score 6.5). *Application deadline:* For fall admission, 1/1 priority date for domestic students; for spring admission, 9/1 for domestic students. Application fee: $56 ($96 for international students). Electronic applications accepted. *Financial support:* Fellowships, research assistantships, teaching assistantships, career-related internships or fieldwork, health care benefits, unspecified assistantships, and project assistantships available. Support available to part-time students. Financial award application deadline: 4/15; financial award applicants required to submit FAFSA. *Application contact:* General Information Contact, 414-229-4721, E-mail: soeinfo@uwm.edu.
Website: http://uwm.edu/education/academics/curriculum-instruction-department/

University of Wisconsin–Milwaukee, Graduate School, School of Education, Department of Exceptional Education, Milwaukee, WI 53201-0413. Offers autism spectrum disorders (Graduate Certificate); exceptional education (MS); transition for students with disabilities (Graduate Certificate); urban education (PhD), including adult, continuing and higher education leadership, art education, curriculum and instruction, exceptional education, mathematics education, multicultural studies, social foundations of education. *Program availability:* Part-time. *Students:* 45 full-time (34 women), 68 part-time (54 women); includes 46 minority (27 Black or African American, non-Hispanic/Latino; 7 Asian, non-Hispanic/Latino; 1 Hispanic/Latino; 11 Two or more races, non-Hispanic/Latino), 4 international. Average age 39. 43 applicants, 53% accepted, 19 enrolled. In 2017, 12 master's, 13 doctorates, 8 other advanced degrees awarded. *Entrance requirements:* Additional exam requirements/recommendations for international students: Required—TOEFL (minimum score 550 paper-based; 79 iBT), IELTS (minimum score 6.5). *Application deadline:* For fall admission, 1/1 priority date for domestic students; for spring admission, 9/1 for domestic students. Application fee: $56 ($96 for international students). Electronic applications accepted. *Financial support:* Fellowships, research assistantships, teaching assistantships, career-related internships or fieldwork, health care benefits, and unspecified assistantships available. Support available to part-time students. Financial award application deadline: 4/15; financial award applicants required to submit FAFSA. *Faculty research:* Emotional disturbance, hearing impairment, learning disabilities, mental retardation. *Application contact:* General Information Contact, 414-229-4721, E-mail: soeinfo@uwm.edu.
Website: http://uwm.edu/education/academics/exceptional-edu-department/

Vanderbilt University, Peabody College, Department of Teaching and Learning, Nashville, TN 37240-1001. Offers elementary education (M Ed); English language learners (M Ed); learning and design (M Ed); learning, diversity, and urban studies (M Ed); reading education (M Ed); secondary education (M Ed). *Accreditation:* NCATE. *Program availability:* Part-time. *Faculty:* 43 full-time (32 women), 28 part-time/adjunct (25 women). *Students:* 139 full-time (110 women), 35 part-time (23 women); includes 31 minority (18 Black or African American, non-Hispanic/Latino; 1 American Indian or Alaska Native, non-Hispanic/Latino; 6 Asian, non-Hispanic/Latino; 4 Hispanic/Latino; 2 Two or more races, non-Hispanic/Latino), 44 international. Average age 26. 510 applicants, 69% accepted, 113 enrolled. In 2017, 87 master's awarded. *Degree requirements:* For master's, comprehensive exam, thesis optional. *Entrance requirements:* For master's, GRE General Test, MAT. Additional exam requirements/recommendations for international students: Required—TOEFL (minimum score 550 paper-based; 80 iBT). *Application deadline:* For fall admission, 12/31 priority date for domestic and international students; for spring admission, 11/1 priority date for domestic and international students. Applications are processed on a rolling basis. Application fee: $0. Electronic applications accepted. *Financial support:* Fellowships with partial tuition reimbursements, research assistantships with partial tuition reimbursements, teaching assistantships with partial tuition reimbursements, Federal Work-Study, institutionally sponsored loans, scholarships/grants, tuition waivers (partial), and unspecified assistantships available. Support available to part-time students. Financial award application deadline: 1/15; financial award applicants required to submit FAFSA. *Faculty research:* Children's learning and development in core conceptual domains (STEM, English language arts, social studies); classroom discourse structures that teachers can learn and use to support students' learning and development K-6; intervention and design-based research on educational improvement at classroom, school, and district levels; design-based and learning sciences research on relations between learning in schools and other settings. *Unit head:* Dr. Deborah Rowe, Chair, 615-322-8100, Fax: 615-322-8999, E-mail: deborah.w.rowe@vanderbilt.edu. *Application contact:* Angela Saylor, Educational Coordinator, 615-322-8092, Fax: 615-322-8999, E-mail: angela.saylor@vanderbilt.edu.

Virginia Commonwealth University, Graduate School, School of Education, Doctoral Program in Education, Richmond, VA 23284-9005. Offers art education (PhD); counselor education and supervision (PhD); curriculum, culture and change (PhD); educational leadership (PhD); educational psychology (PhD); leadership (Ed D); research and evaluation (PhD); special education and disability leadership (PhD); sport leadership (PhD); urban services leadership (PhD). *Accreditation:* NCATE. *Program availability:* Part-time. *Degree requirements:* For doctorate, thesis/dissertation. *Entrance requirements:* For doctorate, GRE (for PhD), MAT (for Ed D), interview, master's degree, writing sample. Additional exam requirements/recommendations for international students: Required—TOEFL (minimum score 600 paper-based; 100 iBT). Electronic applications accepted.

Section 26
Subject Areas

This section contains a directory of institutions offering graduate work in subject areas. Additional information about programs listed in the directory may be obtained by writing directly to the dean of a graduate school or chair of a department at the address given in the directory.

For programs offering related work, see also in this book *Administration, Instruction, and Theory; Business Administration and Management; Education; Instructional Levels; Leisure Studies and Recreation; Physical Education and Kinesiology;* and *Special Focus.* In the other guides in this series:

Graduate Programs in the Humanities, Arts & Social Sciences

See *Art and Art History; Family and Consumer Sciences; Language and Literature; Performing Arts; Psychology and Counseling (School Psychology); Public, Regional, and Industrial Affairs (Urban Studies); Religious Studies;* and *Social Sciences*

Graduate Programs in the Biological/Biomedical Sciences & Health-Related Medical Professions

See *Health-Related Professions*

Graduate Programs in the Physical Sciences, Mathematics, Agricultural Sciences, the Environment & Natural Resources

See *Mathematical Sciences*

Graduate Programs in Engineering & Applied Sciences

See *Computer Science and Information Technology*

CONTENTS

Program Directories

Agricultural Education

Alcorn State University, School of Graduate Studies, School of Psychology and Education, Lorman, MS 39096-7500. Offers agricultural education (MS Ed); elementary education (MS Ed, Ed S); guidance and counseling (MS Ed); industrial education (MS Ed); secondary education (MS Ed), including health and physical education; special education (MS Ed). *Accreditation:* NCATE. *Degree requirements:* For master's, thesis optional.

Arkansas State University, Graduate School, College of Agriculture and Technology, State University, AR 72467. Offers agricultural education (SCCT); agriculture (MSA); vocational-technical administration (SCCT). *Program availability:* Part-time. *Degree requirements:* For master's, comprehensive exam, thesis or alternative; for SCCT, comprehensive exam. *Entrance requirements:* For master's, GRE General Test or MAT, appropriate bachelor's degree, official transcripts, immunization records; for SCCT, GRE General Test or MAT, interview, master's degree, official transcript, immunization records. Additional exam requirements/recommendations for international students: Required—TOEFL (minimum score 550 paper-based; 79 iBT), IELTS (minimum score 6), PTE (minimum score 56). Electronic applications accepted.

California Polytechnic State University, San Luis Obispo, College of Agriculture, Food and Environmental Sciences, Department of Agricultural Education and Communication, San Luis Obispo, CA 93407. Offers MAE. *Program availability:* Part-time. *Faculty:* 3 full-time (2 women), 2 part-time/adjunct (0 women). *Students:* 26 full-time (21 women), 6 part-time (5 women); includes 9 minority (6 Hispanic/Latino; 3 Two or more races, non-Hispanic/Latino), 1 international. Average age 26. 27 applicants, 74% accepted, 13 enrolled. In 2017, 21 master's awarded. *Degree requirements:* For master's, comprehensive exam. *Entrance requirements:* For master's, GRE. Additional exam requirements/recommendations for international students: Required—TOEFL (minimum score 80 iBT). *Application deadline:* For fall admission, 4/1 for domestic and international students; for winter admission, 10/1 for domestic students, 6/30 for international students; for spring admission, 10/1 for domestic students. Applications are processed on a rolling basis. Application fee: $55. Electronic applications accepted. *Expenses:* Tuition, state resident: full-time $7176; part-time $4164 per year. *Required fees:* $3690; $3219 per year. $1073 per trimester. *Financial support:* Teaching assistantships and unspecified assistantships available. Financial award application deadline: 3/2; financial award applicants required to submit FAFSA. *Faculty research:* Agricultural education with emphasis on public school teaching. *Unit head:* Dr. Robert Flores, Department Head, 805-756-2169, E-mail: rflores@calpoly.edu. *Application contact:* Dr. Ann De Lay, Graduate Coordinator, 805-756-7272, E-mail: adelay@calpoly.edu.
Website: http://aged.calpoly.edu/

California State University, Chico, Office of Graduate Studies, College of Agriculture, Chico, CA 95929-0722. Offers agricultural education (MS). *Degree requirements:* For master's, thesis or alternative, oral exam. *Entrance requirements:* For master's, GRE or MAT, 3 letters of recommendation, three departmental recommendation forms, statement of purpose. Additional exam requirements/recommendations for international students: Required—TOEFL (minimum score 550 paper-based; 80 iBT), IELTS (minimum score 6.5), PTE (minimum score 59).

Clemson University, Graduate School, College of Agriculture, Forestry and Life Sciences, Department of Agricultural Sciences, Clemson, SC 29634. Offers agricultural education (M Ag Ed); applied economics (PhD); applied economics and statistics (MS). *Program availability:* Part-time. *Faculty:* 20 full-time (3 women). *Students:* 30 full-time (20 women), 25 part-time (14 women). Average age 27. 72 applicants, 50% accepted, 17 enrolled. In 2017, 6 master's, 1 doctorate awarded. *Degree requirements:* For master's, thesis optional; for doctorate, comprehensive exam, thesis/dissertation. *Entrance requirements:* For master's and doctorate, GRE General Test, unofficial transcripts, letters of recommendation. Additional exam requirements/recommendations for international students: Required—TOEFL (minimum score 80 iBT), IELTS (minimum score 6.5), PTE (minimum score 5). *Application deadline:* For fall admission, 6/1 for domestic students, 7/1 for international students; for spring admission, 10/1 for domestic students, 11/1 for international students. Applications are processed on a rolling basis. Application fee: $80 ($90 for international students). Electronic applications accepted. *Expenses:* $5,174 per semester full-time resident, $9,714 per semester full-time non-resident, $511 per credit hour part-time resident, $1,017 per credit hour part-time non-resident; $741 per credit hour online; other fees may apply per session. *Financial support:* In 2017–18, 11 students received support, including 7 research assistantships with partial tuition reimbursements available (averaging $11,750 per year), 4 teaching assistantships with partial tuition reimbursements available (averaging $8,307 per year); fellowships, career-related internships or fieldwork, and unspecified assistantships also available. Financial award application deadline: 6/1. *Faculty research:* Agricultural education, agricultural economics, agricultural statistics, agribusiness. *Unit head:* Dr. Charles Privette, Interim Department Head, 864-656-6247, E-mail: privett@clemson.edu.
Website: http://www.clemson.edu/cafls/departments/agricultural-sciences/index.html

Colorado State University, College of Agricultural Sciences, Programs in Agricultural Sciences and Extension Education, Fort Collins, CO 80523. Offers agricultural sciences (M Agr); extension education (M Ext Ed). *Program availability:* Part-time, evening/weekend, online only, 100% online. *Faculty:* 1 full-time (0 women), 1 part-time/adjunct (0 women). *Students:* 4 full-time (2 women), 89 part-time (58 women); includes 12 minority (2 Black or African American, non-Hispanic/Latino; 2 American Indian or Alaska Native, non-Hispanic/Latino; 3 Hispanic/Latino; 5 Two or more races, non-Hispanic/Latino), 7 international. Average age 35. 25 applicants, 76% accepted, 17 enrolled. In 2017, 35 master's awarded. *Degree requirements:* For master's, professional paper (for some programs); internship. *Entrance requirements:* For master's, minimum GPA of 3.0, bachelor's degree. Additional exam requirements/recommendations for international students: Required—TOEFL (minimum score 550 paper-based; 80 iBT), IELTS (minimum score 6.5). Application fee: $60 ($70 for international students). Electronic applications accepted. *Expenses:* $624 per credit hour. *Financial support:* Scholarships/grants available. Financial award applicants required to submit FAFSA. *Unit head:* Dr. Ajay Menon, Dean, 970-491-6274, Fax: 970-491-4895, E-mail: ajay.menon@colostate.edu. *Application contact:* Pam Schell, Administrative Assistant, 970-491-2410, Fax: 970-491-4895, E-mail: pam.schell@colostate.edu.

Cornell University, Graduate School, Graduate Fields of Agriculture and Life Sciences, Field of Education, Ithaca, NY 14853. Offers adult and extension education (MPS, MS, PhD); learning, teaching, and social policy (MPS, MS, PhD); mathematics 7-12 (MS). Terminal master's awarded for partial completion of doctoral program. *Degree requirements:* For master's, thesis (MS); for doctorate, comprehensive exam, thesis/dissertation. *Entrance requirements:* For master's and doctorate, GRE General Test, sample of written work (recommended), 2 letters of recommendation. Additional exam

requirements/recommendations for international students: Required—TOEFL (minimum score 550 paper-based; 77 iBT). Electronic applications accepted. *Faculty research:* Moral development and professional ethics, public issues education and community development, socio/political issues in public education, teacher education and curriculum in agricultural science and mathematics, extension research.

Eastern Kentucky University, The Graduate School, College of Education, Department of Curriculum and Instruction, Program in Secondary and Higher Education, Richmond, KY 40475-3102. Offers secondary education (MA Ed), including agricultural education, art education, biological sciences education, business education, English education, geography education, history education, home economics education, industrial education, mathematical sciences education, physical education, school health education. *Accreditation:* NCATE. *Program availability:* Part-time. *Entrance requirements:* For master's, GRE General Test, minimum GPA of 2.5.

Iowa State University of Science and Technology, Department of Agricultural Education and Studies, Ames, IA 50011. Offers MS, PhD. *Entrance requirements:* For master's and doctorate, resume. Additional exam requirements/recommendations for international students: Required—TOEFL (minimum score 550 paper-based; 79 iBT), IELTS (minimum score 6.5). Electronic applications accepted. *Faculty research:* Agricultural extension education, teaching, learning processes, distance education, international education, adult education.

Ithaca College, School of Humanities and Sciences, Program in Agriculture Education, Ithaca, NY 14850. Offers MAT. Program offered in collaboration with Cornell University. *Program availability:* Part-time. *Faculty:* 11 full-time (7 women), 1 part-time/adjunct (0 women). *Students:* 3 full-time (all women); includes 1 minority (Hispanic/Latino). Average age 25. 6 applicants, 50% accepted, 2 enrolled. In 2017, 4 master's awarded. *Degree requirements:* For master's, thesis or alternative, student teaching. *Entrance requirements:* Additional exam requirements/recommendations for international students: Required—TOEFL (minimum score 550 paper-based; 80 iBT). *Application deadline:* For fall admission, 3/19 for domestic and international students. Applications are processed on a rolling basis. Application fee: $40. Electronic applications accepted. *Expenses:* Contact institution. *Financial support:* In 2017–18, 3 students received support, including 3 research assistantships (averaging $7,096 per year); career-related internships or fieldwork, Federal Work-Study, scholarships/grants, and unspecified assistantships also available. Support available to part-time students. Financial award application deadline: 3/1; financial award applicants required to submit FAFSA. *Unit head:* Dr. Peter Martin, Chair, 607-274-1076, E-mail: pmartin@ithaca.edu. *Application contact:* Nicole Eversley Bradwell, Director, Office of Admission, 607-274-3124, Fax: 607-274-1263, E-mail: admission@ithaca.edu.
Website: http://www.ithaca.edu/gradprograms/education/programs/aded

Kansas State University, Graduate School, College of Agriculture, Department of Communications and Agricultural Education, Manhattan, KS 66506. Offers agricultural education and communication (MS). *Program availability:* Part-time, online learning. *Degree requirements:* For master's, comprehensive exam, thesis or alternative. *Entrance requirements:* For master's, GRE if GPA on last 60 undergraduate credits is less than 3.0. Electronic applications accepted. *Faculty research:* Curriculum development, instructional design, strategic communications, risk and crisis communications.

Louisiana State University and Agricultural & Mechanical College, Graduate School, College of Human Sciences and Education, School of Human Resource Education and Workforce Development, Baton Rouge, LA 70803. Offers agriculture and extension education and youth development (MS, PhD); career and technical education (MS, PhD); comprehensive vocational education (MS, PhD); extension and international education (MS, PhD); human resource and leadership development (MS, PhD); industrial education (MS); vocational agriculture education (MS, PhD); vocational business education (MS); vocational home economics education (MS). *Accreditation:* NCATE. *Faculty:* 11 full-time (6 women). *Students:* 102 full-time (71 women), 130 part-time (92 women); includes 89 minority (63 Black or African American, non-Hispanic/Latino; 3 American Indian or Alaska Native, non-Hispanic/Latino; 8 Asian, non-Hispanic/Latino; 14 Hispanic/Latino; 1 Two or more races, non-Hispanic/Latino), 6 international. Average age 35. 98 applicants, 69% accepted, 52 enrolled. In 2017, 94 master's, 15 doctorates awarded. *Financial support:* In 2017–18, 1 fellowship (averaging $18,238 per year), 16 teaching assistantships (averaging $15,341 per year) were awarded. *Total annual research expenditures:* $1,998.

Mississippi State University, College of Agriculture and Life Sciences, School of Human Sciences, Mississippi State, MS 39762. Offers agriculture and extension education (MS), including communication, leadership; agriculture science (PhD), including agriculture and extension education; fashion design and merchandising (MS), including design and product development, merchandising; human development and family studies (MS, PhD). *Accreditation:* NCATE (one or more programs are accredited). *Program availability:* Part-time. *Faculty:* 20 full-time (11 women). *Students:* 31 full-time (23 women), 54 part-time (38 women); includes 19 minority (15 Black or African American, non-Hispanic/Latino; 1 Hispanic/Latino; 3 Two or more races, non-Hispanic/Latino), 5 international. Average age 36. 26 applicants, 65% accepted, 15 enrolled. In 2017, 19 master's, 2 doctorates awarded. *Degree requirements:* For master's, thesis optional, comprehensive oral or written exam. *Entrance requirements:* For master's, GRE, minimum GPA of 2.75 in last 4 semesters of course work; for doctorate, minimum GPA of 3.0 on prior graduate work. Additional exam requirements/recommendations for international students: Required—TOEFL (minimum score 477 paper-based; 53 iBT); Recommended—IELTS (minimum score 4.5). *Application deadline:* For fall admission, 7/1 for domestic students, 5/1 for international students; for spring admission, 11/1 for domestic students, 9/1 for international students. Applications are processed on a rolling basis. Application fee: $60 ($80 for international students). Electronic applications accepted. *Expenses:* Tuition, state resident: full-time $8318; part-time $462.12 per credit hour. Tuition, nonresident: full-time $22,358; part-time $1242.12 per credit hour. *Required fees:* $110; $12.24 per credit hour. $6.12 per semester. *Financial support:* In 2017–18, 13 research assistantships (averaging $13,718 per year) were awarded; Federal Work-Study, institutionally sponsored loans, and unspecified assistantships also available. Financial award application deadline: 4/1; financial award applicants required to submit FAFSA. *Faculty research:* Animal welfare, agroscience, information technology, learning styles, problem solving. *Unit head:* Dr. Michael Newman, Professor and Director, 662-325-2950, E-mail: mnewman@humansci.msstate.edu. *Application contact:* Marina Hunt, Admissions and Enrollment Assistant, 662-325-5188, E-mail: mhunt@grad.msstate.edu.
Website: http://www.humansci.msstate.edu

Montana State University, The Graduate School, College of Agriculture, Division of Agricultural Education, Bozeman, MT 59717. Offers MS. *Program availability:* Part-time, online learning. *Degree requirements:* For master's, comprehensive exam. *Entrance requirements:* For master's, GRE General Test. Additional exam requirements/recommendations for international students: Required—TOEFL (minimum score 550 paper-based). Electronic applications accepted. *Faculty research:* Extension systems, youth leadership, agricultural, adult and youth education in agriculture, international agricultural education, enzymology of vitamins, coenzymes and metal ions, steroid metabolism, protein structure, impact of wolves on big game hunting demand, prescription drug price dispersion in heterogeneous markets, divorce risk and the labor force participation of women with and without children, the economics of terraces in the Peruvian Andes.

Murray State University, Hutson School of Agriculture, Murray, KY 42071. Offers agriculture (MS), including agribusiness economics, agriculture education, sustainable agriculture, veterinary hospital management; veterinary hospital management (Certificate). *Program availability:* Part-time, 100% online, blended/hybrid learning. *Faculty:* 15 full-time (7 women). *Students:* 35 full-time (23 women), 59 part-time (39 women); includes 5 minority (3 Black or African American, non-Hispanic/Latino; 1 Hispanic/Latino; 1 Two or more races, non-Hispanic/Latino), 5 international. Average age 28. 71 applicants, 77% accepted, 29 enrolled. In 2017, 19 master's, 3 other advanced degrees awarded. *Entrance requirements:* For master's, GRE or GMAT, minimum university GPA of 2.75. Additional exam requirements/recommendations for international students: Required—TOEFL (minimum score 527 paper-based; 71 iBT). *Application deadline:* Applications are processed on a rolling basis. Application fee: $40 ($50 for international students). Electronic applications accepted. *Expenses:* Tuition, state resident: full-time $9504. Tuition, nonresident: full-time $26,811. *International tuition:* $14,400 full-time. Tuition and fees vary according to course load, degree level and reciprocity agreements. *Financial support:* In 2017–18, 1 research assistantship, 4 teaching assistantships were awarded; Federal Work-Study also available. *Unit head:* Dr. Tony L. Brannon, Dean, 270-809-6923, Fax: 270-809-5454, E-mail: tbannon@murraystate.edu. *Application contact:* Kaitlyn Burzynski, Interim Assistant Director of Graduate Recruitment and Records, 270-809-5732, Fax: 270-809-3780, E-mail: msu.graduateadmissions@murraystate.edu.
Website: http://www.murraystate.edu/academics/CollegesDepartments/HutsonSchoolOfAgriculture/index.aspx

New Mexico State University, College of Agricultural, Consumer and Environmental Sciences, Department of Agricultural and Extension Education, Las Cruces, NM 88003. Offers MA. *Accreditation:* NCATE. *Program availability:* Part-time, evening/weekend, blended/hybrid learning. *Faculty:* 5 full-time (1 woman). *Students:* 7 full-time (5 women), 14 part-time (9 women); includes 6 minority (1 American Indian or Alaska Native, non-Hispanic/Latino; 5 Hispanic/Latino), 1 international. Average age 33. 7 applicants, 71% accepted, 3 enrolled. In 2017, 13 master's awarded. *Degree requirements:* For master's, comprehensive exam, thesis or creative component. *Entrance requirements:* For master's, 3 letters of recommendation. Additional exam requirements/recommendations for international students: Required—TOEFL (minimum score 550 paper-based; 79 iBT), IELTS (minimum score 6.5). *Application deadline:* For fall admission, 7/1 priority date for domestic and international students; for spring admission, 11/1 priority date for domestic and international students. Applications are processed on a rolling basis. Application fee: $40 ($50 for international students). Electronic applications accepted. *Expenses:* Tuition, state resident: full-time $4390. Tuition, nonresident: full-time $15,309. *Required fees:* $853. *Financial support:* In 2017–18, 10 students received support, including 4 teaching assistantships (averaging $16,964 per year); career-related internships or fieldwork, Federal Work-Study, scholarships/grants, traineeships, and health care benefits also available. Support available to part-time students. Financial award application deadline: 3/1. *Faculty research:* Secondary agricultural education programs, teaching and learning, agricultural technology and safety, youth leadership development, agricultural development, youth development. *Total annual research expenditures:* $218,297. *Unit head:* Dr. April Ulery, Interim Department Head, 575-646-2219, Fax: 575-646-4082, E-mail: aulery@nmsu.edu. *Application contact:* Dr. Brenda S. Seevers, Graduate Program Coordinator, 575-646-4511, Fax: 575-646-4082, E-mail: bseevers@nmsu.edu.
Website: http://aces.nmsu.edu/academics/axed

North Carolina Agricultural and Technical State University, School of Graduate Studies, School of Agriculture and Environmental Sciences, Department of Agribusiness, Applied Economics, and Agriscience Education, Greensboro, NC 27411. Offers agricultural economics (MS); agricultural education (MS). *Accreditation:* NCATE. *Program availability:* Part-time, evening/weekend. *Degree requirements:* For master's, comprehensive exam, thesis or alternative, qualifying exam. *Entrance requirements:* For master's, GRE General Test, minimum GPA of 3.0. *Faculty research:* Aid for small farmers, agricultural technology resources, labor force mobility, agrology.

North Carolina State University, Graduate School, College of Agriculture and Life Sciences, Department of Agricultural and Extension Education, Program in Agricultural Education, Raleigh, NC 27695. Offers MAE, MS, Certificate. *Program availability:* Online learning. *Degree requirements:* For master's, thesis optional. *Entrance requirements:* For master's, GRE or MAT. Electronic applications accepted. *Faculty research:* Instructional methodology, distance education, leadership development, foundations, curriculum development.

North Dakota State University, College of Graduate and Interdisciplinary Studies, College of Human Development and Education, School of Education, Program in Agricultural Education, Fargo, ND 58102. Offers M Ed, MS. *Accreditation:* NCATE. *Program availability:* Part-time. *Degree requirements:* For master's, comprehensive exam, thesis or alternative. *Entrance requirements:* Additional exam requirements/recommendations for international students: Required—TOEFL (minimum score 525 paper-based; 71 iBT). *Faculty research:* Vocational and cooperative extension education, rural leadership, rural education, international extension.

Northwest Missouri State University, Graduate School, School of Agricultural Sciences, Maryville, MO 64468-6001. Offers agricultural economics (MBA); agricultural education (MS Ed); agriculture (MS); teaching: agriculture (MS Ed). *Program availability:* Part-time. *Faculty:* 7 full-time (1 woman). *Students:* 7 full-time (4 women), 4 part-time (1 woman), 3 international. Average age 26. 11 applicants, 64% accepted, 3 enrolled. In 2017, 3 master's awarded. *Degree requirements:* For master's, comprehensive exam, thesis (for some programs). *Entrance requirements:* For master's, GRE General Test, minimum undergraduate GPA of 2.5, writing sample. Additional exam requirements/recommendations for international students: Required—TOEFL (minimum score 550 paper-based). *Application deadline:* For fall admission, 7/1 for domestic and international students; for spring admission, 11/15 for domestic and international students. Applications are processed on a rolling basis. Application fee: $0 ($50 for international students). Electronic applications accepted. *Expenses:* Tuition, state resident: full-time $4551; part-time $252.86 per credit hour. Tuition, nonresident: full-time $9103; part-time $505.72 per credit hour. *Required fees:* $2453; $136.25 per credit hour. Tuition and fees vary according to course load and program. *Financial support:* Research assistantships with full tuition reimbursements, teaching assistantships with full tuition reimbursements, and unspecified assistantships available. Financial award application deadline: 4/1; financial award applicants required to submit FAFSA. *Unit*

head: Rodney Barr, Director, 660-562-1620.
Website: http://www.nwmissouri.edu/ag/

The Ohio State University, Graduate School, College of Food, Agricultural, and Environmental Sciences, Department of Agricultural Communication, Education and Leadership, Program in Agricultural and Extension Education, Columbus, OH 43210. Offers MS. *Program availability:* Part-time, online learning. *Students:* 15 (13 women). Average age 27. In 2017, 4 master's awarded. *Entrance requirements:* For master's, GRE. Additional exam requirements/recommendations for international students: Required—TOEFL (minimum score 550 paper-based; 79 iBT), Michigan English Language Assessment Battery (minimum score 82); Recommended—IELTS (minimum score 7). *Application deadline:* For fall admission, 1/1 priority date for domestic students, 12/1 priority date for international students; for spring admission, 11/11 for domestic and international students; for summer admission, 3/1 for domestic and international students. Applications are processed on a rolling basis. Application fee: $60 ($70 for international students). Electronic applications accepted. *Financial support:* Institutionally sponsored loans available. Support available to part-time students. *Unit head:* Dr. Scott Scheer, Graduate Studies Chair, 614-292-6758, E-mail: scheer.9@osu.edu. *Application contact:* Graduate and Professional Admissions, 614-292-9444, Fax: 614-292-3895, E-mail: gpadmissions@osu.edu.
Website: http://acel.osu.edu/

Oklahoma State University, College of Agricultural Science and Natural Resources, Department of Agricultural Education, Communications and Leadership, Stillwater, OK 74078. Offers M Ag, MS, PhD. *Program availability:* Online learning. *Faculty:* 10 full-time (3 women), 3 part-time/adjunct (2 women). *Students:* 21 full-time (13 women), 41 part-time (30 women); includes 8 minority (4 American Indian or Alaska Native, non-Hispanic/Latino; 4 Hispanic/Latino), 3 international. Average age 29. 25 applicants, 84% accepted, 17 enrolled. In 2017, 17 master's, 2 doctorates awarded. *Entrance requirements:* For master's and doctorate, GRE or GMAT. Additional exam requirements/recommendations for international students: Required—TOEFL (minimum score 550 paper-based; 79 iBT). *Application deadline:* For fall admission, 3/1 priority date for international students; for spring admission, 8/1 priority date for international students. Applications are processed on a rolling basis. Application fee: $40 ($75 for international students). Electronic applications accepted. *Expenses:* Tuition, state resident: full-time $4019; part-time $2679.60 per year. Tuition, nonresident: full-time $15,286; part-time $10,190.40 per year. *Required fees:* $2129; $1419 per unit. Tuition and fees vary according to program. *Financial support:* Research assistantships, teaching assistantships, career-related internships or fieldwork, Federal Work-Study, scholarships/grants, health care benefits, tuition waivers (partial), and unspecified assistantships available. Support available to part-time students. Financial award application deadline: 3/1; financial award applicants required to submit FAFSA. *Faculty research:* Teaching in and learning about agriculture, agriculture teacher evaluation, evaluation of information dissemination delivery methods, agricultural literacy curriculum model development, distance education delivery methods. *Unit head:* Dr. Robert Terry, Department Head, 405-744-8036, Fax: 405-744-5176, E-mail: rob.terry@okstate.edu.
Website: http://aged.okstate.edu/

Oregon State University, College of Agricultural Sciences, Program in Agricultural Education, Corvallis, OR 97331. Offers leadership and communication in agriculture (MS). *Program availability:* Part-time. *Entrance requirements:* Additional exam requirements/recommendations for international students: Required—TOEFL (minimum score 80 iBT), IELTS (minimum score 6.5). *Application deadline:* For fall admission, 8/1 for domestic students, 4/1 for international students; for winter admission, 12/1 for domestic students, 7/1 for international students; for spring admission, 2/1 for domestic students, 10/1 for international students; for summer admission, 5/1 for domestic students, 1/1 for international students. Application fee: $75 ($85 for international students). *Unit head:* John Stewart, Instructor, 541-737-2854. *Application contact:* John Stewart, Instructor, 541-737-2854.
Website: http://agsci.oregonstate.edu/ag-ed

Oregon State University, College of Education, Program in Education, Corvallis, OR 97331. Offers agricultural education (PhD); language equity and education policy (PhD); mathematics education (MS); science education (MS); science/mathematics education (PhD). *Program availability:* Part-time, 100% online, blended/hybrid learning. Terminal master's awarded for partial completion of doctoral program. *Degree requirements:* For master's, variable foreign language requirement, thesis (for some programs); for doctorate, variable foreign language requirement, thesis/dissertation. *Entrance requirements:* Additional exam requirements/recommendations for international students: Required—TOEFL (minimum score 575 paper-based). Application fee: $75 ($85 for international students). *Faculty research:* School administration, educational foundations, research methodology, education policy development, higher education administration. *Unit head:* Nick Cabot, Ecampus Counseling Lead, 541-737-8564, E-mail: cabotn@oregonstate.edu. *Application contact:* Nick Cabot, Ecampus Counseling Lead, 541-737-8564, E-mail: cabotn@oregonstate.edu.

Penn State University Park, Graduate School, College of Agricultural Sciences, Department of Agricultural Economics, Sociology, and Education, University Park, PA 16802. Offers agricultural and extension education (M Ed, MS, PhD, Certificate); applied youth, family and community education (M Ed); energy, environmental, and food economics (MS, PhD); rural sociology (MS, PhD). *Unit head:* Dr. Richard T. Roush, Dean, 814-865-2541, Fax: 814-865-3103. *Application contact:* Lori Hawn, Director, Graduate Student Services, 814-865-1795, Fax: 814-863-4627, E-mail: l-gswww@lists.psu.edu.
Website: http://aese.psu.edu/

Purdue University, Graduate School, College of Agriculture, Department of Youth Development and Agricultural Education, West Lafayette, IN 47907. Offers MA, PhD. *Faculty:* 11 full-time (5 women). *Students:* 17 full-time (14 women), 8 part-time (7 women); includes 6 minority (5 Black or African American, non-Hispanic/Latino; 1 Asian, non-Hispanic/Latino), 3 international. Average age 27. 16 applicants, 69% accepted, 8 enrolled. In 2017, 6 master's, 1 doctorate awarded. *Degree requirements:* For doctorate, comprehensive exam. *Entrance requirements:* For master's and doctorate, GRE General Test (minimum combined score of 1000), minimum undergraduate GPA of 3.0 or equivalent. Additional exam requirements/recommendations for international students: Required—TOEFL (minimum score 550 paper-based; 77 iBT), TWE with minimum score of 5 (recommended for MA, required for PhD). *Application deadline:* For fall admission, 3/15 priority date for domestic students, 3/1 for international students; for spring admission, 10/15 priority date for domestic students, 8/1 for international students; for summer admission, 3/15 for domestic students, 1/1 for international students. Applications are processed on a rolling basis. Application fee: $60 ($75 for international students). Electronic applications accepted. *Unit head:* Mark A. Russell, Head, 765-494-8423, E-mail: mrussell@purdue.edu. *Application contact:* Brenda Pickett, Graduate Contact, 765-494-8439, E-mail: bpicket@purdue.edu.
Website: https://ag.purdue.edu/ydae

Purdue University, Graduate School, College of Education, Department of Curriculum and Instruction, West Lafayette, IN 47907. Offers agricultural and extension education (MS, MS Ed, PhD, Ed S); art education (PhD); career and technical education (MS Ed, PhD, Ed S); curriculum studies (MS Ed, PhD, Ed S); educational technology (MS Ed,

Agricultural Education

PhD, Ed S); elementary education (MS Ed); family and consumer sciences education (MS Ed, PhD, Ed S); foreign language education (MS Ed, PhD, Ed S); industrial technology (PhD, Ed S); language arts (MS Ed, PhD, Ed S); literacy (MS Ed, PhD, Ed S); mathematics education (MS, MS Ed, PhD, Ed S); science education (MS, MS Ed, PhD, Ed S); social studies education (MS Ed, PhD, Ed S). *Accreditation:* NCATE. *Program availability:* Part-time, evening/weekend. *Faculty:* 37 full-time (27 women), 1 (woman) part-time/adjunct. *Students:* 78 full-time (50 women), 286 part-time (195 women); includes 68 minority (25 Black or African American, non-Hispanic/Latino; 3 American Indian or Alaska Native, non-Hispanic/Latino; 10 Asian, non-Hispanic/Latino; 22 Hispanic/Latino; 1 Native Hawaiian or other Pacific Islander, non-Hispanic/Latino; 7 Two or more races, non-Hispanic/Latino), 44 international. Average age 36. 150 applicants, 79% accepted, 73 enrolled. In 2017, 107 master's, 20 doctorates, 2 other advanced degrees awarded. *Degree requirements:* For master's, thesis optional; for doctorate, thesis/dissertation, oral and written exams; for Ed S, oral presentation, project. *Entrance requirements:* For master's, GRE General Test (if undergraduate GPA is below 3.0), minimum undergraduate GPA of 3.0 or equivalent; for doctorate, GRE General Test (minimum combined verbal and quantitative score of 1000, 300 for new scoring), minimum undergraduate GPA of 3.0 or equivalent; master's degree with minimum GPA of 3.0 or equivalent; for Ed S, GRE General Test (minimum combined verbal and quantitative score of 1000, 300 for new scoring), minimum undergraduate GPA of 3.0 or equivalent; master's degree. Additional exam requirements/recommendations for international students: Required—TOEFL (minimum score 550 paper-based; 77 iBT). *Application deadline:* For fall admission, 12/15 for domestic students, 3/1 for international students; for spring admission, 9/15 for domestic students, 8/1 for international students. Application fee: $60 ($75 for international students). Electronic applications accepted. *Financial support:* Fellowships with full tuition reimbursements, research assistantships with full tuition reimbursements, teaching assistantships with full tuition reimbursements, career-related internships or fieldwork, and tuition waivers (full) available. Support available to part-time students. Financial award application deadline: 3/1; financial award applicants required to submit FAFSA. *Faculty research:* Literacy acquisition and development, teacher beliefs and knowledge, recruitment and retention of underrepresented students, economic education, literacy discourse. *Unit head:* Janet M. Alsup, Head, 765-494-9667, E-mail: alsupj@purdue.edu. *Application contact:* Heather Brinkman, Graduate Contact, 765-494-2345, E-mail: hbrinkma@purdue.edu.
Website: http://www.edci.purdue.edu/

Saint Leo University, Graduate Studies in Public Safety Administration, Saint Leo, FL 33574-6665. Offers criminal justice (MS), including behavioral studies, corrections, criminal investigation, criminal justice, emergency and disaster management, forensic science, legal studies; emergency and disaster management (MS), including emergency and disaster management, fire science. *Program availability:* Part-time, evening/weekend, 100% online, blended/hybrid learning. *Faculty:* 8 full-time (3 women), 32 part-time/adjunct (7 women). *Students:* 7 full-time (6 women), 617 part-time (385 women); includes 313 minority (235 Black or African American, non-Hispanic/Latino; 5 American Indian or Alaska Native, non-Hispanic/Latino; 3 Asian, non-Hispanic/Latino; 54 Hispanic/Latino; 1 Native Hawaiian or other Pacific Islander, non-Hispanic/Latino; 15 Two or more races, non-Hispanic/Latino). Average age 36. 336 applicants, 63% accepted, 197 enrolled. In 2017, 267 master's awarded. *Degree requirements:* For master's, comprehensive project. *Entrance requirements:* For master's, official transcripts, bachelor's degree from regionally-accredited university with minimum GPA of 3.0. Additional exam requirements/recommendations for international students: Required—TOEFL (minimum score 550 paper-based; 78 iBT). *Application deadline:* For fall admission, 7/1 priority date for domestic and international students; for spring admission, 11/1 priority date for domestic and international students. Applications are processed on a rolling basis. Application fee: $80. Electronic applications accepted. *Expenses:* $555 per credit hour. *Financial support:* In 2017–18, 21 students received support. Scholarships/grants, health care benefits, unspecified assistantships, and tuition remission for Saint Leo employees and their dependents available. Financial award application deadline: 3/1; financial award applicants required to submit FAFSA. *Faculty research:* Emergency management, fire science, community policing. *Unit head:* Dr. Robert Diemer, Director of Graduate Studies in Safety Administration, 352-588-8974, Fax: 352-588-8289, E-mail: graduatepublicsafety@saintleo.edu. *Application contact:* Mark Russum, Assistant Vice President, Enrollment, 800-707-8846, Fax: 352-588-7873, E-mail: grad.admissions@saintleo.edu.
Website: https://www.saintleo.edu/criminal-justice-master-degree

South Dakota State University, Graduate School, College of Education and Human Sciences, Department of Teaching, Learning and Leadership, Brookings, SD 57007. Offers agricultural education (MS); curriculum and instruction (M Ed); educational administration (M Ed). *Program availability:* Part-time, evening/weekend, online learning. *Degree requirements:* For master's, portfolio, oral exam. *Entrance requirements:* For master's, minimum GPA of 2.75. Additional exam requirements/recommendations for international students: Required—TOEFL (minimum score 550 paper-based; 80 iBT). *Faculty research:* Inclusion school climate, K-12 reform and restructuring, rural development, ESL, leadership.

State University of New York at Oswego, Graduate Studies, School of Education, Department of Vocational Teacher Preparation, Oswego, NY 13126. Offers agriculture (MS Ed); business and marketing (MS Ed); family and consumer sciences (MS Ed); health careers (MS Ed); technical education (MS Ed); trade education (MS Ed). *Accreditation:* NCATE. *Program availability:* Part-time, evening/weekend. *Degree requirements:* For master's, comprehensive exam, thesis or alternative. *Entrance requirements:* Additional exam requirements/recommendations for international students: Required—TOEFL (minimum score 560 paper-based).

Stephen F. Austin State University, Graduate School, College of Forestry and Agriculture, Department of Agriculture, Nacogdoches, TX 75962. Offers MS. *Accreditation:* NCATE. *Degree requirements:* For master's, comprehensive exam, thesis (for some programs). *Entrance requirements:* For master's, GRE General Test, minimum GPA of 2.8 in last half of major, 2.5 overall. Additional exam requirements/recommendations for international students: Required—TOEFL (minimum score 550 paper-based). *Faculty research:* Asian vegetables, soil fertility, animal breeding, animal nutrition.

Tennessee State University, The School of Graduate Studies and Research, College of Agriculture, Human and Natural Sciences, Nashville, TN 37209-1561. Offers agricultural sciences (MS), including agribusiness, agricultural and extension education, animal science, plant and soil science; biological sciences (MS, PhD); biotechnology (PhD); chemistry (MS). *Program availability:* Part-time, evening/weekend. *Degree requirements:* For master's, thesis. *Entrance requirements:* For master's, GRE General Test, GRE Subject Test, MAT. *Faculty research:* Small farm economics, ornamental horticulture, beef cattle production, rural elderly.

Texas A&M University, College of Agriculture and Life Sciences, Department of Agricultural Leadership, Education and Communications, College Station, TX 77843. Offers agricultural development (M Agr); agricultural education (Ed D); agricultural leadership, education and communication (M Ed, MS, PhD). *Program availability:* Part-time, blended/hybrid learning. *Faculty:* 19. *Students:* 55 full-time (45 women), 72 part-

time (47 women); includes 21 minority (7 Black or African American, non-Hispanic/Latino; 1 American Indian or Alaska Native, non-Hispanic/Latino; 3 Asian, non-Hispanic/Latino; 9 Hispanic/Latino; 1 Two or more races, non-Hispanic/Latino), 3 international. Average age 32. 43 applicants, 93% accepted, 33 enrolled. In 2017, 30 master's, 8 doctorates awarded. Terminal master's awarded for partial completion of doctoral program. *Degree requirements:* For master's, comprehensive exam, thesis (for some programs); for doctorate, comprehensive exam, thesis/dissertation. *Entrance requirements:* For master's, GRE General Test, letters of reference, curriculum vitae; for doctorate, GRE General Test, 3 years of professional experience, letters of reference, curriculum vitae. Additional exam requirements/recommendations for international students: Required—TOEFL (minimum score 550 paper-based; 80 iBT), IELTS (minimum score 6), PTE (minimum score 53). *Application deadline:* For fall admission, 3/15 priority date for domestic students; for spring admission, 10/15 for domestic students. Application fee: $50 ($90 for international students). Electronic applications accepted. *Expenses:* Contact institution. *Financial support:* In 2017–18, 71 students received support, including 6 fellowships with tuition reimbursements available (averaging $18,512 per year), 7 research assistantships with tuition reimbursements available (averaging $7,789 per year), 22 teaching assistantships with tuition reimbursements available (averaging $8,558 per year); career-related internships or fieldwork, institutionally sponsored loans, scholarships/grants, traineeships, health care benefits, tuition waivers (full and partial), and unspecified assistantships also available. Support available to part-time students. Financial award application deadline: 3/15; financial award applicants required to submit FAFSA. *Faculty research:* Planning and needs assessment, instructional design, delivery strategies, evaluation and accountability, distance education. *Unit head:* Dr. Jack Elliot, Department Head, 979-862-3003, E-mail: jelliot@tamu.edu. *Application contact:* Clarice Fulton, Graduate Program Coordinator, 979-862-7180, E-mail: cfulton@tamu.edu.
Website: http://alec.tamu.edu/

Texas State University, The Graduate College, College of Applied Arts, Program in Agricultural Education, San Marcos, TX 78666. Offers M Ed. *Program availability:* Part-time, evening/weekend. *Faculty:* 7 full-time (2 women), 1 (woman) part-time/adjunct. *Students:* 12 full-time (9 women), 4 part-time (2 women); includes 6 minority (1 Black or African American, non-Hispanic/Latino; 1 Asian, non-Hispanic/Latino; 4 Hispanic/Latino), 1 international. Average age 28. 8 applicants, 88% accepted, 4 enrolled. In 2017, 6 master's awarded. *Degree requirements:* For master's, comprehensive exam, thesis (for some programs). *Entrance requirements:* For master's, baccalaureate degree from regionally-accredited university in agriculture or closely-related field with minimum GPA of 2.75 in last 60 hours of course work; 3 letters of reference (2 from academia). Additional exam requirements/recommendations for international students: Required—TOEFL (minimum score 550 paper-based; 78 iBT), IELTS (minimum score 6.5). *Application deadline:* For fall admission, 6/15 for domestic students, 6/1 for international students; for spring admission, 10/15 for domestic students, 10/1 for international students; for summer admission, 4/15 for domestic students, 3/15 for international students. Applications are processed on a rolling basis. Application fee: $40 ($90 for international students). Electronic applications accepted. *Expenses:* Tuition, state resident: full-time $7868; part-time $3934 per semester. Tuition, nonresident: full-time $17,828; part-time $8914 per semester. Required fees: $2092; $1435 per semester. Tuition and fees vary according to course load. *Financial support:* In 2017–18, 10 students received support, including 4 research assistantships (averaging $12,354 per year), 3 teaching assistantships (averaging $8,251 per year); career-related internships or fieldwork, Federal Work-Study, institutionally sponsored loans, and scholarships/grants also available. Support available to part-time students. Financial award application deadline: 3/1; financial award applicants required to submit FAFSA. *Faculty research:* Food safety and agroterrorism; sustainable agriculture; soil and water conservation; determining market forces of premium leafy greens in Texas. *Total annual research expenditures:* $253,640. *Unit head:* Dr. Douglas Morrish, Graduate Advisor, 512-245-2130, E-mail: dm43@txstate.edu. *Application contact:* Dr. Andrea Golato, Dean of the Graduate College, 512-245-2581, Fax: 512-245-8365, E-mail: gradcollege@txstate.edu.
Website: http://ag.txstate.edu/

Texas Tech University, Graduate School, College of Agricultural Sciences and Natural Resources, Department of Agricultural Education and Communications, Lubbock, TX 79409. Offers agricultural communications (MS); agricultural communications and education (PhD); agricultural education (MS, Ed D). *Program availability:* Part-time, evening/weekend, 100% online. *Faculty:* 13 full-time (7 women), 2 part-time/adjunct (0 women). *Students:* 38 full-time (32 women), 49 part-time (37 women); includes 10 minority (2 Black or African American, non-Hispanic/Latino; 6 Hispanic/Latino; 2 Two or more races, non-Hispanic/Latino), 9 international. Average age 30. 52 applicants, 58% accepted, 26 enrolled. In 2017, 15 master's, 6 doctorates awarded. Terminal master's awarded for partial completion of doctoral program. *Degree requirements:* For master's, variable foreign language requirement, comprehensive exam, thesis optional; for doctorate, variable foreign language requirement, comprehensive exam, thesis/dissertation, experience plan. *Entrance requirements:* For master's and doctorate, GRE. Additional exam requirements/recommendations for international students: Required—TOEFL (minimum score 550 paper-based; 79 iBT). *Application deadline:* For fall admission, 6/1 priority date for domestic students, 1/15 priority date for international students; for spring admission, 9/1 priority date for domestic students, 6/15 priority date for international students. Applications are processed on a rolling basis. Application fee: $60. Electronic applications accepted. *Expenses:* Contact institution. *Financial support:* In 2017–18, 60 students received support, including 47 fellowships (averaging $3,120 per year), 38 research assistantships (averaging $13,872 per year), 14 teaching assistantships (averaging $6,038 per year); institutionally sponsored loans and scholarships/grants also available. Financial award application deadline: 4/15; financial award applicants required to submit FAFSA. *Faculty research:* Sustainable agriculture, food safety, international development, use of technology in agriculture, improvement of teaching and pedagogy. *Total annual research expenditures:* $361,053. *Unit head:* Dr. Scott Burris, Professor and Interim Chair, 806-834-8689, Fax: 806-742-2880, E-mail: scott.burris@ttu.edu. *Application contact:* Dr. Courtney Meyers, Associate Professor and Graduate Coordinator, 806-834-4364, Fax: 806-742-2880, E-mail: courtney.meyers@ttu.edu.
Website: http://www.aged.ttu.edu

The University of Arizona, College of Agriculture and Life Sciences, Department of Agricultural Education, Tucson, AZ 85721. Offers MAE, MS, Graduate Certificate. *Degree requirements:* For master's, thesis. *Entrance requirements:* For master's, teaching/extension experience or equivalent, minimum GPA of 3.0, 2 letters of recommendation. Additional exam requirements/recommendations for international students: Required—TOEFL (minimum score 550 paper-based; 79 iBT). Electronic applications accepted. *Faculty research:* Career placement, learning styles, noise impact on learning, computer technology, vocational education.

University of Arkansas, Graduate School, Dale Bumpers College of Agricultural, Food and Life Sciences, Department of Agricultural Education, Communications and Technology, Fayetteville, AR 72701. Offers agricultural and extension education (MS). *Accreditation:* NCATE. *Students:* 11 applicants, 100% accepted. In 2017, 8 master's awarded. *Application deadline:* For fall admission, 8/1 for domestic students, 4/1 for international students; for

spring admission, 12/1 for domestic students, 10/1 for international students; for summer admission, 4/15 for domestic students, 3/1 for international students. Applications are processed on a rolling basis. Application fee: $60. Electronic applications accepted. *Expenses:* Tuition, state resident: full-time $3782. Tuition, nonresident: full-time $10,238. *Financial support:* In 2017–18, 3 research assistantships, 4 teaching assistantships were awarded; fellowships, career-related internships or fieldwork, and Federal Work-Study also available. Support available to part-time students. Financial award application deadline: 4/1; financial award applicants required to submit FAFSA. *Unit head:* Dr. George William Wardlow, Department Head, 479-575-2038, E-mail: wardlow@uark.edu. *Application contact:* Dr. Donna Graham, Graduate Coordinator, 479-575-2039, E-mail: dgraham@uark.edu.
Website: https://agricultural-education-communications-and-technology.uark.edu/index.php

University of Connecticut, Graduate School, Neag School of Education, Department of Curriculum and Instruction, Storrs, CT 06269. Offers agriculture (MA), including agriculture education; agriculture education (PhD); bilingual and bicultural education (MA, PhD); elementary education (MA, PhD); English education (MA, PhD); history and social sciences education (MA, PhD); mathematics education (MA, PhD); music education (MA); reading education (MA, PhD); science education (MA, PhD); secondary education (MA, PhD); world languages education (MA, PhD). *Accreditation:* NCATE. Terminal master's awarded for partial completion of doctoral program. *Degree requirements:* For master's, comprehensive exam, thesis or alternative; for doctorate, thesis/dissertation. *Entrance requirements:* For doctorate, GRE General Test. Additional exam requirements/recommendations for international students: Required—TOEFL (minimum score 550 paper-based). Electronic applications accepted.

University of Delaware, College of Agriculture and Natural Resources, Department of Food and Resource Economics, Agricultural Education Program, Newark, DE 19716. Offers MA.

University of Florida, Graduate School, College of Agricultural and Life Sciences, Department of Agricultural Education and Communication, Gainesville, FL 32611. Offers agricultural education and communication (MS, PhD); tropical conservation and development (MS, PhD). *Program availability:* Part-time, evening/weekend, online learning. *Degree requirements:* For master's, comprehensive exam (for some programs), thesis (for some programs); for doctorate, comprehensive exam, thesis/dissertation. *Entrance requirements:* For master's and doctorate, GRE General Test, minimum GPA of 3.0. Additional exam requirements/recommendations for international students: Required—TOEFL (minimum score 550 paper-based; 80 iBT), IELTS (minimum score 6). Electronic applications accepted. *Faculty research:* Teaching and learning in formal and non-formal settings, program evaluation and development, leadership development in agriculture and natural resources, public issues education in agriculture and natural resources.

University of Illinois at Urbana–Champaign, Graduate College, College of Agricultural, Consumer and Environmental Sciences, Agricultural Education Program, Champaign, IL 61820. Offers MS. *Program availability:* Part-time, online learning.

University of Missouri, Office of Research and Graduate Studies, College of Agriculture, Food and Natural Resources, Department of Agricultural Education, Columbia, MO 65211. Offers MS, PhD. *Accreditation:* TEAC. *Degree requirements:* For doctorate, comprehensive exam, thesis/dissertation. *Entrance requirements:* For master's, minimum GPA of 3.0 for last 60 hours of undergraduate coursework; for doctorate, GRE (preferred minimum score of 1000), minimum GPA of 3.5 on prior graduate course work; minimum of 3 years of full-time appropriate teaching or other professional experience; correspondence with one department faculty member in proposed area of concentration. Additional exam requirements/recommendations for international students: Required—TOEFL (minimum score 550 paper-based; 80 iBT). Electronic applications accepted. *Faculty research:* Program and professional development, evaluation, teaching and learning theories and practices, educational methods, organization and administration, leadership and communication.

University of Missouri, Office of Research and Graduate Studies, College of Education, Department of Learning, Teaching and Curriculum, Columbia, MO 65211. Offers agricultural education (M Ed, PhD, Ed S); art education (M Ed, PhD, Ed S); business and office education (M Ed, PhD, Ed S); early childhood education (M Ed, PhD, Ed S); elementary education (M Ed, PhD, Ed S); English education (M Ed, PhD, Ed S); foreign language education (M Ed, PhD, Ed S); health education and promotion (M Ed, PhD); learning and instruction (M Ed); marketing education (M Ed, PhD, Ed S); mathematics education (M Ed, PhD, Ed S); music education (M Ed, PhD, Ed S); reading education (M Ed, PhD, Ed S); science education (M Ed, PhD, Ed S); social studies education (M Ed, PhD, Ed S); vocational education (M Ed, PhD, Ed S). *Program availability:* Part-time. Terminal master's awarded for partial completion of doctoral program. *Degree requirements:* For doctorate, thesis/dissertation. *Entrance requirements:* For master's and Ed S, GRE General Test or MAT, minimum GPA of 3.0; for doctorate, GRE General Test, minimum GPA of 3.0. Additional exam requirements/recommendations for international students: Required—TOEFL (minimum score 600 paper-based; 100 iBT). Electronic applications accepted.

University of Nebraska–Lincoln, Graduate College, College of Agricultural Sciences and Natural Resources, Department of Agricultural Leadership, Education and Communication, Lincoln, NE 68588. Offers leadership development (MS); leadership education (MS); teaching and extension education (MS). *Accreditation:* TEAC. *Degree requirements:* For master's, thesis optional. *Entrance requirements:* For master's, resume. Additional exam requirements/recommendations for international students: Required—TOEFL (minimum score 550 paper-based). Electronic applications accepted. *Faculty research:* Teaching and instruction, extension education, leadership and human resource development, international agricultural education.

University of Puerto Rico–Mayagüez, Graduate Studies, College of Agricultural Sciences, Department of Agricultural Education, Mayagüez, PR 00681-9000. Offers agricultural education (MS); agricultural extension (MS). *Accreditation:* NCATE. *Program availability:* Part-time. *Degree requirements:* For master's, comprehensive exam, thesis. *Entrance requirements:* For master's, BA in home economics; BS in agricultural education, agriculture, home economics, or equivalent. Electronic applications accepted. *Faculty research:* Curricular development and supervision, youth education, rural sociology.

The University of Tennessee, Graduate School, College of Agricultural Sciences and Natural Resources, Department of Agricultural Economics, Knoxville, TN 37996. Offers agricultural education (MS); agricultural extension education (MS). *Accreditation:* NCATE. *Program availability:* Part-time, online learning. *Degree requirements:* For master's, thesis or alternative. *Entrance requirements:* For master's, minimum GPA of 2.7. Additional exam requirements/recommendations for international students: Required—TOEFL. Electronic applications accepted.

University of Wisconsin–River Falls, Outreach and Graduate Studies, College of Agriculture, Food, and Environmental Sciences, Department of Agricultural Education, River Falls, WI 54022. Offers MS. *Program availability:* Part-time. *Degree requirements:* For master's, comprehensive exam, thesis (for some programs). *Entrance requirements:* For master's, minimum GPA of 2.75. Additional exam requirements/recommendations for international students: Required—TOEFL (minimum score 500 paper-based; 65 iBT), IELTS (minimum score 5.5). Electronic applications accepted.

Utah State University, School of Graduate Studies, College of Agriculture and Applied Sciences, School of Applied Sciences, Technology and Education, Logan, UT 84322. Offers agricultural extension and education (MS); family and consumer sciences education and extension (MS); technology and engineering education (MS). *Program availability:* Part-time, online learning. *Degree requirements:* For master's, comprehensive exam (for some programs), thesis (for some programs). *Entrance requirements:* For master's, GRE General Test, MAT, BS in agricultural education, agricultural extension, or related agricultural or science discipline; minimum GPA of 3.0. Additional exam requirements/recommendations for international students: Required—TOEFL. *Faculty research:* Extension and adult education; structures and environment; low-input agriculture; farm safety, systems, and mechanizations.

West Virginia University, Davis College of Agriculture, Forestry and Consumer Sciences, Morgantown, WV 26506. Offers agricultural and extension education (MS, PhD); agriculture and resource management (MS); agriculture, natural resources and design (M Agr); agronomy (MS); animal and food science (PhD); animal physiology (MS); applied and environmental microbiology (MS); design and merchandising (MS); entomology (MS); forest resource science (PhD); forestry (MSF); genetics and developmental biology (MS, PhD); horticulture (MS); human and community development (PhD); landscape architecture (MLA); natural resource economics (PhD); nutritional and food science (MS); plant and soil science (PhD); plant pathology (MS); recreation, parks and tourism resources (MS); reproductive physiology (MS, PhD); wildlife and fisheries resources (PhD). *Program availability:* Part-time. *Students:* 200 full-time (97 women), 53 part-time (32 women); includes 27 minority (6 Black or African American, non-Hispanic/Latino; 1 American Indian or Alaska Native, non-Hispanic/Latino; 4 Asian, non-Hispanic/Latino; 11 Hispanic/Latino; 5 Two or more races, non-Hispanic/Latino), 67 international. *Degree requirements:* For master's, thesis; for doctorate, thesis/dissertation. *Entrance requirements:* Additional exam requirements/recommendations for international students: Required—TOEFL (minimum score 550 paper-based). *Application deadline:* For fall admission, 6/1 priority date for domestic students, 6/1 for international students; for spring admission, 1/5 for domestic and international students. Applications are processed on a rolling basis. Application fee: $60. Electronic applications accepted. *Expenses:* Tuition, state resident: full-time $9450. Tuition, nonresident: full-time $24,390. *Financial support:* Fellowships, research assistantships, teaching assistantships, career-related internships or fieldwork, Federal Work-Study, institutionally sponsored loans, tuition waivers (full and partial), and unspecified assistantships available. Financial award application deadline: 2/1; financial award applicants required to submit FAFSA. *Faculty research:* Reproductive physiology, soil and water quality, human nutrition, aquaculture, wildlife management. *Unit head:* Dr. Dan J. Robison, Dean, 304-293-2395, Fax: 304-293-3740, E-mail: dan.robison@mail.wvu.edu. *Application contact:* Dr. Dennis K. Smith, Associate Dean, 304-293-2275, Fax: 304-293-3740, E-mail: denny.smith@mail.wvu.edu.
Website: https://www.davis.wvu.edu

Art Education

Academy of Art University, Graduate Programs, School of Art Education, San Francisco, CA 94105-3410. Offers MA, MAT. *Program availability:* Part-time, 100% online. *Faculty:* 2 full-time (1 woman), 4 part-time/adjunct (all women). *Students:* 26 full-time (all women), 14 part-time (12 women); includes 6 minority (2 Black or African American, non-Hispanic/Latino; 2 Asian, non-Hispanic/Latino; 2 Hispanic/Latino), 18 international. Average age 31. 27 applicants, 100% accepted, 16 enrolled. In 2017, 19 master's awarded. *Degree requirements:* For master's, final review. *Entrance requirements:* For master's, statement of intent; resume; portfolio/reel; official college transcripts. *Application deadline:* Applications are processed on a rolling basis. Application fee: $50. Electronic applications accepted. *Expenses:* Tuition: Part-time $982 per unit. *Financial support:* Career-related internships or fieldwork, Federal Work-Study, and scholarships/grants available. Financial award application deadline: 8/10; financial award applicants required to submit FAFSA. *Unit head:* 800-544-ARTS, E-mail: info@academyart.edu. *Application contact:* 800-544-ARTS, E-mail: info@academyart.edu.
Website: http://www.academyart.edu/art-education-school/index.html

Adelphi University, Ruth S. Ammon School of Education, Program in Art Education, Garden City, NY 11530-0701. Offers MA. *Program availability:* Part-time. *Students:* 5 full-time (all women), 1 (woman) part-time. Average age 28. 13 applicants, 46% accepted, 2 enrolled. In 2017, 5 master's awarded. *Entrance requirements:* For master's, 2 letters of recommendation, visual arts portfolio, essay. Additional exam requirements/recommendations for international students: Required—TOEFL (minimum score 550 paper-based; 80 iBT), IELTS (minimum score 6.5). *Application deadline:* For fall admission, 4/1 for international students; for spring admission, 11/1 for international students. Application fee: $50. Electronic applications accepted. *Expenses:* Contact institution. *Financial support:* Research assistantships, teaching assistantships, career-related internships or fieldwork, institutionally sponsored loans, scholarships/grants, traineeships, and unspecified assistantships available. Support available to part-time students. Financial award application deadline: 2/15; financial award applicants required to submit FAFSA. *Unit head:* Courtney Lee Weida, Director, 516-877-4105, E-mail: cweida@adelphi.edu. *Application contact:* E-mail: graduateadmissions@adelphi.edu.

Alabama Agricultural and Mechanical University, School of Graduate Studies, College of Education, Humanities, and Behavioral Sciences, Department of Visual, Performing, and Communication Arts, Huntsville, AL 35811. Offers art education (MS); music education (M Ed). *Accreditation:* NCATE. *Program availability:* Part-time, evening/weekend. *Degree requirements:* For master's, comprehensive exam. *Entrance requirements:* For master's, GRE General Test. Additional exam requirements/recommendations for international students: Required—TOEFL (minimum score 500 paper-based; 61 iBT). Electronic applications accepted. *Faculty research:* Jazz and black music, Alabama folk music.

American University of Puerto Rico, Program in Education, Bayamon, PR 00960-2037. Offers art education (M Ed); elementary education 4-6 (M Ed); elementary education K-3 (M Ed); general science education (M Ed); physical education (M Ed); special education (M Ed). *Program availability:* Part-time, evening/weekend. *Faculty:* 17 part-time/adjunct (7 women). *Students:* 22 full-time (18 women), 54 part-time (42 women); all minorities (all Hispanic/Latino). Average age 33. 22 applicants, 86% accepted, 19 enrolled. In 2017, 53 master's awarded. *Entrance requirements:* For master's, EXADEP, GRE, or MAT, 2 letters of recommendation, minimum GPA of 2.5. *Application deadline:* For fall admission, 8/1 for domestic students; for winter admission, 10/18 for domestic students; for spring admission, 3/15 for domestic students. Applications are processed on a rolling basis. Application fee: $25. Tuition and fees vary according to course load and degree level. *Financial support:* In 2017–18, 79 students received support, including 76 fellowships (averaging $400 per year), 55 teaching assistantships (averaging $1,741 per year). Financial award applicants required to submit FAFSA. *Unit head:* Prof. Bolivar Ramirez-Carlo, III, Dean of Faculty, 787-620-2040 Ext. 2010, Fax: 787-620-2958, E-mail: bramirez@aupr.edu. *Application contact:* Keren I. Llanos-Figueroa, Information Contact, 787-620-2040 Ext. 2021, Fax: 787-785-7377, E-mail: oficnaadmisiones@aupr.edu.

Arcadia University, School of Education, Glenside, PA 19038-3295. Offers art education (M Ed); computer education (CAS); curriculum (CAS); curriculum studies (M Ed); early childhood education (M Ed), including individualized, master teacher, research in child development; educational leadership (M Ed, Ed D, CAS); elementary education (M Ed); English education (MA Ed); environmental education (MA Ed); instructional technology (M Ed); language arts (M Ed); library science (M Ed); mathematics education (M Ed, MA Ed); music education (MA Ed); psychology (M Ed); reading (M Ed, CAS); science education (M Ed, CAS); secondary education (M Ed, CAS); special education (M Ed, Ed D, CAS); theater arts (MA Ed); written communication (MA Ed). *Accreditation:* NASAD. *Program availability:* Part-time, evening/weekend, online learning. Electronic applications accepted. *Expenses:* Contact institution.

Arizona State University at the Tempe campus, Herberger Institute for Design and the Arts, School of Art, Tempe, AZ 85287-1505. Offers art education (MA); art history (MA); ceramics (MFA); design, environment and the arts (PhD), including history, theory and criticism; drawing (MFA); fibers (MFA); intermedia (MFA); metals (MFA); museum studies (MA); painting (MFA); printmaking (MFA); sculpture (MFA); wood (MFA); MFA/MA. Terminal master's awarded for partial completion of doctoral program. *Degree requirements:* For master's, thesis/exhibition (MFA, MA in art education); interactive Program of Study (iPOS) submitted before completing 50 percent of required credit hours; for doctorate, comprehensive exam, thesis/dissertation, interactive Program of Study (iPOS) submitted before completing 50 percent of required credit hours. *Entrance requirements:* For master's, GRE or MAT, minimum GPA of 3.0 or equivalent in last 2 years of work leading to bachelor's degree; for doctorate, GRE, master's degree in architecture, graphic design, industrial design, interior design, landscape architecture, or art history or equivalent standing; statement of purpose; 3 letters of recommendation; indication of potential faculty mentor; sample of written work. Additional exam requirements/recommendations for international students: Required—TOEFL, IELTS, or PTE. Electronic applications accepted.

Art Academy of Cincinnati, Program in Art Education, Cincinnati, OH 45202. Offers MAAE. Offered during summer only. *Accreditation:* NASAD. *Program availability:* Part-time. *Degree requirements:* For master's, thesis, portfolio/exhibit. *Entrance requirements:* For master's, 2 letters of recommendation, portfolio, artist statement, undergraduate transcript. Additional exam requirements/recommendations for international students: Required—TOEFL (minimum score 550 paper-based; 80 iBT). Electronic applications accepted.

Avila University, School of Education, Kansas City, MO 64145-1698. Offers advanced classroom management (MA); art K-12 (Teaching Certificate); educational technology (MA, Certificate); elementary education (Teaching Certificate); English as a second language (MA); English language learners (Advanced Certificate); middle school (Teaching Certificate); physical education K-12 (Teaching Certificate); secondary education (Teaching Certificate); special education (Teaching Certificate); special reading (Advanced Certificate); teaching and learning (MA). *Program availability:* Part-time, evening/weekend, online learning. *Faculty:* 6 full-time (5 women), 9 part-time/adjunct (8 women). *Students:* 81 full-time (63 women), 20 part-time (11 women); includes 14 minority (8 Black or African American, non-Hispanic/Latino; 2 Asian, non-Hispanic/Latino; 3 Hispanic/Latino; 1 Two or more races, non-Hispanic/Latino), 4 international. Average age 35. 92 applicants, 62% accepted, 40 enrolled. In 2017, 24 master's awarded. *Entrance requirements:* For master's, minimum GPA of 3.0, writing sample, recommendation, interview; for other advanced degree, foreign language. Additional exam requirements/recommendations for international students: Required—TOEFL (minimum score 580 paper-based; 92 iBT). *Application deadline:* Applications are processed on a rolling basis. Electronic applications accepted. *Expenses:* Contact institution. *Financial support:* In 2017–18, 14 students received support. Unspecified assistantships available. Financial award applicants required to submit FAFSA. *Unit head:* Dr. Stacy Keith, Director of Graduate Education, 816-501-2446, Fax: 816-501-2915, E-mail: stacy.keith@avila.edu. *Application contact:* Cory Roup, Graduate Education Enrollment and Academic Advisor, 816-501-2464, E-mail: cory.roup@avila.edu.
Website: https://www.avila.edu/academics/graduate-studies/grad-education

Boston University, College of Fine Arts, School of Visual Arts, Boston, MA 02215. Offers art education (MA); graphic design (MFA); painting (MFA); sculpture (MFA); studio teaching (MA). *Faculty:* 17 full-time, 4 part-time/adjunct. *Students:* 161 full-time (139 women), 3 part-time (all women); includes 19 minority (2 Black or African American, non-Hispanic/Latino; 6 Asian, non-Hispanic/Latino; 9 Hispanic/Latino; 2 Two or more races, non-Hispanic/Latino), 37 international. Average age 30. 365 applicants, 27% accepted, 21 enrolled. In 2017, 85 master's awarded. *Entrance requirements:* For master's, portfolio. Additional exam requirements/recommendations for international students: Required—TOEFL (minimum score 90 iBT), IELTS (minimum score 7). *Application deadline:* For fall admission, 2/1 for domestic and international students. Applications are processed on a rolling basis. Application fee: $95. *Expenses:* Contact institution. *Financial support:* In 2017–18, 36 students received support. Fellowships, teaching assistantships, scholarships/grants, and unspecified assistantships available. Financial award application deadline: 2/1. *Unit head:* Lynne Allen, Director, 617-353-3371. *Application contact:* Jessica Caccamo, Assistant Director of Admissions, 617-353-3371, E-mail: visuarts@bu.edu.

Bowling Green State University, Graduate College, College of Arts and Sciences, School of Art, Bowling Green, OH 43403. Offers 2-D studio art (MA, MFA); 3-D studio art (MA, MFA); art education (MA); art history (MA); computer art (MA); design (MFA); digital arts (MFA); graphics (MFA). *Accreditation:* NASAD. *Program availability:* Part-time. *Degree requirements:* For master's, thesis or alternative, final exhibit (MFA). *Entrance requirements:* For master's, GRE General Test (for MA), slide portfolio (15-20 slides). Additional exam requirements/recommendations for international students: Required—TOEFL. Electronic applications accepted. *Faculty research:* Computer animation and virtual reality, Spanish still-life painting from 1600 to 1800, art and

psychotherapy, Japanese wood-firing techniques in ceramics, non-toxic printmaking technologies.

Bridgewater State University, College of Graduate Studies, College of Humanities and Social Sciences, Department of Art, Bridgewater, MA 02325. Offers MAT. *Accreditation:* NASAD. *Program availability:* Part-time, evening/weekend. *Degree requirements:* For master's, comprehensive exam. *Entrance requirements:* For master's, GRE General Test.

Brigham Young University, Graduate Studies, College of Fine Arts and Communications, Department of Art, Provo, UT 84602-6414. Offers art education (M Ed); studio arts (MFA). Art education applications accepted biennially. *Accreditation:* NASAD. *Faculty:* 13 full-time (2 women). *Students:* 26 full-time (18 women); includes 4 minority (3 Asian, non-Hispanic/Latino; 1 Hispanic/Latino). Average age 36. 22 applicants, 55% accepted, 10 enrolled. In 2017, 6 master's awarded. *Degree requirements:* For master's, one foreign language, comprehensive exam, thesis, selected project (for MFA); curriculum project (for art education). *Entrance requirements:* For master's, minimum GPA of 3.0 (for MFA, MA in art education), portfolio submitted on a flash drive (for MFA); writing samples (for MA). Additional exam requirements/recommendations for international students: Required—TOEFL (minimum score 580 paper-based, 85 iBT) or IELTS (7). *Application deadline:* For fall admission, 2/1 for domestic and international students. Application fee: $50. Electronic applications accepted. *Expenses:* $10,320 per academic year, $405 per credit hour for members of the Church of Jesus Christ of Latter-day Saints; $20,640 for the year, $810 per credit hour for those who are not members of the Church; lab fees: $25 per credit hour for printmaking, $25 for ceramics, and $15 for sculpture. *Financial support:* In 2017–18, 19 students received support, including 11 teaching assistantships with partial tuition reimbursements available; scholarships/grants also available. Financial award application deadline: 2/1. *Faculty research:* Methodology-standards-assessment, exploration of art making processes, new genre, installation, photography, theory and critical studies, art history. *Unit head:* Prof. Gary C. Barton, Chair, 801-422-4429, Fax: 801-422-0695, E-mail: garold_barton@byu.edu. *Application contact:* Sharon Lyn Heelis, Secretary, 801-422-4429, Fax: 801-422-0695, E-mail: sharon_heelis@byu.edu.
Website: http://art.byu.edu

Brooklyn College of the City University of New York, School of Education, Program in Early Childhood Education, Brooklyn, NY 11210-2889. Offers art teacher (K-12) (MA); birth-grade 2 (MS Ed). *Program availability:* Part-time, evening/weekend. *Entrance requirements:* For master's, LAST, bachelor's degree in early childhood education, resume, 2 letters of recommendation, essay. Additional exam requirements/recommendations for international students: Required—TOEFL (minimum score 500 paper-based; 61 iBT). Electronic applications accepted. *Faculty research:* Children's narrations, language acquisition, culture and education.

Buffalo State College, State University of New York, The Graduate School, Faculty of Arts and Humanities, Department of Art Education, Buffalo, NY 14222-1095. Offers MS Ed. *Accreditation:* NASAD; NCATE. *Program availability:* Part-time, evening/weekend. *Degree requirements:* For master's, thesis or alternative, project. *Entrance requirements:* For master's, New York teaching certificate, interview, minimum GPA of 3.0. Additional exam requirements/recommendations for international students: Required—TOEFL (minimum score 500 paper-based).

California State University, Long Beach, Graduate Studies, College of the Arts, Department of Art, Long Beach, CA 90840. Offers art education (MA); studio art (MFA). *Accreditation:* NASAD. *Program availability:* Part-time. *Degree requirements:* For master's, thesis (for some programs). *Entrance requirements:* For master's, minimum GPA of 3.0 in last 60 hours. Electronic applications accepted.

California State University, Los Angeles, Graduate Studies, College of Arts and Letters, Department of Art, Los Angeles, CA 90032-8530. Offers art (MA), including art education, art history, art therapy, ceramics, metals, and textiles, design (MA, MFA), painting, sculpture, and graphic arts, photography; fine arts (MFA), including crafts, design (MA, MFA), studio arts. *Accreditation:* NASAD (one or more programs are accredited). *Program availability:* Part-time, evening/weekend. *Degree requirements:* For master's, comprehensive exam, project or thesis. *Entrance requirements:* For master's, portfolio. Additional exam requirements/recommendations for international students: Required—TOEFL (minimum score 500 paper-based). Electronic applications accepted. *Faculty research:* The artist and the book, conceptual art, ceramic processes, computer graphics, architectural graphics.

California State University, Northridge, Graduate Studies, Mike Curb College of Arts, Media, and Communication, Department of Art, Northridge, CA 91330. Offers art education (MA); art history (MA); studio art (MA, MFA); visual communications (MA, MFA). *Accreditation:* NASAD. *Students:* 27 full-time (16 women), 9 part-time (4 women); includes 17 minority (1 Black or African American, non-Hispanic/Latino; 2 Asian, non-Hispanic/Latino; 11 Hispanic/Latino; 3 Two or more races, non-Hispanic/Latino). Average age 31. 58 applicants, 34% accepted, 20 enrolled. In 2017, 11 master's awarded. *Application deadline:* For fall admission, 11/30 for domestic students. Application fee: $55. *Financial support:* Application deadline: 3/1. *Unit head:* Prof. Edward Alfano, Chair, 818-677-2242, E-mail: art.dept@csun.edu.
Website: http://www.csun.edu/art/

Carthage College, Division of Teacher Education, Kenosha, WI 53140. Offers classroom guidance and counseling (M Ed); creative arts (M Ed); gifted and talented children (M Ed); language arts (M Ed); modern language (M Ed); natural sciences (M Ed); reading (M Ed, Certificate); social sciences (M Ed); teacher leadership (M Ed). *Program availability:* Part-time, evening/weekend. *Degree requirements:* For master's, thesis optional. *Entrance requirements:* For master's, MAT, minimum B average, letters of reference.

Case Western Reserve University, School of Graduate Studies, Department of Art History and Art, Program in Art Education, Cleveland, OH 44106. Offers MA. Programs offered jointly with The Cleveland Museum of Art. *Accreditation:* TEAC. *Program availability:* Part-time. *Faculty:* 8 full-time (7 women), 2 part-time/adjunct (both women). *Students:* 4 full-time (all women); includes 2 minority (1 Hispanic/Latino; 1 Two or more races, non-Hispanic/Latino). Average age 25. 2 applicants, 50% accepted, 1 enrolled. In 2017, 5 master's awarded. *Degree requirements:* For master's, thesis, art exhibit. *Entrance requirements:* For master's, NTE, interview, portfolio, three letters of recommendation. Additional exam requirements/recommendations for international students: Required—TOEFL (minimum score 577 paper-based; 90 iBT); Recommended—IELTS (minimum score 7). *Application deadline:* For fall admission, 3/1 for domestic students; for spring admission, 11/1 for domestic students. Applications are processed on a rolling basis. Application fee: $50. Electronic applications accepted. *Expenses:* Tuition: Full-time $43,854; part-time $1827 per credit hour. Required fees: $50; $50 per credit hour. Tuition and fees vary according to course load and program. *Faculty research:* Visual and aesthetic education, ethnographic arts, multiculturalism. *Unit head:* Tim Shuckerow, Director of Art Education and Art Studio, 216-368-2714, Fax: 216-368-2715, E-mail: tim.shuckerow@case.edu. *Application contact:* Dawn Rohm, Department Assistant, 216-368-2714, Fax: 216-368-4681, E-mail: dawn.rohm@case.edu.
Website: http://arthistory.case.edu/graduate/art-education/

Central Connecticut State University, School of Graduate Studies, College of Liberal Arts and Social Sciences, Department of Art, New Britain, CT 06050-4010. Offers art education (MS, Certificate). *Program availability:* Part-time, evening/weekend. *Faculty:* 6 full-time (1 woman). *Students:* 18 full-time (16 women), 18 part-time (13 women); includes 3 minority (2 Black or African American, non-Hispanic/Latino; 1 Hispanic/Latino). Average age 31. 18 applicants, 72% accepted, 9 enrolled. In 2017, 6 master's, 6 other advanced degrees awarded. *Degree requirements:* For master's, thesis or alternative, exhibit or special project; for Certificate, qualifying exam. *Entrance requirements:* For master's, portfolio, essay. Additional exam requirements/recommendations for international students: Required—TOEFL (minimum score 550 paper-based; 79 iBT); Recommended—IELTS (minimum score 6.5). *Application deadline:* For fall admission, 8/1 for domestic students, 5/1 for international students; for spring admission, 11/1 for domestic and international students. Applications are processed on a rolling basis. Application fee: $50. Electronic applications accepted. *Expenses: Tuition, area resident:* Full-time $6757. Tuition, state resident: full-time $9750; part-time $374 per credit. Tuition, nonresident: full-time $18,102; part-time $874 per credit. *Required fees:* $4635; $255 per credit. *Financial support:* In 2017–18, 8 students received support. Career-related internships or fieldwork, Federal Work-Study, scholarships/grants, and unspecified assistantships available. Support available to part-time students. Financial award application deadline: 3/1; financial award applicants required to submit FAFSA. *Faculty research:* Visual arts. *Unit head:* Prof. Rachel Siporin, Chair, 860-832-2620, E-mail: siporinr@ccsu.edu. *Application contact:* Patricia Gardner, Associate Director of Graduate Studies, 860-832-2350, Fax: 860-832-2362. Website: http://www.ccsu.edu/art/

Chatham University, Program in Education, Pittsburgh, PA 15232-2826. Offers early childhood education (MAT); elementary education (MAT); environmental education (K-12) (MAT); secondary art (MAT); secondary biology education (MAT); secondary chemistry education (MAT); secondary English education (MAT); secondary math education (MAT); secondary physics education (MAT); secondary social studies education (MAT); special education (MAT). *Faculty:* 1 (woman) full-time, 15 part-time/adjunct (13 women). *Students:* 31 full-time (23 women), 3 part-time (1 woman); includes 9 minority (8 Black or African American, non-Hispanic/Latino; 1 Hispanic/Latino). Average age 30. 25 applicants, 60% accepted, 9 enrolled. In 2017, 23 master's awarded. *Degree requirements:* For master's, thesis, teaching experience. *Entrance requirements:* For master's, minimum GPA of 3.0, sample of written work, recommendation letters. Additional exam requirements/recommendations for international students: Required—TOEFL (minimum score 600 paper-based; 100 iBT), IELTS (minimum score 7), TWE. *Application deadline:* For fall admission, 4/1 priority date for domestic and international students; for spring admission, 11/1 priority date for domestic students, 10/1 priority date for international students. Applications are processed on a rolling basis. Application fee: $45. Electronic applications accepted. Application fee is waived when completed online. *Expenses: Tuition:* Full-time $16,740; part-time $930 per credit. *Required fees:* $486; $27 per credit. $243 per semester. *Financial support:* Career-related internships or fieldwork available. Financial award applicants required to submit FAFSA. *Faculty research:* Gifted education, environmental education, technology in education, writing as learning, class size and achievement. *Application contact:* Katie Noel, Assistant Director of Graduate Admission, 412-365-2758, Fax: 412-365-1609, E-mail: gradadmissions@chatham.edu. Website: http://www.chatham.edu/mat

Cleveland State University, College of Graduate Studies, College of Education and Human Services, Department of Teacher Education, Cleveland, OH 44115. Offers art education (M Ed); early childhood education (M Ed); foreign language education (M Ed); middle childhood mathematics and science education (M Ed); special education (M Ed), including mild/moderate disabilities, moderate/intensive disabilities; teaching English to speakers of other languages (M Ed). *Program availability:* Part-time, evening/weekend. *Faculty:* 19 full-time (14 women), 32 part-time/adjunct (27 women). *Students:* 80 full-time (60 women), 361 part-time (277 women); includes 119 minority (86 Black or African American, non-Hispanic/Latino; 5 Asian, non-Hispanic/Latino; 16 Hispanic/Latino; 12 Two or more races, non-Hispanic/Latino), 20 international. Average age 34. 177 applicants, 55% accepted, 68 enrolled. In 2017, 137 master's awarded. *Degree requirements:* For master's, comprehensive exam (for some programs), thesis or alternative. *Entrance requirements:* For master's, GRE General Test or MAT, minimum GPA of 2.75. Additional exam requirements/recommendations for international students: Required—TOEFL (minimum score 550 paper-based; 78 iBT), IELTS (minimum score 6). *Application deadline:* For fall admission, 7/1 priority date for domestic students, 5/15 for international students; for spring admission, 11/15 for domestic students, 11/1 for international students; for summer admission, 4/1 for domestic students, 3/15 for international students. Applications are processed on a rolling basis. Application fee: $30. *Financial support:* In 2017–18, 13 research assistantships with full tuition reimbursements (averaging $15,845 per year) were awarded; tuition waivers (partial) and unspecified assistantships also available. Financial award application deadline: 2/15; financial award applicants required to submit FAFSA. *Faculty research:* Early childhood education, literacy education, special education: mild/moderate, moderate/intensive, early childhood intervention specialist, teaching English to speakers of other languages (TESOL). *Total annual research expenditures:* $275,907. *Unit head:* Dr. Tachelle Banks, Department Chairperson, 216-687-4600, Fax: 216-687-5379, E-mail: t.i.banks@csuohio.edu. *Application contact:* Rosalyn Adams, Administrative Coordinator, 216-523-7139, Fax: 216-687-5491, E-mail: r.m.adams@csuohio.edu. Website: http://www.csuohio.edu/cehs/te/te

The College of New Rochelle, Graduate School, Division of Education, Program in Art Education, New Rochelle, NY 10805-2308. Offers MS. *Program availability:* Part-time, evening/weekend. *Degree requirements:* For master's, thesis. *Entrance requirements:* For master's, interview, minimum GPA of 3.0 in field, 2.7 overall, portfolio. *Expenses: Tuition:* Full-time $17,406. *Required fees:* $1120. *Faculty research:* Developmental stages in art, assessment and evaluation, curriculum development, multicultural education, art museum education.

The Colorado College, Education Department, Program in Secondary Education, Colorado Springs, CO 80903-3294. Offers art teaching (K-12) (MAT); English teaching (MAT); foreign language teaching (MAT); mathematics teaching (MAT); music teaching (MAT); science teaching (MAT); social studies teaching (MAT). *Degree requirements:* For master's, thesis, internship. Electronic applications accepted.

Colorado State University–Pueblo, College of Education, Engineering and Professional Studies, Education Program, Pueblo, CO 81001-4901. Offers art education (M Ed); foreign language education (M Ed); health and physical education (M Ed); instructional technology (M Ed); linguistically diverse education (M Ed); music education (M Ed); special education (M Ed). *Accreditation:* TEAC. *Program availability:* Part-time. *Degree requirements:* For master's, portfolio. *Entrance requirements:* For master's, 3 recommendations, teaching license. Additional exam requirements/recommendations for international students: Required—TOEFL (minimum score 500 paper-based). Electronic applications accepted. *Faculty research:* Portfolio assessment, math education, science education.

Columbus State University, Graduate Studies, College of the Arts, Department of Art, Columbus, GA 31907-5645. Offers art education (M Ed, MAT). *Accreditation:* NASAD;

NCATE. *Program availability:* Part-time, evening/weekend. *Faculty:* 1 full-time (0 women). *Students:* 1 (woman) full-time, 3 part-time (1 woman); includes 2 minority (both Black or African American, non-Hispanic/Latino). Average age 31. 5 applicants, 20% accepted, 1 enrolled. In 2017, 1 master's awarded. *Degree requirements:* For master's, comprehensive exam, exhibit. *Entrance requirements:* For master's, portfolio, interview. Additional exam requirements/recommendations for international students: Required—TOEFL (minimum score 550 paper-based; 79 iBT). *Application deadline:* For fall admission, 6/30 for domestic students, 5/1 for international students; for spring admission, 11/1 for domestic and international students; for summer admission, 3/1 for domestic and international students. Applications are processed on a rolling basis. Application fee: $50. Electronic applications accepted. *Expenses:* Tuition, state resident: full-time $3708; part-time $2472 per year. Tuition, nonresident: full-time $14,418; part-time $9612 per year. *International tuition:* $19,218 full-time. *Required fees:* $1605. Tuition and fees vary according to program. *Financial support:* In 2017–18, 1 research assistantship was awarded; career-related internships or fieldwork, Federal Work-Study, institutionally sponsored loans, scholarships/grants, tuition waivers (partial), and unspecified assistantships also available. Support available to part-time students. Financial award application deadline: 5/1; financial award applicants required to submit FAFSA. *Unit head:* Prof. Joe Sanders, Department Chair, 706-507-8302, E-mail: sanders_joe@columbusstate.edu. *Application contact:* Catrina Smith-Edmond, Assistant Director for Graduate and Global Admission, 706-507-8824, Fax: 706-568-5091, E-mail: smithedmond_catrina@columbusstate.edu. Website: http://art.columbusstate.edu/

Concordia University, School of Graduate Studies, Faculty of Fine Arts, Department of Art Education, Montréal, QC H3G 1M8, Canada. Offers art education (MA, PhD), including art in education (MA). *Degree requirements:* For master's, thesis (for some programs), practicum; for doctorate, comprehensive exam, thesis/dissertation. *Entrance requirements:* For master's, teaching experience; for doctorate, teaching or related professional experience. *Faculty research:* Vernacular culture, museum education, psychotic art, adults and families.

Concordia University Wisconsin, Graduate Programs, Department of Education, Mequon, WI 53097-2402. Offers art education (MS Ed); early childhood (MS Ed); educational administration (MS Ed); environmental education (MS Ed); family studies (MS Ed); literacy (MS Ed); school counseling (MS Ed); special education (MS Ed). *Program availability:* Part-time, evening/weekend, online learning. *Degree requirements:* For master's, comprehensive exam, thesis or alternative. *Entrance requirements:* For master's, minimum GPA of 3.0, teaching license. Additional exam requirements/recommendations for international students: Required—TOEFL. *Faculty research:* Motivation, developmental learning, learning styles.

Converse College, Program in Art Education, Spartanburg, SC 29302. Offers M Ed, MAT. *Accreditation:* NASAD. *Unit head:* Susanne Gunter, Department Chair, 864-596-9126, E-mail: susanne.gunter@converse.edu. *Application contact:* 864-596-9404, E-mail: graduate@converse.edu.

Delaware State University, Graduate Programs, College of Education, Health and Public Policy, Program in Art Education, Dover, DE 19901-2277. Offers MA. *Entrance requirements:* Additional exam requirements/recommendations for international students: Required—TOEFL (minimum score 550 paper-based). Electronic applications accepted.

East Carolina University, Graduate School, College of Fine Arts and Communication, School of Art and Design, Greenville, NC 27858-4353. Offers art education (MA Ed); ceramics (MFA); graphic design (MFA); illustration (MFA); metal design (MFA); painting and drawing (MFA); photography (MFA); printmaking (MFA); sculpture (MFA); textile design (MFA); wood design (MFA). *Accreditation:* NASAD (one or more programs are accredited). *Program availability:* Part-time, evening/weekend. *Students:* 24 full-time (14 women), 12 part-time (10 women); includes 6 minority (3 Asian, non-Hispanic/Latino; 2 Hispanic/Latino; 1 Two or more races, non-Hispanic/Latino). Average age 33. 27 applicants, 70% accepted, 12 enrolled. In 2017, 16 master's awarded. *Degree requirements:* For master's, comprehensive exam (for some programs), thesis (for some programs). *Entrance requirements:* For master's, portfolio. *Application deadline:* For fall admission, 2/1 for domestic students; for spring admission, 10/1 for domestic students. Applications are processed on a rolling basis. Application fee: $75. Electronic applications accepted. *Expenses:* Tuition, state resident: full-time $4749; part-time $297 per credit hour. Tuition, nonresident: full-time $17,898; part-time $1119 per credit hour. *Required fees:* $2691; $224 per credit hour. Part-time tuition and fees vary according to course load and program. *Financial support:* Research assistantships with partial tuition reimbursements, teaching assistantships with partial tuition reimbursements, and Federal Work-Study available. Support available to part-time students. Financial award application deadline: 6/1. *Unit head:* Michael H. Drought, Director, 252-328-6665, E-mail: droughtm@ecu.edu. *Application contact:* Dr. Linda H. Nelson, Information Contact, 252-328-1286, E-mail: nelsonlh@ecu.edu. Website: http://www.ecu.edu/soad/

Eastern Illinois University, Graduate School, College of Liberal Arts and Sciences, Department of Art, Charleston, IL 61920. Offers art (MA); art education (MA); community arts (MA). *Accreditation:* NASAD. *Program availability:* Part-time, evening/weekend, online learning. *Degree requirements:* For master's, comprehensive exam (for some programs), thesis (for some programs). *Entrance requirements:* For master's, GMAT or GRE. Additional exam requirements/recommendations for international students: Required—TOEFL (minimum score 500 paper-based; 61 iBT), IELTS (minimum score 6). *Application deadline:* For fall admission, 5/15 for domestic and international students; for spring admission, 10/15 for domestic and international students. Applications are processed on a rolling basis. Application fee: $30. Electronic applications accepted. *Financial support:* Teaching assistantships with tuition reimbursements, career-related internships or fieldwork, Federal Work-Study, and unspecified assistantships available. Support available to part-time students. Financial award application deadline: 3/1; financial award applicants required to submit FAFSA. *Unit head:* Chris Kahler, Chair, 217-581-3410, Fax: 217-581-6199, E-mail: cbkahler@eiu.edu. *Application contact:* Patricia K. Belleville, Program Director, 217-581-7009, Fax: 217-581-6199, E-mail: pkbelleville@eiu.edu. Website: http://www.eiu.edu/artgrad/index.php

Eastern Kentucky University, The Graduate School, College of Education, Department of Curriculum and Instruction, Program in Secondary and Higher Education, Richmond, KY 40475-3102. Offers secondary education (MA Ed), including agricultural education, art education, biological sciences education, business education, English education, geography education, history education, home economics education, industrial education, mathematical sciences education, physical education, school health education. *Accreditation:* NCATE. *Program availability:* Part-time. *Entrance requirements:* For master's, GRE General Test, minimum GPA of 2.5.

Eastern Michigan University, Graduate School, College of Arts and Sciences, School of Art and Design, Program in Visual Art Education, Ypsilanti, MI 48197. Offers MA. *Program availability:* Part-time, evening/weekend, online learning. *Students:* 3 part-time (1 woman). Average age 35. 4 applicants, 75% accepted. In 2017, 1 master's awarded. *Entrance requirements:* Additional exam requirements/recommendations for international students: Required—TOEFL. *Application deadline:* Applications are processed on a rolling basis. Application fee: $45. *Financial support:* Fellowships with tuition reimbursements, research assistantships with full tuition reimbursements, teaching assistantships with full tuition reimbursements, career-related internships or fieldwork, Federal Work-Study, institutionally sponsored loans, scholarships/grants, and unspecified assistantships available. Support available to part-time students. Financial award applicants required to submit FAFSA. *Application contact:* Michael Reedy, Advisor, 734-487-1268, Fax: 734-487-2324, E-mail: mreedy@emich.edu.

Edinboro University of Pennsylvania, Department of Art, Edinboro, PA 16444. Offers art education (MA); fine arts (MFA), including ceramics (MA, MFA), metals/jewelry, painting (MA, MFA), printmaking (MA, MFA), sculpture (MA, MFA); studio art (MA), including ceramics (MA, MFA), jewelry/metals, painting (MA, MFA), printmaking (MA, MFA), sculpture (MA, MFA). *Accreditation:* NASAD. *Program availability:* Evening/weekend. *Degree requirements:* For master's, comprehensive exam, thesis or alternative, competency exam, exhibit, portfolio. *Entrance requirements:* For master's, GRE or MAT, interview, minimum QPA of 2.5, portfolio. Electronic applications accepted.

Ferris State University, Kendall College of Art and Design, Grand Rapids, MI 49503. Offers architecture (M Arch); art education (MAE); design (MA); drawing (MFA); painting (MFA); photography (MFA); printmaking (MFA); visual and critical studies (MA). *Program availability:* Part-time. *Faculty:* 21 full-time (15 women), 6 part-time/adjunct (2 women). *Students:* 39 full-time (29 women), 15 part-time (9 women); includes 12 minority (4 Black or African American, non-Hispanic/Latino; 1 American Indian or Alaska Native, non-Hispanic/Latino; 3 Asian, non-Hispanic/Latino; 4 Hispanic/Latino), 6 international. Average age 31. 48 applicants, 60% accepted, 17 enrolled. In 2017, 12 master's awarded. *Degree requirements:* For master's, thesis, seminars. *Entrance requirements:* For master's, portfolio, 3 letters of recommendation, curriculum vitae, artist statement, letter of intent. Additional exam requirements/recommendations for international students: Required—TOEFL (minimum score 79 iBT). *Application deadline:* For fall admission, 2/1 priority date for domestic and international students; for spring admission, 11/1 priority date for domestic and international students. Applications are processed on a rolling basis. Application fee: $0. Electronic applications accepted. *Expenses:* Contact institution. *Financial support:* In 2017–18, 32 students received support, including 8 fellowships (averaging $16,781 per year); scholarships/grants and unspecified assistantships also available. Financial award application deadline: 2/1; financial award applicants required to submit FAFSA. *Unit head:* Leslie Bellavance, President, 616-451-2787. *Application contact:* Thomas Post, Graduate Recruitment Specialist, 616-451-2787, Fax: 616-831-9689, E-mail: thomaspost@ferris.edu. Website: http://www.kcad.edu/

Fitchburg State University, Division of Graduate and Continuing Education, Program in Arts Education, Fitchburg, MA 01420-2697. Offers arts education (M Ed); fine arts director (Certificate). *Accreditation:* NCATE. *Program availability:* Part-time, evening/weekend. *Faculty:* 2 part-time/adjunct (1 woman). *Students:* 2 full-time (both women), 3 part-time (2 women). Average age 34. 1 applicant, 100% accepted, 1 enrolled. In 2017, 5 master's awarded. *Entrance requirements:* Additional exam requirements/recommendations for international students: Required—TOEFL (minimum score 550 paper-based; 79 iBT). *Application deadline:* For fall admission, 7/15 for international students; for spring admission, 12/1 for international students. Applications are processed on a rolling basis. Application fee: $50. Electronic applications accepted. *Expenses:* Contact institution. *Financial support:* In 2017–18, research assistantships with partial tuition reimbursements (averaging $5,500 per year) were awarded; Federal Work-Study, scholarships/grants, and unspecified assistantships also available. Support available to part-time students. Financial award application deadline: 3/1; financial award applicants required to submit FAFSA. *Unit head:* Dr. Petri Flint, Chair, 978-665-3279, Fax: 978-665-3658, E-mail: gce@fitchburgstate.edu. *Application contact:* Jinawa McNeil, Director of Admissions, 978-665-3140, Fax: 978-665-4540, E-mail: admissions@fitchburgstate.edu. Website: http://www.fitchburgstate.edu

Florida Atlantic University, College of Education, Department of Teaching and Learning, Boca Raton, FL 33431-0991. Offers curriculum and instruction (M Ed), including art, biology, chemistry, English, French, German, mathematics, music, physics, Pre-K and primary education, reading, social sciences, Spanish; elementary education (M Ed); environmental education (M Ed); reading education (M Ed); social foundations of education (M Ed), including educational psychology, educational technology, multilingual education. *Accreditation:* NCATE. *Program availability:* Part-time, evening/weekend. *Faculty:* 13 full-time (10 women), 1 part-time/adjunct (0 women). *Students:* 26 full-time (22 women), 43 part-time (39 women); includes 19 minority (9 Black or African American, non-Hispanic/Latino; 1 Asian, non-Hispanic/Latino; 8 Hispanic/Latino; 1 Two or more races, non-Hispanic/Latino), 3 international. Average age 30. 91 applicants, 57% accepted, 33 enrolled. In 2017, 25 master's awarded. *Entrance requirements:* For master's, GRE General Test, minimum GPA of 3.0 in last 2 years of undergraduate course work. Additional exam requirements/recommendations for international students: Required—TOEFL (minimum score 500 paper-based; 61 iBT), IELTS (minimum score 6). *Application deadline:* For fall admission, 7/1 for domestic students, 2/15 for international students; for spring admission, 11/1 for domestic students, 7/15 for international students. Applications are processed on a rolling basis. Application fee: $30. *Expenses:* Tuition, state resident: full-time $7400; part-time $369.82 per credit. Tuition, nonresident: full-time $20,496; part-time $1042.81 per credit. *Financial support:* Fellowships with partial tuition reimbursements, research assistantships with partial tuition reimbursements, teaching assistantships with partial tuition reimbursements, career-related internships or fieldwork, scholarships/grants, and unspecified assistantships available. *Faculty research:* Technology, teaching English to speakers of other languages, math teaching, electronic portfolio assessment, global perspectives through social studies. *Unit head:* Dr. Barbara Ridener, Chairperson, 561-297-3588, E-mail: bridener@fau.edu. *Application contact:* Dr. Eliah Watlington, Associate Dean, 561-296-8520, Fax: 261-297-2991, E-mail: ewatling@fau.edu. Website: http://www.coe.fau.edu/academicdepartments/tl/

Florida International University, College of Arts, Sciences, and Education, Department of Teaching and Learning, Miami, FL 33199. Offers art education (MA, MS); curriculum and instruction (MS, Ed D, PhD, Ed S), including curriculum development (MS); elementary education (MS); English education (MS); learning technologies (MS); mathematics education (MS); modern language education (MS); physical education (MS); science education (MS); social studies education (MS); special education (MS); early childhood education (MS); exceptional student education (Ed D); foreign language education (MS), including foreign language education, teaching English to speakers of other languages (TESOL); language, literacy and culture (PhD); mathematics, science, and learning technologies (PhD); physical education (MS), including sport and fitness; reading education (MS). *Program availability:* Part-time, evening/weekend. *Faculty:* 60 full-time (41 women), 112 part-time/adjunct (77 women). *Students:* 165 full-time (139 women), 191 part-time (148 women); includes 270 minority (56 Black or African American, non-Hispanic/Latino; 12 Asian, non-Hispanic/Latino; 191 Hispanic/Latino; 11 Two or more races, non-Hispanic/Latino), 13 international. Average age 34. 238

applicants, 68% accepted, 107 enrolled. In 2017, 184 master's, 15 doctorates awarded. *Degree requirements:* For doctorate, comprehensive exam, thesis/dissertation. *Entrance requirements:* For master's, GRE General Test, Florida General Knowledge Test or Florida College Level Academic Skills Test; for doctorate and Ed S, GRE General Test. Additional exam requirements/recommendations for international students: Required—TOEFL (minimum score 550 paper-based; 80 iBT), IELTS (minimum score 6.3). *Application deadline:* For fall admission, 6/1 priority date for domestic students, 4/1 for international students; for winter admission, 10/1 priority date for domestic students, 9/1 for international students; for spring admission, 3/1 priority date for domestic students, 2/1 for international students. Applications are processed on a rolling basis. Application fee: $30. Electronic applications accepted. *Expenses:* Tuition, state resident: full-time $8912; part-time $446 per credit hour. Tuition, nonresident: full-time $21,393; part-time $992 per credit hour. *Required fees:* $390; $195 per semester. *Financial support:* Research assistantships with tuition reimbursements and teaching assistantships with tuition reimbursements available. *Unit head:* Dr. Lynn Miller, Chair, 305-348-2005, Fax: 305-348-2086, E-mail: lynne.miller@fiu.edu. *Application contact:* Nanett Rojas, Assistant Director, Graduate Admissions, 305-348-7464, Fax: 305-348-7441, E-mail: gradadm@fiu.edu. Website: https://tl.fiu.edu/

Florida State University, The Graduate School, College of Fine Arts, Department of Art Education, Tallahassee, FL 32306. Offers art education (MA, MS, Ed D, PhD); art therapy (PhD); arts administration (PhD). *Accreditation:* NASAD (one or more programs are accredited). *Program availability:* Part-time, evening/weekend, 100% online. *Faculty:* 9 full-time (6 women), 4 part-time/adjunct (all women). *Students:* 58 full-time (57 women), 20 part-time (15 women); includes 27 minority (8 Black or African American, non-Hispanic/Latino; 1 American Indian or Alaska Native, non-Hispanic/Latino; 1 Asian, non-Hispanic/Latino; 12 Hispanic/Latino; 5 Two or more races, non-Hispanic/Latino), 7 international. Average age 30. 90 applicants, 57% accepted, 38 enrolled. In 2017, 28 master's, 1 doctorate awarded. *Degree requirements:* For master's, comprehensive exam, thesis (for some programs); for doctorate, thesis/dissertation. *Entrance requirements:* For master's, GRE, minimum GPA of 3.0 in last 2 years; for doctorate, GRE. Additional exam requirements/recommendations for international students: Required—TOEFL (minimum score 550 paper-based; 80 iBT). *Application deadline:* For fall admission, 1/15 priority date for domestic and international students; for spring admission, 10/1 priority date for domestic and international students. Application fee: $30. Electronic applications accepted. *Financial support:* In 2017–18, 24 students received support, including 22 research assistantships with full tuition reimbursements available (averaging $5,000 per year), 5 teaching assistantships with full tuition reimbursements available (averaging $8,500 per year); fellowships, career-related internships or fieldwork, scholarships/grants, health care benefits, and unspecified assistantships also available. Financial award application deadline: 1/15; financial award applicants required to submit FAFSA. *Faculty research:* Teaching and learning in art, museum education, art therapy, arts administration, discipline-based art education. *Total annual research expenditures:* $110,000. *Unit head:* Dr. Jeff Broome, Interim Chair, 850-645-9892, Fax: 850-644-5067, E-mail: jbroome@fsu.edu. *Application contact:* Vicki Barr, Academic Support Assistant, 850-644-5473, Fax: 850-644-6067, E-mail: vbarr@fsu.edu. Website: http://arted.fsu.edu/

Fontbonne University, Graduate Programs, St. Louis, MO 63105-3098. Offers accounting (MBA, MS); art (MA); art (K-12) (MAT); business (MBA); computer science (MS); deaf education (MA); early intervention in deaf education (MA); education (MA), including autism spectrum disorders, curriculum and instruction, diverse learners, early childhood education, reading, special education; elementary education (MAT); family and consumer sciences (MA), including multidisciplinary health communication studies; fine arts (MFA); instructional design and technology (MS); management and leadership (MM); middle school education (MAT); secondary education (MAT); special education (MAT); speech-language pathology (MS); supply chain management (MS); theatre (MA). *Program availability:* Part-time, evening/weekend, online learning. *Degree requirements:* For master's, comprehensive exam (for some programs), thesis (for some programs). *Entrance requirements:* Additional exam requirements/recommendations for international students: Required—TOEFL (minimum score 500 paper-based; 65 iBT). Electronic applications accepted.

Framingham State University, Graduate Studies, Program in Art, Framingham, MA 01701-9101. Offers M Ed. *Accreditation:* NASAD. *Unit head:* Brian Bishop, Program Coordinator, E-mail: bbishop@framingham.edu. *Application contact:* Graduate Officer, 508-626-4550, Fax: 508-626-4030, E-mail: dgce@frc.mass.edu.

George Mason University, College of Visual and Performing Arts, Program in Art Education, Fairfax, VA 22030. Offers MAT. *Faculty:* 3 full-time (2 women), 1 (woman) part-time/adjunct. *Students:* 2 full-time (both women), 18 part-time (15 women); includes 6 minority (all Asian, non-Hispanic/Latino). Average age 30. 7 applicants, 86% accepted, 4 enrolled. In 2017, 14 master's awarded. *Degree requirements:* For master's, thesis or alternative, capstone. *Entrance requirements:* Additional exam requirements/recommendations for international students: Required—TOEFL (minimum score 575 paper-based; 88 iBT), IELTS (minimum score 6.5), PTE (minimum score 59). *Application deadline:* For fall admission, 4/1 for domestic and international students. Application fee: $75 ($80 for international students). Electronic applications accepted. *Expenses:* Tuition, state resident: full-time $11,228; part-time $459.50 per credit. Tuition, nonresident: full-time $30,932; part-time $1280.50 per credit. *Required fees:* $3252; $135.50 per credit. Part-time tuition and fees vary according to course load and program. *Financial support:* Career-related internships or fieldwork, Federal Work-Study, and scholarships/grants available. Financial award application deadline: 3/1; financial award applicants required to submit FAFSA. *Faculty research:* Maker spaces and technology; data visualization; teacher preparation licensure; cognition and child development in the arts. *Unit head:* Mary Del Popolo, Program Director, 703-993-8562, Fax: 703-993-8798, E-mail: mdelpopo@gmu.edu. *Application contact:* Nikki Brugnoli-Whipkey, Administrative Assistant for Graduate Study, 703-993-5792, Fax: 703-993-8798, E-mail: nbrugnol@gmu.edu. Website: http://arteducation.gmu.edu/

The George Washington University, Columbian College of Arts and Sciences, Corcoran School of the Arts and Design, Washington, DC 20007. Offers art and the book (MA); art education (MA, MAT); decorative arts and design history (MA); exhibition design (MA); interior design (MA); new media photojournalism (MA). MA in decorative arts and design history offered in partnership with Smithsonian Associates. *Accreditation:* NASAD. *Program availability:* Part-time. *Entrance requirements:* Additional exam requirements/recommendations for international students: Required—TOEFL (minimum score 95 iBT). *Expenses: Tuition:* Full-time $28,800; part-time $1655 per credit hour. *Required fees:* $45; $2.75 per credit hour.

Georgia State University, Ernest G. Welch School of Art and Design, Program in Art Education, Atlanta, GA 30302-3083. Offers MA Ed. *Accreditation:* NASAD. *Program availability:* Part-time. *Entrance requirements:* For master's, GRE. Additional exam requirements/recommendations for international students: Required—TOEFL. Application fee: $50. Electronic applications accepted. *Expenses:* Tuition, state resident: full-time $7020. Tuition, nonresident: full-time $22,518. *Required fees:* $2128.

Tuition and fees vary according to degree level and program. *Financial support:* Tuition waivers (full) and unspecified assistantships available. Financial award application deadline: 4/15; financial award applicants required to submit FAFSA. *Faculty research:* Critical theories, museum education, instructional technology, multi-culture and interdisciplinary art education, Chinese art history. *Unit head:* Michael White, Director, Welch School of Art and Design, 404-413-5221, Fax: 404-413-5261, E-mail: mwhite@gsu.edu. *Application contact:* Hubert Stanley Anderson, Director of Graduate Studies, 404-413-5229, Fax: 404-413-5261, E-mail: artgrad@gsu.edu.
Website: http://artdesign.gsu.edu/graduate/admissions/masters-of-art-education/

Harding University, Cannon-Clary College of Education, Searcy, AR 72149-0001. Offers advanced studies in teaching and learning (M Ed); art (MSE); behavioral science (MSE); counseling (MS, Ed S); early childhood special education (M Ed, MSE); education (MSE); educational leadership (M Ed, Ed S); elementary education (M Ed); English (MSE); French (MSE); history/social science (MSE); kinesiology (MSE); math (MSE); reading (M Ed); secondary education (MSE); Spanish (MSE); teaching (MAT); teaching English as a second language (MSE). *Accreditation:* NCATE. *Program availability:* Part-time, evening/weekend. *Faculty:* 22 full-time (9 women), 51 part-time/adjunct (37 women). *Students:* 135 full-time (95 women), 316 part-time (231 women); includes 77 minority (46 Black or African American, non-Hispanic/Latino; 7 American Indian or Alaska Native, non-Hispanic/Latino; 4 Asian, non-Hispanic/Latino; 9 Hispanic/Latino; 11 Two or more races, non-Hispanic/Latino), 11 international. Average age 34. 128 applicants, 87% accepted, 111 enrolled. In 2017, 153 master's, 24 other advanced degrees awarded. *Degree requirements:* For master's, comprehensive exam (for some programs), thesis optional, portfolio(s); for Ed S, comprehensive exam, portfolio, project. *Entrance requirements:* For master's, GRE, MAT, PRAXIS; for Ed S, MAT or GRE. Additional exam requirements/recommendations for international students: Required—TOEFL (minimum score 550 paper-based; 79 iBT). *Application deadline:* For fall admission, 8/1 for domestic and international students; for spring admission, 1/1 for domestic and international students. Applications are processed on a rolling basis. Application fee: $35. Tuition and fees vary according to course load, degree level, campus/location and program. *Financial support:* In 2017–18, 33 students received support. Unspecified assistantships available. *Faculty research:* Reading, comprehension, school violence, educational technology, behavior, college choice, differentiated instruction, brain-based teaching. *Unit head:* Dr. Clara Carroll, Chair, 501-279-4501, Fax: 501-279-4083, E-mail: ccarroll@harding.edu. *Application contact:* Information Contact, 501-279-4315, E-mail: gradstudiesedu@harding.edu.
Website: http://www.harding.edu/education

Harvard University, Harvard Graduate School of Education, Master's Programs in Education, Cambridge, MA 02138. Offers arts in education (Ed M); education policy and management (Ed M); higher education (Ed M); human development and psychology (Ed M); international education policy (Ed M); language and literacy (Ed M); learning and teaching (Ed M); mind, brain, and education (Ed M); prevention science and practice (Ed M); school leadership (Ed M); special studies (Ed M); teacher education (Ed M); technology, innovation, and education (Ed M). *Program availability:* Part-time. *Entrance requirements:* For master's, GRE General Test, statement of purpose, 3 letters of recommendation, resume, official transcripts. Additional exam requirements/recommendations for international students: Required—TOEFL (minimum score 613 paper-based; 104 iBT), TWE (minimum score 5). Electronic applications accepted. *Faculty research:* Learning and development, educational leadership and organizations, education policy analysis.

Hofstra University, School of Education, Programs in Teacher Education, Hempstead, NY 11549. Offers bilingual education (MA); bilingual extension (Advanced Certificate), including education/speech language pathology, intensive teacher institute; business education (MS Ed); curriculum studies (MS Ed); early childhood and childhood education (MS Ed); early childhood education (MA, MS Ed); educational technology (Advanced Certificate); elementary education (MA, MS Ed), including science, technology, engineering, and mathematics (STEM) (MA); English education (MS Ed); family and consumer science (MS Ed); fine arts and music education (Advanced Certificate); fine arts education (MS Ed); foreign language and TESOL (MS Ed); foreign language education (MA, MS Ed), including Arabic (MS Ed), biology, chemistry, Chinese (MS Ed), earth science, French, German, Italian (MS Ed), Mandarin (MS Ed), physics, Russian, Spanish; foundations of education (Advanced Certificate), including grades 5-6, grades 7-9; languages other than English and teaching English as a second language (MA); learning and teaching (Ed D), including applied linguistics, art education, arts and humanities, early childhood education, English education, human development, math education, math, science, and technology, multicultural education, physical education, science education, social studies education, special education; mathematics education (MA, MS Ed); music education (MA, MS Ed); science education (MA), including biology (MA, MS Ed), chemistry (MA, MS Ed), earth science (MA, MS Ed), physics (MA, MS Ed); secondary education (Advanced Certificate); social studies education (MA, MS Ed); teaching languages other than English and TESOL (MS Ed); technology for learning (MA); TESOL (MS Ed, Advanced Certificate); TESOL with specialization in STEM (MA); work based learning extension (Advanced Certificate). *Program availability:* Part-time, evening/weekend, blended/hybrid learning. *Students:* 119 full-time (83 women), 124 part-time (90 women); includes 54 minority (15 Black or African American, non-Hispanic/Latino; 9 Asian, non-Hispanic/Latino; 29 Hispanic/Latino; 1 Native Hawaiian or other Pacific Islander, non-Hispanic/Latino), 12 international. Average age 29, 205 applicants, 88% accepted, 93 enrolled. In 2017, 103 master's, 4 doctorates, 32 other advanced degrees awarded. *Degree requirements:* For master's, comprehensive exam, thesis (for some programs), exit project, student teaching, fieldwork, electronic portfolio, curriculum project, minimum GPA of 3.0; for doctorate, thesis/dissertation; for Advanced Certificate, 3 foreign languages, comprehensive exam (for some programs), thesis project. *Entrance requirements:* For master's, GRE, 2 letters of recommendation, portfolio, teacher certification (MA), interview, essay; for doctorate, GMAT, GRE, LSAT, or MAT; for Advanced Certificate, 2 letters of recommendation, essay, interview and/or portfolio, teaching certificate. Additional exam requirements/recommendations for international students: Required—TOEFL (minimum score 550 paper-based; 80 iBT). *Application deadline:* Applications are processed on a rolling basis. Application fee: $75. Electronic applications accepted. *Expenses: Tuition:* Full-time $1292. *Required fees:* $970. Tuition and fees vary according to program. *Financial support:* In 2017–18, 112 students received support, including 56 fellowships with full and partial tuition reimbursements available (averaging $4,998 per year), 2 research assistantships with full and partial tuition reimbursements available (averaging $8,753 per year); career-related internships or fieldwork, Federal Work-Study, institutionally sponsored loans, scholarships/grants, traineeships, tuition waivers (full and partial), and unspecified assistantships also available. Support available to part-time students. Financial award applicants required to submit FAFSA. *Faculty research:* Educational interventions that foster critical-thinking skills; teachers' attitudes about professional development; threats to teacher quality. *Unit head:* Dr. Eustace Thompson, Chairperson, 516-463-5749, Fax: 516-463-6275, E-mail: eustace.g.thompson@hofstra.edu. *Application contact:* Sunil Samuel, Assistant Vice President of Admissions, 516-463-4723, Fax: 516-463-4664, E-mail: graduateadmission@hofstra.edu.
Website: http://www.hofstra.edu/education/

Indiana University Bloomington, School of Education, Department of Curriculum and Instruction, Bloomington, IN 47405-7000. Offers art education (MS, Ed D, PhD); curriculum studies (Ed D, PhD); elementary education (MS, Ed D, PhD, Ed S); mathematics education (MS, Ed D, PhD); science education (MS, Ed D, PhD); secondary education (MS, Ed D, PhD); social studies education (MS, PhD); special education (PhD, Ed S). *Accreditation:* NCATE. *Program availability:* Part-time, evening/weekend. Terminal master's awarded for partial completion of doctoral program. *Degree requirements:* For doctorate, thesis/dissertation; for Ed S, comprehensive exam or project. *Entrance requirements:* For master's, doctorate, and Ed S, GRE General Test. Electronic applications accepted.

James Madison University, The Graduate School, College of Visual and Performing Arts, School of Art, Design and Art History, Harrisonburg, VA 22801. Offers art education (MA); studio art (MA, MFA), including ceramics (MFA), drawing/painting (MFA), intermedia (MFA), metal/jewelry (MFA), photography (MFA), sculpture (MFA). *Accreditation:* NASAD. *Program availability:* Part-time. *Students:* 7 full-time (5 women), 1 (woman) part-time. Average age 30. In 2017, 5 master's awarded. Application fee: $55. Electronic applications accepted. *Expenses:* Tuition, state resident: full-time $10,512; part-time $438 per credit hour. Tuition, nonresident: full-time $28,358; part-time $1162 per credit hour. *Required fees:* $1128. *Financial support:* In 2017–18, 7 students received support, including 4 teaching assistantships with full tuition reimbursements available (averaging $9,284 per year); Federal Work-Study and 3 assistantships (averaging $7911) also available. Financial award application deadline: 3/1; financial award applicants required to submit FAFSA. *Unit head:* Dr. Kathy A. Schwartz, Director of School of Art, Design and Art History, 540-568-6216, E-mail: schwarka@jmu.edu. *Application contact:* Lynette D. Michael, Director of Graduate Student Admissions, 540-568-6131 Ext. 6395, Fax: 540-568-7860, E-mail: michaeld@jmu.edu.
Website: http://www.jmu.edu/artandarthistory/

Kean University, College of Liberal Arts, Program in Fine Arts Education, Union, NJ 07083. Offers initial teaching certification (MA); studio (MA); supervision (MA). *Accreditation:* NASAD. *Program availability:* Part-time. *Faculty:* 13 full-time (7 women). *Students:* 8 full-time (7 women), 21 part-time (15 women); includes 10 minority (3 Black or African American, non-Hispanic/Latino; 2 Asian, non-Hispanic/Latino; 4 Hispanic/Latino; 1 Native Hawaiian or other Pacific Islander, non-Hispanic/Latino). Average age 35. 8 applicants, 100% accepted, 6 enrolled. In 2017, 7 master's awarded. *Degree requirements:* For master's, thesis (for some programs), exhibition, 3 years of teaching experience (for supervision), PRAXIS and fieldwork (for initial teaching certification). *Entrance requirements:* For master's, studio portfolio, proficiencies in academic writing, dialogue skills, minimum GPA of 3.0, interview, 2 letters of recommendation, official transcripts from all institutions attended. Additional exam requirements/recommendations for international students: Required—TOEFL (minimum score 550 paper-based; 79 iBT), IELTS (minimum score 6.5). *Application deadline:* For fall admission, 6/30 for domestic and international students; for spring admission, 12/1 for domestic and international students. Applications are processed on a rolling basis. Application fee: $75. Electronic applications accepted. *Expenses:* Tuition, state resident: full-time $13,419; part-time $653 per credit. Tuition, nonresident: full-time $18,188; part-time $801 per credit. *Required fees:* $3382; $154 per credit. Tuition and fees vary according to course level, course load, degree level and program. *Financial support:* Scholarships/grants and unspecified assistantships available. Financial award applicants required to submit FAFSA. *Unit head:* Dr. Joseph Amorino, Program Coordinator, 908-737-4403, Fax: 908-737-4377, E-mail: jamorino@kean.edu. *Application contact:* Amy Clark, Program Assistant, 908-737-7100, E-mail: gradadmissions@kean.edu.
Website: http://grad.kean.edu/masters-programs/initial-teaching-certification

Kennesaw State University, Leland and Clarice C. Bagwell College of Education, Program in Teaching, Kennesaw, GA 30144. Offers art education (MAT); biology (MAT); chemistry (MAT); foreign language education (Chinese and Spanish) (MAT); physics (MAT); secondary English (MAT); secondary mathematics (MAT); special education (MAT); teaching English to speakers of other languages (MAT). *Program availability:* Part-time, evening/weekend. *Entrance requirements:* For master's, GRE, GACE I (state certificate exam), minimum GPA of 2.75, 2 recommendations, resume. Additional exam requirements/recommendations for international students: Required—TOEFL (minimum score 550 paper-based; 80 iBT), IELTS (minimum score 6.5). Electronic applications accepted.

Kent State University, College of the Arts, School of Art, Kent, OH 44242-0001. Offers art education (MA); art history (MA); crafts (MA), including glass (MA, MFA); fine arts (MA), including fashion; studio art (MFA), including ceramics (MA, MFA), drawing, glass (MA, MFA), jewelry, metals and enameling, painting, print media and photography, sculpture, textiles. *Accreditation:* NASAD (one or more programs are accredited). *Program availability:* Part-time, online learning. *Faculty:* 24 full-time (13 women), 3 part-time/adjunct (all women). *Students:* 40 full-time (27 women), 22 part-time (19 women); includes 3 minority (2 Black or African American, non-Hispanic/Latino; 1 Two or more races, non-Hispanic/Latino). Average age 31. 40 applicants, 75% accepted, 23 enrolled. In 2017, 22 master's awarded. *Degree requirements:* For master's, comprehensive exam, thesis (for some programs), 1 foreign language (for art history); final project (for crafts and fine arts). *Entrance requirements:* For master's, transcripts, goal statement, 3 letters of recommendation, curriculum vitae, portfolio. Additional exam requirements/recommendations for international students: Required—TOEFL (minimum score 550 paper-based, 79 iBT), Michigan English Language Assessment Battery (minimum score 77), IELTS (minimum score 6.5) or PTE (minimum score 58). *Application deadline:* For fall admission, 2/2 for domestic and international students; for spring admission, 10/15 for domestic and international students. Applications are processed on a rolling basis. Application fee: $45 ($70 for international students). Electronic applications accepted. *Expenses:* Tuition, state resident: full-time $11,310; part-time $515 per credit hour. Tuition, nonresident: full-time $20,396; part-time $928 per credit hour. *International tuition:* $18,544 full-time. *Financial support:* Career-related internships or fieldwork, scholarships/grants, and unspecified assistantships available. Financial award application deadline: 3/16. *Unit head:* Marie Bukowski, Director, 330-672-2192, E-mail: mbukows1@kent.edu. *Application contact:* Linda Hoeptner Poling, Graduate Coordinator and Associate Professor of Art Education, 330-672-7895, E-mail: lhoeptne@kent.edu.
Website: http://www.kent.edu/art

Kutztown University of Pennsylvania, College of Visual and Performing Arts, Program in Art Education, Kutztown, PA 19530-0730. Offers M Ed. *Accreditation:* NASAD; NCATE. *Program availability:* Part-time. *Faculty:* 5 full-time (4 women), 2 part-time/adjunct (both women). *Students:* 8 full-time (6 women), 34 part-time (32 women); includes 1 minority (Hispanic/Latino). Average age 30. 30 applicants, 90% accepted, 14 enrolled. In 2017, 8 master's awarded. *Degree requirements:* For master's, comprehensive exam, thesis optional. *Entrance requirements:* For master's, PRAXIS II, valid instructional I or II teaching certificate, or GRE, minimum undergraduate GPA of 3.0, 3 letters of recommendation. Additional exam requirements/recommendations for international students: Required—TOEFL (minimum score 550 paper-based, 79 iBT), IELTS (minimum score 6.5), or PTE (minimum score 53). *Application deadline:* For fall

Art Education

admission, 8/1 for domestic and international students; for spring admission, 12/1 for domestic and international students. Application fee: $35. Electronic applications accepted. *Expenses:* Tuition, state resident: part-time $500 per credit. Tuition, nonresident: part-time $750 per credit. *Required fees:* $115 per credit. One-time fee: $50 part-time. Tuition and fees vary according to degree level. *Financial support:* Career-related internships or fieldwork, Federal Work-Study, and unspecified assistantships available. Financial award application deadline: 3/1; financial award applicants required to submit FAFSA. *Faculty research:* Teaching of art history, child development in art, aesthetics and criticism curriculum, multicultural education, assessment in art. *Unit head:* Dr. Julia Hovanec, Department Chair, 610-683-4815, E-mail: hovanec@kutztown.edu.
Website: https://www.kutztown.edu/academics/graduate-programs/art-education.htm

Lake Forest College, Master of Arts in Teaching Program, Lake Forest, IL 60045. Offers elementary education (MAT); K-12 French (MAT); K-12 music (MAT); K-12 Spanish (MAT); K-12 visual art (MAT); secondary biology (MAT); secondary chemistry (MAT); secondary English (MAT); secondary history (MAT); secondary mathematics (MAT). *Degree requirements:* For master's, comprehensive exam, portfolio. *Entrance requirements:* For master's, GRE.

Lesley University, Graduate School of Education, Cambridge, MA 02138-2790. Offers arts, community, and education (M Ed); autism studies (Certificate); curriculum and instruction (M Ed, CAGS); early childhood education (M Ed); ecological teaching and learning (MS); educational studies (PhD), including adult learning, educational leadership, individually designed; elementary education (M Ed); emergent technologies for educators (Certificate); ESLArts: language learning through the arts (M Ed); high school education (M Ed); individually designed (M Ed); integrated teaching through the arts (M Ed); literacy for K-8 classroom teachers (M Ed); mathematics education (M Ed); middle school education (M Ed); moderate disabilities (M Ed); online learning (Certificate); reading (CAGS); science in education (M Ed); severe disabilities (M Ed); special needs (CAGS); specialist teacher of reading (M Ed); teacher of visual art (M Ed); technology in education (M Ed, CAGS). *Accreditation:* TEAC. *Program availability:* Part-time, evening/weekend, online learning. *Degree requirements:* For master's, practicum; for doctorate, thesis/dissertation. *Entrance requirements:* For master's, Massachusetts Tests for Educator Licensure (MTEL), transcripts, statement of purpose, recommendations; interview (for special education); for doctorate, GRE General Test, transcripts, statement of purpose, recommendations, interview, master's degree, resume; for other advanced degree, interview, master's degree. Additional exam requirements/recommendations for international students: Required—TOEFL (minimum score 550 paper-based; 80 iBT). Electronic applications accepted. *Faculty research:* Assessment in literacy, mathematics and science; autism spectrum disorders; instructional technology and online learning; multicultural education and English language learners.

Long Island University–LIU Post, College of Education, Information and Technology, Brookville, NY 11548-1300. Offers adolescence education (MS); adolescence education 7-12 (MS); archives and records management (AC); art education (MS); childhood education (MS); childhood education/literacy B-6 (MS); childhood education/special education (MS); clinical mental health counseling (MS, AC); early childhood education (MS); early childhood education/childhood education (MS); educational leadership (AC); educational technology (MS); information studies (PhD); interdisciplinary educational studies (Ed D); middle childhood education (MS); music education (MS); public library administration (AC); school counselor (MS); special education (MS Ed); speech-language pathology (MA); students with disabilities, 7-12 generalist (AC); TESOL (MA). *Accreditation:* TEAC. *Program availability:* Part-time, 100% online, blended/hybrid learning. *Faculty:* 40 full-time (26 women), 73 part-time/adjunct (38 women). *Students:* 472 full-time (400 women), 696 part-time (543 women); includes 254 minority (93 Black or African American, non-Hispanic/Latino; 46 Asian, non-Hispanic/Latino; 105 Hispanic/Latino; 10 Two or more races, non-Hispanic/Latino), 33 international. Average age 33. 917 applicants, 82% accepted, 357 enrolled. In 2017, 408 master's, 31 other advanced degrees awarded. Terminal master's awarded for partial completion of doctoral program. *Degree requirements:* For master's, variable foreign language requirement, comprehensive exam (for some programs), thesis optional; for doctorate, comprehensive exam, thesis/dissertation. *Entrance requirements:* For master's and AC, GRE (for some programs). Additional exam requirements/recommendations for international students: Required—TOEFL (minimum score 550 paper-based, 75 iBT), IELTS, or PTE. *Application deadline:* Applications are processed on a rolling basis. Application fee: $50. Electronic applications accepted. *Expenses: Tuition:* Full-time $21,618; part-time $1201 per credit. *Required fees:* $1840; $920 per term. Tuition and fees vary according to course load. *Financial support:* In 2017–18, 376 students received support. Career-related internships or fieldwork, Federal Work-Study, institutionally sponsored loans, scholarships/grants, tuition waivers (partial), and unspecified assistantships available. Support available to part-time students. Financial award application deadline: 2/15; financial award applicants required to submit FAFSA. *Faculty research:* Sleep; use of technology to develop executive function by students with disabilities; early childhood literacy development through play; social justice through education; using a structured protocol to discuss Bad News. *Unit head:* Dr. Albert Inserra, Dean, 516-299-2210, E-mail: albert.inserra@liu.edu. *Application contact:* Rita Langdon, Graduate Admissions, 516-299-2900, Fax: 516-299-2137, E-mail: post-enroll@liu.edu.
Website: http://liu.edu/CWPost/Academics/College-of-Education-Information-and-Technology

Manhattanville College, School of Education, Program in Visual Arts Education, Purchase, NY 10577-2132. Offers visual arts (MAT, Certificate). *Program availability:* Part-time, evening/weekend. *Faculty:* 2 part-time/adjunct (1 woman). *Students:* 3 full-time (2 women), 7 part-time (5 women); includes 1 minority (Hispanic/Latino). Average age 38. 1 applicant, 100% accepted. In 2017, 5 master's awarded. *Degree requirements:* For master's, comprehensive exam (for some programs), thesis (for some programs), student teaching, research seminars, portfolios, internships, writing assessment; for Certificate, comprehensive exam (for some programs). *Entrance requirements:* For master's, GRE or MAT (for programs leading to certification), minimum GPA of 3.0, 2 letters of recommendation, interview, essay (2-3 page personal statement that describes reasons for choosing teaching or educational leadership as profession and philosophy of education), proof of immunization (for those born after 1957). Additional exam requirements/recommendations for international students: Required—TOEFL (minimum score 600 paper-based; 110 iBT); Recommended—IELTS (minimum score 8). *Application deadline:* Applications are processed on a rolling basis. Application fee: $75. Electronic applications accepted. *Expenses:* $915 per credit. *Financial support:* Teaching assistantships, career-related internships or fieldwork, Federal Work-Study, institutionally sponsored loans, scholarships/grants, and unspecified assistantships available. Financial award application deadline: 3/15; financial award applicants required to submit FAFSA. *Unit head:* Dr. Shelly Wepner, Dean, 914-323-3153, Fax: 914-323-5493, E-mail: shelly.wepner@mville.edu. *Application contact:* Alissa Wilson, Director, Graduate Admissions, 914-323-3150, Fax: 914-694-1732, E-mail: edschool@mville.edu.
Website: http://www.mville.edu/programs/visual-art-education

Mansfield University of Pennsylvania, Graduate Studies, Department of Art, Mansfield, PA 16933. Offers art education (M Ed). *Program availability:* Part-time. *Degree requirements:* For master's, thesis optional. *Entrance requirements:* For master's, minimum GPA of 3.0, portfolio. Additional exam requirements/recommendations for international students: Required—TOEFL (minimum score 550 paper-based). Electronic applications accepted.

Maryland Institute College of Art, Graduate Studies, MA Program in Art Education, Baltimore, MD 21201. Offers MA. Program offered in summer only. *Accreditation:* NASAD. *Degree requirements:* For master's, thesis, exhibition and documentation. *Entrance requirements:* For master's, portfolio, bachelor's degree in any field. Additional exam requirements/recommendations for international students: Required—TOEFL (minimum score 550 paper-based; 80 iBT), IELTS (minimum score 6.5). Electronic applications accepted. *Expenses:* Contact institution.

Maryland Institute College of Art, Graduate Studies, MAT Program, Baltimore, MD 21201. Offers MAT. *Degree requirements:* For master's, thesis, student teaching, thesis exhibition, thesis writing. *Entrance requirements:* For master's, PRAXIS I, portfolio, writing samples. Additional exam requirements/recommendations for international students: Required—TOEFL (minimum score 550 paper-based; 80 iBT), IELTS (minimum score 6.5). Electronic applications accepted.

Marywood University, Academic Affairs, Insalaco College of Creative and Performing Arts, Art Department, Program in Art Education, Scranton, PA 18509-1598. Offers MA. *Accreditation:* NASAD; NCATE. Electronic applications accepted.

Massachusetts College of Art and Design, Graduate Programs, Program in Art Education, Boston, MA 02115-5882. Offers art education (M Ed, MAT); art teacher preparation (Postbaccalaureate Certificate). *Accreditation:* NASAD. *Faculty:* 2 full-time (both women), 3 part-time/adjunct (all women). *Students:* 8 full-time (all women), 9 part-time (2 women); includes 4 minority (2 Asian, non-Hispanic/Latino; 1 Hispanic/Latino; 1 Two or more races, non-Hispanic/Latino). 26 applicants, 85% accepted, 9 enrolled. In 2017, 7 master's awarded. *Entrance requirements:* For master's and Postbaccalaureate Certificate, portfolio, college transcripts, resume, statement of purpose, letters of reference, interview. Additional exam requirements/recommendations for international students: Required—TOEFL (minimum score 550 paper-based; 85 iBT); Recommended—IELTS (minimum score 6). *Application deadline:* For fall admission, 1/4 priority date for domestic and international students. Application fee: $90. Electronic applications accepted. *Expenses:* $780 per credit. *Financial support:* In 2017–18, 10 students received support, including 4 teaching assistantships (averaging $2,160 per year); research assistantships, career-related internships or fieldwork, scholarships/grants, tuition waivers (partial), and unspecified assistantships also available. Support available to part-time students. Financial award application deadline: 1/4; financial award applicants required to submit FAFSA. *Faculty research:* Cognitive and developmental psychology, research methodologies and synthesis, embodied aesthetics, neuro-aesthetics and neuro-philosophy, interactive art. *Unit head:* Paul Paturzo, Dean of Graduate Studies, 617-879-7166, E-mail: pjpaturzo@massart.edu. *Application contact:* Lauren O'Neill, Assistant Director of Graduate Admissions, 617-879-7222, E-mail: gradadmissions@massart.edu.
Website: http://www.massart.edu/Admissions/Graduate_Programs.html

McNeese State University, Doré School of Graduate Studies, Burton College of Education, Department of Education Professions, Program in Multiple Levels Grades K-12, Lake Charles, LA 70609. Offers multiple levels grades K-12 (Postbaccalaureate Certificate), including art, health and physical education, music - instrumental, music - vocal. *Entrance requirements:* For degree, PRAXIS, 2 letters of recommendation, autobiography. *Application deadline:* For fall admission, 5/15 priority date for domestic and international students; for spring admission, 10/15 priority date for domestic and international students. Applications are processed on a rolling basis. Application fee: $20 ($30 for international students). *Financial support:* Application deadline: 5/1. *Unit head:* Dr. Veronica Faye White, Head, 337-475-5400, Fax: 337-475-5272, E-mail: vfwhite@mcneese.edu. *Application contact:* Dr. Dustin M. Hebert, Director of Dore' School of Graduate Studies, 337-475-5396, Fax: 337-475-5397, E-mail: admissions@mcneese.edu.

Miami University, College of Creative Arts, Department of Art, Oxford, OH 45056. Offers art education (MA); studio art (MFA). *Accreditation:* NASAD (one or more programs are accredited). *Students:* 16 full-time (8 women), 2 part-time (both women); includes 3 minority (1 Black or African American, non-Hispanic/Latino; 1 Asian, non-Hispanic/Latino; 1 Two or more races, non-Hispanic/Latino), 4 international. Average age 33. In 2017, 10 master's awarded. *Expenses:* Tuition, state resident: full-time $13,812; part-time $575 per credit hour. Tuition, nonresident: full-time $30,860; part-time $1286 per credit hour. *Unit head:* Rob Robbins, Chair and Professor, 513-529-2900, E-mail: art@miamioh.edu.
Website: http://www.MiamiOH.edu/art

Millersville University of Pennsylvania, College of Graduate Studies and Adult Learning, College of Arts, Humanities and Social Sciences, Department of Art and Design, Millersville, PA 17551-0302. Offers art education (M Ed). *Accreditation:* NASAD; NCATE. *Program availability:* Part-time. *Faculty:* 3 full-time (all women), 3 part-time/adjunct (2 women). *Students:* 3 full-time (2 women), 11 part-time (9 women); includes 3 minority (2 Asian, non-Hispanic/Latino; 1 Hispanic/Latino). Average age 34. 5 applicants, 100% accepted, 1 enrolled. In 2017, 8 master's awarded. *Degree requirements:* For master's, comprehensive exam, thesis optional. *Entrance requirements:* For master's, teaching certificate (unless enrolled in post baccalaureate certificate at same time); portfolio (if not MU graduate); minimum undergraduate and post baccalaureate GPA of 3.0 cumulative, 3.25 in art and art education courses; three letters of recommendation; professional goals as stated by the applicant. Additional exam requirements/recommendations for international students: Required—TOEFL (minimum score 80 iBT), IELTS (minimum score 6.5), PTE (minimum score 60). *Application deadline:* Applications are processed on a rolling basis. Application fee: $40. Electronic applications accepted. *Expenses:* $500 per credit resident tuition and fees; $750 per credit non-resident tuition and fees; $114.75 per credit general fee (maximum of 12 credits); technology fee $27 per credit (resident), $39 per credit (non-resident). *Financial support:* Unspecified assistantships available. Financial award application deadline: 3/15; financial award applicants required to submit FAFSA. *Faculty research:* Ceramics; representational painting; material investigations involving bronze casting, steel forming and fabrication, mold-making, wood working; art educator's professional learning, assessment in the arts, and postmodern; interactive design fundamentals, interdisciplinary design, interaction, visual storytelling and digital narrative forms and choice-based approaches to teaching art. *Unit head:* Deborah S. Sigel, Chairperson, 717-871-7248, Fax: 717-871-2004, E-mail: deborah.sigel@millersville.edu. *Application contact:* Dr. Victor S. DeSantis, Dean of College of Graduate Studies and Adult Learning/Associate Provost for Civic and Community Engagement, 717-871-7619, Fax: 717-871-7954, E-mail: victor.desantis@millersville.edu.
Website: http://www.millersville.edu/art/

Minnesota State University Mankato, College of Graduate Studies and Research, College of Arts and Humanities, Department of Art, Mankato, MN 56001. Offers art (MA); art education (MAT). *Accreditation:* NASAD (one or more programs are accredited). *Program availability:* Part-time. *Degree requirements:* For master's, one foreign language, comprehensive exam, thesis or alternative. *Entrance requirements:* For master's, portfolio, three letters of reference. Additional exam requirements/recommendations for international students: Required—TOEFL. Electronic applications accepted.

Mississippi College, Graduate School, School of Education, Department of Teacher Education and Leadership, Clinton, MS 39058. Offers art (M Ed); biological science (M Ed); business education (M Ed); computer science (M Ed); dyslexia therapy (M Ed); educational leadership (M Ed, Ed D, Ed S); elementary education (M Ed, Ed S); English (M Ed); higher education administration (MS); mathematics (M Ed); secondary education (M Ed); social studies (history) (M Ed); teaching arts (M Ed). *Program availability:* Part-time, online learning. *Degree requirements:* For master's, comprehensive exam, thesis optional. *Entrance requirements:* For master's, NTE. Additional exam requirements/recommendations for international students: Recommended—TOEFL, IELTS. Electronic applications accepted.

Montclair State University, The Graduate School, College of Education and Human Services, MAT Program in Teaching, Montclair, NJ 07043-1624. Offers art (MAT); biology (MAT); chemistry (MAT); earth science (MAT); English (MAT); French (MAT); health and physical education (MAT); health education (MAT); mathematics (MAT); music (MAT); physical education (MAT); physical science (MAT); social studies (MAT); Spanish (MAT); teacher of English as a second language (MAT). *Degree requirements:* For master's, comprehensive exam, thesis or alternative. *Entrance requirements:* For master's, interview, 2 letters of recommendation. Additional exam requirements/recommendations for international students: Required—TOEFL (minimum score 83 iBT), IELTS (minimum score 6.5). Electronic applications accepted.

Moore College of Art & Design, Program in Art Education, Philadelphia, PA 19103. Offers MA. *Program availability:* Part-time. *Degree requirements:* For master's, thesis, field practicum. *Entrance requirements:* For master's, minimum GPA of 3.0, on-site interview, portfolio, 3 letters of recommendation, resume.

Morehead State University, Graduate Programs, Caudill College of Arts, Humanities and Social Sciences, Department of Art and Design, Morehead, KY 40351. Offers art education (MA); graphic design (MA); studio art (MA). *Accreditation:* NASAD. *Program availability:* Part-time, evening/weekend. *Degree requirements:* For master's, comprehensive exam, thesis (for some programs), oral exam during exhibition. *Entrance requirements:* For master's, GRE General Test, minimum undergraduate GPA of 3.0 in major, 2.5 overall; portfolio; bachelor's degree in art. Additional exam requirements/recommendations for international students: Required—TOEFL (minimum score 500 paper-based). Electronic applications accepted. *Faculty research:* Computer art, painting, drawing, ceramics, photography.

Nazareth College of Rochester, Graduate Studies, Department of Art, Program in Art Education, Rochester, NY 14618. Offers MS Ed. *Accreditation:* TEAC. *Program availability:* Part-time. *Entrance requirements:* For master's, GRE (for speech-language pathology); GRE or MAT (for education programs), minimum GPA of 3.0, portfolio review. Additional exam requirements/recommendations for international students: Required—TOEFL (minimum score 550 paper-based, 79 iBT) or IELTS (6.5). Electronic applications accepted.

New Hampshire Institute of Art, Graduate Studies, Manchester, NH 03104. Offers art education (MA); creative writing (MFA); photography (MFA); teaching visual arts (MAT); visual arts (MFA). *Accreditation:* NASAD. *Faculty:* 31 part-time/adjunct (14 women). *Students:* 59 full-time (42 women), 6 part-time (3 women); includes 2 minority (1 Asian, non-Hispanic/Latino; 1 Hispanic/Latino). Average age 43. 33 applicants, 36% accepted, 5 enrolled. In 2017, 2 master's awarded. *Degree requirements:* For master's, thesis, corresponding exhibition and artist talk. *Entrance requirements:* For master's, writing sample or visual art portfolio; curriculum vitae; transcripts; letters of recommendation. Additional exam requirements/recommendations for international students: Required—TOEFL (minimum score 550 paper-based; 80 iBT), IELTS (minimum score 6.5). *Application deadline:* For fall admission, 5/1 priority date for domestic students; for spring admission, 11/1 priority date for domestic students. Applications are processed on a rolling basis. Application fee: $75. Electronic applications accepted. *Expenses:* Contact institution. *Financial support:* In 2017–18, 2 teaching assistantships (averaging $1,200 per year) were awarded; scholarships/grants and unspecified assistantships also available. Support available to part-time students. Financial award application deadline: 6/1; financial award applicants required to submit FAFSA. *Faculty research:* Fine arts - visual arts, photography, creative writing; art education. *Unit head:* Lucinda Bliss, Dean of Graduate Studies, 603-836-2522, E-mail: lucindabliss@nhia.edu. *Application contact:* Moriah Billups, Graduate Admissions Coordinator, 603-836 2588, E-mail: gradadmissions@nhia.edu.
Website: http://www.nhia.edu/graduate-studies

New Jersey City University, William J. Maxwell College of Arts and Sciences, Department of Art, Jersey City, NJ 07305-1597. Offers art (MFA); art education (MA); studio art (MFA). *Accreditation:* NASAD. *Program availability:* Part-time, evening/weekend. *Degree requirements:* For master's, thesis or alternative, exhibit. *Entrance requirements:* For master's, portfolio. Additional exam requirements/recommendations for international students: Required—TOEFL (minimum score 79 iBT).

New York University, Steinhardt School of Culture, Education, and Human Development, Department of Art and Art Professions, Program in Art Education, New York, NY 10003-5799. Offers art, education, and community practice (MA); teachers of art, all grades (MA); teaching art/social studies 7-12 (MA), including 5-6 extension. *Accreditation:* TEAC. *Program availability:* Part-time. *Students:* Average age 35. 57 applicants, 63% accepted, 22 enrolled. In 2017, 13 master's awarded. *Entrance requirements:* For master's, portfolio. Additional exam requirements/recommendations for international students: Required—TOEFL (minimum score 100 iBT). *Application deadline:* For fall admission, 12/1 priority date for domestic and international students. Applications are processed on a rolling basis. Application fee: $75. Electronic applications accepted. *Expenses: Tuition:* Full-time $41,352; part-time $19,968 per year. *Required fees:* $2496; $1628 per unit. $814 per term. Tuition and fees vary according to course load and program. *Financial support:* Career-related internships or fieldwork, Federal Work-Study, and tuition waivers (partial) available. Support available to part-time students. Financial award application deadline: 2/1; financial award applicants required to submit FAFSA. *Faculty research:* Multicultural aesthetic inquiry, urban art education, feminism, equity and social justice. *Unit head:* Prof. Dipti Desai, Director, 212-998-5700, Fax: 212-995-4320, E-mail: dd25@nyu.edu. *Application contact:* 212-998-5030, Fax: 212-995-4328, E-mail: steinhardt.gradadmissions@nyu.edu.
Website: http://steinhardt.nyu.edu/art/education

New York University, Steinhardt School of Culture, Education, and Human Development, Department of Teaching and Learning, Program in Social Studies Education, New York, NY 10012. Offers teaching art/social studies 7-12 (MA), including 5-6 extension; teaching social studies 7-12 (MA). *Accreditation:* TEAC. *Program availability:* Part-time, evening/weekend. *Students:* Average age 24. 47 applicants, 81% accepted, 11 enrolled. In 2017, 8 master's awarded. *Entrance requirements:* Additional exam requirements/recommendations for international students: Required—TOEFL (minimum score 100 iBT). *Application deadline:* For fall admission, 12/1 priority date for

domestic and international students; for spring admission, 10/1 for domestic and international students. Applications are processed on a rolling basis. Application fee: $75. Electronic applications accepted. *Expenses: Tuition:* Full-time $41,352; part-time $19,968 per year. *Required fees:* $2496; $1628 per unit. $814 per term. Tuition and fees vary according to course load and program. *Financial support:* Career-related internships or fieldwork, Federal Work-Study, institutionally sponsored loans, scholarships/grants, and tuition waivers (partial) available. Support available to part-time students. Financial award application deadline: 2/1; financial award applicants required to submit FAFSA. *Faculty research:* Social studies education reform, ethnography and oral history, civic education, labor history and social studies curriculum, material culture. *Unit head:* Dr. Diana Turk, Chairperson, 212-998-5492, Fax: 212-995-4049, E-mail: dt23@nyu.edu. *Application contact:* 212-998-5030, Fax: 212-995-4328, E-mail: steinhardt.gradadmissions@nyu.edu.
Website: http://steinhardt.nyu.edu/teachlearn/social_studies

The Ohio State University, Graduate School, College of Arts and Sciences, Division of Arts and Humanities, Department of Arts Administration, Education and Policy, Columbus, OH 43210. Offers art education (MA); arts administration, education and policy (PhD); arts policy and administration (MA). *Accreditation:* NASAD; NCATE. *Program availability:* Online learning. *Faculty:* 11. *Students:* 43 full-time (35 women), 20 part-time (15 women), 16 international. Average age 32. In 2017, 12 master's, 5 doctorates awarded. Terminal master's awarded for partial completion of doctoral program. *Degree requirements:* For master's, thesis; for doctorate, thesis/dissertation. *Entrance requirements:* For master's, GRE; for doctorate, GRE General Test. Additional exam requirements/recommendations for international students: Required—TOEFL (minimum score 600 paper-based; 100 iBT); Recommended—IELTS (minimum score 8). *Application deadline:* For fall admission, 11/30 priority date for domestic and international students; for winter admission, 12/1 for domestic students, 11/1 for international students; for spring admission, 11/30 priority date for domestic and international students. Applications are processed on a rolling basis. Application fee: $60 ($70 for international students). Electronic applications accepted. *Financial support:* Fellowships with tuition reimbursements, research assistantships with tuition reimbursements, teaching assistantships with tuition reimbursements, career-related internships or fieldwork, Federal Work-Study, institutionally sponsored loans, and unspecified assistantships available. Support available to part-time students. Financial award applicants required to submit FAFSA. *Unit head:* Dr. Karen Hutzel, Chair and Associate Professor, 614-292-9852, E-mail: hutzel.4@osu.edu. *Application contact:* Graduate Admissions, 614-292-9444, Fax: 614-292-3895, E-mail: gradadmissions@osu.edu.
Website: http://aaep.osu.edu/

Penn State University Park, Graduate School, College of Arts and Architecture, School of Visual Arts, University Park, PA 16802. Offers art (MFA); art education (MS, PhD, Certificate). *Unit head:* Dr. Barbara O. Korner, Dean, 814-865-2592, Fax: 814-865-2018. *Application contact:* Lori Hawn, Director, Graduate Student Services, 814-865-1795, Fax: 814-863-4627, E-mail: l-gswww@lists.psu.edu.
Website: http://sova.psu.edu/

Piedmont College, School of Education, Demorest, GA 30535. Offers art education (MA, MAT); curriculum and instruction (Ed D, Ed S); early childhood education (MA, MAT); instructional technology (MA); middle grades education (MA, MAT); music education (MA, MAT); secondary education (MA, MAT); special education (MA, MAT). *Program availability:* Part-time, evening/weekend. *Students:* 341 full-time (268 women), 682 part-time (571 women); includes 182 minority (136 Black or African American, non-Hispanic/Latino; 2 American Indian or Alaska Native, non-Hispanic/Latino; 11 Asian, non-Hispanic/Latino; 32 Hispanic/Latino; 1 Two or more races, non-Hispanic/Latino). Average age 37. 333 applicants, 77% accepted, 103 enrolled. In 2017, 292 master's, 9 doctorates, 318 other advanced degrees awarded. *Degree requirements:* For master's, thesis, field experience in the classroom teaching; for doctorate, thesis/dissertation. *Entrance requirements:* For master's, GRE General Test, MAT; for Ed S, minimum graduate GPA of 3.5, valid teaching certificate. Additional exam requirements/recommendations for international students: Required—TOEFL (minimum score 550 paper-based). *Application deadline:* For fall admission, 7/15 for domestic students; for spring admission, 12/1 for domestic students. Applications are processed on a rolling basis. Electronic applications accepted. *Expenses: Tuition:* Full-time $9360; part-time $520 per credit hour. *Required fees:* $200; $200 per year. $100 per term. *Financial support:* Career-related internships or fieldwork, Federal Work-Study, and unspecified assistantships available. Support available to part-time students. Financial award applicants required to submit FAFSA. *Unit head:* Dr. Don Gnecco, Dean, 706-778-3000 Ext. 1201, Fax: 706-776-9608, E-mail: dgnecco@piedmont.edu. *Application contact:* Kathleen Carter, Director of Graduate Enrollment Management, 706-778-8500 Ext. 1181, Fax: 706-778-0150, E-mail: kanderson@piedmont.edu.

Plymouth State University, College of Graduate Studies, Graduate Studies in Education, Program in Teaching, Plymouth, NH 03264-1595. Offers art education (MAT); science education (MAT). *Program availability:* Evening/weekend. *Degree requirements:* For master's, internship or teaching experience.

Pratt Institute, School of Art, Program in Art and Design Education, Brooklyn, NY 11205-3899. Offers MA, MS, Adv C. *Accreditation:* NASAD. *Program availability:* Part-time. *Students:* 19 full-time (18 women), 1 (woman) part-time; includes 10 minority (1 Black or African American, non-Hispanic/Latino; 1 Asian, non-Hispanic/Latino; 7 Hispanic/Latino; 1 Two or more races, non-Hispanic/Latino), 2 international. Average age 25. 16 applicants, 88% accepted, 6 enrolled. In 2017, 2 master's, 1 other advanced degree awarded. *Degree requirements:* For master's, thesis. *Entrance requirements:* For master's, portfolio. Additional exam requirements/recommendations for international students: Required—TOEFL (minimum score 600 paper-based; 100 iBT). *Application deadline:* For fall admission, 1/5 for domestic and international students; for spring admission, 10/1 for domestic and international students. Application fee: $50 ($90 for international students). Electronic applications accepted. *Expenses: Tuition:* Full-time $30,834. *Required fees:* $1974. *Financial support:* Career-related internships or fieldwork, Federal Work-Study, institutionally sponsored loans, scholarships/grants, health care benefits, and unspecified assistantships available. Support available to part-time students. Financial award application deadline: 2/1; financial award applicants required to submit FAFSA. *Unit head:* Heather Lewis, Chairperson, 718-636-3637, Fax: 718-636-3632, E-mail: hlewis@pratt.edu. *Application contact:* Natalie Capannelli, Director of Graduate Admissions, 718-636-3551, Fax: 718-399-4242, E-mail: ncapanne@pratt.edu.
Website: https://www.pratt.edu/academics/school-of-art/graduate-school-of-art/art-and-design-education-grad/

Purdue University, Graduate School, College of Education, Department of Curriculum and Instruction, West Lafayette, IN 47907. Offers agricultural and extension education (MS, MS Ed, PhD, Ed S); art education (PhD); career and technical education (MS Ed, PhD, Ed S); curriculum studies (MS Ed, PhD, Ed S); educational technology (MS Ed, PhD, Ed S); elementary education (MS Ed); family and consumer sciences education (MS Ed, PhD, Ed S); foreign language education (MS Ed, PhD, Ed S); industrial technology (PhD, Ed S); language arts (MS Ed, PhD, Ed S); literacy (MS Ed, PhD, Ed S); mathematics education (MS, MS Ed, PhD, Ed S); science education (MS, MS Ed, PhD, Ed S); social

studies education (MS Ed, PhD, Ed S). *Accreditation:* NCATE. *Program availability:* Part-time, evening/weekend. *Faculty:* 37 full-time (27 women), 1 (woman) part-time/adjunct. *Students:* 78 full-time (50 women), 286 part-time (195 women); includes 68 minority (25 Black or African American, non-Hispanic/Latino; 3 American Indian or Alaska Native, non-Hispanic/Latino; 10 Asian, non-Hispanic/Latino; 22 Hispanic/Latino; 1 Native Hawaiian or other Pacific Islander, non-Hispanic/Latino; 7 Two or more races, non-Hispanic/Latino), 44 international. Average age 36. 150 applicants, 79% accepted, 73 enrolled. In 2017, 107 master's, 20 doctorates, 2 other advanced degrees awarded. *Degree requirements:* For master's, thesis optional; for doctorate, thesis/dissertation, oral and written exams; for Ed S, oral presentation, project. *Entrance requirements:* For master's, GRE General Test (if undergraduate GPA is below 3.0), minimum undergraduate GPA of 3.0 or equivalent; for doctorate, GRE General Test (minimum combined verbal and quantitative score of 1000, 300 for new scoring), minimum undergraduate GPA of 3.0 or equivalent; master's degree with minimum GPA of 3.0 or equivalent; for Ed S, GRE General Test (minimum combined verbal and quantitative score of 1000, 300 for new scoring), minimum undergraduate GPA of 3.0 or equivalent; master's degree. Additional exam requirements/recommendations for international students: Required—TOEFL (minimum score 550 paper-based; 77 iBT). *Application deadline:* For fall admission, 12/15 for domestic students, 3/1 for international students; for spring admission, 9/15 for domestic students, 8/1 for international students. Application fee: $60 ($75 for international students). Electronic applications accepted. *Financial support:* Fellowships with full tuition reimbursements, research assistantships with full tuition reimbursements, teaching assistantships with full tuition reimbursements, career-related internships or fieldwork, and tuition waivers (full) available. Support available to part-time students. Financial award application deadline: 3/1; financial award applicants required to submit FAFSA. *Faculty research:* Literacy acquisition and development, teacher beliefs and knowledge, recruitment and retention of underrepresented students, economic education, literacy discourse. *Unit head:* Janet M. Alsup, Head, 765-494-9667, E-mail: alsupj@purdue.edu. *Application contact:* Heather Brinkman, Graduate Contact, 765-494-2345, E-mail: hbrinkma@purdue.edu.
Website: http://www.edci.purdue.edu/

Purdue University, Graduate School, College of Liberal Arts, Department of Art and Design, West Lafayette, IN 47907. Offers art education (MA, PhD); industrial design (MFA); integrated studio arts (MFA); interior design (MFA); photography (MFA); visual communications design (MFA). *Accreditation:* NASAD; NAST. *Program availability:* Part-time. *Students:* 20 full-time (14 women), 1 part-time (0 women); includes 1 minority (Two or more races, non-Hispanic/Latino), 16 international. Average age 26. 97 applicants, 26% accepted, 10 enrolled. In 2017, 6 master's awarded. *Degree requirements:* For master's, terminal exhibit, project, or thesis. *Entrance requirements:* For master's, GRE General Test (for art education), minimum undergraduate GPA of 3.0 or equivalent; 9 undergraduate hours in an art or design history; BA in art (for MA in art education); for doctorate, GRE General Test (minimum scores 600 in verbal and 1000 total), master's degree in art education or art with teaching certification; 3 years of teaching experience at the K-12 level. Additional exam requirements/recommendations for international students: Required—TOEFL (minimum score 550 paper-based; 77 iBT). *Application deadline:* For fall admission, 2/1 for domestic students, 2/1 priority date for international students. Applications are processed on a rolling basis. Application fee: $60 ($75 for international students). Electronic applications accepted. *Financial support:* Teaching assistantships with tuition reimbursements and career-related internships or fieldwork available. Support available to part-time students. Financial award applicants required to submit FAFSA. *Faculty research:* Design, fine arts, photography, acting, directing, theatre technology. *Unit head:* Harry T. Bulow, Head of the Graduate Program, 765-494-3056, E-mail: hbulow@purdue.edu. *Application contact:* Sara J. Unser, Graduate Contact, 765-494-8662, E-mail: sunser@purdue.edu.
Website: https://www.cla.purdue.edu/vpa/ad/

Queens College of the City University of New York, Division of Education, Department of Secondary Education and Youth Services, Queens, NY 11367-1597. Offers adolescent biology (MAT); art (MS Ed); biology (MS Ed, AC); chemistry (MS Ed, AC); earth sciences (MS Ed, AC); English (MS Ed, AC); French (MS Ed); Italian (MS Ed, AC); literacy education (MS Ed); mathematics (MS Ed, AC); music (MS Ed, AC); physics (MS Ed, AC); social studies (MS Ed, AC); Spanish (MS Ed, AC). *Program availability:* Part-time, evening/weekend. *Students:* 28 full-time (16 women), 349 part-time (202 women); includes 165 minority (18 Black or African American, non-Hispanic/Latino; 56 Asian, non-Hispanic/Latino; 83 Hispanic/Latino; 8 Two or more races, non-Hispanic/Latino), 14 international. Average age 29. *Degree requirements:* For master's, research project. *Entrance requirements:* For master's, minimum GPA of 3.0. Additional exam requirements/recommendations for international students: Required—TOEFL, IELTS. *Application deadline:* For fall admission, 4/1 for domestic students; for spring admission, 11/1 for domestic students. Applications are processed on a rolling basis. Application fee: $125. Electronic applications accepted. *Financial support:* Career-related internships or fieldwork available. Financial award application deadline: 4/1; financial award applicants required to submit FAFSA. *Unit head:* Dr. Eleanor Armour-Thomas, Chairperson, 718-997-5150, E-mail: eleanor.armour-thomas@qc.cuny.edu. *Application contact:* Elizabeth D'Amico-Ramirez, Assistant Director of Graduate Admissions, 718-997-5203, E-mail: elizabeth.damicoramirez@qc.cuny.edu.

Rhode Island College, School of Graduate Studies, Faculty of Arts and Sciences, Department of Art, Providence, RI 02908-1991. Offers art education (MA, MAT); media studies (MA). *Accreditation:* NASAD (one or more programs are accredited). *Program availability:* Part-time, evening/weekend. *Faculty:* 3. *Students:* 4 full-time (3 women), 11 part-time (5 women); includes 4 minority (1 Asian, non-Hispanic/Latino; 3 Hispanic/Latino). Average age 33. In 2017, 4 master's awarded. *Degree requirements:* For master's, thesis. *Entrance requirements:* For master's, GRE General Test, portfolio (MA), 3 letters of recommendation, interview. Additional exam requirements/recommendations for international students: Recommended—TOEFL (minimum score 550 paper-based; 79 iBT). *Application deadline:* For fall admission, 3/1 for domestic students. Applications are processed on a rolling basis. Application fee: $50. Electronic applications accepted. *Expenses:* Tuition, state resident: full-time $9768; part-time $407 per credit. Tuition, nonresident: full-time $19,008; part-time $792 per credit. *Required fees:* $696; $29 per credit. One-time fee: $200 full-time; $100 part-time. Tuition and fees vary according to course load. *Financial support:* In 2017–18, 3 teaching assistantships with full tuition reimbursements (averaging $1,500 per year) were awarded; career-related internships or fieldwork, Federal Work-Study, scholarships/grants, health care benefits, and unspecified assistantships also available. Support available to part-time students. Financial award application deadline: 5/15; financial award applicants required to submit FAFSA. *Unit head:* Prof. Richard Whitten, Chair, 401-456-8054.
Website: http://www.ric.edu/art/index.php

Rhode Island School of Design, Department of Teaching and Learning in Art and Design, Providence, RI 02903-2784. Offers art and design education (MA); art education (MAT). *Accreditation:* NASAD. *Faculty:* 2 full-time (0 women), 7 part-time/adjunct (all women). *Students:* 22 full-time (18 women); includes 6 minority (3 Asian, non-Hispanic/Latino; 1 Hispanic/Latino; 2 Two or more races, non-Hispanic/Latino), 4 international. Average age 28. 38 applicants, 79% accepted, 22 enrolled. In 2017, 17 master's awarded. *Degree requirements:* For master's, thesis, exhibition. *Entrance requirements:* For master's, portfolio, statement of purpose, 3 letters of recommendation. Additional

exam requirements/recommendations for international students: Required—TOEFL (minimum score 580 paper-based; 93 iBT). *Application deadline:* For fall admission, 1/10 for domestic and international students. Application fee: $60. Electronic applications accepted. *Expenses:* Tuition: Full-time $48,210. *Required fees:* $260. *Financial support:* Fellowships, research assistantships, teaching assistantships, Federal Work-Study, scholarships/grants, and unspecified assistantships available. Financial award application deadline: 2/15; financial award applicants required to submit FAFSA. *Unit head:* Paul Sproll, Department Head and Graduate Program Director, 401-454-6695, Fax: 401-454-6694, E-mail: teachlearn@risd.edu. *Application contact:* Molly Pettengill, Assistant Director for Graduate Recruitment, 401-454-6312, Fax: 401-454-6309, E-mail: mpetteng@risd.edu.
Website: http://www.risd.edu/academics/tlad/

Rochester Institute of Technology, Graduate Enrollment Services, College of Imaging Arts and Sciences, School of Art, MST Program in Visual Arts-All Grades, Rochester, NY 14623-5603. Offers MST. *Accreditation:* NASAD; TEAC. *Students:* 11 full-time (all women); includes 6 minority (1 Black or African American, non-Hispanic/Latino; 3 Hispanic/Latino; 2 Two or more races, non-Hispanic/Latino). Average age 27. 19 applicants, 74% accepted, 11 enrolled. In 2017, 4 master's awarded. *Degree requirements:* For master's, practicum in student teaching. *Entrance requirements:* For master's, GRE, portfolio, minimum GPA of 3.0 (recommended). Additional exam requirements/recommendations for international students: Required—TOEFL (minimum score 550 paper-based; 79 iBT), IELTS (minimum score 6.5), PTE (minimum score 58). *Application deadline:* For fall admission, 2/15 priority date for domestic and international students. Applications are processed on a rolling basis. Application fee: $65. Electronic applications accepted. *Expenses:* $1,815 per credit hour. *Financial support:* In 2017–18, 10 students received support. Scholarships/grants and unspecified assistantships available. Financial award applicants required to submit FAFSA. *Faculty research:* Innovation and creativity in teaching and learning. *Unit head:* Adam Smith, Graduate Program Director, 585-475-4552, E-mail: adam.smith@rit.edu. *Application contact:* Diane Ellison, Senior Associate Vice President, Graduate Enrollment Services, 585-475-2229, Fax: 585-475-7164, E-mail: gradinfo@rit.edu.
Website: http://cias.rit.edu/schools/art/graduate-teaching-visual-arts

Rocky Mountain College of Art + Design, Program in Education, Leadership + Emerging Technologies, Lakewood, CO 80214. Offers MA. *Accreditation:* NASAD. *Program availability:* Online learning.

Saint Michael's College, Graduate Programs, Program in Education, Colchester, VT 05439. Offers arts in education (CAGS); literacy (M Ed); school leadership (CAGS); special education (M Ed). *Program availability:* Part-time, evening/weekend. *Students:* 7 full-time (3 women), 204 part-time (173 women); includes 8 minority (1 Black or African American, non-Hispanic/Latino; 1 American Indian or Alaska Native, non-Hispanic/Latino; 3 Hispanic/Latino; 3 Two or more races, non-Hispanic/Latino). Average age 38. 23 applicants, 65% accepted, 10 enrolled. In 2017, 32 master's awarded. *Degree requirements:* For master's, thesis. *Entrance requirements:* For master's, minimum GPA of 3.0, official transcripts, essay, interview. *Application deadline:* Applications are processed on a rolling basis. Application fee: $50. Electronic applications accepted. *Expenses:* Tuition: Part-time $590 per credit. *Financial support:* Fellowships with partial tuition reimbursements and scholarships/grants available. Support available to part-time students. Financial award applicants required to submit FAFSA. *Faculty research:* Integrative curriculum, moral and spiritual dimensions of education, learning styles, multiple intelligences, integrating technology into the curriculum. *Unit head:* Jonathan Silverman, Department Chair, 802-654-2306, Fax: 802-654-2664, E-mail: jsilverman@smcvt.edu. *Application contact:* Lindsay A. Damici, Marketing Communications Manager, 802-654-2556, Fax: 802-654-2732.
Website: http://www.smcvt.edu/graduate-programs/academic-programs/education.aspx

Salem College, Graduate Studies, Winston-Salem, NC 27101. Offers art education (MAT); elementary education (M Ed, MAT); language and literacy (M Ed); middle school education (MAT); organ (MM); piano (MM); school counseling (M Ed); second language studies (MAT); secondary education (MAT); special education (M Ed, MAT). *Accreditation:* NCATE. *Program availability:* Part-time, evening/weekend, online learning. *Faculty:* 8 full-time (all women), 11 part-time/adjunct (8 women). In 2017, 17 master's awarded. *Degree requirements:* For master's, practicum (MAT), action research project (M Ed). *Entrance requirements:* For master's, minimum GPA of 3.0, two academic/professional recommendations, acceptable criminal background check. Additional exam requirements/recommendations for international students: Recommended—TOEFL. *Application deadline:* For fall admission, 8/1 for domestic students, 7/15 for international students; for spring admission, 1/15 for domestic students; for summer admission, 5/1 for domestic students. Applications are processed on a rolling basis. Application fee: $30. Electronic applications accepted. *Expenses:* Tuition: Part-time $440 per semester hour. *Financial support:* Scholarships/grants available. Support available to part-time students. Financial award applicants required to submit FAFSA. *Faculty research:* Teacher professional development, adolescent literacy, instructional technology. *Application contact:* Sheryl Long, Director, 336-721-2658, Fax: 336-917-5384, E-mail: sheryl.long@salem.edu.
Website: http://www.salem.edu

Salem State University, School of Graduate Studies, Program in Art, Salem, MA 01970-5353. Offers MAT. *Accreditation:* NASAD. *Program availability:* Part-time, evening/weekend. *Entrance requirements:* For master's, GRE or MAT. Additional exam requirements/recommendations for international students: Required—TOEFL (minimum score 550 paper-based; 80 iBT) or IELTS (minimum score 5.5).

School of the Art Institute of Chicago, Graduate Division, Program in Art Education and Art Teaching, Chicago, IL 60603-3103. Offers MAAE, MAT. *Accreditation:* NASAD. *Entrance requirements:* Additional exam requirements/recommendations for international students: Required—TOEFL (minimum score 600 paper-based; 100 iBT), IELTS (minimum score 7).

School of Visual Arts, Graduate Programs, Art Education Department, New York, NY 10010-3994. Offers MAT. *Program availability:* Part-time. *Degree requirements:* For master's, one foreign language, thesis, 60 credits, including all required courses; minimum cumulative GPA of 3.0; residency of two academic years. *Entrance requirements:* For master's, Liberal Arts and Sciences Test (strongly recommended), CD with 15 to 20 images (jpeg or tiff formats, and at least 600x500 pixels); 30 credits each in studio art and liberal arts and sciences); 12 credits in art history; coursework in language other than English; personal interview. Additional exam requirements/recommendations for international students: Required—TOEFL (minimum score 550 paper-based; 79 iBT). Electronic applications accepted. *Faculty research:* Teaching art to children in pre-kindergarten through grade 12.

School of Visual Arts, Graduate Programs, Program in Art Writing, New York, NY 10010. Offers MFA. *Degree requirements:* For master's, thesis, 60 credits, including all required courses; residency of two academic years. *Entrance requirements:* For master's, typed writing sample between 2,500 and 3,000 words in length; personal interviews. Additional exam requirements/recommendations for international students: Required—TOEFL (minimum score 550 paper-based; 79 iBT). Electronic applications accepted. *Faculty research:* Art, writing, criticism, editing, art history, philosophy.

Simon Fraser University, Office of Graduate Studies and Postdoctoral Fellows, Faculty of Education, Program in Arts Education, Burnaby, BC V5A 1S6, Canada. Offers M Ed, MA, Ed D, PhD. *Program availability:* Part-time, evening/weekend. *Degree requirements:* For master's, comprehensive exam (for some programs), thesis (for some programs); for doctorate, comprehensive exam (for some programs), thesis/dissertation (for some programs). *Entrance requirements:* For master's, minimum GPA of 3.0 (on scale of 4.33) or 3.33 based on last 60 credits of undergraduate courses; for doctorate, minimum GPA of 3.5 (on scale of 4.33). Additional exam requirements/recommendations for international students: Recommended—TOEFL (minimum score 580 paper-based; 93 iBT), IELTS (minimum score 7), TWE (minimum score 5). *Faculty research:* Drama education, poetic and performative inquiry, the integration of the arts in education, art therapy, arts-based narrative and arts-informed research methodologies.

Southern Connecticut State University, School of Graduate Studies, School of Arts and Sciences, Department of Art, New Haven, CT 06515-1355. Offers art education (MS). *Program availability:* Part-time, evening/weekend. *Degree requirements:* For master's, thesis or alternative. *Entrance requirements:* For master's, interview. Electronic applications accepted.

Southwestern Oklahoma State University, College of Arts and Sciences, Department of Art, Weatherford, OK 73096-3098. Offers art education (M Ed). *Program availability:* Part-time. *Degree requirements:* For master's, exam. *Entrance requirements:* For master's, GRE General Test or minimum undergraduate GPA of 3.0. Additional exam requirements/recommendations for international students: Required—TOEFL.

Spalding University, Graduate Studies, College of Education, Programs in Education, Louisville, KY 40203-2188. Offers art teacher education (MAT); business teacher education (MAT); elementary school education (MAT); foreign language (MAT); high school education (MAT); middle school education (MAT); secondary education (MAT); special education (learning and behavioral disorders) (MAT); student guidance counselor (MA); teacher leader (M Ed). *Accreditation:* NCATE. *Program availability:* Part-time, evening/weekend. *Entrance requirements:* For master's, GRE General Test or MAT, interview, letters of recommendation, resume. Additional exam requirements/recommendations for international students: Required—TOEFL (minimum score 535 paper-based). Electronic applications accepted. *Faculty research:* Instructional technology, achievement gap, classroom management, assessment.

State University of New York at New Paltz, Graduate and Extended Learning School, School of Fine and Performing Arts, Department of Art Education, New Paltz, NY 12561. Offers visual arts education (MS Ed). *Accreditation:* NASAD. *Program availability:* Part-time, evening/weekend. *Faculty:* 1 (woman) full-time. *Students:* 1 (woman) full-time, 7 part-time (all women). In 2017, 3 master's awarded. *Degree requirements:* For master's, thesis, portfolio. *Entrance requirements:* For master's, New York state art education teaching certificate, minimum GPA of 3.0, portfolio. Additional exam requirements/recommendations for international students: Required—TOEFL (minimum score 550 paper-based; 80 iBT), IELTS (minimum score 6.5). *Application deadline:* For fall admission, 4/15 for domestic and international students; for summer admission, 3/15 priority date for domestic and international students. Application fee: $50. Electronic applications accepted. *Financial support:* Application deadline: 8/1. *Unit head:* Prof. Beth Thomas, Director, 845-257-2641, E-mail: thomasb@newpaltz.edu. *Application contact:* Vika Shock, Director of Graduate Admissions, 845-257-3286, E-mail: gradschool@newpaltz.edu.
Website: http://www.newpaltz.edu/arted/

State University of New York at Oswego, Graduate Studies, School of Education, Department of Curriculum and Instruction, Oswego, NY 13126. Offers adolescence education (MST); art education (MAT); childhood education (MST); curriculum and instruction (MS Ed); literacy education (MS Ed); special education (MS Ed). *Program availability:* Part-time, evening/weekend. *Degree requirements:* For master's, comprehensive exam (for some programs), thesis optional. *Entrance requirements:* For master's, GRE General Test, minimum GPA of 2.7, provisional teaching certificate. Additional exam requirements/recommendations for international students: Required—TOEFL (minimum score 560 paper-based). *Faculty research:* Classroom applications for microcomputers; classroom questioning, wait-time, and achievement; values clarification and academic achievement.

Sul Ross State University, College of Arts and Sciences, Department of Fine Arts and Communication, Alpine, TX 79832. Offers art history (MA); studio art (MA), including art education. *Program availability:* Part-time. *Degree requirements:* For master's, oral or written exam. *Entrance requirements:* For master's, GRE General Test, minimum GPA of 2.5 in last 60 hours of undergraduate work. *Faculty research:* Ceramic sculpture, watercolor, wood sculpture, rock art.

Syracuse University, School of Education, MS Program in Art Education, Syracuse, NY 13244. Offers MS. *Program availability:* Part-time. *Entrance requirements:* For master's, GRE, strong teacher and/or employer recommendations, portfolio review. Additional exam requirements/recommendations for international students: Required—TOEFL (minimum score 100 iBT). *Application deadline:* For fall admission, 1/15 for domestic and international students. Application fee: $75 ($0 for international students). Electronic applications accepted. *Financial support:* Fellowships with full tuition reimbursements, research assistantships, teaching assistantships, career-related internships or fieldwork, and scholarships/grants available. Financial award application deadline: 1/15. *Faculty research:* Art educational practice, arts and design practices as a means for personal agency and social responsibility, developing art and design curricula for teaching and learning in multiple contexts, interdisciplinary research promoting creative leadership and entrepreneurship. *Unit head:* Dr. James Haywood Rolling, Jr., Director, 315-443-2305, E-mail: jrolling@syr.edu. *Application contact:* Speranza Migliore, Graduate Admissions Recruiter, 315-443-2505, E-mail: gradrcrt@syr.edu.
Website: http://soe.syr.edu/academic/teaching_and_leadership/graduate/masters/art_education/preparation/default.aspx

Teachers College, Columbia University, Department of Arts and Humanities, New York, NY 10027. Offers applied linguistics (MA, Ed D); art and art education (Ed M, MA, Ed D, Ed DCT); arts administration (MA); bilingual and bicultural education (MA); global competence (Certificate); history and education (Ed D, PhD); music and music education (Ed DCT); philosophy and education (MA, Ed D, PhD); social studies education (Ed M, PhD); teaching English to speakers of other languages (Ed M); teaching of English and English education (Ed M, MA, Ed D, PhD), including English education (Ed M, Ed D, PhD), teaching of English (MA); teaching of social studies (MA); TESOL (MA, Ed D). *Program availability:* Part-time, evening/weekend. *Students:* 391 full-time (305 women), 418 part-time (283 women); includes 246 minority (62 Black or African American, non-Hispanic/Latino; 3 American Indian or Alaska Native, non-Hispanic/Latino; 94 Asian, non-Hispanic/Latino; 75 Hispanic/Latino; 12 Two or more races, non-Hispanic/Latino), 209 international. Average age 30. 1,053 applicants, 60% accepted, 334 enrolled. Terminal master's awarded for partial completion of doctoral program. *Financial support:* Fellowships, research assistantships, teaching assistantships, career-related internships or fieldwork, Federal Work-Study, institutionally sponsored loans, tuition waivers (full and partial), and unspecified assistantships available. Support available to part-time students. *Unit head:* Prof. William Gaudelli, Department Chair, E-mail: gaudelli@tc.columbia.edu. *Application*

contact: David Estrella, Director of Admissions, 212-678-3305, Fax: 212-678-4171, E-mail: estrella@tc.columbia.edu.

Temple University, Tyler School of Art, Department of Art Education and Community Arts Practices, Philadelphia, PA 19122-6096. Offers art education (Ed M). *Program availability:* Part-time, evening/weekend. *Faculty:* 2 full-time (0 women), 9 part-time/adjunct (6 women). *Students:* 6 full-time (4 women), 8 part-time (7 women); includes 3 minority (1 Black or African American, non-Hispanic/Latino; 2 Hispanic/Latino). 10 applicants, 50% accepted, 3 enrolled. In 2017, 1 master's awarded. *Entrance requirements:* For master's, GRE or MAT, minimum GPA of 3.0, slide portfolio, 40 credits in studio art, 9 credits in art history, letters of recommendation, resume/curriculum vitae. Additional exam requirements/recommendations for international students: Required—TOEFL (minimum score 550 paper-based; 79 iBT), IELTS (minimum score 6.5). *Application deadline:* For fall admission, 1/15 for domestic and international students; for spring admission, 11/1 for domestic and international students. Applications are processed on a rolling basis. Application fee: $60. Electronic applications accepted. *Expenses:* Contact institution. *Financial support:* Research assistantships, teaching assistantships, and Federal Work-Study available. Support available to part-time students. Financial award application deadline: 1/15; financial award applicants required to submit FAFSA. *Unit head:* Dr. Lisa Kay, Chair, 215-777-9763, E-mail: lisakay@temple.edu. *Application contact:* Tamryn McDermott, Director of Admissions, 215-777-9090, E-mail: tylerart@temple.edu.

Texas Tech University, Graduate School, J.T. and Margaret Talkington College of Visual and Performing Arts, School of Art, Lubbock, TX 79409. Offers art (MFA); art education (MAE); art history (MA). *Accreditation:* NASAD (one or more programs are accredited). *Program availability:* Part-time, blended/hybrid learning. *Faculty:* 31 full-time (13 women), 10 part-time/adjunct (6 women). *Students:* 32 full-time (22 women), 18 part-time (14 women); includes 11 minority (1 Black or African American, non-Hispanic/Latino; 1 Asian, non-Hispanic/Latino; 8 Hispanic/Latino; 1 Two or more races, non-Hispanic/Latino), 6 international. Average age 35. 31 applicants, 45% accepted, 9 enrolled. In 2017, 22 master's awarded. *Degree requirements:* For master's, variable foreign language requirement, comprehensive exam, thesis (for some programs), exhibition (for MFA). *Entrance requirements:* For master's, GRE (for MA). Additional exam requirements/recommendations for international students: Required—TOEFL (minimum score 550 paper-based; 79 iBT), IELTS (minimum score 6.5). *Application deadline:* For fall admission, 6/1 priority date for domestic students, 1/15 priority date for international students; for spring admission, 9/1 priority date for domestic students, 6/15 priority date for international students. Applications are processed on a rolling basis. Application fee: $60. Electronic applications accepted. *Expenses:* Contact institution. *Financial support:* In 2017–18, 37 students received support, including 36 fellowships (averaging $3,227 per year), 32 teaching assistantships (averaging $9,937 per year); research assistantships, Federal Work-Study, institutionally sponsored loans, scholarships/grants, health care benefits, tuition waivers (partial), and unspecified assistantships also available. Financial award application deadline: 2/15; financial award applicants required to submit FAFSA. *Faculty research:* Contemporary Chicano/a art; transformation of multidisciplinary approach to printmaking; letter press posters; intersection of art and science; transmedia. *Total annual research expenditures:* $44,636. *Unit head:* Prof. Lydia Thompson, Director and Professor, 806-742-3825 Ext. 255, E-mail: lydia.thompson@ttu.edu. *Application contact:* Linda Rumbelow, Academic Advisor, 806-742-3825 Ext. 222, E-mail: linda.rumbelow@ttu.edu.
Website: http://www.art.ttu.edu

Texas Woman's University, Graduate School, College of Arts and Sciences, School of the Arts, Department of Visual Arts, Denton, TX 76204. Offers art (MA, MAT, MFA), including art education (MA, MAT), art history (MA), ceramics (MFA), graphic design (MA), intermedia (MFA), painting (MFA), photography (MFA), sculpture (MFA). MFA degrees are granted through the Federation of North Texas Area Universities (The University of North Texas, Texas A&M Commerce, and Texas Woman's University). *Faculty:* 6 full-time (3 women). *Students:* 8 full-time (6 women), 9 part-time (8 women); includes 7 minority (1 Black or African American, non-Hispanic/Latino; 1 American Indian or Alaska Native, non-Hispanic/Latino; 4 Hispanic/Latino; 1 Two or more races, non-Hispanic/Latino). Average age 33. 10 applicants, 50% accepted, 2 enrolled. In 2017, 10 master's awarded. *Degree requirements:* For master's, comprehensive exam, thesis (for some programs), exhibit (MFA), oral exam, thesis or professional paper (MA). *Entrance requirements:* For master's, portfolio, interview, current curriculum vitae, letter of intent, 3 letters of recommendation, artist statement, 2 research papers (for art history or art education). Additional exam requirements/recommendations for international students: Required—TOEFL (minimum score 550 paper-based; 79 iBT); Recommended—IELTS (minimum score 6.5), TSE (minimum score 53). *Application deadline:* For fall admission, 1/31 priority date for domestic and international students; for spring admission, 10/15 priority date for domestic students, 7/1 priority date for international students. Applications are processed on a rolling basis. Application fee: $50 ($75 for international students). Electronic applications accepted. *Expenses:* $7,520 per year full-time in-state; $16,820 per year full-time out-of-state. *Financial support:* In 2017–18, 9 students received support, including 5 teaching assistantships (averaging $9,780 per year); career-related internships or fieldwork, Federal Work-Study, institutionally sponsored loans, scholarships/grants, traineeships, health care benefits, and unspecified assistantships also available. Support available to part-time students. Financial award application deadline: 3/1; financial award applicants required to submit FAFSA. *Faculty research:* Art education and electronic technology, film noir, one-of-a kind art books, new media, early video art from 1960-1980. *Unit head:* Dr. Vagner Whitehead, Chair, 940-898-2530, Fax: 940-898-2496, E-mail: visualarts@twu.edu. *Application contact:* Korie Hawkins, Associate Director of Admissions, Graduate Recruitment, 940-898-3188, Fax: 940-898-3081, E-mail: admissions@twu.edu.
Website: http://www.twu.edu/visual-arts/

Towson University, College of Fine Arts and Communication, Program in Art Education, Towson, MD 21252-0001. Offers M Ed. *Accreditation:* NCATE. *Program availability:* Part-time, evening/weekend. *Students:* 23 part-time (18 women); includes 5 minority (1 Black or African American, non-Hispanic/Latino; 1 Asian, non-Hispanic/Latino; 1 Hispanic/Latino; 2 Two or more races, non-Hispanic/Latino). *Degree requirements:* For master's, thesis optional. *Entrance requirements:* For master's, bachelor's degree and/or certification in art education, minimum GPA of 3.0, resume. *Application deadline:* For fall admission, 1/17 for domestic students, 5/15 for international students; for spring admission, 10/15 for domestic students, 12/1 for international students. Applications are processed on a rolling basis. Application fee: $45. Electronic applications accepted. *Expenses:* Tuition, state resident: full-time $7960; part-time $398 per unit. Tuition, nonresident: full-time $16,480; part-time $824 per unit. *Required fees:* $2600; $130 per year. $390 per term. *Financial support:* Application deadline: 4/1. *Unit head:* Dr. Ray Martens, Graduate Program Director, 410-704-3819, E-mail: rmartens@towson.edu. *Application contact:* Coverley Beidleman, Assistant Director of Graduate Admissions, 410-704-5630, Fax: 410-704-3030, E-mail: cbeidleman@towson.edu.
Website: http://www.towson.edu/cofac/departments/art/grad/education/

Towson University, College of Fine Arts and Communication, Program in Arts Integration, Towson, MD 21252-0001. Offers Postbaccalaureate Certificate. *Program*

offered jointly with Johns Hopkins University, University of Maryland, College Park and University of Maryland, Baltimore County. *Students:* 39 part-time (all women); includes 2 minority (1 Hispanic/Latino; 1 Two or more races, non-Hispanic/Latino). *Entrance requirements:* For degree, bachelor's degree, minimum GPA of 3.0 (based upon last 60 credits of study); teaching experience (preferred). *Application deadline:* For fall admission, 1/17 for domestic students, 5/15 for international students; for winter admission, 10/15 for domestic students; for spring admission, 12/1 for international students. Applications are processed on a rolling basis. Application fee: $45. Electronic applications accepted. *Expenses:* Tuition, state resident: full-time $7960; part-time $398 per unit. Tuition, nonresident: full-time $16,480; part-time $824 per unit. *Required fees:* $2600; $130 per year. $390 per term. *Unit head:* Prof. Susan Rotkovitz, Program Director, 410-704-3658, E-mail: srotkovitz@towson.edu. *Application contact:* Coverley Beidleman, Assistant Director of Graduate Admissions, 410-704-5630, Fax: 410-704-3030, E-mail: cbeidleman@towson.edu.
Website: http://www.towson.edu/cofac/departments/gradartsintegrationpbc/

Towson University, College of Fine Arts and Communication, Program in Interdisciplinary Arts Infusion, Towson, MD 21252-0001. Offers MA. *Students:* 23 part-time (21 women); includes 8 minority (5 Black or African American, non-Hispanic/Latino; 2 Hispanic/Latino; 1 Two or more races, non-Hispanic/Latino). *Application deadline:* For fall admission, 1/17 priority date for domestic students, 5/15 for international students; for spring admission, 10/15 for domestic students, 12/1 for international students. Applications are processed on a rolling basis. Application fee: $45. Electronic applications accepted. *Expenses:* Tuition, state resident: full-time $7960; part-time $398 per unit. Tuition, nonresident: full-time $16,480; part-time $824 per unit. *Required fees:* $2600; $130 per year. $390 per term. *Unit head:* Dr. Kate Collins, Program Director, 410-704-5614, E-mail: maiai@towson.edu. *Application contact:* Coverley Beidleman, Assistant Director of Graduate Admissions, 410-704-5630, Fax: 410-704-3030, E-mail: cbeidleman@towson.edu.
Website: https://www.towson.edu/cofac/departments/gradartsinfusion/

Tufts University, Graduate School of Arts and Sciences, Department of Education, Medford, MA 02155. Offers art education (MAT); education (MA, MAT, MS, PhD), including educational studies (MA), elementary education (MAT), middle and secondary education (MAT), museum education (MA), secondary education (MA), STEM education (MS, PhD); school psychology (MA, Ed S). *Program availability:* Part-time. *Students:* 95 full-time (78 women), 9 part-time (8 women); includes 17 minority (4 Black or African American, non-Hispanic/Latino; 6 Asian, non-Hispanic/Latino; 5 Hispanic/Latino; 2 Two or more races, non-Hispanic/Latino), 4 international. Average age 27. 197 applicants, 57% accepted, 65 enrolled. In 2017, 64 master's, 14 other advanced degrees awarded. *Degree requirements:* For master's, thesis optional; for doctorate, thesis/dissertation. *Entrance requirements:* For master's and doctorate, GRE General Test. Additional exam requirements/recommendations for international students: Required—TOEFL (minimum score 550 paper-based; 80 iBT), IELTS (minimum score 6.5). *Application deadline:* For fall admission, 1/2 for domestic and international students; for spring admission, 10/15 for domestic and international students. Applications are processed on a rolling basis. Application fee: $85. Electronic applications accepted. *Expenses:* Contact institution. *Financial support:* Teaching assistantships, Federal Work-Study, scholarships/grants, and tuition waivers (full and partial) available. Support available to part-time students. Financial award application deadline: 1/2. *Unit head:* Dr. David Hammer, Graduate Program Director, 617-627-2396. *Application contact:* Office of Graduate Admissions, 617-627-3395, E-mail: gradadmissions@tufts.edu.
Website: http://www.ase.tufts.edu/education/

Tufts University, School of the Museum of Fine Arts at Tufts University, Boston, MA 02115. Offers art education (MAT); studio art (MFA, Postbaccalaureate Certificate), including museum studies (MFA). *Faculty:* 31 full-time (19 women), 23 part-time/adjunct (16 women). *Students:* 55 full-time. Average age 25. In 2017, 44 master's, 15 other advanced degrees awarded. Terminal master's awarded for partial completion of doctoral program. *Degree requirements:* For master's, thesis, thesis exhibition. *Entrance requirements:* For master's, BFA (preferred) or bachelor's degree or equivalent in related area; portfolio; for Postbaccalaureate Certificate, portfolio, BFA or equivalent. Additional exam requirements/recommendations for international students: Required—TOEFL (minimum score 85 iBT), IELTS (minimum score 6.5). *Application deadline:* For fall admission, 1/15 priority date for domestic and international students. Applications are processed on a rolling basis. Application fee: $85. Electronic applications accepted. *Expenses:* $45,008 (MFA); $3,995 per credit (Post-Baccalaureate Certificate). *Financial support:* Fellowships, teaching assistantships, Federal Work-Study, and scholarships/grants available. Financial award application deadline: 1/15. *Faculty research:* Public art commissions, National Endowment for the Arts grant recipients, international group and solo exhibitions. *Unit head:* Lisa Bynoe, Associate Director of Graduate Programs, 617-627-0031, E-mail: lisa.bynoe@tufts.edu. *Application contact:* Office of Graduate Admissions, 617-627-3395, E-mail: gradadmissions@tufts.edu.
Website: https://smfa.tufts.edu/

The University of Akron, Graduate School, College of Education, Department of Curricular and Instructional Studies, Program in P-12 Multi-Age Education, Akron, OH 44325. Offers art education (MS); drama/theatre (MS). *Students:* 11 full-time (5 women), 5 part-time (3 women); includes 3 minority (2 Black or African American, non-Hispanic/Latino; 1 Two or more races, non-Hispanic/Latino). Average age 31. 5 applicants, 100% accepted, 5 enrolled. In 2017, 3 master's awarded. *Entrance requirements:* Additional exam requirements/recommendations for international students: Required—TOEFL (minimum score 79 iBT), IELTS (minimum score 6.5). *Unit head:* Dr. Evonn Welton, Interim Department Chair, 330-972-6742, E-mail: ewelton@uakron.edu. *Application contact:* Kelly Chaff, College Program Specialist, 330-972-7028, E-mail: klchaff@uakron.edu.
Website: http://www.uakron.edu/education/academic-programs/graduate-programs.dot

The University of Alabama at Birmingham, School of Education, Program in Arts Education, Birmingham, AL 35294. Offers MA Ed. *Accreditation:* NCATE. *Program availability:* Part-time. *Degree requirements:* For master's, thesis optional. *Entrance requirements:* For master's, MAT (minimum score 388 scaled, 35 raw) or GRE (minimum score 385). Electronic applications accepted.

The University of Arizona, College of Fine Arts, School of Art, Program in Art Education, Tucson, AZ 85721. Offers MA. *Accreditation:* NASAD. *Degree requirements:* For master's, thesis. *Entrance requirements:* For master's, portfolio, resume, autobiography, 3 letters of reference, writing sample. Additional exam requirements/recommendations for international students: Required—TOEFL (minimum score 550 paper-based; 79 iBT). Electronic applications accepted. *Faculty research:* Artistic styles, visual perception, integration of arts into elementary curricula, aesthetics of the vanishing roadsides of America.

The University of Arizona, College of Fine Arts, School of Art, Program in Art History and Education, Tucson, AZ 85721. Offers PhD. *Degree requirements:* For doctorate, thesis/dissertation. *Entrance requirements:* Additional exam requirements/recommendations for international students: Required—TOEFL (minimum score 550 paper-based; 79 iBT). Electronic applications accepted.

University of Arkansas at Little Rock, Graduate School, College of Arts, Letters, and Sciences, Department of Art, Little Rock, AR 72204-1099. Offers art education (MA); art history (MA); studio art (MA). *Accreditation:* NASAD. *Program availability:* Part-time. *Degree requirements:* For master's, 4 foreign languages, oral exam, oral defense of thesis or exhibit. *Entrance requirements:* For master's, portfolio review or term paper evaluation, minimum GPA of 2.7.

The University of British Columbia, Faculty of Education, Department of Curriculum and Pedagogy, Vancouver, BC V6T 1Z4, Canada. Offers art education (M Ed, MA); curriculum studies (M Ed, MA, PhD); home economics education (M Ed, MA); mathematics education (M Ed, MA); media and technology studies education (M Ed, MA); music education (M Ed, MA); physical education (M Ed, MA); science education (M Ed, MA); social studies education (M Ed, MA). *Program availability:* Part-time, online learning. *Degree requirements:* For master's, thesis (MA); for doctorate, comprehensive exam, thesis/dissertation. *Entrance requirements:* Additional exam requirements/recommendations for international students: Required—TOEFL, IELTS. Electronic applications accepted. *Expenses:* Contact institution. *Faculty research:* School subjects, teaching and learning.

University of Central Florida, College of Community Innovation and Education, School of Teacher Education, Program in Teacher Education, Orlando, FL 32816. Offers art education (MAT); English language (MAT); mathematics education (MAT); middle school mathematics (MAT); middle school science (MAT); science education (MAT), including biology, chemistry, physics; social science education (MAT). *Accreditation:* NCATE. *Program availability:* Part-time, evening/weekend. *Students:* 11 full-time (9 women), 28 part-time (23 women); includes 15 minority (5 Black or African American, non-Hispanic/Latino; 2 Asian, non-Hispanic/Latino; 6 Hispanic/Latino; 2 Two or more races, non-Hispanic/Latino), 2 international. Average age 29. In 2017, 6 master's awarded. *Degree requirements:* For master's, thesis or alternative. *Entrance requirements:* For master's, Florida Teacher Certification Examination/General Knowledge Test or GRE General Test. Additional exam requirements/recommendations for international students: Required—TOEFL. *Application deadline:* For spring admission, 12/1 for domestic students; for summer admission, 4/15 for domestic students. Application fee: $30. Electronic applications accepted. *Expenses:* Tuition, state resident: part-time $288.16 per credit hour. Tuition, nonresident: part-time $1073.31 per credit hour. Tuition and fees vary according to program. *Financial support:* Fellowships, research assistantships, teaching assistantships, career-related internships or fieldwork, Federal Work-Study, institutionally sponsored loans, tuition waivers (partial), and unspecified assistantships available. Financial award application deadline: 3/1; financial award applicants required to submit FAFSA. *Unit head:* Dr. Michael Hynes, Director, 407-823-2005, E-mail: mychael.hynes@ucf.edu. *Application contact:* Associate Director, Graduate Admissions, 407-823-2766, Fax: 407-823-6442, E-mail: gradadmissions@ucf.edu.
Website: http://www.graduatecatalog.ucf.edu/programs/program.aspx?id=9727&program=Teacher%20Education%20MAT

University of Cincinnati, Graduate School, College of Design, Architecture, Art, and Planning, School of Art, Program in Visual Arts Education, Cincinnati, OH 45221. Offers MA. *Accreditation:* NASAD; NCATE. *Entrance requirements:* For master's, MAT. Electronic applications accepted. *Expenses: Tuition, area resident:* Full-time $14,468. Tuition, state resident: full-time $14,968; part-time $754 per credit hour. Tuition, nonresident: full-time $24,210; part-time $1311 per credit hour. International student: $26,460 full-time. *Required fees:* $3958; $84 per credit hour. One-time fee: $85 full-time. Tuition and fees vary according to course load, degree level and program.

University of Denver, University College, Denver, CO 80208. Offers arts and culture (MA, Certificate); communication management (MS, Certificate), including translation studies (Certificate), world history and culture (Certificate); environmental policy and management (MS); geographic information systems (MS); global affairs (MA, Certificate), including human capital in organizations (Certificate), philanthropic leadership (Certificate), project management (Certificate), strategic innovation and change (Certificate); healthcare leadership (MS); information communications and technology (MS); leadership and organizations (MS); professional creative writing (MA, Certificate), including emergency planning and response (Certificate), organizational security (Certificate); security management (MS, Certificate); strategic human resources (Certificate). *Program availability:* Part-time, evening/weekend, online learning. *Faculty:* 118 part-time/adjunct (62 women). *Students:* 56 full-time (32 women), 1,287 part-time (707 women); includes 330 minority (99 Black or African American, non-Hispanic/Latino; 7 American Indian or Alaska Native, non-Hispanic/Latino; 43 Asian, non-Hispanic/Latino; 141 Hispanic/Latino; 3 Native Hawaiian or other Pacific Islander, non-Hispanic/Latino; 37 Two or more races, non-Hispanic/Latino), 84 international. Average age 34. 783 applicants, 86% accepted, 420 enrolled. In 2017, 461 master's, 173 other advanced degrees awarded. *Degree requirements:* For master's, capstone project. *Entrance requirements:* For master's, transcripts, two letters of recommendation, personal statement, resume. Additional exam requirements/recommendations for international students: Required—TOEFL (minimum score 550 paper-based; 80 iBT). *Application deadline:* For fall admission, 6/21 priority date for domestic students, 5/1 priority date for international students; for winter admission, 9/14 priority date for domestic students, 9/19 priority date for international students; for spring admission, 1/11 priority date for domestic students, 12/12 priority date for international students; for summer admission, 3/29 priority date for domestic students, 3/6 priority date for international students. Applications are processed on a rolling basis. Application fee: $75. Electronic applications accepted. *Expenses:* $7,968 per year half-time. *Financial support:* In 2017–18, 29 students received support. Teaching assistantships available. Financial award applicants required to submit FAFSA. *Unit head:* Dr. Michael McGuire, Dean, 303-871-3518, Fax: 303-871-3303, E-mail: mmcguire@du.edu. *Application contact:* Information Contact, 303-871-2291, E-mail: ucoladm@du.edu.
Website: http://universitycollege.du.edu/

University of Florida, Graduate School, College of The Arts, School of Art and Art History, Gainesville, FL 32611. Offers art (MA), including digital arts and sciences; art education (MA); art history (MA, PhD); museology (MA), including historic preservation. *Accreditation:* NASAD. *Program availability:* Online learning. *Degree requirements:* For master's, project or thesis (MFA) 1 foreign language (MA in art history); for doctorate, 2 foreign languages, comprehensive exam, thesis/dissertation. *Entrance requirements:* For master's, GRE General Test, portfolio (MFA), writing sample (MA), minimum GPA 3.0; for doctorate, GRE General Test, minimum GPA of 3.0. Additional exam requirements/recommendations for international students: Required—TOEFL (minimum score 550 paper-based; 80 iBT), IELTS (minimum score 6). Electronic applications accepted. *Faculty research:* Studio production, art historical studies of style context.

University of Illinois at Urbana–Champaign, Graduate College, College of Fine and Applied Arts, School of Art and Design, Program in Art Education, Champaign, IL 61820. Offers Ed M, MA, PhD. *Accreditation:* NASAD.

University of Indianapolis, Graduate Programs, School of Education, Indianapolis, IN 46227-3697. Offers art education (MAT); biology (MAT); chemistry (MAT); curriculum and instruction (MA); earth sciences (MAT); education (MA, MAT); educational leadership (MA); elementary education (MA); English (MAT); French (MAT); math (MAT); physical education (MAT); physics (MAT); secondary education (MA), including art education, education, English education, social studies education; social studies (MAT); Spanish (MAT). *Accreditation:* NCATE. *Program availability:* Part-time, evening/weekend. *Entrance requirements:* For master's, GRE Subject Test, PRAXIS I, minimum GPA of 2.5, 3 letters of recommendation, interview. Additional exam requirements/recommendations for international students: Required—TOEFL (minimum score 550 paper-based). *Faculty research:* Assessment of teacher education, perceptions of prospective teachers by parents.

The University of Iowa, Graduate College, College of Education, Department of Teaching and Learning, Program in Education, Iowa City, IA 52242-1316. Offers art education (MA); developmental reading (MA); elementary education (MA); English education (MA, MAT); foreign and second language education (MAT); foreign language education (MA); foreign language/ESL education (PhD); language, literacy and culture (PhD); mathematics education (MA, MAT, PhD); music education (MM, PhD); science education (MA); secondary education (MA); social studies (MA, PhD). *Degree requirements:* For master's, thesis optional, exam; for doctorate, comprehensive exam, thesis/dissertation. *Entrance requirements:* For master's and doctorate, GRE General Test, minimum GPA of 3.0. Additional exam requirements/recommendations for international students: Required—TOEFL (minimum score 550 paper-based; 81 iBT). Electronic applications accepted.

The University of Kansas, Graduate Studies, College of Liberal Arts and Sciences, Department of Visual Art, Program in Visual Art Education, Lawrence, KS 66045. Offers MA. *Program availability:* Part-time. *Students:* 2 full-time (both women), 2 part-time (both women). Average age 31. 6 applicants, 33% accepted. *Entrance requirements:* For master's, portfolio, 3 letters of recommendation, minimum GPA of 3.0. Additional exam requirements/recommendations for international students: Required—TOEFL (minimum score 570 paper-based) or IELTS (minimum score 6.5). *Application deadline:* For fall admission, 5/1 for domestic and international students; for spring admission, 12/1 for domestic and international students. Application fee: $65 ($85 for international students). Electronic applications accepted. *Financial support:* Teaching assistantships, Federal Work-Study, scholarships/grants, and unspecified assistantships available. *Faculty research:* Emphasizing a balance of studio, art history, and education courses. *Unit head:* Mary Anne Jordan, Chairperson, 785-864-2952, E-mail: majordan@ku.edu. *Application contact:* Lauren Chaney, Graduate Admissions Contact, 785-864-2306, E-mail: lkchaney@ku.edu.
Website: http://art.ku.edu/programs/visual_art_education/

University of Kentucky, Graduate School, College of Fine Arts, Program in Art Education, Lexington, KY 40506-0032. Offers MA. *Degree requirements:* For master's, comprehensive exam, thesis optional. *Entrance requirements:* For master's, GRE General Test, minimum undergraduate GPA of 2.75. Additional exam requirements/recommendations for international students: Required—TOEFL (minimum score 550 paper-based). Electronic applications accepted. *Faculty research:* Multicultural art education, women's issues in art education, lifelong learning in the arts, the artist-teacher, art teaching as a form of art, place and art, children's home art and creativity as a basis for school art instruction.

University of Louisville, Graduate School, College of Education and Human Development, Departments of Early Childhood and Elementary Education, Middle and Secondary Education, and Special Education, Louisville, KY 40292-0001. Offers art education (MAT); autism and applied behavior analysis (Certificate); curriculum and instruction (PhD); early elementary education (MAT); exercise physiology (MS); health and physical education (MAT); health professions education (Certificate); higher education (MA); human resources and organization development (MS); instructional technology (M Ed); interdisciplinary early childhood education (MAT); middle school education (MAT); music education (MAT); secondary education (MAT); special education (MAT); sport administration (MS); teacher leadership (M Ed). *Program availability:* Part-time, evening/weekend. *Students:* 114 full-time (73 women), 173 part-time (114 women); includes 49 minority (19 Black or African American, non-Hispanic/Latino; 5 Asian, non-Hispanic/Latino; 13 Hispanic/Latino; 12 Two or more races, non-Hispanic/Latino), 7 international. Average age 29. 132 applicants, 73% accepted, 57 enrolled. In 2017, 70 master's, 2 doctorates, 2 other advanced degrees awarded. *Application deadline:* For spring admission, 1/1 priority date for international students. Application fee: $65. *Expenses:* Tuition, state resident: full-time $12,246; part-time $681 per credit hour. Tuition, nonresident: full-time $25,486; part-time $1417 per credit hour. *Required fees:* $196. Tuition and fees vary according to course load, program and reciprocity agreements. *Financial support:* Application deadline: 6/1; applicants required to submit FAFSA. *Faculty research:* STEM teaching and learning; content literacy for English language learners; social justice in teacher education; adolescent literacy; mathematics teacher development. *Total annual research expenditures:* $1.7 million. *Unit head:* Dr. Ann E. Larson, Dean, College of Education and Human Development, 502-852-6411, Fax: 502-852-1464, E-mail: ann@louisville.edu. *Application contact:* Betty Hampton, Director of Graduate Student Services, 502-852-5597, Fax: 502-852-1465, E-mail: edadvise@louisville.edu.
Website: http://louisville.edu/delphi

University of Maryland, Baltimore County, The Graduate School, College of Arts, Humanities and Social Sciences, Department of Education, Program in Teaching, Baltimore, MD 21250. Offers early childhood education (MAT); elementary education (MAT); teaching (MAT), including art, biology, chemistry, choral music, classical foreign language, dance, earth/space science, English, instrumental music, mathematics, modern foreign language, physical science, physics, social studies, theatre. *Program availability:* Part-time, evening/weekend. *Faculty:* 24 full-time (18 women), 25 part-time/adjunct (19 women). *Students:* 41 full-time (34 women), 27 part-time (18 women); includes 26 minority (6 Black or African American, non-Hispanic/Latino; 9 Asian, non-Hispanic/Latino; 7 Hispanic/Latino; 1 Native Hawaiian or other Pacific Islander, non-Hispanic/Latino; 3 Two or more races, non-Hispanic/Latino), 2 international. Average age 30. 54 applicants, 83% accepted, 35 enrolled. In 2017, 50 master's awarded. *Degree requirements:* For master's, comprehensive exam (for some programs), thesis (for some programs). *Entrance requirements:* For master's, PRAXIS Core Examination or GRE (minimum score of 1000), minimum GPA of 3.0. Additional exam requirements/recommendations for international students: Required—TOEFL. *Application deadline:* For fall admission, 6/1 for domestic and international students; for spring admission, 11/1 for domestic and international students. Applications are processed on a rolling basis. Application fee: $50. Electronic applications accepted. *Expenses: Required fees:* $132. *Financial support:* In 2017–18, 8 students received support, including teaching assistantships with tuition reimbursements available (averaging $12,000 per year); career-related internships or fieldwork, Federal Work-Study, scholarships/grants, tuition waivers, and unspecified assistantships also available. Financial award application deadline: 3/15. *Faculty research:* STEM teacher education, culturally sensitive pedagogy, ESOL/bilingual education, early childhood education, language, literacy and culture. *Total annual research expenditures:* $100,000. *Unit head:* Dr. Susan M. Blunck, Graduate Program Director, 410-455-2869, Fax: 410-455-3986, E-mail: blunck@umbc.edu. *Application contact:* Cheryl Johnson, MAT Program Specialist, 410-455-3388, E-mail: blackwel@umbc.edu.
Website: http://www.umbc.edu/education/

University of Massachusetts Amherst, Graduate School, College of Humanities and Fine Arts, Department of Art, Amherst, MA 01003. Offers art (MA, MFA), including art education (MA), studio art (MFA). *Program availability:* Part-time. *Degree requirements:* For master's, comprehensive exam (for some programs), thesis (for some programs). *Entrance requirements:* For master's, portfolio. Additional exam requirements/recommendations for international students: Required—TOEFL (minimum score 550 paper-based; 80 iBT), IELTS (minimum score 6.5). Electronic applications accepted.

University of Massachusetts Dartmouth, Graduate School, College of Visual and Performing Arts, Department of Art Education, Art History and Media Studies, North Dartmouth, MA 02747-2300. Offers MAE. *Accreditation:* NASAD. *Program availability:* Part-time. *Faculty:* 7 full-time (6 women), 1 (woman) part-time/adjunct. *Students:* 4 full-time (all women), 22 part-time (18 women); includes 2 minority (1 Asian, non-Hispanic/Latino; 1 Hispanic/Latino). Average age 32. 11 applicants, 100% accepted, 9 enrolled. In 2017, 2 master's awarded. *Degree requirements:* For master's, thesis. *Entrance requirements:* For master's, MTEL (Communication Literacy and Visual Arts), statement of purpose (minimum of 300 words), resume, 2 letters of recommendation, official transcripts, portfolio (20 images representing applicant's art work, process of thinking, implementation of concepts and studio production). Additional exam requirements/recommendations for international students: Required—TOEFL (minimum score 533 paper-based; 72 iBT), IELTS (minimum score 6). *Application deadline:* For fall admission, 8/1 priority date for domestic students, 7/1 priority date for international students; for spring admission, 10/15 priority date for domestic students, 9/15 priority date for international students. Application fee: $60. Electronic applications accepted. *Expenses:* Tuition, state resident: full-time $15,449; part-time $643.71 per credit. Tuition, nonresident: full-time $27,880; part-time $1161.67 per credit. *Required fees:* $405; $25.88 per credit. Tuition and fees vary according to course load and reciprocity agreements. *Financial support:* In 2017–18, 1 teaching assistantship (averaging $4,000 per year) was awarded; tuition waivers (partial) and unspecified assistantships also available. Support available to part-time students. Financial award application deadline: 3/1; financial award applicants required to submit FAFSA. *Faculty research:* Contemporary art, design and architectural history, curatorial studies, film studies, theory of photography. *Unit head:* Cathy Smilan, Graduate Program Director, 508-910-6594, Fax: 508-999-8901, E-mail: csmilan@umassd.edu. *Application contact:* Steven Briggs, Director of Marketing and Recruitment for Graduate Studies, 508-999-8604, Fax: 508-999-8183, E-mail: graduate@umassd.edu.
Website: http://www.umassd.edu/cvpa/programs

University of Minnesota, Twin Cities Campus, Graduate School, College of Education and Human Development, Department of Curriculum and Instruction, Program in Teaching, Minneapolis, MN 55455-0213. Offers teaching (M Ed), including arts in education, elementary education, English education, mathematics, science, second language education, social studies. *Students:* 251 full-time (180 women), 136 part-time (82 women); includes 68 minority (16 Black or African American, non-Hispanic/Latino; 25 Asian, non-Hispanic/Latino; 17 Hispanic/Latino; 20 Two or more races, non-Hispanic/Latino), 9 international. Average age 28. 341 applicants, 72% accepted, 229 enrolled. In 2017, 263 master's awarded. Application fee: $75 ($95 for international students). *Unit head:* Dr. Cynthia Lewis, Chair, 612-625-6313, Fax: 612-624-8277, E-mail: lewis@umn.edu. *Application contact:* Dr. Kendall King, Director of Graduate Studies, 612-625-3692, E-mail: roehr013@umn.edu.
Website: http://www.cehd.umn.edu/ci/

University of Missouri, Office of Research and Graduate Studies, College of Education, Department of Learning, Teaching and Curriculum, Columbia, MO 65211. Offers agricultural education (M Ed, PhD, Ed S); art education (M Ed, PhD, Ed S); business and office education (M Ed, PhD, Ed S); early childhood education (M Ed, PhD, Ed S); elementary education (M Ed, PhD, Ed S); English education (M Ed, PhD, Ed S); foreign language education (M Ed, PhD, Ed S); health education and promotion (M Ed, PhD); learning and instruction (M Ed); marketing education (M Ed, PhD, Ed S); mathematics education (M Ed, PhD, Ed S); music education (M Ed, PhD, Ed S); reading education (M Ed, PhD, Ed S); science education (M Ed, PhD, Ed S); social studies education (M Ed, PhD, Ed S); vocational education (M Ed, PhD, Ed S). *Program availability:* Part-time. Terminal master's awarded for partial completion of doctoral program. *Degree requirements:* For doctorate, thesis/dissertation. *Entrance requirements:* For master's and Ed S, GRE General Test or MAT, minimum GPA of 3.0; for doctorate, GRE General Test, minimum GPA of 3.0. Additional exam requirements/recommendations for international students: Required—TOEFL (minimum score 600 paper-based; 100 iBT). Electronic applications accepted.

University of Montana, Graduate School, College of Visual and Performing Arts, Creative Pulse: Master's in Integrated Arts and Education, Missoula, MT 59812. Offers MA. *Degree requirements:* For master's, field project.

University of Nebraska at Kearney, College of Fine Arts and Humanities, Department of Art and Design, Kearney, NE 68849-0001. Offers art education (MA Ed), including classroom education, museum education. *Accreditation:* NCATE. *Program availability:* Part-time, evening/weekend, 100% online. *Degree requirements:* For master's, comprehensive exam, thesis optional. *Entrance requirements:* For master's, two letters of recommendation, resume, statement of purpose, 24 undergraduate hours of art/art history/art education. Additional exam requirements/recommendations for international students: Recommended—TOEFL (minimum score 550 paper-based; 79 iBT), IELTS (minimum score 6.5). Electronic applications accepted. *Faculty research:* Fibers, art education, kiln design construction and low-fire glaze, relationship between environment and photography, digital arts, graphic design, three-dimensional design, atomic testing imagery.

University of New Mexico, Graduate Studies, College of Education, Program in Art Education, Albuquerque, NM 87131-2039. Offers MA. *Accreditation:* NCATE. *Program availability:* Part-time, evening/weekend. *Faculty:* 8 full-time (4 women), 3 part-time/adjunct (all women). *Students:* 12 full-time (10 women), 13 part-time (10 women); includes 10 minority (1 American Indian or Alaska Native, non-Hispanic/Latino; 1 Asian, non-Hispanic/Latino; 6 Hispanic/Latino; 2 Two or more races, non-Hispanic/Latino). Average age 44. 8 applicants, 63% accepted, 4 enrolled. In 2017, 16 master's awarded. *Degree requirements:* For master's, comprehensive exam, thesis optional, participation in art exhibit. *Entrance requirements:* For master's, letter of intent, resume, 3 letters of recommendation, portfolio of 10 samples of art work. Additional exam requirements/recommendations for international students: Required—TOEFL. *Application deadline:* For fall admission, 3/30 for domestic and international students; for spring admission, 10/30 for domestic and international students. Application fee: $50. Electronic applications accepted. *Financial support:* Fellowships, research assistantships with full tuition reimbursements, teaching assistantships, Federal Work-Study, institutionally sponsored loans, scholarships/grants, and unspecified assistantships available. Financial award application deadline: 3/1; financial award applicants required to submit FAFSA. *Faculty research:* Studio in art education, visual culture, curricular issues regarding gender and sexual identity, archetypal thought in art education, teacher preparation. *Unit head:* Prof. Ruth Luckasson, Chair, 505-277-6510, Fax: 505-277-6929, E-mail: ruthl@unm.edu. *Application contact:* Katherine Vazquez, Information Contact, 505-277-4112, Fax: 505-277-0576, E-mail: arted@unm.edu.
Website: http://www.unm.edu/~arted

Art Education

The University of North Carolina at Charlotte, Cato College of Education, Interdisciplinary Education Programs, Charlotte, NC 28223-0001. Offers art education (Graduate Certificate); child and family development: early childhood education (MAT); curriculum and instruction (PhD); elementary education (MAT); foreign language education (MAT); middle grades education (MAT); secondary education (MAT); special education (MAT); teaching (Graduate Certificate); teaching English as a second language (MAT); theatre education (Graduate Certificate). *Program availability:* Part-time, 100% online, blended/hybrid learning. *Students:* 86 full-time (63 women), 533 part-time (423 women); includes 229 minority (169 Black or African American, non-Hispanic/Latino; 1 American Indian or Alaska Native, non-Hispanic/Latino; 7 Asian, non-Hispanic/Latino; 39 Hispanic/Latino; 13 Two or more races, non-Hispanic/Latino), 13 international. Average age 32. 382 applicants, 91% accepted, 253 enrolled. In 2017, 182 master's, 10 doctorates, 172 other advanced degrees awarded. *Degree requirements:* For master's, thesis or alternative, research project/portfolio. *Entrance requirements:* For master's, GRE or MAT, bachelor's degree, or its U.S. equivalent, from regionally-accredited college or university; minimum overall GPA of 3.0 on all previous work beyond high school; statement of purpose (essay); at least three recommendation forms; for doctorate, GRE or MAT, bachelor's degree (or its U.S. equivalent) from regionally-accredited college or university; minimum overall GPA of 3.5 in master's degree program; for Graduate Certificate, bachelor's degree from regionally-accredited university; minimum GPA of 2.75 on all post-secondary work attempted; transcripts; personal statement outlining why the applicant seeks admission to the program. Additional exam requirements/recommendations for international students: Required—TOEFL (minimum score 523 paper-based, 70 iBT) or IELTS (6.5). *Application deadline:* For fall admission, 3/1 priority date for domestic and international students; for spring admission, 10/1 priority date for domestic and international students; for summer admission, 4/1 priority date for domestic and international students. Applications are processed on a rolling basis. Application fee: $75. Electronic applications accepted. *Expenses:* Tuition, state resident: full-time $4337. Tuition, nonresident: full-time $17,771. *Required fees:* $3211. Tuition and fees vary according to course load and program. *Financial support:* Career-related internships or fieldwork, institutionally sponsored loans, scholarships/grants, and unspecified assistantships available. Support available to part-time students. Financial award application deadline: 3/1; financial award applicants required to submit FAFSA. *Unit head:* Dr. Ellen McIntyre, Dean, 704-687-8722, E-mail: ellen.mcintyre@uncc.edu. *Application contact:* Kathy B. Giddings, Director of Graduate Admissions, 704-687-5503, Fax: 704-687-1668, E-mail: gradadm@uncc.edu.
Website: http://education.uncc.edu/academic-programs

The University of North Carolina at Pembroke, The Graduate School, Department of Art, Pembroke, NC 28372-1510. Offers art (MAT); art education (MA). *Program availability:* Part-time, evening/weekend. *Degree requirements:* For master's, comprehensive exam, capstone show. *Entrance requirements:* For master's, GRE or MAT, minimum GPA of 3.0 in major or 2.5 overall. Additional exam requirements/recommendations for international students: Required—TOEFL. *Application deadline:* For fall admission, 7/15 priority date for domestic and international students; for spring admission, 12/1 priority date for domestic and international students. Applications are processed on a rolling basis. Application fee: $45 ($60 for international students). *Expenses:* Contact institution. *Financial support:* Application deadline: 4/15; applicants required to submit FAFSA. *Unit head:* Dr. Ann Horton-Lopez, Director of Graduate Art Education, 910-521-6407, Fax: 910-521-6164, E-mail: ann.lopez@uncp.edu.
Website: http://uncp.edu/art/

University of Northern Colorado, Graduate School, College of Performing and Visual Arts, School of Art and Design, Greeley, CO 80639. Offers art education (MA); art history (MA); studio art (MA). *Accreditation:* NASAD. *Program availability:* Part-time. *Degree requirements:* For master's, comprehensive exam, thesis. *Entrance requirements:* For master's, GRE General Test, portfolio, 3 letters of recommendation, minimum undergraduate GPA of 3.0. Electronic applications accepted.

University of Northern Iowa, Graduate College, College of Humanities, Arts and Sciences, Department of Art, Cedar Falls, IA 50614. Offers art education (MA). *Program availability:* Part-time, evening/weekend. *Degree requirements:* For master's, comprehensive exam (for some programs), thesis or alternative. *Entrance requirements:* For master's, minimum GPA of 3.0, portfolio. Additional exam requirements/recommendations for international students: Required—TOEFL (minimum score 500 paper-based; 61 iBT). Electronic applications accepted.

University of North Texas, Robert B. Toulouse School of Graduate Studies, Denton, TX 76203-5459. Offers accounting (MS); applied anthropology (MA, MS); applied behavior analysis (Certificate); applied geography (MA); applied technology and performance improvement (M Ed, MS); art education (MA); art history (MA); art museum education (Certificate); arts leadership (Certificate); audiology (Au D); behavior analysis (MS); behavioral science (PhD); biochemistry and molecular biology (MS); biology (MA, MS); biomedical engineering (MS); business analysis (MS); chemistry (MS); clinical health psychology (PhD); communication studies (MA, MS); computer engineering (MS); computer science (MS); counseling (M Ed, MS), including clinical mental health counseling (MS), college and university counseling, elementary school counseling, secondary school counseling; creative writing (MA); criminal justice (MS); curriculum and instruction (M Ed); decision sciences (MBA); design (MA, MFA), including fashion design (MFA), innovation studies, interior design (MFA); early childhood studies (PhD); economics (MS); educational leadership (M Ed, Ed D); educational psychology (MS, PhD), including family studies (MS), gifted and talented (MS), human development (MS), learning and cognition (MS), research, measurement and evaluation (MS); electrical engineering (MS); emergency management (MPA); engineering technology (MS); English (MA); English as a second language (MA); environmental science (MS); finance (MBA, MS); financial management (MPA); French (MA); health services management (MBA); higher education (M Ed, Ed D); history (MA, MS); hospitality management (MS); human resources management (MPA); information science (MS); information systems (PhD); information technologies (MBA); interdisciplinary studies (MA, MS); international studies (MA); international sustainable tourism (MS); jazz studies (MM); journalism (MA, MJ, Graduate Certificate), including interactive and virtual digital communication (Graduate Certificate), narrative journalism (Graduate Certificate), public relations (Graduate Certificate); kinesiology (MS); linguistics (MA); local government management (MPA); logistics (PhD); logistics and supply chain management (MBA); long-term care, senior housing, and aging services (MA); management (PhD); marketing (MBA); mathematics (MA, MS); mechanical and energy engineering (MS, PhD); music (MA), including ethnomusicology, music theory, musicology, performance; music composition (PhD); music education (MM Ed, PhD); nonprofit management (MPA); operations and supply chain management (MBA); performance (MM, DMA); philosophy (MA); political science (MA); professional and technical communication (MA); radio, television and film (MA, MFA); rehabilitation counseling (Certificate); sociology (MA); Spanish (MA); special education (M Ed); speech-language pathology (MA); strategic management (MBA); studio art (MFA); teaching (M Ed); MBA/MS. *Program availability:* Part-time, evening/weekend, online learning. Terminal master's awarded for partial completion of doctoral program. *Degree requirements:* For master's, variable foreign language requirement, comprehensive exam (for some programs), thesis (for some programs); for doctorate, variable foreign language requirement, comprehensive exam

(for some programs), thesis/dissertation; for other advanced degree, variable foreign language requirement, comprehensive exam (for some programs). *Entrance requirements:* For master's and doctorate, GRE, GMAT. Additional exam requirements/recommendations for international students: Required—TOEFL (minimum score 550 paper-based; 79 iBT). Electronic applications accepted.

University of Rio Grande, Graduate School, Rio Grande, OH 45674. Offers athletic coaching leadership (M Ed); educational leadership (M Ed); integrated arts (M Ed); intervention specialist in early childhood (M Ed); intervention specialist in mild/moderate (M Ed). *Accreditation:* NCATE. *Program availability:* Part-time. *Degree requirements:* For master's, final research project, portfolio. *Entrance requirements:* For master's, minimum GPA of 2.7 in major, 2.5 overall. Additional exam requirements/recommendations for international students: Required—TOEFL. *Faculty research:* Interagency collaboration, reading and mathematics, learning styles, college access, literacy.

University of St. Francis, College of Education, Joliet, IL 60435-6169. Offers educational leadership (MS, Ed D); elementary education (M Ed); reading (MS); secondary education (M Ed), including English education, math education, science education, social studies education, visual arts education; special education (M Ed); teaching and learning (MS); TESOL (Certificate). *Accreditation:* NCATE. *Program availability:* Part-time, evening/weekend, 100% online, blended/hybrid learning. *Faculty:* 11 full-time (8 women), 52 part-time/adjunct (36 women). *Students:* 39 full-time (32 women), 411 part-time (318 women); includes 106 minority (57 Black or African American, non-Hispanic/Latino; 8 Asian, non-Hispanic/Latino; 37 Hispanic/Latino; 4 Two or more races, non-Hispanic/Latino), 4 international. Average age 37. 277 applicants, 55% accepted, 137 enrolled. In 2017, 199 master's, 28 doctorates awarded. *Degree requirements:* For master's, comprehensive exam; for doctorate, thesis/dissertation. *Entrance requirements:* Additional exam requirements/recommendations for international students: Required—TOEFL (minimum score 550 paper-based; 79 iBT), IELTS (minimum score 6). *Application deadline:* Applications are processed on a rolling basis. Application fee: $30. Electronic applications accepted. Application fee is waived when completed online. *Expenses:* $365 to $748 per credit hour. *Financial support:* In 2017–18, 40 students received support. Scholarships/grants and unspecified assistantships available. Support available to part-time students. Financial award applicants required to submit FAFSA. *Unit head:* Dr. John Gambro, Dean, 815-740-3829, Fax: 815-740-2264, E-mail: jgambro@stfrancis.edu. *Application contact:* Sandra Sloka, Director of Admissions for Graduate and Degree Completion Programs, 800-735-7500, Fax: 815-740-3431, E-mail: ssloka@stfrancis.edu.
Website: http://www.stfrancis.edu/academics/college-of-education/

University of South Alabama, College of Education and Professional Studies, Department of Leadership and Teacher Education, Mobile, AL 36688. Offers art education (M Ed); early childhood education (M Ed); educational leadership (M Ed, Ed D); elementary education (M Ed); reading education (M Ed); science education (M Ed); secondary education (M Ed); special education (M Ed). *Accreditation:* NCATE. *Program availability:* Part-time. *Faculty:* 15 full-time (11 women), 10 part-time/adjunct (6 women). *Students:* 203 full-time (154 women), 90 part-time (68 women); includes 73 minority (54 Black or African American, non-Hispanic/Latino; 3 American Indian or Alaska Native, non-Hispanic/Latino; 4 Asian, non-Hispanic/Latino; 10 Hispanic/Latino; 2 Two or more races, non-Hispanic/Latino). Average age 34. 134 applicants, 55% accepted, 57 enrolled. In 2017, 73 master's, 8 doctorates awarded. *Degree requirements:* For master's, comprehensive exam, thesis (for some programs); for doctorate, comprehensive exam, thesis/dissertation. *Entrance requirements:* For master's, GRE General Test or MAT, minimum GPA of 3.0; for doctorate, GRE, minimum graduate GPA of 3.25, 3 years of experience in field, 3 letters of recommendation, interview, official transcripts. Additional exam requirements/recommendations for international students: Required—TOEFL. *Application deadline:* For fall admission, 7/15 for domestic students, 6/15 for international students; for spring admission, 11/15 for domestic students, 11/1 for international students; for summer admission, 4/15 for domestic students, 4/1 for international students. Applications are processed on a rolling basis. Application fee: $35. Electronic applications accepted. *Expenses:* Tuition, state resident: full-time $10,104; part-time $421 per semester hour. Tuition, nonresident: full-time $20,208; part-time $842 per semester hour. *Financial support:* Fellowships, research assistantships, teaching assistantships, career-related internships or fieldwork, Federal Work-Study, institutionally sponsored loans, scholarships/grants, and unspecified assistantships available. Support available to part-time students. Financial award application deadline: 3/31; financial award applicants required to submit FAFSA. *Unit head:* Dr. Susan Santoli, Chair/Director of Graduate Studies, 251-380-2836, Fax: 251-380-2748, E-mail: ssantoli@southalabama.edu.
Website: http://www.southalabama.edu/colleges/ceps/lte/index.html

University of South Carolina, The Graduate School, College of Arts and Sciences, Department of Art, Program in Art Education, Columbia, SC 29208. Offers IMA, MA, MAT. IMA and MAT offered in cooperation with the College of Education. *Accreditation:* NCATE. *Degree requirements:* For master's, comprehensive exam, thesis (for some programs). *Entrance requirements:* For master's, GRE General Test or MAT, portfolio. Additional exam requirements/recommendations for international students: Required—TOEFL. Electronic applications accepted. *Faculty research:* Teaching art at the primary and secondary levels of education.

University of South Carolina, The Graduate School, College of Education, Department of Instruction and Teacher Education, Program in Secondary Education, Columbia, SC 29208. Offers art education (IMA, MAT); business education (IMA, MAT); English (MAT); foreign language (MAT); health education (MAT); mathematics (MAT); science (IMA, MAT); secondary (Ed D); secondary education (MT, PhD); social studies (MAT); theatre and speech (MAT). IMA and MT offered jointly with the subject areas. *Accreditation:* NCATE. *Degree requirements:* For master's, comprehensive exam, thesis (for some programs), foreign language (MA); for doctorate, one foreign language, comprehensive exam, thesis/dissertation. *Entrance requirements:* For master's, GRE General Test or MAT, teaching certificate (IMA, M Ed), interview; for doctorate, GRE General Test or MAT, interview. *Faculty research:* Middle school programs, professional development, school collaboration.

University of South Dakota, Graduate School, College of Fine Arts, Department of Art, Vermillion, SD 57069. Offers art education (MFA); ceramics (MFA); graphic design (MFA); painting (MFA); photography (MFA); printmaking (MFA); sculpture (MFA). *Accreditation:* NASAD. *Degree requirements:* For master's, thesis or alternative. *Entrance requirements:* For master's, portfolio, minimum GPA of 2.7. Additional exam requirements/recommendations for international students: Required—TOEFL (minimum score 550 paper-based; 79 iBT). *Application deadline:* Applications are processed on a rolling basis. Application fee: $35. Electronic applications accepted. *Financial support:* Research assistantships with partial tuition reimbursements, teaching assistantships with partial tuition reimbursements, Federal Work-Study, and unspecified assistantships available. Support available to part-time students. Financial award applicants required to submit FAFSA. *Application contact:* Graduate School, 605-658-6140, Fax: 605-677-6118, E-mail: grad@usd.edu.
Website: http://www.usd.edu/fine-arts/art

The University of Tennessee, Graduate School, College of Education, Health and Human Sciences, Program in Education, Knoxville, TN 37996. Offers art education (MS); counseling education (PhD); cultural studies in education (PhD); curriculum (MS, Ed S); curriculum, educational research and evaluation (Ed D, PhD); early childhood education (PhD); early childhood special education (MS); education of deaf and hard of hearing (MS); educational administration and policy studies (Ed D, PhD); educational administration and supervision (Ed S); educational psychology (Ed D, PhD); elementary education (MS, Ed S); elementary teaching (MS); English education (MS, Ed S); exercise science (PhD); foreign language/ESL education (MS, Ed S); instructional technology (MS, Ed D, PhD, Ed S); literacy, language and ESL education (PhD); literacy, language education, and ESL education (Ed D); mathematics education (MS, Ed S); modified and comprehensive special education (MS); reading education (MS, Ed S); school counseling (Ed S); school psychology (PhD, Ed S); science education (MS, Ed S); secondary teaching (MS); social foundations (MS); social science education (MS, Ed S); socio-cultural foundations of sports and education (PhD); special education (Ed S); teacher education (Ed D, PhD). *Accreditation:* NCATE. *Program availability:* Part-time, evening/weekend. *Degree requirements:* For master's and Ed S, thesis optional; for doctorate, variable foreign language requirement, thesis/dissertation. *Entrance requirements:* For master's, minimum GPA of 2.7; for doctorate and Ed S, GRE General Test, minimum GPA of 2.7. Additional exam requirements/recommendations for international students: Required—TOEFL. Electronic applications accepted.

The University of Texas at Austin, Graduate School, College of Fine Arts, Department of Art and Art History, Program in Art Education, Austin, TX 78712-1111. Offers MA. *Accreditation:* NASAD. *Program availability:* Part-time. *Degree requirements:* For master's, thesis, oral and written exam. *Entrance requirements:* For master's, GRE General Test, 2 samples of written work, 10 slides of art work. Electronic applications accepted. *Faculty research:* Museum education; community-based, environmental, and multicultural art education; interdisciplinary art education, elementary and secondary art education.

The University of Texas at El Paso, Graduate School, College of Liberal Arts, Department of Art, El Paso, TX 79968-0001. Offers art education (MA); studio art (MA). *Program availability:* Part-time, evening/weekend. *Degree requirements:* For master's, thesis optional. *Entrance requirements:* For master's, minimum GPA of 3.0, digital portfolio, letters of recommendation. Additional exam requirements/recommendations for international students: Required—TOEFL; Recommended—IELTS. Electronic applications accepted.

The University of the Arts, College of Art, Media and Design, Department of Art Education, Philadelphia, PA 19102-4944. Offers art education (MA); visual arts (MAT). *Accreditation:* NASAD (one or more programs are accredited). *Program availability:* Part-time. *Degree requirements:* For master's, student teaching (MAT); thesis (MA). *Entrance requirements:* For master's, portfolio, official transcripts from each undergraduate or graduate school attended, three letters of recommendation, one- to two-page statement of professional plans and goals, personal interview, writing sample. Additional exam requirements/recommendations for international students: Required—TOEFL (minimum score 580 paper-based, 92 iBT) or IELTS (minimum score 6.5). *Faculty research:* Using technology and visual arts concepts to develop critical and creative thinking skills.

The University of Toledo, College of Graduate Studies, Judith Herb College of Education, Department of Curriculum and Instruction, Toledo, OH 43606-3390. Offers art education (ME); career and technical education (ME, Ed S); curriculum and instruction (ME, PhD, Ed S); early childhood education (Ed S); education and anthropology (MAE); education and biology (MES); education and chemistry (MES); education and classics (MAE); education and economics (MAE); education and English (MAE); education and French (MAE); education and geology (MES); education and German (MAE); education and history (MAE); education and mathematics (MAE, MES); education and physics (MES); education and political science (MAE); education and sociology (MAE); education and Spanish (MAE); educational media (PhD); educational technology (ME); educational technology: virtual educator (Certificate); elementary education (PhD); English as a second language (MAE); gifted and talented education (PhD); middle childhood education (ME); secondary education (ME, PhD); special education (PhD). *Accreditation:* NCATE. *Program availability:* Part-time, evening/weekend. *Degree requirements:* For master's, comprehensive exam, thesis or alternative; for doctorate, comprehensive exam, thesis/dissertation; for other advanced degree, thesis optional. *Entrance requirements:* For master's, doctorate, and other advanced degree, minimum cumulative GPA of 2.7 for all previous academic work, letters of recommendation. Additional exam requirements/recommendations for international students: Required—TOEFL (minimum score 550 paper-based; 80 iBT). Electronic applications accepted.

University of Utah, Graduate School, College of Fine Arts, Department of Art and Art History, Salt Lake City, UT 84112-0380. Offers art history (MA); ceramics (MFA); community-based art education (MFA); drawing (MFA); graphic design (MFA); painting (MFA); photography/digital imaging (MFA); printmaking (MFA); sculpture/intermedia (MFA). *Faculty:* 19 full-time (9 women), 23 part-time/adjunct (11 women). *Students:* 6 full-time (3 women); includes 1 minority (Asian, non-Hispanic/Latino). Average age 24. 48 applicants, 31% accepted, 3 enrolled. In 2017, 6 master's awarded. *Degree requirements:* For master's, variable foreign language requirement, comprehensive exam (for some programs), thesis or alternative, exhibit and final project paper (for MFA). *Entrance requirements:* For master's, CD portfolio (MFA), writing sample (MA), curriculum vitae, letters of recommendation, letter of intent. Additional exam requirements/recommendations for international students: Required—TOEFL (minimum score 575 paper-based; 75 iBT). *Application deadline:* For fall admission, 1/15 priority date for domestic and international students. Application fee: $55 ($65 for international students). Electronic applications accepted. *Expenses:* Contact institution. *Financial support:* In 2017–18, 6 students received support, including 2 fellowships, 6 research assistantships with partial tuition reimbursements available, 34 teaching assistantships with partial tuition reimbursements available; Federal Work-Study, institutionally sponsored loans, scholarships/grants, tuition waivers (partial), unspecified assistantships, and stipends also available. Financial award application deadline: 1/15; financial award applicants required to submit FAFSA. *Faculty research:* Studio art, European art history, Asian art history, Latin American art history, twentieth-century/contemporary art history. *Total annual research expenditures:* $54,906. *Unit head:* Prof. Brian Snapp, Chair, 801-581-8677, Fax: 801-585-6171, E-mail: b.snapp@utah.edu. *Application contact:* Prof. Kim Martinez, Director of Graduate Studies, 801-581-8677, Fax: 801-585-6171, E-mail: kim.martinez@art.utah.edu.
Website: http://www.art.utah.edu/

University of Victoria, Faculty of Graduate Studies, Faculty of Education, Department of Curriculum and Instruction, Victoria, BC V8W 2Y2, Canada. Offers art education (M Ed, PhD); curriculum studies (M Ed, MA, PhD); early childhood education (M Ed, PhD); educational studies (PhD); language and literacy (M Ed, MA, PhD); mathematics (M Ed, MA, PhD); music education (M Ed, MA, PhD); science (M Ed, MA, PhD); social studies (M Ed, MA); social, cultural and foundational studies (MA, PhD); technology and environmental education (PhD). *Program availability:* Part-time. *Degree requirements:*

For master's, thesis, project (M Ed); for doctorate, comprehensive exam, thesis/dissertation. *Entrance requirements:* For master's, minimum B average. Additional exam requirements/recommendations for international students: Required—TOEFL (minimum score 575 paper-based), IELTS (minimum score 7). Electronic applications accepted. *Faculty research:* Elementary and secondary English, language arts, curriculum theory and practice, educational media and technology, educational administration and leadership, history and philosophy of education.

University of Wisconsin–Milwaukee, Graduate School, School of Education, Department of Exceptional Education, Milwaukee, WI 53201-0413. Offers autism spectrum disorders (Graduate Certificate); exceptional education (MS); transition for students with disabilities (Graduate Certificate); urban education (PhD), including adult, continuing and higher education leadership, art education, curriculum and instruction, exceptional education, mathematics education, multicultural studies, social foundations of education. *Program availability:* Part-time. *Students:* 45 full-time (34 women), 68 part-time (54 women); includes 46 minority (27 Black or African American, non-Hispanic/Latino; 7 Asian, non-Hispanic/Latino; 1 Hispanic/Latino; 11 Two or more races, non-Hispanic/Latino), 4 international. Average age 39. 43 applicants, 53% accepted, 19 enrolled. In 2017, 12 master's, 13 doctorates, 8 other advanced degrees awarded. *Entrance requirements:* Additional exam requirements/recommendations for international students: Required—TOEFL (minimum score 550 paper-based; 79 iBT), IELTS (minimum score 6.5). *Application deadline:* For fall admission, 1/1 priority date for domestic students; for spring admission, 9/1 for domestic students. Application fee: $56 ($96 for international students). Electronic applications accepted. *Financial support:* Fellowships, research assistantships, teaching assistantships, career-related internships or fieldwork, health care benefits, and unspecified assistantships available. Support available to part-time students. Financial award application deadline: 4/15; financial award applicants required to submit FAFSA. *Faculty research:* Emotional disturbance, hearing impairment, learning disabilities, mental retardation. *Application contact:* General Information Contact, 414-229-4721, E-mail: soeinfo@uwm.edu. Website: http://uwm.edu/education/academics/exceptional-edu-department/

University of Wisconsin–Superior, Graduate Division, Department of Visual Arts, Superior, WI 54880-4500. Offers art education (MA); art history (MA); art therapy (MA); studio arts (MA). *Program availability:* Part-time. *Degree requirements:* For master's, comprehensive exam, exhibit. *Entrance requirements:* For master's, minimum GPA of 2.75, portfolio. Electronic applications accepted.

Vermont College of Fine Arts, Graduate Studies in Art and Design Education, Montpelier, VT 05602. Offers MA, MAT. *Faculty:* 4 full-time (3 women). *Students:* 16 full-time (13 women), 2 part-time (both women); includes 6 minority (2 Black or African American, non-Hispanic/Latino; 1 American Indian or Alaska Native, non-Hispanic/Latino; 1 Asian, non-Hispanic/Latino; 1 Hispanic/Latino; 1 Native Hawaiian or other Pacific Islander, non-Hispanic/Latino). Average age 32. 17 applicants, 94% accepted, 11 enrolled. *Degree requirements:* For master's, thesis. *Entrance requirements:* For master's, SAT, GRE, PRAXIS, bachelor's degree. *Application deadline:* For fall admission, 4/1 priority date for domestic and international students. Applications are processed on a rolling basis. Application fee: $75. Electronic applications accepted. *Expenses:* Contact institution. *Financial support:* In 2017–18, 18 students received support. Scholarships/grants available. Financial award application deadline: 4/1; financial award applicants required to submit FAFSA. *Unit head:* Jennifer Skinder, Director, E-mail: jennifer.skinder@vcfa.edu. *Application contact:* David Markow, Director of Enrollment Management, 802-828-8535, E-mail: admissions@vcfa.edu. Website: http://vcfa.edu/art-design-education

Virginia Commonwealth University, Graduate School, School of Education, Doctoral Program in Education, Richmond, VA 23284-9005. Offers art education (PhD); counselor education and supervision (PhD); curriculum, culture and change (PhD); educational leadership (PhD); educational psychology (PhD); leadership (Ed D); research and evaluation (PhD); special education and disability leadership (PhD); sport leadership (PhD); urban services leadership (PhD). *Accreditation:* NCATE. *Program availability:* Part-time. *Degree requirements:* For doctorate, thesis/dissertation. *Entrance requirements:* For doctorate, GRE (for PhD), MAT (for Ed D), interview, master's degree, writing sample. Additional exam requirements/recommendations for international students: Required—TOEFL (minimum score 600 paper-based; 100 iBT). Electronic applications accepted.

Virginia Commonwealth University, Graduate School, School of the Arts, Department of Art Education, Richmond, VA 23284-9005. Offers MAE, PhD. *Accreditation:* NASAD. *Degree requirements:* For master's, thesis optional. *Entrance requirements:* For master's, GRE if GPA is below 3.0, portfolio. Additional exam requirements/recommendations for international students: Required—TOEFL (minimum score 600 paper-based; 100 iBT). Electronic applications accepted. *Faculty research:* Teaching methods.

Wayne State University, College of Education, Division of Teacher Education, Detroit, MI 48202. Offers art education (M Ed); bilingual/bicultural education (Certificate); curriculum and instruction (Ed D, PhD, Ed S), including English as a second language (MAT, Ed D, Ed S), K-12 curriculum (PhD); elementary education (MAT), including bilingual/bicultural education (M Ed, MAT), early childhood education (M Ed, MAT), English as a second language (MAT, Ed D, Ed S), foreign language education, science education (M Ed, MAT), special education (M Ed, MAT); elementary mathematics specialist (Certificate); English as a second language (Certificate); reading (M Ed, Ed S); reading, language and literature (Ed D); secondary education (MAT), including bilingual/bicultural education (M Ed, MAT), early childhood education (M Ed, MAT), English as a second language (MAT, Ed D, Ed S), English education, foreign language education, mathematics education (M Ed, MAT), science education (M Ed, MAT), social studies education (M Ed, MAT); special education (MAT), including career and technical education; teaching and learning (M Ed), including bilingual/bicultural education (M Ed, MAT), early childhood education (M Ed, MAT), elementary education, foreign language, mathematics education (M Ed, MAT), science education (M Ed, MAT), social studies education (M Ed, MAT), special education (M Ed, MAT). *Program availability:* Part-time, blended/hybrid learning. *Faculty:* 22. 168 full-time (96 women), 317 part-time (258 women); includes 134 minority (95 Black or African American, non-Hispanic/Latino; 1 American Indian or Alaska Native, non-Hispanic/Latino; 8 Asian, non-Hispanic/Latino; 17 Hispanic/Latino; 1 Native Hawaiian or other Pacific Islander, non-Hispanic/Latino; 12 Two or more races, non-Hispanic/Latino), 13 international. Average age 37. 260 applicants, 33% accepted, 57 enrolled. In 2017, 111 master's, 13 doctorates, 7 other advanced degrees awarded. *Degree requirements:* For master's, essay or project (for some M Ed programs), professional field experience (for MAT programs); for doctorate, thesis/dissertation. *Entrance requirements:* For master's, Michigan Test for Teacher Certification (for most programs), verification of participation in group work with children (for MAT programs), Michigan State Police criminal background check; for doctorate, minimum undergraduate GPA of 3.0, graduate 3.5; interview; curriculum vitae; references; master's degree (for most programs). Additional exam requirements/recommendations for international students: Required—TOEFL (minimum score 550 paper-based; 79 iBT), TWE (minimum score 5.5); Recommended—IELTS (minimum score 6.5). *Application deadline:* For fall admission, 6/1 priority date for domestic students, 5/1 priority date for international students; for winter admission, 10/1 priority

date for domestic students, 9/1 priority date for international students; for spring admission, 2/1 priority date for domestic students, 1/1 priority date for international students. Applications are processed on a rolling basis. Application fee: $50. Electronic applications accepted. *Expenses:* Tuition, state resident: full-time $10,224; part-time $638.98 per credit hour. Tuition, nonresident: full-time $22,145; part-time $1384.04 per credit hour. Tuition and fees vary according to course load and program. *Financial support:* In 2017–18, 78 students received support, including 4 fellowships (averaging $13,500 per year), 1 research assistantship with tuition reimbursement available (averaging $16,000 per year); Federal Work-Study, scholarships/grants, and unspecified assistantships also available. Support available to part-time students. Financial award applicants required to submit FAFSA. *Faculty research:* Improving students' skill achievement in mathematics, improving elementary children's understanding of informational text, teachers' use of their pedagogical and mathematical knowledge in the interactive work of teaching, the intersection of identity construction in teaching and learning, identifying effective methods of literacy instruction and assessments for bilingual students in elementary language arts classrooms. *Unit head:* Dr. Thomas Edwards, Interim Associate Dean for Teacher Education, 313-577-3886, E-mail: t.g.edwards@wayne.edu. *Application contact:* 313-577-0902, E-mail: askcoe@wayne.edu.
Website: http://coe.wayne.edu/ted/index.php

Western Kentucky University, Graduate Studies, Potter College of Arts and Letters, Department of Art, Bowling Green, KY 42101. Offers art education (MA Ed). *Accreditation:* NASAD; NCATE. *Program availability:* Part-time, evening/weekend. *Degree requirements:* For master's, comprehensive exam, final exam. *Entrance requirements:* For master's, GRE General Test, minimum GPA of 2.75. Additional exam requirements/recommendations for international students: Required—TOEFL (minimum score 555 paper-based; 79 iBT). *Faculty research:* Nineteenth century Kentucky women artists.

Western Michigan University, Graduate College, College of Fine Arts, Gwen Frostic School of Art, Kalamazoo, MI 49008. Offers art education (MA). *Accreditation:* NASAD. *Degree requirements:* For master's, thesis or alternative.

West Virginia University, College of Creative Arts, Morgantown, WV 26506. Offers acting (MFA); art education (MA); art history (MA); ceramics (MFA); collaborative piano (MM, DMA); composition (MM, DMA); conducting (MM, DMA); costume design and technology (MFA); graphic design (MFA); jazz pedagogy (MM); lighting design and technology (MFA); music (PhD); music education (MM, PhD); music industry (MA); music theory (MM); musicology (MA); painting and printmaking (MFA); performance (MM, DMA); photography (MFA); piano pedagogy (MM); scenic design and technology (MFA); sculpture (MFA); studio art (MA); technical direction (MFA); vocal pedagogy and performance (DMA). *Program availability:* Part-time. *Students:* 114 full-time (64 women), 39 part-time (21 women); includes 19 minority (11 Black or African American, non-Hispanic/Latino; 1 Asian, non-Hispanic/Latino; 6 Hispanic/Latino; 1 Two or more races, non-Hispanic/Latino), 33 international. *Degree requirements:* For master's, thesis, recitals; for doctorate, comprehensive exam, thesis/dissertation, recitals (DMA). *Entrance requirements:* For doctorate, minimum GPA of 3.0, audition. Additional exam

requirements/recommendations for international students: Required—TOEFL. *Application deadline:* For fall admission, 3/1 priority date for domestic students, 2/15 for international students; for spring admission, 11/1 for domestic students, 9/15 for international students. Applications are processed on a rolling basis. Application fee: $60. Electronic applications accepted. *Expenses:* Tuition, state resident: full-time $9450. Tuition, nonresident: full-time $24,390. *Financial support:* Research assistantships, teaching assistantships, career-related internships or fieldwork, Federal Work-Study, institutionally sponsored loans, scholarships/grants, health care benefits, tuition waivers (partial), and administrative assistantships available. Financial award applicants required to submit FAFSA. *Faculty research:* Professional directing, consulting, acting design, music education, jazz history. *Unit head:* Dr. Paul Kreider, Dean, 304-293-4841 Ext. 3109, Fax: 304-293-6896, E-mail: paul.kreider@mail.wvu.edu. *Application contact:* Records Officer, 304-293-4841, Fax: 304-293-2533, E-mail: rachel.hanks@mail.wvu.edu.
Website: http://www.ccarts.wvu.edu

William Carey University, School of Education, Hattiesburg, MS 39401. Offers art education (M Ed); art of teaching (M Ed); elementary education (M Ed, Ed S); English education (M Ed); gifted education (M Ed); history and social science (M Ed); mild/moderate disabilities (M Ed); secondary education (M Ed). *Accreditation:* NCATE. *Program availability:* Part-time. *Degree requirements:* For master's, comprehensive exam. *Entrance requirements:* For master's, GRE, MAT, minimum GPA of 2.5, Class A teacher's license. Additional exam requirements/recommendations for international students: Required—TOEFL (minimum score 550 paper-based).

Winthrop University, College of Visual and Performing Arts, Department of Art, Rock Hill, SC 29733. Offers art (MFA); art administration (MA); art education (MA). *Accreditation:* NASAD. *Program availability:* Part-time. *Students:* 6 full-time (5 women), 27 part-time (21 women); includes 10 minority (7 Black or African American, non-Hispanic/Latino; 2 Asian, non-Hispanic/Latino; 1 Hispanic/Latino), 1 international. Average age 38. In 2017, 12 master's awarded. *Degree requirements:* For master's, comprehensive exam (for some programs), thesis (for some programs), documented exhibit, oral exam. *Entrance requirements:* For master's, GRE General Test or MAT, PRAXIS (for MA), minimum GPA of 3.0, resume, slide portfolio, teaching certificate (MA). Additional exam requirements/recommendations for international students: Required—TOEFL (minimum score 550 paper-based; 79 iBT), IELTS (minimum score 6). *Application deadline:* For fall admission, 3/1 priority date for domestic students; for spring admission, 9/1 for domestic students. Applications are processed on a rolling basis. Application fee: $50. Electronic applications accepted. *Financial support:* Research assistantships with full tuition reimbursements, Federal Work-Study, scholarships/grants, and unspecified assistantships available. Support available to part-time students. Financial award application deadline: 2/1; financial award applicants required to submit FAFSA. *Unit head:* Anne Fiala, Interim Chair, 803-323-2653, E-mail: fialaa@winthrop.edu. *Application contact:* 800-411-7041, Fax: 803-323-2292, E-mail: graduatestu@winthrop.edu.
Website: http://www.winthrop.edu/cvpa/finearts

Business Education

Alabama Agricultural and Mechanical University, School of Graduate Studies, College of Education, Humanities, and Behavioral Sciences, Department of Educational Leadership and Secondary Education, Huntsville, AL 35811. Offers biology (M Ed); business/marketing education (M Ed, Ed S); chemistry (M Ed); collaborative teacher secondary education (M Ed, Ed S); education (M Ed, Ed S); English language arts (M Ed); family/consumer science education (M Ed, Ed S); general science (M Ed); general social science (M Ed); mathematics (M Ed, Ed S); physics (M Ed, Ed S); technology education (M Ed). *Accreditation:* NCATE. *Program availability:* Evening/weekend. *Degree requirements:* For master's, comprehensive exam; for Ed S, thesis. *Entrance requirements:* For master's, GRE General Test. Additional exam requirements/recommendations for international students: Required—TOEFL (minimum score 500 paper-based; 61 iBT). Electronic applications accepted. *Faculty research:* World peace through education, computer-assisted instruction.

Arkansas State University, Graduate School, College of Business, Department of Computer and Information Technology, State University, AR 72467. Offers business administration education (SCCT); business technology education (SCCT). *Program availability:* Part-time. *Entrance requirements:* Additional exam requirements/recommendations for international students: Required—TOEFL (minimum score 550 paper-based; 79 iBT), IELTS (minimum score 6), PTE (minimum score 56). Electronic applications accepted. *Expenses:* Contact institution.

Ball State University, Graduate School, Miller College of Business, Department of Information Systems and Operations Management, Muncie, IN 47306. Offers business education (MA); information systems security management (Certificate). *Accreditation:* NCATE (one or more programs are accredited). *Program availability:* Part-time, online only, 100% online. *Faculty:* 4 full-time (0 women). *Students:* 6 full-time (4 women), 10 part-time (8 women); includes 3 minority (1 Hispanic/Latino; 2 Two or more races, non-Hispanic/Latino). Average age 31. 8 applicants, 88% accepted, 5 enrolled. In 2017, 6 master's awarded. *Entrance requirements:* For master's, minimum baccalaureate GPA of 2.75 or 3.0 in latter half of baccalaureate. Additional exam requirements/recommendations for international students: Required—TOEFL (minimum score 550 paper-based; 79 iBT), IELTS (minimum score 6.5). *Application deadline:* Applications are processed on a rolling basis. Application fee: $60. Electronic applications accepted. *Expenses:* Contact institution. *Financial support:* Application deadline: 3/1; applicants required to submit FAFSA. *Unit head:* Dr. John Ledbetter, Interim Chairperson, 765-285-5109, Fax: 765-285-5308, E-mail: jledbett@bsu.edu.
Website: http://www.bsu.edu/isom

Bloomsburg University of Pennsylvania, School of Graduate Studies, Zeigler College of Business, Program in Business Education, Bloomsburg, PA 17815-1301. Offers M Ed. *Program availability:* Part-time, evening/weekend. *Degree requirements:* For master's, thesis optional, student teaching, minimum QPA of 3.0. *Entrance requirements:* For master's, PRAXIS, minimum QPA of 3.0, 2 letters of recommendation, personal statement, resume. Additional exam requirements/recommendations for international students: Required—TOEFL, IELTS. Electronic applications accepted. *Expenses:* Tuition, state resident: full-time $10,000; part-time $500 per credit hour. Tuition, nonresident: full-time $15,000; part-time $750 per credit hour. *Required fees:* $2484; $110.75 per credit hour. $75 per term. Tuition and fees vary according to program.

Bowling Green State University, Graduate College, College of Education and Human Development, School of Teaching and Learning, Program in Workforce Education and Development, Bowling Green, OH 43403. Offers M Ed. *Accreditation:* NCATE. *Program availability:* Part-time. *Degree requirements:* For master's, thesis or alternative. *Entrance requirements:* For master's, GRE General Test. Additional exam requirements/recommendations for international students: Required—TOEFL. Electronic applications accepted. *Faculty research:* School to work, workforce education, marketing education, contextual teaching and learning.

Buffalo State College, State University of New York, The Graduate School, Faculty of Applied Science and Education, Department of Business Studies, Buffalo, NY 14222-1095. Offers business and marketing education (MS Ed). *Program availability:* Part-time, evening/weekend. *Degree requirements:* For master's, thesis or alternative, project. *Entrance requirements:* For master's, minimum GPA of 2.5, New York teaching certificate.

Canisius College, Graduate Division, School of Education and Human Services, Department of Graduate Education and Leadership, Buffalo, NY 14208-1098. Offers business and marketing education (MS Ed); college student personnel (MS Ed); deaf education (MS Ed); deaf/adolescent education, grades 7-12 (MS Ed); deaf/childhood education, grades 1-6 (MS Ed); differentiated instruction (MS Ed); education administration (MS); educational administration (MS Ed); educational technologies (Certificate); gifted education extension (Certificate); literacy (MS Ed); reading (Certificate); school building leadership (MS Ed, Certificate); school district leadership (Certificate); teacher leader (Certificate); TESOL (MS Ed). *Accreditation:* NCATE. *Program availability:* Part-time, evening/weekend, 100% online, blended/hybrid learning. *Faculty:* 5 full-time (all women), 21 part-time/adjunct (16 women). *Students:* 85 full-time (67 women), 189 part-time (151 women); includes 31 minority (18 Black or African American, non-Hispanic/Latino; 3 American Indian or Alaska Native, non-Hispanic/Latino; 3 Asian, non-Hispanic/Latino; 3 Two or more races, non-Hispanic/Latino; 1 international. Average age 31. 83 applicants, 96% accepted, 74 enrolled. In 2017, 94 master's, 47 other advanced degrees awarded. *Entrance requirements:* For master's, GRE (if cumulative GPA less than 2.7), transcripts, two letters of recommendation. Additional exam requirements/recommendations for international students: Required—TOEFL (minimum score 550 paper-based, 79 iBT), IELTS (minimum score 6.5), or CAEL (minimum score 70). *Application deadline:* Applications are processed on a rolling basis. Application fee: $0. Electronic applications accepted. *Expenses:* Tuition: Full-time $22,860; part-time $820 per credit. *Required fees:* $720; $25 per credit. $65 per semester. One-time fee: $425. *Financial support:* Career-related internships or fieldwork, Federal Work-Study, scholarships/grants, tuition waivers (partial), and unspecified assistantships available. Support available to part-time students. Financial award application deadline: 4/30; financial award applicants required to submit FAFSA. *Faculty research:* Asperger's disease, autism, private higher education, reading strategies. *Unit head:* Dr. Anne Marie Tryjankowski, Chair/Associate Professor of Graduate Education and Leadership, 716-888-3715, Fax: 716-888-3142, E-mail: tryjanka@canisius.edu.

Capella University, School of Business and Technology, Doctoral Programs in Business, Minneapolis, MN 55402. Offers accounting (DBA, PhD); business intelligence (DBA); finance (DBA, PhD); general business management (PhD); human resource management (DBA, PhD); leadership (DBA, PhD); management education (PhD); marketing (DBA, PhD); project management (DBA, PhD); strategy and innovation (DBA, PhD). *Accreditation:* ACBSP.

Chadron State College, School of Professional and Graduate Studies, Department of Education, Chadron, NE 69337. Offers business (MA Ed); community counseling (MA Ed); educational administration (MS Ed, Sp Ed); elementary education (MS Ed); history (MA Ed); language and literature (MA Ed); secondary administration (MS Ed); secondary education (MS Ed). *Accreditation:* NCATE. *Program availability:* Part-time, evening/weekend, online learning. *Degree requirements:* For master's, thesis optional. *Entrance requirements:* For master's, GRE General Test, GRE Writing Test, minimum GPA of 2.75 or 12 graduate hours at CSC with minimum GPA of 3.25. Additional exam requirements/recommendations for international students: Required—TOEFL. Electronic applications accepted. *Faculty research:* Rural education, technology, mental health.

Clemson University, Graduate School, College of Business, Clemson, SC 29634. Offers MA, MBA, MP Acc, MS, PhD. *Program availability:* Part-time, evening/weekend. *Faculty:* 144 full-time (47 women), 27 part-time/adjunct (8 women). *Students:* 667 full-time (280 women), 773 part-time (240 women); includes 194 minority (98 Black or African American, non-Hispanic/Latino; 26 Asian, non-Hispanic/Latino; 48 Hispanic/Latino; 2 Native Hawaiian or other Pacific Islander, non-Hispanic/Latino; 20 Two or more races, non-Hispanic/Latino), 188 international. Average age 31. 937 applicants, 70% accepted, 375 enrolled. In 2017, 626 master's, 27 doctorates awarded. Terminal master's awarded for partial completion of doctoral program. *Degree requirements:* For master's, thesis optional; for doctorate, thesis/dissertation. *Entrance requirements:* For master's and doctorate, GRE General Test, GMAT, unofficial transcripts, letters of recommendation. Additional exam requirements/recommendations for international students: Required—TOEFL (minimum score 80 iBT), IELTS (minimum score 6.5), PTE (minimum score 54). *Application deadline:* Applications are processed on a rolling basis. Application fee: $80 ($90 for international students). Electronic applications accepted. *Expenses:* $6,564 per semester full-time resident, $12,538 per semester full-time non-resident, $743 per credit hour part-time resident, $1,486 per credit hour part-time non-resident, $1,203 per credit hour online, other fees may apply per session. *Financial support:* In 2017–18, 105 students received support, including 20 fellowships with partial tuition reimbursements available (averaging $7,400 per year), 2 research assistantships with partial tuition reimbursements available (averaging $13,392 per year), 18 teaching assistantships with partial tuition reimbursements available (averaging $18,778 per year); career-related internships or fieldwork and unspecified assistantships also available. *Faculty research:* Entrepreneurship, marketing, price theory, information systems, operations management. *Total annual research expenditures:* $164,260. *Unit head:* Wendy York, Dean, 864-656-3178. *Application contact:* Dr. Gregory Pickett, Senior Associate Dean, 864-656-3975, E-mail: pgregor@clemson.edu.
Website: http://www.clemson.edu/business/index.html

Colorado Christian University, Program in Curriculum and Instruction, Lakewood, CO 80226. Offers corporate education (MACI); early childhood educator (MACI); elementary educator (MACI); instructional technology (MACI); master educator (MACI); online course developer (MACI); online teaching and learning (MACI); special education generalist (MACI). *Program availability:* Part-time, evening/weekend. *Degree requirements:* For master's, thesis optional, practicum. *Entrance requirements:* For master's, interviews, letters of recommendation. Additional exam requirements/recommendations for international students: Required—TOEFL. Electronic applications accepted. *Expenses:* Contact institution.

East Carolina University, Graduate School, College of Education, Department of Interdisciplinary Professions, Greenville, NC 27858-4353. Offers adult education (MA Ed); business and marketing education (MA Ed); community college instruction (Certificate); counselor education (MS); education in the healthcare professions (Certificate); library science (MLS); student affairs in higher education (Certificate); vocational education (MS). *Accreditation:* ACA; NCATE. *Program availability:* Part-time, evening/weekend. *Students:* 97 full-time (77 women), 392 part-time (344 women); includes 107 minority (73 Black or African American, non-Hispanic/Latino; 6 American Indian or Alaska Native, non-Hispanic/Latino; 5 Asian, non-Hispanic/Latino; 11 Hispanic/Latino; 12 Two or more races, non-Hispanic/Latino). Average age 36. 148 applicants, 97% accepted, 116 enrolled. In 2017, 148 master's, 23 other advanced degrees awarded. *Degree requirements:* For master's, comprehensive exam, thesis optional. *Entrance requirements:* For master's, GRE General Test or MAT, interview, minimum GPA of 2.5, bachelor's degree in related field, teaching license (MA Ed). Additional exam requirements/recommendations for international students: Required—TOEFL. *Application deadline:* For fall admission, 5/15 priority date for domestic students. Applications are processed on a rolling basis. Application fee: $75. *Expenses:* Tuition, state resident: full-time $4749; part-time $297 per credit hour. Tuition, nonresident: full-time $17,898; part-time $1119 per credit hour. *Required fees:* $2691; $224 per credit hour. Part-time tuition and fees vary according to course load and program. *Financial support:* Research assistantships with partial tuition reimbursements, teaching assistantships with partial tuition reimbursements, and Federal Work-Study available. Support available to part-time students. Financial award application deadline: 6/1. *Unit head:* Dr. Vivian W. Mott, Chair, 252-328-6177, Fax: 252-328-4368, E-mail: mottv@ecu.edu.
Website: http://www.ecu.edu/cs-educ/idp/index.cfm

Eastern Kentucky University, The Graduate School, College of Education, Department of Curriculum and Instruction, Program in Secondary and Higher Education, Richmond, KY 40475-3102. Offers secondary education (MA Ed), including agricultural education, art education, biological sciences education, business education, English education, geography education, history education, home economics education, industrial education, mathematical sciences education, physical education, school health education. *Accreditation:* NCATE. *Program availability:* Part-time. *Entrance requirements:* For master's, GRE General Test, minimum GPA of 2.5.

Florida Agricultural and Mechanical University, Division of Graduate Studies, Research, and Continuing Education, College of Education, Department of Vocational Education, Tallahassee, FL 32307-3200. Offers business education (MBE); industrial education (MS Ed); technology education (M Ed). *Accreditation:* NCATE. *Degree requirements:* For master's, thesis (for some programs). *Entrance requirements:* For master's, GRE General Test, minimum GPA of 3.0. Additional exam requirements/recommendations for international students: Required—TOEFL.

Hofstra University, School of Education, Programs in Teacher Education, Hempstead, NY 11549. Offers bilingual education (MA); bilingual extension (Advanced Certificate), including education/speech language pathology, intensive teacher institute; business education (MS Ed); curriculum studies (MS Ed); early childhood and childhood education (MS Ed); early childhood education (MA, MS Ed); educational technology (Advanced Certificate); elementary education (MA, MS Ed), including science, technology, engineering, and mathematics (STEM) (MA); English education (MS Ed); family and consumer science (MS Ed); fine arts and music education (Advanced Certificate); fine arts education (MS Ed); foreign language and TESOL (MS Ed); foreign language education (MA, MS Ed), including Arabic (MS Ed), biology, chemistry, Chinese (MS Ed), earth science, French, German, Italian (MS Ed), Mandarin (MS Ed), physics, Russian, Spanish; foundations of education (Advanced Certificate), including grades 5-6, grades 7-9; languages other than English and teaching English as a second language

(MA); learning and teaching (Ed D), including applied linguistics, art education, arts and humanities, early childhood education, English education, human development, math education, math, science, and technology, multicultural education, physical education, science education, social studies education, special education; mathematics education (MA, MS Ed); music education (MA, MS Ed); science education (MA), including biology (MA, MS Ed), chemistry (MA, MS Ed), earth science (MA, MS Ed), physics (MA, MS Ed); secondary education (Advanced Certificate); social studies education (MA, MS Ed); teaching languages other than English and TESOL (MS Ed); technology for learning (MA); TESOL (MS Ed, Advanced Certificate); TESOL with specialization in STEM (MA); work based learning extension (Advanced Certificate). *Program availability:* Part-time, evening/weekend, blended/hybrid learning. *Students:* 119 full-time (83 women), 124 part-time (90 women); includes 54 minority (15 Black or African American, non-Hispanic/Latino; 9 Asian, non-Hispanic/Latino; 29 Hispanic/Latino; 1 Native Hawaiian or other Pacific Islander, non-Hispanic/Latino), 12 international. Average age 29. 205 applicants, 88% accepted, 93 enrolled. In 2017, 103 master's, 4 doctorates, 32 other advanced degrees awarded. *Degree requirements:* For master's, comprehensive exam, thesis (for some programs), exit project, student teaching, fieldwork, electronic portfolio, curriculum project, minimum GPA of 3.0; for doctorate, thesis/dissertation; for Advanced Certificate, 3 foreign languages, comprehensive exam (for some programs), thesis project. *Entrance requirements:* For master's, GRE, 2 letters of recommendation, portfolio, teacher certification (MA), interview, essay; for doctorate, GMAT, GRE, LSAT, or MAT; for Advanced Certificate, 2 letters of recommendation, essay, interview and/or portfolio, teaching certificate. Additional exam requirements/recommendations for international students: Required—TOEFL (minimum score 550 paper-based; 80 iBT). *Application deadline:* Applications are processed on a rolling basis. Application fee: $75. Electronic applications accepted. *Expenses: Tuition:* Full-time $1292. *Required fees:* $970. Tuition and fees vary according to program. *Financial support:* In 2017–18, 112 students received support, including 56 fellowships with full and partial tuition reimbursements available (averaging $4,998 per year), 2 research assistantships with full and partial tuition reimbursements available (averaging $8,753 per year); career-related internships or fieldwork, Federal Work-Study, institutionally sponsored loans, scholarships/grants, traineeships, tuition waivers (full and partial), and unspecified assistantships also available. Support available to part-time students. Financial award applicants required to submit FAFSA. *Faculty research:* Educational interventions that foster critical-thinking skills; teachers' attitudes about professional development; threats to teacher quality. *Unit head:* Dr. Eustace Thompson, Chairperson, 516-463-5749, Fax: 516-463-6275, E-mail: eustace.g.thompson@hofstra.edu. *Application contact:* Sunil Samuel, Assistant Vice President of Admissions, 516-463-4723, Fax: 516-463-4664, E-mail: graduateadmission@hofstra.edu.
Website: http://www.hofstra.edu/education/

Indiana University of Pennsylvania, School of Graduate Studies and Research, College of Education and Communications, Department of Adult and Community Education, Program in Business/Business Specialist, Indiana, PA 15705. Offers M Ed. *Program availability:* Part-time. *Faculty:* 2 full-time (both women). *Degree requirements:* For master's, thesis optional. *Entrance requirements:* For master's, GMAT or GRE. Additional exam requirements/recommendations for international students: Required—TOEFL (minimum score 540 paper-based). *Application deadline:* Applications are processed on a rolling basis. Application fee: $50. Electronic applications accepted. *Expenses:* Tuition, state resident: full-time $12,000; part-time $500 per credit. Tuition, nonresident: full-time $18,000; part-time $750 per credit. *Required fees:* $4073; $165.55 per credit. $64 per term. *Financial support:* Research assistantships with tuition reimbursements, career-related internships or fieldwork, Federal Work-Study, scholarships/grants, and unspecified assistantships available. Financial award application deadline: 4/15; financial award applicants required to submit FAFSA. *Unit head:* Prof. Jacqueline McGinty, Coordinator, 724-357-2470, E-mail: jacqueline.mcginty@iup.edu.
Website: http://www.iup.edu/ace/grad/default.aspx

Inter American University of Puerto Rico, Metropolitan Campus, Graduate Programs, Program in Commercial Education, San Juan, PR 00919-1293. Offers MA.

Inter American University of Puerto Rico, San Germán Campus, Graduate Studies Center, Program in Business Education, San Germán, PR 00683-5008. Offers MA. *Accreditation:* TEAC. *Program availability:* Part-time, evening/weekend. *Degree requirements:* For master's, comprehensive exam. *Entrance requirements:* For master's, GRE General Test or EXADEP, minimum GPA of 3.0.

Johnson & Wales University, Graduate Studies, MAT Program in Teacher Education, Providence, RI 02903-3703. Offers business education and secondary special education (MAT); culinary arts education (MAT); elementary education and elementary special education (MAT). *Program availability:* Part-time, evening/weekend. *Entrance requirements:* For master's, MAT, minimum GPA of 2.75. Additional exam requirements/recommendations for international students: Required—TOEFL (minimum score 500 paper-based) or IELTS (recommended). *Application deadline:* For fall admission, 8/21 priority date for domestic students, 6/15 priority date for international students; for winter admission, 11/15 priority date for domestic students, 10/1 priority date for international students. Applications are processed on a rolling basis. Application fee: $0. *Expenses: Tuition:* Full-time $12,636; part-time $702 per credit hour. *Financial support:* Unspecified assistantships available. Financial award application deadline: 5/1. *Faculty research:* Secondary education, student teaching, educational reform, evaluation procedures. *Unit head:* Karen Swoboda, Director, 401-598-1922, Fax: 401-598-1125. *Application contact:* Graduate School Admissions, 401-598-1015, Fax: 401-598-1286, E-mail: gradadm@jwu.edu.

Lehman College of the City University of New York, School of Education, Department of Middle and High School Education, Program in Business Education, Bronx, NY 10468-1589. Offers MS Ed. *Accreditation:* NCATE. *Program availability:* Part-time, evening/weekend. *Degree requirements:* For master's, thesis. *Entrance requirements:* For master's, minimum GPA of 2.7.

Lock Haven University of Pennsylvania, The Stephen Poorman College of Business, Information Systems, and Human Services, Lock Haven, PA 17745-2390. Offers clinical mental health counseling (MS); sport science (MS). *Program availability:* Online learning. *Degree requirements:* For master's, thesis. *Entrance requirements:* For master's, minimum undergraduate GPA of 3.0. Additional exam requirements/recommendations for international students: Required—TOEFL. Electronic applications accepted.

Louisiana State University and Agricultural & Mechanical College, Graduate School, College of Human Sciences and Education, School of Human Resource Education and Workforce Development, Baton Rouge, LA 70803. Offers agriculture and extension education and youth development (MS, PhD); career and technical education (MS, PhD); comprehensive vocational education (MS, PhD); extension and international education (MS, PhD); human resource and leadership development (MS, PhD); industrial education (MS); vocational agriculture education (MS, PhD); vocational business education (MS, PhD); vocational home economics education (MS). *Accreditation:* NCATE. *Faculty:* 11 full-time (6 women). *Students:* 102 full-time (71 women), 130 part-time (92 women); includes 89 minority (63 Black or African American, non-Hispanic/Latino; 3 American Indian or Alaska Native, non-Hispanic/Latino; 8 Asian, non-Hispanic/

Latino; 14 Hispanic/Latino; 1 Two or more races, non-Hispanic/Latino), 6 international. Average age 35. 98 applicants, 69% accepted, 52 enrolled. In 2017, 94 master's, 15 doctorates awarded. *Financial support:* In 2017–18, 1 fellowship (averaging $18,238 per year), 16 teaching assistantships (averaging $15,341 per year) were awarded. *Total annual research expenditures:* $1,998.

Manhattanville College, School of Business, Purchase, NY 10577-2132. Offers MS, Advanced Certificate. *Program availability:* Part-time, evening/weekend. *Faculty:* 28 part-time/adjunct (7 women). *Students:* 94 full-time (41 women), 30 part-time (19 women); includes 40 minority (7 Black or African American, non-Hispanic/Latino; 1 American Indian or Alaska Native, non-Hispanic/Latino; 4 Asian, non-Hispanic/Latino; 27 Hispanic/Latino; 1 Two or more races, non-Hispanic/Latino), 14 international. Average age 30. 130 applicants, 40% accepted, 36 enrolled. In 2017, 61 master's awarded. *Degree requirements:* For master's, thesis (for some programs), final project, internship, portfolio. *Entrance requirements:* For master's, personal essay, transcripts, 2 letters of recommendation (academic or professional), resume, health form with proof of immunization (for those born after 1957). Additional exam requirements/recommendations for international students: Required—TOEFL (minimum score 563 paper-based, 85 iBT), IELTS (7), or iTEP (B2). *Application deadline:* Applications are processed on a rolling basis. Application fee: $75. Electronic applications accepted. *Expenses:* $915 per credit. *Financial support:* Federal Work-Study, institutionally sponsored loans, scholarships/grants, and unspecified assistantships available. Financial award application deadline: 3/15; financial award applicants required to submit FAFSA. *Unit head:* Steve Albanese, Dean, 914-323-5469, E-mail: steve.albanese@mville.edu. *Application contact:* Monika Pottgen, Assistant Director, Recruitment and Admissions, 914-323-5150, E-mail: business@mville.edu.
Website: http://www.mville.edu/business

Maryville University of Saint Louis, The John E. Simon School of Business, St. Louis, MO 63141-7299. Offers accounting (MBA, MS, Certificate); business studies (Certificate); cybersecurity (MBA, MS, Certificate); financial services (MBA, Certificate); healthcare practice management (MBA, Certificate); human resource management (MBA, Certificate); information technology (MBA, Certificate); management (MBA, Certificate); management and leadership (MA); marketing (MBA, Certificate); project management (MBA, Certificate); sport business management (MBA); supply chain management (Certificate); supply chain management/logistics (MBA). *Accreditation:* ACBSP. *Program availability:* Part-time, 100% online, blended/hybrid learning. *Faculty:* 5 full-time (3 women), 51 part-time/adjunct (16 women). *Students:* 222 full-time (96 women), 498 part-time (222 women); includes 185 minority (104 Black or African American, non-Hispanic/Latino; 5 American Indian or Alaska Native, non-Hispanic/Latino; 30 Asian, non-Hispanic/Latino; 37 Hispanic/Latino; 9 Two or more races, non-Hispanic/Latino), 26 international. Average age 33. In 2017, 106 master's awarded. *Degree requirements:* For master's, capstone course (for MBA). *Entrance requirements:* Additional exam requirements/recommendations for international students: Required—TOEFL (minimum score 563 paper-based; 85 iBT). *Application deadline:* Applications are processed on a rolling basis. Electronic applications accepted. *Expenses:* Contact institution. *Financial support:* Career-related internships or fieldwork, Federal Work-Study, tuition waivers (partial), and campus employment available. Financial award application deadline: 4/1; financial award applicants required to submit FAFSA. *Unit head:* Pam Horwitz, Interim Dean, 314-529-9680, Fax: 314-529-9975. *Application contact:* Dustin Loeffler, Director for Graduate Studies in Business, 314-529-9571, Fax: 314-529-9975, E-mail: dloeffler@maryville.edu.
Website: http://www.maryville.edu/bu/business-administration-masters/

Middle Tennessee State University, College of Graduate Studies, Jennings A. Jones College of Business, Department of Business Communication and Entrepreneurship, Murfreesboro, TN 37132. Offers business education (MBE). *Program availability:* Part-time, evening/weekend, online learning. *Degree requirements:* For master's, comprehensive exam. *Entrance requirements:* For master's, GRE or MAT. Additional exam requirements/recommendations for international students: Required—TOEFL (minimum score 525 paper-based; 71 iBT) or IELTS (minimum score 6). Electronic applications accepted.

Milwaukee School of Engineering, MBA Program in Education Leadership, Milwaukee, WI 53202-3109. Offers MBA. *Program availability:* Part-time, evening/weekend. *Students:* 28 part-time (14 women); includes 3 minority (1 Black or African American, non-Hispanic/Latino; 1 Asian, non-Hispanic/Latino; 1 Two or more races, non-Hispanic/Latino). Average age 35. 42 applicants, 86% accepted, 28 enrolled. In 2017, 14 master's awarded. *Degree requirements:* For master's, thesis or alternative. *Entrance requirements:* For master's, GRE or GMAT if college GPA is less than 3.5, teaching license, three years of full-time classroom teaching experience, two letters of recommendation, Professional Educator License or eligibility, personal interview. Additional exam requirements/recommendations for international students: Required—TOEFL (minimum score 90 iBT), IELTS (minimum score 7). *Application deadline:* Applications are processed on a rolling basis. Electronic applications accepted. *Expenses: Tuition:* Part-time $814 per credit hour. *Required fees:* $12.50 per credit hour. *Financial support:* In 2017–18, 15 students received support, including 15 fellowships (averaging $45,552 per year); career-related internships or fieldwork and scholarships/grants also available. Financial award application deadline: 3/15; financial award applicants required to submit FAFSA. *Unit head:* Dr. Ruth Barratt, Program Director, 414-277-2230, E-mail: barratt@msoe.edu. *Application contact:* Brian Rutz, Graduate Admission Counselor, 414-277-7200, E-mail: rutz@msoe.edu.
Website: https://www.msoe.edu/academics/graduate-degrees/business/mba-in-education-leadership/

Mississippi College, Graduate School, School of Business, Clinton, MS 39058. Offers accounting (Certificate); business administration (MBA), including accounting; business education (M Ed); finance (MBA, Certificate); JD/MBA. *Accreditation:* ACBSP. *Program availability:* Part-time, evening/weekend. *Degree requirements:* For master's, comprehensive exam, thesis optional. *Entrance requirements:* For master's, GMAT, minimum GPA of 2.5, 24 hours of undergraduate course work in business. Additional exam requirements/recommendations for international students: Recommended—TOEFL, IELTS. Electronic applications accepted.

Mississippi College, Graduate School, School of Education, Department of Teacher Education and Leadership, Clinton, MS 39058. Offers art (M Ed); biological science (M Ed); business education (M Ed); computer science (M Ed); dyslexia therapy (M Ed); educational leadership (M Ed, Ed D, Ed S); elementary education (M Ed, Ed S); English (M Ed); higher education administration (MS); mathematics (M Ed); secondary education (M Ed); social studies (history) (M Ed); teaching arts (M Ed). *Program availability:* Part-time, online learning. *Degree requirements:* For master's, comprehensive exam, thesis optional. *Entrance requirements:* For master's, NTE. Additional exam requirements/recommendations for international students: Recommended—TOEFL, IELTS. Electronic applications accepted.

Morehead State University, Graduate Programs, College of Education, Department of Foundational and Graduate Studies in Education, Morehead, KY 40351. Offers adult and higher education (MA, Ed S); certified professional counselor (Ed S); counseling P-12 (MA); curriculum and instruction (Ed S); educational technology (MA Ed); instructional leadership (Ed S); school administration (MA); school counseling (Ed S);

teacher leader business and marketing content (MA Ed); teacher leader business and marketing technology (MA Ed); teacher leader educational technology (MA Ed); teacher leader English (MA Ed); teacher leader gifted education (MA Ed); teacher leader IECE certification (MA Ed); teacher leader interdisciplinary education P-5 (MA Ed); teacher leader middle grades (MA Ed); teacher leader non IECE certification (MA Ed); teacher leader reading/writing - non-certification (MA Ed); teacher leader reading/writing certification (MA Ed); teacher leader school communication - certification (MA Ed); teacher leader school communication - non-certification (MA Ed); teacher leader social studies (MA Ed); teacher leader special education (MA Ed). *Accreditation:* NCATE. *Program availability:* Part-time, evening/weekend. *Degree requirements:* For master's, thesis optional, oral and/or written comprehensive exams; for Ed S, thesis, oral exam. *Entrance requirements:* For master's, GRE General Test, minimum overall undergraduate GPA of 2.5; for Ed S, GRE General Test, interview, master's degree, minimum GPA of 3.5, work experience. Additional exam requirements/recommendations for international students: Required—TOEFL (minimum score 500 paper-based). Electronic applications accepted. *Faculty research:* Character education, school accountability, computer applications for school administrators.

Morehead State University, Graduate Programs, College of Education, Department of Middle Grades and Secondary Education, Morehead, KY 40351. Offers business and marketing education (MAT); English/language arts 5-9 (MAT); French (MAT); health P-12 (MAT); mathematics 5-9 (MAT); physical education P-12 (MAT); science 5-9 (MAT); secondary biology (MAT); secondary chemistry (MAT); secondary earth science (MAT); secondary English (MAT); secondary math (MAT); secondary physics (MAT); secondary social studies (MAT); social studies 5-9 (MAT); Spanish (MAT). *Program availability:* Part-time, evening/weekend. *Degree requirements:* For master's, portfolio. *Entrance requirements:* For master's, GRE or PRAXIS II content exam, minimum overall undergraduate GPA of 2.5. Additional exam requirements/recommendations for international students: Required—TOEFL (minimum score 500 paper-based). Electronic applications accepted.

New York University, Steinhardt School of Culture, Education, and Human Development, Department of Administration, Leadership, and Technology, Program in Business Education, New York, NY 10012. Offers business and workplace education (MA, Advanced Certificate); workplace learning (Advanced Certificate). *Accreditation:* TEAC. *Program availability:* Part-time. *Students:* Average age 41. 13 applicants, 62% accepted, 3 enrolled. In 2017, 7 master's awarded. *Entrance requirements:* For degree, master's degree. Additional exam requirements/recommendations for international students: Required—TOEFL (minimum score 100 iBT). *Application deadline:* For fall admission, 12/1 priority date for domestic and international students; for spring admission, 10/1 for domestic and international students. Applications are processed on a rolling basis. Application fee: $75. Electronic applications accepted. *Expenses: Tuition:* Full-time $41,352; part-time $19,968 per year. *Required fees:* $2496; $1628 per unit. $814 per term. Tuition and fees vary according to course load and program. *Financial support:* Career-related internships or fieldwork, Federal Work-Study, institutionally sponsored loans, scholarships/grants, tuition waivers (partial), and unspecified assistantships available. Support available to part-time students. Financial award application deadline: 2/1; financial award applicants required to submit FAFSA. *Faculty research:* Applications of technology to instruction, workplace and corporate education, adult learning. *Unit head:* Dr. Bridget N. O'Connor, Director, 212-998-5488, Fax: 212-995-4041, E-mail: bridget.oconnor@nyu.edu. *Application contact:* 212-998-5030, Fax: 212-995-4328, E-mail: steinhardt.gradadmissions@nyu.edu.
Website: http://steinhardt.nyu.edu/alt/businessed

North Carolina Agricultural and Technical State University, School of Graduate Studies, School of Business and Economics, Greensboro, NC 27411. Offers accounting (MBA); business education (MAT); human resources management (MBA); supply chain systems (MBA).

North Carolina State University, Graduate School, College of Education, Department of Curriculum and Instruction, Program in Business and Marketing Education, Raleigh, NC 27695. Offers M Ed, MS. *Entrance requirements:* For master's, MAT or GRE, minimum GPA of 3.0, teaching license, 3 letters of reference.

Nova Southeastern University, H. Wayne Huizenga College of Business and Entrepreneurship, Fort Lauderdale, FL 33314-7796. Offers accounting (M Acc); business (MBA); business intelligence/analytics (MBA); complex health systems (MBA); enterprise informatics (MBA); entrepreneurship (MBA); finance (MBA); human resource management (MBA); international business (MBA); management (MBA); marketing (MBA); process improvement (MBA); public administration (MPA); real estate development (MS); sport revenue generation (MBA); supply chain management (MBA). *Accreditation:* NASPAA. *Program availability:* Part-time, evening/weekend, 100% online, blended/hybrid learning. *Faculty:* 85 full-time (37 women), 59 part-time/adjunct (19 women). *Students:* 1,999 full-time (1,225 women), 335 part-time (210 women); includes 1,516 minority (597 Black or African American, non-Hispanic/Latino; 4 American Indian or Alaska Native, non-Hispanic/Latino; 92 Asian, non-Hispanic/Latino; 789 Hispanic/Latino; 3 Native Hawaiian or other Pacific Islander, non-Hispanic/Latino; 31 Two or more races, non-Hispanic/Latino), 291 international. Average age 34. 1,269 applicants, 59% accepted, 551 enrolled. In 2017, 1,055 master's awarded. *Entrance requirements:* For master's, GMAT or GRE (depending on undergraduate GPA), official transcripts from all schools attended while in pursuit of bachelor's degree; minimum GPA of 2.5 from regionally-accredited institution. Additional exam requirements/recommendations for international students: Required—TOEFL (minimum score 550 paper-based; 79 iBT), IELTS (minimum score 6), PTE (minimum score 54). *Application deadline:* For fall admission, 8/5 priority date for domestic students, 7/29 priority date for international students; for winter admission, 12/16 priority date for domestic students, 12/9 priority date for international students; for summer admission, 4/21 priority date for domestic and international students. Applications are processed on a rolling basis. Application fee: $50. Electronic applications accepted. *Expenses:* $37,785 (online), $35,640 (in-classroom). *Financial support:* In 2017–18, 325 students received support. Federal Work-Study and scholarships/grants available. Support available to part-time students. Financial award application deadline: 4/15; financial award applicants required to submit FAFSA. *Faculty research:* Entrepreneurship and venture capital, ethics and social responsibility, global commerce and cultures, business process management. *Unit head:* Dr. J. Preston Jones, Dean, 954-262-5127, E-mail: prestonj@nova.edu. *Application contact:* Zeida Rodriguez, Associate Director of Enrollment Services, 954-262-5163, Fax: 954-262-3822, E-mail: zeida@nova.edu.
Website: http://www.huizenga.nova.edu

Old Dominion University, Darden College of Education, Programs in STEM Education and Professional Studies, Norfolk, VA 23529. Offers community college teaching (MS); human resources training (PhD); technology education (PhD). *Accreditation:* NCATE (one or more programs are accredited). *Program availability:* Part-time, evening/weekend, mix of synchronous and asynchronous study. *Faculty:* 6 full-time (2 women). *Students:* 10 full-time (7 women), 35 part-time (24 women); includes 22 minority (18 Black or African American, non-Hispanic/Latino; 1 American Indian or Alaska Native, non-Hispanic/Latino; 2 Hispanic/Latino; 1 Two or more races, non-Hispanic/Latino), 1 international. Average age 41. 3 applicants, 100% accepted, 3 enrolled. In 2017, 4 master's, 3 doctorates awarded. Terminal master's awarded for partial completion of doctoral program. *Degree requirements:* For master's, comprehensive exam, thesis optional, writing exam, candidacy exam; for doctorate, comprehensive exam, thesis/ dissertation, writing exam, candidacy exam. *Entrance requirements:* For master's, GRE General Test or MAT, minimum GPA of 2.8, 2 letters of reference; for doctorate, GRE, minimum GPA of 3.0, 3 letters of reference. Additional exam requirements/ recommendations for international students: Required—TOEFL. *Application deadline:* For fall admission, 6/1 priority date for domestic students, 6/1 for international students; for winter admission, 11/1 priority date for domestic students, 11/1 for international students; for spring admission, 3/1 priority date for domestic students, 3/1 for international students. Applications are processed on a rolling basis. Application fee: $50. Electronic applications accepted. *Expenses:* Tuition, state resident: full-time $8928; part-time $496 per credit. Tuition, nonresident: full-time $22,482; part-time $1249 per credit. *Required fees:* $66 per semester. *Financial support:* In 2017–18, 3 students received support, including 2 teaching assistantships with partial tuition reimbursements available (averaging $15,000 per year). Financial award application deadline: 2/15; financial award applicants required to submit FAFSA. *Faculty research:* Training and development, STEM education, visualization, leadership, technology literacy. *Total annual research expenditures:* $1 million. *Unit head:* Dr. Petros Katsioloudis, Department Chair, 757-683-5323, E-mail: pkatsiol@odu.edu. Website: http://education.odu.edu/ots/

Pepperdine University, Seaver College, Division of Business, Malibu, CA 90263. Offers accounting (MS). *Entrance requirements:* For master's, GRE General Test, statement of purpose and intent for writing as a vocation, script writing sample, letters of recommendation. Additional exam requirements/recommendations for international students: Required—TOEFL. *Application deadline:* For fall admission, 2/1 priority date for domestic students. Application fee: $55. Electronic applications accepted. *Unit head:* Dr. Dean Baim, Divisional Dean/Professor of Economics and Finance, 310-506-4237, E-mail: dean.baim@pepperdine.edu. *Application contact:* Hayley Wolf, Director of Admission, 310-506-4392, E-mail: hayley.wolf@pepperdine.edu. Website: http://seaver.pepperdine.edu/humanities/graduate/screenwriting/

Pontifical Catholic University of Puerto Rico, College of Education, Doctoral Program in Business Teacher Education, Ponce, PR 00717-0777. Offers PhD. *Degree requirements:* For doctorate, thesis/dissertation. *Entrance requirements:* For doctorate, EXADEP, GRE General Test or MAT, 3 letters of recommendation.

Pontifical Catholic University of Puerto Rico, College of Education, Master's Program in Business Teacher Education, Ponce, PR 00717-0777. Offers M Ed. *Degree requirements:* For master's, comprehensive exam, thesis (for some programs). *Entrance requirements:* For master's, GRE, 2 letters of recommendation, interview, minimum GPA of 2.75.

Regis University, College of Business and Economics, Denver, CO 80221-1099. Offers accounting (MS); executive leadership (Certificate); finance (MS); finance and accounting (MBA); health industry leadership (MBA); human resource management and leadership (MSOL); management (MBA); marketing (MBA); nonprofit leadership (Post-Graduate Certificate); nonprofit management (MNM); nonprofit organizational capacity building (Certificate); operations management (MBA); organizational leadership and management (MSOL); project leadership and management (MS, MSOL); strategic business management (Certificate); strategic human resource integration (Certificate); strategic management (MBA). Programs offered at Colorado Springs Campus, Northwest Denver Campus, Southeast Denver Campus, Fort Collins Campus, Broomfield Campus, Henderson (Nevada) Campus, and Summerlin (Nevada) Campus. *Program availability:* Part-time, evening/weekend, 100% online, blended/hybrid learning. *Degree requirements:* For master's, thesis (for some programs), capstone or final research project. *Entrance requirements:* For master's, official transcript reflecting baccalaureate degree awarded from regionally-accredited college or university, interview, 2 years of full-time related work experience, resume, letters of recommendation. Additional exam requirements/recommendations for international students: Required—TOEFL (minimum score 550 paper-based; 82 iBT). Electronic applications accepted. *Expenses:* Contact institution. *Faculty research:* Impact of information technology on small business regulation of accounting, international project financing, mineral development, delivery of healthcare to rural indigenous communities.

Rider University, College of Education and Human Services, Teacher Certification Program, Lawrenceville, NJ 08648-3001. Offers bilingual education (Certificate); business education (Certificate); early childhood education (Certificate); elementary education (Certificate); English as a second language (Certificate); English education (Certificate); mathematics education (Certificate); science education (Certificate); secondary education (Certificate); social studies education (Certificate); world languages (Certificate), including French, German, Spanish. *Program availability:* Part-time, online learning. *Degree requirements:* For Certificate, internship, professional portfolio. *Entrance requirements:* For degree, PRAXIS, resume. Additional exam requirements/recommendations for international students: Required—TOEFL (minimum score 550 paper-based). Electronic applications accepted. *Faculty research:* Conceptual foundations for optimal development of creativity; creative theory, cognitive processes in mathematics learning, teacher collaboration.

Robert Morris University, School of Education and Social Sciences, Moon Township, PA 15108-1189. Offers business education (MS); counseling psychology (MS); education (Postbaccalaureate Certificate); higher education (MS); instructional leadership (MS), including education; instructional management and leadership (PhD); literacy (MS); special education (MS). *Accreditation:* TEAC. *Program availability:* Part-time, evening/weekend, online learning. *Faculty:* 18 full-time (10 women), 5 part-time/ adjunct (2 women). *Students:* 151 part-time (90 women); includes 23 minority (12 Black or African American, non-Hispanic/Latino; 2 Asian, non-Hispanic/Latino; 2 Hispanic/ Latino; 7 Two or more races, non-Hispanic/Latino), 4 international. Average age 34. 51 applicants, 39% accepted, 10 enrolled. In 2017, 31 master's, 16 doctorates awarded. *Degree requirements:* For doctorate, thesis/dissertation. *Entrance requirements:* Additional exam requirements/recommendations for international students: Required— TOEFL (minimum score 550 paper-based; 79 iBT). *Application deadline:* For fall admission, 7/1 priority date for domestic and international students; for spring admission, 11/1 priority date for domestic and international students. Applications are processed on a rolling basis. Application fee: $35. Electronic applications accepted. *Expenses:* $890 per credit tuition, $80 per credit university fee. *Unit head:* Dr. George Semich, Acting Dean, 412-397-6032, Fax: 412-397-6044, E-mail: semich@rmu.edu. *Application contact:* E-mail: graduateadmissions@rmu.edu. Website: http://www.rmu.edu/web/cms/schools/sess/

Salve Regina University, Program in Management, Newport, RI 02840-4192. Offers business studies (CGS); human resource management (CGS); innovation and strategic management (MS); management (CGS); nonprofit management (CGS); social entrepreneurship (CGS). *Program availability:* Part-time, evening/weekend, online learning. *Entrance requirements:* For master's, GMAT, GRE General Test, or MAT. Additional exam requirements/recommendations for international students: Required— TOEFL (minimum score 600 paper-based; 100 iBT). Electronic applications accepted.

South Carolina State University, College of Graduate and Professional Studies, Department of Education, Orangeburg, SC 29117-0001. Offers early childhood education (MAT); education (M Ed); elementary education (M Ed, MAT); English (MAT); general science/biology (MAT); mathematics (MAT); secondary education (M Ed), including biology education, business education, counselor education, English education, home economics education, industrial education, mathematics education, science education, social studies education; special education (M Ed), including emotionally handicapped, learning disabilities, mentally handicapped. *Accreditation:* NCATE. *Program availability:* Part-time, evening/weekend. *Faculty:* 11 full-time (6 women), 4 part-time/adjunct (2 women). *Students:* 26 full-time (18 women), 22 part-time (17 women); includes 41 minority (all Black or African American, non-Hispanic/Latino), 1 international. Average age 33. 25 applicants, 100% accepted, 19 enrolled. In 2017, 6 master's awarded. *Degree requirements:* For master's, thesis optional, departmental qualifying exam. *Entrance requirements:* For master's, GRE General Test, NTE, interview, teaching certificate. *Application deadline:* For fall admission, 6/15 priority date for domestic students, 6/15 for international students; for spring admission, 11/1 for domestic and international students. Application fee: $25. Electronic applications accepted. *Expenses:* Tuition, state resident: full-time $9388; part-time $607 per credit hour. Tuition, nonresident: full-time $19,968; part-time $1194 per credit hour. *Required fees:* $766; $766 per credit hour. *Financial support:* Fellowships, career-related internships or fieldwork, Federal Work-Study, and scholarships/grants available. Financial award application deadline: 6/1. *Unit head:* Dr. Charlie Spell, Interim Chair, Department of Education, 803-536-8963, Fax: 803-516-4568, E-mail: cspell@scsu.edu. *Application contact:* Curtis Foskey, Coordinator of Graduate Studies, 803-536-8419, Fax: 803-536-8812, E-mail: cfoskey@scsu.edu.

Spalding University, Graduate Studies, College of Education, Programs in Education, Louisville, KY 40203-2188. Offers art teacher education (MAT); business teacher education (MAT); elementary school education (MAT); foreign language (MAT); high school education (MAT); middle school education (MAT); secondary education (MAT); special education (learning and behavioral disorders) (MAT); student guidance counselor (MA); teacher leader (M Ed). *Accreditation:* NCATE. *Program availability:* Part-time, evening/weekend. *Entrance requirements:* For master's, GRE General Test or MAT, interview, letters of recommendation, resume. Additional exam requirements/ recommendations for international students: Required—TOEFL (minimum score 535 paper-based). Electronic applications accepted. *Faculty research:* Instructional technology, achievement gap, classroom management, assessment.

State University of New York at Oswego, Graduate Studies, School of Education, Department of Vocational Teacher Preparation, Oswego, NY 13126. Offers agriculture (MS Ed); business and marketing (MS Ed); family and consumer sciences (MS Ed); health careers (MS Ed); technical education (MS Ed); trade education (MS Ed). *Accreditation:* NCATE. *Program availability:* Part-time, evening/weekend. *Degree requirements:* For master's, comprehensive exam, thesis or alternative. *Entrance requirements:* Additional exam requirements/recommendations for international students: Required—TOEFL (minimum score 560 paper-based).

Temple University, College of Education, Department of Teaching and Learning, Philadelphia, PA 19122-6096. Offers career and technical education (Ed M), including business, computing, and information technology, industrial education, marketing education; middle grades education (Ed M), including math and language arts, math and science, science and language arts; secondary education (Ed M), including English, math, social studies; teaching English to speakers of other languages (MS Ed); urban education (Ed M). *Program availability:* Part-time, evening/weekend. *Students:* 218 full-time (144 women), 296 part-time (183 women); includes 128 minority (74 Black or African American, non-Hispanic/Latino; 18 Asian, non-Hispanic/Latino; 25 Hispanic/ Latino; 11 Two or more races, non-Hispanic/Latino), 13 international. 254 applicants, 54% accepted, 102 enrolled. In 2017, 128 master's awarded. Terminal master's awarded for partial completion of doctoral program. *Degree requirements:* For master's, thesis or alternative. *Entrance requirements:* Additional exam requirements/ recommendations for international students: Required—TOEFL (minimum score 550 paper-based; 79 iBT). *Application deadline:* For fall admission, 4/1 for domestic students, 12/15 for international students; for spring admission, 10/1 for domestic students, 8/1 for international students. Application fee: $60. Electronic applications accepted. *Expenses:* Contact institution. *Financial support:* Fellowships, research assistantships, and teaching assistantships available. Financial award application deadline: 1/15; financial award applicants required to submit FAFSA. *Faculty research:* Workforce development, vocational education, technical education, industrial education, professional development, literacy, classroom management, school communities, curriculum development, instruction, applied linguistics, cross linguistic influence, bilingual education, oral proficiency, multilingualism. *Unit head:* Dr. Christine Woyshner, Chairperson, 215-204-6387, E-mail: christine.woyshner@temple.edu. *Application contact:* Sarah Stapleton, Assistant Director, Academic Operations, 215-204-8220, E-mail: sarah.stapleton@temple.edu. Website: http://education.temple.edu/tl

Thomas College, Graduate School, Programs in Business, Waterville, ME 04901-5097. Offers business (MBA); computer technology education (MS); education (MS); human resource management (MBA). *Program availability:* Part-time, evening/weekend. *Entrance requirements:* For master's, GMAT, GRE, MAT or minimum GPA of 3.3 in first 3 graduate-level courses. Additional exam requirements/recommendations for international students: Recommended—TOEFL.

University of Delaware, Alfred Lerner College of Business and Economics, Department of Economics, Newark, DE 19716. Offers economic education (PhD); economics (MA, MS, PhD); economics for entrepreneurship and educators (MA); MA/MBA. *Program availability:* Part-time. *Degree requirements:* For master's, comprehensive exam, thesis (for some programs), mathematics review exam, research project; for doctorate, comprehensive exam, thesis/dissertation, field exam. *Entrance requirements:* For master's, GMAT or GRE General Test, minimum GPA of 2.5; for doctorate, GRE General Test, minimum GPA of 3.5 in graduate economics course work. Additional exam requirements/recommendations for international students: Required—TOEFL (minimum score 550 paper-based). Electronic applications accepted. *Faculty research:* Applied quantitative economics, industrial organization, resource economics, monetary economics, labor economics.

University of Georgia, College of Education, Department of Career and Information Studies, Athens, GA 30602. Offers learning, design, and technology (M Ed, PhD, Ed S), including instructional design and development (M Ed, Ed S); workforce education (MAT, Ed D), including business education (M Ed, Ed S). *Accreditation:* NCATE. *Entrance requirements:* For master's, GRE General Test, MAT; for doctorate, GRE General Test; for Ed S, GRE General Test or MAT. Electronic applications accepted.

University of Missouri, Office of Research and Graduate Studies, College of Education, Department of Learning, Teaching and Curriculum, Columbia, MO 65211. Offers agricultural education (M Ed, PhD, Ed S); art education (M Ed, PhD, Ed S); business and office education (M Ed, PhD, Ed S); early childhood education (M Ed, PhD, Ed S); elementary education (M Ed, PhD, Ed S); English education (M Ed, PhD, Ed S); foreign language education (M Ed, PhD, Ed S); health education and promotion (M Ed, PhD); learning and instruction (M Ed); marketing education (M Ed, PhD, Ed S); mathematics education (M Ed, PhD, Ed S); music education (M Ed, PhD, Ed S); reading education (M Ed, PhD, Ed S); science education (M Ed, PhD, Ed S); social studies

Business Education

education (M Ed, PhD, Ed S); vocational education (M Ed, PhD, Ed S). *Program availability:* Part-time. Terminal master's awarded for partial completion of doctoral program. *Degree requirements:* For doctorate, thesis/dissertation. *Entrance requirements:* For master's and Ed S, GRE General Test or MAT, minimum GPA of 3.0; for doctorate, GRE General Test, minimum GPA of 3.0. Additional exam requirements/recommendations for international students: Required—TOEFL (minimum score 600 paper-based; 100 iBT). Electronic applications accepted.

The University of North Carolina at Charlotte, College of Computing and Informatics, Program in Computing and Information Systems, Charlotte, NC 28223-0001. Offers computing and information systems (PhD), including bioinformatics, business information systems and operations management, computer science, interdisciplinary, software and information systems. *Faculty:* 2 full-time (0 women). *Students:* 103 full-time (33 women), 17 part-time (3 women); includes 6 minority (1 Black or African American, non-Hispanic/Latino; 3 Asian, non-Hispanic/Latino; 1 Hispanic/Latino; 1 Two or more races, non-Hispanic/Latino), 90 international. Average age 30. 86 applicants, 48% accepted, 23 enrolled. In 2017, 15 doctorates awarded. *Degree requirements:* For doctorate, comprehensive exam, thesis/dissertation. *Entrance requirements:* For doctorate, GRE or GMAT, baccalaureate degree, minimum GPA of 3.0 on courses related to the chosen field of PhD study, essay, reference letters. Additional exam requirements/recommendations for international students: Required—TOEFL (minimum score 523 paper-based, 70 iBT) or IELTS (6.5). *Application deadline:* For fall admission, 2/1 for domestic and international students; for spring admission, 9/1 for domestic and international students. Applications are processed on a rolling basis. Application fee: $75. Electronic applications accepted. *Expenses:* Tuition, state resident: full-time $4337. Tuition, nonresident: full-time $17,771. *Required fees:* $3211. Tuition and fees vary according to course load and program. *Financial support:* Career-related internships or fieldwork, institutionally sponsored loans, scholarships/grants, health care benefits, and unspecified assistantships available. Support available to part-time students. Financial award applicants required to submit FAFSA. *Unit head:* Dr. Fatma Mili, Dean. *Application contact:* Kathy B. Giddings, Director of Graduate Admissions, 704-687-5503, Fax: 704-687-1668, E-mail: gradadm@uncc.edu.

University of South Carolina, The Graduate School, College of Education, Department of Instruction and Teacher Education, Program in Secondary Education, Columbia, SC 29208. Offers art education (IMA, MAT); business education (IMA, MAT); English (MAT); foreign language (MAT); health education (MAT); mathematics (MAT); science (IMA, MAT); secondary (Ed D); secondary education (MT, PhD); social studies (MAT); theatre and speech (MAT). IMA and MT offered jointly with the subject areas. *Accreditation:* NCATE. *Degree requirements:* For master's, comprehensive exam, thesis (for some programs), foreign language (MA); for doctorate, one foreign language, comprehensive exam, thesis/dissertation. *Entrance requirements:* For master's, GRE General Test or MAT, teaching certificate (IMA, M Ed), interview; for doctorate, GRE General Test or MAT, interview. *Faculty research:* Middle school programs, professional development, school collaboration.

University of the Cumberlands, Graduate Programs in Education, Williamsburg, KY 40769-1372. Offers all grades (P-12) (M Ed); business and marketing (MA Ed, MAT); counselor education and supervision (Ed D); director of pupil personnel (Certificate); director of special education (Certificate); educational administration and supervision (Ed S); educational leadership (Ed D); elementary education (MA Ed, MAT); instructional leadership - principalship (MA Ed); instructional leadership - school principal (Certificate); middle school education (MA Ed, MAT); reading and writing (MA Ed); school counseling (MA Ed); school superintendent (Certificate); secondary education (MA Ed, MAT); special education (MAT); supervisor of instruction (Certificate); teacher leader (MA Ed). *Program availability:* Part-time, evening/weekend, online learning. *Degree requirements:* For master's, comprehensive exam. Electronic applications accepted.

The University of Toledo, College of Graduate Studies, Judith Herb College of Education, Department of Curriculum and Instruction, Toledo, OH 43606-3390. Offers art education (ME); career and technical education (ME, Ed S); curriculum and instruction (ME, PhD, Ed S); early childhood education (Ed S); education and anthropology (MAE); education and biology (MES); education and chemistry (MES); education and classics (MAE); education and economics (MAE); education and English (MAE); education and French (MAE); education and geology (MES); education and German (MAE); education and history (MAE); education and mathematics (MAE, MES); education and physics (MES); education and political science (MAE); education and sociology (MAE); education and Spanish (MAE); educational media (PhD); educational technology (ME); educational technology: virtual educator (Certificate); elementary education (PhD); English as a second language (MAE); gifted and talented education (PhD); middle childhood education (ME); secondary education (ME, PhD); special education (PhD). *Accreditation:* NCATE. *Program availability:* Part-time, evening/weekend. *Degree requirements:* For master's, comprehensive exam, thesis or alternative; for doctorate, comprehensive exam, thesis/dissertation; for other advanced degree, thesis optional. *Entrance requirements:* For master's, doctorate, and other advanced degree, minimum cumulative GPA of 2.7 for all previous academic work, letters of recommendation. Additional exam requirements/recommendations for international students: Required—TOEFL (minimum score 550 paper-based; 80 iBT). Electronic applications accepted.

University of West Georgia, College of Education, Carrollton, GA 30118. Offers business education (M Ed); early childhood education (M Ed, Ed S); educational leadership (M Ed, Ed S); media (M Ed, Ed S); professional counseling (M Ed, Ed S); professional counseling and supervision (Ed D); reading instruction (M Ed); school improvement (Ed D); secondary education (M Ed); special education (M Ed, Ed S), including teaching (M Ed); speech language pathology (M Ed); teaching (MAT). *Accreditation:* NCATE. *Program availability:* Part-time, evening/weekend, 100% online, blended/hybrid learning. *Faculty:* 45 full-time (28 women). *Students:* 344 full-time (286 women), 1,243 part-time (1,039 women); includes 538 minority (456 Black or African American, non-Hispanic/Latino; 19 Asian, non-Hispanic/Latino; 46 Hispanic/Latino; 1 Native Hawaiian or other Pacific Islander, non-Hispanic/Latino; 16 Two or more races,

non-Hispanic/Latino), 7 international. Average age 36. 685 applicants, 78% accepted, 429 enrolled. In 2017, 299 master's, 30 doctorates, 218 other advanced degrees awarded. *Entrance requirements:* Additional exam requirements/recommendations for international students: Required—TOEFL (minimum score 523 paper-based; 69 iBT); Recommended—IELTS (minimum score 6.5). *Application deadline:* For fall admission, 7/21 for domestic students, 6/1 for international students; for spring admission, 11/30 for domestic students, 10/15 for international students; for summer admission, 4/15 for domestic students, 3/30 for international students. Applications are processed on a rolling basis. Application fee: $40. Electronic applications accepted. Tuition and fees vary according to degree level and program. *Financial support:* Fellowships, research assistantships, teaching assistantships, career-related internships or fieldwork, Federal Work-Study, institutionally sponsored loans, scholarships/grants, and unspecified assistantships available. Support available to part-time students. Financial award application deadline: 4/1; financial award applicants required to submit FAFSA. *Unit head:* Dr. Diane Hoff, Dean, College of Education, 678-839-6570, Fax: 678-839-6098, E-mail: dhoff@westga.edu. *Application contact:* Dr. Toby Ziglar, Assistant Dean of the Graduate School, 678-839-1394, Fax: 678-839-1395, E-mail: graduate@westga.edu. Website: http://www.westga.edu/education/

University of Wisconsin–Whitewater, School of Graduate Studies, College of Business and Economics, Program in Business and Marketing Education, Whitewater, WI 53190-1790. Offers MS. *Accreditation:* NCATE. *Program availability:* Part-time, evening/weekend, online learning. *Degree requirements:* For master's, thesis or alternative. *Entrance requirements:* For master's, interview, teaching license. Additional exam requirements/recommendations for international students: Required—TOEFL (minimum score 550 paper-based; 80 iBT), IELTS (minimum score 6). Electronic applications accepted.

Utah State University, School of Graduate Studies, Emma Eccles Jones College of Education and Human Services, Doctoral Program in Education, Logan, UT 84322. Offers business information systems (Ed D, PhD); curriculum and instruction (Ed D, PhD); research and evaluation (PhD). *Degree requirements:* For doctorate, comprehensive exam, thesis/dissertation. *Entrance requirements:* For doctorate, GRE General Test, minimum GPA of 3.0, master's degree. Additional exam requirements/recommendations for international students: Required—TOEFL. Electronic applications accepted. *Faculty research:* Language and literacy development, math and science education, instructional technology, hearing problems/deafness, domestic violence and animal abuse.

Washington State University, College of Education, Department of Educational Leadership, Sports Studies, and Educational/Counseling Psychology, Pullman, WA 99164-2136. Offers counseling psychology (PhD); educational leadership (Ed M, MA, Ed D, PhD); educational psychology (MA, PhD); sport management (MA). Programs also offered at the Spokane, Tri-Cities, Vancouver and Global (online) campuses. *Program availability:* Part-time, online learning. *Degree requirements:* For master's, comprehensive exam (for some programs), thesis (for some programs), oral or written exam; for doctorate, comprehensive exam, thesis/dissertation, oral and written exam, internship. *Entrance requirements:* For master's and doctorate, GRE General Test, minimum GPA of 3.0, 3 letters of recommendation, transcripts showing all college or university course work, statement of professional objectives, current curriculum vitae/resume. Additional exam requirements/recommendations for international students: Required—TOEFL (minimum score 550 paper-based; 80 iBT). Electronic applications accepted. *Faculty research:* Multicultural counseling and career development, educational and psychological measurement issues, business decision-making process and power relationships, leadership practices and processes as suffused with and constituted by emotion work.

Wayne State College, School of Education and Counseling, Department of Educational Foundations and Leadership, Program in Curriculum and Instruction, Wayne, NE 68787. Offers alternative education (MSE); business and information technology education (MSE); communication arts education (MSE); early childhood education (MSE); elementary education (MSE); English as a second language (MSE); English education (MSE); family and consumer sciences education (MSE); industrial technology and vocational education (MSE); learning communities (MSE); mathematics education (MSE); music education (MSE); science education (MSE); social science education (MSE). *Accreditation:* NCATE. *Program availability:* Part-time, evening/weekend. *Degree requirements:* For master's, comprehensive exam, thesis optional. *Entrance requirements:* For master's, GRE General Test. Additional exam requirements/recommendations for international students: Required—TOEFL (minimum score 550 paper-based).

West Chester University of Pennsylvania, College of Business and Public Management, School of Business, West Chester, PA 19383. Offers business analytics (Certificate); business education (MBA). *Accreditation:* AACSB. *Program availability:* Part-time, evening/weekend, online only, 100% online. *Students:* 41 full-time (17 women), 388 part-time (150 women); includes 69 minority (33 Black or African American, non-Hispanic/Latino; 19 Asian, non-Hispanic/Latino; 14 Hispanic/Latino; 3 Two or more races, non-Hispanic/Latino). Average age 32. 268 applicants, 68% accepted, 153 enrolled. In 2017, 78 master's, 21 other advanced degrees awarded. *Degree requirements:* For master's, minimum GPA of 3.0. *Entrance requirements:* For master's, GMAT or GRE, statement of professional goals, resume, three letters of recommendation, transcripts. Additional exam requirements/recommendations for international students: Required—TOEFL or IELTS. *Application deadline:* For fall admission, 5/15 for international students; for spring admission, 10/15 for international students. Applications are processed on a rolling basis. Application fee: $50. Electronic applications accepted. *Expenses:* Tuition, state resident: full-time $9000; part-time $500 per credit. Tuition, nonresident: full-time $13,500; part-time $750 per credit. *Required fees:* $2959; $149.79 per credit. *Financial support:* Scholarships/grants and unspecified assistantships available. Financial award application deadline: 2/15; financial award applicants required to submit FAFSA. *Unit head:* Dr. Brian Halsey, MBA Director/Graduate Coordinator, 610-425-5000 Ext. 4444, E-mail: mba@wcupa.edu. *Application contact:* Office of Graduate Studies and Extended Education, 610-436-2943, Fax: 610-436-2763, E-mail: gradstudy@wcupa.edu.
Website: http://www.wcupa.edu/mba

Computer Education

Arcadia University, School of Education, Glenside, PA 19038-3295. Offers art education (M Ed); computer education (CAS); curriculum (CAS); curriculum studies (M Ed); early childhood education (M Ed), including individualized, master teacher, research in child development; educational leadership (M Ed, Ed D, CAS); elementary education (M Ed); English education (MA Ed); environmental education (MA Ed); instructional technology (M Ed); language arts (M Ed); library science (M Ed);

mathematics education (M Ed, MA Ed); music education (MA Ed); psychology (MA Ed); reading (M Ed, CAS); science education (M Ed, CAS); secondary education (M Ed, CAS); special education (M Ed, Ed D, CAS); theater arts (MA Ed); written communication (MA Ed). *Accreditation:* NASAD. *Program availability:* Part-time, evening/weekend, online learning. Electronic applications accepted. *Expenses:* Contact institution.

Ball State University, Graduate School, Teachers College, Department of Educational Studies, Muncie, IN 47306. Offers adult education (MA, Ed D, Certificate), including adult and community education (MA), adult, higher and community education (Ed D); college and university teaching (Certificate); community college leadership (Certificate); community education (Certificate); computer education (Certificate); curriculum and educational technology (MA); diversity studies (Certificate); educational studies (PhD), including educational studies; executive development for public service (MA); middle-level education (Certificate); qualitative research in education (Certificate); secondary education (MA); student affairs administration in higher education (MA), including student affairs administration in higher education. *Accreditation:* NCATE. *Program availability:* Part-time, 100% online, blended/hybrid learning. *Faculty:* 17 full-time (13 women), 8 part-time/adjunct (6 women). *Students:* 94 full-time (60 women), 221 part-time (167 women); includes 62 minority (42 Black or African American, non-Hispanic/Latino; 2 Asian, non-Hispanic/Latino; 14 Hispanic/Latino; 4 Two or more races, non-Hispanic/Latino), 6 international. Average age 36. 272 applicants, 46% accepted, 105 enrolled. In 2017, 108 master's, 7 doctorate, 13 other advanced degrees awarded. *Entrance requirements:* For master's, minimum baccalaureate GPA or 2.75 or 3.0 in latter half of baccalaureate; for doctorate, minimum graduate GPA of 3.2. Additional exam requirements/recommendations for international students: Required—TOEFL (minimum score 550 paper-based; 79 iBT), IELTS (minimum score 6.5). *Application deadline:* Applications are processed on a rolling basis. Application fee: $60. Electronic applications accepted. *Financial support:* In 2017–18, 17 students received support, including 14 research assistantships with partial tuition reimbursements available (averaging $10,663 per year), 2 teaching assistantships with partial tuition reimbursements available (averaging $12,000 per year); unspecified assistantships also available. Financial award application deadline: 3/1; financial award applicants required to submit FAFSA. *Unit head:* Dr. Theresa Kruczek, Interim Chair, 765-285-8049, E-mail: tkruczek@bsu.edu.
Website: http://www.bsu.edu/edstudies

Eastern Washington University, Graduate Studies, College of Science, Technology, Engineering and Mathematics, Department of Computer Science, Cheney, WA 99004-2431. Offers computer science (MS). *Program availability:* Part-time. *Faculty:* 6. *Students:* 12 full-time (2 women), 8 part-time (3 women); includes 3 minority (1 American Indian or Alaska Native, non-Hispanic/Latino; 1 Asian, non-Hispanic/Latino; 1 Hispanic/Latino), 2 international. Average age 30. 34 applicants, 35% accepted, 9 enrolled. In 2017, 5 master's awarded. *Degree requirements:* For master's, comprehensive exam, thesis or alternative. *Entrance requirements:* For master's, minimum GPA of 3.0. Additional exam requirements/recommendations for international students: Required—TOEFL (minimum score 580 paper-based; 92 iBT), IELTS (minimum score 7), PTE (minimum score 63). *Application deadline:* For fall admission, 4/1 priority date for domestic students; for spring admission, 1/15 for domestic students. Applications are processed on a rolling basis. Application fee: $75. Electronic applications accepted. *Expenses:* Tuition, state resident: full-time $11,191; part-time $373.06 per credit. Tuition, nonresident: full-time $25,995; part-time $866.52 per credit. *Financial support:* Teaching assistantships with partial tuition reimbursements, career-related internships or fieldwork, Federal Work-Study, institutionally sponsored loans, scholarships/grants, health care benefits, tuition waivers (partial), and unspecified assistantships available. Support available to part-time students. Financial award application deadline: 2/1. *Unit head:* Dr. Carol Taylor, Chair, 509-359-6065, Fax: 509-359-2215, E-mail: ctaylor@ewu.edu.
Website: http://www.ewu.edu/cshe/programs/computer-science.xml

Florida Institute of Technology, College of Science, Program in Computer Education, Melbourne, FL 32901-6975. Offers MS. *Program availability:* Part-time. *Students:* Average age 27. 14 applicants, 43% accepted, 1 enrolled. In 2017, 3 master's awarded. *Entrance requirements:* For master's, 3 letters of recommendation, statement of objectives, resume. Additional exam requirements/recommendations for international students: Required—TOEFL (minimum score 550 paper-based; 79 iBT). *Application deadline:* Applications are processed on a rolling basis. Electronic applications accepted. *Expenses:* Tuition: Part-time $1241 per credit hour. Part-time tuition and fees vary according to campus/location. *Financial support:* Applicants required to submit FAFSA. *Unit head:* Dr. Hamed Kastro, Department Head, 321-674-7206, E-mail: khamed@fit.edu. *Application contact:* Cheryl A. Brown, Associate Director of Graduate Admissions, 321-674-7581, Fax: 321-723-9468, E-mail: cbrown@fit.edu.
Website: http://admission.fit.edu/graduate/documents/doc_mgr/214/computer_education.pdf

Illinois Institute of Technology, Graduate College, College of Science, Department of Computer Science, Chicago, IL 60616. Offers business (MCS); computational intelligence (MCS); computer science (MCS, MS, PhD); cyber-physical systems (MCS); data analytics (MCS); data science (MAS); database systems (MCS); distributed and cloud computing (MCS); education (MCS); finance (MCS); information security and assurance (MCS); networking and communications (MCS); software engineering (MCS); telecommunications and software engineering (MAS); MS/MAS. *Program availability:* Part-time, evening/weekend, online learning. Terminal master's awarded for partial completion of doctoral program. *Degree requirements:* For master's, thesis optional; for doctorate, comprehensive exam, thesis/dissertation. *Entrance requirements:* For master's, GRE General Test with minimum scores of 298 Quantitative and Verbal, 3.0 Analytical Writing (for MS); GRE General Test with minimum scores of 292 Quantitative and Verbal, 2.5 Analytical Writing (for MAS), minimum undergraduate GPA of 3.0; for doctorate, GRE General Test (minimum scores: 304 Quantitative and Verbal, 3.5 Analytical Writing), minimum undergraduate GPA of 3.0. Additional exam requirements/recommendations for international students: Required—TOEFL (minimum score 523 paper-based; 70 iBT). Electronic applications accepted. *Faculty research:* Parallel and distributed processing, high-performance computing, computational linguistics, information retrieval, data mining, grid computing.

Kent State University, College of Education, Health and Human Services, School of Lifespan Development and Educational Sciences, Program in Instructional Technology, Kent, OH 44242-0001. Offers computer technology (M Ed); educational psychology (PhD), including instructional technology; general instructional technology (M Ed). *Accreditation:* NCATE. *Degree requirements:* For master's, thesis (for some programs). *Entrance requirements:* For master's, 2 letters of reference, goals statement, minimum GPA of 2.75. Additional exam requirements/recommendations for international students: Required—TOEFL (minimum score 550 paper-based; 80 iBT). *Expenses:* Tuition, state resident: full-time $11,310; part-time $515 per credit hour. Tuition, nonresident: full-time $20,396; part-time $928 per credit hour. *International tuition:* $18,544 full-time. *Faculty research:* Cooperative learning, aesthetics, computers in schools.

Lesley University, Graduate School of Education, Cambridge, MA 02138-2790. Offers arts, community, and education (M Ed); autism studies (Certificate); curriculum and instruction (M Ed, CAGS); early childhood education (M Ed); ecological teaching and learning (MS); educational studies (PhD), including adult learning, educational leadership, individually designed; elementary education (M Ed); emergent technologies for educators (Certificate); ESLArts: language learning through the arts (M Ed); high school education (M Ed); individually designed (M Ed); integrated teaching through the arts (M Ed); literacy for K-8 classroom teachers (M Ed); mathematics education (M Ed);

middle school education (M Ed); moderate disabilities (M Ed); online learning (Certificate); reading (CAGS); science in education (M Ed); severe disabilities (M Ed); special needs (CAGS); specialist teacher of reading (M Ed); teacher of visual art (M Ed); technology in education (M Ed, CAGS). *Accreditation:* TEAC. *Program availability:* Part-time, evening/weekend, online learning. *Degree requirements:* For master's, practicum; for doctorate, thesis/dissertation. *Entrance requirements:* For master's, Massachusetts Tests for Educator Licensure (MTEL), transcripts, statement of purpose, recommendations; interview (for special education); for doctorate, GRE General Test, transcripts, statement of purpose, recommendations, interview, master's degree, resume; for other advanced degree, interview, master's degree. Additional exam requirements/recommendations for international students: Required—TOEFL (minimum score 550 paper-based; 80 iBT). Electronic applications accepted. *Faculty research:* Assessment in literacy, mathematics and science; autism spectrum disorders; instructional technology and online learning; multicultural education and English language learners.

Mississippi College, Graduate School, School of Education, Department of Teacher Education and Leadership, Clinton, MS 39058. Offers art (M Ed); biological science (M Ed); business education (M Ed); computer science (M Ed); dyslexia therapy (M Ed); educational leadership (M Ed, Ed D, Ed S); elementary education (M Ed, Ed S); English (M Ed); higher education administration (MS); mathematics (M Ed); secondary education (M Ed); social studies (history) (M Ed); teaching arts (M Ed). *Program availability:* Part-time, online learning. *Degree requirements:* For master's, comprehensive exam, thesis optional. *Entrance requirements:* For master's, NTE. Additional exam requirements/recommendations for international students: Recommended—TOEFL, IELTS. Electronic applications accepted.

Ohio University, Graduate College, Gladys W. and David H. Patton College of Education and Human Services, Department of Educational Studies, Athens, OH 45701-2979. Offers computer education and technology (M Ed); educational administration (M Ed, Ed D); educational research and evaluation (M Ed, PhD); instructional technology (PhD). *Program availability:* Part-time, evening/weekend, online learning. *Degree requirements:* For master's, thesis or alternative; for doctorate, comprehensive exam, thesis/dissertation. *Entrance requirements:* For master's, GRE General Test (if GPA less than 2.9); for doctorate, GRE General Test, GRE Subject Test, minimum GPA of 2.9, work experience, 3 letters of reference, autobiography. Additional exam requirements/recommendations for international students: Required—TOEFL (minimum score 550 paper-based; 80 iBT) or IELTS (minimum score 6.5). Electronic applications accepted. *Faculty research:* Race, class and gender; computer programs; development and organization theory; evaluation/development of instruments, leadership.

Stony Brook University, State University of New York, Graduate School, College of Engineering and Applied Sciences, Department of Technology and Society, Program in Educational Technology, Stony Brook, NY 11794. Offers MS. *Accreditation:* NCATE. *Entrance requirements:* For master's, GRE, minimum GPA of 3.0, statement of purpose. Additional exam requirements/recommendations for international students: Required—TOEFL (minimum score 85 iBT), IELTS (minimum score 6.5). *Application deadline:* For fall admission, 8/2 for domestic students, 4/15 for international students; for spring admission, 12/1 for domestic students, 10/5 for international students. Application fee: $100. Electronic applications accepted. *Expenses:* Contact institution. *Financial support:* Research assistantships and teaching assistantships available. *Unit head:* Dr. Wolf Schäfer, Interim Department Chair, 631-632-7924, E-mail: wolf.schafer@stonybrook.edu. *Application contact:* Marypat Taveras, Coordinator, 631-632-8762, Fax: 631-632-7809, E-mail: marypat.taveras@stonybrook.edu.
Website: https://www.stonybrook.edu/commcms/est/masters/msedtech

Teachers College, Columbia University, Department of Mathematics, Science and Technology, New York, NY 10027-6696. Offers biology 7-12 (MA); chemistry 7-12 (MA); communication and education (MA, Ed D); computing in education (MA); earth science 7-12 (MA); instructional technology and media (Ed M, MA, Ed D); mathematics education (Ed M, MA, Ed D, Ed DCT, PhD); physics 7-12 (MA); science and dental education (MA); science education (Ed M, MS, Ed DCT, PhD); supervisor/teacher of science education (MA); technology specialist (MA). *Program availability:* Part-time, evening/weekend, online learning. *Students:* 187 full-time (129 women), 228 part-time (153 women); includes 143 minority (42 Black or African American, non-Hispanic/Latino; 64 Asian, non-Hispanic/Latino; 25 Hispanic/Latino; 12 Two or more races, non-Hispanic/Latino), 125 international. Average age 32. 484 applicants, 59% accepted, 141 enrolled. Terminal master's awarded for partial completion of doctoral program. *Degree requirements:* For doctorate, thesis/dissertation. *Unit head:* Prof. Erica Walker, Chair, E-mail: ewalker@tc.columbia.edu. *Application contact:* David Estrella, Director of Admission, 212-678-3305, E-mail: estrella@tc.columbia.edu.
Website: http://www.tc.columbia.edu/mathematics-science-and-technology/

Thomas College, Graduate School, Programs in Business, Waterville, ME 04901-5097. Offers business (MBA); computer technology education (MS); education (MS); human resource management (MBA). *Program availability:* Part-time, evening/weekend. *Entrance requirements:* For master's, GMAT, GRE, MAT or minimum GPA of 3.3 in first 3 graduate-level courses. Additional exam requirements/recommendations for international students: Recommended—TOEFL.

University of Bridgeport, School of Education, Department of Education, Bridgeport, CT 06604. Offers education (MS); educational management (Ed D, Diploma), including intermediate administrator or supervisor (Diploma), leadership (Ed D); elementary education (MS, Diploma), including early childhood education, elementary education; middle school education (MS); music education (MS); remedial reading and language arts (Diploma); secondary education (MS, Diploma), including computer specialist (Diploma), international education (Diploma), reading specialist, secondary education. *Program availability:* Part-time, evening/weekend. *Degree requirements:* For master's, final exam, final project, or thesis; for doctorate, comprehensive exam, thesis/dissertation; for Diploma, thesis or alternative, final project. *Entrance requirements:* For master's, minimum undergraduate QPA of 2.67; for doctorate, GRE, MAT; for Diploma, GRE General Test or MAT, minimum graduate QPA of 3.0. Additional exam requirements/recommendations for international students: Recommended—TOEFL (minimum score 550 paper-based; 80 iBT), IELTS (minimum score 6.5). Electronic applications accepted. *Expenses:* Contact institution.

University of Illinois at Chicago, Program in Learning Sciences, Chicago, IL 60607-7128. Offers PhD.

University of Phoenix–Central Valley Campus, College of Education, Fresno, CA 93720-1552. Offers curriculum and instruction (MA Ed); curriculum and instruction-computer education (MA Ed); elementary teacher education (MA Ed); secondary teacher education (MA Ed).

University of Phoenix–Online Campus, College of Education, Phoenix, AZ 85034-7209. Offers administration and supervision (MAEd, Certificate); adult education and training (MAEd); curriculum and instruction (MAEd), including computer education, curriculum and instruction, English as a second language, language arts, mathematics, reading; early childhood education (MAEd); educational studies (MAEd); elementary teacher education (MAEd), including early childhood, elementary teacher education, high school middle level, middle level; principal licensure (Certificate); secondary teacher education (MAEd); special education (MAEd, Certificate); teacher education (MAEd), including middle level generalist; teacher education middle level mathematics (MAEd), including middle level mathematics; teacher education middle level science (MAEd), including middle level science; teacher education secondary mathematics (MAEd); teacher education secondary science (MAEd); teacher leadership (MAEd); teachers of English learners (Certificate); transition to teaching (Certificate), including elementary education, secondary education. *Program availability:* Evening/weekend, online learning. *Entrance requirements:* Additional exam requirements/ recommendations for international students: Required—TOEFL, TOEIC (Test of English

as an International Communication), Berlitz Online English Proficiency Exam, PTE, or IELTS. Electronic applications accepted. *Expenses:* Contact institution.

University of Phoenix–San Diego Campus, College of Education, San Diego, CA 92123. Offers curriculum and instruction (MA Ed), including computer education, curriculum and instruction, English as a second language; elementary teacher education (MA Ed); secondary teacher education (MA Ed). *Program availability:* Evening/weekend. *Degree requirements:* For master's, thesis (for some programs). *Entrance requirements:* For master's, 3 years of work experience, minimum undergraduate GPA of 3.0. Additional exam requirements/recommendations for international students: Required— TOEFL (minimum score 550 paper-based; 79 iBT). Electronic applications accepted.

Counselor Education

Acadia University, Faculty of Professional Studies, School of Education, Program in Counseling, Wolfville, NS B4P 2R6, Canada. Offers M Ed. *Program availability:* Part-time. *Entrance requirements:* For master's, B Ed, minimum B average in undergraduate course work, 2 years of teaching or related experience. Additional exam requirements/ recommendations for international students: Required—TOEFL (minimum score 580 paper-based; 93 iBT), IELTS (minimum score 6.5). *Application deadline:* For fall and spring admission, 2/1 priority date for domestic and international students. Application fee: $50. *Financial support:* Application deadline: 2/1. *Faculty research:* Computer-assisted supervision, rural/remote school counseling, non-custodial fathers, spirituality, counseling relationships. *Unit head:* Dr. Ann Vibert, Director, 902-585-1229, E-mail: ann.vibert@acadiau.ca. *Application contact:* Rosie Hare, Administrative Assistant, 902-585-1597, Fax: 902-585-1086, E-mail: rosie.hare@acadiau.ca.
Website: http://education.acadiau.ca/

Adams State University, Office of Graduate Studies, Department of Counselor Education, Alamosa, CO 81101. Offers counselor education (MA), including clinical mental health counseling, school counseling; counselor education and supervision (PhD). *Accreditation:* ACA (one or more programs are accredited). *Program availability:* Part-time. *Degree requirements:* For master's, internship, qualifying exam. *Entrance requirements:* For master's, GRE General Test or MAT, minimum undergraduate GPA of 2.75. *Application deadline:* For fall admission, 5/15 priority date for domestic students; for spring admission, 10/15 for domestic students. Applications are processed on a rolling basis. Application fee: $30. *Expenses:* Tuition, state resident: full-time $4800; part-time $2400 per credit. Tuition, nonresident: full-time $7100; part-time $3550 per credit. *Required fees:* $213; $106 per credit. One-time fee: $100. Tuition and fees vary according to campus/location and program. *Financial support:* In 2017–18, fellowships with partial tuition reimbursements (averaging $4,000 per year), teaching assistantships with partial tuition reimbursements (averaging $4,000 per year) were awarded; career-related internships or fieldwork, Federal Work-Study, institutionally sponsored loans, and unspecified assistantships also available. Support available to part-time students. Financial award application deadline: 4/15; financial award applicants required to submit FAFSA. *Unit head:* Dr. Mark Manzanares, Chair, 719-587-7626, Fax: 719-587-7522, E-mail: ceonline@adams.edu. *Application contact:* Nate Pacheco, Assistant Coordinator, 719-587-8138, Fax: 719-587-7522, E-mail: ceonline@adams.edu.
Website: http://counselored.adams.edu/

Adler Graduate School, Program in Adlerian Counseling and Psychotherapy, Richfield, MN 55423. Offers Adlerian studies (MA); art therapy (MA); clinical mental health counseling (MA); co-occurring substance use and mental health disorders (MA); marriage and family therapy (MA); school counseling (MA). *Program availability:* Part-time, evening/weekend. *Faculty:* 71 part-time/adjunct (55 women). *Students:* 317 part-time (259 women); includes 51 minority (40 Black or African American, non-Hispanic/ Latino; 6 American Indian or Alaska Native, non-Hispanic/Latino; 5 Hispanic/Latino). *Degree requirements:* For master's, thesis or alternative, 500-700 hour internship (depending on license choice). *Entrance requirements:* For master's, interview, official transcripts, minimum cumulative GPA of 3.0. *Application deadline:* Applications are processed on a rolling basis. Application fee: $50. Electronic applications accepted. *Expenses:* $575 per credit tuition. *Financial support:* Career-related internships or fieldwork and tuition waivers available. Support available to part-time students. Financial award applicants required to submit FAFSA. *Unit head:* Dr. Jeffrey Allen, President, 612-767-7048, Fax: 612-861-7559, E-mail: jeffrey.allen@alfredadler.edu. *Application contact:* Christina Hilpipre-Frischman, Director of Admissions, 612-767-7055, Fax: 612-861-7559, E-mail: christina@alfredadler.edu.
Website: http://alfredadler.edu/programs/masters-level-programs

Adler University, Graduate Programs, PhD in Counselor Education and Supervision Program, Chicago, IL 60602. Offers PhD. *Program availability:* Evening/weekend, online learning.

Alabama Agricultural and Mechanical University, School of Graduate Studies, College of Education, Humanities, and Behavioral Sciences, Department of Social Work, Psychology and Counseling, Huntsville, AL 35811. Offers psychology and counseling (MS, Ed S), including clinical psychology (MS), counseling psychology (MS), guidance and counseling, rehabilitation counseling (MS), school counseling (MS), school psychology (MS), school psychometry (MS); social work (MSW). *Accreditation:* CORE; NCATE. *Program availability:* Part-time, evening/weekend. *Degree requirements:* For master's, comprehensive exam. *Entrance requirements:* For master's, GRE General Test. Additional exam requirements/recommendations for international students: Required—TOEFL (minimum score 500 paper-based; 61 iBT). *Faculty research:* Increasing numbers of minorities in special education and speech-language pathology.

Alabama State University, College of Education, Department of Instructional Support Programs, Montgomery, AL 36101-0271. Offers applied technology (MS); counselor education (M Ed, MS, Ed S), including general counseling (MS, Ed S), school counseling (M Ed, Ed S); educational administration (M Ed, Ed D, PhD, Ed S), including educational administration (Ed S), educational leadership, policy and law (Ed D, PhD), instructional leadership (M Ed), teacher leadership (Ed S); library education media (M Ed, Ed S). *Program availability:* Part-time. *Faculty:* 11 full-time (6 women), 7 part-time/adjunct (5 women). *Students:* 35 full-time (20 women), 112 part-time (81 women); includes 139 minority (all Black or African American, non-Hispanic/Latino), 1 international. Average age 37. 48 applicants, 75% accepted, 16 enrolled. In 2017, 31 master's, 4 doctorates awarded. Terminal master's awarded for partial completion of doctoral program. *Degree requirements:* For master's, comprehensive exam; for Ed S, comprehensive exam, thesis. *Entrance requirements:* For master's, GRE General Test, MAT, writing competency test, bachelor's degree or its equivalent from accredited college or university with minimum GPA of 2.5; for Ed S, GRE General Test, MAT, writing competency test, minimum GPA of 3.25. Additional exam requirements/

recommendations for international students: Required—TOEFL (minimum score 500 paper-based). *Application deadline:* For fall admission, 4/15 for domestic and international students; for spring admission, 11/15 for domestic and international students; for summer admission, 3/15 for domestic and international students. Applications are processed on a rolling basis. Application fee: $25. Electronic applications accepted. *Expenses:* Contact institution. *Financial support:* In 2017–18, 3 students received support. Research assistantships and unspecified assistantships available. Financial award application deadline: 6/30; financial award applicants required to submit FAFSA. *Unit head:* Dr. Sonja Harrington, Chair, 334-229-8828, Fax: 334-229-6831, E-mail: sharrington@alasu.edu. *Application contact:* Dr. William Person, Dean of Graduate Studies, 334-229-4275, Fax: 334-229-4928, E-mail: wperson@alasu.edu.
Website: http://www.alasu.edu/academics/colleges—departments/college-of-education/instructional-support-programs/index.aspx

Albany State University, College of Education, Albany, GA 31705-2717. Offers early childhood education (M Ed); educational leadership (Ed S); health and physical education (M Ed); middle grades education (M Ed); school counseling (M Ed); special education (M Ed). *Accreditation:* NCATE. *Program availability:* Part-time, evening/ weekend, online learning. *Degree requirements:* For master's, comprehensive exam, internship, GACE Content Exam. *Entrance requirements:* For master's, GRE or MAT. Electronic applications accepted. *Faculty research:* GACE preparation, STEM (science, technology, engineering, and mathematics), technology education, special education, professional teacher development, health implications liberation philosophy, NET-Q, learning community, disabled or at-risk students.

Alcorn State University, School of Graduate Studies, School of Psychology and Education, Lorman, MS 39096-7500. Offers agricultural education (MS Ed); elementary education (MS Ed, Ed S); guidance and counseling (MS Ed); industrial education (MS Ed); secondary education (MS Ed), including health and physical education; special education (MS Ed). *Accreditation:* NCATE. *Degree requirements:* For master's, thesis optional.

Alfred University, Graduate School, Counseling and School Psychology Program, Alfred, NY 14802-1205. Offers mental health counseling (MS Ed); school counseling (MS Ed, CAS); school psychology (MA, Psy D, CAS). *Accreditation:* APA. *Degree requirements:* For master's, internship; for doctorate, thesis/dissertation, internship. *Entrance requirements:* For master's and doctorate, GRE General Test. Additional exam requirements/recommendations for international students: Required—TOEFL (minimum score 590 paper-based; 90 iBT), IELTS (minimum score 6.5). Electronic applications accepted. *Faculty research:* Family processes, alternative assessment approaches, behavior disorders in children, parent involvement, school psychology training issues.

Alliant International University–San Francisco, California School of Professional Psychology, Program in Clinical Counseling, San Francisco, CA 94133. Offers MA. *Degree requirements:* For master's, comprehensive exam, project. *Entrance requirements:* For master's, minimum GPA of 3.0, recommendations, essay, interview. Additional exam requirements/recommendations for international students: Required— TOEFL (minimum score 550 paper-based; 80 iBT), TWE (minimum score 5). Electronic applications accepted. *Faculty research:* Systems of privilege and oppression, multicultural and social justice advocacy competence, rural issues, LGBTQ affirmative therapy and identity development, college student mental health.

Amberton University, Graduate School, Programs in Counseling, Garland, TX 75041-5595. Offers marriage and family therapy (MA); professional counseling (MA); school counseling (MA). *Entrance requirements:* For master's, minimum GPA of 3.0. *Application deadline:* Applications are processed on a rolling basis. Application fee: $0. *Expenses: Tuition:* Part-time $795 per course. *Unit head:* Dr. Don Hebbard, Academic Dean, 972-635-8641 Ext. 157, Fax: 972-279-9773, E-mail: dhebbard@amberton.edu. *Application contact:* Adviser, 972-279-6511 Ext. 180, Fax: 972-279-9773, E-mail: advisor@amberton.edu.

American International College, School of Education, Springfield, MA 01109-3189. Offers early childhood education (M Ed, CAGS); education (MA, Ed D), including counseling psychology (MA), educational leadership and supervision (Ed D), professional counseling and supervision (Ed D), teaching and learning (Ed D); elementary education (M Ed, CAGS); middle education/secondary education (M Ed, CAGS); moderate disabilities (M Ed, CAGS); reading specialist (M Ed, CAGS); school adjustment counseling (MAEP, CAGS); school guidance counseling (MAEP, CAGS); school leadership (M Ed, CAGS). *Program availability:* Evening/weekend. *Faculty:* 1 (woman) full-time, 151 part-time/adjunct (95 women). *Students:* 1,082 full-time (910 women), 143 part-time (113 women); includes 109 minority (19 Black or African American, non-Hispanic/Latino; 2 American Indian or Alaska Native, non-Hispanic/ Latino; 10 Asian, non-Hispanic/Latino; 58 Hispanic/Latino; 1 Native Hawaiian or other Pacific Islander, non-Hispanic/Latino; 19 Two or more races, non-Hispanic/Latino). Average age 34. 537 applicants, 77% accepted, 327 enrolled. In 2017, 486 master's, 112 other advanced degrees awarded. *Degree requirements:* For master's and CAGS, practicum/culminating experience. *Entrance requirements:* For master's, Communication and Literacy portion of the Massachusetts Tests for Education Licensure, graduate of accredited four-year college with minimum B- average in undergraduate course work; for CAGS, M Ed or master's degree in field related to licensure from accredited institution. *Application deadline:* Applications are processed on a rolling basis. Application fee: $50. Electronic applications accepted. *Expenses:* $439 per credit, $30 per term registration fee, $100 graduation fee, $110 technology fee. *Financial support:* Applicants required to submit FAFSA. *Unit head:* Sylvia Mason, Dean, 413-205-1743, Fax: 413-205-3943, E-mail: sylvia.mason@aic.edu. *Application contact:* Kerry Barnes, Dean of Graduate Admissions, 413-205-3703, Fax: 413-205-3051, E-mail: kerry.barnes@aic.edu.
Website: http://www.aic.edu/school-of-education/

Amridge University, Graduate and Professional Programs, Montgomery, AL 36117. Offers Biblical studies (MA, PhD); Christian ministry (MS); family therapy (D Min); human services (MS); leadership and management (MS); marriage and family therapy (M Div, MA, PhD); ministerial leadership (M Div, MS); New Testament studies (MA); Old Testament studies (MA); professional counseling (M Div, MA, PhD); theology (M Div, D Min). *Program availability:* Part-time, evening/weekend, online learning. *Faculty:* 23 full-time (3 women), 9 part-time/adjunct (5 women). *Students:* 105 full-time (55 women), 250 part-time (152 women); includes 217 minority (167 Black or African American, non-Hispanic/Latino; 4 Asian, non-Hispanic/Latino; 42 Hispanic/Latino; 4 Native Hawaiian or other Pacific Islander, non-Hispanic/Latino). Average age 42. 160 applicants, 100% accepted, 110 enrolled. *Degree requirements:* For master's, one foreign language, comprehensive exam (for some programs), thesis (for some programs); for doctorate, one foreign language, comprehensive exam (for some programs), thesis/dissertation (for some programs). *Entrance requirements:* For master's, official transcript showing an earned 4-year BA or BS from regionally- or nationally-accredited institution; for doctorate, official transcript showing earned graduate degree from regionally- or nationally-accredited institution; writing sample (e.g. career monograph, published journal article, term paper from master's degree or doctoral dissertation); interview. Additional exam requirements/recommendations for international students: Required—TOEFL (minimum score 79 iBT). *Application deadline:* Applications are processed on a rolling basis. Application fee: $50. Electronic applications accepted. *Financial support:* In 2017–18, 33 students received support. Federal Work-Study and scholarships/grants available. Support available to part-time students. Financial award applicants required to submit FAFSA. *Faculty research:* Technology and mental healthcare, resilience in black families, theology and congregational ministry. *Unit head:* Laina Costanza, Vice President, Student Affairs, 888-790-8080 Ext. 1, Fax: 334-387-3878, E-mail: cc@amridgeuniversity.edu. *Application contact:* Brooks Housley, Student Affairs Coordinator, 888-790-8080 Ext. 1, Fax: 334-387-3878, E-mail: admissions@amridgeuniversity.edu.

Angelo State University, College of Graduate Studies and Research, College of Education, Department of Curriculum and Instruction, San Angelo, TX 76909. Offers curriculum and instruction (MA); educational administration (M Ed); guidance and counseling (M Ed); student development and leadership in higher education (M Ed). *Program availability:* Part-time, evening/weekend, online learning. *Students:* 405 full-time (332 women), 449 part-time (380 women); includes 291 minority (98 Black or African American, non-Hispanic/Latino; 3 American Indian or Alaska Native, non-Hispanic/Latino; 3 Asian, non-Hispanic/Latino; 178 Hispanic/Latino; 9 Two or more races, non-Hispanic/Latino), 1 international. Average age 35. *Application deadline:* For fall admission, 7/15 priority date for domestic students, 6/10 for international students; for spring admission, 12/1 priority date for domestic students, 11/1 for international students. Application fee: $40 ($50 for international students). *Expenses:* Tuition, state resident: full-time $3856. Tuition, nonresident: full-time $11,324. *Required fees:* $2650. *Unit head:* Dr. Jim Summerlin, Chair, 325-942-2647, Fax: 325-942-2039, E-mail: james.summerlin@angelo.edu. *Application contact:* Lesley Casarez, Graduate Advisor, 325-486-6775, E-mail: lesley.casarez@angelo.edu.
Website: http://www.angelo.edu/dept/ci/

Antioch University Seattle, Program in Counseling, Therapy and Wellness, Seattle, WA 98121. Offers clinical mental health counseling (MA); counselor education and supervision (PhD); couple and family therapy (MA). *Students:* 258 full-time (220 women), 100 part-time (84 women); includes 81 minority (9 Black or African American, non-Hispanic/Latino; 3 American Indian or Alaska Native, non-Hispanic/Latino; 19 Asian, non-Hispanic/Latino; 30 Hispanic/Latino; 20 Two or more races, non-Hispanic/Latino), 1 international. Average age 35. *Unit head:* Peter Rojcewicz, Vice President of Academic Affairs, 206-268-4108, E-mail: projcewicz@antioch.edu. *Application contact:* Eileen Knight, Recruitment and Admissions Director, 206-268-4200, E-mail: psmithmentz@antiochsea.edu.

Appalachian State University, Cratis D. Williams Graduate School, Department of Human Development and Psychological Counseling, Boone, NC 28608. Offers clinical mental health counseling (MA); college student development (MA); marriage and family therapy (MA); school counseling (MA). *Accreditation:* AAMFT/COAMFTE; ACA; NCATE. *Program availability:* Part-time. *Degree requirements:* For master's, comprehensive exam (for some programs), thesis optional, internships. *Entrance requirements:* For master's, GRE General Test, 3 letters of recommendation. Additional exam requirements/recommendations for international students: Required—TOEFL (minimum score 570 paper-based; 79 iBT), IELTS (minimum score 6.5). Electronic applications accepted. *Faculty research:* Multicultural counseling, addictions counseling, play therapy, expressive arts, child and adolescent therapy, sexual abuse counseling.

Argosy University, Atlanta, Georgia School of Professional Psychology, Atlanta, GA 30328. Offers clinical psychology (MA, Psy D, Postdoctoral Respecialization Certificate), including child and family psychology (Psy D), general adult clinical (Psy D), health psychology (Psy D), neuropsychology/geropsychology (Psy D); community counseling (MA), including marriage and family therapy; counselor education and supervision (Ed D); forensic psychology (MA); industrial organizational psychology (MA); marriage and family therapy (Certificate); sport-exercise psychology (MA). *Accreditation:* APA.

Argosy University, Chicago, Illinois School of Professional Psychology, Program in Counseling Psychology, Chicago, IL 60601. Offers counselor education and supervision (Ed D). *Accreditation:* ACA. *Program availability:* Online learning.

Argosy University, Northern Virginia, American School of Professional Psychology, Arlington, VA 22209. Offers clinical psychology (MA, Psy D), including child and family psychology (Psy D), diversity and multicultural psychology (Psy D), forensic psychology (Psy D), health and neuropsychology (Psy D); community counseling (MA); counseling psychology (Ed D), including counselor education and supervision; counselor education and supervision (Ed D); forensic psychology (MA).

Argosy University, Tampa, College of Education, Tampa, FL 33607. Offers community college executive leadership (Ed D); educational leadership (MA Ed, Ed D, Ed S), including higher education administration (Ed D), K-12 education (Ed D); school counseling (MA); teaching and learning (MA Ed, Ed D, Ed S), including higher education (Ed D), K-12 education (Ed D).

Argosy University, Tampa, Florida School of Professional Psychology, Tampa, FL 33607. Offers clinical psychology (MA, Psy D), including clinical psychology; counselor education and supervision (Ed D); industrial organizational psychology (MA); marriage and family therapy (MA); mental health counseling (MA).

Arizona State University at the Tempe campus, School of Letters and Sciences, Program in Counseling, Tempe, AZ 85287-0811. Offers MC. *Accreditation:* ACA. *Degree requirements:* For master's, comprehensive exam (for some programs), thesis (for some programs), interactive Program of Study (iPOS) submitted before completing 50 percent of required credit hours. *Entrance requirements:* For master's, GRE, minimum GPA of 3.0 or equivalent in last 2 years of work leading to bachelor's degree; 3 letters of recommendation; 3-5 page personal statement with information on significant life experiences, professional experiences and goals. Additional exam requirements/recommendations for international students: Required—TOEFL, IELTS, or PTE. Electronic applications accepted.

Arkansas State University, Graduate School, College of Education and Behavioral Science, Department of Psychology and Counseling, State University, AR 72467. Offers clinical mental health counseling (Graduate Certificate); college student personnel services (MS); dyslexia therapy (Graduate Certificate); psychological science (MS); psychology and counseling (Ed S); rehabilitation counseling (MS); school counseling (MSE); student affairs (Graduate Certificate). *Accreditation:* ACA (one or more programs are accredited); CORE (one or more programs are accredited); NCATE. *Program availability:* Part-time. *Degree requirements:* For master's and other advanced degree, comprehensive exam, thesis or alternative. *Entrance requirements:* For master's, GRE General Test or MAT (for MSE), appropriate bachelor's degree, interview, letters of reference, official transcripts, immunization records, written statement, 2-3 page autobiography; for other advanced degree, GRE General Test, interview, master's degree, letters of reference, official transcript, personal statement, immunization records. Additional exam requirements/recommendations for international students: Required—TOEFL (minimum score 550 paper-based; 79 iBT), IELTS (minimum score 6), PTE (minimum score 56). Electronic applications accepted.

Arkansas Tech University, College of Education, Russellville, AR 72801. Offers college student personnel (MS); educational leadership (M Ed, Ed S); instructional technology (M Ed); school counseling and leadership (M Ed); school leadership (Ed D); special education K-12 (M Ed); strength and conditioning studies (MS); teaching (MAT); teaching, learning, and leadership (M Ed). *Accreditation:* NCATE. *Program availability:* Part-time, evening/weekend, 100% online, blended/hybrid learning. *Students:* 80 full-time (45 women), 433 part-time (328 women); includes 114 minority (81 Black or African American, non-Hispanic/Latino; 4 American Indian or Alaska Native, non-Hispanic/Latino; 1 Asian, non-Hispanic/Latino; 13 Hispanic/Latino; 15 Two or more races, non-Hispanic/Latino), 2 international. Average age 34. In 2017, 132 master's, 8 doctorates, 3 other advanced degrees awarded. *Degree requirements:* For master's, comprehensive exam, thesis optional, action research project; for doctorate, thesis/dissertation. *Entrance requirements:* Additional exam requirements/recommendations for international students: Required—TOEFL (minimum score 550 paper-based; 79 iBT), IELTS (minimum score 6.5), PTE (minimum score 58). *Application deadline:* For fall admission, 3/1 priority date for domestic students, 5/1 priority date for international students; for spring admission, 10/1 priority date for domestic and international students. Applications are processed on a rolling basis. Application fee: $40 ($90 for international students). Electronic applications accepted. *Expenses:* Tuition, state resident: full-time $6816; part-time $284 per credit hour. Tuition, nonresident: full-time $13,632; part-time $568 per credit hour. *Required fees:* $420 per semester. Tuition and fees vary according to course load. *Financial support:* In 2017–18, research assistantships with full and partial tuition reimbursements (averaging $4,800 per year), teaching assistantships with full and partial tuition reimbursements (averaging $4,800 per year) were awarded; career-related internships or fieldwork, Federal Work-Study, scholarships/grants, health care benefits, and unspecified assistantships also available. Support available to part-time students. Financial award application deadline: 4/15; financial award applicants required to submit FAFSA. *Unit head:* Dr. Mary Gunter, Dean, 479-964-3217, E-mail: mgunter@atu.edu.
Website: http://www.atu.edu/education/

Ashland Theological Seminary, Graduate Programs, Ashland, OH 44805. Offers Biblical studies (MA); Christian ministries (MACM), including Black church studies (MACM, D Min), general Christian ministries, leadership, spiritual formation (MACM, D Min); clinical mental health counseling (MA); counseling (MAC); historical and theological studies (MA), including Anabaptism and Pietism, Christian theology, church history, New Testament, Old Testament; ministry (D Min), including Black church studies (MACM, D Min), chaplaincy (M Div, D Min), independent design, spiritual formation (MACM, D Min), transformational leadership; pastoral ministry (M Div), including chaplaincy (M Div, D Min), general ministry. MAC program offered in Detroit, MI. *Accreditation:* ATS. *Program availability:* Part-time. *Degree requirements:* For master's, 2 foreign languages, comprehensive exam (for some programs), thesis (for some programs); for doctorate, thesis/dissertation. *Entrance requirements:* For master's, bachelor's degree from accredited institution with minimum undergraduate GPA of 2.75; for doctorate, M Div, minimum undergraduate GPA of 3.0. Additional exam requirements/recommendations for international students: Required—TOEFL (minimum score 500 paper-based; 65 iBT). Electronic applications accepted. *Faculty research:* Semitic languages and linguistics, rhetorical and social-scientific criticism, Anabaptist studies, inner spiritual healing, African-American clergy in film and literature.

Athabasca University, Program in Counseling, Athabasca, AB T9S 3A3, Canada. Offers applied psychology (Post Master's Certificate); art therapy (MC); career counseling (MC); counseling (Advanced Certificate); counseling psychology (MC); school counseling (MC).

Auburn University at Montgomery, College of Education, Department of Counselor, Leadership, and Special Education, Montgomery, AL 36124-4023. Offers counselor education (M Ed, Ed S), including clinical mental health counseling, school counseling; early childhood special education (M Ed); instructional leadership (M Ed, Ed S); special education/collaborative teacher (M Ed, Ed S). *Accreditation:* ACA; NCATE. *Program availability:* Part-time, evening/weekend. *Faculty:* 7 full-time (4 women), 2 part-time/adjunct (both women). *Students:* 27 full-time (23 women), 57 part-time (51 women); includes 40 minority (38 Black or African American, non-Hispanic/Latino; 2 Hispanic/Latino). Average age 34. 76 applicants, 72% accepted, 26 enrolled. In 2017, 37 master's awarded. *Degree requirements:* For master's and Ed S, comprehensive exam. *Entrance requirements:* For master's, GRE General Test or MAT, certification, BS in teaching; for Ed S, GRE General Test or MAT, certification. Additional exam requirements/recommendations for international students: Recommended—TOEFL (minimum score 500 paper-based; 61 iBT), IELTS (minimum score 5.5), TSE (minimum score 44). *Application deadline:* For fall admission, 7/15 for international students; for spring admission, 11/15 for international students; for summer admission, 4/15 for international students. Applications are processed on a rolling basis. Electronic applications accepted. *Expenses:* Tuition, state resident: full-time $6930; part-time $385 per credit hour. Tuition, nonresident: full-time $15,588; part-time $866 per credit hour. *Required fees:* $640. *Financial support:* Career-related internships or fieldwork and scholarships/grants available. Support available to part-time students. Financial award application deadline: 3/1; financial award applicants required to submit FAFSA. *Unit head:* Dr. Samuel Flynt, Head, 334-244-3835, Fax: 334-244-3101, E-mail: sflynt@aum.edu. *Application contact:* Dr. Rhonda Morton, Associate Dean/Graduate Coordinator, 334-244-3287, Fax: 334-244-3978, E-mail: rmorton@aum.edu.
Website: http://education.aum.edu/academic-departments/counselor-leadership-and-special-education

Augusta University, College of Education, Department of Counselor Education, Leadership, and Research, Augusta, GA 30912. Offers counselor education (M Ed, Ed S), including clinical mental health counseling (M Ed), school counselor (M Ed). *Accreditation:* ACA; NCATE. *Program availability:* Part-time, evening/weekend. *Degree requirements:* For master's, comprehensive exam; for Ed S, comprehensive exam, thesis. *Entrance requirements:* For master's, GRE, MAT, minimum GPA of 2.5; for Ed S, GRE, MAT. *Faculty research:* Restructuring schools, financing education, student transition.

Austin Peay State University, College of Graduate Studies, College of Behavioral and Health Sciences, Department of Psychological Science and Counseling, Clarksville, TN

37044. Offers industrial-organizational psychology (MS); mental health counseling (MS); including clinical mental health, school counseling; school counseling (MS). *Program availability:* Part-time, online learning. *Faculty:* 11 full-time (6 women), 1 (woman) part-time/adjunct. *Students:* 60 full-time (46 women), 12 part-time (10 women); includes 16 minority (11 Black or African American, non-Hispanic/Latino; 4 Hispanic/Latino; 1 Two or more races, non-Hispanic/Latino). Average age 29. 59 applicants, 69% accepted, 31 enrolled. In 2017, 30 master's awarded. *Degree requirements:* For master's, comprehensive exam, thesis (for some programs). *Entrance requirements:* For master's, GRE General Test, minimum undergraduate GPA of 2.5, 3 letters of recommendation, bachelor's degree. Additional exam requirements/recommendations for international students: Required—TOEFL (minimum score 500 paper-based). *Application deadline:* For fall admission, 8/8 priority date for domestic students. Applications are processed on a rolling basis. Application fee: $45 ($55 for international students). Electronic applications accepted. *Expenses:* Tuition, state resident: full-time $7686; part-time $427 per credit hour. Tuition, nonresident: full-time $20,268; part-time $1126 per credit hour. *Required fees:* $1529; $76.45 per credit hour. *Financial support:* Research assistantships with full tuition reimbursements, career-related internships or fieldwork, Federal Work-Study, institutionally sponsored loans, scholarships/grants, and unspecified assistantships available. Support available to part-time students. Financial award application deadline: 4/1; financial award applicants required to submit FAFSA. *Unit head:* Dr. Nicole Knickmeyer, Chair, 931-221-7232, Fax: 931-221-6267, E-mail: knickmeyer@apsu.edu. *Application contact:* Brad Averitt, Coordinator of Graduate Admissions, 800-859-4723, Fax: 931-221-7641, E-mail: gradadmissions@apsu.edu. Website: http://www.apsu.edu/psychology/index.php

Austin Peay State University, College of Graduate Studies, College of Education, Department of Educational Specialties, Clarksville, TN 37044. Offers administration and supervision (Ed S); counseling and guidance (Ed S); curriculum and instruction (MA Ed); education leadership (MA Ed); elementary education (Ed S); reading (MA Ed); secondary education (Ed S). *Program availability:* Part-time, evening/weekend, online learning. *Faculty:* 15 full-time (9 women), 5 part-time/adjunct (4 women). *Students:* 73 full-time (54 women), 139 part-time (106 women); includes 49 minority (23 Black or African American, non-Hispanic/Latino; 4 Asian, non-Hispanic/Latino; 12 Hispanic/Latino; 10 Two or more races, non-Hispanic/Latino), 1 international. Average age 35. 72 applicants, 96% accepted, 42 enrolled. In 2017, 94 master's, 12 Ed Ss awarded. *Degree requirements:* For master's, comprehensive exam, thesis optional. *Entrance requirements:* For master's, GRE General Test, MAT, minimum undergraduate GPA of 2.75. Additional exam requirements/recommendations for international students: Required—TOEFL (minimum score 500 paper-based). *Application deadline:* For fall admission, 8/8 priority date for domestic students. Applications are processed on a rolling basis. Application fee: $45 ($50 for international students). Electronic applications accepted. *Expenses:* Tuition, state resident: full-time $7686; part-time $427 per credit hour. Tuition, nonresident: full-time $20,268; part-time $1126 per credit hour. *Required fees:* $1529; $76.45 per credit hour. *Financial support:* Research assistantships with full tuition reimbursements, career-related internships or fieldwork, Federal Work-Study, institutionally sponsored loans, scholarships/grants, and unspecified assistantships available. Support available to part-time students. Financial award application deadline: 4/1; financial award applicants required to submit FAFSA. *Unit head:* Dr. Moniqueka Gold, Chair, 931-221-7696, Fax: 931-221-1292, E-mail: goldm@apsu.edu. *Application contact:* Megan Mitchell, Coordinator of Graduate Admissions, 800-859-4723, Fax: 931-221-7641, E-mail: gradadmissions@apsu.edu.

Azusa Pacific University, School of Education, Department of School Counseling and School Psychology, Program in Educational Counseling, Azusa, CA 91702-7000. Offers MA Ed.

Ball State University, Graduate School, College of Health, Department of Counseling Psychology, Social Psychology, and Counseling, Program in Counseling Psychology, Muncie, IN 47306. Offers counseling (MA), including clinical mental health counseling, mental health counseling, rehabilitation counseling, school counseling; counseling psychology (PhD). *Accreditation:* ACA; APA. *Program availability:* Part-time. *Students:* 88 full-time (57 women), 29 part-time (24 women); includes 18 minority (3 Black or African American, non-Hispanic/Latino; 1 Asian, non-Hispanic/Latino; 7 Hispanic/Latino; 7 Two or more races, non-Hispanic/Latino), 4 international. Average age 26. 133 applicants, 29% accepted, 39 enrolled. In 2017, 29 master's, 9 doctorates awarded. *Degree requirements:* For doctorate, thesis/dissertation. *Entrance requirements:* For master's, GRE General Test (minimum scores 144 quantitative, 153 verbal), minimum baccalaureate GPA of 2.75 or 3.0 in latter half of baccalaureate, minimum GPA of 3.0 in psychology coursework, three letters of recommendation; for doctorate, GRE General Test, interview, minimum graduate GPA of 3.2, resume. Additional exam requirements/recommendations for international students: Required—TOEFL (minimum score 550 paper-based; 79 iBT), IELTS (minimum score 6.5). *Application deadline:* For fall admission, 3/1 priority date for domestic students, 1/1 for international students. Applications are processed on a rolling basis. Application fee: $60. Electronic applications accepted. *Financial support:* Research assistantships with partial tuition reimbursements, teaching assistantships with partial tuition reimbursements, and unspecified assistantships available. Financial award application deadline: 3/1; financial award applicants required to submit FAFSA. *Unit head:* Dr. Sharon Bowman, Chairperson, 765-285-8040, Fax: 765-285-2067, E-mail: sbowman@bsu.edu. Website: http://www.bsu.edu/teachers/counseling/cpsy/

Barry University, School of Education, Program in Counseling, Miami Shores, FL 33161-6695. Offers MS, PhD, Ed S. *Accreditation:* ACA. *Program availability:* Part-time, evening/weekend. *Degree requirements:* For master's, comprehensive exam. *Entrance requirements:* For master's, GRE General Test or MAT, minimum GPA of 3.0; for doctorate, GRE, minimum GPA of 3.25; for Ed S, GRE General Test, minimum GPA of 3.0.

Barry University, School of Education, Program in Mental Health Counseling, Miami Shores, FL 33161-6695. Offers MS, Ed S. *Accreditation:* ACA. *Program availability:* Part-time, evening/weekend. *Degree requirements:* For master's, comprehensive exam, scholarly paper; for Ed S, comprehensive exam. *Entrance requirements:* For master's, GRE General Test or MAT, minimum GPA of 3.0; for Ed S, GRE General Test or MAT, minimum GPA of 3.0. Electronic applications accepted.

Barry University, School of Education, Program in School Counseling, Miami Shores, FL 33161-6695. Offers MS, Ed S. *Accreditation:* ACA (one or more programs are accredited). *Program availability:* Part-time, evening/weekend. *Degree requirements:* For master's, comprehensive exam, scholarly paper; for Ed S, comprehensive exam. *Entrance requirements:* For master's, GRE General Test or MAT, minimum GPA of 3.0; for Ed S, GRE General Test, minimum GPA of 3.0. Electronic applications accepted.

Bayamón Central University, Graduate Programs, Program in Education, Bayamón, PR 00960-1725. Offers administration and supervision (MA Ed); commercial education (MA Ed); elementary education (K–3) (MA Ed); family counseling (Graduate Certificate); guidance and counseling (MA Ed); pre-elementary teacher (MA Ed); rehabilitation counseling (MA Ed); special education (MA Ed), including attention deficit disorder, education of the autistic, learning disabilities. *Program availability:* Part-time, evening/weekend. *Degree requirements:* For master's, comprehensive exam. *Entrance requirements:* For master's, EXADEP, bachelor's degree in education or related field.

Becker College, Program in Mental Health Counseling, Worcester, MA 01609. Offers community mental health (MA); school consultation (MA). *Entrance requirements:* For master's, GRE, interview, official transcript, three letters of recommendation, essay. Electronic applications accepted.

Bellevue University, Graduate School, College of Arts and Sciences, Bellevue, NE 68005-3098. Offers clinical counseling (MS); healthcare administration (MHA); human services (MA); international security and intelligence studies (MS); managerial communication (MA). *Program availability:* Online learning.

Bloomsburg University of Pennsylvania, School of Graduate Studies, College of Education, Department of Teaching and Learning, Program in Educational Leadership, Bloomsburg, PA 17815-1301. Offers college student affairs (M Ed); PreK-12 curriculum and instruction (M Ed); PreK-12 school counseling (M Ed); PreK-12 school principal (M Ed). *Degree requirements:* For master's, practicum. *Entrance requirements:* For master's, 3 letters of recommendation, resume, minimum QPA of 3.0, personal statement, interview. Additional exam requirements/recommendations for international students: Required—TOEFL, IELTS. Electronic applications accepted. *Expenses:* Tuition, state resident: full-time $10,000; part-time $500 per credit hour. Tuition, nonresident: full-time $15,000; part-time $750 per credit hour. *Required fees:* $2484; $110.75 per credit hour. $75 per term. Tuition and fees vary according to program.

Bob Jones University, Graduate Programs, Greenville, SC 29614. Offers accountancy (MS); Bible (MA); Bible translation (MA); Biblical studies (Certificate); broadcast management (MS); business administration (MBA); church history (MA, PhD); church ministries (MA); church music (MM); cinema and video production (MA); counseling (MS); curriculum and instruction (Ed D); divinity (M Div); dramatic production (MA); educational leadership (MS, Ed D, Ed S); elementary education (M Ed, MAT); English (M Ed, MA, MAT); fine arts (MA); graphic design (MA); history (M Ed, MA); illustration (MA); interpretative speech (MA); mathematics (M Ed, MAT); medical missions (Certificate); ministry (MM, D Min); multi-categorical special education (M Ed, MAT); music (M Ed); New Testament interpretation (PhD); Old Testament interpretation (PhD); orchestral instrument performance (MM); organ performance (MM); pastoral studies (MA); personnel services (MS, Ed S); piano pedagogy (MM); piano performance (MM); platform arts (MA); radio and television broadcasting (MS); rhetoric and public address (MA); secondary education (M Ed); studio art (MA); teaching Bible (MA); theology (MA, PhD); voice performance (MM); youth ministries (MA); M Div/MM.

Boise State University, College of Education, Department of Counselor Education, Boise, ID 83725-0399. Offers MA, Graduate Certificate. *Accreditation:* ACA. *Program availability:* Part-time. *Faculty:* 14. *Students:* 36 full-time (30 women), 30 part-time (25 women); includes 8 minority (1 Asian, non-Hispanic/Latino; 6 Hispanic/Latino; 1 Two or more races, non-Hispanic/Latino). Average age 33. 74 applicants, 45% accepted, 20 enrolled. In 2017, 12 master's, 8 other advanced degrees awarded. *Degree requirements:* For master's, comprehensive exam, comprehensive portfolio, video-recorded evidence of skill. *Entrance requirements:* For master's, minimum GPA of 3.0. Additional exam requirements/recommendations for international students: Required—TOEFL (minimum score 550 paper-based; 80 iBT), IELTS (minimum score 6). *Application deadline:* For fall admission, 2/1 for domestic and international students. Application fee: $65 ($95 for international students). Electronic applications accepted. *Expenses:* Tuition, state resident: full-time $6471; part-time $390 per credit. Tuition, nonresident: full-time $21,787; part-time $685 per credit. *Required fees:* $2283; $100 per term. Part-time tuition and fees vary according to course load and program. *Financial support:* Scholarships/grants and unspecified assistantships available. Financial award application deadline: 2/1; financial award applicants required to submit FAFSA. *Unit head:* Dr. Diana Doumas, Department Chair, 208-426-2646, E-mail: dianadoumas@boisestate.edu. *Application contact:* Dr. Laura Gallo, Program Coordinator, 208-426-1219, E-mail: counseloreducation@boisestate.edu. Website: http://education.boisestate.edu/counselored/

Bowie State University, Graduate Programs, Program in Guidance and Counseling, Bowie, MD 20715-9465. Offers M Ed. *Program availability:* Part-time, evening/weekend. *Degree requirements:* For master's, comprehensive exam, thesis optional, research paper. *Entrance requirements:* For master's, teaching experience, minimum GPA of 2.5, 3 recommendations. Electronic applications accepted.

Bowling Green State University, Graduate College, College of Education and Human Development, School of Intervention Services, Program in Clinical Mental Health Counseling, Bowling Green, OH 43403. Offers clinical mental health counseling (MA); school counseling (M Ed). *Accreditation:* ACA; NCATE. *Program availability:* Part-time. *Degree requirements:* For master's, thesis or alternative. *Entrance requirements:* For master's, GRE General Test. Additional exam requirements/recommendations for international students: Required—TOEFL. Electronic applications accepted. *Faculty research:* Perfectionism, multicultural counseling, suicide, ethics and legal issues related to counseling, play therapy.

Bradley University, The Graduate School, College of Education and Health Sciences, Department of Leadership in Education, Nonprofits and Counseling, Peoria, IL 61625-0002. Offers counseling (MA), including clinical mental health counseling, professional school counseling; leadership in educational administration (MA); nonprofit leadership (MA). *Accreditation:* ACA; NCATE. *Program availability:* Part-time, evening/weekend. *Degree requirements:* For master's, comprehensive exam, thesis optional. *Entrance requirements:* For master's, GRE General Test or MAT, interview, 3 letters of recommendation. Additional exam requirements/recommendations for international students: Required—TOEFL (minimum score 550 paper-based; 79 iBT), IELTS (minimum score 6.5). Electronic applications accepted.

Brandman University, School of Education, Irvine, CA 92618. Offers curriculum and instruction (MAE); educational administration (MAE); educational leadership (MAE); educational leadership and administration (MA); elementary education (MAT); instructional technology: teaching the 21st century learner (MAE); leadership in early childhood education (MAE); organizational leadership (Ed D); school counseling (MA); secondary education (MAT); special education (MA); teaching and learning (MAE). *Expenses: Tuition:* Part-time $640 per credit hour. Tuition and fees vary according to degree level and program. *Unit head:* Dr. Christine G. Zeppos, Dean, 949-341-9948, E-mail: zeppos@brandman.edu. *Application contact:* Dr. Christine G. Zeppos, Dean, 949-341-9948, E-mail: zeppos@brandman.edu. Website: https://www.brandman.edu/academic-programs/education

Brandon University, Faculty of Education, Brandon, MB R7A 6A9, Canada. Offers curriculum and instruction (M Ed, Diploma); educational administration (M Ed, Diploma); guidance and counseling (M Ed, Diploma); special education (M Ed, Diploma). *Degree requirements:* For master's, thesis. *Entrance requirements:* For master's, minimum GPA of 3.0, teaching certificate or equivalent. Additional exam requirements/recommendations for international students: Required—TOEFL. *Faculty research:* Comparative education, environmental studies, parent/school council.

Bridgewater State University, College of Graduate Studies, College of Education and Allied Studies, Department of Secondary Education and Professional Programs, Program in Counseling, Bridgewater, MA 02325. Offers M Ed, CAGS. *Accreditation:* ACA; NCATE. *Program availability:* Part-time, evening/weekend. *Entrance requirements:* For master's, GRE General Test.

Brooklyn College of the City University of New York, School of Education, Program in School Counseling, Brooklyn, NY 11210-2889. Offers MS Ed. *Accreditation:* ACA. *Program availability:* Part-time. *Degree requirements:* For master's, comprehensive exam, internship. *Entrance requirements:* For master's, interview, 2 letters of recommendation, resume, essay. Additional exam requirements/recommendations for international students: Required—TOEFL (minimum score 500 paper-based; 61 iBT). Electronic applications accepted. *Faculty research:* Urban school counseling, parent involvement, multicultural competence and counselor training.

Buena Vista University, School of Education, Storm Lake, IA 50588. Offers curriculum and instruction (M Ed), including effective teaching, TESL; school guidance and counseling (MS Ed). Program offered in summer only. *Program availability:* Part-time, evening/weekend, online learning. *Degree requirements:* For master's, thesis, fieldwork/practicum, capstone portfolio. *Entrance requirements:* For master's, Analytical Writing Assessment (in-house), minimum undergraduate GPA of 2.75. Electronic applications accepted. *Faculty research:* Reading, curriculum, educational psychology, special education.

Butler University, College of Education, Indianapolis, IN 46208-3485. Offers applied educational neuroscience (Certificate); educational administration (MS); effective teaching and leadership (MS); licensed mental health counselor (Certificate); school counseling (MS); wellness and sport leadership (Certificate). *Accreditation:* ACA; NCATE. *Program availability:* Part-time. *Faculty:* 12 full-time (8 women), 10 part-time/adjunct (7 women). *Students:* 3 full-time (2 women), 131 part-time (102 women); includes 13 minority (7 Black or African American, non-Hispanic/Latino; 2 Asian, non-Hispanic/Latino; 2 Hispanic/Latino; 2 Two or more races, non-Hispanic/Latino). Average age 31. 65 applicants, 75% accepted, 41 enrolled. In 2017, 45 master's, 10 other advanced degrees awarded. *Degree requirements:* For master's, thesis. *Entrance requirements:* For master's, GRE (minimum score 291) or MAT (minimum score 396) unless undergraduate GPA is a 3.0 or higher, two letters of recommendation, transcripts, interview, professional resume. Additional exam requirements/recommendations for international students: Required—TOEFL (minimum score 550 paper-based; 79 iBT), IELTS (minimum score 6). *Application deadline:* For fall admission, 2/1 for domestic and international students; for spring admission, 11/1 for domestic and international students; for summer admission, 4/1 for domestic and international students. Applications are processed on a rolling basis. Application fee: $0. Electronic applications accepted. *Expenses:* $560 per credit. *Financial support:* In 2017–18, 64 students received support. Scholarships/grants, tuition waivers (full and partial), and unspecified assistantships available. Financial award application deadline: 7/15; financial award applicants required to submit FAFSA. *Faculty research:* Principals role in school improvement, leadership and school climate, retention of teachers in special education, the neuro-diversity brain, school counseling intervention. *Unit head:* Dr. Ena Shelley, Dean, 317-940-9752, Fax: 317-940-6481. *Application contact:* Diane Dubord, Graduate Student Services Specialist, 317-940-8100, Fax: 317-940-8250, E-mail: ddubord@butler.edu.
Website: https://www.butler.edu/coe/graduate-programs

Caldwell University, School of Psychology and Counseling, Caldwell, NJ 07006-6195. Offers art therapy (MA); counseling (MA), including art therapy, mental health, school counseling; director of school counseling (Post-Master's Certificate); professional counselor (Post-Master's Certificate); school counselor (Post-Master's Certificate). *Accreditation:* ACA. *Program availability:* Part-time. *Faculty:* 16 full-time (13 women), 13 part-time/adjunct (7 women). *Students:* 88 full-time (79 women), 84 part-time (82 women); includes 33 minority (12 Black or African American, non-Hispanic/Latino; 6 Asian, non-Hispanic/Latino; 15 Hispanic/Latino). Average age 30. 104 applicants, 100% accepted, 44 enrolled. In 2017, 31 master's awarded. *Degree requirements:* For master's, comprehensive exam, practicum, internship; for Post-Master's Certificate, comprehensive exam. *Entrance requirements:* For master's, minimum GPA of 3.2; two letters of recommendation; interview; writing sample. Additional exam requirements/recommendations for international students: Required—TOEFL (minimum score 580 paper-based, 92 iBT) or IELTS (7.5). *Application deadline:* For fall admission, 6/1 for domestic students, 7/1 for international students; for spring admission, 12/1 for domestic and international students; for summer admission, 4/1 for domestic and international students. Applications are processed on a rolling basis. Application fee: $50. Electronic applications accepted. *Expenses:* $975 per credit. *Financial support:* 2 general assistantships available. Financial award applicants required to submit FAFSA. *Faculty research:* Mental health counseling, school counseling, art therapy. *Unit head:* Dr. Thomson Ling, Associate Dean, 973-618-3596, E-mail: tling@caldwell.edu. *Application contact:* Tom Disch, Senior Graduate Admissions Counselor, 973-618-3544, E-mail: graduate@caldwell.edu.

California Baptist University, Program in School Counseling, Riverside, CA 92504-3206. Offers MS. *Program availability:* Part-time, evening/weekend. *Faculty:* 2 full-time (both women), 6 part-time/adjunct (3 women). *Students:* 58 part-time (49 women); includes 31 minority (2 Black or African American, non-Hispanic/Latino; 1 American Indian or Alaska Native, non-Hispanic/Latino; 1 Asian, non-Hispanic/Latino; 26 Hispanic/Latino; 1 Two or more races, non-Hispanic/Latino). Average age 32. 46 applicants, 50% accepted, 22 enrolled. In 2017, 9 master's awarded. *Degree requirements:* For master's, 100 hours of introductory fieldwork, 600 hours of field experience/internship, PRAXIS. *Entrance requirements:* For master's, California Basic Educational Skills Test (CBEST), minimum GPA of 3.0, completion of prerequisite courses with minimum C grade, three letters of recommendation, 500-word essay. Additional exam requirements/recommendations for international students: Required—TOEFL (minimum score 80 iBT). *Application deadline:* For fall admission, 8/1 priority date for domestic students, 7/7 priority date for international students; for spring admission, 12/1 priority date for domestic students, 11/1 priority date for international students. Applications are processed on a rolling basis. Application fee: $45. Electronic applications accepted. *Expenses:* Contact institution. *Financial support:* In 2017–18, 17 students received support. Federal Work-Study and scholarships/grants available. Financial award applicants required to submit CSS PROFILE or FAFSA. *Faculty research:* Cultural competence, behavioral assessment, school neuropsychology, learning handicapped, cognitive development. *Unit head:* Dr. John Shoup, Dean, School of Education, 951-343-4205, E-mail: jshoup@calbaptist.edu. *Application contact:* David Little, Graduate Admissions Counselor, 951-552-8093, E-mail: dlittle@calbaptist.edu.
Website: http://www.calbaptist.edu/academics/schools-colleges/school-education/programs/graduate/master-science-school-counseling/

California Lutheran University, Graduate Studies, Graduate School of Education, Thousand Oaks, CA 91360-2787. Offers counseling and guidance (MS), including college student personnel, counseling and guidance; educational leadership (MA, Ed D), including educational leadership (K-12) (Ed D), higher education leadership (Ed D); special education (MS); teacher leadership (M Ed); teaching (M Ed). *Accreditation:* NCATE. *Program availability:* Part-time, evening/weekend. *Faculty:* 21 full-time (18 women), 40 part-time/adjunct (27 women). *Students:* 390 full-time (303 women), 61 part-time (51 women); includes 228 minority (6 Black or African American, non-Hispanic/Latino; 2 American Indian or Alaska Native, non-Hispanic/Latino; 13 Asian, non-Hispanic/Latino; 186 Hispanic/Latino; 1 Native Hawaiian or other Pacific Islander, non-Hispanic/Latino; 20 Two or more races, non-Hispanic/Latino). Average age 31. 201

applicants, 76% accepted, 121 enrolled. In 2017, 129 master's, 19 doctorates awarded. *Degree requirements:* For master's, comprehensive exam or thesis; for doctorate, thesis/dissertation. *Entrance requirements:* For master's, GRE General Test, interview, minimum GPA of 3.0. *Application deadline:* For fall admission, 7/1 priority date for domestic students; for spring admission, 11/1 priority date for domestic students; for summer admission, 4/1 priority date for domestic students. Applications are processed on a rolling basis. Application fee: $50. Electronic applications accepted. *Expenses:* Tuition: Full-time $15,000. Full-time tuition and fees vary according to degree level and program. *Unit head:* Dr. Michael Hillis, Dean, 805-493-3421. *Application contact:* 805-493-3325, Fax: 805-493-3861, E-mail: clugrad@calutheran.edu.

California State University, Bakersfield, Division of Graduate Studies, School of Social Sciences and Education, Program in Counseling, Bakersfield, CA 93311. Offers school counseling (MS); student affairs (MS). *Accreditation:* NCATE. *Faculty:* 2 full-time (both women), 7 part-time/adjunct (6 women). *Students:* 64 full-time (52 women), 5 part-time (3 women); includes 55 minority (1 Black or African American, non-Hispanic/Latino; 1 American Indian or Alaska Native, non-Hispanic/Latino; 2 Asian, non-Hispanic/Latino; 51 Hispanic/Latino), 1 international. Average age 27. 74 applicants, 59% accepted, 38 enrolled. In 2017, 35 master's awarded. *Degree requirements:* For master's, thesis or alternative, culminating projects. *Entrance requirements:* For master's, CBEST (for school counseling). *Application deadline:* Applications are processed on a rolling basis. Application fee: $55. *Expenses:* Tuition, state resident: full-time $7176; part-time $4164 per year. *Financial support:* In 2017–18, fellowships (averaging $1,850 per year) were awarded; Federal Work-Study, scholarships/grants, and tuition waivers (full and partial) also available. Financial award application deadline: 3/2; financial award applicants required to submit FAFSA. *Unit head:* Dr. Karen Haas, Director, 661-654-6214, Fax: 661-654-2479, E-mail: khaas8@csub.edu. *Application contact:* Julia Bavier, Admissions and Graduation Advisor, 661-654-3193, Fax: 661-654-2479, E-mail: jbavier@csub.edu. Website: https://www.csub.edu/psychology/mscounselingpsych/index.html

California State University, Dominguez Hills, College of Education, Division of Graduate Education, Program in Counseling, Carson, CA 90747-0001. Offers college counseling (MS); school counseling (MS). *Program availability:* Part-time, evening/weekend. *Degree requirements:* For master's, comprehensive exam. *Entrance requirements:* For master's, minimum GPA of 3.0. Additional exam requirements/recommendations for international students: Required—TOEFL. *Faculty research:* Social development.

California State University, East Bay, Office of Graduate Studies, College of Education and Allied Studies, Department of Educational Psychology, Counseling Program, Hayward, CA 94542-3000. Offers MS. *Accreditation:* NCATE. *Students:* 106 full-time (94 women); includes 61 minority (4 Black or African American, non-Hispanic/Latino; 20 Asian, non-Hispanic/Latino; 27 Hispanic/Latino; 10 Two or more races, non-Hispanic/Latino), 1 international. Average age 29. 179 applicants, 30% accepted, 44 enrolled. In 2017, 42 master's awarded. *Degree requirements:* For master's, comprehensive exam, project or thesis. *Entrance requirements:* For master's, GRE or MAT, interview, minimum GPA of 2.5 during previous 2 years of course work. Additional exam requirements/recommendations for international students: Required—TOEFL (minimum score 550 paper-based). *Application deadline:* For fall admission, 6/1 for domestic and international students. Application fee: $55. Electronic applications accepted. *Financial support:* Career-related internships or fieldwork, Federal Work-Study, and institutionally sponsored loans available. Support available to part-time students. Financial award application deadline: 3/2; financial award applicants required to submit FAFSA. *Unit head:* Dr. Jack Davis, Chair, Educational Psychology, 510-885-3011, Fax: 510-885-4642, E-mail: jack.davis@csueastbay.edu. *Application contact:* Prof. Greg Jennings, Graduate Coordinator, 510-885-2296, Fax: 510-885-4642, E-mail: greg.jennings@csueastbay.edu.
Website: http://www20.csueastbay.edu/ceas/departments/epsy/

California State University, Fresno, Division of Research and Graduate Studies, Kremen School of Education and Human Development, Department of Counselor Education and Rehabilitation, Program in Student Affairs and College Counseling, Fresno, CA 93740-8027. Offers MS. *Accreditation:* NCATE. *Program availability:* Part-time, evening/weekend. *Degree requirements:* For master's, thesis or alternative. *Entrance requirements:* For master's, GRE General Test, MAT, minimum GPA of 3.0. Additional exam requirements/recommendations for international students: Required—TOEFL. Electronic applications accepted.

California State University, Fullerton, Graduate Studies, College of Health and Human Development, Department of Counseling, Fullerton, CA 92831-3599. Offers MS. *Accreditation:* ACA; NCATE. *Program availability:* Part-time. *Faculty:* 9 full-time (5 women), 9 part-time/adjunct (5 women). *Students:* 127 full-time (107 women), 62 part-time (44 women); includes 84 minority (1 Black or African American, non-Hispanic/Latino; 1 American Indian or Alaska Native, non-Hispanic/Latino; 24 Asian, non-Hispanic/Latino; 54 Hispanic/Latino; 4 Two or more races, non-Hispanic/Latino), 4 international. Average age 30. 294 applicants, 21% accepted, 58 enrolled. *Degree requirements:* For master's, comprehensive exam, project or thesis. *Entrance requirements:* For master's, minimum GPA of 3.0 in behavioral science and for undergraduate degree. Application fee: $55. *Financial support:* Career-related internships or fieldwork, Federal Work-Study, institutionally sponsored loans, and scholarships/grants available. Support available to part-time students. Financial award application deadline: 3/1; financial award applicants required to submit FAFSA. *Unit head:* Dr. Leah Brew, Chair, 657-278-8444. *Application contact:* Admissions/Applications, 657-278-2371.

California State University, Long Beach, Graduate Studies, College of Education, Department of Advanced Studies in Education and Counseling, Long Beach, CA 90840. Offers counseling (MS), including marriage and family therapy, school counseling, student development in higher education; education (MA, Ed D); educational administration (MA, Ed D); educational psychology (MA); special education (MS). *Program availability:* Part-time, evening/weekend. *Entrance requirements:* For master's, GRE General Test, minimum GPA of 2.75. Electronic applications accepted.

California State University, Los Angeles, Graduate Studies, Charter College of Education, Division of Special Education and Counseling, Los Angeles, CA 90032-8530. Offers counseling (MS), including applied behavior analysis, community college counseling, rehabilitation counseling, school counseling, school psychology; special education (MA, PhD). *Accreditation:* ACA. *Program availability:* Part-time, evening/weekend. *Entrance requirements:* For master's, minimum GPA of 2.75 in last 90 units of course work, teaching certificate. Additional exam requirements/recommendations for international students: Required—TOEFL (minimum score 500 paper-based). Electronic applications accepted.

California State University, Northridge, Graduate Studies, Michael D. Eisner College of Education, Department of Educational Psychology and Counseling, Northridge, CA 91330. Offers counseling (MS), including career counseling, college counseling and student services, marriage and family therapy, school counseling, school psychology; educational psychology (MA Ed), including development, learning, and instruction, early childhood education. *Accreditation:* ACA (one or more programs are accredited); NCATE. *Program availability:* Part-time, evening/weekend. *Students:* 288 full-time (244

women), 84 part-time (76 women); includes 190 minority (13 Black or African American, non-Hispanic/Latino; 24 Asian, non-Hispanic/Latino; 139 Hispanic/Latino; 14 Two or more races, non-Hispanic/Latino), 11 international. Average age 29. 427 applicants, 34% accepted, 136 enrolled. In 2017, 103 master's awarded. *Entrance requirements:* For master's, GRE General Test or minimum GPA of 3.0. Additional exam requirements/recommendations for international students: Required—TOEFL. *Application deadline:* For fall admission, 11/30 for domestic students. Application fee: $55. *Financial support:* Scholarships/grants available. Support available to part-time students. Financial award application deadline: 3/1. *Unit head:* Dr. Alberto Restori, Chair, 818-677-2599. *Application contact:* 818-677-3755.
Website: http://www.csun.edu/eisner-education/educational-psychology-counseling

California State University, Sacramento, College of Education, Graduate and Professional Studies in Education, Sacramento, CA 95819. Offers behavioral science and gender equity (MA); child development (MA); counseling (MS); curriculum and instruction (MA); education (Ed D), including K-12 and community college; education leadership and policy studies (MA), including higher education, PreK-12; education specialist (Ed S), including school psychology; educational technology (MA); language and literacy (MA); multicultural education (MA); school psychology (MA); special education (MA); workforce development advocacy (MA). *Program availability:* Part-time, evening/weekend, blended/hybrid learning. *Students:* 381 full-time (294 women), 135 part-time (101 women); includes 296 minority (44 Black or African American, non-Hispanic/Latino; 1 American Indian or Alaska Native, non-Hispanic/Latino; 94 Asian, non-Hispanic/Latino; 153 Hispanic/Latino; 4 Native Hawaiian or other Pacific Islander, non-Hispanic/Latino), 3 international. Average age 32. 553 applicants, 53% accepted, 292 enrolled. In 2017, 147 master's, 13 doctorates, 10 other advanced degrees awarded. *Degree requirements:* For master's, thesis or project; writing proficiency exam; for doctorate, thesis/dissertation. *Entrance requirements:* For master's and doctorate, GRE. Additional exam requirements/recommendations for international students: Required—TOEFL (minimum score 550 paper-based; 80 iBT); Recommended—IELTS (minimum score 7), TSE. *Application deadline:* For fall admission, 2/15 for domestic students, 1/15 for international students. Applications are processed on a rolling basis. Application fee: $55. Electronic applications accepted. *Expenses:* Contact institution. *Financial support:* Career-related internships or fieldwork, Federal Work-Study, and scholarships/grants available. Support available to part-time students. Financial award application deadline: 3/1; financial award applicants required to submit FAFSA. *Unit head:* Dr. Elizabeth Liles, Chair, 916-278-5942, E-mail: coe@csus.edu. *Application contact:* Jose Martinez, Graduate Admissions Supervisor, 916-278-7871, E-mail: martinj@skymail.csus.edu.
Website: http://www.csus.edu/coe/academics/graduate/index.html

California State University, San Bernardino, Graduate Studies, College of Education, Program in Counseling and Guidance, San Bernardino, CA 92407. Offers counseling and guidance (MS); rehabilitation counseling (MA). *Accreditation:* NCATE. *Program availability:* Part-time, evening/weekend. *Students:* 120 full-time (99 women), 6 part-time (3 women); includes 93 minority (6 Black or African American, non-Hispanic/Latino; 4 Asian, non-Hispanic/Latino; 81 Hispanic/Latino; 2 Two or more races, non-Hispanic/Latino), 3 international. Average age 29. 99 applicants, 65% accepted, 49 enrolled. In 2017, 54 master's awarded. *Degree requirements:* For master's, comprehensive exam, thesis or alternative. *Entrance requirements:* Additional exam requirements/recommendations for international students: Required—TOEFL. *Application deadline:* For fall admission, 7/16 for domestic students. Application fee: $55. *Unit head:* Dr. Judith Sylva, Chair, 909-537-5606, E-mail: jsylva@csusb.edu. *Application contact:* Dr. Dorota Huizinga, Dean of Graduate Studies, 909-537-3064, E-mail: dorota.huizinga@csusb.edu.

California State University, Stanislaus, College of Education, Kinesiology and Social Work, MA Program in Education, Turlock, CA 95382. Offers curriculum and instruction (MA), including education technology, elementary education, multilingual education, physical education, reading, secondary education, special education; school administration (MA); school counseling (MA). *Program availability:* Part-time, evening/weekend. *Degree requirements:* For master's, comprehensive exam (for some programs), thesis (for some programs). *Entrance requirements:* For master's, MAT, GRE, or CBEST (varies by concentration), 3 letters of recommendation, personal statement. Additional exam requirements/recommendations for international students: Required—TOEFL (minimum score 550 paper-based). Electronic applications accepted. *Faculty research:* Children's perspectives on historical events, method elementary schools dual language education, K-12 reading programs.

California University of Pennsylvania, School of Graduate Studies and Research, College of Education and Human Services, Department of Counselor Education, California, PA 15419-1394. Offers clinical mental health counseling (MS); school counseling (M Ed). *Accreditation:* ACA; NCATE. *Program availability:* Part-time, evening/weekend. *Degree requirements:* For master's, comprehensive exam, thesis optional. *Entrance requirements:* For master's, MAT, minimum GPA of 3.0, resume, letters of reference. Additional exam requirements/recommendations for international students: Required—TOEFL (minimum score 550 paper-based; 80 iBT). *Application deadline:* For fall admission, 8/1 priority date for domestic and international students. Applications are processed on a rolling basis. Application fee: $25. Electronic applications accepted. *Financial support:* Applicants required to submit FAFSA. *Faculty research:* Mind-body theories and practice, grief issues, career development, supervision, sports counseling. *Unit head:* Dr. Grafton Eliason, Program Coordinator, 724-938-4464, E-mail: eliason@calu.edu. *Application contact:* Suzanne C. Powers, Director of Graduate Admissions and Recruitment, 724-938-4029, Fax: 724-938-5712, E-mail: powers_s@cup.edu.
Website: http://www.calu.edu/academics/colleges/education/counselor-education/

Cambridge College, School of Education, Boston, MA 02129. Offers autism specialist (M Ed); autism/behavior analyst (M Ed); behavior analyst (Post-Master's Certificate); behavioral management (M Ed); early childhood teacher (M Ed); education specialist in curriculum and instruction (CAGS); educational leadership (Ed D); elementary teacher (M Ed); English as a second language (M Ed, Certificate); general science (M Ed); health education (Post-Master's Certificate); health/family and consumer sciences (M Ed); history (M Ed); individualized (M Ed); information technology literacy (M Ed); instructional technology (M Ed); interdisciplinary studies (M Ed); library teacher (M Ed); literacy education (M Ed); mathematics (M Ed); mathematics specialist (Certificate); middle school mathematics and science (M Ed); school administration (M Ed, CAGS); school guidance counselor (M Ed); school nurse education (M Ed); school social worker/school adjustment counselor (M Ed); special education administrator (CAGS); special education/moderate disabilities (M Ed); teaching skills and methodologies (M Ed). *Program availability:* Part-time, evening/weekend, online learning. *Degree requirements:* For master's, thesis, internship/practicum (licensure program only); for doctorate, thesis/dissertation; for other advanced degree, thesis. *Entrance requirements:* For master's, interview, resume, documentation of licensure, 2 professional references; for doctorate, official transcripts, interview, resume, documentation of licensure (if any), written personal statement/essay, portfolio of scholarly and professional work, qualifying assessment, 2 professional references, health insurance, immunizations form; for other advanced degree, official transcripts, interview, resume, documentation of licensure (if

any), written personal statement/essay, 2 professional references, health insurance, immunizations form. Additional exam requirements/recommendations for international students: Required—TOEFL (minimum score 550 paper-based; 79 iBT), Michigan English Language Assessment Battery (minimum score 85); Recommended—IELTS (minimum score 6). Electronic applications accepted. *Expenses:* Contact institution. *Faculty research:* Adult education, accelerated learning, mathematics education, brain compatible learning, special education and law.

Cambridge College, School of Psychology and Counseling, Boston, MA 02129. Offers addiction counseling (M Ed); alcohol and drug counseling (Certificate); counseling psychology (M Ed, CAGS); counseling psychology: forensic counseling (M Ed); marriage and family therapy (M Ed); mental health and addiction counseling (M Ed); mental health counseling (M Ed); mental health counseling for school guidance counselors (Post Master's Certificate); psychological studies (M Ed); school adjustment and mental health counseling (M Ed); school adjustment, mental health and addiction counseling (M Ed); school guidance counselor (M Ed); trauma studies (Certificate). *Program availability:* Part-time, evening/weekend. *Degree requirements:* For master's and other advanced degree, thesis, practicum/internship. *Entrance requirements:* For master's, resume, 2 professional references; for other advanced degree, official transcripts, documents for transfer credit evaluation, resume, written personal statement/essay, 2 professional references, health insurance, immunizations form. Additional exam requirements/recommendations for international students: Required—TOEFL (minimum score 550 paper-based; 79 iBT), Michigan English Language Assessment Battery (minimum score 85); Recommended—IELTS (minimum score 6). Electronic applications accepted. *Expenses:* Contact institution. *Faculty research:* Trauma, drug and alcohol counseling, cross-cultural issues, school counseling, trauma in schools.

Campbell University, Graduate and Professional Programs, School of Education, Buies Creek, NC 27506. Offers elementary education (M Ed); interdisciplinary studies (M Ed); middle grades education (M Ed); physical education (M Ed); school administration (MSA); school counseling (M Ed); secondary education (M Ed). *Accreditation:* NCATE. *Program availability:* Part-time, evening/weekend. *Degree requirements:* For master's, comprehensive exam. *Entrance requirements:* For master's, GRE General Test, minimum GPA of 2.7. *Faculty research:* Spiritual values and wellness issues in counseling, stress and professional burnout among counselors, thinking strategies, leadership, adaptive technology.

Canisius College, Graduate Division, School of Education and Human Services, Programs in Counseling and Human Services, Buffalo, NY 14208-1098. Offers community mental health counseling (MS); counseling and human services (MS); school agency counseling (MS). *Accreditation:* ACA. *Program availability:* Part-time, evening/weekend. *Faculty:* 5 full-time (2 women), 11 part-time/adjunct (8 women). *Students:* 80 full-time (68 women), 40 part-time (31 women); includes 21 minority (13 Black or African American, non-Hispanic/Latino; 6 Hispanic/Latino; 2 Two or more races, non-Hispanic/Latino), 5 international. Average age 29. 89 applicants, 85% accepted, 31 enrolled. In 2017, 39 master's awarded. *Degree requirements:* For master's, thesis, research project. *Entrance requirements:* For master's, GRE (if cumulative GPA less than 2.7), transcripts, two letters of recommendation, interview, BA. Additional exam requirements/recommendations for international students: Required—TOEFL (minimum score 550 paper-based, 79 iBT), IELTS (minimum score 6.5), or CAEL (minimum score 70). *Application deadline:* Applications are processed on a rolling basis. Application fee: $0. Electronic applications accepted. *Expenses:* Tuition: Full-time $22,860; part-time $820 per credit. *Required fees:* $720; $25 per credit. $65 per semester. One-time fee: $425. *Financial support:* Career-related internships or fieldwork, Federal Work-Study, scholarships/grants, tuition waivers (partial), and unspecified assistantships available. Support available to part-time students. Financial award application deadline: 4/30; financial award applicants required to submit FAFSA. *Faculty research:* Impact of trauma on adults, long term psych-social impact on police officers. *Unit head:* Dr. Christine Moll, Chair, 716-888-3287, E-mail: moll@canisius.edu.
Website: http://www.canisius.edu/masters-counseling

Capella University, Harold Abel School of Social and Behavioral Science, Doctoral Programs in Counseling, Minneapolis, MN 55402. Offers general counselor education and supervision (PhD); general social work (DSW). *Accreditation:* ACA.

Capella University, Harold Abel School of Social and Behavioral Science, Master's Programs in Counseling, Minneapolis, MN 55402. Offers child and adolescent development (MS); general addiction counseling (MS); general marriage and family counseling/therapy (MS); general mental health counseling (MS); general school counseling (MS).

Carson-Newman University, Graduate Program in Education, Jefferson City, TN 37760. Offers curriculum and instruction (M Ed); educational leadership (M Ed); elementary education (MAT); school counseling (MS); secondary education (MAT); teaching English as a second language (MATESL). *Accreditation:* NCATE. *Program availability:* Part-time, evening/weekend, 100% online, blended/hybrid learning. *Faculty:* 20 full-time (11 women), 16 part-time/adjunct (13 women). *Students:* 63 full-time (37 women), 488 part-time (362 women); includes 60 minority (46 Black or African American, non-Hispanic/Latino; 2 American Indian or Alaska Native, non-Hispanic/Latino; 1 Asian, non-Hispanic/Latino; 5 Hispanic/Latino; 1 Native Hawaiian or other Pacific Islander, non-Hispanic/Latino; 5 Two or more races, non-Hispanic/Latino), 29 international. Average age 35. 204 applicants, 100% accepted, 188 enrolled. In 2017, 211 master's awarded. *Degree requirements:* For master's, thesis or alternative. *Entrance requirements:* For master's, PRAXIS II or GRE with minimum score of 290 on the verbal and quantitative components (for MAT), minimum GPA of 3.0 in major, 2.5 overall. Additional exam requirements/recommendations for international students: Recommended—TOEFL (minimum score 79 iBT), IELTS (minimum score 6.5), TSE (minimum score 53). *Application deadline:* For fall admission, 7/15 priority date for domestic students. Applications are processed on a rolling basis. Application fee: $50. *Expenses: Tuition:* Full-time $10,516; part-time $478 per credit hour. *Required fees:* $240; $120 per semester. One-time fee: $150. *Financial support:* Federal Work-Study and unspecified assistantships available. Financial award applicants required to submit FAFSA. *Unit head:* Dr. Kim Hawkins, Chair, 865-471-3314, E-mail: khawkins@cn.edu. *Application contact:* Nilma Stewart, Graduate Admissions and Services Adviser, 865-471-3230, Fax: 865-471-3875, E-mail: adults@cn.edu.
Website: http://www.cn.edu/adult-graduate-studies

Carson-Newman University, Program in Counseling, Jefferson City, TN 37760. Offers MSC. *Accreditation:* ACA. *Program availability:* Part-time, evening/weekend. *Faculty:* 3 full-time (2 women), 1 part-time/adjunct (0 women). *Students:* 40 full-time (33 women), 34 part-time (29 women); includes 2 minority (1 Black or African American, non-Hispanic/Latino; 1 Hispanic/Latino), 2 international. Average age 29. 19 applicants, 100% accepted, 14 enrolled. In 2017, 18 master's awarded. *Entrance requirements:* Additional exam requirements/recommendations for international students: Recommended—TOEFL (minimum score 79 iBT), IELTS (minimum score 6.5), TSE (minimum score 53). *Application deadline:* Applications are processed on a rolling basis. Application fee: $50. *Expenses: Tuition:* Full-time $10,516; part-time $478 per credit hour. *Required fees:* $240; $120 per semester. One-time fee: $150. *Financial support:* Federal Work-Study and tuition waivers (full and partial) available. Financial award

applicants required to submit FAFSA. *Unit head:* Dr. Michael L. Bundy, Director, 865-471-2087, E-mail: mbundy@cn.edu. *Application contact:* Nilma Stewart, Graduate Admissions and Services Adviser, 865-471-3230, Fax: 865-471-3875, E-mail: adults@cn.edu.
Website: http://www.cn.edu/graduate-adult-studies/programs/graduate-studies-in-counseling

Carthage College, Division of Teacher Education, Kenosha, WI 53140. Offers classroom guidance and counseling (M Ed); creative arts (M Ed); gifted and talented children (M Ed); language arts (M Ed); modern language (M Ed); natural sciences (M Ed); reading (M Ed, Certificate); social sciences (M Ed); teacher leadership (M Ed). *Program availability:* Part-time, evening/weekend. *Degree requirements:* For master's, thesis optional. *Entrance requirements:* For master's, MAT, minimum B average, letters of reference.

Central Connecticut State University, School of Graduate Studies, School of Education and Professional Studies, Department of Counselor Education and Family Therapy, New Britain, CT 06050-4010. Offers marriage and family therapy (MS); professional counseling (MS, AC, Certificate); school counseling (MS); student development in higher education (MS). *Accreditation:* AAMFT/COAMFTE; ACA. *Program availability:* Part-time, evening/weekend. *Faculty:* 9 full-time (6 women), 27 part-time/adjunct (23 women). *Students:* 184 full-time (141 women), 189 part-time (144 women); includes 131 minority (51 Black or African American, non-Hispanic/Latino; 3 Asian, non-Hispanic/Latino; 66 Hispanic/Latino; 11 Two or more races, non-Hispanic/Latino), 1 international. Average age 34. 217 applicants, 64% accepted, 105 enrolled. In 2017, 94 master's, 7 other advanced degrees awarded. *Degree requirements:* For master's, comprehensive exam, thesis or alternative; for other advanced degree, qualifying exam. *Entrance requirements:* For master's, minimum undergraduate GPA of 2.7, essay, interview, letters of recommendation. Additional exam requirements/recommendations for international students: Required—TOEFL (minimum score 550 paper-based; 79 iBT); Recommended—IELTS (minimum score 6.5). *Application deadline:* For fall admission, 3/1 for domestic and international students; for summer admission, 3/1 for domestic and international students. Applications are processed on a rolling basis. Application fee: $50. Electronic applications accepted. *Expenses: Tuition, area resident:* Full-time $6757. Tuition, state resident: full-time $9750; part-time $374 per credit. Tuition, nonresident: full-time $18,102; part-time $374 per credit. *Required fees:* $4635; $255 per credit. *Financial support:* In 2017–18, 77 students received support. Career-related internships or fieldwork, Federal Work-Study, scholarships/grants, and unspecified assistantships available. Support available to part-time students. Financial award application deadline: 3/1; financial award applicants required to submit FAFSA. *Faculty research:* Elementary and secondary school counseling, marriage and family therapy, rehabilitation counseling, counseling in higher educational settings. *Unit head:* Dr. Cherie King, Chair, 860-832-2154, E-mail: kingche@ccsu.edu. *Application contact:* Patricia Gardner, Associate Director of Graduate Studies, 860-832-2350, Fax: 860-832-2362.
Website: http://www.ccsu.edu/ceft/

Central Methodist University, College of Graduate and Extended Studies, Fayette, MO 65248-1198. Offers clinical counseling (MS); clinical nurse leader (MSN); education (M Ed); music education (MME); nurse educator (MSN). *Program availability:* Part-time, evening/weekend, online learning. *Degree requirements:* For master's, thesis. *Entrance requirements:* For master's, GRE General Test, minimum GPA of 2.75. Electronic applications accepted.

Central Michigan University, Central Michigan University Global Campus, Program in Counseling, Mount Pleasant, MI 48859. Offers professional counseling (MA); school counseling (MA). *Accreditation:* TEAC. *Program availability:* Part-time, evening/weekend. *Entrance requirements:* For master's, MAT, minimum GPA of 2.7. Additional exam requirements/recommendations for international students: Required—TOEFL. Electronic applications accepted.

Central Michigan University, College of Graduate Studies, College of Education and Human Services, Department of Counseling and Special Education, Program in Counseling, Mount Pleasant, MI 48859. Offers counseling (MA), including professional counseling, school counseling. *Accreditation:* TEAC. *Program availability:* Part-time. *Degree requirements:* For master's, comprehensive exam, thesis or alternative. *Entrance requirements:* For master's, MAT, eligible for Michigan Teacher Certification (for school counseling). Electronic applications accepted. *Faculty research:* School counseling, professional counseling.

Chadron State College, School of Professional and Graduate Studies, Department of Education, Chadron, NE 69337. Offers business (MA Ed); community counseling (MA Ed); educational administration (MS Ed, Sp Ed); elementary education (MS Ed); history (MA Ed); language and literature (MA Ed); secondary administration (MS Ed); secondary education (MS Ed). *Accreditation:* NCATE. *Program availability:* Part-time, evening/weekend, online learning. *Degree requirements:* For master's, thesis optional. *Entrance requirements:* For master's, GRE General Test, GRE Writing Test, minimum GPA of 2.75 or 12 graduate hours at CSC with minimum GPA of 3.25. Additional exam requirements/recommendations for international students: Required—TOEFL. Electronic applications accepted. *Faculty research:* Rural education, technology, mental health.

Chapman University, Donna Ford Attallah College of Educational Studies, Orange, CA 92866. Offers counseling (MA), including school counseling (MA, Credential); curriculum and instruction (MA), including elementary education, secondary education; education (PhD), including cultural and curricular studies, disability studies, leadership studies, school psychology (PhD, Credential); educational psychology (MA); leadership development (MA); multiple subjects (Credential), including Spanish/English bilingual; pupil personnel services (Credential), including school counseling (MA, Credential), school psychology (PhD, Credential); school psychology (Ed S); single subject (Credential); special education (MA, Credential), including mild/moderate (Credential), moderate/severe (Credential); teaching (MA), including elementary education, secondary education, secondary music education. *Accreditation:* TEAC. *Program availability:* Part-time, evening/weekend. *Faculty:* 32 full-time (18 women), 37 part-time/adjunct (26 women). *Students:* 170 full-time (140 women), 180 part-time (129 women); includes 164 minority (6 Black or African American, non-Hispanic/Latino; 38 Asian, non-Hispanic/Latino; 101 Hispanic/Latino; 1 Native Hawaiian or other Pacific Islander, non-Hispanic/Latino; 18 Two or more races, non-Hispanic/Latino), 10 international. Average age 28. 143 applicants, 63% accepted, 64 enrolled. In 2017, 126 master's, 18 doctorates awarded. *Application deadline:* Applications are processed on a rolling basis. Application fee: $60. Electronic applications accepted. *Expenses:* Contact institution. *Financial support:* Fellowships and scholarships/grants available. Financial award application deadline: 3/2; financial award applicants required to submit FAFSA. *Unit head:* Dr. Margaret Grogan, Dean, 714-516-5968, E-mail: grogan@chapman.edu. *Application contact:* Shannon McCance, Graduate Admission Counselor, 714-516-5236, E-mail: smccance@chapman.edu.
Website: http://www.chapman.edu/CES/

Chicago State University, School of Graduate and Professional Studies, College of Arts and Sciences, Department of Psychology, Chicago, IL 60628. Offers counseling

(MA), including bilingual specialization, clinical mental health counseling, school counseling. *Accreditation:* ACA; NCATE. *Degree requirements:* For master's, comprehensive exam, thesis optional. *Entrance requirements:* For master's, minimum GPA of 3.0 for last 60 semester hours of course work or essay; interview. *Application deadline:* For fall admission, 3/1 for domestic students; for spring admission, 10/15 for domestic students. Application fee: $30. *Unit head:* Karen McCurtis-Witherspoon, Director of Counseling Graduate Program, 773-995-2359, Fax: 773-995-3513, E-mail: kmccurti@csu.edu. *Application contact:* Anika Miller, Graduate Studies Office, 773-995-2404, E-mail: g-studies1@csu.edu.
Website: http://www.csu.edu/cas/psychology/

The Citadel, The Military College of South Carolina, Citadel Graduate College, School of Humanities and Social Sciences, Department of Psychology, Charleston, SC 29409. Offers psychology (MA), including clinical counseling; school psychology (Ed S). *Program availability:* Part-time, evening/weekend. *Degree requirements:* For master's, comprehensive exam, practicum; internship (written and oral presentation of a case study as part of internship); for Ed S, comprehensive exam, thesis (for some programs), practicum, internship. *Entrance requirements:* For master's, GRE (minimum combined score of 297, 150 on verbal reasoning and 141 on quantitative reasoning) or MAT (minimum score of 410), minimum undergraduate GPA of 3.0; 12 credit hours in psychology or minimum score on GRE Subject Test in psychology of 600; 2 letters of recommendation; for Ed S, GRE (minimum combined score of 297, 150 on verbal reasoning and 147 on quantitative reasoning) or MAT (minimum score of 410), minimum undergraduate or graduate GPA of 3.0; 2 letters of recommendation. Additional exam requirements/recommendations for international students: Required—TOEFL (minimum score 550 paper-based; 79 iBT). Electronic applications accepted. *Expenses:* Tuition, state resident: part-time $587 per credit hour. Tuition, nonresident: part-time $988 per credit hour. *Required fees:* $90 per term.

The Citadel, The Military College of South Carolina, Citadel Graduate College, Zucker Family School of Education, Charleston, SC 29409. Offers elementary/secondary school administration and supervision (M Ed); elementary/secondary school counseling (M Ed); interdisciplinary STEM education (M Ed); literacy education (M Ed, Graduate Certificate); middle grades (MAT), including English, mathematics, science, social studies; physical education (grades K-12) (MAT); school superintendency (Ed S); secondary education (MAT), including biology, English, mathematics, social studies; student affairs (Graduate Certificate); student affairs and college counseling (M Ed). *Accreditation:* NCATE. *Program availability:* Part-time, evening/weekend, 100% online, blended/hybrid learning. *Degree requirements:* For master's, comprehensive exam (for some programs). *Entrance requirements:* For master's, GRE (minimum combined verbal and quantitative score of 290) or MAT (minimum score 396). Additional exam requirements/recommendations for international students: Required—TOEFL (minimum score 550 paper-based; 79 iBT). Electronic applications accepted. *Expenses:* Tuition, state resident: part-time $587 per credit hour. Tuition, nonresident: part-time $988 per credit hour. *Required fees:* $90 per term.

City University of Seattle, Graduate Division, Albright School of Education, Seattle, WA 98121. Offers administrator certification (Certificate); curriculum and instruction (M Ed); elementary education (MIT); guidance and counseling (M Ed); leadership (M Ed); reading and literacy (M Ed); school counseling (M Ed); special education (MIT); superintendent certification (Certificate). *Program availability:* Part-time, evening/weekend, online learning. *Degree requirements:* For master's, comprehensive exam (for some programs), thesis (for some programs). *Entrance requirements:* For master's, baccalaureate degree or equivalent from an accredited or otherwise recognized institution. Additional exam requirements/recommendations for international students: Required—TOEFL (minimum score 567 paper-based; 87 iBT); Recommended—IELTS. Electronic applications accepted. *Expenses:* Contact institution.

Clark Atlanta University, School of Education, Department of Counseling and Psychological Studies, Atlanta, GA 30314. Offers MA. *Accreditation:* ACA. *Program availability:* Part-time. *Faculty:* 4 full-time (2 women), 3 part-time/adjunct (2 women). *Students:* 35 full-time (26 women), 19 part-time (14 women); includes 45 minority (all Black or African American, non-Hispanic/Latino), 6 international. Average age 28. 35 applicants, 100% accepted, 20 enrolled. In 2017, 16 master's awarded. *Degree requirements:* For master's, comprehensive exam. *Entrance requirements:* For master's, GRE General Test, minimum undergraduate GPA of 2.6. Additional exam requirements/recommendations for international students: Required—TOEFL (minimum score 500 paper-based; 61 iBT). *Application deadline:* For fall admission, 4/1 for domestic and international students; for spring admission, 11/1 for domestic and international students. Applications are processed on a rolling basis. Application fee: $40 ($55 for international students). Electronic applications accepted. *Financial support:* Career-related internships or fieldwork, Federal Work-Study, scholarships/grants, and unspecified assistantships available. Support available to part-time students. Financial award application deadline: 4/30; financial award applicants required to submit FAFSA. *Unit head:* Dr. Ken Sanders, Chairperson, 404-880-8519, E-mail: ksanders1@cau.edu.

Clarks Summit University, Online Master's Programs, South Abington Township, PA 18411. Offers Bible (MA); counseling (MA, MS); curriculum and instruction (M Ed); educational administration (M Ed); literature (MA); organizational leadership (MA). *Program availability:* Part-time, evening/weekend, online learning. *Entrance requirements:* Additional exam requirements/recommendations for international students: Required—TOEFL (minimum score 500 paper-based). *Application deadline:* Applications are processed on a rolling basis. Application fee: $30. *Financial support:* Institutionally sponsored loans and scholarships/grants available. Financial award application deadline: 8/20; financial award applicants required to submit FAFSA. *Unit head:* Dr. James Lytle, President, 570-586-2400 Ext. 9222, Fax: 570-586-1753. *Application contact:* Drew Whipple, Vice President for Enrollment Management, 570-585-9370, Fax: 570-585-9299, E-mail: awhipple@clarkssummitu.edu.
Website: https://www.clarkssummitu.edu/online-masters-degrees/

Clemson University, Graduate School, College of Education, Department of Education and Human Development, Clemson, SC 29634. Offers counselor education (M Ed, Ed S), including mental health counseling, school counseling, student affairs (M Ed); learning sciences (PhD); literacy (M Ed); literacy, language and culture (PhD); special education (M Ed, MAT, PhD). *Program availability:* Part-time, evening/weekend, 100% online. *Faculty:* 32 full-time (22 women). *Students:* 445 full-time (355 women), 169 part-time (159 women); includes 126 minority (52 Black or African American, non-Hispanic/Latino; 16 Asian, non-Hispanic/Latino; 34 Hispanic/Latino; 24 Two or more races, non-Hispanic/Latino), 5 international. Average age 28. 401 applicants, 60% accepted, 135 enrolled. In 2017, 212 master's, 1 doctorate, 117 other advanced degrees awarded. *Degree requirements:* For master's, thesis (for some programs); for doctorate, comprehensive exam (for some programs), thesis/dissertation. *Entrance requirements:* For master's and doctorate, GRE General Test, unofficial transcripts, letters of recommendation. Additional exam requirements/recommendations for international students: Required—TOEFL (minimum score 80 iBT), IELTS (minimum score 7), PTE (minimum score 54). *Application deadline:* For fall admission, 3/1 priority date for domestic and international students; for spring admission, 10/1 priority date for domestic and international students. Applications are processed on a rolling basis. Application fee: $80 ($90 for international students). Electronic applications accepted. *Expenses:*

Counselor Education

$5,174 per semester full-time resident, $9,714 per semester full-time non-resident, $511 per credit hour part-time resident, $1,017 per credit hour part-time non-resident; $741 per credit hour online; other fees may apply per session. *Financial support:* In 2017–18, 84 students received support, including 9 fellowships with partial tuition reimbursements available (averaging $8,148 per year), 18 teaching assistantships with partial tuition reimbursements available (averaging $13,707 per year); career-related internships or fieldwork and unspecified assistantships also available. Financial award application deadline: 3/1. *Total annual research expenditures:* $1.2 million. *Unit head:* Dr. Debi Switzer, Department Chair, 864-656-5098, E-mail: debi@clemson.edu. *Application contact:* Julie Jones, Student Services Program Coordinator, 864-656-5096, E-mail: jgambre@clemson.edu.
Website: http://www.clemson.edu/education/departments/education-human-development/index.html

Cleveland State University, College of Graduate Studies, College of Education and Human Services, Department of Counseling, Administration, Supervision and Adult Learning (CASAL), Cleveland, OH 44115. Offers adult learning and development (M Ed); counselor education (PhD); early childhood mental health counseling (Certificate); educational administration and supervision (M Ed). *Accreditation:* ACA (one or more programs are accredited). *Program availability:* Part-time, evening/weekend. *Faculty:* 15 full-time (8 women), 19 part-time/adjunct (10 women). *Students:* 121 full-time (98 women), 272 part-time (198 women); includes 127 minority (106 Black or African American, non-Hispanic/Latino; 1 American Indian or Alaska Native, non-Hispanic/Latino; 4 Asian, non-Hispanic/Latino; 11 Hispanic/Latino; 5 Two or more races, non-Hispanic/Latino), 8 international. Average age 33. 57 applicants, 93% accepted, 51 enrolled. In 2017, 99 master's awarded. *Degree requirements:* For master's, comprehensive exam (for some programs), thesis optional, internship. *Entrance requirements:* For master's, GRE General Test or MAT, letter of recommendation and minimum GPA of 2.75 (for counseling); 2 letters of recommendation and interviews (for organizational leadership). Additional exam requirements/recommendations for international students: Required—TOEFL (minimum score 550 paper-based; 78 iBT), IELTS (minimum score 6). *Application deadline:* For fall admission, 6/21 for domestic students, 5/15 for international students; for spring admission, 8/31 for domestic students, 11/1 for international students. Application fee: $40. Electronic applications accepted. *Financial support:* In 2017–18, 19 students received support, including 10 research assistantships with tuition reimbursements available (averaging $11,882 per year), 5 teaching assistantships with tuition reimbursements available (averaging $11,882 per year); scholarships/grants and unspecified assistantships also available. Support available to part-time students. *Faculty research:* Education law, career development, bullying, psychopharmacology, counseling and spirituality. *Total annual research expenditures:* $225,821. *Unit head:* Dr. R. Ingersoll, Chair/Professor, 216-687-4582, Fax: 216-687-5378, E-mail: r.ingersoll@csuohio.edu. *Application contact:* Deborah L. Brown, Interim Assistant Director, Graduate Admissions, 216-523-7572, Fax: 216-687-5400, E-mail: d.l.brown@csuohio.edu.
Website: http://www.csuohio.edu/cehs/departments/CASAL/casal_dept.html

The College at Brockport, State University of New York, School of Education, Health, and Human Services, Department of Counselor Education, Brockport, NY 14420-2997. Offers college counseling (MS Ed, CAS); mental health counseling (MS, CAS); school counseling (MS Ed, CAS); school counselor supervision (CAS). *Accreditation:* ACA (one or more programs are accredited). *Program availability:* Part-time. *Faculty:* 5 full-time (3 women), 6 part-time/adjunct (4 women). *Students:* 32 full-time (23 women), 74 part-time (63 women); includes 24 minority (13 Black or African American, non-Hispanic/Latino; 1 Asian, non-Hispanic/Latino; 4 Hispanic/Latino; 6 Two or more races, non-Hispanic/Latino). 94 applicants, 60% accepted, 24 enrolled. In 2017, 31 master's, 6 other advanced degrees awarded. *Degree requirements:* For master's, thesis, internship. *Entrance requirements:* For master's, group interview, letters of recommendation, written objectives, audio response; for CAS, master's degree, New York state school counselor certificate. Additional exam requirements/recommendations for international students: Required—TOEFL (minimum score 550 paper-based; 79 iBT), IELTS (minimum score 6.5). *Application deadline:* For fall admission, 2/1 priority date for domestic and international students; for spring admission, 9/1 priority date for domestic and international students; for summer admission, 2/1 priority date for domestic and international students. Application fee: $80. Electronic applications accepted. *Expenses:* Tuition, state resident: full-time $10,870; part-time $453 per credit hour. Tuition, nonresident: full-time $22,210. *Required fees:* $988; $246 per semester. *Financial support:* In 2017–18, 1 fellowship with full tuition reimbursement (averaging $7,500 per year), 1 teaching assistantship with full tuition reimbursement (averaging $6,000 per year) were awarded; Federal Work-Study, scholarships/grants, and unspecified assistantships also available. Support available to part-time students. Financial award application deadline: 3/15; financial award applicants required to submit FAFSA. *Faculty research:* Gender and diversity issues; counseling outcomes; spirituality; school, college and mental health counseling; obesity. *Unit head:* Dr. Susan Seem, Chair, 585-395-5492, Fax: 585-395-2366, E-mail: sseem@brockport.edu. *Application contact:* Danielle A. Welch, Graduate Admissions Counselor, 585-395-5465, Fax: 585-395-2515.
Website: https://www.brockport.edu/academics/counselor_education/

The College of New Jersey, Office of Graduate and Advancing Education, School of Education, Department of Counselor Education, Program in Community Counseling: Human Services Specialization, Ewing, NJ 08628. Offers MA. *Accreditation:* ACA. *Program availability:* Part-time. *Degree requirements:* For master's, comprehensive exam. *Entrance requirements:* For master's, GRE General Test, minimum GPA of 3.0 in field or 2.75 overall, interview. Additional exam requirements/recommendations for international students: Required—TOEFL. Electronic applications accepted.

The College of New Jersey, Office of Graduate and Advancing Education, School of Education, Department of Counselor Education, Program in School Counseling, Ewing, NJ 08628. Offers MA. *Accreditation:* ACA; NCATE. *Program availability:* Part-time. *Degree requirements:* For master's, comprehensive exam. *Entrance requirements:* For master's, GRE General Test, minimum GPA of 3.0 in field or 2.75 overall, interview. Additional exam requirements/recommendations for international students: Required—TOEFL. Electronic applications accepted.

College of St. Joseph, Graduate Programs, Division of Psychology and Human Services, Rutland, VT 05701-3899. Offers alcohol and substance abuse counseling (MS); clinical mental health counseling (MS); clinical psychology (MS); community counseling (MS); school guidance counseling (MS). *Program availability:* Part-time, evening/weekend. *Degree requirements:* For master's, comprehensive exam, thesis optional. *Entrance requirements:* For master's, official college transcripts; 2 letters of reference. Additional exam requirements/recommendations for international students: Required—TOEFL (minimum score 550 paper-based). Electronic applications accepted.

The College of Saint Rose, Graduate Studies, Thelma P. Lally School of Education, Programs in Clinical Mental Health Counseling, Albany, NY 12203-1419. Offers clinical mental health counseling (Certificate); school counseling (MS Ed, Certificate), including mental health counseling (MS Ed). *Students:* 44 full-time (39 women), 20 part-time (17 women); includes 11 minority (6 Black or African American, non-Hispanic/Latino; 2 Asian, non-Hispanic/Latino; 2 Hispanic/Latino; 1 Two or more races, non-Hispanic/Latino), 2 international. Average age 28. 32 applicants, 63% accepted, 12 enrolled. In

2017, 23 master's awarded. *Entrance requirements:* For master's, minimum undergraduate GPA of 3.0. Additional exam requirements/recommendations for international students: Required—TOEFL (minimum score 550 paper-based; 80 iBT), IELTS (minimum score 6), PTE (minimum score 56). *Application deadline:* For fall admission, 4/1 for domestic and international students; for spring admission, 10/15 priority date for domestic and international students; for summer admission, 3/15 for domestic and international students. Applications are processed on a rolling basis. Application fee: $40. Electronic applications accepted. *Expenses:* Tuition: Full-time $7191; part-time $799 per credit hour. *Required fees:* $924; $462 per credit hour. Tuition and fees vary according to course load. *Financial support:* Career-related internships or fieldwork, scholarships/grants, tuition waivers (partial), and unspecified assistantships available. Support available to part-time students. Financial award application deadline: 4/15. *Unit head:* Claudia Lingertat-Putnam, Chair, 518-337-4311, E-mail: lingertc@strose.edu. *Application contact:* Cris Murray, Assistant Vice President for Graduate Recruitment and Enrollment, 518-485-3390, Fax: 518-458-5479, E-mail: grad@strose.edu.
Website: https://www.strose.edu/counseling/

The College of William and Mary, School of Education, Program in Counselor Education, Williamsburg, VA 23187-8795. Offers addictions counseling (M Ed); community counseling (M Ed); counselor education (PhD); family counseling (M Ed); school counseling (M Ed). *Accreditation:* ACA; NCATE. *Program availability:* Part-time, evening/weekend, 100% online with required residency. *Faculty:* 12 full-time (4 women), 6 part-time/adjunct (5 women). *Students:* 64 full-time (50 women), 3 part-time (2 women); includes 14 minority (1 Black or African American, non-Hispanic/Latino; 2 Asian, non-Hispanic/Latino; 6 Hispanic/Latino; 5 Two or more races, non-Hispanic/Latino), 2 international. Average age 28. 163 applicants, 43% accepted, 32 enrolled. In 2017, 33 master's, 8 doctorates awarded. *Degree requirements:* For doctorate, comprehensive exam, thesis/dissertation. *Entrance requirements:* For master's, GRE, minimum GPA of 3.0; for doctorate, GRE, minimum GPA of 3.5. Additional exam requirements/recommendations for international students: Required—TOEFL (minimum score 100 iBT), IELTS (minimum score 7). *Application deadline:* For fall admission, 1/15 for domestic and international students. Application fee: $50. Electronic applications accepted. *Expenses:* $9,630 resident full-time, $535 resident part-time per credit hour; $25,920 nonresident full-time, $1,265 nonresident part-time per credit hour; $5,944 full-time fees. *Financial support:* In 2017–18, 34 students received support, including 26 research assistantships (averaging $18,723 per year); scholarships/grants also available. Financial award application deadline: 1/15; financial award applicants required to submit FAFSA. *Faculty research:* Sexuality, multicultural education, addiction counseling, transpersonal psychology, measurement and evaluation in counseling. *Unit head:* Dr. Charles F. Gressard, Department Chair, 757-221-2352, E-mail: cfgres@wm.edu. *Application contact:* Dorothy Smith Osborne, Assistant Dean for Academic Programs and Student Services, 757-221-2317, E-mail: dsosbo@wm.edu.
Website: http://education.wm.edu

Colorado State University, College of Health and Human Sciences, School of Education, Fort Collins, CO 80523-1588. Offers adult education and training (M Ed); counseling and career development (MA); education and human resources (M Ed); education, equity, and transformation (PhD); higher education leadership (PhD); organizational learning, performance, and change (M Ed, PhD); student affairs in higher education (MS). *Accreditation:* ACA; TEAC. *Program availability:* Part-time, online only, 100% online, blended/hybrid learning. *Faculty:* 33 full-time (23 women), 19 part-time/adjunct (11 women). *Students:* 74 full-time (53 women), 548 part-time (357 women); includes 151 minority (37 Black or African American, non-Hispanic/Latino; 4 American Indian or Alaska Native, non-Hispanic/Latino; 14 Asian, non-Hispanic/Latino; 71 Hispanic/Latino; 25 Two or more races, non-Hispanic/Latino), 16 international. Average age 37. 456 applicants, 31% accepted, 123 enrolled. In 2017, 177 master's, 22 doctorates awarded. *Degree requirements:* For master's, thesis optional, professional portfolio or capstone project; for doctorate, comprehensive exam, thesis/dissertation. *Entrance requirements:* For master's, bachelor's degree; minimum GPA of 3.0 in last degree earned; for doctorate, GRE; GRE or GMAT (for organizational learning, performance and change only), master's degree; minimum GPA of 3.0 in last degree earned. Additional exam requirements/recommendations for international students: Required—TOEFL (minimum score 550 paper-based; 80 iBT), IELTS (minimum score 6.5), PTE (minimum score 58). *Application deadline:* Applications are processed on a rolling basis. Application fee: $60 ($70 for international students). Electronic applications accepted. *Expenses:* Contact institution. *Financial support:* In 2017–18, 4 students received support, including 8 research assistantships with full and partial tuition reimbursements available (averaging $12,758 per year), 4 teaching assistantships with full and partial tuition reimbursements available (averaging $14,256 per year); fellowships with full and partial tuition reimbursements available, Federal Work-Study, scholarships/grants, tuition waivers (full and partial), and unspecified assistantships also available. Financial award applicants required to submit FAFSA. *Faculty research:* Diversity, equity, and inclusion; STEM education; higher education; occupational learning, performance, and change; teacher education. *Total annual research expenditures:* $312,562. *Unit head:* Dr. Louise Jennings, Co-Director, 970-491-6317, Fax: 970-491-1317, E-mail: louise.jennings@colostate.edu. *Application contact:* Kelli Clark, Graduate Programs Coordinator, 970-491-2093, Fax: 970-491-1317, E-mail: kelli.clark@colostate.edu.
Website: http://www.soe.chhs.colostate.edu/

Columbia International University, Columbia Graduate School, Columbia, SC 29203. Offers Bible teaching (MABT); counseling (MACN); early childhood and elementary education (MAT); educational administration (M Ed); educational leadership (PhD); instruction and learning (M Ed); teaching English as a foreign language (Certificate); teaching English as a foreign language and intercultural studies (MATF). *Program availability:* Part-time, evening/weekend, online learning. *Degree requirements:* For master's, internships, professional project. *Entrance requirements:* For master's, MAT, GRE (for some programs), minimum GPA of 2.7. Additional exam requirements/recommendations for international students: Required—TOEFL. Electronic applications accepted.

Columbus State University, Graduate Studies, College of Education and Health Professions, Department of Counseling, Foundations, and Leadership, Columbus, GA 31907-5645. Offers clinical mental health counseling (MS); curriculum and leadership (Ed D), including curriculum, educational leadership, higher education (M Ed, Ed D); educational leadership (M Ed, Ed S), including higher education (M Ed, Ed D); school counseling (M Ed, Ed S). *Accreditation:* ACA; NCATE. *Program availability:* Part-time, evening/weekend, 100% online, blended/hybrid learning. *Faculty:* 18 full-time (8 women), 20 part-time/adjunct (10 women). *Students:* 248 full-time (166 women), 308 part-time (236 women); includes 315 minority (278 Black or African American, non-Hispanic/Latino; 11 Asian, non-Hispanic/Latino; 15 Hispanic/Latino; 1 Native Hawaiian or other Pacific Islander, non-Hispanic/Latino; 10 Two or more races, non-Hispanic/Latino), 2 international. Average age 39. 155 applicants, 38% accepted, 40 enrolled. In 2017, 41 master's, 18 doctorates, 110 other advanced degrees awarded. *Degree requirements:* For master's, thesis, exit exam; for doctorate, comprehensive exam, thesis/dissertation; for Ed S, thesis or alternative. *Entrance requirements:* For master's, GRE General Test, minimum undergraduate GPA of 2.75; for doctorate, GRE General

Test, minimum graduate GPA of 3.5, four years of professional service; for Ed S, GRE General Test, minimum undergraduate GPA of 2.75, graduate 3.0. Additional exam requirements/recommendations for international students: Required—TOEFL (minimum score 550 paper-based; 79 iBT). *Application deadline:* For fall admission, 6/30 for domestic and international students; for spring admission, 11/1 for domestic and international students; for summer admission, 3/1 for domestic and international students. Applications are processed on a rolling basis. Application fee: $50. Electronic applications accepted. *Expenses:* Tuition, state resident: full-time $3708; part-time $2472 per year. Tuition, nonresident: full-time $14,418; part-time $9612 per year. *International tuition:* $19,218 full-time. *Required fees:* $1605. Tuition and fees vary according to program. *Financial support:* In 2017–18, 34 students received support, including 14 research assistantships with partial tuition reimbursements available (averaging $3,000 per year); career-related internships or fieldwork, Federal Work-Study, institutionally sponsored loans, scholarships/grants, tuition waivers (partial), and unspecified assistantships also available. Support available to part-time students. Financial award application deadline: 5/1; financial award applicants required to submit FAFSA. *Unit head:* Dr. Tom Hackett, Department Chair, 706-507-8968, Fax: 706-569-3134, E-mail: hackett_paul@columbusstate.edu. *Application contact:* Catrina Smith-Edmond, Assistant Director for Graduate and Global Admission, 706-507-8824, Fax: 706-568-5091, E-mail: smithedmond_catrina@columbusstate.edu.
Website: http://cfl.columbusstate.edu/

Concordia University Chicago, College of Graduate and Innovative Programs, Program in School Counseling, River Forest, IL 60305-1499. Offers MA, CAS. *Accreditation:* ACA (one or more programs are accredited); NCATE. *Program availability:* Part-time, evening/weekend. *Degree requirements:* For master's, comprehensive exam, thesis optional; for CAS, thesis, final project. *Entrance requirements:* For master's, minimum GPA of 2.9; for CAS, master's degree. Additional exam requirements/recommendations for international students: Required—TOEFL (minimum score 550 paper-based). Electronic applications accepted. *Faculty research:* Development of comprehensive school counseling education, training of school counselors for parochial schools.

Concordia University Irvine, School of Education, Irvine, CA 92612-3299. Offers curriculum and instruction (MA); education and preliminary teaching credential (M Ed); educational administration and preliminary administrative services credential (MA); educational technology (MA); school counseling with pupil personnel services credential (MA). *Program availability:* Part-time, evening/weekend, online learning. *Degree requirements:* For master's, action research project. *Entrance requirements:* For master's, California Basic Educational Skills Test, California Subject Examinations for Teachers (M Ed and MA in educational administration and preliminary administrative services credential), official college transcript(s), signed statement of intent, two references, copy of credential. Additional exam requirements/recommendations for international students: Required—TOEFL. Electronic applications accepted. *Expenses:* Contact institution.

Concordia University Wisconsin, Graduate Programs, Department of Education, Mequon, WI 53097-2402. Offers art education (MS Ed); early childhood (MS Ed); educational administration (MS Ed); environmental education (MS Ed); family studies (MS Ed); literacy (MS Ed); school counseling (MS Ed); special education (MS Ed). *Program availability:* Part-time, evening/weekend, online learning. *Degree requirements:* For master's, comprehensive exam, thesis or alternative. *Entrance requirements:* For master's, minimum GPA of 3.0, teaching license. Additional exam requirements/ recommendations for international students: Required—TOEFL. *Faculty research:* Motivation, developmental learning, learning styles.

Creighton University, Graduate School, College of Arts and Sciences, Department of Education, Program in School Counseling and Preventive Mental Health, Omaha, NE 68178-0001. Offers elementary school guidance (MS); secondary school guidance (MS). *Program availability:* Part-time, online only, 100% online, blended/hybrid learning. *Faculty:* 3 full-time (1 woman), 42 part-time (34 women); includes 4 minority (1 Black or African American, non-Hispanic/Latino; 2 American Indian or Alaska Native, non-Hispanic/Latino; 1 Native Hawaiian or other Pacific Islander, non-Hispanic/Latino), 1 international. Average age 31. In 2017, 18 master's awarded. *Degree requirements:* For master's, comprehensive exam. *Entrance requirements:* For master's, resume, 3 letters of recommendation, personal statement, background check. Additional exam requirements/recommendations for international students: Required—TOEFL (minimum score 90 iBT). *Application deadline:* For fall admission, 7/1 for domestic students, 3/1 for international students; for winter admission, 10/1 for domestic students, 7/1 for international students; for spring admission, 3/1 for domestic students, 9/1 for international students; for summer admission, 3/1 for domestic and international students. Application fee: $50. Electronic applications accepted. Part-time tuition and fees vary according to course load, degree level, campus/location and program. *Financial support:* Scholarships/grants available. Support available to part-time students. Financial award applicants required to submit FAFSA. *Unit head:* Dr. Timothy Dickel, Professor of Education, 402-280-2230, E-mail: ctdickel@creighton.edu. *Application contact:* Lindsay Johnson, Director of Graduate and Adult Recruitment, 402-280-2703, Fax: 402-280-2423, E-mail: gradschool@creighton.edu.

Dallas Baptist University, Dorothy M. Bush College of Education, Program in School Counseling, Dallas, TX 75211-9299. Offers M Ed. *Program availability:* Part-time, evening/weekend. *Application deadline:* Applications are processed on a rolling basis. Application fee: $25. Electronic applications accepted. Application fee is waived when completed online. *Expenses:* Tuition: Full-time $16,308; part-time $906 per credit hour. *Required fees:* $900; $450 per semester. Tuition and fees vary according to course load and degree level. *Unit head:* Dr. Neil Dugger, Dean, 214-333-5202, E-mail: neil@dbu.edu. *Application contact:* Dr. Bonnie Bond, Program Director, 214-333-6838, E-mail: bonnie@dbu.edu.
Website: http://www3.dbu.edu/graduate/education_counseling.asp

Delta State University, Graduate Programs, College of Education, Division of Counselor Education and Psychology, Cleveland, MS 38733-0001. Offers counseling (M Ed). *Accreditation:* ACA (one or more programs are accredited); NCATE. *Program availability:* Part-time, evening/weekend. *Degree requirements:* For master's, thesis optional, practicum. Electronic applications accepted.

Delta State University, Graduate Programs, College of Education, Division of Teacher Education, Leadership, and Research, Program in Professional Studies, Cleveland, MS 38733-0001. Offers counselor education (Ed D); elementary education (Ed D); higher education (Ed D). *Program availability:* Part-time, evening/weekend. *Degree requirements:* For doctorate, thesis/dissertation. *Entrance requirements:* For doctorate, GRE General Test.

DePaul University, College of Education, Chicago, IL 60614. Offers bilingual-bicultural education (M Ed, MA); counseling (M Ed, MA), including clinical mental health counseling, college student development, school counseling; curriculum studies (M Ed, MA, Ed D); early childhood (M Ed, MA, Ed D); educational leadership (M Ed, MA, Ed D), including Catholic leadership (M Ed, MA), general (M Ed, MA), higher education (M Ed, MA), physical education (M Ed, MA), principal preparation (M Ed),

teacher preparation (M Ed); elementary education (M Ed, MA); middle grades education (M Ed); middle school mathematics education (MS); reading specialist (M Ed, MA); secondary education (M Ed, MA); social and cultural foundations in education (M Ed, MA); special education (M Ed); sport, fitness and recreation leadership (MS); value-creating education for global citizenship (M Ed); world languages education (M Ed, MA). *Program availability:* Part-time, evening/weekend, online learning. *Degree requirements:* For doctorate, thesis/dissertation. *Application deadline:* Applications are processed on a rolling basis. Application fee: $40. Electronic applications accepted. *Financial support:* Application deadline: 12/31; applicants required to submit FAFSA. *Unit head:* Dr. Paul Zionts, Dean, 773-325-7581, Fax: 773-325-7713, E-mail: pzionts@depaul.edu. *Application contact:* Dr. Paul Zionts, Dean, 773-325-7581, Fax: 773-325-7713, E-mail: pzionts@depaul.edu.
Website: http://education.depaul.edu

Doane University, Program in Counseling, Crete, NE 68333-2430. Offers MAC. *Program availability:* Evening/weekend. *Faculty:* 2 full-time (1 woman), 15 part-time/ adjunct (11 women). *Students:* 61 full-time (48 women), 20 part-time (14 women); includes 9 minority (1 Black or African American, non-Hispanic/Latino; 1 American Indian or Alaska Native, non-Hispanic/Latino; 6 Hispanic/Latino; 1 Two or more races, non-Hispanic/Latino), 4 international. Average age 34. In 2017, 37 master's awarded. *Degree requirements:* For master's, thesis. *Entrance requirements:* For master's, minimum GPA of 3.0. Additional exam requirements/recommendations for international students: Required—TOEFL. *Application deadline:* Applications are processed on a rolling basis. Application fee: $25. Electronic applications accepted. *Expenses:* Contact institution. *Financial support:* Unspecified assistantships available. Financial award application deadline: 6/1; financial award applicants required to submit FAFSA. *Unit head:* Associate Dean/Director of the Counseling Program, 402-466-4774, Fax: 402-466-4228. *Application contact:* Jean Kilnoski, Assistant Dean, 402-466-4774, Fax: 404-466-4228, E-mail: jean.kilnoski@doane.edu.
Website: http://www.doane.edu/master-of-arts-in-counseling-0

Drake University, School of Education, Des Moines, IA 50311-4516. Offers applied behavior analysis (MS); counseling (MS); education (PhD); education administration (Ed D); educational leadership (MSE, Ed D); effective teaching (MSE); leadership development (MS); literacy (Ed S); literacy education (MSE); rehabilitation administration (MS); rehabilitation placement (MS); special education (MSE); STEM education (MSE); teacher education (5-12) (MAT); teacher education (K-8) (MST); teacher effectiveness and professional development (MSE). *Program availability:* Part-time, evening/weekend. *Degree requirements:* For master's and Ed S, comprehensive exam, internships (for some programs); for doctorate, comprehensive exam, thesis/dissertation, internships (for some programs). *Entrance requirements:* For master's, GRE General Test, MAT, or Drake Writing Assessment, resume, 2 letters of recommendation; for doctorate, GRE General Test or MAT, master's degree, 3 letters of recommendation; for Ed S, GRE General Test or MAT. Additional exam requirements/recommendations for international students: Required—TOEFL (minimum score 550 paper-based). *Application deadline:* For fall admission, 7/1 priority date for domestic students, 6/1 priority date for international students; for spring admission, 11/1 priority date for domestic students, 10/1 priority date for international students. Applications are processed on a rolling basis. Application fee: $25. Electronic applications accepted. *Expenses:* Contact institution. *Financial support:* Research assistantships, career-related internships or fieldwork, and unspecified assistantships available. Support available to part-time students. *Faculty research:* Counseling and rehabilitation, behavioral supports, inquiry-based science methods, teacher quality enhancement. *Unit head:* Dr. Janet McMahill, Dean, 515-271-3829, E-mail: janet.mcmahill@drake.edu.
Website: http://www.drake.edu/soe/

Duquesne University, School of Education, Department of Counseling, Psychology, and Special Education, Program in Counselor Education, Pittsburgh, PA 15282-0001. Offers clinical mental health counseling (MS Ed, Post-Master's Certificate); counselor education and supervision (Ed D); counselor licensure (Post-Master's Certificate); marriage and family counseling (MS Ed); school counseling (MS Ed). *Accreditation:* ACA (one or more programs are accredited). *Program availability:* Part-time, evening/ weekend. *Faculty:* 8 full-time (3 women). *Students:* 194 full-time (140 women), 10 part-time (6 women); includes 41 minority (21 Black or African American, non-Hispanic/ Latino; 1 American Indian or Alaska Native, non-Hispanic/Latino; 5 Asian, non-Hispanic/ Latino; 6 Hispanic/Latino; 8 Two or more races, non-Hispanic/Latino), 8 international. Average age 28. 149 applicants, 78% accepted, 66 enrolled. In 2017, 53 master's, 6 doctorates awarded. *Degree requirements:* For master's, thesis optional; for doctorate, thesis/dissertation. *Entrance requirements:* For master's, letters of recommendation, essay, interview, bachelor's degree; for doctorate, GRE, letters of recommendation, essay, interview, master's degree; for Post-Master's Certificate, GRE, letters of recommendation, essay, interview, bachelor's/master's degree. Additional exam requirements/recommendations for international students: Required—TOEFL (minimum score 550 paper-based), IELTS (minimum score 6.5). *Application deadline:* For fall admission, 4/2 for domestic students; for spring admission, 9/1 for domestic students. Applications are processed on a rolling basis. Application fee: $0. Electronic applications accepted. *Expenses:* $1,259 per credit. *Financial support:* Research assistantships, teaching assistantships, and Federal Work-Study available. Support available to part-time students. *Faculty research:* Trauma counseling, counseling supervision, purpose and meaning, Internet addictions, bullying and relational aggression. *Unit head:* Dr. Jered Kolbert, Professor/Director, 412-396-4471, Fax: 412-396-1340, E-mail: kolbertj@duq.edu. *Application contact:* Kelly McGinley, Graduate Admissions Assistant, 412-396-1559, Fax: 412-396-5585, E-mail: mcginleyk@duq.edu.

East Carolina University, Graduate School, College of Allied Health Sciences, Department of Addictions and Rehabilitation Studies, Greenville, NC 27858-4353. Offers clinical counseling (MS); military and trauma counseling (Certificate); rehabilitation and career counseling (MS); rehabilitation counseling (Certificate); rehabilitation counseling and administration (PhD); substance abuse counseling (Certificate); vocational evaluation (Certificate). *Accreditation:* CORE. *Program availability:* Part-time, evening/ weekend. *Students:* 82 full-time (64 women), 55 part-time (43 women); includes 39 minority (28 Black or African American, non-Hispanic/Latino; 1 American Indian or Alaska Native, non-Hispanic/Latino; 2 Asian, non-Hispanic/Latino; 5 Hispanic/Latino; 3 Two or more races, non-Hispanic/Latino). Average age 33. 51 applicants, 73% accepted, 31 enrolled. In 2017, 19 master's, 5 doctorates, 34 other advanced degrees awarded. *Degree requirements:* For master's, comprehensive exam, thesis or alternative, internship; for doctorate, thesis/dissertation, internship. *Entrance requirements:* For master's and doctorate, GRE General Test or MAT. Additional exam requirements/recommendations for international students: Recommended—TOEFL (minimum score 78 iBT), IELTS (minimum score 6.5). *Application deadline:* For fall admission, 3/1 priority date for domestic students; for spring admission, 10/1 priority date for domestic students. Applications are processed on a rolling basis. Application fee: $75. Electronic applications accepted. *Expenses:* Tuition, state resident: full-time $4749; part-time $297 per credit hour. Tuition, nonresident: full-time $17,898; part-time $1119 per credit hour. *Required fees:* $2691; $224 per credit hour. Part-time tuition and fees vary according to course load and program. *Financial support:* Research assistantships with partial tuition reimbursements, teaching assistantships with partial tuition reimbursements, Federal Work-Study, scholarships/grants, and unspecified

Counselor Education

assistantships available. Support available to part-time students. Financial award application deadline: 3/1; financial award applicants required to submit FAFSA. *Unit head:* Dr. Paul Toriello, Chair, 252-744-6292, E-mail: toriellop@ecu.edu. Website: http://www.ecu.edu/rehb/

East Carolina University, Graduate School, College of Education, Department of Interdisciplinary Professions, Greenville, NC 27858-4353. Offers adult education (MA Ed); business and marketing education (MA Ed); community college instruction (Certificate); counselor education (MS); education in the healthcare professions (Certificate); library science (MLS); student affairs in higher education (Certificate); vocational education (MS). *Accreditation:* ACA; NCATE. *Program availability:* Part-time, evening/weekend. *Students:* 97 full-time (77 women), 392 part-time (344 women); includes 107 minority (73 Black or African American, non-Hispanic/Latino; 6 American Indian or Alaska Native, non-Hispanic/Latino; 5 Asian, non-Hispanic/Latino; 11 Hispanic/Latino; 12 Two or more races, non-Hispanic/Latino). Average age 36. 148 applicants, 97% accepted, 116 enrolled. In 2017, 148 master's, 23 other advanced degrees awarded. *Degree requirements:* For master's, comprehensive exam, thesis optional. *Entrance requirements:* For master's, GRE General Test or MAT, interview, minimum GPA of 2.5, bachelor's degree in related field, teaching license (MA Ed). Additional exam requirements/recommendations for international students: Required—TOEFL. *Application deadline:* For fall admission, 5/15 priority date for domestic students. Applications are processed on a rolling basis. Application fee: $75. *Expenses:* Tuition, state resident: full-time $4749; part-time $297 per credit hour. Tuition, nonresident: full-time $17,898; part-time $1119 per credit hour. *Required fees:* $2691; $224 per credit hour. Part-time tuition and fees vary according to course load and program. *Financial support:* Research assistantships with partial tuition reimbursements, teaching assistantships with partial tuition reimbursements, and Federal Work-Study available. Support available to part-time students. Financial award application deadline: 6/1. *Unit head:* Dr. Vivian W. Mott, Chair, 252-328-6177, Fax: 252-328-4368, E-mail: mottv@ecu.edu.
Website: http://www.ecu.edu/cs-educ/idp/index.cfm

Eastern Illinois University, Graduate School, College of Education and Professional Studies, Department of Counseling and Higher Education, Charleston, IL 61920. Offers college student affairs (MS); counseling (MS). *Accreditation:* ACA; NCATE. *Program availability:* Part-time, evening/weekend. *Degree requirements:* For master's, comprehensive exam (for some programs), thesis (for some programs). *Entrance requirements:* For master's, GMAT or GRE. Additional exam requirements/recommendations for international students: Required—TOEFL (minimum score 500 paper-based; 61 iBT), IELTS (minimum score 6). *Application deadline:* For fall admission, 5/15 for domestic and international students; for spring admission, 10/15 for domestic and international students. Applications are processed on a rolling basis. Application fee: $30. Electronic applications accepted. *Financial support:* Research assistantships with full tuition reimbursements, career-related internships or fieldwork, Federal Work-Study, and unspecified assistantships available. Support available to part-time students. Financial award application deadline: 3/1; financial award applicants required to submit FAFSA. *Unit head:* Richard Roberts, Chair, 217-581-2400, Fax: 217-581-7800, E-mail: rlroberts@eiu.edu. *Application contact:* Richard Roberts, Chair, 217-581-2400, Fax: 217-581-7800, E-mail: rlroberts@eiu.edu.
Website: https://www.eiu.edu/che/

Eastern Kentucky University, The Graduate School, College of Education, Department of Counseling and Educational Leadership, Richmond, KY 40475-3102. Offers human services (MA); instructional leadership (MA Ed); mental health counseling (MA); school counseling (MA Ed). *Accreditation:* ACA (one or more programs are accredited); NCATE. *Program availability:* Part-time, online learning. *Entrance requirements:* For master's, GRE General Test, minimum GPA of 2.5.

Eastern Mennonite University, Master of Arts in Counseling Program, Harrisonburg, VA 22802-2462. Offers MA, M Div/MA. *Accreditation:* ACA (one or more programs are accredited); ACIPE. *Program availability:* Part-time. *Degree requirements:* For master's, practicum, internship. *Entrance requirements:* For master's, minimum GPA of 3.0. Additional exam requirements/recommendations for international students: Required—TOEFL (minimum score 550 paper-based; 79 iBT). *Application deadline:* For fall admission, 3/1 for domestic and international students. Application fee: $50. Electronic applications accepted. *Expenses:* Contact institution. *Financial support:* Scholarships/grants available. Financial award application deadline: 6/30; financial award applicants required to submit FAFSA. *Faculty research:* Career and gender, empathy and consciousness, emotion theory, education models. *Unit head:* Dr. Teresa J. Haase, Director, 540-432-4248, Fax: 540-432-4444, E-mail: teresa.haase@emu.edu. *Application contact:* Amanda Williams, Administrative Assistant, 540-432-4243, Fax: 540-432-4444, E-mail: amanda.k.williams@emu.edu.
Website: http://www.emu.edu/graduate-counseling/

Eastern Michigan University, Graduate School, College of Education, Department of Leadership and Counseling, Programs in Counseling, Ypsilanti, MI 48197. Offers clinical mental health counseling (MA); college counseling (MA); helping interventions in a multicultural society (Graduate Certificate); school counseling (MA); school counselor licensure (Post Master's Certificate). *Program availability:* Part-time, evening/weekend. *Students:* 16 full-time (15 women), 49 part-time (46 women); includes 24 minority (16 Black or African American, non-Hispanic/Latino; 2 Asian, non-Hispanic/Latino; 4 Hispanic/Latino; 2 Two or more races, non-Hispanic/Latino), 1 international. Average age 34. 82 applicants, 55% accepted, 17 enrolled. In 2017, 25 master's, 15 other advanced degrees awarded. *Degree requirements:* For master's, comprehensive exam, internship. *Entrance requirements:* Additional exam requirements/recommendations for international students: Required—TOEFL. *Application deadline:* For fall admission, 5/1 for domestic and international students; for winter admission, 9/15 for domestic and international students; for spring admission, 2/10 for domestic and international students. Applications are processed on a rolling basis. Application fee: $45. *Financial support:* Fellowships, research assistantships with full tuition reimbursements, teaching assistantships with full tuition reimbursements, career-related internships or fieldwork, Federal Work-Study, institutionally sponsored loans, scholarships/grants, tuition waivers (partial), and unspecified assistantships available. Support available to part-time students. Financial award applicants required to submit FAFSA. *Application contact:* Dr. Irene Ametrano, Coordinator of Advising for Programs in Counseling, 734-487-0255, Fax: 734-487-4608, E-mail: iametrano@emich.edu.

Eastern New Mexico University, Graduate School, College of Education and Technology, Department of Educational Studies, Program in Counseling, Portales, NM 88130. Offers MA. *Program availability:* Part-time. *Degree requirements:* For master's, comprehensive exam, thesis optional, 48-hour course work including a 600-hour internship in field placement. *Entrance requirements:* For master's, minimum GPA of 3.0, 3 letters of recommendation, interview. Additional exam requirements/recommendations for international students: Required—TOEFL (minimum score 550 paper-based; 79 iBT), IELTS (minimum score 6). *Application deadline:* For fall admission, 7/20 priority date for domestic students, 6/20 priority date for international students; for spring admission, 12/15 priority date for domestic students, 11/15 priority date for international students. Applications are processed on a rolling basis. Application fee: $10. Electronic applications accepted. *Financial support:* Applicants required to

submit FAFSA. *Unit head:* Dr. ShinHwa Lee, Graduate Coordinator, 575-562-2942, E-mail: shinhwa.lee@enmu.edu. *Application contact:* Cheryl Reeves, Senior Secretary, 575-562-2443, Fax: 575-562-2559, E-mail: cheryl.reeves@enmu.edu.
Website: http://education.enmu.edu/grad/counseling.shtml

Eastern New Mexico University, Graduate School, College of Education and Technology, Department of Educational Studies, Program in School Counseling, Portales, NM 88130. Offers M Ed. *Program availability:* Part-time. *Degree requirements:* For master's, comprehensive exam, thesis optional, 48-hour curriculum, 600-hour internship in field placement. *Entrance requirements:* For master's, minimum GPA of 3.0, three letters of recommendation, interview. Additional exam requirements/recommendations for international students: Required—TOEFL (minimum score 550 paper-based; 79 iBT), IELTS (minimum score 6). *Application deadline:* For fall admission, 7/20 priority date for domestic students, 6/20 priority date for international students; for spring admission, 12/15 priority date for domestic students, 11/15 priority date for international students. Applications are processed on a rolling basis. Application fee: $10. Electronic applications accepted. *Financial support:* Applicants required to submit FAFSA. *Unit head:* Dr. ShinHwa Lee, Graduate Coordinator, 575-562-2942, E-mail: shinhwa.lee@enmu.edu. *Application contact:* Cheryl Reeves, Senior Secretary, 575-562-2443, Fax: 575-562-2559, E-mail: cheryl.reeves@enmu.edu.
Website: http://education.enmu.edu/

Eastern Washington University, Graduate Studies, College of Social Sciences, Department of Psychology, Program in School Counseling, Cheney, WA 99004-2431. Offers applied psychology (MS); school counseling (MS). *Accreditation:* ACA. *Students:* 21 full-time (14 women). Average age 27. 22 applicants, 55% accepted, 10 enrolled. In 2017, 8 master's awarded. *Entrance requirements:* Additional exam requirements/recommendations for international students: Required—TOEFL (minimum score 580 paper-based; 92 iBT), IELTS (minimum score 7). *Expenses:* Tuition, state resident: full-time $11,191; part-time $373.06 per credit. Tuition, nonresident: full-time $25,995; part-time $866.52 per credit.

East Tennessee State University, School of Graduate Studies, College of Education, Department of Counseling and Human Services, Johnson City, TN 37614. Offers clinical mental health counseling (MA); college counseling/student affairs higher education (MA); couples and family therapy (MA); human services (MS); school counseling (MA). *Accreditation:* ACA; NCATE. *Program availability:* Part-time. *Degree requirements:* For master's, comprehensive exam, thesis optional, internship, student teaching, culminating experience. *Entrance requirements:* For master's, GRE General Test, minimum GPA of 3.0, three letters of recommendation, interview, 2-3 page essay detailing experiences that have shaped pursuit of degree, resume. Additional exam requirements/recommendations for international students: Required—TOEFL (minimum score 550 paper-based; 79 iBT). *Application deadline:* For fall admission, 1/31 priority date for domestic and international students. Application fee: $55 ($65 for international students). Electronic applications accepted. *Financial support:* Research assistantships with full tuition reimbursements, teaching assistantships with full tuition reimbursements, career-related internships or fieldwork, institutionally sponsored loans, scholarships/grants, traineeships, and unspecified assistantships available. Financial award application deadline: 7/1; financial award applicants required to submit FAFSA. *Faculty research:* Intervention and assistance with at-risk and under-served youth and high conflict families; service and social justice; women and girls' issues in counseling; counseling competence with LGBTQ individuals; counselor education and supervision. *Unit head:* Dr. Janna Scarborough, Chair, 423-439-4191, Fax: 423-439-7790, E-mail: scarboro@etsu.edu. *Application contact:* Dr. Janna Scarborough, Chair, 423-439-4191, Fax: 423-439-7790, E-mail: scarboro@etsu.edu.
Website: http://www.etsu.edu/coe/chs/

Edinboro University of Pennsylvania, Department of Counseling, School Psychology and Special Education, Edinboro, PA 16444. Offers counseling (MA), including art therapy, clinical mental health counseling, college counseling, rehabilitation counseling, school counseling; educational psychology (M Ed); school psychology (Ed S); special education (M Ed), including autism, behavior management. *Accreditation:* ACA. *Program availability:* Part-time, evening/weekend. *Degree requirements:* For master's, thesis or alternative, competency exam; for Ed S, thesis or alternative. *Entrance requirements:* For master's and Ed S, GRE or MAT, minimum QPA of 2.5. Electronic applications accepted.

Emporia State University, Program in School Counseling, Emporia, KS 66801-5415. Offers MS. *Accreditation:* ACA; NCATE. *Program availability:* Part-time. *Faculty:* 13 full-time (9 women). *Students:* 19 full-time (16 women), 73 part-time (67 women); includes 6 minority (1 Asian, non-Hispanic/Latino; 3 Hispanic/Latino; 2 Two or more races, non-Hispanic/Latino). 28 applicants, 50% accepted, 12 enrolled. In 2017, 23 master's awarded. *Degree requirements:* For master's, comprehensive exam or thesis, practicum. *Entrance requirements:* For master's, GRE or MAT, essay exam, appropriate bachelor's degree, interview, letters of recommendation. *Application deadline:* For fall admission, 8/15 priority date for domestic students. Applications are processed on a rolling basis. Application fee: $30 ($75 for international students). Electronic applications accepted. *Expenses:* Tuition, state resident: full-time $6084; part-time $253.50 per credit hour. Tuition, nonresident: full-time $18,924; part-time $788.50 per credit hour. *Required fees:* $1943; $80.95 per credit hour. Tuition and fees vary according to campus/location. *Financial support:* In 2017–18, 4 research assistantships with full tuition reimbursements (averaging $7,344 per year) were awarded; career-related internships or fieldwork, Federal Work-Study, institutionally sponsored loans, health care benefits, and unspecified assistantships also available. Financial award application deadline: 3/15; financial award applicants required to submit FAFSA. *Unit head:* Dr. Katrina Miller, Chair, 620-341-5791, E-mail: kmille12@emporia.edu. *Application contact:* Mary Sewell, Admissions Coordinator, 800-950-GRAD, Fax: 620-341-5909, E-mail: msewell@emporia.edu.

Evangel University, School Counseling Program, Springfield, MO 65802. Offers MS. *Program availability:* Part-time, evening/weekend. *Faculty:* 17 full-time (12 women), 4 part-time/adjunct (3 women). *Students:* 24 full-time (19 women), 21 part-time (19 women); includes 3 minority (2 Black or African American, non-Hispanic/Latino; 1 Hispanic/Latino). Average age 31. 16 applicants, 100% accepted, 11 enrolled. In 2017, 14 master's awarded. *Degree requirements:* For master's, comprehensive exam. *Entrance requirements:* For master's, MAT (preferred) or GRE. Additional exam requirements/recommendations for international students: Required—TOEFL (minimum score 550 paper-based). *Application deadline:* For fall admission, 7/15 priority date for domestic students, 7/1 for international students; for spring admission, 11/15 priority date for domestic students, 12/1 for international students. Applications are processed on a rolling basis. Application fee: $25. Electronic applications accepted. *Expenses:* Tuition: Full-time $7200; part-time $4800 per credit hour. *Required fees:* $210; $155 per semester. *Financial support:* In 2017–18, 6 students received support. Scholarships/grants and unspecified assistantships available. Financial award application deadline: 4/1; financial award applicants required to submit FAFSA. *Unit head:* Dr. Christine Arnzen, Program Coordinator, 417-865-2815 Ext. 8678, Fax: 417-575-5484, E-mail: arnzenc@evangel.edu. *Application contact:* Michael Mann, Enrollment Coordinator, Graduate Studies, 417-865-2815 Ext. 8276, Fax: 417-575-5484, E-mail: mannm@evangel.edu.
Website: http://www.evangel.edu/academics/graduate-studies/graduate-programs

Fairfield University, Graduate School of Education and Allied Professions, Fairfield, CT 06824. Offers applied behavior analysis (ATC); applied psychology (MA); clinical mental health counseling (MA, CAS); educational technology (MA); elementary education (MA, CAS); family studies (MA); integration of spirituality and religion in counseling (ATC); marriage and family therapy (MA); reading and language development (Sixth Year Certificate); school counseling (MA, CAS); school psychology (MA, CAS); school-based marriage and family therapy (ATC); secondary education (MA); special education (MA, CAS); substance abuse counseling (ATC); teaching (Certificate); teaching and foundations (MA, CAS); TESOL, world languages, and bilingual education (MA, CAS). *Accreditation:* NCATE. *Program availability:* Part-time, evening/weekend. *Faculty:* 23 full-time (17 women), 39 part-time/adjunct (28 women). *Students:* 199 full-time (168 women), 251 part-time (206 women); includes 85 minority (21 Black or African American, non-Hispanic/Latino; 9 Asian, non-Hispanic/Latino; 49 Hispanic/Latino; 6 Two or more races, non-Hispanic/Latino), 4 international. Average age 32. 370 applicants, 56% accepted, 125 enrolled. In 2017, 136 master's, 28 other advanced degrees awarded. *Degree requirements:* For master's, comprehensive exam. *Entrance requirements:* For master's, minimum GPA of 3.0, 2 recommendations, resume. Additional exam requirements/recommendations for international students: Required—TOEFL (minimum score 550 paper-based; 84 iBT) or IELTS (minimum score 7.5). *Application deadline:* For fall admission, 2/15 for international students; for spring admission, 10/1 for international students. Application fee: $60. Electronic applications accepted. *Expenses:* $750 per credit hour. *Financial support:* In 2017–18, 34 students received support. Career-related internships or fieldwork and unspecified assistantships available. Support available to part-time students. Financial award applicants required to submit FAFSA. *Faculty research:* Reading and literacy, writing, social justice and inequality in education, addictions and mental health issues, therapeutic relationships and clinical supervision. *Unit head:* Dr. Robert D. Hannafin, Dean, 203-254-4250, Fax: 203-254-4241, E-mail: rhannafin@fairfield.edu. *Application contact:* Marianne Gumpper, Director of Graduate Admission, 203-254-4184, Fax: 203-254-4073, E-mail: gradadmis@fairfield.edu.
Website: http://www.fairfield.edu/gseap

Faulkner University, College of Education, Montgomery, AL 36109-3398. Offers counseling (MS); curriculum and instruction (M Ed); elementary education (M Ed); school counseling (M Ed). *Program availability:* Part-time, evening/weekend, 100% online, blended/hybrid learning. *Faculty:* 13 full-time (8 women), 6 part-time/adjunct (1 woman). *Students:* 140 full-time (107 women), 16 part-time (13 women); includes 97 minority (92 Black or African American, non-Hispanic/Latino; 1 American Indian or Alaska Native, non-Hispanic/Latino; 1 Asian, non-Hispanic/Latino; 3 Hispanic/Latino). Average age 37. 92 applicants, 55% accepted, 48 enrolled. In 2017, 51 master's awarded. *Degree requirements:* For master's, 5+ hours in clinical training (for MS, M Ed in school counseling). *Entrance requirements:* For master's, MAT (minimum score of 370) or GRE (minimum score of 280) taken within last five years, bachelor's degree from regionally-accredited college or university; official transcripts from all colleges and universities attended; three letters of recommendation; goal statement (approximately 600 words); minimum cumulative GPA of 2.75 in undergraduate courses, 3.0 in graduate courses. Additional exam requirements/recommendations for international students: Required—TOEFL (minimum score 500 paper-based). *Application deadline:* For fall admission, 8/1 for domestic students; for spring admission, 12/1 for domestic students; for summer admission, 5/1 for domestic students. Application fee: $35. Electronic applications accepted. *Financial support:* Applicants required to submit FAFSA. *Unit head:* Dr. Leslie S. Cowell, Dean, College of Education, 334-386-7224, Fax: 334-386-7194, E-mail: lcowell@faulkner.edu. *Application contact:* Rebecca L. Horn, Director, Graduate Education, 334-386-7264, Fax: 334-386-7194, E-mail: rhorn@faulkner.edu.
Website: https://www.faulkner.edu/graduate/graduate_academics/

Fitchburg State University, Division of Graduate and Continuing Education, Program in Interdisciplinary Studies, Fitchburg, MA 01420-2697. Offers applied communications (CAGS); counseling/psychology (CAGS); individualized track (CAGS); reading specialist (CAGS). *Program availability:* Part-time, evening/weekend. *Students:* 11 full-time (all women), 14 part-time (13 women); includes 3 minority (all Hispanic/Latino). Average age 36. 5 applicants, 100% accepted, 5 enrolled. In 2017, 14 CAGSs awarded. *Entrance requirements:* Additional exam requirements/recommendations for international students: Required—TOEFL (minimum score 550 paper-based; 79 iBT). *Application deadline:* For fall admission, 7/15 for international students; for spring admission, 12/1 for international students. Applications are processed on a rolling basis. Application fee: $50. Electronic applications accepted. *Expenses:* Contact institution. *Financial support:* In 2017–18, research assistantships with partial tuition reimbursements (averaging $5,500 per year) were awarded; Federal Work-Study, scholarships/grants, and unspecified assistantships also available. Support available to part-time students. Financial award application deadline: 3/1; financial award applicants required to submit FAFSA. *Unit head:* Dr. Jessica Robey, Chair, 978-665-3386, Fax: 978-665-3658, E-mail: gce@fitchburgstate.edu. *Application contact:* Jinawa McNeil, Director of Admissions, 978-665-3140, Fax: 978-665-4540, E-mail: admissions@fitchburgstate.edu.

Fitchburg State University, Division of Graduate and Continuing Education, Programs in Counseling, Fitchburg, MA 01420-2697. Offers clinical mental health counseling (MS); school guidance counseling (MS). *Accreditation:* NCATE. *Program availability:* Part-time, evening/weekend. *Faculty:* 3 full-time (2 women), 10 part-time/adjunct (6 women). *Students:* 60 full-time (54 women), 6 part-time (5 women); includes 7 minority (2 Black or African American, non-Hispanic/Latino; 1 Asian, non-Hispanic/Latino; 4 Hispanic/Latino). Average age 32. 19 applicants, 100% accepted, 14 enrolled. In 2017, 13 master's awarded. *Entrance requirements:* Additional exam requirements/recommendations for international students: Required—TOEFL (minimum score 550 paper-based; 79 iBT). *Application deadline:* For fall admission, 7/15 for international students; for spring admission, 12/1 for international students. Applications are processed on a rolling basis. Application fee: $50. Electronic applications accepted. *Expenses:* Contact institution. *Financial support:* In 2017–18, research assistantships with partial tuition reimbursements (averaging $5,500 per year) were awarded; Federal Work-Study, scholarships/grants, and unspecified assistantships also available. Support available to part-time students. Financial award application deadline: 3/1; financial award applicants required to submit FAFSA. *Unit head:* Dr. Daneen Deptula, Chair, 978-665-3604, Fax: 978-665-3658, E-mail: gce@fitchburgstate.edu. *Application contact:* Jinawa McNeil, Director of Admissions, 978-665-3140, Fax: 978-665-4540, E-mail: admissions@fitchburgstate.edu.
Website: http://www.fitchburgstate.edu

Florida Agricultural and Mechanical University, Division of Graduate Studies, Research, and Continuing Education, College of Education, Department of Educational Leadership and Human Services, Tallahassee, FL 32307-3200. Offers administration and supervision (M Ed, MS, PhD); adult education (M Ed, MS); educational leadership (PhD); guidance and counseling (M Ed, MS). *Accreditation:* NCATE. *Degree requirements:* For master's, thesis (for some programs); for doctorate, thesis/dissertation. *Entrance requirements:* For master's, GRE General Test, minimum GPA of 3.0. Additional exam requirements/recommendations for international students: Required—TOEFL.

Florida Atlantic University, College of Education, Department of Counselor Education, Boca Raton, FL 33431-0991. Offers MS, PhD. *Accreditation:* ACA; NCATE. *Program availability:* Part-time, evening/weekend. *Faculty:* 8 full-time (4 women), 5 part-time/adjunct (2 women). *Students:* 82 full-time (75 women), 80 part-time (62 women); includes 89 minority (40 Black or African American, non-Hispanic/Latino; 1 Asian, non-Hispanic/Latino; 44 Hispanic/Latino; 4 Two or more races, non-Hispanic/Latino), 3 international. Average age 33. 175 applicants, 38% accepted, 52 enrolled. In 2017, 25 master's, 3 doctorates awarded. *Entrance requirements:* For master's, GRE General Test, minimum GPA of 3.0 during previous 2 years. Additional exam requirements/recommendations for international students: Required—TOEFL (minimum score 500 paper-based; 61 iBT), IELTS (minimum score 6). *Application deadline:* For fall admission, 3/1 for domestic students, 2/1 for international students; for spring admission, 9/15 for domestic students, 7/1 for international students. Applications are processed on a rolling basis. Application fee: $30. *Expenses:* Tuition, state resident: full-time $7400; part-time $369.82 per credit. Tuition, nonresident: full-time $20,496; part-time $1042.81 per credit. *Financial support:* Research assistantships with partial tuition reimbursements, teaching assistantships, career-related internships or fieldwork, scholarships/grants, and unspecified assistantships available. *Faculty research:* Brief therapy, psychological type, marriage and family counseling, international programs, integrated services. *Unit head:* Dr. Paul Peluso, Chair, 561-297-3625, Fax: 561-297-2309, E-mail: ppeluso@fau.edu.
Website: http://www.coe.fau.edu/academicdepartments/ce/

Florida International University, College of Arts, Sciences, and Education, Department of Leadership and Professional Studies, Miami, FL 33199. Offers adult education and human resource development (MS, Ed D); counseling (MS), including rehabilitation counseling, school counseling; counselor education (MS), including clinical mental health counseling; educational administration and supervision (Ed D); educational leadership (MS, Certificate, Ed S); higher education (Ed D); higher education administration (MS); international and comparative education (MS); recreation and sport management (MS), including recreation and sport management, recreational therapy; school psychology (Ed S); urban education (MS), including instruction in urban settings, learning technologies, multicultural/bilingual, multicultural/TESOL, urban education. *Program availability:* Part-time, evening/weekend. *Faculty:* 60 full-time (41 women), 112 part-time/adjunct (77 women). *Students:* 221 full-time (162 women), 301 part-time (239 women); includes 418 minority (127 Black or African American, non-Hispanic/Latino; 9 Asian, non-Hispanic/Latino; 271 Hispanic/Latino; 11 Two or more races, non-Hispanic/Latino), 10 international. Average age 31. 330 applicants, 55% accepted, 100 enrolled. In 2017, 181 master's, 6 doctorates awarded. *Degree requirements:* For doctorate, thesis/dissertation. *Entrance requirements:* For master's, minimum GPA of 3.0; for doctorate and other advanced degree, GRE General Test. Additional exam requirements/recommendations for international students: Required—TOEFL (minimum score 550 paper-based; 80 iBT), IELTS (minimum score 6.3). *Application deadline:* For fall admission, 6/1 priority date for domestic students, 4/1 for international students; for winter admission, 10/1 priority date for domestic students, 9/1 for international students; for spring admission, 3/1 priority date for domestic students, 2/1 for international students. Applications are processed on a rolling basis. Application fee: $30. Electronic applications accepted. *Expenses:* Tuition, state resident: full-time $8912; part-time $446 per credit hour. Tuition, nonresident: full-time $21,393; part-time $992 per credit hour. *Required fees:* $390; $195 per semester. *Financial support:* Fellowships, research assistantships with tuition reimbursements, teaching assistantships with tuition reimbursements, Federal Work-Study, and tuition waivers (full and partial) available. Support available to part-time students. Financial award applicants required to submit FAFSA. *Unit head:* Dr. Benjamin Baez, Chair, 305-348-3214, Fax: 305-348-1515, E-mail: benjamin.baez@fiu.edu. *Application contact:* Nanett Rojas, Assistant Director, Graduate Admissions, 305-348-7464, Fax: 305-348-7441, E-mail: gradadm@fiu.edu.
Website: http://education.fiu.edu

Fordham University, Graduate School of Education, Division of Psychological and Educational Services, New York, NY 10023. Offers counseling and personnel services (MSE); counseling psychology (PhD); school psychology (PhD). *Accreditation:* APA (one or more programs are accredited); NCATE. *Program availability:* Part-time, evening/weekend. Terminal master's awarded for partial completion of doctoral program. *Degree requirements:* For master's, comprehensive exam (for some programs); for doctorate, comprehensive exam (for some programs), thesis/dissertation. *Entrance requirements:* For doctorate, GRE General Test. Additional exam requirements/recommendations for international students: Required—TOEFL (minimum score 577 paper-based; 90 iBT), IELTS (minimum score 7). Electronic applications accepted.

Fort Hays State University, Graduate School, College of Education, Department of Educational Administration and Counseling, Program in Counseling, Hays, KS 67601-4099. Offers MS. *Accreditation:* NCATE. *Program availability:* Part-time. *Degree requirements:* For master's, comprehensive exam, thesis or alternative. *Entrance requirements:* For master's, GRE General Test or MAT, minimum undergraduate GPA of 3.0 in last 60 hours. Additional exam requirements/recommendations for international students: Required—TOEFL (minimum score 550 paper-based). Electronic applications accepted. *Faculty research:* Career education, evaluation and plans, counseling the disabled, marriage and family parenting, underemployment and work in the family.

Fort Valley State University, College of Graduate Studies and Extended Education, Department of Counseling Psychology, Fort Valley, GA 31030. Offers guidance and counseling (Ed S); mental health counseling (MS); rehabilitation counseling (MS). *Program availability:* Part-time. *Degree requirements:* For master's, comprehensive exam (for some programs), thesis optional. *Entrance requirements:* For master's and Ed S, GRE General Test or MAT.

Freed-Hardeman University, Program in Counseling, Henderson, TN 38340-2399. Offers MS. *Program availability:* Part-time, evening/weekend. *Degree requirements:* For master's, comprehensive exam, practicum. *Entrance requirements:* For master's, GRE General Test or MAT. Additional exam requirements/recommendations for international students: Required—TOEFL (minimum score 500 paper-based).

Freed-Hardeman University, Program in Education, Henderson, TN 38340-2399. Offers curriculum and instruction (M Ed); school counseling (M Ed), including administration and supervision, special education; school leadership (Ed S). *Accreditation:* NCATE. *Program availability:* Part-time, evening/weekend. *Degree requirements:* For master's, comprehensive exam, thesis optional; for Ed S, thesis. *Entrance requirements:* For master's, GRE General Test or NTE; for Ed S, 3 years of teaching experience. Additional exam requirements/recommendations for international students: Required—TOEFL (minimum score 500 paper-based).

Fresno Pacific University, Graduate Programs, School of Education, Division of Pupil Personnel Services, Program in School Counseling, Fresno, CA 93702-4709. Offers MA. *Program availability:* Part-time, evening/weekend. *Degree requirements:* For master's, thesis or alternative. *Entrance requirements:* Additional exam requirements/recommendations for international students: Required—TOEFL (minimum score 550 paper-based). *Expenses:* Contact institution.

Counselor Education

Frostburg State University, College of Education, Department of Educational Professions, Program in School Counseling, Frostburg, MD 21532. Offers M Ed. *Accreditation:* NCATE. *Program availability:* Part-time, evening/weekend. *Faculty:* 2. *Students:* 32 full-time (25 women), 12 part-time (8 women); includes 9 minority (8 Black or African American, non-Hispanic/Latino; 1 Hispanic/Latino). Average age 28. 20 applicants, 65% accepted, 12 enrolled. In 2017, 10 master's awarded. *Degree requirements:* For master's, comprehensive exam, thesis or alternative. *Entrance requirements:* For master's, GRE General Test or MAT, interview. Additional exam requirements/recommendations for international students: Required—TOEFL. *Application deadline:* For fall admission, 7/15 priority date for domestic students. Applications are processed on a rolling basis. Application fee: $45. Electronic applications accepted. *Expenses:* Tuition, state resident: part-time $433 per credit hour. Tuition, nonresident: part-time $557 per credit hour. *Required fees:* $121 per credit hour. $27 per term. *Financial support:* In 2017–18, 2 research assistantships with full tuition reimbursements (averaging $5,000 per year) were awarded; career-related internships or fieldwork also available. Financial award application deadline: 4/1; financial award applicants required to submit FAFSA. *Unit head:* Dr. Joyce Henderson, Coordinator, 301-687-4422, E-mail: jhhenderson@frostburg.edu. *Application contact:* Vickie Mazer, Director, Graduate Services, 301-687-7053, Fax: 301-687-4597, E-mail: vmmazer@frostburg.edu.

Gallaudet University, The Graduate School, Washington, DC 20002-3625. Offers American Sign Language/English bilingual early childhood deaf education: birth to 5 (Certificate); audiology (Au D); clinical psychology (PhD); deaf and hard of hearing infants, toddlers, and their families (Certificate); deaf education (MA, Ed S); deaf history (Certificate); deaf studies (Certificate); educating deaf students with disabilities (Certificate); education: teacher preparation (MA), including deaf education, early childhood education and deaf education, elementary education and deaf education, secondary education and deaf education; educational neuroscience (PhD); hearing, speech and language sciences (MS, PhD); international development (MA); interpretation (MA, PhD), including combined interpreting practice and research (MA), interpreting research (MA); linguistics (MA, PhD); mental health counseling (MA); peer mentoring (Certificate); public administration (MPA); school counseling (MA); school psychology (Psy S); sign language teaching (MA); social work (MSW); speech-language pathology (MS). *Program availability:* Part-time. Terminal master's awarded for partial completion of doctoral program. *Degree requirements:* For master's, comprehensive exam (for some programs), thesis optional; for doctorate, comprehensive exam, thesis/dissertation. *Entrance requirements:* For master's and doctorate, GRE General Test or MAT, letters of recommendation, interviews, goals statement, American Sign Language proficiency interview, written English competency. Additional exam requirements/recommendations for international students: Required—TOEFL. Electronic applications accepted. *Faculty research:* Signing math dictionaries, telecommunications access, cancer genetics, linguistics, visual language and visual learning, integrated quantum materials, deaf legal discourse, advance recruitment and retention in geosciences.

Geneva College, Master of Arts in Counseling Program, Beaver Falls, PA 15010-3599. Offers clinical mental health counseling (MA); marriage and family counseling (MA); school counseling (MA). *Accreditation:* ACA. *Program availability:* Part-time, evening/weekend. *Faculty:* 6 full-time (3 women), 3 part-time/adjunct (1 woman). *Students:* 34 full-time (26 women), 20 part-time (16 women); includes 12 minority (11 Black or African American, non-Hispanic/Latino; 1 Hispanic/Latino), 1 international. Average age 33. In 2017, 34 master's awarded. *Degree requirements:* For master's, comprehensive exam, 60 credits including practicum and internship. *Entrance requirements:* For master's, minimum GPA of 3.0 (preferred), 3 letters of recommendation, essay on career goals, resume of educational and professional experiences. Additional exam requirements/recommendations for international students: Required—TOEFL. *Application deadline:* For fall admission, 9/1 for domestic students; for spring admission, 1/10 for domestic students. Applications are processed on a rolling basis. Electronic applications accepted. *Expenses:* $670 per credit. *Financial support:* Research assistantships, teaching assistantships, career-related internships or fieldwork, and unspecified assistantships available. Financial award application deadline: 8/1; financial award applicants required to submit FAFSA. *Faculty research:* Blended family counseling; premarital and newlywed couples; religion in clinical supervision; conceptual mapping in research, supervision, and clinical work. *Unit head:* Dr. Shannan Shiderly, Program Director, 724-847-6649, Fax: 724-847-6101, E-mail: slshider@geneva.edu. *Application contact:* Marina Frazier, Graduate Program Manager, 724-847-6697, E-mail: counseling@geneva.edu.
Website: http://www.geneva.edu/page/grad_counseling

George Fox University, College of Education, Graduate Department of Counseling, Newberg, OR 97132-2697. Offers clinical mental health counseling (MA); marriage, couple and family counseling (MA, Certificate); school counseling (MA, Certificate); school psychology (Ed S). *Program availability:* Part-time. *Degree requirements:* For master's, clinical project. *Entrance requirements:* For master's, MAT or GRE, bachelor's degree from regionally-accredited college or university, minimum cumulative GPA of 3.0, 1 professional and 1 academic reference, resume, on-campus interview, official transcripts. Additional exam requirements/recommendations for international students: Required—TOEFL (minimum score 577 paper-based; 90 iBT), IELTS (minimum score 7). Electronic applications accepted. *Expenses:* Contact institution.

George Mason University, College of Education and Human Development, Program in Counseling and Development, Fairfax, VA 22030. Offers community agency counseling (M Ed); school counseling PK-12 (M Ed). *Accreditation:* NCATE. *Program availability:* Part-time. *Faculty:* 5 full-time (4 women), 9 part-time/adjunct (6 women). *Students:* 50 full-time (43 women), 90 part-time (74 women); includes 77 minority (30 Black or African American, non-Hispanic/Latino; 1 American Indian or Alaska Native, non-Hispanic/Latino; 17 Asian, non-Hispanic/Latino; 23 Hispanic/Latino; 1 Native Hawaiian or other Pacific Islander, non-Hispanic/Latino; 5 Two or more races, non-Hispanic/Latino), 3 international. Average age 31. 98 applicants, 32% accepted, 18 enrolled. In 2017, 55 master's awarded. *Degree requirements:* For master's, thesis (for some programs), degree must be completed within six years of enrollment. *Entrance requirements:* For master's, bachelor's degree from regionally-accredited institution with minimum GPA of 3.0 overall or in last 60 credit hours; 2 copies of official transcripts; expanded goals statement; 2 letters of recommendation; 12 credits of undergraduate behavioral sciences; 1000 hours of counseling or related experience. Additional exam requirements/recommendations for international students: Required—TOEFL (minimum score 575 paper-based; 88 iBT), IELTS (minimum score 6.5), PTE (minimum score 59). *Application deadline:* For fall admission, 2/1 for domestic and international students; for spring admission, 10/1 for domestic and international students. Application fee: $75 ($80 for international students). Electronic applications accepted. *Expenses:* Tuition, state resident: full-time $11,228; part-time $459.50 per credit. Tuition, nonresident: full-time $30,932; part-time $1280.50 per credit. *Required fees:* $3252; $135.50 per credit. Part-time tuition and fees vary according to course load and program. *Financial support:* In 2017–18, 4 students received support, including 3 research assistantships with tuition reimbursements available (averaging $5,979 per year), 1 teaching assistantship; career-related internships or fieldwork, Federal Work-Study, scholarships/grants, unspecified assistantships, and health care benefits (for full-time research or teaching assistantship recipients) also available. Support available to part-time students. Financial award application deadline: 3/1; financial award applicants required to submit FAFSA. *Faculty research:* Leadership, multiculturalism, social justice, and advocacy; global well-being; social psychological, physical, and spiritual health of individuals, families, communities, and organizations. *Unit head:* Fred Bemak, Academic Program Coordinator, 703-993-3941, Fax: 703-993-5577, E-mail: fbemak@gmu.edu.
Website: http://gse.gmu.edu/programs/counseling/

The George Washington University, Graduate School of Education and Human Development, Department of Counseling and Human Development, Program in Counseling, Washington, DC 20052. Offers PhD, Ed S. *Accreditation:* ACA (one or more programs are accredited); NCATE. *Program availability:* Part-time, evening/weekend. *Students:* 15 full-time (12 women), 35 part-time (28 women); includes 20 minority (7 Black or African American, non-Hispanic/Latino; 1 American Indian or Alaska Native, non-Hispanic/Latino; 5 Asian, non-Hispanic/Latino; 5 Hispanic/Latino; 2 Two or more races, non-Hispanic/Latino), 5 international. Average age 34. 57 applicants, 35% accepted, 11 enrolled. In 2017, 5 doctorates, 1 other advanced degree awarded. *Degree requirements:* For doctorate, comprehensive exam, thesis/dissertation; for Ed S, comprehensive exam. *Entrance requirements:* For doctorate, GRE General Test, interview, minimum GPA of 3.3; for Ed S, GRE General Test or MAT, minimum GPA of 3.3. *Application deadline:* For fall admission, 1/15 priority date for domestic students; for spring admission, 10/1 for domestic students. Applications are processed on a rolling basis. Application fee: $75. *Expenses: Tuition:* Full-time $28,800; part-time $1655 per credit hour. *Required fees:* $45; $2.75 per credit hour. *Financial support:* Fellowships, research assistantships, teaching assistantships, career-related internships or fieldwork, Federal Work-Study, and tuition waivers (partial) available. Financial award application deadline: 1/15; financial award applicants required to submit FAFSA. *Faculty research:* Values in counseling, religion and counseling. *Unit head:* Dr. Pat Schwallie-Giddis, Director, 202-994-6856, E-mail: drpat@gwu.edu. *Application contact:* Sarah Lang, Director of Graduate Admissions, 202-994-1447, Fax: 202-994-7207, E-mail: slang@gwu.edu.

The George Washington University, Graduate School of Education and Human Development, Department of Counseling and Human Development, Program in School Counseling, Washington, DC 20052. Offers MA Ed, Graduate Certificate. *Students:* 37 full-time (31 women), 4 part-time (all women); includes 13 minority (7 Black or African American, non-Hispanic/Latino; 1 American Indian or Alaska Native, non-Hispanic/Latino; 3 Asian, non-Hispanic/Latino; 2 Hispanic/Latino), 1 international. Average age 30. 72 applicants, 67% accepted, 22 enrolled. In 2017, 20 master's awarded. *Expenses: Tuition:* Full-time $28,800; part-time $1655 per credit hour. *Required fees:* $45; $2.75 per credit hour. *Unit head:* Dr. Pat Schwallie-Giddis, Chair, 202-994-6856, E-mail: drpat@gwu.edu. *Application contact:* Sarah Lang, Director of Graduate Admissions, 202-994-1447, Fax: 202-994-7207, E-mail: slang@gwu.edu.

Georgian Court University, School of Arts and Sciences, Lakewood, NJ 08701-2697. Offers applied behavior analysis (MA); autism spectrum disorders (Certificate); clinical mental health counseling (MA); criminal justice and human rights (MS); holistic health studies (MA, Certificate); homeland security (Certificate); instructional technology (CPC); mercy spirituality (Certificate); parish business management (Certificate); professional counselor (Certificate); school psychology (MA, Certificate); theology (MA, Certificate). *Program availability:* Part-time, evening/weekend. *Faculty:* 18 full-time (11 women), 8 part-time/adjunct (4 women). *Students:* 100 full-time (86 women), 92 part-time (67 women); includes 34 minority (9 Black or African American, non-Hispanic/Latino; 1 Asian, non-Hispanic/Latino; 20 Hispanic/Latino; 4 Two or more races, non-Hispanic/Latino), 2 international. Average age 34. 187 applicants, 56% accepted, 78 enrolled. In 2017, 58 master's, 20 other advanced degrees awarded. *Degree requirements:* For master's, comprehensive exam (for some programs), thesis (for some programs). *Entrance requirements:* For master's, GRE, GMAT, or NTE/PRAXIS, 3 letters of recommendation. Additional exam requirements/recommendations for international students: Required—TOEFL (minimum score 550 paper-based). *Application deadline:* For fall admission, 8/15 for domestic students, 5/1 for international students; for spring admission, 1/15 for domestic students, 10/1 for international students. Applications are processed on a rolling basis. Application fee: $40. Electronic applications accepted. *Expenses: Tuition:* Part-time $839 per credit. *Required fees:* $248 per semester. Tuition and fees vary according to campus/location and program. *Financial support:* Scholarships/grants, health care benefits, and unspecified assistantships available. Financial award application deadline: 4/15; financial award applicants required to submit FAFSA. *Unit head:* Dr. Mary Chinery, Dean, 732-987-2493, Fax: 732-987-2007, E-mail: mchinery@georgian.edu. *Application contact:* Patrick Givens, Director of Graduate and Professional Studies Admissions, 732-987-2736, Fax: 732-987-2000, E-mail: gps@georgian.edu.
Website: https://georgian.edu/academics/school-of-arts-sciences/

Georgia Southern University, Jack N. Averitt College of Graduate Studies, College of Education, Department of Leadership, Technology, and Human Development, Program in Counselor Education, Statesboro, GA 30460. Offers mental health counseling (M Ed); school counseling (M Ed). *Accreditation:* ACA; NCATE. *Program availability:* Part-time, evening/weekend. *Students:* 39 full-time (30 women), 9 part-time (6 women); includes 21 minority (20 Black or African American, non-Hispanic/Latino; 1 Asian, non-Hispanic/Latino). Average age 28. 34 applicants, 53% accepted, 11 enrolled. In 2017, 22 master's awarded. *Degree requirements:* For master's, comprehensive exam, transition point assessments. *Entrance requirements:* For master's, minimum GPA of 2.5, letters of recommendation, interview. Additional exam requirements/recommendations for international students: Required—TOEFL (minimum score 550 paper-based; 80 iBT), IELTS (minimum score 6). *Application deadline:* For fall admission, 3/2 for domestic students, 3/15 for international students; for spring admission, 3/2 for domestic students, 10/1 for international students. Application fee: $50. Electronic applications accepted. *Expenses:* Tuition, state resident: full-time $4986; part-time $3324 per year. Tuition, nonresident: full-time $21,982; part-time $15,352 per year. *Required fees:* $2092; $1802 per credit hour. $901 per semester. Tuition and fees vary according to course load, campus/location and program. *Financial support:* In 2017–18, 25 students received support, including 3 research assistantships with full tuition reimbursements available (averaging $7,750 per year); career-related internships or fieldwork, scholarships/grants, and unspecified assistantships also available. Financial award application deadline: 4/15; financial award applicants required to submit FAFSA. *Faculty research:* School counseling, test development, gender equity, career counseling, mental health counseling, best practices for preparing counselors. *Unit head:* Dr. Brandon Hunt, Program Director, 912-478-0502, Fax: 912-478-7104, E-mail: bhunt@georgiasouthern.edu. *Application contact:* Dr. Lydia Cross, Graduate Academic Services Center, 912-478-8664, E-mail: lcross@georgiasouthern.edu.
Website: http://coe.georgiasouthern.edu/coun/

Georgia State University, College of Education and Human Development, Department of Counseling and Psychological Services, Program in School Counseling, Atlanta, GA 30302-3083. Offers M Ed, Ed S. *Accreditation:* ACA (one or more programs are accredited); NCATE. *Entrance requirements:* For master's, GRE, goal statement, resume, 3 letters of recommendation, transcripts. Additional exam requirements/recommendations for international students: Required—TOEFL. Application fee: $50. Electronic applications accepted. *Expenses:* Tuition, state resident: full-time $7020.

Tuition, nonresident: full-time $22,518. *Required fees:* $2128. Tuition and fees vary according to degree level and program. *Financial support:* Research assistantships, teaching assistantships, career-related internships or fieldwork, institutionally sponsored loans, scholarships/grants, health care benefits, and unspecified assistantships available. Financial award application deadline: 4/1. *Faculty research:* Mattering, adolescent counseling, school counselor identity, group leadership of school counselors, play therapy. *Unit head:* Dr. Brian Dew, Chairperson, 404-413-8168, Fax: 404-413-8013, E-mail: bdew@gsu.edu. *Application contact:* CPS Admissions Office, 404-413-8200, E-mail: nkeita@gsu.edu.
Website: http://cps.education.gsu.edu/programs/school-counseling/

Grambling State University, School of Graduate Studies and Research, College of Education, Department of Educational Leadership, Grambling, LA 71245. Offers developmental education (MS, Ed D, PMC), including curriculum and instructional design (Ed D), English (MS), guidance and counseling (MS), higher education administration and management (Ed D), mathematics (MS), reading (MS), science (MS), student development and personnel services (Ed D); educational leadership (M Ed). *Program availability:* Part-time, evening/weekend. *Degree requirements:* For master's, comprehensive exam, thesis (for some programs); for doctorate, comprehensive exam, thesis/dissertation. *Entrance requirements:* For master's, GRE, minimum GPA of 2.5 on last degree; for doctorate, GRE (minimum score 1000, 500 on Verbal), master's degree, minimum GPA of 3.0 on last degree. Additional exam requirements/recommendations for international students: Required—TOEFL (minimum score 500 paper-based; 62 iBT). Electronic applications accepted.

Gwynedd Mercy University, School of Education, Gwynedd Valley, PA 19437-0901. Offers education (Ed D); educational administration (MS); master teacher (MS); school counseling (MS); special education (MS). *Program availability:* Part-time, evening/weekend, 100% online. *Faculty:* 8 full-time (5 women), 38 part-time/adjunct (24 women). *Students:* 579 full-time (430 women); includes 130 minority (90 Black or African American, non-Hispanic/Latino; 11 Asian, non-Hispanic/Latino; 26 Hispanic/Latino; 3 Two or more races, non-Hispanic/Latino). Average age 36. 127 applicants, 18% accepted, 9 enrolled. In 2017, 106 master's awarded. *Degree requirements:* For master's, thesis, internship, practicum. *Entrance requirements:* For master's, GRE or MAT; PRAXIS I, minimum GPA of 3.0. *Application deadline:* Applications are processed on a rolling basis. *Expenses:* $550 per credit (master's degrees), $965 per credit (doctoral); $17 part-time fee, $165 graduation fee. *Financial support:* In 2017–18, 2 research assistantships were awarded; career-related internships or fieldwork, Federal Work-Study, institutionally sponsored loans, tuition waivers (full and partial), and unspecified assistantships also available. Financial award applicants required to submit FAFSA. *Faculty research:* Learning and the brain, reading literacy, ethics and moral judgment, leadership, teaching and multicultural education. *Unit head:* Dr. Heather Pfleger, Dean, 215-646-7300 Ext. 21581, E-mail: pfleger.h@gmercyu.edu. *Application contact:* Graduate Program Coordinator, 877-499-6333, E-mail: graduate@gmercyu.edu.
Website: https://www.gmercyu.edu/academics/graduate-education-programs

Hampton University, School of Liberal Arts and Education, Program in Counseling, Hampton, VA 23668. Offers college student development (MA); community agency counseling (MA); counseling (Ed S); counselor education and supervision (PhD); pastoral counseling (MA); school counseling (MA). *Accreditation:* ACA; NCATE. *Program availability:* Part-time, evening/weekend, online learning. *Students:* 30 full-time (28 women), 15 part-time (13 women); includes 39 minority (all Black or African American, non-Hispanic/Latino), 1 international. Average age 33. 28 applicants, 25% accepted, 3 enrolled. In 2017, 16 master's awarded. *Degree requirements:* For master's, comprehensive exam; for doctorate, comprehensive exam, thesis/dissertation. *Entrance requirements:* For master's, GRE General Test, personal statement, two letters of recommendation; for doctorate, GRE General Test, personal statement, writing sample, three letters of recommendation; for Ed S, personal statement, two letters of recommendation. Additional exam requirements/recommendations for international students: Required—TOEFL (minimum score 525 paper-based) or IELTS (6.5). *Application deadline:* For fall admission, 6/1 priority date for domestic students, 4/1 priority date for international students; for winter admission, 9/1 priority date for international students; for spring admission, 11/1 priority date for domestic students, 9/1 for international students; for summer admission, 4/1 priority date for domestic students, 2/1 priority date for international students. Applications are processed on a rolling basis. Application fee: $35. Electronic applications accepted. *Expenses: Tuition:* Full-time $22,630; part-time $575 per semester hour. *Required fees:* $70. Tuition and fees vary according to program. *Financial support:* Fellowships, research assistantships, teaching assistantships, career-related internships or fieldwork, Federal Work-Study, institutionally sponsored loans, and scholarships/grants available. Support available to part-time students. Financial award application deadline: 6/30; financial award applicants required to submit FAFSA. *Faculty research:* Personality development, temperament, post-traumatic stress disorder, continuum of normal to abnormal personality. *Unit head:* Dr. Richard Mason, Chairperson, 757-728-6160, E-mail: richard.mason@hamptonu.edu.
Website: http://edhd.hamptonu.edu/counseling/

Harding University, Cannon-Clary College of Education, Searcy, AR 72149-0001. Offers advanced studies in teaching and learning (M Ed); art (MSE); behavioral science (MSE); counseling (MS, Ed S); early childhood special education (M Ed, MSE); education (MSE); educational leadership (M Ed, Ed S); elementary education (M Ed); English (MSE); French (MSE); history/social science (MSE); kinesiology (MSE); math (MSE); reading (M Ed); secondary education (MSE); Spanish (MSE); teaching (MAT); teaching English as a second language (MSE). *Accreditation:* NCATE. *Program availability:* Part-time, evening/weekend. *Faculty:* 22 full-time (9 women), 51 part-time/adjunct (37 women). *Students:* 135 full-time (95 women), 316 part-time (231 women); includes 77 minority (46 Black or African American, non-Hispanic/Latino; 7 American Indian or Alaska Native, non-Hispanic/Latino; 4 Asian, non-Hispanic/Latino; 9 Hispanic/Latino; 11 Two or more races, non-Hispanic/Latino), 11 international. Average age 34. 128 applicants, 87% accepted, 111 enrolled. In 2017, 153 master's, 24 other advanced degrees awarded. *Degree requirements:* For master's, comprehensive exam (for some programs), thesis optional, portfolio(s); for Ed S, comprehensive exam, portfolio, project. *Entrance requirements:* For master's, GRE, MAT, PRAXIS; for Ed S, MAT or GRE. Additional exam requirements/recommendations for international students: Required—TOEFL (minimum score 550 paper-based; 79 iBT). *Application deadline:* For fall admission, 8/1 for domestic and international students; for spring admission, 1/1 for domestic and international students. Applications are processed on a rolling basis. Application fee: $35. Tuition and fees vary according to course load, degree level, campus/location and program. *Financial support:* In 2017–18, 33 students received support. Unspecified assistantships available. *Faculty research:* Reading, comprehension, school violence, educational technology, behavior, college choice, differentiated instruction, brain-based teaching. *Unit head:* Dr. Clara Carroll, Chair, 501-279-4501, Fax: 501-279-4083, E-mail: ccarroll@harding.edu. *Application contact:* Information Contact, 501-279-4315, E-mail: gradstudiesedu@harding.edu.
Website: http://www.harding.edu/education

Hardin-Simmons University, Graduate School, Irvin School of Education, Department of Counseling and Human Development, Abilene, TX 79698-0001. Offers M Ed. *Program availability:* Part-time. *Faculty:* 3 full-time (1 woman), 1 (woman) part-time/adjunct. *Students:* 16 full-time (8 women), 5 part-time (3 women); includes 8 minority (7 Black or African American, non-Hispanic/Latino; 1 Asian, non-Hispanic/Latino; 2 international. Average age 32. 4 applicants, 100% accepted, 3 enrolled. In 2017, 24 master's awarded. *Degree requirements:* For master's, comprehensive exam, practicum. *Entrance requirements:* For master's, minimum undergraduate GPA of 3.0 in major, 2.7 overall; interview; 3 letters of recommendation; resume. Additional exam requirements/recommendations for international students: Required—TOEFL (minimum score 550 paper-based; 79 iBT). *Application deadline:* For fall admission, 8/15 priority date for domestic students, 4/1 for international students; for spring admission, 1/5 priority date for domestic students, 9/1 for international students. Applications are processed on a rolling basis. Application fee: $50 ($150 for international students). Electronic applications accepted. *Expenses: Tuition:* Full-time $13,500; part-time $750 per semester hour. *Required fees:* $220 per term. One-time fee: $50. Tuition and fees vary according to course load, campus/location and program. *Financial support:* In 2017–18, 16 students received support. Fellowships, career-related internships or fieldwork, and scholarships/grants available. Support available to part-time students. Financial award application deadline: 6/30; financial award applicants required to submit FAFSA. *Unit head:* Dr. Robert C. Barnes, Program Director, 325-670-1451, Fax: 325-670-5859, E-mail: rbarnes@hsutx.edu. *Application contact:* Dr. Nancy Kucinski, Dean of Graduate Studies, 325-670-1298, Fax: 325-670-1564, E-mail: gradoff@hsutx.edu.
Website: http://www.hsutx.edu/academics/irvin/graduate/counseling

Henderson State University, Graduate Studies, Teachers College, Department of Counselor Education, Arkadelphia, AR 71999-0001. Offers clinical mental health counseling (MS); developmental therapy (MS, Graduate Certificate); secondary school counseling (MSE). *Accreditation:* NCATE. *Program availability:* Part-time. *Entrance requirements:* For master's, GRE General Test or MAT, letters of recommendation, minimum GPA of 2.7, teacher certification. Additional exam requirements/recommendations for international students: Required—TOEFL (minimum score 600 paper-based); Recommended—IELTS (minimum score 6.5).

Heritage University, Graduate Programs in Education, Program in Counseling, Toppenish, WA 98948-9599. Offers M Ed. *Program availability:* Part-time. *Degree requirements:* For master's, comprehensive exam. *Entrance requirements:* For master's, interview, letters of recommendation, at least 9 semester-credits of behavioral sciences.

Hofstra University, School of Health Professions and Human Services, Programs in Counseling, Hempstead, NY 11549. Offers counseling (MS Ed, PD); creative arts therapy (MA); interdisciplinary transition specialist (Advanced Certificate); marriage and family therapy (MA); mental health counseling (MA, Advanced Certificate), including alcohol and substance abuse (Advanced Certificate); rehabilitation administration (PD); rehabilitation counseling (MS Ed, Advanced Certificate); rehabilitation counseling in mental health (MS Ed, Advanced Certificate). *Accreditation:* ACA. *Program availability:* Part-time, evening/weekend. *Students:* 103 full-time (87 women), 67 part-time (60 women); includes 50 minority (21 Black or African American, non-Hispanic/Latino; 11 Asian, non-Hispanic/Latino; 15 Hispanic/Latino; 1 Native Hawaiian or other Pacific Islander, non-Hispanic/Latino; 2 Two or more races, non-Hispanic/Latino), 6 international. Average age 30. 131 applicants, 79% accepted, 52 enrolled. In 2017, 66 master's, 4 other advanced degrees awarded. *Degree requirements:* For master's, comprehensive exam (for some programs), thesis (for some programs), internship, practicum, student teaching, seminars, minimum GPA of 3.0. *Entrance requirements:* For master's, GRE, interview, letters of recommendation, portfolio, essay, professional experience, certification; for other advanced degree, GRE, interview, letters of recommendation, essay, professional experience, resume, master's degree. Additional exam requirements/recommendations for international students: Required—TOEFL (minimum score 550 paper-based; 80 iBT). *Application deadline:* Applications are processed on a rolling basis. Application fee: $75. Electronic applications accepted. *Expenses: Tuition:* Full-time $1292. *Required fees:* $970. Tuition and fees vary according to program. *Financial support:* In 2017–18, 78 students received support, including 47 fellowships with full and partial tuition reimbursements available (averaging $3,138 per year), 5 research assistantships with full and partial tuition reimbursements available (averaging $5,702 per year); career-related internships or fieldwork, Federal Work-Study, institutionally sponsored loans, scholarships/grants, traineeships, tuition waivers (full and partial), and unspecified assistantships also available. Support available to part-time students. Financial award applicants required to submit FAFSA. *Faculty research:* Couple and family therapy infidelity; creative arts impact on Parkinson's disease; LGBTQ inclusion; substance abuse/heroin addiction's racial identity, multicultural issues, white privilege, Latinos, school counseling and the intensity of the high school curriculum. *Unit head:* Dr. Jamie Mitus, Chairperson, 516-463-5759, E-mail: jamie.s.mitus@hofstra.edu. *Application contact:* Sunil Samuel, Assistant Vice President of Admissions, 516-463-4723, Fax: 516-463-4664, E-mail: graduateadmission@hofstra.edu.
Website: http://www.hofstra.edu/academics/colleges/healthscienceshumanservices/

Houston Baptist University, College of Education and Behavioral Sciences, Programs in Education, Houston, TX 77074-3298. Offers bilingual education (M Ed); counselor education (M Ed); curriculum and instruction (M Ed); curriculum and instruction (EC-6 bilingual) (M Ed); curriculum and instruction in all-level art, Spanish, music, or physical education (M Ed); curriculum and instruction in EC-6 and special education (EC-12) (M Ed); curriculum and instruction in instructional technology (M Ed); curriculum and instruction in mathematics, science, or social studies (4-8) (M Ed); curriculum and instruction with EC-6 generalist (M Ed); curriculum and instruction with English language arts and reading (4-8) (M Ed); educational administration (M Ed); educational diagnostician (M Ed); executive educational leadership (Ed D); higher education in business management (M Ed); higher education in Christian studies (M Ed); higher education in counseling (M Ed); higher education in educational technology (M Ed); reading (M Ed); special educational leadership (Ed D). *Program availability:* Part-time, evening/weekend, 100% online, blended/hybrid learning. *Students:* 83 full-time (65 women), 187 part-time (156 women); includes 189 minority (114 Black or African American, non-Hispanic/Latino; 2 American Indian or Alaska Native, non-Hispanic/Latino; 9 Asian, non-Hispanic/Latino; 58 Hispanic/Latino; 6 Two or more races, non-Hispanic/Latino), 7 international. Average age 36. 309 applicants, 31% accepted, 70 enrolled. In 2017, 92 master's awarded. *Degree requirements:* For master's, comprehensive exam; for doctorate, thesis/dissertation. *Entrance requirements:* For master's, minimum GPA of 2.75, two recommendations, resume, bachelor's degree conferred transcript; interview (for non-certified teachers); for doctorate, GRE, 5 letters of recommendation. Additional exam requirements/recommendations for international students: Required—TOEFL (minimum score 80 iBT), IELTS (minimum score 6.5). *Application deadline:* For fall admission, 8/1 for domestic students, 6/1 for international students; for spring admission, 1/1 for domestic students, 11/1 for international students; for summer admission, 5/1 for domestic students, 3/1 for international students. Applications are processed on a rolling basis. Application fee: $0 ($100 for international students). Electronic applications accepted. Application fee is waived when completed online. *Expenses:* $22,000 tuition; $4,500 fees (general, technology and parking).

Counselor Education

Financial support: In 2017–18, 59 students received support. Research assistantships, teaching assistantships, Federal Work-Study, and scholarships/grants available. Support available to part-time students. Financial award application deadline: 4/1; financial award applicants required to submit FAFSA. *Faculty research:* Autism and inclusion, integrating technology into instruction, school change and leadership trust. *Unit head:* Dr. Charlotte Fontenot, Director, Graduate Programs, 281-649-3078, Fax: 281-649-3361, E-mail: cfontenot@hbu.edu. *Application contact:* Kristy Wright, Administrative Assistant for Graduate Programs, 281-649-3094, Fax: 281-649-3361, E-mail: kwright@hbu.edu.
Website: http://www.hbu.edu/MED

Howard University, School of Education, Department of Human Development and Psychoeducational Studies, Program in School Psychology and Counseling Services, Washington, DC 20059-0002. Offers M Ed. *Accreditation:* NCATE. *Program availability:* Part-time. *Degree requirements:* For master's, comprehensive exam, expository writing exam, practicum. *Entrance requirements:* Additional exam requirements/recommendations for international students: Required—TOEFL (minimum score 550 paper-based; 79 iBT). Electronic applications accepted. *Faculty research:* Law and forensic evaluation, juvenile justice, ethics, clinical assessment, personality disorders, substance abuse.

Hunter College of the City University of New York, Graduate School, School of Education, Department of Educational Foundations and Counseling, Program in School Counseling, New York, NY 10065-5085. Offers MS Ed. *Accreditation:* ACA; NCATE. *Degree requirements:* For master's, thesis, internship, practicum, research seminar. *Entrance requirements:* For master's, interview, minimum GPA of 2.7. Additional exam requirements/recommendations for international students: Required—TOEFL, TWE.

Husson University, Graduate Programs in Counseling and Human Relations, Bangor, ME 04401-2999. Offers clinical mental health counseling (MS); human relations (MS); school counseling (MS). *Accreditation:* ACA. *Program availability:* Part-time, evening/weekend. *Faculty:* 3 full-time (2 women), 5 part-time/adjunct (all women). *Students:* 21 full-time (18 women), 44 part-time (39 women); includes 2 minority (1 Black or African American, non-Hispanic/Latino; 1 Hispanic/Latino), 1 international. Average age 31. 49 applicants, 41% accepted, 13 enrolled. In 2017, 17 master's awarded. *Degree requirements:* For master's, comprehensive exam (for some programs), thesis optional. *Entrance requirements:* For master's, BS with minimum GPA of 3.0, letters of recommendation, interview. Additional exam requirements/recommendations for international students: Required—TOEFL (minimum score 550 paper-based; 80 iBT), IELTS (minimum score 6.5). *Application deadline:* For fall admission, 2/1 for domestic students. Application fee: $50. Electronic applications accepted. *Expenses:* $577 per credit; fees depend on number of credits. *Financial support:* In 2017–18, 2 students received support. Federal Work-Study, scholarships/grants, and unspecified assistantships available. Financial award application deadline: 4/15; financial award applicants required to submit FAFSA. *Faculty research:* Challenges and rewards of counseling practice in rural, small town and neighborhood settings. *Unit head:* Dr. Deborah Drew, Director, Graduate Counseling Programs, 207-992-4912, Fax: 207-992-4952, E-mail: drewd@husson.edu. *Application contact:* Kristen Card, Director of Graduate Admissions, 207-404-5660, Fax: 207-941-7935, E-mail: cardk@husson.edu. Website: http://www.husson.edu/college-of-health-and-education/school-of-education/graduate-programs/

Idaho State University, Office of Graduate Studies, School of Health Professions, Department of Counseling, Pocatello, ID 83209-8120. Offers counseling (M Coun, Ed S), including marriage and family counseling (M Coun), mental health counseling (M Coun), school counseling (M Coun), student affairs and college counseling (M Coun); counselor education and counseling (PhD). *Accreditation:* ACA (one or more programs are accredited). *Program availability:* Part-time. *Degree requirements:* For master's, comprehensive exam, thesis, 4 semesters resident graduate study, practicum/internship; for doctorate, comprehensive exam, thesis/dissertation, 3 semesters internship, 4 consecutive semesters doctoral-level study on campus; for Ed S, comprehensive exam, thesis, case studies, oral exam. *Entrance requirements:* For master's, GRE General Test, MAT, minimum GPA of 3.0, bachelors degree, interview, 3 letters of recommendation; for doctorate, GRE General Test, MAT, minimum graduate GPA of 3.0, resume, interview, counseling license, master's degree; for Ed S, GRE General Test, minimum graduate GPA of 3.0, master's degree in counseling, 3 letters of recommendation, 2 years work experience. Additional exam requirements/recommendations for international students: Required—TOEFL (minimum score 600 paper-based; 80 iBT). Electronic applications accepted. *Faculty research:* Group counseling, multicultural counseling, family counseling, child therapy, supervision.

Indiana State University, College of Graduate and Professional Studies, Bayh College of Education, Department of Communication Disorders and Counseling, School, and Educational Psychology, Terre Haute, IN 47809. Offers clinical mental health counseling (MS); communication disorders (MS); school counseling (M Ed); school psychology (PhD, Ed S); MA/MS. *Accreditation:* ACA; ASHA; NCATE. *Program availability:* Part-time, evening/weekend. *Degree requirements:* For master's, thesis optional; for doctorate, thesis/dissertation, research tools proficiency tests. *Entrance requirements:* For master's, GRE General Test or MAT, minimum undergraduate GPA of 2.75; for doctorate, GRE General Test, master's degree, minimum undergraduate GPA of 3.5. Electronic applications accepted. *Faculty research:* Vocational development supervision.

Indiana University Bloomington, School of Education, Department of Counseling and Educational Psychology, Bloomington, IN 47405-1006. Offers counseling (MS, PhD, Ed S); counselor education (MS, Ed S); educational psychology (MS, PhD); inquiry methodology (PhD); learning and developmental sciences (MS, PhD); school psychology (PhD, Ed S). *Accreditation:* ACA (one or more programs are accredited); APA (one or more programs are accredited); NCATE. Terminal master's awarded for partial completion of doctoral program. *Degree requirements:* For master's, thesis optional; for doctorate, thesis/dissertation; for Ed S, comprehensive exam or project. *Entrance requirements:* For master's, doctorate, and Ed S, GRE General Test. Additional exam requirements/recommendations for international students: Required—TOEFL. Electronic applications accepted. *Faculty research:* Counseling psychology, inquiry methodology, school psychology, learning sciences, human development, educational psychology.

Indiana University of Pennsylvania, School of Graduate Studies and Research, College of Education and Communications, Department of Counseling, Program in School Counseling, Indiana, PA 15705. Offers M Ed. *Accreditation:* ACA. *Program availability:* Part-time. *Faculty:* 11 full-time (10 women), 5 part-time/adjunct (4 women). *Students:* 31 full-time (28 women), 22 part-time (18 women); includes 9 minority (7 Black or African American, non-Hispanic/Latino; 2 Two or more races, non-Hispanic/Latino). Average age 28. 31 applicants, 81% accepted, 20 enrolled. In 2017, 17 master's awarded. *Entrance requirements:* Additional exam requirements/recommendations for international students: Required—TOEFL (minimum score 540 paper-based). *Application deadline:* Applications areas processed on a rolling basis. Application fee: $50. Electronic applications accepted. *Expenses:* Tuition, state resident: full-time $12,000; part-time $500 per credit. Tuition, nonresident: full-time $18,000; part-time $750 per

credit. *Required fees:* $4073; $165.55 per credit. $64 per term. *Financial support:* In 2017–18, 8 research assistantships with tuition reimbursements (averaging $3,033 per year) were awarded; fellowships with full tuition reimbursements, career-related internships or fieldwork, Federal Work-Study, scholarships/grants, and unspecified assistantships also available. Financial award application deadline: 4/15; financial award applicants required to submit FAFSA. *Unit head:* Dr. Claire Dandeneau, Chairperson/Graduate Coordinator, 724-357-2306, E-mail: candean@iup.edu. Website: http://www.iup.edu/grad/schoolcounseling/default.aspx

Indiana University–Purdue University Fort Wayne, College of Education and Public Policy, Department of Professional Studies, Fort Wayne, IN 46805-1499. Offers couple and family counseling (MS Ed); educational leadership (MS Ed); school counseling (MS Ed); special education (MS Ed, Certificate). *Program availability:* Part-time. *Degree requirements:* For master's, comprehensive exam, practicum, internship, portfolio. *Entrance requirements:* For master's, minimum GPA of 2.5, three professional letters of recommendation. Additional exam requirements/recommendations for international students: Required—TOEFL (minimum score 550 paper-based; 79 iBT). *Faculty research:* Learning opportunities with deafness and the hearing impaired, adolescent emotion, student evaluation of teaching.

Indiana University–Purdue University Indianapolis, School of Education, Indianapolis, IN 46202-5155. Offers curriculum and instruction (MS); early childhood (MS); educational leadership (MS, Certificate); English as a second language (Certificate); kindergarten (Certificate); language education (MS); reading (Certificate); school counseling (MS); special education (MS, Certificate). *Program availability:* Part-time, evening/weekend. Terminal master's awarded for partial completion of doctoral program. *Degree requirements:* For master's, thesis optional. *Entrance requirements:* For master's, GRE General Test, minimum GPA of 2.5; for Certificate, official transcripts. Additional exam requirements/recommendations for international students: Required—TOEFL (minimum score 60 iBT), IELTS (minimum score 5.5). Electronic applications accepted. *Expenses:* Contact institution. *Faculty research:* Educational policies and school leaders' responses to these; issues of intersectionality in the experiences of African American lesbian, gay, and bisexual students attending historically black colleges and universities and those who belong to black Greek-letter organizations; students' experiential knowledge and their evolving disciplinary-specific literacy and understanding; innovative program development; urban ESL teacher preparation; target-based instructional coaching.

Indiana University South Bend, School of Education, South Bend, IN 46615. Offers addiction counseling (MS Ed); alcohol and drug counseling (Graduate Certificate); clinical mental health counseling (MS Ed); educational leadership (MS Ed); elementary education (MS Ed); marriage, couple, and family counseling (MS Ed); school counseling (MS Ed); secondary education (MS Ed); special education (MAT, MS Ed), including intense intervention (MS Ed), mild intervention (MS Ed). *Accreditation:* NCATE. *Program availability:* Part-time, evening/weekend. *Degree requirements:* For master's, thesis or alternative, exit project. *Entrance requirements:* For master's, letters of recommendation, GRE or minimum GPA of 3.0. Additional exam requirements/recommendations for international students: Required—TOEFL. Electronic applications accepted. *Expenses:* Contact institution. *Faculty research:* Professional dispositions, early childhood literacy, online learning, program assessments, problem-based learning.

Indiana University Southeast, School of Education, New Albany, IN 47150. Offers counselor education (MS Ed); elementary education (MS Ed); secondary education (MS Ed). *Accreditation:* NCATE. *Program availability:* Part-time, evening/weekend. *Entrance requirements:* For master's, minimum undergraduate GPA of 2.5, graduate 3.0. Electronic applications accepted. *Faculty research:* Learning styles, technology, constructivism, group process, innovative math strategies.

Indiana Wesleyan University, Graduate School, College of Arts and Sciences, Marion, IN 46953. Offers addictions counseling (MS); clinical mental health counseling (MS); community counseling (MS); marriage and family therapy (MS); school counseling (MS); student development counseling and administration (MS). *Accreditation:* ACA. *Program availability:* Part-time. *Degree requirements:* For master's, thesis or alternative. *Entrance requirements:* For master's, GRE General Test. Additional exam requirements/recommendations for international students: Required—TOEFL. Electronic applications accepted. *Expenses:* Contact institution. *Faculty research:* Community counseling, multicultural counseling, addictions.

Inter American University of Puerto Rico, Arecibo Campus, Programs in Education, Arecibo, PR 00614-4050. Offers administration and educational supervision (MA Ed); counseling and guidance (MA Ed); curriculum and teaching (MA Ed), including biology education, English as a second language, history education, math education, Spanish; elementary education (MA Ed). *Accreditation:* TEAC. *Degree requirements:* For master's, comprehensive exam, thesis optional. *Entrance requirements:* For master's, GRE, EXADEP, bachelor's degree in education or teaching license (administration and supervision) or courses in education and psychology (counseling and guidance), minimum GPA of 2.5 in last 60 credits.

Inter American University of Puerto Rico, Metropolitan Campus, Graduate Programs, Program in Education, San Juan, PR 00919-1293. Offers curriculum and instruction (Ed D); educational administration (Ed D); guidance and counseling (MA, Ed D); special education administration (Ed D). *Accreditation:* TEAC. *Degree requirements:* For doctorate, comprehensive exam, thesis/dissertation. *Entrance requirements:* For doctorate, GRE, MAT, or EXADEP. Electronic applications accepted.

Inter American University of Puerto Rico, San Germán Campus, Graduate Studies Center, Program in Counseling and Guidance, San Germán, PR 00683-5008. Offers education: counseling (MA, PhD). *Accreditation:* TEAC. *Program availability:* Part-time, evening/weekend. *Degree requirements:* For master's, comprehensive exam. *Entrance requirements:* For master's, GRE General Test or EXADEP, minimum GPA of 3.0.

Iowa State University of Science and Technology, Department of Educational Leadership and Policy Studies, Ames, IA 50011. Offers counselor education (M Ed, MS); educational administration (M Ed, MS); educational leadership (PhD); higher education (M Ed, MS); organizational learning and human resource development (M Ed, MS); research and evaluation (MS); student affairs (MS). *Degree requirements:* For master's, thesis or alternative; for doctorate, thesis/dissertation. *Entrance requirements:* For master's and doctorate, GRE General Test. Additional exam requirements/recommendations for international students: Required—TOEFL (minimum score 560 paper-based; 83 iBT), IELTS (minimum score 6.5). Electronic applications accepted.

Jackson State University, Graduate School, College of Education and Human Development, Department of Counseling, Rehabilitation and Psychometric Services, Jackson, MS 39217. Offers clinical mental health (MS); rehabilitation counseling (MS); school counseling (MS Ed). *Accreditation:* ACA; CORE (one or more programs are accredited); NCATE. *Program availability:* Part-time, evening/weekend, 100% online, blended/hybrid learning. *Degree requirements:* For master's, comprehensive exam, thesis. *Entrance requirements:* For master's, GRE General Test. Additional exam requirements/recommendations for international students: Required—TOEFL (minimum score 520 paper-based; 67 iBT). Electronic applications accepted. *Expenses:* Contact institution.

Jacksonville State University, College of Graduate Studies and Continuing Education, College of Education and Professional Studies, Program in Guidance and Counseling, Jacksonville, AL 36265-1602. Offers MS. *Accreditation:* ACA; NCATE. *Program availability:* Part-time, evening/weekend. *Degree requirements:* For master's, comprehensive exam, thesis (for some programs). *Entrance requirements:* For master's, GRE General Test or MAT. Additional exam requirements/recommendations for international students: Required—TOEFL (minimum score 500 paper-based; 61 iBT). Electronic applications accepted.

John Brown University, Graduate Counseling Programs, Siloam Springs, AR 72761-2121. Offers clinical mental health counseling (MS); marriage and family therapy (MS); play therapy (Graduate Certificate); school counseling (MS). *Accreditation:* NCATE. *Program availability:* Part-time, evening/weekend. *Degree requirements:* For master's, practica or internships. *Entrance requirements:* For master's, GRE (minimum score of 300), recommendation forms from three people, 200-word essay describing professional plans and reason for seeking acceptance. Additional exam requirements/recommendations for international students: Required—TOEFL (minimum score 550 paper-based; 79 iBT). Electronic applications accepted. *Expenses:* Contact institution.

John Carroll University, Graduate Studies, Program in Clinical Mental Health Counseling, University Heights, OH 44118. Offers clinical counseling (Certificate); community counseling (MA). *Accreditation:* ACA. *Program availability:* Part-time, evening/weekend. *Faculty:* 5 full-time (4 women), 11 part-time/adjunct (4 women). *Students:* 54 full-time (42 women), 37 part-time (30 women); includes 13 minority (6 Black or African American, non-Hispanic/Latino; 2 Asian, non-Hispanic/Latino; 3 Hispanic/Latino; 2 Two or more races, non-Hispanic/Latino), 2 international. Average age 31. In 2017, 42 master's awarded. *Degree requirements:* For master's, comprehensive exam, internship, practicum. *Entrance requirements:* For master's, MAT or GRE, minimum GPA of 2.75, statement of volunteer experience, interview, 12-18 hours of social science course work. Additional exam requirements/recommendations for international students: Required—TOEFL. *Application deadline:* For fall admission, 8/15 priority date for domestic students; for spring admission, 1/3 for domestic students. Applications are processed on a rolling basis. Application fee: $25 ($35 for international students). Electronic applications accepted. *Expenses: Tuition:* Full-time $16,238; part-time $788 per credit hour. One-time fee: $200. Part-time tuition and fees vary according to course load and program. *Financial support:* In 2017–18, 20 students received support, including 1 teaching assistantship with full tuition reimbursement available (averaging $8,000 per year); career-related internships or fieldwork, institutionally sponsored loans, and unspecified assistantships also available. Financial award application deadline: 3/1; financial award applicants required to submit FAFSA. *Faculty research:* Child and adolescent development, HIV, hypnosis, wellness, women's issues. *Unit head:* Dr. Cecile Brennan, Coordinator, 216-397-1987, Fax: 216-397-3045, E-mail: counseladmin@jcu.edu. *Application contact:* Jennifer L. Tucker, Records Management Assistant, 216-397-1925, Fax: 216-397-1835, E-mail: jtucker@jcu.edu.

John Carroll University, Graduate Studies, Program in School Counseling, University Heights, OH 44118. Offers M Ed. *Accreditation:* ACA; NCATE. *Program availability:* Part-time, evening/weekend. *Faculty:* 1 (woman) full-time, 3 part-time/adjunct (2 women). *Students:* 14 full-time (10 women), 7 part-time (5 women); includes 2 minority (both Black or African American, non-Hispanic/Latino). Average age 29. *Degree requirements:* For master's, comprehensive exam, research essay or thesis (MA only). *Entrance requirements:* For master's, GRE General Test or MAT, minimum GPA of 2.75, interview. Additional exam requirements/recommendations for international students: Required—TOEFL. *Application deadline:* For fall admission, 8/15 priority date for domestic students; for spring admission, 1/3 for domestic students. Applications are processed on a rolling basis. Application fee: $25 ($35 for international students). Electronic applications accepted. *Expenses: Tuition:* Full-time $16,238; part-time $788 per credit hour. One-time fee: $200. Part-time tuition and fees vary according to course load and program. *Financial support:* Scholarships/grants, tuition waivers (partial), and unspecified assistantships available. Financial award application deadline: 3/1; financial award applicants required to submit FAFSA. *Unit head:* Dr. Cecile Brennan, Chair of Department of Counseling, 216-397-1987, E-mail: cbrennan@jcu.edu. *Application contact:* Jennifer L. Tucker, Records Management Assistant, 216-397-1925, Fax: 216-397-1835, E-mail: jtucker@jcu.edu.

Johns Hopkins University, School of Education, Certificate Programs in Education, Baltimore, MD 21218. Offers advanced methods for differentiated instruction and inclusive education (Graduate Certificate); applied behavior analysis (Post-Master's Certificate); clinical mental health counseling (Post-Master's Certificate); counseling (Advanced Certificate); data-based decision making and organizational improvement (Graduate Certificate); early intervention/preschool special education specialist (Graduate Certificate); education of students with autism and other pervasive developmental disorders (Graduate Certificate); educational leadership for independent schools (Graduate Certificate); evidence-based teaching in the health professions (Post-Master's Certificate); gifted education (Graduate Certificate); leadership in technology integration (Graduate Certificate); mind, brain and teaching (Graduate Certificate); school administration and supervision (Graduate Certificate); urban education (Graduate Certificate). *Program availability:* Part-time-only, evening/weekend, 100% online, blended/hybrid learning. *Entrance requirements:* For degree, minimum of bachelor's degree from regionally- or nationally-accredited institution (master's degree for some programs); minimum GPA of 3.0 in all previous programs of study; official transcripts from all post-secondary institutions attended; essay; curriculum vitae/resume; two letters of recommendation; dispositions survey. Electronic applications accepted. *Expenses:* Contact institution.

Johns Hopkins University, School of Education, Master's Programs in Education, Baltimore, MD 21218. Offers counseling (MS), including clinical mental health counseling, school counseling; education (MS), including educational studies, gifted education, reading, school administration and supervision, technology for educators; elementary education (MAT); health professions (M Ed); intelligence analysis (MS); organizational leadership (MS); secondary education (MAT), including biology, chemistry, earth/space science, English, physics, social studies; special education (MS), including early childhood special education, general special education studies, mild to moderate disabilities, severe disabilities. *Program availability:* Part-time, evening/weekend, 100% online, blended/hybrid learning. *Degree requirements:* For master's, comprehensive exam (for some programs), portfolio, capstone project and/or internship; PRAXIS II (subject area assessments) for initial teacher preparation programs that lead to licensure. *Entrance requirements:* For master's, GRE (for full-time programs only); PRAXIS I/core or state-approved alternative (for initial teacher preparation programs that lead to licensure), minimum of bachelor's degree from regionally- or nationally-accredited institution; minimum GPA of 3.0 in all previous programs of study; official transcripts from all post-secondary institutions attended; essay; curriculum vitae/resume; letters of recommendation (3 for full-time programs, 2 for part-time programs); dispositions survey. Additional exam requirements/recommendations for international students: Required—TOEFL (minimum score 600 paper-based; 100 iBT), IELTS (minimum score 7). Electronic applications accepted. *Expenses:* Contact institution.

Johnson University, Graduate and Professional Programs, Knoxville, TN 37998-1001. Offers biblical interpretation (Graduate Certificate); business administration (MBA);

Christian ministries (Graduate Certificate); clinical mental health counseling (MA); educational technology (MA); intercultural studies (MA); leadership (MBA); leadership studies (PhD); New Testament (MA); nonprofit management (MBA); school counseling (MA); spiritual formation and leadership (Graduate Certificate); strategic ministry (MA); teacher education (MA). *Program availability:* Part-time, evening/weekend, 100% online, blended/hybrid learning. *Degree requirements:* For master's, variable foreign language requirement, comprehensive exam, thesis (for some programs), internships; for doctorate, variable foreign language requirement, comprehensive exam, thesis/dissertation, internships. *Entrance requirements:* For master's, PRAXIS (for MA in teacher education); MAT (for counseling); GRE or GMAT (for MBA), interview, 3 references, transcripts, essay, minimum GPA of 2.5 or 3.0 (depending on program); for doctorate, GRE or MAT (taken not less than 5 years prior), interview, 3 references, transcripts, essay, minimum GPA of 3.0; for Graduate Certificate, interview, 3 references, transcripts, essay, minimum GPA of 3.0. Additional exam requirements/recommendations for international students: Required—TOEFL (minimum score 527 paper-based; 71 iBT). Electronic applications accepted. *Expenses:* Contact institution.

Kansas State University, Graduate School, College of Education, Department of Special Education, Counseling and Student Affairs, Manhattan, KS 66506. Offers academic advising (MS, Certificate); counseling and student development (MS), including college student development, school counseling; special education (MS, Ed D); special education, counseling, and student affairs (PhD). *Accreditation:* ACA; NCATE. *Program availability:* Part-time, online learning. *Degree requirements:* For master's, comprehensive exam; for doctorate, comprehensive exam, thesis/dissertation. *Entrance requirements:* For master's, minimum undergraduate GPA of 3.0; for doctorate, GRE General Test, minimum GPA of 3.0 in last 60 hours. Additional exam requirements/recommendations for international students: Required—TOEFL. Electronic applications accepted. *Faculty research:* Counseling supervision, academic advising, career development, student development, universal design for learning, autism, learning disabilities.

Kean University, Nathan Weiss Graduate College, Program in Counselor Education, Union, NJ 07083. Offers alcohol and drug abuse counseling (MA); clinical mental health counseling (MA); school counseling (MA). *Accreditation:* ACA; NCATE. *Program availability:* Part-time. *Faculty:* 9 full-time (5 women). *Students:* 146 full-time (115 women), 138 part-time (111 women); includes 123 minority (56 Black or African American, non-Hispanic/Latino; 1 American Indian or Alaska Native, non-Hispanic/Latino; 7 Asian, non-Hispanic/Latino; 53 Hispanic/Latino; 6 Two or more races, non-Hispanic/Latino), 3 international. Average age 32. 197 applicants, 45% accepted, 55 enrolled. In 2017, 80 master's awarded. *Degree requirements:* For master's, practicum, internship, portfolio. *Entrance requirements:* For master's, minimum GPA of 3.0, 2 letters of recommendation, personal statement, resume. Additional exam requirements/recommendations for international students: Required—TOEFL (minimum score 550 paper-based; 79 iBT), IELTS (minimum score 6.5). *Application deadline:* For fall admission, 3/1 for domestic and international students; for spring admission, 11/1 for domestic and international students. Applications are processed on a rolling basis. Application fee: $75. Electronic applications accepted. *Expenses:* Tuition, state resident: full-time $13,419; part-time $653 per credit. Tuition, nonresident: full-time $18,188; part-time $801 per credit. *Required fees:* $3382; $154 per credit. Tuition and fees vary according to course level, course load, degree level and program. *Financial support:* Scholarships/grants and unspecified assistantships available. Financial award applicants required to submit FAFSA. *Unit head:* Dr. J. Barry Mascari, Program Coordinator, 908-737-5954, E-mail: jmascari@kean.edu. *Application contact:* Pedro Lopes, Admissions Counselor, 908-737-7100, E-mail: gradadmissions@kean.edu. Website: http://grad.kean.edu/counseling

Keene State College, School of Professional and Graduate Studies, Keene, NH 03435. Offers curriculum and instruction (M Ed); education leadership (PMC); educational leadership (M Ed); school counselor (M Ed, PMC); special education (M Ed). *Accreditation:* NCATE. *Program availability:* Part-time, evening/weekend. *Faculty:* 6 full-time (3 women), 7 part-time/adjunct (2 women). *Students:* 20 full-time (14 women), 42 part-time (20 women); includes 2 minority (1 Black or African American, non-Hispanic/Latino; 1 Asian, non-Hispanic/Latino), 1 international. Average age 31. 33 applicants, 58% accepted, 17 enrolled. In 2017, 39 master's awarded. *Degree requirements:* For master's, thesis (for some programs). *Entrance requirements:* For master's, PRAXIS I, 3 references; official transcripts; minimum GPA of 2.5; interview; essay; teacher/educator certificate; work/internship experience. Additional exam requirements/recommendations for international students: Required—TOEFL (minimum score 550 paper-based; 61 iBT). *Application deadline:* For fall admission, 4/1 for domestic and international students; for spring admission, 11/1 for domestic and international students; for summer admission, 3/1 for domestic and international students. Applications are processed on a rolling basis. Application fee: $50. Electronic applications accepted. *Expenses:* Tuition, state resident: full-time $9360; part-time $520 per credit. Tuition, nonresident: full-time $10,260; part-time $570 per credit. *Required fees:* $1908; $106 per credit. Tuition and fees vary according to course load. *Financial support:* In 2017–18, 19 students received support. Career-related internships or fieldwork, Federal Work-Study, institutionally sponsored loans, scholarships/grants, and unspecified assistantships available. Support available to part-time students. Financial award application deadline: 3/1; financial award applicants required to submit FAFSA. *Unit head:* Dr. Karrie Kalich, Dean of Professional and Graduate Studies, 603-358-2885, E-mail: kkalich@keene.edu. *Application contact:* Carl Ditkoff, Graduate Program Assistant, 603-358-2497, E-mail: kscgraduatestudies@keene.edu. Website: http://www.keene.edu/academics/graduate/

Kent State University, College of Education, Health and Human Services, School of Lifespan Development and Educational Sciences, Program in Counseling, Kent, OH 44240-0001. Offers Ed S. *Accreditation:* ACA. *Entrance requirements:* For degree, 2 letters of reference, goals statement, interview. Additional exam requirements/recommendations for international students: Required—TOEFL (minimum score 550 paper-based; 80 iBT). Electronic applications accepted. *Expenses:* Tuition, state resident: full-time $11,310; part-time $515 per credit hour. Tuition, nonresident: full-time $20,396; part-time $928 per credit hour. *International tuition:* $18,544 full-time.

Kent State University, College of Education, Health and Human Services, School of Lifespan Development and Educational Sciences, Program in Counseling and Human Development Services, Kent, OH 44242-0001. Offers PhD. *Accreditation:* ACA; NCATE. *Degree requirements:* For doctorate, comprehensive exam, thesis/dissertation. *Entrance requirements:* For doctorate, GRE General Test, preliminary written exam, 2 letters of reference, resume, interview. Additional exam requirements/recommendations for international students: Required—TOEFL (minimum score 550 paper-based; 80 iBT). Electronic applications accepted. *Expenses:* Tuition, state resident: full-time $11,310; part-time $515 per credit hour. Tuition, nonresident: full-time $20,396; part-time $928 per credit hour. *International tuition:* $18,544 full-time. *Faculty research:* Family/child therapy, clinical supervision, group work, experiential training methods.

Kent State University, College of Education, Health and Human Services, School of Lifespan Development and Educational Sciences, Program in School Counseling, Kent, OH 44242-0001. Offers M Ed. *Accreditation:* ACA; NCATE. *Entrance requirements:* For master's, minimum undergraduate GPA of 2.75, 2 letters of reference, goals statement,

Counselor Education

moral character statement, interview. Additional exam requirements/recommendations for international students: Required—TOEFL (minimum score 550 paper-based; 80 iBT). Electronic applications accepted. *Expenses:* Tuition, state resident: full-time $11,310; part-time $515 per credit hour. Tuition, nonresident: full-time $20,396; part-time $928 per credit hour. *International tuition:* $18,544 full-time. *Faculty research:* Appraisal, diagnosis, group work.

Kutztown University of Pennsylvania, College of Education, Program in School Counseling, Kutztown, PA 19530-0730. Offers MS. *Accreditation:* ACA; NCATE. *Program availability:* Part-time, evening/weekend. *Faculty:* 4 full-time (3 women). *Students:* 25 full-time (21 women), 25 part-time (20 women); includes 11 minority (3 Black or African American, non-Hispanic/Latino; 1 Asian, non-Hispanic/Latino; 7 Hispanic/Latino). Average age 28. 34 applicants, 76% accepted, 15 enrolled. In 2017, 27 master's awarded. *Degree requirements:* For master's, comprehensive exam, thesis optional. *Entrance requirements:* For master's, GRE General Test, 3 letters of recommendation, minimum undergraduate GPA of 3.0, psychobiographical statement, resume. Additional exam requirements/recommendations for international students: Required—TOEFL (minimum score 550 paper-based, 79 iBT), IELTS (minimum score 6.5), or PTE (minimum score 53). *Application deadline:* For fall admission, 3/1 for domestic and international students; for spring admission, 10/1 for domestic and international students. Application fee: $35. Electronic applications accepted. *Expenses:* Tuition, state resident: part-time $500 per credit. Tuition, nonresident: part-time $750 per credit. *Required fees:* $115 per credit. One-time fee: $50 part-time. Tuition and fees vary according to degree level. *Financial support:* Career-related internships or fieldwork, Federal Work-Study, and unspecified assistantships available. Financial award application deadline: 3/1; financial award applicants required to submit FAFSA. *Faculty research:* Family addictions, family roles. *Unit head:* Dr. Helen S. Hamlet, Department Chair, 610-683-4204, Fax: 610-683-1585, E-mail: hamlet@kutztown.edu. Website: https://www.kutztown.edu/academics/graduate-programs/counseling.htm

Lakeland University, Graduate Studies Division, Program in Counseling, Plymouth, WI 53073. Offers MA.

Lamar University, College of Graduate Studies, College of Education and Human Development, Department of Counseling and Special Populations, Beaumont, TX 77701. Offers clinical mental health counseling (M Ed); school counseling (M Ed); special education (M Ed), including special education. *Accreditation:* ACA. *Faculty:* 15 full-time (12 women), 22 part-time/adjunct (18 women). *Students:* 27 full-time (22 women), 1,362 part-time (1,200 women); includes 700 minority (359 Black or African American, non-Hispanic/Latino; 6 American Indian or Alaska Native, non-Hispanic/Latino; 18 Asian, non-Hispanic/Latino; 305 Hispanic/Latino; 1 Native Hawaiian or other Pacific Islander, non-Hispanic/Latino; 11 Two or more races, non-Hispanic/Latino), 2 international. Average age 37. 1,317 applicants, 66% accepted, 234 enrolled. In 2017, 645 master's awarded. *Entrance requirements:* Additional exam requirements/recommendations for international students: Required—TOEFL (minimum score 550 paper-based; 79 iBT), IELTS (minimum score 6.5). *Application deadline:* For fall admission, 8/10 for domestic students, 7/1 for international students; for spring admission, 1/5 for domestic students, 12/1 for international students. Applications are processed on a rolling basis. Application fee: $25 ($50 for international students). Electronic applications accepted. *Expenses:* Contact institution. *Financial support:* Applicants required to submit FAFSA. *Unit head:* Dr. Rebecca Weinbaum, Interim Chair, 409-880-8978, Fax: 409-880-2263. *Application contact:* Deidre Mayer, Interim Director, Admissions and Academic Services, 409-880-8888, Fax: 409-880-7419, E-mail: gradmissions@lamar.edu.
Website: http://education.lamar.edu/counseling-and-special-populations

Lancaster Bible College, Graduate School, Lancaster, PA 17601-5036. Offers adult ministries (MA); Bible (MA); children and family ministry (MA); church planting (MA); consulting resource teacher (M Ed); elementary school counseling (M Ed); leadership (PhD); leadership studies (MA); marriage and family counseling (MA); mental health counseling (MA); pastoral studies (MA); secondary school counseling (M Ed); sports ministry (MA); student ministry (MA); town and country ministry (MA). *Program availability:* Part-time, evening/weekend. *Degree requirements:* For master's, comprehensive exam (for some programs), thesis (for some programs). *Entrance requirements:* For master's, bachelor's degree with a minimum of 30 credits of course work in Bible, minimum undergraduate GPA of 3.0, interview. Additional exam requirements/recommendations for international students: Required—TOEFL.

La Sierra University, School of Education, Department of School Psychology and Counseling, Riverside, CA 92505. Offers counseling (MA); educational psychology (Ed S); school psychology (Ed S). *Program availability:* Part-time, evening/weekend. *Degree requirements:* For master's, thesis optional; for Ed S, practicum (educational psychology). *Entrance requirements:* For master's, California Basic Educational Skills Test, NTE, minimum GPA of 3.0; for Ed S, minimum GPA of 3.3. *Faculty research:* Equivalent score scales, self perception.

Lee University, Graduate Studies in Counseling, Cleveland, TN 37320-3450. Offers holistic child development (MS); marriage and family studies (MS); marriage and family therapy (MS); school counseling (MS). *Program availability:* Part-time, 100% online. *Faculty:* 7 full-time (3 women), 3 part-time/adjunct (0 women). *Students:* 95 full-time (71 women), 24 part-time (18 women); includes 27 minority (5 Black or African American, non-Hispanic/Latino; 19 Hispanic/Latino; 3 Two or more races, non-Hispanic/Latino), 7 international. Average age 30. 47 applicants, 87% accepted, 33 enrolled. In 2017, 32 master's awarded. *Degree requirements:* For master's, variable foreign language requirement, comprehensive exam (for some programs), thesis (for some programs), internship. *Entrance requirements:* For master's, GRE General Test or MAT (waived if undergraduate GPA is greater than 3.0 or if applicant already has a graduate degree), minimum undergraduate GPA of 3.0, 3 letters of recommendation, interview, official transcripts, essay. Additional exam requirements/recommendations for international students: Required—TOEFL (minimum score 61 iBT). *Application deadline:* For fall admission, 4/1 priority date for domestic and international students; for spring admission, 11/1 priority date for domestic and international students. Applications are processed on a rolling basis. Application fee: $25. Electronic applications accepted. *Expenses: Tuition:* Full-time $12,780; part-time $710 per credit hour. *Required fees:* $60; $60 per term. Tuition and fees vary according to program. *Financial support:* In 2017–18, 36 students received support. Career-related internships or fieldwork, Federal Work-Study, institutionally sponsored loans, scholarships/grants, and unspecified assistantships available. Financial award application deadline: 3/1; financial award applicants required to submit FAFSA. *Unit head:* Dr. Trevor Milliron, Director, 423-614-8126, Fax: 423-614-8124, E-mail: tmilliron@leeuniversity.edu.
Website: http://www.leeuniversity.edu/academics/graduate/counseling

Lehigh University, College of Education, Program in Counseling Psychology, Bethlehem, PA 18015. Offers counseling and human services (M Ed); counseling psychology (PhD); international counseling (M Ed, Certificate); school counseling (M Ed). *Accreditation:* APA (one or more programs are accredited). *Faculty:* 7 full-time (5 women), 10 part-time/adjunct (8 women). *Students:* 69 full-time (62 women), 28 part-time (22 women); includes 22 minority (6 Black or African American, non-Hispanic/Latino; 6 Asian, non-Hispanic/Latino; 10 Hispanic/Latino), 13 international. Average age 29. 181 applicants, 30% accepted, 22 enrolled. In 2017, 27 master's, 4 doctorates awarded. *Degree requirements:* For master's, thesis (for some programs); for doctorate, comprehensive exam, thesis/dissertation. *Entrance requirements:* For master's, minimum GPA of 3.0, 2 letters of recommendation, essay, transcript; for doctorate, GRE General Test, 2 letters of recommendation, transcript, essay; for Certificate, minimum GPA of 3.0 (undergraduate), 3.5 (graduate). Additional exam requirements/recommendations for international students: Required—TOEFL (minimum score 600 paper-based, 93 iBT) or IELTS. *Application deadline:* For fall admission, 2/1 for domestic and international students. Application fee: $65. Electronic applications accepted. *Financial support:* In 2017–18, 31 students received support, including 7 research assistantships with full and partial tuition reimbursements available (averaging $15,249 per year); fellowships and unspecified assistantships also available. Financial award application deadline: 2/15. *Faculty research:* Maternal/infant attachment, multicultural training and counseling, career development and health interventions, intersection of identities, community based participatory research, cognitive development, gerontology, multicultural competence, south Asian-Asian American concerns, sexual assault prevention, LGBTQ, intimate partner violence, feminist theory and therapy, sexual and reproductive health, women's health, culture and health, prevention, minority student development, educational access an. *Total annual research expenditures:* $423,020. *Unit head:* Dr. Christopher Liang, Director, 610-758-3253, Fax: 610-758-3227, E-mail: ctl212@lehigh.edu. *Application contact:* Kristi Ball, Coordinator, Counseling Psychology, 610-758-3250, Fax: 610-758-6223, E-mail: kmb618@lehigh.edu.
Website: https://ed.lehigh.edu/academics/programs/counseling-psychology

Lehman College of the City University of New York, School of Education, Department of Specialized Services in Education, Program in Guidance and Counseling, Bronx, NY 10468-1589. Offers MS Ed. *Accreditation:* ACA; NCATE. *Program availability:* Part-time, evening/weekend. *Degree requirements:* For master's, thesis. *Entrance requirements:* For master's, minimum GPA of 2.7. *Faculty research:* Crisis intervention, domestic violence, alcohol abuse, gender issues.

Lenoir-Rhyne University, Graduate Programs, School of Counseling and Human Services, Program in School Counseling, Hickory, NC 28601. Offers MA. *Program availability:* Part-time, evening/weekend. *Degree requirements:* For master's, comprehensive exam, thesis optional. *Entrance requirements:* For master's, GRE General Test, minimum undergraduate GPA of 2.7, graduate 3.0; writing sample. Additional exam requirements/recommendations for international students: Required—TOEFL (minimum score 600 paper-based). Electronic applications accepted. *Expenses:* Contact institution.

Lewis University, College of Arts and Sciences, Program in School Counseling, Romeoville, IL 60446. Offers MA. *Program availability:* Part-time, evening/weekend. *Students:* 37 full-time (32 women), 30 part-time (25 women); includes 9 minority (2 Black or African American, non-Hispanic/Latino; 1 Asian, non-Hispanic/Latino; 5 Hispanic/Latino; 1 Two or more races, non-Hispanic/Latino). Average age 29. *Degree requirements:* For master's, comprehensive exam, internship; practicum. *Entrance requirements:* For master's, Test of Academic Proficiency/Basic Skills Test/ACT/SAT, bachelor's degree, two letters of recommendation, interview, minimum GPA of 2.75. Additional exam requirements/recommendations for international students: Required—TOEFL (minimum score 550 paper-based; 79 iBT), IELTS (minimum score 6). *Application deadline:* For fall admission, 5/1 priority date for international students; for spring admission, 11/15 priority date for international students. Applications are processed on a rolling basis. Application fee: $40. Electronic applications accepted. Tuition and fees vary according to program. *Financial support:* Federal Work-Study, scholarships/grants, tuition waivers (full and partial), and unspecified assistantships available. Financial award application deadline: 5/1; financial award applicants required to submit FAFSA. *Unit head:* Dr. Judith Zito, Director, 815-838-0500 Ext. 5971, E-mail: zitoju@lewisu.edu. *Application contact:* Linda Campbell, Graduate Admission Counselor, 815-836-5610, E-mail: grad@lewisu.edu.

Liberty University, School of Behavioral Sciences, Lynchburg, VA 24515. Offers applied psychology (MA), including developmental psychology (MA, MS), industrial/organizational psychology (MA, MS); clinical mental health counseling (MA); community care and counseling (Ed D), including marriage and family counseling, pastoral care and counseling, traumatology; counselor education and supervision (PhD); human services counseling (MA), including addictions and recovery, business, child and family law, Christian ministries, criminal justice, crisis response and trauma, executive leadership, health and wellness, life coaching, marriage and family, military resilience; marriage and family counseling (MA); marriage and family therapy (MA); military resilience (Certificate); pastoral counseling (MA), including addictions and recovery, community chaplaincy, crisis response and trauma, discipleship and church ministry, leadership, life coaching, marriage and family, marriage and family studies, military resilience, parenting and child/adolescent, pastoral counseling, theology; professional counseling (MA); psychology (MS), including developmental psychology (MA, MS), industrial/organizational psychology (MA, MS); school counseling (M Ed). *Program availability:* Part-time, online learning. *Students:* 2,649 full-time (2,085 women), 5,086 part-time (4,015 women); includes 2,275 minority (1,784 Black or African American, non-Hispanic/Latino; 44 American Indian or Alaska Native, non-Hispanic/Latino; 67 Asian, non-Hispanic/Latino; 200 Hispanic/Latino; 11 Native Hawaiian or other Pacific Islander, non-Hispanic/Latino; 169 Two or more races, non-Hispanic/Latino), 145 international. Average age 39. 5,839 applicants, 51% accepted, 1710 enrolled. In 2017, 1,626 master's, 7 doctorates, 61 other advanced degrees awarded. *Application deadline:* Applications are processed on a rolling basis. Application fee: $50. Electronic applications accepted. *Financial support:* Applicants required to submit FAFSA. *Unit head:* Dr. Ronald Hawkins, Founding Dean, School of Behavioral Sciences. *Application contact:* Jay Bridge, Director of Admissions, 800-424-9595, Fax: 800-628-7977, E-mail: gradadmissions@liberty.edu.

Lincoln Memorial University, Carter and Moyers School of Education, Harrogate, TN 37752-1901. Offers administration and supervision (M Ed, Ed S); counseling and guidance (M Ed); curriculum and instruction (M Ed, Ed D, Ed S); English (M Ed); executive leadership (Ed D); higher education administration (Ed D); human resource development (Ed D); leadership and administration (Ed D). *Program availability:* Part-time, evening/weekend, online learning. *Degree requirements:* For master's, comprehensive exam, thesis optional; for Ed S, comprehensive exam. *Entrance requirements:* For master's, PRAXIS, NTE, GRE, MAT, letters of recommendation; for Ed S, graduate transcripts. Additional exam requirements/recommendations for international students: Recommended—TOEFL. *Faculty research:* Brain compatible teaching and learning; poverty in Appalachia; leadership for change; ethics, moral responsibility and social justice; human and organizational learning.

Lincoln University, Graduate Studies, Jefferson City, MO 65101. Offers business administration (MBA), including accounting, management, management information systems, public administration/policy; elementary teaching (M Ed); environmental science (MS); guidance and counseling (M Ed), including community/agency counseling, elementary school, secondary school; higher education (MA); history (MA); integrated agricultural systems (MS); middle school (M Ed); natural sciences (MS); secondary teaching (M Ed); sociology (MA); sociology/criminal justice (MA). *Program availability:* Part-time, evening/weekend, 100% online, blended/hybrid learning.

Students: 40 full-time (23 women), 64 part-time (32 women); includes 33 minority (30 Black or African American, non-Hispanic/Latino; 2 Hispanic/Latino; 1 Two or more races, non-Hispanic/Latino), 12 international. Average age 33. 48 applicants, 81% accepted, 22 enrolled. In 2017, 46 master's awarded. *Degree requirements:* For master's, comprehensive exam, thesis optional. *Entrance requirements:* For master's, GRE, MAT, or GMAT, minimum GPA of 2.75 overall, 3.0 in courses related to specialization; 3 letters of recommendation; minimum C average in English composition; personal statement of purpose. Additional exam requirements/recommendations for international students: Required—TOEFL (minimum score 500 paper-based; 61 iBT), IELTS (minimum score 5.5), Michigan English Language Assessment Battery (minimum score 80). *Application deadline:* For fall admission, 7/1 priority date for domestic students, 5/1 priority date for international students; for spring admission, 11/1 priority date for domestic students, 10/1 priority date for international students; for summer admission, 6/1 priority date for domestic students. Applications are processed on a rolling basis. Application fee: $30. Electronic applications accepted. *Expenses:* Tuition, state resident: part-time $291 per credit hour. Tuition, nonresident: part-time $541.50 per credit hour. *Financial support:* In 2017–18, 2 fellowships with tuition reimbursements, 3 research assistantships with tuition reimbursements were awarded; Federal Work-Study, scholarships/grants, and unspecified assistantships also available. Support available to part-time students. Financial award application deadline: 3/1; financial award applicants required to submit FAFSA. *Unit head:* Dr. Debra F. Greene, Interim Provost, 573-681-5247, Fax: 573-681-5106, E-mail: gradschool@lincolnu.edu. *Application contact:* Irasema Steck, Administrative Assistant, 573-681-5247, Fax: 573-681-5106, E-mail: gradschool@lincolnu.edu.
Website: http://www.lincolnu.edu/web/graduate-studies/graduate-studies

Lindenwood University–Belleville, Graduate Programs, Belleville, IL 62226. Offers business administration (MBA); communications (MA), including digital and multimedia, media management, promotions, training and development; counseling (MA); criminal justice administration (MS); education (MA); healthcare administration (MS); human resource management (MS); school administration (MA); teaching (MAT).

Lindsey Wilson College, School of Professional Counseling, Columbia, KY 42728. Offers counseling and human development (M Ed); counselor education and supervision (PhD). *Accreditation:* ACA (one or more programs are accredited). *Program availability:* Part-time, evening/weekend, online learning.

Loma Linda University, School of Behavioral Health, Department of Counseling and Family Sciences, Loma Linda, CA 92350. Offers child life specialist (MS); clinical mediation (Certificate); counseling (MS); drug and alcohol counseling (Certificate); family life education (Certificate); marital and family therapy (DMFT); school counseling (Certificate). *Degree requirements:* For master's, comprehensive exam, thesis optional; for doctorate, comprehensive exam, thesis/dissertation (for some programs). *Entrance requirements:* For master's, minimum GPA of 3.0; for doctorate, GRE. Additional exam requirements/recommendations for international students: Required—TOEFL (minimum score 550 paper-based). Electronic applications accepted.

Long Island University–Brentwood Campus, Graduate Programs, Brentwood, NY 11717. Offers childhood education (MS), including grades 1-6; childhood education/literacy B-6 (MS); childhood education/special education (grades 1-6) (MS); clinical mental health counseling (MS, Advanced Certificate); criminal justice (MS); early childhood education (MS); educational leadership (MS Ed); family nurse practitioner (MS, Advanced Certificate); health administration (MPA); library and information science (MS); literacy (B-6) (MS Ed); school counselor (MS, Advanced Certificate); social work (MSW); special education (MS Ed); students with disabilities generalist (grades 7-12) (Advanced Certificate). *Program availability:* Part-time. *Faculty:* 14 full-time (9 women), 22 part-time/adjunct (11 women). *Students:* 111 full-time (89 women), 47 part-time (34 women); includes 35 minority (8 Black or African American, non-Hispanic/Latino; 1 American Indian or Alaska Native, non-Hispanic/Latino; 3 Asian, non-Hispanic/Latino; 22 Hispanic/Latino; 1 Two or more races, non-Hispanic/Latino), 1 international. Average age 30. 110 applicants, 82% accepted, 63 enrolled. In 2017, 58 master's, 5 other advanced degrees awarded. *Entrance requirements:* For master's and Advanced Certificate, GRE. Additional exam requirements/recommendations for international students: Required—TOEFL or IELTS. *Application deadline:* Applications are processed on a rolling basis. Application fee: $50. Electronic applications accepted. *Expenses:* Tuition: Full-time $21,168; part-time $1201 per credit. *Required fees:* $1840; $920 per term. Tuition and fees vary according to course load. *Financial support:* In 2017–18, 121 students received support. Scholarships/grants available. Support available to part-time students. Financial award application deadline: 2/15; financial award applicants required to submit FAFSA. *Unit head:* Dr. Abby Van Vlerah, Dean and Chief Operating Officer, 631-299-3831, E-mail: abagail.vanvlerah@liu.edu. *Application contact:* Scott Aug, Associate Director of Enrollment Management, 631-287-8506, E-mail: scott.aug@liu.edu.
Website: http://liu.edu/brentwood

Long Island University–Hudson, Graduate School, Purchase, NY 10577. Offers autism (Advanced Certificate); bilingual education (Advanced Certificate); childhood education (MS Ed); crisis management (Advanced Certificate); early childhood education (MS Ed); educational leadership (MS Ed); health administration (MPA); literacy (MS Ed); marriage and family therapy (MS); mental health counseling (MS, Advanced Certificate), including credentialed alcoholism and substance abuse counselor (MS); middle childhood and adolescence education (MS Ed); pharmaceutics (MS), including cosmetic science, industrial pharmacy; public administration (MPA); school counseling (MS Ed, Advanced Certificate); school psychology (MS Ed); special education (MS Ed); TESOL (MS Ed); TESOL (all grades) (Advanced Certificate). *Program availability:* Part-time, evening/weekend. *Faculty:* 8 full-time (6 women), 41 part-time/adjunct (24 women). *Students:* 69 full-time (54 women), 249 part-time (200 women); includes 102 minority (29 Black or African American, non-Hispanic/Latino; 1 American Indian or Alaska Native, non-Hispanic/Latino; 9 Asian, non-Hispanic/Latino; 62 Hispanic/Latino; 1 Native Hawaiian or other Pacific Islander, non-Hispanic/Latino). Average age 33. 153 applicants, 96% accepted, 103 enrolled. In 2017, 138 master's, 36 other advanced degrees awarded. *Entrance requirements:* Additional exam requirements/recommendations for international students: Required—TOEFL. *Application deadline:* Applications are processed on a rolling basis. Application fee: $50. Electronic applications accepted. *Expenses:* Contact institution. *Financial support:* In 2017–18, 32 students received support. Scholarships/grants available. Support available to part-time students. Financial award application deadline: 2/15; financial award applicants required to submit FAFSA. *Unit head:* Dr. Sylvia Blake, Dean and Chief Operating Officer, 914-831-2700, E-mail: westchester@liu.edu. *Application contact:* Dr. Sylvia Blake, Dean and Chief Operating Officer, 914-831-2700, E-mail: westchester@liu.edu.

Long Island University–LIU Brooklyn, School of Education, Brooklyn, NY 11201-8423. Offers adolescence urban education (MS Ed); applied behavior analysis (Advanced Certificate); bilingual education (Advanced Certificate); bilingual education in urban setting (MS Ed); bilingual school counselor (MS Ed, Advanced Certificate); childhood urban education (MS Ed); childhood/early childhood education (MS Ed); childhood/early childhood urban education (MS Ed); early childhood urban education (MS Ed, Advanced Certificate); educational leadership (Advanced Certificate); marriage and family therapy (MS, Advanced Certificate); mental health counseling (MS, Advanced Certificate); school building district leader (Advanced Certificate); school counselor (MS Ed, Advanced Certificate); school psychologist (MS Ed); teaching students with disabilities (MS Ed); teaching urban children with disabilities (MS Ed); TESOL (MS Ed, Advanced Certificate). *Accreditation:* TEAC. *Program availability:* Part-time, evening/weekend, 100% online. *Faculty:* 14 full-time (12 women), 42 part-time/adjunct (32 women). *Students:* 140 full-time (130 women), 563 part-time (414 women); includes 417 minority (183 Black or African American, non-Hispanic/Latino; 1 American Indian or Alaska Native, non-Hispanic/Latino; 32 Asian, non-Hispanic/Latino; 187 Hispanic/Latino; 14 Two or more races, non-Hispanic/Latino), 10 international. Average age 31. 449 applicants, 82% accepted, 264 enrolled. In 2017, 408 master's, 31 other advanced degrees awarded. *Entrance requirements:* For master's, GRE. Additional exam requirements/recommendations for international students: Required—TOEFL (minimum score 527 paper-based, 75 iBT), IELTS, or PTE. *Application deadline:* Applications are processed on a rolling basis. Application fee: $50. Electronic applications accepted. *Expenses: Tuition:* Full-time $21,618; part-time $1201 per credit. *Required fees:* $1840; $920 per term. Tuition and fees vary according to course load. *Financial support:* In 2017–18, 58 students received support. Career-related internships or fieldwork, Federal Work-Study, scholarships/grants, and unspecified assistantships available. Support available to part-time students. Financial award application deadline: 2/15; financial award applicants required to submit FAFSA. *Faculty research:* Diversity issues in education and mental health care, inclusion - disability studies, sustainability, teacher professional development. *Unit head:* Dean, 718-488-1055, E-mail: bkln-admissions@liu.edu. *Application contact:* Bayu Sutrisno, Graduate Admissions Counselor, 718-488-1011, Fax: 718-780-6110, E-mail: bkln-admissions@liu.edu.
Website: http://www.liu.edu/Brooklyn/Academics/School-of-Education

Longwood University, College of Graduate and Professional Studies, College of Education and Human Services, Farmville, VA 23909. Offers education (MS), including algebra and middle school mathematics, counselor education, elementary and middle school mathematics, elementary education, elementary education initial licensure, health and physical education, special education general curriculum, special education initial licensure; reading, literacy and learning (M Ed); school librarianship (M Ed); social work and communication sciences and disorders (MS), including communication sciences and disorders. *Accreditation:* NCATE. *Program availability:* Part-time, evening/weekend. *Degree requirements:* For master's, comprehensive exam (for some programs), thesis optional, professional portfolio, internship, clinical experience, or practicum. *Entrance requirements:* For master's, PRAXIS I (for initial teaching licensure programs); GRE (for some programs), bachelor's degree from regionally-accredited institution, 2 recommendations (3 for some programs), minimum 500-word personal essay, official transcripts, minimum GPA of 2.75, valid teaching license (for some programs). Additional exam requirements/recommendations for international students: Required—TOEFL (minimum score 570 paper-based), IELTS (minimum score 6.5). Electronic applications accepted. *Expenses:* Contact institution.

Louisiana State University and Agricultural & Mechanical College, Graduate School, College of Human Sciences and Education, Department of Educational Theory, Policy and Practice, Baton Rouge, LA 70803. Offers counseling (M Ed, MA, Ed S); educational administration (M Ed, MA, PhD, Ed S); educational technology (MA); elementary education (M Ed, MAT); higher education (PhD); research methodology (PhD); secondary education (M Ed, MAT). *Accreditation:* ACA (one or more programs are accredited); NCATE. *Faculty:* 34 full-time (22 women). *Students:* 213 full-time (159 women), 228 part-time (178 women); includes 164 minority (123 Black or African American, non-Hispanic/Latino; 7 Asian, non-Hispanic/Latino; 27 Hispanic/Latino; 1 Native Hawaiian or other Pacific Islander, non-Hispanic/Latino; 6 Two or more races, non-Hispanic/Latino), 13 international. Average age 32. 231 applicants, 61% accepted, 82 enrolled. In 2017, 125 master's, 26 doctorates, 28 other advanced degrees awarded. *Financial support:* In 2017–18, 3 fellowships (averaging $12,129 per year), 2 research assistantships (averaging $16,019 per year), 96 teaching assistantships (averaging $16,061 per year) were awarded. *Total annual research expenditures:* $356,867.

Louisiana State University in Shreveport, College of Business, Education, and Human Development, Program in Counseling, Shreveport, LA 71115-2399. Offers MS. *Students:* 18 full-time (15 women), 8 part-time (6 women); includes 7 minority (5 Black or African American, non-Hispanic/Latino; 2 Hispanic/Latino), 1 international. Average age 30. 26 applicants, 100% accepted, 4 enrolled. In 2017, 16 master's awarded. *Degree requirements:* For master's, comprehensive exam, internship (600 clock hours). *Entrance requirements:* For master's, GRE, references, interview. Additional exam requirements/recommendations for international students: Required—TOEFL (minimum score 550 paper-based; 61 iBT). *Application deadline:* For fall admission, 6/30 for domestic and international students; for spring admission, 11/30 for domestic and international students; for summer admission, 4/30 for domestic and international students. Applications are processed on a rolling basis. Application fee: $20 ($30 for international students). Electronic applications accepted. *Expenses:* Tuition, state resident: full-time $3098; part-time $344 per credit hour. Tuition, nonresident: full-time $9923; part-time $1103 per credit hour. *Required fees:* $384 per semester. Tuition and fees vary according to program. *Financial support:* In 2017–18, 8 research assistantships (averaging $3,500 per year) were awarded. Financial award applicants required to submit FAFSA. *Unit head:* Dr. Meredith G. Nelson, Program Director, 318-797-5199, Fax: 318-798-4171, E-mail: mnelson@pilot.lsus.edu. *Application contact:* Mary Catherine Harvison, Director of Admissions, 318-797-2400, Fax: 318-797-5286, E-mail: mary.harvison@lsus.edu.

Loyola Marymount University, School of Education, Program in Guidance and Counseling, Los Angeles, CA 90045-2659. Offers MA. *Unit head:* Dr. Sheri Atwater, Director, Counseling Program, E-mail: sheri.atwater@lmu.edu. *Application contact:* Chake H. Kouyoumjian, Associate Dean of Graduate Studies, 310-338-2721, Fax: 310-338-6086, E-mail: graduateinfo@lmu.edu.
Website: http://soe.lmu.edu/academics/counseling

Loyola Marymount University, School of Education, Program in School Counseling, Los Angeles, CA 90045-2659. Offers MA. *Unit head:* Dr. Sheri Atwater, Director, E-mail: sheri.atwater@lmu.edu. *Application contact:* Chake H. Kouyoumjian, Associate Dean of Graduate Studies, 310-338-2721, Fax: 310-338-6086, E-mail: graduateinfo@lmu.edu.
Website: http://soe.lmu.edu/academics/counseling

Loyola University Chicago, School of Education, Program in School Counseling, Chicago, IL 60660. Offers M Ed, Certificate. *Accreditation:* NCATE. *Program availability:* Part-time. *Faculty:* 5 full-time (2 women), 5 part-time/adjunct (4 women). *Students:* 18 full-time (17 women), 3 part-time (all women); includes 6 minority (1 Black or African American, non-Hispanic/Latino; 1 Asian, non-Hispanic/Latino; 4 Hispanic/Latino). Average age 27. 19 applicants, 79% accepted, 4 enrolled. In 2017, 10 master's awarded. *Degree requirements:* For master's, comprehensive exam. *Entrance requirements:* For master's, GRE General Test, minimum GPA of 3.0, letters of recommendation, resume. Additional exam requirements/recommendations for international students: Required—TOEFL (minimum score 550 paper-based; 79 iBT). *Application deadline:* For fall admission, 1/1 for domestic and international students. Application fee: $50. Electronic applications accepted. Application fee is waived when completed online. *Expenses:* $949 per semester hour, $2,847 per course, $8,541-$11,388 full-time semester tuition; $432 per semester fees, $225 additional fees (first semester only). *Financial support:* Career-related internships or fieldwork, institutionally sponsored loans, and scholarships/grants available. Support available to part-time students. Financial award application deadline: 2/1; financial award applicants required to submit FAFSA. *Faculty research:* Career development, group counseling, family therapy, child and adolescent development, multicultural counseling. *Unit head:* Dr. Eunju Yoon, Program Chair, 312-915-6461, E-mail: eyoon@luc.edu. *Application contact:* Mirtza Campbell, Information Contact, 312-915-8907, E-mail: mcampbell11@luc.edu.

Loyola University Maryland, Graduate Programs, School of Education, Program in School Counseling, Baltimore, MD 21210-2699. Offers M Ed, MA, CAS. *Accreditation:* ACA; NCATE. *Program availability:* Part-time. *Faculty:* 36 full-time (27 women), 23 part-time/adjunct (15 women). *Students:* 52 full-time (47 women), 88 part-time (76 women); includes 47 minority (35 Black or African American, non-Hispanic/Latino; 1 Asian, non-Hispanic/Latino; 8 Hispanic/Latino; 3 Two or more races, non-Hispanic/Latino). Average age 31. *Degree requirements:* For master's, thesis. *Entrance requirements:* For master's, essay, transcript, 2 letters of recommendation. Additional exam requirements/recommendations for international students: Required—TOEFL (minimum score 550 paper-based), IELTS (minimum score 7). *Application deadline:* For fall admission, 6/15 priority date for domestic students, 3/1 for international students. Applications are processed on a rolling basis. Application fee: $60. Electronic applications accepted. *Expenses:* Contact institution. *Financial support:* Scholarships/grants and unspecified assistantships available. Financial award application deadline: 4/15; financial award applicants required to submit FAFSA. *Unit head:* Jennifer Watkinson, Director, 410-617-1705, E-mail: jswatkinson@loyola.edu. *Application contact:* Office of Graduate Admission, 410-617-5020, E-mail: graduate@loyola.edu.

Malone University, Graduate Program in Counseling and Human Development, Canton, OH 44709. Offers clinical counseling (MA); school counseling (MA). *Accreditation:* ACA; NCATE. *Program availability:* Part-time, evening/weekend. *Entrance requirements:* For master's, minimum undergraduate GPA of 3.0. Additional exam requirements/recommendations for international students: Required—TOEFL (minimum score 550 paper-based; 79 iBT). *Faculty research:* Spirituality and clinical counseling supervision, ethical and legal issues in counseling regarding supervision, resilience in adolescent offenders, protective factors for suicidal clients.

Manhattan College, Graduate Programs, School of Education and Health, Program in School Counseling, Riverdale, NY 10471. Offers bilingual pupil personnel services (Professional Diploma); school counseling (MA, Professional Diploma). *Program availability:* Part-time, evening/weekend. *Faculty:* 2 full-time (both women), 11 part-time/adjunct (7 women). *Students:* 50 full-time (35 women), 15 part-time (11 women); includes 40 minority (14 Black or African American, non-Hispanic/Latino; 2 Asian, non-Hispanic/Latino; 24 Hispanic/Latino). Average age 30. 41 applicants, 95% accepted, 39 enrolled. In 2017, 38 master's, 11 advanced degrees awarded. *Degree requirements:* For master's, thesis, internship. *Entrance requirements:* For master's, minimum GPA of 3.0. Additional exam requirements/recommendations for international students: Required—TOEFL. *Application deadline:* For fall admission, 7/1 priority date for domestic students; for spring admission, 12/20 priority date for domestic students. Applications are processed on a rolling basis. Application fee: $75. Electronic applications accepted. *Expenses:* $925 per credit; $110 registration fee per semester; $180 per semester services fee; $170 per semester information fee; $400 graduation fee. *Financial support:* Federal Work-Study, health care benefits, and unspecified assistantships available. Financial award application deadline: 2/1; financial award applicants required to submit FAFSA. *Faculty research:* Cognitive development, college and career readiness, group counseling, cultural attitudes, bullying, family social environments. *Unit head:* Dr. Corine Fitzpatrick, Director, 718-862-7497, Fax: 718-862-7472, E-mail: corine.fitzpatrick@manhattan.edu. *Application contact:* Suzana Pavisic, Director of Graduate Admissions, 718-862-7825, Fax: 718-862-8019, E-mail: spavisic01@manhattan.edu.

Marian University, Master of Science in Counseling Program, Indianapolis, IN 46222-1997. Offers clinical mental health counseling (MS); school counseling (MS). *Program availability:* Part-time. *Faculty:* 2 full-time (1 woman). *Students:* 8 full-time (7 women); includes 2 minority (both Two or more races, non-Hispanic/Latino). Average age 26. 18 applicants, 44% accepted, 8 enrolled. *Degree requirements:* For master's, 60 credit hours plus 1000 hours of supervised practicum (for clinical mental health counseling track); 48 credit hours plus 700 hours of supervised practicum (for school counseling track). *Entrance requirements:* For master's, GRE (preferred scores: combined 295, verbal 150, quantitative 145, writing 4), bachelor's degree (in related field preferred); minimum undergraduate and major GPA of 3.0; completion of undergraduate psychology courses in development, abnormal psychology, statistics or research methods; official transcripts from all postsecondary institutions attended; personal statement; 3 letters of recommendation; resume; interview. Additional exam requirements/recommendations for international students: Required—TOEFL (minimum score 550 paper-based; 79 iBT). *Application deadline:* For fall admission, 4/13 for domestic students; for spring admission, 11/1 for international students. Applications are processed on a rolling basis. Application fee: $40. Electronic applications accepted. Application fee is waived when completed online. *Expenses:* $505 per credit hour. *Financial support:* Application deadline: 4/15; applicants required to submit FAFSA. *Unit head:* Dr. Sarah Jenkins, 317-955-6399, E-mail: sjenkins@marian.edu. *Application contact:* Bryan Moody, Executive Director of Graduate Admission, 317-955-6284, E-mail: bmoody@marian.edu.
Website: http://www.marian.edu/academics/office-of-graduate-studies/master-of-science-in-counseling

Marquette University, Graduate School, College of Education, Department of Counselor Education and Counseling Psychology, Milwaukee, WI 53201-1881. Offers clinical mental health counseling (MS); community counseling (MA); counseling psychology (PhD); school counseling (MA). *Accreditation:* ACA. *Program availability:* Part-time. Terminal master's awarded for partial completion of doctoral program. *Degree requirements:* For master's, comprehensive exam, thesis (for some programs); for doctorate, thesis/dissertation, qualifying exam. *Entrance requirements:* For master's, GRE General Test or MAT, official transcripts from all current and previous colleges/universities except Marquette, three letters of recommendation, statement of purpose; for doctorate, GRE General Test, MAT, sample of written work, official transcripts from all current and previous colleges/universities except Marquette, three letters of recommendation, statement of purpose, resume/curriculum vitae. Additional exam requirements/recommendations for international students: Required—TOEFL (minimum score 530 paper-based). *Faculty research:* Ethical and legal issues in education, anxiety disorders, multicultural counseling, child psychopathology, group counseling and dynamics.

Marshall University, Academic Affairs Division, College of Education and Professional Development, Program in Counseling, Huntington, WV 25755. Offers MA. *Accreditation:* NCATE. *Program availability:* Part-time, evening/weekend. *Students:* 80 full-time (67 women), 40 part-time (34 women); includes 11 minority (5 Black or African American, non-Hispanic/Latino; 2 Hispanic/Latino; 4 Two or more races, non-Hispanic/Latino). Average age 32. In 2017, 42 master's awarded. *Degree requirements:* For master's, thesis optional, comprehensive or oral assessment. *Entrance requirements:* For master's, GRE General Test, MAT. Application fee: $40. *Financial support:* Career-related internships or fieldwork, Federal Work-Study, tuition waivers (full), and unspecified assistantships available. Support available to part-time students. Financial award applicants required to submit FAFSA. *Unit head:* Dr. Bob Rubenstein, Director, 304-746-1953, E-mail: brubenstein@marshall.edu. *Application contact:* Information Contact, 304-746-1900, Fax: 304-746-1902, E-mail: services@marshall.edu.

Marymount University, School of Education and Human Services, Program in Counseling, Arlington, VA 22207-4299. Offers clinical mental health counseling (MA); pastoral counseling (MA); school counseling (MA); MA/MA. *Accreditation:* ACA (one or more programs are accredited). *Program availability:* Part-time, evening/weekend. *Faculty:* 9 full-time (7 women), 5 part-time/adjunct (all women). *Students:* 108 full-time (97 women), 38 part-time (32 women); includes 61 minority (28 Black or African American, non-Hispanic/Latino; 1 American Indian or Alaska Native, non-Hispanic/Latino; 5 Asian, non-Hispanic/Latino; 20 Hispanic/Latino; 7 Two or more races, non-Hispanic/Latino). Average age 29. 74 applicants, 92% accepted, 59 enrolled. In 2017, 40 master's awarded. *Degree requirements:* For master's, thesis or alternative, capstone/internship. *Entrance requirements:* For master's, GRE, 2 letters of recommendation, interview, resume, personal statement. Additional exam requirements/recommendations for international students: Required—TOEFL (minimum score 600 paper-based; 96 iBT), IELTS (minimum score 6.5). *Application deadline:* For fall admission, 1/15 priority date for domestic and international students. Applications are processed on a rolling basis. Application fee: $40. Electronic applications accepted. *Expenses:* Tuition: Full-time $17,550; part-time $975 per credit hour. *Required fees:* $198; $11 per credit hour. One-time fee: $250. Tuition and fees vary according to program. *Financial support:* In 2017–18, 19 students received support, including 4 research assistantships with full and partial tuition reimbursements available (averaging $8,325 per year), 8 teaching assistantships with full and partial tuition reimbursements available (averaging $8,016 per year); career-related internships or fieldwork, Federal Work-Study, scholarships/grants, and unspecified assistantships also available. Support available to part-time students. Financial award application deadline: 3/1; financial award applicants required to submit FAFSA. *Unit head:* Dr. Lisa Jackson-Cherry, Chair, Counseling, 703-284-1633, Fax: 703-284-5708, E-mail: lisa.jackson-cherry@marymount.edu. *Application contact:* Francesca Reed, Director, Graduate Admissions, 703-284-5901, Fax: 703-527-3815, E-mail: grad.admissions@marymount.edu.
Website: http://www.marymount.edu/Academics/School-of-Education-Human-Services/Graduate-Programs/Counseling-(M-A-)

Marywood University, Academic Affairs, Reap College of Education and Human Development, Department of Psychology and Counseling, Program in Counselor Education, Scranton, PA 18509-1598. Offers MS. *Program availability:* Part-time. Electronic applications accepted.

McDaniel College, Graduate and Professional Studies, Program in Counseling, Westminster, MD 21157-4390. Offers MS. *Program availability:* Part-time, evening/weekend. *Faculty:* 5 full-time (3 women), 13 part-time/adjunct (6 women). *Students:* 52 full-time (41 women), 119 part-time (98 women); includes 37 minority (30 Black or African American, non-Hispanic/Latino; 1 Asian, non-Hispanic/Latino; 4 Hispanic/Latino; 2 Two or more races, non-Hispanic/Latino), 1 international. Average age 30. 47 applicants, 100% accepted, 30 enrolled. In 2017, 41 master's awarded. *Degree requirements:* For master's, thesis optional, internship. *Entrance requirements:* For master's, 3 letters of reference; interview with program faculty. Additional exam requirements/recommendations for international students: Required—TOEFL (minimum score 79 iBT), IELTS (minimum score 6). *Application deadline:* For fall admission, 6/1 priority date for domestic students; for spring admission, 11/1 priority date for domestic students; for summer admission, 3/1 priority date for domestic students. Applications are processed on a rolling basis. Application fee: $75. Electronic applications accepted. *Expenses:* Contact institution. *Financial support:* Application deadline: 3/1; applicants required to submit FAFSA. *Unit head:* Fax: 410-857-2515, E-mail: gradadms@mcdaniel.edu. *Application contact:* Penny Pfeiffer, Senior Graduate Enrollment Management Specialist, 410-857-2513, Fax: 410-857-2515, E-mail: ppfeiffer@mcdaniel.edu.

McNeese State University, Doré School of Graduate Studies, Burton College of Education, Department of Education Professions, Program in School Counseling, Lake Charles, LA 70609. Offers M Ed. *Accreditation:* ACA; NCATE. *Program availability:* Evening/weekend. *Entrance requirements:* For master's, GRE, 18 hours in professional education. *Application deadline:* For fall admission, 5/15 priority date for domestic and international students; for spring admission, 10/15 priority date for domestic and international students. Applications are processed on a rolling basis. Application fee: $20 ($30 for international students). *Financial support:* Application deadline: 5/1. *Unit head:* Dr. Brett C. Welch, Director, 337-475-5405, Fax: 337-475-5272, E-mail: bwelch@mcneese.edu. *Application contact:* Dr. Dustin M. Hebert, Director of Doré School of Graduate Studies, 337-475-5396, Fax: 337-475-5397, E-mail: admissions@mcneese.edu.

Mercer University, Graduate Studies, Cecil B. Day Campus, Penfield College, Atlanta, GA 30341. Offers certified rehabilitation counseling (MS); clinical mental health (MS); counselor education and supervision (PhD); criminal justice and public safety leadership (MS); health informatics (MS); human services (MS), including child and adolescent services, gerontology services; organizational leadership (MS), including leadership for the health care professional, leadership for the nonprofit organization, organizational development and change; school counseling (MS). *Program availability:* Part-time, evening/weekend, 100% online, blended/hybrid learning. *Faculty:* 17 full-time (10 women), 27 part-time/adjunct (24 women). *Students:* 199 full-time (165 women), 266 part-time (218 women); includes 268 minority (226 Black or African American, non-Hispanic/Latino; 1 American Indian or Alaska Native, non-Hispanic/Latino; 19 Asian, non-Hispanic/Latino; 19 Hispanic/Latino; 3 Two or more races, non-Hispanic/Latino). Average age 32. 300 applicants, 45% accepted, 114 enrolled. In 2017, 101 master's, 5 doctorates awarded. *Degree requirements:* For master's, comprehensive exam (for some programs), thesis (for some programs); for doctorate, thesis/dissertation. *Entrance requirements:* For master's, GRE or MAT, Georgia Professional Standards Commission (GPSC) Certification at the SC-5 level; for doctorate, GRE or MAT. Additional exam requirements/recommendations for international students: Recommended—TOEFL (minimum score 550 paper-based; 80 iBT), IELTS (minimum score 6.5). *Application deadline:* For fall admission, 7/1 priority date for domestic and international students; for spring admission, 11/1 priority date for domestic and international students; for summer admission, 4/1 priority date for domestic and international students. Application fee: $35. Electronic applications accepted. Application fee is waived when completed online. *Expenses:* $637 per credit. *Financial support:* In 2017–18, 32 students received support. Federal Work-Study, scholarships/grants, and unspecified assistantships available. Financial award applicants required to submit FAFSA. *Faculty research:* Marriage and families issues, leadership and ethics, cyber-bullying, trauma, narrative counseling and theory. *Total annual research expenditures:* $85,000. *Unit head:* Dr. Priscilla R. Danheiser, Dean, 678-547-6028, Fax: 678-547-6008, E-mail: danheiser_p@mercer.edu. *Application contact:* Dr. Melissa McCants Cruz, Director of Graduate Admissions, 678-547-6024, E-mail: penfield.admissions@mercer.edu.
Website: http://penfield.mercer.edu/programs/graduate-professional/

Mercy College, School of Social and Behavioral Sciences, Dobbs Ferry, NY 10522-1189. Offers counseling (MS, Certificate), including counseling (MS), family counseling (Certificate); health services management (MPA, MS); marriage and family therapy (MS); mental health counseling (MS); psychology (MS); school counseling (Certificate); school psychology (MS). *Program availability:* Part-time, evening/weekend, 100% online, blended/hybrid learning. *Students:* 248 full-time (210 women), 265 part-time (221 women); includes 373 minority (150 Black or African American, non-Hispanic/Latino; 1 American Indian or Alaska Native, non-Hispanic/Latino; 13 Asian, non-Hispanic/Latino; 203 Hispanic/Latino; 1 Native Hawaiian or other Pacific Islander, non-Hispanic/Latino; 5 Two or more races, non-Hispanic/Latino), 7 international. Average age 34. 448 applicants, 48% accepted, 150 enrolled. In 2017, 150 master's, 2 other advanced degrees awarded. *Degree requirements:* For master's, comprehensive exam (for some programs), thesis (for some programs). *Entrance requirements:* For master's, essay, 2 letters of recommendation, interview, resume, undergraduate transcript. Additional exam requirements/recommendations for international students: Required—TOEFL (minimum score 600 paper-based; 100 iBT), IELTS (minimum score 8). *Application deadline:* For fall admission, 8/1 for international students. Applications are processed on a rolling basis. Application fee: $40. Electronic applications accepted. *Expenses:* Tuition: Full-time $15,426; part-time $857 per credit hour. *Required fees:* $630; $158 per term. Tuition and fees vary according to course load, degree level and program. *Financial support:* Career-related internships or fieldwork, Federal Work-Study, scholarships/grants, and unspecified assistantships available. Support available to part-time students. Financial award applicants required to submit FAFSA. *Unit head:* Dr. Karol Dean, Dean, School of Social and Behavioral Sciences, 914-674-7517, E-mail: kdean@mercy.edu. *Application contact:* Allison Gurdineer, Senior Director of Admissions, 877-637-2946, Fax: 914-674-7382, E-mail: admissions@mercy.edu. Website: https://www.mercy.edu/social-and-behavioral-sciences/

Messiah College, Program in Counseling, Mechanicsburg, PA 17055. Offers clinical mental health counseling (MAC); counseling (CAGS); marriage, couple, and family counseling (MAC); school counseling (MAC). *Accreditation:* ACA. *Program availability:* Part-time, online learning. *Entrance requirements:* For master's, minimum undergraduate cumulative GPA of 3.0, 2 recommendations, resume or curriculum vitae, interview; for CAGS, bachelor's degree, minimum undergraduate cumulative GPA of 3.0, essay, two recommendations, resume or curriculum vitae, interview. Electronic applications accepted.

Michigan State University, The Graduate School, College of Education, Department of Counseling, Educational Psychology and Special Education, East Lansing, MI 48824. Offers counseling (MA); educational psychology and educational technology (PhD); educational technology (MA); measurement and quantitative methods (PhD); rehabilitation counseling (MA); rehabilitation counselor education (PhD); school psychology (MA, PhD, Ed S); special education (MA, PhD). *Accreditation:* APA (one or more programs are accredited); CORE (one or more programs are accredited). *Program availability:* Part-time. *Entrance requirements:* Additional exam requirements/recommendations for international students: Required—TOEFL. Electronic applications accepted.

Middle Tennessee State University, College of Graduate Studies, College of Education, Department of Educational Leadership, Program in Professional Counseling, Murfreesboro, TN 37132. Offers mental health counseling (M Ed); school counseling (M Ed). *Accreditation:* ACA; NCATE. *Program availability:* Part-time, evening/weekend, online learning. *Degree requirements:* For master's, comprehensive exam, thesis. *Entrance requirements:* For master's, GRE or MAT. Additional exam requirements/recommendations for international students: Required—TOEFL (minimum score 525 paper-based; 71 iBT) or IELTS (minimum score 6). Electronic applications accepted.

Midwestern State University, Billie Doris McAda Graduate School, West College of Education, Program in Counseling, Wichita Falls, TX 76308. Offers counseling (MA); human resource development (MA); school counseling (M Ed); training and development (MA). *Program availability:* Part-time, evening/weekend. *Degree requirements:* For master's, comprehensive exam, thesis (for some programs). *Entrance requirements:* For master's, GRE General Test, MAT, or GMAT, valid teaching certificate (M Ed). Additional exam requirements/recommendations for international students: Required—TOEFL (minimum score 550 paper-based). Electronic applications accepted. *Faculty research:* Social development of students with disabilities, autism, criminal justice counseling, conflict resolution issues, leadership.

Milligan College, Area of Counselor Education Programs, Milligan College, TN 37682. Offers clinical mental health counseling (MSC); counseling ministry (Graduate Certificate); school counseling (MSC). *Program availability:* Part-time. *Faculty:* 4 full-time (all women), 2 part-time/adjunct (0 women). *Students:* 24 full-time (17 women), 7 part-time (6 women); includes 4 minority (3 Black or African American, non-Hispanic/Latino; 1 Two or more races, non-Hispanic/Latino), 1 international. Average age 32. 30 applicants, 70% accepted, 13 enrolled. In 2017, 9 master's awarded. *Degree requirements:* For master's, thesis or alternative. *Entrance requirements:* For master's, GRE General Test if undergraduate GPA is less than 3.0, undergraduate degree and supporting transcripts, essay/personal statement, professional recommendations, interview. Additional exam requirements/recommendations for international students: Required—TOEFL (minimum score 550 paper-based, 79 iBT) or IELTS (6.5). *Application deadline:* For fall admission, 8/1 for domestic students, 6/1 for international students. Applications are processed on a rolling basis. Application fee: $30. Electronic applications accepted. *Expenses:* $440 per hour tuition; $325 per semester tech/activity fees. *Financial support:* Scholarships/grants available. Financial award application deadline: 12/1; financial award applicants required to submit FAFSA. *Faculty research:* Parent-child interaction therapy/autism; childhood developmental trauma/childhood sexual abuse; poverty and homelessness; social justice advocacy and multicultural competencies; school based mental health. *Unit head:* Dr. Christine Browning, Director of Master of Science in Counseling Program, 423-461-3513, Fax: 423-461-8777, E-mail: cmbrowning@milligan.edu. *Application contact:* Jenni Duran, Graduate Admissions Recruiter, Healthcare Programs, 423-461-8424, Fax: 423-461-8789, E-mail: jduran@milligan.edu.

Minnesota State University Mankato, College of Graduate Studies and Research, College of Education, Department of Counseling and Student Personnel, Mankato, MN 56001. Offers college student affairs (MS); counselor education and supervision (Ed D); mental health counseling (MS); professional school counseling (K-12) (MS). *Accreditation:* ACA (one or more programs are accredited); NCATE. *Degree requirements:* For master's, comprehensive exam, thesis or alternative. *Entrance requirements:* For master's, GRE General Test or MAT (if GPA less than 3.0 for last 2 years), minimum GPA of 3.0 during previous 2 years, 3 letters of reference. Additional exam requirements/recommendations for international students: Required—TOEFL. Electronic applications accepted.

Minnesota State University Moorhead, Graduate Studies, College of Education and Human Services, Moorhead, MN 56563. Offers counseling and student affairs (MS); curriculum and instruction (MS); educational leadership (MS, Ed D, Ed S); special education (MS); speech-language pathology (MS). *Accreditation:* NCATE. *Program availability:* Part-time, 100% online, blended/hybrid learning. *Faculty:* 22. *Students:* 117 full-time (101 women), 337 part-time (253 women). Average age 32. 248 applicants,

49% accepted. In 2017, 149 master's, 16 other advanced degrees awarded. *Degree requirements:* For master's, comprehensive exam (for some programs), thesis, final oral defense; for doctorate, comprehensive exam (for some programs), thesis/dissertation, final oral defense. *Entrance requirements:* For master's, GRE, essay, letter of intent, letters of reference, teaching license, teaching verification, minimum cumulative GPA of 3.0; for doctorate, official transcripts; letter of intent; resume or curriculum vitae; master's degree; personal essay. Additional exam requirements/recommendations for international students: Required—TOEFL (minimum score 550 paper-based); Recommended—IELTS (minimum score 6.5). *Application deadline:* Applications are processed on a rolling basis. Application fee: $20. Electronic applications accepted. *Expenses:* Tuition, state resident: full-time $9000; part-time $374 per credit. Tuition, nonresident: full-time $18,000; part-time $748 per credit. *Required fees:* $1055; $43.96 per credit. Tuition and fees vary according to degree level, program and reciprocity agreements. *Financial support:* Federal Work-Study and unspecified assistantships available. Financial award application deadline: 10/1; financial award applicants required to submit FAFSA. *Unit head:* Dr. Ok-Hee Lee, Dean, 218-477-2095, E-mail: okheelee@mnstate.edu. *Application contact:* Karla Wenger, Office Manager, 218-477-2344, Fax: 218-477-2482, E-mail: wengerk@mnstate.edu.
Website: http://www.mnstate.edu/cehs/

Mississippi College, Graduate School, School of Education, Department of Psychology and Counseling, Clinton, MS 39058. Offers counseling (Ed S); marriage and family counseling (MS); mental health counseling (MS); school counseling (M Ed). *Program availability:* Part-time. *Degree requirements:* For master's and Ed S, comprehensive exam, thesis optional. *Entrance requirements:* For master's, GRE or NTE. Additional exam requirements/recommendations for international students: Recommended—TOEFL, IELTS. Electronic applications accepted.

Mississippi State University, College of Education, Department of Counseling, Educational Psychology, and Foundations, Mississippi State, MS 39762. Offers clinical mental health (MS); college counseling (MS); counseling/mental health (PhD); counseling/school psychology (PhD); counselor education (Ed S); educational psychology/general educational psychology (PhD); educational psychology/school psychology (PhD); general educational psychology (MS); psychometry (MS); rehabilitation counseling (MS); school counseling (MS); school psychology (Ed S); student affairs (MS). *Accreditation:* ACA (one or more programs are accredited); APA; CORE (one or more programs are accredited); NCATE. *Program availability:* Part-time, blended/hybrid learning. *Faculty:* 21 full-time (14 women), 3 part-time/adjunct (2 women). *Students:* 106 full-time (85 women), 51 part-time (43 women); includes 55 minority (44 Black or African American, non-Hispanic/Latino; 1 American Indian or Alaska Native, non-Hispanic/Latino; 1 Asian, non-Hispanic/Latino; 5 Hispanic/Latino; 4 Two or more races, non-Hispanic/Latino), 5 international. Average age 29. 136 applicants, 55% accepted, 54 enrolled. In 2017, 50 master's, 7 doctorates, 10 other advanced degrees awarded. Terminal master's awarded for partial completion of doctoral program. *Degree requirements:* For master's, comprehensive exam, thesis optional; for doctorate, thesis/dissertation, comprehensive oral and written exam. *Entrance requirements:* For master's, GRE (taken within the last five years), BS with minimum GPA of 2.75 on last 60 hours; for doctorate, GRE, MS from CACREP- or CORE-accredited program in counseling; for Ed S, GRE, MS in counseling or related field, minimum GPA of 3.3 on all graduate work. Additional exam requirements/recommendations for international students: Required—TOEFL (minimum score 550 paper-based; 79 iBT); Recommended—IELTS (minimum score 6.5). *Application deadline:* For fall admission, 2/1 priority date for domestic and international students. Applications are processed on a rolling basis. Application fee: $60 ($80 for international students). Electronic applications accepted. *Expenses:* Tuition, state resident: full-time $8318; part-time $462.12 per credit hour. Tuition, nonresident: full-time $22,358; part-time $1242.12 per credit hour. *Required fees:* $110; $12.24 per credit hour. $6.12 per semester. *Financial support:* In 2017–18, 4 research assistantships (averaging $9,000 per year), 10 teaching assistantships with full tuition reimbursements (averaging $8,401 per year) were awarded; career-related internships or fieldwork, Federal Work-Study, institutionally sponsored loans, and unspecified assistantships also available. Financial award application deadline: 2/1; financial award applicants required to submit FAFSA. *Faculty research:* HIV/AIDS in college population, substance abuse in youth and college students, ADHD and conduct disorders in youth, assessment and identification of early childhood disabilities, assessment and vocational transition of the disabled. *Unit head:* Dr. David Morse, Professor and Head, 662-325-3426, Fax: 662-325-3263, E-mail: dmorse@colled.msstate.edu. *Application contact:* Marina Hunt, Admissions and Enrollment Assistant, 662-325-3363, E-mail: mhunt@grad.msstate.edu.
Website: http://www.cep.msstate.edu/

Missouri Baptist University, Graduate Programs, St. Louis, MO 63141-8660. Offers business administration (MBA); Christian ministries (MACM); counseling (MAC); education (MSE); education administration (MEA); educational leadership (MSE, Ed S); teaching (MAT).

Missouri State University, Graduate College, College of Education, Department of Counseling, Leadership, and Special Education, Program in Counseling, Springfield, MO 65897. Offers mental health counseling (MS). *Accreditation:* ACA. *Program availability:* Part-time, evening/weekend. *Faculty:* 9 full-time (6 women), 3 part-time/adjunct (2 women). *Students:* 62 full-time (46 women), 41 part-time (31 women); includes 17 minority (6 Black or African American, non-Hispanic/Latino; 7 Hispanic/Latino; 4 Two or more races, non-Hispanic/Latino), 3 international. Average age 24. 35 applicants, 31% accepted, 11 enrolled. In 2017, 53 master's awarded. *Degree requirements:* For master's, comprehensive exam, thesis or alternative. *Entrance requirements:* For master's, GRE or MAT, minimum GPA of 2.75. Additional exam requirements/recommendations for international students: Required—TOEFL (minimum score 550 paper-based; 79 iBT), IELTS (minimum score 6). *Application deadline:* For fall admission, 2/1 priority date for domestic students, 1/1 priority date for international students; for spring admission, 10/1 priority date for domestic students, 9/1 priority date for international students. Application fee: $35 ($50 for international students). Electronic applications accepted. *Expenses:* Tuition, state resident: full-time $2915; part-time $2021 per credit hour. Tuition, nonresident: full-time $5354; part-time $3647 per credit hour. *International tuition:* $11,992 full-time. *Required fees:* $173; $173 per credit hour. Tuition and fees vary according to class time, course level, course load, degree level, campus/location and program. *Financial support:* Federal Work-Study, institutionally sponsored loans, scholarships/grants, and unspecified assistantships available. Financial award application deadline: 3/31; financial award applicants required to submit FAFSA. *Unit head:* Dr. James Satterfield, Department Head, 417-836-5392, Fax: 417-836-4918, E-mail: clse@missouristate.edu. *Application contact:* Stephanie Praschan, Director, Graduate Enrollment Management, 417-836-5300, Fax: 417-836-6200, E-mail: stephaniepraschan@missouristate.edu.
Website: http://education.missouristate.edu/clse/

Montana State University Billings, College of Education, Department of Educational Theory and Practice, Option in School Counseling, Billings, MT 59101. Offers M Ed. *Accreditation:* NCATE. *Program availability:* Part-time. *Degree requirements:* For master's, thesis or professional paper and/or field experience. *Entrance requirements:* For master's, GRE General Test or MAT, minimum GPA of 3.0, letters of

recommendation, resume, letter of intent. Additional exam requirements/recommendations for international students: Required—TOEFL (minimum score 79 iBT), IELTS (minimum score 6.5). *Application deadline:* Applications are processed on a rolling basis. Application fee: $40. Electronic applications accepted. *Expenses:* Tuition, state resident: full-time $11,740; part-time $7880 per year. Tuition, nonresident: full-time $32,200; part-time $24,140 per year. *Financial support:* Teaching assistantships with partial tuition reimbursements, career-related internships or fieldwork, Federal Work-Study, institutionally sponsored loans, scholarships/grants, tuition waivers (partial), and unspecified assistantships available. Support available to part-time students. Financial award application deadline: 5/1; financial award applicants required to submit FAFSA. *Unit head:* Dr. Cindy Dell, Chair, Educational Theory and Practice, 406-657-1614, E-mail: cdell@msubillings.edu. *Application contact:* Dr. Cindy Dell, Chair, Educational Theory and Practice, 406-657-1614, E-mail: cdell@msubillings.edu.
Website: http://www.msubillings.edu/grad/program-school_counseling_option.htm

Montana State University–Northern, Graduate Programs, Option in Counselor Education, Havre, MT 59501-7751. Offers M Ed. *Program availability:* Part-time, evening/weekend. *Degree requirements:* For master's, comprehensive exam, thesis optional, oral exams, internship. *Entrance requirements:* For master's, GRE General Test or MAT, minimum major and overall GPA of 3.0. Electronic applications accepted.

Montclair State University, The Graduate School, College of Education and Human Services, Doctoral Program in Counselor Education, Montclair, NJ 07043-1624. Offers PhD. *Accreditation:* ACA. *Program availability:* Part-time, evening/weekend. *Degree requirements:* For doctorate, comprehensive exam, thesis/dissertation. *Entrance requirements:* For doctorate, GRE General Test, interview, 3 letters of recommendation. Additional exam requirements/recommendations for international students: Required—TOEFL (minimum score 83 iBT), IELTS (minimum score 6.5). Electronic applications accepted.

Montclair State University, The Graduate School, College of Education and Human Services, Program in Counseling, Montclair, NJ 07043-1624. Offers MA. *Accreditation:* ACA. *Program availability:* Part-time, evening/weekend. *Degree requirements:* For master's, comprehensive exam, thesis or alternative. *Entrance requirements:* For master's, GRE General Test, interview, 2 letters of recommendation. Additional exam requirements/recommendations for international students: Required—TOEFL (minimum score 83 iBT), IELTS (minimum score 6.5). Electronic applications accepted.

Morehead State University, Graduate Programs, College of Education, Department of Foundational and Graduate Studies in Education, Morehead, KY 40351. Offers adult and higher education (MA, Ed S); certified professional counselor (Ed S); counseling P-12 (MA); curriculum and instruction (Ed S); educational technology (MA Ed); instructional leadership (Ed S); school administration (MA); school counseling (Ed S); teacher leader business and marketing content (MA Ed); teacher leader business and marketing technology (MA Ed); teacher leader educational technology (MA Ed); teacher leader English (MA Ed); teacher leader gifted education (MA Ed); teacher leader IECE certification (MA Ed); teacher leader interdisciplinary education P-5 (MA Ed); teacher leader middle grades (MA Ed); teacher leader non IECE certification (MA Ed); teacher leader reading/writing - non-certification (MA Ed); teacher leader reading/writing certification (MA Ed); teacher leader school communication - certification (MA Ed); teacher leader school communication - non-certification (MA Ed); teacher leader social studies (MA Ed); teacher leader special education (MA Ed). *Accreditation:* NCATE. *Program availability:* Part-time, evening/weekend. *Degree requirements:* For master's, thesis optional, oral and/or written comprehensive exams; for Ed S, thesis, oral exam. *Entrance requirements:* For master's, GRE General Test, minimum overall undergraduate GPA of 2.5; for Ed S, GRE General Test, interview, master's degree, minimum GPA of 3.5, work experience. Additional exam requirements/recommendations for international students: Required—TOEFL (minimum score 500 paper-based). Electronic applications accepted. *Faculty research:* Character education, school accountability, computer applications for school administrators.

Mount Mary University, Graduate Programs, Program in Counseling, Milwaukee, WI 53222-4597. Offers clinical mental health counseling (MS, Certificate); clinical rehabilitation counseling (MS, Certificate); school counseling (MS, Certificate); vocational rehabilitation counseling (MS, Certificate). *Accreditation:* ACA. *Program availability:* Part-time, evening/weekend. *Degree requirements:* For master's, comprehensive exam, thesis or alternative. *Entrance requirements:* For master's, minimum GPA of 3.0. Additional exam requirements/recommendations for international students: Required—TOEFL (minimum score 550 paper-based; 80 iBT); Recommended—IELTS (minimum score 6.5). Electronic applications accepted. *Expenses:* Contact institution. *Faculty research:* Cognitive behavioral interventions for depression, eating disorders and compliance, trauma-informed care.

Murray State University, College of Education and Human Services, Department of Educational Studies, Leadership and Counseling, Murray, KY 42071. Offers college advising (Certificate); education administration (MA Ed); human development and leadership (MS, Certificate); library media (MA Ed); middle school teacher leader (MA Ed); P-20 and community leadership (Ed D); postsecondary education administration (MA Ed); school counseling (MA Ed); school guidance and counseling (Ed S); secondary teacher leader (MA Ed). *Program availability:* Part-time, evening/weekend, 100% online, blended/hybrid learning. *Faculty:* 38 full-time (16 women), 3 part-time/adjunct (1 woman). *Students:* 45 full-time (22 women), 190 part-time (140 women); includes 33 minority (25 Black or African American, non-Hispanic/Latino; 4 Asian, non-Hispanic/Latino; 3 Hispanic/Latino; 1 Two or more races, non-Hispanic/Latino), 6 international. Average age 35. 87 applicants, 77% accepted, 51 enrolled. In 2017, 21 master's, 16 doctorates, 12 other advanced degrees awarded. *Entrance requirements:* For master's and other advanced degree, GRE or GMAT, minimum university GPA of 2.75. Additional exam requirements/recommendations for international students: Required—TOEFL (minimum score 527 paper-based; 71 iBT). *Application deadline:* Applications are processed on a rolling basis. Application fee: $40 ($50 for international students). Electronic applications accepted. *Expenses:* Tuition, state resident: full-time $9504. Tuition, nonresident: full-time $26,811. *International tuition:* $14,400 full-time. Tuition and fees vary according to course load, degree level and reciprocity agreements. *Financial support:* Federal Work-Study and unspecified assistantships available. Financial award applicants required to submit FAFSA. *Unit head:* Dr. Susana Bloomdahl, Chair, Department of Educational Studies, Leadership, and Counseling, 270-809-6471, Fax: 270-809-3799, E-mail: sbloomdahl@murraystate.edu. *Application contact:* Kaitlyn Burzynski, Interim Assistant Director for Graduate Admission and Records, 270-809-5732, Fax: 270-809-3780, E-mail: msu.graduateadmissions@murraystate.edu.
Website: http://www.murraystate.edu/academics/CollegesDepartments/CollegeOfEducationandHumanServices/coehsacademicunits/EducationalStudiesLeadershipandCounseli

Naropa University, Graduate Programs, Program in Clinical Mental Health Counseling, Concentration in Mindfulness-based Transpersonal Counseling, Boulder, CO 80302-6697. Offers MA. *Faculty:* 10 full-time (7 women), 25 part-time/adjunct (18 women). *Students:* 113 full-time (89 women), 62 part-time (44 women); includes 33 minority (2 Black or African American, non-Hispanic/Latino; 5 Asian, non-Hispanic/Latino; 15 Hispanic/Latino; 11 Two or more races, non-Hispanic/Latino), 7 international. Average age 33. 106 applicants, 85% accepted, 76 enrolled. In 2017, 32 master's awarded. *Degree requirements:* For master's, internship, counseling practicum. *Entrance*

requirements: For master's, interview, statement of interest, essay, professional experience, resume, 2 letters of recommendation, transcripts. Additional exam requirements/recommendations for international students: Required—TOEFL (minimum score 550 paper-based; 80 iBT). *Application deadline:* For fall admission, 1/15 priority date for domestic and international students. Applications are processed on a rolling basis. Application fee: $60. Electronic applications accepted. *Expenses:* $995 per credit. *Financial support:* In 2017–18, 95 students received support, including 1 research assistantship with partial tuition reimbursement available (averaging $1,500 per year), teaching assistantships with partial tuition reimbursements available (averaging $3,000 per year); career-related internships or fieldwork, scholarships/grants, health care benefits, tuition waivers (partial), and unspecified assistantships also available. Support available to part-time students. Financial award application deadline: 3/1; financial award applicants required to submit FAFSA. *Unit head:* Dr. Kathleen Gregory, Dean, Graduate School of Counseling and Psychology, 303-245-4706, E-mail: kgregory@naropa.edu. *Application contact:* Office of Admissions, 303-546-3572, Fax: 303-546-3583, E-mail: admissions@naropa.edu.
Website: http://www.naropa.edu/academics/masters/clinical-mental-health-counseling/mindfulness-based-counseling-psychology/index.php

National Louis University, College of Arts and Sciences, Chicago, IL 60603. Offers adult education (Ed D); counseling and human services (MS); language and academic development (M Ed, Certificate); psychology (MA, PhD, Certificate); public policy (MA); written communication (MS, Certificate). *Program availability:* Part-time, evening/weekend, online learning. *Degree requirements:* For master's and Certificate, comprehensive exam (for some programs), thesis (for some programs); for doctorate, thesis/dissertation. *Entrance requirements:* For master's, MAT or GRE, 3 professional or academic references, interview, minimum GPA of 3.0; for doctorate, GRE General Test, MAT, or Watson-Glaser Critical Thinking Appraisal, three professional or academic references, statement of academic and professional goals, 3 years of experience in field, interview, master's degree, resume, writing sample; for Certificate, GRE, MAT, or Watson-Glaser Critical Thinking Appraisal, three professional or academic references, statement of academic and professional goals, interview, minimum GPA of 3.0. Additional exam requirements/recommendations for international students: Required—Department of Language Studies Assessment or TOEFL (minimum score 550 paper-based; 79 iBT). Electronic applications accepted.

National University, Academic Affairs, Sanford College of Education, La Jolla, CA 92037-1011. Offers advanced teaching practices (MS); applied behavior analysis (MS); applied school leadership (MS); e-teaching and learning (Certificate); education (MA); educational administration (MS); educational and instructional technology (MS); educational counseling (MS); higher education administration (MS); inspired teaching and learning (M Ed); school psychology (MS); special education (MA, MS). *Program availability:* Part-time, evening/weekend, 100% online, blended/hybrid learning. *Degree requirements:* For master's, thesis (for some programs). *Entrance requirements:* For master's, interview, minimum GPA of 2.5. Additional exam requirements/recommendations for international students: Required—TOEFL (minimum score 550 paper-based; 79 iBT), IELTS (minimum score 6). *Application deadline:* Applications are processed on a rolling basis. Application fee: $60 ($65 for international students). Electronic applications accepted. *Expenses:* Tuition: Part-time $430 per quarter hour. *Financial support:* Career-related internships or fieldwork, institutionally sponsored loans, scholarships/grants, and tuition waivers (partial) available. Support available to part-time students. Financial award application deadline: 6/30. *Faculty research:* Teacher education, special education, educational effectiveness, teaching abroad, school counseling. *Unit head:* Dr. Judy Mantle, Dean, 858-642-8320, E-mail: soe@nu.edu. *Application contact:* Brandon Jouganatos, Vice President for Enrollment Services, 800-628-8648, E-mail: advisor@nu.edu.
Website: http://www.nu.edu/OurPrograms/SchoolOfEducation.html

New Jersey City University, Debra Cannon Partridge Wolfe College of Education, Department of Educational Leadership and Counseling, Counselor Education Program, Jersey City, NJ 07305-1597. Offers MA. *Accreditation:* ACA. *Program availability:* Part-time, evening/weekend. *Entrance requirements:* Additional exam requirements/recommendations for international students: Required—TOEFL (minimum score 79 iBT).

New Mexico Highlands University, Graduate Studies, School of Education, Las Vegas, NM 87701. Offers curriculum and instruction (MA); educational leadership (MA); professional counseling (MA); special education (MA). *Accreditation:* NCATE. *Program availability:* Part-time. *Degree requirements:* For master's, comprehensive exam, thesis or alternative. *Entrance requirements:* For master's, minimum undergraduate GPA of 3.0. Additional exam requirements/recommendations for international students: Required—TOEFL (minimum score 540 paper-based). *Faculty research:* Middle school curriculum, integrated computer applications for pre-service classroom teachers, adolescent literacy, narrative cognitive modes in New Mexico multicultural setting, math and math education.

New Mexico State University, College of Education, Department of Counseling and Educational Psychology, Las Cruces, NM 88003. Offers counseling psychology (PhD); educational diagnostics (MA), including counseling and guidance, educational diagnostics; school psychology (Ed S). *Accreditation:* ACA; APA (one or more programs are accredited); NCATE. *Program availability:* Part-time, evening/weekend. *Faculty:* 11 full-time (9 women), 3 part-time/adjunct (all women). *Students:* 80 full-time (57 women), 23 part-time (17 women); includes 68 minority (3 Black or African American, non-Hispanic/Latino; 3 American Indian or Alaska Native, non-Hispanic/Latino; 5 Asian, non-Hispanic/Latino; 56 Hispanic/Latino; 1 Two or more races, non-Hispanic/Latino), 1 international. Average age 31. 103 applicants, 59% accepted, 34 enrolled. In 2017, 18 master's, 5 doctorates, 6 other advanced degrees awarded. *Degree requirements:* For master's, comprehensive exam, thesis optional, internship; for doctorate, comprehensive exam, thesis/dissertation, internship; for Ed S, comprehensive exam, thesis or alternative, internship. *Entrance requirements:* For master's, doctorate, and Ed S, GRE General Test, minimum GPA of 3.0. Additional exam requirements/recommendations for international students: Required—TOEFL (minimum score 550 paper-based; 79 iBT), IELTS (minimum score 6.5). *Application deadline:* For fall admission, 12/15 for domestic and international students; for spring admission, 2/1 priority date for domestic students, 2/1 for international students. Application fee: $40 ($50 for international students). Electronic applications accepted. *Expenses:* Tuition, state resident: full-time $4390. Tuition, nonresident: full-time $15,309. *Required fees:* $853. *Financial support:* In 2017–18, 72 students received support, including 4 fellowships (averaging $4,390 per year), 2 research assistantships (averaging $15,197 per year), 25 teaching assistantships (averaging $14,416 per year); career-related internships or fieldwork, Federal Work-Study, scholarships/grants, traineeships, health care benefits, and unspecified assistantships also available. Support available to part-time students. Financial award application deadline: 3/1. *Faculty research:* Multicultural counseling and training, school and counseling psychology, social justice, integrated primary care behavioral health training, mental health disparities. *Total annual research expenditures:* $110,485. *Unit head:* Dr. Barbara Gormley, Department Head, 575-646-2121, Fax: 575-646-8035, E-mail: bgormley@nmsu.edu. *Application contact:* Norma Arrieta, Student Program Coordinator, 575-646-2121, Fax: 575-646-8035, E-mail: cep@nmsu.edu.
Website: http://cep.education.nmsu.edu

New York Institute of Technology, School of Interdisciplinary Studies and Education, Department of School Counseling, Old Westbury, NY 11568-8000. Offers bilingual school counseling (Advanced Certificate); school counseling (MS); student behavior management (Advanced Certificate). *Accreditation:* ACA. *Program availability:* Part-time, blended/hybrid learning. *Faculty:* 3 full-time (2 women), 4 part-time/adjunct (3 women). *Students:* 24 full-time (20 women), 22 part-time (19 women); includes 20 minority (6 Black or African American, non-Hispanic/Latino; 2 Asian, non-Hispanic/Latino; 12 Hispanic/Latino). Average age 30. 45 applicants, 42% accepted, 12 enrolled. In 2017, 15 master's awarded. *Degree requirements:* For master's, internship, practicum. *Entrance requirements:* For master's, GRE or MAT, minimum undergraduate GPA of 3.0; BS or equivalent with academic background in psychology, education, sociology, law, or related behavioral science, or work experience in school, social agency, hospital, criminal justice, or community action program; goal statement; 3 letters of reference; signed candidate statement of understanding. Additional exam requirements/recommendations for international students: Required—TOEFL (minimum score 79 iBT), IELTS (minimum score 6). *Application deadline:* Applications are processed on a rolling basis. Application fee: $50. Electronic applications accepted. *Expenses:* $1,285 per credit plus fees. *Financial support:* Career-related internships or fieldwork, Federal Work-Study, scholarships/grants, tuition waivers (full and partial), and unspecified assistantships available. Support available to part-time students. Financial award application deadline: 2/15; financial award applicants required to submit FAFSA. *Faculty research:* School counselor accountability, school counselor-principal relationship, comprehensive school counseling program design and evaluation, cultural competence, college and career readiness. *Unit head:* Dr. Carol Dahir, Department Chair, 516-686-7616, Fax: 516-686-7655, E-mail: cdahir@nyit.edu. *Application contact:* Alice Dolitsky, Director, Graduate Admissions, 516-686-7520, Fax: 516-686-1116, E-mail: nyitgrad@nyit.edu.
Website: http://www.nyit.edu/interdisciplinary/department_school_counseling

New York University, Steinhardt School of Culture, Education, and Human Development, Department of Applied Psychology, Programs in Counseling, New York, NY 10012. Offers counseling and guidance (MA, Advanced Certificate), including bilingual school counseling K-12 (MA), school counseling K-12 (MA); counseling for mental health and wellness (MA); counseling psychology (PhD); LGBT health, education, and social services (Advanced Certificate); Advanced Certificate/MPH; MA/Advanced Certificate. *Accreditation:* APA (one or more programs are accredited). *Program availability:* Part-time. *Students:* Average age 29. 663 applicants, 33% accepted, 74 enrolled. In 2017, 87 master's, 7 doctorates awarded. *Entrance requirements:* For doctorate, GRE General Test, interview. Additional exam requirements/recommendations for international students: Required—TOEFL (minimum score 100 iBT). *Application deadline:* For fall admission, 12/1 priority date for domestic and international students. Applications are processed on a rolling basis. Application fee: $75. Electronic applications accepted. *Expenses:* Tuition: Full-time $41,352; part-time $19,968 per year. *Required fees:* $2496; $1628 per unit. $814 per term. Tuition and fees vary according to course load and program. *Financial support:* Fellowships with full and partial tuition reimbursements, research assistantships, teaching assistantships with partial tuition reimbursements, career-related internships or fieldwork, Federal Work-Study, institutionally sponsored loans, scholarships/grants, tuition waivers (partial), and unspecified assistantships available. Support available to part-time students. Financial award application deadline: 2/1; financial award applicants required to submit FAFSA. *Faculty research:* Sexual and gender identities, group dynamics, psychopathy and personality, multicultural assessment, working people's lives. *Unit head:* Dr. Randolph Mowry, Co-Director, 212-998-5222, Fax: 212-995-4358, E-mail: randolph.mowry@nyu.edu. *Application contact:* 212-998-5030, Fax: 212-995-4328, E-mail: steinhardt.gradadmissions@nyu.edu.
Website: http://steinhardt.nyu.edu/appsych/counseling

Niagara University, Graduate Division of Education, Concentration in Mental Health Counseling, Niagara University, NY 14109. Offers MS, Certificate. *Accreditation:* ACA. *Program availability:* Part-time. *Students:* 46 full-time (39 women), 7 part-time (6 women); includes 4 minority (2 Black or African American, non-Hispanic/Latino; 2 Hispanic/Latino), 18 international. Average age 27. In 2017, 19 master's, 1 other advanced degree awarded. *Entrance requirements:* For master's, GRE General Test or MAT. Additional exam requirements/recommendations for international students: Required—TOEFL (minimum score 550 paper-based; 79 iBT), IELTS (minimum score 6). *Application deadline:* For fall admission, 8/1 for domestic students. Applications are processed on a rolling basis. Application fee: $30. *Expenses:* Contact institution. *Financial support:* Research assistantships with tuition reimbursements, teaching assistantships with tuition reimbursements, career-related internships or fieldwork, Federal Work-Study, scholarships/grants, and unspecified assistantships available. Financial award application deadline: 4/15; financial award applicants required to submit FAFSA. *Unit head:* Dr. Kristine Augustyniak, Coordinator, Clinical Mental Health Counseling Program, 716-286-8548, E-mail: kma@niagara.edu. *Application contact:* Evan Pierce, Associate Director, Graduate Studies, 716-286-8327, E-mail: epierce@niagara.edu.
Website: http://www.niagara.edu/mental-health-counseling

Niagara University, Graduate Division of Education, Concentration in School Counseling, Niagara University, NY 14109. Offers MS Ed, Certificate. *Accreditation:* NCATE. *Program availability:* Part-time, evening/weekend. *Students:* 24 full-time (23 women), 10 part-time (8 women); includes 5 minority (4 Black or African American, non-Hispanic/Latino; 1 Hispanic/Latino), 1 international. Average age 26. In 2017, 7 master's, 1 Certificate awarded. *Entrance requirements:* For master's, GRE General Test or MAT; for Certificate, GRE General Test, GRE Subject Test or MAT. Additional exam requirements/recommendations for international students: Required—TOEFL (minimum score 550 paper-based; 79 iBT), IELTS (minimum score 6). *Application deadline:* For fall admission, 8/1 for domestic students. Applications are processed on a rolling basis. Application fee: $30. *Expenses:* Contact institution. *Financial support:* Research assistantships with tuition reimbursements, teaching assistantships with tuition reimbursements, career-related internships or fieldwork, Federal Work-Study, scholarships/grants, and unspecified assistantships available. Financial award application deadline: 4/15; financial award applicants required to submit FAFSA. *Unit head:* Dr. Jennifer Beebe, Associate Professor of Counseling, 716-286-8182, E-mail: jbeebe@niagara.edu. *Application contact:* Evan Pierce, Associate Director, Graduate Studies, 716-286-8327, E-mail: epierce@niagara.edu.
Website: http://www.niagara.edu/school-counseling

Nicholls State University, Graduate Studies, College of Education, Department of Psychology, Counseling and Family Studies, Thibodaux, LA 70310. Offers clinical mental health counseling (MA); school counseling (M Ed); school psychology (SSP). *Accreditation:* NCATE. *Program availability:* Part-time, evening/weekend. *Degree requirements:* For master's, comprehensive exam; for SSP, comprehensive exam, internship. *Entrance requirements:* For master's, GRE General Test. Electronic applications accepted.

North Carolina Agricultural and Technical State University, School of Graduate Studies, School of Education, Department of Human Development and Services, Greensboro, NC 27411. Offers adult education (MS); counseling (MS); school

administration (MS). *Accreditation:* ACA. *Program availability:* Part-time, evening/weekend. *Degree requirements:* For master's, comprehensive exam, thesis, qualifying exam. *Entrance requirements:* For master's, GRE General Test, minimum GPA of 3.0.

North Carolina Central University, School of Education, Program in Counselor Education, Durham, NC 27707-3129. Offers career counseling (MA); clinical mental health counseling (MA); school counseling (MA). *Accreditation:* ACA; NCATE. *Program availability:* Part-time, evening/weekend. *Degree requirements:* For master's, comprehensive exam, thesis or alternative. *Entrance requirements:* For master's, GRE, minimum GPA of 3.0 in major, 2.5 overall. Additional exam requirements/recommendations for international students: Required—TOEFL. *Application deadline:* For fall admission, 8/1 for domestic students. Application fee: $30. *Expenses:* Tuition, state resident: full-time $2770; part-time $692.50 per credit hour. Tuition, nonresident: full-time $9247; part-time $2311.75 per credit hour. *Financial support:* Application deadline: 5/1; applicants required to submit FAFSA. *Unit head:* Peggy Whiting, Coordinator, 919-530-6182, Fax: 919-530-7522, E-mail: pwhiting@nccu.edu. *Application contact:* Peggy Whiting, Coordinator, 919-530-6182, Fax: 919-530-7522, E-mail: pwhiting@nccu.edu.

North Carolina State University, Graduate School, College of Education, Department of Curriculum and Instruction, Program in Counselor Education, Raleigh, NC 27695. Offers M Ed, MS, PhD. *Accreditation:* ACA. *Degree requirements:* For master's, thesis (for some programs). *Entrance requirements:* For master's, GRE or MAT. Electronic applications accepted. *Faculty research:* Career development, retention of at-risk students in higher education, psycho-social development, multicultural issues, cognitive-developmental interventions.

North Dakota State University, College of Graduate and Interdisciplinary Studies, College of Human Development and Education, School of Education, Program in Counselor Education, Fargo, ND 58102. Offers clinical mental health counseling (M Ed, MS); counselor education and supervision (PhD); school counseling (M Ed, MS). *Accreditation:* ACA; NCATE. *Program availability:* Part-time, online learning. *Degree requirements:* For master's, comprehensive exam, thesis or alternative; for doctorate, comprehensive exam, thesis/dissertation. *Entrance requirements:* For master's, GRE, MAT, interview. Additional exam requirements/recommendations for international students: Required—TOEFL. *Faculty research:* Supervision, program assessment, multicultural issues.

Northeastern Illinois University, College of Graduate Studies and Research, Daniel L. Goodwin College of Education, Program in School Counseling, Chicago, IL 60625. Offers MA. *Accreditation:* ACA. *Expenses:* Tuition, state resident: full-time $7274; part-time $404.11 per credit hour. Tuition, nonresident: full-time $14,548; part-time $808.23 per credit hour. *Required fees:* $1284. *Unit head:* Dr. Charles Pistorio, Department Chair/Advisor, 773-442-5551, E-mail: c-pistorio@neiu.edu. *Application contact:* Martha Narvaez, Graduate Admission Representative, 773-442-6006, E-mail: m-narvaez@neiu.edu.

Northern Arizona University, College of Education, Department of Educational Psychology, Flagstaff, AZ 86011. Offers clinical mental health counseling (MA); combined counseling/school psychology (PhD), including counseling psychology; counseling (M Ed), including school counseling, student affairs; human relations (M Ed); psychology of human development and learning (Graduate Certificate); school psychology (Ed S). *Program availability:* Part-time, 100% online, blended/hybrid learning. *Faculty:* 22 full-time (12 women), 6 part-time/adjunct (4 women). *Students:* 184 full-time (139 women), 175 part-time (131 women); includes 118 minority (14 Black or African American, non-Hispanic/Latino; 10 American Indian or Alaska Native, non-Hispanic/Latino; 5 Asian, non-Hispanic/Latino; 79 Hispanic/Latino; 1 Native Hawaiian or other Pacific Islander, non-Hispanic/Latino; 9 Two or more races, non-Hispanic/Latino), 9 international. Average age 33. 244 applicants, 44% accepted, 108 enrolled. In 2017, 147 master's, 4 doctorates awarded. Terminal master's awarded for partial completion of doctoral program. *Degree requirements:* For master's, variable foreign language requirement, comprehensive exam (for some programs), thesis (for some programs); for doctorate, variable foreign language requirement, comprehensive exam (for some programs), thesis/dissertation (for some programs); for other advanced degree, comprehensive exam (for some programs). *Entrance requirements:* Additional exam requirements/recommendations for international students: Required—TOEFL (minimum score 80 iBT), IELTS (minimum score 6.5). *Application deadline:* For fall admission, 12/1 for domestic and international students; for spring admission, 9/15 for domestic and international students. Applications are processed on a rolling basis. Application fee: $65. Electronic applications accepted. *Expenses:* Tuition, state resident: full-time $9240; part-time $458 per credit hour. Tuition, nonresident: full-time $21,588; part-time $1199 per credit hour. *Required fees:* $1021; $14 per credit hour. $646 per semester. Tuition and fees vary according to course load, campus/location and program. *Financial support:* In 2017–18, 62 students received support, including 1 fellowship with full and partial tuition reimbursement available (averaging $13,927 per year), 2 research assistantships with full and partial tuition reimbursements available (averaging $13,927 per year), 15 teaching assistantships with full and partial tuition reimbursements available (averaging $13,927 per year); institutionally sponsored loans, health care benefits, tuition waivers (full and partial), and unspecified assistantships also available. Financial award application deadline: 2/1; financial award applicants required to submit FAFSA. *Unit head:* Dr. Robert Horn, Chair, 928-523-0545, Fax: 928-523-9284, E-mail: robert.horn@nau.edu. *Application contact:* Hope DeMello, Administrative Assistant, 928-523-7103, Fax: 928-523-9284, E-mail: eps@nau.edu.
Website: https://nau.edu/coe/ed-psych/

Northern Illinois University, Graduate School, College of Education, Department of Counseling, Adult and Higher Education, De Kalb, IL 60115-2854. Offers adult and higher education (MS Ed, Ed D); counseling (MS Ed, Ed D). *Accreditation:* ACA. *Program availability:* Part-time, evening/weekend. *Faculty:* 19 full-time (11 women), 2 part-time/adjunct (1 woman). *Students:* 114 full-time (80 women), 215 part-time (156 women); includes 136 minority (74 Black or African American, non-Hispanic/Latino; 2 American Indian or Alaska Native, non-Hispanic/Latino; 11 Asian, non-Hispanic/Latino; 37 Hispanic/Latino; 12 Two or more races, non-Hispanic/Latino), 8 international. Average age 36. 124 applicants, 77% accepted, 49 enrolled. In 2017, 67 master's, 16 doctorates awarded. Terminal master's awarded for partial completion of doctoral program. *Degree requirements:* For master's, comprehensive exam, thesis optional; for doctorate, thesis/dissertation, candidacy exam, dissertation defense. *Entrance requirements:* For master's, GRE General Test or MAT, minimum undergraduate GPA of 2.75, interview (for counseling); for doctorate, GRE General Test, minimum undergraduate GPA of 2.75, 3.2 graduate; interview (for counseling). Additional exam requirements/recommendations for international students: Required—TOEFL (minimum score 550 paper-based). *Application deadline:* For fall admission, 6/1 for domestic students, 5/1 for international students; for spring admission, 11/1 for domestic students, 10/1 for international students. Applications are processed on a rolling basis. Application fee: $40. Electronic applications accepted. *Financial support:* In 2017–18, 15 research assistantships with full tuition reimbursements, 7 teaching assistantships with full tuition reimbursements were awarded; fellowships with full tuition reimbursements, career-related internships or fieldwork, Federal Work-Study, scholarships/grants, tuition waivers (full), and staff assistantships also available. Support available to part-time

Counselor Education

students. Financial award applicants required to submit FAFSA. *Unit head:* Dr. Suzanne Degges-White, Interim Chair, 815-753-1448, E-mail: cahe@niu.edu. *Application contact:* Graduate School Office, 815-753-0395, E-mail: gradsch@niu.edu. Website: http://www.cedu.niu.edu/cahe/index.html

Northern Kentucky University, Office of Graduate Programs, College of Education and Human Services, Program in School Counseling, Highland Heights, KY 41099. Offers MA. *Accreditation:* ACA. *Program availability:* Part-time, evening/weekend. *Degree requirements:* For master's, portfolio, practicum, internship. *Entrance requirements:* For master's, GRE or MAT, official transcript(s), two essays, three letters of reference, professional resume, KY Statement of Eligibility or teaching certificate, criminal background check, interview. Additional exam requirements/recommendations for international students: Required—TOEFL (minimum score 79 iBT); Recommended—IELTS (minimum score 6.5). Electronic applications accepted. *Faculty research:* Counselor wellness, counseling preferences and expectations, creativity in counseling, integrating mindfulness-based approaches into counseling, evidence-based school counseling.

Northern State University, MS Ed Program in Counseling, Aberdeen, SD 57401-7198. Offers clinical mental health counseling (MS Ed); school counseling (MS Ed). *Accreditation:* ACA; NCATE. *Program availability:* Part-time, online learning. *Degree requirements:* For master's, comprehensive exam, thesis optional. *Entrance requirements:* For master's, minimum GPA of 2.75. Additional exam requirements/ recommendations for international students: Required—TOEFL (minimum score 550 paper-based; 78 iBT), IELTS (minimum score 6). Electronic applications accepted.

Northern Vermont University–Johnson, Program in Counseling, Johnson, VT 05656. Offers addictions counseling (MA); clinical mental health counseling (MA); general counseling (MA); school counseling (MA). *Program availability:* Part-time. *Faculty:* 2 full-time (1 woman), 11 part-time/adjunct (6 women). *Students:* 2 full-time (1 woman), 15 part-time (9 women). In 2017, 50 master's awarded. *Degree requirements:* For master's, comprehensive exam. *Entrance requirements:* For master's, interview. Additional exam requirements/recommendations for international students: Required—TOEFL. *Application deadline:* For fall admission, 7/1 for domestic students, 2/1 for international students; for spring admission, 11/1 for domestic students, 7/1 for international students; for summer admission, 4/1 for domestic students. Applications are processed on a rolling basis. Electronic applications accepted. *Expenses:* Tuition, state resident: part-time $572 per credit hour. Tuition, nonresident: part-time $832 per credit hour. *Financial support:* Career-related internships or fieldwork and unspecified assistantships available. Support available to part-time students. Financial award application deadline: 3/1; financial award applicants required to submit FAFSA. *Unit head:* Dr. Kimberly Donovan, Coordinator, 802-635-1453, Fax: 802-635-1465, E-mail: kimberly.donovan@ northernvermont.edu. *Application contact:* Catherine H. Higley, Administrative Assistant, 800-635-2356 Ext. 1244, Fax: 802-635-1248, E-mail: catherine.higley@jsc.edu.

Northern Vermont University–Lyndon, Graduate Programs in Education, Department of Education, Lyndonville, VT 05851. Offers curriculum and instruction (M Ed); reading specialist (M Ed); special education (M Ed); teaching and counseling (M Ed). *Program availability:* Part-time, evening/weekend. *Degree requirements:* For master's, exam or major field project. *Entrance requirements:* Additional exam requirements/ recommendations for international students: Recommended—TOEFL (minimum score 500 paper-based).

Northwest Christian University, School of Education and Counseling, Eugene, OR 97401-3745. Offers clinical mental health counseling (MA); elementary teaching (MAT); English for speakers of other languages (MAT); physical education (MAT); school counseling (MA); secondary teaching (MAT); special education (MA). *Program availability:* Part-time, evening/weekend, online learning. *Faculty:* 9 full-time (4 women), 14 part-time/adjunct (10 women). *Students:* 77 full-time (60 women), 44 part-time (30 women); includes 19 minority (4 Black or African American, non-Hispanic/Latino; 1 American Indian or Alaska Native, non-Hispanic/Latino; 3 Asian, non-Hispanic/Latino; 3 Hispanic/Latino; 1 Native Hawaiian or other Pacific Islander, non-Hispanic/Latino; 8 Two or more races, non-Hispanic/Latino). Average age 34. In 2017, 58 master's awarded. *Degree requirements:* For master's, thesis (for some programs). *Entrance requirements:* For master's, GRE or MAT, minimum undergraduate GPA of 3.0, interview, 2-3 page statement of purpose, two letters of recommendation, resume, background check. Additional exam requirements/recommendations for international students: Required— TOEFL (minimum score 550 paper-based; 80 iBT). *Application deadline:* Applications are processed on a rolling basis. Electronic applications accepted. *Expenses:* $640 to $660 per credit hour, $90 per semester technology fee. *Financial support:* Applicants required to submit FAFSA. *Unit head:* Elizabeth Wosley-George, Director, 541-349-7465, Fax: 541-684-7310, E-mail: ewosleygeorge@nwcu.edu. *Application contact:* Billy Dorsch, Admission Counselor for Graduate Studies, 541-684-7279, Fax: 541-349-5281, E-mail: wdorsch@nwcu.edu.

Northwestern Oklahoma State University, School of Professional Studies, Program in School Counseling, Alva, OK 73717-2799. Offers M Ed. *Accreditation:* NCATE. *Program availability:* Part-time. *Degree requirements:* For master's, thesis optional, portfolio. *Entrance requirements:* For master's, GRE General Test or MAT, minimum GPA of 2.75.

Northwestern State University of Louisiana, Graduate Studies and Research, College of Education and Human Development, Program in School Counseling, Natchitoches, LA 71497. Offers MA. *Accreditation:* ACA. *Degree requirements:* For master's, comprehensive exam, thesis (for some programs). *Entrance requirements:* For master's, GRE General Test. Additional exam requirements/recommendations for international students: Required—TOEFL. Electronic applications accepted.

Northwestern State University of Louisiana, Graduate Studies and Research, College of Education and Human Development, Programs in Educational Leadership and Instruction, Natchitoches, LA 71497. Offers counseling (Ed S); educational leadership (M Ed, Ed S); educational technology (Ed S); elementary teaching (Ed S); reading (Ed S); secondary teaching (Ed S); special education (Ed S). *Accreditation:* NASAD. *Degree requirements:* For master's, comprehensive exam, thesis (for some programs). *Entrance requirements:* For master's and Ed S, GRE General Test. Additional exam requirements/recommendations for international students: Required— TOEFL. Electronic applications accepted.

Northwest Nazarene University, Program in Counselor Education, Nampa, ID 83686-5897. Offers clinical counseling (MS); marriage and family counseling (MS); school counseling (MS). *Program availability:* Part-time. *Students:* Average age 35. 47 applicants, 66% accepted, 25 enrolled. In 2017, 33 master's awarded. *Entrance requirements:* For master's, minimum GPA of 3.0, BA. Additional exam requirements/ recommendations for international students: Required—TOEFL. *Application deadline:* For fall admission, 2/15 for domestic and international students; for spring admission, 9/15 for domestic and international students. Application fee: $50. Electronic applications accepted. *Unit head:* Dr. Michael Pitts, Chair, 208-467-8040, Fax: 208-467-8339. *Application contact:* Lynette Kingsmore, Graduate Admissions Counselor, 208-467-8107, E-mail: lkingsmore@nnu.edu.

Nova Southeastern University, College of Psychology, Fort Lauderdale, FL 33314-7796. Offers clinical mental health counseling (MS); clinical psychology (PhD, Psy D);

counseling (MS); experimental psychology (MS); forensic psychology (MS); general psychology (MS); school counseling (MS); school psychology (Psy D, Psy S); substance abuse counseling (MS); substance abuse counseling and education (MS). *Accreditation:* APA (one or more programs are accredited). *Program availability:* 100% online, blended/hybrid learning. *Faculty:* 51 full-time (21 women), 120 part-time/adjunct (70 women). *Students:* 751 full-time (618 women), 821 part-time (709 women); includes 787 minority (268 Black or African American, non-Hispanic/Latino; 2 American Indian or Alaska Native, non-Hispanic/Latino; 38 Asian, non-Hispanic/Latino; 431 Hispanic/Latino; 2 Native Hawaiian or other Pacific Islander, non-Hispanic/Latino; 46 Two or more races, non-Hispanic/Latino), 45 international. Average age 31. 1,117 applicants, 38% accepted, 294 enrolled. In 2017, 459 master's, 100 doctorates, 10 other advanced degrees awarded. Terminal master's awarded for partial completion of doctoral program. *Degree requirements:* For master's, comprehensive exam, 3 practica; for doctorate, thesis/dissertation, clinical internship, competency exam; for Psy S, comprehensive exam, internship. *Entrance requirements:* For master's and Psy S, GRE General Test, letters of recommendation, research/personal statement, interview; for doctorate, GRE General Test, GRE Subject Test (recommended), minimum undergraduate GPA of 3.0, letters of recommendation, research/personal statement, interview, curriculum vitae/resume. Additional exam requirements/recommendations for international students: Required—TOEFL (minimum score 550 paper-based). *Application deadline:* Applications are processed on a rolling basis. Application fee: $50. Electronic applications accepted. *Expenses:* Contact institution. *Financial support:* In 2017–18, 197 students received support, including 15 research assistantships (averaging $5,600 per year), 68 teaching assistantships (averaging $2,000 per year); career-related internships or fieldwork, Federal Work-Study, institutionally sponsored loans, scholarships/grants, and unspecified assistantships also available. Support available to part-time students. Financial award application deadline: 4/15; financial award applicants required to submit FAFSA. *Faculty research:* Clinical health psychology, multicultural/diversity psychology, clinical neuropsychology, clinical child psychology, family violence. *Unit head:* Dr. Karen Grosby, Dean, 954-262-5712, Fax: 954-262-3859, E-mail: grosby@nova.edu. *Application contact:* Carlos Perez, Senior Manager of Outreach, 954-262-5702, Fax: 954-262-3893, E-mail: gradschool@ nova.edu.
Website: http://psychology.nova.edu/

Nyack College, Alliance Graduate School of Counseling, Nyack, NY 10960. Offers marriage and family therapy (MA); mental health counseling (MA). *Program availability:* Part-time, evening/weekend, 100% online. *Students:* 66 full-time (50 women), 162 part-time (136 women); includes 183 minority (78 Black or African American, non-Hispanic/ Latino; 45 Asian, non-Hispanic/Latino; 53 Hispanic/Latino; 7 Two or more races, non-Hispanic/Latino), 10 international. Average age 37. In 2017, 48 master's awarded. *Degree requirements:* For master's, comprehensive exam, counselor-in-training therapy, internship, CPCE exam. *Entrance requirements:* For master's, Millon Clinical Multiaxial Inventory-3, Minnesota Multiphasic Personality Inventory-2, transcripts, statement of Christian life and experience, statement of support systems. Additional exam requirements/recommendations for international students: Required—TOEFL (minimum score 550 paper-based; 80 iBT). *Application deadline:* For fall admission, 8/1 for domestic students, 2/15 for international students; for spring admission, 12/15 for domestic students, 7/15 for international students. Applications are processed on a rolling basis. Application fee: $30. Electronic applications accepted. *Expenses:* $800 per credit. *Financial support:* Career-related internships or fieldwork and scholarships/ grants available. Financial award applicants required to submit FAFSA. *Unit head:* Dr. Antoinette Gines-Rivera, Director, 646-378-6160. *Application contact:* Chastity Crespo, Admissions Associate, 646-378-6194, E-mail: admissions.grad@nyack.edu. Website: http://www.nyack.edu/agsc

Ohio University, Graduate College, Gladys W. and David H. Patton College of Education and Human Services, Department of Counseling and Higher Education, Athens, OH 45701-2979. Offers college student personnel (M Ed); community/agency counseling (M Ed); counselor education (PhD); higher education (PhD); rehabilitation counseling (M Ed); school counseling (M Ed). *Accreditation:* ACA; CORE. *Program availability:* Part-time, evening/weekend. *Degree requirements:* For master's, comprehensive exam (for some programs), thesis or alternative; for doctorate, comprehensive exam, thesis/dissertation. *Entrance requirements:* For master's, GRE General Test or MAT (if GPA less than 2.9), 3 letters of reference; for doctorate, GRE General Test, work experience, minimum GPA of 3.4. Additional exam requirements/ recommendations for international students: Required—TOEFL (minimum score 550 paper-based; 80 iBT) or IELTS (minimum score 6.5). Electronic applications accepted. *Faculty research:* Youth violence, gender studies, student affairs, chemical dependency, disabilities issues.

Oklahoma City University, Petree College of Arts and Sciences, Oklahoma City, OK 73106-1402. Offers applied behavioral studies (M Ed); applied sociology: nonprofit leadership (MA); creative writing (MFA); criminology (MS); early childhood education (M Ed); elementary education (M Ed); general studies (MLA); leadership/management (MLA); moving image arts (MFA); professional counseling (M Ed); teaching (MA); teaching English to speakers of other languages (MA). *Program availability:* Part-time, evening/weekend. *Faculty:* 6 full-time (2 women), 16 part-time/adjunct (10 women). *Students:* 84 full-time (61 women), 32 part-time (23 women); includes 31 minority (13 Black or African American, non-Hispanic/Latino; 3 American Indian or Alaska Native, non-Hispanic/Latino; 1 Asian, non-Hispanic/Latino; 9 Hispanic/Latino; 5 Two or more races, non-Hispanic/Latino), 30 international. Average age 34. 192 applicants, 67% accepted, 57 enrolled. In 2017, 65 master's awarded. *Degree requirements:* For master's, capstone/practicum. *Entrance requirements:* For master's, bachelor's degree from accredited institution with minimum GPA of 3.0, essay, recommendation letters. Additional exam requirements/recommendations for international students: Required— TOEFL (minimum score 550 paper-based; 80 iBT). *Application deadline:* Applications are processed on a rolling basis. Application fee: $50. Electronic applications accepted. *Expenses:* $8,580. *Financial support:* In 2017–18, 19 students received support. Federal Work-Study, institutionally sponsored loans, scholarships/grants, and tuition waivers (full and partial) available. Support available to part-time students. Financial award application deadline: 6/1; financial award applicants required to submit FAFSA. *Unit head:* Dr. Amy Cataldi, Dean, 405-208-5446, Fax: 405-208-5447, E-mail: acataldi@ okcu.edu. *Application contact:* Michael Harrington, Director of Graduate Admissions, 800-633-7242, Fax: 405-208-5356, E-mail: gadmissions@okcu.edu. Website: https://www.okcu.edu/artsci/home

Old Dominion University, Darden College of Education, Counseling Program, Norfolk, VA 23529. Offers clinical mental health counseling (MS Ed); college counseling (MS Ed); counseling (Ed S); counselor education (PhD); school counseling (MS Ed). *Accreditation:* ACA. *Program availability:* Part-time, evening/weekend. *Faculty:* 14 full-time (7 women), 9 part-time/adjunct (7 women). *Students:* 134 full-time (113 women), 52 part-time (44 women); includes 72 minority (42 Black or African American, non-Hispanic/ Latino; 1 American Indian or Alaska Native, non-Hispanic/Latino; 4 Asian, non-Hispanic/ Latino; 17 Hispanic/Latino; 8 Two or more races, non-Hispanic/Latino), 6 international. Average age 31. 195 applicants, 57% accepted, 79 enrolled. In 2017, 43 master's, 9 doctorates, 2 other advanced degrees awarded. *Degree requirements:* For master's and Ed S, comprehensive exam; for doctorate, comprehensive exam, thesis/dissertation.

Entrance requirements: For master's and Ed S, GRE General Test, resume, essay, transcripts, recommendations; for doctorate, GRE General Test, resume, interview, essay, transcripts, recommendations. Additional exam requirements/recommendations for international students: Required—TOEFL. *Application deadline:* For fall admission, 3/1 for domestic and international students; for winter admission, 1/10 for domestic students; for spring admission, 10/1 for domestic and international students; for summer admission, 3/1 for domestic students, 2/1 for international students. Application fee: $50. Electronic applications accepted. *Expenses:* $496 per credit hour, plus $9.00 services fee per semester. *Financial support:* In 2017–18, 20 students received support, including 2 fellowships with full tuition reimbursements available (averaging $15,000 per year), 13 research assistantships (averaging $9,000 per year), 20 teaching assistantships with full tuition reimbursements available (averaging $20,000 per year); career-related internships or fieldwork, Federal Work-Study, institutionally sponsored loans, scholarships/grants, tuition waivers (partial), and unspecified assistantships also available. Support available to part-time students. Financial award application deadline: 10/1; financial award applicants required to submit FAFSA. *Faculty research:* Group counseling, counselor education, career counseling, spirituality and counseling, school counseling, LGBT counseling, legal and ethical issues. *Total annual research expenditures:* $75,000. *Unit head:* Dr. Jeff Moe, Director, 757-683-6235, Fax: 757-683-5756, E-mail: jmoe@odu.edu.
Website: http://www.odu.edu/chs

Oregon State University, College of Education, Program in Counseling, Corvallis, OR 97331. Offers clinical mental health counseling (M Coun); counseling (PhD); school counseling (M Coun). *Accreditation:* ACA (one or more programs are accredited); NCATE. *Program availability:* Part-time, blended/hybrid learning. *Degree requirements:* For master's, thesis or alternative; for doctorate, one foreign language, thesis/dissertation. *Entrance requirements:* For master's, minimum GPA of 3.0 in last 90 hours; for doctorate, GRE or MAT, master's degree, minimum GPA of 3.0 in last 90 hours of course work, 2 years of teaching experience. Additional exam requirements/recommendations for international students: Required—TOEFL (minimum score 575 paper-based). *Application deadline:* For fall admission, 1/31 for domestic students. Application fee: $75 ($85 for international students). *Financial support:* Application deadline: 3/1. *Faculty research:* Counseling and guidance improvement in social services agencies, elementary and secondary schools. *Unit head:* Lisa Schulz, Counseling Lead, 541-737-5959, E-mail: lisa.schulz@oregonstate.edu. *Application contact:* Mary Aguilera, Advisor, 541-737-2232, E-mail: mary.aguilera@oregonstate.edu.
Website: http://education.oregonstate.edu/counseling

Ottawa University, Graduate Studies-Arizona, Program in Education, Ottawa, KS 66067-3399. Offers community college counseling (MA); curriculum and instruction (MA); early childhood (MA); education intervention (MA); education leadership (MA); education technology (MA); Montessori early childhood education (MA); Montessori elementary education (MA); professional development (MA); school guidance counseling (MA); special education - cross categorical (MA). Programs offered in Mesa, Phoenix, Tempe and West Valley, AZ. *Accreditation:* NCATE. *Program availability:* Part-time. *Degree requirements:* For master's, thesis or alternative. *Entrance requirements:* For master's, minimum undergraduate GPA of 3.0, copy of current state certification or teaching license. Additional exam requirements/recommendations for international students: Required—TOEFL (minimum score 550 paper-based). Electronic applications accepted. *Expenses:* Contact institution.

Our Lady of the Lake University, College of Professional Studies, Program in School Counseling, San Antonio, TX 78207-4689. Offers M Ed. *Program availability:* Part-time, online only, 100% online. *Faculty:* 2 full-time (1 woman), 6 part-time/adjunct (5 women). *Students:* 72 full-time (69 women), 20 part-time (17 women); includes 60 minority (9 Black or African American, non-Hispanic/Latino; 51 Hispanic/Latino). Average age 33. 17 applicants, 100% accepted, 12 enrolled. In 2017, 9 master's awarded. *Degree requirements:* For master's, comprehensive exam, practicum. *Entrance requirements:* For master's, official transcripts, personal statement, reference form, FERPA Consent to Release Education Records and Information form, current teaching license. Additional exam requirements/recommendations for international students: Required—TOEFL. *Application deadline:* For fall admission, 6/15 priority date for domestic and international students; for spring admission, 11/15 priority date for domestic and international students; for summer admission, 4/15 priority date for domestic students, 4/15 for international students. Applications are processed on a rolling basis. Application fee: $40 ($50 for international students). Electronic applications accepted. Application fee is waived when completed online. *Expenses: Tuition:* Full-time $10,668; part-time $5334 per year. *Required fees:* $816; $816 per year. $408 per semester. *Financial support:* In 2017–18, 3 students received support. Federal Work-Study, scholarships/grants, unspecified assistantships, and tuition discounts available. Support available to part-time students. Financial award application deadline: 5/1; financial award applicants required to submit FAFSA. *Faculty research:* Multicultural issues, career counseling, counselor identity, ethics. *Unit head:* Dr. Alycia Maurer, Education Department Chair, 210-434-6711 Ext. 7152, E-mail: admaurer@ollusa.edu. *Application contact:* Office of Graduate Admissions, 210-431-3995 Ext. 2314, Fax: 210-431-3945, E-mail: gradadm@lake.ollusa.edu.
Website: http://onlineprograms.ollusa.edu/med-school-counseling

Palm Beach Atlantic University, School of Education and Behavioral Studies, West Palm Beach, FL 33416-4708. Offers counseling psychology (MS), including addictions/mental health, general counseling, marriage and family therapy, mental health counseling, school guidance counseling. *Program availability:* Part-time, evening/weekend. *Entrance requirements:* For master's, GRE or MAT, minimum GPA of 3.0; essay. Additional exam requirements/recommendations for international students: Required—TOEFL (minimum score 550 paper-based; 79 iBT). Electronic applications accepted. *Faculty research:* Group dynamics, phenomenology, spirituality, multicultural psychology.

Penn State University Park, Graduate School, College of Education, Department of Educational Psychology, Counseling, and Special Education, University Park, PA 16802. Offers counselor education (M Ed, D Ed, PhD, Certificate); educational psychology (MS, PhD, Certificate); school psychology (M Ed, MS, PhD, Certificate); special education (M Ed, MS, PhD). *Unit head:* Dr. David H. Monk, Dean, 814-865-2523, Fax: 814-865-0555. *Application contact:* Lori Hawn, Director, Graduate Student Services, 814-865-1795, Fax: 814-863-4627, E-mail: l-gswww@lists.psu.edu.
Website: http://ed.psu.edu/epcse

Phillips Graduate University, Master's Program in Psychology, Chatsworth, CA 91311. Offers art therapy (MA); marriage and family therapy (MA); school counseling (MA); school psychology (MA). *Program availability:* Evening/weekend. *Degree requirements:* For master's, comprehensive exam, thesis. *Entrance requirements:* For master's, minimum GPA of 2.5. *Application deadline:* For fall admission, 4/16 priority date for domestic students; for spring admission, 11/15 for domestic students. Applications are processed on a rolling basis. Application fee: $80. Electronic applications accepted. *Expenses: Tuition:* Part-time $897 per unit. *Required fees:* $375 per semester. Part-time tuition and fees vary according to degree level and program. *Financial support:* Federal Work-Study and tuition waivers (full and partial) available.

Financial award application deadline: 8/15; financial award applicants required to submit FAFSA. *Faculty research:* Integration of interpersonal psychological theory, systems approach, firsthand experiential learning. *Application contact:* Christine Montagna, Admissions Advisor, 818-600-4945, Fax: 818-386-5699, E-mail: cmontagna@pgu.edu.

Pittsburg State University, Graduate School, College of Education, Department of Psychology and Counseling, Program in Counselor Education, Pittsburg, KS 66762. Offers school counseling (MS). *Accreditation:* NCATE. *Students:* 18. In 2017, 18 master's awarded. *Degree requirements:* For master's, thesis or alternative. *Entrance requirements:* For master's, GRE General Test, minimum GPA of 2.8. Additional exam requirements/recommendations for international students: Required—TOEFL (minimum score 550 paper-based; 79 iBT), IELTS (minimum score 6.5), PTE (minimum score 53). *Application deadline:* Applications are processed on a rolling basis. Application fee: $35 ($60 for international students). Electronic applications accepted. *Expenses:* Contact institution. *Financial support:* Teaching assistantships, career-related internships or fieldwork, and Federal Work-Study available. Financial award application deadline: 2/1; financial award applicants required to submit FAFSA. *Unit head:* Dr. David Hurford, Chairperson, 620-235-4521. *Application contact:* Lisa Allen, Assistant Director of Graduate and Continuing Studies, 620-235-4218, Fax: 620-235-4219, E-mail: lallen@pittstate.edu.

Plymouth State University, College of Graduate Studies, Graduate Studies in Education, Programs in Counseling, Plymouth, NH 03264-1595. Offers human relations (M Ed); school counseling (M Ed); school psychology (M Ed). *Accreditation:* ACA; NCATE. *Program availability:* Part-time, evening/weekend. *Degree requirements:* For master's, PRAXIS I. *Entrance requirements:* For master's, MAT, minimum GPA of 3.0.

Point Loma Nazarene University, School of Education, Program in Education, San Diego, CA 92106-2899. Offers counseling and guidance (MA); educational administration (MA); leadership in learning (MA). *Program availability:* Part-time, evening/weekend. *Students:* 67 full-time (54 women), 161 part-time (128 women); includes 137 minority (7 Black or African American, non-Hispanic/Latino; 14 Asian, non-Hispanic/Latino; 104 Hispanic/Latino; 3 Native Hawaiian or other Pacific Islander, non-Hispanic/Latino; 9 Two or more races, non-Hispanic/Latino), 2 international. Average age 34. 60 applicants, 98% accepted, 53 enrolled. In 2017, 59 master's awarded. *Entrance requirements:* For master's, interview, letters of recommendation, essay. Additional exam requirements/recommendations for international students: Required—TOEFL. *Application deadline:* For fall admission, 8/4 priority date for domestic students; for spring admission, 12/8 priority date for domestic students; for summer admission, 4/12 priority date for domestic students. Applications are processed on a rolling basis. Application fee: $50. Electronic applications accepted. *Expenses:* Contact institution. *Financial support:* Federal Work-Study and scholarships/grants available. Support available to part-time students. Financial award applicants required to submit FAFSA. *Unit head:* Conni Campbell, Associate Dean of the School of Education, 619-849-2532, Fax: 619-849-2532, E-mail: connicampbell@pointloma.edu. *Application contact:* Joanie Joy, Senior Director of Enrollment Management, 619-329-6785, E-mail: gradinfo@pointloma.edu.
Website: https://www.pointloma.edu/schools-departments-colleges/school-education

Pontifical Catholic University of Puerto Rico, College of Education, Program in Counselor Education, Ponce, PR 00717-0777. Offers M Ed. *Degree requirements:* For master's, comprehensive exam, thesis (for some programs). *Entrance requirements:* For master's, GRE, 2 letters of recommendation, interview, minimum GPA of 2.75.

Prairie View A&M University, College of Education, Department of Educational Leadership and Counseling, Prairie View, TX 77446. Offers M Ed, MA, MS Ed, PhD. *Accreditation:* NCATE. *Program availability:* Part-time, evening/weekend. *Faculty:* 14 full-time (5 women), 5 part-time/adjunct (4 women). *Students:* 73 full-time (55 women), 222 part-time (178 women); includes 277 minority (261 Black or African American, non-Hispanic/Latino; 1 Asian, non-Hispanic/Latino; 15 Hispanic/Latino), 5 international. Average age 37. 136 applicants, 85% accepted, 75 enrolled. In 2017, 125 master's, 11 doctorates awarded. *Degree requirements:* For master's, thesis optional; for doctorate, comprehensive exam, thesis/dissertation. *Entrance requirements:* For master's, GRE General Test, 3 letters of reference, minimum undergraduate GPA of 2.5; for doctorate, GRE General Test, 3 letters of reference. Additional exam requirements/recommendations for international students: Required—TOEFL (minimum score 550 paper-based; 79 iBT). *Application deadline:* For fall admission, 5/1 priority date for domestic students, 5/1 for international students; for spring admission, 10/1 priority date for domestic students, 9/1 for international students; for summer admission, 3/1 for domestic students, 2/1 for international students. Applications are processed on a rolling basis. Application fee: $50. Electronic applications accepted. *Expenses:* Tuition, state resident: part-time $242 per credit. Tuition, nonresident: part-time $695 per credit. *Required fees:* $149 per credit. *Financial support:* Career-related internships or fieldwork available. Support available to part-time students. Financial award application deadline: 4/1; financial award applicants required to submit FAFSA. *Faculty research:* Mentoring, personality assessment, holistic/humanistic education. *Unit head:* Dr. Maduakolam Ireh, Department Head, 936-261-3565, Fax: 936-261-3617, E-mail: maireh@pvamu.edu. *Application contact:* Pauline Walker, Administrative Assistant II, Research and Graduate Studies, 936-261-3521, Fax: 936-261-3529, E-mail: gradadmissions@pvamu.edu.

Prescott College, Graduate Programs, Program in Education, Prescott, AZ 86301. Offers early childhood education (MA); early childhood special education (MA); education (MA); elementary education (MA); environmental education leadership and administration (MA); equine-assisted learning (MA); school guidance counseling (MA); secondary education (MA); special education: learning disabilities (MA); special education: mental retardation (MA); special education: serious emotional disabilities (MA); student-directed independent study (MA); sustainability education (PhD). *Program availability:* Part-time, online learning. *Degree requirements:* For master's, thesis, fieldwork or internship, practicum; for doctorate, thesis/dissertation. *Entrance requirements:* For master's, 2 letters of recommendation, resume; for doctorate, 3 letters of recommendation, resume, official transcripts, personal statement, program proposal. Additional exam requirements/recommendations for international students: Required—TOEFL (minimum score 500 paper-based). Electronic applications accepted.

Providence College, Program in Counseling, Providence, RI 02918. Offers M Ed. *Program availability:* Part-time, evening/weekend. *Degree requirements:* For master's, comprehensive exam, portfolio. *Entrance requirements:* Additional exam requirements/recommendations for international students: Required—TOEFL (minimum score 577 paper-based; 90 iBT).

Purdue University, Graduate School, College of Education, Department of Educational Studies, West Lafayette, IN 47907. Offers administration (MS Ed, PhD, Ed S); counseling and development (MS Ed, PhD); education of the gifted (MS Ed); educational psychology (MS Ed, PhD); foundations of education (MS Ed, PhD); higher education administration (MS Ed, PhD); special education (MS Ed, PhD). *Accreditation:* ACA (one or more programs are accredited); NCATE (one or more programs are accredited). *Program availability:* Part-time, evening/weekend. *Faculty:* 29 full-time (22 women), 1 part-time/adjunct (0 women). *Students:* 78 full-time (60 women), 226 part-time (162 women); includes 45 minority (16 Black or African American, non-Hispanic/

Counselor Education

Latino; 8 Asian, non-Hispanic/Latino; 15 Hispanic/Latino; 6 Two or more races, non-Hispanic/Latino), 45 international. Average age 32. 214 applicants, 53% accepted, 70 enrolled. In 2017, 38 master's, 20 doctorates, 4 other advanced degrees awarded. *Degree requirements:* For master's, thesis optional; for doctorate, thesis/dissertation, oral and written exams; for Ed S, oral presentation, project. *Entrance requirements:* For master's, GRE General Test (except for special education if undergraduate GPA is higher than a 3.0), minimum undergraduate GPA of 3.0; for doctorate and Ed S, GRE General Test (minimum combined score of 1000, 300 for new scoring), minimum undergraduate GPA of 3.0. Additional exam requirements/recommendations for international students: Required—TOEFL (minimum score 550 paper-based; 77 iBT), TWE (minimum score 5). *Application deadline:* Applications are processed on a rolling basis. Application fee: $60 ($75 for international students). Electronic applications accepted. *Financial support:* Fellowships with full tuition reimbursements, research assistantships with full tuition reimbursements, teaching assistantships with full tuition reimbursements, career-related internships or fieldwork, and tuition waivers (full) available. Support available to part-time students. Financial award application deadline: 3/1; financial award applicants required to submit FAFSA. *Faculty research:* Motivation, learning disabilities, school learning, group processes, cognitive development. *Unit head:* F. Richard Olenchak, Head, 765-494-9170, E-mail: olenchak@purdue.edu. *Application contact:* Heather Brinkman, Graduate Contact, 765-494-2345, Fax: 765-494-5832, E-mail: hbrinkma@purdue.edu.
Website: http://www.edst.purdue.edu/

Purdue University Northwest, Graduate Studies Office, School of Education, Program in Counseling, Hammond, IN 46323-2094. Offers human services (MS Ed); mental health counseling (MS Ed); school counseling (MS Ed). *Accreditation:* ACA. *Entrance requirements:* Additional exam requirements/recommendations for international students: Required—TOEFL.

Queens College of the City University of New York, Division of Education, Department of Educational and Community Programs, Queens, NY 11367-1597. Offers bilingual pupil personnel (AC); counselor education (MS Ed); mental health counseling (MS); school building leader (AC); school district leader (AC); school psychologist (MS Ed); special education-childhood education (AC); special education-early childhood (MS Ed); teacher of special education 1-6 (MS Ed); teacher of special education birth-2 (MS Ed); teaching students with disabilities, grades 7-12 (MS Ed, AC). *Program availability:* Part-time. *Faculty:* 20 full-time (14 women), 63 part-time/adjunct (37 women). *Students:* 105 full-time (94 women), 423 part-time (350 women); includes 241 minority (40 Black or African American, non-Hispanic/Latino; 2 American Indian or Alaska Native, non-Hispanic/Latino; 50 Asian, non-Hispanic/Latino; 142 Hispanic/Latino; 1 Native Hawaiian or other Pacific Islander, non-Hispanic/Latino; 6 Two or more races, non-Hispanic/Latino), 5 international. Average age 28. 515 applicants, 57% accepted, 230 enrolled. In 2017, 163 master's, 74 other advanced degrees awarded. *Degree requirements:* For master's, research project; for AC, internship. *Entrance requirements:* For master's, minimum GPA of 3.0. Additional exam requirements/recommendations for international students: Required—TOEFL, IELTS. *Application deadline:* For fall admission, 3/1 for domestic students. Applications are processed on a rolling basis. Application fee: $125. Electronic applications accepted. *Financial support:* Career-related internships or fieldwork available. Financial award application deadline: 4/1; financial award applicants required to submit FAFSA. *Unit head:* Dr. Emilia Lopez, Chair, 718-997-5250, E-mail: emilia.lopez@qc.cuny.edu. *Application contact:* Elizabeth D'Amico-Ramirez, Assistant Director of Graduate Admissions, 718-997-5203, E-mail: elizabeth.damicoramirez@qc.cuny.edu.

Quincy University, Master of Science in Education Counseling Program, Quincy, IL 62301-2699. Offers clinical mental health counseling (MS Ed); college student personnel (MS Ed); school counseling (MS Ed). *Program availability:* Part-time, evening/weekend. *Degree requirements:* For master's, comprehensive exam, practicum, internship. *Entrance requirements:* For master's, MAT or GRE. Additional exam requirements/recommendations for international students: Required—TOEFL (minimum score 550 paper-based; 79 iBT). *Application deadline:* Applications are processed on a rolling basis. Application fee: $25. Electronic applications accepted. *Expenses:* Tuition: Part-time $450 per credit hour. *Financial support:* Applicants required to submit FAFSA. *Unit head:* Dr. Kenneth Oliver, Director, 217-228-5432 Ext. 3113, E-mail: oliveke@quincy.edu. *Application contact:* Office of Admissions, 217-228-5210, Fax: 217-228-5479, E-mail: admissions@quincy.edu.
Website: http://www.quincy.edu/academics/graduate-programs/counseling/

Radford University, College of Graduate Studies and Research, Program in Counselor Education, Radford, VA 24142. Offers MS. *Accreditation:* ACA; NCATE. *Program availability:* Part-time, evening/weekend. *Faculty:* 6 full-time (2 women), 1 (woman) part-time/adjunct. *Students:* 53 full-time (41 women), 12 part-time (10 women); includes 11 minority (6 Black or African American, non-Hispanic/Latino; 1 Asian, non-Hispanic/Latino; 4 Two or more races, non-Hispanic/Latino). Average age 27. 73 applicants, 71% accepted, 27 enrolled. In 2017, 23 master's awarded. *Degree requirements:* For master's, comprehensive exam, thesis optional. *Entrance requirements:* For master's, GRE or MAT, minimum GPA of 2.75, 3 letters of reference, personal essay, resume, official transcripts. Additional exam requirements/recommendations for international students: Required—TOEFL (minimum score 550 paper-based; 79 iBT), IELTS (minimum score 6.5). *Application deadline:* For fall admission, 2/15 priority date for domestic students, 12/1 for international students; for spring admission, 7/1 for international students; for summer admission, 2/15 priority date for domestic students. Applications are processed on a rolling basis. Application fee: $50. Electronic applications accepted. *Expenses:* Tuition, state resident: full-time $8336; part-time $347 per credit hour. Tuition, nonresident: full-time $16,862; part-time $702 per credit hour. *Required fees:* $3220; $135 per credit hour. Tuition and fees vary according to course load and program. *Financial support:* In 2017–18, 5 students received support, including 3 teaching assistantships (averaging $11,000 per year); career-related internships or fieldwork, scholarships/grants, and unspecified assistantships also available. Support available to part-time students. Financial award application deadline: 3/1; financial award applicants required to submit FAFSA. *Unit head:* Dr. Alan Forrest, Chair, 540-831-5214, Fax: 540-831-6755, E-mail: vgoad4@radford.edu.
Website: http://www.radford.edu/content/cehd/home/counselor-education.html

Regent University, Graduate School, School of Psychology and Counseling, Virginia Beach, VA 23464-9800. Offers clinical mental health counseling (MA); clinical psychology (Psy D); counseling and psychological studies - clinical (PhD); counseling and psychological studies - research (PhD); counseling studies (CAGS); counselor education and supervision (PhD); general psychology (MS); human services (MA), including addictions counseling, Biblical counseling, Christian counseling, conflict and mediation ministry, criminal justice and ministry, grief counseling, human services counseling, human services for student affairs, life coaching, marriage and family ministry, trauma and crisis counseling; marriage, couple, and family counseling (MA); pastoral counseling (MA); school counseling (MA); M Div/MA; M Ed/MA; MBA/MA. *Accreditation:* ACA; APA (one or more programs are accredited). *Program availability:* Part-time, evening/weekend, 100% online, blended/hybrid learning. *Faculty:* 28 full-time (16 women), 51 part-time/adjunct (30 women). *Students:* 294 full-time (236 women), 404 part-time (317 women); includes 286 minority (218 Black or African American, non-Hispanic/Latino; 4 American Indian or Alaska Native, non-Hispanic/Latino; 17 Asian, non-Hispanic/Latino; 30 Hispanic/Latino; 17 Two or more races, non-Hispanic/Latino), 13 international. Average age 37. 2,109 applicants, 18% accepted, 233 enrolled. In 2017, 158 master's, 28 doctorates awarded. *Degree requirements:* For master's, thesis or alternative, internship, practicum, written competency exam; for doctorate, thesis/dissertation or alternative. *Entrance requirements:* For master's, GRE General Test (including writing exam) or MAT, minimum undergraduate GPA of 3.0, resume, transcripts, writing sample, personal goals statement; for doctorate, GRE General Test (including writing exam), minimum undergraduate GPA of 3.0, graduate 3.5; writing sample; 3 recommendations; resume; college transcripts; personal goals statement. Additional exam requirements/recommendations for international students: Required—TOEFL (minimum score 577 paper-based). *Application deadline:* For fall admission, 4/1 priority date for domestic students; for spring admission, 11/1 priority date for domestic students. Applications are processed on a rolling basis. Application fee: $50. Electronic applications accepted. *Expenses:* Contact institution. *Financial support:* In 2017–18, 557 students received support, including 5 fellowships (averaging $10,000 per year), 11 research assistantships (averaging $3,200 per year); career-related internships or fieldwork, scholarships/grants, and unspecified assistantships also available. Support available to part-time students. *Faculty research:* Marriage enrichment, clinical psychology, troubled youth, faith and learning, trauma. *Unit head:* Dr. William Hathaway, Dean, 757-352-4294, Fax: 757-352-4282, E-mail: willhat@regent.edu. *Application contact:* Heidi Cece, Assistant Vice President of Enrollment Management, 800-373-5504, Fax: 757-352-4381, E-mail: admissions@regent.edu.
Website: https://www.regent.edu/school-of-psychology-and-counseling/

Regis University, Rueckert-Hartman College for Health Professions, Denver, CO 80221-1099. Offers advanced practice nurse (DNP); counseling (MA); counseling children and adolescents (Post-Graduate Certificate); counseling military families (Post-Graduate Certificate); depth psychotherapy (Post-Graduate Certificate); fellowship in orthopedic manual physical therapy (Certificate); health care business management (Certificate); health care quality and patient safety (Certificate); health industry leadership (MBA); health services administration (MS); marriage and family therapy (MA, Post-Graduate Certificate); neonatal nurse practitioner (MSN); nursing education (MSN); nursing leadership (MSN); occupational therapy (OTD); pharmacy (Pharm D); physical therapy (DPT). *Program availability:* Part-time, evening/weekend, 100% online, blended/hybrid learning. *Degree requirements:* For master's, thesis (for some programs), internship. *Entrance requirements:* For master's, official transcript reflecting baccalaureate degree awarded from regionally-accredited college or university. Additional exam requirements/recommendations for international students: Required—TOEFL (minimum score 550 paper-based; 82 iBT). Electronic applications accepted. *Expenses:* Contact institution. *Faculty research:* Normal and pathological balance and gait research, normal/pathological upper limb motor control/biomechanics, exercise energy/metabolism research, optical treatment protocols for therapeutic modalities.

Rhode Island College, School of Graduate Studies, Feinstein School of Education and Human Development, Department of Counseling, Educational Leadership, and School Psychology, Providence, RI 02908-1991. Offers advanced counseling (CGS); agency counseling (MA); clinical mental health counseling (MS); co-occurring disorders (MA, CGS); educational leadership (M Ed); mental health counseling (CAGS); school counseling (MA); school psychology (CAGS); teacher leadership (CGS). *Accreditation:* ACA; NCATE. *Program availability:* Part-time, evening/weekend. *Faculty:* 10. *Students:* 31 full-time (25 women), 75 part-time (65 women); includes 16 minority (4 Black or African American, non-Hispanic/Latino; 11 Hispanic/Latino; 1 Two or more races, non-Hispanic/Latino). Average age 32. In 2017, 40 master's, 15 other advanced degrees awarded. *Degree requirements:* For master's and other advanced degree, comprehensive exam (for some programs), thesis (for some programs). *Entrance requirements:* For master's, GRE General Test or MAT, undergraduate transcripts; minimum undergraduate GPA of 3.0; for other advanced degree, GRE or MAT (for most programs), undergraduate transcripts; minimum undergraduate GPA of 3.0; 3 letters of recommendation; current resume. Additional exam requirements/recommendations for international students: Recommended—TOEFL (minimum score 550 paper-based; 79 iBT). *Application deadline:* For fall admission, 3/1 for domestic students; for spring admission, 11/1 for domestic students. Applications are processed on a rolling basis. Application fee: $50. Electronic applications accepted. *Expenses:* Tuition, state resident: full-time $9768; part-time $407 per credit. Tuition, nonresident: full-time $19,008; part-time $792 per credit. *Required fees:* $696; $29 per credit. One-time fee: $200 full-time; $100 part-time. Tuition and fees vary according to course load. *Financial support:* In 2017–18, 4 teaching assistantships with full tuition reimbursements (averaging $2,063 per year) were awarded; career-related internships or fieldwork, Federal Work-Study, scholarships/grants, health care benefits, and unspecified assistantships also available. Support available to part-time students. Financial award application deadline: 5/15; financial award applicants required to submit FAFSA. *Unit head:* Dr. John Eagle, Chair, 401-456-8023. *Application contact:* Graduate Studies, 401-456-8700.
Website: http://www.ric.edu/counselingEducationalLeadershipSchoolPsychology/index.php

Richmont Graduate University, School of Counseling, Atlanta, GA 30339. Offers clinical mental health counseling (MA); marriage and family therapy (MA). *Accreditation:* ACA. *Program availability:* Part-time, evening/weekend. *Degree requirements:* For master's, comprehensive exam, thesis optional. *Entrance requirements:* For master's, GRE or MAT. Electronic applications accepted.

Rider University, College of Education and Human Services, Program in Counseling Services, Lawrenceville, NJ 08648-3001. Offers clinical mental health counseling (MA); counseling services (MA, Ed S); director of school counseling services (Certificate); life and career coaching (Certificate); school counseling (Certificate); student assistance coordinator (Certificate); substance awareness coordinator (Certificate). *Accreditation:* ACA; NCATE. *Program availability:* Part-time, evening/weekend. *Degree requirements:* For master's, comprehensive exam, research project; for other advanced degree, specialty seminar. *Entrance requirements:* For master's, GRE or MAT, interview, resume, 2 letters of recommendation; for other advanced degree, GRE or MAT, interview, professional experience, 2 letters of recommendation. Additional exam requirements/recommendations for international students: Required—TOEFL (minimum score 550 paper-based). Electronic applications accepted. *Faculty research:* Diversity in counseling.

Rivier University, School of Graduate Studies, Department of Education, Nashua, NH 03060. Offers curriculum and instruction (M Ed); early childhood education (M Ed); educational administration (M Ed); educational studies (M Ed); elementary education (M Ed); elementary education and general special education (M Ed); emotional and behavioral disorders (M Ed); general social education (M Ed); leadership and learning (Ed D, CAGS); learning disabilities (M Ed); learning disabilities and reading (M Ed); mental health counseling (MA); reading (M Ed); school counseling (M Ed). *Program availability:* Part-time, evening/weekend. *Degree requirements:* For master's, comprehensive exam (for some programs), internships. *Entrance requirements:* For master's, GRE General Test or MAT.

Roberts Wesleyan College, Graduate Psychology Programs, Rochester, NY 14624-1997. Offers clinical/school psychology (Psy D); school counseling (MS); school psychology (MS). *Program availability:* Part-time, evening/weekend. *Degree requirements:* For master's, comprehensive exam, PRAXIS II (for school psychology). *Entrance requirements:* For master's, GRE. Electronic applications accepted. Application fee is waived when completed online. *Faculty research:* Counselor supervision, forgiveness, community health psychology, applied research in group process.

Rollins College, Hamilton Holt School, Master of Arts in Counseling Program, Winter Park, FL 32789-4499. Offers clinical mental health counseling (MA). *Accreditation:* ACA. *Program availability:* Part-time, evening/weekend. *Faculty:* 4 full-time (2 women), 4 part-time/adjunct (3 women). *Students:* 45 full-time (35 women), 53 part-time (47 women); includes 36 minority (8 Black or African American, non-Hispanic/Latino; 2 Asian, non-Hispanic/Latino; 22 Hispanic/Latino; 4 Two or more races, non-Hispanic/Latino), 1 international. Average age 31. In 2017, 30 master's awarded. *Degree requirements:* For master's, satisfactory completion of pre-practicum, practicum, and internship (1,000 hours total). *Entrance requirements:* For master's, GRE General Test or MAT, official transcripts, minimum GPA of 3.0, three letters of recommendation, essay, current resume. Additional exam requirements/recommendations for international students: Required—TOEFL (minimum score 550 paper-based; 80 iBT). *Application deadline:* For fall admission, 3/15 for domestic students. Application fee: $50. *Expenses:* $1,890 per course. *Financial support:* Scholarships/grants and unspecified assistantships available. Support available to part-time students. Financial award applicants required to submit FAFSA. *Unit head:* Dr. Samuel Sanabria, Department Chair, 407-646-2132, E-mail: ssanabria@rollins.edu. *Application contact:* 407-646-1568, Fax: 407-975-6430, E-mail: graduateeducation@rollins.edu.

Rosemont College, Schools of Graduate and Professional Studies, Counseling Psychology Program, Rosemont, PA 19010-1699. Offers human services (MA); school counseling (MA). *Program availability:* Part-time, evening/weekend. *Degree requirements:* For master's, thesis or alternative, practicum. *Entrance requirements:* For master's, minimum undergraduate GPA of 3.0, 3 letters of recommendation. Additional exam requirements/recommendations for international students: Required—TOEFL. Electronic applications accepted. Application fee is waived when completed online. *Expenses:* Contact institution. *Faculty research:* Addictions counseling.

Rowan University, Graduate School, College of Education, Department of Educational Services and Leadership, Program in Counseling in Educational Settings, Glassboro, NJ 08028-1701. Offers MA. *Accreditation:* ACA. *Program availability:* Part-time, evening/weekend. *Degree requirements:* For master's, thesis. *Entrance requirements:* For master's, GRE General Test, minimum GPA of 2.8, 1 year of teaching experience. Additional exam requirements/recommendations for international students: Required—TOEFL. Electronic applications accepted. *Expenses:* Tuition, state resident: full-time $15,020; part-time $751 per semester hour. Tuition, nonresident: full-time $15,020; part-time $751 per semester hour. *Required fees:* $3158; $157.90 per semester hour. Tuition and fees vary according to course load, campus/location and program.

Rutgers University–New Brunswick, Graduate School of Education, Department of Educational Psychology, Programs in School Counseling and Counseling Psychology, Piscataway, NJ 08854-8097. Offers Ed M. *Accreditation:* ACA. *Program availability:* Part-time, evening/weekend. *Entrance requirements:* For master's, GRE General Test, 3 letters of recommendation. Additional exam requirements/recommendations for international students: Required—TOEFL (minimum score 550 paper-based; 83 iBT). Electronic applications accepted. *Faculty research:* Children and family in cross-cultural context, attachment theory, multicultural counseling, therapy relationship.

Sage Graduate School, Esteves School of Education, Professional School Counseling Program, Troy, NY 12180-4115. Offers MS, Post Master's Certificate. *Accreditation:* NCATE. *Program availability:* Part-time, evening/weekend. *Faculty:* 2 full-time (both women), 8 part-time/adjunct (4 women). *Students:* 30 full-time (27 women), 13 part-time (7 women); includes 7 minority (1 American Indian or Alaska Native, non-Hispanic/Latino; 2 Asian, non-Hispanic/Latino; 3 Hispanic/Latino; 1 Two or more races, non-Hispanic/Latino). Average age 26. 47 applicants, 60% accepted, 13 enrolled. In 2017, 19 master's, 7 other advanced degrees awarded. *Entrance requirements:* For master's, minimum GPA of 2.75, current resume, essay, official transcripts, 2 letters of recommendation. Additional exam requirements/recommendations for international students: Required—TOEFL (minimum score 550 paper-based). *Application deadline:* Applications are processed on a rolling basis. Application fee: $30. Tuition and fees vary according to degree level and program. *Financial support:* Fellowships, research assistantships, scholarships/grants, and unspecified assistantships available. Financial award application deadline: 3/1; financial award applicants required to submit FAFSA. *Faculty research:* Roles and responsibilities of guidance personnel, projections of need for guidance counselors. *Unit head:* Dr. John Pelizza, Interim Dean, Esteves School of Education, 518-244-2051, Fax: 518-244-2334, E-mail: pelizj@sage.edu. *Application contact:* Dr. Laurae Coburn, Assistant Professor, Education, 518-244-2401, Fax: 518-244-2334, E-mail: wartil@sage.edu.

St. Bonaventure University, School of Graduate Studies, School of Education, Program in Counselor Education, St. Bonaventure, NY 14778-2284. Offers community mental health counseling (MS Ed); rehabilitation counseling (MS Ed); school counseling (MS Ed); school counselor (Adv C). *Accreditation:* ACA. *Program availability:* Part-time, evening/weekend, 100% online. *Faculty:* 4 full-time (2 women), 5 part-time/adjunct (4 women). *Students:* 35 full-time (27 women), 30 part-time (23 women); includes 8 minority (3 Black or African American, non-Hispanic/Latino; 4 Hispanic/Latino; 1 Two or more races, non-Hispanic/Latino), 1 international. Average age 28. 55 applicants, 82% accepted, 29 enrolled. In 2017, 27 master's, 2 Adv Cs awarded. *Degree requirements:* For master's, comprehensive exam, thesis optional, internship, portfolio; for Adv C, internship. *Entrance requirements:* For master's, statement of intent/writing sample; transcripts from all colleges previously attended, two references; interview; minimum undergraduate GPA of 3.0; for Adv C, interview, writing sample, minimum undergraduate GPA of 3.0, two letters of recommendation, master's degree, transcripts from all colleges previously attended. Additional exam requirements/recommendations for international students: Required—TOEFL (minimum score 550 paper-based; 79 iBT). *Application deadline:* For fall admission, 3/15 priority date for domestic students, 2/1 priority date for international students; for spring admission, 11/15 priority date for domestic students, 7/1 priority date for international students. Applications are processed on a rolling basis. Application fee: $0. Electronic applications accepted. *Expenses:* $733 per credit hour, $100 graduation fee. *Financial support:* Career-related internships or fieldwork, Federal Work-Study, scholarships/grants, health care benefits, and unspecified assistantships available. Support available to part-time students. Financial award application deadline: 4/15; financial award applicants required to submit FAFSA. *Faculty research:* Balance between technology and personal contact in counselor education, special education and cyberbullying, school response to child abuse. *Unit head:* Dr. Chris Siuta, Director, 716-375-2114, Fax: 716-375-2360, E-mail: csiuta@sbu.edu. *Application contact:* Bruce Campbell, Director of Graduate Admissions, 716-375-2429, Fax: 716-375-4015, E-mail: gradsch@sbu.edu. Website: http://www.sbu.edu/academics/msed-in-school-counseling

St. Cloud State University, School of Graduate Studies, School of Education, Department of Educational Leadership and Higher Education, Program in College Counseling and Student Development, St. Cloud, MN 56301-4498. Offers MS. *Degree requirements:* For master's, comprehensive exam, thesis or alternative. *Entrance requirements:* For master's, GRE General Test, minimum GPA of 2.75. Additional exam requirements/recommendations for international students: Required—Michigan English Language Assessment Battery; Recommended—TOEFL (minimum score 550 paper-based); IELTS (minimum score 6.5). Electronic applications accepted.

St. Cloud State University, School of Graduate Studies, School of Education, Department of Educational Leadership and Higher Education, Program in School Counseling, St. Cloud, MN 56301-4498. Offers MS. *Accreditation:* ACA; NCATE. *Degree requirements:* For master's, comprehensive exam (for some programs), thesis or alternative. *Entrance requirements:* For master's, GRE General Test, minimum GPA of 2.75. Additional exam requirements/recommendations for international students: Required—Michigan English Language Assessment Battery; Recommended—TOEFL (minimum score 550 paper-based), IELTS. Electronic applications accepted.

St. John's University, The School of Education, Department of Counselor Education, Program in School Counseling, Queens, NY 11439. Offers MS Ed, Adv C. Master's program admits in fall only; Advanced Certificate in spring only. *Accreditation:* ACA (one or more programs are accredited). *Students:* 29 full-time (19 women), 10 part-time (9 women); includes 11 minority (4 Black or African American, non-Hispanic/Latino; 3 Asian, non-Hispanic/Latino; 4 Hispanic/Latino; 2 international. Average age 27. 52 applicants, 87% accepted, 15 enrolled. In 2017, 20 master's, 1 Adv C awarded. *Entrance requirements:* For master's, 2 letters of recommendation, interview; for Adv C, official master's transcripts, statement of purpose. *Application deadline:* For fall admission, 8/17 for domestic and international students; for summer admission, 5/15 for domestic and international students. Application fee: $70. Electronic applications accepted. *Expenses: Tuition:* Full-time $44,280; part-time $1230 per credit. *Required fees:* $340; $340 per credit. Tuition and fees vary according to course load, degree level and program. *Financial support:* Fellowships, research assistantships, scholarships/grants, and unspecified assistantships available. Support available to part-time students. Financial award application deadline: 2/1; financial award applicants required to submit FAFSA. *Faculty research:* Counseling/client engagement; counseling accountability; pipe-line mentoring from grade 4 to college; stress, coping and resilience for children and adults; helping parents deal with aggressive children; effects of bullying and cyber bullying with adolescents; creative connections through the arts. *Unit head:* Dr. Robert K. Eschenauer, Chair, 718-990-2120, E-mail: eschenar@stjohns.edu. *Application contact:* Dr. Robert K. Eschenauer, Chair, 718-990-2120, E-mail: eschenar@stjohns.edu.
Website: https://www.stjohns.edu/academics/schools-and-colleges/school-education/programs-and-majors/school-counseling-master-science-education

St. Lawrence University, Department of Education, Program in Counseling and Human Development, Canton, NY 13617. Offers mental health counseling (MS); school counseling (M Ed, CAS). *Program availability:* Part-time, evening/weekend. *Entrance requirements:* For master's, GRE General Test. *Faculty research:* Defense mechanisms and mediation.

Saint Mary's College of California, Kalmanovitz School of Education, Program in Counseling, Moraga, CA 94575. Offers career counseling (MA); college student services (Credential); general counseling (MA); marriage and family therapy (MA); pupil personnel services (Credential), including school counseling, school psychology; school counseling (MA); school psychology (MA). *Program availability:* Part-time, evening/weekend. *Degree requirements:* For master's, thesis or alternative. *Entrance requirements:* For master's, interview, minimum GPA of 3.0. *Faculty research:* Counselor training effectiveness, multicultural development, empathy, the interface of spirituality and psychotherapy, gender issues.

St. Mary's University, Graduate Studies, Program in Counselor Education and Supervision, San Antonio, TX 78228. Offers PhD. *Accreditation:* ACA. *Program availability:* Part-time, evening/weekend. *Students:* 16 full-time (10 women), 34 part-time (26 women); includes 18 minority (6 Black or African American, non-Hispanic/Latino; 1 American Indian or Alaska Native, non-Hispanic/Latino; 3 Asian, non-Hispanic/Latino; 8 Hispanic/Latino), 12 international. Average age 40. 27 applicants, 15% accepted, 2 enrolled. In 2017, 3 doctorates awarded. *Degree requirements:* For doctorate, comprehensive exam, thesis/dissertation, internship. *Entrance requirements:* For doctorate, GRE General Test, master's degree in counseling or related area from accredited college or university; recommendations from past employers relating to professional counseling experience, as well as from faculties of previous undergraduate/graduate studies; recommendation from Graduate Admissions Committee. Additional exam requirements/recommendations for international students: Required—TOEFL (minimum score 550 paper-based; 80 iBT), IELTS (minimum score 6). *Application deadline:* For fall admission, 7/1 for domestic students; for spring admission, 11/15 for domestic students; for summer admission, 4/1 for domestic students. Applications are processed on a rolling basis. Application fee: $0. Electronic applications accepted. *Expenses: Tuition:* Full-time $16,200; part-time $900 per credit hour. *Required fees:* $810; $405 per semester. *Financial support:* Fellowships, research assistantships, career-related internships or fieldwork, Federal Work-Study, institutionally sponsored loans, scholarships/grants, health care benefits, and unspecified assistantships available. Financial award application deadline: 3/31; financial award applicants required to submit FAFSA. *Faculty research:* Palliative care, neuroscience of psychology and religion, cranial electrotherapy, EEG biofeedback. *Unit head:* Dr. Melanie Harper, Program Director, 210-438-6400, E-mail: mharper@stmarytx.edu. *Application contact:* Kim Thornton, Director of Graduate Admission, 210-436-3101, E-mail: kthornton@stmarytx.edu.
Website: https://www.stmarytx.edu/academics/programs/doctor-counselor-education-supervision/

Saint Peter's University, Graduate Programs in Education, Program in School Counseling, Jersey City, NJ 07306-5997. Offers MA, Certificate.

St. Thomas University, Biscayne College, Department of Social Sciences and Counseling, Program in Guidance and Counseling, Miami Gardens, FL 33054-6459. Offers MS, Post-Master's Certificate. *Program availability:* Part-time, evening/weekend. *Degree requirements:* For master's, comprehensive exam. *Entrance requirements:* For master's, interview, minimum GPA of 3.0 or GRE. Additional exam requirements/recommendations for international students: Required—TOEFL (minimum score 550 paper-based; 79 iBT). Electronic applications accepted.

Saint Xavier University, Graduate Studies, School of Education, Program in Counseling, Chicago, IL 60655-3105. Offers MA. *Degree requirements:* For master's, practicum, internship. *Entrance requirements:* For master's, 3 letters of recommendation, interview. Additional exam requirements/recommendations for international students: Required—TOEFL. Electronic applications accepted.

Salem College, Graduate Studies, Winston-Salem, NC 27101. Offers art education (MAT); elementary education (M Ed, MAT); language and literacy (M Ed); middle school education (MAT); organ (MM); piano (MM); school counseling (M Ed); second language studies (MAT); secondary education (MAT); special education (M Ed, MAT).

Counselor Education

Accreditation: NCATE. *Program availability:* Part-time, evening/weekend, online learning. *Faculty:* 8 full-time (all women), 11 part-time/adjunct (8 women). In 2017, 17 master's awarded. *Degree requirements:* For master's, practicum (MAT), action research project (M Ed). *Entrance requirements:* For master's, minimum GPA of 3.0, two academic/professional recommendations, acceptable criminal background check. Additional exam requirements/recommendations for international students: Recommended—TOEFL. *Application deadline:* For fall admission, 8/1 for domestic students, 7/15 for international students; for spring admission, 1/15 for domestic students; for summer admission, 5/1 for domestic students. Applications are processed on a rolling basis. Application fee: $30. Electronic applications accepted. *Expenses:* Tuition: Part-time $440 per semester hour. *Financial support:* Scholarships/grants available. Support available to part-time students. Financial award applicants required to submit FAFSA. *Faculty research:* Teacher professional development, adolescent literacy, instructional technology. *Application contact:* Sheryl Long, Director, 336-721-2658, Fax: 336-917-5384, E-mail: sheryl.long@salem.edu.
Website: http://www.salem.edu

Salem State University, School of Graduate Studies, Program in School Counseling, Salem, MA 01970-5353. Offers M Ed. *Accreditation:* NCATE. *Program availability:* Part-time, evening/weekend. *Entrance requirements:* For master's, GRE or MAT. Additional exam requirements/recommendations for international students: Required—TOEFL (minimum score 550 paper-based; 80 iBT) or IELTS (minimum score 5.5).

Sam Houston State University, College of Education, Department of Counseling, Huntsville, TX 77341. Offers M Ed, MA, PhD. *Accreditation:* NCATE. *Program availability:* Part-time, online learning. *Degree requirements:* For master's, thesis optional; for doctorate, comprehensive exam, thesis/dissertation. *Entrance requirements:* For master's, GRE General Test, 3.0 GPA, Three References, Essay, Face-to-Face interview; for doctorate, On-site interview, on-site professional presentation, and on-site writing prompt, Personal statement, Five References, Master's Degree with 3.5 GPA. Additional exam requirements/recommendations for international students: Required—TOEFL (minimum score 550 paper-based; 79 iBT), IELTS (minimum score 6.5). Electronic applications accepted. *Faculty research:* Family counseling, career counseling, business emergent counseling.

San Diego State University, Graduate and Research Affairs, College of Education, Department of Counseling and School Psychology, San Diego, CA 92182. Offers MS. *Accreditation:* NCATE. *Program availability:* Evening/weekend. *Degree requirements:* For master's, comprehensive exam (for some programs), thesis (for some programs). *Entrance requirements:* For master's, GRE General Test, interview, letters of reference. Additional exam requirements/recommendations for international students: Required—TOEFL. Electronic applications accepted. *Faculty research:* Multicultural and cross-cultural counseling and training, AIDS counseling.

San Jose State University, Graduate Studies and Research, Connie L. Lurie College of Education, San Jose, CA 95192-0071. Offers child and adolescent development (MA); education (MA), including counseling and student personnel, curriculum and instruction, speech pathology; educational leadership (MA, Ed D), including administration and supervision (MA), educational leadership (MA); elementary education (MA), including curriculum and instruction. *Accreditation:* NCATE. *Program availability:* Part-time, evening/weekend. *Faculty:* 29 full-time (22 women), 47 part-time/adjunct (40 women). *Students:* 414 full-time (339 women), 115 part-time (93 women); includes 341 minority (14 Black or African American, non-Hispanic/Latino; 87 Asian, non-Hispanic/Latino; 176 Hispanic/Latino; 64 Two or more races, non-Hispanic/Latino), 9 international. Average age 30. 654 applicants, 34% accepted, 161 enrolled. In 2017, 286 master's, 7 doctorates awarded. Terminal master's awarded for partial completion of doctoral program. *Degree requirements:* For master's, project or theses, graduate writing assessment; for doctorate, thesis/dissertation. *Entrance requirements:* For master's, GRE General Test (for some programs). Additional exam requirements/recommendations for international students: Required—TOEFL (minimum score 550 paper-based; 80 iBT), IELTS (minimum score 6.5), PTE (minimum score 53). *Application deadline:* For fall admission, 2/1 for domestic and international students. Applications are processed on a rolling basis. Application fee: $55. Electronic applications accepted. *Expenses:* Tuition, state resident: full-time $7176. Tuition, nonresident: full-time $16,680. Tuition and fees vary according to course load and program. *Financial support:* In 2017–18, 4 research assistantships with partial tuition reimbursements (averaging $2,500 per year) were awarded; fellowships, career-related internships or fieldwork, Federal Work-Study, scholarships/grants, traineeships, and tuition waivers (full and partial) also available. Support available to part-time students. Financial award application deadline: 4/28; financial award applicants required to submit FAFSA. *Faculty research:* Equity and social justice in public education, interdisciplinary practices, teacher training, and effective pedagogy, clinical efficacy, typical and atypical development in children. *Unit head:* Dr. Paul Cascella, Interim Dean, 408-924-3600, Fax: 408-924-3713, E-mail: paul.cascella@sjsu.edu.
Website: http://www.sjsu.edu/education/

Santa Clara University, School of Education and Counseling Psychology, Santa Clara, CA 95053. Offers alternative and correctional education (Certificate); Catholic school teaching (MAT); counseling (MA); counseling psychology (MA); educational leadership (MA); interdisciplinary education (MA); teaching multiple subjects (MAT); teaching single subjects (MAT). *Program availability:* Part-time. *Faculty:* 31 full-time (21 women), 37 part-time/adjunct (25 women). *Students:* 253 full-time (195 women), 350 part-time (283 women); includes 296 minority (10 Black or African American, non-Hispanic/Latino; 1 American Indian or Alaska Native, non-Hispanic/Latino; 80 Asian, non-Hispanic/Latino; 179 Hispanic/Latino; 26 Two or more races, non-Hispanic/Latino), 41 international. Average age 31. 211 applicants, 75% accepted, 142 enrolled. In 2017, 266 master's awarded. *Entrance requirements:* For master's, official transcripts, 2-3 letters of recommendation, statement of purpose, resume or curriculum vitae. Additional exam requirements/recommendations for international students: Required—TOEFL (minimum score 90 iBT) or IELTS (6.5). *Application deadline:* For fall admission, 4/16 for international students; for summer admission, 3/12 for domestic students. Applications are processed on a rolling basis. Application fee: $50. Electronic applications accepted. *Expenses:* $607 per unit. *Financial support:* In 2017–18, 355 students received support. Fellowships, research assistantships, teaching assistantships, Federal Work-Study, scholarships/grants, and health care benefits available. Support available to part-time students. Financial award applicants required to submit FAFSA. *Unit head:* Dr. Sabrina Zirkel, Dean, 408-551-3074, Fax: 408-554-4367, E-mail: szirkel@scu.edu. *Application contact:* Victoria Rodriguez, Graduate Admissions Advisor, 408-554-4723, E-mail: v1rodriguez@scu.edu.
Website: http://www.scu.edu/ecp/

Seattle Pacific University, Master of Education in School Counseling Program, Seattle, WA 98119-1997. Offers M Ed, Certificate. *Accreditation:* ACA; NCATE. *Program availability:* Part-time. *Students:* 42 full-time (30 women), 37 part-time (34 women); includes 20 minority (2 Black or African American, non-Hispanic/Latino; 1 American Indian or Alaska Native, non-Hispanic/Latino; 10 Asian, non-Hispanic/Latino; 5 Hispanic/Latino; 1 Native Hawaiian or other Pacific Islander, non-Hispanic/Latino; 1 Two or more races, non-Hispanic/Latino), 2 international. Average age 29. 56 applicants, 55% accepted, 19 enrolled. In 2017, 16 master's awarded. *Degree requirements:* For

master's, year-long internship. *Entrance requirements:* For master's, GRE General Test or MAT, copy of teaching certificate; official transcript(s) from each college/university attended; resume; personal statement, including long-term professional goals (maximum of 500 words); 2 letters of recommendation. Additional exam requirements/recommendations for international students: Required—TOEFL (minimum score 550 paper-based), IELTS (minimum score 7). *Application deadline:* For fall admission, 4/1 priority date for domestic students. Application fee: $50. Electronic applications accepted. *Expenses:* Contact institution. *Financial support:* Scholarships/grants available. Financial award applicants required to submit FAFSA. *Unit head:* Dr. June Hyun, Chair, 206-281-2671, Fax: 206-281-2756, E-mail: jhyun@spu.edu. *Application contact:* 206-281-2091.
Website: http://spu.edu/academics/school-of-education/graduate-programs/masters-programs/school-counseling-med/program-outline

Seattle Pacific University, PhD in Counselor Education Program, Seattle, WA 98119-1997. Offers PhD. *Students:* 7 part-time (6 women); includes 4 minority (1 Black or African American, non-Hispanic/Latino; 2 Asian, non-Hispanic/Latino; 1 Two or more races, non-Hispanic/Latino). Average age 35. *Entrance requirements:* For doctorate, GRE (minimum revised score of 153 Verbal, 152 Quantitative, taken within five years of application; minimum combined score of 1200 on old test), official transcripts, personal statement, four recent letters of recommendation, writing sample, resume. *Application deadline:* For fall admission, 8/15 for domestic students; for winter admission, 11/15 for domestic students; for spring admission, 2/15 for domestic students; for summer admission, 5/15 for domestic students. Application fee: $50. *Unit head:* Nyaradzo Mvududu, Director, 206-281-2551, E-mail: nyaradzo@spu.edu.
Website: http://spu.edu/academics/school-of-education/graduate-programs/doctoral-programs/doctor-of-philosophy-counselor-education-phd

Seattle University, College of Education, Program in Counseling and School Psychology, Seattle, WA 98122-1090. Offers MA, Certificate, Ed S. *Accreditation:* ACA; NCATE. *Program availability:* Part-time, evening/weekend. *Faculty:* 13 full-time (7 women), 3 part-time/adjunct (2 women). *Students:* 122 full-time (107 women), 90 part-time (74 women); includes 71 minority (8 Black or African American, non-Hispanic/Latino; 3 American Indian or Alaska Native, non-Hispanic/Latino; 21 Asian, non-Hispanic/Latino; 28 Hispanic/Latino; 11 Two or more races, non-Hispanic/Latino), 3 international. Average age 29. 212 applicants, 55% accepted, 54 enrolled. In 2017, 40 master's, 27 other advanced degrees awarded. *Degree requirements:* For master's, comprehensive exam. *Entrance requirements:* For master's, interview; GRE, MAT, or minimum GPA of 3.0; related work experience. Additional exam requirements/recommendations for international students: Required—TOEFL. *Application deadline:* For fall admission, 7/1 for domestic students; for winter admission, 10/20 for domestic students; for spring admission, 1/20 for domestic students. Application fee: $55. *Expenses:* Tuition: Full-time $12,960. *Required fees:* $570. Tuition and fees vary according to program. *Financial support:* In 2017–18, 39 students received support. *Unit head:* Hutch Haney, Director, 206-296-5750, E-mail: schpsy@seattleu.edu. *Application contact:* Janet Shandley, Associate Dean of Graduate Admissions, 206-296-5900, Fax: 206-298-5656, E-mail: grad_admissions@seattleu.edu.
Website: https://www.seattleu.edu/education/psychology/

Seton Hall University, College of Education and Human Services, Department of Professional Psychology and Family Therapy, Program in Counseling Psychology, South Orange, NJ 07079-2697. Offers counseling psychology (PhD); school counseling (MA). *Accreditation:* APA. *Degree requirements:* For doctorate, comprehensive exam, thesis/dissertation, internship. *Entrance requirements:* For master's and doctorate, GRE, interview. *Faculty research:* Vocational indecision, coping skills, cognitive behavioral interventions, vocational development.

Shippensburg University of Pennsylvania, School of Graduate Studies, College of Education and Human Services, Department of Counseling, Shippensburg, PA 17257-2299. Offers college counseling (MS); college student personnel (MS); counselor education and supervision (Ed D); mental health counseling (MS); school counseling (M Ed). *Accreditation:* ACA (one or more programs are accredited); NCATE. *Program availability:* Part-time, evening/weekend, blended/hybrid learning. *Faculty:* 9 full-time (3 women), 1 part-time/adjunct (0 women). *Students:* 75 full-time (64 women), 49 part-time (40 women); includes 28 minority (17 Black or African American, non-Hispanic/Latino; 1 Asian, non-Hispanic/Latino; 7 Hispanic/Latino; 3 Two or more races, non-Hispanic/Latino), 3 international. Average age 29. 94 applicants, 54% accepted, 41 enrolled. In 2017, 56 master's awarded. *Degree requirements:* For master's, fieldwork, research project, internship, candidacy; for doctorate, thesis/dissertation, practicum, internship. *Entrance requirements:* For master's, GRE or MAT (for MS if GPA is less than 2.75), minimum GPA of 2.75 (3.0 for M Ed), resume, 3 letter of recommendation forms, one year of relevant work experience, on-campus interview, autobiographical statement; for doctorate, master's degree in counseling or related discipline; resume; three recommendation letters (1 each from employer, clinical supervisor, and prior graduate school faculty member); personal essay; interview with department chair. Additional exam requirements/recommendations for international students: Required—TOEFL (minimum score 550 paper-based, 68 iBT) or IELTS (minimum score 6). *Application deadline:* Applications are processed on a rolling basis. Application fee: $45. Electronic applications accepted. *Expenses:* Tuition, state resident: part-time $500 per credit. Tuition, nonresident: part-time $750 per credit. *Required fees:* $145 per credit. *Financial support:* In 2017–18, 54 students received support. Career-related internships or fieldwork, scholarships/grants, unspecified assistantships, and resident hall director and student payroll positions available. Support available to part-time students. Financial award application deadline: 3/1; financial award applicants required to submit FAFSA. *Unit head:* Dr. Kurt L. Kraus, Departmental Chair and Program Coordinator, 717-477-1603, Fax: 717-477-4056, E-mail: klkrau@ship.edu. *Application contact:* Maya T. Mapp, Director of Admissions, 717-477-1231, Fax: 717-477-4016, E-mail: mtmapp@ship.edu.
Website: http://www.ship.edu/counsel/

Simon Fraser University, Office of Graduate Studies and Postdoctoral Fellows, Faculty of Education, Program in Counseling Psychology, Burnaby, BC V5A 1S6, Canada. Offers M Ed, MA. *Program availability:* Part-time, evening/weekend. *Degree requirements:* For master's, comprehensive exam (for some programs), thesis (for some programs), practicum. *Entrance requirements:* For master's, minimum GPA of 3.0 (on scale of 4.33) or 3.33 based on last 60 credits of undergraduate courses. Additional exam requirements/recommendations for international students: Recommended—TOEFL (minimum score 580 paper-based; 93 iBT), IELTS (minimum score 7), TWE (minimum score 5). Electronic applications accepted. *Faculty research:* Cultural and personal dimensions in psychological development, and psychology of working; and career development, social justice and multicultural competence issues, traumatic stress studies, counselor education.

Slippery Rock University of Pennsylvania, Graduate Studies (Recruitment), College of Education, Department of Counseling and Development, Slippery Rock, PA 16057-1383. Offers clinical mental health (MA); school counseling (M Ed); student affairs in higher education (MA); student affairs in higher education with college counseling (MA). *Accreditation:* ACA (one or more programs are accredited); NCATE. *Program availability:* Part-time, evening/weekend. *Degree requirements:* For master's, comprehensive exam, thesis (for some programs). *Entrance requirements:* For master's,

GRE General Test or MAT, official transcripts, personal statement, three letters of recommendation, interview. Additional exam requirements/recommendations for international students: Required—TOEFL (minimum score 550 paper-based; 80 iBT). Electronic applications accepted. *Expenses:* Contact institution.

South Carolina State University, College of Graduate and Professional Studies, Department of Education, Orangeburg, SC 29117-0001. Offers early childhood education (MAT); education (M Ed); elementary education (M Ed, MAT); English (MAT); general science/biology (MAT); mathematics (MAT); secondary education (M Ed), including biology education, business education, counselor education, English education, home economics education, industrial education, mathematics education, science education, social studies education; special education (M Ed), including emotionally handicapped, learning disabilities, mentally handicapped. *Accreditation:* NCATE. *Program availability:* Part-time, evening/weekend. *Faculty:* 11 full-time (6 women), 4 part-time/adjunct (2 women). *Students:* 26 full-time (18 women), 22 part-time (17 women); includes 41 minority (all Black or African American, non-Hispanic/Latino), 1 international. Average age 33. 25 applicants, 100% accepted, 19 enrolled. In 2017, 6 master's awarded. *Degree requirements:* For master's, thesis optional, departmental qualifying exam. *Entrance requirements:* For master's, GRE General Test, NTE, interview, teaching certificate. *Application deadline:* For fall admission, 6/15 priority date for domestic students, 6/15 for international students; for spring admission, 11/1 for domestic and international students. Application fee: $25. Electronic applications accepted. *Expenses:* Tuition, state resident: full-time $9388; part-time $607 per credit hour. Tuition, nonresident: full-time $19,968; part-time $1194 per credit hour. *Required fees:* $766; $766 per credit hour. *Financial support:* Fellowships, career-related internships or fieldwork, Federal Work-Study, and scholarships/grants available. Financial award application deadline: 6/1. *Unit head:* Dr. Charlie Spell, Interim Chair, Department of Education, 803-536-8963, Fax: 803-516-4568, E-mail: cspell@scsu.edu. *Application contact:* Curtis Foskey, Coordinator of Graduate Studies, 803-536-8419, Fax: 803-536-8812, E-mail: cfoskey@scsu.edu.

South Carolina State University, College of Graduate and Professional Studies, Department of Human Services, Orangeburg, SC 29117-0001. Offers counselor education (M Ed); rehabilitation counseling (MA). *Accreditation:* CORE. *Program availability:* Part-time, evening/weekend. *Faculty:* 8 full-time (6 women), 3 part-time/adjunct (all women). *Students:* 87 full-time (74 women), 25 part-time (17 women); includes 106 minority (all Black or African American, non-Hispanic/Latino). Average age 32. 60 applicants, 93% accepted, 51 enrolled. In 2017, 38 master's awarded. *Degree requirements:* For master's, comprehensive exam (for some programs), departmental qualifying exam, internship. *Entrance requirements:* For master's, GRE, MAT, minimum GPA of 2.7. *Application deadline:* For fall admission, 6/15 priority date for domestic students, 6/15 for international students; for spring admission, 11/1 for domestic and international students. Application fee: $25. Electronic applications accepted. *Expenses:* Tuition, state resident: full-time $9388; part-time $607 per credit hour. Tuition, nonresident: full-time $19,968; part-time $1194 per credit hour. *Required fees:* $766; $766 per credit hour. *Financial support:* Fellowships, career-related internships or fieldwork, scholarships/grants, and unspecified assistantships available. Financial award application deadline: 6/1. *Unit head:* Dr. Michelle Maultsby-Priester, Interim Chair, Department of Human Services, 803-536-7075, Fax: 803-533-3636, E-mail: mmaultsb@scsu.edu. *Application contact:* Curtis Foskey, Coordinator of Graduate Admissions, 803-536-8419, Fax: 803-536-8812, E-mail: cfoskey@scsu.edu.

South Dakota State University, Graduate School, College of Education and Human Sciences, Department of Counseling and Human Development, Brookings, SD 57007. Offers counseling and human resource development (M Ed, MS); human sciences (MS). *Accreditation:* ACA (one or more programs are accredited); NCATE. *Program availability:* Part-time, evening/weekend. *Degree requirements:* For master's, comprehensive exam, thesis (for some programs), oral exams. *Entrance requirements:* For master's, minimum GPA of 2.75. Additional exam requirements/recommendations for international students: Required—TOEFL (minimum score 525 paper-based; 71 iBT). *Faculty research:* Rural mental health, family issues, character education, student affairs, solution focused therapy.

Southeastern Louisiana University, College of Nursing and Health Sciences, Department of Health and Human Sciences, Hammond, LA 70402. Offers communication sciences and disorders (MS); counseling (MS). *Accreditation:* ACA; ASHA; NCATE. *Program availability:* Part-time. *Faculty:* 15 full-time (14 women), 2 part-time/adjunct (both women). *Students:* 193 full-time (96 women), 41 part-time (38 women); includes 40 minority (13 Black or African American, non-Hispanic/Latino; 1 Asian, non-Hispanic/Latino; 13 Hispanic/Latino; 1 Native Hawaiian or other Pacific Islander, non-Hispanic/Latino; 12 Two or more races, non-Hispanic/Latino). Average age 28. 28 applicants, 57% accepted, 11 enrolled. In 2017, 53 master's awarded. *Degree requirements:* For master's, comprehensive exam, thesis optional, 25 clock hours of clinical observation (for communication sciences and disorders). *Entrance requirements:* For master's, GRE (minimum combined score of 279), minimum GPA of 2.8. Additional exam requirements/recommendations for international students: Required—TOEFL (minimum score 500 paper-based; 61 iBT). *Application deadline:* For fall admission, 3/1 priority date for domestic students, 6/1 priority date for international students; for spring admission, 10/1 priority date for domestic and international students. Applications are processed on a rolling basis. Application fee: $20 ($30 for international students). Electronic applications accepted. *Expenses:* Tuition, state resident: full-time $6684. Tuition, nonresident: full-time $19,162. *Required fees:* $2088. *Financial support:* In 2017–18, 65 students received support. Career-related internships or fieldwork, Federal Work-Study, institutionally sponsored loans, scholarships/grants, and unspecified assistantships available. Support available to part-time students. Financial award application deadline: 5/1; financial award applicants required to submit FAFSA. *Faculty research:* School counseling, play therapy, family counseling, grief counseling, transformational teaching. *Unit head:* Dr. Jacqueline Guendouzi, Department Head, 985-549-2309, Fax: 985-549-3758, E-mail: jguendouzi@southeastern.edu. *Application contact:* Amanda Harper, Graduate Admissions Analyst, 985-549-5620, Fax: 985-549-5632, E-mail: admissions@southeastern.edu.
Website: http://www.southeastern.edu/acad_research/depts/hhs/index.html

Southeastern Oklahoma State University, School of Behavioral Sciences, Durant, OK 74701-0609. Offers clinical mental health counseling (MS). *Accreditation:* ACA. *Program availability:* Part-time, evening/weekend. *Degree requirements:* For master's, comprehensive exam, thesis optional. *Entrance requirements:* For master's, GRE General Test, minimum GPA of 3.0 in last 60 hours or 2.75 overall. Additional exam requirements/recommendations for international students: Required—TOEFL (minimum score 550 paper-based; 79 iBT). Electronic applications accepted.

Southeastern Oklahoma State University, School of Education, Durant, OK 74701-0609. Offers math specialist (M Ed); reading specialist (M Ed); school administration (M Ed); school counseling (M Ed). *Accreditation:* NCATE. *Program availability:* Part-time, evening/weekend. *Degree requirements:* For master's, comprehensive exam, thesis optional, portfolio (M Ed). *Entrance requirements:* For master's, GRE General Test (for school counseling), minimum GPA of 3.0 in last 60 hours or 2.75 overall. Additional exam requirements/recommendations for international students: Required—TOEFL (minimum score 550 paper-based; 79 iBT). Electronic applications accepted.

Southeastern University, College of Behavioral and Social Sciences, Lakeland, FL 33801-6099. Offers human services (MA); international community development (MA); marriage and family counseling (MS); professional counseling (MS); school counseling (MS); social work (MSW). *Program availability:* Evening/weekend. *Faculty:* 9 full-time (6 women), 7 part-time/adjunct (4 women). *Students:* 72 full-time (60 women), 9 part-time (all women); includes 28 minority (12 Black or African American, non-Hispanic/Latino; 2 Asian, non-Hispanic/Latino; 13 Hispanic/Latino; 1 Native Hawaiian or other Pacific Islander, non-Hispanic/Latino), 1 international. Average age 29. Application fee: $50. Electronic applications accepted. *Unit head:* Erica H. Sirrine, Dean, 863-667-5341, E-mail: ehsirrine@seu.edu.
Website: http://www.seu.edu/behavior/

Southeast Missouri State University, School of Graduate Studies, Department of Educational Leadership and Counseling, Counseling Program, Cape Girardeau, MO 63701-4799. Offers career counseling (MA); mental health counseling (MA); school counseling (MA). *Accreditation:* ACA; NCATE. *Program availability:* Part-time, evening/weekend. *Faculty:* 5 full-time (4 women), 2 part-time/adjunct (both women). *Students:* 30 full-time (23 women), 30 part-time (26 women); includes 6 minority (4 Black or African American, non-Hispanic/Latino; 2 American Indian or Alaska Native, non-Hispanic/Latino), 1 international. Average age 33. 45 applicants, 78% accepted, 26 enrolled. In 2017, 49 master's, 4 other advanced degrees awarded. *Degree requirements:* For master's and Ed S, comprehensive exam, thesis or alternative. *Entrance requirements:* For master's, personal essay, interview, minimum GPA of 3.5; for Ed S, minimum graduate GPA of 3.7. Additional exam requirements/recommendations for international students: Required—TOEFL (minimum score 550 paper-based; 79 iBT), IELTS (minimum score 6), PTE (minimum score 53). *Application deadline:* For fall admission, 3/1 for domestic and international students; for spring admission, 11/21 for domestic students, 10/1 for international students; for summer admission, 3/1 for domestic students. Applications are processed on a rolling basis. Application fee: $30 ($40 for international students). Electronic applications accepted. *Expenses:* $270.35 per credit hour in-state tuition, $33.40 per credit hour fees. *Financial support:* In 2017–18, 6 students received support. Career-related internships or fieldwork, Federal Work-Study, scholarships/grants, traineeships, tuition waivers (full), and unspecified assistantships available. Financial award application deadline: 6/30; financial award applicants required to submit FAFSA. *Faculty research:* School counseling, mental health, career and family counseling, social justice and spirituality in counseling. *Unit head:* Dr. C. P. Gause, Department Chair, 573-651-2137, Fax: 573-986-6512, E-mail: cpgause@semo.edu. *Application contact:* Dr. Jan Ward, Program Coordinator/Associate Professor, 573-651-2137, Fax: 573-986-6512, E-mail: jward@semo.edu.
Website: http://www.semo.edu/eduleadcounsel/

Southern Adventist University, School of Education and Psychology, Collegedale, TN 37315-0370. Offers clinical mental health counseling (MS); instructional leadership (MS Ed); literacy education (MS Ed); outdoor education (MS Ed); professional school counseling (MS). *Accreditation:* NCATE. *Program availability:* Part-time, evening/weekend. *Degree requirements:* For master's, comprehensive exam (for some programs), thesis optional, position paper (MS), portfolio (MS Ed in outdoor education). *Entrance requirements:* For master's, interview (MS); 9 semester hours of upper-division course work in psychology or related field, including 1 course in psychology research or statistics; 9 semester hours of education (MS Ed). Additional exam requirements/recommendations for international students: Required—TOEFL (minimum score 600 paper-based; 100 iBT). *Application deadline:* For fall admission, 7/1 priority date for domestic students, 6/1 priority date for international students; for winter admission, 11/1 priority date for domestic students, 10/1 priority date for international students; for spring admission, 4/1 priority date for domestic students, 3/1 priority date for international students. Applications are processed on a rolling basis. Application fee: $40. Electronic applications accepted. *Expenses:* Tuition: Full-time $11,430; part-time $635 per credit hour. Tuition and fees vary according to degree level and program. *Financial support:* Research assistantships with full tuition reimbursements, teaching assistantships with full tuition reimbursements, career-related internships or fieldwork, scholarships/grants, tuition waivers (partial), and unspecified assistantships available. Support available to part-time students. Financial award application deadline: 4/1; financial award applicants required to submit FAFSA. *Unit head:* Bonnie Eder, Interim Dean, 423-236-2759, Fax: 423-236-1765, E-mail: beder@southern.edu. *Application contact:* Mikhaile Spence, Graduate Enrollment Counselor, 423-236-2496, Fax: 423-236-1765, E-mail: maspence@southern.edu.
Website: https://www.southern.edu/academics/edpsych.html

Southern Arkansas University–Magnolia, School of Graduate Studies, Magnolia, AR 71753. Offers agriculture (MS); business administration (MBA), including agribusiness, social entrepreneurship, supply chain management; clinical and mental health counseling (MS); computer and information sciences (MS), including cyber security and privacy, data science, information technology; gifted and talented (M Ed), including curriculum and instruction, educational administration and supervision, gifted and talented P-8/7-12, instructional specialist P-4; higher, adult and lifelong education (M Ed); kinesiology (M Ed), including coaching; library media and information specialist (M Ed); public administration (MPA); school counseling K-12 (M Ed); student affairs and college counseling (M Ed); teaching (MAT). *Accreditation:* NCATE. *Program availability:* Part-time, 100% online, blended/hybrid learning. *Faculty:* 36 full-time (20 women), 31 part-time/adjunct (12 women). *Students:* 242 full-time (89 women), 889 part-time (459 women); includes 167 minority (143 Black or African American, non-Hispanic/Latino; 7 American Indian or Alaska Native, non-Hispanic/Latino; 7 Asian, non-Hispanic/Latino; 3 Hispanic/Latino; 7 Two or more races, non-Hispanic/Latino), 562 international. Average age 28. 400 applicants, 100% accepted, 239 enrolled. In 2017, 875 master's awarded. *Degree requirements:* For master's, comprehensive exam (for some programs), thesis optional. *Entrance requirements:* For master's, GRE, MAT or GMAT, minimum GPA of 2.5. Additional exam requirements/recommendations for international students: Required—TOEFL (minimum score 550 paper-based), IELTS (minimum score 6). *Application deadline:* For fall admission, 7/20 for domestic students, 7/10 for international students; for spring admission, 12/1 for domestic students, 11/15 for international students; for summer admission, 4/1 for domestic students, 5/1 for international students. Applications are processed on a rolling basis. Application fee: $25 ($50 for international students). Electronic applications accepted. *Expenses:* Tuition, state resident: full-time $6038. Tuition, nonresident: full-time $8558. *Required fees:* $804. One-time fee: $110 full-time. Tuition and fees vary according to course load. *Financial support:* Career-related internships or fieldwork, Federal Work-Study, scholarships/grants, tuition waivers (full), and unspecified assistantships available. Financial award applicants required to submit FAFSA. *Faculty research:* Alternative certification for teachers, supervision of instruction, instructional leadership, counseling. *Unit head:* Dr. Kim Bloss, Dean, School of Graduate Studies, 870-235-4150, Fax: 870-235-5227, E-mail: kkbloss@saumag.edu. *Application contact:* Shrijana Malakar, Admissions Specialist, 870-235-4150, Fax: 870-235-5227, E-mail: smalakar@saumag.edu.
Website: http://www.saumag.edu/graduate

Southern Connecticut State University, School of Graduate Studies, School of Education, Department of Counseling and School Psychology, New Haven, CT 06515-1355. Offers community counseling (MS); counseling (Diploma); school counseling

(MS); school psychology (MS, Diploma). *Accreditation:* ACA (one or more programs are accredited); NCATE. *Program availability:* Part-time, evening/weekend. *Degree requirements:* For master's, comprehensive exam. *Entrance requirements:* For master's, interview, previous course work in behavioral sciences, minimum QPA of 2.7. Electronic applications accepted.

Southern Methodist University, Annette Caldwell Simmons School of Education and Human Development, Department of Dispute Resolution and Counseling, Dallas, TX 75275. Offers counseling (MS); dispute resolution (MA). *Program availability:* Part-time. *Degree requirements:* For master's, practica experience, 2 internships (counseling). *Entrance requirements:* For master's, minimum undergraduate GPA of 2.75 (for dispute resolution), 3.0 (for counseling); 3 letters of recommendation. Additional exam requirements/recommendations for international students: Required—TOEFL. Electronic applications accepted.

Southern University and Agricultural and Mechanical College, Graduate School, College of Education, Department of Behavioral Studies and Educational Leadership, Baton Rouge, LA 70813. Offers administration and supervision (M Ed); counselor education (MA); educational leadership (M Ed); mental health counseling (MA). *Accreditation:* ACA; NCATE. *Degree requirements:* For master's, comprehensive exam, thesis optional. *Entrance requirements:* For master's, GRE General Test. Additional exam requirements/recommendations for international students: Required—TOEFL (minimum score 525 paper-based). *Faculty research:* Mental health, computer assisted programs, families relations, head start improvements, careers.

Southwestern Oklahoma State University, College of Professional and Graduate Studies, School of Behavioral Sciences and Education, Specialization in Community Counseling, Weatherford, OK 73096-3098. Offers M Ed. M Ed distance learning degree program offered to Oklahoma residents only. *Accreditation:* NCATE. *Program availability:* Part-time, evening/weekend, online learning. *Degree requirements:* For master's, exam. *Entrance requirements:* For master's, GRE General Test or minimum undergraduate GPA of 3.0. Additional exam requirements/recommendations for international students: Required—TOEFL.

Southwestern Oklahoma State University, College of Professional and Graduate Studies, School of Behavioral Sciences and Education, Specialization in School Counseling, Weatherford, OK 73096-3098. Offers M Ed. M Ed distance learning degree program offered to Oklahoma residents only. *Accreditation:* NCATE. *Program availability:* Part-time, evening/weekend, online learning. *Degree requirements:* For master's, exam. *Entrance requirements:* For master's, GRE General Test or minimum undergraduate GPA of 3.0, portfolio. Additional exam requirements/recommendations for international students: Required—TOEFL.

Spalding University, Graduate Studies, College of Education, Programs in Education, Louisville, KY 40203-2188. Offers art teacher education (MAT); business teacher education (MAT); elementary school education (MAT); foreign language (MAT); high school education (MAT); middle school education (MAT); secondary education (MAT); special education (learning and behavioral disorders) (MAT); student guidance counselor (MA); teacher leader (M Ed). *Accreditation:* NCATE. *Program availability:* Part-time, evening/weekend. *Entrance requirements:* For master's, GRE General Test or MAT, interview, letters of recommendation, resume. Additional exam requirements/recommendations for international students: Required—TOEFL (minimum score 535 paper-based). Electronic applications accepted. *Faculty research:* Instructional technology, achievement gap, classroom management, assessment.

Springfield College, Graduate Programs, Programs in Psychology, Springfield, MA 01109-3797. Offers athletic counseling (MS, CAGS); clinical mental health counseling (M Ed, CAGS); counseling psychology (Psy D); general counseling (M Ed); industrial/organizational psychology (M Ed, CAGS); school counseling (M Ed, CAGS); student personnel administration in higher education (M Ed, CAGS). *Accreditation:* APA. *Program availability:* Part-time. *Students:* 192 applicants, 65% accepted, 64 enrolled. In 2017, 56 master's, 5 doctorates awarded. *Degree requirements:* For master's, research project, portfolio; for doctorate, dissertation project, 1500 hours of counseling psychology practicum, full-year internship. *Entrance requirements:* For doctorate, GRE. Additional exam requirements/recommendations for international students: Required—TOEFL (minimum score 550 paper-based); Recommended—IELTS (minimum score 7). *Application deadline:* For fall admission, 1/15 priority date for domestic students, 1/15 for international students; for winter admission, 11/1 for domestic and international students; for spring admission, 11/1 for domestic and international students. Applications are processed on a rolling basis. Application fee: $50. Electronic applications accepted. *Financial support:* Fellowships with partial tuition reimbursements, teaching assistantships with partial tuition reimbursements, career-related internships or fieldwork, Federal Work-Study, institutionally sponsored loans, scholarships/grants, and unspecified assistantships available. Financial award application deadline: 3/1; financial award applicants required to submit FAFSA. *Unit head:* Dr. Allison Cumming-McCann, Chair, 413-748-3025, Fax: 413-748-3854, E-mail: acumming@springfield.edu. *Application contact:* Anne Griffin, Director of Graduate Admissions, 413-748-3225, E-mail: agriffin2@springfield.edu.
Website: http://springfield.edu/programs

State University of New York at New Paltz, Graduate and Extended Learning School, School of Liberal Arts and Sciences, Department of Psychology, New Paltz, NY 12561. Offers clinical mental health counseling (MS); mental health counseling (AC); psychological science (MS); school counseling (MS); trauma and disaster mental health (AC). *Program availability:* Part-time, evening/weekend. *Faculty:* 12 full-time (9 women), 1 (woman) part-time/adjunct. *Students:* 61 full-time (44 women), 19 part-time (15 women); includes 18 minority (2 Black or African American, non-Hispanic/Latino; 1 Asian, non-Hispanic/Latino; 12 Hispanic/Latino; 1 Native Hawaiian or other Pacific Islander, non-Hispanic/Latino; 2 Two or more races, non-Hispanic/Latino). 109 applicants, 57% accepted, 40 enrolled. In 2017, 16 master's awarded. *Degree requirements:* For master's, comprehensive exam, thesis. *Entrance requirements:* For master's, GRE General Test, minimum GPA of 3.0. Additional exam requirements/recommendations for international students: Required—TOEFL (minimum score 550 paper-based; 80 iBT), IELTS (minimum score 6.5). *Application deadline:* For fall admission, 2/1 priority date for domestic and international students; for spring admission, 11/15 priority date for domestic and international students. Application fee: $50. Electronic applications accepted. *Financial support:* In 2017–18, 6 teaching assistantships with partial tuition reimbursements (averaging $5,000 per year) were awarded. Financial award application deadline: 8/1. *Faculty research:* Disaster mental health, women's objectification, mate selection, cultural psychology, achievement motivation. *Unit head:* Dr. Glenn Geher, Chair, 845-257-3091, E-mail: geherg@newpaltz.edu. *Application contact:* Dr. Tabitha Holmes, Program Coordinator, 845-257-3955, E-mail: holmest@newpaltz.edu.
Website: http://www.newpaltz.edu/psychology/

State University of New York at Plattsburgh, School of Education, Health, and Human Services, Department of Counselor Education, Plattsburgh, NY 12901-2681. Offers clinical mental health counseling (MS, Advanced Certificate); school counselor (MS Ed, CAS); student affairs counseling (MS). *Accreditation:* ACA (one or more programs are accredited); TEAC. *Program availability:* Part-time. *Entrance*

requirements: For master's, GRE General Test or MAT, minimum GPA of 2.8. Additional exam requirements/recommendations for international students: Required—TOEFL. *Faculty research:* Campus violence, program accreditation, substance abuse, vocational assessment, group counseling, divorce.

State University of New York College at Oneonta, Graduate Programs, Division of Education, Department of Educational Psychology, Counseling and Special Education, Oneonta, NY 13820-4015. Offers school counselor K-12 (MS Ed, CAS); special education (MS Ed). *Accreditation:* NCATE. *Program availability:* Part-time, evening/weekend. *Degree requirements:* For master's, comprehensive exam. *Entrance requirements:* For master's, GRE General Test.

Stephen F. Austin State University, Graduate School, College of Education, Department of Human Services, Nacogdoches, TX 75962. Offers counseling (MA); school psychology (MA); special education (M Ed); speech-language pathology (MS). *Accreditation:* ACA (one or more programs are accredited); ASHA (one or more programs are accredited); CORE; NCATE. *Degree requirements:* For master's, comprehensive exam, thesis (for some programs). *Entrance requirements:* For master's, GRE General Test, minimum GPA of 2.8. Additional exam requirements/recommendations for international students: Required—TOEFL.

Stephens College, Division of Graduate and Continuing Studies, Columbia, MO 65215-0002. Offers counseling (M Ed), including addictions counseling, clinical mental health counseling, school counseling; health information administration (Postbaccalaureate Certificate); physician assistant studies (MPAS); TV and screenwriting (MFA). *Program availability:* Part-time, evening/weekend, online learning. *Entrance requirements:* For master's, minimum GPA of 3.0 in last 60 hours. Additional exam requirements/recommendations for international students: Required—TOEFL (minimum score 79 iBT). Electronic applications accepted. *Faculty research:* Educational psychology, outcomes assessment.

Stetson University, College of Arts and Sciences, Division of Education, Department of Counselor Education, DeLand, FL 32723. Offers marriage, couple and family counseling (MS); mental health counseling (MS); school counseling (MS). *Accreditation:* ACA. *Program availability:* Evening/weekend. *Faculty:* 6 full-time (5 women), 5 part-time/adjunct (2 women). *Students:* 100 full-time (82 women), 9 part-time (all women); includes 37 minority (9 Black or African American, non-Hispanic/Latino; 4 American Indian or Alaska Native, non-Hispanic/Latino; 15 Hispanic/Latino; 9 Two or more races, non-Hispanic/Latino), 5 international. Average age 30. 42 applicants, 79% accepted, 22 enrolled. In 2017, 24 master's awarded. *Entrance requirements:* For master's, GRE or MAT, transcripts, three letters of recommendation, group interview. Additional exam requirements/recommendations for international students: Required—TOEFL (minimum score 90 iBT), IELTS (minimum score 7). *Application deadline:* For fall admission, 8/1 priority date for domestic students; for spring admission, 1/1 priority date for domestic students; for summer admission, 5/1 priority date for domestic students. Applications are processed on a rolling basis. Application fee: $50. Electronic applications accepted. *Expenses:* $911 per credit hour. *Financial support:* In 2017–18, 29 students received support. Federal Work-Study, scholarships/grants, unspecified assistantships, and tuition waivers (for staff and dependents) available. Support available to part-time students. Financial award applicants required to submit FAFSA. *Faculty research:* Play therapy, trauma, spirituality and wellness in counseling, gatekeeping and supervision in counselor education, reproductive health in counseling, LBGTQ+ issues in counseling. *Unit head:* Dr. Leila Roach, Chair, 386-822-8992. *Application contact:* Jamie Vanderlip, Director of Admissions for Graduate, Transfer and Adult Programs, 386-822-7100, Fax: 386-822-7112, E-mail: jlvander@stetson.edu.

Suffolk University, College of Arts and Sciences, Department of Psychology, Boston, MA 02108-2770. Offers clinical psychology (PhD); college admission counseling (Certificate); mental health counseling (MS); school counseling (MS). *Accreditation:* APA. *Faculty:* 14 full-time (7 women), 3 part-time/adjunct (all women). *Students:* 52 full-time (47 women), 35 part-time (28 women); includes 17 minority (4 Black or African American, non-Hispanic/Latino; 1 Asian, non-Hispanic/Latino; 11 Hispanic/Latino; 1 Two or more races, non-Hispanic/Latino), 7 international. Average age 27. 266 applicants, 23% accepted, 19 enrolled. In 2017, 23 master's, 7 doctorates, 11 other advanced degrees awarded. Terminal master's awarded for partial completion of doctoral program. *Degree requirements:* For master's, practicum, internship; for doctorate, thesis/dissertation, practicum. *Entrance requirements:* For doctorate, GRE General Test or MAT, 2 letters of recommendation, resume. Additional exam requirements/recommendations for international students: Required—TOEFL (minimum score 550 paper-based; 80 iBT). *Application deadline:* For fall admission, 12/1 for domestic and international students. Applications are processed on a rolling basis. Application fee: $50. Electronic applications accepted. *Expenses:* $36,936 per year full-time, $1,539 per credit part-time (for PhD); $15,675 per year full-time, $1,045 per credit part-time (for MS). *Financial support:* In 2017–18, 57 students received support, including 21 fellowships (averaging $17,193 per year); career-related internships or fieldwork, Federal Work-Study, institutionally sponsored loans, scholarships/grants, and unspecified assistantships also available. Support available to part-time students. Financial award application deadline: 4/1; financial award applicants required to submit FAFSA. *Faculty research:* Assessing exposure in the context of a family-based cognitive behavioral treatment for pediatric OCD, a mindfulness approach to designing and testing the efficacy of a new sexual revictimization prevention program for college women, olfaction and decision-making in substance-dependent individuals, the role of experiential avoidance in Generalized Anxiety Disorder, ego development as a predictor of dogmatism and intolerance in the political right and left. *Unit head:* Dr. Amy Marks, Chairperson, 617-573-8017, E-mail: akmarks@suffolk.edu. *Application contact:* Mara Marzocchi, Associate Director of Graduate Admissions, 617-573-8302, Fax: 617-305-1733, E-mail: grad.admission@suffolk.edu.
Website: http://www.suffolk.edu/college/graduate/69299.php

Sul Ross State University, College of Professional Studies, Department of Education, Program in Counseling, Alpine, TX 79832. Offers M Ed. *Program availability:* Part-time, evening/weekend. *Degree requirements:* For master's, thesis optional. *Entrance requirements:* For master's, GMAT or GRE General Test, minimum GPA of 2.5 in last 60 hours of undergraduate work.

Sul Ross State University, Rio Grande College of Sul Ross State University, Alpine, TX 79832. Offers business administration (MBA); teacher education (M Ed), including bilingual education, counseling, educational diagnostics, elementary education, general education, reading, school administration, secondary education. *Program availability:* Part-time, evening/weekend, online learning. *Degree requirements:* For master's, comprehensive exam, thesis optional, minimum GPA of 3.0. *Entrance requirements:* For master's, GMAT or GRE General Test, minimum GPA of 2.5 in last 60 hours of undergraduate work. Additional exam requirements/recommendations for international students: Required—TOEFL.

Syracuse University, School of Education, MS Program in Student Affairs Counseling, Syracuse, NY 13244. Offers MS. *Program availability:* Part-time. *Students:* Average age 28. *Entrance requirements:* For master's, GRE or MAT, baccalaureate degree from regionally-accredited college/university, three letters of recommendation, personal statement, transcripts, interview. Additional exam requirements/recommendations for

international students: Required—TOEFL (minimum score 100 iBT). *Application deadline:* For fall admission, 6/15 priority date for domestic and international students; for spring admission, 10/15 priority date for domestic and international students; for summer admission, 1/15 priority date for domestic and international students. Applications are processed on a rolling basis. Application fee: $75. Electronic applications accepted. *Financial support:* Fellowships with full tuition reimbursements, research assistantships, teaching assistantships, career-related internships or fieldwork, and scholarships/grants available. Financial award application deadline: 1/15. *Faculty research:* Group work in counseling, theories of counseling and psychotherapy, social and cultural dimensions of counseling, life-span human development, assessment in counseling. *Unit head:* Dr. Derek Seward, Professor/Chair of the Department of Counseling and Human Service, 315-443-2266, E-mail: dxseward@syr.edu. *Application contact:* Speranza Migliore, Graduate Admissions Recruiter, 315-443-2505, E-mail: gradrcrt@syr.edu.
Website: http://soe.syr.edu/academic/counseling_and_human_services/graduate/masters/student_affairs_counseling/default.aspx

Syracuse University, School of Education, PhD Program in Counseling and Counselor Education, Syracuse, NY 13244. Offers PhD. *Accreditation:* ACA. *Program availability:* Part-time. *Degree requirements:* For doctorate, comprehensive exam, thesis/dissertation. *Entrance requirements:* For doctorate, GRE including Writing/Analytic Test, master's degree in counseling or rehabilitation counseling, personal interview, three letters of recommendation, transcripts of all undergraduate and graduate study, personal statement. Additional exam requirements/recommendations for international students: Required—TOEFL (minimum score 600 paper-based; 100 iBT), IELTS (minimum score 7). *Application deadline:* For fall admission, 11/1 for domestic and international students. Applications are processed on a rolling basis. Application fee: $75. Electronic applications accepted. *Financial support:* Fellowships with full tuition reimbursements, research assistantships, teaching assistantships with full tuition reimbursements, career-related internships or fieldwork, and scholarships/grants available. Financial award application deadline: 1/15; financial award applicants required to submit FAFSA. *Faculty research:* Clinical supervision, college mental health counseling, counseling people with disabilities, the future professoriate, social justice and urban youth. *Unit head:* Dr. Derek Seward, Chair, 315-443-2266, Fax: 315-443-5732, E-mail: dxseward@syr.edu. *Application contact:* Speranza Migliore, Graduate Admissions Recruiter, 315-443-2505, E-mail: gradrcrt@syr.edu.
Website: http://soe.syr.edu/academic/counseling_and_human_services/graduate/phd/default.aspx

Texas A&M International University, Office of Graduate Studies and Research, College of Education, Department of Professional Programs, Laredo, TX 78041. Offers educational administration (MS Ed); generic special education (MS Ed); school counseling (MS). *Entrance requirements:* Additional exam requirements/recommendations for international students: Required—TOEFL (minimum score 550 paper-based; 79 iBT).

Texas A&M University–Central Texas, Graduate Studies and Research, Killeen, TX 76549. Offers accounting (MS); business administration (MBA); clinical mental health counseling (MS); criminal justice (MCJ); curriculum and instruction (M Ed); educational administration (M Ed); educational psychology - experimental psychology (MS); history (MA); human resource management (MS); information systems (MS); liberal studies (MS); management and leadership (MS); marriage and family therapy (MS); mathematics (MS); political science (MA); school counseling (M Ed); school psychology (Ed S).

Texas A&M University–Commerce, College of Education and Human Services, Commerce, TX 75429. Offers counseling (M Ed, MS, PhD); early childhood education (M Ed, MS); educational administration (M Ed, MS, Ed D); educational psychology (PhD); educational technology leadership (M Ed, MS); educational technology library science (M Ed, MS); elementary education (M Ed); health, kinesiology and sports studies (MS); higher education (M Ed, MS); psychology (MS); reading (M Ed, MS); secondary education (M Ed, MS); social work (MSW); special education (M Ed, MS); supervision, curriculum and instruction-elementary education (Ed D); training and development (MS). *Program availability:* Part-time, evening/weekend, 100% online, blended/hybrid learning. *Faculty:* 91 full-time (51 women), 38 part-time/adjunct (31 women). *Students:* 1,400 full-time (310 women), 1,400 part-time (1,117 women); includes 724 minority (412 Black or African American, non-Hispanic/Latino; 8 American Indian or Alaska Native, non-Hispanic/Latino; 24 Asian, non-Hispanic/Latino; 220 Hispanic/Latino; 60 Two or more races, non-Hispanic/Latino), 18 international. Average age 37. 951 applicants, 46% accepted, 331 enrolled. In 2017, 564 master's, 24 doctorates awarded. *Degree requirements:* For master's, comprehensive exam, thesis optional, departmental qualifying exams (for some programs); for doctorate, comprehensive exam, thesis/dissertation, departmental qualifying exam; for SSP, comprehensive exam, thesis optional. *Entrance requirements:* For master's and doctorate, GRE General Test. Additional exam requirements/recommendations for international students: Required—TOEFL (minimum score 550 paper-based; 79 iBT), IELTS (minimum score 6). *Application deadline:* For fall admission, 6/1 priority date for international students; for spring admission, 10/15 priority date for international students; for summer admission, 3/15 priority date for international students. Applications are processed on a rolling basis. Application fee: $50. Electronic applications accepted. *Expenses:* Tuition, state resident: full-time $3630. Tuition, nonresident: full-time $11,100. *Required fees:* $2564. Tuition and fees vary according to course load, degree level and program. *Financial support:* In 2017–18, 84 students received support, including 40 research assistantships with partial tuition reimbursements available (averaging $10,800 per year), 12 teaching assistantships with partial tuition reimbursements available (averaging $13,000 per year); career-related internships or fieldwork, Federal Work-Study, institutionally sponsored loans, scholarships/grants, health care benefits, and unspecified assistantships also available. Financial award application deadline: 6/15; financial award applicants required to submit FAFSA. *Faculty research:* Cognitive and bilingual education, positive behavioral intervention, literacy, math readiness. *Total annual research expenditures:* $1.1 million. *Unit head:* Dr. Timothy Letzring, Dean, 903-886-5181, Fax: 903-886-5905, E-mail: tim.letzring@tamuc.edu. *Application contact:* Vicky Turner, Doctoral Degree and Special Programs Coordinator, 903-886-5167, E-mail: vicky.turner@tamuc.edu.
Website: http://www.tamuc.edu/academics/graduateSchool/programs/education/default.aspx

Texas A&M University–Corpus Christi, College of Graduate Studies, College of Education and Human Development, Programs in Counseling, Corpus Christi, TX 78412. Offers MS, PhD. *Accreditation:* ACA. *Program availability:* Part-time, evening/weekend. *Students:* 99 full-time (79 women), 71 part-time (57 women); includes 98 minority (15 Black or African American, non-Hispanic/Latino; 1 Asian, non-Hispanic/Latino; 80 Hispanic/Latino; 2 Two or more races, non-Hispanic/Latino). Average age 33. 94 applicants, 56% accepted, 44 enrolled. In 2017, 25 master's, 6 doctorates awarded. *Degree requirements:* For master's, comprehensive exam; for doctorate, comprehensive exam, thesis/dissertation. *Entrance requirements:* For master's, minimum GPA of 3.0 in last 60 hours, essay (approximately 500-700 words in length), 3 letters of recommendation, interview; for doctorate, GRE (taken within 5 years), master's

degree, essay (2 pages), resume, 3 reference forms, interview. Additional exam requirements/recommendations for international students: Required—TOEFL (minimum score 550 paper-based; 79 iBT), IELTS (minimum score 6.5). *Application deadline:* For fall admission, 6/15 priority date for domestic and international students; for spring admission, 10/15 priority date for domestic students, 9/1 priority date for international students; for summer admission, 2/15 priority date for domestic students, 2/1 priority date for international students. Applications are processed on a rolling basis. Application fee: $50 ($70 for international students). Electronic applications accepted. *Expenses:* Tuition, state resident: full-time $3568; part-time $198.24 per credit hour. Tuition, nonresident: full-time $11,038; part-time $613.24 per credit hour. *Required fees:* $2129; $1422.58 per semester. Tuition and fees vary according to program. *Financial support:* Research assistantships, teaching assistantships, career-related internships or fieldwork, Federal Work-Study, institutionally sponsored loans, scholarships/grants, health care benefits, and unspecified assistantships available. Support available to part-time students. Financial award application deadline: 3/15; financial award applicants required to submit FAFSA. *Unit head:* Dr. Robert Smith, Chair, 361-825-2307, E-mail: robert.smith@tamucc.edu. *Application contact:* Graduate Admissions Coordinator, 361-825-2177, Fax: 361-825-2755, E-mail: gradweb@tamucc.edu.
Website: http://cnep.tamucc.edu/

Texas A&M University–Kingsville, College of Graduate Studies, College of Education and Human Performance, Department of Educational Leadership and Counseling, Program in Counseling and Guidance, Kingsville, TX 78363. Offers MA, MS. MS offered jointly with University of North Texas. *Program availability:* Part-time, evening/weekend. *Degree requirements:* For master's, variable foreign language requirement, comprehensive exam, thesis (for some programs). *Entrance requirements:* For master's, GRE, MAT, GMAT, minimum GPA of 2.6. Additional exam requirements/recommendations for international students: Required—TOEFL (minimum score 550 paper-based; 79 iBT). Electronic applications accepted. *Faculty research:* Diagnostician requirements for certification, teaching methods for adult learners.

Texas A&M University–San Antonio, Department of Counseling, Health and Kinesiology, San Antonio, TX 78224. Offers clinical mental health counseling (MA); counseling and guidance (MS); kinesiology (MS); marriage and family counseling (MA). *Program availability:* Part-time, evening/weekend, online learning. *Faculty:* 12 full-time (5 women), 6 part-time/adjunct (4 women). *Students:* 48 full-time (35 women), 146 part-time (118 women); includes 135 minority (24 Black or African American, non-Hispanic/Latino; 3 Asian, non-Hispanic/Latino; 103 Hispanic/Latino; 5 Two or more races, non-Hispanic/Latino), 2 international. Average age 34. 201 applicants, 56% accepted, 62 enrolled. In 2017, 68 master's awarded. *Degree requirements:* For master's, comprehensive exam, thesis or alternative. *Entrance requirements:* For master's, MAT or GRE (composite quantitative and verbal). Additional exam requirements/recommendations for international students: Required—TOEFL (minimum score 550 paper-based; 79 iBT), IELTS (minimum score 6). *Application deadline:* For fall admission, 3/15 priority date for domestic and international students; for spring admission, 11/1 priority date for domestic and international students; for summer admission, 4/1 priority date for domestic and international students. Applications are processed on a rolling basis. Application fee: $35 ($50 for international students). Electronic applications accepted. *Expenses:* Tuition, state resident: full-time $3475; part-time $1930 per semester. Tuition, nonresident: full-time $10,945; part-time $6080 per semester. *Required fees:* $2148; $1412 per year. $706 per semester. Tuition and fees vary according to course load. *Financial support:* In 2017–18, 10 students received support. Federal Work-Study, scholarships/grants, and tuition waivers available. Financial award application deadline: 3/15; financial award applicants required to submit FAFSA. *Unit head:* Dr. Suzanne Mudge, Department Chair. *Application contact:* Caitie Garza, Graduate Admissions Coordinator, 210-784-1300, E-mail: beajaguar@tamusa.edu.
Website: http://www.tamusa.edu/collegeofeducationandhumandevelopment/counselinghealthkinesiology/index.html

Texas Christian University, College of Education, Doctoral Programs in Education, Fort Worth, TX 76129. Offers counseling and counselor education (PhD); curriculum studies (PhD); educational leadership (Ed D); higher educational leadership (Ed D); science education (PhD); MBA/Ed D. *Program availability:* Part-time, evening/weekend. *Faculty:* 29 full-time (21 women), 3 part-time/adjunct (1 woman). *Students:* 80 full-time (57 women), 26 part-time (13 women); includes 41 minority (15 Black or African American, non-Hispanic/Latino; 6 Asian, non-Hispanic/Latino; 17 Hispanic/Latino; 3 Two or more races, non-Hispanic/Latino), 6 international. Average age 39. 109 applicants, 50% accepted, 23 enrolled. In 2017, 12 doctorates awarded. *Degree requirements:* For doctorate, comprehensive exam, thesis/dissertation. *Entrance requirements:* For doctorate, GRE General Test. Additional exam requirements/recommendations for international students: Required—TOEFL (minimum score 550 paper-based; 80 iBT). *Application deadline:* For fall admission, 2/1 for domestic and international students; for winter admission, 2/1 for domestic and international students; for spring admission, 11/16 for domestic and international students. Application fee: $60. Electronic applications accepted. *Financial support:* In 2017–18, 69 students received support, including 1 fellowship with full tuition reimbursement available (averaging $18,500 per year), 8 research assistantships with full tuition reimbursements available (averaging $18,500 per year), 7 teaching assistantships with full tuition reimbursements available (averaging $18,500 per year); career-related internships or fieldwork, scholarships/grants, health care benefits, and unspecified assistantships also available. Support available to part-time students. Financial award application deadline: 2/1. *Unit head:* Dr. Jan Lacina, Associate Dean, 817-257-6786, Fax: 817-257-7466, E-mail: j.lacina@tcu.edu. *Application contact:* Lori Kimball, Administrative Program Specialist, 817-257-7661, Fax: 817-257-7466, E-mail: l.kimball@tcu.edu.
Website: http://coe.tcu.edu/graduate-overview/

Texas Christian University, College of Education, Master's Programs in Education, Fort Worth, TX 76129. Offers counseling (M Ed); curriculum and instruction (M Ed), including curriculum studies, language and literacy, math education, science education; education (MAT); educational leadership (M Ed); special education (M Ed). *Program availability:* Part-time, evening/weekend. *Faculty:* 29 full-time (21 women), 3 part-time/adjunct (1 woman). *Students:* 124 full-time (94 women), 14 part-time (12 women); includes 52 minority (14 Black or African American, non-Hispanic/Latino; 2 American Indian or Alaska Native, non-Hispanic/Latino; 3 Asian, non-Hispanic/Latino; 28 Hispanic/Latino; 5 Two or more races, non-Hispanic/Latino), 1 international. Average age 28. 172 applicants, 69% accepted, 86 enrolled. In 2017, 62 master's awarded. *Degree requirements:* For master's, comprehensive exam (for some programs), thesis (for some programs). *Entrance requirements:* For master's, GRE General Test; Pre-Admission Content Test (for MAT). Additional exam requirements/recommendations for international students: Required—TOEFL (minimum score 550 paper-based; 80 iBT). *Application deadline:* For fall admission, 3/1 for domestic and international students; for spring admission, 11/16 for domestic and international students; for summer admission, 3/1 for domestic and international students. Application fee: $60. Electronic applications accepted. *Financial support:* In 2017–18, 124 students received support, including 1 research assistantship with full tuition reimbursement available (averaging $15,000 per year), 29 teaching assistantships with full tuition reimbursements available (averaging $15,000 per year); career-related internships or fieldwork, scholarships/grants, and

unspecified assistantships also available. Support available to part-time students. Financial award application deadline: 3/1. *Unit head:* Dr. Jan Lacina, Associate Dean, 817-257-6786, Fax: 817-257-7466, E-mail: j.lacina@tcu.edu. *Application contact:* Lori Kimball, Administrative Program Specialist, 817-257-7661, Fax: 817-257-7466, E-mail: l.kimball@tcu.edu.
Website: http://coe.tcu.edu/graduate-overview/

Texas Southern University, College of Education, Department of Counselor Education, Houston, TX 77004-4584. Offers counseling (M Ed); counselor education (Ed D). *Program availability:* Part-time, evening/weekend. *Degree requirements:* For master's, one foreign language, comprehensive exam; for doctorate, comprehensive exam, thesis/dissertation. *Entrance requirements:* For master's, GRE General Test, minimum GPA of 2.5; for doctorate, GRE General Test or MAT, master's degree, minimum B+ average. Additional exam requirements/recommendations for international students: Required—TOEFL. Electronic applications accepted. *Faculty research:* Clinical and urban psychology.

Texas State University, The Graduate College, College of Education, Program in Professional Counseling, San Marcos, TX 78666. Offers clinical mental health counseling (MA); marriage and family counseling (MA); school counseling (MA). *Accreditation:* ACA. *Program availability:* Part-time. *Faculty:* 12 full-time (11 women), 12 part-time/adjunct (9 women). *Students:* 87 full-time (71 women), 99 part-time (80 women); includes 49 minority (6 Black or African American, non-Hispanic/Latino; 6 Asian, non-Hispanic/Latino; 30 Hispanic/Latino; 7 Two or more races, non-Hispanic/Latino). Average age 31. 144 applicants, 46% accepted, 23 enrolled. In 2017, 57 master's awarded. *Degree requirements:* For master's, comprehensive exam, thesis optional, internship. *Entrance requirements:* For master's, GRE General Test (minimum preferred score of 291 [150 verbal, 141 quantitative]), baccalaureate degree from regionally-accredited institution with minimum GPA of 3.0 in last 60 hours of undergraduate work; resume; statement of purpose addressing professional goals, reasoning for specified emphasis (i.e., community, school, marital), strengths and weaknesses, and perspective on diversity; 3 references. Additional exam requirements/recommendations for international students: Required—TOEFL (minimum iBT scores: 22 listening, 22 reading, 24 speaking, 21 writing). *Application deadline:* For fall admission, 2/15 for domestic and international students; for spring admission, 10/1 for domestic and international students; for summer admission, 2/15 for domestic and international students. Applications are processed on a rolling basis. Application fee: $40 ($90 for international students). Electronic applications accepted. *Expenses:* Tuition, state resident: full-time $7868; part-time $3934 per semester. Tuition, nonresident: full-time 17,828; part-time $8914 per semester. *Required fees:* $2092; $1435 per semester. Tuition and fees vary according to course load. *Financial support:* In 2017–18, 97 students received support, including 11 research assistantships (averaging $7,298 per year); teaching assistantships, Federal Work-Study, institutionally sponsored loans, and scholarships/grants also available. Support available to part-time students. Financial award application deadline: 3/1; financial award applicants required to submit FAFSA. *Unit head:* Dr. Kevin Fall, Graduate Advisor, 512-245-2081, Fax: 512-245-8872, E-mail: kf22@txstate.edu. *Application contact:* Dr. Andrea Golato, Dean of Graduate School, 512-245-2581, Fax: 512-245-8365, E-mail: gradcollege@txstate.edu.
Website: http://www.gradcollege.txstate.edu/programs/counseling.html

Texas Tech University, Graduate School, College of Education, Department of Educational Psychology and Leadership, Lubbock, TX 79409. Offers counselor education (M Ed, PhD); educational leadership (M Ed, Ed D, PhD); educational psychology (M Ed, PhD); higher education (M Ed); higher education administration (Ed D); higher education research (PhD); instructional technology (M Ed, Ed D); special education (M Ed, Ed D, PhD). *Accreditation:* ACA; NCATE. *Program availability:* Part-time, evening/weekend. *Faculty:* 64 full-time (30 women), 6 part-time/adjunct (4 women). *Students:* 263 full-time (193 women), 637 part-time (490 women); includes 307 minority (84 Black or African American, non-Hispanic/Latino; 3 American Indian or Alaska Native, non-Hispanic/Latino; 4 Asian, non-Hispanic/Latino; 193 Hispanic/Latino; 23 Two or more races, non-Hispanic/Latino), 48 international. Average age 36. 510 applicants, 47% accepted, 185 enrolled. In 2017, 209 master's, 64 doctorates awarded. Terminal master's awarded for partial completion of doctoral program. *Degree requirements:* For master's, comprehensive exam, thesis optional; for doctorate, comprehensive exam, thesis/dissertation. *Entrance requirements:* For master's, GRE (for some programs); for doctorate, GRE. Additional exam requirements/recommendations for international students: Required—TOEFL (minimum score 550 paper-based; 79 iBT). *Application deadline:* For fall admission, 6/1 priority date for domestic students, 1/15 priority date for international students; for spring admission, 9/1 priority date for domestic students, 6/15 priority date for international students. Applications are processed on a rolling basis. Application fee: $60. Electronic applications accepted. *Expenses:* Contact institution. *Financial support:* In 2017–18, 366 students received support, including 360 fellowships (averaging $3,231 per year), 63 research assistantships (averaging $11,899 per year); teaching assistantships, scholarships/grants, and unspecified assistantships also available. Support available to part-time students. Financial award application deadline: 1/3; financial award applicants required to submit FAFSA. *Faculty research:* Cognitive, motivational, and developmental processes in learning; counseling education; instructional technology; generic special education and sensory impairment; community college administration; K-12 school administration. *Total annual research expenditures:* $127,956. *Unit head:* Dr. Hansel Burley, Chair, 806-834-5135, Fax: 806-742-2179, E-mail: hansel.burley@ttu.edu. *Application contact:* Pam Smith, Admissions Advisor, 806-834-2969, Fax: 806-742-2179, E-mail: pam.smith@ttu.edu.
Website: http://www.educ.ttu.edu/

Texas Woman's University, Graduate School, College of Professional Education, Department of Family Sciences, Denton, TX 76204. Offers child development (MS); child life (MS); counseling and development (MS); early childhood development and education (PhD); early childhood education (M Ed); family studies (MS, PhD); family therapy (MS, PhD). *Accreditation:* ACA (one or more programs are accredited). *Program availability:* Part-time, evening/weekend. *Faculty:* 24 full-time (19 women), 17 part-time/adjunct (15 women). *Students:* 153 full-time (146 women), 237 part-time (220 women); includes 169 minority (81 Black or African American, non-Hispanic/Latino; 9 Asian, non-Hispanic/Latino; 68 Hispanic/Latino; 11 Two or more races, non-Hispanic/Latino), 10 international. Average age 32. 235 applicants, 55% accepted, 87 enrolled. In 2017, 77 master's, 15 doctorates awarded. Terminal master's awarded for partial completion of doctoral program. *Degree requirements:* For master's, comprehensive exam (for some programs), thesis, professional paper, or coursework; practicums (for some programs); for doctorate, comprehensive exam, thesis/dissertation. *Entrance requirements:* For master's, GRE with preferred minimum score 147 Verbal, 144 Quantitative, 4.0 Analytical (for MS in child development and M Ed), minimum GPA of 3.0 (3.25 for family therapy), 3 letters of recommendations (1 for child life), letter of intent, curriculum vitae/resume, interview, writing sample; for doctorate, GRE (preferred minimum score 147 Verbal, 144 Quantitative, 4.0 Analytical), minimum GPA of 3.5 (3.35 for family studies) on all prior graduate work, curriculum vitae/resume, letter of intent. Additional exam requirements/recommendations for international students: Required—TOEFL (minimum score 550 paper-based; 79 iBT); Recommended—IELTS (minimum score 6.5), TSE (minimum score 53). *Application deadline:* For fall admission, 3/1 priority date for domestic and international students; for spring admission, 11/1 priority date for domestic students, 7/1 priority date for international students. Applications are processed on a rolling basis. Application fee: $50 ($75 for international students). Electronic applications accepted. *Expenses:* $7,520 per year full-time in-state; $16,820 per year full-time out-of-state. *Financial support:* In 2017–18, 104 students received support, including 12 teaching assistantships (averaging $22,972 per year); career-related internships or fieldwork, Federal Work-Study, institutionally sponsored loans, scholarships/grants, traineeships, health care benefits, and unspecified assistantships also available. Support available to part-time students. Financial award application deadline: 3/1; financial award applicants required to submit FAFSA. *Faculty research:* Parenting/parent education, play therapy, healthy relationships, child development, technology integration. *Unit head:* Dr. Jerry Whitworth, Interim Chair, 940-898-2685, Fax: 940-898-2676, E-mail: famsci@twu.edu. *Application contact:* Korie Hawkins, Associate Director of Admissions, Graduate Recruitment, 940-898-3188, Fax: 940-898-3081, E-mail: admissions@twu.edu.
Website: http://www.twu.edu/family-sciences/

Trevecca Nazarene University, Graduate Counseling Program, Nashville, TN 37210-2877. Offers clinical counseling: teaching and supervision (PhD); clinical mental health counseling (MA); marriage and family counseling/therapy (MMFC/T). *Accreditation:* ACA. *Program availability:* Part-time, evening/weekend. *Faculty:* 7 full-time (3 women), 11 part-time/adjunct (8 women). *Students:* 157 full-time (129 women), 73 part-time (50 women); includes 49 minority (38 Black or African American, non-Hispanic/Latino; 5 Hispanic/Latino; 6 Two or more races, non-Hispanic/Latino). Average age 35. In 2017, 47 master's, 3 doctorates awarded. *Degree requirements:* For master's, comprehensive exam; for doctorate, comprehensive exam, thesis/dissertation. *Entrance requirements:* For master's, MAT (minimum score of 380) or GRE (minimum score of 290 combined verbal and quantitative), minimum GPA of 2.7, official transcript from regionally accredited institution, 2 reference assessment forms; for doctorate, GRE (minimum scores: 300 combined verbal and quantitative, 3.5 analytical writing), minimum GPA of 3.25, official transcript of master's degree from regionally accredited institution, 3 recommendation forms, 400-word letter of intent, professional vita, interview. Additional exam requirements/recommendations for international students: Required—TOEFL (minimum score 600 paper-based; 100 iBT). *Application deadline:* Applications are processed on a rolling basis. Application fee: $0. Electronic applications accepted. *Expenses:* $636 per credit hour (MA and MMFC/T); $799 per credit hour (PhD). *Financial support:* Applicants required to submit FAFSA. *Unit head:* Dr. Susan Lahey, Director, 615-248-1384, Fax: 615-248-1662, E-mail: admissions_gradcouns@trevecca.edu. *Application contact:* 615-248-1384, Fax: 615-248-1662, E-mail: admissions_gradcouns@trevecca.edu.
Website: http://trevecca.edu/gradcounseling

Trinity Washington University, School of Education, Washington, DC 20017-1094. Offers clinical mental health counseling (MA); early childhood education (MAT); educating for change (M Ed); educational administration (MSA); elementary education (MAT); reading (M Ed); school counseling (MA); secondary education (MAT), including English, social studies; special education (MAT). *Accreditation:* NCATE. *Program availability:* Part-time, evening/weekend. *Degree requirements:* For master's, thesis (for some programs), capstone project(s). *Entrance requirements:* For master's, PRAXIS I, minimum GPA of 2.8. Additional exam requirements/recommendations for international students: Required—TOEFL (minimum score 550 paper-based). *Faculty research:* Technology, literacy, special education, organizations, inclusion models.

Troy University, Graduate School, College of Education, Program in Counseling and Psychology, Troy, AL 36082. Offers community counseling (MS). *Accreditation:* ACA; CORE; NCATE. *Program availability:* Part-time, evening/weekend. *Faculty:* 7 full-time (4 women), 1 (woman) part-time/adjunct. *Students:* 326 full-time (266 women), 350 part-time (302 women); includes 546 minority (213 Black or African American, non-Hispanic/Latino; 4 American Indian or Alaska Native, non-Hispanic/Latino; 1 Asian, non-Hispanic/Latino; 21 Hispanic/Latino; 12 Native Hawaiian or other Pacific Islander, non-Hispanic/Latino; 295 Two or more races, non-Hispanic/Latino). Average age 32. 196 applicants, 96% accepted, 117 enrolled. In 2017, 255 master's, 13 other advanced degrees awarded. *Degree requirements:* For master's, comprehensive exam, thesis. *Entrance requirements:* For master's, GRE (minimum score of 850 on old exam or 290 on new exam), GMAT (minimum score of 380), or MAT (minimum score of 385), bachelor's degree; minimum undergraduate GPA of 2.5 or 3.0 on last 30 semester hours, letter of recommendation. Additional exam requirements/recommendations for international students: Required—TOEFL (minimum score 523 paper-based; 70 iBT), IELTS (minimum score 6). *Application deadline:* Applications are processed on a rolling basis. Application fee: $50. Electronic applications accepted. *Expenses:* Tuition, state resident: part-time $417 per credit hour. Tuition, nonresident: part-time $834 per credit hour. *Required fees:* $42 per credit hour. $50 per semester. Tuition and fees vary according to campus/location. *Financial support:* Fellowships, career-related internships or fieldwork, and scholarships/grants available. Support available to part-time students. *Unit head:* Dr. Andrew Creamer, Chair, 334-670-3350, Fax: 334-670-3291, E-mail: acreamer@troy.edu. *Application contact:* Jessica A. Kimbro, Director of Graduate Admissions, 334-670-3178, E-mail: jacord@troy.edu.

Troy University, Graduate School, College of Education, Program in School Counseling, Troy, AL 36082. Offers MS, Ed S. *Accreditation:* ACA; CORE; NCATE. *Program availability:* Part-time, evening/weekend. *Faculty:* 22 full-time (12 women), 13 part-time/adjunct (8 women). *Students:* 17 full-time (16 women), 30 part-time (27 women); includes 24 minority (all Black or African American, non-Hispanic/Latino). Average age 34. 13 applicants, 92% accepted, 4 enrolled. In 2017, 5 master's, 3 other advanced degrees awarded. *Degree requirements:* For master's, comprehensive exam, thesis. *Entrance requirements:* For master's, GRE (minimum score of 850 on old exam or 290 on new exam), GMAT (minimum score of 380), or MAT (minimum score of 385), bachelor's degree, minimum undergraduate GPA of 2.5 or 3.0 on last 30 semester hours, letter of recommendation, teaching certification, 2 years of teaching experience. Additional exam requirements/recommendations for international students: Required—TOEFL (minimum score 523 paper-based; 70 iBT), IELTS (minimum score 6). *Application deadline:* Applications are processed on a rolling basis. Application fee: $50. Electronic applications accepted. *Expenses:* Tuition, state resident: part-time $417 per credit hour. Tuition, nonresident: part-time $834 per credit hour. *Required fees:* $42 per credit hour. $50 per semester. Tuition and fees vary according to campus/location. *Financial support:* Fellowships, career-related internships or fieldwork, and scholarships/grants available. Support available to part-time students. *Unit head:* Dr. Andrew Creamer, Chair, 334-670-3350, Fax: 334-670-3291, E-mail: drcreamer@troy.edu. *Application contact:* Jessica A. Kimbro, Director of Graduate Admissions, 334-670-3178, E-mail: jacord@troy.edu.

Universidad del Turabo, Graduate Programs, Programs in Education, Program in Counseling, Gurabo, PR 00778-3030. Offers M Ed. *Program availability:* Part-time, evening/weekend. *Entrance requirements:* For master's, GRE, EXADEP, GMAT, interview, official transcript, essay, recommendation letters. Electronic applications accepted.

Université de Moncton, Faculty of Education, Graduate Studies in Education, Moncton, NB E1A 3E9, Canada. Offers educational psychology (M Ed, MA Ed);

guidance (M Ed, MA Ed); school administration (M Ed, MA Ed); teaching (M Ed, MA Ed). *Program availability:* Part-time. *Degree requirements:* For master's, proficiency in English and French. *Entrance requirements:* For master's, minimum GPA of 3.0. *Faculty research:* Guidance, ethnolinguistic vitality, children's rights, ecological education, entrepreneurship.

Université Laval, Faculty of Education, Department of Foundations and Interventions in Education, Programs in Orientation Sciences, Québec, QC G1K 7P4, Canada. Offers MA, PhD. Terminal master's awarded for partial completion of doctoral program. *Degree requirements:* For master's, thesis (for some programs); for doctorate, comprehensive exam, thesis/dissertation. *Entrance requirements:* For master's, English test (comprehension of written English), knowledge of French; for doctorate, oral exam (subject of thesis), knowledge of French and English. Electronic applications accepted. *Faculty research:* Counseling psychology, psychological education, vocational guidance, growth and development.

University at Buffalo, the State University of New York, Graduate School, Graduate School of Education, Department of Counseling, School, and Educational Psychology, Buffalo, NY 14260. Offers applied statistical analysis (Advanced Certificate); counseling/ school psychology (PhD); counselor education (PhD); education studies (Ed M); educational psychology (MA, PhD); mental health counseling (MS, Certificate); mindful counseling for wellness and engagement (Advanced Certificate); rehabilitation counseling (MS, Advanced Certificate); school counseling (Ed M, Certificate). *Accreditation:* CORE (one or more programs are accredited). *Program availability:* Part-time, 100% online. *Faculty:* 21 full-time (11 women), 53 part-time/adjunct (41 women). *Students:* 173 full-time (140 women), 138 part-time (116 women); includes 32 minority (25 Black or African American, non-Hispanic/Latino; 2 American Indian or Alaska Native, non-Hispanic/Latino; 2 Asian, non-Hispanic/Latino; 3 Hispanic/Latino), 16 international. Average age 32. 328 applicants, 59% accepted, 143 enrolled. In 2017, 74 master's, 12 doctorates, 39 other advanced degrees awarded. *Degree requirements:* For master's, comprehensive exam (for some programs), thesis (for some programs); for doctorate, comprehensive exam, thesis/dissertation. *Entrance requirements:* For master's, GRE General Test, interview, letters of reference; for doctorate, GRE General Test, interview, letters of reference, writing sample. Additional exam requirements/recommendations for international students: Required—TOEFL (minimum score 79 iBT). *Application deadline:* For fall admission, 2/1 priority date for domestic and international students. Application fee: $50. Electronic applications accepted. *Financial support:* In 2017–18, 22 fellowships (averaging $7,823 per year), 41 research assistantships with tuition reimbursements (averaging $10,876 per year) were awarded; teaching assistantships, career-related internships or fieldwork, Federal Work-Study, institutionally sponsored loans, scholarships/grants, tuition waivers (full and partial), and unspecified assistantships also available. Financial award application deadline: 2/1; financial award applicants required to submit FAFSA. *Faculty research:* Multicultural counseling, class size effects, good work in counseling, eating disorders, outcome assessment, change agents and therapeutic factors in group counseling. *Total annual research expenditures:* $1.3 million. *Unit head:* Dr. Jeremy Finn, Chair, 716-645-1126, Fax: 716-645-6616, E-mail: finn@buffalo.edu. *Application contact:* Baylee Richards, Recruitment and Student Services Coordinator, 716-645-2110, Fax: 716-645-7937, E-mail: gse-info@buffalo.edu.
Website: http://gse.buffalo.edu/csep

The University of Akron, Graduate School, College of Health Professions, School of Counseling, Program in Counselor Education and Supervision, Akron, OH 44325. Offers PhD. *Accreditation:* ACA. *Students:* 10 full-time (9 women), 14 part-time (12 women); includes 7 minority (6 Black or African American, non-Hispanic/Latino; 1 Asian, non-Hispanic/Latino). Average age 35. 13 applicants, 54% accepted, 4 enrolled. In 2017, 3 doctorates awarded. *Degree requirements:* For doctorate, comprehensive exam, thesis/ dissertation, written and oral exams. *Entrance requirements:* For doctorate, GRE, minimum GPA of 3.25 on all completed graduate coursework, three letters of recommendation, professional resume, interview. Additional exam requirements/ recommendations for international students: Required—TOEFL (minimum score 79 iBT), IELTS (minimum score 6.5). *Application deadline:* For fall admission, 1/15 for domestic and international students. Application fee: $45 ($70 for international students). Electronic applications accepted. *Unit head:* Dr. Varunee Faii Sangganjanavanich, Interim School Director, 339-972-6851, E-mail: vfs@uakron.edu.
Website: http://www.uakron.edu/soc/doctoral/counselor-education/

The University of Akron, Graduate School, College of Health Professions, School of Counseling, Program in School Counseling, Akron, OH 44325. Offers MA, MS. *Accreditation:* ACA; NCATE. *Students:* 23 full-time (19 women), 23 part-time (14 women); includes 12 minority (9 Black or African American, non-Hispanic/Latino; 1 Asian, non-Hispanic/Latino; 1 Hispanic/Latino; 1 Two or more races, non-Hispanic/ Latino), 1 international. Average age 29. 16 applicants, 63% accepted, 4 enrolled. In 2017, 26 master's awarded. *Degree requirements:* For master's, comprehensive exam. *Entrance requirements:* For master's, minimum GPA of 2.75, three letters of recommendation, Bureau of Criminal Investigation clearance, interview. Additional exam requirements/recommendations for international students: Required—TOEFL (minimum score 79 iBT), IELTS (minimum score 6.5). *Application deadline:* For fall admission, 3/15 for domestic and international students; for spring admission, 10/1 for domestic and international students. Application fee: $45 ($70 for international students). Electronic applications accepted. *Unit head:* Dr. Varunee Faii Sangganjanavanich, Interim School Director, 330-972-6851, E-mail: vfs@uakron.edu. *Application contact:* Dr. Delila Owens, Program Coordinator, 330-972-8635, E-mail: dowens1@uakron.edu.
Website: http://www.uakron.edu/soc/masters/school-counseling/

The University of Alabama, Graduate School, College of Education, Department of Educational Studies in Psychology, Research Methodology and Counseling, Tuscaloosa, AL 35487. Offers MA, Ed D, PhD, Ed S. *Accreditation:* ACA (one or more programs are accredited); CORE; NCATE. *Program availability:* Part-time. *Faculty:* 32 full-time (18 women), 1 part-time/adjunct (0 women). *Students:* 118 full-time (93 women), 100 part-time (90 women); includes 70 minority (50 Black or African American, non-Hispanic/Latino; 6 Asian, non-Hispanic/Latino; 11 Hispanic/Latino; 3 Two or more races, non-Hispanic/Latino), 18 international. Average age 34. 165 applicants, 65% accepted, 64 enrolled. In 2017, 42 master's, 10 doctorates, 4 other advanced degrees awarded. *Degree requirements:* For master's, comprehensive exam, thesis optional; for doctorate, comprehensive exam, thesis/dissertation; for Ed S, comprehensive exam. *Entrance requirements:* For master's and doctorate, GRE General Test, MAT, or NTE, minimum GPA of 3.0; for Ed S, minimum GPA of 3.0 during previous 2 years. Additional exam requirements/recommendations for international students: Required—TOEFL (minimum score 550 paper-based), IELTS (minimum score 6.5). *Application deadline:* For fall admission, 7/1 for domestic students; for spring admission, 11/1 for domestic students. Applications are processed on a rolling basis. Application fee: $50 ($60 for international students). Electronic applications accepted. *Financial support:* In 2017–18, 32 students received support. Research assistantships with tuition reimbursements available, teaching assistantships with tuition reimbursements available, and career-related internships or fieldwork available. Financial award application deadline: 7/14; financial award applicants required to submit FAFSA. *Faculty research:* Moral development, positive psychology, children's fears, digital storytelling. *Total annual research expenditures:* $11,905. *Unit head:* Dr. Aaron Kuntz, Department Head, 205-348-5675, E-mail: amkuntz@ua.edu. *Application contact:* Marie S. Marshall, Office Associate II, 205-348-8362, Fax: 205-348-0683, E-mail: mmarshal@bamaed.ua.edu.
Website: http://education.ua.edu/departments/esprmc/

The University of Alabama at Birmingham, School of Education, Program in Counseling, Birmingham, AL 35294. Offers MA. *Accreditation:* ACA; CORE; NCATE. *Degree requirements:* For master's, comprehensive exam, thesis optional, practicum, internship. *Entrance requirements:* For master's, GRE General Test or MAT, minimum GPA of 2.75, interview. Electronic applications accepted.

University of Alaska Anchorage, College of Education, Program in Counseling and Guidance, Anchorage, AK 99508. Offers M Ed. *Program availability:* Part-time. *Entrance requirements:* For master's, GRE or MAT, interview, resume. Additional exam requirements/recommendations for international students: Required—TOEFL (minimum score 550 paper-based).

University of Alaska Fairbanks, School of Education, Program in Counseling, Fairbanks, AK 99775-7480. Offers community counseling (M Ed). *Program availability:* 100% online, blended/hybrid learning. *Degree requirements:* For master's, comprehensive exam, oral defense of project or thesis. *Entrance requirements:* For master's, bachelor's degree from accredited institution with minimum cumulative undergraduate and major GPA of 3.0; for Graduate Certificate, master's degree from accredited institution with minimum GPA of 3.0. Additional exam requirements/ recommendations for international students: Required—TOEFL (minimum score 550 paper-based; 79 iBT), IELTS (minimum score 6.5). Electronic applications accepted.

University of Alberta, Faculty of Graduate Studies and Research, Department of Educational Psychology, Edmonton, AB T6G 2E1, Canada. Offers counseling psychology (M Ed, PhD); educational psychology (M Ed, PhD); instructional technology (M Ed); school counseling (M Ed); school psychology (M Ed, PhD); special education (M Ed, PhD); special education-deafness studies (M Ed); teaching English as a second language (M Ed). *Program availability:* Part-time. *Degree requirements:* For master's, thesis optional; for doctorate, comprehensive exam, thesis/dissertation. *Entrance requirements:* For master's and doctorate, minimum GPA of 3.0. Additional exam requirements/recommendations for international students: Required—TOEFL. *Faculty research:* Human learning, development and assessment.

The University of Arizona, College of Education, Department of Disability and Psychoeducational Studies, Program in School Counseling, Tucson, AZ 85721. Offers MA. *Accreditation:* ACA. *Program availability:* Part-time. *Degree requirements:* For master's, presentation or thesis. *Entrance requirements:* Additional exam requirements/ recommendations for international students: Required—TOEFL (minimum score 550 paper-based; 79 iBT). Electronic applications accepted.

University of Arkansas, Graduate School, College of Education and Health Professions, Department of Rehabilitation, Human Resources and Communication Disorders, Program in Counselor Education, Fayetteville, AR 72701. Offers MS, PhD. *Accreditation:* ACA; NCATE. *Program availability:* Part-time, evening/weekend. *Students:* 130 part-time (96 women); includes 30 minority (9 Black or African American, non-Hispanic/Latino; 4 American Indian or Alaska Native, non-Hispanic/Latino; 2 Asian, non-Hispanic/Latino; 10 Hispanic/Latino; 5 Two or more races, non-Hispanic/Latino), 3 international. In 2017, 21 master's awarded. *Degree requirements:* For master's, thesis optional; for doctorate, thesis/dissertation. *Entrance requirements:* For master's, GRE General Test or MAT; for doctorate, GRE General Test. *Application deadline:* For fall admission, 8/1 for domestic students, 4/1 for international students; for spring admission, 12/1 for domestic students, 10/1 for international students; for summer admission, 4/15 for domestic students, 3/1 for international students. Applications are processed on a rolling basis. Application fee: $60. Electronic applications accepted. *Expenses:* Tuition, state resident: full-time $3782. Tuition, nonresident: full-time $10,238. *Financial support:* In 2017–18, 15 research assistantships, 2 teaching assistantships were awarded; fellowships with tuition reimbursements, career-related internships or fieldwork, and Federal Work-Study also available. Support available to part-time students. Financial award application deadline: 4/1; financial award applicants required to submit FAFSA. *Unit head:* Dr. Kristin Higgins, Program Coordinator, 479-575-3329, E-mail: kkhiggi@uark.edu. *Application contact:* Dr. Kristin Higgins, Graduate Coordinator, 479-575-3329, E-mail: kkhiggi@uark.edu.
Website: http://cned.uark.edu

University of Arkansas at Little Rock, Graduate School, College of Education and Health Professions, Department of Counseling, Adult and Rehabilitation Education, Program in Counselor Education, Little Rock, AR 72204-1099. Offers M Ed. *Program availability:* Part-time, evening/weekend. *Degree requirements:* For master's, comprehensive exam, portfolio or thesis; PRAXIS II. *Entrance requirements:* For master's, minimum GPA of 2.75, teaching certificate, interview, current resume.

University of Central Arkansas, Graduate School, College of Education, Department of Leadership Studies, Program in School Counseling, Conway, AR 72035-0001. Offers MS. *Accreditation:* NCATE. *Program availability:* Part-time, evening/weekend, online learning. *Degree requirements:* For master's, comprehensive exam, thesis optional. *Entrance requirements:* For master's, GRE General Test, minimum GPA of 2.7. Additional exam requirements/recommendations for international students: Required—TOEFL (minimum score 550 paper-based). Electronic applications accepted.

University of Central Florida, College of Community Innovation and Education, Department of Counselor Education and School Psychology, Program in Counselor Education, Orlando, FL 32816. Offers M Ed, MA, Certificate, Ed S. *Accreditation:* ACA. *Program availability:* Part-time, evening/weekend. *Students:* 147 full-time (122 women), 50 part-time (45 women); includes 74 minority (18 Black or African American, non-Hispanic/Latino; 7 Asian, non-Hispanic/Latino; 44 Hispanic/Latino; 5 Two or more races, non-Hispanic/Latino), 2 international. Average age 26. 202 applicants, 51% accepted, 64 enrolled. In 2017, 56 master's, 8 other advanced degrees awarded. *Degree requirements:* For master's, comprehensive exam, thesis or alternative. *Entrance requirements:* For master's, GRE General Test, minimum GPA of 3.0, letters of recommendation, resume, goal statement. Additional exam requirements/ recommendations for international students: Required—TOEFL. *Application deadline:* For fall admission, 2/15 for domestic students; for spring admission, 9/1 for domestic students. Application fee: $30. Electronic applications accepted. *Expenses:* Tuition, state resident: part-time $288.16 per credit hour. Tuition, nonresident: part-time $1073.31 per credit hour. Tuition and fees vary according to program. *Financial support:* In 2017–18, 16 students received support, including 5 fellowships with partial tuition reimbursements available (averaging $4,631 per year), 10 research assistantships with partial tuition reimbursements available (averaging $6,458 per year), 4 teaching assistantships with partial tuition reimbursements available (averaging $9,233 per year); career-related internships or fieldwork, Federal Work-Study, institutionally sponsored loans, tuition waivers (partial), and unspecified assistantships also available. Financial award application deadline: 3/1; financial award applicants required to submit FAFSA. *Unit head:* Dr. W. Bryce Hagedorn, Program Coordinator, 407-823-2401, E-mail: bryce.hagedorn@ucf.edu. *Application contact:* Associate Director, Graduate Admissions, 407-823-2766, Fax: 407-823-6442, E-mail: gradadmissions@ucf.edu.
Website: http://education.ucf.edu/counselored/

Counselor Education

University of Central Florida, College of Community Innovation and Education, Education Doctoral Programs, Orlando, FL 32816. Offers curriculum and instruction (Ed D); education (PhD), including communication sciences and disorders, counselor education, early childhood education, elementary education, exceptional education, exercise physiology, higher education, instructional design and technology, mathematics education, methodology, measurement and analysis, reading education, science education, social science education, TESOL; educational leadership (Ed D). *Students:* 122 full-time (86 women), 129 part-time (88 women); includes 64 minority (24 Black or African American, non-Hispanic/Latino; 1 American Indian or Alaska Native, non-Hispanic/Latino; 9 Asian, non-Hispanic/Latino; 24 Hispanic/Latino; 6 Two or more races, non-Hispanic/Latino), 26 international. Average age 38. 195 applicants, 47% accepted, 72 enrolled. In 2017, 89 doctorates awarded. *Entrance requirements:* For doctorate, GRE, letters of recommendation, goal statement, resume, writing sample. Application fee: $30. Electronic applications accepted. *Expenses:* Tuition, state resident: part-time $288.16 per credit hour. Tuition, nonresident: part-time $1073.31 per credit hour. Tuition and fees vary according to program. *Financial support:* In 2017–18, 77 students received support, including 28 fellowships with partial tuition reimbursements available (averaging $5,733 per year), 29 research assistantships with partial tuition reimbursements available (averaging $10,230 per year), 54 teaching assistantships with partial tuition reimbursements available (averaging $11,614 per year); health care benefits also available. Financial award application deadline: 3/1; financial award applicants required to submit FAFSA. *Unit head:* Dr. Edward Robinson, Director of Doctoral Programs, 407-823-6106, E-mail: edward.robinson@ucf.edu. *Application contact:* Associate Director, Graduate Admissions, 407-823-2766, Fax: 407-823-6442, E-mail: gradadmissions@ucf.edu.
Website: https://edcollege.ucf.edu/academic-programs/graduate/

University of Central Missouri, The Graduate School, Warrensburg, MO 64093. Offers accountancy (MA); accounting (MBA); applied mathematics (MS); aviation safety (MA); biology (MS); business administration (MBA); career and technical education leadership (MS); college student personnel administration (MS); communication (MA); computer science (MS); counseling (MS); criminal justice (MS); educational leadership (Ed D); educational technology (MS); elementary and early childhood education (MSE); English (MA); environmental studies (MA); finance (MBA); history (MA); human services/educational technology (Ed S); human services/learning resources (Ed S); human services/professional counseling (Ed S); industrial hygiene (MS); industrial management (MS); information systems (MBA); information technology (MS); kinesiology (MS); library science and information services (MS); literacy education (MSE); marketing (MBA); mathematics (MS); music (MA); occupational safety management (MS); psychology (MS); rural family nursing (MS); school administration (MSE); social gerontology (MS); sociology (MA); special education (MSE); speech language pathology (MS); superintendency (Ed S); teaching (MAT); teaching English as a second language (MA); technology (MS); technology management (PhD); theatre (MA). *Program availability:* Part-time, 100% online, blended/hybrid learning. *Students:* 337 full-time (145 women), 41 part-time/adjunct (28 women). *Students:* 785 full-time (398 women), 1,633 part-time (1,063 women); includes 231 minority (102 Black or African American, non-Hispanic/Latino; 4 American Indian or Alaska Native, non-Hispanic/Latino; 16 Asian, non-Hispanic/Latino; 52 Hispanic/Latino; 57 Two or more races, non-Hispanic/Latino), 692 international. Average age 30. In 2017, 2,605 master's, 122 other advanced degrees awarded. *Degree requirements:* For master's and Ed S, comprehensive exam (for some programs), thesis (for some programs). *Entrance requirements:* Additional exam requirements/recommendations for international students: Required—TOEFL (minimum score 550 paper-based; 79 iBT). *Application deadline:* For fall admission, 6/1 priority date for domestic and international students; for spring admission, 10/1 priority date for domestic and international students; for summer admission, 4/1 priority date for domestic and international students. Applications are processed on a rolling basis. Application fee: $30 ($75 for international students). Electronic applications accepted. *Expenses:* Tuition, state resident: full-time $8771; part-time $292.35 per credit hour. Tuition, nonresident: full-time $17,541; part-time $584.70 per credit hour. *Required fees:* $372; $24.78 per credit hour. *Financial support:* In 2017–18, 99 students received support. Research assistantships, teaching assistantships, career-related internships or fieldwork, Federal Work-Study, scholarships/grants, and administrative and laboratory assistantships available. Support available to part-time students. Financial award application deadline: 3/1; financial award applicants required to submit FAFSA. *Unit head:* Shellie Hewitt, Director of Graduate and International Student Services, 660-543-4621, Fax: 660-543-4778, E-mail: hewitt@ucmo.edu. *Application contact:* 660-543-4621, E-mail: admit_intl@ucmo.edu.
Website: http://www.ucmo.edu/graduate/

University of Central Oklahoma, The Jackson College of Graduate Studies, College of Education and Professional Studies, Donna Nigh Department of Advanced Professional and Special Services, Edmond, OK 73034-5209. Offers educational leadership (M Ed); library media education (M Ed); reading (M Ed); school counseling (M Ed); special education (M Ed), including mild/moderate disabilities, severe-profound/multiple disabilities; speech-language pathology (MS). *Accreditation:* ASHA. *Program availability:* Part-time. *Faculty:* 17 full-time (12 women), 8 part-time/adjunct (4 women). *Students:* 73 full-time (65 women), 286 part-time (239 women); includes 91 minority (41 Black or African American, non-Hispanic/Latino; 8 American Indian or Alaska Native, non-Hispanic/Latino; 5 Asian, non-Hispanic/Latino; 20 Hispanic/Latino; 17 Two or more races, non-Hispanic/Latino), 3 international. Average age 35. 146 applicants, 83% accepted, 91 enrolled. In 2017, 128 master's awarded. *Degree requirements:* For master's, comprehensive exam (for some programs), thesis (for some programs). *Entrance requirements:* Additional exam requirements/recommendations for international students: Required—TOEFL (minimum score 550 paper-based; 79 iBT), IELTS (minimum score 6.5). *Application deadline:* For fall admission, 7/15 for international students; for spring admission, 11/15 for international students; for summer admission, 1/31 for domestic students. Applications are processed on a rolling basis. Application fee: $60. Electronic applications accepted. *Expenses:* Tuition, state resident: full-time $5375; part-time $268.75 per credit hour. Tuition, nonresident: full-time $13,295; part-time $664.75 per credit hour. *Required fees:* $626; $31.30 per credit hour. One-time fee: $50. Tuition and fees vary according to program. *Financial support:* In 2017–18, 74 students received support, including 1 research assistantship with partial tuition reimbursement available (averaging $2,958 per year), 1 teaching assistantship with partial tuition reimbursement available (averaging $5,915 per year); career-related internships or fieldwork, scholarships/grants, tuition waivers (partial), and unspecified assistantships also available. Financial award application deadline: 3/31; financial award applicants required to submit FAFSA. *Unit head:* Dr. Cheryl Evans, Chair, 405-974-5437, Fax: 405-974-3857. *Application contact:* Carlie Wellington, Assistant Director, CEPS Graduate Enrollment, 405-974-5105, Fax: 405-974-3851, E-mail: gradcoll@uco.edu.
Website: http://sites.uco.edu/ceps/dept/Education-Programs/apss/index.asp

University of Cincinnati, Graduate School, College of Education, Criminal Justice, and Human Services, School of Human Services, Counseling Program, Cincinnati, OH 45221. Offers counselor education (Ed D); mental health (MA); school counseling (M Ed); substance abuse prevention (Graduate Certificate). *Accreditation:* ACA (one or more programs are accredited); NCATE. *Program availability:* Part-time. Terminal

master's awarded for partial completion of doctoral program. *Degree requirements:* For master's, comprehensive exam, thesis or alternative; for doctorate, comprehensive exam, thesis/dissertation. *Entrance requirements:* For master's and doctorate, GRE General Test, interview. Additional exam requirements/recommendations for international students: Required—TOEFL (minimum score 620 paper-based). Electronic applications accepted. *Expenses:* Tuition, area resident: Full-time $14,468. Tuition, state resident: full-time $14,968; part-time $754 per credit hour. Tuition, nonresident: full-time $24,210; part-time $1311 per credit hour. *International tuition:* $26,460 full-time. *Required fees:* $3958; $84 per credit hour. One-time fee: $85 full-time. Tuition and fees vary according to course load, degree level and program. *Faculty research:* Group work, career development, ecology, prevention, multicultural.

University of Colorado Colorado Springs, College of Education, Colorado Springs, CO 80918. Offers counseling and human services (MA); curriculum and instruction (MA); educational leadership (MA); educational leadership, research and policy (PhD); special education (MA); teaching English to speakers of other languages (MA). *Accreditation:* ACA; NCATE. *Program availability:* Part-time, evening/weekend, 100% online, blended/hybrid learning. *Faculty:* 30 full-time (21 women), 61 part-time/adjunct (38 women). *Students:* 190 full-time (132 women), 286 part-time (202 women); includes 117 minority (20 Black or African American, non-Hispanic/Latino; 2 American Indian or Alaska Native, non-Hispanic/Latino; 12 Asian, non-Hispanic/Latino; 59 Hispanic/Latino; 24 Two or more races, non-Hispanic/Latino), 6 international. Average age 36. 169 applicants, 85% accepted, 113 enrolled. In 2017, 160 master's, 16 doctorates awarded. *Degree requirements:* For master's, comprehensive exam, thesis or alternative, microcomputer proficiency; for doctorate, comprehensive exam, thesis/dissertation, research lab. *Entrance requirements:* For master's and doctorate, GRE General Test. Additional exam requirements/recommendations for international students: Recommended—TOEFL (minimum score 550 paper-based; 80 iBT), IELTS (minimum score 6). *Application deadline:* For fall admission, 1/28 priority date for domestic and international students; for spring admission, 11/1 priority date for domestic and international students. Applications are processed on a rolling basis. Application fee: $60 ($100 for international students). Electronic applications accepted. *Expenses:* $10,350 per year resident tuition, $20,935 nonresident, $11,961 nonresidential online; annual costs vary depending on program, course-load, and residency status. *Financial support:* In 2017–18, 81 students received support. Career-related internships or fieldwork, Federal Work-Study, scholarships/grants, and unspecified assistantships available. Support available to part-time students. Financial award application deadline: 3/1; financial award applicants required to submit FAFSA. *Faculty research:* Linguistically diverse education (LDE), educational policy, evidence-based reading and writing instruction, relational and social aggression, positive behavior supports, inclusive schooling, K-12 education policy. *Total annual research expenditures:* $607,967. *Unit head:* Dr. Valerie Martin Conley, Dean, 719-255-4133, E-mail: vmconley@uccs.edu. *Application contact:* The College of Education Student Resource Office, 719-255-4996, E-mail: education@uccs.edu.
Website: http://www.uccs.edu/coe

University of Colorado Denver, School of Education and Human Development, Program in Counseling Psychology and Counselor Education, Denver, CO 80217. Offers counseling (MA), including clinical mental health counseling, couple and family counseling, multicultural counseling, school counseling; school counseling (MA). *Accreditation:* ACA; NCATE. *Program availability:* Part-time, evening/weekend. *Degree requirements:* For master's, comprehensive exam (for some programs), thesis or alternative, 63-66 hours. *Entrance requirements:* For master's, GRE or MAT (unless applicant already holds a graduate degree), letters of recommendation, interview, resume, transcripts from all colleges/universities attended. Additional exam requirements/recommendations for international students: Required—TOEFL (minimum score 525 paper-based; 71 iBT); Recommended—IELTS (minimum score 6.3). Electronic applications accepted. *Expenses:* Contact institution. *Faculty research:* Spiritual issues in counseling, multicultural and diversity issues in counseling, adolescent suicide, career development.

University of Connecticut, Graduate School, Neag School of Education, Department of Educational Psychology, Program in Counseling Psychology, Storrs, CT 06269. Offers counseling psychology (PhD); school counseling (MA). *Accreditation:* ACA. Terminal master's awarded for partial completion of doctoral program. *Degree requirements:* For master's, comprehensive exam, thesis or alternative; for doctorate, thesis/dissertation. *Entrance requirements:* For doctorate, GRE General Test. Additional exam requirements/recommendations for international students: Required—TOEFL (minimum score 550 paper-based). Electronic applications accepted.

University of Dayton, Department of Counselor Education and Human Services, Dayton, OH 45469. Offers clinical mental health counseling (MS Ed); college student personnel (MS Ed); higher education administration (MS Ed); human services (MS Ed); school counseling (MS Ed); school psychology (MS Ed, Ed S). *Accreditation:* ACA; NCATE. *Program availability:* Part-time. *Faculty:* 11 full-time (6 women), 34 part-time/adjunct (24 women). *Students:* 194 full-time (153 women), 83 part-time (68 women); includes 58 minority (37 Black or African American, non-Hispanic/Latino; 2 Asian, non-Hispanic/Latino; 9 Hispanic/Latino; 10 Two or more races, non-Hispanic/Latino), 3 international. Average age 30. 426 applicants, 28% accepted. In 2017, 107 master's, 6 Ed Ss awarded. *Degree requirements:* For master's, thesis (for some programs); for Ed S, thesis (for some programs), professional portfolio. *Entrance requirements:* For master's, MAT or GRE (if GPA less than 2.75), essays (for some programs). Additional exam requirements/recommendations for international students: Required—TOEFL (minimum score 550 paper-based; 80 iBT). *Application deadline:* For fall admission, 1/10 priority date for domestic and international students; for spring admission, 9/10 priority date for domestic and international students; for summer admission, 11/10 priority date for domestic and international students. Application fee: $0 ($50 for international students). Electronic applications accepted. *Expenses:* Contact institution. *Financial support:* In 2017–18, 5 research assistantships with partial tuition reimbursements (averaging $9,950 per year) were awarded; career-related internships or fieldwork, institutionally sponsored loans, and unspecified assistantships also available. Financial award application deadline: 3/1; financial award applicants required to submit FAFSA. *Faculty research:* Student school bonding, traumatic brain injuries, wellness and counseling, creativity in education. *Unit head:* Dr. Alan Demmitt, Chair, 937-229-3644, Fax: 937-229-1055, E-mail: ademmitt1@udayton.edu. *Application contact:* Kathleen Brown, Administrative Assistant, 937-229-3644, Fax: 937-229-1055, E-mail: kbrown1@udayton.edu.
Website: https://www.udayton.edu/education/departments_and_programs/edc/

University of Florida, Graduate School, College of Education, School of Human Development and Organizational Studies in Education, Gainesville, FL 32611. Offers counseling and counselor education (Ed D, PhD), including counseling and counselor education, marriage and family counseling, mental health counseling, school counseling and guidance; educational leadership (M Ed, MAE, Ed D, PhD, Ed S), including educational leadership (Ed D, PhD); education policy (Ed D, PhD); higher education administration (Ed D, PhD), including education policy (Ed D), educational policy, higher education administration; marriage and family counseling (M Ed, MAE, Ed D, PhD, Ed S); mental health counseling (M Ed, MAE, Ed D, PhD, Ed S); research and evaluation methodology (M Ed, MAE, Ed D, PhD); school counseling and guidance (M Ed, MAE, Ed D, PhD, Ed S); student personnel in higher education (M Ed, MAE). *Accreditation:* ACA (one or more programs are accredited); NCATE. *Program availability:* Part-time, online learning. Terminal master's awarded for partial completion of doctoral program. *Degree requirements:* For master's, thesis optional; for doctorate, comprehensive exam, thesis/dissertation. *Entrance requirements:* For master's and doctorate, GRE General Test, minimum GPA of 3.0 (undergraduate), 3.5 (graduate); for Ed S, GRE General Test. Additional exam requirements/recommendations for international students: Required—TOEFL (minimum score 550 paper-based; 80 iBT), IELTS (minimum score 6). Electronic applications accepted.

University of Georgia, College of Education, Department of Counseling and Human Development Services, Athens, GA 30602. Offers college student affairs administration (M Ed, PhD); professional school counseling (Ed S). *Accreditation:* ACA (one or more programs are accredited); APA (one or more programs are accredited); NCATE. *Degree requirements:* For master's, thesis (MA); for doctorate, variable foreign language requirement, thesis/dissertation. *Entrance requirements:* For master's, GRE General Test or MAT; for doctorate, GRE General Test. Electronic applications accepted.

University of Guam, Office of Graduate Studies, School of Education, Program in Counseling, Mangilao, GU 96923. Offers MA. *Degree requirements:* For master's, comprehensive oral and written exams, special project or thesis. *Entrance requirements:* For master's, GRE General Test. Additional exam requirements/recommendations for international students: Required—TOEFL. *Faculty research:* Drugs in the local schools, standardized teaching procedures in the elementary school, how to address the dropout problems.

University of Hartford, College of Education, Nursing, and Health Professions, Program in Counseling, West Hartford, CT 06117-1599. Offers M Ed, MS, Sixth Year Certificate. *Accreditation:* NCATE. *Program availability:* Part-time, evening/weekend. *Degree requirements:* For master's and Sixth Year Certificate, comprehensive exam. *Entrance requirements:* For master's, GRE General Test or MAT, PRAXIS I or waiver, interview, 2 letters of recommendation; for Sixth Year Certificate, GRE General Test or MAT, PRAXIS I or waiver, interview. Additional exam requirements/recommendations for international students: Required—TOEFL (minimum score 550 paper-based). Electronic applications accepted.

University of Holy Cross, Graduate Programs, New Orleans, LA 70131-7399. Offers biomedical sciences (MS); Catholic theology (MA); counseling (MA, PhD), including community counseling (MA), marriage and family counseling (MA), school counseling (MA); educational leadership (M Ed); executive leadership (Ed D); management (MS), including healthcare management, operations management; teaching and learning (M Ed). *Accreditation:* ACA; NCATE. *Program availability:* Part-time, evening/weekend, online learning. *Faculty:* 7 full-time (4 women), 8 part-time/adjunct (3 women). *Students:* 67 full-time (55 women), 69 part-time (55 women); includes 51 minority (46 Black or African American, non-Hispanic/Latino; 2 American Indian or Alaska Native, non-Hispanic/Latino; 1 Asian, non-Hispanic/Latino; 2 Hispanic/Latino). Average age 30. 20 applicants, 50% accepted. In 2017, 28 degrees awarded. *Degree requirements:* For master's, thesis. *Entrance requirements:* For master's, GRE General Test, minimum GPA of 2.7. *Application deadline:* For fall admission, 9/1 for domestic students. Application fee: $15. *Expenses: Tuition:* Full-time $10,890; part-time $605 per credit hour. *Required fees:* $1624; $812 per semester. One-time fee: $50. *Financial support:* Federal Work-Study and tuition waivers (partial) available. Support available to part-time students. Financial award application deadline: 6/1. *Unit head:* Dr. Myles Seghers, Dean of Humanities, Education, and Counseling, 504-394-7744 Ext. 214, Fax: 504-391-2421, E-mail: mseghers@olhcc.edu. *Application contact:* Anne-Katherine Lene, Director of Student Enrollment, 504-394-7744 Ext. 110, Fax: 504-391-2421, E-mail: aklene@olhcc.edu.

University of Houston–Clear Lake, School of Education, Program in Foundations and Professional Studies, Houston, TX 77058-1002. Offers counseling (MS); instructional technology (MS); multicultural studies (MS). *Program availability:* Part-time, evening/weekend. *Degree requirements:* For master's, thesis optional. *Entrance requirements:* For master's, GRE or minimum GPA of 3.0 in last 60 hours. Additional exam requirements/recommendations for international students: Required—TOEFL (minimum score 550 paper-based). Electronic applications accepted.

University of Houston–Victoria, School of Education, Health Professions and Human Development, Victoria, TX 77901-4450. Offers administration and supervision (M Ed); adult and higher education (M Ed); counselor education (M Ed); curriculum and instruction (M Ed); dyslexia education (Certificate); educational technology (M Ed); special education (M Ed). *Program availability:* Part-time, evening/weekend, online learning. *Degree requirements:* For master's, comprehensive exam, project or thesis. *Entrance requirements:* For master's, GRE General Test. Additional exam requirements/recommendations for international students: Required—TOEFL. Electronic applications accepted. *Faculty research:* Reading and language arts education, evaluation and diagnosis of special children's abilities.

University of Idaho, College of Graduate Studies, College of Education, Health and Human Sciences, Department of Leadership and Counseling, Boise, ID 83844-2282. Offers adult/organizational learning and leadership (Ed S); educational leadership (Ed S); rehabilitation counseling and human services (M Ed); school counseling (M Ed, MS). *Faculty:* 14 full-time, 6 part-time/adjunct. *Students:* 29 full-time (20 women), 147 part-time (78 women). Average age 38. In 2017, 62 master's, 32 other advanced degrees awarded. *Entrance requirements:* For master's, minimum GPA of 3.0, writing sample. Additional exam requirements/recommendations for international students: Required—TOEFL (minimum score 79 iBT). *Application deadline:* Applications are processed on a rolling basis. Application fee: $60. Electronic applications accepted. *Expenses:* Tuition, state resident: full-time $6722; part-time $430 per credit hour. Tuition, nonresident: full-time $23,046; part-time $1337 per credit hour. *Required fees:* $2142; $63 per credit hour. *Financial support:* Applicants required to submit FAFSA. *Unit head:* Dr. Kathy Canfield-Davis, Chair, 208-364-4047, E-mail: lead@uidaho.edu. *Application contact:* Sean Scoggin, Graduate Recruitment Coordinator, 208-885-4723, Fax: 208-885-4406, E-mail: graduateadmissions@uidaho.edu. Website: https://www.uidaho.edu/ed/lc

University of Illinois at Urbana–Champaign, Graduate College, College of Education, Department of Educational Psychology, Champaign, IL 61820. Offers Ed M, MA, MS, PhD, CAS. *Accreditation:* APA (one or more programs are accredited). *Program availability:* Part-time, online learning.

The University of Iowa, Graduate College, College of Education, Department of Rehabilitation and Counselor Education, Iowa City, IA 52242-1316. Offers counselor education and supervision (PhD); couple and family therapy (PhD); rehabilitation and mental health counseling (MA); rehabilitation counselor education (PhD); school counseling (MA). *Accreditation:* ACA (one or more programs are accredited); CORE (one or more programs are accredited). *Degree requirements:* For master's, thesis optional, exam; for doctorate, comprehensive exam, thesis/dissertation. *Entrance requirements:* For master's and doctorate, GRE General Test, minimum GPA of 3.0. Additional exam requirements/recommendations for international students: Required—TOEFL (minimum score 550 paper-based; 81 iBT). Electronic applications accepted.

University of La Verne, LaFetra College of Education, Program in Educational Counseling, La Verne, CA 91750-4443. Offers educational counseling (MS); pupil personnel services (Credential); school psychology (MS). *Program availability:* Part-time. *Students:* 64 full-time (57 women), 123 part-time (101 women); includes 131 minority (8 Black or African American, non-Hispanic/Latino; 5 Asian, non-Hispanic/Latino; 116 Hispanic/Latino; 2 Two or more races, non-Hispanic/Latino), 1 international. Average age 31. *Entrance requirements:* For master's, California Basic Educational Skills Test, minimum undergraduate GPA of 2.75, graduate 3.0; interview; 1 year's experience working with children; 3 letters of reference. Additional exam requirements/recommendations for international students: Required—TOEFL (minimum score 550 paper-based). *Application deadline:* Applications are processed on a rolling basis. Application fee: $50. *Expenses:* Contact institution. *Financial support:* Scholarships/grants and traineeships available. Financial award application deadline: 3/2; financial award applicants required to submit FAFSA. *Unit head:* Everett Lovelace, Assistant Professor, Education Counseling, 909-448-1495, E-mail: elovelace@laverne.edu. *Application contact:* Kristen Ahn, Assistant Director of Graduate Admissions, 909-448-4480, E-mail: sahn@laverne.edu. Website: https://education.laverne.edu/counseling

University of La Verne, Regional and Online Campuses, Graduate Credential Program in Education, California Statewide Campus, La Verne, CA 91750-4443. Offers administration services (preliminary) (Credential); education specialist: mild/moderate (Credential); English (Certificate); multiple subject teaching (Credential); pupil personnel services: school counseling (Credential); single subject teaching (Credential); special education (MS); special emphasis (M Ed). *Accreditation:* NCATE. *Program availability:* Part-time. *Faculty:* 3 full-time (2 women), 25 part-time/adjunct (19 women). *Students:* 120 full-time (95 women), 62 part-time (47 women); includes 47 minority (3 Black or African American, non-Hispanic/Latino; 2 American Indian or Alaska Native, non-Hispanic/Latino; 2 Asian, non-Hispanic/Latino; 40 Hispanic/Latino). Average age 31. In 2017, 25 master's, 61 other advanced degrees awarded. *Entrance requirements:* For degree, California Basic Educational Skills Test, minimum undergraduate GPA of 2.75, 3 letters of recommendation, interview. *Application deadline:* Applications are processed on a rolling basis. Application fee: $50. *Expenses:* Contact institution. *Financial support:* Application deadline: 3/2; applicants required to submit FAFSA. *Unit head:* Pam Bergovoy, Assistant Dean, Regional and Online Campuses/Director, Center for Educators, 909-448-4953, E-mail: pbergovoy@laverne.edu. *Application contact:* 877-468-6858, E-mail: gradadmission@laverne.edu. Website: https://laverne.edu/locations/

University of La Verne, Regional and Online Campuses, Graduate Programs, High Desert Campus, Victorville, CA 92392. Offers business administration for experienced professionals (MBA); educational (special emphasis) (M Ed); educational counseling (MS); leadership and management (MS); multiple subject (elementary) (Credential); preliminary administrative services (Credential); pupil personnel services (Credential); single subject (secondary) (Credential). *Students:* 7 full-time (3 women), 16 part-time (12 women); includes 14 minority (3 Black or African American, non-Hispanic/Latino; 1 American Indian or Alaska Native, non-Hispanic/Latino; 1 Asian, non-Hispanic/Latino; 9 Hispanic/Latino). Average age 41. In 2017, 9 master's awarded. *Application deadline:* Applications are processed on a rolling basis. Application fee: $50. *Expenses:* Contact institution. *Financial support:* Application deadline: 3/2; applicants required to submit FAFSA. *Unit head:* Juli Roberts, Regional Campus Director, 760-955-6448, Fax: 760-843-9505, E-mail: jroberts@laverne.edu. *Application contact:* Admissions, 760-955-6440, Fax: 760-955-6443, E-mail: hdcv@laverne.edu. Website: https://laverne.edu/locations/

University of La Verne, Regional and Online Campuses, Graduate Programs, Kern County Campus, Bakersfield, CA 93301. Offers business administration for experienced professionals (MBA-EP); education (special emphasis) (M Ed); educational counseling (MS); educational leadership (M Ed); health administration (MHA); leadership and management (MS); mild/moderate education specialist (Credential); multiple subject (elementary) (Credential); organizational leadership (Ed D); preliminary administrative services (Credential); single subject (secondary) (Credential); special education studies (MS). *Program availability:* Part-time, evening/weekend. *Students:* Average age 36. In 2017, 3 master's awarded. *Application deadline:* Applications are processed on a rolling basis. Application fee: $50. *Expenses:* Contact institution. *Financial support:* Institutionally sponsored loans available. Financial award application deadline: 3/2; financial award applicants required to submit FAFSA. *Unit head:* Nora Dominguez, Regional Campus Director, 661-861-6802, E-mail: ndominguez@laverne.edu. *Application contact:* Rebecca Murillo, Associate Director of Admissions, 661-861-6807, E-mail: rmurillo@laverne.edu. Website: https://laverne.edu/locations/

University of La Verne, Regional and Online Campuses, Graduate Programs, Orange County Campus, Irvine, CA 92840. Offers business administration for experienced professionals (MBA); educational counseling (MS); educational leadership (M Ed); health administration (MHA); leadership and management (MS); preliminary administrative services (Credential); pupil personnel services (Credential). *Program availability:* Part-time. *Students:* 19 full-time (11 women), 51 part-time (30 women); includes 47 minority (12 Black or African American, non-Hispanic/Latino; 2 American Indian or Alaska Native, non-Hispanic/Latino; 12 Asian, non-Hispanic/Latino; 21 Hispanic/Latino). Average age 39. In 2017, 43 master's awarded. *Application deadline:* Applications are processed on a rolling basis. Application fee: $50. *Expenses:* Contact institution. *Financial support:* Application deadline: 3/2; applicants required to submit FAFSA. *Unit head:* Alison Rodriguez-Balles, Interim Campus Director, 714-505-6943, Fax: 909-505-6937, E-mail: arodriguez2@laverne.edu. *Application contact:* 877-468-6858, E-mail: gradadmission@laverne.edu. Website: https://laverne.edu/locations/

University of La Verne, Regional and Online Campuses, Graduate Programs, San Fernando Valley Campus, Burbank, CA 91505. Offers business administration for experienced professionals (MBA-EP); educational counseling (MS); educational leadership (M Ed); leadership and management (MS); preliminary administrative services (Credential); pupil personnel services (Credential). *Program availability:* Part-time, evening/weekend. *Students:* 43 full-time (26 women), 97 part-time (49 women); includes 88 minority (21 Black or African American, non-Hispanic/Latino; 1 American Indian or Alaska Native, non-Hispanic/Latino; 15 Asian, non-Hispanic/Latino; 49 Hispanic/Latino; 1 Native Hawaiian or other Pacific Islander, non-Hispanic/Latino; 1 Two or more races, non-Hispanic/Latino). Average age 38. In 2017, 65 master's awarded. *Application deadline:* Applications are processed on a rolling basis. Application fee: $50. *Expenses:* Contact institution. *Financial support:* Application deadline: 3/2; applicants required to submit FAFSA. *Unit head:* Dr. Nelly Kazman, Senior Executive Director, 818-295-6502, E-mail: nkazman@laverne.edu. *Application contact:* Debi Hrboka, Associate Director of Admissions, 818-295-6508, E-mail: dhrboka@laverne.edu. Website: https://laverne.edu/locations/

University of La Verne, Regional and Online Campuses, Graduate Programs, Ventura County/Point Mugu Naval Air Station Campuses, Oxnard, CA 93036. Offers business administration for experienced professionals (MS); educational counseling (MS); educational leadership (M Ed); leadership and management (MS); multiple subject

(elementary) (Credential); pupil personnel services (Credential); single subject (secondary) (Credential). *Program availability:* Part-time, evening/weekend. *Students:* Average age 38. In 2017, 19 master's awarded. Application fee: $50. *Expenses:* Contact institution. *Financial support:* Institutionally sponsored loans available. Financial award application deadline: 3/2; financial award applicants required to submit FAFSA. *Unit head:* Kitt Vincent, Senior Executive Director, 805-788-6202, E-mail: kvincent@laverne.edu. *Application contact:* Mike Stadler, Assistant Director/Academic Advisor, 805-986-6909, E-mail: mstadler3@laverne.edu.
Website: https://laverne.edu/locations/

University of La Verne, Regional and Online Campuses, Master's Programs in Education, California Statewide Campus, La Verne, CA 91750-4443. Offers administration services (preliminary) (Credential); education specialist: mild/moderate (Credential); educational counseling (MS); educational leadership (M Ed); multiple subject teaching (Credential); pupil personnel services: school counseling (Credential); single subject teaching (Credential); special education studies (MS); special emphasis (M Ed). *Accreditation:* NCATE. *Students:* 106 full-time (88 women), 75 part-time (55 women); includes 112 minority (4 Black or African American, non-Hispanic/Latino; 5 Asian, non-Hispanic/Latino; 102 Hispanic/Latino; 1 Two or more races, non-Hispanic/Latino). Average age 35. In 2017, 76 master's, 82 other advanced degrees awarded. *Entrance requirements:* For master's, California Basic Educational Skills Test, 3 letters of recommendation, teaching credential. *Application deadline:* Applications are processed on a rolling basis. Application fee: $50. *Expenses:* Contact institution. *Financial support:* Application deadline: 3/2; applicants required to submit FAFSA. *Unit head:* Pam Bergovoy, Assistant Dean, Regional and Online Campuses/Director, Center for Educators, 909-448-4953, E-mail: pbergovoy@laverne.edu. *Application contact:* 877-468-6858, E-mail: gradadmission@laverne.edu. *Application contact:* 877-468-6858, E-mail: gradadmission@laverne.edu.
Website: http://www.laverne.edu/locations

University of Lethbridge, School of Graduate Studies, Lethbridge, AB T1K 3M4, Canada. Offers addictions counseling (M Sc); agricultural biotechnology (M Sc); agricultural studies (M Sc, MA); anthropology (MA); archaeology (M Sc, MA); art (MA, MFA); biochemistry (M Sc); biological sciences (M Sc); biomolecular science (PhD); biosystems and biodiversity (PhD); Canadian studies (MA); chemistry (M Sc); computer science (M Sc); computer science and geographical information science (M Sc); counseling (MC); counseling psychology (M Ed); dramatic arts (MA); earth, space, and physical science (PhD); economics (MA); education (MA, PhD); educational leadership (M Ed); English (MA); environmental science (M Sc); evolution and behavior (PhD); exercise science (M Sc); French (MA); French/German (MA); French/Spanish (MA); general education (M Ed); geography (M Sc, MA); German (MA); health sciences (M Sc); individualized multidisciplinary (M Sc, MA); kinesiology (M Sc, MA); management (M Sc), including accounting, finance, human resource management and labor relations, information systems, international management, marketing, policy and strategy; mathematics (M Sc); music (M Mus, MA); Native American studies (MA); neuroscience (M Sc, PhD); new media (MA, MFA); nursing (M Sc, MN); philosophy (MA); physics (M Sc); political science (MA); psychology (M Sc, MA); religious studies (MA); sociology (MA); theatre and dramatic arts (MFA); theoretical and computational science (PhD); urban and regional studies (MA); women and gender studies (MA). *Program availability:* Part-time, evening/weekend. *Degree requirements:* For master's, thesis (for some programs); for doctorate, comprehensive exam, thesis/dissertation. *Entrance requirements:* For master's, GMAT (for M Sc in management), bachelor's degree in related field, minimum GPA of 3.0 during previous 20 graded semester courses, 2 years' teaching or related experience (M Ed); for doctorate, master's degree, minimum graduate GPA of 3.5. Additional exam requirements/recommendations for international students: Required—TOEFL (minimum score 580 paper-based; 93 iBT). Electronic applications accepted. *Faculty research:* Movement and brain plasticity, gibberellin physiology, photosynthesis, carbon cycling, molecular properties of main-group ring components.

University of Louisiana at Lafayette, Department of Counselor Education, Lafayette, LA 70504. Offers MS. *Accreditation:* ACA. *Entrance requirements:* For master's, GRE General Test, minimum GPA of 2.75. Additional exam requirements/recommendations for international students: Required—TOEFL (minimum score 550 paper-based). Electronic applications accepted.

University of Louisiana at Monroe, Graduate School, College of Health and Pharmaceutical Sciences, Programs in Counseling Studies, Monroe, LA 71209-0001. Offers clinical mental health counseling (MS); school counseling (MS). *Accreditation:* ACA; NCATE. *Program availability:* Part-time, evening/weekend, online learning. *Faculty:* 3 full-time (all women). *Students:* 34 full-time (28 women), 8 part-time (7 women); includes 14 minority (12 Black or African American, non-Hispanic/Latino; 1 Asian, non-Hispanic/Latino; 1 Hispanic/Latino). Average age 32. 18 applicants, 94% accepted, 13 enrolled. In 2017, 19 master's awarded. *Degree requirements:* For master's, comprehensive exam, thesis. *Entrance requirements:* For master's, GRE General Test, minimum GPA of 2.8 in last 60 hours. Additional exam requirements/recommendations for international students: Required—TOEFL (minimum score 500 paper-based; 61 iBT). *Application deadline:* For fall admission, 8/24 priority date for domestic students, 7/1 for international students; for winter admission, 12/14 priority date for domestic students; for spring admission, 1/19 for domestic students, 11/1 for international students. Applications are processed on a rolling basis. Application fee: $20 ($30 for international students). Electronic applications accepted. *Expenses:* Tuition, state resident: full-time $6489; part-time $479 per hour. Tuition, nonresident: full-time $12,100; part-time $479 per hour. *Required fees:* $8860; $802 per hour. $3273 per semester. *Financial support:* In 2017–18, 9 students received support. Career-related internships or fieldwork, Federal Work-Study, and unspecified assistantships available. Financial award application deadline: 4/1; financial award applicants required to submit FAFSA. *Unit head:* Dr. David Hale, Director, 318-342-1349, E-mail: dhale@ulm.edu.
Website: http://www.ulm.edu/counseling/

University of Louisville, Graduate School, College of Education and Human Development, Department of Counseling and Human Development, Louisville, KY 40292-0001. Offers counseling and personnel services (M Ed, PhD), including art therapy (M Ed), clinical mental health counseling (M Ed), college student personnel, counseling psychology, counselor education and supervision (PhD), educational psychology, measurement, and evaluation (PhD), school counseling (M Ed). *Accreditation:* APA; NCATE. *Program availability:* Part-time, evening/weekend. *Students:* 144 full-time (107 women), 63 part-time (44 women); includes 49 minority (32 Black or African American, non-Hispanic/Latino; 1 American Indian or Alaska Native, non-Hispanic/Latino; 3 Asian, non-Hispanic/Latino; 7 Hispanic/Latino; 6 Two or more races, non-Hispanic/Latino), 3 international. Average age 28. 178 applicants, 49% accepted, 51 enrolled. In 2017, 35 master's, 3 doctorates awarded. *Degree requirements:* For doctorate, comprehensive exam, thesis/dissertation. *Entrance requirements:* For master's and doctorate, GRE General Test. Application fee: $65. *Expenses:* Tuition, state resident: full-time $12,246; part-time $681 per credit hour. Tuition, nonresident: full-time $25,486; part-time $1417 per credit hour. *Required fees:* $196. Tuition and fees vary according to course load, program and reciprocity agreements. *Financial support:* Fellowships, research assistantships, teaching

assistantships, career-related internships or fieldwork, Federal Work-Study, scholarships/grants, health care benefits, and unspecified assistantships available. Financial award application deadline: 6/1; financial award applicants required to submit FAFSA. *Faculty research:* Mental health services and under-served populations; health disparities and outcomes; well-being identity development; measurement and evaluation. *Total annual research expenditures:* $295,684. *Unit head:* Dr. Mark M. Leach, Interim Chair/Professor, 502-852-0588, Fax: 502-852-0629, E-mail: m.leach@louisville.edu. *Application contact:* Betty Hampton, Director of Graduate Student Services, 502-852-5597, Fax: 502-852-1465, E-mail: edadvise@louisville.edu.
Website: http://www.louisville.edu/education/departments/ecpy

University of Lynchbua, Graduate Studies, M Ed Program in School Counseling, Lynchburg, VA 24501-3199. Offers M Ed. *Accreditation:* ACA. *Program availability:* Part-time, evening/weekend. *Faculty:* 17 full-time (10 women). *Students:* 8 full-time (all women), 4 part-time (3 women); includes 5 minority (3 Black or African American, non-Hispanic/Latino; 1 Hispanic/Latino; 1 Two or more races, non-Hispanic/Latino). Average age 32. 12 applicants, 100% accepted, 3 enrolled. In 2017, 9 master's awarded. *Degree requirements:* For master's, counseling internship. *Entrance requirements:* For master's, GRE, minimum GPA of 3.0 (preferred), official transcripts (bachelor's, others as relevant), three letters of recommendation, career goals statement, personal interview. Additional exam requirements/recommendations for international students: Required—TOEFL (minimum score 550 paper-based; 80 iBT), IELTS (minimum score 6). *Application deadline:* For fall admission, 7/31 for domestic students, 6/1 for international students; for spring admission, 11/30 for domestic students, 10/15 for international students. Applications are processed on a rolling basis. Application fee: $30. Electronic applications accepted. Application fee is waived when completed online. *Expenses:* $510 per credit tuition, $100 fees. *Financial support:* Federal Work-Study, scholarships/grants, health care benefits, and unspecified assistantships available. Support available to part-time students. Financial award application deadline: 7/31; financial award applicants required to submit FAFSA. *Unit head:* Dr. Jeanne Booth, Program Advisor of M Ed in School Counseling, 434-544-8551, E-mail: booth@lynchburg.edu. *Application contact:* Ellen Thompson, Graduate Admissions Counselor, 434-544-8841, E-mail: thompson_e@lynchburg.edu.
Website: http://www.lynchburg.edu/graduate/master-of-education-in-counselor-education/school-counseling/

University of Manitoba, Faculty of Graduate Studies, Faculty of Education, Department of Educational Administration, Foundations and Psychology, Winnipeg, MB R3T 2N2, Canada. Offers adult and post-secondary education (M Ed); educational administration (M Ed); guidance and counseling (M Ed); inclusive special education (M Ed); social foundations of education (M Ed). *Degree requirements:* For master's, thesis or alternative.

University of Mary Hardin-Baylor, Graduate Studies in Counseling, Belton, TX 76513. Offers clinical and mental health counseling (MA); marriage, family and child counseling (MA); non-clinical professional studies (MA). *Accreditation:* ACA. *Program availability:* Part-time, evening/weekend. *Faculty:* 7 full-time (4 women), 1 part-time/adjunct (0 women). *Students:* 74 full-time (58 women), 13 part-time (8 women); includes 44 minority (23 Black or African American, non-Hispanic/Latino; 18 Hispanic/Latino; 3 Two or more races, non-Hispanic/Latino). Average age 32. 54 applicants, 65% accepted, 29 enrolled. In 2017, 27 master's awarded. *Degree requirements:* For master's, comprehensive exam. *Entrance requirements:* For master's, GRE General Test with minimum cumulative score of 300 on verbal and quantitative portions and 3.0 on analytical section (if overall undergraduate GPA is below a 3.0), minimum cumulative undergraduate GPA of 2.75 or 3.0 on last 60 hours of course work; three letters of recommendation; interview with departmental graduate admissions committee. Additional exam requirements/recommendations for international students: Required—TOEFL (minimum score 60 iBT), IELTS (minimum score 4.5). *Application deadline:* For fall admission, 6/1 for domestic students, 4/30 priority date for international students; for spring admission, 11/1 for domestic students, 9/30 priority date for international students. Applications are processed on a rolling basis. Application fee: $35 ($135 for international students). Electronic applications accepted. *Expenses: Tuition:* Full-time $15,570; part-time $10,380 per credit hour. *Required fees:* $1350; $75 per credit hour. $50 per term. Tuition and fees vary according to course load and degree level. *Financial support:* In 2017–18, 55 students received support. Federal Work-Study, unspecified assistantships, and scholarships for some active duty military personnel available. Support available to part-time students. Financial award applicants required to submit FAFSA. *Faculty research:* Teaching mindfulness skills as part of an interdisciplinary training protocol for doctor of physical therapy students; using symbolic art cards and oracle cards in supervision as a method for teaching appropriate self-disclosure, clinical reflection and counselor development reflection; understanding integral breath therapy. *Unit head:* Dr. Dan Williamson, Director, Graduate Counseling, 254-295-5018, E-mail: dwilliamson@umhb.edu. *Application contact:* Sharon Aguilera, Assistant Director, Graduate Admissions, 254-295-4835, E-mail: saguilera@umhb.edu.
Website: https://go.umhb.edu/graduate/counseling/home

University of Maryland, College Park, Academic Affairs, College of Education, Department of Counseling, Higher Education and Special Education, College Park, MD 20742. Offers college student personnel (M Ed, MA); college student personnel administration (PhD); community counseling (CAGS); community/career counseling (M Ed, MA); counseling and personnel services (M Ed, MA, PhD), including art therapy (M Ed), college student personnel (M Ed), counseling and personnel services (PhD), counseling psychology (M Ed), mental health counseling (M Ed), school counseling (M Ed); counseling psychology (PhD); counselor education (PhD); rehabilitation counseling (M Ed, MA, AGSC); school counseling (M Ed, MA); school psychology (M Ed, MA, PhD). *Accreditation:* APA (one or more programs are accredited); NCATE. *Program availability:* Part-time, evening/weekend, online learning. *Degree requirements:* For master's, thesis (for some programs); for doctorate, thesis/dissertation. *Entrance requirements:* For master's, GRE General Test or MAT, minimum GPA of 3.0, 3 letters of recommendation; for doctorate, GRE General Test or MAT, minimum GPA of 3.5, 3 letters of recommendation. Additional exam requirements/recommendations for international students: Required—TOEFL. Electronic applications accepted. *Faculty research:* Educational psychology, counseling, health.

University of Maryland Eastern Shore, Graduate Programs, Department of Education, Program in Guidance and Counseling, Princess Anne, MD 21853. Offers M Ed. *Program availability:* Evening/weekend. *Degree requirements:* For master's, comprehensive exam, practicum, seminar paper. *Entrance requirements:* For master's, interview, minimum GPA of 3.0. Additional exam requirements/recommendations for international students: Required—TOEFL (minimum score 80 iBT). Electronic applications accepted.

University of Massachusetts Amherst, Graduate School, College of Education, Program in Education, Amherst, MA 01003. Offers bilingual, English as a second language, and multicultural education (M Ed, Ed S); child study and early education (M Ed); children, families and schools (Ed D, Ed S); early childhood and elementary teacher education (M Ed); educational leadership (M Ed); educational policy and leadership (Ed D); higher education (M Ed); international education (M Ed); language, literacy and culture (Ed D); learning, media and technology (M Ed, Ed S); mathematics, science, and learning technologies (Ed D); reading and writing (M Ed); research, educational measurement and psychometrics (Ed D); school counselor education (M Ed, Ed S); school psychology (Ed S); science education (Ed S); secondary teacher education (M Ed); social justice education (M Ed, Ed D, Ed S); special education (M Ed, Ed D, Ed S); teacher education and school improvement (Ed D, Ed S). *Accreditation:* NCATE. *Program availability:* Part-time, online learning. Terminal master's awarded for partial completion of doctoral program. *Degree requirements:* For doctorate, comprehensive exam, thesis/dissertation. *Entrance requirements:* Additional exam requirements/recommendations for international students: Required—TOEFL (minimum score 550 paper-based; 80 iBT), IELTS (minimum score 6.5). Electronic applications accepted.

University of Massachusetts Boston, College of Education and Human Development, Program in School Counseling, Boston, MA 02125-3393. Offers M Ed. *Students:* 55 full-time (46 women), 7 part-time (6 women); includes 11 minority (5 Black or African American, non-Hispanic/Latino; 1 Asian, non-Hispanic/Latino; 2 Hispanic/Latino; 3 Two or more races, non-Hispanic/Latino). Average age 30. 68 applicants, 66% accepted, 28 enrolled. In 2017, 22 master's awarded. *Expenses:* Tuition, state resident: full-time $17,375. Tuition, nonresident: full-time $33,915. *Required fees:* $355. *Unit head:* Dr. Tim Poynton, Associate Professor, 617-287-3326. *Application contact:* Graduate Admissions Coordinator, 617-287-6400, Fax: 617-287-6236, E-mail: bos.gadm@dpc.umassp.edu.

University of Memphis, Graduate School, College of Education, Department of Counseling, Educational Psychology and Research, Memphis, TN 38152. Offers counseling (MS, Ed D), including clinical mental health counseling (MS), clinical rehabilitation counseling (MS), rehabilitation counseling (MS), school counseling (MS); counseling psychology (PhD); educational psychology and research (MS, PhD), including educational psychology, educational research. *Accreditation:* ACA (one or more programs are accredited); APA (one or more programs are accredited); CORE (one or more programs are accredited); NCATE. *Program availability:* Blended/hybrid learning. *Faculty:* 26 full-time (17 women), 8 part-time/adjunct (5 women). *Students:* 132 full-time (111 women), 87 part-time (66 women); includes 71 minority (51 Black or African American, non-Hispanic/Latino; 4 Asian, non-Hispanic/Latino; 10 Hispanic/Latino; 6 Two or more races, non-Hispanic/Latino), 5 international. Average age 31. 146 applicants, 49% accepted, 49 enrolled. In 2017, 39 master's, 13 doctorates awarded. *Degree requirements:* For master's, comprehensive exam, thesis or alternative, internship; for doctorate, comprehensive exam, thesis/dissertation, practicum, internship, residency, scholarly work. *Entrance requirements:* For master's, GRE General Test or MAT, minimum GPA of 2.5, letters of reference, interview; for doctorate, GRE General Test, master's degree or equivalent, letters of reference, interview, curriculum vitae, personal statement. Additional exam requirements/recommendations for international students: Required—TOEFL (minimum score 550 paper-based; 79 iBT). *Application deadline:* For fall admission, 10/1 priority date for domestic students; for spring admission, 4/1 priority date for domestic students. Applications are processed on a rolling basis. Application fee: $35 ($60 for international students). Electronic applications accepted. *Expenses:* Contact institution. *Financial support:* In 2017–18, 130 students received support, including 15 research assistantships with full tuition reimbursements available (averaging $13,426 per year), 12 teaching assistantships with full tuition reimbursements available (averaging $11,976 per year); fellowships with full tuition reimbursements available, career-related internships or fieldwork, Federal Work-Study, scholarships/grants, and unspecified assistantships also available. Financial award application deadline: 2/1; financial award applicants required to submit FAFSA. *Faculty research:* Anger management, aging and disability, supervision, multicultural counseling. *Unit head:* Dr. Steve West, Chair, 901-678-2841, Fax: 901-678-5114, E-mail: slwest@memphis.edu. *Application contact:* Dr. Suzanne Lease, Interim Assistant Dean of Education and Graduate Programs, 901-678-4476, Fax: 901-678-4778, E-mail: slease@memphis.edu.
Website: http://www.memphis.edu/cepr/

University of Miami, Graduate School, School of Education and Human Development, Department of Educational and Psychological Studies, Program in Counseling, Coral Gables, FL 33124. Offers counseling and research (MS Ed); Latino mental health (Certificate); marriage and family therapy (MS Ed); mental health counseling (MS Ed). *Program availability:* Part-time, evening/weekend. *Degree requirements:* For master's, comprehensive exam, personal growth experience. *Entrance requirements:* For master's, GRE General Test. Additional exam requirements/recommendations for international students: Required—TOEFL (minimum score 550 paper-based; 80 iBT); Recommended—IELTS (minimum score 6.5). Electronic applications accepted. *Faculty research:* Cocaine recidivism, HIV, non-traditional families, health psychology, diversity.

University of Minnesota, Twin Cities Campus, Graduate School, College of Education and Human Development, Department of Educational Psychology, Program in Counseling and Student Personnel Psychology, Minneapolis, MN 55455-0213. Offers MA. *Students:* 69 full-time (51 women), 7 part-time (4 women); includes 10 minority (3 Asian, non-Hispanic/Latino; 4 Hispanic/Latino; 3 Two or more races, non-Hispanic/Latino), 8 international. Average age 27. 71 applicants, 52% accepted, 36 enrolled. In 2017, 36 master's awarded. Application fee: $75 ($95 for international students). *Unit head:* Dr. Geoffrey Maruyama, Chair, 612-624-1003, Fax: 612-625-5861, E-mail: geoff@umn.edu. *Application contact:* Dr. Ernest Davenport, Director of Graduate Studies, 612-624-1040, E-mail: lqr6576@umn.edu.
Website: http://www.cehd.umn.edu/EdPsych/Programs/CSPP/default.html

University of Mississippi, Graduate School, School of Education, University, MS 38677. Offers counselor education (M Ed, PhD); counselor education - play therapy (Ed S); early childhood (M Ed); educational leadership K-12 (M Ed, Ed D, PhD, Ed S); elementary education (M Ed, Ed D, Ed S); higher education/student personnel (Ed D, PhD); literacy education (M Ed); math education (Ed D); secondary education (M Ed, PhD, Ed S); special education (M Ed, PhD, Ed S); teacher corporations (MA); teacher education (MA). *Accreditation:* NCATE. *Faculty:* 65 full-time (40 women), 25 part-time/adjunct (5 women). *Students:* 185 full-time (148 women), 410 part-time (310 women); includes 193 minority (168 Black or African American, non-Hispanic/Latino; 7 Asian, non-Hispanic/Latino; 14 Hispanic/Latino; 4 Two or more races, non-Hispanic/Latino), 7 international. Average age 33. In 2017, 176 master's, 20 doctorates, 37 other advanced degrees awarded. *Entrance requirements:* For master's, GRE General Test, minimum GPA of 3.0; for doctorate, GRE General Test. Additional exam requirements/recommendations for international students: Required—TOEFL. *Application deadline:* For fall admission, 3/1 for domestic students; for spring admission, 10/1 for domestic students; for summer admission, 3/1 for domestic students. Applications are processed on a rolling basis. Application fee: $50. Electronic applications accepted. *Financial support:* Scholarships/grants available. Financial award application deadline: 3/1; financial award applicants required to submit FAFSA. *Unit head:* Dr. David Rock, Dean, 662-915-7063, Fax: 662-915-7249, E-mail: soe@olemiss.edu. *Application contact:* Dr. Joe Sumrall, Professor of Elementary Education, 662-915-7350, E-mail: soe@olemiss.edu.

University of Missouri–Kansas City, School of Education, Kansas City, MO 64110-2499. Offers administration (Ed D); counseling and guidance (MA, Ed S), including mental health counseling (Ed S), school counseling (Ed S); counseling psychology (PhD); curriculum and instruction (MA, Ed S), including language and literacy (Ed S);

education (PhD), including higher education administration, PK-12 education administration; educational administration (MA, Ed S), including advanced principal (Ed S), beginning principal (Ed S), district-level administration (Ed S); reading education (MA); special education (MA). PhD in education offered through the School of Graduate Studies. *Accreditation:* NCATE. *Program availability:* Part-time, evening/weekend. *Degree requirements:* For doctorate, thesis/dissertation, internship, practicum. *Entrance requirements:* For master's, GRE, minimum GPA of 2.75, 2 letters of reference, written statement of purpose; for doctorate, GRE, minimum GPA of 3.0; for Ed S, minimum GPA of 3.0. Additional exam requirements/recommendations for international students: Required—TOEFL (minimum score 550 paper-based; 80 iBT). *Faculty research:* Urban education, inquiry-based field study, theories of counseling and psychotherapy, school literacy, educational technology.

University of Missouri–St. Louis, College of Education, Interdisciplinary Doctoral Programs, St. Louis, MO 63121. Offers counseling (PhD); educational leadership and policy studies (PhD); educational psychology (PhD); leadership in educational practice (Ed D); teaching-learning processes (PhD). *Faculty:* 50 full-time (29 women), 82 part-time/adjunct (66 women). *Students:* 131 full-time (98 women), 428 part-time (319 women); includes 174 minority (126 Black or African American, non-Hispanic/Latino; 3 American Indian or Alaska Native, non-Hispanic/Latino; 13 Asian, non-Hispanic/Latino; 27 Hispanic/Latino; 5 Two or more races, non-Hispanic/Latino), 11 international. 187 applicants, 84% accepted, 121 enrolled. *Degree requirements:* For doctorate, thesis/dissertation. *Entrance requirements:* For doctorate, GRE General Test, 3 letters of recommendation; personal interview. Additional exam requirements/recommendations for international students: Recommended—TOEFL (minimum score 550 paper-based; 79 iBT), IELTS (minimum score 6.5). *Application deadline:* For fall admission, 3/1 for domestic and international students; for spring admission, 10/1 for domestic and international students. Application fee: $50 ($40 for international students). Electronic applications accepted. *Expenses:* Tuition, state resident: part-time $476.50 per credit hour. Tuition, nonresident: part-time $1169.70 per credit hour. *Financial support:* Research assistantships and teaching assistantships available. Financial award application deadline: 4/1; financial award applicants required to submit FAFSA. *Faculty research:* Higher education law and policy, gender and higher education, student retention, lifelong learning orientation, school counselor's role in violence prevention. *Unit head:* Dr. Kathleen Haywood, Director of Graduate Studies, 314-516-5483, Fax: 314-516-5227, E-mail: kathleen_haywood@umsl.edu. *Application contact:* 314-516-5458, Fax: 314-516-6996, E-mail: gradadm@umsl.edu.

University of Montana, Graduate School, Phyllis J. Washington College of Education and Human Sciences, Department of Counselor Education, Missoula, MT 59812. Offers clinical mental health counseling (MA); counseling and supervision (Ed D); counselor education (Ed S); intercultural youth and family development (MA); school counseling (MA). *Accreditation:* ACA. *Degree requirements:* For doctorate, thesis/dissertation. *Entrance requirements:* For master's, doctorate, and Ed S, GRE General Test. Additional exam requirements/recommendations for international students: Required—TOEFL.

University of Montevallo, College of Education, Program in Counseling, Montevallo, AL 35115. Offers M Ed. *Accreditation:* ACA; NCATE. *Program availability:* Part-time, evening/weekend. *Students:* 55 full-time (47 women), 49 part-time (35 women); includes 28 minority (18 Black or African American, non-Hispanic/Latino; 6 Hispanic/Latino; 4 Two or more races, non-Hispanic/Latino). *Entrance requirements:* For master's, GRE General Test or MAT, minimum undergraduate GPA of 2.75 in last 60 hours or 2.5 overall, interview. Additional exam requirements/recommendations for international students: Required—TOEFL (minimum score 550 paper-based). *Application deadline:* For fall admission, 7/15 for domestic students; for spring admission, 11/15 for domestic students. Application fee: $30. *Expenses:* Tuition, state resident: full-time $9888. Tuition, nonresident: full-time $21,144. *Required fees:* $1920. *Financial support:* Federal Work-Study, scholarships/grants, and unspecified assistantships available. *Unit head:* Dr. Charlotte Daughhetee, Chair, 205-665-6358, E-mail: daughc@montevallo.edu. *Application contact:* Colleen Kennedy, Graduate Program Assistant, 205-665-6350, E-mail: ckennedy@montevallo.edu.
Website: http://www.montevallo.edu/education/college-of-education/traditional-masters-degrees/counseling/

University of Nebraska at Kearney, College of Education, Department of Counseling and School Psychology, Kearney, NE 68849-0001. Offers clinical mental health counseling (MS Ed); school counseling (MS Ed), including elementary, secondary; school psychology (Ed S); student affairs (MS Ed). *Accreditation:* ACA; NCATE. *Program availability:* Part-time, evening/weekend, 100% online. *Degree requirements:* For master's, comprehensive exam, thesis optional; for Ed S, thesis. *Entrance requirements:* For master's and Ed S, personal statement, recommendations, resume, interview. Additional exam requirements/recommendations for international students: Recommended—TOEFL (minimum score 550 paper-based; 79 iBT), IELTS (minimum score 6.5). Electronic applications accepted. *Faculty research:* Multicultural counseling and diversity issues, team decision-making, adult development, women's issues, brief therapy.

University of Nebraska at Omaha, Graduate Studies, College of Education, Department of Counseling, Omaha, NE 68182. Offers MA, MS. *Accreditation:* ACA (one or more programs are accredited); NCATE. *Program availability:* Part-time, evening/weekend. *Degree requirements:* For master's, comprehensive exam, thesis (for some programs). *Entrance requirements:* For master's, GRE General Test, MAT, interview, minimum GPA of 3.0, 3 letters of recommendation, transcripts. Additional exam requirements/recommendations for international students: Required—TOEFL, IELTS, PTE. Electronic applications accepted.

University of Nevada, Las Vegas, Graduate College, College of Education, Department of Educational and Clinical Studies, Las Vegas, NV 89154-3066. Offers addiction studies (Advanced Certificate); counselor education (M Ed, MS), including clinical mental health (MS), school counseling (M Ed); early childhood education (M Ed); early childhood special education (Certificate), including infancy, preschool; English language learning (M Ed); mental health counseling (Advanced Certificate); special education (M Ed, PhD); PhD/JD. *Program availability:* Part-time. *Faculty:* 18 full-time (9 women), 28 part-time/adjunct (22 women). *Students:* 281 full-time (230 women), 193 part-time (148 women); includes 211 minority (54 Black or African American, non-Hispanic/Latino; 2 American Indian or Alaska Native, non-Hispanic/Latino; 28 Asian, non-Hispanic/Latino; 95 Hispanic/Latino; 4 Native Hawaiian or other Pacific Islander, non-Hispanic/Latino; 28 Two or more races, non-Hispanic/Latino), 13 international. Average age 34. 262 applicants, 76% accepted, 161 enrolled. In 2017, 204 master's, 8 doctorates, 1 other advanced degree awarded. *Degree requirements:* For master's, comprehensive exam (for some programs); for doctorate, comprehensive exam, thesis/dissertation; for other advanced degree, final project. *Entrance requirements:* For master's, bachelor's degree; letter of recommendation; statement of purpose; for doctorate, GRE General Test, statement of purpose; writing sample; 3 letters of recommendation. Additional exam requirements/recommendations for international students: Required—TOEFL (minimum score 550 paper-based; 80 iBT), IELTS (minimum score 7). Application fee: $60 ($95 for international students). Electronic applications accepted. *Expenses:* $275 per credit, $850 per course, $7,969 per year

Counselor Education

resident, $22,157 per year non-resident, $7,094 non-resident fee (7 credits or more), $1,307 annual health insurance fee. *Financial support:* In 2017–18, 35 students received support, including 10 research assistantships with full tuition reimbursements available (averaging $13,775 per year), 25 teaching assistantships with full tuition reimbursements available (averaging $17,140 per year); institutionally sponsored loans, scholarships/grants, health care benefits, and unspecified assistantships also available. Financial award application deadline: 3/15; financial award applicants required to submit FAFSA. *Faculty research:* Multicultural issues in counseling, academic interventions for students with disabilities, establishment of pro-social skills in young children with severe disabilities, inclusive strategies for students with disabilities, language and literacy for English language learners. *Total annual research expenditures:* $1.1 million. *Unit head:* Dr. Monica Brown, Interim Department Chair/Professor, 702-895-3167, Fax: 702-895-3205, E-mail: monica.brown@unlv.edu. *Application contact:* Dr. Joseph Morgan, Graduate Coordinator, 702-895-3329, Fax: 702-895-3205, E-mail: joseph.morgan@unlv.edu.
Website: http://education.unlv.edu/ecs/

University of Nevada, Reno, Graduate School, College of Education, Department of Counseling and Educational Psychology, Reno, NV 89557. Offers M Ed, MA, MS, Ed D, PhD, Ed S. *Accreditation:* ACA (one or more programs are accredited); NCATE. Terminal master's awarded for partial completion of doctoral program. *Degree requirements:* For master's, comprehensive exam, thesis optional; for doctorate, comprehensive exam, thesis/dissertation, qualifying exam. *Entrance requirements:* For master's, GRE, minimum GPA of 2.75; for doctorate, GRE, minimum GPA of 3.0. Additional exam requirements/recommendations for international students: Required—TOEFL (minimum score 500 paper-based; 61 iBT), IELTS (minimum score 6). Electronic applications accepted. *Faculty research:* Marriage and family counseling, substance abuse attitudes of teachers, current supply of counseling educators, HIV-positive services for patients, family counseling for youth at risk.

University of New Mexico, Graduate Studies, College of Education, Program in Counselor Education, Albuquerque, NM 87131. Offers counseling (MA); counselor education (PhD). *Accreditation:* ACA (one or more programs are accredited); NCATE. *Program availability:* Part-time. *Students:* Average age 33. 69 applicants, 26% accepted, 16 enrolled. In 2017, 30 master's, 3 doctorates awarded. *Degree requirements:* For master's, comprehensive exam; for doctorate, comprehensive exam, thesis/dissertation. *Entrance requirements:* For master's, 3 letters of recommendation, personal statement; for doctorate, GRE General Test, 3 letters of recommendation, writing sample, personal statement. Additional exam requirements/recommendations for international students: Required—TOEFL. *Application deadline:* For fall admission, 11/1 for domestic and international students; for spring admission, 9/15 for domestic and international students. Application fee: $50. Electronic applications accepted. *Financial support:* Unspecified assistantships available. Financial award application deadline: 3/1; financial award applicants required to submit FAFSA. *Faculty research:* Counselor education and supervision, school counseling, LGBTQQI, crisis and trauma, multiculturalism. *Unit head:* Dr. Jean Keim, Program Coordinator, 505-277-4535, Fax: 505-277-8361, E-mail: divbse@unm.edu. *Application contact:* Cynthia Salas, Department Administrator, 505-277-4535, Fax: 505-277-8361, E-mail: divbse@unm.edu.
Website: https://coe.unm.edu/departments-programs/ifce/counselor-education/index.html

University of New Orleans, Graduate School, College of Education and Human Development, Department of Educational Leadership, Counseling, and Foundations, Program in Counselor Education, New Orleans, LA 70148. Offers M Ed, PhD. *Accreditation:* ACA (one or more programs are accredited); NCATE. *Program availability:* Evening/weekend. Terminal master's awarded for partial completion of doctoral program. *Degree requirements:* For master's, thesis (for some programs); for doctorate, variable foreign language requirement, thesis/dissertation. *Entrance requirements:* For master's and doctorate, GRE General Test. Additional exam requirements/recommendations for international students: Required—TOEFL (minimum score 550 paper-based; 79 iBT). Electronic applications accepted.

University of North Alabama, College of Education, Department of Counselor Education, Florence, AL 35632-0001. Offers clinical mental health counseling (MA); counseling (MA Ed). *Accreditation:* ACA; NCATE. *Program availability:* Part-time. *Faculty:* 3 full-time (all women), 2 part-time/adjunct (1 woman). *Students:* 13 full-time (12 women), 40 part-time (34 women); includes 7 minority (3 Black or African American, non-Hispanic/Latino; 1 American Indian or Alaska Native, non-Hispanic/Latino; 1 Hispanic/Latino; 2 Two or more races, non-Hispanic/Latino). Average age 30. 34 applicants, 44% accepted, 14 enrolled. In 2017, 11 master's awarded. *Degree requirements:* For master's, comprehensive exam. *Entrance requirements:* For master's, GRE, MAT, or NTE, minimum GPA of 2.5, Alabama Class B Certificate or equivalent, teaching experience. Additional exam requirements/recommendations for international students: Required—TOEFL (minimum score 79 iBT), IELTS (minimum score 6), PTE (minimum score 54). *Application deadline:* Applications are processed on a rolling basis. Application fee: $50 ($100 for international students). Electronic applications accepted. *Expenses:* Tuition, state resident: full-time $7824; part-time $5943 per year. Tuition, nonresident: full-time $15,648; part-time $11,736 per year. *Required fees:* $3064; $2298 per unit. Tuition and fees vary according to course load and reciprocity agreements. *Financial support:* In 2017–18, 2 students received support. Federal Work-Study, scholarships/grants, and unspecified assistantships available. Financial award application deadline: 2/1; financial award applicants required to submit FAFSA. *Unit head:* Dr. Quinn Pearson, Chair, 256-765-4763, Fax: 256-765-4159, E-mail: qmpearson@una.edu. *Application contact:* Hillary N. Coats, Graduate Admissions Coordinator, 256-765-4447, E-mail: graduate@una.edu.
Website: http://www.una.edu/education/departments/counselor-education.html

The University of North Carolina at Chapel Hill, Graduate School, School of Education, Program in School Counseling, Chapel Hill, NC 27599. Offers M Ed. *Accreditation:* ACA; NCATE. *Degree requirements:* For master's, comprehensive exam. *Entrance requirements:* For master's, GRE General Test, minimum GPA of 3.0 during last 2 years of undergraduate course work. Additional exam requirements/recommendations for international students: Required—TOEFL (minimum score 550 paper-based). Electronic applications accepted. *Faculty research:* Career counseling, development and assessment, multicultural counseling, measurement.

The University of North Carolina at Charlotte, Cato College of Education, Department of Counseling, Charlotte, NC 28223-0001. Offers counseling (MA); counselor education and supervision (PhD); play therapy (Postbaccalaureate Certificate); school counseling (Post-Master's Certificate); substance abuse counseling (Postbaccalaureate Certificate). *Accreditation:* ACA. *Program availability:* Part-time, evening/weekend. *Faculty:* 11 full-time (7 women), 9 part-time/adjunct (7 women). *Students:* 144 full-time (120 women), 83 part-time (72 women); includes 72 minority (46 Black or African American, non-Hispanic/Latino; 5 Asian, non-Hispanic/Latino; 18 Hispanic/Latino; 3 Two or more races, non-Hispanic/Latino), 2 international. Average age 30. 260 applicants, 49% accepted, 80 enrolled. In 2017, 59 master's, 6 doctorates, 23 other advanced degrees awarded. Terminal master's awarded for partial completion of doctoral program. *Degree requirements:* For master's, thesis or alternative, practicum, internship; for doctorate, thesis/dissertation; for other advanced degree, internship. *Entrance*

requirements: For master's, GRE or MAT, bachelor's degree from regionally-accredited university, minimum overall GPA of 3.0, brief statement of purpose, professional references, official transcripts; for doctorate, GRE or MAT, master's degree in counseling from a CACREP-accredited program with minimum cumulative GPA of 3.5; one year of experience as a professional counselor (preferred); letters of reference; essay; interview; for other advanced degree, statement of purpose, three reference letters. Additional exam requirements/recommendations for international students: Required—TOEFL (minimum score 523 paper-based, 70 iBT) or IELTS (6.5). *Application deadline:* For fall admission, 12/1 for domestic and international students; for summer admission, 12/1 for domestic and international students. Applications are processed on a rolling basis. Application fee: $75. Electronic applications accepted. *Expenses:* Tuition, state resident: full-time $4337. Tuition, nonresident: full-time $17,771. *Required fees:* $3211. Tuition and fees vary according to course load and program. *Financial support:* In 2017–18, 5 students received support, including 3 research assistantships (averaging $7,000 per year), 2 teaching assistantships (averaging $3,500 per year); career-related internships or fieldwork, institutionally sponsored loans, scholarships/grants, and unspecified assistantships also available. Support available to part-time students. Financial award application deadline: 3/1; financial award applicants required to submit FAFSA. *Total annual research expenditures:* $10,000. *Unit head:* Dr. Henry L. Harris, Chair, 704-687-8960, E-mail: hharris2@uncc.edu. *Application contact:* Kathy B. Giddings, Director of Graduate Admissions, 704-687-5503, Fax: 704-687-1668, E-mail: gradadm@uncc.edu.
Website: http://counseling.uncc.edu/

The University of North Carolina at Greensboro, Graduate School, School of Education, Department of Counseling and Educational Development, Greensboro, NC 27412-5001. Offers advanced school counseling (PMC); counseling and counselor education (PhD); counseling and educational development (MS); couple and family counseling (PMC); school counseling (PMC); MS/Ed S. *Accreditation:* ACA (one or more programs are accredited); NCATE. *Degree requirements:* For master's, comprehensive exam, practicum, internship; for doctorate, comprehensive exam, thesis/dissertation. *Entrance requirements:* For master's, doctorate, and PMC, GRE General Test. Additional exam requirements/recommendations for international students: Required—TOEFL. Electronic applications accepted. *Faculty research:* Gerontology, invitational theory, career development, marriage and family therapy, drug and alcohol abuse prevention.

The University of North Carolina at Pembroke, The Graduate School, School of Education, Programs in Counseling, Pembroke, NC 28372-1510. Offers clinical mental health counseling (MA Ed); professional school counseling (MA Ed). *Accreditation:* NCATE. *Program availability:* Part-time, evening/weekend. *Degree requirements:* For master's, comprehensive exam, thesis optional. *Entrance requirements:* For master's, GRE General Test or MAT, minimum GPA of 3.0 in major, 2.5 overall. Additional exam requirements/recommendations for international students: Required—TOEFL. *Application deadline:* For fall admission, 7/15 priority date for domestic and international students; for spring admission, 12/1 priority date for domestic and international students. Applications are processed on a rolling basis. Application fee: $45 ($60 for international students). *Financial support:* Application deadline: 4/15; applicants required to submit FAFSA. *Unit head:* Dr. Jeffrey M. Warren, Department Chair, 910-775-4414, Fax: 910-521-6165, E-mail: jeffrey.warren@uncp.edu.

University of Northern Colorado, Graduate School, College of Education and Behavioral Sciences, Department of Applied Psychology and Counselor Education, Program in Counselor Education and Supervision, Greeley, CO 80639. Offers PhD. *Accreditation:* ACA. *Program availability:* Part-time. *Degree requirements:* For doctorate, comprehensive exam, thesis/dissertation. *Entrance requirements:* For doctorate, GRE General Test, 3 letters of recommendation.

University of Northern Colorado, Graduate School, College of Education and Behavioral Sciences, Department of Applied Psychology and Counselor Education, Program in School Counseling, Greeley, CO 80639. Offers MA. *Accreditation:* ACA. *Program availability:* Part-time. Electronic applications accepted.

University of Northern Iowa, Graduate College, College of Social and Behavioral Sciences, School of Applied Human Sciences, MA Program in Counseling, Cedar Falls, IA 50614. Offers mental health counseling (MA); school counseling (MA). *Accreditation:* ACA. *Program availability:* Part-time, evening/weekend. *Degree requirements:* For master's, comprehensive exam, thesis or alternative. *Entrance requirements:* For master's, minimum GPA of 3.0. Additional exam requirements/recommendations for international students: Required—TOEFL (minimum score 500 paper-based; 61 iBT). Electronic applications accepted.

University of North Florida, College of Education and Human Services, Department of Leadership, School Counseling and Sport Management, Jacksonville, FL 32224. Offers counselor education (M Ed), including school counseling; educational leadership (M Ed, Ed D), including athletic administration (M Ed), educational leadership, educational technology (M Ed), instructional leadership (M Ed). *Program availability:* Part-time, evening/weekend. *Degree requirements:* For doctorate, thesis/dissertation. *Entrance requirements:* For master's, GRE General Test, minimum GPA of 3.0 in last 60 hours, interview, 3 letters of recommendation; for doctorate, GRE General Test, master's degree, interview, 3 letters of recommendation, writing sample. Additional exam requirements/recommendations for international students: Required—TOEFL (minimum score 500 paper-based). Electronic applications accepted. *Faculty research:* Counseling: ethics; lesbian, bisexual and transgender issues; educational leadership: school culture and climate; educational assessment and accountability; school safety and student discipline.

University of North Texas, Robert B. Toulouse School of Graduate Studies, Denton, TX 76203-5459. Offers accounting (MS); applied anthropology (MA, MS); applied behavior analysis (Certificate); applied geography (MA); applied technology and performance improvement (M Ed, MS); art education (MA); art history (MA); art museum education (Certificate); arts leadership (Certificate); audiology (Au D); behavior analysis (MS); behavioral science (PhD); biochemistry and molecular biology (MS); biology (MA, MS); biomedical engineering (MS); business analysis (MS); chemistry (MS); clinical health psychology (PhD); communication studies (MA, MS); computer engineering (MS); computer science (MS); counseling (M Ed, MS), including clinical mental health counseling (MS), college and university counseling, elementary school counseling, secondary school counseling; creative writing (MA); criminal justice (MS); curriculum and instruction (M Ed); decision sciences (MBA); design (MA, MFA), including fashion design (MFA), innovation studies, interior design (MFA); early childhood studies (MS); economics (MS); educational leadership (M Ed, Ed D); educational psychology (MS, PhD), including family studies (MS), gifted and talented (MS), human development (MS), learning and cognition (MS), research, measurement and evaluation (MS); electrical engineering (MS); emergency management (MPA); engineering technology (MS); English (MA); English as a second language (MA); environmental science (MS); finance (MBA, MS); financial management (MPA); French (MA); health services management (MBA); higher education (M Ed, Ed D); history (MA, MS); hospitality management (MS); human resources management (MPA); information science (MS); information systems (PhD); information technologies (MBA); interdisciplinary studies (MA, MS); international studies (MA); international sustainable tourism (MS); jazz studies (MM); journalism (MA,

MJ, Graduate Certificate), including interactive and virtual digital communication (Graduate Certificate), narrative journalism (Graduate Certificate), public relations (Graduate Certificate); kinesiology (MS); linguistics (MA); local government management (MPA); logistics (PhD); logistics and supply chain management (MBA); long-term care, senior housing, and aging services (MA); management (PhD); marketing (MBA); mathematics (MA, MS); mechanical and energy engineering (MS, PhD); music (MA), including ethnomusicology, music theory, musicology, performance; music composition (PhD); music education (MM Ed, PhD); nonprofit management (MPA); operations and supply chain management (MBA); performance (MM, DMA); philosophy (MA); political science (MA); professional and technical communication (MA); radio, television and film (MA, MFA); rehabilitation counseling (Certificate); sociology (MA); Spanish (MA); special education (M Ed); speech-language pathology (MA); strategic management (MBA); studio art (MFA); teaching (M Ed); MBA/MS. *Program availability:* Part-time, evening/weekend, online learning. Terminal master's awarded for partial completion of doctoral program. *Degree requirements:* For master's, variable foreign language requirement, comprehensive exam (for some programs), thesis (for some programs); for doctorate, variable foreign language requirement, comprehensive exam (for some programs), thesis/dissertation; for other advanced degree, variable foreign language requirement, comprehensive exam (for some programs). *Entrance requirements:* For master's and doctorate, GRE, GMAT. Additional exam requirements/ recommendations for international students: Required—TOEFL (minimum score 550 paper-based; 79 iBT). Electronic applications accepted.

University of North Texas at Dallas, Graduate School, Dallas, TX 75241. Offers accounting (MBA); counseling (M Ed, MS); criminal justice (MS); curriculum and instruction (M Ed); educational administration (M Ed); human resources and organizational behavior (MBA); public leadership (MS); strategic management (MBA).

University of Pennsylvania, Graduate School of Education, Division of Human Development and Quantitative Methods, Program in School and Mental Health Counseling, Philadelphia, PA 19104. Offers MS Ed. *Students:* Average age 31. 59 applicants, 80% accepted, 40 enrolled. In 2017, 29 master's awarded.

University of Phoenix–Las Vegas Campus, College of Human Services, Las Vegas, NV 89135. Offers marriage, family, and child therapy (MSC); mental health counseling (MSC); school counseling (MSC). *Program availability:* Online learning. *Entrance requirements:* For master's, minimum undergraduate GPA of 2.5, 3 years of work experience. Additional exam requirements/recommendations for international students: Required—TOEFL (minimum score 550 paper-based; 79 iBT). Electronic applications accepted.

University of Phoenix–Phoenix Campus, College of Social Sciences, Tempe, AZ 85282-2371. Offers counseling (MS), including clinical mental health counseling, community counseling, counseling, marriage, family and child therapy; psychology (MS). *Program availability:* Evening/weekend, online learning. *Entrance requirements:* Additional exam requirements/recommendations for international students: Required— TOEFL, TOEIC (Test of English as an International Communication), Berlitz Online English Proficiency Exam, PTE, or IELTS. Electronic applications accepted. *Expenses:* Contact institution.

University of Puerto Rico–Río Piedras, College of Education, Program in Guidance and Counseling, San Juan, PR 00931-3300. Offers M Ed and Ed D. *Program availability:* Part-time. *Degree requirements:* For master's, thesis; for doctorate, thesis/dissertation, internship. *Entrance requirements:* For master's, PAEG or GRE, interview, minimum GPA of 3.0, letter of recommendation; for doctorate, GRE or PAEG, master's degree, minimum GPA of 3.0, letter of recommendation (2), interview.

University of Puget Sound, School of Education, Program in Counseling, Tacoma, WA 98416. Offers mental health counseling (M Ed); school counseling (M Ed). *Program availability:* Part-time. *Degree requirements:* For master's, capstone course. *Entrance requirements:* For master's, GRE General Test, interview. Additional exam requirements/recommendations for international students: Required—TOEFL (minimum score 550 paper-based; 90 iBT). Electronic applications accepted. *Expenses:* Contact institution. *Faculty research:* Suicide prevention.

University of Rochester, Margaret Warner Graduate School of Education and Human Development, Doctoral Programs in Education, Rochester, NY 14627. Offers counseling (Ed D); educational administration (Ed D); educational policy and theory (PhD); higher education (PhD); human development in educational context (PhD); teaching, curriculum, and change (PhD).

University of Rochester, Margaret Warner Graduate School of Education and Human Development, Master's Program in Counseling, Rochester, NY 14627. Offers school and community counseling (MS); school counseling (MS).

University of Saint Francis, Graduate School, Department of Behavioral and Social Sciences, Fort Wayne, IN 46808-3994. Offers clinical mental health counseling (MS, Post Master's Certificate); psychology (MS); school counseling (MS Ed). *Program availability:* Part-time, evening/weekend. *Faculty:* 4 full-time (0 women). *Students:* 23 full-time (18 women), 7 part-time (6 women); includes 8 minority (7 Black or African American, non-Hispanic/Latino; 1 Asian, non-Hispanic/Latino), 1 international. Average age 30. 18 applicants, 83% accepted, 12 enrolled. In 2017, 23 master's awarded. *Entrance requirements:* For master's, GRE with minimum score of 150 if undergraduate GPA is below 3.0 (for MS Ed in school counseling), minimum undergraduate GPA of 3.0; undergraduate coursework in psychology; statement of professional goals (for MS); 2 professional recommendations; interview (for mental health counseling and school counseling). Additional exam requirements/recommendations for international students: Required—TOEFL (minimum score 550 paper-based) or IELTS (minimum score 6.5). *Application deadline:* For fall admission, 7/1 for international students; for spring admission, 11/1 for international students; for summer admission, 3/1 for international students. Applications are processed on a rolling basis. Application fee: $0. Electronic applications accepted. *Expenses:* $905 per credit. *Financial support:* In 2017–18, 3 students received support. Federal Work-Study, scholarships/grants, and unspecified assistantships available. Financial award application deadline: 4/15; financial award applicants required to submit FAFSA. *Unit head:* Dr. John Brinkman, Chair of Department of Behavioral and Social Sciences, 260-399-7700 Ext. 8425, E-mail: jbrinkman@sf.edu. *Application contact:* Kyle Richardson, Associate Director of Enrollment Services for Adult Learning, 260-399-7700 Ext. 6310, Fax: 260-399-8152, E-mail: krichardson@sf.edu.
Website: https://bhvscience.sf.edu/

University of Saint Joseph, Department of Counseling and Applied Behavioral Studies, West Hartford, CT 06117-2700. Offers clinical mental health counseling (MA); school counseling (MA). *Accreditation:* ACA. *Program availability:* Part-time, evening/weekend. *Degree requirements:* For master's, comprehensive exam, thesis optional. *Entrance requirements:* For master's, 2 letters of recommendation. *Application deadline:* Applications are processed on a rolling basis. Application fee: $50. Electronic applications accepted. Application fee is waived when completed online. *Financial support:* Career-related internships or fieldwork and unspecified assistantships available. Support available to part-time students. Financial award applicants required to submit FAFSA. Website: https://www.usj.edu/academics/schools/sihs/counseling-and-applied-behavioral-studies/

University of St. Thomas, School of Education and Human Services, Houston, TX 77006-4696. Offers all level education (M Ed); bilingual/dual language (M Ed); Catholic school teaching (M Ed); Catholic/private school leadership (M Ed); counselor education (M Ed); curriculum and instruction (M Ed); education (Ed D); educational leadership (M Ed); elementary teaching (M Ed); English as a second language (M Ed); exceptionality/educational diagnostician (M Ed); exceptionality/special education (M Ed); generalist (M Ed); reading (M Ed); secondary teaching (M Ed); teaching (MAT). *Accreditation:* TEAC. *Program availability:* Part-time, evening/weekend, online learning. *Faculty:* 33 full-time (22 women), 43 part-time/adjunct (26 women). *Students:* 119 full-time (97 women), 597 part-time (529 women); includes 478 minority (166 Black or African American, non-Hispanic/Latino; 29 Asian, non-Hispanic/Latino; 277 Hispanic/Latino; 2 Native Hawaiian or other Pacific Islander, non-Hispanic/Latino; 4 Two or more races, non-Hispanic/Latino), 19 international. Average age 36. 306 applicants, 91% accepted, 181 enrolled. In 2017, 328 master's awarded. *Degree requirements:* For master's, thesis, field experience. *Entrance requirements:* For master's, GRE or MAT if GPA is below 3.0, bachelor's degree; minimum GPA of 2.75 in bachelor's degree or last 60 credit hours; official transcripts from all institutions; goal statement of 250-300 words; 1 reference. Additional exam requirements/recommendations for international students: Required—TOEFL (minimum score 94 iBT), IELTS (minimum score 7), PTE (minimum score 53). *Application deadline:* Applications are processed on a rolling basis. Application fee: $35. Electronic applications accepted. *Expenses:* Contact institution. *Financial support:* In 2017–18, 27 students received support. Federal Work-Study, scholarships/grants, and state work-study, institutional employment available. Support available to part-time students. Financial award application deadline: 4/15; financial award applicants required to submit FAFSA. *Faculty research:* Leadership, diversity, personality traits, second language acquisition. *Unit head:* Dr. Paul C. Paese, Dean, 713-942-5999, Fax: 713-525-3871, E-mail: paesep@stthom.edu. *Application contact:* 713-525-3540, E-mail: education@stthom.edu.
Website: http://www.stthom.edu/Academics/
School_of_Education_and_Human_Services/Index.aqf

University of San Diego, School of Leadership and Education Sciences, Department of Counseling and Marital and Family Therapy, San Diego, CA 92110-2492. Offers clinical mental health counseling (MA); marital and family therapy (MA); school counseling (MA). *Accreditation:* ACA. *Program availability:* Part-time, evening/weekend. *Faculty:* 13 full-time (6 women), 26 part-time/adjunct (18 women). *Students:* 172 full-time (155 women), 50 part-time (42 women); includes 106 minority (13 Black or African American, non-Hispanic/Latino; 1 American Indian or Alaska Native, non-Hispanic/Latino; 20 Asian, non-Hispanic/Latino; 62 Hispanic/Latino; 10 Two or more races, non-Hispanic/Latino), 5 international. Average age 27. 406 applicants, 45% accepted, 92 enrolled. In 2017, 69 master's awarded. *Degree requirements:* For master's, comprehensive exam, international experience. *Entrance requirements:* For master's, GRE or GMAT (minimum overall score in 50th percentile), group interview with faculty. Additional exam requirements/recommendations for international students: Required—TOEFL (minimum score 580 paper-based; 83 iBT), TWE. *Application deadline:* For fall admission, 1/13 priority date for domestic and international students. Applications are processed on a rolling basis. Application fee: $45. Electronic applications accepted. *Financial support:* In 2017–18, 160 students received support. Career-related internships or fieldwork, Federal Work-Study, institutionally sponsored loans, unspecified assistantships, and stipends available. Support available to part-time students. Financial award application deadline: 4/1; financial award applicants required to submit FAFSA. *Faculty research:* Action research, collaboration between family therapists and medical professionals, family therapy training and supervision, multicultural counseling, school counseling. *Unit head:* Dr. Ann Garland, Director, 619-260-7879, E-mail: agarland@sandiego.edu. *Application contact:* Monica Mahon, Director of Admissions and Enrollment, 619-260-4524, Fax: 619-260-4158, E-mail: grads@sandiego.edu.
Website: http://www.sandiego.edu/soles/counseling-and-marital-and-family-therapy//

University of San Francisco, School of Education, Department of Counseling Psychology, San Francisco, CA 94117-1080. Offers counseling (MA), including educational counseling, life transitions counseling, marital and family therapy. *Program availability:* Part-time. *Entrance requirements:* Additional exam requirements/recommendations for international students: Required—TOEFL, IELTS, PTE. Electronic applications accepted.

The University of Scranton, Panuska College of Professional Studies, Department of Counseling and Human Services, Program in School Counseling, Scranton, PA 18510. Offers MS. *Accreditation:* ACA; NCATE. *Program availability:* Part-time, evening/weekend. *Degree requirements:* For master's, comprehensive exam (for some programs), thesis (for some programs), capstone experience. *Entrance requirements:* For master's, minimum GPA of 3.0, three letters of reference. Additional exam requirements/recommendations for international students: Required—TOEFL (minimum score 500 paper-based; 80 iBT), IELTS (minimum score 6.5). Electronic applications accepted.

University of South Africa, College of Human Sciences, Pretoria, South Africa. Offers adult education (M Ed); African languages (MA, PhD); African politics (MA, PhD); Afrikaans (MA, PhD); ancient history (MA, PhD); ancient Near Eastern studies (MA, PhD); anthropology (MA, PhD); applied linguistics (MA); Arabic (MA, PhD); archaeology (MA); art history (MA); Biblical archaeology (MA); Biblical studies (M Th, D Th, PhD); Christian spirituality (M Th, D Th); church history (M Th, D Th); classical studies (MA, PhD); clinical psychology (MA); communication (MA); comparative education (M Ed, Ed D); consulting psychology (D Admin, D Com, PhD); curriculum studies (M Ed, Ed D); development studies (M Admin, MA, D Admin, PhD); didactics (M Ed, Ed D); education (M Tech); education management (M Ed, Ed D); educational psychology (M Ed); English (MA); environmental education (M Ed); French (MA, PhD); German (MA, PhD); Greek (MA); guidance and counseling (M Ed); health studies (MA, PhD), including health sciences education (MA), health services management (MA), medical and surgical nursing science (critical care general) (MA), midwifery and neonatal nursing science (MA), trauma and emergency care (MA); history (MA, PhD); history of education (Ed D); inclusive education (M Ed, Ed D); information and communications technology policy and regulation (MA); information science (MA, MIS, PhD); international politics (MA, PhD); Islamic studies (MA, PhD); Italian (MA, PhD); Judaica (MA, PhD); linguistics (MA, PhD); mathematical education (M Ed); mathematics education (MA); missiology (M Th, D Th); modern Hebrew (MA, PhD); musicology (MA, MMus, D Mus, PhD); natural science education (M Ed); New Testament (M Th, D Th); Old Testament (D Th); pastoral therapy (M Th, D Th); philosophy (MA); philosophy of education (M Ed, Ed D); politics (MA, PhD); Portuguese (MA, PhD); practical theology (M Th, D Th); psychology (MA, MS, PhD); psychology of education (M Ed, Ed D); public health (MA); religious studies (MA, D Th, PhD); Romance languages (MA); Russian (MA, PhD); Semitic languages (MA, PhD); social behavior studies in HIV/AIDS (MA); social science (mental health) (MA); social science in development studies (MA); social science in psychology (MA); social science in social work (MA); social science in sociology (MA); social work (MSW, DSW, PhD); socio-education (M Ed, Ed D); sociolinguistics (MA); sociology (MA, PhD); Spanish (MA, PhD); systematic theology (M Th, D Th); TESOL (teaching English to speakers of other languages) (MA); theological ethics (M Th, D Th); theory of literature (MA, PhD); urban ministries (D Th); urban ministry (M Th).

Counselor Education

University of South Alabama, College of Education and Professional Studies, Department of Counseling and Instructional Sciences, Mobile, AL 36688. Offers clinical mental health counseling (MS); educational media (M Ed); educational media and technology (MS); instructional design and development (MS, PhD); instructional leadership (Ed S); school counseling (M Ed). *Accreditation:* NCATE. *Program availability:* Part-time. *Faculty:* 12 full-time (7 women), 10 part-time/adjunct (9 women). *Students:* 110 full-time (85 women), 39 part-time (32 women); includes 43 minority (33 Black or African American, non-Hispanic/Latino; 4 Asian, non-Hispanic/Latino; 5 Hispanic/Latino; 1 Two or more races, non-Hispanic/Latino), 5 international. Average age 34. 68 applicants, 53% accepted, 31 enrolled. In 2017, 32 master's, 9 doctorates, 10 other advanced degrees awarded. *Degree requirements:* For master's, comprehensive exam; for doctorate, comprehensive exam, thesis/dissertation. *Entrance requirements:* For master's, GRE General Test or MAT, minimum GPA of 3.0, three letters of recommendation; for doctorate, GRE, three letters of recommendation, master's degree in field or completion of prerequisites, resume. Additional exam requirements/recommendations for international students: Required—TOEFL (minimum score 525 paper-based; 71 iBT). *Application deadline:* For fall admission, 6/15 for domestic and international students; for spring admission, 12/1 for domestic students, 11/1 for international students; for summer admission, 4/1 for domestic and international students. Applications are processed on a rolling basis. Application fee: $35. Electronic applications accepted. *Expenses:* Tuition, state resident: full-time $10,104; part-time $421 per semester hour. Tuition, nonresident: full-time $20,208; part-time $842 per semester hour. *Financial support:* Fellowships, research assistantships, teaching assistantships, career-related internships or fieldwork, Federal Work-Study, institutionally sponsored loans, scholarships/grants, and unspecified assistantships available. Support available to part-time students. Financial award application deadline: 3/31; financial award applicants required to submit FAFSA. *Faculty research:* Agency counseling, rehabilitation counseling, school psychometry, juvenile delinquency, mixed methods research. *Unit head:* Dr. Tres Stefurak, Department Chair, 251-380-2734, Fax: 251-380-2713, E-mail: jstefurak@southalabama.edu. *Application contact:* Dr. James Van Haneghan, Graduate Coordinator, 251-380-2760, Fax: 251-380-2713, E-mail: jvanhane@southalabama.edu.
Website: http://www.southalabama.edu/colleges/ceps/cins/

University of South Carolina, The Graduate School, College of Education, Department of Educational Studies, Program in Counseling Education, Columbia, SC 29208. Offers PhD, Ed S. *Accreditation:* ACA (one or more programs are accredited); NCATE. *Program availability:* Part-time. *Degree requirements:* For doctorate, one foreign language, comprehensive exam, thesis/dissertation; for Ed S, comprehensive exam. *Entrance requirements:* For doctorate, GRE General Test or MAT, interview, resume, references; for Ed S, GRE General Test or MAT, interview, resum&e, transcripts, letter of intent, references. Electronic applications accepted. *Faculty research:* Multicultural counseling, children's fears, career development, family counseling.

University of South Dakota, Graduate School, School of Education, Division of Counseling and Psychology in Education, Vermillion, SD 57069. Offers counseling (MA, PhD, Ed S); human development and educational psychology (MA, PhD, Ed S); mental health counseling (Certificate); school psychology (PhD, Ed S). *Accreditation:* ACA (one or more programs are accredited); NCATE. *Program availability:* Part-time. *Degree requirements:* For master's and other advanced degree, comprehensive exam, thesis or alternative; for doctorate, comprehensive exam, thesis/dissertation. *Entrance requirements:* For master's and doctorate, GRE General Test, minimum GPA of 3.0. Additional exam requirements/recommendations for international students: Required—TOEFL (minimum score 550 paper-based; 79 iBT). *Application deadline:* Applications are processed on a rolling basis. Application fee: $35. Electronic applications accepted. *Financial support:* Research assistantships with partial tuition reimbursements, teaching assistantships with partial tuition reimbursements, career-related internships or fieldwork, Federal Work-Study, and unspecified assistantships available. Financial award applicants required to submit FAFSA. *Application contact:* Graduate School, 605-658-6140, Fax: 605-677-6118.
Website: http://www.usd.edu/cpe

University of Southern California, Graduate School, Rossier School of Education, Master's Programs in Education, Los Angeles, CA 90089-4038. Offers educational counseling (ME); marriage, family and child counseling (MMFT); postsecondary administration and student affairs [PASA] (ME); school counseling (ME); teaching (online) (MAT); teaching and teaching credential (MAT); teaching English to speakers of other languages (MAT). *Program availability:* Part-time, evening/weekend, online learning. *Degree requirements:* For master's, thesis optional. *Entrance requirements:* For master's, GRE (for all programs except MAT). Additional exam requirements/recommendations for international students: Required—TOEFL (minimum score 100 iBT). Electronic applications accepted. *Faculty research:* College access and equity, preparing teachers for culturally diverse populations, sociocultural basis of learning as mediated by instruction with focus on reading and literacy in English learners, social and political aspects of teaching and learning English, school counselor development and training.

University of Southern Maine, College of Management and Human Service, School of Education and Human Development, Program in Counselor Education, Portland, ME 04103. Offers clinical mental health counseling (MS); counseling (CAS); culturally responsive practices in education and human development (CGS); mental health rehabilitation technician/community (CGS); rehabilitation counseling (MS); school counseling (MS); substance abuse counseling (CGS). *Accreditation:* ACA (one or more programs are accredited); CORE; TEAC. *Program availability:* Part-time, evening/weekend. *Degree requirements:* For master's, comprehensive exam, thesis or alternative; for other advanced degree, thesis or alternative. *Entrance requirements:* For master's, GRE General Test or MAT, interview; for other advanced degree, master's degree. Additional exam requirements/recommendations for international students: Required—TOEFL (minimum score 550 paper-based; 79 iBT). Electronic applications accepted. *Faculty research:* Counselor licensure, group dynamics, counseling theories, healthy adaptation, counselor educator well-being.

University of South Florida, College of Education, Department of Educational and Psychological Studies, Tampa, FL 33620-9951. Offers college student affairs (M Ed); counselor education (MA, PhD, Ed S); interdisciplinary education (PhD, Ed S); school psychology (PhD, Ed S). *Faculty:* 28 full-time (13 women). *Students:* 115 full-time (77 women), 107 part-time (80 women); includes 59 minority (29 Black or African American, non-Hispanic/Latino; 6 Asian, non-Hispanic/Latino; 18 Hispanic/Latino; 1 Native Hawaiian or other Pacific Islander, non-Hispanic/Latino; 5 Two or more races, non-Hispanic/Latino), 23 international. Average age 33. 163 applicants, 72% accepted, 84 enrolled. In 2017, 46 master's, 5 doctorates, 1 other advanced degree awarded. Application fee: $30. *Faculty research:* College student affairs, counselor education, educational psychology, school psychology, social foundations. *Total annual research expenditures:* $9 million. *Unit head:* Dr. Barabara Shircliff, Chair, 813-974-4001, E-mail: shirclif@usf.edu.

University of South Florida, College of Education, Department of Leadership, Counseling, Adult, Career and Higher Education, Tampa, FL 33620-9951. Offers adult education (MA, Ed D, PhD, Ed S); career and technical education (MA); career and workforce education (PhD); higher education/community college teaching (MA, Ed D, PhD); vocational education (Ed S). *Faculty:* 19 full-time (11 women). *Students:* 129 full-time (91 women), 274 part-time (187 women); includes 147 minority (71 Black or African American, non-Hispanic/Latino; 2 American Indian or Alaska Native, non-Hispanic/Latino; 9 Asian, non-Hispanic/Latino; 59 Hispanic/Latino; 6 Two or more races, non-Hispanic/Latino), 15 international. Average age 35. 158 applicants, 67% accepted, 83 enrolled. In 2017, 89 master's, 7 doctorates, 2 other advanced degrees awarded. Application fee: $30. *Total annual research expenditures:* $157,971. *Unit head:* Dr. Judith Ponticell, Chair, 813-974-4897, Fax: 813-974-5423, E-mail: jponticell@usf.edu.
Website: http://www.coedu.usf.edu/main/departments/ache/ache.html

University of South Florida, Innovative Education, Tampa, FL 33620-9951. Offers adult, career and higher education (Graduate Certificate), including college teaching, leadership in developing human resources, leadership in higher education; Africana studies (Graduate Certificate), including diasporas and health disparities, genocide and human rights; aging studies (Graduate Certificate), including gerontology; art research (Graduate Certificate), including museum studies; business foundations (Graduate Certificate); chemical and biomedical engineering (Graduate Certificate), including materials science and engineering, water, health and sustainability; child and family studies (Graduate Certificate), including positive behavior support; civil and industrial engineering (Graduate Certificate), including transportation systems analysis; community and family health (Graduate Certificate), including maternal and child health, social marketing and public health, violence and injury: prevention and intervention, women's health; criminology (Graduate Certificate), including criminal justice administration; data science for public administration (Graduate Certificate); digital humanities (Graduate Certificate); educational measurement and research (Graduate Certificate), including evaluation; English (Graduate Certificate), including comparative literary studies, creative writing, professional and technical communication; entrepreneurship (Graduate Certificate); environmental health (Graduate Certificate), including safety management; epidemiology and biostatistics (Graduate Certificate), including applied biostatistics, biostatistics, concepts and tools of epidemiology, epidemiology, epidemiology of infectious diseases; geography, environment and planning (Graduate Certificate), including community development, environmental policy and management, geographical information systems; geology (Graduate Certificate), including hydrogeology; global health (Graduate Certificate), including disaster management, global health and Latin American and Caribbean studies, global health practice, humanitarian assistance, infection control; government and international affairs (Graduate Certificate), including Cuban studies, globalization studies; health policy and management (Graduate Certificate), including health management and leadership, public health policy and programs; hearing specialist: early intervention (Graduate Certificate); industrial and management systems engineering (Graduate Certificate), including systems engineering, technology management; information studies (Graduate Certificate), including school library media specialist; information systems/decision sciences (Graduate Certificate), including analytics and business intelligence; instructional technology (Graduate Certificate), including distance education, Florida digital/virtual educator, instructional design, multimedia design, Web design; internal medicine, bioethics and medical humanities (Graduate Certificate), including biomedical ethics; Latin American and Caribbean studies (Graduate Certificate); leadership for coastal resiliency planning (Graduate Certificate); mass communications (Graduate Certificate), including multimedia journalism; mathematics and statistics (Graduate Certificate), including mathematics; medicine (Graduate Certificate), including aging and neuroscience, bioinformatics, biotechnology, brain fitness and memory management, clinical investigation, hand and upper limb rehabilitation, health informatics, health sciences, integrative weight management, intellectual property, medicine and gender, metabolic and nutritional medicine, metabolic cardiology, pharmacy sciences; national and competitive intelligence (Graduate Certificate); nursing (Graduate Certificate), including simulation based academic fellowship in advanced pain management; psychological and social foundations (Graduate Certificate), including career counseling, college teaching, diversity in education, mental health counseling, school counseling; public affairs (Graduate Certificate), including nonprofit management, public management, research administration; public health (Graduate Certificate), including assessing chemical toxicity and public health risks, health equity, pharmacoepidemiology, public health generalist, toxicology, translational research in adolescent behavioral health; public health practices (Graduate Certificate), including planning for healthy communities; rehabilitation and mental health counseling (Graduate Certificate), including integrative mental health care, marriage and family therapy, rehabilitation technology; secondary education (Graduate Certificate), including ESOL, foreign language education: culture and content, foreign language education: professional; social work (Graduate Certificate), including geriatric social work/clinical gerontology; special education (Graduate Certificate), including autism spectrum disorder, disabilities education: severe/profound; world languages (Graduate Certificate), including teaching English as a second language (TESL) or foreign language. *Unit head:* Dr. Cynthia DeLuca, Associate Vice President and Assistant Vice Provost, 813-974-3077, Fax: 813-974-7061, E-mail: deluca@usf.edu. *Application contact:* Owen Hooper, Director, Summer and Alternative Calendar Programs, 813-974-6917, E-mail: hooper@usf.edu.
Website: http://www.usf.edu/innovative-education/

The University of Tennessee, Graduate School, College of Education, Health and Human Sciences, Department of Educational Psychology and Counseling, Knoxville, TN 37996. Offers adult education (MS); applied educational psychology (MS); collaborative learning (Ed D); college student personnel (MS); mental health counseling (MS); rehabilitation counseling (MS); school counseling (MS). *Accreditation:* ACA (one or more programs are accredited); CORE (one or more programs are accredited); NCATE. *Program availability:* Part-time, evening/weekend. *Degree requirements:* For master's, thesis optional. *Entrance requirements:* For master's, GRE General Test, minimum GPA of 2.7. Additional exam requirements/recommendations for international students: Required—TOEFL. Electronic applications accepted.

The University of Tennessee, Graduate School, College of Education, Health and Human Sciences, Program in Education, Knoxville, TN 37996. Offers art education (MS); counseling education (PhD); cultural studies in education (PhD); curriculum (MS, Ed S); curriculum, educational research and evaluation (Ed D, PhD); early childhood education (PhD); early childhood special education (MS); education of deaf and hard of hearing (MS); educational administration and policy studies (Ed D, PhD); educational administration and supervision (Ed S); educational psychology (Ed D, PhD); elementary education (MS, Ed S); elementary teaching (MS); English education (MS, Ed S); exercise science (PhD); foreign language/ESL education (MS, Ed S); instructional technology (MS, Ed D, PhD, Ed S); literacy, language and ESL education (PhD); literacy, language education, and ESL education (Ed D); mathematics education (MS, Ed S); modified and comprehensive special education (MS); reading education (MS, Ed S); school counseling (Ed S); school psychology (PhD, Ed S); science education (MS, Ed S); secondary teaching (MS); social foundations (MS); social science education (MS, Ed S); socio-cultural foundations of sports and education (PhD); special education (Ed S); teacher education (Ed D, PhD). *Accreditation:* NCATE. *Program availability:* Part-time, evening/weekend. *Degree requirements:* For master's and Ed S, thesis optional; for doctorate, variable foreign language requirement, thesis/dissertation.

Entrance requirements: For master's, minimum GPA of 2.7; for doctorate and Ed S, GRE General Test, minimum GPA of 2.7. Additional exam requirements/recommendations for international students: Required—TOEFL. Electronic applications accepted.

The University of Tennessee at Chattanooga, Program in Counseling, Chattanooga, TN 37403. Offers mental health (M Ed); school counseling (M Ed, Post Master's Certificate). *Students:* 44 full-time (36 women), 11 part-time (10 women); includes 13 minority (8 Black or African American, non-Hispanic/Latino; 1 Hispanic/Latino; 4 Two or more races, non-Hispanic/Latino). Average age 26. 49 applicants, 67% accepted, 24 enrolled. In 2017, 13 master's awarded. *Degree requirements:* For master's, comprehensive exam, internship. *Entrance requirements:* For master's, MAT or GRE, 2 letters of reference, interview; for Post Master's Certificate, graduate degree in counseling, 2 letters of reference. Additional exam requirements/recommendations for international students: Required—TOEFL (minimum score 550 paper-based; 79 iBT), IELTS (minimum score 6). *Application deadline:* For fall admission, 6/15 priority date for domestic students, 7/1 for international students; for spring admission, 11/1 priority date for domestic students, 11/1 for international students. Applications are processed on a rolling basis. Application fee: $35 ($40 for international students). Electronic applications accepted. *Expenses:* Tuition, state resident: full-time $8244; part-time $458 per credit hour. Tuition, nonresident: full-time $24,362; part-time $1353 per credit hour. *Required fees:* $1776; $487 per semester. Tuition and fees vary according to course load. *Financial support:* Research assistantships, career-related internships or fieldwork, scholarships/grants, and unspecified assistantships available. Support available to part-time students. Financial award application deadline: 7/1; financial award applicants required to submit FAFSA. *Faculty research:* Play therapy; clinical supervision; technology in marital infidelity; female inmates and recidivism; grief, loss and trauma in children. *Unit head:* Dr. Elizabeth O'Brien, Director, 423-425-4544, E-mail: elizabeth-o'brien@utc.edu. *Application contact:* Dr. Joanne Romagni, Dean of the Graduate School, 423-425-4478, Fax: 423-425-4052, E-mail: joanne-romagni@utc.edu. Website: https://www.utc.edu/counselor-education-program/

The University of Tennessee at Chattanooga, School of Education, Chattanooga, TN 37403. Offers counseling (M Ed), including community counseling, school counseling; education (M Ed, Post-Master's Certificate), including elementary education (M Ed), school leadership (Post-Master's Certificate); elementary education (M Ed); learning and leadership (Ed D), including educational leadership; school leadership (Post-Master's Certificate); school leadership: principal licensure (Ed S); secondary education (M Ed); special education (M Ed). *Accreditation:* ACA; NCATE. *Program availability:* Part-time. *Students:* 43 full-time (30 women), 58 part-time (47 women); includes 18 minority (9 Black or African American, non-Hispanic/Latino; 1 Asian, non-Hispanic/Latino; 1 Hispanic/Latino; 7 Two or more races, non-Hispanic/Latino). Average age 31. 118 applicants, 75% accepted, 33 enrolled. In 2017, 59 master's, 7 other advanced degrees awarded. *Degree requirements:* For master's, comprehensive exam, thesis optional, culminating experience; for other advanced degree, internship. *Entrance requirements:* For master's, GRE General Test, PPST 1, teaching certificate; for other advanced degree, two letters of recommendation, graduate degree in education, teaching certificate with three years of experience. Additional exam requirements/recommendations for international students: Required—TOEFL (minimum score 550 paper-based; 79 iBT), IELTS (minimum score 6). *Application deadline:* For fall admission, 6/15 for domestic students, 7/1 for international students; for spring admission, 11/1 for domestic and international students. Applications are processed on a rolling basis. Application fee: $35 ($40 for international students). Electronic applications accepted. *Expenses:* Contact institution. *Financial support:* Research assistantships, teaching assistantships, career-related internships or fieldwork, institutionally sponsored loans, scholarships/grants, and unspecified assistantships available. Support available to part-time students. Financial award application deadline: 7/1; financial award applicants required to submit FAFSA. *Faculty research:* School counseling, community counseling, elementary and secondary education, school leadership and administration. *Total annual research expenditures:* $576,495. *Unit head:* Dr. Renee Murley, Director, 423-425-4684, Fax: 423-425-5380, E-mail: renee-murley@utc.edu. *Application contact:* Dr. Joanne Romagni, Dean of the Graduate School, 423-425-4478, Fax: 423-425-5223, E-mail: joanne-romagni@utc.edu. Website: https://www.utc.edu/school-education/

The University of Tennessee at Martin, Graduate Programs, College of Education, Health and Behavioral Sciences, Program in Counseling, Martin, TN 38238. Offers addictions counseling (MS Ed); community counseling (MS Ed); school counseling (MS Ed); student affairs and college counseling (MS Ed). *Accreditation:* NCATE. *Program availability:* Part-time, online only, 100% online. *Students:* 17 full-time (15 women), 54 part-time (51 women); includes 7 minority (6 Black or African American, non-Hispanic/Latino; 1 Two or more races, non-Hispanic/Latino). Average age 34. 35 applicants, 54% accepted, 12 enrolled. In 2017, 14 master's awarded. *Degree requirements:* For master's, comprehensive exam. *Entrance requirements:* For master's, GRE General Test, minimum GPA of 2.5, resume, letters of reference. Additional exam requirements/recommendations for international students: Required—TOEFL (minimum score 525 paper-based; 71 iBT). *Application deadline:* For fall admission, 7/27 priority date for domestic and international students; for spring admission, 12/27 priority date for domestic and international students; for summer admission, 5/10 priority date for domestic and international students. Applications are processed on a rolling basis. Application fee: $30 ($130 for international students). Electronic applications accepted. *Expenses:* Tuition, state resident: full-time $8658; part-time $481 per credit hour. Tuition, nonresident: full-time $14,418; part-time $801 per credit hour. *International tuition:* $22,602 full-time. *Required fees:* $1404; $79 per credit hour. Part-time tuition and fees vary according to course load. *Financial support:* In 2017–18, 14 students received support, including 1 research assistantship with full tuition reimbursement available (averaging $7,540 per year), 2 teaching assistantships with full tuition reimbursements available (averaging $6,283 per year); scholarships/grants and tuition waivers (full and partial) also available. Financial award application deadline: 2/1; financial award applicants required to submit FAFSA. *Unit head:* Cynthia West, Dean, 731-881-7125, Fax: 731-881-7975, E-mail: cwest@utm.edu. *Application contact:* Jolene L. Cunningham, Student Services Specialist, 731-881-7012, Fax: 731-881-7499, E-mail: jcunningham@utm.edu.

The University of Texas at Austin, Graduate School, College of Education, Department of Educational Psychology, Austin, TX 78712-1111. Offers academic educational psychology (M Ed, MA); counseling psychology (PhD); counselor education (M Ed); human development, culture and learning sciences (PhD); program evaluation (MA); quantitative methods (M Ed, MA, PhD); school psychology (MA, PhD). *Accreditation:* APA (one or more programs are accredited). *Degree requirements:* For master's, thesis optional; for doctorate, thesis/dissertation. *Entrance requirements:* For master's and doctorate, GRE General Test, 3 letters of recommendation. Additional exam requirements/recommendations for international students: Required—TOEFL.

The University of Texas at El Paso, Graduate School, College of Education, Department of Educational Psychology and Special Services, El Paso, TX 79968-0001. Offers educational diagnostics (M Ed); guidance and counseling (M Ed); special education (M Ed). *Program availability:* Part-time, evening/weekend. *Degree*

requirements: For master's, thesis optional. *Entrance requirements:* For master's, minimum GPA of 3.0. Additional exam requirements/recommendations for international students: Required—TOEFL. Electronic applications accepted.

The University of Texas at San Antonio, College of Education and Human Development, Department of Counseling, San Antonio, TX 78207. Offers counselor education and supervision (PhD); school counseling (M Ed). *Accreditation:* ACA. *Program availability:* Part-time, evening/weekend. *Faculty:* 14 full-time (7 women), 8 part-time/adjunct (5 women). *Students:* 206 full-time (181 women), 222 part-time (189 women); includes 253 minority (32 Black or African American, non-Hispanic/Latino; 2 Asian, non-Hispanic/Latino; 213 Hispanic/Latino; 6 Two or more races, non-Hispanic/Latino), 6 international. Average age 32. 199 applicants, 73% accepted, 115 enrolled. In 2017, 111 master's, 10 doctorates awarded. *Degree requirements:* For master's, comprehensive exam, thesis; for doctorate, comprehensive exam, thesis/dissertation. *Entrance requirements:* For master's, minimum GPA of 3.0 during last 60 hours of undergraduate study; two-page narrative statement; for doctorate, GRE, minimum GPA of 3.0 in master's-level courses in counseling or in related mental health field; resume; three letters of recommendation; statement of purpose; interview. Additional exam requirements/recommendations for international students: Required—TOEFL (minimum score 550 paper-based; 79 iBT), IELTS (minimum score 6.5). *Application deadline:* For fall admission, 6/15 for domestic students, 3/1 for international students; for spring admission, 10/15 for domestic students, 9/15 for international students. Applications are processed on a rolling basis. Application fee: $50 ($90 for international students). Electronic applications accepted. *Expenses:* Contact institution. *Financial support:* Research assistantships, scholarships/grants, and unspecified assistantships available. *Faculty research:* Creativity in counseling, non-suicidal self-injury, family violence, counselor preparation and supervision, technology, ethics, cognitive complexity, counseling outcome research, trauma, body image resiliency. *Unit head:* Dr. Thelma Duffey, Department Chair, 210-458-2600, Fax: 210-458-2605, E-mail: thelma.duffey@utsa.edu. *Application contact:* Kristina Talamantez, Senior Student Development Specialist, 210-458-2723, Fax: 210-458-2605, E-mail: kristina.talamantez@utsa.edu. Website: http://coehd.utsa.edu/counseling

The University of Texas of the Permian Basin, Office of Graduate Studies, School of Education, Program in Counseling, Odessa, TX 79762-0001. Offers MA. *Degree requirements:* For master's, comprehensive exam (for some programs), thesis (for some programs). *Entrance requirements:* For master's, GRE General Test. Additional exam requirements/recommendations for international students: Required—TOEFL (minimum score 550 paper-based).

The University of Texas Rio Grande Valley, College of Education and P-16 Integration, Department of Counseling, Edinburg, TX 78539. Offers clinical mental health counseling (M Ed); school counseling (M Ed). *Program availability:* Part-time. *Faculty:* 12. *Students:* 157. In 2017, 61 master's awarded. *Entrance requirements:* For master's, minimum GPA of 3.0 on undergraduate coursework. Additional exam requirements/recommendations for international students: Required—TOEFL (minimum score 550 paper-based; 79 iBT), IELTS (minimum score 6.5). *Application deadline:* For fall admission, 4/15 for domestic students; for spring admission, 11/1 for domestic students. Applications are processed on a rolling basis. Application fee: $50 ($75 for international students). Electronic applications accepted. *Expenses:* Tuition, state resident: full-time $5550; part-time $417 per credit hour. Tuition, nonresident: full-time $13,020; part-time $832 per credit hour. *Required fees:* $1169. *Financial support:* Research assistantships, institutionally sponsored loans, scholarships/grants, and unspecified assistantships available. Financial award application deadline: 4/15; financial award applicants required to submit FAFSA. *Faculty research:* Counseling, mental health. *Unit head:* Dr. Cynthia Wimberly, Chair, 956-665-2816, E-mail: cynthia.wimberly@utrgv.edu. *Application contact:* Stephanie Ozuna, Graduate Student Recruiter, 956-665-3558, E-mail: stephanie.ozuna@utrgv.edu. Website: http://www.utrgv.edu/cg/

University of the Cumberlands, Graduate Programs in Education, Williamsburg, KY 40769-1372. Offers all grades (P-12) (M Ed); business and marketing (MA Ed, MAT); counselor education and supervision (Ed D); director of pupil personnel (Certificate); director of special education (Certificate); educational administration and supervision (Ed S); educational leadership (Ed D); elementary education (MA Ed, MAT); instructional leadership - principalship (MA Ed); instructional leadership - school principal (Certificate); middle school education (MA Ed, MAT); reading and writing (MA Ed); school counseling (MA Ed); school superintendent (Certificate); secondary education (MA Ed, MAT); special education (MAT); supervisor of instruction (Certificate); teacher leader (MA Ed). *Program availability:* Part-time, evening/weekend, online learning. *Degree requirements:* For master's, comprehensive exam. Electronic applications accepted.

University of the Southwest, Graduate Programs, Hobbs, NM 88240-9129. Offers business administration (MBA); curriculum and instruction (MSE); curriculum and instruction: bilingual (MSE); curriculum and instruction: TESOL (MSE); early childhood education (MSE); educational administration (MSE); mental health counseling (MSE); school counseling (MSE); special education (MSE); sports management (MBA). *Program availability:* Part-time, evening/weekend, online learning. *Degree requirements:* For master's, comprehensive exam, thesis (for some programs). *Entrance requirements:* Additional exam requirements/recommendations for international students: Recommended—TOEFL. Electronic applications accepted.

The University of Toledo, College of Graduate Studies, College of Health and Human Services, School of Intervention and Wellness, Toledo, OH 43606-3390. Offers counselor education (MA, PhD); school psychology (Ed S); speech-language pathology (MA). *Accreditation:* ACA (one or more programs are accredited); NCATE. *Degree requirements:* For master's, seminar paper. *Entrance requirements:* For master's, GRE General Test, interview, minimum GPA of 3.0. Electronic applications accepted. *Faculty research:* Training and supervision, ethics and standards, therapist development, multicultural issues, substance abuse screening.

The University of Toledo, College of Graduate Studies, College of Social Justice and Human Service, Department of School Psychology, Higher Education and Counselor Education, Toledo, OH 43606-3390. Offers counselor education (MA, PhD); higher education (ME, PhD, Certificate); school psychology (MA, Ed S). *Program availability:* Part-time. *Degree requirements:* For master's, comprehensive exam, thesis or alternative; for doctorate, comprehensive exam, thesis/dissertation; for other advanced degree, thesis optional. *Entrance requirements:* For master's, doctorate, and other advanced degree, minimum cumulative GPA of 2.7 for all previous academic work, letters of recommendation. Additional exam requirements/recommendations for international students: Required—TOEFL (minimum score 550 paper-based; 80 iBT). Electronic applications accepted.

University of Utah, Graduate School, College of Education, Department of Educational Psychology, Salt Lake City, UT 84112. Offers clinical mental health counseling (M Ed); counseling psychology (PhD); elementary education (M Ed); instructional design and educational technology (M Ed); instructional design and technology (MS); learning and cognition (MS, PhD); reading and literacy (M Ed, PhD); school counseling (M Ed); school psychology (M Ed, PhD, Ed S); statistics (M Stat). *Accreditation:* APA (one or

Counselor Education

more programs are accredited). *Faculty:* 19 full-time (9 women), 12 part-time/adjunct (8 women). *Students:* 122 full-time (95 women), 97 part-time (68 women); includes 26 minority (4 Asian, non-Hispanic/Latino; 16 Hispanic/Latino; 6 Two or more races, non-Hispanic/Latino), 7 international. Average age 31. 296 applicants, 27% accepted, 73 enrolled. In 2017, 65 master's, 15 doctorates awarded. Terminal master's awarded for partial completion of doctoral program. *Entrance requirements:* For master's and doctorate, GRE General Test, minimum GPA of 3.0. Additional exam requirements/recommendations for international students: Required—TOEFL (minimum score 80 iBT). *Application deadline:* For fall admission, 12/15 for domestic and international students; for winter admission, 11/1 for domestic and international students; for spring admission, 3/15 for domestic and international students. Application fee: $55 ($65 for international students). Electronic applications accepted. *Expenses:* Contact institution. *Financial support:* In 2017–18, 84 students received support, including 12 fellowships with full and partial tuition reimbursements available (averaging $17,000 per year), 16 research assistantships with full and partial tuition reimbursements available (averaging $15,500 per year), 39 teaching assistantships with full and partial tuition reimbursements available (averaging $15,500 per year); career-related internships or fieldwork, scholarships/grants, traineeships, health care benefits, and unspecified assistantships also available. Financial award application deadline: 4/1; financial award applicants required to submit FAFSA. *Faculty research:* Autism, computer technology and instruction, cognitive behavior, aging, group counseling. *Total annual research expenditures:* $620,935. *Unit head:* Dr. Anne E. Cook, Chair, 801-581-7148, Fax: 801-581-5566, E-mail: anne.cook@utah.edu. *Application contact:* JoLynn N. Yates, Academic Coordinator, 801-581-7148, Fax: 801-581-5566, E-mail: jo.yates@utah.edu. Website: http://www.ed.utah.edu/edps/

University of Vermont, Graduate College, College of Education and Social Services, Counseling Program, Burlington, VT 05405. Offers counseling (MS), including clinical mental health, school counseling. *Accreditation:* ACA; NCATE. *Students:* 68 (54 women); includes 4 minority (1 American Indian or Alaska Native, non-Hispanic/Latino; 1 Hispanic/Latino; 2 Two or more races, non-Hispanic/Latino). 99 applicants, 64% accepted, 35 enrolled. In 2017, 11 master's awarded. *Entrance requirements:* For master's, resume. Additional exam requirements/recommendations for international students: Required—TOEFL (minimum score 550 paper-based, 90 iBT) or IELTS (6.5). *Application deadline:* For fall admission, 2/1 for domestic and international students. Application fee: $65. Electronic applications accepted. *Expenses:* Tuition, state resident: full-time $11,628; part-time $646 per credit. Tuition, nonresident: full-time $29,340; part-time $1630 per credit. *Required fees:* $1994; $10 per credit. Tuition and fees vary according to course load and program. *Financial support:* In 2017–18, 1 student received support, including 1 teaching assistantship with partial tuition reimbursement available (averaging $8,000 per year); fellowships and research assistantships also available. Financial award application deadline: 2/1. *Faculty research:* Women and tenure, counseling children and adolescents. *Unit head:* Dr. Aaron Kindsvatter, Program Coordinator, 802-656-3888, E-mail: cslgprog@uvm.edu. Website: https://www.uvm.edu/cess/dlds/counseling

University of Victoria, Faculty of Graduate Studies, Faculty of Education, Department of Educational Psychology and Leadership Studies, Victoria, BC V8W 2Y2, Canada. Offers aboriginal communities counseling (M Ed); counseling (M Ed, MA); educational psychology (M Ed, MA, PhD), including counseling psychology (M Ed, MA), leadership studies (PhD), learning and development (MA, PhD), measurement and evaluation, special education (M Ed, MA); leadership studies (M Ed, MA). *Program availability:* Part-time. *Degree requirements:* For master's, thesis (for some programs), comprehensive exam (M Ed); for doctorate, comprehensive exam, thesis/dissertation, candidacy exam. *Entrance requirements:* For master's, 2 years of work experience in a relevant field; for doctorate, GRE, 2 years of work experience in a relevant field, minimum B average. Additional exam requirements/recommendations for international students: Required—TOEFL (minimum score 575 paper-based), IELTS (minimum score 7). *Faculty research:* Learning and development (child, adolescent and adult), special education and exceptional children.

University of Virginia, Curry School of Education, Department of Human Services, Program in Counselor Education, Charlottesville, VA 22903. Offers M Ed, Ed D, Ed S. *Accreditation:* ACA (one or more programs are accredited). *Students:* 46 full-time (42 women); includes 9 minority (3 Black or African American, non-Hispanic/Latino; 4 Hispanic/Latino; 2 Two or more races, non-Hispanic/Latino), 1 international. Average age 24. 47 applicants, 74% accepted, 23 enrolled. In 2017, 20 master's awarded. *Entrance requirements:* For master's and doctorate, GRE General Test, 2 letters of recommendation; for Ed S, GRE General Test. Additional exam requirements/recommendations for international students: Required—TOEFL (minimum score 600 paper-based; 90 iBT), IELTS. *Application deadline:* For fall admission, 1/5 for domestic and international students. Applications are processed on a rolling basis. Application fee: $60. Electronic applications accepted. *Financial support:* Applicants required to submit FAFSA. *Unit head:* Derick J. Williams, Program Area Director, 434-924-4928, E-mail: dw4pd@virginia.edu. *Application contact:* curry-admissions@virginia.edu. Website: http://curry.edschool.virginia.edu/counselor-ed-home-counslered-347?task-view

University of Virginia, Curry School of Education, Program in Education, Charlottesville, VA 22903. Offers administration and supervision (PhD); applied developmental science (PhD); counselor education (PhD); curriculum and instruction (PhD); early childhood special education (MT); education evaluation (PhD); educational psychology (PhD); educational research (PhD); elementary education (MT); English education (MT, PhD); foreign language education (MT); higher education (PhD); instructional technology (PhD); kinesiology (MT, PhD); math education (PhD); reading education (PhD); research, statistics and evaluation (PhD); school psychology (PhD); science education (PhD); social studies education (MT, PhD); special education (PhD); world languages education (MT). *Students:* 431 full-time (353 women), 15 part-time (14 women); includes 100 minority (32 Black or African American, non-Hispanic/Latino; 33 Asian, non-Hispanic/Latino; 16 Hispanic/Latino; 19 Two or more races, non-Hispanic/Latino), 14 international. Average age 25. 264 applicants, 49% accepted, 83 enrolled. In 2017, 142 master's, 33 doctorates awarded. *Degree requirements:* For master's, comprehensive exam (for some programs), field project; for doctorate, comprehensive exam, thesis/dissertation. *Entrance requirements:* For doctorate, GRE General Test. Additional exam requirements/recommendations for international students: Required—TOEFL (minimum score 600 paper-based; 90 iBT), IELTS (minimum score 7). *Application deadline:* Applications are processed on a rolling basis. Application fee: $60. Electronic applications accepted. *Financial support:* Fellowships, research assistantships, and teaching assistantships available. Financial award application deadline: 1/5; financial award applicants required to submit FAFSA. *Unit head:* Robert C. Pianta, Dean, 434-924-3334, E-mail: pianta@virginia.edu. *Application contact:* E-mail: curry-admissions@virginia.edu. Website: http://curry.virginia.edu/teacher-education

The University of West Alabama, School of Graduate Studies, College of Education, Program in Continuing Education, Livingston, AL 35470. Offers counseling and psychology (MSCE); general (MSCE); library media (MSCE). *Accreditation:* NCATE. *Program availability:* Part-time, evening/weekend, 100% online. *Faculty:* 13 full-time (11 women), 48 part-time/adjunct (36 women). *Students:* 195 (163 women); includes 137 minority (134 Black or African American, non-Hispanic/Latino; 1 American Indian or Alaska Native, non-Hispanic/Latino; 1 Native Hawaiian or other Pacific Islander, non-Hispanic/Latino; 1 Two or more races, non-Hispanic/Latino). Average age 34. 59 applicants, 100% accepted, 40 enrolled. In 2017, 103 master's awarded. *Degree requirements:* For master's, comprehensive exam, thesis optional. *Entrance requirements:* For master's, GRE, minimum GPA of 2.75. Additional exam requirements/recommendations for international students: Required—TOEFL (minimum score 500 paper-based; 61 iBT). *Application deadline:* Applications are processed on a rolling basis. Application fee: $40. Electronic applications accepted. *Expenses:* Tuition, state resident: part-time $371 per credit hour. Tuition, nonresident: part-time $742 per credit hour. *Required fees:* $130 per semester. *Financial support:* Teaching assistantships, Federal Work-Study, scholarships/grants, and unspecified assistantships available. Support available to part-time students. Financial award application deadline: 3/1; financial award applicants required to submit FAFSA. *Unit head:* Dr. Reenay Rogers, Chair of Instructional Leadership and Support, 205-652-5423, Fax: 205-652-3706, E-mail: rrogers@uwa.edu. *Application contact:* Dr. B. J. Kimbrough, Dean of Graduate Studies, 205-652-3647, Fax: 205-652-3670, E-mail: bkimbrough@uwa.edu.

The University of West Alabama, School of Graduate Studies, College of Education, Program in School Counseling, Livingston, AL 35470. Offers guidance and counseling (MS); school counseling (M Ed, Ed S). *Accreditation:* NCATE. *Program availability:* Part-time, evening/weekend, 100% online. *Faculty:* 5 full-time (all women), 10 part-time/adjunct (8 women). *Students:* 397 (371 women); includes 137 minority (122 Black or African American, non-Hispanic/Latino; 5 American Indian or Alaska Native, non-Hispanic/Latino; 1 Asian, non-Hispanic/Latino; 4 Hispanic/Latino; 5 Two or more races, non-Hispanic/Latino). Average age 37. 117 applicants, 94% accepted, 73 enrolled. In 2017, 90 master's, 36 other advanced degrees awarded. *Degree requirements:* For master's, comprehensive exam, thesis optional; for Ed S, comprehensive exam. *Entrance requirements:* For master's, GRE, minimum GPA of 2.75, verification of background clearance/fingerprints, essay, three academic references, resume. Additional exam requirements/recommendations for international students: Required—TOEFL (minimum score 500 paper-based; 61 iBT). *Application deadline:* Applications are processed on a rolling basis. Application fee: $40. Electronic applications accepted. *Expenses:* Tuition, state resident: part-time $371 per credit hour. Tuition, nonresident: part-time $742 per credit hour. *Required fees:* $130 per semester. *Financial support:* Teaching assistantships, Federal Work-Study, scholarships/grants, and unspecified assistantships available. Support available to part-time students. Financial award application deadline: 3/1; financial award applicants required to submit FAFSA. *Unit head:* Dr. Reenay Rogers, Chair of Instructional Leadership and Support, 205-652-5423, Fax: 205-652-3706, E-mail: rrogers@uwa.edu. *Application contact:* Dr. B. J. Kimbrough, Dean of Graduate Studies, 205-652-3647, Fax: 205-652-3670, E-mail: bkimbrough@uwa.edu.

University of West Georgia, College of Education, Carrollton, GA 30118. Offers business education (M Ed); early childhood education (M Ed, Ed S); educational leadership (M Ed, Ed S); media (M Ed, Ed S); professional counseling (M Ed, Ed S); professional counseling and supervision (Ed D); reading instruction (M Ed); school improvement (Ed D); secondary education (M Ed); special education (M Ed, Ed S), including teaching (M Ed); speech language pathology (M Ed); teaching (MAT). *Accreditation:* NCATE. *Program availability:* Part-time, evening/weekend, 100% online, blended/hybrid learning. *Faculty:* 45 full-time (28 women). *Students:* 344 full-time (286 women), 1,243 part-time (1,039 women); includes 538 minority (456 Black or African American, non-Hispanic/Latino; 19 Asian, non-Hispanic/Latino; 46 Hispanic/Latino; 1 Native Hawaiian or other Pacific Islander, non-Hispanic/Latino; 16 Two or more races, non-Hispanic/Latino), 7 international. Average age 36. 685 applicants, 78% accepted, 429 enrolled. In 2017, 299 master's, 30 doctorates, 218 other advanced degrees awarded. *Entrance requirements:* Additional exam requirements/recommendations for international students: Required—TOEFL (minimum score 523 paper-based; 69 iBT); Recommended—IELTS (minimum score 6.5). *Application deadline:* For fall admission, 7/21 for domestic students, 6/1 for international students; for spring admission, 11/30 for domestic students, 10/15 for international students; for summer admission, 4/15 for domestic students, 3/30 for international students. Applications are processed on a rolling basis. Application fee: $40. Electronic applications accepted. Tuition and fees vary according to degree level and program. *Financial support:* Fellowships, research assistantships, teaching assistantships, career-related internships or fieldwork, Federal Work-Study, institutionally sponsored loans, scholarships/grants, and unspecified assistantships available. Support available to part-time students. Financial award application deadline: 4/1; financial award applicants required to submit FAFSA. *Unit head:* Dr. Diane Hoff, Dean, College of Education, 678-839-6570, Fax: 678-839-6098, E-mail: dhoff@westga.edu. *Application contact:* Dr. Toby Ziglar, Assistant Dean of the Graduate School, 678-839-1394, Fax: 678-839-1395, E-mail: graduate@westga.edu. Website: http://www.westga.edu/education/

University of Wisconsin–Madison, Graduate School, School of Education, Department of Counseling Psychology, Program in Counseling, Madison, WI 53706-1380. Offers MS. *Entrance requirements:* For master's, GRE General Test. Electronic applications accepted.

University of Wisconsin–Oshkosh, Graduate Studies, College of Education and Human Services, Department of Professional Counseling, Oshkosh, WI 54901. Offers counseling (MSE). *Accreditation:* ACA. *Program availability:* Part-time, evening/weekend. *Degree requirements:* For master's, thesis optional, practicum. *Entrance requirements:* For master's, MAT, interview, minimum GPA of 3.0, letters of recommendation. Additional exam requirements/recommendations for international students: Required—TOEFL (minimum score 550 paper-based; 79 iBT). Electronic applications accepted. *Faculty research:* Gender issues, grief and loss, addictions, career development, close relationships.

University of Wisconsin–River Falls, Outreach and Graduate Studies, College of Education and Professional Studies, Department of Counseling and School Psychology, River Falls, WI 54022. Offers counseling (MSE); school psychology (MSE, Ed S). *Accreditation:* ACA. *Program availability:* Part-time. *Entrance requirements:* For master's, minimum GPA of 2.75, resume, 3 letters of reference, vita. Additional exam requirements/recommendations for international students: Required—TOEFL (minimum score 500 paper-based; 65 iBT), IELTS (minimum score 5.5). Electronic applications accepted.

University of Wisconsin–Stevens Point, College of Professional Studies, School of Education, Program in Guidance and Counseling, Stevens Point, WI 54481-3897. Offers MSE. Program offered jointly with University of Wisconsin–Oshkosh. *Degree requirements:* For master's, comprehensive exam, thesis or alternative.

University of Wisconsin–Superior, Graduate Division, Department of Counseling and Psychological Professions, Superior, WI 54880-4500. Offers community counseling (MSE); human relations (MSE); school counseling (MSE). *Program availability:* Part-time, evening/weekend. *Degree requirements:* For master's, position paper, practicum. *Entrance requirements:* For master's, GRE and/or MAT, minimum GPA of 2.75. Electronic applications accepted. *Faculty research:* Women and power, intrafamily dynamics.

University of Wyoming, College of Education, Programs in Counselor Education, Laramie, WY 82071. Offers community mental health (MS); counselor education and supervision (PhD); school counseling (MS); student affairs (MS). *Accreditation:* ACA (one or more programs are accredited). *Degree requirements:* For master's, comprehensive exam (for some programs), thesis optional; for doctorate, thesis/dissertation, video demonstration. *Entrance requirements:* For master's, interview, background check; for doctorate, video tape session, interview, writing sample, master's degree, background check. Additional exam requirements/recommendations for international students: Required—TOEFL. *Faculty research:* Wyoming SAGE photovoice project; accountable school counseling programs; GLBT issues; addictions; play therapy-early childhood mental health.

Utah State University, School of Graduate Studies, Emma Eccles Jones College of Education and Human Services, Department of Psychology, Logan, UT 84322. Offers clinical/counseling/school psychology (PhD); research and evaluation methodology (PhD); school counseling (MS); school psychology (MS). *Accreditation:* APA (one or more programs are accredited). *Program availability:* Part-time, evening/weekend, online learning. Terminal master's awarded for partial completion of doctoral program. *Degree requirements:* For master's, thesis (for some programs); for doctorate, thesis/dissertation. *Entrance requirements:* For master's, GRE General Test (school psychology), MAT (school counseling), minimum GPA of 3.5; for doctorate, GRE General Test, minimum GPA of 3.5. Additional exam requirements/recommendations for international students: Required—TOEFL. *Faculty research:* Hearing loss detection in infancy, ADHD, eating disorders, domestic violence, neuropsychology, bilingual/Spanish speaking students/parents.

Valdosta State University, Department of Psychology, Counseling, and Family Therapy, Valdosta, GA 31698. Offers industrial/organizational psychology (MS); marriage and family therapy (MS); school counseling (M Ed, Ed S). *Accreditation:* AAMFT/COAMFTE. *Program availability:* Part-time, evening/weekend, 100% online, blended/hybrid learning. *Degree requirements:* For master's, thesis or alternative, comprehensive written and/or oral exams; for Ed S, thesis. *Entrance requirements:* For master's, GRE General Test or MAT, GACE; for Ed S, GRE General Test or MAT. Additional exam requirements/recommendations for international students: Required—TOEFL (minimum score 523 paper-based); Recommended—IELTS. *Application deadline:* For fall admission, 7/1 for domestic and international students; for spring admission, 11/15 for domestic and international students. Applications are processed on a rolling basis. Application fee: $45. Electronic applications accepted. *Expenses:* Contact institution. *Financial support:* Research assistantships with full tuition reimbursements, institutionally sponsored loans, and unspecified assistantships available. Support available to part-time students. Financial award application deadline: 7/1; financial award applicants required to submit FAFSA. *Unit head:* Dr. Kate Warner, Head, 229-293-6264, Fax: 229-259-5576, E-mail: kwarner@valdosta.edu. *Application contact:* Jessica Powers, Admission Specialist, 229-333-5694, Fax: 229-245-3853, E-mail: jldevane@valdosta.edu.
Website: https://www.valdosta.edu/colleges/education/pcft/

Vanderbilt University, Peabody College, Department of Human and Organizational Development, Nashville, TN 37240-1001. Offers community development and action (M Ed); human development counseling (M Ed). *Accreditation:* ACA; NCATE. *Program availability:* Blended/hybrid learning, on-campus immersion once every semester. *Faculty:* 31 full-time (20 women), 19 part-time/adjunct (9 women). *Students:* 104 full-time (87 women), 21 part-time (20 women); includes 18 minority (8 Black or African American, non-Hispanic/Latino; 2 Asian, non-Hispanic/Latino; 4 Hispanic/Latino; 4 Two or more races, non-Hispanic/Latino), 2 international. Average age 26. 186 applicants, 64% accepted, 55 enrolled. In 2017, 52 master's awarded. *Degree requirements:* For master's, comprehensive exam, thesis optional. *Entrance requirements:* For master's, GRE General Test. Additional exam requirements/recommendations for international students: Required—TOEFL (minimum score 550 paper-based; 80 iBT). *Application deadline:* For fall admission, 12/31 priority date for domestic and international students; for spring admission, 11/1 priority date for domestic and international students. Applications are processed on a rolling basis. Application fee: $0. Electronic applications accepted. *Financial support:* Fellowships with partial tuition reimbursements, research assistantships with partial tuition reimbursements, teaching assistantships with partial tuition reimbursements, Federal Work-Study, institutionally sponsored loans, scholarships/grants, tuition waivers (partial), and unspecified assistantships available. Support available to part-time students. Financial award application deadline: 1/15; financial award applicants required to submit FAFSA. *Faculty research:* Community psychology and community development; counseling and mental health services, prevention and positive youth development; organizational and community change; youth physical and behavioral health in schools and communities. *Unit head:* Dr. Paul Speer, Chair, 615-322-6881, Fax: 615-322-1141, E-mail: paul.w.speer@vanderbilt.edu. *Application contact:* Sherrie Lane, Educational Coordinator, 615-322-8484, Fax: 615-322-1141, E-mail: sherrie.a.lane@vanderbilt.edu.

Villanova University, Graduate School of Liberal Arts and Sciences, Department of Education and Counseling, Villanova, PA 19085-1699. Offers elementary school counseling (MS), including counseling and human relations; teacher leadership (MA). *Program availability:* Part-time, evening/weekend. *Faculty:* 24. *Students:* 80 full-time (58 women), 37 part-time (28 women); includes 15 minority (7 Black or African American, non-Hispanic/Latino; 2 Asian, non-Hispanic/Latino; 5 Hispanic/Latino; 1 Two or more races, non-Hispanic/Latino), 2 international. Average age 30. 62 applicants, 74% accepted, 32 enrolled. In 2017, 49 master's awarded. *Degree requirements:* For master's, comprehensive exam. *Entrance requirements:* For master's, GRE or MAT, minimum GPA of 3.0, statement of goals. *Application deadline:* For fall admission, 3/1 priority date for domestic students, 5/1 for international students; for spring admission, 11/15 priority date for domestic students, 10/15 for international students; for summer admission, 5/1 for domestic students. Applications are processed on a rolling basis. Application fee: $50. Electronic applications accepted. *Financial support:* Research assistantships, teaching assistantships, scholarships/grants, and unspecified assistantships available. Financial award applicants required to submit FAFSA. *Unit head:* Dr. Christopher Schmidt, Chairperson, 610-519-4618. *Application contact:* Dean, Graduate School of Liberal Arts and Sciences.
Website: http://www.education.villanova.edu/

Virginia Commonwealth University, Graduate School, School of Education, Doctoral Program in Education, Richmond, VA 23284-9005. Offers art education (PhD); counselor education and supervision (PhD); curriculum, culture and change (PhD); educational leadership (PhD); educational psychology (PhD); leadership (Ed D); research and evaluation (PhD); special education and disability leadership (PhD); sport leadership (PhD); urban services leadership (PhD). *Accreditation:* NCATE. *Program availability:* Part-time. *Degree requirements:* For doctorate, thesis/dissertation. *Entrance requirements:* For doctorate, GRE (for PhD), MAT (for Ed D), interview, master's degree, writing sample. Additional exam requirements/recommendations for international students: Required—TOEFL (minimum score 600 paper-based; 100 iBT). Electronic applications accepted.

Virginia Commonwealth University, Graduate School, School of Education, Program in Counselor Education, Richmond, VA 23284-9005. Offers college student development and counseling (M Ed); school counseling (M Ed). *Accreditation:* ACA; NCATE. *Entrance requirements:* For master's, GRE General Test or MAT. Additional exam requirements/recommendations for international students: Required—TOEFL (minimum score 600 paper-based; 100 iBT). Electronic applications accepted.

Virginia Polytechnic Institute and State University, Graduate School, College of Liberal Arts and Human Sciences, Blacksburg, VA 24061. Offers career and technical education (MS Ed, Ed S); communication (MA); counselor education (MA); creative writing (MFA); curriculum and instruction (MA Ed, Ed S); educational leadership and policy studies (Ed S); educational research and evaluation (PhD); English (MA); social, political, ethical, and cultural thought (PhD); Ed D/PhD. *Faculty:* 411 full-time (213 women), 3 part-time/adjunct (all women). *Students:* 623 full-time (427 women), 431 part-time (278 women); includes 203 minority (115 Black or African American, non-Hispanic/Latino; 4 American Indian or Alaska Native, non-Hispanic/Latino; 29 Asian, non-Hispanic/Latino; 33 Hispanic/Latino; 2 Native Hawaiian or other Pacific Islander, non-Hispanic/Latino; 20 Two or more races, non-Hispanic/Latino), 87 international. Average age 34. 898 applicants, 50% accepted, 329 enrolled. In 2017, 314 master's, 102 doctorates awarded. *Degree requirements:* For master's, comprehensive exam (for some programs), thesis (for some programs); for doctorate, comprehensive exam (for some programs), thesis/dissertation (for some programs). *Entrance requirements:* For master's and doctorate, GRE/GMAT. Additional exam requirements/recommendations for international students: Required—TOEFL (minimum score 80 iBT). *Application deadline:* For fall admission, 8/1 for domestic students, 4/1 for international students; for spring admission, 1/1 for domestic students, 9/1 for international students. Applications are processed on a rolling basis. Application fee: $75. Electronic applications accepted. *Expenses:* Tuition, state resident: full-time $15,072; part-time $718.50 per credit hour. Tuition, nonresident: full-time $28,810; part-time $1448.25 per credit hour. *Required fees:* $2741; $502 per semester. Tuition and fees vary according to course load, campus/location and program. *Financial support:* In 2017–18, 19 research assistantships with full tuition reimbursements (averaging $19,611 per year), 226 teaching assistantships with full tuition reimbursements (averaging $16,220 per year) were awarded. Financial award application deadline: 3/1; financial award applicants required to submit FAFSA. *Total annual research expenditures:* $7.9 million. *Unit head:* Dr. Rosemary Blieszner, Dean, 540-231-6779, Fax: 540-231-7157, E-mail: rmb@vt.edu. *Application contact:* Chelsea Blanchet, Executive Assistant, 540-231-6779, Fax: 540-231-7157, E-mail: bchels1@vt.edu.
Website: http://www.liberalarts.vt.edu/

Virginia State University, College of Graduate Studies, College of Education, Department of School and Community Counseling, Petersburg, VA 23806-0001. Offers M Ed, MS. *Accreditation:* NCATE. *Degree requirements:* For master's, thesis optional.

Wake Forest University, Graduate School of Arts and Sciences, Counseling Program, Winston-Salem, NC 27109. Offers MA, M Div/MA. *Accreditation:* ACA. *Entrance requirements:* For master's, GRE General Test. Additional exam requirements/recommendations for international students: Required—TOEFL (minimum score 79 iBT). Electronic applications accepted.

Walden University, Graduate Programs, School of Counseling, Minneapolis, MN 55401. Offers addiction counseling (MS), including addictions and public health, child and adolescent counseling, family studies and interventions, forensic counseling, general program, military families and culture, trauma and crisis counseling; clinical mental health counseling (MS), including addiction counseling, forensic counseling, military families and culture, trauma and crisis counseling; counselor education and supervision (PhD), including consultation, counseling and social change, forensic mental health counseling, leadership and program evaluation, trauma and crisis; marriage, couple, and family counseling (MS), including addiction counseling, career counseling, forensic counseling, military families and culture, trauma and crisis counseling; school counseling (MS), including addiction counseling, career counseling, crisis and trauma, military families and culture. *Accreditation:* ACA. *Program availability:* Part-time, evening/weekend, online only, 100% online. *Degree requirements:* For master's, residency, field experience, professional development plan, licensure plan; for doctorate, thesis/dissertation, residency, practicum, internship. *Entrance requirements:* For master's, bachelor's degree or higher; minimum GPA of 2.5; official transcripts; goal statement (for some programs); access to computer and Internet; for doctorate, master's degree or higher; three years of related professional or academic experience (preferred); minimum GPA of 3.0; goal statement and current resume (for select programs); official transcripts; access to computer and Internet. Additional exam requirements/recommendations for international students: Required—TOEFL (minimum score 550 paper-based, 79 iBT), IELTS (minimum score 6.5), Michigan English Language Assessment Battery (minimum score 82), or PTE (minimum score 53). Electronic applications accepted.

Walsh University, Graduate Programs, Program in Counseling and Human Development, North Canton, OH 44720-3396. Offers clinical mental health counseling (MA); school counseling (MA); student affairs in higher education (MA). *Accreditation:* ACA. *Program availability:* Part-time, evening/weekend. *Degree requirements:* For master's, comprehensive exam, internship, practicum. *Entrance requirements:* For master's, GRE (minimum score of 145 verbal and 146 quantitative) or MAT (minimum score of 397), interview, minimum GPA of 3.0, writing sample, reference forms, notarized affidavit of good moral conduct. Additional exam requirements/recommendations for international students: Required—TOEFL (minimum score 500 paper-based; 61 iBT). Electronic applications accepted. Application fee is waived when completed online. *Expenses:* Contact institution. *Faculty research:* Supervision of clinical mental health, clinical mental health practice/issues, clinical mental health skills development, advocacy, teaching and professional development, career development, refugee development in US, supervision in student affairs, offender treatment, domestic violence issues, alcohol and drug treatment issues, Professional identity and advocacy in school counseling, Efficacy in counseling clinic.

Waynesburg University, Graduate and Professional Studies, Canonsburg, PA 15370. Offers business (MBA), including energy management, finance, health systems, human resources, leadership, market development; counseling (MA), including addictions counseling, clinical mental health; counselor education and supervision (PhD); criminal investigation (MA); education (M Ed), including autism, curriculum and instruction, educational leadership, online teaching; nursing (MSN), including administration, education, informatics; nursing practice (DNP); special education (M Ed); technology (M Ed); MSN/MBA. *Accreditation:* AACN. *Program availability:* Part-time, evening/weekend. *Degree requirements:* For doctorate, thesis/dissertation. *Entrance requirements:* Additional exam requirements/recommendations for international students: Required—TOEFL. Electronic applications accepted.

Wayne State College, School of Education and Counseling, Department of Counseling and Special Education, Program in Guidance and Counseling, Wayne, NE 68787. Offers counseling (MSE); counselor education (MSE); school counseling (MSE). *Accreditation:* ACA; NCATE. *Program availability:* Part-time, evening/weekend. *Degree requirements:* For master's, comprehensive exam, thesis optional. *Entrance requirements:* For master's, GRE General Test, minimum GPA of 3.0. Additional exam requirements/recommendations for international students: Required—TOEFL (minimum score 550 paper-based). Electronic applications accepted.

Counselor Education

Wayne State University, College of Education, Division of Theoretical and Behavioral Foundations, Detroit, MI 48202. Offers applied behavior analysis (Certificate); counseling (M Ed, MA, Ed D, Ed S); counseling psychology (MA, PhD); education evaluation and research (M Ed, Ed D); educational psychology (M Ed, PhD), including learning and instruction sciences (PhD); rehabilitation counseling and community inclusion (MA); school and community psychology (MA, Certificate). *Accreditation:* ACA (one or more programs are accredited); CORE (one or more programs are accredited). *Program availability:* Evening/weekend. *Students:* Average age 32. 294 applicants, 34% accepted, 72 enrolled. In 2017, 87 master's, 12 doctorates, 14 other advanced degrees awarded. *Entrance requirements:* For master's, GRE, interview, personal statement, portfolio (art therapy); for doctorate, GRE, department-written exam, interview, curriculum vitae, references, master's degree in closely-related field with minimum GPA of 3.5, demonstration of counseling skills (for Ed D in counseling); for other advanced degree, master's degree in counseling and counseling license (for Ed S); good standing in school and community psychology MA program (for Certificate). Additional exam requirements/recommendations for international students: Required—TOEFL (minimum score 550 paper-based; 79 iBT), Michigan English Language Assessment Battery (minimum score 85); Recommended—IELTS (minimum score 6.5), TWE (minimum score 5.5). *Application deadline:* For fall admission, 6/1 priority date for domestic students, 5/1 priority date for international students; for winter admission, 10/1 priority date for domestic students, 9/1 priority date for international students; for spring admission, 2/1 priority date for domestic students, 1/1 priority date for international students. Applications are processed on a rolling basis. Application fee: $50. Electronic applications accepted. *Expenses:* Contact institution. *Financial support:* In 2017–18, 92 students received support, including 2 research assistantships with tuition reimbursements available (averaging $17,994 per year); fellowships, teaching assistantships, Federal Work-Study, scholarships/grants, health care benefits, and unspecified assistantships also available. Support available to part-time students. Financial award applicants required to submit FAFSA. *Faculty research:* Adolescents at risk, supervision of counseling. *Unit head:* Dr. Cheryl Somers, Assistant Dean, 313-577-1670, E-mail: c.somers@wayne.edu. *Application contact:* Janice Green, Assistant Dean, 313-577-1605, E-mail: jwgreen@wayne.edu.
Website: http://coe.wayne.edu/tbf/index.php

West Chester University of Pennsylvania, College of Education and Social Work, Department of Counselor Education, West Chester, PA 19383. Offers clinical mental health counseling (MS); counseling (Certificate); higher education counseling (Post Master's Certificate); higher education counseling/student affairs (MS, Certificate); school counseling (M Ed). *Accreditation:* ACA; NCATE. *Program availability:* Part-time, evening/weekend. *Students:* 134 full-time (110 women), 40 part-time (32 women); includes 38 minority (17 Black or African American, non-Hispanic/Latino; 2 Asian, non-Hispanic/Latino; 11 Hispanic/Latino; 8 Two or more races, non-Hispanic/Latino), 1 international. Average age 27. 177 applicants, 58% accepted, 58 enrolled. In 2017, 79 master's, 1 other advanced degree awarded. *Degree requirements:* For master's, comprehensive exam. *Entrance requirements:* For master's, minimum GPA of 3.0, three letters of reference. Additional exam requirements/recommendations for international students: Required—TOEFL or IELTS. *Application deadline:* For fall admission, 5/15 for international students; for spring admission, 10/15 for international students. Applications are processed on a rolling basis. Application fee: $50. Electronic applications accepted. *Expenses:* Tuition, state resident: full-time $9000; part-time $500 per credit. Tuition, nonresident: full-time $13,500; part-time $750 per credit. *Required fees:* $2959; $149.79 per credit. *Financial support:* Scholarships/grants and unspecified assistantships available. Financial award application deadline: 2/15; financial award applicants required to submit FAFSA. *Faculty research:* Bullying in the schools, adolescent cognitive development, counseling pedagogy, motivational interviewing. *Unit head:* Dr. Eric Owens, Chair, 610-436-2559, Fax: 610-425-7432, E-mail: eowens@wcupa.edu. *Application contact:* Dr. Cheryl Neale-McFall, Graduate Coordinator, 610-436-2559, Fax: 610-425-7432, E-mail: cneale-mcfall@wcupa.edu.
Website: http://www.wcupa.edu/education-socialWork/counselorEducation/

Western Connecticut State University, Division of Graduate Studies, School of Professional Studies, Department of Education and Educational Psychology, Program in School Counseling, Danbury, CT 06810-6885. Offers MS. *Accreditation:* ACA. *Program availability:* Part-time. *Degree requirements:* For master's, practicum, internship, completion of program in 6 years. *Entrance requirements:* For master's, PRAXIS I, minimum GPA of 2.8, 3 letters of reference, essay, 6 hours of psychology. Additional exam requirements/recommendations for international students: Recommended—TOEFL (minimum score 550 paper-based; 79 iBT), IELTS (minimum score 6). *Expenses:* Tuition, state resident: full-time $6757; part-time $374 per credit hour. Tuition, nonresident: full-time $18,102; part-time $374 per credit hour. *Required fees:* $4994; $190 per credit hour. $60 per term. Tuition and fees vary according to degree level and program. *Faculty research:* The effect of affective factors on cognition and learning, statistics and research methods, interviewing, individual and multicultural counseling.

Western Illinois University, School of Graduate Studies, College of Education and Human Services, Department of Counselor Education, Macomb, IL 61455-1390. Offers counseling (MS Ed). *Accreditation:* ACA. *Program availability:* Part-time. *Students:* 31 full-time (27 women), 41 part-time (37 women); includes 12 minority (5 Black or African American, non-Hispanic/Latino; 1 Asian, non-Hispanic/Latino; 6 Hispanic/Latino). Average age 32. 27 applicants, 56% accepted, 8 enrolled. In 2017, 19 master's awarded. *Degree requirements:* For master's, thesis or alternative. *Entrance requirements:* For master's, GRE, interview. Additional exam requirements/recommendations for international students: Required—TOEFL (minimum score 550 paper-based; 80 iBT). Application fee: $30. Electronic applications accepted. *Financial support:* Unspecified assistantships available. Financial award applicants required to submit FAFSA. *Unit head:* Dr. Holly Nikels, Interim Chairperson, 309-762-1876. *Application contact:* Dr. Nancy Parsons, Assistant Director of Graduate Studies, 309-298-1806, Fax: 309-298-2345, E-mail: grad-office@wiu.edu.
Website: http://wiu.edu/counselored

Western Kentucky University, Graduate Studies, College of Education and Behavioral Sciences, Department of Counseling and Student Affairs, Bowling Green, KY 42101. Offers counseling (MA Ed), including marriage and family therapy, mental health counseling; school counseling (P-12) (MA Ed); student affairs in higher education (MA Ed). *Accreditation:* ACA; NCATE. *Program availability:* Part-time, evening/weekend. *Degree requirements:* For master's, comprehensive exam, thesis optional. *Entrance requirements:* For master's, GRE General Test. Additional exam requirements/recommendations for international students: Required—TOEFL (minimum score 555 paper-based; 79 iBT). *Faculty research:* Counselor education, research for residential workers.

Western Michigan University, Graduate College, College of Education and Human Development, Department of Counselor Education and Counseling Psychology, Kalamazoo, MI 49008. Offers counseling psychology (MA, PhD); counselor education (MA, PhD), including counselor education (MA). *Accreditation:* ACA (one or more programs are accredited); APA (one or more programs are accredited); CORE; NCATE. *Degree requirements:* For doctorate, thesis/dissertation.

Western Washington University, Graduate School, College of Humanities and Social Sciences, Department of Psychology, Program in School Counseling, Bellingham, WA 98225-5996. Offers M Ed. *Accreditation:* ACA. *Degree requirements:* For master's, comprehensive exam. *Entrance requirements:* For master's, GRE General Test, minimum GPA of 3.0 in last 60 semester hours or last 90 quarter hours. Additional exam requirements/recommendations for international students: Required—TOEFL (minimum score 567 paper-based). Electronic applications accepted.

Westfield State University, College of Graduate and Continuing Education, Department of Psychology, Program in Counseling, Westfield, MA 01086. Offers forensic mental health counseling (MA); mental health counseling (MA); school adjustment counseling (MA); school guidance counseling (MA). *Program availability:* Part-time, evening/weekend. *Faculty:* 5 full-time (3 women), 4 part-time/adjunct (1 woman). *Students:* 36 full-time (27 women), 14 part-time (10 women); includes 9 minority (1 Black or African American, non-Hispanic/Latino; 1 Asian, non-Hispanic/Latino; 4 Hispanic/Latino; 3 Two or more races, non-Hispanic/Latino). Average age 28. 29 applicants, 79% accepted, 16 enrolled. In 2017, 10 master's awarded. *Degree requirements:* For master's, comprehensive exam, practicum. *Entrance requirements:* For master's, GRE General Test, MAT, minimum undergraduate GPA of 3.0. Additional exam requirements/recommendations for international students: Recommended—TOEFL (minimum score 550 paper-based; 79 iBT). *Application deadline:* For fall admission, 2/1 for domestic students. Applications are processed on a rolling basis. Application fee: $50. *Expenses:* Tuition, state resident: part-time $332 per credit. Tuition, nonresident: part-time $332 per credit. *Required fees:* $75 per semester. Tuition and fees vary according to program. *Financial support:* Unspecified assistantships available. Financial award application deadline: 4/1; financial award applicants required to submit FAFSA. *Unit head:* Dr. Robert Hayes, Professor, 413-572-5700, Fax: 413-572-5227, E-mail: rhayes@westfield.ma.edu. *Application contact:* Shelly Henrichon, Coordinator of College of Graduate and Continuing Education Admissions, 413-572-8022, Fax: 413-572-5227, E-mail: mhenrichon@westfield.ma.edu.

Westminster College, Graduate School, Program in School Counseling, New Wilmington, PA 16172-0001. Offers clinical mental health counseling (MA); school counselor (M Ed). *Program availability:* Part-time, evening/weekend. *Degree requirements:* For master's, comprehensive exam (for M Ed). *Entrance requirements:* For master's, minimum GPA of 3.0, two recommendations. *Application deadline:* For fall admission, 8/15 priority date for domestic students; for spring admission, 1/8 priority date for domestic students. Applications are processed on a rolling basis. Application fee: $35. *Expenses:* Tuition: Part-time $454 per semester hour. *Required fees:* $235.50 per course. Tuition and fees vary according to course load. *Financial support:* Career-related internships or fieldwork and scholarships/grants available. *Unit head:* Coordinator, 724-946-7874, Fax: 724-946-6158. *Application contact:* Coordinator, 724-946-7874, Fax: 724-946-6158.

West Texas A&M University, College of Education and Social Sciences, Department of Education, Program in Counseling, Canyon, TX 79015. Offers MA. *Program availability:* Part-time. *Degree requirements:* For master's, comprehensive exam. *Entrance requirements:* For master's, GRE General Test, interview, 12 semester hours in education and/or psychology, approval from the Counselor Admissions Committee. Additional exam requirements/recommendations for international students: Required—TOEFL (minimum score 550 paper-based). Electronic applications accepted.

West Virginia University, College of Education and Human Services, Morgantown, WV 26506. Offers audiology (Au D); autism spectrum disorder (MA); clinical rehabilitation and mental health counseling (MS); communication science and disorders (PhD); counseling (MA); counseling psychology (PhD); curriculum and instruction (Ed D); early childhood education (MA); early intervention (MA); education (PhD); educational leadership (MA, Ed D); educational leadership/public school administration (MA); educational psychology (MA, Ed D); elementary education (MA); gifted education (MA); higher education administration (MA, Ed D); higher education curriculum and teaching (MA); institutional design and technology (MA); instructional design and technology (Ed D); literacy education (MA); secondary education (MA); secondary education/English (MA); special education (Ed D); speech pathology (MS). *Accreditation:* NCATE. *Program availability:* Part-time, evening/weekend, online learning. *Students:* 423 full-time (347 women), 367 part-time (316 women); includes 57 minority (14 Black or African American, non-Hispanic/Latino; 7 Asian, non-Hispanic/Latino; 20 Hispanic/Latino; 16 Two or more races, non-Hispanic/Latino), 13 international. *Degree requirements:* For master's, content exams; for doctorate, comprehensive exam, thesis/dissertation. *Entrance requirements:* Additional exam requirements/recommendations for international students: Required—TOEFL (minimum score 500 paper-based; 61 iBT). *Application deadline:* For fall admission, 8/1 for domestic students; for spring admission, 1/1 for domestic students; for summer admission, 5/1 for domestic students. Application fee: $60. Electronic applications accepted. *Expenses:* Tuition, state resident: full-time $9450. Tuition, nonresident: full-time $24,390. *Financial support:* Fellowships, research assistantships, teaching assistantships, career-related internships or fieldwork, Federal Work-Study, institutionally sponsored loans, health care benefits, tuition waivers (full and partial), and administrative assistantships available. Financial award applicants required to submit FAFSA. *Faculty research:* Internet training and integration for teachers, rural education, teacher preparation, organization of schools, evaluation of personnel. *Unit head:* Dr. Gypsy Denzine, Dean, 304-293-5703, Fax: 304-293-7565, E-mail: gypsy.denzine@mail.wvu.edu. *Application contact:* Dr. M. Cecil Smith, Associate Dean for Research and Graduate Education, 304-293-2174, Fax: 304-293-3802, E-mail: mcecil.smith@mail.wvu.edu.
Website: http://cehs.wvu.edu/

Whitworth University, School of Education, Graduate Studies in Education, Program in Counseling, Spokane, WA 99251-0001. Offers school counselors (M Ed); social agency/church setting (M Ed). *Accreditation:* NCATE. *Program availability:* Part-time, evening/weekend. *Degree requirements:* For master's, comprehensive exam, internship, practicum, research project, or thesis. *Entrance requirements:* For master's, GRE General Test, MAT. *Faculty research:* Church counseling service support.

Wichita State University, Graduate School, College of Education, Department of Counseling, Educational Leadership, Educational and School Psychology, Wichita, KS 67260. Offers counseling (M Ed); educational leadership (M Ed, Ed D); educational psychology (M Ed); school psychology (Ed S). *Accreditation:* NCATE. *Program availability:* Part-time, evening/weekend. Application fee: $50 ($65 for international students). *Unit head:* Dr. Jody Fiorini, Department Head, 316-978-3325, Fax: 316-978-3102, E-mail: jody.fiorini@wichita.edu. *Application contact:* Jordan Oleson, Admissions Coordinator, 316-978-3095, Fax: 316-978-3253, E-mail: jordan.oleson@wichita.edu.
Website: http://www.wichita.edu/cles

Widener University, School of Human Service Professions, Center for Education, Chester, PA 19013-5792. Offers adult education (M Ed); counseling in higher education (M Ed); counselor education (M Ed); early childhood education (M Ed); educational foundations (M Ed); educational leadership (M Ed); educational psychology (M Ed); elementary education (M Ed); English and language arts (M Ed); health education (M Ed); higher education leadership (Ed D); home and school visitor (M Ed); human sexuality (M Ed, PhD); mathematics education (M Ed); middle school education (M Ed); principalship (M Ed); reading and language arts (Ed D); reading education (M Ed);

school administration (Ed D); science education (M Ed); social studies education (M Ed); special education (M Ed); technology education (M Ed). *Accreditation:* NCATE. *Program availability:* Part-time, evening/weekend. *Faculty:* 34 full-time (22 women), 37 part-time/adjunct (14 women). *Students:* 131 full-time (112 women), 244 part-time (179 women); includes 94 minority (58 Black or African American, non-Hispanic/Latino; 1 American Indian or Alaska Native, non-Hispanic/Latino; 1 Asian, non-Hispanic/Latino; 22 Hispanic/Latino; 12 Two or more races, non-Hispanic/Latino), 12 international. Average age 37. 140 applicants, 38% accepted, 26 enrolled. In 2017, 45 master's, 21 doctorates awarded. Terminal master's awarded for partial completion of doctoral program. *Degree requirements:* For doctorate, thesis/dissertation. *Entrance requirements:* For master's, minimum GPA of 2.5; for doctorate, GRE or MAT, minimum GPA of 2.0 (undergraduate), 3.5 (graduate). *Application deadline:* Applications are processed on a rolling basis. Application fee: $25 ($300 for international students). Electronic applications accepted. *Expenses:* Contact institution. *Financial support:* Career-related internships or fieldwork, tuition waivers (full and partial), and unspecified assistantships available. Support available to part-time students. Financial award application deadline: 5/1. *Faculty research:* Reading and cognition, adult education, technology education, educational leadership, special education. *Unit head:* Dr. Shawn Fitzgerald, Dean, 610-499-4294, Fax: 610-499-4623, E-mail: smfitzgerald@widener.edu. *Application contact:* Megan Kuft, Director of Graduate Admissions, 610-499-4124, E-mail: gradprograms@widener.edu.
Website: http://www.widener.edu/academics/schools/eics

William Paterson University of New Jersey, College of Education, Wayne, NJ 07470-8420. Offers curriculum and learning (M Ed); early childhood education (Certificate); educational leadership (M Ed); educational media specialist (Certificate); elementary education (MAT, Certificate); elementary education subject area (Certificate); higher education administration (MA); learning disabilities consultant (Certificate); literacy (M Ed); middle level education (M Ed); middle school education subject area (Certificate); professional counseling (M Ed); reading specialist (Certificate); school library media specialist (Certificate); school principal (Certificate); school supervisor (Certificate); secondary education (MAT); special education (M Ed); teacher of students with disabilities (Certificate). *Accreditation:* NCATE. *Program availability:* Part-time, evening/weekend. *Faculty:* 37 full-time (25 women), 21 part-time/adjunct (16 women). *Students:* 73 full-time (54 women), 480 part-time (409 women); includes 153 minority (48 Black or African American, non-Hispanic/Latino; 13 Asian, non-Hispanic/Latino; 81 Hispanic/Latino; 11 Two or more races, non-Hispanic/Latino), 1 international. Average age 35. 347 applicants, 87% accepted, 226 enrolled. In 2017, 136 master's awarded. *Degree requirements:* For master's, comprehensive exam, thesis (for some programs), exit interview (for some programs); practicum/internship; minimum GPA of 3.0 (for some programs); exit portfolio (for some programs). *Entrance requirements:* For master's, GRE/MAT, minimum GPA of 2.75; teaching certificate; essay; interview; 2 letters of recommendation; personal statement. Additional exam requirements/recommendations for international students: Required—TOEFL (minimum score 550 paper-based; 79 iBT), IELTS (minimum score 6). *Application deadline:* For fall admission, 6/1 for domestic students, 3/1 for international students; for spring admission, 11/1 for domestic students, 10/1 for international students. Applications are processed on a rolling basis. Application fee: $50. Electronic applications accepted. *Expenses:* Tuition, state resident: full-time $13,920; part-time $6264 per year. Tuition, nonresident: full-time $21,700; part-time $9765 per year. *Required fees:* $80; $36 per year. Tuition and fees vary according to course load, degree level and program. *Financial support:* In 2017–18, 8,416 students received support. Career-related internships or fieldwork, Federal Work-Study, scholarships/grants, and unspecified assistantships available. Support available to part-time students. Financial award application deadline: 3/15; financial award applicants required to submit FAFSA. *Faculty research:* Code switching and creative writing, language instruction, teacher evaluation, preschools, history of educational theories. *Total annual research expenditures:* $311,226. *Unit head:* Dr. Dorothy Feola, Dean, 973-720-2138, Fax: 973-720-3647, E-mail: feolad@wpunj.edu. *Application contact:* Liana Fornarotto, Director of Education Enrollment and Certification, 973-720-2206, Fax: 973-720-2989, E-mail: fornarottol@wpunj.edu.
Website: http://www.wpunj.edu/coe

Wilmington University, College of Education, New Castle, DE 19720-6491. Offers applied technology in education (M Ed); career and technical education (M Ed); educational leadership (Ed D); elementary and secondary school counseling (M Ed); elementary studies (M Ed); ESOL literacy (M Ed); higher education leadership (Ed D); instruction: gifted and talented (M Ed); instruction: teacher of reading (M Ed); instruction: teaching and learning (M Ed); organizational leadership (Ed D); school leadership (M Ed); secondary education (MAT); special education (M Ed). *Accreditation:* NCATE. *Program availability:* Part-time, evening/weekend. *Faculty:* 23 full-time (13 women), 162 part-time/adjunct (99 women). *Students:* 546 full-time (394 women), 960 part-time (732 women); includes 320 minority (241 Black or African American, non-Hispanic/Latino; 12 American Indian or Alaska Native, non-Hispanic/Latino; 11 Asian, non-Hispanic/Latino; 28 Hispanic/Latino; 3 Native Hawaiian or other Pacific Islander, non-Hispanic/Latino; 25 Two or more races, non-Hispanic/Latino), 7 international. Average age 34. 1,068

applicants, 64% accepted, 582 enrolled. In 2017, 430 master's, 59 doctorates awarded. *Entrance requirements:* For master's, 2 letters of recommendation, interview. Additional exam requirements/recommendations for international students: Required—TOEFL (minimum score 500 paper-based). *Application deadline:* For fall admission, 4/30 for domestic students. Applications are processed on a rolling basis. Application fee: $35. Electronic applications accepted. *Expenses:* Tuition: Part-time $466 per credit. *Required fees:* $25 per semester. Tuition and fees vary according to degree level and campus/location. *Financial support:* Applicants required to submit FAFSA. *Unit head:* Dr. John C. Gray, Dean, 302-295-1139. *Application contact:* Laura Morris, Director of Admissions, 877-967-5464, E-mail: infocenter@wilmu.edu.
Website: http://www.wilmu.edu/education/

Winona State University, College of Education, Department of Counselor Education, Winona, MN 55987. Offers addiction counseling (Certificate); clinical mental health counseling (MS); human services (MS); school counseling (MS). *Accreditation:* ACA (one or more programs are accredited); NCATE. *Program availability:* Part-time, evening/weekend. *Degree requirements:* For master's, thesis or alternative. *Entrance requirements:* For master's, letters of reference, interview, group activity, on-site writing. Electronic applications accepted.

Winthrop University, College of Education, Program in Counseling and Development, Rock Hill, SC 29733. Offers agency counseling (M Ed); school counseling (M Ed). *Accreditation:* ACA; NCATE. *Program availability:* Part-time. *Students:* 132 full-time (108 women), 58 part-time (53 women); includes 57 minority (45 Black or African American, non-Hispanic/Latino; 1 American Indian or Alaska Native, non-Hispanic/Latino; 2 Asian, non-Hispanic/Latino; 6 Hispanic/Latino; 1 Native Hawaiian or other Pacific Islander, non-Hispanic/Latino; 2 Two or more races, non-Hispanic/Latino), 2 international. Average age 37. In 2017, 26 master's awarded. *Degree requirements:* For master's, comprehensive exam. *Entrance requirements:* For master's, GRE General Test or MAT, interview. Additional exam requirements/recommendations for international students: Required—TOEFL (minimum score 550 paper-based; 79 iBT), IELTS (minimum score 6). *Application deadline:* For fall admission, 2/1 for domestic students. Application fee: $50. Electronic applications accepted. *Financial support:* Research assistantships with full tuition reimbursements, career-related internships or fieldwork, Federal Work-Study, scholarships/grants, and unspecified assistantships available. Support available to part-time students. Financial award application deadline: 2/1; financial award applicants required to submit FAFSA. *Unit head:* Dr. Jennifer Jordan, Unit Head, 803-323-2456, E-mail: jordanje@winthrop.edu. *Application contact:* 800-411-7041, Fax: 803-323-2292, E-mail: gradschool@winthrop.edu.
Website: http://www.winthrop.edu/coe/csdv

Wright State University, College of Education and Human Services, Department of Human Services, Programs in Counseling, Dayton, OH 45435. Offers counseling (MA, MS), including business and industrial management; pupil personnel services (M Ed), including school counseling. *Accreditation:* ACA (one or more programs are accredited); NCATE. *Degree requirements:* For master's, comprehensive exam, thesis (for some programs). *Entrance requirements:* For master's, GRE General Test, MAT, interview. Additional exam requirements/recommendations for international students: Required—TOEFL.

Xavier University, College of Social Sciences, Health and Education, School of Education, Department of Counseling, Cincinnati, OH 45207. Offers clinical mental health counseling (MA); school counseling (MA). *Program availability:* Part-time, evening/weekend. *Degree requirements:* For master's, internship. *Entrance requirements:* For master's, GRE or MAT, minimum GPA of 3.0; 2 letters of recommendation; resume; official transcript; statement of purpose. Additional exam requirements/recommendations for international students: Required—TOEFL (minimum score 550 paper-based; 79 iBT). Electronic applications accepted. Application fee is waived when completed online. *Expenses:* Contact institution. *Faculty research:* Supervision, ethics, consultation, self-injury, bullying.

Xavier University of Louisiana, Graduate School, Programs in Education, New Orleans, LA 70125. Offers counseling (MA); curriculum and instruction (MA); educational leadership (MA). *Accreditation:* NCATE. *Program availability:* Part-time, evening/weekend. *Degree requirements:* For master's, comprehensive exam, thesis or alternative. *Entrance requirements:* For master's, GRE General Test, MAT, minimum GPA of 2.5. Additional exam requirements/recommendations for international students: Required—TOEFL.

Youngstown State University, Graduate School, Beeghly College of Education, Department of Counseling, Youngstown, OH 44555-0001. Offers community counseling (MS Ed); school counseling (MS Ed). *Accreditation:* ACA; NCATE. *Program availability:* Part-time, evening/weekend. *Degree requirements:* For master's, comprehensive exam. *Entrance requirements:* For master's, MAT, interview, minimum GPA of 2.7. Additional exam requirements/recommendations for international students: Required—TOEFL. *Faculty research:* Suicide, euthanasia, ethical issues, marriage and family.

Developmental Education

East Tennessee State University, School of Graduate Studies, School of Continuing Studies and Academic Outreach, Johnson City, TN 37614. Offers archival studies (Postbaccalaureate Certificate); liberal studies (MALS); reinforcing education through artistic learning (Postbaccalaureate Certificate); strategic leadership (MPS); training and development (MPS). *Program availability:* Part-time, online learning. In 2017, 9 master's, 1 other advanced degree awarded. *Degree requirements:* For master's, comprehensive exam, thesis (for some programs), professional project. *Entrance requirements:* For master's, GRE General Test, minimum GPA of 2.75, professional portfolio, three letters of recommendation, interview, writing sample; for Postbaccalaureate Certificate, minimum GPA of 2.5, three letters of recommendation, interview. Additional exam requirements/recommendations for international students: Required—TOEFL (minimum score 550 paper-based; 79 iBT). *Application deadline:* For fall admission, 6/1 for domestic students, 4/29 for international students; for spring admission, 11/1 for domestic students, 9/29 for international students. Application fee: $55 ($65 for international students). Electronic applications accepted. *Financial support:* Research assistantships with full tuition reimbursements, teaching assistantships with full tuition reimbursements, institutionally sponsored loans, scholarships/grants, tuition waivers, and unspecified assistantships available. Financial award application deadline: 7/1; financial award applicants required to submit FAFSA. *Faculty research:* Appalachian studies, women's and gender studies, interdisciplinary theory, regional and Southern cultures. *Unit head:* Dr. Rick E. Osborn, Dean, 423-439-4223, Fax: 423-439-

7091, E-mail: osbornr@etsu.edu. *Application contact:* Dr. Rick E. Osborn, Dean, 423-439-4223, Fax: 423-439-7091, E-mail: osbornr@etsu.edu.
Website: http://www.etsu.edu/academicaffairs/scs/

Ferris State University, College of Education and Human Services, School of Education, Big Rapids, MI 49307. Offers curriculum and instruction (M Ed), including special education, subject area; educational leadership (MS); instructor (MSCTE); post-secondary administration (MSCTE); training and development (MSCTE). *Program availability:* Part-time, evening/weekend, blended/hybrid learning. *Faculty:* 7 full-time (4 women), 9 part-time/adjunct (6 women). *Students:* 4 full-time (1 woman), 40 part-time (23 women); includes 7 minority (3 Black or African American, non-Hispanic/Latino; 2 Hispanic/Latino; 2 Two or more races, non-Hispanic/Latino), 4 international. Average age 37. 13 applicants, 92% accepted, 7 enrolled. In 2017, 36 master's awarded. *Degree requirements:* For master's, thesis, research paper or project. *Entrance requirements:* For master's, minimum undergraduate GPA of 3.0. Additional exam requirements/recommendations for international students: Required—TOEFL (minimum score 500 paper-based, 79 iBT) or IELTS. *Application deadline:* For fall admission, 7/1 priority date for domestic and international students; for spring admission, 11/1 priority date for domestic and international students; for summer admission, 3/1 priority date for domestic and international students. Applications are processed on a rolling basis. Application fee: $30. Electronic applications accepted. Application fee is waived when completed online. *Financial support:* Career-related internships or fieldwork and

scholarships/grants available. Support available to part-time students. Financial award applicants required to submit FAFSA. *Faculty research:* Suicide prevention, reading, women in education, special needs, administration. *Unit head:* Arrick L. Jackson, Dean, 231-591-2702, Fax: 231-591-2043, E-mail: arrickjackson@ferris.edu. *Application contact:* Liza Ing, Graduate Program Coordinator, 231-591-5362, Fax: 231-591-2043, E-mail: lizaIng@ferris.edu.
Website: http://www.ferris.edu/education/education/

Grambling State University, School of Graduate Studies and Research, College of Education, Department of Educational Leadership, Grambling, LA 71245. Offers developmental education (MS, Ed D, PMC), including curriculum and instructional design (Ed D), English (MS), guidance and counseling (MS), higher education administration and management (Ed D), mathematics (MS), reading (MS), science (MS), student development and personnel services (Ed D); educational leadership (M Ed). *Program availability:* Part-time, evening/weekend. *Degree requirements:* For master's, comprehensive exam, thesis (for some programs); for doctorate, comprehensive exam, thesis/dissertation. *Entrance requirements:* For master's, GRE, minimum GPA of 2.5 on last degree; for doctorate, GRE (minimum score 1000, 500 on Verbal), master's degree, minimum GPA of 3.0 on last degree. Additional exam requirements/recommendations for international students: Required—TOEFL (minimum score 500 paper-based; 62 iBT). Electronic applications accepted.

Instituto Tecnológico y de Estudios Superiores de Monterrey, Campus Ciudad Obregón, Programs in Education, Program in Cognitive Development, Ciudad Obregón, Mexico. Offers ME.

National Louis University, College of Arts and Sciences, Chicago, IL 60603. Offers adult education (Ed D); counseling and human services (MS); language and academic development (M Ed, Certificate); psychology (MA, PhD, Certificate); public policy (MA); written communication (MS, Certificate). *Program availability:* Part-time, evening/weekend, online learning. *Degree requirements:* For master's and Certificate, comprehensive exam (for some programs), thesis (for some programs); for doctorate, thesis/dissertation. *Entrance requirements:* For master's, MAT or GRE, 3 professional or academic references, interview, minimum GPA of 3.0; for doctorate, GRE General Test, MAT, or Watson-Glaser Critical Thinking Appraisal, three professional or academic references, statement of academic and professional goals, 3 years of experience in field, interview, master's degree, resume, writing sample; for Certificate, GRE, MAT, or Watson-Glaser Critical Thinking Appraisal, three professional or academic references, statement of academic and professional goals, interview, minimum GPA of 3.0. Additional exam requirements/recommendations for international students: Required— Department of Language Studies Assessment or TOEFL (minimum score 550 paper-based; 79 iBT). Electronic applications accepted.

North Carolina State University, Graduate School, College of Education, Department of Adult and Higher Education, Program in Training and Development, Raleigh, NC 27695. Offers M Ed, Ed D, Certificate. *Program availability:* Online learning. *Degree requirements:* For master's, thesis optional. *Entrance requirements:* For master's, GRE General Test or MAT, minimum GPA of 3.0 in major. Electronic applications accepted.

Penn State Harrisburg, Graduate School, School of Behavioral Sciences and Education, Middletown, PA 17057. Offers adult education in the health and medical professions (Certificate); applied behavior analysis (MA); applied clinical psychology (MA); applied psychological research (MA); community psychology and social change (MA); English as a second language (ESL) program specialist and leadership (Certificate); health education (M Ed); lifelong learning and adult education (M Ed, D Ed); literacy education (M Ed); literacy leadership (Certificate); psychology: applications in clinical psychology (Certificate); psychology: health psychology (Certificate); teaching and curriculum (M Ed); training and development (M Ed, Certificate). *Program availability:* Part-time, evening/weekend. *Unit head:* Dr. Mukund S. Kulkarni, Chancellor, 717-948-6105, Fax: 717-948-6452. *Application contact:* Robert W. Coffman, Jr., Director of Enrollment Management, Recruitment and Admissions, 717-948-6250, Fax: 717-948-6325, E-mail: hbgadmit@psu.edu.
Website: https://harrisburg.psu.edu/behavioral-sciences-and-education/

Rutgers University–New Brunswick, Graduate School of Education, Department of Educational Psychology, Program in Learning, Cognition and Development, Piscataway, NJ 08854-8097. Offers Ed M. *Program availability:* Part-time, evening/weekend. *Entrance requirements:* For master's, GRE General Test, 3 letters of recommendation. Additional exam requirements/recommendations for international students: Required— TOEFL (minimum score 550 paper-based; 83 iBT). Electronic applications accepted. *Faculty research:* Cognitive development, gender roles, cognition and instruction, peer learning, infancy and early childhood.

Sam Houston State University, College of Education, Department of Educational Leadership, Huntsville, TX 77341. Offers administration (M Ed); developmental education administration (Ed D); educational leadership (Ed D); higher education administration (MA); higher education leadership (Ed D); instructional leadership (M Ed, MA). *Program availability:* Part-time, evening/weekend, online learning. *Degree requirements:* For master's, comprehensive exam (for some programs), thesis (for some programs); for doctorate, comprehensive exam, thesis/dissertation. *Entrance requirements:* For master's, GRE General Test, references, personal essay, resume, professional statement; for doctorate, GRE General Test, master's degree, references, personal essay, resume. Additional exam requirements/recommendations for international students: Required—TOEFL (minimum score 550 paper-based; 79 iBT), IELTS (minimum score 6.5). Electronic applications accepted.

Texas State University, The Graduate College, College of Education, Program in Developmental Education, San Marcos, TX 78666. Offers MA, PhD. *Program availability:* Part-time. *Faculty:* 6 full-time (4 women). *Students:* 26 full-time (22 women), 21 part-time (17 women); includes 23 minority (5 Black or African American, non-Hispanic/Latino; 2 Asian, non-Hispanic/Latino; 15 Hispanic/Latino; 1 Two or more races, non-Hispanic/Latino), 3 international. Average age 38. 25 applicants, 68% accepted, 8 enrolled. In 2017, 5 master's, 4 doctorates awarded. *Degree requirements:* For master's, comprehensive exam, thesis optional; for doctorate, comprehensive exam, thesis/dissertation. *Entrance requirements:* For master's, baccalaureate degree from regionally-accredited institution with minimum GPA of 2.75 on last 60 hours of undergraduate work, statement of purpose, 3 letters of reference from individuals with knowledge of the candidate as a student or professional; for doctorate, GRE (minimum preferred score of 299 with no less than 150 on the verbal section, 149 on the

quantitative section and 4.0 on the analytical section), baccalaureate and master's degrees from regionally-accredited institution in area relevant to developmental education with minimum graduate GPA of 3.0; statement of purpose; resume; 3 letters of recommendation addressing the applicant's professional and academic background. Additional exam requirements/recommendations for international students: Required— TOEFL (minimum score 78 iBT), IELTS (minimum score 6.5). *Application deadline:* For fall admission, 2/1 priority date for domestic and international students; for spring admission, 10/15 for domestic students, 10/1 for international students; for summer admission, 4/15 for domestic students, 3/15 for international students. Application fee: $40 ($90 for international students). Electronic applications accepted. *Expenses:* Tuition, state resident: full-time $7868; part-time $3934 per semester. Tuition, nonresident: full-time $17,828; part-time $8914 per semester. *Required fees:* $2092; $1435 per semester. Tuition and fees vary according to course load. *Financial support:* In 2017–18, 32 students received support, including 15 research assistantships (averaging $23,584 per year), 6 teaching assistantships (averaging $26,260 per year); scholarships/grants and unspecified assistantships also available. Financial award application deadline: 3/1; financial award applicants required to submit FAFSA. *Faculty research:* Texas adult education content standards and benchmarks; Texas success initiative professional development program;. *Total annual research expenditures:* $413,645. *Unit head:* Dr. Sonya Armstrong, Doctoral Program Director, 512-245-7789, E-mail: sla113@txstate.edu. *Application contact:* Dr. Andrea Golato, Dean of Graduate School, 512-245-2581, Fax: 512-245-8365, E-mail: gradcollege@txstate.edu.
Website: http://www.gradcollege.txstate.edu/programs/developmental-ed-phd.html

The University of Iowa, Graduate College, College of Education, Department of Teaching and Learning, Program in Education, Iowa City, IA 52242-1316. Offers art education (MA); developmental reading (MA); elementary education (MA); English education (MA, MAT); foreign and second language education (MAT); foreign language education (MA); foreign language/ESL education (PhD); language, literacy and culture (PhD); mathematics education (MA, MAT, PhD); music education (MM, PhD); science education (MA); secondary education (MA); social studies (MA, PhD). *Degree requirements:* For master's, thesis optional, exam; for doctorate, comprehensive exam, thesis/dissertation. *Entrance requirements:* For master's and doctorate, GRE General Test, minimum GPA of 3.0. Additional exam requirements/recommendations for international students: Required—TOEFL (minimum score 550 paper-based; 81 iBT). Electronic applications accepted.

Walden University, Graduate Programs, Richard W. Riley College of Education and Leadership, Minneapolis, MN 55401. Offers adult education (Post-Master's Certificate); adult learning (Graduate Certificate); college teaching and learning (Graduate Certificate); community college leadership (Ed D); curriculum, instruction and assessment (Ed D, Ed S, Graduate Certificate); developmental education (Graduate Certificate); early childhood administration, management, and leadership (Graduate Certificate); early childhood education (Ed D, Ed S); early childhood public policy and advocacy (Graduate Certificate); early childhood studies (MS), including administration, management and leadership, early childhood public policy and advocacy, teaching adults in the early childhood field, teaching and diversity in early childhood education; education (MS, PhD), including adolescent literacy and learning (MS), curriculum, instruction, and assessment (grades K-12) (MS), curriculum, instruction, assessment, and evaluation (PhD), early childhood leadership and advocacy (PhD), early childhood special education (PhD), educational leadership (MS), educational leadership and administration (principal preparation) (MS), educational technology and design (PhD), elementary reading and literacy (PreK-6) (MS), elementary reading and mathematics (grades K-6) (MS), global and comparative education (PhD), higher education leadership management and policy (PhD), integrating technology in the classroom (grades K-12) (MS), learning, instruction and innovation (PhD), mathematics (grades 5-8) (MS), mathematics (grades K-6) (MS), mathematics and science (grades K-8) (MS), organizational research, assessment, and evaluation (PhD), reading and literacy with a reading K-12 endorsement (MS), reading literacy assessment and evaluation (PhD), science (grades K-8) (MS), special education (non-licensure) (grades K-12) (MS), teacher leadership (grades K-12) (MS), teaching English language learners (grades K-12) (MS); educational administration and leadership (Ed D); educational leadership and administration (principal preparation) (Ed S); educational technology (Ed D, Ed S, Post Master's Certificate); elementary reading and literacy (Graduate Certificate); engaging culturally diverse learners (Graduate Certificate); enrollment management and institutional marketing (Graduate Certificate); higher education (MS), including adult learning, college teaching and learning, enrollment management and institutional marketing, global higher education, leadership for student success, online and distance learning; higher education and adult learning (Ed D); higher education leadership and management (Ed D); higher education leadership for student success (Graduate Certificate); instructional design and technology (MS, Postbaccalaureate Certificate), including general program (MS), online learning (MS), training and performance improvement (MS); integrating technology in the classroom (Graduate Certificate); mathematics 5-8 (Graduate Certificate); mathematics K-6 (Graduate Certificate); online teaching for adult educators (Graduate Certificate); reading, literacy, and assessment (Ed D, Ed S); science K-8 (Graduate Certificate); special education (Ed D, Ed S, Graduate Certificate); special education (K-age 21) (MAT); teacher leadership (Graduate Certificate); teaching adults English as a second language (Graduate Certificate); teaching adults in the early childhood field (Graduate Certificate); teaching and diversity in early childhood education (Graduate Certificate); teaching English language learners (grades K-12) (Graduate Certificate); teaching K-12 students online (Graduate Certificate). *Accreditation:* NCATE. *Program availability:* Part-time, evening/weekend, online only, 100% online. *Degree requirements:* For doctorate, thesis/dissertation (for some programs), residency; for other advanced degree, residency (for some programs). *Entrance requirements:* For master's, bachelor's degree or higher; minimum GPA of 2.5; official transcripts; goal statement (for some programs); access to computer and Internet; for doctorate, master's degree or higher; three years of related professional or academic experience (preferred); minimum GPA of 3.0; goal statement and current resume (for select programs); official transcripts; access to computer and Internet; for other advanced degree, relevant work experience; access to computer and Internet. Additional exam requirements/recommendations for international students: Required—TOEFL (minimum score 550 paper-based, 79 iBT), IELTS (minimum score 6.5), Michigan English Language Assessment Battery (minimum score 82), or PTE (minimum score 53). Electronic applications accepted.

English Education

Alabama Agricultural and Mechanical University, School of Graduate Studies, College of Education, Humanities, and Behavioral Sciences, Department of Educational Leadership and Secondary Education, Huntsville, AL 35811. Offers biology (M Ed); business/marketing education (M Ed, Ed S); chemistry (M Ed); collaborative teacher secondary education (M Ed, Ed S); education (M Ed, Ed S); English language arts (M Ed); family/consumer science education (M Ed, Ed S); general science (M Ed); general social science (M Ed); mathematics (M Ed, Ed S); physics (M Ed, Ed S); technology education (M Ed). *Accreditation:* NCATE. *Program availability:* Evening/weekend. *Degree requirements:* For master's, comprehensive exam; for Ed S, thesis. *Entrance requirements:* For master's, GRE General Test. Additional exam requirements/recommendations for international students: Required—TOEFL (minimum score 500 paper-based; 61 iBT). Electronic applications accepted. *Faculty research:* World peace through education, computer-assisted instruction.

Alabama State University, College of Education, Department of Curriculum and Instruction, Montgomery, AL 36101-0271. Offers early childhood education (M Ed, Ed S); elementary education (M Ed, Ed S); secondary education (M Ed, Ed S), including biology education, English language arts education (M Ed), history education, math education, music education (M Ed), reading education (M Ed), social science education; special education (M Ed). *Program availability:* Part-time. *Faculty:* 7 full-time (4 women), 7 part-time/adjunct (4 women). *Students:* 43 full-time (35 women), 71 part-time (62 women); includes 112 minority (111 Black or African American, non-Hispanic/Latino; 1 Two or more races, non-Hispanic/Latino). Average age 22. 47 applicants, 66% accepted, 19 enrolled. In 2017, 21 master's, 13 Ed Ss awarded. *Degree requirements:* For master's, comprehensive exam, thesis optional; for Ed S, comprehensive exam, thesis. *Entrance requirements:* For master's, GRE General Test, MAT, writing competency test; for Ed S, writing competency test, GRE, MAT. Additional exam requirements/recommendations for international students: Required—TOEFL (minimum score 500 paper-based). *Application deadline:* For fall admission, 4/15 for domestic and international students; for spring admission, 11/15 for domestic and international students; for summer admission, 3/15 for domestic and international students. Applications are processed on a rolling basis. Application fee: $25. Electronic applications accepted. *Expenses:* Tuition, state resident: part-time $412 per credit hour. Tuition, nonresident: part-time $824 per credit hour. *Required fees:* $685 per semester. *Financial support:* Research assistantships available. Financial award application deadline: 6/30; financial award applicants required to submit FAFSA. *Unit head:* Dr. Joyce Johnson, Acting Chairperson, 334-229-4485, Fax: 334-229-5603, E-mail: jjohnson@alasu.edu. *Application contact:* Dr. William Person, Dean of Graduate Studies, 334-229-4274, Fax: 334-229-4928, E-mail: wperson@alasu.edu. Website: http://www.alasu.edu/academics/colleges—departments/college-of-education/curriculum—instruction/index.aspx

Albany State University, College of Arts and Humanities, Albany, GA 31705-2717. Offers criminal justice (MS); English education (M Ed); public administration (MPA), including community and economic development, criminal justice administration, health administration and policy, human resources management, public management, public policy, water resources management and policy; social work (MSW). *Accreditation:* NASPAA. *Program availability:* Part-time. *Degree requirements:* For master's, comprehensive exam, professional portfolio (for MPA), internship, capstone report. *Entrance requirements:* For master's, GRE, MAT, minimum GPA of 3.0, official transcript, pre-medical record/certificate of immunization, letters of reference. Electronic applications accepted. *Faculty research:* HIV prevention for minority students.

Andrews University, School of Graduate Studies, College of Arts and Sciences, Department of English, Berrien Springs, MI 49104. Offers MA, MAT. *Program availability:* Part-time. *Faculty:* 8 full-time (4 women), 2 part-time/adjunct (1 woman). *Students:* 5 full-time (3 women), 7 part-time (4 women); includes 5 minority (2 Black or African American, non-Hispanic/Latino; 3 Hispanic/Latino), 1 international. Average age 33. 5 applicants, 80% accepted, 4 enrolled. In 2017, 2 master's awarded. *Degree requirements:* For master's, one foreign language, thesis optional. *Entrance requirements:* For master's, GRE Subject Test. Additional exam requirements/recommendations for international students: Required—TOEFL (minimum score 550 paper-based). *Application deadline:* For fall admission, 8/15 for domestic students. Applications are processed on a rolling basis. Application fee: $40. *Financial support:* Fellowships, research assistantships, teaching assistantships, career-related internships or fieldwork, and Federal Work-Study available. *Faculty research:* Shakespearean studies. *Unit head:* Dr. Meredith Jones-Gray, Chairperson, 269-471-3298. *Application contact:* Justina Clayburn, Supervisor of Graduate Admission, 800-253-2874, Fax: 269-471-6321, E-mail: graduate@andrews.edu.

Andrews University, School of Graduate Studies, School of Education, Department of Teaching, Learning, and Curriculum, Berrien Springs, MI 49104. Offers curriculum and instruction (MA, Ed D, PhD, Ed S); elementary education (MAT); secondary education (MAT), including biology, education, English, English as a second language, French, history, physics; teacher education (MAT). *Faculty:* 7 full-time (5 women). *Students:* 14 full-time (8 women), 7 part-time (6 women); includes 5 minority (all Black or African American, non-Hispanic/Latino), 9 international. Average age 39. 29 applicants, 31% accepted, 4 enrolled. In 2017, 5 master's, 3 doctorates awarded. *Entrance requirements:* For master's, GRE Subject Test. Additional exam requirements/recommendations for international students: Required—TOEFL (minimum score 550 paper-based). *Application deadline:* For fall admission, 8/15 for domestic students. Applications are processed on a rolling basis. Application fee: $40. *Unit head:* Dr. Lee C. Davidson, Chair, 269-471-6364. *Application contact:* Justina Clayburn, Supervisor of Graduate Admission, 800-253-2874, Fax: 269-471-6321, E-mail: graduate@andrews.edu.

Anna Maria College, Graduate Division, Program in Education, Paxton, MA 01612. Offers early childhood education (M Ed); education (CAGS); elementary education (M Ed); English language arts (M Ed); visual arts (M Ed). *Program availability:* Part-time, evening/weekend. *Entrance requirements:* For master's, bachelor's degree in liberal arts or sciences, minimum GPA of 3.0. Additional exam requirements/recommendations for international students: Required—TOEFL (minimum score 500 paper-based). Electronic applications accepted.

Appalachian State University, Cratis D. Williams Graduate School, Department of Curriculum and Instruction, Boone, NC 28608. Offers curriculum specialist (MA); educational media (MA); elementary education (MA); middle grades education (MA), including language arts, mathematics, science, social studies. *Accreditation:* NCATE. *Program availability:* Part-time, evening/weekend, online learning. *Degree requirements:* For master's, comprehensive exam, thesis or alternative. *Entrance requirements:* For master's, GRE General Test or MAT, 3 letters of recommendation. Additional exam requirements/recommendations for international students: Required—TOEFL (minimum

score 570 paper-based; 79 iBT), IELTS (minimum score 6.5). Electronic applications accepted. *Faculty research:* Media literacy, elementary teaching, curriculum development, online learning environments.

Arcadia University, School of Education, Glenside, PA 19038-3295. Offers art education (M Ed); computer education (CAS); curriculum (CAS); curriculum studies (M Ed); early childhood education (M Ed), including individualized, master teacher, research in child development; educational leadership (M Ed, Ed D, CAS); elementary education (M Ed); English education (MA Ed); environmental education (MA Ed); instructional technology (M Ed); language arts (M Ed); library science (M Ed); mathematics education (M Ed, MA Ed); music education (MA Ed); psychology (MA Ed); reading (M Ed, CAS); science education (M Ed, CAS); secondary education (M Ed, CAS); special education (M Ed, Ed D, CAS); theater arts (MA Ed); written communication (MA Ed). *Accreditation:* NASAD. *Program availability:* Part-time, evening/weekend, online learning. Electronic applications accepted. *Expenses:* Contact institution.

Arkansas State University, Graduate School, College of Humanities and Social Sciences, Department of English and Philosophy, State University, AR 72467. Offers English (MA); English education (MSE, SCCT). *Program availability:* Part-time. *Degree requirements:* For master's, variable foreign language requirement, comprehensive exam, thesis or alternative, preliminary exam; for SCCT, comprehensive exam. *Entrance requirements:* For master's, GRE General Test or MAT, appropriate bachelor's degree, official transcript, valid teaching certificate (for MSE), immunization records; for SCCT, GRE General Test or MAT, interview, master's degree, official transcript, immunization records. Additional exam requirements/recommendations for international students: Required—TOEFL (minimum score 550 paper-based; 79 iBT), IELTS (minimum score 6), PTE (minimum score 56). Electronic applications accepted.

Arkansas Tech University, College of Arts and Humanities, Russellville, AR 72801. Offers applied sociology (MS); English (M Ed, MA); history (MA); liberal arts (MLA); multi-media journalism (MA); psychology (MS); teaching English as a second language (MA). *Program availability:* Part-time, 100% online, blended/hybrid learning. *Students:* 35 full-time (22 women), 122 part-time (94 women); includes 34 minority (11 Black or African American, non-Hispanic/Latino; 2 Asian, non-Hispanic/Latino; 19 Hispanic/Latino; 2 Two or more races, non-Hispanic/Latino), 19 international. Average age 34. In 2017, 85 master's awarded. *Degree requirements:* For master's, comprehensive exam (for some programs), thesis (for some programs), project. *Entrance requirements:* Additional exam requirements/recommendations for international students: Required—TOEFL (minimum score 550 paper-based; 79 iBT), IELTS (minimum score 6.5), PTE (minimum score 58). *Application deadline:* For fall admission, 3/1 priority date for domestic students, 5/1 priority date for international students; for spring admission, 10/1 priority date for domestic and international students. Applications are processed on a rolling basis. Application fee: $40 ($90 for international students). Electronic applications accepted. *Expenses:* Tuition, state resident: full-time $6816; part-time $284 per credit hour. Tuition, nonresident: full-time $13,632; part-time $568 per credit hour. *Required fees:* $420 per semester. Tuition and fees vary according to course load. *Financial support:* In 2017–18, research assistantships with full and partial tuition reimbursements (averaging $4,800 per year), teaching assistantships with full and partial tuition reimbursements (averaging $4,800 per year) were awarded; career-related internships or fieldwork, Federal Work-Study, scholarships/grants, health care benefits, and unspecified assistantships also available. Support available to part-time students. Financial award application deadline: 4/15; financial award applicants required to submit FAFSA. *Unit head:* Dr. Jeffrey Woods, Dean, 479-968-0274, Fax: 479-964-0812, E-mail: jwoods@atu.edu. *Application contact:* Dr. Mary B. Gunter, Dean of Graduate College, 479-968-0398, Fax: 479-964-0542, E-mail: gradcollege@atu.edu. Website: http://www.atu.edu/humanities/

Binghamton University, State University of New York, Graduate School, College of Community and Public Affairs, Department of Teaching, Learning and Educational Leadership, Program in Adolescence Education, Binghamton, NY 13902-6000. Offers biology education (MAT, MS Ed); chemistry education (MAT, MS Ed); earth science education (MAT, MS Ed); English education (MAT, MS Ed); French education (MAT, MS Ed); mathematical sciences education (MAT, MS Ed); physics (MAT, MS Ed); social studies (MAT, MS Ed); Spanish education (MAT, MS Ed). *Accreditation:* TEAC. *Program availability:* Part-time, evening/weekend. *Students:* 53 full-time (32 women), 9 part-time (3 women); includes 10 minority (2 Black or African American, non-Hispanic/Latino; 1 Asian, non-Hispanic/Latino; 5 Hispanic/Latino; 2 Two or more races, non-Hispanic/Latino). Average age 27. 51 applicants, 88% accepted, 31 enrolled. In 2017, 36 master's awarded. *Degree requirements:* For master's, portfolio. *Entrance requirements:* For master's, GRE General Test, teaching certification. Additional exam requirements/recommendations for international students: Required—TOEFL (minimum score 550 paper-based; 80 iBT). *Application deadline:* For fall admission, 2/1 priority date for domestic and international students; for spring admission, 10/15 priority date for domestic and international students. Application fee: $75. Electronic applications accepted. *Financial support:* In 2017–18, 4 students received support. Research assistantships, teaching assistantships, career-related internships or fieldwork, Federal Work-Study, institutionally sponsored loans, scholarships/grants, health care benefits, tuition waivers (full and partial), and unspecified assistantships available. Financial award applicants required to submit FAFSA. *Unit head:* Dr. Susan Strehle, Dean, 607-777-7329, E-mail: sstrehle@binghamton.edu. *Application contact:* Ben Balkaya, Assistant Dean and Director, 607-777-2151, Fax: 607-777-2501, E-mail: balkaya@binghamton.edu.

Bloomsburg University of Pennsylvania, School of Graduate Studies, College of Education, Department of Teaching and Learning, Program in Middle Level Education Grades 4-8, Bloomsburg, PA 17815-1301. Offers language arts (M Ed); math (M Ed); science (M Ed); social studies (M Ed). *Accreditation:* NCATE. *Degree requirements:* For master's, thesis optional, practicum, student teaching. *Entrance requirements:* For master's, MAT, GRE, or PRAXIS, minimum QPA of 3.0, teaching certificate, U.S. citizenship, related undergraduate coursework, professional liability insurance, recent TB test. Additional exam requirements/recommendations for international students: Required—TOEFL (minimum score 550 paper-based), IELTS. Electronic applications accepted. *Expenses:* Tuition, state resident: full-time $10,000; part-time $500 per credit hour. Tuition, nonresident: full-time $15,000; part-time $750 per credit hour. *Required fees:* $2484; $110.75 per credit hour. $75 per term. Tuition and fees vary according to program.

Bob Jones University, Graduate Programs, Greenville, SC 29614. Offers accountancy (MS); Bible (MA); Bible translation (MA); Biblical studies (Certificate); broadcast management (MS); business administration (MBA); church history (MA, PhD); church ministries (MA); church music (MM); cinema and video production (MA); counseling

(MS); curriculum and instruction (Ed D); divinity (M Div); dramatic production (MA); educational leadership (MS, Ed D, Ed S); elementary education (M Ed, MAT); English (M Ed, MA, MAT); fine arts (MA); graphic design (MA); history (M Ed, MA); illustration (MA); interpretative speech (MA); mathematics (M Ed, MAT); medical missions (Certificate); ministry (MM, D Min); multi-categorical special education (M Ed, MAT); music (M Ed); New Testament interpretation (PhD); Old Testament interpretation (PhD); orchestral instrument performance (MM); organ performance (MM); pastoral studies (MA); personnel services (MS, Ed S); piano pedagogy (MM); piano performance (MM); platform arts (MA); radio and television broadcasting (MS); rhetoric and public address (MA); secondary education (M Ed); studio art (MA); teaching Bible (MA); theology (MA, PhD); voice performance (MM); youth ministries (MA); M Div/MM.

Boise State University, College of Arts and Sciences, Department of English, Boise, ID 83725-0399. Offers English literature (MA); English, rhetoric and composition (MA); teaching English language (MA); technical communication (MA). *Program availability:* Part-time. *Faculty:* 26. *Students:* 44 full-time (28 women), 38 part-time (29 women); includes 6 minority (2 American Indian or Alaska Native, non-Hispanic/Latino; 2 Asian, non-Hispanic/Latino; 1 Hispanic/Latino; 1 Two or more races, non-Hispanic/Latino), 3 international. Average age 33. 242 applicants, 15% accepted, 28 enrolled. In 2017, 29 master's awarded. *Degree requirements:* For master's, thesis (for some programs). *Entrance requirements:* For master's, GRE General Test, minimum GPA of 3.0. Additional exam requirements/recommendations for international students: Required—TOEFL (minimum score 550 paper-based; 80 iBT), IELTS (minimum score 6). *Application deadline:* For fall admission, 4/15 for domestic and international students; for spring admission, 10/15 for domestic and international students. Application fee: $65 ($95 for international students). Electronic applications accepted. *Expenses:* Tuition, state resident: full-time $6471; part-time $390 per credit. Tuition, nonresident: full-time $21,787; part-time $685 per credit. *Required fees:* $2283; $100 per term. Part-time tuition and fees vary according to course load and program. *Financial support:* Teaching assistantships, scholarships/grants, and unspecified assistantships available. Financial award application deadline: 1/15; financial award applicants required to submit FAFSA. *Unit head:* Dr. Michelle Payne, Chair, 208-426-3426, Fax: 208-426-4373, E-mail: mpayne@boisestate.edu. *Application contact:* Dr. Tom Hillard, Director, 208-426-2991, E-mail: thomashillard@boisestate.edu.
Website: http://english.boisestate.edu/graduate-programs/

Brooklyn College of the City University of New York, School of Education, Program in Adolescence Science Education and Special Subjects, Brooklyn, NY 11210-2889. Offers adolescence science education (MAT); biology teacher (7-12) (MA); chemistry teacher (7-12) (MA); earth science teacher (7-12) (MAT); English teacher (7-12) (MA); French teacher (7-12) (MA); mathematics teacher (7-12) (MA); music teacher (MA); physics teacher (7-12) (MA); social studies teacher (7-12) (MA); Spanish teacher (7-12) (MA). *Program availability:* Part-time, evening/weekend. *Degree requirements:* For master's, comprehensive exam (for some programs), thesis (for some programs). *Entrance requirements:* For master's, LAST, previous course work in education, resume, 2 letters of recommendation, essay. Additional exam requirements/recommendations for international students: Required—TOEFL (minimum score 500 paper-based; 61 iBT). Electronic applications accepted. *Faculty research:* Interdisciplinary education, semiotics, discourse analysis, autobiography, teacher identity.

Brown University, Graduate School, Department of Education, Program in Teaching, Providence, RI 02912. Offers elementary education (MAT); English (MAT); history/social studies (MAT); science (MAT); secondary education (MAT). *Degree requirements:* For master's, student teaching, portfolio. *Entrance requirements:* For master's, GRE General Test, transcript, personal statement, 3 letters of recommendation, interview, writing sample (English applicants only). Additional exam requirements/recommendations for international students: Required—TOEFL (minimum score 577 paper-based). Electronic applications accepted. *Faculty research:* Literacy, English language learners, diversity, special education, biodiversity.

Buffalo State College, State University of New York, The Graduate School, Faculty of Arts and Humanities, Department of English, Buffalo, NY 14222-1095. Offers English (MA); secondary education (MS Ed), including English. *Program availability:* Part-time, evening/weekend. *Degree requirements:* For master's, thesis or project, 1 foreign language (MS Ed). *Entrance requirements:* For master's, minimum GPA of 2.75, 36 hours in English, New York teaching certificate (MS Ed). Additional exam requirements/recommendations for international students: Required—TOEFL (minimum score 550 paper-based).

California Baptist University, Program in English, Riverside, CA 92504-3206. Offers English pedagogy (MA); literature (MA); teaching English to speakers of other languages (TESOL) (MA). *Program availability:* Part-time, evening/weekend. *Faculty:* 13 full-time (8 women), 1 (woman) part-time/adjunct. *Students:* 3 full-time (2 women), 26 part-time (19 women); includes 14 minority (4 Black or African American, non-Hispanic/Latino; 1 Asian, non-Hispanic/Latino; 9 Hispanic/Latino), 3 international. Average age 28. 11 applicants, 45% accepted, 4 enrolled. In 2017, 8 master's awarded. *Degree requirements:* For master's, comprehensive exam, project, or thesis. *Entrance requirements:* For master's, GRE (for applicants with a GPA below 2.75) or CSET, minimum undergraduate GPA of 2.75; 18 semester hours of course work in English beyond freshman level; three recommendations; essay; demonstration of writing; interview. Additional exam requirements/recommendations for international students: Required—TOEFL (minimum score 80 iBT). *Application deadline:* For fall admission, 8/1 priority date for domestic students, 7/1 for international students; for spring admission, 12/1 priority date for domestic students, 11/1 for international students. Applications are processed on a rolling basis. Application fee: $45. Electronic applications accepted. *Expenses:* Contact institution. *Financial support:* In 2017-18, 5 students received support. Federal Work-Study and scholarships/grants available. Financial award applicants required to submit CSS PROFILE or FAFSA. *Faculty research:* Classical mythology and folklore, multicultural literature, genre studies, science fiction and fantasy literature, intercultural rhetoric. *Unit head:* Dr. Gayne Anacker, Dean, College of Arts and Sciences, 951-343-4682, E-mail: ganacker@calbaptist.edu. *Application contact:* Dr. Laura Veltman, Director, Master of Arts Program in English, 951-343-4276, Fax: 951-343-4661, E-mail: lveltman@calbaptist.edu.
Website: http://www.calbaptist.edu/maenglish/

California State University, Northridge, Graduate Studies, Michael D. Eisner College of Education, Department of Secondary Education, Northridge, CA 91330. Offers educational technology (MA); English education (MA); mathematics education (MA); secondary science education (MA); teaching and learning (MA). *Accreditation:* NCATE. *Program availability:* Part-time. *Students:* 9 full-time (5 women), 85 part-time (57 women); includes 37 minority (2 Black or African American, non-Hispanic/Latino; 12 Asian, non-Hispanic/Latino; 20 Hispanic/Latino; 1 Native Hawaiian or other Pacific Islander, non-Hispanic/Latino; 2 Two or more races, non-Hispanic/Latino), 1 international. Average age 37. 63 applicants, 78% accepted, 45 enrolled. *Degree requirements:* For master's, thesis optional. *Entrance requirements:* For master's, GRE General Test or minimum GPA of 3.0. Additional exam requirements/recommendations for international students: Required—TOEFL. *Application deadline:* For fall admission, 11/30 for domestic students. Application fee: $55. *Financial support:* Application deadline: 3/1. *Unit head:* Dr. Julie Gainsburg, Chair, 818-677-2580. *Application contact:*

Dr. Michael Rivas, Graduate Advisor, 818-677-6792, E-mail: michael.rivas@csun.edu. Website: http://www.csun.edu/eisner-education/secondary-education

Campbellsville University, School of Education, Campbellsville, KY 42718-2799. Offers education (MA); school counseling (MA); school improvement (MA); special education (MASE); special education-teacher leader (MA); teacher leader (MA); teaching (MAT), including middle grades biology, middle grades chemistry, middle grades English. *Accreditation:* NCATE. *Program availability:* Part-time, evening/weekend, 100% online, blended/hybrid learning. *Faculty:* 15 full-time (10 women), 14 part-time/adjunct (9 women). *Students:* 26 full-time (20 women), 155 part-time (122 women); includes 14 minority (13 Black or African American, non-Hispanic/Latino; 1 Hispanic/Latino). Average age 35. 199 applicants, 34% accepted, 57 enrolled. In 2017, 96 master's awarded. *Degree requirements:* For master's, comprehensive exam (for some programs), thesis, research paper. *Entrance requirements:* For master's, GRE or PRAXIS, minimum undergraduate GPA of 2.75, teaching certificate, professional growth plan, letters of recommendation, interview. Additional exam requirements/recommendations for international students: Recommended—TOEFL (minimum score 550 paper-based; 79 iBT), IELTS (minimum score 6). *Application deadline:* Applications are processed on a rolling basis. Application fee: $25. Electronic applications accepted. Application fee is waived when completed online. *Expenses:* $399 per credit hour. *Financial support:* Unspecified assistantships and employee tuition waivers available. Financial award applicants required to submit FAFSA. *Faculty research:* Professional development, curriculum development, school governance, assessment, special education. *Unit head:* Dr. Beverly Ennis, Dean, 270-789-5344, Fax: 270-789-5206, E-mail: bcennis@campbellsville.edu. *Application contact:* Monica Bamwine, Assistant Director of Graduate Admissions, 270-789-5221, Fax: 270-789-5071, E-mail: mkbamwine@campbellsville.edu.

Caribbean University, Graduate School, Bayamón, PR 00960-0493. Offers administration and supervision (MA Ed); criminal justice (MA); curriculum and instruction (MA Ed, PhD), including elementary education (MA Ed), English education (MA Ed), history education (MA Ed), mathematics education (MA Ed), primary education (MA Ed), science education (MA Ed), Spanish education (MA Ed); educational technology in instructional systems (MA Ed); gerontology (MSN); human resources (MBA); museology, archiving and art history (MA Ed); neonatal pediatrics (MSN); physical education (MA Ed); special education (MA Ed). *Entrance requirements:* For master's, interview, minimum GPA of 2.5.

Carthage College, Division of Teacher Education, Kenosha, WI 53140. Offers classroom guidance and counseling (M Ed); creative arts (M Ed); gifted and talented children (M Ed); language arts (M Ed); modern language (M Ed); natural sciences (M Ed); reading (M Ed, Certificate); social sciences (M Ed); teacher leadership (M Ed). *Program availability:* Part-time, evening/weekend. *Degree requirements:* For master's, thesis optional. *Entrance requirements:* For master's, MAT, minimum B average, letters of reference.

Central Connecticut State University, School of Graduate Studies, College of Liberal Arts and Social Sciences, Department of English, New Britain, CT 06050-4010. Offers English (MA); English education (MAT); teaching English to speakers of other languages (MS, Certificate). *Program availability:* Part-time, evening/weekend. *Faculty:* 6 full-time (4 women), 1 part-time/adjunct (0 women). *Students:* 17 full-time (12 women), 43 part-time (37 women); includes 16 minority (5 Black or African American, non-Hispanic/Latino; 1 Asian, non-Hispanic/Latino; 8 Hispanic/Latino; 2 Two or more races, non-Hispanic/Latino), 2 international. Average age 33. 35 applicants, 77% accepted, 16 enrolled. In 2017, 17 master's, 3 other advanced degrees awarded. *Degree requirements:* For master's, comprehensive exam, thesis or alternative; for Certificate, qualifying exam. *Entrance requirements:* For master's, minimum undergraduate GPA of 3.0, writing sample, letters of recommendation, essay. Additional exam requirements/recommendations for international students: Required—TOEFL (minimum score 550 paper-based; 79 iBT); Recommended—IELTS (minimum score 6.5). *Application deadline:* For fall admission, 8/1 for domestic students, 5/1 for international students; for spring admission, 11/1 for domestic and international students. Applications are processed on a rolling basis. Application fee: $50. Electronic applications accepted. *Expenses: Tuition, area resident:* Full-time $6757. Tuition, state resident: full-time $9750; part-time $374 per credit. Tuition, nonresident: full-time $18,102; part-time $374 per credit. *Required fees:* $4635; $255 per credit. *Financial support:* In 2017-18, 9 students received support. Career-related internships or fieldwork, Federal Work-Study, scholarships/grants, and unspecified assistantships available. Support available to part-time students. Financial award application deadline: 3/1; financial award applicants required to submit FAFSA. *Unit head:* Dr. Stephen Cohen, Chair, 860-832-2795, E-mail: cohens@ccsu.edu. *Application contact:* Patricia Gardner, Associate Director of Graduate Studies, 860-832-2350, Fax: 860-832-2362.
Website: http://www.ccsu.edu/english

Chadron State College, School of Professional and Graduate Studies, Department of Education, Chadron, NE 69337. Offers business (MA Ed); community counseling (MA Ed); educational administration (MS Ed, Sp Ed); elementary education (MS Ed); history (MA Ed); language and literature (MA Ed); secondary administration (MS Ed); secondary education (MS Ed). *Accreditation:* NCATE. *Program availability:* Part-time, evening/weekend, online learning. *Degree requirements:* For master's, thesis optional. *Entrance requirements:* For master's, GRE General Test, GRE Writing Test, minimum GPA of 2.75 or 12 graduate hours at CSC with minimum GPA of 3.25. Additional exam requirements/recommendations for international students: Required—TOEFL. Electronic applications accepted. *Faculty research:* Rural education, technology, mental health.

Chatham University, Program in Education, Pittsburgh, PA 15232-2826. Offers early childhood education (MAT); elementary education (MAT); environmental education (K-12) (MAT); secondary art (MAT); secondary biology education (MAT); secondary chemistry education (MAT); secondary English education (MAT); secondary math education (MAT); secondary physics education (MAT); secondary social studies education (MAT); special education (MAT). *Faculty:* 1 (woman) full-time, 15 part-time/adjunct (13 women). *Students:* 31 full-time (23 women), 3 part-time (1 woman); includes 9 minority (8 Black or African American, non-Hispanic/Latino; 1 Hispanic/Latino). Average age 30. 25 applicants, 60% accepted, 9 enrolled. In 2017, 23 master's awarded. *Degree requirements:* For master's, thesis, teaching experience. *Entrance requirements:* For master's, minimum GPA of 3.0, sample of written work, recommendation letters. Additional exam requirements/recommendations for international students: Required—TOEFL (minimum score 600 paper-based; 100 iBT), IELTS (minimum score 7), TWE. *Application deadline:* For fall admission, 4/1 priority date for domestic and international students; for spring admission, 11/1 priority date for domestic students, 10/1 priority date for international students. Applications are processed on a rolling basis. Application fee: $45. Electronic applications accepted. Application fee is waived when completed online. *Expenses: Tuition:* Full-time $16,740; part-time $930 per credit. *Required fees:* $486; $27 per credit. $243 per semester. *Financial support:* Career-related internships or fieldwork available. Financial award applicants required to submit FAFSA. *Faculty research:* Gifted education, environmental education, technology in education, writing as learning, class size and achievement. *Application contact:* Katie Noel, Assistant Director of Graduate Admission, 412-365-2758, Fax: 412-365-1609, E-mail: gradadmissions@chatham.edu.
Website: http://www.chatham.edu/mat

The Citadel, The Military College of South Carolina, Citadel Graduate College, Zucker Family School of Education, Charleston, SC 29409. Offers elementary/secondary school administration and supervision (M Ed); elementary/secondary school counseling (M Ed); interdisciplinary STEM education (M Ed); literacy education (M Ed, Graduate Certificate); middle grades (MAT), including English, mathematics, science, social studies; physical education (grades K-12) (MAT); school superintendency (Ed S); secondary education (MAT), including biology, English, mathematics, social studies; student affairs (Graduate Certificate); student affairs and college counseling (M Ed). *Accreditation:* NCATE. *Program availability:* Part-time, evening/weekend, 100% online, blended/hybrid learning. *Degree requirements:* For master's, comprehensive exam (for some programs). *Entrance requirements:* For master's, GRE (minimum combined verbal and quantitative score of 290) or MAT (minimum score 396). Additional exam requirements/recommendations for international students: Required—TOEFL (minimum score 550 paper-based; 79 iBT). Electronic applications accepted. *Expenses:* Tuition, state resident: part-time $587 per credit hour. Tuition, nonresident: part-time $988 per credit hour. *Required fees:* $90 per term.

City College of the City University of New York, Graduate School, School of Education, Department of Secondary Education, New York, NY 10031-9198. Offers adolescent mathematics education (MA, AC); English education (MA); middle school mathematics education (MS); science education (MA); social studies education (AC). *Accreditation:* NCATE. *Entrance requirements:* For master's, Liberal Arts and Sciences Test (LAST), Content Specialty Test (CST). Additional exam requirements/recommendations for international students: Required—TOEFL.

Clayton State University, School of Graduate Studies, College of Arts and Sciences, Program in Education, Morrow, GA 30260-0285. Offers biology (MAT); English (MAT); history (MAT); mathematics (MAT). *Accreditation:* NCATE. *Entrance requirements:* For master's, GRE, GACE, 2 official copies of transcripts, 3 recommendation letters, statement of purpose. Additional exam requirements/recommendations for international students: Required—TOEFL (minimum score 550 paper-based). Electronic applications accepted.

The College at Brockport, State University of New York, School of Education, Health, and Human Services, Department of Education and Human Development, Program in Adolescence Education, Brockport, NY 14420-2997. Offers adolescence biology education (MS Ed); adolescence chemistry education (MS Ed); adolescence English (MS Ed); adolescence mathematics (MS Ed); adolescence physics (MS Ed); adolescence social studies education (MS Ed). *Accreditation:* NCATE. *Program availability:* Part-time. *Students:* 50 part-time (28 women); includes 1 minority (Black or African American, non-Hispanic/Latino). 24 applicants, 79% accepted, 11 enrolled. In 2017, 18 master's awarded. *Degree requirements:* For master's, thesis or alternative. *Entrance requirements:* For master's, edTPA, GRE or MAT, minimum GPA of 3.0, letters of recommendation, statement of objectives, current resume. Additional exam requirements/recommendations for international students: Required—TOEFL (minimum score 550 paper-based; 79 iBT), IELTS (minimum score 6.5). *Application deadline:* For fall admission, 3/15 priority date for domestic and international students; for spring admission, 10/15 priority date for domestic and international students; for summer admission, 3/15 priority date for domestic students, 3/13 priority date for international students. Application fee: $80. Electronic applications accepted. *Expenses:* Tuition, state resident: full-time $10,870; part-time $453 per credit hour. Tuition, nonresident: full-time $22,210. *Required fees:* $988; $246 per semester. *Financial support:* Federal Work-Study, scholarships/grants, and unspecified assistantships available. Support available to part-time students. Financial award application deadline: 3/15; financial award applicants required to submit FAFSA. *Unit head:* Dr. Sue Robb, Chairperson, 585-395-5935, Fax: 585-395-2172, E-mail: srobb@brockport.edu. *Application contact:* Anne Walton, Coordinator of Certification and Graduate Advisement, 585-395-2326, Fax: 585-395-2172, E-mail: awalton@brockport.edu.
Website: https://www.brockport.edu/academics/education_human_development/department.html

The College at Brockport, State University of New York, School of Education, Health, and Human Services, Department of Education and Human Development, Program in Inclusive Generalist Education, Brockport, NY 14420-2997. Offers biology (MS Ed, AGC); chemistry (MS Ed, AGC); English (MS Ed, Advanced Certificate); mathematics (MS Ed, Advanced Certificate); science (MS Ed, Advanced Certificate); social studies (MS Ed, Advanced Certificate). *Students:* 61 part-time (30 women); includes 2 minority (1 Black or African American, non-Hispanic/Latino; 1 Asian, non-Hispanic/Latino). 41 applicants, 78% accepted, 25 enrolled. In 2017, 12 master's, 3 AGCs awarded. *Degree requirements:* For master's, thesis or alternative. *Entrance requirements:* For master's, edTPA, GRE or MAT, minimum GPA of 3.0, letters of recommendation, statement of objectives, academic major (or equivalent) in program discipline, current resume. Additional exam requirements/recommendations for international students: Required—TOEFL (minimum score 550 paper-based; 79 iBT), IELTS (minimum score 6.5). *Application deadline:* For fall admission, 3/15 priority date for domestic and international students; for spring admission, 10/15 priority date for domestic and international students; for summer admission, 3/15 for domestic and international students. Application fee: $80. Electronic applications accepted. *Expenses:* Tuition, state resident: full-time $10,870; part-time $453 per credit hour. Tuition, nonresident: full-time $22,210. *Required fees:* $988; $246 per semester. *Financial support:* Federal Work-Study, scholarships/grants, and unspecified assistantships available. Support available to part-time students. Financial award application deadline: 3/15; financial award applicants required to submit FAFSA. *Unit head:* Dr. Sue Robb, Chairperson, 585-395-5935, Fax: 585-395-2171, E-mail: srobb@brockport.edu. *Application contact:* Anne Walton, Coordinator of Graduate Advisement, 585-395-2326, Fax: 585-395-2172, E-mail: awalton@brockport.edu.
Website: https://www.brockport.edu/academics/education_human_development/department.html

College of St. Joseph, Graduate Programs, Division of Education, Program in Secondary Education, Rutland, VT 05701-3899. Offers English (M Ed); social studies (M Ed). *Program availability:* Part-time, evening/weekend. *Degree requirements:* For master's, comprehensive exam. *Entrance requirements:* For master's, PRAXIS I, official college transcripts; 2 letters of reference; minimum GPA of 3.0 (initial licensure) or 2.7 (nonlicensure); interview. Additional exam requirements/recommendations for international students: Required—TOEFL (minimum score 550 paper-based). Electronic applications accepted.

College of Staten Island of the City University of New York, Graduate Programs, School of Education, Program in Adolescence Education, Staten Island, NY 10314-6600. Offers adolescence education (MS Ed), including biology, English, mathematics, social studies. *Program availability:* Part-time, evening/weekend. *Faculty:* 23 full-time, 6 part-time/adjunct. *Students:* 87. 45 applicants, 67% accepted, 23 enrolled. In 2017, 21 master's awarded. *Degree requirements:* For master's, thesis, educational research project supervised by faculty. *Entrance requirements:* For master's, GRE General Test or an approved equivalent examination, relevant bachelor's degree, minimum overall GPA of 3.0, two letters of recommendation, one- or two-page personal statement. Additional exam requirements/recommendations for international students: Required—TOEFL (minimum score 550 paper-based; 79 iBT), IELTS (minimum score 6.5).

Application deadline: For fall admission, 4/25 for domestic and international students; for spring admission, 11/25 for domestic and international students. Applications are processed on a rolling basis. Application fee: $125. Electronic applications accepted. *Expenses:* Tuition, state resident: full-time $10,450; part-time $440 per credit. Tuition, nonresident: full-time $19,320; part-time $440 per credit. *Required fees:* $181.10 per semester. Tuition and fees vary according to program. *Faculty research:* Development and assessment of TPACK (technological pedagogical content knowledge), technology and differentiation in stem classrooms, teacher effectiveness and student achievement, teacher knowledge, knowledge transfer from college to classroom. *Unit head:* Diane Brescia, 718-982-3877, E-mail: diane.brescia@csi.cuny.edu. *Application contact:* Sasha Spence, Associate Director for Graduate Admissions, 718-982-2019, Fax: 718-982-2500, E-mail: sasha.spence@csi.cuny.edu.
Website: http://www.csi.cuny.edu/catalog/graduate/graduate-programs-in-education.htm#o2608

The Colorado College, Education Department, Program in Secondary Education, Colorado Springs, CO 80903-3294. Offers art teaching (K-12) (MAT); English teaching (MAT); foreign language teaching (MAT); mathematics teaching (MAT); music teaching (MAT); science teaching (MAT); social studies teaching (MAT). *Degree requirements:* For master's, thesis, internship. Electronic applications accepted.

Columbus State University, Graduate Studies, College of Education and Health Professions, Department of Teacher Education, Columbus, GA 31907-5645. Offers curriculum and instruction in accomplished teaching (M Ed); early childhood education (M Ed, MAT, Ed S); middle grades education (M Ed, MAT, Ed S); secondary education (M Ed, MAT, Ed S), including biology (MAT), chemistry (MAT), earth and space science (MAT), English/language arts, general science (M Ed), history (MAT), mathematics, science (Ed S), social science (M Ed, Ed S); special education (M Ed, MAT, Ed S), including general curriculum (M Ed, MAT); teacher leadership (M Ed). *Accreditation:* NCATE. *Program availability:* Part-time, evening/weekend, 100% online, blended/hybrid learning. *Faculty:* 19 full-time (12 women), 24 part-time/adjunct (18 women). *Students:* 99 full-time (76 women), 181 part-time (143 women); includes 109 minority (94 Black or African American, non-Hispanic/Latino; 1 American Indian or Alaska Native, non-Hispanic/Latino; 1 Asian, non-Hispanic/Latino; 6 Hispanic/Latino; 7 Two or more races, non-Hispanic/Latino). Average age 34. 136 applicants, 63% accepted, 56 enrolled. In 2017, 119 master's, 8 other advanced degrees awarded. *Degree requirements:* For Ed S, thesis or alternative. *Entrance requirements:* For master's, GRE General Test, minimum undergraduate GPA of 2.75; for Ed S, GRE General Test, minimum undergraduate GPA of 2.75, graduate 3.0. Additional exam requirements/recommendations for international students: Required—TOEFL (minimum score 550 paper-based; 79 iBT). *Application deadline:* For fall admission, 6/30 for domestic students, 5/1 for international students; for spring admission, 11/1 for domestic and international students; for summer admission, 3/1 for domestic and international students. Applications are processed on a rolling basis. Application fee: $50. Electronic applications accepted. *Expenses:* Tuition, state resident: full-time $3708; part-time $2472 per year. Tuition, nonresident: full-time $14,418; part-time $9612 per year. *International tuition:* $19,218 full-time. *Required fees:* $1605. Tuition and fees vary according to program. *Financial support:* In 2017–18, 45 students received support, including 9 research assistantships with partial tuition reimbursements available (averaging $3,000 per year); career-related internships or fieldwork, Federal Work-Study, institutionally sponsored loans, scholarships/grants, tuition waivers (partial), and unspecified assistantships also available. Support available to part-time students. Financial award application deadline: 5/1; financial award applicants required to submit FAFSA. *Unit head:* Dr. Jan Burcham, Department Chair, 706-507-8519, Fax: 706-568-3134, E-mail: burcham_jan@columbusstate.edu. *Application contact:* Catrina Smith-Edmond, Assistant Director for Graduate and Global Admission, 706-507-8824, Fax: 706-568-5091, E-mail: smithedmond_catrina@columbusstate.edu.
Website: http://te.columbusstate.edu

Converse College, Program in Secondary Education, Spartanburg, SC 29302. Offers biology (MAT); chemistry (MAT); English (M Ed, MAT); mathematics (M Ed, MAT); natural sciences (M Ed); social sciences (M Ed, MAT). *Program availability:* Part-time. *Degree requirements:* For master's, capstone paper. *Entrance requirements:* For master's, NTE or PRAXIS II (M Ed), minimum GPA of 2.75, 2 recommendations. *Application deadline:* For fall admission, 8/1 for domestic and international students; for winter admission, 11/15 for domestic and international students; for spring admission, 1/15 for domestic and international students. Applications are processed on a rolling basis. Application fee: $40. Electronic applications accepted. *Financial support:* Available to part-time students. Applicants required to submit FAFSA. *Unit head:* Lienne Medford, Dean of Graduate Studies and Distance Education, 864-596-9082, E-mail: lienne.medford@converse.edu. *Application contact:* 864-596-9404, E-mail: graduate@converse.edu.

Delta State University, Graduate Programs, College of Arts and Sciences, Division of Languages and Literature, Cleveland, MS 38733-0001. Offers secondary education (M Ed), including English. *Program availability:* Part-time. *Degree requirements:* For master's, thesis or alternative.

Duquesne University, School of Education, Department of Instruction and Leadership, Program in Secondary Education, Pittsburgh, PA 15282-0001. Offers biology (MS Ed); chemistry (MS Ed); English (MS Ed); K-12 education (MS Ed), including Latin; mathematics (MS Ed); physics (MS Ed); social studies (MS Ed). *Program availability:* Part-time, evening/weekend. *Faculty:* 5 full-time (4 women). *Students:* 22 full-time (10 women); includes 3 minority (2 Black or African American, non-Hispanic/Latino; 1 Two or more races, non-Hispanic/Latino). Average age 26. 8 applicants, 100% accepted, 5 enrolled. In 2017, 9 master's awarded. *Entrance requirements:* For master's, two letters of recommendation, letter of intent, interview, bachelor's degree. Additional exam requirements/recommendations for international students: Required—TOEFL (minimum score 550 paper-based), IELTS (minimum score 7). *Application deadline:* For fall admission, 9/1 for domestic students; for spring admission, 1/2 for domestic students. Applications are processed on a rolling basis. Application fee: $0. Electronic applications accepted. *Expenses:* $1,259 per credit. *Financial support:* Research assistantships and Federal Work-Study available. Support available to part-time students. *Faculty research:* Factors that create highly effective teachers; how to best support teachers to support students in reform-oriented environments; urban education; models of teacher leadership; improving instruction in mathematics/science/social studies/English. *Unit head:* Dr. Melissa Boston, Associate Dean for Teacher Education/Professor, 412-396.6109, Fax: 412-396-5585, E-mail: bostonm@duq.edu. *Application contact:* Kelly McGinley, Graduate Admissions Assistant, 412-396-1559, Fax: 412-396-5585, E-mail: mcginleyk@duq.edu.
Website: http://www.duq.edu/academics/schools/education/graduate-programs-education/ms-ed-secondary-education

East Carolina University, Graduate School, Thomas Harriot College of Arts and Sciences, Department of English, Greenville, NC 27858-4353. Offers creative writing (MA); English studies (MA); linguistics (MA); literature (MA); multicultural and transnational literatures (MA, Certificate); professional communication (Certificate); rhetoric and composition (MA); rhetoric, writing, and professional communication (PhD); teaching English in the two-year college (Certificate); teaching English to speakers of

other languages (MA, Certificate); technical and professional communication (MA). *Program availability:* Part-time, evening/weekend, online learning. *Students:* 40 full-time (27 women), 74 part-time (57 women); includes 33 minority (23 Black or African American, non-Hispanic/Latino; 2 Asian, non-Hispanic/Latino; 4 Hispanic/Latino; 4 Two or more races, non-Hispanic/Latino). Average age 35. 36 applicants, 94% accepted, 25 enrolled. In 2017, 23 master's, 4 doctorates, 24 other advanced degrees awarded. *Degree requirements:* For master's, comprehensive exam, thesis optional; for doctorate, comprehensive exam, thesis/dissertation. *Entrance requirements:* For master's, GRE General Test or MAT; for doctorate, GRE General Test or MAT, writing samples. Additional exam requirements/recommendations for international students: Recommended—TOEFL (minimum score 78 iBT), IELTS (minimum score 6.5), TWE. *Application deadline:* For fall admission, 7/31 priority date for domestic students, 2/1 priority date for international students; for spring admission, 11/30 priority date for domestic students, 10/1 priority date for international students. Applications are processed on a rolling basis. Application fee: $75. Electronic applications accepted. *Expenses:* Tuition, state resident: full-time $4749; part-time $297 per credit hour. Tuition, nonresident: full-time $17,898; part-time $1119 per credit hour. *Required fees:* $2691; $224 per credit hour. Part-time tuition and fees vary according to course load and program. *Financial support:* Research assistantships with partial tuition reimbursements, teaching assistantships with partial tuition reimbursements, and Federal Work-Study available. Support available to part-time students. Financial award application deadline: 3/1. *Faculty research:* Technical and professional communication, rhetoric/composition, multicultural and transnational literature, creative writing, film studies. *Unit head:* Dr. Marianne Montgomery, Chair, 252-328-6687, E-mail: montgomerym@ecu.edu. *Application contact:* Dean of Graduate School, 252-328-6012, Fax: 252-328-6071, E-mail: gradschool@ecu.edu.
Website: http://www.ecu.edu/cs-cas/engl/

Eastern Kentucky University, The Graduate School, College of Education, Department of Curriculum and Instruction, Program in Secondary and Higher Education, Richmond, KY 40475-3102. Offers secondary education (MA Ed), including agricultural education, art education, biological sciences education, business education, English education, geography education, history education, home economics education, industrial education, mathematical sciences education, physical education, school health education. *Accreditation:* NCATE. *Program availability:* Part-time. *Entrance requirements:* For master's, GRE General Test, minimum GPA of 2.5.

Eastern Michigan University, Graduate School, College of Arts and Sciences, Department of English Language and Literature, Program in English Studies for Teachers, Ypsilanti, MI 48197. Offers MA. *Program availability:* Part-time, evening/weekend. *Students:* 6 part-time (5 women); includes 1 minority (Black or African American, non-Hispanic/Latino). Average age 34. 4 applicants, 100% accepted, 1 enrolled. In 2017, 1 master's awarded. *Entrance requirements:* Additional exam requirements/recommendations for international students: Required—TOEFL. Application fee: $45. *Financial support:* Research assistantships with full tuition reimbursements, teaching assistantships with full tuition reimbursements, career-related internships or fieldwork, Federal Work-Study, institutionally sponsored loans, scholarships/grants, and unspecified assistantships available. Support available to part-time students. *Application contact:* Dr. John Staunton, Program Advisor, 734-487-0135, Fax: 734-487-9744, E-mail: jstaunto@emich.edu.

Eastern University, Graduate Education Programs, St. Davids, PA 19087-3696. Offers ESL program specialist (K-12) (Certificate); general supervisor (PreK-12) (Certificate); health and physical education (K-12) (Certificate); middle level (4-8) (Certificate); multicultural education (M Ed); music (K-12) (Certificate); Pre K-4 (Certificate); Pre K-4 with special education (Certificate); reading (M Ed); reading specialist (K-12) (Certificate); reading supervisor (K-12) (Certificate); school counseling (MA, CAGS); school principalship (preK-12) (Certificate); school psychology (MS, CAGS); secondary biology education (7-12) (Certificate); secondary chemistry education (7-12) (Certificate); secondary communication education (7-12) (Certificate); secondary English education (7-12) (Certificate); secondary math education (7-12) (Certificate); secondary social studies education (7-12) (Certificate); special education (M Ed); special education (7-12) (Certificate); special education (Pre K-8) (Certificate); special education supervisor (K-12) (Certificate); TESOL (M Ed); world language (Certificate), including Spanish. *Program availability:* Part-time, evening/weekend, online learning. *Students:* 46 full-time (40 women), 115 part-time (93 women); includes 65 minority (42 Black or African American, non-Hispanic/Latino; 3 Asian, non-Hispanic/Latino; 14 Hispanic/Latino; 6 Two or more races, non-Hispanic/Latino), 1 international. Average age 32. In 2017, 72 master's awarded. *Entrance requirements:* Additional exam requirements/recommendations for international students: Required—TOEFL. *Application deadline:* Applications are processed on a rolling basis. Application fee: $35. Electronic applications accepted. Application fee is waived when completed online. *Expenses:* Contact institution. *Unit head:* Michael Dziedziak, Executive Director of Enrollment, 800-452-0996, E-mail: gpsadmissions@eastern.edu.
Website: https://www.eastern.edu/academics/programs/education-department-graduate-programs/graduate-programs

Elms College, Division of Education, Chicopee, MA 01013-2839. Offers early childhood education (MAT); education (M Ed, CAGS); elementary education (MAT); English as a second language (MAT); reading (MAT); secondary education (MAT), including biology education, English education, Spanish education; special education (MAT). *Program availability:* Part-time, evening/weekend. *Faculty:* 4 full-time (all women), 8 part-time/adjunct (7 women). *Students:* 6 full-time (4 women), 127 part-time (107 women); includes 8 minority (2 Asian, non-Hispanic/Latino; 6 Hispanic/Latino). Average age 33. 42 applicants, 88% accepted, 36 enrolled. In 2017, 50 master's, 6 other advanced degrees awarded. *Degree requirements:* For master's, thesis (for some programs). *Entrance requirements:* For master's, Massachusetts Educators Certification Test, minimum GPA of 3.0; for CAGS, master's degree in education. Additional exam requirements/recommendations for international students: Required—TOEFL. *Application deadline:* For fall admission, 7/1 priority date for domestic students; for spring admission, 11/1 priority date for domestic students. Applications are processed on a rolling basis. Application fee: $30. *Expenses:* Tuition: Full-time $13,860; part-time $770 per credit hour. *Required fees:* $200. Tuition and fees vary according to degree level and program. *Financial support:* In 2017-18, 2 teaching assistantships with partial tuition reimbursements were awarded. Financial award applicants required to submit FAFSA. *Unit head:* Dr. Mary Janeczek, Chair, Division of Education, 413-594-2761, Fax: 413-592-4871, E-mail: janeczeke@elms.edu. *Application contact:* School of Graduate and Professional Studies, 413-265-2445, E-mail: graduateeducation@elms.edu.

Fitchburg State University, Division of Graduate and Continuing Education, Programs in English and Teaching English (Secondary Level), Fitchburg, MA 01420-2697. Offers MA, MAT, Certificate. *Accreditation:* NCATE. *Program availability:* Part-time, evening/weekend. *Faculty:* 4 full-time (2 women). *Students:* 6 full-time (4 women), 10 part-time (9 women); includes 1 minority (Asian, non-Hispanic/Latino). Average age 28. 6 applicants, 100% accepted, 6 enrolled. In 2017, 5 master's awarded. *Entrance requirements:* Additional exam requirements/recommendations for international students: Required—TOEFL (minimum score 550 paper-based; 79 iBT). *Application deadline:* For fall admission, 7/15 for international students; for spring admission, 12/1 for international

students. Applications are processed on a rolling basis. Application fee: $50. Electronic applications accepted. *Expenses:* Contact institution. *Financial support:* In 2017-18, research assistantships with partial tuition reimbursements (averaging $5,500 per year) were awarded; Federal Work-Study, scholarships/grants, and unspecified assistantships also available. Support available to part-time students. Financial award application deadline: 3/1; financial award applicants required to submit FAFSA. *Unit head:* Dr. Chola Chisunka, Chair, 978-665-3445, Fax: 978-665-3658, E-mail: gce@fitchburgstate.edu. *Application contact:* Jinawa McNeil, Director of Admissions, 978-665-3140, Fax: 978-665-4540, E-mail: admissions@fitchburgstate.edu.

Florida Agricultural and Mechanical University, Division of Graduate Studies, Research, and Continuing Education, College of Education, Program in Secondary Education and Foundation, Tallahassee, FL 32307-3200. Offers biology (M Ed); chemistry (MS Ed); English (MS Ed); history (MS Ed); math (MS Ed); physics (MS Ed). *Accreditation:* NCATE. *Degree requirements:* For master's, thesis (for some programs). *Entrance requirements:* For master's, GRE General Test, minimum GPA of 3.0. Additional exam requirements/recommendations for international students: Required—TOEFL.

Florida Atlantic University, College of Education, Department of Teaching and Learning, Boca Raton, FL 33431-0991. Offers curriculum and instruction (M Ed), including art, biology, chemistry, English, French, German, mathematics, music, physics, Pre-K and primary education, reading, social sciences, Spanish; elementary education (M Ed); environmental education (M Ed); reading education (M Ed); social foundations of education (M Ed), including educational psychology, educational technology, multilingual education. *Accreditation:* NCATE. *Program availability:* Part-time, evening/weekend. *Faculty:* 13 full-time (10 women), 1 part-time/adjunct (0 women). *Students:* 26 full-time (22 women), 43 part-time (39 women); includes 19 minority (9 Black or African American, non-Hispanic/Latino; 1 Asian, non-Hispanic/Latino; 8 Hispanic/Latino; 1 Two or more races, non-Hispanic/Latino), 3 international. Average age 30. 91 applicants, 57% accepted, 33 enrolled. In 2017, 25 master's awarded. *Entrance requirements:* For master's, GRE General Test, minimum GPA of 3.0 in last 2 years of undergraduate course work. Additional exam requirements/recommendations for international students: Required—TOEFL (minimum score 500 paper-based; 61 iBT), IELTS (minimum score 6). *Application deadline:* For fall admission, 7/1 for domestic students, 2/15 for international students; for spring admission, 11/1 for domestic students, 7/15 for international students. Applications are processed on a rolling basis. Application fee: $30. *Expenses:* Tuition, state resident: full-time $7400; part-time $369.82 per credit. Tuition, nonresident: full-time $20,496; part-time $1042.81 per credit. *Financial support:* Fellowships with partial tuition reimbursements, research assistantships with partial tuition reimbursements, teaching assistantships with partial tuition reimbursements, career-related internships or fieldwork, scholarships/grants, and unspecified assistantships available. *Faculty research:* Technology, teaching English to speakers of other languages, math teaching, electronic portfolio assessment, global perspectives through social studies. *Unit head:* Dr. Barbara Ridener, Chairperson, 561-297-3588, E-mail: bridener@fau.edu. *Application contact:* Dr. Eliah Watlington, Associate Dean, 561-296-8520, Fax: 261-297-2991, E-mail: ewatling@fau.edu.
Website: http://www.coe.fau.edu/academicdepartments/tl/

Florida Gulf Coast University, College of Education, Program in Curriculum and Instruction, Fort Myers, FL 33965-6565. Offers elementary education (M Ed); English education (M Ed); English speakers of other languages endorsement (M Ed); gifted education (M Ed); mathematics education (M Ed); middle school education (M Ed); reading education (M Ed); science education (M Ed); social science education (M Ed); special education (M Ed). *Program availability:* Part-time, evening/weekend, online learning. *Faculty:* 27 full-time (19 women), 44 part-time/adjunct (30 women). *Students:* 3 full-time (all women), 16 part-time (14 women); includes 4 minority (2 Black or African American, non-Hispanic/Latino; 2 Hispanic/Latino). Average age 30. 6 applicants, 100% accepted, 5 enrolled. In 2017, 4 master's awarded. *Degree requirements:* For master's, final project or portfolio. *Entrance requirements:* For master's, GRE General Test, MAT, minimum undergraduate GPA of 3.0 in last 2 years. Additional exam requirements/recommendations for international students: Required—TOEFL (minimum score 550 paper-based). *Application deadline:* For fall admission, 2/15 priority date for domestic students, 5/1 for international students; for spring admission, 12/1 for domestic students, 9/15 for international students. Applications are processed on a rolling basis. Application fee: $30. Electronic applications accepted. *Expenses:* Tuition, state resident: part-time $290 per credit hour. Tuition, nonresident: part-time $1173 per credit hour. *Required fees:* $127 per credit hour. Tuition and fees vary according to course load. *Financial support:* In 2017-18, 2 students received support. Application deadline: 6/30; applicants required to submit FAFSA. *Faculty research:* Internet in schools, technology in pre-service and in-service teacher training. *Unit head:* Dr. Vickie Johnston, Instructor, 239-590-7754, Fax: 239-590-7801, E-mail: vjohnston@fgcu.edu. *Application contact:* Keiana Desmore, Adviser/Counselor, 239-590-7759, Fax: 239-590-7801, E-mail: kdesmore@fgcu.edu.
Website: http://coe.fgcu.edu/c-imed/

Florida International University, College of Arts, Sciences, and Education, Department of Teaching and Learning, Miami, FL 33199. Offers art education (MA, MS); curriculum and instruction (MS, Ed D, PhD, Ed S), including curriculum development (MS), elementary education (MS), English education (MS), learning technologies (MS), mathematics education (MS), modern language education (MS), physical education (MS), science education (MS), social studies education (MS), special education (MS); early childhood education (MS); exceptional student education (Ed D); foreign language education (MS), including foreign language education, teaching English to speakers of other languages (TESOL); language, literacy and culture (PhD); mathematics, science, and learning technologies (PhD); physical education (MS), including sport and fitness; reading education (MS). *Program availability:* Part-time, evening/weekend. *Faculty:* 60 full-time (41 women), 112 part-time/adjunct (77 women). *Students:* 165 full-time (139 women), 191 part-time (148 women); includes 270 minority (56 Black or African American, non-Hispanic/Latino; 12 Asian, non-Hispanic/Latino; 191 Hispanic/Latino; 11 Two or more races, non-Hispanic/Latino), 13 international. Average age 34. 238 applicants, 68% accepted, 107 enrolled. In 2017, 184 master's, 15 doctorates awarded. *Degree requirements:* For doctorate, comprehensive exam, thesis/dissertation. *Entrance requirements:* For master's, GRE General Test, Florida General Knowledge Test or Florida College Level Academic Skills Test; for doctorate and Ed S, GRE General Test. Additional exam requirements/recommendations for international students: Required—TOEFL (minimum score 550 paper-based; 80 iBT), IELTS (minimum score 6.3). *Application deadline:* For fall admission, 6/1 priority date for domestic students, 4/1 for international students; for winter admission, 10/1 priority date for domestic students, 9/1 for international students; for spring admission, 3/1 priority date for domestic students, 2/1 for international students. Applications are processed on a rolling basis. Application fee: $30. Electronic applications accepted. *Expenses:* Tuition, state resident: full-time $8912; part-time $446 per credit hour. Tuition, nonresident: full-time $21,393; part-time $992 per credit hour. *Required fees:* $390; $195 per semester. *Financial support:* Research assistantships with tuition reimbursements and teaching assistantships with tuition reimbursements available. *Unit head:* Dr. Lynn Miller, Chair, 305-348-2005, Fax: 305-348-2086, E-mail: lynne.miller@fiu.edu. *Application contact:* Nanett Rojas, Assistant Director, Graduate Admissions, 305-348-7464, Fax: 305-348-7441, E-mail: gradadm@fiu.edu.
Website: https://tl.fiu.edu/

Florida State University, The Graduate School, College of Education, School of Teacher Education, Tallahassee, FL 32306-4450. Offers curriculum and instruction (MS, PhD, Ed S), including early childhood education, elementary education, English education, foreign and second language education, mathematics education, reading and language arts, science education, social science education, special education, visual disabilities education (MS); teaching English to speakers of other languages (Certificate). *Program availability:* Part-time, evening/weekend, 100% online, blended/hybrid learning, asynchronous, minimal on-campus study. *Faculty:* 41 full-time (33 women), 21 part-time/adjunct (18 women). *Students:* 133 full-time (93 women), 84 part-time (69 women); includes 48 minority (20 Black or African American, non-Hispanic/Latino; 2 Asian, non-Hispanic/Latino; 19 Hispanic/Latino; 7 Two or more races, non-Hispanic/Latino), 52 international. Average age 31. 146 applicants, 56% accepted, 52 enrolled. In 2017, 91 master's, 7 doctorates, 1 other advanced degree awarded. Terminal master's awarded for partial completion of doctoral program. *Degree requirements:* For master's and other advanced degree, comprehensive exam, thesis optional; for doctorate, comprehensive exam, thesis/dissertation, diagnostic exam, preliminary exam, prospectus defense, dissertation defense. *Entrance requirements:* For master's, doctorate, and other advanced degree, GRE General Test, minimum upper-division GPA of 3.0. Additional exam requirements/recommendations for international students: Required—TOEFL (minimum score 550 paper-based, 80 iBT), Michigan English Language Assessment Battery (minimum score 77), IELTS (minimum score 6.5) or PTE (minimum score 55). Application fee: $30. Electronic applications accepted. *Financial support:* Fellowships, research assistantships, teaching assistantships, scholarships/grants, tuition waivers (full and partial), and unspecified assistantships available. Financial award application deadline: 1/15; financial award applicants required to submit FAFSA. *Faculty research:* Identifying effective intervention strategies to improve reading skills; improving literacy teaching and learning through technology; understanding of student sense making, problem solving, the history and structure of STEM disciplines, and teacher education to support the development of ambitious instruction that supports the STEM learning of all students; examining practices of international education; identifying ways to support the professional development of teachers. *Unit head:* Dr. Sherry Southerland, Professor/Department Chair, 850-644-6885, Fax: 850-644-2725, E-mail: ssoutherland@admin.fsu.edu. *Application contact:* Britni DeZerga, Academic Program Specialist, 850-644-2122, Fax: 850-644-7736, E-mail: bpurvis@fsu.edu.
Website: http://education.fsu.edu

Gardner-Webb University, Graduate School, Department of English, Boiling Springs, NC 28017. Offers English (MA); English education (MA). *Program availability:* Part-time, evening/weekend. *Faculty:* 4 full-time (all women). *Students:* 27 part-time (19 women); includes 3 minority (2 Black or African American, non-Hispanic/Latino; 1 Two or more races, non-Hispanic/Latino). Average age 31. 27 applicants, 37% accepted, 6 enrolled. In 2017, 6 master's awarded. *Degree requirements:* For master's, comprehensive exam. *Entrance requirements:* For master's, GRE General Test, MAT, or NTE; PRAXIS, minimum GPA of 2.5. *Application deadline:* For fall admission, 8/1 priority date for domestic students. Applications are processed on a rolling basis. Application fee: $0. Electronic applications accepted. *Expenses:* Contact institution. *Financial support:* Unspecified assistantships available. *Unit head:* Jennifer Buckner, Chair, 704-406-4394, E-mail: jbuckner@gardner-webb.edu. *Application contact:* Office of Graduate Admissions, 877-498-4723, Fax: 704-406-3895, E-mail: gradinfo@gardner-webb.edu.

George Mason University, College of Education and Human Development, Programs in Curriculum and Instruction, Fairfax, VA 22030. Offers advanced international baccalaureate (M Ed); assistive technology (M Ed); designing digital learning in schools (M Ed); early childhood education (M Ed); early childhood education for diverse learners (M Ed); elementary education (M Ed); English as a second language (M Ed); gifted child education (M Ed); history (M Ed); literacy (M Ed), including PK-12 classroom teachers, reading specialist; literacy leadership for diverse schools (M Ed), including K-12 reading; physical education (M Ed); science K-12 (M Ed); secondary education (M Ed), including biology, chemistry, earth science, English, history/social science, math, physics; special education (M Ed); teacher leadership (M Ed); teaching culturally, linguistically diverse and exceptional learners (M Ed); transformative teaching (M Ed). *Program availability:* Part-time, evening/weekend, 100% online, blended/hybrid learning. *Faculty:* 41 full-time (36 women), 45 part-time/adjunct (37 women). *Students:* 173 full-time (151 women), 729 part-time (611 women); includes 271 minority (65 Black or African American, non-Hispanic/Latino; 5 American Indian or Alaska Native, non-Hispanic/Latino; 88 Asian, non-Hispanic/Latino; 94 Hispanic/Latino; 1 Native Hawaiian or other Pacific Islander, non-Hispanic/Latino; 18 Two or more races, non-Hispanic/Latino), 28 international. Average age 32. 426 applicants, 91% accepted, 289 enrolled. In 2017, 349 master's awarded. *Degree requirements:* For master's, thesis. *Entrance requirements:* For master's, PRAXIS Core (for some programs), 2 letters of recommendation, interview, program goals statement; 9 hours of complete licensure endorsement requirements (for elementary education); minimum GPA of 3.0 in applicant's last 60 hours of undergraduate coursework (for secondary education); at least 1 year of teaching experience (for literacy). Additional exam requirements/recommendations for international students: Required—TOEFL (minimum score 575 paper-based; 88 iBT), IELTS (minimum score 6.5), PTE (minimum score 59). *Application deadline:* For fall admission, 4/2 priority date for domestic and international students; for spring admission, 11/1 for domestic and international students. Application fee: $75 ($80 for international students). Electronic applications accepted. *Expenses:* Tuition, state resident: full-time $11,228; part-time $459.50 per credit. Tuition, nonresident: full-time $30,932; part-time $1280.50 per credit. *Required fees:* $3252; $135.50 per credit. Part-time tuition and fees vary according to course load and program. *Financial support:* In 2017–18, 2 students received support, including 2 teaching assistantships; career-related internships or fieldwork, Federal Work-Study, scholarships/grants, unspecified assistantships, and health care benefits (for full-time research or teaching assistantship recipients) also available. Support available to part-time students. Financial award application deadline: 3/1; financial award applicants required to submit FAFSA. *Faculty research:* Teacher preparation and professional development; adaptive teaching; wonder in science teacher preparation; literacy (digital, adolescent); site based course instruction. *Unit head:* Rebecca Fox, Professor and Academic Program Coordinator, 703-993-4123, E-mail: rfox@gmu.edu.
Website: http://gse.gmu.edu/programs/gsemasters

George Mason University, College of Humanities and Social Sciences, Department of English, Fairfax, VA 22030. Offers college teaching (Certificate), including higher education pedagogy (MFA), including fiction, nonfiction writing, poetry; English (MA), including cultural studies, linguistics, literature, professional writing and rhetoric, teaching of writing and literature; English pedagogy (Certificate); folklore studies (Certificate); linguistics (PhD); writing and rhetoric (PhD). *Program availability:* Part-time. *Faculty:* 78 full-time (40 women), 45 part-time/adjunct (30 women). *Students:* 120 full-time (84 women), 116 part-time (94 women); includes 43 minority (13 Black or African American, non-Hispanic/Latino; 8 Asian, non-Hispanic/Latino; 14 Hispanic/Latino; 1 Native Hawaiian or other Pacific Islander, non-Hispanic/Latino; 7 Two or more races, non-Hispanic/Latino), 19 international. Average age 32. 224 applicants, 61% accepted, 68 enrolled. In 2017, 60 master's, 1 doctorate, 17 other advanced degrees awarded. *Degree requirements:* For master's, thesis (for some programs), proficiency in

a foreign language by course work or translation test; for doctorate, comprehensive exam, thesis/dissertation, 2 papers. *Entrance requirements:* For master's, official transcripts; expanded goals statement; writing sample; portfolio; 2 letters of recommendation; resume; for doctorate, GRE (for linguistics), expanded goals statement; 2 letters of recommendation (writing and rhetoric); 3 letters of recommendation (linguistics); writing sample; introductory course in linguistics; official transcripts; master's degree in relevant field; for Certificate, official transcripts; expanded goals statement; 2 letters of recommendation; writing sample; resume. Additional exam requirements/recommendations for international students: Required—TOEFL (minimum score 575 paper-based; 88 iBT), IELTS (minimum score 6.5), PTE (minimum score 59). *Application deadline:* For fall admission, 3/15 for domestic and international students; for spring admission, 10/15 for domestic and international students. Application fee: $75 ($80 for international students). Electronic applications accepted. *Expenses:* Tuition, state resident: full-time $11,228; part-time $459.50 per credit. Tuition, nonresident: full-time $30,932; part-time $1280.50 per credit. *Required fees:* $3252; $135.50 per credit. Part-time tuition and fees vary according to course load and program. *Financial support:* In 2017–18, 84 students received support, including 9 research assistantships with tuition reimbursements available (averaging $17,199 per year), 76 teaching assistantships with tuition reimbursements available (averaging $11,917 per year); career-related internships or fieldwork, Federal Work-Study, scholarships/grants, unspecified assistantships, and health care benefits (for full-time research or teaching assistantship recipients) also available. Support available to part-time students. Financial award application deadline: 3/1; financial award applicants required to submit FAFSA. *Faculty research:* Literature, professional writing and editing, writing of fiction or poetry. *Total annual research expenditures:* $68,592. *Unit head:* Debra Lattanzi-Shutika, Chair, 703-993-1170, Fax: 703-993-1161, E-mail: dshutika@gmu.edu. *Application contact:* Ana Walsh, Graduate Admissions Coordinator, 703-993-1185, Fax: 703-993-1161, E-mail: awalsh7@gmu.edu.
Website: http://english.gmu.edu

Georgia Southern University, Jack N. Averitt College of Graduate Studies, College of Education, Department of Teaching and Learning, Program in English Education, Statesboro, GA 30460. Offers MAT. *Accreditation:* NCATE. *Program availability:* Part-time, evening/weekend. *Students:* 7 full-time (6 women); includes 1 minority (Hispanic/Latino). Average age 26. 4 applicants, 100% accepted, 4 enrolled. In 2017, 2 master's awarded. *Degree requirements:* For master's, portfolio, transition point assessments, exit assessment. *Entrance requirements:* For master's, GRE General Test or MAT; GACE Basic Skills and Content Assessments (for MAT), minimum cumulative GPA of 2.5. Additional exam requirements/recommendations for international students: Required—TOEFL (minimum score 550 paper-based; 80 iBT), IELTS (minimum score 6). *Application deadline:* For fall admission, 3/1 priority date for domestic and international students; for spring admission, 10/1 priority date for domestic students, 10/1 for international students. Applications are processed on a rolling basis. Application fee: $50. Electronic applications accepted. *Expenses:* Tuition, state resident: full-time $4986; part-time $3324 per year. Tuition, nonresident: full-time $21,982; part-time $15,352 per year. *Required fees:* $2092; $1802 per credit hour. $901 per semester. Tuition and fees vary according to course load, campus/location and program. *Financial support:* In 2017–18, 1 student received support, including 4 fellowships with full tuition reimbursements available (averaging $7,750 per year); Federal Work-Study, scholarships/grants, tuition waivers (full), and unspecified assistantships also available. Support available to part-time students. Financial award application deadline: 4/15; financial award applicants required to submit FAFSA. *Faculty research:* Literacy for at-risk students. *Unit head:* Dr. Greg Chamblee, Coordinator, 912-478-5783, Fax: 912-478-0026, E-mail: gchamblee@georgiasouthern.edu. *Application contact:* Dr. Lydia Cross, Coordinator for Graduate Academic Services Center, 912-478-8664, E-mail: lcross@georgiasouthern.edu.
Website: http://coe.georgiasouthern.edu/ger/

Georgia Southwestern State University, School of Education, Americus, GA 31709-4693. Offers early childhood education (M Ed, Ed S); middle grades education (Ed S); middle grades language arts (M Ed); middle grades mathematics (M Ed); special education (M Ed). *Accreditation:* NCATE. *Faculty:* 17 full-time (7 women), 7 part-time/adjunct (all women). *Students:* 221 full-time (206 women), 5 part-time (all women); includes 70 minority (all Black or African American, non-Hispanic/Latino). Average age 35. In 2017, 89 master's, 94 Ed Ss awarded. *Degree requirements:* For master's, minimum cumulative GPA of 3.0; maximum of 6 credit hours with C grade; no courses with D grade; degree completed within 7 calendar years; for Ed S, minimum GPA of 3.25 in all courses with no grade less than a B; degree must be completed within 7 calendar years from date of initial enrollment in graduate work. *Entrance requirements:* For master's, undergraduate degree from accredited institution; professional Georgia Teaching Certificate or eligibility; minimum undergraduate GPA of 2.75 as reported on official final transcripts from all accredited institutions attended; 2 confidential Administrative Recommendation Forms; for Ed S, master's degree from accredited college or university; professional Georgia Teaching Certificate or eligibility; minimum graduate GPA of 3.0 as reported on official final graduate transcripts from all accredited institutions attended; 2 confidential Administrative Recommendation Forms. *Application deadline:* For summer admission, 4/15 for domestic students. Application fee: $25. Electronic applications accepted. *Expenses:* $257 per credit hour for online courses plus fees which vary according to number of enrolled credit hours. *Financial support:* Application deadline: 6/1; applicants required to submit FAFSA. *Unit head:* Dr. Rachel Abbott, Dean, 229-931-2145. *Application contact:* Whitney Ford, Admissions Specialist, Office of Graduate Admissions, 800-338-0082, Fax: 229-931-2983.
Website: https://gsw.edu/Academics/Schools-and-Departments/School-of-Education/index

Georgia State University, College of Education and Human Development, Department of Middle and Secondary Education, Atlanta, GA 30302-3083. Offers curriculum and instruction (Ed D); English education (MAT); mathematics education (M Ed, MAT); middle level education (MAT); reading, language and literacy education (M Ed, MAT), including reading instruction (M Ed); science education (M Ed, MAT), including biology (MAT), broad field science (MAT), chemistry (MAT), earth science (MAT), physics (MAT); social studies education (M Ed, MAT), including economics (MAT), geography (MAT), history (MAT), political science (MAT); teaching and learning (PhD), including language and literacy, mathematics education, music education, science education, social studies education, teaching and teacher education. *Accreditation:* NCATE. *Program availability:* Part-time, evening/weekend, online learning. *Faculty:* 24 full-time (18 women). *Students:* 179 full-time (110 women), 192 part-time (133 women); includes 193 minority (130 Black or African American, non-Hispanic/Latino; 1 American Indian or Alaska Native, non-Hispanic/Latino; 23 Asian, non-Hispanic/Latino; 25 Hispanic/Latino; 14 Two or more races, non-Hispanic/Latino), 6 international. Average age 33. 175 applicants, 58% accepted, 83 enrolled. In 2017, 81 master's, 17 doctorates awarded. *Entrance requirements:* For master's, GRE; GACE I (for initial teacher preparation programs), baccalaureate degree or equivalent, resume, goals statement, two letters of recommendation, minimum undergraduate GPA of 2.5; proof of initial teacher certification in the content area (for M Ed); for doctorate, GRE, resume, goals statement, writing sample, two letters of recommendation, minimum graduate GPA of 3.3, interview. *Application deadline:* For fall admission, 1/15 priority date for domestic and international

English Education

students; for spring admission, 10/1 for domestic and international students. Application fee: $50. Electronic applications accepted. *Expenses:* Tuition, state resident: full-time $7020. Tuition, nonresident: full-time $22,518. *Required fees:* $2128. Tuition and fees vary according to degree level and program. *Financial support:* In 2017–18, fellowships with full tuition reimbursements (averaging $19,667 per year), research assistantships with full tuition reimbursements (averaging $5,436 per year), teaching assistantships with full tuition reimbursements (averaging $2,779 per year) were awarded; career-related internships or fieldwork, Federal Work-Study, scholarships/grants, health care benefits, tuition waivers (full and partial), and unspecified assistantships also available. Financial award application deadline: 3/15. *Faculty research:* Teacher education in language and literacy, mathematics, science, and social studies in urban middle and secondary school settings; learning technologies in school, community, and corporate settings; multicultural education and education for social justice; urban education; international education. *Unit head:* Dr. Dana L. Fox, Chair, 404-413-8060, Fax: 404-413-8063, E-mail: dfox@gsu.edu. *Application contact:* Bobbie Turner, Administrative Coordinator, 404-413-8405, Fax: 404-413-8063, E-mail: bnturner@gsu.edu. Website: http://mse.education.gsu.edu/

Grand Valley State University, College of Education, Program in Reading and Language Arts, Allendale, MI 49401-9403. Offers M Ed. *Accreditation:* NCATE. *Program availability:* Part-time, evening/weekend. *Students:* 2 part-time (both women). Average age 35. In 2017, 3 master's awarded. *Degree requirements:* For master's, project or thesis. *Entrance requirements:* For master's, GRE General Test or minimum GPA of 3.0; last 60 credits from regionally-accredited college/university; 3 letters of recommendation. Additional exam requirements/recommendations for international students: Required—TOEFL (minimum iBT score of 80), IELTS (6.5), or Michigan English Language Assessment Battery (77). *Application deadline:* Applications are processed on a rolling basis. Application fee: $30. Electronic applications accepted. *Expenses:* $652 per credit hour. *Financial support:* Career-related internships or fieldwork, Federal Work-Study, scholarships/grants, and unspecified assistantships available. *Faculty research:* Culture of literacy, literacy acquisition, assessment, content area literacy, writing pedagogy. *Unit head:* Dr. Elizabeth Stolle, Graduate Program Director, 616-331-6242, Fax: 616-331-6516, E-mail: stollee@gvsu.edu. *Application contact:* Thomas Owens, Director, Student Information and Services Center, 616-331-6282, Fax: 616-331-6217, E-mail: owenst@gvsu.edu.

Hampton University, School of Liberal Arts and Education, Program in Teaching, Hampton, VA 23668. Offers biology education 6-12 (MT); English education 6-12 (MT); mathematics education 6-12 (MT); music education PreK-12 (MT). *Program availability:* Part-time. *Students:* 5 full-time (4 women); all minorities (all Black or African American, non-Hispanic/Latino). Average age 23. 6 applicants, 67% accepted, 1 enrolled. In 2017, 7 master's awarded. *Entrance requirements:* For master's, GRE General Test. Additional exam requirements/recommendations for international students: Required—TOEFL (minimum score 525 paper-based) or IELTS (6.5). *Application deadline:* For fall admission, 6/1 priority date for domestic students, 4/1 for international students; for spring admission, 11/1 priority date for domestic students, 9/1 for international students; for summer admission, 4/1 priority date for domestic students, 2/1 priority date for international students. Applications are processed on a rolling basis. Application fee: $35. Electronic applications accepted. *Expenses: Tuition:* Full-time $22,630; part-time $575 per semester hour. *Required fees:* $70. Tuition and fees vary according to program. *Financial support:* Application deadline: 6/30; applicants required to submit FAFSA. *Unit head:* Dr. Martha Jallim-Hall, Program Coordinator, 757-727-5793.

Harding University, Cannon-Clary College of Education, Searcy, AR 72149-0001. Offers advanced studies in teaching and learning (M Ed); art (MSE); behavioral science (MSE); counseling (MS, Ed S); early childhood special education (M Ed, MSE); education (MSE); educational leadership (M Ed, Ed S); elementary education (M Ed); English (MSE); French (MSE); history/social science (MSE); kinesiology (MSE); math (MSE); reading (M Ed); secondary education (M Ed); Spanish (MSE); teaching (MAT); teaching English as a second language (MSE). *Accreditation:* NCATE. *Program availability:* Part-time, evening/weekend. *Faculty:* 22 full-time (9 women), 51 part-time/adjunct (37 women). *Students:* 135 full-time (95 women), 316 part-time (231 women); includes 77 minority (46 Black or African American, non-Hispanic/Latino; 7 American Indian or Alaska Native, non-Hispanic/Latino; 4 Asian, non-Hispanic/Latino; 9 Hispanic/Latino; 11 Two or more races, non-Hispanic/Latino), 11 international. Average age 34. 128 applicants, 87% accepted, 111 enrolled. In 2017, 153 master's, 24 other advanced degrees awarded. *Degree requirements:* For master's, comprehensive exam (for some programs), thesis optional, portfolio(s); for Ed S, comprehensive exam, portfolio, project. *Entrance requirements:* For master's, GRE, MAT, PRAXIS; for Ed S, MAT or GRE. Additional exam requirements/recommendations for international students: Required—TOEFL (minimum score 550 paper-based; 79 iBT). *Application deadline:* For fall admission, 8/1 for domestic and international students; for spring admission, 1/1 for domestic and international students. Applications are processed on a rolling basis. Application fee: $35. Tuition and fees vary according to course load, degree level, campus/location and program. *Financial support:* In 2017–18, 33 students received support. Unspecified assistantships available. *Faculty research:* Reading, comprehension, school violence, educational technology, behavior, college choice, differentiated instruction, brain-based teaching. *Unit head:* Dr. Clara Carroll, Chair, 501-279-4501, Fax: 501-279-4083, E-mail: ccarroll@harding.edu. *Application contact:* Information Contact, 501-279-4315, E-mail: gradstudiesedu@harding.edu. Website: http://www.harding.edu/education

Hofstra University, School of Education, Programs in Teacher Education, Hempstead, NY 11549. Offers bilingual education (MA); bilingual extension (Advanced Certificate), including education/speech language pathology, intensive teacher institute; business education (MS Ed); curriculum studies (MS Ed); early childhood and childhood education (MS Ed); early childhood education (MA, MS Ed); educational technology (Advanced Certificate); elementary education (MA, MS Ed), including science, technology, engineering, and mathematics (STEM) (MA); English education (MS Ed); family and consumer science (MS Ed); fine arts and music education (Advanced Certificate); fine arts education (MS Ed); foreign language and TESOL (MS Ed); foreign language education (MA, MS Ed), including Arabic (MS Ed), biology, chemistry, Chinese (MS Ed), earth science, French, German, Italian (MS Ed), Mandarin (MS Ed), physics, Russian, Spanish; foundations of education (Advanced Certificate), including grades 5-6, grades 7-9; languages other than English and teaching English as a second language (MA); learning and teaching (Ed D), including applied linguistics, art education, arts and humanities, early childhood education, English education, human development, math education, math, science, and technology, multicultural education, physical education, science education, social studies education, special education; mathematics education (MA, MS Ed); music education (MA, MS Ed); science education (MA), including biology (MA, MS Ed), chemistry (MA, MS Ed), earth science (MA, MS Ed), physics (MA, MS Ed); secondary education (Advanced Certificate); social studies education (MA, MS Ed); teaching languages other than English and TESOL (MS Ed); technology for learning (MA); TESOL (MS Ed, Advanced Certificate); TESOL with specialization in STEM (MA); work based learning extension (Advanced Certificate). *Program availability:* Part-time, evening/weekend, blended/hybrid learning. *Students:* 119 full-time (83 women), 124 part-time (90 women); includes 54 minority (15 Black or African American, non-Hispanic/Latino; 9 Asian, non-Hispanic/Latino; 29 Hispanic/Latino; 1 Native Hawaiian or other Pacific Islander, non-

Hispanic/Latino), 12 international. Average age 29. 205 applicants, 88% accepted, 93 enrolled. In 2017, 103 master's, 4 doctorates, 32 other advanced degrees awarded. *Degree requirements:* For master's, comprehensive exam, thesis (for some programs), exit project, student teaching, fieldwork, electronic portfolio, curriculum project, minimum GPA of 3.0; for doctorate, thesis/dissertation; for Advanced Certificate, 3 foreign languages, comprehensive exam (for some programs), thesis project. *Entrance requirements:* For master's, GRE, 2 letters of recommendation, portfolio, teacher certification (MA), interview, essay; for doctorate, GMAT, GRE, LSAT, or MAT; for Advanced Certificate, 2 letters of recommendation, essay, interview and/or portfolio, teaching certificate. Additional exam requirements/recommendations for international students: Required—TOEFL (minimum score 550 paper-based; 80 iBT). *Application deadline:* Applications are processed on a rolling basis. Application fee: $75. Electronic applications accepted. *Expenses: Tuition:* Full-time $1292. *Required fees:* $970. Tuition and fees vary according to program. *Financial support:* In 2017–18, 112 students received support, including 56 fellowships with full and partial tuition reimbursements available (averaging $4,998 per year), 2 research assistantships with full and partial tuition reimbursements available (averaging $8,753 per year); career-related internships or fieldwork, Federal Work-Study, institutionally sponsored loans, scholarships/grants, traineeships, tuition waivers (full and partial), and unspecified assistantships also available. Support available to part-time students. Financial award applicants required to submit FAFSA. *Faculty research:* Educational interventions that foster critical-thinking skills; teachers' attitudes about professional development; threats to teacher quality. *Unit head:* Dr. Eustace Thompson, Chairperson, 516-463-5749, Fax: 516-463-6275, E-mail: eustace.g.thompson@hofstra.edu. *Application contact:* Sunil Samuel, Assistant Vice President of Admissions, 516-463-4723, Fax: 516-463-4664, E-mail: graduateadmission@hofstra.edu. Website: http://www.hofstra.edu/education/

Houston Baptist University, School of Christian Thought, Program in Divinity, Houston, TX 77074-3298. Offers Biblical languages (M Div); English languages (M Div). *Program availability:* Part-time, evening/weekend. *Students:* 10 full-time (3 women), 17 part-time (8 women); includes 12 minority (9 Black or African American, non-Hispanic/Latino; 3 Hispanic/Latino), 1 international. Average age 40. 22 applicants, 55% accepted, 9 enrolled. *Entrance requirements:* For master's, bachelor's degree conferred transcript, resume, essay/personal statement. Additional exam requirements/recommendations for international students: Required—TOEFL (minimum score 80 iBT), IELTS (minimum score 6.5). *Application deadline:* For fall admission, 8/1 for domestic students, 6/1 for international students; for spring admission, 1/1 for domestic students, 11/1 for international students; for summer admission, 5/1 for domestic students, 3/1 for international students. Applications are processed on a rolling basis. Application fee: $0 ($100 for international students). Electronic applications accepted. Application fee is waived when completed online. *Expenses:* $36,000 tuition; $6,750 fees (general, technology and parking). *Financial support:* In 2017–18, 7 students received support. Federal Work-Study and scholarships/grants available. Financial award application deadline: 4/1; financial award applicants required to submit FAFSA. *Unit head:* Dr. Jeffrey Green, Interim Dean, 281-649-3197, Fax: 281-649-3012, E-mail: jgreen@hbu.edu. *Application contact:* Celeste Risteski, Administrative Assistant to the Dean, 281-649-3383, Fax: 281-649-3012, E-mail: cristeski@hbu.edu.

Hunter College of the City University of New York, Graduate School, School of Education, Programs in Secondary Education, Concentration in English Education, New York, NY 10065-5085. Offers MA. *Accreditation:* NCATE. *Degree requirements:* For master's, thesis, professional teaching portfolio, New York State Teacher Certification Exam, research project. *Entrance requirements:* For master's, minimum GPA of 2.8, 2 letters of reference, minimum of 21 credits in English. Additional exam requirements/recommendations for international students: Required—TOEFL, TWE.

Indiana University of Pennsylvania, School of Graduate Studies and Research, College of Humanities and Social Sciences, Department of English, PhD Program in Composition and Teaching English to Speakers of Other Languages, Indiana, PA 15705. Offers PhD. *Program availability:* Part-time. *Faculty:* 22 full-time (10 women). *Students:* 18 full-time (11 women), 79 part-time (48 women); includes 9 minority (2 Black or African American, non-Hispanic/Latino; 4 Asian, non-Hispanic/Latino; 2 Hispanic/Latino; 1 Two or more races, non-Hispanic/Latino), 38 international. Average age 38. 108 applicants, 57% accepted, 7 enrolled. In 2017, 22 doctorates awarded. *Degree requirements:* For doctorate, one foreign language, comprehensive exam, thesis/dissertation. *Entrance requirements:* For doctorate, 2 letters of recommendation. Additional exam requirements/recommendations for international students: Required—TOEFL (minimum score 600 paper-based). *Application deadline:* For fall admission, 2/1 priority date for domestic students; for summer admission, 11/1 priority date for domestic students. Applications are processed on a rolling basis. Application fee: $50. Electronic applications accepted. *Expenses:* Contact institution. *Financial support:* In 2017–18, 18 research assistantships with tuition reimbursements (averaging $6,398 per year), 5 teaching assistantships with partial tuition reimbursements (averaging $11,652 per year) were awarded; fellowships with full tuition reimbursements, career-related internships or fieldwork, Federal Work-Study, scholarships/grants, and unspecified assistantships also available. Support available to part-time students. Financial award application deadline: 4/15; financial award applicants required to submit FAFSA. *Unit head:* Dr. Sharon Deckert, Graduate Coordinator, 724-357-2261, E-mail: sharon.deckert@iup.edu. Website: http://www.iup.edu/english/grad/composition-tesol-phd/default.aspx

Indiana University of Pennsylvania, School of Graduate Studies and Research, College of Humanities and Social Sciences, Department of English, Program in Teaching English, Indiana, PA 15705. Offers MA. *Program availability:* Part-time. *Faculty:* 22 full-time (10 women). *Students:* 5 applicants, 100% accepted. *Degree requirements:* For master's, thesis optional. *Entrance requirements:* For master's, two letters of recommendation. Additional exam requirements/recommendations for international students: Required—TOEFL (minimum score 540 paper-based). *Application deadline:* Applications are processed on a rolling basis. Application fee: $50. Electronic applications accepted. *Expenses:* Tuition, state resident: full-time $12,000; part-time $500 per credit. Tuition, nonresident: full-time $18,000; part-time $750 per credit. *Required fees:* $4073; $165.55 per credit. $64 per term. *Financial support:* Fellowships with full tuition reimbursements, research assistantships with tuition reimbursements, career-related internships or fieldwork, Federal Work-Study, scholarships/grants, and unspecified assistantships available. Financial award application deadline: 4/16; financial award applicants required to submit FAFSA. *Unit head:* Dr. Linda Norris, Coordinator, 724-357-2263, E-mail: lnorris@iup.edu. Website: http://www.iup.edu/english/grad/teaching-english-ma/default.aspx

Indiana University–Purdue University Fort Wayne, College of Arts and Sciences, Department of English and Linguistics, Fort Wayne, IN 46805-1499. Offers English (MA, MAT); TENL (teaching English as a new language) (Certificate). *Program availability:* Part-time. *Degree requirements:* For master's, one foreign language, thesis (for some programs), teaching certificate (for MAT). *Entrance requirements:* For master's, GRE General Test, minimum GPA of 3.0, major or minor in English, 3 letters of recommendation; for Certificate, bachelor's degree with minimum GPA of 2.5. Additional exam requirements/recommendations for international students: Required—TOEFL (minimum score 600 paper-based; 79 iBT). *Faculty research:* Hebrew names and the vernacular Savior in Anglo-Saxon England.

Iona College, School of Arts and Science, Department of Education, New Rochelle, NY 10801-1890. Offers adolescence education: biology (MS Ed, MST); adolescence education: English (MS Ed); adolescence education: mathematics (MST); adolescence education: social studies (MS Ed, MST); adolescence education: Spanish (MS Ed); adolescence special education 5-12 (MST); childhood and special education (MST); early childhood and childhood (MST); educational leadership (MS Ed). *Accreditation:* NCATE. *Program availability:* Part-time, evening/weekend. *Faculty:* 7 full-time (5 women), 2 part-time/adjunct (1 woman). *Students:* 23 full-time (18 women), 26 part-time (19 women); includes 16 minority (4 Black or African American, non-Hispanic/Latino; 8 Hispanic/Latino). Average age 26. 33 applicants, 97% accepted, 20 enrolled. In 2017, 31 master's awarded. *Degree requirements:* For master's, thesis or alternative. *Entrance requirements:* For master's, minimum GPA of 3.0, NY State teaching certificate and bachelor's degree (for MS Ed). Additional exam requirements/recommendations for international students: Required—TOEFL (minimum score 550 paper-based; 80 iBT), IELTS (minimum score 6.5). *Application deadline:* For fall admission, 8/1 priority date for domestic students, 5/1 priority date for international students; for spring admission, 1/1 priority date for domestic students, 9/1 priority date for international students. Applications are processed on a rolling basis. Electronic applications accepted. Tuition and fees vary according to program. *Financial support:* In 2017–18, 16 students received support. Unspecified assistantships available. Support available to part-time students. Financial award application deadline: 4/15; financial award applicants required to submit FAFSA. *Faculty research:* Engaging teacher educators in scientific process, cross-national comparisons of mathematics teaching, questioning strategies in the classroom, research methods, literacy development. *Unit head:* Margaret Smith, PhD, Chair, 914-633-2210, Fax: 914-633-2608, E-mail: msmith@iona.edu. *Application contact:* Richard McMahon, Coordinator, Graduate School of Education, 914-633-2552, E-mail: rmcmahon@iona.edu.
Website: http://www.iona.edu/Academics/School-of-Arts-Science/Departments/Education/Graduate-Programs.aspx

Ithaca College, School of Humanities and Sciences, Program in Adolescence Education, Ithaca, NY 14850. Offers English (MAT). *Program availability:* Part-time. *Faculty:* 11 full-time (7 women), 1 part-time/adjunct (0 women). *Students:* 12 full-time (7 women); includes 1 minority (Hispanic/Latino), 1 international. Average age 24. 18 applicants, 72% accepted, 11 enrolled. In 2017, 19 master's awarded. *Degree requirements:* For master's, thesis or alternative, student teaching. *Entrance requirements:* Additional exam requirements/recommendations for international students: Required—TOEFL (minimum score 550 paper-based; 80 iBT). *Application deadline:* For fall admission, 3/19 for domestic and international students. Applications are processed on a rolling basis. Application fee: $40. Electronic applications accepted. *Expenses:* Contact institution. *Financial support:* In 2017–18, 11 students received support, including 11 research assistantships (averaging $8,056 per year); career-related internships or fieldwork, Federal Work-Study, scholarships/grants, and unspecified assistantships also available. Support available to part-time students. Financial award application deadline: 3/1; financial award applicants required to submit FAFSA. *Unit head:* Dr. Peter Martin, Chair, 607-274-1076, E-mail: pmartin@ithaca.edu. *Application contact:* Nicole Eversley Bradwell, Director, Office of Admission, 607-274-3124, Fax: 607-274-1263, E-mail: admission@ithaca.edu.
Website: http://www.ithaca.edu/gradprograms/education/programs/aded

Jackson State University, Graduate School, College of Liberal Arts, Department of English and Modern Foreign Languages, Jackson, MS 39217. Offers English (MA); teaching English (MAT). *Program availability:* Part-time, evening/weekend. *Degree requirements:* For master's, comprehensive exam, thesis or alternative. *Entrance requirements:* For master's, GRE General Test. Additional exam requirements/recommendations for international students: Required—TOEFL (minimum score 520 paper-based; 67 iBT). Electronic applications accepted. *Expenses:* Contact institution.

Kansas State University, Graduate School, College of Education, Department of Curriculum and Instruction, Manhattan, KS 66506. Offers curriculum and instruction (Ed D, PhD); digital teaching and learning (MS); educational computing, design and online learning (MS); elementary/middle level curriculum and instruction (MS); online learning (Certificate); reading specialist endorsement (MS); reading/language arts (MS); teacher leader/school improvement (MS); teaching and learning (Certificate). *Accreditation:* NCATE. *Program availability:* Part-time, online learning. *Degree requirements:* For master's, comprehensive exam, portfolio, project, report or thesis; for doctorate, comprehensive exam, thesis/dissertation, preliminary exam; for Certificate, comprehensive exam, portfolio. *Entrance requirements:* For master's, minimum GPA of 3.0, 3 letters of recommendation; for doctorate, GRE, minimum GPA of 3.0, 3 letters of recommendation, evidence of scholarly writing; for Certificate, minimum GPA of 3.0, letters of recommendation. Additional exam requirements/recommendations for international students: Required—TOEFL (minimum score 550 paper-based; 80 iBT) or IELTS. Electronic applications accepted. *Faculty research:* Literacy and technology, critical race theory and diversity, achievement gaps, school improvement, teacher education.

Kennesaw State University, Leland and Clarice C. Bagwell College of Education, Program in Teaching, Kennesaw, GA 30144. Offers art education (MAT); biology (MAT); chemistry (MAT); foreign language education (Chinese and Spanish) (MAT); physics (MAT); secondary English (MAT); secondary mathematics (MAT); special education (MAT); teaching English to speakers of other languages (MAT). *Program availability:* Part-time, evening/weekend. *Entrance requirements:* For master's, GRE, GACE I (state certificate exam), minimum GPA of 2.75, 2 recommendations, resume. Additional exam requirements/recommendations for international students: Required—TOEFL (minimum score 550 paper-based; 80 iBT), IELTS (minimum score 6.5). Electronic applications accepted.

Kent State University, College of Arts and Sciences, Department of English, Kent, OH 44242-0001. Offers creative writing (MFA); English (MA, PhD); English for teachers (MA); literature and writing (MA); rhetoric and composition (PhD); teaching English as a second language (MA). MFA program offered jointly with Cleveland State University, The University of Akron, and Youngstown State University. *Program availability:* Part-time. *Faculty:* 25 full-time (13 women), 2 part-time/adjunct (1 woman). *Students:* 101 full-time (69 women), 19 part-time (11 women); includes 10 minority (4 Black or African American, non-Hispanic/Latino; 1 Asian, non-Hispanic/Latino; 2 Hispanic/Latino; 3 Two or more races, non-Hispanic/Latino), 20 international. Average age 34. 63 applicants, 76% accepted, 18 enrolled. In 2017, 37 master's, 6 doctorates awarded. *Degree requirements:* For master's, comprehensive exam, portfolio, project, report or thesis (for some programs), final portfolio, final exam, or thesis (for MA in teaching English as a second language); for doctorate, one foreign language, comprehensive exam, thesis/dissertation. *Entrance requirements:* For master's, GRE General Test, goal statement, 3 letters of recommendation, 8-15 page writing sample relevant to the field of study (waived for MA in English for teachers concentration); transcripts; for doctorate, GRE General Test, statement of purpose, 3 letters of recommendation, 8-15 page writing sample relevant to field of study, transcripts. Additional exam requirements/recommendations for international students: Required—TOEFL (minimum score 587 paper-based; 94 iBT), Michigan English Language Assessment Battery (minimum score 82), IELTS (minimum score 7.0) or PTE (minimum score 65). *Application deadline:* For fall admission, 1/15 for domestic and international students. Applications are processed on a rolling basis. Application fee: $45 ($70 for international students). Electronic applications accepted. *Expenses:* Tuition, state resident: full-time $11,310; part-time $515 per credit hour. Tuition, nonresident: full-time $20,396; part-time $928 per credit hour. *International tuition:* $18,544 full-time. *Financial support:* Fellowships with full tuition reimbursements, teaching assistantships with full tuition reimbursements, and unspecified assistantships available. Financial award application deadline: 1/15. *Unit head:* Dr. Robert Trogdon, Chair, 330-672-2676, E-mail: rtrogdon@kent.edu. *Application contact:* Wesley Raabe, Graduate Studies Coordinator, E-mail: wraabe@kent.edu.
Website: http://www.kent.edu/english/

Kutztown University of Pennsylvania, College of Education, Program in Secondary Education, Kutztown, PA 19530-0730. Offers biology (M Ed); curriculum and instruction (M Ed); English (M Ed); mathematics (M Ed); middle level (M Ed); social studies (M Ed); teaching (M Ed); transformational teaching and learning (Ed D). *Accreditation:* NCATE. *Program availability:* Part-time, evening/weekend, 100% online, blended/hybrid learning. *Faculty:* 4 full-time (3 women), 1 part-time/adjunct (0 women). *Students:* 33 full-time (21 women), 76 part-time (49 women); includes 6 minority (3 Black or African American, non-Hispanic/Latino; 3 Hispanic/Latino). Average age 32. 76 applicants, 91% accepted, 43 enrolled. In 2017, 31 master's awarded. *Degree requirements:* For master's, comprehensive exam, thesis optional; for doctorate, thesis/dissertation. *Entrance requirements:* For master's, GRE General Test, minimum undergraduate major GPA of 3.0, 3 letters of recommendation, copy of PRAXIS II or valid instructional I or II teaching certificate; for doctorate, master's or specialist degree in education or related field from regionally-accredited institution of higher learning with minimum graduate GPA of 3.25, significant educational experience, employment in an education setting (preferred). Additional exam requirements/recommendations for international students: Required—TOEFL (minimum score 550 paper-based, 79 iBT), IELTS (minimum score 6.5), or PTE (minimum score 53). *Application deadline:* For fall admission, 8/1 for domestic and international students; for spring admission, 12/1 for domestic and international students. Application fee: $35. Electronic applications accepted. *Expenses:* Tuition, state resident: part-time $500 per credit. Tuition, nonresident: part-time $750 per credit. *Required fees:* $115 per credit. One-time fee: $50 part-time. Tuition and fees vary according to degree level. *Financial support:* Career-related internships or fieldwork, Federal Work-Study, scholarships/grants, and unspecified assistantships available. Financial award application deadline: 3/1; financial award applicants required to submit FAFSA. *Unit head:* Dr. Theresa Stahler, Department Chair, 610-683-4259, Fax: 610-683-1338, E-mail: stahler@kutztown.edu. *Application contact:* Dr. Patricia Walsh Coates, Graduate Coordinator, 610-638-4289, Fax: 610-683-1338, E-mail: coates@kutztown.edu.
Website: https://www.kutztown.edu/academics/graduate-programs/secondary-education.htm

Lake Forest College, Master of Arts in Teaching Program, Lake Forest, IL 60045. Offers elementary education (MAT); K-12 French (MAT); K-12 music (MAT); K-12 Spanish (MAT); K-12 visual art (MAT); secondary biology (MAT); secondary chemistry (MAT); secondary English (MAT); secondary history (MAT); secondary mathematics (MAT). *Degree requirements:* For master's, comprehensive exam, portfolio. *Entrance requirements:* For master's, GRE.

Lehman College of the City University of New York, School of Education, Department of Middle and High School Education, Program in English Education, Bronx, NY 10468-1589. Offers MS Ed. *Accreditation:* NCATE. *Entrance requirements:* For master's, minimum GPA of 3.0 in English, 2.8 overall; teaching certificate.

Le Moyne College, Department of Education, Syracuse, NY 13214. Offers adolescent education (MS Ed, MST); adolescent education/special education (MS Ed, MST); adolescent English (MST), including grades 7-12; adolescent English/special education (MST), including grades 7-12; adolescent foreign language (MST), including grades 7-12; adolescent history (MST), including grades 7-12; childhood education (MS Ed); childhood education/special education (MS Ed); elementary education (MS Ed); general education (MS Ed); inclusive childhood education (MST); literacy education (MS Ed), including birth to grade 6, grades 5-12; school building leader (MS Ed); school building leadership (CAS); school district business leader (MS Ed, CAS); school district leader (MS Ed); school district leadership (CAS); secondary education (MS Ed); special education (MS Ed); teaching English to speakers of other languages (MS Ed); urban studies (MS Ed). *Accreditation:* TEAC. *Program availability:* Part-time, evening/weekend. *Faculty:* 7 full-time (5 women), 20 part-time/adjunct (12 women). *Students:* 30 full-time (19 women), 126 part-time (93 women); includes 15 minority (7 Black or African American, non-Hispanic/Latino; 1 American Indian or Alaska Native, non-Hispanic/Latino; 1 Asian, non-Hispanic/Latino; 6 Hispanic/Latino), 4 international. Average age 29. 139 applicants, 65% accepted, 76 enrolled. In 2017, 82 master's, 43 CASs awarded. *Degree requirements:* For master's, thesis. *Entrance requirements:* For master's, bachelor's degree with minimum undergraduate GPA of 3.0, 2 letters of recommendation, transcripts. Additional exam requirements/recommendations for international students: Required—TOEFL (minimum score 550 paper-based; 79 iBT); Recommended—IELTS (minimum score 6.5). *Application deadline:* For fall admission, 4/1 priority date for domestic and international students; for spring admission, 10/1 priority date for domestic and international students; for summer admission, 3/1 priority date for domestic and international students. Applications are processed on a rolling basis. Application fee: $50. Electronic applications accepted. *Expenses:* $700 per credit hour. *Financial support:* In 2017–18, 30 students received support. Career-related internships or fieldwork, scholarships/grants, and health care benefits available. Support available to part-time students. Financial award applicants required to submit FAFSA. *Faculty research:* Minority teachers, special education, multiculturalism, literacy, technology, media literacy learning, autism, school district organization, service-learning, higher level problem solving, teacher leadership. *Unit head:* Dr. Stephen C. Fleury, Chair, Department of Education, 315-445-4376, Fax: 315-445-4744, E-mail: fleurysc@lemoyne.edu. *Application contact:* Kristen P. Richards, Senior Director of Enrollment Management, 315-445-5444, Fax: 315-445-6092, E-mail: trapaskp@lemoyne.edu.
Website: http://www.lemoyne.edu/education

Lewis University, College of Education, Program in Secondary Education, Romeoville, IL 60446. Offers biology (MA); chemistry (MA); English (MA); history (MA); math (MA); physics (MA); psychology and social science (MA). *Program availability:* Part-time. *Students:* 19 full-time (9 women), 22 part-time (12 women); includes 10 minority (2 Black or African American, non-Hispanic/Latino; 1 Asian, non-Hispanic/Latino; 5 Hispanic/Latino; 2 Two or more races, non-Hispanic/Latino). Average age 27. *Degree requirements:* For master's, comprehensive exam, departmental qualifying exam. *Entrance requirements:* For master's, writing exam, Test of Academic Proficiency/Basic Skills Test/ACT/SAT, bachelor's degree, minimum GPA of 2.75, 2 letters of recommendation. Additional exam requirements/recommendations for international students: Required—TOEFL (minimum score 550 paper-based; 79 iBT), IELTS (minimum score 6). *Application deadline:* For fall admission, 5/1 priority date for international students; for spring admission, 11/15 priority date for international students. Applications are processed on a rolling basis. Application fee: $40. Electronic applications accepted. Tuition and fees vary according to program. *Financial support:* Federal Work-Study, scholarships/grants, and unspecified assistantships available. Financial award application deadline: 5/1; financial award applicants required to submit FAFSA. *Unit head:* Dr. Lauren Rentfro, Program Director, 815-836-5026, E-mail: rentfrla@lewisu.edu. *Application contact:* Kathy Lisak, Graduate Admissions Counselor, 815-836-5610, E-mail: grad@lewisu.edu.

Lincoln Memorial University, Carter and Moyers School of Education, Harrogate, TN 37752-1901. Offers administration and supervision (M Ed, Ed S); counseling and guidance (M Ed); curriculum and instruction (M Ed, Ed D, Ed S); English (M Ed); executive leadership (Ed D); higher education administration (Ed D); human resource development (Ed D); leadership and administration (Ed D). *Program availability:* Part-time, evening/weekend, online learning. *Degree requirements:* For master's, comprehensive exam, thesis optional; for Ed S, comprehensive exam. *Entrance requirements:* For master's, PRAXIS, NTE, GRE, MAT, letters of recommendation; for Ed S, graduate transcripts. Additional exam requirements/recommendations for international students: Recommended—TOEFL. *Faculty research:* Brain compatible teaching and learning; poverty in Appalachia; leadership for change; ethics, moral responsibility and social justice; human and organizational learning.

Lipscomb University, College of Education, Nashville, TN 37204-3951. Offers applied behavior analysis (MS, Certificate); coaching for learning (M Ed, Certificate, Ed S); educational leadership (M Ed, Ed S); English language learning (M Ed, Ed S); instructional coaching (M Ed, Certificate, Ed S); instructional practice (M Ed); learning organizations and strategic change (Ed D); literacy coaching (Certificate, Ed S); reading specialty (M Ed, Ed S); school counseling (M Ed, Ed S); special education (M Ed); teaching, learning, and leading (M Ed); technology integration (M Ed, Ed S); technology integration specialist (Certificate). *Accreditation:* NCATE. *Program availability:* Part-time, evening/weekend, 100% online. *Faculty:* 21 full-time (14 women), 42 part-time/adjunct (29 women). *Students:* 565 full-time (452 women), 59 part-time (45 women); includes 154 minority (102 Black or African American, non-Hispanic/Latino; 2 American Indian or Alaska Native, non-Hispanic/Latino; 8 Asian, non-Hispanic/Latino; 26 Hispanic/Latino; 16 Two or more races, non-Hispanic/Latino). Average age 32. 395 applicants, 54% accepted, 196 enrolled. In 2017, 162 master's, 30 doctorates, 54 other advanced degrees awarded. *Degree requirements:* For master's, comprehensive exam, portfolio, research project and presentation; for doctorate, practical capstone project in experiential setting. *Entrance requirements:* For master's, MAT (minimum score 31) or GRE General Test (minimum score 294), 2 reference letters, goals statement, writing sample, interview; for doctorate, MAT or GRE General Test, 3 reference letters, artifact of demonstrated academic excellence, written personal statements, interview. Additional exam requirements/recommendations for international students: Required—TOEFL (minimum score 570 paper-based; 80 iBT). *Application deadline:* For fall admission, 8/29 priority date for domestic students; for spring admission, 1/15 priority date for domestic students. Applications are processed on a rolling basis. Application fee: $50 ($75 for international students). Electronic applications accepted. *Expenses:* Contact institution. *Financial support:* Scholarships/grants, unspecified assistantships, and partnerships with local school districts available. Financial award applicants required to submit FAFSA. *Faculty research:* Facilitative learning styles, leadership, student assessment, interactive multimedia inclusion, learning organizations and strategic change. *Unit head:* Dr. Deborah Boyd, Director of Graduate Studies, 615-966-6263, E-mail: deborah.boyd@lipscomb.edu. *Application contact:* Amanda Logsdon, Director of Enrollment and Outreach, 615-966-7199, E-mail: amanda.logsdon@lipscomb.edu.
Website: http://www.lipscomb.edu/education/graduate-programs

London Metropolitan University, Graduate Programs, London, United Kingdom. Offers applied psychology (M Sc); architecture (MA); biomedical science (M Sc); blood science (M Sc); cancer pharmacology (M Sc); computer networking and cyber security (M Sc); computing and information systems (M Sc); conference interpreting (MA); counter-terrorism studies (M Sc); creative, digital and professional writing (MA); crime, violence and prevention (M Sc); criminology (M Sc); curating contemporary art (MA); data analytics (MA); digital media (MA); early childhood studies (MA); education (MA, Ed D); financial services law, regulation and compliance (LL M); food science (M Sc); forensic psychology (M Sc); health and social care management and policy (M Sc); human nutrition (M Sc); human resource management (MA); human rights and international conflict (MA); information technology (M Sc); intelligence and security studies (M Sc); international oil, gas and energy law (LL M); international relations (MA); interpreting (MA); learning and teaching in higher education (MA); legal practice (LL M); media and entertainment law (LL M); organizational and consumer psychology (M Sc); psychological therapy (M Sc); psychology of mental health (M Sc); public health (M Sc); public policy and management (MPA); security studies (M Sc); social work (M Sc); spatial planning and urban design (MA); sports therapy (M Sc); supporting older children and young people with dyslexia (MA); teaching languages (MA), including Arabic, English; translation (MA); woman and child abuse (MA).

Manhattanville College, School of Education, Program in Middle Childhood/Adolescence Education (Grades 5-12), Purchase, NY 10577-2132. Offers biology (MAT, Advanced Certificate); biology and special education (MPS); chemistry (MAT, Advanced Certificate); chemistry and special education (MPS); earth science (Advanced Certificate); education for sustainability (Advanced Certificate); English (MAT, Advanced Certificate); English and special education (MPS); literacy and special education (MPS); literacy specialist (MPS); math and special education (MPS); mathematics (MAT, Advanced Certificate); physics (MAT, Advanced Certificate); social studies (MAT); social studies and special education (MPS); special education generalist (MPS). *Program availability:* Part-time, evening/weekend. *Faculty:* 2 full-time (both women), 5 part-time/adjunct (1 woman). *Students:* 8 full-time (7 women), 28 part-time (16 women); includes 4 minority (1 Asian, non-Hispanic/Latino; 2 Hispanic/Latino; 1 Two or more races, non-Hispanic/Latino). Average age 31. 7 applicants, 86% accepted, 4 enrolled. In 2017, 13 master's, 1 other advanced degree awarded. *Degree requirements:* For master's, comprehensive exam (for some programs), thesis (for some programs), student teaching, research seminars, portfolios, internships, writing assessment; for Advanced Certificate, comprehensive exam (for some programs). *Entrance requirements:* For master's, GRE or MAT (for programs leading to certification), minimum GPA of 3.0, 2 letters of recommendation, interview, essay (2-3 page personal statement that describes reasons for choosing teaching or educational leadership as profession and philosophy of education), proof of immunization (for those born after 1957). Additional exam requirements/recommendations for international students: Required—TOEFL (minimum score 600 paper-based; 110 iBT); Recommended—IELTS (minimum score 8). *Application deadline:* Applications are processed on a rolling basis. Application fee: $75. Electronic applications accepted. *Expenses:* $915 per credit. *Financial support:* Teaching assistantships, career-related internships or fieldwork, Federal Work-Study, institutionally sponsored loans, scholarships/grants, and unspecified assistantships available. Financial award application deadline: 3/15; financial award applicants required to submit FAFSA. *Faculty research:* Education for sustainability. *Unit head:* Dr. Shelly Wepner, Dean, 914-323-3153, Fax: 914-323-5493, E-mail: shelly.wepner@mville.edu. *Application contact:* Alissa Wilson, Director, Graduate Admissions, 914-323-3150, Fax: 914-694-1732, E-mail: edschool@mville.edu.
Website: http://www.mville.edu/programs#/search/19

Manhattanville College, School of Education, Program in Special Education, Purchase, NY 10577-2132. Offers childhood (grades 1-6) (MPS); childhood education (grades 1-6) and special education (MPS); early childhood (birth-grade 2) (MPS); early childhood (birth-grade 2) and special education (MPS); early childhood and childhood (birth-grade 6) (MPS); English (5-9 and 7-12) (MPS); grades 7-12 generalist (MPS); literacy (birth-grade 6) and special education childhood (grades 1-6) (MPS); literacy 5-12 (MPS); mathematics (5-9 and 7-12) (MPS); science (biology or chemistry 5-9 and 7-12) (MPS); social studies (5-9 and 7-12) (MPS); special education: childhood (grades 1-6) (Certificate); special education: early childhood (birth-grade 2) and childhood (grades 1-6) (Certificate); special education: early childhood (birth-grade 2) (Certificate); special education: grades 7-12 generalist (Certificate). *Program availability:* Part-time, evening/weekend. *Faculty:* 5 full-time (3 women), 24 part-time/adjunct (16 women). *Students:* 77 full-time (69 women), 154 part-time (132 women); includes 33 minority (9 Black or African American, non-Hispanic/Latino; 2 Asian, non-Hispanic/Latino; 22 Hispanic/Latino; 1 international. Average age 28. 87 applicants, 77% accepted, 57 enrolled. In 2017, 86 master's, 2 Certificates awarded. *Degree requirements:* For master's, comprehensive exam (for some programs), thesis (for some programs), student teaching, research seminars, portfolios, internships, writing assessment; for Certificate, comprehensive exam (for some programs). *Entrance requirements:* For master's, GRE or MAT (for programs leading to certification), minimum GPA of 3.0, 2 letters of recommendation, interview, essay (2-3 page personal statement that describes reasons for choosing teaching or educational leadership as profession and philosophy of education), proof of immunization (for those born after 1957). Additional exam requirements/recommendations for international students: Required—TOEFL (minimum score 600 paper-based; 110 iBT); Recommended—IELTS (minimum score 8). *Application deadline:* Applications are processed on a rolling basis. Application fee: $75. Electronic applications accepted. *Expenses:* $915 per credit. *Financial support:* Teaching assistantships, career-related internships or fieldwork, Federal Work-Study, institutionally sponsored loans, scholarships/grants, and unspecified assistantships available. Financial award application deadline: 3/15; financial award applicants required to submit FAFSA. *Faculty research:* Students with emotional difficulties, literacy and adolescents, mindfulness, studying the effects of the environment on special populations, the most difficult cases, students who are presented with multiple challenges: learning, behavioral and ACE experiences who see criminal behavior as a way to cope; working on giving them the tools they need to succeed emotionally and cognitively despite the odds stacked against them. *Unit head:* Dr. Shelly Wepner, Dean, 914-323-3153, Fax: 914-323-5493, E-mail: shelly.wepner@mville.edu. *Application contact:* Alissa Wilson, Director, Graduate Admissions, 914-323-3150, Fax: 914-694-1732, E-mail: edschool@mville.edu.
Website: http://www.mville.edu/programs/special-education

Marymount University, School of Arts and Sciences, Program in English and the Humanities, Arlington, VA 22207-4299. Offers English and humanities (MA); teaching English at the community college (Certificate). *Program availability:* Part-time, evening/weekend. *Faculty:* 3 full-time (0 women). *Students:* 2 full-time (both women), 10 part-time (6 women); includes 5 minority (2 Black or African American, non-Hispanic/Latino; 1 Asian, non-Hispanic/Latino; 1 Hispanic/Latino; 1 Two or more races, non-Hispanic/Latino). Average age 34. 8 applicants, 100% accepted, 5 enrolled. In 2017, 7 master's, 1 other advanced degree awarded. *Degree requirements:* For master's, thesis, capstone. *Entrance requirements:* For master's, 2 letters of recommendation, resume, bachelor's degree in English or other humanities discipline, writing sample of 8-10 pages. Additional exam requirements/recommendations for international students: Required—TOEFL (minimum score 600 paper-based; 96 iBT), IELTS (minimum score 6.5). *Application deadline:* Applications are processed on a rolling basis. Application fee: $40. Electronic applications accepted. *Expenses:* Tuition: Full-time $975; part-time $975 per credit hour. *Required fees:* $198; $11 per credit hour. One-time fee: $250. Tuition and fees vary according to program. *Financial support:* In 2017–18, 1 student received support, including 1 research assistantship with full and partial tuition reimbursement available (averaging $11,700 per year); teaching assistantships with full and partial tuition reimbursements available, career-related internships or fieldwork, Federal Work-Study, scholarships/grants, and unspecified assistantships also available. Support available to part-time students. Financial award application deadline: 3/1; financial award applicants required to submit FAFSA. *Unit head:* Dr. David Brown, Director, English and the Humanities, 703-284-5762, Fax: 703-284-3859, E-mail: david.brown@marymount.edu. *Application contact:* Francesca Reed, Director, Graduate Admissions, 703-284-5901, Fax: 703-527-3815, E-mail: grad.admissions@marymount.edu.
Website: http://www.marymount.edu/Academics/School-of-Arts-Sciences/Graduate-Programs/English-Humanities-(M-A-)

Millersville University of Pennsylvania, College of Graduate Studies and Adult Learning, College of Education and Human Services, Department of Early, Middle, and Exceptional Education, Program in Language and Literacy, Millersville, PA 17551-0302. Offers M Ed. *Program availability:* Part-time, evening/weekend. *Faculty:* 9 full-time (4 women), 11 part-time/adjunct (8 women). *Students:* 45 part-time (all women); includes 1 minority (Asian, non-Hispanic/Latino). Average age 29. 1 applicant, 100% accepted, 1 enrolled. In 2017, 21 master's awarded. *Degree requirements:* For master's, thesis optional. *Entrance requirements:* For master's, GRE or MAT if undergraduate cumulative GPA is lower than 3.0, teaching certificate. Additional exam requirements/recommendations for international students: Required—TOEFL (minimum score 80 iBT), IELTS (minimum score 6.5), PTE (minimum score 60). *Application deadline:* Applications are processed on a rolling basis. Application fee: $40. Electronic applications accepted. *Expenses:* $500 per credit resident tuition and fees; $750 per credit non-resident tuition and fees; $114.75 per credit general fee (maximum of 12 credits); technology fee $27 per credit (resident), $39 per credit (non-resident). *Financial support:* In 2017–18, 1 student received support. Unspecified assistantships available. Financial award application deadline: 3/15; financial award applicants required to submit FAFSA. *Faculty research:* Literacy and technology, children's literature, literacy leadership, disciplinary literacy, diagnosis and assessment. *Unit head:* Dr. Marcia Nell, Chair, 717-871-7344, E-mail: marcia.nell@millersville.edu. *Application contact:* Dr. Victor S. DeSantis, Dean of College of Graduate Studies and Adult Learning/Associate Provost for Civic and Community Engagement, 717-871-7619, Fax: 717-871-7954, E-mail: victor.desantis@millersville.edu.
Website: http://www.millersville.edu/academics/educ/eled/graduate-programs/language-and-literacy.php

Mississippi College, Graduate School, School of Education, Department of Teacher Education and Leadership, Clinton, MS 39058. Offers art (M Ed); biological science (M Ed); business education (M Ed); computer science (M Ed); dyslexia therapy (M Ed); educational leadership (M Ed, Ed D, Ed S); elementary education (M Ed, Ed S); English (M Ed); higher education administration (MS); mathematics (M Ed); secondary education (M Ed); social studies (history) (M Ed); teaching arts (M Ed). *Program availability:* Part-time, online learning. *Degree requirements:* For master's, comprehensive exam, thesis optional. *Entrance requirements:* For master's, NTE. Additional exam requirements/recommendations for international students: Recommended—TOEFL, IELTS. Electronic applications accepted.

Missouri State University, Graduate College, College of Arts and Letters, Department of English, Springfield, MO 65897. Offers applied second language acquisition

(MASLA); English (MA); English education (MS Ed); teaching English to speakers of other languages (Certificate); writing (MA). MASLA offered with the Department of Modern and Classical Languages. *Program availability:* Part-time, evening/weekend. *Faculty:* 25 full-time (18 women), 5 part-time/adjunct (2 women). *Students:* 34 full-time (26 women), 85 part-time (73 women); includes 9 minority (1 Black or African American, non-Hispanic/Latino; 1 Asian, non-Hispanic/Latino; 3 Hispanic/Latino; 1 Native Hawaiian or other Pacific Islander, non-Hispanic/Latino; 3 Two or more races, non-Hispanic/Latino), 14 international. Average age 26. 97 applicants, 65% accepted, 56 enrolled. In 2017, 57 master's awarded. *Degree requirements:* For master's, one foreign language, comprehensive exam, thesis or alternative. *Entrance requirements:* For master's, GRE (for MA), 9-12 teacher certification (MS Ed); minimum GPA of 3.0 (MA); personal statement (200- to 250-word description of reasons and goals behind interest in English graduate studies); at least two letters of recommendation from individuals able to speak of the applicant's academic achievements and potential; writing sample. Additional exam requirements/recommendations for international students: Required—TOEFL (minimum score 550 paper-based; 79 iBT), IELTS (minimum score 6). *Application deadline:* For fall admission, 3/1 priority date for domestic students, 3/1 for international students; for spring admission, 10/1 priority date for domestic students, 10/1 for international students. Applications are processed on a rolling basis. Application fee: $35 ($50 for international students). Electronic applications accepted. *Expenses:* Tuition, state resident: full-time $2915; part-time $2021 per credit hour. Tuition, nonresident: full-time $5354; part-time $3647 per credit hour. *International tuition:* $11,992 full-time. *Required fees:* $173; $173 per credit hour. Tuition and fees vary according to class time, course level, course load, degree level, campus/location and program. *Financial support:* In 2017–18, 23 teaching assistantships with full tuition reimbursements (averaging $8,772 per year) were awarded; Federal Work-Study, institutionally sponsored loans, scholarships/grants, and unspecified assistantships also available. Financial award application deadline: 3/31; financial award applicants required to submit FAFSA. *Faculty research:* History of rhetoric, modern poetry, African-American literature, digital writing, teaching English to speakers of other languages. *Unit head:* Dr. W. D. Blackmon, Department Head, 417-836-5107, Fax: 417-836-6940, E-mail: english@missouristate.edu. *Application contact:* Stephanie Praschan, Director, Graduate Enrollment Management, 417-836-5330, Fax: 417-836-6200, E-mail: stephaniepraschan@missouristate.edu.
Website: http://english.missouristate.edu/

Molloy College, Graduate Education Program, Rockville Centre, NY 11571-5002. Offers adolescent education in biology (MS); adolescent special education (Advanced Certificate); bilingual extension (Advanced Certificate); childhood education (MS); childhood special education (Advanced Certificate); early childhood education (MS); educational technology (MS); English (MS); mathematics (MS); social studies (MS); Spanish (MS); special education on both childhood and adolescent levels (MS); teaching English to speakers of other languages (TESOL) in grades pre-K to 12 (MS); TESOL (Advanced Certificate). *Accreditation:* NCATE. *Program availability:* Part-time, evening/weekend. *Faculty:* 18 full-time (17 women), 11 part-time/adjunct (9 women). *Students:* 102 full-time (80 women), 217 part-time (167 women); includes 65 minority (16 Black or African American, non-Hispanic/Latino; 7 Asian, non-Hispanic/Latino; 38 Hispanic/Latino; 4 Two or more races, non-Hispanic/Latino), 1 international. Average age 41. 153 applicants, 68% accepted, 85 enrolled. In 2017, 95 master's, 3 other advanced degrees awarded. *Entrance requirements:* Additional exam requirements/recommendations for international students: Required—TOEFL (minimum score 550 paper-based; 79 iBT). *Application deadline:* Applications are processed on a rolling basis. Application fee: $60. Electronic applications accepted. *Expenses: Tuition:* Full-time $19,980; part-time $1110 per credit. *Required fees:* $1040. Tuition and fees vary according to course load and degree level. *Financial support:* Application deadline: 3/1; applicants required to submit FAFSA. *Faculty research:* English Language Learners; social emotional needs of students; gifted education; cultural diversity; collaborative teaching methods. *Unit head:* Joanne O'Brien, Associate Dean and Director of Graduate Education Programs, 516-323-3116, E-mail: jobrien@molloy.edu. *Application contact:* Jaclyn Machowicz, Assistant Director for Admissions, 516-323-4010, E-mail: jmachowicz@molloy.edu.

Montclair State University, The Graduate School, College of Education and Human Services, MAT Program in Teaching, Montclair, NJ 07043-1624. Offers art (MAT); biology (MAT); chemistry (MAT); earth science (MAT); English (MAT); French (MAT); health and physical education (MAT); health education (MAT); mathematics (MAT); music (MAT); physical education (MAT); physical science (MAT); social studies (MAT); Spanish (MAT); teacher of English as a second language (MAT). *Degree requirements:* For master's, comprehensive exam, thesis or alternative. *Entrance requirements:* For master's, interview, 2 letters of recommendation. Additional exam requirements/recommendations for international students: Required—TOEFL (minimum score 83 iBT), IELTS (minimum score 6.5). Electronic applications accepted.

Montclair State University, The Graduate School, College of Humanities and Social Sciences, Teaching Writing Certificate Program, Montclair, NJ 07043-1624. Offers Certificate. *Program availability:* Part-time, evening/weekend. *Entrance requirements:* For degree, 2 letters of recommendation, essay. Additional exam requirements/recommendations for international students: Required—TOEFL (minimum score 83 iBT), IELTS (minimum score 6.5). Electronic applications accepted. *Faculty research:* Pedagogy in writing.

Morehead State University, Graduate Programs, College of Education, Department of Foundational and Graduate Studies in Education, Morehead, KY 40351. Offers adult and higher education (MA, Ed S); certified professional counselor (Ed S); counseling P-12 (MA); curriculum and instruction (Ed S); educational technology (MA Ed); instructional leadership (Ed S); school administration (MA); school counseling (Ed S); teacher leader business and marketing content (MA Ed); teacher leader business and marketing technology (MA Ed); teacher leader educational technology (MA Ed); teacher leader English (MA Ed); teacher leader gifted education (MA Ed); teacher leader IECE certification (MA Ed); teacher leader interdisciplinary education P-5 (MA Ed); teacher leader middle grades (MA Ed); teacher leader non IECE certification (MA Ed); teacher leader reading/writing - non-certification (MA Ed); teacher leader reading/writing certification (MA Ed); teacher leader school communication - certification (MA Ed); teacher leader school communication - non-certification (MA Ed); teacher leader social studies (MA Ed); teacher leader special education (MA Ed). *Accreditation:* NCATE. *Program availability:* Part-time, evening/weekend. *Degree requirements:* For master's, thesis optional, oral and/or written comprehensive exams; for Ed S, thesis, oral exam. *Entrance requirements:* For master's, GRE General Test, minimum overall undergraduate GPA of 2.5; for Ed S, GRE General Test, interview, master's degree, minimum GPA of 3.5, work experience. Additional exam requirements/recommendations for international students: Required—TOEFL (minimum score 500 paper-based). Electronic applications accepted. *Faculty research:* Character education, school accountability, computer applications for school administrators.

Morehead State University, Graduate Programs, College of Education, Department of Middle Grades and Secondary Education, Morehead, KY 40351. Offers business and marketing education (MAT); English/language arts 5-9 (MAT); French (MAT); health P-12 (MAT); mathematics 5-9 (MAT); physical education P-12 (MAT); science 5-9 (MAT); secondary biology (MAT); secondary chemistry (MAT); secondary earth science (MAT);

secondary English (MAT); secondary math (MAT); secondary physics (MAT); secondary social studies (MAT); social studies 5-9 (MAT); Spanish (MAT). *Program availability:* Part-time, evening/weekend. *Degree requirements:* For master's, portfolio. *Entrance requirements:* For master's, GRE or PRAXIS II content exam, minimum overall undergraduate GPA of 2.5. Additional exam requirements/recommendations for international students: Required—TOEFL (minimum score 500 paper-based). Electronic applications accepted.

Murray State University, College of Humanities and Fine Arts, Department of English and Philosophy, Murray, KY 42071. Offers creative writing (MFA); English (MA); English pedagogy and technology (DA); gender studies (Certificate); teaching English to speakers of other languages (TESOL) (MA). *Program availability:* Part-time, 100% online, blended/hybrid learning. *Faculty:* 26 full-time (14 women), 1 part-time/adjunct (0 women). *Students:* 31 full-time (12 women), 91 part-time (61 women); includes 11 minority (5 Black or African American, non-Hispanic/Latino; 2 American Indian or Alaska Native, non-Hispanic/Latino; 2 Asian, non-Hispanic/Latino; 2 Two or more races, non-Hispanic/Latino), 23 international. Average age 36. 55 applicants, 95% accepted, 30 enrolled. In 2017, 21 master's awarded. *Entrance requirements:* For master's, doctorate, and Certificate, GRE or GMAT, minimum university GPA of 2.75. Additional exam requirements/recommendations for international students: Required—TOEFL (minimum score 527 paper-based; 71 iBT). *Application deadline:* Applications are processed on a rolling basis. Application fee: $40 ($50 for international students). Electronic applications accepted. *Expenses:* Tuition, state resident: full-time $9504. Tuition, nonresident: full-time $26,811. *International tuition:* $14,400 full-time. Tuition and fees vary according to course load, degree level and reciprocity agreements. *Financial support:* In 2017–18, 3 teaching assistantships were awarded; Federal Work-Study and unspecified assistantships also available. Financial award applicants required to submit FAFSA. *Unit head:* Dr. Sue Sroda, Chair, Department of English and Philosophy, 270-809-4715, Fax: 270-809-4545, E-mail: msroda@murraystate.edu. *Application contact:* Kaitlyn Burzynski, Interim Assistant Director for Graduate Admission and Records, 270-809-5732, Fax: 270-809-3780, E-mail: msu.graduateadmissions@murraystate.edu.
Website: https://www.murraystate.edu/academics/CollegesDepartments/CollegeOfHumanitiesAndFineArts/EnglishAndPhilosophy/index.aspx

National Louis University, National College of Education, Chicago, IL 60603. Offers administration and supervision (M Ed, Ed D, CAS, Ed S); curriculum and instruction (M Ed, MS Ed, CAS); early childhood administration (M Ed, CAS); early childhood education (M Ed, MAT, MS Ed, CAS); education (Ed D); educational psychology/human learning and development (M Ed, MS Ed, CAS, Ed S); elementary education (MAT); interdisciplinary curriculum and instruction (M Ed); mathematics education (M Ed, MS Ed, CAS); middle grades education (MAT); reading and language (M Ed, MS Ed, CAS); school psychology (M Ed, Ed S); science education (M Ed, MS Ed, CAS); secondary education (MAT); special education (M Ed, MAT, CAS); technology in education (M Ed, CAS). *Accreditation:* NCATE. *Program availability:* Part-time, evening/weekend. *Degree requirements:* For doctorate, comprehensive exam, thesis/dissertation. *Entrance requirements:* For master's, MAT or GRE, minimum GPA of 3.0; for doctorate, GRE General Test, minimum GPA of 3.25, interview, resume, writing sample, 4 recommendations. Additional exam requirements/recommendations for international students: Required—TOEFL (minimum score 550 paper-based; 79 iBT).

New Mexico State University, College of Arts and Sciences, Department of English, Las Cruces, NM 88003. Offers creative writing (MFA); English (MA), including creative writing, English studies for teachers, literature, rhetoric and professional communication; rhetoric and professional communication (PhD). *Program availability:* Part-time. *Faculty:* 17 full-time (9 women), 3 part-time/adjunct (1 woman). *Students:* 50 full-time (32 women), 21 part-time (14 women); includes 19 minority (2 Black or African American, non-Hispanic/Latino; 2 Asian, non-Hispanic/Latino; 14 Hispanic/Latino; 1 Two or more races, non-Hispanic/Latino), 8 international. Average age 35. 68 applicants, 50% accepted, 12 enrolled. In 2017, 13 master's, 1 doctorate awarded. *Entrance requirements:* For master's and doctorate, sample of written work. Additional exam requirements/recommendations for international students: Required—TOEFL (minimum score 500 paper-based; 79 iBT), IELTS (minimum score 6.5). *Application deadline:* For fall admission, 2/1 for domestic and international students. Application fee: $40 ($50 for international students). Electronic applications accepted. *Expenses:* Tuition, state resident: full-time $4390. Tuition, nonresident: full-time $15,309. *Required fees:* $853. *Financial support:* In 2017–18, 49 students received support, including 6 fellowships (averaging $4,390 per year), 41 teaching assistantships (averaging $17,317 per year); career-related internships or fieldwork, Federal Work-Study, scholarships/grants, traineeships, health care benefits, and unspecified assistantships also available. Support available to part-time students. Financial award application deadline: 3/1. *Faculty research:* Composition research, history and theory of rhetoric, technical/professional communication, creative writing, English and American literature. *Total annual research expenditures:* $10,666. *Unit head:* Dr. Elizabeth Schirmer, Interim Department Head, 575-646-3931, Fax: 575-646-7725, E-mail: eschirme@nmsu.edu. *Application contact:* Dr. Tracey Eileen Miller-Tomlinson, Director of Graduate Studies, 575-646-2213, Fax: 575-646-7725, E-mail: tomlin@nmsu.edu.
Website: http://english.nmsu.edu

New York Institute of Technology, School of Interdisciplinary Studies and Education, Department of Teacher Education, Old Westbury, NY 11568-8000. Offers adolescence education (MS), including math (MAT, MS), science; adolescent education (MAT), including biology, chemistry, English, math (MAT, MS), social studies; childhood education (MS); early childhood (MS). *Program availability:* Part-time, evening/weekend, 100% online, blended/hybrid learning. *Faculty:* 2 full-time (both women), 7 part-time/adjunct (3 women). *Students:* 46 full-time (44 women), 30 part-time (22 women); includes 23 minority (8 Black or African American, non-Hispanic/Latino; 6 Asian, non-Hispanic/Latino; 8 Hispanic/Latino; 1 Two or more races, non-Hispanic/Latino), 2 international. Average age 29. 39 applicants, 72% accepted, 15 enrolled. In 2017, 14 master's awarded. *Entrance requirements:* For master's, GRE or MAT, BS or equivalent; minimum cumulative undergraduate GPA of 3.0; NY state provisional or initial certification (for MS in adolescence education); BS with major in biology, chemistry, economics, English, history, life sciences, math, physics, or psychology (for MS in childhood, early childhood education, and MAT); interview; personal statement. Additional exam requirements/recommendations for international students: Required—TOEFL (minimum score 79 iBT), IELTS (minimum score 6). *Application deadline:* Applications are processed on a rolling basis. Application fee: $50. Electronic applications accepted. *Expenses:* $1,285 per credit plus fees. *Financial support:* Career-related internships or fieldwork, Federal Work-Study, scholarships/grants, tuition waivers (full and partial), and unspecified assistantships available. Support available to part-time students. Financial award application deadline: 2/15; financial award applicants required to submit FAFSA. *Faculty research:* Evolving definition of new literacies and its impact on teaching and learning (twenty-first century skills), new literacies practices in teacher education, teachers' professional development, English language and literacy learning through mobile learning, teaching reading to culturally and linguistically diverse children. *Unit head:* Dr. Hui-Yin Hsu, Department Chair, 516-686-1322, Fax: 516-686-7655, E-mail: hhsu02@nyit.edu. *Application contact:* Alice Dolitsky, Director, Graduate Admissions, 516-686-7520, Fax: 516-686-1116, E-mail: nyitgrad@nyit.edu.
Website: http://www.nyit.edu/interdisciplinary/department_teacher_education

English Education

New York University, Steinhardt School of Culture, Education, and Human Development, Department of Music and Performing Arts Professions, Program in Educational Theatre, New York, NY 10012. Offers educational theatre and English 7-12 (MA); educational theatre and social studies 7-12 (MA); educational theatre in colleges and communities (MA, Ed D, PhD); educational theatre, all grades (MA). *Program availability:* Part-time. *Students:* Average age 28. 90 applicants, 76% accepted, 37 enrolled. In 2017, 47 master's, 5 doctorates awarded. *Entrance requirements:* For master's, audition; for doctorate, GRE General Test, interview. Additional exam requirements/recommendations for international students: Required—TOEFL (minimum score 100 iBT). *Application deadline:* For fall admission, 12/1 priority date for domestic and international students; for spring admission, 10/1 for domestic and international students. Applications are processed on a rolling basis. Application fee: $75. Electronic applications accepted. *Expenses: Tuition:* Full-time $41,352; part-time $19,968 per year. *Required fees:* $2496; $1628 per unit. $814 per term. Tuition and fees vary according to course load and program. *Financial support:* Teaching assistantships with partial tuition reimbursements, career-related internships or fieldwork, Federal Work-Study, institutionally sponsored loans, and scholarships/grants available. Support available to part-time students. Financial award application deadline: 2/1; financial award applicants required to submit FAFSA. *Faculty research:* Theatre for young audiences, drama in education, applied theatre, arts education assessment, reflective praxis. *Unit head:* Prof. David Montgomery, Director, 212-998-5869, Fax: 212-995-4043, E-mail: dm635@nyu.edu. *Application contact:* 212-998-5030, Fax: 212-995-4328, E-mail: steinhardt.gradadmissions@nyu.edu.
Website: http://steinhardt.nyu.edu/music/edtheatre

New York University, Steinhardt School of Culture, Education, and Human Development, Department of Teaching and Learning, Program in English Education, New York, NY 10012-1019. Offers clinically-based English education, grades 7-12 (MA); English education (PhD, Advanced Certificate); English education, grades 7-12 (MA). *Accreditation:* TEAC. *Program availability:* Part-time. *Students:* Average age 33. 81 applicants, 78% accepted, 21 enrolled. In 2017, 27 master's, 6 doctorates awarded. *Entrance requirements:* For doctorate, GRE General Test, interview; for Advanced Certificate, master's degree. Additional exam requirements/recommendations for international students: Required—TOEFL (minimum score 100 iBT). *Application deadline:* For fall admission, 12/1 priority date for domestic and international students; for spring admission, 10/1 for domestic and international students. Applications are processed on a rolling basis. Application fee: $75. Electronic applications accepted. *Expenses: Tuition:* Full-time $41,352; part-time $19,968 per year. *Required fees:* $2496; $1628 per unit. $814 per term. Tuition and fees vary according to course load and program. *Financial support:* Fellowships with full and partial tuition reimbursements, teaching assistantships with full and partial tuition reimbursements, career-related internships or fieldwork, Federal Work-Study, institutionally sponsored loans, scholarships/grants, tuition waivers (partial), and unspecified assistantships available. Support available to part-time students. Financial award application deadline: 2/1; financial award applicants required to submit FAFSA. *Faculty research:* Making meaning of literature, teaching of literature, urban adolescent literacy and equity, literacy development and globalization, digital media and literacy. *Unit head:* Prof. Sarah W. Beck, Chairperson, 212-998-5473, Fax: 212-995-4049, E-mail: sarah.beck@nyu.edu. *Application contact:* 212-998-5030, Fax: 212-995-4328, E-mail: steinhardt.gradadmissions@nyu.edu.
Website: http://steinhardt.nyu.edu/teachlearn/english

North Carolina Agricultural and Technical State University, School of Graduate Studies, College of Arts and Sciences, Department of English, Greensboro, NC 27411. Offers English (MA); English and African-American literature (MA); English education (MAT, MS). *Program availability:* Part-time, evening/weekend. *Degree requirements:* For master's, comprehensive exam, qualifying exam. *Entrance requirements:* For master's, GRE General Test, minimum GPA of 3.0.

North Carolina State University, Graduate School, College of Education, Department of Curriculum and Instruction, Program in Secondary English Education, Raleigh, NC 27695. Offers M Ed, MS Ed. *Degree requirements:* For master's, thesis optional.

Northeastern Illinois University, College of Graduate Studies and Research, Daniel L. Goodwin College of Education, MAT Program in Secondary Education, Chicago, IL 60625. Offers language arts (MAT); mathematics (MAT); science (MAT); social science (MAT). *Expenses:* Tuition, state resident: full-time $7274; part-time $404.11 per credit hour. Tuition, nonresident: full-time $14,548; part-time $808.23 per credit hour. *Required fees:* $1284. *Unit head:* Dr. Brian Schultz, Department Chair, 773-442-5327, E-mail: b-schultz@neiu.edu. *Application contact:* Martha Narvaez, Graduate Admission Representative, 773-442-6006, E-mail: m-narvaez@neiu.edu.

Northeastern Illinois University, College of Graduate Studies and Research, Daniel L. Goodwin College of Education, MSI Program in Language Arts - Secondary Education, Chicago, IL 60625-4699. Offers MSI. *Expenses:* Tuition, state resident: full-time $7274; part-time $404.11 per credit hour. Tuition, nonresident: full-time $14,548; part-time $808.23 per credit hour. *Required fees:* $1284. *Unit head:* Dr. Maureen D. Gillette, Dean, 773-442-5500. *Application contact:* Ada Umeh, Admission Director, Graduate College, 773-442-6008, Fax: 773-442-6040, E-mail: a-umeh@neiu.edu.

Northwest Missouri State University, Graduate School, College of Arts and Sciences, Maryville, MO 64468-6001. Offers biology (MS); elementary mathematics specialist (MS Ed); English (MA); English education (MS Ed); English pedagogy (MA); geographic information science (MS, Certificate); history (MS Ed); mathematics (MS); mathematics education (MS Ed); teaching: science (MS Ed). *Program availability:* Part-time. *Faculty:* 67 full-time (21 women). *Students:* 11 full-time (5 women), 70 part-time (39 women); includes 9 minority (2 Black or African American, non-Hispanic/Latino; 1 American Indian or Alaska Native, non-Hispanic/Latino; 3 Hispanic/Latino; 3 Two or more races, non-Hispanic/Latino). Average age 34. 33 applicants, 42% accepted, 10 enrolled. In 2017, 19 master's, 7 other advanced degrees awarded. *Degree requirements:* For master's, comprehensive exam. *Entrance requirements:* For master's, GRE General Test, writing sample. Additional exam requirements/recommendations for international students: Required—TOEFL (minimum score 550 paper-based). *Application deadline:* For fall admission, 7/1 for domestic and international students; for spring admission, 11/15 for domestic and international students. Applications are processed on a rolling basis. Application fee: $0 ($50 for international students). Electronic applications accepted. *Expenses: Tuition:* state resident: full-time $4551; part-time $252.86 per credit hour. Tuition, nonresident: full-time $9103; part-time $505.72 per credit hour. *Required fees:* $2453; $136.25 per credit hour. Tuition and fees vary according to course load and program. *Financial support:* Research assistantships with full tuition reimbursements, teaching assistantships with full tuition reimbursements, and administrative assistantships, tutorial assistantships available. Financial award application deadline: 4/1; financial award applicants required to submit FAFSA. *Unit head:* Dr. Michael Steiner, Dean, 660-562-1197.
Website: https://www.nwmissouri.edu/academics/undergraduate/majors/liberal-arts-sciences.htm

Oregon State University, College of Education, Program in Teaching, Corvallis, OR 97331. Offers clinically based elementary education (MAT); elementary education (MAT); language arts (MAT); mathematics (MAT); music education (MAT); science (MAT); social studies (MAT). *Program availability:* Part-time, blended/hybrid learning. *Entrance requirements:* For master's, CBEST. Additional exam requirements/recommendations for international students: Required—TOEFL (minimum score 575 paper-based). *Application deadline:* For fall admission, 12/1 for domestic students. Application fee: $60. *Expenses:* Contact institution. *Unit head:* Jordon Zardinejad, 541-322-3118, E-mail: jordon.zardinejad@osucascades.edu. *Application contact:* Jordon Zardinejad, 541-322-3118, E-mail: jordon.zardinejad@osucascades.edu.
Website: http://education.oregonstate.edu/mat

Plymouth State University, College of Graduate Studies, Graduate Studies in Education, Program in English Education, Plymouth, NH 03264-1595. Offers M Ed. *Program availability:* Part-time, evening/weekend. *Degree requirements:* For master's, capstone, research, or thesis. *Entrance requirements:* For master's, MAT.

Purdue University, Graduate School, College of Education, Department of Curriculum and Instruction, West Lafayette, IN 47907. Offers agricultural and extension education (MS, MS Ed, PhD, Ed S); art education (PhD); career and technical education (MS Ed, PhD, Ed S); curriculum studies (MS Ed, PhD, Ed S); educational technology (MS Ed, PhD, Ed S); elementary education (MS Ed); family and consumer sciences education (MS Ed, PhD, Ed S); foreign language education (MS Ed, PhD, Ed S); industrial technology (PhD, Ed S); language arts (MS Ed, PhD, Ed S); literacy (MS Ed, PhD, Ed S); mathematics education (MS, MS Ed, PhD, Ed S); science education (MS, MS Ed, PhD, Ed S); social studies education (MS Ed, PhD, Ed S). *Accreditation:* NCATE. *Program availability:* Part-time, evening/weekend. *Faculty:* 37 full-time (27 women), 1 (woman) part-time/adjunct. *Students:* 78 full-time (50 women), 286 part-time (195 women); includes 68 minority (25 Black or African American, non-Hispanic/Latino; 3 American Indian or Alaska Native, non-Hispanic/Latino; 10 Asian, non-Hispanic/Latino; 22 Hispanic/Latino; 1 Native Hawaiian or other Pacific Islander, non-Hispanic/Latino; 7 Two or more races, non-Hispanic/Latino), 44 international. Average age 36. 150 applicants, 79% accepted, 73 enrolled. In 2017, 107 master's, 20 doctorates, 2 other advanced degrees awarded. *Degree requirements:* For master's, thesis optional; for doctorate, thesis/dissertation, oral and written exams; for Ed S, oral presentation, project. *Entrance requirements:* For master's, GRE General Test (if undergraduate GPA is below 3.0), minimum undergraduate GPA of 3.0 or equivalent; for doctorate, GRE General Test (minimum combined verbal and quantitative score of 1000, 300 for new scoring), minimum undergraduate GPA of 3.0 or equivalent; master's degree with minimum GPA of 3.0 or equivalent; for Ed S, GRE General Test (minimum combined verbal and quantitative score of 1000, 300 for new scoring), minimum undergraduate GPA of 3.0 or equivalent; master's degree. Additional exam requirements/recommendations for international students: Required—TOEFL (minimum score 550 paper-based; 77 iBT). *Application deadline:* For fall admission, 12/15 for domestic students, 3/1 for international students; for spring admission, 9/15 for domestic students, 8/1 for international students. Application fee: $60 ($75 for international students). Electronic applications accepted. *Financial support:* Fellowships with full tuition reimbursements, research assistantships with full tuition reimbursements, teaching assistantships with full tuition reimbursements, career-related internships or fieldwork, and tuition waivers (full) available. Support available to part-time students. Financial award application deadline: 3/1; financial award applicants required to submit FAFSA. *Faculty research:* Literacy acquisition and development, teacher beliefs and knowledge, recruitment and retention of underrepresented students, economic education, literacy discourse. *Unit head:* Janet M. Alsup, Head, 765-494-9667, E-mail: alsupj@purdue.edu. *Application contact:* Heather Brinkman, Graduate Contact, 765-494-2345, E-mail: hbrinkma@purdue.edu.
Website: http://www.edci.purdue.edu/

Queens College of the City University of New York, Division of Education, Department of Secondary Education and Youth Services, Queens, NY 11367-1597. Offers adolescent biology (MAT); art (MS Ed); biology (MS Ed, AC); chemistry (MS Ed, AC); earth sciences (MS Ed, AC); English (MS Ed, AC); French (MS Ed); Italian (MS Ed, AC); literacy education (MS Ed); mathematics (MS Ed, AC); music (MS Ed, AC); physics (MS Ed, AC); social studies (MS Ed, AC); Spanish (MS Ed, AC). *Program availability:* Part-time, evening/weekend. *Students:* 28 full-time (16 women), 349 part-time (202 women); includes 165 minority (18 Black or African American, non-Hispanic/Latino; 56 Asian, non-Hispanic/Latino; 83 Hispanic/Latino; 8 Two or more races, non-Hispanic/Latino), 14 international. Average age 29. *Degree requirements:* For master's, research project. *Entrance requirements:* For master's, minimum GPA of 3.0. Additional exam requirements/recommendations for international students: Required—TOEFL, IELTS. *Application deadline:* For fall admission, 4/1 for domestic students; for spring admission, 11/1 for domestic students. Applications are processed on a rolling basis. Application fee: $125. Electronic applications accepted. *Financial support:* Career-related internships or fieldwork available. Financial award application deadline: 4/1; financial award applicants required to submit FAFSA. *Unit head:* Dr. Eleanor Armour-Thomas, Chairperson, 718-997-5150, E-mail: eleanor.armour-thomas@qc.cuny.edu. *Application contact:* Elizabeth D'Amico-Ramirez, Assistant Director of Graduate Admissions, 718-997-5203, E-mail: elizabeth.damicoramirez@qc.cuny.edu.

Quinnipiac University, School of Education, Program in Secondary Education, Hamden, CT 06518-1940. Offers biology (MAT); English (MAT); history (MAT); mathematics (MAT); Spanish (MAT). *Accreditation:* NCATE. *Faculty:* 8 full-time (5 women), 27 part-time/adjunct (19 women). *Students:* 27 full-time (20 women); includes 5 minority (1 Black or African American, non-Hispanic/Latino; 3 Hispanic/Latino; 1 Two or more races, non-Hispanic/Latino). 43 applicants, 98% accepted, 36 enrolled. In 2017, 34 master's awarded. *Entrance requirements:* For master's, PRAXIS I or PRAXIS Core Academic Skills Exam, minimum GPA of 3.0, interview. *Application deadline:* For fall admission, 5/1 priority date for domestic students. Applications are processed on a rolling basis. Application fee: $45. Electronic applications accepted. *Financial support:* Career-related internships or fieldwork, Federal Work-Study, and unspecified assistantships available. Financial award application deadline: 6/1; financial award applicants required to submit FAFSA. *Faculty research:* Multicultural and urban education/leadership, challenges of teaching diverse learners, scholarship of teaching and learning, technology and teaching, humor and education. *Unit head:* Mordechai Gordon, Program Director, 203-582-8442, E-mail: mordechai.gordon@qu.edu. *Application contact:* Office of Graduate Admissions, 203-582-8672, Fax: 203-582-3443, E-mail: graduate@qu.edu.
Website: http://www.qu.edu/gradeducation

Rhode Island College, School of Graduate Studies, Feinstein School of Education and Human Development, Department of Educational Studies, Providence, RI 02908-1991. Offers advanced studies in teaching and learning (M Ed); English (MAT); French (MAT); history (MAT); math (MAT); secondary education (MAT); Spanish (MAT); teaching English as a second language (M Ed). *Accreditation:* NCATE. *Program availability:* Part-time, evening/weekend. *Faculty:* 2. *Students:* 1 (woman) full-time, 62 part-time (58 women); includes 10 minority (1 Black or African American, non-Hispanic/Latino; 2 Asian, non-Hispanic/Latino; 6 Hispanic/Latino; 1 Two or more races, non-Hispanic/Latino). Average age 37. In 2017, 31 master's awarded. *Degree requirements:* For master's, capstone or comprehensive assessment. *Entrance requirements:* For master's, GRE or MAT (for most programs), minimum undergraduate GPA of 3.0; baccalaureate degree in English, French, history, math or Spanish; 3 letters of

recommendation; interview. Additional exam requirements/recommendations for international students: Recommended—TOEFL (minimum score 550 paper-based; 79 iBT). *Application deadline:* For fall admission, 3/1 for domestic students; for spring admission, 11/1 for domestic students. Applications are processed on a rolling basis. Application fee: $50. Electronic applications accepted. *Expenses:* Tuition, state resident: full-time $9768; part-time $407 per credit. Tuition, nonresident: full-time $19,008; part-time $792 per credit. *Required fees:* $696; $29 per credit. One-time fee: $200 full-time; $100 part-time. Tuition and fees vary according to course load. *Financial support:* In 2017–18, 3 teaching assistantships with full tuition reimbursements (averaging $2,500 per year) were awarded; career-related internships or fieldwork, Federal Work-Study, scholarships/grants, health care benefits, and unspecified assistantships also available. Support available to part-time students. Financial award application deadline: 5/15; financial award applicants required to submit FAFSA. *Unit head:* Dr. Leslie Bogad, Chair, 401-456-8170. *Application contact:* Graduate Studies, 401-456-8700.
Website: http://www.ric.edu/educationalStudies/

Rider University, College of Education and Human Services, Teacher Certification Program, Lawrenceville, NJ 08648-3001. Offers bilingual education (Certificate); business education (Certificate); early childhood education (Certificate); elementary education (Certificate); English as a second language (Certificate); English education (Certificate); mathematics education (Certificate); science education (Certificate); secondary education (Certificate); social studies education (Certificate); world languages (Certificate), including French, German, Spanish. *Program availability:* Part-time, online learning. *Degree requirements:* For Certificate, internship, professional portfolio. *Entrance requirements:* For degree, PRAXIS, resume. Additional exam requirements/recommendations for international students: Required—TOEFL (minimum score 550 paper-based). Electronic applications accepted. *Faculty research:* Conceptual foundations for optimal development of creativity; creative theory, cognitive processes in mathematics learning, teacher collaboration.

Rowan University, Graduate School, College of Communication and Creative Arts, Writing, Composition, and Rhetoric Certificate of Graduate Study Program, Glassboro, NJ 08028-1701. Offers CGS. *Expenses:* Tuition, state resident: full-time $15,020; part-time $751 per semester hour. Tuition, nonresident: full-time $15,020; part-time $751 per semester hour. *Required fees:* $3158; $157.90 per semester hour. Tuition and fees vary according to course load, campus/location and program.

Rutgers University–New Brunswick, Graduate School of Education, Department of Learning and Teaching, Program in English Education, Piscataway, NJ 08854-8097. Offers Ed M. *Program availability:* Part-time. *Degree requirements:* For master's, comprehensive exam or paper. *Entrance requirements:* For master's, GRE General Test, minimum GPA of 3.0. Additional exam requirements/recommendations for international students: Required—TOEFL. Electronic applications accepted.

St. John Fisher College, Ralph C. Wilson Jr. School of Education, Program in Adolescence Education and Special Education, Rochester, NY 14618-3597. Offers adolescence education: biology with special education (MS Ed); adolescence education: chemistry with special education (MS Ed); adolescence education: English with special education (MS Ed); adolescence education: French with special education (MS Ed); adolescence education: math with special education (MS Ed); adolescence education: physics with special education (MS Ed); adolescence education: social studies with special education (MS Ed); adolescence education: Spanish with special education (MS Ed). *Program availability:* Part-time, evening/weekend. *Faculty:* 5 full-time (4 women), 7 part-time/adjunct (6 women). *Students:* 15 full-time (3 women), 4 part-time (all women); includes 4 minority (2 Black or African American, non-Hispanic/Latino; 1 Hispanic/Latino; 1 Two or more races, non-Hispanic/Latino). Average age 27. 34 applicants, 85% accepted, 12 enrolled. In 2017, 19 master's awarded. *Degree requirements:* For master's, field experiences, student teaching. *Entrance requirements:* For master's, LAST, 2 letters of recommendation, personal statement, current resume. Additional exam requirements/recommendations for international students: Required—TOEFL (minimum score 575 paper-based; 80 iBT). *Application deadline:* Applications are processed on a rolling basis. Application fee: $30. Electronic applications accepted. *Expenses:* Contact institution. *Financial support:* Scholarships/grants available. Financial award applicants required to submit FAFSA. *Faculty research:* Arts and humanities, urban schools, constructivist learning, at-risk students, mentoring. *Unit head:* Dr. Susan Hildenbrand, Program Director, 585-385-7297, E-mail: shildenbrand@sjfc.edu. *Application contact:* Michelle Gosier, Director of Transfer and Graduate Admissions, 585-385-8064, E-mail: mgosier@sjfc.edu.

San Francisco State University, Division of Graduate Studies, College of Education, Department of Elementary Education, Program in Language and Literacy Education, San Francisco, CA 94132-1722. Offers language and literacy education (MA); reading (Certificate); reading and literacy leadership (Credential). *Unit head:* Dr. Josephine Arce, Chair, 415-338-7636, Fax: 415-338-0567, E-mail: jarce@sfsu.edu. *Application contact:* Dr. Ali Borjian, MA Program Coordinator, 415-338-1838, Fax: 415-338-0567, E-mail: borjian@sfsu.edu.
Website: https://eed.sfsu.edu/

Simon Fraser University, Office of Graduate Studies and Postdoctoral Fellows, Faculty of Arts and Social Sciences, Department of English, Burnaby, BC V5A 1S6, Canada. Offers English (MA, PhD); teachers of English (MA). *Program availability:* Part-time. *Degree requirements:* For master's, one foreign language, thesis or alternative; for doctorate, one foreign language, thesis/dissertation, field exams. *Entrance requirements:* For master's, minimum GPA of 3.0 (on scale of 4.33) or 3.33 based on last 60 credits of undergraduate courses; for doctorate, minimum GPA of 3.5 (on scale of 4.33). Additional exam requirements/recommendations for international students: Recommended—TOEFL (minimum score 580 paper-based; 93 iBT), IELTS (minimum score 7), TWE (minimum score 5). Electronic applications accepted. *Faculty research:* Literary criticism, literature and psychoanalysis, Renaissance drama and poetry, Shakespeare, Canadian and American literature.

Slippery Rock University of Pennsylvania, Graduate Studies (Recruitment), College of Education, Department of Secondary Education/Foundations of Education, Slippery Rock, PA 16057-1383. Offers secondary education (M Ed), including English, math/ science, social studies. *Accreditation:* NCATE. *Program availability:* Part-time, evening/ weekend, 100% online. *Degree requirements:* For master's, comprehensive exam, thesis (for some programs). *Entrance requirements:* For master's, copy of teaching certification and two letters of recommendation (for some programs). Additional exam requirements/recommendations for international students: Required—TOEFL (minimum score 550 paper-based; 80 iBT). Electronic applications accepted. *Expenses:* Contact institution.

Smith College, Graduate and Special Programs, Department of Education and Child Study, Program in Secondary Education, Northampton, MA 01063. Offers secondary education (MAT), including biological sciences education, chemistry education, English education, geology education, government education, history education, mathematics education, physics education. *Program availability:* Part-time. *Students:* 5 full-time (all women), 2 part-time (0 women); includes 3 minority (1 Asian, non-Hispanic/Latino; 2 Hispanic/Latino). Average age 29. 13 applicants, 92% accepted, 5 enrolled. In 2017, 5 master's awarded. *Entrance requirements:* Additional exam requirements/ recommendations for international students: Required—TOEFL (minimum score 595 paper-based; 97 iBT), IELTS. *Application deadline:* For fall admission, 4/15 for domestic students, 1/15 priority date for international students; for spring admission, 12/1 for domestic students. Applications are processed on a rolling basis. Application fee: $60. *Expenses:* Contact institution. *Financial support:* In 2017–18, 5 students received support, including 3 fellowships with full tuition reimbursements available; scholarships/ grants and human resources employee benefit also available. Support available to part-time students. Financial award application deadline: 4/15; financial award applicants required to submit CSS PROFILE or FAFSA. *Unit head:* Rosetta Cohen, Graduate Student Advisor, 413-585-3266, E-mail: rcohen@smith.edu. *Application contact:* Ruth Morgan, Program Assistant, 413-585-3050, Fax: 413-585-3054, E-mail: gradstdy@smith.edu.
Website: http://www.smith.edu/educ/

Smith College, Graduate and Special Programs, Department of English Language and Literature, Northampton, MA 01063. Offers secondary education (MAT), including English education. *Program availability:* Part-time. *Students:* 1 (woman) full-time; minority (Asian, non-Hispanic/Latino). Average age 22. 4 applicants, 75% accepted, 1 enrolled. In 2017, 1 master's awarded. *Entrance requirements:* Additional exam requirements/recommendations for international students: Required—TOEFL (minimum score 595 paper-based; 97 iBT), IELTS. *Application deadline:* For fall admission, 4/15 for domestic students, 1/15 for international students; for spring admission, 12/1 for domestic students. Applications are processed on a rolling basis. Application fee: $60. *Expenses:* Contact institution. *Financial support:* In 2017–18, 1 student received support, including 1 fellowship with full tuition reimbursement available; scholarships/ grants also available. Support available to part-time students. Financial award application deadline: 4/15; financial award applicants required to submit CSS PROFILE or FAFSA. *Unit head:* Craig Davis, Graduate Adviser, 413-585-3327, E-mail: crdavis@smith.edu. *Application contact:* Ruth Morgan, Program Assistant, 413-585-3050, Fax: 413-585-3054, E-mail: gradstdy@smith.edu.
Website: http://www.smith.edu/english/

South Carolina State University, College of Graduate and Professional Studies, Department of Education, Orangeburg, SC 29117-0001. Offers early childhood education (MAT); education (M Ed); elementary education (M Ed, MAT); English (MAT); general science/biology (MAT); mathematics (MAT); secondary education (M Ed), including biology education, business education, counselor education, English education, home economics education, industrial education, mathematics education, science education, social studies education; special education (M Ed), including emotionally handicapped, learning disabilities, mentally handicapped. *Accreditation:* NCATE. *Program availability:* Part-time, evening/weekend. *Faculty:* 11 full-time (6 women), 4 part-time/adjunct (2 women). *Students:* 26 full-time (18 women), 22 part-time (17 women); includes 41 minority (all Black or African American, non-Hispanic/Latino), 1 international. Average age 33. 25 applicants, 100% accepted, 19 enrolled. In 2017, 6 master's awarded. *Degree requirements:* For master's, thesis optional, departmental qualifying exam. *Entrance requirements:* For master's, GRE General Test, NTE, interview, teaching certificate. *Application deadline:* For fall admission, 6/15 priority date for domestic students, 6/15 for international students; for spring admission, 11/1 for domestic and international students. Application fee: $25. Electronic applications accepted. *Expenses:* Tuition, state resident: full-time $9388; part-time $607 per credit hour. Tuition, nonresident: full-time $19,968; part-time $1194 per credit hour. *Required fees:* $766; $766 per credit hour. *Financial support:* Fellowships, career-related internships or fieldwork, Federal Work-Study, and scholarships/grants available. Financial award application deadline: 6/1. *Unit head:* Dr. Charlie Spell, Interim Chair, Department of Education, 803-536-8963, Fax: 803-516-4568, E-mail: cspell@scsu.edu. *Application contact:* Curtis Foskey, Coordinator of Graduate Studies, 803-536-8419, Fax: 803-536-8812, E-mail: cfoskey@scsu.edu.

Southeastern Louisiana University, College of Arts, Humanities and Social Sciences, Department of English, Hammond, LA 70402. Offers creative writing (MA); language and theory (MA); professional writing (MA); publishing studies (MA). *Program availability:* Part-time. *Faculty:* 10 full-time (2 women). *Students:* 11 full-time (9 women), 11 part-time (10 women); includes 5 minority (2 Black or African American, non-Hispanic/Latino; 2 Hispanic/Latino; 1 Two or more races, non-Hispanic/Latino). Average age 25. 8 applicants, 38% accepted, 3 enrolled. In 2017, 8 master's awarded. *Degree requirements:* For master's, comprehensive exam, thesis optional. *Entrance requirements:* For master's, GRE (minimum score of 290 combined verbal and quantitative). Additional exam requirements/recommendations for international students: Required—TOEFL (minimum score 500 paper-based; 61 iBT), IELTS (minimum score 5.5). *Application deadline:* For fall admission, 7/15 priority date for domestic students, 6/ 1 priority date for international students; for spring admission, 12/1 priority date for domestic students, 10/1 priority date for international students. Applications are processed on a rolling basis. Application fee: $20 ($30 for international students). Electronic applications accepted. *Expenses:* Tuition, state resident: full-time $6684. Tuition, nonresident: full-time $19,162. *Required fees:* $2088. *Financial support:* In 2017–18, 16 students received support, including 7 teaching assistantships (averaging $5,415 per year); research assistantships, institutionally sponsored loans, scholarships/ grants, and unspecified assistantships also available. Support available to part-time students. Financial award application deadline: 5/1; financial award applicants required to submit FAFSA. *Faculty research:* John Ruskin, animal studies, linguistics, film studies. *Unit head:* Dr. David Hanson, Department Head, 985-549-2100, Fax: 985-549-5021, E-mail: dhanson@southeastern.edu. *Application contact:* Amanda Harper, Graduate Admissions Analyst, 985-549-5620, Fax: 985-549-5632, E-mail: admissions@southeastern.edu.
Website: http://www.southeastern.edu/acad_research/depts/engl

Southern Illinois University Edwardsville, Graduate School, College of Arts and Sciences, Department of English Language and Literature, Program in Teaching of Writing, Edwardsville, IL 62026. Offers MA, Postbaccalaureate Certificate. *Program availability:* Part-time, evening/weekend. *Degree requirements:* For master's, thesis or alternative, final exam. *Entrance requirements:* Additional exam requirements/ recommendations for international students: Required—TOEFL (minimum score 550 paper-based, 79 iBT), IELTS (minimum score 6.5), Michigan Test of English Language Proficiency or PTE. Electronic applications accepted.

Southwestern Oklahoma State University, College of Arts and Sciences, Specialization in English, Weatherford, OK 73096-3098. Offers M Ed. M Ed distance learning degree program offered to Oklahoma residents only. *Accreditation:* NCATE. *Program availability:* Part-time. *Degree requirements:* For master's, exam. *Entrance requirements:* For master's, GRE General Test or minimum undergraduate GPA of 3.0. Additional exam requirements/recommendations for international students: Required—TOEFL.

State University of New York at Fredonia, College of Liberal Arts and Sciences, Fredonia, NY 14063-1136. Offers biology (MS); English (MA); English education 7-12 (MA); interdisciplinary studies (MA, MS); math education (MS Ed); professional writing (CAS); speech pathology (MS); MA/MS. *Program availability:* Part-time, evening/ weekend. *Students:* 73 full-time (62 women), 9 part-time (6 women); includes 7 minority

(1 Black or African American, non-Hispanic/Latino; 1 Asian, non-Hispanic/Latino; 2 Hispanic/Latino; 1 Native Hawaiian or other Pacific Islander, non-Hispanic/Latino; 2 Two or more races, non-Hispanic/Latino). Average age 24. 200 applicants, 25% accepted, 43 enrolled. In 2017, 41 master's, 1 other advanced degree awarded. *Degree requirements:* For master's, comprehensive exam (for some programs), thesis (for some programs). *Entrance requirements:* For master's, GRE. Additional exam requirements/recommendations for international students: Required—TOEFL (minimum score 79 iBT), IELTS (minimum score 6.5). *Application deadline:* Applications are processed on a rolling basis. Application fee: $75. Electronic applications accepted. *Expenses:* Tuition, state resident: full-time $8154. Tuition, nonresident: full-time $16,650. *Required fees:* $1209. *Financial support:* In 2017–18, 5 students received support, including 14 teaching assistantships with full and partial tuition reimbursements available (averaging $5,957 per year); tuition waivers (full and partial) and unspecified assistantships also available. *Faculty research:* Immunology/microbiology, applied human physiology, ecology and evolution, invertebrate biology, molecular biology, biochemistry, physiology, animal behavior, science education, vertebrate physiology, cell biology, plant biology, developmental biology, aquatic ecology, bilingual language acquisition, bilingual language acquisition and disorders, augmentative and alternate communication with ALS, World War I, Zweig, environmental literature, editing, adolescent literature, pedagogy. *Unit head:* Dr. Andy Karafa, Dean, 716-673-3173, Fax: 716-673-3338, E-mail: andy.karafa@gmail.com. *Application contact:* Wendy S. Dunst, Interim Graduate Recruitment and Admissions Associate, 716-673-3808, Fax: 716-673-3712, E-mail: wendy.dunst@fredonia.edu.
Website: http://www.fredonia.edu/clas/

State University of New York at New Paltz, Graduate and Extended Learning School, School of Education, Department of Teaching and Learning, New Paltz, NY 12561. Offers adolescence education: biology (MAT, MS Ed); adolescence education: chemistry (MAT, MS Ed); adolescence education: earth science (MAT, MS Ed); adolescence education: English (MAT, MS Ed); adolescence education: French (MAT, MS Ed); adolescence education: social studies (MAT, MS Ed); adolescence education: Spanish (MAT, MS Ed); second language education (MS Ed, AC), including second language education (MS Ed), teaching English language learners (AC). *Accreditation:* NCATE. *Program availability:* Part-time, evening/weekend. *Faculty:* 6 full-time (5 women), 10 part-time/adjunct (6 women). *Students:* 48 full-time (27 women), 54 part-time (41 women); includes 24 minority (2 Black or African American, non-Hispanic/Latino; 4 Asian, non-Hispanic/Latino; 15 Hispanic/Latino; 3 Two or more races, non-Hispanic/Latino). 33 applicants, 64% accepted, 12 enrolled. In 2017, 49 master's awarded. *Degree requirements:* For master's, comprehensive exam (for some programs), portfolio. *Entrance requirements:* For master's, minimum GPA of 3.0, New York state teaching certificate (MS Ed). Additional exam requirements/recommendations for international students: Required—TOEFL (minimum score 550 paper-based; 80 iBT), IELTS (minimum score 6.5). *Application deadline:* For fall admission, 3/1 priority date for domestic students, 3/1 for international students; for spring admission, 10/1 priority date for domestic students, 10/1 for international students. Application fee: $50. Electronic applications accepted. *Financial support:* Application deadline: 8/1. *Unit head:* Dr. Laura Dull, Chair, 845-257-2849, E-mail: dullj@newpaltz.edu. *Application contact:* Vika Shock, Director of Graduate Admissions, 845-257-3285, Fax: 845-257-3284, E-mail: gradschool@newpaltz.edu.
Website: http://www.newpaltz.edu/secondaryed/

State University of New York at Plattsburgh, School of Education, Health, and Human Services, Program in Teacher Education: Adolescence Education, Plattsburgh, NY 12901-2681. Offers adolescence education (MST); biology 7-12 (MST); chemistry 7-12 (MST); earth science 7-12 (MST); English 7-12 (MST); French 7-12 (MST); mathematics 7-12 (MST); physics 7-12 (MST); social studies 7-12 (MST); Spanish 7-12 (MST). *Accreditation:* TEAC. *Program availability:* Part-time, evening/weekend. *Entrance requirements:* For master's, minimum GPA of 2.75. Additional exam requirements/recommendations for international students: Required—TOEFL.

State University of New York College at Cortland, Graduate Studies, School of Arts and Sciences, Programs in Adolescence Education, Cortland, NY 13045. Offers biology (MAT); chemistry (MAT); English (MAT, MS Ed); mathematics (MAT); mathematics and physics (MS Ed); physics (MAT, MS Ed). *Accreditation:* NCATE. *Program availability:* Part-time, evening/weekend. *Degree requirements:* For master's, one foreign language, comprehensive exam (for some programs), thesis (for some programs). *Entrance requirements:* For master's, GRE General Test.

State University of New York College at Geneseo, Graduate Studies, School of Education, Program in Adolescence Education, Geneseo, NY 14454-1401. Offers English 7-12 (MS Ed); French 7-12 (MS Ed); social studies 7-12 (MS Ed); Spanish 7-12 (MS Ed). *Program availability:* Part-time, evening/weekend. *Faculty:* 8 full-time (6 women), 1 (woman) part-time/adjunct. *Students:* 3 full-time (2 women), 2 part-time (1 woman). Average age 27. 9 applicants, 56% accepted, 3 enrolled. In 2017, 6 master's awarded. *Degree requirements:* For master's, 2 foreign languages, comprehensive examination, thesis or research project. *Entrance requirements:* For master's, GRE, MAT, EAS, edTPA, PRAXIS, or another substantially equivalent test, proof of New York State initial certification or equivalent certification from another state. Additional exam requirements/recommendations for international students: Required—TOEFL (minimum score 525 paper-based; 71 iBT), IELTS (minimum score 6.5), PTE, iTEP. *Application deadline:* For fall admission, 4/1 priority date for domestic students; for spring admission, 11/1 priority date for domestic students; for summer admission, 4/1 priority date for domestic students. Applications are processed on a rolling basis. Application fee: $50. Electronic applications accepted. *Expenses:* Contact institution. *Financial support:* In 2017–18, 3 students received support. Fellowships, research assistantships, scholarships/grants, health care benefits, tuition waivers (full and partial), and unspecified assistantships available. Support available to part-time students. Financial award application deadline: 4/1; financial award applicants required to submit FAFSA. *Unit head:* Dr. Anjoo Sikka, Dean of School of Education, 585-245-5151, Fax: 585-245-5220, E-mail: sikka@geneseo.edu. *Application contact:* Michael R. George, Director of Graduate Admissions, 585-245-5148, Fax: 585-245-5550, E-mail: georgem@geneseo.edu.

State University of New York College at Old Westbury, School of Education, Old Westbury, NY 11568-0210. Offers biology (MAT, MS); chemistry (MAT, MS); English language arts (MAT, MS); math (MAT, MS); social studies (MAT, MS); Spanish (MAT, MS). *Program availability:* Part-time, evening/weekend. *Students:* 164 full-time (80 women), 112 part-time (52 women); includes 87 minority (14 Black or African American, non-Hispanic/Latino; 38 Asian, non-Hispanic/Latino; 35 Hispanic/Latino; 2 international). Average age 30. 34 applicants, 82% accepted, 25 enrolled. In 2017, 25 master's awarded. *Entrance requirements:* For master's, Liberal Arts and Sciences Test, undergraduate degree with at least 30 semester hours of appropriate coursework as defined by the respective discipline; minimum cumulative undergraduate GPA of 3.0; two letters of recommendation (one from an academic source); essay. Additional exam requirements/recommendations for international students: Required—TOEFL (minimum score 550 paper-based); Recommended—IELTS. Application fee: $50. *Financial support:* Applicants required to submit FAFSA. *Unit head:* Dr. Nancy Brown, Dean, School of Education, 516-876-3275, E-mail: brownn@oldwestbury.edu. *Application*

contact: Philip D'Angelo, Graduate Admissions Office, 516-876-3073, E-mail: enroll@oldwestbury.edu.

State University of New York College at Potsdam, School of Education and Professional Studies, Program in Secondary Education, Potsdam, NY 13676. Offers English education (MST); mathematics education (MST); science education (MST), including biology, chemistry, earth science, physics; social studies education (MST). *Accreditation:* NCATE. *Degree requirements:* For master's, culminating experience. *Entrance requirements:* For master's, minimum GPA of 2.75 in last 60 hours of course work (3.0 for English program). Additional exam requirements/recommendations for international students: Required—TOEFL (minimum score 550 paper-based; 80 iBT), IELTS (minimum score 6). Electronic applications accepted.

Stony Brook University, State University of New York, Graduate School, College of Arts and Sciences, Department of English, Stony Brook, NY 11794. Offers English (MA, PhD); English education (MAT). MAT offered through the School of Professional Development. *Faculty:* 20 full-time (11 women), 5 part-time/adjunct (2 women). *Students:* 45 full-time (23 women), 10 part-time (8 women); includes 10 minority (3 Asian, non-Hispanic/Latino; 5 Hispanic/Latino; 2 Two or more races, non-Hispanic/Latino), 4 international. Average age 31. 69 applicants, 38% accepted, 10 enrolled. In 2017, 9 master's, 8 doctorates awarded. Terminal master's awarded for partial completion of doctoral program. *Degree requirements:* For doctorate, thesis/dissertation. *Entrance requirements:* For master's and doctorate, GRE General Test. Additional exam requirements/recommendations for international students: Required—TOEFL. *Application deadline:* For fall admission, 1/15 for domestic students; for spring admission, 10/1 for domestic students. Application fee: $100. Electronic applications accepted. *Expenses:* Contact institution. *Financial support:* In 2017–18, 25 teaching assistantships were awarded; fellowships and research assistantships also available. *Faculty research:* Humanities, poetry, literary theory, rhetoric, American literature. *Unit head:* Dr. Celia Marshik, Chair, 631-632-7356, E-mail: celia.marshik@stonybrook.edu. *Application contact:* Theresa Spadola, Coordinator, 631-632-7373, E-mail: theresa.spadola@stonybrook.edu.
Website: http://www.stonybrook.edu/english/

Stony Brook University, State University of New York, School of Professional Development, Stony Brook, NY 11794. Offers biology (MAT); chemistry (MAT); coaching (Graduate Certificate); earth science (MAT); educational computing (Graduate Certificate); educational leadership (Advanced Certificate); English (MAT); environmental management (MPS, Graduate Certificate); French (MAT); German (MAT); higher education administration (MA, Certificate); human resource management (MS, Graduate Certificate); industrial management (Graduate Certificate); information systems management (Graduate Certificate); Italian (MAT); liberal studies (MA); mathematics (MAT); operations research (Graduate Certificate); physics (MAT); school district business leadership (Advanced Certificate); social studies (MAT); Spanish (MAT). *Program availability:* Part-time, evening/weekend, online learning. *Faculty:* 3 full-time (2 women), 101 part-time/adjunct (45 women). *Students:* 190 full-time (126 women), 974 part-time (708 women); includes 255 minority (88 Black or African American, non-Hispanic/Latino; 2 American Indian or Alaska Native, non-Hispanic/Latino; 31 Asian, non-Hispanic/Latino; 113 Hispanic/Latino; 1 Native Hawaiian or other Pacific Islander, non-Hispanic/Latino; 20 Two or more races, non-Hispanic/Latino), 6 international. Average age 33. 411 applicants, 91% accepted, 288 enrolled. In 2017, 333 master's, 180 other advanced degrees awarded. *Entrance requirements:* Additional exam requirements/recommendations for international students: Required—TOEFL (minimum score 85 iBT). *Application deadline:* For fall admission, 1/15 for domestic students, 6/1 for international students; for spring admission, 10/1 for domestic and international students. Applications are processed on a rolling basis. Application fee: $100. *Expenses:* Contact institution. *Financial support:* Fellowships, research assistantships, teaching assistantships, and career-related internships or fieldwork available. Support available to part-time students. *Unit head:* Dr. Ken Lindblom, Dean, 631-632-7049, Fax: 631-632-9046, E-mail: kenneth.lindblom@stonybrook.edu. *Application contact:* Melissa Jordan, Assistant Dean, 631-632-7751, E-mail: melissa.jordan@stonybrook.edu.
Website: http://www.stonybrook.edu/spd/

Syracuse University, School of Education, MS Program in English Education Preparation (Grades 7-12), Syracuse, NY 13244. Offers MS. *Program availability:* Part-time. *Entrance requirements:* For master's, GRE, baccalaureate degree from regionally-accredited college/university with an English major or a 30-credit major equivalent determined via transcript review, at least nine credits of writing-intensive coursework, strong teacher and/or employer recommendations, personal statement. Additional exam requirements/recommendations for international students: Required—TOEFL (minimum score 100 iBT). *Application deadline:* For fall admission, 1/15 for domestic and international students. Applications are processed on a rolling basis. Application fee: $75. Electronic applications accepted. *Financial support:* Fellowships with full tuition reimbursements, research assistantships, teaching assistantships, career-related internships or fieldwork, and scholarships/grants available. Financial award application deadline: 1/15. *Faculty research:* Educational theory, research in the field of English education, English and textual studies, composition and cultural rhetoric, teaching youth from diverse backgrounds. *Unit head:* Dr. Kelly Chandler-Olcott, Program Coordinator, 315-443-4755, E-mail: kpchandl@syr.edu. *Application contact:* Speranza Migliore, Graduate Admissions Recruiter, 315-443-2505, E-mail: gradrcrt@syr.edu.
Website: http://soe.syr.edu/academic/reading_language_arts/graduate/masters/english_ed_prep_7_12/default.aspx

Teachers College, Columbia University, Department of Arts and Humanities, New York, NY 10027. Offers applied linguistics (MA, Ed D); art and art education (Ed M, MA, Ed D, Ed DCT); arts administration (MA); bilingual and bicultural education (MA); global competence (Certificate); history and education (Ed D, PhD); music and music education (Ed DCT); philosophy and education (MA, Ed D, PhD); social studies education (Ed M, PhD); teaching English to speakers of other languages (Ed M); teaching of English and English education (Ed M, MA, Ed D, PhD), including English education (Ed M, Ed D, PhD), teaching of English (MA); teaching of social studies (MA); TESOL (MA, Ed D). *Program availability:* Part-time, evening/weekend. *Students:* 391 full-time (305 women), 418 part-time (283 women); includes 246 minority (62 Black or African American, non-Hispanic/Latino; 3 American Indian or Alaska Native, non-Hispanic/Latino; 94 Asian, non-Hispanic/Latino; 75 Hispanic/Latino; 12 Two or more races, non-Hispanic/Latino), 209 international. Average age 30. 1,053 applicants, 60% accepted, 334 enrolled. Terminal master's awarded for partial completion of doctoral program. *Financial support:* Fellowships, research assistantships, teaching assistantships, career-related internships or fieldwork, Federal Work-Study, institutionally sponsored loans, tuition waivers (full and partial), and unspecified assistantships available. Support available to part-time students. *Unit head:* Prof. William Gaudelli, Department Chair, E-mail: gaudelli@tc.columbia.edu. *Application contact:* David Estrella, Director of Admissions, 212-678-3305, Fax: 212-678-4171, E-mail: estrella@tc.columbia.edu.

Temple University, College of Education, Department of Teaching and Learning, Philadelphia, PA 19122-6096. Offers career and technical education (Ed M), including business, computing, and information technology, industrial education, marketing

education; middle grades education (Ed M), including math and language arts, math and science, science and language arts; secondary education (Ed M), including English, math, social studies; teaching English to speakers of other languages (MS Ed); urban education (Ed M). *Program availability:* Part-time, evening/weekend. *Students:* 218 full-time (144 women), 296 part-time (183 women); includes 128 minority (74 Black or African American, non-Hispanic/Latino; 18 Asian, non-Hispanic/Latino; 25 Hispanic/Latino; 11 Two or more races, non-Hispanic/Latino), 13 international. 254 applicants, 54% accepted, 102 enrolled. In 2017, 128 master's awarded. Terminal master's awarded for partial completion of doctoral program. *Degree requirements:* For master's, thesis or alternative. *Entrance requirements:* Additional exam requirements/recommendations for international students: Required—TOEFL (minimum score 550 paper-based; 79 iBT). *Application deadline:* For fall admission, 4/1 for domestic students, 12/15 for international students; for spring admission, 10/1 for domestic students, 8/1 for international students. Application fee: $60. Electronic applications accepted. *Expenses:* Contact institution. *Financial support:* Fellowships, research assistantships, and teaching assistantships available. Financial award application deadline: 1/15; financial award applicants required to submit FAFSA. *Faculty research:* Workforce development, vocational education, technical education, industrial education, professional development, literacy, classroom management, school communities, curriculum development, instruction, applied linguistics, cross linguistic influence, bilingual education, oral proficiency, multilingualism. *Unit head:* Dr. Christine Woyshner, Chairperson, 215-204-6387, E-mail: christine.woyshner@temple.edu. *Application contact:* Sarah Stapleton, Assistant Director, Academic Operations, 215-204-8220, E-mail: sarah.stapleton@temple.edu.
Website: http://education.temple.edu/tl

Texas Woman's University, Graduate School, College of Arts and Sciences, Department of English, Speech, and Foreign Languages, Denton, TX 76204. Offers English (MA, MAT); rhetoric (PhD). *Program availability:* Part-time. *Faculty:* 9 full-time (4 women). *Students:* 6 full-time (5 women), 38 part-time (30 women); includes 10 minority (4 Black or African American, non-Hispanic/Latino; 2 Asian, non-Hispanic/Latino; 2 Hispanic/Latino; 2 Two or more races, non-Hispanic/Latino), 1 international. Average age 39. 8 applicants, 63% accepted, 4 enrolled. In 2017, 7 master's, 4 doctorates awarded. *Degree requirements:* For master's, comprehensive exam, thesis (for some programs), professional paper, thesis or coursework; for doctorate, comprehensive exam, thesis/dissertation, residency for at least 2 consecutive semesters (strongly encouraged). *Entrance requirements:* For master's, GRE General Test (preferred minimum score 153 [500 old version] verbal, 138 [350 old version] quantitative), 3 letters of reference, minimum GPA of 3.0 on previous upper-division and graduate work, writing sample, statement of purpose; for doctorate, GRE General Test (preferred minimum score 153 [500 old version] verbal, 138 [350 old version] quantitative), writing sample, 3 letters of reference, interview (for graduate assistants), minimum GPA of 3.0 on previous upper-division and graduate work, statement of purpose. Additional exam requirements/recommendations for international students: Required—TOEFL (minimum score 600 paper-based; 79 iBT); Recommended—IELTS (minimum score 6.5). *Application deadline:* For fall admission, 7/1 for domestic students, 3/1 priority date for international students; for spring admission, 11/1 for domestic students, 7/1 priority date for international students; for summer admission, 4/1 for domestic students, 2/1 priority date for international students. Applications are processed on a rolling basis. Application fee: $50 ($75 for international students). Electronic applications accepted. *Expenses:* $7,520 per year full-time in-state; $16,820 per year full-time out-of-state. *Financial support:* In 2017–18, 20 students received support, including 13 teaching assistantships (averaging $23,215 per year); career-related internships or fieldwork, Federal Work-Study, institutionally sponsored loans, scholarships/grants, traineeships, health care benefits, and unspecified assistantships also available. Support available to part-time students. Financial award application deadline: 3/1; financial award applicants required to submit FAFSA. *Faculty research:* American literature, medieval literature, history of the English language, rhetoric, world literature. *Unit head:* Dr. Genevieve West, Chair, 940-898-2324, Fax: 940-898-2297, E-mail: engspfl@twu.edu. *Application contact:* Korie Hawkins, Associate Director of Admissions, Graduate Recruitment, 940-898-3188, Fax: 940-898-3081, E-mail: admissions@twu.edu.
Website: http://www.twu.edu/english-speech-foreign-languages/

Trinity Washington University, School of Education, Washington, DC 20017-1094. Offers clinical mental health counseling (MA); early childhood education (MAT); educating for change (M Ed); educational administration (MSA); elementary education (MAT); reading (M Ed); school counseling (MA); secondary education (MAT), including English, social studies; special education (MAT). *Accreditation:* NCATE. *Program availability:* Part-time, evening/weekend. *Degree requirements:* For master's, thesis (for some programs), capstone project(s). *Entrance requirements:* For master's, PRAXIS I, minimum GPA of 2.8. Additional exam requirements/recommendations for international students: Required—TOEFL (minimum score 550 paper-based). *Faculty research:* Technology, literacy, special education, organizations, inclusion models.

University at Buffalo, the State University of New York, Graduate School, Graduate School of Education, Department of Learning and Instruction, Buffalo, NY 14260. Offers biology education (Ed M, Certificate); chemistry education (Ed M, Certificate); childhood education (Ed M); childhood education with bilingual extension (Ed M); college teaching (Advanced Certificate); curriculum, instruction and the science of learning (PhD); early childhood education (Ed M); early childhood education with bilingual extension (Ed M); earth science education (Ed M, Certificate); education and technology (Ed M); educational studies (Ed M); educational technology and new literacies (Certificate); educational technology and new literacies (Advanced Certificate); elementary education (Ed D); English education (Ed M, Certificate); English education studies (Ed M); English for speakers of other languages (Ed M); foreign and second language education (PhD); French education (Ed M, Certificate); German education (Ed M, Certificate); gifted education (Certificate); Latin education (Ed M, Certificate); literacy education studies (Ed M); literacy specialist (Ed M); literacy teaching and learning (Certificate); mathematics education (Ed M, Certificate); music education (Ed M, Certificate); music education studies (Ed M); music learning theory (Advanced Certificate); online education (Advanced Certificate); physics education (Ed M, Certificate); science and the public (Ed M); social studies education (Ed M, Certificate); Spanish education (Ed M, Certificate); special education (PhD); teaching English to speakers of other languages (Ed M). *Program availability:* Part-time, evening/weekend, 100% online. *Faculty:* 26 full-time (19 women), 74 part-time/adjunct (52 women). *Students:* 172 full-time (122 women), 325 part-time (226 women); includes 44 minority (25 Black or African American, non-Hispanic/Latino; 5 American Indian or Alaska Native, non-Hispanic/Latino; 14 Asian, non-Hispanic/Latino), 57 international. Average age 33. 316 applicants, 78% accepted, 174 enrolled. In 2017, 109 master's, 34 doctorates, 15 other advanced degrees awarded. *Degree requirements:* For master's, comprehensive exam; for doctorate, thesis/dissertation, research analysis exam, research experience. *Entrance requirements:* For master's, letters of reference; for doctorate, GRE General Test or MAT, interview, writing sample, letters of recommendation. Additional exam requirements/recommendations for international students: Required—TOEFL (minimum score 600 paper-based; 96 iBT). *Application deadline:* For fall admission, 2/1 priority date for domestic and international students; for spring admission, 11/15 priority date for domestic students, 10/1 for international students. Applications are processed on a

rolling basis. Application fee: $50. Electronic applications accepted. *Financial support:* In 2017–18, 42 fellowships (averaging $5,181 per year), 44 research assistantships with tuition reimbursements (averaging $10,908 per year) were awarded; teaching assistantships, career-related internships or fieldwork, Federal Work-Study, institutionally sponsored loans, scholarships/grants, tuition waivers (full and partial), and unspecified assistantships also available. Financial award application deadline: 2/28; financial award applicants required to submit FAFSA. *Faculty research:* Science assessment, foreign language teaching and learning, early learning, new literacies, gender and education. *Total annual research expenditures:* $413,233. *Unit head:* Dr. David Bruce, Chair, 716-645-4069, Fax: 716-645-3161, E-mail: gse-info@buffalo.edu. *Application contact:* Luann Zak, Admissions Assistant, 716-645-2110, Fax: 716-645-7937, E-mail: luannzak@buffalo.edu.
Website: http://gse.buffalo.edu/lai

The University of Akron, Graduate School, College of Education, Department of Curricular and Instructional Studies, Program in Adolescent to Young Adult Education, Akron, OH 44325. Offers chemistry (MS); chemistry and physics (MS); earth science (MS); earth science and chemistry (MS); earth science and physics (MS); integrated language arts (MS); integrated mathematics (MS); integrated social studies (MS); life science (MS); life science and chemistry (MS); life science and earth science (MS); life science and physics (MS); physics (MS). *Accreditation:* NCATE. *Students:* 16 full-time (6 women), 6 part-time (3 women); includes 6 minority (2 Black or African American, non-Hispanic/Latino; 1 Asian, non-Hispanic/Latino; 3 Two or more races, non-Hispanic/Latino). Average age 30. 8 applicants, 100% accepted, 8 enrolled. In 2017, 8 master's awarded. *Degree requirements:* For master's, comprehensive exam. *Entrance requirements:* For master's, minimum GPA of 3.0. Additional exam requirements/recommendations for international students: Required—TOEFL (minimum score 79 iBT), IELTS (minimum score 6.5). *Application deadline:* For fall admission, 3/1 for domestic and international students; for spring admission, 10/1 for domestic and international students. Applications are processed on a rolling basis. Application fee: $45 ($70 for international students). Electronic applications accepted. *Unit head:* Dr. Evonn Welton, Interim Department Chair, 330-972-6742, E-mail: ewelton@uakron.edu. *Application contact:* Kelly Chaff, College Program Specialist, 330-972-7028, E-mail: klchaff@uakron.edu.
Website: http://www.uakron.edu/education/academic-programs/graduate-programs.dot

The University of Alabama in Huntsville, School of Graduate Studies, College of Arts, Humanities, and Social Sciences, Department of English, Huntsville, AL 35899. Offers education (MA); English (MA); technical writing (Certificate); TESOL (Certificate). *Program availability:* Part-time, evening/weekend. *Degree requirements:* For master's, one foreign language, comprehensive exam, thesis or alternative, oral and written exams. *Entrance requirements:* For master's and Certificate, GRE General Test, minimum GPA of 3.0. Additional exam requirements/recommendations for international students: Required—TOEFL (minimum score 500 paper-based; 80 iBT), IELTS (minimum score 6.5). Electronic applications accepted. *Faculty research:* Fiction and identity, Shakespeare, science fiction, eighteenth-century literature, technical writing.

The University of Alabama in Huntsville, School of Graduate Studies, College of Education, Huntsville, AL 35899. Offers autism spectrum disorders (M Ed, Graduate Certificate); biology (MAT); chemistry (MAT); differentiated instruction in elementary education (M Ed); English language arts (MAT); English speakers of other languages (M Ed, MAT); history (MAT); mathematics (MAT); physics (MAT); reading education (M Ed); secondary education (M Ed).

The University of Arizona, College of Humanities, Department of English, Rhetoric, Composition and the Teaching of English Program, Tucson, AZ 85721. Offers MA, PhD. *Accreditation:* NASM. *Degree requirements:* For master's, one foreign language, comprehensive exam; for doctorate, one foreign language, comprehensive exam, thesis/dissertation. *Entrance requirements:* For doctorate, GRE General Test, 3 letters of recommendation, writing sample. Additional exam requirements/recommendations for international students: Required—TOEFL (minimum score 550 paper-based; 79 iBT). Electronic applications accepted.

University of Arkansas at Pine Bluff, School of Education, Pine Bluff, AR 71601-2799. Offers elementary education (M Ed); secondary education (M Ed), including English education, mathematics education, science education, social studies education; teaching (MAT). *Accreditation:* NCATE. *Program availability:* Part-time, evening/weekend. *Degree requirements:* For master's, comprehensive exam. *Entrance requirements:* For master's, GRE, minimum GPA of 2.75, NTE or Standard Arkansas Teaching Certificate. *Faculty research:* Teacher certification, accreditation, assessment, standards, portfolio development, rehabilitation, technology.

University of Central Florida, College of Community Innovation and Education, School of Teacher Education, Program in Teacher Education, Orlando, FL 32816. Offers art education (MAT); English language (MAT); mathematics education (MAT); middle school mathematics (MAT); middle school science (MAT); science education (MAT), including biology, chemistry, physics; social science education (MAT). *Accreditation:* NCATE. *Program availability:* Part-time, evening/weekend. *Students:* 11 full-time (9 women), 28 part-time (23 women); includes 15 minority (5 Black or African American, non-Hispanic/Latino; 2 Asian, non-Hispanic/Latino; 6 Hispanic/Latino; 2 Two or more races, non-Hispanic/Latino), 2 international. Average age 29. In 2017, 6 master's awarded. *Degree requirements:* For master's, thesis or alternative. *Entrance requirements:* For master's, Florida Teacher Certification Examination/General Knowledge Test or GRE General Test. Additional exam requirements/recommendations for international students: Required—TOEFL. *Application deadline:* For spring admission, 12/1 for domestic students; for summer admission, 4/15 for domestic students. Application fee: $30. Electronic applications accepted. *Expenses:* Tuition, state resident: part-time $288.16 per credit hour. Tuition, nonresident: part-time $1073.31 per credit hour. Tuition and fees vary according to program. *Financial support:* Fellowships, research assistantships, teaching assistantships, career-related internships or fieldwork, Federal Work-Study, institutionally sponsored loans, tuition waivers (partial), and unspecified assistantships available. Financial award application deadline: 3/1; financial award applicants required to submit FAFSA. *Unit head:* Dr. Michael Hynes, Director, 407-823-2005, E-mail: mychael.hynes@ucf.edu. *Application contact:* Associate Director, Graduate Admissions, 407-823-2766, Fax: 407-823-6442, E-mail: gradadmissions@ucf.edu.
Website: http://www.graduatecatalog.ucf.edu/programs/
program.aspx?id=9727&program=Teacher%20Education%20MAT

University of Colorado Denver, College of Liberal Arts and Sciences, Department of English, Denver, CO 80217. Offers applied linguistics (MA); literature (MA); rhetoric and teaching of writing (MA). *Program availability:* Part-time, evening/weekend. *Degree requirements:* For master's, variable foreign language requirement, comprehensive exam (for some programs), thesis (for some programs), minimum of 33 credit hours (for literature program), 30 (for rhetoric and teaching of writing and applied linguistics programs). *Entrance requirements:* For master's, GRE General Test, minimum GPA of 3.0 in undergraduate courses, critical writing sample, letters of recommendation, completion of 24 semester hours in English courses (at least 16 at the upper-division level), statement of purpose. Additional exam requirements/recommendations for international students: Required—TOEFL (minimum score 537 paper-based; 75 iBT); Recommended—IELTS (minimum score 6.5). Electronic applications accepted. *Faculty research:* Literature, rhetoric, teaching of writing, applied linguistics.

English Education

University of Colorado Denver, School of Education and Human Development, Teacher Education Programs, Denver, CO 80217. Offers elementary linguistically diverse education (MA); elementary math and science education (MA); elementary math education (MA); elementary reading and writing (MA); elementary science education (MA); secondary English education (MA); secondary linguistically diverse education (MA); secondary math education (MA); secondary reading and writing (MA); secondary science education (MA); special education (MA). *Accreditation:* NCATE. *Program availability:* Part-time, evening/weekend. *Degree requirements:* For master's, comprehensive exam. *Entrance requirements:* For master's, GRE or MAT (for those with GPA below 2.75), transcripts, resume, letters of recommendation. Additional exam requirements/recommendations for international students: Required—TOEFL (minimum score 537 paper-based; 75 iBT); Recommended—IELTS (minimum score 6.5). Electronic applications accepted. *Expenses:* Contact institution. *Faculty research:* Linguistically diverse education/ESL, elementary reading and writing, elementary teacher education, secondary teacher education, special education.

University of Connecticut, Graduate School, Neag School of Education, Department of Curriculum and Instruction, Program in English Education, Storrs, CT 06269. Offers MA, PhD. *Accreditation:* NCATE. Terminal master's awarded for partial completion of doctoral program. *Degree requirements:* For master's, comprehensive exam, thesis or alternative; for doctorate, thesis/dissertation. *Entrance requirements:* For doctorate, GRE General Test. Additional exam requirements/recommendations for international students: Required—TOEFL (minimum score 550 paper-based). Electronic applications accepted.

University of Florida, Graduate School, College of Education, School of Teaching and Learning, Gainesville, FL 32611. Offers curriculum and instruction (M Ed, MAE, Ed D, PhD, Ed S); elementary education (M Ed, MAE); English education (M Ed, MAE); mathematics education (M Ed, MAE); reading education (M Ed, MAE); science education (M Ed, MAE); social studies education (M Ed, MAE). *Accreditation:* NCATE. *Program availability:* Part-time, evening/weekend, online learning. Terminal master's awarded for partial completion of doctoral program. *Degree requirements:* For master's, comprehensive exam (for some programs), thesis (for some programs); for doctorate, comprehensive exam (for some programs), thesis/dissertation (for some programs). *Entrance requirements:* For master's and doctorate, GRE General Test, minimum GPA of 3.0; for Ed S, GRE General Test. Additional exam requirements/recommendations for international students: Required—TOEFL (minimum score 550 paper-based; 80 iBT), IELTS (minimum score 6). Electronic applications accepted. *Faculty research:* STEM education; curriculum; teaching and teacher education; languages and literacy; schools, culture, and society; theories and processes of learning.

University of Georgia, College of Education, Department of Language and Literacy Education, Athens, GA 30602. Offers English education (M Ed); language and literacy education (PhD). *Accreditation:* NCATE. *Degree requirements:* For doctorate, variable foreign language requirement. *Entrance requirements:* For master's, GRE General Test or MAT; for doctorate, GRE General Test. Additional exam requirements/recommendations for international students: Required—TOEFL (minimum score 550 paper-based). Electronic applications accepted. *Faculty research:* Comprehension, critical literacy, literacy and technology, vocabulary instruction, content area reading.

University of Illinois at Springfield, Graduate Programs, College of Liberal Arts and Sciences, Department of English and Modern Languages, Springfield, IL 62703-5407. Offers English (MA); teaching English (Graduate Certificate). *Program availability:* Part-time, evening/weekend. *Faculty:* 12 full-time (11 women). *Students:* 7 full-time (5 women), 13 part-time (6 women); includes 1 minority (Asian, non-Hispanic/Latino), 1 international. Average age 33. 9 applicants, 56% accepted, 5 enrolled. In 2017, 2 master's awarded. *Degree requirements:* For master's, thesis, critical project, or creative project. *Entrance requirements:* For master's, GRE General Test, minimum overall undergraduate GPA of 3.0; analytical writing sample or sample of creative work; curriculum vitae/academic resume; three references, two of which must be academic references. Additional exam requirements/recommendations for international students: Required—TOEFL (minimum score 500 paper-based; 61 iBT). *Application deadline:* Applications are processed on a rolling basis. Application fee: $60 ($75 for international students). Electronic applications accepted. *Expenses:* Tuition, state resident: full-time $7896; part-time $329 per credit hour. Tuition, nonresident: full-time $16,200; part-time $675 per credit hour. Tuition and fees vary according to program. *Financial support:* In 2017–18, research assistantships with full tuition reimbursements (averaging $10,249 per year), teaching assistantships with full tuition reimbursements (averaging $10,303 per year) were awarded; fellowships, career-related internships or fieldwork, Federal Work-Study, scholarships/grants, health care benefits, and unspecified assistantships also available. Support available to part-time students. Financial award application deadline: 11/15; financial award applicants required to submit FAFSA. *Unit head:* Dr. Lan Dong, Program Administrator, 217-206-6779, Fax: 217-206-6217, E-mail: ldong4@uis.edu.

University of Indianapolis, Graduate Programs, School of Education, Indianapolis, IN 46227-3697. Offers art education (MAT); biology (MAT); chemistry (MAT); curriculum and instruction (MA); earth sciences (MAT); education (MA, MAT); educational leadership (MA); elementary education (MA); English (MAT); French (MAT); math (MAT); physical education (MAT); physics (MAT); secondary education (MA), including art education, education, English education, social studies education; social studies (MAT); Spanish (MAT). *Accreditation:* NCATE. *Program availability:* Part-time, evening/weekend. *Entrance requirements:* For master's, GRE Subject Test, PRAXIS I, minimum GPA of 2.5, 3 letters of recommendation, interview. Additional exam requirements/recommendations for international students: Required—TOEFL (minimum score 550 paper-based). *Faculty research:* Assessment of teacher education, perceptions of prospective teachers by parents.

The University of Iowa, Graduate College, College of Education, Department of Teaching and Learning, Program in Education, Iowa City, IA 52242-1316. Offers art education (MA); developmental reading (MA); elementary education (MA); English education (MA, MAT); foreign and second language education (MAT); foreign language education (MA); foreign language/ESL education (PhD); language, literacy and culture (PhD); mathematics education (MA, MAT, PhD); music education (MM, PhD); science education (MA); secondary education (MA); social studies (MA, PhD). *Degree requirements:* For master's, thesis optional, exam; for doctorate, comprehensive exam, thesis/dissertation. *Entrance requirements:* For master's and doctorate, GRE General Test, minimum GPA of 3.0. Additional exam requirements/recommendations for international students: Required—TOEFL (minimum score 550 paper-based; 81 iBT). Electronic applications accepted.

University of Manitoba, Faculty of Graduate Studies, Faculty of Education, Department of Curriculum, Teaching and Learning, Winnipeg, MB R3T 2N2, Canada. Offers language and literacy (M Ed); second language education (M Ed); studies in curriculum, teaching and learning (M Ed). *Degree requirements:* For master's, thesis or alternative.

University of Maryland, Baltimore County, The Graduate School, College of Arts, Humanities and Social Sciences, Department of Education, Program in Teaching, Baltimore, MD 21250. Offers early childhood education (MAT); elementary education (MAT); teaching (MAT), including art, biology, chemistry, choral music, classical foreign language, dance, earth/space science, English, instrumental music, mathematics, modern foreign language, physical science, physics, social studies, theatre. *Program availability:* Part-time, evening/weekend. *Faculty:* 24 full-time (18 women), 25 part-time/adjunct (19 women). *Students:* 41 full-time (34 women), 27 part-time (18 women); includes 26 minority (6 Black or African American, non-Hispanic/Latino; 9 Asian, non-Hispanic/Latino; 7 Hispanic/Latino; 1 Native Hawaiian or other Pacific Islander, non-Hispanic/Latino; 3 Two or more races, non-Hispanic/Latino), 2 international. Average age 30. 54 applicants, 83% accepted, 35 enrolled. In 2017, 50 master's awarded. *Degree requirements:* For master's, comprehensive exam (for some programs), thesis (for some programs). *Entrance requirements:* For master's, PRAXIS Core Examination or GRE (minimum score of 1000), minimum GPA of 3.0. Additional exam requirements/recommendations for international students: Required—TOEFL. *Application deadline:* For fall admission, 6/1 for domestic and international students; for spring admission, 11/1 for domestic and international students. Applications are processed on a rolling basis. Application fee: $50. Electronic applications accepted. *Expenses: Required fees:* $132. *Financial support:* In 2017–18, 8 students received support, including teaching assistantships with tuition reimbursements available (averaging $12,000 per year); career-related internships or fieldwork, Federal Work-Study, scholarships/grants, tuition waivers, and unspecified assistantships also available. Financial award application deadline: 3/15. *Faculty research:* STEM teacher education, culturally sensitive pedagogy, ESOL/bilingual education, early childhood education, language, literacy and culture. *Total annual research expenditures:* $100,000. *Unit head:* Dr. Susan M. Blunck, Graduate Program Director, 410-455-2869, Fax: 410-455-3986, E-mail: blunck@umbc.edu. *Application contact:* Cheryl Johnson, MAT Program Specialist, 410-455-3388, E-mail: blackwel@umbc.edu.
Website: http://www.umbc.edu/education/

University of Michigan, Rackham Graduate School, Joint PhD Program in English and Education, Ann Arbor, MI 48109. Offers PhD. *Accreditation:* TEAC. *Faculty:* 12 full-time (8 women). *Students:* 25 full-time (19 women); includes 4 minority (2 Asian, non-Hispanic/Latino; 2 Hispanic/Latino). Average age 35. 56 applicants, 14% accepted, 3 enrolled. In 2017, 3 doctorates awarded. *Degree requirements:* For doctorate, one foreign language, comprehensive exam, thesis/dissertation, 3 preliminary exams, oral defense of dissertation. *Entrance requirements:* For doctorate, GRE General Test, master's degree, teaching experience. Additional exam requirements/recommendations for international students: Required—TOEFL. *Application deadline:* For fall admission, 12/30 for domestic and international students. Application fee: $75 ($90 for international students). Electronic applications accepted. *Expenses:* Tuition, state resident: full-time $22,368; part-time $1201 per credit hour. Tuition, nonresident: full-time $45,156; part-time $2467 per credit hour. *Required fees:* $376 per term. Tuition and fees vary according to course load, degree level and program. *Financial support:* In 2017–18, 24 students received support, including 10 fellowships with full tuition reimbursements available, 6 research assistantships with full tuition reimbursements available, 30 teaching assistantships with full tuition reimbursements available; institutionally sponsored loans, scholarships/grants, health care benefits, and tuition waivers (full) also available. Financial award application deadline: 4/15. *Faculty research:* Literacy, teacher education, discourse analysis, rhetoric and composition studies. *Unit head:* Dr. Anne Ruggles Gere, Chair, 734-763-6643, Fax: 734-936-1606, E-mail: argere@umich.edu. *Application contact:* Jeanie Mahoney Laubenthal, Graduate Coordinator, 734-763-6643, Fax: 734-936-1606, E-mail: laubenth@umich.edu.
Website: https://jpee.lsa.umich.edu/

University of Minnesota, Twin Cities Campus, Graduate School, College of Education and Human Development, Department of Curriculum and Instruction, Program in Teaching, Minneapolis, MN 55455-0213. Offers teaching (M Ed), including arts in education, elementary education, English education, mathematics, science, second language education, social studies. *Students:* 251 full-time (180 women), 136 part-time (82 women); includes 68 minority (16 Black or African American, non-Hispanic/Latino; 15 Asian, non-Hispanic/Latino; 17 Hispanic/Latino; 20 Two or more races, non-Hispanic/Latino), 9 international. Average age 28. 341 applicants, 72% accepted, 229 enrolled. In 2017, 263 master's awarded. Application fee: $75 ($95 for international students). *Unit head:* Dr. Cynthia Lewis, Chair, 612-625-6313, Fax: 612-624-8277, E-mail: lewis@umn.edu. *Application contact:* Dr. Kendall King, Director of Graduate Studies, 612-625-3692, E-mail: roehr013@umn.edu.
Website: http://www.cehd.umn.edu/ci/

University of Missouri, Office of Research and Graduate Studies, College of Education, Department of Learning, Teaching and Curriculum, Columbia, MO 65211. Offers agricultural education (M Ed, PhD, Ed S); art education (M Ed, PhD, Ed S); business and office education (M Ed, PhD, Ed S); early childhood education (M Ed, PhD, Ed S); elementary education (M Ed, PhD, Ed S); English education (M Ed, PhD, Ed S); foreign language education (M Ed, PhD, Ed S); health education and promotion (M Ed, PhD); learning and instruction (M Ed); marketing education (M Ed, PhD, Ed S); mathematics education (M Ed, PhD, Ed S); music education (M Ed, PhD, Ed S); reading education (M Ed, PhD, Ed S); science education (M Ed, PhD, Ed S); social studies education (M Ed, PhD, Ed S); vocational education (M Ed, PhD, Ed S). *Program availability:* Part-time. Terminal master's awarded for partial completion of doctoral program. *Degree requirements:* For doctorate, thesis/dissertation. *Entrance requirements:* For master's and Ed S, GRE General Test or MAT, minimum GPA of 3.0; for doctorate, GRE General Test, minimum GPA of 3.0. Additional exam requirements/recommendations for international students: Required—TOEFL (minimum score 600 paper-based; 100 iBT). Electronic applications accepted.

University of Montana, Graduate School, College of Humanities and Sciences, Department of English, Program in Teaching, Missoula, MT 59812. Offers MA. *Entrance requirements:* For master's, GRE General Test, sample of written work.

University of New Mexico, Graduate Studies, College of Education, Program in Language, Literacy and Sociocultural Studies, Albuquerque, NM 87131. Offers American Indian education (MA); bilingual education (MA, PhD); educational linguistics (PhD); educational thought and sociocultural studies (MA, PhD); literacy/language arts (MA, PhD); social studies (MA); TESOL (MA, PhD). *Faculty:* 16 full-time (10 women), 4 part-time/adjunct (all women). *Students:* 56 full-time (34 women), 129 part-time (97 women); includes 93 minority (7 Black or African American, non-Hispanic/Latino; 15 American Indian or Alaska Native, non-Hispanic/Latino; 9 Asian, non-Hispanic/Latino; 56 Hispanic/Latino; 6 Two or more races, non-Hispanic/Latino), 44 international. Average age 40. 61 applicants, 38% accepted, 23 enrolled. In 2017, 36 master's, 4 doctorates awarded. *Degree requirements:* For master's, comprehensive exam, thesis optional; for doctorate, comprehensive exam, thesis/dissertation, research skills. *Entrance requirements:* For master's, letter of intent, 3 letters of recommendation, resume, BA/BS, department demographic form, transcripts; for doctorate, writing sample, letter of intent, 3 letters of recommendation, resume, BA/BS, MA, department demographic form, transcripts. Additional exam requirements/recommendations for international students: Required—TOEFL. *Application deadline:* For fall admission, 12/1 for domestic and international students; for spring admission, 9/15 for domestic and international students. Application fee: $50. Electronic applications accepted. *Financial support:* Fellowships, research assistantships, teaching assistantships, career-related internships or fieldwork, institutionally sponsored loans, scholarships/grants, and

unspecified assistantships available. Support available to part-time students. Financial award application deadline: 3/1; financial award applicants required to submit FAFSA. *Faculty research:* School reform, professional development, history of education, Native American education, politics of education, feminism and issues of sexual identity, critical race theory, bilingualism, literacy reading, adolescent literature, second language acquisition, critical theory and schooling, indigenous languages. *Unit head:* Dr. Lois M. Meyer, Chair, 505-277-7244, Fax: 505-277-8362, E-mail: lsmeyer@unm.edu. *Application contact:* Debra Schaffer, Administrative Assistant, 505-277-0437, Fax: 505-277-8362, E-mail: schaffer@unm.edu.
Website: http://coe.unm.edu/departments-programs/llss/index.html

The University of North Carolina at Chapel Hill, Graduate School, School of Education, Program in Secondary Education, Chapel Hill, NC 27599. Offers English (Grades 9-12) (MAT); English as a second language (MAT); French (Grades K-12) (MAT); German (Grades K-12) (MAT); Japanese (Grades K-12) (MAT); Latin (Grades 9-12) (MAT); mathematics (Grades 9-12) (MAT); music (Grades K-12) (MAT); science (Grades 9-12) (MAT); social studies (Grades 9-12) (MAT); Spanish (Grades K-12) (MAT). *Accreditation:* NCATE. *Degree requirements:* For master's, comprehensive exam. *Entrance requirements:* For master's, GRE General Test, minimum GPA of 3.0 during last 2 years of undergraduate course work. Additional exam requirements/recommendations for international students: Required—TOEFL (minimum score 550 paper-based). Electronic applications accepted.

The University of North Carolina at Greensboro, Graduate School, College of Arts and Sciences, Department of English, Program in English, Greensboro, NC 27412-5001. Offers American literature (PhD); English (M Ed, MA); English literature (PhD); rhetoric and composition (PhD). *Degree requirements:* For master's, comprehensive exam, thesis or alternative; for doctorate, variable foreign language requirement, thesis/dissertation, preliminary exam. *Entrance requirements:* For master's, GRE General Test, GRE Subject Test, minimum GPA of 3.0; for doctorate, GRE General Test, GRE Subject Test, critical writing sample, minimum GPA of 3.0. Additional exam requirements/recommendations for international students: Required—TOEFL. Electronic applications accepted.

The University of North Carolina at Pembroke, The Graduate School, Department of English, Theatre and Foreign Languages, Pembroke, NC 28372-1510. Offers English education (MA, MAT). *Program availability:* Part-time, evening/weekend. *Degree requirements:* For master's, comprehensive exam, thesis optional. *Entrance requirements:* For master's, GRE, MAT, or NTE, minimum GPA of 3.0 in major or 2.5 overall. Additional exam requirements/recommendations for international students: Required—TOEFL. *Application deadline:* For fall admission, 7/15 priority date for domestic students, 7/15 for international students; for spring admission, 12/1 priority date for domestic students, 12/1 for international students. Applications are processed on a rolling basis. Application fee: $45 ($60 for international students). *Financial support:* Application deadline: 4/15; applicants required to submit FAFSA. *Unit head:* Dr. Roger A. Ladd, Program Director, 910-521-6624, Fax: 910-521-6646, E-mail: roger.ladd@uncp.edu.
Website: http://www.uncp.edu/etfl/

University of Northern Colorado, Graduate School, College of Education and Behavioral Sciences, School of Teacher Education, Greeley, CO 80639. Offers curriculum studies (MAT); educational studies (Ed D); elementary education (MAT); English education (MAT); literacy (MA); multilingual education (MA), including TESOL, world languages; teaching diverse learners (MA). *Accreditation:* NCATE. *Program availability:* Part-time, evening/weekend. *Degree requirements:* For master's, comprehensive exam, thesis or alternative; for doctorate, comprehensive exam, thesis/dissertation. *Entrance requirements:* For master's and doctorate, GRE General Test, 3 letters of recommendation. Electronic applications accepted.

University of Northern Iowa, Graduate College, College of Humanities, Arts and Sciences, Department of Languages and Literatures, MA Program in Teaching English in Secondary Schools, Cedar Falls, IA 50614. Offers MA.

University of North Georgia, Master of Arts in Teaching Program, Dahlonega, GA 30597. Offers physical education (MAT); secondary education - English (MAT); secondary education - history (MAT); secondary education - mathematics (MAT); secondary education - middle grades (MAT). *Students:* 27 part-time (20 women). Average age 29. 12 applicants, 75% accepted, 7 enrolled. In 2017, 15 master's awarded. *Degree requirements:* For master's, internship, capstone. *Entrance requirements:* For master's, GRE or MAT, GACE I and II, GA pre-service application, lawful presence verification, official transcripts, GA Educator Ethics Program entry assessment. Additional exam requirements/recommendations for international students: Required—TOEFL (minimum score 550 paper-based; 79 iBT), IELTS (minimum score 6.5). *Application deadline:* For summer admission, 2/1 for domestic students. Application fee: $40. Electronic applications accepted. *Expenses:* Contact institution. *Financial support:* Application deadline: 3/17; applicants required to submit FAFSA. *Unit head:* Dr. Susan Brandenburg-Ayres, Dean, 706-864-1998, E-mail: susan.ayres@ung.edu. *Application contact:* Melinda Maxwell, Director of Graduate Admissions, 706-867-2077, E-mail: melinda.maxwell@ung.edu.
Website: https://ung.edu/teacher-education/graduate/master-of-arts-teaching.php

University of Oklahoma, Jeannine Rainbolt College of Education, Department of Instructional Leadership and Academic Curriculum, Norman, OK 73019. Offers instructional leadership and academic curriculum (M Ed, PhD), including biomedical education (PhD), early childhood education, elementary education, English education, instructional leadership, mathematics education, reading education, science education, social studies education, world languages education (M Ed); reading specialist (M Ed). *Accreditation:* NCATE. *Program availability:* Part-time. *Faculty:* 19 full-time (15 women), 1 (woman) part-time/adjunct. *Students:* 37 full-time (28 women), 121 part-time (98 women); includes 32 minority (7 Black or African American, non-Hispanic/Latino; 4 American Indian or Alaska Native, non-Hispanic/Latino; 5 Asian, non-Hispanic/Latino; 6 Hispanic/Latino; 1 Native Hawaiian or other Pacific Islander, non-Hispanic/Latino; 9 Two or more races, non-Hispanic/Latino), 12 international. Average age 35. 39 applicants, 77% accepted, 22 enrolled. In 2017, 49 master's, 12 doctorates awarded. Terminal master's awarded for partial completion of doctoral program. *Degree requirements:* For master's, comprehensive exam (for some programs), thesis (for some programs); for doctorate, comprehensive exam (for some programs), thesis/dissertation. *Entrance requirements:* For doctorate, GRE. Additional exam requirements/recommendations for international students: Required—TOEFL (minimum score 79 iBT) or IELTS (minimum score 6.5). Application fee: $50 ($100 for international students). Electronic applications accepted. *Expenses:* Tuition, state resident: full-time $5119; part-time $213.30 per credit hour. Tuition, nonresident: full-time $19,778; part-time $824.10 per credit hour. *Required fees:* $3458; $133.55 per credit hour. $126.50 per semester. *Financial support:* In 2017–18, 90 students received support, including 8 research assistantships (averaging $11,248 per year), 6 teaching assistantships (averaging $12,188 per year); fellowships, scholarships/grants, and unspecified assistantships also available. Financial award application deadline: 6/1; financial award applicants required to submit FAFSA. *Faculty research:* Teacher preparation; instruction; curriculum; learning; constructivist theory. *Total annual research expenditures:* $707,690. *Unit head:* Dr. Stacy Reeder, Chair, 405-325-1498, Fax: 405-325-4061, E-mail: reeder@ou.edu.

Application contact: Anna Steele, Graduate Programs Officer, 405-325-4525, E-mail: anna.steele@ou.edu.
Website: http://www.ou.edu/education/ilac

University of Pennsylvania, Graduate School of Education, Division of Literacy, Culture, and International Education, Program in Reading/Writing/Literacy, Philadelphia, PA 19104. Offers MS Ed, Ed D, PhD. *Program availability:* Part-time. *Students:* Average age 32. 101 applicants, 53% accepted, 30 enrolled. In 2017, 15 master's, 7 doctorates awarded. *Financial support:* In 2017–18, 26 students received support.

University of Phoenix–Online Campus, College of Education, Phoenix, AZ 85034-7209. Offers administration and supervision (MAEd, Certificate); adult education and training (MAEd); curriculum and instruction (MAEd), including computer education, curriculum and instruction, English as a second language, language arts, mathematics, reading; early childhood education (MAEd); educational studies (MAEd); elementary teacher education (MAEd), including early childhood, elementary teacher education, high school middle level, middle level; principal licensure (Certificate); secondary teacher education (MAEd); special education (MAEd, Certificate); teacher education (MAEd), including middle level generalist; teacher education middle level mathematics (MAEd), including middle level mathematics; teacher education middle level science (MAEd), including middle level science; teacher education secondary mathematics (MAEd); teacher education secondary science (MAEd); teacher leadership (MAEd); teachers of English learners (Certificate); transition to teaching (Certificate), including elementary education, secondary education. *Program availability:* Evening/weekend, online learning. *Entrance requirements:* Additional exam requirements/recommendations for international students: Required—TOEFL, TOEIC (Test of English as an International Communication), Berlitz Online English Proficiency Exam, PTE, or IELTS. Electronic applications accepted. *Expenses:* Contact institution.

University of Pittsburgh, School of Education, Department of Instruction and Learning, Program in Secondary Education, Pittsburgh, PA 15260. Offers English and communications education (M Ed, MAT); foreign language education (M Ed, MAT); language, literacy and culture education (Ed D, PhD); mathematics education (M Ed, MAT, Ed D, PhD); science education (M Ed, MAT, Ed D, PhD); secondary education (PhD); social studies education (M Ed, MAT); STEM education (Ed D). *Program availability:* Part-time, evening/weekend. *Degree requirements:* For master's, thesis; for doctorate, thesis/dissertation. *Entrance requirements:* For master's, PRAXIS I; for doctorate, GRE General Test. Additional exam requirements/recommendations for international students: Required—TOEFL. Electronic applications accepted.

University of Puerto Rico–Mayagüez, Graduate Studies, College of Arts and Sciences, Department of English, Mayagüez, PR 00681-9000. Offers English education (MA). *Program availability:* Part-time. *Degree requirements:* For master's, one foreign language, comprehensive exam, thesis. *Entrance requirements:* For master's, minimum GPA of 3.0; course work in linguistics or language, American literature, British literature, and structure/grammar or syntax. Additional exam requirements/recommendations for international students: Required—TOEFL (minimum score 550 paper-based; 79 iBT). Electronic applications accepted. *Faculty research:* Multiliteracies and multimodality theorizing and practice, second language writing, Afro-Puerto Rican studies, modern poetry, Puerto Rican culture and folklore.

University of St. Francis, College of Education, Joliet, IL 60435-6169. Offers educational leadership (MS, Ed D); elementary education (M Ed); reading (MS); secondary education (M Ed), including English education, math education, science education, social studies education, visual arts education; special education (M Ed); teaching and learning (MS); TESOL (Certificate). *Accreditation:* NCATE. *Program availability:* Part-time, evening/weekend, 100% online, blended/hybrid learning. *Faculty:* 11 full-time (8 women), 52 part-time/adjunct (36 women). *Students:* 39 full-time (32 women), 411 part-time (318 women); includes 106 minority (57 Black or African American, non-Hispanic/Latino; 8 Asian, non-Hispanic/Latino; 37 Hispanic/Latino; 4 Two or more races, non-Hispanic/Latino), 4 international. Average age 37. 277 applicants, 55% accepted, 137 enrolled. In 2017, 199 master's, 28 doctorates awarded. *Degree requirements:* For master's, comprehensive exam; for doctorate, thesis/dissertation. *Entrance requirements:* Additional exam requirements/recommendations for international students: Required—TOEFL (minimum score 550 paper-based; 79 iBT), IELTS (minimum score 6). *Application deadline:* Applications are processed on a rolling basis. Application fee: $30. Electronic applications accepted. Application fee is waived when completed online. *Expenses:* $365 to $748 per credit hour. *Financial support:* In 2017–18, 40 students received support. Scholarships/grants and unspecified assistantships available. Support available to part-time students. Financial award applicants required to submit FAFSA. *Unit head:* Dr. John Gambro, Dean, 815-740-3829, Fax: 815-740-2264, E-mail: jgambro@stfrancis.edu. *Application contact:* Sandra Sloka, Director of Admissions for Graduate and Degree Completion Programs, 800-735-7500, Fax: 815-740-3431, E-mail: ssloka@stfrancis.edu.
Website: http://www.stfrancis.edu/academics/college-of-education/

University of South Carolina, The Graduate School, College of Arts and Sciences, Department of English Language and Literature, Columbia, SC 29208. Offers creative writing (MFA); English (MA, PhD); English education (MAT); MLIS/MA. MAT offered in cooperation with the College of Education. *Program availability:* Part-time. *Degree requirements:* For master's, one foreign language, comprehensive exam, thesis; for doctorate, 2 foreign languages, comprehensive exam, thesis/dissertation. *Entrance requirements:* For master's, GRE General Test (MFA), GRE Subject Test (MA, MAT), sample of written work; for doctorate, GRE General Test, GRE Subject Test, sample of written work. Additional exam requirements/recommendations for international students: Required—TOEFL. Electronic applications accepted. *Faculty research:* American literature, British literature, composition and rhetoric, linguistics, speech communication.

University of South Carolina, The Graduate School, College of Education, Department of Instruction and Teacher Education, Program in Secondary Education, Columbia, SC 29208. Offers art education (IMA, MAT); business education (IMA, MAT); English (MAT); foreign language (MAT); health education (MAT); mathematics (MAT); science (IMA, MAT); secondary (Ed D); secondary education (MT, PhD); social studies (MAT); theatre and speech (MAT). IMA and MT offered jointly with the subject areas. *Accreditation:* NCATE. *Degree requirements:* For master's, comprehensive exam, thesis (for some programs), foreign language (MA); for doctorate, one foreign language, comprehensive exam, thesis/dissertation. *Entrance requirements:* For master's, GRE General Test or MAT, teaching certificate (IMA, M Ed), interview; for doctorate, GRE General Test or MAT, interview. *Faculty research:* Middle school programs, professional development, school collaboration.

University of Southern Mississippi, College of Arts and Letters, Department of English, Hattiesburg, MS 39406-0001. Offers creative writing (MA, PhD); English education (MA); literature (MA, PhD). *Students:* 16 full-time (12 women), 2 part-time (both women). 48 applicants, 65% accepted, 18 enrolled. In 2017, 73 master's, 16 doctorates awarded. *Degree requirements:* For master's, one foreign language, comprehensive exam, thesis; for doctorate, 2 foreign languages, comprehensive exam, thesis/dissertation. *Entrance requirements:* For master's, GRE General Test, minimum GPA of 3.0 in field of study, 2.75 in last 2 years; for doctorate, GRE General Test, minimum GPA of 3.5. Additional exam requirements/recommendations for international

students: Required—TOEFL, IELTS. *Application deadline:* For fall admission, 3/15 priority date for domestic students, 3/15 for international students. Application fee: $60. Electronic applications accepted. *Expenses:* Tuition, state resident: full-time $3830. *Financial support:* Fellowships, research assistantships with full tuition reimbursements, teaching assistantships with full tuition reimbursements, Federal Work-Study, institutionally sponsored loans, scholarships/grants, and unspecified assistantships available. Financial award application deadline: 3/15; financial award applicants required to submit FAFSA. *Faculty research:* English and American literature, critical theory and cultural studies, creative writing. *Unit head:* Dr. Luis Iglesias, Chair, 601-266-4060, Fax: 601-266-5757, E-mail: luis.iglesias@usm.edu. *Application contact:* Dr. Alexandra Valint, Director, Graduate Studies, 601-266-4070.
Website: https://www.usm.edu/english

University of South Florida, St. Petersburg, College of Education, St. Petersburg, FL 33701. Offers educational leadership development (M Ed); elementary education (MA), including math/science; English education (MA); middle grades STEM education (MS); reading education (MA). *Program availability:* Part-time. *Degree requirements:* For master's, comprehensive exam, practicum, internship, comprehensive portfolio. *Entrance requirements:* For master's, State of Florida General Knowledge Test (GKT), Florida Teaching Certificate (for non-initial certification programs), letters of recommendation. Additional exam requirements/recommendations for international students: Required—TOEFL (minimum score 550 paper-based; 79 iBT); Recommended—IELTS. Electronic applications accepted.

University of South Florida Sarasota-Manatee, College of Liberal Arts and Social Sciences, Sarasota, FL 34243. Offers criminal justice (MA); education (MA); educational leadership (M Ed), including curriculum leadership, K-12 public school leadership, non-public/charter school leadership; elementary education (MAT); English education (MA); social work (MSW). *Program availability:* Part-time, 100% online, blended/hybrid learning. *Faculty:* 15 full-time (12 women), 8 part-time/adjunct (6 women). *Students:* 11 full-time (10 women), 43 part-time (37 women); includes 17 minority (7 Black or African American, non-Hispanic/Latino; 2 Asian, non-Hispanic/Latino; 8 Hispanic/Latino), 1 international. Average age 35. 62 applicants, 27% accepted, 14 enrolled. In 2017, 32 master's awarded. *Degree requirements:* For master's, comprehensive exam (for some programs). *Entrance requirements:* For master's, GRE. Additional exam requirements/recommendations for international students: Required—TOEFL (minimum score 550 paper-based; 79 iBT), IELTS (minimum score 6.5). *Application deadline:* For fall admission, 3/1 priority date for domestic students, 3/1 for international students; for spring admission, 10/1 priority date for domestic students, 10/1 for international students. Applications are processed on a rolling basis. Application fee: $30. Electronic applications accepted. *Expenses:* Tuition, state resident: full-time $8350; part-time $418 per credit hour. Tuition, nonresident: full-time $19,047; part-time $863 per credit hour. *Required fees:* $1689. Tuition and fees vary according to degree level and program. *Financial support:* In 2017–18, 1 student received support. Career-related internships or fieldwork, institutionally sponsored loans, scholarships/grants, health care benefits, and unspecified assistantships available. Support available to part-time students. Financial award application deadline: 3/1; financial award applicants required to submit FAFSA. *Faculty research:* Educational leadership, secondary education, elementary education, criminal justice, social work. *Total annual research expenditures:* $72,000. *Unit head:* Dr. Jane Rose, Dean, 941-359-4469, Fax: 941-359-4778, E-mail: jane.rose@sar.usf.edu. *Application contact:* Brandon Avery, Assistant Director, Admissions, 941-359-4331, E-mail: bavery@sar.usf.edu.

The University of Tennessee, Graduate School, College of Education, Health and Human Sciences, Program in Education, Knoxville, TN 37996. Offers art education (MS); counseling education (PhD); cultural studies in education (PhD); curriculum (MS, Ed S); curriculum, educational research and evaluation (Ed D, PhD); early childhood education (PhD); early childhood special education (PhD); education of deaf and hard of hearing (MS); educational administration and policy studies (Ed D, PhD); educational administration and supervision (Ed S); educational psychology (Ed D, PhD); elementary education (MS, Ed S); elementary teaching (MS); English education (MS, Ed S); exercise science (PhD); foreign language/ESL education (MS, Ed S); instructional technology (MS, Ed D, PhD, Ed S); literacy, language and ESL education (PhD); literacy, language education, and ESL education (Ed D); mathematics education (MS, Ed S); modified and comprehensive special education (MS); reading education (MS, Ed S); school counseling (Ed S); school psychology (PhD, Ed S); science education (MS, Ed S); secondary teaching (MS); social foundations (MS); social science education (MS, Ed S); socio-cultural foundations of sports and education (PhD); special education (Ed S); teacher education (Ed D, PhD). *Accreditation:* NCATE. *Program availability:* Part-time, evening/weekend. *Degree requirements:* For master's and Ed S, thesis optional; for doctorate, variable foreign language requirement, thesis/dissertation. *Entrance requirements:* For master's, minimum GPA of 2.7; for doctorate and Ed S, GRE General Test, minimum GPA of 2.7. Additional exam requirements/recommendations for international students: Required—TOEFL. Electronic applications accepted.

The University of Texas at El Paso, Graduate School, College of Liberal Arts, Department of English, El Paso, TX 79968-0001. Offers bilingual professional writing (Certificate); English and American literature (MA); rhetoric and composition (PhD); rhetoric and writing studies (MA); teaching English (MAT). *Program availability:* Part-time, evening/weekend. *Degree requirements:* For master's, thesis optional. *Entrance requirements:* For master's, GRE General Test, minimum GPA of 3.0. Additional exam requirements/recommendations for international students: Required—TOEFL. Electronic applications accepted. *Faculty research:* Literature, creative writing, literary theory.

University of the District of Columbia, College of Arts and Sciences, Program in Teaching, Washington, DC 20008-1175. Offers elementary education (MAT); middle school mathematics (MAT); secondary English language arts (MAT); secondary social studies (MAT).

University of the Sacred Heart, Graduate Programs, Department of Education, San Juan, PR 00914-0383. Offers early childhood education (M Ed); information technology and multimedia (Certificate); instruction systems and education technology (M Ed), including English, information technology and multimedia, instructional design, mathematics, Spanish. *Program availability:* Part-time, evening/weekend. *Degree requirements:* For master's, thesis. *Entrance requirements:* For master's, EXADEP, minimum undergraduate GPA of 2.75, interview.

The University of Toledo, College of Graduate Studies, Judith Herb College of Education, Department of Curriculum and Instruction, Toledo, OH 43606-3390. Offers art education (ME); career and technical education (ME, Ed S); curriculum and instruction (ME, PhD, Ed S); early childhood education (Ed S); education and anthropology (MAE); education and biology (MES); education and chemistry (MES); education and classics (MAE); education and economics (MAE); education and English (MAE); education and French (MAE); education and geology (MES); education and German (MAE); education and history (MAE); education and mathematics (MAE, MES); education and physics (MES); education and political science (MAE); education and sociology (MAE); education and Spanish (MAE); educational media (PhD); educational technology (ME); educational technology: virtual educator (Certificate); elementary

education (PhD); English as a second language (MAE); gifted and talented education (PhD); middle childhood education (ME); secondary education (ME, PhD); special education (PhD). *Accreditation:* NCATE. *Program availability:* Part-time, evening/weekend. *Degree requirements:* For master's, comprehensive exam, thesis or alternative; for doctorate, comprehensive exam, thesis/dissertation; for other advanced degree, thesis optional. *Entrance requirements:* For master's, doctorate, and other advanced degree, minimum cumulative GPA of 2.7 for all previous academic work, letters of recommendation. Additional exam requirements/recommendations for international students: Required—TOEFL (minimum score 550 paper-based; 80 iBT). Electronic applications accepted.

The University of Tulsa, Graduate School, Kendall College of Arts and Sciences, School of Education, Tulsa, OK 74104-3189. Offers mathematics and science education (MSMSE); teaching arts (MTA), including art, biology, English, history, mathematics; urban education (MA). *Accreditation:* TEAC. *Program availability:* Part-time. *Faculty:* 9 full-time (5 women), 2 part-time/adjunct (both women). *Students:* 38 full-time (4 women), 6 part-time (5 women); includes 4 minority (1 Black or African American, non-Hispanic/Latino; 1 American Indian or Alaska Native, non-Hispanic/Latino; 1 Asian, non-Hispanic/Latino; 1 Two or more races, non-Hispanic/Latino). Average age 31. 22 applicants, 9% accepted. In 2017, 10 master's awarded. *Degree requirements:* For master's, thesis optional. *Entrance requirements:* For master's, GRE General Test. Additional exam requirements/recommendations for international students: Required—TOEFL (minimum score 577 paper-based; 91 iBT), IELTS (minimum score 6.5). *Application deadline:* For fall admission, 2/1 priority date for domestic students. Applications are processed on a rolling basis. Application fee: $55. Electronic applications accepted. *Expenses:* Tuition: Full-time $22,230. *Required fees:* $2000. Tuition and fees vary according to course load and program. *Financial support:* In 2017–18, 3 students received support, including 3 teaching assistantships with full tuition reimbursements available (averaging $13,410 per year); fellowships with tuition reimbursements available, research assistantships with tuition reimbursements available, career-related internships or fieldwork, Federal Work-Study, scholarships/grants, health care benefits, tuition waivers (full and partial), and unspecified assistantships also available. Support available to part-time students. Financial award application deadline: 2/1; financial award applicants required to submit FAFSA. *Faculty research:* Elementary/secondary certification, math/science education, teaching arts. *Unit head:* Dr. Elizabeth Smith, Chair, 918-631-2238, Fax: 918-631-3721, E-mail: elizabeth-smith-43@utulsa.edu. *Application contact:* Dr. David Brown, Advisor, 918-631-2719, Fax: 918-631-2133, E-mail: david-brown@utulsa.edu.
Website: http://artsandsciences.utulsa.edu/academics/departments-schools/urban-education/

University of Victoria, Faculty of Graduate Studies, Faculty of Education, Department of Curriculum and Instruction, Victoria, BC V8W 2Y2, Canada. Offers art education (M Ed, PhD); curriculum studies (M Ed, MA, PhD); early childhood education (M Ed, PhD); educational studies (PhD); language and literacy (M Ed, MA, PhD); mathematics (M Ed, MA, PhD); music education (M Ed, MA, PhD); science (M Ed, MA, PhD); social studies (M Ed, MA); social, cultural and foundational studies (MA, PhD); technology and environmental education (PhD). *Program availability:* Part-time. *Degree requirements:* For master's, thesis, project (M Ed); for doctorate, comprehensive exam, thesis/dissertation. *Entrance requirements:* For master's, minimum B average. Additional exam requirements/recommendations for international students: Required—TOEFL (minimum score 575 paper-based), IELTS (minimum score 7). Electronic applications accepted. *Faculty research:* Elementary and secondary English, language arts, curriculum theory and practice, educational media and technology, educational administration and leadership, history and philosophy of education.

University of Virginia, Curry School of Education, Department of Curriculum, Instruction, and Special Education, Program in Curriculum and Instruction, Charlottesville, VA 22903. Offers curriculum and instruction (M Ed, Ed S); elementary education (M Ed, Ed D); English education (M Ed, Ed D); foreign language education (M Ed); mathematics education (M Ed, Ed D); science education (Ed D); social studies education (M Ed); MBA/M Ed. *Program availability:* 100% online. *Students:* 38 full-time (31 women), 15 part-time (12 women); includes 6 minority (2 Asian, non-Hispanic/Latino; 2 Hispanic/Latino; 2 Two or more races, non-Hispanic/Latino), 2 international. Average age 32. 92 applicants, 64% accepted, 47 enrolled. In 2017, 47 master's, 9 doctorates, 8 other advanced degrees awarded. *Degree requirements:* For master's, comprehensive exam (for some programs); for doctorate, comprehensive exam, thesis/dissertation; for Ed S, comprehensive exam. *Entrance requirements:* For master's, doctorate, and Ed S, GRE General Test, 2 letters of recommendation. Additional exam requirements/recommendations for international students: Required—TOEFL (minimum score 600 paper-based; 90 iBT), IELTS (minimum score 7). *Application deadline:* Applications are processed on a rolling basis. Application fee: $60. Electronic applications accepted. *Financial support:* Fellowships with tuition reimbursements, research assistantships with tuition reimbursements, and teaching assistantships with tuition reimbursements available. Financial award application deadline: 1/5; financial award applicants required to submit FAFSA. *Unit head:* Susan Mintz, Program Area Director, 434-924-3128, E-mail: slm4r@virginia.edu. *Application contact:* E-mail: curry-admissions@virginia.edu.
Website: http://curry.virginia.edu/academics/areas-of-study/curriculum-teaching-learning

University of Virginia, Curry School of Education, Program in Education, Charlottesville, VA 22903. Offers administration and supervision (PhD); applied developmental science (PhD); counselor education (PhD); curriculum and instruction (PhD); early childhood special education (MT); education evaluation (PhD); educational psychology (PhD); educational research (PhD); elementary education (MT); English education (MT, PhD); foreign language education (MT); higher education (PhD); instructional technology (MT); kinesiology (MT, PhD); math education (PhD); reading education (PhD); research, statistics and evaluation (PhD); school psychology (PhD); science education (PhD); social studies education (MT, PhD); special education (PhD); world languages education (MT). *Students:* 431 full-time (353 women), 15 part-time (14 women); includes 100 minority (32 Black or African American, non-Hispanic/Latino; 33 Asian, non-Hispanic/Latino; 16 Hispanic/Latino; 19 Two or more races, non-Hispanic/Latino), 14 international. Average age 25. 264 applicants, 49% accepted, 83 enrolled. In 2017, 142 master's, 33 doctorates awarded. *Degree requirements:* For master's, comprehensive exam (for some programs), field project; for doctorate, comprehensive exam, thesis/dissertation. *Entrance requirements:* For doctorate, GRE General Test. Additional exam requirements/recommendations for international students: Required—TOEFL (minimum score 600 paper-based; 90 iBT), IELTS (minimum score 7). *Application deadline:* Applications are processed on a rolling basis. Application fee: $60. Electronic applications accepted. *Financial support:* Fellowships, research assistantships, and teaching assistantships available. Financial award application deadline: 1/5; financial award applicants required to submit FAFSA. *Unit head:* Robert C. Pianta, Dean, 434-924-3334, E-mail: pianta@virginia.edu. *Application contact:* E-mail: curry-admissions@virginia.edu.
Website: http://curry.virginia.edu/teacher-education

University of Washington, Graduate School, College of Arts and Sciences, Department of English, Seattle, WA 98195. Offers creative writing (MFA); English as a second language (MAT); English literature and language (MA, MAT, PhD). *Program availability:* Part-time. Terminal master's awarded for partial completion of doctoral program. *Degree requirements:* For master's, one foreign language, thesis (for some programs); for doctorate, one foreign language, thesis/dissertation. *Entrance requirements:* For master's, GRE General Test, GRE Subject Test (MA and MAT in English), minimum GPA of 3.0; for doctorate, GRE General Test, GRE Subject Test. Additional exam requirements/recommendations for international students: Required—TOEFL. Electronic applications accepted. *Faculty research:* English and American literature, critical theory, creative writing, language theory.

University of Washington, Graduate School, College of Education, Seattle, WA 98195. Offers curriculum and instruction (M Ed, Ed D, PhD), including educational technology, general curriculum (Ed D, PhD), language, literacy, and culture, mathematics education, multicultural education, reading and language arts education (Ed D), science education, social studies education, teaching and curriculum (M Ed); educational leadership and policy studies (M Ed, Ed D, PhD), including administration (Ed D), educational policy, organization, and leadership (M Ed, PhD), higher education, leadership for learning (Ed D), social and cultural foundations of education (M Ed, PhD); educational psychology (M Ed, PhD), including educational psychology (PhD), human development and cognition (M Ed), learning sciences, measurement, statistics and research design (M Ed), school psychology (M Ed); instructional leadership (M Ed); intercollegiate athletic leadership (M Ed); special education (M Ed, Ed D, PhD), including early childhood special education (M Ed), emotional and behavioral disabilities (M Ed), learning disabilities (M Ed), low-incidence disabilities (M Ed), severe disabilities (M Ed), special education (Ed D, PhD); teacher education (MIT). *Accreditation:* APA. *Program availability:* Part-time, evening/weekend. *Degree requirements:* For master's, thesis optional; for doctorate, thesis/dissertation. *Entrance requirements:* For master's and doctorate, GRE General Test, minimum GPA of 3.0. Additional exam requirements/recommendations for international students: Required—TOEFL. Electronic applications accepted. *Faculty research:* School restructuring/effective schools, special education interventions, literacy and writing, technology, school partnerships, teacher preparation.

The University of West Alabama, School of Graduate Studies, College of Education, Program in Secondary Education, Livingston, AL 35470. Offers biology (MAT); English language arts (MAT); high school 6-12 (M Ed); history (MAT); mathematics (MAT); science (MAT); social science (MAT). *Program availability:* Part-time, evening/weekend, 100% online. *Faculty:* 21 full-time (7 women), 5 part-time/adjunct (1 woman). *Students:* 259 (183 women); includes 61 minority (51 Black or African American, non-Hispanic/Latino; 2 American Indian or Alaska Native, non-Hispanic/Latino; 3 Asian, non-Hispanic/Latino; 2 Hispanic/Latino; 3 Two or more races, non-Hispanic/Latino). Average age 32. 58 applicants, 93% accepted, 45 enrolled. In 2017, 80 master's awarded. *Degree requirements:* For master's, comprehensive exam, thesis optional. *Entrance requirements:* For master's, GRE, minimum GPA of 2.75, verification of background clearance/fingerprints, valid bachelor's-level Professional Educator Certificate in same teaching field. Additional exam requirements/recommendations for international students: Required—TOEFL (minimum score 500 paper-based; 61 iBT). *Application deadline:* Applications are processed on a rolling basis. Application fee: $40. Electronic applications accepted. *Expenses:* Tuition, state resident: part-time $371 per credit hour. Tuition, nonresident: part-time $742 per credit hour. *Required fees:* $130 per semester. *Financial support:* Teaching assistantships, Federal Work-Study, scholarships/grants, and unspecified assistantships available. Support available to part-time students. Financial award application deadline: 3/1; financial award applicants required to submit FAFSA. *Unit head:* Dr. Jodie Winship, Chair of Teaching and Learning, 205-652-5415, Fax: 205-652-3706, E-mail: jwinship@uwa.edu. *Application contact:* Dr. B. J. Kimbrough, Dean of Graduate Studies, 205-652-3647, Fax: 205-652-3670, E-mail: bkimbrough@uwa.edu.

University of Wisconsin–La Crosse, School of Education, La Crosse, WI 54601-3742. Offers English language arts elementary (Graduate Certificate); professional development in education (ME-PD); reading (MS Ed); special education (MS Ed). *Program availability:* Part-time, evening/weekend. *Faculty:* 6 full-time (4 women), 8 part-time/adjunct (6 women). *Students:* 70 part-time (51 women); includes 2 minority (1 Asian, non-Hispanic/Latino; 1 Two or more races, non-Hispanic/Latino). Average age 30. 59 applicants, 100% accepted, 34 enrolled. In 2017, 69 master's, 1 other advanced degree awarded. *Entrance requirements:* For master's, GRE. Additional exam requirements/recommendations for international students: Required—TOEFL (minimum score 550 paper-based; 79 iBT). *Application deadline:* Applications are processed on a rolling basis. Electronic applications accepted. *Financial support:* Research assistantships, Federal Work-Study, scholarships/grants, health care benefits, and tuition waivers (partial) available. Support available to part-time students. Financial award application deadline: 3/15; financial award applicants required to submit FAFSA. *Unit head:* Marcie Wycoff-Horn, Dean, School of Education, 608-785-6786, E-mail: mwycoff-horn@uwlax.edu. *Application contact:* Brandon Schaller, Senior Graduate Student Status Examiner, 608-785-8941, E-mail: admissions@uwlax.edu.
Website: https://www.uwlax.edu/soe/

University of Wisconsin–Milwaukee, Graduate School, College of Letters and Science, Department of English, Milwaukee, WI 53201-0413. Offers English (MA, PhD), including creative writing, English language and linguistics, English secondary education, literary and critical studies, literature and cultural theory (PhD), literature and language studies, literature, culture, and media, media, cinema and digital studies, professional and technical communication (MA), professional and technical writing, professional writing (PhD), rhetoric and composition (PhD), rhetoric and writing. *Students:* 90 full-time (54 women), 42 part-time (17 women); includes 12 minority (2 Black or African American, non-Hispanic/Latino; 1 American Indian or Alaska Native, non-Hispanic/Latino; 4 Asian, non-Hispanic/Latino; 1 Hispanic/Latino; 4 Two or more races, non-Hispanic/Latino), 9 international. Average age 34. 166 applicants, 21% accepted, 27 enrolled. In 2017, 10 master's, 12 doctorates awarded. *Degree requirements:* For master's, thesis or alternative; for doctorate, one foreign language, thesis/dissertation. *Entrance requirements:* For master's, GRE General Test, GRE Subject Test; for doctorate, GRE. Additional exam requirements/recommendations for international students: Required—TOEFL (minimum score 550 paper-based; 79 iBT), IELTS (minimum score 6.5). *Application deadline:* For fall admission, 1/1 priority date for domestic students; for spring admission, 9/1 for domestic students. Application fee: $56 ($96 for international students). Electronic applications accepted. *Financial support:* Fellowships, research assistantships, teaching assistantships, career-related internships or fieldwork, unspecified assistantships, and project assistantships available. Support available to part-time students. Financial award application deadline: 4/15; financial award applicants required to submit FAFSA. *Unit head:* Mark Netzloff, Department Chair, 414-229-4511, E-mail: netzloff@uwm.edu. *Application contact:* General Information Contact, 414-229-4982, Fax: 414-229-6967, E-mail: gradschool@uwm.edu.
Website: https://uwm.edu/english/

University of Wisconsin–Milwaukee, Graduate School, School of Education, Department of Curriculum and Instruction, Milwaukee, WI 53201-0413. Offers curriculum and instruction (MS), including cross-curricular focus, early childhood education, English education, mathematics education, middle childhood/early

adolescence education, reading education, science education, urban social studies education. *Program availability:* Part-time. *Students:* 17 full-time (13 women), 45 part-time (39 women); includes 13 minority (2 Black or African American, non-Hispanic/Latino; 3 Asian, non-Hispanic/Latino; 1 Hispanic/Latino; 7 Two or more races, non-Hispanic/Latino). Average age 33. 32 applicants, 66% accepted, 16 enrolled. In 2017, 26 master's awarded. *Entrance requirements:* Additional exam requirements/recommendations for international students: Required—TOEFL (minimum score 550 paper-based; 79 iBT), IELTS (minimum score 6.5). *Application deadline:* For fall admission, 1/1 priority date for domestic students; for spring admission, 9/1 for domestic students. Application fee: $56 ($96 for international students). Electronic applications accepted. *Financial support:* Fellowships, research assistantships, teaching assistantships, career-related internships or fieldwork, health care benefits, unspecified assistantships, and project assistantships available. Support available to part-time students. Financial award application deadline: 4/15; financial award applicants required to submit FAFSA. *Application contact:* General Information Contact, 414-229-4721, E-mail: soeinfo@uwm.edu.
Website: http://uwm.edu/education/academics/curriculum-instruction-department/

Valdosta State University, Department of English, Valdosta, GA 31698. Offers English (MA); English studies for language arts teachers (MA). *Program availability:* Part-time, 100% online, blended/hybrid learning. *Degree requirements:* For master's, one foreign language, thesis, comprehensive written and/or oral exams. *Entrance requirements:* For master's, GRE General Test, minimum GPA of 3.0. Additional exam requirements/recommendations for international students: Required—TOEFL (minimum score 523 paper-based); Recommended—IELTS. *Application deadline:* For fall admission, 7/1 for domestic and international students; for spring admission, 11/1 for domestic and international students. Applications are processed on a rolling basis. Application fee: $45. Electronic applications accepted. *Expenses:* Contact institution. *Financial support:* Research assistantships with full tuition reimbursements, teaching assistantships with full tuition reimbursements, institutionally sponsored loans, scholarships/grants, and unspecified assistantships available. Support available to part-time students. Financial award application deadline: 7/1; financial award applicants required to submit FAFSA. *Faculty research:* American literature, creative writing. *Unit head:* Dr. Maren Clegg Hyer, Graduate Program Adviser, 229-333-7347, E-mail: mcleggyer@valdosta.edu. *Application contact:* Jessica Powers, Admission Specialist, 229-333-5694, Fax: 229-245-3853, E-mail: jldevane@valdosta.edu.
Website: https://www.valdosta.edu/english/

Valley City State University, Online Graduate Programs, Valley City, ND 58072. Offers elementary education (M Ed); English education (M Ed); library and information technologies (M Ed); teaching (MAT); teaching and technology (M Ed); teaching English language learners (M Ed); technology education (M Ed). *Accreditation:* NCATE. *Program availability:* Part-time, evening/weekend, online only, 100% online. *Faculty:* 21 full-time (12 women), 15 part-time/adjunct (11 women). *Students:* 12 full-time (9 women), 138 part-time (99 women); includes 5 minority (3 Hispanic/Latino; 2 Two or more races, non-Hispanic/Latino). Average age 36. 13 applicants, 92% accepted, 12 enrolled. In 2017, 45 master's awarded. *Degree requirements:* For master's, action research report, comprehensive portfolio. *Entrance requirements:* For master's, GRE, MAT, PRAXIS II or National Teaching Board for Professional Standards (if GPA is less than 3.0). Additional exam requirements/recommendations for international students: Required—TOEFL (minimum score 525 paper-based; 71 iBT); Recommended—IELTS (minimum score 5.5). *Application deadline:* For fall admission, 7/21 for domestic and international students; for spring admission, 12/8 for domestic and international students; for summer admission, 5/5 for domestic and international students. Applications are processed on a rolling basis. Application fee: $35. Electronic applications accepted. *Expenses:* $384.21 per credit. *Financial support:* In 2017–18, 16 students received support. Scholarships/grants, tuition waivers (full and partial), and unspecified assistantships available. Financial award applicants required to submit FAFSA. *Faculty research:* Universal accessibility, instructional design and technology, gender communication, STEM education in K-12, English language learners. *Unit head:* Dr. Sheri Okland, Dean, 701-845-7184, E-mail: sheri.l.okland@vcsu.edu. *Application contact:* Misty Lindgren, Graduate Studies, 701-845-7303, Fax: 701-845-7190, E-mail: misty.lindgren@vcsu.edu.
Website: http://www.vcsu.edu/graduate

Vanderbilt University, Peabody College, Department of Teaching and Learning, Nashville, TN 37240-1001. Offers elementary education (M Ed); English language learners (M Ed); learning and design (M Ed); learning, diversity, and urban studies (M Ed); reading education (M Ed); secondary education (M Ed). *Accreditation:* NCATE. *Program availability:* Part-time. *Faculty:* 43 full-time (32 women), 28 part-time/adjunct (25 women). *Students:* 139 full-time (110 women), 35 part-time (23 women); includes 31 minority (18 Black or African American, non-Hispanic/Latino; 1 American Indian or Alaska Native, non-Hispanic/Latino; 6 Asian, non-Hispanic/Latino; 4 Hispanic/Latino; 2 Two or more races, non-Hispanic/Latino), 44 international. Average age 26. 510 applicants, 69% accepted, 113 enrolled. In 2017, 87 master's awarded. *Degree requirements:* For master's, comprehensive exam, thesis optional. *Entrance requirements:* For master's, GRE General Test, MAT. Additional exam requirements/recommendations for international students: Required—TOEFL (minimum score 550 paper-based; 80 iBT). *Application deadline:* For fall admission, 12/31 priority date for domestic and international students; for spring admission, 11/1 priority date for domestic and international students. Applications are processed on a rolling basis. Application fee: $0. Electronic applications accepted. *Financial support:* Fellowships with partial tuition reimbursements, research assistantships with partial tuition reimbursements, teaching assistantships with partial tuition reimbursements, Federal Work-Study, institutionally sponsored loans, scholarships/grants, tuition waivers (partial), and unspecified assistantships available. Support available to part-time students. Financial award application deadline: 1/15; financial award applicants required to submit FAFSA. *Faculty research:* Children's learning and development in core conceptual domains (STEM, English language arts, social studies); classroom discourse structures that teachers can learn and use to support students' learning and development K-6; intervention and design-based research on educational improvement at classroom, school, and district levels; design-based and learning sciences research on relations between learning in schools and other settings. *Unit head:* Dr. Deborah Rowe, Chair, 615-322-8100, Fax: 615-322-8999, E-mail: deborah.w.rowe@vanderbilt.edu. *Application contact:* Angela Saylor, Educational Coordinator, 615-322-8092, Fax: 615-322-8999, E-mail: angela.saylor@vanderbilt.edu.

Wagner College, Division of Graduate Studies, Education Department, Program in Secondary Education/Students with Disabilities, Staten Island, NY 10301-4495. Offers secondary education 7-12 (MS Ed), including language arts, languages other than English, mathematics and technology, science and technology, social studies. *Program availability:* Evening/weekend. *Faculty:* 2 full-time (1 woman), 7 part-time/adjunct (3 women). *Students:* 17 full-time (14 women), 6 part-time (4 women); includes 2 minority (1 Black or African American, non-Hispanic/Latino; 1 Asian, non-Hispanic/Latino). Average age 24. 15 applicants, 80% accepted, 11 enrolled. In 2017, 8 master's awarded. *Degree requirements:* For master's, thesis (for some programs), completion of state certification exams before student teaching. *Entrance requirements:* For master's, GRE, minimum GPA of 3.0, interview, recommendations. Additional exam requirements/

recommendations for international students: Required—TOEFL (minimum score 550 paper-based; 79 iBT), IELTS (minimum score 6.5). *Application deadline:* For fall admission, 12/1 priority date for domestic and international students. Application fee: $60. Electronic applications accepted. *Expenses:* Contact institution. *Financial support:* Unspecified assistantships and alumni fellowship available. Financial award application deadline: 2/15; financial award applicants required to submit FAFSA. *Unit head:* Dr. Jason Fitzgerald, Department Chair, 718-420-4129, Fax: 718-390-3456, E-mail: jason.fitzgerald@wagner.edu. *Application contact:* Patricia Clancy, Assistant Director of Enrollment, 718-420-4464, Fax: 718-390-3105, E-mail: patricia.clancy@wagner.edu. Website: http://www.wagner.edu/education

Wayland Baptist University, Graduate Programs, Program in Education, Plainview, TX 79072-6998. Offers education administration (M Ed); education diagnostics (M Ed); education literacy (M Ed); elementary certification (M Ed); English (M Ed); English as a second language (M Ed); higher education administration (M Ed); human resources (M Ed); instructional leadership (M Ed); instructional technology (M Ed); leadership training and development (M Ed); science education (M Ed); secondary certification (M Ed); social studies (M Ed); special education (M Ed); sports administration and management (M Ed). *Program availability:* Part-time, evening/weekend, 100% online. *Faculty:* 33 full-time (17 women), 28 part-time/adjunct (17 women). *Students:* 16 full-time (13 women), 221 part-time (143 women); includes 97 minority (26 Black or African American, non-Hispanic/Latino; 1 American Indian or Alaska Native, non-Hispanic/Latino; 5 Asian, non-Hispanic/Latino; 54 Hispanic/Latino; 11 Two or more races, non-Hispanic/Latino), 1 international. Average age 39. 32 applicants, 97% accepted, 23 enrolled. In 2017, 78 master's awarded. *Degree requirements:* For master's, comprehensive exam, capstone course. *Entrance requirements:* For master's, GRE, GMAT or MAT. Additional exam requirements/recommendations for international students: Required—TOEFL (minimum score 500 paper-based; 61 iBT). *Application deadline:* Applications are processed on a rolling basis. Application fee: $50. Electronic applications accepted. *Expenses: Tuition:* Full-time $11,250; part-time $625 per credit hour. *Required fees:* $1200. *Financial support:* Federal Work-Study, institutionally sponsored loans, and scholarships/grants available. Support available to part-time students. Financial award application deadline: 5/1; financial award applicants required to submit FAFSA. *Unit head:* Dr. Gene Whitfill, Dean, 806-291-1047, Fax: 806-291-1951, E-mail: whitfillg@wbu.edu. *Application contact:* Amanda Stanton, Coordinator of Graduate Studies, 806-291-3423, Fax: 806-291-1950, E-mail: stanton@wbu.edu.

Wayne State College, School of Education and Counseling, Department of Educational Foundations and Leadership, Program in Curriculum and Instruction, Wayne, NE 68787. Offers alternative education (MSE); business and information technology education (MSE); communication arts education (MSE); early childhood education (MSE); elementary education (MSE); English as a second language (MSE); English education (MSE); family and consumer sciences education (MSE); industrial technology and vocational education (MSE); learning communities (MSE); mathematics education (MSE); music education (MSE); science education (MSE); social science education (MSE). *Accreditation:* NCATE. *Program availability:* Part-time, evening/weekend. *Degree requirements:* For master's, comprehensive exam, thesis optional. *Entrance requirements:* For master's, GRE General Test. Additional exam requirements/recommendations for international students: Required—TOEFL (minimum score 550 paper-based).

Wayne State University, College of Education, Division of Teacher Education, Detroit, MI 48202. Offers art education (M Ed); bilingual/bicultural education (Certificate); curriculum and instruction (Ed D, PhD, Ed S), including English as a second language (MAT, Ed D, Ed S), K-12 curriculum (PhD); elementary education (MAT), including bilingual/bicultural education (M Ed, MAT), early childhood education (M Ed, MAT), English as a second language (MAT, Ed D, Ed S), foreign language education, science education (M Ed, MAT), special education (M Ed, MAT); elementary mathematics specialist (Certificate); English as a second language (Certificate); reading (M Ed, Ed S); reading, language and literature (Ed D); secondary education (MAT), including bilingual/bicultural education (M Ed, MAT), early childhood education (M Ed, MAT), English as a second language (MAT, Ed D, Ed S), English education, foreign language education, mathematics education (M Ed, MAT), science education (M Ed, MAT), social studies education (M Ed, MAT); special education (MAT), including career and technical education; teaching and learning (M Ed), including bilingual/bicultural education (M Ed, MAT), early childhood education (M Ed, MAT), elementary education, foreign language, mathematics education (M Ed, MAT), science education (M Ed, MAT), social studies education (M Ed, MAT), special education (M Ed, MAT). *Program availability:* Part-time, blended/hybrid learning. *Faculty:* 22. *Students:* 126 full-time (96 women), 317 part-time (258 women); includes 134 minority (95 Black or African American, non-Hispanic/Latino; 1 American Indian or Alaska Native, non-Hispanic/Latino; 8 Asian, non-Hispanic/Latino; 17 Hispanic/Latino; 1 Native Hawaiian or other Pacific Islander, non-Hispanic/Latino; 12 Two or more races, non-Hispanic/Latino), 13 international. Average age 37. 260 applicants, 33% accepted, 57 enrolled. In 2017, 111 master's, 13 doctorates, 7 other advanced degrees awarded. *Degree requirements:* For master's, essay or project (for some M Ed programs), professional field experience (for MAT programs); for doctorate, thesis/dissertation. *Entrance requirements:* For master's, Michigan Test for Teacher Certification (for most programs), verification of participation in group work with children (for MAT programs), Michigan State Police criminal background check; for doctorate, minimum undergraduate GPA of 3.0, graduate 3.5; interview; curriculum vitae; references; master's degree (for most programs). Additional exam requirements/recommendations for international students: Required—TOEFL (minimum score 550 paper-based; 79 iBT), TWE (minimum score 5.5); Recommended—IELTS (minimum score 6.5). *Application deadline:* For fall admission, 6/1 priority date for domestic students, 5/1 priority date for international students; for winter admission, 10/1 priority date for domestic students, 9/1 priority date for international students; for spring admission, 2/1 priority date for domestic students, 1/1 priority date for international students. Applications are processed on a rolling basis. Application fee: $50. Electronic applications accepted. *Expenses:* Tuition, state resident: full-time $10,224; part-time $638.98 per credit hour. Tuition, nonresident: full-time $22,145; part-time $1384.04 per credit hour. Tuition and fees vary according to course load and program. *Financial support:* In 2017–18, 78 students received support, including 4 fellowships (averaging $13,500 per year), 1 research assistantship with tuition reimbursement available (averaging $16,000 per year); Federal Work-Study, scholarships/grants, and unspecified assistantships also available. Support available to part-time students. Financial award applicants required to submit FAFSA. *Faculty research:* Improving students' skill achievement in mathematics, improving elementary children's understanding of informational text, teachers' use of their pedagogical and mathematical knowledge in the interactive work of teaching, the intersection of identity construction in teaching and learning, identifying effective methods of literacy instruction and assessments for bilingual students in elementary language arts classrooms. *Unit head:* Dr. Thomas Edwards, Interim Associate Dean for Teacher Education, 313-577-3886, E-mail: t.g.edwards@wayne.edu. *Application contact:* 313-577-0902, E-mail: askcoe@wayne.edu. Website: http://coe.wayne.edu/ted/index.php

West Chester University of Pennsylvania, College of Arts and Humanities, Department of English, West Chester, PA 19383. Offers English (MA), including creative writing, literature, writing, teaching, and criticism; publishing (Certificate); secondary English (Teaching Certificate). *Program availability:* Part-time, evening/weekend.

Students: 25 full-time (17 women), 47 part-time (27 women); includes 5 minority (1 Black or African American, non-Hispanic/Latino; 1 Asian, non-Hispanic/Latino; 3 Two or more races, non-Hispanic/Latino), 2 international. Average age 29. 43 applicants, 88% accepted, 25 enrolled. In 2017, 10 master's, 1 other advanced degree awarded. *Degree requirements:* For master's, thesis optional; for other advanced degree, capstone internship and e-portfolio (for Certificate in publishing). *Entrance requirements:* For master's, minimum GPA of 2.8, two letters of recommendation, writing sample, goals statement, official transcripts; for other advanced degree, two letters of recommendation, statement of goals, official transcripts; undergraduate degree (for Certificate); minimum GPA of 2.85 and writing sample (for Teaching Certificate). Additional exam requirements/recommendations for international students: Required—TOEFL or IELTS. *Application deadline:* For fall admission, 5/15 for international students; for spring admission, 10/15 for international students. Applications are processed on a rolling basis. Application fee: $50. Electronic applications accepted. *Expenses:* Tuition, state resident: full-time $9000; part-time $500 per credit. Tuition, nonresident: full-time $13,500; part-time $750 per credit. *Required fees:* $2959; $149.79 per credit. *Financial support:* Scholarships/grants and unspecified assistantships available. Financial award application deadline: 2/15; financial award applicants required to submit FAFSA. *Faculty research:* Critical theory, cultural studies, literature, rhetoric and composition, creative writing. *Unit head:* Dr. Rodney Mader, Chair, 610-436-2822, Fax: 610-738-0516, E-mail: rmader@wcupa.edu. *Application contact:* Dr. Eleanor Shevlin, Graduate Coordinator for English, 610-436-2745, Fax: 610-738-0516, E-mail: eshevlin@wcupa.edu. Website: http://www.wcupa.edu/arts-humanities/english/

Western Governors University, Teachers College, Salt Lake City, UT 84107. Offers curriculum and instruction (MS); educational leadership (MS); educational studies (MA); educational studies (5-12) (MA), including mathematics; elementary education (K-8) (MAT, Postbaccalaureate Certificate); elementary education (PreK-8) (MAT); English language learning (K-12) (MA); instructional design (MAT); learning and technology (M Ed, MA); management and innovation (M Ed); mathematics (5-12) (MAT, Postbaccalaureate Certificate); mathematics (5-9) (MAT, Postbaccalaureate Certificate); mathematics education (5-12) (MA); mathematics education (5-9) (MA); mathematics education (K-6) (MA); measurement and evaluation (M Ed); science (5-12) (Postbaccalaureate Certificate); science (5-9) (MAT, Postbaccalaureate Certificate); science education (5-12) (MA), including biology, chemistry, geology, physics; science education (5-9) (MA); social science (5-12) (MAT, Postbaccalaureate Certificate); special education (MAT, MS). *Accreditation:* NCATE. *Program availability:* Evening/weekend, online learning. *Degree requirements:* For master's, capstone project. *Entrance requirements:* For master's and Postbaccalaureate Certificate, Readiness Assessment, transcripts. Additional exam requirements/recommendations for international students: Required—TOEFL (minimum score 450 paper-based; 80 iBT). Electronic applications accepted. *Expenses:* Contact institution.

Western Kentucky University, Graduate Studies, Potter College of Arts and Letters, Department of English, Bowling Green, KY 42101. Offers education (MA); English (MA Ed); literature (MA), including American literature, British literature, literary theory, women writers, world literature; teaching English as a second language (MA); writing (MA). *Program availability:* Part-time, evening/weekend. *Degree requirements:* For master's, comprehensive exam, thesis optional, final exam. *Entrance requirements:* For master's, GRE General Test, minimum GPA of 2.75. Additional exam requirements/recommendations for international students: Required—TOEFL (minimum score 555 paper-based; 79 iBT). *Faculty research:* Improving writing, linking teacher knowledge and performance, Victorian women writers, Kentucky women writers, Kentucky poets.

Western Michigan University, Graduate College, College of Arts and Sciences, Department of English, Kalamazoo, MI 49008. Offers creative writing (MFA, PhD); English (MA, PhD); English teaching (MA). *Degree requirements:* For doctorate, one foreign language, thesis/dissertation.

Western New England University, College of Arts and Sciences, Program in English for Teachers, Springfield, MA 01119. Offers MAET. *Program availability:* Part-time, evening/weekend. *Faculty:* 11 full-time (5 women). *Students:* 15 part-time (8 women); includes 1 minority (Hispanic/Latino), 1 international. Average age 28. 12 applicants, 100% accepted, 6 enrolled. In 2017, 11 master's awarded. *Entrance requirements:* For master's, two letters of recommendation, official transcript, personal statement, resume; provisional or standard state teaching certificate (preferred). Additional exam requirements/recommendations for international students: Required—TOEFL (minimum score 79 iBT). *Application deadline:* Applications are processed on a rolling basis. Application fee: $30. Electronic applications accepted. *Expenses:* Contact institution. *Financial support:* Application deadline: 4/15; applicants required to submit FAFSA. *Unit head:* Dr. Saeed Ghahramani, Dean, 413-782-1218, Fax: 413-796-2118, E-mail: sghahram@wne.edu. *Application contact:* Matthew Fox, Director of Admissions for Graduate Students and Adult Learners, 413-782-1410, Fax: 413-782-1777, E-mail: study@wne.edu. Website: http://www1.wne.edu/academics/graduate/ma-english-teachers.cfm

West Virginia University, College of Education and Human Services, Morgantown, WV 26506. Offers audiology (Au D); autism spectrum disorder (MA); clinical rehabilitation and mental health counseling (MS); communication science and disorders (PhD); counseling (MA); counseling psychology (PhD); curriculum and instruction (Ed D); early childhood education (MA); early intervention (MA); education (PhD); educational leadership (MA, Ed D); educational leadership/public school administration (MA); educational psychology (MA, Ed D); elementary education (MA); gifted education (MA); higher education administration (MA, Ed D); higher education curriculum and teaching (MA); institutional design and technology (MA); instructional design and technology (Ed D); literacy education (MA); secondary education (MA); secondary education/English (MA); special education (MS); speech pathology (MS). *Accreditation:* NCATE. *Program availability:* Part-time, evening/weekend, online learning. *Students:* 423 full-time (347 women), 367 part-time (316 women); includes 57 minority (14 Black or African American, non-Hispanic/Latino; 7 Asian, non-Hispanic/Latino; 20 Hispanic/Latino; 16 Two or more races, non-Hispanic/Latino), 13 international. *Degree requirements:* For master's, content exams; for doctorate, comprehensive exam, thesis/dissertation. *Entrance requirements:* Additional exam requirements/recommendations for international students: Required—TOEFL (minimum score 500 paper-based; 61 iBT). *Application deadline:* For fall admission, 8/1 for domestic students; for spring admission, 1/1 for domestic students; for summer admission, 5/1 for domestic students. Application fee: $60. Electronic applications accepted. *Expenses:* Tuition, state resident: full-time $9450. Tuition, nonresident: full-time $24,390. *Financial support:* Fellowships, research assistantships, teaching assistantships, career-related internships or fieldwork, Federal Work-Study, institutionally sponsored loans, health care benefits, tuition waivers (full and partial), and administrative assistantships available. Financial award applicants required to submit FAFSA. *Faculty research:* Internet training and integration for teachers, rural education, teacher preparation, organization of schools, evaluation of personnel. *Unit head:* Dr. Gypsy Denzine, Dean, 304-293-5703, Fax: 304-293-7565, E-mail: gypsy.denzine@mail.wvu.edu. *Application contact:* Dr. M. Cecil Smith, Associate Dean for Research and Graduate Education, 304-293-2174, Fax: 304-293-3802, E-mail: mcecil.smith@mail.wvu.edu. Website: http://cehs.wvu.edu/

Widener University, School of Human Service Professions, Center for Education, Chester, PA 19013-5792. Offers adult education (M Ed); counseling in higher education (M Ed); counselor education (M Ed); early childhood education (M Ed); educational foundations (M Ed); educational leadership (M Ed); educational psychology (M Ed); elementary education (M Ed); English and language arts (M Ed); health education (M Ed); higher education leadership (Ed D); home and school visitor (M Ed); human sexuality (M Ed, PhD); mathematics education (M Ed); middle school education (M Ed); principalship (M Ed); reading and language arts (Ed D); reading education (M Ed); school administration (Ed D); science education (M Ed); social studies education (M Ed); special education (M Ed); technology education (M Ed). *Accreditation:* NCATE. *Program availability:* Part-time, evening/weekend. *Faculty:* 34 full-time (22 women), 37 part-time/adjunct (14 women). *Students:* 131 full-time (112 women), 244 part-time (179 women); includes 94 minority (58 Black or African American, non-Hispanic/Latino; 1 American Indian or Alaska Native, non-Hispanic/Latino; 1 Asian, non-Hispanic/Latino; 22 Hispanic/Latino; 12 Two or more races, non-Hispanic/Latino), 12 international. Average age 37. 140 applicants, 38% accepted, 26 enrolled. In 2017, 45 master's, 21 doctorates awarded. Terminal master's awarded for partial completion of doctoral program. *Degree requirements:* For doctorate, thesis/dissertation. *Entrance requirements:* For master's, minimum GPA of 2.5; for doctorate, GRE or MAT, minimum GPA of 2.0 (undergraduate), 3.5 (graduate). *Application deadline:* Applications are processed on a rolling basis. Application fee: $25 ($300 for international students). Electronic applications accepted. *Expenses:* Contact institution. *Financial support:* Career-related internships or fieldwork, tuition waivers (full and partial), and unspecified assistantships available. Support available to part-time students. Financial award application deadline: 5/1. *Faculty research:* Reading and cognition, adult education, technology education, educational leadership, special education. *Unit head:* Dr. Shawn Fitzgerald,. Dean, 610-499-4294, Fax: 610-499-4623, E-mail: smfitzgerald@widener.edu. *Application contact:* Megan Kuft, Director of Graduate Admissions, 610-499-4124, E-mail: gradprograms@widener.edu.
Website: http://www.widener.edu/academics/schools/eics

William Carey University, School of Education, Hattiesburg, MS 39401. Offers art education (M Ed); art of teaching (M Ed); elementary education (M Ed, Ed S); English education (M Ed); gifted education (M Ed); history and social science (M Ed); mild/moderate disabilities (M Ed); secondary education (M Ed). *Accreditation:* NCATE. *Program availability:* Part-time. *Degree requirements:* For master's, comprehensive exam. *Entrance requirements:* For master's, GRE, MAT, minimum GPA of 2.5, Class A teacher's license. Additional exam requirements/recommendations for international students: Required—TOEFL (minimum score 550 paper-based).

William Jessup University, Program in Teaching, Rocklin, CA 95765. Offers single subject English (MAT); single subject math (MAT). *Program availability:* Evening/weekend.

Worcester State University, Graduate School, Program in English, Worcester, MA 01602-2597. Offers MA. *Program availability:* Part-time, evening/weekend. *Faculty:* 7 full-time. *Students:* 2 full-time (1 woman), 10 part-time (4 women). Average age 37. 6 applicants, 83% accepted, 3 enrolled. In 2017, 8 master's awarded. *Degree requirements:* For master's, comprehensive exam (for some programs), thesis or exam. *Entrance requirements:* For master's, GRE General Test or MAT, undergraduate degree in English or 18 undergraduate credits in English, excluding composition classes or English for English Language Learners. Additional exam requirements/recommendations for international students: Required—TOEFL (minimum score 550 paper-based; 79 iBT). *Application deadline:* For fall admission, 6/15 for domestic and international students; for spring admission, 11/1 for domestic and international students; for summer admission, 4/1 for domestic and international students. Applications are processed on a rolling basis. Application fee: $50. Electronic applications accepted. *Expenses:* Tuition, state resident: full-time $3042; part-time $169 per credit hour. Tuition, nonresident: full-time $3042; part-time $169 per credit hour. *Required fees:* $2754; $153 per credit hour. *Financial support:* Career-related internships or fieldwork, scholarships/grants, and unspecified assistantships available. Financial award application deadline: 3/1; financial award applicants required to submit FAFSA. *Unit head:* Dr. Dennis Quinn, Coordinator, 508-929-8705, E-mail: dwquinn@worcester.edu. *Application contact:* Sara Grady, Associate Dean, Graduate Studies and Professional Development, 508-929-8130, E-mail: sara.grady@worcester.edu.

Environmental Education

Alaska Pacific University, Graduate Programs, Environmental Science Department, Program in Outdoor and Environmental Education, Anchorage, AK 99508-4672. Offers MSOEE. *Program availability:* Part-time. *Degree requirements:* For master's, thesis. *Entrance requirements:* For master's, MAT or GRE, minimum GPA of 3.0. Additional exam requirements/recommendations for international students: Required—TOEFL (minimum score 550 paper-based).

Antioch University New England, Graduate School, Department of Environmental Studies, Program in Environmental Education, Keene, NH 03431-3552. Offers MS. *Degree requirements:* For master's, practicum. *Entrance requirements:* For master's, previous undergraduate course work in biology, chemistry, and mathematics; resume; 3 letters of recommendation. Additional exam requirements/recommendations for international students: Required—TOEFL (minimum score 550 paper-based). Electronic applications accepted. *Expenses:* Contact institution. *Faculty research:* Sustainability, natural resources inventory.

Arcadia University, School of Education, Glenside, PA 19038-3295. Offers art education (M Ed); computer education (CAS); curriculum (CAS); curriculum studies (M Ed); early childhood education (M Ed), including individualized, master teacher, research in child development; educational leadership (M Ed, Ed D, CAS); elementary education (M Ed); English education (MA Ed); environmental education (MA Ed); instructional technology (M Ed); language arts (M Ed); library science (M Ed); mathematics education (M Ed, MA Ed); music education (MA Ed); psychology (MA Ed); reading (M Ed, CAS); science education (M Ed, CAS); secondary education (M Ed, CAS); special education (M Ed, Ed D, CAS); theater arts (MA Ed); written communication (MA Ed). *Accreditation:* NASAD. *Program availability:* Part-time, evening/weekend, online learning. Electronic applications accepted. *Expenses:* Contact institution.

Ball State University, Graduate School, College of Sciences and Humanities, Department of Natural Resources and Environmental Management, Muncie, IN 47306. Offers emergency management and homeland security (Certificate); natural resources and environmental management (MA, MS). *Program availability:* Part-time. *Faculty:* 5 full-time (2 women). *Students:* 4 full-time (2 women), 9 part-time (5 women); includes 1 minority (Two or more races, non-Hispanic/Latino). Average age 28. 12 applicants, 67% accepted, 4 enrolled. In 2017, 4 master's, 3 other advanced degrees awarded. *Degree requirements:* For master's, thesis (for some programs). *Entrance requirements:* For master's, GRE General Test, minimum baccalaureate GPA of 2.75 or 3.0 in latter half of baccalaureate, two letters of reference. Additional exam requirements/recommendations for international students: Required—TOEFL (minimum score 550 paper-based; 79 iBT), IELTS (minimum score 6.5). *Application deadline:* For fall admission, 3/1 priority date for domestic students. Applications are processed on a rolling basis. Application fee: $60. Electronic applications accepted. *Financial support:* In 2017–18, 8 students received support, including 2 research assistantships with partial tuition reimbursements available (averaging $12,250 per year), 6 teaching assistantships with partial tuition reimbursements available (averaging $9,907 per year); unspecified assistantships also available. Financial award application deadline: 3/1; financial award applicants required to submit FAFSA. *Faculty research:* Acid rain, indoor air pollution, land reclamation. *Unit head:* Dr. Amy Gregg, Chairperson, 765-285-5781, Fax: 765-285-2606, E-mail: algregg2@bsu.edu.
Website: http://www.bsu.edu/nrem/

Brooklyn College of the City University of New York, School of Education, Program in Childhood Education, Brooklyn, NY 11210-2889. Offers bilingual education (MS Ed); liberal arts (MS Ed); mathematics (MS Ed); science and environmental education (MS Ed). *Program availability:* Part-time, evening/weekend. *Entrance requirements:* For master's, LAST, interview, previous course work in education, writing sample, resume, 2 letters of recommendation. Additional exam requirements/recommendations for international students: Required—TOEFL (minimum score 500 paper-based; 61 iBT). Electronic applications accepted. *Faculty research:* Emotional intelligence, multiculturalism, arts immersion, the Holocaust.

Chatham University, Program in Education, Pittsburgh, PA 15232-2826. Offers early childhood education (MAT); elementary education (MAT); environmental education (K-12) (MAT); secondary art (MAT); secondary biology education (MAT); secondary chemistry education (MAT); secondary English education (MAT); secondary math education (MAT); secondary physics education (MAT); secondary social studies education (MAT); special education (MAT). *Faculty:* 1 (woman) full-time, 15 part-time/adjunct (13 women). *Students:* 31 full-time (23 women), 3 part-time (1 woman); includes 9 minority (8 Black or African American, non-Hispanic/Latino; 1 Hispanic/Latino). Average age 30. 25 applicants, 60% accepted, 9 enrolled. In 2017, 23 master's awarded. *Degree requirements:* For master's, thesis, teaching experience. *Entrance requirements:* For master's, minimum GPA of 3.0, sample of written work, recommendation letters. Additional exam requirements/recommendations for international students: Required—TOEFL (minimum score 600 paper-based; 100 iBT), IELTS (minimum score 7), TWE. *Application deadline:* For fall admission, 4/1 priority date for domestic and international students; for spring admission, 11/1 priority date for domestic students, 10/1 priority date for international students. Applications are processed on a rolling basis. Application fee: $45. Electronic applications accepted. Application fee is waived when completed online. *Expenses:* Tuition: Full-time $16,740; part-time $930 per credit. *Required fees:* $486; $27 per credit. $243 per semester. *Financial support:* Career-related internships or fieldwork available. Financial award applicants required to submit FAFSA. *Faculty research:* Gifted education, environmental education, technology in education, writing as learning, class size and achievement. *Application contact:* Katie Noel, Assistant Director of Graduate Admission, 412-365-2758, Fax: 412-365-1609, E-mail: gradadmissions@chatham.edu.
Website: http://www.chatham.edu/mat

Concordia University, College of Education, Portland, OR 97211-6099. Offers career and technical education (M Ed); curriculum and instruction (M Ed), including adolescent literacy, career and technical education, e-learning/technology education, early childhood education, English for speakers of other languages, English language development, environmental education, mathematics, methods and curriculum, reading, science, teacher leadership, the inclusive classroom; early childhood (MAT); education leadership (Ed D); educational administration (M Ed); elementary education (MAT); secondary education (MAT); special education (M Ed); teacher leadership (Ed D). *Program availability:* Part-time, online learning. *Degree requirements:* For master's, comprehensive exam, work samples/portfolio. *Entrance requirements:* For master's, California Basic Educational Skills Test or PRAXIS I, minimum undergraduate GPA of 2.8, graduate 3.0; 2 letters of recommendation. Additional exam requirements/recommendations for international students: Required—TOEFL (minimum score 525 paper-based). Electronic applications accepted. *Faculty research:* Learner-centered classroom, brain-based learning, future of online learning.

Concordia University Wisconsin, Graduate Programs, Department of Education, Mequon, WI 53097-2402. Offers art education (MS Ed); early childhood (MS Ed); educational administration (MS Ed); environmental education (MS Ed); family studies (MS Ed); literacy (MS Ed); school counseling (MS Ed); special education (MS Ed). *Program availability:* Part-time, evening/weekend, online learning. *Degree requirements:* For master's, comprehensive exam, thesis or alternative. *Entrance requirements:* For master's, minimum GPA of 3.0, teaching license. Additional exam requirements/recommendations for international students: Required—TOEFL. *Faculty research:* Motivation, developmental learning, learning styles.

Florida Atlantic University, College of Education, Department of Teaching and Learning, Boca Raton, FL 33431-0991. Offers curriculum and instruction (M Ed), including art, biology, chemistry, English, French, German, mathematics, music, physics, Pre-K and primary education, reading, social sciences, Spanish; elementary education (M Ed); environmental education (M Ed); reading education (M Ed); social foundations of education (M Ed), including educational psychology, educational technology, multilingual education. *Accreditation:* NCATE. *Program availability:* Part-time, evening/weekend. *Faculty:* 13 full-time (10 women), 1 part-time/adjunct (0 women). *Students:* 26 full-time (22 women), 43 part-time (39 women); includes 19 minority (9 Black or African American, non-Hispanic/Latino; 1 Asian, non-Hispanic/Latino; 8 Hispanic/Latino; 1 Two or more races, non-Hispanic/Latino), 3 international. Average age 30. 91 applicants, 57% accepted, 33 enrolled. In 2017, 25 master's awarded. *Entrance requirements:* For master's, GRE General Test, minimum GPA of 3.0 in last 2 years of undergraduate course work. Additional exam requirements/recommendations for international students: Required—TOEFL (minimum score 500 paper-based; 61 iBT), IELTS (minimum score 6). *Application deadline:* For fall

admission, 7/1 for domestic students, 2/15 for international students; for spring admission, 11/1 for domestic students, 7/15 for international students. Applications are processed on a rolling basis. Application fee: $30. *Expenses:* Tuition, state resident: full-time $7400; part-time $369.82 per credit. Tuition, nonresident: full-time $20,496; part-time $1042.81 per credit. *Financial support:* Fellowships with partial tuition reimbursements, research assistantships with partial tuition reimbursements, teaching assistantships with partial tuition reimbursements, career-related internships or fieldwork, scholarships/grants, and unspecified assistantships available. *Faculty research:* Technology, teaching English to speakers of other languages, math teaching, electronic portfolio assessment, global perspectives through social studies. *Unit head:* Dr. Barbara Ridener, Chairperson, 561-297-3588, E-mail: bridener@fau.edu. *Application contact:* Dr. Eliah Watlington, Associate Dean, 561-296-8520, Fax: 261-297-2991, E-mail: ewatling@fau.edu.
Website: http://www.coe.fau.edu/academicdepartments/tl/

Florida Institute of Technology, College of Science, Program in Environmental Education, Melbourne, FL 32901-6975. Offers MS. *Students:* Average age 25. 5 applicants, 60% accepted, 1 enrolled. In 2017, 2 master's awarded. *Degree requirements:* For master's, comprehensive exam (for some programs), thesis optional, 30 credit hours. *Entrance requirements:* For master's, 3 letters of recommendation; resume; statement of objectives; bachelor's degree in science, environmental studies, environmental interpretation, psychology, or K-12 education. Additional exam requirements/recommendations for international students: Required—TOEFL (minimum score 550 paper-based; 79 iBT). *Application deadline:* Applications are processed on a rolling basis. Electronic applications accepted. *Expenses: Tuition:* Part-time $1241 per credit hour. Part-time tuition and fees vary according to campus/location. *Financial support:* Applicants required to submit FAFSA. *Unit head:* Dr. Kastro Hamed, Department Head, 321-674-7206, E-mail: khamed@fit.edu. *Application contact:* Cheryl A. Brown, Associate Director of Graduate Admissions, 321-674-7581, Fax: 321-723-9468, E-mail: cbrown@fit.edu.
Website: http://www.fit.edu/programs/8119/ms-environmental-education#.VT_jzU10ypo

Goshen College, Merry Lea Environmental Learning Center, Goshen, IN 46526-4794. Offers MA. *Accreditation:* NCATE. *Faculty:* 9 full-time (1 woman), 1 part-time/adjunct (0 women). *Students:* 11 full-time (6 women). *Degree requirements:* For master's, thesis. *Entrance requirements:* For master's, resume, official transcripts, three letters of reference. Additional exam requirements/recommendations for international students: Required—TOEFL (minimum score 600 paper-based; 100 iBT), IELTS (minimum score 6.5). *Application deadline:* For fall admission, 3/30 for domestic students. Applications are processed on a rolling basis. Application fee: $25. Electronic applications accepted. *Expenses: Tuition:* Full-time $13,356; part-time $742 per credit hour. Tuition and fees vary according to degree level, campus/location and program. *Financial support:* Application deadline: 9/10. *Faculty research:* Environmental education, climate change, climate justice, landscape ecology, invasive species. *Unit head:* Dr. Luke Gascho, Executive Director, 260-799-5869, E-mail: lukeag@goshen.edu. *Application contact:* Dr. David Ostergren, Director of the Graduate Program in Environmental Education, 260-799-5869, E-mail: daveo@goshen.edu.
Website: http://www.goshen.edu/merrylea/

Hamline University, School of Education, St. Paul, MN 55104-1284. Offers education (MA Ed, Ed D); English as a second language (MA); literacy education (MA); natural science and environmental education (MA Ed); teaching (MAT); teaching English to speakers of other languages (MA). *Accreditation:* NCATE (one or more programs are accredited). *Program availability:* Part-time, evening/weekend, 100% online, blended/hybrid learning. *Faculty:* 23 full-time (15 women), 43 part-time/adjunct (30 women). *Students:* 79 full-time (60 women), 898 part-time (692 women); includes 139 minority (31 Black or African American, non-Hispanic/Latino; 1 American Indian or Alaska Native, non-Hispanic/Latino; 58 Asian, non-Hispanic/Latino; 33 Hispanic/Latino; 16 Two or more races, non-Hispanic/Latino), 8 international. Average age 35. 366 applicants, 78% accepted, 193 enrolled. In 2017, 236 master's, 7 doctorates awarded. *Degree requirements:* For master's, thesis (for some programs), thesis or capstone project; for doctorate, comprehensive exam, thesis/dissertation. *Entrance requirements:* For master's, official transcripts, essay, letters of recommendation, minimum GPA of 3.0 from bachelor's work; resume and/or writing samples (for some programs); for doctorate, personal statement, master's degree with minimum GPA of 3.0, letters of recommendation, writing sample. Additional exam requirements/recommendations for international students: Required—TOEFL (minimum score 550 paper-based; 80 iBT), IELTS (minimum score 6.5). *Application deadline:* For fall admission, 6/1 for domestic and international students; for spring admission, 11/1 for domestic and international students; for summer admission, 3/1 for domestic and international students. Applications are processed on a rolling basis. Application fee: $0 ($100 for international students). Electronic applications accepted. *Expenses:* $466 per credit (for MA Ed), $625 per credit (for MATESOL), $569 per credit (for MAT), $721 per credit plus fees (for EdD). *Financial support:* Career-related internships or fieldwork, Federal Work-Study, and scholarships/grants available. Support available to part-time students. Financial award application deadline: 4/20; financial award applicants required to submit FAFSA. *Faculty research:* Adult basic education, service-learning, teacher dispositions, diversity, technology. *Unit head:* Dr. Marcela Kostihova, Dean, 651-523-2206, Fax: 651-523-2489, E-mail: cladean@hamline.edu. *Application contact:* Shawn Skoog, Director of Graduate Recruitment and Admission, 651-523-2900, Fax: 651-523-3058, E-mail: gradprog@hamline.edu.
Website: http://www.hamline.edu/education

Instituto Tecnologico de Santo Domingo, Graduate School, Area of Basic And Environmental Sciences, Santo Domingo, Dominican Republic. Offers environmental science (M En S), including environmental education, environmental management, marine resources, natural resources management; mathematics (MS, PhD); renewable energy technology (MS, Certificate).

Montclair State University, The Graduate School, College of Science and Mathematics, Program in Environmental Studies, Montclair, NJ 07043-1624. Offers environmental education (MA); environmental management (MA); environmental science (MA). *Program availability:* Part-time, evening/weekend. *Degree requirements:* For master's, thesis. *Entrance requirements:* For master's, GRE General Test, 2 letters of recommendation, essay. Additional exam requirements/recommendations for international students: Required—TOEFL (minimum score 83 iBT), IELTS (minimum score 6.5). Electronic applications accepted. *Faculty research:* Environmental geochemistry/remediation/forensics, environmental law and policy, regional climate modeling, remote sensing, Cenozoic marine sediment records from polar regions, sustainability science.

New York University, Steinhardt School of Culture, Education, and Human Development, Department of Teaching and Learning, Program in Environmental Conservation Education, New York, NY 10012. Offers MA. *Accreditation:* TEAC. *Program availability:* Part-time. *Students:* Average age 27. 36 applicants, 92% accepted, 17 enrolled. In 2017, 23 master's awarded. *Entrance requirements:* Additional exam requirements/recommendations for international students: Required—TOEFL (minimum score 100 iBT). *Application deadline:* For fall admission, 12/1 priority date for domestic and international students; for spring admission, 10/1 for domestic and international

students. Applications are processed on a rolling basis. Application fee: $75. Electronic applications accepted. *Expenses: Tuition:* Full-time $41,352; part-time $19,968 per year. *Required fees:* $2496; $1628 per unit. $814 per term. Tuition and fees vary according to course load and program. *Financial support:* Career-related internships or fieldwork, Federal Work-Study, institutionally sponsored loans, and tuition waivers (partial) available. Support available to part-time students. Financial award application deadline: 2/1; financial award applicants required to submit FAFSA. *Faculty research:* Environmental ethics, values and policy, philosophy and geography. *Unit head:* Dr. Mary Leou, Acting Director, 212-998-5474, Fax: 212-995-4832, E-mail: mary.leou@nyu.edu. *Application contact:* 212-998-5030, Fax: 212-995-4328, E-mail: steinhardt.gradadmissions@nyu.edu.
Website: http://steinhardt.nyu.edu/teachlearn/environmental

Oregon State University, Interdisciplinary/Institutional Programs, Program in Environmental Sciences, Corvallis, OR 97331. Offers biogeochemistry (MA, MS, PSM, PhD); ecology (MA, MS, PSM, PhD); environmental education (MA, MS, PhD); quantitative analysis (PSM); social science (MA, MS, PSM, PhD); water resources (MA, MS, PhD). *Program availability:* Part-time. *Degree requirements:* For master's, variable foreign language requirement, thesis; for doctorate, thesis/dissertation. *Entrance requirements:* For master's and doctorate, GRE. Additional exam requirements/recommendations for international students: Required—TOEFL (minimum score 80 iBT), IELTS (minimum score 6.5). *Application deadline:* For fall admission, 1/15 priority date for domestic and international students. Application fee: $75 ($85 for international students). *Unit head:* Dr. Carolyn Fonyo Boggess, Interim Director, 541-760-4196, E-mail: carolyn.fonyo@oregonstate.edu. *Application contact:* Dr. Carolyn Fonyo Boggess, Interim Director, 541-760-4196, E-mail: carolyn.fonyo@oregonstate.edu.
Website: http://gradschool.oregonstate.edu/environmental-sciences-graduate-program-esgp

Prescott College, Graduate Programs, Program in Education, Prescott, AZ 86301. Offers early childhood education (MA); early childhood special education (MA); education (MA); elementary education (MA); environmental education leadership and administration (MA); equine-assisted learning (MA); school guidance counseling (MA); secondary education (MA); special education: learning disabilities (MA); special education: mental retardation (MA); special education: serious emotional disabilities (MA); student-directed independent study (MA); sustainability education (PhD). *Program availability:* Part-time, online learning. *Degree requirements:* For master's, thesis, fieldwork or internship, practicum; for doctorate, thesis/dissertation. *Entrance requirements:* For master's, 2 letters of recommendation, resume; for doctorate, 3 letters of recommendation, resume, official transcripts, personal statement, program proposal. Additional exam requirements/recommendations for international students: Required—TOEFL (minimum score 500 paper-based). Electronic applications accepted.

Royal Roads University, Graduate Studies, Environment and Sustainability Program, Victoria, BC V9B 5Y2, Canada. Offers environment and management (M Sc, MA); environment and sustainability (MAIS); environmental education and communication (MA, G Dip, Graduate Certificate); MA/MS. *Program availability:* Blended/hybrid learning. *Faculty:* 6 full-time (2 women), 22 part-time/adjunct (13 women). *Degree requirements:* For master's, thesis. *Entrance requirements:* For master's, 5-7 years of related work experience. *Application deadline:* Applications are processed on a rolling basis. Application fee: $120 ($240 for international students). Electronic applications accepted. *Financial support:* Federal Work-Study, institutionally sponsored loans, scholarships/grants, and bursaries available. Support available to part-time students. *Faculty research:* Sustainable development, atmospheric processes, sustainable communities, chemical fate and transport of persistent organic pollutants, educational technology. Total annual research expenditures: $40,000. *Unit head:* Dr. Brigitte Harris, Dean, 250-391-2511. *Application contact:* 250-391-2511, E-mail: admissions@royalroads.ca.

Slippery Rock University of Pennsylvania, Graduate Studies (Recruitment), College of Health, Environment, and Science, Department of Parks and Recreation, Slippery Rock, PA 16057-1383. Offers environmental education (M Ed); park and resource management (MS). *Program availability:* Part-time, evening/weekend, online only, 100% online. *Degree requirements:* For master's, comprehensive exam (for some programs), thesis (for some programs), internship. *Entrance requirements:* For master's, official transcripts, minimum GPA of 2.75, personal statement. Additional exam requirements/recommendations for international students: Required—TOEFL (minimum score 550 paper-based; 80 iBT). Electronic applications accepted. *Expenses:* Contact institution.

Southern Connecticut State University, School of Graduate Studies, School of Arts and Sciences, Department of Environment, Geography and Marine Sciences, New Haven, CT 06515-1355. Offers environmental education (MS); science education (MS, Diploma). *Accreditation:* NCATE. *Program availability:* Part-time, evening/weekend. *Degree requirements:* For master's, thesis or alternative. *Entrance requirements:* For master's, interview; for Diploma, master's degree. Electronic applications accepted.

Southern Oregon University, Graduate Studies, Program in Environmental Education, Ashland, OR 97520. Offers MS. *Program availability:* Part-time, online learning. *Degree requirements:* For master's, thesis (for some programs), comprehensive exam (for MA). *Entrance requirements:* For master's, GRE General Test, minimum cumulative GPA of 3.0 in the last 90 quarter credits (60 semester credits) of undergraduate coursework. Additional exam requirements/recommendations for international students: Required—TOEFL (minimum score 540 paper-based; 76 iBT), IELTS (minimum score 6), ELPT (minimum score 964) or ELS (minimum score 112). Electronic applications accepted.

State University of New York College at Cortland, Graduate Studies, School of Professional Studies, Department of Recreation, Parks and Leisure Studies, Cortland, NY 13045. Offers outdoor education (MS, MS Ed); recreation management (MS, MS Ed); therapeutic recreation (MS, MS Ed). *Program availability:* Part-time, evening/weekend. *Degree requirements:* For master's, comprehensive exam, thesis (for some programs). *Entrance requirements:* Additional exam requirements/recommendations for international students: Required—TOEFL.

Université du Québec à Montréal, Graduate Programs, Program in Education, Montréal, QC H3C 3P8, Canada. Offers education (M Ed, MA, PhD); education of the environmental sciences (Diploma). PhD offered jointly with Université du Québec à Chicoutimi, Université du Québec à Rimouski, Université du Québec à Trois-Rivières, Université du Québec en Outaouais, and Université du Québec en Abitibi-Témiscamingue. *Program availability:* Part-time. *Degree requirements:* For master's, thesis (for some programs); for doctorate, thesis/dissertation. *Entrance requirements:* For master's and Diploma, appropriate bachelor's degree or equivalent, proficiency in French; for doctorate, appropriate master's degree or equivalent, proficiency in French.

University of Colorado Denver, College of Liberal Arts and Sciences, Department of Geography and Environmental Sciences, Denver, CO 80217. Offers environmental sciences (MS), including air quality, ecosystems, environmental health, environmental science education, geospatial analysis, urban agriculture, water quality. *Program availability:* Part-time, evening/weekend. *Degree requirements:* For master's, thesis or alternative, 30 credits including 21 of core requirements and 9 of environmental science electives. *Entrance requirements:* For master's, GRE General Test, BA in one of the natural/physical sciences or engineering (or equivalent background); prerequisite coursework in calculus and physics (one semester each); general chemistry with lab and general biology with lab (two semesters each); three letters of recommendation. Additional exam requirements/recommendations for international students: Required—TOEFL (minimum score 537 paper-based; 75 iBT); Recommended—IELTS (minimum score 6.5). Electronic applications accepted. *Faculty research:* Air quality, environmental health, ecosystems, hazardous waste, water quality, geospatial analysis and environmental science education.

University of Florida, Graduate School, College of Agricultural and Life Sciences, Department of Wildlife Ecology and Conservation, Gainesville, FL 32611. Offers environmental education and communications (Certificate); wildlife ecology and conservation (MS, PhD), including geographic information systems, tropical conservation and development, wetland sciences. *Degree requirements:* For master's, comprehensive exam, thesis optional; for doctorate, comprehensive exam, thesis/dissertation. *Entrance requirements:* For master's and doctorate, GRE General Test (minimum 34th percentile for Quantitative), minimum GPA of 3.3. Additional exam requirements/recommendations for international students: Required—TOEFL (minimum score 550 paper-based; 80 iBT), IELTS (minimum score 6). Electronic applications accepted. *Faculty research:* Conservation biology, spatial ecology, wildlife conservation and management, wetlands ecology and conservation, human dimensions in wildlife conservation.

University of South Africa, College of Human Sciences, Pretoria, South Africa. Offers adult education (M Ed); African languages (MA, PhD); African politics (MA, PhD); Afrikaans (MA, PhD); ancient history (MA, PhD); ancient Near Eastern studies (MA, PhD); anthropology (MA, PhD); applied linguistics (MA); Arabic (MA, PhD); archaeology (MA); art history (MA); Biblical archaeology (MA); Biblical studies (M Th, D Th, PhD); Christian spirituality (M Th, D Th); church history (M Th, D Th); classical studies (MA, PhD); clinical psychology (MA); communication (MA, PhD); comparative education (M Ed, Ed D); consulting psychology (D Admin, D Com, PhD); curriculum studies (M Ed, Ed D); development studies (M Admin, MA, D Admin, PhD); didactics (M Ed, Ed D); education (M Tech); education management (M Ed, Ed D); educational psychology (M Ed); English (MA); environmental education (M Ed); French (MA, PhD); German (MA, PhD); Greek (MA); guidance and counseling (M Ed); health studies (MA, PhD), including health sciences education (MA), health services management (MA), medical and surgical nursing science (critical care general) (MA), midwifery and neonatal nursing science (MA), trauma and emergency care (MA); history (MA, PhD); history of education (Ed D); inclusive education (M Ed, Ed D); information and communications technology policy and regulation (MA); information science (MA, MIS, PhD); international politics (MA, PhD); Islamic studies (MA, PhD); Italian (MA, PhD); Judaica (MA, PhD); linguistics (MA, PhD); mathematical education (M Ed); mathematics education (MA); missiology (M Th, D Th); modern Hebrew (MA, PhD); musicology (MA, MMus, D Mus, PhD); natural science education (M Ed); New Testament (M Th, D Th); Old Testament (D Th); pastoral therapy (M Th, D Th); philosophy (MA); philosophy of education (M Ed, Ed D); politics (MA, PhD); Portuguese (MA, PhD); practical theology (M Th, D Th); psychology (MA, MS, PhD); psychology of education (M Ed, Ed D); public health (MA); religious studies (MA, D Th, PhD); Romance languages (MA); Russian (MA, PhD); Semitic languages (MA, PhD); social behavior studies in HIV/AIDS (MA); social science (mental health) (MA); social science in development studies (MA); social science in psychology (MA); social science in social work (MA); social science in sociology (MA); social work (MSW, DSW, PhD); socio-education (M Ed, Ed D); sociolinguistics (MA); sociology (MA, PhD); Spanish (MA, PhD); systematic theology (M Th, D Th); TESOL (teaching English to speakers of other languages) (MA); theological ethics (M Th, D Th); theory of literature (MA, PhD); urban ministries (D Th); urban ministry (M Th).

University of Victoria, Faculty of Graduate Studies, Faculty of Education, Department of Curriculum and Instruction, Victoria, BC V8W 2Y2, Canada. Offers art education (M Ed, PhD); curriculum studies (M Ed, MA, PhD); early childhood education (M Ed, PhD); educational studies (PhD); language and literacy (M Ed, MA, PhD); mathematics (M Ed, MA, PhD); music education (M Ed, MA, PhD); science (M Ed, MA, PhD); social studies (M Ed, MA); social, cultural and foundational studies (MA, PhD); technology and environmental education (PhD). *Program availability:* Part-time. *Degree requirements:* For master's, thesis, project (M Ed); for doctorate, comprehensive exam, thesis/dissertation. *Entrance requirements:* For master's, minimum B average. Additional exam requirements/recommendations for international students: Required—TOEFL (minimum score 575 paper-based), IELTS (minimum score 7). Electronic applications accepted. *Faculty research:* Elementary and secondary English, language arts, curriculum theory and practice, educational media and technology, educational administration and leadership, history and philosophy of education.

Western Washington University, Graduate School, Huxley College of the Environment, Department of Environmental Studies, Program in Environmental Education, Bellingham, WA 98225-5996. Offers M Ed. *Program availability:* Part-time. *Degree requirements:* For master's, comprehensive exam, thesis optional. *Entrance requirements:* For master's, GRE or MAT, minimum GPA of 3.0 in last 60 semester hours. Additional exam requirements/recommendations for international students: Required—TOEFL (minimum score 567 paper-based). Electronic applications accepted. *Faculty research:* Role of wilderness in national park history; history of the conservation movement and sense of place in environmental education; environmental care and responsibility; conservation psychology and environmental education.

Foreign Languages Education

Andrews University, School of Graduate Studies, School of Education, Department of Teaching, Learning, and Curriculum, Berrien Springs, MI 49104. Offers curriculum and instruction (MA, Ed D, PhD, Ed S); elementary education (MAT); secondary education (MAT), including biology, education, English, English as a second language, French, history, physics; teacher education (MAT). *Faculty:* 7 full-time (5 women). *Students:* 14 full-time (8 women), 7 part-time (6 women); includes 5 minority (all Black or African American, non-Hispanic/Latino), 9 international. Average age 39. 29 applicants, 31% accepted, 4 enrolled. In 2017, 5 master's, 3 doctorates awarded. *Entrance requirements:* For master's, GRE Subject Test. Additional exam requirements/recommendations for international students: Required—TOEFL (minimum score 550 paper-based). *Application deadline:* For fall admission, 8/15 for domestic students. Applications are processed on a rolling basis. Application fee: $40. *Unit head:* Dr. Lee C. Davidson, Chair, 269-471-6364. *Application contact:* Justina Clayburn, Supervisor of Graduate Admission, 800-253-2874, Fax: 269-471-6321, E-mail: graduate@andrews.edu.

Appalachian State University, Cratis D. Williams Graduate School, Department of Languages, Literatures and Cultures, Boone, NC 28608. Offers romance languages (MA), including French teaching, Spanish teaching. *Program availability:* Part-time, online learning. *Degree requirements:* For master's, one foreign language, comprehensive exam, thesis optional. *Entrance requirements:* For master's, GRE General Test, 3 letters of recommendation. Additional exam requirements/recommendations for international students: Required—TOEFL (minimum score 570 paper-based; 79 iBT) or IELTS (minimum score 6.5). Electronic applications accepted. *Faculty research:* French and Spanish literature, Latin American culture, teaching foreign languages.

Arizona State University at the Tempe campus, College of Liberal Arts and Sciences, School of International Letters and Cultures, Program in Spanish, Tempe, AZ 85287-0202. Offers cultural studies (PhD); linguistics (MA), including second language acquisition/applied linguistics, sociolinguistics; literature (PhD); literature and culture (MA). *Program availability:* Part-time. Terminal master's awarded for partial completion of doctoral program. *Degree requirements:* For master's, thesis, oral defense; written comprehensive exam (literature and culture); portfolio review (linguistics); interactive Program of Study (iPOS) submitted before completing 50 percent of required credit hours; for doctorate, comprehensive exam, thesis/dissertation, interactive Program of Study (iPOS) submitted before completing 50 percent of required credit hours. *Entrance requirements:* For master's, GRE (recommended), BA in Spanish or close equivalent from accredited institution with minimum GPA of 3.5, 3 letters of recommendation, personal statement, academic writing sample; for doctorate, GRE (recommended), MA in Spanish or equivalent from accredited institution with minimum GPA of 3.75, 3 letters of recommendation, personal statement, academic writing sample. Additional exam requirements/recommendations for international students: Required—TOEFL (minimum score 550 paper-based; 83 iBT), IELTS (minimum score 6.5). Electronic applications accepted.

Augusta University, College of Education, Program in Curriculum and Instruction, Augusta, GA 30912. Offers curriculum and instruction (Ed S); elementary education (MAT); foreign language education (MAT); instruction (M Ed); middle grades education (MAT); music education (MAT); secondary education (MAT); special education (MAT). *Degree requirements:* For master's, thesis, portfolio. *Entrance requirements:* For master's, GRE, MAT, minimum GPA of 2.5.

Binghamton University, State University of New York, Graduate School, College of Community and Public Affairs, Department of Teaching, Learning and Educational Leadership, Program in Adolescence Education, Binghamton, NY 13902-6000. Offers biology education (MAT, MS Ed); chemistry education (MAT, MS Ed); earth science education (MAT, MS Ed); English education (MAT, MS Ed); French education (MAT, MS Ed); mathematical sciences education (MAT, MS Ed); physics (MAT, MS Ed); social studies (MAT, MS Ed); Spanish education (MAT, MS Ed). *Accreditation:* TEAC. *Program availability:* Part-time, evening/weekend. *Students:* 53 full-time (32 women), 9 part-time (3 women); includes 10 minority (2 Black or African American, non-Hispanic/Latino; 1 Asian, non-Hispanic/Latino; 5 Hispanic/Latino; 2 Two or more races, non-Hispanic/Latino). Average age 27. 51 applicants, 88% accepted, 31 enrolled. In 2017, 36 master's awarded. *Degree requirements:* For master's, portfolio. *Entrance requirements:* For master's, GRE General Test, teaching certification. Additional exam requirements/recommendations for international students: Required—TOEFL (minimum score 550 paper-based; 80 iBT). *Application deadline:* For fall admission, 2/1 priority date for domestic and international students; for spring admission, 10/15 priority date for domestic and international students. Application fee: $75. Electronic applications accepted. *Financial support:* In 2017–18, 4 students received support. Research assistantships, teaching assistantships, career-related internships or fieldwork, Federal Work-Study, institutionally sponsored loans, scholarships/grants, health care benefits, tuition waivers (full and partial), and unspecified assistantships available. Financial award applicants required to submit FAFSA. *Unit head:* Dr. Susan Strehle, Dean, 607-777-7329, E-mail: sstrehle@binghamton.edu. *Application contact:* Ben Balkaya, Assistant Dean and Director, 607-777-2151, Fax: 607-777-2501, E-mail: balkaya@binghamton.edu.

Brandeis University, Graduate School of Arts and Sciences, Program in Teaching Chinese Language and Culture, Waltham, MA 02454-9110. Offers MA. *Students:* 5 full-time (all women), all international. Average age 24. 15 applicants, 80% accepted, 12 enrolled. In 2017, 6 master's awarded. *Degree requirements:* For master's, one foreign language. *Entrance requirements:* For master's, transcripts, letters of recommendation, resume, video of teaching in the classroom, statement of purpose. Additional exam requirements/recommendations for international students: Required—PTE (minimum score 68), TOEFL (minimum score 600 paper-based, 100 iBT) or IELTS (7). *Application deadline:* For fall admission, 1/15 priority date for domestic students. Applications are processed on a rolling basis. Application fee: $75. Electronic applications accepted. *Expenses: Tuition:* Full-time $48,720. *Required fees:* $88. Tuition and fees vary according to course load, degree level, program and student level. *Financial support:* In 2017–18, 2 students received support, including 4 teaching assistantships (averaging $3,200 per year); scholarships/grants also available. Financial award application deadline: 4/15; financial award applicants required to submit FAFSA. *Unit head:* Dr. Yu Feng, Director of Graduate Studies, 781-736-2961, E-mail: yfeng@brandeis.edu. Website: http://www.brandeis.edu/gsas/programs/chinese.html

Brigham Young University, Graduate Studies, College of Humanities, Center for Language Studies, Provo, UT 84602. Offers second language teaching (MA). *Faculty:* 33 full-time (4 women). *Students:* 5 full-time (3 women), 4 part-time (1 woman); includes 2 minority (both Asian, non-Hispanic/Latino). Average age 34. 4 applicants, 50% accepted, 2 enrolled. In 2017, 4 master's awarded. *Degree requirements:* For master's, one foreign language, comprehensive exam, thesis. *Entrance requirements:* For master's, GRE General Test (minimum score in 50th percentile on the verbal section, 4 on analytical/writing section); ACTFL OPI in language of specialization (if student is not a native speaker of the target language), English writing sample, minimum GPA of 3.0, three letters of recommendation, letter of intent, completion of a teaching method class. Additional exam requirements/recommendations for international students: Required—TOEFL (minimum score 580 paper-based; 85 iBT), IELTS (minimum score 7). *Application deadline:* For fall admission, 2/1 for domestic and international students. Application fee: $50. Electronic applications accepted. *Expenses:* $3,440 full-time; $746 per credit part-time. *Financial support:* In 2017–18, 13 students received support. Scholarships/grants available. Financial award application deadline: 2/1. *Faculty research:* Test construct validation, strategy for attaining superior language proficiency, error correction strategies, direct versus indirect testing, eye tracking and reading proficiency. *Unit head:* Dr. Ray T. Clifford, Director, 801-422-3263, E-mail: rayc@byu.edu. *Application contact:* Rebecca L. Brazzale, Graduate Program Manager, 801-422-5199, E-mail: rebecca_brazzale@byu.edu. Website: https://cls.byu.edu/

Foreign Languages Education

Brigham Young University, Graduate Studies, College of Humanities, Department of Spanish and Portuguese, Provo, UT 84602. Offers Portuguese (MA), including Luso-Brazilian literatures, Portuguese linguistics, Portuguese pedagogy; Spanish (MA), including Hispanic linguistics, Hispanic literatures, Spanish pedagogy. *Faculty:* 30 full-time (6 women). *Students:* 32 full-time (17 women), 6 part-time (4 women); includes 16 minority (all Hispanic/Latino). Average age 31. 19 applicants, 68% accepted, 10 enrolled. In 2017, 6 master's awarded. *Degree requirements:* For master's, 2 foreign languages, comprehensive exam, thesis, 1 semester of teaching. *Entrance requirements:* For master's, minimum GPA of 3.5 in Spanish or Portuguese, 3.3 overall. Additional exam requirements/recommendations for international students: Required—TOEFL (minimum score 580 paper-based; 85 iBT), IELTS (minimum score 6.5), PTE (minimum score 53). *Application deadline:* For fall admission, 2/1 for domestic and international students. Application fee: $50. Electronic applications accepted. *Expenses:* Contact institution. *Financial support:* In 2017–18, 23 students received support, including 87 teaching assistantships (averaging $3,200 per year); research assistantships, institutionally sponsored loans, scholarships/grants, tuition waivers (partial), and unspecified assistantships also available. Support available to part-time students. *Faculty research:* Mexican prose; Latin American theater; literature; phonetics, and phonology; pedagogy; classical Portuguese literature. *Unit head:* Dr. Jeffrey S. Turley, Chair, 801-422-7019, Fax: 801-422-0628, E-mail: jeffrey_turley@byu.edu. *Application contact:* Patricia E. Wilson, Graduate Program Manager, 801-422-2838, Fax: 801-422-0628, E-mail: patricia_rubio@byu.edu.
Website: http://spanport.byu.edu/

Brooklyn College of the City University of New York, School of Education, Program in Adolescence Science Education and Special Subjects, Brooklyn, NY 11210-2889. Offers adolescence science education (MAT); biology teacher (7-12) (MA); chemistry teacher (7-12) (MA); earth science teacher (7-12) (MAT); English teacher (7-12) (MA); French teacher (7-12) (MA); mathematics teacher (7-12) (MA); music teacher (MA); physics teacher (7-12) (MA); social studies teacher (7-12) (MA); Spanish teacher (7-12) (MA). *Program availability:* Part-time, evening/weekend. *Degree requirements:* For master's, comprehensive exam (for some programs), thesis (for some programs). *Entrance requirements:* For master's, LAST, previous course work in education, resume, 2 letters of recommendation, essay. Additional exam requirements/recommendations for international students: Required—TOEFL (minimum score 500 paper-based; 61 iBT). Electronic applications accepted. *Faculty research:* Interdisciplinary education, semiotics, discourse analysis, autobiography, teacher identity.

California State University, Sacramento, College of Arts and Letters, Department of World Languages and Literatures, Sacramento, CA 95819. Offers MA. *Program availability:* Part-time. *Students:* 8 full-time (4 women), 15 part-time (12 women); includes 21 minority (all Hispanic/Latino). Average age 34. 8 applicants, 88% accepted, 6 enrolled. In 2017, 10 master's awarded. *Degree requirements:* For master's, comprehensive exam, thesis or project. *Entrance requirements:* For master's, interview, minimum GPA of 3.0 during previous 2 years of course work. Additional exam requirements/recommendations for international students: Required—TOEFL (minimum score 550 paper-based; 80 iBT). *Application deadline:* For fall admission, 3/1 for domestic and international students; for spring admission, 9/30 for international students. Applications are processed on a rolling basis. Application fee: $55. Electronic applications accepted. *Expenses:* Contact institution. *Financial support:* Teaching assistantships, career-related internships or fieldwork, Federal Work-Study, and scholarships/grants available. Support available to part-time students. Financial award application deadline: 3/1; financial award applicants required to submit FAFSA. *Unit head:* Dr. Curtis Smith, Chair, 916-278-6333, Fax: 916-278-5502, E-mail: curtis.smith@csus.edu. *Application contact:* Jose Martinez, Graduate Admissions Supervisor, 916-278-7871, E-mail: martinj@skymail.csus.edu.
Website: http://www.csus.edu/fl

Caribbean University, Graduate School, Bayamón, PR 00960-0493. Offers administration and supervision (MA Ed); criminal justice (MA); curriculum and instruction (MA Ed, PhD), including elementary education (MA Ed), English education (MA Ed), history education (MA Ed), mathematics education (MA Ed), primary education (MA Ed), science education (MA Ed), Spanish education (MA Ed); educational technology in instructional systems (MA Ed); gerontology (MSN); human resources (MBA); museology, archiving and art history (MA Ed); neonatal pediatrics (MSN); physical education (MA Ed); special education (MA Ed). *Entrance requirements:* For master's, interview, minimum GPA of 2.5.

Central Connecticut State University, School of Graduate Studies, College of Liberal Arts and Social Sciences, Department of Modern Languages, New Britain, CT 06050-4010. Offers modern language (MA, Certificate), including French, German (Certificate), Italian, Spanish (MA); Spanish (MS, Certificate). *Program availability:* Part-time, evening/weekend. *Faculty:* 7 full-time (6 women). *Students:* 6 full-time (5 women), 16 part-time (12 women); includes 9 minority (all Hispanic/Latino), 1 international. Average age 32. 8 applicants, 88% accepted, 5 enrolled. In 2017, 12 master's awarded. *Degree requirements:* For master's, one foreign language, comprehensive exam, thesis or alternative; for Certificate, qualifying exam. *Entrance requirements:* For master's, minimum undergraduate GPA of 2.7, 24 credits of undergraduate courses in each language in which graduate work will be undertaken. Additional exam requirements/recommendations for international students: Required—TOEFL (minimum score 550 paper-based; 79 iBT); Recommended—IELTS (minimum score 6.5). *Application deadline:* For fall admission, 8/1 for domestic students, 5/1 for international students; for spring admission, 11/1 for domestic and international students. Applications are processed on a rolling basis. Application fee: $50. Electronic applications accepted. *Expenses:* Tuition, area resident: Full-time $6757. Tuition, state resident: full-time $9750; part-time $374 per credit. Tuition, nonresident: full-time $18,102; part-time $374 per credit. *Required fees:* $4635; $255 per credit. *Financial support:* In 2017–18, 3 students received support. Career-related internships or fieldwork, Federal Work-Study, scholarships/grants, and unspecified assistantships available. Support available to part-time students. Financial award application deadline: 3/1; financial award applicants required to submit FAFSA. *Faculty research:* Quebecois literature, Caribbean literature, modern French/Spanish drama, Puerto Rican novel and drama. *Unit head:* Dr. Carmela Pesca, Chair, 860-832-2875, E-mail: pescac@ccsu.edu. *Application contact:* Patricia Gardner, Associate Director of Graduate Studies, 860-832-2350, Fax: 860-832-2362.
Website: http://www.ccsu.edu/modlang/

City College of the City University of New York, Graduate School, Division of Humanities and the Arts, Department of Classical and Modern Languages and Literatures, New York, NY 10031-9198. Offers Spanish (MA). *Degree requirements:* For master's, one foreign language, comprehensive exam, thesis or alternative. *Entrance requirements:* For master's, minimum GPA of 3.0. Additional exam requirements/recommendations for international students: Required—TOEFL (minimum score 500 paper-based; 61 iBT). Electronic applications accepted.

Cleveland State University, College of Graduate Studies, College of Education and Human Services, Department of Teacher Education, Cleveland, OH 44115. Offers art education (M Ed); early childhood education (M Ed); foreign language education (M Ed); middle childhood mathematics and science education (M Ed); special education (M Ed);

including mild/moderate disabilities, moderate/intensive disabilities; teaching English to speakers of other languages (M Ed). *Program availability:* Part-time, evening/weekend. *Faculty:* 19 full-time (14 women), 32 part-time/adjunct (27 women). *Students:* 80 full-time (60 women), 361 part-time (277 women); includes 119 minority (86 Black or African American, non-Hispanic/Latino; 5 Asian, non-Hispanic/Latino; 16 Hispanic/Latino; 12 Two or more races, non-Hispanic/Latino), 20 international. Average age 34. 177 applicants, 55% accepted, 68 enrolled. In 2017, 137 master's awarded. *Degree requirements:* For master's, comprehensive exam (for some programs), thesis or alternative. *Entrance requirements:* For master's, GRE General Test or MAT, minimum GPA of 2.75. Additional exam requirements/recommendations for international students: Required—TOEFL (minimum score 550 paper-based; 78 iBT), IELTS (minimum score 6). *Application deadline:* For fall admission, 7/1 priority date for domestic students, 5/15 for international students; for spring admission, 11/15 for domestic students, 11/1 for international students; for summer admission, 4/1 for domestic students, 3/15 for international students. Applications are processed on a rolling basis. Application fee: $30. *Financial support:* In 2017–18, 13 research assistantships with full tuition reimbursements (averaging $15,845 per year) were awarded; tuition waivers (partial) and unspecified assistantships also available. Financial award application deadline: 2/15; financial award applicants required to submit FAFSA. *Faculty research:* Early childhood education, literacy education, special education: mild/moderate, moderate/intensive, early childhood intervention specialist; teaching English to speakers of other languages (TESOL). *Total annual research expenditures:* $275,907. *Unit head:* Dr. Tachelle Banks, Department Chairperson, 216-687-4600, Fax: 216-687-5379, E-mail: t.i.banks@csuohio.edu. *Application contact:* Rosalyn Adams, Administrative Coordinator, 216-523-7139, Fax: 216-687-5491, E-mail: r.m.adams@csuohio.edu.
Website: http://www.csuohio.edu/cehs/te/te

College of Charleston, Graduate School, School of Education, Health, and Human Performance, Program in Languages, Charleston, SC 29424-0001. Offers M Ed. *Program availability:* Part-time, evening/weekend. *Degree requirements:* For master's, comprehensive exam or portfolio. *Entrance requirements:* For master's, minimum GPA of 2.5. Additional exam requirements/recommendations for international students: Required—TOEFL (minimum score 81 iBT). Electronic applications accepted.

The College of William and Mary, School of Education, Program in Curriculum and Instruction, Williamsburg, VA 23187-8795. Offers elementary education (MA Ed); English as a second language/bilingual education (MA Ed); gifted education (MA Ed); literacy leadership (MA Ed); math specialist (MA Ed); secondary education (MA Ed), including English, foreign language, math, science, social studies; special education (MA Ed). *Accreditation:* NCATE. *Program availability:* Part-time. *Faculty:* 23 full-time (16 women), 40 part-time/adjunct (32 women). *Students:* 85 full-time (63 women), 16 part-time (15 women); includes 18 minority (5 Black or African American, non-Hispanic/Latino; 4 Asian, non-Hispanic/Latino; 7 Hispanic/Latino; 2 Two or more races, non-Hispanic/Latino), 1 international. Average age 27. 152 applicants, 83% accepted, 90 enrolled. In 2017, 67 master's awarded. *Degree requirements:* For master's, project. *Entrance requirements:* For master's, GRE, MAT, PRAXIS Core Academic Skills for Educators, minimum GPA of 2.5. Additional exam requirements/recommendations for international students: Required—TOEFL (minimum score 100 iBT), IELTS (minimum score 7). *Application deadline:* For fall admission, 1/15 for domestic and international students; for spring admission, 10/1 for domestic and international students. Application fee: $50. Electronic applications accepted. *Expenses:* $9,630 resident full-time, $535 resident part-time per credit hour; $25,920 nonresident full-time, $1,265 nonresident part-time per credit hour; $5,944 full-time fees. *Financial support:* In 2017–18, 35 students received support, including 7 research assistantships (averaging $6,678 per year); scholarships/grants and unspecified assistantships also available. Financial award application deadline: 1/15; financial award applicants required to submit FAFSA. *Faculty research:* Educational technology, professional development and evaluation, inclusive education, rural education, education policy. *Unit head:* Dr. Jeremy D. Stoddard, Department Chair, 757-221-2348, E-mail: jdstod@wm.edu. *Application contact:* Dorothy Smith Osborne, Assistant Dean for Academic Programs and Student Services, 757-221-2317, E-mail: dsosbo@wm.edu.
Website: http://education.wm.edu

The Colorado College, Education Department, Program in Secondary Education, Colorado Springs, CO 80903-3294. Offers art teaching (K-12) (MAT); English teaching (MAT); foreign language teaching (MAT); mathematics teaching (MAT); music teaching (MAT); science teaching (MAT); social studies teaching (MAT). *Degree requirements:* For master's, thesis, internship. Electronic applications accepted.

Colorado State University–Pueblo, College of Education, Engineering and Professional Studies, Education Program, Pueblo, CO 81001-4901. Offers art education (M Ed); foreign language education (M Ed); health and physical education (M Ed); instructional technology (M Ed); linguistically diverse education (M Ed); music education (M Ed); special education (M Ed). *Accreditation:* TEAC. *Program availability:* Part-time. *Degree requirements:* For master's, portfolio. *Entrance requirements:* For master's, 3 recommendations, teaching license. Additional exam requirements/recommendations for international students: Required—TOEFL (minimum score 500 paper-based). Electronic applications accepted. *Faculty research:* Portfolio assessment, math education, science education.

Columbia University, Graduate School of Arts and Sciences, New York, NY 10027. Offers African-American studies (MA); American studies (MA); anthropology (MA, PhD); art history and archaeology (MA, PhD); astronomy (PhD); biological sciences (PhD); biotechnology (MA); chemical physics (PhD); chemistry (PhD); classical studies (MA, PhD); classics (MA, PhD); climate and society (MA); conservation biology (MA); earth and environmental sciences (PhD); East Asia: regional studies (MA); East Asian languages and cultures (MA, PhD); ecology, evolution and environmental biology (MA), including conservation biology; ecology, evolution, and environmental biology (PhD), including ecology and evolutionary biology, evolutionary primatology; economics (MA, PhD); English and comparative literature (MA, PhD); French and Romance philology (MA, PhD); Germanic languages (MA, PhD); global French studies (MA); global thought (MA); Hispanic cultural studies (MA); history (PhD); history and literature (MA); human rights studies (MA); Islamic studies (MA); Italian (MA, PhD); Japanese pedagogy (MA); Jewish studies (MA); Latin America and the Caribbean: regional studies (MA); Latin American and Iberian cultures (PhD); mathematics (MA, PhD), including finance (MA); medieval and Renaissance studies (MA); Middle Eastern, South Asian, and African studies (MA, PhD); modern art: critical and curatorial studies (MA); modern European studies (MA); museum anthropology (MA); music (DMA, PhD); oral history (MA); philosophical foundations of physics (MA); philosophy (MA, PhD); physics (PhD); political science (MA, PhD); psychology (PhD); quantitative methods in the social sciences (MA); religion (MA, PhD); Russia, Eurasia and East Europe: regional studies (MA); Russian translation (MA); Slavic cultures (MA); Slavic languages (MA, PhD); sociology (MA, PhD); South Asian studies (MA); statistics (MA, PhD); theatre (PhD). Dual-degree programs require admission to both Graduate School of Arts and Sciences and another Columbia school. *Program availability:* Part-time. Terminal master's awarded for partial completion of doctoral program. *Degree requirements:* For master's, variable foreign language requirement, comprehensive exam (for some programs), thesis (for some programs); for doctorate, variable foreign language requirement, comprehensive exam (for some programs), thesis/dissertation. *Entrance requirements:* For master's and doctorate, GRE General Test, GRE Subject Test (for some programs). Additional exam requirements/recommendations for international students: Required—TOEFL, IELTS. Electronic applications accepted. *Expenses: Tuition:* Full-time $44,864; part-time $1704 per credit. *Required fees:* $2370 per semester. One-time fee: $105.

Concordia College, Program in Education, Moorhead, MN 56562. Offers world language instruction (M Ed). *Degree requirements:* For master's, thesis/seminar. *Entrance requirements:* For master's, 2 professional references, 1 personal reference.

Cornell University, Graduate School, Graduate Fields of Arts and Sciences, Field of Linguistics, Ithaca, NY 14853. Offers applied linguistics (MA, PhD); East Asian linguistics (MA, PhD); English linguistics (MA, PhD); general linguistics (MA, PhD); Germanic linguistics (MA, PhD); Indo-European linguistics (MA, PhD); phonetics (MA, PhD); phonological theory (MA, PhD); Romance linguistics (MA, PhD); second language acquisition (MA, PhD); semantics (MA, PhD); Slavic linguistics (MA, PhD); sociolinguistics (MA, PhD); South Asian linguistics (MA, PhD); Southeast Asian linguistics (MA, PhD); syntactic theory (MA, PhD). Terminal master's awarded for partial completion of doctoral program. *Degree requirements:* For master's, one foreign language, thesis; for doctorate, one foreign language, comprehensive exam, thesis/dissertation. *Entrance requirements:* For master's and doctorate, GRE General Test, 2 letters of recommendation. Additional exam requirements/recommendations for international students: Required—TOEFL (minimum score 600 paper-based; 77 iBT). Electronic applications accepted. *Faculty research:* Phonology and phonetics, syntax and semantics, historical linguistics, philosophy of language, language acquisition.

Delaware State University, Graduate Programs, Department of English and Foreign Languages, Dover, DE 19901-2277. Offers French (MA); Spanish (MA). *Entrance requirements:* Additional exam requirements/recommendations for international students: Required—TOEFL (minimum score 550 paper-based). Electronic applications accepted.

DePaul University, College of Education, Chicago, IL 60614. Offers bilingual-bicultural education (M Ed, MA); counseling (M Ed, MA), including clinical mental health counseling, college student development, school counseling; curriculum studies (M Ed, MA, Ed D); early childhood education (M Ed, MA, Ed D); educational leadership (M Ed, MA, Ed D), including Catholic leadership (M Ed, MA), general (M Ed, MA), higher education (M Ed, MA), physical education (M Ed, MA), principal preparation (M Ed); teacher preparation (M Ed); elementary education (M Ed, MA); middle grades education (M Ed); middle school mathematics education (MS); reading specialist (M Ed, MA); secondary education (M Ed, MA); social and cultural foundations in education (M Ed, MA); special education (M Ed); sport, fitness and recreation leadership (MS); value-creating education for global citizenship (M Ed); world languages education (M Ed, MA). *Program availability:* Part-time, evening/weekend, online learning. *Degree requirements:* For doctorate, thesis/dissertation. *Application deadline:* Applications are processed on a rolling basis. Application fee: $40. Electronic applications accepted. *Financial support:* Application deadline: 12/31; applicants required to submit FAFSA. *Unit head:* Dr. Paul Zionts, Dean, 773-325-7581, Fax: 773-325-7713, E-mail: pzionts@depaul.edu. *Application contact:* Dr. Paul Zionts, Dean, 773-325-7581, Fax: 773-325-7713, E-mail: pzionts@depaul.edu.
Website: http://education.depaul.edu

Duquesne University, School of Education, Department of Instruction and Leadership, Program in Secondary Education, Pittsburgh, PA 15282-0001. Offers biology (MS Ed); chemistry (MS Ed); English (MS Ed); K-12 education (MS Ed), including Latin; mathematics (MS Ed); physics (MS Ed); social studies (MS Ed). *Program availability:* Part-time, evening/weekend. *Faculty:* 5 full-time (4 women). *Students:* 22 full-time (10 women); includes 3 minority (2 Black or African American, non-Hispanic/Latino; 1 Two or more races, non-Hispanic/Latino). Average age 26. 8 applicants, 100% accepted, 5 enrolled. In 2017, 9 master's awarded. *Entrance requirements:* For master's, two letters of recommendation, letter of intent, interview, bachelor's degree. Additional exam requirements/recommendations for international students: Required—TOEFL (minimum score 550 paper-based), IELTS (minimum score 7). *Application deadline:* For fall admission, 9/1 for domestic students; for spring admission, 1/2 for domestic students. Applications are processed on a rolling basis. Application fee: $0. Electronic applications accepted. *Expenses:* $1,259 per credit. *Financial support:* Research assistantships and Federal Work-Study available. Support available to part-time students. *Faculty research:* Factors that create highly effective teachers; how to best support teachers to support students in reform-oriented environments; urban education; models of teacher leadership; improving instruction in mathematics/science/social studies/English. *Unit head:* Dr. Melissa Boston, Associate Dean for Teacher Education/Professor, 412-396.6109, Fax: 412-396-5585, E-mail: bostonm@duq.edu. *Application contact:* Kelly McGinley, Graduate Admissions Assistant, 412-396-1559, Fax: 412-396-5585, E-mail: mcginleyk@duq.edu.
Website: http://www.duq.edu/academics/schools/education/graduate-programs-education/ms-ed-secondary-education

Eastern Michigan University, Graduate School, College of Arts and Sciences, Department of World Languages, Programs in World Languages, Ypsilanti, MI 48197. Offers MA, Graduate Certificate. *Program availability:* Part-time, evening/weekend, online learning. *Students:* 2 full-time (both women), 12 part-time (9 women); includes 5 minority (1 Black or African American, non-Hispanic/Latino; 4 Hispanic/Latino). Average age 32. 7 applicants, 86% accepted, 2 enrolled. In 2017, 8 master's awarded. *Degree requirements:* For master's, one foreign language, thesis optional. *Entrance requirements:* Additional exam requirements/recommendations for international students: Required—TOEFL. *Application deadline:* Applications are processed on a rolling basis. Application fee: $45. *Financial support:* Fellowships, research assistantships with full tuition reimbursements, teaching assistantships with full tuition reimbursements, career-related internships or fieldwork, Federal Work-Study, institutionally sponsored loans, scholarships/grants, tuition waivers (partial), and unspecified assistantships available. Support available to part-time students. Financial award applicants required to submit FAFSA. *Application contact:* Dr. Genevieve Peden, Program Advisor, 734-487-1498, Fax: 734-487-3411, E-mail: gpeden@emich.edu.

Eastern University, Graduate Education Programs, St. Davids, PA 19087-3696. Offers ESL program specialist (K-12) (Certificate); general supervisor (PreK-12) (Certificate); health and physical education (K-12) (Certificate); middle level (4-8) (Certificate); multicultural education (M Ed); music (K-12) (Certificate); Pre K-4 (Certificate); Pre K-4 with special education (Certificate); reading (M Ed); reading specialist (K-12) (Certificate); reading supervisor (K-12) (Certificate); school counseling (MA, CAGS); school principalship (preK-12) (Certificate); school psychology (MS, CAGS); secondary biology education (7-12) (Certificate); secondary chemistry education (7-12) (Certificate); secondary communication education (7-12) (Certificate); secondary English education (7-12) (Certificate); secondary math education (7-12) (Certificate); secondary social studies education (7-12) (Certificate); special education (M Ed); special education (7-12) (Certificate); special education (Pre K-8) (Certificate); special education supervisor (K-12) (Certificate); TESOL (M Ed); world language (Certificate), including Spanish. *Program availability:* Part-time, evening/weekend, online learning. *Students:* 46 full-time (40 women), 115 part-time (93 women); includes 65 minority (42 Black or African American, non-Hispanic/Latino; 3 Asian, non-Hispanic/Latino; 14

Hispanic/Latino; 6 Two or more races, non-Hispanic/Latino), 1 international. Average age 32. In 2017, 72 master's awarded. *Entrance requirements:* Additional exam requirements/recommendations for international students: Required—TOEFL. *Application deadline:* Applications are processed on a rolling basis. Application fee: $35. Electronic applications accepted. Application fee is waived when completed online. *Expenses:* Contact institution. *Unit head:* Michael Dziedziak, Executive Director of Enrollment, 800-452-0996, E-mail: gpsadmissions@eastern.edu.
Website: https://www.eastern.edu/academics/programs/education-department-graduate-programs/graduate-programs

Elms College, Division of Education, Chicopee, MA 01013-2839. Offers early childhood education (MAT); education (M Ed, CAGS); elementary education (MAT); English as a second language (MAT); reading (MAT); secondary education (MAT), including biology education, English education, Spanish education; special education (MAT). *Program availability:* Part-time, evening/weekend. *Faculty:* 4 full-time (all women), 8 part-time/adjunct (7 women). *Students:* 6 full-time (4 women), 127 part-time (107 women); includes 8 minority (2 Asian, non-Hispanic/Latino; 6 Hispanic/Latino). Average age 33. 42 applicants, 88% accepted, 36 enrolled. In 2017, 50 master's, 6 other advanced degrees awarded. *Degree requirements:* For master's, thesis (for some programs). *Entrance requirements:* For master's, Massachusetts Educators Certification Test, minimum GPA of 3.0; for CAGS, master's degree in education. Additional exam requirements/recommendations for international students: Required—TOEFL. *Application deadline:* For fall admission, 7/1 priority date for domestic students; for spring admission, 11/1 priority date for domestic students. Applications are processed on a rolling basis. Application fee: $30. *Expenses: Tuition:* Full-time $13,860; part-time $770 per credit hour. *Required fees:* $200. Tuition and fees vary according to degree level and program. *Financial support:* In 2017–18, 2 teaching assistantships with partial tuition reimbursements were awarded. Financial award applicants required to submit FAFSA. *Unit head:* Dr. Mary Janeczek, Chair, Division of Education, 413-594-2761, Fax: 413-592-4871, E-mail: janeczeke@elms.edu. *Application contact:* School of Graduate and Professional Studies, 413-265-2445, E-mail: graduateeducation@elms.edu.

Florida International University, College of Arts, Sciences, and Education, Department of Teaching and Learning, Miami, FL 33199. Offers art education (MA, MS); curriculum and instruction (MS, Ed D, PhD, Ed S), including curriculum development (MS), elementary education (MS), English education (MS), learning technologies (MS), mathematics education (MS), modern language education (MS), physical education (MS), science education (MS), social studies education (MS), special education (MS); early childhood education (MS); exceptional student education (Ed D); foreign language education (MS), including foreign language education, teaching English to speakers of other languages (TESOL); language, literacy and culture (PhD); mathematics, science, and learning technologies (PhD); physical education (MS), including sport and fitness; reading education (MS). *Program availability:* Part-time, evening/weekend. *Faculty:* 60 full-time (41 women), 112 part-time/adjunct (77 women). *Students:* 165 full-time (139 women), 191 part-time (148 women); includes 270 minority (56 Black or African American, non-Hispanic/Latino; 12 Asian, non-Hispanic/Latino; 191 Hispanic/Latino; 11 Two or more races, non-Hispanic/Latino), 13 international. Average age 34. 238 applicants, 68% accepted, 107 enrolled. In 2017, 184 master's, 15 doctorates awarded. *Degree requirements:* For doctorate, comprehensive exam, thesis/dissertation. *Entrance requirements:* For master's, GRE General Test, Florida General Knowledge Test or Florida College Level Academic Skills Test; for doctorate and Ed S, GRE General Test. Additional exam requirements/recommendations for international students: Required—TOEFL (minimum score 550 paper-based; 80 iBT), IELTS (minimum score 6.3). *Application deadline:* For fall admission, 6/1 priority date for domestic students, 4/1 for international students; for winter admission, 10/1 priority date for domestic students, 9/1 for international students; for spring admission, 3/1 priority date for domestic students, 2/1 for international students. Applications are processed on a rolling basis. Application fee: $30. Electronic applications accepted. *Expenses: Tuition, state resident:* full-time $8912; part-time $446 per credit hour. *Tuition, nonresident:* full-time $21,393; part-time $992 per credit hour. *Required fees:* $390; $195 per semester. *Financial support:* Research assistantships with tuition reimbursements and teaching assistantships with tuition reimbursements available. *Unit head:* Dr. Lynn Miller, Chair, 305-348-2005, Fax: 305-348-2086, E-mail: lynne.miller@fiu.edu. *Application contact:* Nanett Rojas, Assistant Director, Graduate Admissions, 305-348-7464, Fax: 305-348-7441, E-mail: gradadm@fiu.edu.
Website: https://tl.fiu.edu/

Florida State University, The Graduate School, College of Education, School of Teacher Education, Tallahassee, FL 32306-4450. Offers curriculum and instruction (MS, PhD, Ed S), including early childhood education, elementary education, English education, foreign and second language education, mathematics education, reading and language arts, science education, social science education, special education, visual disabilities education (MS); teaching English to speakers of other languages (Certificate). *Program availability:* Part-time, evening/weekend, 100% online, blended/hybrid learning, asynchronous, minimal on-campus study. *Faculty:* 41 full-time (33 women), 21 part-time/adjunct (18 women). *Students:* 133 full-time (93 women), 84 part-time (69 women); includes 48 minority (20 Black or African American, non-Hispanic/Latino; 2 Asian, non-Hispanic/Latino; 19 Hispanic/Latino; 7 Two or more races, non-Hispanic/Latino), 52 international. Average age 31. 146 applicants, 56% accepted, 52 enrolled. In 2017, 91 master's, 7 doctorates, 1 other advanced degree awarded. Terminal master's awarded for partial completion of doctoral program. *Degree requirements:* For master's and other advanced degree, comprehensive exam, thesis optional; for doctorate, comprehensive exam, thesis/dissertation, diagnostic exam, preliminary exam, prospectus defense, dissertation defense. *Entrance requirements:* For master's, doctorate, and other advanced degree, GRE General Test, minimum upper-division GPA of 3.0. Additional exam requirements/recommendations for international students: Required—TOEFL (minimum score 550 paper-based, 80 iBT), Michigan English Language Assessment Battery (minimum score 77), IELTS (minimum score 6.5) or PTE (minimum score 55). Application fee: $30. Electronic applications accepted. *Financial support:* Fellowships, research assistantships, teaching assistantships, scholarships/grants, tuition waivers (full and partial), and unspecified assistantships available. Financial award application deadline: 1/15; financial award applicants required to submit FAFSA. *Faculty research:* Identifying effective intervention strategies to improve reading skills; improving literacy teaching and learning through technology; understanding of student sense making, problem solving, the history and structure of STEM disciplines, and teacher education to support the development of ambitious instruction that supports the STEM learning of all students; examining practices of international education; identifying ways to support the professional development of teachers. *Unit head:* Dr. Sherry Southerland, Professor/Department Chair, 850-644-6885, Fax: 850-644-2725, E-mail: ssoutherland@admin.fsu.edu. *Application contact:* Britni DeZerga, Academic Program Specialist, 850-644-2122, Fax: 850-644-7736, E-mail: bpurvis@fsu.edu.
Website: http://education.fsu.edu

George Mason University, College of Humanities and Social Sciences, Department of Modern and Classical Languages, Fairfax, VA 22030. Offers foreign languages (MA), including French, Spanish, Spanish and French, Spanish/bilingual-multicultural education. *Faculty:* 33 full-time (23 women), 38 part-time/adjunct (26 women). *Students:*

7 full-time (5 women), 17 part-time (11 women); includes 17 minority (3 Black or African American, non-Hispanic/Latino; 13 Hispanic/Latino; 1 Two or more races, non-Hispanic/Latino), 1 international. Average age 35. 12 applicants, 92% accepted, 6 enrolled. In 2017, 8 master's awarded. *Degree requirements:* For master's, one foreign language, thesis optional, take-home exit exam. *Entrance requirements:* For master's, goals statement, language proficiency statement. Additional exam requirements/recommendations for international students: Required—TOEFL (minimum score 575 paper-based; 88 iBT), IELTS (minimum score 6.5), PTE (minimum score 59). *Application deadline:* For fall admission, 4/15 for domestic students. Application fee: $75 ($80 for international students). Electronic applications accepted. *Expenses:* Tuition, state resident: full-time $11,228; part-time $459.50 per credit. Tuition, nonresident: full-time $30,932; part-time $1280.50 per credit. *Required fees:* $3252; $135.50 per credit. Part-time tuition and fees vary according to course load and program. *Financial support:* In 2017–18, 5 students received support, including 6 teaching assistantships with tuition reimbursements available (averaging $8,415 per year); career-related internships or fieldwork, Federal Work-Study, scholarships/grants, unspecified assistantships, and health care benefits (for full-time research or teaching assistantship recipients) also available. Support available to part-time students. Financial award application deadline: 3/1; financial award applicants required to submit FAFSA. *Faculty research:* Film and media studies; literary analysis, criticism, and theory; applied linguistics and pedagogy, sociolinguistics, interdisciplinary approaches. *Unit head:* Rei Berroa, Chair, 703-993-1220, Fax: 703-993-1245, E-mail: rberroa@gmu.edu. *Application contact:* Jen Barnard, Office Manager, 703-993-1230, Fax: 703-993-1245, E-mail: jbarnard@gmu.edu. Website: http://mcl.gmu.edu/

The George Washington University, Graduate School of Education and Human Development, Department of Curriculum and Pedagogy, Program in Secondary Education, Washington, DC 20052. Offers Arabic (M Ed); Italian (M Ed); math (M Ed); physics (M Ed); Russian (M Ed). Programs also offered in Arlington and Ashburn, VA. *Accreditation:* NCATE. *Students:* 10 full-time (7 women), 26 part-time (16 women); includes 10 minority (5 Black or African American, non-Hispanic/Latino; 2 American Indian or Alaska Native, non-Hispanic/Latino; 1 Asian, non-Hispanic/Latino; 2 Two or more races, non-Hispanic/Latino), 1 international. Average age 31. 66 applicants, 62% accepted, 22 enrolled. In 2017, 17 master's awarded. *Entrance requirements:* For master's, GRE General Test or MAT, interview, minimum GPA of 2.75. *Application deadline:* For fall admission, 1/15 priority date for domestic students; for spring admission, 10/1 for domestic students. Applications are processed on a rolling basis. Application fee: $75. *Expenses: Tuition:* Full-time $28,800; part-time $1655 per credit hour. *Required fees:* $45; $2.75 per credit hour. *Financial support:* Fellowships, career-related internships or fieldwork, Federal Work-Study, tuition waivers (full and partial), and stipends available. Financial award application deadline: 1/15; financial award applicants required to submit FAFSA. *Unit head:* Prof. Curtis Pyke, Chair, 202-994-4516, E-mail: cpyke@gwu.edu. *Application contact:* Sarah Lang, Director of Graduate Admissions, 202-994-1447, Fax: 202-994-7207, E-mail: slang@gwu.edu.

Georgia Southern University, Jack N. Averitt College of Graduate Studies, College of Education, Department of Teaching and Learning, Program in Spanish P-12 Education, Statesboro, GA 30458. Offers MAT. *Program availability:* Part-time. *Students:* 4 full-time (3 women), 4 part-time (3 women); includes 3 minority (all Hispanic/Latino). Average age 29. 4 applicants, 100% accepted. In 2017, 2 master's awarded. *Degree requirements:* For master's, key assessments. *Entrance requirements:* For master's, GACE. Additional exam requirements/recommendations for international students: Required—TOEFL (minimum score 80 iBT). *Application deadline:* For fall admission, 3/15 for domestic and international students; for spring admission, 10/1 for domestic and international students; for summer admission, 3/1 for domestic and international students. *Expenses:* Tuition, state resident: full-time $4986; part-time $3324 per year. Tuition, nonresident: full-time $21,982; part-time $15,352 per year. *Required fees:* $2092; $1802 per credit hour. $901 per semester. Tuition and fees vary according to course load, campus/location and program. *Financial support:* In 2017–18, 3 students received support. Scholarships/grants and unspecified assistantships available. Financial award applicants required to submit FAFSA. *Faculty research:* P-12 preparation of Spanish language education professionals. *Unit head:* Dr. Marcela Ruiz-Funes, Program Director, 912-478-5281, E-mail: mruizfunes@georgiasouthern.edu. *Application contact:* Dr. Lydia Cross, Director for Graduate Academic Services Center, 912-478-8664, E-mail: lcross@georgiasouthern.edu.

Georgia State University, College of Arts and Sciences, Department of World Languages and Cultures, Atlanta, GA 30302-3083. Offers French (MA), including applied linguistics and pedagogy, French studies, literature and culture; Latin American studies (Certificate); Spanish (MA); translation and interpretation (Certificate), including interpretation, translation. *Program availability:* Part-time. *Faculty:* 36 full-time (20 women). *Students:* 25 full-time (19 women), 9 part-time (5 women); includes 19 minority (8 Black or African American, non-Hispanic/Latino; 10 Hispanic/Latino; 1 Two or more races, non-Hispanic/Latino), 4 international. Average age 39. 36 applicants, 86% accepted, 22 enrolled. In 2017, 10 master's, 2 other advanced degrees awarded. *Entrance requirements:* For master's, GRE, statement of purpose, writing sample in the target language, 2 letters of recommendation, official transcripts; for Certificate, entrance examination involving translating one passage from English to the target language and one passage from the target language to English, 3 letters of recommendation, resume/curriculum vitae, official transcripts. Additional exam requirements/recommendations for international students: Required—TOEFL (minimum score 79 iBT). *Application deadline:* For fall admission, 3/15 priority date for domestic and international students; for spring admission, 11/15 priority date for domestic and international students. Application fee: $50. Electronic applications accepted. *Expenses:* Tuition, state resident: full-time $7020. Tuition, nonresident: full-time $22,518. *Required fees:* $2128. Tuition and fees vary according to degree level and program. *Financial support:* Applicants required to submit FAFSA. *Faculty research:* French literature and culture, Francophone literature and culture, Latin American literature and culture, Spanish literature and culture, Hispanic linguistics. *Unit head:* Dr. Fernando Reati, Department Chair, 404-413-5984, Fax: 404-413-5982, E-mail: freati@gsu.edu. *Application contact:* Amber Amari, Director, Graduate and Scheduling Services, 404-413-5037, E-mail: aamari@gsu.edu. Website: http://wlc.gsu.edu/

Harding University, Cannon-Clary College of Education, Searcy, AR 72149-0001. Offers advanced studies in teaching and learning (M Ed); art (MSE); behavioral science (MSE); counseling (MS, Ed S); early childhood special education (M Ed, MSE); education (MSE); educational leadership (M Ed, Ed S); elementary education (M Ed); English (MSE); French (MSE); history/social science (MSE); kinesiology (MSE); math (MSE); reading (M Ed); secondary education (M Ed); Spanish (MSE); teaching (MAT); teaching English as a second language (MSE). *Accreditation:* NCATE. *Program availability:* Part-time, evening/weekend. *Faculty:* 22 full-time (9 women), 51 part-time/adjunct (37 women). *Students:* 135 full-time (95 women), 316 part-time (231 women); includes 77 minority (46 Black or African American, non-Hispanic/Latino; 7 American Indian or Alaska Native, non-Hispanic/Latino; 4 Asian, non-Hispanic/Latino; 9 Hispanic/Latino; 11 Two or more races, non-Hispanic/Latino), 11 international. Average age 34. 128 applicants, 87% accepted, 111 enrolled. In 2017, 153 master's, 24 other advanced degrees awarded. *Degree requirements:* For master's, comprehensive exam (for some

programs), thesis optional, portfolio(s); for Ed S, comprehensive exam, portfolio, project. *Entrance requirements:* For master's, GRE, MAT, PRAXIS; for Ed S, MAT or GRE. Additional exam requirements/recommendations for international students: Required—TOEFL (minimum score 550 paper-based; 79 iBT). *Application deadline:* For fall admission, 8/1 for domestic and international students; for spring admission, 1/1 for domestic and international students. Applications are processed on a rolling basis. Application fee: $35. Tuition and fees vary according to course load, degree level, campus/location and program. *Financial support:* In 2017–18, 33 students received support. Unspecified assistantships available. *Faculty research:* Reading, comprehension, school violence, educational technology, behavior, college choice, differentiated instruction, brain-based teaching. *Unit head:* Dr. Clara Carroll, Chair, 501-279-4501, Fax: 501-279-4083, E-mail: ccarroll@harding.edu. *Application contact:* Information Contact, 501-279-4315, E-mail: gradstudiesedu@harding.edu. Website: http://www.harding.edu/education

Hofstra University, School of Education, Programs in Teacher Education, Hempstead, NY 11549. Offers bilingual education (MA); bilingual extension (Advanced Certificate), including education/speech language pathology, intensive teacher institute; business education (MS Ed); curriculum studies (MS Ed); early childhood and childhood education (MS Ed); early childhood education (MA, MS Ed); educational technology (Advanced Certificate); elementary education (MA, MS Ed), including science, technology, engineering, and mathematics (STEM) (MA); English education (MS Ed); family and consumer science (MS Ed); fine arts and music education (Advanced Certificate); fine arts education (MS Ed); foreign language and TESOL (MS Ed); foreign language education (MA, MS Ed), including Arabic (MS Ed), biology, chemistry, Chinese (MS Ed), earth science, French, German, Italian (MS Ed), Mandarin (MS Ed), physics, Russian, Spanish; foundations of education (Advanced Certificate), including grades 5-6, grades 7-9; languages other than English and teaching English as a second language (MA); learning and teaching (Ed D), including applied linguistics, art education, arts and humanities, early childhood education, English education, human development, math education, math, science, and technology, multicultural education, physical education, science education, social studies education, special education; mathematics education (MA, MS Ed); music education (MA, MS Ed); science education (MA), including biology (MA, MS Ed), chemistry (MA, MS Ed), earth science (MA, MS Ed), physics (MA, MS Ed); secondary education (Advanced Certificate); social studies education (MA, MS Ed); teaching languages other than English and TESOL (MS Ed); technology for learning (MA); TESOL (MS Ed, Advanced Certificate); TESOL with specialization in STEM (MA); work based learning extension (Advanced Certificate). *Program availability:* Part-time, evening/weekend, blended/hybrid learning. *Students:* 119 full-time (83 women), 124 part-time (90 women); includes 54 minority (15 Black or African American, non-Hispanic/Latino; 9 Asian, non-Hispanic/Latino; 29 Hispanic/Latino; 1 Native Hawaiian or other Pacific Islander, non-Hispanic/Latino), 12 international. Average age 29. 205 applicants, 88% accepted, 93 enrolled. In 2017, 103 master's, 4 doctorates, 32 other advanced degrees awarded. *Degree requirements:* For master's, comprehensive exam, thesis (for some programs), exit project, student teaching, fieldwork, electronic portfolio, curriculum project, minimum GPA of 3.0; for doctorate, thesis/dissertation; for Advanced Certificate, 3 foreign languages, comprehensive exam (for some programs), thesis project. *Entrance requirements:* For master's, GRE, 2 letters of recommendation, portfolio, teacher certification (MA), interview, essay; for doctorate, GMAT, GRE, LSAT, or MAT; for Advanced Certificate, 2 letters of recommendation, essay, interview and/or portfolio, teaching certificate. Additional exam requirements/recommendations for international students: Required—TOEFL (minimum score 550 paper-based; 80 iBT). *Application deadline:* Applications are processed on a rolling basis. Application fee: $75. Electronic applications accepted. *Expenses: Tuition:* Full-time $1292. *Required fees:* $970. Tuition and fees vary according to program. *Financial support:* In 2017–18, 112 students received support, including 56 fellowships with full and partial tuition reimbursements available (averaging $4,998 per year), 2 research assistantships with full and partial tuition reimbursements available (averaging $8,753 per year); career-related internships or fieldwork, Federal Work-Study, institutionally sponsored loans, scholarships/grants, traineeships, tuition waivers (full and partial), and unspecified assistantships also available. Support available to part-time students. Financial award applicants required to submit FAFSA. *Faculty research:* Educational interventions that foster critical-thinking skills; teachers' attitudes about professional development; threats to teacher quality. *Unit head:* Dr. Eustace Thompson, Chairperson, 516-463-5749, Fax: 516-463-6275, E-mail: eustace.g.thompson@hofstra.edu. *Application contact:* Sunil Samuel, Assistant Vice President of Admissions, 516-463-4723, Fax: 516-463-4664, E-mail: graduateadmission@hofstra.edu. Website: http://www.hofstra.edu/education/

Hunter College of the City University of New York, Graduate School, School of Education, Programs in Secondary Education, Concentration in French Education, New York, NY 10065-5085. Offers MA. *Accreditation:* NCATE. *Degree requirements:* For master's, thesis, professional teaching portfolio, New York State Teacher Certification Exam. *Entrance requirements:* For master's, 24 credits in French; minimum GPA of 3.0 in French, 2.8 overall; 2 letters of reference; interview. Additional exam requirements/recommendations for international students: Required—TOEFL, TWE.

Hunter College of the City University of New York, Graduate School, School of Education, Programs in Secondary Education, Concentration in Italian Education, New York, NY 10065-5085. Offers MA. *Accreditation:* NCATE. *Degree requirements:* For master's, thesis, professional teaching portfolio, New York State Teacher Certification Exam, research project. *Entrance requirements:* For master's, minimum GPA of 3.0 in Italian, 2.8 overall; 24 credits of course work in Italian; 2 letters of reference; interview. Additional exam requirements/recommendations for international students: Required—TOEFL, TWE.

Hunter College of the City University of New York, Graduate School, School of Education, Programs in Secondary Education, Concentration in Spanish Education, New York, NY 10065-5085. Offers MA. *Accreditation:* NCATE. *Degree requirements:* For master's, thesis, professional teaching portfolio, New York State Teacher Certification Exam. *Entrance requirements:* For master's, minimum GPA of 3.0 in Spanish, 2.8 overall; 24 credits of course work in Spanish; 2 letters of reference; interview. Additional exam requirements/recommendations for international students: Required—TOEFL, TWE.

Indiana State University, College of Graduate and Professional Studies, College of Arts and Sciences, Department of Languages, Literatures, and Linguistics, Terre Haute, IN 47809. Offers applied linguistics/teaching English as a second language (MA); language education (PhD); Spanish/teaching english as a second language (MA); TESL/TEFL (CAS). *Degree requirements:* For master's, comprehensive exam. Electronic applications accepted.

Indiana University Bloomington, University Graduate School, College of Arts and Sciences, Department of French and Italian, Bloomington, IN 47405. Offers French (MA, PhD), including French and Francophone studies (MA), French instruction (MA), French linguistics; Italian (MA, PhD). *Program availability:* Part-time. Terminal master's awarded for partial completion of doctoral program. *Degree requirements:* For master's, variable foreign language requirement, comprehensive exam (for some programs), thesis or alternative; for doctorate, variable foreign language requirement, comprehensive exam, thesis/dissertation. *Entrance requirements:* For master's, GRE General Test, BA or equivalent undergraduate preparation in French or Italian; for doctorate, GRE General Test, MA from degree program at IU; MA in the specific field. Additional exam requirements/recommendations for international students: Required—TOEFL (minimum score 550 paper-based; 79 iBT), GRE General Test (recommended). Electronic applications accepted. *Faculty research:* French and Italian literature, French linguistics, including the novel and political theory, literature and fine arts, literary theory, postcolonialism, French-Creole studies, French literature of Africa and its Diaspora, humanism, Medieval folklore and mythology, humor in Medieval and Renaissance literature, emigration, second language acquisition, syntax, sociolinguistics, phonology, lexicography, media and cultural studies, cinema, drama.

Indiana University Bloomington, University Graduate School, College of Arts and Sciences, Department of Germanic Studies, Bloomington, IN 47405-7000. Offers German philology and linguistics (PhD); German studies (MA, PhD), including German (MA), German literature and culture (MA), German literature and linguistics (MA); medieval German studies (PhD); teaching German (MAT). *Degree requirements:* For master's, one foreign language, project; for doctorate, one foreign language, comprehensive exam, thesis/dissertation. *Entrance requirements:* For master's, GRE General Test, BA in German or equivalent; for doctorate, GRE General Test, MA in German or equivalent. Additional exam requirements/recommendations for international students: Required—TOEFL. Electronic applications accepted. *Faculty research:* German and other European literature: medieval to modern/postmodern, German and culture studies, Germanic philology, literary theory, literature and the other arts.

Indiana University Bloomington, University Graduate School, College of Arts and Sciences, School of Global and International Studies, Department of East Asian Languages and Cultures, Bloomington, IN 47408. Offers Chinese (MA, PhD); Chinese language pedagogy (MA); East Asian studies (MA); Japanese (MA, PhD); Japanese language pedagogy (MA). *Program availability:* Part-time. *Degree requirements:* For master's, one foreign language, thesis; for doctorate, 2 foreign languages, comprehensive exam, thesis/dissertation. *Entrance requirements:* Additional exam requirements/recommendations for international students: Required—TOEFL (minimum score 93 iBT). Electronic applications accepted. *Faculty research:* Modern East Asian history; politics and society; traditional Chinese thought and society; medieval and premodern Japanese history, literature and society; modern Chinese and Japanese film and literature; Chinese, Japanese, Korean language and linguistics.

Indiana University of Pennsylvania, School of Graduate Studies and Research, College of Humanities and Social Sciences, Department of Foreign Languages, Program in Spanish/Applied Linguistics and Teaching Methodology, Indiana, PA 15705. Offers MA. Application fee: $50. *Expenses:* Tuition, state resident: full-time $12,000; part-time $500 per credit. Tuition, nonresident: full-time $18,000; part-time $750 per credit. *Required fees:* $4073; $165.55 per credit. $64 per term. *Financial support:* Fellowships with full tuition reimbursements and research assistantships with tuition reimbursements available. *Unit head:* Dr. Sean McDaniel, Chairperson, 724-357-7532, E-mail: mcdaniel@iup.edu.

Indiana University–Purdue University Indianapolis, School of Education, Indianapolis, IN 46202-5155. Offers curriculum and instruction (MS); early childhood (MS); educational leadership (MS, Certificate); English as a second language (Certificate); kindergarten (Certificate); language education (MS); reading (Certificate); school counseling (MS); special education (MS, Certificate). *Program availability:* Part-time, evening/weekend. Terminal master's awarded for partial completion of doctoral program. *Degree requirements:* For master's, thesis optional. *Entrance requirements:* For master's, GRE General Test, minimum GPA of 2.5; for Certificate, official transcripts. Additional exam requirements/recommendations for international students: Required—TOEFL (minimum score 60 iBT), IELTS (minimum score 5.5). Electronic applications accepted. *Expenses:* Contact institution. *Faculty research:* Educational policies and school leaders' responses to these; issues of intersectionality in the experiences of African American lesbian, gay, and bisexual students attending historically black colleges and universities and those who belong to black Greek-letter organizations; students' experiential knowledge and their evolving disciplinary-specific literacy and understanding; innovative program development; urban ESL teacher preparation; target-based instructional coaching.

Inter American University of Puerto Rico, Arecibo Campus, Programs in Education, Arecibo, PR 00614-4050. Offers administration and educational supervision (MA Ed); counseling and guidance (MA Ed); curriculum and teaching (MA Ed), including biology education, English as a second language, history education, math education, Spanish; elementary education (MA Ed). *Accreditation:* TEAC. *Degree requirements:* For master's, comprehensive exam, thesis optional. *Entrance requirements:* For master's, GRE, EXADEP, bachelor's degree in education or teaching license (administration and supervision) or courses in education and psychology (counseling and guidance), minimum GPA of 2.5 in last 60 credits.

Inter American University of Puerto Rico, Barranquitas Campus, Program in Education, Barranquitas, PR 00794. Offers curriculum and teaching (M Ed), including biology, English as a second language, history, Spanish; educational leadership and management (MA); elementary education (M Ed); information and library service technology (M Ed); special education (MA). *Accreditation:* TEAC. *Program availability:* Part-time, evening/weekend. *Faculty:* 1 full-time (0 women), 3 part-time/adjunct (2 women). *Students:* 17 full-time (16 women), 2 part-time (both women); all minorities (all Hispanic/Latino). Average age 34. 9 applicants, 89% accepted, 8 enrolled. In 2017, 5 master's awarded. *Degree requirements:* For master's, 2 foreign languages, comprehensive exam, thesis (for some programs). *Entrance requirements:* For master's, GRE or EXADEP, bachelor's degree or its equivalent from accredited institution, official academic transcript from institution that conferred bachelor's degree, minimum GPA of 2.5, two recommendation letters, interview (for some programs), essay (for some programs). *Application deadline:* Applications are processed on a rolling basis. Application fee: $31. Electronic applications accepted. *Expenses:* $3,392 full-time tuition plus $652 fees. *Financial support:* Applicants required to submit FAFSA. *Unit head:* Juan A. Negron-Berrios, PhD, Chancellor, 787-857-3600 Ext. 2002, Fax: 787-857-2125, E-mail: janegron@br.inter.edu. *Application contact:* Aramilda Cartagena-Santiago, Dean of Students, 787-857-3600 Ext. 2009, Fax: 787-857-2125, E-mail: aramildacartagena@br.inter.edu.

Inter American University of Puerto Rico, Metropolitan Campus, Graduate Programs, Program in Spanish Education, San Juan, PR 00919-1293. Offers MA.

Iona College, School of Arts and Science, Department of Education, New Rochelle, NY 10801-1890. Offers adolescence education: biology (MS Ed, MST); adolescence education: English (MS Ed); adolescence education: mathematics (MST); adolescence education: social studies (MS Ed, MST); adolescence education: Spanish (MS Ed); adolescence special education 5-12 (MST); childhood and special education (MST); early childhood and childhood (MST); educational leadership (MS Ed). *Accreditation:* NCATE. *Program availability:* Part-time, evening/weekend. *Faculty:* 7 full-time (5 women), 2 part-time/adjunct (1 woman). *Students:* 23 full-time (18 women), 26 part-time (19 women); includes 12 minority (4 Black or African American, non-Hispanic/Latino; 8 Hispanic/Latino). Average age 26. 33 applicants, 97% accepted, 20 enrolled. In 2017,

31 master's awarded. *Degree requirements:* For master's, thesis or alternative. *Entrance requirements:* For master's, minimum GPA of 3.0, NY State teaching certificate and bachelor's degree (for MS Ed). Additional exam requirements/recommendations for international students: Required—TOEFL (minimum score 550 paper-based; 80 iBT), IELTS (minimum score 6.5). *Application deadline:* For fall admission, 8/1 priority date for domestic students, 5/1 priority date for international students; for spring admission, 1/1 priority date for domestic students, 9/1 priority date for international students. Applications are processed on a rolling basis. Electronic applications accepted. Tuition and fees vary according to program. *Financial support:* In 2017–18, 16 students received support. Unspecified assistantships available. Support available to part-time students. Financial award application deadline: 4/15; financial award applicants required to submit FAFSA. *Faculty research:* Engaging teacher educators in scientific process, cross-national comparisons of mathematics teaching, questioning strategies in the classroom, research methods, literacy development. *Unit head:* Margaret Smith, PhD, Chair, 914-633-2210, Fax: 914-633-2608, E-mail: msmith@iona.edu. *Application contact:* Richard McMahon, Coordinator, Graduate School of Education, 914-633-2552, E-mail: rmcmahon@iona.edu.
Website: http://www.iona.edu/Academics/School-of-Arts-Science/Departments/Education/Graduate-Programs.aspx

James Madison University, The Graduate School, College of Education, Program in Education, Harrisonburg, VA 22807. Offers early childhood education (preK-3) (MAT); educational leadership (M Ed); educational technology (M Ed); elementary education (MAT); equity and cultural diversity (M Ed); inclusive early childhood education (MAT); K-8 mathematics specialist (M Ed); middle education (MAT); reading education (M Ed); secondary education (MAT); Spanish language and culture for educators (M Ed); TESOL (MAT). *Accreditation:* NCATE. *Program availability:* Part-time, evening/weekend. *Students:* 260 full-time (233 women), 158 part-time (100 women); includes 48 minority (10 Black or African American, non-Hispanic/Latino; 4 Asian, non-Hispanic/Latino; 26 Hispanic/Latino; 1 Native Hawaiian or other Pacific Islander, non-Hispanic/Latino; 7 Two or more races, non-Hispanic/Latino), 2 international. Average age 30. In 2017, 262 master's awarded. Application fee: $55. Electronic applications accepted. *Expenses:* Tuition, state resident: full-time $10,512; part-time $438 per credit hour. Tuition, nonresident: full-time $28,358; part-time $1162 per credit hour. *Required fees:* $1128. *Financial support:* In 2017–18, 23 students received support, including 1 teaching assistantship; career-related internships or fieldwork, Federal Work-Study, and 22 assistantships (averaging $7911) also available. Financial award application deadline: 3/1; financial award applicants required to submit FAFSA. *Unit head:* Dr. Phillip M. Wishon, Dean, 540-568-6572, E-mail: wishonpm@jmu.edu. *Application contact:* Lynette D. Michael, Director of Graduate Admissions, 540-568-6131 Ext. 6395, Fax: 540-568-7860, E-mail: michaeld@jmu.edu.
Website: http://www.jmu.edu/coe/index.shtml

Kean University, College of Education, Program in Hindi and Urdu Language Pedagogy, Union, NJ 07083. Offers MA. *Program availability:* 100% online. *Faculty:* 3 full-time (0 women). *Students:* 10 part-time (all women); includes 8 minority (all Asian, non-Hispanic/Latino). Average age 45. 1 applicant, 100% accepted. *Degree requirements:* For master's, thesis/action research project. *Entrance requirements:* For master's, ACTFL OPI and WPT in Hindi or Urdu, bachelor's degree, minimum cumulative GPA of 3.0, official transcripts, professional resume or curriculum vitae, personal statement, two letters of recommendation, interview, teaching experience. Additional exam requirements/recommendations for international students: Required—TOEFL (minimum score 550 paper-based, 79 iBT) or IELTS (6.5). *Application deadline:* For fall admission, 6/30 for domestic and international students. Application fee: $75. Electronic applications accepted. *Expenses:* Tuition, state resident: full-time $13,419; part-time $653 per credit. Tuition, nonresident: full-time $18,188; part-time $801 per credit. *Required fees:* $3382; $154 per credit. Tuition and fees vary according to course level, course load, degree level and program. *Financial support:* Scholarships/grants and unspecified assistantships available. Financial award applicants required to submit FAFSA. *Unit head:* Dr. Michael Searson, Director, 908-737-0550, E-mail: msearson@kean.edu. *Application contact:* Brittany Gerstenhaber, Admissions Counselor, 908-737-7100, E-mail: grad-adm@kean.edu.

Kennesaw State University, Leland and Clarice C. Bagwell College of Education, Program in Teaching, Kennesaw, GA 30144. Offers art education (MAT); biology (MAT); chemistry (MAT); foreign language education (Chinese and Spanish) (MAT); physics (MAT); secondary English (MAT); secondary mathematics (MAT); special education (MAT); teaching English to speakers of other languages (MAT). *Program availability:* Part-time, evening/weekend. *Entrance requirements:* For master's, GRE, GACE I (state certificate exam), minimum GPA of 2.75, 2 recommendations, resume. Additional exam requirements/recommendations for international students: Required—TOEFL (minimum score 550 paper-based; 80 iBT), IELTS (minimum score 6.5). Electronic applications accepted.

Lamar University, College of Graduate Studies, College of Arts and Sciences, Department of English and Modern Languages, Beaumont, TX 77701. Offers English (MA); teaching Spanish (MA). *Program availability:* Part-time, evening/weekend. *Faculty:* 30 full-time (18 women), 4 part-time/adjunct (3 women). *Students:* 9 full-time (7 women), 21 part-time (18 women); includes 17 minority (2 Black or African American, non-Hispanic/Latino; 15 Hispanic/Latino), 1 international. Average age 40. 18 applicants, 100% accepted, 10 enrolled. In 2017, 12 master's awarded. *Degree requirements:* For master's, one foreign language, thesis optional, practicum. *Entrance requirements:* For master's, GRE General Test, minimum GPA of 2.5 in last 60 hours of undergraduate course work. Additional exam requirements/recommendations for international students: Required—TOEFL (minimum score 550 paper-based; 79 iBT), IELTS (minimum score 6.5). *Application deadline:* For fall admission, 8/10 for domestic students, 7/1 for international students; for spring admission, 1/5 for domestic students, 12/1 for international students. Applications are processed on a rolling basis. Application fee: $25 ($50 for international students). Electronic applications accepted. *Expenses:* Contact institution. *Financial support:* In 2017–18, 4 teaching assistantships (averaging $8,000 per year) were awarded; career-related internships or fieldwork, Federal Work-Study, and institutionally sponsored loans also available. Support available to part-time students. Financial award application deadline: 4/1; financial award applicants required to submit FAFSA. *Faculty research:* British, Renaissance, nineteenth-century, and American literature; creative writing; modern literature; African-American literature. *Unit head:* Dr. Jim Sanderson, Chair, 409-880-8558, Fax: 409-880-8591. *Application contact:* Deidre Mayer, Interim Director, Admissions and Academic Services, 409-880-8888, Fax: 409-880-7419, E-mail: gradmissions@lamar.edu.
Website: http://artssciences.lamar.edu/english-and-modern-languages

Le Moyne College, Department of Education, Syracuse, NY 13214. Offers adolescent education (MS Ed, MST); adolescent education/special education (MS Ed, MST); adolescent English (MST), including grades 7-12; adolescent English/special education (MST), including grades 7-12; adolescent foreign language (MST), including grades 7-12; adolescent history (MST), including grades 7-12; childhood education (MS Ed); childhood education/special education (MS Ed); elementary education (MS Ed); general education (MS Ed); inclusive childhood education (MST); literacy education (MS Ed), including birth to grade 6, grades 5-12; school building leader (MS Ed); school building

Foreign Languages Education

leadership (CAS); school district business leader (MS Ed, CAS); school district leader (MS Ed); school district leadership (CAS); secondary education (MS Ed); special education (MS Ed); teaching English to speakers of other languages (MS Ed); urban studies (MS Ed). *Accreditation:* TEAC. *Program availability:* Part-time, evening/weekend. *Faculty:* 7 full-time (5 women), 20 part-time/adjunct (12 women). *Students:* 30 full-time (19 women), 126 part-time (93 women); includes 15 minority (7 Black or African American, non-Hispanic/Latino; 1 American Indian or Alaska Native, non-Hispanic/Latino; 1 Asian, non-Hispanic/Latino; 6 Hispanic/Latino), 4 international. Average age 29. 139 applicants, 65% accepted, 76 enrolled. In 2017, 82 master's, 43 CASs awarded. *Degree requirements:* For master's, thesis. *Entrance requirements:* For master's, bachelor's degree with minimum undergraduate GPA of 3.0, 2 letters of recommendation, transcripts. Additional exam requirements/recommendations for international students: Required—TOEFL (minimum score 550 paper-based; 79 iBT); Recommended—IELTS (minimum score 6.5). *Application deadline:* For fall admission, 4/1 priority date for domestic and international students; for spring admission, 10/1 priority date for domestic and international students; for summer admission, 3/1 priority date for domestic and international students. Applications are processed on a rolling basis. Application fee: $50. Electronic applications accepted. *Expenses:* $700 per credit hour. *Financial support:* In 2017–18, 30 students received support. Career-related internships or fieldwork, scholarships/grants, and health care benefits available. Support available to part-time students. Financial award applicants required to submit FAFSA. *Faculty research:* Minority teachers, special education, multiculturalism, literacy, technology, media literacy learning, autism, school district organization, service-learning, higher level problem solving, teacher leadership. *Unit head:* Dr. Stephen C. Fleury, Chair, Department of Education, 315-445-4376, Fax: 315-445-4744, E-mail: fleurysc@lemoyne.edu. *Application contact:* Kristen P. Richards, Senior Director of Enrollment Management, 315-445-5444, Fax: 315-445-6092, E-mail: trapaskp@lemoyne.edu.
Website: http://www.lemoyne.edu/education

Lewis University, College of Education, Program in Foreign Language Instruction, Romeoville, IL 60446. Offers MA. *Program availability:* Part-time. *Students:* 3 full-time (all women), 3 part-time (all women); includes 2 minority (1 Black or African American, non-Hispanic/Latino; 1 Hispanic/Latino). Average age 26. *Degree requirements:* For master's, comprehensive exam. *Entrance requirements:* For master's, writing exam, Test of Academic Proficiency/Basic Skills Test/ACT/SAT, bachelor's degree, minimum GPA of 2.75, 2 letters of recommendation. Additional exam requirements/recommendations for international students: Required—TOEFL (minimum score 550 paper-based; 79 iBT), IELTS (minimum score 6). *Application deadline:* For fall admission, 5/1 for international students; for spring admission, 11/1 for international students. Application fee: $40. Electronic applications accepted. Tuition and fees vary according to program. *Financial support:* Federal Work-Study, scholarships/grants, and unspecified assistantships available. Support available to part-time students. Financial award application deadline: 5/1; financial award applicants required to submit FAFSA. *Unit head:* Dr. Pamela Jessee, Dean, 815-836-5316, E-mail: jesseepa@lewisu.edu. *Application contact:* Kathy Lisak, Graduate Admission Counselor, 815-836-5610, E-mail: grad@lewisu.edu.
Website: http://www.lewisu.edu/academics/mastersforeignlanguage/index.htm

London Metropolitan University, Graduate Programs, London, United Kingdom. Offers applied psychology (M Sc); architecture (MA); biomedical science (M Sc); blood science (M Sc); cancer pharmacology (M Sc); computer networking and cyber security (M Sc); computing and information systems (M Sc); conference interpreting (MA); counter-terrorism studies (M Sc); creative, digital and professional writing (MA); crime, violence and prevention (M Sc); criminology (M Sc); curating contemporary art (MA); data analytics (M Sc); digital media (MA); early childhood studies (MA); education (MA, Ed D); financial services law, regulation and compliance (LL M); food science (M Sc); forensic psychology (M Sc); health and social care management and policy (M Sc); human nutrition (M Sc); human resource management (MA); human rights and international conflict (MA); information technology (M Sc); intelligence and security studies (M Sc); international oil, gas and energy law (LL M); international relations (MA); interpreting (MA); learning and teaching in higher education (MA); legal practice (LL M); media and entertainment law (LL M); organizational and consumer psychology (M Sc); psychological therapy (M Sc); psychology of mental health (M Sc); public health (M Sc); public policy and management (MPA); security studies (M Sc); social work (M Sc); spatial planning and urban design (MA); sports therapy (M Sc); supporting older children and young people with dyslexia (MA); teaching languages (MA), including Arabic, English; translation (MA); woman and child abuse (MA).

Manhattanville College, School of Education, Program in Teaching of Languages Other than English, Purchase, NY 10577-2132. Offers adolescence education (grades 7-12) foreign language (MAT, Advanced Certificate), including French, Italian, Latin (Advanced Certificate), Latin (MAT), Spanish. *Program availability:* Part-time, evening/weekend. *Faculty:* 2 full-time (1 woman). *Students:* 3 part-time (2 women); includes 1 minority (Hispanic/Latino). Average age 31. In 2017, 4 master's, 1 other advanced degree awarded. *Degree requirements:* For master's, comprehensive exam (for some programs), thesis (for some programs), student teaching, research seminars, portfolios, internships, writing assessment; for Advanced Certificate, comprehensive exam (for some programs). *Entrance requirements:* For master's, GRE or MAT (for programs leading to certification), minimum GPA of 3.0, 2 letters of recommendation, interview, essay (2-3 page personal statement that describes reasons for choosing teaching or educational leadership as profession and philosophy of education), proof of immunization (for those born after 1957). Additional exam requirements/recommendations for international students: Required—TOEFL (minimum score 600 paper-based; 110 iBT); Recommended—IELTS (minimum score 8). *Application deadline:* Applications are processed on a rolling basis. Application fee: $75. Electronic applications accepted. *Expenses:* $915 per credit. *Financial support:* Teaching assistantships, career-related internships or fieldwork, Federal Work-Study, institutionally sponsored loans, scholarships/grants, and unspecified assistantships available. Financial award application deadline: 3/15; financial award applicants required to submit FAFSA. *Faculty research:* Changing suburbs institute and community schools. *Unit head:* Dr. Shelly Wepner, Dean, 914-323-3153, Fax: 914-323-5493. *Application contact:* Alissa Wilson, Director, Graduate Admissions, 914-323-3150, Fax: 914-694-1732, E-mail: edschool@mville.edu.
Website: https://www.mville.edu/programs/teaching-languages-other-english

Marquette University, Graduate School, College of Arts and Sciences, Department of Foreign Languages and Literatures, Milwaukee, WI 53201-1881. Offers Spanish (MA). *Program availability:* Part-time, evening/weekend. *Degree requirements:* For master's, one foreign language, comprehensive exam. *Entrance requirements:* For master's, official transcripts from all current and previous colleges/universities except Marquette, three letters of recommendation, tape recording of foreign speaking voice. Additional exam requirements/recommendations for international students: Required—TOEFL. Electronic applications accepted. *Faculty research:* Latin American literature, Afro-Hispanic literature, descriptive Spanish linguistics, inter-American studies, foreign language education.

McGill University, Faculty of Graduate and Postdoctoral Studies, Faculty of Education, Department of Integrated Studies in Education, Montréal, QC H3A 2T5, Canada. Offers culture and values in education (MA, PhD); curriculum studies (MA); educational leadership (MA, Certificate); educational studies (PhD); integrated studies in education (M Ed); second language education (MA, PhD).

Michigan State University, The Graduate School, College of Arts and Letters, Program in Second Language Studies, East Lansing, MI 48824. Offers PhD. *Accreditation:* TEAC. *Entrance requirements:* Additional exam requirements/recommendations for international students: Required—TOEFL, Michigan State University ELT (minimum score 85), Michigan English Language Assessment Battery (minimum score 83). Electronic applications accepted.

Middlebury Institute of International Studies at Monterey, Graduate School of Translation, Interpretation and Language Education, Program in Teaching Foreign Language, Monterey, CA 93940-2691. Offers MATFL. *Degree requirements:* For master's, one foreign language, portfolio, oral defense. *Entrance requirements:* For master's, minimum GPA of 3.0, proficiency in foreign language. Additional exam requirements/recommendations for international students: Required—TOEFL (minimum score 600 paper-based; 100 iBT). Electronic applications accepted.

Middle Tennessee State University, College of Graduate Studies, College of Liberal Arts, Department of Foreign Languages and Literatures, Murfreesboro, TN 37132. Offers foreign languages (MAT), including French, German, Spanish. *Program availability:* Part-time, evening/weekend, online learning. *Degree requirements:* For master's, one foreign language, comprehensive exam, thesis optional. *Entrance requirements:* For master's, GRE. Additional exam requirements/recommendations for international students: Required—TOEFL (minimum score 525 paper-based; 71 iBT) or IELTS (minimum score 6). Electronic applications accepted.

Minnesota State University Mankato, College of Graduate Studies and Research, College of Arts and Humanities, Department of World Languages and Cultures, Program in French, Mankato, MN 56001. Offers French (MS); French education (MS). *Degree requirements:* For master's, one foreign language, comprehensive exam, thesis or alternative. *Entrance requirements:* For master's, minimum GPA of 3.0 during previous 2 years. Additional exam requirements/recommendations for international students: Required—TOEFL. Electronic applications accepted.

Minnesota State University Mankato, College of Graduate Studies and Research, College of Arts and Humanities, Department of World Languages and Cultures, Program in Spanish, Mankato, MN 56001. Offers Spanish (MS); Spanish education (MS); Spanish for the professions (MS). *Degree requirements:* For master's, one foreign language, comprehensive exam, thesis. *Entrance requirements:* For master's, minimum GPA of 3.0 during previous 2 years. Electronic applications accepted.

Mississippi State University, College of Arts and Sciences, Department of Classical and Modern Languages and Literatures, Mississippi State, MS 39762. Offers MA. *Program availability:* Part-time. *Faculty:* 13 full-time (4 women). *Students:* 10 full-time (8 women), 3 part-time (2 women); includes 3 minority (1 Black or African American, non-Hispanic/Latino; 2 Hispanic/Latino), 2 international. Average age 28. 10 applicants, 90% accepted, 7 enrolled. In 2017, 6 master's awarded. *Degree requirements:* For master's, one foreign language, thesis optional, comprehensive oral or written exam. *Entrance requirements:* For master's, minimum GPA of 2.75 on last two years of undergraduate courses. Additional exam requirements/recommendations for international students: Required—TOEFL (minimum score 525 paper-based; 70 iBT); Recommended—IELTS (minimum score 6). *Application deadline:* For fall admission, 7/1 for domestic students, 5/1 for international students; for spring admission, 11/1 for domestic students, 9/1 for international students. Applications are processed on a rolling basis. Application fee: $60 ($80 for international students). Electronic applications accepted. *Expenses:* Tuition, state resident: full-time $8318; part-time $462.12 per credit hour. Tuition, nonresident: full-time $22,358; part-time $1242.12 per credit hour. *Required fees:* $110; $12.24 per credit hour. $6.12 per semester. *Financial support:* In 2017–18, 9 teaching assistantships (averaging $8,766 per year) were awarded; Federal Work-Study, institutionally sponsored loans, and unspecified assistantships also available. Financial award application deadline: 4/1; financial award applicants required to submit FAFSA. *Faculty research:* French, German, Spanish literature from medieval era to present; gender and cultural studies in French; Spanish-American literature; foreign language methodology; linguistics. *Unit head:* Dr. Peter Corrigan, Professor and Department Head, 662-325-3480, Fax: 662-325-8209, E-mail: pc862@msstate.edu. *Application contact:* Lakan Drinker, Admissions and Enrollment Assistant, 662-325-8951, E-mail: ldrinker@grad.msstate.edu.
Website: http://www.cmll.msstate.edu/

Molloy College, Graduate Education Program, Rockville Centre, NY 11571-5002. Offers adolescent education in biology (MS); adolescent special education (Advanced Certificate); bilingual extension (Advanced Certificate); childhood education (MS); childhood special education (Advanced Certificate); early childhood education (MS); educational technology (MS); English (MS); mathematics (MS); social studies (MS); Spanish (MS); special education on both childhood and adolescent levels (MS); teaching English to speakers of other languages (TESOL) in grades pre-K to 12 (MS); TESOL (Advanced Certificate). *Accreditation:* NCATE. *Program availability:* Part-time, evening/weekend. *Faculty:* 18 full-time (17 women), 11 part-time/adjunct (9 women). *Students:* 102 full-time (80 women), 217 part-time (167 women); includes 65 minority (16 Black or African American, non-Hispanic/Latino; 7 Asian, non-Hispanic/Latino; 38 Hispanic/Latino; 4 Two or more races, non-Hispanic/Latino), 1 international. Average age 41. 153 applicants, 68% accepted, 85 enrolled. In 2017, 95 master's, 3 other advanced degrees awarded. *Entrance requirements:* Additional exam requirements/recommendations for international students: Required—TOEFL (minimum score 550 paper-based; 79 iBT). *Application deadline:* Applications are processed on a rolling basis. Application fee: $60. Electronic applications accepted. *Expenses:* Tuition: Full-time $19,980; part-time $1110 per credit. *Required fees:* $1040. Tuition and fees vary according to course load and degree level. *Financial support:* Application deadline: 3/1; applicants required to submit FAFSA. *Faculty research:* English Language Learners; social emotional needs of students; gifted education; cultural diversity; collaborative teaching methods. *Unit head:* Joanne O'Brien, Associate Dean and Director of Graduate Education Programs, 516-323-3116, E-mail: jobrien@molloy.edu. *Application contact:* Jaclyn Machowicz, Assistant Director for Admissions, 516-323-4010, E-mail: jmachowicz@molloy.edu.

Morehead State University, Graduate Programs, College of Education, Department of Middle Grades and Secondary Education, Morehead, KY 40351. Offers business and marketing education (MAT); English/language arts 5-9 (MAT); French (MAT); health P-12 (MAT); mathematics 5-9 (MAT); physical education P-12 (MAT); science 5-9 (MAT); secondary biology (MAT); secondary chemistry (MAT); secondary earth science (MAT); secondary English (MAT); secondary math (MAT); secondary physics (MAT); secondary social studies (MAT); social studies 5-9 (MAT); Spanish (MAT). *Program availability:* Part-time, evening/weekend. *Degree requirements:* For master's, portfolio. *Entrance requirements:* For master's, GRE or PRAXIS II content exam, minimum overall undergraduate GPA of 2.5. Additional exam requirements/recommendations for international students: Required—TOEFL (minimum score 500 paper-based). Electronic applications accepted.

New Mexico State University, College of Education, Department of Curriculum and Instruction, Las Cruces, NM 88003. Offers bilingual education (MA); curriculum and instruction (MA, Ed D, PhD); early childhood education (MA); educational diagnostics (Ed S); language, literacy and culture (MA); learning design and technologies (MA); teaching (MAT), including dance, Spanish; teaching English to speakers of other languages (MA). *Accreditation:* NCATE. *Program availability:* Part-time, evening/weekend, 100% online. *Faculty:* 22 full-time (17 women), 7 part-time/adjunct (2 women). *Students:* 113 full-time (79 women), 194 part-time (138 women); includes 171 minority (15 Black or African American, non-Hispanic/Latino; 3 American Indian or Alaska Native, non-Hispanic/Latino; 4 Asian, non-Hispanic/Latino; 142 Hispanic/Latino; 7 Two or more races, non-Hispanic/Latino), 37 international. Average age 36. 106 applicants, 80% accepted, 56 enrolled. In 2017, 82 master's, 15 doctorates, 1 other advanced degree awarded. *Entrance requirements:* For master's, minimum cumulative GPA of 3.0; for doctorate, portfolio, minimum cumulative GPA of 3.0. Additional exam requirements/recommendations for international students: Required—TOEFL (minimum score 550 paper-based; 79 iBT), IELTS (minimum score 6.5). *Application deadline:* For fall admission, 12/15 priority date for domestic and international students; for spring admission, 11/1 for domestic students. Applications are processed on a rolling basis. Application fee: $40 ($50 for international students). Electronic applications accepted. *Expenses:* Tuition, state resident: full-time $4390. Tuition, nonresident: full-time $15,309. *Required fees:* $853. *Financial support:* In 2017–18, 97 students received support, including 2 fellowships (averaging $4,390 per year), 1 research assistantship (averaging $17,368 per year), 10 teaching assistantships (averaging $17,489 per year); career-related internships or fieldwork, Federal Work-Study, scholarships/grants, traineeships, health care benefits, and unspecified assistantships also available. Support available to part-time students. Financial award application deadline: 3/1. *Faculty research:* STEM education, bilingual and English as a second language education, critical pedagogy/multicultural education, learning design and technology, early childhood education. *Total annual research expenditures:* $13,518. *Unit head:* Dr. David Rutledge, Department Head, 575-646-5411, Fax: 575-646-5436, E-mail: rutledge@nmsu.edu. *Application contact:* Dr. David Rutledge, Associate Department Head for Graduate Programs, 575-646-5411, Fax: 575-646-5436, E-mail: rutledge@nmsu.edu.
Website: http://tpal.nmsu.edu/

New York University, Steinhardt School of Culture, Education, and Human Development, Department of Teaching and Learning, Program in Multilingual/Multicultural Studies, New York, NY 10012. Offers bilingual education (MA, PhD, Advanced Certificate); foreign language education (MA); teaching English to speakers of other languages (MA, PhD); teaching foreign languages, 7-12 (MA), including Chinese, French, Italian, Japanese, Spanish; teaching French as a foreign language (MA), including teaching English to speakers of other languages; teaching Spanish as a foreign language (MA), including teaching English to speakers of other languages. MA in teaching English to speakers of other languages also offered in collaboration with NYU Shanghai. *Accreditation:* TEAC. *Program availability:* Part-time, evening/weekend. *Students:* Average age 29. 431 applicants, 61% accepted, 92 enrolled. In 2017, 121 master's, 1 doctorate, 2 other advanced degrees awarded. *Entrance requirements:* For doctorate, GRE General Test, interview; for Advanced Certificate, master's degree. Additional exam requirements/recommendations for international students: Required—TOEFL (minimum score 100 iBT). *Application deadline:* For fall admission, 12/1 priority date for domestic and international students; for spring admission, 10/1 for domestic and international students. Applications are processed on a rolling basis. Application fee: $75. Electronic applications accepted. *Expenses:* Tuition: Full-time $41,352; part-time $19,968 per year. *Required fees:* $2496; $1628 per unit. $814 per term. Tuition and fees vary according to course load and program. *Financial support:* Fellowships with full and partial tuition reimbursements, career-related internships or fieldwork, Federal Work-Study, institutionally sponsored loans, scholarships/grants, and tuition waivers (partial) available. Support available to part-time students. Financial award application deadline: 2/1; financial award applicants required to submit FAFSA. *Faculty research:* Second language acquisition, cross-cultural communication, technology-enhanced language learning, language variation, action learning. *Unit head:* Prof. Shondel Nero, Director, 212-998-5757, E-mail: shondel.nero@nyu.edu. *Application contact:* 212-998-5030, Fax: 212-995-4328, E-mail: steinhardt.gradadmissions@nyu.edu.
Website: http://steinhardt.nyu.edu/teachlearn/mms

Northern Arizona University, College of Arts and Letters, Department of Global Languages and Cultures, Flagstaff, AZ 86011. Offers Spanish (MAT); Spanish education (MAT). *Program availability:* Part-time. *Faculty:* 33 full-time (21 women), 2 part-time/adjunct (both women). *Students:* 20 full-time (11 women), 2 part-time (1 woman); includes 10 minority (9 Hispanic/Latino; 1 Two or more races, non-Hispanic/Latino), 4 international. Average age 30. 15 applicants, 73% accepted, 11 enrolled. In 2017, 7 master's awarded. *Degree requirements:* For master's, variable foreign language requirement, comprehensive exam (for some programs), thesis (for some programs). *Entrance requirements:* Additional exam requirements/recommendations for international students: Required—TOEFL (minimum score 80 iBT), IELTS (minimum score 7). *Application deadline:* For fall admission, 3/1 for domestic and international students; for spring admission, 10/1 for domestic and international students. Applications are processed on a rolling basis. Application fee: $65. Electronic applications accepted. *Expenses:* Tuition, state resident: full-time $9240; part-time $458 per credit hour. Tuition, nonresident: full-time $21,588; part-time $1199 per credit hour. *Required fees:* $1021; $14 per credit hour. $646 per semester. Tuition and fees vary according to course load, campus/location and program. *Financial support:* In 2017–18, 21 students received support, including 21 teaching assistantships with full and partial tuition reimbursements available (averaging $13,500 per year); institutionally sponsored loans, health care benefits, tuition waivers (full and partial), and unspecified assistantships also available. Financial award application deadline: 2/1; financial award applicants required to submit FAFSA. *Unit head:* Dr. Patricia Frederick, Chair, 928-523-9437, E-mail: patricia.frederick@nau.edu. *Application contact:* Alexandria McConocha, Administrative Associate, 928-523-6237, Fax: 928-523-0963, E-mail: alexandria.mcconocha@nau.edu.
Website: https://nau.edu/cal/modern-languages/

Pace University, School of Education, New York, NY 10038. Offers adolescent education (MST), including biology, chemistry, earth science, English, foreign languages, mathematics, physics, social studies; childhood education (MST); early childhood development, learning and intervention (MST); educational technology studies (MS); inclusive adolescent education (MST), including biology, chemistry, earth science, English, foreign languages, mathematics, physics, social studies; integrated instruction for educational technology (Certificate); integrated instruction for literacy and technology (Certificate); literacy (MS Ed); special education (MS Ed). *Accreditation:* NCATE. *Program availability:* Part-time, evening/weekend, 100% online, blended/hybrid learning. *Faculty:* 19 full-time (13 women), 86 part-time/adjunct (49 women). *Students:* 91 full-time (76 women), 548 part-time (401 women); includes 247 minority (112 Black or African American, non-Hispanic/Latino; 2 American Indian or Alaska Native, non-Hispanic/Latino; 31 Asian, non-Hispanic/Latino; 93 Hispanic/Latino; 1 Native Hawaiian or other Pacific Islander, non-Hispanic/Latino; 8 Two or more races, non-Hispanic/Latino), 6 international. Average age 30. 188 applicants, 86% accepted, 114 enrolled. In

2017, 213 master's, 8 other advanced degrees awarded. *Degree requirements:* For master's and Certificate, certification exams. *Entrance requirements:* For master's, GRE (for initial certification programs only), teaching certificate (for MS Ed in literacy and special education programs only). Additional exam requirements/recommendations for international students: Required—TOEFL (minimum score 88 iBT), IELTS or PTE. *Application deadline:* For fall admission, 8/1 priority date for domestic students, 6/1 for international students; for spring admission, 12/1 priority date for domestic students, 10/1 for international students. Applications are processed on a rolling basis. Application fee: $70. Electronic applications accepted. *Expenses:* Contact institution. *Financial support:* In 2017–18, 17 students received support, including 17 research assistantships with partial tuition reimbursements available (averaging $6,020 per year); career-related internships or fieldwork, Federal Work-Study, scholarships/grants, and unspecified assistantships also available. Financial award application deadline: 9/1; financial award applicants required to submit FAFSA. *Faculty research:* STEM education, TESOL, teacher education, special education, language and literary development. *Total annual research expenditures:* $29,706. *Unit head:* Dr. Xiao-Lei Wang, Dean, School of Education, 914-773-3876, E-mail: xwang@pace.edu. *Application contact:* Susan Ford-Goldschein, Director of Graduate Admissions, 212-346-1531, Fax: 212-346-1585, E-mail: graduateadmission@pace.edu.
Website: http://www.pace.edu/school-of-education

Plymouth State University, College of Graduate Studies, Graduate Studies in Education, Program in Secondary Education, Plymouth, NH 03264-1595. Offers curriculum and instruction (M Ed); language education (M Ed); library media (M Ed); physical education (M Ed); social studies education (M Ed); special education (M Ed). *Program availability:* Part-time, evening/weekend. *Entrance requirements:* For master's, MAT.

Portland State University, Graduate School, College of Liberal Arts and Sciences, Department of World Languages and Literatures, Portland, OR 97207-0751. Offers French (MA); German (MA); Japanese (MA); Spanish (MA); world literature and language (MA). *Program availability:* Part-time. *Faculty:* 61 full-time (37 women), 26 part-time/adjunct (20 women). *Students:* 22 full-time (13 women), 11 part-time (5 women); includes 7 minority (1 Asian, non-Hispanic/Latino; 6 Hispanic/Latino), 8 international. Average age 30. 26 applicants, 73% accepted, 16 enrolled. In 2017, 9 master's awarded. *Degree requirements:* For master's, variable foreign language requirement, thesis (for some programs). *Entrance requirements:* For master's, ACTFL, BA in the major language, minimum GPA of 3.0 in all coursework. Additional exam requirements/recommendations for international students: Required—TOEFL (minimum score 550 paper-based; 80 iBT), IELTS (minimum score 6.5). *Application deadline:* For fall admission, 4/1 for domestic students, 3/1 for international students; for winter admission, 9/1 for domestic students, 7/1 for international students; for spring admission, 11/1 for domestic and international students. Applications are processed on a rolling basis. Application fee: $65. *Expenses:* Tuition, state resident: full-time $14,436; part-time $401 per credit. Tuition, nonresident: full-time $21,780; part-time $605 per credit. *Required fees:* $1380; $22 per credit. $119 per quarter. One-time fee: $325. Tuition and fees vary according to program. *Financial support:* In 2017–18, 22 teaching assistantships with full and partial tuition reimbursements (averaging $11,431 per year) were awarded; research assistantships, Federal Work-Study, scholarships/grants, and unspecified assistantships also available. Support available to part-time students. Financial award application deadline: 3/1; financial award applicants required to submit FAFSA. *Faculty research:* Foreign language pedagogy, applied and social linguistics, literary history and criticism. *Total annual research expenditures:* $522,357. *Unit head:* Dr. Gina Greco, Chair, 503-725-5287, E-mail: grecog@pdx.edu. *Application contact:* Kelli Martin, Graduate Admissions Coordinator, 503-725-3243, E-mail: kmarti@pdx.edu.
Website: http://www.pdx.edu/wll/

Purdue University, Graduate School, College of Education, Department of Curriculum and Instruction, West Lafayette, IN 47907. Offers agricultural and extension education (MS, MS Ed, PhD, Ed S); art education (PhD); career and technical education (MS Ed, PhD, Ed S); curriculum studies (MS Ed, PhD, Ed S); educational technology (MS Ed, PhD, Ed S); elementary education (MS Ed); family and consumer sciences education (MS Ed, PhD, Ed S); foreign language education (MS Ed, PhD, Ed S); industrial technology (PhD, Ed S); language arts (MS Ed, PhD, Ed S); literacy (MS Ed, PhD, Ed S); mathematics education (MS, MS Ed, PhD, Ed S); science education (MS, MS Ed, PhD, Ed S); social studies education (MS Ed, PhD, Ed S). *Accreditation:* NCATE. *Program availability:* Part-time, evening/weekend. *Faculty:* 37 full-time (27 women), 1 (woman) part-time/adjunct. *Students:* 78 full-time (50 women), 286 part-time (195 women); includes 68 minority (25 Black or African American, non-Hispanic/Latino; 3 American Indian or Alaska Native, non-Hispanic/Latino; 10 Asian, non-Hispanic/Latino; 22 Hispanic/Latino; 1 Native Hawaiian or other Pacific Islander, non-Hispanic/Latino; 7 Two or more races, non-Hispanic/Latino), 44 international. Average age 36. 150 applicants, 79% accepted, 73 enrolled. In 2017, 107 master's, 20 doctorates, 2 other advanced degrees awarded. *Degree requirements:* For master's, thesis optional; for doctorate, thesis/dissertation, oral and written exams; for Ed S, oral presentation, project. *Entrance requirements:* For master's, GRE General Test (if undergraduate GPA is below 3.0), minimum undergraduate GPA of 3.0 or equivalent; for doctorate, GRE General Test (minimum combined verbal and quantitative score of 1000, 300 for new scoring), minimum undergraduate GPA of 3.0 or equivalent; master's degree with minimum GPA of 3.0 or equivalent; for Ed S, GRE General Test (minimum combined verbal and quantitative score of 1000, 300 for new scoring), minimum undergraduate GPA of 3.0 or equivalent; master's degree. Additional exam requirements/recommendations for international students: Required—TOEFL (minimum score 550 paper-based; 77 iBT). *Application deadline:* For fall admission, 12/15 for domestic students, 3/1 for international students; for spring admission, 9/15 for domestic students, 8/1 for international students. Application fee: $60 ($75 for international students). Electronic applications accepted. *Financial support:* Fellowships with full tuition reimbursements, research assistantships with full tuition reimbursements, teaching assistantships with full tuition reimbursements, career-related internships or fieldwork, and tuition waivers (full) available. Support available to part-time students. Financial award application deadline: 3/1; financial award applicants required to submit FAFSA. *Faculty research:* Literacy acquisition and development, teacher beliefs and knowledge, recruitment and retention of underrepresented students, economic education, literacy discourse. *Unit head:* Janet M. Alsup, Head, 765-494-9667, E-mail: alsupj@purdue.edu. *Application contact:* Heather Brinkman, Graduate Contact, 765-494-2345, E-mail: hbrinkma@purdue.edu.
Website: http://www.edci.purdue.edu/

Purdue University, Graduate School, College of Liberal Arts, School of Languages and Cultures, West Lafayette, IN 47907. Offers French (MA, MAT, PhD), including French (MA, PhD), French education (MAT); German (MA, MAT, PhD), including German (MA, PhD), German education (MAT); Japanese pedagogy (MA); Spanish (MA, MAT, PhD), including Spanish (MA, PhD), Spanish education (MAT). *Faculty:* 44 full-time (22 women), 1 (woman) part-time/adjunct. *Students:* 37 full-time (18 women), 41 part-time (30 women); includes 9 minority (1 Asian, non-Hispanic/Latino; 8 Hispanic/Latino), 52 international. Average age 32. 49 applicants, 39% accepted, 14 enrolled. In 2017, 11 master's, 5 doctorates awarded. Terminal master's awarded for partial completion of doctoral program. *Degree requirements:* For master's, one foreign language; for

doctorate, 2 foreign languages, thesis/dissertation. *Entrance requirements:* For master's, GRE General Test (minimum score 600, 160 for new scoring), two writing samples, one in English, one in language (French, German, Japanese, or Spanish); sample recording of English and language of study; for doctorate, GRE General Test (minimum score 600, 160 for new scoring), master's degree with minimum GPA of 3.5 or equivalent; two writing samples, one in English, one in language (French, German, Japanese, or Spanish); sample recording of English and language of study. Additional exam requirements/recommendations for international students: Required—TOEFL (minimum score 550 paper-based; 77 iBT); Recommended—TWE. *Application deadline:* For fall admission, 12/12 for domestic and international students; for spring admission, 10/1 for domestic and international students. Applications are processed on a rolling basis. Application fee: $60 ($75 for international students). Electronic applications accepted. *Financial support:* In 2017–18, fellowships with tuition reimbursements (averaging $15,750 per year), teaching assistantships with tuition reimbursements (averaging $13,463 per year) were awarded. Support available to part-time students. Financial award applicants required to submit FAFSA. *Faculty research:* Linguistics, semiotics, literary criticism, pedagogy. *Unit head:* Jennifer M. William, Head, 765-494-3834, E-mail: jmwilliam@purdue.edu. *Application contact:* Joni L. Hipsher, Graduate Contact, 765-494-3841, E-mail: jlhipshe@purdue.edu.
Website: http://www.cla.purdue.edu/slc/main/

Queens College of the City University of New York, Division of Education, Department of Secondary Education and Youth Services, Queens, NY 11367-1597. Offers adolescent biology (MAT); art (MS Ed); biology (MS Ed, AC); chemistry (MS Ed, AC); earth sciences (MS Ed, AC); English (MS Ed, AC); French (MS Ed); Italian (MS Ed, AC); literacy education (MS Ed); mathematics (MS Ed, AC); music (MS Ed, AC); physics (MS Ed, AC); social studies (MS Ed, AC); Spanish (MS Ed, AC). *Program availability:* Part-time, evening/weekend. *Students:* 28 full-time (16 women), 349 part-time (202 women); includes 165 minority (18 Black or African American, non-Hispanic/Latino; 56 Asian, non-Hispanic/Latino; 83 Hispanic/Latino; 8 Two or more races, non-Hispanic/Latino), 14 international. Average age 29. *Degree requirements:* For master's, research project. *Entrance requirements:* For master's, minimum GPA of 3.0. Additional exam requirements/recommendations for international students: Required—TOEFL, IELTS. *Application deadline:* For fall admission, 4/1 for domestic students; for spring admission, 11/1 for domestic students. Applications are processed on a rolling basis. Application fee: $125. Electronic applications accepted. *Financial support:* Career-related internships or fieldwork available. Financial award application deadline: 4/1; financial award applicants required to submit FAFSA. *Unit head:* Dr. Eleanor Armour-Thomas, Chairperson, 718-997-5150, E-mail: eleanor.armour-thomas@qc.cuny.edu. *Application contact:* Elizabeth D'Amico-Ramirez, Assistant Director of Graduate Admissions, 718-997-5203, E-mail: elizabeth.damicoramirez@qc.cuny.edu.

Quinnipiac University, School of Education, Program in Secondary Education, Hamden, CT 06518-1940. Offers biology (MAT); English (MAT); history (MAT); mathematics (MAT); Spanish (MAT). *Accreditation:* NCATE. *Faculty:* 8 full-time (5 women), 27 part-time/adjunct (19 women). *Students:* 27 full-time (20 women); includes 5 minority (1 Black or African American, non-Hispanic/Latino; 3 Hispanic/Latino; 1 Two or more races, non-Hispanic/Latino). 43 applicants, 98% accepted, 36 enrolled. In 2017, 34 master's awarded. *Entrance requirements:* For master's, PRAXIS I or PRAXIS Core Academic Skills Exam, minimum GPA of 3.0, interview. *Application deadline:* For fall admission, 5/1 priority date for domestic students. Applications are processed on a rolling basis. Application fee: $45. Electronic applications accepted. *Financial support:* Career-related internships or fieldwork, Federal Work-Study, and unspecified assistantships available. Financial award application deadline: 6/1; financial award applicants required to submit FAFSA. *Faculty research:* Multicultural and urban education/leadership, challenges of teaching diverse learners, scholarship of teaching and learning, technology and teaching, humor and education. *Unit head:* Mordechai Gordon, Program Director, 203-582-8442, E-mail: mordechai.gordon@qu.edu. *Application contact:* Office of Graduate Admissions, 203-582-8672, Fax: 203-582-3443, E-mail: graduate@qu.edu.
Website: http://www.qu.edu/gradeducation

Rhode Island College, School of Graduate Studies, Feinstein School of Education and Human Development, Department of Educational Studies, Providence, RI 02908-1991. Offers advanced studies in teaching and learning (M Ed); English (MAT); French (MAT); history (MAT); math (MAT); secondary education (MAT); Spanish (MAT); teaching English as a second language (M Ed). *Accreditation:* NCATE. *Program availability:* Part-time, evening/weekend. *Faculty:* 2. *Students:* 1 (woman) full-time, 62 part-time (58 women); includes 10 minority (1 Black or African American, non-Hispanic/Latino; 2 Asian, non-Hispanic/Latino; 6 Hispanic/Latino; 1 Two or more races, non-Hispanic/Latino). Average age 37. In 2017, 31 master's awarded. *Degree requirements:* For master's, capstone or comprehensive assessment. *Entrance requirements:* For master's, GRE or MAT (for most programs), minimum undergraduate GPA of 3.0; baccalaureate degree in English, French, history, math or Spanish; 3 letters of recommendation; interview. Additional exam requirements/recommendations for international students: Recommended—TOEFL (minimum score 550 paper-based; 79 iBT). *Application deadline:* For fall admission, 3/1 for domestic students; for spring admission, 11/1 for domestic students. Applications are processed on a rolling basis. Application fee: $50. Electronic applications accepted. *Expenses:* Tuition, state resident: full-time $9768; part-time $407 per credit. Tuition, nonresident: full-time $19,008; part-time $792 per credit. *Required fees:* $696; $29 per credit. One-time fee: $200 full-time; $100 part-time. Tuition and fees vary according to course load. *Financial support:* In 2017–18, 3 teaching assistantships with full tuition reimbursements (averaging $2,500 per year) were awarded; career-related internships or fieldwork, Federal Work-Study, scholarships/grants, health care benefits, and unspecified assistantships also available. Support available to part-time students. Financial award application deadline: 5/15; financial award applicants required to submit FAFSA. *Unit head:* Dr. Leslie Bogad, Chair, 401-456-8170. *Application contact:* Graduate Studies, 401-456-8700.
Website: http://www.ric.edu/educationalStudies/

Rider University, College of Education and Human Services, Teacher Certification Program, Lawrenceville, NJ 08648-3001. Offers bilingual education (Certificate); business education (Certificate); early childhood education (Certificate); elementary education (Certificate); English as a second language (Certificate); English education (Certificate); mathematics education (Certificate); science education (Certificate); secondary education (Certificate); social studies education (Certificate); world languages (Certificate), including French, German, Spanish. *Program availability:* Part-time, online learning. *Degree requirements:* For Certificate, internship, professional portfolio. *Entrance requirements:* For degree, PRAXIS, resume. Additional exam requirements/recommendations for international students: Required—TOEFL (minimum score 550 paper-based). Electronic applications accepted. *Faculty research:* Conceptual foundations for optimal development of creativity; creative theory, cognitive processes in mathematics learning, teacher collaboration.

Rivier University, School of Graduate Studies, Department of Modern Languages, Nashua, NH 03060. Offers Spanish (MAT). *Program availability:* Part-time, evening/weekend.

Rutgers University–New Brunswick, Graduate School-New Brunswick, Program in French, Piscataway, NJ 08854-8097. Offers French (MA, PhD); French studies (MAT). *Program availability:* Part-time, evening/weekend. Terminal master's awarded for partial completion of doctoral program. *Degree requirements:* For master's, one foreign language, written and oral exams (MA); for doctorate, 3 foreign languages, thesis/dissertation, qualifying exam. *Entrance requirements:* For master's and doctorate, GRE General Test. *Faculty research:* Literatures in French, literary history and theory, rhetoric and poetics.

Rutgers University–New Brunswick, Graduate School-New Brunswick, Program in Italian, Piscataway, NJ 08854-8097. Offers Italian (MA, PhD); Italian literature and literary criticism (MA); language, literature and culture (MAT). *Program availability:* Part-time, evening/weekend. Terminal master's awarded for partial completion of doctoral program. *Degree requirements:* For master's, one foreign language, comprehensive exam (for some programs), thesis optional; for doctorate, 2 foreign languages, thesis/dissertation, qualifying exam. *Entrance requirements:* For master's and doctorate, GRE General Test. Additional exam requirements/recommendations for international students: Required—TOEFL. *Faculty research:* Literature.

Rutgers University–New Brunswick, Graduate School-New Brunswick, Program in Spanish, Piscataway, NJ 08854-8097. Offers bilingualism and second language acquisition (MA, PhD); Spanish (MA, MAT, PhD); Spanish literature (MA, PhD); translation (MA). *Program availability:* Part-time. *Degree requirements:* For master's, comprehensive exam (for some programs), thesis (for some programs); for doctorate, 2 foreign languages, comprehensive exam, thesis/dissertation. *Entrance requirements:* For master's and doctorate, GRE General Test. Additional exam requirements/recommendations for international students: Required—TOEFL. Electronic applications accepted. *Faculty research:* Hispanic literature, Luso-Brazilian literature, Spanish linguistics, Spanish translation.

Rutgers University–New Brunswick, Graduate School of Education, Department of Learning and Teaching, Program in Language Education, Piscataway, NJ 08854-8097. Offers English as a second language education (Ed M); language education (Ed M, Ed D). *Program availability:* Part-time. Terminal master's awarded for partial completion of doctoral program. *Degree requirements:* For master's, comprehensive exam; for doctorate, thesis/dissertation, concept paper, qualifying exam. *Entrance requirements:* For master's, GRE General Test, minimum GPA of 3.0; for doctorate, GRE General Test, minimum GPA of 3.5. Additional exam requirements/recommendations for international students: Required—TOEFL. Electronic applications accepted. *Faculty research:* Linguistics, sociolinguistics, cross-cultural/international communication.

Saginaw Valley State University, College of Education, Program in Teaching Chinese as a Foreign Language, University Center, MI 48710. Offers MAT. *Program availability:* Part-time, evening/weekend. *Students:* 10 full-time (6 women), all international. Average age 26. 10 applicants, 90% accepted, 8 enrolled. In 2017, 4 master's awarded. *Entrance requirements:* For master's, minimum GPA of 3.0. Additional exam requirements/recommendations for international students: Required—TOEFL (minimum score 550 paper-based; 79 iBT). *Application deadline:* For fall admission, 7/15 for international students; for winter admission, 11/15 for international students; for spring admission, 4/15 for international students. Applications are processed on a rolling basis. Application fee: $30 ($90 for international students). Electronic applications accepted. *Expenses:* Tuition, state resident: full-time $10,156; part-time $564.20 per credit hour. Tuition, nonresident: full-time $19,336; part-time $1074.20 per credit hour. *Required fees:* $263; $14.60 per credit hour. Tuition and fees vary according to degree level and program. *Financial support:* Federal Work-Study and scholarships/grants available. Support available to part-time students. Financial award application deadline: 4/1; financial award applicants required to submit FAFSA. *Unit head:* Dr. Craig Douglas, Dean, 989-964-4057, Fax: 989-964-4563, E-mail: coeconnect@svsu.edu. *Application contact:* Jenna Briggs, Director, Graduate and International Admissions, 989-964-6096, Fax: 989-964-2788, E-mail: gradadm@svsu.edu.

St. John Fisher College, Ralph C. Wilson Jr. School of Education, Program in Adolescence Education and Special Education, Rochester, NY 14618-3597. Offers adolescence education: biology with special education (MS Ed); adolescence education: chemistry with special education (MS Ed); adolescence education: English with special education (MS Ed); adolescence education: French with special education (MS Ed); adolescence education: math with special education (MS Ed); adolescence education: physics with special education (MS Ed); adolescence education: social studies with special education (MS Ed); adolescence education: Spanish with special education (MS Ed). *Program availability:* Part-time, evening/weekend. *Faculty:* 5 full-time (4 women), 7 part-time/adjunct (6 women). *Students:* 15 full-time (3 women), 4 part-time (all women); includes 4 minority (2 Black or African American, non-Hispanic/Latino; 1 Hispanic/Latino; 1 Two or more races, non-Hispanic/Latino). Average age 27. 34 applicants, 85% accepted, 12 enrolled. In 2017, 19 master's awarded. *Degree requirements:* For master's, field experiences, student teaching. *Entrance requirements:* For master's, LAST, 2 letters of recommendation, personal statement, current resume. Additional exam requirements/recommendations for international students: Required—TOEFL (minimum score 575 paper-based; 80 iBT). *Application deadline:* Applications are processed on a rolling basis. Application fee: $30. Electronic applications accepted. *Expenses:* Contact institution. *Financial support:* Scholarships/grants available. Financial award applicants required to submit FAFSA. *Faculty research:* Arts and humanities, urban schools, constructivist learning, at-risk students, mentoring. *Unit head:* Dr. Susan Hildenbrand, Program Director, 585-385-7297, E-mail: shildenbrand@sjfc.edu. *Application contact:* Michelle Gosier, Director of Transfer and Graduate Admissions, 585-385-8064, E-mail: mgosier@sjfc.edu.

Saint Xavier University, Graduate Studies, School of Education, Chicago, IL 60655-3105. Offers counseling (MA); curriculum and instruction (MA); early childhood education (MA); educational administration (MA); elementary education (MA); individualized studies (MA), including educational technology, English as a second language (ESL), ISTEM (integrative science, technology, engineering, and math), science education (MA); music education (MA); reading (MA); secondary education (MA); Spanish education (MA); special education (MA); teaching and leadership (MA). *Accreditation:* NCATE. *Program availability:* Part-time, evening/weekend. *Degree requirements:* For master's, thesis or project. *Entrance requirements:* For master's, minimum GPA of 3.0. *Expenses:* Contact institution.

Shippensburg University of Pennsylvania, School of Graduate Studies, College of Education and Human Services, Department of Teacher Education, Shippensburg, PA 17257-2299. Offers curriculum and instruction (M Ed), including biology, early childhood education, elementary education, geography/earth science, history, mathematics, middle school education, modern languages; reading (M Ed). *Accreditation:* NCATE. *Program availability:* Part-time, evening/weekend, 100% online, blended/hybrid learning. *Faculty:* 13 full-time (8 women), 1 (woman) part-time/adjunct. *Students:* 10 full-time (7 women), 94 part-time (81 women); includes 10 minority (3 Black or African American, non-Hispanic/Latino; 2 Asian, non-Hispanic/Latino; 5 Hispanic/Latino), 1 international. Average age 34. 71 applicants, 86% accepted, 35 enrolled. In 2017, 23 master's awarded. *Degree requirements:* For master's, comprehensive exam (for some programs), thesis optional, practicum or internship; capstone seminar (for some programs). *Entrance requirements:* For master's, MAT or GRE (if GPA less than 2.75), interview, 3 letters of reference, questionnaire of teaching background and future goals, resume. Additional exam requirements/recommendations for international students: Required—TOEFL (minimum score 550 paper-based, 68 iBT) or IELTS (minimum score 6). *Application deadline:* For fall admission, 4/1 priority date for domestic students, 4/30 for international students; for spring admission, 9/1 priority date for domestic students, 9/30 for international students; for summer admission, 2/1 priority date for domestic students. Applications are processed on a rolling basis. Application fee: $45. Electronic applications accepted. *Expenses:* Tuition, state resident: part-time $500 per credit. Tuition, nonresident: part-time $750 per credit. *Required fees:* $145 per credit. *Financial support:* In 2017–18, 1 student received support. Career-related internships or fieldwork, scholarships/grants, unspecified assistantships, and resident hall director and student payroll positions available. Support available to part-time students. Financial award application deadline: 3/1; financial award applicants required to submit FAFSA. *Unit head:* Dr. Christine A. Royce, Chairperson, 717-477-1688, Fax: 717-477-4046, E-mail: caroyc@ship.edu. *Application contact:* Maya T. Mapp, Director of Admissions, 717-477-1231, Fax: 717-477-4016, E-mail: mtmapp@ship.edu. Website: http://www.ship.edu/teacher/

Southern Connecticut State University, School of Graduate Studies, School of Arts and Sciences, Department of World Languages and Literatures, New Haven, CT 06515-1355. Offers multicultural-bilingual education/teaching English to speakers of other languages (MS); romance languages (MA). *Program availability:* Part-time, evening/weekend. *Degree requirements:* For master's, one foreign language, thesis or alternative. *Entrance requirements:* For master's, interview, minimum undergraduate GPA of 2.7. Electronic applications accepted.

Southern Oregon University, Graduate Studies, Department of Foreign Languages and Literatures, Ashland, OR 97520. Offers French language teaching (MA); Spanish language teaching (MA). *Program availability:* Part-time, online learning. *Degree requirements:* For master's, thesis (for some programs). *Entrance requirements:* For master's, GRE General Test, minimum cumulative GPA of 3.0 in the last 90 quarter credits (60 semester credits) of undergraduate coursework. Additional exam requirements/recommendations for international students: Required—TOEFL (minimum score 540 paper-based; 76 iBT), IELTS (minimum score 6), ELPT (minimum score 964) or ELS (minimum score 112). Electronic applications accepted.

Spalding University, Graduate Studies, College of Education, Programs in Education, Louisville, KY 40203-2188. Offers art teacher education (MAT); business teacher education (MAT); elementary school education (MAT); foreign language (MAT); high school education (MAT); middle school education (MAT); secondary education (MAT); special education (learning and behavioral disorders) (MAT); student guidance counselor (MA); teacher leader (M Ed). *Accreditation:* NCATE. *Program availability:* Part-time, evening/weekend. *Entrance requirements:* For master's, GRE General Test or MAT, interview, letters of recommendation, resume. Additional exam requirements/recommendations for international students: Required—TOEFL (minimum score 535 paper-based). Electronic applications accepted. *Faculty research:* Instructional technology, achievement gap, classroom management, assessment.

State University of New York at Plattsburgh, School of Education, Health, and Human Services, Program in Teacher Education: Adolescence Education, Plattsburgh, NY 12901-2681. Offers adolescence education (MST); biology 7-12 (MST); chemistry 7-12 (MST); earth science 7-12 (MST); English 7-12 (MST); French 7-12 (MST); mathematics 7-12 (MST); physics 7-12 (MST); social studies 7-12 (MST); Spanish 7-12 (MST). *Accreditation:* TEAC. *Program availability:* Part-time, evening/weekend. *Entrance requirements:* For master's, minimum GPA of 2.75. Additional exam requirements/recommendations for international students: Required—TOEFL.

State University of New York College at Old Westbury, School of Education, Old Westbury, NY 11568-0210. Offers biology (MAT, MS); chemistry (MAT, MS); English language arts (MAT, MS); math (MAT, MS); social studies (MAT, MS); Spanish (MAT, MS). *Program availability:* Part-time, evening/weekend. *Students:* 164 full-time (80 women), 112 part-time (52 women); includes 87 minority (14 Black or African American, non-Hispanic/Latino; 38 Asian, non-Hispanic/Latino; 35 Hispanic/Latino), 2 international. Average age 30. 34 applicants, 82% accepted, 25 enrolled. In 2017, 25 master's awarded. *Entrance requirements:* For master's, Liberal Arts and Sciences Test, undergraduate degree with at least 30 semester hours of appropriate coursework as defined by the respective discipline; minimum cumulative undergraduate GPA of 3.0; two letters of recommendation (one from an academic source); essay. Additional exam requirements/recommendations for international students: Required—TOEFL (minimum score 550 paper-based); Recommended—IELTS. Application fee: $50. *Financial support:* Applicants required to submit FAFSA. *Unit head:* Dr. Nancy Brown, Dean, School of Education, 516-876-3275, E-mail: brownn@oldwestbury.edu. *Application contact:* Philip D'Angelo, Graduate Admissions Office, 516-876-3073, E-mail: enroll@oldwestbury.edu.

Stony Brook University, State University of New York, School of Professional Development, Stony Brook, NY 11794. Offers biology (MAT); chemistry (MAT); coaching (Graduate Certificate); earth science (MAT); educational computing (Graduate Certificate); educational leadership (Advanced Certificate); English (MAT); environmental management (MPS, Graduate Certificate); French (MAT); German (MAT); higher education administration (MA, Certificate); human resource management (MS, Graduate Certificate); industrial management (Graduate Certificate); information systems management (Graduate Certificate); Italian (MAT); liberal studies (MA); mathematics (MAT); operations research (Graduate Certificate); physics (MAT); school district business leadership (Advanced Certificate); social studies (MAT); Spanish (MAT). *Program availability:* Part-time, evening/weekend, online learning. *Faculty:* 3 full-time (2 women), 101 part-time/adjunct (45 women). *Students:* 190 full-time (126 women), 974 part-time (708 women); includes 255 minority (88 Black or African American, non-Hispanic/Latino; 2 American Indian or Alaska Native, non-Hispanic/Latino; 31 Asian, non-Hispanic/Latino; 113 Hispanic/Latino; 1 Native Hawaiian or other Pacific Islander, non-Hispanic/Latino; 20 Two or more races, non-Hispanic/Latino), 6 international. Average age 33. 411 applicants, 91% accepted, 288 enrolled. In 2017, 333 master's, 180 other advanced degrees awarded. *Entrance requirements:* Additional exam requirements/recommendations for international students: Required—TOEFL (minimum score 85 iBT). *Application deadline:* For fall admission, 1/15 for domestic students, 6/1 for international students; for spring admission, 10/1 for domestic and international students. Applications are processed on a rolling basis. Application fee: $100. *Expenses:* Contact institution. *Financial support:* Fellowships, research assistantships, teaching assistantships, and career-related internships or fieldwork available. Support available to part-time students. *Unit head:* Dr. Ken Lindblom, Dean, 631-632-7049, Fax: 631-632-9046, E-mail: kenneth.lindblom@stonybrook.edu. *Application contact:* Melissa Jordan, Assistant Dean, 631-632-7751, E-mail: melissa.jordan@stonybrook.edu. Website: http://www.stonybrook.edu/spd/

Texas A&M International University, Office of Graduate Studies and Research, College of Arts and Sciences, Department of Humanities, Laredo, TX 78041. Offers English (MA); Hispanic studies (PhD); history and political thought (MA); language and translation (MA). *Degree requirements:* For master's, comprehensive exam (for some programs), thesis (for some programs). *Entrance requirements:* For

master's, GRE General Test. Additional exam requirements/recommendations for international students: Required—TOEFL (minimum score 550 paper-based; 79 iBT).

Texas A&M University–Kingsville, College of Graduate Studies, College of Arts and Sciences, Department of Language and Literature, Kingsville, TX 78363. Offers cultural studies (MA); English (MA, MS); Spanish (MA). *Entrance requirements:* Additional exam requirements/recommendations for international students: Required—TOEFL (minimum score 550 paper-based; 79 iBT); Recommended—IELTS. Electronic applications accepted.

Universidad del Este, Graduate School, Carolina, PR 00984. Offers accounting (MBA); adult education (M Ed); agribusiness (MBA); criminal justice and criminology (MA); curriculum and instruction - early education (M Ed); curriculum and instruction - elementary (M Ed); curriculum and instruction - English (M Ed); curriculum and instruction - Spanish (M Ed); human resources (MBA); information security management (MBA); information technology and Web business development (MBA); management (MBA); public policy (MPA); social work (MA), including clinical social work; special education (M Ed); strategic leadership (MBA).

Université du Québec en Outaouais, Graduate Programs, Department of Language Studies, Gatineau, QC J8X 3X7, Canada. Offers second and foreign language teaching (Diploma).

University at Buffalo, the State University of New York, Graduate School, Graduate School of Education, Department of Learning and Instruction, Buffalo, NY 14260. Offers biology education (Ed M, Certificate); chemistry education (Ed M, Certificate); childhood education (Ed M); childhood education with bilingual extension (Ed M); college teaching (Advanced Certificate); curriculum, instruction and the science of learning (PhD); early childhood education (Ed M); early childhood education with bilingual extension (Ed M); earth science education (Ed M, Certificate); education and technology (Ed M); education studies (Ed M); educational technology and new literacies (Certificate); educational technology and new literacies (Advanced Certificate); elementary education (Ed D); English education (Ed M, Certificate); English education studies (Ed M); English for speakers of other languages (Ed M); foreign and second language education (PhD); French education (Ed M, Certificate); German education (Ed M, Certificate); gifted education (Certificate); Latin education (Ed M, Certificate); literacy education studies (Ed M); literacy specialist (Ed M); literacy teaching and learning (Certificate); mathematics education (Ed M, Certificate); music education (Ed M, Certificate); music education studies (Ed M); music learning theory (Advanced Certificate); online education (Advanced Certificate); physics education (Ed M, Certificate); science and the public (Ed M); social studies education (Ed M, Certificate); Spanish education (Ed M, Certificate); special education (PhD); teaching English to speakers of other languages (Ed M). *Program availability:* Part-time, evening/weekend, 100% online. *Faculty:* 26 full-time (19 women), 74 part-time/adjunct (52 women). *Students:* 172 full-time (122 women), 325 part-time (226 women); includes 44 minority (25 Black or African American, non-Hispanic/Latino; 5 American Indian or Alaska Native, non-Hispanic/Latino; 14 Asian, non-Hispanic/Latino), 57 international. Average age 33. 316 applicants, 78% accepted, 174 enrolled. In 2017, 109 master's, 34 doctorates, 15 other advanced degrees awarded. *Degree requirements:* For master's, comprehensive exam; for doctorate, thesis/dissertation, research analysis exam, research experience. *Entrance requirements:* For master's, letters of reference; for doctorate, GRE General Test or MAT, interview, writing sample, letters of recommendation. Additional exam requirements/recommendations for international students: Required—TOEFL (minimum score 600 paper-based; 96 iBT). *Application deadline:* For fall admission, 2/1 priority date for domestic and international students; for spring admission, 11/15 priority date for domestic students, 10/1 for international students. Applications are processed on a rolling basis. Application fee: $50. Electronic applications accepted. *Financial support:* In 2017–18, 42 fellowships (averaging $5,181 per year), 44 research assistantships with tuition reimbursements (averaging $10,908 per year) were awarded; teaching assistantships, career-related internships or fieldwork, Federal Work-Study, institutionally sponsored loans, scholarships/grants, tuition waivers (full and partial), and unspecified assistantships also available. Financial award application deadline: 2/28; financial award applicants required to submit FAFSA. *Faculty research:* Science assessment, foreign language teaching and learning, early learning, new literacies, gender and education. *Total annual research expenditures:* $413,233. *Unit head:* Dr. David Bruce, Chair, 716-645-4069, Fax: 716-645-3161, E-mail: gse-info@buffalo.edu. *Application contact:* Luann Zak, Admissions Assistant, 716-645-2110, Fax: 716-645-7937, E-mail: luannzak@buffalo.edu. Website: http://gse.buffalo.edu/lai

University of Arkansas at Little Rock, Graduate School, College of Arts, Letters, and Sciences, Department of International and Second Language Studies, Little Rock, AR 72204-1099. Offers second languages (MA). *Degree requirements:* For master's, comprehensive exam, thesis. *Entrance requirements:* For master's, GRE or MAT, bachelor's degree; 3 letters of reference; personal interview; minimum overall undergraduate GPA of 2.75, 3.0 in last 60 hours.

University of California, Irvine, School of Humanities, Department of Spanish and Portuguese, Irvine, CA 92697. Offers Spanish (MA, MAT, PhD). *Students:* 28 full-time (21 women), 2 part-time (0 women); includes 21 minority (20 Hispanic/Latino; 1 Two or more races, non-Hispanic/Latino), 4 international. Average age 36. 16 applicants, 44% accepted, 4 enrolled. In 2017, 3 master's, 4 doctorates awarded. *Entrance requirements:* For master's and doctorate, GRE General Test, minimum GPA of 3.0. Additional exam requirements/recommendations for international students: Required—TOEFL (minimum score 550 paper-based). *Application deadline:* For fall admission, 1/2 priority date for domestic students, 1/2 for international students. Applications are processed on a rolling basis. Application fee: $105 ($125 for international students). Electronic applications accepted. *Financial support:* Fellowships, teaching assistantships, institutionally sponsored loans, traineeships, health care benefits, and unspecified assistantships available. Financial award application deadline: 3/1; financial award applicants required to submit FAFSA. *Faculty research:* Latin American literature, Spanish literature, Spanish linguistics in Creole studies, Hispanic literature in the U.S., Luso-Brazilian literature. *Unit head:* Luis Aviles, Department Chair, 949-824-7268, Fax: 949-824-2803, E-mail: laviles@uci.edu. *Application contact:* Evelyn Flores, Graduate Program Coordinator, 949-824-8793, Fax: 949-824-2803, E-mail: evelynf@uci.edu. Website: http://www.hnet.uci.edu/spanishandportuguese/

University of Central Arkansas, Graduate School, College of Liberal Arts, Department of Foreign Languages, Conway, AR 72035-0001. Offers MA. *Program availability:* Part-time. *Degree requirements:* For master's, one foreign language, comprehensive exam, thesis optional. *Entrance requirements:* For master's, GRE General Test, minimum GPA of 2.7. Additional exam requirements/recommendations for international students: Required—TOEFL (minimum score 550 paper-based). Electronic applications accepted.

University of Central Florida, College of Community Innovation and Education, School of Teacher Education, Orlando, FL 32816. Offers applied learning and instruction (MA); curriculum and instruction (M Ed); elementary education (M Ed, MA); exceptional student education (M Ed, MA, Certificate), including autism spectrum disorders (Certificate), exceptional student education (M Ed), exceptional student education K-12 (MA), intervention specialist (Certificate), pre-kindergarten disabilities (Certificate), severe or profound disabilities (Certificate), special education (Certificate); K-8 mathematics and science education (M Ed, Certificate); reading education (M Ed, Certificate); teacher education (MAT), including art education, English language, mathematics education, middle school mathematics, middle school science, science education, social science education; world languages education - English for speakers of other languages (ESOL) (Certificate); world languages education - languages other than English (LOTE) (Certificate). *Program availability:* Part-time, evening/weekend. *Students:* 63 full-time (59 women), 218 part-time (190 women); includes 104 minority (34 Black or African American, non-Hispanic/Latino; 1 American Indian or Alaska Native, non-Hispanic/Latino; 13 Asian, non-Hispanic/Latino; 52 Hispanic/Latino; 4 Two or more races, non-Hispanic/Latino), 5 international. Average age 31. 189 applicants, 78% accepted, 98 enrolled. In 2017, 124 master's, 16 other advanced degrees awarded. *Degree requirements:* For Certificate, thesis or alternative. *Entrance requirements:* For degree, GRE General Test, minimum GPA of 3.0. Additional exam requirements/recommendations for international students: Required—TOEFL. *Application deadline:* For fall admission, 7/15 for domestic students; for spring admission, 12/15 for domestic students. Application fee: $30. Electronic applications accepted. *Expenses:* Tuition, state resident: part-time $288.16 per credit hour. Tuition, nonresident: part-time $1073.31 per credit hour. Tuition and fees vary according to program. *Financial support:* In 2017–18, 5 students received support, including 1 fellowship with partial tuition reimbursement available (averaging $1,000 per year), 4 research assistantships with partial tuition reimbursements available (averaging $5,617 per year), 1 teaching assistantship with partial tuition reimbursement available (averaging $9,086 per year); career-related internships or fieldwork, Federal Work-Study, institutionally sponsored loans, health care benefits, tuition waivers (partial), and unspecified assistantships also available. Financial award application deadline: 3/1; financial award applicants required to submit FAFSA. *Unit head:* Dr. Michael Hynes, Director, 407-823-1768, E-mail: michael.hynes@ucf.edu. *Application contact:* Associate Director, Graduate Admissions, 407-823-2766, Fax: 407-823-6442, E-mail: gradadmissions@ucf.edu. Website: https://ccie.ucf.edu/teachered/

University of Connecticut, Graduate School, Neag School of Education, Department of Curriculum and Instruction, Program in World Languages Education, Storrs, CT 06269. Offers MA, PhD. *Accreditation:* NCATE. Terminal master's awarded for partial completion of doctoral program. *Degree requirements:* For master's, comprehensive exam, thesis or alternative; for doctorate, thesis/dissertation. *Entrance requirements:* For doctorate, GRE General Test. Additional exam requirements/recommendations for international students: Required—TOEFL (minimum score 550 paper-based). Electronic applications accepted.

University of Dayton, Department of Teacher Education, Dayton, OH 45469. Offers adolescence to young adult education (MS Ed); early childhood leadership and advocacy (MS Ed); interdisciplinary education (MS Ed), including visual arts; interdisciplinary education studies (MS Ed); leadership in educational systems (MS Ed); literacy (MS Ed); mathematics education (MS Ed); middle childhood education (MS Ed); multi-age education (MS Ed), including world languages; music education (MS Ed); teacher as leader (MS Ed); teacher education (MS Ed); technology-enhanced learning (MS Ed); trans-disciplinary early childhood education (MS Ed). *Program availability:* Part-time, 100% online. *Faculty:* 23 full-time (20 women), 41 part-time/adjunct (36 women). *Students:* 45 full-time (38 women), 68 part-time (57 women); includes 7 minority (3 Black or African American, non-Hispanic/Latino; 1 Hispanic/Latino; 3 Two or more races, non-Hispanic/Latino), 6 international. Average age 31. 106 applicants, 28% accepted. In 2017, 70 master's awarded. *Degree requirements:* For master's, variable foreign language requirement, thesis or alternative, internship (for teaching licensure or endorsement). *Entrance requirements:* For master's, GRE (minimum score of 149 verbal, 4 on writing) or MAT (minimum score of 396) if undergraduate GPA was under 2.75, minimum GPA of 2.75, 3 letters of recommendation, personal statement or resume, official transcripts. Additional exam requirements/recommendations for international students: Required—TOEFL (minimum score 550 paper-based; 80 iBT); Recommended—IELTS (minimum score 6.5). *Application deadline:* Applications are processed on a rolling basis. Application fee: $0 ($50 for international students). Electronic applications accepted. *Expenses:* Contact institution. *Financial support:* In 2017–18, 5 research assistantships with partial tuition reimbursements (averaging $9,640 per year) were awarded; teaching assistantships, career-related internships or fieldwork, institutionally sponsored loans, and unspecified assistantships also available. Financial award application deadline: 3/1; financial award applicants required to submit FAFSA. *Faculty research:* Social emotional learning, culturally responsive teaching, urban teaching, literacy, instructional strategies, pre-service teacher education preparation. *Unit head:* Dr. Connie L. Bowman, Chair, 937-229-3348, E-mail: cbowman1@udayton.edu. *Application contact:* Gina Seiter, Coordinator of Graduate Programs and Licensing, 937-229-3103, E-mail: gseiter1@udayton.edu. Website: https://www.udayton.edu/education/departments_and_programs/edt

University of Delaware, College of Arts and Sciences, Department of Foreign Languages and Literatures, Newark, DE 19716. Offers foreign languages and literatures (MA), including French, German, Spanish; foreign languages pedagogy (MA), including French, German, Spanish; technical Chinese translation (MA). *Degree requirements:* For master's, one foreign language, comprehensive exam, thesis optional. *Entrance requirements:* For master's, GRE General Test, letters of recommendation, writing sample. Additional exam requirements/recommendations for international students: Required—TOEFL. Electronic applications accepted. *Faculty research:* Medieval to Modern French and Spanish literature, twentieth-century German, French, Spanish literature by women, computer-assisted instruction.

University of Florida, Graduate School, College of Liberal Arts and Sciences, Department of Spanish and Portuguese Studies, Gainesville, FL 32611. Offers Spanish (MA, MAT, PhD). *Program availability:* Part-time. Terminal master's awarded for partial completion of doctoral program. *Degree requirements:* For master's, one foreign language, comprehensive exam, thesis or extended research paper; for doctorate, 2 foreign languages, comprehensive exam, thesis/dissertation, qualifying exam. *Entrance requirements:* For master's and doctorate, GRE General Test, minimum GPA of 3.0. Additional exam requirements/recommendations for international students: Required—TOEFL (minimum score 550 paper-based; 80 iBT), IELTS (minimum score 6). Electronic applications accepted. *Faculty research:* Spanish linguistics; second language acquisition and teaching; Spanish literature, film and culture; Latin American literature, film and culture; Portuguese literature, film and culture.

University of Hawaii at Hilo, Program in Hawaiian and Indigenous Language and Culture Revitalization, Hilo, HI 96720-4091. Offers PhD. *Entrance requirements:* Additional exam requirements/recommendations for international students: Required—TOEFL, IELTS. Electronic applications accepted.

University of Hawaii at Hilo, Program in Hawaiian Language and Literature, Hilo, HI 96720-4091. Offers MA. *Entrance requirements:* Additional exam requirements/recommendations for international students: Required—TOEFL, IELTS. Electronic applications accepted.

University of Hawaii at Hilo, Program in Indigenous Language and Culture Education, Hilo, HI 96720-4091. Offers MA. *Entrance requirements:* Additional exam requirements/recommendations for international students: Required—TOEFL, IELTS. Electronic applications accepted.

University of Hawaii at Manoa, Office of Graduate Education, College of Languages, Linguistics and Literature, Department of Second Language Studies, Honolulu, HI 96822. Offers English as a second language (MA, Graduate Certificate); second language acquisition (PhD). *Program availability:* Part-time. *Degree requirements:* For master's, 2 foreign languages, thesis optional; for doctorate, 2 foreign languages, comprehensive exam, thesis/dissertation. *Entrance requirements:* For master's, GRE General Test, minimum GPA of 3.0; for doctorate, GRE General Test, MA, scholarly publications. Additional exam requirements/recommendations for international students: Required—TOEFL (minimum score 600 paper-based; 100 iBT), IELTS (minimum score 7). *Faculty research:* Second language use, second language analysis, second language pedagogy and testing, second language learning, qualitative and quantitative research methods for second languages.

University of Hawaii at Manoa, Office of Graduate Education, Hawai'inuiakea School of Hawaiian Knowledge, Program in Hawaiian, Honolulu, HI 96822. Offers MA. *Program availability:* Part-time. *Degree requirements:* For master's, thesis optional. *Entrance requirements:* Additional exam requirements/recommendations for international students: Required—TOEFL (minimum score 500 paper-based; 61 iBT), IELTS (minimum score 5).

University of Hawaii at Manoa, Office of Graduate Education, Hawai'inuiakea School of Hawaiian Knowledge, Program in Hawaiian Studies, Honolulu, HI 96822. Offers MA. *Program availability:* Part-time. *Degree requirements:* For master's, thesis optional. *Entrance requirements:* Additional exam requirements/recommendations for international students: Required—TOEFL (minimum score 500 paper-based; 61 iBT), IELTS (minimum score 5).

University of Illinois at Chicago, College of Liberal Arts and Sciences, School of Literatures, Cultural Studies and Linguistics, Chicago, IL 60607-7128. Offers French and Francophone studies (MA); Germanic studies (MA); Hispanic and Italian studies (MAT, PhD), including Hispanic linguistics (PhD), Hispanic literary and cultural studies (PhD), teaching of Spanish (MAT); linguistics (MA), including teaching English to speakers of other languages/applied linguistics; Slavic and Baltic languages and literatures (MA), including Slavic studies (MA, PhD); Slavic and Baltic languages and literatures (PhD), including Slavic studies (MA, PhD). *Program availability:* Part-time. Terminal master's awarded for partial completion of doctoral program. *Degree requirements:* For master's, one foreign language, exam. *Entrance requirements:* For master's, minimum GPA of 2.75. Additional exam requirements/recommendations for international students: Required—TOEFL. Electronic applications accepted. *Faculty research:* International studies, religious (Catholic, Jewish) studies, moving image arts.

University of Illinois at Urbana–Champaign, Graduate College, College of Liberal Arts and Sciences, School of Literatures, Cultures and Linguistics, Department of Spanish, Italian and Portuguese, Champaign, IL 61820. Offers Italian (MA, PhD); Portuguese (MA, PhD); Spanish (MA, PhD).

University of Illinois at Urbana–Champaign, Graduate College, College of Liberal Arts and Sciences, School of Literatures, Cultures and Linguistics, Department of the Classics, Champaign, IL 61820. Offers classical philology (PhD); classics (MA); teaching of Latin (MA).

University of Indianapolis, Graduate Programs, School of Education, Indianapolis, IN 46227-3697. Offers art education (MAT); biology (MAT); chemistry (MAT); curriculum and instruction (MAT); earth sciences (MAT); education (MA, MAT); educational leadership (MA); elementary education (MA); English (MAT); French (MAT); math (MAT); physical education (MAT); physics (MAT); secondary education (MA), including art education, education, English education, social studies education; social studies (MAT); Spanish (MAT). *Accreditation:* NCATE. *Program availability:* Part-time, evening/weekend. *Entrance requirements:* For master's, GRE Subject Test, PRAXIS I, minimum GPA of 2.5, 3 letters of recommendation, interview. Additional exam requirements/recommendations for international students: Required—TOEFL (minimum score 550 paper-based). *Faculty research:* Assessment of teacher education, perceptions of prospective teachers by parents.

The University of Iowa, Graduate College, College of Education, Department of Teaching and Learning, Program in Education, Iowa City, IA 52242-1316. Offers art education (MA); developmental reading (MA); elementary education (MA); English education (MA, MAT); foreign and second language education (MAT); foreign language education (MA); foreign language/ESL education (PhD); language, literacy and culture (PhD); mathematics education (MA, MAT, PhD); music education (MM, PhD); science education (MA); secondary education (MA); social studies (MA, PhD). *Degree requirements:* For master's, thesis optional, exam; for doctorate, comprehensive exam, thesis/dissertation. *Entrance requirements:* For master's and doctorate, GRE General Test, minimum GPA of 3.0. Additional exam requirements/recommendations for international students: Required—TOEFL (minimum score 550 paper-based; 81 iBT). Electronic applications accepted.

The University of Iowa, Graduate College, College of Liberal Arts and Sciences, Program in Second Language Acquisition, Iowa City, IA 52242-1316. Offers PhD. *Degree requirements:* For doctorate, comprehensive exam, thesis/dissertation. *Entrance requirements:* For doctorate, GRE General Test, minimum GPA of 3.0. Additional exam requirements/recommendations for international students: Required—TOEFL (minimum score 600 paper-based; 100 iBT). Electronic applications accepted.

University of Kentucky, Graduate School, College of Arts and Sciences and College of Education, Program in Teaching World Languages, Lexington, KY 40506-0032. Offers MA. *Entrance requirements:* For master's, GRE General Test, minimum undergraduate GPA of 2.75. Additional exam requirements/recommendations for international students: Required—TOEFL (minimum score 550 paper-based). Electronic applications accepted.

University of Maine, Graduate School, College of Liberal Arts and Sciences, Department of Modern Languages and Classics, Orono, ME 04469. Offers French (MA, MAT); Spanish (MAT). *Program availability:* Part-time. *Faculty:* 7 full-time (4 women). *Students:* 4 full-time (3 women), 2 part-time (both women); includes 2 minority (1 Black or African American, non-Hispanic/Latino; 1 Hispanic/Latino). Average age 38. 6 applicants, 100% accepted, 3 enrolled. In 2017, 3 master's awarded. *Degree requirements:* For master's, one foreign language, thesis (for some programs). *Entrance requirements:* For master's, GRE General Test; PRAXIS II (for MAT). Additional exam requirements/recommendations for international students: Required—TOEFL, PRAXIS II. *Application deadline:* For fall admission, 2/1 priority date for domestic and international students. Applications are processed on a rolling basis. Application fee: $65. Electronic applications accepted. *Expenses:* Tuition, state resident: full-time $7722; part-time $429 per credit hour. Tuition, nonresident: full-time $25,146; part-time $1397 per credit hour. Required fees: $1162; $581 per credit hour. *Financial support:* In 2017–18, 4 students received support, including 2 fellowships (averaging $15,000 per year), 2 teaching assistantships with tuition reimbursements available (averaging $15,200 per year); Federal Work-Study and tuition waivers (full and partial) also available. Financial award application deadline: 3/1. *Faculty research:* Contemporary Latin American literature and culture, modern and contemporary Spanish peninsular

literature, North American French linguistics, 20th-century Quebec literature and culture, contemporary French philosophy. *Unit head:* Dr. Jane Smith, Chair, 207-581-2075, Fax: 207-581-1832. *Application contact:* Scott G. Delcourt, Assistant Vice President for Graduate Studies/Senior Associate Dean, 207-581-3291, Fax: 207-581-3232, E-mail: graduate@maine.edu.
Website: https://umaine.edu/mlandc/graduate-programs/

University of Maryland, Baltimore County, The Graduate School, College of Arts, Humanities and Social Sciences, Department of Education, Program in Teaching, Baltimore, MD 21250. Offers early childhood education (MAT); elementary education (MAT); teaching (MAT), including art, biology, chemistry, choral music, classical foreign language, dance, earth/space science, English, instrumental music, mathematics, modern foreign language, physical science, physics, social studies, theatre. *Program availability:* Part-time, evening/weekend. *Faculty:* 24 full-time (18 women), 25 part-time/adjunct (19 women). *Students:* 41 full-time (34 women), 27 part-time (18 women); includes 26 minority (6 Black or African American, non-Hispanic/Latino; 9 Asian, non-Hispanic/Latino; 7 Hispanic/Latino; 1 Native Hawaiian or other Pacific Islander, non-Hispanic/Latino; 3 Two or more races, non-Hispanic/Latino), 2 international. Average age 30. 54 applicants, 83% accepted, 35 enrolled. In 2017, 50 master's awarded. *Degree requirements:* For master's, comprehensive exam (for some programs), thesis (for some programs). *Entrance requirements:* For master's, PRAXIS Core Examination or GRE (minimum score of 1000), minimum GPA of 3.0. Additional exam requirements/recommendations for international students: Required—TOEFL. *Application deadline:* For fall admission, 6/1 for domestic and international students; for spring admission, 11/1 for domestic and international students. Applications are processed on a rolling basis. Application fee: $50. Electronic applications accepted. *Expenses: Required fees:* $132. *Financial support:* In 2017–18, 8 students received support, including teaching assistantships with tuition reimbursements available (averaging $12,000 per year); career-related internships or fieldwork, Federal Work-Study, scholarships/grants, tuition waivers, and unspecified assistantships also available. Financial award application deadline: 3/15. *Faculty research:* STEM teacher education, culturally sensitive pedagogy, ESOL/bilingual education, early childhood education, language, literacy and culture. *Total annual research expenditures:* $100,000. *Unit head:* Dr. Susan M. Blunck, Graduate Program Director, 410-455-2869, Fax: 410-455-3986, E-mail: blunck@umbc.edu. *Application contact:* Cheryl Johnson, MAT Program Specialist, 410-455-3388, E-mail: blackwel@umbc.edu.
Website: http://www.umbc.edu/education/

University of Maryland, College Park, Academic Affairs, College of Arts and Humanities, School of Languages, Literatures, and Cultures, Program in Second Language Acquisition and Application, College Park, MD 20742. Offers second language instruction (PhD); second language learning (PhD); second language measurement and assessment (PhD); second language use (PhD). Electronic applications accepted. *Faculty research:* Second language acquisition, pedagogical perspectives, technological applications, language use in professional contexts.

University of Massachusetts Amherst, Graduate School, College of Humanities and Fine Arts, Department of Languages, Literatures, and Cultures, Program in French and Francophone Studies, Amherst, MA 01003. Offers French (MAT); French and Francophone studies (MA). *Program availability:* Part-time. *Degree requirements:* For master's, thesis or alternative. *Entrance requirements:* For master's, GRE General Test. Additional exam requirements/recommendations for international students: Required—TOEFL (minimum score 550 paper-based; 80 iBT), IELTS (minimum score 6.5). Electronic applications accepted.

University of Michigan, Rackham Graduate School, College of Literature, Science, and the Arts, Department of Classical Studies, Ann Arbor, MI 48109. Offers classical studies (MA, PhD); Greek and Roman history (PhD); Latin (MA); Latin with teaching certification (MAT). *Faculty:* 26 full-time (15 women), 3 part-time/adjunct (2 women). *Students:* 41 full-time (16 women); includes 4 minority (2 Asian, non-Hispanic/Latino; 2 Two or more races, non-Hispanic/Latino), 6 international. Average age 27. 72 applicants, 19% accepted, 10 enrolled. In 2017, 1 master's, 4 doctorates awarded. Terminal master's awarded for partial completion of doctoral program. *Degree requirements:* For master's, one foreign language, comprehensive exam; for doctorate, 4 foreign languages, comprehensive exam, thesis/dissertation, oral defense of dissertation, preliminary exams, qualifying exams. *Entrance requirements:* For master's, GRE General Test, 2-3 years of Latin (for the Latin MAT); for doctorate, GRE General Test, strict minimum of 3 years of college-level Latin and 2 years of college-level Greek. Additional exam requirements/recommendations for international students: Required—TOEFL (minimum score 560 paper-based). *Application deadline:* For fall admission, 12/15 for domestic and international students. Application fee: $75 ($90 for international students). Electronic applications accepted. *Expenses:* Tuition and fees for PhD programs are waived. *Financial support:* In 2017–18, 41 students received support, including 23 fellowships with full tuition reimbursements available (averaging $20,850 per year), 1 research assistantship with full tuition reimbursement available (averaging $20,850 per year), 15 teaching assistantships with full tuition reimbursements available (averaging $20,850 per year); career-related internships or fieldwork, institutionally sponsored loans, scholarships/grants, traineeships, tuition waivers (full), unspecified assistantships, and summer stipends, year-round health care also available. Financial award application deadline: 3/15. *Faculty research:* Greek and Latin literature, ancient history, papyrology, archaeology. *Unit head:* Prof. Artemis Leontis, Chair and Professor, 734-764-0360, Fax: 734-763-4959, E-mail: classics@umich.edu. *Application contact:* Sarah Kandell-Gritzmaker, Student Services Coordinator, 734-615-3181, Fax: 734-763-4959, E-mail: skandell@umich.edu.
Website: http://www.lsa.umich.edu/classics

University of Minnesota, Twin Cities Campus, Graduate School, College of Education and Human Development, Department of Curriculum and Instruction, Program in Teaching, Minneapolis, MN 55455-0213. Offers teaching (M Ed), including arts in education, elementary education, English education, mathematics, science, second language education, social studies. *Students:* 251 full-time (180 women), 136 part-time (82 women); includes 68 minority (16 Black or African American, non-Hispanic/Latino; 15 Asian, non-Hispanic/Latino; 17 Hispanic/Latino; 20 Two or more races, non-Hispanic/Latino), 9 international. Average age 28. 341 applicants, 72% accepted, 229 enrolled. In 2017, 263 master's awarded. Application fee: $75 ($95 for international students). *Unit head:* Dr. Cynthia Lewis, Chair, 612-625-6313, Fax: 612-624-8277, E-mail: lewis@umn.edu. *Application contact:* Dr. Kendall King, Director of Graduate Studies, 612-625-3692, E-mail: roehr013@umn.edu.
Website: http://www.cehd.umn.edu/ci/

University of Mississippi, Graduate School, College of Liberal Arts, University, MS 38677. Offers anthropology (MA); biology (MS, PhD); chemistry (MS, DA, PhD); creative writing (MFA); documentary expression (MFA); economics (MA, PhD); English (MA, PhD); experimental psychology (PhD); history (MA, PhD); mathematics (MS, PhD); modern languages (MA); music (MM); philosophy (MA); physics (MA, MS, PhD); political science (MA, PhD); Southern studies (MA); studio art (MFA). *Program availability:* Part-time. *Faculty:* 465 full-time (207 women), 82 part-time/adjunct (46 women). *Students:* 466 full-time (229 women), 72 part-time (34 women); includes 87 minority (38 Black or African American, non-Hispanic/Latino; 18 Asian, non-Hispanic/Latino; 24 Hispanic/

Latino; 7 Two or more races, non-Hispanic/Latino), 121 international. Average age 29. *Degree requirements:* For doctorate, thesis/dissertation. *Entrance requirements:* For master's, GRE General Test, minimum GPA of 3.0; for doctorate, GRE General Test. Additional exam requirements/recommendations for international students: Required—TOEFL. *Application deadline:* For fall admission, 2/1 priority date for domestic students; for spring admission, 10/1 for domestic students. Applications are processed on a rolling basis. Application fee: $50. Electronic applications accepted. *Financial support:* Fellowships, research assistantships, teaching assistantships, career-related internships or fieldwork, Federal Work-Study, institutionally sponsored loans, scholarships/grants, and unspecified assistantships available. Financial award application deadline: 3/1; financial award applicants required to submit FAFSA. *Unit head:* Dr. Lee Michael Cohen, Dean, 662-915-7177, Fax: 662-915-5792, E-mail: libarts@olemiss.edu. *Application contact:* Dr. Christy M. Wyandt, Associate Dean of Graduate School, 662-915-7474, Fax: 662-915-7577, E-mail: cwyandt@olemiss.edu.

University of Missouri, Office of Research and Graduate Studies, College of Arts and Science, Department of Romance Languages and Literatures, Columbia, MO 65211. Offers French (MA, PhD); literature (MA); Spanish (MA, PhD); teaching (MA). Terminal master's awarded for partial completion of doctoral program. *Degree requirements:* For master's, one foreign language; for doctorate, 4 foreign languages, comprehensive exam, thesis/dissertation. *Entrance requirements:* For master's, GRE General Test, minimum GPA of 3.0 in field of major; bachelor's degree; for doctorate, GRE General Test, minimum GPA of 3.0 in field of major; master's degree. Additional exam requirements/recommendations for international students: Required—TOEFL (minimum score 500 paper-based; 61 iBT). Electronic applications accepted.

University of Missouri, Office of Research and Graduate Studies, College of Education, Department of Learning, Teaching and Curriculum, Columbia, MO 65211. Offers agricultural education (M Ed, PhD, Ed S); art education (M Ed, PhD, Ed S); business and office education (M Ed, PhD, Ed S); early childhood education (M Ed, PhD, Ed S); elementary education (M Ed, PhD, Ed S); English education (M Ed, PhD, Ed S); foreign language education (M Ed, PhD, Ed S); health education and promotion (M Ed, PhD); learning and instruction (M Ed); marketing education (M Ed, PhD, Ed S); mathematics education (M Ed, PhD, Ed S); music education (M Ed, PhD, Ed S); reading education (M Ed, PhD, Ed S); science education (M Ed, PhD, Ed S); social studies education (M Ed, PhD, Ed S); vocational education (M Ed, PhD, Ed S). *Program availability:* Part-time. Terminal master's awarded for partial completion of doctoral program. *Degree requirements:* For doctorate, thesis/dissertation. *Entrance requirements:* For master's and Ed S, GRE General Test or MAT, minimum GPA of 3.0; for doctorate, GRE General Test, minimum GPA of 3.0. Additional exam requirements/recommendations for international students: Required—TOEFL (minimum score 600 paper-based; 100 iBT). Electronic applications accepted.

University of Nebraska at Kearney, College of Fine Arts and Humanities, Department of Modern Languages, Kearney, NE 68849-0001. Offers Spanish education (MA Ed). *Accreditation:* NCATE. *Program availability:* Part-time, evening/weekend. *Degree requirements:* For master's, comprehensive exam, thesis optional. *Entrance requirements:* For master's, 21 semester hours of upper-level Spanish; two-page Spanish essay; one-page English essay; two letters of recommendation. Additional exam requirements/recommendations for international students: Recommended—TOEFL (minimum score 550 paper-based; 79 iBT), IELTS (minimum score 6.5). Electronic applications accepted. *Faculty research:* Translation theory, Spanish linguistics; symotolistic poetry, critical theory and Marxism, French and Francophone film, themes of culture, nationality and ethnicity.

University of Nebraska at Omaha, Graduate Studies, College of Arts and Sciences, Program in Language Teaching, Omaha, NE 68182. Offers MA. *Program availability:* Part-time, evening/weekend. *Degree requirements:* For master's, comprehensive exam, thesis (for some programs). *Entrance requirements:* For master's, minimum GPA of 3.0, official transcripts, 2 letters of recommendation, oral language sample, writing sample. Additional exam requirements/recommendations for international students: Required—TOEFL, IELTS, PTE. Electronic applications accepted.

University of Nevada, Reno, Graduate School, College of Liberal Arts, Department of Foreign Languages and Literatures, Reno, NV 89557. Offers French (MA); German (MA); Spanish (MA). *Degree requirements:* For master's, one foreign language, thesis optional. *Entrance requirements:* For master's, GRE General Test, minimum GPA of 2.75. Additional exam requirements/recommendations for international students: Required—TOEFL (minimum score 500 paper-based; 61 iBT), IELTS (minimum score 6). *Faculty research:* Thirteenth century mysticism, contemporary Spanish and Latin American poetry and theater, French interrelation between narration and photography, exile literature and Holocaust.

The University of North Carolina at Chapel Hill, Graduate School, School of Education, Program in Secondary Education, Chapel Hill, NC 27599. Offers English (Grades 9-12) (MAT); English as a second language (MAT); French (Grades K-12) (MAT); German (Grades K-12) (MAT); Japanese (Grades K-12) (MAT); Latin (Grades 9-12) (MAT); mathematics (Grades 9-12) (MAT); music (Grades K-12) (MAT); science (Grades 9-12) (MAT); social studies (Grades 9-12) (MAT); Spanish (Grades K-12) (MAT). *Accreditation:* NCATE. *Degree requirements:* For master's, comprehensive exam. *Entrance requirements:* For master's, GRE General Test, minimum GPA of 3.0 during last 2 years of undergraduate course work. Additional exam requirements/recommendations for international students: Required—TOEFL (minimum score 550 paper-based). Electronic applications accepted.

The University of North Carolina at Charlotte, Cato College of Education, Interdisciplinary Education Programs, Charlotte, NC 28223-0001. Offers art education (Graduate Certificate); child and family development: early childhood education (MAT); curriculum and instruction (PhD); elementary education (MAT); foreign language education (MAT); middle grades education (MAT); secondary education (MAT); special education (MAT); teaching (Graduate Certificate); teaching English as a second language (MAT); theatre education (Graduate Certificate). *Program availability:* Part-time, 100% online, blended/hybrid learning. *Students:* 86 full-time (63 women), 533 part-time (423 women); includes 229 minority (169 Black or African American, non-Hispanic/Latino; 1 American Indian or Alaska Native, non-Hispanic/Latino; 7 Asian, non-Hispanic/Latino; 39 Hispanic/Latino; 13 Two or more races, non-Hispanic/Latino), 13 international. Average age 32. 382 applicants, 91% accepted, 253 enrolled. In 2017, 182 master's, 10 doctorates, 172 other advanced degrees awarded. *Degree requirements:* For master's, thesis or alternative, research project/portfolio. *Entrance requirements:* For master's, GRE or MAT, bachelor's degree, or its U.S. equivalent, from regionally-accredited college or university; minimum overall GPA of 3.0 on all previous work beyond high school; statement of purpose (essay); at least three recommendation forms; for doctorate, GRE or MAT, bachelor's degree (or its U.S. equivalent) from regionally-accredited college or university; minimum overall GPA of 3.5 in master's degree program; for Graduate Certificate, bachelor's degree from regionally-accredited university; minimum GPA of 2.75 on all post-secondary work attempted; transcripts; personal statement outlining why the applicant seeks admission to the program. Additional exam requirements/recommendations for international students: Required—TOEFL (minimum score 523 paper-based, 70 iBT) or IELTS (6.5). *Application deadline:* For fall admission, 3/1 priority date for domestic and international students; for spring

admission, 10/1 priority date for domestic and international students; for summer admission, 4/1 priority date for domestic and international students. Applications are processed on a rolling basis. Application fee: $75. Electronic applications accepted. *Expenses:* Tuition, state resident: full-time $4337. Tuition, nonresident: full-time $17,771. *Required fees:* $3211. Tuition and fees vary according to course load and program. *Financial support:* Career-related internships or fieldwork, institutionally sponsored loans, scholarships/grants, and unspecified assistantships available. Support available to part-time students. Financial award application deadline: 3/1; financial award applicants required to submit FAFSA. *Unit head:* Dr. Ellen McIntyre, Dean, 704-687-8722, E-mail: ellen.mcintyre@uncc.edu. *Application contact:* Kathy B. Giddings, Director of Graduate Admissions, 704-687-5503, Fax: 704-687-1668, E-mail: gradadm@uncc.edu.
Website: http://education.uncc.edu/academic-programs

The University of North Carolina at Greensboro, Graduate School, School of Education, Department of Teacher Education and Higher Education, Greensboro, NC 27412-5001. Offers college teaching and adult learning (Certificate); curriculum and instruction (M Ed), including chemistry education, elementary education, English as a second language, French education, instructional technology, mathematics education, middle grades education, reading education, science education, social studies education, Spanish education; curriculum and teaching (PhD), including higher education, teacher education and development; English as a second language (Certificate); higher education (M Ed); supervision (M Ed). *Accreditation:* NCATE. *Program availability:* Part-time. *Degree requirements:* For doctorate, thesis/dissertation. *Entrance requirements:* For master's and doctorate, GRE General Test. Additional exam requirements/recommendations for international students: Required—TOEFL. Electronic applications accepted. *Faculty research:* Community college literacy program, middle school mathematics/computer mathematics.

University of Northern Colorado, Graduate School, College of Education and Behavioral Sciences, School of Teacher Education, Greeley, CO 80639. Offers curriculum studies (MAT); educational studies (Ed D); elementary education (MAT); English education (MAT); literacy (MA); multilingual education (MA), including TESOL, world languages; teaching diverse learners (MA). *Accreditation:* NCATE. *Program availability:* Part-time, evening/weekend. *Degree requirements:* For master's, comprehensive exam, thesis or alternative; for doctorate, comprehensive exam, thesis/dissertation. *Entrance requirements:* For master's and doctorate, GRE General Test, 3 letters of recommendation. Electronic applications accepted.

University of Northern Iowa, Graduate College, College of Humanities, Arts and Sciences, Department of Languages and Literatures, MA Program in Spanish, Cedar Falls, IA 50614. Offers Spanish (MA); Spanish teaching (MA). *Program availability:* Part-time, evening/weekend. *Degree requirements:* For master's, one foreign language, comprehensive exam, thesis or alternative. *Entrance requirements:* For master's, minimum GPA of 3.0, valid teaching license, documentation of successful teaching experience. Additional exam requirements/recommendations for international students: Required—TOEFL (minimum score 600 paper-based; 100 iBT). Electronic applications accepted.

University of Northern Iowa, Graduate College, College of Humanities, Arts and Sciences, Department of Languages and Literatures, MA Program in TESOL/Spanish, Cedar Falls, IA 50614. Offers MA.

University of Oklahoma, Jeannine Rainbolt College of Education, Department of Instructional Leadership and Academic Curriculum, Norman, OK 73019. Offers instructional leadership and academic curriculum (M Ed, PhD), including biomedical education (PhD), early childhood education, elementary education, English education, instructional leadership, mathematics education, reading education, science education, social studies education, world languages education (M Ed); reading specialist (M Ed). *Accreditation:* NCATE. *Program availability:* Part-time. *Faculty:* 19 full-time (15 women), 1 (woman) part-time/adjunct. *Students:* 37 full-time (28 women), 121 part-time (98 women); includes 32 minority (7 Black or African American, non-Hispanic/Latino; 4 American Indian or Alaska Native, non-Hispanic/Latino; 5 Asian, non-Hispanic/Latino; 6 Hispanic/Latino; 1 Native Hawaiian or other Pacific Islander, non-Hispanic/Latino; 9 Two or more races, non-Hispanic/Latino), 12 international. Average age 35. 39 applicants, 77% accepted, 22 enrolled. In 2017, 49 master's, 12 doctorates awarded. Terminal master's awarded for partial completion of doctoral program. *Degree requirements:* For master's, comprehensive exam (for some programs), thesis (for some programs); for doctorate, comprehensive exam (for some programs), thesis/dissertation. *Entrance requirements:* For doctorate, GRE. Additional exam requirements/recommendations for international students: Required—TOEFL (minimum score 79 iBT) or IELTS (minimum score 6.5). Application fee: $50 ($100 for international students). Electronic applications accepted. *Expenses:* Tuition, state resident: full-time $5119; part-time $213.30 per credit hour. Tuition, nonresident: full-time $19,778; part-time $824.10 per credit hour. *Required fees:* $3458; $133.55 per credit hour. $126.50 per semester. *Financial support:* In 2017–18, 90 students received support, including 8 research assistantships (averaging $11,248 per year), 6 teaching assistantships (averaging $12,188 per year); fellowships, scholarships/grants, and unspecified assistantships also available. Financial award application deadline: 6/1; financial award applicants required to submit FAFSA. *Faculty research:* Teacher preparation; instruction; curriculum; learning; constructivist theory. *Total annual research expenditures:* $707,690. *Unit head:* Dr. Stacy Reeder, Chair, 405-325-1498, Fax: 405-325-4061, E-mail: reeder@ou.edu. *Application contact:* Anna Steele, Graduate Programs Officer, 405-325-4525, E-mail: anna.steele@ou.edu.
Website: http://www.ou.edu/education/ilac

University of Pittsburgh, School of Education, Department of Instruction and Learning, Program in Secondary Education, Pittsburgh, PA 15260. Offers English and communications education (M Ed, MAT); foreign language education (M Ed, MAT); language, literacy and culture education (Ed D, PhD); mathematics education (M Ed, MAT, Ed D, PhD); science education (M Ed, MAT, Ed D, PhD); secondary education (PhD); social studies education (M Ed, MAT); STEM education (Ed D). *Program availability:* Part-time, evening/weekend. *Degree requirements:* For master's, thesis; for doctorate, thesis/dissertation. *Entrance requirements:* For master's, PRAXIS I; for doctorate, GRE General Test. Additional exam requirements/recommendations for international students: Required—TOEFL. Electronic applications accepted.

University of Puerto Rico–Río Piedras, College of Education, Program in Curriculum and Teaching, San Juan, PR 00931-3300. Offers biology education (M Ed); chemistry education (M Ed); curriculum and teaching (Ed D); history education (M Ed); mathematics education (M Ed); physics education (M Ed); Spanish education (M Ed). *Program availability:* Part-time. *Degree requirements:* For master's, thesis; for doctorate, thesis/dissertation, internship. *Entrance requirements:* For master's, PAEG or GRE, minimum GPA of 3.0, letter of recommendation; for doctorate, GRE or PAEG, master's degree, minimum GPA of 3.0, letter of recommendation (2), interview. *Faculty research:* Curriculum, math teaching.

University of South Carolina, The Graduate School, College of Arts and Sciences, Department of Languages, Literatures, and Cultures, Columbia, SC 29208. Offers comparative literature (MA, PhD); foreign languages (MAT), including French, German, Spanish; French (MA); German (MA); Spanish (MA). MAT offered in cooperation with the College of Education. *Program availability:* Part-time. *Degree requirements:* For master's, one foreign language, comprehensive exam, thesis optional; for doctorate, 2 foreign languages, comprehensive exam, thesis/dissertation. *Entrance requirements:* For master's and doctorate, GRE General Test, writing sample. Additional exam requirements/recommendations for international students: Required—TOEFL (minimum score 75 iBT). Electronic applications accepted. *Faculty research:* Modern literature, linguistics, literature and culture, medieval literature, literary theory.

University of South Carolina, The Graduate School, College of Education, Department of Instruction and Teacher Education, Program in Secondary Education, Columbia, SC 29208. Offers art education (IMA, MAT); business education (IMA, MAT); English (MAT); foreign language (MAT); health education (MAT); mathematics (MAT); science (IMA, MAT); secondary (Ed D); secondary education (MT, PhD); social studies (MAT); theatre and speech (MAT). IMA and MT offered jointly with the subject areas. *Accreditation:* NCATE. *Degree requirements:* For master's, comprehensive exam, thesis (for some programs), foreign language (MA); for doctorate, one foreign language, comprehensive exam, thesis/dissertation. *Entrance requirements:* For master's, GRE General Test or MAT, teaching certificate (IMA, M Ed), interview; for doctorate, GRE General Test or MAT, interview. *Faculty research:* Middle school programs, professional development, school collaboration.

University of Southern Mississippi, College of Arts and Letters, Department of Foreign Languages and Literatures, Hattiesburg, MS 39406-0001. Offers Spanish (MATL). *Program availability:* 100% online. *Students:* 13 applicants, 77% accepted, 8 enrolled. In 2017, 41 master's awarded. *Degree requirements:* For master's, comprehensive exam. *Entrance requirements:* For master's, GRE General Test, minimum GPA of 3.0 in field of study, 2.75 in last 2 years. Additional exam requirements/recommendations for international students: Required—TOEFL, IELTS. *Application deadline:* For fall admission, 3/1 for domestic and international students. Applications are processed on a rolling basis. Application fee: $60. Electronic applications accepted. *Expenses:* Tuition, state resident: full-time $3830. *Financial support:* Teaching assistantships with full tuition reimbursements, Federal Work-Study, institutionally sponsored loans, scholarships/grants, health care benefits, and unspecified assistantships available. Financial award application deadline: 3/15; financial award applicants required to submit FAFSA. *Unit head:* Christopher Miles, Chair, 601-266-4964, Fax: 601-266-4583. *Application contact:* Laurel Abreau, Graduate Director, 601-266-4964.
Website: https://www.usm.edu/foreign-languages-literatures

University of South Florida, Innovative Education, Tampa, FL 33620-9951. Offers adult, career and higher education (Graduate Certificate), including college teaching, leadership in developing human resources, leadership in higher education; Africana studies (Graduate Certificate), including diasporas and health disparities, genocide and human rights; aging studies (Graduate Certificate), including gerontology; art research (Graduate Certificate), including museum studies; business foundations (Graduate Certificate); chemical and biomedical engineering (Graduate Certificate), including materials science and engineering, water, health and sustainability; child and family studies (Graduate Certificate), including positive behavior support; civil and industrial engineering (Graduate Certificate), including transportation systems analysis; community and family health (Graduate Certificate), including maternal and child health, social marketing and public health, violence and injury: prevention and intervention, women's health; criminology (Graduate Certificate), including criminal justice administration; data science for public administration (Graduate Certificate); digital humanities (Graduate Certificate); educational measurement and research (Graduate Certificate), including evaluation; English (Graduate Certificate), including comparative literary studies, creative writing, professional and technical communication; entrepreneurship (Graduate Certificate); environmental health (Graduate Certificate), including safety management; epidemiology and biostatistics (Graduate Certificate), including applied biostatistics, biostatistics, concepts and tools of epidemiology, epidemiology, epidemiology of infectious diseases; geography, environment and planning (Graduate Certificate), including community development, environmental policy and management, geographical information systems; geology (Graduate Certificate), including hydrogeology; global health (Graduate Certificate), including disaster management, global health and Latin American and Caribbean studies, global health practice, humanitarian assistance, infection control; government and international affairs (Graduate Certificate), including Cuban studies, globalization studies; health policy and management (Graduate Certificate), including health management and leadership, public health policy and programs; hearing specialist: early intervention (Graduate Certificate); industrial and management systems engineering (Graduate Certificate), including systems engineering, technology management; information studies (Graduate Certificate), including school library media specialist; information systems/decision sciences (Graduate Certificate), including analytics and business intelligence; instructional technology (Graduate Certificate), including distance education, Florida digital/virtual educator, instructional design, multimedia design, Web design; internal medicine, bioethics and medical humanities (Graduate Certificate), including biomedical ethics; Latin American and Caribbean studies (Graduate Certificate); leadership for coastal resiliency planning (Graduate Certificate); mass communications (Graduate Certificate), including multimedia journalism; mathematics and statistics (Graduate Certificate), including mathematics; medicine (Graduate Certificate), including aging and neuroscience, bioinformatics, biotechnology, brain fitness and memory management, clinical investigation, hand and upper limb rehabilitation, health informatics, health sciences, integrative weight management, intellectual property, medicine and gender, metabolic and nutritional medicine, metabolic cardiology, pharmacy sciences; national and competitive intelligence (Graduate Certificate); nursing (Graduate Certificate), including simulation based academic fellowship in advanced pain management; psychological and social foundations (Graduate Certificate), including career counseling, college teaching, diversity in education, mental health counseling, school counseling; public affairs (Graduate Certificate), including nonprofit management, public management, research administration; public health (Graduate Certificate), including assessing chemical toxicity and public health risks, health equity, pharmacoepidemiology, public health generalist, toxicology, translational research in adolescent behavioral health; public health practices (Graduate Certificate), including planning for healthy communities; rehabilitation and mental health counseling (Graduate Certificate), including integrative mental health care, marriage and family therapy, rehabilitation technology; secondary education (Graduate Certificate), including ESOL, foreign language education: culture and content, foreign language education: professional; social work (Graduate Certificate), including geriatric social work/clinical gerontology; special education (Graduate Certificate), including autism spectrum disorder, disabilities education: severe/profound; world languages (Graduate Certificate), including teaching English as a second language (TESL) or foreign language. *Unit head:* Dr. Cynthia DeLuca, Associate Vice President and Assistant Vice Provost, 813-974-3077, Fax: 813-974-7061, E-mail: deluca@usf.edu. *Application contact:* Owen Hooper, Director, Summer and Alternative Calendar Programs, 813-974-6917, E-mail: hooper@usf.edu.
Website: http://www.usf.edu/innovative-education/

The University of Tennessee, Graduate School, College of Education, Health and Human Sciences, Program in Education, Knoxville, TN 37996. Offers art education (MS); counseling education (PhD); cultural studies in education (PhD); curriculum (MS, Ed S); curriculum, educational research and evaluation (Ed D, PhD); early childhood education (PhD); early childhood special education (MS); education of deaf and hard of hearing (MS); educational administration and policy studies (Ed D, PhD); educational administration and supervision (Ed S); educational psychology (Ed D, PhD); elementary education (MS, Ed S); elementary teaching (MS); English education (MS, Ed S); exercise science (PhD); foreign language/ESL education (MS, Ed S); instructional technology (MS, Ed D, PhD, Ed S); literacy, language and ESL education (PhD); literacy, language education, and ESL education (Ed D); mathematics education (MS, Ed S); modified and comprehensive special education (MS); reading education (MS, Ed S); school counseling (Ed S); school psychology (PhD, Ed S); science education (MS, Ed S); secondary teaching (MS); social foundations (MS); social science education (MS, Ed S); socio-cultural foundations of sports and education (PhD); special education (Ed S); teacher education (Ed D, PhD). *Accreditation:* NCATE. *Program availability:* Part-time, evening/weekend. *Degree requirements:* For master's and Ed S, thesis optional; for doctorate, variable foreign language requirement, thesis/dissertation. *Entrance requirements:* For master's, minimum GPA of 2.7; for doctorate and Ed S, GRE General Test, minimum GPA of 2.7. Additional exam requirements/recommendations for international students: Required—TOEFL. Electronic applications accepted.

University of the Sacred Heart, Graduate Programs, Department of Education, San Juan, PR 00914-0383. Offers early childhood education (M Ed); information technology and multimedia (Certificate); instruction systems and education technology (M Ed), including English, information technology and multimedia, instructional design, mathematics, Spanish. *Program availability:* Part-time, evening/weekend. *Degree requirements:* For master's, thesis. *Entrance requirements:* For master's, EXADEP, minimum undergraduate GPA of 2.75, interview.

The University of Toledo, College of Graduate Studies, Judith Herb College of Education, Department of Curriculum and Instruction, Toledo, OH 43606-3390. Offers art education (ME); career and technical education (ME, Ed S); curriculum and instruction (ME, PhD, Ed S); early childhood education (Ed S); education and anthropology (MAE); education and biology (MES); education and chemistry (MES); education and classics (MAE); education and economics (MAE); education and English (MAE); education and French (MAE); education and geology (MES); education and German (MAE); education and history (MAE); education and mathematics (MAE, MES); education and physics (MES); education and political science (MAE); education and sociology (MAE); education and Spanish (MAE); educational media (PhD); educational technology (ME); educational technology: virtual educator (Certificate); elementary education (PhD); English as a second language (MAE); gifted and talented education (PhD); middle childhood education (ME); secondary education (ME, PhD); special education (PhD). *Accreditation:* NCATE. *Program availability:* Part-time, evening/weekend. *Degree requirements:* For master's, comprehensive exam, thesis or alternative; for doctorate, comprehensive exam, thesis/dissertation; for other advanced degree, thesis optional. *Entrance requirements:* For master's, doctorate, and other advanced degree, minimum cumulative GPA of 2.7 for all previous academic work, letters of recommendation. Additional exam requirements/recommendations for international students: Required—TOEFL (minimum score 550 paper-based; 80 iBT). Electronic applications accepted.

University of Vermont, Graduate College, College of Arts and Sciences, Department of Classics, Burlington, VT 05404. Offers Greek and Latin (MA); Greek and Latin languages (Graduate Certificate); Latin (MAT). *Students:* 4 (3 women). 6 applicants, 83% accepted, 2 enrolled. In 2017, 3 master's awarded. *Degree requirements:* For master's, one foreign language, thesis. *Entrance requirements:* For master's, GRE General Test, writing sample (for MA). Additional exam requirements/recommendations for international students: Required—TOEFL (minimum score 550 paper-based; 90 iBT) or IELTS (6.5). *Application deadline:* For fall admission, 2/15 priority date for domestic and international students. Applications are processed on a rolling basis. Application fee: $65. Electronic applications accepted. *Expenses:* Tuition, state resident: full-time $11,628; part-time $646 per credit. Tuition, nonresident: full-time $29,340; part-time $1630 per credit. *Required fees:* $1994; $10 per credit. Tuition and fees vary according to course load and program. *Financial support:* In 2017–18, 4 students received support, including 4 teaching assistantships with full tuition reimbursements available (averaging $8,000 per year); fellowships and health care benefits also available. Financial award application deadline: 3/1. *Faculty research:* Early Greek literature. *Unit head:* Dr. John C. Franklin, Chair, 802-656-0649, E-mail: john.franklin@uvm.edu. *Application contact:* Prof. Jacques Bailly, Coordinator, 802-656-3210, E-mail: jacques.bailly@uvm.edu.
Website: http://www.uvm.edu/~classics/

University of Victoria, Faculty of Graduate Studies, Faculty of Humanities, Department of French, Victoria, BC V8W 2Y2, Canada. Offers literature (MA); teaching emphasis (MA). *Program availability:* Part-time, evening/weekend. *Degree requirements:* For master's, 2 foreign languages, thesis optional. *Entrance requirements:* For master's, BA in French. Additional exam requirements/recommendations for international students: Required—TOEFL (minimum score 575 paper-based; 7), IELTS (minimum score 7). Electronic applications accepted. *Faculty research:* French-Canadian literature, stylistics, comparative literature, Francophone literature.

University of Virginia, Curry School of Education, Department of Curriculum, Instruction, and Special Education, Program in Curriculum and Instruction, Charlottesville, VA 22903. Offers curriculum and instruction (M Ed, Ed S); elementary education (M Ed, Ed D); English education (M Ed, Ed D); foreign language education (M Ed); mathematics education (M Ed, Ed D); science education (Ed D); social studies education (M Ed); MBA/M Ed. *Program availability:* 100% online. *Students:* 38 full-time (31 women), 15 part-time (12 women); includes 6 minority (2 Asian, non-Hispanic/Latino; 2 Hispanic/Latino; 2 Two or more races, non-Hispanic/Latino), 2 international. Average age 32. 92 applicants, 64% accepted, 47 enrolled. In 2017, 47 master's, 9 doctorates, 8 other advanced degrees awarded. *Degree requirements:* For master's, comprehensive exam (for some programs); for doctorate, comprehensive exam, thesis/dissertation; for Ed S, comprehensive exam. *Entrance requirements:* For master's, doctorate, and Ed S, GRE General Test, 2 letters of recommendation. Additional exam requirements/recommendations for international students: Required—TOEFL (minimum score 600 paper-based; 90 iBT), IELTS (minimum score 7). *Application deadline:* Applications are processed on a rolling basis. Application fee: $60. Electronic applications accepted. *Financial support:* Fellowships with tuition reimbursements, research assistantships with tuition reimbursements, and teaching assistantships with tuition reimbursements available. Financial award application deadline: 1/5; financial award applicants required to submit FAFSA. *Unit head:* Susan Mintz, Program Area Director, 434-924-3128, E-mail: slm4r@virginia.edu. *Application contact:* E-mail: curry-admissions@virginia.edu.
Website: http://curry.virginia.edu/academics/areas-of-study/curriculum-teaching-learning

University of Virginia, Curry School of Education, Program in Education, Charlottesville, VA 22903. Offers administration and supervision (PhD); applied developmental science (PhD); counselor education (PhD); curriculum and instruction (PhD); early childhood special education (MT); education evaluation (PhD); educational psychology (PhD); educational research (PhD); elementary education (MT); English education (MT, PhD); foreign language education (MT); higher education (PhD); instructional technology (PhD); kinesiology (MT, PhD); math education (PhD); reading education (PhD); research, statistics and evaluation (PhD); school psychology (PhD); science education (PhD); social studies education (MT, PhD); special education (PhD); world languages education (MT). *Students:* 431 full-time (353 women), 15 part-time (14 women); includes 100 minority (32 Black or African American, non-Hispanic/Latino; 33 Asian, non-Hispanic/Latino; 16 Hispanic/Latino; 19 Two or more races, non-Hispanic/Latino), 14 international. Average age 25. 264 applicants, 49% accepted, 83 enrolled. In 2017, 142 master's, 33 doctorates awarded. *Degree requirements:* For master's, comprehensive exam (for some programs), field project; for doctorate, comprehensive exam, thesis/dissertation. *Entrance requirements:* For doctorate, GRE General Test. Additional exam requirements/recommendations for international students: Required—TOEFL (minimum score 600 paper-based; 90 iBT), IELTS (minimum score 7). *Application deadline:* Applications are processed on a rolling basis. Application fee: $60. Electronic applications accepted. *Financial support:* Fellowships, research assistantships, and teaching assistantships available. Financial award application deadline: 1/5; financial award applicants required to submit FAFSA. *Unit head:* Robert C. Pianta, Dean, 434-924-3334, E-mail: pianta@virginia.edu. *Application contact:* E-mail: curry-admissions@virginia.edu.
Website: http://curry.virginia.edu/teacher-education

University of Wisconsin–Milwaukee, Graduate School, College of Letters and Science, Department of Foreign Languages and Literature, Milwaukee, WI 53201-0413. Offers foreign languages and literature (MA), including classic Greek, classics, comparative literature, French/Francophone language, literature, and culture, German language, literature, and culture, interpreting, Latin, linguistics, Spanish language, literature, and culture, translation; interpreting (Graduate Certificate); language, literature, and translation (MA, MALLT); translation (Graduate Certificate). *Program availability:* Part-time. *Students:* 11 full-time (6 women), 40 part-time (29 women); includes 10 minority (2 Black or African American, non-Hispanic/Latino; 3 Hispanic/Latino; 5 Two or more races, non-Hispanic/Latino), 4 international. Average age 35. 37 applicants, 68% accepted, 20 enrolled. In 2017, 5 master's awarded. *Degree requirements:* For master's, 2 foreign languages, thesis or alternative. *Entrance requirements:* Additional exam requirements/recommendations for international students: Required—TOEFL (minimum score 550 paper-based; 79 iBT), IELTS (minimum score 6.5). *Application deadline:* For fall admission, 1/1 priority date for domestic students; for spring admission, 9/1 for domestic students. Application fee: $56 ($96 for international students). Electronic applications accepted. *Financial support:* Fellowships, research assistantships, teaching assistantships, career-related internships or fieldwork, health care benefits, unspecified assistantships, and project assistantships available. Support available to part-time students. Financial award application deadline: 4/15; financial award applicants required to submit FAFSA. *Unit head:* Kevin Muse, Department Chair, 414-229-5213, E-mail: kmuse@uwm.edu. *Application contact:* General Information Contact, 414-229-4982, Fax: 414-229-6967, E-mail: gradschool@uwm.edu.
Website: http://uwm.edu/foreign-languages-literature/

Vanderbilt University, Department of French and Italian, Nashville, TN 37240-1001. Offers French (MA, MAT, PhD). *Faculty:* 12 full-time (7 women). *Students:* 13 full-time (8 women); includes 2 minority (1 Hispanic/Latino; 1 Two or more races, non-Hispanic/Latino), 2 international. Average age 28. 17 applicants, 29% accepted, 3 enrolled. In 2017, 1 doctorate awarded. Terminal master's awarded for partial completion of doctoral program. *Degree requirements:* For master's, one foreign language, comprehensive exam; for doctorate, 2 foreign languages, comprehensive exam, thesis/dissertation, final and qualifying exams. *Entrance requirements:* For master's and doctorate, GRE General Test. Additional exam requirements/recommendations for international students: Required—TOEFL (minimum score 570 paper-based; 88 iBT). *Application deadline:* For fall admission, 1/15 for domestic and international students. Electronic applications accepted. *Financial support:* Fellowships, teaching assistantships, career-related internships or fieldwork, Federal Work-Study, institutionally sponsored loans, scholarships/grants, and health care benefits available. Financial award application deadline: 1/15; financial award applicants required to submit CSS PROFILE or FAFSA. *Faculty research:* Baudelaire, Rabelais, voyage literature, postcolonial literature, medieval epic. *Unit head:* Dr. Laura Schneider, Chair, 615-322-6900, Fax: 615-343-6909, E-mail: laura.c.schneider@vanderbilt.edu. *Application contact:* Paul Miller, Director of Graduate Studies, 615-322-6900, Fax: 615-343-6909, E-mail: paul.miller@vanderbilt.edu.
Website: http://as.vanderbilt.edu/french-italian/

Vanderbilt University, Department of Germanic and Slavic Languages, Nashville, TN 37240-1001. Offers German (MA, MAT, PhD). *Faculty:* 6 full-time (3 women). *Students:* 20 full-time (13 women); includes 4 minority (1 Black or African American, non-Hispanic/Latino; 1 Hispanic/Latino; 2 Two or more races, non-Hispanic/Latino), 3 international. Average age 30. 11 applicants, 36% accepted, 2 enrolled. In 2017, 1 master's, 2 doctorates awarded. Terminal master's awarded for partial completion of doctoral program. *Degree requirements:* For master's, one foreign language, comprehensive exam; for doctorate, 2 foreign languages, comprehensive exam, thesis/dissertation, qualifying and final exams. *Entrance requirements:* For master's and doctorate, GRE General Test, sample of written work. Additional exam requirements/recommendations for international students: Required—TOEFL (minimum score 570 paper-based; 88 iBT). *Application deadline:* For fall admission, 1/15 for domestic and international students. Electronic applications accepted. *Financial support:* Fellowships, teaching assistantships, career-related internships or fieldwork, Federal Work-Study, institutionally sponsored loans, scholarships/grants, and health care benefits available. Financial award application deadline: 1/15; financial award applicants required to submit CSS PROFILE or FAFSA. *Faculty research:* 1750 to present, Middle Ages, Baroque, language pedagogy, linguistics. *Unit head:* Dr. Lutz Koepnick, Chair, 615-322-2611, Fax: 615-343-7258, E-mail: lutz.koepnick@vanderbilt.edu. *Application contact:* Christoph Zeller, Director of Graduate Studies, 615-875-9065, Fax: 615-343-7258, E-mail: christoph.zeller@vanderbilt.edu.
Website: http://www.vanderbilt.edu/german/graduate/

Vanderbilt University, Department of Spanish and Portuguese, Nashville, TN 37240-1001. Offers Portuguese (MA); Spanish (MA, MAT, PhD); Spanish and Portuguese (PhD). *Faculty:* 12 full-time (5 women). *Students:* 24 full-time (12 women); includes 7 minority (2 Black or African American, non-Hispanic/Latino; 5 Hispanic/Latino), 12 international. Average age 31. 39 applicants, 18% accepted, 6 enrolled. In 2017, 1 master's, 4 doctorates awarded. *Degree requirements:* For master's, one foreign language, thesis; for doctorate, 2 foreign languages, thesis/dissertation, final and qualifying exams. *Entrance requirements:* For master's, GRE General Test; for doctorate, GRE General Test, writing sample in Spanish. Additional exam requirements/recommendations for international students: Required—TOEFL (minimum score 570 paper-based; 88 iBT). *Application deadline:* For fall admission, 1/15 for domestic and

international students. Electronic applications accepted. *Financial support:* Fellowships, teaching assistantships with full tuition reimbursements, Federal Work-Study, institutionally sponsored loans, and health care benefits available. Financial award application deadline: 1/15; financial award applicants required to submit CSS PROFILE or FAFSA. *Faculty research:* Spanish, Portuguese, and Latin American literatures; foreign language pedagogy; Renaissance and Baroque poetry; nineteenth-century Spanish novel. *Unit head:* Dr. Benigno Trigo, Chair, 615-322-6930, Fax: 615-343-7260, E-mail: benigno.trigo@vanderbilt.edu. *Application contact:* Andres Zamora, Director of Graduate Studies, 615-322-6930, Fax: 615-343-7260, E-mail: andres.zamora@vanderbilt.edu.
Website: http://as.vanderbilt.edu/spanish-portuguese/graduate/index.php

Wagner College, Division of Graduate Studies, Education Department, Program in Secondary Education/Students with Disabilities, Staten Island, NY 10301-4495. Offers secondary education 7-12 (MS Ed), including language arts, languages other than English, mathematics and technology, science and technology, social studies. *Program availability:* Evening/weekend. *Faculty:* 2 full-time (1 woman), 7 part-time/adjunct (3 women). *Students:* 17 full-time (14 women), 6 part-time (4 women); includes 2 minority (1 Black or African American, non-Hispanic/Latino; 1 Asian, non-Hispanic/Latino). Average age 24. 15 applicants, 80% accepted, 11 enrolled. In 2017, 8 master's awarded. *Degree requirements:* For master's, thesis (for some programs), completion of state certification exams before student teaching. *Entrance requirements:* For master's, GRE, minimum GPA of 3.0, interview, recommendations. Additional exam requirements/recommendations for international students: Required—TOEFL (minimum score 550 paper-based; 79 iBT), IELTS (minimum score 6.5). *Application deadline:* For fall admission, 12/1 priority date for domestic and international students. Application fee: $60. Electronic applications accepted. *Expenses:* Contact institution. *Financial support:* Unspecified assistantships and alumni fellowship available. Financial award application deadline: 2/15; financial award applicants required to submit FAFSA. *Unit head:* Dr. Jason Fitzgerald, Department Chair, 718-420-4129, Fax: 718-390-3456, E-mail: jason.fitzgerald@wagner.edu. *Application contact:* Patricia Clancy, Assistant Director of Enrollment, 718-420-4464, Fax: 718-390-3105, E-mail: patricia.clancy@wagner.edu.
Website: http://www.wagner.edu/education

Washington State University, College of Arts and Sciences, Department of Foreign Languages and Cultures, Pullman, WA 99164. Offers MA. Programs offered at the Pullman campus. *Degree requirements:* For master's, comprehensive exam (for some programs), thesis (for some programs), 4 written exams, oral exam, paper. *Entrance requirements:* For master's, three current letters of recommendation; all original transcripts including an official English translation; two writing samples; letter of application stating qualifications and personal goals; brief (3-5 minute) tape recordings of two informal dialogues between applicant and native speaker. Additional exam requirements/recommendations for international students: Required—TOEFL (minimum score 550 paper-based). Electronic applications accepted. *Faculty research:* Spanish and Latin American literature, film, and culture; pedagogy; computer-aided instruction.

Wayne State University, College of Education, Division of Teacher Education, Detroit, MI 48202. Offers art education (M Ed); bilingual/bicultural education (Certificate); curriculum and instruction (Ed D, PhD, Ed S), including English as a second language (MAT, Ed D, Ed S), K-12 curriculum (PhD); elementary education (MAT), including bilingual/bicultural education (M Ed, MAT), early childhood education (M Ed, MAT), English as a second language (MAT, Ed D, Ed S), foreign language education, science education (M Ed, MAT), special education (M Ed, MAT); elementary mathematics specialist (Certificate); English as a second language (Certificate); reading (M Ed, Ed S); reading, language and literature (Ed D); secondary education (MAT), including bilingual/bicultural education (M Ed, MAT), early childhood education (M Ed, MAT), English as a second language (MAT, Ed D, Ed S), English education, foreign language education, mathematics education (M Ed, MAT), science education (M Ed, MAT), social studies education (M Ed, MAT); special education (MAT), including career and technical education; teaching and learning (M Ed), including bilingual/bicultural education (M Ed, MAT), early childhood education (M Ed, MAT), elementary education, foreign language, mathematics education (M Ed, MAT), science education (M Ed, MAT), social studies education (M Ed, MAT), special education (M Ed, MAT). *Program availability:* Part-time, blended/hybrid learning. *Faculty:* 22. *Students:* 126 full-time (96 women), 317 part-time (258 women); includes 134 minority (95 Black or African American, non-Hispanic/Latino; 1 American Indian or Alaska Native, non-Hispanic/Latino; 8 Asian, non-Hispanic/Latino; 17 Hispanic/Latino; 1 Native Hawaiian or other Pacific Islander, non-Hispanic/Latino; 12 Two or more races, non-Hispanic/Latino), 13 international. Average age 37. 260 applicants, 33% accepted, 57 enrolled. In 2017, 111 master's, 13 doctorates, 7 other advanced degrees awarded. *Degree requirements:* For master's, essay or project (for some M Ed programs), professional field experience (for MAT programs); for doctorate, thesis/dissertation. *Entrance requirements:* For master's, Michigan Test for Teacher Certification (for most programs), verification of participation in group work with children (for MAT programs), Michigan State Police criminal background check; for doctorate, minimum undergraduate GPA of 3.0, graduate 3.5; interview; curriculum vitae; references; master's degree (for most programs). Additional exam requirements/recommendations for international students: Required—TOEFL (minimum score 550 paper-based; 79 iBT), TWE (minimum score 5.5); Recommended—IELTS (minimum score 6.5). *Application deadline:* For fall admission, 6/1 priority date for domestic students, 5/1 priority date for international students; for winter admission, 10/1 priority date for domestic students, 9/1 priority date for international students; for spring admission, 2/1 priority date for domestic students, 1/1 priority date for international students. Applications are processed on a rolling basis. Application fee: $50. Electronic applications accepted. *Expenses:* Tuition, state resident: full-time $10,224; part-time $638.98 per credit hour. Tuition, nonresident: full-time $22,145; part-time $1384.04 per credit hour. Tuition and fees vary according to course load and program. *Financial support:* In 2017–18, 78 students received support, including 4 fellowships (averaging $13,500 per year), 1 research assistantship with tuition reimbursement available (averaging $16,000 per year); Federal Work-Study, scholarships/grants, and unspecified assistantships also available. Support available to part-time students. Financial award applicants required to submit FAFSA. *Faculty research:* Improving students' skill achievement in mathematics, improving elementary children's understanding of informational text, teachers' use of their pedagogical and mathematical

knowledge in the interactive work of teaching, the intersection of identity construction in teaching and learning, identifying effective methods of literacy instruction and assessments for bilingual students in elementary language arts classrooms. *Unit head:* Dr. Thomas Edwards, Interim Associate Dean for Teacher Education, 313-577-3886, E-mail: t.g.edwards@wayne.edu. *Application contact:* 313-577-0902, E-mail: askcoe@wayne.edu.
Website: http://coe.wayne.edu/ted/index.php

Wayne State University, College of Liberal Arts and Sciences, Department of Classical and Modern Languages, Literatures, and Cultures, Detroit, MI 48202. Offers classics (MA), including ancient Greek and Latin, ancient studies, classics, Latin; German (MA); language learning (MALL), including Arabic (MA, MALL), French (MA, MALL, PhD), German (MALL, PhD), Italian (MA, MALL), Spanish (MA, MALL, PhD); modern languages (PhD), including French (MA, MALL, PhD), German (MALL, PhD), Spanish (MA, MALL, PhD); Near Eastern languages (MA), including Arabic (MA, MALL), Hebrew; Romance languages (MA), including French (MA, MALL, PhD), Italian (MA, MALL), Spanish (MA, MALL, PhD). *Faculty:* 22. *Students:* 24 full-time (18 women), 21 part-time (15 women); includes 11 minority (4 Black or African American, non-Hispanic/Latino; 1 American Indian or Alaska Native, non-Hispanic/Latino; 2 Asian, non-Hispanic/Latino; 2 Hispanic/Latino; 2 Two or more races, non-Hispanic/Latino), 3 international. Average age 37. 32 applicants, 63% accepted, 14 enrolled. In 2017, 10 master's awarded. *Degree requirements:* For master's, variable foreign language requirement, comprehensive exam (for some programs), thesis (for some programs); for doctorate, one foreign language, comprehensive exam, thesis/dissertation. *Entrance requirements:* Additional exam requirements/recommendations for international students: Required—TOEFL (minimum score 550 paper-based; 79 iBT), TWE (minimum score 5.5), Michigan English Language Assessment Battery (minimum score 85); Recommended—IELTS (minimum score 6.5). Application fee: $50. Electronic applications accepted. *Expenses:* Tuition, state resident: full-time $10,224; part-time $638.98 per credit hour. Tuition, nonresident: full-time $22,145; part-time $1384.04 per credit hour. Tuition and fees vary according to course load and program. *Financial support:* In 2017–18, 25 students received support, including 4 fellowships with tuition reimbursements available (averaging $13,500 per year), 17 teaching assistantships with tuition reimbursements available (averaging $18,591 per year); research assistantships, scholarships/grants, health care benefits, and unspecified assistantships also available. Financial award applicants required to submit FAFSA. *Faculty research:* Classical and modern literature and culture (Greek, Latin, Arabic, Chinese, French, German, Russian, Spanish) including colonial studies and exile and Holocaust studies; critical theory (French, German, Slavic, Spanish); theoretical and applied linguistics (Arabic, Chinese, French, Spanish); area studies (Arabic, Near Eastern, classical, Islamic, and Judaic studies). *Unit head:* Dr. Anne Duggan, Department Chair, 313-577-6244, Fax: 313-577-6243, E-mail: a.duggan@wayne.edu.
Website: http://clas.wayne.edu/languages/

West Chester University of Pennsylvania, College of Arts and Humanities, Department of Languages and Cultures, West Chester, PA 19383. Offers French (Teaching Certificate); German (Teaching Certificate); languages and cultures (MA), including French, German, Spanish; Spanish (Teaching Certificate). *Program availability:* Part-time, evening/weekend, minimal on-campus study. *Students:* 8 full-time (all women), 24 part-time (19 women); includes 10 minority (all Hispanic/Latino), 1 international. Average age 30. 8 applicants, 88% accepted, 7 enrolled. In 2017, 10 master's awarded. *Degree requirements:* For master's, one foreign language, comprehensive exam, portfolio defended at oral exit exam, capstone project; for Teaching Certificate, one foreign language. *Entrance requirements:* For master's and Teaching Certificate, ACTFL OPI and WPT. Additional exam requirements/recommendations for international students: Required—TOEFL or IELTS. *Application deadline:* For fall admission, 5/15 for international students; for spring admission, 10/15 for international students. Applications are processed on a rolling basis. Application fee: $50. Electronic applications accepted. *Expenses:* Tuition, state resident: full-time $9000; part-time $500 per credit. Tuition, nonresident: full-time $13,500; part-time $750 per credit. *Required fees:* $2959; $149.79 per credit. *Financial support:* Scholarships/grants and unspecified assistantships available. Financial award application deadline: 2/15; financial award applicants required to submit FAFSA. *Faculty research:* Language structure, literature, film, culture, pedagogy, technology. *Unit head:* Dr. Mahmoud Amer, Chair, 610-430-5077, Fax: 610-436-3048, E-mail: mamer@wcupa.edu. *Application contact:* Dr. Maria Van Liew, Graduate Coordinator, 610-436-4746, Fax: 610-436-3048, E-mail: mvanliew@wcupa.edu.
Website: http://www.wcupa.edu/arts-humanities/languagesCultures/

Western Kentucky University, Graduate Studies, Potter College of Arts and Letters, Department of Modern Languages, Bowling Green, KY 42101. Offers French (MA Ed); German (MA Ed); Spanish (MA Ed).

Worcester State University, Graduate School, Program in Spanish, Worcester, MA 01602-2597. Offers MA. *Program availability:* Part-time. *Faculty:* 3 full-time. *Students:* 10 part-time (8 women); includes 4 minority (all Hispanic/Latino), 1 international. Average age 35. 5 applicants, 80% accepted. In 2017, 8 master's awarded. *Degree requirements:* For master's, one foreign language, thesis or comprehensive exam. *Entrance requirements:* For master's, GRE, MAT, BA in Spanish or related field and/or interview with faculty member. Additional exam requirements/recommendations for international students: Required—TOEFL (minimum score 550 paper-based; 79 iBT). *Application deadline:* For fall admission, 6/15 for domestic and international students; for spring admission, 11/1 for domestic and international students; for summer admission, 3/1 for domestic students, 4/1 for international students. Applications are processed on a rolling basis. Application fee: $50. Electronic applications accepted. *Expenses:* Tuition, state resident: full-time $3042; part-time $169 per credit hour. Tuition, nonresident: full-time $3042; part-time $169 per credit hour. *Required fees:* $2754; $153 per credit hour. *Financial support:* Career-related internships or fieldwork, scholarships/grants, and unspecified assistantships available. Financial award application deadline: 3/1; financial award applicants required to submit FAFSA. *Unit head:* Dr. Antonio Guijarro-Donadios, Program Coordinator, 508-929-8619, E-mail: aguijarrodonadios@worcester.edu. *Application contact:* Sara Grady, Associate Dean, Graduate Studies and Professional Development, 508-929-8130, E-mail: sara.grady@worcester.edu.

Health Education

Adelphi University, Ruth S. Ammon School of Education, Program in Health Studies, Garden City, NY 11530-0701. Offers community health education (MA, Certificate); school health education (MA). *Program availability:* Part-time, evening/weekend. *Students:* 10 full-time (7 women), 17 part-time (9 women); includes 2 minority (1 Black or African American, non-Hispanic/Latino; 1 Hispanic/Latino), 1 international. Average age 30. 17 applicants, 65% accepted, 7 enrolled. In 2017, 9 master's awarded. *Degree requirements:* For master's, internship. *Entrance requirements:* For master's, 3 letters of recommendation, resume, minimum cumulative GPA of 2.75. Additional exam requirements/recommendations for international students: Required—TOEFL (minimum score 550 paper-based; 80 iBT), IELTS (minimum score 6.5). *Application deadline:* For fall admission, 4/1 for international students; for spring admission, 11/1 for international students. Applications are processed on a rolling basis. Application fee: $50. Electronic applications accepted. *Expenses:* Contact institution. *Financial support:* Research assistantships with partial tuition reimbursements, teaching assistantships, career-related internships or fieldwork, institutionally sponsored loans, scholarships/grants, traineeships, and unspecified assistantships available. Support available to part-time students. Financial award application deadline: 2/15; financial award applicants required to submit FAFSA. *Faculty research:* Alcohol abuse, tobacco cessation, drug abuse, healthy family lives, healthy personal living. *Unit head:* Dr. Ronald Feingold, Director, 516-877-4764, E-mail: feingold@adelphi.edu. *Application contact:* E-mail: graduateadmissions@adelphi.edu.

Alabama State University, College of Education, Department of Health, Physical Education, and Recreation, Montgomery, AL 36101-0271. Offers health education (M Ed); physical education (M Ed). *Program availability:* Part-time. *Students:* 4 full-time (2 women), 6 part-time (2 women); includes 8 minority (all Black or African American, non-Hispanic/Latino), 1 international. Average age 29. 2 applicants, 100% accepted, 2 enrolled. In 2017, 5 master's awarded. *Degree requirements:* For master's, comprehensive exam. *Entrance requirements:* For master's, GRE General Test, MAT, writing competency test, bachelor's degree or its equivalent from accredited college or university with minimum GPA of 2.5. Additional exam requirements/recommendations for international students: Required—TOEFL (minimum score 500 paper-based). *Application deadline:* For fall admission, 4/15 for domestic and international students; for spring admission, 11/15 for domestic and international students; for summer admission, 3/15 for domestic and international students. Applications are processed on a rolling basis. Application fee: $25. Electronic applications accepted. *Expenses:* Contact institution. *Financial support:* Research assistantships available. Financial award application deadline: 6/30; financial award applicants required to submit FAFSA. *Faculty research:* Risk factors for heart disease in the college-age population, cardiovascular reactivity for the Cold Pressor Test. *Unit head:* Dr. Charlie Gibbons, Interim Chair, 334-229-4504, Fax: 334-229-4928, E-mail: cgibbons@alasu.edu. *Application contact:* Dr. William Person, Dean of Graduate Studies, 334-229-4274, Fax: 334-229-4928, E-mail: wperson@alasu.edu.
Website: http://www.alasu.edu/academics/colleges---departments/college-of-education/health-physical-education---recreation/index.aspx

Albany State University, College of Education, Albany, GA 31705-2717. Offers early childhood education (M Ed); educational leadership (Ed S); health and physical education (M Ed); middle grades education (M Ed); school counseling (M Ed); special education (M Ed). *Accreditation:* NCATE. *Program availability:* Part-time, evening/weekend, online learning. *Degree requirements:* For master's, comprehensive exam, internship, GACE Content Exam. *Entrance requirements:* For master's, GRE or MAT. Electronic applications accepted. *Faculty research:* GACE preparation, STEM (science, technology, engineering, and mathematics), technology education, special education, professional teacher development, health implications liberation philosophy, NET-Q, learning community, disabled or at-risk students.

Alcorn State University, School of Graduate Studies, School of Psychology and Education, Lorman, MS 39096-7500. Offers agricultural education (MS Ed); elementary education (MS Ed, Ed S); guidance and counseling (MS Ed); industrial education (MS Ed); secondary education (MS Ed), including health and physical education; special education (MS Ed). *Accreditation:* NCATE. *Degree requirements:* For master's, thesis optional.

Allen College, Graduate Programs, Waterloo, IA 50703. Offers adult-gerontology acute care nurse practitioner (MSN); community/public health nursing (MSN); education (MSN); family nurse practitioner (MSN); health sciences (Ed D); leadership in health care delivery (MSN); leadership in health care informatics (MSN); nursing (DNP); occupational therapy (MS); psychiatric mental health nurse practitioner (MSN). MSN in leadership in healthcare informatics offered in partnership with University of Minnesota. *Accreditation:* AACN; ACEN. *Program availability:* Part-time, 100% online, blended/hybrid learning. *Faculty:* 24 full-time (all women), 8 part-time/adjunct (7 women). *Students:* 106 full-time (91 women), 187 part-time (164 women); includes 22 minority (12 Black or African American, non-Hispanic/Latino; 1 American Indian or Alaska Native, non-Hispanic/Latino; 2 Asian, non-Hispanic/Latino; 3 Hispanic/Latino; 4 Two or more races, non-Hispanic/Latino), 2 international. Average age 33. 352 applicants, 56% accepted, 131 enrolled. In 2017, 73 master's, 2 doctorates awarded. *Entrance requirements:* For master's, minimum GPA of 3.0 in the last 60 hours of undergraduate coursework; for doctorate, minimum GPA of 3.25 in graduate coursework. *Application deadline:* For fall admission, 2/1 priority date for domestic students; for spring admission, 9/1 priority date for domestic students. Applications are processed on a rolling basis. Application fee: $50. Electronic applications accepted. *Expenses:* $17,860 per year. *Financial support:* In 2017–18, 97 students received support. Federal Work-Study, institutionally sponsored loans, scholarships/grants, and traineeships available. Support available to part-time students. Financial award application deadline: 8/1; financial award applicants required to submit FAFSA. *Faculty research:* Poverty. *Unit head:* Dr. Nancy Kramer, Vice Chancellor for Academic Affairs, 319-226-2040, Fax: 319-226-2070, E-mail: nancy.kramer@allencollege.edu. *Application contact:* Molly Quinn, Director of Admissions, 319-226-2001, Fax: 319-226-2010, E-mail: molly.quinn@allencollege.edu.
Website: http://www.allencollege.edu/

American University, College of Arts and Sciences, Department of Health Studies, Program in Nutrition Education, Washington, DC 20016-8001. Offers MS, Certificate. *Program availability:* Part-time, online only, 100% online. *Students:* 1 (woman) full-time, 64 part-time (56 women); includes 2 minority (1 Black or African American, non-Hispanic/Latino; 1 Hispanic/Latino). Average age 35. 50 applicants, 90% accepted, 35 enrolled. In 2017, 37 master's, 2 other advanced degrees awarded. *Entrance requirements:* For master's, GRE; for Certificate, statement of purpose, transcripts, resume. Additional exam requirements/recommendations for international students: Required—TOEFL (minimum score 600 paper-based; 100 iBT), IELTS (minimum score 7). *Application deadline:* For fall admission, 2/1 priority date for domestic students; for

spring admission, 11/1 priority date for domestic students. Application fee: $55. *Expenses:* Contact institution. *Financial support:* Applicants required to submit FAFSA. *Unit head:* Dr. Anastasia Snelling, Chair, Department of Health Studies, 202-885-6278, Fax: 202-885-1187, E-mail: stacey@american.edu. *Application contact:* Jonathan Harper, Assistant Director, Graduate Recruitment, 202-855-3622, E-mail: jharper@american.edu.
Website: http://www.american.edu/cas/nutrition/nutrition-education-ms.cfm

Arcadia University, College of Health Sciences, Department of Public Health, Program in Health Education, Glenside, PA 19038-3295. Offers MSHE. *Program availability:* Part-time, evening/weekend. *Expenses:* Contact institution.

Arizona State University at the Tempe campus, College of Health Solutions, Program in Behavioral Health, Phoenix, AZ 85004-2135. Offers DBH. *Program availability:* Part-time, evening/weekend, online learning. *Degree requirements:* For doctorate, thesis/dissertation or alternative, 16 hours/week practicum (400 hours total), applied research paper focused on design, implementation and evaluation of a clinical intervention in primary care or related setting, interactive Program of Study (iPOS) submitted before completing 50 percent of required credit hours. *Entrance requirements:* For doctorate, minimum GPA of 3.0 or equivalent in last 2 years of work leading to bachelor's degree; 3 professional reference letters; copy of current clinical license(s) to practice behavioral health; interview. Additional exam requirements/recommendations for international students: Required—TOEFL, IELTS, or PTE. Electronic applications accepted. *Expenses:* Contact institution.

Arkansas State University, Graduate School, College of Nursing and Health Professions, School of Nursing, State University, AR 72467. Offers aging studies (Graduate Certificate); health care management (Graduate Certificate); health sciences (MS); health sciences education (Graduate Certificate); nurse anesthesia (MSN); nursing (MSN); nursing practice (DNP). *Accreditation:* AANA/CANAEP (one or more programs are accredited); ACEN. *Program availability:* Part-time. *Degree requirements:* For master's and Graduate Certificate, comprehensive exam, thesis or alternative; for doctorate, comprehensive exam, thesis/dissertation. *Entrance requirements:* For master's, GRE General Test or MAT, appropriate bachelor's degree, current Arkansas nursing license, CPR certification, physical examination, professional liability insurance, critical care experience, ACLS Certification, PALS Certification, interview, immunization records, personal goal statement, health assessment; for doctorate, GRE or MAT, NCLEX-RN Exam, appropriate master's degree, current Arkansas nursing license, CPR certification, physical examination, professional liability insurance, critical care experience, ACLS Certification, PALS Certification, interview, immunization records, personal goal statement, health assessment, TB skin test, background check; for Graduate Certificate, GRE or MAT, appropriate bachelor's degree, official transcripts, immunization records, proof of employment in healthcare, TB Skin Test, TB Mask Fit Test, CPR Certification. Additional exam requirements/recommendations for international students: Required—TOEFL (minimum score 550 paper-based; 79 iBT), IELTS (minimum score 6), PTE (minimum score 56). Electronic applications accepted. *Expenses:* Contact institution.

Auburn University, Graduate School, College of Education, Department of Kinesiology, Auburn University, AL 36849. Offers exercise science (M Ed). *Accreditation:* NCATE. *Program availability:* Part-time. *Faculty:* 21 full-time (10 women), 2 part-time/adjunct (0 women). *Students:* 94 full-time (45 women), 31 part-time (16 women); includes 30 minority (17 Black or African American, non-Hispanic/Latino; 1 Asian, non-Hispanic/Latino; 8 Hispanic/Latino; 4 Two or more races, non-Hispanic/Latino), 8 international. Average age 26. 132 applicants, 68% accepted, 59 enrolled. In 2017, 53 master's, 8 doctorates awarded. *Degree requirements:* For master's, thesis (for some programs); for doctorate, thesis/dissertation; for Ed S, exam, field project. *Entrance requirements:* For master's, GRE General Test; for doctorate and Ed S, GRE General Test, interview, master's degree. *Application deadline:* Applications are processed on a rolling basis. Application fee: $50 ($60 for international students). Electronic applications accepted. *Expenses:* Tuition, state resident: full-time $10,974; part-time $519 per credit hour. Tuition, nonresident: full-time $29,658; part-time $1557 per credit hour. *Required fees:* $816 per semester. Tuition and fees vary according to degree level and program. *Financial support:* Research assistantships, teaching assistantships, and Federal Work-Study available. Support available to part-time students. Financial award application deadline: 3/15; financial award applicants required to submit FAFSA. *Faculty research:* Biomechanics, exercise physiology, motor skill learning, school health, curriculum development. *Unit head:* Dr. Mary E. Rudisill, Director, 334-844-1458. *Application contact:* Dr. George Flowers, Dean of the Graduate School, 334-844-2125.

Austin Peay State University, College of Graduate Studies, College of Behavioral and Health Sciences, Department of Health and Human Performance, Clarksville, TN 37044. Offers public health education (MS); sports and wellness leadership (MS). *Program availability:* Part-time, evening/weekend, online learning. *Faculty:* 8 full-time (4 women). *Students:* 14 full-time (7 women), 38 part-time (27 women); includes 15 minority (10 Black or African American, non-Hispanic/Latino; 1 Asian, non-Hispanic/Latino; 2 Hispanic/Latino; 2 Two or more races, non-Hispanic/Latino), 1 international. Average age 29. 66 applicants, 67% accepted, 33 enrolled. In 2017, 34 master's awarded. *Degree requirements:* For master's, comprehensive exam, thesis optional. *Entrance requirements:* For master's, GRE General Test, 3 letters of recommendation, minimum undergraduate GPA of 2.5. Additional exam requirements/recommendations for international students: Required—TOEFL (minimum score 500 paper-based). *Application deadline:* For fall admission, 8/8 priority date for domestic students. Applications are processed on a rolling basis. Application fee: $45 ($55 for international students). Electronic applications accepted. *Expenses:* Tuition, state resident: full-time $7686; part-time $427 per credit hour. Tuition, nonresident: full-time $20,268; part-time $1126 per credit hour. *Required fees:* $1529; $76.45 per credit hour. *Financial support:* Research assistantships with full tuition reimbursements, career-related internships or fieldwork, Federal Work-Study, institutionally sponsored loans, scholarships/grants, and unspecified assistantships available. Support available to part-time students. Financial award application deadline: 4/1; financial award applicants required to submit FAFSA. *Unit head:* Dr. Marcy Maurer, Chair, 931-221-6105, Fax: 931-221-7040, E-mail: maurerm@apsu.edu. *Application contact:* Megan Mitchell, Coordinator of Graduate Admissions, 931-221-6189, Fax: 931-221-7641, E-mail: mitchellm@apsu.edu.
Website: http://www.apsu.edu/hhp/index.php

Baldwin Wallace University, Graduate Programs, Public Health Program, Berea, OH 44017-2088. Offers health education and disease prevention (MPH); population health leadership and management (MPH). Program offered in partnership with The MetroHealth System. *Program availability:* Part-time, evening/weekend, online learning. *Faculty:* 1 full-time (0 women), 2 part-time/adjunct (0 women). *Students:* 23 full-time (18 women), 1 (woman) part-time; includes 9 minority (2 Black or African American, non-

Health Education

Hispanic/Latino; 3 Asian, non-Hispanic/Latino; 2 Hispanic/Latino; 2 Two or more races, non-Hispanic/Latino), 1 international. Average age 39. 30 applicants, 57% accepted, 13 enrolled. *Entrance requirements:* For master's, GRE. Additional exam requirements/recommendations for international students: Required—TOEFL (minimum score 550 paper-based; 100 iBT). *Application deadline:* For fall admission, 7/15 for domestic students. Applications are processed on a rolling basis. *Expenses:* $921 per credit hour. *Financial support:* Applicants required to submit FAFSA. *Unit head:* Stephen D. Stahl, Provost, Academic Affairs, 440-826-2251, Fax: 440-826-2329, E-mail: sstahl@bw.edu. *Application contact:* Winnie W. Gerhardt, Director of Transfer, Adult and Graduate Admission, 440-826-8002, E-mail: wgerhard@bw.edu.
Website: http://www.bw.edu/academics/master-public-health/

Baylor University, Graduate School, Robbins College of Health and Human Sciences, Department of Health, Human Performance and Recreation, Waco, TX 76798. Offers athletic training (MS); community health (MPH); exercise physiology (MS); kinesiology, exercise nutrition, and health promotion (PhD); sport pedagogy (MS). *Accreditation:* NCATE. *Program availability:* Part-time. *Faculty:* 24 full-time (11 women). *Students:* 86 full-time (52 women), 9 part-time (6 women); includes 24 minority (7 Black or African American, non-Hispanic/Latino; 3 Asian, non-Hispanic/Latino; 10 Hispanic/Latino; 1 Native Hawaiian or other Pacific Islander, non-Hispanic/Latino; 3 Two or more races, non-Hispanic/Latino), 8 international. 109 applicants, 59% accepted, 44 enrolled. In 2017, 30 master's, 3 doctorates awarded. *Degree requirements:* For master's, comprehensive exam, thesis optional; for doctorate, comprehensive exam, thesis/dissertation. *Entrance requirements:* For master's and doctorate, GRE General Test. Additional exam requirements/recommendations for international students: Required—TOEFL (minimum score 550 paper-based; 80 iBT). *Application deadline:* For fall admission, 2/1 priority date for domestic students, 2/1 for international students; for spring admission, 10/1 for domestic and international students. Applications are processed on a rolling basis. Application fee: $25. Electronic applications accepted. *Financial support:* In 2017–18, 60 students received support, including 1 research assistantship with full tuition reimbursement available (averaging $12,700 per year), 33 teaching assistantships with full tuition reimbursements available (averaging $7,650 per year); career-related internships or fieldwork, Federal Work-Study, institutionally sponsored loans, scholarships/grants, tuition waivers (full), and unspecified assistantships also available. Financial award application deadline: 2/1. *Faculty research:* Exercise testing, cardio-metabolic health, resistance exercise and training, nutritional intervention, population health, health promotion, global health epidemiology, coaching, natural resource management, stimulant misuse, diet, microbiome and colon cancer etiology. *Total annual research expenditures:* $250,118. *Unit head:* Dr. Jaeho Shim, Graduate Program Director, 254-710-4009, Fax: 254-710-3527, E-mail: joe_shim@baylor.edu. *Application contact:* Deepa Morris, Graduate Program Coordinator, 254-710-3526, Fax: 254-710-3527, E-mail: deepa_morris@baylor.edu.
Website: http://www.baylor.edu/HHPR/

Benedictine University, Graduate Programs, Program in Public Health, Lisle, IL 60532. Offers administration of health care institutions (MPH); dietetics (MPH); disaster management (MPH); health education (MPH); health information systems (MPH); MBA/MPH; MPH/MS. *Accreditation:* CEPH. *Program availability:* Part-time, evening/weekend, online learning. *Entrance requirements:* For master's, MAT, GRE, or GMAT. Additional exam requirements/recommendations for international students: Required—TOEFL (minimum score 550 paper-based).

Boston University, School of Medicine, Division of Graduate Medical Sciences, Program in Health Sciences Education, Boston, MA 02215. Offers MS.

Brandeis University, The Heller School for Social Policy and Management, Program in Social Policy, Waltham, MA 02454-9110. Offers assets and inequalities (PhD); children, youth and families (PhD); global health and development (PhD); health and behavioral health (PhD). *Degree requirements:* For doctorate, comprehensive exam, thesis/dissertation, qualifying paper, 2-year residency. *Entrance requirements:* For doctorate, GRE General Test, 3 letters of recommendation, statement of purpose, writing sample, at least 3-5 years of professional experience. Additional exam requirements/recommendations for international students: Required—TOEFL (minimum score 600 paper-based; 100 iBT). Electronic applications accepted. *Expenses:* Tuition: Full-time $48,720. *Required fees:* $88. Tuition and fees vary according to course load, degree level, program and student level. *Faculty research:* Health; mental health; substance abuse; children, youth, and families; aging; international and community development; disabilities; work and inequality; hunger and poverty.

California Baptist University, Program in Public Health, Riverside, CA 92504-3206. Offers health education and promotion (MPH); health policy and administration (MPH). *Program availability:* Part-time, evening/weekend. *Faculty:* 9 full-time (5 women), 4 part-time/adjunct (2 women). *Students:* 56 full-time (47 women), 37 part-time (30 women); includes 72 minority (18 Black or African American, non-Hispanic/Latino; 8 Asian, non-Hispanic/Latino; 38 Hispanic/Latino; 8 Two or more races, non-Hispanic/Latino), 4 international. Average age 28. 83 applicants, 64% accepted, 39 enrolled. In 2017, 4 master's awarded. *Degree requirements:* For master's, capstone project; practicum. *Entrance requirements:* For master's, minimum undergraduate GPA of 2.75, two recommendations, 500-word essay, resume. Additional exam requirements/recommendations for international students: Required—TOEFL (minimum score 80 iBT). *Application deadline:* For fall admission, 8/1 priority date for domestic students, 7/1 for international students; for spring admission, 12/1 priority date for domestic students, 11/1 for international students. Applications are processed on a rolling basis. Application fee: $45. Electronic applications accepted. *Expenses:* Contact institution. *Financial support:* In 2017–18, 22 students received support. Federal Work-Study and scholarships/grants available. Financial award applicants required to submit CSS PROFILE or FAFSA. *Faculty research:* Epidemiology, statistical education, exercise and immunity, obesity and chronic disease. *Unit head:* Dr. David Pearson, Dean, College of Health Science, 951-343-4298, E-mail: dpearson@calbaptist.edu. *Application contact:* Tamakia King, Graduate Admissions Counselor, 951-552-8138, E-mail: tking@calbaptist.edu.
Website: http://www.calbaptist.edu/explore-cbu/schools-colleges/college-allied-health/health-sciences/master-public-health/

California State University, Long Beach, Graduate Studies, College of Health and Human Services, Department of Health Science, Long Beach, CA 90840. Offers MPH. *Accreditation:* CEPH; NCATE. *Program availability:* Part-time. *Degree requirements:* For master's, thesis optional. *Entrance requirements:* For master's, GRE, minimum GPA of 3.0 in last 60 units. Electronic applications accepted.

California State University, Northridge, Graduate Studies, College of Health and Human Development, Department of Health Sciences, Northridge, CA 91330. Offers health administration (MS); public health (MPH), including applied epidemiology, community health education. *Accreditation:* CEPH. *Students:* 128 full-time (96 women), 53 part-time (45 women); includes 96 minority (10 Black or African American, non-Hispanic/Latino; 21 Asian, non-Hispanic/Latino; 53 Hispanic/Latino; 1 Native Hawaiian or other Pacific Islander, non-Hispanic/Latino; 11 Two or more races, non-Hispanic/Latino), 6 international. Average age 30. 323 applicants, 38% accepted, 68 enrolled. In 2017, 70 master's awarded. *Entrance requirements:* For master's, GRE General Test or minimum GPA of 3.0. Additional exam requirements/recommendations for international

students: Required—TOEFL. *Application deadline:* For fall admission, 11/30 for domestic students. Application fee: $55. *Financial support:* Teaching assistantships available. Financial award application deadline: 3/1. *Faculty research:* Labor market needs assessment, health education products, dental hygiene, independent practice prototype. *Unit head:* Louis Rubino, Chair, 818-677-3101.
Website: http://www.csun.edu/hhd/hsci/

California State University, Northridge, Graduate Studies, Tseng College, Northridge, CA 91330. Offers business administration (Graduate Certificate); health administration (MPA); health education (MPH); knowledge management (MKM); music industry administration (MA); nonprofit-sector management (Graduate Certificate); public administration (MPA); public sector management and leadership (MPA); social work (MSW); taxation (MS); tourism, hospitality and recreation management (MS). *Students:* 4 part-time (all women); includes 1 minority (Black or African American, non-Hispanic/Latino). Average age 37. In 2017, 2 master's awarded. *Entrance requirements:* For master's, GRE (if cumulative undergraduate GPA less than 3.0). *Unit head:* Joyce Feucht-Haviar, Dean, 866-873-6439.

California State University, San Marcos, College of Education, Health and Human Services, Department of Social Work, San Marcos, CA 92096-0001. Offers behavioral health (MSW); children, youth and families (MSW). *Accreditation:* CSWE. *Degree requirements:* For master's, thesis, capstone project. *Expenses:* Contact institution. *Unit head:* Dr. Blake Beecher, Chair, 760-750-7373.
Website: http://www.csusm.edu/socialwork/

Cambridge College, School of Education, Boston, MA 02129. Offers autism specialist (M Ed); autism/behavior analyst (M Ed); behavior analyst (Post-Master's Certificate); behavioral management (M Ed); early childhood teacher (M Ed); education specialist in curriculum and instruction (CAGS); educational leadership (Ed D); elementary teacher (M Ed); English as a second language (M Ed, Certificate); general science (M Ed); health education (Post-Master's Certificate); health/family and consumer sciences (M Ed); history (M Ed); individualized (M Ed); information technology literacy (M Ed); instructional technology (M Ed); interdisciplinary studies (M Ed); library teacher (M Ed); literacy education (M Ed); mathematics (M Ed); mathematics specialist (Certificate); middle school mathematics and science (M Ed); school administration (M Ed, CAGS); school guidance counselor (M Ed); school nurse education (M Ed); school social worker/school adjustment counselor (M Ed); special education administrator (CAGS); special education/moderate disabilities (M Ed); teaching skills and methodologies (M Ed). *Program availability:* Part-time, evening/weekend, online learning. *Degree requirements:* For master's, thesis, internship/practicum (licensure program only); for doctorate, thesis/dissertation; for other advanced degree, thesis. *Entrance requirements:* For master's, interview, resume, documentation of licensure, 2 professional references; for doctorate, official transcripts, interview, resume, documentation of licensure (if any), written personal statement/essay, portfolio of scholarly and professional work, qualifying assessment, 2 professional references, health insurance, immunizations form; for other advanced degree, official transcripts, interview, resume, documentation of licensure (if any), written personal statement/essay, 2 professional references, health insurance, immunizations form. Additional exam requirements/recommendations for international students: Required—TOEFL (minimum score 550 paper-based; 79 iBT), Michigan English Language Assessment Battery (minimum score 85); Recommended—IELTS (minimum score 6). Electronic applications accepted. *Expenses:* Contact institution. *Faculty research:* Adult education, accelerated learning, mathematics education, brain compatible learning, special education and law.

Central Washington University, School of Graduate Studies and Research, College of Education and Professional Studies, Department of Physical Education, School Health and Movement Studies, Ellensburg, WA 98926. Offers athletic administration (MS); health and physical education (MS). *Program availability:* Part-time. *Degree requirements:* For master's, comprehensive exam, thesis or alternative. *Entrance requirements:* For master's, minimum GPA of 3.0. Additional exam requirements/recommendations for international students: Required—TOEFL (minimum score 550 paper-based; 79 iBT), IELTS. *Application deadline:* For fall admission, 2/1 priority date for domestic students; for winter admission, 10/1 for domestic students; for spring admission, 1/1 for domestic students. Applications are processed on a rolling basis. Application fee: $50. Electronic applications accepted. *Financial support:* Applicants required to submit FAFSA. *Unit head:* Dr. Heidi Henschel Pellett, Chair, 509-963-1483, E-mail: heidi.henschelpellett@cwu.edu. *Application contact:* Justine Eason, Admissions Program Coordinator, 509-963-3103, Fax: 509-963-1799, E-mail: masters@cwu.edu.
Website: http://www.cwu.edu/~pesph/

Clark University, Graduate School, Department of International Development, Community, and Environment, Worcester, MA 01610-1477. Offers community and global health (MHS); community development and planning (MA); environmental science and policy (MS); geographic information science for development and environment (MS); international development and social change (MA); MA/MBA; MBA/MS. *Faculty:* 19 full-time (10 women), 4 part-time/adjunct (3 women). *Students:* 150 full-time (90 women); includes 23 minority (10 Black or African American, non-Hispanic/Latino; 3 Asian, non-Hispanic/Latino; 5 Hispanic/Latino; 5 Two or more races, non-Hispanic/Latino), 38 international. Average age 27. 364 applicants, 86% accepted, 113 enrolled. In 2017, 85 master's awarded. *Entrance requirements:* For master's, 3 references, resume or curriculum vitae. Additional exam requirements/recommendations for international students: Required—TOEFL (minimum score 575 paper-based; 90 iBT) or IELTS (minimum score 6.5). *Application deadline:* For fall admission, 1/15 for domestic students. Application fee: $75. *Financial support:* Fellowships, research assistantships, teaching assistantships, institutionally sponsored loans, and scholarships/grants available. *Faculty research:* Community action research, gender analysis, environmental risk assessment, land-use planning, geographic information systems, HIV and AIDS, global health and social justice, environmental health, climate change and sustainability. *Unit head:* Dr. Ed Carr, Director, 508-421-3895, Fax: 508-793-8820, E-mail: edcarr@clarku.edu. *Application contact:* Erika Paradis, Student and Academic Services Director, 508-793-7201, Fax: 508-793-8820, E-mail: eparadis@clarku.edu.
Website: http://www2.clarku.edu/departments/international-development-community-environment/

Cleveland State University, College of Graduate Studies, College of Education and Human Services, Department of Health and Human Performance, Cleveland, OH 44115. Offers physical education pedagogy (M Ed); public health (MPH). *Program availability:* Part-time. *Faculty:* 7 full-time (4 women), 3 part-time/adjunct (2 women). *Students:* 30 full-time (16 women), 60 part-time (36 women); includes 43 minority (33 Black or African American, non-Hispanic/Latino; 4 Asian, non-Hispanic/Latino; 2 Hispanic/Latino; 1 Native Hawaiian or other Pacific Islander, non-Hispanic/Latino; 3 Two or more races, non-Hispanic/Latino), 5 international. Average age 29. 103 applicants, 72% accepted, 43 enrolled. In 2017, 44 master's awarded. *Degree requirements:* For master's, comprehensive exam, thesis optional. *Entrance requirements:* For master's, GRE General Test or MAT (if undergraduate GPA less than 2.75), minimum undergraduate GPA of 2.75. Additional exam requirements/recommendations for international students: Required—TOEFL (minimum score 550 paper-based; 78 iBT), IELTS (minimum score 6). *Application deadline:* For fall admission, 7/15 priority date for domestic students; for spring admission, 12/15 priority date for domestic students. Applications are processed on a rolling basis. Application fee: $30. Electronic applications accepted. *Financial support:* In 2017–18, 6 research assistantships with tuition reimbursements (averaging $3,480 per year), 1 teaching assistantship with tuition reimbursement (averaging $3,480 per year) were awarded; career-related internships or fieldwork, tuition waivers (full), and unspecified assistantships also available. Financial award application deadline: 3/15; financial award applicants required to submit FAFSA. *Faculty research:* Bone density, marketing fitness centers, motor development of disabled, online learning and survey research. *Unit head:* Dr. Mike Loovis, Associate Professor/Department Chairperson, 216-687-3665, Fax: 216-687-5410, E-mail: e.loovis@csuohio.edu. *Application contact:* David Easler, Director, Graduate Recruitment, 216-687-5047, Fax: 216-687-5400, E-mail: d.easler@csuohio.edu. Website: http://www.csuohio.edu/cehs/departments/HPERD/hperd_dept.html

Cleveland University–Kansas City, Program in Health Education and Promotion, Overland Park, KS 66210. Offers MS. *Program availability:* Part-time. *Entrance requirements:* For master's, professional statement. Additional exam requirements/recommendations for international students: Required—TOEFL (minimum score 550 paper-based; 79 iBT). *Application deadline:* For fall admission, 7/1 for domestic and international students; for winter admission, 10/1 for domestic and international students. Applications are processed on a rolling basis. Electronic applications accepted. *Expenses:* Contact institution. *Financial support:* Applicants required to submit FAFSA. *Application contact:* Melissa Denton, Director of Admissions, 913-234-0744, Fax: 913-234-0906, E-mail: kc.admissions@cleveland.edu. Website: https://www.cleveland.edu/academics/college-of-health-sciences/ms-in-health-promotion

The College at Brockport, State University of New York, School of Education, Health, and Human Services, Department of Public Health and Health Education, Brockport, NY 14420-2997. Offers community health education (MS Ed); health education (MS Ed), including health education K-12. *Faculty:* 2 full-time (0 women), 3 part-time/adjunct (2 women). *Students:* 5 full-time (3 women), 26 part-time (11 women); includes 2 minority (1 Black or African American, non-Hispanic/Latino; 1 Hispanic/Latino). 11 applicants, 82% accepted, 7 enrolled. In 2017, 7 master's awarded. *Degree requirements:* For master's, thesis or alternative. *Entrance requirements:* For master's, minimum GPA of 3.0, letters of recommendation. Additional exam requirements/recommendations for international students: Required—TOEFL (minimum score 500 paper-based; 79 iBT), IELTS (minimum score 6.5). *Application deadline:* For fall admission, 3/1 priority date for domestic and international students; for spring admission, 10/1 priority date for domestic and international students; for summer admission, 3/1 priority date for domestic and international students. Application fee: $80. Electronic applications accepted. *Expenses:* Tuition, state resident: full-time $10,870; part-time $453 per credit hour. Tuition, nonresident: full-time $22,210. *Required fees:* $988; $246 per semester. *Financial support:* In 2017–18, 1 teaching assistantship with full tuition reimbursement (averaging $6,000 per year) was awarded; Federal Work-Study, scholarships/grants, and unspecified assistantships also available. Support available to part-time students. Financial award application deadline: 3/15; financial award applicants required to submit FAFSA. *Faculty research:* Nutrition, substance use, HIV/AIDS, bioethics, worksite health. *Unit head:* Dr. Darson Rhodes, Graduate Director, 585-395-5901, Fax: 585-395-5246, E-mail: drhodes@brockport.edu. *Application contact:* Danielle A. Welch, Graduate Admissions Counselor, 585-395-5465, Fax: 585-395-2515.
Website: https://www.brockport.edu/academics/public_health/

College of Saint Mary, Program in Health Professions Education, Omaha, NE 68106. Offers Ed D. *Program availability:* Part-time.

Colorado State University–Pueblo, College of Education, Engineering and Professional Studies, Education Program, Pueblo, CO 81001-4901. Offers art education (M Ed); foreign language education (M Ed); health and physical education (M Ed); instructional technology (M Ed); linguistically diverse education (M Ed); music education (M Ed); special education (M Ed). *Accreditation:* TEAC. *Program availability:* Part-time. *Degree requirements:* For master's, portfolio. *Entrance requirements:* For master's, 3 recommendations, teaching license. Additional exam requirements/recommendations for international students: Required—TOEFL (minimum score 500 paper-based). Electronic applications accepted. *Faculty research:* Portfolio assessment, math education, science education.

Columbus State University, Graduate Studies, College of Education and Health Professions, Department of Health, Physical Education and Exercise Science, Columbus, GA 31907-5645. Offers exercise science (MS); health and physical education (M Ed, MAT). *Program availability:* Part-time, evening/weekend. *Faculty:* 6 full-time (4 women). *Students:* 19 full-time (8 women), 9 part-time (3 women); includes 13 minority (8 Black or African American, non-Hispanic/Latino; 1 Asian, non-Hispanic/Latino; 3 Hispanic/Latino; 1 Two or more races, non-Hispanic/Latino). Average age 28. 20 applicants, 65% accepted, 9 enrolled. In 2017, 14 master's awarded. *Degree requirements:* For master's, thesis optional. *Entrance requirements:* For master's, GRE, minimum undergraduate GPA of 2.75. Additional exam requirements/recommendations for international students: Required—TOEFL (minimum score 550 paper-based; 79 iBT). *Application deadline:* For fall admission, 5/1 for domestic students, 4/1 for international students; for spring admission, 11/1 for domestic and international students; for summer admission, 2/1 for domestic students, 3/1 for international students. Applications are processed on a rolling basis. Application fee: $50. Electronic applications accepted. *Expenses:* Tuition, state resident: full-time $3708; part-time $2472 per year. Tuition, nonresident: full-time $14,418; part-time $9612 per year. *International tuition:* $19,218 full-time. *Required fees:* $1605. Tuition and fees vary according to program. *Financial support:* In 2017–18, 2 students received support, including 6 research assistantships (averaging $3,000 per year). Financial award application deadline: 5/15; financial award applicants required to submit FAFSA. *Unit head:* Dr. Tara Underwood, Chair, 706-568-2485, E-mail: underwood_tara@columbusstate.edu. *Application contact:* Catrina Smith-Edmond, Assistant Director for Graduate and Global Admission, 706-507-8824, Fax: 706-568-5091, E-mail: smithedmond_catrina@columbusstate.edu.
Website: http://hpex.columbusstate.edu/

Concordia University Wisconsin, Graduate Programs, School of Health Professions, Mequon, WI 53097-2402. Offers MOT, MSRS, DPT.

Daemen College, Program in Public Health, Amherst, NY 14226-3592. Offers community health education (MPH); epidemiology (MPH); generalist (MPH). *Program availability:* Part-time, online learning. *Degree requirements:* For master's, practicum.

Dalhousie University, Faculty of Health Professions, School of Health and Human Performance, Program in Health Promotion, Halifax, NS B3H 3J5, Canada. Offers MA. *Program availability:* Part-time. *Degree requirements:* For master's, thesis. *Entrance requirements:* Additional exam requirements/recommendations for international students: Required—TOEFL, IELTS, CANTEST, CAEL, or Michigan English Language Assessment Battery. Electronic applications accepted. *Faculty research:* AIDS research, health knowledge of adolescents, evaluating health promotion, program evaluation.

Delta State University, Graduate Programs, College of Education, Division of Health, Physical Education, and Recreation, Cleveland, MS 38733-0001. Offers health, physical

education, and recreation (M Ed); sport and human performance (MS). *Program availability:* Part-time, evening/weekend. *Degree requirements:* For master's, thesis optional. *Entrance requirements:* For master's, GRE General Test or MAT, Class A teaching certificate. *Faculty research:* Blood pressure, body fat, power and reaction time, learning disorders of athletes, effects of walking.

Drew University, Caspersen School of Graduate Studies, Madison, NJ 07940-1493. Offers conflict resolution and leadership (Certificate), including community leadership, moderation, peace building; education (M Ed); finance (MA); history and culture (MA, PhD), including American history, book history, British history, European history, Holocaust and genocide (M Litt, MA, D Litt, PhD), intellectual history, Irish history, print culture, public history; K-12 education (MAT), including art, biology, chemistry, elementary education, English, French, Italian, math, secondary education, special education, teacher of students with disabilities; liberal studies (M Litt, D Litt), including history, Holocaust and genocide (M Litt, MA, D Litt, PhD), Irish/Irish-American studies, literature (M Litt, MMH, D Litt, DMH, CMH), religion, spirituality, teaching in the two-year college, writing; medical humanities (MMH, DMH, CMH), including arts, health, healthcare, literature (M Litt, MMH, D Litt, DMH, CMH), scientific research; poetry (MFA). *Program availability:* Part-time, evening/weekend. *Faculty:* 4 full-time (2 women), 29 part-time/adjunct (15 women). *Students:* 77 full-time (42 women), 175 part-time (114 women); includes 39 minority (12 Black or African American, non-Hispanic/Latino; 6 Asian, non-Hispanic/Latino; 16 Hispanic/Latino; 5 Two or more races, non-Hispanic/Latino), 11 international. Average age 41. 126 applicants, 75% accepted, 52 enrolled. In 2017, 38 master's, 23 doctorates, 35 other advanced degrees awarded. Terminal master's awarded for partial completion of doctoral program. *Degree requirements:* For master's and other advanced degree, thesis (for some programs); for doctorate, one foreign language, comprehensive exam (for some programs), thesis/dissertation. *Entrance requirements:* For master's, PRAXIS Core and Subject Area tests (for MAT), GRE/GMAT (for M Fin), resume, transcripts, writing sample, personal statement, letters of recommendation; for doctorate, GRE (PhD in history and culture); resume, transcripts, writing sample, personal statement, letters of recommendation; for other advanced degree, resume, transcripts, personal statement. Additional exam requirements/recommendations for international students: Required—TOEFL (minimum score 587 paper-based; 80 iBT), IELTS (minimum score 6), TWE (minimum score 4). *Application deadline:* For fall admission, 8/1 for domestic students, 6/1 for international students; for spring admission, 12/1 for domestic students, 10/1 for international students. Applications are processed on a rolling basis. Application fee: $35. Electronic applications accepted. *Financial support:* Fellowships, research assistantships, teaching assistantships, career-related internships or fieldwork, Federal Work-Study, scholarships/grants, and unspecified assistantships available. Support available to part-time students. Financial award applicants required to submit FAFSA. *Faculty research:* Irish history and culture, conflict resolution and leadership. *Application contact:* Leanne Horinko, Director of Caspersen Admissions, 973-408-3280, E-mail: gradm@drew.edu. Website: http://www.drew.edu/caspersen

East Carolina University, Graduate School, College of Health and Human Performance, Department of Health Education and Promotion, Greenville, NC 27858-4353. Offers environmental health (MS); health education (MA Ed); health education and promotion (MA). *Accreditation:* CEPH; NCATE. *Students:* 18 full-time (15 women), 54 part-time (42 women); includes 18 minority (11 Black or African American, non-Hispanic/Latino; 2 Asian, non-Hispanic/Latino; 4 Hispanic/Latino; 1 Two or more races, non-Hispanic/Latino). Average age 31. 25 applicants, 80% accepted, 18 enrolled. In 2017, 31 master's awarded. *Degree requirements:* For master's, comprehensive exam, thesis optional. *Entrance requirements:* For master's, GRE General Test or MAT. Additional exam requirements/recommendations for international students: Recommended—TOEFL (minimum score 78 iBT), IELTS (minimum score 6.5). *Application deadline:* For fall admission, 6/1 priority date for domestic students. Applications are processed on a rolling basis. Application fee: $75. *Expenses:* Tuition, state resident: full-time $4749; part-time $297 per credit hour. Tuition, nonresident: full-time $17,898; part-time $1119 per credit hour. *Required fees:* $2691; $224 per credit hour. Part-time tuition and fees vary according to course load and program. *Financial support:* Fellowships, research assistantships, teaching assistantships, and career-related internships or fieldwork available. Support available to part-time students. Financial award application deadline: 6/1. *Faculty research:* Community health education, worksite health promotion, school health education, environmental health. *Unit head:* Dr. J. Don Chaney, Chair, 252-737-4942, E-mail: chaneyj@ecu.edu. Website: https://hhp.ecu.edu/hep/

Eastern Kentucky University, The Graduate School, College of Education, Department of Curriculum and Instruction, Program in Secondary and Higher Education, Richmond, KY 40475-3102. Offers secondary education (MA Ed), including agricultural education, art education, biological sciences education, business education, English education, geography education, history education, home economics education, industrial education, mathematical sciences education, physical education, school health education. *Accreditation:* NCATE. *Program availability:* Part-time. *Entrance requirements:* For master's, GRE General Test, minimum GPA of 2.5.

Eastern Michigan University, Graduate School, College of Health and Human Services, School of Health Promotion and Human Performance, Program in Health Education, Ypsilanti, MI 48197. Offers MS, Graduate Certificate. *Program availability:* Part-time, evening/weekend. *Students:* 1 (woman) full-time, 12 part-time (10 women); includes 1 minority (Black or African American, non-Hispanic/Latino). Average age 29. 6 applicants, 67% accepted, 3 enrolled. In 2017, 8 master's awarded. *Degree requirements:* For master's, thesis or project. *Entrance requirements:* For master's, teaching credential. Additional exam requirements/recommendations for international students: Required—TOEFL. *Application deadline:* For fall admission, 8/1 for domestic students, 5/1 for international students; for winter admission, 12/1 for domestic students, 10/1 for international students; for spring admission, 4/15 for domestic students, 3/1 for international students. Application fee: $45. *Application contact:* Dr. Joan Cowdery, Program Coordinator, 734-487-2811, Fax: 734-487-2024, E-mail: jcowdery@emich.edu.

Eastern University, Department of Nursing, St. Davids, PA 19087-3696. Offers nursing (MSN); school health services (M Ed); school health supervisor (K-12) (Certificate); school nurse (K-12) (Certificate). *Students:* 1 (woman) full-time, 41 part-time (40 women); includes 5 minority (4 Black or African American, non-Hispanic/Latino; 1 Asian, non-Hispanic/Latino). Average age 43. In 2017, 8 master's awarded. *Application deadline:* Applications are processed on a rolling basis. Application fee: $35. Electronic applications accepted. Application fee is waived when completed online. *Expenses:* Contact institution. *Unit head:* Michael Dziedziak, Executive Director of Enrollment, 800-452-0996, E-mail: gpsadmissions@eastern.edu. Website: https://www.eastern.edu/academics/programs/department-nursing-adult-undergraduate-graduate

Eastern University, Graduate Education Programs, St. Davids, PA 19087-3696. Offers ESL program specialist (K-12) (Certificate); general supervisor (PreK-12) (Certificate); health and physical education (K-12) (Certificate); middle level (4-8) (Certificate); multicultural education (M Ed); music (K-12) (Certificate); Pre K-4 (Certificate); Pre K-4 with special education (Certificate); reading (M Ed); reading specialist (K-12) (Certificate); reading supervisor (K-12) (Certificate); school counseling (MA, CAGS);

school principalship (preK-12) (Certificate); school psychology (MS, CAGS); secondary biology education (7-12) (Certificate); secondary chemistry education (7-12) (Certificate); secondary communication education (7-12) (Certificate); secondary English education (7-12) (Certificate); secondary math education (7-12) (Certificate); secondary social studies education (7-12) (Certificate); special education (M Ed); special education (7-12) (Certificate); special education (Pre K-8) (Certificate); special education supervisor (K-12) (Certificate); TESOL (M Ed); world language (Certificate), including Spanish. *Program availability:* Part-time, evening/weekend, online learning. *Students:* 46 full-time (40 women), 115 part-time (93 women); includes 65 minority (42 Black or African American, non-Hispanic/Latino; 3 Asian, non-Hispanic/Latino; 14 Hispanic/Latino; 6 Two or more races, non-Hispanic/Latino), 1 international. Average age 32. In 2017, 72 master's awarded. *Entrance requirements:* Additional exam requirements/recommendations for international students: Required—TOEFL. *Application deadline:* Applications are processed on a rolling basis. Application fee: $35. Electronic applications accepted. Application fee is waived when completed online. *Expenses:* Contact institution. *Unit head:* Michael Dziedziak, Executive Director of Enrollment, 800-452-0996, E-mail: gpsadmissions@eastern.edu.
Website: https://www.eastern.edu/academics/programs/education-department-graduate-programs

East Stroudsburg University of Pennsylvania, Graduate and Extended Studies, College of Health Sciences, Department of Exercise Science, East Stroudsburg, PA 18301-2999. Offers MS. *Program availability:* Part-time, evening/weekend, online learning. *Faculty:* 8 full-time (2 women). *Students:* 59 full-time (22 women), 4 part-time (2 women); includes 16 minority (8 Black or African American, non-Hispanic/Latino; 1 Asian, non-Hispanic/Latino; 4 Hispanic/Latino; 3 Two or more races, non-Hispanic/Latino), 2 international. Average age 25. 19 applicants, 47% accepted, 8 enrolled. In 2017, 40 master's awarded. *Degree requirements:* For master's, comprehensive exam, thesis or alternative, computer literacy. *Entrance requirements:* Additional exam requirements/recommendations for international students: Recommended—TOEFL (minimum score 560 paper-based; 83 iBT), IELTS. *Application deadline:* For fall admission, 3/1 priority date for domestic and international students; for spring admission, 11/30 for domestic students, 10/31 for international students. Applications are processed on a rolling basis. Application fee: $50. Electronic applications accepted. *Expenses:* Tuition, state resident: full-time $4500; part-time $3000 per credit. Tuition, nonresident: full-time $6750; part-time $4500 per credit. *Required fees:* $2642; $1756 per credit. $878 per semester. Tuition and fees vary according to course load, campus/location and program. *Financial support:* Research assistantships with tuition reimbursements, Federal Work-Study, and unspecified assistantships available. Support available to part-time students. Financial award application deadline: 3/1; financial award applicants required to submit FAFSA. *Unit head:* Dr. Chad Witmer, Graduate Coordinator, 570-422-3362, E-mail: cwitmer@esu.edu. *Application contact:* Kevin Quintero, Associate Director, Graduate and Extended Studies, 570-422-3890, Fax: 570-422-2711, E-mail: kquintero@esu.edu.

East Stroudsburg University of Pennsylvania, Graduate and Extended Studies, College of Health Sciences, Department of Health Studies, East Stroudsburg, PA 18301-2999. Offers MPH, MS. *Accreditation:* CEPH (one or more programs are accredited). *Program availability:* Part-time, evening/weekend, online learning. *Faculty:* 5 full-time (all women). *Students:* 19 full-time (14 women), 29 part-time (25 women); includes 9 minority (3 Black or African American, non-Hispanic/Latino; 1 Asian, non-Hispanic/Latino; 3 Hispanic/Latino; 2 Two or more races, non-Hispanic/Latino), 2 international. Average age 31. 39 applicants, 67% accepted, 20 enrolled. In 2017, 17 master's awarded. *Degree requirements:* For master's, oral comprehensive exam. *Entrance requirements:* For master's, GRE General Test, minimum GPA of 3.0 in major, 2.8 overall; undergraduate prerequisites in anatomy and physiology; 3 verifiable letters of recommendation; professional resume. Additional exam requirements/recommendations for international students: Recommended—TOEFL (minimum score 560 paper-based; 83 iBT), IELTS. *Application deadline:* For fall admission, 7/31 priority date for domestic students, 6/30 priority date for international students; for spring admission, 11/30 for domestic students, 10/31 for international students. Applications are processed on a rolling basis. Application fee: $50. Electronic applications accepted. *Expenses:* Tuition, state resident: full-time $4500; part-time $3000 per credit. Tuition, nonresident: full-time $6750; part-time $4500 per credit. *Required fees:* $2642; $1756 per credit. $878 per semester. Tuition and fees vary according to course load, campus/location and program. *Financial support:* Research assistantships with tuition reimbursements, Federal Work-Study, and unspecified assistantships available. Support available to part-time students. Financial award application deadline: 3/1; financial award applicants required to submit FAFSA. *Faculty research:* HIV prevention, wellness, international health issues. *Unit head:* Dr. Kim Razzano, Chair, 570-422-3693, Fax: 570-422-3848, E-mail: krazzano@esu.edu. *Application contact:* Kevin Quintero, Associate Director, Graduate and Extended Studies, 570-422-3890, Fax: 570-422-2711, E-mail: kquintero@esu.edu.

Emory University, Rollins School of Public Health, Department of Behavioral Sciences and Health Education, Atlanta, GA 30322-1100. Offers MPH, PhD. *Accreditation:* CEPH. *Program availability:* Part-time. *Degree requirements:* For master's, comprehensive exam (for some programs), thesis, practicum. *Entrance requirements:* For master's, GRE General Test. Additional exam requirements/recommendations for international students: Required—TOEFL (minimum score 550 paper-based; 80 iBT). Electronic applications accepted.

Excelsior College, School of Health Sciences, Albany, NY 12203-5159. Offers health care administration (MS); health professions education (MSHS); healthcare informatics (MS); organizational development (MS); public health (MSHS). *Program availability:* Part-time, evening/weekend, online learning. *Faculty:* 4 part-time/adjunct (all women). *Students:* 133 part-time (92 women); includes 84 minority (49 Black or African American, non-Hispanic/Latino; 4 American Indian or Alaska Native, non-Hispanic/Latino; 8 Asian, non-Hispanic/Latino; 13 Hispanic/Latino; 2 Native Hawaiian or other Pacific Islander, non-Hispanic/Latino; 8 Two or more races, non-Hispanic/Latino). Average age 40. In 2017, 38 master's awarded. *Application deadline:* Applications are processed on a rolling basis. Application fee: $50. Electronic applications accepted. *Expenses: Tuition:* Part-time $645 per credit. *Required fees:* $265 per credit. *Financial support:* Scholarships/grants available. *Unit head:* Dr. Barbara Pieper, Dean, 518-464-8500, Fax: 518-464-8777. *Application contact:* Admissions Counselor, 518-464-8500, Fax: 518-464-8777, E-mail: gradadmissions@excelsior.edu.

Fairfield University, Marion Peckham Egan School of Nursing and Health Studies, Fairfield, CT 06824. Offers advanced practice (DNP); family nurse practitioner (MSN, DNP); nurse anesthesia (DNP); nursing leadership (MSN); psychiatric nurse practitioner (MSN, DNP). *Accreditation:* AACN; AANA/CANAEP. *Program availability:* Part-time, evening/weekend. *Faculty:* 9 full-time (all women), 11 part-time/adjunct (8 women). *Students:* 50 full-time (42 women), 153 part-time (140 women); includes 48 minority (15 Black or African American, non-Hispanic/Latino; 1 American Indian or Alaska Native, non-Hispanic/Latino; 10 Asian, non-Hispanic/Latino; 19 Hispanic/Latino; 3 Two or more races, non-Hispanic/Latino), 2 international. Average age 34. 160 applicants, 50% accepted, 55 enrolled. In 2017, 26 master's, 36 doctorates awarded. *Degree requirements:* For master's, capstone project. *Entrance requirements:* For master's,

minimum QPA of 3.0, RN license, resume, 2 recommendations; for doctorate, MSN (minimum QPA of 3.2) or BSN (minimum QPA of 3.0); critical care nursing experience (for nurse anesthesia DNP candidates). Additional exam requirements/recommendations for international students: Required—TOEFL (minimum score 550 paper-based; 80 iBT) or IELTS (minimum score 6.5). *Application deadline:* For fall admission, 5/15 for international students; for spring admission, 10/15 for international students. Applications are processed on a rolling basis. Application fee: $60. Electronic applications accepted. *Expenses:* $850 per credit hour (for MSN); $1,000 per credit hour (for DNP). *Financial support:* In 2017–18, 45 students received support. Scholarships/grants and unspecified assistantships available. Financial award applicants required to submit FAFSA. *Faculty research:* Aging, spiritual care, palliative and end of life care, psychiatric mental health, pediatric trauma. *Unit head:* Dr. Meredith Wallace Kazer, Dean, 203-254-4000 Ext. 2701, Fax: 203-254-4126, E-mail: mkazer@fairfield.edu. *Application contact:* Marianne Gumpper, Director of Graduate and Continuing Studies Admission, 203-254-4184, Fax: 203-254-4073, E-mail: gradadmis@fairfield.edu. Website: http://fairfield.edu/son

Florida State University, The Graduate School, College of Human Sciences, Department of Nutrition, Food and Exercise Sciences, Tallahassee, FL 32306-1493. Offers exercise physiology (MS, PhD); nutrition and food science (MS, PhD), including clinical nutrition (MS), food science, human nutrition (PhD), nutrition education and health promotion (MS), nutrition science (MS); sports nutrition (MS); sports sciences (MS). *Program availability:* Part-time. *Faculty:* 21 full-time (8 women). *Students:* 86 full-time (56 women), 5 part-time (2 women); includes 13 minority (1 Black or African American, non-Hispanic/Latino; 1 Asian, non-Hispanic/Latino; 2 Hispanic/Latino; 9 Two or more races, non-Hispanic/Latino), 17 international. 116 applicants, 57% accepted, 29 enrolled. In 2017, 23 master's, 9 doctorates awarded. *Degree requirements:* For master's, thesis optional; for doctorate, thesis/dissertation, preliminary examination, minimum of 24 credit hours dissertation, dissertation defense. *Entrance requirements:* For master's and doctorate, GRE General Test, minimum upper-division GPA of 3.0. Additional exam requirements/recommendations for international students: Required—TOEFL (minimum score 550 paper-based; 80 iBT). *Application deadline:* For fall admission, 4/1 for domestic and international students; for spring admission, 10/1 for domestic and international students. Applications are processed on a rolling basis. Application fee: $30. Electronic applications accepted. *Expenses:* $480 per credit hour in-state; $1,111 per credit hour out-of-state. *Financial support:* In 2017–18, 53 students received support, including 22 research assistantships with full tuition reimbursements available (averaging $9,446 per year), 36 teaching assistantships with full tuition reimbursements available (averaging $14,725 per year); career-related internships or fieldwork, Federal Work-Study, institutionally sponsored loans, scholarships/grants, and unspecified assistantships also available. Financial award application deadline: 2/1; financial award applicants required to submit FAFSA. *Faculty research:* Body composition, functional food, chronic disease and aging response; food safety, food allergy, and safety/quality detection methods; sports nutrition, energy and human performance; strength training, functional performance, cardiovascular physiology, sarcopenia. *Total annual research expenditures:* $613,329. *Unit head:* Dr. Chester Ray, Department Chair, 850-644-1850, Fax: 850-645-5000, E-mail: caray@fsu.edu. *Application contact:* Mary-Sue McLemore, Academic Support Assistant, 850-644-1117, E-mail: mmclemore@fsu.edu.
Website: https://humansciences.fsu.edu/nutrition-food-exercise-sciences/students/graduate-programs/

Fort Hays State University, Graduate School, College of Health and Life Sciences, Department of Health and Human Performance, Hays, KS 67601-4099. Offers MS. *Program availability:* Part-time. *Degree requirements:* For master's, comprehensive exam, thesis optional. *Entrance requirements:* For master's, GRE General Test or MAT. Additional exam requirements/recommendations for international students: Required—TOEFL (minimum score 550 paper-based). Electronic applications accepted. *Faculty research:* Isoproterenol hydrochloride and exercise, dehydrogenase and high-density lipoprotein levels in athletics, venous blood parameters to adipose fat.

Georgia College & State University, Graduate School, College of Health Sciences, School of Health and Human Performance, Milledgeville, GA 31061. Offers health and human performance (MS), including health performance, health promotion; kinesiology/health education (MAT). *Accreditation:* NCATE (one or more programs are accredited). *Program availability:* Part-time, 100% online. *Faculty:* 19 full-time (9 women). *Students:* 35 full-time (20 women), 17 part-time (10 women); includes 9 minority (3 Black or African American, non-Hispanic/Latino; 5 Hispanic/Latino; 1 Two or more races, non-Hispanic/Latino), 2 international. Average age 27. 21 applicants, 100% accepted, 19 enrolled. In 2017, 21 master's awarded. *Degree requirements:* For master's, thesis (for some programs), completed in 6 years with minimum GPA of 3.0 (for MS); minimum GPA of 3.0 and electronic teaching portfolio (for MAT). *Entrance requirements:* For master's, GRE with minimum score of 297 or MAT with minimum score of 385 (for MS); GRE with minimum score of 297, MAT 385, SAT 1000, ACT 43, or GACE with 250 on each section (for MAT), resume, 3 professional references; minimum GPA of 2.75 in upper-level undergraduate courses and undergraduate statistics course (for MS); minimum GPA of 2.75 on upper-division major courses (for MAT). *Application deadline:* For fall admission, 7/15 priority date for domestic students, 4/1 for international students; for spring admission, 11/15 priority date for domestic students, 9/1 for international students; for summer admission, 4/15 priority date for domestic students. Applications are processed on a rolling basis. Application fee: $40. Electronic applications accepted. *Expenses:* Contact institution. *Financial support:* In 2017–18, 22 students received support. Unspecified assistantships available. Support available to part-time students. Financial award application deadline: 3/1; financial award applicants required to submit FAFSA. *Unit head:* Dr. Lisa Griffin, Director, School of Health and Human Performance, 478-445-4072, Fax: 478-445-4074, E-mail: lisa.griffin@gcsu.edu.
Website: http://www.gcsu.edu/health/shhp

Georgia Southern University, Jack N. Averitt College of Graduate Studies, Jiann-Ping Hsu College of Public Health, Program in Public Health, Statesboro, GA 30460. Offers biostatistics (MPH, Dr PH); community health behavior and education (Dr PH); community health education (MPH); environmental health sciences (MPH); epidemiology (MPH); health policy and management (MPH, Dr PH). *Program availability:* Part-time. *Faculty:* 11 full-time (5 women). *Students:* 146 full-time (90 women), 70 part-time (57 women); includes 112 minority (95 Black or African American, non-Hispanic/Latino; 9 Asian, non-Hispanic/Latino; 5 Hispanic/Latino; 3 Two or more races, non-Hispanic/Latino), 47 international. Average age 32. 190 applicants, 78% accepted, 89 enrolled. In 2017, 34 master's, 13 doctorates awarded. *Degree requirements:* For master's, thesis optional, practicum; for doctorate, comprehensive exam, thesis/dissertation, preceptorship. *Entrance requirements:* For master's, GRE General Test, minimum GPA of 2.75, 3 letters of recommendation, statement of purpose, resume or curriculum vitae; for doctorate, GRE, GMAT, MCAT, LSAT, minimum GPA of 3.0, 3 letters of recommendation, statement of purpose, resume or curriculum vitae. Additional exam requirements/recommendations for international students: Required—TOEFL (minimum score 537 paper-based; 75 iBT), IELTS (minimum score 6). *Application deadline:* For fall admission, 6/1 for domestic students, 5/1 for international students. Applications are processed on a rolling basis. Application fee: $135. Electronic applications accepted. *Expenses:* $3,949 in-state, $13,929 out-of-

state (for MPH); $4,014 in-state, $14,159 out-of-state (for Dr PH). *Financial support:* In 2017–18, 106 students received support, including 1 research assistantship with full tuition reimbursement available (averaging $12,350 per year), 6 teaching assistantships with full tuition reimbursements available (averaging $12,350 per year); scholarships/ grants, tuition waivers (full), and unspecified assistantships also available. Financial award application deadline: 4/15; financial award applicants required to submit FAFSA. *Faculty research:* Rural public health best practices, health disparity elimination, community initiatives to enhance public health, cost effectiveness analysis, epidemiology of rural public health, environmental health issues, health care system assessment, rural health care, health policy and healthcare financing, survival analysis, nonparametric statistics and resampling methods, micro-arrays and genomics, data imputation techniques and clinical trial methodology. *Total annual research expenditures:* $415,747. *Unit head:* Dr. Robert Greg Evans, Dean, 912-478-2674, E-mail: rgevans@georgiasouthern.edu. *Application contact:* Shamia Garrett, Coordinator, Office of Student Services, 912-478-2674, Fax: 912-478-5811, E-mail: jphcoph-gradadvisor@georgiasouthern.edu.
Website: http://jphcoph.georgiasouthern.edu/

Georgia State University, College of Education and Human Development, Department of Kinesiology and Health, Program in Health and Physical Education, Atlanta, GA 30302-3083. Offers M Ed. *Program availability:* Part-time, evening/weekend. *Entrance requirements:* For master's, GRE General Test, minimum GPA of 2.5. Application fee: $50. *Expenses:* Tuition, state resident: full-time $7020. Tuition, nonresident: full-time $22,518. *Required fees:* $2128. Tuition and fees vary according to degree level and program. *Financial support:* Teaching assistantships and career-related internships or fieldwork available. *Faculty research:* Exercise science, teacher behavior. *Unit head:* Dr. Jacalyn Lea Lund, Chair, 404-413-8051, E-mail: jlund@gsu.edu. *Application contact:* Dr. Rachel Gurvitch, Program Coordinator, 404-413-8374, E-mail: rgurvitch@gsu.edu.
Website: http://education.gsu.edu/KIN/kh_programs.htm

Harding University, Cannon-Clary College of Education, Searcy, AR 72149-0001. Offers advanced studies in teaching and learning (M Ed); art (MSE); behavioral science (MSE); counseling (MS, Ed S); early childhood special education (M Ed, MSE); education (MSE); educational leadership (M Ed, Ed S); elementary education (M Ed); English (MSE); French (MSE); history/social science (MSE); kinesiology (MSE); math (MSE); reading (M Ed); secondary education (M Ed); Spanish (MSE); teaching (MAT); teaching English as a second language (MSE). *Accreditation:* NCATE. *Program availability:* Part-time, evening/weekend. *Faculty:* 22 full-time (9 women), 51 part-time/ adjunct (37 women). *Students:* 135 full-time (95 women), 316 part-time (231 women); includes 77 minority (46 Black or African American, non-Hispanic/Latino; 7 American Indian or Alaska Native, non-Hispanic/Latino; 4 Asian, non-Hispanic/Latino; 9 Hispanic/ Latino; 11 Two or more races, non-Hispanic/Latino), 11 international. Average age 34. 128 applicants, 87% accepted, 111 enrolled. In 2017, 153 master's, 24 other advanced degrees awarded. *Degree requirements:* For master's, comprehensive exam (for some programs), thesis optional, portfolio(s); for Ed S, comprehensive exam, portfolio, project. *Entrance requirements:* For master's, GRE, MAT, PRAXIS; for Ed S, MAT or GRE. Additional exam requirements/recommendations for international students: Required— TOEFL (minimum score 550 paper-based; 79 iBT). *Application deadline:* For fall admission, 8/1 for domestic and international students; for spring admission, 1/1 for domestic and international students. Applications are processed on a rolling basis. Application fee: $35. Tuition and fees vary according to course load, degree level, campus/location and program. *Financial support:* In 2017–18, 33 students received support. Unspecified assistantships available. *Faculty research:* Reading, comprehension, school violence, educational technology, behavior, college choice, differentiated instruction, brain-based teaching. *Unit head:* Dr. Clara Carroll, Chair, 501-279-4501, Fax: 501-279-4083, E-mail: ccarroll@harding.edu. *Application contact:* Information Contact, 501-279-4315, E-mail: gradstudiesedu@harding.edu.
Website: http://www.harding.edu/education

Hofstra University, School of Education, Specialized Programs in Education, Hempstead, NY 11549. Offers applied behavior analysis (Advanced Certificate); childhood special education (MS Ed); early childhood special education (MS Ed, Advanced Certificate); educational and policy leadership (Ed D); educational leadership (Advanced Certificate), including school building leader/school district business leader; educational leadership and policy studies (MS Ed), including K-12; elementary special education (MS Ed); gifted education (Advanced Certificate), including school building leader/school district business leader; health education (MS); health professions pedagogy and leadership (MS); higher education leadership and policy studies (MS Ed); inclusive early childhood special education (MS Ed); inclusive elementary special education (MS Ed); inclusive secondary special education (MS Ed); literacy studies (MA, MS Ed, Ed D, Advanced Certificate), including birth-grade 6 (MS Ed, Advanced Certificate), grades 5-12 (MS Ed, Advanced Certificate), literacy studies (Ed D); pedagogy for health professions (Advanced Certificate); physical education (MS); school district business leader (Advanced Certificate); secondary education generalist - students with disabilities 7-12 (MS Ed), including students with disabilities 7-12; secondary special education generalist (MS Ed), including extension in secondary education; special education (MS Ed, Advanced Certificate); special education assessment and diagnosis (Advanced Certificate); special education early childhood intervention (MS Ed); special education: international perspectives (MS Ed); teaching students with severe or multiple disabilities (Advanced Certificate). *Program availability:* Part-time, evening/weekend, blended/hybrid learning. *Students:* 148 full-time (110 women), 249 part-time (188 women); includes 105 minority (54 Black or African American, non-Hispanic/Latino; 1 American Indian or Alaska Native, non-Hispanic/ Latino; 13 Asian, non-Hispanic/Latino; 35 Hispanic/Latino; 1 Native Hawaiian or other Pacific Islander, non-Hispanic/Latino; 1 Two or more races, non-Hispanic/Latino), 1 international. Average age 32. 228 applicants, 93% accepted, 132 enrolled. In 2017, 97 master's, 22 doctorates, 31 other advanced degrees awarded. *Degree requirements:* For master's, one foreign language, comprehensive exam (for some programs), thesis (for some programs), electronic portfolio, capstone course, internship, practicum, student teaching, seminars, minimum GPA of 3.0; for doctorate, one foreign language, comprehensive exam, thesis/dissertation, qualifying hearing. *Entrance requirements:* For master's, GRE, interview, letters of recommendation, portfolio, essay, certification; for doctorate, GRE or MAT, interview, resume, essay, master's degree, 3 letters of recommendation, writing sample; for Advanced Certificate, GRE, interview, letters of recommendation, essay, professional experience, resume, master's degree. Additional exam requirements/recommendations for international students: Required—TOEFL (minimum score 550 paper-based; 80 iBT). *Application deadline:* Applications are processed on a rolling basis. Application fee: $75. Electronic applications accepted. *Expenses: Tuition:* Full-time $1292. *Required fees:* $970. Tuition and fees vary according to program. *Financial support:* In 2017–18, 225 students received support, including 118 fellowships with full and partial tuition reimbursements available (averaging $3,887 per year), 12 research assistantships with full and partial tuition reimbursements available (averaging $7,215 per year); career-related internships or fieldwork, Federal Work-Study, institutionally sponsored loans, scholarships/grants, traineeships, tuition waivers (full and partial), and unspecified assistantships also available. Support available to part-time students. Financial award applicants required to submit FAFSA. *Faculty research:* Collaborative teaching and learning; language and

culture; new media literacies; applied behavior analysis; K-12 leadership development. *Unit head:* Dr. Elfreda Blue, Chairperson, 516-463-5762, Fax: 516-463-6184, E-mail: elfreda.blue@hofstra.edu. *Application contact:* Sunil Samuel, Assistant Vice President of Admissions, 516-463-4723, Fax: 516-463-4664, E-mail: graduateadmission@ hofstra.edu.
Website: http://www.hofstra.edu/education/

Howard University, Graduate School, Department of Health, Human Performance and Leisure Studies, Washington, DC 20059-0002. Offers exercise physiology (MS); health education (MS); sports studies (MS), including sociology of sports, sports management; urban recreation (MS), including leisure studies. *Program availability:* Part-time, evening/weekend. *Degree requirements:* For master's, comprehensive exam, thesis. *Entrance requirements:* For master's, BS in human performance or related field. Additional exam requirements/recommendations for international students: Recommended—TOEFL. Electronic applications accepted. *Faculty research:* Health promotion, cardiovascular hypertension, physical activity, sport and human rights issues.

Idaho State University, Office of Graduate Studies, School of Health Professions, Department of Community and Public Health, Program in Health Education, Pocatello, ID 83209-8109. Offers MHE. *Program availability:* Part-time. *Degree requirements:* For master's, comprehensive exam, thesis or project. *Entrance requirements:* For master's, GRE General Test, previous coursework in statistics, natural sciences, tests and measurements. Additional exam requirements/recommendations for international students: Required—TOEFL (minimum score 600 paper-based). Electronic applications accepted. *Faculty research:* Health and wellness.

Illinois State University, Graduate School, College of Applied Science and Technology, School of Kinesiology and Recreation, Normal, IL 61790. Offers health education (MS). *Degree requirements:* For master's, thesis or alternative. *Entrance requirements:* For master's, GRE General Test, minimum GPA of 2.6 in last 60 hours of course work. *Faculty research:* Influences on positive youth development through sport, country-wide health fitness project, graduate practicum in athletic training, perceived exertion and self-selected intensity during resistance exercise in younger and older.

Indiana State University, College of Graduate and Professional Studies, College of Health and Human Services, Department of Applied Health Sciences, Terre Haute, IN 47809. Offers MS, DHS. *Accreditation:* NCATE (one or more programs are accredited). *Degree requirements:* For master's, thesis or alternative. *Entrance requirements:* For master's, GRE General Test. Electronic applications accepted.

Indiana University Bloomington, School of Public Health, Department of Applied Health Science, Bloomington, IN 47405. Offers behavioral, social, and community health (MPH); family health (MPH); health behavior (PhD); nutrition science (MS); professional health education (MPH); public health administration (MPH); safety management (MS); school and college health education (MS). *Degree requirements:* For master's, thesis optional; for doctorate, comprehensive exam, thesis/dissertation. *Entrance requirements:* For master's, GRE (for MS in nutrition science), 3 recommendations; for doctorate, GRE, 3 recommendations. Additional exam requirements/recommendations for international students: Required—TOEFL (minimum score 550 paper-based; 80 iBT). Electronic applications accepted. *Faculty research:* Cancer education, HIV/AIDS and drug education, public health, parent-child interactions, safety education, obesity, public health policy, public health administration, school health, health education, human development, nutrition, human sexuality, chronic disease, early childhood health.

Indiana University of Pennsylvania, School of Graduate Studies and Research, College of Health and Human Services, Department of Kinesiology, Health, and Sport Science, Program in Health and Physical Education, Indiana, PA 15705. Offers M Ed. *Program availability:* Part-time. *Faculty:* 10 full-time (3 women). *Students:* 34 full-time (17 women), 11 part-time (9 women); includes 4 minority (3 Black or African American, non-Hispanic/Latino; 1 Two or more races, non-Hispanic/Latino). Average age 25. 35 applicants, 89% accepted, 21 enrolled. In 2017, 11 master's awarded. *Entrance requirements:* Additional exam requirements/recommendations for international students: Required—TOEFL (minimum score 540 paper-based). *Application deadline:* Applications are processed on a rolling basis. Application fee: $50. Electronic applications accepted. *Expenses: Tuition,* state resident: full-time $12,000; part-time $500 per credit. Tuition, nonresident: full-time $18,000; part-time $750 per credit. *Required fees:* $4073; $165.55 per credit. $64 per term. *Financial support:* In 2017–18, 7 research assistantships with tuition reimbursements (averaging $3,303 per year) were awarded; career-related internships or fieldwork, Federal Work-Study, scholarships/ grants, and unspecified assistantships also available. Support available to part-time students. Financial award application deadline: 4/15; financial award applicants required to submit FAFSA. *Unit head:* Dr. Keri Kulik, Coordinator, 724-357-5656, E-mail: kskulik@iup.edu.
Website: http://www.iup.edu/grad/healthphysed/default.aspx

Indiana University–Purdue University Indianapolis, School of Health and Rehabilitation Sciences, Indianapolis, IN 46202. Offers health and rehabilitation sciences (PhD); health sciences (MS); nutrition and dietetics (MS); occupational therapy (OTD); physical therapy (DPT); physician assistant (MPAS). *Program availability:* Part-time, evening/weekend. *Degree requirements:* For master's, thesis (for some programs). *Entrance requirements:* For master's, GRE General Test, minimum GPA of 3.0 (for MS in health sciences, nutrition and dietetics), 3.2 (for MS in occupational therapy), 3.0 cumulative and prerequisite math/science (for MPAS); for doctorate, GRE, minimum cumulative and prerequisite math/science GPA of 3.2. Additional exam requirements/ recommendations for international students: Required—TOEFL (minimum score 550 paper-based; 79 iBT), IELTS (minimum score 6.5), PTE (minimum score 54). Electronic applications accepted. *Expenses:* Contact institution. *Faculty research:* Function and mobility across the lifespan, pediatric nutrition, driving and mobility rehabilitation, neurorehabilitation and biomechanics, rehabilitation and integrative therapy.

Inter American University of Puerto Rico, Metropolitan Campus, Graduate Programs, Program in Physical Education, San Juan, PR 00919-1293. Offers teaching of physical education (MA); training and sport performance (MA). *Degree requirements:* For master's, comprehensive exam. *Entrance requirements:* For master's, GRE or EXADEP, interview. Electronic applications accepted.

Inter American University of Puerto Rico, San Germán Campus, Graduate Studies Center, Program in Health and Physical Education, San Germán, PR 00683-5008. Offers MA. *Program availability:* Part-time, evening/weekend. *Degree requirements:* For master's, comprehensive exam. *Entrance requirements:* For master's, GRE General Test or EXADEP, minimum GPA of 3.0.

Ithaca College, School of Health Sciences and Human Performance, Program in Health Education, Ithaca, NY 14850. Offers MS. *Program availability:* Part-time. *Faculty:* 3 full-time (2 women). *Students:* 4 full-time (3 women), 1 (woman) part-time; includes 2 minority (both Black or African American, non-Hispanic/Latino). Average age 24. 8 applicants, 88% accepted, 4 enrolled. In 2017, 6 master's awarded. *Degree requirements:* For master's, thesis optional. *Entrance requirements:* Additional exam requirements/recommendations for international students: Required—TOEFL (minimum score 550 paper-based; 80 iBT). *Application deadline:* For fall admission, 3/1 for domestic and international students; for spring admission, 12/1 for domestic and international students. Applications are processed on a rolling basis. Application fee: $40. Electronic applications accepted. *Expenses:* Contact institution. *Financial support:* In 2017–18, 5 students received support, including 4 research assistantships (averaging $10,517 per year); career-related internships or fieldwork, Federal Work-Study, scholarships/grants, and unspecified assistantships also available. Support available to part-time students. Financial award application deadline: 3/1; financial award applicants required to submit FAFSA. *Unit head:* Dr. Stewart Auyash, Chair, 607-274-1312, E-mail: auyash@ithaca.edu. *Application contact:* Nicole Eversley Bradwell, Director, Office of Admission, 607-274-3124, Fax: 607-274-1263, E-mail: admission@ithaca.edu. Website: http://www.ithaca.edu/gradprograms/hppe/programs/healthed

Jackson State University, Graduate School, College of Education and Human Development, Department of Health, Physical Education and Recreation, Jackson, MS 39217. Offers physical education (MS Ed); sport science (MS). *Accreditation:* NCATE. *Program availability:* Part-time, evening/weekend, 100% online, blended/hybrid learning. *Degree requirements:* For master's, comprehensive exam, thesis or alternative. *Entrance requirements:* For master's, GRE General Test. Additional exam requirements/recommendations for international students: Required—TOEFL (minimum score 520 paper-based; 67 iBT). Electronic applications accepted. *Expenses:* Contact institution.

James Madison University, The Graduate School, College of Arts and Letters, Program in Communication and Advocacy, Harrisonburg, VA 22801. Offers environmental communication (MA); health communication (MA); strategic communication (MA). *Program availability:* Part-time, evening/weekend. *Students:* 27 full-time (18 women), 4 part-time (all women); includes 11 minority (6 Black or African American, non-Hispanic/Latino; 2 Asian, non-Hispanic/Latino; 1 Hispanic/Latino; 2 Two or more races, non-Hispanic/Latino), 2 international. Average age 30. In 2017, 7 master's awarded. Application fee: $55. Electronic applications accepted. *Expenses:* Tuition, state resident: full-time $10,512; part-time $438 per credit hour. Tuition, nonresident: full-time $28,358; part-time $1162 per credit hour. *Required fees:* $1128. *Financial support:* In 2017–18, 21 students received support, including 14 fellowships, 7 teaching assistantships with full tuition reimbursements available (averaging $9,284 per year); Federal Work-Study and assistantships (averaging $7911) also available. Financial award application deadline: 3/1; financial award applicants required to submit FAFSA. *Unit head:* Dr. Eric M. Fife, Director of the School of Communication Studies, 540-568-6449, E-mail: fifeem@jmu.edu. *Application contact:* Lynette D. Michael, Director of Graduate Admissions, 540-568-6131 Ext. 6395, Fax: 540-568-7860, E-mail: michaeld@jmu.edu.
Website: http://www.jmu.edu/commstudies/

James Madison University, The Graduate School, College of Health and Behavioral Studies, Program in Kinesiology, Harrisonburg, VA 22801. Offers clinical exercise physiology (MS); exercise physiology (MS); kinesiology (MAT, MS); nutrition and exercise (MS); physical and health education (MAT); sport and recreation leadership (MS). *Program availability:* Part-time, evening/weekend. *Students:* 43 full-time (22 women), 3 part-time (2 women); includes 10 minority (4 Black or African American, non-Hispanic/Latino; 1 Asian, non-Hispanic/Latino; 4 Hispanic/Latino; 1 Two or more races, non-Hispanic/Latino). Average age 30. In 2017, 46 master's awarded. Application fee: $55. Electronic applications accepted. *Expenses:* Tuition, state resident: full-time $10,512; part-time $438 per credit hour. Tuition, nonresident: full-time $28,358; part-time $1162 per credit hour. *Required fees:* $1128. *Financial support:* In 2017–18, 32 students received support, including 13 teaching assistantships with full tuition reimbursements available (averaging $8,837 per year); Federal Work-Study and 19 assistantships (averaging $7911), 20 athletic assistantships (averaging $9284) also available. Financial award application deadline: 3/1; financial award applicants required to submit FAFSA. *Unit head:* Dr. Christopher J. Womack, Department Head, 540-568-6145, E-mail: womackcx@jmu.edu. *Application contact:* Lynette D. Michael, Director of Graduate Admissions, 540-568-6131 Ext. 6395, Fax: 540-568-7860, E-mail: michaeld@jmu.edu.
Website: http://www.jmu.edu/kinesiology/

John F. Kennedy University, Graduate School of Holistic Studies, Department of Integral Studies, Program in Holistic Health Education, Pleasant Hill, CA 94523-4817. Offers MA. *Program availability:* Part-time, evening/weekend. *Degree requirements:* For master's, thesis or alternative. *Entrance requirements:* For master's, interview. Additional exam requirements/recommendations for international students: Required—TOEFL.

Johns Hopkins University, Bloomberg School of Public Health, Department of Health, Behavior and Society, Baltimore, MD 21218. Offers genetic counseling (Sc M); health education and health communication (MSPH); social and behavioral sciences (PhD); social factors in health (MHS). *Students:* 86 full-time (76 women), 5 part-time (4 women); includes 33 minority (8 Black or African American, non-Hispanic/Latino; 13 Asian, non-Hispanic/Latino; 7 Hispanic/Latino; 5 Two or more races, non-Hispanic/Latino), 13 international. Average age 28. 312 applicants, 29% accepted, 28 enrolled. In 2017, 27 master's, 10 doctorates awarded. *Degree requirements:* For master's, comprehensive exam (for some programs), thesis (for some programs); for doctorate, comprehensive exam, thesis/dissertation. *Entrance requirements:* For master's, GRE, curriculum vitae, 3 letters of recommendation; for doctorate, GRE, transcripts, curriculum vitae, 3 recommendation letters. Additional exam requirements/recommendations for international students: Required—TOEFL (minimum score 100 iBT), IELTS (minimum score 7). *Application deadline:* Applications are processed on a rolling basis. Application fee: $135. Electronic applications accepted. *Financial support:* Fellowships with tuition reimbursements, research assistantships, teaching assistantships, career-related internships or fieldwork, Federal Work-Study, scholarships/grants, traineeships, health care benefits, unspecified assistantships, and stipends available. *Faculty research:* Social determinants of health and structural and community-level inventions to improve health, communication and health education, behavioral and social aspects of genetic counseling. *Unit head:* Margaret Ensminger, Interim Chair, 410-502-4076, Fax: 410-502-4080. *Application contact:* Shenay Johnson, Academic Program Administrator, 410-502-4415, E-mail: shejohns@jhu.edu.
Website: http://jhsph.edu/dept/hbs

Johns Hopkins University, School of Education, Master's Programs in Education, Baltimore, MD 21218. Offers counseling (MS), including clinical mental health counseling, school counseling; education (MS), including educational studies, gifted education, reading, school administration and supervision, technology for educators; elementary education (MAT); health professions (M Ed); intelligence analysis (MS); organizational leadership (MS); secondary education (MAT), including biology, chemistry, earth/space science, English, physics, social studies; special education (MS), including early childhood special education, general special education studies, mild to moderate disabilities, severe disabilities. *Program availability:* Part-time, evening/weekend, 100% online, blended/hybrid learning. *Degree requirements:* For master's, comprehensive exam (for some programs), portfolio, capstone project and/or internship; PRAXIS II (subject area assessments) for initial teacher preparation programs that lead to licensure. *Entrance requirements:* For master's, GRE (for full-time programs only); PRAXIS I/core or state-approved alternative (for initial teacher preparation programs that lead to licensure), minimum of bachelor's degree from regionally- or nationally-accredited institution; minimum GPA of 3.0 in all previous programs of study; official

transcripts from all post-secondary institutions attended; essay; curriculum vitae/resume; letters of recommendation (3 for full-time programs, 2 for part-time programs); dispositions survey. Additional exam requirements/recommendations for international students: Required—TOEFL (minimum score 600 paper-based; 100 iBT), IELTS (minimum score 7). Electronic applications accepted. *Expenses:* Contact institution.

Kansas State University, Graduate School, College of Human Ecology, Department of Food, Nutrition, Dietetics and Health, Manhattan, KS 66506. Offers dietetics (MS); human nutrition (PhD); nutrition, dietetics and sensory sciences (MS); nutritional sciences (PhD); public health nutrition (PhD); public health physical activity (PhD); sensory analysis and consumer behavior (PhD). *Program availability:* Part-time. *Degree requirements:* For master's, thesis or alternative, residency; for doctorate, thesis/dissertation, residency. *Entrance requirements:* For master's, GRE General Test, minimum undergraduate GPA of 3.0; for doctorate, GRE General Test, minimum graduate GPA of 3.0. Additional exam requirements/recommendations for international students: Required—TOEFL (minimum score 550 paper-based; 79 iBT), IELTS (minimum score 6.5). Electronic applications accepted. *Faculty research:* Cancer and immunology, obesity, sensory analysis and consumer behavior, nutrient metabolism, clinical and community interventions.

Keiser University, Master of Science in Education Program, Fort Lauderdale, FL 33309. Offers allied health teaching and leadership (MS Ed); career college administration (MS Ed); leadership (MS Ed); online teaching and learning (MS Ed); teaching and learning (MS Ed). *Program availability:* Part-time, online learning. *Unit head:* Brian Keintz, Chair of Graduate Programs.
Website: http://www.keiseruniversity.edu/graduateschool/

Kent State University, College of Education, Health and Human Services, School of Health Sciences, Program in Health Education and Promotion, Kent, OH 44242-0001. Offers M Ed, PhD. *Accreditation:* NCATE. *Degree requirements:* For doctorate, comprehensive exam, thesis/dissertation. *Entrance requirements:* For master's, 2 letters of reference, goals statement; for doctorate, GRE General Test, goals statement, resume, interview. Additional exam requirements/recommendations for international students: Required—TOEFL (minimum score 550 paper-based; 80 iBT). Electronic applications accepted. *Expenses:* Tuition, state resident: full-time $11,310; part-time $515 per credit hour. Tuition, nonresident: full-time $20,396; part-time $928 per credit hour. *International tuition:* $18,544 full-time. *Faculty research:* Substance use/abuse, sexuality, community health assessment, epidemiology, HIV/AIDS.

Lake Erie College of Osteopathic Medicine, Professional Programs, Erie, PA 16509-1025. Offers biomedical sciences (Postbaccalaureate Certificate); medical education (MS); osteopathic medicine (DO); pharmacy (Pharm D). *Accreditation:* ACPE; AOsA. *Degree requirements:* For doctorate, comprehensive exam, National Osteopathic Medical Licensing Exam, Levels 1 and 2; for Postbaccalaureate Certificate, comprehensive exam, North American Pharmacist Licensure Examination (NAPLEX). *Entrance requirements:* For doctorate, MCAT, minimum GPA of 3.2, letters of recommendation; for Postbaccalaureate Certificate, PCAT, letters of recommendation, minimum GPA of 3.5. Electronic applications accepted. *Faculty research:* Cardiac smooth and skeletal muscle mechanics, chemotherapeutics and vitamins, osteopathic manipulation.

Lehman College of the City University of New York, School of Health Sciences, Human Services and Nursing, Department of Health Sciences, Program in Health Education and Promotion, Bronx, NY 10468-1589. Offers MA. *Accreditation:* NCATE. *Program availability:* Part-time, evening/weekend. *Degree requirements:* For master's, thesis or alternative. *Entrance requirements:* For master's, minimum GPA of 2.7.

Lehman College of the City University of New York, School of Health Sciences, Human Services and Nursing, Department of Health Sciences, Program in Health N–12 Teacher, Bronx, NY 10468-1589. Offers MS Ed. *Accreditation:* NCATE. *Degree requirements:* For master's, thesis or alternative.

Lock Haven University of Pennsylvania, College of Natural, Behavioral and Health Sciences, Lock Haven, PA 17745-2390. Offers actuarial science (PSM); athletic training (MS); health promotion/education (MHS); healthcare management (MHS); physician assistant (MHS). Program also offered at the Clearfield, Coudersport, and Harrisburg campuses. *Accreditation:* ARC-PA. *Entrance requirements:* For master's, minimum undergraduate GPA of 3.0. Additional exam requirements/recommendations for international students: Required—TOEFL. Electronic applications accepted.

Logan University, College of Health Sciences, Chesterfield, MO 63017. Offers health informatics (MS); health professionals education (DHPE); nutrition and human performance (MS); sports science and rehabilitation (MS). *Program availability:* Part-time, online only, 100% online. *Faculty:* 4 full-time (1 woman), 25 part-time/adjunct (13 women). *Students:* 84 full-time (63 women), 417 part-time (314 women); includes 75 minority (36 Black or African American, non-Hispanic/Latino; 3 American Indian or Alaska Native, non-Hispanic/Latino; 15 Asian, non-Hispanic/Latino; 17 Hispanic/Latino; 4 Two or more races, non-Hispanic/Latino), 1 international. Average age 36. 238 applicants, 72% accepted, 134 enrolled. In 2017, 61 master's awarded. *Entrance requirements:* For master's, minimum GPA of 2.5; 6 hours of biology and physical science; bachelor's degree and 9 hours of business health administration (for health informatics). Additional exam requirements/recommendations for international students: Required—TOEFL (minimum score 500 paper-based; 79 iBT); Recommended—IELTS (minimum score 6.5). *Application deadline:* Applications are processed on a rolling basis. Application fee: $50. Electronic applications accepted. *Expenses:* $450 per credit hour (for MS), $650 per credit hour (for DHPE), $80 fee per trimester. *Financial support:* In 2017–18, 4 students received support. Federal Work-Study available. Support available to part-time students. Financial award applicants required to submit FAFSA. *Faculty research:* Ankle injury prevention in high school athletes, low back pain in college football players, short arc banding and low back pain, the effects of enzymes on inflammatory blood markers, gait analysis in high school and college athletes. *Unit head:* Dr. Sherri Cole, Dean, College of Health Sciences, 636-227-2100 Ext. 2702, Fax: 636-207-2418, E-mail: sherri.cole@logan.edu. *Application contact:* Natacha Douglas, Executive Director of Admissions, 636-227-2100 Ext. 1718, Fax: 636-207-2425, E-mail: admissions@logan.edu.

Loma Linda University, School of Public Health, Programs in Health Education, Loma Linda, CA 92350. Offers MPH, Dr PH. *Accreditation:* CEPH (one or more programs are accredited). *Degree requirements:* For doctorate, thesis/dissertation. *Entrance requirements:* For doctorate, GRE General Test. Additional exam requirements/recommendations for international students: Required—Michigan English Language Assessment Battery or TOEFL. *Expenses:* Contact institution.

Longwood University, College of Graduate and Professional Studies, College of Education and Human Services, Farmville, VA 23909. Offers education (MS), including algebra and middle school mathematics, counselor education, elementary and middle school mathematics, elementary education, elementary education initial licensure, health and physical education, special education general curriculum, special education initial licensure; reading, literacy and learning (M Ed); school librarianship (M Ed); social work and communication sciences and disorders (MS), including communication sciences and disorders. *Accreditation:* NCATE. *Program availability:* Part-time, evening/weekend. *Degree requirements:* For master's, comprehensive exam (for some programs), thesis optional, professional portfolio, internship, clinical experience, or practicum. *Entrance requirements:* For master's, PRAXIS I (for initial teaching licensure programs); GRE (for some programs), bachelor's degree from regionally-accredited institution, 2 recommendations (3 for some programs), minimum 500-word personal essay, official transcripts, minimum GPA of 2.75, valid teaching license (for some programs). Additional exam requirements/recommendations for international students: Required—TOEFL (minimum score 570 paper-based), IELTS (minimum score 6.5). Electronic applications accepted. *Expenses:* Contact institution.

Marshall University, Academic Affairs Division, College of Information Technology and Engineering, Division of Applied Science and Technology, Program in Safety, Huntington, WV 25755. Offers MS. *Accreditation:* NCATE. *Students:* 8 full-time (1 woman), 28 part-time (7 women); includes 2 minority (1 Black or African American, non-Hispanic/Latino; 1 Hispanic/Latino). Average age 36. In 2017, 11 master's awarded. *Degree requirements:* For master's, thesis optional, comprehensive assessment. Application fee: $40. *Unit head:* Dr. Anthony Szwilski, Division Chair, 304-696-5457, E-mail: szwilski@marshall.edu. *Application contact:* Information Contact, 304-746-1900, Fax: 304-746-1902, E-mail: services@marshall.edu.
Website: http://muwww-new.marshall.edu/cite/dast/safety-technology-graduate-degree-program/

Marymount University, Malek School of Health Professions, Program in Health Education and Promotion, Arlington, VA 22207-4299. Offers MS. *Program availability:* Part-time, evening/weekend. *Faculty:* 4 full-time (3 women). *Students:* 10 full-time (5 women), 5 part-time (all women); includes 3 minority (1 Black or African American, non-Hispanic/Latino; 2 Asian, non-Hispanic/Latino), 3 international. Average age 29. 15 applicants, 100% accepted, 10 enrolled. In 2017, 4 master's awarded. *Degree requirements:* For master's, internship. *Entrance requirements:* For master's, GRE, MAT, minimum cumulative GPA of 3.0, or significant related experience, 2 letters of recommendation, interview, resume, personal statement. Additional exam requirements/recommendations for international students: Required—TOEFL (minimum score 600 paper-based; 96 iBT), IELTS (minimum score 6.5). *Application deadline:* Applications are processed on a rolling basis. Application fee: $40. Electronic applications accepted. *Expenses: Tuition:* Full-time $17,550; part-time $975 per credit hour. *Required fees:* $198; $11 per credit hour. One-time fee: $250. Tuition and fees vary according to program. *Financial support:* In 2017–18, 5 students received support, including 3 teaching assistantships with full and partial tuition reimbursements available (averaging $11,700 per year); research assistantships with full and partial tuition reimbursements available, career-related internships or fieldwork, Federal Work-Study, scholarships/grants, and unspecified assistantships also available. Support available to part-time students. Financial award application deadline: 3/1; financial award applicants required to submit FAFSA. *Unit head:* Dr. Jennifer Tripken, Chair, Health and Human Performance, 703-526-1597, Fax: 703-284-3819, E-mail: jennifer.tripken@marymount.edu. *Application contact:* Francesca Reed, Director, Graduate Admissions, 703-284-5901, Fax: 703-527-3815, E-mail: grad.admissions@marymount.edu.
Website: http://www.marymount.edu/Academics/Malek-School-of-Health-Professions/Graduate-Programs/Health-Education-Promotion-(M-S)

Marywood University, Academic Affairs, Center for Interdisciplinary Studies, Scranton, PA 18509-1598. Offers human development (PhD), including educational administration, health promotion, higher education administration, instructional leadership, social work. *Program availability:* Part-time. Electronic applications accepted. *Expenses:* Contact institution.

Massachusetts College of Liberal Arts, Graduate Programs, North Adams, MA 01247-4100. Offers business (MBA); educational administration (M Ed); educational leadership (CAGS); instruction and curriculum (M Ed); instructional technology (M Ed); physical education and health (M Ed); reading (M Ed); special education (M Ed). *Program availability:* Part-time, evening/weekend. *Degree requirements:* For master's, thesis. *Entrance requirements:* For master's, writing sample.

McNeese State University, Doré School of Graduate Studies, Burton College of Education, Department of Education Professions, Program in Multiple Levels Grades K-12, Lake Charles, LA 70609. Offers multiple levels grades K-12 (Postbaccalaureate Certificate), including art, health and physical education, music - instrumental, music - vocal. *Entrance requirements:* For degree, PRAXIS, 2 letters of recommendation, autobiography. *Application deadline:* For fall admission, 5/15 priority date for domestic and international students; for spring admission, 10/15 priority date for domestic and international students. Applications are processed on a rolling basis. Application fee: $20 ($30 for international students). *Financial support:* Application deadline: 5/1. *Unit head:* Dr. Veronica Faye White, Head, 337-475-5400, Fax: 337-475-5272, E-mail: vfwhite@mcneese.edu. *Application contact:* Dr. Dustin M. Hebert, Director of Doré' School of Graduate Studies, 337-475-5396, Fax: 337-475-5397, E-mail: admissions@mcneese.edu.

Meredith College, School of Education, Health and Human Sciences, Raleigh, NC 27607-5298. Offers academically and intellectually gifted (M Ed); elementary education (M Ed, MAT); English as a second language (M Ed, MAT); health and physical education (MAT); nutrition, health and human performance (MS, Postbaccalaureate Certificate), including dietetic internship (Postbaccalaureate Certificate), nutrition (MS); psychology (MA), including industrial/organizational psychology; reading (M Ed); special education (MAT); special education (general curriculum) (M Ed). *Accreditation:* NCATE. *Program availability:* Part-time, evening/weekend. *Students:* 25 full-time (24 women), 22 part-time (all women); includes 13 minority (8 Black or African American, non-Hispanic/Latino; 1 American Indian or Alaska Native, non-Hispanic/Latino; 1 Asian, non-Hispanic/Latino; 3 Hispanic/Latino). Average age 31. 57 applicants, 54% accepted, 31 enrolled. In 2017, 14 master's awarded. *Degree requirements:* For master's, thesis optional. *Entrance requirements:* For master's, GRE General Test or MAT, minimum GPA of 2.5, teaching license, recommendations. Additional exam requirements/recommendations for international students: Required—TOEFL. *Application deadline:* For fall admission, 7/1 priority date for domestic students; for spring admission, 11/1 priority date for domestic students. Applications are processed on a rolling basis. Application fee: $50. Electronic applications accepted. *Expenses:* Contact institution. *Financial support:* Career-related internships or fieldwork, institutionally sponsored loans, and tuition waivers (partial) available. Support available to part-time students. Financial award application deadline: 2/15; financial award applicants required to submit FAFSA. *Unit head:* Dr. Monica McKinney, Graduate Program Manager, 919-760-8056, Fax: 919-760-2303, E-mail: mckinneym@meredith.edu.
Website: https://www.meredith.edu/school-of-education-health-and-human-sciences

Merrimack College, School of Health Sciences, North Andover, MA 01845-5800. Offers athletic training (MS); community health education (MS); exercise and sport science (MS); health and wellness management (MS). *Program availability:* Part-time, evening/weekend. *Faculty:* 8 full-time, 6 part-time/adjunct. *Students:* 87 full-time (58 women), 4 part-time (all women); includes 10 minority (2 Black or African American, non-Hispanic/Latino; 7 Hispanic/Latino; 1 Two or more races, non-Hispanic/Latino), 3 international. Average age 25. 147 applicants, 90% accepted, 83 enrolled. In 2017, 47 master's awarded. *Degree requirements:* For master's, capstone (for community health education, exercise and sport science, and health and wellness management). *Entrance requirements:* For master's, resume, official college transcripts, personal statement, 2

recommendations. Additional exam requirements/recommendations for international students: Required—TOEFL (minimum score 84 iBT), IELTS (minimum score 6.5), PTE (minimum score 56). *Application deadline:* For fall admission, 8/24 for domestic students, 7/30 for international students; for summer admission, 5/10 for domestic students, 4/10 for international students. Applications are processed on a rolling basis. Electronic applications accepted. *Expenses:* $865 per credit hour tuition; $670 per credit hour (for MAT); comprehensive fees are $165 per semester for 1-8 credit hours and $320 per semester for 9+ credit hours. *Financial support:* Fellowships with partial tuition reimbursements, career-related internships or fieldwork, scholarships/grants, and health care benefits available. Support available to part-time students. Financial award application deadline: 5/1; financial award applicants required to submit FAFSA. *Unit head:* Kyle McInnis, Dean, 978-837-3590, E-mail: mcinnisk@merrimack.edu. *Application contact:* Allison Pena, Office of Graduate Studies, 978-837-3563, E-mail: graduate@merrimack.edu.
Website: http://www.merrimack.edu/academics/health-sciences/

Middle Tennessee State University, College of Graduate Studies, College of Behavioral and Health Sciences, Department of Health and Human Performance, Program in Health, Physical Education and Recreation, Murfreesboro, TN 37132. Offers health and human performance (MS); leisure and sport management (MS). *Program availability:* Part-time, evening/weekend, online learning. *Degree requirements:* For master's, comprehensive exam, thesis optional. *Entrance requirements:* For master's, GRE. Additional exam requirements/recommendations for international students: Required—TOEFL (minimum score 525 paper-based; 71 iBT) or IELTS (minimum score 6). *Faculty research:* Kinesiometrics, leisure behavior, health, lifestyles.

Minnesota State University Mankato, College of Graduate Studies and Research, College of Allied Health and Nursing, Department of Health Science, Mankato, MN 56001. Offers community health education (MS); public health education (Postbaccalaureate Certificate); school health education (MS, Postbaccalaureate Certificate). *Program availability:* Part-time. *Degree requirements:* For master's, comprehensive exam, thesis or alternative. *Entrance requirements:* For master's, minimum GPA of 3.0 during previous 2 years; for Postbaccalaureate Certificate, teaching license. Additional exam requirements/recommendations for international students: Required—TOEFL (minimum score 500 paper-based; 61 iBT). Electronic applications accepted.

Mississippi University for Women, Graduate School, College of Nursing and Health Sciences, Columbus, MS 39701-9998. Offers nursing (MSN, DNP, PMC); public health education (MPH); speech-language pathology (MS). *Accreditation:* AACN; ASHA. *Program availability:* Part-time. *Degree requirements:* For master's, comprehensive exam, thesis. *Entrance requirements:* For master's, GRE General Test, bachelor's degree in nursing, previous course work in statistics, proficiency in English.

Montana State University, The Graduate School, College of Education, Health, and Human Development, Department of Health and Human Development, Bozeman, MT 59717. Offers family and consumer sciences (MS). *Accreditation:* ACA. *Program availability:* Part-time, online learning. *Degree requirements:* For master's, comprehensive exam. *Entrance requirements:* For master's, GRE (minimum scores: verbal 480; quantitative 480). Additional exam requirements/recommendations for international students: Required—TOEFL (minimum score 550 paper-based). Electronic applications accepted. *Faculty research:* Community food systems, ethic of care for teachers and coaches, influence of public policy on families and communities, cost effectiveness of early childhood education, exercise metabolism, winter sport performance enhancement, assessment of physical activity.

Montclair State University, The Graduate School, College of Education and Human Services, MAT Program in Teaching, Montclair, NJ 07043-1624. Offers art (MAT); biology (MAT); chemistry (MAT); earth science (MAT); English (MAT); French (MAT); health and physical education (MAT); health education (MAT); mathematics (MAT); music (MAT); physical education (MAT); physical science (MAT); social studies (MAT); Spanish (MAT); teacher of English as a second language (MAT). *Degree requirements:* For master's, comprehensive exam, thesis or alternative. *Entrance requirements:* For master's, interview, 2 letters of recommendation. Additional exam requirements/recommendations for international students: Required—TOEFL (minimum score 83 iBT), IELTS (minimum score 6.5). Electronic applications accepted.

Morehead State University, Graduate Programs, College of Education, Department of Middle Grades and Secondary Education, Morehead, KY 40351. Offers business and marketing education (MAT); English/language arts 5-9 (MAT); French (MAT); health P-12 (MAT); mathematics 5-9 (MAT); physical education P-12 (MAT); science 5-9 (MAT); secondary biology (MAT); secondary chemistry (MAT); secondary earth science (MAT); secondary English (MAT); secondary math (MAT); secondary physics (MAT); secondary social studies (MAT); social studies 5-9 (MAT); Spanish (MAT). *Program availability:* Part-time, evening/weekend. *Degree requirements:* For master's, portfolio. *Entrance requirements:* For master's, GRE or PRAXIS II content exam, minimum overall undergraduate GPA of 2.5. Additional exam requirements/recommendations for international students: Required—TOEFL (minimum score 500 paper-based). Electronic applications accepted.

Morehead State University, Graduate Programs, College of Science and Technology, Department of Health, Wellness and Human Performance, Morehead, KY 40351. Offers health/physical education (MA). *Accreditation:* NCATE. *Program availability:* Part-time, evening/weekend. *Degree requirements:* For master's, comprehensive exam, thesis, oral exam, written core exam. *Entrance requirements:* For master's, GRE General Test or MAT, minimum GPA of 2.5; undergraduate major/minor in health, physical education, or recreation. Additional exam requirements/recommendations for international students: Required—TOEFL (minimum score 500 paper-based). Electronic applications accepted. *Faculty research:* Child growth and performance, instructional strategies, outdoor leadership qualities, exercise science, athletic training.

New Jersey City University, College of Professional Studies, Department of Health Sciences, Jersey City, NJ 07305-1597. Offers community health education (MS); health administration (MS); school health education (MS). *Program availability:* Part-time, evening/weekend. *Degree requirements:* For master's, thesis or alternative, internship. *Entrance requirements:* Additional exam requirements/recommendations for international students: Required—TOEFL (minimum score 79 iBT).

New Mexico Highlands University, Graduate Studies, College of Arts and Sciences, Department of Exercise and Sport Sciences, Las Vegas, NM 87701. Offers human performance and sport (MA), including human performance and sport sciences, sports administration, teacher education. *Program availability:* Part-time. *Degree requirements:* For master's, comprehensive exam, thesis or alternative. *Entrance requirements:* For master's, minimum undergraduate GPA of 3.0. Additional exam requirements/recommendations for international students: Required—TOEFL (minimum score 540 paper-based). *Faculty research:* Child obesity and physical inactivity, body composition and fitness assessment, motor development, sport marketing, sport finance.

New York Medical College, School of Health Sciences and Practice, Valhalla, NY 10595. Offers behavioral sciences and health promotion (MPH); biostatistics (MS); children with special health care (Graduate Certificate); emergency preparedness (Graduate Certificate); environmental health science (MPH); epidemiology (MPH, MS);

global health (Graduate Certificate); health education (Graduate Certificate); health policy and management (MPH, Dr PH); industrial hygiene (Graduate Certificate); pediatric dysphagia (Post-Graduate Certificate); physical therapy (DPT); public health (Graduate Certificate); speech-language pathology (MS). *Accreditation:* CEPH. *Program availability:* Part-time, evening/weekend, 100% online, blended/hybrid learning. *Faculty:* 48 full-time (33 women), 235 part-time/adjunct (141 women). *Students:* 221 full-time (153 women), 270 part-time (194 women); includes 202 minority (83 Black or African American, non-Hispanic/Latino; 2 American Indian or Alaska Native, non-Hispanic/Latino; 64 Asian, non-Hispanic/Latino; 47 Hispanic/Latino; 1 Native Hawaiian or other Pacific Islander, non-Hispanic/Latino; 5 Two or more races, non-Hispanic/Latino), 19 international. Average age 29. 1,118 applicants, 38% accepted, 169 enrolled. In 2017, 110 master's, 41 doctorates awarded. *Degree requirements:* For master's, comprehensive exam (for some programs), thesis (for some programs); for doctorate, thesis/dissertation. *Entrance requirements:* For master's, GRE (for MS in speech-language pathology); for doctorate, GRE. Additional exam requirements/recommendations for international students: Required—TOEFL, IELTS. *Application deadline:* For fall admission, 8/1 for domestic students, 4/15 for international students; for spring admission, 12/1 for domestic students; for summer admission, 5/1 for domestic students, 4/15 for international students. Application fee: $125. Electronic applications accepted. *Expenses:* $1,125 per credit, $245 fees. *Financial support:* In 2017–18, 10,000 students received support. Scholarships/grants and unspecified assistantships available. Financial award application deadline: 4/30; financial award applicants required to submit FAFSA. *Unit head:* Ben Watson, PhD, Vice Dean, 914-594-4531, E-mail: ben_watson@nymc.edu. *Application contact:* Irene Bundziak, Assistant to Director of Admissions, 914-594-4905, E-mail: irene_bundziak@nymc.edu. Website: http://www.nymc.edu/school-of-health-sciences-and-practice-shsp/

Nicholls State University, Graduate Studies, College of Education, Department of Teacher Education, Thibodaux, LA 70310. Offers curriculum and instruction (M Ed); educational leadership (M Ed); elementary education (MAT); human performance education (MAT); middle school education (MAT); secondary education (MAT). *Accreditation:* NCATE. *Program availability:* Part-time, evening/weekend, online learning. *Degree requirements:* For master's, comprehensive exam, portfolio. *Entrance requirements:* For master's, GRE General Test, teaching license. Electronic applications accepted.

North Carolina Agricultural and Technical State University, School of Graduate Studies, School of Education, Department of Human Performance and Leisure Studies, Greensboro, NC 27411. Offers physical education (MAT, MS). *Accreditation:* NCATE. *Program availability:* Part-time, evening/weekend. *Degree requirements:* For master's, comprehensive exam, thesis or alternative, qualifying exam. *Entrance requirements:* For master's, GRE General Test or MAT.

Northeastern State University, College of Education, Department of Health and Kinesiology, Tahlequah, OK 74464-2399. Offers MS. *Program availability:* Part-time, evening/weekend. *Faculty:* 3 full-time (1 woman). *Students:* 13 full-time (5 women), 25 part-time (16 women); includes 17 minority (2 Black or African American, non-Hispanic/Latino; 7 American Indian or Alaska Native, non-Hispanic/Latino; 2 Hispanic/Latino; 6 Two or more races, non-Hispanic/Latino), 3 international. Average age 26. In 2017, 10 master's awarded. *Entrance requirements:* For master's, MAT or GRE, minimum GPA of 2.5. Additional exam requirements/recommendations for international students: Required—TOEFL. *Application deadline:* For fall admission, 6/1 for domestic and international students; for winter admission, 11/1 for domestic and international students; for spring admission, 3/1 for domestic students, 2/1 for international students. Applications are processed on a rolling basis. Application fee: $25. Electronic applications accepted. *Expenses:* Tuition, state resident: part-time $222 per credit hour. Tuition, nonresident: part-time $501.75 per credit hour. *Required fees:* $37.40 per credit hour. Tuition and fees vary according to degree level. *Unit head:* Dee Gerlach, Department Chair, 918-444-3929, E-mail: gerlach@nsuok.edu. *Application contact:* Josh McCollum, Graduate Coordinator, 918-444-2093, E-mail: mccolluj@nsuok.edu. Website: http://academics.nsuok.edu/education/DegreePrograms/GraduatePrograms/HealthandKinesiology.aspx

Northwestern State University of Louisiana, Graduate Studies and Research, Department of Health and Human Performance, Natchitoches, LA 71497. Offers MS. *Degree requirements:* For master's, comprehensive exam, thesis or alternative. *Entrance requirements:* For master's, GRE General Test, minimum undergraduate GPA of 2.5. Additional exam requirements/recommendations for international students: Required—TOEFL. Electronic applications accepted.

Northwest Missouri State University, Graduate School, School of Health Science and Wellness, Maryville, MO 64468-6001. Offers applied health and sport sciences (MS); guidance and counseling (MS Ed); health and physical education (MS Ed); recreation (MS); sport and exercise psychology (MS). *Accreditation:* NCATE. *Program availability:* Part-time. *Faculty:* 23 full-time (11 women). *Students:* 68 full-time (43 women), 41 part-time (29 women); includes 9 minority (3 Black or African American, non-Hispanic/Latino; 4 Hispanic/Latino; 2 Two or more races, non-Hispanic/Latino), 5 international. Average age 27. 49 applicants, 47% accepted, 16 enrolled. In 2017, 34 master's awarded. *Degree requirements:* For master's, comprehensive exam. *Entrance requirements:* For master's, GRE General Test, minimum undergraduate GPA of 2.75, teaching certificate, writing sample. Additional exam requirements/recommendations for international students: Required—TOEFL (minimum score 550 paper-based). *Application deadline:* For fall admission, 7/1 for domestic and international students; for spring admission, 11/15 for domestic and international students. Applications are processed on a rolling basis. Application fee: $0 ($50 for international students). *Expenses:* Tuition, state resident: full-time $4551; part-time $252.86 per credit hour. Tuition, nonresident: full-time $9103; part-time $505.72 per credit hour. *Required fees:* $2453; $136.25 per credit hour. Tuition and fees vary according to course load and program. *Financial support:* Teaching assistantships with full tuition reimbursements and unspecified assistantships available. Financial award application deadline: 4/1; financial award applicants required to submit FAFSA. *Unit head:* Dr. Terry Long, Director, School of Health Science and Wellness, 660-562-1706, Fax: 660-562-1483, E-mail: tlong@nwmissouri.edu. *Application contact:* Gina Smith, Secretary, 660-562-1297, Fax: 660-562-1963, E-mail: smigina@nwmissouri.edu. Website: http://www.nwmissouri.edu/health/

Nova Southeastern University, Dr. Kiran C. Patel College of Osteopathic Medicine, Fort Lauderdale, FL 33328. Offers biomedical informatics (MS, Graduate Certificate), including biomedical informatics (MS); clinical informatics (Graduate Certificate); public health informatics (Graduate Certificate); disaster and emergency management (MS); medical education (MS); nutrition (MS, Graduate Certificate), including functional nutrition and herbal therapy (Graduate Certificate); osteopathic medicine (DO); public health (MPH, Graduate Certificate), including health education (Graduate Certificate); social medicine (Graduate Certificate); DO/DMD. *Accreditation:* AOsA. *Faculty:* 98 full-time (58 women), 1,484 part-time/adjunct (401 women). *Students:* 1,032 full-time (479 women), 197 part-time (129 women); includes 656 minority (97 Black or African American, non-Hispanic/Latino; 308 Asian, non-Hispanic/Latino; 215 Hispanic/Latino; 1 Native Hawaiian or other Pacific Islander, non-Hispanic/Latino; 35 Two or more races, non-Hispanic/Latino), 67 international. Average age 26. 5,226 applicants, 9% accepted,

248 enrolled. In 2017, 110 master's, 239 doctorates, 7 other advanced degrees awarded. *Degree requirements:* For master's, comprehensive exam (for MPH); field/special projects; for doctorate, comprehensive exam, COMLEX Board Exams; for Graduate Certificate, thesis or alternative. *Entrance requirements:* For master's, GRE; for doctorate, MCAT, coursework in biology, chemistry, organic chemistry, physics (all with labs), biochemistry, and English. *Application deadline:* For fall admission, 1/15 for domestic students. Applications are processed on a rolling basis. Application fee: $50. Electronic applications accepted. *Expenses:* Contact institution. *Financial support:* In 2017–18, 83 students received support, including 24 fellowships with tuition reimbursements available; Federal Work-Study and scholarships/grants also available. Financial award application deadline: 6/1; financial award applicants required to submit FAFSA. *Faculty research:* Teaching strategies, simulated patient use, HIV/AIDS education, minority health issues, immune disorders. *Unit head:* Elaine M. Wallace, Dean, 954-262-1457, Fax: 954-262-2250, E-mail: ewallace@nova.edu. *Application contact:* HPD Admissions, 877-640-0218, E-mail: hpdinfo@nova.edu. Website: https://www.osteopathic.nova.edu/

Nova Southeastern University, Halmos College of Natural Sciences and Oceanography, Fort Lauderdale, FL 33314-7796. Offers biological sciences (MS), including health studies; marine biology and oceanography (PhD), including marine biology, oceanography. *Program availability:* Part-time, evening/weekend, blended/hybrid learning. *Faculty:* 17 full-time (3 women), 22 part-time/adjunct (11 women). *Students:* 29 full-time (18 women), 149 part-time (93 women); includes 29 minority (5 Black or African American, non-Hispanic/Latino; 6 Asian, non-Hispanic/Latino; 12 Hispanic/Latino; 6 Two or more races, non-Hispanic/Latino), 5 international. Average age 30. 78 applicants, 73% accepted, 34 enrolled. In 2017, 46 master's, 1 doctorate awarded. *Degree requirements:* For master's, thesis; for doctorate, comprehensive exam, thesis/dissertation, departmental qualifying exam. *Entrance requirements:* For master's, GRE General Test, 3 letters of recommendation; BS/BA in natural science (for marine biology program); BS/BA in biology (for biological sciences program); minor in the natural sciences or equivalent (for coastal zone management and marine environmental sciences); for doctorate, GRE General Test, master's degree. Additional exam requirements/recommendations for international students: Required—TOEFL (minimum score 550 paper-based); Recommended—IELTS. *Application deadline:* Applications are processed on a rolling basis. Application fee: $50. Electronic applications accepted. *Expenses:* Contact institution. *Financial support:* In 2017–18, 101 students received support, including 6 fellowships with full and partial tuition reimbursements available (averaging $25,000 per year), 40 research assistantships with full and partial tuition reimbursements available (averaging $20,000 per year), 8 teaching assistantships with tuition reimbursements available (averaging $15,000 per year); career-related internships or fieldwork, Federal Work-Study, scholarships/grants, health care benefits, tuition waivers (full and partial), and unspecified assistantships also available. Support available to part-time students. Financial award application deadline: 4/15; financial award applicants required to submit FAFSA. *Faculty research:* Physical and biological oceanography, molecular and microbiology, ecology and evolution, coral reefs, marine ecosystems. *Total annual research expenditures:* $5 million. *Unit head:* Dr. Richard Dodge, Dean, 954-262-3600, Fax: 954-262-4020, E-mail: dodge@nsu.nova.edu. *Application contact:* Dr. Bernhard Riegl, Chair, Department of Marine and Environmental Sciences, 954-262-3600, Fax: 954-262-4020, E-mail: rieglb@nova.edu. Website: http://cnso.nova.edu

Oklahoma State University, College of Education, Health and Aviation, School of Applied Health and Educational Psychology, Stillwater, OK 74078. Offers applied behavioral studies (Ed D); applied health and educational psychology (MS, PhD, Ed S). *Accreditation:* APA (one or more programs are accredited). *Program availability:* Part-time. *Faculty:* 31 full-time (20 women), 9 part-time/adjunct (7 women). *Students:* 169 full-time (119 women), 158 part-time (102 women); includes 98 minority (29 Black or African American, non-Hispanic/Latino; 15 American Indian or Alaska Native, non-Hispanic/Latino; 5 Asian, non-Hispanic/Latino; 24 Hispanic/Latino; 25 Two or more races, non-Hispanic/Latino), 22 international. Average age 30. 140 applicants, 56% accepted, 69 enrolled. In 2017, 71 master's, 24 doctorates awarded. *Entrance requirements:* For master's and doctorate, GRE or GMAT. Additional exam requirements/recommendations for international students: Required—TOEFL (minimum score 550 paper-based; 79 iBT). *Application deadline:* For fall admission, 3/1 priority date for international students; for spring admission, 8/1 priority date for international students. Applications are processed on a rolling basis. Application fee: $40 ($75 for international students). Electronic applications accepted. *Expenses:* Tuition, state resident: full-time $4019; part-time $2679.60 per year. Tuition, nonresident: full-time $15,286; part-time $10,190.40 per year. *Required fees:* $2129; $1419 per unit. Tuition and fees vary according to program. *Financial support:* Research assistantships, teaching assistantships, career-related internships or fieldwork, Federal Work-Study, scholarships/grants, health care benefits, tuition waivers (partial), and unspecified assistantships available. Support available to part-time students. Financial award application deadline: 3/1; financial award applicants required to submit FAFSA. *Unit head:* Dr. Aric Warren, Head, 405-744-6040, Fax: 405-744-6779, E-mail: aric.warren@okstate.edu. Website: http://education.okstate.edu/

Old Dominion University, Darden College of Education, Program in Physical Education, Curriculum and Instruction Emphasis, Norfolk, VA 23529. Offers human movement sciences (PhD), including health and sport pedagogy; physical education (MS Ed), including adapted physical education, coaching education, curriculum and instruction. *Program availability:* Part-time, evening/weekend. *Faculty:* 3 full-time (1 woman). *Students:* 2 full-time (1 woman), 5 part-time (1 woman); includes 2 minority (1 Black or African American, non-Hispanic/Latino; 1 Two or more races, non-Hispanic/Latino). Average age 29. 2 applicants, 50% accepted. In 2017, 2 master's awarded. *Degree requirements:* For master's, comprehensive exam (for some programs), thesis or alternative, internship, research project. *Entrance requirements:* For master's, GRE, PRAXIS tests (for licensure only), minimum GPA of 2.8 overall, 3.0 in major. Additional exam requirements/recommendations for international students: Required—TOEFL (minimum score 500 paper-based; 97 iBT). *Application deadline:* For fall admission, 3/1 priority date for domestic students; for spring admission, 11/1 for domestic students. Applications are processed on a rolling basis. Application fee: $50. Electronic applications accepted. *Expenses:* Tuition, state resident: full-time $8928; part-time $496 per credit. Tuition, nonresident: full-time $22,482; part-time $1249 per credit. *Required fees:* $66 per semester. *Financial support:* Unspecified assistantships available. Financial award application deadline: 4/15. *Faculty research:* Motor development, physical activity and fitness, motivation and learning in physical education, curriculum and instruction, adapted physical education. *Total annual research expenditures:* $104,000. *Unit head:* Dr. Lynn Ridinger, Chair, 757-683-4995, E-mail: lridinge@odu.edu. *Application contact:* William Heffelfinger, Director of Graduate Admissions, 757-683-5554, Fax: 757-683-3255, E-mail: gradadmit@odu.edu. Website: https://www.odu.edu/hms/academics/hpe/graduate

Penn State Harrisburg, Graduate School, School of Behavioral Sciences and Education, Middletown, PA 17057. Offers adult education in the health and medical professions (Certificate); applied behavior analysis (MA); applied clinical psychology (MA); applied psychological research (MA); community psychology and social change

(MA); English as a second language (ESL) program specialist and leadership (Certificate); health education (M Ed); lifelong learning and adult education (M Ed, D Ed); literacy education (M Ed); literacy leadership (Certificate); psychology: applications in clinical psychology (Certificate); psychology: health psychology (Certificate); teaching and curriculum (M Ed); training and development (M Ed, Certificate). *Program availability:* Part-time, evening/weekend. *Unit head:* Dr. Mukund S. Kulkarni, Chancellor, 717-948-6105, Fax: 717-948-6452. *Application contact:* Robert W. Coffman, Jr., Director of Enrollment Management, Recruitment and Admissions, 717-948-6250, Fax: 717-948-6325, E-mail: hbgadmit@psu.edu. Website: https://harrisburg.psu.edu/behavioral-sciences-and-education/

Pennsylvania College of Health Sciences, Graduate Programs, Lancaster, PA 17601. Offers administration (MSN); education (MSHS, MSN); healthcare administration (MHA). *Degree requirements:* For master's, internship (for MHA, MSN in administration); practicum (for MSHS, MSN in education).

Pittsburg State University, Graduate School, College of Education, Department of Health, Physical Education and Recreation, Pittsburg, KS 66762. Offers health, human performance, and recreation (MS), including human performance and wellness, sport and leisure service management. *Program availability:* Part-time, online only, 100% online. *Students:* 66 (25 women); includes 17 minority (5 Black or African American, non-Hispanic/Latino; 2 American Indian or Alaska Native, non-Hispanic/Latino; 4 Hispanic/Latino; 6 Two or more races, non-Hispanic/Latino). In 2017, 33 master's awarded. *Degree requirements:* For master's, thesis or alternative. *Entrance requirements:* For master's, letter of intent. Additional exam requirements/recommendations for international students: Required—TOEFL (minimum score 520 paper-based; 68 iBT), IELTS (minimum score 6), PTE (minimum score 47). *Application deadline:* For fall admission, 6/1 for international students; for spring admission, 10/15 for international students; for summer admission, 4/1 for international students. Applications are processed on a rolling basis. Application fee: $35 ($60 for international students). Electronic applications accepted. *Financial support:* In 2017–18, 9 teaching assistantships with full tuition reimbursements (averaging $5,500 per year) were awarded; career-related internships or fieldwork, Federal Work-Study, and unspecified assistantships also available. Financial award application deadline: 2/1; financial award applicants required to submit FAFSA. *Faculty research:* Personality of athletes, fitness activities for children, aerobic conditioning, fitness evaluation. *Unit head:* Dr. John Oppliger, Chairperson, 620-235-4668, E-mail: joppliger@pittstate.edu. *Application contact:* Lisa Allen, Assistant Director of Graduate and Continuing Studies, 620-235-4223, Fax: 620-235-4219, E-mail: lallen@pittstate.edu.

Plymouth State University, College of Graduate Studies, Graduate Studies in Education, Program in Health Education, Plymouth, NH 03264-1595. Offers M Ed. *Program availability:* Part-time, evening/weekend. *Degree requirements:* For master's, PRAXIS. *Entrance requirements:* For master's, MAT, minimum GPA of 3.0.

Prairie View A&M University, College of Education, Department of Health and Kinesiology, Prairie View, TX 77446. Offers M Ed, MS. *Accreditation:* NCATE. *Program availability:* Part-time, evening/weekend. *Faculty:* 4 full-time (all women). *Students:* 26 full-time (18 women), 4 part-time (1 woman); all minorities (27 Black or African American, non-Hispanic/Latino; 1 Hispanic/Latino; 1 Native Hawaiian or other Pacific Islander, non-Hispanic/Latino; 1 Two or more races, non-Hispanic/Latino). Average age 26. 18 applicants, 100% accepted, 14 enrolled. In 2017, 13 master's awarded. *Degree requirements:* For master's, thesis. *Entrance requirements:* For master's, GRE General Test. Additional exam requirements/recommendations for international students: Required—TOEFL (minimum score 550 paper-based; 79 iBT). *Application deadline:* For fall admission, 5/1 priority date for domestic and international students; for spring admission, 10/1 priority date for domestic students, 9/1 priority date for international students; for summer admission, 3/1 priority date for domestic students, 2/1 priority date for international students. Applications are processed on a rolling basis. Application fee: $50. Electronic applications accepted. *Expenses:* Tuition, state resident: part-time $242 per credit. Tuition, nonresident: part-time $695 per credit. *Required fees:* $149 per credit. *Financial support:* Career-related internships or fieldwork available. Support available to part-time students. Financial award application deadline: 4/1; financial award applicants required to submit FAFSA. *Unit head:* Dr. Angela Branch-Vital, Department Head, 936-261-3900, Fax: 936-261-3905, E-mail: abranch-vital@pvamu.edu. *Application contact:* Pauline Walker, Administrative Assistant II, Research and Graduate Studies, 936-261-3521, Fax: 936-261-3529, E-mail: gradadmissions@pvamu.edu.

Purdue University, Graduate School, College of Health and Human Sciences, Department of Health and Kinesiology, West Lafayette, IN 47907. Offers athletic training education administration (MS, PhD); biomechanics (MS, PhD); exercise physiology (MS, PhD); health education (MS, PhD); history/philosophy of sport (MS, PhD); motor control and development (MS, PhD); physical education pedagogy (PhD); physical education teacher education (MS); recreation and sport management (MS, PhD); sport and exercise psychology (MS, PhD). *Program availability:* Part-time. *Faculty:* 19 full-time (7 women). *Students:* 30 full-time (13 women), 10 part-time (5 women); includes 2 minority (1 Asian, non-Hispanic/Latino; 1 Two or more races, non-Hispanic/Latino), 6 international. Average age 26. 77 applicants, 29% accepted, 18 enrolled. In 2017, 18 master's, 9 doctorates awarded. *Degree requirements:* For master's, thesis optional; for doctorate, comprehensive exam, thesis/dissertation, qualifying examination, preliminary examination. *Entrance requirements:* For master's, GRE General Test (minimum score 1000 combined verbal and quantitative), minimum undergraduate GPA of 3.0 or equivalent; for doctorate, GRE General Test (minimum score 1100 combined verbal and quantitative), minimum undergraduate GPA of 3.0 or equivalent; master's degree with minimum GPA of 3.25 (recommended). Additional exam requirements/recommendations for international students: Required—TOEFL (minimum score 77 iBT); Recommended—TWE. *Application deadline:* For fall admission, 4/30 for domestic and international students; for spring admission, 10/15 for domestic and international students. Applications are processed on a rolling basis. Application fee: $60 ($75 for international students). Electronic applications accepted. *Financial support:* Fellowships with partial tuition reimbursements, research assistantships with partial tuition reimbursements, teaching assistantships with partial tuition reimbursements, and Federal Work-Study available. Support available to part-time students. Financial award applicants required to submit FAFSA. *Faculty research:* Wellness, motivation, teaching effectiveness, learning and development. *Unit head:* Dr. Timothy P. Gavin, Head of the Graduate Program, 765-494-3178, Fax: 765-494-1239, E-mail: gavin1@purdue.edu. *Application contact:* David B. Klenosky, Graduate Contact, 765-494-0865, E-mail: klenosky@purdue.edu. Website: http://www.purdue.edu/hhs/hk/

Purdue University, Graduate School, College of Health and Human Sciences, Department of Nutrition Science, West Lafayette, IN 47907. Offers animal health (MS, PhD); biochemical and molecular nutrition (MS, PhD); growth and development (MS, PhD); human and clinical nutrition (MS, PhD); public health and education (MS, PhD). *Faculty:* 21 full-time (15 women), 1 part-time/adjunct (0 women). *Students:* 40 full-time (29 women), 9 part-time (7 women); includes 5 minority (3 Black or African American, non-Hispanic/Latino; 1 Asian, non-Hispanic/Latino; 1 Two or more races, non-Hispanic/

Latino), 20 international. Average age 28. 66 applicants, 33% accepted, 13 enrolled. In 2017, 2 master's, 6 doctorates awarded. *Degree requirements:* For master's, thesis; for doctorate, thesis/dissertation. *Entrance requirements:* For master's and doctorate, GRE General Test (minimum scores in verbal and quantitative areas of 1000 or 300 on new scoring), minimum undergraduate GPA of 3.0 or equivalent. Additional exam requirements/recommendations for international students: Required—TOEFL (minimum score 600 paper-based; 77 iBT). *Application deadline:* For fall admission, 1/10 for domestic and international students. Applications are processed on a rolling basis. Application fee: $60 ($75 for international students). Electronic applications accepted. *Financial support:* Fellowships, research assistantships, and teaching assistantships available. Support available to part-time students. Financial award applicants required to submit FAFSA. *Faculty research:* Nutrient requirements, nutrient metabolism, nutrition and disease prevention. *Unit head:* Michele R. Forman, Head, 765-494-9921, E-mail: mforman@purdue.edu. *Application contact:* Jon A. Story, Graduate Contact for Admissions, 765-494-6843, E-mail: jastory@purdue.edu. Website: http://www.cfs.purdue.edu/fn/

Rhode Island College, School of Graduate Studies, Feinstein School of Education and Human Development, Department of Health and Physical Education, Providence, RI 02908-1991. Offers health education (M Ed); physical education (CGS). *Accreditation:* NCATE. *Program availability:* Part-time, evening/weekend. *Faculty:* 1. *Students:* 3 part-time (all women); includes 1 minority (Hispanic/Latino). Average age 38. In 2017, 4 master's awarded. *Degree requirements:* For master's, comprehensive assessment. *Entrance requirements:* For master's, GRE General Test or MAT, undergraduate transcripts; minimum undergraduate GPA of 3.0; 3 letters of recommendation; for CGS, GRE or MAT (for most programs), undergraduate transcripts; minimum undergraduate GPA of 3.0; 3 letters of recommendation. Additional exam requirements/recommendations for international students: Recommended—TOEFL (minimum score 550 paper-based; 79 iBT). *Application deadline:* For fall admission, 3/1 for domestic students; for spring admission, 11/1 for domestic students. Applications are processed on a rolling basis. Application fee: $50. Electronic applications accepted. *Expenses:* Tuition, state resident: full-time $9768; part-time $407 per credit. Tuition, nonresident: full-time $19,008; part-time $792 per credit. *Required fees:* $696; $29 per credit. One-time fee: $200 full-time; $100 part-time. Tuition and fees vary according to course load. *Financial support:* In 2017–18, 1 teaching assistantship with full tuition reimbursement (averaging $2,250 per year) was awarded; Federal Work-Study, scholarships/grants, health care benefits, and unspecified assistantships also available. Support available to part-time students. Financial award application deadline: 5/15; financial award applicants required to submit FAFSA. *Unit head:* Dr. Robin Kirkwood Auld, Chair, 401-456-8046. *Application contact:* Graduate Studies, 401-456-8700. Website: http://www.ric.edu/healthPhysicalEducation/

Rosalind Franklin University of Medicine and Science, College of Health Professions, Department of Interprofessional Healthcare Studies, Health Professions Education Program, North Chicago, IL 60064-3095. Offers MS.

Rosalind Franklin University of Medicine and Science, College of Health Professions, Department of Nutrition, North Chicago, IL 60064-3095. Offers clinical nutrition (MS); health promotion and wellness (MS); nutrition education (MS). *Program availability:* Part-time, evening/weekend, online learning. *Degree requirements:* For master's, thesis optional, portfolio. *Entrance requirements:* For master's, minimum GPA of 2.75, registered dietitian (RD), professional certificate or license. Additional exam requirements/recommendations for international students: Required—TOEFL. *Expenses:* Contact institution. *Faculty research:* Nutrition education, distance learning, computer-based graduate education, childhood obesity, nutrition medical education.

Rutgers University–Newark, School of Health Related Professions, Department of Interdisciplinary Studies, Program in Health Sciences, Newark, NJ 07102. Offers health sciences (MS, PhD). *Program availability:* Part-time, evening/weekend, online learning. *Degree requirements:* For doctorate, thesis/dissertation. *Entrance requirements:* For master's, BS, 2 reference letters, statement of career goals, curriculum vitae; for doctorate, GRE, interview, writing sample, 3 reference letters, curriculum vitae. Additional exam requirements/recommendations for international students: Required—TOEFL. Electronic applications accepted.

Rutgers University–New Brunswick, School of Public Health, Piscataway, NJ 08854. Offers biostatistics (MPH, MS, Dr PH, PhD); clinical epidemiology (Certificate); environmental and occupational health (MPH, Dr PH, Certificate); epidemiology (MPH, Dr PH, PhD); general public health (Certificate); health education and behavioral science (MPH, Dr PH, PhD); health systems and policy (MPH, PhD); public health (MPH, Dr PH, PhD); public health preparedness (Certificate); DO/MPH; JD/MPH; MBA/MPH; MD/MPH; MPH/MBA; MPH/MSPA; MS/MPH; Psy D/MPH. *Accreditation:* CEPH. *Program availability:* Part-time, evening/weekend. *Degree requirements:* For master's, thesis, internship; for doctorate, comprehensive exam, thesis/dissertation. *Entrance requirements:* For master's, GRE General Test; for doctorate, GRE General Test, MPH (Dr PH); MA, MPH, or MS (PhD). Additional exam requirements/recommendations for international students: Required—TOEFL. Electronic applications accepted.

Sage Graduate School, Esteves School of Education, Program in School Health Education, Troy, NY 12180-4115. Offers MS. *Accreditation:* NCATE. *Program availability:* Part-time, evening/weekend. *Faculty:* 2 full-time (both women), 8 part-time/adjunct (4 women). *Students:* 5 full-time (3 women), 13 part-time (4 women); includes 1 minority (Black or African American, non-Hispanic/Latino). Average age 27. 17 applicants, 82% accepted, 9 enrolled. In 2017, 8 master's awarded. *Degree requirements:* For master's, thesis optional. *Entrance requirements:* For master's, interview with advisor, assessment of writing skills. Additional exam requirements/recommendations for international students: Required—TOEFL (minimum score 550 paper-based). *Application deadline:* Applications are processed on a rolling basis. Application fee: $30. Electronic applications accepted. Tuition and fees vary according to degree level and program. *Financial support:* Fellowships, research assistantships, scholarships/grants, and unspecified assistantships available. Financial award application deadline: 3/1; financial award applicants required to submit FAFSA. *Faculty research:* Policy development in health education and health care. *Unit head:* Dr. John Pelizza, Interim Dean, Estevez School of Education, 518-244-2051, Fax: 518-244-2334, E-mail: pelizj@sage.edu. *Application contact:* Wendy D. Diefendorf, Director of Graduate and Adult Admission, 518-244-2443, Fax: 518-244-6880, E-mail: diefew@sage.edu.

Saint Francis University, Health Science Program, Loretto, PA 15940-0600. Offers MHS. *Program availability:* Part-time, evening/weekend, 100% online. *Faculty:* 2 full-time (both women), 16 part-time/adjunct (10 women). *Students:* 5 full-time (all women), 64 part-time (55 women); includes 33 minority (19 Black or African American, non-Hispanic/Latino; 5 Asian, non-Hispanic/Latino; 3 Hispanic/Latino; 1 Native Hawaiian or other Pacific Islander, non-Hispanic/Latino; 5 Two or more races, non-Hispanic/Latino). Average age 36. 14 applicants, 100% accepted, 1 enrolled. In 2017, 42 master's awarded. *Degree requirements:* For master's, minimum GPA of 2.8. *Entrance requirements:* For master's, undergraduate transcript, letters of reference, minimum QPA of 2.5, resume. Additional exam requirements/recommendations for international students: Recommended—TOEFL (minimum score 80 iBT). *Application deadline:* For fall admission, 7/19 for domestic and international students; for spring admission, 11/15

for domestic and international students; for summer admission, 3/22 for domestic and international students. Applications are processed on a rolling basis. Application fee: $50. Electronic applications accepted. *Expenses:* Contact institution. *Financial support:* Available to part-time students. Applicants required to submit FAFSA. *Faculty research:* Distance education, health sciences, medical sciences, communication, adult education. *Application contact:* Jean A. Kline, Administrative Assistant, 814-472-3357, Fax: 814-472-3066, E-mail: jkline@francis.edu.
Website: http://onlinemhsc.francis.edu

Saint Joseph's College of Maine, Master of Science in Education Program, Standish, ME 04084. Offers adult education and training (MS Ed); Catholic school leadership (MS Ed); health care educator (MS Ed); school educator (MS Ed). Program available by correspondence. *Program availability:* Part-time, online learning. Electronic applications accepted.

San Francisco State University, Division of Graduate Studies, College of Health and Social Sciences, Department of Health Education, San Francisco, CA 94132-1722. Offers community health education (MPH). *Accreditation:* CEPH. *Program availability:* Part-time. *Students:* Average age 36. *Application deadline:* Applications are processed on a rolling basis. *Unit head:* Dr. Mary Beth Love, Chair, 415-338-1413, Fax: 415-338-0570, E-mail: love@sfsu.edu. *Application contact:* Vincent Lam, Graduate Coordinator, 415-338-1413, Fax: 415-338-0570, E-mail: vlam@sfsu.edu.
Website: http://healthed.sfsu.edu/graduate

San Francisco State University, Division of Graduate Studies, College of Health and Social Sciences, Department of Sexuality Studies, San Francisco, CA 94132-1722. Offers MA. *Unit head:* Dr. Andreana Clay, Chair, 415-338-1090, Fax: 415-338-2653, E-mail: andreana@sfsu.edu. *Application contact:* Dr. Alexis Martinez, Graduate Coordinator, 415-338-2269, Fax: 415-338-2653, E-mail: alexisnm@sfsu.edu.
Website: http://sxs.sfsu.edu/

Shenandoah University, School of Education and Leadership, Winchester, VA 22601. Offers administration and supervision (Certificate); administrative leadership (D Ed); early childhood literacy (MS); educational administration (MSE); elementary school teacher education (Certificate); emphasis in teaching (MSE); health and physical education (Certificate); individualized focus (MS, MSE); literacy education (MS); middle school teacher education (Certificate); organizational leadership (MS, D Prof); reading licensure (MS, Certificate); reading non-licensure (MS); secondary school teacher education (Certificate); special education (MSE); writing (MS). *Accreditation:* TEAC. *Program availability:* Part-time, evening/weekend. *Faculty:* 8 full-time (7 women), 22 part-time/adjunct (16 women). *Students:* 16 full-time (14 women), 221 part-time (167 women); includes 32 minority (17 Black or African American, non-Hispanic/Latino; 1 American Indian or Alaska Native, non-Hispanic/Latino; 6 Asian, non-Hispanic/Latino; 5 Hispanic/Latino; 1 Native Hawaiian or other Pacific Islander, non-Hispanic/Latino; 2 Two or more races, non-Hispanic/Latino), 3 international. Average age 38. 81 applicants, 99% accepted, 63 enrolled. In 2017, 53 master's, 11 doctorates, 49 other advanced degrees awarded. *Degree requirements:* For master's, comprehensive exam (for some programs), thesis (for some programs); for doctorate, comprehensive exam, thesis/dissertation. *Entrance requirements:* For degree, PRAXIS Academic Core, SAT/ACT, PRAXIS Academic Core Math, or VCLA, three letters of recommendation, writing sample, undergraduate degree. Additional exam requirements/recommendations for international students: Required—TOEFL (minimum score 550 paper-based, 79 iBT) or IELTS (6.5). *Application deadline:* For fall admission, 5/1 priority date for domestic students, 5/1 for international students; for spring admission, 10/15 priority date for domestic students, 10/15 for international students; for summer admission, 3/15 priority date for domestic students, 3/15 for international students. Application fee: $30. Electronic applications accepted. *Expenses:* $15,600 tuition plus $1,296 fees (technology and student services). *Financial support:* In 2017–18, 26 students received support. Scholarships/grants and unspecified assistantships available. Financial award applicants required to submit FAFSA. *Faculty research:* Mentoring, behavior support for students, teacher change agency, educational technology in pedagogy, literacy education. *Unit head:* Jill Lindsey, PhD, Director, 540-535-7324, Fax: 540-665-4726, E-mail: jlindsey@su.edu. *Application contact:* Andrew Woodall, Executive Director of Recruitment and Admissions, 540-665-4581, Fax: 540-665-4627, E-mail: admit@su.edu.
Website: http://www.su.edu/education/

Simmons College, School of Nursing and Health Sciences, Boston, MA 02115. Offers didactic dietetics (Certificate); dietetic internship (Certificate); health professions education (PhD, CAGS); nursing (MS, MSN), including family nurse practitioner (MS); nursing practice (DNP); nutrition and health promotion (MS); physical therapy (DPT); sports nutrition (Certificate). *Accreditation:* AACN. *Program availability:* Part-time, 100% online, blended/hybrid learning. *Faculty:* 34 full-time (28 women), 44 part-time/adjunct (40 women). *Students:* 390 full-time (350 women), 1,286 part-time (1,169 women); includes 346 minority (131 Black or African American, non-Hispanic/Latino; 6 American Indian or Alaska Native, non-Hispanic/Latino; 75 Asian, non-Hispanic/Latino; 91 Hispanic/Latino; 3 Native Hawaiian or other Pacific Islander, non-Hispanic/Latino; 40 Two or more races, non-Hispanic/Latino), 9 international. Average age 34. 1,219 applicants, 74% accepted, 481 enrolled. In 2017, 423 master's, 39 doctorates, 55 other advanced degrees awarded. *Entrance requirements:* For doctorate, GRE. Additional exam requirements/recommendations for international students: Required—TOEFL (minimum score 570 paper-based; 88 iBT). *Application deadline:* For fall admission, 6/1 for international students. Application fee: $50. Electronic applications accepted. *Expenses:* $1,278 per credit, $116 activity fee per semester. *Financial support:* In 2017–18, 15 research assistantships with partial tuition reimbursements were awarded; scholarships/grants and unspecified assistantships also available. Financial award applicants required to submit FAFSA. *Unit head:* Dr. Judy Beal, Dean, 617-521-2139. *Application contact:* Brett DiMarzo, Director of Graduate Admission, 617-521-2651, Fax: 617-521-3137, E-mail: brett.dimarzo@simmons.edu.
Website: http://www.simmons.edu/snhs

Southeastern Louisiana University, College of Nursing and Health Sciences, Department of Kinesiology and Health Studies, Hammond, LA 70402. Offers MS. *Accreditation:* NCATE. *Program availability:* Part-time. *Faculty:* 6 full-time (2 women), 1 part-time/adjunct (0 women). *Students:* 26 full-time (14 women), 16 part-time (7 women); includes 19 minority (10 Black or African American, non-Hispanic/Latino; 4 Hispanic/Latino; 1 Native Hawaiian or other Pacific Islander, non-Hispanic/Latino; 4 Two or more races, non-Hispanic/Latino), 1 international. Average age 26. 28 applicants, 57% accepted, 11 enrolled. In 2017, 11 master's awarded. *Degree requirements:* For master's, comprehensive exam (for some programs), thesis (for some programs). *Entrance requirements:* For master's, GRE (minimum combined Verbal and Quantitative score of 286), undergraduate human anatomy and physiology course. Additional exam requirements/recommendations for international students: Required—TOEFL (minimum score 500 paper-based; 61 iBT). *Application deadline:* For fall admission, 7/15 priority date for domestic students, 6/1 priority date for international students; for spring admission, 12/1 priority date for domestic students, 10/1 priority date for international students. Applications are processed on a rolling basis. Application fee: $20 ($30 for international students). Electronic applications accepted. *Expenses:* Tuition, state resident: full-time $6684. Tuition, nonresident: full-time $19,162. *Required fees:* $2088.

Financial support: In 2017–18, 16 students received support, including 7 research assistantships (averaging $9,275 per year), 4 teaching assistantships (averaging $9,550 per year); career-related internships or fieldwork, Federal Work-Study, institutionally sponsored loans, scholarships/grants, and unspecified assistantships also available. Support available to part-time students. Financial award application deadline: 5/1; financial award applicants required to submit FAFSA. *Faculty research:* Exercise physiology, motor learning, sport and exercise psychology, school health, health and aging. *Unit head:* Dr. Eddie Hebert, Department Head, 985-549-2129, Fax: 985-549-5119, E-mail: ehebert@southeastern.edu. *Application contact:* Amanda Harper, Graduate Admissions Analyst, 985-549-5620, Fax: 985-549-5632, E-mail: admissions@southeastern.edu.
Website: http://www.southeastern.edu/acad_research/depts/kin_hs/index.html

Southern Connecticut State University, School of Graduate Studies, School of Health and Human Services, Department of Exercise Science, Program in School Health Education, New Haven, CT 06515-1355. Offers MS. *Accreditation:* NCATE. *Program availability:* Part-time, evening/weekend. *Entrance requirements:* For master's, interview. Electronic applications accepted.

Southern Illinois University Carbondale, Graduate School, College of Education and Human Services, Department of Health Education and Recreation, Program in Community Health Education, Carbondale, IL 62901-4701. Offers MPH, MD/MPH, PhD/MPH. *Accreditation:* CEPH. *Entrance requirements:* Additional exam requirements/recommendations for international students: Required—TOEFL (minimum score 550 paper-based; 80 iBT).

Southern Illinois University Carbondale, Graduate School, College of Education and Human Services, Department of Health Education and Recreation, Program in Health Education, Carbondale, IL 62901-4701. Offers MS Ed, PhD. *Accreditation:* NCATE. *Program availability:* Part-time. *Degree requirements:* For master's, thesis; for doctorate, thesis/dissertation. *Entrance requirements:* For master's, MAT, minimum GPA of 2.7; for doctorate, MAT, minimum GPA of 3.25. Additional exam requirements/recommendations for international students: Required—TOEFL. *Faculty research:* Sexuality education, research design, injury control, program evaluation.

Southern Illinois University Edwardsville, Graduate School, College of Arts and Sciences, Department of Applied Communication Studies, Edwardsville, IL 62026. Offers corporate and organizational communication (MA); health communication (MA); interpersonal communication (MA); public relations (MA). *Program availability:* Part-time, evening/weekend. *Degree requirements:* For master's, comprehensive exam (for some programs), thesis (for some programs), final exam. *Entrance requirements:* Additional exam requirements/recommendations for international students: Required—TOEFL (minimum score 550 paper-based; 79 iBT), IELTS (minimum score 6.5). Electronic applications accepted.

Southern Illinois University Edwardsville, Graduate School, School of Education, Health, and Human Behavior, Edwardsville, IL 62062. Offers MA, MS, MS Ed, Ed D, Ed S, Post-Master's Certificate, Postbaccalaureate Certificate, SD. *Accreditation:* NCATE. *Program availability:* Part-time, evening/weekend. *Degree requirements:* For master's, comprehensive exam (for some programs), thesis (for some programs), final exam, portfolio. *Entrance requirements:* For master's, GRE. Additional exam requirements/recommendations for international students: Required—TOEFL (minimum score 550 paper-based; 79 iBT), IELTS (minimum score 6.5). Electronic applications accepted.

State University of New York College at Cortland, Graduate Studies, School of Professional Studies, Department of Health, Cortland, NY 13045. Offers community health (MS); health education (MST). *Accreditation:* NCATE. *Program availability:* Part-time, evening/weekend. *Entrance requirements:* Additional exam requirements/recommendations for international students: Required—TOEFL.

Stony Brook University, State University of New York, Stony Brook Medicine, School of Medicine, Program in Public Health, Stony Brook, NY 11794. Offers community health (MPH); evaluation sciences (MPH); family violence (MPH); health communication (Certificate); health economics (MPH); health education and promotion (Certificate); population health (MPH); substance abuse (MPH). *Accreditation:* CEPH. *Program availability:* Part-time, evening/weekend. *Students:* 32 full-time (24 women), 11 part-time (10 women); includes 18 minority (4 Black or African American, non-Hispanic/Latino; 10 Asian, non-Hispanic/Latino; 4 Hispanic/Latino), 2 international. Average age 29. 128 applicants, 71% accepted, 29 enrolled. In 2017, 25 master's, 1 other advanced degree awarded. *Entrance requirements:* For master's, GRE, 3 references, bachelor's degree from accredited college or university with minimum GPA of 3.0, essays, interview. Additional exam requirements/recommendations for international students: Required—TOEFL (minimum score 90 iBT). *Application deadline:* For fall admission, 7/15 for domestic students, 3/15 for international students. Application fee: $100. Electronic applications accepted. *Expenses:* Contact institution. *Financial support:* Fellowships available. *Faculty research:* Abnormal psychology, academic achievement, broadcast media, communications, communications systems, public health. *Total annual research expenditures:* $422,408. *Unit head:* Dr. Lisa A. Benz Scott, Director, 631-444-8811, E-mail: lisa.benzscott@stonybrook.edu. *Application contact:* Joanie Maniaci, Assistant Director for Student Affairs, 631-444-2074, Fax: 631-444-6035, E-mail: joanmarie.maniaci@stonybrook.edu.
Website: http://publichealth.stonybrookmedicine.edu/

Teachers College, Columbia University, Department of Health and Behavior Studies, New York, NY 10027-6696. Offers applied behavior analysis (MA, PhD); applied educational psychology: school psychology (Ed M, PhD); behavioral nutrition (PhD), including nutrition (Ed D, PhD); community health education (MS); community nutrition education (Ed M), including community nutrition education; education of deaf and hard of hearing (MA, PhD); health education (MA, Ed D); hearing impairment (Ed D); intellectual disability/autism (MA, Ed D, PhD); nursing education (Ed D, Advanced Certificate); nutrition and education (MS); nutrition and exercise physiology (MS); nutrition and public health (MS); nutrition education (Ed D), including nutrition (Ed D, PhD); physical disabilities (Ed D); reading specialist (MA); severe or multiple disabilities (MA); special education (Ed M, MA, Ed D); teaching of sign language (MA). *Program availability:* Part-time, evening/weekend. *Students:* 245 full-time (226 women), 242 part-time (219 women); includes 167 minority (52 Black or African American, non-Hispanic/Latino; 2 American Indian or Alaska Native, non-Hispanic/Latino; 55 Asian, non-Hispanic/Latino; 48 Hispanic/Latino; 1 Native Hawaiian or other Pacific Islander, non-Hispanic/Latino; 9 Two or more races, non-Hispanic/Latino), 60 international. Average age 30. 480 applicants, 59% accepted, 157 enrolled. Terminal master's awarded for partial completion of doctoral program. *Unit head:* Prof. Dolores Perin, Chair, E-mail: dp111@tc.columbia.edu. *Application contact:* David Estrella, Director of Admission, 212-678-3305, E-mail: estrella@tc.columbia.edu.
Website: http://www.tc.columbia.edu/health-and-behavior-studies/

Tennessee Technological University, College of Graduate Studies, College of Education, Department of Exercise Science, Physical Education and Wellness, Cookeville, TN 38505. Offers adapted physical education (MA); elementary/middle school physical education (MA); lifetime wellness (MA); sport management (MA). *Accreditation:* NCATE. *Program availability:* Part-time, online learning. *Faculty:* 7 full-time (0 women). *Students:* 17 full-time (8 women), 34 part-time (14 women); includes 10 minority (5 Black or African American, non-Hispanic/Latino; 1 Asian, non-Hispanic/Latino; 2 Hispanic/Latino; 2 Two or more races, non-Hispanic/Latino). 35 applicants, 71% accepted, 23 enrolled. In 2017, 28 master's awarded. *Degree requirements:* For master's, comprehensive exam, thesis or alternative. *Entrance requirements:* For master's, MAT or GRE. Additional exam requirements/recommendations for international students: Required—TOEFL (minimum score 527 paper-based; 71 iBT), IELTS (minimum score 5.5), PTE (minimum score 48), or TOEIC (Test of English as an International Communication). *Application deadline:* For fall admission, 8/1 for domestic students, 5/1 for international students; for spring admission, 12/1 for domestic students, 10/1 for international students; for summer admission, 5/1 for domestic students, 2/1 for international students. Applications are processed on a rolling basis. Application fee: $35 ($40 for international students). Electronic applications accepted. *Expenses:* Tuition, state resident: full-time $9925; part-time $565 per credit hour. Tuition, nonresident: full-time $22,993; part-time $1291 per credit hour. *Financial support:* Fellowships, research assistantships, teaching assistantships, and career-related internships or fieldwork available. Financial award application deadline: 4/1. *Unit head:* Dr. Christy Killman, Chairperson, 931-372-3467, Fax: 931-372-6319, E-mail: ckillman@tntech.edu. *Application contact:* Shelia K. Kendrick, Coordinator of Graduate Studies, 931-372-3808, Fax: 931-372-3497, E-mail: skendrick@tntech.edu.

Texas A&M University, College of Education and Human Development, Department of Health and Kinesiology, College Station, TX 77843. Offers athletic training (MS); health education (MS, PhD); kinesiology (MS, PhD); sports management (MS). *Program availability:* Part-time. *Faculty:* 53. *Students:* 223 full-time (120 women), 94 part-time (53 women); includes 106 minority (42 Black or African American, non-Hispanic/Latino; 2 American Indian or Alaska Native, non-Hispanic/Latino; 5 Asian, non-Hispanic/Latino; 50 Hispanic/Latino; 7 Two or more races, non-Hispanic/Latino), 27 international. Average age 29. 161 applicants, 79% accepted, 81 enrolled. In 2017, 126 master's, 13 doctorates awarded. *Degree requirements:* For master's, thesis (for some programs); for doctorate, comprehensive exam, thesis/dissertation. *Entrance requirements:* For master's and doctorate, GRE General Test. Additional exam requirements/recommendations for international students: Required—TOEFL (minimum score 550 paper-based; 80 iBT), IELTS (minimum score 6), PTE (minimum score 53). *Application deadline:* For fall admission, 1/15 for domestic students; for spring admission, 10/1 for domestic students. Applications are processed on a rolling basis. Application fee: $50 ($90 for international students). Electronic applications accepted. *Expenses:* Contact institution. *Financial support:* In 2017–18, 204 students received support, including 2 fellowships with tuition reimbursements available (averaging $43,805 per year), 63 research assistantships with tuition reimbursements available (averaging $10,102 per year), 59 teaching assistantships with tuition reimbursements available (averaging $9,712 per year); career-related internships or fieldwork, institutionally sponsored loans, scholarships/grants, traineeships, health care benefits, tuition waivers (full and partial), and unspecified assistantships also available. Support available to part-time students. Financial award application deadline: 3/15; financial award applicants required to submit FAFSA. *Unit head:* Dr. Richard Kreider, Head, 979-845-1333, Fax: 979-847-8987, E-mail: rkreider@hlkn.tamu.edu. *Application contact:* Jenny Bilski, Academic Advisor, 979-862-4052, E-mail: jenny.bilski@tamu.edu.
Website: http://hlknweb.tamu.edu/

Texas A&M University–Kingsville, College of Graduate Studies, College of Education and Human Performance, Department of Health and Kinesiology, Kingsville, TX 78363. Offers MA, MS. *Degree requirements:* For master's, variable foreign language requirement, comprehensive exam, thesis (for some programs). *Entrance requirements:* For master's, GRE, MAT, GMAT, essay. Additional exam requirements/recommendations for international students: Required—TOEFL (minimum score 550 paper-based; 79 iBT). Electronic applications accepted.

Texas Southern University, College of Education, Department of Health and Kinesiology, Houston, TX 77004-4584. Offers health education (MS); human performance (MS). *Program availability:* Part-time, evening/weekend. *Degree requirements:* For master's, comprehensive exam, thesis optional. *Entrance requirements:* For master's, GRE General Test, minimum GPA of 2.5. Additional exam requirements/recommendations for international students: Required—TOEFL. Electronic applications accepted.

Texas State University, The Graduate College, College of Education, Program in Health Education, San Marcos, TX 78666. Offers M Ed. *Program availability:* Part-time, evening/weekend. *Faculty:* 6 full-time (2 women). *Students:* 16 full-time (all women), 4 part-time (all women); includes 10 minority (2 Black or African American, non-Hispanic/Latino; 2 Asian, non-Hispanic/Latino; 5 Hispanic/Latino; 1 Two or more races, non-Hispanic/Latino). Average age 27. 15 applicants, 93% accepted, 6 enrolled. In 2017, 9 master's awarded. *Degree requirements:* For master's, comprehensive exam, thesis optional. *Entrance requirements:* For master's, baccalaureate degree from regionally-accredited institution with minimum GPA of 2.75 in last 60 hours of course work, 18 hours of health education background courses, statement of purpose. Additional exam requirements/recommendations for international students: Required—TOEFL (minimum score 550 paper-based; 78 iBT), IELTS (minimum score 6.5). *Application deadline:* For fall admission, 2/15 priority date for domestic and international students; for spring admission, 10/15 priority date for domestic students, 10/1 for international students; for summer admission, 4/15 for domestic students, 3/15 for international students. Applications are processed on a rolling basis. Application fee: $40 ($90 for international students). Electronic applications accepted. *Expenses:* Tuition, state resident: full-time $7868; part-time $3934 per semester. Tuition, nonresident: full-time $17,828; part-time $8914 per semester. *Required fees:* $2092; $1435 per semester. Tuition and fees vary according to course load. *Financial support:* In 2017–18, 13 students received support, including 1 research assistantship (averaging $12,152 per year), 7 teaching assistantships (averaging $12,596 per year); career-related internships or fieldwork, Federal Work-Study, institutionally sponsored loans, scholarships/grants, and unspecified assistantships also available. Support available to part-time students. Financial award application deadline: 3/1; financial award applicants required to submit FAFSA. *Faculty research:* AIDS education, employee wellness, isometric strength evaluation, Fresh Start. *Total annual research expenditures:* $4,059. *Unit head:* Dr. David C. Wiley, Graduate Advisor, 512-245-2946, E-mail: dw13@txstate.edu. *Application contact:* Dr. Andrea Golato, Dean of the Graduate College, 512-245-2581, Fax: 512-245-8365, E-mail: gradcollege@txstate.edu.
Website: http://www.gradcollege.txstate.edu/programs/health-ed.html

Texas Woman's University, Graduate School, College of Health Sciences, Department of Health Studies, Denton, TX 76204. Offers health studies (MS, PhD), including dental hygiene (MS). *Program availability:* Part-time, evening/weekend. *Faculty:* 8 full-time (7 women), 5 part-time/adjunct (2 women). *Students:* 35 full-time (32 women), 93 part-time (82 women); includes 68 minority (37 Black or African American, non-Hispanic/Latino; 1 American Indian or Alaska Native, non-Hispanic/Latino; 6 Asian, non-Hispanic/Latino; 20 Hispanic/Latino; 4 Two or more races, non-Hispanic/Latino), 1 international. Average age 34. 49 applicants, 57% accepted, 22 enrolled. In 2017, 8 master's, 3 doctorates awarded. *Degree requirements:* For master's, comprehensive exam, thesis, non-thesis options, or work-site health (for dental hygiene); for doctorate, comprehensive exam,

thesis/dissertation, qualifying exam. *Entrance requirements:* For master's, minimum undergraduate GPA of 3.0 in last 60 credit hours of bachelor's degree, resume/curriculum vitae, 2 letters of recommendation, personal statement letter; for doctorate, GRE General Test (preferred minimum scores 152 [480 old version] Verbal, 140 [400 old version] Quantitative), minimum GPA of 3.5 on all master's course work, 2 letters of recommendation, curriculum vitae, essay, writing sample. Additional exam requirements/recommendations for international students: Required—TOEFL (minimum score 575 paper-based; 79 iBT); Recommended—IELTS (minimum score 6.5), TSE (minimum score 53). *Application deadline:* For fall admission, 3/1 priority date for domestic and international students; for spring admission, 11/1 priority date for domestic students, 7/1 priority date for international students. Applications are processed on a rolling basis. Application fee: $50 ($75 for international students). Electronic applications accepted. *Expenses:* $8,240 per year full-time in-state, $17,540 per year full-time out-of-state. *Financial support:* In 2017–18, 29 students received support, including 2 research assistantships (averaging $11,926 per year), 3 teaching assistantships (averaging $11,926 per year); career-related internships or fieldwork, Federal Work-Study, institutionally sponsored loans, scholarships/grants, traineeships, health care benefits, and unspecified assistantships also available. Support available to part-time students. Financial award application deadline: 3/1; financial award applicants required to submit FAFSA. *Faculty research:* Teen pregnancy prevention, eating disorder and obesity prevention, body image issues, adolescent and women's health, chronic disease prevention. *Total annual research expenditures:* $158,000. *Unit head:* Dr. George King, Chair, 940-898-2860, Fax: 940-898-2859, E-mail: healthstudiesinfo@twu.edu. *Application contact:* Korie Hawkins, Associate Director of Admissions, Graduate Recruitment, 940-898-3188, Fax: 940-898-3081, E-mail: admissions@twu.edu.
Website: http://www.twu.edu/health-studies/

Thomas Jefferson University, Jefferson College of Population Health, Philadelphia, PA 19107. Offers applied health economics and outcomes research (MS, PhD, Certificate); behavioral health science (PhD); health policy (MS, Certificate); healthcare quality and safety (MS, PhD); population health (Certificate); public health (MPH, Certificate). *Program availability:* Part-time, evening/weekend, online learning. Terminal master's awarded for partial completion of doctoral program. *Degree requirements:* For master's, thesis; for doctorate, comprehensive exam, thesis/dissertation. *Entrance requirements:* For master's, GRE or other graduate entrance exam (MCAT, LSAT, DAT, etc.), two letters of recommendation, curriculum vitae, transcripts from all undergraduate and graduate institutions; for doctorate, GRE (taken within the last 5 years), three letters of recommendation, curriculum vitae, transcripts from all undergraduate and graduate institutions. Additional exam requirements/recommendations for international students: Required—TOEFL. Electronic applications accepted. *Faculty research:* Applied health economics and outcomes research, behavioral and health sciences, chronic disease management, health policy, healthcare quality and patient safety, wellness and prevention.

Trident University International, College of Health Sciences, Program in Health Sciences, Cypress, CA 90630. Offers clinical research administration (MS, Certificate); emergency and disaster management (MS, Certificate); environmental health science (Certificate); health care administration (PhD); health care management (MS), including health informatics; health education (MS, Certificate); health informatics (Certificate); health sciences (PhD); international health (MS); international health: educator or researcher option (PhD); international health: practitioner option (PhD); law and expert witness studies (MS, Certificate); public health (MS); quality assurance (Certificate). *Program availability:* Part-time, evening/weekend, online learning. *Degree requirements:* For doctorate, comprehensive exam, thesis/dissertation, defense of dissertation. *Entrance requirements:* For master's, minimum GPA of 2.5 (students with GPA 3.0 or greater may transfer up to 30% of graduate level credits); for doctorate, minimum GPA of 3.4, curriculum vitae, course work in research methods or statistics. Additional exam requirements/recommendations for international students: Required—TOEFL. Electronic applications accepted.

Union College, Graduate Programs, Department of Education, Barbourville, KY 40906-1499. Offers elementary education (MA); health and physical education (MA); middle grades (MA); music education (MA); principalship (MA); reading specialist (MA); secondary education (MA); special education (MA). *Degree requirements:* For master's, thesis optional. *Entrance requirements:* For master's, GRE General Test, NTE.

Union College, Graduate Programs, Department of Health and Physical Education, Barbourville, KY 40906-1499. Offers health (MA Ed). *Degree requirements:* For master's, thesis optional. *Entrance requirements:* For master's, GRE General Test, NTE.

The University of Alabama, Graduate School, College of Human Environmental Sciences, Department of Health Science, Tuscaloosa, AL 35487-0311. Offers health education and promotion (PhD); health studies (MA). *Program availability:* Part-time, online learning. *Faculty:* 11 full-time (7 women). *Students:* 53 full-time (44 women), 102 part-time (86 women); includes 55 minority (40 Black or African American, non-Hispanic/Latino; 2 American Indian or Alaska Native, non-Hispanic/Latino; 2 Asian, non-Hispanic/Latino; 7 Hispanic/Latino; 4 Two or more races, non-Hispanic/Latino), 2 international. Average age 33. 87 applicants, 74% accepted, 46 enrolled. In 2017, 74 master's, 8 doctorates awarded. *Degree requirements:* For master's, comprehensive exam, thesis optional; for doctorate, one foreign language, comprehensive exam, thesis/dissertation. *Entrance requirements:* For master's, minimum GPA of 3.0; for doctorate, GRE General Test, minimum GPA of 3.0, prerequisites in health education. Additional exam requirements/recommendations for international students: Required—TOEFL. *Application deadline:* For fall admission, 3/15 priority date for domestic students, 3/15 for international students. Applications are processed on a rolling basis. Application fee: $50 ($60 for international students). Electronic applications accepted. *Financial support:* In 2017–18, 10 students received support, including research assistantships with full tuition reimbursements available (averaging $10,500 per year), teaching assistantships with full tuition reimbursements available (averaging $10,500 per year); career-related internships or fieldwork, Federal Work-Study, institutionally sponsored loans, health care benefits, and unspecified assistantships also available. Financial award application deadline: 4/14. *Faculty research:* Program planning, substance abuse prevention, obesity prevention, nutrition, physical activity, athletic training, osteoporosis, health behavior. *Unit head:* Dr. David Birch, Department Head and Professor, 205-348-4751, E-mail: dabirch@ches.ua.edu. *Application contact:* Dr. Stuart Usdan, Associate Professor and Doctoral Program Coordinator, 205-348-8373, Fax: 205-348-7568, E-mail: susdan@ches.ua.edu.
Website: http://ches.ua.edu/

The University of Alabama at Birmingham, School of Public Health, Program in Health Education and Health Promotion, Birmingham, AL 35294-0022. Offers PhD. Program offered jointly with the School of Education and The University of Alabama (Tuscaloosa). *Program availability:* Part-time. *Faculty:* 9 full-time (6 women), 4 part-time/adjunct (1 woman). *Students:* 7 full-time (5 women), 19 part-time (15 women); includes 10 minority (all Black or African American, non-Hispanic/Latino), 3 international. Average age 37. 11 applicants, 73% accepted, 6 enrolled. In 2017, 3 doctorates awarded. *Degree requirements:* For doctorate, comprehensive exam, thesis/dissertation, research internship. *Entrance requirements:* For doctorate, GRE, 3 letters

Health Education

of recommendation, transcripts, personal statement, curriculum vitae/resume. Additional exam requirements/recommendations for international students: Required—TOEFL (minimum score 550 paper-based; 80 iBT), IELTS (minimum score 6.5). *Application deadline:* For fall admission, 2/15 priority date for domestic and international students. Applications are processed on a rolling basis. Application fee: $50 ($60 for international students). Electronic applications accepted. *Expenses:* $451 per semester hour in-state; $1,025 per semester hour out-of-state; $250 per online course fee. *Financial support:* In 2017–18, 23 students received support, including 1 fellowship with full tuition reimbursement available (averaging $26,400 per year), 1 research assistantship with full tuition reimbursement available (averaging $20,424 per year), 5 teaching assistantships (averaging $3,000 per year); career-related internships or fieldwork, Federal Work-Study, scholarships/grants, traineeships, health care benefits, and full-time employee tuition coverage also available. Financial award application deadline: 2/15. *Faculty research:* Obesity prevention including lifestyle interventions, family and adolescent health issues, prevention and control of addictive behaviors, sexual health risks including HIV/AIDS prevention and treatment, and mental health issues including issues of homelessness. *Total annual research expenditures:* $574,000. *Unit head:* Dr. Robin G. Lanzi, Graduate Program Director, 205-975-8071, Fax: 205-934-9325, E-mail: rlanzi@uab.edu. *Application contact:* Hannah VanSlambrouck, Director, Enrollment Management, 205-975-8688, E-mail: hannahv@uab.edu.
Website: http://www.soph.uab.edu/hb

University of Arkansas, Graduate School, College of Education and Health Professions, Department of Health, Human Performance and Recreation, Fayetteville, AR 72701. Offers athletic training (MAT); community health promotion (MS, PhD); health science (MS, PhD); kinesiology (MS, PhD); physical education (M Ed, MAT); recreation and sports management (M Ed, Ed D). In 2017, 77 master's, 6 doctorates awarded. *Degree requirements:* For doctorate, thesis/dissertation. *Application deadline:* For fall admission, 8/1 for domestic students, 4/1 for international students; for spring admission, 12/1 for domestic students, 10/1 for international students; for summer admission, 4/15 for domestic students, 3/1 for international students. Applications are processed on a rolling basis. Application fee: $60. Electronic applications accepted. *Expenses:* Tuition, state resident: full-time $3782. Tuition, nonresident: full-time $10,238. *Financial support:* In 2017–18, 13 research assistantships, 10 teaching assistantships were awarded; fellowships with tuition reimbursements, career-related internships or fieldwork, and Federal Work-Study also available. Support available to part-time students. Financial award application deadline: 4/1; financial award applicants required to submit FAFSA. *Unit head:* Dr. Matthew Stueck Ganio, Department Head, 479-575-2956, Fax: 479-575-5778, E-mail: msganio@uark.edu. *Application contact:* Dr. Stephen Dittmore, Coordinator of Graduate Studies, 479-575-6625, E-mail: dittmore@uark.edu.
Website: http://hkrd.uark.edu/

University of Arkansas at Little Rock, Graduate School, College of Education and Health Professions, Department of Educational Leadership, Program in Higher Education, Little Rock, AR 72204-1099. Offers administration (MA); college student affairs (MA); health professions teaching and learning (MA); higher education (Ed D); two-year college teaching (MA). *Degree requirements:* For doctorate, comprehensive exam, oral defense of dissertation, residency. *Entrance requirements:* For master's, GRE General Test or MAT, interview, minimum graduate GPA of 3.0; for doctorate, GRE General Test, interview, minimum graduate GPA of 3.5, teaching certificate, three years of work experience.

University of Arkansas at Little Rock, Graduate School, College of Education and Health Professions, Department of Health, Human Performance and Sport Management, Little Rock, AR 72204-1099. Offers exercise science (MS); health education and promotion (MS); sport management (MS). *Program availability:* Part-time, evening/weekend. *Degree requirements:* For master's, directed study or residency. *Entrance requirements:* For master's, GRE General Test, minimum GPA of 3.0, 3 reference letters.

University of Arkansas for Medical Sciences, College of Public Health, Little Rock, AR 72205-7199. Offers biostatistics (MPH); environmental and occupational health (MPH, Certificate); epidemiology (MPH, PhD); health behavior and health education (MPH); health policy and management (MPH); health promotion and prevention research (PhD); health services administration (MHSA); health systems research (PhD); public health (Certificate); public health leadership (Dr PH). *Accreditation:* CEPH. *Program availability:* Part-time. *Degree requirements:* For master's, preceptorship, culminating experience, internship; for doctorate, comprehensive exam, capstone. *Entrance requirements:* For master's, GRE, GMAT, LSAT, PCAT, MCAT, DAT; for doctorate, GRE. Additional exam requirements/recommendations for international students: Required—TOEFL (minimum score 80 iBT), IELTS. Electronic applications accepted. *Expenses:* Contact institution. *Faculty research:* Health systems, tobacco prevention control, obesity prevention, environmental and occupational exposure, cancer prevention.

University of Central Arkansas, Graduate School, College of Health and Behavioral Sciences, Department of Health Sciences, Conway, AR 72035-0001. Offers health education (MS). *Program availability:* Part-time, evening/weekend, online learning. *Degree requirements:* For master's, comprehensive exam, thesis optional. *Entrance requirements:* For master's, GRE General Test, minimum GPA of 2.7. Additional exam requirements/recommendations for international students: Required—TOEFL (minimum score 550 paper-based). Electronic applications accepted.

University of Cincinnati, Graduate School, College of Education, Criminal Justice, and Human Services, School of Human Services, Health Promotion and Education Program, Cincinnati, OH 45221. Offers exercise and fitness (MS); health education (PhD); public and community health (MS); public health (MPH). *Accreditation:* NCATE. *Program availability:* Part-time, evening/weekend. *Degree requirements:* For master's, thesis or alternative; for doctorate, thesis/dissertation. *Entrance requirements:* For master's and doctorate, GRE General Test. Additional exam requirements/recommendations for international students: Required—TOEFL (minimum score 580 paper-based). Electronic applications accepted. *Expenses:* Tuition, area resident: Full-time $14,468. Tuition, state resident: full-time $14,968; part-time $754 per credit hour. Tuition, nonresident: full-time $24,210; part-time $1311 per credit hour. *International tuition:* $26,460 full-time. *Required fees:* $3958; $84 per credit hour. One-time fee: $85 full-time. Tuition and fees vary according to course load, degree level and program.

University of Colorado Denver, College of Liberal Arts and Sciences, Program in Health and Behavioral Sciences, Denver, CO 80217. Offers PhD. *Program availability:* Part-time, evening/weekend. *Degree requirements:* For doctorate, comprehensive exam, thesis/dissertation, minimum of 62 credit hours of course work. *Entrance requirements:* For doctorate, GRE (minimum scores in the top 30th percentile), master's or equivalent graduate degree; prior coursework or experience in social or behavioral sciences (minimum 15 semester hours), human biology or physiology (minimum six semester hours), and statistics and epidemiology (minimum three semester hours each); minimum undergraduate GPA of 3.25, graduate 3.5; three letters of recommendation; essay. Additional exam requirements/recommendations for international students: Required—TOEFL (minimum score 525 paper-based; 71 iBT). Electronic applications accepted. *Faculty research:* HIV/AIDS prevention, tobacco

control, globalization and primary health care, social inequality and health, maternal and child health.

University of Colorado Denver, Colorado School of Public Health, Program in Public Health, Aurora, CO 80206. Offers community and behavioral health (MPH, Dr PH); environmental and occupational health (MPH); epidemiology (MPH); health systems, management and policy (MPH). *Program availability:* Part-time, evening/weekend. *Degree requirements:* For master's, thesis or alternative, 42 credit hours; for doctorate, comprehensive exam, thesis/dissertation, 67 credit hours. *Entrance requirements:* For master's, GRE, MCAT, DAT, LSAT, PCAT, GMAT or master's degree from accredited institution, baccalaureate degree or equivalent; minimum GPA of 3.0; transcripts; references; resume; essay; for doctorate, GRE, MCAT, DAT, LSAT, PCAT or GMAT, MPH or master's or higher degree in related field or equivalent; 2 years of previous work experience in public health; essay; resume. Additional exam requirements/recommendations for international students: Required—TOEFL (minimum score 550 paper-based; 80 iBT). Electronic applications accepted. *Expenses:* Contact institution. *Faculty research:* Cancer prevention by nutrition, cancer survivorship outcomes, social and cultural factors related to health.

University of Colorado Denver, School of Medicine, Physician Assistant Program, Aurora, CO 80045. Offers child health associate (MPAS), including global health, leadership, education, advocacy, development, and scholarship, pediatric critical and acute care, rural health, urban/underserved populations. *Accreditation:* ARC-PA. *Degree requirements:* For master's, comprehensive exam. *Entrance requirements:* For master's, GRE General Test, minimum GPA of 2.8; 3 letters of recommendation; prerequisite courses in chemistry, biology, general genetics, psychology and statistics; interview. Additional exam requirements/recommendations for international students: Required—TOEFL (minimum score 550 paper-based; 80 iBT). Electronic applications accepted. *Expenses:* Contact institution. *Faculty research:* Clinical genetics and genetic counseling, evidence-based medicine, pediatric allergy and asthma, childhood diabetes, standardized patient assessment.

University of Florida, Graduate School, College of Health and Human Performance, Department of Health Education and Behavior, Gainesville, FL 32611. Offers health and human performance (PhD), including health behavior; health communication (Graduate Certificate); health education and behavior (MS). *Accreditation:* NCATE (one or more programs are accredited). *Program availability:* Part-time. Terminal master's awarded for partial completion of doctoral program. *Degree requirements:* For master's, comprehensive exam, thesis (for some programs); for doctorate, comprehensive exam, thesis/dissertation. *Entrance requirements:* For master's and doctorate, GRE General Test (minimum score 293), minimum GPA of 3.0. Additional exam requirements/recommendations for international students: Required—TOEFL (minimum score 550 paper-based; 80 iBT), IELTS (minimum score 6). Electronic applications accepted. *Faculty research:* Community-based participatory research; health disparities issues; health; cancer prevention and control; obesity-related issues; community capacity building; training community health workers; use of community based research principles to design, implement, an evaluate community health worker interventions; obesity; weight management; health literacy; health disparities (ethnic, gender, age, urban/rural); tailored health messages; entertainment education; COPD.

University of Georgia, Biomedical and Health Sciences Institute, Athens, GA 30602. Offers neuroscience (PhD). *Entrance requirements:* For doctorate, GRE, official transcripts, 3 letters of recommendation, statement of interest. Additional exam requirements/recommendations for international students: Required—TOEFL.

University of Georgia, College of Public Health, Department of Health Promotion and Behavior, Athens, GA 30602. Offers MA, MPH, Dr PH, PhD. *Accreditation:* NCATE (one or more programs are accredited). *Degree requirements:* For master's, thesis (MA); for doctorate, thesis/dissertation. *Entrance requirements:* For master's, GRE General Test or MAT; for doctorate, GRE General Test. Electronic applications accepted.

University of Houston, College of Liberal Arts and Social Sciences, Department of Health and Human Performance, Houston, TX 77204. Offers exercise science (MS); human nutrition (MS); human space exploration sciences (MS); kinesiology (PhD); physical education (M Ed). *Accreditation:* NCATE (one or more programs are accredited). *Program availability:* Part-time, evening/weekend. *Degree requirements:* For master's, comprehensive exam (for some programs), thesis (for some programs); for doctorate, comprehensive exam, thesis/dissertation, qualifying exam, candidacy paper. *Entrance requirements:* For master's, GRE (minimum 35th percentile on each section), minimum cumulative GPA of 3.0; for doctorate, GRE (minimum 35th percentile on each section), minimum cumulative GPA of 3.3. Additional exam requirements/recommendations for international students: Required—TOEFL (minimum score 550 paper-based; 79 iBT). Electronic applications accepted. *Faculty research:* Biomechanics, exercise physiology, obesity, nutrition, space exploration science.

University of Illinois at Chicago, College of Medicine and Graduate College, Graduate Programs in Medicine, Department of Medical Education, Chicago, IL 60607-7128. Offers MHPE. *Program availability:* Part-time. *Degree requirements:* For master's, thesis. *Entrance requirements:* For master's, GRE General Test. Additional exam requirements/recommendations for international students: Required—TOEFL. Electronic applications accepted.

University of Illinois at Springfield, Graduate Programs, College of Public Affairs and Administration, Program in Public Health, Springfield, IL 62703-5407. Offers community health education (Graduate Certificate); emergency preparedness and homeland security (Graduate Certificate); environmental health (MPH, Graduate Certificate); environmental risk assessment (Graduate Certificate); epidemiology (Graduate Certificate); public health (MPH). *Program availability:* Part-time, evening/weekend, 100% online. *Faculty:* 7 full-time (4 women). *Students:* 38 full-time (23 women), 46 part-time (34 women); includes 27 minority (16 Black or African American, non-Hispanic/Latino; 4 Asian, non-Hispanic/Latino; 5 Hispanic/Latino; 2 Two or more races, non-Hispanic/Latino), 22 international. Average age 32. 47 applicants, 51% accepted, 18 enrolled. In 2017, 28 master's, 17 other advanced degrees awarded. *Degree requirements:* For master's, comprehensive exam, internship. *Entrance requirements:* For master's, GRE, minimum undergraduate GPA of 3.0, 3 letters of recommendation, statement of personal goals. Additional exam requirements/recommendations for international students: Required—TOEFL (minimum score 500 paper-based; 61 iBT). *Application deadline:* Applications are processed on a rolling basis. Application fee: $60 ($75 for international students). Electronic applications accepted. *Expenses:* Tuition, state resident: full-time $7896; part-time $329 per credit hour. Tuition, nonresident: full-time $16,200; part-time $675 per credit hour. Tuition and fees vary according to program. *Financial support:* In 2017–18, research assistantships with full tuition reimbursements (averaging $10,249 per year), teaching assistantships with full tuition reimbursements (averaging $10,303 per year) were awarded; fellowships, career-related internships or fieldwork, Federal Work-Study, scholarships/grants, health care benefits, and unspecified assistantships also available. Support available to part-time students. Financial award application deadline: 11/15; financial award applicants required to submit FAFSA. *Unit head:* Dr. Josiah Alamu, Program Administrator, 217-206-7874, Fax: 217-206-7279, E-mail: jalam3@uis.edu.
Website: http://www.uis.edu/publichealth/

The University of Kansas, University of Kansas Medical Center, School of Nursing, Kansas City, KS 66160. Offers adult/gerontological clinical nurse specialist (PMC); adult/gerontological nurse practitioner (PMC); health care informatics (PMC); health professions educator (PMC); nurse midwife (PMC); nursing (MS, DNP, PhD); organizational leadership (PMC); psychiatric/mental health nurse practitioner (PMC); public health nursing (PMC). *Accreditation:* AACN; ACNM/ACME. *Program availability:* Part-time, 100% online, blended/hybrid learning. *Faculty:* 56. *Students:* 48 full-time (44 women), 260 part-time (235 women); includes 50 minority (12 Black or African American, non-Hispanic/Latino; 2 American Indian or Alaska Native, non-Hispanic/Latino; 16 Asian, non-Hispanic/Latino; 8 Hispanic/Latino; 12 Two or more races, non-Hispanic/Latino). Average age 36. 87 applicants, 95% accepted, 61 enrolled. In 2017, 37 master's, 18 doctorates, 3 other advanced degrees awarded. Terminal master's awarded for partial completion of doctoral program. *Degree requirements:* For master's, comprehensive exam, thesis (for some programs), general oral exam; for doctorate, thesis/dissertation or alternative, comprehensive oral exam (for DNP); comprehensive written and oral exam, or three publications (for PhD). *Entrance requirements:* For master's, bachelor's degree in nursing, minimum GPA of 3.0, 1 year of clinical experience, RN license in KS and MO; for doctorate, GRE General Test (for PhD only), bachelor's degree in nursing, minimum GPA of 3.5, RN license in KS and MO. Additional exam requirements/recommendations for international students: Required—TOEFL. *Application deadline:* For fall admission, 4/1 for domestic and international students; for spring admission, 9/1 for domestic and international students. Application fee: $75. Electronic applications accepted. *Financial support:* In 2017–18, 5 research assistantships with tuition reimbursements (averaging $20,000 per year), 30 teaching assistantships with tuition reimbursements (averaging $20,000 per year) were awarded; scholarships/grants and traineeships also available. Financial award application deadline: 3/1; financial award applicants required to submit FAFSA. *Faculty research:* Breastfeeding practices of teen mothers, national database of nursing quality indicators, caregiving of families of patients using technology in the home, simulation in nursing education, diaphragm fatigue. *Total annual research expenditures:* $1.4 million. *Unit head:* Dr. Sally Maliski, Dean, 913-588-1601, Fax: 913-588-1660, E-mail: smaliski@kumc.edu. *Application contact:* Dr. Pamela K. Barnes, Associate Dean, Student Affairs, 913-588-1619, Fax: 913-588-1615, E-mail: pbarnes2@kumc.edu.
Website: http://nursing.kumc.edu

University of Louisville, Graduate School, College of Education and Human Development, Department of Educational Leadership, Evaluation and Organizational Development, Louisville, KY 40292-0001. Offers educational leadership and organizational development (Ed D, PhD), including evaluation (PhD), human resource development (PhD), P-12 administration (PhD), post-secondary administration (PhD), sport administration (PhD); health professions education (Certificate); higher education administration (MA); human resources and organization development (MS), including health professions education, human resource leadership, workplace learning and performance; P-12 educational administration (Ed S), including principalship, supervisor of instruction. *Accreditation:* NCATE. *Program availability:* Part-time, evening/weekend, online learning. *Students:* 190 full-time (64 women), 516 part-time (298 women); includes 218 minority (131 Black or African American, non-Hispanic/Latino; 1 American Indian or Alaska Native, non-Hispanic/Latino; 16 Asian, non-Hispanic/Latino; 47 Hispanic/Latino; 2 Native Hawaiian or other Pacific Islander, non-Hispanic/Latino; 21 Two or more races, non-Hispanic/Latino), 3 international. Average age 36. 232 applicants, 84% accepted, 141 enrolled. In 2017, 68 master's, 2 doctorates, 17 other advanced degrees awarded. Application fee: $65. *Expenses:* Tuition, state resident: full-time $12,246; part-time $681 per credit hour. Tuition, nonresident: full-time $25,486; part-time $1417 per credit hour. *Required fees:* $196. Tuition and fees vary according to course load, program and reciprocity agreements. *Financial support:* Application deadline: 6/1; applicants required to submit FAFSA. *Faculty research:* Urban educational leadership and policy, human resource and organizational development, program evaluation, community and military partnerships, higher education, and economic education. *Total annual research expenditures:* $256,111. *Unit head:* Dr. Jeffrey Sun, Chair and Professor, 502-852-0618, E-mail: jeffrey.sun@louisville.edu. *Application contact:* Betty Hampton, Director of Graduate Student Services, 502-852-5597, Fax: 502-852-1465, E-mail: edadvise@louisville.edu.
Website: http://louisville.edu/education/departments/eleod

University of Louisville, Graduate School, College of Education and Human Development, Department of Health and Sport Sciences, Louisville, KY 40292-0001. Offers community health education (M Ed); exercise physiology (MS), including health and sport sciences, strength and conditioning; health and physical education (MAT); sport administration (MS). *Program availability:* Part-time, evening/weekend. *Students:* 35 full-time (11 women), 6 part-time (4 women); includes 10 minority (5 Black or African American, non-Hispanic/Latino; 4 Hispanic/Latino; 1 Two or more races, non-Hispanic/Latino), 1 international. Average age 28. 46 applicants, 67% accepted, 20 enrolled. In 2017, 21 master's awarded. Application fee: $65. *Expenses:* Tuition, state resident: full-time $12,246; part-time $681 per credit hour. Tuition, nonresident: full-time $25,486; part-time $1417 per credit hour. *Required fees:* $196. Tuition and fees vary according to course load, program and reciprocity agreements. *Financial support:* Applicants required to submit FAFSA. *Faculty research:* Sport administration, exercise physiology, exercise science, physical education, health education. *Total annual research expenditures:* $91,688. *Unit head:* Dr. Margaret Hancock, Interim Chair/Assistant Professor, 502-852-6645, E-mail: meg.hancock@louisville.edu. *Application contact:* Betty Hampton, Director of Graduate Student Services, 502-852-5597, Fax: 502-852-1465, E-mail: edadvise@louisville.edu.
Website: http://www.louisville.edu/education/departments/hss

University of Louisville, Graduate School, College of Education and Human Development, Departments of Early Childhood and Elementary Education, Middle and Secondary Education, and Special Education, Louisville, KY 40292-0001. Offers art education (MAT); autism and applied behavior analysis (Certificate); curriculum and instruction (PhD); early elementary education (MAT); exercise physiology (MS); health and physical education (MAT); health professions education (Certificate); higher education (MA); human resources and organization development (MS); instructional technology (M Ed); interdisciplinary early childhood education (MAT); middle school education (MAT); music education (MAT); secondary education (MAT); special education (MAT); sport administration (MS); teacher leadership (M Ed). *Program availability:* Part-time, evening/weekend. *Students:* 114 full-time (73 women), 173 part-time (114 women); includes 49 minority (19 Black or African American, non-Hispanic/Latino; 5 Asian, non-Hispanic/Latino; 13 Hispanic/Latino; 12 Two or more races, non-Hispanic/Latino), 7 international. Average age 29. 132 applicants, 73% accepted, 57 enrolled. In 2017, 70 master's, 2 doctorates, 2 other advanced degrees awarded. *Application deadline:* For spring admission, 1/1 priority date for international students. Application fee: $65. *Expenses:* Tuition, state resident: full-time $12,246; part-time $681 per credit hour. Tuition, nonresident: full-time $25,486; part-time $1417 per credit hour. *Required fees:* $196. Tuition and fees vary according to course load, program and reciprocity agreements. *Financial support:* Application deadline: 6/1; applicants required to submit FAFSA. *Faculty research:* STEM teaching and learning; content literacy for English language learners; social justice in teacher education; adolescent literacy; mathematics teacher development. *Total annual research expenditures:* $1.7 million.

Unit head: Dr. Ann E. Larson, Dean, College of Education and Human Development, 502-852-6411, Fax: 502-852-1464, E-mail: ann@louisville.edu. *Application contact:* Betty Hampton, Director of Graduate Student Services, 502-852-5597, Fax: 502-852-1465, E-mail: edadvise@louisville.edu.
Website: http://louisville.edu/delphi

University of Maryland, College Park, Academic Affairs, School of Public Health, Department of Behavioral and Community Health, College Park, MD 20742. Offers community health education (MPH); public/community health (PhD). *Accreditation:* CEPH. *Program availability:* Part-time, evening/weekend. *Degree requirements:* For master's, thesis optional; for doctorate, comprehensive exam, thesis/dissertation. *Entrance requirements:* For master's, GRE General Test, minimum GPA of 3.0, 3 letters of recommendation; for doctorate, GRE General Test, minimum GPA of 3.5, 3 letters of recommendation. Additional exam requirements/recommendations for international students: Required—TOEFL. Electronic applications accepted. *Faculty research:* Controlling stress and tension, women's health, aging and public policy, adolescent health, long-term care.

University of Massachusetts Amherst, Graduate School, School of Public Health and Health Sciences, Department of Public Health, Amherst, MA 01003. Offers biostatistics (MPH, MS, PhD); community health education (MPH, MS, PhD); environmental health sciences (MPH, MS, PhD); epidemiology (MPH, MS, PhD); health policy and management (MPH, MS, PhD); nutrition (MPH, PhD); public health practice (MPH); MPH/MPPA. *Program availability:* Part-time, evening/weekend, online learning. Terminal master's awarded for partial completion of doctoral program. *Degree requirements:* For master's, thesis (for some programs); for doctorate, comprehensive exam, thesis/dissertation. *Entrance requirements:* For master's and doctorate, GRE General Test. Additional exam requirements/recommendations for international students: Required—TOEFL (minimum score 550 paper-based; 80 iBT), IELTS (minimum score 6.5). Electronic applications accepted.

University of Michigan, School of Public Health, Department of Health Behavior and Health Education, Ann Arbor, MI 48109. Offers MPH, PhD, MPH/MSW. PhD offered through the Rackham Graduate School. *Accreditation:* CEPH (one or more programs are accredited). Terminal master's awarded for partial completion of doctoral program. *Degree requirements:* For doctorate, oral defense of dissertation, preliminary exam. *Entrance requirements:* For master's, GRE General Test (preferred); MCAT; for doctorate, GRE General Test. Additional exam requirements/recommendations for international students: Required—TOEFL (minimum score 100 iBT). Electronic applications accepted. *Expenses:* Tuition, state resident: full-time $22,368; part-time $1201 per credit hour. Tuition, nonresident: full-time $45,156; part-time $2467 per credit hour. *Required fees:* $376 per term. Tuition and fees vary according to course load, degree level and program. *Faculty research:* Empowerment theory; structure, culture, and health; health disparities; community-based participatory research; health and medical decision-making.

University of Michigan–Flint, School of Health Professions and Studies, Program in Public Health, Flint, MI 48501-1950. Offers health administration (MPH); health education (MPH). *Program availability:* Part-time. *Faculty:* 16 full-time (11 women), 36 part-time/adjunct (19 women). *Students:* 14 full-time (11 women), 37 part-time (32 women); includes 15 minority (9 Black or African American, non-Hispanic/Latino; 2 American Indian or Alaska Native, non-Hispanic/Latino; 2 Asian, non-Hispanic/Latino; 2 Two or more races, non-Hispanic/Latino), 7 international. Average age 31. 38 applicants, 50% accepted, 9 enrolled. In 2017, 18 master's awarded. *Degree requirements:* For master's, thesis, public health capstone. *Entrance requirements:* For master's, GRE, bachelor's degree from accredited institution with sufficient preparation in algebra to succeed in epidemiology and biostatistics; minimum overall undergraduate GPA of 3.0. Additional exam requirements/recommendations for international students: Required—TOEFL (minimum score 84 iBT), IELTS (minimum score 6.5). *Application deadline:* For fall admission, 8/1 for domestic students, 5/1 for international students; for winter admission, 11/15 for domestic students, 9/1 for international students; for spring admission, 3/15 for domestic students, 1/1 for international students. Applications are processed on a rolling basis. Application fee: $55. Electronic applications accepted. *Expenses:* Contact institution. *Financial support:* Federal Work-Study, institutionally sponsored loans, scholarships/grants, and unspecified assistantships available. Support available to part-time students. Financial award application deadline: 3/1; financial award applicants required to submit FAFSA. *Unit head:* Dr. Shan Parker, Director, 810-762-3172, E-mail: shanpark@umflint.edu. *Application contact:* Bradley T. Maki, Director of Graduate Admissions, 810-762-3171, Fax: 810-766-6789, E-mail: bmaki@umflint.edu.
Website: http://www.umflint.edu/graduateprograms/public-health-mph

University of Missouri, Office of Research and Graduate Studies, College of Education, Department of Learning, Teaching and Curriculum, Columbia, MO 65211. Offers agricultural education (M Ed, PhD, Ed S); art education (M Ed, PhD, Ed S); business and office education (M Ed, PhD, Ed S); early childhood education (M Ed, PhD, Ed S); elementary education (M Ed, PhD, Ed S); English education (M Ed, PhD, Ed S); foreign language education (M Ed, PhD, Ed S); health education and promotion (M Ed, PhD); learning and instruction (M Ed); marketing education (M Ed, PhD, Ed S); mathematics education (M Ed, PhD, Ed S); music education (M Ed, PhD, Ed S); reading education (M Ed, PhD, Ed S); science education (M Ed, PhD, Ed S); social studies education (M Ed, PhD, Ed S); vocational education (M Ed, PhD, Ed S). *Program availability:* Part-time. Terminal master's awarded for partial completion of doctoral program. *Degree requirements:* For doctorate, thesis/dissertation. *Entrance requirements:* For master's and Ed S, GRE General Test or MAT, minimum GPA of 3.0; for doctorate, GRE General Test, minimum GPA of 3.0. Additional exam requirements/recommendations for international students: Required—TOEFL (minimum score 600 paper-based; 100 iBT). Electronic applications accepted.

University of Missouri–Kansas City, School of Medicine, Kansas City, MO 64110-2499. Offers health professions education (MS); MD/PhD. *Accreditation:* LCME/AMA. *Degree requirements:* For doctorate, one foreign language, United States Medical Licensing Exam Step 1 and 2. *Entrance requirements:* For doctorate, interview. *Expenses:* Contact institution. *Faculty research:* Cardiovascular disease, women's and children's health, trauma and infectious diseases, neurological, metabolic disease.

University of Montana, Graduate School, Phyllis J. Washington College of Education and Human Sciences, Department of Health and Human Performance, Missoula, MT 59812. Offers community health (MS); exercise science (MS); health and human performance generalist (MS). *Program availability:* Part-time. *Entrance requirements:* For master's, GRE General Test. Additional exam requirements/recommendations for international students: Required—TOEFL. *Faculty research:* Exercise physiology, performance psychology, nutrition, pre-employment physical screening, program evaluation.

University of Nebraska at Omaha, Graduate Studies, College of Education, School of Health and Kinesiology, Omaha, NE 68182. Offers athletic training (MA); exercise science (PhD); health, physical education, and recreation (MA, MS). *Program availability:* Part-time, evening/weekend. *Degree requirements:* For master's, comprehensive exam, thesis (for some programs). *Entrance requirements:* For master's,

Health Education

GRE; entrance exam, minimum GPA of 3.0, official transcripts, statement of purpose, 2 letters of recommendation; for doctorate, GRE, minimum GPA of 3.2, official transcripts, statement of purpose, 3 letters of recommendation, resume, writing sample. Additional exam requirements/recommendations for international students: Required—TOEFL, IELTS, PTE. Electronic applications accepted.

University of New Mexico, Graduate Studies, College of Education, Program in Health Education, Albuquerque, NM 87131-2039. Offers community health education (MS). *Accreditation:* NCATE. *Program availability:* Part-time. *Faculty:* 4 full-time (3 women), 1 (woman) part-time/adjunct. *Students:* 10 full-time (all women), 8 part-time (7 women); includes 12 minority (2 Black or African American, non-Hispanic/Latino; 5 American Indian or Alaska Native, non-Hispanic/Latino; 5 Hispanic/Latino), 1 international. Average age 32. 8 applicants, 75% accepted, 6 enrolled. In 2017, 11 master's awarded. *Degree requirements:* For master's, comprehensive exam, thesis optional. *Entrance requirements:* For master's, 3 letters of reference, resume, minimum cumulative GPA of 3.0 in last 2 years of bachelor's degree, letter of intent. Additional exam requirements/recommendations for international students: Required—TOEFL (minimum score 550 paper-based). *Application deadline:* For fall admission, 6/15 priority date for domestic students; for spring admission, 11/1 priority date for domestic students. Applications are processed on a rolling basis. Application fee: $50. Electronic applications accepted. *Financial support:* Fellowships, teaching assistantships with full tuition reimbursements, career-related internships or fieldwork, institutionally sponsored loans, scholarships/grants, and health care benefits available. Financial award application deadline: 3/1; financial award applicants required to submit FAFSA. *Faculty research:* Alcohol and families, health behaviors and sexuality, multicultural health behavior, health promotion policy, school/community-based prevention, health and aging. *Unit head:* Dr. Elias Duryea, Coordinator, 505-277-5151, Fax: 505-277-6227, E-mail: duryea@unm.edu. *Application contact:* Carol Catania, Graduate Coordinator, 505-277-5151, Fax: 505-277-6227, E-mail: catania@unm.edu.

The University of North Carolina at Pembroke, The Graduate School, School of Education, Department of Health and Human Performance, Pembroke, NC 28372-1510. Offers health/physical education (MAT); physical education (MA), including exercise/sports administration, physical education advanced licensure. *Program availability:* Part-time, evening/weekend. *Degree requirements:* For master's, comprehensive exam, thesis optional. *Entrance requirements:* For master's, MAT or GRE, minimum GPA of 3.0 in major, 2.5 overall. Additional exam requirements/recommendations for international students: Required—TOEFL. *Application deadline:* For fall admission, 7/15 priority date for domestic and international students; for spring admission, 12/1 priority date for domestic and international students. Applications are processed on a rolling basis. Application fee: $45 ($60 for international students). *Financial support:* Application deadline: 4/15; applicants required to submit FAFSA. *Unit head:* Dr. Leah Fiorentino, Program Director, 910-775-4354, E-mail: leah.fiorentino@uncp.edu. Website: https://www.uncp.edu/departments/health-and-human-performance

University of Northern Colorado, Graduate School, College of Natural and Health Sciences, School of Human Sciences, Program in Public Health, Greeley, CO 80639. Offers community health education (MPH); global health and community health education (MPH); healthy aging and community health education (MPH). *Degree requirements:* For master's, comprehensive exam, thesis or alternative. *Entrance requirements:* For master's, GRE General Test, 2 letters of recommendation. Electronic applications accepted.

University of Northern Iowa, Graduate College, College of Education, School of Kinesiology, Allied Health and Human Services, MA Program in Health Education, Cedar Falls, IA 50614. Offers community health education (MA); health promotion/fitness management (MA); school health education (MA). *Program availability:* Part-time, evening/weekend. *Degree requirements:* For master's, comprehensive exam, thesis or alternative. *Entrance requirements:* For master's, minimum GPA of 3.0. Additional exam requirements/recommendations for international students: Required—TOEFL (minimum score 500 paper-based; 61 iBT). Electronic applications accepted.

University of Oklahoma Health Sciences Center, Graduate College, College of Allied Health, Department of Allied Health Sciences, Oklahoma City, OK 73190. Offers PhD. *Degree requirements:* For doctorate, one foreign language, comprehensive exam, thesis/dissertation optional. *Entrance requirements:* For doctorate, GRE General Test, 3 letters of recommendation, master's degree. Additional exam requirements/recommendations for international students: Required—TOEFL (minimum score 550 paper-based).

University of Phoenix–Online Campus, College of Health Sciences and Nursing, Phoenix, AZ 85034-7209. Offers family nurse practitioner (Certificate); health care (Certificate); health care education (Certificate); health care informatics (Certificate); informatics (MSN); nursing (MSN); nursing and health care education (MSN); MSN/MBA; MSN/MHA. *Accreditation:* AACN. *Program availability:* Evening/weekend, online learning. *Entrance requirements:* Additional exam requirements/recommendations for international students: Required—TOEFL, TOEIC (Test of English as an International Communication), Berlitz Online English Proficiency Exam, PTE, or IELTS. Electronic applications accepted. *Expenses:* Contact institution.

University of Pittsburgh, Graduate School of Public Health, Department of Infectious Diseases and Microbiology, Pittsburgh, PA 15261. Offers infectious diseases and microbiology (MS, PhD); management, intervention, and community practice (MPH); pathogenesis, eradication, and laboratory practice (MPH). *Program availability:* Part-time. *Faculty:* 21 full-time (7 women), 5 part-time/adjunct (2 women). *Students:* 55 full-time (34 women), 19 part-time (12 women); includes 17 minority (2 Black or African American, non-Hispanic/Latino; 8 Asian, non-Hispanic/Latino; 1 Hispanic/Latino; 6 Two or more races, non-Hispanic/Latino), 8 international. Average age 26. 152 applicants, 51% accepted, 27 enrolled. In 2017, 34 master's, 2 doctorates awarded. Terminal master's awarded for partial completion of doctoral program. *Degree requirements:* For master's, thesis, comprehensive exam (for MS); for doctorate, comprehensive exam, thesis/dissertation, preliminary exam, dissertation defense. *Entrance requirements:* For master's, GRE General Test, MCAT, or DAT, minimum GPA of 3.0, 6 credits of behavioral science; for doctorate, GRE General Test, MCAT, DAT, minimum GPA of 3.0; research experience; knowledge of biology or microbiology, chemistry, and algebra. Additional exam requirements/recommendations for international students: Required—TOEFL (minimum score 550 paper-based, 80 iBT) or IELTS (minimum score 6.5). *Application deadline:* For fall admission, 1/15 priority date for domestic students, 3/15 priority date for international students. Applications are processed on a rolling basis. Application fee: $135. Electronic applications accepted. *Expenses:* $26,136 per year in-state tuition, $43,392 out-of-state, $850 fees. *Financial support:* In 2017–18, 38 students received support, including 19 research assistantships with full tuition reimbursements available; fellowships, teaching assistantships, scholarships/grants, and tuition waivers (full) also available. Financial award applicants required to submit FAFSA. *Faculty research:* Development of HIV vaccines, complications of antiretroviral therapy, emerging infections, herpes viruses. *Unit head:* Robin Tierno, Department Administrator, 412-624-3105, Fax: 412-624-4953, E-mail: rtierno@pitt.edu. *Application contact:* Abby Kincaid, Student Services Coordinator, 412-624-3331, E-mail: abbykincaid@pitt.edu. Website: http://www.publichealth.pitt.edu/idm

University of Puerto Rico–Medical Sciences Campus, Graduate School of Public Health, Department of Social Sciences, Program in Public Health Education, San Juan, PR 00936-5067. Offers MPHE. *Program availability:* Part-time, evening/weekend. *Degree requirements:* For master's, thesis. *Entrance requirements:* For master's, GRE, previous course work in education, social sciences, algebra, and natural sciences.

University of Rhode Island, Graduate School, College of Health Sciences, Department of Kinesiology, Kingston, RI 02881. Offers cultural studies of sport and physical culture (MS); exercise science (MS); psychosocial/behavioral aspects of physical activity (MS). *Accreditation:* NCATE. *Program availability:* Part-time. *Faculty:* 14 full-time (9 women). *Students:* 10 full-time (4 women), 3 part-time (1 woman), 1 international. 8 applicants, 100% accepted, 6 enrolled. In 2017, 7 master's awarded. *Entrance requirements:* Additional exam requirements/recommendations for international students: Required—TOEFL. *Application deadline:* For fall admission, 7/15 for domestic students, 2/1 for international students; for spring admission, 11/15 for domestic students, 7/15 for international students. Application fee: $65. Electronic applications accepted. *Expenses:* Tuition, state resident: full-time $12,706; part-time $786 per credit. Tuition, nonresident: full-time $25,216; part-time $1401 per credit. *Required fees:* $1598; $45 per credit. One-time fee: $30 part-time. *Financial support:* In 2017–18, 5 teaching assistantships with tuition reimbursements (averaging $11,078 per year) were awarded. Financial award application deadline: 2/1; financial award applicants required to submit FAFSA. *Unit head:* Dr. Disa Hatfield, Interim Chair, 401-874-5183, E-mail: doch@uri.edu. *Application contact:* Dr. Matthew Delmonico, Graduate Program Director, 401-874-5440, E-mail: delmonico@uri.edu. Website: http://web.uri.edu/kinesiology/

University of St. Augustine for Health Sciences, Graduate Programs, Master of Health Science Program, San Marcos, CA 92069. Offers athletic training (MHS); executive leadership (MHS); informatics (MHS); teaching and learning (MHS). *Program availability:* Online learning. *Degree requirements:* For master's, comprehensive project.

University of St. Augustine for Health Sciences, Graduate Programs, Post Professional Programs, San Marcos, CA 92069. Offers health science (DH Sc); health sciences education (Ed D); occupational therapy (TOTD); physical therapy (TDPT). *Program availability:* Part-time, online learning. *Entrance requirements:* For doctorate, GRE General Test, master's degree in related field. Additional exam requirements/recommendations for international students: Required—TOEFL.

University of South Africa, College of Human Sciences, Pretoria, South Africa. Offers adult education (M Ed); African languages (MA, PhD); African politics (MA, PhD); Afrikaans (MA, PhD); ancient history (MA, PhD); ancient Near Eastern studies (MA, PhD); anthropology (MA, PhD); applied linguistics (MA); Arabic (MA, PhD); archaeology (MA); art history (MA); Biblical archaeology (MA); Biblical studies (M Th, D Th, PhD); Christian spirituality (M Th, D Th); church history (M Th, D Th); classical studies (MA, PhD); clinical psychology (MA); communication (MA, PhD); comparative education (M Ed, Ed D); consulting psychology (D Admin, D Com, PhD); curriculum studies (M Ed, Ed D); development studies (M Admin, MA, D Admin, PhD); didactics (M Ed, Ed D); education (M Tech); education management (M Ed, Ed D); educational psychology (M Ed); English (MA); environmental education (M Ed); French (MA, PhD); German (MA, PhD); Greek (MA); guidance and counseling (M Ed); health studies (MA, PhD), including health sciences education (MA), health services management (MA), medical and surgical nursing science (critical care general) (MA), midwifery and neonatal nursing science (MA), trauma and emergency care (MA); history (MA, PhD); history of education (Ed D); inclusive education (M Ed, Ed D); information and communications technology policy and regulation (MA); information science (MA, MIS, PhD); international politics (MA, PhD); Islamic studies (MA, PhD); Italian (MA, PhD); Judaica (MA, PhD); linguistics (MA, PhD); mathematical education (M Ed); mathematics education (MA); missiology (M Th, D Th); modern Hebrew (MA, PhD); musicology (MA, MMus, D Mus, PhD); natural science education (M Ed); New Testament (M Th, D Th); Old Testament (D Th); pastoral therapy (M Th, D Th); philosophy (MA); philosophy of education (M Ed, Ed D); politics (MA, PhD); Portuguese (MA, PhD); practical theology (M Th, D Th); psychology (MA, MS, PhD); psychology of education (M Ed, Ed D); public health (MA); religious studies (MA, D Th, PhD); Romance languages (MA); Russian (MA, PhD); Semitic languages (MA, PhD); social behavior studies in HIV/AIDS (MA); social science (mental health) (MA); social science in development studies (MA); social science in psychology (MA); social science in social work (MA); social science in sociology (MA); social work (MSW, DSW, PhD); socio-education (M Ed, Ed D); sociolinguistics (MA); sociology (MA, PhD); Spanish (MA, PhD); systematic theology (M Th, D Th); TESOL (teaching English to speakers of other languages) (MA); theological ethics (M Th, D Th); theory of literature (MA, PhD); urban ministries (D Th); urban ministry (M Th).

University of South Alabama, College of Education and Professional Studies, Department of Health, Kinesiology, and Sport, Mobile, AL 36688. Offers exercise science (MS); health education (M Ed, MS); physical education (M Ed); sport management (MS). *Accreditation:* NCATE (one or more programs are accredited). *Program availability:* Part-time. *Faculty:* 7 full-time (2 women). *Students:* 47 full-time (15 women), 7 part-time (3 women); includes 23 minority (19 Black or African American, non-Hispanic/Latino; 1 American Indian or Alaska Native, non-Hispanic/Latino; 2 Asian, non-Hispanic/Latino; 1 Hispanic/Latino), 4 international. Average age 25. 48 applicants, 54% accepted, 19 enrolled. In 2017, 23 master's awarded. *Degree requirements:* For master's, comprehensive exam, thesis optional. *Entrance requirements:* For master's, GRE General Test or MAT, Alabama Class B certificate or the equivalent (for students seeking the master's-level/Class A certification). Additional exam requirements/recommendations for international students: Required—TOEFL. *Application deadline:* For fall admission, 7/1 priority date for domestic students, 6/15 priority date for international students; for spring admission, 11/15 priority date for domestic students, 11/1 priority date for international students; for summer admission, 4/15 for domestic students, 4/1 for international students. Applications are processed on a rolling basis. Application fee: $35. Electronic applications accepted. *Expenses:* Tuition, state resident: full-time $10,104; part-time $421 per semester hour. Tuition, nonresident: full-time $20,208; part-time $842 per semester hour. *Financial support:* Fellowships, research assistantships, teaching assistantships with partial tuition reimbursements, career-related internships or fieldwork, Federal Work-Study, institutionally sponsored loans, scholarships/grants, and unspecified assistantships available. Support available to part-time students. Financial award application deadline: 3/31; financial award applicants required to submit FAFSA. *Unit head:* Dr. John Kovaleski, Department Chair, 251-461-1622, Fax: 251-460-7222, E-mail: jkovales@southalabama.edu. *Application contact:* Dr. Susan Santoli, Director of Graduate Studies, 251-380-2836, Fax: 251-380-2748, E-mail: ssantoli@southalabama.edu. Website: http://www.southalabama.edu/colleges/ceps/hks/index.html

University of South Carolina, The Graduate School, Arnold School of Public Health, Department of Health Promotion, Education, and Behavior, Columbia, SC 29208. Offers health education (MAT); health promotion, education, and behavior (MPH, MS, MSPH, Dr PH, PhD); school health education (Certificate); MSW/MPH. MAT offered in cooperation with the College of Education. *Accreditation:* CEPH (one or more programs are accredited); NCATE (one or more programs are accredited). *Program availability:* Part-time. *Degree requirements:* For master's, comprehensive exam, thesis or alternative, practicum (MPH), project (MS); for doctorate, comprehensive exam, thesis/

dissertation. *Entrance requirements:* For master's and doctorate, GRE General Test. Additional exam requirements/recommendations for international students: Required— TOEFL (minimum score 570 paper-based; 75 iBT). Electronic applications accepted. *Faculty research:* Health disparities and inequalities in communities, global health and nutrition, cancer and HIV/AIDS prevention, health communication, policy and program design.

University of South Carolina, The Graduate School, College of Education, Department of Instruction and Teacher Education, Program in Secondary Education, Columbia, SC 29208. Offers art education (IMA, MAT); business education (IMA, MAT); English (MAT); foreign language (MAT); health education (MAT); mathematics (MAT); science (IMA, MAT); secondary (Ed D); secondary education (MT, PhD); social studies (MAT); theatre and speech (MAT). IMA and MT offered jointly with the subject areas. *Accreditation:* NCATE. *Degree requirements:* For master's, comprehensive exam, thesis (for some programs), foreign language (MA); for doctorate, one foreign language, comprehensive exam, thesis/dissertation. *Entrance requirements:* For master's, GRE General Test or MAT, teaching certificate (IMA, M Ed), interview; for doctorate, GRE General Test or MAT, interview. *Faculty research:* Middle school programs, professional development, school collaboration.

University of Southern California, Keck School of Medicine and Graduate School, Graduate Programs in Medicine, Department of Preventive Medicine, Master of Public Health Program, Los Angeles, CA 90032. Offers biostatistics and epidemiology (MPH); child and family health (MPH); environmental health (MPH); geohealth (MPH); global health leadership (MPH); health communication (MPH); health education and promotion (MPH); public health policy (MPH). *Accreditation:* CEPH. *Program availability:* Part-time, evening/weekend. *Faculty:* 47 full-time (35 women), 13 part-time/adjunct (8 women). *Students:* 258 full-time (204 women), 61 part-time (50 women); includes 167 minority (28 Black or African American, non-Hispanic/Latino; 1 American Indian or Alaska Native, non-Hispanic/Latino; 61 Asian, non-Hispanic/Latino; 64 Hispanic/Latino; 4 Native Hawaiian or other Pacific Islander, non-Hispanic/Latino; 9 Two or more races, non-Hispanic/Latino), 28 international. Average age 26. 378 applicants, 53% accepted, 87 enrolled. In 2017, 91 master's awarded. *Degree requirements:* For master's, practicum, final report, oral presentation. *Entrance requirements:* For master's, GRE General Test, MCAT, GMAT, minimum GPA of 3.0. Additional exam requirements/recommendations for international students: Required—TOEFL (minimum score 600 paper-based; 90 iBT). *Application deadline:* For fall admission, 12/1 priority date for domestic students, 5/1 priority date for international students; for spring admission, 9/1 priority date for domestic and international students; for summer admission, 3/1 for domestic and international students. Applications are processed on a rolling basis. Application fee: $90. Electronic applications accepted. *Expenses:* Contact institution. *Financial support:* Career-related internships or fieldwork, Federal Work-Study, institutionally sponsored loans, and scholarships/grants available. Support available to part-time students. Financial award application deadline: 5/4; financial award applicants required to submit CSS PROFILE or FAFSA. *Faculty research:* Cancer and heart disease epidemiology and prevention, mass media and health communication research, effects of air pollution on health, tobacco control, global health. *Total annual research expenditures:* $7 million. *Unit head:* Dr. Louise A. Rohrbach, Director, 323-442-8237, Fax: 323-442-8297, E-mail: rohrbac@usc.edu. *Application contact:* Valerie Burris, Admissions Counselor, 323-442-7257, Fax: 323-442-8297, E-mail: valeriem@usc.edu.
Website: http://mph.usc.edu/

University of South Florida, College of Pharmacy, Tampa, FL 33620-9951. Offers pharmaceutical nanotechnology (MS), including biomedical engineering, drug discovery, delivery, development and manufacturing; pharmacy (Pharm D), including pharmacy and health education. *Accreditation:* ACPE. *Faculty:* 39 full-time (28 women), 1 part-time/adjunct (0 women). *Students:* 381 full-time (226 women), 3 part-time (1 woman); includes 172 minority (27 Black or African American, non-Hispanic/Latino; 70 Asian, non-Hispanic/Latino; 59 Hispanic/Latino; 4 Native Hawaiian or other Pacific Islander, non-Hispanic/Latino; 12 Two or more races, non-Hispanic/Latino), 4 international. Average age 25. 678 applicants, 31% accepted, 105 enrolled. In 2017, 111 doctorates awarded. *Degree requirements:* For master's, comprehensive exam, thesis optional. *Entrance requirements:* For master's, GRE, MCAT or DAT, minimum GPA of 3.0, letters of reference, resume; for doctorate, PCAT, minimum GPA of 2.75 overall (preferred), completion of 72 prerequisite credit hours; U.S. citizenship or permanent resident. Additional exam requirements/recommendations for international students: Required— TOEFL (minimum score 550 paper-based; 79 iBT), IELTS (minimum score 6.5). *Application deadline:* For fall admission, 2/1 priority date for domestic students, 2/1 for international students; for spring admission, 10/15 for domestic students, 9/15 for international students; for summer admission, 2/15 for domestic and international students. Electronic applications accepted. *Financial support:* In 2017–18, 91 students received support. *Total annual research expenditures:* $1.7 million. *Unit head:* Dr. Kevin Sneed, Dean, 813-974-5699, E-mail: ksneed@health.usf.edu. *Application contact:* Dr. Amy Schwartz, Associate Dean, 813-974-2251, E-mail: aschwar1@health.usf.edu.

The University of Tennessee, Graduate School, College of Education, Health and Human Sciences, Program in Health Promotion and Health Education, Knoxville, TN 37996. Offers MS. *Program availability:* Part-time. *Degree requirements:* For master's, thesis optional. *Entrance requirements:* For master's, minimum GPA of 2.7. Additional exam requirements/recommendations for international students: Required—TOEFL. Electronic applications accepted.

The University of Tennessee, Graduate School, College of Education, Health and Human Sciences, Program in Safety, Knoxville, TN 37996. Offers MS. *Accreditation:* NCATE. *Program availability:* Part-time. *Degree requirements:* For master's, thesis optional. *Entrance requirements:* For master's, minimum GPA of 2.7. Additional exam requirements/recommendations for international students: Required—TOEFL. Electronic applications accepted.

The University of Texas at Austin, Graduate School, College of Education, Department of Kinesiology and Health Education, Austin, TX 78712-1111. Offers behavioral health (PhD); exercise and sport psychology (M Ed, MA); exercise science (M Ed, MS, PhD); health education (M Ed, MS, Ed D, PhD). *Program availability:* Part-time. Terminal master's awarded for partial completion of doctoral program. *Degree requirements:* For master's, thesis (for some programs); for doctorate, thesis/ dissertation. *Entrance requirements:* For master's and doctorate, GRE General Test. Additional exam requirements/recommendations for international students: Required— TOEFL. Electronic applications accepted. *Faculty research:* Health promotion, human performance and exercise biochemistry, motor behavior and biomechanics, sport management, aging and pediatric development.

The University of Texas at San Antonio, College of Education and Human Development, Department of Kinesiology, Health, and Nutrition, San Antonio, TX 78249-0617. Offers health and kinesiology (MS). *Program availability:* Part-time, evening/ weekend. *Faculty:* 10 full-time (4 women), 1 (woman) part-time/adjunct. *Students:* 68 full-time (41 women), 42 part-time (22 women); includes 76 minority (11 Black or African American, non-Hispanic/Latino; 7 Asian, non-Hispanic/Latino; 56 Hispanic/Latino; 2 Two or more races, non-Hispanic/Latino), 1 international. Average age 27. 67 applicants, 78% accepted, 25 enrolled. In 2017, 56 master's awarded. *Degree requirements:* For master's, comprehensive exam, thesis optional. *Entrance requirements:* For master's,

bachelor's degree with minimum GPA of 3.0 in last 60 hours of coursework; resume; statement of purpose; two letters of recommendation. Additional exam requirements/ recommendations for international students: Required—TOEFL (minimum score 550 paper-based; 79 iBT), IELTS (minimum score 6.5). *Application deadline:* For fall admission, 6/15 for domestic students, 3/1 for international students; for spring admission, 10/15 for domestic students, 9/15 for international students; for summer admission, 4/15 for domestic students, 2/15 for international students. Applications are processed on a rolling basis. Application fee: $50 ($90 for international students). Electronic applications accepted. *Expenses:* Contact institution. *Financial support:* Unspecified assistantships available. Financial award applicants required to submit FAFSA. *Faculty research:* Childhood obesity, health disparities, community health, exercise physiology, sport psychology. *Total annual research expenditures:* $767,220. *Unit head:* Dr. Sara Oswalt, Chair, 210-458-6227, E-mail: sara.oswalt@utsa.edu.
Website: http://education.utsa.edu/health_and_kinesiology

The University of Texas at Tyler, College of Nursing and Health Sciences, Department of Health and Kinesiology, Tyler, TX 75799-0001. Offers health and kinesiology (M Ed, MA); health sciences (MS); kinesiology (MS). *Accreditation:* TEAC. *Program availability:* Part-time, online learning. *Degree requirements:* For master's, comprehensive exam (for some programs), thesis (for some programs). *Entrance requirements:* Additional exam requirements/recommendations for international students: Required—TOEFL. Electronic applications accepted. *Faculty research:* Osteoporosis, muscle soreness, economy of locomotion, adoption of rehabilitation programs, effect of inactivity and aging on muscle blood vessels, territoriality.

The University of Toledo, College of Graduate Studies, College of Health and Human Services, School of Population Health, Toledo, OH 43606-3390. Offers health education (PhD); occupational health-industrial hygiene (MS); public health (MPH).

The University of Toledo, College of Graduate Studies, College of Medicine and Life Sciences, Department of Public Health and Preventative Medicine, Toledo, OH 43606-3390. Offers biostatistics and epidemiology (Certificate); contemporary gerontological practice (Certificate); environmental and occupational health and safety (MPH); epidemiology (Certificate); global public health (Certificate); health promotion and education (MPH); industrial hygiene (MSOH); medical and health science teaching and learning (Certificate); occupational health (Certificate); public health administration (MPH); public health and emergency response (Certificate); public health epidemiology (MPH); public health nutrition (MPH); MD/MPH. *Program availability:* Part-time, evening/ weekend. *Degree requirements:* For master's, thesis or alternative. *Entrance requirements:* For master's, GRE, minimum undergraduate GPA of 3.0, three letters of recommendation, statement of purpose, transcripts from all prior institutions attended, resume; for Certificate, minimum undergraduate GPA of 3.0, three letters of recommendation, statement of purpose, transcripts from all prior institutions attended, resume. Additional exam requirements/recommendations for international students: Required—TOEFL (minimum score 550 paper-based; 80 iBT), IELTS (minimum score 6.5). Electronic applications accepted.

University of Utah, Graduate School, College of Health, Health Promotion and Education Program, Salt Lake City, UT 84112. Offers M Phil, MS, PhD. *Program availability:* Part-time. *Faculty:* 5 full-time (2 women), 9 part-time/adjunct (5 women). *Students:* 38 full-time (32 women), 3 part-time (1 woman); includes 5 minority (1 Black or African American, non-Hispanic/Latino; 1 American Indian or Alaska Native, non-Hispanic/Latino; 2 Asian, non-Hispanic/Latino; 1 Hispanic/Latino), 2 international. Average age 29. 26 applicants, 69% accepted, 16 enrolled. In 2017, 24 master's, 3 doctorates awarded. *Degree requirements:* For master's, comprehensive exam, thesis or alternative, field experience; for doctorate, comprehensive exam, thesis/dissertation, field experience. *Entrance requirements:* For master's, GRE, minimum GPA of 3.0; for doctorate, GRE, minimum GPA of 3.2. Additional exam requirements/recommendations for international students: Required—TOEFL (minimum score 550 paper-based; 80 iBT). *Application deadline:* For fall admission, 1/15 for domestic and international students. Application fee: $55 ($65 for international students). Electronic applications accepted. *Financial support:* In 2017–18, 11 students received support, including 3 research assistantships with full tuition reimbursements available (averaging $14,500 per year), 6 teaching assistantships with full tuition reimbursements available (averaging $14,500 per year); health care benefits and unspecified assistantships also available. Financial award application deadline: 3/1; financial award applicants required to submit FAFSA. *Faculty research:* Health behavior and counseling, health service administration, evaluation of health programs. *Unit head:* Dr. Tim Brusseau, Program Director, 801-581-7558, Fax: 801-585-3992, E-mail: tim.brusseau@utah.edu. *Application contact:* Dr. Maria Newton, Director of Graduate Studies, 801-581-7558, Fax: 801-585-3992, E-mail: maria.newton@health.utah.edu.
Website: http://www.health.utah.edu/healthed/index.htm

University of Waterloo, Graduate Studies, Faculty of Applied Health Sciences, School of Public Health and Health Systems, Waterloo, ON N2L 3G1, Canada. Offers health evaluation (MHE); health informatics (MHI); health studies and gerontology (M Sc, PhD); public health (MPH). *Program availability:* Part-time. *Degree requirements:* For master's, thesis; for doctorate, comprehensive exam, thesis/dissertation. *Entrance requirements:* For master's, honors degree, minimum B average, resume, writing sample; for doctorate, GRE (recommended), master's degree, minimum B average, resume, writing sample. Additional exam requirements/recommendations for international students: Required—TOEFL, IELTS, PTE. Electronic applications accepted. *Faculty research:* Population health, health promotion and disease prevention, healthy aging, health policy, planning and evaluation, health information management and health informatics, aging, health and well-being, work and health.

University of Wisconsin–La Crosse, College of Science and Health, Department of Health Education and Health Promotion, Program in Community Health Education, La Crosse, WI 54601-3742. Offers community health education (MS); public health (MPH). *Students:* 16 full-time (11 women), 9 part-time (7 women); includes 4 minority (2 Asian, non-Hispanic/Latino; 2 Two or more races, non-Hispanic/Latino). Average age 31. 15 applicants, 93% accepted, 10 enrolled. In 2017, 8 master's awarded. *Degree requirements:* For master's, thesis. *Entrance requirements:* For master's, GRE General Test, GRE Subject Test (for MPH), 3 letters of recommendation. Additional exam requirements/recommendations for international students: Required—TOEFL (minimum score 550 paper-based; 79 iBT). Electronic applications accepted. *Financial support:* Research assistantships with partial tuition reimbursements, Federal Work-Study, scholarships/grants, health care benefits, and tuition waivers (partial) available. Support available to part-time students. Financial award applicants required to submit FAFSA. *Unit head:* Dr. Gary Gilmore, Director, 608-785-8163, E-mail: gilmore.gary@uwlax.edu. *Application contact:* Brandon Schaller, Senior Graduate Student Status Examiner, 608-785-8941, E-mail: admissions@uwlax.edu.

University of Wisconsin–La Crosse, College of Science and Health, Department of Health Education and Health Promotion, Program in School Health Education, La Crosse, WI 54601-3742. Offers MS. In 2017, 1 master's awarded. *Entrance requirements:* For master's, GRE General Test, minimum GPA of 2.85. Additional exam requirements/recommendations for international students: Required—TOEFL (minimum score 550 paper-based; 79 iBT). *Application deadline:* Applications are processed on a rolling basis. Electronic applications accepted. *Financial support:* Federal Work-Study

and scholarships/grants available. Support available to part-time students. Financial award applicants required to submit FAFSA. *Faculty research:* Adolescent health issues, heath education, human sexuality, mental health, stress management, comprehensive school health pedagogy (curriculum, instructional methodology and assessment), PK-12 health literacy, K-12 education, relationship management, substance use and abuse, skill development within health education. *Unit head:* Dr. Tracy Caravella, Director, 608-785-6788, E-mail: caravell.trac@uwlax.edu. *Application contact:* Brandon Schaller, Senior Graduate Student Status Examiner, 608-785-8941, E-mail: admissions@uwlax.edu.
Website: http://www.uwlax.edu/sah/hehp/html/gr_she.htm

University of Wyoming, College of Health Sciences, Division of Kinesiology and Health, Laramie, WY 82071. Offers MS. *Accreditation:* NCATE. *Program availability:* Part-time, online learning. *Degree requirements:* For master's, comprehensive exam (for some programs), thesis (for some programs). *Entrance requirements:* For master's, GRE General Test, minimum GPA of 3.0. Additional exam requirements/recommendations for international students: Required—TOEFL. Electronic applications accepted. *Faculty research:* Teacher effectiveness, effects of exercising on heart function, physiological responses of overtraining, psychological benefits of physical activity, health behavior.

Utah State University, School of Graduate Studies, Emma Eccles Jones College of Education and Human Services, Department of Kinesiology and Health Science, Logan, UT 84322. Offers fitness promotion (MS); health and human movement (MS); pathokinesiology (PhD); physical and sport eductaion (M Ed); public health (MPH). *Program availability:* Part-time, evening/weekend, online learning. *Degree requirements:* For master's, thesis (for some programs). *Entrance requirements:* For master's, GRE General Test or MAT, minimum GPA of 3.0. Additional exam requirements/recommendations for international students: Required—TOEFL. *Faculty research:* Sport psychology intervention, motor learning biomechanics, pedagogy, physiology.

Virginia State University, College of Graduate Studies, College of Natural and Health Sciences, Department of Psychology, Petersburg, VA 23806-0001. Offers behavioral and community health sciences (PhD); clinical health psychology (PhD); clinical psychology (MS); general psychology (MS). *Degree requirements:* For master's, one foreign language, thesis. *Entrance requirements:* For master's, GRE General Test.

Walden University, Graduate Programs, School of Health Sciences, Minneapolis, MN 55401. Offers clinical research administration (MS, Graduate Certificate); health education and promotion (MS, PhD), including behavioral health (PhD); disease surveillance (PhD); emergency preparedness (MS); general (MHA, MS); global health (PhD); health policy (PhD); health policy and advocacy (MS); population health (PhD); health informatics (MS); health services (PhD), including community health, healthcare administration, leadership, public health policy, self-designed; healthcare administration (MHA, DHA), including general (MHA, MS); leadership and organizational development (MHA); public health (MPH, Dr PH, PhD, Graduate Certificate), including community health education (PhD), epidemiology (PhD); systems policy (MHA). *Program availability:* Part-time, evening/weekend, online only, 100% online. *Degree requirements:* For doctorate, thesis/dissertation, residency. *Entrance requirements:* For master's, bachelor's degree or higher; minimum GPA of 2.5; official transcripts; goal statement (for some programs); access to computer and Internet; for doctorate, master's degree or higher; three years of related professional or academic experience (preferred); minimum GPA of 3.0; goal statement and current resume (for select programs); official transcripts; access to computer and Internet; for Graduate Certificate, relevant work experience; access to computer and Internet. Additional exam requirements/recommendations for international students: Required—TOEFL (minimum score 550 paper-based, 79 iBT), IELTS (minimum score 6.5), Michigan English Language Assessment Battery (minimum score 82), or PTE (minimum score 53). Electronic applications accepted.

Washburn University, School of Applied Studies, Department of Allied Health, Topeka, KS 66621. Offers health care education (MHS). *Program availability:* Part-time. *Degree requirements:* For master's, internship, practicum. *Entrance requirements:* For master's, bachelor's degree, two years of professional work experience in a health care environment, official transcripts, personal statement, resume, college algebra course with grade no lower than a C. Additional exam requirements/recommendations for international students: Required—TOEFL (minimum score 80 iBT).

Wayne State University, College of Education, Division of Kinesiology, Health and Sports Studies, Detroit, MI 48202. Offers athletic training (MSAT); health education (M Ed); kinesiology (M Ed, PhD), including exercise and sport science (PhD), physical education and physical activity leadership (PhD); sports administration (MA). *Program availability:* Part-time, 100% online. *Faculty:* 9. *Students:* 65 full-time (33 women), 109 part-time (56 women); includes 70 minority (59 Black or African American, non-Hispanic/Latino; 3 Hispanic/Latino; 8 Two or more races, non-Hispanic/Latino), 8 international. Average age 30. 182 applicants, 53% accepted, 56 enrolled. In 2017, 62 master's, 3 doctorates awarded. *Degree requirements:* For master's, thesis (for some programs); for doctorate, thesis/dissertation. *Entrance requirements:* For master's, minimum undergraduate GPA of 3.0; undergraduate degree directly relating to the field of specialization being applied for or one accompanied by extensive educational background in closely-related field; teaching certificates in specific areas (for some programs); for doctorate, minimum undergraduate GPA of 3.0; undergraduate degree directly relating to the field of specialization being applied for or one accompanied by extensive educational background in closely-related field. Additional exam requirements/recommendations for international students: Required—TOEFL (minimum score 79 iBT), TWE (minimum score 5.5); Recommended—IELTS (minimum score 6.5). *Application deadline:* For fall admission, 6/1 priority date for domestic students, 5/1 priority date for international students; for winter admission, 10/1 priority date for domestic students, 9/1 priority date for international students; for spring admission, 2/1 priority date for domestic students, 1/1 priority date for international students. Application fee: $50. Electronic applications accepted. *Expenses:* Contact institution. *Financial support:* In 2017–18, 47 students received support, including 6 research assistantships with tuition reimbursements available (averaging $18,534 per year), 5 teaching assistantships with tuition reimbursements available (averaging $18,534 per year); fellowships with tuition reimbursements available, scholarships/grants, health care benefits, and unspecified assistantships also available. Support available to part-time students. Financial award applicants required to submit FAFSA. *Faculty research:* Exercise and sport science, nutrition and physical activity interventions, school and community health, obesity prevention. *Unit head:* Dr. Nate McCaughtry, Assistant Dean, Division of Kinesiology, Health and Sport Studies/Director, Center for School Health, 313-577-0014, Fax: 313-577-5002, E-mail: aj4391@wayne.edu. *Application contact:* 313-577-4249, E-mail: askcoe@wayne.edu.
Website: http://coe.wayne.edu/kinesiology/index.php

Wayne State University, School of Medicine, Office of Biomedical Graduate Programs, Detroit, MI 48202. Offers anatomy and cell biology (MS, PhD); basic medical sciences (MS); biochemistry and molecular biology (MS, PhD); cancer biology (MS, PhD); clinical and translational science (Graduate Certificate); family medicine and public health sciences (MPH, Graduate Certificate), including public health practice; genetic

counseling (MS); immunology and microbiology (MS, PhD); medical physics (MS, PhD, Graduate Certificate); medical research (MS); molecular medicine and genomics (MS, PhD), including molecular genetics and genomics; pathology (PhD); pharmacology (MS, PhD); physiology (MS, PhD), including physiology, reproductive sciences (PhD); psychiatry and behavioral neurosciences (PhD), including translational neuroscience; MD/MPH; MD/PhD; MPH/MA; MSW/MPH. *Program availability:* Part-time, evening/weekend. *Students:* 268 full-time (152 women), 117 part-time (59 women); includes 108 minority (19 Black or African American, non-Hispanic/Latino; 1 American Indian or Alaska Native, non-Hispanic/Latino; 62 Asian, non-Hispanic/Latino; 9 Hispanic/Latino; 17 Two or more races, non-Hispanic/Latino), 48 international. Average age 26. 1,133 applicants, 21% accepted, 151 enrolled. In 2017, 70 master's, 25 doctorates, 10 other advanced degrees awarded. Terminal master's awarded for partial completion of doctoral program. *Degree requirements:* For master's, thesis (for some programs); for doctorate, thesis/dissertation. *Entrance requirements:* For master's, doctorate, and Graduate Certificate, GRE. Additional exam requirements/recommendations for international students: Required—TOEFL (minimum score 550 paper-based; 100 iBT), Michigan English Language Assessment Battery (minimum score 85); Recommended—IELTS (minimum score 6.5), TWE (minimum score 5.5). *Application deadline:* For fall admission, 2/1 for domestic and international students. Applications are processed on a rolling basis. Application fee: $50. Electronic applications accepted. *Expenses:* Contact institution. *Financial support:* In 2017–18, 177 students received support, including 64 fellowships with full tuition reimbursements available (averaging $24,388 per year), 79 research assistantships with full tuition reimbursements available (averaging $26,894 per year); scholarships/grants, traineeships, and health care benefits also available. *Faculty research:* Cancer biology, neurosciences, vision sciences, molecular biology, pathology, physiology, pharmacology, public health, medical physics. *Unit head:* Dr. Daniel A. Walz, Associate Dean for Biomedical Graduate Programs, 313-577-1455, Fax: 313-577-8796, E-mail: gradprogs@med.wayne.edu.
Website: https://www.med.wayne.edu/biomedical-graduate-programs/

Western Illinois University, School of Graduate Studies, College of Education and Human Services, Department of Health Sciences and Social Work, Macomb, IL 61455-1390. Offers health sciences (MS), including public health, school health. *Accreditation:* NCATE. *Program availability:* Part-time. *Degree requirements:* For master's, comprehensive exam, thesis or alternative. *Entrance requirements:* Additional exam requirements/recommendations for international students: Required—TOEFL (minimum score 550 paper-based; 80 iBT). *Application deadline:* Applications are processed on a rolling basis. Application fee: $30. Electronic applications accepted. *Financial support:* Unspecified assistantships available. Financial award applicants required to submit FAFSA. *Unit head:* Dr. Lorette Oden, Chairperson, 309-298-1076. *Application contact:* Dr. Nancy Parsons, Associate Provost and Director of Graduate Studies, 309-298-1806, Fax: 309-298-2345, E-mail: grad-office@wiu.edu.
Website: http://www.wiu.edu/coehs/health_sciences/

Western Michigan University, Graduate College, College of Health and Human Services, Department of Interdisciplinary Health and Human Services, Kalamazoo, MI 49008. Offers interdisciplinary health services (PhD).

Western Oregon University, Graduate Programs, College of Education, Division of Teacher Education, Program in Secondary Education, Monmouth, OR 97361. Offers bilingual education (MS Ed); health (MS Ed); humanities (MAT, MS Ed); initial licensure (MAT); mathematics (MAT, MS Ed); science (MAT, MS Ed); social science (MAT, MS Ed). *Accreditation:* NCATE. *Program availability:* Part-time, evening/weekend. *Degree requirements:* For master's, thesis optional, written exam. *Entrance requirements:* For master's, minimum GPA of 3.0, teaching license. Additional exam requirements/recommendations for international students: Required—TOEFL (minimum score 550 paper-based; 79 iBT), IELTS (minimum score 6.5). *Faculty research:* Literacy, science in primary grades, geography education, retention, teacher burnout.

Western University of Health Sciences, College of Allied Health Professions, Program in Health Sciences, Pomona, CA 91766-1854. Offers MS. *Program availability:* Blended/hybrid learning. *Faculty:* 3 full-time (all women). *Students:* 14 full-time (13 women), 12 part-time (9 women); includes 16 minority (4 Black or African American, non-Hispanic/Latino; 3 Asian, non-Hispanic/Latino; 5 Hispanic/Latino; 4 Two or more races, non-Hispanic/Latino), 3 international. Average age 32. 14 applicants, 14% accepted, 2 enrolled. In 2017, 11 master's awarded. *Entrance requirements:* For master's, GRE (minimum score of 3.5 on analytical writing), bachelor's degree (preferred); minimum undergraduate GPA of 2.7, graduate 3.0; letters of recommendation; statement of purpose; current curriculum vitae. Additional exam requirements/recommendations for international students: Required—TOEFL. *Application deadline:* For fall admission, 6/30 priority date for domestic students, 6/30 for international students. Applications are processed on a rolling basis. Application fee: $35. Electronic applications accepted. *Expenses:* $3,732 per year tuition and fees; $622 per unit. *Financial support:* In 2017–18, 5 students received support. Scholarships/grants available. Financial award application deadline: 3/2; financial award applicants required to submit FAFSA. *Faculty research:* Women's health, community based participatory research, global health, central Asia health and politics. *Unit head:* Dr. Tina Meyer, Chair, 909-469-5397, Fax: 909-469-5407, E-mail: tmeyer@westernu.edu. *Application contact:* Susan Hanson, Executive Director of Admissions for the College of Osteopathic Medicine of the Pacific and for Health Professions Education, 909-469-5335, Fax: 909-469-5570, E-mail: admissions@westernu.edu.
Website: http://prospective.westernu.edu/health-sciences/welcome-3/

Widener University, School of Human Service Professions, Center for Education, Chester, PA 19013-5792. Offers adult education (M Ed); counseling in higher education (M Ed); counselor education (M Ed); early childhood education (M Ed); educational foundations (M Ed); educational leadership (M Ed); educational psychology (M Ed); elementary education (M Ed); English and language arts (M Ed); health education (M Ed); higher education leadership (Ed D); home and school visitor (M Ed); human sexuality (M Ed, PhD); mathematics education (M Ed); middle school education (M Ed); principalship (M Ed); reading and language arts (Ed D); reading education (M Ed); school administration (Ed D); science education (M Ed); social studies education (M Ed); special education (M Ed); technology education (M Ed). *Accreditation:* NCATE. *Program availability:* Part-time, evening/weekend. *Faculty:* 34 full-time (22 women), 37 part-time/adjunct (14 women). *Students:* 131 full-time (112 women), 244 part-time (179 women); includes 94 minority (58 Black or African American, non-Hispanic/Latino; 1 American Indian or Alaska Native, non-Hispanic/Latino; 1 Asian, non-Hispanic/Latino; 22 Hispanic/Latino; 12 Two or more races, non-Hispanic/Latino), 12 international. Average age 37. 140 applicants, 38% accepted, 26 enrolled. In 2017, 45 master's, 21 doctorates awarded. Terminal master's awarded for partial completion of doctoral program. *Degree requirements:* For doctorate, thesis/dissertation. *Entrance requirements:* For master's, minimum GPA of 2.5; for doctorate, GRE or MAT, minimum GPA of 2.0 (undergraduate), 3.5 (graduate). *Application deadline:* Applications are processed on a rolling basis. Application fee: $25 ($300 for international students). Electronic applications accepted. *Expenses:* Contact institution. *Financial support:* Career-related internships or fieldwork, tuition waivers (full and partial), and unspecified assistantships available. Support available to part-time students. Financial award

application deadline: 5/1. *Faculty research:* Reading and cognition, adult education, technology education, educational leadership, special education. *Unit head:* Dr. Shawn Fitzgerald, Dean, 610-499-4294, Fax: 610-499-4623, E-mail: smfitzgerald@widener.edu. *Application contact:* Megan Kuft, Director of Graduate Admissions, 610-499-4124, E-Mail: gradprograms@widener.edu.
Website: http://www.widener.edu/academics/schools/eics

Worcester State University, Graduate School, Department of Education, Program in Health Education, Worcester, MA 01602-2597. Offers M Ed. *Program availability:* Part-time. *Students:* 5 part-time (2 women); includes 1 minority (Black or African American, non-Hispanic/Latino). Average age 29. 3 applicants. In 2017, 8 master's awarded. *Degree requirements:* For master's, comprehensive exam (for some programs), thesis optional, Certified Health Education Specialist exam. *Entrance requirements:* For master's, GRE General Test or MAT. Additional exam requirements/recommendations for international students: Required—TOEFL (minimum score 550 paper-based; 79 iBT). *Application deadline:* For fall admission, 6/15 for domestic and international students; for

spring admission, 11/1 for domestic and international students; for summer admission, 4/1 for domestic and international students. Applications are processed on a rolling basis. Application fee: $50. Electronic applications accepted. *Expenses:* Tuition, state resident: full-time $3042; part-time $169 per credit hour. Tuition, nonresident: full-time $3042; part-time $169 per credit hour. *Required fees:* $2754; $153 per credit hour. *Financial support:* Career-related internships or fieldwork, scholarships/grants, and unspecified assistantships available. Financial award application deadline: 3/1; financial award applicants required to submit FAFSA. *Unit head:* Dr. Andrew Piazza, Coordinator, 508-929-8137, E-mail: apiazza@worcester.edu. *Application contact:* Sara Grady, Associate Dean for Graduate Studies and Professional Development, 508-929-8130, E-mail: sara.grady@worcester.edu.

Wright State University, Boonshoft School of Medicine, Department of Population and Public Health Sciences, Dayton, OH 45435. Offers health promotion and education (MPH).

Home Economics Education

Alabama Agricultural and Mechanical University, School of Graduate Studies, College of Education, Humanities, and Behavioral Sciences, Department of Educational Leadership and Secondary Education, Huntsville, AL 35811. Offers biology (M Ed); business/marketing education (M Ed, Ed S); chemistry (M Ed); collaborative teacher secondary education (M Ed, Ed S); education (M Ed, Ed S); English language arts (M Ed); family/consumer science education (M Ed, Ed S); general science (M Ed); general social science (M Ed); mathematics (M Ed, Ed S); physics (M Ed, Ed S); technology education (M Ed). *Accreditation:* NCATE. *Program availability:* Evening/weekend. *Degree requirements:* For master's, comprehensive exam; for Ed S, thesis. *Entrance requirements:* For master's, GRE General Test. Additional exam requirements/recommendations for international students: Required—TOEFL (minimum score 500 paper-based; 61 iBT). Electronic applications accepted. *Faculty research:* World peace through education, computer-assisted instruction.

Cambridge College, School of Education, Boston, MA 02129. Offers autism specialist (M Ed); autism/behavior analyst (M Ed); behavior analyst (Post-Master's Certificate); behavioral management (M Ed); early childhood teacher (M Ed); education specialist in curriculum and instruction (CAGS); educational leadership (Ed D); elementary teacher (M Ed); English as a second language (M Ed, Certificate); general science (M Ed); health education (Post-Master's Certificate); health/family and consumer sciences (M Ed); history (M Ed); individualized (M Ed); information technology literacy (M Ed); instructional technology (M Ed); interdisciplinary studies (M Ed); library teacher (M Ed); literacy education (M Ed); mathematics (M Ed); mathematics specialist (Certificate); middle school mathematics and science (M Ed); school administration (M Ed, CAGS); school guidance counselor (M Ed); school nurse education (M Ed); school social worker/school adjustment counselor (M Ed); special education administrator (CAGS); special education/moderate disabilities (M Ed); teaching skills and methodologies (M Ed). *Program availability:* Part-time, evening/weekend, online learning. *Degree requirements:* For master's, thesis, internship/practicum (licensure program only); for doctorate, thesis/dissertation; for other advanced degree, thesis. *Entrance requirements:* For master's, interview, resume, documentation of licensure, 2 professional references; for doctorate, official transcripts, interview, resume, documentation of licensure (if any), written personal statement/essay, portfolio of scholarly and professional work, qualifying assessment, 2 professional references, health insurance, immunizations form; for other advanced degree, official transcripts, interview, resume, documentation of licensure (if any), written personal statement/essay, 2 professional references, health insurance, immunizations form. Additional exam requirements/recommendations for international students: Required—TOEFL (minimum score 550 paper-based; 79 iBT), Michigan English Language Assessment Battery (minimum score 85); Recommended—IELTS (minimum score 6). Electronic applications accepted. *Expenses:* Contact institution. *Faculty research:* Adult education, accelerated learning, mathematics education, brain compatible learning, special education and law.

Central Washington University, School of Graduate Studies and Research, College of Education and Professional Studies, Department of Family and Consumer Sciences, Ellensburg, WA 98926. Offers career and technical education (MS); family and child life (MS); family and consumer sciences education (MS). *Program availability:* Part-time. *Entrance requirements:* For master's, minimum GPA of 3.0. Additional exam requirements/recommendations for international students: Required—TOEFL (minimum score 550 paper-based; 79 iBT). *Application deadline:* For fall admission, 2/1 priority date for domestic students; for winter admission, 10/1 for domestic students; for spring admission, 1/1 for domestic students. Applications are processed on a rolling basis. Application fee: $50. Electronic applications accepted. *Financial support:* Application deadline: 3/1; applicants required to submit FAFSA. *Unit head:* Dr. Duane Dowd, Department Chair, 509-963-2740, E-mail: duane.dowd@cwu.edu. *Application contact:* Justine Eason, Admissions Program Coordinator, 509-963-3103, Fax: 509-963-1799, E-mail: masters@cwu.edu.
Website: http://www.cwu.edu/~fandcs/

Eastern Kentucky University, The Graduate School, College of Education, Department of Curriculum and Instruction, Program in Secondary and Higher Education, Richmond, KY 40475-3102. Offers secondary education (MA Ed), including agricultural education, art education, biological sciences education, business education, English education, geography education, history education, home economics education, industrial education, mathematical sciences education, physical education, school health education. *Accreditation:* NCATE. *Program availability:* Part-time. *Entrance requirements:* For master's, GRE General Test, minimum GPA of 2.5.

Louisiana State University and Agricultural & Mechanical College, Graduate School, College of Human Sciences and Education, School of Human Resource Education and Workforce Development, Baton Rouge, LA 70803. Offers agriculture and extension education and youth development (MS, PhD); career and technical education (MS, PhD); comprehensive vocational education (MS, PhD); extension and international education (MS, PhD); human resource and leadership development (MS, PhD); industrial education (MS); vocational agriculture education (MS, PhD); vocational business education (MS); vocational home economics education (MS). *Accreditation:* NCATE. *Faculty:* 11 full-time (6 women). *Students:* 102 full-time (71 women), 130 part-time (92 women); includes 89 minority (63 Black or African American, non-Hispanic/Latino; 3 American Indian or Alaska Native, non-Hispanic/Latino; 8 Asian, non-Hispanic/Latino; 14 Hispanic/Latino; 1 Two or more races, non-Hispanic/Latino), 6 international. Average age 35. 98 applicants, 69% accepted, 52 enrolled. In 2017, 94 master's, 15 doctorates awarded. *Financial support:* In 2017–18, 1 fellowship (averaging $18,238

per year), 16 teaching assistantships (averaging $15,341 per year) were awarded. *Total annual research expenditures:* $1,998.

Montana State University, The Graduate School, College of Education, Health, and Human Development, Department of Health and Human Development, Bozeman, MT 59717. Offers family and consumer sciences (MS). *Accreditation:* ACA. *Program availability:* Part-time, online learning. *Degree requirements:* For master's, comprehensive exam. *Entrance requirements:* For master's, GRE (minimum scores: verbal 480; quantitative 480). Additional exam requirements/recommendations for international students: Required—TOEFL (minimum score 550 paper-based). Electronic applications accepted. *Faculty research:* Community food systems, ethic of care for teachers and coaches, influence of public policy on families and communities, cost effectiveness of early childhood education, exercise metabolism, winter sport performance enhancement, assessment of physical activity.

Purdue University, Graduate School, College of Education, Department of Curriculum and Instruction, West Lafayette, IN 47907. Offers agricultural and extension education (MS, MS Ed, PhD, Ed S); art education (PhD); career and technical education (MS Ed, PhD, Ed S); curriculum studies (MS Ed, PhD, Ed S); educational technology (MS Ed, PhD, Ed S); elementary education (MS Ed); family and consumer sciences education (MS Ed, PhD, Ed S); foreign language education (MS Ed, PhD, Ed S); industrial technology (PhD, Ed S); language arts (MS Ed, PhD, Ed S); literacy (MS Ed, PhD, Ed S); mathematics education (MS, MS Ed, PhD, Ed S); science education (MS, MS Ed, PhD, Ed S); social studies education (MS Ed, PhD, Ed S). *Accreditation:* NCATE. *Program availability:* Part-time, evening/weekend. *Faculty:* 37 full-time (27 women), 1 (woman) part-time/adjunct. *Students:* 78 full-time (50 women), 286 part-time (195 women); includes 68 minority (25 Black or African American, non-Hispanic/Latino; 3 American Indian or Alaska Native, non-Hispanic/Latino; 10 Asian, non-Hispanic/Latino; 22 Hispanic/Latino; 1 Native Hawaiian or other Pacific Islander, non-Hispanic/Latino; 7 Two or more races, non-Hispanic/Latino), 44 international. Average age 36. 150 applicants, 79% accepted, 73 enrolled. In 2017, 107 master's, 20 doctorates, 2 other advanced degrees awarded. *Degree requirements:* For master's, thesis optional; for doctorate, thesis/dissertation, oral and written exams; for Ed S, oral presentation, project. *Entrance requirements:* For master's, GRE General Test (if undergraduate GPA is below 3.0), minimum undergraduate GPA of 3.0 or equivalent; for doctorate, GRE General Test (minimum combined verbal and quantitative score of 1000, 300 for new scoring), minimum undergraduate GPA of 3.0 or equivalent; master's degree with minimum GPA of 3.0 or equivalent; for Ed S, GRE General Test (minimum combined verbal and quantitative score of 1000, 300 for new scoring), minimum undergraduate GPA of 3.0 or equivalent; master's degree. Additional exam requirements/recommendations for international students: Required—TOEFL (minimum score 550 paper-based; 77 iBT). *Application deadline:* For fall admission, 12/15 for domestic students, 3/1 for international students; for spring admission, 9/15 for domestic students, 8/1 for international students. Application fee: $60 ($75 for international students). Electronic applications accepted. *Financial support:* Fellowships with full tuition reimbursements, research assistantships with full tuition reimbursements, teaching assistantships with full tuition reimbursements, career-related internships or fieldwork, and tuition waivers (full) available. Support available to part-time students. Financial award application deadline: 3/1; financial award applicants required to submit FAFSA. *Faculty research:* Literacy acquisition and development, teacher beliefs and knowledge, recruitment and retention of underrepresented students, economic education, literacy discourse. *Unit head:* Janet M. Alsup, Head, 765-494-9667, E-mail: alsupj@purdue.edu. *Application contact:* Heather Brinkman, Graduate Contact, 765-494-2345, E-mail: hbrinkma@purdue.edu.
Website: http://www.edci.purdue.edu/

South Carolina State University, College of Graduate and Professional Studies, Department of Education, Orangeburg, SC 29117-0001. Offers early childhood education (MAT); education (M Ed); elementary education (M Ed, MAT); English (MAT); general science/biology (MAT); mathematics (MAT); secondary education (M Ed), including biology education, business education, counselor education, English education, home economics education, industrial education, mathematics education, science education, social studies education; special education (M Ed), including emotionally handicapped, learning disabilities, mentally handicapped. *Accreditation:* NCATE. *Program availability:* Part-time, evening/weekend. *Faculty:* 11 full-time (6 women), 4 part-time/adjunct (2 women). *Students:* 26 full-time (18 women), 22 part-time (17 women); includes 41 minority (all Black or African American, non-Hispanic/Latino), 1 international. Average age 33. 25 applicants, 100% accepted, 19 enrolled. In 2017, 6 master's awarded. *Degree requirements:* For master's, thesis optional, departmental qualifying exam. *Entrance requirements:* For master's, GRE General Test, NTE, interview, teaching certificate. *Application deadline:* For fall admission, 6/15 priority date for domestic students, 6/15 for international students; for spring admission, 11/1 for domestic and international students. Application fee: $25. Electronic applications accepted. *Expenses:* Tuition, state resident: full-time $9388; part-time $607 per credit hour. Tuition, nonresident: full-time $19,968; part-time $1194 per credit hour. *Required fees:* $766; $766 per credit hour. *Financial support:* Fellowships, career-related internships or fieldwork, Federal Work-Study, and scholarships/grants available. Financial award application deadline: 6/1. *Unit head:* Dr. Charlie Spell, Interim Chair, Department of Education, 803-536-8963, Fax: 803-516-4568, E-mail: cspell@scsu.edu. *Application contact:* Curtis Foskey, Coordinator of Graduate Studies, 803-536-8419, Fax: 803-536-8812, E-mail: cfoskey@scsu.edu.

Texas Tech University, Graduate School, College of Human Sciences, Program in Family and Consumer Sciences Education, Lubbock, TX 79409-1162. Offers MS, PhD. *Program availability:* Part-time, evening/weekend, 100% online, blended/hybrid learning. *Students:* 6 full-time (all women), 32 part-time (29 women); includes 4 minority (1 Asian, non-Hispanic/Latino; 3 Hispanic/Latino). Average age 39. 14 applicants, 57% accepted, 2 enrolled. In 2017, 8 master's, 1 doctorate awarded. *Degree requirements:* For master's, comprehensive exam, thesis or alternative; for doctorate, comprehensive exam, thesis/dissertation. *Entrance requirements:* Additional exam requirements/recommendations for international students: Required—TOEFL (minimum score 550 paper-based; 79 iBT). *Application deadline:* For fall admission, 6/1 priority date for domestic students, 1/15 priority date for international students; for spring admission, 9/1 priority date for domestic students, 6/15 priority date for international students. Applications are processed on a rolling basis. Application fee: $60. Electronic applications accepted. *Expenses:* Contact institution. *Financial support:* In 2017–18, 16 students received support, including 16 fellowships (averaging $4,293 per year); research assistantships, teaching assistantships, and scholarships/grants also available. Financial award application deadline: 1/15; financial award applicants required to submit FAFSA. *Faculty research:* Content literacy, implementation of programs of study, instructional practices for working with limited English proficiency students in FCS, mobile technologies with FCS instruction. *Total annual research expenditures:* $158,457. *Unit head:* Dr. Karen Alexander, Program Chair, 806-834-2212, Fax: 806-742-1849, E-mail: karen.alexander@ttu.edu. *Application contact:* Ashlee Murden, Business Coordinator, 806-834-4140, Fax: 806-742-1849, E-mail: ashlee.murden@ttu.edu.
Website: http://www.depts.ttu.edu/hs/fcse/

The University of British Columbia, Faculty of Education, Department of Curriculum and Pedagogy, Vancouver, BC V6T 1Z4, Canada. Offers art education (M Ed, MA); curriculum studies (M Ed, MA, PhD); home economics education (M Ed, MA); mathematics education (M Ed, MA); media and technology studies education (M Ed, MA); music education (M Ed, MA); physical education (M Ed, MA); science education (M Ed, MA); social studies education (M Ed, MA). *Program availability:* Part-time, online learning. *Degree requirements:* For master's, thesis (MA); for doctorate, comprehensive exam, thesis/dissertation. *Entrance requirements:* Additional exam requirements/recommendations for international students: Required—TOEFL, IELTS. Electronic applications accepted. *Expenses:* Contact institution. *Faculty research:* School subjects, teaching and learning.

University of Nebraska–Lincoln, Graduate College, College of Education and Human Sciences, Department of Child, Youth and Family Studies, Lincoln, NE 68588. Offers child development/early childhood education (MS, PhD); child, youth and family studies (MS); family and consumer sciences education (MS, PhD); family financial planning (MS); family science (MS, PhD); gerontology (PhD); human sciences (PhD), including child, youth and family studies, gerontology, medical family therapy; marriage and family therapy (MS); medical family therapy (PhD); youth development (MS). *Accreditation:* AAMFT/COAMFTE (one or more programs are accredited). *Program availability:* Online learning. *Degree requirements:* For master's, thesis optional. *Entrance requirements:* For master's, GRE. Additional exam requirements/recommendations for international students: Required—TOEFL (minimum score 550 paper-based). Electronic applications accepted. *Faculty research:* Marriage and family therapy, child development/early childhood education, family financial management.

Utah State University, School of Graduate Studies, College of Agriculture and Applied Sciences, School of Applied Sciences, Technology and Education, Logan, UT 84322. Offers agricultural extension and education (MS); family and consumer sciences education and extension (MS); technology and engineering education (MS). *Program availability:* Part-time, online learning. *Degree requirements:* For master's, comprehensive exam (for some programs), thesis (for some programs). *Entrance requirements:* For master's, GRE General Test, MAT, BS in agricultural education, agricultural extension, or related agricultural or science discipline; minimum GPA of 3.0. Additional exam requirements/recommendations for international students: Required—TOEFL. *Faculty research:* Extension and adult education; structures and environment; low-input agriculture; farm safety, systems, and mechanizations.

Wayne State College, School of Education and Counseling, Department of Educational Foundations and Leadership, Program in Curriculum and Instruction, Wayne, NE 68787. Offers alternative education (MSE); business and information technology education (MSE); communication arts education (MSE); early childhood education (MSE); elementary education (MSE); English as a second language (MSE); English education (MSE); family and consumer sciences education (MSE); industrial technology and vocational education (MSE); learning communities (MSE); mathematics education (MSE); music education (MSE); science education (MSE); social science education (MSE). *Accreditation:* NCATE. *Program availability:* Part-time, evening/weekend. *Degree requirements:* For master's, comprehensive exam, thesis optional. *Entrance requirements:* For master's, GRE General Test. Additional exam requirements/recommendations for international students: Required—TOEFL (minimum score 550 paper-based).

Mathematics Education

Adams State University, Office of Graduate Studies, Department of Teacher Education, Alamosa, CO 81101. Offers teacher education (MA), including adaptive leadership, curriculum and instruction, curriculum and instruction-STEM, educational leadership. *Program availability:* Part-time, online learning. *Degree requirements:* For master's, qualifying exam. *Entrance requirements:* For master's, GRE General Test or MAT, minimum undergraduate GPA of 3.0. *Application deadline:* For fall admission, 5/15 priority date for domestic students; for spring admission, 10/15 for domestic students. Applications are processed on a rolling basis. Application fee: $30. *Expenses:* Tuition, state resident: full-time $4800; part-time $2400 per credit. Tuition, nonresident: full-time $7100; part-time $3550 per credit. *Required fees:* $213; $106 per credit. One-time fee: $100. Tuition and fees vary according to campus/location and program. *Financial support:* In 2017–18, fellowships with partial tuition reimbursements (averaging $4,000 per year), teaching assistantships with partial tuition reimbursements (averaging $4,000 per year) were awarded; career-related internships or fieldwork, Federal Work-Study, institutionally sponsored loans, and unspecified assistantships also available. Support available to part-time students. Financial award application deadline: 4/15; financial award applicants required to submit FAFSA. *Unit head:* Dr. Cheri Meder, Interim Chair, 719-587-7934, Fax: 719-587-8145, E-mail: teachered@adams.edu. *Application contact:* Information Contact, 719-587-7776, Fax: 719-587-8145, E-mail: teachered@adams.edu.
Website: http://teachered.adams.edu

Alabama Agricultural and Mechanical University, School of Graduate Studies, College of Education, Humanities, and Behavioral Sciences, Department of Educational Leadership and Secondary Education, Huntsville, AL 35811. Offers biology (M Ed); business/marketing education (M Ed, Ed S); chemistry (M Ed); collaborative teacher secondary education (M Ed, Ed S); education (M Ed, Ed S); English language arts (M Ed); family/consumer science education (M Ed); general science (M Ed); general social science (M Ed); mathematics (M Ed, Ed S); physics (M Ed, Ed S); technology education (M Ed). *Accreditation:* NCATE. *Program availability:* Evening/weekend. *Degree requirements:* For master's, comprehensive exam; for Ed S, thesis. *Entrance requirements:* For master's, GRE General Test. Additional exam requirements/recommendations for international students: Required—TOEFL (minimum score 500 paper-based; 61 iBT). Electronic applications accepted. *Faculty research:* World peace through education, computer-assisted instruction.

Alabama State University, College of Education, Department of Curriculum and Instruction, Montgomery, AL 36101-0271. Offers early childhood education (M Ed, Ed S); elementary education (M Ed, Ed S); secondary education (M Ed, Ed S), including biology education, English language arts education (M Ed), history education, math education, music education (M Ed), reading education (M Ed), social science education; special education (M Ed). *Program availability:* Part-time. *Faculty:* 7 full-time (4 women), 7 part-time/adjunct (4 women). *Students:* 43 full-time (35 women), 71 part-time (62 women); includes 112 minority (111 Black or African American, non-Hispanic/Latino; 1 Two or more races, non-Hispanic/Latino). Average age 22. 47 applicants, 66% accepted, 19 enrolled. In 2017, 21 master's, 13 Ed Ss awarded. *Degree requirements:* For master's, comprehensive exam, thesis optional; for Ed S, comprehensive exam, thesis. *Entrance requirements:* For master's, GRE General Test, MAT, writing competency test; for Ed S, writing competency test, GRE, MAT. Additional exam requirements/recommendations for international students: Required—TOEFL (minimum score 500 paper-based). *Application deadline:* For fall admission, 4/15 for domestic and international students; for spring admission, 11/15 for domestic and international students; for summer admission, 3/15 for domestic and international students. Applications are processed on a rolling basis. Application fee: $25. Electronic applications accepted. *Expenses:* Tuition, state resident: part-time $412 per credit hour. Tuition, nonresident: part-time $824 per credit hour. *Required fees:* $685 per semester. *Financial support:* Research assistantships available. Financial award application deadline: 6/30; financial award applicants required to submit FAFSA. *Unit head:* Dr.

Joyce Johnson, Acting Chairperson, 334-229-4485, Fax: 334-229-5603, E-mail: jjohnson@alasu.edu. *Application contact:* Dr. William Person, Dean of Graduate Studies, 334-229-4274, Fax: 334-229-4928, E-mail: wperson@alasu.edu.
Website: http://www.alasu.edu/academics/colleges—departments/college-of-education/curriculum—instruction/index.aspx

American University of Beirut, Graduate Programs, Faculty of Arts and Sciences, 1107 2020, Lebanon. Offers anthropology (MA); Arab and Middle Eastern history (PhD); Arabic language and literature (MA, PhD); archaeology (MA); art history and curating (MA); biology (MS); cell and molecular biology (PhD); chemistry (MS); clinical psychology (MA); computational sciences (MS); computer science (MS); economics (MA); education (MA), including administration and policy studies, elementary education, mathematics education, psychology school guidance, psychology test and measurements, science education, teaching English as a foreign language; English language (MA); English literature (MA); environmental policy planning (MS); financial economics (MAFE); general psychology (MA); geology (MS); history (MA); Islamic studies (MA); mathematics (MS); media studies (MA); Middle East studies (MA); philosophy (MA); physics (MS); political studies (MA); public administration (MA); public policy and international affairs (MA); sociology (MA); theoretical physics (PhD). *Program availability:* Part-time. *Faculty:* 108 full-time (36 women), 5 part-time/adjunct (4 women). *Students:* 251 full-time (180 women), 233 part-time (172 women). Average age 26. 425 applicants, 65% accepted, 121 enrolled. In 2017, 47 master's, 2 doctorates awarded. *Degree requirements:* For master's, one foreign language, comprehensive exam, thesis (for some programs), project; for doctorate, one foreign language, comprehensive exam, thesis/dissertation. *Entrance requirements:* For master's, GRE General Test (for some programs); for doctorate, GRE General Test (GRE Subject Test for theoretical physics). Additional exam requirements/recommendations for international students: Required—TOEFL (minimum score 583 paper-based; 97 iBT), IELTS (minimum score 7). *Application deadline:* For fall admission, 2/8 for domestic students; for spring admission, 11/3 for domestic students. Application fee: $50. Electronic applications accepted. *Expenses:* Contact institution. *Financial support:* In 2017–18, 29 fellowships, 40 research assistantships were awarded; teaching assistantships, scholarships/grants, tuition waivers (full and partial), and unspecified assistantships also available. Financial award application deadline: 4/4. *Unit head:* Dr. Nadia Maria El Cheikh, Dean, Faculty of Arts and Sciences, 961-1-374374 Ext. 3800, Fax: 961-1-744461, E-mail: nmcheikh@aub.edu.lb. *Application contact:* Rima Rassi, Graduate Studies Officer, 961-1-350000 Ext. 3833, Fax: 961-1-744461, E-mail: rr46@aub.edu.lb.
Website: http://www.aub.edu.lb/fas/pages/default.aspx

Appalachian State University, Cratis D. Williams Graduate School, Department of Curriculum and Instruction, Boone, NC 28608. Offers curriculum specialist (MA); educational media (MA); elementary education (MA); middle grades education (MA), including language arts, mathematics, science, social studies. *Accreditation:* NCATE. *Program availability:* Part-time, evening/weekend, online learning. *Degree requirements:* For master's, comprehensive exam, thesis or alternative. *Entrance requirements:* For master's, GRE General Test or MAT, 3 letters of recommendation. Additional exam requirements/recommendations for international students: Required—TOEFL (minimum score 570 paper-based; 79 iBT), IELTS (minimum score 6.5). Electronic applications accepted. *Faculty research:* Media literacy, elementary teaching, curriculum development, online learning environments.

Arcadia University, School of Education, Glenside, PA 19038-3295. Offers art education (M Ed); computer education (CAS); curriculum (CAS); curriculum studies (M Ed); early childhood education (M Ed), including individualized, master teacher, research in child development; educational leadership (M Ed, Ed D, CAS); elementary education (M Ed); English education (MA Ed); environmental education (MA Ed); instructional technology (M Ed); language arts (M Ed); library science (M Ed); mathematics education (M Ed, MA Ed); music education (MA Ed); psychology (MA Ed); reading (M Ed, CAS); science education (M Ed, CAS); secondary education (M Ed,

CAS); special education (M Ed, Ed D, CAS); theater arts (MA Ed); written communication (MA Ed). *Accreditation:* NASAD. *Program availability:* Part-time, evening/weekend, online learning. Electronic applications accepted. *Expenses:* Contact institution.

Arizona State University at the Tempe campus, College of Liberal Arts and Sciences, School of Mathematical and Statistical Sciences, Tempe, AZ 85287-1804. Offers applied mathematics (PhD); mathematics (MA, PhD); mathematics education (PhD); statistics (MS, PhD, Graduate Certificate). *Program availability:* Part-time. Terminal master's awarded for partial completion of doctoral program. *Degree requirements:* For master's, thesis or alternative, interactive Program of Study (iPOS) submitted before completing 50 percent of required credit hours; for doctorate, comprehensive exam, thesis/dissertation, interactive Program of Study (iPOS) submitted before completing 50 percent of required credit hours. *Entrance requirements:* For master's and doctorate, GRE General Test, minimum GPA of 3.0 or equivalent in last 2 years of work leading to bachelor's degree. Additional exam requirements/recommendations for international students: Required—TOEFL, IELTS, or PTE. Electronic applications accepted. *Expenses:* Contact institution.

Arkansas State University, Graduate School, College of Sciences and Mathematics, Department of Mathematics and Statistics, State University, AR 72467. Offers mathematics (MS); mathematics education (MSE). *Program availability:* Part-time. *Degree requirements:* For master's, comprehensive exam, thesis or alternative. *Entrance requirements:* For master's, GRE General Test or MAT, appropriate bachelor's degree, official transcripts, immunization records, valid teaching certificate (for MSE). Additional exam requirements/recommendations for international students: Required— TOEFL (minimum score 550 paper-based; 79 iBT), IELTS (minimum score 6), PTE (minimum score 56). Electronic applications accepted.

Asbury University, School of Graduate and Professional Studies, Wilmore, KY 40390-1198. Offers biology: alternative certificate (MA Ed); chemistry: alternative certificate (MA Ed); English (MA Ed); English as a second language (MA Ed); ESL (MA Ed); French (MA Ed); Latin: alternative certificate (MA Ed); mathematics: alternative certificate (MA Ed); reading/writing endorsement (MA Ed); social studies (MA Ed); social work (MSW), including child and family services; Spanish (MA Ed); special education (MA Ed); special education: alternative certificate (MA Ed); teacher as leader endorsement (MA Ed). *Accreditation:* NCATE. *Program availability:* Part-time. *Degree requirements:* For master's, action research project, portfolio. *Entrance requirements:* For master's, PRAXIS/NTE, minimum GPA of 2.75, letters of recommendation. Additional exam requirements/recommendations for international students: Required— TOEFL (minimum score 550 paper-based). Electronic applications accepted.

Aurora University, College of Arts and Sciences, Aurora, IL 60506-4892. Offers homeland security (MS); mathematics (MS); mathematics and science education for elementary teachers (MA); mathematics educaton (MA); science education (MA). *Program availability:* Part-time, evening/weekend, 100% online. *Faculty:* 3 full-time (2 women), 6 part-time/adjunct (3 women). *Students:* 47 full-time (28 women), 45 part-time (10 women); includes 12 minority (5 Black or African American, non-Hispanic/Latino; 4 Asian, non-Hispanic/Latino; 3 Hispanic/Latino). Average age 36. 68 applicants, 96% accepted, 15 enrolled. *Degree requirements:* For master's, research seminars. *Entrance requirements:* For master's, bachelor's degree in mathematics or in some other field with extensive course work in mathematics (for MS in mathematics). Additional exam requirements/recommendations for international students: Required—TOEFL (minimum score 550 paper-based; 79 iBT). *Application deadline:* For fall admission, 6/1 for international students; for spring admission, 10/1 for international students. Applications are processed on a rolling basis. Application fee: $0. Electronic applications accepted. *Expenses:* Contact institution. *Financial support:* Federal Work-Study, scholarships/ grants, and unspecified assistantships available. Support available to part-time students. Financial award application deadline: 4/1; financial award applicants required to submit FAFSA. *Unit head:* Dr. Frank Buscher, Vice President for Academic Affairs, 630-844-5252, E-mail: fbuscher@aurora.edu. *Application contact:* Judson Curry, Dean of Adult and Graduate Studies, 630-947-8946, E-mail: jcurry@aurora.edu.

Austin Peay State University, College of Graduate Studies, College of Science, Technology, Engineering and Mathematics, Professional Science Master's Program, Clarksville, TN 37044. Offers data management and analysis (MS, PSM); information assurance and security (MS, PSM); mathematical finance (MS, PSM); mathematics instruction (MS); predictive analytics (MS, PSM). *Program availability:* Part-time, online learning. *Faculty:* 5 full-time (0 women), 1 part-time/adjunct (0 women). *Students:* 23 full-time (6 women), 41 part-time (15 women); includes 17 minority (6 Black or African American, non-Hispanic/Latino; 3 Asian, non-Hispanic/Latino; 4 Two or more races, non-Hispanic/Latino), 9 international. Average age 34. 48 applicants, 98% accepted, 35 enrolled. In 2017, 6 master's awarded. *Entrance requirements:* For master's, GRE, minimum undergraduate GPA of 2.5. Additional exam requirements/ recommendations for international students: Required—TOEFL (minimum score 500 paper-based). *Application deadline:* For fall admission, 8/8 priority date for domestic students. Applications are processed on a rolling basis. Application fee: $45 ($55 for international students). Electronic applications accepted. *Expenses:* Tuition, state resident: full-time $7686; part-time $427 per credit hour. Tuition, nonresident: full-time $20,268; part-time $1126 per credit hour. *Required fees:* $1529; $76.45 per credit hour. *Financial support:* Research assistantships with full tuition reimbursements, career-related internships or fieldwork, Federal Work-Study, institutionally sponsored loans, scholarships/grants, and unspecified assistantships available. Support available to part-time students. Financial award application deadline: 4/1; financial award applicants required to submit FAFSA. *Unit head:* Dr. Matt Jones, 931-221-7814, E-mail: gradpsm@ apsu.edu. *Application contact:* Megan Mitchell, Coordinator of Graduate Admissions, 800-859-4723, Fax: 931-221-7641, E-mail: gradadmissions@apsu.edu. Website: http://www.apsu.edu/csci/masters_degrees/index.php

Ball State University, Graduate School, College of Sciences and Humanities, Department of Mathematical Sciences, Program in Mathematics Education, Muncie, IN 47306. Offers mathematics education (MA), including elementary and middle school mathematics, elementary and middle school mathematics specialist, secondary mathematics. *Program availability:* Part-time, 100% online, blended/hybrid learning. *Students:* 54 part-time (38 women); includes 5 minority (2 Black or African American, non-Hispanic/Latino; 1 Asian, non-Hispanic/Latino; 1 Hispanic/Latino; 1 Two or more races, non-Hispanic/Latino). Average age 34. 15 applicants, 73% accepted, 10 enrolled. In 2017, 8 master's awarded. *Entrance requirements:* For master's, minimum baccalaureate GPA of 2.75 or 3.0 in latter half of baccalaureate. Additional exam requirements/recommendations for international students: Required—TOEFL (minimum score 550 paper-based; 79 iBT), IELTS (minimum score 6.5). *Application deadline:* Applications are processed on a rolling basis. Application fee: $60. Electronic applications accepted. *Financial support:* Teaching assistantships with partial tuition reimbursements available. Financial award application deadline: 3/1; financial award applicants required to submit FAFSA. *Unit head:* Dr. Michael Karls, Chairperson, 765-285-8640, Fax: 765-285-1721, E-mail: mkarls@bsu.edu. Website: http://www.bsu.edu/math

Bank Street College of Education, Graduate School, Programs in Educational Leadership, New York, NY 10025. Offers early childhood leadership (MS Ed);

educational leadership (MS Ed); leadership for educational change (Ed M, MS Ed); leadership in community-based learning (MS Ed); leadership in mathematics education (MS Ed); leadership in museum education (MS Ed); leadership in the arts: creative writing (MS Ed); leadership in the arts: visual arts (MS Ed). *Degree requirements:* For master's, thesis. *Entrance requirements:* For master's, interview, essays, minimum of 2 years experience as a classroom teacher. Additional exam requirements/ recommendations for international students: Required—TOEFL (minimum score 600 paper-based; 100 iBT), IELTS (minimum score 7). Electronic applications accepted. *Faculty research:* Leadership in urban schools, leadership in small schools, mathematics in elementary schools, professional development in early childhood, leadership in arts education, leadership in special education, museum leadership, community-based leadership.

Bard College, Master of Arts in Teaching Program, Annandale-on-Hudson, NY 12504. Offers secondary education (MAT), including biology, history, literature, mathematics, Spanish; MS/MAT. *Program availability:* Part-time. *Degree requirements:* For master's, year-long teaching residencies in area middle and high schools. *Entrance requirements:* For master's, GRE General Test, resume, 3 letters of recommendation, personal statement, official transcripts. Additional exam requirements/recommendations for international students: Required—TOEFL. Electronic applications accepted. Application fee is waived when completed online.

Bemidji State University, School of Graduate Studies, Bemidji, MN 56601. Offers biology (MS); education (MS); English (MA, MS); environmental studies (MS); mathematics (MS); mathematics (elementary and middle level education) (MS); special education (M Sp Ed). *Program availability:* Part-time, online learning. *Degree requirements:* For master's, comprehensive exam, thesis (for some programs). *Entrance requirements:* For master's, GRE; GMAT, letters of recommendation, letters of interest. Additional exam requirements/recommendations for international students: Required— TOEFL (minimum score 550 paper-based; 80 iBT). Electronic applications accepted. *Expenses:* Contact institution. *Faculty research:* Human performance, sport, and health: physical education teacher education, continuum models, spiritual health, intellectual health, resiliency, health priorities; psychology: health psychology, college student drinking behavior, micro-aggressions, infant cognition, false memories, leadership assessment; biology: structure and dynamics of forest communities, aquatic and riverine ecology, interaction between animal populations and aquatic environments, cellular motility.

Binghamton University, State University of New York, Graduate School, College of Community and Public Affairs, Department of Teaching, Learning and Educational Leadership, Program in Adolescence Education, Binghamton, NY 13902-6000. Offers biology education (MAT, MS Ed); chemistry education (MAT, MS Ed); earth science education (MAT, MS Ed); English education (MAT, MS Ed); French education (MAT, MS Ed); mathematical sciences education (MAT, MS Ed); physics (MAT, MS Ed); social studies (MAT, MS Ed); Spanish education (MAT, MS Ed). *Accreditation:* TEAC. *Program availability:* Part-time, evening/weekend. *Students:* 53 full-time (32 women), 9 part-time (3 women); includes 10 minority (2 Black or African American, non-Hispanic/ Latino; 1 Asian, non-Hispanic/Latino; 5 Hispanic/Latino; 2 Two or more races, non-Hispanic/Latino). Average age 27. 51 applicants, 88% accepted, 31 enrolled. In 2017, 36 master's awarded. *Degree requirements:* For master's, portfolio. *Entrance requirements:* For master's, GRE General Test, teaching certification. Additional exam requirements/recommendations for international students: Required—TOEFL (minimum score 550 paper-based; 80 iBT). *Application deadline:* For fall admission, 2/1 priority date for domestic and international students; for spring admission, 10/15 priority date for domestic and international students. Application fee: $75. Electronic applications accepted. *Financial support:* In 2017–18, 4 students received support. Research assistantships, teaching assistantships, career-related internships or fieldwork, Federal Work-Study, institutionally sponsored loans, scholarships/grants, health care benefits, tuition waivers (full and partial), and unspecified assistantships available. Financial award applicants required to submit FAFSA. *Unit head:* Dr. Susan Strehle, Dean, 607-777-7329, E-mail: sstrehle@binghamton.edu. *Application contact:* Ben Balkaya, Assistant Dean and Director, 607-777-2151, Fax: 607-777-2501, E-mail: balkaya@ binghamton.edu.

Bloomsburg University of Pennsylvania, School of Graduate Studies, College of Education, Department of Teaching and Learning, Program in Middle Level Education, Grades 4-8, Bloomsburg, PA 17815-1301. Offers language arts (M Ed); math (M Ed); science (M Ed); social studies (M Ed). *Accreditation:* NCATE. *Degree requirements:* For master's, thesis optional, practicum, student teaching. *Entrance requirements:* For master's, MAT, GRE, or PRAXIS, minimum QPA of 3.0, teaching certificate, U.S. citizenship, related undergraduate coursework, professional liability insurance, recent TB test. Additional exam requirements/recommendations for international students: Required—TOEFL (minimum score 550 paper-based), IELTS. Electronic applications accepted. *Expenses:* Tuition, state resident: full-time $10,000; part-time $500 per credit hour. Tuition, nonresident: full-time $15,000; part-time $750 per credit hour. *Required fees:* $2484; $110.75 per credit hour. $75 per term. Tuition and fees vary according to program.

Bob Jones University, Graduate Programs, Greenville, SC 29614. Offers accountancy (MS); Bible (MA); Bible translation (MA); Biblical studies (Certificate); broadcast management (MS); business administration (MBA); church history (MA, PhD); church ministries (MA); church music (MM); cinema and video production (MA); counseling (MS); curriculum and instruction (Ed D); divinity (M Div); dramatic production (MA); educational leadership (M Ed, Ed D, Ed S); elementary education (M Ed, MAT); English (M Ed, MA, MAT); fine arts (MA); graphic design (MA); history (M Ed, MA); illustration (MA); interpretative speech (MA); mathematics (M Ed, MAT); medical missions (Certificate); ministry (MM, D Min); multi-categorical special education (M Ed, MAT); music (M Ed); New Testament interpretation (PhD); Old Testament interpretation (PhD); orchestral instrument performance (MM); organ performance (MM); pastoral studies (MA); personnel services (MS, Ed S); piano pedagogy (MM); piano performance (MM); platform arts (MA); radio and television broadcasting (MS); rhetoric and public address (MA); secondary education (M Ed); studio art (MA); teaching Bible (MA); theology (MA, PhD); voice performance (MM); youth ministries (MA); M Div/MM.

Boise State University, College of Arts and Sciences, Department of Mathematics, Boise, ID 83725-0399. Offers mathematics (MS); mathematics education (MS). *Program availability:* Part-time. *Faculty:* 12. *Students:* 16 full-time (8 women), 9 part-time (5 women); includes 3 minority (all Asian, non-Hispanic/Latino), 3 international. Average age 31. 33 applicants, 33% accepted, 10 enrolled. In 2017, 4 master's awarded. *Degree requirements:* For master's, thesis optional. *Entrance requirements:* For master's, GRE General Test. Additional exam requirements/recommendations for international students: Required—TOEFL (minimum score 550 paper-based; 80 iBT), IELTS (minimum score 6). *Application deadline:* For fall admission, 2/1 priority date for domestic and international students. Application fee: $65 ($95 for international students). Electronic applications accepted. *Expenses:* Tuition, state resident: full-time $6471; part-time $390 per credit. Tuition, nonresident: full-time $21,787; part-time $685 per credit. *Required fees:* $2283; $100 per term. Part-time tuition and fees vary according to course load and program. *Financial support:* Teaching assistantships, scholarships/grants, and unspecified assistantships available. Financial award

application deadline: 2/1; financial award applicants required to submit FAFSA. *Unit head:* Dr. Leming Qu, Chair, 208-426-1172, E-mail: lqu@boisestate.edu. *Application contact:* Dr. Jens Harlander, Graduate Program Coordinator, 208-426-3312, E-mail: mathematicsgrad@boisestate.edu.
Website: http://math.boisestate.edu/

Bowling Green State University, Graduate College, College of Arts and Sciences, Department of Mathematics and Statistics, Bowling Green, OH 43403. Offers mathematics (MA, MAT, PhD); statistics (PhD). *Program availability:* Part-time. *Degree requirements:* For master's, thesis or alternative; for doctorate, comprehensive exam, thesis/dissertation. *Entrance requirements:* For master's and doctorate, GRE General Test. Additional exam requirements/recommendations for international students: Required—TOEFL. Electronic applications accepted. *Faculty research:* Statistics and probability, algebra, analysis.

Bridgewater State University, College of Graduate Studies, Bartlett College of Science and Mathematics, Department of Mathematics, Bridgewater, MA 02325. Offers MAT. *Program availability:* Part-time, evening/weekend. *Entrance requirements:* For master's, GRE General Test.

Brigham Young University, Graduate Studies, College of Physical and Mathematical Sciences, Department of Mathematics Education, Provo, UT 84602-1001. Offers MA. *Program availability:* Part-time. *Faculty:* 8 full-time (2 women). *Students:* 10 full-time (all women), 4 part-time (2 women). Average age 31. 5 applicants, 100% accepted, 5 enrolled. In 2017, 6 master's awarded. *Degree requirements:* For master's, comprehensive exam, project or thesis. *Entrance requirements:* For master's, GRE General Test, teaching certificate, bachelor's degree in math education or equivalent. Additional exam requirements/recommendations for international students: Required—TOEFL. *Application deadline:* For fall admission, 3/1 priority date for domestic and international students; for summer admission, 3/1 priority date for domestic and international students. Application fee: $50. Electronic applications accepted. *Expenses:* $405 per credit hour. *Financial support:* In 2017–18, 14 students received support, including 5 research assistantships with full tuition reimbursements available (averaging $13,000 per year), 15 teaching assistantships with full tuition reimbursements available (averaging $13,000 per year); scholarships/grants also available. Financial award application deadline: 3/1. *Faculty research:* Understanding the characteristics of high-quality mathematics instruction, teaching mathematics for social justice, applying mathematics to science and engineering, technology in teaching and learning mathematics, how preservice teachers learn to teach mathematics, discourse and literacy in mathematics classrooms, how national policy influences mathematics teachers. *Total annual research expenditures:* $150,000. *Unit head:* Dr. Blake E. Peterson, Chair, 801-422-7784, E-mail: blake@byu.edu. *Application contact:* Kathy Lee Garrett, Administrative Assistant, 801-422-1840, E-mail: kathylee@mathed.byu.edu.
Website: https://mathed.byu.edu/

Brooklyn College of the City University of New York, School of Education, Program in Adolescence Science Education and Special Subjects, Brooklyn, NY 11210-2889. Offers adolescence science education (MAT); biology teacher (7-12) (MA); chemistry teacher (7-12) (MA); earth science teacher (7-12) (MAT); English teacher (7-12) (MA); French teacher (7-12) (MA); mathematics teacher (7-12) (MA); music teacher (MA); physics teacher (7-12) (MA); social studies teacher (7-12) (MA); Spanish teacher (7-12) (MA). *Program availability:* Part-time, evening/weekend. *Degree requirements:* For master's, comprehensive exam (for some programs), thesis (for some programs). *Entrance requirements:* For master's, LAST, previous course work in education, resume, 2 letters of recommendation, essay. Additional exam requirements/recommendations for international students: Required—TOEFL (minimum score 500 paper-based; 61 iBT). Electronic applications accepted. *Faculty research:* Interdisciplinary education, semiotics, discourse analysis, autobiography, teacher identity.

Brooklyn College of the City University of New York, School of Education, Program in Childhood Education, Brooklyn, NY 11210-2889. Offers bilingual education (MS Ed); liberal arts (MS Ed); mathematics (MS Ed); science and environmental education (MS Ed). *Program availability:* Part-time, evening/weekend. *Entrance requirements:* For master's, LAST, interview, previous course work in education, writing sample, resume, 2 letters of recommendation. Additional exam requirements/recommendations for international students: Required—TOEFL (minimum score 500 paper-based; 61 iBT). Electronic applications accepted. *Faculty research:* Emotional intelligence, multiculturalism, arts immersion, the Holocaust.

Brooklyn College of the City University of New York, School of Education, Program in Middle Childhood Mathematics Education, Brooklyn, NY 11210-2889. Offers MS Ed. *Entrance requirements:* For master's, LAST, 2 letters of recommendation, essay, resume. Additional exam requirements/recommendations for international students: Required—TOEFL (minimum score 500 paper-based; 61 iBT). Electronic applications accepted.

Buffalo State College, State University of New York, The Graduate School, Faculty of Natural and Social Sciences, Department of Mathematics, Buffalo, NY 14222-1095. Offers mathematics education (MS Ed). *Accreditation:* NCATE. *Program availability:* Part-time, evening/weekend. *Degree requirements:* For master's, thesis or alternative. *Entrance requirements:* For master's, 18 undergraduate hours in upper-level mathematics, minimum GPA of 2.5 in undergraduate math courses. Additional exam requirements/recommendations for international students: Required—TOEFL (minimum score 550 paper-based).

California State University, Bakersfield, Division of Graduate Studies, School of Natural Sciences, Mathematics, and Engineering, Program in Teaching Mathematics, Bakersfield, CA 93311. Offers MA. *Entrance requirements:* For master's, minimum GPA of 2.5 for last 90 quarter units. *Expenses:* Tuition, state resident: full-time $7176; part-time $4164 per year. *Unit head:* Sophia Raczkowski, Chair, 661-654-3151, Fax: 661-664-2039. *Application contact:* Debbie Blowers, Assistant Director of Admissions and Evaluations, 661-654-3381, E-mail: dblowers@csub.edu.
Website: https://www.csub.edu/math/info/index.html

California State University, Chico, Office of Graduate Studies, College of Natural Sciences, Program in Mathematics Education, Chico, CA 95929-0722. Offers mathematics in education (MS). *Program availability:* Part-time. *Degree requirements:* For master's, thesis or project. *Entrance requirements:* For master's, GRE, teaching credential in mathematics, statement of purpose. Additional exam requirements/recommendations for international students: Required—TOEFL (minimum score 550 paper-based; 80 iBT), IELTS (minimum score 6.5), PTE (minimum score 59). Electronic applications accepted.

California State University, East Bay, Office of Graduate Studies, College of Science, Department of Mathematics, Hayward, CA 94542-3000. Offers mathematics teaching (MS); pure mathematics (MS). *Program availability:* Part-time, evening/weekend. *Students:* 27 full-time (10 women), 25 part-time (10 women); includes 29 minority (3 Black or African American, non-Hispanic/Latino; 11 Asian, non-Hispanic/Latino; 12 Hispanic/Latino; 1 Native Hawaiian or other Pacific Islander, non-Hispanic/Latino; 2 Two or more races, non-Hispanic/Latino), 8 international. Average age 34. 37 applicants, 86% accepted, 18 enrolled. In 2017, 11 master's awarded. *Degree requirements:* For master's, comprehensive exam or thesis. *Entrance requirements:* For master's, minimum GPA of 3.0 in field. Additional exam requirements/recommendations for international students: Required—TOEFL (minimum score 550 paper-based). *Application deadline:* For fall admission, 6/1 for domestic and international students. Application fee: $55. Electronic applications accepted. *Financial support:* Fellowships, research assistantships, teaching assistantships, Federal Work-Study, institutionally sponsored loans, and scholarships/grants available. Support available to part-time students. Financial award application deadline: 3/1; financial award applicants required to submit FAFSA. *Unit head:* Julie Glass, Chair, 510-885-2159, E-mail: julie.glass@csueastbay.edu. *Application contact:* Dr. Donald Wolitzer, Math Graduate Advisor, 510-885-3467, E-mail: donald.wolitzer@csueastbay.edu.
Website: http://www.csueastbay.edu/csci/departments/math/index.html

California State University, Fresno, Division of Research and Graduate Studies, College of Science and Mathematics, Department of Mathematics, Fresno, CA 93740-8027. Offers mathematics (MA); mathematics teaching (MA). *Program availability:* Part-time. *Degree requirements:* For master's, thesis or alternative. *Entrance requirements:* For master's, GRE General Test. Additional exam requirements/recommendations for international students: Required—TOEFL. Electronic applications accepted. *Faculty research:* Diagnostic testing project.

California State University, Fullerton, Graduate Studies, College of Education, Department of Secondary Education, Fullerton, CA 92831-3599. Offers teacher instruction (MS); teaching foundational mathematics (MS). *Program availability:* Part-time. *Faculty:* 4 full-time (3 women), 1 (woman) part-time/adjunct. *Students:* 38 part-time (24 women); includes 15 minority (1 Black or African American, non-Hispanic/Latino; 3 Asian, non-Hispanic/Latino; 9 Hispanic/Latino; 2 Two or more races, non-Hispanic/Latino). Average age 29. 29 applicants, 76% accepted, 21 enrolled. Application fee: $55. *Financial support:* Career-related internships or fieldwork, Federal Work-Study, institutionally sponsored loans, and scholarships/grants available. Support available to part-time students. Financial award application deadline: 3/1; financial award applicants required to submit FAFSA. *Unit head:* Dr. Grace Cho, Chair, 657-278-3283, E-mail: gcho@fullerton.edu. *Application contact:* Admissions/Applications, 657-278-2371.

California State University, Fullerton, Graduate Studies, College of Natural Science and Mathematics, Department of Mathematics, Fullerton, CA 92831-3599. Offers applied mathematics (MA); mathematics education (MA). *Program availability:* Part-time. *Faculty:* 9 full-time (3 women). *Students:* 7 full-time (6 women), 119 part-time (56 women); includes 56 minority (2 Black or African American, non-Hispanic/Latino; 28 Asian, non-Hispanic/Latino; 23 Hispanic/Latino; 3 Two or more races, non-Hispanic/Latino), 16 international. Average age 30. 175 applicants, 70% accepted, 63 enrolled. *Entrance requirements:* For master's, minimum GPA of 2.5 in last 60 units of course work, major in mathematics or related field. Application fee: $55. *Financial support:* Research assistantships, teaching assistantships, career-related internships or fieldwork, Federal Work-Study, institutionally sponsored loans, and scholarships/grants available. Support available to part-time students. Financial award application deadline: 3/1; financial award applicants required to submit FAFSA. *Unit head:* Dr. Stephen W. Goode, Chair, 657-278-3631. *Application contact:* Admissions/Applications, 657-278-2371.

California State University, Long Beach, Graduate Studies, College of Natural Sciences and Mathematics, Department of Mathematics and Statistics, Long Beach, CA 90840. Offers mathematics (MS), including applied mathematics, applied statistics, mathematics education for secondary school teachers. *Program availability:* Part-time. *Degree requirements:* For master's, comprehensive exam or thesis. Electronic applications accepted. *Faculty research:* Algebra, functional analysis, partial differential equations, operator theory, numerical analysis.

California State University, Northridge, Graduate Studies, Michael D. Eisner College of Education, Department of Secondary Education, Northridge, CA 91330. Offers educational technology (MA); English education (MA); mathematics education (MA); secondary science education (MA); teaching and learning (MA). *Accreditation:* NCATE. *Program availability:* Part-time. *Students:* 9 full-time (5 women), 85 part-time (57 women); includes 37 minority (2 Black or African American, non-Hispanic/Latino; 12 Asian, non-Hispanic/Latino; 20 Hispanic/Latino; 1 Native Hawaiian or other Pacific Islander, non-Hispanic/Latino; 2 Two or more races, non-Hispanic/Latino), 1 international. Average age 37. 63 applicants, 78% accepted, 45 enrolled. *Degree requirements:* For master's, thesis optional. *Entrance requirements:* For master's, GRE General Test or minimum GPA of 3.0. Additional exam requirements/recommendations for international students: Required—TOEFL. *Application deadline:* For fall admission, 11/30 for domestic students. Application fee: $55. *Financial support:* Application deadline: 3/1. *Unit head:* Dr. Julie Gainsburg, Chair, 818-677-2580. *Application contact:* Dr. Michael Rivas, Graduate Advisor, 818-677-6792, E-mail: michael.rivas@csun.edu.
Website: http://www.csun.edu/eisner-education/secondary-education

California State University, San Bernardino, Graduate Studies, College of Natural Sciences, Program in Mathematics, San Bernardino, CA 92407. Offers mathematics (MA); teaching mathematics (MAT). *Program availability:* Part-time. *Faculty:* 6 full-time (2 women). *Students:* 4 full-time (2 women), 29 part-time (14 women); includes 23 minority (1 Black or African American, non-Hispanic/Latino; 22 Hispanic/Latino), 1 international. Average age 30. 22 applicants, 55% accepted, 11 enrolled. In 2017, 6 master's awarded. *Degree requirements:* For master's, advancement to candidacy. *Entrance requirements:* Additional exam requirements/recommendations for international students: Required—TOEFL. *Application deadline:* For fall admission, 7/16 for domestic students; for winter admission, 10/16 for domestic students; for spring admission, 1/22 for domestic students. Application fee: $55. *Faculty research:* Mathematics education, technology in education, algebra, combinatorics, real analysis. *Unit head:* Dr. Charles Stanton, Chair, 909-537-5361, E-mail: cstanton@csusb.edu. *Application contact:* Dr. Dorota Huizinga, Assistant Dean of Graduate Studies, 909-537-3064, E-mail: dorota.huizinga@csusb.edu.

California University of Pennsylvania, School of Graduate Studies and Research, College of Education and Human Services, Department of Childhood Education, California, PA 15419-1394. Offers early childhood education (M Ed); elementary education (M Ed); STEM education (M Ed). *Accreditation:* NCATE. *Program availability:* Part-time, evening/weekend. *Degree requirements:* For master's, comprehensive exam, thesis optional. *Entrance requirements:* For master's, MAT, PRAXIS, minimum GPA of 3.0, state police clearances. Additional exam requirements/recommendations for international students: Required—TOEFL (minimum score 550 paper-based; 80 iBT). *Application deadline:* For fall admission, 8/1 priority date for domestic and international students; for spring admission, 5/1 priority date for domestic and international students. Applications are processed on a rolling basis. Application fee: $25. Electronic applications accepted. *Financial support:* Applicants required to submit FAFSA. *Faculty research:* English as a second language, adult literacy, emerging literacy, diagnosis and remediation, phonemic awareness. *Unit head:* Dr. Diane H. Nettles, Department Chair, 724-938-4497, E-mail: nettles@calu.edu. *Application contact:* Suzanne C. Powers, Director of Graduate Admissions and Recruitment, 724-938-4029, Fax: 724-938-5712, E-mail: powers_s@cup.edu.
Website: http://www.calu.edu/academics/graduate-programs/elementary/

Cambridge College, School of Education, Boston, MA 02129. Offers autism specialist (M Ed); autism/behavior analyst (M Ed); behavior analyst (Post-Master's Certificate); behavioral management (M Ed); early childhood teacher (M Ed); education specialist in curriculum and instruction (CAGS); educational leadership (Ed D); elementary teacher (M Ed); English as a second language (M Ed, Certificate); general science (M Ed); health education (Post-Master's Certificate); health/family and consumer sciences (M Ed); history (M Ed); individualized (M Ed); information technology literacy (M Ed); instructional technology (M Ed); interdisciplinary studies (M Ed); library teacher (M Ed); literacy education (M Ed); mathematics (M Ed); mathematics specialist (Certificate); middle school mathematics and science (M Ed, CAGS); school administration (M Ed, CAGS); school guidance counselor (M Ed); school nurse education (M Ed); school social worker/school adjustment counselor (M Ed); special education administrator (CAGS); special education/moderate disabilities (M Ed); teaching skills and methodologies (M Ed). *Program availability:* Part-time, evening/weekend, online learning. *Degree requirements:* For master's, thesis, internship/practicum (licensure program only); for doctorate, thesis/dissertation; for other advanced degree, thesis. *Entrance requirements:* For master's, interview, resume, documentation of licensure, 2 professional references; for doctorate, official transcripts, interview, resume, documentation of licensure (if any), written personal statement/essay, portfolio of scholarly and professional work, qualifying assessment, 2 professional references, health insurance, immunizations form; for other advanced degree, official transcripts, interview, resume, documentation of licensure (if any), written personal statement/essay, 2 professional references, health insurance, immunizations form. Additional exam requirements/recommendations for international students: Required—TOEFL (minimum score 550 paper-based; 79 iBT), Michigan English Language Assessment Battery (minimum score 85); Recommended—IELTS (minimum score 6). Electronic applications accepted. *Expenses:* Contact institution. *Faculty research:* Adult education, accelerated learning, mathematics education, brain compatible learning, special education and law.

Caribbean University, Graduate School, Bayamón, PR 00960-0493. Offers administration and supervision (MA Ed); criminal justice (MA); curriculum and instruction (MA Ed, PhD), including elementary education (MA Ed), English education (MA Ed), history education (MA Ed), mathematics education (MA Ed), primary education (MA Ed), science education (MA Ed), Spanish education (MA Ed); educational technology in instructional systems (MA Ed); gerontology (MSN); human resources (MBA); museology, archiving and art history (MA Ed); neonatal pediatrics (MSN); physical education (MA Ed); special education (MA Ed). *Entrance requirements:* For master's, interview, minimum GPA of 2.5.

Central Michigan University, College of Graduate Studies, College of Science and Technology, Department of Mathematics, Mount Pleasant, MI 48859. Offers mathematics (MA, PhD), including teaching of college mathematics (PhD). *Program availability:* Part-time. *Degree requirements:* For master's, thesis or alternative; for doctorate, thesis/dissertation. *Entrance requirements:* For master's, minimum GPA of 2.7, 20 hours of course work in mathematics; for doctorate, GRE, minimum GPA of 3.0, 20 hours of course work in mathematics. Electronic applications accepted. *Faculty research:* Combinatorics, approximation theory, applied mathematics, statistics, functional analysis and operator theory.

Chatham University, Program in Education, Pittsburgh, PA 15232-2826. Offers early childhood education (MAT); elementary education (MAT); environmental education (K-12) (MAT); secondary art (MAT); secondary biology education (MAT); secondary chemistry education (MAT); secondary English education (MAT); secondary math education (MAT); secondary physics education (MAT); secondary social studies education (MAT); special education (MAT). *Faculty:* 1 (woman) full-time, 15 part-time/adjunct (13 women). *Students:* 31 full-time (23 women), 3 part-time (1 woman); includes 9 minority (8 Black or African American, non-Hispanic/Latino; 1 Hispanic/Latino). Average age 30. 25 applicants, 60% accepted, 9 enrolled. In 2017, 23 master's awarded. *Degree requirements:* For master's, thesis, teaching experience. *Entrance requirements:* For master's, minimum GPA of 3.0, sample of written work, recommendation letters. Additional exam requirements/recommendations for international students: Required—TOEFL (minimum score 600 paper-based; 100 iBT), IELTS (minimum score 7), TWE. *Application deadline:* For fall admission, 4/1 priority date for domestic and international students; for spring admission, 11/1 priority date for domestic students, 10/1 priority date for international students. Applications are processed on a rolling basis. Application fee: $45. Electronic applications accepted. Application fee is waived when completed online. *Expenses: Tuition:* Full-time $16,740; part-time $930 per credit. *Required fees:* $486; $27 per credit. $243 per semester. *Financial support:* Career-related internships or fieldwork available. Financial award applicants required to submit FAFSA. *Faculty research:* Gifted education, environmental education, technology in education, writing as learning, class size and achievement. *Application contact:* Katie Noel, Assistant Director of Graduate Admission, 412-365-2758, Fax: 412-365-1609, E-mail: gradadmissions@chatham.edu.
Website: http://www.chatham.edu/mat

The Citadel, The Military College of South Carolina, Citadel Graduate College, Zucker Family School of Education, Charleston, SC 29409. Offers elementary/secondary school administration and supervision (M Ed); elementary/secondary school counseling (M Ed); interdisciplinary STEM education (M Ed); literacy education (M Ed, Graduate Certificate); middle grades (MAT), including English, mathematics, science, social studies; physical education (grades K-12) (MAT); school superintendency (Ed S); secondary education (MAT), including biology, English, mathematics, social studies; student affairs (Graduate Certificate); student affairs and college counseling (M Ed). *Accreditation:* NCATE. *Program availability:* Part-time, evening/weekend, 100% online, blended/hybrid learning. *Degree requirements:* For master's, comprehensive exam (for some programs). *Entrance requirements:* For master's, GRE (minimum combined verbal and quantitative score of 290) or MAT (minimum score 396). Additional exam requirements/recommendations for international students: Required—TOEFL (minimum score 550 paper-based; 79 iBT). Electronic applications accepted. *Expenses:* Tuition, state resident: part-time $587 per credit hour. Tuition, nonresident: part-time $988 per credit hour. *Required fees:* $90 per term.

City College of the City University of New York, Graduate School, School of Education, Department of Secondary Education, New York, NY 10031-9198. Offers adolescent mathematics education (MA, AC); English education (MA); middle school mathematics education (MS); science education (MA); social studies education (AC). *Accreditation:* NCATE. *Entrance requirements:* For master's, Liberal Arts and Sciences Test (LAST), Content Specialty Test (CST). Additional exam requirements/recommendations for international students: Required—TOEFL.

Clarion University of Pennsylvania, College of Arts, Education and Sciences, Master of Education Program, Clarion, PA 16214. Offers curriculum and instruction (M Ed); early childhood (M Ed); math education (M Ed); reading (M Ed); science education (M Ed); special education (M Ed); technology (M Ed). *Accreditation:* NCATE. *Program availability:* Part-time, evening/weekend, online only, 100% online, blended/hybrid learning. *Faculty:* 6 full-time (3 women). *Students:* 11 full-time (all women), 101 part-time (82 women); includes 4 minority (2 Black or African American, non-Hispanic/Latino; 1 Hispanic/Latino; 1 Two or more races, non-Hispanic/Latino). Average age 30. 80 applicants, 98% accepted, 33 enrolled. In 2017, 52 master's awarded. *Degree*

requirements: For master's, comprehensive exam, thesis, or portfolio. *Entrance requirements:* For master's, minimum QPA of 3.0. Additional exam requirements/recommendations for international students: Required—TOEFL (minimum score 550 paper-based, 80 iBT) or IELTS (7). *Application deadline:* For fall admission, 8/15 priority date for domestic students, 7/15 priority date for international students; for winter admission, 11/1 priority date for domestic students; for spring admission, 1/7 priority date for domestic students, 11/15 priority date for international students; for summer admission, 4/1 priority date for domestic students. Applications are processed on a rolling basis. Application fee: $40. Electronic applications accepted. *Expenses:* $655.05 per credit. *Financial support:* Career-related internships or fieldwork and scholarships/grants available. Support available to part-time students. Financial award application deadline: 3/1; financial award applicants required to submit FAFSA. *Unit head:* Dr. John McCullough, Chair, Department of Education, 814-393-2404, Fax: 814-393-2446, E-mail: gradstudies@clarion.edu. *Application contact:* Dana Bearer, Associate Director for Transfer, Adult, and Graduate Programs, 814-393-2337, Fax: 814-393-2722, E-mail: gradstudies@clarion.edu.

Clark Atlanta University, School of Education, Department of Curriculum and Instruction, Atlanta, GA 30314. Offers special education general education (MA); teaching math and science (MAT). *Program availability:* Part-time. *Faculty:* 5 full-time (4 women), 6 part-time/adjunct (2 women). *Students:* 8 full-time (2 women), 4 part-time (1 woman); includes 6 minority (all Black or African American, non-Hispanic/Latino), 5 international. Average age 34. 10 applicants, 90% accepted, 3 enrolled. In 2017, 1 master's awarded. *Degree requirements:* For master's, one foreign language, comprehensive exam. *Entrance requirements:* For master's, GRE General Test, minimum undergraduate GPA of 2.6. Additional exam requirements/recommendations for international students: Required—TOEFL (minimum score 500 paper-based; 61 iBT). *Application deadline:* For fall admission, 4/1 for domestic and international students; for spring admission, 11/1 for domestic and international students. Applications are processed on a rolling basis. Application fee: $40 ($55 for international students). *Financial support:* Career-related internships or fieldwork, Federal Work-Study, scholarships/grants, and unspecified assistantships available. Support available to part-time students. Financial award application deadline: 4/30; financial award applicants required to submit FAFSA. *Unit head:* Dr. James Young, Chairperson, 404-880-6079, E-mail: jyoung@cau.edu.
Website: http://www.cau.edu/school-of-education/Dept-of-Curriculum-and-Instruction/index.html

Clayton State University, School of Graduate Studies, College of Arts and Sciences, Program in Education, Morrow, GA 30260-0285. Offers biology (MAT); English (MAT); history (MAT); mathematics (MAT). *Accreditation:* NCATE. *Entrance requirements:* For master's, GRE, GACE, 2 official copies of transcripts, 3 recommendation letters, statement of purpose. Additional exam requirements/recommendations for international students: Required—TOEFL (minimum score 550 paper-based). Electronic applications accepted.

Clemson University, Graduate School, College of Education, Department of Teaching and Learning, Clemson, SC 29634. Offers curriculum and instruction (PhD); middle level education (MAT); secondary math and science (MAT); STEAM education (Certificate); teaching and learning (M Ed). *Program availability:* Part-time, evening/weekend, 100% online. *Faculty:* 21 full-time (17 women). *Students:* 41 full-time (27 women), 94 part-time (78 women); includes 16 minority (8 Black or African American, non-Hispanic/Latino; 6 Hispanic/Latino; 1 Native Hawaiian or other Pacific Islander, non-Hispanic/Latino; 1 Two or more races, non-Hispanic/Latino), 3 international. Average age 29. 65 applicants, 62% accepted, 33 enrolled. In 2017, 74 master's awarded. *Degree requirements:* For master's, comprehensive exam; for doctorate, comprehensive exam, thesis/dissertation. *Entrance requirements:* For master's, doctorate, and Certificate, GRE General Test, unofficial transcripts, letters of recommendation. Additional exam requirements/recommendations for international students: Required—TOEFL (minimum score 540 paper-based; 80 iBT), IELTS (minimum score 7), PTE (minimum score 45). *Application deadline:* For fall admission, 4/15 for domestic and international students. Applications are processed on a rolling basis. Application fee: $80 ($90 for international students). Electronic applications accepted. *Expenses:* $5,767 per semester full-time resident, $10,918 per semester full-time non-resident, $656 per credit hour part-time resident, $1,310 per credit hour part-time non-resident, $915 per credit hour online; other fees may apply per session. *Financial support:* In 2017–18, 8 students received support, including 2 fellowships with partial tuition reimbursements available (averaging $3,500 per year), 1 research assistantship with partial tuition reimbursement available (averaging $18,000 per year), 5 teaching assistantships with partial tuition reimbursements available (averaging $18,000 per year); career-related internships or fieldwork also available. Financial award application deadline: 4/1. *Faculty research:* STEAM education, inquiry-based instruction, cultural hegemony and mathematics, equity and ethics, teacher effectiveness. *Total annual research expenditures:* $1.6 million. *Unit head:* Dr. Jeff Marshall, Department Chair, 864-656-2059, E-mail: marsha9@clemson.edu. *Application contact:* Alison Search, Student Services Coordinator, 864-250-8880, E-mail: alisonp@clemson.edu.
Website: http://www.clemson.edu/education/departments/teaching-learning/index.html

Cleveland State University, College of Graduate Studies, College of Education and Human Services, Department of Teacher Education, Cleveland, OH 44115. Offers art education (M Ed); early childhood education (M Ed); foreign language education (M Ed); middle childhood mathematics and science education (M Ed); special education (M Ed), including mild/moderate disabilities, moderate/intensive disabilities; teaching English to speakers of other languages (M Ed). *Program availability:* Part-time, evening/weekend. *Faculty:* 19 full-time (14 women), 32 part-time/adjunct (27 women). *Students:* 80 full-time (60 women), 361 part-time (277 women); includes 119 minority (86 Black or African American, non-Hispanic/Latino; 5 Asian, non-Hispanic/Latino; 16 Hispanic/Latino; 12 Two or more races, non-Hispanic/Latino), 20 international. Average age 34. 177 applicants, 55% accepted, 68 enrolled. In 2017, 137 master's awarded. *Degree requirements:* For master's, comprehensive exam (for some programs), thesis or alternative. *Entrance requirements:* For master's, GRE General Test or MAT, minimum GPA of 2.75. Additional exam requirements/recommendations for international students: Required—TOEFL (minimum score 550 paper-based; 78 iBT), IELTS (minimum score 6). *Application deadline:* For fall admission, 7/1 priority date for domestic students, 5/15 for international students; for spring admission, 11/15 for domestic students, 11/1 for international students; for summer admission, 4/1 for domestic students, 3/15 for international students. Applications are processed on a rolling basis. Application fee: $30. *Financial support:* In 2017–18, 13 research assistantships with full tuition reimbursements (averaging $15,845 per year) were awarded; tuition waivers (partial) and unspecified assistantships also available. Financial award application deadline: 2/15; financial award applicants required to submit FAFSA. *Faculty research:* Early childhood education, literacy education, special education: mild/moderate, moderate/intensive, early childhood intervention specialist), teaching English to speakers of other languages (TESOL). *Total annual research expenditures:* $275,907. *Unit head:* Dr. Tachelle Banks, Department Chairperson, 216-687-4600, Fax: 216-687-5379, E-mail: t.i.banks@csuohio.edu. *Application contact:* Rosalyn Adams, Administrative Coordinator, 216-523-7139, Fax: 216-687-5491, E-mail: r.m.adams@csuohio.edu.
Website: http://www.csuohio.edu/cehs/te/te

The College at Brockport, State University of New York, School of Education, Health, and Human Services, Department of Education and Human Development, Program in Adolescence Education, Brockport, NY 14420-2997. Offers adolescence biology education (MS Ed); adolescence chemistry education (MS Ed); adolescence English (MS Ed); adolescence mathematics (MS Ed); adolescence physics (MS Ed); adolescence social studies education (MS Ed). *Accreditation:* NCATE. *Program availability:* Part-time. *Students:* 50 part-time (28 women); includes 1 minority (Black or African American, non-Hispanic/Latino). 24 applicants, 79% accepted, 11 enrolled. In 2017, 18 master's awarded. *Degree requirements:* For master's, thesis or alternative. *Entrance requirements:* For master's, edTPA, GRE or MAT, minimum GPA of 3.0, letters of recommendation, statement of objectives, current resume. Additional exam requirements/recommendations for international students: Required—TOEFL (minimum score 550 paper-based; 79 iBT), IELTS (minimum score 6.5). *Application deadline:* For fall admission, 3/15 priority date for domestic and international students; for spring admission, 10/15 priority date for domestic and international students; for summer admission, 3/15 priority date for domestic students, 3/13 priority date for international students. Application fee: $80. Electronic applications accepted. *Expenses:* Tuition, state resident: full-time $10,870; part-time $453 per credit hour. Tuition, nonresident: full-time $22,210. *Required fees:* $988; $246 per semester. *Financial support:* Federal Work-Study, scholarships/grants, and unspecified assistantships available. Support available to part-time students. Financial award application deadline: 3/15; financial award applicants required to submit FAFSA. *Unit head:* Dr. Sue Robb, Chairperson, 585-395-5935, Fax: 585-395-2172, E-mail: srobb@brockport.edu. *Application contact:* Anne Walton, Coordinator of Certification and Graduate Advisement, 585-395-2326, Fax: 585-395-2172, E-mail: awalton@brockport.edu.
Website: https://www.brockport.edu/academics/education_human_development/department.html

The College at Brockport, State University of New York, School of Education, Health, and Human Services, Department of Education and Human Development, Program in Inclusive Generalist Education, Brockport, NY 14420-2997. Offers biology (MS Ed, AGC); chemistry (MS Ed, AGC); English (MS Ed, Advanced Certificate); mathematics (MS Ed, Advanced Certificate); science (MS Ed, Advanced Certificate); social studies (MS Ed, Advanced Certificate). *Students:* 61 part-time (30 women); includes 2 minority (1 Black or African American, non-Hispanic/Latino; 1 Asian, non-Hispanic/Latino). 41 applicants, 78% accepted, 25 enrolled. In 2017, 12 master's, 3 AGCs awarded. *Degree requirements:* For master's, thesis or alternative. *Entrance requirements:* For master's, edTPA, GRE or MAT, minimum GPA of 3.0, letters of recommendation, statement of objectives, academic major (or equivalent) in program discipline, current resume. Additional exam requirements/recommendations for international students: Required—TOEFL (minimum score 550 paper-based; 79 iBT), IELTS (minimum score 6.5). *Application deadline:* For fall admission, 3/15 priority date for domestic and international students; for spring admission, 10/15 priority date for domestic and international students; for summer admission, 3/15 for domestic and international students. Application fee: $80. Electronic applications accepted. *Expenses:* Tuition, state resident: full-time $10,870; part-time $453 per credit hour. Tuition, nonresident: full-time $22,210. *Required fees:* $988; $246 per semester. *Financial support:* Federal Work-Study, scholarships/grants, and unspecified assistantships available. Support available to part-time students. Financial award application deadline: 3/15; financial award applicants required to submit FAFSA. *Unit head:* Dr. Sue Robb, Chairperson, 585-395-5935, Fax: 585-395-2171, E-mail: srobb@brockport.edu. *Application contact:* Anne Walton, Coordinator of Graduate Advisement, 585-395-2326, Fax: 585-395-2172, E-mail: awalton@brockport.edu.
Website: https://www.brockport.edu/academics/education_human_development/department.html

College of Charleston, Graduate School, School of Education, Health, and Human Performance, Program in Science and Mathematics for Teachers, Charleston, SC 29424-0001. Offers M Ed. *Accreditation:* NCATE. *Program availability:* Part-time, evening/weekend. *Degree requirements:* For master's, capstone project. *Entrance requirements:* For master's, GRE or PRAXIS, 2 letters of recommendation, copy of teaching certificate. Additional exam requirements/recommendations for international students: Required—TOEFL (minimum score 81 iBT). Electronic applications accepted.

College of Staten Island of the City University of New York, Graduate Programs, School of Education, Program in Adolescence Education, Staten Island, NY 10314-6600. Offers adolescence education (MS Ed), including biology, English, mathematics, social studies. *Program availability:* Part-time, evening/weekend. *Faculty:* 23 full-time, 6 part-time/adjunct. *Students:* 87. 45 applicants, 67% accepted, 23 enrolled. In 2017, 21 master's awarded. *Degree requirements:* For master's, educational research project supervised by faculty. *Entrance requirements:* For master's, GRE General Test or an approved equivalent examination, relevant bachelor's degree, minimum overall GPA of 3.0, two letters of recommendation, one- or two-page personal statement. Additional exam requirements/recommendations for international students: Required—TOEFL (minimum score 550 paper-based; 79 iBT), IELTS (minimum score 6.5). *Application deadline:* For fall admission, 4/25 for domestic and international students; for spring admission, 11/25 for domestic and international students. Applications are processed on a rolling basis. Application fee: $125. Electronic applications accepted. *Expenses:* Tuition, state resident: full-time $10,450; part-time $440 per credit. Tuition, nonresident: full-time $19,320; part-time $440 per credit. *Required fees:* $181.10 per semester. Tuition and fees vary according to program. *Faculty research:* Development and assessment of TPACK (technological pedagogical content knowledge), technology and differentiation in stem classrooms, teacher effectiveness and student achievement, teacher knowledge, knowledge transfer from college to classroom. *Unit head:* Diane Brescia, 718-982-3877, E-mail: diane.brescia@csi.cuny.edu. *Application contact:* Sasha Spence, Associate Director for Graduate Admissions, 718-982-2019, Fax: 718-982-2500, E-mail: sasha.spence@csi.cuny.edu.
Website: http://www.csi.cuny.edu/catalog/graduate/graduate-programs-in-education.htm#o2608

The College of William and Mary, School of Education, Program in Curriculum and Instruction, Williamsburg, VA 23187-8795. Offers elementary education (MA Ed); English as a second language/bilingual education (MA Ed); gifted education (MA Ed); literacy leadership (MA Ed); math specialist (MA Ed); secondary education (MA Ed), including English, foreign language, math, science, social studies; special education (MA Ed). *Accreditation:* NCATE. *Program availability:* Part-time. *Faculty:* 23 full-time (16 women), 40 part-time/adjunct (32 women). *Students:* 85 full-time (63 women), 16 part-time (15 women); includes 18 minority (5 Black or African American, non-Hispanic/Latino; 4 Asian, non-Hispanic/Latino; 7 Hispanic/Latino; 2 Two or more races, non-Hispanic/Latino), 1 international. Average age 27. 152 applicants, 83% accepted, 90 enrolled. In 2017, 67 master's awarded. *Degree requirements:* For master's, project. *Entrance requirements:* For master's, GRE, MAT, PRAXIS Core Academic Skills for Educators, minimum GPA of 2.5. Additional exam requirements/recommendations for international students: Required—TOEFL (minimum score 100 iBT), IELTS (minimum score 7). *Application deadline:* For fall admission, 1/15 for domestic and international students; for spring admission, 10/1 for domestic and international students. Application fee: $50. Electronic applications accepted. *Expenses:* $9,630 resident full-time, $535 resident part-time per credit hour; $25,920 nonresident full-time, $1,265 nonresident

part-time per credit hour; $5,944 full-time fees. *Financial support:* In 2017–18, 35 students received support, including 7 research assistantships (averaging $6,678 per year); scholarships/grants and unspecified assistantships also available. Financial award application deadline: 1/15; financial award applicants required to submit FAFSA. *Faculty research:* Educational technology, professional development and evaluation, inclusive education, rural education, education policy. *Unit head:* Dr. Jeremy D. Stoddard, Department Chair, 757-221-2348, E-mail: jdstod@wm.edu. *Application contact:* Dorothy Smith Osborne, Assistant Dean for Academic Programs and Student Services, 757-221-2317, E-mail: dsosbo@wm.edu.
Website: http://education.wm.edu

The Colorado College, Education Department, Program in Secondary Education, Colorado Springs, CO 80903-3294. Offers art teaching (K-12) (MAT); English teaching (MAT); foreign language teaching (MAT); mathematics teaching (MAT); music teaching (MAT); science teaching (MAT); social studies teaching (MAT). *Degree requirements:* For master's, thesis, internship. Electronic applications accepted.

Columbus State University, Graduate Studies, College of Education and Health Professions, Department of Teacher Education, Columbus, GA 31907-5645. Offers curriculum and instruction in accomplished teaching (M Ed); early childhood education (M Ed, MAT, Ed S); middle grades education (M Ed, MAT, Ed S); secondary education (M Ed, MAT, Ed S), including biology (MAT), chemistry (MAT), earth and space science (MAT), English/language arts, general science (M Ed), history (MAT), mathematics, science (Ed S), social science (M Ed, Ed S); special education (M Ed, MAT, Ed S), including general curriculum (M Ed, MAT); teacher leadership (M Ed). *Accreditation:* NCATE. *Program availability:* Part-time, evening/weekend, 100% online, blended/hybrid learning. *Faculty:* 19 full-time (12 women), 24 part-time/adjunct (18 women). *Students:* 99 full-time (76 women), 181 part-time (143 women); includes 109 minority (94 Black or African American, non-Hispanic/Latino; 1 American Indian or Alaska Native, non-Hispanic/Latino; 1 Asian, non-Hispanic/Latino; 6 Hispanic/Latino; 7 Two or more races, non-Hispanic/Latino). Average age 34. 136 applicants, 63% accepted, 56 enrolled. In 2017, 119 master's, 8 other advanced degrees awarded. *Degree requirements:* For Ed S, thesis or alternative. *Entrance requirements:* For master's, GRE General Test, minimum undergraduate GPA of 2.75; for Ed S, GRE General Test, minimum undergraduate GPA of 2.75, graduate 3.0. Additional exam requirements/recommendations for international students: Required—TOEFL (minimum score 550 paper-based; 79 iBT). *Application deadline:* For fall admission, 6/30 for domestic students, 5/1 for international students; for spring admission, 11/1 for domestic and international students; for summer admission, 3/1 for domestic and international students. Applications are processed on a rolling basis. Application fee: $50. Electronic applications accepted. *Expenses:* Tuition, state resident: full-time $3708; part-time $2472 per year. Tuition, nonresident: full-time $14,418; part-time $9612 per year. *International tuition:* $19,218 full-time. *Required fees:* $1605. Tuition and fees vary according to program. *Financial support:* In 2017–18, 45 students received support, including 9 research assistantships with partial tuition reimbursements available (averaging $3,000 per year); career-related internships or fieldwork, Federal Work-Study, institutionally sponsored loans, scholarships/grants, tuition waivers (partial), and unspecified assistantships also available. Support available to part-time students. Financial award application deadline: 5/1; financial award applicants required to submit FAFSA. *Unit head:* Dr. Jan Burcham, Department Chair, 706-507-8519, Fax: 706-568-3134, E-mail: burcham_jan@columbusstate.edu. *Application contact:* Catrina Smith-Edmond, Assistant Director for Graduate and Global Admission, 706-507-8824, Fax: 706-568-5091, E-mail: smithedmond_catrina@columbusstate.edu.
Website: http://te.columbusstate.edu/

Concordia University, College of Education, Portland, OR 97211-6099. Offers career and technical education (M Ed); curriculum and instruction (M Ed), including adolescent literacy, career and technical education, e-learning/technology education, early childhood education, English for speakers of other languages, English language development, environmental education, mathematics, methods and curriculum, reading, science, teacher leadership, the inclusive classroom; early childhood (MAT); education leadership (Ed D); educational administration (M Ed); elementary education (MAT); secondary education (MAT); special education (M Ed); teacher leadership (Ed D). *Program availability:* Part-time, online learning. *Degree requirements:* For master's, comprehensive exam, work samples/portfolio. *Entrance requirements:* For master's, California Basic Educational Skills Test or PRAXIS I, minimum undergraduate GPA of 2.8, graduate 3.0; 2 letters of recommendation. Additional exam requirements/recommendations for international students: Required—TOEFL (minimum score 525 paper-based). Electronic applications accepted. *Faculty research:* Learner-centered classroom, brain-based learning, future of online learning.

Concordia University, School of Graduate Studies, Faculty of Arts and Science, Department of Mathematics and Statistics, Montréal, QC H3G 1M8, Canada. Offers mathematics (PhD); mathematics and statistics (M Sc, MA); teaching of mathematics (MTM). *Degree requirements:* For master's, thesis optional; for doctorate, comprehensive exam, thesis/dissertation. *Entrance requirements:* For master's, honors degree in mathematics or equivalent. *Faculty research:* Number theory, computational algebra, mathematical physics, differential geometry, dynamical systems and statistics.

Converse College, Program in Middle Level Education, Spartanburg, SC 29302. Offers language arts/English (MAT); mathematics (MAT); middle level education (M Ed); science (MAT); social studies (MAT). *Unit head:* Lienne Medford, Dean of Graduate Studies and Distance Education, 864-596-9082, E-mail: lienne.medford@converse.edu. *Application contact:* 864-596-9404, E-mail: graduate@converse.edu.

Converse College, Program in Secondary Education, Spartanburg, SC 29302. Offers biology (MAT); chemistry (MAT); English (M Ed, MAT); mathematics (M Ed, MAT); natural sciences (M Ed); social sciences (M Ed, MAT). *Program availability:* Part-time. *Degree requirements:* For master's, capstone paper. *Entrance requirements:* For master's, NTE or PRAXIS II (M Ed), minimum GPA of 2.75, 2 recommendations. *Application deadline:* For fall admission, 8/1 for domestic and international students; for winter admission, 11/15 for domestic and international students; for spring admission, 1/15 for domestic and international students. Applications are processed on a rolling basis. Application fee: $40. Electronic applications accepted. *Financial support:* Available to part-time students. Applicants required to submit FAFSA. *Unit head:* Lienne Medford, Dean of Graduate Studies and Distance Education, 864-596-9082, E-mail: lienne.medford@converse.edu. *Application contact:* 864-596-9404, E-mail: graduate@converse.edu.

Cornell University, Graduate School, Graduate Fields of Agriculture and Life Sciences, Field of Education, Ithaca, NY 14853. Offers adult and extension education (MPS, MS, PhD); learning, teaching, and social policy (MPS, MS, PhD); mathematics 7-12 (MS). Terminal master's awarded for partial completion of doctoral program. *Degree requirements:* For master's, thesis (MS); for doctorate, comprehensive exam, thesis/dissertation. *Entrance requirements:* For master's and doctorate, GRE General Test, sample of written work (recommended), 2 letters of recommendation. Additional exam requirements/recommendations for international students: Required—TOEFL (minimum score 550 paper-based; 77 iBT). Electronic applications accepted. *Faculty research:* Moral development and professional ethics, public issues education and community development, socio/political issues in public education, teacher education and curriculum in agricultural science and mathematics, extension research.

Delaware State University, Graduate Programs, Department of Mathematics, Program in Mathematics Education, Dover, DE 19901-2277. Offers MS. *Entrance requirements:* Additional exam requirements/recommendations for international students: Required—TOEFL (minimum score 550 paper-based). Electronic applications accepted.

DePaul University, College of Science and Health, Chicago, IL 60604. Offers applied mathematics (MS); applied statistics (MS); biological sciences (MA, MS); chemistry (MS); environmental science (MS); mathematics education (MA); mathematics for teaching (MS); nursing (MS); nursing practice (DNP); physics (MS); polymer and coatings science (MS); psychology (MS); pure mathematics (MS); science education (MS); MA/PhD. *Accreditation:* AACN. *Application deadline:* Applications are processed on a rolling basis. Application fee: $40. Electronic applications accepted. *Financial support:* Applicants required to submit FAFSA. *Unit head:* Dr. Gerald P. Koocher, Dean, 773-325-8300. *Application contact:* Ann Spittle, Director of Graduate Admission, 773-325-7315, Fax: 312-476-3244, E-mail: graddepaul@depaul.edu. Website: http://csh.depaul.edu/

Drake University, School of Education, Des Moines, IA 50311-4516. Offers applied behavior analysis (MS); counseling (MS); education (PhD); education administration (Ed D); educational leadership (MSE, Ed D); effective teaching (MSE); leadership development (MS); literacy (Ed S); literacy education (MSE); rehabilitation administration (MS); rehabilitation placement (MS); special education (MSE); STEM education (MSE); teacher education (5-12) (MAT); teacher education (K-8) (MST); teacher effectiveness and professional development (MSE). *Program availability:* Part-time, evening/weekend. *Degree requirements:* For master's and Ed S, comprehensive exam, internships (for some programs); for doctorate, comprehensive exam, thesis/dissertation, internships (for some programs). *Entrance requirements:* For master's, GRE General Test, MAT, or Drake Writing Assessment, resume, 2 letters of recommendation; for doctorate, GRE General Test or MAT, master's degree, 3 letters of recommendation; for Ed S, GRE General Test or MAT. Additional exam requirements/recommendations for international students: Required—TOEFL (minimum score 550 paper-based). *Application deadline:* For fall admission, 7/1 priority date for domestic students, 6/1 priority date for international students; for spring admission, 11/1 priority date for domestic students, 10/1 priority date for international students. Applications are processed on a rolling basis. Application fee: $25. Electronic applications accepted. *Expenses:* Contact institution. *Financial support:* Research assistantships, career-related internships or fieldwork, and unspecified assistantships available. Support available to part-time students. *Faculty research:* Counseling and rehabilitation, behavioral supports, inquiry-based science methods, teacher quality enhancement. *Unit head:* Dr. Janet McMahill, Dean, 515-271-3829, E-mail: janet.mcmahill@drake.edu. Website: http://www.drake.edu/soe/

Duquesne University, School of Education, Department of Instruction and Leadership, Program in Secondary Education, Pittsburgh, PA 15282-0001. Offers biology (MS Ed); chemistry (MS Ed); English (MS Ed); K-12 education (MS Ed), including Latin; mathematics (MS Ed); physics (MS Ed); social studies (MS Ed). *Program availability:* Part-time, evening/weekend. *Faculty:* 5 full-time (4 women). *Students:* 22 full-time (10 women); includes 3 minority (2 Black or African American, non-Hispanic/Latino; 1 Two or more races, non-Hispanic/Latino). Average age 26. 8 applicants, 100% accepted, 5 enrolled. In 2017, 9 master's awarded. *Entrance requirements:* For master's, two letters of recommendation, letter of intent, interview, bachelor's degree. Additional exam requirements/recommendations for international students: Required—TOEFL (minimum score 550 paper-based), IELTS (minimum score 7). *Application deadline:* For fall admission, 9/1 for domestic students; for spring admission, 1/2 for domestic students. Applications are processed on a rolling basis. Application fee: $0. Electronic applications accepted. *Expenses:* $1,259 per credit. *Financial support:* Research assistantships and Federal Work-Study available. Support available to part-time students. *Faculty research:* Factors that create highly effective teachers; how to best support teachers to support students in reform-oriented environments; urban education; models of teacher leadership; improving instruction in mathematics/science/social studies/English. *Unit head:* Dr. Melissa Boston, Associate Dean for Teacher Education/Professor, 412-396.6109, Fax: 412-396-5585, E-mail: bostonm@duq.edu. *Application contact:* Kelly McGinley, Graduate Admissions Assistant, 412-396-1559, Fax: 412-396-5585, E-mail: mcginleyk@duq.edu.
Website: http://www.duq.edu/academics/schools/education/graduate-programs-education/ms-ed-secondary-education

East Carolina University, Graduate School, College of Education, Department of Mathematics, Science, and Instructional Technology Education, Greenville, NC 27858-4353. Offers distance learning and administration (Certificate); elementary mathematics education (Certificate); instructional technology (MA Ed, MS); mathematics education (MA Ed); science education (MA Ed, MAT); special endorsement in computer education (Certificate). *Program availability:* Part-time, evening/weekend. *Students:* 12 full-time (10 women), 202 part-time (153 women); includes 49 minority (31 Black or African American, non-Hispanic/Latino; 2 American Indian or Alaska Native, non-Hispanic/Latino; 2 Asian, non-Hispanic/Latino; 9 Hispanic/Latino; 5 Two or more races, non-Hispanic/Latino). Average age 38. 56 applicants, 100% accepted, 50 enrolled. In 2017, 76 master's, 30 other advanced degrees awarded. *Degree requirements:* For master's, comprehensive exam, thesis optional. *Entrance requirements:* For master's, GRE General Test or MAT, interview, minimum GPA of 2.5, bachelor's degree in related field, teaching license (MA Ed). Additional exam requirements/recommendations for international students: Required—TOEFL. *Application deadline:* For fall admission, 6/1 priority date for domestic students. Applications are processed on a rolling basis. Application fee: $75. *Expenses:* Tuition, state resident: full-time $4749; part-time $297 per credit hour. Tuition, nonresident: full-time $17,898; part-time $1119 per credit hour. *Required fees:* $2691; $224 per credit hour. Part-time tuition and fees vary according to course load and program. *Financial support:* Research assistantships, teaching assistantships, and Federal Work-Study available. Support available to part-time students. Financial award application deadline: 6/1. *Unit head:* Susan Ganter, Chair, 252-737-3001, E-mail: ganters@ecu.edu.
Website: http://www.ecu.edu/cs-educ/msite/

Eastern Illinois University, Graduate School, College of Liberal Arts and Sciences, Department of Mathematics and Computer Science, Charleston, IL 61920. Offers elementary/middle school mathematics education (MA); mathematics (MA); secondary mathematics education (MA). *Program availability:* Part-time, evening/weekend. *Degree requirements:* For master's, comprehensive exam (for some programs), thesis (for some programs). *Entrance requirements:* For master's, GMAT or GRE. Additional exam requirements/recommendations for international students: Required—TOEFL (minimum score 500 paper-based; 61 iBT), IELTS (minimum score 6). *Application deadline:* For fall admission, 5/15 for domestic and international students; for spring admission, 10/15 for domestic and international students. Applications are processed on a rolling basis. Application fee: $30. Electronic applications accepted. *Financial support:* Teaching assistantships with full tuition reimbursements, career-related internships or fieldwork, Federal Work-Study, and unspecified assistantships available. Support available to part-time students. Financial award application deadline: 3/1; financial award applicants required to submit FAFSA. *Unit head:* Marshall B. Lassak, Chair, 217-581-6450, Fax: 217-581-6284, E-mail: mblassak@eiu.edu. *Application contact:* Peter S. Wiles,

Graduate Coordinator, 217-581-6275, Fax: 217-581-6284, E-mail: pswiles@eiu.edu. Website: http://www.eiu.edu/mathgrad/

Eastern Kentucky University, The Graduate School, College of Education, Department of Curriculum and Instruction, Program in Secondary and Higher Education, Richmond, KY 40475-3102. Offers secondary education (MA Ed), including agricultural education, art education, biological sciences education, business education, English education, geography education, history education, home economics education, industrial education, mathematical sciences education, physical education, school health education. *Accreditation:* NCATE. *Program availability:* Part-time. *Entrance requirements:* For master's, GRE General Test, minimum GPA of 2.5.

Eastern University, Graduate Education Programs, St. Davids, PA 19087-3696. Offers ESL program specialist (K-12) (Certificate); general supervisor (PreK-12) (Certificate); health and physical education (K-12) (Certificate); middle level (4-8) (Certificate); multicultural education (M Ed) (Certificate); music (K-12) (Certificate); Pre K-4 (Certificate); Pre K-4 with special education (Certificate); reading (M Ed); reading specialist (K-12) (Certificate); reading supervisor (K-12) (Certificate); school counseling (MA, CAGS); school principalship (preK-12) (Certificate); school psychology (MS, CAGS); secondary biology education (7-12) (Certificate); secondary chemistry education (7-12) (Certificate); secondary communication education (7-12) (Certificate); secondary English education (7-12) (Certificate); secondary math education (7-12) (Certificate); secondary social studies education (7-12) (Certificate); special education (M Ed); special education (7-12) (Certificate); special education (Pre K-8) (Certificate); special education supervisor (K-12) (Certificate); TESOL (M Ed); world language (K-12) (Certificate), including Spanish. *Program availability:* Part-time, evening/weekend, online learning. *Students:* 46 full-time (40 women), 115 part-time (93 women); includes 65 minority (42 Black or African American, non-Hispanic/Latino; 3 Asian, non-Hispanic/Latino; 14 Hispanic/Latino; 6 Two or more races, non-Hispanic/Latino), 1 international. Average age 32. In 2017, 72 master's awarded. *Entrance requirements:* Additional exam requirements/recommendations for international students: Required—TOEFL. *Application deadline:* Applications are processed on a rolling basis. Application fee: $35. Electronic applications accepted. Application fee is waived when completed online. *Expenses:* Contact institution. *Unit head:* Michael Dziedziak, Executive Director of Enrollment, 800-452-0996, E-mail: gpsadmissions@eastern.edu.
Website: https://www.eastern.edu/academics/programs/education-department-graduate-programs/graduate-programs

Elizabeth City State University, Department of Mathematics and Computer Science, Master of Science in Mathematics Program, Elizabeth City, NC 27909-7806. Offers applied mathematics (MS); community college teaching (MS); mathematics education (MS); remote sensing (MS). *Program availability:* Part-time, evening/weekend. *Faculty:* 7 full-time (2 women). *Students:* 25 part-time (13 women); includes 19 minority (all Black or African American, non-Hispanic/Latino). Average age 25. 5 applicants, 80% accepted, 4 enrolled. In 2017, 18 master's awarded. *Degree requirements:* For master's, thesis. *Entrance requirements:* For master's, MAT and/or GRE, minimum GPA of 3.0, 3 letters of recommendation, two official transcripts from all undergraduate/graduate schools attended, typewritten one-page request for entry into program that includes description of student's educational preparation. Additional exam requirements/recommendations for international students: Required—TOEFL (minimum score 550 paper-based, 80 iBT) or IELTS (minimum score 6.5). *Application deadline:* For fall admission, 7/15 priority date for domestic and international students; for spring admission, 11/15 priority date for domestic and international students; for summer admission, 3/15 priority date for domestic and international students. Applications are processed on a rolling basis. Application fee: $30. Electronic applications accepted. Tuition and fees vary according to course load and program. *Financial support:* In 2017–18, 22 students received support, including 3 research assistantships (averaging $19,000 per year), 2 teaching assistantships (averaging $18,000 per year); scholarships/grants and tuition waivers also available. Financial award application deadline: 6/30; financial award applicants required to submit FAFSA. *Faculty research:* Oceanic temperature effects, mathematics strategies in elementary schools, multimedia, Antarctic temperature mapping, computer networks, water quality, remote sensing, polar ice, satellite imagery. *Total annual research expenditures:* $25,000. *Unit head:* Dr. Kenneth L. Jones, Chair, 252-335-3858, E-mail: kljones@ecsu.edu. *Application contact:* Dr. Sharon D. Raynor, Director, Graduate Education Program, 252-335-3945, E-mail: sdraynor@ecsu.edu.
Website: http://www.ecsu.edu/academics/mathsciencetechnology/

Fitchburg State University, Division of Graduate and Continuing Education, Program in Middle School Education, Fitchburg, MA 01420-2697. Offers English (M Ed); general science (M Ed); history (M Ed); math (M Ed). *Accreditation:* NCATE. *Program availability:* Part-time, evening/weekend. *Students:* 15 full-time (7 women), 5 part-time (2 women); includes 3 minority (2 Black or African American, non-Hispanic/Latino; 1 Two or more races, non-Hispanic/Latino). Average age 32. 11 applicants, 100% accepted, 10 enrolled. In 2017, 4 master's awarded. *Entrance requirements:* Additional exam requirements/recommendations for international students: Required—TOEFL (minimum score 550 paper-based; 79 iBT). *Application deadline:* For fall admission, 7/15 for international students; for spring admission, 12/1 for international students. Applications are processed on a rolling basis. Application fee: $50. Electronic applications accepted. *Expenses:* Contact institution. *Financial support:* In 2017–18, research assistantships with partial tuition reimbursements (averaging $5,500 per year) were awarded; Federal Work-Study, scholarships/grants, and unspecified assistantships also available. Support available to part-time students. Financial award application deadline: 3/1; financial award applicants required to submit FAFSA. *Unit head:* William Cortezia, Chair, 978-665-3193, Fax: 978-665-3658, E-mail: gce@fitchburgstate.edu. *Application contact:* Jinawa McNeil, Director of Admissions, 978-665-3140, Fax: 978-665-4540, E-mail: admissions@fitchburgstate.edu.
Website: http://www.fitchburgstate.edu

Florida Agricultural and Mechanical University, Division of Graduate Studies, Research, and Continuing Education, College of Education, Program in Secondary Education and Foundation, Tallahassee, FL 32307-3200. Offers biology (M Ed); chemistry (MS Ed); English (MS Ed); history (MS Ed); math (MS Ed); physics (MS Ed). *Accreditation:* NCATE. *Degree requirements:* For master's, thesis (for some programs). *Entrance requirements:* For master's, GRE General Test, minimum GPA of 3.0. Additional exam requirements/recommendations for international students: Required—TOEFL.

Florida Atlantic University, College of Education, Department of Teaching and Learning, Boca Raton, FL 33431-0991. Offers curriculum and instruction (M Ed), including art, biology, chemistry, English, French, German, mathematics, music, physics, Pre-K and primary education, reading, social sciences, Spanish; elementary education (M Ed); environmental education (M Ed); reading education (M Ed); social foundations of education (M Ed), including educational psychology, educational technology, multilingual education. *Accreditation:* NCATE. *Program availability:* Part-time, evening/weekend. *Faculty:* 13 full-time (10 women), 1 part-time/adjunct (0 women). *Students:* 26 full-time (22 women), 43 part-time (39 women); includes 19 minority (9 Black or African American, non-Hispanic/Latino; 1 Asian, non-Hispanic/Latino; 8 Hispanic/Latino; 1 Two or more races, non-Hispanic/Latino), 3 international.

Mathematics Education

Average age 30. 91 applicants, 57% accepted, 33 enrolled. In 2017, 25 master's awarded. *Entrance requirements:* For master's, GRE General Test, minimum GPA of 3.0 in last 2 years of undergraduate course work. Additional exam requirements/recommendations for international students: Required—TOEFL (minimum score 500 paper-based; 61 iBT), IELTS (minimum score 6). *Application deadline:* For fall admission, 7/1 for domestic students, 2/15 for international students; for spring admission, 11/1 for domestic students, 7/15 for international students. Applications are processed on a rolling basis. Application fee: $30. *Expenses:* Tuition, state resident: full-time $7400; part-time $369.82 per credit. Tuition, nonresident: full-time $20,496; part-time $1042.81 per credit. *Financial support:* Fellowships with partial tuition reimbursements, research assistantships with partial tuition reimbursements, teaching assistantships with partial tuition reimbursements, career-related internships or fieldwork, scholarships/grants, and unspecified assistantships available. *Faculty research:* Technology, teaching English to speakers of other languages, math teaching, electronic portfolio assessment, global perspectives through social studies. *Unit head:* Dr. Barbara Ridener, Chairperson, 561-297-3588, E-mail: bridener@fau.edu. *Application contact:* Dr. Eliah Watlington, Associate Dean, 561-296-8520, Fax: 261-297-2991, E-mail: ewatling@fau.edu.
Website: http://www.coe.fau.edu/academicdepartments/tl/

Florida Gulf Coast University, College of Education, Program in Curriculum and Instruction, Fort Myers, FL 33965-6565. Offers elementary education (M Ed); English education (M Ed); English speakers of other languages endorsement (M Ed); gifted education (M Ed); mathematics education (M Ed); middle school education (M Ed); reading education (M Ed); science education (M Ed); social science education (M Ed); special education (M Ed). *Program availability:* Part-time, evening/weekend, online learning. *Faculty:* 27 full-time (19 women), 44 part-time/adjunct (30 women). *Students:* 3 full-time (all women), 16 part-time (14 women); includes 4 minority (2 Black or African American, non-Hispanic/Latino; 2 Hispanic/Latino). Average age 30. 6 applicants, 100% accepted, 5 enrolled. In 2017, 4 master's awarded. *Degree requirements:* For master's, final project or portfolio. *Entrance requirements:* For master's, GRE General Test, MAT, minimum undergraduate GPA of 3.0 in last 2 years. Additional exam requirements/recommendations for international students: Required—TOEFL (minimum score 550 paper-based). *Application deadline:* For fall admission, 2/15 priority date for domestic students, 5/1 for international students; for spring admission, 12/1 for domestic students, 9/15 for international students. Applications are processed on a rolling basis. Application fee: $30. Electronic applications accepted. *Expenses:* Tuition, state resident: part-time $290 per credit hour. Tuition, nonresident: part-time $1173 per credit hour. *Required fees:* $127 per credit hour. Tuition and fees vary according to course load. *Financial support:* In 2017–18, 2 students received support. Application deadline: 6/30; applicants required to submit FAFSA. *Faculty research:* Internet in schools, technology in pre-service and in-service teacher training. *Unit head:* Dr. Vickie Johnston, Instructor, 239-590-7754, Fax: 239-590-7801, E-mail: vjohnston@fgcu.edu. *Application contact:* Keiana Desmore, Adviser/Counselor, 239-590-7759, Fax: 239-590-7801, E-mail: kdesmore@fgcu.edu.
Website: http://coe.fgcu.edu/c-imed/

Florida Institute of Technology, College of Science, Program in Mathematics Education, Melbourne, FL 32901-6975. Offers MS, PhD, Ed S. *Students:* Average age 33. 15 applicants, 60% accepted, 2 enrolled. In 2017, 1 doctorate, 1 other advanced degree awarded. *Degree requirements:* For master's, comprehensive exam (for some programs), thesis optional, minimum of 30 credit hours; for doctorate, comprehensive exam, thesis/dissertation, minimum of 42 credit hours; for Ed S, comprehensive exam, minimum of 30 credit hours, minimum GPA of 3.0. *Entrance requirements:* For master's, resume, statement of objectives, bachelor's degree in either mathematics or middle/secondary school mathematics education; for doctorate, master's degree in mathematics or mathematics education with minimum GPA of 3.2, 3 letters of recommendation, resume, statement of objectives; for Ed S, master's degree in mathematics or mathematics education, 3 letters of recommendation, resume, statement of objectives. Additional exam requirements/recommendations for international students: Required—TOEFL (minimum score 550 paper-based; 79 iBT). *Application deadline:* Applications are processed on a rolling basis. Electronic applications accepted. *Expenses:* Tuition: Part-time $1241 per credit hour. Part-time tuition and fees vary according to campus/location. *Unit head:* Dr. Kastro Hamed, Department Head, 321-674-7206, E-mail: khmed@fit.edu. *Application contact:* Cheryl A. Brown, Associate Director of Graduate Admissions, 321-674-7581, Fax: 321-723-9468, E-mail: cbrown@fit.edu.
Website: http://www.fit.edu/programs/8127/ms-mathematics-education/career#.VT_qdU10ypo

Florida International University, College of Arts, Sciences, and Education, Department of Teaching and Learning, Miami, FL 33199. Offers art education (MA, MS); curriculum and instruction (MS, Ed D, PhD, Ed S), including curriculum development (MS), elementary education (MS), English education (MS), learning technologies (MS), mathematics education (MS), modern language education (MS), physical education (MS), science education (MS), social studies education (MS), special education (MS); early childhood education (MS); exceptional student education (Ed D); foreign language education (MS), including foreign language education, teaching English to speakers of other languages (TESOL); language, literacy and culture (PhD); mathematics, science, and learning technologies (PhD); physical education (MS), including sport and fitness; reading education (MS). *Program availability:* Part-time, evening/weekend. *Faculty:* 60 full-time (41 women), 112 part-time/adjunct (77 women). *Students:* 165 full-time (139 women), 191 part-time (148 women); includes 270 minority (56 Black or African American, non-Hispanic/Latino; 12 Asian, non-Hispanic/Latino; 191 Hispanic/Latino; 11 Two or more races, non-Hispanic/Latino), 13 international. Average age 34. 238 applicants, 68% accepted, 107 enrolled. In 2017, 184 master's, 15 doctorates awarded. *Degree requirements:* For doctorate, comprehensive exam, thesis/dissertation. *Entrance requirements:* For master's, GRE General Test, Florida General Knowledge Test or Florida College Level Academic Skills Test; for doctorate and Ed S, GRE General Test. Additional exam requirements/recommendations for international students: Required—TOEFL (minimum score 550 paper-based; 80 iBT), IELTS (minimum score 6.3). *Application deadline:* For fall admission, 6/1 priority date for domestic students, 4/1 for international students; for winter admission, 10/1 priority date for domestic students, 9/1 for international students; for spring admission, 3/1 priority date for domestic students, 2/1 for international students. Applications are processed on a rolling basis. Application fee: $30. Electronic applications accepted. *Expenses:* Tuition, state resident: full-time $8912; part-time $446 per credit hour. Tuition, nonresident: full-time $21,393; part-time $992 per credit hour. *Required fees:* $390; $195 per semester. *Financial support:* Research assistantships with tuition reimbursements and teaching assistantships with tuition reimbursements available. *Unit head:* Dr. Lynn Miller, Chair, 305-348-2005, Fax: 305-348-2086, E-mail: lynne.miller@fiu.edu. *Application contact:* Nanett Rojas, Assistant Director, Graduate Admissions, 305-348-7464, Fax: 305-348-7441, E-mail: gradadm@fiu.edu.
Website: https://tl.fiu.edu/

Florida State University, The Graduate School, College of Education, School of Teacher Education, Tallahassee, FL 32306-4450. Offers curriculum and instruction (MS, PhD, Ed S), including early childhood education, elementary education, English education, foreign and second language education, mathematics education, reading and

language arts, science education, social science education, special education, visual disabilities education (MS); teaching English to speakers of other languages (Certificate). *Program availability:* Part-time, evening/weekend, 100% online, blended/hybrid learning, asynchronous, minimal on-campus study. *Faculty:* 41 full-time (33 women), 21 part-time/adjunct (18 women). *Students:* 133 full-time (93 women), 84 part-time (69 women); includes 48 minority (20 Black or African American, non-Hispanic/Latino; 2 Asian, non-Hispanic/Latino; 19 Hispanic/Latino; 7 Two or more races, non-Hispanic/Latino), 52 international. Average age 31. 146 applicants, 56% accepted, 52 enrolled. In 2017, 91 master's, 7 doctorates, 1 other advanced degree awarded. Terminal master's awarded for partial completion of doctoral program. *Degree requirements:* For master's and other advanced degree, comprehensive exam, thesis optional; for doctorate, comprehensive exam, thesis/dissertation, diagnostic exam, preliminary exam, prospectus defense, dissertation defense. *Entrance requirements:* For master's, doctorate, and other advanced degree, GRE General Test, minimum upper-division GPA of 3.0. Additional exam requirements/recommendations for international students: Required—TOEFL (minimum score 550 paper-based; 80 iBT), Michigan English Language Assessment Battery (minimum score 77), IELTS (minimum score 6.5) or PTE (minimum score 55). Application fee: $30. Electronic applications accepted. *Financial support:* Fellowships, research assistantships, teaching assistantships, scholarships/grants, tuition waivers (full and partial), and unspecified assistantships available. Financial award application deadline: 1/15; financial award applicants required to submit FAFSA. *Faculty research:* Identifying effective intervention strategies to improve reading skills; improving literacy teaching and learning through technology; understanding of student sense making, problem solving, the history and structure of STEM disciplines, and teacher education to support the development of ambitious instruction that supports the STEM learning of all students; examining practices of international education; identifying ways to support the professional development of teachers. *Unit head:* Dr. Sherry Southerland, Professor/Department Chair, 850-644-6885, Fax: 850-644-2725, E-mail: ssoutherland@admin.fsu.edu. *Application contact:* Britni DeZerga, Academic Program Specialist, 850-644-2122, Fax: 850-644-7736, E-mail: bpurvis@fsu.edu.
Website: http://education.fsu.edu

Framingham State University, Graduate Studies, Program in Mathematics, Framingham, MA 01701-9101. Offers M Ed. *Entrance requirements:* For master's, GRE General Test, minimum GPA of 3.0. *Unit head:* Dr. Julie Levandosky, Program Coordinator, E-mail: jlevandosky@framingham.edu. *Application contact:* 508-626-4550, Fax: 508-626-4030, E-mail: dgce@frc.mass.edu.

Fresno Pacific University, Graduate Programs, School of Education, Program in STEM Education, Fresno, CA 93702-4709. Offers MA Ed. *Program availability:* Part-time, evening/weekend. *Degree requirements:* For master's, thesis or alternative. *Entrance requirements:* Additional exam requirements/recommendations for international students: Required—TOEFL (minimum score 550 paper-based). *Expenses:* Contact institution.

George Mason University, College of Education and Human Development, Programs in Curriculum and Instruction, Fairfax, VA 22030. Offers advanced international baccalaureate (M Ed); assistive technology (M Ed); designing digital learning in schools (M Ed); early childhood education (M Ed); early childhood education for diverse learners (M Ed); elementary education (M Ed); English as a second language (M Ed); gifted child education (M Ed); history (M Ed); literacy (M Ed), including PK-12 classroom teachers, reading specialist; literacy leadership for diverse schools (M Ed), including K-12 reading; physical education (M Ed); science K-12 (M Ed); secondary education (M Ed), including biology, chemistry, earth science, English, history/social science, math, physics; special education (M Ed); teacher leadership (M Ed); teaching culturally, linguistically diverse and exceptional learners (M Ed); transformative teaching (M Ed). *Program availability:* Part-time, evening/weekend, 100% online, blended/hybrid learning. *Faculty:* 41 full-time (36 women), 45 part-time/adjunct (37 women). *Students:* 173 full-time (151 women), 729 part-time (611 women); includes 271 minority (65 Black or African American, non-Hispanic/Latino; 5 American Indian or Alaska Native, non-Hispanic/Latino; 88 Asian, non-Hispanic/Latino; 94 Hispanic/Latino; 1 Native Hawaiian or other Pacific Islander, non-Hispanic/Latino; 18 Two or more races, non-Hispanic/Latino), 28 international. Average age 32. 426 applicants, 91% accepted, 289 enrolled. In 2017, 349 master's awarded. *Degree requirements:* For master's, thesis. *Entrance requirements:* For master's, PRAXIS Core (for some programs), 2 letters of recommendation, interview, program goals statement; 9 hours of complete licensure endorsement requirements (for elementary education); minimum GPA of 3.0 in applicant's last 60 hours of undergraduate coursework (for secondary education); at least 1 year of teaching experience (for literacy). Additional exam requirements/recommendations for international students: Required—TOEFL (minimum score 575 paper-based; 88 iBT), IELTS (minimum score 6.5), PTE (minimum score 59). *Application deadline:* For fall admission, 4/2 priority date for domestic and international students; for spring admission, 11/1 for domestic and international students. Application fee: $75 ($80 for international students). Electronic applications accepted. *Expenses:* Tuition, state resident: full-time $11,228; part-time $459.50 per credit. Tuition, nonresident: full-time $30,932; part-time $1280.50 per credit. *Required fees:* $3252; $135.50 per credit. Part-time tuition and fees vary according to course load and program. *Financial support:* In 2017–18, 2 students received support, including 2 teaching assistantships; career-related internships or fieldwork, Federal Work-Study, scholarships/grants, unspecified assistantships, and health care benefits (for full-time research or teaching assistantship recipients) also available. Support available to part-time students. Financial award application deadline: 3/1; financial award applicants required to submit FAFSA. *Faculty research:* Teacher preparation and professional development; adaptive teaching; wonder in science teacher preparation; literacy (digital, adolescent); site based course instruction. *Unit head:* Rebecca Fox, Professor and Academic Program Coordinator, 703-993-4123, E-mail: rfox@gmu.edu.
Website: http://gse.gmu.edu/programs/gsemasters

The George Washington University, Graduate School of Education and Human Development, Department of Curriculum and Pedagogy, Program in Secondary Education, Washington, DC 20052. Offers Arabic (M Ed); Italian (M Ed); math (M Ed); physics (M Ed); Russian (M Ed). Programs also offered in Arlington and Ashburn, VA. *Accreditation:* NCATE. *Students:* 10 full-time (7 women), 26 part-time (16 women); includes 10 minority (5 Black or African American, non-Hispanic/Latino; 2 American Indian or Alaska Native, non-Hispanic/Latino; 1 Asian, non-Hispanic/Latino; 2 Two or more races, non-Hispanic/Latino), 1 international. Average age 31. 66 applicants, 62% accepted, 22 enrolled. In 2017, 17 master's awarded. *Entrance requirements:* For master's, GRE General Test or MAT, interview, minimum GPA of 2.75. *Application deadline:* For fall admission, 1/15 priority date for domestic students; for spring admission, 10/1 for domestic students. Applications are processed on a rolling basis. Application fee: $75. *Expenses:* Tuition: Full-time $28,800; part-time $1655 per credit hour. *Required fees:* $45; $2.75 per credit hour. *Financial support:* Fellowships, career-related internships or fieldwork, Federal Work-Study, tuition waivers (full and partial), and stipends available. Financial award application deadline: 1/15; financial award applicants required to submit FAFSA. *Unit head:* Prof. Curtis Pyke, Chair, 202-994-4516, E-mail: cpyke@gwu.edu. *Application contact:* Sarah Lang, Director of Graduate Admissions, 202-994-1447, Fax: 202-994-7207, E-mail: slang@gwu.edu.

Georgia Southwestern State University, School of Education, Americus, GA 31709-4693. Offers early childhood education (M Ed, Ed S); middle grades education (Ed S); middle grades language arts (M Ed); middle grades mathematics (M Ed); special education (M Ed). *Accreditation:* NCATE. *Faculty:* 17 full-time (7 women), 7 part-time/adjunct (all women). *Students:* 221 full-time (206 women), 5 part-time (all women); includes 70 minority (all Black or African American, non-Hispanic/Latino). Average age 35. In 2017, 89 master's, 94 Ed Ss awarded. *Degree requirements:* For master's, minimum cumulative GPA of 3.0; maximum of 6 credit hours with C grade; no courses with D grade; degree completed within 7 calendar years; for Ed S, minimum GPA of 3.25 in all courses with no grade less than a B; degree must be completed within 7 calendar years from date of initial enrollment in graduate work. *Entrance requirements:* For master's, undergraduate degree from accredited institution; professional Georgia Teaching Certificate or eligibility; minimum undergraduate GPA of 2.75 as reported on official final transcripts from all accredited institutions attended; 2 confidential Administrative Recommendation Forms; for Ed S, master's degree from accredited college or university; professional Georgia Teaching Certificate or eligibility; minimum graduate GPA of 3.0 as reported on official final graduate transcripts from all accredited institutions attended; 2 confidential Administrative Recommendation Forms. *Application deadline:* For summer admission, 4/15 for domestic students. Application fee: $25. Electronic applications accepted. *Expenses:* $257 per credit hour for online courses plus fees which vary according to number of enrolled credit hours. *Financial support:* Application deadline: 6/1; applicants required to submit FAFSA. *Unit head:* Dr. Rachel Abbott, Dean, 229-931-2145. *Application contact:* Whitney Ford, Admissions Specialist, Office of Graduate Admissions, 800-338-0082, Fax: 229-931-2983.
Website: https://gsw.edu/Academics/Schools-and-Departments/School-of-Education/index

Georgia State University, College of Education and Human Development, Department of Early Childhood Education, Atlanta, GA 30302-3083. Offers early childhood and elementary education (PhD); early childhood education (M Ed, Ed S); mathematics education (M Ed); urban education (M Ed). *Accreditation:* NCATE. *Program availability:* Part-time, evening/weekend. *Faculty:* 27 full-time (22 women). *Students:* 74 full-time (68 women), 22 part-time (21 women); includes 49 minority (41 Black or African American, non-Hispanic/Latino; 4 Asian, non-Hispanic/Latino; 2 Hispanic/Latino; 2 Two or more races, non-Hispanic/Latino), 3 international. Average age 30. 49 applicants, 65% accepted, 25 enrolled. In 2017, 27 master's, 3 doctorates awarded. *Entrance requirements:* For master's, GRE, undergraduate diploma; for doctorate and Ed S, GRE, master's degree. *Application deadline:* Applications are processed on a rolling basis. Application fee: $50. Electronic applications accepted. *Expenses:* Tuition, state resident: full-time $7020. Tuition, nonresident: full-time $22,518. *Required fees:* $2128. Tuition and fees vary according to degree level and program. *Financial support:* In 2017–18, fellowships with full tuition reimbursements (averaging $24,000 per year), research assistantships with full tuition reimbursements (averaging $4,000 per year), teaching assistantships with full tuition reimbursements (averaging $2,000 per year) were awarded; career-related internships or fieldwork, Federal Work-Study, institutionally sponsored loans, scholarships/grants, traineeships, health care benefits, tuition waivers (partial), and unspecified assistantships also available. Support available to part-time students. Financial award applicants required to submit FAFSA. *Faculty research:* Teacher development; language arts/literacy education; mathematics education; intersection of science, urban, and multicultural education; diversity in education. *Unit head:* Dr. Barbara Meyers, Department Chair, 404-413-8021, Fax: 404-413-8023, E-mail: barbara@gsu.edu. *Application contact:* Elaine King Jones, Administrative Curriculum Specialist, 404-413-8234, Fax: 404-413-8023, E-mail: ekjones@gsu.edu.
Website: http://ecee.education.gsu.edu/

Georgia State University, College of Education and Human Development, Department of Middle and Secondary Education, Atlanta, GA 30302-3083. Offers curriculum and instruction (Ed D); English education (MAT); mathematics education (M Ed, MAT); middle level education (MAT); reading, language and literacy education (M Ed, MAT), including reading instruction (M Ed); science education (M Ed, MAT), including biology (MAT), broad field science (MAT), chemistry (MAT), earth science (MAT), physics (MAT); social studies education (M Ed, MAT), including economics (MAT), geography (MAT), history (MAT), political science (MAT); teaching and learning (PhD), including language and literacy, mathematics education, music education, science education, social studies education, teaching and teacher education. *Accreditation:* NCATE. *Program availability:* Part-time, evening/weekend, online learning. *Faculty:* 24 full-time (18 women). *Students:* 179 full-time (110 women), 192 part-time (133 women); includes 193 minority (130 Black or African American, non-Hispanic/Latino; 1 American Indian or Alaska Native, non-Hispanic/Latino; 23 Asian, non-Hispanic/Latino; 25 Hispanic/Latino; 14 Two or more races, non-Hispanic/Latino), 6 international. Average age 33. 175 applicants, 58% accepted, 83 enrolled. In 2017, 81 master's, 17 doctorates awarded. *Entrance requirements:* For master's, GRE; GACE I (for initial teacher preparation programs), baccalaureate degree or equivalent, resume, goals statement, two letters of recommendation, minimum undergraduate GPA of 2.5; proof of initial teacher certification in the content area (for M Ed); for doctorate, GRE, resume, goals statement, writing sample, two letters of recommendation, minimum graduate GPA of 3.3, interview. *Application deadline:* For fall admission, 1/15 priority date for domestic and international students; for spring admission, 10/1 for domestic and international students. Application fee: $50. Electronic applications accepted. *Expenses:* Tuition, state resident: full-time $7020. Tuition, nonresident: full-time $22,518. *Required fees:* $2128. Tuition and fees vary according to degree level and program. *Financial support:* In 2017–18, fellowships with full tuition reimbursements (averaging $19,667 per year), research assistantships with full tuition reimbursements (averaging $5,436 per year), teaching assistantships with full tuition reimbursements (averaging $2,779 per year) were awarded; career-related internships or fieldwork, Federal Work-Study, scholarships/grants, health care benefits, tuition waivers (full and partial), and unspecified assistantships also available. Financial award application deadline: 3/15. *Faculty research:* Teacher education in language and literacy, mathematics, science, and social studies in urban middle and secondary school settings; learning technologies in school, community, and corporate settings; multicultural education and education for social justice; urban education; international education. *Unit head:* Dr. Dana L. Fox, Chair, 404-413-8060, Fax: 404-413-8063, E-mail: dfox@gsu.edu. *Application contact:* Bobbie Turner, Administrative Coordinator, 404-413-8405, Fax: 404-413-8063, E-mail: bnturner@gsu.edu.
Website: http://mse.education.gsu.edu/

Gordon College, Graduate Education Program, Wenham, MA 01984-1899. Offers early childhood (M Ed); educational leadership (M Ed, Ed S); elementary education (M Ed); English as a second language (M Ed, Ed S); math specialist (M Ed); mathematics specialist (Ed S); middle school education (M Ed); moderate disabilities (M Ed); Montessori education (M Ed); reading (M Ed, Ed S); secondary education (M Ed). *Program availability:* Part-time, evening/weekend. *Faculty:* 23 full-time (17 women), 32 part-time/adjunct (23 women). *Students:* 68 full-time (50 women), 114 part-time (99 women); includes 24 minority (2 Black or African American, non-Hispanic/Latino; 8 Asian, non-Hispanic/Latino; 13 Hispanic/Latino; 1 Two or more races, non-Hispanic/Latino), 10 international. Average age 34. 248 applicants, 100% accepted, 182 enrolled. In 2017, 99 master's, 16 Ed Ss awarded. *Degree requirements:* For master's, action

research or clinical experience (for most programs); for Ed S, action research or clinical experience (for some programs). *Entrance requirements:* For master's, minimum undergraduate GPA of 3.0; 2 official undergraduate transcripts; professional resume; 3 recommendation letters (one professional reference, one academic reference, one personal reference); 500-700 word statement of purpose; for Ed S, minimum master's GPA of 3.3; 2 official transcripts from undergraduate and graduate schools; professional resume; 3 recommendation letters (one professional reference, one academic reference, one personal reference); 500-700 word statement of purpose. Additional exam requirements/recommendations for international students: Required—TOEFL (minimum score 550 paper-based, 80 iBT) or IELTS (minimum score 6.5). *Application deadline:* Applications are processed on a rolling basis. Application fee: $75. *Expenses:* $325 per credit tuition; $75 per semester administrative fee. *Financial support:* Applicants required to submit FAFSA. *Faculty research:* Reading, early childhood development, English language learners, universal design for learning. *Unit head:* Dr. Janet Arndt, Director of Graduate Studies, 978-867-4355, Fax: 978-867-4663. *Application contact:* Julie Lenocker, Program Administrator, 978-867-4322, Fax: 978-867-4663, E-mail: graduate-education@gordon.edu.
Website: http://www.gordon.edu/graduate

Grambling State University, School of Graduate Studies and Research, College of Education, Department of Educational Leadership, Grambling, LA 71245. Offers developmental education (MS, Ed D, PMC), including curriculum and instructional design (Ed D), English (MS), guidance and counseling (MS), higher education administration and management (Ed D), mathematics (MBA), reading (MS), science (MS), student development and personnel services (Ed D); educational leadership (M Ed). *Program availability:* Part-time, evening/weekend. *Degree requirements:* For master's, comprehensive exam, thesis (for some programs); for doctorate, comprehensive exam, thesis/dissertation. *Entrance requirements:* For master's, GRE, minimum GPA of 2.5 on last degree; for doctorate, GRE (minimum score 1000, 500 on Verbal), master's degree, minimum GPA of 3.0 on last degree. Additional exam requirements/recommendations for international students: Required—TOEFL (minimum score 500 paper-based; 62 iBT). Electronic applications accepted.

Hampton University, School of Liberal Arts and Education, Program in Teaching, Hampton, VA 23668. Offers biology education 6-12 (MT); English education 6-12 (MT); mathematics education 6-12 (MT); music education PreK-12 (MT). *Program availability:* Part-time. *Students:* 5 full-time (4 women); all minorities (all Black or African American, non-Hispanic/Latino). Average age 23. 6 applicants, 67% accepted, 1 enrolled. In 2017, 7 master's awarded. *Entrance requirements:* For master's, GRE General Test. Additional exam requirements/recommendations for international students: Required—TOEFL (minimum score 525 paper-based) or IELTS (6.5). *Application deadline:* For fall admission, 6/1 priority date for domestic students, 4/1 for international students; for spring admission, 11/1 priority date for domestic students, 9/1 for international students; for summer admission, 4/1 priority date for domestic students, 2/1 priority date for international students. Applications are processed on a rolling basis. Application fee: $35. Electronic applications accepted. *Expenses:* Tuition: Full-time $22,630; part-time $575 per semester hour. *Required fees:* $70. Tuition and fees vary according to program. *Financial support:* Application deadline: 6/30; applicants required to submit FAFSA. *Unit head:* Dr. Martha Jallim-Hall, Program Coordinator, 757-727-5793.

Harding University, Cannon-Clary College of Education, Searcy, AR 72149-0001. Offers advanced studies in teaching and learning (M Ed); art (MSE); behavioral science (MSE); counseling (MS, Ed S); early childhood special education (M Ed, MSE); education (MSE); educational leadership (M Ed, Ed S); elementary education (M Ed); English (MSE); French (MSE); history/social science (MSE); kinesiology (MSE); math (MSE); reading (M Ed); secondary education (M Ed); Spanish (MSE); teaching (MAT); teaching English as a second language (MSE). *Accreditation:* NCATE. *Program availability:* Part-time, evening/weekend. *Faculty:* 22 full-time (9 women), 51 part-time/adjunct (37 women). *Students:* 135 full-time (95 women), 316 part-time (231 women); includes 77 minority (46 Black or African American, non-Hispanic/Latino; 7 American Indian or Alaska Native, non-Hispanic/Latino; 4 Asian, non-Hispanic/Latino; 9 Hispanic/Latino; 11 Two or more races, non-Hispanic/Latino), 11 international. Average age 34. 128 applicants, 87% accepted, 111 enrolled. In 2017, 153 master's, 24 other advanced degrees awarded. *Degree requirements:* For master's, comprehensive exam (for some programs), thesis optional, portfolio(s); for Ed S, comprehensive exam, portfolio, project. *Entrance requirements:* For master's, GRE, MAT, PRAXIS; for Ed S, MAT or GRE. Additional exam requirements/recommendations for international students: Required—TOEFL (minimum score 550 paper-based; 79 iBT). *Application deadline:* For fall admission, 8/1 for domestic and international students; for spring admission, 1/1 for domestic and international students. Applications are processed on a rolling basis. Application fee: $35. Tuition and fees vary according to course load, degree level, campus/location and program. *Financial support:* In 2017–18, 33 students received support. Unspecified assistantships available. *Faculty research:* Reading, comprehension, school violence, educational technology, behavior, college choice, differentiated instruction, brain-based teaching. *Unit head:* Dr. Clara Carroll, Chair, 501-279-4501, Fax: 501-279-4083, E-mail: ccarroll@harding.edu. *Application contact:* Information Contact, 501-279-4315, E-mail: gradstudiesedu@harding.edu.
Website: http://www.harding.edu/education

Harvard University, Extension School, Cambridge, MA 02138-3722. Offers applied sciences (CAS); biotechnology (ALM); educational technologies (ALM); educational technology (CET); English for graduate and professional studies (DGP); environmental management (ALM, CEM); information technology (ALM); journalism (ALM); liberal arts (ALM); management (ALM, CM); mathematics for teaching (ALM); museum studies (ALM); premedical studies (Diploma); publication and communication (CPC). *Program availability:* Part-time, evening/weekend. *Degree requirements:* For master's, thesis. *Entrance requirements:* For master's, 3 completed graduate courses with grade of B or higher. Additional exam requirements/recommendations for international students: Required—TOEFL (minimum score 600 paper-based), TWE (minimum score 5). *Expenses:* Contact institution.

High Point University, Norcross Graduate School, High Point, NC 27268. Offers athletic training (MSAT); business administration (MBA); educational leadership (M Ed, Ed D); elementary education (M Ed, MAT); pharmacy (Pharm D); physical therapy (DPT); physician assistant studies (MPAS); secondary mathematics (M Ed, MAT); special education (M Ed); strategic communication (MA). *Accreditation:* NCATE. *Program availability:* Part-time, evening/weekend. *Degree requirements:* For master's, comprehensive exam (for some programs), thesis (for some programs). *Entrance requirements:* For master's, GMAT (MBA), GRE, MAT, minimum GPA of 3.0. Additional exam requirements/recommendations for international students: Required—TOEFL (minimum score 550 paper-based). Electronic applications accepted.

Hofstra University, School of Education, Programs in Teacher Education, Hempstead, NY 11549. Offers bilingual education (MA); bilingual extension (Advanced Certificate), including education/speech language pathology, intensive teacher institute; business education (MS Ed); curriculum studies (MS Ed); early childhood and childhood education (MS Ed); early childhood education (MA, MS Ed); educational technology (Advanced Certificate); elementary education (MA, MS Ed), including science, technology, engineering, and mathematics (STEM) (MA); English education (MS Ed);

Mathematics Education

family and consumer science (MS Ed); fine arts and music education (Advanced Certificate); fine arts education (MS Ed); foreign language and TESOL (MS Ed); foreign language education (MA, MS Ed), including Arabic (MS Ed), biology, chemistry, Chinese (MS Ed), earth science, French, German, Italian (MS Ed), Mandarin (MS Ed), physics, Russian, Spanish; foundations of education (Advanced Certificate), including grades 5-6, grades 7-9; languages other than English and teaching English as a second language (MA); learning and teaching (Ed D), including applied linguistics, art education, arts and humanities, early childhood education, English education, human development, math education, math, science, and technology, multicultural education, physical education, science education, social studies education, special education; mathematics education (MA, MS Ed); music education (MA, MS Ed); science education (MA), including biology (MA, MS Ed), chemistry (MA, MS Ed), earth science (MA, MS Ed), physics (MA, MS Ed); secondary education (Advanced Certificate); social studies education (MA, MS Ed); teaching languages other than English and TESOL (MS Ed); technology for learning (MA); TESOL (MS Ed, Advanced Certificate); TESOL with specialization in STEM (MA); work based learning extension (Advanced Certificate). *Program availability:* Part-time, evening/weekend, blended/hybrid learning. *Students:* 119 full-time (83 women), 124 part-time (90 women); includes 54 minority (15 Black or African American, non-Hispanic/Latino; 9 Asian, non-Hispanic/Latino; 29 Hispanic/Latino; 1 Native Hawaiian or other Pacific Islander, non-Hispanic/Latino), 12 international. Average age 29. 205 applicants, 88% accepted, 93 enrolled. In 2017, 103 master's, 4 doctorates, 32 other advanced degrees awarded. *Degree requirements:* For master's, comprehensive exam, thesis (for some programs), exit project, student teaching, fieldwork, electronic portfolio, curriculum project, minimum GPA of 3.0; for doctorate, thesis/dissertation; for Advanced Certificate, 3 foreign languages, comprehensive exam (for some programs), thesis project. *Entrance requirements:* For master's, GRE, 2 letters of recommendation, portfolio, teacher certification (MA), interview, essay; for doctorate, GMAT, GRE, LSAT, or MAT; for Advanced Certificate, 2 letters of recommendation, essay, interview and/or portfolio, teaching certificate. Additional exam requirements/recommendations for international students: Required—TOEFL (minimum score 550 paper-based; 80 iBT). *Application deadline:* Applications are processed on a rolling basis. Application fee: $75. Electronic applications accepted. *Expenses: Tuition:* Full-time $1292. *Required fees:* $970. Tuition and fees vary according to program. *Financial support:* In 2017–18, 112 students received support, including 56 fellowships with full and partial tuition reimbursements available (averaging $4,998 per year), 2 research assistantships with full and partial tuition reimbursements available (averaging $8,753 per year); career-related internships or fieldwork, Federal Work-Study, institutionally sponsored loans, scholarships/grants, traineeships, tuition waivers (full and partial), and unspecified assistantships also available. Support available to part-time students. Financial award applicants required to submit FAFSA. *Faculty research:* Educational interventions that foster critical-thinking skills; teachers' attitudes about professional development; threats to teacher quality. *Unit head:* Dr. Eustace Thompson, Chairperson, 516-463-5749, Fax: 516-463-6275, E-mail: eustace.g.thompson@hofstra.edu. *Application contact:* Sunil Samuel, Assistant Vice President of Admissions, 516-463-4723, Fax: 516-463-4664, E-mail: graduateadmission@hofstra.edu.
Website: http://www.hofstra.edu/education/

Hood College, Graduate School, Department of Education, Frederick, MD 21701-8575. Offers curriculum and instruction (MS), including elementary education, elementary science and mathematics education, secondary education, special education; education, multidisciplinary studies (MS); educational leadership (MS, Certificate); reading specialization (MS); STEM education (Certificate). *Accreditation:* NCATE. *Program availability:* Part-time-only, evening/weekend. *Faculty:* 6 full-time (4 women), 35 part-time/adjunct (27 women). *Students:* 3 full-time (all women), 329 part-time (265 women); includes 62 minority (35 Black or African American, non-Hispanic/Latino; 4 Asian, non-Hispanic/Latino; 14 Hispanic/Latino; 9 Two or more races, non-Hispanic/Latino), 3 international. Average age 33. 76 applicants, 100% accepted, 63 enrolled. In 2017, 53 master's, 58 other advanced degrees awarded. *Degree requirements:* For master's, action research project, portfolio (for reading specialization); for Certificate, STEM capstone activity. *Entrance requirements:* For master's, minimum GPA of 2.75, teaching certification, writing sample during interview, letter of recommendation from principal (for educational leadership program only). Additional exam requirements/recommendations for international students: Required—TOEFL (minimum score 575 paper-based; 89 iBT), IELTS (minimum score 6.5). *Application deadline:* For fall admission, 8/15 priority date for domestic students, 8/5 for international students; for spring admission, 12/1 priority date for domestic students, 12/1 for international students; for summer admission, 5/1 priority date for domestic students, 4/15 for international students. Applications are processed on a rolling basis. Application fee: $35. Electronic applications accepted. *Expenses:* $465 per credit plus $110 comprehensive fee per semester. *Financial support:* Tuition waivers (partial) and unspecified assistantships available. Financial award applicants required to submit FAFSA. *Faculty research:* Leadership, action research, brain research, learning styles. *Unit head:* Dr. April M. Boulton, Dean of the Graduate School, 301-696-3612, E-mail: gofurther@hood.edu. *Application contact:* Jan Marcus, Assistant Director of Graduate Admissions, 301-696-3600, E-mail: gofurther@hood.edu.
Website: http://www.hood.edu/academics/education/index.html

Hood College, Graduate School, Program in Secondary Mathematics Education, Frederick, MD 21701-8575. Offers high school (MS); middle school (MS); secondary mathematics education (Certificate). *Program availability:* Part-time, evening/weekend. *Faculty:* 2 full-time (1 woman), 3 part-time/adjunct (2 women). *Students:* 29 part-time (20 women); includes 2 minority (1 Black or African American, non-Hispanic/Latino; 1 Hispanic/Latino). Average age 32. 6 applicants, 100% accepted, 6 enrolled. In 2017, 8 master's awarded. *Degree requirements:* For master's, exitfolio, capstone/research project. *Entrance requirements:* For master's, minimum GPA of 2.75, initial teacher certification, essay. Additional exam requirements/recommendations for international students: Required—TOEFL (minimum score 575 paper-based; 89 iBT), IELTS (minimum score 6.5). *Application deadline:* For fall admission, 8/15 priority date for domestic students, 8/15 for international students; for spring admission, 12/1 priority date for domestic students, 12/1 for international students; for summer admission, 5/1 priority date for domestic students, 4/15 for international students. Applications are processed on a rolling basis. Application fee: $35. Electronic applications accepted. *Expenses:* $465 per credit hour plus $110 comprehensive fee per semseter. *Financial support:* Tuition waivers (partial) and unspecified assistantships available. Financial award applicants required to submit FAFSA. *Unit head:* Dr. April M. Boulton, Dean of the Graduate School, 301-696-3600, E-mail: gofurther@hood.edu. *Application contact:* Jan Marcus, Assistant Director of Graduate Admissions, 301-696-3600, E-mail: gofurther@hood.edu.
Website: http://www.hood.edu/graduate

Hunter College of the City University of New York, Graduate School, School of Arts and Sciences, Department of Mathematics and Statistics, New York, NY 10065-5085. Offers adolescent mathematics education (MA); applied mathematics (MA); bioinformatics (MA); pure mathematics (MA); statistics (MA). *Program availability:* Part-time, evening/weekend. *Degree requirements:* For master's, one foreign language, comprehensive exam, thesis (for some programs). *Entrance requirements:* For master's, GRE General Test, 24 credits in mathematics. Additional exam requirements/

recommendations for international students: Required—TOEFL. *Faculty research:* Data analysis, dynamical systems, computer graphics, topology, statistical decision theory.

Hunter College of the City University of New York, Graduate School, School of Education, Programs in Secondary Education, Concentration in Mathematics Education, New York, NY 10065-5085. Offers MA. *Accreditation:* NCATE. *Degree requirements:* For master's, thesis, professional teaching portfolio, New York State Teacher Certification Exam, research project. *Entrance requirements:* For master's, minimum GPA of 2.8 overall, 2.7 in mathematics courses; 24 credits of course work in mathematics. Additional exam requirements/recommendations for international students: Required—TOEFL, TWE.

Idaho State University, Office of Graduate Studies, College of Science and Engineering, Department of Mathematics and Statistics, Pocatello, ID 83209-8085. Offers mathematics (MS, DA); mathematics for secondary teachers (MA). *Program availability:* Part-time. *Degree requirements:* For master's, comprehensive exam, thesis (for some programs), oral and written exams; for doctorate, comprehensive exam, thesis/dissertation, teaching internships. *Entrance requirements:* For master's, GRE General Test, GRE Subject Test, course work in modern algebra, differential equations, advanced calculus, introductory analysis; for doctorate, GRE General Test, GRE Subject Test, minimum graduate GPA of 3.5, MS in mathematics, teaching experience, 3 letters of recommendation. Additional exam requirements/recommendations for international students: Required—TOEFL (minimum score 550 paper-based; 80 iBT). Electronic applications accepted. *Faculty research:* Algebra, analysis geometry, statistics, applied mathematics.

Illinois Institute of Technology, Graduate College, College of Science, Department of Mathematics and Science Education, Chicago, IL 60616. Offers mathematics education (MAS, PhD); science education (MAS, PhD). *Degree requirements:* For master's, comprehensive exam (for some programs), thesis optional; for doctorate, comprehensive exam, thesis/dissertation. *Entrance requirements:* For master's, GRE General Test (minimum score 900 quantitative and verbal; 2.5 analytical writing), minimum undergraduate GPA of 3.0; two-page professional statement of goals/objectives; curriculum vita; three letters of recommendation; for doctorate, GRE General Test (minimum score 1000 quantitative and verbal; 3.0 analytical writing), minimum GPA of 3.0, 3 years of teaching experience. Additional exam requirements/recommendations for international students: Required—TOEFL (minimum score 600 paper-based; 80 iBT). Electronic applications accepted. *Faculty research:* Informal science/math education, curriculum development, integration of science/math disciplines and across disciplines, instructional methods, students' and teachers' conceptions of scientific/mathematical inquiry and the nature of science/math, instructional models, evaluation, and research design.

Illinois State University, Graduate School, College of Arts and Sciences, Department of Mathematics, Program in Mathematics Education, Normal, IL 61790. Offers MA, PhD. *Degree requirements:* For doctorate, variable foreign language requirement, comprehensive exam, thesis/dissertation, 2 terms of residency. *Entrance requirements:* For doctorate, GRE General Test.

Indiana University Bloomington, School of Education, Department of Curriculum and Instruction, Bloomington, IN 47405-7000. Offers art education (MS, Ed D, PhD); curriculum studies (Ed D, PhD); elementary education (MS, Ed D, PhD, Ed S); mathematics education (MS, Ed D, PhD); science education (MS, Ed D, PhD); secondary education (MS, Ed D, PhD); social studies education (MS, PhD); special education (PhD, Ed S). *Accreditation:* NCATE. *Program availability:* Part-time, evening/weekend. Terminal master's awarded for partial completion of doctoral program. *Degree requirements:* For doctorate, thesis/dissertation; for Ed S, comprehensive exam or project. *Entrance requirements:* For master's, doctorate, and Ed S, GRE General Test. Electronic applications accepted.

Indiana University Bloomington, University Graduate School, College of Arts and Sciences, Department of Mathematics, Bloomington, IN 47405. Offers applied mathematics (MA); mathematical physics (PhD); mathematics education (MAT); pure mathematics (MA, PhD). Terminal master's awarded for partial completion of doctoral program. *Degree requirements:* For doctorate, one foreign language, thesis/dissertation. *Entrance requirements:* For master's and doctorate, GRE General Test, GRE Subject Test. Additional exam requirements/recommendations for international students: Required—TOEFL. Electronic applications accepted. *Expenses:* Contact institution. *Faculty research:* Topology, geometry, algebra, applied mathematics, analysis.

Indiana University of Pennsylvania, School of Graduate Studies and Research, College of Natural Sciences and Mathematics, Department of Mathematics, Program in Elementary and Middle School Mathematics Education, Indiana, PA 15705. Offers M Ed. *Accreditation:* NCATE. *Program availability:* Part-time. *Faculty:* 10 full-time (3 women). *Students:* 8 part-time (6 women). Average age 26. 7 applicants, 57% accepted, 4 enrolled. In 2017, 2 master's awarded. *Entrance requirements:* For master's, 2 letters of recommendation. Additional exam requirements/recommendations for international students: Required—TOEFL (minimum score 540 paper-based). *Application deadline:* Applications are processed on a rolling basis. Application fee: $50. Electronic applications accepted. *Expenses:* Tuition, state resident: full-time $12,000; part-time $500 per credit. Tuition, nonresident: full-time $18,000; part-time $750 per credit. *Required fees:* $4073; $165.55 per credit. $64 per term. *Financial support:* Research assistantships, career-related internships or fieldwork, and Federal Work-Study available. Support available to part-time students. Financial award application deadline: 4/15; financial award applicants required to submit FAFSA. *Unit head:* Dr. Mary Lou Metz, Graduate Coordinator, 724-357-4759, E-mail: mlmetz@iup.edu.
Website: http://www.iup.edu/grad/mathed/default.aspx

Indiana University of Pennsylvania, School of Graduate Studies and Research, College of Natural Sciences and Mathematics, Department of Mathematics, Program in Secondary Mathematics Education, Indiana, PA 15705. Offers M Ed. *Accreditation:* NCATE. *Program availability:* Part-time. *Faculty:* 10 full-time (3 women). *Students:* 18 part-time (10 women); includes 2 minority (both Black or African American, non-Hispanic/Latino). Average age 31. 4 applicants, 100% accepted, 4 enrolled. In 2017, 3 master's awarded. *Entrance requirements:* For master's, 2 letters of recommendation. Additional exam requirements/recommendations for international students: Required—TOEFL (minimum score 540 paper-based). *Application deadline:* Applications are processed on a rolling basis. Application fee: $50. Electronic applications accepted. *Expenses:* Tuition, state resident: full-time $12,000; part-time $500 per credit. Tuition, nonresident: full-time $18,000; part-time $750 per credit. *Required fees:* $4073; $165.55 per credit. $64 per term. *Financial support:* Fellowships, research assistantships, career-related internships or fieldwork, Federal Work-Study, scholarships/grants, and unspecified assistantships available. Support available to part-time students. Financial award application deadline: 4/15; financial award applicants required to submit FAFSA. *Unit head:* Dr. Margaret Stempien, Graduate Coordinator, 724-357-3791, E-mail: margaret.stempien@iup.edu. *Application contact:* Dr. Yu-Ju Kuo, Graduate Coordinator, 724-357-3797, E-mail: yjkuo@iup.edu.
Website: http://www.iup.edu/math/grad/mathematics-education-med/

Indiana University–Purdue University Fort Wayne, College of Arts and Sciences, Department of Mathematical Sciences, Fort Wayne, IN 46805-1499. Offers applied

1352 www.petersons.com

mathematics (MS); applied statistics (Certificate); mathematics (MS); operations research (MS); teaching (MAT). *Program availability:* Part-time, evening/weekend. *Entrance requirements:* For master's, minimum GPA of 3.0, major or minor in mathematics, three letters of recommendation. Additional exam requirements/ recommendations for international students: Required—TOEFL (minimum score 550 paper-based; 79 iBT); Recommended—TWE. Electronic applications accepted. *Faculty research:* Eves' Theorem, paired-placements for student teaching, holomorphic maps.

Indiana University–Purdue University Indianapolis, School of Science, Department of Mathematical Sciences, Indianapolis, IN 46202-3216. Offers mathematics (MS, PhD), including applied mathematics, applied statistics (MS), mathematical statistics (PhD), mathematics, mathematics education (MS). *Program availability:* Part-time, evening/ weekend. *Degree requirements:* For master's, thesis optional; for doctorate, one foreign language, comprehensive exam, thesis/dissertation. *Entrance requirements:* For doctorate, GRE General Test (recommended). Additional exam requirements/ recommendations for international students: Required—TOEFL (minimum score 79 iBT), IELTS (minimum score 6.5), GRE General Test. Electronic applications accepted. *Faculty research:* Mathematical physics, integral systems, partial differential equations, noncommutative geometry, biomathematics, computational neurosciences.

Instituto Tecnológico y de Estudios Superiores de Monterrey, Campus Ciudad Obregón, Programs in Education, Program in Mathematics, Ciudad Obregón, Mexico. Offers ME.

Inter American University of Puerto Rico, Arecibo Campus, Programs in Education, Arecibo, PR 00614-4050. Offers administration and educational supervision (MA Ed); counseling and guidance (MA Ed); curriculum and teaching (MA Ed), including biology education, English as a second language, history education, math education, Spanish; elementary education (MA Ed). *Accreditation:* TEAC. *Degree requirements:* For master's, comprehensive exam, thesis optional. *Entrance requirements:* For master's, GRE, EXADEP, bachelor's degree in education or teaching license (administration and supervision) or courses in education and psychology (counseling and guidance), minimum GPA of 2.5 in last 60 credits.

Inter American University of Puerto Rico, Metropolitan Campus, Graduate Programs, Program in Teaching of Math, San Juan, PR 00919-1293. Offers MA.

Inter American University of Puerto Rico, Ponce Campus, Graduate School, Mercedita, PR 00715-1602. Offers accounting (MBA); biology (M Ed); chemistry (M Ed); criminal justice (MA); elementary education (M Ed); English as a Second Language (M Ed); finance (MBA); history (M Ed); human resources (MBA); marketing (MBA); mathematics (M Ed); Spanish (M Ed). *Entrance requirements:* For master's, minimum GPA of 2.5.

Inter American University of Puerto Rico, San Germán Campus, Graduate Studies Center, Program in Mathematics Education, San Germán, PR 00683-5008. Offers applied mathematics (MA). *Program availability:* Part-time, evening/weekend. *Degree requirements:* For master's, comprehensive exam. *Entrance requirements:* For master's, EXADEP or GRE General Test, minimum GPA of 3.0.

Iona College, School of Arts and Science, Department of Education, New Rochelle, NY 10801-1890. Offers adolescence education: biology (MS Ed, MST); adolescence education: English (MS Ed); adolescence education: mathematics (MST); adolescence education: social studies (MS Ed, MST); adolescence education: Spanish (MS Ed); adolescence special education 5-12 (MST); childhood and special education (MST); early childhood and childhood (MST); educational leadership (MS Ed). *Accreditation:* NCATE. *Program availability:* Part-time, evening/weekend. *Faculty:* 7 full-time (5 women), 2 part-time/adjunct (1 woman). *Students:* 23 full-time (18 women), 26 part-time (19 women); includes 12 minority (4 Black or African American, non-Hispanic/Latino; 8 Hispanic/Latino). Average age 26. 33 applicants, 97% accepted, 20 enrolled. In 2017, 31 master's awarded. *Degree requirements:* For master's, thesis or alternative. *Entrance requirements:* For master's, minimum GPA of 3.0, NY State teaching certificate and bachelor's degree (for MS Ed). Additional exam requirements/ recommendations for international students: Required—TOEFL (minimum score 550 paper-based; 80 iBT), IELTS (minimum score 6.5). *Application deadline:* For fall admission, 8/1 priority date for domestic students, 5/1 priority date for international students; for spring admission, 1/1 priority date for domestic students, 9/1 priority date for international students. Applications are processed on a rolling basis. Electronic applications accepted. Tuition and fees vary according to program. *Financial support:* In 2017–18, 16 students received support. Unspecified assistantships available. Support available to part-time students. Financial award application deadline: 4/15; financial award applicants required to submit FAFSA. *Faculty research:* Engaging teacher educators in scientific process, cross-national comparisons of mathematics teaching, questioning strategies in the classroom, research methods, literacy development. *Unit head:* Margaret Smith, PhD, Chair, 914-633-2210, Fax: 914-633-2608, E-mail: msmith@ iona.edu. *Application contact:* Richard McMahon, Coordinator, Graduate School of Education, 914-633-2552, E-mail: rmcmahon@iona.edu.
Website: http://www.iona.edu/Academics/School-of-Arts-Science/Departments/ Education/Graduate-Programs.aspx

Iowa State University of Science and Technology, Department of Mathematics, Ames, IA 50011. Offers applied mathematics (MS, PhD); mathematics (MS, PhD); school mathematics (MSM). *Degree requirements:* For master's, thesis or alternative; for doctorate, thesis/dissertation. *Entrance requirements:* For master's and doctorate, GRE General Test. Additional exam requirements/recommendations for international students: Required—TOEFL (minimum score 550 paper-based; 79 iBT), IELTS (minimum score 6.5). Electronic applications accepted.

Iowa State University of Science and Technology, Program in School Mathematics, Ames, IA 50011. Offers MSM. *Entrance requirements:* For master's, official academic transcripts, resume, three letters of recommendation, statement of purpose. Additional exam requirements/recommendations for international students: Required—TOEFL (minimum score 550 paper-based; 79 iBT), IELTS (minimum score 6.5). Electronic applications accepted.

Jackson State University, Graduate School, College of Science, Engineering and Technology, Department of Mathematics and Statistical Sciences, Jackson, MS 39217. Offers applied mathematics (MS); mathematics education (MST); pure mathematics (MS). *Program availability:* Part-time, evening/weekend. *Degree requirements:* For master's, comprehensive exam, thesis (for some programs). *Entrance requirements:* For master's, GRE General Test. Additional exam requirements/recommendations for international students: Required—TOEFL (minimum score 520 paper-based; 67 iBT).

James Madison University, The Graduate School, College of Education, Program in Education, Harrisonburg, VA 22807. Offers early childhood education (preK-3) (MAT); educational leadership (M Ed); educational technology (M Ed); elementary education (MAT); equity and cultural diversity (M Ed); inclusive early childhood education (MAT); K-8 mathematics specialist (M Ed); middle education (MAT); reading education (M Ed); secondary education (MAT); Spanish language and culture for educators (M Ed); TESOL (MAT). *Accreditation:* NCATE. *Program availability:* Part-time, evening/ weekend. *Students:* 260 full-time (233 women), 158 part-time (100 women); includes 48 minority (10 Black or African American, non-Hispanic/Latino; 4 Asian, non-Hispanic/

Latino; 26 Hispanic/Latino; 1 Native Hawaiian or other Pacific Islander, non-Hispanic/ Latino; 7 Two or more races, non-Hispanic/Latino), 2 international. Average age 30. In 2017, 262 master's awarded. Application fee: $55. Electronic applications accepted. *Expenses:* Tuition, state resident: full-time $10,512; part-time $438 per credit hour. Tuition, nonresident: full-time $28,358; part-time $1162 per credit hour. *Required fees:* $1128. *Financial support:* In 2017–18, 23 students received support, including 1 teaching assistantship; career-related internships or fieldwork, Federal Work-Study, and 22 assistantships (averaging $7911) also available. Financial award application deadline: 3/1; financial award applicants required to submit FAFSA. *Unit head:* Dr. Phillip M. Wishon, Dean, 540-568-6572, E-mail: wishonpm@jmu.edu. *Application contact:* Lynette D. Michael, Director of Graduate Admissions, 540-568-6131 Ext. 6395, Fax: 540-568-7860, E-mail: michaeld@jmu.edu.
Website: http://www.jmu.edu/coe/index.shtml

James Madison University, The Graduate School, College of Education, Program in Mathematics Education, Harrisonburg, VA 22801. Offers K-8 math specialist (M Ed); mathematics (M Ed). *Students:* Average age 27. Application fee: $55. Electronic applications accepted. *Expenses:* Tuition, state resident: full-time $10,512; part-time $438 per credit hour. Tuition, nonresident: full-time $28,358; part-time $1162 per credit hour. *Required fees:* $1128. *Financial support:* In 2017–18, 17 students received support. Fellowships and 11 assistantships (averaging $4450) available. Financial award application deadline: 3/1; financial award applicants required to submit FAFSA. *Unit head:* Dr. Steven L. Purcell, Department Head, 540-568-6793. *Application contact:* Lynette D. Michael, Director of Graduate Admissions and Student Records, 540-568-6131 Ext. 6395, Fax: 540-568-7860, E-mail: michaeld@jmu.edu.
Website: http://www.jmu.edu/coe/msme/index.shtml

James Madison University, The Graduate School, College of Science and Mathematics, Program in Mathematics, Harrisonburg, VA 22801. Offers M Ed. *Program availability:* Part-time. *Students:* 18 part-time (14 women); includes 1 minority (Asian, non-Hispanic/Latino). Average age 30. In 2017, 1 master's awarded. Application fee: $55. Electronic applications accepted. *Expenses:* Tuition, state resident: full-time $10,512; part-time $438 per credit hour. Tuition, nonresident: full-time $28,358; part-time $1162 per credit hour. *Required fees:* $1128. *Financial support:* Federal Work-Study and unspecified assistantships available. Financial award application deadline: 3/ 1; financial award applicants required to submit FAFSA. *Unit head:* Dr. David C. Carothers, Department Head, 540-568-6184, E-mail: carothdc@jmu.edu. *Application contact:* Lynette D. Michael, Director of Graduate Admissions, 540-568-6395, Fax: 540-568-7860, E-mail: michaeld@jmu.edu.
Website: http://www.jmu.edu/mathstat/

Kennesaw State University, Leland and Clarice C. Bagwell College of Education, Program in Teaching, Kennesaw, GA 30144. Offers art education (MAT); biology (MAT); chemistry (MAT); foreign language education (Chinese and Spanish) (MAT); physics (MAT); secondary English (MAT); secondary mathematics (MAT); special education (MAT); teaching English to speakers of other languages (MAT). *Program availability:* Part-time, evening/weekend. *Entrance requirements:* For master's, GRE, GACE I (state certificate exam), minimum GPA of 2.75, 2 recommendations, resume. Additional exam requirements/recommendations for international students: Required—TOEFL (minimum score 550 paper-based; 80 iBT), IELTS (minimum score 6.5). Electronic applications accepted.

Kent State University, College of Arts and Sciences, Department of Mathematical Sciences, Kent, OH 44242-0001. Offers applied mathematics (MA, MS, PhD); mathematics for secondary teachers (MA); pure mathematics (MA, MS, PhD). *Program availability:* Part-time. *Faculty:* 24 full-time (7 women). *Students:* 71 full-time (27 women), 33 part-time (12 women); includes 7 minority (1 Black or African American, non-Hispanic/Latino; 5 Asian, non-Hispanic/Latino; 1 Hispanic/Latino), 45 international. Average age 29. 77 applicants, 75% accepted, 22 enrolled. In 2017, 13 master's, 7 doctorates awarded. *Degree requirements:* For master's, comprehensive exam (for some programs), thesis (for some programs); for doctorate, comprehensive exam, thesis/dissertation. *Entrance requirements:* For master's, bachelor's degree with proficiency in numerical analysis and statistics, goal statement, resume or vita, 3 letters of recommendation; for doctorate, official transcript(s), goal statement, three letters of recommendation, resume or vita, passage of the departmental qualifying examination at the master's level. Additional exam requirements/recommendations for international students: Required—TOEFL (minimum score 525 paper-based, 71 iBT), Michigan English Language Assessment Battery (minimum score 74), IELTS (minimum score 6.0) or PTE (minimum score 50). *Application deadline:* For fall admission, 5/1 for domestic and international students; for spring admission, 10/1 for domestic and international students; for summer admission, 2/1 for domestic and international students. Applications are processed on a rolling basis. Application fee: $45 ($70 for international students). Electronic applications accepted. *Expenses:* Tuition, state resident: full-time $11,310; part-time $515 per credit hour. Tuition, nonresident: full-time $20,396; part-time $928 per credit hour. *International tuition:* $18,544 full-time. *Financial support:* Fellowships with full tuition reimbursements, research assistantships with full tuition reimbursements, teaching assistantships with full tuition reimbursements, scholarships/ grants, and unspecified assistantships available. Financial award application deadline: 1/31. *Unit head:* Dr. Brian Hayashi, Professor and Chair, 330-672-8914, E-mail: bhayashi@kent.edu. *Application contact:* Artem Zvavitch, Professor and Graduate Coordinator, 330-672-3316, E-mail: zvavitch@math.kent.edu.
Website: http://www.kent.edu/math/

Lake Forest College, Master of Arts in Teaching Program, Lake Forest, IL 60045. Offers elementary education (MAT); K-12 French (MAT); K-12 music (MAT); K-12 Spanish (MAT); K-12 visual art (MAT); secondary biology (MAT); secondary chemistry (MAT); secondary English (MAT); secondary history (MAT); secondary mathematics (MAT). *Degree requirements:* For master's, comprehensive exam, portfolio. *Entrance requirements:* For master's, GRE.

Lebanon Valley College, Program in Science Education, Annville, PA 17003. Offers integrative STEM education (Certificate); STEM education (MSE). *Program availability:* Part-time-only, evening/weekend, 100% online, blended/hybrid learning. *Faculty:* 14 part-time/adjunct (7 women). *Students:* 3 part-time (all women). Average age 42. 4 applicants, 100% accepted, 3 enrolled. In 2017, 10 master's awarded. *Degree requirements:* For master's, thesis or capstone project. *Entrance requirements:* For master's, baccalaureate degree, minimum GPA of 3.0, teacher certification, 3 letters of recommendation, transcripts, goal statement. Additional exam requirements/ recommendations for international students: Required—TOEFL (minimum score 80 iBT). *Application deadline:* Applications are processed on a rolling basis. Application fee: $0. Electronic applications accepted. *Expenses:* $618 per credit hour. *Financial support:* Scholarships/grants available. Financial award application deadline: 3/1; financial award applicants required to submit FAFSA. *Faculty research:* Teacher quality and student achievement, STEM reform, STEM education, effective teaching. *Unit head:* Carrie Coryer, Director of MSE and STEM-based programs, 717-867-6190, Fax: 717-867-6018, E-mail: coryer@lvc.edu.
Website: http://www.lvc.edu/academics/graduate-studies/master-of-science-in-stem-education/

Mathematics Education

Lee University, Program in Education, Cleveland, TN 37320-3450. Offers art (MAT); curriculum and instruction (M Ed, Ed S); early childhood (MAT); educational leadership (M Ed, Ed S); elementary education (MAT); English and math (MAT); English and science (MAT); English and social studies (MAT); higher education administration (MS); history (MAT); history and economics (MAT); math and science (MAT); math and social studies (MAT); middle grades (MAT); science and social studies (MASW); secondary education (MAT); Spanish (MAT); special education (M Ed, MAT); TESOL (MAT). *Accreditation:* NCATE. *Program availability:* Part-time. *Faculty:* 15 full-time (7 women), 8 part-time/adjunct (3 women). *Students:* 28 full-time (21 women), 77 part-time (48 women); includes 12 minority (7 Black or African American, non-Hispanic/Latino; 2 Hispanic/Latino; 3 Two or more races, non-Hispanic/Latino), 1 international. Average age 31. 35 applicants, 83% accepted, 22 enrolled. In 2017, 54 master's, 4 other advanced degrees awarded. *Degree requirements:* For master's, variable foreign language requirement, thesis optional, internship. *Entrance requirements:* For master's, MAT or GRE General Test, minimum undergraduate GPA of 2.75, 3 letters of recommendation, interview, writing sample, official transcripts, background check; for Ed S, minimum undergraduate and master's GPA of 2.75, official transcripts for undergraduate and master's degrees. Additional exam requirements/recommendations for international students: Required—TOEFL (minimum score 61 iBT). *Application deadline:* For fall admission, 6/1 priority date for domestic and international students; for spring admission, 11/1 priority date for domestic and international students; for summer admission, 4/1 priority date for domestic and international students. Applications are processed on a rolling basis. Application fee: $25. Electronic applications accepted. *Expenses: Tuition:* Full-time $12,780; part-time $710 per credit hour. *Required fees:* $60; $60 per term. Tuition and fees vary according to program. *Financial support:* In 2017–18, 32 students received support. Career-related internships or fieldwork, Federal Work-Study, institutionally sponsored loans, scholarships/grants, and unspecified assistantships available. Financial award application deadline: 3/1; financial award applicants required to submit FAFSA. *Unit head:* Dr. William Kamm, Director, 423-614-8544, E-mail: wkamm@leeuniversity.edu. *Application contact:* Crystal Keeter, Graduate Education Secretary, 423-614-8544, E-mail: ckeeter@leeuniversity.edu. Website: http://www.leeuniversity.edu/academics/graduate/education

Lehman College of the City University of New York, School of Education, Department of Middle and High School Education, Program in Mathematics 7–12, Bronx, NY 10468-1589. Offers MS Ed. *Accreditation:* NCATE. *Program availability:* Part-time, evening/weekend. *Degree requirements:* For master's, comprehensive exam or thesis. *Entrance requirements:* For master's, 18 credits in mathematics, 12 credits in education. *Faculty research:* Mathematical problem solving, Piagetian cognitive theory.

Lesley University, Graduate School of Education, Cambridge, MA 02138-2790. Offers arts, community, and education (M Ed); autism studies (Certificate); curriculum and instruction (M Ed, CAGS); early childhood education (M Ed); ecological teaching and learning (MS); educational studies (PhD), including adult learning, educational leadership, individually designed; elementary education (M Ed); emergent technologies for educators (Certificate); ESLArts: language learning through the arts (M Ed); high school education (M Ed); individually designed (M Ed); integrated teaching through the arts (M Ed); literacy for K-8 classroom teachers (M Ed); mathematics education (M Ed); middle school education (M Ed); moderate disabilities (M Ed); online learning (Certificate); reading (CAGS); science in education (M Ed); severe disabilities (M Ed); special needs (CAGS); specialist teacher of reading (M Ed); teacher of visual art (M Ed); technology in education (M Ed, CAGS). *Accreditation:* TEAC. *Program availability:* Part-time, evening/weekend, online learning. *Degree requirements:* For master's, practicum; for doctorate, thesis/dissertation. *Entrance requirements:* For master's, Massachusetts Tests for Educator Licensure (MTEL), transcripts, statement of purpose, recommendations; interview (for special education); for doctorate, GRE General Test, transcripts, statement of purpose, recommendations, interview, master's degree, resume; for other advanced degree, interview, master's degree. Additional exam requirements/recommendations for international students: Required—TOEFL (minimum score 550 paper-based; 80 iBT). Electronic applications accepted. *Faculty research:* Assessment in literacy, mathematics and science; autism spectrum disorders; instructional technology and online learning; multicultural education and English language learners.

Lewis University, College of Education, Program in Secondary Education, Romeoville, IL 60446. Offers biology (MA); chemistry (MA); English (MA); history (MA); math (MA); physics (MA); psychology and social science (MA). *Program availability:* Part-time. *Students:* 19 full-time (9 women), 22 part-time (12 women); includes 10 minority (2 Black or African American, non-Hispanic/Latino; 1 Asian, non-Hispanic/Latino; 5 Hispanic/Latino; 2 Two or more races, non-Hispanic/Latino). Average age 27. *Degree requirements:* For master's, comprehensive exam, departmental qualifying exam. *Entrance requirements:* For master's, writing exam, Test of Academic Proficiency/Basic Skills Test/ACT/SAT, bachelor's degree, minimum GPA of 2.75, 2 letters of recommendation. Additional exam requirements/recommendations for international students: Required—TOEFL (minimum score 550 paper-based; 79 iBT), IELTS (minimum score 6). *Application deadline:* For fall admission, 5/1 priority date for international students; for spring admission, 11/15 priority date for international students. Applications are processed on a rolling basis. Application fee: $40. Electronic applications accepted. Tuition and fees vary according to program. *Financial support:* Federal Work-Study, scholarships/grants, and unspecified assistantships available. Financial award application deadline: 5/1; financial award applicants required to submit FAFSA. *Unit head:* Dr. Lauren Rentfro, Program Director, 815-836-5026, E-mail: rentfrla@lewisu.edu. *Application contact:* Kathy Lisak, Graduate Admissions Counselor, 815-836-5610, E-mail: grad@lewisu.edu.

Liberty University, School of Education, Lynchburg, VA 24515. Offers curriculum and instruction (Ed D, Ed S), including elementary education, middle grades education, secondary education, special education; educational leadership (Ed D); gifted education (Certificate); math specialist (M Ed); middle grades (MAT, Certificate); reading specialist (M Ed); school leadership (Certificate); secondary education (MAT); sport management (MS), including coaching and athletic administration, outdoor adventure sport, sport administration, tourism. *Accreditation:* NCATE. *Program availability:* Part-time, online learning. *Students:* 1,966 full-time (1,428 women), 3,484 part-time (2,528 women); includes 1,323 minority (1,026 Black or African American, non-Hispanic/Latino; 29 American Indian or Alaska Native, non-Hispanic/Latino; 49 Asian, non-Hispanic/Latino; 100 Hispanic/Latino; 9 Native Hawaiian or other Pacific Islander, non-Hispanic/Latino; 110 Two or more races, non-Hispanic/Latino), 58 international. Average age 37. 3,748 applicants, 58% accepted, 1167 enrolled. In 2017, 656 master's, 110 doctorates, 316 other advanced degrees awarded. *Degree requirements:* For doctorate, comprehensive exam, thesis/dissertation. *Entrance requirements:* For master's, GRE General Test or MAT (if taken in or before 1999), 2 letters of recommendation, minimum undergraduate GPA of 3.0, curriculum vitae; for doctorate and other advanced degree, GRE General Test or MAT (if taken before 1999), minimum master's GPA of 3.0, 3 years of teaching experience. Additional exam requirements/recommendations for international students: Required—TOEFL (minimum score 600 paper-based; 100 iBT). *Application deadline:* For fall admission, 6/1 for domestic students; for spring admission, 11/1 for domestic students. Applications are processed on a rolling basis. Application fee: $50. Electronic applications accepted. *Expenses:* Contact institution. *Financial support:* Federal Work-

Study and tuition waivers (partial) available. *Faculty research:* Self-determination, character education, bibliotherapy, learning styles, distance education. *Unit head:* Dr. Heather Schoffstall, Dean, 434-582-2445, Fax: 434-582-2468, E-mail: awgunter@liberty.edu. *Application contact:* Jay Bridge, Director of Graduate Admissions, 800-424-9595, Fax: 800-628-7977, E-mail: gradadmissions@liberty.edu. Website: http://www.liberty.edu/academics/education/graduate/

Longwood University, College of Graduate and Professional Studies, College of Education and Human Services, Farmville, VA 23909. Offers education (MS), including algebra and middle school mathematics, counselor education, elementary and middle school mathematics, elementary education, elementary education initial licensure, health and physical education, special education general curriculum, special education initial licensure; reading, literacy and learning (M Ed); school librarianship (M Ed); social work and communication sciences and disorders (MS), including communication sciences and disorders. *Accreditation:* NCATE. *Program availability:* Part-time, evening/weekend. *Degree requirements:* For master's, comprehensive exam (for some programs), thesis optional, professional portfolio, internship, clinical experience, or practicum. *Entrance requirements:* For master's, PRAXIS I (for initial teaching licensure programs); GRE (for some programs), bachelor's degree from regionally-accredited institution, 2 recommendations (3 for some programs), minimum 500-word personal essay, official transcripts, minimum GPA of 2.75, valid teaching license (for some programs). Additional exam requirements/recommendations for international students: Required—TOEFL (minimum score 570 paper-based), IELTS (minimum score 6.5). Electronic applications accepted. *Expenses:* Contact institution.

Loyola Marymount University, Frank R. Seaver College of Science and Engineering, Program in Teaching Mathematics, Los Angeles, CA 90045-2659. Offers MAT. *Unit head:* Dr. Anna E. Bargagliotti, Graduate Program Director, Mathematics for Teaching, 310-338-4582, E-mail: abargagl@lmu.edu. *Application contact:* Chake H. Kouyoumjian, Associate Dean of Graduate Studies, 310-338-2721, Fax: 310-338-6086, E-mail: graduateinfo@lmu.edu. Website: http://cse.lmu.edu/graduateprograms/teachingmathematics

Manhattanville College, School of Education, Program in Middle Childhood/Adolescence Education (Grades 5-12), Purchase, NY 10577-2132. Offers biology (MAT, Advanced Certificate); biology and special education (MPS); chemistry (MAT, Advanced Certificate); chemistry and special education (MPS); earth science (Advanced Certificate); education for sustainability (Advanced Certificate); English (MAT, Advanced Certificate); English and special education (MPS); literacy and special education (MPS); literacy specialist (MPS); math and special education (MPS); mathematics (MAT, Advanced Certificate); physics (MAT, Advanced Certificate); social studies (MAT); social studies and special education (MPS); special education generalist (MPS). *Program availability:* Part-time, evening/weekend. *Faculty:* 2 full-time (both women), 5 part-time/adjunct (1 woman). *Students:* 8 full-time (7 women), 28 part-time (16 women); includes 4 minority (1 Asian, non-Hispanic/Latino; 2 Hispanic/Latino; 1 Two or more races, non-Hispanic/Latino). Average age 31. 7 applicants, 86% accepted, 4 enrolled. In 2017, 13 master's, 1 other advanced degree awarded. *Degree requirements:* For master's, comprehensive exam (for some programs), thesis (for some programs), student teaching, research seminars, portfolios, internships, writing assessment; for Advanced Certificate, comprehensive exam (for some programs). *Entrance requirements:* For master's, GRE or MAT (for programs leading to certification), minimum GPA of 3.0, 2 letters of recommendation, interview, essay (2-3 page personal statement that describes reasons for choosing teaching or educational leadership as profession and philosophy of education), proof of immunization (for those born after 1957). Additional exam requirements/recommendations for international students: Required—TOEFL (minimum score 600 paper-based; 110 iBT); Recommended—IELTS (minimum score 8). *Application deadline:* Applications are processed on a rolling basis. Application fee: $75. Electronic applications accepted. *Expenses:* $915 per credit. *Financial support:* Teaching assistantships, career-related internships or fieldwork, Federal Work-Study, institutionally sponsored loans, scholarships/grants, and unspecified assistantships available. Financial award application deadline: 3/15; financial award applicants required to submit FAFSA. *Faculty research:* Education for sustainability. *Unit head:* Dr. Shelly Wepner, Dean, 914-323-3153, Fax: 914-323-5493, E-mail: shelly.wepner@mville.edu. *Application contact:* Alissa Wilson, Director, Graduate Admissions, 914-323-3150, Fax: 914-694-1732, E-mail: edschool@mville.edu. Website: http://www.mville.edu/programs#/search/19

Manhattanville College, School of Education, Program in Special Education, Purchase, NY 10577-2132. Offers childhood (grades 1-6) (MPS); childhood education (grades 1-6) and special education (MPS); early childhood (birth-grade 2) (MPS); early childhood (birth-grade 2) and special education (MPS); early childhood and childhood (birth-grade 6) (MPS); English (5-9 and 7-12) (MPS); grades 7-12 generalist (MPS); literacy (birth-grade 6) and special education childhood (grades 1-6) (MPS); literacy 5-12 (MPS); mathematics (5-9 and 7-12) (MPS); science (biology or chemistry 5-9 and 7-12) (MPS); social studies (5-9 and 7-12) (MPS); special education: childhood (grades 1-6) (Certificate); special education: early childhood (birth-grade 2) and childhood (grades 1-6) (Certificate); special education: early childhood (birth-grade 2) (Certificate); special education: grades 7-12 generalist (Certificate). *Program availability:* Part-time, evening/weekend. *Faculty:* 5 full-time (3 women), 24 part-time/adjunct (16 women). *Students:* 77 full-time (69 women), 154 part-time (132 women); includes 33 minority (9 Black or African American, non-Hispanic/Latino; 2 Asian, non-Hispanic/Latino; 22 Hispanic/Latino), 1 international. Average age 28. 87 applicants, 77% accepted, 57 enrolled. In 2017, 86 master's, 2 Certificates awarded. *Degree requirements:* For master's, comprehensive exam (for some programs), thesis (for some programs), student teaching, research seminars, portfolios, internships, writing assessment; for Certificate, comprehensive exam (for some programs). *Entrance requirements:* For master's, GRE or MAT (for programs leading to certification), minimum GPA of 3.0, 2 letters of recommendation, interview, essay (2-3 page personal statement that describes reasons for choosing teaching or educational leadership as profession and philosophy of education), proof of immunization (for those born after 1957). Additional exam requirements/recommendations for international students: Required—TOEFL (minimum score 600 paper-based; 110 iBT); Recommended—IELTS (minimum score 8). *Application deadline:* Applications are processed on a rolling basis. Application fee: $75. Electronic applications accepted. *Expenses:* $915 per credit. *Financial support:* Teaching assistantships, career-related internships or fieldwork, Federal Work-Study, institutionally sponsored loans, scholarships/grants, and unspecified assistantships available. Financial award application deadline: 3/15; financial award applicants required to submit FAFSA. *Faculty research:* Students with emotional difficulties, literacy and adolescents, mindfulness, studying the effects of the environment on special populations, the most difficult cases, students who are presented with multiple challenges: learning, behavioral and ACE experiences who see criminal behavior as a way to cope; working on giving them the tools they need to succeed emotionally and cognitively despite the odds stacked against them. *Unit head:* Dr. Shelly Wepner, Dean, 914-323-3153, Fax: 914-323-5493, E-mail: shelly.wepner@mville.edu. *Application contact:* Alissa Wilson, Director, Graduate Admissions, 914-323-3150, Fax: 914-694-1732, E-mail: edschool@mville.edu. Website: http://www.mville.edu/programs/special-education

Marquette University, Graduate School, College of Arts and Sciences, Department of Mathematics, Statistics, and Computer Science, Milwaukee, WI 53201-1881. Offers bioinformatics (MS); computational sciences (MS, PhD); computing (MS); mathematics education (MS). *Program availability:* Part-time, evening/weekend, online learning. Terminal master's awarded for partial completion of doctoral program. *Degree requirements:* For master's, thesis (for some programs), essay with oral presentation; for doctorate, comprehensive exam, thesis/dissertation, qualifying examination. *Entrance requirements:* For master's, official transcripts from all current and previous colleges/universities except Marquette, three letters of recommendation; for doctorate, GRE General Test, official transcripts from all current and previous colleges/universities except Marquette, three letters of recommendation. Additional exam requirements/recommendations for international students: Required—TOEFL (minimum score 530 paper-based). Electronic applications accepted. *Faculty research:* Models of physiological systems, mathematical immunology, computational group theory, mathematical logic, computational science.

McDaniel College, Graduate and Professional Studies, Program in Elementary and Secondary Education, Westminster, MD 21157-4390. Offers elementary education (MS); elementary STEM instructional leader (Postbaccalaureate Certificate); equity and excellence in education (Postbaccalaureate Certificate); learning technology specialist (Postbaccalaureate Certificate); secondary education (MS). *Accreditation:* NCATE. *Program availability:* Part-time, evening/weekend. *Faculty:* 3 full-time (2 women), 27 part-time/adjunct (22 women). *Students:* 16 full-time (8 women), 148 part-time (114 women); includes 30 minority (17 Black or African American, non-Hispanic/Latino; 5 Asian, non-Hispanic/Latino; 7 Hispanic/Latino; 1 Two or more races, non-Hispanic/Latino), 1 international. Average age 34. 34 applicants, 97% accepted, 18 enrolled. In 2017, 24 master's, 47 other advanced degrees awarded. *Degree requirements:* For master's, comprehensive exam (for some programs), thesis optional. *Entrance requirements:* For master's, PRAXIS, 2 references. Additional exam requirements/recommendations for international students: Required—TOEFL (minimum score 79 iBT), IELTS (minimum score 6). *Application deadline:* For fall admission, 6/1 priority date for domestic students; for spring admission, 11/1 priority date for domestic students; for summer admission, 3/1 priority date for domestic students. Applications are processed on a rolling basis. Application fee: $75. Electronic applications accepted. *Expenses: Tuition:* Full-time $11,760; part-time $490 per credit hour. Tuition and fees vary according to course load and program. *Financial support:* Application deadline: 3/1; applicants required to submit FAFSA. *Unit head:* Fax: 410-857-2515, E-mail: gradadms@mcdaniel.edu. *Application contact:* Penny Pfeiffer, Senior Graduate Enrollment Management Specialist, 410-857-2513, Fax: 410-857-2515, E-mail: ppfeiffer@mcdaniel.edu.

McNeese State University, Doré School of Graduate Studies, Burton College of Education, Department of Education Professions, Program in Middle School Education Grades 4-8, Lake Charles, LA 70609. Offers middle school education grades 4-8 (Postbaccalaureate Certificate), including mathematics, science. *Entrance requirements:* For degree, PRAXIS, 2 letters of recommendation, autobiography. *Application deadline:* For fall admission, 5/15 priority date for domestic and international students; for spring admission, 10/15 priority date for domestic and international students. Applications are processed on a rolling basis. Application fee: $20 ($30 for international students). *Financial support:* Application deadline: 5/1. *Unit head:* Dr. Veronica Faye White, Head, 337-475-5400, Fax: 337-475-5272, E-mail: vfwhite@mcneese.edu. *Application contact:* Dr. Dustin M. Hebert, Director of Doré' School of Graduate Studies, 337-475-5396, Fax: 337-475-5397, E-mail: admissions@mcneese.edu.

Miami University, College of Arts and Science, Department of Mathematics, Oxford, OH 45056. Offers MA, MAT, MS. *Students:* 21 full-time (9 women), 1 (woman) part-time, 8 international. Average age 24. In 2017, 10 master's awarded. *Expenses:* Tuition, state resident: full-time $13,812; part-time $575 per credit hour. Tuition, nonresident: full-time $30,860; part-time $1286 per credit hour. *Unit head:* Dr. Patrick Dowling, Department Chair, 513-529-5831, E-mail: dowlinpn@miamioh.edu. *Application contact:* Dr. Doug Ward, Director of Graduate Studies, 513-529-3534, E-mail: wardde@miamioh.edu. Website: http://www.MiamiOH.edu/mathematics

Michigan State University, The Graduate School, College of Natural Science, Department of Mathematics, East Lansing, MI 48824. Offers applied mathematics (MS, PhD); industrial mathematics (MS); mathematics (MAT, MS, PhD). *Entrance requirements:* Additional exam requirements/recommendations for international students: Required—TOEFL. Electronic applications accepted.

Michigan State University, The Graduate School, College of Natural Science and College of Education, Division of Science and Mathematics Education, East Lansing, MI 48824. Offers biological, physical and general science for teachers (MAT, MS), including biological science (MS), general science (MAT), physical science (MS); mathematics education (MS, PhD).

Middle Tennessee State University, College of Graduate Studies, College of Basic and Applied Sciences, Department of Mathematical Sciences, Murfreesboro, TN 37132. Offers mathematics (MS, MST). *Program availability:* Part-time, evening/weekend, online learning. *Degree requirements:* For master's, comprehensive exam, thesis optional. *Entrance requirements:* For master's, GRE General Test or MAT. Additional exam requirements/recommendations for international students: Required—TOEFL (minimum score 525 paper-based; 71 iBT) or IELTS (minimum score 6). Electronic applications accepted.

Middle Tennessee State University, College of Graduate Studies, Interdisciplinary Program in Mathematics and Science Education, Murfreesboro, TN 37132. Offers PhD. *Program availability:* Part-time, evening/weekend, online learning. *Entrance requirements:* For doctorate, GRE. Additional exam requirements/recommendations for international students: Required—TOEFL (minimum score 525 paper-based; 71 iBT) or IELTS (minimum score 6). Electronic applications accepted.

Millersville University of Pennsylvania, College of Graduate Studies and Adult Learning, College of Education and Human Services, Department of Educational Foundations, Program in Assessment, Curriculum and Teaching - STEM Education Option, Millersville, PA 17551-0302. Offers assessment, curriculum, and teaching (M Ed), including integrative STEM education. *Program availability:* Part-time, evening/weekend, online only, 100% online. *Faculty:* 9 full-time (8 women), 8 part-time/adjunct (5 women). *Students:* 1 (woman) full-time, 31 part-time (20 women). Average age 31. 17 applicants, 100% accepted, 9 enrolled. *Degree requirements:* For master's, comprehensive exam, thesis/capstone experience. *Entrance requirements:* For master's, GRE or MAT (if undergraduate cumulative GPA is lower than 2.8), teaching certificate. Additional exam requirements/recommendations for international students: Required—TOEFL (minimum score 80 iBT), IELTS (minimum score 6.5), PTE (minimum score 60). *Application deadline:* Applications are processed on a rolling basis. Application fee: $40. Electronic applications accepted. *Expenses:* $500 per credit resident tuition, $581.75 per credit non-resident tuition, $59.25 academic support fee. *Financial support:* Unspecified assistantships available. Financial award application deadline: 3/15; financial award applicants required to submit FAFSA. *Faculty research:* Pedagogical content knowledge in instructional technology and stem, watershed

development and management, on-line teaching enhancement. *Unit head:* Dr. Tim E. Mahoney, Coordinator, 717-871-7202, E-mail: tim.mahoney@millersville.edu. *Application contact:* Dr. Victor S. DeSantis, Dean of College of Graduate Studies and Adult Learning/Associate Provost for Civic and Community Engagement, 717-871-7619, Fax: 717-871-7954, E-mail: victor.desantis@millersville.edu. Website: http://millersville.edu/academics/educ/edfoundations/master-stem.php

Millersville University of Pennsylvania, College of Graduate Studies and Adult Learning, College of Science and Technology, Department of Mathematics, Millersville, PA 17551-0302. Offers M Ed. *Accreditation:* NCATE. *Program availability:* Part-time, evening/weekend. *Faculty:* 7 full-time (3 women). *Students:* 4 full-time (2 women), 7 part-time (4 women); includes 1 minority (Asian, non-Hispanic/Latino). Average age 32. 5 applicants, 80% accepted, 1 enrolled. In 2017, 6 master's awarded. *Degree requirements:* For master's, thesis optional, field experience (thesis or research project). *Entrance requirements:* For master's, prerequisite math courses, three letters of recommendation, written statement of academic and professional goals. Additional exam requirements/recommendations for international students: Required—TOEFL (minimum score 80 iBT), IELTS (minimum score 6.5), PTE (minimum score 60). *Application deadline:* Applications are processed on a rolling basis. Application fee: $40. Electronic applications accepted. *Expenses:* $500 per credit resident tuition and fees; $750 per credit non-resident tuition and fees; $114.75 per credit general fee (maximum of 12 credits); technology fee $27 per credit (resident), $39 per credit (non-resident). *Financial support:* In 2017–18, 1 student received support. Unspecified assistantships available. Financial award application deadline: 3/15; financial award applicants required to submit FAFSA. *Faculty research:* Training of secondary mathematics teachers, the use of technology in mathematics classes, equity in mathematics, middle school mathematics, questioning techniques of teacher educators. *Unit head:* Dr. Delray J. Schultz, Chairperson, 717-871-7668, Fax: 717-871-7948, E-mail: delray.schultz@millersville.edu. *Application contact:* Dr. Victor S. DeSantis, Dean of College of Graduate Studies and Adult Learning/Associate Provost for Civic and Community Engagement, 717-871-7619, Fax: 717-871-7954, E-mail: victor.desantis@millersville.edu. Website: http://www.millersville.edu/math/

Minnesota State University Mankato, College of Graduate Studies and Research, College of Science, Engineering and Technology, Department of Mathematics and Statistics, Program in Mathematics, Mankato, MN 56001. Offers mathematics (MA); mathematics education (MS). *Degree requirements:* For master's, one foreign language, comprehensive exam (for some programs), thesis or alternative. *Entrance requirements:* For master's, GRE General Test, minimum GPA of 3.0 during previous 2 years. Additional exam requirements/recommendations for international students: Required—TOEFL. Electronic applications accepted.

Minot State University, Graduate School, Department of Mathematics and Computer Science, Minot, ND 58707-0002. Offers mathematics (MAT). *Degree requirements:* For master's, thesis or alternative. *Entrance requirements:* For master's, GRE General Test, minimum GPA of 2.75, undergraduate major in mathematics, teaching certificate. Additional exam requirements/recommendations for international students: Required—TOEFL (minimum score 79 iBT), IELTS (minimum score 6). *Faculty research:* Mathematics education.

Mississippi College, Graduate School, School of Education, Department of Teacher Education and Leadership, Clinton, MS 39058. Offers art (M Ed); biological science (M Ed); business education (M Ed); computer science (M Ed); dyslexia therapy (M Ed); educational leadership (M Ed, Ed D, Ed S); elementary education (M Ed, Ed S); English (M Ed); higher education administration (MS); mathematics (M Ed); secondary education (M Ed); social studies (history) (M Ed); teaching arts (M Ed). *Program availability:* Part-time, online learning. *Degree requirements:* For master's, comprehensive exam, thesis optional. *Entrance requirements:* For master's, NTE. Additional exam requirements/recommendations for international students: Recommended—TOEFL, IELTS. Electronic applications accepted.

Missouri State University, Graduate College, College of Natural and Applied Sciences, Department of Mathematics, Springfield, MO 65897. Offers mathematics (MS); natural and applied science (MNAS), including mathematics (MNAS, MS Ed); secondary education (MS Ed), including mathematics (MNAS, MS Ed). *Program availability:* Part-time. *Faculty:* 21 full-time (4 women). *Students:* 12 full-time (3 women), 19 part-time (8 women); includes 1 minority (Black or African American, non-Hispanic/Latino), 7 international. Average age 29. 18 applicants, 72% accepted, 8 enrolled. In 2017, 7 master's awarded. *Degree requirements:* For master's, comprehensive exam, thesis or alternative. *Entrance requirements:* For master's, GRE (MS, MNAS), minimum undergraduate GPA of 3.0 (MS, MNAS), 9-12 teacher certification (MS Ed). Additional exam requirements/recommendations for international students: Required—TOEFL (minimum score 550 paper-based; 79 iBT), IELTS (minimum score 6). *Application deadline:* For fall admission, 7/20 priority date for domestic students, 5/1 for international students; for spring admission, 12/20 priority date for domestic students, 9/1 for international students. Applications are processed on a rolling basis. Application fee: $35 ($50 for international students). Electronic applications accepted. *Expenses:* Tuition, state resident: full-time $2915; part-time $2021 per credit hour. Tuition, nonresident: full-time $5354; part-time $3647 per credit hour. *International tuition:* $11,992 full-time. *Required fees:* $173; $173 per credit hour. Tuition and fees vary according to class time, course level, course load, degree level, campus/location and program. *Financial support:* In 2017–18, 11 teaching assistantships with full tuition reimbursements (averaging $10,672 per year) were awarded; Federal Work-Study, institutionally sponsored loans, scholarships/grants, and unspecified assistantships also available. Financial award application deadline: 3/31; financial award applicants required to submit FAFSA. *Faculty research:* Harmonic analysis, commutative algebra, number theory, K-theory, probability. *Unit head:* Dr. William Bray, Department Head, 417-836-5112, Fax: 417-836-6966, E-mail: mathematics@missouristate.edu. *Application contact:* Stephanie Praschan, Director, Graduate Enrollment Management, 417-836-5330, Fax: 417-836-6200, E-mail: stephaniepraschan@missouristate.edu. Website: http://math.missouristate.edu

Missouri University of Science and Technology, Department of Mathematics and Statistics, Rolla, MO 65401. Offers applied mathematics (MS); mathematics (MST, PhD), including mathematics (PhD); mathematics education (MST); statistics (PhD). *Faculty:* 21 full-time (9 women), 1 part-time/adjunct (0 women). *Students:* 38 full-time (16 women), 5 part-time (0 women), 33 international. Average age 29. 37 applicants, 68% accepted, 8 enrolled. In 2017, 5 master's, 3 doctorates awarded. Terminal master's awarded for partial completion of doctoral program. *Degree requirements:* For master's, thesis or alternative; for doctorate, one foreign language, thesis/dissertation. *Entrance requirements:* For master's and doctorate, GRE General Test, GRE Subject Test. Additional exam requirements/recommendations for international students: Required—TOEFL (minimum score 550 paper-based). *Application deadline:* For fall admission, 7/1 for domestic students. Applications are processed on a rolling basis. Application fee: $55 ($75 for international students). Electronic applications accepted. *Expenses:* Tuition, state resident: full-time $7391; part-time $3696 per year. Tuition, nonresident: full-time $21,712; part-time $10,857 per year. *Required fees:* $728; $564 per unit. Tuition and fees vary according to course load. *Financial support:* In 2017–18, 5 fellowships, 1 research assistantship with partial tuition reimbursement (averaging

$1,814 per year), 19 teaching assistantships with partial tuition reimbursements (averaging $1,813 per year) were awarded; institutionally sponsored loans also available. *Faculty research:* Analysis, differential equations, topology, statistics. *Total annual research expenditures:* $223,299. *Unit head:* Dr. Stephen L. Clark, Chair, 573-341-4912, Fax: 573-341-4741, E-mail: sclark@mst.edu. *Application contact:* Dr. V. A. Samaranayake, Director of Graduate Studies, 573-341-4658, Fax: 573-341-4741, E-mail: vsam@mst.edu.
Website: http://math.mst.edu/

Molloy College, Graduate Education Program, Rockville Centre, NY 11571-5002. Offers adolescent education in biology (MS); adolescent special education (Advanced Certificate); bilingual extension (Advanced Certificate); childhood education (MS); childhood special education (Advanced Certificate); early childhood education (MS); educational technology (MS); English (MS); mathematics (MS); social studies (MS); Spanish (MS); special education on both childhood and adolescent levels (MS); teaching English to speakers of other languages (TESOL) in grades pre-K to 12 (MS); TESOL (Advanced Certificate). *Accreditation:* NCATE. *Program availability:* Part-time, evening/weekend. *Faculty:* 18 full-time (17 women), 11 part-time/adjunct (9 women). *Students:* 102 full-time (80 women), 217 part-time (167 women); includes 65 minority (16 Black or African American, non-Hispanic/Latino; 7 Asian, non-Hispanic/Latino; 38 Hispanic/Latino; 4 Two or more races, non-Hispanic/Latino), 1 international. Average age 41. 153 applicants, 68% accepted, 85 enrolled. In 2017, 95 master's, 3 other advanced degrees awarded. *Entrance requirements:* Additional exam requirements/recommendations for international students: Required—TOEFL (minimum score 550 paper-based; 79 iBT). *Application deadline:* Applications are processed on a rolling basis. Application fee: $60. Electronic applications accepted. *Expenses: Tuition:* Full-time $19,980; part-time $1110 per credit. *Required fees:* $1040. Tuition and fees vary according to course load and degree level. *Financial support:* Application deadline: 3/1; applicants required to submit FAFSA. *Faculty research:* English Language Learners; social emotional needs of students; gifted education; cultural diversity; collaborative teaching methods. *Unit head:* Joanne O'Brien, Associate Dean and Director of Graduate Education Programs, 516-323-3116, E-mail: jobrien@molloy.edu. *Application contact:* Jaclyn Machowicz, Assistant Director for Admissions, 516-323-4010, E-mail: jmachowicz@molloy.edu.

Montana State University, The Graduate School, College of Letters and Science, Department of Mathematical Sciences, Bozeman, MT 59717. Offers mathematics (MS, PhD), including mathematics education option (MS); statistics (MS, PhD). *Program availability:* Part-time, online learning. *Degree requirements:* For master's, comprehensive exam, thesis (for some programs); for doctorate, comprehensive exam, thesis/dissertation. *Entrance requirements:* For master's and doctorate, GRE General Test. Additional exam requirements/recommendations for international students: Required—TOEFL (minimum score 550 paper-based). Electronic applications accepted. *Faculty research:* Applied mathematics, dynamical systems, statistics, mathematics education, mathematical and computational biology.

Montclair State University, The Graduate School, College of Education and Human Services, MAT Program in Teaching, Montclair, NJ 07043-1624. Offers art (MAT); biology (MAT); chemistry (MAT); earth science (MAT); English (MAT); French (MAT); health and physical education (MAT); health education (MAT); mathematics (MAT); music (MAT); physical education (MAT); physical science (MAT); social studies (MAT); Spanish (MAT); teacher of English as a second language (MAT). *Degree requirements:* For master's, comprehensive exam, thesis or alternative. *Entrance requirements:* For master's, interview, 2 letters of recommendation. Additional exam requirements/recommendations for international students: Required—TOEFL (minimum score 83 iBT), IELTS (minimum score 6.5). Electronic applications accepted.

Montclair State University, The Graduate School, College of Science and Mathematics, Program in Mathematics, Montclair, NJ 07043-1624. Offers mathematics education (MS); pure and applied mathematics (MS). *Program availability:* Part-time, evening/weekend. *Degree requirements:* For master's, comprehensive exam. *Entrance requirements:* For master's, GRE General Test, 2 letters of recommendation, essay. Additional exam requirements/recommendations for international students: Required—TOEFL (minimum score 83 iBT), IELTS (minimum score 6.5). Electronic applications accepted. *Faculty research:* Computation, applied analysis.

Montclair State University, The Graduate School, College of Science and Mathematics, Program in Mathematics Education, Montclair, NJ 07043-1624. Offers Ed D. *Degree requirements:* For doctorate, thesis/dissertation. *Entrance requirements:* For doctorate, GRE General Test, 2 letters of recommendation, essay. Additional exam requirements/recommendations for international students: Required—TOEFL (minimum score 83 iBT), IELTS (minimum score 6.5). Electronic applications accepted. *Faculty research:* Teacher development, student thinking.

Montclair State University, The Graduate School, College of Science and Mathematics, Program in Teaching Middle Grades Mathematics, Montclair, NJ 07043-1624. Offers MA. *Program availability:* Part-time, evening/weekend. *Degree requirements:* For master's, comprehensive exam, thesis or alternative. *Entrance requirements:* For master's, GRE General Test, 2 letters of recommendation, essay. Additional exam requirements/recommendations for international students: Required—TOEFL (minimum score 83 iBT), IELTS (minimum score 6.5). Electronic applications accepted. *Faculty research:* Teacher knowledge, curriculum.

Montclair State University, The Graduate School, College of Science and Mathematics, Teaching Middle Grades Mathematics Certificate Program, Montclair, NJ 07043-1624. Offers Certificate.

Morehead State University, Graduate Programs, College of Education, Department of Middle Grades and Secondary Education, Morehead, KY 40351. Offers business and marketing education (MAT); English/language arts 5-9 (MAT); French (MAT); health P-12 (MAT); mathematics 5-9 (MAT); physical education P-12 (MAT); science 5-9 (MAT); secondary biology (MAT); secondary chemistry (MAT); secondary earth science (MAT); secondary English (MAT); secondary math (MAT); secondary physics (MAT); secondary social studies (MAT); social studies 5-9 (MAT); Spanish (MAT). *Program availability:* Part-time, evening/weekend. *Degree requirements:* For master's, portfolio. *Entrance requirements:* For master's, GRE or PRAXIS II content exam, minimum overall undergraduate GPA of 2.5. Additional exam requirements/recommendations for international students: Required—TOEFL (minimum score 500 paper-based). Electronic applications accepted.

Morgan State University, School of Graduate Studies, School of Education and Urban Studies, Department of Advanced Studies, Leadership and Policy, Program in Mathematics Education, Baltimore, MD 21251. Offers MS, Ed D. *Degree requirements:* For doctorate, comprehensive exam, thesis/dissertation. *Entrance requirements:* For doctorate, GRE General Test or MAT. Additional exam requirements/recommendations for international students: Required—TOEFL (minimum score 550 paper-based). *Application deadline:* For fall admission, 2/1 priority date for domestic students; for spring admission, 10/1 priority date for domestic students. Application fee: $0. *Expenses:* Tuition, state resident: part-time $433 per credit. Tuition, nonresident: part-time $851 per credit. *Required fees:* $81.50 per credit. *Financial support:* Application deadline: 2/1. *Unit head:* Dr. Xiao-Xiong Gan, Program Coordinator, 443-885-3079,

E-mail: xiao-xiong.gan@morgan.edu. *Application contact:* Dr. Dean Campbell, Graduate Recruitment Specialist, 443-885-3185, Fax: 443-885-8226, E-mail: dean.campbell@morgan.edu.

Mount Holyoke College, Professional and Graduate Education (PaGE), South Hadley, MA 01075. Offers mathematics teaching (MAMT); teacher leadership (MATL); teaching (MAT). *Program availability:* Part-time, 100% online, blended/hybrid learning. *Faculty:* 39 part-time/adjunct. *Students:* 20 full-time (18 women), 104 part-time (88 women); includes 18 minority (6 Black or African American, non-Hispanic/Latino; 2 Asian, non-Hispanic/Latino; 8 Hispanic/Latino; 2 Two or more races, non-Hispanic/Latino), 8 international. Average age 34. 100 applicants, 94% accepted, 68 enrolled. In 2017, 32 master's awarded. *Degree requirements:* For master's, practicum (for MAT); capstone project (for MATL); capstone portfolio (for MAMT). *Entrance requirements:* For master's, MTEL (for MAT initial licensure), bachelor's degree; subject area knowledge in desired teaching discipline; personal statement; essay; official transcripts; two letters of recommendation; history of effective classroom teaching (for MATL). Additional exam requirements/recommendations for international students: Required—TOEFL, IELTS. *Application deadline:* For fall admission, 8/15 for domestic students, 8/16 for international students; for winter admission, 12/15 for domestic and international students; for spring admission, 1/8 for domestic and international students; for summer admission, 5/15 for domestic and international students. Applications are processed on a rolling basis. Application fee: $50. Electronic applications accepted. *Expenses: Tuition:* Full-time $24,500; part-time $766 per credit hour. *Required fees:* $100. Tuition and fees vary according to course load and program. *Financial support:* Fellowships, research assistantships, scholarships/grants, and unspecified assistantships available. Support available to part-time students. *Faculty research:* Social justice; special education/moderate disabilities; English language learners and literacy; research and assessment; professional development and facilitating professional learning. *Unit head:* Dr. Tiffany Espinosa, Executive Director of Professional and Graduate Education, 413-538-3478, Fax: 413-538-3098, E-mail: tespinos@mtholyoke.edu.
Website: https://www.mtholyoke.edu/professional-graduate

Murray State University, Jesse D. Jones College of Science, Engineering and Technology, Department of Mathematics and Statistics, Murray, KY 42071. Offers mathematics (MA, MS); mathematics teacher leader (MAT). *Program availability:* Part-time. *Faculty:* 16 full-time (2 women). *Students:* 5 full-time (3 women), 3 part-time (1 woman), 1 international. Average age 27. 17 applicants, 47% accepted, 1 enrolled. In 2017, 1 master's awarded. *Entrance requirements:* For master's, GRE or GMAT, minimum university GPA of 2.75. Additional exam requirements/recommendations for international students: Required—TOEFL (minimum score 527 paper-based; 71 iBT). *Application deadline:* Applications are processed on a rolling basis. Application fee: $40 ($50 for international students). Electronic applications accepted. *Expenses:* Tuition, state resident: full-time $9504. Tuition, nonresident: full-time $26,811. International tuition: $14,400 full-time. Tuition and fees vary according to course load, degree level and reciprocity agreements. *Financial support:* In 2017–18, 3 teaching assistantships were awarded; Federal Work-Study and scholarships/grants also available. Financial award applicants required to submit FAFSA. *Unit head:* Dr. Ed Thome, Chair, Department of Mathematics and Statistics, 270-809-2311, Fax: 270-809-3780, E-mail: ethome@murraystate.edu. *Application contact:* Kaitlyn Burzynski, Interim Assistant Director of Graduate Recruitment and Records, 270-809-5732, Fax: 270-809-3780, E-mail: msu.graduateadmissions@murraystate.edu.
Website: http://www.murraystate.edu/academics/CollegesDepartments/CollegeOfScienceEngineeringandTechnology/CollegeOfSciencePrograms/mathStats/mathstatsgraduate

National Louis University, National College of Education, Chicago, IL 60603. Offers administration and supervision (M Ed, Ed D, CAS, Ed S); curriculum and instruction (M Ed, MS Ed, CAS); early childhood administration (M Ed, CAS); early childhood education (M Ed, MAT, MS Ed, CAS); education (Ed D); educational psychology/human learning and development (M Ed, MS Ed, CAS, Ed S); elementary education (MAT); interdisciplinary curriculum and instruction (M Ed); mathematics education (M Ed, MS Ed, CAS); middle grades education (MAT); reading and language (M Ed, MS Ed, CAS); school psychology (M Ed, Ed S); science education (M Ed, MS Ed, CAS); secondary education (MAT); special education (M Ed, MAT, CAS); technology in education (M Ed, CAS). *Accreditation:* NCATE. *Program availability:* Part-time, evening/weekend. *Degree requirements:* For doctorate, comprehensive exam, thesis/dissertation. *Entrance requirements:* For master's, MAT or GRE, minimum GPA of 3.0; for doctorate, GRE General Test, minimum GPA of 3.25, interview, resume, writing sample, 4 recommendations. Additional exam requirements/recommendations for international students: Required—TOEFL (minimum score 550 paper-based; 79 iBT).

National University, Academic Affairs, College of Letters and Sciences, La Jolla, CA 92037-1011. Offers biology (MS); counseling psychology (MA), including licensed professional clinical counseling, marriage and family therapy; creative writing (MFA); english (MA); film studies (MA); forensic and crime scene investigations (Certificate); forensic sciences (MFS); human behavior (MA); mathematics for educators (MS); performance psychology (MA); strategic communications (MA). *Program availability:* Part-time, evening/weekend, 100% online, blended/hybrid learning. *Degree requirements:* For master's, thesis (for some programs). *Entrance requirements:* For master's, interview, minimum GPA of 2.5. Additional exam requirements/recommendations for international students: Required—TOEFL (minimum score 550 paper-based; 79 iBT), IELTS (minimum score 6). *Application deadline:* Applications are processed on a rolling basis. Application fee: $60 ($65 for international students). Electronic applications accepted. *Expenses: Tuition:* Part-time $430 per quarter hour. *Financial support:* Career-related internships or fieldwork, institutionally sponsored loans, scholarships/grants, and tuition waivers (partial) available. Support available to part-time students. Financial award application deadline: 6/30; financial award applicants required to submit FAFSA. *Unit head:* Dr. Carol Richardson, Dean, 858-642-8450, E-mail: cols@nu.edu. *Application contact:* Brandon Jouganatos, Interim Vice President for Enrollment Services, 800-628-8648, E-mail: advisor@nu.edu.
Website: http://www.nu.edu/OurPrograms/CollegeOfLettersAndSciences.html

New Jersey City University, William J. Maxwell College of Arts and Sciences, Department of Mathematics, Jersey City, NJ 07305-1597. Offers mathematics education (MA). *Accreditation:* TEAC. *Program availability:* Part-time, evening/weekend. *Degree requirements:* For master's, comprehensive exam, thesis optional. *Entrance requirements:* Additional exam requirements/recommendations for international students: Required—TOEFL (minimum score 79 iBT).

New York Institute of Technology, School of Interdisciplinary Studies and Education, Department of Instructional Technology, Old Westbury, NY 11568-8000. Offers emerging technologies for trainers (Advanced Certificate); instructional design for global e-learning (Advanced Certificate); instructional technology (MS), including educators, trainers; STEM education (Advanced Certificate). *Program availability:* Part-time, evening/weekend, 100% online, blended/hybrid learning. *Faculty:* 6 full-time (3 women), 6 part-time/adjunct (4 women). *Students:* 7 full-time (2 women), 105 part-time (73 women); includes 15 minority (5 Black or African American, non-Hispanic/Latino; 4 Asian, non-Hispanic/Latino; 4 Hispanic/Latino; 2 Two or more races, non-Hispanic/Latino), 1 international. Average age 33. 47 applicants, 83% accepted, 30 enrolled. In

2017, 53 master's, 13 other advanced degrees awarded. *Entrance requirements:* For master's, GRE (minimum combined score of 300) or MAT (minimum score of 400) within the last five years; bachelor's degree; minimum undergraduate GPA of 3.0; demonstrated proficiency in basic uses of instructional technologies; initial/provisional or permanent/professional NY state certification in any teaching area (for educators option); for Advanced Certificate, GRE or MAT (within last 5 years), BS; minimum undergraduate GPA of 3.0; demonstrated proficiency in basic uses of instructional technologies. Additional exam requirements/recommendations for international students: Required—TOEFL (minimum score 79 iBT), IELTS (minimum score 6). *Application deadline:* Applications are processed on a rolling basis. Application fee: $50. Electronic applications accepted. *Expenses:* $1,285 per credit plus fees. *Financial support:* Career-related internships or fieldwork, scholarships/grants, health care benefits, tuition waivers (full and partial), and unspecified assistantships available. Support available to part-time students. Financial award application deadline: 2/15; financial award applicants required to submit FAFSA. *Faculty research:* Integration of information and communication technologies (ICTs) and media literacy education into learning environments; urban K-12 teachers' effective use of technology to enhance student achievement; instructional design and transdisciplinary curriculum studies for online instruction; STEM and computing partnerships for K-12 teachers; experiential, collaborative, and performance-based approaches to pedagogy and technology integration in the K-12 classroom. *Unit head:* Dr. Melda Yildiz, Department Chair, 516-686-1053, Fax: 516-686-7655, E-mail: myildiz@nyit.edu. *Application contact:* Alice Dolitsky, Director, Graduate Admissions, 516-686-7520, Fax: 516-686-1116, E-mail: nyitgrad@nyit.edu.
Website: http://www.nyit.edu/interdisciplinary/department_instructional_technology

New York Institute of Technology, School of Interdisciplinary Studies and Education, Department of Teacher Education, Old Westbury, NY 11568-8000. Offers adolescence education (MS), including math (MAT, MS), science; adolescent education (MAT), including biology, chemistry, English, math (MAT, MS), social studies; childhood education (MS); early childhood (MS). *Program availability:* Part-time, evening/weekend, 100% online, blended/hybrid learning. *Faculty:* 2 full-time (both women), 7 part-time/adjunct (3 women). *Students:* 46 full-time (44 women), 30 part-time (22 women); includes 23 minority (8 Black or African American, non-Hispanic/Latino; 6 Asian, non-Hispanic/Latino; 8 Hispanic/Latino; 1 Two or more races, non-Hispanic/Latino), 2 international. Average age 29. 39 applicants, 72% accepted, 15 enrolled. In 2017, 14 master's awarded. *Entrance requirements:* For master's, GRE or MAT, BS or equivalent; minimum cumulative undergraduate GPA of 3.0; NY state provisional or initial certification (for MS in adolescence education); BS with major in biology, chemistry, economics, English, history, life sciences, math, physics, or psychology (for MS in childhood, early childhood education, and MAT); interview; personal statement. Additional exam requirements/recommendations for international students: Required—TOEFL (minimum score 79 iBT), IELTS (minimum score 6). *Application deadline:* Applications are processed on a rolling basis. Application fee: $50. Electronic applications accepted. *Expenses:* $1,285 per credit plus fees. *Financial support:* Career-related internships or fieldwork, Federal Work-Study, scholarships/grants, tuition waivers (full and partial), and unspecified assistantships available. Support available to part-time students. Financial award application deadline: 2/15; financial award applicants required to submit FAFSA. *Faculty research:* Evolving definition of new literacies and its impact on teaching and learning (twenty-first century skills), new literacies practices in teacher education, teachers' professional development, English language and literacy learning through mobile learning, teaching reading to culturally and linguistically diverse children. *Unit head:* Dr. Hui-Yin Hsu, Department Chair, 516-686-1322, Fax: 516-686-7655, E-mail: hhsu02@nyit.edu. *Application contact:* Alice Dolitsky, Director, Graduate Admissions, 516-686-7520, Fax: 516-686-1116, E-mail: nyitgrad@nyit.edu.
Website: http://www.nyit.edu/interdisciplinary/department_teacher_education

New York University, Steinhardt School of Culture, Education, and Human Development, Department of Teaching and Learning, Program in Mathematics Education, New York, NY 10012. Offers MA. *Accreditation:* TEAC. *Program availability:* Part-time, evening/weekend. *Students:* Average age 30. 28 applicants, 82% accepted, 4 enrolled. In 2017, 6 master's awarded. *Entrance requirements:* Additional exam requirements/recommendations for international students: Required—TOEFL (minimum score 100 iBT). *Application deadline:* For fall admission, 2/1 priority date for domestic and international students; for spring admission, 11/1 for domestic and international students. Applications are processed on a rolling basis. Application fee: $75. Electronic applications accepted. *Expenses:* Tuition: Full-time $41,352; part-time $19,968 per year. *Required fees:* $2496; $1628 per unit. $814 per term. Tuition and fees vary according to course load and program. *Financial support:* Career-related internships or fieldwork, Federal Work-Study, institutionally sponsored loans, scholarships/grants, and tuition waivers (partial) available. Support available to part-time students. Financial award application deadline: 2/1; financial award applicants required to submit FAFSA. *Faculty research:* Race, gender and mathematics learning; developing mathematical concepts through activity; innovative secondary school mathematics materials. *Unit head:* Dr. Orit Zaslavsky, Director, 212-998-5476, Fax: 212-995-4049, E-mail: oz2@nyu.edu. *Application contact:* 212-998-5030, Fax: 212-995-4328, E-mail: steinhardt.gradadmissions@nyu.edu.
Website: http://steinhardt.nyu.edu/teachlearn/math

North Carolina State University, Graduate School, College of Education, Department of Mathematics, Science, and Technology Education, Program in Mathematics Education, Raleigh, NC 27695. Offers M Ed, MS, PhD. *Accreditation:* NCATE. *Program availability:* Part-time. *Degree requirements:* For master's, thesis (for some programs), oral exam; for doctorate, one foreign language, thesis/dissertation, oral and written exams. *Entrance requirements:* For master's, GRE General Test or MAT, minimum GPA of 3.0; for doctorate, GRE General Test, minimum GPA of 3.0, interview. Electronic applications accepted. *Faculty research:* Teacher education using technology, curriculum development, scientific visualization, problem solving.

North Dakota State University, College of Graduate and Interdisciplinary Studies, College of Engineering, Doctoral Program in Engineering, Fargo, ND 58102. Offers environmental and conservation science (PhD); materials and nanotechnology (PhD); natural resource management (PhD); science, technology, engineering, mathematics education (STEM) (PhD); transportation and logistics (PhD). *Degree requirements:* For doctorate, comprehensive exam, thesis/dissertation. *Entrance requirements:* For doctorate, bachelor's degree in engineering, minimum GPA of 3.0. Additional exam requirements/recommendations for international students: Required—TOEFL. Electronic applications accepted. *Expenses:* Contact institution.

North Dakota State University, College of Graduate and Interdisciplinary Studies, College of Human Development and Education, School of Education, Fargo, ND 58102. Offers agricultural education (M Ed, MS), including agricultural education; counselor education (M Ed, MS, PhD), including clinical mental health counseling (M Ed, MS), counselor education and supervision (PhD), school counseling (M Ed, MS); curriculum and instruction (M Ed, MS); education (PhD); educational leadership (M Ed, MS, Ed S); family and consumer sciences education (M Ed, MS); history education (M Ed, MS); institutional analysis (Ed D); mathematics education (M Ed, MS); music education (M Ed, MS); occupational and adult education (Ed D); science education (M Ed, MS).

Accreditation: NCATE. *Program availability:* Part-time, evening/weekend, online learning. *Degree requirements:* For master's, comprehensive exam; for doctorate, thesis/dissertation; for Ed S, thesis. *Entrance requirements:* For degree, GRE General Test, master's degree, minimum GPA of 3.25. Additional exam requirements/recommendations for international students: Required—TOEFL.

North Dakota State University, College of Graduate and Interdisciplinary Studies, Program in STEM Education, Fargo, ND 58102. Offers PhD. Electronic applications accepted.

Northeastern Illinois University, College of Graduate Studies and Research, College of Arts and Sciences, Program in Secondary Education Mathematics, Chicago, IL 60625-4699. Offers MS. *Expenses:* Tuition, state resident: full-time $7274; part-time $404.11 per credit hour. Tuition, nonresident: full-time $14,548; part-time $808.23 per credit hour. *Required fees:* $1284. *Unit head:* Dr. Paul P. O'Hara, Department Chair, 708-442-5783. *Application contact:* Ada Umeh, Admission Director, Graduate College, 773-442-6008, Fax: 773-442-6040, E-mail: a-umeh@neiu.edu.

Northeastern Illinois University, College of Graduate Studies and Research, Daniel L. Goodwin College of Education, MAT Program in Secondary Education, Chicago, IL 60625. Offers language arts (MAT); mathematics (MAT); science (MAT); social science (MAT). *Expenses:* Tuition, state resident: full-time $7274; part-time $404.11 per credit hour. Tuition, nonresident: full-time $14,548; part-time $808.23 per credit hour. *Required fees:* $1284. *Unit head:* Dr. Brian Schultz, Department Chair, 773-442-5327, E-mail: b-schultz@neiu.edu. *Application contact:* Martha Narvaez, Graduate Admission Representative, 773-442-6006, E-mail: m-narvaez@neiu.edu.

Northeastern State University, College of Science and Health Professions, Program in Mathematics Education, Tahlequah, OK 74464-2399. Offers M Ed. *Faculty:* 2 full-time (1 woman). *Students:* 4 full-time (2 women), 18 part-time (17 women); includes 5 minority (4 American Indian or Alaska Native, non-Hispanic/Latino; 1 Asian, non-Hispanic/Latino). Average age 36. In 2017, 10 master's awarded. *Entrance requirements:* For master's, GRE or MAT, minimum GPA of 2.5. Additional exam requirements/recommendations for international students: Required—TOEFL. *Application deadline:* For fall admission, 8/19 for domestic students; for spring admission, 1/7 for domestic students. Applications are processed on a rolling basis. Application fee: $25. Electronic applications accepted. *Expenses:* Tuition, state resident: full-time $222 per credit hour. Tuition, nonresident: part-time $501.75 per credit hour. *Required fees:* $37.40 per credit hour. Tuition and fees vary according to degree level. *Unit head:* Dr. Darryl Linde, Department Chair, 918-444-3809, E-mail: linded@nsuok.edu. *Application contact:* Josh McCollum, Graduate Coordinator, 918-444-2093, E-mail: mccolluj@nsuok.edu.
Website: http://academics.nsuok.edu/mathematics/DegreesMajors/Graduate/MEdMathematicsEducation.aspx

Northern Arizona University, College of Engineering, Forestry, and Natural Sciences, Department of Mathematics and Statistics, Flagstaff, AZ 86011. Offers applied statistics (Graduate Certificate); mathematics (MS); mathematics education (Graduate Certificate); statistics (MS); teaching introductory community college mathematics (Graduate Certificate). *Program availability:* Part-time. *Faculty:* 45 full-time (18 women), 1 part-time/adjunct (0 women). *Students:* 41 full-time (21 women), 22 part-time (15 women); includes 7 minority (3 Asian, non-Hispanic/Latino; 4 Hispanic/Latino), 18 international. Average age 29. 85 applicants, 39% accepted, 29 enrolled. In 2017, 22 master's, 2 other advanced degrees awarded. *Degree requirements:* For master's, variable foreign language requirement, comprehensive exam (for some programs), thesis (for some programs); for Graduate Certificate, comprehensive exam (for some programs). *Entrance requirements:* Additional exam requirements/recommendations for international students: Required—TOEFL (minimum score 80 iBT), IELTS (minimum score 6.5), TOEFL minimum iBT score of 89 (for MS and Graduate Certificate). *Application deadline:* For fall admission, 3/1 for domestic and international students; for spring admission, 10/1 for domestic and international students. Applications are processed on a rolling basis. Application fee: $65. Electronic applications accepted. *Expenses:* Tuition, state resident: full-time $9240; part-time $458 per credit hour. Tuition, nonresident: full-time $21,588; part-time $1199 per credit hour. *Required fees:* $1021; $14 per credit hour. $646 per semester. Tuition and fees vary according to course load, campus/location and program. *Financial support:* In 2017–18, 35 students received support, including 35 teaching assistantships with full and partial tuition reimbursements available (averaging $14,213 per year); institutionally sponsored loans, health care benefits, and unspecified assistantships also available. Financial award application deadline: 2/1; financial award applicants required to submit FAFSA. *Unit head:* Dr. Terry Crites, Chair, 928-523-6883, Fax: 928-523-5847, E-mail: terry.crites@nau.edu. *Application contact:* Tina Sutton, Coordinator, Graduate College, 928-523-4348, Fax: 928-523-8950, E-mail: graduate@nau.edu.
Website: https://nau.edu/cefns/natsci/math/

Northwest Missouri State University, Graduate School, College of Arts and Sciences, Maryville, MO 64468-6001. Offers biology (MS); elementary mathematics specialist (MS Ed); English (MA); English education (MS Ed); English pedagogy (MA); geographic information science (MS, Certificate); history (MS Ed); mathematics (MS); mathematics education (MS Ed); teaching: science (MS Ed). *Program availability:* Part-time. *Faculty:* 67 full-time (21 women). *Students:* 11 full-time (5 women), 70 part-time (39 women); includes 9 minority (2 Black or African American, non-Hispanic/Latino; 1 American Indian or Alaska Native, non-Hispanic/Latino; 3 Hispanic/Latino; 3 Two or more races, non-Hispanic/Latino). Average age 34. 33 applicants, 42% accepted, 10 enrolled. In 2017, 19 master's, 7 other advanced degrees awarded. *Degree requirements:* For master's, comprehensive exam. *Entrance requirements:* For master's, GRE General Test, writing sample. Additional exam requirements/recommendations for international students: Required—TOEFL (minimum score 550 paper-based). *Application deadline:* For fall admission, 7/1 for domestic and international students; for spring admission, 11/15 for domestic and international students. Applications are processed on a rolling basis. Application fee: $0 ($50 for international students). Electronic applications accepted. *Expenses:* Tuition, state resident: full-time $4551; part-time $252.86 per credit hour. Tuition, nonresident: full-time $9103; part-time $505.72 per credit hour. *Required fees:* $2453; $136.25 per credit hour. Tuition and fees vary according to course load and program. *Financial support:* Research assistantships with full tuition reimbursements, teaching assistantships with full tuition reimbursements, and administrative assistantships, tutorial assistantships available. Financial award application deadline: 4/1; financial award applicants required to submit FAFSA. *Unit head:* Dr. Michael Steiner, Dean, 660-562-1197.
Website: https://www.nwmissouri.edu/academics/undergraduate/majors/liberal-arts-sciences.htm

Northwest Missouri State University, Graduate School, School of Education, Maryville, MO 64468-6001. Offers early childhood education (MS Ed); education leadership (MS Ed), including elementary, K-12, secondary; educational leadership (Ed S), including elementary school principalship, secondary school principalship, superintendency; educational leadership and policy analysis (Ed D); elementary education (MS Ed); elementary mathematics (MS Ed); higher education leadership (MS); middle school education (MS Ed); reading (MS Ed); special education (MS Ed); teacher leadership (MS Ed); teaching English language learners (MS Ed). *Accreditation:* NCATE. *Program availability:* Part-time. *Faculty:* 15 full-time (8 women). *Students:* 28 full-time (20 women), 170 part-time (114 women); includes 20 minority (7 Black or

Mathematics Education

African American, non-Hispanic/Latino; 1 Asian, non-Hispanic/Latino; 8 Hispanic/Latino; 4 Two or more races, non-Hispanic/Latino). Average age 33. 168 applicants, 73% accepted, 114 enrolled. In 2017, 67 master's, 21 other advanced degrees awarded. *Degree requirements:* For master's, comprehensive exam; for Ed S, comprehensive exam, thesis. *Entrance requirements:* For master's, GRE General Test, writing sample; for Ed S, minimum graduate GPA of 3.25. Additional exam requirements/recommendations for international students: Required—TOEFL (minimum score 550 paper-based). *Application deadline:* For fall admission, 7/1 for domestic and international students; for spring admission, 11/15 for domestic and international students. Applications are processed on a rolling basis. Application fee: $0 ($50 for international students). Electronic applications accepted. *Expenses:* $389.11 per credit hour in-state tuition and fees, $641.97 out-of-state; $9,750 total cost (for online-based education program). *Financial support:* Research assistantships with full tuition reimbursements, teaching assistantships with full tuition reimbursements, and unspecified assistantships available. Financial award application deadline: 4/1; financial award applicants required to submit FAFSA. *Unit head:* Dr. Tim Wall, Director, 660-562-1179, E-mail: timwall@nwmissouri.edu.
Website: https://www.nwmissouri.edu/education/index.htm

The Ohio State University, Graduate School, College of Arts and Sciences, Division of Natural and Mathematical Sciences, Department of Mathematics, Columbus, OH 43210. Offers actuarial and quantitative risk management (MAQRM); computational sciences (MMS); mathematical biosciences (MMS); mathematics (PhD); mathematics for educators (MMS). *Faculty:* 64. *Students:* 142 full-time (22 women); includes 7 minority (all Asian, non-Hispanic/Latino), 75 international. Average age 25. In 2017, 33 master's, 11 doctorates awarded. *Degree requirements:* For master's, thesis optional; for doctorate, one foreign language, thesis/dissertation. *Entrance requirements:* For master's, GRE General Test; for doctorate, GRE General Test (recommended), GRE Subject Test (mathematics). Additional exam requirements/recommendations for international students: Required—TOEFL (minimum score 550 paper-based; 79 iBT), Michigan English Language Assessment Battery (minimum score 82); Recommended—IELTS (minimum score 7). *Application deadline:* For fall admission, 12/15 priority date for domestic and international students. Applications are processed on a rolling basis. Application fee: $60 ($70 for international students). Electronic applications accepted. *Financial support:* Fellowships, research assistantships, teaching assistantships, Federal Work-Study, institutionally sponsored loans, and unspecified assistantships available. Support available to part-time students. *Unit head:* Dr. Luis Casian, Chair and Professor, 614-292-7173, E-mail: casian.1@osu.edu. *Application contact:* Erin Anthony, Graduate Studies Coordinator, 614-292-6274, Fax: 614-292-1479, E-mail: grad-info@math.osu.edu.
Website: http://www.math.osu.edu/

Oregon State University, College of Education, Program in Education, Corvallis, OR 97331. Offers agricultural education (PhD); language equity and education policy (PhD); mathematics education (MS); science education (MS); science/mathematics education (PhD). *Program availability:* Part-time, 100% online, blended/hybrid learning. Terminal master's awarded for partial completion of doctoral program. *Degree requirements:* For master's, variable foreign language requirement, thesis (for some programs); for doctorate, variable foreign language requirement, thesis/dissertation. *Entrance requirements:* Additional exam requirements/recommendations for international students: Required—TOEFL (minimum score 575 paper-based). Application fee: $75 ($85 for international students). *Faculty research:* School administration, educational foundations, research methodology, education policy development, higher education administration. *Unit head:* Nick Cabot, Ecampus Counseling Lead, 541-737-8564, E-mail: cabotn@oregonstate.edu. *Application contact:* Nick Cabot, Ecampus Counseling Lead, 541-737-8564, E-mail: cabotn@oregonstate.edu.

Oregon State University, College of Science, Program in Mathematics, Corvallis, OR 97331. Offers differential geometry (MA, MS, PhD); financial and actuarial mathematics (MA, MS, PhD); mathematical biology (MA, MS, PhD); mathematics education (MA, MS, PhD); number theory (MA, MS, PhD); numerical analysis (MA, MS, PhD); probability (MA). Terminal master's awarded for partial completion of doctoral program. *Degree requirements:* For master's, thesis or alternative; for doctorate, thesis/dissertation, qualifying exams. *Entrance requirements:* For master's and doctorate, GRE. Additional exam requirements/recommendations for international students: Required—TOEFL (minimum score 100 iBT). *Application deadline:* For fall admission, 1/15 for domestic and international students. Application fee: $75 ($85 for international students). Electronic applications accepted. *Financial support:* Application deadline: 1/15. *Unit head:* Malgorzata Peszynska, Graduate Chair, 541-737-9847, E-mail: mpesz@math.oregonstate.edu. *Application contact:* Mathematics Advisor, 541-737-4686, E-mail: gradinfo@math.oregonstate.edu.
Website: http://www.math.oregonstate.edu/

Plymouth State University, College of Graduate Studies, Graduate Studies in Education, Program in Mathematics Education, Plymouth, NH 03264-1595. Offers M Ed. *Program availability:* Part-time, evening/weekend. *Degree requirements:* For master's, comprehensive exam, thesis optional, internship or practicum. *Entrance requirements:* For master's, MAT, minimum GPA of 3.0.

Portland State University, Graduate Studies, College of Liberal Arts and Sciences, Fariborz Maseeh Department of Mathematics and Statistics, Portland, OR 97207-0751. Offers applied statistics (Certificate); mathematical sciences (PhD); mathematics education (PhD); mathematics for middle school (Certificate); mathematics for teachers (MS); statistics (MS); MA/MS. *Faculty:* 35 full-time (10 women), 16 part-time/adjunct (5 women). *Students:* 82 full-time (30 women), 67 part-time (31 women); includes 37 minority (2 Black or African American, non-Hispanic/Latino; 1 American Indian or Alaska Native, non-Hispanic/Latino; 12 Asian, non-Hispanic/Latino; 18 Hispanic/Latino; 1 Native Hawaiian or other Pacific Islander, non-Hispanic/Latino; 3 Two or more races, non-Hispanic/Latino), 15 international. Average age 33. 108 applicants, 65% accepted, 46 enrolled. In 2017, 25 master's, 4 doctorates awarded. *Degree requirements:* For master's, comprehensive exam, thesis or alternative, 2 written examinations; for doctorate, thesis/dissertation, preliminary and comprehensive examinations. *Entrance requirements:* For master's, GRE General Test, GRE Subject Test, minimum GPA of 3.0 in upper-division course work or 2.75 cumulative undergraduate; for doctorate, GRE General Test. Additional exam requirements/recommendations for international students: Required—TOEFL (minimum score 550 paper-based; 80 iBT). *Application deadline:* For fall admission, 4/1 for domestic students, 3/1 for international students; for winter admission, 9/1 for domestic students, 7/1 for international students; for spring admission, 11/1 for domestic and international students; for summer admission, 2/1 for domestic and international students. Applications are processed on a rolling basis. Application fee: $65. *Expenses:* Tuition, state resident: full-time $14,436; part-time $401 per credit. Tuition, nonresident: full-time $21,780; part-time $605 per credit. *Required fees:* $1380; $22 per credit. $119 per quarter. One-time fee: $325. Tuition and fees vary according to program. *Financial support:* In 2017–18, 44 students received support, including 7 research assistantships with full and partial tuition reimbursements available (averaging $16,418 per year), 30 teaching assistantships with full and partial tuition reimbursements available (averaging $14,943 per year); Federal Work-Study, scholarships/grants, tuition waivers (full and partial), and unspecified assistantships also available. Support available to part-time students. Financial award application deadline:

3/1; financial award applicants required to submit FAFSA. *Faculty research:* Algebra, topology, statistical distribution theory, control theory, statistical robustness. *Total annual research expenditures:* $1.7 million. *Unit head:* Dr. John Caughman, Chair, 503-725-3634, E-mail: caughman@pdx.edu. *Application contact:* Kathie Leck, Graduate Program Administrator, 503-725-3604, Fax: 503-725-8244, E-mail: leck@pdx.edu.
Website: https://www.pdx.edu/math/

Providence College, Program in Teaching Mathematics, Providence, RI 02918. Offers MA. *Program availability:* Part-time, evening/weekend. *Entrance requirements:* Additional exam requirements/recommendations for international students: Required—TOEFL (minimum score 577 paper-based; 90 iBT). *Expenses:* Contact institution.

Purdue University, Graduate School, College of Education, Department of Curriculum and Instruction, West Lafayette, IN 47907. Offers agricultural and extension education (MS, MS Ed, PhD, Ed S); art education (PhD); career and technical education (MS Ed, PhD, Ed S); curriculum studies (MS Ed, PhD, Ed S); educational technology (MS Ed, PhD, Ed S); elementary education (MS Ed); family and consumer sciences education (MS Ed, PhD, Ed S); foreign language education (MS Ed, PhD, Ed S); industrial technology (PhD, Ed S); language arts (MS Ed, PhD, Ed S); literacy (MS Ed, PhD, Ed S); mathematics education (MS, MS Ed, PhD, Ed S); science education (MS, MS Ed, PhD, Ed S); social studies education (MS Ed, PhD, Ed S). *Accreditation:* NCATE. *Program availability:* Part-time, evening/weekend. *Faculty:* 37 full-time (27 women), 1 (woman) part-time/adjunct. *Students:* 78 full-time (50 women), 286 part-time (195 women); includes 68 minority (25 Black or African American, non-Hispanic/Latino; 3 American Indian or Alaska Native, non-Hispanic/Latino; 10 Asian, non-Hispanic/Latino; 22 Hispanic/Latino; 1 Native Hawaiian or other Pacific Islander, non-Hispanic/Latino; 7 Two or more races, non-Hispanic/Latino), 44 international. Average age 36. 150 applicants, 79% accepted, 73 enrolled. In 2017, 107 master's, 20 doctorates, 2 other advanced degrees awarded. *Degree requirements:* For master's, thesis optional; for doctorate, thesis/dissertation, oral and written exams; for Ed S, oral presentation, project. *Entrance requirements:* For master's, GRE General Test (if undergraduate GPA is below 3.0), minimum undergraduate GPA of 3.0 or equivalent; for doctorate, GRE General Test (minimum combined verbal and quantitative score of 1000, 300 for new scoring), minimum undergraduate GPA of 3.0 or equivalent; master's degree with minimum GPA of 3.0 or equivalent; for Ed S, GRE General Test (minimum combined verbal and quantitative score of 1000, 300 for new scoring), minimum undergraduate GPA of 3.0 or equivalent; master's degree. Additional exam requirements/recommendations for international students: Required—TOEFL (minimum score 550 paper-based; 77 iBT). *Application deadline:* For fall admission, 12/15 for domestic students, 3/1 for international students; for spring admission, 9/15 for domestic students, 8/1 for international students. Application fee: $60 ($75 for international students). Electronic applications accepted. *Financial support:* Fellowships with full tuition reimbursements, research assistantships with full tuition reimbursements, teaching assistantships with full tuition reimbursements, career-related internships or fieldwork, and tuition waivers (full) available. Support available to part-time students. Financial award application deadline: 3/1; financial award applicants required to submit FAFSA. *Faculty research:* Literacy acquisition and development, teacher beliefs and knowledge, recruitment and retention of underrepresented students, economic education, literacy discourse. *Unit head:* Janet M. Alsup, Head, 765-494-9667, E-mail: alsupj@purdue.edu. *Application contact:* Heather Brinkman, Graduate Contact, 765-494-2345, E-mail: hbrinkma@purdue.edu.
Website: http://www.edci.purdue.edu/

Purdue University Global, School of Teacher Education, Davenport, IA 52807. Offers education (M Ed); secondary education (M Ed); teaching and learning (MA); teaching literacy and language: grades 6-12 (MA); teaching literacy and language: grades K-6 (MA); teaching mathematics: grades 6-8 (MA); teaching mathematics: grades 9-12 (MA); teaching mathematics: grades K-5 (MA); teaching science: grades 6-12 (MA); teaching science: grades K-6 (MA); teaching students with special needs (MA); teaching with technology (MA). *Program availability:* Part-time, evening/weekend, online learning. *Entrance requirements:* Additional exam requirements/recommendations for international students: Required—TOEFL (minimum score 550 paper-based; 80 iBT).

Purdue University Northwest, Graduate Studies Office, School of Engineering, Mathematics, and Science, Department of Mathematics, Computer Science, and Statistics, Hammond, IN 46323-2094. Offers computer science (MS); mathematics (MAT, MS). *Program availability:* Part-time. *Entrance requirements:* Additional exam requirements/recommendations for international students: Required—TOEFL. *Faculty research:* Topology, analysis, algebra, mathematics education.

Queens College of the City University of New York, Division of Education, Department of Secondary Education and Youth Services, Queens, NY 11367-1597. Offers adolescent biology (MAT); art (MS Ed); biology (MS Ed, AC); chemistry (MS Ed, AC); earth sciences (MS Ed, AC); English (MS Ed, AC); French (MS Ed); Italian (MS Ed, AC); literacy education (MS Ed); mathematics (MS Ed, AC); music (MS Ed, AC); physics (MS Ed, AC); social studies (MS Ed, AC); Spanish (MS Ed, AC). *Program availability:* Part-time, evening/weekend. *Students:* 58 full-time (16 women), 349 part-time (202 women); includes 165 minority (18 Black or African American, non-Hispanic/Latino; 56 Asian, non-Hispanic/Latino; 83 Hispanic/Latino; 8 Two or more races, non-Hispanic/Latino), 14 international. Average age 29. *Degree requirements:* For master's, research project. *Entrance requirements:* For master's, minimum GPA of 3.0. Additional exam requirements/recommendations for international students: Required—TOEFL, IELTS. *Application deadline:* For fall admission, 4/1 for domestic students; for spring admission, 11/1 for domestic students. Applications are processed on a rolling basis. Application fee: $125. Electronic applications accepted. *Financial support:* Career-related internships or fieldwork available. Financial award application deadline: 4/1; financial award applicants required to submit FAFSA. *Unit head:* Dr. Eleanor Armour-Thomas, Chairperson, 718-997-5150, E-mail: eleanor.armour-thomas@qc.cuny.edu. *Application contact:* Elizabeth D'Amico-Ramirez, Assistant Director of Graduate Admissions, 718-997-5203, E-mail: elizabeth.damicoramirez@qc.cuny.edu.

Quinnipiac University, School of Education, Program in Secondary Education, Hamden, CT 06518-1940. Offers biology (MAT); English (MAT); history (MAT); mathematics (MAT); Spanish (MAT). *Accreditation:* NCATE. *Faculty:* 8 full-time (5 women), 27 part-time/adjunct (19 women). *Students:* 27 full-time (20 women); includes 5 minority (1 Black or African American, non-Hispanic/Latino; 3 Hispanic/Latino; 1 Two or more races, non-Hispanic/Latino). 43 applicants, 98% accepted, 36 enrolled. In 2017, 34 master's awarded. *Entrance requirements:* For master's, PRAXIS I or PRAXIS Core Academic Skills Exam, minimum GPA of 3.0, interview. *Application deadline:* For fall admission, 5/1 priority date for domestic students. Applications are processed on a rolling basis. Application fee: $45. Electronic applications accepted. *Financial support:* Career-related internships or fieldwork, Federal Work-Study, and unspecified assistantships available. Financial award application deadline: 6/1; financial award applicants required to submit FAFSA. *Faculty research:* Multicultural and urban education/leadership, challenges of teaching diverse learners, scholarship of teaching and learning, technology and teaching, humor and education. *Unit head:* Mordechai Gordon, Program Director, 203-582-8442, E-mail: mordechai.gordon@qu.edu. *Application contact:* Office of Graduate Admissions, 203-582-8672, Fax: 203-582-3443, E-mail: graduate@qu.edu.
Website: http://www.qu.edu/gradeducation

Radford University, College of Graduate Studies and Research, Program in Education, Radford, VA 24142. Offers early childhood education (MS); mathematics education (MS). *Accreditation:* NCATE. *Program availability:* Part-time, evening/weekend. *Faculty:* 18 full-time (13 women), 9 part-time/adjunct (7 women). *Students:* 33 full-time (26 women), 61 part-time (47 women); includes 11 minority (2 Black or African American, non-Hispanic/Latino; 2 Asian, non-Hispanic/Latino; 6 Hispanic/Latino; 1 Two or more races, non-Hispanic/Latino). Average age 31. 28 applicants, 100% accepted, 22 enrolled. In 2017, 33 master's awarded. *Degree requirements:* For master's, comprehensive exam. *Entrance requirements:* For master's, GRE (waived for any applicant with advanced degree), minimum GPA of 3.0, 2 letters of professional reference, personal statement, resume, official transcripts. Additional exam requirements/recommendations for international students: Required—TOEFL (minimum score 550 paper-based; 79 iBT), IELTS (minimum score 6.5). *Application deadline:* For fall admission, 2/15 priority date for domestic students, 12/1 for international students; for spring admission, 7/1 for international students. Applications are processed on a rolling basis. Application fee: $50. Electronic applications accepted. *Expenses:* Tuition, state resident: full-time $8336; part-time $347 per credit hour. Tuition, nonresident: full-time $16,862; part-time $702 per credit hour. *Required fees:* $3220; $135 per credit hour. Tuition and fees vary according to course load and program. *Financial support:* In 2017–18, 7 students received support, including 1 research assistantship (averaging $10,000 per year); career-related internships or fieldwork, scholarships/grants, and unspecified assistantships also available. Support available to part-time students. Financial award application deadline: 3/1; financial award applicants required to submit FAFSA. *Unit head:* Dr. Wendy Eckenrod-Green, Coordinator, 540-831-5302, E-mail: stel@radford.edu.
Website: http://www.radford.edu/content/cehd/home/teacher-ed/programs/education-master.html

Rhode Island College, School of Graduate Studies, Feinstein School of Education and Human Development, Department of Educational Studies, Providence, RI 02908-1991. Offers advanced studies in teaching and learning (M Ed); English (MAT); French (MAT); history (MAT); math (MAT); secondary education (MAT); Spanish (MAT); teaching English as a second language (M Ed). *Accreditation:* NCATE. *Program availability:* Part-time, evening/weekend. *Faculty:* 2. *Students:* 1 (woman) full-time, 62 part-time (58 women); includes 10 minority (1 Black or African American, non-Hispanic/Latino; 2 Asian, non-Hispanic/Latino; 6 Hispanic/Latino; 1 Two or more races, non-Hispanic/Latino). Average age 37. In 2017, 31 master's awarded. *Degree requirements:* For master's, capstone or comprehensive assessment. *Entrance requirements:* For master's, GRE or MAT (for most programs), minimum undergraduate GPA of 3.0; baccalaureate degree in English, French, history, math or Spanish; 3 letters of recommendation; interview. Additional exam requirements/recommendations for international students: Recommended—TOEFL (minimum score 550 paper-based; 79 iBT). *Application deadline:* For fall admission, 3/1 for domestic students; for spring admission, 11/1 for domestic students. Applications are processed on a rolling basis. Application fee: $50. Electronic applications accepted. *Expenses:* Tuition, state resident: full-time $9768; part-time $407 per credit. Tuition, nonresident: full-time $19,008; part-time $792 per credit. *Required fees:* $696; $29 per credit. One-time fee: $200 full-time; $100 part-time. Tuition and fees vary according to course load. *Financial support:* In 2017–18, 3 teaching assistantships with full tuition reimbursements (averaging $2,500 per year) were awarded; career-related internships or fieldwork, Federal Work-Study, scholarships/grants, health care benefits, and unspecified assistantships also available. Support available to part-time students. Financial award application deadline: 5/15; financial award applicants required to submit FAFSA. *Unit head:* Dr. Leslie Bogad, Chair, 401-456-8170. *Application contact:* Graduate Studies, 401-456-8700.
Website: http://www.ric.edu/educationalStudies/

Rider University, College of Education and Human Services, Teacher Certification Program, Lawrenceville, NJ 08648-3001. Offers bilingual education (Certificate); business education (Certificate); early childhood education (Certificate); elementary education (Certificate); English as a second language (Certificate); English education (Certificate); mathematics education (Certificate); science education (Certificate); secondary education (Certificate); social studies education (Certificate); world languages (Certificate), including French, German, Spanish. *Program availability:* Part-time, online learning. *Degree requirements:* For Certificate, internship, professional portfolio. *Entrance requirements:* For degree, PRAXIS, resume. Additional exam requirements/recommendations for international students: Required—TOEFL (minimum score 550 paper-based). Electronic applications accepted. *Faculty research:* Conceptual foundations for optimal development of creativity; creative theory, cognitive processes in mathematics learning, teacher collaboration.

Rowan University, Graduate School, College of Education, Department of Science, Technology, Engineering, Art and Math Education, Glassboro, NJ 08028-1701. Offers educational technology (CGS); STEM education (MA). *Program availability:* Part-time, evening/weekend. *Degree requirements:* For master's, thesis. *Entrance requirements:* For master's, GRE General Test. Additional exam requirements/recommendations for international students: Required—TOEFL. Electronic applications accepted. *Expenses:* Tuition, state resident: full-time $15,020; part-time $751 per semester hour. Tuition, nonresident: full-time $15,020; part-time $751 per semester hour. *Required fees:* $3158; $157.90 per semester hour. Tuition and fees vary according to course load, campus/location and program.

Rowan University, Graduate School, College of Science and Mathematics, Department of Mathematics, Program in Middle Grades Math Education, Glassboro, NJ 08028-1701. Offers CGS. Electronic applications accepted. *Expenses:* Tuition, state resident: full-time $15,020; part-time $751 per semester hour. Tuition, nonresident: full-time $15,020; part-time $751 per semester hour. *Required fees:* $3158; $157.90 per semester hour. Tuition and fees vary according to course load, campus/location and program.

Rutgers University–Camden, Graduate School of Arts and Sciences, Program in Mathematical Sciences, Camden, NJ 08102. Offers industrial mathematics (MBS); industrial/applied mathematics (MS); mathematical computer science (MS); pure mathematics (MS); teaching in mathematical sciences (MS). *Program availability:* Part-time, evening/weekend. *Degree requirements:* For master's, comprehensive exam, thesis optional, survey paper, 30 credits. *Entrance requirements:* For master's, GRE, BS/BA in math or related subject, 2 letters of recommendation. Additional exam requirements/recommendations for international students: Required—TOEFL (minimum score 550 paper-based), IELTS. Electronic applications accepted. *Faculty research:* Differential geometry, dynamical systems, vertex operator algebra, automorphic forms, CR-structures.

Rutgers University–New Brunswick, Graduate School of Education, Department of Learning and Teaching, Program in Mathematics Education, Piscataway, NJ 08854-8097. Offers Ed M, Ed D. *Program availability:* Part-time. Terminal master's awarded for partial completion of doctoral program. *Degree requirements:* For master's, comprehensive exam (for some programs); for doctorate, thesis/dissertation, qualifying exam. *Entrance requirements:* For master's, GRE General Test, minimum GPA of 3.0; for doctorate, GRE General Test, minimum GPA of 3.5. Additional exam requirements/recommendations for international students: Required—TOEFL. Electronic applications accepted.

Rutgers University–New Brunswick, Graduate School of Education, Doctoral Program in Education, New Brunswick, NJ 08901. Offers educational policy (PhD); educational psychology (PhD); literacy education (PhD); mathematics education (PhD). *Program availability:* Part-time. *Degree requirements:* For doctorate, dissertation, qualifying exam. *Entrance requirements:* For doctorate, GRE General Test, GRE Subject Test (mathematics education). Additional exam requirements/recommendations for international students: Required—TOEFL (minimum score 575 paper-based; 83 iBT). Electronic applications accepted. *Faculty research:* Literacy education, math education, educational psychology, educational policy, learning sciences.

St. John Fisher College, Ralph C. Wilson Jr. School of Education, Program in Adolescence Education and Special Education, Rochester, NY 14618-3597. Offers adolescence education: biology with special education (MS Ed); adolescence education: chemistry with special education (MS Ed); adolescence education: English with special education (MS Ed); adolescence education: French with special education (MS Ed); adolescence education: math with special education (MS Ed); adolescence education: physics with special education (MS Ed); adolescence education: social studies with special education (MS Ed); adolescence education: Spanish with special education (MS Ed). *Program availability:* Part-time, evening/weekend. *Faculty:* 5 full-time (4 women), 7 part-time/adjunct (6 women). *Students:* 15 full-time (3 women), 4 part-time (all women); includes 4 minority (2 Black or African American, non-Hispanic/Latino; 1 Hispanic/Latino; 1 Two or more races, non-Hispanic/Latino). Average age 27. 34 applicants, 85% accepted, 12 enrolled. In 2017, 19 master's awarded. *Degree requirements:* For master's, field experiences, student teaching. *Entrance requirements:* For master's, LAST, 2 letters of recommendation, personal statement, current resume. Additional exam requirements/recommendations for international students: Required—TOEFL (minimum score 575 paper-based; 80 iBT). *Application deadline:* Applications are processed on a rolling basis. Application fee: $30. Electronic applications accepted. *Expenses:* Contact institution. *Financial support:* Scholarships/grants available. Financial award applicants required to submit FAFSA. *Faculty research:* Arts and humanities, urban schools, constructivist learning, at-risk students, mentoring. *Unit head:* Dr. Susan Hildenbrand, Program Director, 585-385-7297, E-mail: shildenbrand@sjfc.edu. *Application contact:* Michelle Gosier, Director of Transfer and Graduate Admissions, 585-385-8064, E-mail: mgosier@sjfc.edu.

St. John Fisher College, School of Arts and Sciences, Program in Math, Science, and Technology Education, Rochester, NY 14618-3597. Offers MS. *Program availability:* Part-time, evening/weekend. *Faculty:* 1 full-time (0 women). *Students:* 9 part-time (6 women); includes 2 minority (1 Black or African American, non-Hispanic/Latino; 1 Asian, non-Hispanic/Latino). Average age 32. 9 applicants, 100% accepted, 9 enrolled. In 2017, 6 master's awarded. *Degree requirements:* For master's, directed research project. *Entrance requirements:* For master's, 2 letters of recommendation, personal statement, current resume. Additional exam requirements/recommendations for international students: Required—TOEFL (minimum score 575 paper-based; 80 iBT). Application fee: $30. *Expenses: Tuition:* Part-time $920 per credit hour. *Required fees:* $10 per credit hour. Tuition and fees vary according to degree level and program. *Financial support:* Scholarships/grants available. *Unit head:* Dr. Bernard Ricca, Director, 585-899-3866, E-mail: bricca@sjfc.edu. *Application contact:* Michelle Gosier, Director of Transfer and Graduate Admissions, 585-385-8064, E-mail: mgosier@sjfc.edu.
Website: https://www.sjfc.edu/graduate-programs/ms-in-applied-data-science/

St. John's University, The School of Education, Department of Curriculum and Instruction, PhD in Curriculum and Instruction Program, Queens, NY 11439. Offers early childhood (PhD); global education (PhD); STEM education (PhD); teaching, learning, and knowing (PhD). *Program availability:* Part-time-only. *Degree requirements:* For doctorate, comprehensive exam, thesis/dissertation. *Entrance requirements:* For doctorate, teacher certification (or equivalent), at least three years' teaching experience or the equivalent in informal learning environments, master's degree. Additional exam requirements/recommendations for international students: Required—TOEFL. *Application deadline:* Applications are processed on a rolling basis. Application fee: $70. Electronic applications accepted. *Expenses: Tuition:* Full-time $44,280; part-time $1230 per credit. *Required fees:* $340; $340 per credit. Tuition and fees vary according to course load, degree level and program. *Financial support:* Fellowships, research assistantships, and scholarships/grants available. Support available to part-time students. Financial award application deadline: 2/1; financial award applicants required to submit FAFSA. *Faculty research:* Literacies, early childhood, STEM, school culture, global education. *Unit head:* Dr. Sandra Schamroth Abrams, PhD Program Director, 718-990-8313, E-mail: abramss@stjohns.edu. *Application contact:* Dr. Sandra Schamroth Abrams, PhD Program Director, 718-990-8313, E-mail: abramss@stjohns.edu.
Website: https://www.stjohns.edu/academics/schools-and-colleges/school-education/programs-and-majors/phd-curriculum-and-instruction

St. Joseph's College, Long Island Campus, Programs in Education, Field in Mathematics Education, Patchogue, NY 11772-2399. Offers MA. *Program availability:* Part-time, evening/weekend. *Faculty:* 1 (woman) full-time, 1 part-time/adjunct (0 women). *Students:* 14 part-time (10 women); includes 2 minority (1 Native Hawaiian or other Pacific Islander, non-Hispanic/Latino; 1 Two or more races, non-Hispanic/Latino). Average age 24. 5 applicants, 100% accepted, 5 enrolled. In 2017, 16 master's awarded. *Entrance requirements:* For master's, LAST, ATS-W, CST, resume, two letters of recommendation, copies of certificates granted by the New York State Education Department, official transcripts, completed medical form. Application fee: $25. *Expenses: Tuition:* Full-time $17,550; part-time $975 per credit. *Required fees:* $362. *Financial support:* In 2017–18, 6 students received support. *Unit head:* Elana Reiser, Director of Master's in Mathematics Education/Professor, 631-687-5170, E-mail: ereiser@sjcny.edu.

Saint Peter's University, Graduate Programs in Education, Jersey City, NJ 07306-5997. Offers director of school counseling services (Certificate); educational leadership (MA Ed, Ed D); higher education (Ed D); middle school mathematics (Certificate); professional/associate counselor (Certificate); reading (MA Ed); school business administrator (Certificate); school counseling (MA, Certificate); special education (MA Ed, Certificate), including applied behavioral analysis (MA Ed), literacy (MA Ed), teacher of students with disabilities (Certificate); teaching (MA Ed, Certificate), including 6-8 middle school education, K-12 secondary education, K-5 elementary education. *Accreditation:* TEAC. *Program availability:* Part-time, evening/weekend. *Degree requirements:* For master's, comprehensive exam; for doctorate, comprehensive exam, thesis/dissertation. *Entrance requirements:* For master's and doctorate, GRE or MAT. Additional exam requirements/recommendations for international students: Required—TOEFL. Electronic applications accepted.

Salem State University, School of Graduate Studies, Program in Middle School Education, Salem, MA 01970-5353. Offers humanities (M Ed); math/science (MAT). *Program availability:* Part-time, evening/weekend. *Entrance requirements:* For master's, GRE or MAT. Additional exam requirements/recommendations for international students: Required—TOEFL (minimum score 550 paper-based; 80 iBT) or IELTS (minimum score 5.5).

Mathematics Education

Salem State University, School of Graduate Studies, Program in Middle School Math, Salem, MA 01970-5353. Offers MAT. *Program availability:* Part-time, evening/weekend. *Entrance requirements:* For master's, GRE or MAT. Additional exam requirements/recommendations for international students: Required—TOEFL (minimum score 550 paper-based; 80 iBT) or IELTS (minimum score 5.5).

Salisbury University, Program in Mathematics Education, Salisbury, MD 21801-6837. Offers mathematics (MSME), including high school, middle school. *Program availability:* Part-time, evening/weekend. *Faculty:* 4 full-time (2 women), 2 part-time/adjunct (1 woman). *Students:* 1 (woman) full-time, 7 part-time (5 women). Average age 27. 5 applicants, 80% accepted, 4 enrolled. In 2017, 5 master's awarded. *Entrance requirements:* For master's, two letters of recommendation; transcripts from colleges and universities attended; personal statement. Additional exam requirements/recommendations for international students: Required—TOEFL (minimum score 550 paper-based; 79 iBT), IELTS (minimum score 6.5). *Application deadline:* For fall admission, 8/1 priority date for domestic and international students; for spring admission, 10/1 priority date for domestic and international students. Applications are processed on a rolling basis. Application fee: $65. Electronic applications accepted. *Expenses:* $392 per credit hour resident; $703 per credit hour non-resident; $92 per credit hour fees. *Financial support:* In 2017–18, 1 teaching assistantship with full tuition reimbursement (averaging $8,000 per year) was awarded; career-related internships or fieldwork and scholarships/grants also available. Support available to part-time students. Financial award application deadline: 3/1; financial award applicants required to submit FAFSA. *Faculty research:* Conceptual development of multiplicative reasoning; early childhood mathematics; teachers' attitudes towards mathematics. *Unit head:* Dr. Jennifer Bergner, Graduate Program Director, Mathematics Education, 410-677-5429, E-mail: jabergner@salisbury.edu. Website: http://www.salisbury.edu/gsr/gradstudies/MSMEpage.html

San Diego State University, Graduate and Research Affairs, College of Sciences, Department of Mathematics and Statistics, San Diego, CA 92182. Offers applied mathematics (MS); mathematics (MA); mathematics and science education (PhD); statistics (MS). PhD offered jointly wtih University of California, San Diego. *Program availability:* Part-time. *Degree requirements:* For doctorate, thesis/dissertation. *Entrance requirements:* For master's, GRE General Test; for doctorate, GRE, minimum GPA of 3.25 in last 30 undergraduate semester units, minimum graduate GPA of 3.5, MSE recommendation form, 3 letters of recommendation. Additional exam requirements/recommendations for international students: Required—TOEFL. Electronic applications accepted. *Faculty research:* Teacher education in mathematics.

San Francisco State University, Division of Graduate Studies, College of Education, Department of Elementary Education, Program in Mathematics Education, San Francisco, CA 94132-1722. Offers MA. *Accreditation:* NCATE. *Unit head:* Dr. Josephine Arce, Chair, 415-338-7636, Fax: 415-338-0567, E-mail: jarce@sfsu.edu. *Application contact:* Dr. Maria Zavala, MA Program Coordinator, 415-405-0465, Fax: 415-338-0567, E-mail: mza@sfsu.edu. Website: https://eed.sfsu.edu/

San Francisco State University, Division of Graduate Studies, College of Education, Department of Secondary Education, San Francisco, CA 94132-1722. Offers mathematics education (MA); secondary education (MA, Credential). *Accreditation:* NCATE. *Unit head:* Dr. Maika Watanabe, Chair, 415-338-1622, Fax: 415-338-0914, E-mail: watanabe@sfsu.edu. *Application contact:* Administrative Office Coordinator, 415-338-7649, Fax: 415-338-0914, E-mail: seced@sfsu.edu. Website: http://secondaryed.sfsu.edu/

San Jose State University, Graduate Studies and Research, College of Science, San Jose, CA 95192-0099. Offers bioinformatics (MS); biological sciences (MA, MS), including ecology and evolution (MS), molecular biology and microbiology (MS), physiology (MS); biotechnology (MBT); chemistry (MA, MS); computer science (MS); geology (MS); marine science (MS); mathematics (MA, MS), including mathematics education (MA); medical products development management (MS); meteorology (MS); physics (MS), including computational physics, modern optics, physics; statistics (MS). MS in marine science offered through Moss Landing Marine Labs. *Program availability:* Part-time. *Faculty:* 78 full-time (27 women), 25 part-time/adjunct (13 women). *Students:* 154 full-time (76 women), 212 part-time (102 women); includes 135 minority (4 Black or African American, non-Hispanic/Latino; 78 Asian, non-Hispanic/Latino; 27 Hispanic/Latino; 1 Native Hawaiian or other Pacific Islander, non-Hispanic/Latino; 25 Two or more races, non-Hispanic/Latino), 135 international. Average age 28. 1,156 applicants, 26% accepted, 179 enrolled. In 2017, 196 master's awarded. *Degree requirements:* For master's, comprehensive exam (for some programs), thesis (for some programs), directed reading, colloquium, project, writing project, statistical consulting. *Entrance requirements:* Additional exam requirements/recommendations for international students: Required—TOEFL (minimum score 550 paper-based; 80 iBT), IELTS (minimum score 6.5), TWE, PTE (minimum score 53). *Application deadline:* For fall admission, 2/1 for domestic and international students. Applications are processed on a rolling basis. Application fee: $55. Electronic applications accepted. *Expenses:* Tuition, state resident: full-time $7176. Tuition, nonresident: full-time $16,680. Tuition and fees vary according to course load and program. *Financial support:* Fellowships, research assistantships, career-related internships or fieldwork, Federal Work-Study, scholarships/grants, traineeships, tuition waivers (full and partial), and unspecified assistantships available. Support available to part-time students. Financial award application deadline: 4/28; financial award applicants required to submit FAFSA. *Unit head:* Dr. Michael Kaufman, Dean, 408-924-4800, Fax: 408-924-4815, E-mail: michael.kaufman@sjsu.edu. Website: http://www.sjsu.edu/science/

Seattle Pacific University, Program in Teaching Mathematics and Science, Seattle, WA 98119-1997. Offers MTMS. *Students:* 19 full-time (8 women), 2 part-time (1 woman); includes 4 minority (1 Asian, non-Hispanic/Latino; 2 Hispanic/Latino; 1 Two or more races, non-Hispanic/Latino). Average age 32. In 2017, 20 master's awarded. *Degree requirements:* For master's, internship. *Application deadline:* For fall admission, 8/15 for domestic students; for winter admission, 11/15 for domestic students; for spring admission, 2/15 for domestic students; for summer admission, 5/15 for domestic students. *Unit head:* David W. Dento, Graduate Teacher Education Chair, 206-281-2504, E-mail: dentod@spu.edu. Website: http://spu.edu/academics/school-of-education/graduate-programs/masters-programs/master-in-teaching-mathematics-and-science

Shippensburg University of Pennsylvania, School of Graduate Studies, College of Education and Human Services, Department of Teacher Education, Shippensburg, PA 17257-2299. Offers curriculum and instruction (M Ed), including biology, early childhood education, elementary education, geography/earth science, history, mathematics, middle school education, modern languages; reading (M Ed). *Accreditation:* NCATE. *Program availability:* Part-time, evening/weekend, 100% online, blended/hybrid learning. *Faculty:* 13 full-time (8 women), 1 (woman) part-time/adjunct. *Students:* 10 full-time (7 women), 94 part-time (81 women); includes 10 minority (3 Black or African American, non-Hispanic/Latino; 2 Asian, non-Hispanic/Latino; 5 Hispanic/Latino), 1 international. Average age 34. 71 applicants, 86% accepted, 35 enrolled. In 2017, 23 master's awarded. *Degree requirements:* For master's, comprehensive exam (for some programs), thesis optional, practicum or internship; capstone seminar (for some

programs). *Entrance requirements:* For master's, MAT or GRE (if GPA less than 2.75), interview, 3 letters of reference, questionnaire of teaching background and future goals, resume. Additional exam requirements/recommendations for international students: Required—TOEFL (minimum score 550 paper-based, 68 iBT) or IELTS (minimum score 6). *Application deadline:* For fall admission, 4/1 priority date for domestic students, 4/30 for international students; for spring admission, 9/1 priority date for domestic students, 9/30 for international students; for summer admission, 2/1 priority date for domestic students. Applications are processed on a rolling basis. Application fee: $45. Electronic applications accepted. *Expenses:* Tuition, state resident: part-time $500 per credit. Tuition, nonresident: part-time $750 per credit. *Required fees:* $145 per credit. *Financial support:* In 2017–18, 1 student received support. Career-related internships or fieldwork, scholarships/grants, unspecified assistantships, and resident hall director and student payroll positions available. Support available to part-time students. Financial award application deadline: 3/1; financial award applicants required to submit FAFSA. *Unit head:* Dr. Christine A. Royce, Chairperson, 717-477-1688, Fax: 717-477-4046, E-mail: caroyc@ship.edu. *Application contact:* Maya T. Mapp, Director of Admissions, 717-477-1231, Fax: 717-477-4016, E-mail: mtmapp@ship.edu. Website: http://www.ship.edu/teacher/

Simon Fraser University, Office of Graduate Studies and Postdoctoral Fellows, Faculty of Education, Program in Mathematics Education, Burnaby, BC V5A 1S6, Canada. Offers mathematics education (PhD); secondary mathematics education (M Ed, M Sc). *Program availability:* Part-time, evening/weekend. *Degree requirements:* For master's, comprehensive exam (for some programs), thesis; for doctorate, comprehensive exam, thesis/dissertation. *Entrance requirements:* For master's, minimum GPA of 3.0 (on scale of 4.33) or 3.33 based on last 60 credits of undergraduate courses; for doctorate, minimum GPA of 3.5 (on scale of 4.33). Additional exam requirements/recommendations for international students: Recommended—TOEFL (minimum score 580 paper-based; 93 iBT), IELTS (minimum score 7), TWE (minimum score 5). Electronic applications accepted. *Faculty research:* Historical and psychological development of mathematical thinking, math anxiety and concept formation, mathematical problem solving, numeracy, instructional design, cognition in mathematics thinking and learning, undergraduate math education.

Slippery Rock University of Pennsylvania, Graduate Studies (Recruitment), College of Education, Department of Elementary Education and Early Childhood, Slippery Rock, PA 16057-1383. Offers instructional coach (M Ed); K-12 reading (M Ed); K-12 science and math (M Ed); reading specialist (M Ed). *Accreditation:* NCATE. *Program availability:* Part-time, evening/weekend, online only, 100% online. *Degree requirements:* For master's, comprehensive exam (for some programs), thesis optional. *Entrance requirements:* For master's, minimum GPA of 3.0, resume, teaching certification, transcripts, letters of recommendation (depending on program). Additional exam requirements/recommendations for international students: Required—TOEFL (minimum score 550 paper-based; 80 iBT). Electronic applications accepted. *Expenses:* Contact institution.

Slippery Rock University of Pennsylvania, Graduate Studies (Recruitment), College of Education, Department of Secondary Education/Foundations of Education, Slippery Rock, PA 16057-1383. Offers secondary education (M Ed), including English, math/science, social studies. *Accreditation:* NCATE. *Program availability:* Part-time, evening/weekend, 100% online. *Degree requirements:* For master's, comprehensive exam, thesis (for some programs). *Entrance requirements:* For master's, copy of teaching certification and two letters of recommendation (for some programs). Additional exam requirements/recommendations for international students: Required—TOEFL (minimum score 550 paper-based; 80 iBT). Electronic applications accepted. *Expenses:* Contact institution.

Smith College, Graduate and Special Programs, Department of Education and Child Study, Program in Secondary Education, Northampton, MA 01063. Offers secondary education (MAT), including biological sciences education, chemistry education, English education, geology education, government education, history education, mathematics education, physics education. *Program availability:* Part-time. *Students:* 5 full-time (all women), 2 part-time (0 women); includes 3 minority (1 Asian, non-Hispanic/Latino; 2 Hispanic/Latino). Average age 29. 13 applicants, 92% accepted, 5 enrolled. In 2017, 5 master's awarded. *Entrance requirements:* Additional exam requirements/recommendations for international students: Required—TOEFL (minimum score 595 paper-based; 97 iBT), IELTS. *Application deadline:* For fall admission, 4/15 for domestic students, 1/15 priority date for international students; for spring admission, 12/1 for domestic students. Applications are processed on a rolling basis. Application fee: $60. *Expenses:* Contact institution. *Financial support:* In 2017–18, 5 students received support, including 3 fellowships with full tuition reimbursements available; scholarships/grants and human resources employee benefit also available. Support available to part-time students. Financial award application deadline: 4/15; financial award applicants required to submit CSS PROFILE or FAFSA. *Unit head:* Rosetta Cohen, Graduate Student Advisor, 413-585-3266, E-mail: rcohen@smith.edu. *Application contact:* Ruth Morgan, Program Assistant, 413-585-3050, Fax: 413-585-3054, E-mail: gradstdy@smith.edu. Website: http://www.smith.edu/educ/

Smith College, Graduate and Special Programs, Department of Mathematics, Northampton, MA 01063. Offers secondary education (MAT), including mathematics education. *Program availability:* Part-time. *Students:* 1 applicant, 100% accepted. In 2017, 1 master's awarded. *Entrance requirements:* Additional exam requirements/recommendations for international students: Required—TOEFL (minimum score 595 paper-based; 97 iBT), IELTS. *Application deadline:* For fall admission, 4/15 for domestic students, 1/15 for international students; for spring admission, 12/1 for domestic students. Applications are processed on a rolling basis. Application fee: $60. *Expenses:* Contact institution. *Financial support:* Scholarships/grants available. Support available to part-time students. Financial award application deadline: 4/15; financial award applicants required to submit CSS PROFILE or FAFSA. *Unit head:* Julianna Tymoczko, Department Chair, 413-585-3775, E-mail: jtymoczko@smith.edu. *Application contact:* Ruth Morgan, Program Assistant, 413-585-3050, Fax: 413-585-3054, E-mail: gradstdy@smith.edu. Website: http://www.math.smith.edu/

South Carolina State University, College of Graduate and Professional Studies, Department of Education, Orangeburg, SC 29117-0001. Offers early childhood education (MAT); education (M Ed); elementary education (M Ed, MAT); English (MAT); general science/biology (MAT); mathematics (MAT); secondary education (M Ed), including biology education, business education, counselor education, English education, home economics education, industrial education, mathematics education, science education, social studies education; special education (M Ed), including emotionally handicapped, learning disabilities, mentally handicapped. *Accreditation:* NCATE. *Program availability:* Part-time, evening/weekend. *Faculty:* 11 full-time (6 women), 4 part-time/adjunct (2 women). *Students:* 26 full-time (18 women), 22 part-time (17 women); includes 41 minority (all Black or African American, non-Hispanic/Latino), 1 international. Average age 33. 25 applicants, 100% accepted, 19 enrolled. In 2017, 6 master's awarded. *Degree requirements:* For master's, thesis optional, departmental qualifying exam. *Entrance requirements:* For master's, GRE General Test, NTE, interview, teaching certificate. *Application deadline:* For fall admission, 6/15 priority date for domestic students, 6/15 for international students; for spring admission, 11/1 for domestic and international students. Application fee: $25. Electronic applications accepted. *Expenses:* Tuition, state resident: full-time $9388; part-time $607 per credit hour. Tuition, nonresident: full-time $19,968; part-time $1194 per credit hour. *Required fees:* $766; $766 per credit hour. *Financial support:* Fellowships, career-related internships or fieldwork, Federal Work-Study, and scholarships/grants available. Financial award application deadline: 6/1. *Unit head:* Dr. Charlie Spell, Interim Chair, Department of Education, 803-536-8963, Fax: 803-516-4568, E-mail: cspell@scsu.edu. *Application contact:* Curtis Foskey, Coordinator of Graduate Studies, 803-536-8419, Fax: 803-536-8812, E-mail: cfoskey@scsu.edu.

Southeastern Oklahoma State University, School of Education, Durant, OK 74701-0609. Offers math specialist (M Ed); reading specialist (M Ed); school administration (M Ed); school counseling (M Ed). *Accreditation:* NCATE. *Program availability:* Part-time, evening/weekend. *Degree requirements:* For master's, comprehensive exam, thesis optional, portfolio (M Ed). *Entrance requirements:* For master's, GRE General Test (for school counseling), minimum GPA of 3.0 in last 60 hours or 2.75 overall. Additional exam requirements/recommendations for international students: Required—TOEFL (minimum score 550 paper-based; 79 iBT). Electronic applications accepted.

Southern Illinois University Edwardsville, Graduate School, College of Arts and Sciences, Department of Mathematics and Statistics, Program in Postsecondary Mathematics Education, Edwardsville, IL 62026. Offers MS. *Program availability:* Part-time. *Degree requirements:* For master's, thesis (for some programs), special project. *Entrance requirements:* Additional exam requirements/recommendations for international students: Required—TOEFL (minimum score 550 paper-based, 79 iBT), IELTS (minimum score 6.5), Michigan Test of English Language Proficiency or PTE. Electronic applications accepted.

Southern University and Agricultural and Mechanical College, Graduate School, Department of Science/Mathematics Education, Baton Rouge, LA 70813. Offers PhD. *Accreditation:* NCATE. *Degree requirements:* For doctorate, thesis/dissertation. *Entrance requirements:* For doctorate, GRE General Test. Additional exam requirements/recommendations for international students: Required—TOEFL (minimum score 525 paper-based). *Faculty research:* Performance assessment in science/mathematics education, equity in science/mathematics education, technology and distance learning, science/mathematics concept formation, cognitive themes, problem solving in science/mathematics education.

Southwestern Oklahoma State University, College of Arts and Sciences, Department of Mathematics, Weatherford, OK 73096-3098. Offers M Ed. *Program availability:* Part-time. *Degree requirements:* For master's, exam. *Entrance requirements:* For master's, GRE General Test or minimum undergraduate GPA of 3.0. Additional exam requirements/recommendations for international students: Required—TOEFL.

Southwest Minnesota State University, Department of Education, Marshall, MN 56258. Offers ESL (MS); math (MS); reading (MS); special education (MS), including developmental disabilities, early childhood education, emotional behavioral disorders, learning disabilities; teaching, learning and leadership (MS). *Program availability:* Part-time, evening/weekend, online learning. *Entrance requirements:* Additional exam requirements/recommendations for international students: Required—TOEFL or IELTS; Recommended—TOEFL (minimum score 550 paper-based; 80 iBT), IELTS.

State University of New York at Fredonia, College of Liberal Arts and Sciences, Fredonia, NY 14063-1136. Offers biology (MS); English (MA); English education 7-12 (MA); interdisciplinary studies (MA, MS); math education (MS Ed); professional writing (CAS); speech pathology (MS); MA/MS. *Program availability:* Part-time, evening/weekend. *Students:* 73 full-time (62 women), 9 part-time (6 women); includes 7 minority (1 Black or African American, non-Hispanic/Latino; 1 Asian, non-Hispanic/Latino; 2 Hispanic/Latino; 1 Native Hawaiian or other Pacific Islander, non-Hispanic/Latino; 2 Two or more races, non-Hispanic/Latino). Average age 24. 200 applicants, 25% accepted, 43 enrolled. In 2017, 41 master's, 1 other advanced degree awarded. *Degree requirements:* For master's, comprehensive exam (for some programs), thesis (for some programs). *Entrance requirements:* For master's, GRE. Additional exam requirements/recommendations for international students: Required—TOEFL (minimum score 79 iBT), IELTS (minimum score 6.5). *Application deadline:* Applications are processed on a rolling basis. Application fee: $75. Electronic applications accepted. *Expenses:* Tuition, state resident: full-time $8154. Tuition, nonresident: full-time $16,650. *Required fees:* $1209. *Financial support:* In 2017–18, 5 students received support, including 14 teaching assistantships with full and partial tuition reimbursements available (averaging $5,957 per year); tuition waivers (full and partial) and unspecified assistantships also available. *Faculty research:* Immunology/microbiology, applied human physiology, ecology and evolution, invertebrate biology, molecular biology, biochemistry, physiology, animal behavior, science education, vertebrate physiology, cell biology, plant biology, developmental biology, aquatic ecology, bilingual language acquisition, bilingual language acquisition and disorders, augmentative and alternate communication with ALS, World War I, Zweig, environmental literature, editing, adolescent literature, pedagogy. *Unit head:* Dr. Andy Karafa, Dean, 716-673-3173, Fax: 716-673-3338, E-mail: andy.karafa@gmail.com. *Application contact:* Wendy S. Dunst, Interim Graduate Recruitment and Admissions Associate, 716-673-3808, Fax: 716-673-3712, E-mail: wendy.dunst@fredonia.edu.
Website: http://www.fredonia.edu/clas/

State University of New York at Plattsburgh, School of Education, Health, and Human Services, Program in Teacher Education: Adolescence Education, Plattsburgh, NY 12901-2681. Offers adolescence education (MST); biology 7-12 (MST); chemistry 7-12 (MST); earth science 7-12 (MST); English 7-12 (MST); French 7-12 (MST); mathematics 7-12 (MST); physics 7-12 (MST); social studies 7-12 (MST); Spanish 7-12 (MST). *Accreditation:* TEAC. *Program availability:* Part-time, evening/weekend. *Entrance requirements:* For master's, minimum GPA of 2.75. Additional exam requirements/recommendations for international students: Required—TOEFL.

State University of New York College at Cortland, Graduate Studies, School of Arts and Sciences, Programs in Adolescence Education, Cortland, NY 13045. Offers biology (MAT); chemistry (MAT); English (MAT, MS Ed); mathematics (MAT); mathematics and physics (MS Ed); physics (MAT, MS Ed). *Accreditation:* NCATE. *Program availability:* Part-time, evening/weekend. *Degree requirements:* For master's, one foreign language, comprehensive exam (for some programs), thesis (for some programs). *Entrance requirements:* For master's, GRE General Test.

State University of New York College at Old Westbury, School of Education, Old Westbury, NY 11568-0210. Offers biology (MAT, MS); chemistry (MAT, MS); English language arts (MAT, MS); math (MAT, MS); social studies (MAT, MS); Spanish (MAT, MS). *Program availability:* Part-time, evening/weekend. *Students:* 164 full-time (80 women), 112 part-time (52 women); includes 87 minority (14 Black or African American, non-Hispanic/Latino; 38 Asian, non-Hispanic/Latino; 35 Hispanic/Latino), 2 international. Average age 30. 34 applicants, 82% accepted, 25 enrolled. In 2017, 25 master's awarded. *Entrance requirements:* For master's, Liberal Arts and Sciences Test, undergraduate degree with at least 30 semester hours of appropriate coursework as defined by the respective discipline; minimum cumulative undergraduate GPA of 3.0;

two letters of recommendation (one from an academic source); essay. Additional exam requirements/recommendations for international students: Required—TOEFL (minimum score 550 paper-based); Recommended—IELTS. Application fee: $50. *Financial support:* Applicants required to submit FAFSA. *Unit head:* Dr. Nancy Brown, Dean, School of Education, 516-876-3275, E-mail: brownn@oldwestbury.edu. *Application contact:* Philip D'Angelo, Graduate Admissions Office, 516-876-3073, E-mail: enroll@oldwestbury.edu.

State University of New York College at Potsdam, School of Education and Professional Studies, Program in Secondary Education, Potsdam, NY 13676. Offers English education (MST); mathematics education (MST); science education (MST), including biology, chemistry, earth science, physics; social studies education (MST). *Accreditation:* NCATE. *Degree requirements:* For master's, culminating experience. *Entrance requirements:* For master's, minimum GPA of 2.75 in last 60 hours of course work (3.0 for English program). Additional exam requirements/recommendations for international students: Required—TOEFL (minimum score 550 paper-based; 80 iBT), IELTS (minimum score 6). Electronic applications accepted.

Stephen F. Austin State University, Graduate School, College of Sciences and Mathematics, Department of Mathematics and Statistics, Nacogdoches, TX 75962. Offers mathematics (MS); mathematics education (MS); statistics (MS). *Degree requirements:* For master's, comprehensive exam, thesis optional. *Entrance requirements:* For master's, GRE General Test, minimum GPA of 2.8 in last 60 hours, 2.5 overall. Additional exam requirements/recommendations for international students: Required—TOEFL. *Faculty research:* Kernel type estimators, fractal mappings, spline curve fitting, robust regression continua theory.

Stevenson University, Master of Arts in Teaching Program, Stevenson, MD 21153. Offers secondary biology (MAT); secondary chemistry (MAT); secondary mathematics (MAT). *Program availability:* Part-time, blended/hybrid learning. *Faculty:* 5 part-time/adjunct (all women). *Students:* 18 part-time (11 women); includes 6 minority (2 Black or African American, non-Hispanic/Latino; 2 Asian, non-Hispanic/Latino; 1 Hispanic/Latino; 1 Two or more races, non-Hispanic/Latino). Average age 31. 8 applicants, 100% accepted, 8 enrolled. *Degree requirements:* For master's, internship, portfolio, action research project. *Entrance requirements:* For master's, PRAXIS, GRE, SAT, or ACT, official transcripts from each college or university attended verifying completion of baccalaureate degree in a science or math discipline from regionally-accredited institution. *Application deadline:* Applications are processed on a rolling basis. Electronic applications accepted. *Expenses:* Contact institution. *Financial support:* Unspecified assistantships available. Financial award applicants required to submit FAFSA. *Unit head:* Anne P. Davis, Associate Dean of Teacher Education. *Application contact:* Amanda Courter, Senior Enrollment Counselor, 443-352-4243, Fax: 443-352-4440, E-mail: acourter@stevenson.edu.
Website: http://www.stevenson.edu/online/academics/online-graduate-programs/master-arts-teaching/

Stony Brook University, State University of New York, School of Professional Development, Stony Brook, NY 11794. Offers biology (MAT); chemistry (MAT); coaching (Graduate Certificate); earth science (MAT); educational computing (Graduate Certificate); educational leadership (Advanced Certificate); English (MAT); environmental management (MPS, Graduate Certificate); French (MAT); German (MAT); higher education administration (MA, Certificate); human resource management (MS, Graduate Certificate); industrial management (Graduate Certificate); information systems management (Graduate Certificate); Italian (MAT); liberal studies (MA); mathematics (MAT); operations research (Graduate Certificate); physics (MAT); school district business leadership (Advanced Certificate); social studies (MAT); Spanish (MAT). *Program availability:* Part-time, evening/weekend, online learning. *Faculty:* 3 full-time (2 women), 101 part-time/adjunct (45 women). *Students:* 190 full-time (126 women), 974 part-time (708 women); includes 255 minority (88 Black or African American, non-Hispanic/Latino; 2 American Indian or Alaska Native, non-Hispanic/Latino; 31 Asian, non-Hispanic/Latino; 113 Hispanic/Latino; 1 Native Hawaiian or other Pacific Islander, non-Hispanic/Latino; 20 Two or more races, non-Hispanic/Latino), 6 international. Average age 33. 411 applicants, 91% accepted, 288 enrolled. In 2017, 333 master's, 180 other advanced degrees awarded. *Entrance requirements:* Additional exam requirements/recommendations for international students: Required—TOEFL (minimum score 85 iBT). *Application deadline:* For fall admission, 1/15 for domestic students, 6/1 for international students; for spring admission, 10/1 for domestic and international students. Applications are processed on a rolling basis. Application fee: $100. *Expenses:* Contact institution. *Financial support:* Fellowships, research assistantships, teaching assistantships, and career-related internships or fieldwork available. Support available to part-time students. *Unit head:* Dr. Ken Lindblom, Dean, 631-632-7049, Fax: 631-632-9046, E-mail: kenneth.lindblom@stonybrook.edu. *Application contact:* Melissa Jordan, Assistant Dean, 631-632-7751, E-mail: melissa.jordan@stonybrook.edu.
Website: http://www.stonybrook.edu/spd/

Syracuse University, College of Arts and Sciences, Department of Mathematics, Syracuse, NY 13244. Offers math education (PhD); mathematics (MS, PhD); mathematics education (MS). *Program availability:* Part-time. In 2017, 11 master's, 3 doctorates awarded. Terminal master's awarded for partial completion of doctoral program. *Degree requirements:* For doctorate, 2 foreign languages, comprehensive exam, thesis/dissertation. *Entrance requirements:* For master's and doctorate, GRE General Test, GRE Subject Test (recommended), brief (about 500 words) statement indicating why applicant wishes to pursue graduate study and why Syracuse is a good fit, curriculum vitae or resume, transcripts from each post-secondary institution, three letters of recommendation. Additional exam requirements/recommendations for international students: Required—TOEFL (minimum score 100 iBT). *Application deadline:* For fall admission, 1/20 priority date for domestic and international students. Application fee: $75. Electronic applications accepted. *Financial support:* Teaching assistantships with tuition reimbursements, scholarships/grants, and tuition waivers available. Financial award applicants required to submit FAFSA. *Faculty research:* Pure mathematics, numerical mathematics, computing statistics. *Unit head:* Dr. Uday Banerjee, Chair, 315-443-1471, E-mail: banerjee@syr.edu. *Application contact:* Graham Leuschke, Professor and Associate Chair for Graduate Affairs, 315-443-1500, E-mail: gjleusch@syr.edu.
Website: http://math.syr.edu

Syracuse University, School of Education, Programs in Mathematics Education, Syracuse, NY 13244. Offers MS, PhD. *Program availability:* Part-time. *Students:* Average age 30. *Degree requirements:* For master's, thesis or alternative; for doctorate, comprehensive exam, thesis/dissertation. *Entrance requirements:* For master's, GRE or MAT, baccalaureate degree from regionally-accredited college/university, transcripts, personal essay; for doctorate, GRE, master's degree, transcripts. Additional exam requirements/recommendations for international students: Required—TOEFL (minimum score 100 iBT). *Application deadline:* For fall admission, 1/15 priority date for domestic and international students; for spring admission, 10/15 priority date for domestic and international students. Applications are processed on a rolling basis. Application fee: $75. Electronic applications accepted. *Financial support:* Fellowships with full tuition reimbursements, research assistantships, teaching assistantships, career-related

internships or fieldwork, and scholarships/grants available. Financial award application deadline: 1/15. *Unit head:* Dr. Joanna Masingila, Dean and Professor, 315-443-4751, E-mail: jomasing@syr.edu. *Application contact:* Speranza Migliore, Graduate Admissions Recruiter, 315-443-2505, E-mail: gradrcrt@syr.edu.
Website: http://soe.syr.edu/academic/teaching_and_leadership/graduate/masters/mathematics_education/

Teachers College, Columbia University, Department of Mathematics, Science and Technology, New York, NY 10027-6696. Offers biology 7-12 (MA); chemistry 7-12 (MA); communication and education (MA, Ed D); computing in education (MA); earth science 7-12 (MA); instructional technology and media (Ed M, MA, Ed D); mathematics education (Ed M, MA, Ed D, Ed DCT, PhD); physics 7-12 (MA); science and dental education (MA); science education (Ed M, MS, Ed DCT, PhD); supervisor/teacher of science education (MA); technology specialist (MA). *Program availability:* Part-time, evening/weekend, online learning. *Students:* 187 full-time (129 women), 228 part-time (153 women); includes 143 minority (42 Black or African American, non-Hispanic/Latino; 64 Asian, non-Hispanic/Latino; 25 Hispanic/Latino; 12 Two or more races, non-Hispanic/Latino; 125 international. Average age 32. 484 applicants, 59% accepted, 141 enrolled. Terminal master's awarded for partial completion of doctoral program. *Degree requirements:* For doctorate, thesis/dissertation. *Unit head:* Prof. Erica Walker, Chair, E-mail: ewalker@tc.columbia.edu. *Application contact:* David Estrella, Director of Admission, 212-678-3305, E-mail: estrella@tc.columbia.edu.
Website: http://www.tc.columbia.edu/mathematics-science-and-technology/

Teachers College of San Joaquin, Master's Program in Education, Stockton, CA 95206. Offers early education (M Ed); educational inquiry (M Ed); educational leadership and school development (M Ed); science, technology, engineering, and mathematics (M Ed); special education (M Ed).

Temple University, College of Education, Department of Teaching and Learning, Philadelphia, PA 19122-6096. Offers career and technical education (Ed M), including business, computing, and information technology, industrial education, marketing education; middle grades education (Ed M), including math and language arts, math and science, science and language arts; secondary education (Ed M), including English, math, social studies; teaching English to speakers of other languages (MS Ed); urban education (Ed M). *Program availability:* Part-time, evening/weekend. *Students:* 218 full-time (144 women), 296 part-time (183 women); includes 128 minority (74 Black or African American, non-Hispanic/Latino; 18 Asian, non-Hispanic/Latino; 25 Hispanic/Latino; 11 Two or more races, non-Hispanic/Latino), 13 international. 254 applicants, 54% accepted, 102 enrolled. In 2017, 128 master's awarded. Terminal master's awarded for partial completion of doctoral program. *Degree requirements:* For master's, thesis or alternative. *Entrance requirements:* Additional exam requirements/recommendations for international students: Required—TOEFL (minimum score 550 paper-based; 79 iBT). *Application deadline:* For fall admission, 4/1 for domestic students, 12/15 for international students; for spring admission, 10/1 for domestic students, 8/1 for international students. Application fee: $60. Electronic applications accepted. *Expenses:* Contact institution. *Financial support:* Fellowships, research assistantships, and teaching assistantships available. Financial award application deadline: 1/15; financial award applicants required to submit FAFSA. *Faculty research:* Workforce development, vocational education, technical education, industrial education, professional development, literacy, classroom management, school communities, curriculum development, instruction, applied linguistics, cross linguistic influence, bilingual education, oral proficiency, multilingualism. *Unit head:* Dr. Christine Woyshner, Chairperson, 215-204-6387, E-mail: christine.woyshner@temple.edu. *Application contact:* Sarah Stapleton, Assistant Director, Academic Operations, 215-204-8220, E-mail: sarah.stapleton@temple.edu.
Website: http://education.temple.edu/tl

Tennessee Technological University, College of Graduate Studies, College of Education, Department of Curriculum and Instruction, Program in STEM Education, Cookeville, TN 38505. Offers MA, Ed S. *Program availability:* Part-time, evening/weekend. *Students:* 2 full-time (1 woman), 4 part-time (3 women); includes 1 minority (Two or more races, non-Hispanic/Latino). 4 applicants, 100% accepted, 3 enrolled. In 2017, 2 master's awarded. *Degree requirements:* For master's, comprehensive exam, thesis or alternative. *Entrance requirements:* For master's, GRE, MAT. Additional exam requirements/recommendations for international students: Required—TOEFL (minimum score 527 paper-based; 71 iBT), IELTS (minimum score 5.5) or PTE (48). *Application deadline:* For fall admission, 8/1 for domestic students, 5/1 for international students; for spring admission, 2/1 for domestic students, 10/1 for international students; for summer admission, 5/1 for domestic students, 2/1 for international students. Applications are processed on a rolling basis. Application fee: $35 ($40 for international students). Electronic applications accepted. *Expenses:* Tuition, state resident: full-time $9925; part-time $565 per credit hour. Tuition, nonresident: full-time $22,993; part-time $1291 per credit hour. *Financial support:* Application deadline: 4/1. *Unit head:* Dr. Jeremy Wendt, Interim Chairperson, 931-372-3181, E-mail: jwendt@tntech.edu. *Application contact:* Shelia K. Kendrick, Coordinator of Graduate Studies, 931-372-3808, Fax: 931-372-3497, E-mail: skendrick@tntech.edu.

Texas Christian University, College of Education, Master's Programs in Education, Fort Worth, TX 76129. Offers counseling (M Ed); curriculum and instruction (M Ed), including curriculum studies, language and literacy, math education, science education; education (MAT); educational leadership (M Ed); special education (M Ed). *Program availability:* Part-time, evening/weekend. *Faculty:* 29 full-time (21 women), 3 part-time/adjunct (1 woman). *Students:* 124 full-time (94 women), 14 part-time (12 women); includes 52 minority (14 Black or African American, non-Hispanic/Latino; 2 American Indian or Alaska Native, non-Hispanic/Latino; 3 Asian, non-Hispanic/Latino; 28 Hispanic/Latino; 5 Two or more races, non-Hispanic/Latino), 1 international. Average age 28. 172 applicants, 69% accepted, 86 enrolled. In 2017, 62 master's awarded. *Degree requirements:* For master's, comprehensive exam (for some programs), thesis (for some programs). *Entrance requirements:* For master's, GRE General Test; Pre-Admission Content Test (for MAT). Additional exam requirements/recommendations for international students: Required—TOEFL (minimum score 550 paper-based; 80 iBT). *Application deadline:* For fall admission, 3/1 for domestic and international students; for spring admission, 11/16 for domestic and international students; for summer admission, 3/1 for domestic and international students. Application fee: $60. Electronic applications accepted. *Financial support:* In 2017-18, 124 students received support, including 1 research assistantship with full tuition reimbursement available (averaging $15,000 per year), 29 teaching assistantships with full tuition reimbursements available (averaging $15,000 per year); career-related internships or fieldwork, scholarships/grants, and unspecified assistantships also available. Support available to part-time students. Financial award application deadline: 3/1. *Unit head:* Dr. Jan Lacina, Associate Dean, 817-257-6786, Fax: 817-257-7466, E-mail: j.lacina@tcu.edu. *Application contact:* Lori Kimball, Administrative Program Specialist, 817-257-7661, Fax: 817-257-7466, E-mail: l.kimball@tcu.edu.
Website: http://coe.tcu.edu/graduate-overview/

Texas State University, The Graduate College, College of Science and Engineering, PhD Program in Mathematics Education, San Marcos, TX 78666. Offers PhD. *Program availability:* Part-time. *Faculty:* 9 full-time (2 women), 1 part-time/adjunct (0 women).

Students: 22 full-time (16 women), 5 part-time (3 women); includes 4 minority (1 Black or African American, non-Hispanic/Latino; 1 Hispanic/Latino; 2 Two or more races, non-Hispanic/Latino), 8 international. Average age 35. 15 applicants, 67% accepted, 5 enrolled. In 2017, 4 doctorates awarded. *Degree requirements:* For doctorate, comprehensive exam, thesis/dissertation. *Entrance requirements:* For doctorate, GRE (minimum preferred score of 300 verbal and quantitative combined), baccalaureate degree from regionally-accredited university with minimum GPA of 3.0 on last 60 undergraduate semester hours, 500-word statement of purpose, current curriculum vitae, 3 letters of recommendation, interview with faculty, 2 years of teaching experience. Additional exam requirements/recommendations for international students: Required—TOEFL (minimum score 550 paper-based; 78 iBT), IELTS (minimum score 6.5). *Application deadline:* For fall admission, 1/10 for domestic and international students; for spring admission, 8/10 for domestic and international students. Application fee: $40 ($90 for international students). Electronic applications accepted. *Expenses:* Tuition, state resident: full-time $7868; part-time $3934 per semester. Tuition, nonresident: full-time $17,828; part-time $8914 per semester. *Required fees:* $2092; $1435 per semester. Tuition and fees vary according to course load. *Financial support:* In 2017–18, 18 students received support, including 23 teaching assistantships (averaging $27,095 per year); research assistantships, Federal Work-Study, institutionally sponsored loans, scholarships/grants, health care benefits, and unspecified assistantships also available. Support available to part-time students. Financial award application deadline: 3/1; financial award applicants required to submit FAFSA. *Faculty research:* Characterizing critical aspects of mathematics classroom discourse, enhancing mathematics teaching and learning in urban elementary schools, meadows foundation - math works algebra program, Mathematics Instruction for English Language Learners (MI-ELL), dynamic geometry in classrooms. *Total annual research expenditures:* $323,014. *Unit head:* Dr. Alexander White, PhD Program Director, 512-245-2551, E-mail: aw22@txstate.edu. *Application contact:* Dr. Andrea Golato, Dean of the Graduate College, 512-245-2581, Fax: 512-245-8365, E-mail: gradcollege@txstate.edu.
Website: http://www.math.txstate.edu/math-ed/

Texas State University, The Graduate College, College of Science and Engineering, Program in Middle School Mathematics Teaching, San Marcos, TX 78666. Offers M Ed. *Program availability:* Part-time. *Faculty:* 9 full-time (2 women), 1 part-time/adjunct (0 women). *Students:* 1 applicant. In 2017, 5 master's awarded. *Degree requirements:* For master's, comprehensive exam. *Entrance requirements:* For master's, GRE (minimum preferred score of 300 verbal and quantitative combined), baccalaureate degree in mathematics or related field from regionally-accredited university with minimum GPA of 2.75 on last 60 undergraduate semester hours, resume, statement of purpose, 3 letters of recommendation addressing the substance and quality of preparation for graduate study. Additional exam requirements/recommendations for international students: Required—TOEFL (minimum score 550 paper-based; 78 iBT), IELTS (minimum score 6.5). *Application deadline:* For fall admission, 2/1 priority date for domestic and international students; for spring admission, 10/15 for domestic students, 10/1 for international students; for summer admission, 4/15 for domestic students, 3/15 for international students. Applications are processed on a rolling basis. Application fee: $40 ($90 for international students). Electronic applications accepted. *Expenses:* Tuition, state resident: full-time $7868; part-time $3934 per semester. Tuition, nonresident: full-time $17,828; part-time $8914 per semester. *Required fees:* $2092; $1435 per semester. Tuition and fees vary according to course load. *Financial support:* Teaching assistantships, Federal Work-Study, institutionally sponsored loans, health care benefits, and unspecified assistantships available. Support available to part-time students. Financial award application deadline: 3/1; financial award applicants required to submit FAFSA. *Faculty research:* Characterizing critical aspects of mathematics classroom discourse. *Total annual research expenditures:* $68,208. *Unit head:* Dr. Gregory Passty, Graduate Advisor, 512-245-2551, Fax: 512-245-3425, E-mail: gp02@txstate.edu. *Application contact:* Dr. Andrea Golato, Dean of the Graduate College, 512-245-2581, E-mail: gradcollege@txstate.edu.
Website: http://www.txstate.edu/math/degrees-programs/masters/middle-school.html

Texas Woman's University, Graduate School, College of Arts and Sciences, Department of Mathematics and Computer Science, Denton, TX 76204. Offers emphasis in mathematics or computer science (MAT); informatics (MS); mathematics (MS); mathematics teaching (MS). *Program availability:* Part-time, evening/weekend. *Faculty:* 12 full-time (7 women). *Students:* 21 full-time (15 women), 59 part-time (43 women); includes 40 minority (15 Black or African American, non-Hispanic/Latino; 14 Asian, non-Hispanic/Latino; 9 Hispanic/Latino; 2 Two or more races, non-Hispanic/Latino), 3 international. Average age 37. 30 applicants, 90% accepted, 22 enrolled. In 2017, 10 master's awarded. *Degree requirements:* For master's, comprehensive exam, thesis (for some programs), professional paper, capstone or thesis (depending on degree). *Entrance requirements:* For master's, minimum GPA of 3.0 in last 60 undergraduate credit hours, 2 semesters of calculus, 2 additional advanced math courses, 2 letters of reference (for MS in mathematics, mathematics teaching); minimum GPA of 3.0, statement of intent, resume, 2 letters of recommendation (for MS in informatics). Additional exam requirements/recommendations for international students: Required—TOEFL (minimum score 550 paper-based; 79 iBT); Recommended—IELTS (minimum score 6.5), TSE (minimum score 53). *Application deadline:* For fall admission, 3/1 priority date for domestic and international students; for spring admission, 11/1 priority date for domestic students, 7/1 priority date for international students. Applications are processed on a rolling basis. Application fee: $50 ($75 for international students). Electronic applications accepted. *Expenses:* $7,520 per year full-time in-state; $16,820 per year full-time out-of-state. *Financial support:* In 2017–18, 16 students received support, including 3 teaching assistantships (averaging $22,300 per year); career-related internships or fieldwork, Federal Work-Study, institutionally sponsored loans, scholarships/grants, traineeships, health care benefits, and unspecified assistantships also available. Support available to part-time students. Financial award application deadline: 3/1; financial award applicants required to submit FAFSA. *Faculty research:* Optimal control theory and differential games, information security, statistics and modern approaches, knot theory, math education. *Total annual research expenditures:* $55,000. *Unit head:* Dr. Don E. Edwards, Chair, 940-898-2166, Fax: 940-898-2179, E-mail: mathcs@twu.edu. *Application contact:* Korie Hawkins, Associate Director of Admissions, Graduate Recruitment, 940-898-3188, Fax: 940-898-3081, E-mail: admissions@twu.edu.
Website: http://www.twu.edu/math-computer-science/

Touro College, Graduate School of Education, New York, NY 10010. Offers education and special education (MS); instructional technology (MS); mathematics education (MS); school leadership (MS); teaching English to speakers of other languages (MS); teaching literacy (MS). *Accreditation:* TEAC. *Program availability:* Part-time, evening/weekend, online learning. *Faculty:* 52 full-time (34 women), 199 part-time/adjunct (136 women). *Students:* 756 full-time (686 women), 3,833 part-time (3,492 women). Average age 33. 1,422 applicants, 50% accepted, 675 enrolled. In 2017, 6 master's awarded. *Entrance requirements:* Additional exam requirements/recommendations for international students: Required—TOEFL (minimum score 83 iBT), IELTS (minimum score 6.5). *Application deadline:* For fall admission, 8/26 for domestic students, 7/15 for international students; for spring admission, 12/31 for domestic students, 12/15 for international students. Applications are processed on a rolling basis. Application fee: $50. *Financial support:* Federal Work-Study available. Financial award applicants required to submit FAFSA. *Faculty research:* Equity assistance, language development, scholarly communications, Latin American studies and cultural sensitivity, behavior management techniques and strategies in special education. *Unit head:* Dr. Jacob Easley, III, Dean, 212-463-0400 Ext. 5561, Fax: 212-462-4889, E-mail: jeasley@touro.edu. *Application contact:* Sharmilee Hoopnarine, Admissions, 212-463-0400.

Towson University, Jess and Mildred Fisher College of Science and Mathematics, Program in Mathematics Education, Towson, MD 21252-0001. Offers MS. *Accreditation:* NCATE. *Program availability:* Part-time, evening/weekend. *Students:* 1 (woman) full-time, 32 part-time (27 women); includes 4 minority (3 Black or African American, non-Hispanic/Latino; 1 Asian, non-Hispanic/Latino), 1 international. *Entrance requirements:* For master's, undergraduate degree in mathematics or elementary education, current certification for teaching secondary school or elementary school mathematics, minimum GPA of 3.0. *Application deadline:* For fall admission, 1/17 for domestic students, 5/15 for international students; for spring admission, 10/15 for domestic students, 12/1 for international students. Applications are processed on a rolling basis. Application fee: $45. Electronic applications accepted. *Expenses:* Tuition, state resident: full-time $7960; part-time $398 per unit. Tuition, nonresident: full-time $16,480; part-time $824 per unit. *Required fees:* $2600; $130 per year. $390 per term. *Financial support:* Application deadline: 4/1. *Unit head:* Dr. Sandy Spitzer, Graduate Program Director, 410-704-2062, E-mail: sspitzer@towson.edu. *Application contact:* Coverley Beidleman, Assistant Director of Graduate Admissions, 410-704-5630, Fax: 410-704-3030, E-mail: cbeidleman@towson.edu.
Website: http://www.towson.edu/fcsm/departments/mathematics/grad/education/

Tufts University, Graduate School of Arts and Sciences, Department of Education, Program in Education, Medford, MA 02155. Offers educational studies (MA); elementary education (MAT); middle and secondary education (MAT); museum education (MA); secondary education (MA); STEM education (MS, PhD). *Program availability:* Part-time. *Students:* 50 full-time (38 women), 9 part-time (8 women); includes 9 minority (2 Black or African American, non-Hispanic/Latino; 2 Asian, non-Hispanic/Latino; 4 Hispanic/Latino; 1 Two or more races, non-Hispanic/Latino), 4 international. Average age 28. 120 applicants, 71% accepted, 49 enrolled. In 2017, 51 master's awarded. *Degree requirements:* For master's, thesis optional. *Entrance requirements:* For master's, GRE General Test, portfolio (for art education only); for doctorate, GRE General Test, writing sample. Additional exam requirements/recommendations for international students: Required—TOEFL (minimum score 550 paper-based; 80 iBT), IELTS (minimum score 6.5). *Application deadline:* For fall admission, 1/2 for domestic and international students; for spring admission, 10/15 for domestic and international students. Applications are processed on a rolling basis. Application fee: $85. Electronic applications accepted. *Expenses:* Contact institution. *Financial support:* Research assistantships, teaching assistantships, Federal Work-Study, scholarships/grants, and tuition waivers (full and partial) available. Support available to part-time students. Financial award application deadline: 1/2. *Unit head:* Dr. David Hammer, Graduate Program Director, 617-627-2396. *Application contact:* Office of Graduate Admissions, 617-627-3395, E-mail: gradadmissions@tufts.edu.

Universidad Autonoma de Guadalajara, Graduate Programs, Guadalajara, Mexico. Offers administrative law and justice (LL M); advertising and corporate communications (MA); architecture (M Arch); business (MBA); computational science (MCC); education (Ed M, Ed D); English-Spanish translation (MA); entrepreneurship and management (MBA); integrated management of digital animation (MA); international business (MIB); international corporate law (LL M); internet technologies (MS); manufacturing systems (MMS); occupational health (MS); philosophy (MA, PhD); power electronics (MS); quality systems (MQS); renewable energy (MS); social evaluation of projects (MBA); strategic market research (MBA); tax law (MA); teaching mathematics (MA).

University at Buffalo, the State University of New York, Graduate School, Graduate School of Education, Department of Learning and Instruction, Buffalo, NY 14260. Offers biology education (Ed M, Certificate); chemistry education (Ed M, Certificate); childhood education (Ed M); childhood education with bilingual extension (Ed M); college teaching (Advanced Certificate); curriculum, instruction and the science of learning (PhD); early childhood education (Ed M); early childhood education with bilingual extension (Ed M); earth science education (Ed M, Certificate); education and technology (Ed M); education studies (Ed M); educational technology and new literacies (Certificate); educational technology and new literacies (Advanced Certificate); elementary education (Ed D); English education (Ed M, Certificate); English education studies (Ed M); English for speakers of other languages (Ed M); foreign and second language education (PhD); French education (Ed M, Certificate); German education (Ed M, Certificate); gifted education (Certificate); Latin education (Ed M, Certificate); literacy education studies (Ed M); literacy specialist (Ed M); literacy teaching and learning (Certificate); mathematics education (Ed M, Certificate); music education (Ed M, Certificate); music education studies (Ed M); music learning theory (Advanced Certificate); online education (Advanced Certificate); physics education (Ed M, Certificate); science and the public (Ed M); social studies education (Ed M, Certificate); Spanish education (Ed M, Certificate); special education (PhD); teaching English to speakers of other languages (Ed M). *Program availability:* Part-time, evening/weekend, 100% online. *Faculty:* 26 full-time (19 women), 74 part-time/adjunct (52 women). *Students:* 172 full-time (122 women), 325 part-time (226 women); includes 44 minority (25 Black or African American, non-Hispanic/Latino; 5 American Indian or Alaska Native, non-Hispanic/Latino; 14 Asian, non-Hispanic/Latino), 57 international. Average age 33. 316 applicants, 78% accepted, 174 enrolled. In 2017, 109 master's, 34 doctorates, 15 other advanced degrees awarded. *Degree requirements:* For master's, comprehensive exam; for doctorate, thesis/dissertation, research analysis exam, research experience. *Entrance requirements:* For master's, letters of reference; for doctorate, GRE General Test or MAT, interview, writing sample, letters of recommendation. Additional exam requirements/recommendations for international students: Required—TOEFL (minimum score 600 paper-based; 96 iBT). *Application deadline:* For fall admission, 2/1 priority date for domestic and international students; for spring admission, 11/15 priority date for domestic students, 10/1 for international students. Applications are processed on a rolling basis. Application fee: $50. Electronic applications accepted. *Financial support:* In 2017–18, 42 fellowships (averaging $5,181 per year), 44 research assistantships with tuition reimbursements (averaging $10,908 per year) were awarded; teaching assistantships, career-related internships or fieldwork, Federal Work-Study, institutionally sponsored loans, scholarships/grants, tuition waivers (full and partial), and unspecified assistantships also available. Financial award application deadline: 2/28; financial award applicants required to submit FAFSA. *Faculty research:* Science assessment, foreign language teaching and learning, early learning, new literacies, gender and education. *Total annual research expenditures:* $413,233. *Unit head:* Dr. David Bruce, Chair, 716-645-4069, Fax: 716-645-3161, E-mail: gse-info@buffalo.edu. *Application contact:* Luann Zak, Admissions Assistant, 716-645-2110, Fax: 716-645-7937, E-mail: luannzak@buffalo.edu.
Website: http://gse.buffalo.edu/lai

The University of Akron, Graduate School, College of Education, Department of Curricular and Instructional Studies, Program in Adolescent to Young Adult Education, Akron, OH 44325. Offers chemistry (MS); chemistry and physics (MS); earth science

(MS); earth science and chemistry (MS); earth science and physics (MS); integrated language arts (MS); integrated mathematics (MS); integrated social studies (MS); life science (MS); life science and chemistry (MS); life science and earth science (MS); life science and physics (MS); physics (MS). *Accreditation:* NCATE. *Students:* 16 full-time (6 women), 6 part-time (3 women); includes 6 minority (2 Black or African American, non-Hispanic/Latino; 1 Asian, non-Hispanic/Latino; 3 Two or more races, non-Hispanic/Latino). Average age 30. 8 applicants, 100% accepted, 8 enrolled. In 2017, 8 master's awarded. *Degree requirements:* For master's, comprehensive exam. *Entrance requirements:* For master's, minimum GPA of 3.0. Additional exam requirements/recommendations for international students: Required—TOEFL (minimum score 79 iBT), IELTS (minimum score 6.5). *Application deadline:* For fall admission, 3/1 for domestic and international students; for spring admission, 10/1 for domestic and international students. Applications are processed on a rolling basis. Application fee: $45 ($70 for international students). Electronic applications accepted. *Unit head:* Dr. Evonn Welton, Interim Department Chair, 330-972-6742, E-mail: ewelton@uakron.edu. *Application contact:* Kelly Chaff, College Program Specialist, 330-972-7028, E-mail: klchaff@uakron.edu.
Website: http://www.uakron.edu/education/academic-programs/graduate-programs.dot

The University of Alabama in Huntsville, School of Graduate Studies, College of Education, Huntsville, AL 35899. Offers autism spectrum disorders (M Ed, Graduate Certificate); biology (MAT); chemistry (MAT); differentiated instruction in elementary education (M Ed); English language arts (MAT); English speakers of other languages (M Ed, MAT); history (MAT); mathematics (MAT); physics (MAT); reading education (M Ed); secondary education (M Ed).

The University of Alabama in Huntsville, School of Graduate Studies, College of Science, Department of Mathematical Sciences, Huntsville, AL 35899. Offers applied mathematics (PhD); education (MA); mathematics (MA, MS). PhD offered jointly with The University of Alabama (Tuscaloosa) and The University of Alabama at Birmingham. *Program availability:* Part-time, evening/weekend. *Degree requirements:* For master's, comprehensive exam, thesis or alternative, oral and written exams; for doctorate, comprehensive exam, thesis/dissertation, oral and written exams. *Entrance requirements:* For master's and doctorate, GRE General Test, minimum GPA of 3.0. Additional exam requirements/recommendations for international students: Required—TOEFL (minimum score 550 paper-based; 80 iBT), IELTS (minimum score 6.5). Electronic applications accepted. *Faculty research:* Combinatorics and graph theory, computational mathematics, differential equations and applications, mathematical biology, probability and stochastic processes.

University of Alaska Southeast, Graduate Programs, Program in Education, Juneau, AK 99801. Offers educational leadership (M Ed); elementary education (MAT); learning design and technology (M Ed); mathematics education (M Ed); reading specialist (M Ed); secondary education (MAT); special education (M Ed, MAT). *Accreditation:* NCATE. *Program availability:* Part-time, evening/weekend, online learning. *Degree requirements:* For master's, comprehensive exam or project, portfolio. *Entrance requirements:* For master's, PRAXIS, minimum GPA of 3.0, writing sample, letters of recommendation. Electronic applications accepted. *Faculty research:* Applied classroom research, culturally responsive practices, action research, teaching effectiveness.

The University of Arizona, College of Science, Department of Mathematics, Program in Secondary Mathematics Education, Tucson, AZ 85721. Offers MA. *Program availability:* Part-time. *Degree requirements:* For master's, thesis, internships, colloquium, business courses. *Entrance requirements:* For master's, GRE, minimum GPA of 3.0, statement of purpose. Additional exam requirements/recommendations for international students: Required—TOEFL (minimum score 550 paper-based). *Faculty research:* Algebra, coding theory, graph theory, combinatorics, probability.

University of Arkansas, Graduate School, J. William Fulbright College of Arts and Sciences, Department of Mathematical Sciences, Program in Secondary Mathematics, Fayetteville, AR 72701. Offers MA. *Accreditation:* NCATE. In 2017, 2 master's awarded. *Degree requirements:* For master's, written exam. *Application deadline:* For fall admission, 8/1 for domestic students, 4/1 for international students; for spring admission, 12/1 for domestic students, 10/1 for international students; for summer admission, 4/15 for domestic students, 3/1 for international students. Applications are processed on a rolling basis. Application fee: $60. Electronic applications accepted. *Expenses:* Tuition, state resident: full-time $3782. Tuition, nonresident: full-time $10,238. *Financial support:* In 2017–18, 1 teaching assistantship was awarded; fellowships, research assistantships, career-related internships or fieldwork, and Federal Work-Study also available. Support available to part-time students. Financial award application deadline: 4/1; financial award applicants required to submit FAFSA. *Unit head:* Dr. Mark Johnson, Chair, 479-575-3351, Fax: 479-575-8630, E-mail: markj@uark.edu. *Application contact:* Dr. Maria Tjani, Graduate Coordinator, 479-575-3351, Fax: 479-575-8630, E-mail: mtjani@uark.edu.
Website: https://fulbright.uark.edu/departments/math/C

University of Arkansas at Pine Bluff, School of Education, Pine Bluff, AR 71601-2799. Offers elementary education (M Ed); secondary education (M Ed), including English education, mathematics education, science education, social studies education; teaching (MAT). *Accreditation:* NCATE. *Program availability:* Part-time, evening/weekend. *Degree requirements:* For master's, comprehensive exam. *Entrance requirements:* For master's, GRE, minimum GPA of 2.75, NTE or Standard Arkansas Teaching Certificate. *Faculty research:* Teacher certification, accreditation, assessment, standards, portfolio development, rehabilitation, technology.

The University of British Columbia, Faculty of Education, Department of Curriculum and Pedagogy, Vancouver, BC V6T 1Z4, Canada. Offers art education (M Ed, MA); curriculum studies (M Ed, MA, PhD); home economics education (M Ed, MA); mathematics education (M Ed, MA); media and technology studies education (M Ed, MA); music education (M Ed, MA); physical education (M Ed, MA); science education (M Ed, MA); social studies education (M Ed, MA). *Program availability:* Part-time, online learning. *Degree requirements:* For master's, thesis (MA); for doctorate, comprehensive exam, thesis/dissertation. *Entrance requirements:* For master's, Additional exam requirements/recommendations for international students: Required—TOEFL, IELTS. Electronic applications accepted. *Expenses:* Contact institution. *Faculty research:* School subjects, teaching and learning.

University of California, Berkeley, Graduate Division, School of Education, Group in Science and Mathematics Education, Berkeley, CA 94720-1500. Offers PhD, MA/Credential. Electronic applications accepted.

University of California, Berkeley, Graduate Division, School of Education, Programs in Education, Berkeley, CA 94720-1500. Offers development in mathematics and science (MA); education in mathematics, science, and technology (MA, PhD); human development and education (MA, PhD); leadership education (MA); special education (PhD); teacher education (MA); MA/Credential; PhD/Credential; PhD/MA. Terminal master's awarded for partial completion of doctoral program. *Degree requirements:* For master's, exam or thesis; for doctorate, thesis/dissertation, oral qualifying exam. *Entrance requirements:* For master's and doctorate, GRE General Test, minimum GPA of 3.0 during last 2 years of undergraduate course work. Electronic applications accepted. *Faculty research:* Human development, social and moral educational psychology, developmental teacher preparation.

University of California, San Diego, Graduate Division, Program in Mathematics and Science Education, La Jolla, CA 92093. Offers PhD. Program offered jointly with San Diego State University. *Students:* 12 part-time (10 women). In 2017, 3 doctorates awarded. *Degree requirements:* For doctorate, thesis/dissertation, teaching practicum. *Entrance requirements:* For doctorate, GRE General Test, minimum GPA of 3.25. Additional exam requirements/recommendations for international students: Required—TOEFL (minimum score 550 paper-based; 80 iBT), IELTS (minimum score 7). Electronic applications accepted. *Financial support:* Scholarships/grants and stipends available. Financial award applicants required to submit FAFSA. *Faculty research:* Effective teaching of rational numbers, teacher development, development of number sense and estimation. *Unit head:* Gabriele Wienhausen, Chair, 858-534-3105, E-mail: gwienhausen@ucsd.edu. *Application contact:* Sherry Seethaler, Graduate Coordinator, 858-534-4656, E-mail: sseethaler@ucsd.edu.
Website: http://sci.sdsu.edu/CRMSE/msed

University of Central Arkansas, Graduate School, College of Natural Sciences and Math, Department of Mathematics, Conway, AR 72035-0001. Offers applied mathematics (MS); math education (MA). *Program availability:* Part-time. *Degree requirements:* For master's, comprehensive exam, thesis optional. *Entrance requirements:* For master's, GRE General Test, minimum GPA of 2.7. Additional exam requirements/recommendations for international students: Required—TOEFL (minimum score 550 paper-based; 80 iBT). Electronic applications accepted.

University of Central Florida, College of Community Innovation and Education, Education Doctoral Programs, Orlando, FL 32816. Offers curriculum and instruction (Ed D); education (PhD), including communication sciences and disorders, counselor education, early childhood education, elementary education, exceptional education, exercise physiology, higher education, instructional design and technology, mathematics education, methodology, measurement and analysis, reading education, science education, social science education, TESOL; educational leadership (Ed D). *Students:* 122 full-time (86 women), 129 part-time (88 women); includes 64 minority (24 Black or African American, non-Hispanic/Latino; 1 American Indian or Alaska Native, non-Hispanic/Latino; 9 Asian, non-Hispanic/Latino; 24 Hispanic/Latino; 6 Two or more races, non-Hispanic/Latino), 26 international. Average age 38. 195 applicants, 47% accepted, 72 enrolled. In 2017, 89 doctorates awarded. *Entrance requirements:* For doctorate, GRE, letters of recommendation, goal statement, resume, writing sample. Application fee: $30. Electronic applications accepted. *Expenses:* Tuition, state resident: part-time $288.16 per credit hour. Tuition, nonresident: part-time $1073.31 per credit hour. Tuition and fees vary according to program. *Financial support:* In 2017–18, 77 students received support, including 28 fellowships with partial tuition reimbursements available (averaging $5,733 per year), 29 research assistantships with partial tuition reimbursements available (averaging $10,230 per year), 54 teaching assistantships with partial tuition reimbursements available (averaging $11,614 per year); health care benefits also available. Financial award application deadline: 3/1; financial award applicants required to submit FAFSA. *Unit head:* Dr. Edward Robinson, Director of Doctoral Programs, 407-823-6106, E-mail: edward.robinson@ucf.edu. *Application contact:* Associate Director, Graduate Admissions, 407-823-2766, Fax: 407-823-6442, E-mail: gradadmissions@ucf.edu.
Website: https://edcollege.ucf.edu/academic-programs/graduate/

University of Central Florida, College of Community Innovation and Education, School of Teacher Education, Program in K-8 Mathematics and Science Education, Orlando, FL 32816. Offers M Ed, Certificate. *Accreditation:* NCATE. *Program availability:* Part-time. *Students:* 1 full-time (0 women), 16 part-time (15 women); includes 10 minority (3 Black or African American, non-Hispanic/Latino; 7 Hispanic/Latino). Average age 36. 3 applicants, 100% accepted, 3 enrolled. In 2017, 11 master's awarded. *Degree requirements:* For master's, thesis or alternative. *Entrance requirements:* Additional exam requirements/recommendations for international students: Required—TOEFL. *Application deadline:* For summer admission, 4/15 for domestic students. Application fee: $30. Electronic applications accepted. *Expenses:* Tuition, state resident: part-time $288.16 per credit hour. Tuition, nonresident: part-time $1073.31 per credit hour. Tuition and fees vary according to program. *Financial support:* In 2017–18, 1 student received support, including 2 research assistantships with partial tuition reimbursements available (averaging $5,522 per year). Financial award application deadline: 3/1; financial award applicants required to submit FAFSA. *Unit head:* Dr. Malcolm Butler, Program Coordinator, 407-823-3272, E-mail: malcolm.butler@ucf.edu. *Application contact:* Associate Director, Graduate Admissions, 407-823-2766, Fax: 407-823-6442, E-mail: gradadmissions@ucf.edu.
Website: http://education.ucf.edu/mathed/

University of Central Florida, College of Community Innovation and Education, School of Teacher Education, Program in Teacher Education, Orlando, FL 32816. Offers art education (MAT); English language (MAT); mathematics education (MAT); middle school mathematics (MAT); middle school science (MAT); science education (MAT), including biology, chemistry, physics; social science education (MAT). *Accreditation:* NCATE. *Program availability:* Part-time, evening/weekend. *Students:* 11 full-time (9 women), 28 part-time (23 women); includes 15 minority (5 Black or African American, non-Hispanic/Latino; 2 Asian, non-Hispanic/Latino; 6 Hispanic/Latino; 2 Two or more races, non-Hispanic/Latino), 2 international. Average age 29. In 2017, 6 master's awarded. *Degree requirements:* For master's, thesis or alternative. *Entrance requirements:* For master's, Florida Teacher Certification Examination/General Knowledge Test or GRE General Test. Additional exam requirements/recommendations for international students: Required—TOEFL. *Application deadline:* For spring admission, 12/1 for domestic students; for summer admission, 4/15 for domestic students. Application fee: $30. Electronic applications accepted. *Expenses:* Tuition, state resident: part-time $288.16 per credit hour. Tuition, nonresident: part-time $1073.31 per credit hour. Tuition and fees vary according to program. *Financial support:* Fellowships, research assistantships, teaching assistantships, career-related internships or fieldwork, Federal Work-Study, institutionally sponsored loans, tuition waivers (partial), and unspecified assistantships available. Financial award application deadline: 3/1; financial award applicants required to submit FAFSA. *Unit head:* Dr. Michael Hynes, Director, 407-823-2005, E-mail: mychael.hynes@ucf.edu. *Application contact:* Associate Director, Graduate Admissions, 407-823-2766, Fax: 407-823-6442, E-mail: gradadmissions@ucf.edu.
Website: http://www.graduatecatalog.ucf.edu/programs/program.aspx?id=9727&program=Teacher%20Education%20MAT

University of Cincinnati, Graduate School, McMicken College of Arts and Sciences, Department of Mathematical Sciences, Cincinnati, OH 45221. Offers applied mathematics (MS, PhD); mathematics education (MAT); pure mathematics (MS, PhD); statistics (MS, PhD). *Program availability:* Part-time. Terminal master's awarded for partial completion of doctoral program. *Degree requirements:* For master's, comprehensive exam, thesis or alternative; for doctorate, one foreign language, comprehensive exam, thesis/dissertation. *Entrance requirements:* For master's, GRE, teacher certification (for MAT); for doctorate, GRE. Additional exam requirements/recommendations for international students: Required—TOEFL. Electronic applications accepted. *Expenses: Tuition, area resident:* Full-time $14,468. *Tuition, state resident:* full-time $14,968; part-time $754 per credit hour. *Tuition, nonresident:* full-time $24,210;

part-time $1311 per credit hour. *International tuition:* $26,460 full-time. *Required fees:* $3958; $84 per credit hour. One-time fee: $85 full-time. Tuition and fees vary according to course load, degree level and program. *Faculty research:* Algebra, analysis, differential equations, numerical analysis, statistics.

University of Colorado Denver, College of Liberal Arts and Sciences, Department of Mathematical and Statistical Sciences, Denver, CO 80217. Offers applied mathematics (MS, PhD), including applied mathematics, applied probability (MS), applied statistics (MS), computational biology, computational mathematics (PhD), discrete mathematics, finite geometry (PhD), mathematics education (PhD), mathematics of engineering and science (MS), numerical analysis, operations research (MS), optimization and operations research (PhD), probability (PhD), statistics (PhD). *Program availability:* Part-time. *Degree requirements:* For master's, comprehensive exam, thesis optional, 30 hours of course work with minimum GPA of 3.0; for doctorate, comprehensive exam, thesis/dissertation, 42 hours of course work with minimum GPA of 3.25. *Entrance requirements:* For master's, GRE General Test; GRE Subject Test in math (recommended), 30 hours of course work in mathematics (24 of which must be upper-division mathematics), bachelor's degree with minimum GPA of 3.0; for doctorate, GRE General Test; GRE Subject Test in math (recommended), 30 hours of course work in mathematics (24 of which must be upper-division mathematics), master's degree with minimum GPA of 3.25. Additional exam requirements/recommendations for international students: Required—TOEFL (minimum score 537 paper-based; 75 iBT); Recommended—IELTS (minimum score 6.5). Electronic applications accepted. *Faculty research:* Computational mathematics, computational biology, discrete mathematics and geometry, probability and statistics, optimization.

University of Colorado Denver, School of Education and Human Development, Program in Educational Leadership and Innovation, Denver, CO 80217. Offers educational studies and research (PhD), including administrative leadership and policy, early childhood special education, math education, research, assessment and evaluation, science education, urban ecologies. *Program availability:* Part-time, evening/weekend. *Degree requirements:* For doctorate, comprehensive exam, thesis/dissertation, 75 credit hours (for PhD). *Entrance requirements:* For doctorate, GRE or equivalent, resume or curriculum vitae, letters of recommendation, master's degree or equivalent, completion of basic or advanced statistics course with minimum B grade. Additional exam requirements/recommendations for international students: Required—TOEFL (minimum score 537 paper-based; 75 iBT); Recommended—IELTS (minimum score 6.5). Electronic applications accepted. *Expenses:* Contact institution. *Faculty research:* Administrative leadership and policy studies, early childhood education, research in diversity, paraprofessionals in education, urban schools lab.

University of Colorado Denver, School of Education and Human Development, Program in Mathematics Education, Denver, CO 80217. Offers MS Ed. *Degree requirements:* For master's, thesis or alternative, 36 semester hours. *Entrance requirements:* For master's, GRE or MAT, resume or curriculum vitae, three letters of recommendation, transcripts from all colleges/universities attended. Additional exam requirements/recommendations for international students: Required—TOEFL (minimum score 75 iBT). Electronic applications accepted.

University of Colorado Denver, School of Education and Human Development, Teacher Education Programs, Denver, CO 80217. Offers elementary linguistically diverse education (MA); elementary math and science education (MA); elementary math education (MA); elementary reading and writing (MA); elementary science education (MA); secondary English education (MA); secondary linguistically diverse education (MA); secondary math education (MA); secondary reading and writing (MA); secondary science education (MA); special education (MA). *Accreditation:* NCATE. *Program availability:* Part-time, evening/weekend. *Degree requirements:* For master's, comprehensive exam. *Entrance requirements:* For master's, GRE or MAT (for those with GPA below 2.75), transcripts, resume, letters of recommendation. Additional exam requirements/recommendations for international students: Required—TOEFL (minimum score 537 paper-based; 75 iBT); Recommended—IELTS (minimum score 6.5). Electronic applications accepted. *Expenses:* Contact institution. *Faculty research:* Linguistically diverse education/ESL, elementary reading and writing, elementary teacher education, secondary teacher education, special education.

University of Connecticut, Graduate School, Neag School of Education, Department of Curriculum and Instruction, Program in Mathematics Education, Storrs, CT 06269. Offers MA, PhD. *Accreditation:* NCATE. Terminal master's awarded for partial completion of doctoral program. *Degree requirements:* For master's, comprehensive exam; for doctorate, thesis/dissertation. *Entrance requirements:* For doctorate, GRE General Test. Additional exam requirements/recommendations for international students: Required—TOEFL (minimum score 550 paper-based). Electronic applications accepted.

University of Dayton, Department of Teacher Education, Dayton, OH 45469. Offers adolescence to young adult education (MS Ed); early childhood leadership and advocacy (MS Ed); interdisciplinary education (MS Ed), including visual arts; interdisciplinary education studies (MS Ed); leadership in educational systems (MS Ed); literacy (MS Ed); mathematics education (MS Ed); middle childhood education (MS Ed); multi-age education (MS Ed), including world languages; music education (MS Ed); teacher as leader (MS Ed); teacher education (MS Ed); technology-enhanced learning (MS Ed); trans-disciplinary early childhood education (MS Ed). *Program availability:* Part-time, 100% online. *Faculty:* 23 full-time (20 women), 41 part-time/adjunct (36 women). *Students:* 45 full-time (38 women), 68 part-time (57 women); includes 7 minority (3 Black or African American, non-Hispanic/Latino; 1 Hispanic/Latino; 3 Two or more races, non-Hispanic/Latino), 6 international. Average age 31. 106 applicants, 28% accepted. In 2017, 70 master's awarded. *Degree requirements:* For master's, variable foreign language requirement, thesis or alternative, internship (for teaching licensure or endorsement). *Entrance requirements:* For master's, GRE (minimum score of 149 verbal, 4 on writing) or MAT (minimum score of 396) if undergraduate GPA was under 2.75, minimum GPA of 2.75, 3 letters of recommendation, personal statement or resume, official transcripts. Additional exam requirements/recommendations for international students: Required—TOEFL (minimum score 550 paper-based; 80 iBT); Recommended—IELTS (minimum score 6.5). *Application deadline:* Applications are processed on a rolling basis. Application fee: $0 ($50 for international students). Electronic applications accepted. *Expenses:* Contact institution. *Financial support:* In 2017–18, 5 research assistantships with partial tuition reimbursements (averaging $9,640 per year) were awarded; teaching assistantships, career-related internships or fieldwork, institutionally sponsored loans, and unspecified assistantships also available. Financial award application deadline: 3/1; financial award applicants required to submit FAFSA. *Faculty research:* Social emotional learning, culturally responsive teaching, urban teaching, literacy, instructional strategies, pre-service teacher education preparation. *Unit head:* Dr. Connie L. Bowman, Chair, 937-229-3348, E-mail: cbowman1@udayton.edu. *Application contact:* Gina Seiter, Coordinator of Graduate Programs and Licensing, 937-229-3103, E-mail: gseiter1@udayton.edu.
Website: https://www.udayton.edu/education/departments_and_programs/edt

University of Detroit Mercy, College of Engineering and Science, Detroit, MI 48221. Offers chemistry (MS); civil and environmental engineering (DE); electrical and computer engineering (ME); electrical engineering (DE); engineering management

(M Eng Mgt); environmental engineering (MEE); mechanical engineering (MME, DE); product development (MS); software engineering (MSSE); teaching of mathematics (MATM). *Program availability:* Part-time, evening/weekend. *Degree requirements:* For doctorate, thesis/dissertation. Electronic applications accepted. Application fee is waived when completed online. *Expenses:* Contact institution.

University of Florida, Graduate School, College of Education, School of Teaching and Learning, Gainesville, FL 32611. Offers curriculum and instruction (M Ed, MAE, Ed D, PhD, Ed S); elementary education (M Ed, MAE); English education (M Ed, MAE); mathematics education (M Ed, MAE); reading education (M Ed, MAE); science education (M Ed, MAE); social studies education (M Ed, MAE). *Accreditation:* NCATE. *Program availability:* Part-time, evening/weekend, online learning. Terminal master's awarded for partial completion of doctoral program. *Degree requirements:* For master's, comprehensive exam (for some programs), thesis (for some programs); for doctorate, comprehensive exam (for some programs), thesis/dissertation (for some programs). *Entrance requirements:* For master's and doctorate, GRE General Test, minimum GPA of 3.0; for Ed S, GRE General Test. Additional exam requirements/recommendations for international students: Required—TOEFL (minimum score 550 paper-based; 80 iBT), IELTS (minimum score 6). Electronic applications accepted. *Faculty research:* STEM education; curriculum; teaching and teacher education; languages and literacy; schools, culture, and society; theories and processes of learning.

University of Georgia, College of Education, Department of Mathematics and Science Education, Athens, GA 30602. Offers mathematics education (M Ed, PhD, Ed S).

University of Illinois at Chicago, College of Liberal Arts and Sciences, Department of Mathematics, Statistics, and Computer Science, Program in Secondary School Mathematics, Chicago, IL 60607-7128. Offers MST. *Program availability:* Part-time. *Degree requirements:* For master's, comprehensive exam. *Entrance requirements:* For master's, GRE General Test, minimum GPA of 2.75. Additional exam requirements/recommendations for international students: Required—TOEFL. Electronic applications accepted.

University of Illinois at Chicago, Program in Learning Sciences, Chicago, IL 60607-7128. Offers PhD.

University of Illinois at Urbana–Champaign, Graduate College, College of Liberal Arts and Sciences, Department of Mathematics, Champaign, IL 61820. Offers applied mathematics (MS); applied mathematics: actuarial science (MS); mathematics (MS, PhD); teaching of mathematics (MS).

University of Indianapolis, Graduate Programs, School of Education, Indianapolis, IN 46227-3697. Offers art education (MAT); biology (MAT); chemistry (MAT); curriculum and instruction (MA); earth sciences (MAT); education (MA, MAT); educational leadership (MA); elementary education (MA); English (MAT); French (MAT); math (MAT); physical education (MAT); physics (MAT); secondary education (MA), including art education, education, English education, social studies education; social studies (MAT); Spanish (MAT). *Accreditation:* NCATE. *Program availability:* Part-time, evening/weekend. *Entrance requirements:* For master's, GRE Subject Test, PRAXIS I, minimum GPA of 2.5, 3 letters of recommendation, interview. Additional exam requirements/recommendations for international students: Required—TOEFL (minimum score 550 paper-based). *Faculty research:* Assessment of teacher education, perceptions of prospective teachers by parents.

The University of Iowa, Graduate College, College of Education, Department of Teaching and Learning, Program in Education, Iowa City, IA 52242-1316. Offers art education (MA); developmental reading (MA); elementary education (MA); English education (MA, MAT); foreign and second language education (MAT); foreign language education (MA); foreign language/ESL education (PhD); language, literacy and culture (PhD); mathematics education (MA, MAT, PhD); music education (MM, PhD); science education (MA); secondary education (MA); social studies (MA, PhD). *Degree requirements:* For master's, thesis optional, exam; for doctorate, comprehensive exam, thesis/dissertation. *Entrance requirements:* For master's and doctorate, GRE General Test, minimum GPA of 3.0. Additional exam requirements/recommendations for international students: Required—TOEFL (minimum score 550 paper-based; 81 iBT). Electronic applications accepted.

University of Maryland, Baltimore County, The Graduate School, College of Arts, Humanities and Social Sciences, Department of Education, Master of Arts in Education Program, Baltimore, MD 21250. Offers K-8 mathematics instructional leadership (MAE); K-8 science education (MAE); K-8 STEM education (MAE); secondary mathematics education (MAE); secondary science education (MAE); secondary STEM education (MAE). *Program availability:* Part-time-only, evening/weekend, 100% online, blended/hybrid learning. *Faculty:* 4 full-time (3 women), 9 part-time/adjunct (7 women). *Students:* 142 part-time (110 women); includes 16 minority (5 Black or African American, non-Hispanic/Latino; 1 American Indian or Alaska Native, non-Hispanic/Latino; 7 Asian, non-Hispanic/Latino; 3 Hispanic/Latino; 2 Two or more races, non-Hispanic/Latino). Average age 32. 15 applicants, 100% accepted, 13 enrolled. *Degree requirements:* For master's, comprehensive exam (for some programs), thesis (for some programs). *Application deadline:* For fall admission, 6/1 for domestic students; for spring admission, 11/1 for domestic students. Application fee: $50. Electronic applications accepted. *Expenses:* $1,050 tuition per 3-credit course; $195 fees per 3-credit course. *Financial support:* In 2017–18, 1 student received support. Application deadline: 3/1; applicants required to submit FAFSA. *Unit head:* Jerri Frick, Graduate Program Director, Fax: 410-455-6182, E-mail: frick@umbc.edu.
Website: http://mae.umbc.edu

University of Maryland, Baltimore County, The Graduate School, College of Arts, Humanities and Social Sciences, Department of Education, Program in Teaching, Baltimore, MD 21250. Offers early childhood education (MAT); elementary education (MAT); teaching (MAT), including art, biology, chemistry, choral music, classical foreign language, dance, earth/space science, English, instrumental music, mathematics, modern foreign language, physical science, physics, social studies, theatre. *Program availability:* Part-time, evening/weekend. *Faculty:* 24 full-time (18 women), 25 part-time/adjunct (19 women). *Students:* 41 full-time (34 women), 27 part-time (18 women); includes 26 minority (6 Black or African American, non-Hispanic/Latino; 9 Asian, non-Hispanic/Latino; 7 Hispanic/Latino; 1 Native Hawaiian or other Pacific Islander, non-Hispanic/Latino; 3 Two or more races, non-Hispanic/Latino), 2 international. Average age 30. 54 applicants, 83% accepted, 35 enrolled. In 2017, 50 master's awarded. *Degree requirements:* For master's, comprehensive exam (for some programs), thesis (for some programs). *Entrance requirements:* For master's, PRAXIS Core Examination or GRE (minimum score of 1000), minimum GPA of 3.0. Additional exam requirements/recommendations for international students: Required—TOEFL. *Application deadline:* For fall admission, 6/1 for domestic and international students; for spring admission, 11/1 for domestic and international students. Applications are processed on a rolling basis. Application fee: $50. Electronic applications accepted. *Expenses: Required fees:* $132. *Financial support:* In 2017–18, 8 students received support, including teaching assistantships with tuition reimbursements available (averaging $12,000 per year); career-related internships or fieldwork, Federal Work-Study, scholarships/grants, tuition waivers, and unspecified assistantships also available. Financial award application deadline: 3/15. *Faculty research:* STEM teacher education, culturally sensitive

pedagogy, ESOL/bilingual education, early childhood education, language, literacy and culture. *Total annual research expenditures:* $100,000. *Unit head:* Dr. Susan M. Blunck, Graduate Program Director, 410-455-2869, Fax: 410-455-3986, E-mail: blunck@umbc.edu. *Application contact:* Cheryl Johnson, MAT Program Specialist, 410-455-3388, E-mail: blackwel@umbc.edu.
Website: http://www.umbc.edu/education/

University of Massachusetts Dartmouth, Graduate School, College of Arts and Sciences, School of Education, Department of STEM Education and Teacher Development, North Dartmouth, MA 02747-2300. Offers English as a second language (Postbaccalaureate Certificate); mathematics education (PhD); middle school education (MAT); secondary school education (MAT). *Program availability:* Part-time. *Faculty:* 9 full-time (6 women), 11 part-time/adjunct (7 women). *Students:* 26 full-time (15 women), 102 part-time (60 women); includes 16 minority (2 Black or African American, non-Hispanic/Latino; 2 Asian, non-Hispanic/Latino; 6 Hispanic/Latino; 6 Two or more races, non-Hispanic/Latino), 2 international. Average age 32. 60 applicants, 92% accepted, 51 enrolled. In 2017, 41 master's, 2 doctorates awarded. *Degree requirements:* For doctorate, thesis/dissertation. *Entrance requirements:* For master's, statement of purpose (minimum of 300 words), resume, 2 letters of recommendation, official transcripts; for doctorate, GRE, statement of purpose (minimum of 300 words), resume, official transcripts, 3 letters of recommendation. Additional exam requirements/recommendations for international students: Required—TOEFL (minimum score 533 paper-based; 72 iBT), IELTS (minimum score 6). *Application deadline:* For fall admission, 2/15 priority date for domestic students, 1/15 priority date for international students; for spring admission, 1/15 priority date for domestic students, 12/15 priority date for international students. Application fee: $60. Electronic applications accepted. *Expenses:* Tuition, state resident: full-time $15,449; part-time $643.71 per credit. Tuition, nonresident: full-time $27,880; part-time $1161.67 per credit. *Required fees:* $405; $25.88 per credit. Tuition and fees vary according to course load and reciprocity agreements. *Financial support:* In 2017–18, 2 fellowships (averaging $16,000 per year), 4 research assistantships (averaging $20,656 per year), 2 teaching assistantships (averaging $16,000 per year) were awarded; tuition waivers (full) and unspecified assistantships also available. Support available to part-time students. Financial award application deadline: 3/1; financial award applicants required to submit FAFSA. *Faculty research:* Mindfulness in education, literacies, assessment of teacher knowledge, curriculum tools for supporting mathematics learning. *Total annual research expenditures:* $1.6 million. *Unit head:* Traci Almeida, Coordinator of Graduate Admissions and Licensure, 508-999-8098, Fax: 508-910-8183, E-mail: talmeida@umassd.edu. *Application contact:* Steven Briggs, Director of Marketing and Recruitment for Graduate Studies, 508-999-8604, Fax: 508-999-8183, E-mail: graduate@umassd.edu.
Website: http://www.umassd.edu/cas/schoolofeducation/departments/stemeducationandteacherdevelopment/

University of Memphis, Graduate School, College of Arts and Sciences, Department of Mathematical Sciences, Memphis, TN 38152. Offers applied mathematics (MS); applied statistics (PhD); mathematics (MS, PhD); statistics (MS); teaching of mathematics (MS). *Program availability:* Part-time. *Faculty:* 20 full-time (8 women), 1 (woman) part-time/adjunct. *Students:* 32 full-time (7 women), 20 part-time (8 women); includes 18 minority (5 Black or African American, non-Hispanic/Latino; 9 Asian, non-Hispanic/Latino; 3 Hispanic/Latino; 1 Two or more races, non-Hispanic/Latino), 17 international. Average age 32. 32 applicants, 84% accepted, 9 enrolled. In 2017, 6 master's, 6 doctorates awarded. Terminal master's awarded for partial completion of doctoral program. *Degree requirements:* For master's, comprehensive exam, thesis or alternative; for doctorate, one foreign language, comprehensive exam, thesis/dissertation, qualifying exam, final exam. *Entrance requirements:* For master's, GRE General Test, minimum GPA of 2.5, undergraduate degree in math or statistics, two letters of recommendation; for doctorate, GRE General Test, minimum GPA of 2.5, three letters of recommendation. Additional exam requirements/recommendations for international students: Required—TOEFL (minimum score 550 paper-based; 79 iBT). *Application deadline:* For fall admission, 8/1 for domestic students, 5/1 priority date for international students; for spring admission, 12/1 for domestic students, 9/1 priority date for international students. Applications are processed on a rolling basis. Application fee: $35 ($60 for international students). Electronic applications accepted. *Expenses:* Contact institution. *Financial support:* In 2017–18, 22 students received support, including 4 research assistantships with full tuition reimbursements available (averaging $25,500 per year), 21 teaching assistantships with full tuition reimbursements available (averaging $24,438 per year); fellowships with full tuition reimbursements available, career-related internships or fieldwork, Federal Work-Study, scholarships/grants, and unspecified assistantships also available. Financial award application deadline: 2/1; financial award applicants required to submit FAFSA. *Faculty research:* Combinatorics, ergodic theory, graph theory, Ramsey theory, applied statistics. *Unit head:* Dr. Irena Lasiecka, Chair, 901-678-2482, Fax: 901-678-2480, E-mail: lasiecka@memphis.edu. *Application contact:* Dr. Fernanda Botelho, Director of Graduate Studies, 901-678-3131, Fax: 901-678-2480, E-mail: mbotelho@memphis.edu.
Website: http://www.MSCI.memphis.edu/

University of Miami, Graduate School, School of Education and Human Development, Department of Teaching and Learning, Program in Teaching and Learning, Coral Gables, FL 33124. Offers language and literacy learning in multilingual settings (PhD); science, technology, engineering and mathematics (PhD); special education (PhD). *Degree requirements:* For doctorate, thesis/dissertation, qualifying exam, electronic portfolio. *Entrance requirements:* For doctorate, GRE General Test. Additional exam requirements/recommendations for international students: Required—TOEFL (minimum score 550 paper-based; 80 iBT); Recommended—IELTS (minimum score 6.5). Electronic applications accepted. *Faculty research:* Teacher education, multicultural education, special education, second language acquisition, math and science education.

University of Minnesota, Twin Cities Campus, Graduate School, College of Education and Human Development, Department of Curriculum and Instruction, Minneapolis, MN 55455-0213. Offers art education (M Ed, MA, PhD); curriculum and instruction (M Ed, MA, PhD); elementary education (MA, PhD); English education (PhD); language and immersion education (Certificate); learning technologies (MA, PhD); literacy education (MA, PhD); second language education (MA, PhD); social studies education (MA, PhD); STEM education (MA, PhD); teaching (M Ed), including mathematics, science, social studies, teaching; teaching English to speakers of other languages (MA); technology enhanced learning (Certificate). *Faculty:* 37 full-time (21 women). *Students:* 401 full-time (282 women), 303 part-time (212 women); includes 139 minority (26 Black or African American, non-Hispanic/Latino; 4 American Indian or Alaska Native, non-Hispanic/Latino; 34 Asian, non-Hispanic/Latino; 45 Hispanic/Latino; 1 Native Hawaiian or other Pacific Islander, non-Hispanic/Latino; 29 Two or more races, non-Hispanic/Latino), 43 international. Average age 32. 596 applicants, 61% accepted, 330 enrolled. In 2017, 316 master's, 30 doctorates, 19 other advanced degrees awarded. Application fee: $75 ($95 for international students). *Financial support:* In 2017–18, 3 fellowships, 56 research assistantships with full tuition reimbursements (averaging $11,118 per year), 67 teaching assistantships with full tuition reimbursements (averaging $11,975 per year) were awarded. *Faculty research:* Teaching and learning; influence of cultural, linguistic, social, political, and technological

factors on teaching, learning and educational research; relationship between educational practice and a democratic and just society; urban education; immigrant education, racial justice and education. *Total annual research expenditures:* $2.2 million. *Unit head:* Dr. Cynthia Lewis, Chair, 612-625-6313, E-mail: lewis@umn.edu. *Application contact:* Dr. Gillian Roehrig, Director of Graduate Studies, 612-625-0561, E-mail: roehr013@umn.edu.
Website: http://www.cehd.umn.edu/ci

University of Mississippi, Graduate School, School of Education, University, MS 38677. Offers counselor education (M Ed, PhD); counselor education - play therapy (Ed S); early childhood (M Ed); educational leadership K-12 (M Ed, Ed D, PhD, Ed S); elementary education (M Ed, Ed D, Ed S); higher education/student personnel (Ed D, PhD); literacy education (M Ed); math education (Ed D); secondary education (M Ed, PhD, Ed S); special education (M Ed, PhD, Ed S); teacher corporations (MA); teacher education (MA). *Accreditation:* NCATE. *Faculty:* 65 full-time (40 women), 25 part-time/adjunct (5 women). *Students:* 185 full-time (148 women), 410 part-time (310 women); includes 193 minority (168 Black or African American, non-Hispanic/Latino; 7 Asian, non-Hispanic/Latino; 14 Hispanic/Latino; 4 Two or more races, non-Hispanic/Latino), 7 international. Average age 33. In 2017, 176 master's, 20 doctorates, 37 other advanced degrees awarded. *Entrance requirements:* For master's, GRE General Test, minimum GPA of 3.0; for doctorate, GRE General Test. Additional exam requirements/recommendations for international students: Required—TOEFL. *Application deadline:* For fall admission, 3/1 for domestic students; for spring admission, 10/1 for domestic students; for summer admission, 3/1 for domestic students. Applications are processed on a rolling basis. Application fee: $50. Electronic applications accepted. *Financial support:* Scholarships/grants available. Financial award application deadline: 3/1; financial award applicants required to submit FAFSA. *Unit head:* Dr. David Rock, Dean, 662-915-7063, Fax: 662-915-7249, E-mail: soe@olemiss.edu. *Application contact:* Dr. Joe Sumrall, Professor of Elementary Education, 662-915-7350, E-mail: soe@olemiss.edu.

University of Missouri, Office of Research and Graduate Studies, College of Arts and Science, Department of Mathematics, Columbia, MO 65211. Offers applied mathematics (MS); mathematics (MA, MST, PhD). *Degree requirements:* For doctorate, 2 foreign languages, comprehensive exam, thesis/dissertation. *Entrance requirements:* For master's and doctorate, GRE General Test, minimum GPA 3.0; bachelor's degree from accredited institution. Additional exam requirements/recommendations for international students: Required—TOEFL (minimum score 500 paper-based; 61 iBT). Electronic applications accepted. *Faculty research:* Algebraic geometry, analysis (real, complex, functional and harmonic), analytic functions, applied mathematics, financial mathematics and mathematics of insurance, commutative rings, scattering theory, differential equations (ordinary and partial), differential geometry, dynamical systems, general relativity, mathematical physics, number theory, probabilistic analysis and topology.

University of Missouri, Office of Research and Graduate Studies, College of Education, Department of Learning, Teaching and Curriculum, Columbia, MO 65211. Offers agricultural education (M Ed, PhD, Ed S); art education (M Ed, PhD, Ed S); business and office education (M Ed, PhD, Ed S); early childhood education (M Ed, PhD, Ed S); elementary education (M Ed, PhD, Ed S); English education (M Ed, PhD, Ed S); foreign language education (M Ed, PhD, Ed S); health education and promotion (M Ed, PhD); learning and instruction (M Ed); marketing education (M Ed, PhD, Ed S); mathematics education (M Ed, PhD, Ed S); music education (M Ed, PhD, Ed S); reading education (M Ed, PhD, Ed S); science education (M Ed, PhD, Ed S); social studies education (M Ed, PhD, Ed S); vocational education (M Ed, PhD, Ed S). *Program availability:* Part-time. Terminal master's awarded for partial completion of doctoral program. *Degree requirements:* For doctorate, thesis/dissertation. *Entrance requirements:* For master's and Ed S, GRE General Test or MAT, minimum GPA of 3.0; for doctorate, GRE General Test, minimum GPA of 3.0. Additional exam requirements/recommendations for international students: Required—TOEFL (minimum score 600 paper-based; 100 iBT). Electronic applications accepted.

University of Montana, Graduate School, College of Humanities and Sciences, Department of Mathematical Sciences, Missoula, MT 59812. Offers mathematics (MA, PhD), including college mathematics teaching (PhD), mathematical sciences research (PhD); mathematics education (MA). *Program availability:* Part-time. Terminal master's awarded for partial completion of doctoral program. *Degree requirements:* For doctorate, thesis/dissertation. *Entrance requirements:* For master's and doctorate, GRE General Test. Additional exam requirements/recommendations for international students: Required—TOEFL (minimum score 525 paper-based).

University of Nebraska at Kearney, College of Natural and Social Sciences, Department of Biology, Kearney, NE 68849. Offers biology (MS); science/math education (MA Ed). *Program availability:* Part-time, evening/weekend, 100% online. *Degree requirements:* For master's, comprehensive exam, thesis option optional. *Entrance requirements:* For master's, GRE (for thesis option and for online program applicants if undergraduate GPA is below 2.75), letter of interest. Additional exam requirements/recommendations for international students: Recommended—TOEFL (minimum score 550 paper-based; 79 iBT), IELTS (minimum score 6.5). Electronic applications accepted. *Expenses:* Contact institution. *Faculty research:* Pollution injury, molecular biology-viral gene expression, prairie range condition modeling, evolution of symbiotic nitrogen fixation, geographic information systems (GIS), molecular genetics of aging.

University of Nevada, Reno, Graduate School, College of Science, Department of Mathematics and Statistics, Reno, NV 89557. Offers mathematics (MS); teaching mathematics (MATM). *Degree requirements:* For master's, thesis optional. *Entrance requirements:* For master's, GRE General Test, minimum GPA of 2.75. Additional exam requirements/recommendations for international students: Required—TOEFL (minimum score 500 paper-based; 61 iBT), IELTS (minimum score 6). Electronic applications accepted. *Faculty research:* Operator algebra, nonlinear systems, differential equations.

University of New Hampshire, Graduate School, College of Engineering and Physical Sciences, Department of Mathematics and Statistics, Durham, NH 03824. Offers applied mathematics (PhD); industrial statistics (Certificate); mathematics (MS, MST, PhD); mathematics education (PhD); mathematics: applied mathematics (MS); mathematics: statistics (MS, PhD). *Students:* 39 full-time (16 women), 24 part-time (7 women); includes 6 minority (1 Black or African American, non-Hispanic/Latino; 1 American Indian or Alaska Native, non-Hispanic/Latino; 3 Asian, non-Hispanic/Latino; 1 Hispanic/Latino), 23 international. Average age 29. 111 applicants, 54% accepted, 13 enrolled. In 2017, 16 master's, 9 doctorates, 1 other advanced degree awarded. Terminal master's awarded for partial completion of doctoral program. *Entrance requirements:* Additional exam requirements/recommendations for international students: Required—TOEFL (minimum score 550 paper-based; 80 iBT). *Application deadline:* For fall admission, 4/1 priority date for domestic students, 4/1 for international students; for spring admission, 12/1 for domestic students. Application fee: $65. Electronic applications accepted. *Financial support:* In 2017–18, 49 students received support, including 4 research assistantships, 45 teaching assistantships; fellowships, Federal Work-Study, scholarships/grants, and tuition waivers (full and partial) also available. Support available to part-time students. Financial award application deadline: 2/15. *Unit head:* Dr. Karen Graham, Chairperson, 603-862-2688. *Application contact:* Jennifer Cooke, Administrative Assistant, 603-862-1943, E-mail: jennifer.cooke@unh.edu. Website: http://www.ceps.unh.edu/mathematics-statistics

The University of North Carolina at Chapel Hill, Graduate School, School of Education, Program in Secondary Education, Chapel Hill, NC 27599. Offers English (Grades 9-12) (MAT); English as a second language (MAT); French (Grades K-12) (MAT); German (Grades K-12) (MAT); Japanese (Grades K-12) (MAT); Latin (Grades 9-12) (MAT); mathematics (Grades 9-12) (MAT); music (Grades K-12) (MAT); science (Grades 9-12) (MAT); social studies (Grades 9-12) (MAT); Spanish (Grades K-12) (MAT). *Accreditation:* NCATE. *Degree requirements:* For master's, comprehensive exam. *Entrance requirements:* For master's, GRE General Test, minimum GPA of 3.0 during last 2 years of undergraduate course work. Additional exam requirements/recommendations for international students: Required—TOEFL (minimum score 550 paper-based). Electronic applications accepted.

The University of North Carolina at Greensboro, Graduate School, School of Education, Department of Teacher Education and Higher Education, Greensboro, NC 27412-5001. Offers college teaching and adult learning (Certificate); curriculum and instruction (M Ed), including chemistry education, elementary education, English as a second language, French education, instructional technology, mathematics education, middle grades education, reading education, science education, social studies education, Spanish education; curriculum and teaching (PhD), including higher education, teacher education and development; English as a second language (Certificate); higher education (M Ed); supervision (M Ed). *Accreditation:* NCATE. *Program availability:* Part-time. *Degree requirements:* For doctorate, thesis/dissertation. *Entrance requirements:* For master's and doctorate, GRE General Test. Additional exam requirements/recommendations for international students: Required—TOEFL. Electronic applications accepted. *Faculty research:* Community college literacy program, middle school mathematics/computer mathematics.

The University of North Carolina at Pembroke, The Graduate School, Department of Mathematics and Computer Science, Pembroke, NC 28372-1510. Offers mathematics education (MA). *Program availability:* Part-time, evening/weekend. *Degree requirements:* For master's, comprehensive exam, thesis option. *Entrance requirements:* For master's, GRE General Test or MAT, bachelor's degree in mathematics or mathematics education; minimum GPA of 3.0 in major, 2.5 overall. Additional exam requirements/recommendations for international students: Required—TOEFL. *Application deadline:* For fall admission, 7/15 priority date for domestic and international students; for spring admission, 12/1 priority date for domestic and international students. Applications are processed on a rolling basis. Application fee: $45 ($60 for international students). *Financial support:* Application deadline: 4/15; applicants required to submit FAFSA. *Unit head:* Mary B. Klinikowski, Interim Director, 910-521-6417, E-mail: mary.klinikowski@uncp.edu. Website: http://www.uncp.edu/mathcs/

University of Northern Colorado, Graduate School, College of Natural and Health Sciences, School of Mathematical Sciences, Greeley, CO 80639. Offers educational mathematics (PhD); mathematical teaching (MA); mathematics (MA). *Program availability:* Part-time. *Degree requirements:* For master's, comprehensive exam, thesis or alternative; for doctorate, comprehensive exam, thesis/dissertation. *Entrance requirements:* For master's, GRE General Test (for liberal arts), 3 letters of recommendation; for doctorate, GRE General Test, 3 letters of recommendation. Electronic applications accepted.

University of Northern Iowa, Graduate College, College of Humanities, Arts and Sciences, Department of Mathematics, MA Program in Mathematics, Cedar Falls, IA 50614. Offers community college teaching (MA); mathematics (MA); secondary teaching (MA).

University of Northern Iowa, Graduate College, College of Humanities, Arts and Sciences, Department of Mathematics, MA Program in Mathematics for the Middle Grades, Cedar Falls, IA 50614. Offers MA.

University of North Georgia, Master of Arts in Teaching Program, Dahlonega, GA 30597. Offers physical education (MAT); secondary education - English (MAT); secondary education - history (MAT); secondary education - mathematics (MAT); secondary education - middle grades (MAT). *Students:* 27 part-time (20 women). Average age 29. 12 applicants, 75% accepted, 7 enrolled. In 2017, 15 master's awarded. *Degree requirements:* For master's, internship, capstone. *Entrance requirements:* For master's, GRE or MAT, GACE I and II, GA pre-service application, lawful presence verification, official transcripts, GA Educator Ethics Program entry assessment. Additional exam requirements/recommendations for international students: Required—TOEFL (minimum score 550 paper-based; 79 iBT), IELTS (minimum score 6.5). *Application deadline:* For summer admission, 2/1 for domestic students. Application fee: $40. Electronic applications accepted. *Expenses:* Contact institution. *Financial support:* Application deadline: 3/17; applicants required to submit FAFSA. *Unit head:* Dr. Susan Brandenburg-Ayres, Dean, 706-864-1998, E-mail: susan.ayres@ung.edu. *Application contact:* Melinda Maxwell, Director of Graduate Admissions, 706-867-2077, E-mail: melinda.maxwell@ung.edu.
Website: https://ung.edu/teacher-education/graduate/master-of-arts-teaching.php

University of North Georgia, Program in Middle Grades Math and Science, Dahlonega, GA 30597. Offers M Ed. *Program availability:* Part-time, evening/weekend, online only, 100% online. *Students:* 6 full-time (all women), 12 part-time (8 women); includes 1 minority (Black or African American, non-Hispanic/Latino). Average age 29. 4 applicants, 75% accepted, 3 enrolled. In 2017, 8 master's awarded. *Degree requirements:* For master's, teaching practicum. *Entrance requirements:* For master's, baccalaureate degree from regionally-accredited, four-year institution with minimum cumulative GPA of 2.75; employment as teacher in middle grades classroom working with students at least 20 hours per week; clear/renewable teaching certificate in middle grades math or science in the state of Georgia or equivalent. Additional exam requirements/recommendations for international students: Required—TOEFL (minimum score 550 paper-based; 79 iBT), IELTS (minimum score 6.5). *Application deadline:* For fall admission, 7/24 for domestic students; for spring admission, 12/12 for domestic students; for summer admission, 4/26 for domestic students. Application fee: $40. Electronic applications accepted. *Expenses:* Contact institution. *Financial support:* Application deadline: 3/17; applicants required to submit FAFSA. *Unit head:* Dr. Susan Brandenburg-Ayres, Dean, 706-864-1998, E-mail: susan.ayres@ung.edu. *Application contact:* Melinda Maxwell, Director of Graduate Studies, 706-867-2077, E-mail: melinda.maxwell@ung.edu.
Website: https://ung.edu/teacher-education/graduate/master-education-middle-grades.php

University of Oklahoma, Jeannine Rainbolt College of Education, Department of Instructional Leadership and Academic Curriculum, Norman, OK 73019. Offers instructional leadership and academic curriculum (M Ed, PhD), including biomedical education (PhD), early childhood education, elementary education, English education, instructional leadership, mathematics education, reading education, science education, social studies education, world languages education (M Ed); reading specialist (M Ed). *Accreditation:* NCATE. *Program availability:* Part-time. *Faculty:* 19 full-time (15 women), 1 (woman) part-time/adjunct. *Students:* 37 full-time (28 women), 121 part-time (98 women); includes 32 minority (7 Black or African American, non-Hispanic/Latino; 4 American Indian or Alaska Native, non-Hispanic/Latino; 5 Asian, non-Hispanic/Latino; 6

Hispanic/Latino; 1 Native Hawaiian or other Pacific Islander, non-Hispanic/Latino; 9 Two or more races, non-Hispanic/Latino), 12 international. Average age 35. 39 applicants, 77% accepted, 22 enrolled. In 2017, 49 master's, 12 doctorates awarded. Terminal master's awarded for partial completion of doctoral program. *Degree requirements:* For master's, comprehensive exam (for some programs), thesis (for some programs); for doctorate, comprehensive exam (for some programs), thesis/dissertation. *Entrance requirements:* For doctorate, GRE. Additional exam requirements/recommendations for international students: Required—TOEFL (minimum score 79 iBT) or IELTS (minimum score 6.5). Application fee: $50 ($100 for international students). Electronic applications accepted. *Expenses:* Tuition, state resident: full-time $5119; part-time $213.30 per credit hour. Tuition, nonresident: full-time $19,778; part-time $824.10 per credit hour. *Required fees:* $3458; $133.55 per credit hour. $126.50 per semester. *Financial support:* In 2017–18, 90 students received support, including 8 research assistantships (averaging $11,248 per year), 6 teaching assistantships (averaging $12,188 per year); fellowships, scholarships/grants, and unspecified assistantships also available. Financial award application deadline: 6/1; financial award applicants required to submit FAFSA. *Faculty research:* Teacher preparation; instruction; curriculum; learning; constructivist theory. *Total annual research expenditures:* $707,690. *Unit head:* Dr. Stacy Reeder, Chair, 405-325-1498, Fax: 405-325-4061, E-mail: reeder@ou.edu. *Application contact:* Anna Steele, Graduate Programs Officer, 405-325-4525, E-mail: anna.steele@ou.edu.
Website: http://www.ou.edu/education/ilac

University of Phoenix–Online Campus, College of Education, Phoenix, AZ 85034-7209. Offers administration and supervision (MAEd, Certificate); adult education and training (MAEd); curriculum and instruction (MAEd), including computer education, curriculum and instruction, English as a second language, language arts, mathematics, reading; early childhood education (MAEd); educational studies (MAEd); elementary teacher education (MAEd), including early childhood, elementary teacher education, high school middle level, middle level; principal licensure (Certificate); secondary teacher education (MAEd); special education (MAEd, Certificate); teacher education (MAEd), including middle level generalist; teacher education middle level mathematics (MAEd), including middle level mathematics; teacher education middle level science (MAEd), including middle level science; teacher education secondary mathematics (MAEd); teacher education secondary science (MAEd); teacher leadership (MAEd); teachers of English learners (Certificate); transition to teaching (Certificate), including elementary education, secondary education. *Program availability:* Evening/weekend, online learning. *Entrance requirements:* Additional exam requirements/recommendations for international students: Required—TOEFL, TOEIC (Test of English as an International Communication), Berlitz Online English Proficiency Exam, PTE, or IELTS. Electronic applications accepted. *Expenses:* Contact institution.

University of Pittsburgh, School of Education, Department of Instruction and Learning, Program in Secondary Education, Pittsburgh, PA 15260. Offers English and communications education (M Ed, MAT); foreign language education (M Ed, MAT); language, literacy and culture education (Ed D, PhD); mathematics education (M Ed, MAT, Ed D, PhD); science education (M Ed, MAT, Ed D, PhD); secondary education (PhD); social studies education (M Ed, MAT); STEM education (Ed D). *Program availability:* Part-time, evening/weekend. *Degree requirements:* For master's, thesis; for doctorate, thesis/dissertation. *Entrance requirements:* For master's, PRAXIS I; for doctorate, GRE General Test. Additional exam requirements/recommendations for international students: Required—TOEFL. Electronic applications accepted.

University of Puerto Rico–Mayagüez, Graduate Studies, College of Arts and Sciences, Department of Mathematical Sciences, Mayagüez, PR 00681-9000. Offers applied mathematics (MS); pre-college math education (MS); pure mathematics (MS); scientific computing (MS); statistics (MS). *Program availability:* Part-time. *Degree requirements:* For master's, one foreign language, comprehensive exam, thesis. *Entrance requirements:* For master's, undergraduate degree in mathematics or its equivalent. Electronic applications accepted. *Faculty research:* Automata theory, linear algebra, logic.

University of Puerto Rico–Río Piedras, College of Education, Program in Curriculum and Teaching, San Juan, PR 00931-3300. Offers biology education (M Ed); chemistry education (M Ed); curriculum and teaching (Ed D); history education (M Ed); mathematics education (M Ed); physics education (M Ed); Spanish education (M Ed). *Program availability:* Part-time. *Degree requirements:* For master's, thesis; for doctorate, thesis/dissertation, internship. *Entrance requirements:* For master's, PAEG or GRE, minimum GPA of 3.0, letter of recommendation; for doctorate, GRE or PAEG, master's degree, minimum GPA of 3.0, letter of recommendation (2), interview. *Faculty research:* Curriculum, math teaching.

University of St. Francis, College of Education, Joliet, IL 60435-6169. Offers educational leadership (MS, Ed D); elementary education (M Ed); reading (MS); secondary education (M Ed), including English education, math education, science education, social studies education, visual arts education; special education (M Ed); teaching and learning (MS); TESOL (Certificate). *Accreditation:* NCATE. *Program availability:* Part-time, evening/weekend, 100% online, blended/hybrid learning. *Faculty:* 11 full-time (8 women), 52 part-time/adjunct (36 women). *Students:* 39 full-time (32 women), 411 part-time (318 women); includes 106 minority (57 Black or African American, non-Hispanic/Latino; 8 Asian, non-Hispanic/Latino; 37 Hispanic/Latino; 4 Two or more races, non-Hispanic/Latino), 4 international. Average age 37. 277 applicants, 55% accepted, 137 enrolled. In 2017, 199 master's, 28 doctorates awarded. *Degree requirements:* For master's, comprehensive exam; for doctorate, thesis/dissertation. *Entrance requirements:* Additional exam requirements/recommendations for international students: Required—TOEFL (minimum score 550 paper-based; 79 iBT), IELTS (minimum score 6). *Application deadline:* Applications are processed on a rolling basis. Application fee: $30. Electronic applications accepted. Application fee is waived when completed online. *Expenses:* $365 to $748 per credit hour. *Financial support:* In 2017–18, 40 students received support. Scholarships/grants and unspecified assistantships available. Support available to part-time students. Financial award applicants required to submit FAFSA. *Unit head:* Dr. John Gambro, Dean, 815-740-3829, Fax: 815-740-2264, E-mail: jgambro@stfrancis.edu. *Application contact:* Sandra Sloka, Director of Admissions for Graduate and Degree Completion Programs, 800-735-7500, Fax: 815-740-3431, E-mail: ssloka@stfrancis.edu.
Website: http://www.stfrancis.edu/academics/college-of-education/

University of South Africa, College of Human Sciences, Pretoria, South Africa. Offers adult education (M Ed); African languages (MA, PhD); African politics (MA, PhD); Afrikaans (MA, PhD); ancient history (MA, PhD); ancient Near Eastern studies (MA, PhD); anthropology (MA, PhD); applied linguistics (MA); Arabic (MA, PhD); archaeology (MA); art history (MA); Biblical archaeology (MA); Biblical studies (M Th, D Th, PhD); Christian spirituality (M Th, D Th); church history (M Th, D Th); classical studies (MA, PhD); clinical psychology (MA); communication (MA); comparative education (M Ed, Ed D); consulting psychology (D Admin, D Com, PhD); curriculum studies (M Ed, Ed D); development studies (M Admin, MA, D Admin, PhD); didactics (M Ed, Ed D); education (M Tech); education management (M Ed, Ed D); educational psychology (M Ed); English (MA); environmental education (M Ed); French (MA, PhD); German (MA, PhD); Greek (MA); guidance and counseling (M Ed); health studies (MA, PhD);

including health sciences education (MA), health services management (MA), medical and surgical nursing science (critical care general) (MA), midwifery and neonatal nursing science (MA), trauma and emergency care (MA); history (MA, PhD); history of education (Ed D); inclusive education (M Ed, Ed D); information and communications technology policy and regulation (MA); information science (MA, MIS, PhD); international politics (MA, PhD); Islamic studies (MA, PhD); Italian (MA, PhD); Judaica (MA, PhD); linguistics (MA, PhD); mathematical education (M Ed); mathematics education (MA); missiology (M Th, D Th); modern Hebrew (MA, PhD); musicology (MA, MMus, D Mus, PhD); natural science education (M Ed); New Testament (M Th, D Th); Old Testament (D Th); pastoral therapy (M Th, D Th); philosophy (MA); philosophy of education (M Ed, Ed D); politics (MA, PhD); Portuguese (MA, PhD); practical theology (M Th, D Th); psychology (MA, MS, PhD); psychology of education (M Ed, Ed D); public health (MA); religious studies (MA, D Th, PhD); Romance languages (MA); Russian (MA, PhD); Semitic languages (MA, PhD); social behavior studies in HIV/AIDS (MA); social science (mental health) (MA); social science in development studies (MA); social science in psychology (MA); social science in social work (MA); social science in sociology (MA); social work (MSW, DSW, PhD); socio-education (M Ed, Ed D); sociolinguistics (MA); sociology (MA, PhD); Spanish (MA, PhD); systematic theology (M Th, D Th); TESOL (teaching English to speakers of other languages) (MA); theological ethics (M Th, D Th); theory of literature (MA, PhD); urban ministries (D Th); urban ministry (M Th).

University of South Africa, Institute for Science and Technology Education, Pretoria, South Africa. Offers mathematics, science and technology education (M Sc, PhD).

University of South Carolina, The Graduate School, College of Arts and Sciences, Department of Mathematics, Columbia, SC 29208. Offers mathematics (MA, MS, PhD); mathematics education (M Math, MAT). MAT offered in cooperation with the College of Education. *Program availability:* Part-time. Terminal master's awarded for partial completion of doctoral program. *Degree requirements:* For master's, comprehensive exam, thesis (for some programs); for doctorate, one foreign language, comprehensive exam, thesis/dissertation, admission to candidacy exam, residency. *Entrance requirements:* For master's and doctorate, GRE General Test. Additional exam requirements/recommendations for international students: Required—TOEFL (minimum score 600 paper-based; 100 iBT). Electronic applications accepted. *Faculty research:* Computational mathematics, analysis (classical/modern), discrete mathematics, algebra, number theory.

University of South Carolina, The Graduate School, College of Education, Department of Instruction and Teacher Education, Program in Secondary Education, Columbia, SC 29208. Offers art education (IMA, MAT); business education (IMA, MAT); English (MAT); foreign language (MAT); health education (MAT); mathematics (MAT); science (IMA, MAT); secondary (Ed D); secondary education (MT, PhD); social studies (MAT); theatre and speech (MAT). IMA and MT offered jointly with the subject areas. *Accreditation:* NCATE. *Degree requirements:* For master's, comprehensive exam, thesis (for some programs), foreign language (MA); for doctorate, one foreign language, comprehensive exam, thesis/dissertation. *Entrance requirements:* For master's, GRE General Test or MAT, teaching certificate (IMA, M Ed), interview; for doctorate, GRE General Test or MAT, interview. *Faculty research:* Middle school programs, professional development, school collaboration.

University of South Dakota, Graduate School, School of Education, Division of Curriculum and Instruction, Program in Elementary Education, Vermillion, SD 57069. Offers elementary education (MA), including early childhood education, English language learning, reading specialist/literacy coach, science, technology and math (STEM). *Accreditation:* NCATE. *Program availability:* Part-time, 100% online, blended/hybrid learning. *Degree requirements:* For master's, comprehensive exam, thesis or alternative. *Entrance requirements:* For master's, GRE General Test, MAT, minimum GPA of 2.7. Additional exam requirements/recommendations for international students: Required—TOEFL (minimum score 550 paper-based; 79 iBT). *Application deadline:* Applications are processed on a rolling basis. Application fee: $35. Electronic applications accepted. *Financial support:* Research assistantships with partial tuition reimbursements, teaching assistantships with partial tuition reimbursements, career-related internships or fieldwork, Federal Work-Study, and unspecified assistantships available. Financial award applicants required to submit FAFSA. *Application contact:* Graduate School, 605-658-6140, Fax: 605-677-6118, E-mail: grad@usd.edu.
Website: http://www.usd.edu/ci

University of South Dakota, Graduate School, School of Education, Division of Curriculum and Instruction, Program in Secondary Education, Vermillion, SD 57069. Offers secondary education (MA), including English language learning, science, technology and math (STEM), secondary education plus certification. *Accreditation:* NCATE. *Program availability:* Part-time, online learning. *Degree requirements:* For master's, comprehensive exam, thesis or alternative. *Entrance requirements:* For master's, GRE General Test, MAT, minimum GPA of 2.7. Additional exam requirements/recommendations for international students: Required—TOEFL (minimum score 550 paper-based; 79 iBT). *Application deadline:* Applications are processed on a rolling basis. Application fee: $35. Electronic applications accepted. *Financial support:* Research assistantships with partial tuition reimbursements, teaching assistantships with partial tuition reimbursements, career-related internships or fieldwork, Federal Work-Study, and unspecified assistantships available. Financial award applicants required to submit FAFSA. *Application contact:* Graduate School, 605-658-6140, Fax: 605-677-6118.
Website: http://www.usd.edu/ci

University of Southern Indiana, Graduate Studies, Pott College of Science, Engineering, and Education, Department of Teacher Education, Program in Secondary Education, Evansville, IN 47712-3590. Offers secondary education (MSE), including mathematics teaching. *Accreditation:* NCATE. *Program availability:* Part-time, evening/weekend. *Faculty:* 4 full-time (3 women), 2 part-time/adjunct (1 woman). *Students:* 1 (woman) full-time. Average age 30. In 2017, 3 master's awarded. *Entrance requirements:* For master's, PRAXIS II, bachelor's degree with minimum cumulative GPA of 2.75 from college or university accredited by NCATE or comparable association; minimum GPA of 3.0 in all courses taken at graduate level at all schools attended; teaching license. Additional exam requirements/recommendations for international students: Required—TOEFL (minimum score 550 paper-based; 79 iBT), IELTS (minimum score 6). *Application deadline:* For fall admission, 7/1 priority date for domestic students, 1/1 priority date for international students. Applications are processed on a rolling basis. Application fee: $40. Electronic applications accepted. *Expenses:* Tuition, state resident: full-time $9394. Tuition, nonresident: full-time $17,917. *Required fees:* $510. *Financial support:* In 2017–18, 6 students received support. Federal Work-Study, institutionally sponsored loans, scholarships/grants, tuition waivers (full and partial), and unspecified assistantships available. Financial award application deadline: 3/1; financial award applicants required to submit FAFSA. *Unit head:* Dr. Bonnie Beach, Associate Dean, 812-465-1620, E-mail: blbeach@usi.edu. *Application contact:* Dr. Mayola Rowser, Director, Graduate Studies, 812-465-7015, Fax: 812-464-1956, E-mail: mrowser@usi.edu.
Website: http://www.usi.edu/science/teacher-education/programs/mse

University of South Florida, St. Petersburg, College of Education, St. Petersburg, FL 33701. Offers educational leadership development (M Ed); elementary education (MA),

Mathematics Education

including math/science; English education (MA); middle grades STEM education (MS); reading education (MA). *Program availability:* Part-time. *Degree requirements:* For master's, comprehensive exam, practicum, internship, comprehensive portfolio. *Entrance requirements:* For master's, State of Florida General Knowledge Test (GKT), Florida Teaching Certificate (for non-initial certification programs), letters of recommendation. Additional exam requirements/recommendations for international students: Required—TOEFL (minimum score 550 paper-based; 79 iBT); Recommended—IELTS. Electronic applications accepted.

The University of Tennessee, Graduate School, College of Education, Health and Human Sciences, Program in Education, Knoxville, TN 37996. Offers art education (MS); counseling education (PhD); cultural studies in education (PhD); curriculum (MS, Ed S); curriculum, educational research and evaluation (Ed D, PhD); early childhood education (PhD); early childhood special education (MS); education of deaf and hard of hearing (MS); educational administration and policy studies (Ed D, PhD); educational administration and supervision (Ed S); educational psychology (Ed D, PhD); elementary education (MS, Ed S); elementary teaching (MS); English education (MS, Ed S); exercise science (PhD); foreign language/ESL education (MS, Ed S); instructional technology (MS, Ed D, PhD, Ed S); literacy, language and ESL education (PhD); literacy, language education, and ESL education (Ed D); mathematics education (MS, Ed S); modified and comprehensive special education (MS); reading education (MS, Ed S); school counseling (Ed S); school psychology (PhD, Ed S); science education (MS, Ed S); secondary teaching (MS); social foundations (MS); social science education (MS, Ed S); socio-cultural foundations of sports and education (PhD); special education (Ed S); teacher education (Ed D, PhD). *Accreditation:* NCATE. *Program availability:* Part-time, evening/weekend. *Degree requirements:* For master's and Ed S, thesis optional; for doctorate, variable foreign language requirement, thesis/dissertation. *Entrance requirements:* For master's, minimum GPA of 2.7; for doctorate and Ed S, GRE General Test, minimum GPA of 2.7. Additional exam requirements/recommendations for international students: Required—TOEFL. Electronic applications accepted.

The University of Tennessee at Chattanooga, Program in Mathematics, Chattanooga, TN 37403. Offers applied mathematics (MS); applied statistics (MS); mathematics education (MS); pre-professional mathematics (MS). *Program availability:* Part-time. *Students:* 10 full-time (2 women), 6 part-time (3 women); includes 4 minority (1 Hispanic/Latino; 3 Two or more races, non-Hispanic/Latino), 1 international. Average age 27. 6 applicants, 100% accepted, 5 enrolled. In 2017, 9 master's awarded. *Degree requirements:* For master's, internship or thesis. *Entrance requirements:* For master's, GRE (if applying for an assistantship), two letters of recommendation. Additional exam requirements/recommendations for international students: Required—TOEFL (minimum score 550 paper-based; 61 iBT), IELTS (minimum score 6). *Application deadline:* For fall admission, 6/15 for domestic students, 7/1 for international students; for spring admission, 11/1 for domestic and international students. Applications are processed on a rolling basis. Application fee: $35 ($40 for international students). Electronic applications accepted. *Expenses:* Contact institution. *Financial support:* Research assistantships and teaching assistantships available. Financial award application deadline: 7/1; financial award applicants required to submit FAFSA. *Total annual research expenditures:* $131,880. *Unit head:* Dr. Francesco Barioli, Graduate Program Coordinator, 423-425-2198, E-mail: francesco-barioli@utc.edu. *Application contact:* Dr. Joanne Romagni, Dean of the Graduate School, 423-425-4478, Fax: 423-425-5223, E-mail: joanne-romagni@utc.edu.
Website: http://www.utc.edu/mathematics/

The University of Texas at Arlington, Graduate School, College of Education, Department of Curriculum and Instruction, Arlington, TX 76019. Offers curriculum and instruction (M Ed), including literacy studies, mathematics education, mind, brain, and education, science education; teaching (with certification) (M Ed T). *Accreditation:* NCATE. *Program availability:* Part-time, evening/weekend, online learning. *Degree requirements:* For master's, comprehensive exam (for some programs), comprehensive activity, research project. *Entrance requirements:* For master's, GRE General Test, minimum undergraduate GPA of 3.0 in last 60 hours of course work, writing sample, 3 letters of recommendation. Additional exam requirements/recommendations for international students: Required—TOEFL (minimum score 550 paper-based). Electronic applications accepted.

The University of Texas at Arlington, Graduate School, College of Science, Department of Mathematics, Arlington, TX 76019. Offers applied math (MS); mathematics (PhD); mathematics education (MA). *Program availability:* Part-time, evening/weekend. *Degree requirements:* For master's, comprehensive exam, thesis or alternative; for doctorate, comprehensive exam, thesis/dissertation, preliminary examinations. *Entrance requirements:* For master's, GRE General Test (minimum score 350 verbal, 650 quantitative); for doctorate, GRE General Test (minimum score 350 verbal, 700 quantitative), 30 hours of graduate course work in mathematics, minimum GPA of 3.0 in last 60 hours of course work. Additional exam requirements/recommendations for international students: Required—TOEFL (minimum score 550 paper-based; 79 iBT). Electronic applications accepted. *Faculty research:* Algebra, combinatorics and geometry, applied mathematics and mathematical biology, computational mathematics, mathematics education, probability and statistics.

The University of Texas at Dallas, School of Natural Sciences and Mathematics, Department of Science/Mathematics Education, Richardson, TX 75080. Offers mathematics education (MAT); science education (MAT). *Program availability:* Part-time, evening/weekend, online learning. *Faculty:* 4 full-time (1 woman). *Students:* 4 full-time (2 women), 29 part-time (19 women); includes 14 minority (1 Black or African American, non-Hispanic/Latino; 6 Asian, non-Hispanic/Latino; 5 Hispanic/Latino; 2 Two or more races, non-Hispanic/Latino), 1 international. Average age 33. 28 applicants, 61% accepted, 13 enrolled. In 2017, 16 master's awarded. *Degree requirements:* For master's, thesis optional. *Entrance requirements:* For master's, GRE General Test, minimum GPA of 3.0 in upper-level coursework in field. Additional exam requirements/recommendations for international students: Required—TOEFL (minimum score 550 paper-based). *Application deadline:* For fall admission, 7/15 for domestic students, 5/1 priority date for international students; for spring admission, 11/15 for domestic students, 9/1 priority date for international students. Applications are processed on a rolling basis. Application fee: $50 ($100 for international students). Electronic applications accepted. *Expenses:* Tuition, state resident: full-time $12,916; part-time $718 per credit hour. Tuition, nonresident: full-time $25,252; part-time $1403 per credit hour. *Financial support:* In 2017–18, 20 students received support, including 3 teaching assistantships with partial tuition reimbursements available (averaging $17,100 per year); fellowships, research assistantships with partial tuition reimbursements available, career-related internships or fieldwork, Federal Work-Study, institutionally sponsored loans, scholarships/grants, and unspecified assistantships also available. Support available to part-time students. Financial award application deadline: 4/30; financial award applicants required to submit FAFSA. *Faculty research:* Innovative science/math education programs. *Unit head:* Dr. Mary Urquhart Kelly, Department Head, 972-883-2496, Fax: 972-883-6796, E-mail: scimathed@utdallas.edu.
Website: http://www.utdallas.edu/sme/

The University of Texas at El Paso, Graduate School, College of Science, Department of Mathematical Sciences, El Paso, TX 79968-0001. Offers mathematical sciences (MS); mathematics (teaching) (MAT); statistics (MS). *Program availability:* Part-time, evening/weekend. *Degree requirements:* For master's, thesis optional. *Entrance requirements:* For master's, minimum GPA of 3.0, letters of recommendation. Additional exam requirements/recommendations for international students: Required—TOEFL; Recommended—IELTS. Electronic applications accepted.

The University of Texas at San Antonio, College of Sciences, Department of Mathematics, San Antonio, TX 78249-0617. Offers applied mathematics (MS), including industrial mathematics; mathematics (MS); mathematics education (MS). *Program availability:* Part-time, evening/weekend. *Faculty:* 9 full-time (0 women). *Students:* 4 full-time (1 woman), 22 part-time (9 women); includes 15 minority (13 Hispanic/Latino; 2 Two or more races, non-Hispanic/Latino). Average age 32. 15 applicants, 93% accepted, 11 enrolled. In 2017, 12 master's awarded. *Degree requirements:* For master's, comprehensive exam (for some programs), thesis or alternative. *Entrance requirements:* For master's, GRE General Test, minimum GPA of 3.0 in last 60 hours. Additional exam requirements/recommendations for international students: Required—TOEFL (minimum score 550 paper-based; 79 iBT), IELTS (minimum score 6.5). *Application deadline:* For fall admission, 6/15 for domestic students, 3/1 for international students; for spring admission, 10/15 for domestic students, 9/15 for international students. Applications are processed on a rolling basis. Application fee: $50 ($90 for international students). Electronic applications accepted. *Expenses:* Tuition, state resident: full-time $5495. Tuition, nonresident: full-time $21,938. *Required fees:* $1915. Tuition and fees vary according to program. *Financial support:* Applicants required to submit FAFSA. *Faculty research:* Differential equations, functional analysis, numerical analysis, number theory, logic. *Total annual research expenditures:* $190,853. *Unit head:* Dr. Sandy Norman, Department Chair, 210-458-5735, E-mail: sandy.norman@utsa.edu. *Application contact:* Monica Rodriguez, Director of Graduate Admissions, 210-458-4331, Fax: 210-458-4332, E-mail: graduate.admissions@utsa.edu.
Website: http://math.utsa.edu

University of the District of Columbia, College of Arts and Sciences, Program in Teaching, Washington, DC 20008-1175. Offers elementary education (MAT); middle school mathematics (MAT); secondary English language arts (MAT); secondary social studies (MAT).

University of the Incarnate Word, School of Mathematics, Science, and Engineering, San Antonio, TX 78209-6397. Offers applied statistics (MS); biology (MA, MS); mathematics (MA), including teaching; multidisciplinary sciences (MA); nutrition (MS). *Program availability:* Part-time, evening/weekend. *Faculty:* 9 full-time (4 women), 3 part-time/adjunct (1 woman). *Students:* 42 full-time (33 women), 6 part-time (5 women); includes 27 minority (2 Black or African American, non-Hispanic/Latino; 1 American Indian or Alaska Native, non-Hispanic/Latino; 1 Asian, non-Hispanic/Latino; 23 Hispanic/Latino), 6 international. In 2017, 13 master's awarded. *Degree requirements:* For master's, comprehensive exam (for some programs), thesis optional, capstone. *Entrance requirements:* For master's, GRE, recommendation letter. Additional exam requirements/recommendations for international students: Required—TOEFL (minimum score 560 paper-based; 83 iBT). *Application deadline:* Applications are processed on a rolling basis. Application fee: $20. Electronic applications accepted. *Expenses: Tuition:* Full-time $16,470; part-time $915 per credit hour. Tuition and fees vary according to degree level, program and student level. *Financial support:* In 2017–18, 1 research assistantship (averaging $5,000 per year) was awarded; Federal Work-Study, scholarships/grants, tuition waivers (partial), and unspecified assistantships also available. Financial award applicants required to submit FAFSA. *Faculty research:* Neural morphallaxis in lumbriculus variegatus, igneous and metamorphic petrology, applied cloud and precipitation physics, DNA-protein interactions, evolution of adenoviruses and picornaviruses. *Unit head:* Dr. Carlos A. Garcia, Dean, 210-829-2717, Fax: 210-829-3153, E-mail: cagarci9@uiwtx.edu. *Application contact:* Johnny Garcia, Graduate Admissions Counselor, 210-805-3554, Fax: 210-829-3921, E-mail: admis@uiwtx.edu.
Website: http://www.uiw.edu/smse/index.htm

University of the Sacred Heart, Graduate Programs, Department of Education, San Juan, PR 00914-0383. Offers early childhood education (M Ed); information technology and multimedia (Certificate); instruction systems and education technology (M Ed), including English, information technology and multimedia, instructional design, mathematics, Spanish. *Program availability:* Part-time, evening/weekend. *Degree requirements:* For master's, thesis. *Entrance requirements:* For master's, EXADEP, minimum undergraduate GPA of 2.75, interview.

University of the Virgin Islands, College of Science and Mathematics, St. Thomas, VI 00802. Offers marine and environmental science (MS); mathematics for secondary teachers (MA). *Program availability:* Part-time, online learning. *Degree requirements:* For master's, comprehensive exam, thesis. *Entrance requirements:* For master's, GRE, minimum GPA of 2.5. Additional exam requirements/recommendations for international students: Required—TOEFL (minimum score 550 paper-based). Electronic applications accepted.

The University of Toledo, College of Graduate Studies, Judith Herb College of Education, Department of Curriculum and Instruction, Toledo, OH 43606-3390. Offers art education (ME); career and technical education (ME, Ed S); curriculum and instruction (ME, PhD, Ed S); early childhood education (Ed S); education and anthropology (MAE); education and biology (MES); education and chemistry (MES); education and classics (MAE); education and economics (MAE); education and English (MAE); education and French (MAE); education and geology (MES); education and German (MAE); education and history (MAE); education and mathematics (MAE, MES); education and physics (MES); education and political science (MAE); education and sociology (MAE); education and Spanish (MAE); educational media (PhD); educational technology (ME); educational technology: virtual educator (Certificate); elementary education (PhD); English as a second language (MAE); gifted and talented education (PhD); middle childhood education (ME); secondary education (ME, PhD); special education (PhD). *Accreditation:* NCATE. *Program availability:* Part-time, evening/weekend. *Degree requirements:* For master's, comprehensive exam, thesis or alternative; for doctorate, comprehensive exam, thesis/dissertation; for other advanced degree, thesis optional. *Entrance requirements:* For master's, doctorate, and other advanced degree, minimum cumulative GPA of 2.7 for all previous academic work, letters of recommendation. Additional exam requirements/recommendations for international students: Required—TOEFL (minimum score 550 paper-based; 80 iBT). Electronic applications accepted.

The University of Tulsa, Graduate School, Kendall College of Arts and Sciences, School of Education, Tulsa, OK 74104-3189. Offers mathematics and science education (MSMSE); teaching arts (MTA), including art, biology, English, history, mathematics; urban education (MA). *Accreditation:* TEAC. *Program availability:* Part-time. *Faculty:* 9 full-time (5 women), 2 part-time/adjunct (both women). *Students:* 8 full-time (4 women), 6 part-time (5 women); includes 4 minority (1 Black or African American, non-Hispanic/Latino; 1 American Indian or Alaska Native, non-Hispanic/Latino; 1 Asian, non-Hispanic/Latino; 1 Two or more races, non-Hispanic/Latino). Average age 31. 22 applicants, 9% accepted. In 2017, 10 master's awarded. *Degree requirements:* For master's, thesis optional. *Entrance requirements:* For master's, GRE General Test. Additional exam requirements/recommendations for international students: Required—TOEFL (minimum score 577 paper-based; 91 iBT), IELTS (minimum score 6.5). *Application deadline:* For fall admission, 2/1 priority date for domestic students. Applications are processed on a rolling basis. Application fee: $55. Electronic applications accepted. *Expenses: Tuition:* Full-time $22,230. *Required fees:* $2000. Tuition and fees vary according to course load and program. *Financial support:* In 2017–18, 3 students received support, including 3 teaching assistantships with full tuition reimbursements available (averaging $13,410 per year); fellowships with tuition reimbursements available, research assistantships with tuition reimbursements available, career-related internships or fieldwork, Federal Work-Study, scholarships/grants, health care benefits, tuition waivers (full and partial), and unspecified assistantships also available. Support available to part-time students. Financial award application deadline: 2/1; financial award applicants required to submit FAFSA. *Faculty research:* Elementary/secondary certification, math/science education, teaching arts. *Unit head:* Dr. Elizabeth Smith, Chair, 918-631-2238, Fax: 918-631-3721, E-mail: elizabeth-smith-43@utulsa.edu. *Application contact:* Dr. David Brown, Advisor, 918-631-2719, Fax: 918-631-2133, E-mail: david-brown@utulsa.edu. Website: http://artsandsciences.utulsa.edu/academics/departments-schools/urban-education/

University of Utah, Graduate School, College of Science, Department of Mathematics, Salt Lake City, UT 84112-0090. Offers mathematics (MA, MS, PhD); mathematics teaching (MS); statistics (M Stat). *Program availability:* Part-time. *Faculty:* 39 full-time (4 women), 30 part-time/adjunct (8 women). *Students:* 97 full-time (31 women), 28 part-time (11 women); includes 12 minority (5 Asian, non-Hispanic/Latino; 5 Hispanic/Latino; 2 Two or more races, non-Hispanic/Latino), 37 international. Average age 26. 195 applicants, 32% accepted, 27 enrolled. In 2017, 12 master's, 12 doctorates awarded. Terminal master's awarded for partial completion of doctoral program. *Degree requirements:* For master's, comprehensive exam, thesis or alternative, written or oral exam; for doctorate, comprehensive exam, thesis/dissertation, written and oral exams. *Entrance requirements:* For master's and doctorate, GRE Subject Test in math (recommended), minimum undergraduate GPA of 3.0. Additional exam requirements/recommendations for international students: Required—TOEFL (minimum score 550 paper-based; 80 iBT), GRE (recommended). *Application deadline:* For fall admission, 4/1 for domestic and international students; for spring admission, 11/1 for domestic and international students; for summer admission, 3/15 for domestic and international students. Application fee: $55 ($65 for international students). Electronic applications accepted. *Expenses:* Contact institution. *Financial support:* In 2017–18, 118 students received support, including 1 fellowship (averaging $34,000 per year), 29 research assistantships with full tuition reimbursements available (averaging $19,350 per year), 81 teaching assistantships with full tuition reimbursements available (averaging $20,000 per year); health care benefits and unspecified assistantships also available. Financial award application deadline: 1/1; financial award applicants required to submit FAFSA. *Faculty research:* Algebraic geometry, applied mathematics, commutative algebra, data science, geometry and topology, materials and microstructure, mathematical biology, number theory, probability, statistics. *Total annual research expenditures:* $3.4 million. *Unit head:* Dr. Davar Khoshnevisan, Chair, 801-581-7870, E-mail: chair@math.utah.edu. *Application contact:* Dr. Elena Cherkaev, Director of Graduate Studies, 801-581-7315, Fax: 801-581-6841, E-mail: elena@math.utah.edu. Website: http://www.math.utah.edu/

University of Victoria, Faculty of Graduate Studies, Faculty of Education, Department of Curriculum and Instruction, Victoria, BC V8W 2Y2, Canada. Offers art education (M Ed, PhD); curriculum studies (M Ed, MA, PhD); early childhood education (M Ed, PhD); educational studies (PhD); language and literacy (M Ed, MA, PhD); mathematics (M Ed, MA, PhD); music education (M Ed, MA, PhD); science (M Ed, MA, PhD); social studies (M Ed, MA); social, cultural and foundational studies (MA, PhD); technology and environmental education (PhD). *Program availability:* Part-time. *Degree requirements:* For master's, thesis, project (M Ed); for doctorate, comprehensive exam, thesis/dissertation. *Entrance requirements:* For master's, minimum B average. Additional exam requirements/recommendations for international students: Required—TOEFL (minimum score 575 paper-based), IELTS (minimum score 7). Electronic applications accepted. *Faculty research:* Elementary and secondary English, language arts, curriculum theory and practice, educational media and technology, educational administration and leadership, history and philosophy of education.

University of Virginia, Curry School of Education, Department of Curriculum, Instruction, and Special Education, Program in Curriculum and Instruction, Charlottesville, VA 22903. Offers curriculum and instruction (M Ed, Ed S); elementary education (M Ed, Ed D); English education (M Ed, Ed D); foreign language education (M Ed); mathematics education (M Ed, Ed D); science education (Ed D); social studies education (M Ed); MBA/M Ed. *Program availability:* 100% online. *Students:* 38 full-time (31 women), 15 part-time (12 women); includes 6 minority (2 Asian, non-Hispanic/Latino; 2 Hispanic/Latino; 2 Two or more races, non-Hispanic/Latino), 2 international. Average age 32. 92 applicants, 64% accepted, 47 enrolled. In 2017, 47 master's, 9 doctorates, 8 other advanced degrees awarded. *Degree requirements:* For master's, comprehensive exam (for some programs); for doctorate, comprehensive exam, thesis/dissertation; for Ed S, comprehensive exam. *Entrance requirements:* For master's, doctorate, and Ed S, GRE General Test, 2 letters of recommendation. Additional exam requirements/recommendations for international students: Required—TOEFL (minimum score 600 paper-based; 90 iBT), IELTS (minimum score 7). *Application deadline:* Applications are processed on a rolling basis. Application fee: $60. Electronic applications accepted. *Financial support:* Fellowships with tuition reimbursements, research assistantships with tuition reimbursements, and teaching assistantships with tuition reimbursements available. Financial award application deadline: 1/5; financial award applicants required to submit FAFSA. *Unit head:* Susan Mintz, Program Area Director, 434-924-3128, E-mail: slm4r@virginia.edu. *Application contact:* E-mail: curry-admissions@virginia.edu. Website: http://curry.virginia.edu/academics/areas-of-study/curriculum-teaching-learning

University of Virginia, Curry School of Education, Program in Education, Charlottesville, VA 22903. Offers administration and supervision (PhD); applied developmental science (PhD); counselor education (PhD); curriculum and instruction (PhD); early childhood special education (MT); education evaluation (PhD); educational psychology (PhD); educational research (PhD); elementary education (MT); English education (MT, PhD); foreign language education (MT); higher education (PhD); instructional technology (PhD); kinesiology (MT, PhD); math education (PhD); reading education (PhD); research, statistics and evaluation (PhD); school psychology (PhD); science education (PhD); social studies education (MT, PhD); special education (PhD); world languages education (MT). *Students:* 431 full-time (353 women), 15 part-time (14 women); includes 100 minority (32 Black or African American, non-Hispanic/Latino; 33 Asian, non-Hispanic/Latino; 16 Hispanic/Latino; 19 Two or more races, non-Hispanic/Latino), 14 international. Average age 25. 264 applicants, 49% accepted, 83 enrolled. In 2017, 142 master's, 33 doctorates awarded. *Degree requirements:* For master's, comprehensive exam (for some programs), field project; for doctorate, comprehensive exam, thesis/dissertation. *Entrance requirements:* For doctorate, GRE General Test. Additional exam requirements/recommendations for international students: Required—

TOEFL (minimum score 600 paper-based; 90 iBT), IELTS (minimum score 7). *Application deadline:* Applications are processed on a rolling basis. Application fee: $60. Electronic applications accepted. *Financial support:* Fellowships, research assistantships, and teaching assistantships available. Financial award application deadline: 1/5; financial award applicants required to submit FAFSA. *Unit head:* Robert C. Pianta, Dean, 434-924-3334, E-mail: pianta@virginia.edu. *Application contact:* E-mail: curry-admissions@virginia.edu. Website: http://curry.virginia.edu/teacher-education

University of Washington, Graduate School, College of Education, Seattle, WA 98195. Offers curriculum and instruction (M Ed, Ed D, PhD), including educational technology, general curriculum (Ed D, PhD), language, literacy, and culture, mathematics education, multicultural education, reading and language arts education (Ed D), science education, social studies education, teaching and curriculum (M Ed); educational leadership and policy studies (M Ed, Ed D, PhD), including administration (Ed D), educational policy, organization, and leadership (M Ed, PhD), higher education, leadership for learning (Ed D), social and cultural foundations of education (M Ed, PhD); educational psychology (M Ed, PhD), including educational psychology (PhD), human development and cognition (M Ed), learning sciences, measurement, statistics and research design (M Ed), school psychology (M Ed); instructional leadership (M Ed); intercollegiate athletic leadership (M Ed); special education (M Ed, Ed D, PhD), including early childhood special education (M Ed), emotional and behavioral disabilities (M Ed), learning disabilities (M Ed), low-incidence disabilities (M Ed), severe disabilities (M Ed), special education (Ed D, PhD); teacher education (MIT). *Accreditation:* APA. *Program availability:* Part-time, evening/weekend. *Degree requirements:* For master's, thesis optional; for doctorate, thesis/dissertation. *Entrance requirements:* For master's and doctorate, GRE General Test, minimum GPA of 3.0. Additional exam requirements/recommendations for international students: Required—TOEFL. Electronic applications accepted. *Faculty research:* School restructuring/effective schools, special education interventions, literacy and writing, technology, school partnerships, teacher preparation.

University of Washington, Tacoma, Graduate Programs, Program in Education, Tacoma, WA 98402-3100. Offers education (M Ed); educational administration (principal or program administrator certification) (M Ed); elementary education teacher certification (M Ed); elementary education/special education teacher certification (M Ed); secondary science or math teacher certification (M Ed). *Program availability:* Part-time, evening/weekend. *Degree requirements:* For master's, culminating project. *Entrance requirements:* For master's, WEST-B, WEST-E (teacher certification programs only), official sealed transcript from every college/university attended, personal goal statement, letters of recommendation, copy of valid teaching certificate. Additional exam requirements/recommendations for international students: Required—TOEFL (minimum score 580 paper-based; 92 iBT). Electronic applications accepted. *Faculty research:* Global learning communities for English/Chinese languages, evaluation of mathematics and reading intervention programs, response to intervention, school-wide behavioral and emotional support, mathematics education and culturally responsive mathematics education.

The University of West Alabama, School of Graduate Studies, College of Education, Program in Secondary Education, Livingston, AL 35470. Offers biology (MAT); English language arts (MAT); high school 6-12 (M Ed); history (MAT); mathematics (MAT); science (MAT); social science (MAT). *Program availability:* Part-time, evening/weekend, 100% online. *Faculty:* 21 full-time (7 women), 5 part-time/adjunct (1 woman). *Students:* 259 (183 women); includes 61 minority (51 Black or African American, non-Hispanic/Latino; 2 American Indian or Alaska Native, non-Hispanic/Latino; 3 Asian, non-Hispanic/Latino; 2 Hispanic/Latino; 3 Two or more races, non-Hispanic/Latino). Average age 32. 58 applicants, 93% accepted, 45 enrolled. In 2017, 80 master's awarded. *Degree requirements:* For master's, comprehensive exam, thesis optional. *Entrance requirements:* For master's, GRE, minimum GPA of 2.75, verification of background clearance/fingerprints, valid bachelor's-level Professional Educator Certificate in same teaching field. Additional exam requirements/recommendations for international students: Required—TOEFL (minimum score 500 paper-based; 61 iBT). *Application deadline:* Applications are processed on a rolling basis. Application fee: $40. Electronic applications accepted. *Expenses:* Tuition, state resident: part-time $371 per credit hour. Tuition, nonresident: part-time $742 per credit hour. *Required fees:* $130 per semester. *Financial support:* Teaching assistantships, Federal Work-Study, scholarships/grants, and unspecified assistantships available. Support available to part-time students. Financial award application deadline: 3/1; financial award applicants required to submit FAFSA. *Unit head:* Dr. Jodie Winship, Chair of Teaching and Learning, 205-652-5415, Fax: 205-652-3706, E-mail: jwinship@uwa.edu. *Application contact:* Dr. B. J. Kimbrough, Dean of Graduate Studies, 205-652-3647, Fax: 205-652-3670, E-mail: bkimbrough@uwa.edu.

University of Wisconsin–Milwaukee, Graduate School, School of Education, Department of Curriculum and Instruction, Milwaukee, WI 53201-0413. Offers curriculum and instruction (MS), including cross-curricular focus, early childhood education, English education, mathematics education, middle childhood/early adolescence education, reading education, science education, urban social studies education. *Program availability:* Part-time. *Students:* 17 full-time (13 women), 45 part-time (39 women); includes 13 minority (2 Black or African American, non-Hispanic/Latino; 3 Asian, non-Hispanic/Latino; 1 Hispanic/Latino; 7 Two or more races, non-Hispanic/Latino). Average age 33. 32 applicants, 66% accepted, 16 enrolled. In 2017, 26 master's awarded. *Entrance requirements:* Additional exam requirements/recommendations for international students: Required—TOEFL (minimum score 550 paper-based; 79 iBT), IELTS (minimum score 6.5). *Application deadline:* For fall admission, 1/1 priority date for domestic students; for spring admission, 9/1 for domestic students. Application fee: $56 ($96 for international students). Electronic applications accepted. *Financial support:* Fellowships, research assistantships, teaching assistantships, career-related internships or fieldwork, health care benefits, unspecified assistantships, and project assistantships available. Support available to part-time students. Financial award application deadline: 4/15; financial award applicants required to submit FAFSA. *Application contact:* General Information Contact, 414-229-4721, E-mail: soeinfo@uwm.edu. Website: http://uwm.edu/education/academics/curriculum-instruction-department/

University of Wisconsin–Milwaukee, Graduate School, School of Education, Department of Exceptional Education, Milwaukee, WI 53201-0413. Offers autism spectrum disorders (Graduate Certificate); exceptional education (MS); transition for students with disabilities (Graduate Certificate); urban education (PhD), including adult, continuing and higher education leadership, art education, curriculum and instruction, exceptional education, mathematics education, multicultural studies, social foundations of education. *Program availability:* Part-time. *Students:* 45 full-time (34 women), 68 part-time (54 women); includes 46 minority (27 Black or African American, non-Hispanic/Latino; 7 Asian, non-Hispanic/Latino; 1 Hispanic/Latino; 11 Two or more races, non-Hispanic/Latino), 4 international. Average age 39. 43 applicants, 53% accepted, 19 enrolled. In 2017, 12 master's, 13 doctorates, 8 other advanced degrees awarded. *Entrance requirements:* Additional exam requirements/recommendations for international students: Required—TOEFL (minimum score 550 paper-based; 79 iBT), IELTS (minimum score 6.5). *Application deadline:* For fall admission, 1/1 priority date for domestic students; for spring admission, 9/1 for domestic students. Application fee: $56 ($96 for international students). Electronic applications accepted. *Financial support:* Fellowships, research assistantships, teaching assistantships, career-related internships or fieldwork, health care benefits, and unspecified assistantships available. Support available to part-time students. Financial award application deadline: 4/15; financial award applicants required to submit FAFSA. *Faculty research:* Emotional disturbance, hearing impairment, learning disabilities, mental retardation. *Application contact:* General Information Contact, 414-229-4721, E-mail: soeinfo@uwm.edu. Website: http://uwm.edu/education/academics/exceptional-edu-department/

University of Wisconsin–Oshkosh, Graduate Studies, College of Letters and Science, Department of Mathematics, Oshkosh, WI 54901. Offers mathematics education (MS). *Program availability:* Part-time. *Degree requirements:* For master's, comprehensive exam, thesis optional. *Entrance requirements:* For master's, 30 undergraduate credits in mathematics. Additional exam requirements/recommendations for international students: Required—TOEFL (minimum score 550 paper-based; 79 iBT). Electronic applications accepted. *Faculty research:* Problem solving, number theory, discrete mathematics, statistics.

University of Wisconsin–River Falls, Outreach and Graduate Studies, College of Arts and Science, Program in Mathematics, River Falls, WI 54022. Offers mathematics education (MSE). *Program availability:* Part-time. *Degree requirements:* For master's, thesis (for some programs). *Entrance requirements:* For master's, minimum GPA of 2.75. Additional exam requirements/recommendations for international students: Required—TOEFL (minimum score 500 paper-based; 65 iBT), IELTS (minimum score 5.5). Electronic applications accepted.

University of Wyoming, College of Arts and Sciences, Department of Mathematics, Laramie, WY 82071. Offers mathematics (MA, MAT, MS, MST, PhD); mathematics/computer science (PhD). *Program availability:* Part-time. Terminal master's awarded for partial completion of doctoral program. *Degree requirements:* For master's, comprehensive exam, thesis, qualifying exam; for doctorate, comprehensive exam, thesis/dissertation, preliminary exam. *Entrance requirements:* For master's and doctorate, GRE General Test, minimum GPA of 3.0. Additional exam requirements/recommendations for international students: Required—TOEFL (minimum score 540 paper-based; 76 iBT). *Faculty research:* Numerical analysis, classical analysis, mathematical modeling, algebraic combinations.

Utah Valley University, Program in Education, Orem, UT 84058-5999. Offers educational technology (M Ed); elementary mathematics (M Ed); elementary STEM (M Ed); English as a second language (M Ed); reading (M Ed); teachers as leaders (M Ed). *Accreditation:* TEAC. *Program availability:* Part-time. *Degree requirements:* For master's, project. *Entrance requirements:* For master's, GRE, 3 letters of recommendation, interview, essay. Additional exam requirements/recommendations for international students: Required—TOEFL (minimum score 83 iBT). Electronic applications accepted. *Expenses:* Contact institution.

Virginia State University, College of Graduate Studies, College of Engineering and Technology, Department of Mathematics and Computer Science, Petersburg, VA 23806-0001. Offers computer science (MS); mathematics (MS); mathematics education (MS). *Degree requirements:* For master's, thesis (for some programs).

Wagner College, Division of Graduate Studies, Education Department, Program in Secondary Education/Students with Disabilities, Staten Island, NY 10301-4495. Offers secondary education 7-12 (MS Ed), including language arts, languages other than English, mathematics and technology, science and technology, social studies. *Program availability:* Evening/weekend. *Faculty:* 2 full-time (1 woman), 7 part-time/adjunct (3 women). *Students:* 17 full-time (14 women), 6 part-time (4 women); includes 2 minority (1 Black or African American, non-Hispanic/Latino; 1 Asian, non-Hispanic/Latino). Average age 24. 15 applicants, 80% accepted, 11 enrolled. In 2017, 8 master's awarded. *Degree requirements:* For master's, thesis (for some programs), completion of state certification exams before student teaching. *Entrance requirements:* For master's, GRE, minimum GPA of 3.0, interview, recommendations. Additional exam requirements/recommendations for international students: Required—TOEFL (minimum score 550 paper-based; 79 iBT), IELTS (minimum score 6.5). *Application deadline:* For fall admission, 12/1 priority date for domestic and international students. Application fee: $60. Electronic applications accepted. *Expenses:* Contact institution. *Financial support:* Unspecified assistantships and alumni fellowship available. Financial award application deadline: 2/15; financial award applicants required to submit FAFSA. *Unit head:* Dr. Jason Fitzgerald, Department Chair, 718-420-4129, Fax: 718-390-3456, E-mail: jason.fitzgerald@wagner.edu. *Application contact:* Patricia Clancy, Assistant Director of Enrollment, 718-420-4464, Fax: 718-390-3105, E-mail: patricia.clancy@wagner.edu. Website: http://www.wagner.edu/education

Walden University, Graduate Programs, Richard W. Riley College of Education and Leadership, Minneapolis, MN 55401. Offers adult education (Post-Master's Certificate); adult learning (Graduate Certificate); college teaching and learning (Graduate Certificate); community college leadership (Ed D); curriculum, instruction and assessment (Ed D, Ed S, Graduate Certificate); developmental education (Graduate Certificate); early childhood administration, management, and leadership (Graduate Certificate); early childhood education (Ed D, Ed S); early childhood public policy and advocacy (Graduate Certificate); early childhood studies (MS), including administration, management and leadership, early childhood public policy and advocacy, teaching adults in the early childhood field, teaching and diversity in early childhood education; education (MS, PhD), including adolescent literacy and learning (MS), curriculum, instruction, and assessment (grades K-12) (MS), curriculum, instruction, assessment, and evaluation (PhD), early childhood leadership and advocacy (PhD), early childhood special education (PhD), educational leadership (MS), educational leadership and administration (principal preparation) (MS), educational technology and design (PhD), elementary reading and literacy (PreK-6) (MS), elementary reading and mathematics (grades K-6) (MS), global and comparative education (PhD), higher education leadership management and policy (PhD), integrating technology in the classroom (grades K-12) (MS), learning, instruction and innovation (PhD), mathematics (grades 5-8) (MS), mathematics (grades K-6) (MS), mathematics and science (grades K-8) (MS), organizational research, assessment, and evaluation (PhD), reading and literacy with a reading K-12 endorsement (MS), reading literacy assessment and evaluation (PhD), science (grades K-8) (MS), special education (non-licensure) (grades K-12) (MS), teacher leadership (grades K-12) (MS), teaching English language learners (grades K-12) (MS); educational administration and leadership (Ed D); educational leadership and administration (principal preparation) (Ed S); educational technology (Ed D, Ed S, Post Master's Certificate); elementary reading and literacy (Graduate Certificate); engaging culturally diverse learners (Graduate Certificate); enrollment management and institutional marketing (Graduate Certificate); higher education (MS), including adult learning, college teaching and learning, enrollment management and institutional marketing, global higher education, leadership for student success, online and distance learning; higher education and adult learning (Ed D); higher education leadership and management (Ed D); higher education leadership for student success (Graduate Certificate); instructional design and technology (MS, Postbaccalaureate Certificate), including general program (MS), online learning (MS), training and performance improvement (MS); integrating technology in the classroom (Graduate Certificate);

mathematics 5-8 (Graduate Certificate); mathematics K-6 (Graduate Certificate); online teaching for adult educators (Graduate Certificate); reading, literacy, and assessment (Ed D, Ed S); science K-8 (Graduate Certificate); special education (Ed D, Ed S, Graduate Certificate); special education (K-age 21) (MAT); teacher leadership (Graduate Certificate); teaching adults English as a second language (Graduate Certificate); teaching adults in the early childhood field (Graduate Certificate); teaching and diversity in early childhood education (Graduate Certificate); teaching English language learners (grades K-12) (Graduate Certificate); teaching K-12 students online (Graduate Certificate). *Accreditation:* NCATE. *Program availability:* Part-time, evening/weekend, online only, 100% online. *Degree requirements:* For doctorate, thesis/dissertation (for some programs), residency; for other advanced degree, residency (for some programs). *Entrance requirements:* For master's, bachelor's degree or higher; minimum GPA of 2.5; official transcripts; goal statement (for some programs); access to computer and Internet; for doctorate, master's degree or higher; three years of related professional or academic experience (preferred); minimum GPA of 3.0; goal statement and current resume (for select programs); official transcripts; access to computer and Internet; for other advanced degree, relevant work experience; access to computer and Internet. Additional exam requirements/recommendations for international students: Required—TOEFL (minimum score 550 paper-based, 79 iBT), IELTS (minimum score 6.5), Michigan English Language Assessment Battery (minimum score 82), or PTE (minimum score 53). Electronic applications accepted.

Washington State University, College of Arts and Sciences, Department of Mathematics, Pullman, WA 99164. Offers applied mathematics (MS, PhD); mathematics (MS, PhD); mathematics teaching (MS, PhD). Programs offered at the Pullman campus. *Program availability:* Part-time. Terminal master's awarded for partial completion of doctoral program. *Degree requirements:* For master's, comprehensive exam (for some programs), thesis or alternative, oral exam, project; for doctorate, 2 foreign languages, comprehensive exam, thesis/dissertation, oral exam, written exam. *Entrance requirements:* For master's and doctorate, minimum GPA of 3.0, 3 letters of recommendation. Additional exam requirements/recommendations for international students: Required—TOEFL (minimum score 600 paper-based; 100 iBT) or IELTS (minimum score 7). Electronic applications accepted. *Faculty research:* Computational mathematics, operations research, modeling in the natural sciences, applied statistics.

Washington State University, College of Education, Department of Teaching and Learning, Pullman, WA 99164-2132. Offers cultural studies and social thought in education (PhD); curriculum and instruction (Ed M, MA); English language learners (Ed M, MA); language, literacy and technology (PhD); literacy education (Ed M, MA); mathematics education (PhD); special education (Ed M, MA, PhD); teacher leadership (Ed D); teaching (MIT), including elementary education, secondary education. Programs offered at the Pullman, Spokane, Tri-cities, Vancouver and Global (online) campuses. *Program availability:* Part-time, online learning. *Degree requirements:* For master's, comprehensive exam, thesis, oral or written exam; for doctorate, comprehensive exam, thesis/dissertation, oral and written exam. *Entrance requirements:* For master's, GRE General Test, minimum GPA of 3.0, 3 letters of recommendation, letter of intent, transcripts, resume/curriculum vitae; for doctorate, GRE General Test, minimum GPA of 3.0, 3 letters of recommendation, letter of intent, transcripts, writing sample, resume/curriculum vitae. Additional exam requirements/recommendations for international students: Required—TOEFL (minimum score 550 paper-based; 80 iBT). Electronic applications accepted. *Faculty research:* Intersection of gender, youth cultures and schooling; examination of ideology of power in children's literature; early childhood special education; analyzing pre-service and in-service teacher development; second language acquisition.

Wayne State College, School of Education and Counseling, Department of Educational Foundations and Leadership, Program in Curriculum and Instruction, Wayne, NE 68787. Offers alternative education (MSE); business and information technology education (MSE); communication arts education (MSE); early childhood education (MSE); elementary education (MSE); English as a second language (MSE); English education (MSE); family and consumer sciences education (MSE); industrial technology and vocational education (MSE); learning communities (MSE); mathematics education (MSE); music education (MSE); science education (MSE); social science education (MSE). *Accreditation:* NCATE. *Program availability:* Part-time, evening/weekend. *Degree requirements:* For master's, comprehensive exam, thesis optional. *Entrance requirements:* For master's, GRE General Test. Additional exam requirements/recommendations for international students: Required—TOEFL (minimum score 550 paper-based).

Wayne State University, College of Education, Division of Teacher Education, Detroit, MI 48202. Offers art education (M Ed); bilingual/bicultural education (Certificate); curriculum and instruction (Ed D, PhD, Ed S), including English as a second language (MAT, Ed D, Ed S), K-12 curriculum (PhD); elementary education (MAT), including bilingual/bicultural education (M Ed, MAT), early childhood education (M Ed, MAT), English as a second language (MAT, Ed D, Ed S), foreign language education, science education (M Ed, MAT), special education (M Ed, MAT); elementary mathematics specialist (Certificate); English as a second language (Certificate); reading (M Ed, Ed S); reading, language and literature (Ed D); secondary education (MAT), including bilingual/bicultural education (M Ed, MAT), early childhood education (M Ed, MAT), English as a second language (MAT, Ed D, Ed S), English education, foreign language education, mathematics education (M Ed, MAT), science education (M Ed, MAT), social studies education (M Ed, MAT); special education (MAT), including career and technical education; teaching and learning (M Ed), including bilingual/bicultural education (M Ed, MAT), early childhood education (M Ed, MAT), elementary education, foreign language, mathematics education (M Ed, MAT), science education (M Ed, MAT), social studies education (M Ed, MAT), special education (M Ed, MAT). *Program availability:* Part-time, blended/hybrid learning. *Faculty:* 22. *Students:* 126 full-time (96 women), 317 part-time (258 women); includes 134 minority (95 Black or African American, non-Hispanic/Latino; 1 American Indian or Alaska Native, non-Hispanic/Latino; 8 Asian, non-Hispanic/Latino; 17 Hispanic/Latino; 1 Native Hawaiian or other Pacific Islander, non-Hispanic/Latino; 12 Two or more races, non-Hispanic/Latino), 13 international. Average age 37. 260 applicants, 33% accepted, 57 enrolled. In 2017, 111 master's, 13 doctorates, 7 other advanced degrees awarded. *Degree requirements:* For master's, essay or project (for some M Ed programs), professional field experience (for MAT programs); for doctorate, thesis/dissertation. *Entrance requirements:* For master's, Michigan Test for Teacher Certification (for most programs), verification of participation in group work with children (for MAT programs), Michigan State Police criminal background check; for doctorate, minimum undergraduate GPA of 3.0, graduate 3.5; interview; curriculum vitae; references; master's degree (for most programs). Additional exam requirements/recommendations for international students: Required—TOEFL (minimum score 550 paper-based; 79 iBT), TWE (minimum score 5.5). Recommended—IELTS (minimum score 6.5). *Application deadline:* For fall admission, 6/1 priority date for domestic students, 5/1 priority date for international students; for winter admission, 10/1 priority date for domestic students, 9/1 priority date for international students; for spring admission, 2/1 priority date for domestic students, 1/1 priority date for international students. Applications are processed on a rolling basis. Application fee: $50. Electronic applications accepted. *Expenses:* Tuition, state resident: full-time $10,224; part-time $638.98 per credit hour. Tuition, nonresident: full-time $22,145; part-time $1384.04 per

credit hour. Tuition and fees vary according to course load and program. *Financial support:* In 2017–18, 78 students received support, including 4 fellowships (averaging $13,500 per year), 1 research assistantship with tuition reimbursement available (averaging $16,000 per year); Federal Work-Study, scholarships/grants, and unspecified assistantships also available. Support available to part-time students. Financial award applicants required to submit FAFSA. *Faculty research:* Improving students' skill achievement in mathematics, improving elementary children's understanding of informational text, teachers' use of their pedagogical and mathematical knowledge in the interactive work of teaching, the intersection of identity construction in teaching and learning, identifying effective methods of literacy instruction and assessments for bilingual students in elementary language arts classrooms. *Unit head:* Dr. Thomas Edwards, Interim Associate Dean for Teacher Education, 313-577-3886, E-mail: t.g.edwards@wayne.edu. *Application contact:* 313-577-0902, E-mail: askcoe@wayne.edu.
Website: http://coe.wayne.edu/ted/index.php

Webster University, School of Education, Department of Multidisciplinary Studies, St. Louis, MO 63119-3194. Offers applied educational psychology (MA, Ed S); communication arts (MA); early childhood education (MA, MAT); education and innovation (MA); educational technology (MET); elementary education (MAT); mathematics for educators (MA); middle school education (MAT); multidisciplinary studies (MAT); multimodal literacy for global impact (MA); reading (MA); secondary school education (MAT); special education (MA, MAT); teaching English as a second language (MA); transformative learning in the global community (Ed S). *Program availability:* Part-time. *Entrance requirements:* For master's, minimum GPA of 2.5. Additional exam requirements/recommendations for international students: Required—TOEFL.

West Chester University of Pennsylvania, College of the Sciences and Mathematics, Department of Mathematics, West Chester, PA 19383. Offers applied and computational mathematics (MS); applied statistics (MS, Certificate); mathematics (MA, Teaching Certificate); mathematics education (MA). *Program availability:* Part-time, evening/weekend. *Students:* 17 full-time (6 women), 99 part-time (45 women); includes 25 minority (5 Black or African American, non-Hispanic/Latino; 18 Asian, non-Hispanic/Latino; 2 Two or more races, non-Hispanic/Latino), 14 international. Average age 31. 73 applicants, 95% accepted, 53 enrolled. In 2017, 41 master's awarded. *Degree requirements:* For master's, comprehensive exam or thesis (for MA). *Entrance requirements:* For master's, GMAT or GRE General Test (for MA in mathematics, may be waived under certain circumstances), interview (for MA in mathematics); for other advanced degree, GMAT or GRE General Test (for Certificate in applied statistics). Additional exam requirements/recommendations for international students: Required—TOEFL or IELTS. *Application deadline:* For fall admission, 5/15 for international students; for spring admission, 10/15 for international students. Applications are processed on a rolling basis. Application fee: $50. Electronic applications accepted. *Expenses:* Tuition, state resident: full-time $9000; part-time $500 per credit. Tuition, nonresident: full-time $13,500; part-time $750 per credit. *Required fees:* $2959; $149.79 per credit. *Financial support:* Scholarships/grants and unspecified assistantships available. Financial award application deadline: 2/15; financial award applicants required to submit FAFSA. *Faculty research:* Teachers teaching with technology in service training program, biostatistics, hierarchical linear models, clustered binary outcome data, mathematics biology, stochastic analysis. *Unit head:* Dr. Peter Glidden, Chair, 610-436-2440, Fax: 610-738-0578, E-mail: pglidden@wcupa.edu. *Application contact:* Dr. Gail Gallitano, Graduate Coordinator, 610-436-2452, Fax: 610-738-0578, E-mail: ggallitano@wcupa.edu.
Website: http://www.wcupa.edu/sciences-mathematics/mathematics/

Western Governors University, Teachers College, Salt Lake City, UT 84107. Offers curriculum and instruction (MS); educational leadership (MS); educational studies (MA); educational studies (5-12) (MA), including mathematics; elementary education (K-8) (MAT, Postbaccalaureate Certificate); elementary education (PreK-8) (MAT); English language learning (K-12) (MA); instructional design (MAT); learning and technology (M Ed, MA); management and innovation (M Ed); mathematics (5-12) (MAT, Postbaccalaureate Certificate); mathematics (5-9) (MAT, Postbaccalaureate Certificate); mathematics education (5-12) (MA); mathematics education (5-9) (MA); mathematics education (K-6) (MA); measurement and evaluation (M Ed); science (5-12) (Postbaccalaureate Certificate); science (5-9) (MAT, Postbaccalaureate Certificate); science education (5-12) (MA), including biology, chemistry, geology, physics; science education (5-9) (MA); social science (5-12) (MAT, Postbaccalaureate Certificate); special education (MAT, MS). *Accreditation:* NCATE. *Program availability:* Evening/weekend, online learning. *Degree requirements:* For master's, capstone project. *Entrance requirements:* For master's and Postbaccalaureate Certificate, Readiness Assessment, transcripts. Additional exam requirements/recommendations for international students: Required—TOEFL (minimum score 450 paper-based; 80 iBT). Electronic applications accepted. *Expenses:* Contact institution.

Western Michigan University, Graduate College, College of Arts and Sciences, Department of Mathematics, Kalamazoo, MI 49008. Offers applied and computational mathematics (MS); mathematics education (MA, PhD), including collegiate mathematics education (PhD). *Degree requirements:* For doctorate, one foreign language, thesis/dissertation.

Western New England University, College of Arts and Sciences, Program in Mathematics for Teachers, Springfield, MA 01119. Offers MAMT. *Program availability:* Part-time, evening/weekend. *Faculty:* 16 full-time (7 women). *Students:* 16 part-time (10 women); includes 1 minority (Asian, non-Hispanic/Latino), 1 international. Average age 35. 15 applicants, 80% accepted, 9 enrolled. In 2017, 5 master's awarded. *Entrance requirements:* For master's, two letters of recommendation, official transcript, personal statement, resume. Additional exam requirements/recommendations for international students: Required—TOEFL (minimum score 79 iBT). *Application deadline:* Applications are processed on a rolling basis. Application fee: $30. Electronic applications accepted. *Expenses:* Contact institution. *Financial support:* Application deadline: 4/15; applicants required to submit FAFSA. *Unit head:* Dr. David Mazur, Chair and Professor of Mathematics, 413-782-1696, E-mail: dmazur@wne.edu. *Application contact:* Matthew Fox, Director of Admissions for Graduate Students and Adult Learners, 413-782-1410, Fax: 413-782-1777, E-mail: study@wne.edu.
Website: http://www1.wne.edu/academics/graduate/ma-mathematics-teachers.cfm

Western Oregon University, Graduate Programs, College of Education, Division of Teacher Education, Program in Secondary Education, Monmouth, OR 97361. Offers bilingual education (MS Ed); health (MS Ed); humanities (MAT, MS Ed); initial licensure (MAT); mathematics (MAT, MS Ed); science (MAT, MS Ed); social science (MAT, MS Ed). *Accreditation:* NCATE. *Program availability:* Part-time, evening/weekend. *Degree requirements:* For master's, thesis optional, written exam. *Entrance requirements:* For master's, minimum GPA of 3.0, teaching license. Additional exam requirements/recommendations for international students: Required—TOEFL (minimum

score 550 paper-based; 79 iBT), IELTS (minimum score 6.5). *Faculty research:* Literacy, science in primary grades, geography education, retention, teacher burnout.

Westfield State University, College of Graduate and Continuing Education, Department of Education, Westfield, MA 01086. Offers early childhood education (M Ed); elementary education (M Ed); reading specialist (M Ed); secondary education (M Ed), including biology teacher education, chemistry teacher education, general science teacher education, history teacher education, mathematics teacher education, physical education teacher education; special education (M Ed), including moderate disabilities, 5-12, moderate disabilities, preK-8; vocational technical education (M Ed). *Accreditation:* NCATE. *Program availability:* Part-time, evening/weekend. *Faculty:* 6 full-time (all women), 17 part-time/adjunct (13 women). *Students:* 12 full-time (8 women), 137 part-time (110 women); includes 5 minority (1 Black or African American, non-Hispanic/Latino; 1 Asian, non-Hispanic/Latino; 1 Hispanic/Latino; 2 Two or more races, non-Hispanic/Latino). Average age 31. 65 applicants, 98% accepted, 50 enrolled. In 2017, 60 master's awarded. *Degree requirements:* For master's, comprehensive exam, practicum. *Entrance requirements:* For master's, GRE General Test or MAT, minimum undergraduate GPA of 2.8. Additional exam requirements/recommendations for international students: Recommended—TOEFL (minimum score 550 paper-based; 79 iBT). *Application deadline:* For fall admission, 7/1 for domestic students; for spring admission, 11/1 for domestic students; for summer admission, 4/1 for domestic students. Applications are processed on a rolling basis. Application fee: $50. *Expenses:* Tuition, state resident: part-time $332 per credit. Tuition, nonresident: part-time $332 per credit. *Required fees:* $75 per semester. Tuition and fees vary according to program. *Financial support:* Unspecified assistantships and SOS scholarships (for education majors only) available. Financial award application deadline: 3/1; financial award applicants required to submit FAFSA. *Faculty research:* Collaborative teacher education, developmental early childhood education. *Unit head:* Dr. Laura Baker, Department Chair, 413-572-5324, E-mail: lbaker@westfield.ma.edu. *Application contact:* Shelly Henrichon, Coordinator of College of Graduate and Continuing Education Admissions, 413-572-8022, Fax: 413-572-5227, E-mail: mhenrichon@westfield.ma.edu.
Website: http://www.westfield.ma.edu/academics/degrees/education-graduate-programs

Westfield State University, College of Graduate and Continuing Education, Department of Education, Programs in Secondary Education, Program in Mathematics Teacher Education, Westfield, MA 01086. Offers secondary education-mathematics (M Ed). *Program availability:* Part-time, evening/weekend. *Faculty:* 5 full-time (1 woman). *Students:* 4 part-time (3 women). Average age 28. 2 applicants, 100% accepted. In 2017, 7 master's awarded. *Degree requirements:* For master's, comprehensive exam, thesis (for some programs). *Entrance requirements:* For master's, GRE General Test or MAT, minimum undergraduate GPA of 2.8. Additional exam requirements/recommendations for international students: Recommended—TOEFL (minimum score 550 paper-based; 79 iBT). *Application deadline:* For fall admission, 7/1 for domestic students; for spring admission, 11/1 for domestic students; for summer admission, 4/1 for domestic students. Applications are processed on a rolling basis. Application fee: $50. *Expenses:* Tuition, state resident: part-time $332 per credit. Tuition, nonresident: part-time $332 per credit. *Required fees:* $75 per semester. Tuition and fees vary according to program. *Financial support:* Unspecified assistantships and SOS scholarships (for education majors only) available. Financial award application deadline: 3/1; financial award applicants required to submit FAFSA. *Unit head:* Dr. Laura Baker, Department Chair, 413-572-5324, E-mail: lbaker@westfield.ma.edu. *Application contact:* Shelly Henrichon, Coordinator of College of Graduate and Continuing Education Admissions, 413-572-8022, Fax: 413-572-5227, E-mail: mhenrichon@westfield.ma.edu.

Widener University, School of Human Service Professions, Center for Education, Chester, PA 19013-5792. Offers adult education (M Ed); counseling in higher education (M Ed); counselor education (M Ed); early childhood education (M Ed); educational foundations (M Ed); educational leadership (M Ed); educational psychology (M Ed); elementary education (M Ed); English and language arts (M Ed); health education (M Ed); higher education leadership (Ed D); home and school visitor (M Ed); human sexuality (M Ed, PhD); mathematics education (M Ed); middle school education (M Ed); principalship (M Ed); reading and language arts (Ed D); reading education (M Ed); school administration (Ed D); science education (M Ed); social studies education (M Ed); special education (M Ed); technology education (M Ed). *Accreditation:* NCATE. *Program availability:* Part-time, evening/weekend. *Faculty:* 34 full-time (22 women), 37 part-time/adjunct (14 women). *Students:* 131 full-time (112 women), 244 part-time (179 women); includes 94 minority (58 Black or African American, non-Hispanic/Latino; 1 American Indian or Alaska Native, non-Hispanic/Latino; 1 Asian, non-Hispanic/Latino; 22 Hispanic/Latino; 12 Two or more races, non-Hispanic/Latino), 12 international. Average age 37. 140 applicants, 38% accepted, 26 enrolled. In 2017, 45 master's, 21 doctorates awarded. Terminal master's awarded for partial completion of doctoral program. *Degree requirements:* For doctorate, thesis/dissertation. *Entrance requirements:* For master's, minimum GPA of 2.5; for doctorate, GRE or MAT, minimum GPA of 2.0 (undergraduate), 3.5 (graduate). *Application deadline:* Applications are processed on a rolling basis. Application fee: $25 ($300 for international students). Electronic applications accepted. *Expenses:* Contact institution. *Financial support:* Career-related internships or fieldwork, tuition waivers (full and partial), and unspecified assistantships available. Support available to part-time students. Financial award application deadline: 5/1. *Faculty research:* Reading and cognition, adult education, technology education, educational leadership, special education. *Unit head:* Dr. Shawn Fitzgerald, Dean, 610-499-4294, Fax: 610-499-4623, E-mail: smfitzgerald@widener.edu. *Application contact:* Megan Kuft, Director of Graduate Admissions, 610-499-4124, E-mail: gradprograms@widener.edu.
Website: http://www.widener.edu/academics/schools/eics

William Jessup University, Program in Teaching, Rocklin, CA 95765. Offers single subject English (MAT); single subject math (MAT). *Program availability:* Evening/weekend.

Wright State University, Graduate School, College of Science and Mathematics, Interdisciplinary Program in Science and Mathematics, Dayton, OH 45435. Offers PhD.

Youngstown State University, Graduate School, College of Science, Technology, Engineering and Mathematics, Department of Mathematics and Statistics, Youngstown, OH 44555-0001. Offers applied mathematics (MS); computer science (MS); secondary mathematics (MS); statistics (MS). *Program availability:* Part-time. *Degree requirements:* For master's, comprehensive exam, thesis optional. *Entrance requirements:* For master's, minimum GPA of 2.7 in computer science and mathematics. Additional exam requirements/recommendations for international students: Required—TOEFL. *Faculty research:* Regression analysis, numerical analysis, statistics, Markov chain, topology and fuzzy sets.

Museum Education

Bank Street College of Education, Graduate School, Program in Museum Education, New York, NY 10025. Offers museum education (MS Ed); museum education: elementary education certification (MS Ed). *Degree requirements:* For master's, thesis. *Entrance requirements:* For master's, interview, essays. Additional exam requirements/recommendations for international students: Required—TOEFL (minimum score 600 paper-based; 100 iBT), IELTS (minimum score 7). Electronic applications accepted. *Faculty research:* Equitable access and openness to diversity in museum settings, exhibition display and development, museum and school partnerships.

Bank Street College of Education, Graduate School, Programs in Educational Leadership, New York, NY 10025. Offers early childhood leadership (MS Ed); educational leadership (MS Ed); leadership for educational change (Ed M, MS Ed); leadership in community-based learning (MS Ed); leadership in mathematics education (MS Ed); leadership in museum education (MS Ed); leadership in the arts: creative writing (MS Ed); leadership in the arts: visual arts (MS Ed). *Degree requirements:* For master's, thesis. *Entrance requirements:* For master's, interview, essays, minimum of 2 years experience as a classroom teacher. Additional exam requirements/recommendations for international students: Required—TOEFL (minimum score 600 paper-based; 100 iBT), IELTS (minimum score 7). Electronic applications accepted. *Faculty research:* Leadership in urban schools, leadership in small schools, mathematics in elementary schools, professional development in early childhood, leadership in arts education, leadership in special education, museum leadership, community-based leadership.

Eastern Michigan University, Graduate School, College of Arts and Sciences, Department of Sociology, Anthropology and Criminology, Program in Cultural Museum Studies, Ypsilanti, MI 48197. Offers Graduate Certificate. *Program availability:* Part-time, evening/weekend, online learning. *Students:* 2 part-time (both women). Average age 39. 4 applicants, 50% accepted, 1 enrolled. In 2017, 2 Graduate Certificates awarded. *Entrance requirements:* Additional exam requirements/recommendations for international students: Required—TOEFL. *Application deadline:* Applications are processed on a rolling basis. Application fee: $45. *Financial support:* Fellowships, research assistantships with full tuition reimbursements, teaching assistantships with full tuition reimbursements, career-related internships or fieldwork, Federal Work-Study, institutionally sponsored loans, scholarships/grants, tuition waivers (partial), and unspecified assistantships available. Support available to part-time students. Financial award applicants required to submit FAFSA. *Application contact:* Dr. Liza Cerroni-Long, Advisor, 734-487-0012, Fax: 734-487-9666, E-mail: liza.cerroni-long@emich.edu.

The George Washington University, Graduate School of Education and Human Development, Department of Educational Leadership, Program in Museum Education, Washington, DC 20052. Offers MAT. *Students:* 15 full-time (14 women); includes 4 minority (2 Black or African American, non-Hispanic/Latino; 1 American Indian or Alaska Native, non-Hispanic/Latino; 1 Asian, non-Hispanic/Latino), 1 international. Average age 26. 37 applicants, 73% accepted, 15 enrolled. In 2017, 15 master's awarded. *Entrance requirements:* For master's, GRE General Test or MAT, minimum GPA of 2.75. *Application deadline:* For fall admission, 1/15 priority date for domestic students; for spring admission, 10/1 for domestic students. Applications are processed on a rolling basis. Application fee: $75. *Expenses: Tuition:* Full-time $28,800; part-time $1655 per credit hour. *Required fees:* $45; $2.75 per credit hour. *Financial support:* In 2017–18, 7 students received support. Fellowships, career-related internships or fieldwork, Federal Work-Study, and tuition waivers available. Financial award application deadline: 1/15; financial award applicants required to submit FAFSA. *Unit head:* Michael Feuer, Dean, 202-994-6161, E-mail: mjfeuer@gwu.edu. *Application contact:* Sarah Lang, Director of Graduate Admissions, 202-994-1447, Fax: 202-994-7207, E-mail: slang@gwu.edu. Website: http://gsehd.gwu.edu/MEP

Tufts University, Graduate School of Arts and Sciences, Department of Education, Program in Education, Medford, MA 02155. Offers educational studies (MA); elementary education (MAT); middle and secondary education (MAT); museum education (MA); secondary education (MA); STEM education (MS, PhD). *Program availability:* Part-time. *Students:* 50 full-time (38 women), 9 part-time (8 women); includes 9 minority (2 Black or African American, non-Hispanic/Latino; 2 Asian, non-Hispanic/Latino; 4 Hispanic/Latino; 1 Two or more races, non-Hispanic/Latino), 4 international. Average age 28. 120 applicants, 71% accepted, 49 enrolled. In 2017, 51 master's awarded. *Degree requirements:* For master's, thesis optional. *Entrance requirements:* For master's, GRE General Test, portfolio (for art education only); for doctorate, GRE General Test, writing sample. Additional exam requirements/recommendations for international students: Required—TOEFL (minimum score 550 paper-based; 80 iBT), IELTS (minimum score 6.5). *Application deadline:* For fall admission, 1/2 for domestic and international students; for spring admission, 10/15 for domestic and international students. Applications are processed on a rolling basis. Application fee: $85. Electronic applications accepted. *Expenses:* Contact institution. *Financial support:* Research assistantships, teaching assistantships, Federal Work-Study, scholarships/grants, and tuition waivers (full and partial) available. Support available to part-time students. Financial award application deadline: 1/2. *Unit head:* Dr. David Hammer, Graduate Program Director, 617-627-2396. *Application contact:* Office of Graduate Admissions, 617-627-3395, E-mail: gradadmissions@tufts.edu.

The University of the Arts, College of Art, Media and Design, Department of Museum Studies, Philadelphia, PA 19102-4944. Offers museum communication (MA); museum education (MA); museum exhibition planning and design (MFA). *Accreditation:* NASAD. *Degree requirements:* For master's, thesis, internship. *Entrance requirements:* For master's, official transcripts, three letters of recommendation, one- to two-page statement, personal interview; academic writing sample and examples of work (for museum communication); two examples of academic and professional writing (for museum education); portfolio and/or writing samples (for museum exhibition planning and design). Additional exam requirements/recommendations for international students: Required—TOEFL (minimum score 580 paper-based, 92 iBT) or IELTS (minimum score 6.5).

Music Education

Acadia University, Faculty of Professional Studies, School of Education, Program in Curriculum Studies, Wolfville, NS B4P 2R6, Canada. Offers curriculum studies (M Ed); interprofessional health practice (M Ed); music education (M Ed). *Program availability:* Part-time. *Entrance requirements:* For master's, B Ed or the equivalent, minimum B average in undergraduate course work, 2 years of teaching experience. Additional exam requirements/recommendations for international students: Required—TOEFL (minimum score 580 paper-based; 93 iBT), IELTS (minimum score 6.5). *Application deadline:* For fall admission, 3/15 priority date for domestic and international students. Applications are processed on a rolling basis. Application fee: $50. *Financial support:* Application deadline: 3/15. *Faculty research:* Literacy development, postmodern philosophy and curriculum theory, historiography, philosophy of education, learning and technology. *Unit head:* Dr. Ann Vibert, Director, 902-585-1229, E-mail: ann.vibert@acadiau.ca. *Application contact:* Rosie Hare, Administrative Assistant, 902-585-1597, Fax: 902-585-1086, E-mail: rosie.hare@acadiau.ca. Website: http://education.acadiau.ca/

Adams State University, Office of Graduate Studies, Department of Music, Alamosa, CO 81101. Offers music education (MA). *Expenses:* Tuition, state resident: full-time $4800; part-time $2400 per credit. Tuition, nonresident: full-time $7100; part-time $3550 per credit. *Required fees:* $213; $106 per credit. One-time fee: $100. Tuition and fees vary according to campus/location and program.

Alabama Agricultural and Mechanical University, School of Graduate Studies, College of Education, Humanities, and Behavioral Sciences, Department of Visual, Performing, and Communication Arts, Huntsville, AL 35811. Offers art education (MS); music education (M Ed). *Accreditation:* NCATE. *Program availability:* Part-time, evening/weekend. *Degree requirements:* For master's, comprehensive exam. *Entrance requirements:* For master's, GRE General Test. Additional exam requirements/recommendations for international students: Required—TOEFL (minimum score 500 paper-based; 61 iBT). Electronic applications accepted. *Faculty research:* Jazz and black music, Alabama folk music.

Alabama State University, College of Education, Department of Curriculum and Instruction, Montgomery, AL 36101-0271. Offers early childhood education (M Ed, Ed S); elementary education (M Ed, Ed S); secondary education (M Ed, Ed S), including biology education, English language arts education (M Ed), history education, math education, music education (M Ed), reading education (M Ed), social science education; special education (M Ed). *Program availability:* Part-time. *Faculty:* 7 full-time (4 women), 7 part-time/adjunct (4 women). *Students:* 43 full-time (35 women), 71 part-time (62 women); includes 112 minority (111 Black or African American, non-Hispanic/Latino; 1 Two or more races, non-Hispanic/Latino). Average age 22. 47 applicants, 66% accepted, 19 enrolled. In 2017, 21 master's, 13 Ed Ss awarded. *Degree requirements:* For master's, comprehensive exam, thesis optional; for Ed S, comprehensive exam, thesis. *Entrance requirements:* For master's, GRE General Test, MAT, writing competency test; for Ed S, writing competency test, GRE, MAT. Additional exam requirements/recommendations for international students: Required—TOEFL (minimum

score 500 paper-based). *Application deadline:* For fall admission, 4/15 for domestic and international students; for spring admission, 11/15 for domestic and international students; for summer admission, 3/15 for domestic and international students. Applications are processed on a rolling basis. Application fee: $25. Electronic applications accepted. *Expenses:* Tuition, state resident: part-time $412 per credit hour. Tuition, nonresident: part-time $824 per credit hour. *Required fees:* $685 per semester. *Financial support:* Research assistantships available. Financial award application deadline: 6/30; financial award applicants required to submit FAFSA. *Unit head:* Dr. Joyce Johnson, Acting Chairperson, 334-229-4485, Fax: 334-229-5603, E-mail: jjohnson@alasu.edu. *Application contact:* Dr. William Person, Dean of Graduate Studies, 334-229-4274, Fax: 334-229-4928, E-mail: wperson@alasu.edu. Website: http://www.alasu.edu/academics/colleges—departments/college-of-education/curriculum—instruction/index.aspx

Anderson University, South Carolina School of the Arts, Anderson, SC 29621-4035. Offers music education (MM). *Program availability:* Online learning. *Degree requirements:* For master's, comprehensive exam. *Expenses: Tuition:* Full-time $24,290; part-time $650 per credit hour. Full-time tuition and fees vary according to degree level and program. *Unit head:* David Larson, Dean, 864-231-2002, E-mail: dlarson@andersonuniversity.edu. *Application contact:* Chris Woodlief, Associate Director of Adult and Graduate Programs, 864-231-5531, E-mail: cwoodlief@andersonuniversity.edu. Website: http://www.andersonuniversity.edu/school-of-the-arts

Arcadia University, School of Education, Glenside, PA 19038-3295. Offers art education (M Ed); computer education (CAS); curriculum (CAS); curriculum studies (M Ed); early childhood education (M Ed), including individualized, master teacher, research in child development; educational leadership (M Ed, Ed D, CAS); elementary education (M Ed); English education (MA Ed); environmental education (MA Ed); instructional technology (M Ed); language arts (M Ed); library science (M Ed); mathematics education (M Ed, MA Ed); music education (MA Ed); psychology (MA Ed); reading (M Ed, CAS); science education (M Ed, CAS); secondary education (M Ed, CAS); special education (M Ed, Ed D, CAS); theater arts (MA Ed); written communication (MA Ed). *Accreditation:* NASAD. *Program availability:* Part-time, evening/weekend, online learning. Electronic applications accepted. *Expenses:* Contact institution.

Arizona State University at the Tempe campus, Herberger Institute for Design and the Arts, School of Music, Tempe, AZ 85287-0405. Offers composition (MM, DMA); conducting (DMA); ethnomusicology (MA); interdisciplinary digital media/performance (DMA); music education (MM, PhD); music history and literature (MA); music therapy (MM); performance (MM, DMA). *Accreditation:* NASM. Terminal master's awarded for partial completion of doctoral program. *Degree requirements:* For master's, thesis (for some programs), interactive Program of Study (iPOS) submitted before completing 50 percent of required credit hours; for doctorate, comprehensive exam, thesis/dissertation, interactive Program of Study (iPOS) submitted before completing 50 percent of required credit hours. *Entrance requirements:* For master's, minimum GPA of 3.0 or equivalent in last 2 years of work leading to bachelor's degree, 3 letters of recommendation, resume; for doctorate, GRE or MAT, minimum GPA of 3.0 or equivalent in last 2 years of work leading to bachelor's degree, 3 letters of recommendation, curriculum vitae, statement of intent. Additional exam requirements/recommendations for international students: Required—TOEFL, IELTS, or PTE. Electronic applications accepted.

Arkansas State University, Graduate School, College of Fine Arts, Department of Music, State University, AR 72467. Offers music education (MME, SCCT); music performance (MM). *Accreditation:* NASM (one or more programs are accredited). *Program availability:* Part-time. *Degree requirements:* For master's, 2 foreign languages, comprehensive exam, thesis or alternative; for SCCT, comprehensive exam. *Entrance requirements:* For master's, GRE General Test or MAT, university entrance exam, appropriate bachelor's degree, audition, letters of recommendation, teaching experience, official transcripts, immunization records, valid teaching certificate; for SCCT, GRE General Test or MAT, interview, master's degree, official transcript, immunization records, letters of recommendation. Additional exam requirements/recommendations for international students: Required—TOEFL (minimum score 550 paper-based; 79 iBT), IELTS (minimum score 6), PTE (minimum score 56). Electronic applications accepted.

Augusta University, College of Education, Program in Curriculum and Instruction, Augusta, GA 30912. Offers curriculum and instruction (Ed S); elementary education (MAT); foreign language education (MAT); instruction (M Ed); middle grades education (MAT); music education (MAT); secondary education (MAT); special education (MAT). *Degree requirements:* For master's, thesis, portfolio. *Entrance requirements:* For master's, GRE, MAT, minimum GPA of 2.5.

Austin Peay State University, College of Graduate Studies, College of Arts and Letters, Department of Music, Clarksville, TN 37044. Offers music education (M Mu); music performance (M Mu). *Accreditation:* NASM. *Program availability:* Part-time. *Faculty:* 17 full-time (7 women), 5 part-time/adjunct (3 women). *Students:* 18 full-time (6 women), 5 part-time (1 woman); includes 1 minority (Black or African American, non-Hispanic/Latino), 3 international. Average age 28. 25 applicants, 72% accepted, 15 enrolled. In 2017, 6 master's awarded. *Degree requirements:* For master's, comprehensive exam, thesis optional. *Entrance requirements:* For master's, GRE General Test, diagnostic exams, audition, interview, bachelor's degree, 3 letters of recommendation. Additional exam requirements/recommendations for international students: Required—TOEFL (minimum score 500 paper-based). *Application deadline:* For fall admission, 8/8 priority date for domestic students. Applications are processed on a rolling basis. Application fee: $45 ($55 for international students). Electronic applications accepted. *Expenses:* Tuition, state resident: full-time $7686; part-time $427 per credit hour. Tuition, nonresident: full-time $20,268; part-time $1126 per credit hour. *Required fees:* $1529; $76.45 per credit hour. *Financial support:* Research assistantships with full tuition reimbursements, career-related internships or fieldwork, Federal Work-Study, institutionally sponsored loans, scholarships/grants, and unspecified assistantships available. Support available to part-time students. Financial award application deadline: 4/1; financial award applicants required to submit FAFSA. *Unit head:* Dr. Eric Branscome, Chair, 931-221-7811, Fax: 931-221-7529, E-mail: branscomee@apsu.edu. *Application contact:* Megan Mitchell, Coordinator of Graduate Admissions, 931-221-6189, Fax: 931-221-7641, E-mail: mitchellm@apsu.edu. Website: http://www.apsu.edu/music/

Azusa Pacific University, College of Music and the Arts, Azusa, CA 91702-7000. Offers composition (M Mus); conducting (M Mus); education (M Mus); modern art history, theory, and criticism (MA); music entrepreneurial studies (MA); performance (M Mus); screenwriting (MA); visual art (MFA). *Accreditation:* NASAD; NASM. *Program availability:* Part-time, evening/weekend. *Degree requirements:* For master's, recital. *Entrance requirements:* For master's, interview, audition. Additional exam requirements/recommendations for international students: Required—TOEFL (minimum score 550 paper-based).

Ball State University, Graduate School, College of Fine Arts, School of Music, Muncie, IN 47306. Offers music (MA, MM, DA, Artist Diploma), including conducting (MM, DA), music education (MA, MM, DA), music history and musicology (MA, MM, DA), music performance (MA, MM, DA), music theory (MA), music theory and composition (DA), piano chamber music/accompanying (MM, DA), piano performance and pedagogy (MM), woodwinds (MM). *Accreditation:* NASM; NCATE (one or more programs are accredited). *Faculty:* 50 full-time (19 women), 3 part-time/adjunct (2 women). *Students:* 42 full-time, 47 part-time; includes 10 minority (5 Black or African American, non-Hispanic/Latino; 2 Asian, non-Hispanic/Latino; 3 Hispanic/Latino), 27 international. Average age 30. 75 applicants, 56% accepted, 26 enrolled. In 2017, 12 master's, 6 doctorates, 2 other advanced degrees awarded. *Degree requirements:* For doctorate, thesis/dissertation. *Entrance requirements:* For master's, placement tests in history and theory, minimum baccalaureate GPA of 2.75 or 3.0 in latter half of baccalaureate, resume, audition; for doctorate, GRE General Test, minimum graduate GPA of 3.2, interview, audition, resume, three professional letters of reference. Additional exam requirements/recommendations for international students: Required—TOEFL (minimum score 550 paper-based; 79 iBT), IELTS (minimum score 6.5). *Application deadline:* For fall admission, 2/15 for domestic students. Applications are processed on a rolling basis. Application fee: $60. Electronic applications accepted. *Expenses:* Contact institution. *Financial support:* In 2017–18, 58 students received support, including 39 teaching assistantships with partial tuition reimbursements available (averaging $10,361 per year); unspecified assistantships also available. Financial award application deadline: 3/1; financial award applicants required to submit FAFSA. *Unit head:* Dr. Ryan Hourigan, Director, 765-285-5501, Fax: 765-285-5401, E-mail: rmhourigan@bsu.edu. *Application contact:* Dr. Linda Pohly, Graduate Advisor, 765-285-5502, Fax: 765-285-5401, E-mail: lpohly@bsu.edu. Website: http://www.bsu.edu/

Bob Jones University, Graduate Programs, Greenville, SC 29614. Offers accountancy (MS); Bible (MA); Bible translation (MA); Biblical studies (Certificate); broadcast management (MS); business administration (MBA); church history (MA, PhD); church ministries (MA); church music (MM); cinema and video production (MA); counseling (MS); curriculum and instruction (Ed D); divinity (M Div); dramatic production (MA); educational leadership (MS, Ed D, Ed S); elementary education (M Ed, MAT); English (M Ed, MA, MAT); fine arts (MA); graphic design (MA); history (M Ed, MA); illustration (MA); interpretative speech (MA); mathematics (M Ed, MAT); medical missions (Certificate); ministry (MM, D Min); multi-categorical special education (M Ed, MAT); music (M Ed); New Testament interpretation (PhD); Old Testament interpretation (PhD); orchestral instrument performance (MM); organ performance (MM); pastoral studies (MA); personnel services (MS, Ed S); piano pedagogy (MM); piano performance (MM); platform arts (MA); radio and television broadcasting (MS); rhetoric and public address (MA); secondary education (M Ed); studio art (MA); teaching Bible (MA); theology (MA, PhD); voice performance (MM); youth ministries (MA); M Div/MM.

Boise State University, College of Arts and Sciences, Department of Music, Boise, ID 83725-0399. Offers music education (MM); music performance (MM). *Accreditation:* NASM. *Program availability:* Part-time. *Faculty:* 14. *Students:* 11 full-time (3 women), 6 part-time (3 women); includes 2 minority (1 Asian, non-Hispanic/Latino; 1 Hispanic/

Latino), 2 international. Average age 27. 9 applicants, 78% accepted, 5 enrolled. In 2017, 10 master's awarded. *Degree requirements:* For master's, thesis optional. *Entrance requirements:* For master's, minimum GPA of 3.0, performance demonstration. Additional exam requirements/recommendations for international students: Required—TOEFL (minimum score 550 paper-based; 80 iBT), IELTS (minimum score 6). *Application deadline:* For fall admission, 2/9 priority date for domestic and international students. Application fee: $65 ($95 for international students). Electronic applications accepted. *Expenses:* Tuition, state resident: full-time $6471; part-time $390 per credit. Tuition, nonresident: full-time $21,787; part-time $685 per credit. *Required fees:* $2283; $100 per term. Part-time tuition and fees vary according to course load and program. *Financial support:* Teaching assistantships, scholarships/grants, and unspecified assistantships available. Financial award application deadline: 2/9; financial award applicants required to submit FAFSA. *Unit head:* Dr. Linda Kline, Chair, 208-426-3665, E-mail: lkline@boisestate.edu. *Application contact:* Dr. Jeanne Belfy, Graduate Program Coordinator, 208-426-1216, E-mail: jbelfy@boisestate.edu. Website: http://music.boisestate.edu/graduate/

Boston University, College of Fine Arts, School of Music, Program in Music Education, Boston, MA 02215. Offers MM, DMA. *Accreditation:* NASM. *Program availability:* Part-time, 100% online. *Faculty:* 9 full-time (3 women). *Students:* 359 full-time (183 women), 9 part-time (3 women); includes 67 minority (23 Black or African American, non-Hispanic/Latino; 2 American Indian or Alaska Native, non-Hispanic/Latino; 11 Asian, non-Hispanic/Latino; 20 Hispanic/Latino; 1 Native Hawaiian or other Pacific Islander, non-Hispanic/Latino; 10 Two or more races, non-Hispanic/Latino), 21 international. Average age 35. 36 applicants, 56% accepted, 7 enrolled. In 2017, 75 master's, 23 doctorates awarded. *Degree requirements:* For master's, thesis; for doctorate, 2 foreign languages, thesis/dissertation. *Entrance requirements:* Additional exam requirements/recommendations for international students: Required—TOEFL (minimum score 90 iBT), IELTS (minimum score 7). *Application deadline:* For fall admission, 12/1 priority date for domestic and international students. Application fee: $95. Electronic applications accepted. *Expenses:* Contact institution. *Financial support:* Fellowships, teaching assistantships, scholarships/grants, and unspecified assistantships available. Financial award application deadline: 12/1. *Unit head:* Shiela Kibbe, Director, 617-353-8789, Fax: 617-353-7455, E-mail: cfamusic@bu.edu. *Application contact:* Katie Luellen, Assistant Director, School of Music Admissions and Student Affairs, 617-353-3341, E-mail: arts@bu.edu.

Bowling Green State University, Graduate College, College of Musical Arts, Bowling Green, OH 43403. Offers composition (MM); contemporary music (DMA), including composition, performance; ethnomusicology (MM); music education (MM), including choral music education, comprehensive music education, instrumental music education; music history (MM); music theory (MM); performance (MM). *Accreditation:* NASM. *Program availability:* Part-time. *Degree requirements:* For master's, thesis or alternative, recitals; for doctorate, comprehensive exam, thesis/dissertation. *Entrance requirements:* For master's, GRE General Test, diagnostic placement exams in music history and theory, audition, interview. Additional exam requirements/recommendations for international students: Required—TOEFL. Electronic applications accepted. *Faculty research:* Ethnomusicology.

Brandon University, School of Music, Brandon, MB R7A 6A9, Canada. Offers composition (M Mus); music education (M Mus); performance and literature (M Mus), including clarinet, conducting, jazz, low brass, piano, strings, trumpet. *Program availability:* Part-time. *Degree requirements:* For master's, comprehensive exam (for some programs), thesis (for some programs), 2 recitals. *Entrance requirements:* For master's, B Mus. Additional exam requirements/recommendations for international students: Required—TOEFL (minimum score 580 paper-based), IELTS (minimum score 7). Electronic applications accepted. *Expenses:* Contact institution. *Faculty research:* Composition, evaluation and assessment, performance anxiety, philosophy of music, teacher education.

Brigham Young University, Graduate Studies, College of Fine Arts and Communications, School of Music, Provo, UT 84602. Offers composition (MM); conducting (MM), including band and orchestral conducting, choral conducting; music education (MA, MM); performance (MM), including keyboard performance, orchestral instrument, vocal performance. *Accreditation:* NASM. *Faculty:* 51 full-time (10 women), 60 part-time/adjunct (38 women). *Students:* 18 full-time (10 women), 24 part-time (15 women); includes 6 minority (3 Asian, non-Hispanic/Latino; 2 Hispanic/Latino; 1 Native Hawaiian or other Pacific Islander, non-Hispanic/Latino). Average age 24. 44 applicants, 43% accepted, 16 enrolled. In 2017, 16 master's awarded. *Degree requirements:* For master's, comprehensive exam (for some programs), thesis (for some programs), recital, project, or composition (for some programs). *Entrance requirements:* For master's, School of Music Entrance Exam, minimum GPA of 3.0, undergraduate degree in music. Additional exam requirements/recommendations for international students: Required—TOEFL (minimum score 85 iBT), IELTS (minimum score 7). *Application deadline:* For fall admission, 12/15 priority date for domestic and international students. Application fee: $50. Electronic applications accepted. *Expenses:* Contact institution. *Financial support:* In 2017–18, 43 students received support, including 43 research assistantships (averaging $3,000 per year), 43 teaching assistantships (averaging $3,500 per year); career-related internships or fieldwork, institutionally sponsored loans, scholarships/grants, tuition waivers (partial), and unspecified assistantships also available. Support available to part-time students. Financial award application deadline: 12/15; financial award applicants required to submit FAFSA. *Faculty research:* Max Steiner film archive study; liturgical compositions; music education undergraduate curriculum; Mormon music; jazz history. *Unit head:* Dr. Kirt R. Saville, Director, 801-422-6304, Fax: 801-422-0533, E-mail: kirt_saville@byu.edu. *Application contact:* Dr. A. Claudine Bigelow, Graduate Coordinator, 801-422-1315, Fax: 801-422-0533, E-mail: claudine_bigelow@byu.edu. Website: https://cfac.byu.edu/music/

Brooklyn College of the City University of New York, School of Education, Program in Adolescence Science Education and Special Subjects, Brooklyn, NY 11210-2889. Offers adolescence science education (MA); biology teacher (7-12) (MA); chemistry teacher (7-12) (MA); earth science teacher (7-12) (MAT); English teacher (7-12) (MA); French teacher (7-12) (MA); mathematics teacher (7-12) (MA); music teacher (MA); physics teacher (7-12) (MA); social studies teacher (7-12) (MA); Spanish teacher (7-12) (MA). *Program availability:* Part-time, evening/weekend. *Degree requirements:* For master's, comprehensive exam (for some programs), thesis (for some programs). *Entrance requirements:* For master's, LAST, previous course work in education, resume, 2 letters of recommendation, essay. Additional exam requirements/recommendations for international students: Required—TOEFL (minimum score 500 paper-based; 61 iBT). Electronic applications accepted. *Faculty research:* Interdisciplinary education, semiotics, discourse analysis, autobiography, teacher identity.

Brooklyn College of the City University of New York, School of Visual, Media and Performing Arts, Conservatory of Music, Brooklyn, NY 11210-2889. Offers composition (MM); music teacher (MA); musicology (MM); performance (MM). *Program availability:* Part-time. *Degree requirements:* For master's, one foreign language, comprehensive exam, thesis. *Entrance requirements:* For master's, placement exam, 36 credits in

Music Education

music, audition, completed composition, writing sample. Additional exam requirements/recommendations for international students: Required—TOEFL (minimum score 550 paper-based; 79 iBT). Electronic applications accepted. *Faculty research:* American music, computer music.

Butler University, Jordan College of the Arts, Indianapolis, IN 46208-3485. Offers composition (MM); conducting (MM), including choral, instrumental; music education (MM); musicology (MA); performance (MM); piano pedagogy (MM). *Accreditation:* NASM. *Program availability:* Part-time. *Faculty:* 25 full-time (7 women), 35 part-time/adjunct (18 women). *Students:* 12 full-time (3 women), 25 part-time (9 women); includes 8 minority (3 Black or African American, non-Hispanic/Latino; 2 Asian, non-Hispanic/Latino; 1 Hispanic/Latino; 2 Two or more races, non-Hispanic/Latino), 1 international. Average age 27. 36 applicants, 67% accepted, 14 enrolled. In 2017, 10 master's awarded. *Degree requirements:* For master's, variable foreign language requirement, comprehensive exam, thesis (for some programs). *Entrance requirements:* For master's, GRE General Test (for MA in musicology), audition, interview, three letters of recommendation, transcripts, sample works. Additional exam requirements/recommendations for international students: Required—TOEFL (minimum score 550 paper-based; 79 iBT), IELTS (minimum score 6). *Application deadline:* For fall admission, 2/1 for domestic and international students; for spring admission, 12/15 for domestic and international students; for summer admission, 4/15 for domestic and international students. Applications are processed on a rolling basis. Application fee: $0. Electronic applications accepted. *Expenses:* $560 per credit. *Financial support:* In 2017–18, 19 students received support. Scholarships/grants, tuition waivers (full and partial), and unspecified assistantships available. Financial award application deadline: 7/15; financial award applicants required to submit FAFSA. *Faculty research:* Music neuroscience; woodwind pedagogy and repertoire; Johannes Kepler and Carolus Luython; music criticism in early 20th-century Germany and Austria; Arabic choral music; pedagogy of music theory. *Unit head:* Wendy Meaden, Dean, 317-940-9229, E-mail: wmeaden@butler.edu. *Application contact:* Diane Dubord, Graduate Student Services Specialist, 317-940-8107, E-mail: ddubord@butler.edu. Website: http://www.butler.edu/jca/

California Baptist University, Program in Music, Riverside, CA 92504-3206. Offers conducting (MM); music education (MM); performance (MM). *Accreditation:* NASM. *Program availability:* Part-time, evening/weekend. *Faculty:* 13 full-time (6 women), 18 part-time/adjunct (9 women). *Students:* 13 full-time (6 women), 6 part-time (5 women); includes 5 minority (2 Black or African American, non-Hispanic/Latino; 2 Asian, non-Hispanic/Latino; 1 Hispanic/Latino), 9 international. Average age 27. 10 applicants, 70% accepted, 5 enrolled. In 2017, 8 master's awarded. *Degree requirements:* For master's, comprehensive exam or thesis. *Entrance requirements:* For master's, minimum undergraduate GPA of 2.75; bachelor's degree in music; three recommendations; comprehensive essay; interview/audition. Additional exam requirements/recommendations for international students: Required—TOEFL (minimum score 80 iBT). *Application deadline:* For fall admission, 8/1 priority date for domestic students, 7/1 for international students; for spring admission, 12/1 priority date for domestic students, 11/1 for international students. Applications are processed on a rolling basis. Application fee: $45. Electronic applications accepted. *Expenses:* Contact institution. *Financial support:* In 2017–18, 8 students received support. Federal Work-Study and scholarships/grants available. Financial award applicants required to submit CSS PROFILE or FAFSA. *Faculty research:* Choral conducting, church music, choir building, hymnology, music technology. *Unit head:* Dr. Joseph Bolin, Dean, School of Music, 951-343-4714, Fax: 951-343-4570, E-mail: jbolin@calbaptist.edu. *Application contact:* Rudy Villarruel, Graduate Admissions Counselor, 951-552-8132, E-mail: rvillarruel@calbaptist.edu.
Website: http://www.calbaptist.edu/masterofmusic/

California State University, Fresno, Division of Research and Graduate Studies, College of Arts and Humanities, Department of Music, Fresno, CA 93740-8027. Offers music (MA); music education (MA); performance (MA). *Accreditation:* NASM. *Program availability:* Part-time. *Degree requirements:* For master's, thesis or alternative. *Entrance requirements:* For master's, GRE General Test, BA in music, minimum GPA of 3.0. Additional exam requirements/recommendations for international students: Required—TOEFL. Electronic applications accepted. *Faculty research:* Technology transfer, folk art.

California State University, Fullerton, Graduate Studies, College of the Arts, Department of Music, Fullerton, CA 92831-3599. Offers music education (MA); performance (MM). *Accreditation:* NASM. *Program availability:* Part-time. *Faculty:* 13 full-time (3 women), 18 part-time/adjunct (2 women). *Students:* 20 full-time (10 women), 30 part-time (9 women); includes 17 minority (9 Asian, non-Hispanic/Latino; 5 Hispanic/Latino; 3 Two or more races, non-Hispanic/Latino), 8 international. Average age 28. 69 applicants, 46% accepted, 17 enrolled. *Degree requirements:* For master's, comprehensive exam, project or thesis. *Entrance requirements:* For master's, audition, major in music or related field, minimum GPA of 2.5 in last 60 units of course work. Application fee: $55. *Financial support:* Career-related internships or fieldwork, Federal Work-Study, institutionally sponsored loans, and scholarships/grants available. Support available to part-time students. Financial award application deadline: 3/1; financial award applicants required to submit FAFSA. *Unit head:* Dr. Marc Dickey, Chair, 657-278-3511. *Application contact:* Admissions/Applications, 657-278-2371.

California State University, Los Angeles, Graduate Studies, College of Arts and Letters, Department of Music, Los Angeles, CA 90032-8530. Offers music composition (MM); music education (MA); musicology (MA); performance (MM). *Accreditation:* NASM. *Program availability:* Part-time, evening/weekend. *Degree requirements:* For master's, comprehensive exam, project or thesis. *Entrance requirements:* For master's, audition. Additional exam requirements/recommendations for international students: Required—TOEFL (minimum score 500 paper-based). Electronic applications accepted. *Faculty research:* Gregorian semiology, Baroque opera.

California State University, Northridge, Graduate Studies, Mike Curb College of Arts, Media, and Communication, Department of Music, Northridge, CA 91330. Offers composition (MM); conducting (MM); music education (MA); performance (MM). *Accreditation:* NASM. *Students:* 32 full-time (21 women), 35 part-time (18 women); includes 18 minority (1 Black or African American, non-Hispanic/Latino; 7 Asian, non-Hispanic/Latino; 7 Hispanic/Latino; 3 Two or more races, non-Hispanic/Latino), 21 international. Average age 28. 149 applicants, 48% accepted, 23 enrolled. In 2017, 71 master's awarded. *Degree requirements:* For master's, thesis. *Entrance requirements:* For master's, audition, GRE General Test or minimum GPA of 3.0. Additional exam requirements/recommendations for international students: Required—TOEFL. *Application deadline:* For fall admission, 11/30 for domestic students. Application fee: $55. *Financial support:* Application deadline: 3/1. *Unit head:* Ron Borczon, Chair, 816-677-4752. *Application contact:* 818-677-3184.
Website: http://www.csun.edu/music/

Campbellsville University, School of Music, Campbellsville, KY 42718-2799. Offers music (MA, MM), including conducting (MM), instrumental performance (MM), music education (MM), vocal performance and pedagogy (MM); musicology (MM); worship (MA). *Accreditation:* NASM. *Program availability:* Part-time, 100% online, blended/hybrid learning. *Faculty:* 14 full-time (6 women), 9 part-time/adjunct (4 women). *Students:* 25

part-time (11 women); includes 1 minority (Black or African American, non-Hispanic/Latino), 6 international. Average age 31. 13 applicants, 38% accepted, 5 enrolled. In 2017, 3 master's awarded. *Degree requirements:* For master's, comprehensive exam, thesis (for some programs), paper or recital. *Entrance requirements:* For master's, GRE General Test or PRAXIS, minimum GPA of 2.75, college transcripts. Additional exam requirements/recommendations for international students: Required—TOEFL (minimum score 550 paper-based; 79 iBT); Recommended—IELTS (minimum score 6). *Application deadline:* Applications are processed on a rolling basis. Application fee: $25. Electronic applications accepted. Application fee is waived when completed online. *Expenses:* $399 per credit hour. *Financial support:* In 2017–18, 14 students received support. Unspecified assistantships and employee tuition waivers available. Financial award application deadline: 6/1; financial award applicants required to submit FAFSA. *Unit head:* Dr. Tony Cunha, Dean, 270-789-5240, Fax: 270-789-5524, E-mail: accunha@campbellsville.edu. *Application contact:* Monica Bamwine, Assistant Director of Graduate Admissions, 270-789-5221, Fax: 270-789-5071, E-mail: mkbamwine@campbellsville.edu.
Website: http://www.campbellsville.edu/music

Capital University, Conservatory of Music, Columbus, OH 43209-2394. Offers music education (MM), including instrumental emphasis, Kodály emphasis. Program offered only in summer. *Accreditation:* NASM. *Program availability:* Part-time. *Degree requirements:* For master's, comprehensive exam, thesis or alternative, chamber performance exam. *Entrance requirements:* For master's, music theory exam, minimum undergraduate GPA of 3.0. Additional exam requirements/recommendations for international students: Required—TOEFL (minimum score 550 paper-based; 80 iBT). Electronic applications accepted. *Expenses:* Contact institution. *Faculty research:* Folk song research, Kodály method, performance, composition.

Carnegie Mellon University, College of Fine Arts, School of Music, Pittsburgh, PA 15213-3891. Offers collaborative piano (MM); composition (MM); instrumental performance (MM); music and technology (MS); music education (MM); vocal performance (MM). *Accreditation:* NASM. *Program availability:* Part-time. *Degree requirements:* For master's, comprehensive exam, recital. *Entrance requirements:* For master's, audition. *Faculty research:* Computer music, music history.

Case Western Reserve University, School of Graduate Studies, Department of Music, Program in Music Education, Cleveland, OH 44106. Offers MA, PhD. *Accreditation:* NASM; TEAC. *Faculty:* 4 full-time (2 women). *Students:* 7 full-time (5 women), 9 part-time (4 women); includes 1 minority (Hispanic/Latino). Average age 35. 6 applicants, 50% accepted, 3 enrolled. In 2017, 3 master's, 2 doctorates awarded. *Degree requirements:* For master's, comprehensive exam (for some programs), thesis (for some programs); for doctorate, comprehensive exam, thesis/dissertation. *Entrance requirements:* For master's, GRE, resume, PDF of teaching license/certificate, audition/interview, writing sample, 1 year of teaching; for doctorate, GRE, resume, PDF of teaching license/certificate, audition/interview, writing sample, 3 years of teaching. Additional exam requirements/recommendations for international students: Required—TOEFL (minimum score 577 paper-based; 90 iBT); Recommended—IELTS (minimum score 7). *Application deadline:* For fall admission, 1/15 priority date for domestic students. Application fee: $50. Electronic applications accepted. *Expenses: Tuition:* Full-time $43,854; part-time $1827 per credit hour. *Required fees:* $50; $50 per credit hour. Tuition and fees vary according to course load and program. *Financial support:* Fellowships, teaching assistantships, career-related internships or fieldwork, tuition waivers (full), unspecified assistantships, and stipends available. Financial award application deadline: 1/15; financial award applicants required to submit CSS PROFILE or FAFSA. *Faculty research:* Psychology of music, creative thinking, computer applications, educational psychology. *Unit head:* David J. Rothenberg, Associate Professor/Department Chair, 216-368-6046, Fax: 216-368-6557, E-mail: music@case.edu. *Application contact:* Laura Stauffer, Department Administrator, 216-368-0117, Fax: 216-368-6557, E-mail: music@case.edu.
Website: http://music.case.edu/

The Catholic University of America, Benjamin T. Rome School of Music, Washington, DC 20064. Offers cello (Artist Diploma); chamber music (piano) (MM, DMA); composition (MM, DMA), including concert music (MM), stage music (MM); music (MAT); musicology (MA, PhD); orchestral conducting (MM, DMA, Artist Diploma); orchestral instruments/guitar (MM, DMA); piano (Artist Diploma); piano pedagogy (MM, DMA); piano performance (MM, DMA); sacred music (MMSM, DMA); violin (Artist Diploma); vocal accompanying (MM, DMA); vocal pedagogy (MM, DMA); vocal performance (MM, DMA); voice (Artist Diploma); MA/MSLIS. MA/MSLIS offered in partnership with Department of Library and Information Science. *Accreditation:* NASM. *Program availability:* Part-time. *Faculty:* 19 full-time (4 women), 43 part-time/adjunct (18 women). *Students:* 30 full-time (19 women), 61 part-time (27 women); includes 25 minority (7 Black or African American, non-Hispanic/Latino; 10 Asian, non-Hispanic/Latino; 5 Hispanic/Latino; 3 Two or more races, non-Hispanic/Latino), 22 international. Average age 33. 104 applicants, 76% accepted, 26 enrolled. In 2017, 14 master's, 18 doctorates awarded. *Degree requirements:* For master's, variable foreign language requirement, comprehensive exam (for some programs), thesis (for some programs); for doctorate, variable foreign language requirement, comprehensive exam (for some programs), thesis/dissertation (for some programs), final recital (for some programs); for Artist Diploma, variable foreign language requirement, final recital (for some programs). *Entrance requirements:* For master's, music theory and music history placement examinations, statement of purpose, 2 letters of recommendation, minimum undergraduate B average, audition (for all performance degrees), official copy of academic transcript showing completed and conferred BM; for doctorate, music theory and music history placement examinations, 2 letters of recommendation, minimum B average in all previous course work and degrees, official copies of academic transcripts showing completion and conferral of all previous degrees, audition (for all performance degrees); for Artist Diploma, music theory and music history placement examinations, statement of purpose, 2 letters of recommendation, minimum B average in all previous course work and degrees, BM, audition, official copies of academic transcripts showing completion and conferral of all previous degrees. Additional exam requirements/recommendations for international students: Required—TOEFL (minimum score 550 paper-based; 80 iBT). *Application deadline:* For fall admission, 7/15 priority date for domestic students, 7/1 for international students; for spring admission, 11/15 priority date for domestic students, 11/1 for international students. Applications are processed on a rolling basis. Application fee: $55. Electronic applications accepted. *Expenses:* Contact institution. *Financial support:* Fellowships, research assistantships, teaching assistantships, Federal Work-Study, scholarships/grants, tuition waivers (full and partial), and unspecified assistantships available. Financial award application deadline: 2/1; financial award applicants required to submit FAFSA. *Faculty research:* Composition, sacred music, orchestral instruments, piano and vocal performance, piano and vocal pedagogy. *Unit head:* Dr. Grayson Wagstaff, Dean, 202-319-5417, Fax: 202-319-6280, E-mail: cua-music@cua.edu. *Application contact:* Dr. Steven Brown, Director of Graduate Admissions, 202-319-5247, Fax: 202-319-6174, E-mail: cua-graduatestudies@cua.edu.
Website: https://music.catholic.edu/

Central Connecticut State University, School of Graduate Studies, College of Liberal Arts and Social Sciences, Department of Music, New Britain, CT 06050-4010. Offers music education (MS, Certificate). *Accreditation:* NASM. *Program availability:* Part-time, evening/weekend. *Faculty:* 1 full-time (0 women). *Students:* 3 full-time (2 women), 1 part-time (0 women). Average age 27. 7 applicants, 57% accepted, 1 enrolled. In 2017, 4 master's awarded. *Degree requirements:* For master's, comprehensive exam, thesis or alternative, special project; for Certificate, qualifying exam. *Entrance requirements:* For master's, theory examination, audition, minimum undergraduate GPA of 2.7, essay, portfolio, evidence of proficiency in technology. Additional exam requirements/recommendations for international students: Required—TOEFL (minimum score 550 paper-based; 79 iBT); Recommended—IELTS (minimum score 6.5). *Application deadline:* For fall admission, 4/1 for domestic and international students; for spring admission, 11/1 for domestic and international students. Applications are processed on a rolling basis. Application fee: $50. Electronic applications accepted. *Expenses: Tuition, area resident:* Full-time $6757. Tuition, state resident: full-time $9750; part-time $374 per credit. Tuition, nonresident: full-time $18,102; part-time $374 per credit. *Required fees:* $4635; $255 per credit. *Financial support:* In 2017–18, 1 student received support. Career-related internships or fieldwork, Federal Work-Study, scholarships/grants, and unspecified assistantships available. Support available to part-time students. Financial award application deadline: 3/1. *Faculty research:* Applied music. *Unit head:* Dr. Carlotta Parr, Chair, 860-832-2912, E-mail: parrc@ccsu.edu. *Application contact:* Patricia Gardner, Associate Director of Graduate Studies, 860-832-2350, Fax: 860-832-2362. Website: http://www.ccsu.edu/music/

Central Methodist University, College of Graduate and Extended Studies, Fayette, MO 65248-1198. Offers clinical counseling (MS); clinical nurse leader (MSN); education (M Ed); music education (MME); nurse educator (MSN). *Program availability:* Part-time, evening/weekend, online learning. *Degree requirements:* For master's, thesis. *Entrance requirements:* For master's, GRE General Test, minimum GPA of 2.75. Electronic applications accepted.

Central Michigan University, College of Graduate Studies, College of Communication and Fine Arts, School of Music, Mount Pleasant, MI 48859. Offers composition (MM); conducting (MM); music education (MM); performance (MM). *Accreditation:* NASM. *Program availability:* Part-time. *Degree requirements:* For master's, thesis or alternative. Electronic applications accepted. *Faculty research:* Music education, music composition, conducting, music performance.

Central Washington University, School of Graduate Studies and Research, College of Arts and Humanities, Department of Music, Ellensburg, WA 98926. Offers composition (MM); conducting (MM); music education (MM); pedagogy (MM); performance (MM). *Accreditation:* NASM. *Entrance requirements:* For master's, minimum GPA of 3.0. Additional exam requirements/recommendations for international students: Required—TOEFL (minimum score 550 paper-based; 79 iBT) or IELTS (minimum score 6.5). *Application deadline:* For fall admission, 2/1 priority date for domestic students; for winter admission, 10/1 for domestic students; for spring admission, 1/1 for domestic students. Applications are processed on a rolling basis. Application fee: $50. Electronic applications accepted. *Financial support:* Application deadline: 3/1; applicants required to submit FAFSA. *Unit head:* Bret P. Smith, Associate Chair, 509-963-1548, E-mail: bpsmith@cwu.edu. *Application contact:* Justine Eason, Admissions Program Coordinator, 509-963-3103, Fax: 509-963-1799, E-mail: masters@cwu.edu. Website: http://www.cwu.edu/~music/

Cleveland State University, College of Graduate Studies, College of Liberal Arts and Social Sciences, Department of Music, Cleveland, OH 44115. Offers composition (MM); music education (MM). *Accreditation:* NASM. *Program availability:* Part-time, evening/weekend. *Faculty:* 9 full-time (2 women), 19 part-time/adjunct (6 women). *Students:* 17 full-time (6 women), 19 part-time (8 women); includes 5 minority (1 Black or African American, non-Hispanic/Latino; 3 Hispanic/Latino; 1 Two or more races, non-Hispanic/Latino), 8 international. Average age 26. 34 applicants, 91% accepted, 19 enrolled. In 2017, 8 master's awarded. *Entrance requirements:* For master's, departmental assessment in music history, minimum undergraduate GPA of 2.75, audition on primary instrument, or submission of composition portfolio or written samples (for music education). Additional exam requirements/recommendations for international students: Required—TOEFL (minimum score 550 paper-based; 78 iBT). *Application deadline:* For fall admission, 7/1 priority date for domestic students, 5/15 for international students; for spring admission, 11/15 for domestic students, 11/1 for international students; for summer admission, 4/1 for domestic students, 3/15 for international students. Applications are processed on a rolling basis. Application fee: $40. Electronic applications accepted. *Financial support:* In 2017–18, 14 students received support. Scholarships/grants, tuition waivers (partial), and unspecified assistantships available. Financial award application deadline: 3/15; financial award applicants required to submit FAFSA. *Faculty research:* Performance, music education, music composition. *Total annual research expenditures:* $26. *Unit head:* Dr. John Perrine, Chairperson/Associate Professor, 216-687-3959, Fax: 216-687-9279, E-mail: j.m.perrine@csuohio.edu. *Application contact:* Kate Bill, Music Admission Specialist, 216-687-5039, Fax: 216-687-9279, E-mail: m.c.bill@csuohio.edu. Website: http://www.csuohio.edu/music/

College of Charleston, Graduate School, School of Education, Health, and Human Performance, Department of Foundations, Secondary, and Special Education, Program in Performing Arts Education, Charleston, SC 29424-0001. Offers MAT. *Accreditation:* NASM. *Program availability:* Part-time, evening/weekend. *Entrance requirements:* For master's, GRE, minimum GPA of 2.5 overall, 3.0 in last 60 hours of undergraduate coursework; 2 letters of recommendation; audition/interview. Additional exam requirements/recommendations for international students: Required—TOEFL (minimum score 81 iBT). Electronic applications accepted.

The Colorado College, Education Department, Program in Secondary Education, Colorado Springs, CO 80903-3294. Offers art teaching (K-12) (MAT); English teaching (MAT); foreign language teaching (MAT); mathematics teaching (MAT); music teaching (MAT); science teaching (MAT); social studies teaching (MAT). *Degree requirements:* For master's, thesis, internship. Electronic applications accepted.

Colorado State University–Pueblo, College of Education, Engineering and Professional Studies, Education Program, Pueblo, CO 81001-4901. Offers art education (M Ed); foreign language education (M Ed); health and physical education (M Ed); instructional technology (M Ed); linguistically diverse education (M Ed); music education (M Ed); special education (M Ed). *Accreditation:* TEAC. *Program availability:* Part-time. *Degree requirements:* For master's, portfolio. *Entrance requirements:* For master's, 3 recommendations, teaching license. Additional exam requirements/recommendations for international students: Required—TOEFL (minimum score 500 paper-based). Electronic applications accepted. *Faculty research:* Portfolio assessment, math education, science education.

Columbus State University, Graduate Studies, College of the Arts, Schwob School of Music, Columbus, GA 31907-5645. Offers music (Artist Diploma); music education (MM); music performance (MM). *Accreditation:* NASM; NCATE (one or more programs are accredited). *Program availability:* Part-time. *Faculty:* 25 full-time (10 women), 4 part-time/adjunct (2 women). *Students:* 44 full-time (15 women), 7 part-time (3 women); includes 11 minority (5 Black or African American, non-Hispanic/Latino; 4 Asian, non-Hispanic/Latino; 1 Hispanic/Latino; 1 Native Hawaiian or other Pacific Islander, non-Hispanic/Latino), 20 international. Average age 27. 59 applicants, 44% accepted, 17 enrolled. In 2017, 11 master's, 5 Artist Diplomas awarded. *Degree requirements:* For master's, exit exam. *Entrance requirements:* For master's, audition, letters of recommendation, undergraduate degree in music with minimum GPA of 2.5. Additional exam requirements/recommendations for international students: Required—TOEFL (minimum score 550 paper-based; 79 iBT). *Application deadline:* For fall admission, 6/30 for domestic students, 5/1 for international students; for spring admission, 11/1 for domestic and international students; for summer admission, 3/1 for domestic and international students. Applications are processed on a rolling basis. Application fee: $50. Electronic applications accepted. *Expenses:* Tuition, state resident: full-time $3708; part-time $2472 per year. Tuition, nonresident: full-time $14,418; part-time $9612 per year. International tuition: $19,218 full-time. *Required fees:* $1605. Tuition and fees vary according to program. *Financial support:* In 2017–18, 43 students received support, including 26 research assistantships with partial tuition reimbursements available (averaging $3,000 per year); career-related internships or fieldwork, Federal Work-Study, institutionally sponsored loans, scholarships/grants, tuition waivers (partial), and unspecified assistantships also available. Support available to part-time students. Financial award application deadline: 5/1; financial award applicants required to submit FAFSA. *Unit head:* Dr. Edwin Scott Harris, Director, 706-507-8419, E-mail: harris_scott@columbusstate.edu. *Application contact:* Catrina Smith-Edmond, Assistant Director for Graduate and Global Admission, 706-507-8824, Fax: 706-568-5091, E-mail: smithedmond_catrina@columbusstate.edu. Website: http://music.columbusstate.edu/

Conservatorio de Musica de Puerto Rico, Program in Music Education, San Juan, PR 00907. Offers MM Ed. *Entrance requirements:* For master's, EXADEP, 3 letters of recommendation, audition, bachelor's degree in music education, interview, minimum GPA of 2.5, performance video, teaching video. Additional exam requirements/recommendations for international students: Required—TOEFL.

Converse College, Petrie School of Music, Spartanburg, SC 29302. Offers music education (M Mus); performance (M Mus). *Accreditation:* NASM. *Program availability:* Part-time, evening/weekend. *Degree requirements:* For master's, variable foreign language requirement, comprehensive exam, thesis (for some programs), recitals. *Entrance requirements:* For master's, NTE (music education), audition, 3 letters of recommendation. Additional exam requirements/recommendations for international students: Required—TOEFL. *Application deadline:* For spring admission, 3/1 priority date for domestic and international students. Applications are processed on a rolling basis. Application fee: $40. Electronic applications accepted. *Financial support:* Career-related internships or fieldwork, Federal Work-Study, institutionally sponsored loans, and unspecified assistantships available. Support available to part-time students. Financial award application deadline: 4/15. *Faculty research:* Chamber music, opera, performance, composition, recording. *Unit head:* Chris Vaneman, Head, Petrie School of Music/Associate Professor of Flute and Musicology, 864-596-9038, E-mail: chris.vaneman@converse.edu. Website: http://www.converse.edu/academics/school-arts/petrie-school-music

DePaul University, School of Music, Chicago, IL 60614. Offers composition (MM); jazz studies (MM); music education (MM); music performance (MM); performance (Certificate). *Accreditation:* NASM (one or more programs are accredited). *Program availability:* Part-time, evening/weekend. *Degree requirements:* For master's, comprehensive exam. *Entrance requirements:* For master's, bachelor's degree in music or related field, minimum GPA of 3.0, auditions (performance), scores (composition); for Certificate, master's degree in performance or related field, auditions (for performance majors). Additional exam requirements/recommendations for international students: Required—TOEFL (minimum score 550 paper-based; 80 iBT). *Application deadline:* For fall admission, 12/1 priority date for domestic and international students. Applications are processed on a rolling basis. Application fee: $40. Electronic applications accepted. *Expenses:* Contact institution. *Financial support:* Application deadline: 12/1; applicants required to submit FAFSA. *Unit head:* Ronald Caltabiano, Dean, 773-325-7256, Fax: 773-325-7429, E-mail: rcalt@depaul.edu. *Application contact:* Ross Beacraft, Director of Admission, 773-325-7444, Fax: 773-325-7429, E-mail: musicadmissions@depaul.edu. Website: http://www.depaul.edu

Duquesne University, Mary Pappert School of Music, Pittsburgh, PA 15282-0001. Offers music education (MM). *Accreditation:* NASM. *Program availability:* Part-time. *Faculty:* 26 full-time (9 women), 77 part-time/adjunct (22 women). *Students:* 54 full-time (21 women), 9 part-time (3 women); includes 4 minority (1 Black or African American, non-Hispanic/Latino; 1 Asian, non-Hispanic/Latino; 2 Hispanic/Latino), 23 international. Average age 26. 76 applicants, 95% accepted, 31 enrolled. In 2017, 47 master's, 12 ADs awarded. *Degree requirements:* For master's, comprehensive exam, thesis (for some programs), recital (music performance); for AD, recital. *Entrance requirements:* For master's, audition, minimum undergraduate QPA of 3.0 in music, portfolio of original compositions, or music education experience; for AD, audition. Additional exam requirements/recommendations for international students: Required—TOEFL (minimum score 550 paper-based; 79 iBT), IELTS (minimum score 6.5). *Application deadline:* For fall admission, 7/1 for domestic and international students; for spring admission, 12/1 for domestic and international students; for summer admission, 6/1 for domestic students, 5/1 for international students. Applications are processed on a rolling basis. Application fee: $50. Electronic applications accepted. Application fee is waived when completed online. *Expenses:* $1,525 per credit. *Financial support:* In 2017–18, 76 students received support. Scholarships/grants and unspecified assistantships available. Financial award application deadline: 4/1. *Faculty research:* Assessment of music education and professional dispositions; music philosophy; curricular design, pedagogy, and assessment; music composition; music performance. *Unit head:* Dr. Seth Beckman, Dean/Professor, 412-396-6082, Fax: 412-396-1524, E-mail: beckmans@duq.edu. *Application contact:* Thomas Carsecka, Director of Music Admissions, 412-396-5983, Fax: 412-396-5719, E-mail: carseckat@duq.edu. Website: http://duq.edu/music

East Carolina University, Graduate School, College of Fine Arts and Communication, School of Music, Greenville, NC 27858-4353. Offers advanced performance studies (Certificate); composition (MM); music education (MM), including choral conducting, instrumental conducting, music theory/composition, music therapy, performance, Suzuki pedagogy; music therapy (MM); Suzuki pedagogy (Certificate); theory (MM); woodwind specialist (MM), including accompanying, choral conducting, instrumental, instrumental conducting, jazz studies, keyboard, organ, piano pedagogy, Suzuki string pedagogy, vocal pedagogy, voice, woodwind specialist. *Accreditation:* NASM. *Program availability:* Part-time. *Students:* 31 full-time (16 women), 18 part-time (8 women); includes 11 minority (4 Black or African American, non-Hispanic/Latino; 5 Asian, non-Hispanic/Latino; 2 Two or more races, non-Hispanic/Latino), 1 international. Average age 28. 39 applicants, 85% accepted, 21 enrolled. In 2017, 10 master's, 2 Certificates awarded. *Degree requirements:* For master's, comprehensive exam, thesis optional. *Application deadline:* For fall admission, 6/1 priority date for domestic students. Applications are processed on a rolling basis. Application fee: $75. *Expenses:* Tuition, state resident: full-time $4749; part-time $297 per credit hour. Tuition, nonresident: full-time $17,898;

part-time $1119 per credit hour. *Required fees:* $2691; $224 per credit hour. Part-time tuition and fees vary according to course load and program. *Financial support:* Fellowships, research assistantships, teaching assistantships, and Federal Work-Study available. Support available to part-time students. Financial award application deadline: 6/1. *Unit head:* Christopher Ulffers, Director, 252-328-4270, E-mail: ulffersj@ecu.edu. Website: http://www.ecu.edu/music/

Eastern Illinois University, Graduate School, College of Liberal Arts and Sciences, Department of Music, Charleston, IL 61920. Offers composition (MA); conducting (MA); music education (MA); performance (MA). *Accreditation:* NASM. *Program availability:* Part-time, evening/weekend, online learning. *Degree requirements:* For master's, comprehensive exam (for some programs), thesis (for some programs). *Entrance requirements:* For master's, personal statement, resume, three letters of recommendation. Additional exam requirements/recommendations for international students: Required—TOEFL (minimum score 500 paper-based; 61 iBT), IELTS (minimum score 6). *Application deadline:* For fall admission, 5/15 for domestic and international students; for spring admission, 10/15 for domestic and international students. Applications are processed on a rolling basis. Application fee: $30. Electronic applications accepted. *Financial support:* Teaching assistantships with full tuition reimbursements, career-related internships or fieldwork, Federal Work-Study, and unspecified assistantships available. Support available to part-time students. Financial award application deadline: 3/1; financial award applicants required to submit FAFSA. *Unit head:* Shellie L. Gregorich, Chair, 217-581-3010, Fax: 217-581-7137, E-mail: slgregorich@eiu.edu. *Application contact:* Shellie L. Gregorich, Chair, 217-581-3010, Fax: 217-581-7137, E-mail: slgregorich@eiu.edu.
Website: http://www.eiu.edu/musicgrad

Eastern Kentucky University, The Graduate School, College of Education, Department of Curriculum and Instruction, Richmond, KY 40475-3102. Offers elementary education (MA Ed), including early elementary education, reading; library science (MA Ed); music education (MA Ed); secondary and higher education (MA Ed), including secondary education; teaching (MAT). *Accreditation:* NCATE. *Program availability:* Part-time. *Degree requirements:* For master's, portfolio is part of exam. *Entrance requirements:* For master's, GRE General Test, PRAXIS II (KY), minimum GPA of 2.5. *Faculty research:* Technology in education, reading instruction, e-portfolios, induction to teacher education, dispositions of teachers.

Eastern Washington University, Graduate Studies, College of Arts, Letters and Education, Department of Music, Cheney, WA 99004-2431. Offers composition (MA); instrumental/vocal performance (MA); jazz pedagogy (MA); liberal arts (MA); music education (MA). *Accreditation:* NASM. *Program availability:* Part-time. *Faculty:* 17. *Students:* 10 full-time (4 women), 3 part-time (0 women), 1 international. Average age 31. 12 applicants, 58% accepted, 5 enrolled. In 2017, 7 master's awarded. *Degree requirements:* For master's, comprehensive exam, thesis or alternative. *Entrance requirements:* For master's, GRE General Test, minimum GPA of 3.0. Additional exam requirements/recommendations for international students: Required—TOEFL (minimum score 580 paper-based; 92 iBT), IELTS (minimum score 7), TWE, PTE (minimum score 63). *Application deadline:* For fall admission, 4/1 priority date for domestic students; for spring admission, 1/15 for domestic students. Applications are processed on a rolling basis. Application fee: $75. Electronic applications accepted. *Expenses:* Tuition, state resident: full-time $11,191; part-time $373.06 per credit. Tuition, nonresident: full-time $25,995; part-time $866.52 per credit. *Financial support:* In 2017–18, 8 students received support, including teaching assistantships with partial tuition reimbursements available (averaging $10,000 per year); career-related internships or fieldwork, Federal Work-Study, institutionally sponsored loans, scholarships/grants, health care benefits, tuition waivers (partial), and unspecified assistantships also available. Support available to part-time students. Financial award application deadline: 2/1; financial award applicants required to submit FAFSA. *Unit head:* Dr. Jody Graves, 509-359-6119, E-mail: jgraves@ewu.edu.
Website: http://www.ewu.edu/cale/programs/music.xml

Five Towns College, Graduate Programs, Dix Hills, NY 11746-6055. Offers childhood education (MS Ed); composition and arranging (DMA); jazz/commercial music (MM); music education (MM, DMA); music history and literature (DMA); music performance (DMA). *Program availability:* Part-time. *Faculty:* 12 full-time (3 women), 6 part-time/adjunct (0 women). *Students:* 18 full-time (7 women), 6 part-time (2 women); includes 9 minority (3 Black or African American, non-Hispanic/Latino; 4 Asian, non-Hispanic/Latino; 1 Hispanic/Latino; 1 Two or more races, non-Hispanic/Latino), 1 international. Average age 35. 63 applicants, 11% accepted, 7 enrolled. In 2017, 4 master's, 2 doctorates awarded. *Degree requirements:* For master's, thesis, exams, major composition or capstone project, recital; for doctorate, comprehensive exam, thesis/dissertation, final oral exam. *Entrance requirements:* For master's, audition (for MM); New York state teaching certification (for MS Ed); personal statement, two letters of recommendation; for doctorate, 3 letters of recommendation, audition, essay. Additional exam requirements/recommendations for international students: Required—TOEFL (minimum score 520 paper-based; 85 iBT); Recommended—IELTS (minimum score 7). *Application deadline:* For fall admission, 9/1 for domestic and international students; for spring admission, 1/25 for domestic and international students. Applications are processed on a rolling basis. Application fee: $50. Electronic applications accepted. *Financial support:* Fellowships with tuition reimbursements, teaching assistantships with tuition reimbursements, and tuition waivers (partial) available. Financial award applicants required to submit FAFSA. *Faculty research:* Teaching methods, teaching strategies and techniques, analysis of modern music, jazz. *Application contact:* Ronnie MacDonald, Director of Admissions, 631-656-2110, Fax: 631-656-2172, E-mail: admissions@ftc.edu.
Website: http://www.ftc.edu

Florida Atlantic University, College of Education, Department of Teaching and Learning, Boca Raton, FL 33431-0991. Offers curriculum and instruction (M Ed), including art, biology, chemistry, English, French, German, mathematics, music, physics, Pre-K and primary education, reading, social sciences, Spanish; elementary education (M Ed); environmental education (M Ed); reading education (M Ed); social foundations of education (M Ed), including educational psychology, educational technology, multilingual education. *Accreditation:* NCATE. *Program availability:* Part-time, evening/weekend. *Faculty:* 13 full-time (10 women), 1 part-time/adjunct (0 women). *Students:* 26 full-time (22 women), 43 part-time (39 women); includes 19 minority (9 Black or African American, non-Hispanic/Latino; 1 Asian, non-Hispanic/Latino; 8 Hispanic/Latino; 1 Two or more races, non-Hispanic/Latino), 3 international. Average age 30. 91 applicants, 57% accepted, 33 enrolled. In 2017, 25 master's awarded. *Entrance requirements:* For master's, GRE General Test, minimum GPA of 3.0 in last 2 years of undergraduate course work. Additional exam requirements/recommendations for international students: Required—TOEFL (minimum score 500 paper-based; 61 iBT), IELTS (minimum score 6). *Application deadline:* For fall admission, 7/1 for domestic students, 2/15 for international students; for spring admission, 11/1 for domestic students, 7/15 for international students. Applications are processed on a rolling basis. Application fee: $30. *Expenses:* Tuition, state resident: full-time $7400; part-time $369.82 per credit. Tuition, nonresident: full-time $20,496; part-time $1042.81 per credit. *Financial support:* Fellowships with partial tuition

reimbursements, research assistantships with partial tuition reimbursements, teaching assistantships with partial tuition reimbursements, career-related internships or fieldwork, scholarships/grants, and unspecified assistantships available. *Faculty research:* Technology, teaching English to speakers of other languages, math teaching, electronic portfolio assessment, global perspectives through social studies. *Unit head:* Dr. Barbara Ridener, Chairperson, 561-297-3588, E-mail: bridener@fau.edu. *Application contact:* Dr. Eliah Watlington, Associate Dean, 561-296-8520, Fax: 261-297-2991, E-mail: ewatling@fau.edu.
Website: http://www.coe.fau.edu/academicdepartments/tl/

Florida International University, College of Communication, Architecture and The Arts, School of Music, Miami, FL 33199. Offers music (MM); music education (MS). *Accreditation:* NASM. *Program availability:* Part-time, evening/weekend. *Faculty:* 22 full-time (4 women), 27 part-time/adjunct (7 women). *Students:* 27 full-time (11 women), 10 part-time (5 women); includes 23 minority (6 Black or African American, non-Hispanic/Latino; 1 Asian, non-Hispanic/Latino; 15 Hispanic/Latino; 1 Two or more races, non-Hispanic/Latino), 4 international. Average age 32. 46 applicants, 61% accepted, 14 enrolled. In 2017, 24 master's awarded. *Degree requirements:* For master's, thesis (for some programs). *Entrance requirements:* For master's, GRE (depending on program), statement of intent; 2 letters of recommendation; audition, interview and/or writing sample (depending on the area). Additional exam requirements/recommendations for international students: Required—TOEFL (minimum score 550 paper-based; 80 iBT). *Application deadline:* For fall admission, 6/1 for domestic students, 4/1 for international students; for spring admission, 10/1 for domestic students, 9/1 for international students. Applications are processed on a rolling basis. Application fee: $30. Electronic applications accepted. *Expenses:* Tuition, state resident: full-time $8912; part-time $446 per credit hour. Tuition, nonresident: full-time $21,393; part-time $992 per credit hour. *Required fees:* $390; $195 per semester. *Financial support:* Institutionally sponsored loans and scholarships/grants available. Financial award application deadline: 3/1; financial award applicants required to submit FAFSA. *Unit head:* Robert Dundas, Interim Chair, 305-348-3587, Fax: 305-348-4073, E-mail: robert.dundas@fiu.edu. *Application contact:* Joel Galand, Graduate Program Director, 305-348-7078, E-mail: galandj@fiu.edu.
Website: http://carta.fiu.edu/music/

George Mason University, College of Visual and Performing Arts, School of Music, Program in Music, Fairfax, VA 22030. Offers composition (MM); conducting (MM); jazz studies (MM); music education (MM); pedagogy (MM); performance (MM). *Accreditation:* NASM. *Faculty:* 21 full-time (10 women), 38 part-time/adjunct (11 women). *Students:* 14 full-time (8 women), 25 part-time (13 women); includes 10 minority (3 Black or African American, non-Hispanic/Latino; 3 Asian, non-Hispanic/Latino; 3 Hispanic/Latino; 1 Two or more races, non-Hispanic/Latino), 1 international. Average age 32. 46 applicants, 59% accepted, 14 enrolled. In 2017, 17 master's awarded. *Degree requirements:* For master's, comprehensive exam. *Entrance requirements:* For master's, expanded goals statement; 2 letters of recommendation; official transcript. Additional exam requirements/recommendations for international students: Required—TOEFL (minimum score 575 paper-based; 88 iBT), IELTS (minimum score 6.5), PTE (minimum score 59). Application fee: $75 ($80 for international students). Electronic applications accepted. *Expenses:* Tuition, state resident: full-time $11,228; part-time $459.50 per credit. Tuition, nonresident: full-time $30,932; part-time $1280.50 per credit. *Required fees:* $3252; $135.50 per credit. Part-time tuition and fees vary according to course load and program. *Financial support:* In 2017–18, 1 student received support, including 1 teaching assistantship; career-related internships or fieldwork, Federal Work-Study, scholarships/grants, and unspecified assistantships also available. Financial award application deadline: 3/1; financial award applicants required to submit FAFSA. *Unit head:* Dr. Linda Apple Monson, Managing Director, 703-993-3580, Fax: 703-993-1394, E-mail: lmonson@gmu.edu. *Application contact:* Dr. Lisa A. Billingham, Director of Graduate Studies, 703-993-3778, Fax: 703-993-1394, E-mail: lbillin1@gmu.edu.
Website: http://music.gmu.edu

Georgia College & State University, Graduate School, College of Arts and Sciences, Department of Music, Milledgeville, GA 31061. Offers MM Ed. *Accreditation:* NASM. *Program availability:* Part-time, evening/weekend, online only, 100% online. *Faculty:* 10 full-time (6 women). *Students:* 2 full-time (both women), 1 (woman) part-time; includes 2 minority (both Black or African American, non-Hispanic/Latino). Average age 35. 1 applicant, 100% accepted. In 2017, 3 master's awarded. *Degree requirements:* For master's, comprehensive exam, publication or presentation of a capstone project. *Entrance requirements:* For master's, bachelor's degree in music education, 3 letters of recommendation, interview, resume, video recorded lesson or rehearsal with written lesson plan, transcript. *Application deadline:* For fall admission, 8/1 priority date for domestic students; for spring admission, 11/1 priority date for domestic students; for summer admission, 4/1 priority date for domestic students. Applications are processed on a rolling basis. Application fee: $40. Electronic applications accepted. *Expenses:* $288 per semester hour full-time, $2,592 per term; $343 per semester fees. *Financial support:* In 2017–18, 1 student received support. Unspecified assistantships available. Financial award applicants required to submit FAFSA. *Unit head:* Dr. Tina Holmes-Davis, Graduate Coordinator for Music Education, 478-445-6289, Fax: 478-445-1336, E-mail: tina.holmes-davis@gcsu.edu. *Application contact:* Kate Marshall, Graduate Admissions Coordinator, 478-445-1184, Fax: 478-445-1336, E-mail: grad-admit@gcsu.edu.
Website: http://www.gcsu.edu/artsandsciences/music/music-education-mmed

Georgia Southern University, Jack N. Averitt College of Graduate Studies, College of Liberal Arts and Social Sciences, Program in Music, Statesboro, GA 30460. Offers composition (MM); conducting (MM); music education (MM); music technology (MM); performance (MM). *Accreditation:* NASM. *Program availability:* Part-time, evening/weekend. *Faculty:* 26 full-time (16 women), 3 part-time/adjunct (0 women). *Students:* 10 full-time (3 women), 16 part-time (6 women); includes 9 minority (4 Black or African American, non-Hispanic/Latino; 1 Asian, non-Hispanic/Latino; 2 Hispanic/Latino; 2 Two or more races, non-Hispanic/Latino), 3 international. Average age 27. 18 applicants, 94% accepted, 11 enrolled. In 2017, 8 master's awarded. *Degree requirements:* For master's, comprehensive exam, recital or final project. *Entrance requirements:* For master's, minimum GPA of 2.5, audition, letters of recommendation. Additional exam requirements/recommendations for international students: Required—TOEFL (minimum score 550 paper-based; 80 iBT), IELTS (minimum score 6). *Application deadline:* For fall admission, 3/1 priority date for domestic and international students; for spring admission, 10/1 priority date for domestic students, 10/1 for international students. Applications are processed on a rolling basis. Application fee: $50. Electronic applications accepted. *Expenses:* Tuition, state resident: full-time $4986; part-time $3324 per year. Tuition, nonresident: full-time $21,982; part-time $15,352 per year. *Required fees:* $2092; $1802 per credit hour. $901 per semester. Tuition and fees vary according to course load, campus/location and program. *Financial support:* In 2017–18, 19 students received support, including 10 fellowships with full tuition reimbursements available (averaging $7,750 per year), 3 teaching assistantships with full tuition reimbursements available (averaging $7,750 per year); Federal Work-Study, scholarships/grants, tuition waivers (full), and unspecified assistantships also available. Support available to part-time students. Financial award application deadline: 4/15;

financial award applicants required to submit FAFSA. *Faculty research:* Performance, conducting, composition, technology, education. *Unit head:* Dr. Greg Harwood, Graduate Director, 912-478-5813, Fax: 912-478-1295, E-mail: gharwood@georgiasouthern.edu.
Website: http://class.georgiasouthern.edu/music/

Georgia State University, College of Education and Human Development, Department of Middle and Secondary Education, Atlanta, GA 30302-3083. Offers curriculum and instruction (Ed D); English education (MAT); mathematics education (M Ed, MAT); middle level education (MAT); reading, language and literacy education (M Ed, MAT), including reading instruction (M Ed); science education (M Ed, MAT), including biology (MAT), broad field science (MAT), chemistry (MAT), earth science (MAT), physics (MAT); social studies education (M Ed, MAT), including economics (MAT), geography (MAT), history (MAT), political science (MAT); teaching and learning (PhD), including language and literacy, mathematics education, music education, science education, social studies education, teaching and teacher education. *Accreditation:* NCATE. *Program availability:* Part-time, evening/weekend, online learning. *Faculty:* 24 full-time (18 women). *Students:* 179 full-time (110 women), 192 part-time (133 women); includes 193 minority (130 Black or African American, non-Hispanic/Latino; 1 American Indian or Alaska Native, non-Hispanic/Latino; 23 Asian, non-Hispanic/Latino; 25 Hispanic/Latino; 14 Two or more races, non-Hispanic/Latino), 6 international. Average age 33. 175 applicants, 58% accepted, 83 enrolled. In 2017, 81 master's, 17 doctorates awarded. *Entrance requirements:* For master's, GRE; GACE I (for initial teacher preparation programs), baccalaureate degree or equivalent, resume, goals statement, two letters of recommendation, minimum undergraduate GPA of 2.5; proof of initial teacher certification in the content area (for M Ed); for doctorate, GRE, resume, goals statement, writing sample, two letters of recommendation, minimum graduate GPA of 3.3, interview. *Application deadline:* For fall admission, 1/15 priority date for domestic and international students; for spring admission, 10/1 for domestic and international students. Application fee: $50. Electronic applications accepted. *Expenses:* Tuition, state resident: full-time $7020. Tuition, nonresident: full-time $22,518. *Required fees:* $2128. Tuition and fees vary according to degree level and program. *Financial support:* In 2017–18, fellowships with full tuition reimbursements (averaging $19,667 per year), research assistantships with full tuition reimbursements (averaging $5,436 per year), teaching assistantships with full tuition reimbursements (averaging $2,779 per year) were awarded; career-related internships or fieldwork, Federal Work-Study, scholarships/grants, health care benefits, tuition waivers (full and partial), and unspecified assistantships also available. Financial award application deadline: 3/15. *Faculty research:* Teacher education in language and literacy, mathematics, science, and social studies in urban middle and secondary school settings; learning technologies in school, community, and corporate settings; multicultural education and education for social justice; urban education; international education. *Unit head:* Dr. Dana L. Fox, Chair, 404-413-8060, Fax: 404-413-8063, E-mail: dfox@gsu.edu. *Application contact:* Bobbie Turner, Administrative Coordinator, 404-413-8405, Fax: 404-413-8063, E-mail: bnturner@gsu.edu.
Website: http://mse.education.gsu.edu/

Georgia State University, School of Music, Atlanta, GA 30303. Offers choral conducting (MM); jazz studies (MM); music (Certificate); music composition (MM); music education (PhD); orchestral conducting (MM); performance (MM), including guitar, orchestral, piano, vocal; piano pedagogy (MM); wind band conducting (MM). *Accreditation:* NASM. *Program availability:* Part-time, evening/weekend. *Faculty:* 40 full-time (13 women). *Students:* 80 full-time (36 women), 10 part-time (4 women); includes 32 minority (19 Black or African American, non-Hispanic/Latino; 5 Asian, non-Hispanic/Latino; 8 Hispanic/Latino), 13 international. Average age 30. 84 applicants, 69% accepted, 42 enrolled. In 2017, 25 master's, 2 other advanced degrees awarded. *Degree requirements:* For master's, comprehensive exam, thesis (for some programs), recital; for doctorate, comprehensive exam, thesis/dissertation; for Certificate, recital. *Entrance requirements:* For master's, GRE (for music education, composition only), BM; for doctorate, GRE, MM; for Certificate, MM. Additional exam requirements/recommendations for international students: Required—TOEFL (minimum score 550 paper-based; 80 iBT). *Application deadline:* For fall admission, 3/1 priority date for domestic and international students; for spring admission, 10/1 priority date for domestic and international students. Applications are processed on a rolling basis. Application fee: $50. Electronic applications accepted. *Expenses:* Tuition, state resident: full-time $7020. Tuition, nonresident: full-time $22,518. *Required fees:* $2128. Tuition and fees vary according to degree level and program. *Financial support:* In 2017–18, research assistantships with full tuition reimbursements (averaging $4,000 per year) were awarded; Federal Work-Study, scholarships/grants, health care benefits, tuition waivers (partial), and unspecified assistantships also available. Financial award application deadline: 3/1; financial award applicants required to submit FAFSA. *Faculty research:* Male changing voice, nineteenth-century chamber music, improvisation and learning, Garibunda, African-American classical musicians. *Unit head:* William Dwight Coleman, Director, School of Music, 404-413-5953, Fax: 404-413-5910, E-mail: wcoleman@gsu.edu. *Application contact:* Dr. Steven Andrew Harper, Graduate Director, 404-413-5943, Fax: 404-413-5910, E-mail: sharper@gsu.edu.
Website: http://www.music.gsu.edu/

Gordon College, Graduate Music Education Program, Wenham, MA 01984-1899. Offers MM Ed. *Accreditation:* NASM. *Program availability:* Part-time. *Faculty:* 2 full-time (1 woman), 6 part-time/adjunct (3 women). *Students:* 13 full-time (7 women), 11 part-time (10 women); includes 5 minority (3 Asian, non-Hispanic/Latino; 1 Hispanic/Latino; 1 Two or more races, non-Hispanic/Latino). Average age 34. 9 applicants, 100% accepted, 9 enrolled. In 2017, 10 master's awarded. *Degree requirements:* For master's, comprehensive exam, thesis or alternative, field-based experience, capstone research project. *Entrance requirements:* For master's, music theory and music history diagnostic exams, 15-20 minute video-recorded demonstration of current classroom teaching; letter of introduction; at least one year of teaching experience; initial license in music (for professional licensure); professional resume; 3-4 page essay; two letters of recommendation; two official transcripts. Additional exam requirements/recommendations for international students: Required—TOEFL (minimum score 550 paper-based with minimum of 50 on each test area), Oral Proficiency Interview. *Application deadline:* For summer admission, 4/1 for domestic and international students. Applications are processed on a rolling basis. Application fee: $50. *Expenses:* $600 tuition per credit; $125 comprehensive fee per semester. *Financial support:* Applicants required to submit FAFSA. *Faculty research:* Medium-high security prison education through choral music instruction; healthy vocal development in adolescents; healthy use of the singing voice; national common music assessment initiative; choral literature and techniques to incorporate the new national standards for music education. *Unit head:* Dr. Sandra Doneski, Associate Professor, 978-867-4818, E-mail: sandra.doneski@gordon.edu. *Application contact:* Kristen Harrington, Program Administrator, 978-867-4429, Fax: 978-867-4663, E-mail: kristen.harrington@gordon.edu.
Website: http://www.gordon.edu/gradmusic

Hampton University, School of Liberal Arts and Education, Program in Teaching, Hampton, VA 23668. Offers biology education 6-12 (MT); English education 6-12 (MT); mathematics education 6-12 (MT); music education PreK-12 (MT). *Program availability:* Part-time. *Students:* 5 full-time (4 women); all minorities (all Black or African American,

non-Hispanic/Latino). Average age 23. 6 applicants, 67% accepted, 1 enrolled. In 2017, 7 master's awarded. *Entrance requirements:* For master's, GRE General Test. Additional exam requirements/recommendations for international students: Required—TOEFL (minimum score 525 paper-based) or IELTS (6.5). *Application deadline:* For fall admission, 6/1 priority date for domestic students, 4/1 for international students; for spring admission, 11/1 priority date for domestic students, 9/1 for international students; for summer admission, 4/1 priority date for domestic students, 2/1 priority date for international students. Applications are processed on a rolling basis. Application fee: $35. Electronic applications accepted. *Expenses: Tuition:* Full-time $22,630; part-time $575 per semester hour. *Required fees:* $70. Tuition and fees vary according to program. *Financial support:* Application deadline: 6/30; applicants required to submit FAFSA. *Unit head:* Dr. Martha Jallim-Hall, Program Coordinator, 757-727-5793.

Hardin-Simmons University, Graduate School, College of Fine Arts, Abilene, TX 79698-0001. Offers church music (MM); music education (MM); music performance (MM); theory and composition (MM). *Accreditation:* NASM. *Program availability:* Part-time. *Faculty:* 14 full-time (4 women), 1 part-time/adjunct (0 women). *Students:* 4 full-time (2 women), 2 part-time (0 women); includes 3 minority (1 Hispanic/Latino; 2 Two or more races, non-Hispanic/Latino). Average age 29. 2 applicants, 50% accepted, 1 enrolled. In 2017, 3 master's awarded. *Degree requirements:* For master's, comprehensive exam, thesis (for some programs). *Entrance requirements:* For master's, minimum undergraduate GPA of 3.0 in major, 2.7 overall; writing sample; demonstrated knowledge in chosen area. Additional exam requirements/recommendations for international students: Required—TOEFL (minimum score 550 paper-based; 79 iBT). *Application deadline:* For fall admission, 8/15 priority date for domestic students, 4/1 for international students; for spring admission, 1/5 priority date for domestic students, 9/1 for international students. Applications are processed on a rolling basis. Application fee: $50 ($150 for international students). Electronic applications accepted. *Expenses: Tuition:* Full-time $13,500; part-time $750 per semester hour. *Required fees:* $220 per term. One-time fee: $50. Tuition and fees vary according to course load, campus/location and program. *Financial support:* In 2017–18, 6 students received support, including 3 fellowships (averaging $1,213 per year); career-related internships or fieldwork and scholarships/grants also available. Support available to part-time students. Financial award application deadline: 6/30; financial award applicants required to submit FAFSA. *Unit head:* Dr. Lynnette Chambers, Program Director, 325-670-1430, Fax: 325-670-5873, E-mail: lchambers@hsutx.edu. *Application contact:* Dr. Nancy Kucinski, Dean of Graduate Studies, 325-670-1298, Fax: 325-670-1564, E-mail: gradoff@hsutx.edu.
Website: http://www.hsutx.edu/academics/cofa/

Hebrew College, Program in Jewish Studies, Newton Centre, MA 02459. Offers Jewish liturgical music (Certificate); Jewish music education (Certificate); Jewish studies (MA). *Program availability:* Part-time, evening/weekend, online learning. *Degree requirements:* For master's, one foreign language. *Entrance requirements:* For master's, GRE, interview. Additional exam requirements/recommendations for international students: Required—TOEFL.

Heidelberg University, Master of Music Education Program, Tiffin, OH 44883-2462. Offers MME. Program offered in summer only. *Accreditation:* NASM. *Program availability:* Part-time. In 2017, 2 master's awarded. *Entrance requirements:* For master's, bachelor's degree in music education; minimum cumulative GPA of 2.9; 3 letters of recommendation; copy of U.S. teaching license in music education. Additional exam requirements/recommendations for international students: Required—TOEFL (minimum score 550 paper-based; 79 iBT), IELTS (minimum score 6.5). *Application deadline:* For fall admission, 6/1 for domestic students. Applications are processed on a rolling basis. Application fee: $0. Electronic applications accepted. *Expenses:* $525 per hour. *Financial support:* Unspecified assistantships available. Financial award applicants required to submit FAFSA. *Unit head:* Dr. Carol Dusdieker, Director, 419-448-2080, E-mail: cdusdiek@heidelberg.edu. *Application contact:* Katie Zeyen, Graduate Studies Coordinator, 419-448-2602, Fax: 419-448-2565, E-mail: kzeyen@heidelberg.edu.
Website: https://www.heidelberg.edu/academics/programs/master-music-education

Hofstra University, School of Education, Programs in Teacher Education, Hempstead, NY 11549. Offers bilingual education (MA); bilingual extension (Advanced Certificate), including education/speech language pathology, intensive teacher institute; business education (MS Ed); curriculum studies (MS Ed); early childhood and childhood education (MS Ed); early childhood education (MA, MS Ed); educational technology (Advanced Certificate); elementary education (MA, MS Ed), including science, technology, engineering, and mathematics (STEM) (MA); English education (MS Ed); family and consumer science (MS Ed); fine arts and music education (Advanced Certificate); fine arts education (MS Ed); foreign language and TESOL (MS Ed); foreign language education (MA, MS Ed), including Arabic (MS Ed), biology, chemistry, Chinese (MS Ed), earth science, French, German, Italian (MS Ed), Mandarin (MS Ed), physics, Russian, Spanish; foundations of education (Advanced Certificate), including grades 5-6, grades 7-9; languages other than English and teaching English as a second language (MA); learning and teaching (Ed D), including applied linguistics, art education, arts and humanities, early childhood education, English education, human development, math education, math, science, and technology, multicultural education, physical education, science education, social studies education, special education; mathematics education (MA, MS Ed); music education (MA, MS Ed); science education (MA), including biology (MA, MS Ed), chemistry (MA, MS Ed), earth science (MA, MS Ed), physics (MA, MS Ed); secondary education (Advanced Certificate); social studies education (MA, MS Ed); teaching languages other than English and TESOL (MS Ed); technology for learning (MA); TESOL (MS Ed, Advanced Certificate); TESOL with specialization in STEM (MA); work based learning extension (Advanced Certificate). *Program availability:* Part-time, evening/weekend, blended/hybrid learning. *Students:* 119 full-time (83 women), 124 part-time (90 women); includes 54 minority (15 Black or African American, non-Hispanic/Latino; 9 Asian, non-Hispanic/Latino; 29 Hispanic/Latino; 1 Native Hawaiian or other Pacific Islander, non-Hispanic/Latino), 12 international. Average age 29. 205 applicants, 88% accepted, 93 enrolled. In 2017, 103 master's, 4 doctorates, 32 other advanced degrees awarded. *Degree requirements:* For master's, comprehensive exam, thesis (for some programs), exit project, student teaching, fieldwork, electronic portfolio, curriculum project, minimum GPA of 3.0; for doctorate, thesis/dissertation; for Advanced Certificate, 3 foreign languages, comprehensive exam (for some programs), thesis project. *Entrance requirements:* For master's, GRE, 2 letters of recommendation, portfolio, teacher certification (MA), interview, essay; for doctorate, GMAT, GRE, LSAT, or MAT; for Advanced Certificate, 2 letters of recommendation, essay, interview and/or portfolio, teaching certificate. Additional exam requirements/recommendations for international students: Required—TOEFL (minimum score 550 paper-based; 80 iBT). *Application deadline:* Applications are processed on a rolling basis. Application fee: $75. Electronic applications accepted. *Expenses: Tuition:* Full-time $1292. *Required fees:* $970. Tuition and fees vary according to program. *Financial support:* In 2017–18, 112 students received support, including 56 fellowships with full and partial tuition reimbursements available (averaging $4,998 per year), 2 research assistantships with full and partial tuition reimbursements available (averaging $8,753 per year); career-related internships or fieldwork, Federal Work-Study, institutionally sponsored loans, scholarships/grants, traineeships, tuition waivers (full and partial), and unspecified assistantships also available. Support available to part-time students. Financial award

applicants required to submit FAFSA. *Faculty research:* Educational interventions that foster critical-thinking skills; teachers' attitudes about professional development; threats to teacher quality. *Unit head:* Dr. Eustace Thompson, Chairperson, 516-463-5749, Fax: 516-463-6275, E-mail: eustace.g.thompson@hofstra.edu. *Application contact:* Sunil Samuel, Assistant Vice President of Admissions, 516-463-4723, Fax: 516-463-4664, E-mail: graduateadmission@hofstra.edu.
Website: http://www.hofstra.edu/education/

Holy Names University, Graduate Division, Department of Music, Oakland, CA 94619-1699. Offers Kodaly (Certificate); music education with Kodaly emphasis (MM); piano pedagogy (MM); vocal pedagogy (MM). *Degree requirements:* For master's, comprehensive exam, recital. *Entrance requirements:* For master's, audition; minimum undergraduate GPA of 2.6 overall, 3.0 in major. Additional exam requirements/recommendations for international students: Required—TOEFL (minimum score 550 paper-based; 79 iBT). Electronic applications accepted. *Faculty research:* Performance practice with special interest in Baroque, Romantic, and twentieth-century instrumental and vocal music; choral pedagogy; Hungarian music education.

Howard University, Graduate School, Division of Fine Arts, Department of Music, Washington, DC 20059-0002. Offers applied music (MM); instrument (MM Ed); jazz studies (MM); organ (MM Ed); piano (MM Ed); voice (MM Ed). *Accreditation:* NASM. *Program availability:* Part-time. *Degree requirements:* For master's, comprehensive exam, thesis or alternative, departmental qualifying exam, recital. *Entrance requirements:* For master's, minimum GPA of 3.0, bachelor's degree in music or music education. Additional exam requirements/recommendations for international students: Required—TOEFL.

Hunter College of the City University of New York, Graduate School, School of Education, Program in Music Education, New York, NY 10065-5085. Offers MA. *Accreditation:* NCATE. *Degree requirements:* For master's, one foreign language, comprehensive exam, thesis, professional teaching portfolio, New York State Teacher Certification Exams. *Entrance requirements:* For master's, minimum GPA of 2.8, 2 letters of reference. Additional exam requirements/recommendations for international students: Required—TOEFL, TWE.

Idaho State University, Office of Graduate Studies, College of Education, Department of Teaching and Educational Studies, Pocatello, ID 83209-8059. Offers deaf education (M Ed); elementary education (M Ed); human exceptionality (M Ed); literacy (M Ed); music education (M Ed); secondary education (M Ed). *Program availability:* Part-time. *Degree requirements:* For master's, comprehensive exam, thesis (for some programs), oral thesis defense or written comprehensive exam and oral exam. *Entrance requirements:* For master's, GRE or MAT, minimum undergraduate GPA of 3.0, bachelor's degree, professional experience in an educational context. Additional exam requirements/recommendations for international students: Required—TOEFL (minimum score 550 paper-based; 80 iBT). Electronic applications accepted. *Faculty research:* Literacy, school psychology, special education.

Indiana State University, College of Graduate and Professional Studies, College of Arts and Sciences, School of Music, Terre Haute, IN 47809. Offers conducting (MM); music education (MM); music performance (MM). *Accreditation:* NASM. *Degree requirements:* For master's, comprehensive exam, thesis, qualifying exam. Electronic applications accepted.

Indiana University of Pennsylvania, School of Graduate Studies and Research, College of Fine Arts, Department of Music, Program in Music Education, Indiana, PA 15705. Offers MA. *Faculty:* 15 full-time (5 women). *Students:* 19 part-time (10 women). Average age 25. 9 applicants, 89% accepted, 8 enrolled. In 2017, 6 master's awarded. *Application deadline:* Applications are processed on a rolling basis. Application fee: $50. Electronic applications accepted. *Expenses:* Tuition, state resident: full-time $12,000; part-time $500 per credit. Tuition, nonresident: full-time $18,000; part-time $750 per credit. *Required fees:* $4073; $165.55 per credit. $64 per term. *Financial support:* Federal Work-Study and scholarships/grants available. *Unit head:* Dr. Matthew Baumer, Coordinator, 724-357-5646, E-mail: mbaumer@iup.edu.
Website: http://www.iup.edu/music/grad/music-education-ma/

Inter American University of Puerto Rico, Metropolitan Campus, Graduate Programs, Program in Music Education, San Juan, PR 00919-1293. Offers MM.

Inter American University of Puerto Rico, San Germán Campus, Graduate Studies Center, Program in Music Education, San Germán, PR 00683-5008. Offers music (MA); music teacher education (MA). *Accreditation:* TEAC. *Program availability:* Part-time, evening/weekend.

Ithaca College, School of Music, Programs in Music and Music Education, Ithaca, NY 14850. Offers composition (MM); conducting (MM); music education (MM, MS); performance (MM); Suzuki pedagogy (MM). *Accreditation:* NASM. *Program availability:* Part-time. *Faculty:* 66 full-time (22 women), 9 part-time/adjunct (4 women). *Students:* 18 full-time (10 women), 29 part-time (11 women); includes 12 minority (3 Black or African American, non-Hispanic/Latino; 4 Asian, non-Hispanic/Latino; 4 Hispanic/Latino; 1 Two or more races, non-Hispanic/Latino), 5 international. Average age 25. 147 applicants, 44% accepted, 23 enrolled. In 2017, 31 master's awarded. *Degree requirements:* For master's, comprehensive exam (for some programs), thesis (for some programs). *Entrance requirements:* For master's, GRE (for music education applicants). Additional exam requirements/recommendations for international students: Required—TOEFL (minimum score 550 paper-based; 80 iBT). *Application deadline:* For fall admission, 12/1 for domestic and international students. Applications are processed on a rolling basis. Application fee: $40. Electronic applications accepted. *Expenses:* Contact institution. *Financial support:* In 2017–18, 44 students received support, including 43 teaching assistantships (averaging $10,191 per year); career-related internships or fieldwork, Federal Work-Study, scholarships/grants, and unspecified assistantships also available. Support available to part-time students. Financial award application deadline: 12/1; financial award applicants required to submit FAFSA. *Unit head:* Dr. Les Black, Chair, Graduate Studies in Music, 607-274-7997, E-mail: lblack@ithaca.edu. *Application contact:* Nicole Eversley Bradwell, Director, Office of Admission, 607-274-3124, Fax: 607-274-1263, E-mail: admission@ithaca.edu.
Website: http://www.ithaca.edu/gradprograms/music

Jackson State University, Graduate School, College of Liberal Arts, Department of Music, Jackson, MS 39217. Offers music education (MM Ed). *Accreditation:* NASM. *Program availability:* Part-time, evening/weekend. *Degree requirements:* For master's, comprehensive exam, thesis or alternative. *Entrance requirements:* For master's, GRE General Test. Additional exam requirements/recommendations for international students: Required—TOEFL (minimum score 520 paper-based; 67 iBT).

James Madison University, The Graduate School, College of Visual and Performing Arts, Master of Music Program, Harrisonburg, VA 22801. Offers composition (MM); conducting (MM); music education (MM); performance (MM). *Accreditation:* NASM. *Program availability:* Part-time. *Students:* 18 full-time (9 women), 3 part-time (all women); includes 5 minority (2 Black or African American, non-Hispanic/Latino; 2 Hispanic/Latino; 1 Two or more races, non-Hispanic/Latino), 2 international. Average age 30. In 2017, 11 master's awarded. Application fee: $55. Electronic applications accepted. *Expenses:* Tuition, state resident: full-time $10,512; part-time $438 per credit

hour. Tuition, nonresident: full-time $28,358; part-time $1162 per credit hour. *Required fees:* $1128. *Financial support:* In 2017–18, 13 students received support, including 1 teaching assistantship with full tuition reimbursement available (averaging $8,837 per year); fellowships, Federal Work-Study, and 12 assistantships (averaging $7911) also available. Financial award application deadline: 3/1; financial award applicants required to submit FAFSA. *Unit head:* Dr. Jeffrey Bush, Director of the School of Music, 540-568-3614, E-mail: bushje@jmu.edu. *Application contact:* Lynette D. Michael, Director of Graduate Admissions, 540-568-6131 Ext. 6395, Fax: 540-568-7860, E-mail: michaeld@jmu.edu.
Website: http://www.jmu.edu/music/

Kent State University, College of the Arts, Hugh A. Glauser School of Music, Kent, OH 44242-0001. Offers conducting (MM), including choral conducting; ethnomusicology (MA); music composition (MA); music education (MM, PhD); music theory (MA); music theory-composition (PhD); performance (MM), including chamber music. *Accreditation:* NASM. *Program availability:* Part-time, online learning. *Faculty:* 34 full-time (11 women), 22 part-time/adjunct (15 women). *Students:* 64 full-time (36 women), 178 part-time (125 women); includes 22 minority (8 Black or African American, non-Hispanic/Latino; 2 Asian, non-Hispanic/Latino; 6 Hispanic/Latino; 6 Two or more races, non-Hispanic/Latino), 31 international. Average age 31. 106 applicants, 92% accepted, 79 enrolled. In 2017, 78 master's, 2 doctorates awarded. *Degree requirements:* For master's, comprehensive exam (for some programs), thesis (for some programs), capstone project or thesis (for MM in music education); for doctorate, comprehensive exam, thesis/dissertation. *Entrance requirements:* For master's, transcripts; minimum GPA of 3.0; 3 letters of recommendation; goal statement; resume; writing sample (for MA in ethnomusicology); portfolio of original composition (for MA in composition); audition (for MM in conducting, performance); prior degree, teaching certificate, and 1 year of teaching experience (for MM in music education); for doctorate, writing sample; 3 letters of recommendation; curriculum vitae/resume; transcripts; minimum GPA of 3.0; prior degree in music education, teaching license, statement of purpose, video of teaching sample, 3 years of teaching, and interview (for music education); goal statement and 3 original compositions (for music theory-composition). Additional exam requirements/recommendations for international students: Required—TOEFL (minimum score 525 paper-based, 71 iBT), Michigan English Language Assessment Battery (minimum score 74), IELTS (minimum score 6.0) or PTE (minimum score 50). *Application deadline:* Applications are processed on a rolling basis. Application fee: $45 ($70 for international students). Electronic applications accepted. *Expenses:* Tuition, state resident: full-time $11,310; part-time $515 per credit hour. Tuition, nonresident: full-time $20,396; part-time $928 per credit hour. *International tuition:* $18,544 full-time. *Financial support:* Unspecified assistantships available. Financial award application deadline: 4/1. *Unit head:* Jane Dressler, Interim Director, 330-672-2172, E-mail: jdressle@kent.edu. *Application contact:* Michael Chunn, Graduate Coordinator/Trumpet Professor, 330-672-9234, Fax: 330-672-7837, E-mail: mchunn@kent.edu.
Website: http://www.kent.edu/music/

Lake Forest College, Master of Arts in Teaching Program, Lake Forest, IL 60045. Offers elementary education (MAT); K-12 French (MAT); K-12 music (MAT); K-12 Spanish (MAT); K-12 visual art (MAT); secondary biology (MAT); secondary chemistry (MAT); secondary English (MAT); secondary history (MAT); secondary mathematics (MAT). *Degree requirements:* For master's, comprehensive exam, portfolio. *Entrance requirements:* For master's, GRE.

Lebanon Valley College, Program in Music Education, Annville, PA 17003-1400. Offers MME. *Accreditation:* NASM. *Program availability:* Part-time-only, evening/weekend. *Faculty:* 11 part-time/adjunct (3 women). *Students:* 2 part-time (1 woman). Average age 40. 1 applicant, 100% accepted, 1 enrolled. In 2017, 9 master's awarded. *Degree requirements:* For master's, thesis or project. *Entrance requirements:* For master's, teaching certification, 2 years of teaching experience, bachelor's degree, current resume, professional statement. Additional exam requirements/recommendations for international students: Required—TOEFL (minimum score 80 iBT). *Application deadline:* Applications are processed on a rolling basis. Application fee: $0. Electronic applications accepted. *Expenses:* $618 per credit hour. *Financial support:* Career-related internships or fieldwork and scholarships/grants available. Financial award application deadline: 3/1; financial award applicants required to submit FAFSA. *Faculty research:* Modern band, popular music pedagogy. *Unit head:* Cherie Van Zant, Graduate and Community Programs Administrator, 717-867-6383, E-mail: vanzant@lvc.edu. *Application contact:* Cherie VanZant, Graduate and Community Programs Administrator, 717-867-6383, E-mail: vanzant@lvc.edu.
Website: http://www.lvc.edu/academics/graduate-studies/master-of-music-education

Lee University, Program in Music, Cleveland, TN 37320-3450. Offers conducting (MM); music education (MM); music performance (MM); religious studies (MCM); sacred music (MCM). *Accreditation:* NASM. *Program availability:* Part-time. *Faculty:* 23 full-time (6 women), 6 part-time/adjunct (3 women). *Students:* 24 full-time (10 women), 9 part-time (6 women); includes 3 minority (2 Black or African American, non-Hispanic/Latino; 1 Asian, non-Hispanic/Latino), 5 international. Average age 27. 19 applicants, 89% accepted, 12 enrolled. In 2017, 9 master's awarded. *Degree requirements:* For master's, variable foreign language requirement, comprehensive exam, thesis, internship. *Entrance requirements:* For master's, placement exercises in music theory, music history, diction, and piano proficiency, audition, resume, interview, minimum GPA of 2.75, official transcripts, essay, 3 recommendations, immunization forms. Additional exam requirements/recommendations for international students: Required—TOEFL (minimum score 61 iBT). *Application deadline:* For fall admission, 4/1 priority date for domestic and international students; for spring admission, 10/1 priority date for domestic and international students. Applications are processed on a rolling basis. Application fee: $25. Electronic applications accepted. *Expenses:* Tuition: Full-time $12,780; part-time $710 per credit hour. *Required fees:* $60; $60 per term. Tuition and fees vary according to program. *Financial support:* In 2017–18, 31 students received support. Career-related internships or fieldwork, Federal Work-Study, institutionally sponsored loans, scholarships/grants, and unspecified assistantships available. Financial award application deadline: 3/1; financial award applicants required to submit FAFSA. *Unit head:* Dr. Brad J. Moffett, Director, 423-614-8240, Fax: 423-614-8245, E-mail: gradmusic@leeuniversity.edu.
Website: http://www.leeuniversity.edu/academics/graduate/music

Lehman College of the City University of New York, School of Arts and Humanities, Department of Music, Bronx, NY 10468-1589. Offers MAT. *Accreditation:* NCATE. *Program availability:* Part-time, evening/weekend. *Entrance requirements:* For master's, audition. *Faculty research:* Music and music education.

Lehman College of the City University of New York, School of Education, Department of Middle and High School Education, Program in Music Education, Bronx, NY 10468-1589. Offers MS Ed. *Program availability:* Part-time, evening/weekend.

Liberty University, School of Music, Lynchburg, VA 24515. Offers ethnomusicology (MA); music and worship (MA); music education (MA); worship studies (MA, DWS), including ethnomusicology (MA), leadership (MA), pastoral counseling (MA), worship techniques (MA). *Accreditation:* NASM. *Program availability:* Part-time, online learning. *Students:* 93 full-time (43 women), 181 part-time (89 women); includes 69 minority (44 Black or African American, non-Hispanic/Latino; 1 American Indian or Alaska Native,

non-Hispanic/Latino; 6 Asian, non-Hispanic/Latino; 12 Hispanic/Latino; 6 Two or more races, non-Hispanic/Latino), 9 international. Average age 37. 307 applicants, 43% accepted, 69 enrolled. In 2017, 26 master's, 2 doctorates awarded. *Entrance requirements:* For master's, minimum GPA of 3.0; interview; letter of recommendation; statement of purpose; bachelor's/master's degree in music, worship, or related field, or 5 years of experience. Additional exam requirements/recommendations for international students: Required—TOEFL (minimum score 600 paper-based; 100 iBT). *Application deadline:* Applications are processed on a rolling basis. Application fee: $50. Electronic applications accepted. *Financial support:* Applicants required to submit FAFSA. *Unit head:* Dr. Vernon Whaley, Dean, 434-592-3463, E-mail: vwhaley@liberty.edu. *Application contact:* Jay Bridge, Director of Admissions, 800-424-9595, Fax: 800-628-7977, E-mail: gradadmissions@liberty.edu.
Website: http://www.liberty.edu/academics/music/

Long Island University–LIU Post, College of Education, Information and Technology, Brookville, NY 11548-1300. Offers adolescence education (MS); adolescence education 7-12 (MS); archives and records management (AC); art education (MS); childhood education (MS); childhood education/literacy B-6 (MS); childhood education/special education (MS); clinical mental health counseling (MS, AC); early childhood education (MS); early childhood education/childhood education (MS); educational leadership (AC); educational technology (MS); information studies (PhD); interdisciplinary educational studies (Ed D); middle childhood education (MS); music education (MS); public library administration (AC); school counselor (MS); special education (MS Ed); speech-language pathology (MA); students with disabilities, 7-12 generalist (AC); TESOL (MA). *Accreditation:* TEAC. *Program availability:* Part-time, 100% online, blended/hybrid learning. *Faculty:* 40 full-time (26 women), 73 part-time/adjunct (38 women). *Students:* 472 full-time (400 women), 696 part-time (543 women); includes 254 minority (93 Black or African American, non-Hispanic/Latino; 46 Asian, non-Hispanic/Latino; 105 Hispanic/Latino; 10 Two or more races, non-Hispanic/Latino), 33 international. Average age 33. 917 applicants, 82% accepted, 357 enrolled. In 2017, 408 master's, 31 other advanced degrees awarded. Terminal master's awarded for partial completion of doctoral program. *Degree requirements:* For master's, variable foreign language requirement, comprehensive exam (for some programs), thesis optional; for doctorate, comprehensive exam, thesis/dissertation. *Entrance requirements:* For master's and AC, GRE (for some programs). Additional exam requirements/recommendations for international students: Required—TOEFL (minimum score 550 paper-based, 75 iBT), IELTS, or PTE. *Application deadline:* Applications are processed on a rolling basis. Application fee: $50. Electronic applications accepted. *Expenses: Tuition:* Full-time $21,618; part-time $1201 per credit. *Required fees:* $1840; $920 per term. Tuition and fees vary according to course load. *Financial support:* In 2017–18, 376 students received support. Career-related internships or fieldwork, Federal Work-Study, institutionally sponsored loans, scholarships/grants, tuition waivers (partial), and unspecified assistantships available. Support available to part-time students. Financial award application deadline: 2/15; financial award applicants required to submit FAFSA. *Faculty research:* Sleep; use of technology to develop executive function by students with disabilities; early childhood literacy development through play; social justice through education; using a structured protocol to discuss Bad News. *Unit head:* Dr. Albert Inserra, Dean, 516-299-2210, E-mail: albert.inserra@liu.edu. *Application contact:* Rita Langdon, Graduate Admissions, 516-299-2900, Fax: 516-299-2137, E-mail: post-enroll@liu.edu.
Website: http://liu.edu/CWPost/Academics/College-of-Education-Information-and-Technology

Louisiana State University and Agricultural & Mechanical College, Graduate School, College of Music and Dramatic Arts, School of Music, Baton Rouge, LA 70803. Offers music (MM, DMA, PhD); music education (PhD). *Accreditation:* NASM. *Faculty:* 54 full-time (16 women), 1 (woman) part-time/adjunct. *Students:* 163 full-time (72 women), 21 part-time (7 women); includes 36 minority (14 Black or African American, non-Hispanic/Latino; 1 American Indian or Alaska Native, non-Hispanic/Latino; 6 Asian, non-Hispanic/Latino; 14 Hispanic/Latino; 1 Two or more races, non-Hispanic/Latino), 53 international. Average age 29. 199 applicants, 45% accepted, 59 enrolled. In 2017, 35 master's, 27 doctorates awarded. *Financial support:* In 2017–18, 2 fellowships (averaging $27,547 per year), 2 research assistantships (averaging $25,682 per year), 107 teaching assistantships (averaging $14,277 per year) were awarded.

Loyola University Maryland, Graduate Programs, School of Education, Program in Kodaly Music Education, Baltimore, MD 21210-2699. Offers M Ed. *Students:* 42 full-time (34 women); includes 3 minority (all Black or African American, non-Hispanic/Latino). Average age 31. *Entrance requirements:* For master's, essay, letter of recommendation, resume, transcript. Additional exam requirements/recommendations for international students: Required—TOEFL (minimum score 80 iBT), IELTS (minimum score 7). *Application deadline:* For summer admission, 5/1 for domestic students, 4/1 for international students. Applications are processed on a rolling basis. Application fee: $60. Electronic applications accepted. *Expenses:* Contact institution. *Financial support:* Scholarships/grants available. Financial award application deadline: 4/15; financial award applicants required to submit FAFSA. *Unit head:* Lauren McDougle, Program Director, 410-617-5343, E-mail: lkmcdougle@loyola.edu. *Application contact:* Office of Graduate Admission, 410-617-5020, E-mail: graduate@loyola.edu.
Website: https://www.loyola.edu/school-education/academics/graduate/kodaly-music-education

Manhattanville College, School of Education, Program in Music Education, Purchase, NY 10577-2132. Offers MAT, Advanced Certificate. *Program availability:* Part-time, evening/weekend. *Faculty:* 1 full-time (0 women), 3 part-time/adjunct (0 women). *Students:* 6 full-time (3 women), 1 part-time (0 women); includes 1 minority (Black or African American, non-Hispanic/Latino). Average age 24. 1 applicant, 100% accepted, 1 enrolled. In 2017, 3 master's, 1 other advanced degree awarded. *Degree requirements:* For master's, comprehensive exam (for some programs), thesis (for some programs), student teaching, research seminars, portfolios, internships, writing assessment; for Advanced Certificate, comprehensive exam (for some programs). *Entrance requirements:* For master's, one-hour written music theory exam (including analysis, figured bass realization, and general fundamentals); one-hour written music history and literature exam (covering significant musical developments, compositions, and key figures from Renaissance-present); GRE or MAT (for programs leading to certification), audition (performance of three compositions from different periods of music on major performing medium, test of sight-reading skills at piano, test of sight-singing skills, and test of skills involving the harmonization of a melody at piano); minimum GPA of 3.0; 2 letters of recommendation; interview; essay; proof of immunization. Additional exam requirements/recommendations for international students: Required—TOEFL (minimum score 600 paper-based; 110 iBT); Recommended—IELTS (minimum score 8). *Application deadline:* Applications are processed on a rolling basis. Application fee: $75. Electronic applications accepted. *Expenses:* $915 per credit. *Financial support:* Teaching assistantships, career-related internships or fieldwork, Federal Work-Study, institutionally sponsored loans, scholarships/grants, and unspecified assistantships available. Financial award application deadline: 3/15; financial award applicants required to submit FAFSA. *Unit head:* Dr. Shelly Wepner, Dean, 914-323-3153, Fax: 914-323-5493, E-mail: shelly.wepner@mville.edu. *Application contact:* Alissa Wilson, Director, Graduate Admissions, 914-323-3150, Fax: 914-694-1732, E-mail: edschool@mville.edu.
Website: http://www.mville.edu/programs/music-education-graduate

Marywood University, Academic Affairs, Insalaco College of Creative and Performing Arts, Music, Theatre and Dance Department, Scranton, PA 18509-1598. Offers music education (MA). *Accreditation:* NASM. *Program availability:* Part-time. Electronic applications accepted.

McGill University, Faculty of Graduate and Postdoctoral Studies, Schulich School of Music, Montréal, QC H3A 2T5, Canada. Offers composition (M Mus, D Mus, PhD); music education (MA, PhD); music technology (MA, PhD); musicology (MA, PhD); performance (M Mus); performance studies (D Mus); sound recording (M Mus, PhD); theory (MA, PhD).

McKendree University, Graduate Programs, Programs in Education, Lebanon, IL 62254-1299. Offers curriculum design and instruction (Ed D, Ed S); educational administration and leadership (MA Ed); educational studies (MA Ed); higher education administrative services (MA Ed); music education (MA Ed); reading (MA Ed); special education (MA Ed); teacher leadership (MA Ed); teaching certification (MA Ed). *Accreditation:* NCATE. *Program availability:* Part-time, evening/weekend, online learning. *Entrance requirements:* For master's, official transcripts from all institutions previously attended, minimum GPA of 3.0, resume, references; for doctorate, GRE (within the past 5 years), master's degree in education and Ed S, or the equivalent, from regionally-accredited institution; official transcripts from all institutions previously attended; curriculum vitae/resume; essay/personal statement; two years of teaching/professional experience; for Ed S, GRE (within the past 5 years), master's degree in education from regionally-accredited institution of higher education; official transcripts from all institutions previously attended; curriculum vitae/resume; essay/personal statement; two years of teaching/professional experience. Additional exam requirements/recommendations for international students: Required—TOEFL. Electronic applications accepted.

McNeese State University, Doré School of Graduate Studies, Burton College of Education, Department of Education Professions, Program in Multiple Levels Grades K-12, Lake Charles, LA 70609. Offers multiple levels grades K-12 (Postbaccalaureate Certificate), including art, health and physical education, music - instrumental, music - vocal. *Entrance requirements:* For degree, PRAXIS, 2 letters of recommendation, autobiography. *Application deadline:* For fall admission, 5/15 priority date for domestic and international students; for spring admission, 10/15 priority date for domestic and international students. Applications are processed on a rolling basis. Application fee: $20 ($30 for international students). *Financial support:* Application deadline: 5/1. *Unit head:* Dr. Veronica Faye White, Head, 337-475-5400, Fax: 337-475-5272, E-mail: vfwhite@mcneese.edu. *Application contact:* Dr. Dustin M. Hebert, Director of Doré' School of Graduate Studies, 337-475-5396, Fax: 337-475-5397, E-mail: admissions@mcneese.edu.

Miami University, College of Creative Arts, Department of Music, Oxford, OH 45056. Offers music education (MM); music performance (MM). *Accreditation:* NASM. *Students:* 15 full-time (8 women), 1 (woman) part-time; includes 2 minority (both Asian, non-Hispanic/Latino), 5 international. Average age 26. In 2017, 12 master's awarded. *Expenses:* Tuition, state resident: full-time $13,812; part-time $575 per credit hour. Tuition, nonresident: full-time $30,860; part-time $1286 per credit hour. *Unit head:* Dr. Chris Tanner, Interim Chair, 513-529-3082, E-mail: tannerc@miamioh.edu. *Application contact:* Dr. Brenda Mitchell, Associate Professor of Music/Director of Graduate Studies, 513-529-1228, E-mail: mitchebs@miamioh.edu.
Website: http://www.miamioh.edu/music

Michigan State University, The Graduate School, College of Music, East Lansing, MI 48824. Offers collaborative piano (M Mus); jazz studies (M Mus); music (PhD); music composition (M Mus, DMA); music conducting (M Mus, DMA); music education (M Mus); music performance (M Mus, DMA); music theory (M Mus); music therapy (M Mus); musicology (MA); piano pedagogy (M Mus). *Accreditation:* NASM. *Entrance requirements:* Additional exam requirements/recommendations for international students: Required—TOEFL. Electronic applications accepted.

Minnesota State University Mankato, College of Graduate Studies and Research, College of Arts and Humanities, Department of Music, Mankato, MN 56001. Offers choral conducting (MM); music education (MAT); piano performance (MM); wind band conducting (MM). *Accreditation:* NASM. *Degree requirements:* For master's, comprehensive exam, thesis or alternative. *Entrance requirements:* For master's, minimum GPA of 3.0 during previous 2 years, audition or test. Additional exam requirements/recommendations for international students: Required—TOEFL. Electronic applications accepted.

Mississippi College, Graduate School, College of Arts and Sciences, School of Christian Studies and the Arts, Department of Music, Clinton, MS 39058. Offers applied music performance (MM); conducting (MM); music education (MM); music performance: organ (MM); vocal pedagogy (MM). *Accreditation:* NASM. *Program availability:* Part-time, evening/weekend. *Degree requirements:* For master's, comprehensive exam, recital. *Entrance requirements:* For master's, GRE, minimum GPA of 2.5. Additional exam requirements/recommendations for international students: Recommended—TOEFL, IELTS. Electronic applications accepted.

Montclair State University, The Graduate School, College of Education and Human Services, MAT Program in Teaching, Montclair, NJ 07043-1624. Offers art (MAT); biology (MAT); chemistry (MAT); earth science (MAT); English (MAT); French (MAT); health and physical education (MAT); health education (MAT); mathematics (MAT); music (MAT); physical education (MAT); physical science (MAT); social studies (MAT); Spanish (MAT); teacher of English as a second language (MAT). *Degree requirements:* For master's, comprehensive exam, thesis or alternative. *Entrance requirements:* For master's, interview, 2 letters of recommendation. Additional exam requirements/recommendations for international students: Required—TOEFL (minimum score 83 iBT), IELTS (minimum score 6.5). Electronic applications accepted.

Montclair State University, The Graduate School, College of the Arts, John J. Cali School of Music, Program in Music, Montclair, NJ 07043-1624. Offers music education (MA); music therapy (MA); performance (MA); theory/composition (MA). *Program availability:* Part-time, evening/weekend. *Degree requirements:* For master's, thesis. *Entrance requirements:* For master's, GRE General Test, 2 letters of recommendation, essay. Additional exam requirements/recommendations for international students: Required—TOEFL (minimum score 83 iBT), IELTS (minimum score 6.5). Electronic applications accepted.

Morehead State University, Graduate Programs, Caudill College of Arts, Humanities and Social Sciences, Department of Music, Theatre and Dance, Morehead, KY 40351. Offers music education (MM); music performance (MM). *Accreditation:* NASM. *Program availability:* Part-time, evening/weekend. *Degree requirements:* For master's, comprehensive exam, oral and written exams. *Entrance requirements:* For master's, music entrance exam, BA in music with minimum GPA of 3.0, 2.5 overall; audition. Additional exam requirements/recommendations for international students: Required—TOEFL (minimum score 550 paper-based). Electronic applications accepted. *Faculty research:* Musical instrument digital interface (MIDI) applications, tonal concepts of euphonium and baritone horn, digital synthesis, computer-assisted instruction in music, musical composition.

Music Education

Murray State University, College of Humanities and Fine Arts, Department of Music, Murray, KY 42071. Offers music education (MME). *Accreditation:* NASM. *Program availability:* Part-time. *Faculty:* 10 full-time (3 women), 2 part-time/adjunct (1 woman). *Students:* 1 (woman) full-time, 3 part-time (2 women). Average age 27. In 2017, 3 master's awarded. *Entrance requirements:* For master's, GRE or GMAT, minimum university GPA of 2.75. Additional exam requirements/recommendations for international students: Required—TOEFL (minimum score 527 paper-based; 71 iBT). *Application deadline:* Applications are processed on a rolling basis. Application fee: $40 ($50 for international students). Electronic applications accepted. *Expenses:* Tuition, state resident: full-time $9504. Tuition, nonresident: full-time $26,811. *International tuition:* $14,400 full-time. Tuition and fees vary according to course load, degree level and reciprocity agreements. *Financial support:* Federal Work-Study and unspecified assistantships available. Financial award applicants required to submit FAFSA. *Unit head:* Dr. Lucia Unrau, Chair, Department of Music, 270-809-4288, Fax: 270-809-3965, E-mail: lunrauterry@murraystate.edu. *Application contact:* Kaitlyn Burzynski, Interim Assistant Director for Graduate Admission and Records, 270-809-5732, Fax: 270-809-3780, E-mail: msu.graduateadmissions@murraystate.edu. Website: https://www.murraystate.edu/academics/CollegesDepartments/CollegeOfHumanitiesAndFineArts/Music/index.aspx

Nazareth College of Rochester, Graduate Studies, Department of Music, Program in Music Education, Rochester, NY 14618. Offers MS Ed. *Accreditation:* NASM; TEAC. *Program availability:* Part-time, evening/weekend. *Entrance requirements:* For master's, audition, minimum GPA of 3.0. Additional exam requirements/recommendations for international students: Required—TOEFL or IELTS.

New Jersey City University, William J. Maxwell College of Arts and Sciences, Department of Music, Dance and Theatre, Jersey City, NJ 07305-1597. Offers music education (MA); performance (MA). *Accreditation:* NASM. *Program availability:* Part-time, evening/weekend. *Degree requirements:* For master's, thesis optional, recital. *Entrance requirements:* Additional exam requirements/recommendations for international students: Required—TOEFL (minimum score 79 iBT).

New Mexico State University, College of Arts and Sciences, Department of Music, Las Cruces, NM 88003. Offers conducting (MM); music education (MM); performance (MM). *Accreditation:* NASM. *Program availability:* Part-time-only, online learning. *Faculty:* 16 full-time (5 women), 3 part-time/adjunct (0 women). *Students:* 13 full-time (10 women), 12 part-time (5 women); includes 13 minority (all Hispanic/Latino), 4 international. Average age 31. 10 applicants, 70% accepted, 5 enrolled. In 2017, 3 master's awarded. *Degree requirements:* For master's, comprehensive exam, thesis (for some programs), recital. *Entrance requirements:* For master's, audition, bachelor's degree or equivalent from an accredited institution. Additional exam requirements/recommendations for international students: Required—TOEFL (minimum score 550 paper-based; 79 iBT), IELTS (minimum score 6.5). *Application deadline:* For fall admission, 7/1 priority date for domestic students; for spring admission, 11/1 for domestic students; for summer admission, 3/1 for domestic students. Applications are processed on a rolling basis. Application fee: $40 ($50 for international students). Electronic applications accepted. *Expenses:* Tuition, state resident: full-time $4390. Tuition, nonresident: full-time $15,309. *Required fees:* $853. *Financial support:* In 2017–18, 13 students received support, including 1 fellowship (averaging $788 per year), 8 teaching assistantships (averaging $14,844 per year); career-related internships or fieldwork, Federal Work-Study, scholarships/grants, traineeships, health care benefits, and unspecified assistantships also available. Support available to part-time students. Financial award application deadline: 3/1. *Faculty research:* Music education, contemporary wind band literature, performance, music history, composition. *Total annual research expenditures:* $2,606. *Unit head:* Dr. Lon W. Chaffin, Department Head, 575-646-2421, Fax: 575-646-8199, E-mail: lchaffin@nmsu.edu. *Application contact:* Dr. James Shearer, Coordinator of Graduate Studies, 575-646-2601, Fax: 575-646-8199, E-mail: jshearer@nmsu.edu. Website: http://music.nmsu.edu

New York University, Steinhardt School of Culture, Education, and Human Development, Department of Music and Performing Arts Professions, Program in Music Education, New York, NY 10012. Offers MA, Ed D, PhD. *Accreditation:* TEAC. *Program availability:* Part-time. *Students:* Average age 28. 48 applicants, 81% accepted, 24 enrolled. In 2017, 23 master's, 2 doctorates awarded. *Entrance requirements:* For master's, audition; for doctorate, GRE General Test, interview. Additional exam requirements/recommendations for international students: Required—TOEFL (minimum score 100 iBT). *Application deadline:* For fall admission, 12/1 priority date for domestic and international students; for spring admission, 10/1 for domestic and international students. Applications are processed on a rolling basis. Application fee: $75. Electronic applications accepted. *Expenses:* Tuition: Full-time $41,352; part-time $19,968 per year. *Required fees:* $2496; $1628 per unit. $814 per term. Tuition and fees vary according to course load and program. *Financial support:* Fellowships with full and partial tuition reimbursements, career-related internships or fieldwork, Federal Work-Study, scholarships/grants, and tuition waivers (partial) available. Support available to part-time students. Financial award application deadline: 2/1; financial award applicants required to submit FAFSA. *Faculty research:* Music education philosophy; community music education; integrated curriculum; multiple intelligences; technology in arts education; cognition, emotion, and music. *Unit head:* Dr. John Gilbert, Director, 212-998-5424, E-mail: john.gilbert@nyu.edu. *Application contact:* 212-998-5030, Fax: 212-995-4328, E-mail: steinhardt.gradadmissions@nyu.edu. Website: http://steinhardt.nyu.edu/music/education

New York University, Steinhardt School of Culture, Education, and Human Development, Department of Music and Performing Arts Professions, Program in Music Performance and Composition, New York, NY 10012. Offers instrumental performance (MM), including instrumental performance, jazz instrumental performance; music performance and composition (PhD), including music performance and composition; music theory and composition (MM), including composition for film and multimedia, composition for music theater, computer music composition, music theory and composition, songwriting; piano performance (MM), including collaborative piano, solo piano; vocal pedagogy (Advanced Certificate); vocal performance (MM), including classical voice, musical theatre performance. *Program availability:* Part-time. *Students:* Average age 27. 534 applicants, 50% accepted, 141 enrolled. In 2017, 130 master's, 2 doctorates, 12 other advanced degrees awarded. *Entrance requirements:* For master's, audition; for doctorate, GRE General Test, audition, interview. Additional exam requirements/recommendations for international students: Required—TOEFL (minimum score 100 iBT). *Application deadline:* For fall admission, 12/1 priority date for domestic and international students; for spring admission, 10/1 for domestic and international students. Applications are processed on a rolling basis. Application fee: $75. Electronic applications accepted. *Expenses:* Tuition: Full-time $41,352; part-time $19,968 per year. *Required fees:* $2496; $1628 per unit. $814 per term. Tuition and fees vary according to course load and program. *Financial support:* Fellowships with full and partial tuition reimbursements, Federal Work-Study, scholarships/grants, and tuition waivers (partial) available. Support available to part-time students. Financial award application deadline: 2/1; financial award applicants required to submit FAFSA. *Faculty research:* Aesthetics, performance analysis, twentieth century music, music methodologies for arts criticism and analysis. *Unit head:* Dr. Tae Hong Park, Director, 212-998-5424, Fax: 212-995-

4043, E-mail: tae.hong.park@nyu.edu. *Application contact:* 212-998-5030, Fax: 212-995-4328, E-mail: steinhardt.gradadmissions@nyu.edu. Website: http://steinhardt.nyu.edu/music/composition/programs/graduate

Norfolk State University, School of Graduate Studies, School of Liberal Arts, Department of Music, Norfolk, VA 23504. Offers music (MM); music education (MM); performance (MM); theory and composition (MM). *Accreditation:* NASM. *Program availability:* Part-time. *Degree requirements:* For master's, thesis or alternative. *Entrance requirements:* For master's, minimum GPA of 2.7, letters of recommendation. Additional exam requirements/recommendations for international students: Required—TOEFL.

North Dakota State University, College of Graduate and Interdisciplinary Studies, College of Arts, Humanities and Social Sciences, Challey School of Music, Fargo, ND 58102. Offers conducting (MM, DMA); music education (MM); performance (MM, DMA). *Accreditation:* NASM. *Degree requirements:* For master's, 2 foreign languages, comprehensive exam, thesis or alternative, recitals; for doctorate, 2 foreign languages, comprehensive exam, thesis/dissertation or alternative, recitals. *Entrance requirements:* For master's and doctorate, music history, music theory, performance audition. Additional exam requirements/recommendations for international students: Required—TOEFL (minimum score 525 paper-based; 71 iBT). Electronic applications accepted. *Faculty research:* Performance, conducting.

North Dakota State University, College of Graduate and Interdisciplinary Studies, College of Human Development and Education, School of Education, Fargo, ND 58102. Offers agricultural education (M Ed, MS), including agricultural education; counselor education (M Ed, MS, PhD), including clinical mental health counseling (M Ed, MS), counselor education and supervision (PhD); school counseling (M Ed, MS); curriculum and instruction (M Ed, MS); education (PhD); educational leadership (M Ed, MS, Ed S); family and consumer sciences education (M Ed, MS); history education (M Ed, MS); institutional analysis (Ed D); mathematics education (M Ed, MS); music education (M Ed, MS); occupational and adult education (Ed D); science education (M Ed, MS). *Accreditation:* NCATE. *Program availability:* Part-time, evening/weekend, online learning. *Degree requirements:* For master's, comprehensive exam; for doctorate, thesis/dissertation; for Ed S, thesis. *Entrance requirements:* For degree, GRE General Test, master's degree, minimum GPA of 3.25. Additional exam requirements/recommendations for international students: Required—TOEFL.

Northeastern Illinois University, College of Graduate Studies and Research, College of Arts and Sciences, Program in Music, Chicago, IL 60625. Offers music (MA), including applied music pedagogy. *Accreditation:* NASM. *Program availability:* Part-time, evening/weekend. *Degree requirements:* For master's, comprehensive exam, thesis optional. *Entrance requirements:* For master's, departmental exam, audition, minimum GPA of 2.75. Additional exam requirements/recommendations for international students: Required—TOEFL (minimum score 550 paper-based; 79 iBT). *Application deadline:* Applications are processed on a rolling basis. Application fee: $30. Electronic applications accepted. *Expenses:* Tuition, state resident: full-time $7274; part-time $404.11 per credit hour. Tuition, nonresident: full-time $14,548; part-time $808.23 per credit hour. *Required fees:* $1284. *Financial support:* Applicants required to submit FAFSA. *Faculty research:* World music, computers as applied instruments, vocal pedagogy, vocal interpretation, jazz repertory. *Unit head:* Dr. Shayne Cofer, Department Chair, 773-442-5919, E-mail: r-shaynecofer@neiu.edu. *Application contact:* Martha Narvaez, Graduate Admission Representative, 773-442-6006, E-mail: m-narvaez@neiu.edu.

Northern State University, MME Program in Music Education, Aberdeen, SD 57401-7198. Offers MME. *Accreditation:* NASM. *Program availability:* Part-time, online learning. *Entrance requirements:* For master's, minimum GPA of 2.75. Additional exam requirements/recommendations for international students: Required—TOEFL (minimum score 550 paper-based; 78 iBT), IELTS (minimum score 6). Electronic applications accepted.

Northwestern University, Henry and Leigh Bienen School of Music, Department of Music Performance, Evanston, IL 60208. Offers brass performance (MM, DMA); conducting (MM, DMA); jazz studies (MM); percussion performance (MM, DMA); performance (MM); piano pedagogy (MME); piano performance (MM, DMA); piano performance and collaborative arts (MM, DMA); piano performance and pedagogy (MM, DMA); string performance (MM, DMA); voice and opera performance (MM, DMA); woodwind performance (MM, DMA). *Accreditation:* NASM. *Degree requirements:* For master's, recital; for doctorate, comprehensive exam, thesis/dissertation, 3 recitals. *Entrance requirements:* For master's, audition, prescreening auditions where required; for doctorate, audition, preliminary tapes. Additional exam requirements/recommendations for international students: Required—TOEFL (minimum score 80 iBT).

Northwestern University, Henry and Leigh Bienen School of Music, Department of Music Studies, Evanston, IL 60208. Offers composition (DMA); music education (MME, PhD); music theory and cognition (PhD); musicology (MM, PhD); theory (MM). PhD admissions and degree offered through The Graduate School. *Accreditation:* NASM. *Degree requirements:* For doctorate, comprehensive exam, thesis/dissertation. *Entrance requirements:* For master's, portfolio or research papers; for doctorate, GRE General Test (for PhD), portfolio, research papers. Additional exam requirements/recommendations for international students: Required—TOEFL (minimum score 600 paper-based; 80 iBT). *Faculty research:* Music cognition, cognitive learning, aesthetic education, computer music, technology in education.

Oakland University, Graduate Study and Lifelong Learning, College of Arts and Sciences, Department of Music, Rochester, MI 48309-4401. Offers music (MM); music education (PhD). *Accreditation:* NASM. *Entrance requirements:* For master's, minimum GPA of 3.0. Additional exam requirements/recommendations for international students: Required—TOEFL (minimum score 550 paper-based). Electronic applications accepted. *Expenses:* Contact institution.

Ohio University, Graduate College, College of Fine Arts, School of Music, Athens, OH 45701-2979. Offers accompanying (MM); composition (MM); conducting (MM); history/literature (MM); music education (MM); music therapy (MM); performance (MM, Certificate); performance/pedagogy (MM); theory (MM). *Accreditation:* NASM. *Program availability:* Part-time, evening/weekend, online learning. *Degree requirements:* For master's, comprehensive exam, thesis (for some programs), oral exam. *Entrance requirements:* For master's, audition, interview, portfolio, recordings (varies by program). Additional exam requirements/recommendations for international students: Required—TOEFL (minimum score 550 paper-based; 80 iBT) or IELTS (minimum score 6.5). Electronic applications accepted.

Oklahoma State University, College of Arts and Sciences, Michael and Anne Greenwood School of Music, Stillwater, OK 74078. Offers pedagogy and performance (MM). *Accreditation:* NASM. *Faculty:* 33 full-time (14 women), 9 part-time/adjunct (2 women). *Students:* 15 full-time (6 women), 7 part-time (2 women); includes 4 minority (2 Black or African American, non-Hispanic/Latino; 1 Hispanic/Latino; 1 Two or more races, non-Hispanic/Latino), 3 international. Average age 26. 37 applicants, 49% accepted, 13 enrolled. In 2017, 5 master's awarded. *Entrance requirements:* For master's, GRE, audition. Additional exam requirements/recommendations for international students: Required—TOEFL (minimum score 550 paper-based; 79 iBT). *Application deadline:* For

fall admission, 3/1 priority date for international students; for spring admission, 8/1 priority date for international students. Applications are processed on a rolling basis. Application fee: $40 ($75 for international students). Electronic applications accepted. *Expenses:* Tuition, state resident: full-time $4019; part-time $2679.60 per year. Tuition, nonresident: full-time $15,286; part-time $10,190.40 per year. *Required fees:* $2129; $1419 per unit. Tuition and fees vary according to program. *Financial support:* Teaching assistantships, career-related internships or fieldwork, Federal Work-Study, scholarships/grants, health care benefits, tuition waivers (partial), and unspecified assistantships available. Support available to part-time students. Financial award application deadline: 3/1; financial award applicants required to submit FAFSA. *Faculty research:* Discovery and presentation of music literature of other countries, transportation of ancient music literature to modern notation. *Unit head:* Dr. Howard Potter, Department Head, 405-744-8997, Fax: 405-744-9324, E-mail: osumusic@okstate.edu.
Website: http://music.okstate.edu/

Old Dominion University, College of Arts and Letters, Master of Music Education Program, Norfolk, VA 23529. Offers applied studies or conducting (MME); pedagogy (MME); research (MME). *Accreditation:* NASM. *Program availability:* Part-time, evening/weekend. *Faculty:* 13 full-time (2 women), 3 part-time/adjunct (2 women). *Students:* 9 full-time (5 women), 10 part-time (7 women); includes 7 minority (3 Black or African American, non-Hispanic/Latino; 1 Asian, non-Hispanic/Latino; 3 Hispanic/Latino). Average age 35. 8 applicants, 88% accepted, 7 enrolled. In 2017, 11 master's awarded. *Degree requirements:* For master's, comprehensive exam, thesis (for some programs), performance recital (for applied studies or conducting), ePortfolio (for pedagogy). *Entrance requirements:* For master's, music theory exam, diagnostic examination, GRE or MAT, baccalaureate degree in music education, music theory, music history, or applied music; audition (for applied music areas). Additional exam requirements/recommendations for international students: Required—TOEFL. *Application deadline:* Applications are processed on a rolling basis. Application fee: $50. Electronic applications accepted. *Expenses:* Contact institution. *Financial support:* In 2017–18, 6 students received support, including 6 teaching assistantships (averaging $10,000 per year); scholarships/grants and unspecified assistantships also available. Financial award application deadline: 3/30; financial award applicants required to submit FAFSA. *Faculty research:* Performance, composition, conducting, music education research. *Unit head:* Dr. Douglas T. Owens, Graduate Program Director, 757-683-6562, Fax: 757-683-5056, E-mail: dtowens@odu.edu.
Website: http://www.odu.edu/musicdept/programs/graduate

Oregon State University, College of Education, Program in Teaching, Corvallis, OR 97331. Offers clinically based elementary education (MAT); elementary education (MAT); language arts (MAT); mathematics (MAT); music education (MAT); science (MAT); social studies (MAT). *Program availability:* Part-time, blended/hybrid learning. *Entrance requirements:* For master's, CBEST. Additional exam requirements/recommendations for international students: Required—TOEFL (minimum score 575 paper-based). *Application deadline:* For fall admission, 12/1 for domestic students. Application fee: $60. *Expenses:* Contact institution. *Unit head:* Jordon Zardinejad, 541-322-3118, E-mail: jordon.zardinejad@osucascades.edu. *Application contact:* Jordon Zardinejad, 541-322-3118, E-mail: jordon.zardinejad@osucascades.edu.
Website: http://education.oregonstate.edu/mat

Penn State University Park, Graduate School, College of Arts and Architecture, School of Music, University Park, PA 16802. Offers composition-theory (M Mus); conducting (M Mus); music (MA); music education (MME, PhD, Certificate); pedagogy and performance (M Mus); piano performance (DMA). *Accreditation:* NASM. *Unit head:* Dr. Barbara O. Korner, Dean, 814-865-2592, Fax: 814-865-2018. *Application contact:* Lori Hawn, Director, Graduate Student Services, 814-865-1795, Fax: 814-863-4627, E-mail: l-gswww@lists.psu.edu.
Website: http://music.psu.edu/

Piedmont College, School of Education, Demorest, GA 30535. Offers art education (MA, MAT); curriculum and instruction (Ed D, Ed S); early childhood education (MA, MAT); instructional technology (MA); middle grades education (MA, MAT); music education (MA, MAT); secondary education (MA, MAT); special education (MA, MAT). *Program availability:* Part-time, evening/weekend. *Students:* 341 full-time (268 women), 682 part-time (571 women); includes 182 minority (136 Black or African American, non-Hispanic/Latino; 2 American Indian or Alaska Native, non-Hispanic/Latino; 11 Asian, non-Hispanic/Latino; 32 Hispanic/Latino; 1 Two or more races, non-Hispanic/Latino). Average age 37. 333 applicants, 77% accepted, 103 enrolled. In 2017, 292 master's, 9 doctorates, 318 other advanced degrees awarded. *Degree requirements:* For master's, thesis, field experience in the classroom teaching; for doctorate, thesis/dissertation. *Entrance requirements:* For master's, GRE General Test, MAT; for Ed S, minimum graduate GPA of 3.5, valid teaching certificate. Additional exam requirements/recommendations for international students: Required—TOEFL (minimum score 550 paper-based). *Application deadline:* For fall admission, 7/15 for domestic students; for spring admission, 12/1 for domestic students. Applications are processed on a rolling basis. Electronic applications accepted. *Expenses: Tuition:* Full-time $9360; part-time $520 per credit hour. *Required fees:* $200; $200 per year. $100 per term. *Financial support:* Career-related internships or fieldwork, Federal Work-Study, and unspecified assistantships available. Support available to part-time students. Financial award applicants required to submit FAFSA. *Unit head:* Dr. Don Gnecco, Dean, 706-778-3000 Ext. 1201, Fax: 706-776-9608, E-mail: dgnecco@piedmont.edu. *Application contact:* Kathleen Carter, Director of Graduate Enrollment Management, 706-778-8500 Ext. 1181, Fax: 706-778-0150, E-mail: kanderson@piedmont.edu.

Pittsburg State University, Graduate School, College of Arts and Sciences, Department of Music, Pittsburg, KS 66762. Offers conducting (MM), including choral, instrumental - orchestral, instrumental - wind, organ, piano, voice; education (MM), including instrumental, vocal; performance (MM), including harpsichord, percussion, strings, winds. *Accreditation:* NASM. *Students:* 8 (3 women); includes 1 minority (Two or more races, non-Hispanic/Latino), 1 international. In 2017, 7 master's awarded. *Degree requirements:* For master's, thesis or alternative. *Entrance requirements:* Additional exam requirements/recommendations for international students: Required—TOEFL (minimum score 520 paper-based; 68 iBT), IELTS (minimum score 6), PTE (minimum score 47). *Application deadline:* For fall admission, 7/15 for domestic students, 6/1 for international students; for spring admission, 12/15 for domestic students, 10/15 for international students; for summer admission, 5/15 for domestic students, 4/1 for international students. Applications are processed on a rolling basis. Application fee: $35 ($60 for international students). Electronic applications accepted. *Expenses:* Contact institution. *Financial support:* In 2017–18, 5 teaching assistantships with full tuition reimbursements (averaging $5,500 per year) were awarded; career-related internships or fieldwork, Federal Work-Study, and unspecified assistantships also available. Financial award application deadline: 2/1; financial award applicants required to submit FAFSA. *Unit head:* Dr. Susan Marchant, Chairperson, 620-235-4466, E-mail: smarchant@pittstate.edu. *Application contact:* Lisa Allen, Assistant Director of Graduate and Continuing Studies, 620-235-4223, Fax: 620-235-4219, E-mail: lallen@pittstate.edu.

Plymouth State University, College of Graduate Studies, Graduate Studies in Education, Program in Music Education, Plymouth, NH 03264-1595. Offers M Ed. *Program availability:* Evening/weekend.

Queens College of the City University of New York, Arts and Humanities Division, Aaron Copland School of Music, Queens, NY 11367-1597. Offers classical performance (MM, Advanced Diploma); jazz studies (MM); music (MM); music education (MS Ed, Advanced Certificate). *Program availability:* Part-time. *Students:* 23 full-time (5 women), 162 part-time (72 women); includes 49 minority (8 Black or African American, non-Hispanic/Latino; 16 Asian, non-Hispanic/Latino; 17 Hispanic/Latino; 8 Two or more races, non-Hispanic/Latino), 46 international. Average age 30. *Degree requirements:* For master's, qualifying exams, recital. *Entrance requirements:* For master's, audition, bachelor's degree in music, minimum GPA of 3.0. Additional exam requirements/recommendations for international students: Required—TOEFL, IELTS. *Application deadline:* For fall admission, 4/1 for domestic students; for spring admission, 11/1 for domestic students. Applications are processed on a rolling basis. Application fee: $125. Electronic applications accepted. *Financial support:* Career-related internships or fieldwork, Federal Work-Study, institutionally sponsored loans, and tuition waivers (partial) available. Support available to part-time students. Financial award application deadline: 4/1; financial award applicants required to submit FAFSA. *Unit head:* Dr. David Schober, Chair, 718-997-3800, E-mail: david.schober@qc.cuny.edu. *Application contact:* Elizabeth D'Amico-Ramirez, Assistant Director of Graduate Admissions, 718-997-5203, E-mail: elizabeth.damicoramirez@qc.cuny.edu.
Website: http://qcpages.qc.cuny.edu/music/

Queens College of the City University of New York, Division of Education, Department of Secondary Education and Youth Services, Queens, NY 11367-1597. Offers adolescent biology (MAT); art (MS Ed); biology (MS Ed, AC); chemistry (MS Ed, AC); earth sciences (MS Ed, AC); English (MS Ed, AC); French (MS Ed); Italian (MS Ed, AC); literacy education (MS Ed); mathematics (MS Ed, AC); music (MS Ed, AC); physics (MS Ed, AC); social studies (MS Ed, AC); Spanish (MS Ed, AC). *Program availability:* Part-time, evening/weekend. *Students:* 28 full-time (16 women), 349 part-time (202 women); includes 165 minority (18 Black or African American, non-Hispanic/Latino; 56 Asian, non-Hispanic/Latino; 83 Hispanic/Latino; 8 Two or more races, non-Hispanic/Latino), 14 international. Average age 29. *Degree requirements:* For master's, research project. *Entrance requirements:* For master's, minimum GPA of 3.0. Additional exam requirements/recommendations for international students: Required—TOEFL, IELTS. *Application deadline:* For fall admission, 4/1 for domestic students; for spring admission, 11/1 for domestic students. Applications are processed on a rolling basis. Application fee: $125. Electronic applications accepted. *Financial support:* Career-related internships or fieldwork available. Financial award application deadline: 4/1; financial award applicants required to submit FAFSA. *Unit head:* Dr. Eleanor Armour-Thomas, Chairperson, 718-997-5150, E-mail: eleanor.armour-thomas@qc.cuny.edu. *Application contact:* Elizabeth D'Amico-Ramirez, Assistant Director of Graduate Admissions, 718-997-5203, E-mail: elizabeth.damicoramirez@qc.cuny.edu.

Rhode Island College, School of Graduate Studies, Faculty of Arts and Sciences, Department of Music, Theatre, and Dance, Providence, RI 02908-1991. Offers music education (MAT, MM Ed). *Program availability:* Part-time, evening/weekend. *Faculty:* 2. *Students:* 1 (woman) part-time. Average age 47. In 2017, 1 master's awarded. *Degree requirements:* For master's, comprehensive exam, thesis, final project (MFA). *Entrance requirements:* For master's, GRE General Test or MAT; exams in music education, theory, history and literature, audition, 3 letters of recommendation, evidence of musicianship, interview. Additional exam requirements/recommendations for international students: Recommended—TOEFL (minimum score 550 paper-based; 79 iBT). *Application deadline:* For fall admission, 3/1 for domestic students; for spring admission, 11/1 for domestic students. Applications are processed on a rolling basis. Application fee: $50. Electronic applications accepted. *Expenses:* Tuition, state resident: full-time $9768; part-time $407 per credit. Tuition, nonresident: full-time $19,008; part-time $792 per credit. *Required fees:* $696; $29 per credit. One-time fee: $200 full-time; $100 part-time. Tuition and fees vary according to course load. *Financial support:* In 2017–18, 1 teaching assistantship with full tuition reimbursement (averaging $3,500 per year) was awarded; Federal Work-Study, scholarships/grants, health care benefits, and unspecified assistantships also available. Support available to part-time students. Financial award application deadline: 5/15; financial award applicants required to submit FAFSA. *Unit head:* Prof. Ian Greitzer, Chair, 401-456-9883. *Application contact:* Graduate Studies, 401-456-8700.
Website: http://www.ric.edu/mtd/index.php

Rider University, Westminster Choir College, Program in Music Education, Lawrenceville, NJ 08648-3001. Offers MAT, MM, MME. *Program availability:* Part-time, online learning. *Entrance requirements:* For master's, audition, interview, repertoire list, 2 letters of reference, resume. Additional exam requirements/recommendations for international students: Required—TOEFL (minimum score 525 paper-based). Electronic applications accepted.

Rider University, Westminster Choir College, Programs in Music, Lawrenceville, NJ 08648-3001. Offers American and public musicology (MM); choral conducting (MM); composition (MM); organ performance (MM); piano accompanying and coaching (MM); piano pedagogy and performance (MM); piano performance (MM); sacred music (MM); voice pedagogy and performance (MM, MVP). *Program availability:* Part-time. *Degree requirements:* For master's, variable foreign language requirement, departmental qualifying exam. *Entrance requirements:* For master's, audition, interview, repertoire list, 2 letters of reference, resume. Additional exam requirements/recommendations for international students: Required—TOEFL (minimum score 525 paper-based). Electronic applications accepted.

Rutgers University–New Brunswick, Mason Gross School of the Arts, Music Department, New Brunswick, NJ 08901. Offers collaborative piano (MM, DMA); conducting: choral (MM, DMA); conducting: instrumental (MM, DMA); conducting: orchestral (MM, DMA); jazz studies (MM); music (DMA, AD); music education (MM, DMA); music performance (MM). *Accreditation:* NASM. *Degree requirements:* For doctorate, one foreign language. *Entrance requirements:* For master's and doctorate, audition. Additional exam requirements/recommendations for international students: Required—TOEFL (minimum score 550 paper-based), IELTS (minimum score 7). Electronic applications accepted. *Faculty research:* Performance, twentieth-century music, jazz, music education.

St. Cloud State University, School of Graduate Studies, College of Liberal Arts, Department of Music, St. Cloud, MN 56301-4498. Offers conducting and literature (MM); music education (MM); piano pedagogy (MM). *Degree requirements:* For master's, comprehensive exam (for some programs), thesis or alternative. *Entrance requirements:* For master's, GRE General Test, minimum GPA of 2.75. Additional exam requirements/recommendations for international students: Required—TOEFL (minimum score 550 paper-based; 79 iBT), IELTS (minimum score 6.5), Michigan English Language Assessment Battery. Electronic applications accepted.

Saint Xavier University, Graduate Studies, School of Education, Chicago, IL 60655-3105. Offers counseling (MA); curriculum and instruction (MA); early childhood education (MA); educational administration (MA); elementary education (MA);

individualized studies (MA), including educational technology, English as a second language (ESL), ISTEM (integrative science, technology, engineering, and math), science education; music education (MA); reading (MA); secondary education (MA); Spanish education (MA); special education (MA); teaching and leadership (MA). *Accreditation:* NCATE. *Program availability:* Part-time, evening/weekend. *Degree requirements:* For master's, thesis or project. *Entrance requirements:* For master's, minimum GPA of 3.0. *Expenses:* Contact institution.

Samford University, School of the Arts, Birmingham, AL 35229. Offers church music (MM), including conducting, performance, thesis; instrumental performance (MM); piano performance and pedagogy (MM); vocal performance (MM); vocal/choral or instrumental music (MME). MME program offered in traditional, fifth-year non-traditional, and national board cohort formats. *Accreditation:* NASM. *Program availability:* Part-time. *Faculty:* 13 full-time (4 women), 2 part-time/adjunct (1 woman). *Students:* 13 full-time (5 women), 2 part-time (both women); includes 5 minority (all Black or African American, non-Hispanic/Latino), 1 international. Average age 29. 7 applicants, 86% accepted, 4 enrolled. In 2017, 1 master's awarded. *Degree requirements:* For master's, comprehensive exam, recital. *Entrance requirements:* For master's, 3 letters of recommendation, audition. Additional exam requirements/recommendations for international students: Required—TOEFL (minimum score 550 paper-based; 79 iBT). *Application deadline:* For fall admission, 2/28 priority date for domestic and international students; for winter admission, 10/1 priority date for domestic and international students; for spring admission, 2/28 priority date for domestic and international students; for summer admission, 5/1 priority date for domestic and international students. Applications are processed on a rolling basis. Application fee: $35. Electronic applications accepted. *Expenses:* Tuition: Full-time $19,058; part-time $813 per credit hour. *Required fees:* $550. Tuition and fees vary according to course load, degree level, program and student level. *Financial support:* In 2017–18, 13 students received support. Scholarships/grants available. Financial award application deadline: 2/15; financial award applicants required to submit FAFSA. *Unit head:* Dr. Joseph Hopkin, Dean of the School of the Arts/Professor, 205-726-2778, E-mail: jhopkins@samford.edu. *Application contact:* Dr. Mark Lackey, Assistant Professor, 205-726-4623, Fax: 205-726-2615, E-mail: mlckey@samford.edu.
Website: http://www.samford.edu/arts

San Diego State University, Graduate and Research Affairs, College of Professional Studies and Fine Arts, School of Music and Dance, San Diego, CA 92182. Offers composition (acoustic and electronic) (MM); conducting (MM); ethnomusicology (MA); jazz studies (MM); musicology (MA); performance (MM); piano pedagogy (MA); theory (MA). *Degree requirements:* For master's, comprehensive exam (for some programs), thesis (for some programs). *Entrance requirements:* For master's, GRE General Test, bachelor's degree in related field, 2 letters of reference. Additional exam requirements/recommendations for international students: Required—TOEFL. Electronic applications accepted.

San Francisco Conservatory of Music, Graduate Division, San Francisco, CA 94102. Offers brass (MM), including bass trombone, horn, tenor trombone, trumpet, tuba; chamber music (MM, Artist Certificate), including cello (MM, Artist Certificate, Artist Diploma), piano (MM, Artist Certificate, Artist Diploma), preformed string quartet, viola (MM, Artist Certificate, Artist Diploma), violin (MM, Artist Certificate, Artist Diploma); composition (MM); conducting (MM); guitar (MM); harp (MM); historical performance (MM), including harpsichord (MM, MM); percussion (MM), including percussion; piano (MM, MM, Artist Diploma), including collaborative piano (MM), harpsichord (MM, MM), organ (MM), piano (MM, Artist Certificate, Artist Diploma); strings (MM, Artist Diploma), including cello (MM, Artist Certificate, Artist Diploma), double bass (MM), viola (MM, Artist Certificate, Artist Diploma), violin (MM, Artist Certificate, Artist Diploma); voice (MM, Postgraduate Diploma); woodwinds (MM), including bassoon, clarinet, flute, oboe. *Faculty:* 27 full-time (7 women), 107 part-time/adjunct (36 women). *Students:* 208 full-time (120 women), 1 (woman) part-time; includes 37 minority (7 Black or African American, non-Hispanic/Latino; 13 Asian, non-Hispanic/Latino; 7 Hispanic/Latino; 10 Two or more races, non-Hispanic/Latino), 82 international. Average age 25. 709 applicants, 36% accepted, 117 enrolled. In 2017, 74 master's, 41 Artist Diplomas awarded. *Degree requirements:* For master's and other advanced degree, variable foreign language requirement, 1-2 recitals, 1-3 juried performances. *Entrance requirements:* For master's and other advanced degree, recommendations, transcripts, audition. Additional exam requirements/recommendations for international students: Required—TOEFL (minimum score 500 paper-based; 80 iBT). *Application deadline:* For fall admission, 12/1 for domestic and international students; for spring admission, 10/1 for domestic and international students. Application fee: $110. Electronic applications accepted. *Expenses:* $43,700 full-time, $1,924 per credit part-time, $1,110 fees. *Financial support:* In 2017–18, 214 students received support. Federal Work-Study, scholarships/grants, tuition waivers (partial), and unspecified assistantships available. Financial award application deadline: 2/15; financial award applicants required to submit FAFSA. *Unit head:* Kate Sheeran, Provost and Dean, 415-503-6251, Fax: 415-503-6205, E-mail: snedel@sfcm.edu. *Application contact:* Melissa Cocco-Mitten, Director of Admission, 415-503-6231, Fax: 415-503-6299, E-mail: admit@sfcm.edu.

San Francisco State University, Division of Graduate Studies, College of Liberal and Creative Arts, School of Music, San Francisco, CA 94132-1722. Offers chamber music (MM); classical performance (MM); composition (MA); conducting (MM); music education (MA); music history (MA). *Accreditation:* NASM. *Unit head:* Dr. Cyrus Ginwala, Director, 415-338-7613, E-mail: cginwala@sfsu.edu. *Application contact:* E-mail: music@sfsu.edu.
Website: http://music.sfsu.edu/

San Jose State University, Graduate Studies and Research, College of Humanities and the Arts, San Jose, CA 95192-0088. Offers art (MA, MFA), including digital media art (MFA), history and visual culture (MA), photography (MFA), pictorial art (MFA), spatial art (MFA); English (MA, MFA), including creative writing (MFA); linguistics (MA); music (MM); music education (MA); philosophy (MA); Spanish (MA); teaching English to speakers of other languages (MA). *Program availability:* Part-time. *Faculty:* 35 full-time (17 women), 19 part-time/adjunct (11 women). *Students:* 129 full-time (79 women), 106 part-time (71 women); includes 117 minority (5 Black or African American, non-Hispanic/Latino; 29 Asian, non-Hispanic/Latino; 44 Hispanic/Latino; 39 Two or more races, non-Hispanic/Latino), 28 international. Average age 35. 204 applicants, 65% accepted, 79 enrolled. In 2017, 85 master's awarded. *Degree requirements:* For master's, one foreign language, comprehensive exam (for some programs), thesis (for some programs), graduate writing assessment, special study/project, recital. *Entrance requirements:* Additional exam requirements/recommendations for international students: Required—TOEFL (minimum score 550 paper-based; 80 iBT), IELTS (minimum score 6.5), PTE (minimum score 53). *Application deadline:* For fall admission, 2/1 for domestic and international students. Applications are processed on a rolling basis. Application fee: $55. Electronic applications accepted. *Expenses:* Tuition, state resident: full-time $7176. Tuition, nonresident: full-time $16,680. Tuition and fees vary according to course load and program. *Financial support:* Fellowships, research assistantships, Federal Work-Study, scholarships/grants, traineeships, tuition waivers (full and partial), and unspecified assistantships available. Support available to part-time students. Financial award application deadline: 4/28; financial award applicants required to submit

FAFSA. *Unit head:* Dr. Shannon Miller, Dean, 408-924-4300, Fax: 408-924-4365, E-mail: shannon.miller@sjsu.edu.
Website: http://www.sjsu.edu/humanitiesandarts/

Shenandoah University, Shenandoah Conservatory, Winchester, VA 22601-5195. Offers church music (MM, Certificate); collaborative piano (MM); composition (MM); conducting (MM); music (Artist Diploma); music education (MME); music therapy (MMT, Certificate); pedagogy - voice (MM, DMA); performance (MM, DMA); performing arts leadership and management (MS). *Accreditation:* NASM. *Program availability:* Part-time. *Faculty:* 32 full-time (11 women), 12 part-time/adjunct (6 women). *Students:* 70 full-time (38 women), 69 part-time (44 women); includes 20 minority (6 Black or African American, non-Hispanic/Latino; 1 American Indian or Alaska Native, non-Hispanic/Latino; 2 Asian, non-Hispanic/Latino; 11 Hispanic/Latino), 18 international. Average age 30. 135 applicants, 77% accepted, 49 enrolled. In 2017, 32 master's, 13 doctorates, 11 other advanced degrees awarded. *Degree requirements:* For master's, comprehensive exam, minimum GPA of 3.0, internship (MS), recital (MM), research teaching project or thesis (MME), project (MA); for doctorate, comprehensive exam, minimum GPA of 3.0, dissertation or teaching project, recital; for other advanced degree, minimum GPA of 3.0, research project, recital. *Entrance requirements:* For master's, music theory diagnostic exam, bachelor's degree with minimum of GPA of 2.5, performance audition, writing sample, resume, all academic transcripts; for doctorate, music theory diagnostic exam; music history diagnostic exam; vocal diction proficiency exam, master's degree with minimum GPA of 3.25, performance audition, 2 letters of recommendation, writing sample, resume, all academic transcripts; for other advanced degree, bachelor's or master's degree; minimum GPA of 2.5; performance audition (for Artist Diploma). Additional exam requirements/recommendations for international students: Required—TOEFL (minimum score 550 paper-based, 79 iBT) or IELTS (6.5). *Application deadline:* For fall and spring admission, 1/15 for domestic and international students; for summer admission, 4/15 for domestic and international students. Application fee: $30. Electronic applications accepted. *Expenses:* $15,600 tuition, $2,400 fees (applied major lesson fee, conservatory fee, technology fee, and student services fee). *Financial support:* In 2017–18, 42 students received support. Scholarships/grants and unspecified assistantships available. Financial award applicants required to submit FAFSA. *Faculty research:* Brahms, Scriabin, arts as inquiry. *Unit head:* Dr. Michael J. Stepniak, Dean, 540-542-6201, Fax: 540-665-5402, E-mail: mstepnia@su.edu. *Application contact:* Andrew Woodall, Executive Director of Recruitment and Advancement, 540-665-4581, Fax: 540-665-4627, E-mail: admit@su.edu.
Website: http://www.su.edu/conservatory/

Southern Illinois University Edwardsville, Graduate School, College of Arts and Sciences, Department of Music, Program in Music, Edwardsville, IL 62026. Offers music education (MM); music performance (MM). *Accreditation:* NASM. *Program availability:* Part-time. *Degree requirements:* For master's, one foreign language, thesis (for some programs), recital. *Entrance requirements:* Additional exam requirements/recommendations for international students: Required—TOEFL (minimum score 550 paper-based; 79 iBT), IELTS (minimum score 6.5). Electronic applications accepted.

Southern Illinois University Edwardsville, Graduate School, College of Arts and Sciences, Department of Music, Program in Piano Pedagogy, Edwardsville, IL 62026. Offers Postbaccalaureate Certificate. *Program availability:* Part-time. *Entrance requirements:* Additional exam requirements/recommendations for international students: Required—TOEFL (minimum score 550 paper-based; 79 iBT), IELTS (minimum score 6.5). Electronic applications accepted.

Southern Illinois University Edwardsville, Graduate School, College of Arts and Sciences, Department of Music, Program in Vocal Pedagogy, Edwardsville, IL 62026. Offers Postbaccalaureate Certificate. *Program availability:* Part-time. *Entrance requirements:* Additional exam requirements/recommendations for international students: Required—TOEFL (minimum score 550 paper-based; 79 iBT), IELTS (minimum score 6.5). Electronic applications accepted.

Southern Methodist University, Meadows School of the Arts, Division of Music, Dallas, TX 75275. Offers composition (MM); conducting (MM), including choral, instrumental; music education (MM); music history and literature (MM); performance (MM), including harpsichord, orchestral instrument, organ, piano, voice; piano performance and pedagogy (MM); theory pedagogy (MM). *Accreditation:* NASM. *Program availability:* Part-time. *Degree requirements:* For master's, variable foreign language requirement, comprehensive exam, project, recital, or thesis. *Entrance requirements:* For master's, placement exams in music history and theory, audition; bachelor's degree in music or equivalent; minimum GPA of 3.0; research paper in history, theory, education. Additional exam requirements/recommendations for international students: Required—TOEFL (minimum score 550 paper-based; 80 iBT). Electronic applications accepted. *Faculty research:* Music perception and cognition, computer-based instruction, music medicine and therapy, theoretical and historical analysis-medieval to contemporary.

Southwestern Oklahoma State University, College of Arts and Sciences, Department of Music, Weatherford, OK 73096-3098. Offers music education (MM); performance (MM). *Accreditation:* NASM. *Program availability:* Part-time. *Degree requirements:* For master's, comprehensive exam, recital (music performance). *Entrance requirements:* For master's, minimum GPA of 2.5. Additional exam requirements/recommendations for international students: Required—TOEFL.

State University of New York at Fredonia, School of Music, Fredonia, NY 14063-1136. Offers music education (MM); music performance (MM); music theory/composition (MM); music therapy (MM). *Accreditation:* NASM. *Program availability:* Part-time. *Faculty:* 36 full-time (16 women), 14 part-time/adjunct (10 women). *Students:* 34 full-time (17 women), 21 part-time (16 women); includes 6 minority (2 Black or African American, non-Hispanic/Latino; 2 Asian, non-Hispanic/Latino; 2 Hispanic/Latino), 12 international. Average age 25. 46 applicants, 72% accepted, 14 enrolled. In 2017, 25 master's awarded. *Degree requirements:* For master's, comprehensive exam (for some programs), thesis or final project/recital. *Entrance requirements:* For master's, audition. Additional exam requirements/recommendations for international students: Required—TOEFL (minimum score 79 iBT), IELTS (minimum score 6.5). *Application deadline:* For fall admission, 4/1 priority date for domestic and international students; for spring admission, 11/1 priority date for domestic students, 11/1 for international students. Applications are processed on a rolling basis. Application fee: $75. Electronic applications accepted. *Expenses:* Tuition, state resident: full-time $8154. Tuition, nonresident: full-time $16,650. *Required fees:* $1209. *Financial support:* In 2017–18, 14 students received support, including 4 fellowships (averaging $7,314 per year). Financial award application deadline: 3/15; financial award applicants required to submit FAFSA. *Faculty research:* Schenkerian analysis, early American Music, music pedagogy, music therapy, professional performance. *Unit head:* Dr. Melvin Unger, Director, School of Music, 716-673-3151, E-mail: melvin.unger@fredonia.edu. *Application contact:* Dr. Barry Kilpatrick, Admissions Coordinator, School of Music, 716-673-4635, E-mail: barry.kilpatrick@fredonia.edu.
Website: http://www.fredonia.edu/music/

State University of New York College at Potsdam, Crane School of Music, Potsdam, NY 13676. Offers music education (MM); music performance (MM). *Program availability:*

Part-time. *Degree requirements:* For master's, variable foreign language requirement, thesis (for some programs). *Entrance requirements:* For master's, audition, minimum GPA of 3.0. Additional exam requirements/recommendations for international students: Required—TOEFL (minimum score 550 paper-based; 80 iBT), IELTS (minimum score 6). Electronic applications accepted.

Syracuse University, College of Visual and Performing Arts, MM Program in Voice Pedagogy, Syracuse, NY 13244. Offers MM. *Degree requirements:* For master's, thesis or alternative. *Entrance requirements:* For master's, audition, three letters of recommendation, academic transcript, personal statement/essay, resume. Additional exam requirements/recommendations for international students: Required—TOEFL (minimum score 100 iBT). *Application deadline:* For fall admission, 2/1 priority date for domestic and international students. Application fee: $75. Electronic applications accepted. *Financial support:* Fellowships with full tuition reimbursements and teaching assistantships with tuition reimbursements available. Financial award application deadline: 1/1; financial award applicants required to submit FAFSA. *Faculty research:* Voice pedagogy, voice science, pedagogical issues, repertoire, diction, career planning methods, voice study, performance, experience in teaching. *Unit head:* Prof. Kathleen Roland-Silverstein, Assistant Professor, Applied Music and Performance, 315-443-5898, E-mail: krolands@syr.edu. *Application contact:* Caitlin Jarvis, Graduate Recruitment Specialist, 315-443-2769, E-mail: admissg@syr.edu.
Website: http://vpa.syr.edu/academics/setnor/graduate/voice-pedagogy/

Syracuse University, School of Education, MM/MS Programs in Music Education, Syracuse, NY 13255. Offers MM, MS. *Accreditation:* NASM. *Program availability:* Part-time. *Students:* Average age 23. *Entrance requirements:* For master's, GRE, bachelor's degree in music from institution accredited by the National Association of Schools of Music (NASM). Additional exam requirements/recommendations for international students: Required—TOEFL (minimum score 100 iBT). *Application deadline:* For fall admission, 1/15 priority date for domestic and international students; for spring admission, 10/15 priority date for domestic and international students; for summer admission, 4/1 priority date for domestic and international students. Applications are processed on a rolling basis. Application fee: $75. Electronic applications accepted. *Financial support:* Fellowships with full tuition reimbursements, research assistantships, teaching assistantships, career-related internships or fieldwork, and scholarships/grants available. Financial award application deadline: 1/15. *Faculty research:* Developing optimal teaching competencies, artistry and musicianship, philosophical perspectives of music, theoretical and historical perspectives of music and music education. *Unit head:* Dr. Benjamin Dotger, Department Chair, 315-443-2685, E-mail: bdotger@syr.edu. *Application contact:* Speranza Migliore, Graduate Admissions Recruiter, 315-443-2505, E-mail: gradrcrt@syr.edu.
Website: http://soe.syr.edu/academic/teaching_and_leadership/graduate/masters/music_education/default.aspx

Tarleton State University, College of Graduate Studies, College of Liberal and Fine Arts, Department of Fine Arts, Stephenville, TX 76402. Offers music education (MM). *Accreditation:* NASM. *Program availability:* Part-time, evening/weekend. *Faculty:* 1 (woman) part-time/adjunct. *Students:* 29 part-time (15 women); includes 11 minority (6 Black or African American, non-Hispanic/Latino; 5 Hispanic/Latino). Average age 33. 16 applicants, 94% accepted, 13 enrolled. In 2017, 6 master's awarded. *Degree requirements:* For master's, comprehensive exam, thesis optional. *Entrance requirements:* For master's, GRE, minimum GPA of 3.0. Additional exam requirements/recommendations for international students: Required—TOEFL (minimum score 550 paper-based; 80 iBT), IELTS (minimum score 6). *Application deadline:* For fall admission, 8/15 priority date for domestic students; for spring admission, 1/7 for domestic students. Applications are processed on a rolling basis. Application fee: $45 ($145 for international students). Electronic applications accepted. *Expenses:* Contact institution. *Financial support:* Research assistantships, institutionally sponsored loans, and scholarships/grants available. Financial award application deadline: 5/1; financial award applicants required to submit FAFSA. *Application contact:* Information Contact, 254-968-9104, Fax: 254-968-9670, E-mail: gradoffice@tarleton.edu.

Teachers College, Columbia University, Department of Arts and Humanities, New York, NY 10027. Offers applied linguistics (MA, Ed D); art and art education (Ed M, MA, Ed D, Ed DCT); arts administration (MA); bilingual and bicultural education (MA); global competence (Certificate); history and education (Ed D, PhD); music and music education (Ed DCT); philosophy and education (MA, Ed D, PhD); social studies education (Ed M, PhD); teaching English to speakers of other languages (Ed M); teaching of English and English education (Ed M, MA, Ed D, PhD), including English education (Ed M, Ed D, PhD), teaching of English (MA); teaching of social studies (MA); TESOL (MA, Ed D). *Program availability:* Part-time, evening/weekend. *Students:* 391 full-time (305 women), 418 part-time (283 women); includes 246 minority (62 Black or African American, non-Hispanic/Latino; 3 American Indian or Alaska Native, non-Hispanic/Latino; 94 Asian, non-Hispanic/Latino; 75 Hispanic/Latino; 12 Two or more races, non-Hispanic/Latino), 209 international. Average age 30. 1,053 applicants, 60% accepted, 334 enrolled. Terminal master's awarded for partial completion of doctoral program. *Financial support:* Fellowships, research assistantships, teaching assistantships, career-related internships or fieldwork, Federal Work-Study, institutionally sponsored loans, tuition waivers (full and partial), and unspecified assistantships available. Support available to part-time students. *Unit head:* Prof. William Gaudelli, Department Chair, E-mail: gaudelli@tc.columbia.edu. *Application contact:* David Estrella, Director of Admissions, 212-678-3305, Fax: 212-678-4171, E-mail: estrella@tc.columbia.edu.

Temple University, Center for the Performing and Cinematic Arts, Boyer College of Music and Dance, Department of Music, Philadelphia, PA 19122-6096. Offers choral conducting (MM); collaborative piano/chamber music (MM); collaborative piano/opera coaching (MM); composition (MM, PhD); instrumental conducting (MM); music education (MM, PhD); music history (MM); music performance (MM, DMA), including instrumental studies (MM), keyboard (DMA), keyboard studies (MM), voice (DMA), voice and opera (MM); music studies (PhD); music theory (MM, PhD); music therapy (MMT, PhD); musicology (MM, PhD); opera (MM); piano pedagogy (MM); string pedagogy (MM). *Accreditation:* NASM. *Program availability:* Part-time, online learning. *Faculty:* 42 full-time (17 women), 35 part-time/adjunct (13 women). *Students:* 193 full-time (108 women), 51 part-time (33 women); includes 38 minority (13 Black or African American, non-Hispanic/Latino; 8 Asian, non-Hispanic/Latino; 9 Hispanic/Latino; 8 Two or more races, non-Hispanic/Latino), 85 international. 394 applicants, 49% accepted, 77 enrolled. In 2017, 67 master's, 2 doctorates awarded. Terminal master's awarded for partial completion of doctoral program. *Degree requirements:* For doctorate, thesis/dissertation. *Entrance requirements:* Additional exam requirements/recommendations for international students: Required—TOEFL. *Application deadline:* For fall admission, 11/15 for international students; for spring admission, 8/1 for international students. Applications are processed on a rolling basis. Application fee: $60. Electronic applications accepted. *Expenses:* Tuition, state resident: full-time $16,164; part-time $898 per credit hour. Tuition, nonresident: full-time $22,158; part-time $1231 per credit hour. *Required fees:* $890; $445 per semester. Full-time tuition and fees vary according to course load, degree level, campus/location and program. *Financial support:* Fellowships with tuition reimbursements, research assistantships with tuition reimbursements, teaching assistantships with tuition reimbursements, career-related internships or fieldwork, Federal Work-Study, scholarships/grants, health care benefits, and unspecified assistantships available. Financial award application deadline: 3/1; financial award applicants required to submit FAFSA. *Unit head:* Dr. Robert Stroker, Dean, 215-204-8598, Fax: 215-204-4957, E-mail: rstroker@temple.edu. *Application contact:* James Short, Assistant Dean, Undergraduate and Graduate Admissions, 215-204-8301, Fax: 215-204-8598, E-mail: james.short@temple.edu.
Website: http://www.temple.edu/boyer/academicprograms/

Tennessee Technological University, College of Graduate Studies, College of Education, Department of Curriculum and Instruction, Program in Music, Cookeville, TN 38505. Offers MA. *Accreditation:* NASM. *Program availability:* Part-time, evening/weekend. *Students:* 2 full-time (1 woman), 3 part-time (0 women); includes 1 minority (Two or more races, non-Hispanic/Latino). 4 applicants, 100% accepted, 4 enrolled. In 2017, 2 master's awarded. *Degree requirements:* For master's, comprehensive exam, thesis or alternative. *Entrance requirements:* For master's, MAT or GRE. Additional exam requirements/recommendations for international students: Required—TOEFL (minimum score 527 paper-based; 71 iBT), IELTS (minimum score 5.5), PTE (minimum score 48), or TOEIC (Test of English as an International Communication). *Application deadline:* For fall admission, 8/1 for domestic students, 5/1 for international students; for spring admission, 12/1 for domestic students, 10/1 for international students; for summer admission, 5/1 for domestic students, 2/1 for international students. Applications are processed on a rolling basis. Application fee: $35 ($40 for international students). Electronic applications accepted. *Expenses:* Tuition, state resident: full-time $9925; part-time $565 per credit hour. Tuition, nonresident: full-time $22,993; part-time $1291 per credit hour. *Financial support:* Career-related internships or fieldwork available. Financial award application deadline: 4/1; financial award applicants required to submit FAFSA. *Unit head:* Dr. Jeremy Wendt, Interim Chairperson, 931-372-3181, Fax: 931-372-6270, E-mail: jwendt@tntech.edu. *Application contact:* Shelia K. Kendrick, Coordinator of Graduate Studies, 931-372-3808, Fax: 931-372-3497, E-mail: skendrick@tntech.edu.

Texas A&M University–Commerce, College of Humanities, Social Sciences and Arts, Commerce, TX 75429. Offers applied criminology (MS); applied linguistics (MA, MS); art (MA, MFA); computational linguistics (Graduate Certificate); creative writing (Graduate Certificate); criminal justice management (Graduate Certificate); criminal justice studies (Graduate Certificate); English (MA, MS, PhD); film studies (Graduate Certificate); history (MA, MS); history of Christianity (Graduate Certificate); Holocaust studies (Graduate Certificate); homeland security (Graduate Certificate); music education (MM); music performance (MM); political science (MA, MS); public history (Graduate Certificate); sociology (MS); Spanish (MA); studies in children's and adolescent literature and culture (Graduate Certificate); teaching English to speakers of other languages (Graduate Certificate); theater (MA, MS); world history (Graduate Certificate). *Program availability:* Part-time. *Faculty:* 56 full-time (26 women), 10 part-time/adjunct (5 women). *Students:* 133 full-time (85 women), 439 part-time (311 women); includes 204 minority (79 Black or African American, non-Hispanic/Latino; 4 American Indian or Alaska Native, non-Hispanic/Latino; 9 Asian, non-Hispanic/Latino; 98 Hispanic/Latino; 14 Two or more races, non-Hispanic/Latino), 26 international. Average age 36. 261 applicants, 50% accepted, 113 enrolled. In 2017, 105 master's, 5 doctorates awarded. *Degree requirements:* For master's, one foreign language, comprehensive exam, thesis (for some programs); for doctorate, one foreign language, comprehensive exam, thesis/dissertation, departmental qualifying exam. *Entrance requirements:* For master's and doctorate, GRE General Test. Additional exam requirements/recommendations for international students: Required—TOEFL (minimum score 550 paper-based; 79 iBT), IELTS (minimum score 6). *Application deadline:* Applications are processed on a rolling basis. Application fee: $50. Electronic applications accepted. *Expenses:* Contact institution. *Financial support:* In 2017–18, 43 students received support, including 9 research assistantships with partial tuition reimbursements available (averaging $9,000 per year), 68 teaching assistantships with partial tuition reimbursements available (averaging $9,000 per year); Federal Work-Study, institutionally sponsored loans, scholarships/grants, health care benefits, and unspecified assistantships also available. Financial award application deadline: 5/1; financial award applicants required to submit FAFSA. *Unit head:* Dr. William F. Kuracina, Interim Dean, 903-886-5166, Fax: 903-886-5774, E-mail: william.kuracina@tamuc.edu. *Application contact:* Vicky Turner, Doctoral Degree and Special Programs Coordinator, 903-886-5167, E-mail: vicky.turner@tamuc.edu.
Website: http://www.tamuc.edu/academics/graduateSchool/programs/humanitiesSocialScienceArts/default.aspx

Texas A&M University–Kingsville, College of Graduate Studies, College of Arts and Sciences, Department of Music, Program in Music Education, Kingsville, TX 78363. Offers elementary music (MM); instrumental (MM); vocal (MM).

Texas Christian University, College of Fine Arts, School of Music, Doctoral Programs in Music, Fort Worth, TX 76129. Offers composition (DMA), including music history; conducting (DMA), including music history, music theory; performance (DMA), including music history, music theory, piano pedagogy; piano pedagogy (DMA). *Accreditation:* NASM. *Faculty:* 43 full-time (10 women), 15 part-time/adjunct (7 women). *Students:* 10 full-time (2 women), 3 part-time (1 woman); includes 1 minority (Two or more races, non-Hispanic/Latino), 5 international. Average age 33. 44 applicants, 25% accepted, 2 enrolled. In 2017, 3 doctorates awarded. *Degree requirements:* For doctorate, comprehensive exam, thesis/dissertation. *Entrance requirements:* For doctorate, GRE General Test. Additional exam requirements/recommendations for international students: Required—TOEFL (minimum score 100 iBT). *Application deadline:* For spring admission, 12/1 for domestic and international students. Application fee: $80. Electronic applications accepted. *Financial support:* In 2017–18, 9 students received support, including 10 research assistantships with full tuition reimbursements available (averaging $10,000 per year); career-related internships or fieldwork, institutionally sponsored loans, scholarships/grants, tuition waivers (full and partial), and unspecified assistantships also available. Financial award application deadline: 12/1; financial award applicants required to submit CSS PROFILE or FAFSA. *Unit head:* Dr. Richard C. Gipson, Director, 817-257-6606, Fax: 817-257-5818, E-mail: r.gipson@tcu.edu. *Application contact:* Donna Smolik, TCU College of Fine Arts Graduate Office, 817-257-7603, Fax: 817-257-5672, E-mail: cfagradinfo@tcu.edu.
Website: http://www.music.tcu.edu

Texas Christian University, College of Fine Arts, School of Music, Master's Programs in Music, Fort Worth, TX 76129. Offers conducting (M Mus); music education (MM Ed). *Faculty:* 43 full-time (10 women), 15 part-time/adjunct (7 women). *Students:* 39 full-time (16 women), 1 part-time (0 women); includes 6 minority (4 Hispanic/Latino; 2 Two or more races, non-Hispanic/Latino), 11 international. Average age 24. 62 applicants, 47% accepted, 20 enrolled. In 2017, 21 master's awarded. *Degree requirements:* For master's, comprehensive exam. *Entrance requirements:* For master's, GRE General Test. Additional exam requirements/recommendations for international students: Required—TOEFL (minimum score 80 iBT). *Application deadline:* For fall admission, 3/1 for domestic and international students. Application fee: $80. Electronic applications accepted. *Financial support:* In 2017–18, 41 students received support, including 41 research assistantships with full tuition reimbursements available (averaging $6,000 per

Music Education

year); career-related internships or fieldwork, institutionally sponsored loans, scholarships/grants, tuition waivers (full and partial), and unspecified assistantships also available. Financial award application deadline: 3/1; financial award applicants required to submit CSS PROFILE or FAFSA. *Unit head:* Dr. Richard C. Gipson, Director, 817-257-6606, Fax: 817-257-5818, E-mail: music@tcu.edu. *Application contact:* Donna Smolik, TCU College of Fine Arts Graduate Office, 817-257-7603, Fax: 817-257-5672, E-mail: cfagradinfo@tcu.edu.
Website: http://www.music.tcu.edu

Texas State University, The Graduate College, College of Fine Arts and Communication, Program in Music Education, San Marcos, TX 78666. Offers MM. *Accreditation:* NASM. *Program availability:* Part-time. *Faculty:* 10 full-time (5 women). *Students:* 1 full-time (0 women), 4 part-time (2 women); includes 3 minority (1 Black or African American, non-Hispanic/Latino; 2 Hispanic/Latino). Average age 36. 2 applicants. In 2017, 5 master's awarded. *Degree requirements:* For master's, comprehensive exam. *Entrance requirements:* For master's, baccalaureate degree in music from regionally-accredited institution with minimum GPA of 2.75 in last 60 hours of undergraduate course work, statement of purpose, resume, 3 letters of reference, music portfolio. Additional exam requirements/recommendations for international students: Required—TOEFL (minimum score 550 paper-based; 78 iBT), IELTS (minimum score 6). *Application deadline:* For fall admission, 1/15 priority date for domestic students, 1/1 priority date for international students; for spring admission, 10/15 for domestic students, 10/1 for international students; for summer admission, 4/15 for domestic students, 3/15 for international students. Applications are processed on a rolling basis. Application fee: $40 ($90 for international students). Electronic applications accepted. *Expenses:* Tuition, state resident: full-time $7868; part-time $3934 per semester. Tuition, nonresident: full-time $17,828; part-time $8914 per semester. *Required fees:* $2092; $1435 per semester. Tuition and fees vary according to course load. *Financial support:* In 2017–18, 3 students received support, including 1 teaching assistantship (averaging $6,232 per year); career-related internships or fieldwork, Federal Work-Study, institutionally sponsored loans, scholarships/grants, and unspecified assistantships also available. Support available to part-time students. Financial award application deadline: 3/1; financial award applicants required to submit FAFSA. *Unit head:* Dr. Jason Kwak, Graduate Advisor, 512-245-3390, Fax: 512-245-8181, E-mail: jk45@txstate.edu. *Application contact:* Dr. Andrea Golato, Dean of Graduate School, 512-245-2581, Fax: 512-245-8365, E-mail: gradcollege@txstate.edu.
Website: http://www.finearts.txstate.edu/music/

Texas Tech University, Graduate School, J.T. and Margaret Talkington College of Visual and Performing Arts, School of Music, Lubbock, TX 79409-2033. Offers music (MM, DMA); music education (MM Ed). *Accreditation:* NASM. *Program availability:* Part-time. *Faculty:* 56 full-time (22 women), 7 part-time/adjunct (4 women). *Students:* 112 full-time (46 women), 30 part-time (12 women); includes 20 minority (5 Black or African American, non-Hispanic/Latino; 14 Hispanic/Latino; 1 Two or more races, non-Hispanic/Latino), 42 international. Average age 30. 112 applicants, 69% accepted, 43 enrolled. In 2017, 25 master's, 15 doctorates awarded. *Degree requirements:* For master's, thesis or alternative; for doctorate, comprehensive exam (for some programs), thesis/dissertation. *Entrance requirements:* Additional exam requirements/recommendations for international students: Required—TOEFL (minimum score 550 paper-based; 79 iBT). *Application deadline:* For fall admission, 6/1 priority date for domestic students, 1/15 priority date for international students; for spring admission, 9/1 priority date for domestic students, 6/15 priority date for international students. Applications are processed on a rolling basis. Application fee: $60. Electronic applications accepted. *Expenses:* Contact institution. *Financial support:* In 2017–18, 160 students received support, including 142 fellowships (averaging $2,547 per year), 101 teaching assistantships (averaging $10,247 per year); research assistantships, Federal Work-Study, institutionally sponsored loans, scholarships/grants, health care benefits, tuition waivers (partial), and unspecified assistantships also available. Financial award application deadline: 4/15; financial award applicants required to submit FAFSA. *Faculty research:* Strategies for music pedagogy in grades K-12, performance practice of traditional music, role of the woman piano virtuoso, vernacular music center, voice health and culture. *Total annual research expenditures:* $10,747. *Unit head:* Dr. Keith Dye, Interim Director and Professor, 806-834-2497, E-mail: keith.dye@ttu.edu. *Application contact:* Emily Gifford, Graduate Student Coordinator, 806-834-5076, Fax: 806-742-2294, E-mail: emily.gifford@ttu.edu.
Website: http://www.depts.ttu.edu/music

Texas Woman's University, Graduate School, College of Arts and Sciences, School of the Arts, Department of Music and Drama, Denton, TX 76204. Offers drama (MA); music (MA), including music education, music therapy, pedagogy, performance. *Accreditation:* NASM. *Program availability:* Part-time. *Faculty:* 15 full-time (7 women), 8 part-time/adjunct (4 women). *Students:* 54 full-time (41 women), 43 part-time (30 women); includes 32 minority (6 Black or African American, non-Hispanic/Latino; 2 Asian, non-Hispanic/Latino; 21 Hispanic/Latino; 3 Two or more races, non-Hispanic/Latino), 6 international. Average age 30. 42 applicants, 98% accepted, 33 enrolled. In 2017, 21 master's awarded. *Degree requirements:* For master's, comprehensive exam, thesis (for some programs), project recital, professional paper or thesis (for music education). *Entrance requirements:* For master's, music history/theory placement exam (for music only), audition and/or design portfolio, interview, resume, writing sample (for drama only), letter of intent, minimum undergraduate GPA of 3.0. Additional exam requirements/recommendations for international students: Required—TOEFL (minimum score 550 paper-based; 79 iBT); Recommended—IELTS (minimum score 6.5), TSE (minimum score 53). *Application deadline:* For fall admission, 3/1 priority date for domestic and international students; for spring admission, 11/1 priority date for domestic students, 7/1 priority date for international students; for summer admission, 5/1 priority date for domestic students, 2/1 priority date for international students. Applications are processed on a rolling basis. Application fee: $50 ($75 for international students). Electronic applications accepted. *Expenses:* $8,150 per year full-time in-state, $17,450 per year full-time out-of-state (for music). *Financial support:* In 2017–18, 31 students received support, including 5 teaching assistantships (averaging $11,736 per year); career-related internships or fieldwork, Federal Work-Study, institutionally sponsored loans, scholarships/grants, traineeships, health care benefits, and unspecified assistantships also available. Support available to part-time students. Financial award application deadline: 3/1; financial award applicants required to submit FAFSA. *Faculty research:* Musical development in early childhood, little known or neglected compositions for flute (especially by women composers), pedagogical development of the singing voice, music therapy, music and neuroscience technology. *Unit head:* Dr. Pamela Youngblood, Chair of Music and Drama, 940-898-2500, Fax: 940-898-2494, E-mail: music@twu.edu. *Application contact:* Korie Hawkins, Associate Director of Admissions, Graduate Recruitment, 940-898-3188, Fax: 940-898-3081, E-mail: admissions@twu.edu.

Towson University, College of Fine Arts and Communication, Program in Music Education, Towson, MD 21252-0001. Offers MS. *Accreditation:* NASM; NCATE. *Program availability:* Part-time, evening/weekend. *Students:* 7 full-time (4 women), 19 part-time (9 women); includes 3 minority (1 Black or African American, non-Hispanic/Latino; 2 Hispanic/Latino), 1 international. *Degree requirements:* For master's, thesis optional. *Entrance requirements:* For master's, placement examination in music history

and music theory, bachelor's degree in music education or certification as public school music teacher, minimum GPA of 3.0. *Application deadline:* For fall admission, 1/17 for domestic students, 5/15 for international students; for spring admission, 10/15 for domestic students, 12/1 for international students. Applications are processed on a rolling basis. Application fee: $45. Electronic applications accepted. *Expenses:* Tuition, state resident: full-time $7960; part-time $398 per unit. Tuition, nonresident: full-time $16,480; part-time $824 per unit. *Required fees:* $2600; $130 per year. $390 per term. *Financial support:* Application deadline: 4/1. *Unit head:* Dr. Kathryn Evans, Program Coordinator, 410-704-2257, E-mail: kevans@towson.edu. *Application contact:* Coverley Beidleman, Assistant Director of Graduate Admissions, 410-704-5630, Fax: 410-704-3030, E-mail: cbeidleman@towson.edu.
Website: http://www.towson.edu/cofac/departments/music/grad/education/

Union College, Graduate Programs, Department of Education, Barbourville, KY 40906-1499. Offers elementary education (MA); health and physical education (MA); middle grades (MA); music education (MA); principalship (MA); reading specialist (MA); secondary education (MA); special education (MA). *Degree requirements:* For master's, thesis optional. *Entrance requirements:* For master's, GRE General Test, NTE.

Université Laval, Faculty of Music, Programs in Music, Québec, QC G1K 7P4, Canada. Offers composition (M Mus); instrumental didactics (M Mus); interpretation (M Mus); music education (M Mus, PhD); musicology (M Mus, PhD). Terminal master's awarded for partial completion of doctoral program. *Degree requirements:* For master's, thesis (for some programs); for doctorate, comprehensive exam, thesis/dissertation. *Entrance requirements:* For master's, English exam, audition, knowledge of French; for doctorate, English exam, knowledge of French, third language. Electronic applications accepted.

University at Buffalo, the State University of New York, Graduate School, Graduate School of Education, Department of Learning and Instruction, Buffalo, NY 14260. Offers biology education (Ed M, Certificate); chemistry education (Ed M, Certificate); childhood education (Ed M); childhood education with bilingual extension (Ed M); college teaching (Advanced Certificate); curriculum, instruction and the science of learning (PhD); early childhood education (Ed M); early childhood education with bilingual extension (Ed M); earth science education (Ed M, Certificate); education and technology (Ed M); education studies (Ed M); educational technology and new literacies (Certificate); educational technology and new literacies (Advanced Certificate); elementary education (Ed D); English education (Ed M, Certificate); English education studies (Ed M); English for speakers of other languages (Ed M); foreign and second language education (PhD); French education (Ed M, Certificate); German education (Ed M, Certificate); gifted education (Certificate); Latin education (Ed M, Certificate); literacy education studies (Ed M); literacy specialist (Ed M); literacy teaching and learning (Certificate); mathematics education (Ed M, Certificate); music education (Ed M, Certificate); music education studies (Ed M); music learning theory (Advanced Certificate); online education (Advanced Certificate); physics education (Ed M, Certificate); science and the public (Ed M); social studies education (Ed M, Certificate); Spanish education (Ed M, Certificate); special education (PhD); teaching English to speakers of other languages (Ed M). *Program availability:* Part-time, evening/weekend, 100% online. *Faculty:* 26 full-time (19 women), 74 part-time/adjunct (52 women). *Students:* 172 full-time (122 women), 325 part-time (226 women); includes 44 minority (25 Black or African American, non-Hispanic/Latino; 5 American Indian or Alaska Native, non-Hispanic/Latino; 14 Asian, non-Hispanic/Latino), 57 international. Average age 33. 316 applicants, 78% accepted, 174 enrolled. In 2017, 109 master's, 34 doctorates, 15 other advanced degrees awarded. *Degree requirements:* For master's, comprehensive exam; for doctorate, thesis/dissertation, research analysis exam, research experience. *Entrance requirements:* For master's, letters of reference; for doctorate, GRE General Test or MAT, interview, writing sample, letters of recommendation. Additional exam requirements/recommendations for international students: Required—TOEFL (minimum score 600 paper-based; 96 iBT). *Application deadline:* For fall admission, 2/1 priority date for domestic and international students; for spring admission, 11/15 priority date for domestic students, 10/1 for international students. Applications are processed on a rolling basis. Application fee: $50. Electronic applications accepted. *Financial support:* In 2017–18, 42 fellowships (averaging $5,181 per year), 44 research assistantships with tuition reimbursements (averaging $10,908 per year) were awarded; teaching assistantships, career-related internships or fieldwork, Federal Work-Study, institutionally sponsored loans, scholarships/grants, tuition waivers (full and partial), and unspecified assistantships also available. Financial award application deadline: 2/28; financial award applicants required to submit FAFSA. *Faculty research:* Science assessment, foreign language teaching and learning, early learning, new literacies, gender and education. *Total annual research expenditures:* $413,233. *Unit head:* Dr. David Bruce, Chair, 716-645-4069, Fax: 716-645-3161, E-mail: gse-info@buffalo.edu. *Application contact:* Luann Zak, Admissions Assistant, 716-645-2110, Fax: 716-645-7937, E-mail: luannzak@buffalo.edu.
Website: http://gse.buffalo.edu/lai

The University of Akron, Graduate School, Buchtel College of Arts and Sciences, School of Music, Program in Music Education, Akron, OH 44325. Offers MM. *Accreditation:* NCATE. *Students:* 7 full-time (3 women), 2 part-time (0 women); includes 1 minority (Hispanic/Latino). Average age 25. 4 applicants, 100% accepted, 3 enrolled. In 2017, 4 master's awarded. *Degree requirements:* For master's, comprehensive exam, thesis optional. *Entrance requirements:* For master's, minimum GPA of 2.75, interview, three letters of recommendation. Additional exam requirements/recommendations for international students: Required—TOEFL (minimum score 79 iBT), IELTS (minimum score 6.5). *Application deadline:* Applications are processed on a rolling basis. Application fee: $45 ($70 for international students). Electronic applications accepted. *Unit head:* Dr. J Thomas Dukes, Interim Director, 330-972-5761, E-mail: jtdukes@uakron.edu. *Application contact:* Dr. Ann Usher, Program Coordinator, 330-972-6923, E-mail: ausher@uakron.edu.
Website: http://www.uakron.edu/academics_majors/graduate/programs_detail.dot?programId=52411&pageTitle=Graduate programs&crumbTitle=Music - Education

The University of Alabama, Graduate School, College of Arts and Sciences, School of Music, Tuscaloosa, AL 35487. Offers arranging (MM); choral conducting (MM, DMA); church music (MM); composition (MM, DMA); music education (MA, PhD); musicology (MM); performance (MM, DMA); theory (MM); wind conducting (MM, DMA). *Accreditation:* NASM. *Faculty:* 38 full-time (13 women), 2 part-time/adjunct (both women). *Students:* 56 full-time (26 women), 15 part-time (3 women); includes 15 minority (6 Black or African American, non-Hispanic/Latino; 1 American Indian or Alaska Native, non-Hispanic/Latino; 6 Hispanic/Latino; 2 Two or more races, non-Hispanic/Latino), 11 international. Average age 30. 67 applicants, 64% accepted, 22 enrolled. In 2017, 10 master's, 6 doctorates awarded. *Degree requirements:* For master's, variable foreign language requirement, comprehensive exam (for some programs), thesis (for some programs), recital; for doctorate, variable foreign language requirement, comprehensive exam, thesis/dissertation, oral exam; recital (for some majors). *Entrance requirements:* For master's and doctorate, audition exam, audition in the major instrument or area. Additional exam requirements/recommendations for international students: Required—PTE (minimum score 59), TOEFL (minimum score 550 paper-based, 79 iBT) or IELTS (minimum score 6.5). *Application deadline:* For fall admission,

3/15 priority date for domestic and international students; for winter admission, 9/1 priority date for domestic and international students; for spring admission, 9/1 priority date for domestic and international students. Applications are processed on a rolling basis. Application fee: $50 ($60 for international students). Electronic applications accepted. *Financial support:* In 2017–18, 37 students received support, including fellowships with full tuition reimbursements available (averaging $10,000 per year), teaching assistantships with tuition reimbursements available (averaging $10,161 per year); institutionally sponsored loans, scholarships/grants, health care benefits, and unspecified assistantships also available. Financial award application deadline: 3/15. *Faculty research:* Performance practice, musicology, theory, composition. *Unit head:* Charles G. Snead, Director, 205-348-7110, Fax: 205-348-1473, E-mail: ssnead@music.ua.edu. *Application contact:* Dr. Jon Noffsinger, Director of Graduate Studies, 205-348-1475, Fax: 205-348-1473, E-mail: jnoffsin@ua.edu.
Website: http://music.ua.edu/

The University of Alabama, Graduate School, College of Education, Department of Music Education, Tuscaloosa, AL 35487-0366. Offers choral music education (MA); instrumental music education (MA); music education (Ed D, PhD, Ed S). *Accreditation:* NASM. *Program availability:* Part-time. *Faculty:* 4 full-time (1 woman), 1 (woman) part-time/adjunct. *Degree requirements:* For master's, comprehensive exam, thesis optional; for doctorate, comprehensive exam, thesis/dissertation, oral exam (for PhD). *Entrance requirements:* For master's, GRE or MAT, video of teaching, letters of recommendation; for doctorate, GRE or MAT, interview, writing sample, video of teaching, letters of recommendation; for Ed S, GRE or MAT. Additional exam requirements/recommendations for international students: Required—TOEFL (minimum score 550 paper-based). *Application deadline:* For fall admission, 7/1 priority date for domestic students; for spring admission, 11/1 priority date for domestic students. Applications are processed on a rolling basis. Application fee: $50 ($60 for international students). Electronic applications accepted. *Financial support:* In 2017–18, 3 students received support. Research assistantships with tuition reimbursements available and teaching assistantships with tuition reimbursements available available. Financial award application deadline: 3/1. *Faculty research:* Elementary music, music for students with special needs, choral music. *Unit head:* Dr. Marvin E. Latimer, Department Head and Associate Professor, 205-348-0393, Fax: 205-348-1675, E-mail: mlatimer@music.ua.edu. *Application contact:* Jessica M. Westbrook, Senior Office Associate, 205-348-6054, Fax: 205-348-1675, E-mail: jessica.westbrook@ua.edu.
Website: http://www.musiceducation.ua.edu

The University of Arizona, College of Fine Arts, School of Music, Program in Music, Tucson, AZ 85721. Offers composition (MM); ethnomusicology (MM); music education (MM, PhD); music theory (MM, PhD); musicology (MM); performance (MM), including conducting - choral, conducting - instrumental, instrumental, keyboard, piano accompanying, piano and dance accompanying, vocal. *Entrance requirements:* Additional exam requirements/recommendations for international students: Required—TOEFL (minimum score 550 paper-based; 79 iBT). Electronic applications accepted. *Faculty research:* Music in general education, psychology of music learning, innovation in string music education, Zarzuela, Franz Liszt's work.

University of Bridgeport, School of Education, Department of Education, Bridgeport, CT 06604. Offers education (MS); educational management (Ed D, Diploma), including intermediate administrator or supervisor (Diploma), leadership (Ed D); elementary education (MS, Diploma), including early childhood education, elementary education; middle school education (MS); music education (MS); remedial reading and language arts (Diploma); secondary education (MS, Diploma), including computer specialist (Diploma), international education (Diploma), reading specialist, secondary education. *Program availability:* Part-time, evening/weekend. *Degree requirements:* For master's, final exam, final project, or thesis; for doctorate, comprehensive exam, thesis/dissertation; for Diploma, thesis or alternative, final project. *Entrance requirements:* For master's, minimum undergraduate QPA of 2.67; for doctorate, GRE, MAT; for Diploma, GRE General Test or MAT, minimum graduate QPA of 3.0. Additional exam requirements/recommendations for international students: Recommended—TOEFL (minimum score 550 paper-based; 80 iBT), IELTS (minimum score 6.5). Electronic applications accepted. *Expenses:* Contact institution.

The University of British Columbia, Faculty of Education, Department of Curriculum and Pedagogy, Vancouver, BC V6T 1Z4, Canada. Offers art education (M Ed, MA); curriculum studies (M Ed, MA, PhD); home economics education (M Ed, MA); mathematics education (M Ed, MA); media and technology studies education (M Ed, MA); music education (M Ed, MA); physical education (M Ed, MA); science education (M Ed, MA); social studies education (M Ed, MA). *Program availability:* Part-time, online learning. *Degree requirements:* For master's, thesis (MA); for doctorate, comprehensive exam, thesis/dissertation. *Entrance requirements:* Additional exam requirements/recommendations for international students: Required—TOEFL, IELTS. Electronic applications accepted. *Expenses:* Contact institution. *Faculty research:* School subjects, teaching and learning.

University of Central Arkansas, Graduate School, College of Fine Arts and Communication, Department of Music, Conway, AR 72035-0001. Offers choral conducting (MM); instrumental conducting (MM); music (PC); music education (MM); music theory (MM); performance (MM). *Accreditation:* NASM. *Program availability:* Part-time. *Degree requirements:* For master's, comprehensive exam, thesis optional. *Entrance requirements:* For master's, GRE General Test, minimum GPA of 2.7. Additional exam requirements/recommendations for international students: Required—TOEFL (minimum score 550 paper-based). Electronic applications accepted.

University of Central Oklahoma, The Jackson College of Graduate Studies, College of Fine Arts and Design, Department of Music, Edmond, OK 73034-5209. Offers jazz studies (MM), including music production, performance; music (MM), including collaborative piano, composition, conducting, instrumental performance, music education, musical theatre, piano pedagogy, piano performance, vocal pedagogy, vocal performance. *Accreditation:* NASM. *Program availability:* Part-time. *Faculty:* 25 full-time (10 women), 18 part-time/adjunct (6 women). *Students:* 46 full-time (21 women), 15 part-time (9 women); includes 10 minority (4 Black or African American, non-Hispanic/Latino; 1 American Indian or Alaska Native, non-Hispanic/Latino; 4 Hispanic/Latino; 1 Two or more races, non-Hispanic/Latino), 19 international. Average age 29. 44 applicants, 66% accepted, 21 enrolled. In 2017, 21 master's awarded. *Degree requirements:* For master's, comprehensive exam, recital or project. *Entrance requirements:* For master's, interview, audition. Additional exam requirements/recommendations for international students: Required—TOEFL (minimum score 550 paper-based; 79 iBT), IELTS (minimum score 6.5). *Application deadline:* For fall admission, 7/15 for international students; for spring admission, 11/15 for international students. Applications are processed on a rolling basis. Application fee: $60. Electronic applications accepted. *Expenses:* Tuition, state resident: full-time $5375; part-time $268.75 per credit hour. Tuition, nonresident: full-time $13,295; part-time $664.75 per credit hour. *Required fees:* $626; $31.30 per credit hour. One-time fee: $50. Tuition and fees vary according to program. *Financial support:* In 2017–18, 25 students received support, including 1 research assistantship with partial tuition reimbursement available (averaging $2,958 per year), 16 teaching assistantships with partial tuition reimbursements available (averaging $6,765 per year); career-related internships or

fieldwork, Federal Work-Study, scholarships/grants, tuition waivers (partial), and unspecified assistantships also available. Financial award application deadline: 3/31; financial award applicants required to submit FAFSA. *Unit head:* Dr. Brian Lamb, Director of the School of Music, 405-974-5004. *Application contact:* Dr. Samuel Magrill, Graduate Advisor, 405-974-5684, E-mail: gradcoll@uco.edu.
Website: http://sites.uco.edu/cfad/academics/music/index.asp

University of Cincinnati, Graduate School, College-Conservatory of Music, Division of Music Education, Cincinnati, OH 45221. Offers MM. *Accreditation:* NASM; NCATE. *Degree requirements:* For master's, comprehensive exam, paper or thesis. *Entrance requirements:* For master's, GRE General Test, interview. Additional exam requirements/recommendations for international students: Required—TOEFL (minimum score 520 paper-based). Electronic applications accepted. *Expenses:* Tuition, area resident: Full-time $14,468. Tuition, state resident: full-time $14,968; part-time $754 per credit hour. Tuition, nonresident: full-time $24,210; part-time $1311 per credit hour. *International tuition:* $26,460 full-time. *Required fees:* $3958; $84 per credit hour. One-time fee: $85 full-time. Tuition and fees vary according to course load, degree level and program. *Faculty research:* Choral, orchestral, and wind conducting; Kodaly; Orff-Schulwerk; jazz studies; string education.

University of Colorado Boulder, Graduate School, College of Music, Boulder, CO 80309. Offers composition (M Mus, D Mus A); conducting (M Mus); instrumental conducting and literature (D Mus A); literature and performance of choral music (D Mus A); music education (M Mus Ed, PhD), including choral or wind instrument conducting (M Mus Ed), general (M Mus Ed), Kodaly concepts (M Mus Ed), piano pedagogy (M Mus Ed), primary instruments (M Mus Ed), secondary instruments (M Mus Ed), voice pedagogy (M Mus Ed); music theory (M Mus); performance (M Mus, D Mus A); performance and pedagogy (M Mus, D Mus A). *Accreditation:* NASM. *Faculty:* 64 full-time (19 women). *Students:* 165 full-time (79 women), 35 part-time (12 women); includes 22 minority (3 Black or African American, non-Hispanic/Latino; 3 Asian, non-Hispanic/Latino; 10 Hispanic/Latino; 6 Two or more races, non-Hispanic/Latino), 19 international. Average age 29. 459 applicants, 41% accepted, 65 enrolled. In 2017, 46 master's, 22 doctorates awarded. Terminal master's awarded for partial completion of doctoral program. *Degree requirements:* For master's, variable foreign language requirement, comprehensive exam, thesis or alternative, recital; for doctorate, variable foreign language requirement, thesis/dissertation. *Entrance requirements:* For master's, GRE General Test, GRE Subject Test (music literature), minimum undergraduate GPA of 2.75; for doctorate, GRE General Test, GRE Subject Test, audition, sample of research. *Application deadline:* For fall admission, 12/1 for domestic and international students; for spring admission, 10/1 for domestic and international students. Applications are processed on a rolling basis. Application fee: $60 ($80 for international students). Electronic applications accepted. Application fee is waived when completed online. *Financial support:* In 2017–18, 546 students received support, including 250 fellowships (averaging $2,731 per year), 116 teaching assistantships with full and partial tuition reimbursements available (averaging $19,272 per year); research assistantships, institutionally sponsored loans, scholarships/grants, health care benefits, and unspecified assistantships also available. Financial award application deadline: 2/15; financial award applicants required to submit FAFSA. *Faculty research:* Music; instrumental music; performing arts; chamber music; musicology/music theory. *Total annual research expenditures:* $30,622. *Application contact:* E-mail: gradmusc@colorado.edu.
Website: http://music.colorado.edu/

University of Connecticut, Graduate School, Neag School of Education, Department of Curriculum and Instruction, Storrs, CT 06269. Offers agriculture (MA), including agriculture education; agriculture education (PhD); bilingual and bicultural education (MA, PhD); elementary education (MA, PhD); English education (MA, PhD); history and social sciences education (MA, PhD); mathematics education (MA, PhD); music education (MA); reading education (MA, PhD); science education (MA, PhD); secondary education (MA, PhD); world languages education (MA, PhD). *Accreditation:* NCATE. Terminal master's awarded for partial completion of doctoral program. *Degree requirements:* For master's, comprehensive exam, thesis or alternative; for doctorate, thesis/dissertation. *Entrance requirements:* For doctorate, GRE General Test. Additional exam requirements/recommendations for international students: Required—TOEFL (minimum score 550 paper-based). Electronic applications accepted.

University of Dayton, Department of Teacher Education, Dayton, OH 45469. Offers adolescence to young adult education (MS Ed); early childhood leadership and advocacy (MS Ed); interdisciplinary education (MS Ed), including visual arts; interdisciplinary education studies (MS Ed); leadership in educational systems (MS Ed); literacy (MS Ed); mathematics education (MS Ed); middle childhood education (MS Ed); multi-age education (MS Ed), including world languages; music education (MS Ed); teacher as leader (MS Ed); teacher education (MS Ed); technology-enhanced learning (MS Ed); trans-disciplinary early childhood education (MS Ed). *Program availability:* Part-time, 100% online. *Faculty:* 23 full-time (20 women), 41 part-time/adjunct (36 women). *Students:* 45 full-time (38 women), 68 part-time (57 women); includes 7 minority (3 Black or African American, non-Hispanic/Latino; 1 Hispanic/Latino; 3 Two or more races, non-Hispanic/Latino), 6 international. Average age 31. 106 applicants, 28% accepted. In 2017, 70 master's awarded. *Degree requirements:* For master's, variable foreign language requirement, thesis or alternative, internship (for teaching licensure or endorsement). *Entrance requirements:* For master's, GRE (minimum score of 149 verbal, 4 on writing) or MAT (minimum score of 396) if undergraduate GPA was under 2.75, minimum GPA of 2.75, 3 letters of recommendation, personal statement or resume, official transcripts. Additional exam requirements/recommendations for international students: Required—TOEFL (minimum score 550 paper-based; 80 iBT); Recommended—IELTS (minimum score 6.5). *Application deadline:* Applications are processed on a rolling basis. Application fee: $50 ($50 for international students). Electronic applications accepted. *Expenses:* Contact institution. *Financial support:* In 2017–18, 5 research assistantships with partial tuition reimbursements (averaging $9,640 per year) were awarded; teaching assistantships, career-related internships or fieldwork, institutionally sponsored loans, and unspecified assistantships also available. Financial award application deadline: 3/1; financial award applicants required to submit FAFSA. *Faculty research:* Social emotional learning, culturally responsive teaching, urban teaching, literacy, instructional strategies, pre-service teacher education preparation. *Unit head:* Dr. Connie L. Bowman, Chair, 937-229-3348, E-mail: cbowman1@udayton.edu. *Application contact:* Gina Seiter, Coordinator of Graduate Programs and Licensing, 937-229-3103, E-mail: gseiter1@udayton.edu.
Website: https://www.udayton.edu/education/departments_and_programs/edt

University of Delaware, College of Arts and Sciences, Department of Music, Newark, DE 19716. Offers composition (MM); music education (MM); performance (MM). *Accreditation:* NASM. *Program availability:* Part-time. *Entrance requirements:* For master's, audition. Additional exam requirements/recommendations for international students: Required—TOEFL. Electronic applications accepted. *Faculty research:* Teaching of music.

University of Denver, Division of Arts, Humanities and Social Sciences, Lamont School of Music, Denver, CO 80208. Offers composition (MM); composition - jazz emphasis (MM); conducting (MM, Certificate); jazz studies (Certificate); music theory (MA);

Music Education

musicology (MA); orchestral studies (Certificate); pedagogy (MM); performance (MM, Certificate); performance - jazz emphasis (MM); Suzuki teaching (Certificate). *Accreditation:* NASM. *Program availability:* Part-time. *Faculty:* 32 full-time (9 women), 33 part-time/adjunct (15 women). *Students:* 27 full-time (9 women), 76 part-time (38 women); includes 20 minority (3 Black or African American, non-Hispanic/Latino; 3 Asian, non-Hispanic/Latino; 7 Hispanic/Latino; 7 Two or more races, non-Hispanic/Latino), 14 international. Average age 28. 149 applicants, 79% accepted, 54 enrolled. In 2017, 37 master's, 3 other advanced degrees awarded. *Degree requirements:* For master's, one foreign language, comprehensive exam, recital or project (for performance), thesis (for musicology, music theory, piano pedagogy). *Entrance requirements:* For master's, GRE General Test (for MA only), bachelor's degree, transcripts, personal statement, resume, three letters of recommendation, pre-screen audition (for performance), portfolio (for composition), essay or research paper (for MA only); for Certificate, bachelor's degree, transcripts, personal statement, resume, letters of recommendation, pre-screen video recording or music audition. Additional exam requirements/recommendations for international students: Required—TOEFL (minimum score 550 paper-based; 80 iBT). *Application deadline:* For fall admission, 1/15 priority date for domestic and international students. Applications are processed on a rolling basis. Application fee: $65. Electronic applications accepted. *Expenses:* $31,935 per year full-time. *Financial support:* In 2017–18, 89 students received support, including 7 teaching assistantships with tuition reimbursements available (averaging $6,917 per year); career-related internships or fieldwork, Federal Work-Study, institutionally sponsored loans, scholarships/grants, tuition waivers, and unspecified assistantships also available. Support available to part-time students. Financial award application deadline: 2/15; financial award applicants required to submit FAFSA. *Faculty research:* Performance, jazz studies and commercial music, musicology, music theory, composition, music pedagogy, music recording and production. *Unit head:* Dr. Nancy Cochran, Professor and Director, 303-871-6986, Fax: 303-871-3118, E-mail: nancy.cochran@du.edu. *Application contact:* Stephen Campbell, Director of Admission, 303-871-6973, Fax: 303-871-3118, E-mail: stephen.l.campbell@du.edu. Website: http://www.du.edu/ahss/lamont/index.html

University of Florida, Graduate School, College of The Arts, School of Music, Gainesville, FL 32611. Offers choral conducting (MM); composition (MM, PhD); electronic music (MM); ethnomusicology (MM); instrumental conducting (MM); music (MM, PhD); music education (MM, PhD), including choral conducting (MM), composition (MM), electronic music (MM), ethnomusicology (MM), instrumental conducting (MM), music education (MM), music history and literature (MM), music theory (MM), performance (MM), piano pedagogy (MM); music history and literature (MM, PhD); music theory (MM); performance (MM); sacred music (MM). *Accreditation:* NASM. *Degree requirements:* For master's, variable foreign language requirement, comprehensive exam, thesis, recital; for doctorate, thesis/dissertation. *Entrance requirements:* For master's and doctorate, GRE General Test, audition, minimum GPA of 3.0. Additional exam requirements/recommendations for international students: Required—TOEFL (minimum score 550 paper-based; 80 iBT), IELTS (minimum score 6). Electronic applications accepted.

University of Georgia, Franklin College of Arts and Sciences, Hugh Hodgson School of Music, Athens, GA 30602. Offers composition (MM, DMA); conducting (MM, DMA); music (PhD); music education (MM Ed, Ed D); musicology (MA); performance (MM, DMA). Ed D offered jointly with College of Education. *Accreditation:* NASM. *Degree requirements:* For master's, variable foreign language requirement, thesis (MA); for doctorate, variable foreign language requirement, thesis/dissertation. *Entrance requirements:* For master's and doctorate, GRE General Test. Electronic applications accepted.

University of Hartford, The Hartt School, West Hartford, CT 06117-1599. Offers choral conducting (MM Ed); composition (MM, DMA, Artist Diploma, Diploma); conducting (MM, DMA, Artist Diploma, Diploma), including choral (MM, Diploma), instrumental (MM, Diploma); early childhood education (MM Ed); instrumental conducting (MM Ed); Kodály (MM Ed); music (CAGS); music education (DMA, PhD); music history (MM); music theory (MM); pedagogy (MM Ed); performance (MM, MM Ed, DMA, Artist Diploma, Diploma); research (MM Ed); technology (MM Ed). *Program availability:* Part-time. *Degree requirements:* For master's, variable foreign language requirement, thesis (for some programs), recital; for doctorate, variable foreign language requirement, thesis/dissertation (for some programs), recital; for other advanced degree, recital. *Entrance requirements:* For master's, audition, letters of recommendation; for doctorate, proficiency exam, audition, interview, research paper; for other advanced degree, audition. Additional exam requirements/recommendations for international students: Required—TOEFL. Electronic applications accepted. *Expenses:* Contact institution.

University of Houston, Kathrine G. McGovern College of the Arts, Moores School of Music, Houston, TX 77204. Offers accompanying and chamber music (MM); applied music (MM); composition (MM); music education (DMA); music theory (MM); performance (DMA). *Accreditation:* NASM. *Program availability:* Part-time. *Degree requirements:* For master's, one foreign language, comprehensive exam, recital; for doctorate, one foreign language, comprehensive exam, thesis/dissertation. *Entrance requirements:* For master's, audition, resume, 3 letters of recommendation; for doctorate, writing sample, audition, statement of purpose, resume. Additional exam requirements/recommendations for international students: Required—TOEFL (minimum score 550 paper-based; 79 iBT), IELTS (minimum score 6.5). Electronic applications accepted. *Faculty research:* Twentieth century music, Baroque music, history of music theory, music analysis.

University of Illinois at Urbana–Champaign, Graduate College, College of Fine and Applied Arts, School of Music, Champaign, IL 61820. Offers music (M Mus, AD, DMA); music education (MME, PhD); musicology (PhD). *Accreditation:* NASM.

The University of Iowa, Graduate College, College of Education, Department of Teaching and Learning, Program in Education, Iowa City, IA 52242-1316. Offers art education (MA); developmental reading (MA); elementary education (MA); English education (MA, MAT); foreign and second language education (MAT); foreign language education (MA); foreign language/ESL education (PhD); language, literacy and culture (PhD); mathematics education (MA, MAT, PhD); music education (MM, PhD); science education (MA); secondary education (MA); social studies (MA, PhD). *Degree requirements:* For master's, thesis optional, exam; for doctorate, comprehensive exam, thesis/dissertation. *Entrance requirements:* For master's and doctorate, GRE General Test, minimum GPA of 3.0. Additional exam requirements/recommendations for international students: Required—TOEFL (minimum score 550 paper-based; 81 iBT). Electronic applications accepted.

The University of Kansas, Graduate Studies, School of Music, Program in Music Education, Lawrence, KS 66045. Offers MME, PhD. *Accreditation:* NASM. *Program availability:* Part-time. *Students:* 15 full-time (11 women), 8 part-time (6 women); includes 2 minority (both Asian, non-Hispanic/Latino), 2 international. Average age 34. 19 applicants, 79% accepted, 12 enrolled. In 2017, 8 master's, 3 doctorates awarded. *Entrance requirements:* For master's, GRE General Test, minimum undergraduate GPA of 3.0, video, letters of reference, transcripts; for doctorate, GRE General Test, MEMT Diagnostic Exam, minimum graduate GPA of 3.5, video, reference letters, transcripts, writing sample, proof of professional experience. *Application deadline:* For fall

admission, 12/1 priority date for domestic students, 12/15 priority date for international students. Application fee: $65 ($85 for international students). Electronic applications accepted. *Financial support:* Fellowships, research assistantships, teaching assistantships, institutionally sponsored loans, scholarships/grants, and unspecified assistantships available. Financial award application deadline: 12/15; financial award applicants required to submit FAFSA. *Faculty research:* Philosophy of music and music education; choral/voice pedagogy, choir acoustics; classroom management, teacher stress; the child voice, children's choirs; string pedagogy, history of string education in American public school systems. *Unit head:* Dr. Chris Johnson, Director, 785-864-9633, E-mail: cmj@ku.edu. *Application contact:* Lois Elmer, Administrative Professional, 785-864-2862, Fax: 785-864-9640, E-mail: elmer@ku.edu. Website: http://music.ku.edu/memt

University of Kentucky, Graduate School, College of Fine Arts, Program in Music, Lexington, KY 40506-0032. Offers composition (MM, DMA); conducting (MM, DMA); music education (MM, PhD); music theory (MA, PhD); music therapy (MM); musicology (MA, PhD); performance (MM, DMA); sacred music (MM). *Accreditation:* NASM. *Program availability:* Part-time, evening/weekend. *Degree requirements:* For master's, variable foreign language requirement, comprehensive exam, thesis (for some programs); for doctorate, variable foreign language requirement, comprehensive exam, thesis/dissertation. *Entrance requirements:* For master's, GRE General Test, minimum undergraduate GPA of 2.75; for doctorate, GRE General Test, minimum undergraduate GPA of 2.75, graduate 3.0. Additional exam requirements/recommendations for international students: Required—TOEFL (minimum score 550 paper-based). Electronic applications accepted. *Faculty research:* Musicology, music theory, jazz, music education, performance and conducting.

University of Louisiana at Lafayette, College of the Arts, School of Music, Lafayette, LA 70504. Offers conducting (MM); pedagogy (MM); vocal and instrumental performance (MM). *Accreditation:* NASM. *Degree requirements:* For master's, thesis or alternative. *Entrance requirements:* For master's, GRE General Test, minimum GPA of 2.75. Additional exam requirements/recommendations for international students: Required—TOEFL (minimum score 550 paper-based). Electronic applications accepted. *Faculty research:* Nineteenth century American music, trumpet pedagogy, fifteenth century Renaissance polyphony, Charles Ives.

University of Louisville, Graduate School, College of Education and Human Development, Departments of Early Childhood and Elementary Education, Middle and Secondary Education, and Special Education, Louisville, KY 40292-0001. Offers art education (MAT); autism and applied behavior analysis (Certificate); curriculum and instruction (PhD); early elementary education (MAT); exercise physiology (MS); health and physical education (MAT); health professions education (Certificate); higher education (MA); human resources and organization development (MS); instructional technology (M Ed); interdisciplinary early childhood education (MAT); middle school education (MAT); music education (MAT); secondary education (MAT); special education (MAT); sport administration (MS); teacher leadership (M Ed). *Program availability:* Part-time, evening/weekend. *Students:* 114 full-time (73 women), 173 part-time (114 women); includes 49 minority (19 Black or African American, non-Hispanic/Latino; 5 Asian, non-Hispanic/Latino; 13 Hispanic/Latino; 12 Two or more races, non-Hispanic/Latino), 7 international. Average age 29. 132 applicants, 73% accepted, 57 enrolled. In 2017, 70 master's, 2 doctorates, 2 other advanced degrees awarded. *Application deadline:* For spring admission, 1/1 priority date for international students. Application fee: $65. *Expenses:* Tuition, state resident: full-time $12,246; part-time $681 per credit hour. Tuition, nonresident: full-time $25,486; part-time $1417 per credit hour. *Required fees:* $196. Tuition and fees vary according to course load, program and reciprocity agreements. *Financial support:* Application deadline: 6/1; applicants required to submit FAFSA. *Faculty research:* STEM teaching and learning; content literacy for English language learners; social justice in teacher education; adolescent literacy; mathematics teacher development. *Total annual research expenditures:* $1.7 million. *Unit head:* Dr. Ann E. Larson, Dean, College of Education and Human Development, 502-852-6411, Fax: 502-852-1464, E-mail: ann@louisville.edu. *Application contact:* Betty Hampton, Director of Graduate Student Services, 502-852-5597, Fax: 502-852-1465, E-mail: edadvise@louisville.edu. Website: http://louisville.edu/delphi

University of Louisville, Graduate School, School of Music, Louisville, KY 40292-0001. Offers composition (MM); electronic composition (MM); music education (MME); music history and literature (MM); music performance (MM), including choral conducting, instrumental, jazz composition, jazz performance, orchestral conducting, organ performance, piano pedagogy, piano performance, string pedagogy, vocal performance, wind band performance, wind conducting; music theory (MM). *Accreditation:* NASM. *Program availability:* Part-time. *Students:* 38 full-time (11 women), 39 part-time/adjunct (16 women). *Students:* 51 full-time (14 women), 3 part-time (2 women); includes 8 minority (3 Black or African American, non-Hispanic/Latino; 2 Asian, non-Hispanic/Latino; 2 Hispanic/Latino; 1 Two or more races, non-Hispanic/Latino), 7 international. Average age 26. 73 applicants, 53% accepted, 29 enrolled. In 2017, 29 master's awarded. *Degree requirements:* For master's, variable foreign language requirement, comprehensive exam, thesis (for some programs), recital (for performance), paper or thesis (for music education), major composition (for composition). *Entrance requirements:* For master's, music history and theory entrance exams, jazz history and theory entrance exam (for jazz majors), audition, portfolio. Additional exam requirements/recommendations for international students: Required—TOEFL (minimum score 79 iBT) or IELTS (6.5). Application fee: $60. Electronic applications accepted. *Expenses:* Contact institution. *Financial support:* In 2017–18, 1 fellowship with full tuition reimbursement (averaging $12,000 per year), 12 teaching assistantships with full tuition reimbursements (averaging $12,000 per year) were awarded; Federal Work-Study, scholarships/grants, health care benefits, and unspecified assistantships also available. Financial award application deadline: 3/1. *Faculty research:* Composition, musicology, performance, pedagogy, analysis and theoretical application. *Total annual research expenditures:* $87,500. *Unit head:* Dr. Christopher P. Doane, Dean, 502-852-6907, Fax: 502-852-0520, E-mail: c0doan01@louisville.edu. *Application contact:* Laura Angermeier, Admissions Counselor/Senior Advising Counselor, 502-852-1623, Fax: 502-852-0520, E-mail: leange01@louisville.edu. Website: http://www.louisville.edu/music/

University of Maryland, Baltimore County, The Graduate School, College of Arts, Humanities and Social Sciences, Department of Education, Program in Teaching, Baltimore, MD 21250. Offers early childhood education (MAT); elementary education (MAT); teaching (MAT), including art, biology, chemistry, choral music, classical foreign language, dance, earth/space science, English, instrumental music, mathematics, modern foreign language, physical science, physics, social studies, theatre. *Program availability:* Part-time, evening/weekend. *Faculty:* 24 full-time (9 women), 25 part-time/adjunct (19 women). *Students:* 41 full-time (34 women), 27 part-time (18 women); includes 26 minority (6 Black or African American, non-Hispanic/Latino; 9 Asian, non-Hispanic/Latino; 7 Hispanic/Latino; 1 Native Hawaiian or other Pacific Islander, non-Hispanic/Latino; 3 Two or more races, non-Hispanic/Latino), 2 international. Average age 30. 54 applicants, 83% accepted, 35 enrolled. In 2017, 50 master's awarded. *Degree requirements:* For master's, comprehensive exam (for some programs), thesis

(for some programs). *Entrance requirements:* For master's, PRAXIS Core Examination or GRE (minimum score of 1000), minimum GPA of 3.0. Additional exam requirements/recommendations for international students: Required—TOEFL. *Application deadline:* For fall admission, 6/1 for domestic and international students; for spring admission, 11/1 for domestic and international students. Applications are processed on a rolling basis. Application fee: $50. Electronic applications accepted. *Expenses: Required fees:* $132. *Financial support:* In 2017–18, 8 students received support, including teaching assistantships with tuition reimbursements available (averaging $12,000 per year); career-related internships or fieldwork, Federal Work-Study, scholarships/grants, tuition waivers, and unspecified assistantships also available. Financial award application deadline: 3/15. *Faculty research:* STEM teacher education, culturally sensitive pedagogy, ESOL/bilingual education, early childhood education, language, literacy and culture. *Total annual research expenditures:* $100,000. *Unit head:* Dr. Susan M. Blunck, Graduate Program Director, 410-455-2869, Fax: 410-455-3986, E-mail: blunck@umbc.edu. *Application contact:* Cheryl Johnson, MAT Program Specialist, 410-455-3388, E-mail: blackwel@umbc.edu.
Website: http://www.umbc.edu/education/

University of Maryland, College Park, Academic Affairs, College of Arts and Humanities, School of Music, Program in Music, College Park, MD 20742. Offers M Ed, MA, MM, DMA, Ed D, PhD. *Accreditation:* NASM. *Entrance requirements:* For master's, GRE General Test (for ethnomusicology, historical musicology and music theory), 3 letters of recommendation, audition/interview. Additional exam requirements/recommendations for international students: Required—TOEFL.

University of Massachusetts Amherst, Graduate School, College of Humanities and Fine Arts, Department of Music and Dance, Amherst, MA 01003. Offers collaborative piano (MM); composition (MM); conducting (MM); jazz composition/arranging (MM); music education (MM, PhD); music history (MM); music theory (PhD); performance (MM). *Accreditation:* NASM. *Program availability:* Part-time. Terminal master's awarded for partial completion of doctoral program. *Degree requirements:* For master's, thesis or alternative; for doctorate, comprehensive exam, thesis/dissertation. *Entrance requirements:* For master's and doctorate, placement tests, original scores, research, audition or tape. Additional exam requirements/recommendations for international students: Required—TOEFL (minimum score 550 paper-based; 80 iBT), IELTS (minimum score 6.5). Electronic applications accepted.

University of Massachusetts Lowell, College of Fine Arts, Humanities and Social Sciences, Department of Music, Lowell, MA 01854. Offers music education (MM). *Accreditation:* NASM. *Program availability:* Part-time. *Degree requirements:* For master's, one foreign language, thesis. *Entrance requirements:* For master's, MAT, audition. Electronic applications accepted.

University of Memphis, Graduate School, College of Communication and Fine Arts, Rudi E. Scheidt School of Music, Memphis, TN 38152. Offers composition (M Mu, DMA); conducting (M Mu, DMA); jazz and studio music (M Mu); music education (M Mu, PhD); music theory (DCC); musicology (PhD); Orff-Schulwerk (M Mu); pedagogy (M Mu); performance (M Mu, DMA). *Accreditation:* NASM. *Program availability:* Part-time. *Faculty:* 32 full-time (8 women), 5 part-time/adjunct (1 woman). *Students:* 62 full-time (27 women), 46 part-time (21 women); includes 25 minority (11 Black or African American, non-Hispanic/Latino; 2 Asian, non-Hispanic/Latino; 8 Hispanic/Latino; 4 Two or more races, non-Hispanic/Latino), 10 international. Average age 31. 71 applicants, 82% accepted, 28 enrolled. In 2017, 22 master's, 7 doctorates awarded. Terminal master's awarded for partial completion of doctoral program. *Degree requirements:* For master's, variable foreign language requirement, comprehensive exam, thesis or alternative; for doctorate, one foreign language, comprehensive exam, thesis/dissertation, qualifying exam. *Entrance requirements:* For master's, audition; for doctorate, GRE General Test or MAT, proficiency exam, audition, work sample, master's degree. Additional exam requirements/recommendations for international students: Required—TOEFL (minimum score 550 paper-based; 79 iBT). *Application deadline:* For fall admission, 8/1 for domestic students; for spring admission, 12/1 for domestic students. Applications are processed on a rolling basis. Application fee: $35 ($60 for international students). Electronic applications accepted. *Expenses:* Contact institution. *Financial support:* In 2017–18, 73 students received support, including 26 research assistantships with tuition reimbursements available (averaging $10,250 per year), 26 teaching assistantships with tuition reimbursements available (averaging $11,288 per year); Federal Work-Study, scholarships/grants, and unspecified assistantships also available. Financial award application deadline: 2/1; financial award applicants required to submit FAFSA. *Faculty research:* Spanish Renaissance, twentieth-century music, Project OPTIMUS, composition, musical performance, regional music, performance, performance practice, composition. *Unit head:* Dr. John Chiego, Director, 901-678-3773, Fax: 901-678-3096, E-mail: jchiego@memphis.edu. *Application contact:* Dr. Dave Spencer, Assistant Director for Graduate Studies, 901-678-3779, Fax: 901-678-3096, E-mail: dspencer@memphis.edu.
Website: http://www.memphis.edu/music/

University of Miami, Graduate School, Frost School of Music, Department of Music Education and Music Therapy, Coral Gables, FL 33124. Offers music education (MM, PhD, Spec M); music therapy (MM). *Accreditation:* NASM. *Degree requirements:* For master's, thesis; for doctorate, thesis/dissertation, 2 research tools; for Spec M, thesis, research project. *Entrance requirements:* For master's and doctorate, GRE General Test. Additional exam requirements/recommendations for international students: Required—TOEFL (minimum score 550 paper-based; 59 iBT). Electronic applications accepted. *Faculty research:* Motivation, quantitative research, early childhood, instrumental music, elementary music.

University of Michigan, Rackham Graduate School, School of Music, Theatre, and Dance, Program in Music Education, Ann Arbor, MI 48109-2085. Offers MM, PhD, Spec M. *Accreditation:* NASM; TEAC. *Degree requirements:* For doctorate, thesis/dissertation, oral and preliminary exams. *Entrance requirements:* For doctorate, MAT, writing sample, portfolio. Additional exam requirements/recommendations for international students: Required—TOEFL. Electronic applications accepted. *Expenses:* Tuition, state resident: full-time $22,368; part-time $1201 per credit hour. Tuition, nonresident: full-time $45,156; part-time $2467 per credit hour. *Required fees:* $376 per term. Tuition and fees vary according to course load, degree level and program.

University of Minnesota, Duluth, Graduate School, School of Fine Arts, Department of Music, Duluth, MN 55812-2496. Offers music education (MM); performance (MM). *Accreditation:* NASM. *Program availability:* Part-time. *Degree requirements:* For master's, comprehensive exam, thesis (for some programs), recital (MM in performance). *Entrance requirements:* For master's, audition, minimum GPA of 3.0, sample of written work, interview, bachelor's degree in music, video of teaching. Additional exam requirements/recommendations for international students: Required—TOEFL (minimum score 550 paper-based). *Faculty research:* Band composition, music aesthetics, learning theory, value theory, music advocacy.

University of Missouri, Office of Research and Graduate Studies, College of Education, Department of Learning, Teaching and Curriculum, Columbia, MO 65211. Offers agricultural education (M Ed, PhD, Ed S); art education (M Ed, PhD, Ed S); business and office education (M Ed, PhD, Ed S); early childhood education (M Ed,

PhD, Ed S); elementary education (M Ed, PhD, Ed S); English education (M Ed, PhD, Ed S); foreign language education (M Ed, PhD, Ed S); health education and promotion (M Ed, PhD); learning and instruction (M Ed); marketing education (M Ed, PhD, Ed S); mathematics education (M Ed, PhD, Ed S); music education (M Ed, PhD, Ed S); reading education (M Ed, PhD, Ed S); science education (M Ed, PhD, Ed S); social studies education (M Ed, PhD, Ed S); vocational education (M Ed, PhD, Ed S). *Program availability:* Part-time. Terminal master's awarded for partial completion of doctoral program. *Degree requirements:* For doctorate, thesis/dissertation. *Entrance requirements:* For master's and Ed S, GRE General Test or MAT, minimum GPA of 3.0; for doctorate, GRE General Test, minimum GPA of 3.0. Additional exam requirements/recommendations for international students: Required—TOEFL (minimum score 600 paper-based; 100 iBT). Electronic applications accepted.

University of Missouri–Kansas City, Conservatory of Music and Dance, Kansas City, MO 64110-2499. Offers composition (MM, DMA); conducting (MM, DMA); music (MA); music education (MME, PhD); music history and literature (MM); music theory (MM); music therapy (MA); performance (MM, DMA). PhD (interdisciplinary) offered through the School of Graduate Studies. *Accreditation:* NASM. *Program availability:* Part-time. *Degree requirements:* For master's, variable foreign language requirement, comprehensive exam, thesis (for some programs); for doctorate, variable foreign language requirement, comprehensive exam, thesis/dissertation or alternative. *Entrance requirements:* For master's, minimum GPA of 3.0 in major, auditions (for MM in performance); for doctorate, minimum graduate GPA of 3.5, auditions (for DMA in performance), portfolio of compositions. Additional exam requirements/recommendations for international students: Required—TOEFL (minimum score 550 paper-based; 80 iBT). *Faculty research:* Electro-acoustic composition, affective music responses, American music theatre, Russian choral music, music therapy and Alzheimer's.

University of Nebraska at Kearney, College of Fine Arts and Humanities, Department of Music, Kearney, NE 68849-0001. Offers music education (MA Ed). *Accreditation:* NASM; NCATE. *Program availability:* Part-time, evening/weekend, 100% online. *Degree requirements:* For master's, comprehensive exam, thesis optional. *Entrance requirements:* For master's, undergraduate degree in music, resume, philosophy of teaching, three letters of recommendation. Additional exam requirements/recommendations for international students: Recommended—TOEFL (minimum score 550 paper-based; 79 iBT), IELTS (minimum score 6.5). Electronic applications accepted. *Faculty research:* Contemporary American music, musical theater, opera, woodwind performance and pedagogy, percussion pedagogy, historic and contemporary American piano, dramatic mezzo-soprano, violin performance, piano performance and pedagogy, music composition, opera, healing effects of music, Chamber music, diction.

University of Nebraska–Lincoln, Graduate College, College of Fine and Performing Arts, School of Music, Lincoln, NE 68588. Offers composition (MM, DMA); conducting (MM, DMA); music education (MM, PhD); music history (MM); music theory (MM); performance (MM, DMA); piano pedagogy (MM); woodwind specialties (MM). *Accreditation:* NASM. *Degree requirements:* For master's, thesis optional; for doctorate, comprehensive exam, thesis/dissertation. *Entrance requirements:* For master's and doctorate, audition. Additional exam requirements/recommendations for international students: Required—TOEFL. Electronic applications accepted. *Faculty research:* Mozart, Tchaikovsky, Josquin des Prez, practice of J.S. Bach's organ works, instructional strategies in music education.

University of New Mexico, Graduate Studies, College of Fine Arts, Program in Music, Albuquerque, NM 87131-0001. Offers collaborative piano (M Mu); conducting (M Mu); music education (M Mu); music history and literature (M Mu); performance (M Mu); theory and composition (M Mu). *Accreditation:* NASM. *Program availability:* Part-time. *Students:* Average age 29. 75 applicants, 76% accepted, 36 enrolled. In 2017, 30 master's awarded. *Degree requirements:* For master's, variable foreign language requirement, comprehensive exam, thesis (for some programs), recital (for some programs). *Entrance requirements:* For master's, placement exams in music history and theory. Additional exam requirements/recommendations for international students: Required—TOEFL (minimum score 550 paper-based). *Application deadline:* For fall admission, 7/1 for domestic students, 5/1 for international students; for spring admission, 11/1 for domestic students, 10/1 for international students. Applications are processed on a rolling basis. Application fee: $50. Electronic applications accepted. *Financial support:* Research assistantships, teaching assistantships, Federal Work-Study, scholarships/grants, and unspecified assistantships available. Support available to part-time students. Financial award application deadline: 2/1; financial award applicants required to submit FAFSA. *Faculty research:* Opera, twentieth-century and contemporary music, performance, conducting. *Unit head:* Dr. Steven Block, Chair, 505-277-2127, Fax: 505-277-4202, E-mail: sblock@unm.edu. *Application contact:* Colleen M. Sheinberg, Graduate Coordinator, 505-277-8401, Fax: 505-277-4202, E-mail: colleens@unm.edu.
Website: http://music.unm.edu/

The University of North Carolina at Chapel Hill, Graduate School, School of Education, Program in Secondary Education, Chapel Hill, NC 27599. Offers English (Grades 9-12) (MAT); English as a second language (MAT); French (Grades K-12) (MAT); German (Grades K-12) (MAT); Japanese (Grades K-12) (MAT); Latin (Grades 9-12) (MAT); mathematics (Grades 9-12) (MAT); music (Grades K-12) (MAT); science (Grades 9-12) (MAT); social studies (Grades 9-12) (MAT); Spanish (Grades K-12) (MAT). *Accreditation:* NCATE. *Degree requirements:* For master's, comprehensive exam. *Entrance requirements:* For master's, GRE General Test, minimum GPA of 3.0 during last 2 years of undergraduate course work. Additional exam requirements/recommendations for international students: Required—TOEFL (minimum score 550 paper-based). Electronic applications accepted.

The University of North Carolina at Greensboro, Graduate School, School of Music, Theatre and Dance, Greensboro, NC 27412-5001. Offers composition (MM); dance (MA, MFA); education (MM); music education (PhD); performance (MM, DMA); theatre (M Ed, MFA), including acting (MFA), design (MFA), directing (MFA), theatre education (M Ed), theatre for youth (MFA); theory (MM). *Accreditation:* NASM. *Degree requirements:* For master's, variable foreign language requirement, thesis (for some programs), recital; for doctorate, comprehensive exam, thesis/dissertation, diagnostic exam, recital. *Entrance requirements:* For master's, GRE General Test, NTE, audition; for doctorate, GRE General Test, GRE Subject Test (music), audition. Additional exam requirements/recommendations for international students: Required—TOEFL. Electronic applications accepted.

University of North Dakota, Graduate School, College of Arts and Sciences, Department of Music, Grand Forks, ND 58202. Offers music (MM); music education (PhD). *Accreditation:* NASM. *Program availability:* Part-time. *Degree requirements:* For master's, comprehensive exam, thesis or alternative. *Entrance requirements:* For master's, minimum GPA of 3.0. Additional exam requirements/recommendations for international students: Required—TOEFL (minimum score 550 paper-based; 79 iBT), IELTS (minimum score 6.5). Electronic applications accepted.

University of Northern Colorado, Graduate School, College of Performing and Visual Arts, School of Music, Greeley, CO 80639. Offers collaborative piano (MM, DA); composition (DA); conducting (MM, DA); instrumental performance (MM); jazz studies (MM, DA); music education (MM, DA); music history and literature (MM, DA); music theory and composition (MM); performance (DA); vocal performance (MM). *Accreditation:* NASM; NCATE (one or more programs are accredited). *Program availability:* Part-time. *Degree requirements:* For master's, comprehensive exam, thesis or alternative; for doctorate, comprehensive exam, thesis/dissertation. *Entrance requirements:* For master's, audition; for doctorate, GRE General Test, audition, 3 letters of recommendation. Electronic applications accepted.

University of Northern Iowa, Graduate College, College of Humanities, Arts and Sciences, School of Music, MM Program in Jazz Pedagogy, Cedar Falls, IA 50614. Offers MM. *Degree requirements:* For master's, comprehensive exam. *Entrance requirements:* For master's, audition, interview, essay.

University of Northern Iowa, Graduate College, College of Humanities, Arts and Sciences, School of Music, MM Program in Music Education, Cedar Falls, IA 50614. Offers MM. *Accreditation:* NASM. *Program availability:* Part-time, evening/weekend. *Degree requirements:* For master's, comprehensive exam, thesis or alternative. *Entrance requirements:* For master's, written diagnostic exam in theory, music history, expository writing skills, and in the area of claimed competency, portfolio, tape recordings of compositions, in-person auditions, minimum GPA of 3.0. Additional exam requirements/recommendations for international students: Required—TOEFL (minimum score 500 paper-based; 61 iBT). Electronic applications accepted.

University of Northern Iowa, Graduate College, College of Humanities, Arts and Sciences, School of Music, MM Program in Piano Performance and Pedagogy, Cedar Falls, IA 50614. Offers MM.

University of North Texas, Robert B. Toulouse School of Graduate Studies, Denton, TX 76203-5459. Offers accounting (MS); applied anthropology (MA, MS); applied behavior analysis (Certificate); applied geography (MA); applied technology and performance improvement (M Ed, MS); art education (MA); art history (MA); art museum education (Certificate); arts leadership (Certificate); audiology (Au D); behavior analysis (MS); behavioral science (PhD); biochemistry and molecular biology (MA, MS); biomedical engineering (MS); business analysis (MS); chemistry (MS); clinical health psychology (PhD); communication studies (MA, MS); computer engineering (MS); computer science (MS); counseling (M Ed, MS), including clinical mental health counseling (MS), college and university counseling, elementary school counseling, secondary school counseling; creative writing (MA); criminal justice (MS); curriculum and instruction (M Ed); decision sciences (MBA); design (MA, MFA), including fashion design (MFA), innovation studies, interior design (MFA); early childhood studies (MS); economics (MS); educational leadership (M Ed, Ed D); educational psychology (MS, PhD), including family studies (MS), gifted and talented (MS), human development (MS), learning and cognition (MS), research, measurement and evaluation (MS); electrical engineering (MS); emergency management (MPA); engineering technology (MS); English (MA); English as a second language (MA); environmental science (MS); finance (MBA, MS); financial management (MPA); French (MA); health services management (MBA); higher education (M Ed, Ed D); history (MS); hospitality management (MS); human resources management (MPA); information science (MS); information systems (PhD); information technologies (MBA); interdisciplinary studies (MA, MS); international studies (MA); international sustainable tourism (MS); jazz studies (MM); journalism (MA, MJ, Graduate Certificate), including interactive and virtual digital communication (Graduate Certificate), narrative journalism (Graduate Certificate), public relations (Graduate Certificate); kinesiology (MS); linguistics (MA); local government management (MPA); logistics (PhD); logistics and supply chain management (MBA); long-term care, senior housing, and aging services (MA); management (PhD); marketing (MBA); mathematics (MA, MS); mechanical and energy engineering (MS, PhD); music (MA), including ethnomusicology, music theory, musicology, performance; music composition (PhD); music education (MM Ed, PhD); nonprofit management (MPA); operations and supply chain management (MBA); performance (MM, DMA); philosophy (MA); political science (MA); professional and technical communication (MA); radio, television and film (MA, MFA); rehabilitation counseling (Certificate); sociology (MA); Spanish (MA); special education (M Ed); speech-language pathology (MA); strategic management (MBA); studio art (MFA); teaching (M Ed); MBA/MS. *Program availability:* Part-time, evening/weekend, online learning. Terminal master's awarded for partial completion of doctoral program. *Degree requirements:* For master's, variable foreign language requirement, comprehensive exam (for some programs), thesis (for some programs); for doctorate, variable foreign language requirement, comprehensive exam (for some programs), thesis/dissertation; for other advanced degree, variable foreign language requirement, comprehensive exam (for some programs). *Entrance requirements:* For master's and doctorate, GRE, GMAT. Additional exam requirements/recommendations for international students: Required—TOEFL (minimum score 550 paper-based; 79 iBT). Electronic applications accepted.

University of Oklahoma, Weitzenhoffer Family College of Fine Arts, School of Music, Norman, OK 73019. Offers choral conducting (M Mus), including church music (M Mus, DMA), standard (M Mus, DMA, PhD); composition (M Mus, DMA); conducting (M Mus Ed, DMA), including choral, church music (M Mus, DMA), instrumental (M Mus Ed), orchestral (DMA), wind (DMA); general (M Mus Ed), including Kodaly concepts (M Mus Ed, PhD), vocal/general; instrumental (M Mus Ed), including primary instrument, secondary instrument; instrumental conducting (M Mus); music education (PhD), including conducting, Kodaly concepts (M Mus Ed, PhD), piano pedagogy, standard (M Mus, DMA, PhD); music performance (Graduate Certificate); music theory (M Mus); musicology (M Mus); organ (M Mus, DMA), including church music, organ technology (M Mus), standard (M Mus, DMA, PhD); piano (M Mus, DMA), including performance, performance and pedagogy; piano pedagogy (M Mus Ed); voice (M Mus, DMA), including opera (M Mus); performance; wind/percussion/string instruments (M Mus, DMA). *Accreditation:* NASM. *Faculty:* 56 full-time (13 women). *Students:* 104 full-time (43 women), 70 part-time (29 women); includes 26 minority (3 Black or African American, non-Hispanic/Latino; 5 American Indian or Alaska Native, non-Hispanic/Latino; 5 Asian, non-Hispanic/Latino; 8 Hispanic/Latino; 5 Two or more races, non-Hispanic/Latino), 26 international. Average age 29. 182 applicants, 42% accepted, 48 enrolled. In 2017, 41 master's, 15 doctorates awarded. *Degree requirements:* For master's, variable foreign language requirement, comprehensive exam (for some programs), thesis (for some programs), final recital (for M Mus performance, conducting, and composition degrees); for doctorate, variable foreign language requirement, comprehensive exam, thesis/dissertation, three recitals and/or workshops (two recitals for DMA in composition); for Graduate Certificate, variable foreign language requirement, two recitals. *Entrance requirements:* For master's, bachelor's degree in music, music education, or the equivalent; transcripts; resume; personal statement; 3 letters of recommendation; audition and/or other practical application materials as appropriate to intended degree; sample of scholarly writing (for M Mus in musicology and in music theory); for doctorate, master's degree in music, music education, or the equivalent; transcripts; resume; personal statement; 3 letters of recommendation; sample of scholarly writing; audition and/or other practical application materials as appropriate to intended degree; for Graduate Certificate, bachelor's degree in music,

music education, or the equivalent; transcripts; resume; personal statement; 3 letters of recommendation; audition. Additional exam requirements/recommendations for international students: Required—TOEFL (minimum score 79 iBT) or IELTS (minimum score 6.5). *Application deadline:* For fall admission, 2/1 for domestic and international students; for spring admission, 10/1 for domestic students, 9/1 for international students; for summer admission, 2/1 for domestic and international students. Applications are processed on a rolling basis. Application fee: $50 ($100 for international students). Electronic applications accepted. *Expenses:* Tuition, state resident: full-time $5119; part-time $213.30 per credit hour. Tuition, nonresident: full-time $19,778; part-time $824.10 per credit hour. *Required fees:* $3458; $133.55 per credit hour. $126.50 per semester. *Financial support:* In 2017–18, 123 students received support, including 2 fellowships with full tuition reimbursements available (averaging $5,000 per year), 35 research assistantships with full tuition reimbursements available (averaging $10,515 per year), 62 teaching assistantships with full tuition reimbursements available (averaging $10,452 per year); health care benefits, tuition waivers, and unspecified assistantships also available. Financial award application deadline: 6/1; financial award applicants required to submit FAFSA. *Faculty research:* Piano pedagogy, performance practice, music education, musicology, music theory. *Unit head:* Dr. Roland Barrett, Director, 405-325-2081, Fax: 405-325-7574, E-mail: rcbarrett@ou.edu. *Application contact:* Jan Russell, Graduate Admissions and Recruiting Advisor, 405-325-5393, Fax: 405-325-7574, E-mail: jrussell@ou.edu.
Website: http://music.ou.edu

University of Oregon, Graduate School, School of Music, Program in Music Education, Eugene, OR 97403. Offers M Mus, DMA, PhD. *Accreditation:* NASM. *Program availability:* Part-time. Terminal master's awarded for partial completion of doctoral program. *Degree requirements:* For master's, variable foreign language requirement, thesis (for some programs); for doctorate, one foreign language, comprehensive exam, thesis/dissertation. *Entrance requirements:* For master's, minimum GPA of 3.0, videotape or interview; for doctorate, GRE General Test, minimum GPA of 3.0, videotape or interview. Additional exam requirements/recommendations for international students: Required—TOEFL. *Faculty research:* Psalms of DeLasso, stress and muscular tension in stringed instrument performance, piano music of Stravinsky, learning aptitudes in elementary music.

University of Ottawa, Faculty of Graduate and Postdoctoral Studies, Faculty of Arts, Department of Music, Ottawa, ON K1N 6N5, Canada. Offers music (M Mus, MA); orchestral studies (Certificate); piano pedagogy research (Certificate). *Degree requirements:* For master's, thesis optional. *Entrance requirements:* For master's, honors degree or equivalent, minimum B+ average. Electronic applications accepted. *Faculty research:* Performance, theory, musicology.

University of Rhode Island, Graduate School, College of Arts and Sciences, Department of Music, Kingston, RI 02881. Offers music education (MM), including composition, conducting, performance, thesis; music performance (MM), including composition, conducting, voice or instrument. Program offered in partnership with School of Education. *Accreditation:* NASM. *Program availability:* Part-time. *Faculty:* 12 full-time (6 women). *Students:* 11 full-time (4 women), 1 (woman) part-time; includes 2 minority (both Black or African American, non-Hispanic/Latino). 12 applicants, 75% accepted, 6 enrolled. In 2017, 3 master's awarded. *Entrance requirements:* For master's, 2 letters of recommendation, audition. Additional exam requirements/recommendations for international students: Required—TOEFL. *Application deadline:* For fall admission, 7/15 for domestic students, 2/1 for international students; for spring admission, 11/15 for domestic students, 7/15 for international students. Application fee: $65. Electronic applications accepted. *Expenses:* Tuition, state resident: full-time $12,706; part-time $786 per credit. Tuition, nonresident: full-time $25,216; part-time $1401 per credit. *Required fees:* $1598; $45 per credit. One-time fee: $30 part-time. *Financial support:* In 2017–18, 3 teaching assistantships with tuition reimbursements (averaging $18,054 per year) were awarded. Financial award application deadline: 2/1; financial award applicants required to submit FAFSA. *Unit head:* Dr. Mark Conley, Chair, 401-874-2431, E-mail: mconley@uri.edu. *Application contact:* Dr. Joe Parillo, Director of Graduate Studies, 401-874-2431, E-mail: jmparillo@uri.edu.
Website: https://web.uri.edu/music/

University of Rochester, Eastman School of Music, Programs in Music Education, Rochester, NY 14627. Offers MA, MM, DMA, PhD.

University of St. Thomas, College of Arts and Sciences, Graduate Programs in Music Education, St. Paul, MN 55105-1096. Offers choral (MA); instrumental (MA); Kodaly (MA); leadership in music education (Ed D); Orff Schulwerk (MA); piano pedagogy (MA). *Accreditation:* NASM; NCATE. *Program availability:* Part-time. *Faculty:* 11 full-time (5 women), 16 part-time/adjunct (9 women). *Students:* 153 part-time (117 women). 3 applicants, 100% accepted, 3 enrolled. In 2017, 19 master's awarded. *Degree requirements:* For master's, comprehensive exam, thesis, music history theory and diagnostic exam, piano recital (for piano pedagogy students), oral exam. *Entrance requirements:* For master's, performance assessment hearing, interview. Additional exam requirements/recommendations for international students: Required—TOEFL (minimum score 550 paper-based; 80 iBT). *Application deadline:* For fall admission, 7/1 for domestic and international students; for winter admission, 12/1 for domestic and international students; for spring admission, 4/1 for domestic and international students. Applications are processed on a rolling basis. Application fee: $0. Electronic applications accepted. *Expenses:* $875.50 per credit. *Financial support:* In 2017–18, 23 students received support. Federal Work-Study, institutionally sponsored loans, and scholarships/grants available. Financial award application deadline: 4/1; financial award applicants required to submit FAFSA. *Faculty research:* Kodaly, choral, piano pedagogy, Orff, instrumental, world music. *Unit head:* Dr. Douglas C. Orzolek, Director, 651-962-5878, Fax: 651-962-5886, E-mail: dcorzolek@stthomas.edu. *Application contact:* Bev Johnson, Program Coordinator, 651-962-5870, Fax: 651-962-5886, E-mail: bhjohnson@stthomas.edu.
Website: http://www.stthomas.edu/music/graduate

University of South Alabama, College of Arts and Sciences, Department of Music, Mobile, AL 36688. Offers collaborative keyboard (MM); music education (MM); performance (MM). *Faculty:* 4 full-time (1 woman). *Students:* 2 full-time (both women), 2 part-time (0 women). Average age 34. 4 applicants. *Degree requirements:* For master's, comprehensive exam, final project. *Entrance requirements:* For master's, GRE/GMAT, undergraduate degree in music with minimum GPA of 3.0, official transcript, resume, 3 recommendation letters; teaching certificate (for music education). Additional exam requirements/recommendations for international students: Required—TOEFL (minimum score 525 paper-based; 71 iBT). *Application deadline:* For fall admission, 7/1 priority date for domestic students, 6/1 priority date for international students; for spring admission, 12/1 priority date for domestic students, 11/1 priority date for international students; for summer admission, 5/1 priority date for domestic students, 4/1 priority date for international students. Applications are processed on a rolling basis. Application fee: $35. Electronic applications accepted. *Expenses:* Tuition, state resident: full-time $10,104; part-time $421 per semester hour. Tuition, nonresident: full-time $20,208; part-time $842 per semester hour. *Financial support:* Fellowships, research assistantships, teaching assistantships, career-related internships or fieldwork, Federal Work-Study, institutionally sponsored loans, scholarships/grants, and unspecified

assistantships available. Support available to part-time students. Financial award application deadline: 3/31; financial award applicants required to submit FAFSA. *Unit head:* Dr. Greg Gruner, Chair, Music, 251-460-6804, Fax: 251-460-7328, E-mail: ggruner@southalabama.edu. *Application contact:* Dr. Jeannette Fresne, Graduate Coordinator, Music, 251-460-6697, Fax: 251-460-7328, E-mail: jfresne@ southalabama.edu.
Website: http://www.southalabama.edu/colleges/music/

University of South Carolina, The Graduate School, School of Music, Columbia, SC 29208. Offers composition (MM, DMA); conducting (MM, DMA); jazz studies (MM); music education (MM Ed, PhD); music history (MM); music performance (Certificate); music theory (MM); opera theater (MM); performance (MM, DMA); piano pedagogy (MM, DMA). *Accreditation:* NASM. *Program availability:* Part-time. *Degree requirements:* For master's, 5 foreign languages, comprehensive exam, thesis (for some programs); for doctorate, one foreign language, comprehensive exam, thesis/dissertation; for Certificate, recitals. *Entrance requirements:* For master's and doctorate, GRE General Test or MAT, music diagnostic exam. Additional exam requirements/recommendations for international students: Required—TOEFL (minimum score 570 paper-based). Electronic applications accepted. *Expenses:* Contact institution. *Faculty research:* Music skills in pre-school children, evaluation of school performing ensembles.

University of South Dakota, Graduate School, College of Fine Arts, Department of Music, Vermillion, SD 57069. Offers collaborative piano (MM); conducting (MM); history of musical instruments (MM); music education (MM); music history (MM); music performance (MM). *Accreditation:* NASM. *Degree requirements:* For master's, thesis or alternative. *Entrance requirements:* For master's, minimum GPA of 2.7, audition or performance tape. Additional exam requirements/recommendations for international students: Required—TOEFL (minimum score 550 paper-based; 79 iBT). *Application deadline:* Applications are processed on a rolling basis. Application fee: $35. Electronic applications accepted. *Financial support:* Research assistantships with partial tuition reimbursements, teaching assistantships with partial tuition reimbursements, and scholarships/grants available. Financial award applicants required to submit FAFSA. *Application contact:* Graduate School, 605-658-6140, Fax: 605-677-6118, E-mail: grad@usd.edu.
Website: http://www.usd.edu/fine-arts/music

University of Southern California, Graduate School, Thornton School of Music, Los Angeles, CA 90089. Offers brass performance (MM, DMA, Graduate Certificate); choral and sacred music (MM, DMA); classical guitar (MM, DMA, Graduate Certificate); composition (MM, DMA); early music (MA, DMA); harp performance (MM, DMA, Graduate Certificate); historical musicology (PhD); jazz studies (MM, DMA, Graduate Certificate); keyboard collaborative arts (MM, DMA, Graduate Certificate); music education (MM, DMA); organ performance (MM, DMA, Graduate Certificate); percussion performance (MM, DMA, Graduate Certificate); piano performance (MM, DMA, Graduate Certificate); scoring for motion pictures and television (Graduate Certificate); strings performance (MM, DMA, Graduate Certificate); studio jazz guitar (MM, DMA, Graduate Certificate); teaching music (MA); vocal arts (classical voice/opera) (MM, DMA, Graduate Certificate); woodwind performance (MM, DMA, Graduate Certificate). *Program availability:* Part-time, evening/weekend. Terminal master's awarded for partial completion of doctoral program. *Degree requirements:* For master's, variable foreign language requirement, comprehensive exam (for some programs), thesis (for some programs); for doctorate, variable foreign language requirement, comprehensive exam, thesis/dissertation (for some programs). *Entrance requirements:* For master's, GRE (for MA in early music and MM in music education); for doctorate, GRE (for DMA). Additional exam requirements/recommendations for international students: Required—TOEFL (minimum score 560 paper-based; 83 iBT). Electronic applications accepted. *Expenses:* Contact institution. *Faculty research:* Early Modern musical improvisation and composition, maternal sound stimulation of the premature infant, physiological characteristics of jazz guitarists, the musical experience of the very young child, electronic music.

University of Southern Maine, College of Arts, Humanities, and Social Sciences, School of Music, Portland, ME 04103. Offers composition (MM); conducting (MM); jazz studies (MM); music education (MM); performance (MM). *Accreditation:* NASM.

University of Southern Mississippi, College of Arts and Letters, School of Music, Hattiesburg, MS 39406-0001. Offers conducting (DMA); music education (MME); performance and pedagogy (DMA); piano accompanying (MM); theory (MM); woodwind performance and pedagogy (MM). *Accreditation:* NASM. *Program availability:* Blended/hybrid learning. *Students:* 37 full-time (14 women), 2 part-time (0 women). 89 applicants, 74% accepted, 39 enrolled. In 2017, 3 master's, 1 doctorate awarded. Terminal master's awarded for partial completion of doctoral program. *Degree requirements:* For master's, comprehensive exam, thesis (for some programs); for doctorate, comprehensive exam, thesis/dissertation. *Entrance requirements:* For master's, GRE General Test, minimum GPA of 2.75 in last 60 hours; for doctorate, GRE General Test, minimum GPA of 3.5. Additional exam requirements/recommendations for international students: Required—TOEFL, IELTS. *Application deadline:* For fall admission, 6/1 for domestic students; for spring admission, 11/1 for domestic students; for summer admission, 3/1 for domestic students. Applications are processed on a rolling basis. Application fee: $60. *Expenses:* Tuition, state resident: full-time $3830. *Financial support:* Fellowships with full tuition reimbursements, research assistantships, teaching assistantships with full tuition reimbursements, Federal Work-Study, institutionally sponsored loans, scholarships/grants, health care benefits, tuition waivers (partial), and unspecified assistantships available. Financial award application deadline: 2/1; financial award applicants required to submit FAFSA. *Faculty research:* Music theory, composition, music performance. *Unit head:* Dr. Richard Kravchak, Director, 601-266-5543, Fax: 601-266-6427.
Website: https://www.usm.edu/music

University of South Florida, College of The Arts, School of Music, Tampa, FL 33620-9951. Offers music (MM, PhD), including chamber music (MM); choral conducting (MM); composition (MM); electro-acoustic music (MM); instrumental conducting (MM); jazz composition (MM); jazz performance (MM); music education (PhD); performance (MM); piano pedagogy (MM); theory (MM); music education (MA). *Accreditation:* NASM. *Program availability:* Part-time, evening/weekend. *Faculty:* 27 full-time (8 women), 1 part-time/adjunct (0 women). *Students:* 62 full-time (28 women), 20 part-time (7 women); includes 13 minority (3 Black or African American, non-Hispanic/Latino; 1 Asian, non-Hispanic/Latino; 7 Hispanic/Latino; 2 Two or more races, non-Hispanic/Latino), 21 international. Average age 30. 59 applicants, 61% accepted, 27 enrolled. In 2017, 27 master's, 2 doctorates awarded. *Degree requirements:* For master's, comprehensive exam, thesis optional; for doctorate, comprehensive exam, thesis/dissertation. *Entrance requirements:* For master's, minimum GPA of 3.0 in upper-division courses and music courses for bachelor's degree; resume; three letters of recommendation; at least 2 years of K-12 music teaching experience (for MA in music education); audition or interview (for MM); for doctorate, GRE General Test, master's degree from accredited institution with minimum GPA of 3.5, 3.0 in upper-division undergraduate courses; at least 2 years of K-12 music teaching experience; interview with faculty; 3 letters of recommendation; academic writing sample; curriculum vitae; personal goals statement; 15-20 minute video of applicant teaching music. Additional exam requirements/recommendations for international students: Required—TOEFL (minimum score 550 paper-based; 79 iBT) or

IELTS (minimum score 6.5). *Application deadline:* For fall admission, 2/15 priority date for domestic students, 2/1 for international students; for spring admission, 10/15 for domestic students, 9/15 for international students; for summer admission, 2/15 for domestic students, 1/15 for international students. Application fee: $30. Electronic applications accepted. *Financial support:* In 2017–18, 39 students received support, including 1 research assistantship with tuition reimbursement available (averaging $15,724 per year), 46 teaching assistantships with tuition reimbursements available (averaging $10,099 per year); unspecified assistantships also available. Financial award application deadline: 2/15. *Faculty research:* Music education: alternate methods, community collaboration, contemporary changes, early childhood, general music, international perspectives, multicultural issues, technology, teacher behaviors, philosophy, psychology, sociology; music: chamber music, composition, conducting, jazz studies, music performance, music theory, pedagogy, electronic music. *Total annual research expenditures:* $43,461. *Unit head:* Dr. Karen Bryan, Director, 813-974-2311, Fax: 813-974-8721, E-mail: kmbryan@usf.edu. *Application contact:* Dr. David Williams, Associate Director/Associate Professor of Music Education, 813-974-9166, Fax: 813-974-8721, E-mail: davidw@usf.edu.
Website: http://music.arts.usf.edu/

The University of Tennessee, Graduate School, College of Arts and Sciences, School of Music, Knoxville, TN 37996. Offers accompanying (MM); choral conducting (MM); composition (MM); instrumental conducting (MM); jazz (MM); music education (MM); music theory (MM); musicology (MM); performance (MM); piano pedagogy and literature (MM). *Accreditation:* NASM. *Program availability:* Part-time. *Degree requirements:* For master's, thesis (for some programs). *Entrance requirements:* For master's, audition, minimum GPA of 2.7. Additional exam requirements/recommendations for international students: Required—TOEFL. Electronic applications accepted.

The University of Tennessee at Chattanooga, Program in Music, Chattanooga, TN 37403. Offers music education (MM); performance (MM). *Accreditation:* NASM. In 2017, 6 master's awarded. *Degree requirements:* For master's, comprehensive exam, thesis or alternative, recital. *Entrance requirements:* For master's, GRE General Test, bachelor's degree in music. Additional exam requirements/recommendations for international students: Required—TOEFL (minimum score 550 paper-based; 79 iBT), IELTS (minimum score 6). *Application deadline:* For fall admission, 6/15 priority date for domestic students, 7/1 for international students; for spring admission, 11/1 priority date for domestic students, 11/1 for international students. Applications are processed on a rolling basis. Application fee: $35 ($40 for international students). Electronic applications accepted. *Expenses:* Contact institution. *Financial support:* Research assistantships, Federal Work-Study, scholarships/grants, and unspecified assistantships available. Financial award application deadline: 7/1; financial award applicants required to submit FAFSA. *Faculty research:* Music education, conducting, opera, vocal instruction, orchestras. *Total annual research expenditures:* $1,400. *Unit head:* Dr. Stuart Benkert, Interim Department Head, 423-425-4614, Fax: 423-425-4603, E-mail: stuart-benkert@ utc.edu. *Application contact:* Dr. Joanne Romagni, Dean of the Graduate School, 423-425-4478, Fax: 423-425-5223, E-mail: joanne-romagni@utc.edu.
Website: http://www.utc.edu/music/

The University of Texas at Arlington, Graduate School, College of Liberal Arts, Department of Music, Arlington, TX 76019. Offers education (MM); performance (MM). *Accreditation:* NASM. *Program availability:* Part-time, evening/weekend. *Degree requirements:* For master's, comprehensive exam, thesis optional. *Entrance requirements:* For master's, GRE, 3 letters of recommendation, minimum GPA of 3.0 in last 60 hours of course work. Additional exam requirements/recommendations for international students: Required—TOEFL (minimum score 550 paper-based). Electronic applications accepted.

The University of Texas at Austin, Graduate School, College of Fine Arts, Sarah and Ernest Butler School of Music, Austin, TX 78712-1111. Offers band and wind conducting (M Music, DMA); brass/woodwind/percussion (MM, DMA); chamber music (MM); choral conducting (MM, DMA); collaborative piano (MM, DMA); composition (MM, DMA), including composition, jazz, jazz (DMA); ethnomusicology (MM, PhD); literature and pedagogy (MM); music and human learning (MM, PhD); music and human learning (DMA), including jazz (MM, DMA), piano pedagogy; musicology (MM, PhD); opera performance (MM, DMA); orchestral conducting (MM, DMA); organ (MM), including sacred music; organ performance (MM, DMA); performance (MM), including jazz (MM, DMA); performance (DMA), including jazz (MM, DMA), piano (DMA), including jazz (MM, DMA); piano literature and pedagogy (MM); piano performance (MM, DMA); string performance (MM, DMA); theory (MM, PhD); vocal performance (MM, DMA); voice (DMA), including opera; voice performance pedagogy (DMA); woodwind, brass, percussion performance (MM, DMA). *Accreditation:* NASM. *Program availability:* Part-time. *Degree requirements:* For master's, one foreign language, comprehensive exam, thesis (for some programs), recital (performance or composition majors); for doctorate, one foreign language, comprehensive exam, thesis/dissertation (for some programs), recital (for performance or composition majors). *Entrance requirements:* For master's and doctorate, GRE General Test (except for performance or composition majors), audition (performance majors). Electronic applications accepted.

The University of Texas at El Paso, Graduate School, College of Liberal Arts, Department of Music, El Paso, TX 79968-0001. Offers music education (MM); music performance (MM). *Accreditation:* NASM. *Program availability:* Part-time, evening/weekend. *Degree requirements:* For master's, thesis optional. *Entrance requirements:* For master's, audition, interview, letters of recommendation. Additional exam requirements/recommendations for international students: Required—TOEFL; Recommended—IELTS. Electronic applications accepted.

The University of the Arts, College of Performing Arts, School of Music, Division of Music Education, Philadelphia, PA 19102-4944. Offers MAT, MM. MM program offered in conjunction with Villanova University's Summer Music Studies program with summer enrollment only and priority application date of January 1. *Degree requirements:* For master's, student teaching (for MAT); thesis/project (for MM). *Entrance requirements:* For master's, official transcripts, three letters of recommendation, one- to two-page statement, personal interview, undergraduate degree with minimum cumulative GPA of 3.0, DVD/CD or link to uploaded film on YouTube or related site (or VHS video tape for MM), live or taped performance audition (for MAT). Additional exam requirements/recommendations for international students: Required—TOEFL (minimum score 580 paper-based, 92 iBT) or IELTS (minimum score 6.5).

University of the Pacific, Conservatory of Music, Stockton, CA 95211-0197. Offers music education (MM); music therapy (MA). *Faculty:* 4 full-time (2 women), 3 part-time/ adjunct (all women). *Students:* 8 full-time (4 women), 17 part-time (11 women); includes 9 minority (1 Black or African American, non-Hispanic/Latino; 4 Asian, non-Hispanic/ Latino; 2 Hispanic/Latino; 2 Two or more races, non-Hispanic/Latino), 3 international. Average age 31. 36 applicants, 42% accepted, 9 enrolled. In 2017, 5 master's awarded. *Entrance requirements:* For master's, GRE General Test. Additional exam requirements/ recommendations for international students: Required—TOEFL. *Application deadline:* For fall admission, 3/1 priority date for domestic students; for spring admission, 10/1 priority date for domestic students. Applications are processed on a rolling basis. Application fee: $75. *Financial support:* Teaching assistantships and institutionally sponsored loans available. Support available to part-time students. Financial award application deadline: 3/1; financial award applicants required to submit FAFSA. *Unit head:* Dr. Daniel Ebbers, Interim Dean, 209-946-2415, E-mail: musicdean@pacific.edu. *Application contact:* 209-946-2415, Fax: 209-946-2770.

The University of Toledo, College of Graduate Studies, College of Communication and the Arts, Toledo, OH 43606-3390. Offers ME, MME, MMP, Certificate. *Accreditation:* NASM. *Degree requirements:* For master's, comprehensive exam, diagnostic theory and history exam. *Entrance requirements:* For master's, GRE if GPA is less than 3.0, minimum cumulative point-hour ratio of 2.7 for all previous academic work, audition. Additional exam requirements/recommendations for international students: Required—TOEFL (minimum score 550 paper-based; 80 iBT). Electronic applications accepted.

University of Toronto, School of Graduate Studies, Faculty of Music, Toronto, ON M5S 1A1, Canada. Offers composition (M Mus, DMA); ethnomusicology (MA, PhD); jazz (M Mus); music education (MA, PhD); musicology/theory (MA, PhD); opera (M Mus); performance (M Mus, DMA). *Program availability:* Part-time. *Degree requirements:* For master's, comprehensive exam (for some programs), oral examination (M Mus in composition), 1 foreign language (MA); for doctorate, recital of original works (DMA), thesis (PhD). *Entrance requirements:* For master's, BM in area of specialization with minimum B average in final 2 years, original compositions (M Mus in composition); for doctorate, master's degree in area of specialization, minimum B+ average, at least 2 extended compositions (DMA). Additional exam requirements/recommendations for international students: Required—TOEFL (minimum score 580 paper-based; 93 iBT), TWE (minimum score 5). Electronic applications accepted.

University of Utah, Graduate School, College of Fine Arts, School of Music, Salt Lake City, UT 84112. Offers choral conducting (M Mus, DMA); collaborative piano (M Mus); composition (M Mus, PhD); instrumental conducting (M Mus, DMA); instrumental performance (M Mus, DMA); jazz studies (M Mus); music education (M Mus, PhD); music history and literature (M Mus); musicology (MA); organ performance (M Mus); piano performance (M Mus, DMA); piano performance and pedagogy (M Mus); string performance and pedagogy (M Mus); theory (M Mus); vocal performance (DMA). *Accreditation:* NASM. *Faculty:* 23 full-time (5 women), 59 part-time/adjunct (22 women). *Students:* 68 full-time (31 women), 21 part-time (12 women); includes 12 minority (5 Asian, non-Hispanic/Latino; 4 Hispanic/Latino; 1 Native Hawaiian or other Pacific Islander, non-Hispanic/Latino; 2 Two or more races, non-Hispanic/Latino), 18 international. Average age 25. 121 applicants, 55% accepted, 31 enrolled. In 2017, 28 master's, 10 doctorates awarded. *Entrance requirements:* For master's, placement exams, minimum GPA of 3.0, audition, bachelor's degree in music; for doctorate, placement exams, minimum GPA of 3.0, audition, master's degree in music. Additional exam requirements/recommendations for international students: Required—TOEFL (minimum score 85 iBT). *Application deadline:* For fall admission, 2/15 for domestic students, 1/15 for international students; for spring admission, 10/1 for domestic students, 9/1 for international students; for summer admission, 3/15 for domestic students, 2/15 for international students. Applications are processed on a rolling basis. Application fee: $55 ($65 for international students). Electronic applications accepted. *Expenses:* Contact institution. *Financial support:* In 2017–18, 62 students received support, including 52 teaching assistantships with full and partial tuition reimbursements available (averaging $10,875 per year); scholarships/grants, health care benefits, tuition waivers (full and partial), and unspecified assistantships also available. Financial award application deadline: 2/15. *Faculty research:* Music education, conducting, musicology, composition, performance. *Total annual research expenditures:* $25,000. *Unit head:* Miguel Chuaqui, Director, 801-585-3720, E-mail: m.chauqui@utah.edu. *Application contact:* Cassie Wagstaff, Academic Coordinator, 801-585-6972, Fax: 801-581-5683, E-mail: cassandra.wagstaff@utah.edu.
Website: http://www.music.utah.edu/

University of Victoria, Faculty of Graduate Studies, Faculty of Education, Department of Curriculum and Instruction, Victoria, BC V8W 2Y2, Canada. Offers art education (M Ed, PhD); curriculum studies (M Ed, MA, PhD); early childhood education (M Ed, PhD); educational studies (PhD); language and literacy (M Ed, MA, PhD); mathematics (M Ed, MA, PhD); music education (M Ed, MA, PhD); science (M Ed, MA, PhD); social studies (M Ed, MA); social, cultural and foundational studies (MA, PhD); technology and environmental education (PhD). *Program availability:* Part-time. *Degree requirements:* For master's, thesis, project (M Ed); for doctorate, comprehensive exam, thesis/dissertation. *Entrance requirements:* For master's, minimum B average. Additional exam requirements/recommendations for international students: Required—TOEFL (minimum score 575 paper-based), IELTS (minimum score 7). Electronic applications accepted. *Faculty research:* Elementary and secondary English, language arts, curriculum theory and practice, educational media and technology, educational administration and leadership, history and philosophy of education.

University of Washington, Graduate School, College of Arts and Sciences, School of Music, Concentration in Music Education, Seattle, WA 98195. Offers MA, PhD. *Degree requirements:* For doctorate, thesis/dissertation. *Entrance requirements:* For master's, GRE General Test, GRE Subject Test, minimum GPA of 3.0; for doctorate, GRE General Test, GRE Subject Test, minimum GPA of 3.0, sample of scholarly writing, videotape of teaching, 1 year of teaching experience. Additional exam requirements/recommendations for international students: Required—TOEFL. Electronic applications accepted. *Faculty research:* Multiethnic issues in music instruction, affective responses to music.

University of West Georgia, College of Arts and Humanities, Carrollton, GA 30118. Offers English (MA); history (MA); museum studies (Postbaccalaureate Certificate); music performance (M Mus); music teacher education (M Mus); public history (Postbaccalaureate Certificate). *Program availability:* Part-time, evening/weekend, 100% online, blended/hybrid learning. *Faculty:* 69 full-time (38 women). *Students:* 25 full-time (15 women), 51 part-time (34 women); includes 16 minority (7 Black or African American, non-Hispanic/Latino; 1 American Indian or Alaska Native, non-Hispanic/Latino; 2 Asian, non-Hispanic/Latino; 5 Hispanic/Latino; 1 Two or more races, non-Hispanic/Latino), 1 international. Average age 30. 23 applicants, 96% accepted, 16 enrolled. In 2017, 29 master's, 6 other advanced degrees awarded. *Entrance requirements:* Additional exam requirements/recommendations for international students: Required—TOEFL (minimum score 523 paper-based; 69 iBT); Recommended—IELTS (minimum score 6.5). *Application deadline:* For fall admission, 8/1 for domestic students, 6/1 for international students; for spring admission, 11/15 for domestic students, 10/15 for international students; for summer admission, 5/15 for domestic students, 3/30 for international students. Applications are processed on a rolling basis. Application fee: $40. Electronic applications accepted. Tuition and fees vary according to degree level and program. *Financial support:* Fellowships, research assistantships, teaching assistantships, career-related internships or fieldwork, Federal Work-Study, institutionally sponsored loans, scholarships/grants, and unspecified assistantships available. Support available to part-time students. Financial award application deadline: 4/1; financial award applicants required to submit FAFSA. *Unit head:* Dr. Pauline D. Gagnon, Dean of Arts and Humanities, 678-839-5450, Fax: 678-839-5451, E-mail: pgagnon@westga.edu. *Application contact:* Dr. Toby Ziglar, Assistant Dean of the Graduate School, 678-839-1394, Fax: 678-839-1395, E-mail: graduate@westga.edu.
Website: http://www.westga.edu/coah

University of Wisconsin–Madison, Graduate School, College of Letters and Science, School of Music, Program in Music Education, Madison, WI 53706-1380. Offers curriculum and instruction (MS, PhD); music education (MM). *Accreditation:* NASM. *Degree requirements:* For doctorate, 2 foreign languages, thesis/dissertation. *Entrance requirements:* For doctorate, GRE General Test.

University of Wisconsin–Stevens Point, College of Fine Arts and Communication, Department of Music, Stevens Point, WI 54481-3897. Offers elementary/secondary (MM Ed); studio pedagogy (MM Ed); Suzuki talent education (MM Ed). *Accreditation:* NASM. *Program availability:* Part-time. *Degree requirements:* For master's, thesis or alternative. *Entrance requirements:* For master's, teaching certificate. *Faculty research:* Music education, music composition, music performance.

University of Wyoming, College of Arts and Sciences, Department of Music, Laramie, WY 82071. Offers music education (MME); performance (MM). *Accreditation:* NASM. *Degree requirements:* For master's, comprehensive exam, thesis or alternative. *Entrance requirements:* For master's, minimum GPA of 3.0. Additional exam requirements/recommendations for international students: Required—TOEFL (minimum score 540 paper-based). Electronic applications accepted.

Utah State University, School of Graduate Studies, Caine College of the Arts, Department of Music, Logan, UT 84322. Offers guitar performance (MM); piano performance and pedagogy (MM).

VanderCook College of Music, Master of Music Education Program, Chicago, IL 60616-3731. Offers MM Ed. *Accreditation:* NASM. *Program availability:* Part-time. *Degree requirements:* For master's, thesis, written comprehensive exam or professional teaching portfolio. *Entrance requirements:* For master's, minimum of one year of teaching experience, or its equivalent, in music; official transcripts; 3 letters of recommendation; bachelor's degree in music education from accredited college or university or minimum of 60 credits in undergraduate music and music education coursework. Additional exam requirements/recommendations for international students: Required—TOEFL (minimum score 500 paper-based; 70 iBT).

Virginia Commonwealth University, Graduate School, School of the Arts, Department of Music, Richmond, VA 23284-9005. Offers music education (MM). *Accreditation:* NASM. *Degree requirements:* For master's, departmental qualifying exam, recital. *Entrance requirements:* For master's, department examination, audition or tapes, portfolio. Additional exam requirements/recommendations for international students: Required—TOEFL (minimum score 600 paper-based; 100 iBT). Electronic applications accepted. *Faculty research:* Composition, conducting, education, performance.

Wayne State College, School of Education and Counseling, Department of Educational Foundations and Leadership, Program in Curriculum and Instruction, Wayne, NE 68787. Offers alternative education (MSE); business and information technology education (MSE); communication arts education (MSE); early childhood education (MSE); elementary education (MSE); English as a second language (MSE); English education (MSE); family and consumer sciences education (MSE); industrial technology and vocational education (MSE); learning communities (MSE); mathematics education (MSE); music education (MSE); science education (MSE); social science education (MSE). *Accreditation:* NCATE. *Program availability:* Part-time, evening/weekend. *Degree requirements:* For master's, comprehensive exam, thesis optional. *Entrance requirements:* For master's, GRE General Test. Additional exam requirements/recommendations for international students: Required—TOEFL (minimum score 550 paper-based).

Wayne State University, College of Fine, Performing and Communication Arts, Department of Music, Detroit, MI 48202. Offers composition/theory (MA, MM); conducting (MA, MM); jazz performance (MA, MM); music education (MA, MM); orchestral studies (Certificate); performance (MA, MM). *Accreditation:* NASM. *Faculty:* 29. *Students:* 13 full-time (2 women), 9 part-time (2 women); includes 4 minority (2 Black or African American, non-Hispanic/Latino; 1 American Indian or Alaska Native, non-Hispanic/Latino; 1 Two or more races, non-Hispanic/Latino), 1 international. Average age 32. 41 applicants, 59% accepted, 10 enrolled. In 2017, 8 master's awarded. *Degree requirements:* For master's, thesis (for some programs), oral examination (for some programs), recital with program notes (for some programs). *Entrance requirements:* For master's, diagnostic exam in theory and history, undergraduate degree in same field as desired field of graduate study or equivalent in course work, private study, or experience; audition/interview; for Certificate, undergraduate degree in same field as desired field of graduate study or equivalent in course work, private study, or experience; audition/interview. Additional exam requirements/recommendations for international students: Required—TOEFL (minimum score 550 paper-based; 79 iBT), Michigan English Language Assessment Battery (minimum score 85); Recommended—IELTS (minimum score 6.5), TWE (minimum score 5.5). *Application deadline:* Applications are processed on a rolling basis. Application fee: $50. Electronic applications accepted. *Expenses:* Contact institution. *Financial support:* In 2017–18, 19 students received support. Career-related internships or fieldwork, institutionally sponsored loans, and scholarships/grants available. Support available to part-time students. Financial award applicants required to submit FAFSA. *Faculty research:* Teacher training, pedagogy, musicology, composition/theory, conducting/performance practice. *Unit head:* Dr. Norah Duncan, Professor and Chair, 313-577-1775, E-mail: norah.duncan@wayne.edu. *Application contact:* E-mail: music@wayne.edu.
Website: http://music.wayne.edu/

Webster University, Leigh Gerdine College of Fine Arts, Department of Music, St. Louis, MO 63119-3194. Offers church music (MM); composition (MM); jazz studies (MM); music (MA); music education (MM); organ (MM); performance (MM); piano (MM); voice (MM). *Accreditation:* NASM. *Entrance requirements:* Additional exam requirements/recommendations for international students: Required—TOEFL.

West Chester University of Pennsylvania, School of Music, Department of Applied Music, West Chester, PA 19383. Offers performance (MM), including conducting, instrumental, keyboard, voice; piano pedagogy (MM, Certificate). *Program availability:* Part-time, evening/weekend. *Students:* 16 full-time (9 women), 14 part-time (4 women); includes 4 minority (1 Asian, non-Hispanic/Latino; 1 Hispanic/Latino; 2 Two or more races, non-Hispanic/Latino), 5 international. Average age 28. 24 applicants, 75% accepted, 15 enrolled. In 2017, 13 master's awarded. *Degree requirements:* For master's, comprehensive exam, thesis optional, recital. *Entrance requirements:* For master's and Certificate, School of Music Graduate Placement Test (GPT), audition, interview. Additional exam requirements/recommendations for international students: Required—TOEFL or IELTS. *Application deadline:* For fall admission, 5/15 for international students; for spring admission, 10/15 for international students. Applications are processed on a rolling basis. Application fee: $50. Electronic applications accepted. *Expenses:* Tuition, state resident: full-time $9000; part-time $500 per credit. Tuition, nonresident: full-time $13,500; part-time $750 per credit. *Required fees:* $2959; $149.79 per credit. *Financial support:* Scholarships/grants and unspecified assistantships available. Financial award application deadline: 2/15; financial award applicants required to submit FAFSA. *Faculty research:* Performance, historical perspective, pedagogy. *Unit head:* Christopher Hanning, Chair, 610-436-4178, Fax: 610-436-2873, E-mail: channing@wcupa.edu. *Application contact:* Dr. M. Gregory Martin, Graduate Coordinator, 610-436-2070, Fax: 610-436-2873, E-mail: mmartin@wcupa.edu.
Website: http://www.wcupa.edu/arts-humanities/music/appliedMusic/

West Chester University of Pennsylvania, School of Music, Department of Music Education, West Chester, PA 19383. Offers Kodaly methodology (Certificate); music education (MM, Teaching Certificate), including Kodaly methodology (MM), music technology (MM), Orff-Schulwerk (MM), performance (MM); music technology (Certificate); Orff-Schulwerk (Certificate). *Accreditation:* NASM; NCATE. *Program availability:* Part-time, evening/weekend. *Students:* 4 full-time (all women), 13 part-time (8 women); includes 1 minority (Asian, non-Hispanic/Latino). Average age 28. 11 applicants, 91% accepted, 6 enrolled. In 2017, 14 master's, 6 Certificates awarded. *Degree requirements:* For master's, comprehensive exam, thesis (for some programs), recital (performance option only). *Entrance requirements:* For master's, School of Music Graduate Placement Test (GPT), audition (performance track only), interview; for other advanced degree, audition, interview. Additional exam requirements/recommendations for international students: Required—TOEFL or IELTS. *Application deadline:* For fall admission, 5/15 for international students; for spring admission, 10/15 for international students. Applications are processed on a rolling basis. Application fee: $50. Electronic applications accepted. *Expenses:* Tuition, state resident: full-time $9000; part-time $500 per credit. Tuition, nonresident: full-time $13,500; part-time $750 per credit. *Required fees:* $2959; $149.79 per credit. *Financial support:* Scholarships/grants and unspecified assistantships available. Financial award application deadline: 2/15; financial award applicants required to submit FAFSA. *Faculty research:* Music education in other cultures, educational advocacy and pedagogy, research in music education, special needs learners in music education, developing music listening skills. *Unit head:* Dr. Marci Major, Chair, 610-436-3030, Fax: 610-436-2873, E-mail: mmajor@wcupa.edu. *Application contact:* Dr. M. Gregory Martin, Graduate Coordinator, 610-436-2070, E-mail: mmartin@wcupa.edu.
Website: http://www.wcupa.edu/arts-humanities/music/musicEducation/

Western Connecticut State University, Division of Graduate Studies, School of Visual and Performing Arts, Department of Music, Danbury, CT 06810-6885. Offers music education (MS). *Accreditation:* NASM. *Program availability:* Part-time. *Degree requirements:* For master's, thesis or comprehensive exam, completion of program within 6 years. *Entrance requirements:* For master's, minimum GPA of 2.8, teaching certificate. Additional exam requirements/recommendations for international students: Recommended—TOEFL (minimum score 550 paper-based; 79 iBT), IELTS (minimum score 6). *Expenses:* Tuition, state resident: full-time $6757; part-time $374 per credit hour. Tuition, nonresident: full-time $18,102; part-time $374 per credit hour. *Required fees:* $4994; $190 per credit hour. $60 per term. Tuition and fees vary according to degree level and program. *Faculty research:* Ear training.

Western Kentucky University, Graduate Studies, Potter College of Arts and Letters, Department of Music, Bowling Green, KY 42101. Offers MA Ed. *Accreditation:* NASM; NCATE. *Program availability:* Part-time, evening/weekend. *Degree requirements:* For master's, comprehensive exam, written exam. *Entrance requirements:* For master's, GRE General Test, minimum GPA of 3.0. Additional exam requirements/recommendations for international students: Required—TOEFL (minimum score 555 paper-based; 79 iBT). *Faculty research:* Music education, music technology, performance.

Western Michigan University, Graduate College, College of Fine Arts, School of Music, Kalamazoo, MI 49008. Offers music (MA); music composition (MM); music conducting (MM); music education (MM); music performance (MM); music therapy (MM). *Accreditation:* NASM.

West Virginia University, College of Creative Arts, Morgantown, WV 26506. Offers acting (MFA); art education (MA); art history (MA); ceramics (MFA); collaborative piano (MM, DMA); composition (MM, DMA); conducting (MM, DMA); costume design and technology (MFA); graphic design (MFA); jazz pedagogy (MM); lighting design and technology (MFA); music (PhD); music education (MM, PhD); music industry (MA); music theory (MM); musicology (MA); painting and printmaking (MFA); performance (MM, DMA); photography (MFA); piano pedagogy (MM); scenic design and technology (MFA); sculpture (MFA); studio art (MA); technical direction (MFA); vocal pedagogy and performance (DMA). *Program availability:* Part-time. *Students:* 114 full-time (64 women), 39 part-time (21 women); includes 19 minority (11 Black or African American, non-Hispanic/Latino; 1 Asian, non-Hispanic/Latino; 6 Hispanic/Latino; 1 Two or more races,

non-Hispanic/Latino), 33 international. *Degree requirements:* For master's, thesis, recitals; for doctorate, comprehensive exam, thesis/dissertation, recitals (DMA). *Entrance requirements:* For doctorate, minimum GPA of 3.0, audition. Additional exam requirements/recommendations for international students: Required—TOEFL. *Application deadline:* For fall admission, 3/1 priority date for domestic students, 2/15 for international students; for spring admission, 11/1 for domestic students, 9/15 for international students. Applications are processed on a rolling basis. Application fee: $60. Electronic applications accepted. *Expenses:* Tuition, state resident: full-time $9450. Tuition, nonresident: full-time $24,390. *Financial support:* Research assistantships, teaching assistantships, career-related internships or fieldwork, Federal Work-Study, institutionally sponsored loans, scholarships/grants, health care benefits, tuition waivers (partial), and administrative assistantships available. Financial award applicants required to submit FAFSA. *Faculty research:* Professional directing, consulting, acting design, music education, jazz history. *Unit head:* Dr. Paul Kreider, Dean, 304-293-4841 Ext. 3109, Fax: 304-293-6896, E-mail: paul.kreider@mail.wvu.edu. *Application contact:* Records Officer, 304-293-4841, Fax: 304-293-2533, E-mail: rachel.hanks@mail.wvu.edu.
Website: http://www.ccarts.wvu.edu

Wichita State University, Graduate School, College of Fine Arts, School of Music, Wichita, KS 67260. Offers music (MM); music education (MME). *Accreditation:* NASM. *Program availability:* Part-time. *Unit head:* Dr. Aleks Sternfeld-Dunn, Director, 316-978-6272, Fax: 316-978-3625, E-mail: aleks.sternfeld-dunn@wichita.edu. *Application contact:* Jordan Oleson, Admissions Coordinator, 316-978-3095, Fax: 316-978-3253, E-mail: jordan.oleson@wichita.edu.
Website: http://www.wichita.edu/music

Winthrop University, College of Visual and Performing Arts, Department of Music, Rock Hill, SC 29733. Offers conducting (MM); music education (MME); performance (MM). *Accreditation:* NASM. *Program availability:* Part-time. *Students:* 8 full-time (4 women), 6 part-time (3 women); includes 4 minority (all Black or African American, non-Hispanic/Latino). Average age 33. In 2017, 8 master's awarded. *Degree requirements:* For master's, comprehensive exam (for some programs), oral and written exams, recital (MM). *Entrance requirements:* For master's, GRE General Test, audition, minimum GPA of 3.0, 2 recitals. Additional exam requirements/recommendations for international students: Required—TOEFL (minimum score 550 paper-based; 79 iBT), IELTS (minimum score 6). *Application deadline:* For fall admission, 7/15 priority date for domestic students; for spring admission, 12/1 for domestic students. Applications are processed on a rolling basis. Application fee: $50. Electronic applications accepted. *Financial support:* Research assistantships with full tuition reimbursements, Federal Work-Study, scholarships/grants, and unspecified assistantships available. Support available to part-time students. Financial award application deadline: 2/1; financial award applicants required to submit FAFSA. *Unit head:* Donald Rogers, Graduate Program Director, E-mail: rogersd@winthrop.edu. *Application contact:* 803-411-7041, E-mail: gradschool@winthrop.edu.
Website: http://www.winthrop.edu/cvpa/music

Wright State University, Graduate School, College of Liberal Arts, Department of Music, Dayton, OH 45435. Offers MM. *Accreditation:* NASM. *Program availability:* Part-time. *Degree requirements:* For master's, thesis or alternative, oral exam. *Entrance requirements:* For master's, theory placement test, BA in music. Additional exam requirements/recommendations for international students: Required—TOEFL. *Faculty research:* General music, current needs, role of teacher, expectations in music education.

Youngstown State University, Graduate School, College of Fine and Performing Arts, Dana School of Music, Youngstown, OH 44555-0001. Offers jazz studies (MM); music education (MM); music history and literature (MM); music theory and composition (MM); performance (MM). *Accreditation:* NASM. *Program availability:* Part-time, evening/weekend. *Degree requirements:* For master's, one foreign language, thesis optional, final qualifying exam. *Entrance requirements:* For master's, audition; GRE General Test or minimum GPA of 2.7. Additional exam requirements/recommendations for international students: Required—TOEFL. *Faculty research:* Teaching education, use of computers, conducting.

Reading Education

Abilene Christian University, Graduate Programs, College of Education and Human Services, Teaching and Learning Program, Abilene, TX 79699. Offers initial certification (M Ed); reading teacher (M Ed). *Faculty:* 8 part-time/adjunct (5 women). *Students:* 7 full-time (all women), 13 part-time (all women); includes 4 minority (1 Black or African American, non-Hispanic/Latino; 3 Hispanic/Latino). 29 applicants, 72% accepted, 20 enrolled. In 2017, 10 master's awarded. *Entrance requirements:* Additional exam requirements/recommendations for international students: Required—TOEFL (minimum score 80 iBT), IELTS (minimum score 6), PTE. *Application deadline:* For fall admission, 11/15 for domestic students. Application fee: $50. Electronic applications accepted. *Expenses:* $100 per hour. *Financial support:* In 2017–18, 20 students received support. Scholarships/grants available. Financial award application deadline: 4/1; financial award applicants required to submit FAFSA. *Unit head:* Dr. Dana Pemberton, Department Chair, 325-674-2112, Fax: 325-674-2123, E-mail: dlp94a@acu.edu. *Application contact:* Graduate Admissions, 325-674-6911, Fax: 325-674-6717, E-mail: gradinfo@acu.edu.
Website: http://www.acu.edu/graduate/academics/teaching-and-learning.html

Adelphi University, Ruth S. Ammon School of Education, Program in Literacy, Garden City, NY 11530-0701. Offers birth-grade 12 (MS); birth-grade 6 (MS); grades 5-12 (MS). *Program availability:* Part-time, evening/weekend. *Students:* 2 full-time (both women), 15 part-time (14 women); includes 4 minority (3 Black or African American, non-Hispanic/Latino; 1 Hispanic/Latino). Average age 34. 14 applicants, 71% accepted, 6 enrolled. In 2017, 2 master's awarded. *Entrance requirements:* For master's, 2 letters of recommendation, resume, valid New York state teaching certification. Additional exam requirements/recommendations for international students: Required—TOEFL (minimum score 550 paper-based; 80 iBT), IELTS (minimum score 6.5). *Application deadline:* For fall admission, 4/1 priority date for domestic students, 4/1 for international students; for spring admission, 11/1 priority date for domestic students, 11/1 for international students. Applications are processed on a rolling basis. Application fee: $50. Electronic applications accepted. *Expenses:* Contact institution. *Financial support:* Research assistantships, teaching assistantships, career-related internships or fieldwork, institutionally sponsored loans, scholarships/grants, traineeships, and unspecified assistantships available. Support available to part-time students. Financial award application deadline: 2/15; financial award applicants required to submit FAFSA. *Faculty research:* Assessment and intervention, literacy education and development, higher and

teacher education, human and adult development, achieving styles and human motivation. *Unit head:* Dr. Lori Wolf, Director, 516-877-4104, E-mail: wolf@adelphi.edu. *Application contact:* E-mail: graduateadmissions@adelphi.edu.

Alabama Agricultural and Mechanical University, School of Graduate Studies, College of Education, Humanities, and Behavioral Sciences, Department of Reading, Elementary, Early Childhood and Special Education, Huntsville, AL 35811. Offers early childhood education (MS Ed, Ed S); elementary education (MS Ed, Ed S); reading/literacy (PhD); special education collaborative teacher training (MS Ed, Ed S). *Accreditation:* NCATE. *Program availability:* Evening/weekend. *Degree requirements:* For master's, comprehensive exam; for Ed S, thesis. *Entrance requirements:* For master's, GRE General Test. Additional exam requirements/recommendations for international students: Required—TOEFL (minimum score 500 paper-based; 61 iBT). Electronic applications accepted. *Faculty research:* Multicultural education, learning styles, diagnostic-prescriptive instruction.

Alabama State University, College of Education, Department of Curriculum and Instruction, Montgomery, AL 36101-0271. Offers early childhood education (M Ed, Ed S); elementary education (M Ed, Ed S); secondary education (M Ed, Ed S), including biology education, English language arts education (M Ed), history education, math education, music education (M Ed), reading education (M Ed), social science education; special education (M Ed). *Program availability:* Part-time. *Faculty:* 7 full-time (4 women), 7 part-time/adjunct (4 women). *Students:* 43 full-time (35 women), 71 part-time (62 women); includes 112 minority (111 Black or African American, non-Hispanic/Latino; 1 Two or more races, non-Hispanic/Latino). Average age 22. 47 applicants, 66% accepted, 19 enrolled. In 2017, 21 master's, 13 Ed Ss awarded. *Degree requirements:* For master's, comprehensive exam, thesis optional; for Ed S, comprehensive exam, thesis. *Entrance requirements:* For master's, GRE General Test, MAT, writing competency test; for Ed S, writing competency test, GRE, MAT. Additional exam requirements/recommendations for international students: Required—TOEFL (minimum score 500 paper-based). *Application deadline:* For fall admission, 4/15 for domestic and international students; for spring admission, 11/15 for domestic and international students; for summer admission, 3/15 for domestic and international students. Applications are processed on a rolling basis. Application fee: $25. Electronic applications accepted. *Expenses:* Tuition, state resident: part-time $412 per credit hour.

Tuition, nonresident: part-time $824 per credit hour. *Required fees:* $685 per semester. *Financial support:* Research assistantships available. Financial award application deadline: 6/30; financial award applicants required to submit FAFSA. *Unit head:* Dr. Joyce Johnson, Acting Chairperson, 334-229-4485, Fax: 334-229-5603, E-mail: jjohnson@alasu.edu. *Application contact:* Dr. William Person, Dean of Graduate Studies, 334-229-4274, Fax: 334-229-4928, E-mail: wperson@alasu.edu. Website: http://www.alasu.edu/academics/colleges—departments/college-of-education—instruction/index.aspx

Alfred University, Graduate School, Division of Education, Alfred, NY 14802-1205. Offers college student development (MS Ed); literacy (MS Ed). *Accreditation:* TEAC. *Program availability:* Part-time. *Entrance requirements:* For master's, Liberal Arts and Sciences Test (LAST), Assessment of Teaching Skills (written) (ATS-W), Content Specialty Test (CST). Additional exam requirements/recommendations for international students: Required—TOEFL (minimum score 590 paper-based; 90 iBT), IELTS (minimum score 6.5). Electronic applications accepted.

Alverno College, School of Professional Studies - Education Division, Milwaukee, WI 53234-3922. Offers adaptive education (MA); administrative leadership (MA); adult education and organizational development (MA); adult educational and instructional design (MA); adult educational and instructional technology (MA); global connections in the humanities (MA); instructional leadership (MA); instructional technology for K-12 settings (MA); professional development (MA); reading education (MA); reading education with adaptive education (MA); science education (MA); special education (MA); teaching in alternative schools (MA). *Accreditation:* NCATE. *Program availability:* Part-time, evening/weekend. *Faculty:* 3 full-time (2 women), 23 part-time/adjunct (17 women). *Students:* 37 full-time (34 women), 68 part-time (65 women); includes 27 minority (16 Black or African American, non-Hispanic/Latino; 1 American Indian or Alaska Native, non-Hispanic/Latino; 1 Asian, non-Hispanic/Latino; 7 Hispanic/Latino; 2 Two or more races, non-Hispanic/Latino). Average age 35. 67 applicants, 100% accepted, 51 enrolled. In 2017, 68 master's awarded. *Degree requirements:* For master's, presentation/defense of proposal, conference presentation of inquiry projects. *Entrance requirements:* For master's, bachelor's degree in related field, communication samples from work setting, 3 letters of recommendation. Additional exam requirements/recommendations for international students: Required—TOEFL. *Application deadline:* For fall admission, 7/15 priority date for domestic and international students; for spring admission, 12/15 priority date for domestic and international students. Applications are processed on a rolling basis. Application fee: $0. Electronic applications accepted. *Expenses:* Contact institution. *Financial support:* Federal Work-Study and scholarships/grants available. Support available to part-time students. Financial award applicants required to submit FAFSA. *Faculty research:* Student self-assessment, self-reflection, integration of curriculum, identifying needs of students in strategic situations and designing appropriate classroom strategies. *Unit head:* Dr. Patricia Luebke, Dean, School of Professional Studies, 414-382-6368, Fax: 414-382-6354, E-mail: patricia.luebke@alverno.edu. *Application contact:* Katie Kipp, Graduate Admissions Counselor, 414-382-6045, Fax: 414-382-6354, E-mail: katie.kipp@alverno.edu.

American International College, School of Education, Springfield, MA 01109-3189. Offers early childhood education (M Ed, CAGS); education (MA, Ed D), including counseling psychology (MA), educational leadership and supervision (Ed D), professional counseling and supervision (Ed D), teaching and learning (Ed D); elementary education (M Ed, CAGS); middle education/secondary education (M Ed, CAGS); moderate disabilities (M Ed, CAGS); reading specialist (M Ed, CAGS); school adjustment counseling (MAEP, CAGS); school guidance counseling (MAEP, CAGS); school leadership (M Ed, CAGS). *Program availability:* Evening/weekend. *Faculty:* 1 (woman) full-time, 151 part-time/adjunct (95 women). *Students:* 1,082 full-time (910 women), 143 part-time (113 women); includes 109 minority (19 Black or African American, non-Hispanic/Latino; 2 American Indian or Alaska Native, non-Hispanic/Latino; 10 Asian, non-Hispanic/Latino; 58 Hispanic/Latino; 1 Native Hawaiian or other Pacific Islander, non-Hispanic/Latino; 19 Two or more races, non-Hispanic/Latino). Average age 34. 537 applicants, 77% accepted, 327 enrolled. In 2017, 486 master's, 112 other advanced degrees awarded. *Degree requirements:* For master's and CAGS, practicum/culminating experience. *Entrance requirements:* For master's, Communication and Literacy portion of the Massachusetts Tests for Education Licensure, graduate of accredited four-year college with minimum B- average in undergraduate course work; for CAGS, M Ed or master's degree in field related to licensure from accredited institution. *Application deadline:* Applications are processed on a rolling basis. Application fee: $50. Electronic applications accepted. *Expenses:* $439 per credit, $30 per term registration fee, $100 graduation fee, $110 technology fee. *Financial support:* Applicants required to submit FAFSA. *Unit head:* Sylvia Mason, Dean, 413-205-1743, Fax: 413-205-3943, E-mail: sylvia.mason@aic.edu. *Application contact:* Kerry Barnes, Dean of Graduate Admissions, 413-205-3703, Fax: 413-205-3051, E-mail: kerry.barnes@aic.edu.
Website: http://www.aic.edu/school-of-education/

Appalachian State University, Cratis D. Williams Graduate School, Department of Reading Education and Special Education, Boone, NC 28608. Offers reading education (MA); special education (MA). *Accreditation:* ASHA. *Program availability:* Part-time, evening/weekend, online learning. *Degree requirements:* For master's, comprehensive exam, thesis optional. *Entrance requirements:* For master's, GRE General Test or MAT, 3 letters of recommendation. Additional exam requirements/recommendations for international students: Required—TOEFL (minimum score 570 paper-based; 79 iBT), IELTS (minimum score 6.5). Electronic applications accepted. *Faculty research:* Special education, language arts, reading.

Arcadia University, School of Education, Glenside, PA 19038-3295. Offers art education (M Ed); computer education (CAS); curriculum (CAS); curriculum studies (M Ed); early childhood education (M Ed), including individualized, master teacher, research in child development; educational leadership (M Ed, Ed D, CAS); elementary education (M Ed); English education (MA Ed); environmental education (MA Ed); instructional technology (M Ed); language arts (M Ed); library science (M Ed); mathematics education (M Ed, MA Ed); music education (MA Ed); psychology (M Ed); reading (M Ed, CAS); science education (M Ed, CAS); secondary education (M Ed, CAS); special education (M Ed, Ed D, CAS); theater arts (MA Ed); written communication (MA Ed). *Accreditation:* NASAD. *Program availability:* Part-time, evening/weekend, online learning. Electronic applications accepted. *Expenses:* Contact institution.

Arkansas State University, Graduate School, College of Education and Behavioral Science, School of Teacher Education and Leadership, State University, AR 72467. Offers community college administration (SCCT); curriculum and instruction (MSE); early childhood education (MSE); early childhood services (MS); educational leadership (MSE, Ed D, Ed S); educational theory and practice (MSE); middle level education (MAT, MSE); reading (MSE, Ed S); special education - gifted, talented, and creative (MSE); special education - instructional specialist grades 4-12 (MSE); special education - instructional specialist grades P-4 (MSE); special education, K-12 (MSE). *Accreditation:* NCATE. *Program availability:* Part-time, online learning. *Degree requirements:* For master's, comprehensive exam, thesis or alternative; for doctorate, comprehensive exam, thesis/dissertation; for other advanced degree, comprehensive

exam. *Entrance requirements:* For master's, GRE General Test or MAT, appropriate bachelor's degree, official transcripts, immunization records, letters of reference, interview; for doctorate, GRE General Test or MAT, interview, master's degree, letters of reference, official transcript, personal statement, writing sample, immunization records; for other advanced degree, GRE General Test or MAT, interview, master's degree, official transcript, immunization records, letters of reference, 3 years of teaching experience, teaching license. Additional exam requirements/recommendations for international students: Required—TOEFL (minimum score 550 paper-based; 79 iBT), IELTS (minimum score 6), PTE (minimum score 56). Electronic applications accepted.

Asbury University, School of Graduate and Professional Studies, Wilmore, KY 40390-1198. Offers biology: alternative certificate (MA Ed); chemistry: alternative certificate (MA Ed); English (MA Ed); English as a second language (MA Ed); ESL (MA Ed); French (MA Ed); Latin: alternative certificate (MA Ed); mathematics: alternative certificate (MA Ed); reading/writing endorsement (MA Ed); social studies (MA Ed); social work (MSW), including child and family services; Spanish (MA Ed); special education (MA Ed); special education: alternative certificate (MA Ed); teacher as leader endorsement (MA Ed). *Accreditation:* NCATE. *Program availability:* Part-time. *Degree requirements:* For master's, action research project, portfolio. *Entrance requirements:* For master's, PRAXIS/NTE, minimum GPA of 2.75, letters of recommendation. Additional exam requirements/recommendations for international students: Required—TOEFL (minimum score 550 paper-based). Electronic applications accepted.

Augustana University, MA in Education Program, Sioux Falls, SD 57197. Offers instructional strategies (MA); reading (MA); special populations (MA); STEM (MA); technology (MA). *Accreditation:* NCATE. *Program availability:* Part-time-only, evening/weekend, online only, 100% online. *Faculty:* 7 full-time (5 women), 6 part-time/adjunct (5 women). *Students:* 288 part-time (250 women); includes 20 minority (2 Black or African American, non-Hispanic/Latino; 2 American Indian or Alaska Native, non-Hispanic/Latino; 1 Asian, non-Hispanic/Latino; 11 Hispanic/Latino; 1 Native Hawaiian or other Pacific Islander, non-Hispanic/Latino; 3 Two or more races, non-Hispanic/Latino), 3 international. Average age 32. 47 applicants, 77% accepted, 35 enrolled. In 2017, 84 master's awarded. *Degree requirements:* For master's, thesis. *Entrance requirements:* For master's, appropriate bachelor's degree, minimum GPA of 3.0, teaching certificate. Additional exam requirements/recommendations for international students: Required—TOEFL (minimum score 550 paper-based). *Application deadline:* For fall admission, 8/1 for domestic and international students; for spring admission, 11/1 for domestic and international students; for summer admission, 4/1 for domestic and international students. Applications are processed on a rolling basis. Application fee: $60. Electronic applications accepted. *Expenses:* Contact institution. *Financial support:* Application deadline: 3/1; applicants required to submit FAFSA. *Faculty research:* Multicultural education, education of students with autism, well-being in school settings, factors that predict academic hopefulness. *Unit head:* Dr. Laurie Daily, Chair, 605-274-5211, E-mail: laurie.daily@augie.edu. *Application contact:* Julia Paulich, Graduate Coordinator, 605-274-4043, Fax: 605-274-4450, E-mail: graduate@augie.edu.
Website: http://www.augie.edu/master-arts-education

Aurora University, School of Education and Human Performance, Aurora, IL 60506-4892. Offers applied behavioral analysis (MS); bilingual-ESL education (MA); educational leadership with principal endorsement (MA); educational technology (MA); leadership in adult learning higher education (Ed D); leadership in curriculum and instruction (Ed D); leadership in educational administration (Ed D); reading instruction (MA); special education (MA). *Accreditation:* NCATE. *Program availability:* Part-time, evening/weekend. *Faculty:* 15 full-time (8 women), 39 part-time/adjunct (20 women). *Students:* 421 full-time (299 women), 142 part-time (89 women); includes 90 minority (25 Black or African American, non-Hispanic/Latino; 7 Asian, non-Hispanic/Latino; 50 Hispanic/Latino; 2 Native Hawaiian or other Pacific Islander, non-Hispanic/Latino; 6 Two or more races, non-Hispanic/Latino). Average age 37. 169 applicants, 95% accepted, 59 enrolled. In 2017, 175 master's, 36 doctorates awarded. *Degree requirements:* For master's, student teaching; for doctorate, comprehensive exam, thesis/dissertation. *Entrance requirements:* For master's, 2 years of teaching experience, valid teaching certificate, resume; for doctorate, appropriate master's degree, two references, curriculum vitae, personal statement, professional project, reflective essay. Additional exam requirements/recommendations for international students: Required—TOEFL (minimum score 550 paper-based; 79 iBT). *Application deadline:* For fall admission, 6/1 for international students; for spring admission, 10/1 for international students. Applications are processed on a rolling basis. Application fee: $0. Electronic applications accepted. *Financial support:* In 2017–18, 34 students received support. Federal Work-Study, scholarships/grants, and unspecified assistantships available. Support available to part-time students. Financial award applicants required to submit FAFSA. *Unit head:* Dr. Jen Buckley, Dean, School of Education and Human Performance, 630-844-1542, Fax: 630-844-6155, E-mail: jbuckley@aurora.edu. *Application contact:* Elizabeth Botica, Graduate Education Recruiter, 630-947-8918, E-mail: ebotica@aurora.edu.
Website: http://aurora.edu/education

Austin Peay State University, College of Graduate Studies, College of Education, Department of Educational Specialties, Clarksville, TN 37044. Offers administration and supervision (Ed S); counseling and guidance (Ed S); curriculum and instruction (MA Ed); education leadership (MA Ed); elementary education (Ed S); reading (MA Ed); secondary education (Ed S). *Program availability:* Part-time, evening/weekend, online learning. *Faculty:* 15 full-time (9 women), 5 part-time/adjunct (4 women). *Students:* 73 full-time (54 women), 139 part-time (106 women); includes 49 minority (23 Black or African American, non-Hispanic/Latino; 4 Asian, non-Hispanic/Latino; 12 Hispanic/Latino; 10 Two or more races, non-Hispanic/Latino), 1 international. Average age 35. 72 applicants, 96% accepted, 42 enrolled. In 2017, 94 master's, 12 Ed Ss awarded. *Degree requirements:* For master's, comprehensive exam, thesis optional. *Entrance requirements:* For master's, GRE General Test, MAT, minimum undergraduate GPA of 2.75. Additional exam requirements/recommendations for international students: Required—TOEFL (minimum score 500 paper-based). *Application deadline:* For fall admission, 8/8 priority date for domestic students. Applications are processed on a rolling basis. Application fee: $45 ($50 for international students). Electronic applications accepted. *Expenses:* Tuition, state resident: full-time $7686; part-time $427 per credit hour. Tuition, nonresident: full-time $20,268; part-time $1126 per credit hour. *Required fees:* $1529; $76.45 per credit hour. *Financial support:* Research assistantships with full tuition reimbursements, career-related internships or fieldwork, Federal Work-Study, institutionally sponsored loans, scholarships/grants, and unspecified assistantships available. Support available to part-time students. Financial award application deadline: 4/1; financial award applicants required to submit FAFSA. *Unit head:* Dr. Moniqueka Gold, Chair, 931-221-7696, Fax: 931-221-1292, E-mail: goldm@apsu.edu. *Application contact:* Megan Mitchell, Coordinator of Graduate Admissions, 800-859-4723, Fax: 931-221-7641, E-mail: gradadmissions@apsu.edu.

Avila University, School of Education, Kansas City, MO 64145-1698. Offers advanced classroom management (MA); art K-12 (Teaching Certificate); educational technology (MA, Certificate); elementary education (Teaching Certificate); English as a second language (MA); English language learners (Advanced Certificate); middle school (Teaching Certificate); physical education K-12 (Teaching Certificate); secondary

education (Teaching Certificate); special education (Teaching Certificate); special reading (Advanced Certificate); teaching and learning (MA). *Program availability:* Part-time, evening/weekend, online learning. *Faculty:* 6 full-time (5 women), 9 part-time/adjunct (8 women). *Students:* 81 full-time (63 women), 20 part-time (11 women); includes 14 minority (8 Black or African American, non-Hispanic/Latino; 2 Asian, non-Hispanic/Latino; 3 Hispanic/Latino; 1 Two or more races, non-Hispanic/Latino), 4 international. Average age 35. 92 applicants, 62% accepted, 40 enrolled. In 2017, 24 master's awarded. *Entrance requirements:* For master's, minimum GPA of 3.0, writing sample, recommendation, interview; for other advanced degree, foreign language. Additional exam requirements/recommendations for international students: Required—TOEFL (minimum score 580 paper-based; 92 iBT). *Application deadline:* Applications are processed on a rolling basis. Electronic applications accepted. *Expenses:* Contact institution. *Financial support:* In 2017–18, 14 students received support. Unspecified assistantships available. Financial award applicants required to submit FAFSA. *Unit head:* Dr. Stacy Keith, Director of Graduate Education, 816-501-2446, Fax: 816-501-2915, E-mail: stacy.keith@avila.edu. *Application contact:* Cory Roup, Graduate Education Enrollment and Academic Advisor, 816-501-2464, E-mail: cory.roup@avila.edu.
Website: https://www.avila.edu/academics/graduate-studies/grad-education

Baldwin Wallace University, Graduate Programs, School of Education, Specialization in Literacy, Berea, OH 44017-2088. Offers MA Ed. *Accreditation:* NCATE. *Program availability:* Part-time, evening/weekend, blended/hybrid learning. *Students:* 14 full-time (all women), 24 part-time (22 women); includes 7 minority (5 Black or African American, non-Hispanic/Latino; 1 Hispanic/Latino; 1 Two or more races, non-Hispanic/Latino). Average age 29. 12 applicants, 75% accepted, 6 enrolled. In 2017, 21 master's awarded. *Degree requirements:* For master's, capstone practicum. *Entrance requirements:* For master's, bachelor's degree in field, MAT or minimum GPA of 3.0. Additional exam requirements/recommendations for international students: Required—TOEFL (minimum score 550 paper-based; 79 iBT). *Application deadline:* For fall admission, 8/15 priority date for domestic students; for spring admission, 12/15 priority date for domestic students. Applications are processed on a rolling basis. Application fee: $25. Electronic applications accepted. Application fee is waived when completed online. *Expenses:* $721 per credit hour. *Financial support:* Career-related internships or fieldwork available. Financial award applicants required to submit FAFSA. *Faculty research:* Metacognition and the reading process, language acquisition, genres and the reader response theory, cultural responsiveness, content area literacy. *Unit head:* Dr. Rochelle Berndt, Chair, 440-826-2168, Fax: 440-826-3779, E-mail: kkaye@bw.edu. *Application contact:* Winnie W. Gerhardt, Director of Transfer, Adult and Graduate Admission, 440-826-2222, Fax: 440-826-3830, E-mail: admission@bw.edu.
Website: http://www.bw.edu/academics/master-of-arts-in-education/maed-in-literacy/

Ball State University, Graduate School, Teachers College, Department of Elementary Education, Muncie, IN 47306. Offers early childhood administration (Certificate); elementary education (MAE, Ed D, PhD); enhanced teaching practices for elementary teachers (Certificate); literacy instruction (Certificate). *Accreditation:* NCATE. *Program availability:* Part-time, 100% online. *Faculty:* 11 full-time (all women), 2 part-time/adjunct (both women). *Students:* 17 full-time (15 women), 193 part-time (189 women); includes 31 minority (21 Black or African American, non-Hispanic/Latino; 1 Asian, non-Hispanic/Latino; 3 Hispanic/Latino; 6 Two or more races, non-Hispanic/Latino), 1 international. Average age 36. 152 applicants, 79% accepted, 83 enrolled. In 2017, 53 master's, 1 doctorate, 12 other advanced degrees awarded. *Entrance requirements:* For master's, minimum baccalaureate GPA of 2.75 or 3.0 in latter half of baccalaureate; for doctorate, GRE General Test, minimum graduate GPA of 3.2. Additional exam requirements/recommendations for international students: Required—TOEFL (minimum score 550 paper-based; 79 iBT), IELTS (minimum score 6.5). *Application deadline:* For fall admission, 7/15 for domestic students; for spring admission, 11/15 for domestic students; for summer admission, 4/15 for domestic students. Applications are processed on a rolling basis. Application fee: $60. Electronic applications accepted. *Financial support:* In 2017–18, 11 students received support, including 5 research assistantships with partial tuition reimbursements available (averaging $7,831 per year), 4 teaching assistantships with partial tuition reimbursements available (averaging $8,723 per year). Financial award application deadline: 3/1; financial award applicants required to submit FAFSA. *Unit head:* Dr. Pat Clark, Chairperson, 765-285-8564, Fax: 765-285-8793, E-mail: pclark@bsu.edu.
Website: http://www.bsu.edu/elementaryeducation/

Bank Street College of Education, Graduate School, Program in Reading and Literacy, New York, NY 10025. Offers advanced literacy specialization (Ed M); reading and literacy (MS Ed); teaching literacy (MS Ed); teaching literacy and childhood general education (MS Ed). *Degree requirements:* For master's, thesis. *Entrance requirements:* For master's, interview, essays. Additional exam requirements/recommendations for international students: Required—TOEFL (minimum score 600 paper-based; 100 iBT), IELTS (minimum score 7). Electronic applications accepted. *Faculty research:* Language development, children's literature, whole language, the reading and writing processes, reading difficulties in multicultural classrooms.

Barry University, School of Education, Program in Curriculum and Instruction, Miami Shores, FL 33161-6695. Offers accomplished teacher (Ed S); culture, language and literacy (TESOL) (PhD); curriculum evaluation and research (PhD); early childhood (Ed S); early childhood education (PhD); elementary (Ed S); elementary education (PhD); ESOL (Ed S); gifted (Ed S); Montessori (Ed S); PKP/elementary (Ed S); reading (Ed S); reading, language and cognition (PhD). *Entrance requirements:* For doctorate, GRE, minimum GPA of 3.25.

Barry University, School of Education, Program in Reading, Miami Shores, FL 33161-6695. Offers MS, Ed S. *Program availability:* Part-time, evening/weekend. *Degree requirements:* For master's, comprehensive exam, practicum; for Ed S, practicum. *Entrance requirements:* For master's, GRE General Test or MAT, minimum GPA of 3.0, course work in children's literature; for Ed S, GRE General Test, minimum GPA of 3.0. Electronic applications accepted.

Belhaven University, School of Education, Jackson, MS 39202-1789. Offers education (M Ed, MAT); educational leadership (Ed D, Ed S); reading literacy (M Ed). *Program availability:* Part-time, evening/weekend, 100% online, blended/hybrid learning. *Faculty:* 7 full-time (all women), 34 part-time/adjunct (23 women). *Students:* 4 full-time (all women), 505 part-time (413 women); includes 273 minority (257 Black or African American, non-Hispanic/Latino; 1 Asian, non-Hispanic/Latino; 5 Hispanic/Latino; 10 Two or more races, non-Hispanic/Latino). Average age 35. 203 applicants, 48% accepted, 92 enrolled. In 2017, 82 master's awarded. *Degree requirements:* For master's, comprehensive exam, portfolio; for doctorate, thesis/dissertation. *Entrance requirements:* For master's, PRAXIS I and II, minimum GPA of 2.8; for doctorate, MAT or GRE, master's degree in education or related field with minimum GPA of 3.0; essay; three professional letters of recommendation; minimum three years' experience in a PK-12 education context. *Application deadline:* Applications are processed on a rolling basis. Application fee: $25. Electronic applications accepted. *Expenses:* Contact institution. *Financial support:* Applicants required to submit FAFSA. *Unit head:* Dr. David Hand, Dean, 601-965-7020, E-mail: dhand@belhaven.edu. *Application contact:*

Sean Kirnan, Assistant Vice President for Adult and Graduate Enrollment and Student Services, 601-968-8727, Fax: 601-968-5953, E-mail: gradadmission@belhaven.edu.

Bellarmine University, Annsley Frazier Thornton School of Education, Louisville, KY 40205. Offers education and district leadership (Ed D); education and social change (PhD); elementary education (MA Ed, MAT); leadership in higher education (PhD); middle school education (MA Ed, MAT); principalship (Ed S); reading and writing (MA Ed); secondary education (MAT); teacher leadership (MA Ed). *Accreditation:* NCATE. *Program availability:* Part-time, evening/weekend. *Faculty:* 19 full-time (10 women), 36 part-time/adjunct (29 women). *Students:* 34 full-time (27 women), 204 part-time (158 women); includes 60 minority (43 Black or African American, non-Hispanic/Latino; 7 Asian, non-Hispanic/Latino; 7 Hispanic/Latino; 3 Two or more races, non-Hispanic/Latino). Average age 33. In 2017, 50 master's, 8 doctorates, 42 other advanced degrees awarded. *Degree requirements:* For master's, comprehensive exam (for some programs), thesis (for some programs); for doctorate, comprehensive exam (for some programs), thesis/dissertation; for Ed S, comprehensive exam (for some programs). *Entrance requirements:* For master's, GRE, baccalaureate degree from accredited institution; minimum cumulative GPA of 2.75; recommendations from employers, supervisors, or professors attesting to applicant's potential as graduate student; statement of intent to pursue graduate degree; for doctorate, GRE, minimum GPA of 3.5 in all graduate coursework; baccalaureate and master's degrees in education or fields directly relevant to education; three letters of recommendation; two essays (no more than 1,000 words each); resume or curriculum vitae; interview; for Ed S, master's degree in education; valid teaching certificate; three years of experience in teaching; three recommendations; minimum GPA of 3.0 in all graduate work; interview; essays; personal goal statement. Additional exam requirements/recommendations for international students: Required—TOEFL (minimum score 550 paper-based, 68 iBT), IELTS (minimum score 6), or Michigan English Language Assessment Battery. *Application deadline:* For fall admission, 8/1 priority date for domestic and international students; for spring admission, 12/1 priority date for domestic and international students; for summer admission, 4/10 priority date for domestic and international students. Applications are processed on a rolling basis. Application fee: $40. Electronic applications accepted. Tuition and fees vary according to program. *Financial support:* Scholarships/grants available. Financial award applicants required to submit FAFSA. *Faculty research:* Literacy, service-learning, dispositions, educational technology, special education. *Unit head:* Dr. Elizabeth Dinkins, Interim Dean, 502-272-7958, Fax: 502-272-8189, E-mail: edinkins@bellarmine.edu. *Application contact:* Sarah Schuble, Senior Graduate Admissions Recruiter, 502-272-8271, Fax: 502-272-8002, E-mail: sschuble@bellarmine.edu.
Website: http://www.bellarmine.edu/education/graduate

Benedictine University, Graduate Programs, Program in Education, Lisle, IL 60532. Offers curriculum and instruction and collaborative teaching (M Ed); elementary education (MA Ed); leadership and administration (M Ed); reading and literacy (M Ed); secondary education (MA Ed); special education (MA Ed). *Program availability:* Part-time, evening/weekend. *Degree requirements:* For master's, comprehensive exam, thesis (for some programs). *Entrance requirements:* For master's, GRE or MAT. Additional exam requirements/recommendations for international students: Required—TOEFL (minimum score 550 paper-based). Electronic applications accepted. *Expenses:* Contact institution.

Berry College, Graduate Programs, Graduate Programs in Education, Program in Middle-Grades Education and Reading, Mount Berry, GA 30149-0159. Offers middle grades education (MAT); middle-grades education (M Ed); reading (M Ed). *Accreditation:* NCATE. *Program availability:* Part-time. In 2017, 1 master's awarded. *Degree requirements:* For master's, thesis, portfolio, oral exams. *Entrance requirements:* For master's, GRE General Test or MAT, minimum GPA of 2.5. Additional exam requirements/recommendations for international students: Required—TOEFL (minimum score 550 paper-based). *Application deadline:* For fall admission, 7/20 for domestic students, 5/1 for international students; for spring admission, 12/1 for domestic students, 10/1 for international students. Applications are processed on a rolling basis. Application fee: $25 ($30 for international students). Electronic applications accepted. *Expenses:* $8,370 full-time tuition plus $176 fees per year; $465 per credit hour part-time tuition. *Financial support:* Research assistantships with full tuition reimbursements, scholarships/grants, tuition waivers (partial), and unspecified assistantships available. Support available to part-time students. Financial award application deadline: 3/1; financial award applicants required to submit FAFSA. *Unit head:* Dr. Jacqueline McDowell, Dean, 706-236-1717, Fax: 706-238-5827, E-mail: jmcdowell@berry.edu. *Application contact:* Brett Kennedy, Assistant Vice President of Enrollment Management, 706-236-2215, Fax: 706-290-2178, E-mail: admissions@berry.edu.

Binghamton University, State University of New York, Graduate School, College of Community and Public Affairs, Department of Teaching, Learning and Educational Leadership, Program in Literacy Education, Binghamton, NY 13902-6000. Offers MS Ed. *Accreditation:* TEAC. *Program availability:* Part-time, evening/weekend. *Students:* 4 full-time (all women), 16 part-time (13 women); includes 1 minority (Two or more races, non-Hispanic/Latino). Average age 31. 8 applicants, 100% accepted, 3 enrolled. In 2017, 13 master's awarded. *Degree requirements:* For master's, thesis. *Entrance requirements:* For master's, GRE General Test, teaching certification. Additional exam requirements/recommendations for international students: Required—TOEFL (minimum score 550 paper-based; 80 iBT). *Application deadline:* For fall admission, 2/1 priority date for domestic and international students; for spring admission, 10/15 priority date for domestic and international students. Application fee: $75. Electronic applications accepted. *Financial support:* In 2017–18, 4 students received support. Teaching assistantships, career-related internships or fieldwork, Federal Work-Study, institutionally sponsored loans, scholarships/grants, health care benefits, tuition waivers (full and partial), and unspecified assistantships available. Financial award applicants required to submit FAFSA. *Unit head:* Dr. Susan Strehle, Dean, 607-777-7329, E-mail: sstrehle@binghamton.edu. *Application contact:* Ben Balkaya, Assistant Dean and Director, 607-777-2151, Fax: 607-777-2501, E-mail: balkaya@binghamton.edu.

Bloomsburg University of Pennsylvania, School of Graduate Studies, College of Education, Department of Teaching and Learning, Program in Reading, Bloomsburg, PA 17815-1301. Offers M Ed. *Degree requirements:* For master's, thesis, PRAXIS II. *Entrance requirements:* For master's, baccalaureate degree, letter of intent, two letters of recommendation, teaching certificate. Additional exam requirements/recommendations for international students: Required—TOEFL, IELTS. Electronic applications accepted. *Expenses:* Tuition, state resident: full-time $10,000; part-time $500 per credit hour. Tuition, nonresident: full-time $15,000; part-time $750 per credit hour. *Required fees:* $2484; $110.75 per credit hour. $75 per term. Tuition and fees vary according to program.

Blue Mountain College, Program in Literacy/Reading (K-12), Blue Mountain, MS 38610. Offers M Ed. *Program availability:* Part-time, evening/weekend. *Faculty:* 3 part-time/adjunct (2 women). *Students:* 3 full-time (all women), 8 part-time (all women); includes 1 minority (Black or African American, non-Hispanic/Latino). Average age 34. 3 applicants, 33% accepted. In 2017, 13 master's awarded. *Degree requirements:* For master's, comprehensive exam. *Entrance requirements:* For master's, PRAXIS, GRE or

Reading Education

MAT, official transcripts, bachelor's degree in a field of education from an accredited university or college, permanent teaching license, three recommendations. Additional exam requirements/recommendations for international students: Required—TOEFL (minimum score 550 paper-based). *Application deadline:* For fall admission, 7/15 priority date for domestic students; for spring admission, 12/1 priority date for domestic students; for summer admission, 5/1 priority date for domestic students. Applications are processed on a rolling basis. Electronic applications accepted. *Expenses: Tuition:* Full-time $6030; part-time $335 per semester hour. *Required fees:* $790; $790 per semester hour. *Financial support:* Scholarships/grants available. Financial award application deadline: 6/30; financial award applicants required to submit FAFSA. *Unit head:* Dr. Jenetta R. Waddell, Dean of Graduate Studies, 662-685-4771 Ext. 118, Fax: 662-815-2919, E-mail: jwaddell@bmc.edu. *Application contact:* Jean Harrington, Administrative Assistant, Department of Education, 662-685-4771 Ext. 238, Fax: 662-815-2919, E-mail: jharrington@bmc.edu.
Website: http://www.bmc.edu/master_of_education.asp

Bluffton University, Programs in Education, Bluffton, OH 45817. Offers intervention specialist (MA Ed); leadership (MA Ed); reading (MA Ed). *Accreditation:* NCATE. *Program availability:* Part-time, 100% online, blended/hybrid learning, videoconference. *Faculty:* 2 full-time (1 woman), 1 part-time/adjunct (0 women). *Students:* 7 full-time (4 women), 11 part-time (10 women); includes 1 minority (Black or African American, non-Hispanic/Latino). Average age 29. 14 applicants, 64% accepted, 9 enrolled. In 2017, 7 master's awarded. *Degree requirements:* For master's, action research project, public presentation. *Entrance requirements:* For master's, PRAXIS I, bachelor's degree, minimum GPA of 3.0. Additional exam requirements/recommendations for international students: Required—TOEFL. *Application deadline:* For fall admission, 8/15 priority date for domestic students, 6/15 priority date for international students; for spring admission, 12/15 priority date for domestic students, 9/15 priority date for international students. Applications are processed on a rolling basis. Electronic applications accepted. *Expenses:* $456 per credit hour tuition, $50 per semester technology fee ($100 for more than 6 hours). *Financial support:* In 2017–18, 2 students received support. Unspecified assistantships available. Financial award application deadline: 9/15; financial award applicants required to submit FAFSA. *Unit head:* Dr. Amy K. Mullins, Director of Graduate Programs in Education, 419-358-3457, E-mail: mullinsa@bluffton.edu. *Application contact:* Nancey Schortgen, Program Representative, 419-358-3202, Fax: 419-358-3399, E-mail: schortgenn@bluffton.edu.
Website: http://www.bluffton.edu/grad/

Boise State University, College of Education, Department of Literacy, Language and Culture, Boise, ID 83725-0399. Offers bilingual education (M Ed); English as a new language (M Ed); literacy (MA). *Accreditation:* NCATE. *Program availability:* Part-time, evening/weekend. *Faculty:* 11 full-time (6 women). *Students:* 10 full-time (9 women), 53 part-time (46 women); includes 9 minority (1 Black or African American, non-Hispanic/Latino; 2 Asian, non-Hispanic/Latino; 5 Hispanic/Latino; 1 Native Hawaiian or other Pacific Islander, non-Hispanic/Latino), 6 international. Average age 36. 20 applicants, 75% accepted, 12 enrolled. In 2017, 26 master's awarded. *Degree requirements:* For master's, thesis optional. *Entrance requirements:* For master's, minimum GPA of 3.0. Additional exam requirements/recommendations for international students: Required—TOEFL (minimum score 550 paper-based; 80 iBT), IELTS (minimum score 6). Application fee: $65 ($95 for international students). Electronic applications accepted. *Expenses:* Tuition, state resident: full-time $6471; part-time $390 per credit. Tuition, nonresident: full-time $21,787; part-time $685 per credit. *Required fees:* $2283; $100 per term. Part-time tuition and fees vary according to course load and program. *Financial support:* Scholarships/grants and unspecified assistantships available. Financial award applicants required to submit FAFSA. *Unit head:* Dr. Maggie Chase, Department Chair, 208-426-3206, E-mail: maggiechase@boisestate.edu. *Application contact:* Dr. Arturo Rodriguez, Program Coordinator, 208-426-2243, E-mail: arturorodriguez@boisestate.edu.
Website: https://education.boisestate.edu/literacy/master-of-arts/

Boston College, Lynch School of Education, Program in Reading and Literacy, Chestnut Hill, MA 02467-3800. Offers M Ed, MAT, CAES. *Accreditation:* TEAC. *Program availability:* Part-time, evening/weekend. *Students:* 3 full-time (all women), 7 part-time (all women); includes 1 minority (Black or African American, non-Hispanic/Latino). Average age 25. 22 applicants, 82% accepted, 9 enrolled. In 2017, 7 master's awarded. *Degree requirements:* For master's and CAES, comprehensive exam. *Entrance requirements:* For master's, GRE General Test or MAT, general licensure, one year of teaching experience; for CAES, GRE General Test or MAT. Additional exam requirements/recommendations for international students: Required—TOEFL (minimum score 100 iBT). *Application deadline:* For fall admission, 12/1 priority date for domestic students, 12/1 for international students; for spring admission, 11/1 priority date for domestic and international students. Application fee: $65. Electronic applications accepted. *Financial support:* Fellowships with tuition reimbursements, research assistantships with tuition reimbursements, teaching assistantships with tuition reimbursements, Federal Work-Study, scholarships/grants, and tuition waivers (full and partial) available. Financial award applicants required to submit FAFSA. *Unit head:* Dr. Susan Bruce, Chairperson, 617-552-4214, Fax: 617-552-0398. *Application contact:* Kimberly Rose, Graduate Admission Assistant, 617-552-4214, Fax: 617-552-0398, E-mail: roseki@bc.edu.

Bowie State University, Graduate Programs, Program in Reading Education, Bowie, MD 20715-9465. Offers M Ed. *Accreditation:* NCATE. *Program availability:* Part-time, evening/weekend. *Degree requirements:* For master's, comprehensive exam, thesis optional, research paper. *Entrance requirements:* For master's, minimum GPA of 2.5, teaching certificate, teaching experience. *Faculty research:* Literacy education, multicultural education.

Bowling Green State University, Graduate College, College of Education and Human Development, School of Teaching and Learning, Program in Reading, Bowling Green, OH 43403. Offers M Ed, Ed S. *Accreditation:* NCATE. *Program availability:* Part-time. *Degree requirements:* For master's, thesis or alternative; for Ed S, practicum or field experience. *Entrance requirements:* For master's and Ed S, GRE General Test. Additional exam requirements/recommendations for international students: Required—TOEFL. Electronic applications accepted. *Faculty research:* Children's literature, attention deficit disorder (ADD)/reading correlation, content area reading, reading instruction, reading/writing connection.

Bridgewater State University, College of Graduate Studies, College of Education and Allied Studies, Department of Elementary and Early Childhood Education, Program in Reading, Bridgewater, MA 02325. Offers M Ed, CAGS. *Accreditation:* NCATE. *Program availability:* Part-time, evening/weekend. *Entrance requirements:* For master's, GRE General Test, 1 year of teaching experience.

Buffalo State College, State University of New York, The Graduate School, Faculty of Applied Science and Education, Department of Elementary Education and Reading, Programs in Literacy Specialist, Buffalo, NY 14222-1095. Offers literacy specialist (birth-grade 6) (MS Ed); literacy specialist (grades 5-12) (MPS). *Accreditation:* NCATE. *Program availability:* Part-time, evening/weekend. *Degree requirements:* For master's, project. *Entrance requirements:* For master's, minimum GPA of 3.0 in last 60 hours.

Additional exam requirements/recommendations for international students: Required—TOEFL (minimum score 550 paper-based).

Cabrini University, Academic Affairs, Radnor, PA 19087. Offers accounting (M Acc); autism spectrum disorder (M Ed); biological sciences (MS), including civic leadership; criminology and criminal justice (MA); curriculum, instruction, and assessment (M Ed); educational leadership (M Ed, Ed D), including curriculum and instructional leadership (Ed D), preK-12 leadership (Ed D); English as a second language (M Ed); organizational leadership (DBA, PhD); preK to 4 (M Ed); reading specialist (M Ed); secondary education (M Ed), including biology, chemistry, English, English/communication, mathematics, social studies; special education grades 7-12 (M Ed); special education preK-8 (M Ed); teaching and learning (M Ed). *Program availability:* Part-time, evening/weekend. *Faculty:* 23 full-time (17 women), 46 part-time/adjunct (38 women). *Students:* 60 full-time (35 women), 559 part-time (435 women); includes 93 minority (66 Black or African American, non-Hispanic/Latino; 1 American Indian or Alaska Native, non-Hispanic/Latino; 8 Asian, non-Hispanic/Latino; 15 Hispanic/Latino; 3 Two or more races, non-Hispanic/Latino), 4 international. Average age 33. 290 applicants, 82% accepted, 154 enrolled. In 2017, 283 master's awarded. *Degree requirements:* For master's, comprehensive exam (for some programs), thesis (for some programs); for doctorate, comprehensive exam (for some programs), thesis/dissertation. *Entrance requirements:* For master's, professional resume, personal statement, two recommendations, official transcripts; for doctorate, official transcripts, minimum master's GPA of 3.0, two recommendations, interview with admissions committee. Additional exam requirements/recommendations for international students: Required—TOEFL (minimum score 80 iBT). *Application deadline:* For fall admission, 8/26 for domestic students, 8/1 for international students; for winter admission, 1/13 for domestic students, 12/20 for international students; for spring admission, 1/13 for domestic students, 12/20 for international students; for summer admission, 5/20 for domestic students, 4/30 for international students. Applications are processed on a rolling basis. Application fee: $50. Electronic applications accepted. Application fee is waived when completed online. *Expenses:* Contact institution. *Financial support:* In 2017–18, 1,459 students received support. Tuition waivers and unspecified assistantships available. Financial award application deadline: 5/1; financial award applicants required to submit FAFSA. *Unit head:* Dr. Maliha Zaman, 610-902-8502, Fax: 610-902-8797, E-mail: msz37@cabrini.edu. *Application contact:* Diane Greenwood, Director of Graduate Admissions, 610-902-8291, E-mail: diane.l.greenwood@cabrini.edu.
Website: http://cabrini.edu/graduate

Caldwell University, School of Education, Caldwell, NJ 07006-6195. Offers curriculum and instruction (MA); education leadership (Ed D); educational administration (MA); elementary, secondary or preschool endorsement, special ed, ESL (Postbaccalaureate Certificate); learning disabilities teacher-consultant (Post-Master's Certificate); literacy instruction (MA); principal (Post-Master's Certificate); reading specialist (Post-Master's Certificate); special education (MA), including special education, teaching of students with disabilities, teaching of students with disabilities and learning disabilities teacher-consultant; superintendent (Post-Master's Certificate); supervisor (Post-Master's Certificate). *Program availability:* Part-time, evening/weekend. *Faculty:* 10 full-time (6 women), 21 part-time/adjunct (12 women). *Students:* 37 full-time (30 women), 225 part-time (177 women); includes 47 minority (19 Black or African American, non-Hispanic/Latino; 3 Asian, non-Hispanic/Latino; 23 Hispanic/Latino; 2 Two or more races, non-Hispanic/Latino). Average age 35. 189 applicants, 57% accepted, 85 enrolled. In 2017, 47 master's awarded. *Degree requirements:* For master's, comprehensive exam (for some programs), thesis (for some programs); for doctorate, thesis/dissertation. *Entrance requirements:* For master's, PRAXIS, 3 years of work experience, prior teaching certification; for doctorate, GRE or MAT; for other advanced degree, two letters of recommendation; interview (for some programs). Additional exam requirements/recommendations for international students: Required—TOEFL (minimum score 580 paper-based, 70 iBT), IELTS (6), or ELS Level 112 Certification of Completion. *Application deadline:* For fall admission, 6/1 for domestic students; for spring admission, 12/1 for domestic students; for summer admission, 4/1 for domestic students. Applications are processed on a rolling basis. Application fee: $50. Electronic applications accepted. *Expenses:* $950 per credit (for master's and certificate programs); $1,125 per credit (for doctoral programs). *Financial support:* Unspecified assistantships available. Financial award applicants required to submit FAFSA. *Faculty research:* Curriculum and instruction, secondary education, special education, education and technology, literacy instruction, higher education administration, education leadership. *Unit head:* Dr. Joan Moriarity, Associate Dean, 973-618-3626, E-mail: jmoriarity@caldwell.edu. *Application contact:* Tom Disch, Senior Admissions Counselor, 973-618-3544, E-mail: graduate@caldwell.edu.

California Baptist University, Program in Education, Riverside, CA 92504-3206. Offers educational leadership (MS); educational leadership for faith-based institutions (MS); educational leadership for public institutions (MS); educational technology (MS); instructional computer applications (MS); international education (MS); leadership and adult learning (MS); leadership and organizational studies (MS); online teaching and learning (MS); reading (MS); science education (MA); special education in mild/moderate disabilities (MS); special education in moderate/severe disabilities (MS); teacher leadership (MS); teaching (MS); teaching and learning (MS). *Program availability:* Part-time, evening/weekend, 100% online, blended/hybrid learning. *Faculty:* 19 full-time (11 women), 36 part-time/adjunct (22 women). *Students:* 232 full-time (182 women), 315 part-time (247 women); includes 264 minority (33 Black or African American, non-Hispanic/Latino; 4 American Indian or Alaska Native, non-Hispanic/Latino; 11 Asian, non-Hispanic/Latino; 186 Hispanic/Latino; 7 Native Hawaiian or other Pacific Islander, non-Hispanic/Latino; 23 Two or more races, non-Hispanic/Latino). Average age 31. 217 applicants, 64% accepted, 129 enrolled. In 2017, 196 master's awarded. *Entrance requirements:* For master's, minimum undergraduate GPA of 2.75; 500-word essay; three letters of recommendation; two prerequisite courses completed with minimum C grade. Additional exam requirements/recommendations for international students: Required—TOEFL (minimum score 80 iBT). *Application deadline:* For fall admission, 8/1 priority date for domestic students, 7/1 for international students; for spring admission, 12/1 priority date for domestic students, 11/1 for international students. Applications are processed on a rolling basis. Application fee: $45. Electronic applications accepted. *Expenses:* Contact institution. *Financial support:* In 2017–18, 162 students received support. Federal Work-Study and scholarships/grants available. Financial award applicants required to submit CSS PROFILE or FAFSA. *Faculty research:* Leadership development, complexity theory, faith and learning, special education, social and philosophical contexts of education. *Unit head:* Dr. John Shoup, Dean, School of Education, 951-343-4516, E-mail: jshoup@calbaptist.edu. *Application contact:* Gavin Andrew, Graduate Admissions Counselor, 951-552-8437, E-mail: gandrew@calbaptist.edu.
Website: http://www.calbaptist.edu/mastersined/

California State Polytechnic University, Pomona, Master's Programs in Education, Pomona, CA 91768-2557. Offers curriculum and instruction (MA), including literacy studies. *Program availability:* Part-time, evening/weekend. *Students:* 19 full-time (14 women), 71 part-time (43 women); includes 58 minority (6 Black or African American, non-Hispanic/Latino; 10 Asian, non-Hispanic/Latino; 39 Hispanic/Latino; 3 Two or more races, non-Hispanic/Latino), 5 international. Average age 35. 45 applicants, 56% accepted, 13 enrolled. In 2017, 43 master's awarded. *Entrance requirements:* Additional exam requirements/recommendations for international students: Required—TOEFL (minimum score 550 paper-based). *Application deadline:* Applications are processed on a rolling basis. Application fee: $55. Electronic applications accepted. *Expenses:* Contact institution. *Financial support:* Application deadline: 3/2; applicants required to submit FAFSA. *Unit head:* Dr. Richard A. Navarro, Professor/Graduate Coordinator, 909-869-2081, Fax: 909-869-4822, E-mail: ranavarro@cpp.edu. *Application contact:* Deborah L. Brandon, Executive Director of Admissions and Enrollment Planning, 909-869-3427, Fax: 909-869-5315, E-mail: dlbrandon@cpp.edu. Website: http://www.cpp.edu/~ceis/education/masters-programs/index.shtml

California State University, East Bay, Office of Graduate Studies, College of Education and Allied Studies, Department of Teacher Education, Hayward, CA 94542-3000. Offers education (MS), including curriculum, early childhood education, educational technology and leadership, reading instruction. *Program availability:* Online learning. *Faculty:* 11 full-time (8 women), 56 part-time/adjunct (40 women). *Students:* 49 full-time (35 women), 15 part-time (13 women); includes 31 minority (5 Black or African American, non-Hispanic/Latino; 13 Asian, non-Hispanic/Latino; 11 Hispanic/Latino; 2 Two or more races, non-Hispanic/Latino), 7 international. Average age 31. 76 applicants, 82% accepted, 33 enrolled. In 2017, 83 master's awarded. *Degree requirements:* For master's, project or thesis. *Entrance requirements:* For master's, minimum GPA of 3.0 in field, 2.5 overall; teaching experience; baccalaureate degree; 3 letters of recommendation. Additional exam requirements/recommendations for international students: Required—TOEFL (minimum score 550 paper-based), IELTS. *Application deadline:* For fall admission, 6/1 for domestic and international students. Application fee: $55. Electronic applications accepted. *Financial support:* Career-related internships or fieldwork, Federal Work-Study, and institutionally sponsored loans available. Support available to part-time students. Financial award application deadline: 3/2; financial award applicants required to submit FAFSA. *Faculty research:* Online, pedagogy, writing, learning, teaching. *Unit head:* Dr. Eric Engdahl, Chair, 510-885-4599, E-mail: eric.engdahl@csueastbay.edu. *Application contact:* Prof. Valerie Helgren-Lempesis, Education Graduate Advisor, 510-885-3006, Fax: 510-885-4632, E-mail: valerie.helgren-lempesis@csueastbay.edu. Website: http://www20.csueastbay.edu/ceas/departments/ted/index.html

California State University, Fresno, Division of Research and Graduate Studies, Kremen School of Education and Human Development, Department of Literacy, Early, Bilingual, and Special Education, Fresno, CA 93740-8027. Offers education (MA), including early childhood education, reading/language arts; special education (MA). *Accreditation:* NCATE. *Program availability:* Part-time, evening/weekend. *Degree requirements:* For master's, thesis or alternative. *Entrance requirements:* For master's, GRE General Test, MAT, minimum GPA of 2.75. Additional exam requirements/recommendations for international students: Required—TOEFL. Electronic applications accepted. *Faculty research:* Reading recovery, monitoring/tutoring programs, character and academics, professional ethics, low-performing partnership schools.

California State University, Fullerton, Graduate Studies, College of Education, Department of Literacy and Reading Education, Fullerton, CA 92831-3599. Offers MS. *Program availability:* Part-time. *Faculty:* 4 full-time (2 women), 4 part-time/adjunct (3 women). *Students:* 4 full-time (all women), 104 part-time (98 women); includes 55 minority (4 Black or African American, non-Hispanic/Latino; 1 American Indian or Alaska Native, non-Hispanic/Latino; 16 Asian, non-Hispanic/Latino; 31 Hispanic/Latino; 3 Two or more races, non-Hispanic/Latino), 3 international. Average age 37. 49 applicants, 80% accepted, 31 enrolled. In 2017, 25 master's awarded. Application fee: $55. *Financial support:* Career-related internships or fieldwork, Federal Work-Study, institutionally sponsored loans, and scholarships/grants available. Support available to part-time students. Financial award application deadline: 3/1; financial award applicants required to submit FAFSA. *Unit head:* Dr. Ula Manzo, Chair, 657-278-3357. *Application contact:* Admissions/Applications, 657-278-2371. Website: http://ed.fullerton.edu/reading/

California State University, Northridge, Graduate Studies, Michael D. Eisner College of Education, Department of Elementary Education, Northridge, CA 91330. Offers curriculum and instruction (MA); language and literacy (MA); multilingual/multicultural education (MA). *Accreditation:* NCATE. *Program availability:* Part-time, evening/weekend. *Students:* 3 full-time (all women), 62 part-time (56 women); includes 37 minority (7 Asian, non-Hispanic/Latino; 26 Hispanic/Latino; 4 Two or more races, non-Hispanic/Latino). Average age 30. 42 applicants, 50% accepted, 19 enrolled. In 2017, 103 master's awarded. *Degree requirements:* For master's, comprehensive exam. *Entrance requirements:* For master's, GRE General Test or minimum GPA of 3.0. Additional exam requirements/recommendations for international students: Required—TOEFL. *Application deadline:* For fall admission, 11/30 for domestic students. Application fee: $55. *Financial support:* Federal Work-Study available. Financial award application deadline: 3/1. *Unit head:* Dr. Joyce Burstein, Chair, 818-677-2621. Website: http://www.csun.edu/eisner-education/elementary-education

California State University, Sacramento, College of Education, Graduate and Professional Studies in Education, Sacramento, CA 95819. Offers behavioral science and gender equity (MA); child development (MA); counseling (MS); curriculum and instruction (MA); education (Ed D), including K-12 and community college; education leadership and policy studies (MA), including higher education, PreK-12; education specialist (Ed S), including school psychology; educational technology (MA); language and literacy (MA); multicultural education (MA); school psychology (MA); special education (MA); workforce development advocacy (MA). *Program availability:* Part-time, evening/weekend, blended/hybrid learning. *Students:* 381 full-time (294 women), 135 part-time (101 women); includes 296 minority (44 Black or African American, non-Hispanic/Latino; 1 American Indian or Alaska Native, non-Hispanic/Latino; 94 Asian, non-Hispanic/Latino; 153 Hispanic/Latino; 4 Native Hawaiian or other Pacific Islander, non-Hispanic/Latino), 3 international. Average age 32. 553 applicants, 53% accepted, 292 enrolled. In 2017, 147 master's, 13 doctorates, 10 other advanced degrees awarded. *Degree requirements:* For master's, thesis or project; writing proficiency exam; for doctorate, thesis/dissertation. *Entrance requirements:* For master's and doctorate, GRE. Additional exam requirements/recommendations for international students: Required—TOEFL (minimum score 550 paper-based; 80 iBT); Recommended—IELTS (minimum score 7), TSE. *Application deadline:* For fall admission, 2/15 for domestic students, 1/15 for international students. Applications are processed on a rolling basis. Application fee: $55. Electronic applications accepted. *Expenses:* Contact institution. *Financial support:* Career-related internships or fieldwork, Federal Work-Study, and scholarships/grants available. Support available to part-time students. Financial award application deadline: 3/1; financial award applicants required to submit FAFSA. *Unit head:* Dr. Elizabeth Liles, Chair, 916-278-5942, E-mail: coe@csus.edu. *Application contact:* Jose Martinez, Graduate Admissions Supervisor, 916-278-7871, E-mail: martinj@skymail.csus.edu. Website: http://www.csus.edu/coe/academics/graduate/index.html

California State University, San Marcos, College of Education, Health and Human Services, School of Education, San Marcos, CA 92096-0001. Offers education (MA); educational administration (MA); educational leadership (Ed D); literacy education (MA); special education (MA). *Accreditation:* NCATE (one or more programs are accredited).

Program availability: Part-time, evening/weekend. *Entrance requirements:* For master's, minimum GPA of 3.0, teaching credentials, 1 year of teaching experience. *Application deadline:* For fall admission, 2/1 priority date for domestic students. Applications are processed on a rolling basis. Application fee: $55. *Expenses:* Tuition, state resident: full-time $7176. Tuition, nonresident: full-time $9504. *Financial support:* Applicants required to submit FAFSA. *Faculty research:* Multicultural literature, art as knowledge, poetry and second language acquisition, restructuring K–12 education and improving the training of K–8 science teachers. *Unit head:* Pat Stall, Director, 760-750-4386, E-mail: pstall@csusm.edu. Website: http://www.csusm.edu/education/

California State University, Stanislaus, College of Education, Kinesiology and Social Work, MA Program in Education, Turlock, CA 95382. Offers curriculum and instruction (MA), including education technology, elementary education, multilingual education, physical education, reading, secondary education, special education; school administration (MA); school counseling (MA). *Program availability:* Part-time, evening/weekend. *Degree requirements:* For master's, comprehensive exam (for some programs), thesis (for some programs). *Entrance requirements:* For master's, MAT, GRE, or CBEST (varies by concentration), 3 letters of recommendation, personal statement. Additional exam requirements/recommendations for international students: Required—TOEFL (minimum score 550 paper-based). Electronic applications accepted. *Faculty research:* Children's perspectives on historical events, method elementary schools dual language education, K-12 reading programs.

California University of Pennsylvania, School of Graduate Studies and Research, College of Education and Human Services, Program in Reading Specialist, California, PA 15419-1394. Offers M Ed. *Accreditation:* NCATE. *Program availability:* Part-time, evening/weekend. *Degree requirements:* For master's, comprehensive exam, thesis optional, practicum. *Entrance requirements:* For master's, MAT, PRAXIS, minimum GPA of 3.0, teaching certificate. Additional exam requirements/recommendations for international students: Required—TOEFL (minimum score 550 paper-based; 80 iBT). *Application deadline:* For fall admission, 8/1 priority date for domestic and international students; for spring admission, 5/1 priority date for domestic and international students. Applications are processed on a rolling basis. Application fee: $25. Electronic applications accepted. *Financial support:* Applicants required to submit FAFSA. *Faculty research:* Online education in reading supervision, phonetics education, remedial reading, injury and reading remediation in brain patients. *Unit head:* Dr. Diane Fine, Graduate Coordinator, 724-938-4495, E-mail: fine@calu.edu. *Application contact:* Suzanne C. Powers, Director of Graduate Admissions and Recruitment, 724-938-4029, Fax: 724-938-5712, E-mail: powers_s@cup.edu. Website: http://www.calu.edu/academics/graduate-programs/reading-specialist/index.htm

Cambridge College, School of Education, Boston, MA 02129. Offers autism specialist (M Ed); autism/behavior analyst (M Ed); behavior analyst (Post-Master's Certificate); behavioral management (M Ed); early childhood teacher (M Ed); education specialist in curriculum and instruction (CAGS); educational leadership (Ed D); elementary teacher (M Ed); English as a second language (M Ed, Certificate); general science (M Ed); health education (Post-Master's Certificate); health/family and consumer sciences (M Ed); history (M Ed); individualized (M Ed); information technology literacy (M Ed); instructional technology (M Ed); interdisciplinary studies (M Ed); library teacher (M Ed); literacy education (M Ed); mathematics (M Ed); mathematics specialist (Certificate); middle school mathematics and science (M Ed); school administration (M Ed, CAGS); school guidance counselor (M Ed); school nurse education (M Ed); school social worker/school adjustment counselor (M Ed); special education administrator (CAGS); special education/moderate disabilities (M Ed); teaching skills and methodologies (M Ed). *Program availability:* Part-time, evening/weekend, online learning. *Degree requirements:* For master's, thesis, internship/practicum (licensure program only); for doctorate, thesis/dissertation; for other advanced degree, thesis. *Entrance requirements:* For master's, interview, resume, documentation of licensure, 2 professional references; for doctorate, official transcripts, interview, resume, documentation of licensure (if any), written personal statement/essay, portfolio of scholarly and professional work, qualifying assessment, 2 professional references, health insurance, immunizations form; for other advanced degree, official transcripts, interview, resume, documentation of licensure (if any), written personal statement/essay, 2 professional references, health insurance, immunizations form. Additional exam requirements/recommendations for international students: Required—TOEFL (minimum score 550 paper-based; 79 iBT), Michigan English Language Assessment Battery (minimum score 85); Recommended—IELTS (minimum score 6). Electronic applications accepted. *Expenses:* Contact institution. *Faculty research:* Adult education, accelerated learning, mathematics education, brain compatible learning, special education and law.

Canisius College, Graduate Division, School of Education and Human Services, Department of Graduate Education and Leadership, Buffalo, NY 14208-1098. Offers business and marketing education (MS Ed); college student personnel (MS Ed); deaf education (MS Ed); deaf/adolescent education, grades 7-12 (MS Ed); deaf/childhood education, grades 1-6 (MS Ed); differentiated instruction (MS Ed); education administration (MS); educational administration (MS Ed); educational technologies (Certificate); gifted education extension (Certificate); literacy (MS Ed); reading (Certificate); school building leadership (MS Ed, Certificate); school district leadership (Certificate); teacher leader (Certificate); TESOL (MS Ed). *Accreditation:* NCATE. *Program availability:* Part-time, evening/weekend, 100% online, blended/hybrid learning. *Faculty:* 5 full-time (all women), 21 part-time/adjunct (16 women). *Students:* 85 full-time (67 women), 189 part-time (151 women); includes 31 minority (18 Black or African American, non-Hispanic/Latino; 3 American Indian or Alaska Native, non-Hispanic/Latino; 3 Asian, non-Hispanic/Latino; 4 Hispanic/Latino; 3 Two or more races, non-Hispanic/Latino), 1 international. Average age 31. 83 applicants, 96% accepted, 74 enrolled. In 2017, 94 master's, 47 other advanced degrees awarded. *Entrance requirements:* For master's, GRE (if cumulative GPA less than 2.7), transcripts, two letters of recommendation. Additional exam requirements/recommendations for international students: Required—TOEFL (minimum score 550 paper-based, 79 iBT), IELTS (minimum score 6.5), or CAEL (minimum score 70). *Application deadline:* Applications are processed on a rolling basis. Application fee: $0. Electronic applications accepted. *Expenses:* Tuition: Full-time $22,860; part-time $820 per credit. *Required fees:* $720; $25 per credit. $65 per semester. One-time fee: $425. *Financial support:* Career-related internships or fieldwork, Federal Work-Study, scholarships/grants, tuition waivers (partial), and unspecified assistantships available. Support available to part-time students. Financial award application deadline: 4/30; financial award applicants required to submit FAFSA. *Faculty research:* Asperger's disease, autism, private higher education, reading strategies. *Unit head:* Dr. Anne Marie Tryjankowski, Chair/Associate Professor of Graduate Education and Leadership, 716-888-3715, Fax: 716-888-3142, E-mail: tryjanka@canisius.edu.

Capella University, School of Education, Doctoral Programs in Education, Minneapolis, MN 55402. Offers curriculum and instruction (PhD); educational leadership and management (Ed D); instructional design for online learning (PhD); K-12 studies in education (PhD); leadership for higher education (PhD); leadership in educational administration (PhD); postsecondary and adult education (PhD); professional studies in education (PhD); reading and literacy (Ed D); special education leadership (PhD); training and performance improvement (PhD).

Reading Education

Capella University, School of Education, Master's Programs in Education, Minneapolis, MN 55402. Offers adult education (MS); curriculum and instruction (MS); early childhood education (MS); enrollment management (MS); higher education leadership and management (MS); instructional design for online learning (MS); integrative studies (MS); K-12 studies in education (MS); leadership in educational administration (MS); reading and literacy (MS); special education teaching (MS).

Cardinal Stritch University, College of Education and Leadership, Department of Literacy, Milwaukee, WI 53217-3985. Offers language and literacy (MA, PhD). *Accreditation:* NCATE. *Program availability:* Part-time, evening/weekend. *Students:* 23 part-time (22 women); includes 3 minority (1 American Indian or Alaska Native, non-Hispanic/Latino; 2 Hispanic/Latino), 1 international. Average age 40. 8 applicants, 100% accepted, 6 enrolled. In 2017, 13 master's, 2 doctorates awarded. *Degree requirements:* For master's, comprehensive exam, thesis, faculty recommendation, research project; for doctorate, thesis/dissertation. *Entrance requirements:* For master's, 2 letters of recommendation, minimum GPA of 2.75; for doctorate, 3 letters of recommendation, minimum GPA of 3.5. Additional exam requirements/recommendations for international students: Required—TOEFL (minimum score 550 paper-based; 79 iBT), IELTS (minimum score 6.5). *Application deadline:* For fall admission, 7/15 priority date for domestic students; for spring admission, 12/15 priority date for domestic students. Applications are processed on a rolling basis. Electronic applications accepted. *Expenses:* Tuition varies by program. *Financial support:* Research assistantships with partial tuition reimbursements, Federal Work-Study, and scholarships/grants available. Financial award applicants required to submit FAFSA. *Unit head:* 414-410-4000. *Application contact:* 800-347-8822 Ext. 4042, E-mail: admissions@stritch.edu.

Carthage College, Division of Teacher Education, Kenosha, WI 53140. Offers classroom guidance and counseling (M Ed); creative arts (M Ed); gifted and talented children (M Ed); language arts (M Ed); modern language (M Ed); natural sciences (M Ed); reading (M Ed, Certificate); social sciences (M Ed); teacher leadership (M Ed). *Program availability:* Part-time, evening/weekend. *Degree requirements:* For master's, thesis optional. *Entrance requirements:* For master's, MAT, minimum B average, letters of reference.

Castleton University, Division of Graduate Studies, Department of Education, Program in Language Arts and Reading, Castleton, VT 05735. Offers MA Ed, CAGS. *Program availability:* Part-time, evening/weekend. *Degree requirements:* For master's, thesis or alternative; for CAGS, publishable paper, written exams. *Entrance requirements:* For master's, GRE General Test, MAT, interview, minimum undergraduate GPA of 3.0; for CAGS, educational research, master's degree, minimum undergraduate GPA of 3.0.

Centenary University, Program in Education, Hackettstown, NJ 07840-2100. Offers education practice (M Ed); educational leadership (MA, Ed D); instructional leadership (MA); reading (M Ed); special education (MA). *Accreditation:* TEAC. *Program availability:* Part-time, evening/weekend, online learning. *Degree requirements:* For master's, thesis. *Entrance requirements:* For master's, interview, minimum undergraduate GPA of 2.8.

Central Connecticut State University, School of Graduate Studies, School of Education and Professional Studies, Department of Literacy, Elementary, and Early Childhood Education, New Britain, CT 06050-4010. Offers MS, AC, Sixth Year Certificate. *Program availability:* Part-time, evening/weekend. *Faculty:* 7 full-time (6 women), 1 (woman) part-time/adjunct. *Students:* 9 full-time (7 women), 109 part-time (101 women); includes 7 minority (1 Black or African American, non-Hispanic/Latino; 5 Hispanic/Latino; 1 Two or more races, non-Hispanic/Latino). Average age 31. 49 applicants, 73% accepted, 26 enrolled. In 2017, 44 master's, 10 other advanced degrees awarded. *Degree requirements:* For master's, comprehensive exam, thesis or alternative; for other advanced degree, qualifying exam. *Entrance requirements:* For master's, minimum undergraduate GPA of 2.7, teacher certification, interview, essay, letters of recommendation; for other advanced degree, master's degree, essay, teacher certification, interview, letters of recommendation. Additional exam requirements/recommendations for international students: Required—TOEFL (minimum score 550 paper-based; 79 iBT); Recommended—IELTS (minimum score 6.5). *Application deadline:* For fall admission, 8/1 for domestic students, 5/1 for international students; for spring admission, 11/1 for domestic and international students. Applications are processed on a rolling basis. Application fee: $50. Electronic applications accepted. *Expenses: Tuition, area resident:* Full-time $6757. Tuition, state resident: full-time $9750; part-time $374 per credit. Tuition, nonresident: full-time $18,102; part-time $374 per credit. *Required fees:* $4635; $255 per credit. *Financial support:* In 2017–18, 6 students received support. Career-related internships or fieldwork, Federal Work-Study, scholarships/grants, and unspecified assistantships available. Support available to part-time students. Financial award application deadline: 3/1. *Faculty research:* Developmental, clinical, and administrative aspects of reading and language arts instruction. *Unit head:* Dr. Helen Abadiano, Chair, 860-832-2175, E-mail: abadiano@ccsu.edu. *Application contact:* Patricia Gardner, Associate Director of Graduate Studies, 860-832-2350, Fax: 860-832-2362.
Website: http://www.ccsu.edu/leece/index.html

Central Michigan University, Central Michigan University Global Campus, Program in Education, Mount Pleasant, MI 48859. Offers college teaching (Graduate Certificate); community college (MA); curriculum and instruction (MA); educational technology (MA, DET); reading and literacy K-12 (MA); school principalship (MA), including charter school leadership; training and development (MA). *Accreditation:* TEAC. *Program availability:* Part-time, evening/weekend. *Entrance requirements:* For master's, minimum GPA of 2.7 in major. Additional exam requirements/recommendations for international students: Required—TOEFL. Electronic applications accepted.

Central Michigan University, College of Graduate Studies, College of Education and Human Services, Department of Teacher Education and Professional Development, Mount Pleasant, MI 48859. Offers educational technology (MA, Graduate Certificate); elementary education (MA), including classroom teaching, early childhood; reading and literacy K-12 (MA); secondary education (MA). *Program availability:* Part-time, evening/weekend. *Degree requirements:* For master's, thesis or alternative. Electronic applications accepted. *Faculty research:* Integrating literacy across the curriculum, science teaching and aesthetic learning in science, diversity education, educational technology, educational psychology and child development.

Central Washington University, School of Graduate Studies and Research, College of Education and Professional Studies, Department of Education, Development, Teaching, and Learning, Ellensburg, WA 98926. Offers literacy (M Ed). *Program availability:* Part-time. *Faculty:* 11 full-time (8 women). *Students:* 1 (woman) full-time, 3 part-time (2 women). 5 applicants, 100% accepted, 3 enrolled. In 2017, 2 master's awarded. *Degree requirements:* For master's, thesis or alternative. *Entrance requirements:* For master's, minimum GPA of 3.0. Additional exam requirements/recommendations for international students: Required—TOEFL (minimum score 550 paper-based; 79 iBT), IELTS (minimum score 6.5). *Application deadline:* For fall admission, 2/1 priority date for domestic students; for winter admission, 10/1 for domestic students; for spring admission, 1/1 for domestic students. Applications are processed on a rolling basis. Application fee: $50. Electronic applications accepted. *Financial support:* Federal Work-Study, health care benefits, and unspecified assistantships available. Financial award

application deadline: 3/1; financial award applicants required to submit FAFSA. *Unit head:* Dr. Dan Fennerty, Co-Chair, 509-963-2737. *Application contact:* Justine Eason, Admissions Program Coordinator, 509-963-3103, Fax: 509-963-1799, E-mail: masters@cwu.edu.
Website: http://www.cwu.edu/~llse/

Chestnut Hill College, School of Graduate Studies, Department of Education, Program in Reading, Philadelphia, PA 19118-2693. Offers reading specialist (M Ed), including K-12, special education 7-12, special education PreK-8. *Program availability:* Part-time, evening/weekend. *Degree requirements:* For master's, thesis optional. *Entrance requirements:* Additional exam requirements/recommendations for international students: Required—TOEFL (minimum score 500 paper-based) or IELTS (minimum score 6). Electronic applications accepted. *Expenses:* Contact institution. *Faculty research:* Inclusive education, cultural issues in education.

Chicago State University, School of Graduate and Professional Studies, College of Education, Department of Reading, Elementary Education, Library Information and Media Studies, Program in Reading, Chicago, IL 60628. Offers teaching of reading (MS Ed). *Accreditation:* NCATE. *Entrance requirements:* For master's, minimum GPA of 2.75. *Application deadline:* For fall admission, 7/1 for domestic students; for spring admission, 11/10 for domestic students. Application fee: $25. *Unit head:* Dr. Cathryn Busch. *Application contact:* Anika Miller, Graduate Studies Office, 773-995-2404, E-mail: g-studies1@csu.edu.

The Citadel, The Military College of South Carolina, Citadel Graduate College, Zucker Family School of Education, Charleston, SC 29409. Offers elementary/secondary school administration and supervision (M Ed); elementary/secondary school counseling (M Ed); interdisciplinary STEM education (M Ed); literacy education M Ed, Graduate Certificate); middle grades (MAT), including English, mathematics, science, social studies; physical education (grades K-12) (MAT); school superintendency (Ed S); secondary education (MAT), including biology, English, mathematics, social studies; student affairs (Graduate Certificate); student affairs and college counseling (M Ed). *Accreditation:* NCATE. *Program availability:* Part-time, evening/weekend, 100% online, blended/hybrid learning. *Degree requirements:* For master's, comprehensive exam (for some programs). *Entrance requirements:* For master's, GRE (minimum combined verbal and quantitative score of 290) or MAT (minimum score 396). Additional exam requirements/recommendations for international students: Required—TOEFL (minimum score 550 paper-based; 79 iBT). Electronic applications accepted. *Expenses:* Tuition, state resident: part-time $587 per credit hour. Tuition, nonresident: part-time $988 per credit hour. *Required fees:* $90 per term.

City College of the City University of New York, Graduate School, Division of Humanities and the Arts, Department of English, Program in Language and Literacy, New York, NY 10031-9198. Offers MA. *Accreditation:* NCATE. *Entrance requirements:* For master's, 2 writing samples. Additional exam requirements/recommendations for international students: Required—TOEFL (minimum score 600 paper-based; 100 iBT). Electronic applications accepted.

City College of the City University of New York, Graduate School, School of Education, Department of Teaching, Learning and Culture, New York, NY 10031-9198. Offers bilingual education (MS); childhood education (MS); early childhood education (MS); educational theatre (MS); literacy (MS); TESOL (MS). *Accreditation:* NCATE. *Degree requirements:* For master's, thesis. *Entrance requirements:* For master's, Liberal Arts and Sciences Test (LAST), Content Specialty Test (CST). Additional exam requirements/recommendations for international students: Required—TOEFL.

City University of Seattle, Graduate Division, Albright School of Education, Seattle, WA 98121. Offers administrator certification (Certificate); curriculum and instruction (M Ed); elementary education (MIT); guidance and counseling (M Ed); leadership (M Ed); reading and literacy (M Ed); school counseling (M Ed); special education (MIT); superintendent certification (Certificate). *Program availability:* Part-time, evening/weekend, online learning. *Degree requirements:* For master's, comprehensive exam (for some programs), thesis (for some programs). *Entrance requirements:* For master's, baccalaureate degree or equivalent from an accredited or otherwise recognized institution. Additional exam requirements/recommendations for international students: Required—TOEFL (minimum score 567 paper-based; 87 iBT); Recommended—IELTS. Electronic applications accepted. *Expenses:* Contact institution.

Clarion University of Pennsylvania, College of Arts, Education and Sciences, Master of Education Program, Clarion, PA 16214. Offers curriculum and instruction (M Ed); early childhood (M Ed); math education (M Ed); reading (M Ed); science education (M Ed); special education (M Ed); technology (M Ed). *Accreditation:* NCATE. *Program availability:* Part-time, evening/weekend, online only, 100% online, blended/hybrid learning. *Faculty:* 6 full-time (3 women). *Students:* 11 full-time (all women), 101 part-time (82 women); includes 4 minority (2 Black or African American, non-Hispanic/Latino; 1 Hispanic/Latino; 1 Two or more races, non-Hispanic/Latino). Average age 30. 80 applicants, 98% accepted, 33 enrolled. In 2017, 52 master's awarded. *Degree requirements:* For master's, comprehensive exam, thesis, or portfolio. *Entrance requirements:* For master's, minimum QPA of 3.0. Additional exam requirements/recommendations for international students: Required—TOEFL (minimum score 550 paper-based, 80 iBT) or IELTS (7). *Application deadline:* For fall admission, 8/15 priority date for domestic students, 7/15 priority date for international students; for winter admission, 11/1 priority date for domestic students; for spring admission, 1/7 priority date for domestic students, 11/15 priority date for international students; for summer admission, 4/1 priority date for domestic students. Applications are processed on a rolling basis. Application fee: $40. Electronic applications accepted. *Expenses:* $655.05 per credit. *Financial support:* Career-related internships or fieldwork and scholarships/grants available. Support available to part-time students. Financial award application deadline: 3/1; financial award applicants required to submit FAFSA. *Unit head:* Dr. John McCullough, Chair, Department of Education, 814-393-2404, Fax: 814-393-2446, E-mail: gradstudies@clarion.edu. *Application contact:* Dana Bearer, Associate Director for Transfer, Adult, and Graduate Programs, 814-393-2337, Fax: 814-393-2722, E-mail: gradstudies@clarion.edu.

Clemson University, Graduate School, College of Education, Department of Education and Human Development, Clemson, SC 29634. Offers counselor education (M Ed, Ed S), including mental health counseling, school counseling, student affairs (M Ed); learning sciences (PhD); literacy (M Ed); literacy, language and culture (PhD); special education (M Ed, MAT, PhD). *Program availability:* Part-time, evening/weekend, 100% online. *Faculty:* 32 full-time (22 women). *Students:* 445 full-time (355 women), 169 part-time (159 women); includes 126 minority (52 Black or African American, non-Hispanic/Latino; 16 Asian, non-Hispanic/Latino; 34 Hispanic/Latino; 24 Two or more races, non-Hispanic/Latino), 5 international. Average age 28. 401 applicants, 60% accepted, 135 enrolled. In 2017, 212 master's, 1 doctorate, 117 other advanced degrees awarded. *Degree requirements:* For master's, thesis (for some programs); for doctorate, comprehensive exam (for some programs), thesis/dissertation. *Entrance requirements:* For master's and doctorate, GRE General Test, unofficial transcripts, letters of recommendation. Additional exam requirements/recommendations for international students: Required—TOEFL (minimum score 80 iBT), IELTS (minimum score 7), PTE (minimum score 54). *Application deadline:* For fall admission, 3/1 priority date for

domestic and international students; for spring admission, 10/1 priority date for domestic and international students. Applications are processed on a rolling basis. Application fee: $80 ($90 for international students). Electronic applications accepted. *Expenses:* $5,174 per semester full-time resident, $9,714 per semester full-time non-resident, $511 per credit hour part-time resident, $1,017 per credit hour part-time non-resident; $741 per credit hour online; other fees may apply per session. *Financial support:* In 2017–18, 84 students received support, including 9 fellowships with partial tuition reimbursements available (averaging $8,148 per year), 18 teaching assistantships with partial tuition reimbursements available (averaging $13,707 per year); career-related internships or fieldwork and unspecified assistantships also available. Financial award application deadline: 3/1. *Total annual research expenditures:* $1.2 million. *Unit head:* Dr. Debi Switzer, Department Chair, 864-656-5098, E-mail: debi@clemson.edu. *Application contact:* Julie Jones, Student Services Program Coordinator, 864-656-5096, E-mail: jgambre@clemson.edu.
Website: http://www.clemson.edu/education/departments/education-human-development/index.html

Coastal Carolina University, Spadoni College of Education, Conway, SC 29528-6054. Offers education (MAT); educational leadership (M Ed, Ed S); English for speakers of other languages (Certificate); instructional technology (M Ed, Ed S); language, literacy and culture (M Ed); learning and teaching (M Ed); online teaching and training (Certificate); special education (M Ed). *Accreditation:* NCATE. *Program availability:* Part-time, evening/weekend, 100% online, blended/hybrid learning. *Faculty:* 16 full-time (9 women), 22 part-time/adjunct (15 women). *Students:* 43 full-time (22 women), 345 part-time (290 women); includes 70 minority (51 Black or African American, non-Hispanic/Latino; 3 American Indian or Alaska Native, non-Hispanic/Latino; 3 Asian, non-Hispanic/Latino; 8 Hispanic/Latino; 1 Native Hawaiian or other Pacific Islander, non-Hispanic/Latino; 4 Two or more races, non-Hispanic/Latino). Average age 33. 288 applicants, 77% accepted, 157 enrolled. In 2017, 151 master's, 28 other advanced degrees awarded. *Degree requirements:* For master's and other advanced degree, comprehensive exam. *Entrance requirements:* For master's, GRE, GMAT, 2 letters of recommendation, evidence of teacher certification, official transcripts; for other advanced degree, official transcripts, 3 letters of reference, master's degree in related field with minimum overall cumulative GPA of 3.0. Additional exam requirements/recommendations for international students: Required—TOEFL (minimum score 550 paper-based; 79 iBT), IELTS (minimum score 6.5). *Application deadline:* For fall admission, 5/1 priority date for domestic and international students; for spring admission, 11/1 priority date for domestic and international students; for summer admission, 3/1 priority date for domestic and international students. Applications are processed on a rolling basis. Application fee: $45. Electronic applications accepted. *Expenses:* Tuition, state resident: full-time $5184; part-time $576 per credit hour. Tuition, nonresident: full-time $9369; part-time $1041 per credit hour. *Required fees:* $90; $5 per credit hour. *Financial support:* Fellowships, research assistantships, teaching assistantships, and tuition waivers available. Financial award application deadline: 3/1; financial award applicants required to submit FAFSA. *Unit head:* Dr. Edward Jadallah, Dean/Vice President for Online Education and Teaching Excellence, 843-349-2773, Fax: 843-349-2106, E-mail: ejadalla@coastal.edu. *Application contact:* Dr. James O. Luken, Associate Provost for Graduate Program/Vice-Dean of the Coastal Environment, 843-349-2235, Fax: 843-349-6444, E-mail: joluken@coastal.edu.
Website: https://www.coastal.edu/education/

Coker College, Graduate Programs, Hartsville, SC 29550. Offers college athletic administration (MS); criminal and social justice policy (MS); curriculum and instructional technology (M Ed); literacy studies (M Ed); management and leadership (MS). *Program availability:* Part-time, 100% online. *Faculty:* 9 full-time (4 women), 3 part-time/adjunct (2 women). *Students:* 77 full-time (47 women), 9 part-time (4 women); includes 21 minority (15 Black or African American, non-Hispanic/Latino; 1 American Indian or Alaska Native, non-Hispanic/Latino; 1 Hispanic/Latino; 4 Two or more races, non-Hispanic/Latino), 1 international. Average age 30. *Degree requirements:* For master's, comprehensive exam, portfolio. *Entrance requirements:* For master's, GRE or GMAT, minimum overall GPA of 2.85 in bachelor's program, official transcripts, resume, three letters of recommendation, teacher licensure. *Application deadline:* Applications are processed on a rolling basis. Application fee: $25. Electronic applications accepted. *Expenses: Tuition:* Full-time $14,424; part-time $601 per credit hour. *Required fees:* $176; $176 per credit hour. Tuition and fees vary according to course load and program. *Financial support:* Unspecified assistantships available. Financial award application deadline: 6/30; financial award applicants required to submit FAFSA. *Application contact:* Lacey Rice-Serafin, Director of Graduate Programs, 843-857-4128, E-mail: lriceserafin@coker.edu.

The College at Brockport, State University of New York, School of Education, Health, and Human Services, Department of Education and Human Development, Literacy Education B-12 Program, Brockport, NY 14420-2997. Offers MS Ed. *Accreditation:* NCATE. *Program availability:* Part-time. *Students:* 103 part-time (89 women); includes 2 minority (1 Black or African American, non-Hispanic/Latino; 1 American Indian or Alaska Native, non-Hispanic/Latino). 38 applicants, 89% accepted, 25 enrolled. In 2017, 53 master's awarded. *Degree requirements:* For master's, thesis or alternative. *Entrance requirements:* For master's, minimum GPA of 3.0, letters of recommendation, interview. Additional exam requirements/recommendations for international students: Required—TOEFL (minimum score 550 paper-based; 79 iBT), IELTS (minimum score 6.5). *Application deadline:* For fall admission, 3/15 priority date for domestic and international students; for spring admission, 10/15 priority date for domestic and international students; for summer admission, 3/15 priority date for domestic and international students. Application fee: $80. Electronic applications accepted. *Expenses:* Tuition, state resident: full-time $10,870; part-time $453 per credit hour. Tuition, nonresident: full-time $22,210. *Required fees:* $988; $246 per semester. *Financial support:* Federal Work-Study and scholarships/grants available. Support available to part-time students. Financial award application deadline: 3/15; financial award applicants required to submit FAFSA. *Unit head:* Dr. Sue Robb, Chairperson, 585-395-5935, Fax: 585-395-2172, E-mail: srobb@brockport.edu. *Application contact:* Anne Walton, Coordinator of Graduate Advisement, 585-395-2326, Fax: 585-395-2172, E-mail: awalton@brockport.edu.
Website: https://www.brockport.edu/academics/education_human_development/graduate/literacy_masters.html

The College of New Jersey, Office of Graduate and Advancing Education, School of Education, Department of Special Education, Language and Literacy, Program in Developmental Reading, Ewing, NJ 08628. Offers M Ed. *Accreditation:* NCATE. *Program availability:* Part-time. *Degree requirements:* For master's, comprehensive exam. *Entrance requirements:* For master's, GRE General Test, minimum GPA of 3.0 in field or 2.75 overall. Additional exam requirements/recommendations for international students: Required—TOEFL. Electronic applications accepted.

The College of New Jersey, Office of Graduate and Advancing Education, School of Education, Department of Special Education, Language and Literacy, Program in Reading Certification, Ewing, NJ 08628. Offers Certificate. *Program availability:* Part-time. *Entrance requirements:* Additional exam requirements/recommendations for international students: Required—TOEFL. Electronic applications accepted.

The College of New Rochelle, Graduate School, Division of Education, Program in Literacy Education, New Rochelle, NY 10805-2308. Offers MS Ed. *Program availability:* Part-time, evening/weekend. *Degree requirements:* For master's, practicum. *Entrance requirements:* For master's, interview, minimum GPA of 3.0 in field, 2.7 overall, early elementary teacher certification. *Expenses: Tuition:* Full-time $17,406. *Required fees:* $1120.

College of St. Joseph, Graduate Programs, Division of Education, Program in Reading, Rutland, VT 05701-3899. Offers M Ed. *Program availability:* Part-time, evening/weekend. *Degree requirements:* For master's, comprehensive exam. *Entrance requirements:* For master's, PRAXIS I, official college transcripts; 2 letters of reference; minimum GPA of 3.0 (initial licensure) or 2.7 (nonlicensure); interview. Additional exam requirements/recommendations for international students: Required—TOEFL (minimum score 550 paper-based). Electronic applications accepted.

The College of Saint Rose, Graduate Studies, Thelma P. Lally School of Education, Programs in Literacy, Albany, NY 12203-1419. Offers literacy: birth-grade 6 (MS Ed, Advanced Certificate); literacy: grades 5-12 (MS Ed, Advanced Certificate). *Students:* 11 full-time (all women), 13 part-time (all women); includes 2 minority (both Hispanic/Latino). Average age 24. 21 applicants, 71% accepted, 10 enrolled. In 2017, 24 master's, 2 Advanced Certificates awarded. *Degree requirements:* For master's, field and clinical experiences. *Entrance requirements:* For master's, minimum undergraduate GPA of 3.0, current classroom teaching certification, baccalaureate degree from accredited institution, official transcripts from all colleges/universities attended. Additional exam requirements/recommendations for international students: Required—TOEFL (minimum score 550 paper-based; 80 iBT), IELTS (minimum score 6), PTE (minimum score 56). *Application deadline:* For fall admission, 4/1 priority date for domestic and international students; for spring admission, 10/15 priority date for domestic and international students. Applications are processed on a rolling basis. Application fee: $40. Electronic applications accepted. *Expenses: Tuition:* Full-time $7191; part-time $799 per credit hour. *Required fees:* $924; $462 per credit hour. Tuition and fees vary according to course load. *Financial support:* Career-related internships or fieldwork, scholarships/grants, tuition waivers (partial), and unspecified assistantships available. Support available to part-time students. Financial award application deadline: 4/15. *Unit head:* Ekaterina Midgette, Co-Chair, 518-485-3797, E-mail: midgette@strose.edu. *Application contact:* Cris Murray, Assistant Vice President for Graduate Recruitment and Enrollment, 518-485-3390, E-mail: grad@strose.edu.
Website: https://www.strose.edu/literacy/

The College of William and Mary, School of Education, Program in Curriculum and Instruction, Williamsburg, VA 23187-8795. Offers elementary education (MA Ed); English as a second language/bilingual education (MA Ed); gifted education (MA Ed); literacy leadership (MA Ed); math specialist (MA Ed); secondary education (MA Ed), including English, foreign language, math, science, social studies; special education (MA Ed). *Accreditation:* NCATE. *Program availability:* Part-time. *Faculty:* 23 full-time (16 women), 40 part-time/adjunct (32 women). *Students:* 85 full-time (63 women), 16 part-time (15 women); includes 18 minority (5 Black or African American, non-Hispanic/Latino; 4 Asian, non-Hispanic/Latino; 7 Hispanic/Latino; 2 Two or more races, non-Hispanic/Latino), 1 international. Average age 27. 152 applicants, 83% accepted, 90 enrolled. In 2017, 67 master's awarded. *Degree requirements:* For master's, project. *Entrance requirements:* For master's, GRE, MAT, PRAXIS Core Academic Skills for Educators, minimum GPA of 2.5. Additional exam requirements/recommendations for international students: Required—TOEFL (minimum score 100 iBT), IELTS (minimum score 7). *Application deadline:* For fall admission, 1/15 for domestic and international students; for spring admission, 10/1 for domestic and international students. Application fee: $50. Electronic applications accepted. *Expenses:* $9,630 resident full-time, $535 resident part-time per credit hour; $25,920 nonresident full-time, $1,265 nonresident part-time per credit hour; $5,944 full-time fees. *Financial support:* In 2017–18, 35 students received support, including 7 research assistantships (averaging $6,678 per year); scholarships/grants and unspecified assistantships also available. Financial award application deadline: 1/15; financial award applicants required to submit FAFSA. *Faculty research:* Educational technology, professional development and evaluation, inclusive education, rural education, education policy. *Unit head:* Dr. Jeremy D. Stoddard, Department Chair, 757-221-2348, E-mail: jdstod@wm.edu. *Application contact:* Dorothy Smith Osborne, Assistant Dean for Academic Programs and Student Services, 757-221-2317, E-mail: dsosbo@wm.edu.
Website: http://education.wm.edu

Concordia University, College of Education, Portland, OR 97211-6099. Offers career and technical education (M Ed); curriculum and instruction (M Ed), including adolescent literacy, career and technical education, e-learning/technology education, early childhood education, English for speakers of other languages, English language development, environmental education, mathematics, methods and curriculum, reading, science, teacher leadership, the inclusive classroom; early childhood (MAT); education leadership (Ed D); educational administration (M Ed); elementary education (MAT); secondary education (MAT); special education (M Ed); teacher leadership (Ed D). *Program availability:* Part-time, online learning. *Degree requirements:* For master's, comprehensive exam, work samples/portfolio. *Entrance requirements:* For master's, California Basic Educational Skills Test or PRAXIS I, minimum undergraduate GPA of 2.8, graduate 3.0; 2 letters of recommendation. Additional exam requirements/recommendations for international students: Required—TOEFL (minimum score 525 paper-based). Electronic applications accepted. *Faculty research:* Learner-centered classroom, brain-based learning, future of online learning.

Concordia University Chicago, College of Education, Program in Reading Education, River Forest, IL 60305-1499. Offers MA. *Program availability:* Part-time, evening/weekend. *Degree requirements:* For master's, comprehensive exam, thesis optional. *Entrance requirements:* For master's, minimum GPA of 2.9. Additional exam requirements/recommendations for international students: Required—TOEFL (minimum score 550 paper-based). Electronic applications accepted. *Faculty research:* Early literacy, classroom management and organization in reading, minority students and reading.

Concordia University, Nebraska, Graduate Programs in Education, Program in Reading Education, Seward, NE 68434. Offers M Ed. *Accreditation:* NCATE. *Program availability:* Part-time. *Degree requirements:* For master's, thesis or alternative. *Entrance requirements:* For master's, GRE, MAT, or NTE, minimum GPA of 3.0, BS in education or equivalent.

Concordia University, St. Paul, College of Education, St. Paul, MN 55104-5494. Offers classroom instruction (MA Ed), including K-12 reading; differentiated instruction (MA Ed); early childhood education (MA Ed); education (Ed D); educational leadership (MA Ed); educational technology (MA Ed, Certificate); K-12 principal licensure (Ed S); special education (MA Ed), including autism spectrum disorder, emotional and behavioral disorders, learning disabilities; superintendent (Ed S); teaching (MAT). *Accreditation:* NCATE. *Program availability:* Part-time, evening/weekend, 100% online, blended/hybrid learning. *Faculty:* 15 full-time (8 women), 86 part-time/adjunct (56 women). *Students:* 955 full-time (731 women), 42 part-time (28 women); includes 105 minority (35 Black or African American, non-Hispanic/Latino; 5 American Indian or Alaska Native, non-Hispanic/Latino; 31 Asian, non-Hispanic/Latino; 19 Hispanic/Latino;

15 Two or more races, non-Hispanic/Latino), 9 international. Average age 34. 409 applicants, 87% accepted, 347 enrolled. In 2017, 386 master's, 104 other advanced degrees awarded. *Degree requirements:* For master's, thesis (for some programs); for doctorate, thesis/dissertation, capstone projects; for other advanced degree, e-folio review of competencies. *Entrance requirements:* For master's, official transcripts from regionally-accredited institution stating the conferral of a bachelor's degree with minimum cumulative GPA of 3.0; personal statement; professional resume; practitioner in field through work or volunteerism; resume; for doctorate, minimum master's or specialist degree GPA of 3.25; transcript; writing sample; three letters of recommendation; current resume; on-campus interview; for other advanced degree, minimum master's or specialist degree GPA of 3.25; transcript; statement covering employment history and long-term academic and professional goals; two letters of recommendation; interview with program director. Additional exam requirements/recommendations for international students: Recommended—TOEFL (minimum score 547 paper-based; 78 iBT), IELTS (minimum score 6). *Application deadline:* For fall admission, 8/1 for domestic and international students; for spring admission, 12/1 for domestic and international students; for summer admission, 5/1 for domestic and international students. Applications are processed on a rolling basis. Application fee: $0. Electronic applications accepted. *Expenses:* $395 per credit (for MA in education); $440 per credit (for MAT); $615 per credit (for EdD). *Financial support:* In 2017–18, 105 students received support. Scholarships/grants and unspecified assistantships available. Financial award applicants required to submit FAFSA. *Faculty research:* Differentiated instruction in K-12 educational settings; educational leadership; effective online pedagogy in higher education; equine-assisted learning; faculty development in higher education. *Unit head:* Lonn Maly, Dean, 651-641-8203, E-mail: maly@csp.edu. *Application contact:* Amber Faletti, Director of Enrollment Management, 651-641-8838, Fax: 651-603-6320, E-mail: faletti@csp.edu.

Concordia University Wisconsin, Graduate Programs, Department of Education, Program in Literacy, Mequon, WI 53097-2402. Offers MS Ed. *Program availability:* Part-time, evening/weekend, online learning. *Degree requirements:* For master's, comprehensive exam, thesis or alternative. *Entrance requirements:* For master's, minimum GPA of 3.0. Additional exam requirements/recommendations for international students: Required—TOEFL.

Concord University, Graduate Studies, Athens, WV 24712-1000. Offers educational leadership and supervision (M Ed); health promotion (MA); reading specialist (M Ed); social work (MSW); special education (M Ed); teaching (MAT). *Program availability:* Part-time, evening/weekend, 100% online. *Faculty:* 16 full-time (10 women), 7 part-time/adjunct (4 women). *Students:* 146 full-time (117 women), 195 part-time (161 women); includes 26 minority (15 Black or African American, non-Hispanic/Latino; 1 American Indian or Alaska Native, non-Hispanic/Latino; 4 Asian, non-Hispanic/Latino; 1 Hispanic/Latino; 5 Two or more races, non-Hispanic/Latino). Average age 34. 591 applicants, 99% accepted, 144 enrolled. In 2017, 114 master's awarded. *Degree requirements:* For master's, thesis (for some programs). *Entrance requirements:* For master's, GRE or MAT, baccalaureate degree with minimum GPA of 2.5 from regionally-accredited institution; teaching license; 2 letters of recommendation; completed disposition assessment form. *Application deadline:* Applications are processed on a rolling basis. Application fee: $30. Electronic applications accepted. *Expenses:* Tuition, state resident: full-time $8132; part-time $453 per semester hour. Tuition, nonresident: full-time $14,180; part-time $788 per semester hour. *Financial support:* Tuition waivers and unspecified assistantships available. Financial award applicants required to submit FAFSA. *Unit head:* Dr. Cheryl Barnes, Director, 304-384-6306, E-mail: cbarnes@concord.edu. *Application contact:* Debra Moore, Special Events Assistant, 304-384-5113, E-mail: dlm@concord.edu.
Website: http://www.concord.edu/graduate

Converse College, Education Specialist Program, Spartanburg, SC 29302. Offers administration and leadership (Ed S); administration and supervision (Ed S); literacy (Ed S). *Accreditation:* AAMFT/COAMFTE. *Program availability:* Part-time. *Entrance requirements:* For degree, GRE or MAT (marriage and family therapy), minimum GPA of 3.0. *Application deadline:* For fall admission, 8/1 for domestic and international students; for winter admission, 11/15 for domestic and international students; for spring admission, 1/15 for domestic and international students. Applications are processed on a rolling basis. Application fee: $40. Electronic applications accepted. *Unit head:* Lienne Medford, Dean of Graduate Studies and Distance Education, 864-596-9082, E-mail: lienne.medford@converse.edu. *Application contact:* Kimberly Newton-Burgess, Director of Post-Traditional and Online Admissions, 864-596-9746, E-mail: kimberly.newton-burgess@converse.edu.

Coppin State University, Division of Graduate Studies, Division of Education, Department of Curriculum and Instruction, Program in Reading Education, Baltimore, MD 21216-3698. Offers MS. *Program availability:* Part-time. *Degree requirements:* For master's, 3 hours of capstone experience in urban literacy. *Entrance requirements:* For master's, MAT or GRE, resume, references, teacher certification, 3 years of teaching experience.

Crandall University, Graduate Programs, Moncton, NB E1C 9L7, Canada. Offers literacy education (M Ed); organizational management (MOM); resource education (M Ed).

Curry College, Graduate Studies, Program in Education, Milton, MA 02186-9984. Offers elementary education (M Ed); foundations (non-license) (M Ed); reading (M Ed, Certificate); special education (M Ed). *Program availability:* Part-time, evening/weekend. *Degree requirements:* For master's, project or thesis. *Entrance requirements:* For master's, interview, recommendations, resume, written statement. Additional exam requirements/recommendations for international students: Required—TOEFL (minimum score 550 paper-based; 80 iBT). *Expenses:* Contact institution. *Faculty research:* Classroom trauma, therapeutic writing, inclusionary practices.

Dallas Baptist University, Dorothy M. Bush College of Education, Program in Reading and English as a Second Language, Dallas, TX 75211-9299. Offers bilingual education (M Ed); reading and English as a second language (M Ed). *Program availability:* Part-time, evening/weekend. *Application deadline:* Applications are processed on a rolling basis. Application fee: $25. Electronic applications accepted. Application fee is waived when completed online. *Expenses: Tuition:* Full-time $16,308; part-time $906 per credit hour. *Required fees:* $900; $450 per semester. Tuition and fees vary according to course load and degree level. *Unit head:* Dr. Neil Dugger, Dean, 214-333-5202, E-mail: neil@dbu.edu. *Application contact:* Dr. Adelita Baker, Program Director, 214-333-5515, E-mail: adelita@dbu.edu.
Website: http://www3.dbu.edu/graduate/english_reading.asp

Delaware State University, Graduate Programs, College of Education, Health and Public Policy, Program in Adult Literacy and Basic Education, Dover, DE 19901-2277. Offers MA. *Entrance requirements:* Additional exam requirements/recommendations for international students: Required—TOEFL (minimum score 550 paper-based). Electronic applications accepted.

DePaul University, College of Education, Chicago, IL 60614. Offers bilingual-bicultural education (M Ed, MA); counseling (M Ed, MA), including clinical mental health counseling, college student development, school counseling; curriculum studies (M Ed,

MA, Ed D); early childhood education (M Ed, MA, Ed D); educational leadership (M Ed, MA, Ed D), including Catholic leadership (M Ed, MA), general (M Ed, MA), higher education (M Ed, MA), physical education (M Ed, MA), principal preparation (M Ed), teacher preparation (M Ed); elementary education (M Ed, MA); middle grades education (M Ed); middle school mathematics education (MS); reading specialist (M Ed, MA); secondary education (M Ed, MA); social and cultural foundations in education (M Ed, MA); special education (M Ed); sport, fitness and recreation leadership (MS); value-creating education for global citizenship (M Ed); world languages education (M Ed, MA). *Program availability:* Part-time, evening/weekend, online learning. *Degree requirements:* For doctorate, thesis/dissertation. *Application deadline:* Applications are processed on a rolling basis. Application fee: $40. Electronic applications accepted. *Financial support:* Application deadline: 12/31; applicants required to submit FAFSA. *Unit head:* Dr. Paul Zionts, Dean, 773-325-7581, Fax: 773-325-7713, E-mail: pzionts@depaul.edu. *Application contact:* Dr. Paul Zionts, Dean, 773-325-7581, Fax: 773-325-7713, E-mail: pzionts@depaul.edu.
Website: http://education.depaul.edu

Dominican University, School of Education, River Forest, IL 60305-1099. Offers child life studies (MS); early childhood education (MS); education (MAT); elementary education (MA Ed); English as a second language (MA Ed); reading (MA Ed); secondary education (MAT); special education (MS). *Accreditation:* NCATE. *Program availability:* Part-time, evening/weekend, 100% online, blended/hybrid learning. *Faculty:* 8 full-time (6 women), 42 part-time/adjunct (38 women). *Students:* 5 full-time (all women), 261 part-time (206 women); includes 45 minority (16 Black or African American, non-Hispanic/Latino; 1 American Indian or Alaska Native, non-Hispanic/Latino; 5 Asian, non-Hispanic/Latino; 18 Hispanic/Latino; 5 Two or more races, non-Hispanic/Latino), 1 international. Average age 32. 95 applicants, 98% accepted, 72 enrolled. In 2017, 206 master's awarded. *Entrance requirements:* For master's, Illinois Test of Basic Skills. Additional exam requirements/recommendations for international students: Required—TOEFL (minimum score 550 paper-based; 79 iBT). *Application deadline:* Applications are processed on a rolling basis. Application fee: $25. *Expenses:* Contact institution. *Financial support:* Career-related internships or fieldwork, scholarships/grants, tuition waivers (partial), and unspecified assistantships available. Support available to part-time students. Financial award application deadline: 8/15; financial award applicants required to submit FAFSA. *Faculty research:* Governance of private education institutions, reading and language arts, inclusion, organizational planning, leadership and vision. *Unit head:* Dr. Colleen Reardon, Interim Executive Director, School of Education, 708-524-6643, Fax: 708-524-6665, E-mail: creardon@dom.edu. *Application contact:* Benjamin Mueller, Senior Graduate Marketing and Recruitment Coordinator, 708-524-6456, Fax: 708-524-6665, E-mail: bmueller@dom.edu.
Website: http://educate.dom.edu/

Drake University, School of Education, Des Moines, IA 50311-4516. Offers applied behavior analysis (MS); counseling (MS); education (PhD); education administration (Ed D); educational leadership (MSE, Ed D); effective teaching (MSE); leadership development (MS); literacy (Ed S); literacy education (MSE); rehabilitation administration (MS); rehabilitation placement (MS); special education (MSE); STEM education (MSE); teacher education (5-12) (MAT); teacher education (K-8) (MST); teacher effectiveness and professional development (MSE). *Program availability:* Part-time, evening/weekend. *Degree requirements:* For master's and Ed S, comprehensive exam, internships (for some programs); for doctorate, comprehensive exam, thesis/dissertation, internships (for some programs). *Entrance requirements:* For master's, GRE General Test, MAT, or Drake Writing Assessment, resume, 2 letters of recommendation; for doctorate, GRE General Test or MAT, master's degree, 3 letters of recommendation; for Ed S, GRE General Test or MAT. Additional exam requirements/recommendations for international students: Required—TOEFL (minimum score 550 paper-based). *Application deadline:* For fall admission, 7/1 priority date for domestic students, 6/1 priority date for international students; for spring admission, 11/1 priority date for domestic students, 10/1 priority date for international students. Applications are processed on a rolling basis. Application fee: $25. Electronic applications accepted. *Expenses:* Contact institution. *Financial support:* Research assistantships, career-related internships or fieldwork, and unspecified assistantships available. Support available to part-time students. *Faculty research:* Counseling and rehabilitation, behavioral supports, inquiry-based science methods, teacher quality enhancement. *Unit head:* Dr. Janet McMahill, Dean, 515-271-3829, E-mail: janet.mcmahill@drake.edu.
Website: http://www.drake.edu/soe/

Drury University, Master in Education Program, Springfield, MO 5802. Offers curriculum and instruction (M Ed), including elementary, middle school, secondary; gifted education (M Ed); instructional leadership (M Ed); instructional technology (M Ed); integrated learning (M Ed); online teaching (M Ed); special education (M Ed); special reading (M Ed). *Accreditation:* NCATE. *Program availability:* Part-time, evening/weekend, 100% online, blended/hybrid learning. *Entrance requirements:* For master's, GRE, bachelor's degree with minimum GPA of 2.75. Additional exam requirements/recommendations for international students: Recommended—TOEFL (minimum score 80 iBT), IELTS (minimum score 6.5). Electronic applications accepted. *Expenses:* Contact institution. *Faculty research:* Gifted students, instructional technology, autism, diversity and social justice.

Duquesne University, School of Education, Department of Instruction and Leadership, Program in Reading and Language Arts, Pittsburgh, PA 15282-0001. Offers MS Ed. *Program availability:* Part-time, evening/weekend. *Faculty:* 1 (woman) full-time. *Students:* 4 full-time (all women), 3 part-time (all women); includes 1 minority (Asian, non-Hispanic/Latino). Average age 24. 9 applicants, 100% accepted, 3 enrolled. In 2017, 5 master's awarded. *Degree requirements:* For master's, thesis optional. *Entrance requirements:* For master's, bachelor's degree; undergraduate degree with minimum GPA of 3.0 overall or on most recent 48 credits, or minimum overall GPA of 2.8 and PRAXIS I PPST or PAPA exams. Additional exam requirements/recommendations for international students: Required—TOEFL (minimum score 550 paper-based), IELTS (minimum score 7). *Application deadline:* For fall admission, 9/1 for domestic students; for spring admission, 1/2 for domestic students. Applications are processed on a rolling basis. Application fee: $0. Electronic applications accepted. *Expenses:* $1,259 per credit. *Financial support:* Research assistantships and Federal Work-Study available. Support available to part-time students. *Faculty research:* Adolescent literacy; multi-modal texts including graphic novels; struggling readers and why they struggle; family engagement and community partnerships; factors that create highly effective teachers;. *Unit head:* Dr. Carla Meyer, Assistant Professor, 412-396.5837, Fax: 412-396-1759, E-mail: meyerc2@duq.edu. *Application contact:* Kelly McGinley, Graduate Admissions Assistant, 412-396-1559, Fax: 412-396-5585, E-mail: mcginleyk@duq.edu.
Website: http://www.duq.edu/academics/schools/education/graduate-programs-education/ms-reading-language-arts

East Carolina University, Graduate School, College of Education, Department of Literacy Studies, English and History Education, Greenville, NC 27858-4353. Offers curriculum and instruction (MA Ed); English education (MAT); history education (MAT); reading education (MA Ed). *Accreditation:* NCATE. *Program availability:* Part-time, evening/weekend, online learning. *Students:* 4 full-time (3 women), 50 part-time (47 women); includes 4 minority (2 Black or African American, non-Hispanic/Latino; 1 Hispanic/Latino; 1 Two or more races, non-Hispanic/Latino). Average age 33. 18 applicants, 94% accepted, 17 enrolled. In 2017, 17 master's awarded. *Degree requirements:* For master's, comprehensive exam, thesis optional. *Entrance requirements:* For master's, GRE General Test or MAT, interview, minimum GPA of 2.5, bachelor's degree in related field, teaching license (MA Ed). Additional exam requirements/recommendations for international students: Required—TOEFL. *Application deadline:* For fall admission, 6/1 priority date for domestic students. Applications are processed on a rolling basis. Application fee: $75. *Expenses:* Tuition, state resident: full-time $4749; part-time $297 per credit hour. Tuition, nonresident: full-time $17,898; part-time $1119 per credit hour. *Required fees:* $2691; $224 per credit hour. Part-time tuition and fees vary according to course load and program. *Financial support:* Research assistantships, teaching assistantships, and Federal Work-Study available. Support available to part-time students. Financial award application deadline: 6/1. *Unit head:* Katherine Misulis, Chair, 252-328-6128, E-mail: misulisk@ecu.edu. Website: http://www.ecu.edu/cs-educ/libs/index.cfm

Eastern Mennonite University, Program in Teacher Education, Harrisonburg, VA 22802-2462. Offers curriculum and instruction (MA Ed); diverse needs (MA Ed); literacy (MA Ed); restorative justice in education (MA Ed). *Accreditation:* NCATE. *Program availability:* Part-time. *Degree requirements:* For master's, portfolio, research projects. *Entrance requirements:* For master's, 1 year of teaching experience, interview, minimum undergraduate GPA of 2.75. Additional exam requirements/recommendations for international students: Required—TOEFL (minimum score 550 paper-based). *Application deadline:* Applications are processed on a rolling basis. Application fee: $50. Electronic applications accepted. *Expenses:* Contact institution. *Financial support:* Federal Work-Study and scholarships/grants available. Financial award application deadline: 6/30; financial award applicants required to submit FAFSA. *Faculty research:* Effective literacy instruction for middle school English language learners, beginning teacher's emotional experiences, constructivist learning environments, restorative discipline. *Unit head:* Cathy Smeltzer Erb, Chair, 540-432-4638. *Application contact:* Yvonne Martin, Office Assistant, 540-432-4350, Fax: 540-432-4071, E-mail: yvonne.martin@emu.edu. Website: http://www.emu.edu/maed/

Eastern Michigan University, Graduate School, College of Education, Department of Teacher Education, Program in Reading, Ypsilanti, MI 48197. Offers MA. *Accreditation:* NCATE. *Program availability:* Part-time, evening/weekend, online learning. *Students:* 2 full-time (both women), 22 part-time (all women); includes 1 minority (Hispanic/Latino). Average age 30. 11 applicants, 82% accepted, 6 enrolled. In 2017, 8 master's awarded. *Entrance requirements:* For master's, GRE. Additional exam requirements/recommendations for international students: Required—TOEFL. *Application deadline:* Applications are processed on a rolling basis. Application fee: $45. *Financial support:* Fellowships, research assistantships with full tuition reimbursements, teaching assistantships with full tuition reimbursements, career-related internships or fieldwork, Federal Work-Study, institutionally sponsored loans, scholarships/grants, tuition waivers (partial), and unspecified assistantships available. Support available to part-time students. Financial award applicants required to submit FAFSA. *Application contact:* Dr. Linda Lewis-White, Coordinator, 734-487-3260, Fax: 734-487-2101, E-mail: llewiswh@emich.edu.

Eastern Michigan University, Graduate School, College of Education, Department of Teacher Education, Programs in Curriculum and Instruction, Ypsilanti, MI 48197. Offers advanced teaching and learning (MA); early literacy instruction (Graduate Certificate); instructional leadership (MA); learning, motivation and creativity (Graduate Certificate); literacy coaching (Graduate Certificate); online teaching (Certificate); secondary literacy instruction (Graduate Certificate); urban and diversity education (MA). *Students:* 1 full-time (0 women), 22 part-time (19 women); includes 6 minority (2 Black or African American, non-Hispanic/Latino; 1 Hispanic/Latino; 3 Two or more races, non-Hispanic/Latino). Average age 31. 15 applicants, 67% accepted, 7 enrolled. In 2017, 15 master's, 1 other advanced degree awarded. Application fee: $45. *Application contact:* Dr. Virginia Harder, Graduate Coordinator/Advisor, 734-487-2729, Fax: 734-487-2101, E-mail: vharder1@emich.edu.

Eastern Nazarene College, Adult and Graduate Studies, Division of Teacher Education, Quincy, MA 02170. Offers administration (M Ed); early childhood education (M Ed, Certificate); elementary education (M Ed, Certificate); English as a second language (Certificate); instructional enrichment and development (Certificate); middle school education (M Ed, Certificate); moderate special needs education (Certificate); principal (Certificate); program development and supervision (Certificate); secondary education (M Ed, Certificate); special education administrator (Certificate); special needs (M Ed); supervisor (Certificate); teacher of reading (M Ed, Certificate). M Ed also available through weekend program for administration, special needs, and teacher of reading only. *Program availability:* Part-time, evening/weekend. *Entrance requirements:* Additional exam requirements/recommendations for international students: Required—TOEFL (minimum score 550 paper-based).

Eastern New Mexico University, Graduate School, College of Education and Technology, Department of Curriculum and Instruction, Portales, NM 88130. Offers alternative licensure in elementary education (M Ed); bilingual education (M Ed); career and technical education (M Ed); educational technology (M Ed); elementary education (M Ed); English as a second language (M Ed); pedagogy and learning (M Ed); reading/literacy (M Ed). *Program availability:* Part-time, online learning. *Degree requirements:* For master's, comprehensive exam, thesis optional. *Entrance requirements:* For master's, writing assessment, minimum GPA of 3.0, photocopy of teaching license, letter of recommendation. Additional exam requirements/recommendations for international students: Required—TOEFL (minimum score 550 paper-based; 79 iBT), IELTS (minimum score 6). *Application deadline:* For fall admission, 7/20 priority date for domestic students, 6/20 priority date for international students; for spring admission, 12/15 priority date for domestic students, 11/15 priority date for international students. Applications are processed on a rolling basis. Application fee: $10. Electronic applications accepted. *Financial support:* Applicants required to submit FAFSA. *Unit head:* Dr. Mary Daughrity, Graduate Coordinator, 575-562-2481, Fax: 575-562-2559, E-mail: mary.daughrity@enmu.edu. *Application contact:* Cheryl Reeves, Senior Secretary, 575-562-2443, E-mail: cheryl.reeves@enmu.edu. Website: http://education.enmu.edu

Eastern University, Graduate Education Programs, St. Davids, PA 19087-3696. Offers ESL program specialist (K-12) (Certificate); general supervisor (PreK-12) (Certificate); health and physical education (K-12) (Certificate); middle level (4-8) (Certificate); multicultural education (M Ed); music (K-12) (Certificate); Pre K-4 (Certificate); Pre K-4 with special education (Certificate); reading (M Ed); reading specialist (K-12) (Certificate); reading supervisor (K-12) (Certificate); school counseling (MA, CAGS); school principalship (preK-12) (Certificate); school psychology (MS, CAGS); secondary biology education (7-12) (Certificate); secondary chemistry education (7-12) (Certificate); secondary communication education (7-12) (Certificate); secondary English education (7-12) (Certificate); secondary math education (7-12) (Certificate); secondary social studies education (7-12) (Certificate); special education (M Ed); special education (7-12) (Certificate); special education (Pre K-8) (Certificate); special

education supervisor (K-12) (Certificate); TESOL (M Ed); world language (Certificate), including Spanish. *Program availability:* Part-time, evening/weekend, online learning. *Students:* 46 full-time (40 women), 115 part-time (93 women); includes 65 minority (42 Black or African American, non-Hispanic/Latino; 3 Asian, non-Hispanic/Latino; 14 Hispanic/Latino; 6 Two or more races, non-Hispanic/Latino), 1 international. Average age 32. In 2017, 72 master's awarded. *Entrance requirements:* Additional exam requirements/recommendations for international students: Required—TOEFL. *Application deadline:* Applications are processed on a rolling basis. Application fee: $35. Electronic applications accepted. Application fee is waived when completed online. *Expenses:* Contact institution. *Unit head:* Michael Dziedziak, Executive Director of Enrollment, 800-452-0996, E-mail: gpsadmissions@eastern.edu. Website: https://www.eastern.edu/academics/programs/education-department-graduate-programs

Eastern Washington University, Graduate Studies, College of Arts, Letters and Education, Department of Education, Program in Literacy, Cheney, WA 99004-2431. Offers M Ed. *Students:* 1 (woman) full-time, 2 part-time (1 woman); includes 1 minority (Hispanic/Latino). Average age 27. 2 applicants, 50% accepted, 1 enrolled. In 2017, 1 master's awarded. *Degree requirements:* For master's, comprehensive exam. *Entrance requirements:* For master's, minimum GPA of 3.0. Additional exam requirements/recommendations for international students: Required—TOEFL (minimum score 580 paper-based; 92 iBT), IELTS (minimum score 7), PTE (minimum score 63). *Application deadline:* For fall admission, 4/1 priority date for domestic students; for spring admission, 1/15 for domestic students. Applications are processed on a rolling basis. Application fee: $75. Electronic applications accepted. *Expenses:* Tuition, state resident: full-time $11,191; part-time $373.06 per credit. Tuition, nonresident: full-time $25,995; part-time $866.52 per credit. *Financial support:* In 2017–18, teaching assistantships with partial tuition reimbursements (averaging $10,000 per year) were awarded; career-related internships or fieldwork, Federal Work-Study, institutionally sponsored loans, scholarships/grants, health care benefits, tuition waivers (partial), and unspecified assistantships also available. Support available to part-time students. Financial award application deadline: 2/1; financial award applicants required to submit FAFSA. *Unit head:* Dr. Vince Aleccia, Program Coordinator, 509-359-7024, E-mail: valeccia@ewu.edu.

East Stroudsburg University of Pennsylvania, Graduate and Extended Studies, College of Education, Department of Reading, East Stroudsburg, PA 18301-2999. Offers M Ed. *Program availability:* Part-time, evening/weekend, online only, 100% online. *Faculty:* 2 full-time (both women). *Students:* 2 full-time (both women), 62 part-time (60 women); includes 3 minority (1 Black or African American, non-Hispanic/Latino; 1 Hispanic/Latino; 1 Two or more races, non-Hispanic/Latino). Average age 31. 19 applicants, 79% accepted, 8 enrolled. In 2017, 8 master's awarded. *Degree requirements:* For master's, comprehensive exam, research paper, electronic program portfolio. *Entrance requirements:* For master's, PRAXIS/teacher certification, letter of recommendation, Pennsylvania Department of Education requirements. Additional exam requirements/recommendations for international students: Recommended—TOEFL (minimum score 560 paper-based; 83 iBT), IELTS. *Application deadline:* For fall admission, 7/31 priority date for domestic students, 6/30 priority date for international students; for spring admission, 11/30 for domestic students, 10/31 for international students. Applications are processed on a rolling basis. Application fee: $50. Electronic applications accepted. *Expenses:* Tuition, state resident: full-time $4500; part-time $3000 per credit. Tuition, nonresident: full-time $6750; part-time $4500 per credit. *Required fees:* $2642; $1756 per credit. $878 per semester. Tuition and fees vary according to course load, campus/location and program. *Financial support:* Research assistantships with tuition reimbursements, Federal Work-Study, and unspecified assistantships available. Support available to part-time students. Financial award application deadline: 3/1; financial award applicants required to submit FAFSA. *Faculty research:* Portfolio assessment, reading assessment. *Unit head:* Shawn Watkins, Department Chair, 570-422-3416, Fax: 570-422-3920, E-mail: swatkins1@esu.edu. *Application contact:* Kevin Quintero, Associate Director, Graduate and Extended Studies, 570-422-3890, Fax: 570-422-2791, E-mail: kquintero@esu.edu.

East Tennessee State University, School of Graduate Studies, College of Education, Department of Curriculum and Instruction, Johnson City, TN 37614. Offers advanced studies in teaching and learning (M Ed), including childhood literacy; educational technology (M Ed), including educational communications and technology, school library media; elementary education (M Ed); reading (M Ed, MA), including reading education (MA); storytelling (MA); response to intervention (Post-Master's Certificate); school library professional (Post-Master's Certificate); secondary education (M Ed); STEAM K-12 education (Postbaccalaureate Certificate); storytelling (Postbaccalaureate Certificate); teacher education (MAT), including elementary education K-5, middle grades education 4-8, middle grades education 6-8, secondary education 6-12 and preK-12, secondary education K-12. *Accreditation:* NCATE. *Program availability:* Part-time, evening/weekend, online learning. *Degree requirements:* For master's, comprehensive exam, thesis optional, student teaching, practicum; for other advanced degree, field work (school library); culminating experience (storytelling). *Entrance requirements:* For master's, GRE, SAT, ACT, PRAXIS, minimum GPA of 3.0, interview, 3 letters of recommendation, background check; for other advanced degree, master's degree, TN teaching license. Additional exam requirements/recommendations for international students: Required—TOEFL (minimum score 550 paper-based; 79 iBT). *Application deadline:* For fall admission, 6/1 for domestic students, 4/29 for international students; for spring admission, 11/1 for domestic students, 4/29 for international students. Application fee: $55 ($65 for international students). Electronic applications accepted. *Financial support:* Research assistantships with full tuition reimbursements, teaching assistantships with tuition reimbursements, career-related internships or fieldwork, institutionally sponsored loans, scholarships/grants, and unspecified assistantships available. Financial award application deadline: 7/1; financial award applicants required to submit FAFSA. *Faculty research:* Critical thinking; curriculum development in reading, math, and science education; cultural diversity; cognitive processes; effective teaching strategies. *Unit head:* Dr. Karin Keith, Chair, 423-439-7598, Fax: 423-439-8362, E-mail: keithkj@etsu.edu. *Application contact:* Dr. Aimee Govett, Graduate Coordinator, 423-439-7804, Fax: 423-439-5624, E-mail: govett@etsu.edu. Website: http://www.etsu.edu/coe/cuai/

Edinboro University of Pennsylvania, Department of Early Childhood and Reading, Edinboro, PA 16444. Offers arts infusion (Graduate Certificate); early childhood education (M Ed); reading (M Ed); reading specialist (Graduate Certificate). *Program availability:* Part-time, evening/weekend. *Degree requirements:* For master's, thesis or alternative, competency exam; for Graduate Certificate, thesis or alternative. *Entrance requirements:* For master's and Graduate Certificate, GRE or MAT, minimum QPA of 2.5. Electronic applications accepted.

Elms College, Division of Education, Chicopee, MA 01013-2839. Offers early childhood education (MAT); education (M Ed, CAGS); elementary education (MAT); English as a second language (MAT); reading (MAT); secondary education (MAT), including biology education, English education, Spanish education; special education (MAT). *Program availability:* Part-time, evening/weekend. *Faculty:* 4 full-time (all women), 8 part-time/

adjunct (7 women). *Students:* 6 full-time (4 women), 127 part-time (107 women); includes 8 minority (2 Asian, non-Hispanic/Latino; 6 Hispanic/Latino). Average age 33. 42 applicants, 88% accepted, 36 enrolled. In 2017, 50 master's, 6 other advanced degrees awarded. *Degree requirements:* For master's, thesis (for some programs). *Entrance requirements:* For master's, Massachusetts Educators Certification Test, minimum GPA of 3.0; for CAGS, master's degree in education. Additional exam requirements/recommendations for international students: Required—TOEFL. *Application deadline:* For fall admission, 7/1 priority date for domestic students; for spring admission, 11/1 priority date for domestic students. Applications are processed on a rolling basis. Application fee: $30. *Expenses: Tuition:* Full-time $13,860; part-time $770 per credit hour. *Required fees:* $200. Tuition and fees vary according to degree level and program. *Financial support:* In 2017–18, 2 teaching assistantships with partial tuition reimbursements were awarded. Financial award applicants required to submit FAFSA. *Unit head:* Dr. Mary Janeczek, Chair, Division of Education, 413-594-2761, Fax: 413-592-4871, E-mail: janeczeke@elms.edu. *Application contact:* School of Graduate and Professional Studies, 413-265-2445, E-mail: graduateeducation@elms.edu.

Emory & Henry College, Graduate Programs, Emory, VA 24327. Offers American history (MA Ed); education professional studies (M Ed); occupational therapy (MOT); organizational leadership (MCOL); physical therapy (DPT); physician assistant studies (MPAS); reading specialist (MA Ed). *Program availability:* Part-time. *Faculty:* 7 full-time (3 women). *Students:* 194 full-time (128 women), 4 part-time (2 women); includes 6 minority (2 Black or African American, non-Hispanic/Latino; 1 American Indian or Alaska Native, non-Hispanic/Latino; 1 Asian, non-Hispanic/Latino; 2 Hispanic/Latino). Average age 25. 525 applicants, 21% accepted, 74 enrolled. In 2017, 24 master's awarded. *Degree requirements:* For master's, thesis optional; for doctorate, thesis/dissertation optional. *Entrance requirements:* For master's, GRE or PRAXIS I, official transcripts from all colleges previously attended, three professional recommendations, essay. Additional exam requirements/recommendations for international students: Recommended—TOEFL, IELTS (minimum score 6). *Application deadline:* Applications are processed on a rolling basis. Electronic applications accepted. *Expenses:* Contact institution. *Financial support:* Application deadline: 10/15; applicants required to submit FAFSA. *Unit head:* Dr. Michael Puglisi, Associate Dean for Academic Affairs, 276-944-6662, E-mail: mpuglisi@ehc.edu. *Application contact:* Mary Bolt, Director of Transfer and Graduate Admission, 276-944-6135, E-mail: mbolt@ehc.edu.

Emporia State University, Program in Instructional Specialist, Emporia, KS 66801-5415. Offers elementary subject matter (MS); reading (MS). *Accreditation:* NCATE. *Program availability:* Part-time. *Faculty:* 30 full-time (24 women), 1 part-time/adjunct (0 women). *Students:* 2 full-time (1 woman), 88 part-time (80 women); includes 3 minority (1 Black or African American, non-Hispanic/Latino; 1 Asian, non-Hispanic/Latino; 1 Two or more races, non-Hispanic/Latino). 14 applicants, 93% accepted, 11 enrolled. In 2017, 15 master's awarded. *Degree requirements:* For master's, comprehensive exam or thesis, practicum. *Entrance requirements:* For master's, GRE General Test or MAT, essay exam, appropriate bachelor's degree, letters of recommendation. Additional exam requirements/recommendations for international students: Required—TOEFL (minimum score 520 paper-based; 68 iBT). *Application deadline:* For fall admission, 8/15 priority date for domestic students. Applications are processed on a rolling basis. Application fee: $30 ($75 for international students). Electronic applications accepted. *Expenses:* Tuition, state resident: full-time $6084; part-time $253.50 per credit hour. Tuition, nonresident: full-time $18,924; part-time $788.50 per credit hour. *Required fees:* $1943; $80.95 per credit hour. Tuition and fees vary according to campus/location. *Financial support:* Federal Work-Study, institutionally sponsored loans, health care benefits, and unspecified assistantships available. Financial award application deadline: 3/15; financial award applicants required to submit FAFSA. *Unit head:* Dr. Matt Siemears, Chair, 620-341-6057, E-mail: msiemear@emporia.edu. *Application contact:* Mary Sewell, Admissions Coordinator, 800-950-GRAD, Fax: 620-341-5909, E-mail: msewell@emporia.edu.

Endicott College, Van Loan School of Graduate and Professional Studies, Program in Reading and Literacy, Beverly, MA 01915-2096. Offers M Ed. *Program availability:* Part-time, evening/weekend, 100% online, blended/hybrid learning. *Faculty:* 2 full-time (1 woman), 3 part-time/adjunct (all women). *Students:* 11 full-time (all women), 6 part-time (all women). Average age 28. 2 applicants, 100% accepted, 1 enrolled. In 2017, 17 master's awarded. *Degree requirements:* For master's, comprehensive exam, practicum, seminar. *Entrance requirements:* For master's, MAT or GRE, Massachusetts Tests for Educator Licensure (MTEL), Massachusetts teaching certificate, letters of recommendation. Additional exam requirements/recommendations for international students: Required—TOEFL. *Application deadline:* Applications are processed on a rolling basis. Application fee: $50. Electronic applications accepted. *Expenses:* Contact institution. *Financial support:* Career-related internships or fieldwork available. Financial award applicants required to submit FAFSA. *Unit head:* Dr. Aubry Threlkeld, Director of Graduate Licensure Programs, 978-232-2408, E-mail: athrelke@endicott.edu. *Application contact:* Ian Menchini, Director, Graduate Enrollment and Advising, 978-232-5292, Fax: 978-232-3000, E-mail: imenchin@endicott.edu.
Website: https://vanloan.endicott.edu/programs-of-study/masters-programs/educator-preparation-program/reading-and-literacy-program

Evangel University, Department of Education, Springfield, MO 65802. Offers curriculum and instruction (M Ed); educational leadership (M Ed); literacy (M Ed); secondary teaching (M Ed). *Accreditation:* NCATE. *Program availability:* Part-time, evening/weekend, 100% online, blended/hybrid learning. *Faculty:* 8 full-time (5 women), 8 part-time/adjunct (5 women). *Students:* 1 (woman) full-time, 47 part-time (41 women); includes 2 minority (both Hispanic/Latino). Average age 37. 16 applicants, 100% accepted, 14 enrolled. In 2017, 14 master's awarded. *Entrance requirements:* For master's, PRAXIS II (preferred) or GRE, minimum undergraduate GPA of 3.0. Additional exam requirements/recommendations for international students: Required—TOEFL (minimum score 550 paper-based). *Application deadline:* For fall admission, 7/15 priority date for domestic students, 8/1 for international students; for spring admission, 11/15 priority date for domestic students, 12/1 for international students. Applications are processed on a rolling basis. Application fee: $25. Electronic applications accepted. Application fee is waived when completed online. *Expenses: Tuition:* Full-time $7200; part-time $4800 per credit hour. *Required fees:* $210; $155 per semester. *Financial support:* In 2017–18, 23 students received support. Scholarships/grants and unspecified assistantships available. Financial award application deadline: 4/1; financial award applicants required to submit FAFSA. *Unit head:* Dr. Susan Langston, Program Coordinator, 417-865-2815 Ext. 8552, E-mail: langstons@evangel.edu. *Application contact:* Michael Mann, Enrollment Coordinator, Graduate Studies, 417-865-2815 Ext. 8276, Fax: 417-575-5484, E-mail: mannm@evangel.edu.
Website: http://www.evangel.edu/academics/graduate-studies/graduate-programs

Fairleigh Dickinson University, Florham Campus, University College: Arts, Sciences, and Professional Studies, Peter Sammartino School of Education, Madison, NJ 07940-1099. Offers education for certified teachers (MA, Certificate); educational leadership (MA); instructional technology (Certificate); literacy/reading (Certificate); teaching (MAT).

Fairleigh Dickinson University, Metropolitan Campus, University College: Arts, Sciences, and Professional Studies, Peter Sammartino School of Education, Teaneck,

NJ 07666-1914. Offers dyslexia specialist (Certificate); education for certified teachers (MA); educational leadership (MA); instructional technology (Certificate); learning disabilities (MA); literacy/reading (Certificate); multilingual education (MA); teacher of the handicapped (Certificate); teaching (MAT). *Accreditation:* TEAC. *Program availability:* Part-time. *Degree requirements:* For master's, research project (MAT).

Fairmont State University, Programs in Education, Fairmont, WV 26554. Offers digital media, new literacies and learning (M Ed); education (MAT); exercise science, fitness and wellness (M Ed); professional studies (M Ed); reading (M Ed); special education (M Ed). *Accreditation:* NCATE. *Program availability:* Part-time, evening/weekend, 100% online. *Entrance requirements:* For master's, GRE. Additional exam requirements/recommendations for international students: Required—TOEFL (minimum score 80 iBT), IELTS (minimum score 6.5). Electronic applications accepted.

Fitchburg State University, Division of Graduate and Continuing Education, Program in Interdisciplinary Studies, Fitchburg, MA 01420-2697. Offers applied communications (CAGS); counseling/psychology (CAGS); individualized track (CAGS); reading specialist (CAGS). *Program availability:* Part-time, evening/weekend. *Students:* 11 full-time (all women), 14 part-time (13 women); includes 3 minority (all Hispanic/Latino). Average age 36. 5 applicants, 100% accepted, 5 enrolled. In 2017, 14 CAGSs awarded. *Entrance requirements:* Additional exam requirements/recommendations for international students: Required—TOEFL (minimum score 550 paper-based; 79 iBT). *Application deadline:* For fall admission, 7/15 for international students; for spring admission, 12/1 for international students. Applications are processed on a rolling basis. Application fee: $50. Electronic applications accepted. *Expenses:* Contact institution. *Financial support:* In 2017–18, research assistantships with partial tuition reimbursements (averaging $5,500 per year) were awarded; Federal Work-Study, scholarships/grants, and unspecified assistantships also available. Support available to part-time students. Financial award application deadline: 3/1; financial award applicants required to submit FAFSA. *Unit head:* Dr. Jessica Robey, Chair, 978-665-3386, Fax: 978-665-3658, E-mail: gce@fitchburgstate.edu. *Application contact:* Jinawa McNeil, Director of Admissions, 978-665-3140, Fax: 978-665-4540, E-mail: admissions@fitchburgstate.edu.

Florida Atlantic University, College of Education, Department of Teaching and Learning, Boca Raton, FL 33431-0991. Offers curriculum and instruction (M Ed), including art, biology, chemistry, English, French, German, mathematics, music, physics, Pre-K and primary education, reading, social sciences, Spanish; elementary education (M Ed); environmental education (M Ed); reading education (M Ed); social foundations of education (M Ed), including educational psychology, educational technology, multilingual education. *Accreditation:* NCATE. *Program availability:* Part-time, evening/weekend. *Faculty:* 13 full-time (10 women), 1 part-time/adjunct (0 women). *Students:* 26 full-time (22 women), 43 part-time (39 women); includes 19 minority (9 Black or African American, non-Hispanic/Latino; 1 Asian, non-Hispanic/Latino; 8 Hispanic/Latino; 1 Two or more races, non-Hispanic/Latino), 3 international. Average age 30. 91 applicants, 57% accepted, 33 enrolled. In 2017, 25 master's awarded. *Entrance requirements:* For master's, GRE General Test, minimum GPA of 3.0 in last 2 years of undergraduate course work. Additional exam requirements/recommendations for international students: Required—TOEFL (minimum score 500 paper-based; 61 iBT), IELTS (minimum score 6). *Application deadline:* For fall admission, 7/1 for domestic students, 2/15 for international students; for spring admission, 11/1 for domestic students, 7/15 for international students. Applications are processed on a rolling basis. Application fee: $30. *Expenses:* Tuition, state resident: full-time $7400; part-time $369.82 per credit. Tuition, nonresident: full-time $20,496; part-time $1042.81 per credit. *Financial support:* Fellowships with partial tuition reimbursements, research assistantships with partial tuition reimbursements, teaching assistantships with partial tuition reimbursements, career-related internships or fieldwork, scholarships/grants, and unspecified assistantships available. *Faculty research:* Technology, teaching English to speakers of other languages, math teaching, electronic portfolio assessment, global perspectives through social studies. *Unit head:* Dr. Barbara Ridener, Chairperson, 561-297-3588, E-mail: bridener@fau.edu. *Application contact:* Dr. Eliah Watlington, Associate Dean, 561-296-8520, Fax: 261-297-2991, E-mail: ewatling@fau.edu.
Website: http://www.coe.fau.edu/academicdepartments/tl/

Florida Gulf Coast University, College of Education, Program in Curriculum and Instruction, Fort Myers, FL 33965-6565. Offers elementary education (M Ed); English education (M Ed); English speakers of other languages endorsement (M Ed); gifted education (M Ed); mathematics education (M Ed); middle school education (M Ed); reading education (M Ed); science education (M Ed); social science education (M Ed); special education (M Ed). *Program availability:* Part-time, evening/weekend, online learning. *Faculty:* 27 full-time (19 women), 44 part-time/adjunct (30 women). *Students:* 3 full-time (all women), 16 part-time (14 women); includes 4 minority (2 Black or African American, non-Hispanic/Latino; 2 Hispanic/Latino). Average age 30. 6 applicants, 100% accepted, 5 enrolled. In 2017, 4 master's awarded. *Degree requirements:* For master's, final project or portfolio. *Entrance requirements:* For master's, GRE General Test, MAT, minimum undergraduate GPA of 3.0 in last 2 years. Additional exam requirements/recommendations for international students: Required—TOEFL (minimum score 550 paper-based). *Application deadline:* For fall admission, 2/15 priority date for domestic students, 5/1 for international students; for spring admission, 12/1 for domestic students, 9/15 for international students. Applications are processed on a rolling basis. Application fee: $30. Electronic applications accepted. *Expenses:* Tuition, state resident: part-time $290 per credit hour. Tuition, nonresident: part-time $1173 per credit hour. *Required fees:* $127 per credit hour. Tuition and fees vary according to course load. *Financial support:* In 2017–18, 2 students received support. Application deadline: 6/30; applicants required to submit FAFSA. *Faculty research:* Internet in schools, technology in pre-service and in-service teacher training. *Unit head:* Dr. Vickie Johnston, Instructor, 239-590-7754, Fax: 239-590-7801, E-mail: vjohnston@fgcu.edu. *Application contact:* Keiana Desmore, Adviser/Counselor, 239-590-7759, Fax: 239-590-7801, E-mail: kdesmore@fgcu.edu.
Website: http://coe.fgcu.edu/c-imed/

Florida International University, College of Arts, Sciences, and Education, Department of Teaching and Learning, Miami, FL 33199. Offers art education (MA, MS); curriculum and instruction (MS, Ed D, PhD, Ed S), including curriculum development (MS), elementary education (MS), English education (MS), learning technologies (MS), mathematics education (MS), modern language education (MS), physical education (MS), science education (MS), social studies education (MS), special education (MS); early childhood education (MS); exceptional student education (Ed D); foreign language education (MS), including foreign language education, teaching English to speakers of other languages (TESOL); language, literacy and culture (PhD); mathematics, science, and learning technologies (PhD); physical education (MS), including sport and fitness; reading education (MS). *Program availability:* Part-time, evening/weekend. *Faculty:* 60 full-time (41 women), 112 part-time/adjunct (77 women). *Students:* 165 full-time (139 women), 191 part-time (148 women); includes 270 minority (56 Black or African American, non-Hispanic/Latino; 12 Asian, non-Hispanic/Latino; 191 Hispanic/Latino; 11 Two or more races, non-Hispanic/Latino), 13 international. Average age 34. 238 applicants, 68% accepted, 107 enrolled. In 2017, 184 master's, 15 doctorates awarded.

Degree requirements: For doctorate, comprehensive exam, thesis/dissertation. *Entrance requirements:* For master's, GRE General Test, Florida General Knowledge Test or Florida College Level Academic Skills Test; for doctorate and Ed S, GRE General Test. Additional exam requirements/recommendations for international students: Required—TOEFL (minimum score 550 paper-based; 80 iBT), IELTS (minimum score 6.3). *Application deadline:* For fall admission, 6/1 priority date for domestic students, 4/1 for international students; for winter admission, 10/1 priority date for domestic students, 9/1 for international students; for spring admission, 3/1 priority date for domestic students, 2/1 for international students. Applications are processed on a rolling basis. Application fee: $30. Electronic applications accepted. *Expenses:* Tuition, state resident: full-time $8912; part-time $446 per credit hour. Tuition, nonresident: full-time $21,393; part-time $992 per credit hour. *Required fees:* $390; $195 per semester. *Financial support:* Research assistantships with tuition reimbursements and teaching assistantships with tuition reimbursements available. *Unit head:* Dr. Lynn Miller, Chair, 305-348-2005, Fax: 305-348-2086, E-mail: lynne.miller@fiu.edu. *Application contact:* Nanett Rojas, Assistant Director, Graduate Admissions, 305-348-7464, Fax: 305-348-7441, E-mail: gradadm@fiu.edu. Website: https://tl.fiu.edu/

Florida Memorial University, School of Education, Miami-Dade, FL 33054. Offers elementary education (MS); exceptional student education (MS); reading (MS). *Degree requirements:* For master's, comprehensive exam or thesis, field and clinical experiences, exit exam. *Entrance requirements:* For master's, GRE, CLAST, PRAXIS I, baccalaureate or graduate degree with minimum GPA of 3.0 in last 60 hours, 3 recommendations. Additional exam requirements/recommendations for international students: Recommended—TOEFL.

Florida State University, The Graduate School, College of Education, School of Teacher Education, Tallahassee, FL 32306-4450. Offers curriculum and instruction (MS, PhD, Ed S), including early childhood education, elementary education, English education, foreign and second language education, mathematics education, reading and language arts, science education, social science education, special education, visual disabilities education (MS); teaching English to speakers of other languages (Certificate). *Program availability:* Part-time, evening/weekend, 100% online, blended/hybrid learning, asynchronous, minimal on-campus study. *Faculty:* 41 full-time (33 women), 21 part-time/adjunct (18 women). *Students:* 133 full-time (93 women), 84 part-time (69 women); includes 48 minority (20 Black or African American, non-Hispanic/Latino; 2 Asian, non-Hispanic/Latino; 19 Hispanic/Latino; 7 Two or more races, non-Hispanic/Latino), 52 international. Average age 31. 146 applicants, 56% accepted, 52 enrolled. In 2017, 91 master's, 7 doctorates, 1 other advanced degree awarded. Terminal master's awarded for partial completion of doctoral program. *Degree requirements:* For master's and other advanced degree, comprehensive exam, thesis optional; for doctorate, comprehensive exam, thesis/dissertation, diagnostic exam, preliminary exam, prospectus defense, dissertation defense. *Entrance requirements:* For master's, doctorate, and other advanced degree, GRE General Test, minimum upper-division GPA of 3.0. Additional exam requirements/recommendations for international students: Required—TOEFL (minimum score 550 paper-based, 80 iBT), Michigan English Language Assessment Battery (minimum score 77), IELTS (minimum score 6.5) or PTE (minimum score 55). Application fee: $30. Electronic applications accepted. *Financial support:* Fellowships, research assistantships, teaching assistantships, scholarships/grants, tuition waivers (full and partial), and unspecified assistantships available. Financial award application deadline: 1/15; financial award applicants required to submit FAFSA. *Faculty research:* Identifying effective intervention strategies to improve reading skills; improving literacy teaching and learning through technology; understanding of student sense making, problem solving, the history and structure of STEM disciplines, and teacher education to support the development of ambitious instruction that supports the STEM learning of all students; examining practices of international education; identifying ways to support the professional development of teachers. *Unit head:* Dr. Sherry Southerland, Professor/Department Chair, 850-644-6885, Fax: 850-644-2725, E-mail: ssoutherland@admin.fsu.edu. *Application contact:* Britni DeZerga, Academic Program Specialist, 850-644-2122, Fax: 850-644-7736, E-mail: bpurvis@fsu.edu. Website: http://education.fsu.edu

Fontbonne University, Graduate Programs, St. Louis, MO 63105-3098. Offers accounting (MBA, MS); art (MA); art (K-12) (MAT); business (MBA); computer science (MS); deaf education (MA); early intervention in deaf education (MA); education (MA), including autism spectrum disorders, curriculum and instruction, diverse learners, early childhood education, reading, special education; elementary education (MAT); family and consumer sciences (MA), including multidisciplinary health communication studies; fine arts (MFA); instructional design and technology (MS); management and leadership (MM); middle school education (MAT); secondary education (MAT); special education (MAT); speech-language pathology (MS); supply chain management (MS); theatre (MA). *Program availability:* Part-time, evening/weekend, online learning. *Degree requirements:* For master's, comprehensive exam (for some programs), thesis (for some programs). *Entrance requirements:* Additional exam requirements/recommendations for international students: Required—TOEFL (minimum score 500 paper-based; 65 iBT). Electronic applications accepted.

Framingham State University, Graduate Studies, Program in Literacy and Language, Framingham, MA 01701-9101. Offers M Ed. *Program availability:* Part-time, evening/weekend. *Entrance requirements:* For master's, MAT. *Unit head:* Dr. Diane Lowe, Program Coordinator, 508-626-4550, Fax: 508-626-4030, E-mail: dlowe@frc.mass.edu. *Application contact:* 508-626-4550, Fax: 508-626-4030, E-mail: dgce@frc.mass.edu.

Fresno Pacific University, Graduate Programs, School of Education, Program in Reading and Language Arts, Fresno, CA 93702-4709. Offers reading (Certificate); reading/English as a second language (MA Ed); reading/language arts (MA Ed). *Program availability:* Part-time, evening/weekend. *Degree requirements:* For master's, thesis or alternative. *Entrance requirements:* For master's, three references. Additional exam requirements/recommendations for international students: Required—TOEFL (minimum score 550 paper-based). Electronic applications accepted. *Expenses:* Contact institution.

Frostburg State University, College of Education, Department of Educational Professions, Program in Reading, Frostburg, MD 21532. Offers M Ed, Ed D. *Accreditation:* NCATE. *Faculty:* 5. *Students:* 7 full-time (all women), 30 part-time (all women); includes 4 minority (2 Black or African American, non-Hispanic/Latino; 2 Two or more races, non-Hispanic/Latino), 1 international. Average age 32. 14 applicants, 100% accepted, 9 enrolled. In 2017, 8 master's, 1 doctorate awarded. *Degree requirements:* For master's, thesis or alternative, in-service. *Entrance requirements:* For master's, teaching certificate. Additional exam requirements/recommendations for international students: Required—TOEFL. *Application deadline:* For fall admission, 7/15 priority date for domestic students. Applications are processed on a rolling basis. Application fee: $45. Electronic applications accepted. *Expenses:* Tuition, state resident: part-time $433 per credit hour. Tuition, nonresident: part-time $557 per credit hour. *Required fees:* $121 per credit hour. $27 per term. *Financial support:* In 2017–18, 1 research assistantship with full tuition reimbursement (averaging $5,000 per year) was awarded; career-related internships or fieldwork also available. Financial award

application deadline: 4/1; financial award applicants required to submit FAFSA. *Unit head:* Dr. Kris McGee, Coordinator, 240-527-2730, E-mail: kmcgee@frostburg.edu. *Application contact:* Vickie Mazer, Director, Graduate Services, 301-687-7053, Fax: 301-687-4597, E-mail: vmmazer@frostburg.edu.

Furman University, Graduate Division, Department of Education, Greenville, SC 29613. Offers curriculum and instruction (MA); early childhood education (MA); educational leadership (Ed S); English as a second language (MA); literacy (MA); school leadership (MA); special education (MA). *Accreditation:* NCATE. *Program availability:* Part-time, online learning. *Degree requirements:* For master's, comprehensive exam (for some programs), thesis or alternative. *Entrance requirements:* For master's, PRAXIS II. *Faculty research:* Literacy, pedagogy and practice, social justice, advanced leadership, achievement in high poverty schools.

Gannon University, School of Graduate Studies, College of Humanities, Education, and Social Sciences, School of Education, Program in Reading, Erie, PA 16541-0001. Offers M Ed. *Program availability:* Part-time, evening/weekend, 100% online. *Degree requirements:* For master's, comprehensive exam, thesis or alternative, portfolio project. *Entrance requirements:* For master's, 3 letters of recommendation, transcript, bachelor's degree from regionally-accredited college or university with minimum GPA of 3.0. Additional exam requirements/recommendations for international students: Required—TOEFL (minimum score 79 iBT). Electronic applications accepted. Application fee is waived when completed online. *Expenses:* Contact institution.

Gannon University, School of Graduate Studies, College of Humanities, Education, and Social Sciences, School of Education, Program in Reading Specialist, Erie, PA 16541-0001. Offers Certificate. *Program availability:* Part-time, evening/weekend, 100% online. *Entrance requirements:* For degree, 3 letters of recommendation, transcript, bachelor's degree from regionally-accredited college or university with minimum GPA of 3.0, valid instructional I or II teaching certificate. Additional exam requirements/recommendations for international students: Required—TOEFL (minimum score 79 iBT). Application fee is waived when completed online.

George Fox University, College of Education, Graduate Teaching and Leading Program, Newberg, OR 97132-2697. Offers administrative leadership (Ed S); continuing administrator license (Certificate); educational leadership (M Ed); educational technology (M Ed); English for speakers of other languages (M Ed); ESOL (Certificate); initial administrator license (Certificate); reading (M Ed, Certificate); special education (M Ed); teaching (MAT). *Accreditation:* NCATE. *Program availability:* Part-time, evening/weekend, online learning. *Degree requirements:* For master's, thesis (for some programs). *Entrance requirements:* For master's, minimum undergraduate GPA of 3.0 during previous 2 years of course work, resume, 3 professional recommendations on university forms, official transcripts. Additional exam requirements/recommendations for international students: Required—TOEFL (minimum score 577 paper-based; 90 iBT). Electronic applications accepted. *Expenses:* Contact institution.

George Mason University, College of Education and Human Development, Programs in Curriculum and Instruction, Fairfax, VA 22030. Offers advanced international baccalaureate (M Ed); assistive technology (M Ed); designing digital learning in schools (M Ed); early childhood education (M Ed); early childhood education for diverse learners (M Ed); elementary education (M Ed); English as a second language (M Ed); gifted child education (M Ed); history (M Ed); literacy (M Ed), including PK-12 classroom teachers, reading specialist; literacy leadership for diverse schools (M Ed), including K-12 reading; physical education (M Ed); science K-12 (M Ed); secondary education (M Ed), including biology, chemistry, earth science, English, history/social science, math, physics; special education (M Ed); teacher leadership (M Ed); teaching culturally, linguistically diverse and exceptional learners (M Ed); transformative teaching (M Ed). *Program availability:* Part-time, evening/weekend, 100% online, blended/hybrid learning. *Faculty:* 41 full-time (36 women), 45 part-time/adjunct (37 women). *Students:* 173 full-time (151 women), 729 part-time (611 women); includes 271 minority (65 Black or African American, non-Hispanic/Latino; 5 American Indian or Alaska Native, non-Hispanic/Latino; 88 Asian, non-Hispanic/Latino; 94 Hispanic/Latino; 1 Native Hawaiian or other Pacific Islander, non-Hispanic/Latino; 18 Two or more races, non-Hispanic/Latino), 28 international. Average age 32. 426 applicants, 91% accepted, 289 enrolled. In 2017, 349 master's awarded. *Degree requirements:* For master's, thesis. *Entrance requirements:* For master's, PRAXIS Core (for some programs), 2 letters of recommendation, interview, program goals statement; 9 hours of complete licensure endorsement requirements (for elementary education); minimum GPA of 3.0 in applicant's last 60 hours of undergraduate coursework (for secondary education); at least 1 year of teaching experience (for literacy). Additional exam requirements/recommendations for international students: Required—TOEFL (minimum score 575 paper-based; 88 iBT), IELTS (minimum score 6.5), PTE (minimum score 59). *Application deadline:* For fall admission, 4/2 priority date for domestic and international students; for spring admission, 11/1 for domestic and international students. Application fee: $75 ($80 for international students). Electronic applications accepted. *Expenses:* Tuition, state resident: full-time $11,228; part-time $459.50 per credit. Tuition, nonresident: full-time $30,932; part-time $1280.50 per credit. *Required fees:* $3252; $135.50 per credit. Part-time tuition and fees vary according to course load and program. *Financial support:* In 2017–18, 2 students received support, including 2 teaching assistantships; career-related internships or fieldwork, Federal Work-Study, scholarships/grants, unspecified assistantships, and health care benefits (for full-time research or teaching assistantship recipients) also available. Support available to part-time students. Financial award application deadline: 3/1; financial award applicants required to submit FAFSA. *Faculty research:* Teacher preparation and professional development; adaptive teaching; wonder in science teacher preparation; literacy (digital, adolescent); site based course instruction. *Unit head:* Rebecca Fox, Professor and Academic Program Coordinator, 703-993-4123, E-mail: rfox@gmu.edu. Website: http://gse.gmu.edu/programs/gsemasters

Georgetown College, Department of Education, Georgetown, KY 40324-1696. Offers reading and writing (MA Ed); special education (MA Ed); teaching (MA Ed). *Accreditation:* NCATE. *Program availability:* Part-time. *Degree requirements:* For master's, portfolio. *Entrance requirements:* For master's, teaching certificate, minimum GPA of 2.7 or GRE General Test.

Georgia Southern University, Jack N. Averitt College of Graduate Studies, College of Education, Department of Curriculum, Foundations, and Reading, Program in Reading Education, Statesboro, GA 30460. Offers M Ed, Ed S. *Accreditation:* NCATE. *Program availability:* Part-time, evening/weekend. *Students:* 4 full-time (3 women), 25 part-time (all women); includes 5 minority (4 Black or African American, non-Hispanic/Latino; 1 Two or more races, non-Hispanic/Latino). Average age 34. 6 applicants, 100% accepted, 6 enrolled. In 2017, 13 master's, 2 Ed Ss awarded. *Degree requirements:* For master's, comprehensive exam, transition point assessments. *Entrance requirements:* For master's, minimum GPA of 2.5. Additional exam requirements/recommendations for international students: Required—TOEFL (minimum score 550 paper-based; 80 iBT), IELTS (minimum score 6). *Application deadline:* For fall admission, 3/15 priority date for domestic students, 3/1 priority date for international students; for spring admission, 10/1 priority date for domestic students, 10/1 for international students; for summer admission, 3/1 for domestic students. Applications are processed on a rolling basis. Application fee: $50. Electronic applications accepted. *Expenses:* Tuition, state

Reading Education

resident: full-time $4986; part-time $3324 per year. Tuition, nonresident: full-time $21,982; part-time $15,352 per year. *Required fees:* $2092; $1802 per credit hour. $901 per semester. Tuition and fees vary according to course load, campus/location and program. *Financial support:* Research assistantships with partial tuition reimbursements, teaching assistantships with full tuition reimbursements, career-related internships or fieldwork, scholarships/grants, and unspecified assistantships available. Support available to part-time students. Financial award application deadline: 4/15; financial award applicants required to submit FAFSA. *Faculty research:* Emerging literacy, content literacy, digital literacies, English language learners, literature groups, phonics/whole language, interpreting literacy policy. *Unit head:* Dr. Sally Brown, Director, 912-478-7268, Fax: 912-478-5382, E-mail: sallybrown@georgiasouthern.edu. *Application contact:* Dr. Lydia Cross, Coordinator for Graduate Student Recruitment, 912-478-8664, E-mail: lcross@georgiasouthern.edu.
Website: http://coe.georgiasouthern.edu/reading

Georgia Southern University–Armstrong Campus, College of Graduate Studies, Department of Childhood and Exceptional Student Education, Savannah, GA 31419-1997. Offers early childhood education (M Ed, MAT); reading (Certificate); special education (M Ed, MAT); special education transition specialist (Certificate). *Accreditation:* NCATE. *Program availability:* Part-time, evening/weekend. *Faculty:* 14 full-time (11 women), 1 (woman) part-time/adjunct. *Students:* 7 full-time (6 women), 214 part-time (195 women); includes 79 minority (63 Black or African American, non-Hispanic/Latino; 3 Asian, non-Hispanic/Latino; 6 Hispanic/Latino; 7 Two or more races, non-Hispanic/Latino). Average age 34. 159 applicants, 50% accepted, 69 enrolled. In 2017, 72 master's, 3 other advanced degrees awarded. *Degree requirements:* For master's, portfolio. *Entrance requirements:* For master's, MAT, Georgia Assessment for the Certification of Educators. Additional exam requirements/recommendations for international students: Required—TOEFL (minimum score 523 paper-based; 70 iBT). *Application deadline:* For fall admission, 7/1 priority date for domestic students, 5/1 priority date for international students; for spring admission, 11/15 priority date for domestic students, 9/15 priority date for international students; for summer admission, 4/15 priority date for domestic students, 9/15 for international students. Applications are processed on a rolling basis. Application fee: $30. Electronic applications accepted. *Expenses:* Tuition, state resident: part-time $211 per credit hour. Tuition, nonresident: part-time $782 per credit hour. *Required fees:* $737 per semester. Tuition and fees vary according to course load, degree level, campus/location and program. *Financial support:* In 2017–18, research assistantships with full tuition reimbursements (averaging $5,000 per year) were awarded; career-related internships or fieldwork, Federal Work-Study, and scholarships/grants also available. Support available to part-time students. Financial award application deadline: 3/15; financial award applicants required to submit FAFSA. *Faculty research:* Literacy, instructional design, poetry, working with local schools. *Unit head:* Dr. John Hobe, Department Head, 912-344-2619, Fax: 912-344-3443, E-mail: john.hobe@armstrong.edu. *Application contact:* McKenzie Peterman, Assistant Director of Graduate Admissions, 912-344-2503, Fax: 912-344-3417, E-mail: graduate@armstrong.edu.
Website: https://www.armstrong.edu/academic-departments/education-ceed

Georgia State University, College of Education and Human Development, Department of Middle and Secondary Education, Atlanta, GA 30302-3083. Offers curriculum and instruction (Ed D); English education (MAT); mathematics education (M Ed, MAT); middle level education (MAT); reading, language and literacy education (M Ed, MAT), including reading instruction (M Ed); science education (M Ed, MAT), including biology (MAT), broad field science (MAT), chemistry (MAT), earth science (MAT), physics (MAT); social studies education (M Ed, MAT), including economics (MAT), geography (MAT), history (MAT), political science (MAT); teaching and learning (PhD), including language and literacy, mathematics education, music education, science education, social studies education, teaching and teacher education. *Accreditation:* NCATE. *Program availability:* Part-time, evening/weekend, online learning. *Faculty:* 24 full-time (18 women). *Students:* 179 full-time (110 women), 192 part-time (133 women); includes 193 minority (130 Black or African American, non-Hispanic/Latino; 1 American Indian or Alaska Native, non-Hispanic/Latino; 23 Asian, non-Hispanic/Latino; 25 Hispanic/Latino; 14 Two or more races, non-Hispanic/Latino), 6 international. Average age 33. 175 applicants, 58% accepted, 83 enrolled. In 2017, 81 master's, 17 doctorates awarded. *Entrance requirements:* For master's, GRE, GACE I (for initial teacher preparation programs), baccalaureate degree or equivalent, resume, goals statement, two letters of recommendation, minimum undergraduate GPA of 2.5; proof of initial teacher certification in the content area (for M Ed); for doctorate, GRE, resume, goals statement, writing sample, two letters of recommendation, minimum graduate GPA of 3.3, interview. *Application deadline:* For fall admission, 1/15 priority date for domestic and international students; for spring admission, 10/1 for domestic and international students. Application fee: $50. Electronic applications accepted. *Expenses:* Tuition, state resident: full-time $7020. Tuition, nonresident: full-time $22,518. *Required fees:* $2128. Tuition and fees vary according to degree level and program. *Financial support:* In 2017–18, fellowships with full tuition reimbursements (averaging $19,667 per year), research assistantships with full tuition reimbursements (averaging $5,436 per year), teaching assistantships with full tuition reimbursements (averaging $2,779 per year) were awarded; career-related internships or fieldwork, Federal Work-Study, scholarships/grants, health care benefits, tuition waivers (full and partial), and unspecified assistantships also available. Financial award application deadline: 3/15. *Faculty research:* Teacher education in language and literacy, mathematics, science, and social studies in urban middle and secondary school settings; learning technologies in school, community, and corporate settings; multicultural education and education for social justice; urban education; international education. *Unit head:* Dr. Dana L. Fox, Chair, 404-413-8060, Fax: 404-413-8063, E-mail: dfox@gsu.edu. *Application contact:* Bobbie Turner, Administrative Coordinator, 404-413-8405, Fax: 404-413-8063, E-mail: bnturner@gsu.edu.
Website: http://mse.education.gsu.edu/

Gordon College, Graduate Education Program, Wenham, MA 01984-1899. Offers early childhood (M Ed); educational leadership (M Ed, Ed S); elementary education (M Ed); English as a second language (M Ed, Ed S); math specialist (M Ed); mathematics specialist (Ed S); middle school education (M Ed); moderate disabilities (M Ed); Montessori education (M Ed); reading (M Ed, Ed S); secondary education (M Ed). *Program availability:* Part-time, evening/weekend. *Faculty:* 23 full-time (17 women), 32 part-time/adjunct (23 women). *Students:* 68 full-time (50 women), 114 part-time (99 women); includes 24 minority (2 Black or African American, non-Hispanic/Latino; 8 Asian, non-Hispanic/Latino; 13 Hispanic/Latino; 1 Two or more races, non-Hispanic/Latino), 10 international. Average age 34. 248 applicants, 100% accepted, 182 enrolled. In 2017, 99 master's, 16 Ed Ss awarded. *Degree requirements:* For master's, action research or clinical experience (for most programs); for Ed S, action research or clinical experience (for some programs). *Entrance requirements:* For master's, minimum undergraduate GPA of 3.0; 2 official undergraduate transcripts; professional resume; 3 recommendation letters (one professional reference, one academic reference, one personal reference); 500-700 word statement of purpose; for Ed S, minimum master's GPA of 3.3; 2 official transcripts from undergraduate and graduate schools; professional resume; 3 recommendation letters (one professional reference, one academic reference, one personal reference); 500-700 word statement of purpose. Additional exam requirements/recommendations for international students: Required—TOEFL

(minimum score 550 paper-based, 80 iBT) or IELTS (minimum score 6.5). *Application deadline:* Applications are processed on a rolling basis. Application fee: $75. *Expenses:* $325 per credit tuition; $75 per semester administrative fee. *Financial support:* Applicants required to submit FAFSA. *Faculty research:* Reading, early childhood development, English language learners, universal design for learning. *Unit head:* Dr. Janet Arndt, Director of Graduate Studies, 978-867-4355, Fax: 978-867-4663. *Application contact:* Julie Lenocker, Program Administrator, 978-867-4322, Fax: 978-867-4663, E-mail: graduate-education@gordon.edu.
Website: http://www.gordon.edu/graduate

Goucher College, Graduate Programs in Education, Baltimore, MD 21204-2794. Offers at-risk and diverse learners (M Ed, Certificate); athletic program leadership and administration (M Ed, Certificate); elementary education (MAT); literacy strategies for content learning (M Ed); middle school (M Ed, Certificate); Montessori studies (M Ed); reading instruction (M Ed, Certificate); reducing student, classroom, and school disruption (M Ed); school improvement leadership (M Ed); secondary education (MAT); special education (MAT), including elementary education; special education for certified elementary and secondary teachers (M Ed); teacher as leader in technology (M Ed). *Program availability:* Part-time, evening/weekend. *Degree requirements:* For master's, thesis (M Ed), final presentation (MAT). *Entrance requirements:* For master's, minimum GPA of 3.0. Additional exam requirements/recommendations for international students: Required—TOEFL (minimum score 550 paper-based; 80 iBT), IELTS (minimum score 7). *Application deadline:* For fall admission, 9/1 for domestic students; for spring admission, 1/15 for domestic students. Applications are processed on a rolling basis. Application fee: $75. Electronic applications accepted. *Expenses:* Contact institution. *Financial support:* Career-related internships or fieldwork and unspecified assistantships available. Support available to part-time students. Financial award application deadline: 4/15; financial award applicants required to submit FAFSA. *Faculty research:* Urban education, middle school, school improvement, teacher education, at-risk student achievement. *Unit head:* Dr. Phyllis Sunshine, Assistant Provost, 410-337-6047, Fax: 410-337-6394, E-mail: psunshin@goucher.edu. *Application contact:* Carlton E. Surbeck, III, Director of Admissions, 410-337-6100, Fax: 410-337-6085, E-mail: admissions@goucher.edu.
Website: http://www.goucher.edu/graduate-programs/graduate-programs-in-education

Governors State University, College of Education, Program in Reading, University Park, IL 60484. Offers MA. *Accreditation:* NCATE. *Program availability:* Part-time. *Faculty:* 20 full-time (12 women), 40 part-time/adjunct (28 women). *Students:* 1 (woman) part-time; minority (Black or African American, non-Hispanic/Latino). Average age 42. 4 applicants, 50% accepted, 1 enrolled. In 2017, 2 master's awarded. *Application deadline:* For fall admission, 4/1 for domestic students. Applications are processed on a rolling basis. Application fee: $50. Electronic applications accepted. *Expenses:* Tuition, state resident: full-time $8472; part-time $353 per credit hour. Tuition, nonresident: full-time $16,944; part-time $706 per credit hour. *Required fees:* $1824; $76 per credit hour. $38 per term. Tuition and fees vary according to course load, degree level and program. *Financial support:* Application deadline: 5/1; applicants required to submit FAFSA. *Unit head:* Timothy Harrington, Chair, Division of Education, 708-534-5000 Ext. 4361, E-mail: tharrington2@govst.edu.

Graceland University, Gleazer School of Education, Independence, MO 64050. Offers curriculum and instruction: collaborative learning and teaching (M Ed); differentiated instruction (M Ed); instructional leadership (M Ed); literacy instruction (M Ed); management in a quality classroom (M Ed); special education (M Ed); technology integration (M Ed). *Accreditation:* NCATE. *Program availability:* Part-time, 100% online. *Faculty:* 2 full-time (both women), 13 part-time/adjunct (10 women). *Students:* 117 full-time (102 women), 62 part-time (54 women); includes 8 minority (3 Black or African American, non-Hispanic/Latino; 1 Asian, non-Hispanic/Latino; 2 Hispanic/Latino; 1 Native Hawaiian or other Pacific Islander, non-Hispanic/Latino; 1 Two or more races, non-Hispanic/Latino), 1 international. Average age 35. 28 applicants, 100% accepted, 19 enrolled. In 2017, 64 master's awarded. *Degree requirements:* For master's, action research capstone. *Entrance requirements:* For master's, minimum GPA of 3.0, teaching certificate, current teaching contract and license, two letters of reference, statement of professional goals, verification of ongoing access to computer technology, including email and Internet. Additional exam requirements/recommendations for international students: Required—TOEFL (minimum score 550 paper-based; 79 iBT). *Application deadline:* For fall admission, 10/1 for domestic students; for winter admission, 11/15 for domestic students; for spring admission, 2/15 priority date for domestic students; for summer admission, 6/1 for domestic students. Application fee: $50. Electronic applications accepted. *Expenses:* Contact institution. *Financial support:* In 2017–18, 3 students received support. Tuition waivers available. Financial award applicants required to submit FAFSA. *Faculty research:* Literacy, technology, faculty mentoring, adult literacy, e-learning, online teaching. *Unit head:* Dr. Lee Bash, Interim Dean, 641-784-5072, E-mail: bash@graceland.edu. *Application contact:* Jeanette Calipetro, Admissions Representative, 816-423-4716, Fax: 816-833-2990, E-mail: jcali1@graceland.edu.
Website: http://www.graceland.edu/education

Grambling State University, School of Graduate Studies and Research, College of Education, Department of Educational Leadership, Grambling, LA 71245. Offers developmental education (MS, Ed D, PMC), including curriculum and instructional design (Ed D), English (MS), guidance and counseling (MS), higher education administration and management (Ed D), mathematics (MS), reading (MS), science (MS), student development and personnel services (Ed D); educational leadership (M Ed). *Program availability:* Part-time, evening/weekend. *Degree requirements:* For master's, comprehensive exam, thesis (for some programs); for doctorate, comprehensive exam, thesis/dissertation. *Entrance requirements:* For master's, GRE, minimum GPA of 2.5 on last degree; for doctorate, GRE (minimum score 1000, 500 on Verbal), master's degree, minimum GPA of 3.0 on last degree. Additional exam requirements/recommendations for international students: Required—TOEFL (minimum score 500 paper-based; 62 iBT). Electronic applications accepted.

Grand Canyon University, College of Education, Phoenix, AZ 85017-1097. Offers autism spectrum disorders (MA); curriculum and instruction (MA); early childhood education (M Ed); educational administration (M Ed); educational leadership (M Ed); elementary education (M Ed); gifted education (MA); instructional technology (MS); K-12 leadership (Ed S); reading (MA); secondary education (M Ed); secondary humanities education (M Ed); secondary STEM education (M Ed); special education (M Ed); teaching and learning (Ed D); teaching English to speakers of other languages (MA). *Program availability:* Part-time, evening/weekend, online learning. *Degree requirements:* For master's, publishable research paper (M Ed), e-portfolio. *Entrance requirements:* For master's, undergraduate degree from accredited, GCU-approved college, university, or program with minimum GPA 2.8. Additional exam requirements/recommendations for international students: Required—TOEFL (minimum score 550 paper-based; 79 iBT), IELTS (minimum score 6). Electronic applications accepted.

Grand Valley State University, College of Education, Program in Literacy Studies, Allendale, MI 49401-9403. Offers M Ed. *Program availability:* Part-time, evening/weekend. *Students:* 3 full-time (all women), 112 part-time (106 women); includes 10 minority (4 Black or African American, non-Hispanic/Latino; 2 American Indian or Alaska

Native, non-Hispanic/Latino; 1 Asian, non-Hispanic/Latino; 2 Hispanic/Latino; 1 Two or more races, non-Hispanic/Latino), 2 international. Average age 31. 19 applicants, 95% accepted, 10 enrolled. In 2017, 24 master's awarded. *Degree requirements:* For master's, project or thesis. *Entrance requirements:* For master's, minimum GPA 3.0 or GRE General Test, last 60 credits from regionally-accredited college/university, 3 letters of recommendation. Additional exam requirements/recommendations for international students: Required—TOEFL (minimum iBT score of 80), IELTS (6.5), or Michigan English Language Assessment Battery (77). *Application deadline:* Applications are processed on a rolling basis. Application fee: $30. Electronic applications accepted. *Expenses:* $652 per credit hour. *Financial support:* In 2017–18, 21 students received support, including 21 fellowships; unspecified assistantships also available. *Unit head:* Dr. Elizabeth Stolle, Program Coordinator, 616-331-6241, Fax: 616-331-6515, E-mail: stollee@gvsu.edu. *Application contact:* Thomas Owens, Director, Student Information and Services Center, 616-331-6282, Fax: 616-331-6217, E-mail: owenst@gvsu.edu. Website: http://www.gvsu.edu/grad/literacy.

Grand Valley State University, College of Education, Program in Reading and Language Arts, Allendale, MI 49401-9403. Offers M Ed. *Accreditation:* NCATE. *Program availability:* Part-time, evening/weekend. *Students:* 2 part-time (both women). Average age 35. In 2017, 3 master's awarded. *Degree requirements:* For master's, project or thesis. *Entrance requirements:* For master's, GRE General Test or minimum GPA of 3.0; last 60 credits from regionally-accredited college/university; 3 letters of recommendation. Additional exam requirements/recommendations for international students: Required—TOEFL (minimum iBT score of 80), IELTS (6.5), or Michigan English Language Assessment Battery (77). *Application deadline:* Applications are processed on a rolling basis. Application fee: $30. Electronic applications accepted. *Expenses:* $652 per credit hour. *Financial support:* Career-related internships or fieldwork, Federal Work-Study, scholarships/grants, and unspecified assistantships available. *Faculty research:* Culture of literacy, literacy acquisition, assessment, content area literacy, writing pedagogy. *Unit head:* Dr. Elizabeth Stolle, Graduate Program Director, 616-331-6242, Fax: 616-331-6516, E-mail: stollee@gvsu.edu. *Application contact:* Thomas Owens, Director, Student Information and Services Center, 616-331-6282, Fax: 616-331-6217, E-mail: owenst@gvsu.edu.

Hamline University, School of Education, St. Paul, MN 55104-1284. Offers education (MA Ed, Ed D); English as a second language (MA); literacy education (MA); natural science and environmental education (MA Ed); teaching (MAT); teaching English to speakers of other languages (MA). *Accreditation:* NCATE (one or more programs are accredited). *Program availability:* Part-time, evening/weekend, 100% online, blended/hybrid learning. *Faculty:* 23 full-time (15 women), 43 part-time/adjunct (30 women). *Students:* 79 full-time (60 women), 898 part-time (692 women); includes 139 minority (31 Black or African American, non-Hispanic/Latino; 1 American Indian or Alaska Native, non-Hispanic/Latino; 58 Asian, non-Hispanic/Latino; 33 Hispanic/Latino; 16 Two or more races, non-Hispanic/Latino), 8 international. Average age 35. 366 applicants, 78% accepted, 193 enrolled. In 2017, 236 master's, 7 doctorates awarded. *Degree requirements:* For master's, thesis (for some programs), thesis or capstone project; for doctorate, comprehensive exam, thesis/dissertation. *Entrance requirements:* For master's, official transcripts, essay, letters of recommendation, minimum GPA of 3.0 from bachelor's work; resume and/or writing samples (for some programs); for doctorate, personal statement, master's degree with minimum GPA of 3.0, letters of recommendation, writing sample. Additional exam requirements/recommendations for international students: Required—TOEFL (minimum score 550 paper-based; 80 iBT), IELTS (minimum score 6.5). *Application deadline:* For fall admission, 6/1 for domestic and international students; for spring admission, 11/1 for domestic and international students; for summer admission, 3/1 for domestic and international students. Applications are processed on a rolling basis. Application fee: $0 ($100 for international students). Electronic applications accepted. *Expenses:* $466 per credit (for MA Ed), $625 per credit (for MATESOL), $569 per credit (for MAT), $721 per credit plus fees (for EdD). *Financial support:* Career-related internships or fieldwork, Federal Work-Study, and scholarships/grants available. Support available to part-time students. Financial award application deadline: 4/20; financial award applicants required to submit FAFSA. *Faculty research:* Adult basic education, service-learning, teacher dispositions, diversity, technology. *Unit head:* Dr. Marcela Kostihova, Dean, 651-523-2206, Fax: 651-523-2489, E-mail: cladean@hamline.edu. *Application contact:* Shawn Skoog, Director of Graduate Recruitment and Admission, 651-523-2900, Fax: 651-523-3058, E-mail: gradprog@hamline.edu.
Website: http://www.hamline.edu/education

Hannibal-LaGrange University, Program in Education, Hannibal, MO 63401-1999. Offers literacy (MS Ed); teaching and learning (MS Ed). *Program availability:* Part-time, evening/weekend. *Degree requirements:* For master's, thesis, portfolio, documenting of program outcomes, public sharing of research. *Entrance requirements:* For master's, copy of current teaching certificate; minimum GPA of 2.75. *Faculty research:* Reading assessment, reading remediation, handwriting instruction, early childhood intervention.

Harding University, Cannon-Clary College of Education, Searcy, AR 72149-0001. Offers advanced studies in teaching and learning (M Ed); art (MSE); behavioral science (MSE); counseling (MS, Ed S); early childhood special education (M Ed, MSE); education (MSE); educational leadership (M Ed, Ed S); elementary education (M Ed); English (MSE); French (MSE); history/social science (MSE); kinesiology (MSE); math (MSE); reading (M Ed); secondary education (M Ed); Spanish (MSE); teaching (MAT); teaching English as a second language (MSE). *Accreditation:* NCATE. *Program availability:* Part-time, evening/weekend. *Faculty:* 22 full-time (9 women), 51 part-time/adjunct (37 women). *Students:* 135 full-time (95 women), 316 part-time (231 women); includes 77 minority (46 Black or African American, non-Hispanic/Latino; 7 American Indian or Alaska Native, non-Hispanic/Latino; 4 Asian, non-Hispanic/Latino; 9 Hispanic/Latino; 11 Two or more races, non-Hispanic/Latino), 11 international. Average age 34. 128 applicants, 87% accepted, 111 enrolled. In 2017, 153 master's, 24 other advanced degrees awarded. *Degree requirements:* For master's, comprehensive exam (for some programs), thesis optional, portfolio(s); for Ed S, comprehensive exam, portfolio, project. *Entrance requirements:* For master's, GRE, MAT, PRAXIS; for Ed S, MAT or GRE. Additional exam requirements/recommendations for international students: Required—TOEFL (minimum score 550 paper-based; 79 iBT). *Application deadline:* For fall admission, 8/1 for domestic and international students; for spring admission, 1/1 for domestic and international students. Applications are processed on a rolling basis. Application fee: $35. Tuition and fees vary according to course load, degree level, campus/location and program. *Financial support:* In 2017–18, 33 students received support. Unspecified assistantships available. *Faculty research:* Reading, comprehension, school violence, educational technology, behavior, college choice, differentiated instruction, brain-based teaching. *Unit head:* Dr. Clara Carroll, Chair, 501-279-4501, Fax: 501-279-4083, E-mail: ccarroll@harding.edu. *Application contact:* Information Contact, 501-279-4315, E-mail: gradstudiesedu@harding.edu.
Website: http://www.harding.edu/education

Hardin-Simmons University, Graduate School, Irvin School of Education, Department of Educational Studies, Program in Reading Specialist Education, Abilene, TX 79698-0001. Offers reading education (M Ed). *Program availability:* Part-time. *Faculty:* 1 (woman) full-time, 1 (woman) part-time/adjunct. *Students:* 3 part-time (all women).

Average age 38. 4 applicants, 100% accepted, 2 enrolled. *Degree requirements:* For master's, comprehensive exam. *Entrance requirements:* For master's, minimum undergraduate GPA of 3.0 in major or all upper-level coursework, 2.7 overall. Additional exam requirements/recommendations for international students: Required—TOEFL (minimum score 550 paper-based; 79 iBT). *Application deadline:* For fall admission, 8/15 priority date for domestic students, 4/1 for international students; for spring admission, 1/5 priority date for domestic students, 9/1 for international students. Applications are processed on a rolling basis. Application fee: $50 ($150 for international students). Electronic applications accepted. *Expenses: Tuition:* Full-time $13,500; part-time $750 per semester hour. *Required fees:* $220 per term. One-time fee: $50. Tuition and fees vary according to course load, campus/location and program. *Financial support:* In 2017–18, 1 student received support. Fellowships and scholarships/grants available. Support available to part-time students. Financial award application deadline: 6/30; financial award applicants required to submit FAFSA. *Faculty research:* Social networking as a gatekeeper, reflective process of teachers, growth of reflective practice in pre-service teachers, multicultural children's literature. *Unit head:* Dr. Emily Dean, Program Director, 325-671-5784, Fax: 325-670-5859, E-mail: emily.o.dean@hsutx.edu. *Application contact:* Dr. Nancy Kucinski, Dean of Graduate Studies, 325-670-1298, Fax: 325-670-1564, E-mail: gradoff@hsutx.edu.
Website: http://www.hsutx.edu/academics/irvin/graduate/readinged

Harvard University, Harvard Graduate School of Education, Master's Programs in Education, Cambridge, MA 02138. Offers arts in education (Ed M); education policy and management (Ed M); higher education (Ed M); human development and psychology (Ed M); international education policy (Ed M); language and literacy (Ed M); learning and teaching (Ed M); mind, brain, and education (Ed M); prevention science and practice (Ed M); school leadership (Ed M); special studies (Ed M); teacher education (Ed M); technology, innovation, and education (Ed M). *Program availability:* Part-time. *Entrance requirements:* For master's, GRE General Test, statement of purpose, 3 letters of recommendation, resume, official transcripts. Additional exam requirements/recommendations for international students: Required—TOEFL (minimum score 613 paper-based; 104 iBT), TWE (minimum score 5). Electronic applications accepted. *Faculty research:* Learning and development, educational leadership and organizations, education policy analysis.

Heritage University, Graduate Programs in Education, Program in Professional Studies, Toppenish, WA 98948-9599. Offers bilingual education/ESL (M Ed); biology (M Ed); English and literature (M Ed); reading/literacy (M Ed); special education (M Ed). *Program availability:* Part-time, evening/weekend. *Degree requirements:* For master's, comprehensive exam (for some programs), thesis (for some programs).

Hofstra University, School of Education, Specialized Programs in Education, Hempstead, NY 11549. Offers applied behavior analysis (Advanced Certificate); childhood special education (MS Ed); early childhood special education (MS Ed, Advanced Certificate); educational and policy leadership (Ed D); educational leadership (Advanced Certificate), including school building leader/school district business leader; educational leadership and policy studies (MS Ed), including K-12; elementary special education (MS Ed); gifted education (Advanced Certificate), including school building leader/school district business leader; health education (MS); health professions pedagogy and leadership (MS); higher education leadership and policy studies (MS Ed); inclusive early childhood special education (MS Ed); inclusive elementary special education (MS Ed); inclusive secondary special education (MS Ed); literacy studies (MA, MS Ed, Ed D, Advanced Certificate), including birth-grade 6 (MS Ed, Advanced Certificate), grades 5-12 (MS Ed, Advanced Certificate), literacy studies (Ed D); pedagogy for health professions (Advanced Certificate); physical education (MS); school district business leader (Advanced Certificate); secondary education generalist - students with disabilities 7-12 (MS Ed), including students with disabilities 7-12; secondary special education generalist (MS Ed), including extension in secondary education; special education (MS Ed, Advanced Certificate); special education assessment and diagnosis (Advanced Certificate); special education early childhood intervention (MS Ed); special education: international perspectives (MS Ed); teaching students with severe or multiple disabilities (Advanced Certificate). *Program availability:* Part-time, evening/weekend, blended/hybrid learning. *Students:* 148 full-time (110 women), 249 part-time (188 women); includes 105 minority (54 Black or African American, non-Hispanic/Latino; 1 American Indian or Alaska Native, non-Hispanic/Latino; 13 Asian, non-Hispanic/Latino; 35 Hispanic/Latino; 1 Native Hawaiian or other Pacific Islander, non-Hispanic/Latino; 1 Two or more races, non-Hispanic/Latino), 1 international. Average age 32. 228 applicants, 93% accepted, 132 enrolled. In 2017, 97 master's, 22 doctorates, 31 other advanced degrees awarded. *Degree requirements:* For master's, one foreign language, comprehensive exam (for some programs), thesis (for some programs), electronic portfolio, capstone course, internship, practicum, student teaching, seminars, minimum GPA of 3.0; for doctorate, one foreign language, comprehensive exam, thesis/dissertation, qualifying hearing. *Entrance requirements:* For master's, GRE, interview, letters of recommendation, portfolio, essay, certification; for doctorate, GRE or MAT, interview, resume, essay, master's degree, 3 letters of recommendation, writing sample; for Advanced Certificate, GRE, interview, letters of recommendation, essay, professional experience, resume, master's degree. Additional exam requirements/recommendations for international students: Required—TOEFL (minimum score 550 paper-based; 80 iBT). *Application deadline:* Applications are processed on a rolling basis. Application fee: $75. Electronic applications accepted. *Expenses: Tuition:* Full-time $1292. *Required fees:* $970. Tuition and fees vary according to program. *Financial support:* In 2017–18, 225 students received support, including 118 fellowships with full and partial tuition reimbursements available (averaging $3,887 per year), 12 research assistantships with full and partial tuition reimbursements available (averaging $7,215 per year); career-related internships or fieldwork, Federal Work-Study, institutionally sponsored loans, scholarships/grants, traineeships, tuition waivers (full and partial), and unspecified assistantships also available. Support available to part-time students. Financial award applicants required to submit FAFSA. *Faculty research:* Collaborative teaching and learning; language and culture; new media literacies; applied behavior analysis; K-12 leadership development. *Unit head:* Dr. Elfreda Blue, Chairperson, 516-463-5762, Fax: 516-463-6184, E-mail: elfreda.blue@hofstra.edu. *Application contact:* Sunil Samuel, Assistant Vice President of Admissions, 516-463-4723, Fax: 516-463-4664, E-mail: graduateadmission@hofstra.edu.
Website: http://www.hofstra.edu/education/

Holy Family University, Graduate and Professional Programs, School of Education, Master of Education Programs, Philadelphia, PA 19114. Offers early elementary education (PreK-Grade 4) (M Ed); education leadership (M Ed); general education (M Ed); reading specialist (M Ed); special education (M Ed); TESOL and literacy (M Ed). *Program availability:* Part-time. *Degree requirements:* For master's, thesis optional. Electronic applications accepted. *Expenses: Tuition:* Full-time $13,518; part-time $9012 per credit hour. Tuition and fees vary according to degree level and program.

Hood College, Graduate School, Department of Education, Frederick, MD 21701-8575. Offers curriculum and instruction (MS), including elementary education, elementary science and mathematics education, secondary education, special education; education, multidisciplinary studies (MS); educational leadership (MS, Certificate);

reading specialization (MS); STEM education (Certificate). *Accreditation:* NCATE. *Program availability:* Part-time-only, evening/weekend. *Faculty:* 6 full-time (4 women), 35 part-time/adjunct (27 women). *Students:* 3 full-time (all women), 329 part-time (265 women); includes 62 minority (35 Black or African American, non-Hispanic/Latino; 4 Asian, non-Hispanic/Latino; 14 Hispanic/Latino; 9 Two or more races, non-Hispanic/Latino), 3 international. Average age 33. 76 applicants, 100% accepted, 63 enrolled. In 2017, 53 master's, 58 other advanced degrees awarded. *Degree requirements:* For master's, action research project, portfolio (for reading specialization); for Certificate, STEM capstone activity. *Entrance requirements:* For master's, minimum GPA of 2.75, teaching certification, writing sample during interview, letter of recommendation from principal (for educational leadership program only). Additional exam requirements/recommendations for international students: Required—TOEFL (minimum score 575 paper-based; 89 iBT), IELTS (minimum score 6.5). *Application deadline:* For fall admission, 8/15 priority date for domestic students, 8/5 for international students; for spring admission, 12/1 priority date for domestic students, 12/1 for international students; for summer admission, 5/1 priority date for domestic students, 4/15 for international students. Applications are processed on a rolling basis. Application fee: $35. Electronic applications accepted. *Expenses:* $465 per credit plus $110 comprehensive fee per semester. *Financial support:* Tuition waivers (partial) and unspecified assistantships available. Financial award applicants required to submit FAFSA. *Faculty research:* Leadership, action research, brain research, learning styles. *Unit head:* Dr. April M. Boulton, Dean of the Graduate School, 301-696-3612, E-mail: gofurther@hood.edu. *Application contact:* Jan Marcus, Assistant Director of Graduate Admissions, 301-696-3600, E-mail: gofurther@hood.edu.
Website: http://www.hood.edu/academics/education/index.html

Houston Baptist University, College of Education and Behavioral Sciences, Programs in Education, Houston, TX 77074-3298. Offers bilingual education (M Ed); counselor education (M Ed); curriculum and instruction (M Ed); curriculum and instruction (EC-6 bilingual) (M Ed); curriculum and instruction in all-level art, Spanish, music, or physical education (M Ed); curriculum and instruction in EC-6 and special education (EC-12) (M Ed); curriculum and instruction in instructional technology (M Ed); curriculum and instruction in mathematics, science, or social studies (4-8) (M Ed); curriculum and instruction with EC-6 generalist (M Ed); curriculum and instruction with English language arts and reading (4-8) (M Ed); educational administration (M Ed); educational diagnostician (M Ed); executive educational leadership (Ed D); higher education in business management (M Ed); higher education in Christian studies (M Ed); higher education in counseling (M Ed); higher education in educational technology (M Ed); reading (M Ed); special educational leadership (Ed D). *Program availability:* Part-time, evening/weekend, 100% online, blended/hybrid learning. *Students:* 83 full-time (65 women), 187 part-time (156 women); includes 189 minority (114 Black or African American, non-Hispanic/Latino; 2 American Indian or Alaska Native, non-Hispanic/Latino; 9 Asian, non-Hispanic/Latino; 58 Hispanic/Latino; 6 Two or more races, non-Hispanic/Latino), 7 international. Average age 36. 309 applicants, 31% accepted, 70 enrolled. In 2017, 92 master's awarded. *Degree requirements:* For master's, comprehensive exam; for doctorate, thesis/dissertation. *Entrance requirements:* For master's, minimum GPA of 2.75, two recommendations, resume, bachelor's degree conferred transcript; interview (for non-certified teachers); for doctorate, GRE, 5 letters of recommendation. Additional exam requirements/recommendations for international students: Required—TOEFL (minimum score 80 iBT), IELTS (minimum score 6.5). *Application deadline:* For fall admission, 8/1 for domestic students, 6/1 for international students; for spring admission, 1/1 for domestic students, 11/1 for international students; for summer admission, 5/1 for domestic students, 3/1 for international students. Applications are processed on a rolling basis. Application fee: $0 ($100 for international students). Electronic applications accepted. Application fee is waived when completed online. *Expenses:* $22,000 tuition; $4,500 fees (general, technology and parking). *Financial support:* In 2017–18, 59 students received support. Research assistantships, teaching assistantships, Federal Work-Study, and scholarships/grants available. Support available to part-time students. Financial award application deadline: 4/1; financial award applicants required to submit FAFSA. *Faculty research:* Autism and inclusion, integrating technology into instruction, school change and leadership trust. *Unit head:* Dr. Charlotte Fontenot, Director, Graduate Programs, 281-649-3078, Fax: 281-649-3361, E-mail: cfontenot@hbu.edu. *Application contact:* Kristy Wright, Administrative Assistant for Graduate Programs, 281-649-3094, Fax: 281-649-3361, E-mail: kwright@hbu.edu.
Website: http://www.hbu.edu/MED

Idaho State University, Office of Graduate Studies, College of Education, Department of Teaching and Educational Studies, Pocatello, ID 83209-8059. Offers deaf education (M Ed); elementary education (M Ed); human exceptionality (M Ed); literacy (M Ed); music education (M Ed); secondary education (M Ed). *Program availability:* Part-time. *Degree requirements:* For master's, comprehensive exam, thesis (for some programs), oral thesis defense or written comprehensive exam and oral exam. *Entrance requirements:* For master's, GRE or MAT, minimum undergraduate GPA of 3.0, bachelor's degree, professional experience in an educational context. Additional exam requirements/recommendations for international students: Required—TOEFL (minimum score 550 paper-based; 80 iBT). Electronic applications accepted. *Faculty research:* Literacy, school psychology, special education.

Illinois State University, Graduate School, College of Education, Department of Curriculum and Instruction, Program in Reading, Normal, IL 61790. Offers MS Ed. *Accreditation:* NCATE. *Degree requirements:* For master's, practicum. *Entrance requirements:* For master's, GRE General Test, minimum GPA of 3.0 in last 60 hours of course work, course work in reading.

Indiana University Bloomington, School of Education, Department of Literacy, Culture, and Language Education, Bloomington, IN 47405-7000. Offers MS, Ed D, PhD, Ed S. *Accreditation:* NCATE. *Program availability:* Part-time, evening/weekend, online learning. Terminal master's awarded for partial completion of doctoral program. *Degree requirements:* For doctorate, thesis/dissertation, internship; for Ed S, comprehensive exam or project. *Entrance requirements:* For master's, GRE General Test or minimum GPA of 3.0; for doctorate, GRE General Test, minimum graduate GPA of 3.5; for Ed S, GRE General Test. Additional exam requirements/recommendations for international students: Required—TOEFL. *Faculty research:* Discourse analysis, sociolinguistics, critical literacy, cultural studies.

Indiana University of Pennsylvania, School of Graduate Studies and Research, College of Education and Communications, Department of Professional Studies in Education, Program in Literacy, Indiana, PA 15705. Offers literacy (M Ed); reading (Certificate). *Accreditation:* NCATE. *Program availability:* Part-time. *Faculty:* 13 full-time (11 women), 3 part-time/adjunct (2 women). *Students:* 12 full-time (all women), 13 part-time (9 women). Average age 25. 21 applicants, 95% accepted, 13 enrolled. In 2017, 11 master's awarded. *Degree requirements:* For master's, thesis optional. *Entrance requirements:* For master's, 2 letters of recommendation. Additional exam requirements/recommendations for international students: Required—TOEFL (minimum score 540 paper-based). *Application deadline:* For fall admission, 7/1 for domestic students; for spring admission, 11/1 for domestic students. Applications are processed on a rolling basis. Application fee: $50. Electronic applications accepted. *Expenses:* Tuition, state resident: full-time $12,000; part-time $500 per credit. Tuition, nonresident: full-time

$18,000; part-time $750 per credit. *Required fees:* $4073; $165.55 per credit. $64 per term. *Financial support:* In 2017–18, 12 research assistantships with tuition reimbursements (averaging $5,679 per year) were awarded; fellowships, career-related internships or fieldwork, Federal Work-Study, scholarships/grants, and unspecified assistantships also available. Support available to part-time students. Financial award application deadline: 4/15; financial award applicants required to submit FAFSA. *Unit head:* Dr. Deanna Laverick, Graduate Co-Coordinator, 724-357-5597, E-mail: d.m.laverick@iup.edu. *Application contact:* Dr. Kelli Paquette, Graduate Co-Coordinator, 724-357-2400, E-mail: kpaquette@iup.edu.
Website: http://www.iup.edu/pse/grad/literacy-med-reading-specialist-certification/default.aspx

Indiana University–Purdue University Indianapolis, School of Education, Indianapolis, IN 46202-5155. Offers curriculum and instruction (MS); early childhood (MS); educational leadership (MS, Certificate); English as a second language (Certificate); kindergarten (Certificate); language education (MS); reading (Certificate); school counseling (MS); special education (MS, Certificate). *Program availability:* Part-time, evening/weekend. Terminal master's awarded for partial completion of doctoral program. *Degree requirements:* For master's, thesis optional. *Entrance requirements:* For master's, GRE General Test, minimum GPA of 2.5; for Certificate, official transcripts. Additional exam requirements/recommendations for international students: Required—TOEFL (minimum score 60 iBT), IELTS (minimum score 5.5). Electronic applications accepted. *Expenses:* Contact institution. *Faculty research:* Educational policies and school leaders' responses to these; issues of intersectionality in the experiences of African American lesbian, gay, and bisexual students attending historically black colleges and universities and those who belong to black Greek-letter organizations; students' experiential knowledge and their evolving disciplinary-specific literacy and understanding; innovative program development; urban ESL teacher preparation; target-based instructional coaching.

Jackson State University, Graduate School, College of Education and Human Development, Department of Elementary and Early Childhood Education, Jackson, MS 39217. Offers early childhood education (MS Ed, Ed D); elementary education (MS Ed, Ed S); reading education (MS Ed). *Accreditation:* NCATE. *Program availability:* Part-time, evening/weekend, 100% online, blended/hybrid learning. Terminal master's awarded for partial completion of doctoral program. *Degree requirements:* For master's, comprehensive exam, thesis or alternative; for doctorate, comprehensive exam, thesis/dissertation. *Entrance requirements:* For master's, GRE General Test; for doctorate, MAT, teaching experience. Additional exam requirements/recommendations for international students: Required—TOEFL (minimum score 520 paper-based; 67 iBT). Electronic applications accepted. *Expenses:* Contact institution.

Jacksonville State University, College of Graduate Studies and Continuing Education, College of Education and Professional Studies, Program in Reading Specialist, Jacksonville, AL 36265-1602. Offers MS Ed. *Program availability:* Part-time, evening/weekend. *Degree requirements:* For master's, comprehensive exam, thesis (for some programs). *Entrance requirements:* Additional exam requirements/recommendations for international students: Required—TOEFL (minimum score 500 paper-based; 61 iBT). Electronic applications accepted.

James Madison University, The Graduate School, College of Education, Program in Education, Harrisonburg, VA 22807. Offers early childhood education (preK-3) (MAT); educational leadership (M Ed); educational technology (M Ed); elementary education (MAT); equity and cultural diversity (M Ed); inclusive early childhood education (MAT); K-8 mathematics specialist (M Ed); middle education (MAT); reading education (M Ed); secondary education (MAT); Spanish language and culture for educators (M Ed); TESOL (MAT). *Accreditation:* NCATE. *Program availability:* Part-time, evening/weekend. *Students:* 260 full-time (233 women), 158 part-time (100 women); includes 48 minority (10 Black or African American, non-Hispanic/Latino; 4 Asian, non-Hispanic/Latino; 26 Hispanic/Latino; 1 Native Hawaiian or other Pacific Islander, non-Hispanic/Latino; 7 Two or more races, non-Hispanic/Latino), 2 international. Average age 30. In 2017, 262 master's awarded. Application fee: $55. Electronic applications accepted. *Expenses:* Tuition, state resident: full-time $10,512; part-time $438 per credit hour. Tuition, nonresident: full-time $28,358; part-time $1162 per credit hour. *Required fees:* $1128. *Financial support:* In 2017–18, 23 students received support, including 1 teaching assistantship; career-related internships or fieldwork, Federal Work-Study, and 22 assistantships (averaging $7911) also available. Financial award application deadline: 3/1; financial award applicants required to submit FAFSA. *Unit head:* Dr. Phillip M. Wishon, Dean, 540-568-6572, E-mail: wishonpm@jmu.edu. *Application contact:* Lynette D. Michael, Director of Graduate Admissions, 540-568-6131 Ext. 6395, Fax: 540-568-7860, E-mail: michaeld@jmu.edu.
Website: http://www.jmu.edu/coe/index.shtml

James Madison University, The Graduate School, College of Education, Program in Reading Education, Harrisonburg, VA 22807. Offers M Ed. *Accreditation:* NCATE. *Program availability:* Part-time. *Students:* Average age 27. *Entrance requirements:* For master's, GRE General Test. Additional exam requirements/recommendations for international students: Required—TOEFL. *Application deadline:* For fall admission, 5/1 priority date for domestic students; for spring admission, 9/1 priority date for domestic students. Applications are processed on a rolling basis. Application fee: $55. Electronic applications accepted. *Expenses:* Tuition, state resident: full-time $10,512; part-time $438 per credit hour. Tuition, nonresident: full-time $28,358; part-time $1162 per credit hour. *Required fees:* $1128. *Financial support:* Federal Work-Study and unspecified assistantships available. Financial award application deadline: 3/1; financial award applicants required to submit FAFSA. *Unit head:* Dr. Martha Ross, Academic Unit Head, 540-568-6255. *Application contact:* Lynette M. Bible, Director of Graduate Admissions, 540-568-6395, Fax: 540-568-7860, E-mail: biblelm@jmu.edu.

Johns Hopkins University, School of Education, Master's Programs in Education, Baltimore, MD 21218. Offers counseling (MS), including clinical mental health counseling, school counseling; education (MS), including educational studies, gifted education, reading, school administration and supervision, technology for educators; elementary education (MAT); health professions (M Ed); intelligence analysis (MS); organizational leadership (MS); secondary education (MAT), including biology, chemistry, earth/space science, English, physics, social studies; special education (MS), including early childhood special education, general special education studies, mild to moderate disabilities, severe disabilities. *Program availability:* Part-time, evening/weekend, 100% online, blended/hybrid learning. *Degree requirements:* For master's, comprehensive exam (for some programs), portfolio, capstone project and/or internship; PRAXIS II (subject area assessments) for initial teacher preparation programs that lead to licensure. *Entrance requirements:* For master's, GRE (for full-time programs only); PRAXIS I/core or state-approved alternative (for initial teacher preparation programs that lead to licensure), minimum of bachelor's degree from regionally- or nationally-accredited institution; minimum GPA of 3.0 in all previous programs of study; official transcripts from all post-secondary institutions attended; essay; curriculum vitae/resume; letters of recommendation (3 for full-time programs, 2 for part-time programs); dispositions survey. Additional exam requirements/recommendations for international students: Required—TOEFL (minimum score 600 paper-based; 100 iBT), IELTS (minimum score 7). Electronic applications accepted. *Expenses:* Contact institution.

Judson University, Doctor of Education in Literacy Program, Elgin, IL 60123-1498. Offers Ed D. *Faculty:* 5 full-time (3 women), 10 part-time/adjunct (all women). *Students:* 15 full-time (12 women), 21 part-time (18 women); includes 2 minority (1 Black or African American, non-Hispanic/Latino; 1 Hispanic/Latino). Average age 40. 9 applicants, 100% accepted, 9 enrolled. In 2017, 9 doctorates awarded. *Degree requirements:* For doctorate, thesis/dissertation, 4 authentic benchmark assessments. *Entrance requirements:* For doctorate, resume/curriculum vitae; official transcript(s) of all master's work; three letters of recommendation; minimum GPA of 3.35; essay; interview; live writing sample. *Application deadline:* For fall admission, 11/15 for domestic and international students. Application fee: $200. *Expenses:* Contact institution. *Financial support:* Teaching assistantships available. Financial award application deadline: 11/15; financial award applicants required to submit FAFSA. *Faculty research:* Literacy, social justice, linguistics, communication theory, higher education. *Unit head:* Dr. Steven L. Layne, Director, 847-628-1093, E-mail: slayne@judsonu.edu. *Application contact:* Maria Aguirre, Student Academic Advisor, 847-628-1160, E-mail: maguirre@judsonu.edu. Website: http://www.judsonu.edu/literacydoctor/

Judson University, Master of Education in Literacy Program, Elgin, IL 60123-1498. Offers M Ed. *Faculty:* 4 full-time (2 women), 10 part-time/adjunct (9 women). *Students:* 14 part-time (all women). Average age 42. 12 applicants, 100% accepted, 12 enrolled. In 2017, 16 master's awarded. *Degree requirements:* For master's, completion and submission of a feature article to a peer-reviewed journal in the field. *Entrance requirements:* For master's, copy of official teaching certificate; official transcript(s) of all college coursework; bachelor's degree with minimum GPA of 3.0; 2 letters of reference; essay; interview; live writing sample. *Application deadline:* For fall admission, 4/15 for domestic and international students. Applications are processed on a rolling basis. Application fee: $55. *Expenses:* Contact institution. *Financial support:* Tuition discounts available. Financial award application deadline: 4/15; financial award applicants required to submit FAFSA. *Faculty research:* Affective domain in reading, children's and adolescent literature, cross-curricular writing, critical thinking, administration in higher education, linguistics. *Unit head:* Dr. Steven L. Layne, Director, 847-628-1093, E-mail: slayne@judsonu.edu. *Application contact:* Maria Aguirre, Student Academic Advisor, 847-628-1160, E-mail: maguirre@judsonu.edu.

Kansas State University, Graduate School, College of Education, Department of Curriculum and Instruction, Manhattan, KS 66506. Offers curriculum and instruction (Ed D, PhD); digital teaching and learning (MS); educational computing, design and online learning (MS); elementary/middle level curriculum and instruction (MS); online learning (Certificate); reading specialist endorsement (MS); reading/language arts (MS); teacher leader/school improvement (MS); teaching and learning (Certificate). *Accreditation:* NCATE. *Program availability:* Part-time, online learning. *Degree requirements:* For master's, comprehensive exam, portfolio, project, report or thesis; for doctorate, comprehensive exam, thesis/dissertation, preliminary exam; for Certificate, comprehensive exam, portfolio. *Entrance requirements:* For master's, minimum GPA of 3.0, 3 letters of recommendation; for doctorate, GRE, minimum GPA of 3.0, 3 letters of recommendation, evidence of scholarly writing; for Certificate, minimum GPA of 3.0, letters of recommendation. Additional exam requirements/recommendations for international students: Required—TOEFL (minimum score 550 paper-based; 80 iBT) or IELTS. Electronic applications accepted. *Faculty research:* Literacy and technology, critical race theory and diversity, achievement gaps, school improvement, teacher education.

Kennesaw State University, Leland and Clarice C. Bagwell College of Education, Program in Graduate Education, Kennesaw, GA 30144. Offers educational leadership (M Ed); educational leadership technology (M Ed); elementary and early childhood education (M Ed); instructional technology (M Ed); middle grades education (M Ed); reading (M Ed); secondary education (M Ed); special education (M Ed); teaching English to speakers of other languages (M Ed). *Accreditation:* NCATE. *Program availability:* Part-time. *Degree requirements:* For master's, thesis or alternative. *Entrance requirements:* For master's, GRE General Test, T-4 state certification, minimum GPA of 2.75. Additional exam requirements/recommendations for international students: Required—TOEFL (minimum score 550 paper-based; 80 iBT), IELTS (minimum score 6.5). Electronic applications accepted.

Kent State University, College of Education, Health and Human Services, School of Teaching, Learning and Curriculum Studies, Program in Reading Specialization, Kent, OH 44242-0001. Offers M Ed, MA. *Accreditation:* NCATE. *Program availability:* Part-time, evening/weekend. *Degree requirements:* For master's, thesis (for some programs). *Entrance requirements:* For master's, 2 letters of reference, goals statement. Additional exam requirements/recommendations for international students: Required—TOEFL (minimum score 550 paper-based; 80 iBT). Electronic applications accepted. *Expenses:* Tuition, state resident: full-time $11,310; part-time $515 per credit hour. Tuition, nonresident: full-time $20,396; part-time $928 per credit hour. *International tuition:* $18,544 full-time. *Faculty research:* Adolescent literacy, adult and family literacy, school change in literacy education, struggling readers.

Kutztown University of Pennsylvania, College of Education, Program in Reading, Kutztown, PA 19530-0730. Offers M Ed. *Accreditation:* NCATE. *Program availability:* Part-time, evening/weekend. *Students:* 2 full-time (both women), 53 part-time (49 women); includes 2 minority (1 Asian, non-Hispanic/Latino; 1 Two or more races, non-Hispanic/Latino). Average age 36. 29 applicants, 100% accepted, 20 enrolled. In 2017, 21 master's awarded. *Degree requirements:* For master's, comprehensive project. *Entrance requirements:* For master's, GRE General Test, PRAXIS II, NTE, or 10 years' experience in elementary or secondary school with appropriate certification, valid PA instructional I or II teaching certificate, 3 graduate evaluation forms from professionals in education. Additional exam requirements/recommendations for international students: Required—TOEFL (minimum score 550 paper-based, 79 iBT), IELTS (minimum score 6.5), or PTE (minimum score 53). *Application deadline:* For fall admission, 8/1 for domestic and international students; for spring admission, 12/1 for domestic and international students. Application fee: $35. Electronic applications accepted. *Expenses:* Tuition, state resident: part-time $500 per credit. Tuition, nonresident: part-time $750 per credit. *Required fees:* $115 per credit. One-time fee: $50 part-time. Tuition and fees vary according to degree level. *Financial support:* Career-related internships or fieldwork, Federal Work-Study, and unspecified assistantships available. Financial award application deadline: 3/1; financial award applicants required to submit FAFSA. *Unit head:* Dr. Sandy Chambers, Associate Professor, 610-683-4270, E-mail: chambers@kutztown.edu. Website: https://www.kutztown.edu/academics/graduate-programs/reading.htm

La Salle University, School of Arts and Sciences, Program in Education, Philadelphia, PA 19141-1199. Offers autism spectrum disorders (MA, Certificate); bilingual/bicultural studies (MA); classroom management (MA); dual early childhood and special education (MA); dual middle-level science and math and special education (MA); education (MA); English (MA); English as a second language (Certificate); history (MA); instructional coach (Certificate); instructional leadership (MA); reading specialist (MA, Certificate); secondary education (MA); special education (MA, Certificate). *Program availability:* Part-time, evening/weekend. *Faculty:* 5 full-time (4 women), 8 part-time/adjunct (5 women). *Students:* 2 full-time (1 woman), 110 part-time (81 women); includes 23 minority (11 Black or African American, non-Hispanic/Latino; 1 Asian, non-Hispanic/

Latino; 7 Hispanic/Latino; 4 Two or more races, non-Hispanic/Latino). Average age 33. 137 applicants, 70% accepted, 63 enrolled. In 2017, 148 master's awarded. *Degree requirements:* For master's, comprehensive exam. *Entrance requirements:* For master's, MAT or GRE, 2 letters of recommendation; for Certificate, GMAT or GRE, 2 letters of recommendation. Additional exam requirements/recommendations for international students: Required—TOEFL. *Application deadline:* For fall admission, 8/15 priority date for domestic students, 7/15 for international students; for spring admission, 12/15 priority date for domestic students, 11/15 for international students; for summer admission, 4/15 priority date for domestic students, 3/15 for international students. Applications are processed on a rolling basis. Application fee: $35. Electronic applications accepted. Application fee is waived when completed online. *Expenses:* Contact institution. *Financial support:* In 2017–18, 19 students received support. Scholarships/grants available. Support available to part-time students. Financial award application deadline: 8/31; financial award applicants required to submit FAFSA. *Unit head:* Dr. Greer Richardson, Director, 215-951-1806, Fax: 215-951-1843, E-mail: graded@lasalle.edu. *Application contact:* Elizabeth Heenan, Director, Graduate and Adult Enrollment, 215-951-1100, Fax: 215-951-1462, E-mail: heenan@lasalle.edu. Website: http://www.lasalle.edu/grad-education-programs/

Lehman College of the City University of New York, School of Education, Department of Specialized Services in Education, Program in Reading Teacher, Bronx, NY 10468-1589. Offers MS Ed. *Accreditation:* NCATE. *Program availability:* Evening/weekend. *Entrance requirements:* For master's, interview, minimum GPA of 2.7. *Faculty research:* Emergent literacy, language-based classrooms, primary and secondary social contexts of language and literacy, innovative in-service education models, adult literacy.

Le Moyne College, Department of Education, Syracuse, NY 13214. Offers adolescent education (MS Ed, MST); adolescent education/special education (MS Ed, MST); adolescent English (MST), including grades 7-12; adolescent English/special education (MST), including grades 7-12; adolescent foreign language (MST), including grades 7-12; adolescent history (MST), including grades 7-12; childhood education (MS Ed); childhood education/special education (MS Ed); elementary education (MS Ed); general education (MS Ed); inclusive childhood education (MST); literacy education (MS Ed), including birth to grade 6, grades 5-12; school building leader (MS Ed); school building leadership (CAS); school district business leader (MS Ed, CAS); school district leader (MS Ed); school district leadership (CAS); secondary education (MS Ed); special education (MS Ed); teaching English to speakers of other languages (MS Ed); urban studies (MS Ed). *Accreditation:* TEAC. *Program availability:* Part-time, evening/weekend. *Faculty:* 7 full-time (5 women), 20 part-time/adjunct (12 women). *Students:* 30 full-time (19 women), 126 part-time (93 women); includes 15 minority (7 Black or African American, non-Hispanic/Latino; 1 American Indian or Alaska Native, non-Hispanic/Latino; 1 Asian, non-Hispanic/Latino; 6 Hispanic/Latino), 4 international. Average age 29. 139 applicants, 65% accepted, 76 enrolled. In 2017, 82 master's, 43 CASs awarded. *Degree requirements:* For master's, thesis. *Entrance requirements:* For master's, bachelor's degree with minimum undergraduate GPA of 3.0, 2 letters of recommendation, transcripts. Additional exam requirements/recommendations for international students: Required—TOEFL (minimum score 550 paper-based; 79 iBT); Recommended—IELTS (minimum score 6.5). *Application deadline:* For fall admission, 4/1 priority date for domestic and international students; for spring admission, 10/1 priority date for domestic and international students; for summer admission, 3/1 priority date for domestic and international students. Applications are processed on a rolling basis. Application fee: $50. Electronic applications accepted. *Expenses:* $700 per credit hour. *Financial support:* In 2017–18, 30 students received support. Career-related internships or fieldwork, scholarships/grants, and health care benefits available. Support available to part-time students. Financial award applicants required to submit FAFSA. *Faculty research:* Minority teachers, special education, multiculturalism, literacy, technology, media literacy learning, autism, school district organization, service-learning, higher level problem solving, teacher leadership. *Unit head:* Dr. Stephen C. Fleury, Chair, Department of Education, 315-445-4376, Fax: 315-445-4744, E-mail: fleurysc@lemoyne.edu. *Application contact:* Kristen P. Richards, Senior Director of Enrollment Management, 315-445-5444, Fax: 315-445-6092, E-mail: trapaskp@lemoyne.edu. Website: http://www.lemoyne.edu/education

Lesley University, Graduate School of Education, Cambridge, MA 02138-2790. Offers arts, community, and education (M Ed); autism studies (Certificate); curriculum and instruction (M Ed, CAGS); early childhood education (M Ed); ecological teaching and learning (MS); educational studies (PhD), including adult learning, educational leadership, individually designed; elementary education (M Ed); emergent technologies for educators (Certificate); ESLArts: language learning through the arts (M Ed); high school education (M Ed); individually designed (M Ed); integrated teaching through the arts (M Ed); literacy for K-8 classroom teachers (M Ed); mathematics education (M Ed); middle school education (M Ed); moderate disabilities (M Ed); online learning (Certificate); reading (CAGS); science in education (M Ed); severe disabilities (M Ed); special needs (CAGS); specialist teacher of reading (M Ed); teacher of visual art (M Ed); technology in education (M Ed, CAGS). *Accreditation:* TEAC. *Program availability:* Part-time, evening/weekend, online learning. *Degree requirements:* For master's, practicum; for doctorate, thesis/dissertation. *Entrance requirements:* For master's, Massachusetts Tests for Educator Licensure (MTEL), transcripts, statement of purpose, recommendations; interview (for special education); for doctorate, GRE General Test, transcripts, statement of purpose, recommendations, interview, master's degree; for other advanced degree, interview, master's degree. Additional exam requirements/recommendations for international students: Required—TOEFL (minimum score 550 paper-based; 80 iBT). Electronic applications accepted. *Faculty research:* Assessment in literacy, mathematics and science; autism spectrum disorders; instructional technology and online learning; multicultural education and English language learners.

Lewis University, College of Education, Program in Curriculum and Instruction: Literacy and English Language Learning, Romeoville, IL 60446. Offers M Ed. *Program availability:* Part-time. *Degree requirements:* For master's, comprehensive exam. *Entrance requirements:* For master's, Test of Academic Proficiency/Basic Skills Test/ACT/SAT, bachelor's degree, minimum undergraduate GPA of 2.75, state licensure with teaching endorsement. Additional exam requirements/recommendations for international students: Required—TOEFL (minimum score 550 paper-based; 79 iBT), IELTS (minimum score 6). *Application deadline:* For fall admission, 5/1 priority date for international students; for spring admission, 11/1 for international students. Application fee: $40. Electronic applications accepted. Tuition and fees vary according to program. *Financial support:* Federal Work-Study and unspecified assistantships available. Financial award application deadline: 5/1; financial award applicants required to submit FAFSA. *Unit head:* Dr. Pamela Jessee, Dean, 815-836-5316, E-mail: jesseepa@lewisu.edu. *Application contact:* Kathy Lisak, Graduate Admission Counselor, 815-836-5610, E-mail: grad@lewisu.edu. Website: http://www.lewisu.edu/academics/literacy-ELL/index.htm

Lewis University, College of Education, Programs in Reading and Literacy, Romeoville, IL 60446. Offers M Ed, MA. *Program availability:* Part-time. *Students:* 4 part-time (all women). Average age 30. *Degree requirements:* For master's, comprehensive exam, departmental qualifying exam. *Entrance requirements:* For master's, writing exam, Test of Academic Proficiency/Basic Skills Test/ACT/SAT, bachelor's degree, minimum GPA of 2.75, 2 letters of recommendation, professional educator license. Additional exam requirements/recommendations for international students: Required—TOEFL (minimum score 550 paper-based; 79 iBT), IELTS (minimum score 6). *Application deadline:* For fall admission, 5/1 priority date for international students; for spring admission, 11/15 priority date for international students. Applications are processed on a rolling basis. Application fee: $40. Electronic applications accepted. Tuition and fees vary according to program. *Financial support:* Federal Work-Study, scholarships/grants, and unspecified assistantships available. Financial award application deadline: 5/1; financial award applicants required to submit FAFSA. *Unit head:* Dr. Deb Augsburger, Program Director, 815-838-0500 Ext. 5883, E-mail: augsbude@lewisu.edu. *Application contact:* Kathy Lisak, Graduate Admission Counselor, 815-836-5610, E-mail: grad@lewisu.edu.

Liberty University, School of Education, Lynchburg, VA 24515. Offers curriculum and instruction (Ed D, Ed S), including elementary education, middle grades education, secondary education, special education; educational leadership (Ed D); gifted education (Certificate); math specialist (M Ed); middle grades (MAT, Certificate); reading specialist (M Ed); school leadership (Certificate); secondary education (MAT); sport management (MS), including coaching and athletic administration, outdoor adventure sport, sport administration, tourism. *Accreditation:* NCATE. *Program availability:* Part-time, online learning. *Students:* 1,966 full-time (1,428 women), 3,484 part-time (2,528 women); includes 1,323 minority (1,026 Black or African American, non-Hispanic/Latino; 29 American Indian or Alaska Native, non-Hispanic/Latino; 49 Asian, non-Hispanic/Latino; 100 Hispanic/Latino; 9 Native Hawaiian or other Pacific Islander, non-Hispanic/Latino; 110 Two or more races, non-Hispanic/Latino), 58 international. Average age 37. 3,748 applicants, 58% accepted, 1167 enrolled. In 2017, 656 master's, 110 doctorates, 316 other advanced degrees awarded. *Degree requirements:* For doctorate, comprehensive exam, thesis/dissertation. *Entrance requirements:* For master's, GRE General Test or MAT (if taken in or before 1999), 2 letters of recommendation, minimum undergraduate GPA of 3.0, curriculum vitae; for doctorate and other advanced degree, GRE General Test or MAT (if taken before 1999), minimum master's GPA of 3.0, 3 years of teaching experience. Additional exam requirements/recommendations for international students: Required—TOEFL (minimum score 600 paper-based; 100 iBT). *Application deadline:* For fall admission, 6/1 for domestic students; for spring admission, 11/1 for domestic students. Applications are processed on a rolling basis. Application fee: $50. Electronic applications accepted. *Expenses:* Contact institution. *Financial support:* Federal Work-Study and tuition waivers (partial) available. *Faculty research:* Self-determination, character education, bibliotherapy, learning styles, distance education. *Unit head:* Dr. Heather Schoffstall, Dean, 434-582-2445, Fax: 434-582-2468, E-mail: awgunter@liberty.edu. *Application contact:* Jay Bridge, Director of Graduate Admissions, 800-424-9595, Fax: 800-628-7977, E-mail: gradadmissions@liberty.edu.
Website: http://www.liberty.edu/academics/education/graduate/

Lipscomb University, College of Education, Nashville, TN 37204-3951. Offers applied behavior analysis (MS, Certificate); coaching for learning (M Ed, Certificate, Ed S); educational leadership (M Ed, Ed S); English language learning (M Ed, Ed S); instructional coaching (M Ed, Certificate, Ed S); instructional practice (M Ed); learning organizations and strategic change (Ed D); literacy coaching (Certificate, Ed S); reading specialty (M Ed, Ed S); school counseling (M Ed, Ed S); special education (M Ed); teaching, learning, and leading (M Ed); technology integration (M Ed, Ed S); technology integration specialist (Certificate). *Accreditation:* NCATE. *Program availability:* Part-time, evening/weekend, 100% online. *Faculty:* 21 full-time (14 women), 42 part-time/adjunct (29 women). *Students:* 565 full-time (452 women), 59 part-time (45 women); includes 154 minority (102 Black or African American, non-Hispanic/Latino; 2 American Indian or Alaska Native, non-Hispanic/Latino; 8 Asian, non-Hispanic/Latino; 26 Hispanic/Latino; 16 Two or more races, non-Hispanic/Latino). Average age 32. 395 applicants, 54% accepted, 196 enrolled. In 2017, 162 master's, 30 doctorates, 54 other advanced degrees awarded. *Degree requirements:* For master's, comprehensive exam, portfolio, research project and presentation; for doctorate, practical capstone project in experiential setting. *Entrance requirements:* For master's, MAT (minimum score 31) or GRE General Test (minimum score 294), 2 reference letters, goals statement, writing sample, interview; for doctorate, MAT or GRE General Test, 3 reference letters, artifact of demonstrated academic excellence, written personal statements, interview. Additional exam requirements/recommendations for international students: Required—TOEFL (minimum score 570 paper-based; 80 iBT). *Application deadline:* For fall admission, 8/29 priority date for domestic students; for spring admission, 1/15 priority date for domestic students. Applications are processed on a rolling basis. Application fee: $50 ($75 for international students). Electronic applications accepted. *Expenses:* Contact institution. *Financial support:* Scholarships/grants, unspecified assistantships, and partnerships with local school districts available. Financial award applicants required to submit FAFSA. *Faculty research:* Facilitative learning styles, leadership, student assessment, interactive multimedia inclusion, learning organizations and strategic change. *Unit head:* Dr. Deborah Boyd, Director of Graduate Studies, 615-966-6263, E-mail: deborah.boyd@lipscomb.edu. *Application contact:* Amanda Logsdon, Director of Enrollment and Outreach, 615-966-7199, E-mail: amanda.logsdon@lipscomb.edu.
Website: http://www.lipscomb.edu/education/graduate-programs

Long Island University–Brentwood Campus, Graduate Programs, Brentwood, NY 11717. Offers childhood education (MS), including grades 1-6; childhood education/literacy B-6 (MS); childhood education/special education (grades 1-6) (MS); clinical mental health counseling (MS, Advanced Certificate); criminal justice (MS); early childhood education (MS); educational leadership (MS Ed); family nurse practitioner (MS, Advanced Certificate); health administration (MPA); library and information science (MS); literacy (B-6) (MS Ed); school counselor (MS, Advanced Certificate); social work (MSW); special education (MS Ed); students with disabilities generalist (grades 7-12) (Advanced Certificate). *Program availability:* Part-time. *Faculty:* 14 full-time (9 women), 22 part-time/adjunct (11 women). *Students:* 111 full-time (89 women), 47 part-time (34 women); includes 35 minority (8 Black or African American, non-Hispanic/Latino; 1 American Indian or Alaska Native, non-Hispanic/Latino; 3 Asian, non-Hispanic/Latino; 22 Hispanic/Latino; 1 Two or more races, non-Hispanic/Latino), 1 international. Average age 30. 110 applicants, 82% accepted, 63 enrolled. In 2017, 58 master's, 5 other advanced degrees awarded. *Entrance requirements:* For master's and Advanced Certificate, GRE. Additional exam requirements/recommendations for international students: Required—TOEFL or IELTS. *Application deadline:* Applications are processed on a rolling basis. Application fee: $50. Electronic applications accepted. *Expenses:* Tuition: Full-time $21,168; part-time $1201 per credit. *Required fees:* $1840; $920 per term. Tuition and fees vary according to course load. *Financial support:* In 2017–18, 121 students received support. Scholarships/grants available. Support available to part-time students. Financial award application deadline: 2/15; financial award applicants required to submit FAFSA. *Unit head:* Dr. Abby Van Vlerah, Dean and Chief Operating Officer, 631-299-3831, E-mail: abagail.vanvlerah@liu.edu. *Application contact:* Scott Aug, Associate Director of Enrollment Management, 631-287-8506, E-mail: scott.aug@liu.edu.
Website: http://liu.edu/brentwood

Long Island University–Hudson, Graduate School, Purchase, NY 10577. Offers autism (Advanced Certificate); bilingual education (Advanced Certificate); childhood education (MS Ed); crisis management (Advanced Certificate); early childhood education (MS Ed); educational leadership (MS Ed); health administration (MPA); literacy (MS Ed); marriage and family therapy (MS); mental health counseling (MS, Advanced Certificate), including credentialed alcoholism and substance abuse counselor (MS); middle childhood and adolescence education (MS Ed); pharmaceutics (MS), including cosmetic science, industrial pharmacy; public administration (MPA); school counseling (MS Ed, Advanced Certificate); school psychology (MS Ed); special education (MS Ed); TESOL (MS Ed); TESOL (all grades) (Advanced Certificate). *Program availability:* Part-time, evening/weekend. *Faculty:* 8 full-time (6 women), 41 part-time/adjunct (24 women). *Students:* 69 full-time (54 women), 249 part-time (200 women); includes 102 minority (29 Black or African American, non-Hispanic/Latino; 1 American Indian or Alaska Native, non-Hispanic/Latino; 9 Asian, non-Hispanic/Latino; 62 Hispanic/Latino; 1 Native Hawaiian or other Pacific Islander, non-Hispanic/Latino). Average age 33. 153 applicants, 96% accepted, 103 enrolled. In 2017, 138 master's, 36 other advanced degrees awarded. *Entrance requirements:* Additional exam requirements/recommendations for international students: Required—TOEFL. *Application deadline:* Applications are processed on a rolling basis. Application fee: $50. Electronic applications accepted. *Expenses:* Contact institution. *Financial support:* In 2017–18, 32 students received support. Scholarships/grants available. Support available to part-time students. Financial award application deadline: 2/15; financial award applicants required to submit FAFSA. *Unit head:* Dr. Sylvia Blake, Dean and Chief Operating Officer, 914-831-2700, E-mail: westchester@liu.edu. *Application contact:* Dr. Sylvia Blake, Dean and Chief Operating Officer, 914-831-2700, E-mail: westchester@liu.edu.

Long Island University–LIU Post, College of Education, Information and Technology, Brookville, NY 11548-1300. Offers adolescence education (MS); adolescence education 7-12 (MS); archives and records management (AC); art education (MS); childhood education (MS); childhood education/literacy B-6 (MS); childhood education/special education (MS); clinical mental health counseling (MS, AC); early childhood education (MS); early childhood education/childhood education (MS); educational leadership (AC); educational technology (MS); information studies (PhD); interdisciplinary educational studies (Ed D); middle childhood education (MS); music education (MS); public library administration (AC); school counselor (MS); special education (MS Ed); speech-language pathology (MA); students with disabilities, 7-12 generalist (AC); TESOL (MA). *Accreditation:* TEAC. *Program availability:* Part-time, 100% online, blended/hybrid learning. *Faculty:* 40 full-time (26 women), 73 part-time/adjunct (38 women). *Students:* 472 full-time (400 women), 696 part-time (543 women); includes 254 minority (93 Black or African American, non-Hispanic/Latino; 46 Asian, non-Hispanic/Latino; 105 Hispanic/Latino; 10 Two or more races, non-Hispanic/Latino), 33 international. Average age 33. 917 applicants, 82% accepted, 357 enrolled. In 2017, 408 master's, 31 other advanced degrees awarded. Terminal master's awarded for partial completion of doctoral program. *Degree requirements:* For master's, variable foreign language requirement, comprehensive exam (for some programs), thesis optional; for doctorate, comprehensive exam, thesis/dissertation. *Entrance requirements:* For master's and AC, GRE (for some programs). Additional exam requirements/recommendations for international students: Required—TOEFL (minimum score 550 paper-based, 75 iBT), IELTS, or PTE. *Application deadline:* Applications are processed on a rolling basis. Application fee: $50. Electronic applications accepted. *Expenses:* Tuition: Full-time $21,618; part-time $1201 per credit. *Required fees:* $1840; $920 per term. Tuition and fees vary according to course load. *Financial support:* In 2017–18, 376 students received support. Career-related internships or fieldwork, Federal Work-Study, institutionally sponsored loans, scholarships/grants, tuition waivers (partial), and unspecified assistantships available. Support available to part-time students. Financial award application deadline: 2/15; financial award applicants required to submit FAFSA. *Faculty research:* Sleep; use of technology to develop executive function by students with disabilities; early childhood literacy development through play; social justice through education; using a structured protocol to discuss Bad News. *Unit head:* Dr. Albert Inserra, Dean, 516-299-2210, E-mail: albert.inserra@liu.edu. *Application contact:* Rita Langdon, Graduate Admissions, 516-299-2900, Fax: 516-299-2137, E-mail: post-enroll@liu.edu.
Website: http://liu.edu/CWPost/Academics/College-of-Education-Information-and-Technology

Long Island University–Riverhead, Graduate Programs, Riverhead, NY 11901. Offers applied behavior analysis (Advanced Certificate); childhood education (MS), including grades 1-6; cybersecurity policy (Advanced Certificate); homeland security management (MS, Advanced Certificate); literacy education (MS); literacy education B-6 (MS); teaching students with disabilities (MS), including grades 1-6; TESOL (Advanced Certificate). *Accreditation:* TEAC. *Program availability:* Part-time. *Faculty:* 4 full-time (1 woman), 11 part-time/adjunct (5 women). *Students:* 17 full-time (14 women), 58 part-time (36 women); includes 14 minority (4 Black or African American, non-Hispanic/Latino; 1 American Indian or Alaska Native, non-Hispanic/Latino; 1 Asian, non-Hispanic/Latino; 6 Hispanic/Latino; 2 Two or more races, non-Hispanic/Latino). Average age 32. 68 applicants, 79% accepted, 26 enrolled. In 2017, 30 master's, 7 other advanced degrees awarded. *Entrance requirements:* Additional exam requirements/recommendations for international students: Required—TOEFL or IELTS. *Application deadline:* Applications are processed on a rolling basis. Application fee: $50. Electronic applications accepted. *Expenses:* Contact institution. *Financial support:* In 2017–18, 53 students received support. Scholarships/grants available. Support available to part-time students. Financial award application deadline: 2/15; financial award applicants required to submit FAFSA. *Unit head:* Dr. Abagail VanVlerah, Dean and Chief Operating Officer, 631-299-3831, E-mail: abagail.vanvlerah@liu.edu. *Application contact:* Jean Conroy, Associate Dean, 631-287-8301, E-mail: jean.conroy@liu.edu.

Longwood University, College of Graduate and Professional Studies, College of Education and Human Services, Program in Reading, Literacy and Learning, Farmville, VA 23909. Offers M Ed. *Program availability:* Part-time, evening/weekend. *Degree requirements:* For master's, professional portfolio. *Entrance requirements:* For master's, bachelor's degree from regionally-accredited institution, 2 recommendations, minimum 500-word personal essay, official transcripts, minimum GPA of 2.75, valid teaching license. Additional exam requirements/recommendations for international students: Required—TOEFL (minimum score 570 paper-based; 80 iBT), IELTS (minimum score 6.5). Electronic applications accepted. *Expenses:* Contact institution.

Lourdes University, Graduate School, Sylvania, OH 43560-2898. Offers business (MBA); leadership (M Ed); nurse anesthesia (MSN); nurse educator (MSN); nurse leader (MSN); organizational leadership (MOL); reading (M Ed); teaching and curriculum (M Ed); theology (MA). *Program availability:* Evening/weekend. *Entrance requirements:* Additional exam requirements/recommendations for international students: Required—TOEFL.

Loyola Marymount University, School of Education, Program in Literacy Education, Los Angeles, CA 90045-2659. Offers MA. *Unit head:* Dr. Candace Poindexter, Director, Literacy and Educational Studies, 310-338-7314, E-mail: cpoindex@lmu.edu. *Application contact:* Chake H. Kouyoumjian, Associate Dean of Graduate Studies, 310-338-2721, Fax: 310-338-6086, E-mail: graduateinfo@lmu.edu.
Website: http://soe.lmu.edu

Loyola Marymount University, School of Education, Program in Literacy Instruction for Urban Environments, Los Angeles, CA 90045-2659. Offers MA. *Unit head:* Dr. Candace Poindexter, Director, Literacy and Educational Studies, 310-338-7314, E-mail: cpoindex@lmu.edu. *Application contact:* Chake H. Kouyoumjian, Associate Dean of Graduate Studies, 310-338-2721, Fax: 310-338-6086, E-mail: graduateinfo@lmu.edu. Website: http://soe.lmu.edu/academics/literacyinstructionforurbanenvironmentsonline

Loyola Marymount University, School of Education, Program in Literacy/Language Arts, Los Angeles, CA 90045-2659. Offers MA. *Unit head:* Dr. Candace Poindexter, Director, Literacy and Educational Studies, 310-338-7314, E-mail: cpoindex@lmu.edu. *Application contact:* Chake H. Kouyoumjian, Associate Dean of Graduate Studies, 310-338-2721, Fax: 310-338-6086, E-mail: graduateinfo@lmu.edu. Website: http://soe.lmu.edu

Loyola Marymount University, School of Education, Program in Reading Instruction, Los Angeles, CA 90045-2659. Offers MA. *Unit head:* Dr. Candace Poindexter, Director, Literacy and Educational Studies, 310-338-7314, E-mail: cpoindex@lmu.edu. *Application contact:* Chake H. Kouyoumjian, Associate Dean of Graduate Studies, 310-338-2721, Fax: 310-338-6086, E-mail: graduateinfo@lmu.edu. Website: http://soe.lmu.edu/academics/readinginstruction

Loyola University Maryland, Graduate Programs, School of Education, Program in Literacy/Reading, Baltimore, MD 21210-2699. Offers literacy teacher (M Ed); reading specialist (M Ed). *Accreditation:* NCATE. *Program availability:* Part-time. *Faculty:* 36 full-time (27 women), 23 part-time/adjunct (15 women). *Students:* 1 (woman) full-time, 114 part-time (109 women); includes 48 minority (39 Black or African American, non-Hispanic/Latino; 2 Asian, non-Hispanic/Latino; 3 Hispanic/Latino; 1 Native Hawaiian or other Pacific Islander, non-Hispanic/Latino; 3 Two or more races, non-Hispanic/Latino). Average age 33. *Entrance requirements:* For master's, essay, 2 letters of recommendation, resume, transcripts. Additional exam requirements/recommendations for international students: Required—TOEFL (minimum score 550 paper-based), IELTS (minimum score 7). *Application deadline:* For fall admission, 6/15 for domestic students; for winter admission, 11/1 for domestic students; for spring admission, 3/15 for domestic students. Applications are processed on a rolling basis. Application fee: $60. Electronic applications accepted. *Expenses:* Contact institution. *Financial support:* Unspecified assistantships available. Financial award application deadline: 4/15; financial award applicants required to submit FAFSA. *Unit head:* Wendy Smith, Co-Director, 410-617-2194, E-mail: wmsmith@loyola.edu. *Application contact:* Office of Graduate Admission, 410-617-5020, E-mail: graduate@loyola.edu. Website: http://www.loyola.edu/soe/academics/graduate/literacy-reading.aspx

Madonna University, Programs in Education, Livonia, MI 48150-1173. Offers Catholic school leadership (MSA); educational leadership (MSA); learning disabilities (MAT); literacy education (MAT); teaching and learning (MAT). *Accreditation:* NCATE. *Program availability:* Part-time, evening/weekend. *Degree requirements:* For master's, thesis or alternative. Electronic applications accepted.

Manhattanville College, School of Education, Program in Literacy Education, Purchase, NY 10577-2132. Offers literacy (birth-grade 6) and special education childhood (grades 1-6) (MPS); literacy 5-12 (MPS); literacy specialist (birth-grade 6) (MPS); literacy specialist (grades 5-12) (MPS); science of reading: multisensory instruction (Advanced Certificate). *Program availability:* Part-time, evening/weekend. *Faculty:* 4 full-time (all women), 8 part-time/adjunct (5 women). *Students:* 1 (woman) full-time, 21 part-time (20 women). Average age 31. 12 applicants, 92% accepted, 8 enrolled. In 2017, 7 master's, 3 Advanced Certificates awarded. *Degree requirements:* For master's, comprehensive exam (for some programs), thesis (for some programs), student teaching, research seminars, portfolios, internships, writing assessment; for Advanced Certificate, comprehensive exam (for some programs). *Entrance requirements:* For master's, GRE or MAT (for programs leading to certification), minimum GPA of 3.0, 2 letters of recommendation, interview, essay (2-3 page personal statement that describes reasons for choosing teaching or educational leadership as profession and philosophy of education), proof of immunization (for those born after 1957). Additional exam requirements/recommendations for international students: Required—TOEFL (minimum score 600 paper-based; 110 iBT); Recommended—IELTS (minimum score 8). *Application deadline:* Applications are processed on a rolling basis. Application fee: $75. Electronic applications accepted. *Expenses:* $915 per credit. *Financial support:* Teaching assistantships, career-related internships or fieldwork, Federal Work-Study, institutionally sponsored loans, scholarships/grants, and unspecified assistantships available. Financial award application deadline: 3/15; financial award applicants required to submit FAFSA. *Faculty research:* Power of story for literacy development, English learners. *Total annual research expenditures:* $800. *Unit head:* Dr. Shelly Wepner, Dean, 914-323-3153, Fax: 914-323-5493, E-mail: shelly.wepner@mville.edu. *Application contact:* Alissa Wilson, Director, Graduate Admissions, 914-323-3150, Fax: 914-694-1732, E-mail: edschool@mville.edu. Website: http://www.mville.edu/programs/literacy-education

Manhattanville College, School of Education, Program in Middle Childhood/Adolescence Education (Grades 5-12), Purchase, NY 10577-2132. Offers biology (MAT, Advanced Certificate); biology and special education (MPS); chemistry (MAT, Advanced Certificate); chemistry and special education (MPS); earth science (Advanced Certificate); education for sustainability (Advanced Certificate); English (MAT, Advanced Certificate); English and special education (MPS); literacy and special education (MPS); literacy specialist (MPS); math and special education (MPS); mathematics (MAT, Advanced Certificate); physics (MAT, Advanced Certificate); social studies (MAT); social studies and special education (MPS); special education generalist (MPS). *Program availability:* Part-time, evening/weekend. *Faculty:* 2 full-time (both women), 5 part-time/adjunct (1 woman). *Students:* 8 full-time (7 women), 28 part-time (16 women); includes 4 minority (1 Asian, non-Hispanic/Latino; 2 Hispanic/Latino; 1 Two or more races, non-Hispanic/Latino). Average age 31. 7 applicants, 86% accepted, 4 enrolled. In 2017, 13 master's, 1 other advanced degree awarded. *Degree requirements:* For master's, comprehensive exam (for some programs), thesis (for some programs), student teaching, research seminars, portfolios, internships, writing assessment; for Advanced Certificate, comprehensive exam (for some programs). *Entrance requirements:* For master's, GRE or MAT (for programs leading to certification), minimum GPA of 3.0, 2 letters of recommendation, interview, essay (2-3 page personal statement that describes reasons for choosing teaching or educational leadership as profession and philosophy of education), proof of immunization (for those born after 1957). Additional exam requirements/recommendations for international students: Required—TOEFL (minimum score 600 paper-based; 110 iBT); Recommended—IELTS (minimum score 8). *Application deadline:* Applications are processed on a rolling basis. Application fee: $75. Electronic applications accepted. *Expenses:* $915 per credit. *Financial support:* Teaching assistantships, career-related internships or fieldwork, Federal Work-Study, institutionally sponsored loans, scholarships/grants, and unspecified assistantships available. Financial award application deadline: 3/15; financial award applicants required to submit FAFSA. *Faculty research:* Education for sustainability. *Unit head:* Dr. Shelly Wepner, Dean, 914-323-3153, Fax: 914-323-5493, E-mail: shelly.wepner@mville.edu. *Application contact:* Alissa Wilson, Director, Graduate Admissions, 914-323-3150, Fax: 914-694-1732, E-mail: edschool@mville.edu. Website: http://www.mville.edu/programs#/search/19

Manhattanville College, School of Education, Program in Special Education, Purchase, NY 10577-2132. Offers childhood (grades 1-6) (MPS); childhood education (grades 1-6) and special education (MPS); early childhood (birth-grade 2) (MPS); early childhood (birth-grade 2) and special education (MPS); early childhood and childhood (birth-grade 6) (MPS); English (5-9 and 7-12) (MPS); grades 7-12 generalist (MPS); literacy (birth-grade 6) and special education childhood (grades 1-6) (MPS); literacy 5-12 (MPS); mathematics (5-9 and 7-12) (MPS); science (biology or chemistry 5-9 and 7-12) (MPS); social studies (5-9 and 7-12) (MPS); special education: childhood (grades 1-6) (Certificate); special education: early childhood (birth-grade 2) and childhood (grades 1-6) (Certificate); special education: early childhood (birth-grade 2) (Certificate); special education: grades 7-12 generalist (Certificate). *Program availability:* Part-time, evening/weekend. *Faculty:* 5 full-time (3 women), 24 part-time/adjunct (16 women). *Students:* 77 full-time (69 women), 154 part-time (132 women); includes 33 minority (9 Black or African American, non-Hispanic/Latino; 2 Asian, non-Hispanic/Latino; 22 Hispanic/Latino), 1 international. Average age 28. 87 applicants, 77% accepted, 57 enrolled. In 2017, 86 master's, 2 Certificates awarded. *Degree requirements:* For master's, comprehensive exam (for some programs), thesis (for some programs), student teaching, research seminars, portfolios, internships, writing assessment; for Certificate, comprehensive exam (for some programs). *Entrance requirements:* For master's, GRE or MAT (for programs leading to certification), minimum GPA of 3.0, 2 letters of recommendation, interview, essay (2-3 page personal statement that describes reasons for choosing teaching or educational leadership as profession and philosophy of education), proof of immunization (for those born after 1957). Additional exam requirements/recommendations for international students: Required—TOEFL (minimum score 600 paper-based; 110 iBT); Recommended—IELTS (minimum score 8). *Application deadline:* Applications are processed on a rolling basis. Application fee: $75. Electronic applications accepted. *Expenses:* $915 per credit. *Financial support:* Teaching assistantships, career-related internships or fieldwork, Federal Work-Study, institutionally sponsored loans, scholarships/grants, and unspecified assistantships available. Financial award application deadline: 3/15; financial award applicants required to submit FAFSA. *Faculty research:* Students with emotional difficulties, literacy and adolescents, mindfulness, studying the effects of the environment on special populations, the most difficult cases, students who are presented with multiple challenges: learning, behavioral and ACE experiences who see criminal behavior as a way to cope; working on giving them the tools they need to succeed emotionally and cognitively despite the odds stacked against them. *Unit head:* Dr. Shelly Wepner, Dean, 914-323-3153, Fax: 914-323-5493, E-mail: shelly.wepner@mville.edu. *Application contact:* Alissa Wilson, Director, Graduate Admissions, 914-323-3150, Fax: 914-694-1732, E-mail: edschool@mville.edu. Website: http://www.mville.edu/programs/special-education

Marquette University, Graduate School, College of Education, Department of Educational Policy and Leadership, Milwaukee, WI 53201-1881. Offers college student personnel administration (M Ed); curriculum and instruction (MA); education (MA); educational administration (M Ed); educational policy and foundations (MA); elementary education (Certificate); literacy (MA); principal (Certificate); reading specialist (Certificate); reading teacher (Certificate); secondary education (Certificate); superintendent (Certificate). *Program availability:* Part-time, evening/weekend. Terminal master's awarded for partial completion of doctoral program. *Degree requirements:* For master's, comprehensive exam, thesis (for some programs); for doctorate, thesis/dissertation, qualifying exam. *Entrance requirements:* For master's, GRE General Test or MAT, official transcripts from all current and previous colleges/universities except Marquette, three letters of recommendation, statement of purpose; for doctorate, GRE General Test, MAT, sample of written work, official transcripts from all current and previous colleges/universities except Marquette, three letters of recommendation, statement of purpose, resume/curriculum vitae; for Certificate, GRE General Test or MAT, master's degree. Additional exam requirements/recommendations for international students: Required—TOEFL (minimum score 530 paper-based). *Expenses:* Contact institution. *Faculty research:* Leadership; social justice in education; development of lifelong learners; race, class, and schooling in historical perspective; urban teacher education.

Marshall University, Academic Affairs Division, College of Education and Professional Development, Program in Literacy Education, Huntington, WV 25755. Offers MA. *Accreditation:* NCATE. *Program availability:* Part-time, evening/weekend. *Students:* 6 full-time (5 women), 59 part-time (58 women). Average age 34. In 2017, 22 master's awarded. *Degree requirements:* For master's, thesis optional, comprehensive or oral assessment, final project. *Entrance requirements:* For master's, GRE General Test or MAT. Application fee: $40. *Financial support:* Federal Work-Study, tuition waivers (full and partial), and unspecified assistantships available. Support available to part-time students. Financial award applicants required to submit FAFSA. *Unit head:* Dr. Barbara O'Byrne, Program Director, 304-746-1986, E-mail: bobyrne@marshall.edu. *Application contact:* Information Contact, 304-746-1900, Fax: 304-746-1902, E-mail: services@marshall.edu.

Marygrove College, Graduate Studies, Detroit, MI 48221-2599. Offers autism spectrum disorders (M Ed, Certificate); curriculum instruction and assessment (MAT); educational leadership (MA); educational technology (M Ed); effective teaching in the 21st century-classroom focus (MAT); effective teaching in the 21st century-technology focus (MAT); human resource management (MA, Certificate); mathematics 6-8 (MAT); mathematics K-5 (MAT); reading and literacy K-6 (MAT); reading specialist (M Ed); school administrator (Certificate); social justice (MA); special education (MAT); special education - learning disabilities (M Ed); teaching - pre-elementary education (M Ed); teaching - pre-secondary education (M Ed). *Program availability:* Part-time, evening/weekend, 100% online, blended/hybrid learning. *Students:* 163 full-time (123 women), 264 part-time (186 women). Average age 34. *Entrance requirements:* For master's, all official bachelor's transcripts. Additional exam requirements/recommendations for international students: Required—TOEFL (minimum score 550 paper-based; 80 iBT). *Application deadline:* Applications are processed on a rolling basis. Electronic applications accepted. *Expenses: Tuition:* Part-time $590 per credit hour. *Required fees:* $120 per semester. One-time fee: $25 part-time. *Financial support:* Applicants required to submit FAFSA. *Unit head:* Marygrove College Admissions, 313-927-1240, E-mail: info@marygrove.edu. *Application contact:* Marygrove College Admissions, 313-927-1240, E-mail: info@marygrove.edu.

Maryville University of Saint Louis, School of Education, St. Louis, MO 63141-7299. Offers early childhood education (MA Ed); educational leadership (Ed D); elementary education (MA Ed); higher education leadership (Ed D); literacy specialist (MA Ed); middle grades education (MA Ed); secondary teaching and inquiry (MA Ed); teacher as leader (MA Ed, Ed D). *Accreditation:* NCATE. *Program availability:* Part-time, 100% online, blended/hybrid learning. *Faculty:* 20 full-time (14 women), 19 part-time/adjunct (13 women). *Students:* 6 full-time (4 women), 337 part-time (250 women); includes 101 minority (85 Black or African American, non-Hispanic/Latino; 4 Asian, non-Hispanic/Latino; 8 Hispanic/Latino; 4 Two or more races, non-Hispanic/Latino), 3 international. Average age 38. In 2017, 34 master's, 67 doctorates awarded. *Degree requirements:* For master's, thesis, project. *Entrance requirements:* For master's, minimum cumulative GPA of 3.0, 3 professional recommendations, essays, interview with program faculty; for doctorate, minimum GPA of 3.0, 3 professional recommendations, essay, interview, on-site writing sample. Additional exam requirements/recommendations for international students: Required—TOEFL (minimum score 550 paper-based). *Application deadline:* Applications are processed on a rolling basis. Electronic applications accepted. *Expenses:* Contact institution. *Financial support:* Career-related internships or fieldwork, Federal Work-Study, tuition waivers (partial), and professional educator discounts available. Financial award application deadline: 4/1; financial award applicants required to submit FAFSA. *Faculty research:* Collaboration with public schools, pre-service program development, mathematics, diversity, literacy. *Unit head:* Dr. Cathy Bear, Dean, 314-529-9692, Fax: 314-529-9921, E-mail: cbear@maryville.edu. *Application contact:* Stacey Ruffin, Coordinator of Clinical Experiences and Graduate Programs, 314-529-9542, Fax: 314-529-9921, E-mail: teachered@maryville.edu. Website: http://www.maryville.edu/ed/graduate-programs/

Marywood University, Academic Affairs, Reap College of Education and Human Development, Department of Education, Program in Reading Education, Scranton, PA 18509-1598. Offers MS. *Accreditation:* NCATE. *Program availability:* Part-time. Electronic applications accepted.

Massachusetts College of Liberal Arts, Graduate Programs, North Adams, MA 01247-4100. Offers business (MBA); educational administration (M Ed); educational leadership (CAGS); instruction and curriculum (M Ed); instructional technology (M Ed); physical education and health (M Ed); reading (M Ed); special education (M Ed). *Program availability:* Part-time, evening/weekend. *Degree requirements:* For master's, thesis. *Entrance requirements:* For master's, writing sample.

McDaniel College, Graduate and Professional Studies, Program for Reading Specialists: Literacy Leadership, Westminster, MD 21157-4390. Offers MS. *Accreditation:* NCATE. *Program availability:* Part-time-only, evening/weekend. *Faculty:* 2 full-time (both women), 3 part-time/adjunct (all women). *Students:* 26 part-time (all women); includes 1 minority (Black or African American, non-Hispanic/Latino). Average age 28. 3 applicants, 100% accepted, 2 enrolled. In 2017, 5 master's awarded. *Degree requirements:* For master's, comprehensive exam, thesis optional. *Entrance requirements:* For master's, PRAXIS I, 3 references, teaching certificate. Additional exam requirements/recommendations for international students: Required—TOEFL (minimum score 79 iBT), IELTS (minimum score 6). *Application deadline:* For fall admission, 6/1 priority date for domestic students; for spring admission, 11/1 priority date for domestic students; for summer admission, 3/1 priority date for domestic students. Applications are processed on a rolling basis. Application fee: $75. Electronic applications accepted. *Expenses: Tuition:* Full-time $11,760; part-time $490 per credit hour. Tuition and fees vary according to course load and program. *Financial support:* Application deadline: 3/1; applicants required to submit FAFSA. *Unit head:* Fax: 410-857-2515, E-mail: gradadms@mcdaniel.edu. *Application contact:* Penny Pfeiffer, Senior Graduate Enrollment Management Specialist, 410-857-2513, Fax: 410-857-2515, E-mail: ppfeiffer@mcdaniel.edu.

McKendree University, Graduate Programs, Programs in Education, Lebanon, IL 62254-1299. Offers curriculum design and instruction (Ed D, Ed S); educational administration and leadership (MA Ed); educational studies (MA Ed); higher education administrative services (MA Ed); music education (MA Ed); reading (MA Ed); special education (MA Ed); teacher leadership (MA Ed); teaching certification (MA Ed). *Accreditation:* NCATE. *Program availability:* Part-time, evening/weekend, online learning. *Entrance requirements:* For master's, official transcripts from all institutions previously attended, minimum GPA of 3.0, resume, references; for doctorate, GRE (within the past 5 years), master's degree in education and Ed S, or the equivalent, from regionally-accredited institution; official transcripts from all institutions previously attended; curriculum vitae/resume; essay/personal statement; two years of teaching/professional experience; for Ed S, GRE (within the past 5 years), master's degree in education from regionally-accredited institution of higher education; official transcripts from all institutions previously attended; curriculum vitae/resume; essay/personal statement; two years of teaching/professional experience. Additional exam requirements/recommendations for international students: Required—TOEFL. Electronic applications accepted.

McNeese State University, Doré School of Graduate Studies, Burton College of Education, Department of Education Professions, Program in Curriculum and Instruction, Lake Charles, LA 70609. Offers academically gifted education (M Ed); elementary education (M Ed); reading (M Ed); secondary education (M Ed); special education (M Ed). *Program availability:* Evening/weekend. *Entrance requirements:* For master's, GRE, teaching certificate. *Application deadline:* For fall admission, 5/15 priority date for domestic and international students; for spring admission, 10/15 priority date for domestic and international students. Applications are processed on a rolling basis. Application fee: $20 ($30 for international students). *Financial support:* Application deadline: 5/1. *Unit head:* Dr. Brett C. Welch, Director, 337-475-5405, Fax: 337-475-5272, E-mail: bwelch@mcneese.edu. *Application contact:* Dr. Dustin M. Hebert, Director of Doré School of Graduate Studies, 337-475-5396, Fax: 337-475-5397, E-mail: admissions@mcneese.edu.

Medaille College, Program in Education, Buffalo, NY 14214-2695. Offers adolescent education (MS Ed); curriculum and instruction (MS Ed); education preparation (MS Ed); literacy (MS Ed); special education (MS). *Accreditation:* TEAC. *Program availability:* Part-time, evening/weekend. *Degree requirements:* For master's, comprehensive exam (for some programs), thesis or alternative. *Entrance requirements:* For master's, minimum undergraduate GPA of 2.7. Additional exam requirements/recommendations for international students: Required—TOEFL (minimum score 550 paper-based). Electronic applications accepted. *Faculty research:* Curriculum planning, truancy, tracking minority students, curriculum design, mentoring students.

Mercy College, School of Education, Program in Teaching Literacy, Dobbs Ferry, NY 10522-1189. Offers teaching literacy (Advanced Certificate); teaching literacy, birth-6 (MS); teaching literacy, grades 5-12 (MS). *Program availability:* Part-time, evening/weekend. *Students:* 3 full-time (all women), 36 part-time (33 women); includes 10 minority (3 Black or African American, non-Hispanic/Latino; 1 Asian, non-Hispanic/Latino; 6 Hispanic/Latino). Average age 32. 28 applicants, 43% accepted, 8 enrolled. In 2017, 17 master's awarded. *Degree requirements:* For master's, comprehensive exam (for some programs), thesis (for some programs). *Entrance requirements:* For master's, GRE, resume, undergraduate transcript. Additional exam requirements/recommendations for international students: Required—TOEFL (minimum score 600 paper-based; 100 iBT), IELTS (minimum score 8). *Application deadline:* For fall admission, 8/1 for international students. Applications are processed on a rolling basis. Application fee: $40. Electronic applications accepted. *Expenses: Tuition:* Full-time $15,426; part-time $857 per credit hour. *Required fees:* $630; $158 per term. Tuition and fees vary according to course load, degree level and program. *Financial support:* Career-related internships or fieldwork, Federal Work-Study, scholarships/grants, and unspecified assistantships available. Support available to part-time students. Financial award applicants required to submit FAFSA. *Unit head:* Dr. Rose Rudnitski, Dean for the School of Education, 914-674-7447, Fax: 914-674-7352, E-mail: rrudnitski@mercy.edu. *Application contact:* Allison Gurdineer, Senior Director of Admissions, 877-637-2946, Fax: 914-674-7382, E-mail: admissions@mercy.edu. Website: https://www.mercy.edu/education/literacy-and-multilingual-studies

Meredith College, School of Education, Health and Human Sciences, Raleigh, NC 27607-5298. Offers academically and intellectually gifted (M Ed); elementary education (M Ed, MAT); English as a second language (M Ed, MAT); health and physical education (MAT); nutrition, health and human performance (MS, Postbaccalaureate Certificate), including dietetic internship (Postbaccalaureate Certificate), nutrition (MS); psychology (MA), including industrial/organizational psychology; reading (M Ed); special education (MAT); special education (general curriculum) (M Ed). *Accreditation:* NCATE. *Program availability:* Part-time, evening/weekend. *Students:* 25 full-time (24 women), 22 part-time (all women); includes 13 minority (8 Black or African American, non-Hispanic/Latino; 1 American Indian or Alaska Native, non-Hispanic/Latino; 1 Asian, non-Hispanic/Latino; 3 Hispanic/Latino). Average age 31. 57 applicants, 54% accepted, 31 enrolled. In 2017, 14 master's awarded. *Degree requirements:* For master's, thesis optional. *Entrance requirements:* For master's, GRE General Test or MAT, minimum GPA of 2.5, teaching license, recommendations. Additional exam requirements/recommendations for international students: Required—TOEFL. *Application deadline:* For fall admission, 7/1 priority date for domestic students; for spring admission, 11/1 priority date for domestic students. Applications are processed on a rolling basis. Application fee: $50. Electronic applications accepted. *Expenses:* Contact institution. *Financial support:* Career-related internships or fieldwork, institutionally sponsored loans, and tuition waivers (partial) available. Support available to part-time students. Financial award application deadline: 2/15; financial award applicants required to submit FAFSA. *Unit head:* Dr. Monica McKinney, Graduate Program Manager, 919-760-8056, Fax: 919-760-2303, E-mail: mckinneym@meredith.edu. Website: https://www.meredith.edu/school-of-education-health-and-human-sciences

MGH Institute of Health Professions, School of Health and Rehabilitation Sciences, Department of Communication Sciences and Disorders, Boston, MA 02129. Offers reading (Certificate); speech-language pathology (MS). *Accreditation:* ASHA (one or more programs are accredited). *Program availability:* Part-time. *Degree requirements:* For master's, thesis or alternative, research proposal. *Entrance requirements:* For master's, GRE General Test, bachelor's degree from regionally-accredited college or university. Additional exam requirements/recommendations for international students: Required—TOEFL (minimum score 550 paper-based; 80 iBT). Electronic applications accepted. *Faculty research:* Children's language disorders, reading, speech disorders, voice disorders, augmentative communication, autism.

Michigan State University, The Graduate School, College of Education, Program in Literacy Instruction, East Lansing, MI 48824. Offers MA. *Accreditation:* TEAC. *Program availability:* Part-time. *Degree requirements:* For master's, comprehensive exam (for some programs), final exam or portfolio. *Entrance requirements:* Additional exam requirements/recommendations for international students: Required—TOEFL, Michigan State University ELT (minimum score 85), Michigan English Language Assessment Battery (minimum score 83). Electronic applications accepted.

MidAmerica Nazarene University, Professional and Graduate Studies in Education, Olathe, KS 66062-1899. Offers ESOL (M Ed); reading specialist (M Ed); technology enhanced teaching (M Ed). *Accreditation:* NCATE. *Program availability:* Part-time, evening/weekend, online only, 100% online. *Entrance requirements:* For master's, bachelor's degree from an accredited college or university, minimum undergraduate GPA of 3.0, valid teaching license. Additional exam requirements/recommendations for international students: Required—TOEFL (minimum score 81 iBT), IELTS (minimum score 6). Electronic applications accepted. *Expenses:* Contact institution.

Middle Tennessee State University, College of Graduate Studies, College of Education, Department of Elementary and Special Education, Major in Reading, Murfreesboro, TN 37132. Offers M Ed. *Accreditation:* NCATE. *Program availability:* Part-time, evening/weekend, online learning. *Degree requirements:* For master's, comprehensive exam. *Entrance requirements:* For master's, GRE, MAT or PRAXIS. Additional exam requirements/recommendations for international students: Required—TOEFL (minimum score 525 paper-based; 71 iBT) or IELTS (minimum score 6). Electronic applications accepted.

Middle Tennessee State University, College of Graduate Studies, College of Education, PhD in Literacy Studies Program, Murfreesboro, TN 37132. Offers PhD. *Program availability:* Part-time, evening/weekend, online learning. *Degree requirements:* For doctorate, comprehensive exam, thesis/dissertation. *Entrance requirements:* For doctorate, GRE. Additional exam requirements/recommendations for international students: Required—TOEFL (minimum score 525 paper-based; 71 iBT) or IELTS (minimum score 6).

Middle Tennessee State University, College of Graduate Studies, University College, Murfreesboro, TN 37132. Offers advanced studies in teaching and learning (M Ed); human resources leadership (MPS); nursing administration (MSN); nursing education (MSN); strategic leadership (MPS); training and development (MPS). *Program availability:* Part-time, evening/weekend, online learning. *Entrance requirements:* Additional exam requirements/recommendations for international students: Required—TOEFL (minimum score 525 paper-based; 71 iBT) or IELTS (minimum score 6).

Midwestern State University, Billie Doris McAda Graduate School, West College of Education, Program in Reading, Wichita Falls, TX 76308. Offers M Ed. *Program availability:* Part-time, evening/weekend. *Degree requirements:* For master's, comprehensive exam. *Entrance requirements:* For master's, GRE General Test, MAT or GMAT. Additional exam requirements/recommendations for international students: Required—TOEFL (minimum score 550 paper-based). Electronic applications accepted. *Faculty research:* Collective learning, school culture, early literacy development, family literacy, brain-based learning.

Millersville University of Pennsylvania, College of Graduate Studies and Adult Learning, College of Education and Human Services, Department of Early, Middle, and Exceptional Education, Program in Language and Literacy: Reading Specialist, Millersville, PA 17551-0302. Offers M Ed. *Accreditation:* NCATE. *Program availability:* Part-time, evening/weekend. *Faculty:* 9 full-time (4 women), 11 part-time/adjunct (8 women). *Students:* 10 part-time (all women). Average age 27. 19 applicants, 100% accepted, 10 enrolled. *Degree requirements:* For master's, thesis optional. *Entrance requirements:* For master's, GRE or MAT if undergraduate cumulative GPA is lower than 3.0, teaching certificate. Additional exam requirements/recommendations for international students: Required—TOEFL (minimum score 80 iBT), IELTS (minimum score 6.5), PTE (minimum score 60). *Application deadline:* Applications are processed on a rolling basis. Application fee: $40. Electronic applications accepted. *Expenses:* $500 per credit resident tuition and fees; $750 per credit non-resident tuition and fees; $114.75 per credit general fee (maximum of 12 credits); technology fee $27 per credit (resident), $39 per credit (non-resident). *Financial support:* Unspecified assistantships available. Financial award application deadline: 3/15; financial award applicants required to submit FAFSA. *Faculty research:* Literacy and technology, children's literature, literacy leadership, disciplinary literacy, diagnosis and assessment. *Unit head:* Dr. Marcia Nell, Department Chairperson, 717-871-7344, E-mail: marcia.nell@millersville.edu. *Application contact:* Dr. Victor S. DeSantis, Dean of College of Graduate Studies and Adult Learning/Associate Provost for Civic and Community Engagement, 717-871-7619, Fax: 717-871-7954, E-mail: victor.desantis@millersville.edu. Website: http://www.millersville.edu/academics/educ/eled/graduate-programs/language-and-literacy.php

Misericordia University, College of Health Sciences and Education, Program in Education, Dallas, PA 18612-1098. Offers instructional technology (MS); reading specialist (MS); special education (MS). *Program availability:* Part-time, evening/weekend. *Entrance requirements:* For master's, minimum undergraduate GPA of 3.0. Additional exam requirements/recommendations for international students: Required—TOEFL. Electronic applications accepted.

Mississippi State University, College of Education, Department of Curriculum, Instruction and Special Education, Mississippi State, MS 39762. Offers early childhood education (PhD); elementary education (MS, PhD, Ed S), including early childhood education (MS), general elementary education (MS), middle level education (MS); general curriculum and instruction (PhD); reading education (PhD); secondary education (MAT, MS, PhD, Ed S); special education (MAT, MS, PhD, Ed S). *Accreditation:* NCATE. *Program availability:* Part-time, evening/weekend. *Faculty:* 22 full-time (16 women), 1 (woman) part-time/adjunct. *Students:* 38 full-time (26 women), 170 part-time (131 women); includes 46 minority (37 Black or African American, non-Hispanic/Latino; 4 American Indian or Alaska Native, non-Hispanic/Latino; 2 Hispanic/Latino; 1 Native Hawaiian or other Pacific Islander, non-Hispanic/Latino; 2 Two or more races, non-Hispanic/Latino), 4 international. Average age 32. 88 applicants, 53% accepted, 39 enrolled. In 2017, 68 master's, 4 doctorates, 5 other advanced degrees awarded. *Degree requirements:* For master's, comprehensive exam; for doctorate, thesis/dissertation; for Ed S, comprehensive exam, thesis or alternative. *Entrance requirements:* For master's, GRE, minimum GPA of 2.75 in junior and senior year, eligibility for initial teacher certification; for doctorate, GRE, minimum GPA of 3.4 on previous graduate work; for Ed S, GRE, minimum GPA of 3.2 on master's degree. Additional exam requirements/recommendations for international students: Required—TOEFL (minimum score 550 paper-based; 79 iBT); Recommended—IELTS (minimum score 6.5). *Application deadline:* For fall admission, 3/1 priority date for domestic students, 5/1 for international students; for spring admission, 9/1 priority date for domestic students, 9/1 for international students. Applications are processed on a rolling basis. Application fee: $60 ($80 for international students). Electronic applications accepted. *Expenses:* Tuition, state resident: full-time $8318; part-time $462.12 per credit hour. Tuition, nonresident: full-time $22,358; part-time $1242.12 per credit hour. *Required fees:* $110; $12.24 per credit hour. $6.12 per semester. *Financial support:* In 2017–18, 6 research assistantships with partial tuition reimbursements (averaging $11,307 per year) were awarded; Federal Work-Study, institutionally sponsored loans, scholarships/grants, and unspecified assistantships also available. Financial award application deadline: 4/1; financial award applicants required to submit FAFSA. *Faculty research:* Early childhood education, reading, rural schools, multicultural education, use of technology in instruction. *Unit head:* Dr. Linda Cornelious, Professor and Interim Head, 662-325-3747, Fax: 662-325-7857, E-mail: lcornelious@colled.msstate.edu. *Application contact:* Laken Drinker, Admissions and Enrollment Assistant, 662-325-8951, E-mail: ldrinker@grad.msstate.edu.
Website: http://www.cise.msstate.edu/

Mississippi University for Women, Graduate School, College of Education and Human Sciences, Columbus, MS 39701-9998. Offers differentiated instruction (M Ed); educational leadership (M Ed); gifted studies (M Ed); reading/literacy (M Ed); teaching (MAT). *Accreditation:* ASHA; NCATE. *Program availability:* Part-time. *Degree requirements:* For master's, comprehensive exam, thesis optional. *Entrance requirements:* For master's, GRE General Test or NTE (M Ed in gifted education or MS in speech/language pathology), MAT (M Ed in instructional management), minimum QPA of 3.0.

Missouri State University, Graduate College, College of Education, Department of Reading, Foundations, and Technology, Program in Literacy, Springfield, MO 65897. Offers MS Ed, Graduate Certificate. *Program availability:* Part-time, 100% online, blended/hybrid learning. *Faculty:* 6 full-time (all women). *Students:* 5 full-time (all women), 84 part-time (79 women); includes 2 minority (both Hispanic/Latino). Average age 26. 27 applicants, 78% accepted, 18 enrolled. In 2017, 29 master's awarded. *Degree requirements:* For master's, comprehensive exam, thesis or alternative. *Entrance requirements:* For master's, GRE or minimum GPA of 3.0, teaching certificate. Additional exam requirements/recommendations for international students: Required—TOEFL (minimum score 550 paper-based; 79 iBT), IELTS (minimum score 6). *Application deadline:* For fall admission, 7/20 priority date for domestic students, 5/1 for international students; for spring admission, 12/20 priority date for domestic students, 9/1 for international students; for summer admission, 5/20 priority date for domestic students. Applications are processed on a rolling basis. Application fee: $35 ($50 for international students). Electronic applications accepted. *Expenses:* Tuition, state resident: full-time $2915; part-time $2021 per credit hour. Tuition, nonresident: full-time $5354; part-time $3647 per credit hour. International tuition: $11,992 full-time. *Required fees:* $173; $173 per credit hour. Tuition and fees vary according to class time, course level, course load, degree level, campus/location and program. *Financial support:* Federal Work-Study, institutionally sponsored loans, scholarships/grants, and unspecified assistantships available. Financial award application deadline: 3/31; financial award applicants required to submit FAFSA. *Unit head:* Dr. Emmett Sawyer, Interim Department Head, 417-836-6769, E-mail: rft@missouristate.edu. *Application contact:* Stephanie Praschan, Director, Graduate Enrollment Management, 417-836-5330, Fax: 417-836-6200, E-mail: stephaniepraschan@missouristate.edu.
Website: http://education.missouristate.edu/rft/

Monmouth University, Graduate Studies, School of Education, West Long Branch, NJ 07764-1898. Offers applied behavior analysis (Certificate); autism (Certificate); director of school counseling services (Post-Master's Certificate); early childhood (M Ed); educational leadership (Ed D); elementary education (MAT), including elementary level, secondary level; English as a second language (M Ed); learning disabilities teacher-consultant (Post-Master's Certificate); literacy (MS Ed); school counseling (MS Ed); special education (MS Ed), including autism, learning disabilities teacher-consultant, teacher of students with disabilities, teaching in inclusive settings; speech-language pathology (MS Ed); student affairs and college counseling (MS Ed); supervisor (Post-Master's Certificate); teaching English to speakers of other languages (Certificate). *Accreditation:* NCATE. *Program availability:* Part-time, evening/weekend, 100% online, blended/hybrid learning. *Faculty:* 23 full-time (19 women), 33 part-time/adjunct (25 women). *Students:* 175 full-time (163 women), 168 part-time (142 women); includes 54 minority (10 Black or African American, non-Hispanic/Latino; 4 Asian, non-Hispanic/Latino; 32 Hispanic/Latino; 8 Two or more races, non-Hispanic/Latino). Average age 27. In 2017, 160 master's, 3 other advanced degrees awarded. *Entrance requirements:* For master's, GRE taken within last 5 years (for MS Ed in speech-language pathology), SAT (minimum combined score of 1660 in 3 sections), ACT (23), GRE (minimum score of 4.0 on analytical writing section and minimum combined score of 310 on quantitative and verbal sections), or passing scores on 3 parts of Core Academic Skills Educators, minimum GPA of 3.0 in major; 2 letters of recommendation (for some programs); resume, personal statement or essay (depending on program). Additional exam requirements/recommendations for international students: Required—TOEFL (minimum score 550 paper-based; 79 iBT), IELTS (minimum score 6), Michigan English Language Assessment Battery (minimum score 77) or Certificate of Advanced English (minimum score 160). *Application deadline:* For fall admission, 7/15 priority date for domestic students, 7/1 for international students; for spring admission, 12/1 priority date for domestic students, 11/1 for international students; for summer admission, 5/1 for domestic students. Applications are processed on a rolling basis. Application fee: $50. Electronic applications accepted. *Expenses: Tuition:* Full-time $21,366; part-time $7122 per credit. *Required fees:* $700; $175 per term. *Financial support:* In 2017–18, 125 students received support. Institutionally sponsored loans, scholarships/grants, and unspecified assistantships available. Support available to part-time students. Financial award applicants required to submit FAFSA. *Faculty research:* Multicultural literacy, science and mathematics teaching strategies, teacher as reflective practitioner, children with disabilities. *Unit head:* Dr. John E. Henning, Dean, 732-263-5513, Fax: 732-263-5277. *Application contact:* Laurie Kuhn, Associate Director of Graduate Admission, 732-571-3452, Fax: 732-263-5123, E-mail: gradadm@monmouth.edu.
Website: http://www.monmouth.edu/academics/schools/education/default.asp

Montana State University Billings, College of Education, Department of Educational Theory and Practice, Option in Reading, Billings, MT 59101. Offers M Ed. *Accreditation:* NCATE. *Program availability:* Part-time. *Degree requirements:* For master's, thesis or professional paper and/or field experience. *Entrance requirements:* For master's, GRE General Test or MAT, minimum GPA of 3.0. Additional exam requirements/recommendations for international students: Required—TOEFL (minimum score 79 iBT), IELTS (minimum score 6.5). *Application deadline:* Applications are processed on a rolling basis. Application fee: $40. Electronic applications accepted. *Expenses:* Tuition, state resident: full-time $11,740; part-time $7880 per year. Tuition, nonresident: full-time $32,200; part-time $24,140 per year. *Financial support:* Teaching assistantships with partial tuition reimbursements, career-related internships or fieldwork, Federal Work-Study, institutionally sponsored loans, scholarships/grants, tuition waivers (partial), and unspecified assistantships available. Support available to part-time students. Financial award application deadline: 5/1; financial award applicants required to submit FAFSA. *Unit head:* Rachael Waller, Assistant Professor, 406-657-2335, E-mail: rachael.waller@msubillings.edu. *Application contact:* Rachael Waller, Assistant Professor, 406-657-2335, E-mail: rachael.waller@msubillings.edu.
Website: http://www.msubillings.edu/grad/program-med_reading.htm

Montclair State University, The Graduate School, College of Education and Human Services, Program in Reading, Montclair, NJ 07043-1624. Offers MA. *Program availability:* Part-time, evening/weekend. *Entrance requirements:* For master's, GRE General Test, interview, essay, 2 letters of recommendation. Additional exam requirements/recommendations for international students: Required—TOEFL (minimum score 83 iBT), IELTS (minimum score 6.5). Electronic applications accepted.

Morehead State University, Graduate Education, College of Education, Department of Curriculum and Instruction, Morehead, KY 40351. Offers curriculum and instruction (Ed S); elementary education (MA Ed), including elementary education, international education, middle school education, reading; secondary education (MA Ed); special education (MA Ed); teaching (MAT). *Program availability:* Part-time, evening/weekend. *Degree requirements:* For master's, comprehensive exam, thesis optional; for Ed S, thesis, oral exam. *Entrance requirements:* For master's, GRE General Test, minimum GPA of 2.75, teaching certificate; for Ed S, GRE General Test, interview, master's degree, minimum GPA of 3.5, work experience. Additional exam requirements/recommendations for international students: Required—TOEFL (minimum score 500 paper-based). Electronic applications accepted. *Faculty research:* Communicative competence of learning-disabled students, teaching social studies in elementary schools, ungraded primary school organization, study skills.

Morehead State University, Graduate Programs, College of Education, Department of Foundational and Graduate Studies in Education, Morehead, KY 40351. Offers adult and higher education (MA, Ed S); certified professional counselor (MA); counseling P-12 (MA); curriculum and instruction (Ed S); educational technology (MA Ed); instructional leadership (Ed S); school administration (MA); school counseling (Ed S); teacher leader business and marketing content (MA Ed); teacher leader business and marketing technology (MA Ed); teacher leader educational technology (MA Ed); teacher leader English (MA Ed); teacher leader gifted education (MA Ed); teacher leader IECE certification (MA Ed); teacher leader interdisciplinary education P-5 (MA Ed); teacher leader middle grades (MA Ed); teacher leader non IECE certification (MA Ed); teacher leader reading/writing - non-certification (MA Ed); teacher leader reading/writing certification (MA Ed); teacher leader school communication - certification (MA Ed); teacher leader school communication - non-certification (MA Ed); teacher leader social studies (MA Ed); teacher leader special education (MA Ed). *Accreditation:* NCATE. *Program availability:* Part-time, evening/weekend. *Degree requirements:* For master's, thesis optional, oral and/or written comprehensive exams; for Ed S, thesis, oral exam. *Entrance requirements:* For master's, GRE General Test, minimum overall undergraduate GPA of 2.5; for Ed S, GRE General Test, interview, master's degree, minimum GPA of 3.5, work experience. Additional exam requirements/recommendations for international students: Required—TOEFL (minimum score 500 paper-based). Electronic applications accepted. *Faculty research:* Character education, school accountability, computer applications for school administrators.

Mount Mercy University, Program in Education, Cedar Rapids, IA 52402-4797. Offers reading (MA Ed); special education (MA Ed); teacher leadership (MA Ed). *Entrance requirements:* For master's, minimum cumulative GPA of 3.0, 2 letters of recommendation, resume, valid teaching license. Additional exam requirements/recommendations for international students: Required—TOEFL (minimum score 570 paper-based; 88 iBT). Electronic applications accepted.

Mount St. Joseph University, Graduate Education Program, Cincinnati, OH 45233-1670. Offers adolescent to young adult education (MA); dyslexia (Certificate); inclusive early childhood education (MA); middle childhood education (MA); multicultural special education (MA); reading science (MA). *Accreditation:* TEAC. *Program availability:* Part-time, evening/weekend, 100% online, blended/hybrid learning. *Faculty:* 6 full-time (5 women), 11 part-time/adjunct (8 women). *Students:* 37 full-time (30 women), 91 part-time (83 women); includes 13 minority (11 Black or African American, non-Hispanic/Latino; 1 Hispanic/Latino; 1 Two or more races, non-Hispanic/Latino). Average age 34. In 2017, 79 master's awarded. *Degree requirements:* For master's, comprehensive exam, thesis, research project, student teaching, clinical and field-based experiences. *Entrance requirements:* For master's, GRE (if GPA is below 3.0), letter of intent, 2 referrals, background check, interview, resume, minimum undergraduate GPA of 3.0. Additional exam requirements/recommendations for international students: Required—TOEFL (minimum score 560 paper-based; 83 iBT). *Application deadline:* Applications are processed on a rolling basis. Application fee: $50. Electronic applications accepted. *Expenses:* $600 per credit hour. *Financial support:* Applicants required to submit FAFSA. *Faculty research:* Foreign and second language learning problems/reading disabilities, multicultural/bilingual special education, science education, pedagogical content knowledge, early childhood, response to intervention. *Unit head:* Dr. Laura Saylor, Dean, 513-244-3263, E-mail: laura.saylor@msj.edu. *Application contact:* Mary Brigham, Assistant Director of Graduate Recruitment, 513-244-4233, Fax: 513-244-4629, E-mail: mary.brigham@msj.edu.
Website: http://www.msj.edu/academics/graduate-programs/master-of-arts-initial-teacher-licensure-programs/

Mount Saint Mary College, Division of Education, Newburgh, NY 12550-3494. Offers adolescence and special education (MS Ed); childhood education (MS Ed); literacy

education (MS Ed); middle school (7-9) (MS Ed). *Accreditation:* NCATE. *Program availability:* Part-time, evening/weekend. *Faculty:* 10 full-time (9 women), 3 part-time/adjunct (all women). *Students:* 11 full-time (9 women), 83 part-time (62 women); includes 9 minority (1 American Indian or Alaska Native, non-Hispanic/Latino; 6 Hispanic/Latino; 2 Two or more races, non-Hispanic/Latino). Average age 28. 20 applicants, 100% accepted, 16 enrolled. In 2017, 57 master's awarded. *Entrance requirements:* Additional exam requirements/recommendations for international students: Required—TOEFL (minimum score 80 iBT). *Application deadline:* Applications are processed on a rolling basis. Application fee: $45. Electronic applications accepted. Application fee is waived when completed online. *Expenses: Tuition:* Full-time $14,454; part-time $803 per credit. *Required fees:* $172; $86 per semester. *Financial support:* In 2017–18, 15 students received support. Unspecified assistantships available. Financial award application deadline: 4/15; financial award applicants required to submit FAFSA. *Faculty research:* Learning and teaching styles, computers in special education, language development. *Unit head:* Dr. Monica Merritt, Graduate Coordinator, 845-569-3430, Fax: 845-569-3535, E-mail: monica.merritt@msmc.edu. *Application contact:* Lisa Alvarez, Director of Admissions for Graduate Programs and Adult Degree Completion, 845-569-3166, Fax: 845-569-3450, E-mail: lisa.gallina@msmc.edu.
Website: http://www.msmc.edu/Academics/Graduate_Programs/Master_of_Science_in_Education

Mount Saint Vincent University, Graduate Programs, Faculty of Education, Program in Literacy Education, Halifax, NS B3M 2J6, Canada. Offers M Ed, MA Ed, MA-R. *Program availability:* Part-time, evening/weekend, online learning. *Degree requirements:* For master's, thesis (for some programs). *Entrance requirements:* For master's, minimum B average, 1 year of teaching experience, bachelor's degree in related field. Electronic applications accepted. *Faculty research:* Writing processes and instruction, assessment and evaluation of literacy education, critical literacy, early literacy development, gender and literacy.

National Louis University, National College of Education, Chicago, IL 60603. Offers administration and supervision (M Ed, Ed D, CAS, Ed S); curriculum and instruction (M Ed, MS Ed, CAS); early childhood administration (M Ed, CAS); early childhood education (M Ed, MAT, MS Ed, CAS); education (Ed D); educational psychology/human learning and development (M Ed, MS Ed, CAS, Ed S); elementary education (MAT); interdisciplinary curriculum and instruction (M Ed); mathematics education (M Ed, MS Ed, CAS); middle grades education (MAT); reading and language (M Ed, MS Ed, CAS); school psychology (M Ed, Ed S); science education (M Ed, MS Ed, CAS); secondary education (MAT); special education (M Ed, MAT, CAS); technology in education (M Ed, CAS). *Accreditation:* NCATE. *Program availability:* Part-time, evening/weekend. *Degree requirements:* For doctorate, comprehensive exam, thesis/dissertation. *Entrance requirements:* For master's, MAT or GRE, minimum GPA of 3.0; for doctorate, GRE General Test, minimum GPA of 3.25, interview, resume, writing sample, 4 recommendations. Additional exam requirements/recommendations for international students: Required—TOEFL (minimum score 550 paper-based; 79 iBT).

Nazareth College of Rochester, Graduate Studies, Department of Education, Program in Literacy Education, Rochester, NY 14618. Offers MS Ed. *Accreditation:* TEAC. *Program availability:* Part-time, evening/weekend. *Entrance requirements:* For master's, minimum GPA of 3.0. Additional exam requirements/recommendations for international students: Required—TOEFL or IELTS.

Newman University, Master of Science in Education Program, Wichita, KS 67213-2097. Offers building leadership (MS Ed); curriculum and instruction (MS Ed), including English as a second language, reading specialist; organizational leadership (MS Ed). *Accreditation:* NCATE. *Program availability:* Part-time, evening/weekend, online learning. *Degree requirements:* For master's, thesis optional. *Entrance requirements:* For master's, 3 years' full-time teaching experience, minimum GPA of 3.0, writing sample, 2 letters of recommendation, evidence of teaching certification. Additional exam requirements/recommendations for international students: Required—TOEFL (minimum score 600 paper-based; 100 iBT). Electronic applications accepted. *Expenses:* Contact institution. *Faculty research:* Online course design and deliver, staff engagement, classroom action.

New Mexico State University, College of Education, Department of Curriculum and Instruction, Las Cruces, NM 88003. Offers bilingual education (MA); curriculum and instruction (MA, Ed D, PhD); early childhood education (MA); educational diagnostics (Ed S); language, literacy and culture (MA); learning design and technologies (MA); teaching (MAT), including dance, Spanish; teaching English to speakers of other languages (MA). *Accreditation:* NCATE. *Program availability:* Part-time, evening/weekend, 100% online. *Faculty:* 22 full-time (17 women), 7 part-time/adjunct (2 women). *Students:* 113 full-time (79 women), 194 part-time (138 women); includes 171 minority (15 Black or African American, non-Hispanic/Latino; 3 American Indian or Alaska Native, non-Hispanic/Latino; 4 Asian, non-Hispanic/Latino; 142 Hispanic/Latino; 7 Two or more races, non-Hispanic/Latino), 37 international. Average age 36. 106 applicants, 80% accepted, 56 enrolled. In 2017, 82 master's, 15 doctorates, 1 other advanced degree awarded. *Entrance requirements:* For master's, minimum cumulative GPA of 3.0; for doctorate, portfolio, minimum cumulative GPA of 3.0. Additional exam requirements/recommendations for international students: Required—TOEFL (minimum score 550 paper-based; 79 iBT), IELTS (minimum score 6.5). *Application deadline:* For fall admission, 12/15 priority date for domestic and international students; for spring admission, 11/1 for domestic students. Applications are processed on a rolling basis. Application fee: $40 ($50 for international students). Electronic applications accepted. *Expenses: Tuition,* state resident: full-time $4390. *Tuition,* nonresident: full-time $15,309. *Required fees:* $853. *Financial support:* In 2017–18, 97 students received support, including 2 fellowships (averaging $4,390 per year), 1 research assistantship (averaging $17,368 per year), 10 teaching assistantships (averaging $17,489 per year); career-related internships or fieldwork, Federal Work-Study, scholarships/grants, traineeships, health care benefits, and unspecified assistantships also available. Support available to part-time students. Financial award application deadline: 3/1. *Faculty research:* STEM education, bilingual and English as a second language education, critical pedagogy/multicultural education, learning design and technology, early childhood education. *Total annual research expenditures:* $13,518. *Unit head:* Dr. David Rutledge, Department Head, 575-646-5411, Fax: 575-646-5436, E-mail: rutledge@nmsu.edu. *Application contact:* Dr. David Rutledge, Associate Department Head for Graduate Programs, 575-646-5411, Fax: 575-646-5436, E-mail: rutledge@nmsu.edu.
Website: http://tpal.nmsu.edu/

New York University, Steinhardt School of Culture, Education, and Human Development, Department of Teaching and Learning, Program in Literacy Education, New York, NY 10012-1019. Offers MA. *Accreditation:* TEAC. *Program availability:* Part-time. *Students:* Average age 24. 36 applicants, 89% accepted, 12 enrolled. In 2017, 18 master's awarded. *Degree requirements:* For master's, thesis (for some programs), fieldwork. *Entrance requirements:* For master's, teacher certification. Additional exam requirements/recommendations for international students: Required—TOEFL (minimum score 100 iBT). *Application deadline:* For fall admission, 12/1 priority date for domestic and international students. Applications are processed on a rolling basis. Application fee: $75. Electronic applications accepted. *Expenses: Tuition:* Full-time $41,352; part-

time $19,968 per year. *Required fees:* $2496; $1628 per unit. $814 per term. Tuition and fees vary according to course load and program. *Financial support:* Career-related internships or fieldwork, Federal Work-Study, institutionally sponsored loans, scholarships/grants, and tuition waivers (partial) available. Support available to part-time students. Financial award application deadline: 2/1; financial award applicants required to submit FAFSA. *Faculty research:* Early literacy intervention and development, psycho and sociolinguistics, multicultural education, literacy assessment and instruction. *Unit head:* Prof. Kay D. Stahl, Director, 212-998-5204, Fax: 212-995-4049, E-mail: kay.stahl@nyu.edu. *Application contact:* Office of Graduate Admissions, 212-998-5030, Fax: 212-995-4328, E-mail: steinhardt.gradadmissions@nyu.edu.
Website: http://steinhardt.nyu.edu/teachlearn/literacy

Niagara University, Graduate Division of Education, Concentration in Literacy Instruction, Niagara University, NY 14109. Offers MS Ed. *Program availability:* Part-time. *Students:* 9 full-time (all women), 21 part-time (20 women); includes 2 minority (both Black or African American, non-Hispanic/Latino). Average age 26. In 2017, 22 master's awarded. *Entrance requirements:* For master's, GRE. Additional exam requirements/recommendations for international students: Required—TOEFL (minimum score 550 paper-based; 79 iBT), IELTS (minimum score 6). *Application deadline:* For fall admission, 8/1 for domestic students. Application fee: $30. *Expenses:* Contact institution. *Financial support:* Research assistantships with tuition reimbursements, teaching assistantships with tuition reimbursements, career-related internships or fieldwork, Federal Work-Study, scholarships/grants, and unspecified assistantships available. Financial award application deadline: 4/15. *Unit head:* Dr. Robin Erwin, Chair, 716-286-8551, E-mail: rerwin@niagara.edu. *Application contact:* Evan Pierce, Associate Director for Graduate Recruitment, 716-286-8769, Fax: 716-286-8170, E-mail: epierce@niagara.edu.
Website: http://www.niagara.edu/literacy-instruction

North Carolina Agricultural and Technical State University, School of Graduate Studies, School of Education, Department of Curriculum and Instruction, Program in Reading Education, Greensboro, NC 27411. Offers MA Ed. *Accreditation:* NCATE. *Program availability:* Part-time, evening/weekend. *Degree requirements:* For master's, comprehensive exam, comprehensive portfolio. *Entrance requirements:* For master's, GRE General Test, minimum GPA of 3.0.

Northeastern Illinois University, College of Graduate Studies and Research, Daniel L. Goodwin College of Education, Program in Literacy Education, Chicago, IL 60625. Offers MA. *Program availability:* Part-time, evening/weekend. *Degree requirements:* For master's, comprehensive exam, thesis optional. *Entrance requirements:* For master's, previous course work in psychology or tests and measurements, minimum GPA of 2.75. Additional exam requirements/recommendations for international students: Required—TOEFL (minimum score 550 paper-based; 79 iBT). *Application deadline:* For fall admission, 4/1 priority date for domestic students; for spring admission, 8/15 for domestic students. Applications are processed on a rolling basis. Application fee: $30. Electronic applications accepted. *Expenses: Tuition,* state resident: full-time $7274; part-time $404.11 per credit hour. *Tuition,* nonresident: full-time $14,548; part-time $808.23 per credit hour. *Required fees:* $1284. *Financial support:* Applicants required to submit FAFSA. *Faculty research:* Early literacy, reading disabilities, cognitive processes, multicultural and linguistic diversity, use of literature in the classroom. *Unit head:* Dr. Joyce H. Jennings, Department Chair, 773-442-5398, E-mail: j-jennings@neiu.edu. *Application contact:* Martha Narvaez, Graduate Admission Representative, 773-442-6006, E-mail: m-narvaez@neiu.edu.

Northeastern State University, College of Education, Department of Curriculum and Instruction, Program in Reading, Tahlequah, OK 74464-2399. Offers M Ed. *Program availability:* Part-time, evening/weekend. *Faculty:* 5 full-time (4 women). *Students:* 7 full-time (6 women), 67 part-time (64 women); includes 22 minority (5 American Indian or Alaska Native, non-Hispanic/Latino; 1 Asian, non-Hispanic/Latino; 3 Hispanic/Latino; 13 Two or more races, non-Hispanic/Latino), 1 international. Average age 35. In 2017, 68 master's awarded. *Degree requirements:* For master's, thesis. *Entrance requirements:* For master's, MAT or GRE, minimum GPA of 2.5. Additional exam requirements/recommendations for international students: Required—TOEFL. *Application deadline:* For fall admission, 6/1 priority date for domestic students. Applications are processed on a rolling basis. Application fee: $25. Electronic applications accepted. *Expenses:* Tuition, state resident: part-time $222 per credit hour. Tuition, nonresident: part-time $501.75 per credit hour. *Required fees:* $37.40 per credit hour. Tuition and fees vary according to degree level. *Financial support:* Teaching assistantships and Federal Work-Study available. Financial award application deadline: 3/1. *Unit head:* Dr. Meagan Moreland, Reading Chair, 918-449-6441, E-mail: morela02@nsuok.edu. *Application contact:* Josh McCollum, Graduate Coordinator, 918-444-2093, E-mail: mccolluj@nsuok.edu.
Website: https://academics.nsuok.edu/education/EducationHome/COEDepartments/CurriculumInstruction.aspx

Northern Michigan University, Office of Graduate Education and Research, College of Health Sciences and Professional Studies, School of Education, Leadership and Public Service, Marquette, MI 49855-5301. Offers administration and supervision (MAE); instruction (MAE); learning disabilities (MAE); postsecondary biology education (MS); reading education (MAE), including reading, reading specialist. *Accreditation:* TEAC. *Program availability:* Part-time, online learning. *Degree requirements:* For master's, thesis (for some programs). *Entrance requirements:* For master's, minimum GPA of 3.0. Additional exam requirements/recommendations for international students: Required—TOEFL (minimum score 550 paper-based; 79 iBT), IELTS (minimum score 6.5). *Application deadline:* For fall admission, 7/1 priority date for domestic students; for winter admission, 11/15 for domestic students; for spring admission, 3/17 for domestic students. Applications are processed on a rolling basis. Application fee: $50. Electronic applications accepted. *Expenses:* Tuition, state resident: full-time $9417; part-time $542 per credit hour. Tuition, nonresident: full-time $12,873; part-time $758 per credit hour. Tuition and fees vary according to course load, degree level and program. *Financial support:* Research assistantships with full tuition reimbursements, career-related internships or fieldwork, Federal Work-Study, institutionally sponsored loans, and unspecified assistantships available. Support available to part-time students. Financial award application deadline: 3/1; financial award applicants required to submit FAFSA. *Unit head:* Dr. Joseph Lubig, Associate Dean for Teacher Education, 906-227-1880, Fax: 906-227-2764, E-mail: jlubig@nmu.edu. *Application contact:* Dr. Joseph Lubig, Associate Dean for Teacher Education, 906-227-1880, Fax: 906-227-2764, E-mail: jlubig@nmu.edu.
Website: http://www.nmu.edu/education/

Northern Vermont University–Lyndon, Graduate Programs in Education, Department of Education, Lyndonville, VT 05851. Offers curriculum and instruction (M Ed); reading specialist (M Ed); special education (M Ed); teaching and counseling (M Ed). *Program availability:* Part-time, evening/weekend. *Degree requirements:* For master's, exam or major field project. *Entrance requirements:* Additional exam requirements/recommendations for international students: Recommended—TOEFL (minimum score 500 paper-based).

Northwestern Oklahoma State University, School of Professional Studies, Reading Specialist Program, Alva, OK 73717-2799. Offers M Ed. *Accreditation:* NCATE. *Program availability:* Part-time. *Degree requirements:* For master's, thesis optional, portfolio. *Entrance requirements:* For master's, GRE General Test or MAT, minimum GPA of 2.75.

Northwestern State University of Louisiana, Graduate Studies and Research, College of Education and Human Development, Programs in Educational Leadership and Instruction, Natchitoches, LA 71497. Offers counseling (Ed S); educational leadership (M Ed, Ed S); educational technology (Ed S); elementary teaching (Ed S); reading (Ed S); secondary teaching (Ed S); special education (Ed S). *Accreditation:* NASAD. *Degree requirements:* For master's, comprehensive exam, thesis (for some programs). *Entrance requirements:* For master's and Ed S, GRE General Test. Additional exam requirements/recommendations for international students: Required—TOEFL. Electronic applications accepted.

Northwest Missouri State University, Graduate School, School of Education, Maryville, MO 64468-6001. Offers early childhood education (MS Ed); education leadership (MS Ed), including elementary, K-12, secondary; educational leadership (Ed S), including elementary school principalship, secondary school principalship, superintendency; educational leadership and policy analysis (Ed D); elementary education (MS Ed); elementary mathematics (MS Ed); higher education leadership (MS); middle school education (MS Ed); reading (MS Ed); special education (MS Ed); teacher leadership (MS Ed); teaching English language learners (MS Ed). *Accreditation:* NCATE. *Program availability:* Part-time. *Faculty:* 15 full-time (8 women). *Students:* 28 full-time (20 women), 170 part-time (114 women); includes 20 minority (7 Black or African American, non-Hispanic/Latino; 1 Asian, non-Hispanic/Latino; 8 Hispanic/Latino; 4 Two or more races, non-Hispanic/Latino). Average age 33. 168 applicants, 73% accepted, 114 enrolled. In 2017, 67 master's, 21 other advanced degrees awarded. *Degree requirements:* For master's, comprehensive exam; for Ed S, comprehensive exam, thesis. *Entrance requirements:* For master's, GRE General Test, writing sample; for Ed S, minimum graduate GPA of 3.25. Additional exam requirements/ recommendations for international students: Required—TOEFL (minimum score 550 paper-based). *Application deadline:* For fall admission, 7/1 for domestic and international students; for spring admission, 11/15 for domestic and international students. Applications are processed on a rolling basis. Application fee: $0 ($50 for international students). Electronic applications accepted. *Expenses:* $389.11 per credit hour in-state tuition and fees, $641.97 out-of-state; $9,750 total cost (for online-based education program). *Financial support:* Research assistantships with full tuition reimbursements, teaching assistantships with full tuition reimbursements, and unspecified assistantships available. Financial award application deadline: 4/1; financial award applicants required to submit FAFSA. *Unit head:* Dr. Tim Wall, Director, 660-562-1179, E-mail: timwall@nwmissouri.edu.
Website: https://www.nwmissouri.edu/education/index.htm

Notre Dame College, Graduate Programs, South Euclid, OH 44121-4293. Offers mild/ moderate needs (M Ed); reading (M Ed); security policy studies (MA, Graduate Certificate); technology (M Ed). *Program availability:* Part-time, evening/weekend. *Degree requirements:* For master's, thesis. *Entrance requirements:* For master's, GRE General Test, MAT, minimum undergraduate GPA of 2.75, valid teaching certificate, bachelor's degree in an education-related field from accredited college or university, official transcripts of most recent college work. *Faculty research:* Cognitive psychology, teaching critical thinking in the classroom.

Oakland University, Graduate Study and Lifelong Learning, School of Education and Human Services, Department of Reading and Language Arts, Rochester, MI 48309-4401. Offers advanced microcomputer applications (Graduate Certificate); digital literacies and learning (Graduate Certificate); microcomputer applications (Graduate Certificate); reading and language arts (MAT); reading education (PhD); reading, language arts and literature (PMC). *Accreditation:* TEAC. *Degree requirements:* For doctorate, thesis/dissertation. *Entrance requirements:* For master's, minimum GPA of 3.0; for doctorate, MAT, minimum GPA of 3.0. Electronic applications accepted. *Expenses:* Tuition, state resident: full-time $16,950; part-time $706.25 per credit. Tuition, nonresident: full-time $24,648; part-time $1027 per credit.

Ohio University, Graduate College, Gladys W. and David H. Patton College of Education and Human Services, Department of Teacher Education, Athens, OH 45701-2979. Offers adolescent to young adult education (M Ed); curriculum and instruction (M Ed, PhD); early childhood/special education (M Ed); intervention specialist/mild-moderate needs (M Ed); intervention specialist/moderate-intensive needs (M Ed); middle childhood education (M Ed); reading education (M Ed). *Program availability:* Part-time, evening/weekend. *Degree requirements:* For master's, thesis or alternative; for doctorate, comprehensive exam, thesis/dissertation. *Entrance requirements:* For master's, GRE General Test or MAT (if GPA is below 2.9); for doctorate, GRE General Test, minimum GPA of 3.4, work experience. Additional exam requirements/ recommendations for international students: Required—TOEFL (minimum score 550 paper-based; 80 iBT) or IELTS (minimum score 6.5). Electronic applications accepted. *Faculty research:* Cognition literacy, character education, teacher's education reform, disabilities.

Old Dominion University, Darden College of Education, Program in Literacy Leadership, Norfolk, VA 23529. Offers PhD. *Program availability:* Part-time, evening/ weekend. *Faculty:* 6 full-time (4 women). *Students:* 2 full-time (both women), 2 part-time (both women); includes 1 minority (Black or African American, non-Hispanic/Latino). Average age 38. 2 applicants, 100% accepted, 2 enrolled. *Degree requirements:* For doctorate, comprehensive exam, thesis/dissertation. *Entrance requirements:* For doctorate, GRE, minimum GPA of 3.0, MS in reading or related degree, letters of recommendation. Additional exam requirements/recommendations for international students: Required—TOEFL (minimum score 600 paper-based). *Application deadline:* For fall admission, 6/1 for domestic students, 4/15 for international students; for winter admission, 11/1 for domestic students, 10/1 for international students; for spring admission, 11/1 for domestic students, 10/1 for international students; for summer admission, 2/1 for domestic and international students. Applications are processed on a rolling basis. Application fee: $50. Electronic applications accepted. *Expenses:* Tuition, state resident: full-time $8928; part-time $496 per credit. Tuition, nonresident: full-time $22,482; part-time $1249 per credit. *Required fees:* $66 per semester. *Financial support:* In 2017–18, 1 teaching assistantship with full tuition reimbursement (averaging $20,000 per year) was awarded. Financial award applicants required to submit FAFSA. *Faculty research:* Literacy for students with special needs, children's reading first instruction, reading in the content area. *Unit head:* Dr. Sue Kimmel, Graduate Program Director, 757-683-3284, E-mail: skimmel@odu.edu. *Application contact:* William Heffelfinger, Director of Graduate Admissions, 757-683-5554, Fax: 757-683-3255, E-mail: gradadmit@odu.edu.
Website: http://education.odu.edu/eci/litphd/

Old Dominion University, Darden College of Education, Program in Reading Education, Norfolk, VA 23529. Offers reading specialist (MS Ed). *Accreditation:* NCATE. *Program availability:* Part-time, evening/weekend, 100% online, blended/hybrid learning. *Faculty:* 7 full-time (6 women), 12 part-time/adjunct (11 women). *Students:* 1 (woman) full-time, 70 part-time (68 women); includes 16 minority (13 Black or African American, non-Hispanic/Latino; 2 Hispanic/Latino; 1 Two or more races, non-Hispanic/Latino). Average age 36. 24 applicants, 75% accepted, 18 enrolled. In 2017, 5 master's awarded. *Degree requirements:* For master's, thesis optional, Virginia Reading Specialist Exam. *Entrance requirements:* For master's, minimum GPA of 3.0 in major, 2.8 overall; 5-year renewable teaching certificate; official transcripts; 2 letters of

reference; essay. Additional exam requirements/recommendations for international students: Required—TOEFL (minimum score 550 paper-based; 80 iBT). *Application deadline:* For fall admission, 6/1 for domestic students, 4/15 for international students; for spring admission, 11/1 for domestic students, 10/1 for international students; for summer admission, 3/1 for domestic students, 2/1 for international students. Applications are processed on a rolling basis. Application fee: $18 ($0 for international students). Electronic applications accepted. *Expenses:* Tuition, state resident: full-time $8928; part-time $496 per credit. Tuition, nonresident: full-time $22,482; part-time $1249 per credit. *Required fees:* $66 per semester. *Financial support:* In 2017–18, 7 students received support. Unspecified assistantships available. Financial award application deadline: 2/15; financial award applicants required to submit FAFSA. *Faculty research:* Metacognition and reading, strategies for improving comprehension in reading science, reading in content areas, vocabulary instruction for adolescents, literacy with special needs children, Reading First instruction, reading in the content area, vocabulary, diversity and literacy. *Total annual research expenditures:* $150,000. *Unit head:* Dr. Tami Al-Hazza, Graduate Program Director, 757-683-3228, Fax: 757-683-5862, E-mail: reading@odu.edu.
Website: https://www.odu.edu/teaching/academics/reading/masters

Olivet Nazarene University, Graduate School, Division of Education, Program in Reading Specialist, Bourbonnais, IL 60914. Offers MAE.

Pace University, School of Education, New York, NY 10038. Offers adolescent education (MST), including biology, chemistry, earth science, English, foreign languages, mathematics, physics, social studies; childhood education (MST); early childhood development, learning and intervention (MST); educational technology studies (MS); inclusive adolescent education (MST), including biology, chemistry, earth science, English, foreign languages, mathematics, physics, social studies; integrated instruction for educational technology (Certificate); integrated instruction for literacy and technology (Certificate); literacy (MS Ed); special education (MS Ed). *Accreditation:* NCATE. *Program availability:* Part-time, evening/weekend, 100% online, blended/hybrid learning. *Faculty:* 19 full-time (13 women), 86 part-time/adjunct (49 women). *Students:* 91 full-time (76 women), 548 part-time (401 women); includes 247 minority (112 Black or African American, non-Hispanic/Latino; 2 American Indian or Alaska Native, non-Hispanic/Latino; 31 Asian, non-Hispanic/Latino; 93 Hispanic/Latino; 1 Native Hawaiian or other Pacific Islander, non-Hispanic/Latino; 8 Two or more races, non-Hispanic/Latino), 6 international. Average age 30. 188 applicants, 86% accepted, 114 enrolled. In 2017, 213 master's, 8 other advanced degrees awarded. *Degree requirements:* For master's and Certificate, certification exams. *Entrance requirements:* For master's, GRE (for initial certification programs only), teaching certificate (for MS Ed in literacy and special education programs only). Additional exam requirements/recommendations for international students: Required—TOEFL (minimum score 88 iBT), IELTS or PTE. *Application deadline:* For fall admission, 8/1 priority date for domestic students, 6/1 for international students; for spring admission, 12/1 priority date for domestic students, 10/ 1 for international students. Applications are processed on a rolling basis. Application fee: $70. Electronic applications accepted. *Expenses:* Contact institution. *Financial support:* In 2017–18, 17 students received support, including 17 research assistantships with partial tuition reimbursements available (averaging $6,020 per year); career-related internships or fieldwork, Federal Work-Study, scholarships/grants, and unspecified assistantships also available. Financial award application deadline: 9/1; financial award applicants required to submit FAFSA. *Faculty research:* STEM education, TESOL, teacher education, special education, language and literary development. *Total annual research expenditures:* $29,706. *Unit head:* Dr. Xiao-Lei Wang, Dean, School of Education, 914-773-3876, E-mail: xwang@pace.edu. *Application contact:* Susan Ford-Goldschein, Director of Graduate Admissions, 212-346-1531, Fax: 212-346-1585, E-mail: graduateadmission@pace.edu.
Website: http://www.pace.edu/school-of-education

Park University, School of Graduate and Professional Studies, Kansas City, MO 54105. Offers adult education (M Ed); business and government leadership (Graduate Certificate); business, government, and global society (MPA); communication and leadership (MA); creative and life writing (Graduate Certificate); disaster and emergency management (MPA, Graduate Certificate); educational leadership (M Ed); finance (MBA, Graduate Certificate); general business (MBA); global business (Graduate Certificate); healthcare administration (MHA); healthcare services management and leadership (Graduate Certificate); international business (MBA); language and literacy (M Ed), including English for speakers of other languages, special reading teacher/ literacy coach; leadership of international healthcare organizations (Graduate Certificate); management information systems (MBA, Graduate Certificate); music performance (ADP, Graduate Certificate), including cello (MM, ADP), piano (MM, ADP), viola (MM, ADP), violin (MM, ADP); nonprofit and community services management (MPA); nonprofit leadership (Graduate Certificate); performance (MM), including cello (MM, ADP), piano (MM, ADP), viola (MM, ADP), violin (MM, ADP); public management (MPA); social work (MSW); teacher leadership (M Ed), including curriculum and assessment, instructional leader. *Program availability:* Part-time, evening/weekend, online learning. *Degree requirements:* For master's, comprehensive exam (for some programs), thesis (for some programs), internship (for some programs); exam (for some programs). *Entrance requirements:* For master's, GRE or GMAT (for some programs), teacher certification (for some M Ed programs), letters of recommendation, essay, resume (for some programs). Additional exam requirements/recommendations for international students: Required—TOEFL (minimum score 550 paper-based; 79 iBT), IELTS (minimum score 6). Electronic applications accepted.

Penn State Harrisburg, Graduate School, School of Behavioral Sciences and Education, Middletown, PA 17057. Offers adult education in the health and medical professions (Certificate); applied behavior analysis (MA); applied clinical psychology (MA); applied psychological research (MA); community psychology and social change (MA); English as a second language (ESL) program specialist and leadership (Certificate); health education (M Ed); lifelong learning and adult education (M Ed, D Ed); literacy education (M Ed); literacy leadership (Certificate); psychology: applications in clinical psychology (Certificate); psychology: health psychology (Certificate); teaching and curriculum (M Ed); training and development (M Ed, Certificate). *Program availability:* Part-time, evening/weekend. *Unit head:* Dr. Mukund S. Kulkarni, Chancellor, 717-948-6105, Fax: 717-948-6452. *Application contact:* Robert W. Coffman, Jr., Director of Enrollment Management, Recruitment and Admissions, 717-948-6250, Fax: 717-948-6325, E-mail: hbgadmit@psu.edu.
Website: https://harrisburg.psu.edu/behavioral-sciences-and-education/

Plymouth State University, College of Graduate Studies, Graduate Studies in Education, Program in Reading and Writing, Plymouth, NH 03264-1595. Offers M Ed. *Program availability:* Part-time, evening/weekend. *Degree requirements:* For master's, PRAXIS. *Entrance requirements:* For master's, GRE General Test or MAT, minimum GPA of 3.0.

Providence College, Program in Literacy, Providence, RI 02918. Offers M Ed. *Program availability:* Part-time, evening/weekend. *Degree requirements:* For master's, portfolio. *Entrance requirements:* Additional exam requirements/recommendations for international students: Required—TOEFL (minimum score 577 paper-based; 90 iBT).

Purdue University, Graduate School, College of Education, Department of Curriculum and Instruction, West Lafayette, IN 47907. Offers agricultural and extension education (MS, MS Ed, PhD, Ed S); art education (PhD); career and technical education (MS Ed, PhD, Ed S); curriculum studies (MS Ed, PhD, Ed S); educational technology (MS Ed, PhD, Ed S); elementary education (MS Ed); family and consumer sciences education (MS Ed, PhD, Ed S); foreign language education (MS Ed, PhD, Ed S); industrial technology (PhD, Ed S); language arts (MS Ed, PhD, Ed S); literacy (MS Ed, PhD, Ed S); mathematics education (MS, MS Ed, PhD, Ed S); science education (MS, MS Ed, PhD, Ed S); social studies education (MS Ed, PhD, Ed S). *Accreditation:* NCATE. *Program availability:* Part-time, evening/weekend. *Faculty:* 37 full-time (27 women), 1 (woman) part-time/adjunct. *Students:* 78 full-time (50 women), 286 part-time (195 women); includes 68 minority (25 Black or African American, non-Hispanic/Latino; 3 American Indian or Alaska Native, non-Hispanic/Latino; 10 Asian, non-Hispanic/Latino; 22 Hispanic/Latino; 1 Native Hawaiian or other Pacific Islander, non-Hispanic/Latino; 7 Two or more races, non-Hispanic/Latino), 44 international. Average age 36. 150 applicants, 79% accepted, 73 enrolled. In 2017, 107 master's, 20 doctorates, 2 other advanced degrees awarded. *Degree requirements:* For master's, thesis optional; for doctorate, thesis/dissertation, oral and written exams; for Ed S, oral presentation, project. *Entrance requirements:* For master's, GRE General Test (if undergraduate GPA is below 3.0), minimum undergraduate GPA of 3.0 or equivalent; for doctorate, GRE General Test (minimum combined verbal and quantitative score of 1000, 300 for new scoring), minimum undergraduate GPA of 3.0 or equivalent; master's degree with minimum GPA of 3.0 or equivalent; for Ed S, GRE General Test (minimum combined verbal and quantitative score of 1000, 300 for new scoring), minimum undergraduate GPA of 3.0 or equivalent; master's degree. Additional exam requirements/ recommendations for international students: Required—TOEFL (minimum score 550 paper-based; 77 iBT). *Application deadline:* For fall admission, 12/15 for domestic students, 3/1 for international students; for spring admission, 9/15 for domestic students, 8/1 for international students. Application fee: $60 ($75 for international students). Electronic applications accepted. *Financial support:* Fellowships with full tuition reimbursements, research assistantships with full tuition reimbursements, teaching assistantships with full tuition reimbursements, career-related internships or fieldwork, and tuition waivers (full) available. Support available to part-time students. Financial award application deadline: 3/1; financial award applicants required to submit FAFSA. *Faculty research:* Literacy acquisition and development, teacher beliefs and knowledge, recruitment and retention of underrepresented students, economic education, literacy discourse. *Unit head:* Janet M. Alsup, Head, 765-494-9667, E-mail: alsupj@purdue.edu. *Application contact:* Heather Brinkman, Graduate Contact, 765-494-2345, E-mail: hbrinkma@purdue.edu.
Website: http://www.edci.purdue.edu/

Purdue University Global, School of Teacher Education, Davenport, IA 52807. Offers education (M Ed); secondary education (M Ed); teaching and learning (MA); teaching literacy and language: grades 6-12 (MA); teaching literacy and language: grades K-6 (MA); teaching mathematics: grades 6-8 (MA); teaching mathematics: grades 9-12 (MA); teaching mathematics: grades K-5 (MA); teaching science: grades 6-12 (MA); teaching science: grades K-6 (MA); teaching students with special needs (MA); teaching with technology (MA). *Program availability:* Part-time, evening/weekend, online learning. *Entrance requirements:* Additional exam requirements/recommendations for international students: Required—TOEFL (minimum score 550 paper-based; 80 iBT).

Queens College of the City University of New York, Division of Education, Department of Elementary and Early Childhood Education, Queens, NY 11367-1597. Offers bilingual education (MAT, MS Ed, AC); childhood education (MAT, MS Ed); early childhood education birth-2 (MAT, MS Ed, AC); literacy education birth-grade 6 (MS Ed, AC). *Program availability:* Part-time, evening/weekend. *Students:* 112 full-time (98 women), 342 part-time (312 women); includes 243 minority (39 Black or African American, non-Hispanic/Latino; 87 Asian, non-Hispanic/Latino; 110 Hispanic/Latino; 7 Two or more races, non-Hispanic/Latino), 12 international. Average age 29. *Degree requirements:* For master's, research project. *Entrance requirements:* For master's, minimum GPA of 3.0. Additional exam requirements/recommendations for international students: Required—TOEFL, IELTS. *Application deadline:* For fall admission, 4/1 for domestic students. Applications are processed on a rolling basis. Application fee: $125. Electronic applications accepted. *Financial support:* Career-related internships or fieldwork available. Financial award application deadline: 4/1; financial award applicants required to submit FAFSA. *Unit head:* Daisuke Akiba, Chair, 718-997-5300, E-mail: daisuke.akiba@qc.cuny.edu. *Application contact:* Elizabeth D'Amico-Ramirez, Assistant Director of Graduate Admissions, 718-997-5203, E-mail: elizabeth.damicoramirez@ qc.cuny.edu.

Queens College of the City University of New York, Division of Education, Department of Secondary Education and Youth Services, Queens, NY 11367-1597. Offers adolescent biology (MAT); art (MS Ed); biology (MS Ed, AC); chemistry (MS Ed, AC); earth sciences (MS Ed, AC); English (MS Ed, AC); French (MS Ed); Italian (MS Ed, AC); literacy education (MS Ed); mathematics (MS Ed, AC); music (MS Ed, AC); physics (MS Ed, AC); social studies (MS Ed, AC); Spanish (MS Ed, AC). *Program availability:* Part-time, evening/weekend. *Students:* 28 full-time (16 women), 349 part-time (202 women); includes 165 minority (18 Black or African American, non-Hispanic/Latino; 56 Asian, non-Hispanic/Latino; 83 Hispanic/Latino; 8 Two or more races, non-Hispanic/Latino), 14 international. Average age 29. *Degree requirements:* For master's, research project. *Entrance requirements:* For master's, minimum GPA of 3.0. Additional exam requirements/recommendations for international students: Required—TOEFL, IELTS. *Application deadline:* For fall admission, 4/1 for domestic students; for spring admission, 11/1 for domestic students. Applications are processed on a rolling basis. Application fee: $125. Electronic applications accepted. *Financial support:* Career-related internships or fieldwork available. Financial award application deadline: 4/1; financial award applicants required to submit FAFSA. *Unit head:* Dr. Eleanor Armour-Thomas, Chairperson, 718-997-5150, E-mail: eleanor.armour-thomas@qc.cuny.edu. *Application contact:* Elizabeth D'Amico-Ramirez, Assistant Director of Graduate Admissions, 718-997-5203, E-mail: elizabeth.damicoramirez@qc.cuny.edu.

Queens University of Charlotte, Wayland H. Cato, Jr. School of Education, Charlotte, NC 28274-0002. Offers educational leadership (MA); K-6 (MAT); literacy K-12 (M Ed). *Accreditation:* NCATE. *Program availability:* Part-time, evening/weekend, online learning. *Degree requirements:* For master's, comprehensive exam. *Entrance requirements:* For master's, GRE General Test. *Expenses:* Contact institution.

Quincy University, Master of Science in Education Programs, Quincy, IL 62301-2699. Offers curriculum and instruction (MS Ed), including bilingual/English as a second language; education studies (MS Ed); leadership (MS Ed); reading education (MS Ed); teacher leader (MS Ed). *Program availability:* Part-time, evening/weekend, online learning. *Degree requirements:* For master's, comprehensive exam, (for some programs), thesis optional. *Entrance requirements:* For master's, MAT or GRE, personal resume. Additional exam requirements/recommendations for international students: Required—TOEFL (minimum score 550 paper-based; 79 iBT). *Application deadline:* Applications are processed on a rolling basis. Application fee: $25. Electronic applications accepted. Application fee is waived when completed online. *Expenses:* Tuition: Part-time $450 per credit hour. *Financial support:* Applicants required to submit

FAFSA. *Unit head:* Dr. Bruce Alan Spitzer, Director, 217-228-5432 Ext. 3106, E-mail: spitzbr@quincy.edu. *Application contact:* Office of Admissions, 217-228-5210, Fax: 217-228-5479, E-mail: admissions@quincy.edu.
Website: http://www.quincy.edu/academics/graduate-programs/education

Radford University, College of Graduate Studies and Research, Program in Literacy Education, Radford, VA 24142. Offers MS. *Accreditation:* NCATE. *Program availability:* Part-time, evening/weekend. *Faculty:* 3 full-time (2 women), 1 (woman) part-time/adjunct. *Students:* 12 part-time (all women); includes 1 minority (Two or more races, non-Hispanic/Latino). Average age 38. In 2017, 4 master's awarded. *Degree requirements:* For master's, comprehensive exam. *Entrance requirements:* For master's, minimum GPA of 2.75; copy of teaching license; 2 letters of reference; personal essay; resume; official transcripts. Additional exam requirements/ recommendations for international students: Required—TOEFL (minimum score 550 paper-based; 79 iBT), IELTS (minimum score 6.5). *Application deadline:* For fall admission, 2/15 priority date for domestic students, 12/1 for international students; for spring admission, 7/1 for international students. Applications are processed on a rolling basis. Application fee: $50. Electronic applications accepted. *Expenses:* Tuition, state resident: full-time $8336; part-time $347 per credit hour. Tuition, nonresident: full-time $16,862; part-time $702 per credit hour. *Required fees:* $3220; $135 per credit hour. Tuition and fees vary according to course load and program. *Financial support:* In 2017–18, 3 students received support. Career-related internships or fieldwork, scholarships/grants, and unspecified assistantships available. Support available to part-time students. Financial award application deadline: 3/1; financial award applicants required to submit FAFSA. *Unit head:* Dr. Jennifer Jones-Powell, Graduate Program Coordinator, 540-831-5311, E-mail: jjones292@radford.edu.
Website: http://www.radford.edu/content/cehd/home/teacher-ed/programs/master-literacy.html

Regent University, Graduate School, School of Education, Virginia Beach, VA 23464-9800. Offers education (M Ed, Ed D, PhD), including adult education (Ed D, PhD, Ed S); advanced educational leadership (Ed D, PhD, Ed S); character education (Ed D, PhD, Ed S); Christian education leadership (Ed D, PhD, Ed S); Christian school administration (M Ed); curriculum and instruction (Ed D, PhD, Ed S); curriculum and instruction - adult education (M Ed); curriculum and instruction - Christian school (M Ed); curriculum and instruction - gifted and talented (M Ed); curriculum and instruction - STEM education (M Ed); curriculum and instruction - teacher leader (M Ed); discipleship for ministry (M Ed); educational leadership (M Ed); educational psychology (Ed D, PhD, Ed S); educational technology and online learning (Ed D, PhD, Ed S); elementary education (M Ed); exceptional education executive leadership (Ed D, PhD, Ed S); higher education (Ed D, PhD, Ed S); higher education leadership and management (Ed D, PhD, Ed S); instructional design and technology (M Ed); K-12 school leadership (Ed D, PhD, Ed S); K-12 special education (M Ed); leadership in mathematics education (M Ed); reading specialist (M Ed); special education (Ed D, PhD, Ed S); student affairs (M Ed); TESOL - adult education (M Ed); TESOL - K-12 (M Ed); educational specialist (Ed S), including adult education (Ed D, PhD, Ed S); advanced educational leadership (Ed D, PhD, Ed S); character education (Ed D, PhD, Ed S); Christian education leadership (Ed D, PhD, Ed S); curriculum and instruction (Ed D, PhD, Ed S); educational psychology (Ed D, PhD, Ed S); educational technology and online learning (Ed D, PhD, Ed S); exceptional education executive leadership (Ed D, PhD, Ed S); higher education (Ed D, PhD, Ed S); higher education leadership and management (Ed D, PhD, Ed S); K-12 school leadership (Ed D, PhD, Ed S); special education (Ed D, PhD, Ed S). *Accreditation:* TEAC. *Program availability:* Part-time, evening/weekend, 100% online, blended/hybrid learning. *Faculty:* 22 full-time (10 women), 44 part-time/adjunct (32 women). *Students:* 80 full-time (59 women), 945 part-time (750 women); includes 432 minority (352 Black or African American, non-Hispanic/Latino; 4 American Indian or Alaska Native, non-Hispanic/Latino; 14 Asian, non-Hispanic/Latino; 43 Hispanic/Latino; 19 Two or more races, non-Hispanic/Latino), 12 international. Average age 40. 1,125 applicants, 49% accepted, 436 enrolled. In 2017, 316 master's, 24 doctorates awarded. *Degree requirements:* For master's, thesis or alternative; for doctorate, comprehensive exam, thesis/dissertation. *Entrance requirements:* For master's, Virginia Communication and Literacy Assessment (VCLA), PRAXIS, college transcripts, writing sample, interview; for doctorate, GRE, writing sample, resume, transcripts, interview. Additional exam requirements/recommendations for international students: Required—TOEFL (minimum score 577 paper-based). *Application deadline:* For fall admission, 4/1 priority date for domestic students; for spring admission, 10/15 priority date for domestic students. Applications are processed on a rolling basis. Application fee: $50. Electronic applications accepted. *Expenses:* Contact institution. *Financial support:* In 2017–18, 669 students received support, including 1 fellowship (averaging $10,000 per year); career-related internships or fieldwork, scholarships/grants, and unspecified assistantships also available. Support available to part-time students. *Faculty research:* Christian school administration, curriculum and instruction, educational technology and online learning, higher education, special education. *Unit head:* Dr. Donald Finn, Dean, 757-352-4278, Fax: 757-352-4318, E-mail: dfinn@regent.edu. *Application contact:* Heidi Cece, Assistant Vice President of Enrollment Management, 800-373-5504, Fax: 757-352-4381, E-mail: admissions@regent.edu.
Website: https://www.regent.edu/school-of-education/

Regis University, College of Contemporary Liberal Studies, Denver, CO 80221-1099. Offers creative writing (MFA); criminology (M Sc); curriculum, instruction and assessment (M Ed); education - teacher leadership (M Ed); educational leadership (M Ed); elementary education (M Ed); literacy (Certificate); reading (M Ed); secondary education (M Ed); special education (M Ed); teacher academic leadership (Certificate); teacher leadership (MA); teacher/educational leadership (M Ed); teaching the linguistically diverse (M Ed). *Program availability:* Part-time, evening/weekend, 100% online, blended/hybrid learning. *Degree requirements:* For master's, thesis (for some programs). *Entrance requirements:* For master's, official transcript reflecting baccalaureate degree awarded from regionally-accredited college or university, work experience, resume, letters of recommendation. Additional exam requirements/ recommendations for international students: Required—TOEFL (minimum score 550 paper-based; 82 iBT). Electronic applications accepted. *Expenses:* Contact institution.

Rhode Island College, School of Graduate Studies, Feinstein School of Education and Human Development, Department of Elementary Education, Providence, RI 02908-1991. Offers early childhood education (M Ed); elementary education (M Ed, MAT); reading (M Ed). *Accreditation:* NCATE. *Program availability:* Part-time, evening/weekend. *Faculty:* 9. *Students:* 19 full-time (18 women), 24 part-time (23 women). Average age 33. In 2017, 21 master's awarded. *Degree requirements:* For master's, comprehensive exam (for some programs), comprehensive assessment. *Entrance requirements:* For master's, GRE General Test or MAT, PRAXIS II (elementary content knowledge), undergraduate transcripts; minimum undergraduate GPA of 3.0; 3 letters of recommendation. Additional exam requirements/recommendations for international students: Recommended—TOEFL (minimum score 550 paper-based; 79 iBT). *Application deadline:* For fall admission, 3/1 for domestic students; for spring admission, 11/1 for domestic students. Applications are processed on a rolling basis. Application fee: $50. Electronic applications accepted. *Expenses:* Tuition, state resident: full-time $9768; part-time $407 per credit. Tuition, nonresident: full-time $19,008; part-time $792 per credit. *Required fees:* $696; $29 per credit. One-time fee: $200 full-time; $100 part-

time. Tuition and fees vary according to course load. *Financial support:* Teaching assistantships with full tuition reimbursements, Federal Work-Study, scholarships/grants, and health care benefits available. Support available to part-time students. Financial award application deadline: 5/15; financial award applicants required to submit FAFSA. *Unit head:* Dr. Carolyn Obel-Omia, Chair, 401-456-8016. *Application contact:* Graduate Studies, 401-456-8700.
Website: http://www.ric.edu/elementaryEducation/

Rider University, College of Education and Human Services, Program in Literacy, Lawrenceville, NJ 08648-3001. Offers MA, Certificate. *Accreditation:* NCATE. *Program availability:* Part-time, evening/weekend, online learning. *Degree requirements:* For master's, comprehensive exam, research project. *Entrance requirements:* For master's, interview, resume. Additional exam requirements/recommendations for international students: Required—TOEFL (minimum score 550 paper-based). Electronic applications accepted. *Faculty research:* Ethnography in the reading/language arts process.

Rivier University, School of Graduate Studies, Department of Education, Nashua, NH 03060. Offers curriculum and instruction (M Ed); early childhood education (M Ed); educational administration (M Ed); educational studies (M Ed); elementary education (M Ed); elementary education and general special education (M Ed); emotional and behavioral disorders (M Ed); general social education (M Ed); leadership and learning (Ed D, CAGS); learning disabilities (M Ed); learning disabilities and reading (M Ed); mental health counseling (MA); reading (M Ed); school counseling (M Ed). *Program availability:* Part-time, evening/weekend. *Degree requirements:* For master's, comprehensive exam (for some programs), internships. *Entrance requirements:* For master's, GRE General Test or MAT.

Robert Morris University, School of Education and Social Sciences, Moon Township, PA 15108-1189. Offers business education (MS); counseling psychology (MS); education (Postbaccalaureate Certificate); higher education (MS); instructional leadership (MS), including education; instructional management and leadership (PhD); literacy (MS); special education (MS). *Accreditation:* TEAC. *Program availability:* Part-time, evening/weekend, online learning. *Faculty:* 18 full-time (10 women), 5 part-time/adjunct (2 women). *Students:* 151 part-time (90 women); includes 23 minority (12 Black or African American, non-Hispanic/Latino; 2 Asian, non-Hispanic/Latino; 2 Hispanic/Latino; 7 Two or more races, non-Hispanic/Latino), 4 international. Average age 34. 51 applicants, 39% accepted, 10 enrolled. In 2017, 31 master's, 16 doctorates awarded. *Degree requirements:* For doctorate, thesis/dissertation. *Entrance requirements:* Additional exam requirements/recommendations for international students: Required—TOEFL (minimum score 550 paper-based; 79 iBT). *Application deadline:* For fall admission, 7/1 priority date for domestic and international students; for spring admission, 11/1 priority date for domestic and international students. Applications are processed on a rolling basis. Application fee: $35. Electronic applications accepted. *Expenses:* $890 per credit tuition, $80 per credit university fee. *Unit head:* Dr. George Semich, Acting Dean, 412-397-6032, Fax: 412-397-6044, E-mail: semich@rmu.edu. *Application contact:* E-mail: graduateadmission@rmu.edu.
Website: http://www.rmu.edu/web/cms/schools/sess/

Roberts Wesleyan College, Graduate Teacher Education Programs, Rochester, NY 14624-1997. Offers adolescence and special education (M Ed); childhood and special education (M Ed); literacy education (M Ed); special education (M Ed). *Program availability:* Part-time, evening/weekend. *Degree requirements:* For master's, thesis. Electronic applications accepted.

Rockford University, Graduate Studies, Department of Education, Program in Reading, Rockford, IL 61108-2393. Offers MAT. *Program availability:* Part-time, evening/weekend. *Degree requirements:* For master's, thesis optional. *Entrance requirements:* For master's, GRE General Test, 3 letters of recommendation. Additional exam requirements/recommendations for international students: Required—TOEFL (minimum score 550 paper-based; 79 iBT). Electronic applications accepted.

Roger Williams University, Feinstein School of Humanities, Arts and Education, Bristol, RI 02809. Offers literacy education (MA); middle school certification (Certificate). *Program availability:* Part-time-only, evening/weekend. *Faculty:* 3 full-time (all women), 5 part-time/adjunct (4 women). *Students:* 14 part-time (all women); includes 1 minority (Hispanic/Latino). Average age 33. 10 applicants, 100% accepted, 7 enrolled. In 2017, 10 master's awarded. *Entrance requirements:* For master's, resume, 2 letters of recommendation, college transcript, letter of intent, verification of active teaching license. Additional exam requirements/recommendations for international students: Required—TOEFL (minimum score 85 iBT), IELTS (minimum score 6.5). *Application deadline:* Applications are processed on a rolling basis. Application fee: $50. Electronic applications accepted. *Expenses:* $573 per credit hour, $258 graduation fee. *Financial support:* Application deadline: 4/1; applicants required to submit FAFSA. *Unit head:* Jeffrey Meriwether, Interim Dean, 401-254-3780, E-mail: jmeriwether@rwu.edu. *Application contact:* Marcus Hanscom, Director of Graduate Admissions, 401-254-3345, Fax: 401-254-3557, E-mail: gradadmit@rwu.edu.
Website: http://www.rwu.edu/academics/schools-and-colleges/fshae

Roosevelt University, Graduate Division, College of Education, Program in Reading, Chicago, IL 60605. Offers reading teacher education (MA). *Program availability:* Part-time, evening/weekend. *Students:* 17 part-time (14 women); includes 4 minority (2 Black or African American, non-Hispanic/Latino; 1 Asian, non-Hispanic/Latino; 1 Hispanic/Latino). Average age 29. 5 applicants, 100% accepted, 5 enrolled. In 2017, 12 master's awarded. *Application deadline:* Applications are processed on a rolling basis. Application fee: $40. Electronic applications accepted. *Financial support:* Scholarships/grants available. *Unit head:* Margaret Policastro, Director, 312-281-3199. *Application contact:* Laura Lag, Associate Dean for Graduate Admission, 312-853-4753, E-mail: llag@roosevelt.edu.
Website: https://www.roosevelt.edu/

Rowan University, Graduate School, College of Education, Department of Language, Literacy, and Sociocultural Education, Program in Reading Education, Glassboro, NJ 08028-1701. Offers MA, CGS. Electronic applications accepted. *Expenses:* Tuition, state resident: full-time $15,020; part-time $751 per semester hour. Tuition, nonresident: full-time $15,020; part-time $751 per semester hour. *Required fees:* $3158; $157.90 per semester hour. Tuition and fees vary according to course load, campus/location and program.

Rutgers University–New Brunswick, Graduate School of Education, Department of Learning and Teaching, Program in Literacy Education, Piscataway, NJ 08854-8097. Offers Ed M, Ed D. *Program availability:* Part-time. Terminal master's awarded for partial completion of doctoral program. *Degree requirements:* For master's, comprehensive exam; for doctorate, thesis/dissertation, qualifying exam. *Entrance requirements:* For master's, GRE General Test, minimum undergraduate GPA of 3.0; for doctorate, GRE General Test, 2 years of teaching experience, certification, minimum graduate GPA of 3.5. Additional exam requirements/recommendations for international students: Required—TOEFL. Electronic applications accepted. *Faculty research:* Early childhood literacy development, discourse analysis-adult literacy.

Rutgers University–New Brunswick, Graduate School of Education, Department of Learning and Teaching, Program in Reading Education, Piscataway, NJ 08854-8097. Offers Ed M. *Program availability:* Part-time. *Degree requirements:* For master's,

comprehensive exam or paper. *Entrance requirements:* For master's, GRE General Test. Electronic applications accepted.

Rutgers University–New Brunswick, Graduate School of Education, Doctoral Program in Education, New Brunswick, NJ 08901. Offers educational policy (PhD); educational psychology (PhD); literacy education (PhD); mathematics education (PhD). *Program availability:* Part-time. *Degree requirements:* For doctorate, thesis/dissertation, qualifying exam. *Entrance requirements:* For doctorate, GRE General Test, GRE Subject Test (mathematics education). Additional exam requirements/recommendations for international students: Required—TOEFL (minimum score 575 paper-based; 83 iBT). Electronic applications accepted. *Faculty research:* Literacy education, math education, educational psychology, educational policy, learning sciences.

Sacred Heart University, Graduate Programs, Isabelle Farrington College of Education, Department of Leadership/Literacy, Fairfield, CT 06825. Offers advanced studies in administration (Professional Certificate); advanced studies in literacy (Professional Certificate). *Program availability:* Part-time, evening/weekend. *Faculty:* 7 full-time (3 women), 17 part-time/adjunct (8 women). *Students:* 70 part-time (67 women); includes 5 minority (2 Black or African American, non-Hispanic/Latino; 1 American Indian or Alaska Native, non-Hispanic/Latino; 1 Asian, non-Hispanic/Latino; 1 Hispanic/Latino). Average age 37. 162 applicants, 98% accepted, 143 enrolled. In 2017, 59 Professional Certificates awarded. *Degree requirements:* For Professional Certificate, thesis or alternative. *Entrance requirements:* For degree, CT teacher certification. *Application deadline:* Applications are processed on a rolling basis. Application fee: $75. Electronic applications accepted. *Expenses:* Contact institution. *Financial support:* Unspecified assistantships available. Financial award applicants required to submit FAFSA. *Unit head:* Randall Glading, Chair/Assistant Professor, 203-396-8312, E-mail: gladingr@sacredheart.edu. *Application contact:* Tara Chudy, Executive Director of Graduate Admissions, 203-365-4735, E-mail: chudyt@sacredheart.edu.

Sage Graduate School, Esteves School of Education, Program in Childhood Education/Literacy, Troy, NY 12180-4115. Offers MS. *Program availability:* Part-time, evening/weekend. *Faculty:* 2 full-time (both women), 8 part-time/adjunct (4 women). *Students:* 11 full-time (all women). Average age 28. 13 applicants, 15% accepted, 1 enrolled. In 2017, 1 master's awarded. *Degree requirements:* For master's, thesis optional. *Entrance requirements:* For master's, GRE (minimum scores: Verbal Reasoning 145, Quantitative Reasoning 145, Analytical Writing 3.5) or MAT (minimum score: 350), bachelor's degree in a liberal arts or science area, minimum cumulative GPA of 3.0. Additional exam requirements/recommendations for international students: Required—TOEFL (minimum score 550 paper-based). *Application deadline:* Applications are processed on a rolling basis. Application fee: $30. Electronic applications accepted. Tuition and fees vary according to degree level and program. *Financial support:* Fellowships, research assistantships, scholarships/grants, and unspecified assistantships available. Financial award application deadline: 3/1; financial award applicants required to submit FAFSA. *Unit head:* Dr. John Pelizza, Interim Dean, Esteves School of Education, 518-244-2051, Fax: 518-244-2334, E-mail: pelizj@sage.edu. *Application contact:* Dr. Kathleen Gormley, Chair and Professor of Education, 518-244-2403, Fax: 518-244-2334, E-mail: gormlk@sage.edu.

Sage Graduate School, Esteves School of Education, Program in Literacy, Troy, NY 12180-4115. Offers MS Ed. *Accreditation:* NCATE. *Program availability:* Part-time, evening/weekend. *Faculty:* 2 full-time (both women), 8 part-time/adjunct (4 women). *Students:* 2 full-time (both women), 4 part-time (all women). Average age 32. 8 applicants, 63% accepted, 3 enrolled. In 2017, 5 master's awarded. *Entrance requirements:* For master's, minimum GPA of 2.75, resume, 2 letters of recommendation. Additional exam requirements/recommendations for international students: Required—TOEFL (minimum score 550 paper-based). *Application deadline:* Applications are processed on a rolling basis. Application fee: $30. Tuition and fees vary according to degree level and program. *Financial support:* Fellowships, research assistantships, scholarships/grants, and unspecified assistantships available. Financial award application deadline: 3/1; financial award applicants required to submit FAFSA. *Faculty research:* Literacy development in at-risk children. *Unit head:* Dr. John Pelizza, Interim Dean, Esteves School of Education, 518-244-2051, Fax: 518-244-2334, E-mail: pelizj@sage.edu. *Application contact:* Dr. Kathleen Gormley, Chair/Professor of Education, 518-244-2403, Fax: 518-244-2334, E-mail: gormlk@sage.edu.

Sage Graduate School, Esteves School of Education, Program in Literacy/Childhood Special Education, Troy, NY 12180-4115. Offers MS Ed. *Accreditation:* NCATE. *Program availability:* Part-time, evening/weekend. *Faculty:* 2 full-time (both women), 8 part-time/adjunct (4 women). *Students:* 1 (woman) full-time, 7 part-time (6 women). Average age 28. 6 applicants. In 2017, 3 master's awarded. *Entrance requirements:* For master's, current teacher certification, interview with appropriate advisor, assessment of writing. Additional exam requirements/recommendations for international students: Required—TOEFL (minimum score 550 paper-based). *Application deadline:* Applications are processed on a rolling basis. Application fee: $30. Electronic applications accepted. Tuition and fees vary according to degree level and program. *Financial support:* Fellowships, research assistantships, scholarships/grants, and unspecified assistantships available. Financial award application deadline: 3/1; financial award applicants required to submit FAFSA. *Faculty research:* Commonalities in the roles of reading specialists and resource/consultant teachers. *Unit head:* Dr. John Pelizza, Interim Dean, Esteves School of Education, 518-244-2051, Fax: 518-244-2334, E-mail: pelizj@sage.edu. *Application contact:* Dr. Kathleen Gormley, Chair and Professor of Education, 518-244-2403, Fax: 518-244-2334, E-mail: gormlk@sage.edu.

Saginaw Valley State University, College of Education, Program in K-12 Literacy Specialist, University Center, MI 48710. Offers MAT. *Program availability:* Part-time, evening/weekend. *Students:* 1 (woman) full-time, 27 part-time (25 women); includes 2 minority (both Black or African American, non-Hispanic/Latino). Average age 33. 4 applicants, 100% accepted, 4 enrolled. In 2017, 10 master's awarded. *Degree requirements:* For master's, capstone course. *Entrance requirements:* For master's, minimum GPA of 3.0. Additional exam requirements/recommendations for international students: Required—TOEFL (minimum score 550 paper-based; 79 iBT). *Application deadline:* For fall admission, 7/15 for international students; for winter admission, 11/15 for international students; for spring admission, 4/15 for international students. Applications are processed on a rolling basis. Application fee: $30 ($90 for international students). Electronic applications accepted. *Expenses:* Tuition, state resident: full-time $10,156; part-time $564.20 per credit hour. Tuition, nonresident: full-time $19,336; part-time $1074.20 per credit hour. *Required fees:* $263; $14.60 per credit hour. Tuition and fees vary according to degree level and program. *Financial support:* Federal Work-Study and scholarships/grants available. Support available to part-time students. Financial award applicants required to submit FAFSA. *Unit head:* Dr. Gretchen Owocki, Professor of Teacher Education, 989-964-7393, Fax: 989-964-4563, E-mail: coeconnect@svsu.edu. *Application contact:* Jenna Briggs, Director, Graduate and International Admissions, 989-964-6096, Fax: 989-964-2788, E-mail: gradadm@svsu.edu.

Saginaw Valley State University, College of Education, Program in Reading Education, University Center, MI 48710. Offers MAT. *Accreditation:* NCATE. *Program availability:* Part-time, evening/weekend. *Degree requirements:* For master's, capstone course, practicum. *Entrance requirements:* For master's, minimum GPA of 3.0, teaching

Reading Education

certificate. Additional exam requirements/recommendations for international students: Required—TOEFL (minimum score 550 paper-based; 79 iBT). *Application deadline:* For fall admission, 7/15 for international students; for winter admission, 11/15 for international students; for spring admission, 4/15 for international students. Applications are processed on a rolling basis. Application fee: $30 ($90 for international students). Electronic applications accepted. *Expenses:* Tuition, state resident: full-time $10,156; part-time $564.20 per credit hour. Tuition, nonresident: full-time $19,336; part-time $1074.20 per credit hour. *Required fees:* $263; $14.60 per credit hour. Tuition and fees vary according to degree level and program. *Financial support:* Federal Work-Study and scholarships/grants available. Support available to part-time students. Financial award applicants required to submit FAFSA. *Faculty research:* Pre-service, middle school, secondary teacher, literacy education. *Unit head:* Dr. Craig Douglas, Dean, 989-964-4057, Fax: 989-964-4385, E-mail: coeconnect@svsu.edu. *Application contact:* Jenna Briggs, Director, Graduate and International Admissions, 989-964-6096, Fax: 989-964-2788, E-mail: gradadm@svsu.edu.

St. Bonaventure University, School of Graduate Studies, School of Education, Literacy Programs, St. Bonaventure, NY 14778-2284. Offers adolescent literacy 5-12 (MS Ed); childhood literacy B-6 (MS Ed). *Accreditation:* NCATE. *Program availability:* Part-time, evening/weekend. *Faculty:* 2 part-time/adjunct (both women). *Students:* 7 full-time (all women), 3 part-time (1 woman); includes 2 minority (1 Black or African American, non-Hispanic/Latino; 1 Hispanic/Latino). Average age 23. 3 applicants, 100% accepted, 3 enrolled. In 2017, 13 master's awarded. *Degree requirements:* For master's, comprehensive exam, thesis optional, minimum cumulative GPA of 3.0, clinical practicum, literacy coaching internship, electronic portfolio. *Entrance requirements:* For master's, GRE or MAT, teaching certificate in matching area in-hand or pending, transcripts from all previous colleges, minimum GPA of 3.0, 2 references, interview, writing sample. Additional exam requirements/recommendations for international students: Required—TOEFL (minimum score 550 paper-based; 80 iBT). *Application deadline:* For fall admission, 6/15 priority date for domestic students, 2/1 for international students; for spring admission, 11/15 priority date for domestic students, 7/1 for international students. Applications are processed on a rolling basis. Application fee: $0. Electronic applications accepted. *Expenses:* $733 per credit hour, $100 graduation fee. *Financial support:* Federal Work-Study, scholarships/grants, health care benefits, and unspecified assistantships available. Support available to part-time students. Financial award application deadline: 4/15; financial award applicants required to submit FAFSA. *Unit head:* Dr. Lisa Buenaventura, Interim Program Director, 716-375-2394, Fax: 716-375-2360, E-mail: lbuenave@sbu.edu. *Application contact:* Bruce Campbell, Director of Graduate Admissions, 716-375-2429, Fax: 716-375-4015, E-mail: gradsch@sbu.edu. Website: http://www.sbu.edu/academics/schools/education/graduate-degrees-certificates/msed-in-childhood-literacy

Saint Francis University, Graduate Education Program, Loretto, PA 15940-0600. Offers education (M Ed); leadership (M Ed); reading (M Ed). *Program availability:* Part-time, 100% online, blended/hybrid learning. *Faculty:* 1 full-time (0 women), 15 part-time/adjunct (9 women). *Students:* 13 full-time (6 women), 96 part-time (65 women); includes 3 minority (2 Black or African American, non-Hispanic/Latino; 1 Hispanic/Latino). Average age 35. 22 applicants, 100% accepted, 16 enrolled. In 2017, 33 master's awarded. *Degree requirements:* For master's, comprehensive exam, thesis optional. *Entrance requirements:* For master's, GRE or MAT (if undergraduate GPA less than 3.0). Additional exam requirements/recommendations for international students: Required—TOEFL (minimum score 550 paper-based; 75 iBT), IELTS (minimum score 6.5), International Test of English proficiency (minimum score 4). *Application deadline:* Applications are processed on a rolling basis. Application fee: $30. Electronic applications accepted. *Financial support:* Applicants required to submit FAFSA. *Unit head:* Dr. Janette D. Kelly, Director, 814-472-3068, Fax: 814-472-3864, E-mail: jkelly@francis.edu. *Application contact:* Sherri L. Toth, Coordinator, 814-472-3058, Fax: 814-472-3864, E-mail: stoth@francis.edu. Website: http://www.francis.edu/master-of-education/

St. John Fisher College, Ralph C. Wilson Jr. School of Education, Program in Literacy Education, Rochester, NY 14618-3597. Offers literacy birth to grade 6 (MS); literacy grades 5 to 12 (MS). *Program availability:* Part-time, evening/weekend. *Faculty:* 3 full-time (all women), 2 part-time/adjunct (both women). *Students:* 1 (woman) full-time, 18 part-time (14 women). Average age 24. 9 applicants, 89% accepted, 2 enrolled. In 2017, 21 master's awarded. *Degree requirements:* For master's, capstone project, practicum. *Entrance requirements:* For master's, teacher certification, 2 letters of recommendation, personal statement, current resume. Additional exam requirements/recommendations for international students: Required—TOEFL (minimum score 575 paper-based; 80 iBT). *Application deadline:* Applications are processed on a rolling basis. Application fee: $30. Electronic applications accepted. *Expenses:* Contact institution. *Financial support:* Scholarships/grants available. Financial award applicants required to submit FAFSA. *Faculty research:* Adolescent use of new literacies (instant messaging), referral practices, at risk early literacy, new literacies (Internet, technology), equity in education. *Unit head:* Dr. Kathleen Broikou, Program Director, 585-385-8112, E-mail: kbroikou@sjfc.edu. *Application contact:* Michelle Gosier, Director of Transfer and Graduate Admissions, 585-385-8064, E-mail: mgosier@sjfc.edu. Website: https://www.sjfc.edu/graduate-programs/ms-in-literacy-education/

St. John's University, The School of Education, Department of Education Specialties, Program in Literacy, Queens, NY 11439. Offers literacy (PhD); literacy leadership (Adv C); teaching literacy (MS Ed, Adv C); teaching literacy (5-12) and TESOL (K-12) (MS Ed); teaching literacy (B-6) and teaching children with disabilities in childhood education (MS Ed); teaching literacy (B-6) and TESOL (K-12) (MS Ed). *Program availability:* Part-time, evening/weekend, 100% online. *Students:* 21 full-time (20 women), 66 part-time (59 women); includes 33 minority (12 Black or African American, non-Hispanic/Latino; 2 Asian, non-Hispanic/Latino; 16 Hispanic/Latino; 3 Two or more races, non-Hispanic/Latino). Average age 35. 63 applicants, 92% accepted, 52 enrolled. In 2017, 28 master's, 2 doctorates, 4 other advanced degrees awarded. *Degree requirements:* For master's, comprehensive exam, practicum completion of 50-hours of field work; for doctorate, comprehensive exam, thesis/dissertation. *Entrance requirements:* For doctorate, GRE, resume, statement of goals, official master's transcripts. *Application deadline:* For fall admission, 8/17 for domestic and international students; for summer admission, 5/15 for domestic and international students. Applications are processed on a rolling basis. Application fee: $70. Electronic applications accepted. *Expenses: Tuition:* Full-time $44,280; part-time $1230 per credit. *Required fees:* $340; $340 per credit. Tuition and fees vary according to course load, degree level and program. *Financial support:* Fellowships, research assistantships, scholarships/grants, and unspecified assistantships available. Support available to part-time students. Financial award application deadline: 2/1; financial award applicants required to submit FAFSA. *Faculty research:* Literacy and language; diversity; urban education; reading and writing; digital literacies. *Unit head:* Dr. John Spiridakis, Chair, 718-990-5591, E-mail: spiridaj@stjohns.edu. *Application contact:* Dr. John Spiridakis, Chair, 718-990-5591, E-mail: spiridaj@stjohns.edu. Website: https://www.stjohns.edu/academics/schools-and-colleges/school-education/programs-and-majors/literacy-doctor-philosophy

St. Joseph's College, Long Island Campus, Programs in Education, Field of Literacy and Cognition, Patchogue, NY 11772-2399. Offers literacy 5-12 (MA); literacy and cognition birth-6 (MA); literacy birth-12 (MA); literacy/cognition and special education (MA). *Program availability:* Part-time, evening/weekend. *Faculty:* 8 full-time (6 women), 7 part-time/adjunct (3 women). *Students:* 5 full-time (all women), 110 part-time (106 women); includes 10 minority (1 Black or African American, non-Hispanic/Latino; 1 American Indian or Alaska Native, non-Hispanic/Latino; 1 Asian, non-Hispanic/Latino; 5 Hispanic/Latino; 2 Two or more races, non-Hispanic/Latino). Average age 24. 71 applicants, 85% accepted, 54 enrolled. In 2017, 47 master's awarded. *Entrance requirements:* For master's, GRE, PRAXIS Core Academic Skills, or MAT, resume, two completed letter of reference forms, copies of certificates granted by the New York State Education Department, official transcripts. Additional exam requirements/ recommendations for international students: Recommended—TOEFL (minimum score 550 paper-based; 79 iBT), IELTS (minimum score 7). *Application deadline:* Applications are processed on a rolling basis. Application fee: $25. Electronic applications accepted. *Expenses: Tuition:* Full-time $17,550; part-time $975 per credit. *Required fees:* $362. *Financial support:* In 2017–18, 53 students received support. Federal Work-Study available. *Unit head:* Karen Megay-Nespoli, Associate Professor/Director of MA in Literacy and Cognition, 631-687-1212, E-mail: kmegay-nespoli@sjcny.edu.

St. Joseph's College, New York, Programs in Education, Field of Literacy and Cognition, Brooklyn, NY 11205-3688. Offers MA. *Program availability:* Part-time, evening/weekend. *Faculty:* 2 full-time (both women), 2 part-time/adjunct (both women). *Students:* 16 part-time (all women); includes 4 minority (all Hispanic/Latino). Average age 23. 10 applicants, 90% accepted, 7 enrolled. In 2017, 9 master's awarded. *Entrance requirements:* For master's, GRE, PRAXIS or MAT, official transcripts, two letters of recommendation, resume, copy of teaching certification. Additional exam requirements/ recommendations for international students: Required—TOEFL (minimum score 80 iBT). *Application deadline:* Applications are processed on a rolling basis. Application fee: $25. Electronic applications accepted. *Expenses: Tuition:* Full-time $17,550; part-time $975 per credit. *Required fees:* $362. *Financial support:* In 2017–18, 12 students received support. *Unit head:* Esther Berkowitz, Associate Professor/Director of the Literacy and Cognition Program, 718-940-5692, E-mail: eberkowitz@sjcny.edu. Website: http://www.sjcny.edu

Saint Joseph's University, College of Arts and Sciences, Graduate Programs in Education, Philadelphia, PA 19131-1395. Offers curriculum supervisor (Certificate); educational leadership (MS, Ed D); elementary education (MS, Certificate); elementary/ middle school education (Certificate); organizational development and leadership (MS); principal (Certificate); professional education (MS); reading specialist (MS, Certificate); reading supervisor (Certificate); secondary education (MS, Certificate); special education (MS); special education 7-12 (Certificate); special education PK-8 (Certificate); superintendent's letter of eligibility (Certificate); supervisor of special education (Certificate); teacher of the deaf and hard of hearing (Certificate). *Program availability:* Part-time, evening/weekend, blended/hybrid learning. *Faculty:* 18 full-time (16 women), 63 part-time/adjunct (44 women). *Students:* 79 full-time (60 women), 793 part-time (604 women); includes 179 minority (125 Black or African American, non-Hispanic/Latino; 5 American Indian or Alaska Native, non-Hispanic/Latino; 15 Asian, non-Hispanic/Latino; 27 Hispanic/Latino; 1 Native Hawaiian or other Pacific Islander, non-Hispanic/Latino; 6 Two or more races, non-Hispanic/Latino), 12 international. Average age 34. 375 applicants, 75% accepted, 189 enrolled. In 2017, 340 master's, 13 doctorates, 3 other advanced degrees awarded. *Degree requirements:* For master's, thesis or alternative; for doctorate, comprehensive exam, thesis/dissertation. *Entrance requirements:* For master's, 2 letters of recommendation, minimum GPA of 3.0, official transcripts, personal statement; for doctorate, GRE, master's degree from accredited institution, minimum graduate GPA of 3.5, computer competence, interview with program director. Additional exam requirements/recommendations for international students: Required—TOEFL (minimum score 550 paper-based; 80 iBT), IELTS (minimum score 6.5), PTE (minimum score 60). *Application deadline:* For fall admission, 7/15 for international students; for spring admission, 11/1 for international students. Applications are processed on a rolling basis. Application fee: $35. Electronic applications accepted. *Expenses:* Contact institution. *Financial support:* Scholarships/ grants and unspecified assistantships available. Financial award application deadline: 5/ 1; financial award applicants required to submit FAFSA. *Faculty research:* Factors predicting early mathematics skills for low income children, early child care and development, preschool quality, parent communication and home-school collaboration issues, education of terminally ill children, preparing literacy teachers for urban schools. *Unit head:* Dr. John Vacca, Associate Dean, Education, 610-660-3131, E-mail: gradcas@sju.edu. *Application contact:* Graduate Admissions, College of Arts and Sciences, 610-660-3131, E-mail: gradcas@sju.edu. Website: https://sites.sju.edu/education/graduate-programs/

Saint Leo University, Graduate Studies in Education, Saint Leo, FL 33574-6665. Offers educational leadership (M Ed), including Catholic school administration; exceptional student education (M Ed); instructional design (MS, Certificate); instructional leadership (M Ed); reading (M Ed, Certificate); school leadership (Ed S). *Program availability:* Part-time, evening/weekend, online only, 100% online. *Faculty:* 8 full-time (all women), 18 part-time/adjunct (11 women). *Students:* 1 (woman) full-time, 360 part-time (282 women); includes 95 minority (56 Black or African American, non-Hispanic/Latino; 1 American Indian or Alaska Native, non-Hispanic/Latino; 1 Asian, non-Hispanic/Latino; 31 Hispanic/Latino; 6 Two or more races, non-Hispanic/Latino), 1 international. Average age 37. 214 applicants, 69% accepted, 125 enrolled. In 2017, 158 master's, 5 other advanced degrees awarded. *Degree requirements:* For master's, appropriate State of Florida certification tests, internship. *Entrance requirements:* For master's, GRE (minimum score of 1000), MAT (minimum score of 410), or minimum undergraduate GPA of 3.0 in final 2 years, official transcripts, current resumé, 2 professional recommendations, personal statement, bachelor's degree from regionally-accredited university, valid professional teaching certificate; for other advanced degree, valid professional teaching certificate (for Ed S). Additional exam requirements/ recommendations for international students: Required—TOEFL (minimum score 550 paper-based; 78 iBT). *Application deadline:* For fall admission, 7/1 priority date for domestic students, 7/1 for international students; for winter admission, 7/1 for international students; for spring admission, 11/1 priority date for domestic students. Applications are processed on a rolling basis. Application fee: $80. Electronic applications accepted. *Expenses:* $480 per credit (for M Ed), $670 per credit (for Ed S). *Financial support:* In 2017–18, 17 students received support. Career-related internships or fieldwork, scholarships/grants, health care benefits, and tuition remission for Saint Leo employees and their dependents available. Financial award application deadline: 3/ 1; financial award applicants required to submit FAFSA. *Faculty research:* Impact of partnerships with K-12 school and university programs. *Unit head:* Dr. Fern Aefsky, Director of Graduate Studies in Education, 352-588-8309, Fax: 352-588-8861, E-mail: kara.winkler@saintleo.edu. *Application contact:* Mark Russum, Assistant Vice President, Enrollment, 800-707-8846, Fax: 352-588-7873, E-mail: grad.admissions@saintleo.edu. Website: https://www.saintleo.edu/education-master-degree

Saint Mary's University of Minnesota, Schools of Graduate and Professional Programs, Graduate School of Education, Literacy Education Program, Winona, MN 55987-1399. Offers K-12 reading teacher (Certificate); literacy education (MA). *Unit*

head: Cindy Kronebusch, Assistant Program Director, 507-457-6637, E-mail: ckronebu@smumn.edu. *Application contact:* James Callinan, Director of Admissions for Graduate and Professional Programs, 612-728-5158, Fax: 612-728-5121, E-mail: jcallina@smumn.edu.
Website: http://www.smumn.edu/graduate-home/areas-of-study/graduate-school-of-education/ma-in-literacy-education

Saint Michael's College, Graduate Programs, Program in Education, Colchester, VT 05439. Offers arts in education (CAGS); literacy (M Ed); school leadership (CAGS); special education (M Ed). *Program availability:* Part-time, evening/weekend. *Students:* 7 full-time (3 women), 204 part-time (173 women); includes 8 minority (1 Black or African American, non-Hispanic/Latino; 1 American Indian or Alaska Native, non-Hispanic/Latino; 3 Hispanic/Latino; 3 Two or more races, non-Hispanic/Latino). Average age 38. 23 applicants, 65% accepted, 10 enrolled. In 2017, 32 master's awarded. *Degree requirements:* For master's, thesis. *Entrance requirements:* For master's, minimum GPA of 3.0, official transcripts, essay, interview. *Application deadline:* Applications are processed on a rolling basis. Application fee: $50. Electronic applications accepted. *Expenses: Tuition:* Part-time $590 per credit. *Financial support:* Fellowships with partial tuition reimbursements and scholarships/grants available. Support available to part-time students. Financial award applicants required to submit FAFSA. *Faculty research:* Integrative curriculum, moral and spiritual dimensions of education, learning styles, multiple intelligences, integrating technology into the curriculum. *Unit head:* Jonathan Silverman, Department Chair, 802-654-2306, Fax: 802-654-2664, E-mail: jsilverman@smcvt.edu. *Application contact:* Lindsay A. Damici, Marketing Communications Manager, 802-654-2556, Fax: 802-654-2732.
Website: http://www.smcvt.edu/graduate-programs/academic-programs/education.aspx

Saint Peter's University, Graduate Programs in Education, Program in Special Education, Jersey City, NJ 07306-5997. Offers literacy (MA Ed). *Program availability:* Part-time, evening/weekend. *Degree requirements:* For master's, comprehensive exam. *Entrance requirements:* For master's, GRE or MAT. Additional exam requirements/recommendations for international students: Required—TOEFL. Electronic applications accepted.

Saint Peter's University, Graduate Programs in Education, Reading Program, Jersey City, NJ 07306-5997. Offers MA Ed. *Accreditation:* TEAC. *Program availability:* Part-time, evening/weekend. *Degree requirements:* For master's, comprehensive exam. *Entrance requirements:* For master's, GRE or MAT. Additional exam requirements/recommendations for international students: Required—TOEFL. Electronic applications accepted.

St. Thomas Aquinas College, Division of Teacher Education, Sparkill, NY 10976. Offers adolescence education (MST); childhood and special education (MST); childhood education (MST); educational leadership (MS Ed); reading (MS Ed, PMC); special education (MS Ed, PMC); teaching (MS Ed), including elementary education, middle school education, secondary education. *Accreditation:* NCATE. *Program availability:* Part-time, evening/weekend. *Degree requirements:* For master's, comprehensive exam, comprehensive professional portfolio; for PMC, action research project. *Entrance requirements:* For master's, New York State Qualifying Exam, GRE General Test or minimum GPA of 3.0, teaching certificate; for PMC, GRE General Test or minimum GPA of 3.0. Electronic applications accepted. *Faculty research:* Computer applications in education, adolescent special education students, literacy development, inclusive practices for special education students.

St. Thomas University, School of Leadership Studies, Institute for Education, Miami Gardens, FL 33054-6459. Offers earth/space science (Certificate); educational administration (MS, Certificate); educational leadership (Ed D); elementary education (MS); ESOL (Certificate); gifted education (Certificate); instructional technology (MS, Certificate); professional/studies (Certificate); reading (MS, Certificate); special education (MS). *Program availability:* Part-time, evening/weekend. *Degree requirements:* For master's, comprehensive exam; for doctorate, comprehensive exam, thesis/dissertation. *Entrance requirements:* For master's, interview, minimum GPA of 3.0 or GRE; for doctorate, GRE or MAT. Additional exam requirements/recommendations for international students: Required—TOEFL (minimum score 550 paper-based; 79 iBT). Electronic applications accepted.

Saint Xavier University, Graduate Studies, School of Education, Chicago, IL 60655-3105. Offers counseling (MA); curriculum and instruction (MA); early childhood education (MA); educational administration (MA); elementary education (MA); individualized studies (MA), including educational technology, English as a second language (ESL), ISTEM (integrative science, technology, engineering, and math), science education; music education (MA); reading (MA); secondary education (MA); Spanish education (MA); special education (MA); teaching and leadership (MA). *Accreditation:* NCATE. *Program availability:* Part-time, evening/weekend. *Degree requirements:* For master's, thesis or project. *Entrance requirements:* For master's, minimum GPA of 3.0. *Expenses:* Contact institution.

Salem College, Graduate Studies, Winston-Salem, NC 27101. Offers art education (MAT); elementary education (M Ed, MAT); language and literacy (M Ed); middle school education (MAT); organ (MM); piano (MM); school counseling (M Ed); second language studies (MAT); secondary education (MAT); special education (M Ed, MAT). *Accreditation:* NCATE. *Program availability:* Part-time, evening/weekend, online learning. *Faculty:* 8 full-time (all women), 11 part-time/adjunct (8 women). In 2017, 17 master's awarded. *Degree requirements:* For master's, practicum (MAT), action research project (M Ed). *Entrance requirements:* For master's, minimum GPA of 3.0, two academic/professional recommendations, acceptable criminal background check. Additional exam requirements/recommendations for international students: Recommended—TOEFL. *Application deadline:* For fall admission, 8/1 for domestic students, 7/15 for international students; for spring admission, 1/15 for domestic students; for summer admission, 5/1 for domestic students. Applications are processed on a rolling basis. Application fee: $30. Electronic applications accepted. *Expenses: Tuition:* Part-time $440 per semester hour. *Financial support:* Scholarships/grants available. Support available to part-time students. Financial award applicants required to submit FAFSA. *Faculty research:* Teacher professional development, adolescent literacy, instructional technology. *Application contact:* Sheryl Long, Director, 336-721-2658, Fax: 336-917-5384, E-mail: sheryl.long@salem.edu.
Website: http://www.salem.edu

Salem State University, School of Graduate Studies, Program in Reading, Salem, MA 01970-5353. Offers M Ed. *Accreditation:* NCATE. *Program availability:* Part-time, evening/weekend. *Entrance requirements:* For master's, GRE or MAT. Additional exam requirements/recommendations for international students: Required—TOEFL (minimum score 550 paper-based; 80 iBT) or IELTS (minimum score 5.5).

Salisbury University, Program in Contemporary Curriculum Theory and Instruction: Literacy, Salisbury, MD 21801-6837. Offers Ed D. *Program availability:* Part-time. *Faculty:* 4 full-time (2 women). *Students:* 22 full-time (17 women), 18 part-time (17 women); includes 2 minority (1 Black or African American, non-Hispanic/Latino; 1 Two or more races, non-Hispanic/Latino). Average age 39. 14 applicants, 86% accepted, 12 enrolled. *Degree requirements:* For doctorate, comprehensive exam, thesis/dissertation. *Entrance requirements:* For doctorate, three letters of recommendation; transcripts from

all colleges and universities attended; written statement; writing sample. Additional exam requirements/recommendations for international students: Required—TOEFL (minimum score 550 paper-based; 79 iBT), IELTS (minimum score 6.5). *Application deadline:* For fall admission, 3/31 priority date for domestic and international students. Applications are processed on a rolling basis. Application fee: $65. Electronic applications accepted. *Expenses:* $540 per credit hour resident; $940 per credit hour non-resident; $92 per credit hour fees. *Financial support:* In 2017–18, 4 students received support, including 2 teaching assistantships with full tuition reimbursements available (averaging $10,000 per year); career-related internships or fieldwork and scholarships/grants also available. Support available to part-time students. Financial award application deadline: 3/1; financial award applicants required to submit FAFSA. *Faculty research:* Education policy; research in reading; eye movement miscue analysis; writing pedagogy; English education. *Unit head:* Dr. Judith Franzak, Graduate Program Director, 410-677-0238, E-mail: jkfranzak@salisbury.edu. *Application contact:* Stefani Hoffman, Administrative Assistant II, 410-677-0236, E-mail: slhoffman@salisbury.edu.
Website: http://www.salisbury.edu/gsr/gradstudies/EDDpage.html

Salisbury University, Program in Reading Specialist, Salisbury, MD 21801-6837. Offers M Ed. *Program availability:* Part-time, evening/weekend. *Faculty:* 2 full-time (both women), 1 (woman) part-time/adjunct. *Students:* 1 (woman) full-time, 23 part-time (21 women); includes 2 minority (both Asian, non-Hispanic/Latino). Average age 31. 8 applicants, 63% accepted, 5 enrolled. In 2017, 8 master's awarded. *Entrance requirements:* For master's, two letters of recommendation; transcripts from colleges and universities attended; personal statement; minimum GPA of 3.0; resume; current teaching certificate. Additional exam requirements/recommendations for international students: Required—TOEFL (minimum score 550 paper-based; 79 iBT), IELTS (minimum score 6.5). *Application deadline:* For fall admission, 3/1 priority date for domestic and international students; for spring admission, 10/1 priority date for domestic and international students; for summer admission, 3/1 priority date for domestic and international students. Applications are processed on a rolling basis. Application fee: $65. Electronic applications accepted. *Expenses:* $392 per credit hour resident; $703 per credit hour non-resident; $92 per credit hour fees. *Financial support:* In 2017–18, 6 students received support, including 1 teaching assistantship with full tuition reimbursement available (averaging $9,000 per year); career-related internships or fieldwork and scholarships/grants also available. Support available to part-time students. Financial award application deadline: 3/1; financial award applicants required to submit FAFSA. *Faculty research:* Literacy intervention; literacy assessment; emergent literacy; diversity and literacy; literacy achievement gap. *Unit head:* Dr. Joyce Wiencek, Graduate Program Director, Reading Specialist, 410-543-6288, E-mail: bjwiencek@salisbury.edu.
Website: http://www.salisbury.edu/gsr/gradstudies/MEDpage.html

Sam Houston State University, College of Education, Department of Language, Literacy, and Special Populations, Huntsville, TX 77341. Offers international literacy (M Ed); reading (M Ed); special education (M Ed, MA), including low incidence disabilities and autism. *Program availability:* Part-time, evening/weekend, online learning. *Degree requirements:* For master's, comprehensive exam (for some programs), thesis optional, comprehensive portfolio; for doctorate, comprehensive exam, thesis/dissertation. *Entrance requirements:* For master's, GRE General Test, MAT, writing sample, recommendations; for doctorate, GRE General Test, MAT, master's degree, personal statement, recommendations. Additional exam requirements/recommendations for international students: Required—TOEFL (minimum score 550 paper-based; 79 iBT), IELTS (minimum score 6.5). Electronic applications accepted.

San Diego State University, Graduate and Research Affairs, College of Education, School of Teacher Education, Program in Reading Education, San Diego, CA 92182. Offers MA. *Accreditation:* NCATE. *Program availability:* Part-time. *Entrance requirements:* For master's, GRE General Test, letters of reference. Additional exam requirements/recommendations for international students: Required—TOEFL. Electronic applications accepted. *Faculty research:* Literacy, writing, reading/writing connection, class size reduction in reading, book clubs, evaluation instruments in reading/language arts.

San Francisco State University, Division of Graduate Studies, College of Education, Department of Elementary Education, Program in Language and Literacy Education, San Francisco, CA 94132-1722. Offers language and literacy education (MA); reading (Certificate); reading and literacy leadership (Credential). *Unit head:* Dr. Josephine Arce, Chair, 415-338-7636, Fax: 415-338-0567, E-mail: jarce@sfsu.edu. *Application contact:* Dr. Ali Borjian, MA Program Coordinator, 415-338-1838, Fax: 415-338-0567, E-mail: borjian@sfsu.edu.
Website: https://eed.sfsu.edu/

San Francisco State University, Division of Graduate Studies, College of Liberal and Creative Arts, Department of English Language and Literature, San Francisco, CA 94132-1722. Offers composition (MA, Certificate); immigrant literacies (Certificate); linguistics (MA); literature (MA); teaching English to speakers of other languages (MA); teaching post-secondary reading (Certificate). *Program availability:* Part-time. *Application deadline:* Applications are processed on a rolling basis. *Unit head:* Dr. Sugie Goen-Salter, Chair, 415-338-7582, Fax: 415-338-6159, E-mail: sgoen@sfsu.edu. *Application contact:* Cynthia Losinsky, Graduate Programs Coordinator, 415-338-2660, Fax: 415-338-6159, E-mail: cynthia@sfsu.edu.
Website: http://english.sfsu.edu/

Seattle Pacific University, Master of Education in Literacy Program, Seattle, WA 98119-1997. Offers M Ed. *Program availability:* Part-time. *Students:* 17 part-time (all women); includes 2 minority (1 Asian, non-Hispanic/Latino; 1 Hispanic/Latino). Average age 28. 9 applicants, 100% accepted, 7 enrolled. In 2017, 5 master's awarded. *Degree requirements:* For master's, comprehensive exam. *Entrance requirements:* For master's, MAT or GRE (unless minimum undergraduate GPA of 3.4 or master's degree from accredited university), copy of teaching certificate, official transcript(s) from each college/university attended, personal statement (1-2 pages), two letters of recommendation, moral and character fitness policy form, resume. *Application deadline:* For fall admission, 8/15 for domestic students; for winter admission, 11/15 for domestic students; for spring admission, 2/15 for domestic students; for summer admission, 5/15 for domestic students. Applications are processed on a rolling basis. Application fee: $50. Electronic applications accepted. *Financial support:* Scholarships/grants available. Financial award applicants required to submit FAFSA. *Unit head:* Dr. Scott F. Beers, Chair, 206-281-2707, E-mail: sbeers@spu.edu. *Application contact:* The Graduate Center, 206-281-2091.
Website: http://spu.edu/academics/school-of-education/graduate-programs/masters-programs/literacy

Shenandoah University, School of Education and Leadership, Winchester, VA 22601. Offers administration and supervision (Certificate); administrative leadership (D Ed); early childhood literacy (MS); educational administration (MSE); elementary school teacher education (Certificate); emphasis in teaching (MSE); health and physical education (Certificate); individualized focus (MS, MSE); literacy education (MS); middle school teacher education (Certificate); organizational leadership (MS, D Prof); reading licensure (MS, Certificate); reading non-licensure (MS); secondary school teacher education (Certificate); special education (MSE); writing (MS). *Accreditation:* TEAC. *Program availability:* Part-time, evening/weekend. *Faculty:* 8 full-time (7 women), 22

Reading Education

part-time/adjunct (16 women). *Students:* 16 full-time (14 women), 221 part-time (167 women); includes 32 minority (17 Black or African American, non-Hispanic/Latino; 1 American Indian or Alaska Native, non-Hispanic/Latino; 6 Asian, non-Hispanic/Latino; 5 Hispanic/Latino; 1 Native Hawaiian or other Pacific Islander, non-Hispanic/Latino; 2 Two or more races, non-Hispanic/Latino), 3 international. Average age 38. 81 applicants, 99% accepted, 63 enrolled. In 2017, 53 master's, 11 doctorates, 49 other advanced degrees awarded. *Degree requirements:* For master's, comprehensive exam (for some programs), thesis (for some programs); for doctorate, comprehensive exam, thesis/dissertation. *Entrance requirements:* For degree, PRAXIS Academic Core, SAT/ACT, PRAXIS Academic Core Math, or VCLA, three letters of recommendation, writing sample, undergraduate degree. Additional exam requirements/recommendations for international students: Required—TOEFL (minimum score 550 paper-based, 79 iBT) or IELTS (6.5). *Application deadline:* For fall admission, 5/1 priority date for domestic students, 5/1 for international students; for spring admission, 10/15 priority date for domestic students, 10/15 for international students; for summer admission, 3/15 priority date for domestic students, 3/15 for international students. Application fee: $30. Electronic applications accepted. *Expenses:* $15,600 tuition plus $1,296 fees (technology and student services). *Financial support:* In 2017–18, 26 students received support. Scholarships/grants and unspecified assistantships available. Financial award applicants required to submit FAFSA. *Faculty research:* Mentoring, behavior support for students, teacher change agency, educational technology in pedagogy, literacy education. *Unit head:* Jill Lindsey, PhD, Director, 540-535-7324, Fax: 540-665-4726, E-mail: jlindsey@su.edu. *Application contact:* Andrew Woodall, Executive Director of Recruitment and Admissions, 540-665-4581, Fax: 540-665-4627, E-mail: admit@su.edu.
Website: http://www.su.edu/education/

Shippensburg University of Pennsylvania, School of Graduate Studies, College of Education and Human Services, Department of Teacher Education, Shippensburg, PA 17257-2299. Offers curriculum and instruction (M Ed), including biology, early childhood education, elementary education, geography/earth science, history, mathematics, middle school education, modern languages; reading (M Ed). *Accreditation:* NCATE. *Program availability:* Part-time, evening/weekend, 100% online, blended/hybrid learning. *Faculty:* 13 full-time (8 women), 1 (woman) part-time/adjunct. *Students:* 10 full-time (7 women), 94 part-time (81 women); includes 10 minority (3 Black or African American, non-Hispanic/Latino; 2 Asian, non-Hispanic/Latino; 5 Hispanic/Latino), 1 international. Average age 34. 71 applicants, 86% accepted, 35 enrolled. In 2017, 23 master's awarded. *Degree requirements:* For master's, comprehensive exam (for some programs), thesis optional, practicum or internship; capstone seminar (for some programs). *Entrance requirements:* For master's, MAT or GRE (if GPA less than 2.75), interview, 3 letters of reference, questionnaire of teaching background and future goals, resume. Additional exam requirements/recommendations for international students: Required—TOEFL (minimum score 550 paper-based, 68 iBT) or IELTS (minimum score 6). *Application deadline:* For fall admission, 4/1 priority date for domestic students, 4/30 for international students; for spring admission, 9/1 priority date for domestic students, 9/30 for international students; for summer admission, 2/1 priority date for domestic students. Applications are processed on a rolling basis. Application fee: $45. Electronic applications accepted. *Expenses:* Tuition, state resident: part-time $500 per credit. Tuition, nonresident: part-time $750 per credit. *Required fees:* $145 per credit. *Financial support:* In 2017–18, 1 student received support. Career-related internships or fieldwork, scholarships/grants, unspecified assistantships, and resident hall director and student payroll positions available. Support available to part-time students. Financial award application deadline: 3/1; financial award applicants required to submit FAFSA. *Unit head:* Dr. Christine A. Royce, Chairperson, 717-477-1688, Fax: 717-477-4046, E-mail: caroyc@ship.edu. *Application contact:* Maya T. Mapp, Director of Admissions, 717-477-1231, Fax: 717-477-4016, E-mail: mtmapp@ship.edu.
Website: http://www.ship.edu/teacher/

Siena Heights University, Graduate College, Adrian, MI 49221-1796. Offers clinical mental health counseling (MA); educational leadership (Specialist); leadership (MA), including health care leadership, organizational leadership; teacher education (MA), including early childhood education, early childhood education: Montessori, education leadership: principal, elementary education: reading K-12, leadership: higher education, secondary education: reading K-12, special education: cognitive impairment, special education: learning disabilities. *Program availability:* Part-time, evening/weekend. *Degree requirements:* For master's, thesis, presentation. *Entrance requirements:* For master's, minimum GPA of 3.0, current resume, essay, all post-secondary transcripts, 3 letters of reference, conviction disclosure form; copy of teaching certificate (for some education programs); for Specialist, master's degree, minimum GPA of 3.0, current resume, essay, all post-secondary transcripts, 3 letters of reference, conviction disclosure form; copy of teaching certificate (for some education programs). Electronic applications accepted.

Simmons College, School of Library and Information Science, Boston, MA 02115. Offers children's literature (MA); library and information science (MS, PhD, Certificate), including archives management (MS), cultural heritage (MS), information science and technology (MS), school library teacher (MS); writing for children (MFA); MA/MA; MA/MAT; MA/MFA; MS/MA. *Accreditation:* ALA (one or more programs are accredited). *Program availability:* Part-time, evening/weekend, 100% online, blended/hybrid learning. *Faculty:* 28 full-time (21 women), 34 part-time/adjunct (25 women). *Students:* 339 full-time (287 women), 509 part-time (415 women); includes 91 minority (15 Black or African American, non-Hispanic/Latino; 18 Asian, non-Hispanic/Latino; 35 Hispanic/Latino; 23 Two or more races, non-Hispanic/Latino), 12 international. Average age 30. 533 applicants, 98% accepted, 268 enrolled. In 2017, 300 master's, 10 doctorates, 5 other advanced degrees awarded. *Degree requirements:* For master's, thesis optional, capstone project experience; for doctorate, comprehensive exam, thesis/dissertation, 36 credit hours. *Entrance requirements:* For master's, GRE when applicants' GPA is below 3.0 for all degrees, statement of purpose, current resume or curriculum vitae, college transcripts, three letters of recommendation; for doctorate, GRE or MTEL, transcripts, personal statement, resume, recommendations, master's degree. Additional exam requirements/recommendations for international students: Required—TOEFL (minimum score 550 paper-based; 79 iBT), IELTS (minimum score 7). *Application deadline:* For fall admission, 3/1 for domestic and international students; for spring admission, 9/1 for domestic and international students; for summer admission, 2/1 for domestic and international students. Applications are processed on a rolling basis. Application fee: $65. Electronic applications accepted. *Expenses:* $1,135 per credit, $3,405 per course, $55 activity fee per semester. *Financial support:* In 2017–18, 10 fellowships with partial tuition reimbursements were awarded; scholarships/grants and unspecified assistantships also available. Support available to part-time students. Financial award application deadline: 6/1; financial award applicants required to submit FAFSA. *Faculty research:* Archives and social justice, information-seeking behavior, information retrieval, organization of information, cultural heritage informatics. *Unit head:* Dr. Eileen G. Abels, Dean, 617-521-2869. *Application contact:* Kate Benson, Director, SLIS Admission, 617-521-2801, Fax: 617-521-3192, E-mail: slisadm@simmons.edu.
Website: http://www.simmons.edu/slis/

Simon Fraser University, Office of Graduate Studies and Postdoctoral Fellows, Faculty of Education, Program in Languages, Cultures, and Literacies, Burnaby, BC V5A 1S6, Canada. Offers PhD.

Slippery Rock University of Pennsylvania, Graduate Studies (Recruitment), College of Education, Department of Elementary Education and Early Childhood, Slippery Rock, PA 16057-1383. Offers instructional coach (M Ed); K-12 reading (M Ed); K-12 science and math (M Ed); reading specialist (M Ed). *Accreditation:* NCATE. *Program availability:* Part-time, evening/weekend, online only, 100% online. *Degree requirements:* For master's, comprehensive exam (for some programs), thesis optional. *Entrance requirements:* For master's, minimum GPA of 3.0, resume, teaching certification, transcripts, letters of recommendation (depending on program). Additional exam requirements/recommendations for international students: Required—TOEFL (minimum score 550 paper-based; 80 iBT). Electronic applications accepted. *Expenses:* Contact institution.

Sonoma State University, School of Education, Rohnert Park, CA 94928. Offers administrative services (Credential); curriculum, teaching, and learning (MA); early childhood education (MA); education specialist (Credential); educational leadership (MA); multiple subject (Credential); reading and literacy (MA, Credential); single subject (Credential); special education (MA). *Accreditation:* NCATE. *Program availability:* Part-time, evening/weekend. *Entrance requirements:* For master's, minimum GPA of 2.5. Additional exam requirements/recommendations for international students: Required—TOEFL (minimum score 500 paper-based). Application fee: $55. *Financial support:* Fellowships, research assistantships, career-related internships or fieldwork, and Federal Work-Study available. Support available to part-time students. Financial award application deadline: 3/2; financial award applicants required to submit FAFSA. *Unit head:* Dr. Carlos Ayala, Dean, 707-664-4412, E-mail: carlos.ayala@sonoma.edu. *Application contact:* Dr. Karen Grady, Coordinator of Graduate Studies, 707-664-3328, E-mail: karen.grady@sonoma.edu.
Website: http://www.sonoma.edu/education/

Southeastern Louisiana University, College of Arts, Humanities and Social Sciences, Department of English, Hammond, LA 70402. Offers creative writing (MA); language and theory (MA); professional writing (MA); publishing studies (MA). *Program availability:* Part-time. *Faculty:* 10 full-time (2 women). *Students:* 11 full-time (9 women), 11 part-time (10 women); includes 5 minority (2 Black or African American, non-Hispanic/Latino; 2 Hispanic/Latino; 1 Two or more races, non-Hispanic/Latino). Average age 25. 8 applicants, 38% accepted, 3 enrolled. In 2017, 8 master's awarded. *Degree requirements:* For master's, comprehensive exam, thesis optional. *Entrance requirements:* For master's, GRE (minimum score of 290 combined verbal and quantitative). Additional exam requirements/recommendations for international students: Required—TOEFL (minimum score 500 paper-based; 61 iBT), IELTS (minimum score 5.5). *Application deadline:* For fall admission, 7/15 priority date for domestic students, 6/1 priority date for international students; for spring admission, 12/1 priority date for domestic students, 10/1 priority date for international students. Applications are processed on a rolling basis. Application fee: $20 ($30 for international students). Electronic applications accepted. *Expenses:* Tuition, state resident: full-time $6684. Tuition, nonresident: full-time $19,162. *Required fees:* $2088. *Financial support:* In 2017–18, 16 students received support, including 7 teaching assistantships (averaging $5,415 per year); research assistantships, institutionally sponsored loans, scholarships/grants, and unspecified assistantships also available. Support available to part-time students. Financial award application deadline: 5/1; financial award applicants required to submit FAFSA. *Faculty research:* John Ruskin, animal studies, linguistics, film studies. *Unit head:* Dr. David Hanson, Department Head, 985-549-2100, Fax: 985-549-5021, E-mail: dhanson@southeastern.edu. *Application contact:* Amanda Harper, Graduate Admissions Analyst, 985-549-5620, Fax: 985-549-5632, E-mail: admissions@southeastern.edu.
Website: http://www.southeastern.edu/acad_research/depts/engl

Southeastern Oklahoma State University, School of Education, Durant, OK 74701-0609. Offers math specialist (M Ed); reading specialist (M Ed); school administration (M Ed); school counseling (M Ed). *Accreditation:* NCATE. *Program availability:* Part-time, evening/weekend. *Degree requirements:* For master's, comprehensive exam, thesis optional, portfolio (M Ed). *Entrance requirements:* For master's, GRE General Test (for school counseling), minimum GPA of 3.0 in last 60 hours or 2.75 overall. Additional exam requirements/recommendations for international students: Required—TOEFL (minimum score 550 paper-based; 79 iBT). Electronic applications accepted.

Southeastern University, College of Education, Lakeland, FL 33801-6099. Offers curriculum and instruction (Ed D); educational leadership (M Ed); elementary education (M Ed); exceptional student education (M Ed); exceptional student education/educational therapy (M Ed); kinesiology (M Ed); organizational leadership (Ed D); reading education (M Ed); teaching English to speakers of other languages (M Ed). *Faculty:* 8 full-time (5 women), 12 part-time/adjunct (7 women). *Students:* 139 full-time (109 women), 225 part-time (172 women); includes 107 minority (57 Black or African American, non-Hispanic/Latino; 2 Asian, non-Hispanic/Latino; 48 Hispanic/Latino), 4 international. Average age 40. Application fee: $50. Electronic applications accepted. *Unit head:* James A. Anderson, Dean, 863-667-5366, E-mail: jaanderson2@seu.edu.
Website: http://www.seu.edu/education/

Southern Adventist University, School of Education and Psychology, Collegedale, TN 37315-0370. Offers clinical mental health counseling (MS); instructional leadership (MS Ed); literacy education (MS Ed); outdoor education (MS Ed); professional school counseling (MS). *Accreditation:* NCATE. *Program availability:* Part-time, evening/weekend. *Degree requirements:* For master's, comprehensive exam (for some programs), thesis optional, position paper (MS), portfolio (MS Ed in outdoor education). *Entrance requirements:* For master's, interview (MS); 9 semester hours of upper-division course work in psychology or related field, including 1 course in psychology research or statistics; 9 semester hours of education (MS Ed). Additional exam requirements/recommendations for international students: Required—TOEFL (minimum score 600 paper-based; 100 iBT). *Application deadline:* For fall admission, 7/1 priority date for domestic students, 6/1 priority date for international students; for winter admission, 11/1 priority date for domestic students, 10/1 priority date for international students; for spring admission, 4/1 priority date for domestic students, 3/1 priority date for international students. Applications are processed on a rolling basis. Application fee: $40. Electronic applications accepted. *Expenses:* Tuition: Full-time $11,430; part-time $635 per credit hour. Tuition and fees vary according to degree level and program. *Financial support:* Research assistantships with full tuition reimbursements, teaching assistantships with full tuition reimbursements, career-related internships or fieldwork, scholarships/grants, tuition waivers (partial), and unspecified assistantships available. Support available to part-time students. Financial award application deadline: 4/1; financial award applicants required to submit FAFSA. *Unit head:* Bonnie Eder, Interim Dean, 423-236-2759, Fax: 423-236-1765, E-mail: beder@southern.edu. *Application contact:* Mikhaile Spence, Graduate Enrollment Counselor, 423-236-2496, Fax: 423-236-1765, E-mail: maspence@southern.edu.
Website: https://www.southern.edu/academics/edpsych.html

Southern Connecticut State University, School of Graduate Studies, School of Education, Program in Reading, New Haven, CT 06515-1355. Offers MS, Diploma. *Program availability:* Part-time, evening/weekend. *Degree requirements:* For master's, thesis or alternative. *Entrance requirements:* For master's, interview, teaching certificate; for Diploma, master's degree. Electronic applications accepted.

Southern Illinois University Edwardsville, Graduate School, School of Education, Health, and Human Behavior, Department of Curriculum and Instruction, Program in Literacy Education, Edwardsville, IL 62026. Offers MS Ed. *Program availability:* Part-time, evening/weekend. *Degree requirements:* For master's, comprehensive exam, research paper. *Entrance requirements:* Additional exam requirements/recommendations for international students: Required—TOEFL (minimum score 550 paper-based; 79 iBT), IELTS (minimum score 6.5). Electronic applications accepted.

Southern Illinois University Edwardsville, Graduate School, School of Education, Health, and Human Behavior, Department of Curriculum and Instruction, Program in Literacy Specialist, Edwardsville, IL 62026. Offers Post-Master's Certificate. *Program availability:* Part-time. *Entrance requirements:* Additional exam requirements/recommendations for international students: Required—TOEFL (minimum score 550 paper-based; 79 iBT), IELTS (minimum score 6.5). Electronic applications accepted.

Southern Methodist University, Annette Caldwell Simmons School of Education and Human Development, Department of Teaching and Learning, Dallas, TX 75275. Offers bilingual/ESL education (MBE); education (M Ed, PhD); gifted education (MBE); reading and writing (M Ed); special education (MBE). *Program availability:* Part-time, evening/weekend. Terminal master's awarded for partial completion of doctoral program. *Degree requirements:* For master's, comprehensive exam, minimum GPA of 3.0; for doctorate, thesis/dissertation, qualifying exams, major area paper, evidence of teaching competency, dissemination of research (e.g., conference presentation), professional portfolio. *Entrance requirements:* For master's, minimum GPA of 3.0 or GRE, 3 letters of recommendation; for doctorate, GRE, minimum GPA of 3.3, 3 years of full-time teaching, 3 letters of recommendation, interview. Additional exam requirements/recommendations for international students: Required—TOEFL. Electronic applications accepted. *Faculty research:* Reading intervention, mathematics intervention, bilingual education, new literacies.

Southern New Hampshire University, School of Education, Manchester, NH 03106-1045. Offers curriculum and instruction (M Ed), including dyslexia studies and language-based learning disabilities, educational leadership, reading, special education, technology integration; dyslexia studies and language-based learning disabilities (Certificate); early childhood and special education (M Ed); educational leadership (M Ed, Ed D); educational studies (M Ed); elementary and special education (M Ed); field based education (M Ed); higher education administration (MS); teaching English as a foreign language (MS). *Program availability:* Part-time, evening/weekend, online learning. *Degree requirements:* For master's, comprehensive exam (for some programs), thesis or alternative. *Entrance requirements:* For master's, PRAXIS I, minimum GPA of 2.75. Additional exam requirements/recommendations for international students: Required—TOEFL (minimum score 550 paper-based). *Application deadline:* Applications are processed on a rolling basis. Application fee: $40. Electronic applications accepted. *Expenses:* Contact institution. *Financial support:* Institutionally sponsored loans available. Financial award applicants required to submit FAFSA. *Unit head:* Raymond McNulty, Dean, 603-668-2211, Fax: 603-629-4673. *Application contact:* Office of Graduate Admission, 888-327-SNHU, Fax: 603-644-3144, E-mail: enroll@snhu.edu.

Southern Oregon University, Graduate Studies, School of Education, Ashland, OR 97520. Offers elementary education (MA Ed, MS Ed), including classroom teacher, early childhood, handicapped learner, reading, supervision; secondary education (MA Ed, MS Ed), including classroom teacher, handicapped learner, reading, supervision; teaching (MAT). *Program availability:* Online learning. *Degree requirements:* For master's, thesis optional. *Entrance requirements:* For master's, GRE General Test, minimum cumulative GPA of 3.0 in the last 90 quarter credits (60 semester credits) of undergraduate coursework. Additional exam requirements/recommendations for international students: Required—TOEFL (minimum score 540 paper-based; 76 iBT), IELTS (minimum score 6), ELPT (minimum score 964) or ELS (minimum score 112). Electronic applications accepted.

Southwestern Adventist University, Education Department, Keene, TX 76059. Offers curriculum and instruction with reading emphasis (M Ed); educational leadership (M Ed). *Program availability:* Part-time, evening/weekend. *Degree requirements:* For master's, thesis or alternative, professional paper. *Entrance requirements:* For master's, GRE General Test.

Southwest Minnesota State University, Department of Education, Marshall, MN 56258. Offers ESL (MS); math (MS); reading (MS); special education (MS), including developmental disabilities, early childhood education, emotional behavioral disorders, learning disabilities; teaching, learning and leadership (MS). *Program availability:* Part-time, evening/weekend, online learning. *Entrance requirements:* Additional exam requirements/recommendations for international students: Required—TOEFL or IELTS; Recommended—TOEFL (minimum score 550 paper-based; 80 iBT), IELTS.

Spring Arbor University, School of Education, Spring Arbor, MI 49283-9799. Offers education (MAE); reading (MAR); special education (MSE). *Accreditation:* TEAC. *Program availability:* Part-time, evening/weekend, online learning. *Degree requirements:* For master's, thesis. *Entrance requirements:* For master's, official transcripts from all institutions attended, including evidence of an earned bachelor's degree from regionally-accredited college or university with minimum cumulative GPA of 3.0 for the last two years of the bachelor's degree; two professional letters of recommendation. Additional exam requirements/recommendations for international students: Required—TOEFL (minimum score 600 paper-based). Electronic applications accepted.

State University of New York at Fredonia, College of Education, Fredonia, NY 14063-1136. Offers curriculum and instruction (MS Ed); literacy education (MS Ed), including birth-grade 12, grades 5-12; TESOL (MS Ed). *Accreditation:* NCATE. *Program availability:* Part-time. *Faculty:* 11 full-time (9 women), 1 part-time/adjunct (0 women). *Students:* Average age 29. 60 applicants, 97% accepted, 39 enrolled. In 2017, 33 master's awarded. *Degree requirements:* For master's, thesis. *Entrance requirements:* For master's, GRE, minimum undergraduate GPA of 3.0. Additional exam requirements/recommendations for international students: Required—TOEFL (minimum score 79 iBT), IELTS (minimum score 6.5). *Application deadline:* For fall admission, 4/1 priority date for domestic and international students; for spring admission, 11/1 priority date for domestic students, 11/1 for international students. Applications are processed on a rolling basis. Application fee: $75. Electronic applications accepted. *Expenses:* Tuition, state resident: full-time $8154. Tuition, nonresident: full-time $16,650. *Required fees:* $1209. *Financial support:* In 2017–18, 4 teaching assistantships with full and partial tuition reimbursements (averaging $7,075 per year) were awarded. Financial award application deadline: 3/15; financial award applicants required to submit FAFSA. *Faculty research:* Positive behavioral intervention and support (PBIS), place-based science education, peer support for education, primary source material for social studies education, policies and practices in learning English language. *Unit head:* Dr. Christine Givner, Dean, 716-673-3311, E-mail: christine.givner@fredonia.edu. *Application contact:* Wendy S. Dunst, Interim Graduate Recruitment and Admissions Associate, 716-673-3808, Fax: 716-673-3712, E-mail: wendy.dunst@fredonia.edu. Website: http://www.fredonia.edu/coe/

State University of New York at New Paltz, Graduate and Extended Learning School, School of Education, Department of Educational Studies and Leadership, Program in Special Education, New Paltz, NY 12561. Offers adolescence special education (7-12) (MS Ed); adolescence special education and literacy (MS Ed); childhood special education (1-6) (MS Ed); childhood special education and literacy (MS Ed); early childhood special education (B-2) (MS Ed). *Accreditation:* NCATE. *Program availability:* Part-time, evening/weekend. *Faculty:* 5 full-time (all women). *Students:* 11 full-time (7 women), 37 part-time (31 women); includes 4 minority (1 Asian, non-Hispanic/Latino; 3 Hispanic/Latino). 29 applicants, 93% accepted, 24 enrolled. In 2017, 28 master's awarded. *Entrance requirements:* For master's, minimum GPA of 3.0 (3.2 for special education and literacy programs), New York state teaching certificate. Additional exam requirements/recommendations for international students: Required—TOEFL (minimum score 550 paper-based; 80 iBT), IELTS (minimum score 6.5). *Application deadline:* For fall admission, 3/15 priority date for domestic students, 3/15 for international students; for spring admission, 11/1 for domestic and international students. Application fee: $50. Electronic applications accepted. *Financial support:* Application deadline: 8/1. *Unit head:* Dr. Jane Sileo, Coordinator, 845-257-2835, E-mail: sileoj@newpaltz.edu. *Application contact:* Vika Shock, Director of Graduate Admissions, 845-257-3286, E-mail: gradschool@newpaltz.edu. Website: http://www.newpaltz.edu/schoolofed/department-of-teaching—learning/special_ed.html

State University of New York at Oswego, Graduate Studies, School of Education, Department of Curriculum and Instruction, Oswego, NY 13126. Offers adolescence education (MST); art education (MAT); childhood education (MST); curriculum and instruction (MS Ed); literacy education (MS Ed); special education (MS Ed). *Program availability:* Part-time, evening/weekend. *Degree requirements:* For master's, comprehensive exam (for some programs), thesis optional. *Entrance requirements:* For master's, GRE General Test, minimum GPA of 2.7, provisional teaching certificate. Additional exam requirements/recommendations for international students: Required—TOEFL (minimum score 560 paper-based). *Faculty research:* Classroom applications for microcomputers; classroom questioning, wait-time, and achievement; values clarification and academic achievement.

State University of New York at Plattsburgh, School of Education, Health, and Human Services, Program in Teacher Education: Literacy Education, Plattsburgh, NY 12901-2681. Offers birth-grade 6 (MS Ed); grades 5-12 (MS Ed). *Accreditation:* TEAC. *Program availability:* Part-time, evening/weekend. *Entrance requirements:* For master's, minimum GPA of 2.75. Additional exam requirements/recommendations for international students: Required—TOEFL. *Faculty research:* Reading pedagogy, early childhood literacy, children's literature, integrated language arts.

State University of New York College at Cortland, Graduate Studies, School of Education, Program in Literacy Education, Cortland, NY 13045. Offers MS Ed. *Accreditation:* NCATE. *Program availability:* Part-time, evening/weekend. *Degree requirements:* For master's, one foreign language, comprehensive exam, thesis (for some programs). *Entrance requirements:* Additional exam requirements/recommendations for international students: Required—TOEFL.

State University of New York College at Geneseo, Graduate Studies, School of Education, Program in Reading and Literacy, Geneseo, NY 14454-1401. Offers reading and literacy B-12 (MS Ed). *Program availability:* Part-time. *Faculty:* 6 full-time (5 women), 1 (woman) part-time/adjunct. *Students:* 24 full-time (22 women), 30 part-time (24 women); includes 3 minority (1 Asian, non-Hispanic/Latino; 2 Hispanic/Latino). Average age 25. 36 applicants, 97% accepted, 35 enrolled. In 2017, 49 master's awarded. *Degree requirements:* For master's, thesis optional, two reading clinics (practicum), action research project. *Entrance requirements:* For master's, GRE, MAT, EAS, edTPA, PRAXIS, or another substantially equivalent test, proof of New York State initial certification or equivalent certification from another state. Additional exam requirements/recommendations for international students: Required—TOEFL (minimum score 525 paper-based; 71 iBT), IELTS (minimum score 6.5), PTE, iTEP. *Application deadline:* For fall admission, 4/1 priority date for domestic students; for spring admission, 11/1 priority date for domestic students; for summer admission, 4/1 priority date for domestic students. Applications are processed on a rolling basis. Application fee: $50. Electronic applications accepted. *Expenses:* Contact institution. *Financial support:* In 2017–18, 10 students received support, including 9 fellowships with full tuition reimbursements available (averaging $8,823 per year); career-related internships or fieldwork, scholarships/grants, health care benefits, tuition waivers (full), and unspecified assistantships also available. Support available to part-time students. Financial award application deadline: 4/1; financial award applicants required to submit FAFSA. *Unit head:* Dr. Anjoo Sikka, Dean of School of Education, 585-245-5151, Fax: 585-245-5220, E-mail: sikka@geneseo.edu. *Application contact:* Michael R. George, Director of Graduate Admissions, 585-245-5148, Fax: 585-245-5550, E-mail: georgem@geneseo.edu.

State University of New York College at Oneonta, Graduate Programs, Division of Education, Department of Elementary Education and Reading, Oneonta, NY 13820-4015. Offers childhood education (MS Ed); literacy education (MS Ed). *Accreditation:* NCATE. *Program availability:* Part-time, evening/weekend. *Entrance requirements:* For master's, GRE General Test.

State University of New York College at Potsdam, School of Education and Professional Studies, Program in Literacy, Potsdam, NY 13676. Offers literacy educator (MS Ed); literacy specialist (MS Ed), including birth-grade 6, grades 5-12. *Accreditation:* NCATE. *Program availability:* Part-time, online learning. *Entrance requirements:* For master's, minimum GPA of 2.75 in last 60 hours of course work. Additional exam requirements/recommendations for international students: Required—TOEFL (minimum score 550 paper-based; 80 iBT), IELTS (minimum score 6). Electronic applications accepted.

Sul Ross State University, College of Professional Studies, Department of Education, Program in Reading Specialist, Alpine, TX 79832. Offers master reading teacher (Certificate); Texas reading specialist (M Ed). *Program availability:* Part-time, evening/weekend. *Degree requirements:* For master's, thesis optional. *Entrance requirements:* For master's, GMAT or GRE General Test, minimum GPA of 2.5 in last 60 hours of undergraduate work.

Sul Ross State University, Rio Grande College of Sul Ross State University, Alpine, TX 79832. Offers business administration (MBA); teacher education (M Ed), including bilingual education, counseling, educational diagnostics, elementary education, general education, reading, school administration, secondary education. *Program availability:* Part-time, evening/weekend, online learning. *Degree requirements:* For master's, comprehensive exam, thesis optional, minimum GPA of 3.0. *Entrance requirements:* For master's, GMAT or GRE General Test, minimum GPA of 2.5 in last 60 hours of undergraduate work. Additional exam requirements/recommendations for international students: Required—TOEFL.

Syracuse University, School of Education, MS Program in Literacy Education (Birth - Grade 12), Syracuse, NY 13244. Offers MS. *Program availability:* Part-time. *Students:* Average age 24. *Entrance requirements:* For master's, GRE, baccalaureate degree from regionally-accredited college/university, New York State teaching certification, strong writing skills, letters of recommendation, personal statement. Additional exam requirements/recommendations for international students: Required—TOEFL (minimum

Reading Education

score 100 iBT). *Application deadline:* For fall admission, 1/15 priority date for domestic and international students. Applications are processed on a rolling basis. Application fee: $75. Electronic applications accepted. *Financial support:* Fellowships with full tuition reimbursements, research assistantships, teaching assistantships, career-related internships or fieldwork, and scholarships/grants available. Financial award application deadline: 1/15. *Faculty research:* Literacy, knowledge modeling, assessment, teaching of literature, writing. *Unit head:* Dr. Marcelle Haddix, Chair of Reading and Language Arts/Associate Professor, 315-443-7642, E-mail: mhaddix@syr.edu. *Application contact:* Speranza Migliore, Graduate Admissions Recruiter, 315-443-2505, E-mail: gradrcrt@syr.edu.
Website: http://soe.syr.edu/academic/reading_language_arts/graduate/masters/literacy_education/default.aspx

Syracuse University, School of Education, PhD Program in Literacy Education, Syracuse, NY 13244. Offers PhD. *Program availability:* Part-time. *Entrance requirements:* For doctorate, GRE, master's degree, three references, personal statement, college/university transcripts. Additional exam requirements/recommendations for international students: Required—TOEFL (minimum score 100 iBT). *Application deadline:* For fall admission, 1/15 priority date for domestic and international students; for spring admission, 10/15 priority date for domestic and international students. Applications are processed on a rolling basis. Application fee: $75. Electronic applications accepted. *Financial support:* Fellowships with full tuition reimbursements, research assistantships, teaching assistantships, career-related internships or fieldwork, and scholarships/grants available. Financial award application deadline: 1/15. *Faculty research:* Social and critical perspectives toward language and literacy development, instruction and teacher education, programs and curriculum development related to childhood or adolescent reading and writing instruction, literacy across the curriculum, multimodal literacies. *Unit head:* Dr. Marcelle Haddix, Chair of Reading and Language Arts/Associate Professor, 315-443-7642, E-mail: mhaddix@syr.edu. *Application contact:* Speranza Migliore, Graduate Admissions Recruiter, 315-443-2505, E-mail: gradrcrt@syr.edu.
Website: http://soe.syr.edu/academic/reading_language_arts/graduate/phd/default.aspx

Teachers College, Columbia University, Department of Curriculum and Teaching, New York, NY 10027-6696. Offers curriculum and teaching (Ed M, MA, Ed D); curriculum and teaching: elementary education (MA); curriculum and teaching: secondary education (MA); early childhood education (MA, Ed D); early childhood education: special education (MA); elementary education-gifted extension (MA); elementary inclusive education (MA); gifted education (MA); literacy specialist (MA); secondary inclusive education (MA); special inclusive elementary education (MA). *Program availability:* Part-time, evening/weekend. *Students:* 196 full-time (181 women), 181 part-time (161 women); includes 141 minority (45 Black or African American, non-Hispanic/Latino; 2 American Indian or Alaska Native, non-Hispanic/Latino; 45 Asian, non-Hispanic/Latino; 35 Hispanic/Latino; 14 Two or more races, non-Hispanic/Latino), 37 international. Average age 30. 509 applicants, 72% accepted, 155 enrolled. Terminal master's awarded for partial completion of doctoral program. *Degree requirements:* For doctorate, thesis/dissertation. *Unit head:* Prof. Daniel Friedrich, Chair, E-mail: friedrich@exchange.tc.columbia.edu. *Application contact:* David Estrella, Director of Admission, 212-678-3305, Fax: 212-678-4171, E-mail: estrella@tc.columbia.edu.

Teachers College, Columbia University, Department of Health and Behavior Studies, New York, NY 10027-6696. Offers applied behavior analysis (MA, PhD); applied educational psychology: school psychology (Ed M, PhD); behavioral nutrition (PhD), including nutrition (Ed D, PhD); community health education (MS); community nutrition education (Ed M), including community nutrition education; education of deaf and hard of hearing (MA, PhD); health education (MA, Ed D); hearing impairment (Ed D); intellectual disability/autism (MA, Ed D, PhD); nursing education (Ed D, Advanced Certificate); nutrition and education (MS); nutrition and exercise physiology (MS); nutrition and public health (MS); nutrition education (Ed D), including nutrition (Ed D, PhD); physical disabilities (Ed D); reading specialist (MA); severe or multiple disabilities (MA); special education (Ed M, MA, Ed D); teaching of sign language (MA). *Program availability:* Part-time, evening/weekend. *Students:* 245 full-time (226 women), 242 part-time (219 women); includes 167 minority (52 Black or African American, non-Hispanic/Latino; 2 American Indian or Alaska Native, non-Hispanic/Latino; 55 Asian, non-Hispanic/Latino; 48 Hispanic/Latino; 1 Native Hawaiian or other Pacific Islander, non-Hispanic/Latino; 9 Two or more races, non-Hispanic/Latino), 60 international. Average age 30. 480 applicants, 59% accepted, 157 enrolled. Terminal master's awarded for partial completion of doctoral program. *Unit head:* Prof. Dolores Perin, Chair, E-mail: dp111@tc.columbia.edu. *Application contact:* David Estrella, Director of Admission, 212-678-3305, E-mail: estrella@tc.columbia.edu.
Website: http://www.tc.columbia.edu/health-and-behavior-studies/

Tennessee Technological University, College of Graduate Studies, College of Education, Department of Curriculum and Instruction, Program in Exceptional Learning, Cookeville, TN 38505. Offers applied behavior analysis (PhD); literacy (PhD); program planning and evaluation (PhD); STEM education (PhD). *Program availability:* Part-time, evening/weekend. *Students:* 9 full-time (4 women), 32 part-time (24 women); includes 2 minority (1 Black or African American, non-Hispanic/Latino; 1 Two or more races, non-Hispanic/Latino), 4 international. 24 applicants, 54% accepted, 11 enrolled. In 2017, 10 doctorates awarded. *Degree requirements:* For doctorate, comprehensive exam, thesis/dissertation. *Entrance requirements:* For doctorate, GRE, minimum GPA of 3.0. Additional exam requirements/recommendations for international students: Required—TOEFL (minimum score 550 paper-based; 79 iBT), IELTS (minimum score 5.5), PTE (minimum score 53), or TOEIC (Test of English as an International Communication). *Application deadline:* For fall admission, 8/1 for domestic students, 5/1 for international students; for spring admission, 12/1 for domestic students, 10/1 for international students; for summer admission, 5/1 for domestic students, 2/1 for international students. Applications are processed on a rolling basis. Application fee: $35 ($40 for international students). Electronic applications accepted. *Expenses:* Tuition, state resident: full-time $9925; part-time $565 per credit hour. Tuition, nonresident: full-time $22,993; part-time $1291 per credit hour. *Financial support:* Fellowships, research assistantships, and teaching assistantships available. Financial award application deadline: 4/1. *Unit head:* Dr. Lisa Zagumny, Director, 931-372-3078, Fax: 931-372-3517, E-mail: lzagumny@tntech.edu. *Application contact:* Shelia K. Kendrick, Coordinator of Graduate Studies, 931-372-3808, Fax: 931-372-3497, E-mail: skendrick@tntech.edu.
Website: https://www.tntech.edu/education/elphd/

Tennessee Technological University, College of Graduate Studies, College of Education, Department of Curriculum and Instruction, Program in Reading, Cookeville, TN 38505. Offers MA, Ed S. *Accreditation:* NCATE. *Program availability:* Part-time, evening/weekend. *Faculty:* 2 full-time (both women). *Students:* 6 part-time (all women). 3 applicants, 100% accepted, 1 enrolled. In 2017, 3 master's, 2 other advanced degrees awarded. *Degree requirements:* For master's and Ed S, comprehensive exam, thesis or alternative. *Entrance requirements:* For master's and Ed S, MAT or GRE. Additional exam requirements/recommendations for international students: Required—TOEFL (minimum score 527 paper-based; 71 iBT), IELTS (minimum score 5.5), PTE (minimum score 48), or TOEIC (Test of English as an International Communication). *Application*

deadline: For fall admission, 8/1 for domestic students, 5/1 for international students; for spring admission, 12/1 for domestic students, 10/1 for international students; for summer admission, 5/1 for domestic students, 2/1 for international students. Applications are processed on a rolling basis. Application fee: $35 ($40 for international students). Electronic applications accepted. *Expenses:* Tuition, state resident: full-time $9925; part-time $565 per credit hour. Tuition, nonresident: full-time $22,993; part-time $1291 per credit hour. *Financial support:* Fellowships, research assistantships, teaching assistantships, and career-related internships or fieldwork available. Financial award application deadline: 4/1. *Unit head:* Dr. Jeremy Wendt, Interim Chairperson, 931-372-3181, Fax: 931-372-6270, E-mail: jwendt@tntech.edu. *Application contact:* Shelia K. Kendrick, Coordinator of Graduate Studies, 931-372-3808, Fax: 931-372-3497, E-mail: skendrick@tntech.edu.

Texas A&M University–Commerce, College of Education and Human Services, Commerce, TX 75429. Offers counseling (M Ed, MS, PhD); early childhood education (M Ed, MS); educational administration (M Ed, MS, Ed D); educational psychology (PhD); educational technology leadership (M Ed, MS); educational technology library science (M Ed, MS); elementary education (M Ed); health, kinesiology and sports studies (MS); higher education (MS, Ed D); psychology (MS); reading (M Ed, MS); secondary education (M Ed, MS); social work (MSW); special education (M Ed, MS); supervision, curriculum and instruction-elementary education (Ed D); training and development (MS). *Program availability:* Part-time, evening/weekend, 100% online, blended/hybrid learning. *Faculty:* 91 full-time (51 women), 38 part-time/adjunct (31 women). *Students:* 400 full-time (310 women), 1,400 part-time (1,117 women); includes 724 minority (412 Black or African American, non-Hispanic/Latino; 8 American Indian or Alaska Native, non-Hispanic/Latino; 24 Asian, non-Hispanic/Latino; 220 Hispanic/Latino; 60 Two or more races, non-Hispanic/Latino), 18 international. Average age 37. 951 applicants, 46% accepted, 331 enrolled. In 2017, 564 master's, 24 doctorates awarded. *Degree requirements:* For master's, comprehensive exam, thesis optional, departmental qualifying exams (for some programs); for doctorate, comprehensive exam, thesis/dissertation, departmental qualifying exam; for SSP, comprehensive exam, thesis optional. *Entrance requirements:* For master's and doctorate, GRE General Test. Additional exam requirements/recommendations for international students: Required—TOEFL (minimum score 550 paper-based; 79 iBT), IELTS (minimum score 6). *Application deadline:* For fall admission, 6/1 priority date for international students; for spring admission, 10/15 priority date for international students; for summer admission, 3/15 priority date for international students. Applications are processed on a rolling basis. Application fee: $50. Electronic applications accepted. *Expenses:* Tuition, state resident: full-time $3630. Tuition, nonresident: full-time $11,100. *Required fees:* $2564. Tuition and fees vary according to course load, degree level and program. *Financial support:* In 2017–18, 84 students received support, including 40 research assistantships with partial tuition reimbursements available (averaging $10,800 per year), 12 teaching assistantships with partial tuition reimbursements available (averaging $13,000 per year); career-related internships or fieldwork, Federal Work-Study, institutionally sponsored loans, scholarships/grants, health care benefits, and unspecified assistantships also available. Financial award application deadline: 6/15; financial award applicants required to submit FAFSA. *Faculty research:* Cognitive and bilingual education, positive behavioral intervention, literacy, math readiness. *Total annual research expenditures:* $1.1 million. *Unit head:* Dr. Timothy Letzring, Dean, 903-886-5181, Fax: 903-886-5905, E-mail: tim.letzring@tamuc.edu. *Application contact:* Vicky Turner, Doctoral Degree and Special Programs Coordinator, 903-886-5167, E-mail: vicky.turner@tamuc.edu.
Website: http://www.tamuc.edu/academics/graduateSchool/programs/education/default.aspx

Texas A&M University–Corpus Christi, College of Graduate Studies, College of Education and Human Development, Corpus Christi, TX 78412. Offers counseling (MS), including counseling; counselor education (PhD); curriculum and instruction (MS, PhD); early childhood education (MS); educational administration (MS); educational leadership (Ed D); elementary education (MS); instructional design and educational technology (MS); kinesiology (MS); reading (MS); secondary education (MS); special education (MS). *Program availability:* Part-time, evening/weekend, blended/hybrid learning. *Faculty:* 50 full-time (29 women), 29 part-time/adjunct (18 women). *Students:* 160 full-time (127 women), 366 part-time (293 women); includes 279 minority (40 Black or African American, non-Hispanic/Latino; 3 Asian, non-Hispanic/Latino; 228 Hispanic/Latino; 8 Two or more races, non-Hispanic/Latino), 18 international. Average age 35. 296 applicants, 65% accepted, 155 enrolled. In 2017, 103 master's, 27 doctorates awarded. *Degree requirements:* For master's, comprehensive exam, capstone; for doctorate, thesis/dissertation. *Entrance requirements:* For master's, GRE General Test, essay (300 words); for doctorate, GRE, essay, resume, 3-4 reference forms. *Application deadline:* For fall admission, 7/15 priority date for domestic students, 5/1 priority date for international students; for spring admission, 11/15 priority date for domestic students, 9/1 priority date for international students. Applications are processed on a rolling basis. Application fee: $50 ($70 for international students). Electronic applications accepted. *Expenses:* Tuition, state resident: full-time $3568; part-time $198.24 per credit hour. Tuition, nonresident: full-time $11,038; part-time $613.24 per credit hour. *Required fees:* $2129; $1422.58 per semester. Tuition and fees vary according to program. *Financial support:* Research assistantships, teaching assistantships, career-related internships or fieldwork, Federal Work-Study, institutionally sponsored loans, scholarships/grants, health care benefits, and unspecified assistantships available. Support available to part-time students. Financial award application deadline: 3/15; financial award applicants required to submit FAFSA. *Unit head:* Dr. David Scott, Dean, 361-825-2660, E-mail: david.scott@tamucc.edu. *Application contact:* Graduate Admissions Coordinator, 361-825-2177, Fax: 361-825-2755, E-mail: gradweb@tamucc.edu.
Website: http://education.tamucc.edu/

Texas A&M University–Kingsville, College of Graduate Studies, College of Education and Human Performance, Department of Teacher and Bilingual Education, Program in Reading Specialization, Kingsville, TX 78363. Offers MS. *Program availability:* Part-time, evening/weekend. *Degree requirements:* For master's, variable foreign language requirement, comprehensive exam, thesis (for some programs). *Entrance requirements:* For master's, GRE, MAT, GMAT. Additional exam requirements/recommendations for international students: Required—TOEFL (minimum score 550 paper-based; 79 iBT). Electronic applications accepted.

Texas A&M University–San Antonio, Department of Educator and Leadership Preparation, San Antonio, TX 78224. Offers bilingual education (MS); early childhood education (M Ed); educational administration (MA); reading specialization (MS); special education (M Ed), including educational diagnostician. *Program availability:* Part-time, evening/weekend, online learning. *Faculty:* 19 full-time (14 women), 8 part-time/adjunct (2 women). *Students:* 24 full-time (21 women), 188 part-time (143 women); includes 163 minority (7 Black or African American, non-Hispanic/Latino; 1 Asian, non-Hispanic/Latino; 149 Hispanic/Latino; 6 Two or more races, non-Hispanic/Latino), 1 international. Average age 36. 191 applicants, 62% accepted, 67 enrolled. In 2017, 70 master's awarded. *Degree requirements:* For master's, comprehensive exam, thesis or alternative. *Entrance requirements:* For master's, GRE (Quantitative and Verbal) or MAT. Additional exam requirements/recommendations for international students: Required—TOEFL (minimum score 550 paper-based; 79 iBT), IELTS (minimum

6). *Application deadline:* For fall admission, 3/15 priority date for domestic and international students; for spring admission, 11/1 priority date for domestic and international students; for summer admission, 4/1 priority date for domestic and international students. Applications are processed on a rolling basis. Application fee: $35 ($50 for international students). Electronic applications accepted. *Expenses:* Tuition, state resident: full-time $3475; part-time $1930 per semester. Tuition, nonresident: full-time $10,945; part-time $6080 per semester. *Required fees:* $2148; $1412 per year. $706 per semester. Tuition and fees vary according to course load. *Financial support:* In 2017–18, 16 students received support. Research assistantships, Federal Work-Study, scholarships/grants, and tuition waivers available. Financial award application deadline: 3/15; financial award applicants required to submit FAFSA. *Faculty research:* Equity in education, biliteracy practices among Latina and immigrants, academic achievement of low socio-economic students, equity practices in instruction and educational leadership in diverse settings, racial identity development and multicultural education. *Unit head:* Dr. Debbie Vera, Department Chair. *Application contact:* Caitie Garza, Graduate Admissions Coordinator, 210-784-1300, E-mail: beajaguar@tamusa.edu.
Website: http://www.tamusa.edu/collegeofeducationandhumandevelopment/educatorleadershippreparation/index.html

Texas Christian University, College of Education, Master's Programs in Education, Fort Worth, TX 76129. Offers counseling (M Ed); curriculum and instruction (M Ed), including curriculum studies, language and literacy, math education, science education; education (MAT); educational leadership (M Ed); special education (M Ed). *Program availability:* Part-time, evening/weekend. *Faculty:* 29 full-time (21 women), 3 part-time/adjunct (1 woman). *Students:* 124 full-time (94 women), 14 part-time (12 women); includes 52 minority (14 Black or African American, non-Hispanic/Latino; 2 American Indian or Alaska Native, non-Hispanic/Latino; 3 Asian, non-Hispanic/Latino; 28 Hispanic/Latino; 5 Two or more races, non-Hispanic/Latino), 1 international. Average age 28. 172 applicants, 69% accepted, 86 enrolled. In 2017, 62 master's awarded. *Degree requirements:* For master's, comprehensive exam (for some programs), thesis (for some programs). *Entrance requirements:* For master's, GRE General Test; Pre-Admission Content Test (for MAT). Additional exam requirements/recommendations for international students: Required—TOEFL (minimum score 550 paper-based; 80 iBT). *Application deadline:* For fall admission, 3/1 for domestic and international students; for spring admission, 11/16 for domestic and international students; for summer admission, 3/1 for domestic and international students. Application fee: $60. Electronic applications accepted. *Financial support:* In 2017–18, 124 students received support, including 1 research assistantship with full tuition reimbursement available (averaging $15,000 per year), 29 teaching assistantships with full tuition reimbursements available (averaging $15,000 per year); career-related internships or fieldwork, scholarships/grants, and unspecified assistantships also available. Support available to part-time students. Financial award application deadline: 3/1. *Unit head:* Dr. Jan Lacina, Associate Dean, 817-257-6786, Fax: 817-257-7466, E-mail: j.lacina@tcu.edu. *Application contact:* Lori Kimball, Administrative Program Specialist, 817-257-7661, Fax: 817-257-7466, E-mail: l.kimball@tcu.edu.
Website: http://coe.tcu.edu/graduate-overview/

Texas State University, The Graduate College, College of Education, Program in Reading Education, San Marcos, TX 78666. Offers early childhood-12 reading specialist (M Ed). *Program availability:* Part-time, evening/weekend. *Faculty:* 10 full-time (9 women), 2 part-time/adjunct (1 woman). *Students:* 1 (woman) full-time, 24 part-time (23 women); includes 12 minority (all Hispanic/Latino). Average age 37. 4 applicants, 75% accepted. In 2017, 7 master's awarded. *Degree requirements:* For master's, comprehensive exam. *Entrance requirements:* For master's, baccalaureate degree from regionally-accredited institution with minimum GPA of 3.0 in last 60 hours of course work, statement of purpose, official teaching certificate. Additional exam requirements/recommendations for international students: Required—IELTS, TOEFL (minimum iBT scores: 22 listening, 22 reading, 24 speaking, 21 writing). *Application deadline:* For fall admission, 2/15 priority date for domestic and international students; for spring admission, 10/15 priority date for domestic students, 10/1 for international students; for summer admission, 4/15 for domestic students, 3/15 for international students. Applications are processed on a rolling basis. Application fee: $40 ($90 for international students). Electronic applications accepted. *Expenses:* Tuition, state resident: full-time $7868; part-time $3934 per semester. Tuition, nonresident: full-time $17,828; part-time $8914 per semester. *Required fees:* $2092; $1435 per semester. Tuition and fees vary according to course load. *Financial support:* In 2017–18, 15 students received support, including 1 research assistantship (averaging $12,152 per year); teaching assistantships, career-related internships or fieldwork, Federal Work-Study, institutionally sponsored loans, scholarships/grants, and unspecified assistantships also available. Support available to part-time students. Financial award application deadline: 3/1; financial award applicants required to submit FAFSA. *Faculty research:* Impact of developmental integrated reading and writing. *Total annual research expenditures:* $64,880. *Unit head:* Dr. Jane Saunders, Graduate Advisor, 512-245-1512, Fax: 512-245-8365, E-mail: js99@txstate.edu. *Application contact:* Dr. Andrea Golato, Dean of Graduate School, 512-245-2581, Fax: 512-245-8365, E-mail: gradcollege@txstate.edu.
Website: http://www.education.txstate.edu/ci/degrees-certifications/graduate/reading.html

Texas Tech University, Graduate School, College of Education, Department of Curriculum and Instruction, Lubbock, TX 79409. Offers bilingual education (M Ed); curriculum and instruction (M Ed); elementary education (M Ed); language/literacy education (M Ed); multidisciplinary science (MS); secondary education (M Ed). *Accreditation:* NCATE. *Program availability:* Part-time, evening/weekend, online learning. *Faculty:* 22 full-time (14 women), 2 part-time/adjunct (1 woman). *Students:* 64 full-time (50 women), 247 part-time (205 women); includes 100 minority (26 Black or African American, non-Hispanic/Latino; 1 American Indian or Alaska Native, non-Hispanic/Latino; 11 Asian, non-Hispanic/Latino; 54 Hispanic/Latino; 8 Two or more races, non-Hispanic/Latino), 39 international. Average age 39. 157 applicants, 56% accepted, 71 enrolled. In 2017, 20 master's, 21 doctorates awarded. Terminal master's awarded for partial completion of doctoral program. *Degree requirements:* For master's, comprehensive exam (for some programs), thesis optional; for doctorate, comprehensive exam, thesis/dissertation. *Entrance requirements:* For master's, bachelor's degree; resume; letter of intent; academic writing sample; 2 letters of recommendation; for doctorate, GRE, master's degree; resume; letter of intent; academic writing sample; 3 letters of recommendation. Additional exam requirements/recommendations for international students: Required—TOEFL (minimum score 550 paper-based; 79 iBT). *Application deadline:* For fall admission, 6/1 priority date for domestic students, 1/15 priority date for international students; for spring admission, 9/1 priority date for domestic students, 6/15 priority date for international students. Applications are processed on a rolling basis. Application fee: $60. Electronic applications accepted. *Expenses:* Contact institution. *Financial support:* In 2017–18, 96 students received support, including 92 fellowships (averaging $3,321 per year), 37 research assistantships (averaging $12,336 per year); teaching assistantships, Federal Work-Study, institutionally sponsored loans, scholarships/grants, health care benefits, and unspecified assistantships also available. Support available to part-time students. Financial award application deadline: 2/1; financial award applicants required to submit

FAFSA. *Faculty research:* Teacher education, curriculum studies, bilingual education, science and math education, language and literacy education. *Total annual research expenditures:* $107,999. *Unit head:* Dr. Fanni Liu Coward, Interim Chairperson, 806-834-4475, Fax: 806-742-2179, E-mail: fanni.coward@ttu.edu. *Application contact:* Brianna Sanchez, Coordinator, 806-834-2353, Fax: 806-742-2179, E-mail: brianna.sanchez@ttu.edu.
Website: http://www.educ.ttu.edu

Texas Woman's University, Graduate School, College of Professional Education, Department of Reading, Denton, TX 76204. Offers reading education (M Ed, MA, PhD); Texas all-level (K-12) reading specialist (Certificate); Texas master reading teacher (Certificate). *Program availability:* Part-time, evening/weekend. *Faculty:* 9 full-time (all women), 3 part-time/adjunct (all women). *Students:* 62 part-time (59 women); includes 27 minority (10 Black or African American, non-Hispanic/Latino; 15 Hispanic/Latino; 2 Two or more races, non-Hispanic/Latino). Average age 41. 27 applicants, 81% accepted, 19 enrolled. In 2017, 10 master's, 5 doctorates awarded. Terminal master's awarded for partial completion of doctoral program. *Degree requirements:* For master's, comprehensive exam, thesis (for some programs), thesis or portfolio; for doctorate, comprehensive exam, thesis/dissertation; for Certificate, comprehensive exam, thesis (for some programs). *Entrance requirements:* For master's, minimum GPA of 3.0 for last 60 semester credit hours of undergraduate study and all prior graduate work; for doctorate, GRE General Test (preferred minimum score 153 [500 old version] Verbal, 144 [500 old version] Quantitative), master's degree, minimum GPA of 3.5, on-site writing sample, interview, 3 letters of reference, curriculum vitae/resume, 1-2 page statement of professional experience and goals, 3 years of teaching experience; for Certificate, TExES (for Texas all-level K-12 reading specialist), teacher certification, master's degree, and 2 years' classroom teaching experience (for Texas all-level K-12 reading specialist); previous certification, 3 years' teaching experience, and MRT certification (for Texas master reading teacher). Additional exam requirements/recommendations for international students: Required—TOEFL (minimum score 550 paper-based; 79 iBT); Recommended—IELTS (minimum score 6.5), TSE (minimum score 53). *Application deadline:* For fall admission, 3/1 priority date for domestic and international students; for spring admission, 11/1 priority date for domestic students, 7/1 priority date for international students. Applications are processed on a rolling basis. Application fee: $50 ($75 for international students). Electronic applications accepted. *Expenses:* $7,520 per year full-time in-state; $16,820 per year full-time out-of-state. *Financial support:* In 2017–18, 9 students received support. Career-related internships or fieldwork, Federal Work-Study, institutionally sponsored loans, scholarships/grants, traineeships, health care benefits, and unspecified assistantships available. Support available to part-time students. Financial award application deadline: 3/1; financial award applicants required to submit FAFSA. *Faculty research:* Effective literacy practices, home/school partnerships, literacy language acquisitions, multicultural education, children's literature. *Total annual research expenditures:* $349,396. *Unit head:* Dr. Connie Briggs, Chair, 940-898-2227, Fax: 940-898-2224, E-mail: reading@twu.edu. *Application contact:* Korie Hawkins, Associate Director of Admissions, Graduate Recruitment, 940-898-3188, Fax: 940-898-3081, E-mail: admissions@twu.edu.
Website: http://www.twu.edu/reading

Touro College, Graduate School of Education, New York, NY 10010. Offers education and special education (MS); instructional technology (MS); mathematics education (MS); school leadership (MS); teaching English to speakers of other languages (MS); teaching literacy (MS). *Accreditation:* TEAC. *Program availability:* Part-time, evening/weekend, online learning. *Faculty:* 52 full-time (34 women), 199 part-time/adjunct (136 women). *Students:* 756 full-time (686 women), 3,833 part-time (3,492 women). Average age 33. 1,422 applicants, 50% accepted, 675 enrolled. In 2017, 6 master's awarded. *Entrance requirements:* Additional exam requirements/recommendations for international students: Required—TOEFL (minimum score 83 iBT), IELTS (minimum score 6.5). *Application deadline:* For fall admission, 8/26 for domestic students, 7/15 for international students; for spring admission, 12/31 for domestic students, 12/15 for international students. Applications are processed on a rolling basis. Application fee: $50. *Financial support:* Federal Work-Study available. Financial award applicants required to submit FAFSA. *Faculty research:* Equity assistance, language development, scholarly communications, Latin American studies and cultural sensitivity, behavior management techniques and strategies in special education. *Unit head:* Dr. Jacob Easley, III, Dean, 212-463-0400 Ext. 5561, Fax: 212-462-4889, E-mail: jeasley@touro.edu. *Application contact:* Sharmilee Hoopnarine, Admissions, 212-463-0400.

Towson University, College of Education, Program in Reading, Towson, MD 21252-0001. Offers reading (M Ed); reading education (CAS). *Accreditation:* NCATE. *Program availability:* Part-time, evening/weekend. *Students:* 170 part-time (162 women); includes 13 minority (6 Black or African American, non-Hispanic/Latino; 1 Asian, non-Hispanic/Latino; 2 Hispanic/Latino; 4 Two or more races, non-Hispanic/Latino). *Entrance requirements:* For master's, minimum GPA of 3.0, essay; for CAS, 3 letters of reference, portfolio, master's degree in reading or related field. *Application deadline:* For fall admission, 1/17 for domestic students, 5/15 for international students; for spring admission, 10/15 for domestic students, 12/1 for international students. Applications are processed on a rolling basis. Application fee: $45. Electronic applications accepted. *Expenses:* Tuition, state resident: full-time $7960; part-time $398 per unit. Tuition, nonresident: full-time $16,480; part-time $824 per unit. *Required fees:* $2600; $130 per year. $390 per term. *Financial support:* Application deadline: 4/1. *Unit head:* Dr. Gilda Martinez-Alba, Graduate Program Director, 410-704-2480, E-mail: gmartinez@towson.edu. *Application contact:* Coverley Beidleman, Assistant Director of Graduate Admissions, 410-704-5630, Fax: 410-704-3030, E-mail: cbeidleman@towson.edu.
Website: http://www.towson.edu/coe/departments/elementary/grad/reading

Trident University International, College of Education, Program in Education, Cypress, CA 90630. Offers adult education (MA Ed); aviation education (MA Ed); children's literacy development (MA Ed); e-learning (MA Ed); early childhood education (MA Ed); enrollment management (MA Ed); higher education (MA Ed); teaching and instruction (MA Ed); training and development (MA Ed). *Program availability:* Part-time, evening/weekend, online learning. *Degree requirements:* For master's, capstone project with integrative paper. *Entrance requirements:* For master's, minimum GPA of 2.5 (students with GPA 3.0 or greater may transfer up to 30% of graduate level credits). Additional exam requirements/recommendations for international students: Required—TOEFL (minimum score 525 paper-based). Electronic applications accepted.

Trinity Washington University, School of Education, Washington, DC 20017-1094. Offers clinical mental health counseling (MA); early childhood education (MAT); educating for change (M Ed); educational administration (MSA); elementary education (MAT); reading (M Ed); school counseling (MA); secondary education (MAT), including English, social studies; special education (MAT). *Accreditation:* NCATE. *Program availability:* Part-time, evening/weekend. *Degree requirements:* For master's, thesis (for some programs), capstone project(s). *Entrance requirements:* For master's, PRAXIS I, minimum GPA of 2.8. Additional exam requirements/recommendations for international students: Required—TOEFL (minimum score 550 paper-based). *Faculty research:* Technology, literacy, special education, organizations, inclusion models.

Union College, Graduate Programs, Department of Education, Barbourville, KY 40906-1499. Offers elementary education (MA); health and physical education (MA); middle grades (MA); music education (MA); principalship (MA); reading specialist (MA); secondary education (MA); special education (MA). *Degree requirements:* For master's, thesis optional. *Entrance requirements:* For master's, GRE General Test, NTE.

University at Albany, State University of New York, School of Education, Department of Literacy Teaching and Learning, Albany, NY 12222-0001. Offers MS, PhD, CAS. *Program availability:* Evening/weekend. *Faculty:* 8 full-time (all women), 6 part-time/adjunct (all women). *Students:* 14 full-time (13 women), 115 part-time (113 women); includes 8 minority (2 Black or African American, non-Hispanic/Latino; 2 Asian, non-Hispanic/Latino; 4 Hispanic/Latino), 1 international. Average age 33. 65 applicants, 74% accepted, 44 enrolled. In 2017, 38 master's, 2 doctorates, 2 other advanced degrees awarded. *Degree requirements:* For doctorate, one foreign language, thesis/dissertation. *Entrance requirements:* For doctorate, GRE General Test. Additional exam requirements/recommendations for international students: Required—TOEFL (minimum score 550 paper-based). *Application deadline:* For fall admission, 3/1 for domestic students. Applications are processed on a rolling basis. Application fee: $75. Electronic applications accepted. *Expenses:* Tuition, state resident: full-time $10,870; part-time $453 per credit hour. Tuition, nonresident: full-time $22,210; part-time $925 per credit hour. *Required fees:* $84.68 per credit hour. $508.06 per semester. Part-time tuition and fees vary according to course load and program. *Financial support:* Fellowships available. Financial award application deadline: 4/15. *Unit head:* Dr. Virginia Goatley, Chair, 518-442-5104, E-mail: vgoatley@albany.edu.

University at Buffalo, the State University of New York, Graduate School, Graduate School of Education, Department of Learning and Instruction, Buffalo, NY 14260. Offers biology education (Ed M, Certificate); chemistry education (Ed M, Certificate); childhood education (Ed M); childhood education with bilingual extension (Ed M); college teaching (Advanced Certificate); curriculum, instruction and the science of learning (PhD); early childhood education (Ed M); early childhood education with bilingual extension (Ed M); earth science education (Ed M, Certificate); education and technology (Ed M); education studies (Ed M); educational technology and new literacies (Certificate); educational technology and new literacies (Advanced Certificate); elementary education (Ed D); English education (Ed M, Certificate); English education studies (Ed M); English for speakers of other languages (Ed M); foreign and second language education (PhD); French education (Ed M, Certificate); German education (Ed M, Certificate); gifted education (Certificate); Latin education (Ed M, Certificate); literacy education studies (Ed M); literacy specialist (Ed M); literacy teaching and learning (Certificate); mathematics education (Ed M, Certificate); music education (Ed M, Certificate); music education studies (Ed M); music learning theory (Advanced Certificate); online education (Advanced Certificate); physics education (Ed M, Certificate); science and the public (Ed M); social studies education (Ed M, Certificate); Spanish education (Ed M, Certificate); special education (PhD); teaching English to speakers of other languages (Ed M). *Program availability:* Part-time, evening/weekend, 100% online. *Faculty:* 26 full-time (19 women), 74 part-time/adjunct (52 women). *Students:* 172 full-time (122 women), 325 part-time (226 women); includes 44 minority (25 Black or African American, non-Hispanic/Latino; 5 American Indian or Alaska Native, non-Hispanic/Latino; 14 Asian, non-Hispanic/Latino), 57 international. Average age 33. 316 applicants, 78% accepted, 174 enrolled. In 2017, 109 master's, 34 doctorates, 15 other advanced degrees awarded. *Degree requirements:* For master's, comprehensive exam; for doctorate, thesis/dissertation, research analysis exam, research experience. *Entrance requirements:* For master's, letters of reference; for doctorate, GRE General Test or MAT, interview, writing sample, letters of recommendation. Additional exam requirements/recommendations for international students: Required—TOEFL (minimum score 600 paper-based; 96 iBT). *Application deadline:* For fall admission, 2/1 priority date for domestic and international students; for spring admission, 11/15 priority date for domestic students, 10/1 for international students. Applications are processed on a rolling basis. Application fee: $50. Electronic applications accepted. *Financial support:* In 2017–18, 42 fellowships (averaging $5,181 per year), 44 research assistantships with tuition reimbursements (averaging $10,908 per year) were awarded; teaching assistantships, career-related internships or fieldwork, Federal Work-Study, institutionally sponsored loans, scholarships/grants, tuition waivers (full and partial), and unspecified assistantships also available. Financial award application deadline: 2/28; financial award applicants required to submit FAFSA. *Faculty research:* Science assessment, foreign language teaching and learning, early learning, new literacies, gender and education. *Total annual research expenditures:* $413,233. *Unit head:* Dr. David Bruce, Chair, 716-645-4069, Fax: 716-645-3161, E-mail: gse-info@buffalo.edu. *Application contact:* Luann Zak, Admissions Assistant, 716-645-2110, Fax: 716-645-7937, E-mail: luannzak@buffalo.edu.
Website: http://gse.buffalo.edu/lai

The University of Akron, Graduate School, College of Education, Department of Curricular and Instructional Studies, Program in Elementary Education - Literacy Option, Akron, OH 44325. Offers MA. *Accreditation:* NCATE. *Students:* 4 full-time (3 women), 17 part-time (16 women); includes 2 minority (both Black or African American, non-Hispanic/Latino), 3 international. Average age 37. 2 applicants, 100% accepted, 2 enrolled. In 2017, 19 master's awarded. *Degree requirements:* For master's, comprehensive exam, thesis optional. *Entrance requirements:* For master's, valid teaching license. Additional exam requirements/recommendations for international students: Required—TOEFL (minimum score 79 iBT), IELTS (minimum score 6.5). *Application deadline:* Applications are processed on a rolling basis. Application fee: $45 ($70 for international students). Electronic applications accepted. *Unit head:* Dr. Evonn Welton, Interim Department Chair, 330-972-6742, E-mail: ewelton@uakron.edu. *Application contact:* Kelly Chaff, College Program Specialist, 330-972-7028, E-mail: klchaff@uakron.edu.
Website: http://www.uakron.edu/education/academic-programs/graduate-programs.dot

The University of Alabama at Birmingham, School of Education, Program in Reading, Birmingham, AL 35294. Offers MA Ed. *Program availability:* Online learning. *Entrance requirements:* For master's, two years' teaching experience, teaching certificate.

The University of Alabama in Huntsville, School of Graduate Studies, College of Education, Huntsville, AL 35899. Offers autism spectrum disorders (M Ed, Graduate Certificate); biology (MAT); chemistry (MAT); differentiated instruction in elementary education (M Ed); English language arts (MAT); English speakers of other languages (M Ed, MAT); history (MAT); mathematics (MAT); physics (MAT); reading education (M Ed); secondary education (M Ed).

University of Alaska Southeast, Graduate Programs, Program in Education, Juneau, AK 99801. Offers educational leadership (M Ed); elementary education (MAT); learning design and technology (M Ed); mathematics education (M Ed); reading specialist (M Ed); secondary education (MAT); special education (M Ed, MAT). *Accreditation:* NCATE. *Program availability:* Part-time, evening/weekend, online learning. *Degree requirements:* For master's, comprehensive exam or project, portfolio. *Entrance requirements:* For master's, PRAXIS, minimum GPA of 3.0, writing sample, letters of recommendation. Electronic applications accepted. *Faculty research:* Applied classroom research, culturally responsive practices, action research, teaching effectiveness.

The University of Arizona, College of Education, Department of Teaching, Learning and Sociocultural Studies, Program in Language, Reading and Culture, Tucson, AZ 85721. Offers MA, Ed D, PhD, Ed S. *Program availability:* Part-time. *Entrance requirements:* Additional exam requirements/recommendations for international students: Required—TOEFL (minimum score 550 paper-based; 79 iBT); Recommended—IELTS (minimum score 7). Electronic applications accepted. *Faculty research:* Literacy acquisition, sociocultural theory, indigenous education, heritage-language revitalization, the study of households and community settings, children's and adolescent literatures and literacy.

University of Arkansas at Little Rock, Graduate School, College of Education and Health Professions, Department of Teacher Education, Program in Reading Education, Little Rock, AR 72204-1099. Offers M Ed, PhD, Ed S.

University of Bridgeport, School of Education, Department of Education, Bridgeport, CT 06604. Offers education (MS); educational management (Ed D, Diploma), including intermediate administrator or supervisor (Diploma), leadership (Ed D); elementary education (MS, Diploma), including early childhood education, elementary education; middle school education (MS); music education (MS); remedial reading and language arts (Diploma); secondary education (MS, Diploma), including computer specialist (Diploma), international education (Diploma), reading specialist, secondary education. *Program availability:* Part-time, evening/weekend. *Degree requirements:* For master's, final exam, final project, or thesis; for doctorate, comprehensive exam, thesis/dissertation; for Diploma, thesis or alternative, final project. *Entrance requirements:* For master's, minimum undergraduate QPA of 2.67; for doctorate, GRE, MAT; for Diploma, GRE General Test or MAT, minimum graduate QPA of 3.0. Additional exam requirements/recommendations for international students: Recommended—TOEFL (minimum score 550 paper-based; 80 iBT), IELTS (minimum score 6.5). Electronic applications accepted. *Expenses:* Contact institution.

The University of British Columbia, Faculty of Education, Department of Language and Literacy Education, Vancouver, BC V6T 1Z2, Canada. Offers literacy education (M Ed, MA, PhD); modern languages education (M Ed, MA); teaching English as a second language (M Ed, MA, PhD). *Program availability:* Part-time, evening/weekend. *Degree requirements:* For master's, thesis (MA); for doctorate, thesis/dissertation. *Entrance requirements:* For master's and doctorate, minimum B+ average in last 2 years with minimum 2 courses at A standing. Additional exam requirements/recommendations for international students: Required—TOEFL, TWE. Electronic applications accepted. *Expenses:* Contact institution. *Faculty research:* Language and literacy development, second language acquisition, Asia Pacific language curriculum, children's literature, whole language instruction.

University of Central Arkansas, Graduate School, College of Education, Department of Early Childhood and Special Education, Program in Reading Education, Conway, AR 72035-0001. Offers MSE. *Accreditation:* NCATE. *Program availability:* Part-time, evening/weekend, online learning. *Degree requirements:* For master's, comprehensive exam, thesis optional. *Entrance requirements:* For master's, GRE General Test, minimum GPA of 2.7. Additional exam requirements/recommendations for international students: Required—TOEFL (minimum score 550 paper-based; 80 iBT).

University of Central Florida, College of Community Innovation and Education, Education Doctoral Programs, Orlando, FL 32816. Offers curriculum and instruction (Ed D); education (PhD), including communication sciences and disorders, counselor education, early childhood education, elementary education, exceptional education, exercise physiology, higher education, instructional design and technology, mathematics education, methodology, measurement and analysis, reading education, science education, social science education, TESOL; educational leadership (Ed D). *Students:* 122 full-time (86 women), 129 part-time (88 women); includes 64 minority (24 Black or African American, non-Hispanic/Latino; 1 American Indian or Alaska Native, non-Hispanic/Latino; 9 Asian, non-Hispanic/Latino; 24 Hispanic/Latino; 6 Two or more races, non-Hispanic/Latino), 26 international. Average age 38. 195 applicants, 47% accepted, 72 enrolled. In 2017, 89 doctorates awarded. *Entrance requirements:* For doctorate, GRE, letters of recommendation, goal statement, resume, writing sample. Application fee: $30. Electronic applications accepted. *Expenses:* Tuition, state resident: part-time $288.16 per credit hour. Tuition, nonresident: part-time $1073.91 per credit hour. Tuition and fees vary according to program. *Financial support:* In 2017–18, 77 students received support, including 28 fellowships with partial tuition reimbursements available (averaging $5,733 per year), 29 research assistantships with partial tuition reimbursements available (averaging $10,230 per year), 54 teaching assistantships with partial tuition reimbursements available (averaging $11,614 per year); health care benefits also available. Financial award application deadline: 3/1; financial award applicants required to submit FAFSA. *Unit head:* Dr. Edward Robinson, Director of Doctoral Programs, 407-823-6106, E-mail: edward.robinson@ucf.edu. *Application contact:* Associate Director, Graduate Admissions, 407-823-2766, Fax: 407-823-6442, E-mail: gradadmissions@ucf.edu.
Website: https://edcollege.ucf.edu/academic-programs/graduate/

University of Central Florida, College of Community Innovation and Education, School of Teacher Education, Program in Reading Education, Orlando, FL 32816. Offers M Ed, Certificate. *Accreditation:* NCATE. *Program availability:* Part-time, evening/weekend. *Students:* 3 full-time (all women), 16 part-time (all women); includes 6 minority (3 Black or African American, non-Hispanic/Latino; 3 Hispanic/Latino). Average age 30. 7 applicants, 100% accepted, 4 enrolled. In 2017, 14 master's, 1 Certificate awarded. *Degree requirements:* For master's, comprehensive exam, thesis or alternative, portfolio, Reading K-12 Subject Area Exam of the Florida Teacher Certification Examination. *Entrance requirements:* Additional exam requirements/recommendations for international students: Required—TOEFL. *Application deadline:* For fall admission, 7/15 for domestic students; for spring admission, 12/1 for domestic students; for summer admission, 4/15 for domestic students. Application fee: $30. Electronic applications accepted. *Expenses:* Tuition, state resident: part-time $288.16 per credit hour. Tuition, nonresident: part-time $1073.91 per credit hour. Tuition and fees vary according to program. *Financial support:* In 2017–18, 1 student received support, including 1 research assistantship with partial tuition reimbursement available (averaging $9,896 per year); career-related internships or fieldwork, Federal Work-Study, institutionally sponsored loans, tuition waivers (partial), and unspecified assistantships also available. Financial award application deadline: 3/1; financial award applicants required to submit FAFSA. *Unit head:* Dr. Karri J. Williams, Program Coordinator, 321-433-7922, E-mail: karri.williams@ucf.edu. *Application contact:* Associate Director, Graduate Admissions, 407-823-2766, Fax: 407-823-6442, E-mail: gradadmissions@ucf.edu.
Website: http://www.education.ucf.edu/readinged/

University of Central Missouri, The Graduate School, Warrensburg, MO 64093. Offers accountancy (MA); accounting (MBA); applied mathematics (MS); aviation safety (MA); biology (MS); business administration (MBA); career and technical education leadership (MS); college student personnel administration (MS); communication (MA); computer science (MS); counseling (MS); criminal justice (MS); educational leadership (Ed D); educational technology (MS); elementary and early childhood education (MSE); English (MA); environmental studies (MA); finance (MBA); history (MA); human services/educational technology (Ed S); human services/learning resources (Ed S); human services/professional counseling (Ed S); industrial hygiene (MS); industrial management

(MS); information systems (MBA); information technology (MS); kinesiology (MS); library science and information services (MS); literacy education (MSE); marketing (MBA); mathematics (MS); music (MA); occupational safety management (MS); psychology (MS); rural family nursing (MS); school administration (MSE); social gerontology (MS); sociology (MA); special education (MSE); speech language pathology (MS); superintendency (Ed S); teaching (MAT); teaching English as a second language (MA); technology (MS); technology management (PhD); theatre (MA). *Program availability:* Part-time, 100% online, blended/hybrid learning. *Faculty:* 337 full-time (145 women), 41 part-time/adjunct (28 women). *Students:* 785 full-time (398 women), 1,633 part-time (1,063 women); includes 231 minority (102 Black or African American, non-Hispanic/Latino; 4 American Indian or Alaska Native, non-Hispanic/Latino; 16 Asian, non-Hispanic/Latino; 52 Hispanic/Latino; 57 Two or more races, non-Hispanic/Latino), 692 international. Average age 30. In 2017, 2,605 master's, 122 other advanced degrees awarded. *Degree requirements:* For master's and Ed S, comprehensive exam (for some programs), thesis (for some programs). *Entrance requirements:* Additional exam requirements/recommendations for international students: Required—TOEFL (minimum score 550 paper-based; 79 iBT). *Application deadline:* For fall admission, 6/1 priority date for domestic and international students; for spring admission, 10/1 priority date for domestic and international students; for summer admission, 4/1 priority date for domestic and international students. Applications are processed on a rolling basis. Application fee: $30 ($75 for international students). Electronic applications accepted. *Expenses:* Tuition, state resident: full-time $8771; part-time $292.35 per credit hour. Tuition, nonresident: full-time $17,541; part-time $584.70 per credit hour. *Required fees:* $372; $24.78 per credit hour. *Financial support:* In 2017–18, 99 students received support. Research assistantships, teaching assistantships, career-related internships or fieldwork, Federal Work-Study, scholarships/grants, and administrative and laboratory assistantships available. Support available to part-time students. Financial award application deadline: 3/1; financial award applicants required to submit FAFSA. *Unit head:* Shellie Hewitt, Director of Graduate and International Student Services, 660-543-4621, Fax: 660-543-4778, E-mail: hewitt@ucmo.edu. *Application contact:* 660-543-4621, E-mail: admit_intl@ucmo.edu.
Website: http://www.ucmo.edu/graduate/

University of Central Oklahoma, The Jackson College of Graduate Studies, College of Education and Professional Studies, Donna Nigh Department of Advanced Professional and Special Services, Edmond, OK 73034-5209. Offers educational leadership (M Ed); library media education (M Ed); reading (M Ed); school counseling (M Ed); special education (M Ed), including mild/moderate disabilities, severe-profound/multiple disabilities; speech-language pathology (MS). *Accreditation:* ASHA. *Program availability:* Part-time. *Faculty:* 17 full-time (12 women), 8 part-time/adjunct (4 women). *Students:* 73 full-time (65 women), 286 part-time (239 women); includes 91 minority (41 Black or African American, non-Hispanic/Latino; 8 American Indian or Alaska Native, non-Hispanic/Latino; 5 Asian, non-Hispanic/Latino; 20 Hispanic/Latino; 17 Two or more races, non-Hispanic/Latino), 3 international. Average age 35. 146 applicants, 83% accepted, 91 enrolled. In 2017, 128 master's awarded. *Degree requirements:* For master's, comprehensive exam (for some programs), thesis (for some programs). *Entrance requirements:* Additional exam requirements/recommendations for international students: Required—TOEFL (minimum score 550 paper-based; 79 iBT), IELTS (minimum score 6.5). *Application deadline:* For fall admission, 7/15 for international students; for spring admission, 11/15 for international students; for summer admission, 1/31 for domestic students. Applications are processed on a rolling basis. Application fee: $60. Electronic applications accepted. *Expenses:* Tuition, state resident: full-time $5375; part-time $268.75 per credit hour. Tuition, nonresident: full-time $13,295; part-time $664.75 per credit hour. *Required fees:* $626; $31.30 per credit hour. One-time fee: $50. Tuition and fees vary according to program. *Financial support:* In 2017–18, 74 students received support, including 1 research assistantship with partial tuition reimbursement available (averaging $2,958 per year), 1 teaching assistantship with partial tuition reimbursement available (averaging $5,915 per year); career-related internships or fieldwork, scholarships/grants, tuition waivers (partial), and unspecified assistantships also available. Financial award application deadline: 3/31; financial award applicants required to submit FAFSA. *Unit head:* Dr. Cheryl Evans, Chair, 405-974-5437, Fax: 405-974-3857. *Application contact:* Carlie Wellington, Assistant Director, CEPS Graduate Enrollment, 405-974-5105, Fax: 405-974-3851, E-mail: gradcoll@uco.edu.
Website: http://sites.uco.edu/ceps/dept/Education-Programs/apss/index.asp

University of Cincinnati, Graduate School, College of Education, Criminal Justice, and Human Services, School of Education, Program in Literacy and Second Language Studies, Cincinnati, OH 45221. Offers M Ed, Ed D. *Accreditation:* NCATE. *Program availability:* Part-time. *Degree requirements:* For master's, thesis or alternative; for doctorate, thesis/dissertation. *Entrance requirements:* For master's, GRE General Test. Additional exam requirements/recommendations for international students: Required—TOEFL (minimum score 550 paper-based), TWE (minimum score 4.5), OEPT. Electronic applications accepted. *Expenses: Tuition, area resident:* Full-time $14,468. Tuition, state resident: full-time $14,968; part-time $754 per credit hour. Tuition, nonresident: full-time $24,210; part-time $1311 per credit hour. *International tuition:* $26,460 full-time. *Required fees:* $3958; $84 per credit hour. One-time fee: $85 full-time. Tuition and fees vary according to course load, degree level and program.

University of Colorado Denver, School of Education and Human Development, Teacher Education Programs, Denver, CO 80217. Offers elementary linguistically diverse education (MA); elementary math and science education (MA); elementary math education (MA); elementary reading and writing (MA); elementary science education (MA); secondary English education (MA); secondary linguistically diverse education (MA); secondary math education (MA); secondary reading and writing (MA); secondary science education (MA); special education (MA). *Accreditation:* NCATE. *Program availability:* Part-time, evening/weekend. *Degree requirements:* For master's, comprehensive exam. *Entrance requirements:* For master's, GRE or MAT (for those with GPA below 2.75), transcripts, resume, letters of recommendation. Additional exam requirements/recommendations for international students: Required—TOEFL (minimum score 537 paper-based; 75 iBT); Recommended—IELTS (minimum score 6.5). Electronic applications accepted. *Expenses:* Contact institution. *Faculty research:* Linguistically diverse education/ESL, elementary reading and writing, elementary teacher education, secondary teacher education, special education.

University of Connecticut, Graduate School, Neag School of Education, Department of Curriculum and Instruction, Program in Reading Education, Storrs, CT 06269. Offers MA, PhD. *Accreditation:* NCATE. Terminal master's awarded for partial completion of doctoral program. *Degree requirements:* For master's, comprehensive exam, thesis or alternative; for doctorate, thesis/dissertation. *Entrance requirements:* For doctorate, GRE General Test. Additional exam requirements/recommendations for international students: Required—TOEFL (minimum score 550 paper-based). Electronic applications accepted.

University of Dayton, Department of Teacher Education, Dayton, OH 45469. Offers adolescence to young adult education (MS Ed); early childhood leadership and advocacy (MS Ed); interdisciplinary education (MS Ed), including visual arts; interdisciplinary education studies (MS Ed); leadership in educational systems (MS Ed); literacy education (MS Ed); mathematics education (MS Ed); middle childhood education (MS Ed); multi-age education (MS Ed), including world languages; music education (MS Ed);

teacher as leader (MS Ed); teacher education (MS Ed); technology-enhanced learning (MS Ed); trans-disciplinary early childhood education (MS Ed). *Program availability:* Part-time, 100% online. *Faculty:* 23 full-time (20 women), 41 part-time/adjunct (36 women). *Students:* 45 full-time (38 women), 68 part-time (57 women); includes 7 minority (3 Black or African American, non-Hispanic/Latino; 1 Hispanic/Latino; 3 Two or more races, non-Hispanic/Latino), 6 international. Average age 31. 106 applicants, 28% accepted. In 2017, 70 master's awarded. *Degree requirements:* For master's, variable foreign language requirement, thesis or alternative, internship (for teaching licensure or endorsement). *Entrance requirements:* For master's, GRE (minimum score of 149 verbal, 4 on writing) or MAT (minimum score of 396) if undergraduate GPA was under 2.75, minimum GPA of 2.75, 3 letters of recommendation, personal statement or resume, official transcripts. Additional exam requirements/recommendations for international students: Required—TOEFL (minimum score 550 paper-based; 80 iBT); Recommended—IELTS (minimum score 6.5). *Application deadline:* Applications are processed on a rolling basis. Application fee: $0 ($50 for international students). Electronic applications accepted. *Expenses:* Contact institution. *Financial support:* In 2017–18, 5 research assistantships with partial tuition reimbursements (averaging $9,640 per year) were awarded; teaching assistantships, career-related internships or fieldwork, institutionally sponsored loans, and unspecified assistantships also available. Financial award application deadline: 3/1; financial award applicants required to submit FAFSA. *Faculty research:* Social emotional learning, culturally responsive teaching, urban teaching, literacy, instructional strategies, pre-service teacher education preparation. *Unit head:* Dr. Connie L. Bowman, Chair, 937-229-3348, E-mail: cbowman1@udayton.edu. *Application contact:* Gina Seiter, Coordinator of Graduate Programs and Licensing, 937-229-3103, E-mail: gseiter1@udayton.edu.
Website: https://www.udayton.edu/education/departments_and_programs/edt

The University of Findlay, Office of Graduate Admissions, Findlay, OH 45840. Offers applied security and analytics (MSAS); athletic training (MAT); business (MBA), including certified management accountant, certified public accountant, health care management, hospitality management; education (MA Ed, Ed D), including children's literature (MA Ed), curriculum and teaching (MA Ed), education (MA Ed), educational administration (MA Ed), human resource development (MA Ed), mathematics (MA Ed), reading (MA Ed), science education (MA Ed), superintendent (Ed D), teaching (Ed D), technology (MA Ed); environmental, safety, and health management (MSEM); health informatics (MS); occupational therapy (MOT); pharmacy (Pharm D); physical therapy (DPT); physician assistant (MPA); rhetoric and writing (MA); teaching English to speakers of other languages (TESOL) and applied linguistics (MA). *Program availability:* Part-time, evening/weekend, 100% online, blended/hybrid learning. *Students:* 688 full-time (430 women), 553 part-time (308 women), 170 international. Average age 28. In 2017, 366 master's, 137 doctorates awarded. *Degree requirements:* For master's, comprehensive exam (for some programs), thesis (for some programs), cumulative project, capstone project; for doctorate, thesis/dissertation (for some programs). *Entrance requirements:* For master's, GRE/GMAT, bachelor's degree from accredited institution, minimum undergraduate GPA of 2.5 in last 64 hours of course work; for doctorate, GRE, MAT, minimum cumulative GPA of 3.0. Additional exam requirements/ recommendations for international students: Required—TOEFL (minimum score 79 iBT), IELTS (minimum score 7), PTE (minimum score 61). *Application deadline:* Applications are processed on a rolling basis. Electronic applications accepted. *Financial support:* In 2017–18, 10 research assistantships with partial tuition reimbursements (averaging $7,200 per year), 35 teaching assistantships with partial tuition reimbursements (averaging $7,200 per year) were awarded; Federal Work-Study, institutionally sponsored loans, and unspecified assistantships also available. Financial award applicants required to submit FAFSA. *Unit head:* Christopher M. Harris, Director of Admissions, 419-434-4347, E-mail: harrisc1@findlay.edu. *Application contact:* Madeline Fauser Brennan, Graduate Admissions Counselor, 419-434-4636, Fax: 419-434-4898, E-mail: fauserbrennan@findlay.edu.
Website: http://www.findlay.edu/admissions/graduate/Pages/default.aspx

University of Florida, Graduate School, College of Education, School of Teaching and Learning, Gainesville, FL 32611. Offers curriculum and instruction (M Ed, MAE, Ed D, PhD, Ed S); elementary education (M Ed, MAE); English education (M Ed, MAE); mathematics education (M Ed, MAE); reading education (M Ed, MAE); science education (M Ed, MAE); social studies education (M Ed, MAE). *Accreditation:* NCATE. *Program availability:* Part-time, evening/weekend, online learning. Terminal master's awarded for partial completion of doctoral program. *Degree requirements:* For master's, comprehensive exam (for some programs), thesis (for some programs); for doctorate, comprehensive exam (for some programs), thesis/dissertation (for some programs). *Entrance requirements:* For master's and doctorate, GRE General Test, minimum GPA of 3.0; for Ed S, GRE General Test. Additional exam requirements/recommendations for international students: Required—TOEFL (minimum score 550 paper-based; 80 iBT), IELTS (minimum score 6). Electronic applications accepted. *Faculty research:* STEM education; curriculum; teaching and teacher education; languages and literacy; schools, culture, and society; theories and processes of learning.

University of Georgia, College of Education, Department of Language and Literacy Education, Athens, GA 30602. Offers English education (M Ed); language and literacy education (PhD). *Accreditation:* NCATE. *Degree requirements:* For doctorate, variable foreign language requirement. *Entrance requirements:* For master's, GRE General Test or MAT; for doctorate, GRE General Test. Additional exam requirements/ recommendations for international students: Required—TOEFL (minimum score 550 paper-based). Electronic applications accepted. *Faculty research:* Comprehension, critical literacy, literacy and technology, vocabulary instruction, content area reading.

University of Guam, Office of Graduate Studies, School of Education, Program in Language and Literacy, Mangilao, GU 96923. Offers M Ed. *Program availability:* Part-time. *Degree requirements:* For master's, comprehensive oral and written exams, special project or thesis. *Entrance requirements:* For master's, GRE General Test. Additional exam requirements/recommendations for international students: Required—TOEFL.

University of Houston–Clear Lake, School of Education, Program in Curriculum and Instruction, Houston, TX 77058-1002. Offers curriculum and instruction (MS); early childhood education (MS); reading (MS); school library and information science (MS). *Program availability:* Part-time, evening/weekend. *Degree requirements:* For master's, thesis (for some programs). *Entrance requirements:* For master's, GRE or minimum GPA of 3.0 in last 60 hours. Additional exam requirements/recommendations for international students: Required—TOEFL (minimum score 550 paper-based). Electronic applications accepted.

University of Houston–Victoria, School of Education, Health Professions and Human Development, Victoria, TX 77901-4450. Offers administration and supervision (M Ed); adult and higher education (M Ed); counselor education (M Ed); curriculum and instruction (M Ed); dyslexia education (Certificate); educational technology (M Ed); special education (M Ed). *Program availability:* Part-time, evening/weekend, online learning. *Degree requirements:* For master's, comprehensive exam, project or thesis. *Entrance requirements:* For master's, GRE General Test. Additional exam requirements/ recommendations for international students: Required—TOEFL. Electronic applications accepted. *Faculty research:* Reading and language arts education, evaluation and diagnosis of special children's abilities.

Reading Education

University of Kentucky, Graduate School, College of Education, Program in Curriculum and Instruction, Lexington, KY 40506-0032. Offers curriculum and instruction (Ed D, PhD); elementary education (MA Ed); instructional system design (MS Ed); literacy (MA Ed); middle school education (MA Ed, MS Ed); secondary education (MA Ed, MS Ed). *Accreditation:* NCATE. *Degree requirements:* For master's, comprehensive exam, thesis optional; for doctorate, comprehensive exam, thesis/dissertation. *Entrance requirements:* For master's, GRE General Test, minimum undergraduate GPA of 2.75; for doctorate, GRE General Test, minimum graduate GPA of 3.0. Additional exam requirements/recommendations for international students: Required—TOEFL (minimum score 550 paper-based). Electronic applications accepted. *Faculty research:* Educational reform, multicultural education, classroom instructional practices, performance based assessment, primary school programs.

University of La Verne, LaFetra College of Education, Program in Reading, La Verne, CA 91750-4443. Offers reading (M Ed, Certificate); reading and language arts specialist (Credential). *Faculty:* 1 (woman) full-time, 1 (woman) part-time/adjunct. *Students:* 9 part-time (all women); includes 4 minority (all Hispanic/Latino). Average age 43. *Entrance requirements:* For master's, MAT, California Basic Educational Skills Test, minimum GPA of 3.0, basic teaching credential, interview, 3 letters of reference. *Application deadline:* Applications are processed on a rolling basis. Application fee: $50. *Expenses:* Contact institution. *Financial support:* Institutionally sponsored loans and scholarships/grants available. Financial award application deadline: 3/2; financial award applicants required to submit FAFSA. *Unit head:* Niki Elliott, Co-Director, Center for Neurodiversity, Learning, and Wellness/Visiting Professor, 909-448-1472, E-mail: nelliott@laverne.edu. *Application contact:* Kristen Ahn, Assistant Director of Graduate Admission, 909-448-4480, Fax: 909-971-2295, E-mail: sahn@laverne.edu.
Website: https://education.laverne.edu/graduate/

University of Lynchburg, Graduate Studies, M Ed Program in Reading, Lynchburg, VA 24501-3199. Offers reading instruction (M Ed); reading specialist (M Ed). *Program availability:* Part-time, evening/weekend. *Faculty:* 17 full-time (10 women). *Students:* 1 (woman) full-time, 16 part-time (15 women); includes 1 minority (Black or African American, non-Hispanic/Latino). Average age 38. 9 applicants, 100% accepted, 4 enrolled. In 2017, 1 master's awarded. *Degree requirements:* For master's, comprehensive exam (for some programs), practicum; portfolio or state license exam. *Entrance requirements:* For master's, GRE, minimum GPA of 3.0 (preferred), three letters of recommendation, official transcripts (bachelor's, others as relevant), career goals statement. Additional exam requirements/recommendations for international students: Required—TOEFL (minimum score 550 paper-based; 80 iBT), IELTS (minimum score 6). *Application deadline:* For fall admission, 7/31 for domestic students, 6/1 for international students; for spring admission, 11/30 for domestic students, 10/15 for international students. Applications are processed on a rolling basis. Application fee: $30. Electronic applications accepted. Application fee is waived when completed online. *Expenses:* $510 per credit tuition, $100 fees. *Financial support:* Federal Work-Study, scholarships/grants, health care benefits, and unspecified assistantships available. Support available to part-time students. Financial award application deadline: 7/31; financial award applicants required to submit FAFSA. *Unit head:* Dr. Gail Brown, Program Director/Professor, Reading, 434-544.8768, E-mail: brown.g@lynchburg.edu. *Application contact:* Ellen Thompson, Graduate Admissions Counselor, 434-544-8841, E-mail: thompson_e@lynchburg.edu.
Website: http://www.lynchburg.edu/graduate/master-of-education-in-reading/

University of Maine, Graduate School, College of Education and Human Development, School of Learning and Teaching, Orono, ME 04469. Offers counselor education (M Ed, MA, MS, CAS); early childhood teacher (CGS); education (PhD), including counselor education, literacy education, prevention and intervention studies; elementary education (M Ed, CAS); individualized education (M Ed); literacy education (CAS); response to intervention for behavior (CGS); secondary education (M Ed, CAS); social studies education (M Ed); special education (M Ed, CAS). *Program availability:* Part-time. *Faculty:* 21 full-time (12 women), 37 part-time/adjunct (29 women). *Students:* 84 full-time (73 women), 190 part-time (165 women); includes 19 minority (1 Black or African American, non-Hispanic/Latino; 9 American Indian or Alaska Native, non-Hispanic/Latino; 2 Asian, non-Hispanic/Latino; 4 Hispanic/Latino; 3 Two or more races, non-Hispanic/Latino), 4 international. Average age 38. 141 applicants, 94% accepted, 91 enrolled. In 2017, 74 master's, 3 doctorates, 36 other advanced degrees awarded. *Degree requirements:* For master's, thesis (for some programs); for doctorate, comprehensive exam, thesis/dissertation. *Entrance requirements:* For master's, GRE General Test, MAT. Additional exam requirements/recommendations for international students: Required—TOEFL (minimum score 550 paper-based; 80 iBT), IELTS (minimum score 6.5). *Application deadline:* For fall admission, 2/1 priority date for domestic students. Applications are processed on a rolling basis. Application fee: $65. Electronic applications accepted. *Expenses:* Tuition, state resident: full-time $7722; part-time $429 per credit hour. Tuition, nonresident: full-time $25,146; part-time $1397 per credit hour. *Required fees:* $1162; $581 per credit hour. *Financial support:* In 2017-18, 14 students received support, including 11 teaching assistantships (averaging $15,200 per year); Federal Work-Study, scholarships/grants, and unspecified assistantships also available. Financial award application deadline: 3/1. *Faculty research:* Gender and leadership, virtual reality, using writing to improve performance in athletics, digital citizenship, professional development for special and general education. *Total annual research expenditures:* $5 million. *Unit head:* Dr. Jim Artesani, Associate Dean of Accreditation and Graduate Affairs, 207-581-4061. *Application contact:* Scott G. Delcourt, Assistant Vice President for Graduate Studies and Senior Associate Dean, 207-581-3291, Fax: 207-581-3232, E-mail: graduate@maine.edu.
Website: http://umaine.edu/edhd/

University of Mary, Liffrig Family School of Education and Behavioral Sciences, Department of Education, Bismarck, ND 58504-9652. Offers curriculum, instruction and assessment (M Ed); education (Ed D); elementary administration (M Ed); reading (M Ed); secondary administration (M Ed); special education strategist (M Ed). *Program availability:* Part-time. *Degree requirements:* For master's, portfolio or thesis. *Entrance requirements:* For master's, interview, letters of reference, minimum GPA of 2.5. Additional exam requirements/recommendations for international students: Required—TOEFL (minimum score 500 paper-based; 71 iBT). Electronic applications accepted.

University of Maryland, College Park, Academic Affairs, College of Education, Department of Teaching, Learning, Policy and Leadership, College Park, MD 20742. Offers reading (M Ed, MA, PhD, CAGS); secondary education (M Ed, MA, Ed D, PhD, CAGS); teaching English to speakers of other languages (M Ed). *Accreditation:* NCATE. *Program availability:* Part-time, evening/weekend, online learning. *Degree requirements:* For master's, comprehensive exam, seminar paper; for doctorate, comprehensive exam, thesis/dissertation, published paper, oral exam. *Entrance requirements:* For master's, GRE General Test or MAT, minimum GPA of 3.0, 3 letters of recommendation; for doctorate, GRE General Test or MAT, minimum undergraduate GPA of 3.0, graduate 3.5; 3 letters of recommendation. Electronic applications accepted. *Faculty research:* Teacher preparation, curriculum study, in-service education.

University of Massachusetts Amherst, Graduate School, College of Education, Program in Education, Amherst, MA 01003. Offers bilingual, English as a second language, and multicultural education (M Ed, Ed S); child study and early education

(M Ed); children, families and schools (Ed D, Ed S); early childhood and elementary teacher education (M Ed); educational leadership (M Ed); educational policy and leadership (Ed D); higher education (M Ed); international education (M Ed); language, literacy and culture (Ed D); learning, media and technology (M Ed, Ed S); mathematics, science, and learning technologies (Ed D); reading and writing (M Ed); research, educational measurement and psychometrics (Ed D); school counselor education (M Ed, Ed S); school psychology (Ed S); science education (Ed S); secondary teacher education (M Ed); social justice education (M Ed, Ed D, Ed S); special education (M Ed, Ed D, Ed S); teacher education and school improvement (Ed D, Ed S). *Accreditation:* NCATE. *Program availability:* Part-time, online learning. Terminal master's awarded for partial completion of doctoral program. *Degree requirements:* For doctorate, comprehensive exam, thesis/dissertation. *Entrance requirements:* Additional exam requirements/recommendations for international students: Required—TOEFL (minimum score 550 paper-based; 80 iBT), IELTS (minimum score 6.5). Electronic applications accepted.

University of Memphis, Graduate School, College of Education, Department of Instruction and Curriculum Leadership, Memphis, TN 38152. Offers advanced studies in teaching and learning (M Ed); applied behavior analysis (Graduate Certificate); autism studies (Graduate Certificate); early childhood education (MAT, MS, Ed D); elementary education (MAT); instruction and curriculum (MS, Ed D); instruction design and technology (MS, Ed D); instructional design and technology (Graduate Certificate); literacy, leadership, and coaching (Graduate Certificate); reading (MS, Ed D); school library information specialist (Graduate Certificate); secondary education (MAT); special education (MAT, MS, Ed D); STEM teacher leadership (Graduate Certificate); urban education (Graduate Certificate). *Accreditation:* NCATE (one or more programs are accredited). *Program availability:* Part-time. *Faculty:* 22 full-time (14 women), 14 part-time/adjunct (10 women). *Students:* 36 full-time (27 women), 351 part-time (271 women); includes 159 minority (132 Black or African American, non-Hispanic/Latino; 1 American Indian or Alaska Native, non-Hispanic/Latino; 7 Asian, non-Hispanic/Latino; 10 Hispanic/Latino; 9 Two or more races, non-Hispanic/Latino), 4 international. Average age 35. 170 applicants, 85% accepted, 111 enrolled. In 2017, 84 master's, 14 doctorates, 32 other advanced degrees awarded. Terminal master's awarded for partial completion of doctoral program. *Degree requirements:* For master's, comprehensive exam, thesis or alternative; for doctorate, comprehensive exam, thesis/dissertation. *Entrance requirements:* For master's, GRE General Test, PRAXIS, minimum GPA of 2.5, letters of reference; for doctorate, GRE General Test, GRE Subject Test, 2 years of teaching experience, letters of reference, statement of purpose, interview. Additional exam requirements/recommendations for international students: Required—TOEFL (minimum score 550 paper-based; 79 iBT). *Application deadline:* For fall admission, 4/1 priority date for domestic students; for spring admission, 10/1 priority date for domestic students; for summer admission, 2/1 priority date for domestic students. Applications are processed on a rolling basis. Application fee: $35 ($60 for international students). Electronic applications accepted. *Expenses:* Contact institution. *Financial support:* In 2017–18, 2 research assistantships with full tuition reimbursements (averaging $10,000 per year), 3 teaching assistantships with full tuition reimbursements (averaging $10,666 per year) were awarded; career-related internships or fieldwork, Federal Work-Study, institutionally sponsored loans, scholarships/grants, traineeships, and unspecified assistantships also available. Support available to part-time students. Financial award application deadline: 2/1; financial award applicants required to submit FAFSA. *Faculty research:* Effective urban teachers, preparation and retention of urban teachers, technology utilization in schools, field-based teacher preparation programs, effective use of online instruction. *Unit head:* Dr. Angiline Powell, Interim Chair, 901-678-3310, E-mail: apowell3@memphis.edu. *Application contact:* Dr. James Meindl, Coordinator of Graduate Studies, 901-678-3310, E-mail: jnmeindl@memphis.edu.
Website: http://www.memphis.edu/icl/

University of Miami, Graduate School, School of Education and Human Development, Department of Teaching and Learning, Program in Teaching and Learning, Coral Gables, FL 33124. Offers language and literacy learning in multilingual settings (PhD); science, technology, engineering and mathematics (PhD); special education (PhD). *Degree requirements:* For doctorate, thesis/dissertation, qualifying exam, electronic portfolio. *Entrance requirements:* For doctorate, GRE General Test. Additional exam requirements/recommendations for international students: Required—TOEFL (minimum score 550 paper-based; 80 iBT); Recommended—IELTS (minimum score 6.5). Electronic applications accepted. *Faculty research:* Teacher education, multicultural education, special education, second language acquisition, math and science education.

University of Michigan–Flint, School of Education and Human Services, Department of Education, Flint, MI 48502-1950. Offers curriculum and instruction (Ed S); early childhood education (MA); education (Ed D); educational leadership (Ed S); educational technology (MA), including curriculum and instruction, developer; literacy education (MA); secondary education with certification (MA). *Program availability:* Part-time, evening/weekend, 100% online, mixed mode format (for some programs). *Faculty:* 18 full-time (11 women), 26 part-time/adjunct (13 women). *Students:* 34 full-time (23 women), 192 part-time (137 women); includes 61 minority (46 Black or African American, non-Hispanic/Latino; 2 Asian, non-Hispanic/Latino; 5 Hispanic/Latino; 2 Native Hawaiian or other Pacific Islander, non-Hispanic/Latino; 6 Two or more races, non-Hispanic/Latino), 2 international. Average age 39. 124 applicants, 87% accepted, 81 enrolled. In 2017, 89 master's, 3 doctorates awarded. *Degree requirements:* For master's, thesis optional; for doctorate, thesis/dissertation. *Entrance requirements:* For master's, bachelor's degree from regionally-accredited institution, minimum overall undergraduate GPA of 3.0; for doctorate, Ed S; minimum overall graduate GPA of 3.3 (6.0 on a 9.0 scale) or equivalent; at least 3 years of work experience in a P-16 educational institution or in an education-related position; for Ed S, MA or MS in education-related field from accredited institution; minimum overall graduate GPA of 3.0 (6.0 on a 9.0 scale) or equivalent; at least 3 years of work experience in an educational setting. Additional exam requirements/recommendations for international students: Required—TOEFL (minimum score 84 iBT), IELTS (minimum score 6.5). *Application deadline:* For fall admission, 8/1 for domestic students, 5/1 for international students; for winter admission, 11/15 for domestic students, 9/15 for international students; for spring admission, 3/15 for domestic students, 1/15 for international students; for summer admission, 5/15 for domestic students. Applications are processed on a rolling basis. Application fee: $55. Electronic applications accepted. *Expenses:* Contact institution. *Financial support:* Federal Work-Study, scholarships/grants, and unspecified assistantships available. Financial award application deadline: 3/1; financial award applicants required to submit FAFSA. *Unit head:* Dr. Mary Jo Finney, Department Chair/Associate Professor, 810-766-6617, E-mail: mjfinney@umflint.edu. *Application contact:* Bradley T. Maki, Director of Graduate Admissions, 810-762-3171, Fax: 810-766-6789, E-mail: bmaki@umflint.edu.
Website: https://www.umflint.edu/education/graduate-programs

University of Minnesota, Twin Cities Campus, Graduate School, College of Education and Human Development, Department of Curriculum and Instruction, Minneapolis, MN 55455-0213. Offers art education (M Ed, MA, PhD); curriculum and instruction (M Ed, MA, PhD); elementary education (MA, PhD); English education (PhD); language and immersion education (Certificate); learning technologies (MA, PhD); literacy education (MA, PhD); second language education (MA, PhD); social studies

education (MA, PhD); STEM education (MA, PhD); teaching (M Ed), including mathematics, science, social studies, teaching; teaching English to speakers of other languages (MA); technology enhanced learning (Certificate). *Faculty:* 37 full-time (21 women). *Students:* 401 full-time (282 women), 303 part-time (212 women); includes 139 minority (26 Black or African American, non-Hispanic/Latino; 4 American Indian or Alaska Native, non-Hispanic/Latino; 34 Asian, non-Hispanic/Latino; 45 Hispanic/Latino; 1 Native Hawaiian or other Pacific Islander, non-Hispanic/Latino; 29 Two or more races, non-Hispanic/Latino), 43 international. Average age 32. 596 applicants, 61% accepted, 330 enrolled. In 2017, 316 master's, 30 doctorates, 19 other advanced degrees awarded. Application fee: $75 ($95 for international students). *Financial support:* In 2017–18, 3 fellowships, 56 research assistantships with full tuition reimbursements (averaging $11,118 per year), 67 teaching assistantships with full tuition reimbursements (averaging $11,975 per year) were awarded. *Faculty research:* Teaching and learning; influence of cultural, linguistic, social, political, and technological factors on teaching, learning and educational research; relationship between educational practice and a democratic and just society; urban education; immigrant education, racial justice and education. *Total annual research expenditures:* $2.2 million. *Unit head:* Dr. Cynthia Lewis, Chair, 612-625-6313, E-mail: lewis@umn.edu. *Application contact:* Dr. Gillian Roehrig, Director of Graduate Studies, 612-625-0561, E-mail: roehr013@umn.edu.
Website: http://www.cehd.umn.edu/ci

University of Minnesota, Twin Cities Campus, Graduate School, College of Education and Human Development, Department of Organizational Leadership, Policy and Development, Minneapolis, MN 55455-0213. Offers adult literacy (Certificate); comparative and international development education (MA, PhD); disability policy and services (Certificate); education policy and leadership (M Ed, MA, Ed D, PhD), including educational policy and leadership (MA, Ed D, PhD), leadership in education (M Ed); evaluation studies (MA, PhD); higher education (MA, Ed D, PhD), including higher education (MA, PhD), multicultural college teaching and learning (MA); human resource development (M Ed, MA, Ed D, PhD, Certificate); PK-12 administrative licensure (Certificate); private college leadership (Certificate); professional development (Certificate); program evaluation (Certificate); technical education (Certificate); undergraduate multicultural teaching and learning (Certificate). *Faculty:* 32 full-time (14 women). *Students:* 289 full-time (210 women), 251 part-time (157 women); includes 114 minority (41 Black or African American, non-Hispanic/Latino; 4 American Indian or Alaska Native, non-Hispanic/Latino; 27 Asian, non-Hispanic/Latino; 22 Hispanic/Latino; 1 Native Hawaiian or other Pacific Islander, non-Hispanic/Latino; 19 Two or more races, non-Hispanic/Latino), 77 international. Average age 36. 419 applicants, 58% accepted, 204 enrolled. In 2017, 79 master's, 36 doctorates, 49 other advanced degrees awarded. Application fee: $75 ($95 for international students). *Financial support:* In 2017–18, 2 fellowships, 30 research assistantships with full tuition reimbursements (averaging $9,944 per year), 27 teaching assistantships with full tuition reimbursements (averaging $10,036 per year) were awarded; scholarships/grants also available. *Faculty research:* Organizational issues in schools, universities, and other organizations; international education and development; program evaluation and research on applied evaluation methods; international human resource development and change; gender and race/ethnicity in relation to learning and leadership. *Total annual research expenditures:* $930,589. *Unit head:* Dr. Heidi Barajas, Chair, 612-625-4823, Fax: 612-624-3377, E-mail: hbarajas@umn.edu. *Application contact:* Dr. Jeremy J. Hernandez, Coordinator of Graduate Studies, 612-626-9377, E-mail: herna220@umn.edu.
Website: http://www.cehd.umn.edu/olpd/

University of Mississippi, Graduate School, School of Education, University, MS 38677. Offers counselor education (M Ed, PhD); counselor education - play therapy (Ed S); early childhood (M Ed); educational leadership K-12 (M Ed, Ed D, PhD, Ed S); elementary education (M Ed, Ed D, Ed S); higher education/student personnel (Ed D, PhD); literacy education (M Ed); math education (Ed D); secondary education (M Ed, PhD, Ed S); special education (M Ed, PhD, Ed S); teacher corporations (MA); teacher education (MA). *Accreditation:* NCATE. *Faculty:* 65 full-time (40 women), 25 part-time/adjunct (5 women). *Students:* 185 full-time (148 women), 410 part-time (310 women); includes 193 minority (168 Black or African American, non-Hispanic/Latino; 7 Asian, non-Hispanic/Latino; 14 Hispanic/Latino; 4 Two or more races, non-Hispanic/Latino), 7 international. Average age 33. In 2017, 176 master's, 20 doctorates, 37 other advanced degrees awarded. *Entrance requirements:* For master's, GRE General Test, minimum GPA of 3.0; for doctorate, GRE General Test. Additional exam requirements/recommendations for international students: Required—TOEFL. *Application deadline:* For fall admission, 3/1 for domestic students; for spring admission, 10/1 for domestic students; for summer admission, 3/1 for domestic students. Applications are processed on a rolling basis. Application fee: $50. Electronic applications accepted. *Financial support:* Scholarships/grants available. Financial award application deadline: 3/1; financial award applicants required to submit FAFSA. *Unit head:* Dr. David Rock, Dean, 662-915-7063, Fax: 662-915-7249, E-mail: soe@olemiss.edu. *Application contact:* Dr. Joe Sumrall, Professor of Elementary Education, 662-915-7350, E-mail: soe@olemiss.edu.

University of Missouri, Office of Research and Graduate Studies, College of Education, Department of Learning, Teaching and Curriculum, Columbia, MO 65211. Offers agricultural education (M Ed, PhD, Ed S); art education (M Ed, PhD, Ed S); business and office education (M Ed, PhD, Ed S); early childhood education (M Ed, PhD, Ed S); elementary education (M Ed, PhD, Ed S); English education (M Ed, PhD, Ed S); foreign language education (M Ed, PhD, Ed S); health education and promotion (M Ed, PhD); learning and instruction (M Ed); marketing education (M Ed, PhD, Ed S); mathematics education (M Ed, PhD, Ed S); music education (M Ed, PhD, Ed S); reading education (M Ed, PhD, Ed S); science education (M Ed, PhD, Ed S); social studies education (M Ed, PhD, Ed S); vocational education (M Ed, PhD, Ed S). *Program availability:* Part-time. Terminal master's awarded for partial completion of doctoral program. *Degree requirements:* For master's, thesis/dissertation. *Entrance requirements:* For master's and Ed S, GRE General Test or MAT, minimum GPA of 3.0; for doctorate, GRE General Test, minimum GPA of 3.0. Additional exam requirements/recommendations for international students: Required—TOEFL (minimum score 600 paper-based; 100 iBT). Electronic applications accepted.

University of Missouri–Kansas City, School of Education, Kansas City, MO 64110-2499. Offers administration (Ed D); counseling and guidance (MA, Ed S), including mental health counseling (Ed S), school counseling (Ed S); counseling psychology (PhD); curriculum and instruction (MA, Ed S), including language and literacy (Ed S); education (PhD), including higher education administration, PK-12 education administration; educational administration (MA, Ed S), including advanced principal (Ed S), beginning principal (Ed S), district-level administration (Ed S); reading education (MA); special education (MA). PhD in education offered through the School of Graduate Studies. *Accreditation:* NCATE. *Program availability:* Part-time, evening/weekend. *Degree requirements:* For doctorate, thesis/dissertation, internship, practicum. *Entrance requirements:* For master's, GRE, minimum GPA of 2.75, 2 letters of reference, written statement of purpose; for doctorate, GRE, minimum GPA of 3.0; for Ed S, minimum GPA of 3.0. Additional exam requirements/recommendations for international students: Required—TOEFL (minimum score 550 paper-based; 80 iBT). *Faculty research:* Urban

education, inquiry-based field study, theories of counseling and psychotherapy, school literacy, educational technology.

University of Missouri–St. Louis, College of Education, Department of Educator Preparation, Innovation and Research, St. Louis, MO 63121. Offers elementary education (M Ed), including early childhood, general, reading; secondary education (M Ed), including curriculum and instruction, general, middle level education, reading, teaching English to speakers of other languages (TESOL); special education (M Ed), including autism and developmental disabilities, early childhood special education. *Program availability:* Part-time, evening/weekend. *Students:* 75 full-time (63 women), 462 part-time (363 women); includes 127 minority (85 Black or African American, non-Hispanic/Latino; 2 American Indian or Alaska Native, non-Hispanic/Latino; 8 Asian, non-Hispanic/Latino; 24 Hispanic/Latino; 8 Two or more races, non-Hispanic/Latino), 1 international. 247 applicants, 92% accepted, 153 enrolled. *Degree requirements:* For master's, comprehensive exam. *Entrance requirements:* Additional exam requirements/recommendations for international students: Recommended—TOEFL (minimum score 550 paper-based; 79 iBT), IELTS (minimum score 6.5). *Application deadline:* For fall admission, 7/1 priority date for domestic and international students; for spring admission, 12/1 priority date for domestic and international students. Application fee: $50 ($40 for international students). Electronic applications accepted. *Expenses:* Tuition, state resident: part-time $476.50 per credit hour. Tuition, nonresident: part-time $1169.70 per credit hour. *Financial support:* Application deadline: 4/1; applicants required to submit FAFSA. *Unit head:* Dr. Gayle Wilkinson, Chair, 314-516-5791. *Application contact:* 314-516-5458, Fax: 314-516-6996, E-mail: gadadm@umsl.edu.
Website: https://coe.umsl.edu/dept/epir.html

University of Nebraska at Kearney, College of Education, Department of Teacher Education, Kearney, NE 68849-0001. Offers curriculum and instruction (MA Ed), including early childhood education, elementary education, English as a second language, instructional effectiveness, reading/special education, secondary education; instructional technology (MS Ed), including information technology, instructional technology, school librarian; reading PK-12 (MA Ed); special education (MA Ed), including advanced practitioner: assistive technology specialist, advanced practitioner: behavioral interventionist, advanced practitioner: inclusive collaboration specialist, gifted, teacher education. *Program availability:* Part-time, evening/weekend, online only, 100% online. *Degree requirements:* For master's, comprehensive exam, thesis optional. *Entrance requirements:* For master's, portfolio or GRE. Additional exam requirements/recommendations for international students: Recommended—TOEFL (minimum score 550 paper-based; 79 iBT), IELTS (minimum score 6.5). Electronic applications accepted. *Expenses:* Contact institution.

University of Nevada, Reno, Graduate School, College of Education, Department of Educational Specialties, Program in Literacy Studies, Reno, NV 89557. Offers M Ed, MA, Ed D, PhD. Terminal master's awarded for partial completion of doctoral program. *Degree requirements:* For master's, thesis optional; for doctorate, thesis/dissertation. *Entrance requirements:* For master's, minimum GPA of 2.75; for doctorate, GRE General Test, minimum GPA of 3.0. Additional exam requirements/recommendations for international students: Required—TOEFL (minimum score 500 paper-based; 61 iBT), IELTS (minimum score 6). Electronic applications accepted. *Faculty research:* Cognitive language process, literacy.

University of New England, College of Graduate and Professional Studies, Portland, ME 04005-9526. Offers advanced educational leadership (CAGS); applied nutrition (MS); career and technical education (MS Ed); curriculum and instruction (MS Ed); education (CAGS, Post-Master's Certificate); educational leadership (MS Ed, Ed D); generalist (MS Ed); health informatics (MS, Graduate Certificate); inclusion education (MS Ed); literacy K-12 (MS Ed); medical education leadership (MMEL); public health (MPH); public health (Graduate Certificate); reading specialist (MS Ed); social work (MSW). *Program availability:* Part-time, evening/weekend, online only, 100% online. *Faculty:* 125 part-time/adjunct (94 women). *Students:* 1,403 full-time (1,128 women), 594 part-time (475 women); includes 474 minority (332 Black or African American, non-Hispanic/Latino; 13 American Indian or Alaska Native, non-Hispanic/Latino; 83 Asian, non-Hispanic/Latino; 27 Hispanic/Latino; 11 Native Hawaiian or other Pacific Islander, non-Hispanic/Latino; 8 Two or more races, non-Hispanic/Latino). Average age 35. 3,153 applicants, 41% accepted, 990 enrolled. In 2017, 307 master's, 59 doctorates, 124 other advanced degrees awarded. *Application deadline:* Applications are processed on a rolling basis. Electronic applications accepted. Tuition and fees vary according to degree level, program and student level. *Financial support:* Application deadline: 5/1; applicants required to submit FAFSA. *Unit head:* Dr. Martha Wilson, Associate Provost for Online Worldwide Learning/Dean of the College of Graduate and Professional Studies, 207-221-4985, E-mail: mwilson13@une.edu.
Website: http://online.une.edu

University of New Mexico, Graduate Studies, College of Education, Program in Language, Literacy and Sociocultural Studies, Albuquerque, NM 87131. Offers American Indian education (MA); bilingual education (MA, PhD); educational linguistics (PhD); educational thought and sociocultural studies (MA, PhD); literacy/language arts (MA, PhD); social studies (MA); TESOL (MA, PhD). *Faculty:* 16 full-time (10 women), 4 part-time/adjunct (all women). *Students:* 56 full-time (34 women), 129 part-time (97 women); includes 93 minority (7 Black or African American, non-Hispanic/Latino; 15 American Indian or Alaska Native, non-Hispanic/Latino; 9 Asian, non-Hispanic/Latino; 56 Hispanic/Latino; 6 Two or more races, non-Hispanic/Latino), 44 international. Average age 40. 61 applicants, 38% accepted, 23 enrolled. In 2017, 36 master's, 4 doctorates awarded. *Degree requirements:* For master's, comprehensive exam, thesis optional; for doctorate, comprehensive exam, thesis/dissertation, research skills. *Entrance requirements:* For master's, letter of intent, 3 letters of recommendation, resume, BA/BS, department demographic form, transcripts; for doctorate, writing sample, letter of intent, 3 letters of recommendation, resume, BA/BS, MA, department demographic form, transcripts. Additional exam requirements/recommendations for international students: Required—TOEFL. *Application deadline:* For fall admission, 12/1 for domestic and international students; for spring admission, 9/15 for domestic and international students. Application fee: $50. Electronic applications accepted. *Financial support:* Fellowships, research assistantships, teaching assistantships, career-related internships or fieldwork, institutionally sponsored loans, scholarships/grants, and unspecified assistantships available. Support available to part-time students. Financial award application deadline: 3/1; financial award applicants required to submit FAFSA. *Faculty research:* School reform, professional development, history of education, Native American education, politics of education, feminism and issues of sexual identity, critical race theory, bilingualism, literacy reading, adolescent literature, second language acquisition, critical theory and schooling, indigenous languages. *Unit head:* Dr. Lois M. Meyer, Chair, 505-277-7244, Fax: 505-277-8362, E-mail: lsmeyer@unm.edu. *Application contact:* Debra Schaffer, Administrative Assistant, 505-277-0437, Fax: 505-277-8362, E-mail: schaffer@unm.edu.
Website: http://coe.unm.edu/departments-programs/llss/index.html

The University of North Carolina at Chapel Hill, Graduate School, School of Education, Program in Education, Chapel Hill, NC 27599. Offers culture, curriculum and change (MA, PhD); early childhood, intervention and literacy (MA, PhD); educational psychology, measurement and evaluation (MA, PhD). *Accreditation:* NCATE. *Degree* *requirements:* For master's, thesis; for doctorate, comprehensive exam, thesis/dissertation. *Entrance requirements:* For master's, GRE General Test, minimum GPA of 3.0 during last 2 years of undergraduates course work; for doctorate, GRE General Test, minimum GPA of 3.0 during last 2 years of undergraduate course work. Additional exam requirements/recommendations for international students: Required—TOEFL (minimum score 550 paper-based). Electronic applications accepted.

The University of North Carolina at Charlotte, Cato College of Education, Department of Reading and Elementary Education, Charlotte, NC 28223-0001. Offers elementary education (M Ed, Graduate Certificate); elementary mathematics education (Graduate Certificate); reading education (M Ed). *Program availability:* Part-time, evening/weekend, 100% online, blended/hybrid learning. *Faculty:* 26 full-time (13 women), 1 part-time/adjunct (0 women). *Students:* 4 full-time (all women), 52 part-time (all women); includes 12 minority (8 Black or African American, non-Hispanic/Latino; 1 American Indian or Alaska Native, non-Hispanic/Latino; 2 Hispanic/Latino; 1 Two or more races, non-Hispanic/Latino). Average age 29. 26 applicants, 100% accepted, 21 enrolled. In 2017, 18 master's, 2 other advanced degrees awarded. *Degree requirements:* For master's, thesis or alternative, capstone project. *Entrance requirements:* For master's, GRE or MAT, three letters of recommendation, official transcripts, academic and professional goals statement, valid teacher's license, bachelor's degree in elementary education; NC A-level license or its equivalent in another state (for reading education). Additional exam requirements/recommendations for international students: Required—TOEFL (minimum score 523 paper-based, 70 iBT) or IELTS (6.5). *Application deadline:* For fall admission, 3/1 priority date for domestic students, 3/1 for international students; for spring admission, 10/1 priority date for domestic students, 10/1 for international students; for summer admission, 4/1 priority date for domestic students, 4/1 for international students. Applications are processed on a rolling basis. Application fee: $75. Electronic applications accepted. *Expenses:* Tuition, state resident: full-time $4337. Tuition, nonresident: full-time $17,771. *Required fees:* $3211. Tuition and fees vary according to course load and program. *Financial support:* In 2017–18, 4 students received support, including 4 research assistantships (averaging $15,000 per year); career-related internships or fieldwork, institutionally sponsored loans, scholarships/grants, and unspecified assistantships also available. Support available to part-time students. Financial award application deadline: 3/1; financial award applicants required to submit FAFSA. *Total annual research expenditures:* $163,549. *Unit head:* Dr. Mike Putman, Chair, 704-687-8019, E-mail: michael.putman@uncc.edu. *Application contact:* Kathy B. Giddings, Director of Graduate Admissions, 704-687-5503, Fax: 704-687-1668, E-mail: gradadm@uncc.edu.
Website: http://reel.uncc.edu/

The University of North Carolina at Greensboro, Graduate School, School of Education, Department of Teacher Education and Higher Education, Greensboro, NC 27412-5001. Offers college teaching and adult learning (Certificate); curriculum and instruction (M Ed), including chemistry education, elementary education, English as a second language, French education, instructional technology, mathematics education, middle grades education, reading education, science education, social studies education, Spanish education; curriculum and teaching (PhD), including higher education, teacher education and development; English as a second language (Certificate); higher education (M Ed); supervision (M Ed). *Accreditation:* NCATE. *Program availability:* Part-time. *Degree requirements:* For doctorate, thesis/dissertation. *Entrance requirements:* For master's and doctorate, GRE General Test. Additional exam requirements/recommendations for international students: Required—TOEFL. Electronic applications accepted. *Faculty research:* Community college literacy program, middle school mathematics/computer mathematics.

The University of North Carolina at Pembroke, The Graduate School, School of Education, Program in Reading Education, Pembroke, NC 28372-1510. Offers MA Ed. *Accreditation:* NCATE. *Program availability:* Part-time, evening/weekend. *Degree requirements:* For master's, comprehensive exam, thesis optional. *Entrance requirements:* For master's, GRE General Test or MAT, minimum GPA of 3.0 in major, 2.5 overall; teaching license; one year of teaching experience; three professional references. Additional exam requirements/recommendations for international students: Required—TOEFL. *Application deadline:* For fall admission, 7/15 priority date for domestic and international students; for spring admission, 12/1 priority date for domestic and international students. Applications are processed on a rolling basis. Application fee: $45 ($60 for international students). *Financial support:* Application deadline: 4/15; applicants required to submit FAFSA. *Unit head:* Dr. Heather Kimberly Sellers, Program Director, 910-521-6636, Fax: 910-521-6165, E-mail: heather.sellers@uncp.edu.

The University of North Carolina Wilmington, Watson College of Education, Department of Early Childhood, Elementary, Middle, Literacy and Special Education, Wilmington, NC 28403-3297. Offers educational leadership, policy, and advocacy (M Ed); elementary education (M Ed, MAT); language and literacy (M Ed); middle grades education (MAT). *Accreditation:* NCATE. *Program availability:* Part-time, blended/hybrid learning. *Faculty:* 22 full-time (15 women), 2 part-time/adjunct (both women). *Students:* 82 full-time (70 women), 91 part-time (84 women); includes 51 minority (33 Black or African American, non-Hispanic/Latino; 3 American Indian or Alaska Native, non-Hispanic/Latino; 1 Asian, non-Hispanic/Latino; 8 Hispanic/Latino; 6 Two or more races, non-Hispanic/Latino). Average age 32. 68 applicants, 82% accepted, 45 enrolled. In 2017, 83 master's awarded. *Degree requirements:* For master's, thesis or alternative, exit portfolio, oral presentation, internship, research project (depending on specialization). *Entrance requirements:* For master's, 3 letters of recommendations, NC Class A teacher license in related field, education statement of interest essay. Additional exam requirements/recommendations for international students: Required—TOEFL (minimum score 550 paper-based; 79 iBT), IELTS (minimum score 6.5). *Application deadline:* For fall admission, 5/15 for domestic students; for spring admission, 10/15 for domestic students; for summer admission, 3/15 for domestic students. Applications are processed on a rolling basis. Application fee: $75. Electronic applications accepted. *Expenses:* Tuition, state resident: full-time $4626; part-time $226.76 per credit hour. Tuition, nonresident: full-time $17,834; part-time $874.22 per credit hour. *Required fees:* $2124. Tuition and fees vary according to program. *Financial support:* Scholarships/grants and unspecified assistantships available. Financial award application deadline: 1/1; financial award applicants required to submit FAFSA. *Unit head:* Dr. Kathy Fox, Chair, 910-962-3240, Fax: 910-962-3988, E-mail: foxk@uncw.edu. *Application contact:* Dr. Elizabeth Crawford, Graduate Program Coordinator, 910-962-2916, Fax: 910-962-3988, E-mail: crawforde@uncw.edu.
Website: http://www.uncw.edu/ed/eemls/index.html

University of North Dakota, Graduate School, College of Education and Human Development, Program in Reading Education, Grand Forks, ND 58202. Offers M Ed, MS. *Accreditation:* NCATE. *Program availability:* Part-time, online learning. *Degree requirements:* For master's, comprehensive exam, thesis or alternative. *Entrance requirements:* For master's, minimum GPA of 3.0. Additional exam requirements/recommendations for international students: Required—TOEFL (minimum score 550 paper-based; 79 iBT), IELTS (minimum score 6.5). Electronic applications accepted. *Faculty research:* Whole language, multicultural education, child-focused learning, experiential science, cooperative learning.

University of Northern Colorado, Graduate School, College of Education and Behavioral Sciences, School of Teacher Education, Program in Literacy, Greeley, CO 80639. Offers MA. *Accreditation:* NCATE. *Program availability:* Part-time, evening/weekend, online learning. *Degree requirements:* For master's, comprehensive exam, thesis or alternative. *Entrance requirements:* For master's, GRE General Test (if undergraduate GPA less than 3.0), resume, letters of reference. Electronic applications accepted.

University of Northern Iowa, Graduate College, College of Education, Department of Curriculum and Instruction, MAE Program in Literacy Education, Cedar Falls, IA 50614. Offers MAE. *Program availability:* Part-time, evening/weekend. *Degree requirements:* For master's, comprehensive exam, thesis or alternative. *Entrance requirements:* For master's, writing exam, minimum GPA of 3.0, two recommendations from professional educators. Additional exam requirements/recommendations for international students: Required—TOEFL (minimum score 500 paper-based; 61 iBT). Electronic applications accepted.

University of North Florida, College of Education and Human Services, Department of Childhood Education, Literacy, and TESOL, Jacksonville, FL 32224. Offers literacy (M Ed); professional education (M Ed); TESOL (M Ed). *Accreditation:* NCATE. *Program availability:* Part-time, evening/weekend. *Entrance requirements:* For master's, GRE General Test, minimum GPA of 3.0 in last 60 hours, 3 letters of recommendation, interview. Additional exam requirements/recommendations for international students: Required—TOEFL (minimum score 500 paper-based). Electronic applications accepted. *Faculty research:* Social context of and processes in learning, inter-disciplinary instruction, cross-cultural conflict resolution, the Vygotskian perspective on literacy diagnosis and instruction, performance poetry and teaching the language arts through drama.

University of Oklahoma, College of Arts and Sciences, Department of English, Norman, OK 73019. Offers literary and cultural studies (MA, PhD); writing and rhetoric studies (MA, PhD). *Program availability:* Part-time. *Faculty:* 25 full-time (13 women), 1 part-time/adjunct (0 women). *Students:* 29 full-time (21 women), 17 part-time (8 women); includes 9 minority (1 American Indian or Alaska Native, non-Hispanic/Latino; 2 Asian, non-Hispanic/Latino; 5 Hispanic/Latino; 1 Two or more races, non-Hispanic/Latino), 2 international. Average age 31. 34 applicants, 71% accepted, 18 enrolled. In 2017, 7 master's, 4 doctorates awarded. *Degree requirements:* For master's, one foreign language, comprehensive exam (for some programs), thesis (for some programs), exam or thesis; for doctorate, one foreign language, comprehensive exam, thesis/dissertation. *Entrance requirements:* For master's, GRE, BA in English or related field; for doctorate, GRE, MA in English or related field. Additional exam requirements/recommendations for international students: Required—TOEFL (minimum score 79 iBT) or IELTS (minimum score 6.5). *Application deadline:* For fall admission, 1/5 priority date for domestic and international students. Application fee: $50 ($100 for international students). Electronic applications accepted. *Expenses:* Tuition, state resident: full-time $5119; part-time $213.30 per credit hour. Tuition, nonresident: full-time $19,778; part-time $824.10 per credit hour. *Required fees:* $3458; $133.55 per credit hour. $126.50 per semester. *Financial support:* In 2017–18, 40 students received support, including 6 research assistantships with full tuition reimbursements available (averaging $14,515 per year), 31 teaching assistantships with full tuition reimbursements available (averaging $12,496 per year); fellowships with full tuition reimbursements available, scholarships/grants, health care benefits, and unspecified assistantships also available. Financial award application deadline: 6/1; financial award applicants required to submit FAFSA. *Faculty research:* American Indian literature and culture; composition and rhetoric; American literature; British literature; postcolonial literature and culture. *Total annual research expenditures:* $101. *Unit head:* Dr. Daniela Garofalo, Professor and Chair, 405-325-4661, Fax: 405-325-0831, E-mail: dg@ou.edu. *Application contact:* Sara Day, Graduate Assistant, 405-325-0489, Fax: 405-325-0831, E-mail: redpanda@ou.edu.
Website: http://cas.ou.edu/english

University of Oklahoma, Jeannine Rainbolt College of Education, Department of Instructional Leadership and Academic Curriculum, Norman, OK 73019. Offers instructional leadership and academic curriculum (M Ed, PhD), including biomedical education (PhD), early childhood education, elementary education, English education, instructional leadership, mathematics education, reading education, science education, social studies education, world languages education (M Ed); reading specialist (M Ed). *Accreditation:* NCATE. *Program availability:* Part-time. *Faculty:* 19 full-time (15 women), 1 (woman) part-time/adjunct. *Students:* 37 full-time (28 women), 121 part-time (98 women); includes 32 minority (7 Black or African American, non-Hispanic/Latino; 4 American Indian or Alaska Native, non-Hispanic/Latino; 5 Asian, non-Hispanic/Latino; 6 Hispanic/Latino; 1 Native Hawaiian or other Pacific Islander, non-Hispanic/Latino; 9 Two or more races, non-Hispanic/Latino), 12 international. Average age 35. 39 applicants, 77% accepted, 22 enrolled. In 2017, 49 master's, 12 doctorates awarded. Terminal master's awarded for partial completion of doctoral program. *Degree requirements:* For master's, comprehensive exam (for some programs), thesis (for some programs); for doctorate, comprehensive exam (for some programs), thesis/dissertation. *Entrance requirements:* For doctorate, GRE. Additional exam requirements/recommendations for international students: Required—TOEFL (minimum score 79 iBT) or IELTS (minimum score 6.5). Application fee: $50 ($100 for international students). Electronic applications accepted. *Expenses:* Tuition, state resident: full-time $5119; part-time $213.30 per credit hour. Tuition, nonresident: full-time $19,778; part-time $824.10 per credit hour. *Required fees:* $3458; $133.55 per credit hour. $126.50 per semester. *Financial support:* In 2017–18, 90 students received support, including 8 research assistantships (averaging $11,248 per year), 6 teaching assistantships (averaging $12,188 per year); fellowships, scholarships/grants, and unspecified assistantships also available. Financial award application deadline: 6/1; financial award applicants required to submit FAFSA. *Faculty research:* Teacher preparation; instruction; curriculum; learning; constructivist theory. *Total annual research expenditures:* $707,690. *Unit head:* Dr. Stacy Reeder, Chair, 405-325-1498, Fax: 405-325-4061, E-mail: reeder@ou.edu. *Application contact:* Anna Steele, Graduate Programs Officer, 405-325-4525, E-mail: anna.steele@ou.edu.
Website: http://www.ou.edu/education/ilac

University of Oklahoma Health Sciences Center, Graduate College, College of Allied Health, Department of Communication Sciences and Disorders, Oklahoma City, OK 73190. Offers audiology (MS, Au D, PhD); communication sciences and disorders (Certificate), including reading, speech-language pathology; education of the deaf (MS); speech-language pathology (MS, PhD). *Accreditation:* ASHA (one or more programs are accredited). *Program availability:* Part-time. Terminal master's awarded for partial completion of doctoral program. *Degree requirements:* For master's, comprehensive exam, thesis optional; for doctorate, one foreign language, comprehensive exam, thesis/dissertation. *Entrance requirements:* For master's and doctorate, GRE General Test, 3 letters of recommendation. Additional exam requirements/recommendations for international students: Required—TOEFL (minimum score 550 paper-based). *Faculty research:* Event-related potentials, cleft palate, fluency disorders, language disorders, hearing and speech science.

University of Pennsylvania, Graduate School of Education, Division of Literacy, Culture, and International Education, Program in Language and Literacy, Philadelphia, PA 19104. Offers MS Ed. *Students:* Average age 27. 15 applicants, 67% accepted, 2 enrolled. In 2017, 2 master's awarded.

University of Phoenix–Online Campus, College of Education, Phoenix, AZ 85034-7209. Offers administration and supervision (MAEd, Certificate); adult education and training (MAEd); curriculum and instruction (MAEd), including computer education, curriculum and instruction, English as a second language, language arts, mathematics, reading; early childhood education (MAEd); educational studies (MAEd); elementary teacher education (MAEd), including early childhood, elementary teacher education, high school middle level, middle level; principal licensure (Certificate); secondary teacher education (MAEd); special education (MAEd, Certificate); teacher education (MAEd), including middle level generalist; teacher education middle level mathematics (MAEd), including middle level mathematics; teacher education middle level science (MAEd), including middle level science; teacher education secondary mathematics (MAEd); teacher education secondary science (MAEd); teacher leadership (MAEd); teachers of English learners (Certificate); transition to teaching (Certificate), including elementary education, secondary education. *Program availability:* Evening/weekend, online learning. *Entrance requirements:* Additional exam requirements/recommendations for international students: Required—TOEFL, TOEIC (Test of English as an International Communication), Berlitz Online English Proficiency Exam, PTE, or IELTS. Electronic applications accepted. *Expenses:* Contact institution.

University of Phoenix–Phoenix Campus, College of Education, Tempe, AZ 85282-2371. Offers administration and supervision (MA Ed); adult education and training (MA Ed); curriculum and instruction reading (MA Ed); early childhood education (MA Ed); education studies (MA Ed); elementary teacher education (MA Ed); secondary teacher education (MA Ed); special education (MA Ed); teacher leadership (MA Ed). *Program availability:* Evening/weekend, online learning. *Entrance requirements:* Additional exam requirements/recommendations for international students: Required—TOEFL, TOEIC (Test of English as an International Communication), Berlitz Online English Proficiency Exam, PTE, or IELTS. Electronic applications accepted. *Expenses:* Contact institution.

University of Pittsburgh, School of Education, Department of Instruction and Learning, Program in Reading Education, Pittsburgh, PA 15260. Offers M Ed, Ed D, PhD. *Degree requirements:* For master's, thesis; for doctorate, thesis/dissertation. *Entrance requirements:* For master's, PRAXIS I; for doctorate, GRE General Test. Additional exam requirements/recommendations for international students: Required—TOEFL.

University of Pittsburgh, School of Education, Department of Instruction and Learning, Program in Secondary Education, Pittsburgh, PA 15260. Offers English and communications education (M Ed, MAT); foreign language education (M Ed, MAT); language, literacy and culture education (Ed D, PhD); mathematics education (M Ed, MAT, Ed D, PhD); science education (M Ed, MAT, Ed D, PhD); secondary education (PhD); social studies education (M Ed, MAT); STEM education (Ed D). *Program availability:* Part-time, evening/weekend. *Degree requirements:* For master's, thesis; for doctorate, thesis/dissertation. *Entrance requirements:* For master's, PRAXIS I; for doctorate, GRE General Test. Additional exam requirements/recommendations for international students: Required—TOEFL. Electronic applications accepted.

University of Portland, School of Education, Portland, OR 97203-5798. Offers education (MA, MAT); educational leadership (M Ed); English for speakers of other languages (M Ed); initial administrator licensure (M Ed); neuroeducation (M Ed, Ed D); organizational leadership and development (Ed D); reading (M Ed); school leadership and development (Ed D); special education (M Ed). M Ed also available through the Graduate Outreach Program for teachers residing in the Oregon and Washington state areas. *Accreditation:* NCATE. *Program availability:* Part-time, evening/weekend. *Entrance requirements:* For master's, minimum GPA of 3.0, teaching certificate, letters of recommendation, resume, statement of goals, official transcripts. Additional exam requirements/recommendations for international students: Required—TOEFL (minimum score 550 paper-based; 80 iBT), IELTS (minimum score 7). *Faculty research:* Multicultural education, supervision/leadership.

University of Rhode Island, Graduate School, Alan Shawn Feinstein College of Education and Professional Studies, School of Education, Kingston, RI 02881. Offers education (PhD); reading (MA); special education (MA). *Accreditation:* NCATE. *Program availability:* Part-time, evening/weekend. *Faculty:* 18 full-time (12 women). *Students:* 59 full-time (44 women), 145 part-time (114 women); includes 24 minority (6 Black or African American, non-Hispanic/Latino; 6 American Indian or Alaska Native, non-Hispanic/Latino; 7 Asian, non-Hispanic/Latino; 3 Hispanic/Latino; 2 Two or more races, non-Hispanic/Latino), 6 international. 91 applicants, 65% accepted, 53 enrolled. In 2017, 50 master's, 9 doctorates awarded. *Entrance requirements:* For master's, 2 letters of recommendation; personal statement; two official transcripts; interview and minimum undergraduate GPA of 3.0 (for special education applicants); for doctorate, GRE, 3 letters of recommendation, resume, personal statement, two copies of official transcripts. Additional exam requirements/recommendations for international students: Required—TOEFL. Application fee: $65. Electronic applications accepted. *Expenses:* Tuition, state resident: full-time $12,706; part-time $786 per credit. Tuition, nonresident: full-time $25,216; part-time $1401 per credit. *Required fees:* $1598; $45 per credit. One-time fee: $30 part-time. *Financial support:* In 2017–18, 1 research assistantship with tuition reimbursement (averaging $8,862 per year), 5 teaching assistantships with tuition reimbursements (averaging $17,795 per year) were awarded. Financial award applicants required to submit FAFSA. *Unit head:* Dr. David Byrd, Director, School of Education, 401-874-5484, Fax: 401-874-5471, E-mail: dbyrd@uri.edu. *Application contact:* Graduate Admissions, 401-874-2262, E-mail: gradadm@etal.uri.edu. Website: http://www.uri.edu/hss/education/

University of St. Francis, College of Education, Joliet, IL 60435-6169. Offers educational leadership (MS, Ed D); elementary education (M Ed); reading (MS); secondary education (M Ed), including English education, math education, science education, social studies education, visual arts education; special education (M Ed); teaching and learning (MS); TESOL (Certificate). *Accreditation:* NCATE. *Program availability:* Part-time, evening/weekend, 100% online, blended/hybrid learning. *Faculty:* 11 full-time (8 women), 52 part-time/adjunct (36 women). *Students:* 39 full-time (32 women), 411 part-time (318 women); includes 106 minority (57 Black or African American, non-Hispanic/Latino; 8 Asian, non-Hispanic/Latino; 37 Hispanic/Latino; 4 Two or more races, non-Hispanic/Latino), 4 international. Average age 37. 277 applicants, 55% accepted, 137 enrolled. In 2017, 199 master's, 28 doctorates awarded. *Degree requirements:* For master's, comprehensive exam; for doctorate, thesis/dissertation. *Entrance requirements:* Additional exam requirements/recommendations for international students: Required—TOEFL (minimum score 550 paper-based; 79 iBT), IELTS (minimum score 6). *Application deadline:* Applications are processed on a rolling basis. Application fee: $30. Electronic applications accepted. Application fee is waived when completed online. *Expenses:* $365 to $748 per credit hour. *Financial support:* In 2017–18, 40 students received support. Scholarships/grants and unspecified assistantships available. Support available to part-time students. Financial award applicants required to submit FAFSA. *Unit head:* Dr. John Gambro, Dean, 815-740-3829, Fax: 815-740-2264, E-mail: jgambro@stfrancis.edu. *Application contact:* Sandra Sloka, Director of Admissions for Graduate and Degree Completion Programs, 800-735-7500, Fax: 815-740-3431, E-mail: ssloka@stfrancis.edu. Website: http://www.stfrancis.edu/academics/college-of-education/

University of Saint Joseph, Department of Education, West Hartford, CT 06117-2700. Offers curriculum and instruction (MA); elementary education (MAT); instructional technology (MA); literacy (MA); secondary education (MAT); TESOL (MA). *Program availability:* Part-time, evening/weekend. *Degree requirements:* For master's, comprehensive exam, thesis or alternative. *Entrance requirements:* For master's, 2 letters of recommendation. *Application deadline:* Applications are processed on a rolling basis. Application fee: $50. Electronic applications accepted. Application fee is waived when completed online. *Financial support:* Career-related internships or fieldwork and unspecified assistantships available. Support available to part-time students. Financial award applicants required to submit FAFSA. Website: https://www.usj.edu/academics/schools/sasbe/education/

University of St. Thomas, School of Education and Human Services, Houston, TX 77006-4696. Offers all level education (M Ed); bilingual/dual language (M Ed); Catholic school teaching (M Ed); Catholic/private school leadership (M Ed); counselor education (M Ed); curriculum and instruction (M Ed); education (Ed D); educational leadership (M Ed); elementary teaching (M Ed); English as a second language (M Ed); exceptionality/educational diagnostician (M Ed); exceptionality/special education (M Ed); generalist (M Ed); reading (M Ed); secondary teaching (M Ed); teaching (MAT). *Accreditation:* TEAC. *Program availability:* Part-time, evening/weekend, online learning. *Faculty:* 33 full-time (22 women), 43 part-time/adjunct (26 women). *Students:* 119 full-time (97 women), 597 part-time (529 women); includes 478 minority (166 Black or African American, non-Hispanic/Latino; 29 Asian, non-Hispanic/Latino; 277 Hispanic/Latino; 2 Native Hawaiian or other Pacific Islander, non-Hispanic/Latino; 4 Two or more races, non-Hispanic/Latino), 19 international. Average age 36. 306 applicants, 91% accepted, 181 enrolled. In 2017, 328 master's awarded. *Degree requirements:* For master's, thesis, field experience. *Entrance requirements:* For master's, GRE or MAT if GPA is below 3.0, bachelor's degree; minimum GPA of 2.75 in bachelor's degree or last 60 credit hours; official transcripts from all institutions; goal statement of 250-300 words; 1 reference. Additional exam requirements/recommendations for international students: Required—TOEFL (minimum score 94 iBT), IELTS (minimum score 7), PTE (minimum score 53). *Application deadline:* Applications are processed on a rolling basis. Application fee: $35. Electronic applications accepted. *Expenses:* Contact institution. *Financial support:* In 2017–18, 27 students received support. Federal Work-Study, scholarships/grants, and state work-study, institutional employment available. Support available to part-time students. Financial award application deadline: 4/15; financial award applicants required to submit FAFSA. *Faculty research:* Leadership, diversity, personality traits, second language acquisition. *Unit head:* Dr. Paul C. Paese, Dean, 713-942-5999, Fax: 713-525-3871, E-mail: paesep@stthom.edu. *Application contact:* 713-525-3540, E-mail: education@stthom.edu. Website: http://www.stthom.edu/Academics/ School_of_Education_and_Human_Services/Index.aqf

University of San Diego, School of Leadership and Education Sciences, Department of Learning and Teaching, San Diego, CA 92110-2492. Offers curriculum and instruction (M Ed); inclusive learning (M Ed); literacy and digital learning (M Ed); school leadership (M Ed); special education (M Ed); STEAM (science, technology, engineering, arts, and mathematics) (M Ed); TESOL, literacy and culture (M Ed). *Program availability:* Part-time, evening/weekend. *Faculty:* 9 full-time (7 women), 30 part-time/adjunct (24 women). *Students:* 160 full-time (128 women), 221 part-time (176 women); includes 131 minority (10 Black or African American, non-Hispanic/Latino; 24 Asian, non-Hispanic/Latino; 83 Hispanic/Latino; 1 Native Hawaiian or other Pacific Islander, non-Hispanic/Latino; 13 Two or more races, non-Hispanic/Latino), 20 international. Average age 33. 398 applicants, 84% accepted, 196 enrolled. In 2017, 151 master's awarded. *Degree requirements:* For master's, thesis (for some programs), international experience. *Entrance requirements:* For master's, California Basic Educational Skills Test, California Subject Examination for Teachers. Additional exam requirements/recommendations for international students: Required—TOEFL (minimum score 580 paper-based; 83 iBT), TWE. *Application deadline:* Applications are processed on a rolling basis. Application fee: $45. Electronic applications accepted. *Financial support:* In 2017–18, 65 students received support. Career-related internships or fieldwork, Federal Work-Study, institutionally sponsored loans, and stipends available. Financial award application deadline: 4/1; financial award applicants required to submit FAFSA. *Faculty research:* Action research methodology, cultural studies, instructional theories and practices, second language acquisition, school reform. *Unit head:* Dr. Maya Kalyanpur, Chair, 619-260-7655, E-mail: mkalyanpur@sandiego.edu. *Application contact:* Monica Mahon, Associate Director of Graduate Admissions, 619-260-4524, Fax: 619-260-4158, E-mail: grads@sandiego.edu. Website: http://www.sandiego.edu/soles/learning-and-teaching/

University of San Francisco, School of Education, Department of Learning and Instruction, San Francisco, CA 94117-1080. Offers digital technologies for teaching and learning (MA); learning and instruction (MA, Ed D); special education (MA, Ed D); teaching reading (MA). *Program availability:* Part-time, evening/weekend. *Degree requirements:* For doctorate, thesis/dissertation. *Entrance requirements:* Additional exam requirements/recommendations for international students: Required—TOEFL, IELTS, PTE. Electronic applications accepted.

University of San Francisco, School of Education, Department of Teacher Education, San Francisco, CA 94117-1080. Offers digital media and learning (MA); teaching (MA); teaching reading (MA); teaching urban education and social justice (MA). *Program availability:* Part-time. *Entrance requirements:* Additional exam requirements/recommendations for international students: Required—TOEFL, IELTS, PTE. Electronic applications accepted.

The University of Scranton, Panuska College of Professional Studies, Department of Education, Program in Reading Education, Scranton, PA 18510. Offers MS. *Accreditation:* NCATE. *Program availability:* Part-time, evening/weekend. *Degree requirements:* For master's, comprehensive exam (for some programs), thesis (for some programs), capstone experience. *Entrance requirements:* For master's, minimum GPA of 3.0, three letters of reference. Additional exam requirements/recommendations for international students: Required—TOEFL (minimum score 500 paper-based; 80 iBT), IELTS (minimum score 6.5). Electronic applications accepted.

University of Sioux Falls, Fredrikson School of Education, Sioux Falls, SD 57105-1699. Offers educational administration (Ed S), including principal leadership, superintendent and district leadership; leadership in reading (M Ed); leadership in schools (M Ed); leadership in technology (M Ed); teaching (M Ed). Admission in summer only. *Accreditation:* NCATE. *Program availability:* Part-time, evening/weekend. *Degree requirements:* For master's, comprehensive exam (for some programs), research application project; for Ed S, comprehensive exam, portfolio. *Entrance requirements:* For master's, minimum GPA of 3.0, 1 year of teaching experience; for Ed S, minimum 3 years of teaching experience, minimum cumulative GPA of 3.5, 1 year of administrative experience. Additional exam requirements/recommendations for international students: Required—TOEFL. *Faculty research:* Reading, literacy, leadership.

University of South Alabama, College of Education and Professional Studies, Department of Leadership and Teacher Education, Mobile, AL 36688. Offers art education (M Ed); early childhood education (M Ed); educational leadership (M Ed, Ed D); elementary education (M Ed); reading education (M Ed); science education

(M Ed); secondary education (M Ed); special education (M Ed). *Accreditation:* NCATE. *Program availability:* Part-time. *Faculty:* 15 full-time (11 women), 10 part-time/adjunct (6 women). *Students:* 203 full-time (154 women), 90 part-time (68 women); includes 73 minority (54 Black or African American, non-Hispanic/Latino; 3 American Indian or Alaska Native, non-Hispanic/Latino; 4 Asian, non-Hispanic/Latino; 10 Hispanic/Latino; 2 Two or more races, non-Hispanic/Latino). Average age 34. 134 applicants, 55% accepted, 57 enrolled. In 2017, 73 master's, 8 doctorates awarded. *Degree requirements:* For master's, comprehensive exam, thesis (for some programs); for doctorate, comprehensive exam, thesis/dissertation. *Entrance requirements:* For master's, GRE General Test or MAT, minimum GPA of 3.0; for doctorate, GRE, minimum graduate GPA of 3.25, 3 years of experience in field, 3 letters of recommendation, interview, official transcripts. Additional exam requirements/recommendations for international students: Required—TOEFL. *Application deadline:* For fall admission, 7/15 for domestic students, 6/15 for international students; for spring admission, 11/15 for domestic students, 11/1 for international students; for summer admission, 4/15 for domestic students, 4/1 for international students. Applications are processed on a rolling basis. Application fee: $35. Electronic applications accepted. *Expenses:* Tuition, state resident: full-time $10,104; part-time $421 per semester hour. Tuition, nonresident: full-time $20,208; part-time $842 per semester hour. *Financial support:* Fellowships, research assistantships, teaching assistantships, career-related internships or fieldwork, Federal Work-Study, institutionally sponsored loans, scholarships/grants, and unspecified assistantships available. Support available to part-time students. Financial award application deadline: 3/31; financial award applicants required to submit FAFSA. *Unit head:* Dr. Susan Santoli, Chair/Director of Graduate Studies, 251-380-2836, Fax: 251-380-2748, E-mail: ssantoli@southalabama.edu. Website: http://www.southalabama.edu/colleges/ceps/lte/index.html

University of South Carolina, The Graduate School, College of Education, Department of Instruction and Teacher Education, Program in Language and Literacy, Columbia, SC 29208. Offers M Ed, PhD. *Accreditation:* NCATE. *Degree requirements:* For master's, comprehensive exam; for doctorate, one foreign language, comprehensive exam, thesis/dissertation. *Entrance requirements:* For master's, GRE General Test, Miller Analogies Test, teaching certificate, resume, letters of reference, letter of intent; for doctorate, GRE General Test, Miller Analogies Test, resumé, letters of reference, letter of intent, interview. *Faculty research:* Remedial and compensatory education, metacognition and learning, literacy, learning, teacher change.

University of South Dakota, Graduate School, School of Education, Division of Curriculum and Instruction, Program in Elementary Education, Vermillion, SD 57069. Offers elementary education (MA), including early childhood education, English language learning, reading specialist/literacy coach, science, technology and math (STEM). *Accreditation:* NCATE. *Program availability:* Part-time, 100% online, blended/hybrid learning. *Degree requirements:* For master's, comprehensive exam, thesis or alternative. *Entrance requirements:* For master's, GRE General Test, MAT, minimum GPA of 2.7. Additional exam requirements/recommendations for international students: Required—TOEFL (minimum score 550 paper-based; 79 iBT). *Application deadline:* Applications are processed on a rolling basis. Application fee: $35. Electronic applications accepted. *Financial support:* Research assistantships with partial tuition reimbursements, teaching assistantships with partial tuition reimbursements, career-related internships or fieldwork, Federal Work-Study, and unspecified assistantships available. Financial award applicants required to submit FAFSA. *Application contact:* Graduate School, 605-658-6140, Fax: 605-677-6118, E-mail: grad@usd.edu. Website: http://www.usd.edu/ci

University of Southern Maine, College of Management and Human Service, School of Education and Human Development, Program in Literacy Education, Portland, ME 04103. Offers applied literacy (MS Ed); English as a second language (MS Ed, CAS, CGS); literacy education (MS Ed, CAS, CGS). *Accreditation:* TEAC. *Program availability:* Part-time, evening/weekend. *Degree requirements:* For master's, comprehensive exam, thesis or alternative; for other advanced degree, thesis or alternative. *Entrance requirements:* For master's, teacher certification; for other advanced degree, master's degree. Additional exam requirements/recommendations for international students: Required—TOEFL (minimum score 550 paper-based; 79 iBT). Electronic applications accepted. *Faculty research:* Teacher research in literacy, multiliteracies, learning to teach culturally and linguistically diverse students, motivation to read.

University of South Florida, College of Education, Department of Teaching and Learning, Tampa, FL 33620-9951. Offers early childhood education (M Ed, MA, PhD); elementary education (MA, MAT, PhD); reading/language arts (MA, PhD, Ed S). *Accreditation:* NCATE. *Faculty:* 37 full-time (28 women). *Students:* 219 full-time (174 women), 302 part-time (217 women); includes 135 minority (65 Black or African American, non-Hispanic/Latino; 3 American Indian or Alaska Native, non-Hispanic/Latino; 12 Asian, non-Hispanic/Latino; 49 Hispanic/Latino; 6 Two or more races, non-Hispanic/Latino), 63 international. Average age 35. 195 applicants, 84% accepted, 138 enrolled. In 2017, 77 master's, 13 doctorates awarded. Application fee: $30. *Total annual research expenditures:* $940,639. *Unit head:* Dr. Denisse Thompson, Chair, 813-974-4110. Website: http://www.coedu.usf.edu/main/departments/ce/ce.html

University of South Florida, St. Petersburg, College of Education, St. Petersburg, FL 33701. Offers educational leadership development (M Ed); elementary education (MA), including math/science; English education (MA); middle grades STEM education (MS); reading education (MA). *Program availability:* Part-time. *Degree requirements:* For master's, comprehensive exam, practicum, internship, comprehensive portfolio. *Entrance requirements:* For master's, State of Florida General Knowledge Test (GKT), Florida Teaching Certificate (for non-initial certification programs), letters of recommendation. Additional exam requirements/recommendations for international students: Required—TOEFL (minimum score 550 paper-based; 79 iBT); Recommended—IELTS. Electronic applications accepted.

The University of Tennessee, Graduate School, College of Education, Health and Human Sciences, Program in Education, Knoxville, TN 37996. Offers art education (MS); counseling education (PhD); cultural studies in education (PhD); curriculum (MS, Ed S); curriculum, educational research and evaluation (Ed D, PhD); early childhood education (PhD); early childhood special education (MS); education of deaf and hard of hearing (MS); educational administration and policy studies (Ed D, PhD); educational administration and supervision (Ed S); educational psychology (Ed D, PhD); elementary education (MS, Ed S); elementary teaching (MS); English education (MS, Ed S); exercise science (PhD); foreign language/ESL education (MS, Ed S); instructional technology (MS, Ed D, PhD, Ed S); literacy, language and ESL education (PhD); literacy, language education, and ESL education (Ed D); mathematics education (MS, Ed S); modified and comprehensive special education (MS); reading education (MS, Ed S); school counseling (Ed S); school psychology (PhD, Ed S); science education (MS, Ed S); secondary teaching (MS); social foundations (MS); social science education (MS, Ed S); socio-cultural foundations of sports and education (PhD); special education (Ed S); teacher education (Ed D, PhD). *Accreditation:* NCATE. *Program availability:* Part-time, evening/weekend. *Degree requirements:* For master's and Ed S, thesis optional; for doctorate, variable foreign language requirement, thesis/dissertation. *Entrance requirements:* For

master's, minimum GPA of 2.7; for doctorate and Ed S, GRE General Test, minimum GPA of 2.7. Additional exam requirements/recommendations for international students: Required—TOEFL. Electronic applications accepted.

The University of Texas at Arlington, Graduate School, College of Education, Department of Curriculum and Instruction, Arlington, TX 76019. Offers curriculum and instruction (M Ed), including literacy studies, mathematics education, mind, brain, and education, science education; teaching (with certification) (M Ed T). *Accreditation:* NCATE. *Program availability:* Part-time, evening/weekend, online learning. *Degree requirements:* For master's, comprehensive exam (for some programs), comprehensive activity, research project. *Entrance requirements:* For master's, GRE General Test, minimum undergraduate GPA of 3.0 in last 60 hours of course work, writing sample, 3 letters of recommendation. Additional exam requirements/recommendations for international students: Required—TOEFL (minimum score 550 paper-based). Electronic applications accepted.

The University of Texas at Austin, Graduate School, College of Education, Department of Curriculum and Instruction, Austin, TX 78712-1111. Offers bilingual/bicultural education (M Ed, MA, PhD); cultural studies in education (M Ed, MA, PhD); early childhood education (M Ed, MA, PhD); language and literacy studies (M Ed, PhD); learning technologies (M Ed, MA, PhD); physical education (M Ed, MA, PhD). Terminal master's awarded for partial completion of doctoral program. *Degree requirements:* For doctorate, thesis/dissertation. *Entrance requirements:* For master's and doctorate, GRE General Test. Electronic applications accepted.

The University of Texas at El Paso, Graduate School, College of Education, Department of Teacher Education, El Paso, TX 79968-0001. Offers education (MA); instruction (M Ed); reading education (M Ed); teaching, learning, and culture (PhD). *Program availability:* Part-time, evening/weekend. *Degree requirements:* For master's, thesis optional. *Entrance requirements:* For master's, GRE General Test, minimum GPA of 3.0. Additional exam requirements/recommendations for international students: Required—TOEFL. Electronic applications accepted.

The University of Texas at San Antonio, College of Education and Human Development, Department of Bicultural and Bilingual Studies, San Antonio, TX 78249-0617. Offers bicultural and bilingual studies (MA), including bicultural and bilingual education, bicultural studies; culture, literacy, and language (PhD); teaching English as a second language (MA). *Program availability:* Part-time, evening/weekend. *Faculty:* 18 full-time (16 women). *Students:* 40 full-time (29 women), 82 part-time (68 women); includes 77 minority (2 Black or African American, non-Hispanic/Latino; 2 Asian, non-Hispanic/Latino; 72 Hispanic/Latino; 1 Two or more races, non-Hispanic/Latino), 9 international. Average age 35. 64 applicants, 80% accepted, 28 enrolled. In 2017, 34 master's, 13 doctorates awarded. *Degree requirements:* For master's, one foreign language, comprehensive exam, thesis optional; for doctorate, one foreign language, comprehensive exam, thesis/dissertation. *Entrance requirements:* For master's, bachelor's degree with 18 credit hours in field of study or in another appropriate field of study; for doctorate, GRE General Test, resume or curriculum vitae, 3 letters of recommendation, statement of purpose, master's degree. Additional exam requirements/recommendations for international students: Required—TOEFL (minimum score 550 paper-based; 79 iBT), IELTS (minimum score 6.5). *Application deadline:* For fall admission, 6/15 for domestic students, 3/15 for international students; for spring admission, 10/15 for domestic students, 9/15 for international students. Applications are processed on a rolling basis. Application fee: $50 ($90 for international students). Electronic applications accepted. *Expenses:* Contact institution. *Financial support:* Fellowships, research assistantships, teaching assistantships, scholarships/grants, and unspecified assistantships available. Financial award application deadline: 4/15. *Faculty research:* Bilingual and ESL teacher preparation; transnational communities; applied linguistics; cultural studies; bilingualism, biliteracy and second language acquisition. *Total annual research expenditures:* $2,246. *Unit head:* Dr. Patricia Sanchez, Chair, 210-458-4426, Fax: 210-458-5962, E-mail: patricia.sanchez@utsa.edu. *Application contact:* Rahnuma Islam, Student Development Specialist, 210-458-6619, Fax: 210-458-5576, E-mail: rahnuma.islam@utsa.edu. Website: http://education.utsa.edu/bicultural-bilingual_studies

The University of Texas at San Antonio, College of Education and Human Development, Department of Interdisciplinary Learning and Teaching, San Antonio, TX 78249-0617. Offers education (MA), including curriculum and instruction, early childhood and elementary education, instructional technology, reading and literacy, special education; interdisciplinary learning and teaching (PhD). *Program availability:* Part-time, evening/weekend. *Faculty:* 24 full-time (16 women), 5 part-time/adjunct (3 women). *Students:* 73 full-time (57 women), 227 part-time (206 women); includes 179 minority (25 Black or African American, non-Hispanic/Latino; 10 Asian, non-Hispanic/Latino; 140 Hispanic/Latino; 1 Native Hawaiian or other Pacific Islander, non-Hispanic/Latino; 3 Two or more races, non-Hispanic/Latino), 7 international. Average age 34. 107 applicants, 88% accepted, 70 enrolled. In 2017, 103 master's, 5 doctorates awarded. *Degree requirements:* For master's, comprehensive exam, thesis optional, 36 hours of course work without thesis (33 with thesis); for doctorate, comprehensive exam, thesis/dissertation, minimum of 60 semester credit hours. *Entrance requirements:* For master's, bachelor's degree with minimum GPA of 3.0 in last 60 hours of coursework; 18 hours of undergraduate coursework in education or related field; for doctorate, GRE, transcripts from all colleges and universities attended, professional vitae demonstrating experience in work environment where education was primary professional emphasis, 3 letters of recommendation, statement of purpose, minimum GPA of 3.5. Additional exam requirements/recommendations for international students: Required—TOEFL (minimum score 550 paper-based; 79 iBT), IELTS (minimum score 6.5). *Application deadline:* For fall admission, 6/15 for domestic students, 3/1 for international students; for spring admission, 10/15 for domestic students, 9/15 for international students. Applications are processed on a rolling basis. Application fee: $50 ($90 for international students). Electronic applications accepted. *Expenses:* Tuition, state resident: full-time $5495. Tuition, nonresident: full-time $21,938. *Required fees:* $1915. Tuition and fees vary according to program. *Financial support:* Career-related internships or fieldwork, Federal Work-Study, and scholarships/grants available. Support available to part-time students. *Faculty research:* Explorations of science, learning and teaching, family involvement in early childhood, culturally-responsive literacy instruction in diverse settings, STEM education, autism spectrum disorder. *Total annual research expenditures:* $511,331. *Unit head:* Dr. Mari R. Cortez, Department Chair, 210-458-4414, Fax: 210-458-7281, E-mail: mari.cortez@utsa.edu. *Application contact:* Elizabeth Narvaez, Student Development Specialist, 210-458-7443, E-mail: elizabeth.narvaez@utsa.edu. Website: http://education.utsa.edu/interdisciplinary_learning_and_teaching/

The University of Texas at Tyler, College of Education and Psychology, School of Education, Tyler, TX 75799-0001. Offers early childhood education (M Ed, MA); reading (M Ed, MA); special education (M Ed, MA). *Program availability:* Part-time, evening/weekend. *Degree requirements:* For master's, comprehensive exam, thesis (for some programs), research project. *Entrance requirements:* For master's, GRE General Test. Additional exam requirements/recommendations for international students: Required—TOEFL. Electronic applications accepted. *Faculty research:* Improving quality in childcare settings, play and creativity, teacher interactions, effects of modeling on early childhood teachers, biofeedback, literacy instruction.

The University of Texas of the Permian Basin, Office of Graduate Studies, School of Education, Program in Reading, Odessa, TX 79762-0001. Offers MA. *Degree requirements:* For master's, comprehensive exam (for some programs), thesis (for some programs). *Entrance requirements:* For master's, GRE General Test. Additional exam requirements/recommendations for international students: Required—TOEFL (minimum score 550 paper-based).

The University of Texas Rio Grande Valley, College of Education and P-16 Integration, Department of Bilingual and Literacy Studies, Edinburg, TX 78539. Offers bilingual education (M Ed), including dual language, ESL; reading and literacy (M Ed), including adolescent literacy, biliteracy, digital literacy, reading specialist. *Program availability:* Part-time, evening/weekend. *Faculty:* 17 full-time (13 women). *Students:* 29. In 2017, 11 master's awarded. *Degree requirements:* For master's, comprehensive exam (for some programs), thesis optional. *Entrance requirements:* For master's, minimum GPA of 3.0 in undergraduate coursework. Additional exam requirements/recommendations for international students: Required—TOEFL (minimum score 550 paper-based; 79 iBT), IELTS (minimum score 6.5). *Application deadline:* For fall admission, 4/15 for domestic students; for spring admission, 11/1 for domestic students; for summer admission, 3/1 for domestic students. Application fee: $50 ($75 for international students). Electronic applications accepted. *Expenses:* Tuition, state resident: full-time $5550; part-time $417 per credit hour. Tuition, nonresident: full-time $13,020; part-time $832 per credit hour. *Required fees:* $1169. *Financial support:* Research assistantships, institutionally sponsored loans, scholarships/grants, and unspecified assistantships available. Financial award application deadline: 4/15; financial award applicants required to submit FAFSA. *Faculty research:* Bilingual education, reading instruction, multicultural education, English as a second language. *Unit head:* Dr. Janine M. Schall, Chair, 956-665-5106, E-mail: janine.schall@utrgv.edu. *Application contact:* Stephanie Ozuna, Graduate Student Recruiter, 956-665-3558, E-mail: stephanie.ozuna@utrgv.edu.

University of the Cumberlands, Graduate Programs in Education, Williamsburg, KY 40769-1372. Offers all grades (P-12) (M Ed); business and marketing (MA Ed, MAT); counselor education and supervision (Ed D); director of pupil personnel (Certificate); director of special education (Certificate); educational administration and supervision (Ed S); educational leadership (Ed D); elementary education (MA Ed, MAT); instructional leadership - principalship (MA Ed); instructional leadership - school principal (Certificate); middle school education (MA Ed, MAT); reading and writing (MA Ed); school counseling (MA Ed); school superintendent (Certificate); secondary education (MA Ed, MAT); special education (MAT); supervisor of instruction (Certificate); teacher leader (MA Ed). *Program availability:* Part-time, evening/weekend, online learning. *Degree requirements:* For master's, comprehensive exam. Electronic applications accepted.

University of Utah, Graduate School, College of Education, Department of Educational Psychology, Salt Lake City, UT 84112. Offers clinical mental health counseling (M Ed); counseling psychology (PhD); elementary education (M Ed); instructional design and educational technology (M Ed); instructional design and technology (MS); learning and cognition (MS, PhD); reading and literacy (M Ed, PhD); school counseling (M Ed); school psychology (M Ed, PhD, Ed S); statistics (M Stat). *Accreditation:* APA (one or more programs are accredited). *Faculty:* 19 full-time (9 women), 12 part-time/adjunct (8 women). *Students:* 122 full-time (95 women), 97 part-time (68 women); includes 26 minority (4 Asian, non-Hispanic/Latino; 16 Hispanic/Latino; 6 Two or more races, non-Hispanic/Latino), 7 international. Average age 31. 296 applicants, 27% accepted, 73 enrolled. In 2017, 65 master's, 15 doctorates awarded. Terminal master's awarded for partial completion of doctoral program. *Entrance requirements:* For master's and doctorate, GRE General Test, minimum GPA of 3.0. Additional exam requirements/recommendations for international students: Required—TOEFL (minimum score 80 iBT). *Application deadline:* For fall admission, 12/15 for domestic and international students; for winter admission, 11/1 for domestic and international students; for spring admission, 3/15 for domestic and international students. Application fee: $55 ($65 for international students). Electronic applications accepted. *Expenses:* Contact institution. *Financial support:* In 2017–18, 84 students received support, including 12 fellowships with full and partial tuition reimbursements available (averaging $17,000 per year), 16 research assistantships with full and partial tuition reimbursements available (averaging $15,500 per year), 39 teaching assistantships with full and partial tuition reimbursements available (averaging $15,500 per year); career-related internships or fieldwork, scholarships/grants, traineeships, health care benefits, and unspecified assistantships also available. Financial award application deadline: 4/1; financial award applicants required to submit FAFSA. *Faculty research:* Autism, computer technology and instruction, cognitive behavior, aging, group counseling. *Total annual research expenditures:* $620,935. *Unit head:* Dr. Anne E. Cook, Chair, 801-581-7148, Fax: 801-581-5566, E-mail: anne.cook@utah.edu. *Application contact:* JoLynn N. Yates, Academic Coordinator, 801-581-7148, Fax: 801-581-5566, E-mail: jo.yates@utah.edu. Website: http://www.ed.utah.edu/edps/

University of Victoria, Faculty of Graduate Studies, Faculty of Education, Department of Curriculum and Instruction, Victoria, BC V8W 2Y2, Canada. Offers art education (M Ed, PhD); curriculum studies (M Ed, MA, PhD); early childhood education (M Ed, PhD); educational studies (PhD); language and literacy (M Ed, MA, PhD); mathematics (M Ed, MA, PhD); music education (M Ed, MA, PhD); science (M Ed, MA, PhD); social studies (M Ed, MA); social, cultural and foundational studies (MA, PhD); technology and environmental education (PhD). *Program availability:* Part-time. *Degree requirements:* For master's, thesis, project (M Ed); for doctorate, comprehensive exam, thesis/dissertation. *Entrance requirements:* For master's, minimum B average. Additional exam requirements/recommendations for international students: Required—TOEFL (minimum score 575 paper-based), IELTS (minimum score 7). Electronic applications accepted. *Faculty research:* Elementary and secondary English, language arts, curriculum theory and practice, educational media and technology, educational administration and leadership, history and philosophy of education.

University of Virginia, Curry School of Education, Program in Education, Charlottesville, VA 22903. Offers administration and supervision (PhD); applied developmental science (PhD); counselor education (PhD); curriculum and instruction (PhD); early childhood special education (MT); education evaluation (PhD); educational psychology (PhD); educational research (PhD); elementary education (MT); English education (MT, PhD); foreign language education (MT); higher education (PhD); instructional technology (PhD); kinesiology (MT, PhD); math education (PhD); reading education (PhD); research, statistics and evaluation (PhD); school psychology (PhD); science education (PhD); social studies education (MT, PhD); special education (PhD); world languages education (MT). *Students:* 431 full-time (353 women), 15 part-time (14 women); includes 100 minority (32 Black or African American, non-Hispanic/Latino; 33 Asian, non-Hispanic/Latino; 16 Hispanic/Latino; 19 Two or more races, non-Hispanic/Latino), 14 international. Average age 25. 264 applicants, 49% accepted, 83 enrolled. In 2017, 142 master's, 33 doctorates awarded. *Degree requirements:* For master's, comprehensive exam (for some programs), field project; for doctorate, comprehensive exam, thesis/dissertation. *Entrance requirements:* For doctorate, GRE General Test. Additional exam requirements/recommendations for international students: Required—TOEFL (minimum score 600 paper-based; 90 iBT), IELTS (minimum score 7).

Application deadline: Applications are processed on a rolling basis. Application fee: $60. Electronic applications accepted. *Financial support:* Fellowships, research assistantships, and teaching assistantships available. Financial award application deadline: 1/5; financial award applicants required to submit FAFSA. *Unit head:* Robert C. Pianta, Dean, 434-924-3334, E-mail: pianta@virginia.edu. *Application contact:* E-mail: curry-admissions@virginia.edu. Website: http://curry.virginia.edu/teacher-education

University of Washington, Graduate School, College of Education, Seattle, WA 98195. Offers curriculum and instruction (M Ed, Ed D, PhD), including educational technology, general curriculum (Ed D, PhD), language, literacy, and culture, mathematics education, multicultural education, reading and language arts education (Ed D), science education, social studies education, teaching and curriculum (M Ed); educational leadership and policy studies (M Ed, Ed D, PhD), including administration (Ed D), educational policy, organization, and leadership (M Ed, PhD), higher education, leadership for learning (Ed D), social and cultural foundations of education (M Ed, PhD); educational psychology (M Ed, PhD), including educational psychology (PhD), human development and cognition (M Ed), learning sciences, measurement, statistics and research design (M Ed), school psychology (M Ed); instructional leadership (M Ed); intercollege athletic leadership (M Ed); special education (M Ed, Ed D, PhD), including early childhood special education (M Ed), emotional and behavioral disabilities (M Ed), learning disabilities (M Ed), low-incidence disabilities (M Ed), severe disabilities (M Ed), special education (Ed D, PhD); teacher education (MIT). *Accreditation:* APA. *Program availability:* Part-time, evening/weekend. *Degree requirements:* For master's, thesis optional; for doctorate, thesis/dissertation. *Entrance requirements:* For master's and doctorate, GRE General Test, minimum GPA of 3.0. Additional exam requirements/recommendations for international students: Required—TOEFL. Electronic applications accepted. *Faculty research:* School restructuring/effective schools, special education interventions, literacy and writing, technology, school partnerships, teacher preparation.

University of West Florida, College of Education and Professional Studies, Department of Teacher Education and Educational Leadership, Program in Reading Education, Pensacola, FL 32514-5750. Offers M Ed. *Program availability:* Part-time, evening/weekend. *Degree requirements:* For master's, portfolio, teacher certification exams (general knowledge, professional, reading subject area). *Entrance requirements:* For master's, GRE (minimum score 450 verbal) or MAT (minimum score 396) if bachelor's GPA less than 3.0, state teaching certification; letter of intent; two professional references. Additional exam requirements/recommendations for international students: Required—TOEFL (minimum score 550 paper-based).

University of West Georgia, College of Education, Carrollton, GA 30118. Offers business education (M Ed); early childhood education (M Ed, Ed S); educational leadership (M Ed, Ed S); media (M Ed, Ed S); professional counseling (M Ed, Ed S); professional counseling and supervision (Ed D); reading instruction (M Ed); school improvement (Ed D); secondary education (M Ed); special education (M Ed, Ed S), including teaching (M Ed); speech language pathology (M Ed); teaching (MAT). *Accreditation:* NCATE. *Program availability:* Part-time, evening/weekend, 100% online, blended/hybrid learning. *Faculty:* 45 full-time (28 women). *Students:* 344 full-time (286 women), 1,243 part-time (1,039 women); includes 538 minority (456 Black or African American, non-Hispanic/Latino; 19 Asian, non-Hispanic/Latino; 46 Hispanic/Latino; 1 Native Hawaiian or other Pacific Islander, non-Hispanic/Latino; 16 Two or more races, non-Hispanic/Latino), 7 international. Average age 36. 685 applicants, 78% accepted, 429 enrolled. In 2017, 299 master's, 30 doctorates, 218 other advanced degrees awarded. *Entrance requirements:* Additional exam requirements/recommendations for international students: Required—TOEFL (minimum score 523 paper-based; 69 iBT); Recommended—IELTS (minimum score 6.5). *Application deadline:* For fall admission, 7/21 for domestic students, 6/1 for international students; for spring admission, 11/30 for domestic students, 10/15 for international students; for summer admission, 4/15 for domestic students, 3/30 for international students. Applications are processed on a rolling basis. Application fee: $40. Electronic applications accepted. Tuition and fees vary according to degree level and program. *Financial support:* Fellowships, research assistantships, teaching assistantships, career-related internships or fieldwork, Federal Work-Study, institutionally sponsored loans, scholarships/grants, and unspecified assistantships available. Support available to part-time students. Financial award application deadline: 4/1; financial award applicants required to submit FAFSA. *Unit head:* Dr. Diane Hoff, Dean, College of Education, 678-839-6570, Fax: 678-839-6098, E-mail: dhoff@westga.edu. *Application contact:* Dr. Toby Ziglar, Assistant Dean of the Graduate School, 678-839-1394, Fax: 678-839-1395, E-mail: graduate@westga.edu. Website: http://www.westga.edu/education/

University of Wisconsin–Eau Claire, College of Education and Human Sciences, Program in Reading, Eau Claire, WI 54702-4004. Offers MST. *Program availability:* Part-time. *Degree requirements:* For master's, comprehensive exam, portfolio with an oral examination. *Entrance requirements:* For master's, certification to teach. Additional exam requirements/recommendations for international students: Required—TOEFL (minimum score 79 iBT).

University of Wisconsin–La Crosse, School of Education, La Crosse, WI 54601-3742. Offers English language arts elementary (Graduate Certificate); professional development in education (ME-PD); reading (MS Ed); special education (MS Ed). *Program availability:* Part-time, evening/weekend. *Faculty:* 6 full-time (4 women), 8 part-time/adjunct (6 women). *Students:* 70 part-time (51 women); includes 2 minority (1 Asian, non-Hispanic/Latino; 1 Two or more races, non-Hispanic/Latino). Average age 30. 59 applicants, 100% accepted, 34 enrolled. In 2017, 69 master's, 1 other advanced degree awarded. *Entrance requirements:* For master's, GRE. Additional exam requirements/recommendations for international students: Required—TOEFL (minimum score 550 paper-based; 79 iBT). *Application deadline:* Applications are processed on a rolling basis. Electronic applications accepted. *Financial support:* Research assistantships, Federal Work-Study, scholarships/grants, health care benefits, and tuition waivers (partial) available. Support available to part-time students. Financial award application deadline: 3/15; financial award applicants required to submit FAFSA. *Unit head:* Marcie Wycoff-Horn, Dean, School of Education, 608-785-6786, E-mail: mwycoff-horn@uwlax.edu. *Application contact:* Brandon Schaller, Senior Graduate Student Status Examiner, 608-785-8941, E-mail: admissions@uwlax.edu. Website: https://www.uwlax.edu/soe/

University of Wisconsin–Milwaukee, Graduate School, School of Education, Department of Curriculum and Instruction, Milwaukee, WI 53201-0413. Offers curriculum and instruction (MS), including cross-curricular focus, early childhood education, English education, mathematics education, middle childhood/early adolescence education, reading education, science education, urban social studies education. *Program availability:* Part-time. *Students:* 17 full-time (13 women), 45 part-time (39 women); includes 13 minority (2 Black or African American, non-Hispanic/Latino; 3 Asian, non-Hispanic/Latino; 1 Hispanic/Latino; 7 Two or more races, non-Hispanic/Latino). Average age 33. 32 applicants, 66% accepted, 16 enrolled. In 2017, 26 master's awarded. *Entrance requirements:* Additional exam requirements/recommendations for international students: Required—TOEFL (minimum score 550 paper-based; 79 iBT), IELTS (minimum score 6.5). *Application deadline:* For fall admission, 1/1 priority date for domestic students; for spring admission, 9/1 for domestic students. Application fee: $56 ($96 for international

students). Electronic applications accepted. *Financial support:* Fellowships, research assistantships, teaching assistantships, career-related internships or fieldwork, health care benefits, unspecified assistantships, and project assistantships available. Support available to part-time students. Financial award application deadline: 4/15; financial award applicants required to submit FAFSA. *Application contact:* General Information Contact, 414-229-4721, E-mail: soeinfo@uwm.edu.
Website: http://uwm.edu/education/academics/curriculum-instruction-department/

University of Wisconsin–Oshkosh, Graduate Studies, College of Education and Human Services, Department of Reading Education, Oshkosh, WI 54901. Offers MSE. Program offered jointly with University of Wisconsin–Green Bay. *Program availability:* Part-time. *Degree requirements:* For master's, thesis or alternative, reflective journey course. *Entrance requirements:* For master's, interview, teaching certificate, undergraduate degree in teacher education, letters of recommendation. Additional exam requirements/recommendations for international students: Required—TOEFL (minimum score 550 paper-based; 79 iBT). Electronic applications accepted. *Faculty research:* Writing and reading, assessment, learner-centered instruction, multicultural literature, family literacy.

University of Wisconsin–River Falls, Outreach and Graduate Studies, College of Education and Professional Studies, Department of Teacher Education, River Falls, WI 54022. Offers elementary education (MSE); professional development shared inquiry communities (MSE); reading (MSE). *Program availability:* Part-time. *Degree requirements:* For master's, comprehensive exam, thesis or alternative. *Entrance requirements:* For master's, minimum GPA of 2.75. Additional exam requirements/recommendations for international students: Required—TOEFL (minimum score 500 paper-based; 65 iBT), IELTS (minimum score 5.5). Electronic applications accepted.

University of Wisconsin–Stevens Point, College of Professional Studies, School of Education, Program in Education—General/Reading, Stevens Point, WI 54481-3897. Offers MSE. *Program availability:* Part-time. *Degree requirements:* For master's, comprehensive exam, thesis or alternative. *Entrance requirements:* For master's, minimum undergraduate GPA of 3.0, teacher certification, 2 years teaching experience, letters of recommendation. Additional exam requirements/recommendations for international students: Required—TOEFL (minimum score 523 paper-based). *Faculty research:* Reading strategies in the content areas, gifted education, curriculum and instruction, standards-based education.

University of Wisconsin–Superior, Graduate Division, Department of Teacher Education, Program in Teaching Reading, Superior, WI 54880-4500. Offers MSE. *Program availability:* Part-time, evening/weekend. *Degree requirements:* For master's, comprehensive exam, thesis or alternative, research project. *Entrance requirements:* For master's, minimum GPA of 2.75, teaching certificate. Electronic applications accepted.

Upper Iowa University, Master of Education Program, Fayette, IA 52142-1857. Offers early childhood (M Ed); English as a second language (M Ed); higher education (M Ed); instructional strategist (M Ed); reading (M Ed); teacher leadership (M Ed).

Utah Valley University, Program in Education, Orem, UT 84058-5999. Offers educational technology (M Ed); elementary mathematics (M Ed); elementary STEM (M Ed); English as a second language (M Ed); reading (M Ed); teachers as leaders (M Ed). *Accreditation:* TEAC. *Program availability:* Part-time. *Degree requirements:* For master's, project. *Entrance requirements:* For master's, GRE, 3 letters of recommendation, interview, essay. Additional exam requirements/recommendations for international students: Required—TOEFL (minimum score 83 iBT). Electronic applications accepted. *Expenses:* Contact institution.

Vanderbilt University, Peabody College, Department of Teaching and Learning, Nashville, TN 37240-1001. Offers elementary education (M Ed); English language learners (M Ed); learning and design (M Ed); learning, diversity, and urban studies (M Ed); reading education (M Ed); secondary education (M Ed). *Accreditation:* NCATE. *Program availability:* Part-time. *Faculty:* 43 full-time (32 women), 28 part-time/adjunct (25 women). *Students:* 139 full-time (110 women), 35 part-time (23 women); includes 31 minority (18 Black or African American, non-Hispanic/Latino; 1 American Indian or Alaska Native, non-Hispanic/Latino; 6 Asian, non-Hispanic/Latino; 4 Hispanic/Latino; 2 Two or more races, non-Hispanic/Latino), 44 international. Average age 26. 510 applicants, 69% accepted, 113 enrolled. In 2017, 87 master's awarded. *Degree requirements:* For master's, comprehensive exam, thesis optional. *Entrance requirements:* For master's, GRE General Test, MAT. Additional exam requirements/recommendations for international students: Required—TOEFL (minimum score 550 paper-based; 80 iBT). *Application deadline:* For fall admission, 12/31 priority date for domestic and international students; for spring admission, 11/1 priority date for domestic and international students. Applications are processed on a rolling basis. Application fee: $0. Electronic applications accepted. *Financial support:* Fellowships with partial tuition reimbursements, research assistantships with partial tuition reimbursements, teaching assistantships with partial tuition reimbursements, Federal Work-Study, institutionally sponsored loans, scholarships/grants, tuition waivers (partial), and unspecified assistantships available. Support available to part-time students. Financial award application deadline: 1/15; financial award applicants required to submit FAFSA. *Faculty research:* Children's learning and development in core conceptual domains (STEM, English language arts, social studies); classroom discourse structures that teachers can learn and use to support students' learning and development K-6; intervention and design-based research on educational improvement at classroom, school, and district levels; design-based and learning sciences research on relations between learning in schools and other settings. *Unit head:* Dr. Deborah Rowe, Chair, 615-322-8100, Fax: 615-322-8999, E-mail: deborah.w.rowe@vanderbilt.edu. *Application contact:* Angela Saylor, Educational Coordinator, 615-322-8092, Fax: 615-322-8999, E-mail: angela.saylor@vanderbilt.edu.

Virginia Commonwealth University, Graduate School, School of Education, Program in Adult Learning, Richmond, VA 23284-9005. Offers adult literacy (M Ed); human resource development (M Ed); teaching and learning with technology (M Ed). *Accreditation:* NCATE. *Program availability:* Part-time. *Entrance requirements:* For master's, GRE General Test or MAT. Additional exam requirements/recommendations for international students: Required—TOEFL (minimum score 600 paper-based; 100 iBT). Electronic applications accepted. *Faculty research:* Adult development and learning, program planning and evaluation.

Virginia Commonwealth University, Graduate School, School of Education, Program in Reading, Richmond, VA 23284-9005. Offers reading (M Ed); reading specialist (Certificate). *Accreditation:* NCATE. *Degree requirements:* For master's, comprehensive exam. *Entrance requirements:* For master's, GRE General Test or MAT. Additional exam requirements/recommendations for international students: Required—TOEFL (minimum score 600 paper-based; 100 iBT). Electronic applications accepted.

Viterbo University, Graduate Programs in Education, La Crosse, WI 54601-4797. Offers cross-categorical special education (Certificate); director of instruction (Certificate); director of special education and pupil services (Certificate); early childhood (Certificate); education (MAE); literacy coaching (Certificate); PreK-12 principal/supervisor of special education (Certificate); principal (Certificate); reading specialist endorsement (Certificate); reading teacher (Certificate); reading teacher 5-12 endorsement (Certificate); reading teacher K-8 endorsement (Certificate);

superintendent (Certificate); talented and gifted endorsement (Certificate); Wisconsin school business administrator (Certificate). Weekend courses available in summer. *Accreditation:* NCATE. *Program availability:* Part-time, evening/weekend. *Degree requirements:* For master's, comprehensive exam, thesis, 30 credits of course work. *Entrance requirements:* For master's, transcripts, teaching license, written narrative. Electronic applications accepted. *Expenses:* Contact institution.

Walden University, Graduate Programs, Richard W. Riley College of Education and Leadership, Minneapolis, MN 55401. Offers adult education (Post-Master's Certificate); adult learning (Graduate Certificate); college teaching and learning (Graduate Certificate); community college leadership (Ed D); curriculum, instruction and assessment (Ed D, Ed S, Graduate Certificate); developmental education (Graduate Certificate); early childhood administration, management, and leadership (Graduate Certificate); early childhood education (Ed D, Ed S); early childhood public policy and advocacy (Graduate Certificate); early childhood studies (MS), including administration, management and leadership, early childhood public policy and advocacy, teaching adults in the early childhood field, teaching and diversity in early childhood education; education (MS, PhD), including adolescent literacy and learning (MS), curriculum, instruction, and assessment (grades K-12) (MS), curriculum, instruction, assessment, and evaluation (PhD), early childhood leadership and advocacy (PhD), early childhood special education (PhD), educational leadership (MS), educational leadership and administration (principal preparation) (MS), educational technology and design (PhD), elementary reading and literacy (PreK-6) (MS), elementary reading and mathematics (grades K-6) (MS), global and comparative education (PhD), higher education leadership management and policy (PhD), integrating technology in the classroom (grades K-12) (MS), learning, instruction and innovation (PhD), mathematics (grades 5-8) (MS), mathematics (grades K-6) (MS), mathematics and science (grades K-8) (MS), organizational research, assessment, and evaluation (PhD), reading and literacy with a reading K-12 endorsement (MS), reading literacy assessment and evaluation (PhD), science (grades K-8) (MS), special education (non-licensure) (grades K-12) (MS), teacher leadership (grades K-12) (MS), teaching English language learners (grades K-12) (MS); educational administration and leadership (Ed D); educational leadership and administration (principal preparation) (Ed S); educational technology (Ed D, Ed S, Post Master's Certificate); elementary reading and literacy (Graduate Certificate); engaging culturally diverse learners (Graduate Certificate); enrollment management and institutional marketing (Graduate Certificate); higher education (MS), including adult learning, college teaching and learning, enrollment management and institutional marketing, global higher education, leadership for student success, online and distance learning; higher education and adult learning (Ed D); higher education leadership and management (Ed D); higher education leadership for student success (Graduate Certificate); instructional design and technology (MS, Postbaccalaureate Certificate), including general program (MS), online learning (MS), training and performance improvement (MS); integrating technology in the classroom (Graduate Certificate); mathematics 5-8 (Graduate Certificate); mathematics K-6 (Graduate Certificate); online teaching for adult educators (Graduate Certificate); reading, literacy, and assessment (Ed D, Ed S); science K-8 (Graduate Certificate); special education (Ed D, Ed S, Graduate Certificate); special education (K-age 21) (MAT); teacher leadership (Graduate Certificate); teaching adults English as a second language (Graduate Certificate); teaching adults in the early childhood field (Graduate Certificate); teaching and diversity in early childhood education (Graduate Certificate); teaching English language learners (grades K-12) (Graduate Certificate); teaching K-12 students online (Graduate Certificate). *Accreditation:* NCATE. *Program availability:* Part-time, evening/weekend, online only, 100% online. *Degree requirements:* For doctorate, thesis/dissertation (for some programs), residency; for other advanced degree, residency for some programs). *Entrance requirements:* For master's, bachelor's degree or higher; minimum GPA of 2.5; official transcripts; goal statement (for some programs); access to computer and Internet; for doctorate, master's degree or higher; three years of related professional or academic experience (preferred); minimum GPA of 3.0; goal statement and current resume (for select programs); official transcripts; access to computer and Internet; for other advanced degree, relevant work experience; access to computer and Internet. Additional exam requirements/recommendations for international students: Required—TOEFL (minimum score 550 paper-based, 79 iBT), IELTS (minimum score 6.5), Michigan English Language Assessment Battery (minimum score 82), or PTE (minimum score 53). Electronic applications accepted.

Walla Walla University, Graduate Studies, School of Education and Psychology, College Place, WA 99324. Offers curriculum and instruction (M Ed, MAT); educational leadership (M Ed, MAT); literacy instruction (M Ed, MAT); special education (M Ed, MAT). *Program availability:* Part-time. *Entrance requirements:* For master's, GRE General Test, minimum GPA of 2.75. Additional exam requirements/recommendations for international students: Required—TOEFL (minimum score 550 paper-based; 79 iBT). *Application deadline:* For fall admission, 4/1 priority date for domestic students. Applications are processed on a rolling basis. Application fee: $50. Electronic applications accepted. *Financial support:* Research assistantships, teaching assistantships, Federal Work-Study, and tuition waivers (partial) available. Support available to part-time students. Financial award application deadline: 4/30; financial award applicants required to submit FAFSA. *Faculty research:* Admissions/retention, instructional psychology, moral development, teaching of reading. *Unit head:* Dr. Debbie Muthersbaugh, Dean, 509-527-2212, Fax: 509-527-2248, E-mail: debbie.muthersbaugh@wallawalla.edu. *Application contact:* Dr. Joe G. Galusha, Dean of Graduate Studies, 509-527-2421, Fax: 509-527-2237, E-mail: joe.galusha@wallawalla.edu.
Website: https://wallawalla.edu/academics/areas-of-study/undergraduate-programs/education-and-psychology/

Walsh University, Graduate Programs, Program in Education, North Canton, OH 44720-3396. Offers leadership with principal license (MA Ed); reading literacy (MA Ed). *Accreditation:* NCATE. *Program availability:* Part-time, evening/weekend. *Degree requirements:* For master's, comprehensive exam (for some programs), thesis optional, action research project or comprehensive exam. *Entrance requirements:* For master's, MAT (minimum score 396), GRE (minimum scores: verbal 145, quantitative 146, combined 291, writing 3.0), or minimum GPA of 3.0 on the baccalaureate transcript, interview, minimum GPA of 3.0, writing sample, 3 recommendation forms, notarized affidavit of good moral character. Additional exam requirements/recommendations for international students: Required—TOEFL (minimum score 500 paper-based; 61 iBT). Electronic applications accepted. Application fee is waived when completed online. *Expenses:* Contact institution. *Faculty research:* Learning and the brain, primary STEM, effective assessment practices, literacy.

Washburn University, College of Arts and Sciences, Department of Education, Topeka, KS 66621. Offers curriculum and instruction (M Ed); educational leadership (M Ed); reading (M Ed); special education (M Ed). *Accreditation:* NCATE. *Program availability:* Part-time. *Degree requirements:* For master's, comprehensive exam, thesis or alternative, portfolio, comprehensive paper, or action research project. *Entrance requirements:* For master's, department exam, GRE General Test or MAT, minimum GPA of 3.0 in graduate coursework or last 60 hours of undergraduate coursework. Additional exam requirements/recommendations for international students: Required—TOEFL (minimum score 80 iBT). *Faculty research:* Reading/literature/literacy, foundations, special education, diversity, teaching and technology.

Washington State University, College of Education, Department of Teaching and Learning, Pullman, WA 99164-2132. Offers cultural studies and social thought in education (PhD); curriculum and instruction (Ed M, MA); English language learners (Ed M, MA); language, literacy and technology (PhD); literacy education (Ed M, MA); mathematics education (PhD); special education (Ed M, MA, PhD); teacher leadership (Ed D); teaching (MIT), including elementary education, secondary education. Programs offered at the Pullman, Spokane, Tri-cities, Vancouver and Global (online) campuses. *Program availability:* Part-time, online learning. *Degree requirements:* For master's, comprehensive exam, thesis, oral or written exam; for doctorate, comprehensive exam, thesis/dissertation, oral and written exam. *Entrance requirements:* For master's, GRE General Test, minimum GPA of 3.0, 3 letters of recommendation, letter of intent, transcripts, resume/curriculum vitae; for doctorate, GRE General Test, minimum GPA of 3.0, 3 letters of recommendation, letter of intent, transcripts, writing sample, resume/curriculum vitae. Additional exam requirements/recommendations for international students: Required—TOEFL (minimum score 550 paper-based; 80 iBT). Electronic applications accepted. *Faculty research:* Intersection of gender, youth cultures and schooling; examination of ideology of power in children's literature; early childhood special education; analyzing pre-service and in-service teacher development; second language acquisition.

Wayne State University, College of Education, Division of Teacher Education, Detroit, MI 48202. Offers art education (M Ed); bilingual/bicultural education (Certificate); curriculum and instruction (Ed D, PhD, Ed S), including English as a second language (MAT, Ed D, Ed S), K-12 curriculum (PhD); elementary education (MAT), including bilingual/bicultural education (M Ed, MAT), early childhood education (M Ed, MAT), English as a second language education (MAT, Ed D, Ed S), foreign language education, science education (M Ed, MAT), special education (M Ed, MAT); elementary mathematics specialist (Certificate); English as a second language (Certificate); reading (M Ed, Ed S); reading, language and literature (Ed D); secondary education (MAT), including bilingual/bicultural education (M Ed, MAT), early childhood education (M Ed, MAT), English as a second language (MAT, Ed D, Ed S), English education, foreign language education, mathematics education (M Ed, MAT), science education (M Ed, MAT), social studies education (M Ed, MAT); special education (MAT), including career and technical education; teaching and learning (M Ed), including bilingual/bicultural education (M Ed, MAT), early childhood education (M Ed, MAT), elementary education, foreign language, mathematics education (M Ed, MAT), science education (M Ed, MAT), social studies education (M Ed, MAT), special education (M Ed, MAT). *Program availability:* Part-time, blended/hybrid learning. *Faculty:* 22. *Students:* 126 full-time (96 women), 317 part-time (258 women); includes 134 minority (95 Black or African American, non-Hispanic/Latino; 1 American Indian or Alaska Native, non-Hispanic/Latino; 8 Asian, non-Hispanic/Latino; 17 Hispanic/Latino; 1 Native Hawaiian or other Pacific Islander, non-Hispanic/Latino; 12 Two or more races, non-Hispanic/Latino), 13 international. Average age 37. 260 applicants, 33% accepted, 57 enrolled. In 2017, 111 master's, 13 doctorates, 7 other advanced degrees awarded. *Degree requirements:* For master's, essay or project (for some M Ed programs), professional field experience (for MAT programs); for doctorate, thesis/dissertation. *Entrance requirements:* For master's, Michigan Test for Teacher Certification (for most programs), verification of participation in group work with children (for MAT programs), Michigan State Police criminal background check; for doctorate, minimum undergraduate GPA of 3.0, graduate 3.5; interview; curriculum vitae; references; master's degree (for most programs). Additional exam requirements/recommendations for international students: Required—TOEFL (minimum score 550 paper-based; 79 iBT), TWE (minimum score 5.5); Recommended—IELTS (minimum score 6.5). *Application deadline:* For fall admission, 6/1 priority date for domestic students, 5/1 priority date for international students; for winter admission, 10/1 priority date for domestic students, 9/1 priority date for international students; for spring admission, 2/1 priority date for domestic students, 1/1 priority date for international students. Applications are processed on a rolling basis. Application fee: $50. Electronic applications accepted. *Expenses:* Tuition, state resident: full-time $10,224; part-time $638.98 per credit hour. Tuition, nonresident: full-time $22,145; part-time $1384.04 per credit hour. Tuition and fees vary according to course load and program. *Financial support:* In 2017–18, 78 students received support, including 4 fellowships (averaging $13,500 per year), 1 research assistantship with tuition reimbursement available (averaging $16,000 per year); Federal Work-Study, scholarships/grants, and unspecified assistantships also available. Support available to part-time students. Financial award applicants required to submit FAFSA. *Faculty research:* Improving students' skill achievement in mathematics, improving elementary children's understanding of informational text, teachers' use of their pedagogical and mathematical knowledge in the interactive work of teaching, the intersection of identity construction in teaching and learning, identifying effective methods of literacy instruction and assessments for bilingual students in elementary language arts classrooms. *Unit head:* Dr. Thomas Edwards, Interim Associate Dean for Teacher Education, 313-577-3886, E-mail: t.g.edwards@wayne.edu. *Application contact:* 313-577-0902, E-mail: askcoe@wayne.edu.
Website: http://coe.wayne.edu/ted/index.php

Webster University, School of Education, Department of Communication Arts, Reading and Early Childhood, St. Louis, MO 63119-3194. Offers communication arts (MAT); reading (MA). *Entrance requirements:* For master's, minimum GPA of 2.5. Additional exam requirements/recommendations for international students: Required—TOEFL.

Webster University, School of Education, Department of Multidisciplinary Studies, St. Louis, MO 63119-3194. Offers applied educational psychology (MA, Ed S); communication arts (MA); early childhood education (MA, MAT); education and innovation (MA); educational technology (MET); elementary education (MAT); mathematics for educators (MA); middle school education (MAT); multidisciplinary studies (MAT); multimodal literacy for global impact (MA); reading (MA); secondary school education (MAT); special education (MA, MAT); teaching English as a second language (MA); transformative learning in the global community (Ed S). *Program availability:* Part-time. *Entrance requirements:* For master's, minimum GPA of 2.5. Additional exam requirements/recommendations for international students: Required—TOEFL.

West Chester University of Pennsylvania, College of Education and Social Work, Department of Literacy, West Chester, PA 19383. Offers literacy (Certificate); literacy coaching (Certificate); literacy (M Ed); reading specialist (Teaching Certificate). *Program availability:* Part-time, evening/weekend. *Students:* 1 (woman) full-time, 134 part-time (131 women); includes 4 minority (1 Black or African American, non-Hispanic/Latino; 3 Hispanic/Latino). Average age 31. 41 applicants, 95% accepted, 31 enrolled. In 2017, 31 master's, 1 Certificate awarded. *Degree requirements:* For master's, minimum GPA of 3.0, portfolio assessment; for other advanced degree, comprehensive exam. *Entrance requirements:* For master's, GRE or MAT if GPA is below 3.0, minimum GPA of 3.0, teaching certificate, two letters of reference. Additional exam requirements/recommendations for international students: Required—TOEFL or IELTS. *Application deadline:* For fall admission, 5/15 for international students; for spring admission, 10/15 for international students. Applications are processed on a rolling basis. Application fee: $50. Electronic applications accepted. *Expenses:* Tuition, state resident: full-time $9000; part-time $500 per credit. Tuition, nonresident: full-time $13,500; part-time $750 per credit. *Required fees:* $2959; $149.79 per credit. *Financial support:* Scholarships/

grants and unspecified assistantships available. Financial award application deadline: 2/15; financial award applicants required to submit FAFSA. *Faculty research:* Teaching and mentoring pre-service and in-service teachers to teach literacy in urban settings, literacy and technology, children's and young adult literature, literacy and diversity, developmental word knowledge. *Unit head:* Dr. Carol Smith, Chair, 610-430-5601, Fax: 610-436-3102, E-mail: csmith@wcupa.edu. *Application contact:* Dr. Diane Santori, Graduate Coordinator, 610-436-6905, Fax: 610-436-3102, E-mail: dsantori@wcupa.edu.
Website: http://www.wcupa.edu/education-socialWork/literacy/

Western Connecticut State University, Division of Graduate Studies, School of Professional Studies, Department of Education and Educational Psychology, Reading Option, Danbury, CT 06810-6885. Offers MS. *Program availability:* Part-time. *Degree requirements:* For master's, thesis or research project, completion of program in 6 years. *Entrance requirements:* For master's, minimum GPA of 2.8, teaching certificate in elementary education. Additional exam requirements/recommendations for international students: Recommended—TOEFL (minimum score 550 paper-based; 79 iBT), IELTS (minimum score 6). *Expenses:* Tuition, state resident: full-time $6757; part-time $374 per credit hour. Tuition, nonresident: full-time $18,102; part-time $374 per credit hour. *Required fees:* $4994; $190 per credit hour. $60 per term. Tuition and fees vary according to degree level and program. *Faculty research:* Training guides for educators.

Western Illinois University, School of Graduate Studies, College of Education and Human Services, Department of Curriculum and Instruction, Program in Reading, Macomb, IL 61455-1390. Offers MS Ed. *Accreditation:* NCATE. *Program availability:* Part-time. *Students:* 1 (woman) full-time, 24 part-time (22 women). Average age 34. 1 applicant, 100% accepted, 1 enrolled. In 2017, 15 master's awarded. *Degree requirements:* For master's, thesis or alternative. *Entrance requirements:* For master's, teacher certification. Additional exam requirements/recommendations for international students: Required—TOEFL (minimum score 550 paper-based; 80 iBT). *Application deadline:* Applications are processed on a rolling basis. Application fee: $30. Electronic applications accepted. *Financial support:* Applicants required to submit FAFSA. *Unit head:* Dr. Barry Witten, Interim Chairperson, 309-298-1961. *Application contact:* Dr. Nancy Parsons, Assistant Director of Graduate Studies, 309-298-1806, Fax: 309-298-2345, E-mail: grad-office@wiu.edu.
Website: http://wiu.edu/curriculum

Western Kentucky University, Graduate Studies, College of Education and Behavioral Sciences, School of Teacher Education, Bowling Green, KY 42101. Offers elementary education (MAE, Ed S); exceptional education: learning and behavioral disorders (MAE); exceptional education: moderate and severe disabilities (MAE); instructional design (MS); interdisciplinary early childhood education (MAE); library media education (MS); literacy education (MAE); middle grades education (MAE); secondary education (MAE, Ed S). *Program availability:* Part-time, evening/weekend, online learning. *Degree requirements:* For master's, comprehensive exam. *Entrance requirements:* For master's, GRE General Test. Additional exam requirements/recommendations for international students: Required—TOEFL (minimum score 555 paper-based; 79 iBT). *Faculty research:* Teacher preparation in moderate/severe disabilities.

Western Michigan University, Graduate College, College of Education and Human Development, Department of Special Education and Literacy Studies, Kalamazoo, MI 49008. Offers literacy studies (MA); special education (MA, Ed D), including clinical teacher (MA); teaching children with visual impairments (MA).

Western New Mexico University, Graduate Division, School of Education, Silver City, NM 88062-0680. Offers bilingual education (MAT); educational leadership (MA); elementary education (MAT); reading (MAT); secondary education (MAT); special education (MAT); TESOL (teaching English to speakers of other languages) (MAT). *Accreditation:* NCATE. *Program availability:* Part-time, online learning. *Degree requirements:* For master's, comprehensive exam. *Entrance requirements:* For master's, minimum GPA of 3.0 in last 64 hours of undergraduate study. Additional exam requirements/recommendations for international students: Required—TOEFL (minimum score 550 paper-based; 79 iBT). Electronic applications accepted. *Faculty research:* International education, electronic reading assessment, developing STEM teachers.

Western State Colorado University, Graduate Programs in Education, Gunnison, CO 81231. Offers education administrator leadership (MA); reading leadership (MA); teacher leadership (MA). *Program availability:* Online learning. *Degree requirements:* For master's, capstone.

Westfield State University, College of Graduate and Continuing Education, Department of Education, Program in Reading Specialist, Westfield, MA 01086. Offers M Ed. *Accreditation:* NCATE. *Program availability:* Part-time, evening/weekend. *Faculty:* 1 (woman) full-time, 3 part-time/adjunct (2 women). *Students:* 1 (woman) full-time, 26 part-time (25 women). Average age 29. 7 applicants, 100% accepted, 6 enrolled. In 2017, 6 master's awarded. *Degree requirements:* For master's, comprehensive exam, practicum. *Entrance requirements:* For master's, GRE General Test or MAT, minimum undergraduate GPA of 2.8. Additional exam requirements/recommendations for international students: Recommended—TOEFL (minimum score 550 paper-based; 79 iBT). *Application deadline:* For fall admission, 7/1 for domestic students; for spring admission, 11/1 for domestic students; for summer admission, 4/1 for domestic students. Applications are processed on a rolling basis. Application fee: $50. *Expenses:* Tuition, state resident: part-time $332 per credit. Tuition, nonresident: part-time $332 per credit. *Required fees:* $75 per semester. Tuition and fees vary according to program. *Financial support:* Unspecified assistantships and SOS scholarships (for education majors only) available. Financial award application deadline: 3/1; financial award applicants required to submit FAFSA. *Unit head:* Dr. Laura Baker, Department Chair, 413-572-5324, E-mail: lbaker@westfield.ma.edu. *Application contact:* Shelly Henrichon, Coordinator of College of Graduate and Continuing Education Admissions, 413-572-8022, Fax: 413-572-5227, E-mail: mhenrichon@westfield.ma.edu.

West Liberty University, College of Education and Human Performance, West Liberty, WV 26074. Offers community education research and leadership (MA Ed); innovative instruction (MA Ed); leadership in disability services (MA Ed); leadership studies (MA Ed); multi-categorical special education (MA Ed); reading specialist (MA Ed); sports leadership and coaching (MA Ed). *Accreditation:* NCATE. *Program availability:* Part-time, evening/weekend. *Students:* 18 full-time (12 women), 74 part-time (60 women); includes 2 minority (1 Black or African American, non-Hispanic/Latino; 1 Native Hawaiian or other Pacific Islander, non-Hispanic/Latino). Average age 32. *Degree requirements:* For master's, capstone experience. *Entrance requirements:* For master's, minimum GPA of 2.5 or 3.0 (depending on track). Additional exam requirements/recommendations for international students: Required—TOEFL. *Application deadline:* Applications are processed on a rolling basis. Application fee: $0. Electronic applications accepted. Tuition and fees vary according to course load and program. *Financial support:* Teaching assistantships and unspecified assistantships available. *Unit head:* Dr. Catherine Monteroso, Interim Dean, 304-336-8247, E-mail: cmonteroso@westliberty.edu. *Application contact:* Sara Sweeney, Director, Office of Graduate Studies, 304-336-8545, E-mail: sara.sweeney@westliberty.edu.
Website: http://westliberty.edu/education/

Reading Education

Westminster College, Graduate School, Program in Special Education and Reading Specialist, New Wilmington, PA 16172-0001. Offers M Ed. *Program availability:* Part-time, evening/weekend. *Degree requirements:* For master's, comprehensive exam, portfolio. *Entrance requirements:* For master's, minimum GPA of 3.0. *Application deadline:* For fall admission, 8/15 priority date for domestic students; for spring admission, 1/8 priority date for domestic students. Applications are processed on a rolling basis. Application fee: $35. *Expenses: Tuition:* Part-time $454 per semester hour. *Required fees:* $235.50 per course. Tuition and fees vary according to course load. *Financial support:* Career-related internships or fieldwork and scholarships/grants available. *Unit head:* Dr. Amy Camardese, Chair, 724-946-7183. *Application contact:* Dr. Amy Camardese, Chair, 724-946-7183.

West Texas A&M University, College of Education and Social Sciences, Department of Education, Program in Reading Education, Canyon, TX 79015. Offers M Ed. *Program availability:* Part-time, evening/weekend. *Degree requirements:* For master's, comprehensive exam. *Entrance requirements:* For master's, GRE General Test, interview with master's committee chairperson, state certification as a reading specialist with 3 years of teaching experience. Electronic applications accepted. *Faculty research:* Multicultural child and adolescent literature, bilingual, dual language, monolingual classrooms.

West Virginia University, College of Education and Human Services, Morgantown, WV 26506. Offers audiology (Au D); autism spectrum disorder (MA); clinical rehabilitation and mental health counseling (MS); communication science and disorders (PhD); counseling (MA); counseling psychology (PhD); curriculum and instruction (Ed D); early childhood education (MA); early intervention (MA); education (PhD); educational leadership (MA, Ed D); educational leadership/public school administration (MA); educational psychology (MA, Ed D); elementary education (MA); gifted education (MA); higher education administration (MA, Ed D); higher education curriculum and teaching (MA); institutional design and technology (MA); instructional design and technology (Ed D); literacy education (MA); secondary education (MA); secondary education/English (MA); special education (Ed D); speech pathology (MS). *Accreditation:* NCATE. *Program availability:* Part-time, evening/weekend, online learning. *Students:* 423 full-time (347 women), 367 part-time (316 women); includes 57 minority (14 Black or African American, non-Hispanic/Latino; 7 Asian, non-Hispanic/Latino; 20 Hispanic/Latino; 16 Two or more races, non-Hispanic/Latino), 13 international. *Degree requirements:* For master's, content exams; for doctorate, comprehensive exam, thesis/dissertation. *Entrance requirements:* Additional exam requirements/recommendations for international students: Required—TOEFL (minimum score 500 paper-based; 61 iBT). *Application deadline:* For fall admission, 8/1 for domestic students; for spring admission, 1/1 for domestic students; for summer admission, 5/1 for domestic students. Application fee: $60. Electronic applications accepted. *Expenses:* Tuition, state resident: full-time $9450. Tuition, nonresident: full-time $24,390. *Financial support:* Fellowships, research assistantships, teaching assistantships, career-related internships or fieldwork, Federal Work-Study, institutionally sponsored loans, health care benefits, tuition waivers (full and partial), and administrative assistantships available. Financial award applicants required to submit FAFSA. *Faculty research:* Internet training and integration for teachers, rural education, teacher preparation, organization of schools, evaluation of personnel. *Unit head:* Dr. Gypsy Denzine, Dean, 304-293-5703, Fax: 304-293-7565, E-mail: gypsy.denzine@mail.wvu.edu. *Application contact:* Dr. M. Cecil Smith, Associate Dean for Research and Graduate Education, 304-293-2174, Fax: 304-293-3802, E-mail: mcecil.smith@mail.wvu.edu.
Website: http://cehs.wvu.edu/

Widener University, School of Human Service Professions, Center for Education, Chester, PA 19013-5792. Offers adult education (M Ed); counseling in higher education (M Ed); counselor education (M Ed); early childhood education (M Ed); educational foundations (M Ed); educational leadership (M Ed); educational psychology (M Ed); elementary education (M Ed); English and language arts (M Ed); health education (M Ed); higher education leadership (Ed D); home and school visitor (M Ed); human sexuality (M Ed, PhD); mathematics education (M Ed); middle school education (M Ed); principalship (M Ed); reading and language arts (Ed D); reading education (M Ed); school administration (Ed D); science education (M Ed); social studies education (M Ed); special education (M Ed); technology education (M Ed). *Accreditation:* NCATE. *Program availability:* Part-time, evening/weekend. *Faculty:* 34 full-time (22 women), 37 part-time/adjunct (14 women). *Students:* 131 full-time (112 women), 244 part-time (179 women); includes 94 minority (58 Black or African American, non-Hispanic/Latino; 1 American Indian or Alaska Native, non-Hispanic/Latino; 1 Asian, non-Hispanic/Latino; 22 Hispanic/Latino; 12 Two or more races, non-Hispanic/Latino), 12 international. Average age 37. 140 applicants, 38% accepted, 26 enrolled. In 2017, 45 master's, 21 doctorates awarded. Terminal master's awarded for partial completion of doctoral program. *Degree requirements:* For doctorate, thesis/dissertation. *Entrance requirements:* For master's, minimum GPA of 2.5; for doctorate, GRE or MAT, minimum GPA of 2.0 (undergraduate), 3.5 (graduate). *Application deadline:* Applications are processed on a rolling basis. Application fee: $25 ($300 for international students). Electronic applications accepted. *Expenses:* Contact institution. *Financial support:* Career-related internships or fieldwork, tuition waivers (full and partial), and unspecified assistantships available. Support available to part-time students. Financial award application deadline: 5/1. *Faculty research:* Reading and cognition, adult education, technology education, educational leadership, special education. *Unit head:* Dr. Shawn Fitzgerald, Dean, 610-499-4294, Fax: 610-499-4623, E-mail: smfitzgerald@widener.edu. *Application contact:* Megan Kuft, Director of Graduate Admissions, 610-499-4124, E-mail: gradprograms@widener.edu.
Website: http://www.widener.edu/academics/schools/eics

Wilkes University, College of Graduate and Professional Studies, School of Education, Wilkes-Barre, PA 18766-0002. Offers educational development and strategies (MS Ed); educational leadership (MS Ed, Ed D); effective teaching (MS Ed); instructional media (MS Ed); instructional technology (MS Ed); international school leadership (MS Ed); international teaching and learning (MS Ed); literacy specialist (MS Ed); middle level education (MS Ed); online teaching (MS Ed); school business leadership (MS Ed); special education (MS Ed); teaching English to speakers of other languages (MS Ed). *Program availability:* Part-time, evening/weekend, 100% online, blended/hybrid learning. *Students:* 76 full-time (57 women), 1,586 part-time (1,204 women); includes 82 minority (10 Black or African American, non-Hispanic/Latino; 12 Asian, non-Hispanic/Latino; 41 Hispanic/Latino; 1 Native Hawaiian or other Pacific Islander, non-Hispanic/Latino; 18 Two or more races, non-Hispanic/Latino). Average age 34. In 2017, 619 master's, 23 doctorates awarded. *Entrance requirements:* Additional exam requirements/recommendations for international students: Required—TOEFL (minimum score 550 paper-based; 79 iBT). *Application deadline:* Applications are processed on a rolling basis. Application fee: $45 ($65 for international students). Electronic applications accepted. *Expenses:* Contact institution. *Financial support:* Unspecified assistantships available. Financial award application deadline: 3/1; financial award applicants required to submit FAFSA. *Unit head:* Dr. Rhonda Rabbitt, Dean, 570-408-4680, Fax: 570-408-7872, E-mail: rhonda.rabbitt@wilkes.edu. *Application contact:* Stephanie Wasmanski, Associate Director of Graduate Admissions, 570-408-5535, Fax: 570-408-7846, E-mail: stephanie.wasmanski@wilkes.edu.
Website: http://www.wilkes.edu/academics/graduate-programs/masters-programs/graduate-education/index.aspx

William Paterson University of New Jersey, College of Education, Wayne, NJ 07470-8420. Offers curriculum and learning (M Ed); early childhood education (Certificate); educational leadership (M Ed); educational media specialist (Certificate); elementary education (MAT, Certificate); elementary education subject area (Certificate); higher education administration (MA); learning disabilities consultant (Certificate); literacy (M Ed); middle level education (M Ed); middle school education subject area (Certificate); professional counseling (M Ed); reading specialist (Certificate); school library media specialist (Certificate); school principal (Certificate); school supervisor (Certificate); secondary education (MAT); special education (M Ed); teacher of students with disabilities (Certificate). *Accreditation:* NCATE. *Program availability:* Part-time, evening/weekend. *Faculty:* 37 full-time (25 women), 21 part-time/adjunct (16 women). *Students:* 73 full-time (54 women), 480 part-time (409 women); includes 153 minority (48 Black or African American, non-Hispanic/Latino; 13 Asian, non-Hispanic/Latino; 81 Hispanic/Latino; 11 Two or more races, non-Hispanic/Latino), 1 international. Average age 35. 347 applicants, 87% accepted, 226 enrolled. In 2017, 136 master's awarded. *Degree requirements:* For master's, comprehensive exam, thesis (for some programs), exit interview (for some programs), practicum/internship; minimum GPA of 3.0 (for some programs); exit portfolio (for some programs). *Entrance requirements:* For master's, GRE/MAT, minimum GPA of 2.75; teaching certificate; essay; interview; 2 letters of recommendation; personal statement. Additional exam requirements/recommendations for international students: Required—TOEFL (minimum score 550 paper-based; 79 iBT), IELTS (minimum score 6). *Application deadline:* For fall admission, 6/1 for domestic students, 3/1 for international students; for spring admission, 11/1 for domestic students, 10/1 for international students. Applications are processed on a rolling basis. Application fee: $50. Electronic applications accepted. *Expenses:* Tuition, state resident: full-time $13,920; part-time $6264 per year. Tuition, nonresident: full-time $21,700; part-time $9765 per year. *Required fees:* $80; $36 per year. Tuition and fees vary according to course load, degree level and program. *Financial support:* In 2017–18, 8,416 students received support. Career-related internships or fieldwork, Federal Work-Study, scholarships/grants, and unspecified assistantships available. Support available to part-time students. Financial award application deadline: 3/15; financial award applicants required to submit FAFSA. *Faculty research:* Code switching and creative writing, language instruction, teacher evaluation, preschools, history of educational theories. *Total annual research expenditures:* $311,226. *Unit head:* Dr. Dorothy Feola, Dean, 973-720-2138, Fax: 973-720-3647, E-mail: feolad@wpunj.edu. *Application contact:* Liana Fornarotto, Director of Education Enrollment and Certification, 973-720-2206, Fax: 973-720-2989, E-mail: fornarottol@wpunj.edu.
Website: http://www.wpunj.edu/coe

Wilmington College, Department of Education, Wilmington, OH 45177. Offers reading (M Ed); special education (M Ed). *Accreditation:* TEAC. *Program availability:* Part-time. *Degree requirements:* For master's, comprehensive exam. *Entrance requirements:* For master's, GRE or MAT, minimum GPA of 3.0, 2 letters of recommendation. Additional exam requirements/recommendations for international students: Required—TOEFL. *Faculty research:* Reading instruction, special education practices, conflict resolution in the schools, models of higher education for teachers.

Wilmington University, College of Education, New Castle, DE 19720-6491. Offers applied technology in education (M Ed); career and technical education (M Ed); educational leadership (Ed D); elementary and secondary school counseling (M Ed); elementary studies (M Ed); ESOL literacy (M Ed); higher education leadership (Ed D); instruction: gifted and talented (M Ed); instruction: teacher of reading (M Ed); instruction: teaching and learning (M Ed); organizational leadership (Ed D); school leadership (M Ed); secondary education (MAT); special education (M Ed). *Accreditation:* NCATE. *Program availability:* Part-time, evening/weekend. *Faculty:* 23 full-time (13 women), 162 part-time/adjunct (99 women). *Students:* 546 full-time (394 women), 960 part-time (732 women); includes 320 minority (241 Black or African American, non-Hispanic/Latino; 12 American Indian or Alaska Native, non-Hispanic/Latino; 11 Asian, non-Hispanic/Latino; 28 Hispanic/Latino; 3 Native Hawaiian or other Pacific Islander, non-Hispanic/Latino; 25 Two or more races, non-Hispanic/Latino), 7 international. Average age 34. 1,068 applicants, 64% accepted, 582 enrolled. In 2017, 430 master's, 59 doctorates awarded. *Entrance requirements:* For master's, 2 letters of recommendation, interview. Additional exam requirements/recommendations for international students: Required—TOEFL (minimum score 500 paper-based). *Application deadline:* For fall admission, 4/30 for domestic students. Applications are processed on a rolling basis. Application fee: $35. Electronic applications accepted. *Expenses: Tuition:* Part-time $466 per credit. *Required fees:* $25 per semester. Tuition and fees vary according to degree level and campus/location. *Financial support:* Applicants required to submit FAFSA. *Unit head:* Dr. John C. Gray, Dean, 302-295-1139. *Application contact:* Laura Morris, Director of Admissions, 877-967-5464, E-mail: infocenter@wilmu.edu.
Website: http://www.wilmu.edu/education/

Worcester State University, Graduate School, Department of Education, Program in Reading, Worcester, MA 01602-2597. Offers M Ed, Postbaccalaureate Certificate. *Program availability:* Part-time, evening/weekend. *Students:* 22 part-time (21 women); includes 1 minority (Hispanic/Latino). Average age 29. 12 applicants, 100% accepted, 10 enrolled. In 2017, 3 master's, 1 other advanced degree awarded. *Degree requirements:* For master's, comprehensive exam (for some programs), thesis optional, portfolio; capstone. *Entrance requirements:* For master's, GRE General Test or MAT, MTEL Communication and Literacy test, teaching license at the initial or professional level; for Postbaccalaureate Certificate, Massachusetts Tests for Educator Licensure (MTEL). Additional exam requirements/recommendations for international students: Required—TOEFL (minimum score 550 paper-based; 79 iBT). *Application deadline:* For fall admission, 6/15 for domestic and international students; for spring admission, 11/1 for domestic and international students; for summer admission, 4/1 for domestic and international students. Applications are processed on a rolling basis. Application fee: $50. Electronic applications accepted. *Expenses:* Tuition, state resident: full-time $3042; part-time $169 per credit hour. Tuition, nonresident: full-time $3042; part-time $169 per credit hour. *Required fees:* $2754; $153 per credit hour. *Financial support:* Career-related internships or fieldwork, scholarships/grants, and unspecified assistantships available. Financial award application deadline: 3/1; financial award applicants required to submit FAFSA. *Unit head:* Dr. Pamela Hollander, Coordinator, 508-929-8347. *Application contact:* Sara Grady, Associate Dean for Graduate Studies and Professional Development, 508-929-8130, E-mail: sara.grady@worcester.edu.

Xavier University, College of Social Sciences, Health and Education, School of Education, Department of Childhood Education and Literacy, Cincinnati, OH 45207. Offers children's multicultural literature (M Ed); elementary education (M Ed); Montessori education (M Ed); reading (M Ed). *Program availability:* Part-time. *Degree requirements:* For master's, comprehensive exam, thesis, 30 semester hours. *Entrance requirements:* For master's, GRE, MAT, official transcript, 3 letters of recommendation (for Montessori education); resume; statement of purpose. Additional exam requirements/recommendations for international students: Required—TOEFL (minimum score 550 paper-based; 79 iBT). Electronic applications accepted. Application fee is waived when completed online. *Expenses:* Contact institution. *Faculty research:* Multicultural literacy/fluency, early literacy development, writing/creative and across curriculum, assessment of reading abilities.

York College of Pennsylvania, Master of Education Program, York, PA 17403-3651. Offers educational leadership (M Ed); educational technology (M Ed); reading specialist (M Ed). *Program availability:* Part-time-only, evening/weekend. *Faculty:* 2 full-time (1 woman), 7 part-time/adjunct (3 women). *Students:* 87 part-time (62 women); includes 2 minority (1 Hispanic/Latino; 1 Two or more races, non-Hispanic/Latino), 1 international. Average age 33. 57 applicants, 79% accepted, 39 enrolled. In 2017, 7 master's awarded. *Degree requirements:* For master's, comprehensive exam (for some programs), thesis (for some programs). *Entrance requirements:* For master's, PRAXIS, statement of applicant's professional and academic goals, 2 letters of recommendation, letter from current supervisor, official undergraduate and graduate transcript(s), copy of teaching certificate(s), current professional resume, interview. *Application deadline:* For fall admission, 7/15 priority date for domestic students; for spring admission, 11/15 priority date for domestic students; for summer admission, 4/15 priority date for domestic students. Applications are processed on a rolling basis. Application fee: $0. Electronic applications accepted. *Expenses:* $620 per credit. *Financial support:* Scholarships/grants available. Financial award applicants required to submit FAFSA. *Faculty*

research: Classroom technology, assessment, educational leadership, professional development, literacy. *Unit head:* Dr. Joshua D. DeSantis, Director, Master of Education Program, 717-815-1936, E-mail: jdesant1@ycp.edu.
Website: https://www.ycp.edu/med

Youngstown State University, Graduate School, Beeghly College of Education, Department of Teacher Education, Youngstown, OH 44555-0001. Offers adolescent/young adult education (MS Ed); content area concentration (MS Ed); early childhood education (MS Ed); educational technology (MS Ed); literacy (MS Ed); middle childhood education (MS Ed); special education (MS Ed), including gifted and talented education, special education. *Accreditation:* NCATE. *Program availability:* Part-time, evening/weekend. *Degree requirements:* For master's, comprehensive exam. *Entrance requirements:* For master's, GRE, MAT, or teaching certificate; minimum GPA of 2.7. Additional exam requirements/recommendations for international students: Required—TOEFL. *Faculty research:* Multicultural literacy, hands-on mathematics teaching, integrated instruction, reading comprehension, emergent curriculum.

Religious Education

Andrews University, School of Graduate Studies, Seventh-day Adventist Theological Seminary, Program in Religious Education, Berrien Springs, MI 49104. Offers MA, Ed D, PhD, and Ed S. *Program availability:* Part-time. *Faculty:* 3 full-time (1 woman). *Students:* 6 full-time (4 women), 5 part-time (3 women); includes 3 minority (2 Black or African American, non-Hispanic/Latino; 1 Asian, non-Hispanic/Latino), 7 international. Average age 43. 6 applicants, 83% accepted, 1 enrolled. In 2017, 5 master's, 1 doctorate awarded. Terminal master's awarded for partial completion of doctoral program. *Degree requirements:* For doctorate, thesis/dissertation. *Entrance requirements:* For master's, GRE Subject Test. Additional exam requirements/recommendations for international students: Required—TOEFL (minimum score 550 paper-based). *Application deadline:* For fall admission, 8/31 for domestic students. Applications are processed on a rolling basis. Application fee: $40. *Financial support:* Fellowships, research assistantships, teaching assistantships, and career-related internships or fieldwork available. Financial award application deadline: 6/1. *Faculty research:* Marriage and family, spiritual gifts and temperament. *Application contact:* Justina Clayburn, Supervisor of Graduate Admission, 800-253-2874, Fax: 269-471-6321, E-mail: graduate@andrews.edu.

Asbury Theological Seminary, Graduate and Professional Programs, Wilmore, KY 40390-1199. Offers M Div, MA, MAAS, MACE, MACL, MACM, MACP, MAMFC, MAMHC, MAPC, MASF, MAYM, Th M, D Min, PhD, Certificate. *Accreditation:* ATS. *Program availability:* Part-time, online learning. Terminal master's awarded for partial completion of doctoral program. *Degree requirements:* For master's, thesis (for some programs); for doctorate, dissertation, qualifying exam. *Entrance requirements:* For master's, minimum GPA of 2.75; for doctorate, minimum GPA of 3.0. Additional exam requirements/recommendations for international students: Required—TOEFL, IELTS. Electronic applications accepted.

Baptist Theological Seminary at Richmond, Graduate and Professional Programs, Richmond, VA 23228. Offers Biblical interpretation (M Div); Christian education formation (M Div); Christian ministry (MCM); justice and peacebuilding (M Div); ministry (D Min); religious freedom (M Div); theological studies (MTS, Graduate Certificate); theology (M Div); youth and student ministries (M Div); M Div/MBA; M Div/MS; M Div/MSW. *Accreditation:* ATS. *Program availability:* Part-time, 100% online, blended/hybrid learning. *Faculty:* 2 full-time (1 woman), 8 part-time/adjunct (2 women). *Students:* 38 full-time (14 women), 31 part-time (22 women); includes 11 minority (11 Black or African American, non-Hispanic/Latino; 4 Asian, non-Hispanic/Latino). Average age 46. In 2017, 15 master's, 2 doctorates awarded. *Degree requirements:* For master's and Graduate Certificate, thesis optional; for doctorate, comprehensive exam, thesis/dissertation, field study, independent study. *Entrance requirements:* For master's, BA/BS, minimum GPA of 2.2, 2 references, resume, official transcripts, writing sample; for doctorate, MAT (minimum score of 400), M Div with minimum GPA of 2.75, 3 years of full-time ministry experience, 3 references, resume, official transcripts, writing sample, personal statement. Additional exam requirements/recommendations for international students: Required—TOEFL (minimum score 550 paper-based), IELTS (minimum score 5.5). *Application deadline:* For fall admission, 7/1 for domestic students, 5/1 for international students; for winter admission, 12/15 for domestic students, 9/1 for international students; for spring admission, 1/15 for domestic students, 10/1 for international students. Applications are processed on a rolling basis. Application fee: $35. Electronic applications accepted. *Financial support:* In 2017–18, 46 students received support, including 9 teaching assistantships (averaging $3,300 per year); scholarships/grants also available. Financial award application deadline: 2/1. *Faculty research:* Biblical studies, pastoral care, church history, theology, ministry. *Unit head:* Dr. Linda M. Bridges, President, 804-204-1201, Fax: 804-355-8182, E-mail: lmbridges@btsr.edu. *Application contact:* Melissa Fallen, Director of Admissions and Recruitment, 804-204-1208, E-mail: admissions@btsr.edu.
Website: http://www.btsr.edu/programs/degree-programs

Biola University, Talbot School of Theology, La Mirada, CA 90639-0001. Offers adult/family ministry (MACE); Bible exposition (MA, Th M); Biblical and theological studies (Certificate); children's ministry (MACE); Christian education (M Div); cross-cultural education ministry (MACE); educational studies (Ed D, PhD); evangelism and discipleship (M Div); general Christian education (MACE); Messianic Jewish studies (M Div, Certificate); missions and intercultural studies (M Div); New Testament (MA, Th M); Old Testament (MA); Old Testament and Semitics (Th M); pastoral and general ministry (M Div); pastoral care and counseling (M Div, MACML); philosophy (MA); preaching and pastoral ministry (MACML); spiritual formation (M Div, Certificate); spiritual formation and soul care (MA); sports ministry (MACML); theology (MA, Th M, D Min, Certificate); youth ministry (MACE). *Program availability:* Part-time, evening/weekend. *Students:* 475 full-time (113 women), 603 part-time (176 women); includes 541 minority (39 Black or African American, non-Hispanic/Latino; 2 American Indian or Alaska Native, non-Hispanic/Latino; 378 Asian, non-Hispanic/Latino; 84 Hispanic/Latino; 1 Native Hawaiian or other Pacific Islander, non-Hispanic/Latino; 37 Two or more races, non-Hispanic/Latino), 105 international. 437 applicants, 78% accepted, 241 enrolled. In 2017, 177 master's, 24 doctorates awarded. *Entrance requirements:* For master's, bachelor's degree from accredited college or university; minimum GPA of 2.6 (for M Div), 3.0 (for MA); for doctorate, M Div or MA. Additional exam requirements/recommendations for international students: Required—TOEFL (minimum score 600 paper-based; 88 iBT). *Application deadline:* For fall admission, 7/1 for domestic students, 6/1 for international students; for spring admission, 12/1 priority date for domestic students. Applications are processed on a rolling basis. Application fee: $65. Electronic applications accepted. *Financial support:* Scholarships/grants and

unspecified assistantships available. Support available to part-time students. Financial award applicants required to submit FAFSA. *Faculty research:* New Testament, Old Testament, spiritual formation, Christian education, theological studies, Christian ministry, preaching and pastoral ministry, language and literature, bible exposition, Christian leadership. *Unit head:* Dr. Clint Arnold, Dean, 562-903-4816, Fax: 562-903-4748. *Application contact:* Graduate Admissions Office, 562-903-4752, E-mail: graduate.admissions@biola.edu.
Website: http://www.talbot.edu/

Boston College, School of Theology and Ministry, Chestnut Hill, MA 02467-3800. Offers church leadership (MA); divinity (M Div); pastoral ministry (MA), including Hispanic ministry, liturgy and worship, pastoral care and counseling, spirituality; religious education (MA, PhD); sacred theology (STD, STL); social justice/social ministry (MA); spiritual direction (MA); theological studies (MTS); theology (Th M, PhD); youth ministry (MA); MA/MA; MS/MA; MSW/MA. *Accreditation:* TEAC. *Program availability:* Part-time. *Degree requirements:* For doctorate, one foreign language, thesis/dissertation. *Entrance requirements:* For doctorate, GRE. Additional exam requirements/recommendations for international students: Required—TOEFL (minimum score 550 paper-based). Electronic applications accepted. *Faculty research:* Philosophy and practice of religious education, pastoral psychology, liturgical and spiritual theology, spiritual formation for the practice of ministry.

Boston University, School of Theology, Boston, MA 02215. Offers chaplaincy (M Div); choral conducting (MSM); church and the arts (M Div); community and global engagement (M Div); constructive theology and ethics (PhD), including constructive theology, theological ethics; history and hermeneutics (PhD), including biblical studies, church history and world Christianity, liturgical studies, mission studies; organ (MSM); pastoral ministry (M Div); practical theology (PhD), including church and society, congregation and community, evangelism and missiology, homiletics, leadership and administration, pastoral theology and psychology, religious education, spirituality studies; worship; religion and the academy (M Div); transformational leadership (D Min); M Div/MSM; M Div/MSW; MTS/MSW. PhD in mission studies offered in collaboration with Gordon-Conwell Theological Seminary. *Accreditation:* ACIPE; ATS. *Program availability:* Part-time, blended/hybrid learning. *Faculty:* 39 full-time (17 women), 11 part-time/adjunct (5 women). *Students:* 256 full-time (135 women), 87 part-time (40 women); includes 82 minority (38 Black or African American, non-Hispanic/Latino; 10 Asian, non-Hispanic/Latino; 23 Hispanic/Latino; 1 Native Hawaiian or other Pacific Islander, non-Hispanic/Latino; 10 Two or more races, non-Hispanic/Latino), 66 international. Average age 34. 334 applicants, 69% accepted, 106 enrolled. In 2017, 62 master's, 9 doctorates awarded. *Degree requirements:* For master's, comprehensive exam (for some programs), thesis optional, contextual education; for doctorate, 2 languages, dissertation, and comprehensive exam (for PhD). *Entrance requirements:* For master's, minimum GPA of 3.0; for doctorate, GRE General Test, minimum GPA of 3.3. Additional exam requirements/recommendations for international students: Required—TOEFL (minimum score 570 paper-based; 89 iBT). *Application deadline:* For fall admission, 1/15 priority date for domestic and international students; for spring admission, 10/15 priority date for domestic and international students. Applications are processed on a rolling basis. Application fee: $95. Electronic applications accepted. *Expenses:* $20,100 tuition. *Financial support:* In 2017–18, 236 students received support, including 102 fellowships with full tuition reimbursements available (averaging $7,500 per year), 11 research assistantships with full tuition reimbursements available (averaging $22,000 per year), 12 teaching assistantships with full tuition reimbursements available (averaging $22,000 per year); career-related internships or fieldwork, Federal Work-Study, scholarships/grants, and health care benefits also available. Support available to part-time students. Financial award application deadline: 7/15. *Faculty research:* Practical theology, ethics, environmental theology, religion and conflict transformation, chaplaincy. *Total annual research expenditures:* $2.5 million. *Unit head:* Rev. Dr. Mary Elizabeth Moore, Dean, 617-353-3050, Fax: 617-353-3061, E-mail: memoore@bu.edu. *Application contact:* Rev. Dr. Anastasia Kidd, Director of Enrollment, 617-353-3036, Fax: 617-358-0140, E-mail: sthadmis@bu.edu.
Website: http://www.bu.edu/sth

Brandeis University, Graduate School of Arts and Sciences, Program in Education, Waltham, MA 02454-9110. Offers Jewish day schools (MAT); public elementary education (MAT); secondary education (MAT), including Bible, biology, chemistry, Chinese, English, history, Jewish day schools, math, physics; teacher leadership (Ed M, AGC). *Faculty:* 4 full-time (2 women), 11 part-time/adjunct (10 women). *Students:* 21 full-time (19 women), 38 part-time (33 women); includes 5 minority (1 Black or African American, non-Hispanic/Latino; 3 Asian, non-Hispanic/Latino; 1 Hispanic/Latino), 8 international. Average age 34. 93 applicants, 78% accepted, 55 enrolled. In 2017, 43 master's, 10 other advanced degrees awarded. *Degree requirements:* For master's, thesis or alternative, internship; research project. *Entrance requirements:* For master's, GRE General Test or MAT, transcripts, letters of recommendation, resume, statement of purpose. Additional exam requirements/recommendations for international students: Required—PTE (minimum score 68), TOEFL (minimum score 600 paper-based, 100 iBT) or IELTS (7). *Application deadline:* For fall admission, 12/1 priority date for domestic students. Applications are processed on a rolling basis. Application fee: $75. Electronic applications accepted. *Expenses:* $32,440 (MAT), $17,520 (M Ed), $23,360 (AGS); $88 fees. *Financial support:* In 2017–18, 61 students received support. Scholarships/grants available. Financial award application deadline: 4/15; financial award applicants required to submit FAFSA. *Faculty research:* Teacher education, education, teaching, elementary

education, secondary education, Jewish education, English, history, biology, chemistry, physics, math, Chinese, Bible/Tanakh. *Unit head:* Marya Levenson, Director, 781-736-2002, E-mail: mlevenso@brandeis.edu. *Application contact:* Manuel Tuan, Department Coordinator, 781-736-2002, E-mail: tuan@brandeis.edu.
Website: http://www.brandeis.edu/gsas/programs/education.html

Brigham Young University, Graduate Studies, College of Religious Education, Provo, UT 84602. Offers MA. *Faculty:* 42 full-time (4 women), 2 part-time/adjunct (0 women). *Students:* 17 full-time (2 women); includes 1 minority (Two or more races, non-Hispanic/Latino). Average age 32. 16 applicants, 75% accepted, 12 enrolled. In 2017, 7 master's awarded. *Degree requirements:* For master's, thesis. *Entrance requirements:* For master's, GRE, minimum GPA of 3.0 in last 60 hours, letter of recommendation. *Application deadline:* For fall admission, 12/1 for domestic and international students. Application fee: $50. Electronic applications accepted. *Expenses:* Contact institution. *Financial support:* In 2017–18, 4 students received support. Scholarships/grants available. *Unit head:* Dr. Brent L. Top, Dean, 801-422-2736, Fax: 801-422-0616, E-mail: brent_top@byu.edu. *Application contact:* Dr. Terry B. Ball, Professor of Ancient Scripture, 801-422-3357, Fax: 801-422-0616, E-mail: terry_ball@byu.edu.

Calvary University, Graduate School and Seminary, Kansas City, MO 64147. Offers Bible and theology (MS); Biblical counseling (MA); education (MS), including administration and leadership, Christian education, curriculum and instruction, elementary education; organizational development (MS); pastoral studies (M Div); worship arts (MS). *Program availability:* Part-time, evening/weekend. *Faculty:* 6 full-time (2 women), 2 part-time/adjunct (1 woman). *Students:* 11 full-time (3 women), 29 part-time (15 women); includes 12 minority (4 Black or African American, non-Hispanic/Latino; 1 American Indian or Alaska Native, non-Hispanic/Latino; 6 Asian, non-Hispanic/Latino; 1 Native Hawaiian or other Pacific Islander, non-Hispanic/Latino). Average age 39. *Degree requirements:* For master's, variable foreign language requirement, comprehensive exam, thesis or alternative. *Entrance requirements:* For master's, minimum GPA of 2.5, BA or BS, doctrine agreement. Additional exam requirements/recommendations for international students: Required—TOEFL (minimum score 550 paper-based). *Application deadline:* Applications are processed on a rolling basis. Application fee: $0. Electronic applications accepted. *Expenses:* Contact institution. *Financial support:* Scholarships/grants available. Financial award application deadline: 11/5; financial award applicants required to submit FAFSA. *Unit head:* Dr. Thomas Baurain, Director of Seminary, 816-322-0110 Ext. 1502, Fax: 816-331-4474, E-mail: thomas.baurain@calvary.edu. *Application contact:* Ann Rogers, Admissions Office Assistant, 800-326-3960 Ext. 1321, Fax: 816-331-4474, E-mail: admissions@calvary.edu.
Website: http://www.calvary.edu

Calvin Theological Seminary, Graduate and Professional Programs, Grand Rapids, MI 49546-4387. Offers Bible and theology (MA); divinity (M Div), including ancient near eastern languages and literature, contextual ministry, evangelism and teaching, history of Christianity, new church development, New Testament, Old Testament, pastoral care and leadership, preaching and worship, theological studies, youth and family ministries; educational ministry (MA); historical theology (PhD); missions and evangelism (MA); pastoral care (MA); philosophical and moral theology (PhD); systematic theology (PhD); theological studies (MTS); theology (Th M); worship (MA); youth and family ministries (MA). *Accreditation:* ACIPE; ATS. *Program availability:* Part-time. *Degree requirements:* For master's, variable foreign language requirement, thesis (for some programs); for doctorate, 4 foreign languages, comprehensive exam, thesis/dissertation. *Entrance requirements:* For doctorate, GRE General Test, Hebrew, Greek, and a modern foreign language. Additional exam requirements/recommendations for international students: Required—TOEFL (minimum score 550 paper-based), TWE (minimum score 4). Electronic applications accepted. *Faculty research:* Recent Trinity theory, Christian anthropology, Proverbs, reformed confessions, Paul's view of law.

Carolina Christian College, Program in Religious Education, Winston-Salem, NC 27102-0777. Offers Christian education (MRE); pastoral care (MRE). *Entrance requirements:* For master's, bachelor's degree from accredited institution, minimum undergraduate "B" average.

Claremont School of Theology, Graduate and Professional Programs, Program in Religion, Claremont, CA 91711-3199. Offers practical theology (PhD), including religious education and formation, spiritual care and counseling; religion (MA, PhD), including comparative theology and philosophy (PhD), Hebrew Bible and Jewish studies (PhD), New Testament and Christian origins (PhD), process studies (PhD), religion, ethics, and society (PhD). *Accreditation:* ACIPE; ATS. Terminal master's awarded for partial completion of doctoral program. *Degree requirements:* For master's, thesis; for doctorate, 2 foreign languages, thesis/dissertation. *Entrance requirements:* For doctorate, GRE General Test. Additional exam requirements/recommendations for international students: Required—TOEFL. Electronic applications accepted.

Clarks Summit University, Baptist Bible Seminary, South Abington Township, PA 18411. Offers Biblical apologetics (MA); Biblical studies (MA); church education (M Min); church planting (M Div, M Min); communication (D Min); counseling and spiritual development (D Min); global ministry (M Min, D Min); ministry (PhD); missions (M Min); organizational leadership (M Min); outreach pastor (M Min); pastoral counseling (M Min); pastoral leadership (M Div, M Min); pastoral ministry (D Min); theological studies (D Min); theology (Th M); youth ministry (M Min). M Min in missions available only for Association of Baptists for World Evangelism missionary personnel. *Program availability:* Part-time, evening/weekend, online learning. Terminal master's awarded for partial completion of doctoral program. *Degree requirements:* For master's, 2 foreign languages, thesis, oral exam (for M Div); for doctorate, 2 foreign languages, comprehensive exam (for some programs), thesis/dissertation, oral exam. *Entrance requirements:* For doctorate, Greek and Hebrew entrance exams (for PhD). *Application deadline:* Applications are processed on a rolling basis. Application fee: $30. Electronic applications accepted. *Financial support:* Career-related internships or fieldwork and scholarships/grants available. Support available to part-time students. *Unit head:* Dr. Wayne Slusser, Dean, 570-585-9348, Fax: 570-585-4057, E-mail: wslusser@clarkssummitu.edu. *Application contact:* Dr. Wayne Slusser, Dean, 570-585-9348, Fax: 570-585-4057, E-mail: wslusser@clarkssummitu.edu.
Website: https://www.clarkssummitu.edu/seminary/

Clarks Summit University, Online Master's Programs, South Abington Township, PA 18411. Offers Bible (MA); counseling (MA, MS); curriculum and instruction (M Ed); educational administration (M Ed); literature (MA); organizational leadership (MA). *Program availability:* Part-time, evening/weekend, online learning. *Entrance requirements:* Additional exam requirements/recommendations for international students: Required—TOEFL (minimum score 500 paper-based). *Application deadline:* Applications are processed on a rolling basis. Application fee: $30. *Financial support:* Institutionally sponsored loans and scholarships/grants available. Financial award application deadline: 8/20; financial award applicants required to submit FAFSA. *Unit head:* Dr. James Lytle, President, 570-586-2400 Ext. 9222, Fax: 570-586-1753. *Application contact:* Drew Whipple, Vice President for Enrollment Management, 570-585-9370, Fax: 570-585-9299, E-mail: awhipple@clarkssummitu.edu.
Website: https://www.clarkssummitu.edu/online-masters-degrees/

Columbia International University, Columbia Graduate School, Columbia, SC 29203. Offers Bible teaching (MABT); counseling (MACN); early childhood and elementary education (MAT); educational administration (M Ed); educational leadership (PhD); instruction and learning (M Ed); teaching English as a foreign language (Certificate); teaching English as a foreign language and intercultural studies (MATF). *Program availability:* Part-time, evening/weekend, online learning. *Degree requirements:* For master's, internships, professional project. *Entrance requirements:* For master's, MAT; GRE (for some programs), minimum GPA of 2.7. Additional exam requirements/recommendations for international students: Required—TOEFL. Electronic applications accepted.

Concordia University Chicago, College of Education, Program in Christian Education, River Forest, IL 60305-1499. Offers MA. *Entrance requirements:* Additional exam requirements/recommendations for international students: Required—TOEFL (minimum score 550 paper-based). Electronic applications accepted.

Concordia University, Nebraska, Graduate Programs in Education, Program in Parish Education, Seward, NE 68434. Offers MPE. *Accreditation:* NCATE. *Program availability:* Part-time, evening/weekend. *Degree requirements:* For master's, thesis or alternative. *Entrance requirements:* For master's, GRE, MAT, or NTE, minimum GPA of 3.0, BS in education or equivalent.

Dallas Baptist University, Graduate School of Ministry, Program in Children's Ministry, Dallas, TX 75211-9299. Offers general (MA); special needs children ministry (MA). *Program availability:* Part-time, evening/weekend. *Application deadline:* Applications are processed on a rolling basis. Application fee: $25. Electronic applications accepted. Application fee is waived when completed online. *Expenses: Tuition:* Full-time $16,308; part-time $906 per credit hour. *Required fees:* $900; $450 per semester. Tuition and fees vary according to course load and degree level. *Unit head:* Dr. Robert R. Brooks, Dean, 214-333-5494, Fax: 214-333-5673, E-mail: bobb@dbu.edu. *Application contact:* Shelly Melia, Program Director, 214-333-5943, E-mail: shelly@dbu.edu.
Website: http://www.dbu.edu/ministry/degree-programs/ma-in-childrens-ministry

Dallas Baptist University, Graduate School of Ministry, Program in Student Ministry, Dallas, TX 75211-9299. Offers MA. *Program availability:* Part-time, evening/weekend. *Application deadline:* Applications are processed on a rolling basis. Application fee: $25. Electronic applications accepted. Application fee is waived when completed online. *Expenses: Tuition:* Full-time $16,308; part-time $906 per credit hour. *Required fees:* $900; $450 per semester. Tuition and fees vary according to course load and degree level. *Unit head:* Dr. Robert R. Brooks, Dean, 214-333-5494, Fax: 214-333-5673, E-mail: bobb@dbu.edu. *Application contact:* Dr. Chris Shirley, Program Director, 214-333-5256, Fax: 214-333-5689, E-mail: chrissh@dbu.edu.
Website: http://www.dbu.edu/ministry/degree-programs/m-a-in-student-ministry

Dallas Theological Seminary, Graduate Programs, Dallas, TX 75204-6499. Offers adult education (Th M); apologetics (Th M); Bible backgrounds (Th M); Bible translation (Th M); Biblical and theological studies (Certificate); biblical counseling (MA); biblical exegesis and linguistics (MA); biblical exposition (PhD); biblical studies (MA); Biblical theology (Th M); children's education (Th M); Christian education (MA, D Min); Christian leadership (MA); cross-cultural ministries (MA); educational administration (Th M); educational leadership (Th M); evangelism and discipleship (Th M); exposition of Biblical books (Th M); family life education (Th M); general studies (Th M); Hebrew and cognate studies (Th M); hermeneutics (Th M); historical theology (Th M); homiletics (Th M); intercultural ministries (Th M); Jesus studies (Th M); leadership studies (Th M); media and communication (MA); media arts (Th M); ministry (D Min); ministry with women (Th M); New Testament studies (Th M, PhD); Old Testament studies (Th M, PhD); parachurch ministries (Th M); pastoral care and counseling (Th M); pastoral theology and practice (Th M); philosophy (Th M); sacred theology (STM); spiritual formation (Th M); systematic theology (Th M); teaching in Christian institutions (Th M); theological studies (PhD); urban ministries (Th M); worship studies (Th M); youth education (Th M). *Program availability:* Part-time, online learning. *Degree requirements:* For master's, variable foreign language requirement, thesis (for some programs); for doctorate, 2 foreign languages, thesis/dissertation. *Entrance requirements:* For master's, GRE or MAT (if minimum undergraduate cumulative GPA is below 2.5 or undergraduate degree is unaccredited). Additional exam requirements/recommendations for international students: Required—TOEFL (minimum score 575 paper-based; 85 iBT), TWE. Electronic applications accepted.

Felician University, Program in Religious Education, Lodi, NJ 07644-2117. Offers MA, Certificate. *Accreditation:* TEAC. *Program availability:* Part-time, evening/weekend, online only, 100% online. *Faculty:* 1 (woman) full-time, 5 part-time/adjunct (2 women). *Students:* 1 (woman) full-time, 12 part-time (8 women); includes 2 minority (1 Asian, non-Hispanic/Latino; 1 Hispanic/Latino), 2 international. Average age 45. 5 applicants, 100% accepted, 5 enrolled. In 2017, 7 master's awarded. *Degree requirements:* For master's, thesis, presentation; for Certificate, thesis, capstone project. *Entrance requirements:* For master's, letter of recommendation, interview, reading/writing sample, ministerial discount form, notarized copy of valid passport, graduation from accredited baccalaureate program. Additional exam requirements/recommendations for international students: Required—TOEFL (minimum score 550 paper-based; 79 iBT), IELTS (minimum score 6.5), PTE (minimum score 56). *Application deadline:* Applications are processed on a rolling basis. Application fee: $40. Electronic applications accepted. Application fee is waived when completed online. *Expenses:* Contact institution. *Financial support:* In 2017–18, 12 students received support. Federal Work-Study, scholarships/grants, and tuition waivers (partial) available. Financial award applicants required to submit FAFSA. *Faculty research:* Catechesis and evangelization, education ministry, religious education, church leadership, faith formation. *Unit head:* Dr. Dolores M. Henchy, Dean of Academic Success Programs, 201-355-1133, E-mail: henchyd@felician.edu. *Application contact:* Michael Szarek, Director of Graduate Admissions, 201-355-1450, E-mail: szarekm@felician.edu.

Fordham University, Graduate School of Religion and Religious Education, New York, NY 10458. Offers pastoral counseling and spiritual care (MA); pastoral ministry/spirituality/pastoral counseling (D Min); religion and religious education (MA); religious education (MS, PhD, PD); spiritual direction (Certificate). *Program availability:* Part-time. Terminal master's awarded for partial completion of doctoral program. *Degree requirements:* For master's, research paper; for doctorate, comprehensive exam, thesis/dissertation. *Entrance requirements:* For doctorate, MAT. Electronic applications accepted. *Expenses:* Contact institution. *Faculty research:* Spirituality and spiritual direction, pastoral care and counseling, adult family and community, growth and young adult.

Gardner-Webb University, School of Divinity, Boiling Springs, NC 28017. Offers biblical studies (M Div); Christian education and formation (M Div); intercultural studies (M Div); ministry (D Min); missiology (M Div); pastoral care and counseling (M Div); pastoral care and counseling/member care for missionaries (D Min); pastoral studies (M Div); M Div/MA; M Div/MBA. *Accreditation:* ACIPE. *Program availability:* Part-time. *Faculty:* 10 full-time (1 woman), 4 part-time/adjunct (2 women). *Students:* 102 full-time (47 women), 56 part-time (15 women); includes 67 minority (63 Black or African American, non-Hispanic/Latino; 3 Asian, non-Hispanic/Latino; 1 Hispanic/Latino). Average age 38. *Entrance requirements:* For master's, minimum GPA of 2.6; for

doctorate, minimum GPA of 2.75. Additional exam requirements/recommendations for international students: Required—TOEFL (minimum score 500 paper-based; 61 iBT). *Application deadline:* Applications are processed on a rolling basis. Electronic applications accepted. *Expenses:* Contact institution. *Financial support:* Fellowships, institutionally sponsored loans, and unspecified assistantships available. Support available to part-time students. Financial award application deadline: 5/15. *Faculty research:* Jewish-Christian dialogue, Islam. *Unit head:* Dr. Robert W. Canoy, Sr., Dean, 704-406-4400, Fax: 704-406-3935, E-mail: rcanoy@gardner-webb.edu. *Application contact:* Kheresa Harmon, Director of Admissions, 704-406-3205, Fax: 704-406-3895, E-mail: kharmon@gardner-webb.edu.
Website: http://gardner-webb.edu/academic-programs-and-resources/colleges-and-schools/divinity/index

Garrett-Evangelical Theological Seminary, Graduate and Professional Programs, Evanston, IL 60201-3298. Offers Bible and culture (PhD); Christian education (MA); Christian education and congregational studies (PhD); contemporary theology and culture (PhD); divinity (M Div); ethics, church, and society (MA); liturgical studies (PhD); ministry (D Min); music ministry (MA); pastoral care and counseling (MA); pastoral theology, personality, and culture (PhD); spiritual formation and evangelism (MA); theological studies (MTS); M Div/MSW. M Div/MSW offered jointly with Loyola University Chicago. *Accreditation:* ACIPE; ATS (one or more programs are accredited). *Program availability:* Part-time. *Degree requirements:* For master's, thesis (for some programs); for doctorate, thesis/dissertation. *Entrance requirements:* For doctorate, GRE (PhD). Additional exam requirements/recommendations for international students: Required—TOEFL (minimum score 560 paper-based). Electronic applications accepted.

Global University, Graduate School of Theology, Springfield, MO 65804. Offers bible and theology (D Min); biblical language (M Div); biblical studies (MA); Christian ministry (M Div, D Min); ministerial studies (MA), including education, leadership, missions, New Testament, Old Testament. *Program availability:* Part-time, evening/weekend, online learning. *Degree requirements:* For master's, thesis (for some programs). *Entrance requirements:* For master's, minimum undergraduate GPA of 3.0. Electronic applications accepted. *Faculty research:* Higher education, cross-cultural missions.

Gratz College, Graduate Programs, Program in Jewish Education, Melrose Park, PA 19027. Offers education leadership (Ed D); Jewish instructional education (MA); MA/MA. *Program availability:* Part-time, evening/weekend, online learning. *Degree requirements:* For master's, one foreign language, internship. *Entrance requirements:* For master's, interview.

Hebrew College, Shoolman Graduate School of Jewish Education, Newton Centre, MA 02459. Offers early childhood Jewish education (Certificate); Jewish day school education (Certificate); Jewish education (MJ Ed); Jewish family education (Certificate); Jewish special education (Certificate); Jewish youth education, informal education and camping (Certificate). *Program availability:* Part-time, evening/weekend, online learning. *Degree requirements:* For master's, one foreign language. *Entrance requirements:* For master's, GRE, interview. Additional exam requirements/recommendations for international students: Required—TOEFL.

Hebrew Union College–Jewish Institute of Religion, School of Education, New York, NY 10012-1186. Offers MARE. *Program availability:* Part-time. *Degree requirements:* For master's, one foreign language, thesis. *Entrance requirements:* For master's, GRE, minimum 2 years of college-level Hebrew.

Houston Baptist University, College of Education and Behavioral Sciences, Programs in Education, Houston, TX 77074-3298. Offers bilingual education (M Ed); counselor education (M Ed); curriculum and instruction (M Ed); curriculum and instruction (EC-6 bilingual) (M Ed); curriculum and instruction in all-level art, Spanish, music, or physical education (M Ed); curriculum and instruction in EC-6 special education (EC-12) (M Ed); curriculum and instruction in instructional technology (M Ed); curriculum and instruction in mathematics, science, or social studies (4-8) (M Ed); curriculum and instruction with EC-6 generalist (M Ed); curriculum and instruction with English language arts and reading (4-8) (M Ed); educational administration (M Ed); educational diagnostician (M Ed); executive educational leadership (Ed D); higher education in business management (M Ed); higher education in Christian studies (M Ed); higher education in counseling (M Ed); higher education in educational technology (M Ed); reading (M Ed); special educational leadership (Ed D). *Program availability:* Part-time, evening/weekend, 100% online, blended/hybrid learning. *Students:* 83 full-time (65 women), 187 part-time (156 women); includes 189 minority (114 Black or African American, non-Hispanic/Latino; 2 American Indian or Alaska Native, non-Hispanic/Latino; 9 Asian, non-Hispanic/Latino; 58 Hispanic/Latino; 6 Two or more races, non-Hispanic/Latino), 7 international. Average age 36. 309 applicants, 31% accepted, 70 enrolled. In 2017, 92 master's awarded. *Degree requirements:* For master's, comprehensive exam; for doctorate, thesis/dissertation. *Entrance requirements:* For master's, minimum GPA of 2.75, two recommendations, resume, bachelor's degree conferred transcript; interview (for non-certified teachers); for doctorate, GRE, 5 letters of recommendation. Additional exam requirements/recommendations for international students: Required—TOEFL (minimum score 80 iBT), IELTS (minimum score 6.5). *Application deadline:* For fall admission, 8/1 for domestic students, 6/1 for international students; for spring admission, 1/1 for domestic students, 11/1 for international students; for summer admission, 5/1 for domestic students, 3/1 for international students. Applications are processed on a rolling basis. Application fee: $0 ($100 for international students). Electronic applications accepted. Application fee is waived when completed online. *Expenses:* $22,000 tuition; $4,500 fees (general, technology and parking). *Financial support:* In 2017–18, 59 students received support. Research assistantships, teaching assistantships, Federal Work-Study, and scholarships/grants available. Support available to part-time students. Financial award application deadline: 4/1; financial award applicants required to submit FAFSA. *Faculty research:* Autism and inclusion, integrating technology into instruction, school change and leadership trust. *Unit head:* Dr. Charlotte Fontenot, Director, Graduate Programs, 281-649-3078, Fax: 281-649-3361, E-mail: cfontenot@hbu.edu. *Application contact:* Kristy Wright, Administrative Assistant for Graduate Programs, 281-649-3094, Fax: 281-649-3361, E-mail: kwright@hbu.edu.
Website: http://www.hbu.edu/MED

Inter American University of Puerto Rico, Metropolitan Campus, Graduate Programs, Program in Christian Education, San Juan, PR 00919-1293. Offers PhD.

Interdenominational Theological Center, Graduate and Professional Programs, Atlanta, GA 30314-4112. Offers Christian education (MACE); ministry (D Min); pastoral counseling (Th D); theology (M Div); M Div/MACE. D Min and Th D programs offered in collaboration with the Atlanta Theological Association. *Accreditation:* ACIPE; ATS (one or more programs are accredited). *Program availability:* Part-time, evening/weekend, blended/hybrid learning. *Degree requirements:* For doctorate, thesis/dissertation. *Entrance requirements:* For doctorate, master's degree. Electronic applications accepted.

The Jewish Theological Seminary, William Davidson Graduate School of Jewish Education, New York, NY 10027-4649. Offers MA, Ed D. Offered in conjunction with The Rabbinical School; H. L. Miller Cantorial School and College of Jewish Music; Teacher's College, Columbia University; and Union Theological Seminary. *Program availability:*

Part-time, online learning. *Degree requirements:* For master's, one foreign language, thesis optional; for doctorate, one foreign language, comprehensive exam, thesis/dissertation. *Entrance requirements:* For master's, GRE or MAT, 3 letters of recommendation; for doctorate, GRE or MAT, writing sample, 3 letters of recommendation. Additional exam requirements/recommendations for international students: Recommended—TOEFL.

Lancaster Theological Seminary, Graduate and Professional Programs, Lancaster, PA 17603-2812. Offers biblical studies (MAR); Christian education (MAR); Christianity and the arts (MAR); church history (MAR); congregational life (MAR); lay leadership (Certificate); theological studies (M Div); theology (D Min); theology and ethics (MAR). *Accreditation:* ACIPE; ATS. *Degree requirements:* For doctorate, thesis/dissertation.

La Sierra University, School of Religion, Riverside, CA 92505. Offers pastoral ministry (M Div); religion (MA); religious education (MA); religious studies (MA). *Program availability:* Part-time. *Degree requirements:* For master's, one foreign language, thesis or alternative. *Entrance requirements:* For master's, GRE General Test, minimum GPA of 3.0.

Liberty University, School of Divinity, Lynchburg, VA 24515. Offers Biblical exposition (MA); Biblical languages (M Div); Biblical studies (M Div, MA, MAR, Th M, D Min); chaplaincy (M Div, D Min); Christian apologetics (M Div, MA, MAR, Th M); Christian leadership and church ministries (M Div); Christian ministries (M Div); Christian ministry (MA); Christian thought (M Div); church history (M Div, MAR, Th M); community chaplaincy (M Div, MAR); discipleship (D Min); discipleship and church ministry (M Div, MAR, MCM); evangelism and church planting (MAR, MCM, D Min); expository preaching (D Min); global ministry (MA); global studies (M Div, MAR, MCM, MGS, Th M); healthcare chaplaincy (M Div); homiletics (M Div, MAR, Th M); leadership (M Div, MAR); marketplace chaplaincy (M Div, MCM); ministry leadership (Ed D); pastoral counseling (M Div, MA, MAR, D Min), including addictions and recovery (MA), crisis response and trauma (MA), discipleship and church ministries (MA), leadership (MA), life coaching (MA), marketplace chaplaincy (MA), marriage and family (MA), military resilience (MA), pastoral counseling (MA); pastoral leadership (D Min); pastoral ministries (M Div, M Serv Soc, MCM); religious education (MRE); sports chaplaincy (MA); theology (M Div, MAR, MTS, Th M); theology and apologetics (D Min, PhD); worship (M Div, MAR, MCM, D Min); youth and family ministries (M Div). *Program availability:* Part-time, online learning. *Students:* 2,140 full-time (615 women), 3,020 part-time (906 women); includes 1,312 minority (1,016 Black or African American, non-Hispanic/Latino; 9 American Indian or Alaska Native, non-Hispanic/Latino; 100 Asian, non-Hispanic/Latino; 90 Hispanic/Latino; 7 Native Hawaiian or other Pacific Islander, non-Hispanic/Latino; 90 Two or more races, non-Hispanic/Latino), 158 international. Average age 42. 4,673 applicants, 33% accepted, 977 enrolled. In 2017, 904 master's, 54 doctorates awarded. *Degree requirements:* For master's, 2 foreign languages, thesis (for some programs); for doctorate, 2 foreign languages, thesis/dissertation. *Entrance requirements:* For master's, minimum undergraduate GPA of 2.0; for doctorate, GRE General Test or MAT, minimum graduate GPA of 3.0. Additional exam requirements/recommendations for international students: Required—TOEFL (minimum score 600 paper-based; 100 iBT). *Application deadline:* For fall admission, 6/1 for domestic students; for spring admission, 11/1 for domestic students. Applications are processed on a rolling basis. Application fee: $50. Electronic applications accepted. *Expenses:* Contact institution. *Financial support:* Teaching assistantships with tuition reimbursements, career-related internships or fieldwork, and Federal Work-Study available. Financial award applicants required to submit FAFSA. *Unit head:* Dr. Ed Hindson, Dean, 434-592-4140, Fax: 434-522-0415, E-mail: ehindson@liberty.edu. *Application contact:* Jay Bridge, Director of Graduate Admissions, 800-424-9595, Fax: 800-628-7977, E-mail: gradadmissions@liberty.edu.
Website: https://www.liberty.edu/divinity/

Lincoln Christian Seminary, Graduate and Professional Programs, Lincoln, IL 62656-2167. Offers Bible and theology (MA); Christian ministries (MA); counseling (MA); divinity (M Div); leadership ministry (D Min); religious education (MRE). *Accreditation:* ACIPE; ATS. *Program availability:* Part-time. *Degree requirements:* For master's, 2 foreign languages, thesis; for doctorate, thesis/dissertation. *Entrance requirements:* For master's, minimum GPA of 2.5; for doctorate, M Div or equivalent. Additional exam requirements/recommendations for international students: Required—TOEFL (minimum score 550 paper-based). Electronic applications accepted.

Loyola University Chicago, Institute of Pastoral Studies, Chicago, IL 60611. Offers Christian spirituality (MA), including spiritual direction; church management (Certificate); counseling for ministry (MA); divinity (M Div); health care ministry leadership (Certificate); health care mission leadership (MA); pastoral counseling (MA, Certificate); pastoral studies (MA); religious education (Certificate); social justice (MA, Certificate); spiritual direction (Certificate); M Div/MA; M Div/MSW; MSW/MA. MSW/MA offered with School of Social Work. *Accreditation:* ACIPE. *Program availability:* Part-time, evening/weekend, 100% online, blended/hybrid learning. *Faculty:* 11 full-time (5 women), 20 part-time/adjunct (9 women). *Students:* 80 full-time (51 women), 150 part-time (107 women); includes 58 minority (24 Black or African American, non-Hispanic/Latino; 7 Asian, non-Hispanic/Latino; 27 Hispanic/Latino), 29 international. Average age 45. 128 applicants, 79% accepted, 72 enrolled. In 2017, 53 master's, 5 other advanced degrees awarded. *Degree requirements:* For master's, thesis optional, project. *Entrance requirements:* Additional exam requirements/recommendations for international students: Required—TOEFL (minimum score 550 paper-based; 79 iBT), IELTS (minimum score 6.5). *Application deadline:* Applications are processed on a rolling basis. Application fee: $50. Electronic applications accepted. Application fee is waived when completed online. *Expenses:* Contact institution. *Financial support:* In 2017–18, 111 students received support. Career-related internships or fieldwork, Federal Work-Study, scholarships/grants, and unspecified assistantships available. Support available to part-time students. Financial award application deadline: 3/15. *Faculty research:* Catholic theology, skills of religious ministry, family ministries, spirituality and divorced men. *Unit head:* Dr. Brian J. Schmisek, Dean, 312-915-7400, Fax: 312-915-7410, E-mail: bschmisek@luc.edu. *Application contact:* Dr. M. Therese Lysaught, Associate Dean, 312-915-7485, Fax: 312-915-7410, E-mail: mlysaught@luc.edu.
Website: http://www.luc.edu/ips/

Maple Springs Baptist Bible College and Seminary, Graduate and Professional Programs, Capitol Heights, MD 20743. Offers biblical studies (MA, Certificate); Christian counseling (MA); church administration (MA); divinity (M Div); ministry (D Min); religious education (MRE).

Midwestern Baptist Theological Seminary, Graduate and Professional Programs, Kansas City, MO 64118-4697. Offers Christian education (MACE); Christian foundations (Graduate Certificate); church music (MCM); counseling (MA); ministry (D Ed Min, D Min); Old or New Testament studies (PhD); theology (M Div). *Accreditation:* ATS. *Program availability:* Part-time, online learning. *Degree requirements:* For doctorate, thesis/dissertation. *Entrance requirements:* For doctorate, MAT. Electronic applications accepted. *Faculty research:* Ministerial studies, Biblical and theological studies, missions, counseling.

Milligan College, Emmanuel Christian Seminary at Milligan College, Milligan College, TN 37682. Offers Christian care and counseling (M Div); Christian education (M Div);

Christian ministries (MACM, Graduate Certificate); Christian ministry (M Div); Christian theology (M Div, MAR); church history (MAR); church history/historical theology (M Div); general studies (M Div); ministry (D Min); New Testament (M Div, MAR); Old Testament (M Div, MAR); urban ministry (M Div); world missions (M Div). *Accreditation:* ACIPE; ATS. *Program availability:* Part-time, blended/hybrid learning. *Faculty:* 10 full-time (1 woman), 8 part-time/adjunct (0 women). *Students:* 52 full-time (23 women), 57 part-time (18 women); includes 11 minority (7 Black or African American, non-Hispanic/Latino; 1 Asian, non-Hispanic/Latino; 3 Hispanic/Latino), 7 international. Average age 35. 62 applicants, 89% accepted, 39 enrolled. In 2017, 19 master's, 3 doctorates awarded. *Degree requirements:* For master's, 2 foreign languages, thesis or alternative, portfolio; for doctorate, thesis/dissertation. *Entrance requirements:* For master's, undergraduate degree and supporting transcripts, essay/personal statement, professional recommendations, interview; for doctorate, M Div or equivalent, essay/personal statement, professional recommendations. Additional exam requirements/recommendations for international students: Required—TOEFL (minimum score 550 paper-based, 79 iBT) or IELTS (6.5). *Application deadline:* For fall admission, 8/1 for domestic students, 6/1 for international students; for spring admission, 12/15 for domestic students, 8/1 for international students. Applications are processed on a rolling basis. Application fee: $30 ($0 for international students). Electronic applications accepted. *Expenses:* Contact institution. *Financial support:* In 2017–18, 124 students received support. Scholarships/grants and unspecified assistantships available. Financial award application deadline: 12/1; financial award applicants required to submit FAFSA. *Faculty research:* Theology of Old Testament prophets; performance criticism of New Testament texts; practical theology and spiritual formation for Christian leaders; church history and missions; constructive theology, art and imagination. *Unit head:* Dr. Rollin Ramsaran, Academic Dean, Emmanuel Christian Seminary, 423-461-1524, Fax: 423-926-6198, E-mail: raramsaran@milligan.edu. *Application contact:* Lauren Gullett, Director of Admissions and Recruitment for Emmanuel Christian Seminary, 423-461-1535, Fax: 423-926-6198, E-mail: lwgullett@milligan.edu.
Website: http://ecs.milligan.edu/

Moody Theological Seminary–Michigan, Graduate Programs, Plymouth, MI 48170. Offers Bible (Graduate Certificate); Christian education (MA); counseling psychology (MA); divinity (M Div); theological studies (MA). *Accreditation:* ATS. *Program availability:* Part-time, evening/weekend. *Degree requirements:* For master's, one foreign language, thesis. *Faculty research:* Judaism, cults, world religions.

Newman Theological College, Religious Education Programs, Edmonton, AB T6V 1H3, Canada. Offers MRE, Graduate Certificate. *Program availability:* Part-time, blended/hybrid learning. *Faculty:* 5 full-time (2 women), 9 part-time/adjunct (4 women). *Students:* 103 part-time (81 women). Average age 40. 35 applicants, 100% accepted, 34 enrolled. In 2017, 19 master's awarded. *Degree requirements:* For master's, thesis or alternative. *Entrance requirements:* For master's, 2 years of teaching experience, graduate diploma in religious education; for Graduate Certificate, bachelor's degree in education, teaching certificate. Additional exam requirements/recommendations for international students: Required—TOEFL (minimum score 560 paper-based; 86 iBT), IELTS (minimum score 6.5). *Application deadline:* For fall admission, 8/21 priority date for domestic students; for winter admission, 11/22 priority date for domestic students; for spring admission, 4/18 priority date for domestic students. Applications are processed on a rolling basis. Application fee: $45 ($250 for international students). *Expenses:* $639 per course; $200 per field education course; $35 administrative fee per semester; $10 library fee per course; $40 full-time/$25 part-time student association fee. *Financial support:* In 2017–18, 9 students received support. Tuition bursaries available. Support available to part-time students. Financial award application deadline: 5/31. *Unit head:* Sandra Talarico, Director, 780-392-2450 Ext. 2214, Fax: 780-462-4013, E-mail: sandra.talarico@newman.edu. *Application contact:* Maria Saulnier, Registrar, 780-392-2451, Fax: 780-462-4013, E-mail: registrar@newman.edu.
Website: http://www.newman.edu/

New Orleans Baptist Theological Seminary, Graduate and Professional Programs, Division of Christian Education Ministries, New Orleans, LA 70126-4858. Offers Christian education (M Div, MACE, D Min, DEM, PhD). *Program availability:* Evening/weekend, online learning. *Degree requirements:* For master's, 2 foreign languages; for doctorate, 3 foreign languages, comprehensive exam, thesis/dissertation. *Entrance requirements:* For doctorate, GRE General Test.

Oral Roberts University, School of Theology and Missions, Tulsa, OK 74171. Offers biblical literature (MA), including advanced languages, Judaic-Christian studies; church ministries and leadership (D Min); clinical pastoral education (M Div); missions (MA); pastoral care and chaplaincy (M Div, D Min); practical theology (MA), including teaching ministries, urban ministries; professional counseling (MA), including addiction studies, marriage and family therapy; theological/historical studies (MA). *Accreditation:* ATS. *Program availability:* Part-time, online learning. *Faculty:* 17 full-time (2 women). *Students:* 371 full-time (156 women), 110 part-time (65 women); includes 177 minority (127 Black or African American, non-Hispanic/Latino; 5 American Indian or Alaska Native, non-Hispanic/Latino; 20 Asian, non-Hispanic/Latino; 25 Hispanic/Latino), 82 international. Average age 36. 159 applicants, 95% accepted, 124 enrolled. In 2017, 52 master's, 10 doctorates awarded. *Degree requirements:* For master's, thesis (for some programs), practicum/internship; for doctorate, thesis/dissertation, applied research project. *Entrance requirements:* For master's, GRE General Test or MAT (waived for those with undergraduate degree from regionally accredited institution and 3.0 or higher GPA), minimum GPA of 2.5 (professional) or 3.0 (academic); for doctorate, M Div, minimum GPA of 3.0, 3 years of full-time ministry experience. Additional exam requirements/recommendations for international students: Recommended—TOEFL (minimum score 550 paper-based; 79 iBT), IELTS (minimum score 7). *Application deadline:* Applications are processed on a rolling basis. Application fee: $35. Electronic applications accepted. Application fee is waived when completed online. *Financial support:* Fellowships and scholarships/grants available. Financial award application deadline: 6/1. *Unit head:* Dr. Bill Buker, Chair, 918-495-6493, E-mail: bbuker@oru.edu. *Application contact:* Michael Thomas, Enrollment Counselor, 918-495-6618, E-mail: mthomas@oru.edu.
Website: http://www.gradtheology.oru.edu/

Palm Beach Atlantic University, School of Ministry, West Palm Beach, FL 33416-4708. Offers Christian studies (MA); ministry (M Div). *Program availability:* Part-time. *Degree requirements:* For master's, one foreign language, comprehensive exam (for some programs), thesis optional, 8 credits of biblical language (for M Div). *Entrance requirements:* For master's, minimum GPA of 2.75; writing samples. Additional exam requirements/recommendations for international students: Required—TOEFL (minimum score 550 paper-based; 79 iBT). Electronic applications accepted. *Faculty research:* Ethics, apologetics, spiritual formation, theology.

Pfeiffer University, Program in Practical Theology, Misenheimer, NC 28109-0960. Offers MA. *Program availability:* Part-time, evening/weekend. *Entrance requirements:* For master's, minimum GPA of 2.75.

Phillips Theological Seminary, Programs in Theology, Tulsa, OK 74116. Offers administration of church agencies (M Div); campus ministry (M Div); church-related social work (M Div); college and seminary teaching (M Div); global mission work (M Div); institutional chaplaincy (M Div); ministerial vocations in Christian education (M Div);

ministry (D Min), including parish ministry, pastoral counseling, practices of ministry; ministry and culture (MAMC), including Christian education, congregational leadership, history and practice of Christian spirituality, theology, ethics, and culture; ministry of music (M Div); pastoral care and counseling (M Div); pastoral ministry (M Div); theological studies (MTS). *Accreditation:* ATS. *Program availability:* Part-time, online learning. *Degree requirements:* For master's, thesis (for some programs); for doctorate, thesis/dissertation. *Entrance requirements:* For master's, minimum GPA of 2.5; for doctorate, M Div, minimum GPA of 3.0. *Faculty research:* Biblical studies, historical studies, theology and culture, practical theology, theology and film.

Pontifical Catholic University of Puerto Rico, College of Education, Program in Religious Education, Ponce, PR 00717-0777. Offers MRE.

Providence University College & Theological Seminary, Theological Seminary, Otterburne, MB R0A 1G0, Canada. Offers children's ministry (Certificate); Christian studies (MA, Certificate); counseling (MA); cross-cultural discipleship (Certificate); divinity (M Div); educational studies (MA), including counseling psychology, educational ministries, student development, teaching English to speakers of other languages, training teachers of English to speakers of other languages; global studies (MA); lay counseling (Diploma); ministry (D Min); teaching English to speakers of other languages (Certificate); theological studies (MA); training teacher of English to speakers of other languages (Certificate); youth ministry (Certificate). *Accreditation:* ATS. *Program availability:* Part-time. *Degree requirements:* For master's, variable foreign language requirement, thesis (for some programs); for doctorate, thesis/dissertation. *Entrance requirements:* Additional exam requirements/recommendations for international students: Recommended—TOEFL (minimum score 550 paper-based). *Faculty research:* Studies in Isaiah, theology of sin.

Reformed Theological Seminary–Jackson Campus, Graduate and Professional Programs, Jackson, MS 39209-3004. Offers Bible, theology, and missions (Certificate); Biblical exegesis (M Div); biblical studies (MA); Christian education (MA); counseling (M Div); marriage and family therapy (MA); ministry (D Min); missions (M Div, MA, D Min); theological studies (MA). *Accreditation:* AAMFT/COAMFTE (one or more programs are accredited); ATS (one or more programs are accredited). *Degree requirements:* For master's, thesis (for some programs), fieldwork; for doctorate, 2 foreign languages, thesis/dissertation. *Entrance requirements:* For master's, minimum GPA of 2.6; for doctorate, minimum GPA of 3.0. Additional exam requirements/recommendations for international students: Required—TOEFL.

Regent University, Graduate School, School of Divinity, Virginia Beach, VA 23464-9800. Offers Christian spirituality and formation (MA); divinity (M Div), including Biblical studies (M Div, MTS, Th M, PhD), chaplain ministry, Christian theology (M Div, MTS, Th M, PhD), church and ministry (M Div, MA), history of Christianity (M Div, MTS, Th M, PhD), inter-cultural studies (M Div, MA), interdisciplinary studies (M Div, MA, MTS), marketplace ministry (M Div, MA), missional discipleship, practical healing ministry (M Div, MA), worship and media (M Div, MA); leadership and renewal (D Min), including Christian leadership and renewal, clinical pastoral education, community transformation, military ministry, ministry leadership coaching; practical theology (MA), including church and ministry (M Div, MA), cosmogony, inter-cultural studies (M Div, MA), interdisciplinary studies (M Div, MA, MTS), marketplace ministry (M Div, MA), practical healing ministry (M Div, MA), worship and media (M Div, MA); renewal theology (PhD), including Biblical studies (M Div, MTS, Th M, PhD), Christian theology (M Div, MTS, Th M, PhD), history of Christianity (M Div, MTS, Th M, PhD), practical theology; theological studies (MTS), including Biblical studies (M Div, MTS, Th M, PhD), Christian theology (M Div, MTS, Th M, PhD), history of Christianity (M Div, MTS, Th M, PhD), interdisciplinary studies (M Div, MA, MTS); theology (Th M), including Biblical studies (M Div, MTS, Th M, PhD), Christian theology (M Div, MTS, Th M, PhD), history of Christianity (M Div, MTS, Th M, PhD). *Accreditation:* ACIPE; ATS. *Program availability:* Part-time, evening/weekend, 100% online, blended/hybrid learning. *Faculty:* 17 full-time (3 women), 66 part-time/adjunct (9 women). *Students:* 146 full-time (54 women), 917 part-time (404 women); includes 563 minority (470 Black or African American, non-Hispanic/Latino; 1 American Indian or Alaska Native, non-Hispanic/Latino; 17 Asian, non-Hispanic/Latino; 56 Hispanic/Latino; 1 Native Hawaiian or other Pacific Islander, non-Hispanic/Latino; 18 Two or more races, non-Hispanic/Latino), 27 international. Average age 44. 1,321 applicants, 39% accepted, 295 enrolled. In 2017, 146 master's, 25 doctorates awarded. *Degree requirements:* For master's, comprehensive exam, thesis or alternative, internship; for doctorate, thesis/dissertation or alternative. *Entrance requirements:* For master's, minimum undergraduate GPA of 2.75, writing sample, personal goal statement, college transcripts; for doctorate, GRE, minimum graduate GPA of 3.5 (PhD), 3.0 (D Min); clergy recommendations; writing sample; transcripts; resume; interview. Additional exam requirements/recommendations for international students: Required—TOEFL (minimum score 577 paper-based). *Application deadline:* For fall admission, 5/1 priority date for domestic students. Applications are processed on a rolling basis. Application fee: $50. Electronic applications accepted. *Expenses:* $495 per credit (master's); $595 per credit (D Min); $650 per credit (PhD); $300 per semester technology fee. *Financial support:* In 2017–18, 721 students received support. Career-related internships or fieldwork, scholarships/grants, and unspecified assistantships available. Support available to part-time students. *Faculty research:* Greek and Hebrew, theology, spiritual formation, global missions and world Christianity, women in ministry leadership. *Unit head:* Dr. Cornelius Bekker, Dean, 757-352-4401, Fax: 757-352-4597, E-mail: clbekker@regent.edu. *Application contact:* Heidi Cece, Assistant Vice President of Enrollment Management, 800-373-5504, Fax: 757-352-4381, E-mail: admissions@regent.edu.
Website: https://www.regent.edu/school-of-divinity/

Regent University, Graduate School, School of Education, Virginia Beach, VA 23464-9800. Offers education (M Ed, Ed D, PhD), including adult education (Ed D, PhD, Ed S), advanced educational leadership (Ed D, PhD, Ed S), character education (Ed D, PhD, Ed S), Christian education leadership (Ed D, PhD, Ed S), Christian school administration (M Ed), curriculum and instruction (Ed D, PhD, Ed S), curriculum and instruction - adult education (M Ed), curriculum and instruction - Christian school (M Ed), curriculum and instruction - gifted and talented (M Ed), curriculum and instruction - STEM education (M Ed), curriculum and instruction - teacher leader (M Ed), discipleship for ministry (M Ed), educational leadership (M Ed), educational psychology (Ed D, PhD, Ed S), educational technology and online learning (Ed D, PhD, Ed S), elementary education (M Ed), exceptional education executive leadership (Ed D, PhD, Ed S), higher education (Ed D, PhD, Ed S), higher education leadership and management (Ed D, PhD, Ed S), instructional design and technology (M Ed), K-12 school leadership (Ed D, PhD, Ed S), K-12 special education (M Ed), leadership in mathematics education (M Ed), reading specialist (M Ed), special education (Ed D, PhD, Ed S), student affairs (M Ed), TESOL - adult education (M Ed), TESOL - K-12 (M Ed); educational specialist (Ed S), including adult education (Ed D, PhD, Ed S), advanced educational leadership (Ed D, PhD, Ed S), character education (Ed D, PhD, Ed S), Christian education leadership (Ed D, PhD, Ed S), curriculum and instruction (Ed D, PhD, Ed S), educational psychology (Ed D, PhD, Ed S), educational technology and online learning (Ed D, PhD, Ed S), exceptional education executive leadership (Ed D, PhD, Ed S), higher education (Ed D, PhD, Ed S), higher education leadership and management (Ed D, PhD, Ed S), K-12 school leadership (Ed D, PhD, Ed S), special education (Ed D, PhD, Ed S). *Accreditation:*

TEAC. *Program availability:* Part-time, evening/weekend, 100% online, blended/hybrid learning. *Faculty:* 22 full-time (10 women), 44 part-time/adjunct (32 women). *Students:* 80 full-time (59 women), 945 part-time (750 women); includes 432 minority (352 Black or African American, non-Hispanic/Latino; 4 American Indian or Alaska Native, non-Hispanic/Latino; 14 Asian, non-Hispanic/Latino; 43 Hispanic/Latino; 19 Two or more races, non-Hispanic/Latino), 12 international. Average age 40. 1,125 applicants, 49% accepted, 436 enrolled. In 2017, 316 master's, 24 doctorates awarded. *Degree requirements:* For master's, thesis or alternative; for doctorate, comprehensive exam, thesis/dissertation. *Entrance requirements:* For master's, Virginia Communication and Literacy Assessment (VCLA), PRAXIS, college transcripts, writing sample, interview; for doctorate, GRE, writing sample, resume, transcripts, interview. Additional exam requirements/recommendations for international students: Required—TOEFL (minimum score 577 paper-based). *Application deadline:* For fall admission, 4/1 priority date for domestic students; for spring admission, 10/15 priority date for domestic students. Applications are processed on a rolling basis. Application fee: $50. Electronic applications accepted. *Expenses:* Contact institution. *Financial support:* In 2017–18, 669 students received support, including 1 fellowship (averaging $10,000 per year); career-related internships or fieldwork, scholarships/grants, and unspecified assistantships also available. Support available to part-time students. *Faculty research:* Christian school administration, curriculum and instruction, educational technology and online learning, higher education, special education. *Unit head:* Dr. Donald Finn, Dean, 757-352-4278, Fax: 757-352-4318, E-mail: dfinn@regent.edu. *Application contact:* Heidi Cece, Assistant Vice President of Enrollment Management, 800-373-5504, Fax: 757-352-4381, E-mail: admissions@regent.edu.
Website: https://www.regent.edu/school-of-education/

Rochester College, Center for Missional Leadership, Rochester Hills, MI 48307-2764. Offers MRE.

St. Augustine's Seminary of Toronto, Graduate and Professional Programs, Scarborough, ON M1M 1M3, Canada. Offers divinity (M Div); lay ministry (Diploma); religious education (MRE); theological studies (MTS, Diploma). *Accreditation:* ATS. *Program availability:* Part-time, evening/weekend. *Entrance requirements:* Additional exam requirements/recommendations for international students: Required—TOEFL (minimum score 580 paper-based), TWE (minimum score 5).

Saint Mary's University of Minnesota, Schools of Graduate and Professional Programs, Graduate School of Education, Institute for LaSallian Studies, Winona, MN 55987-1399. Offers LaSallian leadership (MA); LaSallian studies (MA). *Unit head:* Dr. Roxanne Eubank, Director, 612-728-5217, E-mail: reubank@smumn.edu. *Application contact:* James Callinan, Director of Admissions for Graduate and Professional Programs, 612-728-5158, Fax: 612-728-5121, E-mail: jcallina@smumn.edu.
Website: http://www.smumn.edu/graduate-home/areas-of-study/graduate-school-of-education/ma-in-lasallian-studies

Saints Cyril and Methodius Seminary, Graduate and Professional Programs, Orchard Lake, MI 48324. Offers pastoral ministry (MAPM); religious education (MARE); theology (M Div, MA). *Program availability:* Part-time.

Selma University, Graduate Programs, Selma, AL 36701-5299. Offers Bible and Christian education (MA); Bible and pastoral ministry (MA).

Shasta Bible College, Program in Biblical Counseling, Redding, CA 96002. Offers biblical counseling and Christian family life education (MA). *Program availability:* Part-time. *Degree requirements:* For master's, comprehensive exam (for some programs), thesis or alternative. *Entrance requirements:* For master's, minimum GPA of 2.5. Additional exam requirements/recommendations for international students: Required—TOEFL (minimum score 550 paper-based).

Southeastern Baptist Theological Seminary, Graduate and Professional Programs, Wake Forest, NC 27587. Offers advanced biblical studies (M Div); Christian education (M Div, MACE); Christian ethics (PhD); Christian ministry (M Div); Christian planting (M Div); church music (MACM); counseling (MACO); evangelism (PhD); language (M Div); ministry (D Min); New Testament (PhD); Old Testament (PhD); philosophy (PhD); theology (Th M, PhD); women's studies (M Div). *Accreditation:* ACIPE; ATS (one or more programs are accredited). *Degree requirements:* For master's, thesis (for some programs), oral exam; for doctorate, thesis/dissertation, fieldwork. *Entrance requirements:* For master's, Cooperative English Test, minimum GPA of 2.0, M Div or equivalent (Th M); for doctorate, GRE General Test or MAT, Cooperative English Test, M Div or equivalent, 3 years of professional experience.

Southern Adventist University, School of Religion, Collegedale, TN 37315-0370. Offers Biblical and theological studies (MA); church leadership and management (M Min); church ministry and homiletics (M Min); evangelism and world mission (M Min); religious studies (MA). *Program availability:* Part-time. *Degree requirements:* For master's, comprehensive exam, thesis (for some programs). *Entrance requirements:* For master's, GRE. Additional exam requirements/recommendations for international students: Required—TOEFL (minimum score 600 paper-based). *Application deadline:* For spring admission, 5/1 priority date for domestic students, 4/30 for international students. Applications are processed on a rolling basis. Application fee: $40. *Expenses:* Tuition: Full-time $11,430; part-time $635 per credit hour. Tuition and fees vary according to degree level and program. *Financial support:* Tuition waivers (full) available. Support available to part-time students. Financial award application deadline: 4/1; financial award applicants required to submit FAFSA. *Faculty research:* Biblical archaeology. *Unit head:* Dr. Greg A. King, Dean, 423-236-2975, Fax: 423-236-1976, E-mail: gking@southern.edu. *Application contact:* Susan L. Brown, Administrative Assistant, 423-236-2033, Fax: 423-236-1977, E-mail: sbrown@southern.edu.
Website: https://www.southern.edu/academics/academic-sites/religion/

Southern Evangelical Seminary, Graduate Programs, Matthews, NC 28105. Offers apologetics (MA, D Min, Certificate); Christian education (MA); church ministry (MA, Certificate); divinity (Certificate), including apologetics (M Div, Certificate); Islamic studies (MA, Certificate); Jewish studies (MA); philosophy (MA); philosophy of religion (PhD); religion (MA); theology (M Div), including apologetics (M Div, Certificate); Biblical studies; youth ministry (MA). *Program availability:* Part-time, evening/weekend, online learning. *Degree requirements:* For master's, thesis (for some programs); for doctorate, 2 foreign languages, comprehensive exam (for some programs), thesis/dissertation. *Entrance requirements:* Additional exam requirements/recommendations for international students: Required—TOEFL (minimum score 600 paper-based).

Southwestern Assemblies of God University, Thomas F. Harrison School of Graduate Studies, Program in Education, Waxahachie, TX 75165-5735. Offers Christian school administration (MS); curriculum development (MS); early education administration (M Ed); middle and secondary education (M Ed). *Degree requirements:* For master's, comprehensive written and oral exams. *Entrance requirements:* For master's, GRE General Test, minimum GPA of 2.5. Electronic applications accepted.

Southwestern Baptist Theological Seminary, Jack D. Terry School of Church and Family Ministries, Fort Worth, TX 76122-0000. Offers MA, MACE, MACSE, DEM, PhD. *Program availability:* Part-time, evening/weekend. Terminal master's awarded for partial completion of doctoral program. *Degree requirements:* For master's, thesis; for doctorate, thesis/dissertation, statistics comprehensive exam. *Entrance requirements:*

For doctorate, GRE or MAT, MACE or equivalent, minimum GPA of 3.0. Additional exam requirements/recommendations for international students: Required—TOEFL, TWE. Electronic applications accepted.

Trinity International University, Trinity Evangelical Divinity School, Deerfield, IL 60015-1284. Offers academic ministry (M Div); Biblical and Near Eastern archaeology and languages (MA); chaplaincy and ministry care (MA); Christian studies (Certificate); church and parachurch ministry (M Div); church history (MA, Th M); counseling (Th M); educational ministries (MA); educational ministry (Th M); educational studies (PhD); intercultural studies (MA, PhD); leadership and management (D Min); mental health counseling (MA); military chaplaincy (D Min); ministry (MA); missions (Th M); missions and evangelism (D Min); New Testament (MA, Th M); Old Testament (MA); Old Testament and Semitic languages (MA); pastoral ministry and care (D Min); pastoral theology (Th M); preaching and teaching (D Min); spiritual formation and education (D Min); systematic theology (MA, Th M); theological studies (MA, PhD); urban ministry (MA). *Program availability:* Part-time, online learning. *Degree requirements:* For master's, comprehensive exam, thesis, fieldwork; for doctorate, comprehensive exam (for some programs), thesis/dissertation; for Certificate, comprehensive exam, integrative papers. *Entrance requirements:* For master's, GRE, MAT, minimum cumulative undergraduate GPA of 3.0; for doctorate, GRE, minimum cumulative graduate GPA of 3.2; for Certificate, GRE, MAT, minimum undergraduate GPA of 2.5. Additional exam requirements/recommendations for international students: Required—TOEFL (minimum score 580 paper-based), TWE (minimum score 4). Electronic applications accepted.

Trinity Lutheran Seminary, Graduate and Professional Programs, Columbus, OH 43209-2334. Offers African American studies (MTS); Biblical studies (MTS, STM); Christian education (MA); Christian spirituality (STM); church in the world (MTS); church music (MA); divinity (M Div); general theological studies (MTS); mission and evangelism (STM); pastoral leadership and practice (STM); youth and family ministry (MA); MSN/MTS; MTS/JD. *Accreditation:* ACIPE; ATS. *Program availability:* Part-time. *Degree requirements:* For master's, variable foreign language requirement, comprehensive exam (for some programs), thesis (for some programs), field experience (for some programs). *Entrance requirements:* For master's, BA or equivalent (for MA, M Div, MTS); M Div, MTS, or equivalent (for STM); audition (for MACM). Additional exam requirements/recommendations for international students: Required—TOEFL. Electronic applications accepted. *Expenses:* Contact institution.

Unification Theological Seminary, Graduate Programs, Barrytown, NY 12507. Offers family and educational ministry (D Min); interfaith peacebuilding (MRE); peace and justice ministry (D Min); religious education (MRE), including interfaith peacebuilding; religious studies (MA); theology (M Div). *Program availability:* Part-time, evening/weekend, online learning. *Degree requirements:* For master's, variable foreign language requirement, thesis (for some programs); for doctorate, thesis/dissertation. *Entrance requirements:* For master's, bachelor's degree; for doctorate, M Div or equivalency. Additional exam requirements/recommendations for international students: Required—TOEFL (minimum score 550 paper-based). *Application deadline:* For fall admission, 3/15 priority date for domestic and international students; for spring admission, 9/15 priority date for domestic and international students. Applications are processed on a rolling basis. Application fee: $30. Electronic applications accepted. *Expenses:* Tuition: Full-time $12,000; part-time $500 per credit. *Required fees:* $260; $210 per year. $105 per semester. Tuition and fees vary according to campus/location. *Financial support:* Scholarships/grants available. Financial award application deadline: 6/15; financial award applicants required to submit FAFSA. *Faculty research:* Church leadership, church history, world religions, ecumenism, interfaith peace building, service-learning. *Unit head:* Michael Mickler, Vice-President for Administration, 845-752-3235, Fax: 845-752-3014, E-mail: mm@uts.edu. *Application contact:* Henry Christopher, Director of Admissions and Financial Aid, 212-563-6647 Ext. 105, Fax: 845-752-3014, E-mail: admissions@uts.edu.
Website: http://www.uts.edu/academics/academic-programs

Union Presbyterian Seminary, Graduate and Professional Programs, Richmond, VA 23227-4597. Offers M Div, MACE, Th M, PhD, M Div/MACE. *Program availability:* Part-time, evening/weekend, online learning. *Degree requirements:* For master's, oral and written exams. *Entrance requirements:* For master's, three references, transcripts, background check; for doctorate, GRE General Test, three references, transcripts, background check, statement of goals, essay. Additional exam requirements/recommendations for international students: Required—TOEFL (minimum score 550 paper-based), TWE (minimum score 4). Electronic applications accepted.

University of Detroit Mercy, College of Liberal Arts and Education, Detroit, MI 48221. Offers addiction counseling (MA); addiction studies (Certificate); clinical mental health counseling (MA); clinical psychology (MA, PhD); computer and information systems (MS); criminal justice (MA); curriculum and instruction (MA); economics (MA); educational administration (MA); financial economics (MA); industrial/organizational psychology (MA); information assurance (MS); intelligence analysis (MA); liberal studies (MALS); religious studies (MA); school counseling (MA, Certificate); school psychology (Spec); security administration (MS); special education: emotionally impaired/behaviorally disordered (MA); special education: learning disabilities (MA). *Program availability:* Part-time, evening/weekend. *Degree requirements:* For doctorate, departmental qualifying exam. *Faculty research:* Psychology of aging, history of technology, Renaissance humanism, U.S. and Japanese economic relations.

University of St. Michael's College, Faculty of Theology, Toronto, ON M5S 1J4, Canada. Offers Catholic leadership (MA); eastern Christian studies (Diploma); religious education (Diploma); theological studies (Diploma); theology (M Div, MA, MRE, MTS, D Min, PhD, Th D); theology and Jewish studies (MA). Th D offered jointly with University of Toronto. *Accreditation:* ATS (one or more programs are accredited). *Program availability:* Part-time. *Degree requirements:* For master's, thesis (for some programs), 1 foreign language (MA), 2 foreign languages (Th M); for doctorate, 3 foreign languages, comprehensive exam, thesis/dissertation; for other advanced degree, thesis optional. *Entrance requirements:* For master's, M Div or BA, course work in an ancient or modern language, minimum GPA of 3.3; for doctorate, MA in theology, Th M, or M Div with thesis, minimum GPA of 3.7; for other advanced degree, minimum GPA of 2.7. Additional exam requirements/recommendations for international students: Required—TOEFL (minimum score 600 paper-based). Electronic applications accepted. *Expenses:* Contact institution. *Faculty research:* Patristics, eastern Christianity, ecology and theology, ecumenism, Jewish Christian studies.

University of St. Thomas, The Saint Paul Seminary School of Divinity, St. Paul, MN 55105. Offers pastoral ministry (MAPM); religious education (MARE); theology (MA). *Accreditation:* ACIPE; ATS. *Program availability:* Part-time, evening/weekend. *Degree requirements:* For master's, one foreign language, comprehensive exam (for some programs), thesis (for some programs). *Entrance requirements:* For master's, GRE, 3 letters of recommendation, interview. Additional exam requirements/recommendations for international students: Required—TOEFL (minimum score 550 paper-based). *Application deadline:* For fall admission, 6/1 priority date for domestic students. Applications are processed on a rolling basis. Application fee: $40. Electronic applications accepted. *Expenses:* Contact institution. *Financial support:* Fellowships, research assistantships, institutionally sponsored loans, and scholarships/grants available. Support available to part-time students. Financial award application deadline: 4/1; financial award applicants required to submit FAFSA. *Faculty research:* Theological education. *Unit head:* Rev. Msgr. Aloysius R. Callaghan, Rector/Vice President, 651-962-5052, Fax: 651-962-5790, E-mail: arcallaghan@stthomas.edu. *Application contact:* Ana Theisen, Recruiter/Admissions Counselor, 651-962-5069, Fax: 651-962-5790, E-mail: aztheisen@stthomas.edu. Website: http://www.stthomas.edu/spssod/

University of St. Thomas, School of Education and Human Services, Houston, TX 77006-4696. Offers all level education (M Ed); bilingual/dual language (M Ed); Catholic school teaching (M Ed); Catholic/private school leadership (M Ed); counselor education (M Ed); curriculum and instruction (M Ed); education (Ed D); educational leadership (M Ed); elementary teaching (M Ed); English as a second language (M Ed); exceptionality/educational diagnostician (M Ed); exceptionality/special education (M Ed); generalist (M Ed); reading (M Ed); secondary teaching (M Ed); teaching (MAT). *Accreditation:* TEAC. *Program availability:* Part-time, evening/weekend, online learning. *Faculty:* 33 full-time (22 women), 43 part-time/adjunct (26 women). *Students:* 119 full-time (97 women), 597 part-time (529 women); includes 478 minority (166 Black or African American, non-Hispanic/Latino; 29 Asian, non-Hispanic/Latino; 277 Hispanic/Latino; 2 Native Hawaiian or other Pacific Islander, non-Hispanic/Latino; 4 Two or more races, non-Hispanic/Latino), 19 international. Average age 36. 306 applicants, 91% accepted, 181 enrolled. In 2017, 328 master's awarded. *Degree requirements:* For master's, thesis, field experience. *Entrance requirements:* For master's, GRE or MAT if GPA is below 3.0, bachelor's degree; minimum GPA of 2.75 in bachelor's degree or last 60 credit hours; official transcripts from all institutions; goal statement of 250-300 words; 1 reference. Additional exam requirements/recommendations for international students: Required—TOEFL (minimum score 94 iBT), IELTS (minimum score 7), PTE (minimum score 53). *Application deadline:* Applications are processed on a rolling basis. Application fee: $35. Electronic applications accepted. *Expenses:* Contact institution. *Financial support:* In 2017–18, 27 students received support. Federal Work-Study, scholarships/grants, and state work-study, institutional employment available. Support available to part-time students. Financial award application deadline: 4/15; financial award applicants required to submit FAFSA. *Faculty research:* Leadership, diversity, personality traits, second language acquisition. *Unit head:* Dr. Paul C. Paese, Dean, 713-942-5999, Fax: 713-525-3871, E-mail: paesep@stthom.edu. *Application contact:* 713-525-3540, E-mail: education@stthom.edu. Website: http://www.stthom.edu/Academics/School_of_Education_and_Human_Services/Index.aqf

University of San Francisco, School of Education, Catholic Educational Leadership Program, San Francisco, CA 94117-1080. Offers Catholic school leadership (Ed D). *Program availability:* Part-time, evening/weekend. *Degree requirements:* For doctorate, thesis/dissertation. *Entrance requirements:* Additional exam requirements/recommendations for international students: Required—TOEFL, IELTS, PTE. Electronic applications accepted.

Vancouver School of Theology, Graduate and Professional Programs, Vancouver, BC V6T 1Z1, Canada. Offers denominational studies (Diploma); indigenous and inter-religious studies (MA, Diploma); public and pastoral leadership (MA); public and pastoral leadership in spiritual care (MA); theological studies (MATS, Diploma, Graduate Diploma); theology (M Div, Th M). *Accreditation:* ATS. *Program availability:* Part-time, online learning. *Degree requirements:* For master's, comprehensive exam (for some programs), thesis (for some programs); for other advanced degree, one foreign language, thesis. *Entrance requirements:* Additional exam requirements/recommendations for international students: Required—TOEFL (minimum score 80 iBT); Recommended—IELTS (minimum score 6.5). *Application deadline:* For fall admission, 10/15 for domestic and international students; for spring admission, 3/15 for domestic and international students. Application fee: $75 Canadian dollars. Electronic applications accepted. One-time fee: $426 Canadian dollars full-time. *Financial support:* Research assistantships with partial tuition reimbursements, teaching assistantships with partial tuition reimbursements, career-related internships or fieldwork, scholarships/grants, and tuition waivers (partial) available. Support available to part-time students. Financial award application deadline: 3/15. *Faculty research:* Old Testament studies, pastoral theology, New Testament studies, field education, church history, systematic theology, spirituality. *Unit head:* Rev. Dr. Richard Topping, Principal, 604-822-9808, Fax: 604-822-9212. *Application contact:* Anita Fast, Registrar, 604-822-9563, Fax: 604-822-9212, E-mail: afast@vst.edu. Website: https://vst.edu/students/prospective/degree-programs/graduate-degrees

Walsh University, Graduate Programs, Master of Arts in Theology Program, North Canton, OH 44720-3396. Offers parish administration (MA); pastoral ministry (MA); religious education (MA). *Program availability:* Part-time, evening/weekend. *Degree requirements:* For master's, thesis or alternative, culminating assignment. *Entrance requirements:* For master's, MAT or GRE (minimum scores: Verbal 145, Quantitative 146, Combined 291, Writing 3.0), minimum GPA of 3.0. Additional exam requirements/recommendations for international students: Required—TOEFL. Electronic applications accepted. Application fee is waived when completed online. *Expenses:* Contact institution. *Faculty research:* Cardinal Newman, phenomenological method, Flavius Josephus, post-conciliar moral teaching.

Wesley Biblical Seminary, Graduate Programs, Jackson, MS 39206. Offers apologetics (MA); Biblical languages (M Div); Biblical literature (MA); Christian studies (MA); context and mission (M Div); honors research (M Div); interpretation (M Div); ministry (M Div); spiritual formation (M Div); teaching (M Div); theology (MA). *Accreditation:* ATS. *Program availability:* Part-time. *Degree requirements:* For master's, thesis. *Entrance requirements:* Additional exam requirements/recommendations for international students: Required—TOEFL. Electronic applications accepted. *Faculty research:* Patristics, missiology, culture, hermeneutics.

Wheaton College, Graduate School, Department of Christian Formation and Ministry, Wheaton, IL 60187-5593. Offers MA. *Program availability:* Part-time. *Faculty:* 1 full-time (0 women), 2 part-time/adjunct (both women). *Students:* 14 full-time (10 women), 21 part-time (10 women); includes 8 minority (3 Asian, non-Hispanic/Latino; 3 Hispanic/Latino; 2 Two or more races, non-Hispanic/Latino), 4 international. Average age 26. 30 applicants, 87% accepted, 13 enrolled. In 2017, 21 master's awarded. *Degree requirements:* For master's, thesis or alternative. *Entrance requirements:* For master's, GRE General Test or MAT. Additional exam requirements/recommendations for international students: Required—TOEFL (minimum score 550 paper-based; 80 iBT), IELTS (minimum score 6.5). *Application deadline:* For fall admission, 5/1 for domestic students, 1/1 for international students; for spring admission, 11/1 for domestic students. Applications are processed on a rolling basis. Application fee: $30. Electronic applications accepted. *Expenses: Tuition:* Full-time $19,800; part-time $825 per credit hour. Tuition and fees vary according to degree level and program. *Financial support:* Career-related internships or fieldwork, scholarships/grants, and unspecified assistantships available. Financial award application deadline: 3/1; financial award applicants required to submit FAFSA. *Unit head:* Dr. Laura Barwegen, Chair, 630-752-5196, E-mail: cfm@wheaton.edu. *Application contact:* Director of Graduate Admissions, 630-752-5195, Fax: 630-752-7047, E-mail: graduate.admissions@wheaton.edu. Website: https://www.wheaton.edu/graduate-school/degrees/ma-in-christian-formation-and-ministry/

Xavier University, College of Arts and Sciences, Department of Theology, Cincinnati, OH 45207. Offers health care mission integration (MA); theology (MA), including religious education, social and pastoral ministry, theology. *Program availability:* Part-time, evening/weekend. *Degree requirements:* For master's, final paper (or thesis) and defense or comprehension exam. *Entrance requirements:* For master's, MAT or GRE, 2 letters of recommendation; statement of reasons and goals for enrolling in program (1,000-2,000 words); resume; transcript. Additional exam requirements/recommendations for international students: Required—TOEFL (minimum score 550 paper-based; 79 iBT). Electronic applications accepted. Application fee is waived when completed online. *Expenses:* Contact institution. *Faculty research:* Scripture, ethics, constructive theology, historical theology.

Yeshiva University, Azrieli Graduate School of Jewish Education and Administration, New York, NY 10033-4391. Offers MS, Ed D, Specialist. *Accreditation:* TEAC. *Program availability:* Part-time, evening/weekend. Terminal master's awarded for partial completion of doctoral program. *Degree requirements:* For master's, one foreign language, student teaching experience, comprehensive exam or thesis; for doctorate, one foreign language, comprehensive exam, thesis/dissertation, certifying exams, internship; for Specialist, one foreign language, comprehensive exam, certifying exams, internship. *Entrance requirements:* For master's, GRE General Test, BA in Jewish studies or equivalent; for doctorate and Specialist, GRE General Test, master's degree in Jewish education, 2 years of teaching experience. *Expenses:* Contact institution. *Faculty research:* Social patterns of American and Israeli Jewish population, special education, adult education, technology in education, return to religious values.

Science Education

Adams State University, Office of Graduate Studies, Department of Teacher Education, Alamosa, CO 81101. Offers teacher education (MA), including adaptive leadership, curriculum and instruction, curriculum and instruction-STEM, educational leadership. *Program availability:* Part-time, online learning. *Degree requirements:* For master's, qualifying exam. *Entrance requirements:* For master's, GRE General Test or MAT, minimum undergraduate GPA of 3.0. *Application deadline:* For fall admission, 5/15 priority date for domestic students; for spring admission, 10/15 for domestic students. Applications are processed on a rolling basis. Application fee: $30. *Expenses:* Tuition, state resident: full-time $4800; part-time $2400 per credit. Tuition, nonresident: full-time $7100; part-time $3550 per credit. *Required fees:* $213; $106 per credit. One-time fee: $100. Tuition and fees vary according to campus/location and program. *Financial support:* In 2017–18, fellowships with partial tuition reimbursements (averaging $4,000 per year), teaching assistantships with partial tuition reimbursements (averaging $4,000 per year) were awarded; career-related internships or fieldwork, Federal Work-Study, institutionally sponsored loans, and unspecified assistantships also available. Support available to part-time students. Financial award application deadline: 4/15; financial award applicants required to submit FAFSA. *Unit head:* Dr. Cheri Meder, Interim Chair, 719-587-7934, Fax: 719-587-8145, E-mail: teachered@adams.edu. *Application contact:* Information Contact, 719-587-7776, Fax: 719-587-8145, E-mail: teachered@adams.edu. Website: http://teachered.adams.edu

Alabama Agricultural and Mechanical University, School of Graduate Studies, College of Education, Humanities, and Behavioral Sciences, Department of Educational Leadership and Secondary Education, Huntsville, AL 35811. Offers biology (M Ed); business/marketing education (M Ed, Ed S); chemistry (M Ed); collaborative teacher secondary education (M Ed, Ed S); education (M Ed, Ed S); English language arts (M Ed); family/consumer science education (M Ed, Ed S); general science (M Ed); general social science (M Ed); mathematics (M Ed); physics (M Ed, Ed S); technology education (M Ed). *Accreditation:* NCATE. *Program availability:* Evening/weekend. *Degree requirements:* For master's, comprehensive exam; for Ed S, thesis. *Entrance requirements:* For master's, GRE General Test. Additional exam requirements/

recommendations for international students: Required—TOEFL (minimum score 500 paper-based; 61 iBT). Electronic applications accepted. *Faculty research:* World peace through education, computer-assisted instruction.

Alabama State University, College of Education, Department of Curriculum and Instruction, Montgomery, AL 36101-0271. Offers early childhood education (M Ed, Ed S); elementary education (M Ed, Ed S); secondary education (M Ed, Ed S), including biology education, English language arts education (M Ed), history education, math education, music education (M Ed), reading education (M Ed), social science education; special education (M Ed). *Program availability:* Part-time. *Faculty:* 7 full-time (4 women), 7 part-time/adjunct (4 women). *Students:* 43 full-time (35 women), 71 part-time (62 women); includes 112 minority (111 Black or African American, non-Hispanic/Latino; 1 Two or more races, non-Hispanic/Latino). Average age 22. 47 applicants, 66% accepted, 19 enrolled. In 2017, 21 master's, 13 Ed Ss awarded. *Degree requirements:* For master's, comprehensive exam, thesis optional; for Ed S, comprehensive exam, thesis. *Entrance requirements:* For master's, GRE General Test, MAT, writing competency test; for Ed S, writing competency test, GRE, MAT. Additional exam requirements/recommendations for international students: Required—TOEFL (minimum score 500 paper-based). *Application deadline:* For fall admission, 4/15 for domestic and international students; for spring admission, 11/15 for domestic and international students; for summer admission, 3/15 for domestic and international students. Applications are processed on a rolling basis. Application fee: $25. Electronic applications accepted. *Expenses:* Tuition, state resident: part-time $412 per credit hour. Tuition, nonresident: part-time $824 per credit hour. *Required fees:* $685 per semester. *Financial support:* Research assistantships available. Financial award application deadline: 6/30; financial award applicants required to submit FAFSA. *Unit head:* Dr. Joyce Johnson, Acting Chairperson, 334-229-4485, Fax: 334-229-5603, E-mail: jjohnson@alasu.edu. *Application contact:* Dr. William Person, Dean of Graduate Studies, 334-229-4274, Fax: 334-229-4928, E-mail: wperson@alasu.edu. Website: http://www.alasu.edu/academics/colleges—departments/college-of-education/curriculum—instruction/index.aspx

Alverno College, School of Professional Studies - Education Division, Milwaukee, WI 53234-3922. Offers adaptive education (MA); administrative leadership (MA); adult education and organizational development (MA); adult education and instructional design (MA); adult educational and instructional technology (MA); global connections in the humanities (MA); instructional leadership (MA); instructional technology for K-12 settings (MA); professional development (MA); reading education (MA); reading education with adaptive education (MA); science education (MA); special education (MA); teaching in alternative schools (MA). *Accreditation:* NCATE. *Program availability:* Part-time, evening/weekend. *Faculty:* 3 full-time (2 women), 23 part-time/adjunct (17 women). *Students:* 37 full-time (34 women), 68 part-time (65 women); includes 27 minority (16 Black or African American, non-Hispanic/Latino; 1 American Indian or Alaska Native, non-Hispanic/Latino; 1 Asian, non-Hispanic/Latino; 7 Hispanic/Latino; 2 Two or more races, non-Hispanic/Latino). Average age 35. 67 applicants, 100% accepted, 51 enrolled. In 2017, 68 master's awarded. *Degree requirements:* For master's, presentation/defense of proposal, conference presentation of inquiry projects. *Entrance requirements:* For master's, bachelor's degree in related field, communication samples from work setting, 3 letters of recommendation. Additional exam requirements/recommendations for international students: Required—TOEFL. *Application deadline:* For fall admission, 7/15 priority date for domestic and international students; for spring admission, 12/15 priority date for domestic and international students. Applications are processed on a rolling basis. Application fee: $0. Electronic applications accepted. *Expenses:* Contact institution. *Financial support:* Federal Work-Study and scholarships/grants available. Support available to part-time students. Financial award applicants required to submit FAFSA. *Faculty research:* Student self-assessment, self-reflection, integration of curriculum, identifying needs of students in strategic situations and designing appropriate classroom strategies. *Unit head:* Dr. Patricia Luebke, Dean, School of Professional Studies, 414-382-6368, Fax: 414-382-6354, E-mail: patricia.luebke@alverno.edu. *Application contact:* Katie Kipp, Graduate Admissions Counselor, 414-382-6045, Fax: 414-382-6354, E-mail: katie.kipp@alverno.edu.

American University of Beirut, Graduate Programs, Faculty of Arts and Sciences, 1107 2020, Lebanon. Offers anthropology (MA); Arab and Middle Eastern history (PhD); Arabic language and literature (MA, PhD); archaeology (MA); art history and curating (MA); biology (MS); cell and molecular biology (PhD); chemistry (MS); clinical psychology (MA); computational sciences (MS); computer science (MS); economics (MA); education (MA), including administration and policy studies, elementary education, mathematics education, psychology school guidance, psychology test and measurements, science education, teaching English as a foreign language; English language (MA); English literature (MA); environmental policy planning (MS); financial economics (MAFE); general psychology (MA); geology (MS); history (MA); Islamic studies (MA); mathematics (MS); media studies (MA); Middle East studies (MA); philosophy (MA); physics (MS); political studies (MA); public administration (MA); public policy and international affairs (MA); sociology (MA); theoretical physics (PhD). *Program availability:* Part-time. *Faculty:* 108 full-time (36 women), 5 part-time/adjunct (4 women). *Students:* 251 full-time (180 women), 233 part-time (172 women). Average age 26. 425 applicants, 65% accepted, 121 enrolled. In 2017, 47 master's, 2 doctorates awarded. *Degree requirements:* For master's, one foreign language, comprehensive exam, thesis (for some programs), project; for doctorate, one foreign language, comprehensive exam, thesis/dissertation. *Entrance requirements:* For master's, GRE General Test (for some programs); for doctorate, GRE General Test (GRE Subject Test for theoretical physics). Additional exam requirements/recommendations for international students: Required—TOEFL (minimum score 583 paper-based; 97 iBT), IELTS (minimum score 7). *Application deadline:* For fall admission, 2/8 for domestic students; for spring admission, 11/3 for domestic students. Application fee: $50. Electronic applications accepted. *Expenses:* Contact institution. *Financial support:* In 2017–18, 29 fellowships, 40 research assistantships were awarded; teaching assistantships, scholarships/grants, tuition waivers (full and partial), and unspecified assistantships also available. Financial award application deadline: 4/4. *Unit head:* Dr. Nadia Maria El Cheikh, Dean, Faculty of Arts and Sciences, 961-1-374374 Ext. 3800, Fax: 961-1-744461, E-mail: nmcheikh@aub.edu.lb. *Application contact:* Rima Rassi, Graduate Studies Officer, 961-1-350000 Ext. 3833, Fax: 961-1-744461, E-mail: rr46@aub.edu.lb.
Website: http://www.aub.edu.lb/fas/pages/default.aspx

American University of Puerto Rico, Program in Education, Bayamon, PR 00960-2037. Offers art education (M Ed); elementary education 4-6 (M Ed); elementary education K-3 (M Ed); general science education (M Ed); physical education (M Ed); special education (M Ed). *Program availability:* Part-time, evening/weekend. *Faculty:* 17 part-time/adjunct (7 women). *Students:* 22 full-time (18 women), 54 part-time (42 women); all minorities (all Hispanic/Latino). Average age 33. 22 applicants, 86% accepted, 19 enrolled. In 2017, 53 master's awarded. *Entrance requirements:* For master's, EXADEP, GRE, or MAT, 2 letters of recommendation, minimum GPA of 2.5. *Application deadline:* For fall admission, 8/1 for domestic students; for winter admission, 10/18 for domestic students; for spring admission, 3/15 for domestic students. Applications are processed on a rolling basis. Application fee: $25. Tuition and fees vary according to course load and degree level. *Financial support:* In 2017–18, 79 students received support, including 76 fellowships (averaging $400 per year), 55 teaching assistantships (averaging $1,741 per year). Financial award applicants required to submit FAFSA. *Unit head:* Prof. Bolivar Ramirez-Carlo, III, Dean of Faculty, 787-620-2040 Ext. 2010, Fax: 787-620-2958, E-mail: bramirez@aupr.edu. *Application contact:* Keren I. Llanos-Figueroa, Information Contact, 787-620-2040 Ext. 2021, Fax: 787-785-7377, E-mail: oficnaadmisiones@aupr.edu.

Andrews University, School of Graduate Studies, College of Arts and Sciences, Department of Biology, Berrien Springs, MI 49104. Offers MAT, MS. *Faculty:* 7 full-time (3 women). *Students:* 7 full-time (3 women), 1 (woman) part-time; includes 1 minority (Hispanic/Latino), 2 international. Average age 27. 10 applicants, 60% accepted, 6 enrolled. In 2017, 2 master's awarded. *Degree requirements:* For master's, comprehensive exam, thesis. *Entrance requirements:* For master's, GRE Subject Test. Additional exam requirements/recommendations for international students: Required—TOEFL (minimum score 550 paper-based). *Application deadline:* Applications are processed on a rolling basis. Application fee: $40. *Financial support:* Fellowships, research assistantships, teaching assistantships, career-related internships or fieldwork, Federal Work-Study, and institutionally sponsored loans available. Financial award application deadline: 3/15. *Faculty research:* Manatee habitat characterization, seabird habitat dynamics. *Unit head:* Dr. Thomas Goodwin, Chairman, 269-471-3243. *Application contact:* Justina Clayburn, Supervisor of Graduate Admission, 800-253-2874, Fax: 269-471-6321, E-mail: graduate@andrews.edu.

Andrews University, School of Graduate Studies, School of Education, Department of Teaching, Learning, and Curriculum, Berrien Springs, MI 49104. Offers curriculum and instruction (MA, Ed D, PhD, Ed S); elementary education (MAT); secondary education (MAT), including biology, education, English, English as a second language, French, history, physics; teacher education (MAT). *Faculty:* 7 full-time (5 women). *Students:* 14 full-time (8 women), 7 part-time (6 women); includes 5 minority (all Black or African American, non-Hispanic/Latino), 9 international. Average age 39. 29 applicants, 31% accepted, 4 enrolled. In 2017, 5 master's, 3 doctorates awarded. *Entrance requirements:* For master's, GRE Subject Test. Additional exam requirements/recommendations for international students: Required—TOEFL (minimum score 550

paper-based). *Application deadline:* For fall admission, 8/15 for domestic students. Applications are processed on a rolling basis. Application fee: $40. *Unit head:* Dr. Lee C. Davidson, Chair, 269-471-6364. *Application contact:* Justina Clayburn, Supervisor of Graduate Admission, 800-253-2874, Fax: 269-471-6321, E-mail: graduate@andrews.edu.

Antioch University New England, Graduate School, Department of Education, Integrated Learning Program, Keene, NH 03431-3552. Offers early childhood education (M Ed); elementary education (M Ed), including arts and humanities, science and environmental education; special education (M Ed). *Degree requirements:* For master's, internship. *Entrance requirements:* For master's, previous course work or work experience in education. Additional exam requirements/recommendations for international students: Required—TOEFL (minimum score 550 paper-based). Electronic applications accepted. *Expenses:* Contact institution. *Faculty research:* Problem-based learning, place-based education, mathematics education, democratic classrooms, art education.

Antioch University New England, Graduate School, Department of Environmental Studies, Science Teacher Certification Program, Keene, NH 03431-3552. Offers MS. *Degree requirements:* For master's, practicum, seminar, student teaching. *Entrance requirements:* Additional exam requirements/recommendations for international students: Required—TOEFL (minimum score 550 paper-based). Electronic applications accepted.

Appalachian State University, Cratis D. Williams Graduate School, Department of Curriculum and Instruction, Boone, NC 28608. Offers curriculum specialist (MA); educational media (MA); elementary education (MA); middle grades education (MA), including language arts, mathematics, science, social studies. *Accreditation:* NCATE. *Program availability:* Part-time, evening/weekend, online learning. *Degree requirements:* For master's, comprehensive exam, thesis or alternative. *Entrance requirements:* For master's, GRE General Test or MAT, 3 letters of recommendation. Additional exam requirements/recommendations for international students: Required—TOEFL (minimum score 570 paper-based; 79 iBT), IELTS (minimum score 6.5). Electronic applications accepted. *Faculty research:* Media literacy, elementary teaching, curriculum development, online learning environments.

Arcadia University, School of Education, Glenside, PA 19038-3295. Offers art education (M Ed); computer education (CAS); curriculum (CAS); curriculum studies (M Ed); early childhood education (M Ed), including individualized, master teacher, research in child development; educational leadership (M Ed, Ed D, CAS); elementary education (M Ed); English education (MA Ed); environmental education (MA Ed); instructional technology (M Ed); language arts (M Ed); library science (M Ed); mathematics education (M Ed, MA Ed); music education (MA Ed); psychology (MA Ed); reading (M Ed, CAS); science education (M Ed, CAS); secondary education (M Ed, CAS); special education (M Ed, Ed D, CAS); theater arts (MA Ed); written communication (MA Ed). *Accreditation:* NASAD. *Program availability:* Part-time, evening/weekend, online learning. Electronic applications accepted. *Expenses:* Contact institution.

Arkansas State University, Graduate School, College of Sciences and Mathematics, Department of Biological Sciences, State University, AR 72467. Offers biological sciences (MA); biology (MS); biology education (MSE, SCCT); biotechnology (PSM). *Program availability:* Part-time. *Degree requirements:* For master's, comprehensive exam, thesis (for some programs); for SCCT, comprehensive exam. *Entrance requirements:* For master's, GRE General Test, appropriate bachelor's degree, letters of reference, interview, official transcripts, immunization records, statement of educational objectives and career goals, teaching certificate (for MSE); for SCCT, GRE General Test or MAT, interview, master's degree, letters of reference, official transcript, personal statement, immunization records. Additional exam requirements/recommendations for international students: Required—TOEFL (minimum score 550 paper-based; 79 iBT), IELTS (minimum score 6), PTE (minimum score 56). Electronic applications accepted.

Arkansas State University, Graduate School, College of Sciences and Mathematics, Department of Chemistry and Physics, State University, AR 72467. Offers chemistry (MS); chemistry education (MSE, SCCT). *Program availability:* Part-time. *Degree requirements:* For master's, comprehensive exam, thesis or alternative; for SCCT, comprehensive exam. *Entrance requirements:* For master's, GRE General Test or MAT, appropriate bachelor's degree, official transcript, immunization records, valid teaching certificate (for MSE); for SCCT, GRE General Test or MAT, interview, master's degree, official transcript, immunization records. Additional exam requirements/recommendations for international students: Required—TOEFL (minimum score 550 paper-based; 79 iBT), IELTS (minimum score 6), PTE (minimum score 56). Electronic applications accepted.

Asbury University, School of Graduate and Professional Studies, Wilmore, KY 40390-1198. Offers biology: alternative certificate (MA Ed); chemistry: alternative certificate (MA Ed); English (MA Ed); English as a second language (MA Ed); ESL (MA Ed); French (MA Ed); Latin: alternative certificate (MA Ed); mathematics: alternative certificate (MA Ed); reading/writing endorsement (MA Ed); social studies (MA Ed); social work (MSW), including child and family services; Spanish (MA Ed); special education (MA Ed); special education: alternative certificate (MA Ed); teacher as leader endorsement (MA Ed). *Accreditation:* NCATE. *Program availability:* Part-time. *Degree requirements:* For master's, action research project, portfolio. *Entrance requirements:* For master's, PRAXIS/NTE, minimum GPA of 2.75, letters of recommendation. Additional exam requirements/recommendations for international students: Required—TOEFL (minimum score 550 paper-based). Electronic applications accepted.

Athabasca University, Faculty of Science and Technology, Athabasca, AB T9S 3A3, Canada. Offers architecture (Postgraduate Diploma); information systems (M Sc). *Program availability:* Part-time, online learning. *Degree requirements:* For master's, thesis optional. *Entrance requirements:* For master's, B Sc in computing or other bachelor's degree and IT experience. Electronic applications accepted. *Expenses:* Contact institution. *Faculty research:* Distributed systems multimedia, computer science education, e-services.

Augustana University, MA in Education Program, Sioux Falls, SD 57197. Offers instructional strategies (MA); reading (MA); special populations (MA); STEM (MA); technology (MA). *Accreditation:* NCATE. *Program availability:* Part-time-only, evening/weekend, online only, 100% online. *Faculty:* 7 full-time (5 women), 6 part-time/adjunct (5 women). *Students:* 288 part-time (250 women); includes 20 minority (2 Black or African American, non-Hispanic/Latino; 2 American Indian or Alaska Native, non-Hispanic/Latino; 1 Asian, non-Hispanic/Latino; 11 Hispanic/Latino; 1 Native Hawaiian or other Pacific Islander, non-Hispanic/Latino; 3 Two or more races, non-Hispanic/Latino), 3 international. Average age 32. 47 applicants, 77% accepted, 35 enrolled. In 2017, 84 master's awarded. *Degree requirements:* For master's, thesis. *Entrance requirements:* For master's, appropriate bachelor's degree, minimum GPA of 3.0, teaching certificate. Additional exam requirements/recommendations for international students: Required—TOEFL (minimum score 550 paper-based). *Application deadline:* For fall admission, 8/1 for domestic and international students; for spring admission, 11/1 for domestic and international students; for summer admission, 4/1 for domestic and international students. Applications are processed on a rolling basis. Application fee: $60. Electronic

Science Education

applications accepted. *Expenses:* Contact institution. *Financial support:* Application deadline: 3/1; applicants required to submit FAFSA. *Faculty research:* Multicultural education, education of students with autism, well-being in school settings, factors that predict academic hopefulness. *Unit head:* Dr. Laurie Daily, Chair, 605-274-5211, E-mail: laurie.daily@augie.edu. *Application contact:* Julia Paulich, Graduate Coordinator, 605-274-4043, Fax: 605-274-4450, E-mail: graduate@augie.edu.
Website: http://www.augie.edu/master-arts-education

Aurora University, College of Arts and Sciences, Aurora, IL 60506-4892. Offers homeland security (MS); mathematics (MS); mathematics and science education for elementary teachers (MA); mathematics educaton (MA); science education (MA). *Program availability:* Part-time, evening/weekend, 100% online. *Faculty:* 3 full-time (2 women), 6 part-time/adjunct (3 women). *Students:* 47 full-time (28 women), 45 part-time (10 women); includes 12 minority (5 Black or African American, non-Hispanic/Latino; 4 Asian, non-Hispanic/Latino; 3 Hispanic/Latino). Average age 36. 68 applicants, 96% accepted, 15 enrolled. *Degree requirements:* For master's, research seminars. *Entrance requirements:* For master's, bachelor's degree in mathematics or in some other field with extensive course work in mathematics (for MS in mathematics). Additional exam requirements/recommendations for international students: Required—TOEFL (minimum score 550 paper-based; 79 iBT). *Application deadline:* For fall admission, 6/1 for international students; for spring admission, 10/1 for international students. Applications are processed on a rolling basis. Application fee: $0. Electronic applications accepted. *Expenses:* Contact institution. *Financial support:* Federal Work-Study, scholarships/grants, and unspecified assistantships available. Support available to part-time students. Financial award application deadline: 4/1; financial award applicants required to submit FAFSA. *Unit head:* Dr. Frank Buscher, Vice President for Academic Affairs, 630-844-5252, E-mail: fbuscher@aurora.edu. *Application contact:* Judson Curry, Dean of Adult and Graduate Studies, 630-947-8946, E-mail: jcurry@aurora.edu.

Austin Peay State University, College of Graduate Studies, College of Science, Technology, Engineering and Mathematics, Clarksville, TN 37044. Offers MS, PSM. *Program availability:* Part-time, online learning. *Faculty:* 32 full-time (10 women), 1 part-time/adjunct (0 women). *Students:* 25 full-time (6 women), 76 part-time (31 women); includes 24 minority (7 Black or African American, non-Hispanic/Latino; 3 Asian, non-Hispanic/Latino; 6 Hispanic/Latino; 8 Two or more races, non-Hispanic/Latino), 10 international. Average age 33. 78 applicants, 90% accepted, 49 enrolled. In 2017, 24 master's awarded. *Degree requirements:* For master's, comprehensive exam, thesis optional. *Entrance requirements:* For master's, GRE General Test, 3 letters of recommendation, minimum undergraduate GPA of 2.5. Additional exam requirements/recommendations for international students: Required—TOEFL (minimum score 500 paper-based). *Application deadline:* For fall admission, 8/8 priority date for domestic students. Applications are processed on a rolling basis. Application fee: $45 ($50 for international students). Electronic applications accepted. *Expenses:* Tuition, state resident: full-time $7686; part-time $427 per credit hour. Tuition, nonresident: full-time $20,268; part-time $1126 per credit hour. *Required fees:* $1529; $76.45 per credit hour. *Financial support:* Research assistantships with full tuition reimbursements, career-related internships or fieldwork, Federal Work-Study, institutionally sponsored loans, scholarships/grants, and unspecified assistantships available. Support available to part-time students. Financial award application deadline: 4/1; financial award applicants required to submit FAFSA. *Unit head:* Dr. Karen Meisch, Interim Dean, 931-221-7780, Fax: 931-221-7984, E-mail: meischk@apsu.edu. *Application contact:* Megan Mitchell, Coordinator of Graduate Admissions, 931-221-6189, Fax: 931-221-7641, E-mail: mitchellm@apsu.edu.
Website: http://www.apsu.edu/costem/index.php

Bard College, Master of Arts in Teaching Program, Annandale-on-Hudson, NY 12504. Offers secondary education (MAT), including biology, history, literature, mathematics, Spanish; MS/MAT. *Program availability:* Part-time. *Degree requirements:* For master's, year-long teaching residencies in area middle and high schools. *Entrance requirements:* For master's, GRE General Test, resume, 3 letters of recommendation, personal statement, official transcripts. Additional exam requirements/recommendations for international students: Required—TOEFL. Electronic applications accepted. Application fee is waived when completed online.

Benedictine University, Graduate Programs, Program in Science Content and Process, Lisle, IL 60532. Offers MS.

Binghamton University, State University of New York, Graduate School, College of Community and Public Affairs, Department of Teaching, Learning and Educational Leadership, Program in Adolescence Education, Binghamton, NY 13902-6000. Offers biology education (MAT, MS Ed); chemistry education (MAT, MS Ed); earth science education (MAT, MS Ed); English education (MAT, MS Ed); French education (MAT, MS Ed); mathematical sciences education (MAT, MS Ed); physics (MAT, MS Ed); social studies (MAT, MS Ed); Spanish education (MAT, MS Ed). *Accreditation:* TEAC. *Program availability:* Part-time, evening/weekend. *Students:* 53 full-time (32 women), 9 part-time (3 women); includes 10 minority (2 Black or African American, non-Hispanic/Latino; 1 Asian, non-Hispanic/Latino; 5 Hispanic/Latino; 2 Two or more races, non-Hispanic/Latino). Average age 27. 51 applicants, 88% accepted, 31 enrolled. In 2017, 36 master's awarded. *Degree requirements:* For master's, portfolio. *Entrance requirements:* For master's, GRE General Test, teaching certification. Additional exam requirements/recommendations for international students: Required—TOEFL (minimum score 550 paper-based; 80 iBT). *Application deadline:* For fall admission, 2/1 priority date for domestic and international students; for spring admission, 10/15 priority date for domestic and international students. Application fee: $75. Electronic applications accepted. *Financial support:* In 2017–18, 4 students received support. Research assistantships, teaching assistantships, career-related internships or fieldwork, Federal Work-Study, institutionally sponsored loans, scholarships/grants, health care benefits, tuition waivers (full and partial), and unspecified assistantships available. Financial award applicants required to submit FAFSA. *Unit head:* Dr. Susan Strehle, Dean, 607-777-7329, E-mail: sstrehle@binghamton.edu. *Application contact:* Ben Balkaya, Assistant Dean and Director, 607-777-2151, Fax: 607-777-2501, E-mail: balkaya@binghamton.edu.

Biola University, School of Arts and Sciences, La Mirada, CA 90639-0001. Offers Christian apologetics (MA, Certificate); science and religion (MA); speech language pathology (MA). *Program availability:* Part-time, evening/weekend, online learning. *Faculty:* 20. *Students:* 24 full-time (7 women), 251 part-time (49 women); includes 80 minority (21 Black or African American, non-Hispanic/Latino; 1 American Indian or Alaska Native, non-Hispanic/Latino; 31 Asian, non-Hispanic/Latino; 19 Hispanic/Latino; 8 Two or more races, non-Hispanic/Latino), 15 international. 168 applicants, 70% accepted, 77 enrolled. In 2017, 64 master's awarded. *Entrance requirements:* For master's, minimum GPA of 3.0, bachelor's degree from accredited college or university (in science-related field for science and religion program). Additional exam requirements/recommendations for international students: Required—TOEFL (minimum score 600 paper-based; 100 iBT). *Application deadline:* For fall admission, 7/1 for domestic students, 6/1 for international students; for spring admission, 12/1 for domestic students. Applications are processed on a rolling basis. Application fee: $65. Electronic applications accepted. *Financial support:* Scholarships/grants and unspecified assistantships available. Support available to part-time students. Financial award

applicants required to submit FAFSA. *Faculty research:* Apologetics, science and religion, intelligent design. *Application contact:* Graduate Admissions Office, 562-903-4752, E-mail: graduate.admissions@biola.edu.
Website: http://www.biola.edu/academics/sas/

Bloomsburg University of Pennsylvania, School of Graduate Studies, College of Education, Department of Teaching and Learning, Program in Middle Level Education Grades 4-8, Bloomsburg, PA 17815-1301. Offers language arts (M Ed); math (M Ed); science (M Ed); social studies (M Ed). *Accreditation:* NCATE. *Degree requirements:* For master's, thesis optional, practicum, student teaching. *Entrance requirements:* For master's, MAT, GRE, or PRAXIS, minimum QPA of 3.0, teaching certificate, U.S. citizenship, related undergraduate coursework, professional liability insurance, recent TB test. Additional exam requirements/recommendations for international students: Required—TOEFL (minimum score 550 paper-based), IELTS. Electronic applications accepted. *Expenses:* Tuition, state resident: full-time $10,000; part-time $500 per credit hour. Tuition, nonresident: full-time $15,000; part-time $750 per credit hour. *Required fees:* $2484; $110.75 per credit hour. $75 per term. Tuition and fees vary according to program.

Blue Mountain College, Program in Secondary Education - Biology, Blue Mountain, MS 38610. Offers M Ed. *Program availability:* Part-time, evening/weekend. *Faculty:* 1 part-time/adjunct (0 women). *Students:* 1 (woman) part-time. Average age 31. *Degree requirements:* For master's, comprehensive exam. *Entrance requirements:* For master's, PRAXIS, GRE, or MAT, official transcripts; bachelor's degree in a field of education from an accredited college or university; teaching certificate; three recommendations. Additional exam requirements/recommendations for international students: Required—TOEFL (minimum score 550 paper-based). *Application deadline:* For fall admission, 7/15 priority date for domestic students; for spring admission, 12/1 priority date for domestic students; for summer admission, 5/1 priority date for domestic students. Applications are processed on a rolling basis. Electronic applications accepted. *Expenses: Tuition:* Full-time $6030; part-time $335 per semester hour. *Required fees:* $790; $790 per semester hour. *Financial support:* Scholarships/grants available. Financial award application deadline: 6/30; financial award applicants required to submit FAFSA. *Unit head:* Dr. Jenetta R. Waddell, Dean of Graduate Studies, 662-685-4771 Ext. 118, Fax: 662-815-2919, E-mail: jwaddell@bmc.edu. *Application contact:* Jean Harrington, Administrative Assistant in Department of Education, 662-685-4771 Ext. 238, Fax: 662-815-2919, E-mail: jharrington@bmc.edu.
Website: http://www.bmc.edu/master_of_education.asp

Boston College, Graduate School of Arts and Sciences, Department of Chemistry, Chestnut Hill, MA 02467-3800. Offers biochemistry (PhD); inorganic chemistry (PhD); organic chemistry (PhD); physical chemistry (PhD); science education (MST). *Degree requirements:* For doctorate, thesis/dissertation, qualifying exam. *Entrance requirements:* For doctorate, GRE General Test, GRE Subject Test. Additional exam requirements/recommendations for international students: Required—TOEFL (minimum score 600 paper-based; 100 iBT), IELTS (minimum score 8). Electronic applications accepted. *Faculty research:* Organic and organometallic chemistry, chemical biology and biochemistry, physical and theoretical chemistry, inorganic chemistry.

Bowling Green State University, Graduate College, College of Arts and Sciences, Department of Physics and Astronomy, Bowling Green, OH 43403. Offers geophysics (MS); physics (MAT, MS). *Degree requirements:* For master's, thesis or alternative. *Entrance requirements:* For master's, GRE General Test. Additional exam requirements/recommendations for international students: Required—TOEFL. Electronic applications accepted. *Faculty research:* Computational physics, solid-state physics, materials science, theoretical physics.

Bridgewater State University, College of Graduate Studies, Bartlett College of Science and Mathematics, Department of Biological Sciences, Bridgewater, MA 02325. Offers biology (MAT). *Program availability:* Part-time, evening/weekend. *Entrance requirements:* For master's, GRE General Test.

Bridgewater State University, College of Graduate Studies, Bartlett College of Science and Mathematics, Department of Physics, Bridgewater, MA 02325. Offers MAT. *Accreditation:* NCATE. *Program availability:* Part-time, evening/weekend. *Entrance requirements:* For master's, GRE General Test.

Bridgewater State University, College of Graduate Studies, College of Humanities and Social Sciences, Program in Physical Sciences, Bridgewater, MA 02325. Offers MAT. *Accreditation:* NCATE. *Program availability:* Part-time, evening/weekend. *Entrance requirements:* For master's, GRE General Test.

Brigham Young University, Graduate Studies, College of Life Sciences, Department of Biology, Provo, UT 84602. Offers biological science education (MS); biology (MS, PhD). *Faculty:* 25 full-time (2 women). *Students:* 36 full-time (14 women); includes 5 minority (3 Hispanic/Latino; 2 Native Hawaiian or other Pacific Islander, non-Hispanic/Latino), 5 international. Average age 29. 22 applicants, 50% accepted, 9 enrolled. In 2017, 5 master's, 3 doctorates awarded. *Degree requirements:* For master's, comprehensive exam, thesis, prospectus, defense of research, defense of thesis; for doctorate, comprehensive exam, thesis/dissertation, prospectus, defense of research, defense of dissertation. *Entrance requirements:* For master's and doctorate, GRE General Test, minimum cumulative GPA of 3.0 for undergraduate degree. Additional exam requirements/recommendations for international students: Required—TOEFL (minimum score 580 paper-based; 85 iBT). *Application deadline:* For fall admission, 1/15 for domestic and international students. Application fee: $50. Electronic applications accepted. *Expenses:* $10,320 per academic year, $405 per credit hour for members of the Church of Jesus Christ of Latter-day Saints; $20,640 for the year, $810 per credit hour for those who are not members of the Church. *Financial support:* In 2017–18, 32 students received support, including 2 fellowships with full tuition reimbursements available (averaging $30,000 per year), 62 research assistantships with full and partial tuition reimbursements available (averaging $6,494 per year), 35 teaching assistantships with full and partial tuition reimbursements available (averaging $6,653 per year); career-related internships or fieldwork, institutionally sponsored loans, scholarships/grants, tuition waivers (full and partial), and unspecified assistantships also available. Financial award application deadline: 3/1; financial award applicants required to submit FAFSA. *Faculty research:* Systematics, bioinformatics, ecology, evolution. *Unit head:* Dr. Dennis K. Shiozawa, Chair, 801-422-4972, E-mail: dennis_shiozawa@byu.edu. *Application contact:* Gentri Glaittli, Graduate Program Manager, 801-422-7137, E-mail: biogradmanager@byu.edu.
Website: http://biology.byu.edu/

Brooklyn College of the City University of New York, School of Education, Program in Adolescence Science Education and Special Subjects, Brooklyn, NY 11210-2889. Offers adolescence science education (MAT); biology teacher (7-12) (MA); chemistry teacher (7-12) (MA); earth science teacher (7-12) (MAT); English teacher (7-12) (MA); French teacher (7-12) (MA); mathematics teacher (7-12) (MA); music teacher (MA); physics teacher (7-12) (MA); social studies teacher (7-12) (MA); Spanish teacher (7-12) (MA). *Program availability:* Part-time, evening/weekend. *Degree requirements:* For master's, comprehensive exam (for some programs), thesis (for some programs). *Entrance requirements:* For master's, LAST, previous course work in education, resume, 2 letters of recommendation, essay. Additional exam requirements/recommendations for international students: Required—TOEFL (minimum score 500 paper-based; 61 iBT). Electronic applications accepted. *Faculty research:* Interdisciplinary education, semiotics, discourse analysis, autobiography, teacher identity.

Brooklyn College of the City University of New York, School of Education, Program in Childhood Education, Brooklyn, NY 11210-2889. Offers bilingual education (MS Ed); liberal arts (MS Ed); mathematics (MS Ed); science and environmental education (MS Ed). *Program availability:* Part-time, evening/weekend. *Entrance requirements:* For master's, LAST, interview, previous course work in education, writing sample, resume, 2 letters of recommendation. Additional exam requirements/recommendations for international students: Required—TOEFL (minimum score 500 paper-based; 61 iBT). Electronic applications accepted. *Faculty research:* Emotional intelligence, multiculturalism, arts immersion, the Holocaust.

Brooklyn College of the City University of New York, School of Education, Program in Middle Childhood Science Education, Brooklyn, NY 11210-2889. Offers biology (MA); chemistry (MA); earth science (MA); general science (MA); physics (MA). *Program availability:* Part-time, evening/weekend. *Entrance requirements:* For master's, LAST, interview, previous course work in education and mathematics, resume, 2 letters of recommendation, essay. Additional exam requirements/recommendations for international students: Required—TOEFL (minimum score 500 paper-based; 61 iBT). Electronic applications accepted. *Faculty research:* Geometric thinking, mastery of basic facts, problem-solving strategies, history of mathematics.

Brown University, Graduate School, Department of Education, Program in Teaching, Providence, RI 02912. Offers elementary education (MAT); English (MAT); history/social studies (MAT); science (MAT); secondary education (MAT). *Degree requirements:* For master's, student teaching, portfolio. *Entrance requirements:* For master's, GRE General Test, transcript, personal statement, 3 letters of recommendation, interview, writing sample (English applicants only). Additional exam requirements/recommendations for international students: Required—TOEFL (minimum score 577 paper-based). Electronic applications accepted. *Faculty research:* Literacy, English language learners, diversity, special education, biodiversity.

Buffalo State College, State University of New York, The Graduate School, Faculty of Natural and Social Sciences, Department of Biology, Buffalo, NY 14222-1095. Offers biology (MA); secondary education (MS Ed), including biology. *Program availability:* Evening/weekend. *Degree requirements:* For master's, thesis (for some programs), project. *Entrance requirements:* For master's, minimum GPA of 2.75. Additional exam requirements/recommendations for international students: Required—TOEFL (minimum score 550 paper-based).

Buffalo State College, State University of New York, The Graduate School, Faculty of Natural and Social Sciences, Department of Chemistry, Buffalo, NY 14222-1095. Offers chemistry (MA); secondary education (MS Ed), including chemistry. *Program availability:* Part-time, evening/weekend. *Degree requirements:* For master's, thesis (for some programs), project. *Entrance requirements:* For master's, minimum GPA of 2.6, New York teaching certificate (MS Ed). Additional exam requirements/recommendations for international students: Required—TOEFL (minimum score 550 paper-based).

Buffalo State College, State University of New York, The Graduate School, Faculty of Natural and Social Sciences, Department of Earth Science and Science Education, Buffalo, NY 14222-1095. Offers secondary education (MS Ed), including geoscience, science. *Accreditation:* NCATE. *Program availability:* Part-time, evening/weekend. *Degree requirements:* For master's, thesis or alternative, project. *Entrance requirements:* For master's, 36 undergraduate hours in mathematics and science. Additional exam requirements/recommendations for international students: Required—TOEFL (minimum score 550 paper-based).

Buffalo State College, State University of New York, The Graduate School, Faculty of Natural and Social Sciences, Department of Physics, Buffalo, NY 14222-1095. Offers secondary education physics (MS Ed). *Degree requirements:* For master's, project. *Entrance requirements:* For master's, minimum GPA of 2.5, New York State teaching certification. Additional exam requirements/recommendations for international students: Required—TOEFL (minimum score 550 paper-based).

California Baptist University, Program in Education, Riverside, CA 92504-3206. Offers educational leadership (MS); educational leadership for faith-based institutions (MS); educational leadership for public institutions (MS); educational technology (MS); instructional computer applications (MS); international education (MS); leadership and adult learning (MS); leadership and organizational studies (MS); online teaching and learning (MS); reading (MS); science education (MA); special education in mild/moderate disabilities (MS); special education in moderate/severe disabilities (MS); teacher leadership (MS); teaching (MS); teaching and learning (MS). *Program availability:* Part-time, evening/weekend, 100% online, blended/hybrid learning. *Faculty:* 19 full-time (11 women), 36 part-time/adjunct (22 women). *Students:* 232 full-time (182 women), 315 part-time (247 women); includes 264 minority (33 Black or African American, non-Hispanic/Latino; 4 American Indian or Alaska Native, non-Hispanic/Latino; 11 Asian, non-Hispanic/Latino; 186 Hispanic/Latino; 7 Native Hawaiian or other Pacific Islander, non-Hispanic/Latino; 23 Two or more races, non-Hispanic/Latino). Average age 31. 217 applicants, 64% accepted, 129 enrolled. In 2017, 196 master's awarded. *Degree requirements:* For master's, comprehensive exam, project, or thesis. *Entrance requirements:* For master's, minimum undergraduate GPA of 2.75; 500-word essay; three letters of recommendation; two prerequisite courses completed with minimum C grade. Additional exam requirements/recommendations for international students: Required—TOEFL (minimum score 80 iBT). *Application deadline:* For fall admission, 8/1 priority date for domestic students, 7/1 for international students; for spring admission, 12/1 priority date for domestic students, 11/1 for international students. Applications are processed on a rolling basis. Application fee: $45. Electronic applications accepted. *Expenses:* Contact institution. *Financial support:* In 2017–18, 162 students received support. Federal Work-Study and scholarships/grants available. Financial award applicants required to submit CSS PROFILE or FAFSA. *Faculty research:* Leadership development, complexity theory, faith and learning, special education, social and philosophical contexts of education. *Unit head:* Dr. John Shoup, Dean, School of Education, 951-343-4516, E-mail: jshoup@calbaptist.edu. *Application contact:* Gavin Andrew, Graduate Admissions Counselor, 951-552-8437, E-mail: gandrew@calbaptist.edu.
Website: http://www.calbaptist.edu/mastersined/

California State University, Bakersfield, Division of Graduate Studies, School of Natural Sciences, Mathematics, and Engineering, Program in Geological Sciences, Bakersfield, CA 93311. Offers geological sciences (MS); hydrogeology (MS); petroleum geology (MS); science education (MS). *Program availability:* Part-time, evening/weekend. *Faculty:* 5 full-time (0 women). *Students:* 5 full-time (2 women), 10 part-time (3 women); includes 8 minority (1 Black or African American, non-Hispanic/Latino; 1 American Indian or Alaska Native, non-Hispanic/Latino; 6 Hispanic/Latino). Average age 29. 11 applicants, 82% accepted, 7 enrolled. In 2017, 21 master's awarded. *Degree requirements:* For master's, thesis. *Entrance requirements:* For master's, GRE General Test, BS in geology. *Application deadline:* Applications are processed on a rolling basis. Application fee: $55. *Expenses:* Tuition, state resident: full-time $7176; part-time $4164 per year. *Financial support:* In 2017–18, fellowships (averaging $1,850 per year) were awarded; Federal Work-Study, scholarships/grants, and tuition waivers (full and partial)

also available. Financial award application deadline: 3/2; financial award applicants required to submit FAFSA. *Unit head:* Dr. William Krugh, Graduate Coordinator, 661-654-3126, Fax: 661-664-2040, E-mail: wkrugh@csub.edu. *Application contact:* Debbie Blowers, Assistant Director of Admissions and Evaluations, 661-654-3381, E-mail: dblowers@csub.edu.
Website: https://www.csub.edu/geology/Academic%20Programs%20in%20Geology/Graduate%20Students/index.html

California State University, Long Beach, Graduate Studies, College of Natural Sciences and Mathematics, Department of Science Education, Long Beach, CA 90840. Offers MS.

California State University, Northridge, Graduate Studies, Michael D. Eisner College of Education, Department of Secondary Education, Northridge, CA 91330. Offers educational technology (MA); English education (MA); mathematics education (MA); secondary science education (MA); teaching and learning (MA). *Accreditation:* NCATE. *Program availability:* Part-time. *Students:* 9 full-time (5 women), 85 part-time (57 women); includes 37 minority (2 Black or African American, non-Hispanic/Latino; 12 Asian, non-Hispanic/Latino; 20 Hispanic/Latino; 1 Native Hawaiian or other Pacific Islander, non-Hispanic/Latino; 2 Two or more races, non-Hispanic/Latino); 1 international. Average age 37. 63 applicants, 78% accepted, 45 enrolled. *Degree requirements:* For master's, thesis optional. *Entrance requirements:* For master's, GRE General Test or minimum GPA of 3.0. Additional exam requirements/recommendations for international students: Required—TOEFL. *Application deadline:* For fall admission, 11/30 for domestic students. Application fee: $55. *Financial support:* Application deadline: 3/1. *Unit head:* Dr. Julie Gainsburg, Chair, 818-677-2580. *Application contact:* Dr. Michael Rivas, Graduate Advisor, 818-677-6792, E-mail: michael.rivas@csun.edu.
Website: http://www.csun.edu/eisner-education/secondary-education

California University of Pennsylvania, School of Graduate Studies and Research, College of Education and Human Services, Department of Childhood Education, California, PA 15419-1394. Offers early childhood education (M Ed); elementary education (M Ed); STEM education (M Ed). *Accreditation:* NCATE. *Program availability:* Part-time, evening/weekend. *Degree requirements:* For master's, comprehensive exam, thesis optional. *Entrance requirements:* For master's, MAT, PRAXIS, minimum GPA of 3.0, state police clearances. Additional exam requirements/recommendations for international students: Required—TOEFL (minimum score 550 paper-based; 80 iBT). *Application deadline:* For fall admission, 8/1 priority date for domestic and international students; for spring admission, 5/1 priority date for domestic and international students. Applications are processed on a rolling basis. Application fee: $25. Electronic applications accepted. *Financial support:* Applicants required to submit FAFSA. *Faculty research:* English as a second language, adult literacy, emerging literacy, diagnosis and remediation, phonemic awareness. *Unit head:* Dr. Diane H. Nettles, Department Chair, 724-938-4497, E-mail: nettles@calu.edu. *Application contact:* Suzanne C. Powers, Director of Graduate Admissions and Recruitment, 724-938-4029, Fax: 724-938-5712, E-mail: powers_s@cup.edu.
Website: http://www.calu.edu/academics/graduate-programs/elementary/

Cambridge College, School of Education, Boston, MA 02129. Offers autism specialist (M Ed); autism/behavior analyst (M Ed); behavior analyst (Post-Master's Certificate); behavioral management (M Ed); early childhood teacher (M Ed); education specialist in curriculum and instruction (CAGS); educational leadership (Ed D); elementary teacher (M Ed); English as a second language (M Ed, Certificate); general science (M Ed); health education (Post-Master's Certificate); health/family and consumer sciences (M Ed); history (M Ed); individualized (M Ed); information technology literacy (M Ed); instructional technology (M Ed); interdisciplinary studies (M Ed); library teacher (M Ed); literacy education (M Ed); mathematics (M Ed); mathematics specialist (Certificate); middle school mathematics and science (M Ed); school administration (M Ed, CAGS); school guidance counselor (M Ed); school nurse education (M Ed); school social worker/school adjustment counselor (M Ed); special education administrator (CAGS); special education/moderate disabilities (M Ed); teaching skills and methodologies (M Ed). *Program availability:* Part-time, evening/weekend, online learning. *Degree requirements:* For master's, thesis, internship/practicum (licensure program only); for doctorate, thesis/dissertation; for other advanced degree, thesis. *Entrance requirements:* For master's, interview, resume, documentation of licensure, 2 professional references; for doctorate, official transcripts, interview, resume, documentation of licensure (if any), written personal statement/essay, portfolio of scholarly and professional work, qualifying assessment, 2 professional references, health insurance, immunizations form; for other advanced degree, official transcripts, interview, resume, documentation of licensure (if any), written personal statement/essay, 2 professional references, health insurance, immunizations form. Additional exam requirements/recommendations for international students: Required—TOEFL (minimum score 550 paper-based; 79 iBT), Michigan English Language Assessment Battery (minimum score 85); Recommended—IELTS (minimum score 6). Electronic applications accepted. *Expenses:* Contact institution. *Faculty research:* Adult education, accelerated learning, mathematics education, brain compatible learning, special education and law.

Campbellsville University, School of Education, Campbellsville, KY 42718-2799. Offers education (MA); school counseling (MA); school improvement (MA); special education (MASE); special education-teacher leader (MA); teacher leader (MA); teaching (MAT), including middle grades biology, middle grades chemistry, middle grades English. *Accreditation:* NCATE. *Program availability:* Part-time, evening/weekend, 100% online, blended/hybrid learning. *Faculty:* 15 full-time (10 women), 14 part-time/adjunct (9 women). *Students:* 26 full-time (20 women), 155 part-time (122 women); includes 14 minority (13 Black or African American, non-Hispanic/Latino; 1 Hispanic/Latino). Average age 35. 199 applicants, 34% accepted, 57 enrolled. In 2017, 96 master's awarded. *Degree requirements:* For master's, comprehensive exam (for some programs), thesis, research paper. *Entrance requirements:* For master's, GRE or PRAXIS, minimum undergraduate GPA of 2.75, teaching certificate, professional growth plan, letters of recommendation, interview. Additional exam requirements/recommendations for international students: Recommended—TOEFL (minimum score 550 paper-based; 79 iBT), IELTS (minimum score 6). *Application deadline:* Applications are processed on a rolling basis. Application fee: $25. Electronic applications accepted. Application fee is waived when completed online. *Expenses:* $399 per credit hour. *Financial support:* Unspecified assistantships and employee tuition waivers available. Financial award applicants required to submit FAFSA. *Faculty research:* Professional development, curriculum development, school governance, assessment, special education. *Unit head:* Dr. Beverly Ennis, Dean, 270-789-5344, Fax: 270-789-5206, E-mail: bcennis@campbellsville.edu. *Application contact:* Monica Bamwine, Assistant Director of Graduate Admissions, 270-789-5221, Fax: 270-789-5071, E-mail: mkbamwine@campbellsville.edu.

Caribbean University, Graduate School, Bayamón, PR 00960-0493. Offers administration and supervision (MA Ed); criminal justice (MA); curriculum and instruction (MA Ed, PhD), including elementary education (MA Ed), English education (MA Ed), history education (MA Ed), mathematics education (MA Ed), primary education (MA Ed), science education (MA Ed), Spanish education (MA Ed); educational technology in instructional systems (MA Ed); gerontology (MSN); human resources (MBA); museology, archiving and art history (MA Ed); neonatal pediatrics (MSN); physical education (MA Ed); special education (MA Ed). *Entrance requirements:* For master's, interview, minimum GPA of 2.5.

Science Education

Carlow University, College of Learning and Innovation, Program in Curriculum and Instruction, Pittsburgh, PA 15213-3165. Offers autism (M Ed); early childhood leadership (M Ed); online learning instructional design (M Ed); STEM (M Ed). *Program availability:* Part-time, evening/weekend. *Entrance requirements:* For master's, personal essay; resume or curriculum vitae; two recommendations; official transcripts; interview; minimum undergraduate GPA of 3.0. Additional exam requirements/recommendations for international students: Required—TOEFL (minimum score 550 paper-based). *Application deadline:* Applications are processed on a rolling basis. Electronic applications accepted. *Expenses: Tuition:* Full-time $12,103; part-time $825 per credit hour. Tuition and fees vary according to program. *Financial support:* Application deadline: 4/1; applicants required to submit FAFSA. *Unit head:* Dr. Keeley Baronak, Chair, 412-578-6135, Fax: 412-578-6326, E-mail: kobaronak@carlow.edu. *Application contact:* 412-578-6059, Fax: 412-578-6321, E-mail: gradstudies@carlow.edu.
Website: http://www.carlow.edu/Curriculum_and_Instruction_MEd.aspx

Carthage College, Division of Teacher Education, Kenosha, WI 53140. Offers classroom guidance and counseling (M Ed); creative arts (M Ed); gifted and talented children (M Ed); language arts (M Ed); modern language (M Ed); natural sciences (M Ed); reading (M Ed, Certificate); social sciences (M Ed); teacher leadership (M Ed). *Program availability:* Part-time, evening/weekend. *Degree requirements:* For master's, thesis optional. *Entrance requirements:* For master's, MAT, minimum B average, letters of reference.

Catawba College, Department of Teacher Education, Salisbury, NC 28144-2488. Offers STEM education (M Ed). *Accreditation:* NCATE. *Program availability:* Part-time-only. *Faculty:* 3 full-time (2 women), 4 part-time/adjunct (3 women). *Students:* 14 part-time (13 women); includes 1 minority (Black or African American, non-Hispanic/Latino). Average age 30. 7 applicants, 100% accepted, 7 enrolled. *Degree requirements:* For master's, portfolio. *Entrance requirements:* For master's, NTE, PRAXIS II, minimum undergraduate GPA of 3.0, valid teaching license, official transcripts, 3 references, essay, interview, practicing teacher. *Application deadline:* For spring admission, 10/1 for domestic students. Applications are processed on a rolling basis. Application fee: $25. Electronic applications accepted. *Expenses:* $190 per semester hour; $25 per semester parking fee. *Financial support:* In 2017–18, 12 students received support. Scholarships/grants and free tuition (for Rowan-Salisbury teachers only) available. Financial award application deadline: 10/1. *Unit head:* Dr. Kimberly Creamer, Director, Graduate Program, 704-637-4462, Fax: 704-637-4732, E-mail: kcreamer14@catawba.edu. *Application contact:* Jane V. Snider, Administrative Assistant, 704-637-4461, Fax: 704-637-4732, E-mail: jvsnider@catawba.edu.
Website: http://catawba.edu/academics/schools/education/teacher-education/

Central Connecticut State University, School of Graduate Studies, School of Engineering, Science and Technology, Department of Geological Sciences, New Britain, CT 06050-4010. Offers STEM education (MS). *Program availability:* Part-time, evening/weekend. *Students:* 2 applicants, 50% accepted. In 2017, 1 master's awarded. *Degree requirements:* For master's, thesis or alternative, special project. *Entrance requirements:* For master's, minimum undergraduate GPA of 2.7. Additional exam requirements/recommendations for international students: Required—TOEFL (minimum score 550 paper-based; 79 iBT); Recommended—IELTS (minimum score 6.5). *Application deadline:* For fall admission, 8/1 for domestic students, 5/1 for international students; for spring admission, 11/1 for domestic and international students. Applications are processed on a rolling basis. Application fee: $50. Electronic applications accepted. *Expenses: Tuition, area resident:* Full-time $6757. Tuition, state resident: full-time $9750; part-time $374 per credit. Tuition, nonresident: full-time $18,102; part-time $374 per credit. *Required fees:* $4635; $255 per credit. *Financial support:* Application deadline: 3/1; applicants required to submit FAFSA. *Unit head:* Dr. Mark Evans, Chair, 860-832-2930, E-mail: evansmaa@ccsu.edu. *Application contact:* Patricia Gardner, Associate Director of Graduate Studies, 860-832-2350, Fax: 860-832-2362.
Website: http://www.ccsu.edu/geolsci/

Central Connecticut State University, School of Graduate Studies, School of Engineering, Science and Technology, Department of Physics and Engineering Physics, New Britain, CT 06050-4010. Offers science education (Certificate). *Program availability:* Part-time, evening/weekend. *Students:* 2 applicants, 100% accepted. *Degree requirements:* For Certificate, qualifying exam. *Entrance requirements:* Additional exam requirements/recommendations for international students: Required—TOEFL (minimum score 550 paper-based; 79 iBT); Recommended—IELTS (minimum score 6.5). *Application deadline:* For fall admission, 8/1 for domestic students, 5/1 for international students; for spring admission, 11/1 for domestic and international students. Applications are processed on a rolling basis. Application fee: $50. Electronic applications accepted. *Expenses: Tuition, area resident:* Full-time $6757. Tuition, state resident: full-time $9750; part-time $374 per credit. Tuition, nonresident: full-time $18,102; part-time $374 per credit. *Required fees:* $4635; $255 per credit. *Financial support:* Application deadline: 3/1. *Faculty research:* Elementary and secondary science education, particle and solid states, weather patterns, planetary studies. *Unit head:* Dr. Peter LeMaire, Chair, 860-832-2930, E-mail: lemaire@ccsu.edu. *Application contact:* Patricia Gardner, Associate Director of Graduate Studies, 860-832-2350, Fax: 860-832-2362, E-mail: graduateadmissions@ccsu.edu.
Website: http://www.ccsu.edu/physics/

Central Connecticut State University, School of Graduate Studies, School of Engineering, Science and Technology, Department of Technology and Engineering Education, New Britain, CT 06050-4010. Offers STEM education (MS). *Program availability:* Part-time, evening/weekend. *Faculty:* 5 full-time (2 women), 1 part-time/adjunct (0 women). *Students:* 7 full-time (2 women), 30 part-time (18 women); includes 2 minority (both Hispanic/Latino). Average age 35. 16 applicants, 81% accepted, 6 enrolled. In 2017, 25 master's awarded. *Degree requirements:* For master's, thesis or alternative, special project. *Entrance requirements:* For master's, minimum undergraduate GPA of 2.7. Additional exam requirements/recommendations for international students: Required—TOEFL (minimum score 550 paper-based; 79 iBT); Recommended—IELTS (minimum score 6.5). *Application deadline:* For fall admission, 8/1 for domestic students, 5/1 for international students; for spring admission, 11/1 for domestic and international students. Applications are processed on a rolling basis. Application fee: $50. Electronic applications accepted. *Expenses: Tuition, area resident:* Full-time $6757. Tuition, state resident: full-time $9750; part-time $374 per credit. Tuition, nonresident: full-time $18,102; part-time $374 per credit. *Required fees:* $4635; $255 per credit. *Financial support:* In 2017–18, 4 students received support. Career-related internships or fieldwork, Federal Work-Study, scholarships/grants, and unspecified assistantships available. Support available to part-time students. Financial award application deadline: 3/1; financial award applicants required to submit FAFSA. *Faculty research:* Instruction, curriculum development, administration, occupational training. *Unit head:* Dr. James DeLaura, Chair, 860-832-1850, E-mail: delaura@ccsu.edu. *Application contact:* Patricia Gardner, Associate Director of Graduate Studies, 860-832-2350, Fax: 860-832-2362.
Website: http://www.ccsu.edu/teched/

Central Michigan University, College of Graduate Studies, College of Science and Technology, Department of Chemistry, Mount Pleasant, MI 48859. Offers chemistry (MS); teaching chemistry (MA), including teaching college chemistry, teaching high

school chemistry. *Program availability:* Part-time. *Degree requirements:* For master's, comprehensive exam, thesis or alternative. *Entrance requirements:* For master's, GRE. Electronic applications accepted. *Faculty research:* Analytical and organic-inorganic chemistry, biochemistry, catalysis, dendrimer and polymer studies, nanotechnology.

Chatham University, Program in Education, Pittsburgh, PA 15232-2826. Offers early childhood education (MAT); elementary education (MAT); environmental education (K-12) (MAT); secondary art (MAT); secondary biology education (MAT); secondary chemistry education (MAT); secondary English education (MAT); secondary math education (MAT); secondary physics education (MAT); secondary social studies education (MAT); special education (MAT). *Faculty:* 1 (woman) full-time, 15 part-time/adjunct (13 women). *Students:* 31 full-time (23 women), 3 part-time (1 woman); includes 9 minority (8 Black or African American, non-Hispanic/Latino; 1 Hispanic/Latino). Average age 30. 25 applicants, 60% accepted, 9 enrolled. In 2017, 23 master's awarded. *Degree requirements:* For master's, thesis, teaching experience. *Entrance requirements:* For master's, minimum GPA of 3.0, sample of written work, recommendation letters. Additional exam requirements/recommendations for international students: Required—TOEFL (minimum score 600 paper-based; 100 iBT), IELTS (minimum score 7), TWE. *Application deadline:* For fall admission, 4/1 priority date for domestic and international students; for spring admission, 11/1 priority date for domestic students, 10/1 priority date for international students. Applications are processed on a rolling basis. Application fee: $45. Electronic applications accepted. Application fee is waived when completed online. *Expenses: Tuition:* Full-time $16,740; part-time $930 per credit. *Required fees:* $486; $27 per credit. $243 per semester. *Financial support:* Career-related internships or fieldwork available. Financial award applicants required to submit FAFSA. *Faculty research:* Gifted education, environmental education, technology in education, writing as learning, class size and achievement. *Application contact:* Katie Noel, Assistant Director of Graduate Admission, 412-365-2758, Fax: 412-365-1609, E-mail: gradadmission@chatham.edu.
Website: http://www.chatham.edu/mat

The Citadel, The Military College of South Carolina, Citadel Graduate College, Zucker Family School of Education, Charleston, SC 29409. Offers elementary/secondary school administration and supervision (M Ed); elementary/secondary school counseling (M Ed); interdisciplinary STEM education (M Ed); literacy education (M Ed, Graduate Certificate); middle grades (MAT), including English, mathematics, science, social studies; physical education (grades K-12) (MAT); school superintendency (Ed S); secondary education (MAT), including biology, English, mathematics, social studies; student affairs (Graduate Certificate); student affairs and college counseling (M Ed). *Accreditation:* NCATE. *Program availability:* Part-time, evening/weekend, 100% online, blended/hybrid learning. *Degree requirements:* For master's, comprehensive exam (for some programs). *Entrance requirements:* For master's, GRE (minimum combined verbal and quantitative score of 290) or MAT (minimum score 396). Additional exam requirements/recommendations for international students: Required—TOEFL (minimum score 550 paper-based; 79 iBT). Electronic applications accepted. *Expenses:* Tuition, state resident: part-time $587 per credit hour. Tuition, nonresident: part-time $988 per credit hour. *Required fees:* $90 per term.

City College of the City University of New York, Graduate School, School of Education, Department of Secondary Education, Program in Science Education, New York, NY 10031-9198. Offers MA. *Accreditation:* NCATE. *Entrance requirements:* For master's, Liberal Arts and Sciences Test (LAST), Content Specialty Test (CST). Additional exam requirements/recommendations for international students: Required—TOEFL.

Clarion University of Pennsylvania, College of Arts, Education and Sciences, Master of Education Program, Clarion, PA 16214. Offers curriculum and instruction (M Ed); early childhood (M Ed); math education (M Ed); reading (M Ed); science education (M Ed); special education (M Ed); technology (M Ed). *Accreditation:* NCATE. *Program availability:* Part-time, evening/weekend, online only, 100% online, blended/hybrid learning. *Faculty:* 6 full-time (3 women). *Students:* 11 full-time (all women), 101 part-time (82 women); includes 4 minority (2 Black or African American, non-Hispanic/Latino; 1 Hispanic/Latino; 1 Two or more races, non-Hispanic/Latino). Average age 30. 80 applicants, 98% accepted, 33 enrolled. In 2017, 52 master's awarded. *Degree requirements:* For master's, comprehensive exam, thesis, or portfolio. *Entrance requirements:* For master's, minimum QPA of 3.0. Additional exam requirements/recommendations for international students: Required—TOEFL (minimum score 550 paper-based, 80 iBT) or IELTS (7). *Application deadline:* For fall admission, 8/15 priority date for domestic students, 7/15 priority date for international students; for winter admission, 11/1 priority date for domestic students; for spring admission, 1/7 priority date for domestic students, 11/15 priority date for international students; for summer admission, 4/1 priority date for domestic students. Applications are processed on a rolling basis. Application fee: $40. Electronic applications accepted. *Expenses:* $655.05 per credit. *Financial support:* Career-related internships or fieldwork and scholarships/grants available. Support available to part-time students. Financial award application deadline: 3/1; financial award applicants required to submit FAFSA. *Unit head:* Dr. John McCullough, Chair, Department of Education, 814-393-2404, Fax: 814-393-2446, E-mail: gradstudies@clarion.edu. *Application contact:* Dana Bearer, Associate Director for Transfer, Adult, and Graduate Programs, 814-393-2337, Fax: 814-393-2722, E-mail: gradstudies@clarion.edu.

Clark Atlanta University, School of Education, Department of Curriculum and Instruction, Atlanta, GA 30314. Offers special education general curriculum (MA); teaching math and science (MAT). *Program availability:* Part-time. *Faculty:* 5 full-time (4 women), 6 part-time/adjunct (2 women). *Students:* 8 full-time (2 women), 4 part-time (1 woman); includes 6 minority (all Black or African American, non-Hispanic/Latino), 5 international. Average age 34. 10 applicants, 90% accepted, 3 enrolled. In 2017, 1 master's awarded. *Degree requirements:* For master's, one foreign language, comprehensive exam. *Entrance requirements:* For master's, GRE General Test, minimum undergraduate GPA of 2.6. Additional exam requirements/recommendations for international students: Required—TOEFL (minimum score 500 paper-based; 61 iBT). *Application deadline:* For fall admission, 4/1 for domestic and international students; for spring admission, 11/1 for domestic and international students. Applications are processed on a rolling basis. Application fee: $40 ($55 for international students). *Financial support:* Career-related internships or fieldwork, Federal Work-Study, scholarships/grants, and unspecified assistantships available. Support available to part-time students. Financial award application deadline: 4/30; financial award applicants required to submit FAFSA. *Unit head:* Dr. James Young, Chairperson, 404-880-6079, E-mail: jyoung@cau.edu.
Website: http://www.cau.edu/school-of-education/Dept-of-Curriculum-and-Instruction/index.html

Clemson University, Graduate School, College of Engineering, Computing and Applied Sciences, Department of Engineering and Science Education, Clemson, SC 29634. Offers PhD, Certificate. *Faculty:* 7 full-time (all women). *Students:* 8 full-time (all women), 1 (woman) part-time; includes 2 minority (1 Black or African American, non-Hispanic/Latino; 1 Asian, non-Hispanic/Latino). Average age 29. 7 applicants, 57% accepted, 3 enrolled. In 2017, 3 doctorates, 4 other advanced degrees awarded. *Degree requirements:* For doctorate, comprehensive exam, thesis/dissertation, qualifying exam.

Entrance requirements: For doctorate and Certificate, GRE General Test, unofficial transcripts, letters of recommendation. Additional exam requirements/recommendations for international students: Required—TOEFL (minimum score 550 paper-based; 80 iBT), IELTS (minimum score 6.5), PTE (minimum score 54). *Application deadline:* Applications are processed on a rolling basis. Application fee: $80 ($90 for international students). Electronic applications accepted. *Expenses:* $5,767 per semester full-time resident, $10,918 per semester full-time non-resident, $656 per credit hour part-time resident, $1,310 per credit hour part-time non-resident, $915 per credit hour online; other fees may apply per session. *Financial support:* In 2017–18, 11 students received support, including 2 fellowships with partial tuition reimbursements available (averaging $17,000 per year), 6 research assistantships with partial tuition reimbursements available (averaging $20,819 per year), 1 teaching assistantship with partial tuition reimbursement available (averaging $22,000 per year); career-related internships or fieldwork and unspecified assistantships also available. *Total annual research expenditures:* $402,221. *Unit head:* Dr. Cindy Lee, Department Chair, 864-656-1006, E-mail: lc@clemson.edu. *Application contact:* Dr. Lisa Benson, Program Coordinator, 864-656-0417, E-mail: lbenson@clemson.edu.
Website: http://www.clemson.edu/cecas/departments/ese/

Cleveland State University, College of Graduate Studies, College of Education and Human Services, Department of Teacher Education, Cleveland, OH 44115. Offers art education (M Ed); early childhood education (M Ed); foreign language education (M Ed); middle childhood mathematics and science education (M Ed); special education (M Ed), including mild/moderate disabilities, moderate/intensive disabilities; teaching English to speakers of other languages (M Ed). *Program availability:* Part-time, evening/weekend. *Faculty:* 19 full-time (14 women), 32 part-time/adjunct (27 women). *Students:* 80 full-time (60 women), 361 part-time (277 women); includes 119 minority (86 Black or African American, non-Hispanic/Latino; 5 Asian, non-Hispanic/Latino; 16 Hispanic/Latino; 12 Two or more races, non-Hispanic/Latino), 20 international. Average age 34. 177 applicants, 55% accepted, 68 enrolled. In 2017, 137 master's awarded. *Degree requirements:* For master's, comprehensive exam (for some programs), thesis or alternative. *Entrance requirements:* For master's, GRE General Test or MAT, minimum GPA of 2.75. Additional exam requirements/recommendations for international students: Required—TOEFL (minimum score 550 paper-based; 78 iBT), IELTS (minimum score 6). *Application deadline:* For fall admission, 7/1 priority date for domestic students, 5/15 for international students; for spring admission, 11/15 for domestic students, 11/1 for international students; for summer admission, 4/1 for domestic students, 3/15 for international students. Applications are processed on a rolling basis. Application fee: $30. *Financial support:* In 2017–18, 13 research assistantships with full tuition reimbursements (averaging $15,845 per year) were awarded; tuition waivers (partial) and unspecified assistantships also available. Financial award application deadline: 2/15; financial award applicants required to submit FAFSA. *Faculty research:* Early childhood education, literacy education, special education: mild/moderate, moderate/intensive, early childhood intervention specialist; teaching English to speakers of other languages (TESOL). *Total annual research expenditures:* $275,907. *Unit head:* Dr. Tachelle Banks, Department Chairperson, 216-687-4600, Fax: 216-687-5379, E-mail: t.i.banks@csuohio.edu. *Application contact:* Rosalyn Adams, Administrative Coordinator, 216-523-7139, Fax: 216-687-5491, E-mail: r.m.adams@csuohio.edu.
Website: http://www.csuohio.edu/cehs/te/te

The College at Brockport, State University of New York, School of Education, Health, and Human Services, Department of Education and Human Development, Program in Adolescence Education, Brockport, NY 14420-2997. Offers adolescence biology education (MS Ed); adolescence chemistry education (MS Ed); adolescence English (MS Ed); adolescence mathematics (MS Ed); adolescence physics (MS Ed); adolescence social studies education (MS Ed). *Accreditation:* NCATE. *Program availability:* Part-time. *Students:* 50 part-time (28 women); includes 1 minority (Black or African American, non-Hispanic/Latino). 24 applicants, 79% accepted, 11 enrolled. In 2017, 18 master's awarded. *Degree requirements:* For master's, thesis or alternative. *Entrance requirements:* For master's, edTPA, GRE or MAT, minimum GPA of 3.0, letters of recommendation, statement of objectives, current resume. Additional exam requirements/recommendations for international students: Required—TOEFL (minimum score 550 paper-based; 79 iBT), IELTS (minimum score 6.5). *Application deadline:* For fall admission, 3/15 priority date for domestic and international students; for spring admission, 10/15 priority date for domestic and international students; for summer admission, 3/15 priority date for domestic students, 3/13 priority date for international students. Application fee: $80. Electronic applications accepted. *Expenses:* Tuition, state resident: full-time $10,870; part-time $453 per credit hour. Tuition, nonresident: full-time $22,210. *Required fees:* $988; $246 per semester. *Financial support:* Federal Work-Study, scholarships/grants, and unspecified assistantships available. Support available to part-time students. Financial award application deadline: 3/15; financial award applicants required to submit FAFSA. *Unit head:* Dr. Sue Robb, Chairperson, 585-395-5935, Fax: 585-395-2172, E-mail: srobb@brockport.edu. *Application contact:* Anne Walton, Coordinator of Certification and Graduate Advisement, 585-395-2326, Fax: 585-395-2172, E-mail: awalton@brockport.edu.
Website: https://www.brockport.edu/academics/education_human_development/department.html

The College at Brockport, State University of New York, School of Education, Health, and Human Services, Department of Education and Human Development, Program in Inclusive Generalist Education, Brockport, NY 14420-2997. Offers biology (MS Ed, AGC); chemistry (MS Ed, AGC); English (MS Ed, Advanced Certificate); mathematics (MS Ed, Advanced Certificate); science (MS Ed, Advanced Certificate); social studies (MS Ed, Advanced Certificate). *Students:* 61 part-time (30 women); includes 2 minority (1 Black or African American, non-Hispanic/Latino; 1 Asian, non-Hispanic/Latino). 41 applicants, 78% accepted, 25 enrolled. In 2017, 12 master's, 3 AGCs awarded. *Degree requirements:* For master's, thesis or alternative. *Entrance requirements:* For master's, edTPA, GRE or MAT, minimum GPA of 3.0, letters of recommendation, statement of objectives, academic major (or equivalent) in program discipline, current resume. Additional exam requirements/recommendations for international students: Required—TOEFL (minimum score 550 paper-based; 79 iBT), IELTS (minimum score 6.5). *Application deadline:* For fall admission, 3/15 priority date for domestic and international students; for spring admission, 10/15 priority date for domestic and international students; for summer admission, 3/15 for domestic and international students. Application fee: $80. Electronic applications accepted. *Expenses:* Tuition, state resident: full-time $10,870; part-time $453 per credit hour. Tuition, nonresident: full-time $22,210. *Required fees:* $988; $246 per semester. *Financial support:* Federal Work-Study, scholarships/grants, and unspecified assistantships available. Support available to part-time students. Financial award application deadline: 3/15; financial award applicants required to submit FAFSA. *Unit head:* Dr. Sue Robb, Chairperson, 585-395-5935, Fax: 585-395-2171, E-mail: srobb@brockport.edu. *Application contact:* Anne Walton, Coordinator of Graduate Advisement, 585-395-2326, Fax: 585-395-2172, E-mail: awalton@brockport.edu.
Website: https://www.brockport.edu/academics/education_human_development/department.html

College of Charleston, Graduate School, School of Education, Health, and Human Performance, Program in Science and Mathematics for Teachers, Charleston, SC 29424-0001. Offers M Ed. *Accreditation:* NCATE. *Program availability:* Part-time, evening/weekend. *Degree requirements:* For master's, capstone project. *Entrance requirements:* For master's, GRE or PRAXIS, 2 letters of recommendation, copy of teaching certificate. Additional exam requirements/recommendations for international students: Required—TOEFL (minimum score 81 iBT). Electronic applications accepted.

The College of William and Mary, School of Education, Program in Curriculum and Instruction, Williamsburg, VA 23187-8795. Offers elementary education (MA Ed); English as a second language/bilingual education (MA Ed); gifted education (MA Ed); literacy leadership (MA Ed); math specialist (MA Ed); secondary education (MA Ed), including English, foreign language, math, science, social studies; special education (MA Ed). *Accreditation:* NCATE. *Program availability:* Part-time. *Faculty:* 23 full-time (16 women), 40 part-time/adjunct (32 women). *Students:* 85 full-time (63 women), 16 part-time (15 women); includes 18 minority (5 Black or African American, non-Hispanic/Latino; 4 Asian, non-Hispanic/Latino; 7 Hispanic/Latino; 2 Two or more races, non-Hispanic/Latino), 1 international. Average age 27. 152 applicants, 83% accepted, 90 enrolled. In 2017, 67 master's awarded. *Degree requirements:* For master's, project. *Entrance requirements:* For master's, GRE, MAT, PRAXIS Core Academic Skills for Educators, minimum GPA of 2.5. Additional exam requirements/recommendations for international students: Required—TOEFL (minimum score 100 iBT), IELTS (minimum score 7). *Application deadline:* For fall admission, 1/15 for domestic and international students; for spring admission, 10/1 for domestic and international students. Application fee: $50. Electronic applications accepted. *Expenses:* $9,630 resident full-time, $535 resident part-time per credit hour; $25,920 nonresident full-time, $1,265 nonresident part-time per credit hour; $5,944 full-time fees. *Financial support:* In 2017–18, 35 students received support, including 7 research assistantships (averaging $6,678 per year); scholarships/grants and unspecified assistantships also available. Financial award application deadline: 1/15; financial award applicants required to submit FAFSA. *Faculty research:* Educational technology, professional development and evaluation, inclusive education, rural education, education policy. *Unit head:* Dr. Jeremy D. Stoddard, Department Chair, 757-221-2348, E-mail: jdstod@wm.edu. *Application contact:* Dorothy Smith Osborne, Assistant Dean for Academic Programs and Student Services, 757-221-2317, E-mail: dsosbo@wm.edu.
Website: http://education.wm.edu

The Colorado College, Education Department, Experienced Teacher Program, Colorado Springs, CO 80903-3294. Offers arts and humanities (MAT); integrated natural sciences (MAT); liberal arts (MAT); Southwest studies (MAT). Programs offered during summer only. *Program availability:* Part-time. *Degree requirements:* For master's, thesis, oral exam, 50-page paper. *Expenses:* Contact institution.

The Colorado College, Education Department, Program in Secondary Education, Colorado Springs, CO 80903-3294. Offers art teaching (K-12) (MAT); English teaching (MAT); foreign language teaching (MAT); mathematics teaching (MAT); music teaching (MAT); science teaching (MAT); social studies teaching (MAT). *Degree requirements:* For master's, thesis, internship. Electronic applications accepted.

Columbia University, College of Dental Medicine and Graduate School of Arts and Sciences, Programs in Dental Specialties, New York, NY 10027. Offers advanced education in general dentistry (Certificate); biomedical informatics (MA, PhD); endodontics (Certificate); orthodontics (MS, Certificate); periodontics (MS, Certificate); prosthodontics (MS, Certificate); science education (MA). *Degree requirements:* For master's, thesis, presentation of seminar. *Entrance requirements:* For master's, GRE General Test, DDS or equivalent. *Expenses:* Contact institution. *Faculty research:* Analysis of growth/form, pulpal microcirculation, implants, microbiology of oral environment, calcified tissues.

Columbus State University, Graduate Studies, College of Education and Health Professions, Department of Teacher Education, Columbus, GA 31907-5645. Offers curriculum and instruction in accomplished teaching (M Ed); early childhood education (M Ed, MAT, Ed S); middle grades education (M Ed, MAT, Ed S); secondary education (M Ed, MAT, Ed S), including biology (MAT), chemistry (MAT), earth and space science (MAT), English/language arts, general science (M Ed), history (MAT), mathematics, science (Ed S), social science (M Ed, Ed S); special education (M Ed, MAT, Ed S), including general curriculum (M Ed, MAT); teacher leadership (M Ed). *Accreditation:* NCATE. *Program availability:* Part-time, evening/weekend, 100% online, blended/hybrid learning. *Faculty:* 19 full-time (12 women), 24 part-time/adjunct (18 women). *Students:* 99 full-time (76 women), 181 part-time (143 women); includes 109 minority (94 Black or African American, non-Hispanic/Latino; 1 American Indian or Alaska Native, non-Hispanic/Latino; 1 Asian, non-Hispanic/Latino; 6 Hispanic/Latino; 7 Two or more races, non-Hispanic/Latino). Average age 34. 136 applicants, 63% accepted, 56 enrolled. In 2017, 119 master's, 8 other advanced degrees awarded. *Degree requirements:* For Ed S, thesis or alternative. *Entrance requirements:* For master's, GRE General Test, minimum undergraduate GPA of 2.75; for Ed S, GRE General Test, minimum undergraduate GPA of 2.75, graduate 3.0. Additional exam requirements/recommendations for international students: Required—TOEFL (minimum score 550 paper-based; 79 iBT). *Application deadline:* For fall admission, 6/30 for domestic students, 5/1 for international students; for spring admission, 11/1 for domestic and international students; for summer admission, 3/1 for domestic and international students. Applications are processed on a rolling basis. Application fee: $50. Electronic applications accepted. *Expenses:* Tuition, state resident: full-time $3708; part-time $2472 per year. Tuition, nonresident: full-time $14,418; part-time $9612 per year. *International tuition:* $19,218 full-time. *Required fees:* $1605. Tuition and fees vary according to program. *Financial support:* In 2017–18, 45 students received support, including 9 research assistantships with partial tuition reimbursements available (averaging $3,000 per year); career-related internships or fieldwork, Federal Work-Study, institutionally sponsored loans, scholarships/grants, tuition waivers (partial), and unspecified assistantships also available. Support available to part-time students. Financial award application deadline: 5/1; financial award applicants required to submit FAFSA. *Unit head:* Dr. Jan Burcham, Department Chair, 706-507-8519, Fax: 706-568-3134, E-mail: burcham_jan@columbusstate.edu. *Application contact:* Catrina Smith-Edmond, Assistant Director for Graduate and Global Admission, 706-507-8824, Fax: 706-568-5091, E-mail: smithedmond_catrina@columbusstate.edu.
Website: http://te.columbusstate.edu/

Columbus State University, Graduate Studies, College of Letters and Sciences, Department of Earth and Space Sciences, Columbus, GA 31907-5645. Offers natural sciences (MS), including biology, chemistry, environmental science, geosciences. *Program availability:* Part-time, evening/weekend. *Faculty:* 5 full-time (2 women), 4 part-time/adjunct (0 women). *Students:* 15 full-time (9 women), 6 part-time (4 women); includes 4 minority (2 Black or African American, non-Hispanic/Latino; 1 Hispanic/Latino; 1 Two or more races, non-Hispanic/Latino). Average age 26. 25 applicants, 40% accepted, 5 enrolled. In 2017, 5 master's awarded. *Degree requirements:* For master's, thesis. *Entrance requirements:* For master's, GRE General Test, minimum GPA of 3.0. Additional exam requirements/recommendations for international students: Required—TOEFL (minimum score 550 paper-based; 79 iBT). *Application deadline:* For fall admission, 6/30 priority date for domestic students, 5/1 for international students; for spring admission, 11/1 for domestic and international students; for summer admission, 3/1 for domestic and international students. Applications are processed on a rolling

basis. Application fee: $50. Electronic applications accepted. *Expenses:* Tuition, state resident: full-time $3708; part-time $2472 per year. Tuition, nonresident: full-time $14,418; part-time $9612 per year. *International tuition:* $19,218 full-time. *Required fees:* $1605. Tuition and fees vary according to program. *Financial support:* In 2017–18, 2 students received support, including 14 research assistantships with partial tuition reimbursements available (averaging $3,000 per year); career-related internships or fieldwork, Federal Work-Study, institutionally sponsored loans, scholarships/grants, and unspecified assistantships also available. Support available to part-time students. Financial award application deadline: 5/1; financial award applicants required to submit FAFSA. *Unit head:* Dr. Clint Barineau, Department Chair, 706-569-3026, E-mail: barineau_clinton@columbusstate.edu. *Application contact:* Catrina Smith-Edmond, Assistant Director for Graduate and Global Admission, 706-507-8824, Fax: 706-568-5091, E-mail: smithedmond_catrina@columbusstate.edu.
Website: http://ess.columbusstate.edu/

Concordia University, College of Education, Portland, OR 97211-6099. Offers career and technical education (M Ed); curriculum and instruction (M Ed), including adolescent literacy, career and technical education, e-learning/technology education, early childhood education, English for speakers of other languages, English language development, environmental education, mathematics, methods and curriculum, reading, science, teacher leadership, the inclusive classroom; early childhood (MAT); education leadership (Ed D); educational administration (M Ed); elementary education (MAT); secondary education (MAT); special education (M Ed); teacher leadership (Ed D). *Program availability:* Part-time, online learning. *Degree requirements:* For master's, comprehensive exam, work samples/portfolio. *Entrance requirements:* For master's, California Basic Educational Skills Test or PRAXIS I, minimum undergraduate GPA of 2.8, graduate 3.0; 2 letters of recommendation. Additional exam requirements/recommendations for international students: Required—TOEFL (minimum score 525 paper-based). Electronic applications accepted. *Faculty research:* Learner-centered classroom, brain-based learning, future of online learning.

Converse College, Program in Middle Level Education, Spartanburg, SC 29302. Offers language arts/English (MAT); mathematics (MAT); middle level education (M Ed); science (MAT); social studies (MAT). *Unit head:* Lienne Medford, Dean of Graduate Studies and Distance Education, 864-596-9082, E-mail: lienne.medford@converse.edu. *Application contact:* 864-596-9404, E-mail: graduate@converse.edu.

Converse College, Program in Secondary Education, Spartanburg, SC 29302. Offers biology (MAT); chemistry (MAT); English (M Ed, MAT); mathematics (M Ed, MAT); natural sciences (M Ed); social sciences (M Ed, MAT). *Program availability:* Part-time. *Degree requirements:* For master's, capstone paper. *Entrance requirements:* For master's, NTE or PRAXIS II (M Ed), minimum GPA of 2.75, 2 recommendations. *Application deadline:* For fall admission, 8/1 for domestic and international students; for winter admission, 11/15 for domestic and international students; for spring admission, 1/15 for domestic and international students. Applications are processed on a rolling basis. Application fee: $40. Electronic applications accepted. *Financial support:* Available to part-time students. Applicants required to submit FAFSA. *Unit head:* Lienne Medford, Dean of Graduate Studies and Distance Education, 864-596-9082, E-mail: lienne.medford@converse.edu. *Application contact:* 864-596-9404, E-mail: graduate@converse.edu.

Delaware State University, Graduate Programs, College of Education, Health and Public Policy, Program in Science Education, Dover, DE 19901-2277. Offers MA. *Program availability:* Part-time, evening/weekend. *Degree requirements:* For master's, comprehensive exam, thesis optional. *Entrance requirements:* For master's, GRE General Test, minimum GPA of 3.0 in major, 2.75 overall. Electronic applications accepted. *Faculty research:* Science reform in schools, inquiry science.

Delaware State University, Graduate Programs, Department of Biological Sciences, Program in Biology Education, Dover, DE 19901-2277. Offers MS. *Entrance requirements:* Additional exam requirements/recommendations for international students: Required—TOEFL (minimum score 550 paper-based).

Delaware State University, Graduate Programs, Department of Physics, Dover, DE 19901-2277. Offers applied optics (MS); optics (PhD); physics (MS); physics teaching (MS). *Program availability:* Part-time, evening/weekend. *Entrance requirements:* For master's, minimum GPA of 3.0 in major, 2.75 overall. Additional exam requirements/recommendations for international students: Required—TOEFL. Electronic applications accepted. *Faculty research:* Thermal properties of solids, nuclear physics, radiation damage in solids.

DePaul University, College of Science and Health, Chicago, IL 60604. Offers applied mathematics (MS); applied statistics (MS); biological sciences (MA, MS); chemistry (MS); environmental science (MS); mathematics education (MA); mathematics for teaching (MS); nursing (MS); nursing practice (DNP); physics (MS); polymer and coatings science (MS); psychology (MS); pure mathematics (MS); science education (MS); MA/PhD. *Accreditation:* AACN. *Application deadline:* Applications are processed on a rolling basis. Application fee: $40. Electronic applications accepted. *Financial support:* Applicants required to submit FAFSA. *Unit head:* Dr. Gerald P. Koocher, Dean, 773-325-8300. *Application contact:* Ann Spittle, Director of Graduate Admission, 773-325-7315, Fax: 312-476-3244, E-mail: graddepaul@depaul.edu.
Website: http://csh.depaul.edu/

Drake University, School of Education, Des Moines, IA 50311-4516. Offers applied behavior analysis (MS); counseling (MS); education (PhD); education administration (Ed D); educational leadership (MSE, Ed D); effective teaching (MSE); leadership development (MS); literacy (Ed S); literacy education (MSE); rehabilitation administration (MS); rehabilitation placement (MS); special education (MSE); STEM education (MSE); teacher education (5-12) (MAT); teacher education (K-8) (MST); teacher effectiveness and professional development (MSE). *Program availability:* Part-time, evening/weekend. *Degree requirements:* For master's and Ed S, comprehensive exam, internships (for some programs); for doctorate, comprehensive exam, thesis/dissertation, internships (for some programs). *Entrance requirements:* For master's, GRE General Test, MAT, or Drake Writing Assessment, resume, 2 letters of recommendation; for doctorate, GRE General Test or MAT, master's degree, 3 letters of recommendation; for Ed S, GRE General Test or MAT. Additional exam requirements/recommendations for international students: Required—TOEFL (minimum score 550 paper-based). *Application deadline:* For fall admission, 7/1 priority date for domestic students, 6/1 priority date for international students; for spring admission, 11/1 priority date for domestic students, 10/1 priority date for international students. Applications are processed on a rolling basis. Application fee: $25. Electronic applications accepted. *Expenses:* Contact institution. *Financial support:* Research assistantships, career-related internships or fieldwork, and unspecified assistantships available. Support available to part-time students. *Faculty research:* Counseling and rehabilitation, behavioral supports, inquiry-based science methods, teacher quality enhancement. *Unit head:* Dr. Janet McMahill, Dean, 515-271-3829, E-mail: janet.mcmahill@drake.edu.
Website: http://www.drake.edu/soe/

Duquesne University, School of Education, Department of Instruction and Leadership, Program in Secondary Education, Pittsburgh, PA 15282-0001. Offers biology (MS Ed); chemistry (MS Ed); English (MS Ed); K-12 education (MS Ed), including Latin;

mathematics (MS Ed); physics (MS Ed); social studies (MS Ed). *Program availability:* Part-time, evening/weekend. *Faculty:* 5 full-time (4 women). *Students:* 22 full-time (10 women); includes 3 minority (2 Black or African American, non-Hispanic/Latino; 1 Two or more races, non-Hispanic/Latino). Average age 26. 8 applicants, 100% accepted, 5 enrolled. In 2017, 9 master's awarded. *Entrance requirements:* For master's, two letters of recommendation, letter of intent, interview, bachelor's degree. Additional exam requirements/recommendations for international students: Required—TOEFL (minimum score 550 paper-based), IELTS (minimum score 7). *Application deadline:* For fall admission, 9/1 for domestic students; for spring admission, 1/2 for domestic students. Applications are processed on a rolling basis. Application fee: $0. Electronic applications accepted. *Expenses:* $1,259 per credit. *Financial support:* Research assistantships and Federal Work-Study available. Support available to part-time students. *Faculty research:* Factors that create highly effective teachers; how to best support teachers to support students in reform-oriented environments; urban education; models of teacher leadership; improving instruction in mathematics/science/social studies/English. *Unit head:* Dr. Melissa Boston, Associate Dean for Teacher Education/Professor, 412-396.6109, Fax: 412-396-5585, E-mail: bostonm@duq.edu. *Application contact:* Kelly McGinley, Graduate Admissions Assistant, 412-396-1559, Fax: 412-396-5585, E-mail: mcginleyk@duq.edu.
Website: http://www.duq.edu/academics/schools/education/graduate-programs-education/ms-ed-secondary-education

East Carolina University, Graduate School, College of Education, Department of Mathematics, Science, and Instructional Technology Education, Greenville, NC 27858-4353. Offers distance learning and administration (Certificate); elementary mathematics education (Certificate); instructional technology (MA Ed, MS); mathematics education (MA Ed); science education (MA Ed, MAT); special endorsement in computer education (Certificate). *Program availability:* Part-time, evening/weekend. *Students:* 12 full-time (10 women), 202 part-time (153 women); includes 49 minority (31 Black or African American, non-Hispanic/Latino; 2 American Indian or Alaska Native, non-Hispanic/Latino; 2 Asian, non-Hispanic/Latino; 9 Hispanic/Latino; 5 Two or more races, non-Hispanic/Latino). Average age 38. 56 applicants, 100% accepted, 50 enrolled. In 2017, 76 master's, 30 other advanced degrees awarded. *Degree requirements:* For master's, comprehensive exam, thesis optional. *Entrance requirements:* For master's, GRE General Test or MAT, interview, minimum GPA of 2.5, bachelor's degree in related field, teaching license (MA Ed). Additional exam requirements/recommendations for international students: Required—TOEFL. *Application deadline:* For fall admission, 6/1 priority date for domestic students. Applications are processed on a rolling basis. Application fee: $75. *Expenses:* Tuition, state resident: full-time $4749; part-time $297 per credit hour. Tuition, nonresident: full-time $17,898; part-time $1119 per credit hour. *Required fees:* $2691; $224 per credit hour. Part-time tuition and fees vary according to course load and program. *Financial support:* Research assistantships, teaching assistantships, and Federal Work-Study available. Support available to part-time students. Financial award application deadline: 6/1. *Unit head:* Susan Ganter, Chair, 252-737-3001, E-mail: ganters@ecu.edu.
Website: http://www.ecu.edu/cs-educ/msite/

Eastern Kentucky University, The Graduate School, College of Education, Department of Curriculum and Instruction, Program in Secondary and Higher Education, Richmond, KY 40475-3102. Offers secondary education (MA Ed), including agricultural education, art education, biological sciences education, business education, English education, geography education, history education, home economics education, industrial education, mathematical sciences education, physical education, school health education. *Accreditation:* NCATE. *Program availability:* Part-time. *Entrance requirements:* For master's, GRE General Test, minimum GPA of 2.5.

Eastern Michigan University, Graduate School, College of Arts and Sciences, Department of Biology, Ypsilanti, MI 48197. Offers community college biology teaching (MS); general biology (MS). *Program availability:* Part-time, evening/weekend, online learning. *Faculty:* 24 full-time (7 women). *Students:* 7 full-time (3 women), 26 part-time (11 women); includes 7 minority (1 Black or African American, non-Hispanic/Latino; 3 Asian, non-Hispanic/Latino; 1 Hispanic/Latino; 2 Two or more races, non-Hispanic/Latino), 3 international. Average age 27. 57 applicants, 61% accepted, 18 enrolled. In 2017, 23 master's awarded. *Entrance requirements:* For master's, GRE General Test, GRE Subject Test. Additional exam requirements/recommendations for international students: Required—TOEFL. *Application deadline:* Applications are processed on a rolling basis. Application fee: $45. *Financial support:* Fellowships, research assistantships with full tuition reimbursements, teaching assistantships with full tuition reimbursements, career-related internships or fieldwork, Federal Work-Study, institutionally sponsored loans, scholarships/grants, tuition waivers (partial), and unspecified assistantships available. Support available to part-time students. Financial award applicants required to submit FAFSA. *Unit head:* Dr. Marianne Laporte, Department Head, 734-487-4242, E-mail: mlaporte@emich.edu. *Application contact:* Dr. David Kass, Graduate Coordinator, 734-487-4242, Fax: 734-487-9235, E-mail: dkass@emich.edu.
Website: http://www.emich.edu/biology

Eastern Michigan University, Graduate School, College of Arts and Sciences, Department of Geography and Geology, Ypsilanti, MI 48197. Offers earth science education (MS); geographic information systems (MS, Graduate Certificate), including geographic information systems (MS), geographic information systems for educators (Graduate Certificate), geographic information systems for professionals (Graduate Certificate); historic preservation (MS, Graduate Certificate), including heritage interpretation and museum practice (MS), historic preservation (Graduate Certificate), preservation planning and administration (MS), recording, documentation and digital cultural heritage (MS); urban and regional planning (MS, Graduate Certificate), including transportation planning and modeling (Graduate Certificate), urban and regional planning (MS). *Program availability:* Part-time, evening/weekend, online learning. *Faculty:* 20 full-time (5 women). *Students:* 18 full-time (10 women), 67 part-time (37 women); includes 15 minority (5 Black or African American, non-Hispanic/Latino; 1 Asian, non-Hispanic/Latino; 4 Hispanic/Latino; 5 Two or more races, non-Hispanic/Latino), 14 international. Average age 34. 51 applicants, 75% accepted, 20 enrolled. In 2017, 34 master's, 4 other advanced degrees awarded. *Entrance requirements:* Additional exam requirements/recommendations for international students: Required—TOEFL. *Application deadline:* Applications are processed on a rolling basis. Application fee: $45. *Financial support:* Fellowships, research assistantships with full tuition reimbursements, teaching assistantships with full tuition reimbursements, career-related internships or fieldwork, Federal Work-Study, institutionally sponsored loans, scholarships/grants, tuition waivers (partial), and unspecified assistantships available. Support available to part-time students. Financial award applicants required to submit FAFSA. *Unit head:* Dr. Richard Sambroo, Department Head, 734-487-0218, Fax: 734-487-6979, E-mail: rsambroo@emich.edu.
Website: http://www.emich.edu/geo/

Eastern University, Graduate Education Programs, St. Davids, PA 19087-3696. Offers ESL program specialist (K-12) (Certificate); general supervisor (PreK-12) (Certificate); health and physical education (K-12) (Certificate); middle level (4-8) (Certificate); multicultural education (M Ed) (Certificate); music (K-12) (Certificate); Pre K-4 (Certificate); Pre K-4

with special education (Certificate); reading (M Ed); reading specialist (K-12) (Certificate); reading supervisor (K-12) (Certificate); school counseling (MA, CAGS); school principalship (preK-12) (Certificate); school psychology (MA, CAGS); secondary biology education (7-12) (Certificate); secondary chemistry education (7-12) (Certificate); secondary communication education (7-12) (Certificate); secondary English education (7-12) (Certificate); secondary math education (7-12) (Certificate); secondary social studies education (7-12) (Certificate); special education (M Ed); special education (7-12) (Certificate); special education (Pre K-8) (Certificate); special education supervisor (K-12) (Certificate); TESOL (M Ed); world language (Certificate), including Spanish. *Program availability:* Part-time, evening/weekend, online learning. *Students:* 46 full-time (40 women), 115 part-time (93 women); includes 65 minority (42 Black or African American, non-Hispanic/Latino; 3 Asian, non-Hispanic/Latino; 14 Hispanic/Latino; 6 Two or more races, non-Hispanic/Latino), 1 international. Average age 32. In 2017, 72 master's awarded. *Entrance requirements:* Additional exam requirements/recommendations for international students: Required—TOEFL. *Application deadline:* Applications are processed on a rolling basis. Application fee: $35. Electronic applications accepted. Application fee is waived when completed online. *Expenses:* Contact institution. *Unit head:* Michael Dziedziak, Executive Director of Enrollment, 800-452-0996, E-mail: gpsadmissions@eastern.edu.
Website: https://www.eastern.edu/academics/programs/education-department-graduate-programs/graduate-programs

Elizabeth City State University, Department of Mathematics and Computer Science, Master of Science in Biology Program, Elizabeth City, NC 27909-7806. Offers biological sciences (MS); biology education (MS). *Program availability:* Part-time, evening/weekend. *Faculty:* 8 full-time (1 woman), 1 (woman) part-time/adjunct. *Students:* 3 full-time (1 woman), 17 part-time (11 women); includes 14 minority (12 Black or African American, non-Hispanic/Latino; 1 Asian, non-Hispanic/Latino; 1 Two or more races, non-Hispanic/Latino). Average age 30. 10 applicants, 70% accepted, 5 enrolled. In 2017, 10 master's awarded. *Degree requirements:* For master's, thesis. *Entrance requirements:* For master's, GRE, minimum GPA of 3.0, 3 letters of recommendation, 2 official transcripts from all undergraduate/graduate schools attended, typewritten one-page expository description of student educational preparation, research interests and career aspirations. Additional exam requirements/recommendations for international students: Required—TOEFL (minimum score 550 paper-based, 80 iBT) or IELTS (minimum score 6.5). *Application deadline:* For fall admission, 7/15 priority date for domestic and international students; for spring admission, 11/15 priority date for domestic and international students; for summer admission, 3/15 priority date for domestic and international students. Applications are processed on a rolling basis. Application fee: $30. Electronic applications accepted. Tuition and fees vary according to course load and program. *Financial support:* In 2017–18, 18 students received support. Scholarships/grants available. Financial award application deadline: 6/30; financial award applicants required to submit FAFSA. *Faculty research:* Apoptosis and cancer, plant bioengineering, development of biofuels, microbial degradation, developmental toxicology. *Unit head:* Dr. Gloria Payne, Chair, 252-335-3595, Fax: 252-335-3697, E-mail: gepayne@ecsu.edu.

Elms College, Division of Education, Chicopee, MA 01013-2839. Offers early childhood education (MAT); education (M Ed, CAGS); elementary education (MAT); English as a second language (MAT); reading (MAT); secondary education (MAT), including biology education, English education, Spanish education; secondary education (MAT). *Program availability:* Part-time, evening/weekend. *Faculty:* 4 full-time (all women), 8 part-time/adjunct (7 women). *Students:* 6 full-time (4 women), 127 part-time (107 women); includes 8 minority (2 Asian, non-Hispanic/Latino; 6 Hispanic/Latino). Average age 33. 42 applicants, 88% accepted, 36 enrolled. In 2017, 50 master's, 6 other advanced degrees awarded. *Degree requirements:* For master's, thesis (for some programs). *Entrance requirements:* For master's, Massachusetts Educators Certification Test, minimum GPA of 3.0; for CAGS, master's degree in education. Additional exam requirements/recommendations for international students: Required—TOEFL. *Application deadline:* For fall admission, 7/1 priority date for domestic students; for spring admission, 11/1 priority date for domestic students. Applications are processed on a rolling basis. Application fee: $30. *Expenses: Tuition:* Full-time $13,860; part-time $770 per credit hour. *Required fees:* $200. Tuition and fees vary according to degree level and program. *Financial support:* In 2017–18, 2 teaching assistantships with partial tuition reimbursements were awarded. Financial award applicants required to submit FAFSA. *Unit head:* Dr. Mary Janeczek, Chair, Division of Education, 413-594-2761, Fax: 413-592-4871, E-mail: janeczeke@elms.edu. *Application contact:* School of Graduate and Professional Studies, 413-265-2445, E-mail: graduateeducation@elms.edu.

Fairleigh Dickinson University, Metropolitan Campus, University College: Arts, Sciences, and Professional Studies, School of Natural Sciences, Program in Science, Teaneck, NJ 07666-1914. Offers MA. *Accreditation:* TEAC.

Fitchburg State University, Division of Graduate and Continuing Education, Program in Middle School Education, Fitchburg, MA 01420-2697. Offers English (M Ed); general science (M Ed); history (M Ed); math (M Ed). *Accreditation:* NCATE. *Program availability:* Part-time, evening/weekend. *Students:* 15 full-time (7 women), 5 part-time (2 women); includes 3 minority (2 Black or African American, non-Hispanic/Latino; 1 Two or more races, non-Hispanic/Latino). Average age 32. 11 applicants, 100% accepted, 10 enrolled. In 2017, 4 master's awarded. *Entrance requirements:* Additional exam requirements/recommendations for international students: Required—TOEFL (minimum score 550 paper-based; 79 iBT). *Application deadline:* For fall admission, 7/15 for international students; for spring admission, 12/1 for international students. Applications are processed on a rolling basis. Application fee: $50. Electronic applications accepted. *Expenses:* Contact institution. *Financial support:* In 2017–18, research assistantships with partial tuition reimbursements (averaging $5,500 per year) were awarded; Federal Work-Study, scholarships/grants, and unspecified assistantships also available. Support available to part-time students. Financial award application deadline: 3/1; financial award applicants required to submit FAFSA. *Unit head:* William Cortezia, Chair, 978-665-3193, Fax: 978-665-3658, E-mail: gce@fitchburgstate.edu. *Application contact:* Jinawa McNeil, Director of Admissions, 978-665-3140, Fax: 978-665-4540, E-mail: admissions@fitchburgstate.edu.
Website: http://www.fitchburgstate.edu

Fitchburg State University, Division of Graduate and Continuing Education, Program in Science Education, Fitchburg, MA 01420-2697. Offers M Ed. *Accreditation:* NCATE. *Program availability:* Part-time, evening/weekend. *Faculty:* 1 (woman) full-time. *Students:* 3 part-time (0 women); includes 1 minority (Two or more races, non-Hispanic/Latino). Average age 29. 5 applicants, 100% accepted, 3 enrolled. In 2017, 3 master's awarded. *Entrance requirements:* Additional exam requirements/recommendations for international students: Required—TOEFL (minimum score 550 paper-based; 79 iBT). *Application deadline:* For fall admission, 7/15 for international students; for spring admission, 12/1 for international students. Applications are processed on a rolling basis. Application fee: $50. Electronic applications accepted. *Expenses:* Contact institution. *Financial support:* In 2017–18, research assistantships with partial tuition reimbursements (averaging $5,500 per year) were awarded; Federal Work-Study, scholarships/grants, and unspecified assistantships also available. Support available to part-time students. Financial award application deadline: 3/1; financial award applicants

required to submit FAFSA. *Unit head:* Dr. Lisa Grimm, Chair, 978-665-3245, Fax: 978-665-3658, E-mail: gce@fitchburgstate.edu. *Application contact:* Jinawa McNeil, Director of Admissions, 978-665-3140, Fax: 978-665-4540, E-mail: admissions@fitchburgstate.edu.
Website: http://www.fitchburgstate.edu

Fitchburg State University, Division of Graduate and Continuing Education, Programs in Biology and Teaching Biology (Secondary Level), Fitchburg, MA 01420-2697. Offers biology (MA). *Accreditation:* NCATE. *Program availability:* Part-time, evening/weekend. *Faculty:* 1 (woman) full-time. *Students:* 4 part-time (1 woman); includes 1 minority (Black or African American, non-Hispanic/Latino). Average age 34. 1 applicant, 100% accepted, 1 enrolled. In 2017, 5 master's awarded. *Entrance requirements:* Additional exam requirements/recommendations for international students: Required—TOEFL (minimum score 550 paper-based; 79 iBT). *Application deadline:* For fall admission, 7/15 for international students; for spring admission, 12/1 for international students. Applications are processed on a rolling basis. Application fee: $50. Electronic applications accepted. *Expenses:* Contact institution. *Financial support:* In 2017–18, research assistantships with partial tuition reimbursements (averaging $5,500 per year) were awarded; Federal Work-Study, scholarships/grants, and unspecified assistantships also available. Support available to part-time students. Financial award application deadline: 3/1; financial award applicants required to submit FAFSA. *Unit head:* Dr. Lisa Grimm, Chair, 978-665-3245, Fax: 978-665-3658, E-mail: gce@fitchburgstate.edu. *Application contact:* Jinawa McNeil, Director of Admissions, 978-665-3140, Fax: 978-665-4540, E-mail: admissions@fitchburgstate.edu.

Florida Agricultural and Mechanical University, Division of Graduate Studies, Research, and Continuing Education, College of Education, Program in Secondary Education and Foundation, Tallahassee, FL 32307-3200. Offers biology (M Ed); chemistry (MS Ed); English (MS Ed); history (MS Ed); math (MS Ed); physics (MS Ed). *Accreditation:* NCATE. *Degree requirements:* For master's, thesis (for some programs). *Entrance requirements:* For master's, GRE General Test, minimum GPA of 3.0. Additional exam requirements/recommendations for international students: Required—TOEFL.

Florida Atlantic University, Charles E. Schmidt College of Science, Department of Biological Sciences, Boca Raton, FL 33431-0991. Offers biology (MS, MST). *Program availability:* Part-time. *Faculty:* 42 full-time (16 women), 1 part-time/adjunct (0 women). *Students:* 88 full-time (47 women), 65 part-time (38 women); includes 43 minority (6 Black or African American, non-Hispanic/Latino; 7 Asian, non-Hispanic/Latino; 20 Hispanic/Latino; 10 Two or more races, non-Hispanic/Latino), 13 international. Average age 28. 113 applicants, 30% accepted, 34 enrolled. In 2017, 44 master's awarded. *Degree requirements:* For master's, thesis (for some programs). *Entrance requirements:* For master's, GRE General Test, minimum GPA of 3.0. Additional exam requirements/recommendations for international students: Required—TOEFL (minimum score 500 paper-based; 61 iBT), IELTS (minimum score 6). *Application deadline:* For fall admission, 3/15 for domestic and international students; for spring admission, 10/1 for domestic and international students. Application fee: $30. *Expenses:* Tuition, state resident: full-time $7400; part-time $369.82 per credit. Tuition, nonresident: full-time $20,496; part-time $1042.81 per credit. *Financial support:* Fellowships, research assistantships, teaching assistantships, career-related internships or fieldwork, and Federal Work-Study available. *Faculty research:* Ecology of the Everglades, molecular biology and biotechnology, marine biology. *Unit head:* Rodney K. Murphey, Chair, E-mail: rmurphey@fau.edu.
Website: http://www.science.fau.edu/biology/

Florida Atlantic University, Charles E. Schmidt College of Science, Department of Physics, Boca Raton, FL 33431-0991. Offers physics (MS, MST, PhD). *Program availability:* Part-time. *Faculty:* 13 full-time (1 woman), 3 part-time/adjunct (1 woman). *Students:* 24 full-time (10 women), 17 part-time (5 women); includes 3 minority (all Hispanic/Latino), 27 international. Average age 31. 31 applicants, 55% accepted, 15 enrolled. In 2017, 8 master's, 5 doctorates awarded. *Entrance requirements:* For master's, GRE General Test, minimum GPA of 3.0; for doctorate, GRE General Test. Additional exam requirements/recommendations for international students: Required—TOEFL (minimum score 500 paper-based; 61 iBT), IELTS (minimum score 6). *Application deadline:* For fall admission, 7/1 for domestic students, 2/15 for international students; for spring admission, 11/1 for domestic students, 7/15 for international students. Applications are processed on a rolling basis. Application fee: $30. *Expenses:* Tuition, state resident: full-time $7400; part-time $369.82 per credit. Tuition, nonresident: full-time $20,496; part-time $1042.81 per credit. *Financial support:* Fellowships, research assistantships, teaching assistantships, Federal Work-Study, and unspecified assistantships available. *Faculty research:* Astrophysics, spectroscopy, mathematical physics, theory of metals, superconductivity. *Unit head:* Luc Wille, Professor/Chair. *Application contact:* Zia Smith, 561-297-3380, E-mail: zasmith@fau.edu.
Website: http://physics.fau.edu/

Florida Atlantic University, College of Education, Department of Teaching and Learning, Boca Raton, FL 33431-0991. Offers curriculum and instruction (M Ed), including art, biology, chemistry, English, French, German, mathematics, music, physics, Pre-K and primary education, reading, social sciences, Spanish; elementary education (M Ed); environmental education (M Ed); reading education (M Ed); social foundations of education (M Ed), including educational psychology, educational technology, multilingual education. *Accreditation:* NCATE. *Program availability:* Part-time, evening/weekend. *Faculty:* 13 full-time (10 women), 1 part-time/adjunct (0 women). *Students:* 26 full-time (22 women), 43 part-time (39 women); includes 19 minority (9 Black or African American, non-Hispanic/Latino; 1 Asian, non-Hispanic/Latino; 8 Hispanic/Latino; 1 Two or more races, non-Hispanic/Latino), 3 international. Average age 30. 91 applicants, 57% accepted, 33 enrolled. In 2017, 25 master's awarded. *Entrance requirements:* For master's, GRE General Test, minimum GPA of 3.0 in last 2 years of undergraduate course work. Additional exam requirements/recommendations for international students: Required—TOEFL (minimum score 500 paper-based; 61 iBT), IELTS (minimum score 6). *Application deadline:* For fall admission, 7/1 for domestic students, 2/15 for international students; for spring admission, 11/1 for domestic students, 7/15 for international students. Applications are processed on a rolling basis. Application fee: $30. *Expenses:* Tuition, state resident: full-time $7400; part-time $369.82 per credit. Tuition, nonresident: full-time $20,496; part-time $1042.81 per credit. *Financial support:* Fellowships with partial tuition reimbursements, research assistantships with partial tuition reimbursements, teaching assistantships with partial tuition reimbursements, career-related internships or fieldwork, scholarships/grants, and unspecified assistantships available. *Faculty research:* Technology, teaching English to speakers of other languages, math teaching, electronic portfolio assessment, global perspectives through social studies. *Unit head:* Dr. Barbara Ridener, Chairperson, 561-297-3588, E-mail: bridener@fau.edu. *Application contact:* Dr. Eliah Watlington, Associate Dean, 561-296-8520, Fax: 261-297-2991, E-mail: ewatling@fau.edu.
Website: http://www.coe.fau.edu/academicdepartments/tl/

Florida Gulf Coast University, College of Education, Program in Curriculum and Instruction, Fort Myers, FL 33965-6565. Offers elementary education (M Ed); English

Science Education

education (M Ed); English speakers of other languages endorsement (M Ed); gifted education (M Ed); mathematics education (M Ed); middle school education (M Ed); reading education (M Ed); science education (M Ed); social science education (M Ed); special education (M Ed). *Program availability:* Part-time, evening/weekend, online learning. *Faculty:* 27 full-time (19 women), 44 part-time/adjunct (30 women). *Students:* 3 full-time (all women), 16 part-time (14 women); includes 4 minority (2 Black or African American, non-Hispanic/Latino; 2 Hispanic/Latino). Average age 30. 6 applicants, 100% accepted, 5 enrolled. In 2017, 4 master's awarded. *Degree requirements:* For master's, final project or portfolio. *Entrance requirements:* For master's, GRE General Test, MAT, minimum undergraduate GPA of 3.0 in last 2 years. Additional exam requirements/recommendations for international students: Required—TOEFL (minimum score 550 paper-based). *Application deadline:* For fall admission, 2/15 priority date for domestic students, 5/1 for international students; for spring admission, 12/1 for domestic students, 9/15 for international students. Applications are processed on a rolling basis. Application fee: $30. Electronic applications accepted. *Expenses:* Tuition, state resident: part-time $290 per credit hour. Tuition, nonresident: part-time $1173 per credit hour. *Required fees:* $127 per credit hour. Tuition and fees vary according to course load. *Financial support:* In 2017–18, 2 students received support. Application deadline: 6/30; applicants required to submit FAFSA. *Faculty research:* Internet in schools, technology in pre-service and in-service teacher training. *Unit head:* Dr. Vickie Johnston, Instructor, 239-590-7754, Fax: 239-590-7801, E-mail: vjohnston@fgcu.edu. *Application contact:* Keiana Desmore, Adviser/Counselor, 239-590-7759, Fax: 239-590-7801, E-mail: kdesmore@fgcu.edu. Website: http://coe.fgcu.edu/c-imed/

Florida Institute of Technology, College of Science, Program in Elementary Science Education, Melbourne, FL 32901-6975. Offers M Ed. *Program availability:* Part-time. *Students:* Average age 25. 2 applicants. *Degree requirements:* For master's, comprehensive exam, thesis or alternative, 30 credit hours, minimum GPA of 3.0. *Entrance requirements:* For master's, minimum GPA of 3.0, 3 letters of recommendation, resume, statement of objectives. Additional exam requirements/recommendations for international students: Required—TOEFL (minimum score 550 paper-based; 79 iBT). *Application deadline:* Applications are processed on a rolling basis. Electronic applications accepted. *Expenses: Tuition:* Part-time $1241 per credit hour. Part-time tuition and fees vary according to campus/location. *Financial support:* Applicants required to submit FAFSA. *Unit head:* Dr. Kastro Hamed, Department Head, 321-674-7206, E-mail: khamed@fit.edu. *Application contact:* Cheryl A. Brown, Associate Director of Graduate Admissions, 321-674-7581, Fax: 321-723-9468, E-mail: cbrown@fit.edu. Website: http://www.fit.edu/programs/8118/med-elementary-science-education#.VT_jIU10ypo

Florida Institute of Technology, College of Science, Program in Science Education, Melbourne, FL 32901-6975. Offers MS, PhD, Ed S. *Students:* Average age 38. 24 applicants, 46% accepted, 6 enrolled. In 2017, 1 master's, 3 doctorates, 2 other advanced degrees awarded. *Degree requirements:* For master's, comprehensive exam (for some programs), thesis optional, minimum of 30 credit hours; for doctorate, comprehensive exam, thesis/dissertation, minimum of 42 credit hours; for Ed S, comprehensive exam, thesis or alternative, minimum GPA of 3.0, minimum of 30 credit hours. *Entrance requirements:* For master's, resume, statement of objectives; for doctorate, master's degree in science, technology, aeronautics, or science education with minimum GPA of 3.2 (aeronautics degree must have FAA certification and experience); 3 letters of recommendation; resume; statement of objectives; for Ed S, master's degree in science or education, 3 letters of recommendation, resume, statement of objectives. Additional exam requirements/recommendations for international students: Required—TOEFL (minimum score 550 paper-based; 79 iBT). *Application deadline:* Applications are processed on a rolling basis. Electronic applications accepted. *Expenses: Tuition:* Part-time $1241 per credit hour. Part-time tuition and fees vary according to campus/location. *Financial support:* Applicants required to submit FAFSA. *Unit head:* Dr. Kastro Hamed, Department Head, 321-674-7206, E-mail: khamed@fit.edu. *Application contact:* Cheryl A. Brown, Associate Director of Graduate Admissions, 321-674-7581, Fax: 321-723-9468, E-mail: cbrown@fit.edu. Website: http://cos.fit.edu/education/

Florida Institute of Technology, College of Science, Program in Science Education: Informal Science Education, Melbourne, FL 32901-6975. Offers MS. *Students:* 2 applicants, 50% accepted. *Degree requirements:* For master's, comprehensive exam (for some programs), thesis optional, minimum of 30 credit hours. *Entrance requirements:* For master's, resume, statement of objectives, bachelor's degree in either science or secondary school science education. Additional exam requirements/recommendations for international students: Required—TOEFL (minimum score 550 paper-based; 79 iBT). *Application deadline:* Applications are processed on a rolling basis. Electronic applications accepted. *Expenses: Tuition:* Part-time $1241 per credit hour. Part-time tuition and fees vary according to campus/location. *Financial support:* Applicants required to submit FAFSA. *Unit head:* Dr. Kastro Hamed, Department Head, 321-674-7206, E-mail: khamed@fit.edu. *Application contact:* Cheryl A. Brown, Associate Director of Graduate Admissions, 321-674-7581, Fax: 321-723-9468, E-mail: cbrown@fit.edu. Website: http://cos.fit.edu/education/

Florida International University, College of Arts, Sciences, and Education, Department of Teaching and Learning, Miami, FL 33199. Offers art education (MA, MS); curriculum and instruction (MS, Ed D, PhD, Ed S), including curriculum development (MS), elementary education (MS), English education (MS), learning technologies (MS), mathematics education (MS), modern language education (MS), physical education (MS), science education (MS), social studies education (MS), special education (MS); early childhood education (MS); exceptional student education (Ed D); foreign language education (MS), including foreign language education, teaching English to speakers of other languages (TESOL); language, literacy and culture (PhD); mathematics, science, and learning technologies (PhD); physical education (MS), including sport and fitness; reading education (MS). *Program availability:* Part-time, evening/weekend. *Faculty:* 60 full-time (41 women), 112 part-time/adjunct (77 women). *Students:* 165 full-time (139 women), 191 part-time (148 women); includes 270 minority (56 Black or African American, non-Hispanic/Latino; 12 Asian, non-Hispanic/Latino; 191 Hispanic/Latino; 11 Two or more races, non-Hispanic/Latino), 13 international. Average age 34. 238 applicants, 68% accepted, 107 enrolled. In 2017, 184 master's, 15 doctorates awarded. *Degree requirements:* For doctorate, comprehensive exam, thesis/dissertation. *Entrance requirements:* For master's, GRE General Test, Florida General Knowledge Test or Florida College Level Academic Skills Test; for doctorate and Ed S, GRE General Test. Additional exam requirements/recommendations for international students: Required—TOEFL (minimum score 550 paper-based; 80 iBT), IELTS (minimum score 6.3). *Application deadline:* For fall admission, 6/1 priority date for domestic students, 4/1 for international students; for winter admission, 10/1 priority date for domestic students, 9/1 for international students; for spring admission, 3/1 priority date for domestic students, 2/1 for international students. Applications are processed on a rolling basis. Application fee: $30. Electronic applications accepted. *Expenses:* Tuition, state resident: full-time $8912; part-time $446 per credit hour. Tuition, nonresident: full-time $21,393; part-time $992 per credit hour. *Required fees:* $390; $195 per semester. *Financial support:* Research assistantships with tuition reimbursements and teaching assistantships with tuition reimbursements available. *Unit*

head: Dr. Lynn Miller, Chair, 305-348-2005, Fax: 305-348-2086, E-mail: lynne.miller@fiu.edu. *Application contact:* Nanett Rojas, Assistant Director, Graduate Admissions, 305-348-7464, Fax: 305-348-7441, E-mail: gradadm@fiu.edu. Website: https://tl.fiu.edu/

Florida State University, The Graduate School, College of Arts and Sciences, Department of Biological Science, Master's in Science Teaching Program, Tallahassee, FL 32306. Offers MST. *Faculty:* 2 full-time (both women). *Students:* 5 full-time (all women); includes 1 minority (Hispanic/Latino). Average age 27. In 2017, 3 master's awarded. *Degree requirements:* For master's, thesis or alternative, teacher work sample (action research). *Entrance requirements:* For master's, GRE, minimum upper-level undergraduate GPA of 3.0. *Application deadline:* For fall admission, 7/1 for domestic students; for spring admission, 11/1 for domestic students; for summer admission, 3/1 for domestic students. Applications are processed on a rolling basis. Application fee: $30. Electronic applications accepted. *Faculty research:* Science and mathematics education, science and mathematics teacher preparation. *Unit head:* Dr. D. Ellen Granger, Director, Office of Science Teaching Activities, 850-644-6747, Fax: 850-644-0643, E-mail: granger@bio.fsu.edu. *Application contact:* Dr. Erica M. Staehling, Director, Master's in Science Teaching Program, 850-644-6747, Fax: 850-644-0643, E-mail: staehling@bio.fsu.edu. Website: http://bio.fsu.edu/osta/tpp.php

Florida State University, The Graduate School, College of Education, School of Teacher Education, Tallahassee, FL 32306-4450. Offers curriculum and instruction (MS, PhD, Ed S), including early childhood education, elementary education, English education, foreign and second language education, mathematics education, reading and language arts, science education, social science education, special education, visual disabilities education (MS); teaching English to speakers of other languages (Certificate). *Program availability:* Part-time, evening/weekend, 100% online, blended/hybrid learning, asynchronous, minimal on-campus study. *Faculty:* 41 full-time (33 women), 21 part-time/adjunct (18 women). *Students:* 133 full-time (93 women), 84 part-time (69 women); includes 48 minority (20 Black or African American, non-Hispanic/Latino; 2 Asian, non-Hispanic/Latino; 19 Hispanic/Latino; 7 Two or more races, non-Hispanic/Latino), 52 international. Average age 31. 146 applicants, 56% accepted, 52 enrolled. In 2017, 91 master's, 7 doctorates, 1 other advanced degree awarded. Terminal master's awarded for partial completion of doctoral program. *Degree requirements:* For master's and other advanced degree, comprehensive exam, thesis optional; for doctorate, comprehensive exam, thesis/dissertation, diagnostic exam, preliminary exam, prospectus defense, dissertation defense. *Entrance requirements:* For master's, doctorate, and other advanced degree, GRE General Test, minimum upper-division GPA of 3.0. Additional exam requirements/recommendations for international students: Required—TOEFL (minimum score 550 paper-based, 80 iBT), Michigan English Language Assessment Battery (minimum score 77), IELTS (minimum score 6.5) or PTE (minimum score 55). Application fee: $30. Electronic applications accepted. *Financial support:* Fellowships, research assistantships, teaching assistantships, scholarships/grants, tuition waivers (full and partial), and unspecified assistantships available. Financial award application deadline: 1/15; financial award applicants required to submit FAFSA. *Faculty research:* Identifying effective intervention strategies to improve reading skills; improving literacy teaching and learning through technology; understanding of student sense making, problem solving, the history and structure of STEM disciplines, and teacher education to support the development of ambitious instruction that supports the STEM learning of all students; examining practices of international education; identifying ways to support the professional development of teachers. *Unit head:* Dr. Sherry Southerland, Professor/Department Chair, 850-644-6885, Fax: 850-644-2725, E-mail: ssoutherland@admin.fsu.edu. *Application contact:* Britni DeZerga, Academic Program Specialist, 850-644-2122, Fax: 850-644-7736, E-mail: bpurvis@fsu.edu. Website: http://education.fsu.edu

Fresno Pacific University, Graduate Programs, School of Education, Program in STEM Education, Fresno, CA 93702-4709. Offers MA Ed. *Program availability:* Part-time, evening/weekend. *Degree requirements:* For master's, thesis or alternative. *Entrance requirements:* Additional exam requirements/recommendations for international students: Required—TOEFL (minimum score 550 paper-based). *Expenses:* Contact institution.

George Mason University, College of Education and Human Development, Programs in Curriculum and Instruction, Fairfax, VA 22030. Offers advanced international baccalaureate (M Ed); assistive technology (M Ed); designing digital learning in schools (M Ed); early childhood education (M Ed); early childhood education for diverse learners (M Ed); elementary education (M Ed); English as a second language (M Ed); gifted child education (M Ed); history (M Ed); literacy (M Ed), including PK-12 classroom teachers, reading specialist; literacy leadership for diverse schools (M Ed), including K-12 reading; physical education (M Ed); science K-12 (M Ed); secondary education (M Ed), including biology, chemistry, earth science, English, history/social science, math, physics; special education (M Ed); teacher leadership (M Ed); teaching culturally, linguistically diverse and exceptional learners (M Ed); transformative teaching (M Ed). *Program availability:* Part-time, evening/weekend, 100% online, blended/hybrid learning. *Faculty:* 41 full-time (36 women), 45 part-time/adjunct (37 women). *Students:* 173 full-time (151 women), 729 part-time (611 women); includes 271 minority (65 Black or African American, non-Hispanic/Latino; 5 American Indian or Alaska Native, non-Hispanic/Latino; 88 Asian, non-Hispanic/Latino; 94 Hispanic/Latino; 1 Native Hawaiian or other Pacific Islander, non-Hispanic/Latino; 18 Two or more races, non-Hispanic/Latino), 28 international. Average age 32. 426 applicants, 91% accepted, 289 enrolled. In 2017, 349 master's awarded. *Degree requirements:* For master's, thesis. *Entrance requirements:* For master's, PRAXIS Core (for some programs), 2 letters of recommendation, interview, program goals statement; 9 hours of complete licensure endorsement requirements (for elementary education); minimum GPA of 3.0 in applicant's last 60 hours of undergraduate coursework (for secondary education); at least 1 year of teaching experience (for literacy). Additional exam requirements/recommendations for international students: Required—TOEFL (minimum score 575 paper-based; 88 iBT), IELTS (minimum score 6.5), PTE (minimum score 59). *Application deadline:* For fall admission, 4/2 priority date for domestic and international students; for spring admission, 11/1 for domestic and international students. Application fee: $75 ($80 for international students). Electronic applications accepted. *Expenses:* Tuition, state resident: full-time $11,228; part-time $459.50 per credit. Tuition, nonresident: full-time $30,932; part-time $1280.50 per credit. *Required fees:* $3252; $135.50 per credit. Part-time tuition and fees vary according to course load and program. *Financial support:* In 2017–18, 2 students received support, including 2 teaching assistantships; career-related internships or fieldwork, Federal Work-Study, scholarships/grants, unspecified assistantships, and health care benefits (for full-time research or teaching assistantship recipients) also available. Support available to part-time students. Financial award application deadline: 3/1; financial award applicants required to submit FAFSA. *Faculty research:* Teacher preparation and professional development; adaptive teaching; wonder in science teacher preparation; literacy (digital, adolescent); site based course instruction. *Unit head:* Rebecca Fox, Professor and Academic Program Coordinator, 703-993-4123, E-mail: rfox@gmu.edu. Website: http://gse.gmu.edu/programs/gsemasters

The George Washington University, Graduate School of Education and Human Development, Department of Curriculum and Pedagogy, Program in Secondary Education, Washington, DC 20052. Offers Arabic (M Ed); Italian (M Ed); math (M Ed); physics (M Ed); Russian (M Ed). Programs also offered in Arlington and Ashburn, VA. *Accreditation:* NCATE. *Students:* 10 full-time (7 women), 26 part-time (16 women); includes 10 minority (5 Black or African American, non-Hispanic/Latino; 2 American Indian or Alaska Native, non-Hispanic/Latino; 1 Asian, non-Hispanic/Latino; 2 Two or more races, non-Hispanic/Latino), 1 international. Average age 31. 66 applicants, 62% accepted, 22 enrolled. In 2017, 17 master's awarded. *Entrance requirements:* For master's, GRE General Test or MAT, interview, minimum GPA of 2.75. *Application deadline:* For fall admission, 1/15 priority date for domestic students; for spring admission, 10/1 for domestic students. Applications are processed on a rolling basis. Application fee: $75. *Expenses: Tuition:* Full-time $28,800; part-time $1655 per credit hour. *Required fees:* $45; $2.75 per credit hour. *Financial support:* Fellowships, career-related internships or fieldwork, Federal Work-Study, tuition waivers (full and partial), and stipends available. Financial award application deadline: 1/15; financial award applicants required to submit FAFSA. *Unit head:* Prof. Curtis Pyke, Chair, 202-994-4516, E-mail: cpyke@gwu.edu. *Application contact:* Sarah Lang, Director of Graduate Admissions, 202-994-1447, Fax: 202-994-7207, E-mail: slang@gwu.edu.

Georgia State University, College of Education and Human Development, Department of Middle and Secondary Education, Atlanta, GA 30302-3083. Offers curriculum and instruction (Ed D); English education (MAT); mathematics education (M Ed, MAT); middle level education (MAT); reading, language and literacy education (M Ed, MAT), including reading instruction (M Ed); science education (M Ed, MAT), including biology (MAT), broad field science (MAT), chemistry (MAT), earth science (MAT), physics (MAT); social studies education (M Ed, MAT), including economics (MAT), geography (MAT), history (MAT), political science (MAT); teaching and learning (PhD), including language and literacy, mathematics education, music education, science education, social studies education, teaching and teacher education. *Accreditation:* NCATE. *Program availability:* Part-time, evening/weekend, online learning. *Faculty:* 24 full-time (18 women). *Students:* 179 full-time (110 women), 192 part-time (133 women); includes 193 minority (130 Black or African American, non-Hispanic/Latino; 1 American Indian or Alaska Native, non-Hispanic/Latino; 23 Asian, non-Hispanic/Latino; 25 Hispanic/Latino; 14 Two or more races, non-Hispanic/Latino), 6 international. Average age 33. 175 applicants, 58% accepted, 83 enrolled. In 2017, 81 master's, 17 doctorates awarded. *Entrance requirements:* For master's, GRE; GACE I (for initial teacher preparation programs), baccalaureate degree or equivalent, resume, goals statement, two letters of recommendation, minimum undergraduate GPA of 2.5; proof of initial teacher certification in the content area (for M Ed); for doctorate, GRE, resume, goals statement, writing sample, two letters of recommendation, minimum graduate GPA of 3.3, interview. *Application deadline:* For fall admission, 1/15 priority date for domestic and international students; for spring admission, 10/1 for domestic and international students. Application fee: $50. Electronic applications accepted. *Expenses:* Tuition, state resident: full-time $7020. Tuition, nonresident: full-time $22,518. *Required fees:* $2128. Tuition and fees vary according to degree level and program. *Financial support:* In 2017–18, fellowships with full tuition reimbursements (averaging $19,667 per year), research assistantships with full tuition reimbursements (averaging $5,436 per year), teaching assistantships with full tuition reimbursements (averaging $2,779 per year) were awarded; career-related internships or fieldwork, Federal Work-Study, scholarships/grants, health care benefits, tuition waivers (full and partial), and unspecified assistantships also available. Financial award application deadline: 3/15. *Faculty research:* Teacher education in language and literacy, mathematics, science, and social studies in urban middle and secondary school settings; learning technologies in school, community, and corporate settings; multicultural education and education for social justice; urban education; international education. *Unit head:* Dr. Dana L. Fox, Chair, 404-413-8060, Fax: 404-413-8063, E-mail: dfox@gsu.edu. *Application contact:* Bobbie Turner, Administrative Coordinator, 404-413-8405, Fax: 404-413-8063, E-mail: bnturner@gsu.edu.
Website: http://mse.education.gsu.edu/

Grambling State University, School of Graduate Studies and Research, College of Education, Department of Educational Leadership, Grambling, LA 71245. Offers developmental education (MS, Ed D, PMC), including curriculum and instructional design (Ed D); English (MS); guidance and counseling (MS); higher education administration and management (Ed D); mathematics (MS); reading (MS); science (MS); student development and personnel services (Ed D); educational leadership (M Ed). *Program availability:* Part-time, evening/weekend. *Degree requirements:* For master's, comprehensive exam, thesis (for some programs); for doctorate, comprehensive exam, thesis/dissertation. *Entrance requirements:* For master's, GRE, minimum GPA of 2.5 on last degree; for doctorate, GRE (minimum score 1000, 500 on Verbal), master's degree, minimum GPA of 3.0 on last degree. Additional exam requirements/recommendations for international students: Required—TOEFL (minimum score 500 paper-based; 62 iBT). Electronic applications accepted.

Grand Canyon University, College of Education, Phoenix, AZ 85017-1097. Offers autism spectrum disorders (MA); curriculum and instruction (MA); early childhood education (M Ed); educational administration (M Ed); educational leadership (M Ed); elementary education (M Ed); gifted education (MA); instructional technology (MS); K-12 leadership (Ed S); reading (MA); secondary education (M Ed); secondary humanities education (M Ed); secondary STEM education (M Ed); special education (M Ed); teaching and learning (Ed D); teaching English to speakers of other languages (MA). *Program availability:* Part-time, evening/weekend, online learning. *Degree requirements:* For master's, publishable research paper (M Ed), e-portfolio. *Entrance requirements:* For master's, undergraduate degree from accredited, GCU-approved college, university, or program with minimum GPA 2.8. Additional exam requirements/recommendations for international students: Required—TOEFL (minimum score 550 paper-based; 79 iBT), IELTS (minimum score 6). Electronic applications accepted.

Hamline University, School of Education, St. Paul, MN 55104-1284. Offers education (MA Ed, Ed D); English as a second language (MA); literacy education (MA); natural science and environmental education (MA Ed); teaching (MAT); teaching English to speakers of other languages (MA). *Accreditation:* NCATE (one or more programs are accredited). *Program availability:* Part-time, evening/weekend, 100% online, blended/hybrid learning. *Faculty:* 23 full-time (15 women), 43 part-time/adjunct (30 women). *Students:* 79 full-time (60 women), 898 part-time (692 women); includes 139 minority (31 Black or African American, non-Hispanic/Latino; 1 American Indian or Alaska Native, non-Hispanic/Latino; 58 Asian, non-Hispanic/Latino; 33 Hispanic/Latino; 16 Two or more races, non-Hispanic/Latino), 8 international. Average age 35. 366 applicants, 78% accepted, 193 enrolled. In 2017, 236 master's, 7 doctorates awarded. *Degree requirements:* For master's, thesis (for some programs), thesis or capstone project; for doctorate, comprehensive exam, thesis/dissertation. *Entrance requirements:* For master's, official transcripts, essay, letters of recommendation, minimum GPA of 3.0 from bachelor's work; resume and/or writing samples (for some programs); for doctorate, personal statement, master's degree with minimum GPA of 3.0, letters of recommendation, writing sample. Additional exam requirements/recommendations for international students: Required—TOEFL (minimum score 550 paper-based; 80 iBT), IELTS (minimum score 6.5). *Application deadline:* For fall admission, 6/1 for domestic and international students; for spring admission, 11/1 for domestic and international students; for summer admission,

3/1 for domestic and international students. Applications are processed on a rolling basis. Application fee: $0 ($100 for international students). Electronic applications accepted. *Expenses:* $466 per credit (for MA Ed), $625 per credit (for MATESOL), $569 per credit (for MAT), $721 per credit plus fees (for EdD). *Financial support:* Career-related internships or fieldwork, Federal Work-Study, and scholarships/grants available. Support available to part-time students. Financial award application deadline: 4/20; financial award applicants required to submit FAFSA. *Faculty research:* Adult basic education, service-learning, teacher dispositions, diversity, technology. *Unit head:* Dr. Marcela Kostihova, Dean, 651-523-2206, Fax: 651-523-2489, E-mail: cladean@hamline.edu. *Application contact:* Shawn Skoog, Director of Graduate Recruitment and Admission, 651-523-2900, Fax: 651-523-3058, E-mail: gradprog@hamline.edu.
Website: http://www.hamline.edu/education

Hampton University, School of Liberal Arts and Education, Program in Teaching, Hampton, VA 23668. Offers biology education 6-12 (MT); English education 6-12 (MT); mathematics education 6-12 (MT); music education PreK-12 (MT). *Program availability:* Part-time. *Students:* 5 full-time (4 women); all minorities (all Black or African American, non-Hispanic/Latino). Average age 23. 6 applicants, 67% accepted, 1 enrolled. In 2017, 7 master's awarded. *Entrance requirements:* For master's, GRE General Test. Additional exam requirements/recommendations for international students: Required—TOEFL (minimum score 525 paper-based) or IELTS (6.5). *Application deadline:* For fall admission, 6/1 priority date for domestic students, 4/1 for international students; for spring admission, 11/1 priority date for domestic students, 9/1 for international students; for summer admission, 4/1 priority date for domestic students, 2/1 priority date for international students. Applications are processed on a rolling basis. Application fee: $35. Electronic applications accepted. *Expenses: Tuition:* Full-time $22,630; part-time $575 per semester hour. *Required fees:* $70. Tuition and fees vary according to program. *Financial support:* Application deadline: 6/30; applicants required to submit FAFSA. *Unit head:* Dr. Martha Jallim-Hall, Program Coordinator, 757-727-5793.

Hardin-Simmons University, Graduate School, Holland School of Sciences and Mathematics, Abilene, TX 79698-0001. Offers environmental management (MS); mathematics (MS); physical therapy (DPT); physician assistant studies (MPAS). *Program availability:* Part-time. *Faculty:* 29 full-time (15 women), 6 part-time/adjunct (4 women). *Students:* 115 full-time (77 women), 8 part-time (6 women); includes 25 minority (6 Black or African American, non-Hispanic/Latino; 2 Asian, non-Hispanic/Latino; 17 Hispanic/Latino), 1 international. Average age 25. 1,156 applicants, 7% accepted, 62 enrolled. In 2017, 10 master's, 29 doctorates awarded. *Degree requirements:* For master's, comprehensive exam, thesis or alternative, internship; for doctorate, comprehensive exam, thesis/dissertation or alternative. *Entrance requirements:* For master's, minimum undergraduate GPA of 3.0 in major, 2.7 overall; 2 semesters of course work each in biology, chemistry and geology; interview; writing sample; occupational experience; for doctorate, letters of recommendation, interview, writing sample. Additional exam requirements/recommendations for international students: Required—TOEFL (minimum score 550 paper-based; 79 iBT). *Application deadline:* For fall admission, 8/15 priority date for domestic students, 4/1 for international students; for spring admission, 1/5 priority date for domestic students, 9/1 for international students. Applications are processed on a rolling basis. Application fee: $50 ($150 for international students). Electronic applications accepted. *Expenses: Tuition:* Full-time $13,500; part-time $750 per semester hour. *Required fees:* $220 per term. One-time fee: $50. Tuition and fees vary according to course load, campus/location and program. *Financial support:* In 2017–18, 108 students received support. Fellowships, career-related internships or fieldwork, and scholarships/grants available. Support available to part-time students. Financial award application deadline: 6/30; financial award applicants required to submit FAFSA. *Unit head:* Dr. Christopher McNair, Dean, 325-670-1401, Fax: 325-670-1385, E-mail: cmcnair@hsutx.edu. *Application contact:* Dr. Nancy Kucinski, Dean of Graduate Studies, 325-670-1298, Fax: 325-670-1564, E-mail: gradoff@hsutx.edu.
Website: http://www.hsutx.edu/academics/holland

Harrison Middleton University, Graduate Program, Tempe, AZ 85282. Offers education (MA, Ed D); humanities (MA); imaginative literature (MA); interdisciplinary studies (DA); jurisprudence (MA); natural science (MA); philosophy and religion (MA); social science (MA). *Program availability:* Part-time, evening/weekend, online learning. *Degree requirements:* For master's and doctorate, capstone project. *Entrance requirements:* For master's, interview; for doctorate, 2 academic letters of reference, interview, essay. Additional exam requirements/recommendations for international students: Required—TOEFL (minimum score 550 paper-based; 80 iBT). Electronic applications accepted. *Faculty research:* Japanese animation, educational leadership, war art, John Muir's wilderness.

Heritage University, Graduate Programs in Education, Program in Professional Studies, Toppenish, WA 98948-9599. Offers bilingual education/ESL (M Ed); biology (M Ed); English and literature (M Ed); reading/literacy (M Ed); special education (M Ed). *Program availability:* Part-time, evening/weekend. *Degree requirements:* For master's, comprehensive exam (for some programs), thesis (for some programs).

Hofstra University, School of Education, Programs in Teacher Education, Hempstead, NY 11549. Offers bilingual education (MA); bilingual extension (Advanced Certificate), including education/speech language pathology, intensive teacher institute; business education (MS Ed); curriculum studies (MS Ed); early childhood and childhood education (MS Ed); early childhood education (MA, MS Ed); educational technology (Advanced Certificate); elementary education (MA, MS Ed), including science, technology, engineering, and mathematics (STEM) (MA); English education (MS Ed); family and consumer science (MS Ed); fine arts and music education (Advanced Certificate); fine arts education (MS Ed); foreign language and TESOL (MS Ed); foreign language education (MA, MS Ed), including Arabic (MS Ed), biology, chemistry, Chinese (MS Ed), earth science, French, German, Italian (MS Ed), Mandarin (MS Ed), physics, Russian, Spanish; foundations of education (Advanced Certificate), including grades 5-6, grades 7-9; languages other than English and teaching English as a second language (MA); learning and teaching (Ed D), including applied linguistics, art education, arts and humanities, early childhood education, English education, human development, math education, math, science, and technology, multicultural education, physical education, science education, social studies education, special education; mathematics education (MA, MS Ed); music education (MA, MS Ed); science education (MA), including biology (MA, MS Ed), chemistry (MA, MS Ed), earth science (MA, MS Ed), physics (MA, MS Ed); secondary education (Advanced Certificate); social studies education (MA, MS Ed); teaching languages other than English and TESOL (MS Ed); technology for learning (MA); TESOL (MS Ed, Advanced Certificate); TESOL with specialization in STEM (MA); work based learning extension (Advanced Certificate). *Program availability:* Part-time, evening/weekend, blended/hybrid learning. *Students:* 119 full-time (83 women), 124 part-time (90 women); includes 54 minority (15 Black or African American, non-Hispanic/Latino; 9 Asian, non-Hispanic/Latino; 29 Hispanic/Latino; 1 Native Hawaiian or other Pacific Islander, non-Hispanic/Latino), 12 international. Average age 29. 205 applicants, 88% accepted, 93 enrolled. In 2017, 103 master's, 4 doctorates, 32 other advanced degrees awarded. *Degree requirements:* For master's, comprehensive exam, thesis (for some programs), exit project, student teaching, fieldwork, electronic portfolio, curriculum project, minimum GPA of 3.0; for doctorate, thesis/dissertation; for

Advanced Certificate, 3 foreign languages, comprehensive exam (for some programs), thesis project. *Entrance requirements:* For master's, GRE, 2 letters of recommendation, portfolio, teacher certification (MA), interview, essay; for doctorate, GMAT, GRE, LSAT, or MAT; for Advanced Certificate, 2 letters of recommendation, essay, interview and/or portfolio, teaching certificate. Additional exam requirements/recommendations for international students: Required—TOEFL (minimum score 550 paper-based; 80 iBT). *Application deadline:* Applications are processed on a rolling basis. Application fee: $75. Electronic applications accepted. *Expenses:* Tuition: Full-time $1292. *Required fees:* $970. Tuition and fees vary according to program. *Financial support:* In 2017–18, 112 students received support, including 56 fellowships with full and partial tuition reimbursements available (averaging $4,998 per year), 2 research assistantships with full and partial tuition reimbursements available (averaging $8,753 per year); career-related internships or fieldwork, Federal Work-Study, institutionally sponsored loans, scholarships/grants, traineeships, tuition waivers (full and partial), and unspecified assistantships also available. Support available to part-time students. Financial award applicants required to submit FAFSA. *Faculty research:* Educational interventions that foster critical-thinking skills; teachers' attitudes about professional development; threats to teacher quality. *Unit head:* Dr. Eustace Thompson, Chairperson, 516-463-5749, Fax: 516-463-6275, E-mail: eustace.g.thompson@hofstra.edu. *Application contact:* Sunil Samuel, Assistant Vice President of Admissions, 516-463-4723, Fax: 516-463-4664, E-mail: graduateadmission@hofstra.edu.
Website: http://www.hofstra.edu/education/

Hood College, Graduate School, Department of Education, Frederick, MD 21701-8575. Offers curriculum and instruction (MS), including elementary education, elementary science and mathematics education, secondary education, special education; education, multidisciplinary studies (MS); educational leadership (MS, Certificate); reading specialization (MS); STEM education (Certificate). *Accreditation:* NCATE. *Program availability:* Part-time-only, evening/weekend. *Faculty:* 6 full-time (4 women), 35 part-time/adjunct (27 women). *Students:* 3 full-time (all women), 329 part-time (265 women); includes 62 minority (35 Black or African American, non-Hispanic/Latino; 4 Asian, non-Hispanic/Latino; 14 Hispanic/Latino; 9 Two or more races, non-Hispanic/Latino), 3 international. Average age 33. 76 applicants, 100% accepted, 63 enrolled. In 2017, 53 master's, 58 other advanced degrees awarded. *Degree requirements:* For master's, action research project, portfolio (for reading specialization); for Certificate, STEM capstone activity. *Entrance requirements:* For master's, minimum GPA of 2.75, teaching certification, writing sample during interview, letter of recommendation from principal (for educational leadership program only). Additional exam requirements/recommendations for international students: Required—TOEFL (minimum score 575 paper-based; 89 iBT), IELTS (minimum score 6.5). *Application deadline:* For fall admission, 8/15 priority date for domestic students, 8/5 for international students; for spring admission, 12/1 priority date for domestic students, 12/1 for international students; for summer admission, 5/1 priority date for domestic students, 4/15 for international students. Applications are processed on a rolling basis. Application fee: $35. Electronic applications accepted. *Expenses:* $465 per credit plus $110 comprehensive fee per semester. *Financial support:* Tuition waivers (partial) and unspecified assistantships available. Financial award applicants required to submit FAFSA. *Faculty research:* Leadership, action research, brain research, learning styles. *Unit head:* Dr. April M. Boulton, Dean of the Graduate School, 301-696-3612, E-mail: gofurther@hood.edu. *Application contact:* Jan Marcus, Assistant Director of Graduate Admissions, 301-696-3600, E-mail: gofurther@hood.edu.
Website: http://www.hood.edu/academics/education/index.html

Houston Baptist University, College of Education and Behavioral Sciences, Programs in Education, Houston, TX 77074-3298. Offers bilingual education (M Ed); counselor education (M Ed); curriculum and instruction (M Ed); curriculum and instruction (EC-6 bilingual) (M Ed); curriculum and instruction in all-level art, Spanish, music, or physical education (M Ed); curriculum and instruction in EC-6 and special education (EC-12) (M Ed); curriculum and instruction in instructional technology (M Ed); curriculum and instruction in mathematics, science, or social studies (4-8) (M Ed); curriculum and instruction with EC-6 generalist (M Ed); curriculum and instruction with English language arts and reading (4-8) (M Ed); educational administration (M Ed); educational diagnostician (M Ed); executive educational leadership (Ed D); higher education in business management (M Ed); higher education in Christian studies (M Ed); higher education in counseling (M Ed); higher education in educational technology (M Ed); reading (M Ed); special educational leadership (Ed D). *Program availability:* Part-time, evening/weekend, 100% online, blended/hybrid learning. *Students:* 83 full-time (65 women), 187 part-time (156 women); includes 189 minority (114 Black or African American, non-Hispanic/Latino; 2 American Indian or Alaska Native, non-Hispanic/Latino; 9 Asian, non-Hispanic/Latino; 58 Hispanic/Latino; 6 Two or more races, non-Hispanic/Latino), 7 international. Average age 36. 309 applicants, 31% accepted, 70 enrolled. In 2017, 92 master's awarded. *Degree requirements:* For master's, comprehensive exam; for doctorate, thesis/dissertation. *Entrance requirements:* For master's, minimum GPA of 2.75, two recommendations, resume, bachelor's degree conferred transcript; interview (for non-certified teachers); for doctorate, GRE, 5 letters of recommendation. Additional exam requirements/recommendations for international students: Required—TOEFL (minimum score 80 iBT), IELTS (minimum score 6.5). *Application deadline:* For fall admission, 8/1 for domestic students, 6/1 for international students; for spring admission, 1/1 for domestic students, 11/1 for international students; for summer admission, 5/1 for domestic students, 3/1 for international students. Applications are processed on a rolling basis. Application fee: $0 ($100 for international students). Electronic applications accepted. Application fee is waived when completed online. *Expenses:* $22,000 tuition; $4,500 fees (general, technology and parking). *Financial support:* In 2017–18, 59 students received support. Research assistantships, teaching assistantships, Federal Work-Study, and scholarships/grants available. Support available to part-time students. Financial award application deadline: 4/1; financial award applicants required to submit FAFSA. *Faculty research:* Autism and inclusion, integrating technology into instruction, school change and leadership trust. *Unit head:* Dr. Charlotte Fontenot, Director, Graduate Programs, 281-649-3078, Fax: 281-649-3361, E-mail: cfontenot@hbu.edu. *Application contact:* Kristy Wright, Administrative Assistant for Graduate Programs, 281-649-3094, Fax: 281-649-3361, E-mail: kwright@hbu.edu.
Website: http://www.hbu.edu/MED

Hunter College of the City University of New York, Graduate School, School of Education, Programs in Secondary Education, Concentration in Biology Education, New York, NY 10065-5085. Offers MA. *Accreditation:* NCATE. *Degree requirements:* For master's, thesis, professional teaching portfolio, New York State Teacher Certification Exams, research project. *Entrance requirements:* For master's, minimum GPA of 2.8, 2 letters of reference, 21 credits of course work in biology. Additional exam requirements/recommendations for international students: Required—TOEFL, TWE.

Hunter College of the City University of New York, Graduate School, School of Education, Programs in Secondary Education, Concentration in Chemistry Education, New York, NY 10065-5085. Offers MA. *Accreditation:* NCATE. *Degree requirements:* For master's, thesis, professional teaching portfolio, New York State Teacher Certification Exam. *Entrance requirements:* For master's, minimum GPA of 2.8, 2 letters of reference, minimum of 29 credits in science and mathematics.

Illinois Institute of Technology, Graduate College, College of Science, Department of Mathematics and Science Education, Chicago, IL 60616. Offers mathematics education (MAS, PhD); science education (MAS, PhD). *Degree requirements:* For master's, comprehensive exam (for some programs), thesis optional; for doctorate, comprehensive exam, thesis/dissertation. *Entrance requirements:* For master's, GRE General Test (minimum score 900 quantitative and verbal; 2.5 analytical writing), minimum undergraduate GPA of 3.0; two-page professional statement of goals/objectives; curriculum vita; three letters of recommendation; for doctorate, GRE General Test (minimum score 1000 quantitative and verbal; 3.0 analytical writing), minimum GPA of 3.0, 3 years of teaching experience. Additional exam requirements/recommendations for international students: Required—TOEFL (minimum score 600 paper-based; 80 iBT). Electronic applications accepted. *Faculty research:* Informal science/math education, curriculum development, integration of science/math disciplines and across disciplines, instructional methods, students' and teachers' conceptions of scientific/mathematical inquiry and the nature of science/math, instructional models, evaluation, and research design.

Indiana State University, College of Graduate and Professional Studies, College of Arts and Sciences, Department of Biology, Terre Haute, IN 47809. Offers cellular and molecular biology (PhD); ecology, systematics and evolution (PhD); life sciences (MS); physiology (PhD); science education (MS). *Degree requirements:* For master's, thesis optional; for doctorate, comprehensive exam, thesis/dissertation. *Entrance requirements:* For master's and doctorate, GRE General Test. Electronic applications accepted.

Indiana University Bloomington, School of Education, Department of Curriculum and Instruction, Bloomington, IN 47405-7000. Offers art education (MS, Ed D, PhD); curriculum studies (Ed D, PhD); elementary education (MS, Ed D, PhD, Ed S); mathematics education (MS, Ed D, PhD); science education (MS, Ed D, PhD); secondary education (MS, Ed D, PhD); social studies education (MS, PhD); special education (PhD, Ed S). *Accreditation:* NCATE. *Program availability:* Part-time, evening/weekend. Terminal master's awarded for partial completion of doctoral program. *Degree requirements:* For doctorate, thesis/dissertation; for Ed S, comprehensive exam or project. *Entrance requirements:* For master's, doctorate, and Ed S, GRE General Test. Electronic applications accepted.

Indiana University Bloomington, University Graduate School, College of Arts and Sciences, Department of Biology, Bloomington, IN 47405. Offers biology teaching (MAT); biotechnology (MA); evolution, ecology, and behavior (MA, PhD); genetics (PhD); microbiology (MA, PhD); molecular, cellular, and developmental biology (PhD); plant sciences (MA, PhD); zoology (MA, PhD). Terminal master's awarded for partial completion of doctoral program. *Degree requirements:* For master's, thesis, oral defense; for doctorate, thesis/dissertation, oral defense. *Entrance requirements:* For master's and doctorate, GRE General Test. Additional exam requirements/recommendations for international students: Required—TOEFL (minimum score 100 iBT). Electronic applications accepted. *Faculty research:* Evolution, ecology and behavior; microbiology; molecular biology and genetics; plant biology.

Indiana University Bloomington, University Graduate School, College of Arts and Sciences, Department of Chemistry, Bloomington, IN 47405. Offers analytical chemistry (PhD); chemical biology (PhD); chemistry (MAT); inorganic chemistry (PhD); materials chemistry (PhD); organic chemistry (PhD); physical chemistry (PhD); MSES/MS. Terminal master's awarded for partial completion of doctoral program. *Degree requirements:* For master's, thesis; for doctorate, thesis/dissertation. *Entrance requirements:* For master's and doctorate, GRE General Test, GRE Subject Test. Additional exam requirements/recommendations for international students: Required—TOEFL. Electronic applications accepted. *Faculty research:* Synthesis of complex natural products, organic reaction mechanisms, organic electrochemistry, transitive-metal chemistry, solid-state and surface chemistry.

Instituto Tecnológico y de Estudios Superiores de Monterrey, Campus Monterrey, Graduate and Research Division, Program in Natural and Social Sciences, Monterrey, Mexico. Offers biotechnology (MS); chemistry (MS, PhD); communications (MS); education (MA). *Program availability:* Part-time. *Degree requirements:* For master's, one foreign language, thesis; for doctorate, one foreign language, thesis/dissertation. *Entrance requirements:* For master's, EXADEP; for doctorate, EXADEP, master's degree in related field. Additional exam requirements/recommendations for international students: Required—TOEFL. *Faculty research:* Cultural industries, mineral substances, bioremediation, food processing, CQ in industrial chemical processing.

Inter American University of Puerto Rico, Arecibo Campus, Programs in Education, Arecibo, PR 00614-4050. Offers administration and educational supervision (MA Ed); counseling and guidance (MA Ed); curriculum and teaching (MA Ed), including biology education, English as a second language, history education, math education, Spanish; elementary education (MA Ed). *Accreditation:* TEAC. *Degree requirements:* For master's, comprehensive exam, thesis optional. *Entrance requirements:* For master's, GRE, EXADEP, bachelor's degree in education or teaching license (administration and supervision) or courses in education and psychology (counseling and guidance), minimum GPA of 2.5 in last 60 credits.

Inter American University of Puerto Rico, Metropolitan Campus, Graduate Programs, Program in Teaching of Science, San Juan, PR 00919-1293. Offers MA. *Degree requirements:* For master's, comprehensive exam. *Entrance requirements:* For master's, GRE or EXADEP, interview. Electronic applications accepted.

Inter American University of Puerto Rico, Ponce Campus, Graduate School, Mercedita, PR 00715-1602. Offers accounting (MBA); biology (M Ed); chemistry (M Ed); criminal justice (MA); elementary education (M Ed); English as a Second Language (M Ed); finance (MBA); history (M Ed); human resources (MBA); marketing (MBA); mathematics (M Ed); Spanish (M Ed). *Entrance requirements:* For master's, minimum GPA of 2.5.

Inter American University of Puerto Rico, San Germán Campus, Graduate Studies Center, Program in Science Education, San Germán, PR 00683-5008. Offers MA. *Accreditation:* TEAC. *Program availability:* Part-time, evening/weekend. *Degree requirements:* For master's, comprehensive exam. *Entrance requirements:* For master's, GRE General Test or EXADEP, minimum GPA of 3.0.

Iona College, School of Arts and Science, Department of Education, New Rochelle, NY 10801-1890. Offers adolescence education: biology (MS Ed, MST); adolescence education: English (MS Ed); adolescence education: mathematics (MST); adolescence education: social studies (MS Ed, MST); adolescence education: Spanish (MS Ed); adolescence special education 5-12 (MST); childhood and special education (MST); early childhood and childhood (MST); educational leadership (MS Ed). *Accreditation:* NCATE. *Program availability:* Part-time, evening/weekend. *Faculty:* 7 full-time (5 women), 2 part-time/adjunct (1 woman). *Students:* 23 full-time (18 women), 26 part-time (19 women); includes 12 minority (4 Black or African American, non-Hispanic/Latino; 8 Hispanic/Latino). Average age 26. 33 applicants, 97% accepted, 20 enrolled. In 2017, 31 master's awarded. *Degree requirements:* For master's, thesis or alternative. *Entrance requirements:* For master's, minimum GPA of 3.0, NY State teaching certificate and bachelor's degree (for MS Ed). Additional exam requirements/recommendations for international students: Required—TOEFL (minimum score 550

paper-based; 80 iBT), IELTS (minimum score 6.5). *Application deadline:* For fall admission, 8/1 priority date for domestic students, 5/1 priority date for international students; for spring admission, 1/1 priority date for domestic students, 9/1 priority date for international students. Applications are processed on a rolling basis. Electronic applications accepted. Tuition and fees vary according to program. *Financial support:* In 2017–18, 16 students received support. Unspecified assistantships available. Support available to part-time students. Financial award application deadline: 4/15; financial award applicants required to submit FAFSA. *Faculty research:* Engaging teacher educators in scientific process, cross-national comparisons of mathematics teaching, questioning strategies in the classroom, research methods, literacy development. *Unit head:* Margaret Smith, PhD, Chair, 914-633-2210, Fax: 914-633-2608, E-mail: msmith@iona.edu. *Application contact:* Richard McMahon, Coordinator, Graduate School of Education, 914-633-2552, E-mail: rmcmahon@iona.edu.
Website: http://www.iona.edu/Academics/School-of-Arts-Science/Departments/Education/Graduate-Programs.aspx

Iowa State University of Science and Technology, Program in Science Education, Ames, IA 50011. Offers MAT. *Entrance requirements:* For master's, GRE, three letters of recommendation, undergraduate degree in sciences (preferred). Additional exam requirements/recommendations for international students: Required—TOEFL (minimum score 560 paper-based; 83 iBT), IELTS (minimum score 6.5). Electronic applications accepted.

Jackson State University, Graduate School, College of Science, Engineering and Technology, Department of Physics, Atmospheric Sciences, and Geoscience, Jackson, MS 39217. Offers physical science (MS, PhD); science education (MST). *Program availability:* Part-time, evening/weekend. *Degree requirements:* For master's, comprehensive exam. *Entrance requirements:* For master's, GRE General Test. Additional exam requirements/recommendations for international students: Required—TOEFL (minimum score 520 paper-based; 67 iBT).

Lake Forest College, Master of Arts in Teaching Program, Lake Forest, IL 60045. Offers elementary education (MAT); K-12 French (MAT); K-12 music (MAT); K-12 Spanish (MAT); K-12 visual art (MAT); secondary biology (MAT); secondary chemistry (MAT); secondary English (MAT); secondary history (MAT); secondary mathematics (MAT). *Degree requirements:* For master's, comprehensive exam, portfolio. *Entrance requirements:* For master's, GRE.

Laurentian University, School of Graduate Studies and Research, Programme in Science Communication, Sudbury, ON P3E 2C6, Canada. Offers G Dip.

Lawrence Technological University, College of Arts and Sciences, Southfield, MI 48075-1058. Offers bioinformatics (Graduate Certificate); computer science (MS), including data science, big data, and data mining, intelligent systems; educational technology (MA), including robotics; instructional design, communication, and presentation (Graduate Certificate); integrated science (MA); science education (MA); technical and professional communication (MS, Graduate Certificate); writing for the digital age (Graduate Certificate). *Program availability:* Part-time, evening/weekend. *Faculty:* 6 full-time (2 women), 7 part-time/adjunct (3 women). *Students:* 34 part-time (15 women); includes 4 minority (1 Black or African American, non-Hispanic/Latino; 2 Asian, non-Hispanic/Latino; 1 Hispanic/Latino), 7 international. Average age 31. 84 applicants, 15% accepted, 10 enrolled. In 2017, 14 master's awarded. *Degree requirements:* For master's, thesis (for some programs). *Entrance requirements:* Additional exam requirements/recommendations for international students: Required—TOEFL (minimum score 550 paper-based; 79 iBT), IELTS (minimum score 6.5). *Application deadline:* For fall admission, 5/27 for international students; for spring admission, 10/8 for international students; for summer admission, 2/14 for international students. Applications are processed on a rolling basis. Application fee: $50. Electronic applications accepted. *Expenses:* Tuition: Full-time $15,274; part-time $1091 per credit. One-time fee: $150. *Financial support:* In 2017–18, 8 students received support. Scholarships/grants and tuition reduction available. Financial award application deadline: 4/1; financial award applicants required to submit FAFSA. *Faculty research:* Computer analysis of music, machine learning of literature and lyrics, customer sentiments and response analysis through social media, peta-scale computing in astronomical databases, early detection of diseases with pattern recognition. *Total annual research expenditures:* $242,460. *Unit head:* Glen Bauer, Interim Dean, 248-204-3532, Fax: 248-204-3518, E-mail: scidean@ltu.edu. *Application contact:* Jane Rohrback, Director of Admissions, 248-204-3160, Fax: 248-204-2228, E-mail: admissions@ltu.edu.

Lebanon Valley College, Program in Science Education, Annville, PA 17003. Offers integrative STEM education (Certificate); STEM education (MSE). *Program availability:* Part-time-only, evening/weekend, 100% online, blended/hybrid learning. *Faculty:* 14 part-time/adjunct (7 women). *Students:* 3 part-time (all women). Average age 42. 4 applicants, 100% accepted, 3 enrolled. In 2017, 10 master's awarded. *Degree requirements:* For master's, thesis or capstone project. *Entrance requirements:* For master's, baccalaureate degree, minimum GPA of 3.0, teacher certification, 3 letters of recommendation, transcripts, goal statement. Additional exam requirements/recommendations for international students: Required—TOEFL (minimum score 80 iBT). *Application deadline:* Applications are processed on a rolling basis. Application fee: $0. Electronic applications accepted. *Expenses:* $618 per credit hour. *Financial support:* Scholarships/grants available. Financial award application deadline: 3/1; financial award applicants required to submit FAFSA. *Faculty research:* Teacher quality and student achievement, STEM reform, STEM education, effective teaching. *Unit head:* Carrie Coryer, Director of MSE and STEM-based programs, 717-867-6190, Fax: 717-867-6018, E-mail: coryer@lvc.edu.
Website: http://www.lvc.edu/academics/graduate-studies/master-of-science-in-stem-education/

Lehman College of the City University of New York, School of Education, Department of Middle and High School Education, Program in Science Education, Bronx, NY 10468-1589. Offers MS Ed. *Accreditation:* NCATE.

Lesley University, Graduate School of Education, Cambridge, MA 02138-2790. Offers arts, community, and education (M Ed); autism studies (Certificate); curriculum and instruction (M Ed, CAGS); early childhood education (M Ed); ecological teaching and learning (MS); educational studies (PhD), including adult learning, educational leadership, individually designed; elementary education (M Ed); emergent technologies for educators (Certificate); ESLArts: language learning through the arts (M Ed); high school education (M Ed); individually designed (M Ed); integrated teaching through the arts (M Ed); literacy for K-8 classroom teachers (M Ed); mathematics education (M Ed); middle school education (M Ed); moderate disabilities (M Ed); online learning (Certificate); reading (CAGS); science in education (M Ed); severe disabilities (M Ed); special needs (CAGS); specialist teacher of reading (M Ed); teacher of visual art (M Ed); technology in education (M Ed, CAGS). *Accreditation:* TEAC. *Program availability:* Part-time, evening/weekend, online learning. *Degree requirements:* For master's, practicum; for doctorate, thesis/dissertation. *Entrance requirements:* For master's, Massachusetts Tests for Educator Licensure (MTEL), transcripts, statement of purpose, recommendations; interview (for special education); for doctorate, GRE General Test, transcripts, statement of purpose, recommendations, interview, master's degree; for other advanced degree, interview, master's degree. Additional exam

requirements/recommendations for international students: Required—TOEFL (minimum score 550 paper-based; 80 iBT). Electronic applications accepted. *Faculty research:* Assessment in literacy, mathematics and science; autism spectrum disorders; instructional technology and online learning; multicultural education and English language learners.

Lewis University, College of Education, Program in Secondary Education, Romeoville, IL 60446. Offers biology (MA); chemistry (MA); English (MA); history (MA); math (MA); physics (MA); psychology and social science (MA). *Program availability:* Part-time. *Students:* 19 full-time (9 women), 22 part-time (12 women); includes 10 minority (2 Black or African American, non-Hispanic/Latino; 1 Asian, non-Hispanic/Latino; 5 Hispanic/Latino; 2 Two or more races, non-Hispanic/Latino). Average age 27. *Degree requirements:* For master's, comprehensive exam, departmental qualifying exam. *Entrance requirements:* For master's, writing exam, Test of Academic Proficiency/Basic Skills Test/ACT/SAT, bachelor's degree, minimum GPA of 2.75, 2 letters of recommendation. Additional exam requirements/recommendations for international students: Required—TOEFL (minimum score 550 paper-based; 79 iBT), IELTS (minimum score 6). *Application deadline:* For fall admission, 5/1 priority date for international students; for spring admission, 11/15 priority date for international students. Applications are processed on a rolling basis. Application fee: $40. Electronic applications accepted. Tuition and fees vary according to program. *Financial support:* Federal Work-Study, scholarships/grants, and unspecified assistantships available. Financial award application deadline: 5/1; financial award applicants required to submit FAFSA. *Unit head:* Dr. Lauren Rentfro, Program Director, 815-836-5026, E-mail: rentfrla@lewisu.edu. *Application contact:* Kathy Lisak, Graduate Admissions Counselor, 815-836-5610, E-mail: grad@lewisu.edu.

Manhattanville College, School of Education, Jump Start Program, Purchase, NY 10577-2132. Offers childhood education and special education (grades 1-6) (MPS); early childhood education (birth-grade 2) (MAT); education (Advanced Certificate); English and special education (grades 5-12) (MPS); mathematics and special education (grades 5-12) (MPS); science and special education (grades 5-12) (MPS); social studies and special education (grades 5-12) (MPS); Spanish (grades 7-12) (MAT); TESOL (all grades) (MPS). *Program availability:* Part-time, evening/weekend. *Faculty:* 10 full-time (7 women), 39 part-time/adjunct (27 women). *Students:* 3 full-time (2 women), 40 part-time (24 women); includes 11 minority (3 Black or African American, non-Hispanic/Latino; 6 Hispanic/Latino; 1 Native Hawaiian or other Pacific Islander, non-Hispanic/Latino; 1 Two or more races, non-Hispanic/Latino). Average age 33. 25 applicants, 60% accepted, 7 enrolled. In 2017, 17 master's, 2 other advanced degrees awarded. *Degree requirements:* For master's, comprehensive exam (for some programs), thesis (for some programs), student teaching, research seminars, portfolios, internships, writing assessment; for Advanced Certificate, comprehensive exam (for some programs). *Entrance requirements:* For master's, GRE or MAT (for programs leading to certification), minimum GPA of 3.0, 2 letters of recommendation, interview, essay (2-3 page personal statement that describes reasons for choosing teaching or educational leadership as profession and philosophy of education), proof of immunization (for those born after 1957). Additional exam requirements/recommendations for international students: Required—TOEFL (minimum score 600 paper-based; 110 iBT); Recommended—IELTS (minimum score 8). *Application deadline:* Applications are processed on a rolling basis. Application fee: $75. Electronic applications accepted. *Expenses:* $915 per credit. *Financial support:* Teaching assistantships, career-related internships or fieldwork, Federal Work-Study, institutionally sponsored loans, scholarships/grants, and unspecified assistantships available. Financial award application deadline: 3/15; financial award applicants required to submit FAFSA. *Faculty research:* Early childhood and technology, professional development schools and community schools, students with emotional difficulties, literacy and adolescents, mindfulness, changing suburbs institute, and community schools, studying the effects of the environment on special populations, the most difficult cases, students who are presented with multiple challenges: learning, behavioral and ACE experiences who see criminal behavior as a way to cope; working on giving them the tools they need to succeed. *Unit head:* Dr. Shelly Wepner, Dean, 914-323-3153, E-mail: shelly.wepner@mville.edu. *Application contact:* Alissa Wilson, Director, Graduate Admissions, 914-323-3150, Fax: 914-694-1732, E-mail: edschool@mville.edu.
Website: http://www.mville.edu/programs/jump-start

Manhattanville College, School of Education, Program in Middle Childhood/Adolescence Education (Grades 5-12), Purchase, NY 10577-2132. Offers biology (MAT, Advanced Certificate); biology and special education (MPS); chemistry (MAT, Advanced Certificate); chemistry and special education (MPS); earth science (Advanced Certificate); education for sustainability (Advanced Certificate); English (MAT, Advanced Certificate); English and special education (MPS); literacy and special education (MPS); literacy specialist (MPS); math and special education (MPS); mathematics (MAT, Advanced Certificate); physics (MAT, Advanced Certificate); social studies (MAT); social studies and special education (MPS); special education generalist (MPS). *Program availability:* Part-time, evening/weekend. *Faculty:* 2 full-time (both women), 5 part-time/adjunct (1 woman). *Students:* 8 full-time (7 women), 28 part-time (16 women); includes 4 minority (1 Asian, non-Hispanic/Latino; 2 Hispanic/Latino; 1 Two or more races, non-Hispanic/Latino). Average age 31. 7 applicants, 86% accepted, 4 enrolled. In 2017, 13 master's, 1 other advanced degree awarded. *Degree requirements:* For master's, comprehensive exam (for some programs), thesis (for some programs), student teaching, research seminars, portfolios, internships, writing assessment; for Advanced Certificate, comprehensive exam (for some programs). *Entrance requirements:* For master's, GRE or MAT (for programs leading to certification), minimum GPA of 3.0, 2 letters of recommendation, interview, essay (2-3 page personal statement that describes reasons for choosing teaching or educational leadership as profession and philosophy of education), proof of immunization (for those born after 1957). Additional exam requirements/recommendations for international students: Required—TOEFL (minimum score 600 paper-based; 110 iBT); Recommended—IELTS (minimum score 8). *Application deadline:* Applications are processed on a rolling basis. Application fee: $75. Electronic applications accepted. *Expenses:* $915 per credit. *Financial support:* Teaching assistantships, career-related internships or fieldwork, Federal Work-Study, institutionally sponsored loans, scholarships/grants, and unspecified assistantships available. Financial award application deadline: 3/15; financial award applicants required to submit FAFSA. *Faculty research:* Education for sustainability. *Unit head:* Dr. Shelly Wepner, Dean, 914-323-3153, Fax: 914-323-5493, E-mail: shelly.wepner@mville.edu. *Application contact:* Alissa Wilson, Director, Graduate Admissions, 914-323-3150, Fax: 914-694-1732, E-mail: edschool@mville.edu.
Website: http://www.mville.edu/programs#/search/19

Manhattanville College, School of Education, Program in Special Education, Purchase, NY 10577-2132. Offers childhood (grades 1-6) (MPS); childhood education (grades 1-6) and special education (MPS); early childhood (birth-grade 2) (MPS); early childhood (birth-grade 2) and special education (MPS); early childhood and childhood (birth-grade 6) (MPS); English (5-9 and 7-12) (MPS); grades 7-12 generalist (MPS); literacy (birth-grade 6) and special education childhood (grades 1-6) (MPS); literacy 5-12 (MPS); mathematics (5-9 and 7-12) (MPS); science (biology or chemistry 5-9 and 7-12) (MPS); social studies (5-9 and 7-12) (MPS); special education: childhood (grades 1-6) (Certificate); special education: early childhood (birth-grade 2) and childhood (grades 1-

Science Education

6) (Certificate); special education: early childhood (birth-grade 2) (Certificate); special education: grades 7-12 generalist (Certificate). *Program availability:* Part-time, evening/weekend. *Faculty:* 5 full-time (3 women), 24 part-time/adjunct (16 women). *Students:* 77 full-time (69 women), 154 part-time (132 women); includes 33 minority (9 Black or African American, non-Hispanic/Latino; 2 Asian, non-Hispanic/Latino; 22 Hispanic/Latino), 1 international. Average age 28. 87 applicants, 77% accepted, 57 enrolled. In 2017, 86 master's, 2 Certificates awarded. *Degree requirements:* For master's, comprehensive exam (for some programs), thesis (for some programs), student teaching, research seminars, portfolios, internships, writing assessment; for Certificate, comprehensive exam (for some programs). *Entrance requirements:* For master's, GRE or MAT (for programs leading to certification), minimum GPA of 3.0, 2 letters of recommendation, interview, essay (2-3 page personal statement that describes reasons for choosing teaching or educational leadership as profession and philosophy of education), proof of immunization (for those born after 1957). Additional exam requirements/recommendations for international students: Required—TOEFL (minimum score 600 paper-based; 110 iBT); Recommended—IELTS (minimum score 8). *Application deadline:* Applications are processed on a rolling basis. Application fee: $75. Electronic applications accepted. *Expenses:* $915 per credit. *Financial support:* Teaching assistantships, career-related internships or fieldwork, Federal Work-Study, institutionally sponsored loans, scholarships/grants, and unspecified assistantships available. Financial award application deadline: 3/15; financial award applicants required to submit FAFSA. *Faculty research:* Students with emotional difficulties, literacy and adolescents, mindfulness, studying the effects of the environment on special populations, the most difficult cases, students who are presented with multiple challenges: learning, behavioral and ACE experiences who see criminal behavior as a way to cope; working on giving them the tools they need to succeed emotionally and cognitively despite the odds stacked against them. *Unit head:* Dr. Shelly Wepner, Dean, 914-323-3153, Fax: 914-323-5493, E-mail: shelly.wepner@mville.edu. *Application contact:* Alissa Wilson, Director, Graduate Admissions, 914-323-3150, Fax: 914-694-1732, E-mail: edschool@mville.edu.
Website: http://www.mville.edu/programs/special-education

McDaniel College, Graduate and Professional Studies, Program in Elementary and Secondary Education, Westminster, MD 21157-4390. Offers elementary education (MS); elementary STEM instructional leader (Postbaccalaureate Certificate); equity and excellence in education (Postbaccalaureate Certificate); learning technology specialist (Postbaccalaureate Certificate); secondary education (MS). *Accreditation:* NCATE. *Program availability:* Part-time, evening/weekend. *Faculty:* 3 full-time (2 women), 24 part-time/adjunct (22 women). *Students:* 16 full-time (8 women), 148 part-time (114 women); includes 30 minority (17 Black or African American, non-Hispanic/Latino; 5 Asian, non-Hispanic/Latino; 7 Hispanic/Latino; 1 Two or more races, non-Hispanic/Latino), 1 international. Average age 34. 34 applicants, 97% accepted, 18 enrolled. In 2017, 24 master's, 47 other advanced degrees awarded. *Degree requirements:* For master's, comprehensive exam (for some programs), thesis optional. *Entrance requirements:* For master's, PRAXIS, 2 references. Additional exam requirements/recommendations for international students: Required—TOEFL (minimum score 79 iBT), IELTS (minimum score 6). *Application deadline:* For fall admission, 6/1 priority date for domestic students; for spring admission, 11/1 priority date for domestic students; for summer admission, 3/1 priority date for domestic students. Applications are processed on a rolling basis. Application fee: $75. Electronic applications accepted. *Expenses:* Tuition: Full-time $11,760; part-time $490 per credit hour. Tuition and fees vary according to course load and program. *Financial support:* Application deadline: 3/1; applicants required to submit FAFSA. *Unit head:* Fax: 410-857-2515, E-mail: gradadms@mcdaniel.edu. *Application contact:* Penny Pfeiffer, Senior Graduate Enrollment Management Specialist, 410-857-2513, Fax: 410-857-2515, E-mail: ppfeiffer@mcdaniel.edu.

McNeese State University, Doré School of Graduate Studies, Burton College of Education, Department of Education Professions, Program in Middle School Education Grades 4-8, Lake Charles, LA 70609. Offers middle school education grades 4-8 (Postbaccalaureate Certificate), including mathematics, science. *Entrance requirements:* For degree, PRAXIS, 2 letters of recommendation, autobiography. *Application deadline:* For fall admission, 5/15 priority date for domestic and international students; for spring admission, 10/15 priority date for domestic and international students. Applications are processed on a rolling basis. Application fee: $20 ($30 for international students). *Financial support:* Application deadline: 5/1. *Unit head:* Dr. Veronica Faye White, Head, 337-475-5400, Fax: 337-475-5272, E-mail: vfwhite@mcneese.edu. *Application contact:* Dr. Dustin M. Hebert, Director of Dore' School of Graduate Studies, 337-475-5396, Fax: 337-475-5397, E-mail: admissions@mcneese.edu.

Mercer University, Graduate Studies, Macon Campus, Tift College of Education (Macon), Macon, GA 31207. Offers curriculum and instruction (PhD); early childhood education (M Ed, Ed S); educational leadership (M Ed, PhD, Ed S), including higher education (PhD), P-12; higher education leadership (M Ed); independent and charter school leadership (M Ed); secondary education (MAT), including STEM; teacher leadership (Ed S). *Accreditation:* NCATE. *Program availability:* Part-time, evening/weekend, 100% online, blended/hybrid learning. *Faculty:* 13 full-time (8 women), 1 part-time/adjunct (0 women). *Students:* 33 full-time (18 women), 51 part-time (37 women); includes 49 minority (44 Black or African American, non-Hispanic/Latino; 2 Asian, non-Hispanic/Latino; 2 Hispanic/Latino; 1 Two or more races, non-Hispanic/Latino), 1 international. Average age 32. In 2017, 22 master's, 17 doctorates awarded. *Degree requirements:* For master's, research project report; for doctorate, comprehensive exam, thesis/dissertation. *Entrance requirements:* For master's, GRE or MAT, minimum GPA of 2.75; for doctorate, GRE, minimum GPA of 3.5; interview; writing sample; 3 recommendations; for Ed S, GRE or MAT, minimum GPA of 3.5 (for teacher leadership), 3.0 (for educational leadership). Additional exam requirements/recommendations for international students: Required—TOEFL (minimum score 80 iBT). *Application deadline:* For fall admission, 8/1 for domestic and international students; for spring admission, 12/1 for domestic and international students. Applications are processed on a rolling basis. Application fee: $35. Electronic applications accepted. *Expenses:* Contact institution. *Financial support:* Federal Work-Study, institutionally sponsored loans, and unspecified assistantships available. Support available to part-time students. Financial award application deadline: 5/1; financial award applicants required to submit FAFSA. *Faculty research:* Teacher effectiveness, specific learning disabilities, inclusion. *Unit head:* Dr. Scott Davis, Dean, 478-301-2110, Fax: 478-301-5576, E-mail: davis_ds@mercer.edu.
Website: http://education.mercer.edu/

Michigan State University, The Graduate School, College of Natural Science and College of Education, Division of Science and Mathematics Education, East Lansing, MI 48824. Offers biological, physical and general science for teachers (MAT, MS), including biological science (MS), general science (MAT), physical science (MS); mathematics education (MS, PhD).

Michigan Technological University, Graduate School, College of Sciences and Arts, Department of Cognitive and Learning Sciences, Houghton, MI 49931. Offers applied cognitive science and human factors (MS, PhD); applied science education (MS); post-secondary STEM education (Graduate Certificate). *Program availability:* Part-time,

blended/hybrid learning. *Faculty:* 23 full-time (9 women), 7 part-time/adjunct. *Students:* 12 full-time (7 women), 17 part-time (9 women); includes 2 minority (1 Black or African American, non-Hispanic/Latino; 1 Two or more races, non-Hispanic/Latino), 2 international. Average age 37. 37 applicants, 32% accepted, 3 enrolled. In 2017, 7 master's, 1 doctorate awarded. Terminal master's awarded for partial completion of doctoral program. *Degree requirements:* For master's, comprehensive exam (for some programs), thesis (for some programs); for doctorate, comprehensive exam, thesis/dissertation, applied internship experience. *Entrance requirements:* For master's, GRE (for applied cognitive science and human factors program only), statement of purpose, personal statement, official transcripts, 3 letters of recommendation, resume/curriculum vitae; for doctorate, GRE, statement of purpose, personal statement, official transcripts, 3 letters of recommendation, resume/curriculum vitae. Additional exam requirements/recommendations for international students: Required—TOEFL (recommended minimum score 90 iBT) or IELTS. *Application deadline:* For fall admission, 2/1 priority date for domestic and international students. Applications are processed on a rolling basis. Electronic applications accepted. *Expenses:* Tuition, state resident: full-time $17,100; part-time $950 per credit. Tuition, nonresident: full-time $17,100; part-time $950 per credit. *Required fees:* $248; $124 per term. Tuition and fees vary according to course load and program. *Financial support:* In 2017–18, 14 students received support, including 5 fellowships (averaging $15,790 per year), 5 research assistantships with tuition reimbursements available (averaging $15,790 per year), 1 teaching assistantship (averaging $15,790 per year); career-related internships or fieldwork, Federal Work-Study, scholarships/grants, health care benefits, unspecified assistantships, and adjunct instructor positions also available. Financial award application deadline: 12/15; financial award applicants required to submit FAFSA. *Faculty research:* Applied science education, applied cognitive science, human factors, STEM education, human-computer interaction. *Total annual research expenditures:* $410,074. *Unit head:* Dr. Susan L. Amato-Henderson, Chair, 906-487-2536, Fax: 906-487-2468, E-mail: slamato@mtu.edu. *Application contact:* Kelly S. Steelman, Graduate Program Director, 906-487-2792, Fax: 906-487-2468, E-mail: steelman@mtu.edu.
Website: http://www.mtu.edu/cls/

Middle Tennessee State University, College of Graduate Studies, College of Basic and Applied Sciences, Department of Aerospace, Murfreesboro, TN 37132. Offers aerospace education (M Ed); aviation administration (MS). *Program availability:* Part-time, evening/weekend, online learning. *Degree requirements:* For master's, comprehensive exam, thesis optional. *Entrance requirements:* For master's, GRE General Test or MAT. Additional exam requirements/recommendations for international students: Required—TOEFL (minimum score 525 paper-based; 71 iBT) or IELTS (minimum score 6). Electronic applications accepted.

Middle Tennessee State University, College of Graduate Studies, Interdisciplinary Program in Mathematics and Science Education, Murfreesboro, TN 37132. Offers PhD. *Program availability:* Part-time, evening/weekend, online learning. *Entrance requirements:* For doctorate, GRE. Additional exam requirements/recommendations for international students: Required—TOEFL (minimum score 525 paper-based; 71 iBT) or IELTS (minimum score 6). Electronic applications accepted.

Millersville University of Pennsylvania, College of Graduate Studies and Adult Learning, College of Education and Human Services, Department of Educational Foundations, Program in Assessment, Curriculum and Teaching - STEM Education Option, Millersville, PA 17551-0302. Offers assessment, curriculum, and teaching (M Ed), including integrative STEM education. *Program availability:* Part-time, evening/weekend, online only, 100% online. *Faculty:* 9 full-time (8 women), 8 part-time/adjunct (5 women). *Students:* 1 (woman) full-time, 31 part-time (20 women). Average age 31. 17 applicants, 100% accepted, 9 enrolled. *Degree requirements:* For master's, comprehensive exam, thesis/capstone experience. *Entrance requirements:* For master's, GRE or MAT (if undergraduate cumulative GPA is lower than 2.8), teaching certificate. Additional exam requirements/recommendations for international students: Required—TOEFL (minimum score 80 iBT), IELTS (minimum score 6.5), PTE (minimum score 60). *Application deadline:* Applications are processed on a rolling basis. Application fee: $40. Electronic applications accepted. *Expenses:* $500 per credit resident tuition, $581.75 per credit non-resident tuition, $59.25 academic support fee. *Financial support:* Unspecified assistantships available. Financial award application deadline: 3/15; financial award applicants required to submit FAFSA. *Faculty research:* Pedagogical content knowledge in instructional technology and stem, watershed development and management, on-line teaching enhancement. *Unit head:* Dr. Tim E. Mahoney, Coordinator, 717-871-7202, E-mail: tim.mahoney@millersville.edu. *Application contact:* Dr. Victor S. DeSantis, Dean of College of Graduate Studies and Adult Learning/Associate Provost for Civic and Community Engagement, 717-871-7619, Fax: 717-871-7954, E-mail: victor.desantis@millersville.edu.
Website: http://millersville.edu/academics/educ/edfoundations/master-stem.php

Millersville University of Pennsylvania, College of Graduate Studies and Adult Learning, College of Science and Technology, Millersville, PA 17551-0302. Offers M Ed, MS, MSN, DNP. *Program availability:* Part-time, evening/weekend, 100% online, blended/hybrid learning. *Faculty:* 18 full-time (9 women), 13 part-time/adjunct (7 women). *Students:* 25 full-time (13 women), 174 part-time (113 women); includes 17 minority (5 Black or African American, non-Hispanic/Latino; 1 American Indian or Alaska Native, non-Hispanic/Latino; 4 Asian, non-Hispanic/Latino; 7 Hispanic/Latino), 4 international. Average age 34. 80 applicants, 88% accepted, 47 enrolled. In 2017, 63 master's awarded. *Degree requirements:* For master's, comprehensive exam (for some programs), thesis optional, graded portfolio (educational foundations); field practicum; internship, applied research or scholarly project; for doctorate, thesis/dissertation, scholarly project, clinical hours. *Entrance requirements:* For master's, GRE or MAT (if undergraduate cumulative GPA is 3.0 or lower), letters of recommendation, transcripts, resume, goal statement (for some programs). Additional exam requirements/recommendations for international students: Required—TOEFL (minimum score 80 iBT), IELTS (minimum score 6.5), PTE (minimum score 60). *Application deadline:* Applications are processed on a rolling basis. Application fee: $40. Electronic applications accepted. *Expenses:* $500 per credit resident tuition and fees; $750 per credit non-resident tuition and fees; $114.75 per credit general fee (maximum of 12 credits); technology fee $27 per credit (resident), $39 per credit (non-resident). *Financial support:* In 2017–18, 19 students received support. Unspecified assistantships available. Financial award application deadline: 3/15; financial award applicants required to submit FAFSA. *Faculty research:* Engineering design, emergency management, continuity of operations, regional planning, disaster law and policy, community preparedness and mitigation efforts, climatology and meteorology, weather derivatives, risk management, environmental economics and policy, business operations analysis, training of secondary mathematics teachers, the use of technology and equity in mathematics, questioning techniques of teacher educators, family nurse practitioner, nurse education, primary care, health promo. *Total annual research expenditures:* $141,856. *Unit head:* Dr. Michael Jackson, Dean, College of Science and Technology, 717-871-4292, E-mail: michael.jackson@millersville.edu. *Application contact:* Dr. Victor S. DeSantis, Dean of College of Graduate Studies and Adult Learning/Associate Provost for Civic and Community Engagement, 717-871-7619, Fax: 717-871-7954, E-mail: victor.desantis@millersville.edu.
Website: http://www.millersville.edu/academics/scma/scienceandmath/index.php

Minnesota State University Mankato, College of Graduate Studies and Research, College of Science, Engineering and Technology, Department of Biological Sciences, Mankato, MN 56001. Offers biology (MS); biology education (MS); environmental sciences (MS). *Program availability:* Part-time. *Degree requirements:* For master's, one foreign language, comprehensive exam, thesis or alternative. *Entrance requirements:* For master's, minimum GPA of 3.0 during previous 2 years of course work. Additional exam requirements/recommendations for international students: Required—TOEFL. Electronic applications accepted.

Minnesota State University Mankato, College of Graduate Studies and Research, College of Science, Engineering and Technology, Department of Physics and Astronomy, Mankato, MN 56001. Offers physics (MS); physics education (MS). *Degree requirements:* For master's, one foreign language, comprehensive exam, thesis or alternative. *Entrance requirements:* For master's, minimum GPA of 2.75, two recommendation letters, one-page personal statement. Additional exam requirements/recommendations for international students: Required—TOEFL (minimum score 530 paper-based; 72 iBT). Electronic applications accepted.

Minot State University, Graduate School, Program in Biological and Agricultural Sciences, Minot, ND 58707-0002. Offers science (MAT). *Degree requirements:* For master's, thesis. *Entrance requirements:* For master's, minimum GPA of 3.0 or GRE General Test, secondary teaching certificate. Additional exam requirements/recommendations for international students: Required—TOEFL (minimum score 79 iBT), IELTS (minimum score 6). *Faculty research:* Science education.

Mississippi College, Graduate School, School of Education, Department of Teacher Education and Leadership, Clinton, MS 39058. Offers art (M Ed); biological science (M Ed); business education (M Ed); computer science (M Ed); dyslexia therapy (M Ed); educational leadership (M Ed, Ed D, Ed S); elementary education (M Ed, Ed S); English (M Ed); higher education administration (MS); mathematics (M Ed); secondary education (M Ed); social studies (history) (M Ed); teaching arts (M Ed). *Program availability:* Part-time, online learning. *Degree requirements:* For master's, comprehensive exam, thesis optional. *Entrance requirements:* For master's, NTE. Additional exam requirements/recommendations for international students: Recommended—TOEFL, IELTS. Electronic applications accepted.

Missouri State University, Graduate School, College of Natural and Applied Sciences, Department of Biology, Springfield, MO 65897. Offers biology (MS); natural and applied science (MNAS), including biology (MNAS, MS Ed); secondary education (MS Ed), including biology (MNAS, MS Ed). *Faculty:* 18 full-time (3 women), 7 part-time/adjunct (2 women). *Students:* 21 full-time (12 women), 26 part-time (16 women); includes 5 minority (1 Asian, non-Hispanic/Latino; 3 Hispanic/Latino; 1 Two or more races, non-Hispanic/Latino), 5 international. Average age 26. 28 applicants, 46% accepted, 13 enrolled. In 2017, 20 master's awarded. *Degree requirements:* For master's, comprehensive exam, thesis or alternative. *Entrance requirements:* For master's, GRE (MS, MNAS), 24 hours of course work in biology (MS); minimum GPA of 3.0 (MS, MNAS); 9-12 teacher certification (MS Ed). Additional exam requirements/recommendations for international students: Required—TOEFL (minimum score 550 paper-based; 79 iBT), IELTS (minimum score 6). *Application deadline:* For fall admission, 7/20 priority date for domestic students, 5/1 for international students; for spring admission, 12/20 priority date for domestic students, 9/1 for international students; for summer admission, 5/20 priority date for domestic students. Applications are processed on a rolling basis. Application fee: $35 ($50 for international students). Electronic applications accepted. *Expenses:* Tuition, state resident: full-time $2915; part-time $2021 per credit hour. Tuition, nonresident: full-time $5354; part-time $3647 per credit hour. International tuition: $11,992 full-time. Required fees: $173; $173 per credit hour. Tuition and fees vary according to class time, course level, course load, degree level, campus/location and program. *Financial support:* In 2017–18, 2 research assistantships with full tuition reimbursements (averaging $10,672 per year), 26 teaching assistantships with full tuition reimbursements (averaging $9,746 per year) were awarded; Federal Work-Study, institutionally sponsored loans, scholarships/grants, and unspecified assistantships also available. Financial award application deadline: 3/31; financial award applicants required to submit FAFSA. *Faculty research:* Hibernation physiology of bats, behavioral ecology of salamanders, mussel conservation, plant evolution and systematics, cellular/molecular mechanisms involved in migraine pathology. *Unit head:* Dr. S. Alicia Mathis, Department Head, 417-836-5126, Fax: 417-836-6934, E-mail: biology@missouristate.edu. *Application contact:* Stephanie Praschan, Director, Graduate Enrollment Management, 417-836-5330, Fax: 417-836-6200, E-mail: stephaniepraschan@missouristate.edu.
Website: http://biology.missouristate.edu/

Missouri State University, Graduate College, College of Natural and Applied Sciences, Department of Geography, Geology, and Planning, Springfield, MO 65897. Offers geography, geology, and planning (Certificate); natural and applied science (MNAS), including geography, geology and planning; secondary education (MS Ed), including earth science, physical geography. *Program availability:* Part-time, evening/weekend. *Faculty:* 18 full-time (4 women), 1 part-time/adjunct (0 women). *Students:* 27 full-time (10 women), 7 part-time (6 women); includes 2 minority (both Two or more races, non-Hispanic/Latino), 3 international. Average age 29. 27 applicants, 48% accepted, 13 enrolled. In 2017, 32 master's awarded. *Degree requirements:* For master's, comprehensive exam, thesis (for some programs). *Entrance requirements:* For master's, GRE General Test (MS, MNAS), minimum undergraduate GPA of 3.0 (MS, MNAS), 9-12 teacher certification (MS Ed). Additional exam requirements/recommendations for international students: Required—TOEFL (minimum score 550 paper-based; 79 iBT), IELTS (minimum score 6). *Application deadline:* For fall admission, 7/20 priority date for domestic students, 5/1 for international students; for spring admission, 12/20 priority date for domestic students, 9/1 for international students. Applications are processed on a rolling basis. Application fee: $35 ($50 for international students). Electronic applications accepted. *Expenses:* Tuition, state resident: full-time $2915; part-time $2021 per credit hour. Tuition, nonresident: full-time $5354; part-time $3647 per credit hour. International tuition: $11,992 full-time. Required fees: $173; $173 per credit hour. Tuition and fees vary according to class time, course level, course load, degree level, campus/location and program. *Financial support:* In 2017–18, 3 research assistantships with full tuition reimbursements (averaging $11,574 per year), 15 teaching assistantships with full tuition reimbursements (averaging $9,365 per year) were awarded; career-related internships or fieldwork, Federal Work-Study, institutionally sponsored loans, scholarships/grants, and unspecified assistantships also available. Financial award application deadline: 3/31; financial award applicants required to submit FAFSA. *Faculty research:* Stratigraphy and ancient meteorite impacts, environmental geochemistry of karst, hyperspectral image processing, water quality, small town planning. *Unit head:* Dr. Toby Dogwiler, Department Head, 417-836-5800, Fax: 417-836-6934, E-mail: tobydogwiler@missouristate.edu. *Application contact:* Stephanie Praschan, Director, Graduate Enrollment Management, 417-836-5330, Fax: 417-836-6200, E-mail: stephaniepraschan@missouristate.edu.
Website: http://geosciences.missouristate.edu/

Missouri State University, Graduate College, College of Natural and Applied Sciences, Department of Physics, Astronomy, and Materials Science, Springfield, MO 65897. Offers materials science (MS); natural and applied science (MNAS), including physics (MNAS, MS Ed); secondary education (MS Ed), including physics (MNAS, MS Ed). *Program availability:* Part-time. *Faculty:* 9 full-time (0 women). *Students:* 10 full-time (1 woman), 5 part-time (0 women), 10 international. Average age 26. 12 applicants, 92% accepted, 5 enrolled. In 2017, 14 master's awarded. *Degree requirements:* For master's, comprehensive exam, thesis. *Entrance requirements:* For master's, GRE (MS, MNAS), minimum undergraduate GPA of 3.0 (MS and MNAS), 9-12 teaching certification (MS Ed). Additional exam requirements/recommendations for international students: Required—TOEFL (minimum score 550 paper-based; 79 iBT), IELTS (minimum score 6). *Application deadline:* For fall admission, 7/20 priority date for domestic students, 5/1 for international students; for spring admission, 12/20 priority date for domestic students, 9/1 for international students. Applications are processed on a rolling basis. Application fee: $35 ($50 for international students). Electronic applications accepted. *Expenses:* Tuition, state resident: full-time $2021 per credit hour. Tuition, nonresident: full-time $5354; part-time $3647 per credit hour. International tuition: $11,992 full-time. Required fees: $173; $173 per credit hour. Tuition and fees vary according to class time, course level, course load, degree level, campus/location and program. *Financial support:* In 2017–18, 6 research assistantships with full tuition reimbursements (averaging $10,672 per year), 11 teaching assistantships with full tuition reimbursements (averaging $10,672 per year) were awarded; Federal Work-Study, institutionally sponsored loans, scholarships/grants, and unspecified assistantships also available. Financial award application deadline: 3/31; financial award applicants required to submit FAFSA. *Faculty research:* Nanocomposites, ferroelectricity, infrared focal plane array sensors, biosensors, pulsating stars. *Unit head:* Dr. David Cornelison, Department Head, 417-836-4467, Fax: 417-836-6226, E-mail: physics@missouristate.edu. *Application contact:* Stephanie Praschan, Director, Graduate Enrollment Management, 417-836-5330, Fax: 417-836-6200, E-mail: stephaniepraschan@missouristate.edu.
Website: http://physics.missouristate.edu/

Molloy College, Graduate Education Program, Rockville Centre, NY 11571-5002. Offers adolescent education in biology (MS); adolescent special education (Advanced Certificate); bilingual extension (Advanced Certificate); childhood education (MS); childhood special education (Advanced Certificate); early childhood education (MS); educational technology (MS); English (MS); mathematics (MS); social studies (MS); Spanish (MS); special education on both childhood and adolescent levels (MS); teaching English to speakers of other languages (TESOL) in grades pre-K to 12 (MS); TESOL (Advanced Certificate). *Accreditation:* NCATE. *Program availability:* Part-time, evening/weekend. *Faculty:* 18 full-time (17 women), 11 part-time/adjunct (9 women). *Students:* 102 full-time (80 women), 217 part-time (167 women); includes 65 minority (16 Black or African American, non-Hispanic/Latino; 7 Asian, non-Hispanic/Latino; 38 Hispanic/Latino; 4 Two or more races, non-Hispanic/Latino), 1 international. Average age 41. 153 applicants, 68% accepted, 85 enrolled. In 2017, 95 master's, 3 other advanced degrees awarded. *Entrance requirements:* Additional exam requirements/recommendations for international students: Required—TOEFL (minimum score 550 paper-based; 79 iBT). *Application deadline:* Applications are processed on a rolling basis. Application fee: $60. Electronic applications accepted. *Expenses: Tuition:* Full-time $19,980; part-time $1110 per credit. Required fees: $1040. Tuition and fees vary according to course load and degree level. *Financial support:* Application deadline: 3/1; applicants required to submit FAFSA. *Faculty research:* English Language Learners; social emotional needs of students; gifted education; cultural diversity; collaborative teaching methods. *Unit head:* Joanne O'Brien, Associate Dean and Director of Graduate Education Programs, 516-323-3116, E-mail: jobrien@molloy.edu. *Application contact:* Jaclyn Machowicz, Assistant Director for Admissions, 516-323-4010, E-mail: jmachowicz@molloy.edu.

Montclair State University, The Graduate School, College of Education and Human Services, MAT Program in Teaching, Montclair, NJ 07043-1624. Offers art (MAT); biology (MAT); chemistry (MAT); earth science (MAT); English (MAT); French (MAT); health and physical education (MAT); health education (MAT); mathematics (MAT); music (MAT); physical education (MAT); physical science (MAT); social studies (MAT); Spanish (MAT); teacher of English as a second language (MAT). *Degree requirements:* For master's, comprehensive exam, thesis or alternative. *Entrance requirements:* For master's, interview, 2 letters of recommendation. Additional exam requirements/recommendations for international students: Required—TOEFL (minimum score 83 iBT), IELTS (minimum score 6.5). Electronic applications accepted.

Montclair State University, The Graduate School, College of Science and Mathematics, Program in Biology, Montclair, NJ 07043-1624. Offers biological science/education (MS); biology (MS); ecology and evolution (MS); physiology (MS).

Morehead State University, Graduate Programs, College of Education, Department of Middle Grades and Secondary Education, Morehead, KY 40351. Offers business and marketing education (MAT); English/language arts 5-9 (MAT); French (MAT); health P-12 (MAT); mathematics 5-9 (MAT); physical education P-12 (MAT); science 5-9 (MAT); secondary biology (MAT); secondary chemistry (MAT); secondary earth science (MAT); secondary English (MAT); secondary math (MAT); secondary physics (MAT); secondary social studies (MAT); social studies 5-9 (MAT); Spanish (MAT). *Program availability:* Part-time, evening/weekend. *Degree requirements:* For master's, portfolio. *Entrance requirements:* For master's, GRE or PRAXIS II content exam, minimum overall undergraduate GPA of 2.5. Additional exam requirements/recommendations for international students: Required—TOEFL (minimum score 500 paper-based). Electronic applications accepted.

Morgan State University, School of Graduate Studies, School of Education and Urban Studies, Department of Advanced Studies, Leadership and Policy, Program in Science Education, Baltimore, MD 21251. Offers MS, Ed D. *Entrance requirements:* Additional exam requirements/recommendations for international students: Required—TOEFL (minimum score 550 paper-based). *Application deadline:* For fall admission, 2/1 priority date for domestic students; for spring admission, 10/1 priority date for domestic students. *Expenses:* Tuition, state resident: part-time $433 per credit. Tuition, nonresident: part-time $851 per credit. Required fees: $81.50 per credit. *Unit head:* Whitney Johnson, Graduate Coordinator, E-mail: whitney.johnson@morgan.edu. *Application contact:* Dr. Dean Campbell, Graduate Recruitment Specialist, 443-885-3185, Fax: 443-885-8226, E-mail: dean.campbell@morgan.edu.

National Louis University, National College of Education, Chicago, IL 60603. Offers administration and supervision (M Ed, Ed D, CAS, Ed S); curriculum and instruction (M Ed, MS Ed, CAS); early childhood administration (M Ed, CAS); early childhood education (M Ed, MAT, MS Ed, CAS); education (Ed D); educational psychology/human learning and development (M Ed, MS Ed, CAS, Ed S); elementary education (MAT); interdisciplinary curriculum and instruction (M Ed); mathematics education (M Ed, MS Ed, CAS); middle grades education (MAT); reading and language (M Ed, MS Ed, CAS); school psychology (M Ed, Ed S); science education (M Ed, MS Ed, CAS); secondary education (MAT); special education (M Ed, MAT, CAS); technology in education (M Ed, CAS). *Accreditation:* NCATE. *Program availability:* Part-time, evening/weekend. *Degree requirements:* For doctorate, comprehensive exam, thesis/dissertation. *Entrance requirements:* For master's, MAT or GRE, minimum GPA of 3.0; for doctorate, GRE General Test, minimum GPA of 3.25, interview, resume, writing sample, 4 recommendations. Additional exam requirements/recommendations for international students: Required—TOEFL (minimum score 550 paper-based; 79 iBT).

New Mexico Institute of Mining and Technology, Center for Graduate Studies, Department of Management, Socorro, NM 87801. Offers STEM education (MEM). *Program availability:* Part-time. *Expenses:* Tuition, state resident: full-time $6406; part-time $356 per credit. Tuition, nonresident: full-time $21,190; part-time $1177 per credit. *Required fees:* $1030.

New Mexico Institute of Mining and Technology, Center for Graduate Studies, Master of Science for Teachers Interdepartmental Program, Socorro, NM 87801. Offers MST. *Degree requirements:* For master's, thesis optional. *Entrance requirements:* For master's, GRE General Test. Additional exam requirements/recommendations for international students: Required—TOEFL (minimum score 540 paper-based). Electronic applications accepted. *Expenses:* Tuition, state resident: full-time $6406; part-time $356 per credit. Tuition, nonresident: full-time $21,190; part-time $1177 per credit. *Required fees:* $1030. *Faculty research:* Teaching secondary school science and/or mathematics.

New York Institute of Technology, School of Interdisciplinary Studies and Education, Department of Instructional Technology, Old Westbury, NY 11568-8000. Offers emerging technologies for trainers (Advanced Certificate); instructional design for global e-learning (Advanced Certificate); instructional technology (MS), including educators, trainers; STEM education (Advanced Certificate). *Program availability:* Part-time, evening/weekend, 100% online, blended/hybrid learning. *Faculty:* 6 full-time (3 women), 6 part-time/adjunct (4 women). *Students:* 7 full-time (2 women), 105 part-time (73 women); includes 15 minority (5 Black or African American, non-Hispanic/Latino; 4 Asian, non-Hispanic/Latino; 4 Hispanic/Latino; 2 Two or more races, non-Hispanic/Latino), 1 international. Average age 33. 47 applicants, 83% accepted, 30 enrolled. In 2017, 53 master's, 13 other advanced degrees awarded. *Entrance requirements:* For master's, GRE (minimum combined score of 300) or MAT (minimum score of 400) within the last five years, bachelor's degree; minimum undergraduate GPA of 3.0; demonstrated proficiency in basic uses of instructional technologies; initial/provisional or permanent/professional NY state certification in any teaching area (for educators option); for Advanced Certificate, GRE or MAT (within last 5 years), BS; minimum undergraduate GPA of 3.0; demonstrated proficiency in basic uses of instructional technologies. Additional exam requirements/recommendations for international students: Required—TOEFL (minimum score 79 iBT), IELTS (minimum score 6). *Application deadline:* Applications are processed on a rolling basis. Application fee: $50. Electronic applications accepted. *Expenses:* $1,285 per credit plus fees. *Financial support:* Career-related internships or fieldwork, scholarships/grants, health care benefits, tuition waivers (full and partial), and unspecified assistantships available. Support available to part-time students. Financial award application deadline: 2/15; financial award applicants required to submit FAFSA. *Faculty research:* Integration of information and communication technologies (ICTs) and media literacy education into learning environments; urban K-12 teachers' effective use of technology to enhance student achievement; instructional design and transdisciplinary curriculum studies for online instruction; STEM and computing partnerships for K-12 teachers; experiential, collaborative, and performance-based approaches to pedagogy and technology integration in the K-12 classroom. *Unit head:* Dr. Melda Yildiz, Department Chair, 516-686-1053, Fax: 516-686-7655, E-mail: myildiz@nyit.edu. *Application contact:* Alice Dolitsky, Director, Graduate Admissions, 516-686-7520, Fax: 516-686-1116, E-mail: nyitgrad@nyit.edu.
Website: http://www.nyit.edu/interdisciplinary/department_instructional_technology

New York Institute of Technology, School of Interdisciplinary Studies and Education, Department of Teacher Education, Old Westbury, NY 11568-8000. Offers adolescence education (MS), including math (MAT, MS); science; adolescent education (MAT), including biology, chemistry, English, math (MAT, MS), social studies; childhood education (MS); early childhood (MS). *Program availability:* Part-time, evening/weekend, 100% online, blended/hybrid learning. *Faculty:* 2 full-time (both women), 7 part-time/adjunct (3 women). *Students:* 46 full-time (44 women), 30 part-time (22 women); includes 23 minority (8 Black or African American, non-Hispanic/Latino; 6 Asian, non-Hispanic/Latino; 8 Hispanic/Latino; 1 Two or more races, non-Hispanic/Latino), 2 international. Average age 29. 39 applicants, 72% accepted, 15 enrolled. In 2017, 14 master's awarded. *Entrance requirements:* For master's, GRE or MAT, BS or equivalent; minimum cumulative undergraduate GPA of 3.0; NY state provisional or initial certification (for MS in adolescence education); BS with major in biology, chemistry, economics, English, history, life sciences, math, physics, or psychology (for MS in childhood, early childhood education, and MAT); interview; personal statement. Additional exam requirements/recommendations for international students: Required—TOEFL (minimum score 79 iBT), IELTS (minimum score 6). *Application deadline:* Applications are processed on a rolling basis. Application fee: $50. Electronic applications accepted. *Expenses:* $1,285 per credit plus fees. *Financial support:* Career-related internships or fieldwork, Federal Work-Study, scholarships/grants, tuition waivers (full and partial), and unspecified assistantships available. Support available to part-time students. Financial award application deadline: 2/15; financial award applicants required to submit FAFSA. *Faculty research:* Evolving definition of new literacies and its impact on teaching and learning (twenty-first century skills), new literacies practices in teacher education, teachers' professional development, English language and literacy learning through mobile learning, teaching reading to culturally and linguistically diverse children. *Unit head:* Dr. Hui-Yin Hsu, Department Chair, 516-686-1322, Fax: 516-686-7655, E-mail: hhsu02@nyit.edu. *Application contact:* Alice Dolitsky, Director, Graduate Admissions, 516-686-7520, Fax: 516-686-1116, E-mail: nyitgrad@nyit.edu.
Website: http://www.nyit.edu/interdisciplinary/department_teacher_education

New York University, Steinhardt School of Culture, Education, and Human Development, Department of Teaching and Learning, New York, NY 10012. Offers clinically rich integrated science (MA), including clinically rich integrated science, teaching biology grades 7-12, teaching chemistry 7-12, teaching physics 7-12; early childhood and childhood education (MA), including childhood education, early childhood education, early childhood education/early childhood special education; English education (MA, PhD, Advanced Certificate), including clinically-based English education, grades 7-12 (MA), English education (PhD, Advanced Certificate), English education, grades 7-12 (MA); environmental conservation education (MA); literacy education (MA), including literacy 5-12, literacy B-6; mathematics education (MA), including teachers of mathematics 7-12; multilingual/multicultural studies (MA, PhD, Advanced Certificate), including bilingual education, foreign language education (MA), teaching English to speakers of other languages (MA, PhD), teaching foreign languages, 7-12 (MA), teaching French as a foreign language (MA), teaching Spanish as a foreign language (MA); social studies education (MA), including teaching art/social studies 7-12, teaching social studies 7-12; special education (MA), including childhood, early childhood; teaching and learning (Ed D, PhD). *Program availability:* Part-time. *Students:* Average age 25. 926 applicants, 68% accepted, 210 enrolled. In 2017, 290 master's, 10 doctorates, 2 other advanced degrees awarded. *Entrance requirements:* For doctorate, GRE General Test, interview; for Advanced Certificate, master's degree. Additional exam requirements/recommendations for international students: Required—TOEFL (minimum score 100 iBT). *Application deadline:* For fall admission, 12/1 priority date for domestic and international students; for spring admission, 10/1 for domestic and international students. Applications are processed on a rolling basis. Application fee: $75. Electronic applications accepted. *Expenses: Tuition:* Full-time $41,352; part-time

$19,968 per year. *Required fees:* $2496; $1628 per unit. $814 per term. Tuition and fees vary according to course load and program. *Financial support:* Fellowships with full and partial tuition reimbursements, research assistantships with full and partial tuition reimbursements, teaching assistantships with full and partial tuition reimbursements, career-related internships or fieldwork, Federal Work-Study, institutionally sponsored loans, scholarships/grants, tuition waivers (partial), and unspecified assistantships available. Support available to part-time students. Financial award application deadline: 2/1; financial award applicants required to submit FAFSA. *Faculty research:* Cultural contexts for literacy learning, school restructuring, parenting and education, teacher learning, language assessment. *Unit head:* Dr. Susan Neuman, Chairperson, 212-998-5460, Fax: 212-995-4049. *Application contact:* 212-998-5030, Fax: 212-995-4328, E-mail: steinhardt.gradadmissions@nyu.edu.
Website: http://steinhardt.nyu.edu/teachlearn/

North Carolina Agricultural and Technical State University, School of Graduate Studies, College of Arts and Sciences, Department of Biology, Greensboro, NC 27411. Offers biology (MS); biology education (MAT). *Program availability:* Part-time, evening/weekend. *Degree requirements:* For master's, comprehensive exam, thesis (for some programs), qualifying exam. *Entrance requirements:* For master's, GRE General Test, personal statement. *Faculty research:* Physical ecology, cytochemistry, botany, parasitology, microbiology.

North Carolina State University, Graduate School, College of Education, Department of Mathematics, Science, and Technology Education, Program in Science Education, Raleigh, NC 27695. Offers M Ed, MS, PhD. *Accreditation:* NCATE. *Program availability:* Part-time. *Degree requirements:* For master's, thesis (for some programs), oral exam; for doctorate, one foreign language, thesis/dissertation, oral and written exams. *Entrance requirements:* For master's, GRE General Test or MAT, minimum GPA of 3.0; for doctorate, GRE General Test, minimum GPA of 3.0, interview. Electronic applications accepted. *Faculty research:* Teacher development, sociocultural issues in learning, student science misconceptions, technical applications to science teaching.

North Dakota State University, College of Graduate and Interdisciplinary Studies, College of Engineering, Doctoral Program in Science, Fargo, ND 58102. Offers environmental and conservation science (PhD); materials and nanotechnology (PhD); natural resource management (PhD); science, technology, engineering, mathematics education (STEM) (PhD); transportation and logistics (PhD). *Degree requirements:* For doctorate, comprehensive exam, thesis/dissertation. *Entrance requirements:* For doctorate, bachelor's degree in engineering, minimum GPA of 3.0. Additional exam requirements/recommendations for international students: Required—TOEFL. Electronic applications accepted. *Expenses:* Contact institution.

North Dakota State University, College of Graduate and Interdisciplinary Studies, College of Human Development and Education, School of Education, Fargo, ND 58102. Offers agricultural education (M Ed, MS), including agricultural education; counselor education (M Ed, MS), including clinical mental health counseling (M Ed, MS), counselor education and supervision (PhD), school counseling (M Ed, MS); curriculum and instruction (M Ed, MS); education (PhD); educational leadership (M Ed, MS, Ed S); family and consumer sciences education (M Ed, MS); history education (M Ed, MS); institutional analysis (Ed D); mathematics education (M Ed, MS); music education (M Ed, MS); occupational and adult education (Ed D); science education (M Ed, MS). *Accreditation:* NCATE. *Program availability:* Part-time, evening/weekend, online learning. *Degree requirements:* For master's, comprehensive exam; for doctorate, thesis/dissertation; for Ed S, thesis. *Entrance requirements:* For degree, GRE General Test, master's degree, minimum GPA of 3.25. Additional exam requirements/recommendations for international students: Required—TOEFL.

North Dakota State University, College of Graduate and Interdisciplinary Studies, Program in STEM Education, Fargo, ND 58102. Offers PhD. Electronic applications accepted.

Northeastern Illinois University, College of Graduate Studies and Research, Daniel L. Goodwin College of Education, MAT Program in Secondary Education, Chicago, IL 60625. Offers language arts (MAT); mathematics (MAT); science (MAT); social science (MAT). *Expenses:* Tuition, state resident: full-time $7274; part-time $404.11 per credit hour. Tuition, nonresident: full-time $14,548; part-time $808.23 per credit hour. *Required fees:* $1284. *Unit head:* Dr. Brian Schultz, Department Chair, 773-442-5327, E-mail: b-schultz@neiu.edu. *Application contact:* Martha Narvaez, Graduate Admission Representative, 773-442-6006, E-mail: m-narvaez@neiu.edu.

Northeastern State University, College of Science and Health Professions, Department of Natural Sciences, Program in Science Education, Tahlequah, OK 74464-2399. Offers M Ed. *Program availability:* Part-time, evening/weekend. *Faculty:* 6 full-time (all women), 4 part-time/adjunct (1 woman). *Students:* 28 part-time (24 women); includes 7 minority (1 American Indian or Alaska Native, non-Hispanic/Latino; 2 Asian, non-Hispanic/Latino; 4 Hispanic/Latino). Average age 37. In 2017, 15 master's awarded. *Entrance requirements:* For master's, MAT or GRE, minimum GPA of 2.5. *Application deadline:* For fall admission, 6/1 for domestic students. Applications are processed on a rolling basis. Application fee: $25. Electronic applications accepted. *Expenses:* Tuition, state resident: part-time $222 per credit hour. Tuition, nonresident: part-time $501.75 per credit hour. *Required fees:* $37.40 per credit hour. Tuition and fees vary according to degree level. *Unit head:* Dr. Pamela Christol, Program Chair, 918-449-6539, E-mail: christol@nsuok.edu. *Application contact:* Josh McCollum, Graduate Coordinator, 918-444-2093, E-mail: mccolluj@nsuok.edu.
Website: http://academics.nsuok.edu/naturalsciences/Degrees/Graduate/MEdScienceEducation.aspx

Northern Arizona University, College of Engineering, Forestry, and Natural Sciences, Center for Science Teaching and Learning, Flagstaff, AZ 86011. Offers science teaching (MA); science with certification (MAT). *Program availability:* Part-time, 100% online, blended/hybrid learning. *Faculty:* 8 full-time (4 women). *Students:* 15 full-time (10 women), 15 part-time (10 women); includes 4 minority (1 Black or African American, non-Hispanic/Latino; 2 Hispanic/Latino; 1 Two or more races, non-Hispanic/Latino). Average age 29. 15 applicants, 100% accepted, 15 enrolled. In 2017, 21 master's awarded. *Degree requirements:* For master's, variable foreign language requirement, comprehensive exam (for some programs), thesis (for some programs). *Entrance requirements:* Additional exam requirements/recommendations for international students: Required—TOEFL (minimum score 80 iBT), IELTS (minimum score 6.5). *Application deadline:* For fall admission, 3/1 for domestic and international students; for spring admission, 10/1 for domestic and international students. Application fee: $65. Electronic applications accepted. *Expenses:* Tuition, state resident: full-time $9240; part-time $458 per credit hour. Tuition, nonresident: full-time $21,588; part-time $1199 per credit hour. *Required fees:* $1021; $14 per credit hour. $646 per semester. Tuition and fees vary according to course load, campus/location and program. *Financial support:* In 2017–18, 7 students received support, including 4 research assistantships with full and partial tuition reimbursements available (averaging $17,500 per year), 3 teaching assistantships with full and partial tuition reimbursements available (averaging $17,500 per year); institutionally sponsored loans, health care benefits, tuition waivers (full and partial), and unspecified assistantships also available. Financial award application deadline: 2/1; financial award applicants required to submit FAFSA. *Unit*

head: Dr. Max Dass, Director, 928-523-7120, E-mail: pradeep.dass@nau.edu. *Application contact:* Lillie Giffen, Administrative Associate, 928-523-7187, E-mail: lillie.giffen@nau.edu.
Website: https://nau.edu/CEFNS/CSTL/

Northern Michigan University, Office of Graduate Education and Research, College of Health Sciences and Professional Studies, School of Education, Leadership and Public Service, Marquette, MI 49855-5301. Offers administration and supervision (MAE); instruction (MAE); learning disabilities (MAE); postsecondary biology education (MS); reading education (MAE), including reading, reading specialist. *Accreditation:* TEAC. *Program availability:* Part-time, online learning. *Degree requirements:* For master's, thesis (for some programs). *Entrance requirements:* For master's, minimum GPA of 3.0. Additional exam requirements/recommendations for international students: Required—TOEFL (minimum score 550 paper-based; 79 iBT), IELTS (minimum score 6.5). *Application deadline:* For fall admission, 7/1 priority date for domestic students; for winter admission, 11/15 for domestic students; for spring admission, 3/17 for domestic students. Applications are processed on a rolling basis. Application fee: $50. Electronic applications accepted. *Expenses:* Tuition, state resident: full-time $9417; part-time $542 per credit hour. Tuition, nonresident: full-time $12,873; part-time $758 per credit hour. Tuition and fees vary according to course load, degree level and program. *Financial support:* Research assistantships with full tuition reimbursements, career-related internships or fieldwork, Federal Work-Study, institutionally sponsored loans, and unspecified assistantships available. Support available to part-time students. Financial award application deadline: 3/1; financial award applicants required to submit FAFSA. *Unit head:* Dr. Joseph Lubig, Associate Dean for Teacher Education, 906-227-1880, Fax: 906-227-2764, E-mail: jlubig@nmu.edu. *Application contact:* Dr. Joseph Lubig, Associate Dean for Teacher Education, 906-227-1880, Fax: 906-227-2764, E-mail: jlubig@nmu.edu.
Website: http://www.nmu.edu/education/

Northern Vermont University–Lyndon, Graduate Programs in Education, Department of Natural Sciences, Lyndonville, VT 05851. Offers science education (MST). *Program availability:* Part-time. *Degree requirements:* For master's, exam or major field project. *Entrance requirements:* Additional exam requirements/recommendations for international students: Recommended—TOEFL (minimum score 500 paper-based). *Faculty research:* Fern genetics, comparative butterfly research.

Northwest Missouri State University, Graduate School, College of Arts and Sciences, Maryville, MO 64468-6001. Offers biology (MS); elementary mathematics specialist (MS Ed); English (MA); English education (MS Ed); English pedagogy (MA); geographic information science (MS, Certificate); history (MS Ed); mathematics (MS); mathematics education (MS Ed); teaching: science (MS Ed). *Program availability:* Part-time. *Faculty:* 67 full-time (21 women). *Students:* 11 full-time (5 women), 70 part-time (39 women); includes 9 minority (2 Black or African American, non-Hispanic/Latino; 1 American Indian or Alaska Native, non-Hispanic/Latino; 3 Hispanic/Latino; 3 Two or more races, non-Hispanic/Latino). Average age 34. 33 applicants, 42% accepted, 10 enrolled. In 2017, 19 master's, 7 other advanced degrees awarded. *Degree requirements:* For master's, comprehensive exam. *Entrance requirements:* For master's, GRE General Test, writing sample. Additional exam requirements/recommendations for international students: Required—TOEFL (minimum score 550 paper-based). *Application deadline:* For fall admission, 7/1 for domestic and international students; for spring admission, 11/15 for domestic and international students. Applications are processed on a rolling basis. Application fee: $0 ($50 for international students). Electronic applications accepted. *Expenses:* Tuition, state resident: full-time $4551; part-time $252.86 per credit hour. Tuition, nonresident: full-time $9103; part-time $505.72 per credit hour. *Required fees:* $2453; $136.25 per credit hour. Tuition and fees vary according to course load and program. *Financial support:* Research assistantships with full tuition reimbursements, teaching assistantships with full tuition reimbursements, and administrative assistantships, tutorial assistantships available. Financial award application deadline: 4/1; financial award applicants required to submit FAFSA. *Unit head:* Dr. Michael Steiner, Dean, 660-562-1197.
Website: https://www.nwmissouri.edu/academics/undergraduate/majors/liberal-arts-sciences.htm

Oregon State University, College of Education, Program in Education, Corvallis, OR 97331. Offers agricultural education (PhD); language equity and education policy (PhD); mathematics education (MS); science education (MS); science/mathematics education (PhD). *Program availability:* Part-time, 100% online, blended/hybrid learning. Terminal master's awarded for partial completion of doctoral program. *Degree requirements:* For master's, variable foreign language requirement, thesis (for some programs); for doctorate, variable foreign language requirement, thesis/dissertation. *Entrance requirements:* Additional exam requirements/recommendations for international students: Required—TOEFL (minimum score 575 paper-based). Application fee: $75 ($85 for international students). *Faculty research:* School administration, educational foundations, research methodology, education policy development, higher education administration. *Unit head:* Nick Cabot, Ecampus Counseling Lead, 541-737-8564, E-mail: cabotn@oregonstate.edu. *Application contact:* Nick Cabot, Ecampus Counseling Lead, 541-737-8564, E-mail: cabotn@oregonstate.edu.

Oregon State University, College of Education, Program in Teaching, Corvallis, OR 97331. Offers clinically based elementary education (MAT); elementary education (MAT); language arts (MAT); mathematics (MAT); music education (MAT); science (MAT); social studies (MAT). *Program availability:* Part-time, blended/hybrid learning. *Entrance requirements:* For master's, CBEST. Additional exam requirements/recommendations for international students: Required—TOEFL (minimum score 575 paper-based). *Application deadline:* For fall admission, 12/1 for domestic students. Application fee: $60. *Expenses:* Contact institution. *Unit head:* Jordon Zardinejad, 541-322-3118, E-mail: jordon.zardinejad@osucascades.edu. *Application contact:* Jordon Zardinejad, 541-322-3118, E-mail: jordon.zardinejad@osucascades.edu.
Website: http://education.oregonstate.edu/mat

Our Lady of the Lake University, College of Professional Studies, Program in Curriculum and Instruction, San Antonio, TX 78207-4689. Offers integrated science teaching (M Ed). *Program availability:* Part-time, evening/weekend. *Faculty:* 4 full-time (all women), 3 part-time/adjunct (2 women). *Students:* 20 part-time (17 women); includes 14 minority (all Hispanic/Latino). Average age 39. In 2017, 1 master's awarded. *Degree requirements:* For master's, comprehensive exam. *Entrance requirements:* For master's, GRE General Test or MAT, official transcripts demonstrating bachelor's degree with minimum cumulative GPA of 2.75, personal statement, 2 references, completed FERPA Consent to Release Education Records and Information form, interview. Additional exam requirements/recommendations for international students: Required—TOEFL. *Application deadline:* For fall admission, 6/15 for domestic and international students; for spring admission, 11/15 for domestic and international students; for summer admission, 4/15 for domestic and international students. Applications are processed on a rolling basis. Application fee: $40 ($50 for international students). Electronic applications accepted. Application fee is waived when completed online. *Expenses:* Tuition: Full-time $10,668; part-time $5334 per year. *Required fees:* $816; $816 per year. $408 per semester. *Financial support:* Federal Work-Study, scholarships/grants, unspecified assistantships, and tuition discounts available. Support available to part-time students. Financial award application deadline: 5/1; financial

award applicants required to submit FAFSA. *Faculty research:* Multicultural Issues, technology integration, mentoring teachers, teacher retention. *Unit head:* Dr. Alycia Maurer, Chair, Education Department, 210-434-6711 Ext. 7152, E-mail: admaurer@ollusa.edu. *Application contact:* Office of Graduate Admissions, 210-431-3995, Fax: 210-431-3945, E-mail: gradadm@lake.ollusa.edu.
Website: http://www.ollusa.edu/s/1190/hybrid/default-hybrid-ollu.aspx?sid-1190&gid-1&pgid-7883

Pacific University, College of Education, Forest Grove, OR 97116-1797. Offers early childhood education (MAT); education (MAE); elementary education (MAT); ESOL (MAT); high school education (MAT); middle school education (MAT); special education (MAT); speech-language pathology (MS); STEM education (MAT); talented and gifted (M Ed); visual function in learning (M Ed). *Accreditation:* ASHA; NCATE. *Program availability:* Part-time, evening/weekend. *Degree requirements:* For master's, research project. *Entrance requirements:* For master's, California Basic Educational Skills Test, PRAXIS II, minimum undergraduate GPA of 2.75, 3.0 graduate. Additional exam requirements/recommendations for international students: Required—TOEFL. Electronic applications accepted. *Expenses:* Contact institution. *Faculty research:* Defining a culturally competent classroom, technology in the K-12 classroom, Socratic seminars, social studies education.

Pepperdine University, Graduate School of Education and Psychology, Division of Education, Los Angeles, CA 90263. Offers administration and preliminary administrative services (MS); education (MA); educational leadership, administration, and policy (Ed D); global leadership and change (PhD); learning technologies (MA, Ed D); organizational leadership (Ed D); social entrepreneurship and change (MA); teaching (MA); teaching: TESOL (MA). *Program availability:* Part-time, evening/weekend, blended/hybrid learning. *Students:* 214 full-time (139 women), 327 part-time (216 women); includes 248 minority (113 Black or African American, non-Hispanic/Latino; 2 American Indian or Alaska Native, non-Hispanic/Latino; 48 Asian, non-Hispanic/Latino; 61 Hispanic/Latino; 6 Native Hawaiian or other Pacific Islander, non-Hispanic/Latino; 18 Two or more races, non-Hispanic/Latino), 49 international. Average age 39. 410 applicants, 91% accepted, 160 enrolled. In 2017, 151 master's, 88 doctorates awarded. *Degree requirements:* For doctorate, thesis/dissertation. *Entrance requirements:* For master's, GRE General Test; for doctorate, GRE General Test, MAT. Additional exam requirements/recommendations for international students: Required—TOEFL. *Application deadline:* Applications are processed on a rolling basis. Application fee: $55. Electronic applications accepted. *Expenses:* Contact institution. *Financial support:* Research assistantships, teaching assistantships, career-related internships or fieldwork, institutionally sponsored loans, and scholarships/grants available. Support available to part-time students. Financial award application deadline: 7/1; financial award applicants required to submit FAFSA. *Unit head:* Dr. Martine Jago, Associate Dean, Education Division, 310-568-2828, E-mail: martine.jago@pepperdine.edu. *Application contact:* Chris Costa, Director of Enrollment, 310-568-2850, E-mail: chris.costa@pepperdine.edu.
Website: http://gsep.pepperdine.edu/masters-education/

Plymouth State University, College of Graduate Studies, Graduate Studies in Education, Program in Science, Plymouth, NH 03264-1595. Offers applied meteorology (MS); biology (MS); clinical mental health counseling (MS); environmental science and policy (MS); science education (MS).

Plymouth State University, College of Graduate Studies, Graduate Studies in Education, Program in Teaching, Plymouth, NH 03264-1595. Offers art education (MAT); science education (MAT). *Program availability:* Evening/weekend. *Degree requirements:* For master's, internship or teaching experience.

Portland State University, Graduate Studies, College of Liberal Arts and Sciences, Department of Geology, Portland, OR 97207-0751. Offers environmental science and resources (PhD); geology (MA, MS, Certificate); science/geology (MAT, MST). *Program availability:* Part-time. *Faculty:* 12 full-time (3 women), 5 part-time/adjunct (2 women). *Students:* 17 full-time (13 women), 10 part-time (5 women); includes 4 minority (1 American Indian or Alaska Native, non-Hispanic/Latino; 2 Hispanic/Latino; 1 Two or more races, non-Hispanic/Latino). Average age 32. 36 applicants, 36% accepted, 7 enrolled. In 2017, 9 master's awarded. *Degree requirements:* For master's, comprehensive exam, thesis or alternative, field comprehensive; for doctorate, thesis/dissertation. *Entrance requirements:* For master's, GRE General Test, GRE Subject Test, BA/BS in geology, minimum GPA of 3.0 in geology-related and allied sciences, resume, statement of intent, 2 letters of recommendation. Additional exam requirements/recommendations for international students: Required—TOEFL (minimum score 550 paper-based; 80 iBT). *Application deadline:* 1/31 priority date for domestic and international students. Application fee: $65. Electronic applications accepted. *Expenses:* Tuition, state resident: full-time $14,436; part-time $401 per credit. Tuition, nonresident: full-time $21,780; part-time $605 per credit. *Required fees:* $1380; $22 per credit. $119 per quarter. One-time fee: $325. Tuition and fees vary according to program. *Financial support:* In 2017–18, 13 students received support, including 7 research assistantships with full and partial tuition reimbursements available (averaging $15,914 per year), 8 teaching assistantships with full and partial tuition reimbursements available (averaging $15,000 per year); career-related internships or fieldwork, Federal Work-Study, scholarships/grants, and unspecified assistantships also available. Support available to part-time students. Financial award application deadline: 3/1; financial award applicants required to submit FAFSA. *Faculty research:* Sediment transport, volcanic environmental geology, coastal and fluvial processes. *Total annual research expenditures:* $819,730. *Unit head:* Dr. Martin Streck, Chair, 503-725-3379, Fax: 503-725-3025, E-mail: streckm@pdx.edu. *Application contact:* Dr. Andrew Fountain, Graduate Committee Chair, 503-725-3386, Fax: 503-725-3025, E-mail: andrew@pdx.edu.
Website: https://www.pdx.edu/geology/

Portland State University, Graduate Studies, College of Liberal Arts and Sciences, Interdisciplinary Programs in General Science, General Social Science, and General Arts and Letters, Portland, OR 97207-0751. Offers general arts and letters education (MAT, MST); general science education (MAT, MST); general social science education (MAT, MST). *Program availability:* Part-time, evening/weekend. *Students:* 2 full-time (both women); includes 1 minority (Two or more races, non-Hispanic/Latino). Average age 46. 5 applicants, 80% accepted, 2 enrolled. *Degree requirements:* For master's, variable foreign language requirement, written exam. *Entrance requirements:* For master's, minimum GPA of 3.0 in upper-division course work or 2.75 overall. Additional exam requirements/recommendations for international students: Required—TOEFL (minimum score 550 paper-based; 80 iBT), IELTS (minimum score 6.5). *Application deadline:* For fall admission, 4/1 priority date for domestic students, 3/1 priority date for international students. *Expenses:* Tuition, state resident: full-time $14,436; part-time $401 per credit. Tuition, nonresident: full-time $21,780; part-time $605 per credit. *Required fees:* $1380; $22 per credit. $119 per quarter. One-time fee: $325. Tuition and fees vary according to program. *Financial support:* Federal Work-Study and unspecified assistantships available. Support available to part-time students. Financial award application deadline: 3/1; financial award applicants required to submit FAFSA. *Unit head:* Robert Mercer, Associate Dean, 503-725-5059, Fax: 503-725-3693, E-mail: mercerr@pdx.edu. *Application contact:* CLAS Advising Office, 503-725-3822, E-mail: askclas@pdx.edu.

Science Education

Purdue University, College of Engineering, School of Engineering Education, West Lafayette, IN 47907. Offers PhD. *Faculty:* 34. *Students:* 67. In 2017, 15 doctorates awarded. *Degree requirements:* For doctorate, thesis/dissertation. *Entrance requirements:* For doctorate, GRE General Test, minimum GPA of 3.0. *Application deadline:* For fall admission, 12/15 for domestic and international students; for spring admission, 9/15 for domestic and international students; for summer admission, 12/15 for domestic and international students. Applications are processed on a rolling basis. Application fee: $60 ($75 for international students). Electronic applications accepted. *Financial support:* Fellowships with full and partial tuition reimbursements, research assistantships with full and partial tuition reimbursements, teaching assistantships with full and partial tuition reimbursements, health care benefits, and unspecified assistantships available. Financial award applicants required to submit FAFSA. *Faculty research:* Engineering teaching and learning, learning environments, problem solving, technology, teaming, diversity. *Unit head:* Dr. Donna Riley, Head of the School of Engineering Education, E-mail: riley@purdue.edu. *Application contact:* Loretta McKinniss, Secretary V, 765-494-3331, E-mail: lmckinni@purdue.edu.
Website: https://engineering.purdue.edu/ENE

Purdue University, Graduate School, College of Education, Department of Curriculum and Instruction, West Lafayette, IN 47907. Offers agricultural and extension education (MS, MS Ed, PhD, Ed S); art education (PhD); career and technical education (MS Ed, PhD, Ed S); curriculum studies (MS Ed, PhD, Ed S); educational technology (MS Ed, PhD, Ed S); elementary education (MS Ed); family and consumer sciences education (MS Ed, PhD, Ed S); foreign language education (MS Ed, PhD, Ed S); industrial technology (PhD, Ed S); language arts (MS Ed, PhD, Ed S); literacy (MS Ed, PhD, Ed S); mathematics education (MS, MS Ed, PhD, Ed S); science education (MS, MS Ed, PhD, Ed S); social studies education (MS Ed, PhD, Ed S). *Accreditation:* NCATE. *Program availability:* Part-time, evening/weekend. *Faculty:* 37 full-time (27 women), 1 (woman) part-time/adjunct. *Students:* 78 full-time (50 women), 286 part-time (195 women); includes 68 minority (25 Black or African American, non-Hispanic/Latino; 3 American Indian or Alaska Native, non-Hispanic/Latino; 10 Asian, non-Hispanic/Latino; 22 Hispanic/Latino; 1 Native Hawaiian or other Pacific Islander, non-Hispanic/Latino; 7 Two or more races, non-Hispanic/Latino), 44 international. Average age 36. 150 applicants, 79% accepted, 73 enrolled. In 2017, 107 master's, 20 doctorates, 2 other advanced degrees awarded. *Degree requirements:* For master's, thesis optional; for doctorate, thesis/dissertation, oral and written exams; for Ed S, oral presentation, project. *Entrance requirements:* For master's, GRE General Test (if undergraduate GPA is below 3.0), minimum undergraduate GPA of 3.0 or equivalent; for doctorate, GRE General Test (minimum combined verbal and quantitative score of 1000, 300 for new scoring), minimum undergraduate GPA of 3.0 or equivalent; master's degree with minimum GPA of 3.0 or equivalent; for Ed S, GRE General Test (minimum combined verbal and quantitative score of 1000, 300 for new scoring), minimum undergraduate GPA of 3.0 or equivalent; master's degree. Additional exam requirements/recommendations for international students: Required—TOEFL (minimum score 550 paper-based; 77 iBT). *Application deadline:* For fall admission, 12/15 for domestic students, 3/1 for international students; for spring admission, 9/15 for domestic students, 8/1 for international students. Application fee: $60 ($75 for international students). Electronic applications accepted. *Financial support:* Fellowships with full tuition reimbursements, research assistantships with full tuition reimbursements, teaching assistantships with full tuition reimbursements, career-related internships or fieldwork, and tuition waivers (full) available. Support available to part-time students. Financial award application deadline: 3/1; financial award applicants required to submit FAFSA. *Faculty research:* Literacy acquisition and development, teacher beliefs and knowledge, recruitment and retention of underrepresented students, economic education, literacy discourse. *Unit head:* Janet M. Alsup, Head, 765-494-9667, E-mail: alsupj@purdue.edu. *Application contact:* Heather Brinkman, Graduate Contact, 765-494-2345, E-mail: hbrinkma@purdue.edu.
Website: http://www.edci.purdue.edu/

Purdue University, Graduate School, College of Science, Department of Chemistry, West Lafayette, IN 47907. Offers analytical chemistry (MS, PhD); biochemistry (MS, PhD); chemical education (MS, PhD); inorganic chemistry (MS, PhD); organic chemistry (MS, PhD); physical chemistry (MS, PhD). *Faculty:* 46 full-time (14 women), 2 part-time/adjunct (0 women). *Students:* 320 full-time (129 women), 11 part-time (3 women); includes 60 minority (15 Black or African American, non-Hispanic/Latino; 18 Asian, non-Hispanic/Latino; 20 Hispanic/Latino; 7 Two or more races, non-Hispanic/Latino), 114 international. Average age 26. 719 applicants, 22% accepted, 57 enrolled. In 2017, 11 master's, 53 doctorates awarded. Terminal master's awarded for partial completion of doctoral program. *Degree requirements:* For master's, thesis; for doctorate, comprehensive exam, thesis/dissertation. *Entrance requirements:* For master's and doctorate, minimum undergraduate GPA of 3.0. Additional exam requirements/recommendations for international students: Required—TOEFL (minimum score 550 paper-based; 77 iBT); Recommended—TWE. *Application deadline:* For fall admission, 2/15 priority date for domestic students, 1/1 for international students. Applications are processed on a rolling basis. Application fee: $60 ($75 for international students). Electronic applications accepted. *Financial support:* In 2017–18, 2 fellowships with partial tuition reimbursements (averaging $18,000 per year), 55 teaching assistantships with partial tuition reimbursements (averaging $18,000 per year) were awarded; research assistantships with partial tuition reimbursements and tuition waivers (partial) also available. Support available to part-time students. Financial award applicants required to submit FAFSA. *Unit head:* Christine A. Hrycyna, Head, 765-494-5203, E-mail: hrycyna@purdue.edu. *Application contact:* Betty L. Hatfield, Director of Graduate Admissions, 765-494-5208, E-mail: bettyh@purdue.edu.
Website: https://www.chem.purdue.edu/

Purdue University Global, School of Teacher Education, Davenport, IA 52807. Offers education (M Ed); secondary education (M Ed); teaching and learning (MA); teaching literacy and language: grades 6-12 (MA); teaching literacy and language: grades K-6 (MA); teaching mathematics: grades 6-8 (MA); teaching mathematics: grades 9-12 (MA); teaching mathematics: grades K-5 (MA); teaching science: grades 6-12 (MA); teaching science: grades K-6 (MA); teaching students with special needs (MA); teaching with technology (MA). *Program availability:* Part-time, evening/weekend, online learning. *Entrance requirements:* Additional exam requirements/recommendations for international students: Required—TOEFL (minimum score 550 paper-based; 80 iBT).

Purdue University Northwest, Graduate Studies Office, School of Engineering, Mathematics, and Science, Department of Biological Sciences, Hammond, IN 46323-2094. Offers biology (MS); biology teaching (MS); biotechnology (MS). *Entrance requirements:* For master's, GRE. Additional exam requirements/recommendations for international students: Required—TOEFL. Electronic applications accepted. *Faculty research:* Cell biology, molecular biology, genetics, microbiology, neurophysiology.

Queens College of the City University of New York, Division of Education, Department of Secondary Education and Youth Services, Queens, NY 11367-1597. Offers adolescent biology (MAT); art (MS Ed); biology (MS Ed, AC); chemistry (MS Ed, AC); earth sciences (MS Ed, AC); English (MS Ed, AC); French (MS Ed); Italian (MS Ed, AC); literacy education (MS Ed); mathematics (MS Ed, AC); music (MS Ed, AC); physics (MS Ed, AC); social studies (MS Ed, AC); Spanish (MS Ed, AC). *Program availability:* Part-time, evening/weekend. *Students:* 28 full-time (16 women), 349 part-time (202 women); includes 165 minority (18 Black or African American, non-Hispanic/Latino; 56 Asian, non-Hispanic/Latino; 83 Hispanic/Latino; 8 Two or more races, non-Hispanic/Latino), 14 international. Average age 29. *Degree requirements:* For master's, research project. *Entrance requirements:* For master's, minimum GPA of 3.0. Additional exam requirements/recommendations for international students: Required—TOEFL, IELTS. *Application deadline:* For fall admission, 4/1 for domestic students; for spring admission, 11/1 for domestic students. Applications are processed on a rolling basis. Application fee: $125. Electronic applications accepted. *Financial support:* Career-related internships or fieldwork available. Financial award application deadline: 4/1; financial award applicants required to submit FAFSA. *Unit head:* Dr. Eleanor Armour-Thomas, Chairperson, 718-997-5150, E-mail: eleanor.armour-thomas@qc.cuny.edu. *Application contact:* Elizabeth D'Amico-Ramirez, Assistant Director of Graduate Admissions, 718-997-5203, E-mail: elizabeth.damicoramirez@qc.cuny.edu.

Quinnipiac University, School of Education, Program in Secondary Education, Hamden, CT 06518-1940. Offers biology (MAT); English (MAT); history (MAT); mathematics (MAT); Spanish (MAT). *Accreditation:* NCATE. *Faculty:* 8 full-time (5 women), 27 part-time/adjunct (19 women). *Students:* 27 full-time (20 women); includes 5 minority (1 Black or African American, non-Hispanic/Latino; 3 Hispanic/Latino; 1 Two or more races, non-Hispanic/Latino). 43 applicants, 98% accepted, 36 enrolled. In 2017, 34 master's awarded. *Entrance requirements:* For master's, PRAXIS I or PRAXIS Core Academic Skills Exam, minimum GPA of 3.0, interview. *Application deadline:* For fall admission, 5/1 priority date for domestic students. Applications are processed on a rolling basis. Application fee: $45. Electronic applications accepted. *Financial support:* Career-related internships or fieldwork, Federal Work-Study, and unspecified assistantships available. Financial award application deadline: 6/1; financial award applicants required to submit FAFSA. *Faculty research:* Multicultural and urban education/leadership, challenges of teaching diverse learners, scholarship of teaching and learning, technology and teaching, humor and education. *Unit head:* Mordechai Gordon, Program Director, 203-582-8442, E-mail: mordechai.gordon@qu.edu. *Application contact:* Office of Graduate Admissions, 203-582-8672, Fax: 203-582-3443, E-mail: graduate@qu.edu.
Website: http://www.qu.edu/gradeducation

Regent University, Graduate School, School of Education, Virginia Beach, VA 23464-9800. Offers education (M Ed, Ed D, PhD), including adult education (Ed D, PhD, Ed S), advanced educational leadership (Ed D, PhD, Ed S), character education (Ed D, PhD, Ed S), Christian education leadership (Ed D, PhD, Ed S), Christian school administration (M Ed), curriculum and instruction (Ed D, PhD, Ed S), curriculum and instruction - adult education (M Ed), curriculum and instruction - Christian school (M Ed), curriculum and instruction - gifted and talented (M Ed), curriculum and instruction - STEM education (M Ed), curriculum and instruction - teacher leader (M Ed), discipleship for ministry (M Ed), educational leadership (M Ed), educational psychology (Ed D, PhD, Ed S), educational technology and online learning (Ed D, PhD, Ed S), elementary education (M Ed), exceptional education executive leadership (Ed D, PhD, Ed S), higher education (Ed D, PhD, Ed S), higher education leadership and management (Ed D, PhD, Ed S), instructional design and technology (M Ed), K-12 school leadership (Ed D, PhD, Ed S), K-12 special education (M Ed), leadership in mathematics education (M Ed), reading specialist (M Ed), special education (Ed D, PhD, Ed S), student affairs (M Ed), TESOL - adult education (M Ed), TESOL - K-12 (M Ed); educational specialist (Ed S), including adult education (Ed D, PhD, Ed S), advanced educational leadership (Ed D, PhD, Ed S), character education (Ed D, PhD, Ed S), Christian education leadership (Ed D, PhD, Ed S), curriculum and instruction (Ed D, PhD, Ed S), educational psychology (Ed D, PhD, Ed S), educational technology and online learning (Ed D, PhD, Ed S), exceptional education executive leadership (Ed D, PhD, Ed S), higher education (Ed D, PhD, Ed S), higher education leadership and management (Ed D, PhD, Ed S), K-12 school leadership (Ed D, PhD, Ed S), special education (Ed D, PhD, Ed S). *Accreditation:* TEAC. *Program availability:* Part-time, evening/weekend, 100% online, blended/hybrid learning. *Faculty:* 22 full-time (10 women), 44 part-time/adjunct (32 women). *Students:* 80 full-time (59 women), 945 part-time (750 women); includes 432 minority (352 Black or African American, non-Hispanic/Latino; 4 American Indian or Alaska Native, non-Hispanic/Latino; 14 Asian, non-Hispanic/Latino; 43 Hispanic/Latino; 19 Two or more races, non-Hispanic/Latino), 12 international. Average age 40. 1,125 applicants, 49% accepted, 436 enrolled. In 2017, 316 master's, 24 doctorates awarded. *Degree requirements:* For master's, thesis or alternative; for doctorate, comprehensive exam, thesis/dissertation. *Entrance requirements:* For master's, Virginia Communication and Literacy Assessment (VCLA), PRAXIS, college transcripts, writing sample, interview; for doctorate, GRE, writing sample, resume, transcripts, interview. Additional exam requirements/recommendations for international students: Required—TOEFL (minimum score 577 paper-based). *Application deadline:* For fall admission, 4/1 priority date for domestic students; for spring admission, 10/15 priority date for domestic students. Applications are processed on a rolling basis. Application fee: $50. Electronic applications accepted. *Expenses:* Contact institution. *Financial support:* In 2017–18, 669 students received support, including 1 fellowship (averaging $10,000 per year); career-related internships or fieldwork, scholarships/grants, and unspecified assistantships also available. Support available to part-time students. *Faculty research:* Christian school administration, curriculum and instruction, educational technology and online learning, higher education, special education. *Unit head:* Dr. Donald Finn, Dean, 757-352-4278, Fax: 757-352-4318, E-mail: dfinn@regent.edu. *Application contact:* Heidi Cece, Assistant Vice President of Enrollment Management, 800-373-5504, Fax: 757-352-4381, E-mail: admissions@regent.edu.
Website: https://www.regent.edu/school-of-education/

Rice University, Graduate Programs, Wiess School of Natural Sciences, Department of Physics and Astronomy, Houston, TX 77251-1892. Offers nanoscale physics (MS); physics and astronomy (PhD); science teaching (MST). *Program availability:* Part-time. *Degree requirements:* For master's, thesis (for some programs); for doctorate, thesis/dissertation, minimum B average. *Entrance requirements:* For master's, GRE General Test; for doctorate, GRE General Test, GRE Subject Test. Additional exam requirements/recommendations for international students: Required—TOEFL (minimum score 600 paper-based; 90 iBT). Electronic applications accepted. *Faculty research:* Optical physics; ultra cold atoms; membrane electr-statics, peptides, proteins and lipids; solar astrophysics; stellar activity; magnetic fields; young stars.

Rider University, College of Education and Human Services, Teacher Certification Program, Lawrenceville, NJ 08648-3001. Offers bilingual education (Certificate); business education (Certificate); early childhood education (Certificate); elementary education (Certificate); English as a second language (Certificate); English education (Certificate); mathematics education (Certificate); science education (Certificate); secondary education (Certificate); social studies education (Certificate); world languages (Certificate), including French, German, Spanish. *Program availability:* Part-time, online learning. *Degree requirements:* For Certificate, internship, professional portfolio. *Entrance requirements:* For degree, PRAXIS, resume. Additional exam requirements/recommendations for international students: Required—TOEFL (minimum score 550 paper-based). Electronic applications accepted. *Faculty research:* Conceptual foundations for optimal development of creativity; creative theory, cognitive processes in mathematics learning, teacher collaboration.

Rowan University, Graduate School, College of Education, Department of Science, Technology, Engineering, Art and Math Education, Glassboro, NJ 08028-1701. Offers educational technology (CGS); STEM education (MA). *Program availability:* Part-time, evening/weekend. *Degree requirements:* For master's, thesis. *Entrance requirements:* For master's, GRE General Test. Additional exam requirements/recommendations for international students: Required—TOEFL. Electronic applications accepted. *Expenses:* Tuition, state resident: full-time $15,020; part-time $751 per semester hour. Tuition, nonresident: full-time $15,020; part-time $751 per semester hour. *Required fees:* $3158; $157.90 per semester hour. Tuition and fees vary according to course load, campus/location and program.

Rutgers University–New Brunswick, Graduate School of Education, Department of Learning and Teaching, Program in Science Education, Piscataway, NJ 08854-8097. Offers Ed M, Ed D. *Program availability:* Part-time. Terminal master's awarded for partial completion of doctoral program. *Degree requirements:* For master's, comprehensive exam (for some programs); for doctorate, thesis/dissertation, qualifying exam. *Entrance requirements:* For master's, GRE General Test, minimum GPA of 3.0; for doctorate, GRE General Test, minimum GPA of 3.5. Additional exam requirements/recommendations for international students: Required—TOEFL. Electronic applications accepted.

St. John Fisher College, School of Arts and Sciences, Program in Math, Science, and Technology Education, Rochester, NY 14618-3597. Offers MS. *Program availability:* Part-time, evening/weekend. *Faculty:* 1 full-time (0 women). *Students:* 9 part-time (6 women); includes 2 minority (1 Black or African American, non-Hispanic/Latino; 1 Asian, non-Hispanic/Latino). Average age 32. 9 applicants, 100% accepted, 9 enrolled. In 2017, 6 master's awarded. *Degree requirements:* For master's, directed research project. *Entrance requirements:* For master's, 2 letters of recommendation, personal statement, current resume. Additional exam requirements/recommendations for international students: Required—TOEFL (minimum score 575 paper-based; 80 iBT). Application fee: $30. *Expenses: Tuition:* Part-time $920 per credit hour. *Required fees:* $10 per credit hour. Tuition and fees vary according to degree level and program. *Financial support:* Scholarships/grants available. *Unit head:* Dr. Bernard Ricca, Director, 585-899-3866, E-mail: bricca@sjfc.edu. *Application contact:* Michelle Gosier, Director of Transfer and Graduate Admissions, 585-385-8064, E-mail: mgosier@sjfc.edu.
Website: https://www.sjfc.edu/graduate-programs/ms-in-applied-data-science/

St. John's University, The School of Education, Department of Curriculum and Instruction, PhD in Curriculum and Instruction Program, Queens, NY 11439. Offers early childhood (PhD); global education (PhD); STEM education (PhD); teaching, learning, and knowing (PhD). *Program availability:* Part-time-only. *Degree requirements:* For doctorate, comprehensive exam, thesis/dissertation. *Entrance requirements:* For doctorate, teacher certification (or equivalent), at least three years' teaching experience or the equivalent in informal learning environments, master's degree. Additional exam requirements/recommendations for international students: Required—TOEFL. *Application deadline:* Applications are processed on a rolling basis. Application fee: $70. Electronic applications accepted. *Expenses: Tuition:* Full-time $44,280; part-time $1230 per credit. *Required fees:* $340; $340 per credit. Tuition and fees vary according to course load, degree level and program. *Financial support:* Fellowships, research assistantships, and scholarships/grants available. Support available to part-time students. Financial award application deadline: 2/1; financial award applicants required to submit FAFSA. *Faculty research:* Literacies, early childhood, STEM, school culture, global education. *Unit head:* Dr. Sandra Schamroth Abrams, PhD Program Director, 718-990-8313, E-mail: abramss@stjohns.edu. *Application contact:* Dr. Sandra Schamroth Abrams, PhD Program Director, 718-990-8313, E-mail: abramss@stjohns.edu.
Website: https://www.stjohns.edu/academics/schools-and-colleges/school-education/programs-and-majors/phd-curriculum-and-instruction

Saint Xavier University, Graduate Studies, School of Education, Chicago, IL 60655-3105. Offers counseling (MA); curriculum and instruction (MA); early childhood education (MA); educational administration (MA); elementary education (MA); individualized studies (MA), including educational technology, English as a second language (ESL); ISTEM (integrative science, technology, engineering, and math); science education; music education (MA); reading (MA); secondary education (MA); Spanish education (MA); special education (MA); teaching and leadership (MA). *Accreditation:* NCATE. *Program availability:* Part-time, evening/weekend. *Degree requirements:* For master's, thesis or project. *Entrance requirements:* For master's, minimum GPA of 3.0. *Expenses:* Contact institution.

Salem State University, School of Graduate Studies, Program in Chemistry, Salem, MA 01970-5353. Offers MAT. *Program availability:* Part-time, evening/weekend. *Entrance requirements:* For master's, GRE or MAT. Additional exam requirements/recommendations for international students: Required—TOEFL (minimum score 550 paper-based; 80 iBT) or IELTS (minimum score 5.5).

Salem State University, School of Graduate Studies, Program in Middle School General Science, Salem, MA 01970-5353. Offers MAT. *Program availability:* Part-time, evening/weekend. *Entrance requirements:* For master's, GRE or MAT. Additional exam requirements/recommendations for international students: Required—TOEFL (minimum score 550 paper-based; 80 iBT) or IELTS (minimum score 5.5).

San Diego State University, Graduate and Research Affairs, College of Sciences, Department of Mathematics and Statistics, San Diego, CA 92182. Offers applied mathematics (MS); mathematics (MA); mathematics and science education (PhD); statistics (MS). PhD offered jointly wtih University of California, San Diego. *Program availability:* Part-time. *Degree requirements:* For doctorate, thesis/dissertation. *Entrance requirements:* For master's, GRE General Test; for doctorate, GRE, minimum GPA of 3.25 in last 30 undergraduate semester units, minimum graduate GPA of 3.5, MSE recommendation form, 3 letters of recommendation. Additional exam requirements/recommendations for international students: Required—TOEFL. Electronic applications accepted. *Faculty research:* Teacher education in mathematics.

Seattle Pacific University, Program in Teaching Mathematics and Science, Seattle, WA 98119-1997. Offers MTMS. *Students:* 19 full-time (8 women), 2 part-time (1 woman); includes 4 minority (1 Asian, non-Hispanic/Latino; 2 Hispanic/Latino; 1 Two or more races, non-Hispanic/Latino). Average age 32. In 2017, 20 master's awarded. *Degree requirements:* For master's, internship. *Application deadline:* For fall admission, 8/15 for domestic students; for winter admission, 11/15 for domestic students; for spring admission, 2/15 for domestic students; for summer admission, 5/15 for domestic students. *Unit head:* David W. Dento, Graduate Teacher Education Chair, 206-281-2504, E-mail: dentod@spu.edu.
Website: http://spu.edu/academics/school-of-education/graduate-programs/masters-programs/master-in-teaching-mathematics-and-science

Shippensburg University of Pennsylvania, School of Graduate Studies, College of Education and Human Services, Department of Teacher Education, Shippensburg, PA 17257-2299. Offers curriculum and instruction (M Ed), including biology, early childhood education, elementary education, geography/earth science, history, mathematics, middle school education, modern languages; reading (M Ed). *Accreditation:* NCATE.

Program availability: Part-time, evening/weekend, 100% online, blended/hybrid learning. *Faculty:* 13 full-time (8 women), 1 (woman) part-time/adjunct. *Students:* 10 full-time (7 women), 94 part-time (81 women); includes 10 minority (3 Black or African American, non-Hispanic/Latino; 2 Asian, non-Hispanic/Latino; 5 Hispanic/Latino), 1 international. Average age 34. 71 applicants, 86% accepted, 35 enrolled. In 2017, 23 master's awarded. *Degree requirements:* For master's, comprehensive exam (for some programs), thesis optional, practicum or internship; capstone seminar (for some programs). *Entrance requirements:* For master's, MAT or GRE (if GPA less than 2.75), interview, 3 letters of reference, questionnaire of teaching background and future goals, resume. Additional exam requirements/recommendations for international students: Required—TOEFL (minimum score 550 paper-based, 68 iBT) or IELTS (minimum score 6). *Application deadline:* For fall admission, 4/1 priority date for domestic students, 4/30 for international students; for spring admission, 9/1 priority date for domestic students, 9/30 for international students; for summer admission, 2/1 priority date for domestic students. Applications are processed on a rolling basis. Application fee: $45. Electronic applications accepted. *Expenses:* Tuition, state resident: part-time $500 per credit. Tuition, nonresident: part-time $750 per credit. *Required fees:* $145 per credit. *Financial support:* In 2017–18, 1 student received support. Career-related internships or fieldwork, scholarships/grants, unspecified assistantships, and resident hall director and student payroll positions available. Support available to part-time students. Financial award application deadline: 3/1; financial award applicants required to submit FAFSA. *Unit head:* Dr. Christine A. Royce, Chairperson, 717-477-1688, Fax: 717-477-4046, E-mail: caroyc@ship.edu. *Application contact:* Maya T. Mapp, Director of Admissions, 717-477-1231, Fax: 717-477-4016, E-mail: mtmapp@ship.edu.
Website: http://www.ship.edu/teacher/

Shippensburg University of Pennsylvania, School of Graduate Studies, College of Education and Human Services, Master of Arts in Teaching STEM Education Program, Shippensburg, PA 17257-2299. Offers MAT. *Program availability:* Part-time, evening/weekend, blended/hybrid learning. *Students:* 10 full-time (5 women), 10 part-time (4 women); includes 2 minority (1 Asian, non-Hispanic/Latino; 1 Hispanic/Latino). Average age 32. 17 applicants, 94% accepted, 12 enrolled. *Degree requirements:* For master's, 12-week student teaching practicum (12 credits), two capstone projects which include professional portfolio and the results of a research project. *Entrance requirements:* For master's, Pre-Service Academic Performance Assessment (PAPA), PRAXIS II Subject Assessment, statement of intent summarizing motivations and goals for entering the teaching profession, two letters of recommendation. Additional exam requirements/recommendations for international students: Required—TOEFL (minimum score 550 paper-based, 68 iBT) or IELTS (minimum score 6). *Application deadline:* For fall admission, 4/30 for international students; for spring admission, 9/30 for international students. Applications are processed on a rolling basis. Application fee: $45. Electronic applications accepted. *Expenses:* Tuition, state resident: part-time $500 per credit. Tuition, nonresident: part-time $750 per credit. *Required fees:* $145 per credit. *Financial support:* In 2017–18, 1 student received support. Career-related internships or fieldwork and resident hall director and student payroll positions available. Support available to part-time students. Financial award application deadline: 3/1; financial award applicants required to submit FAFSA. *Unit head:* Dr. Joseph W. Shane, Professor and Program Coordinator, 717-477-1572, Fax: 717-477-4048, E-mail: jwshan@ship.edu. *Application contact:* Maya T. Mapp, Director of Admissions, 717-477-1231, Fax: 717-477-4016, E-mail: mtmapp@ship.edu.
Website: http://www.ship.edu/STEM/

Slippery Rock University of Pennsylvania, Graduate Studies (Recruitment), College of Education, Department of Elementary Education and Early Childhood, Slippery Rock, PA 16057-1383. Offers instructional coach (M Ed); K-12 reading (M Ed); K-12 science and math (M Ed); reading specialist (M Ed). *Accreditation:* NCATE. *Program availability:* Part-time, evening/weekend, online only, 100% online. *Degree requirements:* For master's, comprehensive exam (for some programs), thesis optional. *Entrance requirements:* For master's, minimum GPA of 3.0, resume, teaching certification, transcripts, letters of recommendation (depending on program). Additional exam requirements/recommendations for international students: Required—TOEFL (minimum score 550 paper-based; 80 iBT). Electronic applications accepted. *Expenses:* Contact institution.

Slippery Rock University of Pennsylvania, Graduate Studies (Recruitment), College of Education, Department of Secondary Education/Foundations of Education, Slippery Rock, PA 16057-1383. Offers secondary education (M Ed), including English, math/science, social studies. *Accreditation:* NCATE. *Program availability:* Part-time, evening/weekend, 100% online. *Degree requirements:* For master's, comprehensive exam, thesis (for some programs). *Entrance requirements:* For master's, copy of teaching certification and two letters of recommendation (for some programs). Additional exam requirements/recommendations for international students: Required—TOEFL (minimum score 550 paper-based; 80 iBT). Electronic applications accepted. *Expenses:* Contact institution.

Smith College, Graduate and Special Programs, Department of Education and Child Study, Program in Secondary Education, Northampton, MA 01063. Offers secondary education (MAT), including biological sciences education, chemistry education, English education, geology education, government education, history education, mathematics education, physics education. *Program availability:* Part-time. *Students:* 5 full-time (all women), 2 part-time (0 women); includes 3 minority (1 Asian, non-Hispanic/Latino; 2 Hispanic/Latino). Average age 29. 13 applicants, 92% accepted, 5 enrolled. In 2017, 5 master's awarded. *Entrance requirements:* Additional exam requirements/recommendations for international students: Required—TOEFL (minimum score 595 paper-based; 97 iBT), IELTS. *Application deadline:* For fall admission, 4/15 for domestic students, 1/15 priority date for international students; for spring admission, 12/1 for domestic students. Applications are processed on a rolling basis. Application fee: $60. *Expenses:* Contact institution. *Financial support:* In 2017–18, 5 students received support, including 3 fellowships with full tuition reimbursements available; scholarships/grants and human resources employee benefit also available. Support available to part-time students. Financial award application deadline: 4/15; financial award applicants required to submit CSS PROFILE or FAFSA. *Unit head:* Rosetta Cohen, Graduate Student Advisor, 413-585-3266, E-mail: rcohen@smith.edu. *Application contact:* Ruth Morgan, Program Assistant, 413-585-3050, Fax: 413-585-3054, E-mail: gradstdy@smith.edu.
Website: http://www.smith.edu/educ/

Smith College, Graduate and Special Programs, Department of Physics, Northampton, MA 01063. Offers secondary education (MAT), including physics education. *Program availability:* Part-time. *Students:* 1 part-time (0 women). Average age 37. 1 applicant, 100% accepted, 1 enrolled. In 2017, 1 master's awarded. *Entrance requirements:* Additional exam requirements/recommendations for international students: Required—TOEFL (minimum score 595 paper-based; 97 iBT), IELTS. *Application deadline:* For fall admission, 4/15 for domestic students, 1/15 for international students; for spring admission, 12/1 for domestic students. Applications are processed on a rolling basis. Application fee: $60. *Expenses:* Contact institution. *Financial support:* In 2017–18, 1 student received support. Scholarships/grants available. Support available to part-time students. Financial award application deadline: 4/15; financial award applicants required to submit CSS PROFILE or FAFSA. *Unit head:* Gary Felder, Chair, 413-585-4489, E-mail: gfelder@smith.edu. *Application contact:* Ruth Morgan, Program Assistant, 413-585-3050, Fax: 413-585-3054, E-mail: gradstdy@smith.edu.

South Carolina State University, College of Graduate and Professional Studies, Department of Education, Orangeburg, SC 29117-0001. Offers early childhood education (MAT); education (M Ed); elementary education (M Ed, MAT); English (MAT); general science/biology (MAT); mathematics (MAT); secondary education (M Ed), including biology education, business education, counselor education, English education, home economics education, industrial education, mathematics education, science education, social studies education; special education (M Ed), including emotionally handicapped, learning disabilities, mentally handicapped. *Accreditation:* NCATE. *Program availability:* Part-time, evening/weekend. *Faculty:* 11 full-time (6 women), 4 part-time/adjunct (2 women). *Students:* 26 full-time (18 women), 22 part-time (17 women); includes 41 minority (all Black or African American, non-Hispanic/Latino), 1 international. Average age 33. 25 applicants, 100% accepted, 19 enrolled. In 2017, 6 master's awarded. *Degree requirements:* For master's, thesis optional, departmental qualifying exam. *Entrance requirements:* For master's, GRE General Test, NTE, interview, teaching certificate. *Application deadline:* For fall admission, 6/15 priority date for domestic students, 6/15 for international students; for spring admission, 11/1 for domestic and international students. Application fee: $25. Electronic applications accepted. *Expenses:* Tuition, state resident: full-time $9388; part-time $607 per credit hour. Tuition, nonresident: full-time $19,968; part-time $1194 per credit hour. *Required fees:* $766; $766 per credit hour. *Financial support:* Fellowships, career-related internships or fieldwork, Federal Work-Study, and scholarships/grants available. Financial award application deadline: 6/1. *Unit head:* Dr. Charlie Spell, Interim Chair, Department of Education, 803-536-8963, Fax: 803-516-4568, E-mail: cspell@scsu.edu. *Application contact:* Curtis Foskey, Coordinator of Graduate Studies, 803-536-8419, Fax: 803-536-8812, E-mail: cfoskey@scsu.edu.

Southern Connecticut State University, School of Graduate Studies, School of Arts and Sciences, Department of Environment, Geography and Marine Sciences, New Haven, CT 06515-1355. Offers environmental education (MS); science education (MS, Diploma). *Accreditation:* NCATE. *Program availability:* Part-time, evening/weekend. *Degree requirements:* For master's, thesis or alternative. *Entrance requirements:* For master's, interview; for Diploma, master's degree. Electronic applications accepted.

Southern University and Agricultural and Mechanical College, Graduate School, Department of Science/Mathematics Education, Baton Rouge, LA 70813. Offers PhD. *Accreditation:* NCATE. *Degree requirements:* For doctorate, thesis/dissertation. *Entrance requirements:* For doctorate, GRE General Test. Additional exam requirements/recommendations for international students: Required—TOEFL (minimum score 525 paper-based). *Faculty research:* Performance assessment in science/mathematics education, equity in science/mathematics education, technology and distance learning, science/mathematics concept formation, cognitive themes, problem solving in science/mathematics education.

Southwestern Oklahoma State University, College of Arts and Sciences, Specialization in Natural Sciences, Weatherford, OK 73096-3098. Offers M Ed. *Program availability:* Part-time. *Degree requirements:* For master's, exam. *Entrance requirements:* For master's, GRE General Test or minimum undergraduate GPA of 3.0. Additional exam requirements/recommendations for international students: Required—TOEFL.

State University of New York at New Paltz, Graduate and Extended Learning School, School of Education, Department of Teaching and Learning, New Paltz, NY 12561. Offers adolescence education: biology (MAT, MS Ed); adolescence education: chemistry (MAT, MS Ed); adolescence education: earth science (MAT, MS Ed); adolescence education: English (MAT, MS Ed); adolescence education: French (MAT, MS Ed); adolescence education: social studies (MAT, MS Ed); adolescence education: Spanish (MAT, MS Ed); second language education (MS Ed, AC), including second language education (MS Ed), teaching English language learners (AC). *Accreditation:* NCATE. *Program availability:* Part-time, evening/weekend. *Faculty:* 6 full-time (5 women), 10 part-time/adjunct (6 women). *Students:* 48 full-time (27 women), 54 part-time (41 women); includes 24 minority (2 Black or African American, non-Hispanic/Latino; 4 Asian, non-Hispanic/Latino; 15 Hispanic/Latino; 3 Two or more races, non-Hispanic/Latino). 33 applicants, 64% accepted, 12 enrolled. In 2017, 49 master's awarded. *Degree requirements:* For master's, comprehensive exam (for some programs), portfolio. *Entrance requirements:* For master's, minimum GPA of 3.0, New York state teaching certificate (MS Ed). Additional exam requirements/recommendations for international students: Required—TOEFL (minimum score 550 paper-based; 80 iBT), IELTS (minimum score 6.5). *Application deadline:* For fall admission, 3/1 priority date for domestic students, 3/1 for international students; for spring admission, 10/1 priority date for domestic students, 10/1 for international students. Application fee: $50. Electronic applications accepted. *Financial support:* Application deadline: 8/1. *Unit head:* Dr. Laura Dull, Chair, 845-257-2849, E-mail: dullj@newpaltz.edu. *Application contact:* Vika Shock, Director of Graduate Admissions, 845-257-3285, Fax: 845-257-3284, E-mail: gradschool@newpaltz.edu.
Website: http://www.newpaltz.edu/secondaryed/

State University of New York at Plattsburgh, School of Arts and Sciences, Program in Natural Science, Plattsburgh, NY 12901-2681. Offers MS, PSM. *Accreditation:* TEAC. *Program availability:* Part-time. *Entrance requirements:* For master's, GRE General Test (minimum score of 1200), bachelor's degree in science discipline, minimum GPA of 3.0. Additional exam requirements/recommendations for international students: Required—TOEFL.

State University of New York at Plattsburgh, School of Education, Health, and Human Services, Program in Teacher Education: Adolescence Education, Plattsburgh, NY 12901-2681. Offers adolescence education (MST); biology 7-12 (MST); chemistry 7-12 (MST); earth science 7-12 (MST); English 7-12 (MST); French 7-12 (MST); mathematics 7-12 (MST); physics 7-12 (MST); social studies 7-12 (MST); Spanish 7-12 (MST). *Accreditation:* TEAC. *Program availability:* Part-time, evening/weekend. *Entrance requirements:* For master's, minimum GPA of 2.75. Additional exam requirements/recommendations for international students: Required—TOEFL.

State University of New York College at Cortland, Graduate Studies, School of Arts and Sciences, Programs in Adolescence Education, Cortland, NY 13045. Offers biology (MAT); chemistry (MAT); English (MAT, MS Ed); mathematics (MAT); mathematics and physics (MS Ed); physics (MAT, MS Ed). *Accreditation:* NCATE. *Program availability:* Part-time, evening/weekend. *Degree requirements:* For master's, one foreign language, comprehensive exam (for some programs), thesis (for some programs). *Entrance requirements:* For master's, GRE General Test.

State University of New York College at Old Westbury, School of Education, Old Westbury, NY 11568-0210. Offers biology (MAT, MS); chemistry (MAT, MS); English language arts (MAT, MS); math (MAT, MS); social studies (MAT, MS); Spanish (MAT, MS). *Program availability:* Part-time, evening/weekend. *Students:* 164 full-time (80 women), 112 part-time (52 women); includes 87 minority (14 Black or African American, non-Hispanic/Latino; 38 Asian, non-Hispanic/Latino; 35 Hispanic/Latino), 2 international. Average age 30. 34 applicants, 82% accepted, 25 enrolled. In 2017, 25 master's

awarded. *Entrance requirements:* For master's, Liberal Arts and Sciences Test, undergraduate degree with at least 30 semester hours of appropriate coursework as defined by the respective discipline; minimum cumulative undergraduate GPA of 3.0; two letters of recommendation (one from an academic source); essay. Additional exam requirements/recommendations for international students: Required—TOEFL (minimum score 550 paper-based); Recommended—IELTS. Application fee: $50. *Financial support:* Applicants required to submit FAFSA. *Unit head:* Dr. Nancy Brown, Dean, School of Education, 516-876-3275, E-mail: brownn@oldwestbury.edu. *Application contact:* Philip D'Angelo, Graduate Admissions Office, 516-876-3073, E-mail: enroll@oldwestbury.edu.

State University of New York College at Potsdam, School of Education and Professional Studies, Program in Secondary Education, Potsdam, NY 13676. Offers English education (MST); mathematics education (MST); science education (MST), including biology, chemistry, earth science, physics; social studies education (MST). *Accreditation:* NCATE. *Degree requirements:* For master's, culminating experience. *Entrance requirements:* For master's, minimum GPA of 2.75 in last 60 hours of course work (3.0 for English program). Additional exam requirements/recommendations for international students: Required—TOEFL (minimum score 550 paper-based; 80 iBT), IELTS (minimum score 6). Electronic applications accepted.

Stevenson University, Master of Arts in Teaching Program, Stevenson, MD 21153. Offers secondary biology (MAT); secondary chemistry (MAT); secondary mathematics (MAT). *Program availability:* Part-time, blended/hybrid learning. *Faculty:* 5 part-time/adjunct (all women). *Students:* 18 part-time (11 women); includes 6 minority (2 Black or African American, non-Hispanic/Latino; 2 Asian, non-Hispanic/Latino; 1 Hispanic/Latino; 1 Two or more races, non-Hispanic/Latino). Average age 31. 8 applicants, 100% accepted, 8 enrolled. *Degree requirements:* For master's, internship, portfolio, action research project. *Entrance requirements:* For master's, PRAXIS, GRE, SAT, or ACT, official transcripts from each college or university attended verifying completion of baccalaureate degree in a science or math discipline from regionally-accredited institution. *Application deadline:* Applications are processed on a rolling basis. Electronic applications accepted. *Expenses:* Contact institution. *Financial support:* Unspecified assistantships available. Financial award applicants required to submit FAFSA. *Unit head:* Anne P. Davis, Associate Dean of Teacher Education. *Application contact:* Amanda Courter, Senior Enrollment Counselor, 443-352-4243, Fax: 443-352-4440, E-mail: acourter@stevenson.edu.
Website: http://www.stevenson.edu/online/academics/online-graduate-programs/master-arts-teaching

Stony Brook University, State University of New York, Graduate School, College of Arts and Sciences, Department of Physics and Astronomy, Program in Physics, Stony Brook, NY 11794. Offers modern research instrumentation (MS); physics (MA, PhD); physics education (MAT). *Faculty:* 49 full-time (6 women), 4 part-time/adjunct (1 woman). *Students:* 199 full-time (32 women); includes 16 minority (2 Black or African American, non-Hispanic/Latino; 6 Asian, non-Hispanic/Latino; 7 Hispanic/Latino; 1 Two or more races, non-Hispanic/Latino), 139 international. 570 applicants, 47% accepted, 59 enrolled. In 2017, 14 master's, 23 doctorates awarded. *Degree requirements:* For doctorate, one foreign language, thesis/dissertation. *Entrance requirements:* For master's and doctorate, GRE General Test. Additional exam requirements/recommendations for international students: Required—TOEFL (minimum score 90 iBT). *Application deadline:* For fall admission, 1/15 for domestic students; for spring admission, 10/1 for domestic students. Application fee: $100. Electronic applications accepted. *Expenses:* Contact institution. *Financial support:* In 2017–18, 5 fellowships, 64 research assistantships, 51 teaching assistantships were awarded. Financial award application deadline: 2/1. *Total annual research expenditures:* $12.2 million. *Unit head:* Dr. Axel Drees, Chair, 631-632-8114, E-mail: axel.drees@stonybrook.edu. *Application contact:* Donald Sheehan, Coordinator, 631-632-1046, Fax: 631-632-8176, E-mail: donald.j.sheehan@stonybrook.edu.

Stony Brook University, State University of New York, Graduate School, College of Arts and Sciences, Institute for STEM Education, Stony Brook, NY 11794. Offers PhD. *Faculty:* 5 full-time (4 women), 4 part-time/adjunct (1 woman). *Students:* 28 part-time (19 women); includes 1 minority (Black or African American, non-Hispanic/Latino). Average age 45. In 2017, 2 doctorates awarded. *Degree requirements:* For doctorate, comprehensive exam, thesis/dissertation. *Entrance requirements:* For doctorate, GRE. Additional exam requirements/recommendations for international students: Required—TOEFL (minimum score 550 paper-based; 90 iBT), IELTS (minimum score 6.5), TOEFL with minimum iBT score of 85 (for master's programs). *Application deadline:* For fall admission, 1/15 for domestic students; for spring admission, 10/1 for domestic students. Application fee: $100. *Expenses:* Tuition, state resident: full-time $10,870; part-time $453 per credit. Tuition, nonresident: full-time $22,210; part-time $925 per credit. *Faculty research:* Educational evaluation or assessment, educational improvement, educational psychology. *Unit head:* Dr. Keith Sheppard, Director, 631-632-2989, E-mail: keith.sheppard@stonybrook.edu. *Application contact:* Judith Nimmo, Coordinator, 631-632-9750, E-mail: judith.nimmo@stonybrook.edu.
Website: https://www.stonybrook.edu/istem/

Stony Brook University, State University of New York, School of Professional Development, Stony Brook, NY 11794. Offers biology (MAT); chemistry (MAT); coaching (Graduate Certificate); earth science (MAT); educational computing (Graduate Certificate); educational leadership (Advanced Certificate); English (MAT); environmental management (MPS, Graduate Certificate); French (MAT); German (MAT); higher education administration (MA, Certificate); human resource management (MS, Graduate Certificate); industrial management (Graduate Certificate); information systems management (Graduate Certificate); Italian (MAT); liberal studies (MA); mathematics (MAT); operations research (Graduate Certificate); physics (MAT); school district business leadership (Advanced Certificate); social studies (MAT); Spanish (MAT). *Program availability:* Part-time, evening/weekend, online learning. *Faculty:* 3 full-time (2 women), 101 part-time/adjunct (45 women). *Students:* 190 full-time (126 women), 974 part-time (708 women); includes 255 minority (88 Black or African American, non-Hispanic/Latino; 2 American Indian or Alaska Native, non-Hispanic/Latino; 31 Asian, non-Hispanic/Latino; 113 Hispanic/Latino; 1 Native Hawaiian or other Pacific Islander, non-Hispanic/Latino; 20 Two or more races, non-Hispanic/Latino), 6 international. Average age 33. 411 applicants, 91% accepted, 288 enrolled. In 2017, 333 master's, 180 other advanced degrees awarded. *Entrance requirements:* Additional exam requirements/recommendations for international students: Required—TOEFL (minimum score 85 iBT). *Application deadline:* For fall admission, 1/15 for domestic students, 6/1 for international students; for spring admission, 10/1 for domestic and international students. Applications are processed on a rolling basis. Application fee: $100. *Expenses:* Contact institution. *Financial support:* Fellowships, research assistantships, teaching assistantships, and career-related internships or fieldwork available. Support available to part-time students. *Unit head:* Dr. Ken Lindblom, Dean, 631-632-7049, Fax: 631-632-9046, E-mail: kenneth.lindblom@stonybrook.edu. *Application contact:* Melissa Jordan, Assistant Dean, 631-632-7751, E-mail: melissa.jordan@stonybrook.edu.
Website: http://www.stonybrook.edu/spd/

Syracuse University, College of Arts and Sciences, Program in College Science Teaching, Syracuse, NY 13244. Offers PhD. *Program availability:* Part-time. *Degree requirements:* For doctorate, thesis/dissertation. *Entrance requirements:* For doctorate, GRE General Test, three letters of recommendation, personal statement, transcripts, scholarly writing sample. Additional exam requirements/recommendations for international students: Required—TOEFL (minimum score 100 iBT). *Application deadline:* For fall admission, 2/1 priority date for domestic and international students. Applications are processed on a rolling basis. Application fee: $75. Electronic applications accepted. *Financial support:* Fellowships with full tuition reimbursements, research assistantships with tuition reimbursements, teaching assistantships with tuition reimbursements, and scholarships/grants available. Financial award application deadline: 1/15; financial award applicants required to submit FAFSA. *Faculty research:* Philosophy of science, methods of teaching science in higher education, research focused on the problems of college teaching, curriculum development. *Unit head:* Dr. John W. Tillotson, Department Chairperson, 315-443-9137, E-mail: jwtillot@syr.edu. *Application contact:* Heather Thompson, Administrative Assistant, Earth Sciences and Science Teaching, 315-443-2672, E-mail: hethomps@syr.edu.
Website: http://sciteach.syr.edu/academics/program-science-teaching-phd.html

Syracuse University, School of Education, Programs in Science Education, Syracuse, NY 13244. Offers biology (MS); chemistry (MS, PhD). *Program availability:* Part-time. *Students:* Average age 38. In 2017, 4 doctorates awarded. *Degree requirements:* For doctorate, comprehensive exam, thesis/dissertation. *Entrance requirements:* For master's, GRE General Test or MAT, official transcripts from previous academic institutions, 3 letters of recommendation (preferably from faculty), personal statement that makes a clear and compelling argument for why applicant wants to teach secondary science; for doctorate, GRE General Test or MAT, master's degree, interview. Additional exam requirements/recommendations for international students: Required—TOEFL (minimum score 100 iBT). *Application deadline:* For fall admission, 1/15 priority date for domestic and international students; for spring admission, 10/15 priority date for domestic and international students. Applications are processed on a rolling basis. Application fee: $75. Electronic applications accepted. *Financial support:* Fellowships with full tuition reimbursements, research assistantships, teaching assistantships, and scholarships/grants available. Financial award application deadline: 1/15. *Faculty research:* Diverse field experiences and theoretical and practical knowledge in research-based science teaching, biology, chemistry, earth science, and physics. *Unit head:* Dr. Sharon Dotger, Program Coordinator, 315-443-9138, E-mail: sdotger@syr.edu. *Application contact:* Speranza Migliore, Graduate Admissions Recruiter, 315-443-2505, E-mail: gradrcrt@syr.edu.
Website: http://soe.syr.edu/academic/teaching_and_leadership/graduate/masters/science_education/

Teachers College, Columbia University, Department of Mathematics, Science and Technology, New York, NY 10027-6696. Offers biology 7-12 (MA); chemistry 7-12 (MA); communication and education (MA, Ed D); computing in education (MA); earth science 7-12 (MA); instructional technology and media (Ed M, MA, Ed D); mathematics education (Ed M, MA, Ed D, Ed DCT, PhD); physics 7-12 (MA); science and dental education (MA); science education (Ed M, MS, Ed DCT, PhD); supervisor/teacher of science education (MA); technology specialist (MA). *Program availability:* Part-time, evening/weekend, online learning. *Students:* 187 full-time (129 women), 228 part-time (153 women); includes 143 minority (42 Black or African American, non-Hispanic/Latino; 64 Asian, non-Hispanic/Latino; 25 Hispanic/Latino; 12 Two or more races, non-Hispanic/Latino), 125 international. Average age 32. 484 applicants, 59% accepted, 141 enrolled. Terminal master's awarded for partial completion of doctoral program. *Degree requirements:* For doctorate, thesis/dissertation. *Unit head:* Prof. Erica Walker, Chair, E-mail: ewalker@tc.columbia.edu. *Application contact:* David Estrella, Director of Admission, 212-678-3305, E-mail: estrella@tc.columbia.edu.
Website: http://www.tc.columbia.edu/mathematics-science-and-technology/

Teachers College of San Joaquin, Master's Program in Education, Stockton, CA 95206. Offers early education (M Ed); educational inquiry (M Ed); educational leadership and school development (M Ed); science, technology, engineering, and mathematics (M Ed); special education (M Ed).

Temple University, College of Education, Department of Teaching and Learning, Philadelphia, PA 19122-6096. Offers career and technical education (Ed M), including business, computing, and information technology, industrial education, marketing education; middle grades education (Ed M), including math and language arts, math and science, science and language arts; secondary education (Ed M), including English, math, social studies; teaching English to speakers of other languages (MS Ed); urban education (Ed M). *Program availability:* Part-time, evening/weekend. *Students:* 218 full-time (144 women), 296 part-time (183 women); includes 128 minority (74 Black or African American, non-Hispanic/Latino; 18 Asian, non-Hispanic/Latino; 25 Hispanic/Latino; 11 Two or more races, non-Hispanic/Latino), 13 international. 254 applicants, 54% accepted, 102 enrolled. In 2017, 128 master's awarded. Terminal master's awarded for partial completion of doctoral program. *Degree requirements:* For master's, thesis or alternative. *Entrance requirements:* Additional exam requirements/recommendations for international students: Required—TOEFL (minimum score 550 paper-based; 79 iBT). *Application deadline:* For fall admission, 4/1 for domestic students, 12/15 for international students; for spring admission, 10/1 for domestic students, 8/1 for international students. Application fee: $60. Electronic applications accepted. *Expenses:* Contact institution. *Financial support:* Fellowships, research assistantships, and teaching assistantships available. Financial award application deadline: 1/15; financial award applicants required to submit FAFSA. *Faculty research:* Workforce development, vocational education, technical education, industrial education, professional development, literacy, classroom management, school communities, curriculum development, instruction, applied linguistics, cross linguistic influence, bilingual education, oral proficiency, multilingualism. *Unit head:* Dr. Christine Woyshner, Chairperson, 215-204-6387, E-mail: christine.woyshner@temple.edu. *Application contact:* Sarah Stapleton, Assistant Director, Academic Operations, 215-204-8220, E-mail: sarah.stapleton@temple.edu.
Website: http://education.temple.edu/tl

Tennessee Technological University, College of Graduate Studies, College of Education, Department of Curriculum and Instruction, Program in STEM Education, Cookeville, TN 38505. Offers MA, Ed S. *Program availability:* Part-time, evening/weekend. *Students:* 2 full-time (1 woman), 4 part-time (3 women); includes 1 minority (Two or more races, non-Hispanic/Latino). 4 applicants, 100% accepted, 3 enrolled. In 2017, 2 master's awarded. *Degree requirements:* For master's, comprehensive exam, thesis or alternative. *Entrance requirements:* For master's, GRE, MAT. Additional exam requirements/recommendations for international students: Required—TOEFL (minimum score 527 paper-based; 71 iBT), IELTS (minimum score 5.5) or PTE (48). *Application deadline:* For fall admission, 8/1 for domestic students, 5/1 for international students; for spring admission, 2/1 for domestic students, 10/1 for international students; for summer admission, 5/1 for domestic students, 2/1 for international students. Applications are processed on a rolling basis. Application fee: $35 ($40 for international students). Electronic applications accepted. *Expenses:* Tuition, state resident: full-time $9925; part-time $565 per credit hour. Tuition, nonresident: full-time $22,993; part-time $1291

per credit hour. *Financial support:* Application deadline: 4/1. *Unit head:* Dr. Jeremy Wendt, Interim Chairperson, 931-372-3181, E-mail: jwendt@tntech.edu. *Application contact:* Shelia K. Kendrick, Coordinator of Graduate Studies, 931-372-3808, Fax: 931-372-3497, E-mail: skendrick@tntech.edu.

Texas A&M University–Kingsville, College of Graduate Studies, College of Education and Human Performance, Department of Teacher and Bilingual Education, Program in Science in Education, Kingsville, TX 78363. Offers MS. *Program availability:* Part-time, evening/weekend. *Degree requirements:* For master's, comprehensive exam, thesis or alternative, research report. *Entrance requirements:* For master's, GRE General Test, MAT, minimum GPA of 3.0. *Faculty research:* Professional development/technology, interdisciplinary teaming, educational restructuring.

Texas Christian University, College of Education, Doctoral Programs in Education, Fort Worth, TX 76129. Offers counseling and counselor education (PhD); curriculum studies (PhD); educational leadership (Ed D); higher educational leadership (Ed D); science education (PhD); MBA/Ed D. *Program availability:* Part-time, evening/weekend. *Faculty:* 29 full-time (21 women), 3 part-time/adjunct (1 woman). *Students:* 80 full-time (57 women), 26 part-time (13 women); includes 41 minority (15 Black or African American, non-Hispanic/Latino; 6 Asian, non-Hispanic/Latino; 17 Hispanic/Latino; 3 Two or more races, non-Hispanic/Latino), 6 international. Average age 39. 109 applicants, 50% accepted, 23 enrolled. In 2017, 12 doctorates awarded. *Degree requirements:* For doctorate, comprehensive exam, thesis/dissertation. *Entrance requirements:* For doctorate, GRE General Test. Additional exam requirements/recommendations for international students: Required—TOEFL (minimum score 550 paper-based; 80 iBT). *Application deadline:* For fall admission, 2/1 for domestic and international students; for winter admission, 2/1 for domestic and international students; for spring admission, 11/16 for domestic and international students. Application fee: $60. Electronic applications accepted. *Financial support:* In 2017–18, 69 students received support, including 1 fellowship with full tuition reimbursement available (averaging $18,500 per year), 8 research assistantships with full tuition reimbursements available (averaging $18,500 per year), 7 teaching assistantships with full tuition reimbursements available (averaging $18,500 per year); career-related internships or fieldwork, scholarships/grants, health care benefits, and unspecified assistantships also available. Support available to part-time students. Financial award application deadline: 2/1. *Unit head:* Dr. Jan Lacina, Associate Dean, 817-257-6786, Fax: 817-257-7466, E-mail: j.lacina@tcu.edu. *Application contact:* Lori Kimball, Administrative Program Specialist, 817-257-7661, Fax: 817-257-7466, E-mail: l.kimball@tcu.edu.
Website: http://coe.tcu.edu/graduate-overview/

Texas Christian University, College of Education, Master's Programs in Education, Fort Worth, TX 76129. Offers counseling (M Ed); curriculum and instruction (M Ed), including curriculum studies, language and literacy, math education, science education; education (MAT); educational leadership (M Ed); special education (M Ed). *Program availability:* Part-time, evening/weekend. *Faculty:* 29 full-time (21 women), 3 part-time/adjunct (1 woman). *Students:* 124 full-time (94 women), 14 part-time (12 women); includes 52 minority (14 Black or African American, non-Hispanic/Latino; 2 American Indian or Alaska Native, non-Hispanic/Latino; 3 Asian, non-Hispanic/Latino; 28 Hispanic/Latino; 5 Two or more races, non-Hispanic/Latino), 1 international. Average age 28. 172 applicants, 69% accepted, 86 enrolled. In 2017, 62 master's awarded. *Degree requirements:* For master's, comprehensive exam (for some programs), thesis (for some programs). *Entrance requirements:* For master's, GRE General Test; Pre-Admission Content Test (for MAT). Additional exam requirements/recommendations for international students: Required—TOEFL (minimum score 550 paper-based; 80 iBT). *Application deadline:* For fall admission, 3/1 for domestic and international students; for spring admission, 11/16 for domestic and international students; for summer admission, 3/1 for domestic and international students. Application fee: $60. Electronic applications accepted. *Financial support:* In 2017–18, 124 students received support, including 1 research assistantship with full tuition reimbursement available (averaging $15,000 per year), 29 teaching assistantships with full tuition reimbursements available (averaging $15,000 per year); career-related internships or fieldwork, scholarships/grants, and unspecified assistantships also available. Support available to part-time students. Financial award application deadline: 3/1. *Unit head:* Dr. Jan Lacina, Associate Dean, 817-257-6786, Fax: 817-257-7466, E-mail: j.lacina@tcu.edu. *Application contact:* Lori Kimball, Administrative Program Specialist, 817-257-7661, Fax: 817-257-7466, E-mail: l.kimball@tcu.edu.
Website: http://coe.tcu.edu/graduate-overview/

Texas Tech University, Graduate School, College of Education, Department of Curriculum and Instruction, Lubbock, TX 79409. Offers bilingual education (M Ed); curriculum and instruction (M Ed); elementary education (M Ed); language/literacy education (M Ed); multidisciplinary science (MS); secondary education (M Ed). *Accreditation:* NCATE. *Program availability:* Part-time, evening/weekend, online learning. *Faculty:* 22 full-time (14 women), 2 part-time/adjunct (1 woman). *Students:* 64 full-time (50 women), 247 part-time (205 women); includes 100 minority (26 Black or African American, non-Hispanic/Latino; 1 American Indian or Alaska Native, non-Hispanic/Latino; 11 Asian, non-Hispanic/Latino; 54 Hispanic/Latino; 8 Two or more races, non-Hispanic/Latino), 39 international. Average age 39. 157 applicants, 56% accepted, 71 enrolled. In 2017, 20 master's, 21 doctorates awarded. Terminal master's awarded for partial completion of doctoral program. *Degree requirements:* For master's, comprehensive exam (for some programs), thesis optional; for doctorate, comprehensive exam, thesis/dissertation. *Entrance requirements:* For master's, bachelor's degree; resume; letter of intent; academic writing sample; 2 letters of recommendation; for doctorate, GRE, master's degree; resume; letter of intent; academic writing sample; 3 letters of recommendation. Additional exam requirements/recommendations for international students: Required—TOEFL (minimum score 550 paper-based; 79 iBT). *Application deadline:* For fall admission, 6/1 priority date for domestic students, 1/15 priority date for international students; for spring admission, 9/1 priority date for domestic students, 6/15 priority date for international students. Applications are processed on a rolling basis. Application fee: $60. Electronic applications accepted. *Expenses:* Contact institution. *Financial support:* In 2017–18, 96 students received support, including 92 fellowships (averaging $3,321 per year), 37 research assistantships (averaging $12,336 per year); teaching assistantships, Federal Work-Study, institutionally sponsored loans, scholarships/grants, health care benefits, and unspecified assistantships also available. Support available to part-time students. Financial award application deadline: 2/1; financial award applicants required to submit FAFSA. *Faculty research:* Teacher education, curriculum studies, bilingual education, science and math education, language and literacy education. *Total annual research expenditures:* $107,999. *Unit head:* Dr. Fanni Liu Coward, Interim Chairperson, 806-834-4475, Fax: 806-742-2179, E-mail: fanni.coward@ttu.edu. *Application contact:* Brianna Sanchez, Coordinator, 806-834-2353, Fax: 806-742-2179, E-mail: brianna.sanchez@ttu.edu.
Website: http://www.educ.ttu.edu

Tufts University, Graduate School of Arts and Sciences, Department of Education, Program in Education, Medford, MA 02155. Offers educational studies (MA); elementary education (MAT); middle and secondary education (MAT); museum education (MA); secondary education (MA); STEM education (MS, PhD). *Program availability:* Part-time.

Science Education

Students: 50 full-time (38 women), 9 part-time (8 women); includes 9 minority (2 Black or African American, non-Hispanic/Latino; 2 Asian, non-Hispanic/Latino; 4 Hispanic/Latino; 1 Two or more races, non-Hispanic/Latino), 4 international. Average age 28. 120 applicants, 71% accepted, 49 enrolled. In 2017, 51 master's awarded. *Degree requirements:* For master's, thesis optional. *Entrance requirements:* For master's, GRE General Test, portfolio (for art education only); for doctorate, GRE General Test, writing sample. Additional exam requirements/recommendations for international students: Required—TOEFL (minimum score 550 paper-based; 80 iBT), IELTS (minimum score 6.5). *Application deadline:* For fall admission, 1/2 for domestic and international students; for spring admission, 10/15 for domestic and international students. Applications are processed on a rolling basis. Application fee: $85. Electronic applications accepted. *Expenses:* Contact institution. *Financial support:* Research assistantships, teaching assistantships, Federal Work-Study, scholarships/grants, and tuition waivers (full and partial) available. Support available to part-time students. Financial award application deadline: 1/2. *Unit head:* Dr. David Hammer, Graduate Program Director, 617-627-2396. *Application contact:* Office of Graduate Admissions, 617-627-3395, E-mail: gradadmissions@tufts.edu.

Tufts University, Graduate School of Arts and Sciences, Department of Physics and Astronomy, Medford, MA 02155. Offers astrophysics (MS, PhD); chemical physics (PhD); physics (MS, PhD); physics education (PhD). *Students:* 31 full-time (6 women); includes 1 minority (Asian, non-Hispanic/Latino), 13 international. Average age 27. 126 applicants, 17% accepted, 9 enrolled. In 2017, 8 master's, 8 doctorates awarded. Terminal master's awarded for partial completion of doctoral program. *Degree requirements:* For master's, thesis optional; for doctorate, thesis/dissertation, oral qualifying exam. *Entrance requirements:* For master's and doctorate, GRE General Test. Additional exam requirements/recommendations for international students: Required—TOEFL (minimum score 550 paper-based; 80 iBT), IELTS (minimum score 6.5). *Application deadline:* For fall admission, 1/15 for domestic and international students. Applications are processed on a rolling basis. Application fee: $85. Electronic applications accepted. *Expenses:* Contact institution. *Financial support:* Fellowships, research assistantships, teaching assistantships, Federal Work-Study, scholarships/grants, tuition waivers (full and partial), and unspecified assistantships available. Financial award application deadline: 1/15. *Unit head:* Dr. Danilo Marchesini, Graduate Program Director, 617-627-2756. *Application contact:* Office of Graduate Admissions, 617-627-3395, E-mail: gradadmissions@tufts.edu.
Website: http://www.tufts.edu/as/physics/

Universidad Nacional Pedro Henriquez Urena, Graduate School, Santo Domingo, Dominican Republic. Offers agricultural diversity (MS), including horticultural/fruit production, tropical animal production; conservation of monuments and cultural assets (M Arch); ecology and environment (MS); environmental engineering (MEE); international relations (MA); natural resource management (MS); political science (MA); project optimization (MPM); project feasibility (MPM); project management (MPM); sanitation engineering (ME); science for teachers (MS); tropical Caribbean architecture (M Arch).

University at Buffalo, the State University of New York, Graduate School, Graduate School of Education, Department of Learning and Instruction, Buffalo, NY 14260. Offers biology education (Ed M, Certificate); chemistry education (Ed M, Certificate); childhood education (Ed M); childhood education with bilingual extension (Ed M); college teaching (Advanced Certificate); curriculum, instruction and the science of learning (PhD); early childhood education (Ed M); early childhood education with bilingual extension (Ed M); earth science education (Ed M, Certificate); education and technology (Ed M); education studies (Ed M); educational technology and new literacies (Certificate); educational technology and new literacies (Advanced Certificate); elementary education (Ed D); English education (Ed M, Certificate); English education studies (Ed M); English for speakers of other languages (Ed M); foreign and second language education (PhD); French education (Ed M, Certificate); German education (Ed M, Certificate); gifted education (Certificate); Latin education (Ed M, Certificate); literacy education studies (Ed M); literacy specialist (Ed M); literacy teaching and learning (Certificate); mathematics education (Ed M, Certificate); music education (Ed M, Certificate); music education studies (Ed M); music learning theory (Advanced Certificate); online education (Advanced Certificate); physics education (Ed M, Certificate); science and the public (Ed M); social studies education (Ed M, Certificate); Spanish education (Ed M, Certificate); special education (PhD); teaching English to speakers of other languages (Ed M). *Program availability:* Part-time, evening/weekend, 100% online. *Faculty:* 26 full-time (19 women), 74 part-time/adjunct (52 women). *Students:* 172 full-time (122 women), 325 part-time (226 women); includes 44 minority (25 Black or African American, non-Hispanic/Latino; 5 American Indian or Alaska Native, non-Hispanic/Latino; 14 Asian, non-Hispanic/Latino; 57 international. Average age 33. 316 applicants, 78% accepted, 174 enrolled. In 2017, 109 master's, 34 doctorates, 15 other advanced degrees awarded. *Degree requirements:* For master's, comprehensive exam; for doctorate, thesis/dissertation, research analysis exam, research experience. *Entrance requirements:* For master's, letters of reference; for doctorate, GRE General Test or MAT, interview, writing sample, letters of recommendation. Additional exam requirements/recommendations for international students: Required—TOEFL (minimum score 600 paper-based; 96 iBT). *Application deadline:* For fall admission, 2/1 priority date for domestic and international students; for spring admission, 11/15 priority date for domestic students, 10/1 for international students. Applications are processed on a rolling basis. Application fee: $50. Electronic applications accepted. *Financial support:* In 2017–18, 42 fellowships (averaging $5,181 per year), 44 research assistantships with tuition reimbursements (averaging $10,908 per year) were awarded; teaching assistantships, career-related internships or fieldwork, Federal Work-Study, institutionally sponsored loans, scholarships/grants, tuition waivers (full and partial), and unspecified assistantships also available. Financial award application deadline: 2/28; financial award applicants required to submit FAFSA. *Faculty research:* Science assessment, foreign language teaching and learning, early learning, new literacies, gender and education. *Total annual research expenditures:* $413,233. *Unit head:* Dr. David Bruce, Chair, 716-645-4069, Fax: 716-645-3161, E-mail: gse-info@buffalo.edu. *Application contact:* Luann Zak, Admissions Assistant, 716-645-2110, Fax: 716-645-7937, E-mail: luannzak@buffalo.edu.
Website: http://gse.buffalo.edu/lai

The University of Akron, Graduate School, College of Education, Department of Curricular and Instructional Studies, Program in Adolescent to Young Adult Education, Akron, OH 44325. Offers chemistry (MS); chemistry and physics (MS); earth science (MS); earth science and chemistry (MS); earth science and physics (MS); integrated language arts (MS); integrated mathematics (MS); integrated social studies (MS); life science (MS); life science and chemistry (MS); life science and earth science (MS); life science and physics (MS); physics (MS). *Accreditation:* NCATE. *Students:* 16 full-time (6 women), 6 part-time (3 women); includes 6 minority (2 Black or African American, non-Hispanic/Latino; 1 Asian, non-Hispanic/Latino; 3 Two or more races, non-Hispanic/Latino). Average age 30. 8 applicants, 100% accepted, 8 enrolled. In 2017, 8 master's awarded. *Degree requirements:* For master's, comprehensive exam. *Entrance requirements:* For master's, minimum GPA of 3.0. Additional exam requirements/recommendations for international students: Required—TOEFL (minimum score 79 iBT), IELTS (minimum score 6.5). *Application deadline:* For fall admission, 3/1 for

domestic and international students; for spring admission, 10/1 for domestic and international students. Applications are processed on a rolling basis. Application fee: $45 ($70 for international students). Electronic applications accepted. *Unit head:* Dr. Evonn Welton, Interim Department Chair, 330-972-6742, E-mail: ewelton@uakron.edu. *Application contact:* Kelly Chaff, College Program Specialist, 330-972-7028, E-mail: klchaff@uakron.edu.
Website: http://www.uakron.edu/education/academic-programs/graduate-programs.dot

The University of Alabama in Huntsville, School of Graduate Studies, College of Education, Huntsville, AL 35899. Offers autism spectrum disorders (M Ed, Graduate Certificate); biology (MAT); chemistry (MAT); differentiated instruction in elementary education (M Ed); English language arts (MAT); English speakers of other languages (M Ed, MAT); history (MAT); mathematics (MAT); physics (MAT); reading education (M Ed); secondary education (M Ed).

The University of Alabama in Huntsville, School of Graduate Studies, College of Science, Department of Biological Sciences, Huntsville, AL 35899. Offers biology (MS); biotechnology science and engineering (PhD); education (MS). *Program availability:* Part-time, evening/weekend. *Degree requirements:* For master's, comprehensive exam, thesis or alternative, oral and written exams. *Entrance requirements:* For master's, GRE General Test, previous course work in biochemistry and organic chemistry, minimum GPA of 3.0. Additional exam requirements/recommendations for international students: Required—TOEFL (minimum score 550 paper-based; 80 iBT), IELTS (minimum score 6.5). Electronic applications accepted. *Faculty research:* Physiology, microbiology, genomics and protemics, ecology and evolution, drug discovery.

The University of Alabama in Huntsville, School of Graduate Studies, College of Science, Department of Chemistry, Huntsville, AL 35899. Offers biotechnology science and engineering (PhD); chemistry (MS); education (MS); materials science (MS, PhD). *Program availability:* Part-time, evening/weekend. *Degree requirements:* For master's, comprehensive exam, thesis or alternative, oral and written exams. *Entrance requirements:* For master's, GRE General Test, minimum GPA of 3.0. Additional exam requirements/recommendations for international students: Required—TOEFL (minimum score 550 paper-based; 80 iBT), IELTS (minimum score 6.5). Electronic applications accepted. *Faculty research:* Natural products drug discovery, protein biochemistry, macromolecular biophysics, polymer synthesis, surface modification and analysis of materials.

The University of Alabama in Huntsville, School of Graduate Studies, College of Science, Department of Physics, Huntsville, AL 35899. Offers education (MS); optics and photonics technology (MS); physics (MS, PhD). *Program availability:* Part-time, evening/weekend. *Degree requirements:* For master's, comprehensive exam, thesis or alternative, oral and written exams; for doctorate, comprehensive exam, thesis/dissertation, oral and written exams. *Entrance requirements:* For master's and doctorate, GRE General Test, minimum GPA of 3.0. Additional exam requirements/recommendations for international students: Required—TOEFL (minimum score 550 paper-based; 80 iBT), IELTS (minimum score 6.5). Electronic applications accepted. *Faculty research:* Space and solar physics, computational physics, optics, high energy astrophysics.

University of Arkansas at Pine Bluff, School of Education, Pine Bluff, AR 71601-2799. Offers elementary education (M Ed); secondary education (M Ed), including English education, mathematics education, science education, social studies education; teaching (MAT). *Accreditation:* NCATE. *Program availability:* Part-time, evening/weekend. *Degree requirements:* For master's, comprehensive exam. *Entrance requirements:* For master's, GRE, minimum GPA of 2.75, NTE or Standard Arkansas Teaching Certificate. *Faculty research:* Teacher certification, accreditation, assessment, standards, portfolio development, rehabilitation, technology.

The University of British Columbia, Faculty of Education, Department of Curriculum and Pedagogy, Vancouver, BC V6T 1Z4, Canada. Offers art education (M Ed, MA); curriculum studies (M Ed, MA, PhD); home economics education (M Ed, MA); mathematics education (M Ed, MA); media and technology studies education (M Ed, MA); music education (M Ed, MA); physical education (M Ed, MA); science education (M Ed, MA); social studies education (M Ed, MA). *Program availability:* Part-time, online learning. *Degree requirements:* For master's, thesis (MA); for doctorate, comprehensive exam, thesis/dissertation. *Entrance requirements:* Additional exam requirements/recommendations for international students: Required—TOEFL, IELTS. Electronic applications accepted. *Expenses:* Contact institution. *Faculty research:* School subjects, teaching and learning.

University of California, Berkeley, Graduate Division, School of Education, Group in Science and Mathematics Education, Berkeley, CA 94720-1500. Offers PhD, MA/Credential. Electronic applications accepted.

University of California, Berkeley, Graduate Division, School of Education, Programs in Education, Berkeley, CA 94720-1500. Offers development in mathematics and science (MA); education in mathematics, science, and technology (MA, PhD); human development and education (MA, PhD); leadership education (MA); special education (PhD); teacher education (MA); MA/Credential; PhD/Credential; PhD/MA. Terminal master's awarded for partial completion of doctoral program. *Degree requirements:* For master's, exam or thesis; for doctorate, thesis/dissertation, oral qualifying exam. *Entrance requirements:* For master's and doctorate, GRE General Test, minimum GPA of 3.0 during last 2 years of undergraduate course work. Electronic applications accepted. *Faculty research:* Human development, social and moral educational psychology, developmental teacher preparation.

University of California, San Diego, Graduate Division, Program in Mathematics and Science Education, La Jolla, CA 92093. Offers PhD. Program offered jointly with San Diego State University. *Students:* 12 part-time (10 women). In 2017, 3 doctorates awarded. *Degree requirements:* For doctorate, thesis/dissertation, teaching practicum. *Entrance requirements:* For doctorate, GRE General Test, minimum GPA of 3.25. Additional exam requirements/recommendations for international students: Required—TOEFL (minimum score 550 paper-based; 80 iBT), IELTS (minimum score 7). Electronic applications accepted. *Financial support:* Scholarships/grants and stipends available. Financial award applicants required to submit FAFSA. *Faculty research:* Effective teaching of rational numbers, teacher development, development of number sense and estimation. *Unit head:* Gabriele Wienhausen, Chair, 858-534-3105, E-mail: gwienhausen@ucsd.edu. *Application contact:* Sherry Seethaler, Graduate Coordinator, 858-534-4656, E-mail: sseethaler@ucsd.edu.
Website: http://sci.sdsu.edu/CRMSE/msed/

University of Central Florida, College of Community Innovation and Education, Education Doctoral Programs, Orlando, FL 32816. Offers curriculum and instruction (Ed D); education (PhD), including communication sciences and disorders, counselor education, early childhood education, elementary education, exceptional education, exercise physiology, higher education, instructional design and technology, mathematics education, methodology, measurement and analysis, reading education, science education, social science education, TESOL; educational leadership (Ed D). *Students:* 122 full-time (86 women), 129 part-time (88 women); includes 64 minority (24 Black or African American, non-Hispanic/Latino; 1 American Indian or Alaska Native, non-Hispanic/Latino; 9 Asian, non-Hispanic/Latino; 24 Hispanic/Latino; 6 Two or more

races, non-Hispanic/Latino), 26 international. Average age 38. 195 applicants, 47% accepted, 72 enrolled. In 2017, 89 doctorates awarded. *Entrance requirements:* For doctorate, GRE, letters of recommendation, goal statement, resume, writing sample. Application fee: $30. Electronic applications accepted. *Expenses:* Tuition, state resident: part-time $288.16 per credit hour. Tuition, nonresident: part-time $1073.31 per credit hour. Tuition and fees vary according to program. *Financial support:* In 2017–18, 77 students received support, including 28 fellowships with partial tuition reimbursements available (averaging $5,733 per year), 29 research assistantships with partial tuition reimbursements available (averaging $10,230 per year), 54 teaching assistantships with partial tuition reimbursements available (averaging $11,614 per year); health care benefits also available. Financial award application deadline: 3/1; financial award applicants required to submit FAFSA. *Unit head:* Dr. Edward Robinson, Director of Doctoral Programs, 407-823-6106, E-mail: edward.robinson@ucf.edu. *Application contact:* Associate Director, Graduate Admissions, 407-823-2766, Fax: 407-823-6442, E-mail: gradadmissions@ucf.edu.
Website: https://edcollege.ucf.edu/academic-programs/graduate/

University of Central Florida, College of Community Innovation and Education, School of Teacher Education, Program in K-8 Mathematics and Science Education, Orlando, FL 32816. Offers M Ed, Certificate. *Accreditation:* NCATE. *Program availability:* Part-time. *Students:* 1 full-time (0 women), 16 part-time (15 women); includes 10 minority (3 Black or African American, non-Hispanic/Latino; 7 Hispanic/Latino). Average age 36. 3 applicants, 100% accepted, 3 enrolled. In 2017, 11 master's awarded. *Degree requirements:* For master's, thesis or alternative. *Entrance requirements:* Additional exam requirements/recommendations for international students: Required—TOEFL. *Application deadline:* For summer admission, 4/15 for domestic students. Application fee: $30. Electronic applications accepted. *Expenses:* Tuition, state resident: part-time $288.16 per credit hour. Tuition, nonresident: part-time $1073.31 per credit hour. Tuition and fees vary according to program. *Financial support:* In 2017–18, 1 student received support, including 2 research assistantships with partial tuition reimbursements available (averaging $5,522 per year). Financial award application deadline: 3/1; financial award applicants required to submit FAFSA. *Unit head:* Dr. Malcolm Butler, Program Coordinator, 407-823-3272, E-mail: malcolm.butler@ucf.edu. *Application contact:* Associate Director, Graduate Admissions, 407-823-2766, Fax: 407-823-6442, E-mail: gradadmissions@ucf.edu.
Website: http://education.ucf.edu/mathed/

University of Central Florida, College of Community Innovation and Education, School of Teacher Education, Program in Teacher Education, Orlando, FL 32816. Offers art education (MAT); English language (MAT); mathematics education (MAT); middle school mathematics (MAT); middle school science (MAT); science education (MAT), including biology, chemistry, physics; social science education (MAT). *Accreditation:* NCATE. *Program availability:* Part-time, evening/weekend. *Students:* 11 full-time (9 women), 28 part-time (23 women); includes 15 minority (5 Black or African American, non-Hispanic/Latino; 2 Asian, non-Hispanic/Latino; 6 Hispanic/Latino; 2 Two or more races, non-Hispanic/Latino), 2 international. Average age 29. In 2017, 6 master's awarded. *Degree requirements:* For master's, thesis or alternative. *Entrance requirements:* For master's, Florida Teacher Certification Examination/General Knowledge Test or GRE General Test. Additional exam requirements/recommendations for international students: Required—TOEFL. *Application deadline:* For spring admission, 12/1 for domestic students; for summer admission, 4/15 for domestic students. Application fee: $30. Electronic applications accepted. *Expenses:* Tuition, state resident: part-time $288.16 per credit hour. Tuition, nonresident: part-time $1073.31 per credit hour. Tuition and fees vary according to program. *Financial support:* Fellowships, research assistantships, teaching assistantships, career-related internships or fieldwork, Federal Work-Study, institutionally sponsored loans, tuition waivers (partial), and unspecified assistantships available. Financial award application deadline: 3/1; financial award applicants required to submit FAFSA. *Unit head:* Dr. Michael Hynes, Director, 407-823-2005, E-mail: mychael.hynes@ucf.edu. *Application contact:* Associate Director, Graduate Admissions, 407-823-2766, Fax: 407-823-6442, E-mail: gradadmissions@ucf.edu.
Website: http://www.graduatecatalog.ucf.edu/programs/program.aspx?id=9727&program=Teacher%20Education%20MAT

University of Chicago, Division of the Social Sciences, Committee on Conceptual and Historical Studies of Science, Chicago, IL 60637. Offers PhD. *Faculty:* 17. *Students:* 9 full-time (6 women). 31 applicants, 13% accepted, 1 enrolled. In 2017, 1 doctorate awarded. *Degree requirements:* For doctorate, one foreign language, thesis/dissertation, 2 oral exams. *Entrance requirements:* For doctorate, GRE General Test, 3 letters of recommendation, statement of purpose, transcripts, resume or curriculum vitae, writing sample (dependent on department). Additional exam requirements/recommendations for international students: Required—TOEFL (minimum score 104 iBT), IELTS (minimum score 7). *Application deadline:* For fall admission, 12/15 priority date for domestic and international students. Application fee: $90. Electronic applications accepted. *Financial support:* In 2017–18, 2 students received support, including 2 fellowships with full tuition reimbursements available (averaging $27,000 per year); research assistantships, teaching assistantships, career-related internships or fieldwork, Federal Work-Study, institutionally sponsored loans, scholarships/grants, and health care benefits also available. Financial award application deadline: 12/15. *Unit head:* Prof. Adrian Johns, Chair, 773-702-2334, E-mail: johns@uchicago.edu. *Application contact:* Office of the Dean of Students, 773-702-8415, E-mail: ssd-admissions@uchicago.edu.
Website: http://chss.uchicago.edu/

University of Colorado Denver, School of Education and Human Development, Program in Educational Leadership and Innovation, Denver, CO 80217. Offers educational studies and research (PhD), including administrative leadership and policy, early childhood special education, math education, research, assessment and evaluation, science education, urban ecologies. *Program availability:* Part-time, evening/weekend. *Degree requirements:* For doctorate, comprehensive exam, thesis/dissertation, 75 credit hours (for PhD). *Entrance requirements:* For doctorate, GRE or equivalent, resume or curriculum vitae, letters of recommendation, master's degree or equivalent, completion of basic or advanced statistics course with minimum B grade. Additional exam requirements/recommendations for international students: Required—TOEFL (minimum score 537 paper-based; 75 iBT); Recommended—IELTS (minimum score 6.5). Electronic applications accepted. *Expenses:* Contact institution. *Faculty research:* Administrative leadership and policy studies, early childhood education, research in diversity, paraprofessionals in education, urban schools lab.

University of Colorado Denver, School of Education and Human Development, Teacher Education Programs, Denver, CO 80217. Offers elementary linguistically diverse education (MA); elementary math and science education (MA); elementary math education (MA); elementary reading and writing (MA); elementary science education (MA); secondary English education (MA); secondary linguistically diverse education (MA); secondary math education (MA); secondary reading and writing (MA); secondary science education (MA); special education (MA). *Accreditation:* NCATE. *Program availability:* Part-time, evening/weekend. *Degree requirements:* For master's, comprehensive exam. *Entrance requirements:* For master's, GRE or MAT (for those with

GPA below 2.75), transcripts, resume, letters of recommendation. Additional exam requirements/recommendations for international students: Required—TOEFL (minimum score 537 paper-based; 75 iBT); Recommended—IELTS (minimum score 6.5). Electronic applications accepted. *Expenses:* Contact institution. *Faculty research:* Linguistically diverse education/ESL, elementary reading and writing, elementary teacher education, secondary teacher education, special education.

University of Connecticut, Graduate School, Neag School of Education, Department of Curriculum and Instruction, Program in Science Education, Storrs, CT 06269. Offers MA, PhD. *Accreditation:* NCATE. Terminal master's awarded for partial completion of doctoral program. *Degree requirements:* For master's, comprehensive exam, thesis or alternative; for doctorate, thesis/dissertation. *Entrance requirements:* For doctorate, GRE General Test. Additional exam requirements/recommendations for international students: Required—TOEFL (minimum score 550 paper-based). Electronic applications accepted.

The University of Findlay, Office of Graduate Admissions, Findlay, OH 45840. Offers applied security and analytics (MSAS); athletic training (MAT); business (MBA), including certified management accountant, certified public accountant, health care management, hospitality management; education (MA Ed, Ed D), including children's literature (MA Ed), curriculum and teaching (MA Ed), education (MA Ed), educational administration (MA Ed), human resource development (MA Ed), mathematics (MA Ed), reading (MA Ed), science education (MA Ed), superintendent (Ed D), teaching (Ed D), technology (MA Ed); environmental, safety, and health management (MSEM); health informatics (MS); occupational therapy (MOT); pharmacy (Pharm D); physical therapy (DPT); physician assistant (MPA); rhetoric and writing (MA); teaching English to speakers of other languages (TESOL) and applied linguistics (MA). *Program availability:* Part-time, evening/weekend, 100% online, blended/hybrid learning. *Students:* 688 full-time (430 women), 553 part-time (308 women), 170 international. Average age 28. In 2017, 366 master's, 137 doctorates awarded. *Degree requirements:* For master's, comprehensive exam (for some programs), thesis (for some programs), cumulative project, capstone project; for doctorate, thesis/dissertation (for some programs). *Entrance requirements:* For master's, GRE/GMAT, bachelor's degree from accredited institution, minimum undergraduate GPA of 2.5 in last 64 hours of course work; for doctorate, GRE, MAT, minimum cumulative GPA of 3.0. Additional exam requirements/recommendations for international students: Required—TOEFL (minimum score 79 iBT), IELTS (minimum score 7), PTE (minimum score 61). *Application deadline:* Applications are processed on a rolling basis. Electronic applications accepted. *Financial support:* In 2017–18, 10 research assistantships with partial tuition reimbursements (averaging $7,200 per year), 35 teaching assistantships with partial tuition reimbursements (averaging $7,200 per year) were awarded; Federal Work-Study, institutionally sponsored loans, and unspecified assistantships also available. Financial award applicants required to submit FAFSA. *Unit head:* Christopher M. Harris, Director of Admissions, 419-434-4347, E-mail: harrisc1@findlay.edu. *Application contact:* Madeline Fauser Brennan, Graduate Admissions Counselor, 419-434-4636, Fax: 419-434-4898, E-mail: fauserbrennan@findlay.edu.
Website: http://www.findlay.edu/admissions/graduate/Pages/default.aspx

University of Florida, Graduate School, College of Education, School of Teaching and Learning, Gainesville, FL 32611. Offers curriculum and instruction (M Ed, MAE, Ed D, PhD, Ed S); elementary education (M Ed, MAE); English education (M Ed, MAE); mathematics education (M Ed, MAE); reading education (M Ed, MAE); science education (M Ed, MAE); social studies education (M Ed, MAE). *Accreditation:* NCATE. *Program availability:* Part-time, evening/weekend, online learning. Terminal master's awarded for partial completion of doctoral program. *Degree requirements:* For master's, comprehensive exam (for some programs), thesis (for some programs); for doctorate, comprehensive exam (for some programs), thesis/dissertation (for some programs). *Entrance requirements:* For master's and doctorate, GRE General Test, minimum GPA of 3.0; for Ed S, GRE General Test. Additional exam requirements/recommendations for international students: Required—TOEFL (minimum score 550 paper-based; 80 iBT), IELTS (minimum score 6). Electronic applications accepted. *Faculty research:* STEM education; curriculum; teaching and teacher education; languages and literacy; schools, culture, and society; theories and processes of learning.

University of Georgia, College of Education, Department of Mathematics and Science Education, Athens, GA 30602. Offers mathematics education (M Ed, PhD, Ed S).

University of Illinois at Chicago, Program in Learning Sciences, Chicago, IL 60607-7128. Offers PhD.

University of Illinois at Urbana–Champaign, Graduate College, College of Engineering, Department of Physics, Champaign, IL 61820. Offers physics (MS, PhD); teaching of physics (MS).

University of Illinois at Urbana–Champaign, Graduate College, College of Liberal Arts and Sciences, School of Chemical Sciences, Department of Chemistry, Champaign, IL 61820. Offers astrochemistry (PhD); chemical physics (PhD); chemistry (MA, MS, PhD); teaching of chemistry (MS); MS/JD; MS/MBA.

University of Illinois at Urbana–Champaign, Graduate College, College of Liberal Arts and Sciences, School of Earth, Society and Environment, Department of Geology, Champaign, IL 61820. Offers geology (MS, PhD); teaching of earth sciences (MS). Terminal master's awarded for partial completion of doctoral program.

University of Indianapolis, Graduate Programs, School of Education, Indianapolis, IN 46227-3697. Offers art education (MAT); biology (MAT); chemistry (MAT); curriculum and instruction (MA); earth sciences (MAT); education (MA, MAT); educational leadership (MA); elementary education (MA); English (MAT); French (MAT); math (MAT); physical education (MAT); physics (MAT); secondary education (MA), including art education, education, English education, social studies education; social studies (MAT); Spanish (MAT). *Accreditation:* NCATE. *Program availability:* Part-time, evening/weekend. *Entrance requirements:* For master's, GRE Subject Test, PRAXIS I, minimum GPA of 2.5, 3 letters of recommendation, interview. Additional exam requirements/recommendations for international students: Required—TOEFL (minimum score 550 paper-based). *Faculty research:* Assessment of teacher education, perceptions of prospective teachers by parents.

The University of Iowa, Graduate College, College of Education, Department of Teaching and Learning, Program in Education, Iowa City, IA 52242-1316. Offers art education (MA); developmental reading (MA); elementary education (MA); English education (MA, MAT); foreign and second language education (MAT); foreign language education (MA); foreign language/ESL education (PhD); language, literacy and culture (PhD); mathematics education (MA, MAT, PhD); music education (MM, PhD); science education (MA); secondary education (MA); social studies (MA, PhD). *Degree requirements:* For master's, thesis optional, exam; for doctorate, comprehensive exam, thesis/dissertation. *Entrance requirements:* For master's and doctorate, GRE General Test, minimum GPA of 3.0. Additional exam requirements/recommendations for international students: Required—TOEFL (minimum score 550 paper-based; 81 iBT). Electronic applications accepted.

University of Lynchburg, Graduate Studies, M Ed Program in Science Education, Lynchburg, VA 24501-3199. Offers science education (M Ed), including earth science,

math. *Program availability:* Part-time, evening/weekend. *Faculty:* 17 full-time (10 women), 12 part-time/adjunct (6 women). *Students:* 8 full-time (6 women), 5 part-time (3 women); includes 1 minority (Asian, non-Hispanic/Latino), 2 international. Average age 28. 13 applicants, 100% accepted, 7 enrolled. In 2017, 2 master's awarded. *Degree requirements:* For master's, comprehensive exam. *Entrance requirements:* For master's, GRE, minimum GPA of 3.0 (preferred), official transcripts (bachelor's, others as relevant), three letters of recommendation, career goals statement. Additional exam requirements/recommendations for international students: Required—TOEFL (minimum score 550 paper-based; 80 iBT), IELTS (minimum score 6). *Application deadline:* For fall admission, 7/31 for domestic students, 6/1 for international students; for spring admission, 11/30 for domestic students, 10/15 for international students. Applications are processed on a rolling basis. Application fee: $30. Electronic applications accepted. Application fee is waived when completed online. *Expenses:* $510 per credit hour tuition, $100 fees. *Financial support:* Federal Work-Study, scholarships/grants, health care benefits, and unspecified assistantships available. Support available to part-time students. Financial award application deadline: 7/31; financial award applicants required to submit FAFSA. *Unit head:* Dr. David Perault, Professor/Director of M Ed in Science Education, 434-544-8370, E-mail: perault@lynchburg.edu. *Application contact:* Ellen Thompson, Graduate Admissions Counselor, 434-544-8841, E-mail: thompson_e@lynchburg.edu.
Website: http://www.lynchburg.edu/graduate/master-of-education-in-science-education/

University of Maryland, Baltimore County, The Graduate School, College of Arts, Humanities and Social Sciences, Department of Education, Master of Arts in Education Program, Baltimore, MD 21250. Offers K-8 mathematics instructional leadership (MAE); K-8 science education (MAE); K-8 STEM education (MAE); secondary mathematics education (MAE); secondary science education (MAE); secondary STEM education (MAE). *Program availability:* Part-time-only, evening/weekend, 100% online, blended/hybrid learning. *Faculty:* 4 full-time (3 women), 9 part-time/adjunct (7 women). *Students:* 142 part-time (110 women); includes 18 minority (5 Black or African American, non-Hispanic/Latino; 1 American Indian or Alaska Native, non-Hispanic/Latino; 7 Asian, non-Hispanic/Latino; 3 Hispanic/Latino; 2 Two or more races, non-Hispanic/Latino). Average age 32. 15 applicants, 100% accepted, 13 enrolled. *Degree requirements:* For master's, comprehensive exam (for some programs), thesis (for some programs). *Application deadline:* For fall admission, 6/1 for domestic students; for spring admission, 11/1 for domestic students. Application fee: $50. Electronic applications accepted. *Expenses:* $1,050 tuition per 3-credit course; $195 fees per 3-credit course. *Financial support:* In 2017–18, 1 student received support. *Application deadline:* 3/1; applicants required to submit FAFSA. *Unit head:* Jerri Frick, Graduate Program Director, 410-455-1356, Fax: 410-455-6182, E-mail: frick@umbc.edu.
Website: http://mae.umbc.edu

University of Maryland, Baltimore County, The Graduate School, College of Arts, Humanities and Social Sciences, Department of Education, Program in Teaching, Baltimore, MD 21250. Offers early childhood education (MAT); elementary education (MAT); teaching (MAT), including art, biology, chemistry, choral music, classical foreign language, dance, earth/space science, English, instrumental music, mathematics, modern foreign language, physical science, physics, social studies, theatre. *Program availability:* Part-time, evening/weekend. *Faculty:* 24 full-time (18 women), 25 part-time/adjunct (19 women). *Students:* 41 full-time (34 women), 27 part-time (18 women); includes 26 minority (6 Black or African American, non-Hispanic/Latino; 9 Asian, non-Hispanic/Latino; 7 Hispanic/Latino; 1 Native Hawaiian or other Pacific Islander, non-Hispanic/Latino; 3 Two or more races, non-Hispanic/Latino), 2 international. Average age 30. 54 applicants, 83% accepted, 35 enrolled. In 2017, 50 master's awarded. *Degree requirements:* For master's, comprehensive exam (for some programs), thesis (for some programs). *Entrance requirements:* For master's, PRAXIS Core Examination or GRE (minimum score of 1000), minimum GPA of 3.0. Additional exam requirements/recommendations for international students: Required—TOEFL. *Application deadline:* For fall admission, 6/1 for domestic and international students; for spring admission, 11/1 for domestic and international students. Applications are processed on a rolling basis. Application fee: $50. Electronic applications accepted. *Expenses:* Required fees: $132. *Financial support:* In 2017–18, 8 students received support, including teaching assistantships with tuition reimbursements available (averaging $12,000 per year); career-related internships or fieldwork, Federal Work-Study, scholarships/grants, tuition waivers, and unspecified assistantships also available. Financial award application deadline: 3/15. *Faculty research:* STEM teacher education, culturally sensitive pedagogy, ESOL/bilingual education, early childhood education, language, literacy and culture. Total annual research expenditures: $100,000. *Unit head:* Dr. Susan M. Blunck, Graduate Program Director, 410-455-2869, Fax: 410-455-3986, E-mail: blunck@umbc.edu. *Application contact:* Cheryl Johnson, MAT Program Specialist, 410-455-3388, E-mail: blackwel@umbc.edu.
Website: http://www.umbc.edu/education/

University of Massachusetts Amherst, Graduate School, College of Education, Program in Education, Amherst, MA 01003. Offers bilingual, English as a second language, and multicultural education (M Ed, Ed S); child study and early education (M Ed); children, families and schools (Ed D, Ed S); early childhood and elementary teacher education (M Ed); educational leadership (M Ed); educational policy and leadership (Ed D); higher education (M Ed); international education (M Ed); language, literacy and culture (Ed D); learning, media and technology (M Ed, Ed S); mathematics, science, and learning technologies (Ed D); reading and writing (M Ed); research, educational measurement and psychometrics (Ed D); school counselor education (M Ed, Ed S); school psychology (Ed S); science education (Ed S); secondary teacher education (M Ed); social justice education (M Ed, Ed D, Ed S); special education (M Ed, Ed D, Ed S); teacher education and school improvement (Ed D, Ed S). *Accreditation:* NCATE. *Program availability:* Part-time, online learning. Terminal master's awarded for partial completion of doctoral program. *Degree requirements:* For doctorate, comprehensive exam, thesis/dissertation. *Entrance requirements:* Additional exam requirements/recommendations for international students: Required—TOEFL (minimum score 550 paper-based; 80 iBT), IELTS (minimum score 6.5). Electronic applications accepted.

University of Massachusetts Dartmouth, Graduate School, College of Arts and Sciences, School of Education, Department of STEM Education and Teacher Development, North Dartmouth, MA 02747-2300. Offers English as a second language (Postbaccalaureate Certificate); mathematics education (PhD); middle school education (MAT); secondary school education (MAT). *Program availability:* Part-time. *Faculty:* 9 full-time (6 women), 11 part-time/adjunct (7 women). *Students:* 26 full-time (15 women), 102 part-time (60 women); includes 16 minority (2 Black or African American, non-Hispanic/Latino; 2 Asian, non-Hispanic/Latino; 6 Hispanic/Latino; 6 Two or more races, non-Hispanic/Latino), 2 international. Average age 32. 60 applicants, 92% accepted, 51 enrolled. In 2017, 41 master's, 2 doctorates awarded. *Degree requirements:* For doctorate, thesis/dissertation. *Entrance requirements:* For master's, statement of purpose (minimum of 300 words), resume, 2 letters of recommendation, official transcripts; for doctorate, GRE, statement of purpose (minimum of 300 words), resume, official transcripts, 3 letters of recommendation. Additional exam requirements/recommendations for international students: Required—TOEFL (minimum score 533 paper-based; 72 iBT), IELTS (minimum score 6). *Application deadline:* For fall admission, 2/15 priority date for domestic students, 1/15 priority date for international students; for spring admission, 1/15

priority date for domestic students, 12/15 priority date for international students. Application fee: $60. Electronic applications accepted. *Expenses:* Tuition, state resident: full-time $15,449; part-time $643.71 per credit. Tuition, nonresident: full-time $27,880; part-time $1161.67 per credit. Required fees: $405; $25.88 per credit. Tuition and fees vary according to course load and reciprocity agreements. *Financial support:* In 2017–18, 2 fellowships (averaging $16,000 per year), 4 research assistantships (averaging $20,656 per year), 2 teaching assistantships (averaging $16,000 per year) were awarded; tuition waivers (full) and unspecified assistantships also available. Support available to part-time students. Financial award application deadline: 3/1; financial award applicants required to submit FAFSA. *Faculty research:* Mindfulness in education, literacies, assessment of teacher knowledge, curriculum tools for supporting mathematics learning. Total annual research expenditures: $1.6 million. *Unit head:* Traci Almeida, Coordinator of Graduate Admissions and Licensure, 508-999-8098, Fax: 508-910-8183, E-mail: talmeida@umassd.edu. *Application contact:* Steven Briggs, Director of Marketing and Recruitment for Graduate Studies, 508-999-8604, Fax: 508-999-8183, E-mail: graduate@umassd.edu.
Website: http://www.umassd.edu/cas/schoolofeducation/departments/stemeducationandteacherdevelopment/

University of Memphis, Graduate School, College of Education, Department of Instruction and Curriculum Leadership, Memphis, TN 38152. Offers advanced studies in teaching and learning (M Ed); applied behavior analysis (Graduate Certificate); autism studies (Graduate Certificate); early childhood education (MAT, MS, Ed D); elementary education (MAT); instruction and curriculum (MS, Ed D); instruction design and technology (MS, Ed D); instructional design and technology (Graduate Certificate); literacy, leadership, and coaching (Graduate Certificate); reading (MS, Ed D); school library information specialist (Graduate Certificate); secondary education (MAT); special education (MAT, MS, Ed D); STEM teacher leadership (Graduate Certificate); urban education (Graduate Certificate). *Accreditation:* NCATE. One or more programs are accredited). *Program availability:* Part-time. *Faculty:* 22 full-time (14 women), 14 part-time/adjunct (10 women). *Students:* 36 full-time (27 women), 351 part-time (271 women); includes 159 minority (132 Black or African American, non-Hispanic/Latino; 1 American Indian or Alaska Native, non-Hispanic/Latino; 7 Asian, non-Hispanic/Latino; 10 Hispanic/Latino; 9 Two or more races, non-Hispanic/Latino), 4 international. Average age 35. 170 applicants, 85% accepted, 111 enrolled. In 2017, 84 master's, 14 doctorates, 32 other advanced degrees awarded. Terminal master's awarded for partial completion of doctoral program. *Degree requirements:* For master's, comprehensive exam, thesis or alternative; for doctorate, comprehensive exam, thesis/dissertation. *Entrance requirements:* For master's, GRE General Test, PRAXIS, minimum GPA of 2.5, letters of reference; for doctorate, GRE General Test, GRE Subject Test, 2 years of teaching experience, letters of reference, statement of purpose, interview. Additional exam requirements/recommendations for international students: Required—TOEFL (minimum score 550 paper-based; 79 iBT). *Application deadline:* For fall admission, 4/1 priority date for domestic students; for spring admission, 10/1 priority date for domestic students; for summer admission, 2/1 priority date for domestic students. Applications are processed on a rolling basis. Application fee: $35 ($60 for international students). Electronic applications accepted. *Expenses:* Contact institution. *Financial support:* In 2017–18, 2 research assistantships with full tuition reimbursements (averaging $10,000 per year), 3 teaching assistantships with full tuition reimbursements (averaging $10,666 per year) were awarded; career-related internships or fieldwork, Federal Work-Study, institutionally sponsored loans, scholarships/grants, traineeships, and unspecified assistantships also available. Support available to part-time students. Financial award application deadline: 2/1; financial award applicants required to submit FAFSA. *Faculty research:* Effective urban teachers, preparation and retention of urban teachers, technology utilization in schools, field-based teacher preparation programs, effective use of online instruction. *Unit head:* Dr. Angiline Powell, Interim Chair, 901-678-3310, E-mail: apowell3@memphis.edu. *Application contact:* Dr. James Meindl, Coordinator of Graduate Studies, 901-678-3310, E-mail: jnmeindl@memphis.edu.
Website: http://www.memphis.edu/icl/

University of Miami, Graduate School, School of Education and Human Development, Department of Teaching and Learning, Program in Teaching and Learning, Coral Gables, FL 33124. Offers language and literacy learning in multilingual settings (PhD); science, technology, engineering and mathematics (PhD); special education (PhD). *Degree requirements:* For doctorate, thesis/dissertation, qualifying exam, electronic portfolio. *Entrance requirements:* For doctorate, GRE General Test. Additional exam requirements/recommendations for international students: Required—TOEFL (minimum score 550 paper-based; 80 iBT); Recommended—IELTS (minimum score 6.5). Electronic applications accepted. *Faculty research:* Teacher education, multicultural education, special education, second language acquisition, math and science education.

University of Michigan–Dearborn, College of Education, Health, and Human Services, Master of Science Program in Science Education, Dearborn, MI 48126. Offers MS. *Accreditation:* TEAC. *Program availability:* Part-time, evening/weekend. *Faculty:* 3 full-time (2 women). *Students:* 5 part-time (all women). Average age 37. In 2017, 4 master's awarded. *Entrance requirements:* For master's, minimum GPA of 3.0, bachelor's degree from accredited institution, official transcripts from all post-secondary institutions attended, three professional letters of recommendation, personal statement, valid state of Michigan teaching certificate (if seeking a science endorsement). Additional exam requirements/recommendations for international students: Required—TOEFL (minimum score 560 paper-based; 84 iBT), IELTS (minimum score 6.5). *Application deadline:* For fall admission, 8/1 priority date for domestic students, 5/1 priority date for international students; for winter admission, 12/1 priority date for domestic students, 9/1 priority date for international students; for spring admission, 4/1 priority date for domestic students, 1/1 priority date for international students. Applications are processed on a rolling basis. Application fee: $60. Electronic applications accepted. *Expenses:* $683 per credit hour in-state; $1,176 per credit hour out-state. *Financial support:* Scholarships/grants available. Financial award application deadline: 3/1; financial award applicants required to submit FAFSA. *Faculty research:* STEM teaching and learning, science education, community based education, ecojustice education, pedagogy and interventions. *Unit head:* Dr. Stein Brunvand, Director, Master's Programs, 313-583-6415, E-mail: sbrunvan@umich.edu. *Application contact:* Office of Graduate Studies, 313-583-6321, E-mail: umd-graduatestudies@umich.edu.
Website: http://umdearborn.edu/cehhs/cehhs_msse/

University of Minnesota, Twin Cities Campus, Graduate School, College of Education and Human Development, Department of Curriculum and Instruction, Program in Teaching, Minneapolis, MN 55455-0213. Offers teaching (M Ed), including arts in education, elementary education, English education, mathematics, science, second language education, social studies. *Students:* 251 full-time (180 women), 136 part-time (82 women); includes 68 minority (16 Black or African American, non-Hispanic/Latino; 15 Asian, non-Hispanic/Latino; 17 Hispanic/Latino; 20 Two or more races, non-Hispanic/Latino), 9 international. Average age 28. 341 applicants, 72% accepted, 229 enrolled. In 2017, 263 master's awarded. Application fee: $75 ($95 for international students). *Unit head:* Dr. Cynthia Lewis, Chair, 612-625-6313, Fax: 612-624-8277, E-mail: lewis@umn.edu. *Application contact:* Dr. Kendall King, Director of Graduate Studies, 612-625-3692, E-mail: roehr013@umn.edu.
Website: http://www.cehd.umn.edu/ci/

University of Missouri, Office of Research and Graduate Studies, College of Education, Department of Learning, Teaching and Curriculum, Columbia, MO 65211. Offers agricultural education (M Ed, PhD, Ed S); art education (M Ed, PhD, Ed S); business and office education (M Ed, PhD, Ed S); early childhood education (M Ed, PhD, Ed S); elementary education (M Ed, PhD, Ed S); English education (M Ed, PhD, Ed S); foreign language education (M Ed, PhD, Ed S); health education and promotion (M Ed, PhD); learning and instruction (M Ed); marketing education (M Ed, PhD, Ed S); mathematics education (M Ed, PhD, Ed S); music education (M Ed, PhD, Ed S); reading education (M Ed, PhD, Ed S); science education (M Ed, PhD, Ed S); social studies education (M Ed, PhD, Ed S); vocational education (M Ed, PhD, Ed S). *Program availability:* Part-time. Terminal master's awarded for partial completion of doctoral program. *Degree requirements:* For doctorate, thesis/dissertation. *Entrance requirements:* For master's and Ed S, GRE General Test or MAT, minimum GPA of 3.0; for doctorate, GRE General Test, minimum GPA of 3.0. Additional exam requirements/recommendations for international students: Required—TOEFL (minimum score 600 paper-based; 100 iBT). Electronic applications accepted.

University of Nebraska at Kearney, College of Natural and Social Sciences, Department of Biology, Kearney, NE 68849. Offers biology (MS); science/math education (MA Ed). *Program availability:* Part-time, evening/weekend, 100% online. *Degree requirements:* For master's, comprehensive exam, thesis optional. *Entrance requirements:* For master's, GRE (for thesis option and for online program applicants if undergraduate GPA is below 2.75), letter of interest. Additional exam requirements/recommendations for international students: Recommended—TOEFL (minimum score 550 paper-based; 79 iBT), IELTS (minimum score 6.5). Electronic applications accepted. *Expenses:* Contact institution. *Faculty research:* Pollution injury, molecular biology-viral gene expression, prairie range condition modeling, evolution of symbiotic nitrogen fixation, geographic information systems (GIS), molecular genetics of aging.

University of Nebraska at Omaha, Graduate Studies, College of Arts and Sciences, Department of Biology, Omaha, NE 68182. Offers biology (MS); business for bioscientists (Certificate). *Program availability:* Part-time. *Degree requirements:* For master's, comprehensive exam (for some programs), thesis (for some programs). *Entrance requirements:* For master's, GRE General Test, minimum GPA of 3.0, transcripts, 24 undergraduate biology hours, 3 letters of recommendation, statement of purpose. Additional exam requirements/recommendations for international students: Required—TOEFL, IELTS, PTE. Electronic applications accepted.

University of New Hampshire, Graduate School, College of Engineering and Physical Sciences, Department of Chemistry, Durham, NH 03824. Offers chemistry (MS, PhD); chemistry education (PhD). *Students:* 46 full-time (17 women), 8 part-time (2 women); includes 2 minority (1 Asian, non-Hispanic/Latino; 1 Two or more races, non-Hispanic/Latino), 21 international. Average age 27. 83 applicants, 48% accepted, 17 enrolled. In 2017, 3 master's, 9 doctorates awarded. Terminal master's awarded for partial completion of doctoral program. *Entrance requirements:* For master's and doctorate, GRE. Additional exam requirements/recommendations for international students: Required—TOEFL (minimum score 550 paper-based; 80 iBT). *Application deadline:* For fall admission, 4/1 priority date for domestic students, 4/1 for international students; for spring admission, 12/1 for domestic students. Application fee: $65. Electronic applications accepted. *Financial support:* In 2017–18, 47 students received support, including 6 research assistantships, 40 teaching assistantships; fellowships, Federal Work-Study, scholarships/grants, and tuition waivers (full and partial) also available. Support available to part-time students. Financial award application deadline: 2/15. *Unit head:* Margaret Greenslade, Chair, 603-862-2475. *Application contact:* Laura Bicknell, Administrative Assistant, 603-862-1550, E-mail: chem.dept@unh.edu.
Website: http://www.ceps.unh.edu/chemistry

University of New Mexico, School of Medicine, Program in University Science Teaching, Albuquerque, NM 87131-2039. Offers Certificate.

The University of North Carolina at Chapel Hill, Graduate School, School of Education, Program in Secondary Education, Chapel Hill, NC 27599. Offers English (Grades 9-12) (MAT); English as a second language (MAT); French (Grades K-12) (MAT); German (Grades K-12) (MAT); Japanese (Grades K-12) (MAT); Latin (Grades 9-12) (MAT); mathematics (Grades 9-12) (MAT); music (Grades K-12) (MAT); science (Grades 9-12) (MAT); social studies (Grades 9-12) (MAT); Spanish (Grades K-12) (MAT). *Accreditation:* NCATE. *Degree requirements:* For master's, comprehensive exam. *Entrance requirements:* For master's, GRE General Test, minimum GPA of 3.0 during last 2 years of undergraduate course work. Additional exam requirements/recommendations for international students: Required—TOEFL (minimum score 550 paper-based). Electronic applications accepted.

The University of North Carolina at Greensboro, Graduate School, School of Education, Department of Teacher Education and Higher Education, Greensboro, NC 27412-5001. Offers college teaching and adult learning (Certificate); curriculum and instruction (M Ed), including chemistry education, elementary education, English as a second language, French education, instructional technology, mathematics education, middle grades education, reading education, science education, social studies education, Spanish education; curriculum and teaching (PhD), including higher education, teacher education and development; English as a second language (Certificate); higher education (M Ed); supervision (M Ed). *Accreditation:* NCATE. *Program availability:* Part-time. *Degree requirements:* For doctorate, thesis/dissertation. *Entrance requirements:* For master's and doctorate, GRE General Test. Additional exam requirements/recommendations for international students: Required—TOEFL. Electronic applications accepted. *Faculty research:* Community college literacy program, middle school mathematics/computer mathematics.

The University of North Carolina at Pembroke, The Graduate School, Department of Biology, Pembroke, NC 28372-1510. Offers science education (MA, MAT). *Program availability:* Part-time, evening/weekend. *Entrance requirements:* For master's, GRE or MAT, minimum GPA of 3.0 in major or 2.5 overall. *Application deadline:* For fall admission, 7/15 priority date for domestic and international students; for spring admission, 12/1 priority date for domestic and international students. Applications are processed on a rolling basis. Application fee: $45 ($60 for international students). *Financial support:* Application deadline: 4/15; applicants required to submit FAFSA. *Unit head:* Dr. Rita Hagevik, Director of Graduate Programs in Science Education, 910-521-6652, Fax: 910-521-6567, E-mail: rita.hagevik@uncp.edu.
Website: http://www.uncp.edu/biology

University of Northern Colorado, Graduate School, College of Natural and Health Sciences, Department of Chemistry and Biochemistry, Greeley, CO 80639. Offers chemical education (MS, PhD); chemistry (MS). *Program availability:* Part-time. *Degree requirements:* For master's, comprehensive exam, thesis or alternative; for doctorate, comprehensive exam, thesis/dissertation. *Entrance requirements:* For master's, 3 letters of reference; for doctorate, GRE General Test, 3 letters of reference. Electronic applications accepted.

University of Northern Colorado, Graduate School, College of Natural and Health Sciences, School of Biology, Program in Biology Education, Greeley, CO 80639. Offers PhD. *Program availability:* Part-time. *Degree requirements:* For doctorate,

comprehensive exam, thesis/dissertation. *Entrance requirements:* For doctorate, GRE General Test, 3 letters of recommendation. Electronic applications accepted.

University of Northern Iowa, Graduate College, College of Humanities, Arts and Sciences, MA Program in Science Education, Cedar Falls, IA 50614. Offers earth science education (MA); physics education (MA); science education (MA). *Degree requirements:* For master's, comprehensive exam (for some programs), thesis or alternative. *Entrance requirements:* For master's, minimum GPA of 3.0. Additional exam requirements/recommendations for international students: Required—TOEFL (minimum score 500 paper-based; 61 iBT). Electronic applications accepted.

University of North Georgia, Program in Middle Grades Math and Science, Dahlonega, GA 30597. Offers M Ed. *Program availability:* Part-time, evening/weekend, online only, 100% online. *Students:* 6 full-time (all women), 12 part-time (8 women); includes 1 minority (Black or African American, non-Hispanic/Latino). Average age 29. 4 applicants, 75% accepted, 3 enrolled. In 2017, 8 master's awarded. *Degree requirements:* For master's, teaching practicum. *Entrance requirements:* For master's, baccalaureate degree from regionally-accredited, four-year institution with minimum cumulative GPA of 2.75; employment as teacher in middle grades classroom working with students at least 20 hours per week; clear/renewable teaching certificate in middle grades math or science in the state of Georgia or equivalent. Additional exam requirements/recommendations for international students: Required—TOEFL (minimum score 550 paper-based; 79 iBT), IELTS (minimum score 6.5). *Application deadline:* For fall admission, 7/24 for domestic students; for spring admission, 12/12 for domestic students; for summer admission, 4/26 for domestic students. Application fee: $40. Electronic applications accepted. *Expenses:* Contact institution. *Financial support:* Application deadline: 3/17; applicants required to submit FAFSA. *Unit head:* Dr. Susan Brandenburg-Ayres, Dean, 706-864-1998, E-mail: susan.ayres@ung.edu. *Application contact:* Melinda Maxwell, Director of Graduate Studies, 706-867-2077, E-mail: melinda.maxwell@ung.edu.
Website: https://ung.edu/teacher-education/graduate/master-education-middle-grades.php

University of Oklahoma, Jeannine Rainbolt College of Education, Department of Instructional Leadership and Academic Curriculum, Norman, OK 73019. Offers instructional leadership and academic curriculum (M Ed, PhD), including biomedical education (PhD), early childhood education, elementary education, English education, instructional leadership, mathematics education, reading education, science education, social studies education, world languages education (M Ed); reading specialist (M Ed). *Accreditation:* NCATE. *Program availability:* Part-time. *Faculty:* 19 full-time (15 women), 1 (woman) part-time/adjunct. *Students:* 37 full-time (28 women), 121 part-time (98 women); includes 32 minority (7 Black or African American, non-Hispanic/Latino; 4 American Indian or Alaska Native, non-Hispanic/Latino; 5 Asian, non-Hispanic/Latino; 6 Hispanic/Latino; 1 Native Hawaiian or other Pacific Islander, non-Hispanic/Latino; 9 Two or more races, non-Hispanic/Latino), 12 international. Average age 35. 39 applicants, 77% accepted, 22 enrolled. In 2017, 49 master's, 12 doctorates awarded. Terminal master's awarded for partial completion of doctoral program. *Degree requirements:* For master's, comprehensive exam (for some programs), thesis (for some programs); for doctorate, comprehensive exam (for some programs), thesis/dissertation. *Entrance requirements:* For doctorate, GRE. Additional exam requirements/recommendations for international students: Required—TOEFL (minimum score 79 iBT) or IELTS (minimum score 6.5). Application fee: $50 ($100 for international students). Electronic applications accepted. *Expenses:* Tuition, state resident: full-time $5119; part-time $213.30 per credit hour. Tuition, nonresident: full-time $19,778; part-time $824.10 per credit hour. *Required fees:* $3458; $133.55 per credit hour. $126.50 per semester. *Financial support:* In 2017–18, 90 students received support, including 8 research assistantships (averaging $11,248 per year), 6 teaching assistantships (averaging $12,188 per year); fellowships, scholarships/grants, and unspecified assistantships also available. Financial award application deadline: 6/1; financial award applicants required to submit FAFSA. *Faculty research:* Teacher preparation; instruction; curriculum; learning; constructivist theory. *Total annual research expenditures:* $707,690. *Unit head:* Dr. Stacy Reeder, Chair, 405-325-1498, Fax: 405-325-4061, E-mail: reeder@ou.edu. *Application contact:* Anna Steele, Graduate Programs Officer, 405-325-4525, E-mail: anna.steele@ou.edu.
Website: http://www.ou.edu/education/ilac

University of Pennsylvania, Graduate School of Education, Medical Education Program, Philadelphia, PA 19104. Offers MS Ed, Certificate. Program offered jointly with Perelman School of Medicine and The Children's Hospital of Philadelphia. *Program availability:* Evening/weekend. *Students:* Average age 38. 45 applicants, 78% accepted, 33 enrolled. In 2017, 5 master's awarded. *Entrance requirements:* For master's, bachelor's degree; professional health care experience. Additional exam requirements/recommendations for international students: Required—TOEFL, IELTS. *Application deadline:* Applications are processed on a rolling basis. Application fee: $75. Electronic applications accepted. *Faculty research:* Strategic leadership, workplace learning, evidenced-best decision making, technology in the work place. *Unit head:* Elizabeth Ulivella, Associate Director, 215-573-0591, E-mail: ulivella@upenn.edu.
Website: http://www.gse.upenn.edu/med-ed/

University of Phoenix–Online Campus, College of Education, Phoenix, AZ 85034-7209. Offers administration and supervision (MAEd, Certificate); adult education and training (MAEd); curriculum and instruction (MAEd), including computer education, curriculum and instruction, English as a second language, language arts, mathematics, reading; early childhood education (MAEd); educational studies (MAEd); elementary teacher education (MAEd), including early childhood, elementary teacher education, high school middle level, middle level; principal licensure (Certificate); secondary teacher education (MAEd); special education (MAEd, Certificate); teacher education (MAEd), including middle level generalist; teacher education middle level mathematics (MAEd), including middle level mathematics; teacher education middle level science (MAEd), including middle level science; teacher education secondary mathematics (MAEd); teacher education secondary science (MAEd); teacher leadership (MAEd); teachers of English learners (Certificate); transition to teaching (Certificate), including elementary education, secondary education. *Program availability:* Evening/weekend, online learning. *Entrance requirements:* Additional exam requirements/recommendations for international students: Required—TOEFL, TOEIC (Test of English as an International Communication), Berlitz Online English Proficiency Exam, PTE, or IELTS. Electronic applications accepted. *Expenses:* Contact institution.

University of Pittsburgh, School of Education, Department of Instruction and Learning, Program in Secondary Education, Pittsburgh, PA 15260. Offers English and communications education (M Ed, MAT); foreign language education (M Ed, MAT); language, literacy and culture education (Ed D, PhD); mathematics education (M Ed, MAT, Ed D, PhD); science education (M Ed, MAT, Ed D, PhD); secondary education (PhD); social studies education (M Ed, MAT); STEM education (Ed D). *Program availability:* Part-time, evening/weekend. *Degree requirements:* For master's, thesis; for doctorate, thesis/dissertation. *Entrance requirements:* For master's, PRAXIS I; for doctorate, GRE General Test. Additional exam requirements/recommendations for international students: Required—TOEFL. Electronic applications accepted.

Science Education

University of Puerto Rico–Río Piedras, College of Education, Program in Curriculum and Teaching, San Juan, PR 00931-3300. Offers biology education (M Ed); chemistry education (M Ed); curriculum and teaching (Ed D); history education (M Ed); mathematics education (M Ed); physics education (M Ed); Spanish education (M Ed). *Program availability:* Part-time. *Degree requirements:* For master's, thesis; for doctorate, thesis/dissertation, internship. *Entrance requirements:* For master's, PAEG or GRE, minimum GPA of 3.0, letter of recommendation; for doctorate, GRE or PAEG, master's degree, minimum GPA of 3.0, letter of recommendation (2), interview. *Faculty research:* Curriculum, math teaching.

University of St. Francis, College of Education, Joliet, IL 60435-6169. Offers educational leadership (MS, Ed D); elementary education (M Ed); reading (MS); secondary education (M Ed), including English education, math education, science education, social studies education, visual arts education; special education (M Ed); teaching and learning (MS); TESOL (Certificate). *Accreditation:* NCATE. *Program availability:* Part-time, evening/weekend, 100% online, blended/hybrid learning. *Faculty:* 11 full-time (8 women), 52 part-time/adjunct (36 women). *Students:* 39 full-time (32 women), 411 part-time (318 women); includes 106 minority (57 Black or African American, non-Hispanic/Latino; 8 Asian, non-Hispanic/Latino; 37 Hispanic/Latino; 4 Two or more races, non-Hispanic/Latino), 4 international. Average age 37. 277 applicants, 55% accepted, 137 enrolled. In 2017, 199 master's, 28 doctorates awarded. *Degree requirements:* For master's, comprehensive exam; for doctorate, thesis/dissertation. *Entrance requirements:* Additional exam requirements/recommendations for international students: Required—TOEFL (minimum score 550 paper-based; 79 iBT), IELTS (minimum score 6). *Application deadline:* Applications are processed on a rolling basis. Application fee: $30. Electronic applications accepted. Application fee is waived when completed online. *Expenses:* $365 to $748 per credit hour. *Financial support:* In 2017–18, 40 students received support. Scholarships/grants and unspecified assistantships available. Support available to part-time students. Financial award applicants required to submit FAFSA. *Unit head:* Dr. John Gambro, Dean, 815-740-3829, Fax: 815-740-2264, E-mail: jgambro@stfrancis.edu. *Application contact:* Sandra Sloka, Director of Admissions for Graduate and Degree Completion Programs, 800-735-7500, Fax: 815-740-3431, E-mail: ssloka@stfrancis.edu.
Website: http://www.stfrancis.edu/academics/college-of-education/

University of San Diego, School of Leadership and Education Sciences, Department of Learning and Teaching, San Diego, CA 92110-2492. Offers curriculum and instruction (M Ed); inclusive learning (M Ed); literacy and digital learning (M Ed); school leadership (M Ed); special education (M Ed); STEAM (science, technology, engineering, arts, and mathematics) (M Ed); TESOL, literacy and culture (M Ed). *Program availability:* Part-time, evening/weekend. *Faculty:* 9 full-time (7 women), 30 part-time/adjunct (24 women). *Students:* 160 full-time (128 women), 221 part-time (176 women); includes 131 minority (10 Black or African American, non-Hispanic/Latino; 24 Asian, non-Hispanic/Latino; 83 Hispanic/Latino; 1 Native Hawaiian or other Pacific Islander, non-Hispanic/Latino; 13 Two or more races, non-Hispanic/Latino), 20 international. Average age 33. 398 applicants, 84% accepted, 196 enrolled. In 2017, 151 master's awarded. *Degree requirements:* For master's, thesis (for some programs), international experience. *Entrance requirements:* For master's, California Basic Educational Skills Test, California Subject Examination for Teachers. Additional exam requirements/recommendations for international students: Required—TOEFL (minimum score 580 paper-based; 83 iBT), TWE. *Application deadline:* Applications are processed on a rolling basis. Application fee: $45. Electronic applications accepted. *Financial support:* In 2017–18, 65 students received support. Career-related internships or fieldwork, Federal Work-Study, institutionally sponsored loans, and stipends available. Financial award application deadline: 4/1; financial award applicants required to submit FAFSA. *Faculty research:* Action research methodology, cultural studies, instructional theories and practices, second language acquisition, school reform. *Unit head:* Dr. Maya Kalyanpur, Chair, 619-260-7655, E-mail: mkalyanpur@sandiego.edu. *Application contact:* Monica Mahon, Associate Director of Graduate Admissions, 619-260-4524, Fax: 619-260-4158, E-mail: grads@sandiego.edu.
Website: http://www.sandiego.edu/soles/learning-and-teaching/

University of South Africa, College of Human Sciences, Pretoria, South Africa. Offers adult education (M Ed); African languages (MA, PhD); African politics (MA, PhD); Afrikaans (MA, PhD); ancient history (MA, PhD); ancient Near Eastern studies (MA, PhD); anthropology (MA, PhD); applied linguistics (MA); Arabic (MA, PhD); archaeology (MA); art history (MA); Biblical archaeology (MA); Biblical studies (M Th, D Th, PhD); Christian spirituality (M Th, D Th); church history (M Th, D Th); classical studies (MA, PhD); clinical psychology (MA); communication (MA, PhD); comparative education (M Ed, Ed D); consulting psychology (D Admin, D Com, PhD); curriculum studies (M Ed, Ed D); development studies (M Admin, MA, D Admin, PhD); didactics (M Ed, Ed D); education (M Tech); education management (M Ed, Ed D); educational psychology (M Ed); English (MA); environmental education (M Ed); French (MA, PhD); German (MA, PhD); Greek (MA); guidance and counseling (M Ed); health studies (MA, PhD), including health sciences education (MA), health services management (MA), medical and surgical nursing science (critical care general) (MA), midwifery and neonatal nursing science (MA), trauma and emergency care (MA); history (MA, PhD); history of education (Ed D); inclusive education (M Ed, Ed D); information and communications technology policy and regulation (MA); information science (MA, MIS, PhD); international politics (MA, PhD); Islamic studies (MA, PhD); Italian (MA, PhD); Judaica (MA, PhD); linguistics (MA, PhD); mathematical education (M Ed); mathematics education (MA); missiology (M Th, D Th); modern Hebrew (MA, PhD); musicology (MA, MMus, D Mus, PhD); natural science education (M Ed); New Testament (M Th, D Th); Old Testament (D Th); pastoral therapy (M Th, D Th); philosophy (MA); philosophy of education (M Ed, Ed D); politics (MA, PhD); Portuguese (MA, PhD); practical theology (M Th, D Th); psychology (MA, MS, PhD); psychology of education (M Ed, Ed D); public health (MA); religious studies (MA, D Th, PhD); Romance languages (MA); Russian (MA, PhD); Semitic languages (MA, PhD); social behavior studies in HIV/AIDS (MA); social science (mental health) (MA); social science in development studies (MA); social science in psychology (MA); social science in social work (MA); social science in sociology (MA); social work (MSW, DSW, PhD); socio-education (M Ed, Ed D); sociolinguistics (MA); sociology (MA, PhD); Spanish (MA, PhD); systematic theology (M Th, D Th); TESOL (teaching English to speakers of other languages) (MA); theological ethics (M Th, D Th); theory of literature (MA, PhD); urban ministries (D Th); urban ministry (M Th).

University of South Africa, Institute for Science and Technology Education, Pretoria, South Africa. Offers mathematics, science and technology education (M Sc, PhD).

University of South Alabama, College of Education and Professional Studies, Department of Leadership and Teacher Education, Mobile, AL 36688. Offers art education (M Ed); early childhood education (M Ed); educational leadership (M Ed, Ed D); elementary education (M Ed); reading education (M Ed); science education (M Ed); secondary education (M Ed); special education (M Ed). *Accreditation:* NCATE. *Program availability:* Part-time. *Faculty:* 15 full-time (11 women), 10 part-time/adjunct (6 women). *Students:* 203 full-time (154 women), 90 part-time (68 women); includes 73 minority (54 Black or African American, non-Hispanic/Latino; 3 American Indian or Alaska Native, non-Hispanic/Latino; 4 Asian, non-Hispanic/Latino; 10 Hispanic/Latino; 2 Two or more races, non-Hispanic/Latino). Average age 34. 134 applicants, 55%

accepted, 57 enrolled. In 2017, 73 master's, 8 doctorates awarded. *Degree requirements:* For master's, comprehensive exam, thesis (for some programs); for doctorate, comprehensive exam, thesis/dissertation. *Entrance requirements:* For master's, GRE General Test or MAT, minimum GPA of 3.0; for doctorate, GRE, minimum graduate GPA of 3.25, 3 years of experience in field, 3 letters of recommendation, interview, official transcripts. Additional exam requirements/recommendations for international students: Required—TOEFL. *Application deadline:* For fall admission, 7/15 for domestic students, 6/15 for international students; for spring admission, 11/15 for domestic students, 11/1 for international students; for summer admission, 4/15 for domestic students, 4/1 for international students. Applications are processed on a rolling basis. Application fee: $35. Electronic applications accepted. *Expenses:* Tuition, state resident: full-time $10,104; part-time $421 per semester hour. Tuition, nonresident: full-time $20,208; part-time $842 per semester hour. *Financial support:* Fellowships, research assistantships, teaching assistantships, career-related internships or fieldwork, Federal Work-Study, institutionally sponsored loans, scholarships/grants, and unspecified assistantships available. Support available to part-time students. Financial award application deadline: 3/31; financial award applicants required to submit FAFSA. *Unit head:* Dr. Susan Santoli, Chair/Director of Graduate Studies, 251-380-2836, Fax: 251-380-2748, E-mail: ssantoli@southalabama.edu.
Website: http://www.southalabama.edu/colleges/ceps/lte/index.html

University of South Carolina, The Graduate School, College of Arts and Sciences, Department of Biological Sciences, Columbia, SC 29208. Offers biology (MS, PhD); biology education (IMA, MAT); ecology, evolution and organismal biology (MS, PhD); molecular, cellular, and developmental biology (MS, PhD). IMA and MAT offered in cooperation with the College of Education. Terminal master's awarded for partial completion of doctoral program. *Degree requirements:* For master's, one foreign language, thesis (for some programs); for doctorate, one foreign language, thesis/dissertation. *Entrance requirements:* For master's and doctorate, GRE General Test, minimum GPA of 3.0 in science. Electronic applications accepted. *Faculty research:* Marine ecology, population and evolutionary biology, molecular biology and genetics, development.

University of South Carolina, The Graduate School, College of Arts and Sciences, Department of Geography, Columbia, SC 29208. Offers geography (MA, MS, PhD); geography education (IMA). IMA and MAT offered in cooperation with the College of Education. *Program availability:* Part-time. *Degree requirements:* For master's, comprehensive exam, thesis (for some programs); for doctorate, comprehensive exam, thesis/dissertation. *Entrance requirements:* For master's, GRE General Test; for doctorate, GRE General Test, master's degree. Electronic applications accepted. *Faculty research:* Geographic information processing; economic, cultural, physical, and environmental geography.

University of South Carolina, The Graduate School, College of Education, Department of Instruction and Teacher Education, Program in Secondary Education, Columbia, SC 29208. Offers art education (IMA, MAT); business education (IMA, MAT); English (MAT); foreign language (MAT); health education (MAT); mathematics (MAT); science (IMA, MAT); secondary (Ed D); secondary education (MT, PhD); social studies (MAT); theatre and speech (MAT). IMA and MT offered jointly with the subject areas. *Accreditation:* NCATE. *Degree requirements:* For master's, comprehensive exam, thesis (for some programs), foreign language (MA); for doctorate, one foreign language, comprehensive exam, thesis/dissertation. *Entrance requirements:* For master's, GRE General Test or MAT, teaching certificate (IMA, M Ed), interview; for doctorate, GRE General Test or MAT, interview. *Faculty research:* Middle school programs, professional development, school collaboration.

University of South Dakota, Graduate School, School of Education, Division of Curriculum and Instruction, Program in Elementary Education, Vermillion, SD 57069. Offers elementary education (MA), including early childhood education, English language learning, reading specialist/literacy coach, science, technology and math (STEM). *Accreditation:* NCATE. *Program availability:* Part-time, 100% online, blended/hybrid learning. *Degree requirements:* For master's, comprehensive exam, thesis or alternative. *Entrance requirements:* For master's, GRE General Test, MAT, minimum GPA of 2.7. Additional exam requirements/recommendations for international students: Required—TOEFL (minimum score 550 paper-based; 79 iBT). *Application deadline:* Applications are processed on a rolling basis. Application fee: $35. Electronic applications accepted. *Financial support:* Research assistantships with partial tuition reimbursements, teaching assistantships with partial tuition reimbursements, career-related internships or fieldwork, Federal Work-Study, and unspecified assistantships available. Financial award applicants required to submit FAFSA. *Application contact:* Graduate School, 605-658-6140, Fax: 605-677-6118, E-mail: grad@usd.edu.
Website: http://www.usd.edu/ci

University of South Dakota, Graduate School, School of Education, Division of Curriculum and Instruction, Program in Secondary Education, Vermillion, SD 57069. Offers secondary education (MA), including English language learning, science, technology and math (STEM), secondary education plus certification. *Accreditation:* NCATE. *Program availability:* Part-time, online learning. *Degree requirements:* For master's, comprehensive exam, thesis or alternative. *Entrance requirements:* For master's, GRE General Test, MAT, minimum GPA of 2.7. Additional exam requirements/recommendations for international students: Required—TOEFL (minimum score 550 paper-based; 79 iBT). *Application deadline:* Applications are processed on a rolling basis. Application fee: $35. Electronic applications accepted. *Financial support:* Research assistantships with partial tuition reimbursements, teaching assistantships with partial tuition reimbursements, career-related internships or fieldwork, Federal Work-Study, and unspecified assistantships available. Financial award applicants required to submit FAFSA. *Application contact:* Graduate School, 605-658-6140, Fax: 605-677-6118.
Website: http://www.usd.edu/ci

University of South Florida, St. Petersburg, College of Education, St. Petersburg, FL 33701. Offers educational leadership development (M Ed); elementary education (MA), including math/science; English education (MA); middle grades STEM education (MS); reading education (MA). *Program availability:* Part-time. *Degree requirements:* For master's, comprehensive exam, practicum, internship, comprehensive portfolio. *Entrance requirements:* For master's, State of Florida General Knowledge Test (GKT), Florida Teaching Certificate (for non-initial certification programs), letters of recommendation. Additional exam requirements/recommendations for international students: Required—TOEFL (minimum score 550 paper-based; 79 iBT); Recommended—IELTS. Electronic applications accepted.

The University of Tennessee, Graduate School, College of Education, Health and Human Sciences, Program in Education, Knoxville, TN 37996. Offers art education (MS); counseling education (PhD); cultural studies in education (PhD); curriculum (MS, Ed S); curriculum, educational research and evaluation (Ed D, PhD); early childhood education (PhD); early childhood special education (MS); education of deaf and hard of hearing (MS); educational administration and policy studies (Ed D, PhD); educational administration and supervision (Ed S); educational psychology (Ed D, PhD); elementary education (MS, Ed S); elementary teaching (MS); English education (MS, Ed S); exercise science (PhD); foreign language/ESL education (MS, Ed S); instructional technology (MS, Ed D, PhD, Ed S); literacy, language and ESL education (PhD); literacy, language education, and ESL education (Ed D); mathematics education (MS, Ed S); modified and comprehensive special education (MS); reading education (MS, Ed S); school counseling (Ed S); school psychology (PhD, Ed S); science education (MS, Ed S); secondary teaching (MS); social foundations (MS); social science education (MS, Ed S); socio-cultural foundations of sports and education (PhD); special education (Ed S); teacher education (Ed D, PhD). *Accreditation:* NCATE. *Program availability:* Part-time, evening/weekend. *Degree requirements:* For master's and Ed S, thesis optional; for doctorate, variable foreign language requirement, thesis/dissertation. *Entrance requirements:* For master's, minimum GPA of 2.7; for doctorate and Ed S, GRE General Test, minimum GPA of 2.7. Additional exam requirements/recommendations for international students: Required—TOEFL. Electronic applications accepted.

The University of Texas at Arlington, Graduate School, College of Education, Department of Curriculum and Instruction, Arlington, TX 76019. Offers curriculum and instruction (M Ed), including literacy studies, mathematics education, mind, brain, and education, science education; teaching (with certification) (M Ed T). *Accreditation:* NCATE. *Program availability:* Part-time, evening/weekend, online learning. *Degree requirements:* For master's, comprehensive exam (for some programs), comprehensive activity, research project. *Entrance requirements:* For master's, GRE General Test, minimum undergraduate GPA of 3.0 in last 60 hours of course work, writing sample, 3 letters of recommendation. Additional exam requirements/recommendations for international students: Required—TOEFL (minimum score 550 paper-based). Electronic applications accepted.

The University of Texas at Dallas, School of Natural Sciences and Mathematics, Department of Science/Mathematics Education, Richardson, TX 75080. Offers mathematics education (MAT); science education (MAT). *Program availability:* Part-time, evening/weekend, online learning. *Faculty:* 4 full-time (1 woman). *Students:* 4 full-time (2 women), 29 part-time (19 women); includes 14 minority (1 Black or African American, non-Hispanic/Latino; 6 Asian, non-Hispanic/Latino; 5 Hispanic/Latino; 2 Two or more races, non-Hispanic/Latino), 1 international. Average age 33. 28 applicants, 61% accepted, 13 enrolled. In 2017, 16 master's awarded. *Degree requirements:* For master's, thesis optional. *Entrance requirements:* For master's, GRE General Test, minimum GPA of 3.0 in upper-level coursework in field. Additional exam requirements/recommendations for international students: Required—TOEFL (minimum score 550 paper-based). *Application deadline:* For fall admission, 7/15 for domestic students, 5/1 priority date for international students; for spring admission, 11/15 for domestic students, 9/1 priority date for international students. Applications are processed on a rolling basis. Application fee: $50 ($100 for international students). Electronic applications accepted. *Expenses:* Tuition, state resident: full-time $12,916; part-time $718 per credit hour. Tuition, nonresident: full-time $25,252; part-time $1403 per credit hour. *Financial support:* In 2017–18, 20 students received support, including 3 teaching assistantships with partial tuition reimbursements available (averaging $17,100 per year); fellowships, research assistantships with partial tuition reimbursements available, career-related internships or fieldwork, Federal Work-Study, institutionally sponsored loans, scholarships/grants, and unspecified assistantships also available. Support available to part-time students. Financial award application deadline: 4/30; financial award applicants required to submit FAFSA. *Faculty research:* Innovative science/math education programs. *Unit head:* Dr. Mary Urquhart Kelly, Department Head, 972-883-2496, Fax: 972-883-6796, E-mail: scimathed@utdallas.edu.
Website: http://www.utdallas.edu/sme/

The University of Texas at El Paso, Graduate School, College of Science, Master of Arts in Teaching Science Program, El Paso, TX 79968-0001. Offers MAT. *Program availability:* Part-time, evening/weekend. *Degree requirements:* For master's, thesis optional. *Entrance requirements:* For master's, minimum GPA of 3.0. Additional exam requirements/recommendations for international students: Required—TOEFL; Recommended—IELTS. Electronic applications accepted.

The University of Toledo, College of Graduate Studies, Judith Herb College of Education, Department of Curriculum and Instruction, Toledo, OH 43606-3390. Offers art education (ME); career and technical education (ME, Ed S); curriculum and instruction (ME, PhD, Ed S); early childhood education (Ed S); education and anthropology (MAE); education and biology (MES); education and chemistry (MES); education and classics (MAE); education and economics (MAE); education and English (MAE); education and French (MAE); education and geology (MES); education and German (MAE); education and history (MAE); education and mathematics (MAE, MES); education and physics (MES); education and political science (MAE); education and sociology (MAE); education and Spanish (MAE); educational media (PhD); educational technology (ME); educational educator: virtual educator (Certificate); elementary education (PhD); English as a second language (MAE); gifted and talented education (PhD); middle childhood education (ME); secondary education (ME, PhD); special education (PhD). *Accreditation:* NCATE. *Program availability:* Part-time, evening/weekend. *Degree requirements:* For master's, comprehensive exam, thesis or alternative; for doctorate, comprehensive exam, thesis/dissertation; for other advanced degree, thesis optional. *Entrance requirements:* For master's, doctorate, and other advanced degree, minimum cumulative GPA of 2.7 for all previous academic work, letters of recommendation. Additional exam requirements/recommendations for international students: Required—TOEFL (minimum score 550 paper-based; 80 iBT). Electronic applications accepted.

The University of Tulsa, Graduate School, Kendall College of Arts and Sciences, School of Education, Tulsa, OK 74104-3189. Offers mathematics and science education (MSMSE); teaching arts (MTA), including art, biology, English, history, mathematics; urban education (MA). *Accreditation:* TEAC. *Program availability:* Part-time. *Faculty:* 9 full-time (5 women), 2 part-time/adjunct (both women). *Students:* 8 full-time (4 women), 6 part-time (5 women); includes 4 minority (1 Black or African American, non-Hispanic/Latino; 1 American Indian or Alaska Native, non-Hispanic/Latino; 1 Asian, non-Hispanic/Latino; 1 Two or more races, non-Hispanic/Latino). Average age 31. 22 applicants, 9% accepted. In 2017, 10 master's awarded. *Degree requirements:* For master's, thesis optional. *Entrance requirements:* For master's, GRE General Test. Additional exam requirements/recommendations for international students: Required—TOEFL (minimum score 577 paper-based; 91 iBT), IELTS (minimum score 6.5). *Application deadline:* For fall admission, 2/1 priority date for domestic students. Applications are processed on a rolling basis. Application fee: $55. Electronic applications accepted. *Expenses:* Tuition: Full-time $22,230. *Required fees:* $2000. Tuition and fees vary according to course load and program. *Financial support:* In 2017–18, 3 students received support, including 3 teaching assistantships with full tuition reimbursements available (averaging $13,410 per year); fellowships with tuition reimbursements available, research assistantships with tuition reimbursements available, career-related internships or fieldwork, Federal Work-Study, scholarships/grants, health care benefits, tuition waivers (full and partial), and unspecified assistantships also available. Support available to part-time students. Financial award application deadline: 2/1; financial award applicants required to submit FAFSA. *Faculty research:* Elementary/secondary certification, math/science education, teaching arts. *Unit head:* Dr. Elizabeth Smith, Chair, 918-631-2238, Fax: 918-631-3721, E-mail: elizabeth-smith-43@utulsa.edu. *Application contact:* Dr. David Brown, Advisor, 918-631-2719, Fax: 918-631-2133, E-mail: david-brown@utulsa.edu.
Website: http://artsandsciences.utulsa.edu/academics/departments-schools/urban-education/

University of Utah, Graduate School, College of Science, Department of Chemistry, Salt Lake City, UT 84112-0850. Offers chemistry (MS, PhD); science teacher education (MS). *Program availability:* Part-time, online learning. *Faculty:* 32 full-time (9 women), 10 part-time/adjunct (1 woman). *Students:* 144 full-time (67 women), 27 part-time (7 women); includes 19 minority (2 Black or African American, non-Hispanic/Latino; 1 American Indian or Alaska Native, non-Hispanic/Latino; 8 Asian, non-Hispanic/Latino; 7 Hispanic/Latino; 1 Two or more races, non-Hispanic/Latino), 46 international. Average age 25. 298 applicants, 34% accepted, 37 enrolled. In 2017, 12 master's, 19 doctorates awarded. Terminal master's awarded for partial completion of doctoral program. *Degree requirements:* For master's, thesis optional, 20 hours of course work, 10 hours of research; for doctorate, thesis/dissertation, 18 hours of course work, 14 hours of research. *Entrance requirements:* For master's and doctorate, GRE General Test, minimum GPA of 3.0. Additional exam requirements/recommendations for international students: Required—TOEFL (minimum score 620 paper-based; 105 iBT). *Application deadline:* For fall admission, 4/1 for domestic students, 2/1 for international students; for spring admission, 11/1 for domestic and international students. Application fee: $55 ($65 for international students). Electronic applications accepted. Application fee is waived when completed online. *Expenses:* $10,348. *Financial support:* In 2017–18, 175 students received support, including 1 fellowship with full tuition reimbursement available (averaging $25,000 per year), 119 research assistantships with tuition reimbursements available (averaging $25,500 per year), 55 teaching assistantships with tuition reimbursements available (averaging $25,000 per year); scholarships/grants and tuition waivers (full) also available. Financial award application deadline: 4/1; financial award applicants required to submit FAFSA. *Faculty research:* Analytical, biological, inorganic, materials, organic, physical and theoretical chemistry. *Unit head:* Dr. Cynthia J. Burrows, Chair, 801-585-7290, Fax: 801-581-8433, E-mail: chair@chemistry.utah.edu. *Application contact:* Jo Vallejo, Graduate Coordinator, 801-581-4393, E-mail: jvallejo@chem.utah.edu.
Website: http://www.chem.utah.edu/

University of Utah, Graduate School, College of Science, Department of Physics and Astronomy, Salt Lake City, UT 84112. Offers chemical physics (PhD); medical physics (MS, PhD); physics (MA, MS, PhD); physics teaching (PhD). *Program availability:* Part-time. *Faculty:* 34 full-time (5 women), 16 part-time/adjunct (1 woman). *Students:* 71 full-time (22 women), 29 part-time (12 women); includes 5 minority (1 Asian, non-Hispanic/Latino; 3 Hispanic/Latino; 1 Two or more races, non-Hispanic/Latino), 58 international. Average age 25. 137 applicants, 31% accepted, 19 enrolled. In 2017, 14 master's, 12 doctorates awarded. Terminal master's awarded for partial completion of doctoral program. *Entrance requirements:* For master's and doctorate, GRE Subject Test, minimum GPA of 3.0. Additional exam requirements/recommendations for international students: Required—TOEFL (minimum score 550 paper-based; 85 iBT). *Application deadline:* Applications are processed on a rolling basis. Application fee: $55 ($65 for international students). Electronic applications accepted. *Expenses:* Contact institution. *Financial support:* In 2017–18, 76 students received support, including 23 research assistantships with full tuition reimbursements available (averaging $23,500 per year), 52 teaching assistantships with full tuition reimbursements available (averaging $20,641 per year); unspecified assistantships also available. Financial award application deadline: 2/15; financial award applicants required to submit FAFSA. *Faculty research:* High-energy, cosmic-ray, medical physics, condensed matter, relativity applied physics, biophysics, astronomy and astrophysics. *Total annual research expenditures:* $5.6 million. *Unit head:* Dr. Benjamin Bromley, Chair, 801-581-3538, Fax: 801-581-4801, E-mail: bromley@physics.utah.edu. *Application contact:* Krista Perkins, Academic Coordinator, 801-581-6861, Fax: 801-581-4801, E-mail: krista@physics.utah.edu.
Website: http://www.physics.utah.edu/

University of Vermont, Graduate College, College of Arts and Sciences, Department of Biology, Burlington, VT 05405. Offers biology (MS, PhD); biology education (MST). *Students:* 31 (21 women); includes 2 minority (both Hispanic/Latino), 6 international. 26 applicants, 35% accepted, 2 enrolled. In 2017, 1 master's, 3 doctorates awarded. *Degree requirements:* For master's, thesis; for doctorate, thesis/dissertation. *Entrance requirements:* For master's and doctorate, GRE General Test. Additional exam requirements/recommendations for international students: Required—TOEFL (minimum score 550 paper-based, 90 iBT) or IELTS (6.5). *Application deadline:* For fall admission, 12/15 for domestic and international students. Application fee: $65. Electronic applications accepted. *Expenses:* Tuition, state resident: full-time $11,628; part-time $646 per credit. Tuition, nonresident: full-time $29,340; part-time $1630 per credit. *Required fees:* $1994; $10 per credit. Tuition and fees vary according to course load and program. *Financial support:* In 2017–18, 30 students received support, including 5 research assistantships with full tuition reimbursements available (averaging $22,000 per year), 25 teaching assistantships with full tuition reimbursements available (averaging $20,000 per year); fellowships and health care benefits also available. Financial award application deadline: 3/1. *Application contact:* Dr. Nicholas Gotelli, Coordinator, 802-656-2922, E-mail: nicholas.gotelli@uvm.edu.
Website: https://www.uvm.edu/cas/biology/graduate-programs-overview

University of Victoria, Faculty of Graduate Studies, Faculty of Education, Department of Curriculum and Instruction, Victoria, BC V8W 2Y2, Canada. Offers art education (M Ed, PhD); curriculum studies (M Ed, MA, PhD); early childhood education (M Ed, PhD); educational studies (PhD); language and literacy (M Ed, MA, PhD); mathematics (M Ed, MA, PhD); music education (M Ed, MA, PhD); science (M Ed, MA, PhD); social studies (M Ed, MA); social, cultural and foundational studies (MA, PhD); technology and environmental education (PhD). *Program availability:* Part-time. *Degree requirements:* For master's, thesis, project (M Ed); for doctorate, comprehensive exam, thesis/dissertation. *Entrance requirements:* For master's, minimum B average. Additional exam requirements/recommendations for international students: Required—TOEFL (minimum score 575 paper-based), IELTS (minimum score 7). Electronic applications accepted. *Faculty research:* Elementary and secondary English, language arts, curriculum theory and practice, educational media and technology, educational administration and leadership, history and philosophy of education.

University of Virginia, College and Graduate School of Arts and Sciences, Department of Physics, Charlottesville, VA 22903. Offers physics (MA, PhD); physics education (MAPE). *Faculty:* 31 full-time (3 women). *Students:* 102 full-time (21 women), 1 part-time (0 women); includes 9 minority (1 Black or African American, non-Hispanic/Latino; 5 Asian, non-Hispanic/Latino; 2 Hispanic/Latino; 1 Two or more races, non-Hispanic/Latino), 62 international. Average age 27. 169 applicants, 37% accepted, 18 enrolled. In 2017, 8 master's, 11 doctorates awarded. *Degree requirements:* For master's, thesis (for some programs); for doctorate, comprehensive exam, thesis/dissertation. *Entrance requirements:* For master's and doctorate, GRE General Test, GRE Subject Test, 2 or more letters of recommendation. Additional exam requirements/recommendations for international students: Required—TOEFL (minimum score 600 paper-based; 90 iBT), IELTS. *Application deadline:* For fall admission, 1/7 for domestic and international students. Applications are processed on a rolling basis. Application fee: $60. Electronic applications accepted. *Financial support:* Fellowships, research assistantships, and teaching assistantships available. Financial award applicants required to submit FAFSA. *Unit head:* Joe Poon, Chair, 434-924-3781, Fax: 434-924-4576, E-mail: phys-chair@physics.virginia.edu. *Application contact:* Olivier Pfister, Director of Graduate Studies, 434-924-3781, Fax: 434-924-4576, E-mail: grad-info-request@physics.virginia.edu. Website: http://www.phys.virginia.edu/

University of Virginia, Curry School of Education, Department of Curriculum, Instruction, and Special Education, Program in Curriculum and Instruction, Charlottesville, VA 22903. Offers curriculum and instruction (M Ed, Ed S); elementary education (M Ed, Ed D); English education (M Ed, Ed D); foreign language education (M Ed); mathematics education (M Ed, Ed D); science education (Ed D); social studies education (M Ed); MBA/M Ed. *Program availability:* 100% online. *Students:* 38 full-time (31 women), 15 part-time (12 women); includes 6 minority (2 Asian, non-Hispanic/Latino; 2 Hispanic/Latino; 2 Two or more races, non-Hispanic/Latino), 2 international. Average age 32. 92 applicants, 64% accepted, 47 enrolled. In 2017, 47 master's, 9 doctorates, 8 other advanced degrees awarded. *Degree requirements:* For master's, comprehensive exam (for some programs); for doctorate, comprehensive exam, thesis/dissertation; for Ed S, comprehensive exam. *Entrance requirements:* For master's, doctorate, and Ed S, GRE General Test, 2 letters of recommendation. Additional exam requirements/recommendations for international students: Required—TOEFL (minimum score 600 paper-based; 90 iBT), IELTS (minimum score 7). *Application deadline:* Applications are processed on a rolling basis. Application fee: $60. Electronic applications accepted. *Financial support:* Fellowships with tuition reimbursements, research assistantships with tuition reimbursements, and teaching assistantships with tuition reimbursements available. Financial award application deadline: 1/5; financial award applicants required to submit FAFSA. *Unit head:* Susan Mintz, Program Area Director, 434-924-3128, E-mail: slm4r@virginia.edu. *Application contact:* E-mail: curry-admissions@virginia.edu. Website: http://curry.virginia.edu/academics/areas-of-study/curriculum-teaching-learning

University of Virginia, Curry School of Education, Program in Education, Charlottesville, VA 22903. Offers administration and supervision (PhD); applied developmental science (PhD); counselor education (PhD); curriculum and instruction (PhD); early childhood special education (MT); education evaluation (PhD); educational psychology (PhD); educational research (PhD); elementary education (MT); English education (MT, PhD); foreign language education (MT); higher education (PhD); instructional technology (PhD); kinesiology (MT, PhD); math education (PhD); reading education (PhD); research, statistics and evaluation (PhD); school psychology (PhD); science education (PhD); social studies education (MT, PhD); special education (PhD); world languages education (MT). *Students:* 431 full-time (353 women), 15 part-time (14 women); includes 100 minority (32 Black or African American, non-Hispanic/Latino; 33 Asian, non-Hispanic/Latino; 16 Hispanic/Latino; 19 Two or more races, non-Hispanic/Latino), 14 international. Average age 25. 264 applicants, 49% accepted, 83 enrolled. In 2017, 142 master's, 33 doctorates awarded. *Degree requirements:* For master's, comprehensive exam (for some programs), field project; for doctorate, comprehensive exam, thesis/dissertation. *Entrance requirements:* For doctorate, GRE General Test. Additional exam requirements/recommendations for international students: Required—TOEFL (minimum score 600 paper-based; 90 iBT), IELTS (minimum score 7). *Application deadline:* Applications are processed on a rolling basis. Application fee: $60. Electronic applications accepted. *Financial support:* Fellowships, research assistantships, and teaching assistantships available. Financial award application deadline: 1/5; financial award applicants required to submit FAFSA. *Unit head:* Robert C. Pianta, Dean, 434-924-3334, E-mail: pianta@virginia.edu. *Application contact:* E-mail: curry-admissions@virginia.edu. Website: http://curry.virginia.edu/teacher-education

University of Washington, Graduate School, College of Education, Seattle, WA 98195. Offers curriculum and instruction (M Ed, Ed D, PhD), including educational technology, general curriculum (Ed D), language, literacy, and culture, mathematics education, multicultural education, reading and language arts education (Ed D), science education, social studies education, teaching and curriculum (M Ed); educational leadership and policy studies (M Ed, Ed D, PhD), including administration (Ed D), educational policy, organization, and leadership (M Ed, PhD), higher education, leadership for learning (Ed D), social and cultural foundations of education (M Ed, PhD); educational psychology (M Ed, PhD), including educational psychology (PhD), human development and cognition (M Ed), learning sciences, measurement, statistics and research design (M Ed), school psychology (M Ed); instructional leadership (M Ed); intercollegiate athletic leadership (M Ed); special education (M Ed, Ed D, PhD), including early childhood special education (M Ed), emotional and behavioral disabilities (M Ed), learning disabilities (M Ed), low-incidence disabilities (M Ed), severe disabilities (M Ed), special education (Ed D, PhD); teacher education (MIT). *Accreditation:* APA. *Program availability:* Part-time, evening/weekend. *Degree requirements:* For master's, thesis optional; for doctorate, thesis/dissertation. *Entrance requirements:* For master's and doctorate, GRE General Test, minimum GPA of 3.0. Additional exam requirements/recommendations for international students: Required—TOEFL. Electronic applications accepted. *Faculty research:* School restructuring/effective schools, special education interventions, literacy and writing, technology, school partnerships, teacher preparation.

University of Washington, Graduate School, Interdisciplinary Program in Biology for Teachers, Seattle, WA 98195. Offers MS. *Program availability:* Part-time. *Degree requirements:* For master's, research project and oral exam. *Entrance requirements:* For master's, GRE General Test, minimum GPA of 3.0, teaching certificate or professional teaching experience. Electronic applications accepted.

University of Washington, Tacoma, Graduate Programs, Program in Education, Tacoma, WA 98402-3100. Offers education (M Ed); educational administration (principal or program administrator certification) (M Ed); elementary education teacher certification (M Ed); elementary education/special education teacher certification (M Ed); secondary science or math teacher certification (M Ed). *Program availability:* Part-time, evening/weekend. *Degree requirements:* For master's, culminating project. *Entrance requirements:* For master's, WEST-B, WEST-E (teacher certification programs only), official sealed transcript from every college/university attended, personal goal statement, letters of recommendation, copy of valid teaching certificate. Additional exam requirements/recommendations for international students: Required—TOEFL (minimum score 580 paper-based; 92 iBT). Electronic applications accepted. *Faculty research:* Global learning communities for English/Chinese languages, evaluation of mathematics and reading intervention programs, response to intervention, school-wide behavioral and emotional support, mathematics education and culturally responsive mathematics education.

The University of West Alabama, School of Graduate Studies, College of Education, Program in Secondary Education, Livingston, AL 35470. Offers biology (MAT); English language arts (MAT); high school 6-12 (M Ed); history (MAT); mathematics (MAT); science (MAT); social science (MAT). *Program availability:* Part-time, evening/weekend, 100% online. *Faculty:* 21 full-time (7 women), 5 part-time/adjunct (1 woman). *Students:* 259 (183 women); includes 61 minority (51 Black or African American, non-Hispanic/Latino; 2 American Indian or Alaska Native, non-Hispanic/Latino; 3 Asian, non-Hispanic/Latino; 2 Hispanic/Latino; 3 Two or more races, non-Hispanic/Latino). Average age 32.

58 applicants, 93% accepted, 45 enrolled. In 2017, 80 master's awarded. *Degree requirements:* For master's, comprehensive exam, thesis optional. *Entrance requirements:* For master's, GRE, minimum GPA of 2.75, verification of background clearance/fingerprints, valid bachelor's-level Professional Educator Certificate in same teaching field. Additional exam requirements/recommendations for international students: Required—TOEFL (minimum score 500 paper-based; 61 iBT). *Application deadline:* Applications are processed on a rolling basis. Application fee: $40. Electronic applications accepted. *Expenses:* Tuition, state resident: part-time $371 per credit hour. Tuition, nonresident: part-time $742 per credit hour. *Required fees:* $130 per semester. *Financial support:* Teaching assistantships, Federal Work-Study, scholarships/grants, and unspecified assistantships available. Support available to part-time students. Financial award application deadline: 3/1; financial award applicants required to submit FAFSA. *Unit head:* Dr. Jodie Winship, Chair of Teaching and Learning, 205-652-5415, Fax: 205-652-3706, E-mail: jwinship@uwa.edu. *Application contact:* Dr. B. J. Kimbrough, Dean of Graduate Studies, 205-652-3647, Fax: 205-652-3670, E-mail: bkimbrough@uwa.edu.

University of Wisconsin–Milwaukee, Graduate School, School of Education, Department of Curriculum and Instruction, Milwaukee, WI 53201-0413. Offers curriculum and instruction (MS), including cross-curricular focus, early childhood education, English education, mathematics education, middle childhood/early adolescence education, reading education, science education, urban social studies education. *Program availability:* Part-time. *Students:* 17 full-time (13 women), 45 part-time (39 women); includes 13 minority (2 Black or African American, non-Hispanic/Latino; 3 Asian, non-Hispanic/Latino; 1 Hispanic/Latino; 7 Two or more races, non-Hispanic/Latino). Average age 33. 32 applicants, 66% accepted, 16 enrolled. In 2017, 26 master's awarded. *Entrance requirements:* Additional exam requirements/recommendations for international students: Required—TOEFL (minimum score 550 paper-based; 79 iBT), IELTS (minimum score 6.5). *Application deadline:* For fall admission, 1/1 priority date for domestic students; for spring admission, 9/1 for domestic students. Application fee: $56 ($96 for international students). Electronic applications accepted. *Financial support:* Fellowships, research assistantships, teaching assistantships, career-related internships or fieldwork, health care benefits, unspecified assistantships, and project assistantships available. Support available to part-time students. Financial award application deadline: 4/15; financial award applicants required to submit FAFSA. *Application contact:* General Information Contact, 414-229-4721, E-mail: soeinfo@uwm.edu. Website: http://uwm.edu/education/academics/curriculum-instruction-department/

University of Wisconsin–River Falls, Outreach and Graduate Studies, College of Arts and Science, Program in Science, River Falls, WI 54022. Offers science education (MSE). *Program availability:* Part-time. *Degree requirements:* For master's, comprehensive exam, thesis or alternative. *Entrance requirements:* For master's, minimum GPA of 2.75. Additional exam requirements/recommendations for international students: Required—TOEFL (minimum score 500 paper-based; 65 iBT), IELTS (minimum score 5.5). Electronic applications accepted.

University of Wisconsin–Stevens Point, College of Letters and Science, Department of Biology, Stevens Point, WI 54481-3897. Offers MST. *Degree requirements:* For master's, thesis or alternative. *Entrance requirements:* For master's, minimum undergraduate GPA of 2.75 overall, 3.0 in biology; bachelor's degree; teacher's license.

University of Wyoming, College of Education, Science and Mathematics Teaching Center, Laramie, WY 82071. Offers MS, MST. *Degree requirements:* For master's, thesis. *Entrance requirements:* For master's, GRE General Test, minimum GPA of 3.0, writing sample, 3 letters of recommendation. Electronic applications accepted.

Vanderbilt University, Department of Physics and Astronomy, Nashville, TN 37240-1001. Offers astronomy (MS); health physics (MA); physics (MAT, MS, PhD). *Faculty:* 25 full-time (4 women). *Students:* 42 full-time (8 women), 1 part-time (0 women); includes 5 minority (1 Black or African American, non-Hispanic/Latino; 1 Asian, non-Hispanic/Latino; 2 Hispanic/Latino; 1 Two or more races, non-Hispanic/Latino), 13 international. Average age 27. 89 applicants, 26% accepted, 9 enrolled. In 2017, 3 master's, 16 doctorates awarded. *Degree requirements:* For master's, thesis; for doctorate, comprehensive exam, thesis/dissertation, final and qualifying exams. *Entrance requirements:* For master's, GRE General Test; for doctorate, GRE General Test, GRE Subject Test. Additional exam requirements/recommendations for international students: Required—TOEFL (minimum score 570 paper-based; 88 iBT). *Application deadline:* For fall admission, 1/1 for domestic and international students. Electronic applications accepted. *Financial support:* Fellowships, research assistantships with full tuition reimbursements, teaching assistantships with full tuition reimbursements, career-related internships or fieldwork, Federal Work-Study, and institutionally sponsored loans available. Financial award application deadline: 1/15; financial award applicants required to submit CSS PROFILE or FAFSA. *Faculty research:* Experimental and theoretical physics, free electron laser, living-state physics, heavy-ion physics, nuclear structure. *Unit head:* Dr. Robert Sherrer, Chair, 615-322-2828, E-mail: robert.scherrer@vanderbilt.edu. *Application contact:* Julia Velkovska, Director of Graduate Studies, 615-322-2828, E-mail: julia.velkovska@vanderbilt.edu. Website: http://www.vanderbilt.edu/physics/

Wagner College, Division of Graduate Studies, Education Department, Program in Secondary Education/Students with Disabilities, Staten Island, NY 10301-4495. Offers secondary education 7-12 (MS Ed), including language arts, languages other than English, mathematics and technology, science and technology, social studies. *Program availability:* Evening/weekend. *Faculty:* 2 full-time (1 woman), 7 part-time/adjunct (3 women). *Students:* 17 full-time (14 women), 6 part-time (4 women); includes 2 minority (1 Black or African American, non-Hispanic/Latino; 1 Asian, non-Hispanic/Latino). Average age 24. 15 applicants, 80% accepted, 11 enrolled. In 2017, 8 master's awarded. *Degree requirements:* For master's, thesis (for some programs), completion of state certification exams before student teaching. *Entrance requirements:* For master's, GRE, minimum GPA of 3.0, interview, recommendations. Additional exam requirements/recommendations for international students: Required—TOEFL (minimum score 550 paper-based; 79 iBT), IELTS (minimum score 6.5). *Application deadline:* For fall admission, 12/1 priority date for domestic and international students. Application fee: $60. Electronic applications accepted. *Expenses:* Contact institution. *Financial support:* Unspecified assistantships and alumni fellowship available. Financial award application deadline: 2/15; financial award applicants required to submit FAFSA. *Unit head:* Dr. Jason Fitzgerald, Department Chair, 718-420-4129, Fax: 718-390-3456, E-mail: jason.fitzgerald@wagner.edu. *Application contact:* Patricia Clancy, Assistant Director of Enrollment, 718-420-4464, Fax: 718-390-3105, E-mail: patricia.clancy@wagner.edu. Website: http://www.wagner.edu/education

Walden University, Graduate Programs, Richard W. Riley College of Education and Leadership, Minneapolis, MN 55401. Offers adult education (Post-Master's Certificate); adult learning (Graduate Certificate); college teaching and learning (Graduate Certificate); community college leadership (Ed D); curriculum, instruction and assessment (Ed D, Ed S, Graduate Certificate); developmental education (Graduate Certificate); early childhood administration, management, and leadership (Graduate Certificate); early childhood education (Ed D, Ed S); early childhood public policy and advocacy (Graduate Certificate); early childhood studies (MS), including administration, management and leadership, early childhood public policy and advocacy, teaching adults in the early childhood field, teaching and diversity in early childhood education; education (MS, PhD), including adolescent literacy and learning (MS), curriculum, instruction, and assessment (grades K-12) (MS), curriculum, instruction, assessment, and evaluation (PhD), early childhood leadership and advocacy (PhD), early childhood special education (PhD), educational leadership (MS), educational leadership and administration (principal preparation) (MS), educational technology and design (PhD), elementary reading and literacy (PreK-6) (MS), elementary reading and mathematics (grades K-6) (MS), global and comparative education (PhD), higher education leadership management and policy (PhD), integrating technology in the classroom (grades K-12) (MS), learning, instruction and innovation (PhD), mathematics (grades 5-8) (MS), mathematics (grades K-6) (MS), mathematics and science (grades K-8) (MS), organizational research, assessment, and evaluation (PhD), reading and literacy with a reading K-12 endorsement (MS), reading literacy assessment and evaluation (PhD), science (grades K-8) (MS), special education (non-licensure) (grades K-12) (MS), teacher leadership (grades K-12) (MS), teaching English language learners (grades K-12) (MS); educational administration and leadership (Ed D); educational leadership and administration (principal preparation) (Ed S); educational technology (Ed D, Ed S, Post Master's Certificate); elementary reading and literacy (Graduate Certificate); engaging culturally diverse learners (Graduate Certificate); enrollment management and institutional marketing (Graduate Certificate); higher education (MS), including adult learning, college teaching and learning, enrollment management and institutional marketing, global higher education, leadership for student success, online and distance learning; higher education and adult learning (Ed D); higher education leadership and management (Ed D); higher education leadership for student success (Graduate Certificate); instructional design and technology (MS, Postbaccalaureate Certificate), including general program (MS), online learning (MS), training and performance improvement (MS); integrating technology in the classroom (Graduate Certificate); mathematics 5-8 (Graduate Certificate); mathematics K-6 (Graduate Certificate); online teaching for adult educators (Graduate Certificate); reading, literacy, and assessment (Ed D, Ed S); science K-8 (Graduate Certificate); special education (Ed D, Ed S, Graduate Certificate); special education (K-age 21) (MAT); teacher leadership (Graduate Certificate); teaching adults English as a second language (Graduate Certificate); teaching adults in the early childhood field (Graduate Certificate); teaching and diversity in early childhood education (Graduate Certificate); teaching English language learners (grades K-12) (Graduate Certificate); teaching K-12 students online (Graduate Certificate). *Accreditation:* NCATE. *Program availability:* Part-time, evening/weekend, online only, 100% online. *Degree requirements:* For doctorate, thesis/dissertation (for some programs), residency; for other advanced degree, residency for some programs). *Entrance requirements:* For master's, bachelor's degree or higher; minimum GPA of 2.5; official transcripts; goal statement (for some programs); access to computer and Internet; for doctorate, master's degree or higher; three years of related professional or academic experience (preferred); minimum GPA of 3.0; goal statement and current resume (for select programs); official transcripts; access to computer and Internet; for other advanced degree, relevant work experience; access to computer and Internet. Additional exam requirements/recommendations for international students: Required—TOEFL (minimum score 550 paper-based; 79 iBT), IELTS (minimum score 6.5), Michigan English Language Assessment Battery (minimum score 82), or PTE (minimum score 53). Electronic applications accepted.

Warner University, School of Education, Lake Wales, FL 33859. Offers curriculum and instruction (MAEd); elementary education (MAEd); science, technology, engineering, and mathematics (STEM) (MAEd). *Program availability:* Part-time, evening/weekend, online learning. *Degree requirements:* For master's, thesis, accomplished practices portfolio. *Entrance requirements:* For master's, minimum GPA of 3.0 in last 60 hours of undergraduate coursework; 2 letters of recommendation. Additional exam requirements/ recommendations for international students: Required—TOEFL (minimum score 550 paper-based). Electronic applications accepted.

Wayland Baptist University, Graduate Programs, Program in Education, Plainview, TX 79072-6998. Offers education administration (M Ed); education diagnostics (M Ed); education literacy (M Ed); elementary certification (M Ed); English (M Ed); English as a second language (M Ed); higher education administration (M Ed); human resources (M Ed); instructional leadership (M Ed); instructional technology (M Ed); leadership training and development (M Ed); science education (M Ed); secondary certification (M Ed); social studies (M Ed); special education (M Ed); sports administration and management (M Ed). *Program availability:* Part-time, evening/weekend, 100% online. *Faculty:* 33 full-time (17 women), 28 part-time/adjunct (17 women). *Students:* 16 full-time (13 women), 221 part-time (143 women); includes 97 minority (26 Black or African American, non-Hispanic/Latino; 1 American Indian or Alaska Native, non-Hispanic/Latino; 5 Asian, non-Hispanic/Latino; 54 Hispanic/Latino; 11 Two or more races, non-Hispanic/Latino), 1 international. Average age 39. 32 applicants, 97% accepted, 23 enrolled. In 2017, 78 master's awarded. *Degree requirements:* For master's, comprehensive exam, capstone course. *Entrance requirements:* For master's, GRE, GMAT or MAT. Additional exam requirements/recommendations for international students: Required—TOEFL (minimum score 500 paper-based; 61 iBT). *Application deadline:* Applications are processed on a rolling basis. Application fee: $50. Electronic applications accepted. *Expenses: Tuition:* Full-time $11,250; part-time $625 per credit hour. *Required fees:* $1200. *Financial support:* Federal Work-Study, institutionally sponsored loans, and scholarships/grants available. Support available to part-time students. Financial award application deadline: 5/1; financial award applicants required to submit FAFSA. *Unit head:* Dr. Gene Whitfill, Dean, 806-291-1047, Fax: 806-291-1951, E-mail: whitfillg@wbu.edu. *Application contact:* Amanda Stanton, Coordinator of Graduate Studies, 806-291-3423, Fax: 806-291-1950, E-mail: stanton@wbu.edu.

Wayne State College, School of Education and Counseling, Department of Educational Foundations and Leadership, Program in Curriculum and Instruction, Wayne, NE 68787. Offers alternative education (MSE); business and information technology education (MSE); communication arts education (MSE); early childhood education (MSE); elementary education (MSE); English as a second language (MSE); English education (MSE); family and consumer sciences education (MSE); industrial technology and vocational education (MSE); learning communities (MSE); mathematics education (MSE); music education (MSE); science education (MSE); social science education (MSE). *Accreditation:* NCATE. *Program availability:* Part-time, evening/weekend. *Degree requirements:* For master's, comprehensive exam, thesis optional. *Entrance requirements:* For master's, GRE General Test. Additional exam requirements/ recommendations for international students: Required—TOEFL (minimum score 550 paper-based).

Wayne State University, College of Education, Division of Teacher Education, Detroit, MI 48202. Offers art education (M Ed); bilingual/bicultural education (Certificate); curriculum and instruction (Ed D, PhD, Ed S), including English as a second language (MAT, Ed D, Ed S), K-12 curriculum (PhD); elementary education (MAT), including bilingual/bicultural education (M Ed, MAT), early childhood education (M Ed, MAT), English as a second language (MAT, Ed D, Ed S), foreign language education, science education (M Ed, MAT), special education (M Ed, MAT); elementary mathematics specialist (Certificate); English as a second language (Certificate); reading (M Ed, Ed S); reading, language and literature (Ed D); secondary education (MAT), including bilingual/bicultural education

(M Ed, MAT), early childhood education (M Ed, MAT), English as a second language (MAT, Ed D, Ed S), English education, foreign language education, mathematics education (M Ed, MAT), science education (M Ed, MAT), social studies education (M Ed, MAT); special education (MAT), including career and technical education; teaching and learning (M Ed), including bilingual/bicultural education (M Ed, MAT), early childhood education (M Ed, MAT), elementary education, foreign language, mathematics education (M Ed, MAT), science education (M Ed, MAT), social studies education (M Ed, MAT), special education (M Ed, MAT). *Program availability:* Part-time, blended/hybrid learning. *Faculty:* 22. *Students:* 126 full-time (96 women), 317 part-time (258 women); includes 134 minority (95 Black or African American, non-Hispanic/Latino; 1 American Indian or Alaska Native, non-Hispanic/Latino; 8 Asian, non-Hispanic/Latino; 17 Hispanic/Latino; 1 Native Hawaiian or other Pacific Islander, non-Hispanic/Latino; 12 Two or more races, non-Hispanic/Latino), 13 international. Average age 37. 260 applicants, 33% accepted, 57 enrolled. In 2017, 111 master's, 13 doctorates, 7 other advanced degrees awarded. *Degree requirements:* For master's, essay or project (for some M Ed programs), professional field experience (for MAT programs); for doctorate, thesis/dissertation. *Entrance requirements:* For master's, Michigan Test for Teacher Certification (for most programs), verification of participation in group work with children (for MAT programs), Michigan State Police criminal background check; for doctorate, minimum undergraduate GPA of 3.0, graduate 3.5; interview; curriculum vitae; references; master's degree (for most programs). Additional exam requirements/recommendations for international students: Required—TOEFL (minimum score 550 paper-based; 79 iBT), TWE (minimum score 5.5); Recommended—IELTS (minimum score 6.5). *Application deadline:* For fall admission, 6/1 priority date for domestic students, 5/1 priority date for international students; for winter admission, 10/1 priority date for domestic students, 9/1 priority date for international students; for spring admission, 2/1 priority date for domestic students, 1/1 priority date for international students. Applications are processed on a rolling basis. Application fee: $50. Electronic applications accepted. *Expenses: Tuition,* state resident: full-time $10,224; part-time $638.98 per credit hour. Tuition, nonresident: full-time $22,145; part-time $1384.04 per credit hour. Tuition and fees vary according to course load and program. *Financial support:* In 2017–18, 78 students received support, including 4 fellowships (averaging $13,500 per year), 1 research assistantship with tuition reimbursement available (averaging $16,000 per year); Federal Work-Study, scholarships/ grants, and unspecified assistantships also available. Support available to part-time students. Financial award applicants required to submit FAFSA. *Faculty research:* Improving students' skill achievement in mathematics, improving elementary children's understanding of informational text, teachers' use of their pedagogical and mathematical knowledge in the interactive work of teaching, the intersection of identity construction in teaching and learning, identifying effective methods of literacy instruction and assessments for bilingual students in elementary language arts classrooms. *Unit head:* Dr. Thomas Edwards, Interim Associate Dean for Teacher Education, 313-577-3886, E-mail: t.g.edwards@wayne.edu. *Application contact:* 313-577-0902, E-mail: askcoe@wayne.edu.
Website: http://coe.wayne.edu/ted/index.php

West Chester University of Pennsylvania, College of the Sciences and Mathematics, Department of Biology, West Chester, PA 19383. Offers MS, Teaching Certificate. *Program availability:* Part-time, evening/weekend. *Students:* 7 full-time (all women), 11 part-time (7 women); includes 2 minority (both Black or African American, non-Hispanic/ Latino), 1 international. Average age 29. 12 applicants, 50% accepted, 1 enrolled. In 2017, 10 master's, 1 other advanced degree awarded. *Degree requirements:* For master's, comprehensive exam (for some programs), thesis (for some programs). *Entrance requirements:* For master's, two letters of reference. Additional exam requirements/recommendations for international students: Required—TOEFL or IELTS. *Application deadline:* For fall admission, 5/15 for international students; for spring admission, 10/15 for international students. Applications are processed on a rolling basis. Application fee: $50. Electronic applications accepted. *Expenses:* Tuition, state resident: full-time $9000; part-time $500 per credit. Tuition, nonresident: full-time $13,500; part-time $750 per credit. *Required fees:* $2959; $149.79 per credit. *Financial support:* Scholarships/grants and unspecified assistantships available. Financial award application deadline: 2/15; financial award applicants required to submit FAFSA. *Faculty research:* Medical microbiology, molecular genetics and physiology of living systems, mammalian biomechanics, invertebrate and vertebrate animal systems, aquatic and terrestrial ecology. *Unit head:* Dr. Giovanni Casotti, Department Chair, 610-436-2538, E-mail: gcasotti@wcupa.edu. *Application contact:* Dr. Anne Boettger, Graduate Coordinator, 610-430-4601, E-mail: aboettger@wcupa.edu.
Website: http://bio.wcupa.edu/biology/index.php

West Chester University of Pennsylvania, College of the Sciences and Mathematics, Department of Physics, West Chester, PA 19383. Offers Teaching Certificate. *Entrance requirements:* For degree, bachelor's degree or higher, minimum GPA of 3.0. Additional exam requirements/recommendations for international students: Required—TOEFL or IELTS. *Application deadline:* For fall admission, 5/15 for international students; for spring admission, 10/15 for international students. Applications are processed on a rolling basis. Application fee: $50. Electronic applications accepted. *Expenses:* Tuition, state resident: full-time $9000; part-time $500 per credit. Tuition, nonresident: full-time $13,500; part-time $750 per credit. *Required fees:* $2959; $149.79 per credit. *Financial support:* Scholarships/grants and unspecified assistantships available. Financial award application deadline: 2/15; financial award applicants required to submit FAFSA. *Unit head:* Dr. Anthony J. Nicastro, Chairperson, 610-436-2497, Fax: 610-436-3013. *Application contact:* Dr. Jeffrey J. Sudol, Graduate Coordinator, 610-436-2592, Fax: 610-436-3013, E-mail: jsudol@wcupa.edu.
Website: http://www.wcupa.edu/sciences-mathematics/physics/

Western Governors University, Teachers College, Salt Lake City, UT 84107. Offers curriculum and instruction (MS); educational leadership (MS); educational studies (MA); educational studies (5-12) (MA), including mathematics; elementary education (K-8) (MAT, Postbaccalaureate Certificate); elementary education (PreK-8) (MAT); English language learning (K-12) (MA); instructional design (MAT); learning and technology (M Ed, MA); management and innovation (M Ed); mathematics (5-12) (MAT, Postbaccalaureate Certificate); mathematics (5-9) (MAT, Postbaccalaureate Certificate); mathematics education (5-12) (MA); mathematics education (5-9) (MA); mathematics education (K-6) (MA); measurement and evaluation (M Ed); science (5-12) (Postbaccalaureate Certificate); science (5-9) (MAT, Postbaccalaureate Certificate); science education (5-12) (MA), including biology, chemistry, geology, physics; science education (5-9) (MA); social science (5-12) (MAT, Postbaccalaureate Certificate); special education (MAT, MS). *Accreditation:* NCATE. *Program availability:* Evening/ weekend, online learning. *Degree requirements:* For master's, capstone project. *Entrance requirements:* For master's and Postbaccalaureate Certificate, Readiness Assessment, transcripts. Additional exam requirements/recommendations for international students: Required—TOEFL (minimum score 450 paper-based; 80 iBT). Electronic applications accepted. *Expenses:* Contact institution.

Western Michigan University, Graduate College, College of Arts and Sciences, Department of Interdisciplinary Arts and Sciences, Kalamazoo, MI 49008. Offers science education (MA, PhD), including biological sciences (PhD), chemistry (PhD), geosciences (PhD), physical geography (PhD), physics (PhD), science education (PhD). *Degree requirements:* For doctorate, thesis/dissertation.

Western Oregon University, Graduate Programs, College of Education, Division of Teacher Education, Program in Secondary Education, Monmouth, OR 97361. Offers bilingual education (MS Ed); health (MS Ed); humanities (MAT, MS Ed); initial licensure (MAT); mathematics (MAT, MS Ed); science (MAT, MS Ed); social science (MAT, MS Ed). *Accreditation:* NCATE. *Program availability:* Part-time, evening/weekend. *Degree requirements:* For master's, thesis optional, written exam. *Entrance requirements:* For master's, minimum GPA of 3.0, teaching license. Additional exam requirements/recommendations for international students: Required—TOEFL (minimum score 550 paper-based; 79 iBT), IELTS (minimum score 6.5). *Faculty research:* Literacy, science in primary grades, geography education, retention, teacher burnout.

Western Washington University, Graduate School, College of Sciences and Technology, Program in Natural Science/Science Education, Bellingham, WA 98225-5996. Offers M Ed. Electronic applications accepted. *Faculty research:* Science education reform.

Westfield State University, College of Graduate and Continuing Education, Department of Education, Westfield, MA 01086. Offers early childhood education (M Ed); elementary education (M Ed); reading specialist (M Ed); secondary education (M Ed), including biology teacher education, chemistry teacher education, general science teacher education, history teacher education, mathematics teacher education, physical education teacher education; special education (M Ed), including moderate disabilities, 5-12, moderate disabilities, preK-8; vocational technical education (M Ed). *Accreditation:* NCATE. *Program availability:* Part-time, evening/weekend. *Faculty:* 6 full-time (all women), 17 part-time/adjunct (13 women). *Students:* 12 full-time (8 women), 137 part-time (110 women); includes 5 minority (1 Black or African American, non-Hispanic/Latino; 1 Asian, non-Hispanic/Latino; 1 Hispanic/Latino; 2 Two or more races, non-Hispanic/Latino). Average age 31. 65 applicants, 98% accepted, 50 enrolled. In 2017, 60 master's awarded. *Degree requirements:* For master's, comprehensive exam, practicum. *Entrance requirements:* For master's, GRE General Test or MAT, minimum undergraduate GPA of 2.8. Additional exam requirements/recommendations for international students: Recommended—TOEFL (minimum score 550 paper-based; 79 iBT). *Application deadline:* For fall admission, 7/1 for domestic students; for spring admission, 11/1 for domestic students; for summer admission, 4/1 for domestic students. Applications are processed on a rolling basis. Application fee: $50. *Expenses:* Tuition, state resident: part-time $332 per credit. Tuition, nonresident: part-time $332 per credit. *Required fees:* $75 per semester. Tuition and fees vary according to program. *Financial support:* Unspecified assistantships and SOS scholarships (for education majors only) available. Financial award application deadline: 3/1; financial award applicants required to submit FAFSA. *Faculty research:* Collaborative teacher education, developmental early childhood education. *Unit head:* Dr. Laura Baker, Department Chair, 413-572-5324, E-mail: lbaker@westfield.ma.edu. *Application contact:* Shelly Henrichon, Coordinator of College of Graduate and Continuing Education Admissions, 413-572-8022, Fax: 413-572-5227, E-mail: mhenrichon@westfield.ma.edu.
Website: http://www.westfield.ma.edu/academics/degrees/education-graduate-programs

Westfield State University, College of Graduate and Continuing Education, Department of Education, Programs in Secondary Education, Program in Biology Teacher Education, Westfield, MA 01086. Offers secondary education-biology (M Ed). *Program availability:* Part-time, evening/weekend. *Faculty:* 1 (woman) full-time. *Students:* 3 part-time (2 women). Average age 38. In 2017, 1 master's awarded. *Degree requirements:* For master's, comprehensive exam, thesis (for some programs). *Entrance requirements:* For master's, GRE General Test or MAT, minimum undergraduate GPA of 2.8. Additional exam requirements/recommendations for international students: Recommended—TOEFL (minimum score 550 paper-based; 79 iBT). *Application deadline:* For fall admission, 7/1 for domestic students; for spring admission, 11/1 for domestic students; for summer admission, 4/1 for domestic students. Applications are processed on a rolling basis. Application fee: $50. *Expenses:* Tuition, state resident: part-time $332 per credit. Tuition, nonresident: part-time $332 per credit. *Required fees:* $75 per semester. Tuition and fees vary according to program. *Financial support:* Unspecified assistantships and SOS scholarships (for education majors only) available. Financial award application deadline: 3/1; financial award applicants required to submit FAFSA. *Unit head:* Dr. Laura Baker, Department Chair, 413-572-5324, E-mail: lbaker@westfield.ma.edu. *Application contact:* Shelly Henrichon, Coordinator of College of Graduate and Continuing Education Admissions, 413-572-8022, Fax: 413-572-5227, E-mail: mhenrichon@westfield.ma.edu.

Widener University, School of Human Service Professions, Center for Education, Chester, PA 19013-5792. Offers adult education (M Ed); counseling in higher education (M Ed); counselor education (M Ed); early childhood education (M Ed); educational foundations (M Ed); educational leadership (M Ed); educational psychology (M Ed); elementary education (M Ed); English and language arts (M Ed); health education (M Ed); higher education leadership (Ed D); home and school visitor (M Ed); human sexuality (M Ed, PhD); mathematics education (M Ed); middle school education (M Ed); principalship (M Ed); reading and language arts (Ed D); reading education (M Ed); school administration (Ed D); science education (M Ed); social studies education (M Ed); special education (M Ed); technology education (M Ed). *Accreditation:* NCATE. *Program availability:* Part-time, evening/weekend. *Faculty:* 34 full-time (22 women), 37 part-time/adjunct (14 women). *Students:* 131 full-time (112 women), 244 part-time (179 women); includes 94 minority (58 Black or African American, non-Hispanic/Latino; 1 American Indian or Alaska Native, non-Hispanic/Latino; 1 Asian, non-Hispanic/Latino; 22 Hispanic/Latino; 12 Two or more races, non-Hispanic/Latino), 12 international. Average age 37. 140 applicants, 38% accepted, 26 enrolled. In 2017, 45 master's, 21 doctorates awarded. Terminal master's awarded for partial completion of doctoral program. *Degree requirements:* For doctorate, thesis/dissertation. *Entrance requirements:* For master's, minimum GPA of 2.5; for doctorate, GRE or MAT, minimum GPA of 2.0 (undergraduate), 3.5 (graduate). *Application deadline:* Applications are processed on a rolling basis. Application fee: $25 ($300 for international students). Electronic applications accepted. *Expenses:* Contact institution. *Financial support:* Career-related internships or fieldwork, tuition waivers (full and partial), and unspecified assistantships available. Support available to part-time students. Financial award application deadline: 5/1. *Faculty research:* Reading and cognition, adult education, technology education, educational leadership, special education. *Unit head:* Dr. Shawn Fitzgerald, Dean, 610-499-4294, Fax: 610-499-4623, E-mail: smfitzgerald@widener.edu. *Application contact:* Megan Kuft, Director of Graduate Admissions, 610-499-4124, E-mail: gradprograms@widener.edu.
Website: http://www.widener.edu/academics/schools/eics

Wisconsin Lutheran College, College of Adult and Graduate Studies, Milwaukee, WI 53226-9942. Offers high performance instruction (MA Ed); instructional technology (MA Ed); leadership and innovation (MA Ed); science instruction (MA Ed).

Wright State University, Graduate School, College of Science and Mathematics, Department of Earth and Environmental Sciences, Program in Earth Science Education, Dayton, OH 45435. Offers MST. *Entrance requirements:* For master's, GRE General Test. Additional exam requirements/recommendations for international students: Required—TOEFL. *Faculty research:* Pedagogy.

Wright State University, Graduate School, College of Science and Mathematics, Interdisciplinary Program in Science and Mathematics, Dayton, OH 45435. Offers PhD.

Youngstown State University, Graduate School, College of Science, Technology, Engineering and Mathematics, Department of Chemistry, Youngstown, OH 44555-0001. Offers analytical chemistry (MS); biochemistry (MS); chemistry education (MS); inorganic chemistry (MS); organic chemistry (MS); physical chemistry (MS). *Program availability:* Part-time. *Degree requirements:* For master's, thesis. *Entrance requirements:* For master's, bachelor's degree in chemistry, minimum GPA of 2.7. Additional exam requirements/recommendations for international students: Required—TOEFL. *Faculty research:* Analysis of antioxidants, chromatography, defects and disorder in crystalline oxides, hydrogen bonding, novel organic and organometallic materials.

Social Sciences Education

Alabama Agricultural and Mechanical University, School of Graduate Studies, College of Education, Humanities, and Behavioral Sciences, Department of Educational Leadership and Secondary Education, Huntsville, AL 35811. Offers biology (M Ed); business/marketing education (M Ed, Ed S); chemistry (M Ed); collaborative teacher secondary education (M Ed, Ed S); education (M Ed, Ed S); English language arts (M Ed); family/consumer science education (M Ed, Ed S); general science (M Ed); general social science (M Ed); mathematics (M Ed, Ed S); physics (M Ed, Ed S); technology education (M Ed). *Accreditation:* NCATE. *Program availability:* Evening/weekend. *Degree requirements:* For master's, comprehensive exam; for Ed S, thesis. *Entrance requirements:* For master's, GRE General Test. Additional exam requirements/recommendations for international students: Required—TOEFL (minimum score 500 paper-based; 61 iBT). Electronic applications accepted. *Faculty research:* World peace through education, computer-assisted instruction.

Alabama State University, College of Education, Department of Curriculum and Instruction, Montgomery, AL 36101-0271. Offers early childhood education (M Ed, Ed S); elementary education (M Ed, Ed S); secondary education (M Ed, Ed S), including biology education, English language arts education (M Ed), history education, math education, music education (M Ed), reading education (M Ed), social science education; special education (M Ed). *Program availability:* Part-time. *Faculty:* 7 full-time (4 women), 7 part-time/adjunct (4 women). *Students:* 43 full-time (35 women), 71 part-time (62 women); includes 112 minority (111 Black or African American, non-Hispanic/Latino; 1 Two or more races, non-Hispanic/Latino). Average age 22. 47 applicants, 66% accepted, 19 enrolled. In 2017, 21 master's, 13 Ed Ss awarded. *Degree requirements:* For master's, comprehensive exam, thesis optional; for Ed S, comprehensive exam, thesis. *Entrance requirements:* For master's, GRE General Test, MAT, writing competency test; for Ed S, writing competency test, GRE, MAT. Additional exam requirements/recommendations for international students: Required—TOEFL (minimum score 500 paper-based). *Application deadline:* For fall admission, 4/15 for domestic and international students; for spring admission, 11/15 for domestic and international students; for summer admission, 3/15 for domestic and international students. Applications are processed on a rolling basis. Application fee: $25. Electronic applications accepted. *Expenses:* Tuition, state resident: part-time $412 per credit hour. Tuition, nonresident: part-time $824 per credit hour. *Required fees:* $685 per semester. *Financial support:* Research assistantships available. Financial award application deadline: 6/30; financial award applicants required to submit FAFSA. *Unit head:* Dr. Joyce Johnson, Acting Chairperson, 334-229-4485, Fax: 334-229-5603, E-mail: jjohnson@alasu.edu. *Application contact:* Dr. William Person, Dean of Graduate Studies, 334-229-4274, Fax: 334-229-4928, E-mail: wperson@alasu.edu.
Website: http://www.alasu.edu/academics/colleges—departments/college-of-education/curriculum—instruction/index.aspx

Andrews University, School of Graduate Studies, School of Education, Department of Teaching, Learning, and Curriculum, Berrien Springs, MI 49104. Offers curriculum and instruction (MA, Ed D, PhD, Ed S); elementary education (MAT); secondary education (MAT), including biology, education, English, English as a second language, French, history, physics; teacher education (MAT). *Faculty:* 7 full-time (5 women). *Students:* 14 full-time (8 women), 7 part-time (6 women); includes 5 minority (all Black or African American, non-Hispanic/Latino), 9 international. Average age 39. 29 applicants, 31% accepted, 4 enrolled. In 2017, 5 master's, 3 doctorates awarded. *Entrance requirements:* For master's, GRE Subject Test. Additional exam requirements/recommendations for international students: Required—TOEFL (minimum score 550 paper-based). *Application deadline:* For fall admission, 8/15 for domestic students. Applications are processed on a rolling basis. Application fee: $40. *Unit head:* Dr. Lee C. Davidson, Chair, 269-471-6364. *Application contact:* Justina Clayburn, Supervisor of Graduate Admission, 800-253-2874, Fax: 269-471-6321, E-mail: graduate@andrews.edu.

Appalachian State University, Cratis D. Williams Graduate School, Department of Curriculum and Instruction, Boone, NC 28608. Offers curriculum specialist (MA); educational media (MA); elementary education (MA); middle grades education (MA), including language arts, mathematics, science, social studies. *Accreditation:* NCATE. *Program availability:* Part-time, evening/weekend, online learning. *Degree requirements:* For master's, comprehensive exam, thesis or alternative. *Entrance requirements:* For master's, GRE General Test or MAT, 3 letters of recommendation. Additional exam requirements/recommendations for international students: Required—TOEFL (minimum score 570 paper-based; 79 iBT), IELTS (minimum score 6.5). Electronic applications accepted. *Faculty research:* Media literacy, elementary teaching, curriculum development, online learning environments.

Arkansas State University, Graduate School, College of Humanities and Social Sciences, Department of Criminology, Sociology, and Geography, State University, AR 72467. Offers criminal justice (MA); sociology (MA); sociology education (SCCT). *Program availability:* Part-time. *Degree requirements:* For master's, one foreign language, comprehensive exam, thesis or alternative; for SCCT, comprehensive exam. *Entrance requirements:* For master's, GRE General Test or MAT, appropriate bachelor's degree, letters of recommendation, official transcripts, immunization records; for SCCT, GRE General Test or MAT, interview, master's degree, official transcript, immunization records. Additional exam requirements/recommendations for international students: Required—TOEFL (minimum score 550 paper-based; 79 iBT), IELTS (minimum score 6), PTE (minimum score 56). Electronic applications accepted.

Arkansas State University, Graduate School, College of Humanities and Social Sciences, Department of History, State University, AR 72467. Offers history (MA); history education (SCCT); social science education (MSE). *Program availability:* Part-time. *Degree requirements:* For master's, comprehensive exam, thesis or alternative; for SCCT, comprehensive exam. *Entrance requirements:* For master's, GRE General Test or MAT, GMAT, appropriate bachelor's degree, letters of reference, official transcript, valid teaching certificate (for MSE), immunization records; for SCCT, GRE General Test or MAT, interview, master's degree, letters of reference, official transcript, immunization records. Additional exam requirements/recommendations for international students: Required—TOEFL (minimum score 550 paper-based; 79 iBT), IELTS (minimum score 6), PTE (minimum score 56). Electronic applications accepted.

Arkansas State University, Graduate School, College of Humanities and Social Sciences, Department of Political Science, State University, AR 72467. Offers political science (MA); political science education (SCCT); public administration (MPA). *Accreditation:* NASPAA (one or more programs are accredited). *Program availability:* Part-time. *Degree requirements:* For master's, comprehensive exam, thesis or alternative; for SCCT, comprehensive exam. *Entrance requirements:* For master's, GRE General Test or MAT, GMAT, appropriate bachelor's degree, letters of recommendation, official transcripts, immunization records, statement of purpose; for SCCT, GRE General Test or MAT, GMAT, interview, master's degree, official transcript, letters of recommendation, immunization records. Additional exam requirements/recommendations for international students: Required—TOEFL (minimum score 550 paper-based; 79 iBT), IELTS (minimum score 6), PTE (minimum score 56). Electronic applications accepted.

Arkansas State University, Graduate School, College of Humanities and Social Sciences, Heritage Studies Program, State University, AR 72467. Offers heritage studies (MA, PhD). *Program availability:* Part-time. *Degree requirements:* For master's, comprehensive exam, thesis or alternative, portfolio; for doctorate, comprehensive exam, thesis/dissertation, portfolio. *Entrance requirements:* For master's, GRE, MAT or GMAT, appropriate bachelor's degree, letters of reference, official transcript, interview, letter of interest, writing sample, immunization records; for doctorate, GRE, MAT, or GMAT, appropriate bachelor's or master's degree, interview, letters of reference, official transcript, letter of interest, writing sample, immunization records. Additional exam requirements/recommendations for international students: Required—TOEFL (minimum score 550 paper-based; 79 iBT), IELTS (minimum score 6), PTE (minimum score 56). Electronic applications accepted.

Asbury University, School of Graduate and Professional Studies, Wilmore, KY 40390-1198. Offers biology: alternative certificate (MA Ed); chemistry: alternative certificate (MA Ed); English (MA Ed); English as a second language (MA Ed); ESL (MA Ed); French (MA Ed); Latin: alternative certificate (MA Ed); mathematics: alternative certificate (MA Ed); reading/writing endorsement (MA Ed); social studies (MA Ed); social work (MSW), including child and family services; Spanish (MA Ed); special education (MA Ed); special education: alternative certificate (MA Ed); teacher as leader endorsement (MA Ed). *Accreditation:* NCATE. *Program availability:* Part-time. *Degree requirements:* For master's, action research project, portfolio. *Entrance requirements:* For master's, PRAXIS/NTE, minimum GPA of 2.75, letters of recommendation. Additional exam requirements/recommendations for international students: Required—TOEFL (minimum score 550 paper-based). Electronic applications accepted.

Binghamton University, State University of New York, Graduate School, College of Community and Public Affairs, Department of Teaching, Learning and Educational Leadership, Program in Adolescence Education, Binghamton, NY 13902-6000. Offers biology education (MAT, MS Ed); chemistry education (MAT, MS Ed); earth science education (MAT, MS Ed); English education (MAT, MS Ed); French education (MAT, MS Ed); mathematical sciences education (MAT, MS Ed); physics (MAT, MS Ed); social studies (MAT, MS Ed); Spanish education (MAT, MS Ed). *Accreditation:* TEAC. *Program availability:* Part-time, evening/weekend. *Students:* 53 full-time (32 women), 9 part-time (3 women); includes 10 minority (2 Black or African American, non-Hispanic/Latino; 1 Asian, non-Hispanic/Latino; 5 Hispanic/Latino; 2 Two or more races, non-Hispanic/Latino). Average age 27. 51 applicants, 88% accepted, 31 enrolled. In 2017, 36 master's awarded. *Degree requirements:* For master's, portfolio. *Entrance requirements:* For master's, GRE General Test, teaching certification. Additional exam requirements/recommendations for international students: Required—TOEFL (minimum score 550 paper-based; 80 iBT). *Application deadline:* For fall admission, 2/1 priority date for domestic and international students; for spring admission, 10/15 priority date for domestic and international students. Application fee: $75. Electronic applications accepted. *Financial support:* In 2017–18, 4 students received support. Research assistantships, teaching assistantships, career-related internships or fieldwork, Federal Work-Study, institutionally sponsored loans, scholarships/grants, health care benefits, tuition waivers (full and partial), and unspecified assistantships available. Financial award applicants required to submit FAFSA. *Unit head:* Dr. Susan Strehle, Dean, 607-777-7329, E-mail: sstrehle@binghamton.edu. *Application contact:* Ben Balkaya, Assistant Dean and Director, 607-777-2151, Fax: 607-777-2501, E-mail: balkaya@binghamton.edu.

Bloomsburg University of Pennsylvania, School of Graduate Studies, College of Education, Department of Teaching and Learning, Program in Middle Level Education Grades 4-8, Bloomsburg, PA 17815-1301. Offers language arts (M Ed); math (M Ed); science (M Ed); social studies (M Ed). *Accreditation:* NCATE. *Degree requirements:* For master's, thesis optional, practicum, student teaching. *Entrance requirements:* For master's, MAT, GRE, or PRAXIS, minimum QPA of 3.0, teaching certificate, U.S. citizenship, related undergraduate coursework, professional liability insurance, recent TB test. Additional exam requirements/recommendations for international students: Required—TOEFL (minimum score 550 paper-based), IELTS. Electronic applications accepted. *Expenses:* Tuition, state resident: full-time $10,000; part-time $500 per credit hour. Tuition, nonresident: full-time $15,000; part-time $750 per credit hour. *Required fees:* $2484; $110.75 per credit hour. $75 per term. Tuition and fees vary according to program.

Bob Jones University, Graduate Programs, Greenville, SC 29614. Offers accountancy (MS); Bible (MA); Bible translation (MA); Biblical studies (Certificate); broadcast management (MS); business administration (MBA); church history (MA, PhD); church ministries (MA); church music (MM); cinema and video production (MA); counseling (MS); curriculum and instruction (Ed D); divinity (M Div); dramatic production (MA); educational leadership (MS, Ed D, Ed S); elementary education (M Ed, MAT); English (M Ed, MA, MAT); fine arts (MA); graphic design (MA); history (M Ed, MA); illustration (MA); interpretative speech (MA); mathematics (M Ed, MAT); medical missions (Certificate); ministry (MM, D Min); multi-categorical special education (M Ed, MAT); music (M Ed); New Testament interpretation (PhD); Old Testament interpretation (PhD);

orchestral instrument performance (MM); organ performance (MM); pastoral studies (MA); personnel services (MS, Ed S); piano pedagogy (MM); piano performance (MM); platform arts (MA); radio and television broadcasting (MS); rhetoric and public address (MA); secondary education (M Ed); studio art (MA); teaching Bible (MA); theology (MA, PhD); voice performance (MM); youth ministries (MA); M Div/MM.

Bridgewater State University, College of Graduate Studies, College of Humanities and Social Sciences, Department of History, Bridgewater, MA 02325. Offers MAT. *Program availability:* Part-time, evening/weekend. *Entrance requirements:* For master's, GRE General Test.

Brooklyn College of the City University of New York, School of Education, Program in Adolescence Science Education and Special Subjects, Brooklyn, NY 11210-2889. Offers adolescence science education (MAT); biology teacher (7-12) (MA); chemistry teacher (7-12) (MA); earth science teacher (7-12) (MAT); English teacher (7-12) (MA); French teacher (7-12) (MA); mathematics teacher (7-12) (MA); music teacher (MA); physics teacher (7-12) (MA); social studies teacher (7-12) (MA); Spanish teacher (7-12) (MA). *Program availability:* Part-time, evening/weekend. *Degree requirements:* For master's, comprehensive exam (for some programs), thesis (for some programs). *Entrance requirements:* For master's, LAST, previous course work in education, resume, 2 letters of recommendation, essay. Additional exam requirements/recommendations for international students: Required—TOEFL (minimum score 500 paper-based; 61 iBT). Electronic applications accepted. *Faculty research:* Interdisciplinary education, semiotics, discourse analysis, autobiography, teacher identity.

Brown University, Graduate School, Department of Education, Program in Teaching, Providence, RI 02912. Offers elementary education (MAT); English (MAT); history/social studies (MAT); science (MAT); secondary education (MAT). *Degree requirements:* For master's, student teaching, portfolio. *Entrance requirements:* For master's, GRE General Test, transcript, personal statement, 3 letters of recommendation, interview, writing sample (English applicants only). Additional exam requirements/recommendations for international students: Required—TOEFL (minimum score 577 paper-based). Electronic applications accepted. *Faculty research:* Literacy, English language learners, diversity, special education, biodiversity.

Buffalo State College, State University of New York, The Graduate School, Faculty of Natural and Social Sciences, Department of History and Social Studies, Buffalo, NY 14222-1095. Offers history (MA); secondary education (MS Ed), including social studies. *Program availability:* Part-time, evening/weekend. *Degree requirements:* For master's, one foreign language, thesis (for some programs), project (MS Ed). *Entrance requirements:* For master's, minimum GPA of 2.75, 30 hours in history (MA), 36 hours in history or social sciences (MS Ed). Additional exam requirements/recommendations for international students: Required—TOEFL (minimum score 550 paper-based).

California State University, East Bay, Office of Graduate Studies, College of Letters, Arts, and Social Sciences, Department of History, Hayward, CA 94542-3000. Offers history (MA); public history (MA); teaching (MA). *Program availability:* Part-time, evening/weekend. *Faculty:* 9 full-time (6 women), 11 part-time/adjunct (4 women). *Students:* 1 (woman) full-time, 17 part-time (9 women); includes 4 minority (1 Black or African American, non-Hispanic/Latino; 2 Hispanic/Latino; 1 Two or more races, non-Hispanic/Latino). Average age 39. 17 applicants, 47% accepted, 4 enrolled. In 2017, 6 master's awarded. *Degree requirements:* For master's, one foreign language, comprehensive exam, project, thesis, or exam. *Entrance requirements:* For master's, GRE (strongly recommended), minimum GPA of 3.0 in field, 3.3 in history; 2 letters of recommendation; writing sample. Additional exam requirements/recommendations for international students: Required—TOEFL (minimum score 550 paper-based). *Application deadline:* For fall admission, 5/19 for domestic and international students. Applications are processed on a rolling basis. Application fee: $55. Electronic applications accepted. *Financial support:* Fellowships, teaching assistantships, career-related internships or fieldwork, Federal Work-Study, institutionally sponsored loans, and scholarships/grants available. Support available to part-time students. Financial award application deadline: 3/2; financial award applicants required to submit FAFSA. *Faculty research:* Digital history, American women, early America, Native Americans, medieval colonial India. *Unit head:* Dr. Linda L. Ivey, Chair, 510-885-4015, E-mail: linda.ivey@csueastbay.edu. *Application contact:* Dr. Khal Schneider, Graduate Coordinator, 510-885-3237, Fax: 510-885-4791, E-mail: khal.schneider@csueastbay.edu.
Website: http://www20.csueastbay.edu/class/departments/history/

California State University, Fresno, Division of Research and Graduate Studies, College of Social Sciences, Department of History, Fresno, CA 93740-8027. Offers history (MA); history teaching (MA). *Program availability:* Part-time, evening/weekend. *Degree requirements:* For master's, project; thesis or comprehensive examination. *Entrance requirements:* For master's, GRE General Test, minimum GPA of 3.0. Additional exam requirements/recommendations for international students: Required—TOEFL. Electronic applications accepted. *Faculty research:* International education, classical art history, improving teacher quality.

Cambridge College, School of Education, Boston, MA 02129. Offers autism specialist (M Ed); autism/behavior analyst (M Ed); behavior analyst (Post-Master's Certificate); behavioral management (M Ed); early childhood teacher (M Ed); education specialist in curriculum and instruction (CAGS); educational leadership (Ed D); elementary teacher (M Ed); English as a second language (M Ed, Certificate); general science (M Ed); health education (Post-Master's Certificate); health/family and consumer sciences (M Ed); history (M Ed); individualized (M Ed); information technology literacy (M Ed); instructional technology (M Ed); interdisciplinary studies (M Ed); library teacher (M Ed); literacy education (M Ed); mathematics (M Ed); mathematics specialist (Certificate); middle school mathematics and science (M Ed); school administration (M Ed, CAGS); school guidance counselor (M Ed); school nurse education (M Ed); school social worker/school adjustment counselor (M Ed); special education administrator (CAGS); special education/moderate disabilities (M Ed); teaching skills and methodologies (M Ed). *Program availability:* Part-time, evening/weekend, online learning. *Degree requirements:* For master's, thesis, internship/practicum (licensure program only); for doctorate, thesis/dissertation; for other advanced degree, thesis. *Entrance requirements:* For master's, interview, resume, documentation of licensure, 2 professional references; for doctorate, official transcripts, interview, resume, documentation of licensure (if any), written personal statement/essay, portfolio of scholarly and professional work, qualifying assessment, 2 professional references, health insurance, immunizations form; for other advanced degree, official transcripts, interview, resume, documentation of licensure (if any), written personal statement/essay, 2 professional references, health insurance, immunizations form. Additional exam requirements/recommendations for international students: Required—TOEFL (minimum score 550 paper-based; 79 iBT), Michigan English Language Assessment Battery (minimum score 85); Recommended—IELTS (minimum score 6). Electronic applications accepted. *Expenses:* Contact institution. *Faculty research:* Adult education, accelerated learning, mathematics education, brain compatible learning, special education and law.

Caribbean University, Graduate School, Bayamón, PR 00960-0493. Offers administration and supervision (MA Ed); criminal justice (MA); curriculum and instruction

Social Sciences Education

(MA Ed, PhD), including elementary education (MA Ed), English education (MA Ed), history education (MA Ed), mathematics education (MA Ed), primary education (MA Ed), science education (MA Ed), Spanish education (MA Ed); educational technology in instructional systems (MA Ed); gerontology (MSN); human resources (MBA); museology, archiving and art history (MA Ed); neonatal pediatrics (MSN); physical education (MA Ed); special education (MA Ed). *Entrance requirements:* For master's, interview, minimum GPA of 2.5.

Carthage College, Division of Teacher Education, Kenosha, WI 53140. Offers classroom guidance and counseling (M Ed); creative arts (M Ed); gifted and talented children (M Ed); language arts (M Ed); modern language (M Ed); natural sciences (M Ed); reading (M Ed, Certificate); social sciences (M Ed); teacher leadership (M Ed). *Program availability:* Part-time, evening/weekend. *Degree requirements:* For master's, thesis optional. *Entrance requirements:* For master's, MAT, minimum B average, letters of reference.

Chadron State College, School of Professional and Graduate Studies, Department of Education, Chadron, NE 69337. Offers business (MA Ed); community counseling (MA Ed); educational administration (MS Ed, Sp Ed); elementary education (MS Ed); history (MA Ed); language and literature (MA Ed); secondary administration (MS Ed); secondary education (MS Ed). *Accreditation:* NCATE. *Program availability:* Part-time, evening/weekend, online learning. *Degree requirements:* For master's, thesis optional. *Entrance requirements:* For master's, GRE General Test, GRE Writing Test, minimum GPA of 2.75 or 12 graduate hours at CSC with minimum GPA of 3.25. Additional exam requirements/recommendations for international students: Required—TOEFL. Electronic applications accepted. *Faculty research:* Rural education, technology, mental health.

Chatham University, Program in Education, Pittsburgh, PA 15232-2826. Offers early childhood education (MAT); elementary education (MAT); environmental education (K-12) (MAT); secondary art (MAT); secondary biology education (MAT); secondary chemistry education (MAT); secondary English education (MAT); secondary math education (MAT); secondary physics education (MAT); secondary social studies education (MAT); special education (MAT). *Faculty:* 1 (woman) full-time, 15 part-time/adjunct (13 women). *Students:* 31 full-time (23 women), 3 part-time (1 woman); includes 9 minority (8 Black or African American, non-Hispanic/Latino; 1 Hispanic/Latino). Average age 30. 25 applicants, 60% accepted, 9 enrolled. In 2017, 23 master's awarded. *Degree requirements:* For master's, thesis, teaching experience. *Entrance requirements:* For master's, minimum GPA of 3.0, sample of written work, recommendation letters. Additional exam requirements/recommendations for international students: Required—TOEFL (minimum score 600 paper-based; 100 iBT), IELTS (minimum score 7), TWE. *Application deadline:* For fall admission, 4/1 priority date for domestic and international students; for spring admission, 11/1 priority date for domestic students, 10/1 priority date for international students. Applications are processed on a rolling basis. Application fee: $45. Electronic applications accepted. Application fee is waived when completed online. *Expenses: Tuition:* Full-time $16,740; part-time $930 per credit. *Required fees:* $486; $27 per credit. $243 per semester. *Financial support:* Career-related internships or fieldwork available. Financial award applicants required to submit FAFSA. *Faculty research:* Gifted education, environmental education, technology in education, writing as learning, class size and achievement. *Application contact:* Katie Noel, Assistant Director of Graduate Admission, 412-365-2758, Fax: 412-365-1609, E-mail: gradadmissions@chatham.edu. Website: http://www.chatham.edu/mat

The Citadel, The Military College of South Carolina, Citadel Graduate College, Zucker Family School of Education, Charleston, SC 29409. Offers elementary/secondary school administration and supervision (M Ed); elementary/secondary school counseling (M Ed); interdisciplinary STEM education (M Ed); literacy education (M Ed, Graduate Certificate); middle grades (MAT), including English, mathematics, science, social studies; physical education (grades K-12) (MAT); school superintendency (Ed S); secondary education (MAT), including biology, English, mathematics, social studies; student affairs (Graduate Certificate); student affairs and college counseling (M Ed). *Accreditation:* NCATE. *Program availability:* Part-time, evening/weekend, 100% online, blended/hybrid learning. *Degree requirements:* For master's, comprehensive exam (for some programs). *Entrance requirements:* For master's, GRE (minimum combined verbal and quantitative score of 290) or MAT (minimum score 396). Additional exam requirements/recommendations for international students: Required—TOEFL (minimum score 550 paper-based; 79 iBT). Electronic applications accepted. *Expenses:* Tuition, state resident: part-time $587 per credit hour. Tuition, nonresident: part-time $988 per credit hour. *Required fees:* $90 per term.

City College of the City University of New York, Graduate School, School of Education, Department of Secondary Education, New York, NY 10031-9198. Offers adolescent mathematics education (MA, AC); English education (MA); middle school mathematics education (MS); science education (MA); social studies education (AC). *Accreditation:* NCATE. *Entrance requirements:* For master's, Liberal Arts and Sciences Test (LAST), Content Specialty Test (CST). Additional exam requirements/recommendations for international students: Required—TOEFL.

The College at Brockport, State University of New York, School of Education, Health, and Human Services, Department of Education and Human Development, Program in Adolescence Education, Brockport, NY 14420-2997. Offers adolescence biology education (MS Ed); adolescence chemistry education (MS Ed); adolescence English (MS Ed); adolescence mathematics (MS Ed); adolescence physics (MS Ed); adolescence social studies education (MS Ed). *Accreditation:* NCATE. *Program availability:* Part-time. *Students:* 50 part-time (28 women); includes 1 minority (Black or African American, non-Hispanic/Latino). 24 applicants, 79% accepted, 11 enrolled. In 2017, 18 master's awarded. *Degree requirements:* For master's, thesis or alternative. *Entrance requirements:* For master's, edTPA, GRE or MAT, minimum GPA of 3.0, letters of recommendation, statement of objectives, current resume. Additional exam requirements/recommendations for international students: Required—TOEFL (minimum score 550 paper-based; 79 iBT), IELTS (minimum score 6.5). *Application deadline:* For fall admission, 3/15 priority date for domestic and international students; for spring admission, 10/15 priority date for domestic and international students; for summer admission, 3/15 priority date for domestic and international students, 3/13 priority date for international students. Application fee: $80. Electronic applications accepted. *Expenses:* Tuition, state resident: full-time $10,870; part-time $453 per credit hour. Tuition, nonresident: full-time $22,210. *Required fees:* $988; $246 per semester. *Financial support:* Federal Work-Study, scholarships/grants, and unspecified assistantships available. Support available to part-time students. Financial award application deadline: 3/15; financial award applicants required to submit FAFSA. *Unit head:* Dr. Sue Robb, Chairperson, 585-395-5935, Fax: 585-395-2172, E-mail: srobb@brockport.edu. *Application contact:* Anne Walton, Coordinator of Certification and Graduate Advisement, 585-395-2326, Fax: 585-395-2172, E-mail: awalton@brockport.edu. Website: https://www.brockport.edu/academics/education_human_development/department.html

The College at Brockport, State University of New York, School of Education, Health, and Human Services, Department of Education and Human Development, Program in Inclusive Generalist Education, Brockport, NY 14420-2997. Offers biology (MS Ed, AGC); chemistry (MS Ed, AGC); English (MS Ed, Advanced Certificate); mathematics (MS Ed, Advanced Certificate); science (MS Ed, Advanced Certificate); social studies (MS Ed, Advanced Certificate). *Students:* 61 part-time (30 women); includes 2 minority (1 Black or African American, non-Hispanic/Latino; 1 Asian, non-Hispanic/Latino). 41 applicants, 78% accepted, 25 enrolled. In 2017, 12 master's, 3 AGCs awarded. *Degree requirements:* For master's, thesis or alternative. *Entrance requirements:* For master's, edTPA, GRE or MAT, minimum GPA of 3.0, letters of recommendation, statement of objectives, academic major (or equivalent) in program discipline, current resume. Additional exam requirements/recommendations for international students: Required—TOEFL (minimum score 550 paper-based; 79 iBT), IELTS (minimum score 6.5). *Application deadline:* For fall admission, 3/15 priority date for domestic and international students; for spring admission, 10/15 priority date for domestic and international students; for summer admission, 3/15 for domestic and international students. Application fee: $80. Electronic applications accepted. *Expenses:* Tuition, state resident: full-time $10,870; part-time $453 per credit hour. Tuition, nonresident: full-time $22,210. *Required fees:* $988; $246 per semester. *Financial support:* Federal Work-Study, scholarships/grants, and unspecified assistantships available. Support available to part-time students. Financial award application deadline: 3/15; financial award applicants required to submit FAFSA. *Unit head:* Dr. Sue Robb, Chairperson, 585-395-5935, Fax: 585-395-2171, E-mail: srobb@brockport.edu. *Application contact:* Anne Walton, Coordinator of Graduate Advisement, 585-395-2326, Fax: 585-395-2172, E-mail: awalton@brockport.edu. Website: https://www.brockport.edu/academics/education_human_development/department.html

College of St. Joseph, Graduate Programs, Division of Education, Program in Secondary Education, Rutland, VT 05701-3899. Offers English (M Ed); social studies (M Ed). *Program availability:* Part-time, evening/weekend. *Degree requirements:* For master's, comprehensive exam. *Entrance requirements:* For master's, PRAXIS I, official college transcripts; 2 letters of reference; minimum GPA of 3.0 (initial licensure) or 2.7 (nonlicensure); interview. Additional exam requirements/recommendations for international students: Required—TOEFL (minimum score 550 paper-based). Electronic applications accepted.

The Colorado College, Education Department, Program in Secondary Education, Colorado Springs, CO 80903-3294. Offers art teaching (K-12) (MAT); English teaching (MAT); foreign language teaching (MAT); mathematics teaching (MAT); music teaching (MAT); science teaching (MAT); social studies teaching (MAT). *Degree requirements:* For master's, thesis, internship. Electronic applications accepted.

Columbus State University, Graduate Studies, College of Education and Health Professions, Department of Teacher Education, Columbus, GA 31907-5645. Offers curriculum and instruction in accomplished teaching (M Ed); early childhood education (M Ed, MAT, Ed S); middle grades education (M Ed, MAT, Ed S); secondary education (M Ed, MAT, Ed S), including biology (MAT), chemistry (MAT), earth and space science (MAT), English/language arts, general science (M Ed), history (MAT), mathematics, science (Ed S), social science (M Ed, Ed S); special education (M Ed, MAT, Ed S), including general curriculum (M Ed, MAT); teacher leadership (M Ed). *Accreditation:* NCATE. *Program availability:* Part-time, evening/weekend, 100% online, blended/hybrid learning. *Faculty:* 19 full-time (12 women), 24 part-time/adjunct (18 women). *Students:* 99 full-time (76 women), 181 part-time (143 women); includes 109 minority (94 Black or African American, non-Hispanic/Latino; 1 American Indian or Alaska Native, non-Hispanic/Latino; 1 Asian, non-Hispanic/Latino; 6 Hispanic/Latino; 7 Two or more races, non-Hispanic/Latino). Average age 34. 136 applicants, 63% accepted, 56 enrolled. In 2017, 119 master's, 8 other advanced degrees awarded. *Degree requirements:* For Ed S, thesis or alternative. *Entrance requirements:* For master's, GRE General Test, minimum undergraduate GPA of 2.75; for Ed S, GRE General Test, minimum undergraduate GPA of 2.75, graduate 3.0. Additional exam requirements/recommendations for international students: Required—TOEFL (minimum score 550 paper-based; 79 iBT). *Application deadline:* For fall admission, 6/30 for domestic students, 5/1 for international students; for spring admission, 11/1 for domestic and international students; for summer admission, 3/1 for domestic and international students. Applications are processed on a rolling basis. Application fee: $50. Electronic applications accepted. *Expenses:* Tuition, state resident: full-time $3708; part-time $2472 per year. Tuition, nonresident: full-time $14,418; part-time $9612 per year. *International tuition:* $19,218 full-time. *Required fees:* $1605. Tuition and fees vary according to program. *Financial support:* In 2017–18, 45 students received support, including 9 research assistantships with partial tuition reimbursements available (averaging $3,000 per year); career-related internships or fieldwork, Federal Work-Study, institutionally sponsored loans, scholarships/grants, tuition waivers (partial), and unspecified assistantships also available. Support available to part-time students. Financial award application deadline: 5/1; financial award applicants required to submit FAFSA. *Unit head:* Dr. Jan Burcham, Department Chair, 706-507-8519, Fax: 706-568-3134, E-mail: burcham_jan@columbusstate.edu. *Application contact:* Catrina Smith-Edmond, Assistant Director for Graduate and Global Admission, 706-507-8824, Fax: 706-568-5091, E-mail: smithedmond_catrina@columbusstate.edu. Website: http://te.columbusstate.edu/

Converse College, Program in Middle Level Education, Spartanburg, SC 29302. Offers language arts/English (MAT); mathematics (MAT); middle level education (MAT); science (MAT); social studies (MAT). *Unit head:* Lienne Medford, Dean of Graduate Studies and Distance Education, 864-596-9082, E-mail: lienne.medford@converse.edu. *Application contact:* 864-596-9404, E-mail: graduate@converse.edu.

Converse College, Program in Secondary Education, Spartanburg, SC 29302. Offers biology (MAT); chemistry (MAT); English (M Ed, MAT); mathematics (M Ed, MAT); natural sciences (M Ed); social sciences (M Ed, MAT). *Program availability:* Part-time. *Degree requirements:* For master's, capstone paper. *Entrance requirements:* For master's, NTE or PRAXIS II (M Ed), minimum GPA of 2.75, 2 recommendations. *Application deadline:* For fall admission, 8/1 for domestic and international students; for winter admission, 11/15 for domestic and international students; for spring admission, 1/15 for domestic and international students. Applications are processed on a rolling basis. Application fee: $40. Electronic applications accepted. *Financial support:* Available to part-time students. Applicants required to submit FAFSA. *Unit head:* Lienne Medford, Dean of Graduate Studies and Distance Education, 864-596-9082, E-mail: lienne.medford@converse.edu. *Application contact:* 864-596-9404, E-mail: graduate@converse.edu.

Delta State University, Graduate Programs, College of Arts and Sciences, Division of Social Sciences and History, Cleveland, MS 38733-0001. Offers community development (MS); social justice and criminology (MSJC); social science secondary education (M Ed), including history, social sciences. *Program availability:* Part-time, online learning. *Degree requirements:* For master's, thesis or alternative.

Duquesne University, School of Education, Department of Instruction and Leadership, Program in Secondary Education, Pittsburgh, PA 15282-0001. Offers biology (MS Ed); chemistry (MS Ed); English (MS Ed); K-12 education (MS Ed), including Latin; mathematics (MS Ed); physics (MS Ed); social studies (MS Ed). *Program availability:* Part-time, evening/weekend. *Faculty:* 5 full-time (4 women). *Students:* 22 full-time (10 women); includes 3 minority (2 Black or African American, non-Hispanic/Latino; 1 Two or more races, non-Hispanic/Latino). Average age 26. 8 applicants, 100% accepted, 5 enrolled. In 2017, 9 master's awarded. *Entrance requirements:* For master's, two letters of recommendation, letter of intent, interview, bachelor's degree. Additional exam requirements/recommendations for international students: Required—TOEFL (minimum score 550 paper-based), IELTS (minimum score 7). *Application deadline:* For fall admission, 9/1 for domestic students; for spring admission, 1/2 for domestic students. Applications are processed on a rolling basis. Application fee: $0. Electronic applications accepted. *Expenses:* $1,259 per credit. *Financial support:* Research assistantships and Federal Work-Study available. Support available to part-time students. *Faculty research:* Factors that create highly effective teachers; how to best support teachers to support students in reform-oriented environments; urban education; models of teacher leadership; improving instruction in mathematics/science/social studies/English. *Unit head:* Dr. Melissa Boston, Associate Dean for Teacher Education/Professor, 412-396-6109, Fax: 412-396-5585, E-mail: bostonm@duq.edu. *Application contact:* Kelly McGinley, Graduate Admissions Assistant, 412-396-1559, Fax: 412-396-5585, E-mail: mcginleyk@duq.edu. Website: http://www.duq.edu/academics/schools/education/graduate-programs-education/ms-ed-secondary-education

East Carolina University, Graduate School, College of Education, Department of Literacy Studies, English and History Education, Greenville, NC 27858-4353. Offers curriculum and instruction (MA Ed); English education (MAT); history education (MAT); reading education (MA Ed). *Accreditation:* NCATE. *Program availability:* Part-time, evening/weekend, online learning. *Students:* 4 full-time (3 women), 50 part-time (47 women); includes 4 minority (2 Black or African American, non-Hispanic/Latino; 1 Hispanic/Latino; 1 Two or more races, non-Hispanic/Latino). Average age 33. 18 applicants, 94% accepted, 17 enrolled. In 2017, 17 master's awarded. *Degree requirements:* For master's, comprehensive exam, thesis optional. *Entrance requirements:* For master's, GRE General Test or MAT, interview, minimum GPA of 2.5, bachelor's degree in related field, teaching license (MA Ed). Additional exam requirements/recommendations for international students: Required—TOEFL. *Application deadline:* For fall admission, 6/1 priority date for domestic students. Applications are processed on a rolling basis. Application fee: $75. *Expenses:* Tuition, state resident: full-time $4749; part-time $297 per credit hour. Tuition, nonresident: full-time $17,898; part-time $1119 per credit hour. *Required fees:* $2691; $224 per credit hour. Part-time tuition and fees vary according to course load and program. *Financial support:* Research assistantships, teaching assistantships, and Federal Work-Study available. Support available to part-time students. Financial award application deadline: 6/1. *Unit head:* Katherine Misulis, Chair, 252-328-6128, E-mail: misulisk@ecu.edu. Website: http://www.ecu.edu/cs-educ/libs/index.cfm

Eastern Kentucky University, The Graduate School, College of Education, Department of Curriculum and Instruction, Program in Secondary and Higher Education, Richmond, KY 40475-3102. Offers secondary education (MA Ed), including agricultural education, art education, biological sciences education, business education, English education, geography education, history education, home economics education, industrial education, mathematical sciences education, physical education, school health education. *Accreditation:* NCATE. *Program availability:* Part-time. *Entrance requirements:* For master's, GRE General Test, minimum GPA of 2.5.

Eastern University, Graduate Education Programs, St. Davids, PA 19087-3696. Offers ESL program specialist (K-12) (Certificate); general supervisor (PreK-12) (Certificate); health and physical education (K-12) (Certificate); middle level (4-8) (Certificate); multicultural education (M Ed); music (K-12) (Certificate); Pre K-4 (Certificate); Pre K-4 with special education (Certificate); reading (M Ed); reading specialist (K-12) (Certificate); reading supervisor (K-12) (Certificate); school counseling (MA, CAGS); school principalship (preK-12) (Certificate); school psychology (MS, CAGS); secondary biology education (7-12) (Certificate); secondary chemistry education (7-12) (Certificate); secondary communication education (7-12) (Certificate); secondary English education (7-12) (Certificate); secondary math education (7-12) (Certificate); secondary social studies education (7-12) (Certificate); special education (M Ed); special education (7-12) (Certificate); special education (Pre K-8) (Certificate); special education supervisor (K-12) (Certificate); TESOL (M Ed); world language (Certificate), including Spanish. *Program availability:* Part-time, evening/weekend, online learning. *Students:* 46 full-time (40 women), 115 part-time (93 women); includes 65 minority (42 Black or African American, non-Hispanic/Latino; 3 Asian, non-Hispanic/Latino; 14 Hispanic/Latino; 6 Two or more races, non-Hispanic/Latino), 1 international. Average age 32. In 2017, 72 master's awarded. *Entrance requirements:* Additional exam requirements/recommendations for international students: Required—TOEFL. *Application deadline:* Applications are processed on a rolling basis. Application fee: $35. Electronic applications accepted. Application fee is waived when completed online. *Expenses:* Contact institution. *Unit head:* Michael Dziedziak, Executive Director of Enrollment, 800-452-0996, E-mail: gpsadmissions@eastern.edu. Website: https://www.eastern.edu/academics/programs/education-department-graduate-programs/graduate-programs

Fayetteville State University, Graduate School, Programs in Middle Grades, Secondary, Special and Elementary Education, Fayetteville, NC 28301-4298. Offers middle grades (MA Ed); sociology (MA Ed); special education (MA Ed), including behavioral-emotional handicaps, mentally handicapped, specific training disability. *Accreditation:* NCATE. *Program availability:* Part-time, evening/weekend. *Faculty:* 8 full-time (5 women). *Students:* 14 full-time (7 women), 8 part-time (6 women); includes 16 minority (13 Black or African American, non-Hispanic/Latino; 1 Asian, non-Hispanic/Latino; 2 Hispanic/Latino). Average age 35. 10 applicants, 80% accepted, 7 enrolled. In 2017, 9 master's awarded. *Degree requirements:* For master's, comprehensive exam, internship. *Entrance requirements:* Additional exam requirements/recommendations for international students: Required—TOEFL. *Application deadline:* For fall admission, 4/15 for domestic students; for spring admission, 10/15 for domestic students. Applications are processed on a rolling basis. Application fee: $40. Electronic applications accepted. *Expenses:* Tuition, state resident: full-time $8604. Tuition, nonresident: full-time $19,669. *Financial support:* Application deadline: 3/1; applicants required to submit FAFSA. *Faculty research:* Students with disabilities and selected leadership behaviors, new vision for professional development, gifted and talented students, emotional and behavioral disabilities, professional development for high school biology teachers. *Unit head:* Dr. Cynthia Shamberger, Chair of Middle Grades, Secondary and Specialized Subjects, 910-672-1181, Fax: 910-672-1941, E-mail: cshamber@uncfsu.edu. *Application contact:* Debra D. Brown, Administrative Support Associate, 910-672-1181, Fax: 910-672-1596, E-mail: ddbrown@uncfsu.edu.

Fitchburg State University, Division of Graduate and Continuing Education, Programs in History and Teaching History (Secondary Level), Fitchburg, MA 01420-2697. Offers MA. *Accreditation:* NCATE. *Program availability:* Part-time, evening/weekend. *Faculty:* 4 full-time (0 women). *Students:* 1 (woman) full-time, 8 part-time (2 women). Average age 31. 3 applicants, 100% accepted, 2 enrolled. In 2017, 2 master's awarded. *Entrance requirements:* Additional exam requirements/recommendations for international students: Required—TOEFL (minimum score 550 paper-based; 79 iBT). *Application deadline:* For fall admission, 7/15 for international students; for spring admission, 12/1 for international students. Applications are processed on a rolling basis. Application fee: $50. Electronic applications accepted. *Expenses:* Contact institution. *Financial support:* In 2017–18,

research assistantships with partial tuition reimbursements (averaging $5,500 per year) were awarded; Federal Work-Study, scholarships/grants, and unspecified assistantships also available. Support available to part-time students. Financial award application deadline: 3/1; financial award applicants required to submit FAFSA. *Unit head:* Dr. Daniel Sarefield, Chair, 978-665-3379, Fax: 978-665-3658, E-mail: gce@fitchburgstate.edu. *Application contact:* Jinawa McNeil, Director of Admissions, 978-665-3140, Fax: 978-665-4540, E-mail: admissions@fitchburgstate.edu.

Florida Agricultural and Mechanical University, Division of Graduate Studies, Research, and Continuing Education, College of Education, Program in Secondary Education and Foundation, Tallahassee, FL 32307-3200. Offers biology (M Ed); chemistry (MS Ed); English (MS Ed); history (MS Ed); math (MS Ed); physics (MS Ed). *Accreditation:* NCATE. *Degree requirements:* For master's, thesis (for some programs). *Entrance requirements:* For master's, GRE General Test, minimum GPA of 3.0. Additional exam requirements/recommendations for international students: Required—TOEFL.

Florida Atlantic University, College of Education, Department of Teaching and Learning, Boca Raton, FL 33431-0991. Offers curriculum and instruction (M Ed), including art, biology, chemistry, English, French, German, mathematics, music, physics, Pre-K and primary education, reading, social sciences, Spanish; elementary education (M Ed); environmental education (M Ed); reading education (M Ed); social foundations of education (M Ed), including educational psychology, educational technology, multilingual education. *Accreditation:* NCATE. *Program availability:* Part-time, evening/weekend. *Faculty:* 13 full-time (10 women), 1 part-time/adjunct (0 women). *Students:* 26 full-time (22 women), 43 part-time (39 women); includes 19 minority (9 Black or African American, non-Hispanic/Latino; 1 Asian, non-Hispanic/Latino; 8 Hispanic/Latino; 1 Two or more races, non-Hispanic/Latino), 3 international. Average age 30. 91 applicants, 57% accepted, 33 enrolled. In 2017, 25 master's awarded. *Entrance requirements:* For master's, GRE General Test, minimum GPA of 3.0 in last 2 years of undergraduate course work. Additional exam requirements/recommendations for international students: Required—TOEFL (minimum score 500 paper-based; 61 iBT), IELTS (minimum score 6). *Application deadline:* For fall admission, 7/1 for domestic students, 2/15 for international students; for spring admission, 11/1 for domestic students, 7/15 for international students. Applications are processed on a rolling basis. Application fee: $30. *Expenses:* Tuition, state resident: full-time $7400; part-time $369.82 per credit. Tuition, nonresident: full-time $20,496; part-time $1042.81 per credit. *Financial support:* Fellowships with partial tuition reimbursements, research assistantships with partial tuition reimbursements, teaching assistantships with partial tuition reimbursements, career-related internships or fieldwork, scholarships/grants, and unspecified assistantships available. *Faculty research:* Technology, teaching English to speakers of other languages, math teaching, electronic portfolio assessment, global perspectives through social studies. *Unit head:* Dr. Barbara Ridener, Chairperson, 561-297-3588, E-mail: bridener@fau.edu. *Application contact:* Dr. Eliah Watlington, Associate Dean, 561-296-8520, Fax: 261-297-2991, E-mail: ewatling@fau.edu. Website: http://www.coe.fau.edu/academicdepartments/tl/

Florida Gulf Coast University, College of Education, Program in Curriculum and Instruction, Fort Myers, FL 33965-6565. Offers elementary education (M Ed); English education (M Ed); English speakers of other languages endorsement (M Ed); gifted education (M Ed); mathematics education (M Ed); middle school education (M Ed); reading education (M Ed); science education (M Ed); social science education (M Ed); special education (M Ed). *Program availability:* Part-time, evening/weekend, online learning. *Faculty:* 27 full-time (19 women), 44 part-time/adjunct (30 women). *Students:* 3 full-time (all women), 16 part-time (14 women); includes 4 minority (2 Black or African American, non-Hispanic/Latino; 2 Hispanic/Latino). Average age 30. 6 applicants, 100% accepted, 5 enrolled. In 2017, 4 master's awarded. *Degree requirements:* For master's, final project or portfolio. *Entrance requirements:* For master's, GRE General Test, MAT, minimum undergraduate GPA of 3.0 in last 2 years. Additional exam requirements/recommendations for international students: Required—TOEFL (minimum score 550 paper-based). *Application deadline:* For fall admission, 2/15 priority date for domestic students, 5/1 for international students; for spring admission, 12/1 for domestic students, 9/15 for international students. Applications are processed on a rolling basis. Application fee: $30. Electronic applications accepted. *Expenses:* Tuition, state resident: part-time $290 per credit hour. Tuition, nonresident: part-time $1173 per credit hour. *Required fees:* $127 per credit hour. Tuition and fees vary according to course load. *Financial support:* In 2017–18, 2 students received support. Application deadline: 6/30; applicants required to submit FAFSA. *Faculty research:* Internet in schools, technology in pre-service and in-service teacher training. *Unit head:* Dr. Vickie Johnston, Instructor, 239-590-7754, Fax: 239-590-7801, E-mail: vjohnston@fgcu.edu. *Application contact:* Keiana Desmore, Adviser/Counselor, 239-590-7759, Fax: 239-590-7801, E-mail: kdesmore@fgcu.edu. Website: http://coe.fgcu.edu/c-imed/

Florida International University, College of Arts, Sciences, and Education, Department of Teaching and Learning, Miami, FL 33199. Offers art education (MA, MS); curriculum and instruction (MS, Ed D, PhD, Ed S), including curriculum development (MS), elementary education (MS), English education (MS), learning technologies (MS), mathematics education (MS), modern language education (MS), physical education (MS), science education (MS), social studies education (MS), special education (MS); early childhood education (MS); exceptional student education (Ed D); foreign language education (MS), including foreign language education, teaching English to speakers of other languages (TESOL); language, literacy and culture (PhD); mathematics, science, and learning technologies (PhD); physical education (MS), including sport and fitness; reading education (MS). *Program availability:* Part-time, evening/weekend. *Faculty:* 60 full-time (41 women), 112 part-time/adjunct (77 women). *Students:* 165 full-time (139 women), 191 part-time (148 women); includes 270 minority (56 Black or African American, non-Hispanic/Latino; 12 Asian, non-Hispanic/Latino; 191 Hispanic/Latino; 11 Two or more races, non-Hispanic/Latino), 13 international. Average age 34. 238 applicants, 68% accepted, 107 enrolled. In 2017, 184 master's, 15 doctorates awarded. *Degree requirements:* For doctorate, comprehensive exam, thesis/dissertation. *Entrance requirements:* For master's, GRE General Test, Florida General Knowledge Test or Florida College Level Academic Skills Test; for doctorate and Ed S, GRE General Test. Additional exam requirements/recommendations for international students: Required—TOEFL (minimum score 550 paper-based; 80 iBT), IELTS (minimum score 6.3). *Application deadline:* For fall admission, 6/1 priority date for domestic students, 4/1 for international students; for winter admission, 10/1 priority date for domestic students, 9/1 for international students; for spring admission, 3/1 priority date for domestic students, 2/1 for international students. Applications are processed on a rolling basis. Application fee: $30. Electronic applications accepted. *Expenses:* Tuition, state resident: full-time $8912; part-time $446 per credit hour. Tuition, nonresident: full-time $21,393; part-time $992 per credit hour. *Required fees:* $390; $195 per semester. *Financial support:* Research assistantships with tuition reimbursements and teaching assistantships with tuition reimbursements available. *Unit head:* Dr. Lynn Miller, Chair, 305-348-2005, Fax: 305-348-2086, E-mail: lynne.miller@fiu.edu. *Application contact:* Nanett Rojas, Assistant Director, Graduate Admissions, 305-348-7464, Fax: 305-348-7441, E-mail: gradadm@fiu.edu. Website: https://tl.fiu.edu/

Florida State University, The Graduate School, College of Education, School of Teacher Education, Tallahassee, FL 32306-4450. Offers curriculum and instruction (MS, PhD, Ed S), including early childhood education, elementary education, English education, foreign and second language education, mathematics education, reading and language arts, science education, social science education, special education, visual disabilities education (MS); teaching English to speakers of other languages (Certificate). *Program availability:* Part-time, evening/weekend, 100% online, blended/hybrid learning, asynchronous, minimal on-campus study. *Faculty:* 41 full-time (33 women), 21 part-time/adjunct (18 women). *Students:* 133 full-time (93 women), 84 part-time (69 women); includes 48 minority (20 Black or African American, non-Hispanic/Latino; 2 Asian, non-Hispanic/Latino; 19 Hispanic/Latino; 7 Two or more races, non-Hispanic/Latino), 52 international. Average age 31. 146 applicants, 56% accepted, 52 enrolled. In 2017, 91 master's, 7 doctorates, 1 other advanced degree awarded. Terminal master's awarded for partial completion of doctoral program. *Degree requirements:* For master's and other advanced degree, comprehensive exam, thesis optional; for doctorate, comprehensive exam, thesis/dissertation, diagnostic exam, preliminary exam, prospectus defense, dissertation defense. *Entrance requirements:* For master's, doctorate, and other advanced degree, GRE General Test, minimum upper-division GPA of 3.0. Additional exam requirements/recommendations for international students: Required—TOEFL (minimum score 550 paper-based, 80 iBT), Michigan English Language Assessment Battery (minimum score 77), IELTS (minimum score 6.5) or PTE (minimum score 55). Application fee: $30. Electronic applications accepted. *Financial support:* Fellowships, research assistantships, teaching assistantships, scholarships/grants, tuition waivers (full and partial), and unspecified assistantships available. Financial award application deadline: 1/15; financial award applicants required to submit FAFSA. *Faculty research:* Identifying effective intervention strategies to improve reading skills; improving literacy teaching and learning through technology; understanding of student sense making, problem solving, the history and structure of STEM disciplines, and teacher education to support the development of ambitious instruction that supports the STEM learning of all students; examining practices of international education; identifying ways to support the professional development of teachers. *Unit head:* Dr. Sherry Southerland, Professor/Department Chair, 850-644-6885, Fax: 850-644-2725, E-mail: ssoutherland@admin.fsu.edu. *Application contact:* Britni DeZerga, Academic Program Specialist, 850-644-2122, Fax: 850-644-7736, E-mail: bpurvis@fsu.edu.
Website: http://education.fsu.edu

George Mason University, College of Education and Human Development, Programs in Curriculum and Instruction, Fairfax, VA 22030. Offers advanced international baccalaureate (M Ed); assistive technology (M Ed); designing digital learning in schools (M Ed); early childhood education (M Ed); early childhood education for diverse learners (M Ed); elementary education (M Ed); English as a second language (M Ed); gifted child education (M Ed); history (M Ed); literacy (M Ed), including PK-12 classroom teachers, reading specialist; literacy leadership for diverse schools (M Ed), including K-12 reading; physical education (M Ed); science K-12 (M Ed); secondary education (M Ed), including biology, chemistry, earth science, English, history/social science, math, physics; special education (M Ed); teacher leadership (M Ed); teaching culturally, linguistically diverse and exceptional learners (M Ed); transformative teaching (M Ed). *Program availability:* Part-time, evening/weekend, 100% online, blended/hybrid learning. *Faculty:* 41 full-time (36 women), 45 part-time/adjunct (37 women). *Students:* 173 full-time (151 women), 729 part-time (611 women); includes 271 minority (65 Black or African American, non-Hispanic/Latino; 5 American Indian or Alaska Native, non-Hispanic/Latino; 88 Asian, non-Hispanic/Latino; 94 Hispanic/Latino; 1 Native Hawaiian or other Pacific Islander, non-Hispanic/Latino; 18 Two or more races, non-Hispanic/Latino), 28 international. Average age 32. 426 applicants, 91% accepted, 289 enrolled. In 2017, 349 master's awarded. *Degree requirements:* For master's. *Entrance requirements:* For master's, PRAXIS Core (for some programs), 2 letters of recommendation, interview, program goals statement; 9 hours of complete licensure endorsement requirements (for elementary education); minimum GPA of 3.0 in applicant's last 60 hours of undergraduate coursework (for secondary education); at least 1 year of teaching experience (for literacy). Additional exam requirements/recommendations for international students: Required—TOEFL (minimum score 575 paper-based; 88 iBT), IELTS (minimum score 6.5), PTE (minimum score 59). *Application deadline:* For fall admission, 4/2 priority date for domestic and international students; for spring admission, 11/1 for domestic and international students. Application fee: $75 ($80 for international students). Electronic applications accepted. *Expenses:* Tuition, state resident: full-time $11,228; part-time $459.50 per credit. Tuition, nonresident: full-time $30,932; part-time $1280.50 per credit. *Required fees:* $3252; $135.50 per credit. Part-time tuition and fees vary according to course load and program. *Financial support:* In 2017–18, 2 students received support, including 2 teaching assistantships; career-related internships or fieldwork, Federal Work-Study, scholarships/grants, unspecified assistantships, and health care benefits (for full-time research or teaching assistantship recipients) also available. Support available to part-time students. Financial award application deadline: 3/1; financial award applicants required to submit FAFSA. *Faculty research:* Teacher preparation and professional development; adaptive teaching; wonder in science teacher preparation; literacy (digital, adolescent); site based course instruction. *Unit head:* Rebecca Fox, Professor and Academic Program Coordinator, 703-993-4123, E-mail: rfox@gmu.edu.
Website: http://gse.gmu.edu/programs/gsemasters

Georgia State University, College of Education and Human Development, Department of Middle and Secondary Education, Atlanta, GA 30302-3083. Offers curriculum and instruction (Ed D); English education (MAT); mathematics education (M Ed, MAT); middle level education (MAT); reading, language and literacy education (M Ed, MAT), including reading instruction (M Ed); science education (M Ed, MAT), including biology (MAT), broad field science (MAT), chemistry (MAT), earth science (MAT), physics (MAT); social studies education (M Ed, MAT), including economics (MAT), geography (MAT), history (MAT), political science (MAT); teaching and learning (PhD), including language and literacy, mathematics education, music education, science education, social studies education, teaching and teacher education. *Accreditation:* NCATE. *Program availability:* Part-time, evening/weekend, online learning. *Faculty:* 24 full-time (18 women). *Students:* 179 full-time (110 women), 192 part-time (133 women); includes 193 minority (130 Black or African American, non-Hispanic/Latino; 1 American Indian or Alaska Native, non-Hispanic/Latino; 23 Asian, non-Hispanic/Latino; 25 Hispanic/Latino; 14 Two or more races, non-Hispanic/Latino), 6 international. Average age 33. 175 applicants, 58% accepted, 83 enrolled. In 2017, 81 master's, 17 doctorates awarded. *Entrance requirements:* For master's, GRE; GACE I (for initial teacher preparation programs), baccalaureate degree or equivalent, resume, goals statement, two letters of recommendation, minimum undergraduate GPA of 2.5; proof of initial teacher certification in the content area (for M Ed); for doctorate, GRE, resume, goals statement, writing sample, two letters of recommendation, minimum graduate GPA of 3.3, interview. *Application deadline:* For fall admission, 1/15 priority date for domestic and international students; for spring admission, 10/1 for domestic and international students. Application fee: $50. Electronic applications accepted. *Expenses:* Tuition, state resident: full-time $7020. Tuition, nonresident: full-time $22,518. *Required fees:* $2128. Tuition and fees vary according to degree level and program. *Financial support:* In 2017–18, fellowships

with full tuition reimbursements (averaging $19,667 per year), research assistantships with full tuition reimbursements (averaging $5,436 per year), teaching assistantships with full tuition reimbursements (averaging $2,779 per year) were awarded; career-related internships or fieldwork, Federal Work-Study, scholarships/grants, health care benefits, tuition waivers (full and partial), and unspecified assistantships also available. Financial award application deadline: 3/15. *Faculty research:* Teacher education in language and literacy, mathematics, science, and social studies in urban middle and secondary school settings; learning technologies in school, community, and corporate settings; multicultural education and education for social justice; urban education; international education. *Unit head:* Dr. Dana L. Fox, Chair, 404-413-8060, Fax: 404-413-8063, E-mail: dfox@gsu.edu. *Application contact:* Bobbie Turner, Administrative Coordinator, 404-413-8405, Fax: 404-413-8063, E-mail: bnturner@gsu.edu.
Website: http://mse.education.gsu.edu/

Grambling State University, School of Graduate Studies and Research, College of Arts and Sciences, Department of History and Geography, Grambling, LA 71245. Offers social sciences (MA). *Program availability:* Part-time. *Degree requirements:* For master's, comprehensive exam (for some programs), thesis optional. *Entrance requirements:* For master's, GRE, minimum GPA of 3.0 on last degree. Additional exam requirements/recommendations for international students: Required—TOEFL (minimum score 500 paper-based; 62 iBT). Electronic applications accepted.

Harding University, Cannon-Clary College of Education, Searcy, AR 72149-0001. Offers advanced studies in teaching and learning (M Ed); art (MSE); behavioral science (MSE); counseling (MS, Ed S); early childhood special education (M Ed, MSE); education (MSE); educational leadership (M Ed, Ed S); elementary education (M Ed); English (MSE); French (MSE); history/social science (MSE); kinesiology (MSE); math (MSE); reading (M Ed); secondary education (M Ed); Spanish (MSE); teaching (MAT); teaching English as a second language (MSE). *Accreditation:* NCATE. *Program availability:* Part-time, evening/weekend. *Faculty:* 22 full-time (9 women), 51 part-time/adjunct (37 women). *Students:* 135 full-time (95 women), 316 part-time (231 women); includes 77 minority (46 Black or African American, non-Hispanic/Latino; 7 American Indian or Alaska Native, non-Hispanic/Latino; 4 Asian, non-Hispanic/Latino; 9 Hispanic/Latino; 11 Two or more races, non-Hispanic/Latino), 11 international. Average age 34. 128 applicants, 87% accepted, 111 enrolled. In 2017, 153 master's, 24 other advanced degrees awarded. *Degree requirements:* For master's, comprehensive exam (for some programs), thesis optional, portfolio(s); for Ed S, comprehensive exam, portfolio, project. *Entrance requirements:* For master's, GRE, MAT, PRAXIS; for Ed S, MAT or GRE. Additional exam requirements/recommendations for international students: Required—TOEFL (minimum score 550 paper-based; 79 iBT). *Application deadline:* For fall admission, 8/1 for domestic and international students; for spring admission, 1/1 for domestic and international students. Applications are processed on a rolling basis. Application fee: $35. Tuition and fees vary according to course load, degree level, campus/location and program. *Financial support:* In 2017–18, 33 students received support. Unspecified assistantships available. *Faculty research:* Reading, comprehension, school violence, educational technology, behavior, college choice, differentiated instruction, brain-based teaching. *Unit head:* Dr. Clara Carroll, Chair, 501-279-4501, Fax: 501-279-4083, E-mail: ccarroll@harding.edu. *Application contact:* Information Contact, 501-279-4315, E-mail: gradstudiesedu@harding.edu.
Website: http://www.harding.edu/education

Hofstra University, School of Education, Programs in Teacher Education, Hempstead, NY 11549. Offers bilingual education (MA); bilingual extension (Advanced Certificate), including education/speech language pathology, intensive teacher institute; business education (MS Ed); curriculum studies (MS Ed); early childhood and childhood education (MS Ed); early childhood education (MA, MS Ed); educational technology (Advanced Certificate); elementary education (MA, MS Ed), including science, technology, engineering, and mathematics (STEM) (MA); English education (MS Ed); family and consumer science (MS Ed); fine arts and music education (Advanced Certificate); fine arts education (MS Ed); foreign language and TESOL (MS Ed); foreign language education (MA, MS Ed), including Arabic (MS Ed), biology, chemistry, Chinese (MS Ed), earth science, French, German, Italian (MS Ed), Mandarin (MS Ed), physics, Russian, Spanish; foundations of education (Advanced Certificate), including grades 5-6, grades 7-9; languages other than English and teaching English as a second language (MA); learning and teaching (Ed D), including applied linguistics, art education, arts and humanities, early childhood education, English education, human development, math education, math, science, and technology, multicultural education, physical education, science education, social studies education, special education; mathematics education (MA, MS Ed); music education (MA, MS Ed); science education (MA), including biology (MA, MS Ed), chemistry (MA, MS Ed), earth science (MA, MS Ed), physics (MA, MS Ed); secondary education (Advanced Certificate); social studies education (MA, MS Ed); teaching languages other than English and TESOL (MS Ed); technology for learning (MA); TESOL (MS Ed, Advanced Certificate); TESOL with specialization in STEM (MA); work based learning extension (Advanced Certificate). *Program availability:* Part-time, evening/weekend, blended/hybrid learning. *Students:* 119 full-time (83 women), 124 part-time (90 women); includes 54 minority (15 Black or African American, non-Hispanic/Latino; 9 Asian, non-Hispanic/Latino; 29 Hispanic/Latino; 1 Native Hawaiian or other Pacific Islander, non-Hispanic/Latino), 12 international. Average age 29. 205 applicants, 88% accepted, 93 enrolled. In 2017, 103 master's, 4 doctorates, 32 other advanced degrees awarded. *Degree requirements:* For master's, comprehensive exam, thesis (for some programs), exit project, student teaching, fieldwork, electronic portfolio, curriculum project, minimum GPA of 3.0; for doctorate, thesis/dissertation; for Advanced Certificate, 3 foreign languages, comprehensive exam (for some programs), thesis project. *Entrance requirements:* For master's, GRE, 2 letters of recommendation, portfolio, teacher certification (MA), interview, essay; for doctorate, GMAT, GRE, LSAT, or MAT; for Advanced Certificate, 2 letters of recommendation, essay, interview and/or portfolio, teaching certificate. Additional exam requirements/recommendations for international students: Required—TOEFL (minimum score 550 paper-based; 80 iBT). *Application deadline:* Applications are processed on a rolling basis. Application fee: $75. Electronic applications accepted. *Expenses:* Tuition: Full-time $1292. *Required fees:* $970. Tuition and fees vary according to program. *Financial support:* In 2017–18, 112 students received support, including 56 fellowships with full and partial tuition reimbursements available (averaging $4,998 per year), 2 research assistantships with full and partial tuition reimbursements available (averaging $8,753 per year); career-related internships or fieldwork, Federal Work-Study, institutionally sponsored loans, scholarships/grants, traineeships, tuition waivers (full and partial), and unspecified assistantships also available. Support available to part-time students. Financial award applicants required to submit FAFSA. *Faculty research:* Educational interventions that foster critical-thinking skills; teachers' attitudes about professional development; threats to teacher quality. *Unit head:* Dr. Eustace Thompson, Chairperson, 516-463-5749, Fax: 516-463-6275, E-mail: eustace.g.thompson@hofstra.edu. *Application contact:* Sunil Samuel, Assistant Vice President of Admissions, 516-463-4723, Fax: 516-463-4664, E-mail: graduateadmission@hofstra.edu.
Website: http://www.hofstra.edu/education/

Hunter College of the City University of New York, Graduate School, School of Education, Programs in Secondary Education, Concentration in Social Studies Education, New York, NY 10065-5085. Offers MA. *Accreditation:* NCATE. *Degree* *requirements:* For master's, thesis, professional teaching portfolio, New York State Teacher Certification Exam, research project. *Entrance requirements:* For master's, minimum GPA of 3.0 in history, 2.8 overall; 2 letters of reference; minimum of 30 credits in social studies areas. Additional exam requirements/recommendations for international students: Required—TOEFL, TWE.

Indiana University Bloomington, School of Education, Department of Curriculum and Instruction, Bloomington, IN 47405-7000. Offers art education (MS, Ed D, PhD); curriculum studies (Ed D, PhD); elementary education (MS, Ed D, PhD, Ed S); mathematics education (MS, Ed D, PhD); science education (MS, Ed D, PhD); secondary education (MS, Ed D, PhD); social studies education (MS, PhD); special education (PhD, Ed S). *Accreditation:* NCATE. *Program availability:* Part-time, evening/weekend. Terminal master's awarded for partial completion of doctoral program. *Degree requirements:* For doctorate, thesis/dissertation; for Ed S, comprehensive exam or project. *Entrance requirements:* For master's, doctorate, and Ed S, GRE General Test. Electronic applications accepted.

Instituto Tecnologico de Santo Domingo, Graduate School, Area of Humanities and Social Sciences, Santo Domingo, Dominican Republic. Offers accounting (Certificate); adult education (Certificate); applied linguistics (MA); economics (MA); education (M Ed); educational psychology (MA, Certificate); gender and development (MA, Certificate); humanistic studies (MA); international marketing management (Certificate); international relations in the Caribbean basin (Certificate); intervention systems in family therapy (MA); linguistic and literary communication (Certificate); pedagogical support (MA); social science education (M Ed); sustainable human development (MA); terminal illness and death psychology (Certificate); youth and adult education (M Ed).

Inter American University of Puerto Rico, Arecibo Campus, Programs in Education, Arecibo, PR 00614-4050. Offers administration and educational supervision (MA Ed); counseling and guidance (MA Ed); curriculum and teaching (MA Ed), including biology education, English as a second language, history education, math education, Spanish; elementary education (MA Ed). *Accreditation:* TEAC. *Degree requirements:* For master's, comprehensive exam, thesis optional. *Entrance requirements:* For master's, GRE, EXADEP, bachelor's degree in education or teaching license (administration and supervision) or courses in education and psychology (counseling and guidance), minimum GPA of 2.5 in last 60 credits.

Inter American University of Puerto Rico, Metropolitan Campus, Graduate Programs, Program in History Education, San Juan, PR 00919-1293. Offers MA.

Inter American University of Puerto Rico, Ponce Campus, Graduate School, Mercedita, PR 00715-1602. Offers accounting (MBA); biology (M Ed); chemistry (M Ed); criminal justice (MA); elementary education (M Ed); English as a Second Language (M Ed); finance (MBA); history (M Ed); human resources (MBA); marketing (MBA); mathematics (M Ed); Spanish (M Ed). *Entrance requirements:* For master's, minimum GPA of 2.5.

Iona College, School of Arts and Science, Department of Education, New Rochelle, NY 10801-1890. Offers adolescence education: biology (MS Ed, MST); adolescence education: English (MS Ed); adolescence education: mathematics (MST); adolescence education: social studies (MS Ed, MST); adolescence education: Spanish (MS Ed); adolescence special education 5-12 (MST); childhood and special education (MST); early childhood and childhood (MST); educational leadership (MS Ed). *Accreditation:* NCATE. *Program availability:* Part-time, evening/weekend. *Faculty:* 7 full-time (5 women), 2 part-time/adjunct (1 woman). *Students:* 23 full-time (18 women), 26 part-time (19 women); includes 12 minority (4 Black or African American, non-Hispanic/Latino; 8 Hispanic/Latino). Average age 26. 33 applicants, 97% accepted, 20 enrolled. In 2017, 31 master's awarded. *Degree requirements:* For master's, thesis or alternative. *Entrance requirements:* For master's, minimum GPA of 3.0, NY State teaching certificate and bachelor's degree (for MS Ed). Additional exam requirements/recommendations for international students: Required—TOEFL (minimum score 550 paper-based; 80 iBT), IELTS (minimum score 6.5). *Application deadline:* For fall admission, 8/1 priority date for domestic students, 5/1 priority date for international students; for spring admission, 1/1 priority date for domestic students, 9/1 priority date for international students. Applications are processed on a rolling basis. Electronic applications accepted. Tuition and fees vary according to program. *Financial support:* In 2017–18, 16 students received support. Unspecified assistantships available. Support available to part-time students. Financial award application deadline: 4/15; financial award applicants required to submit FAFSA. *Faculty research:* Engaging teacher educators in scientific process, cross-national comparisons of mathematics teaching, questioning strategies in the classroom, research methods, literacy development. *Unit head:* Margaret Smith, PhD, Chair, 914-633-2210, Fax: 914-633-2608, E-mail: msmith@iona.edu. *Application contact:* Richard McMahon, Coordinator, Graduate School of Education, 914-633-2552, E-mail: rmcmahon@iona.edu.
Website: http://www.iona.edu/Academics/School-of-Arts-Science/Departments/Education/Graduate-Programs.aspx

Johns Hopkins University, School of Education, Master's Programs in Education, Baltimore, MD 21218. Offers counseling (MS), including clinical mental health counseling, school counseling; education (MS), including educational studies, gifted education, reading, school administration and supervision, technology for educators; elementary education (MAT); health professions (M Ed); intelligence analysis (MS); organizational leadership (MS); secondary education (MAT), including biology, chemistry, earth/space science, English, physics, social studies; special education (MS), including early childhood special education, general special education studies, mild to moderate disabilities, severe disabilities. *Program availability:* Part-time, evening/weekend, 100% online, blended/hybrid learning. *Degree requirements:* For master's, comprehensive exam (for some programs), portfolio, capstone project and/or internship; PRAXIS II (subject area assessments) for initial teacher preparation programs that lead to licensure. *Entrance requirements:* For master's, GRE (for full-time programs only); PRAXIS I/core or state-approved alternative (for initial teacher preparation programs that lead to licensure), minimum of bachelor's degree from regionally- or nationally-accredited institution; minimum GPA of 3.0 in all previous programs of study; official transcripts from all post-secondary institutions attended; essay; curriculum vitae/resume; letters of recommendation (3 for full-time programs, 2 for part-time programs); dispositions survey. Additional exam requirements/recommendations for international students: Required—TOEFL (minimum score 600 paper-based; 100 iBT), IELTS (minimum score 7). Electronic applications accepted. *Expenses:* Contact institution.

Kent State University, College of Arts and Sciences, Department of History, Kent, OH 44242-0001. Offers history (MA, PhD), including history (MA), history for teachers (MA). *Program availability:* Part-time. *Faculty:* 13 full-time (5 women), 1 part-time/adjunct (0 women). *Students:* 23 full-time (6 women), 3 part-time (2 women); includes 4 minority (2 Black or African American, non-Hispanic/Latino; 1 Hispanic/Latino; 1 Two or more races, non-Hispanic/Latino). Average age 35. 12 applicants, 50% accepted, 3 enrolled. In 2017, 5 master's, 1 doctorate awarded. *Degree requirements:* For master's, one foreign language, thesis (for some programs); for doctorate, one foreign language, comprehensive exam, thesis/dissertation. *Entrance requirements:* For master's, GRE General Test, official transcript(s), statement of purpose describing professional objectives and proposed field of study, significant piece of written work, three letters of recommendation (preferably academic); for doctorate, GRE General Test, official transcript(s), master's degree in history

or related discipline, statement of purpose describing professional objectives and proposed field of study, significant piece of written work, three letters of recommendation (preferably academic). Additional exam requirements/recommendations for international students: Required—TOEFL (minimum score 550 paper-based, 79 iBT), Michigan English Language Assessment Battery (minimum score 77), IELTS (minimum score 6.5) or PTE (minimum score 58). *Application deadline:* For fall admission, 2/1 for domestic and international students. Applications are processed on a rolling basis. Application fee: $45 ($70 for international students). Electronic applications accepted. *Expenses:* Tuition, state resident: full-time $11,310; part-time $515 per credit hour. Tuition, nonresident: full-time $20,396; part-time $928 per credit hour. *International tuition:* $18,544 full-time. *Financial support:* Teaching assistantships with full tuition reimbursements and unspecified assistantships available. Financial award application deadline: 2/1. *Unit head:* Dr. Brian Hayashi, Professor and Chair, 330-672-8914, E-mail: bhayashi@kent.edu. *Application contact:* Kevin Adams, Associate Professor and Graduate Coordinator, 330-672-8902, E-mail: kadams9@kent.edu.
Website: https://www.kent.edu/history/

Kutztown University of Pennsylvania, College of Education, Program in Secondary Education, Kutztown, PA 19530-0730. Offers biology (M Ed); curriculum and instruction (M Ed); English (M Ed); mathematics (M Ed); middle level (M Ed); social studies (M Ed); teaching (M Ed); transformational teaching and learning (Ed D). *Accreditation:* NCATE. *Program availability:* Part-time, evening/weekend, 100% online, blended/hybrid learning. *Faculty:* 4 full-time (3 women), 1 part-time/adjunct (0 women). *Students:* 33 full-time (21 women), 76 part-time (49 women); includes 6 minority (3 Black or African American, non-Hispanic/Latino; 3 Hispanic/Latino). Average age 32. 76 applicants, 91% accepted, 43 enrolled. In 2017, 31 master's awarded. *Degree requirements:* For master's, comprehensive exam, thesis optional; for doctorate, thesis/dissertation. *Entrance requirements:* For master's, GRE General Test, minimum undergraduate major GPA of 3.0, 3 letters of recommendation, copy of PRAXIS II or valid instructional I or II teaching certificate; for doctorate, master's or specialist degree in education or related field from regionally-accredited institution of higher learning with minimum graduate GPA of 3.25, significant educational experience, employment in an education setting (preferred). Additional exam requirements/recommendations for international students: Required—TOEFL (minimum score 550 paper-based, 79 iBT), IELTS (minimum score 6.5), or PTE (minimum score 53). *Application deadline:* For fall admission, 8/1 for domestic and international students; for spring admission, 12/1 for domestic and international students. Application fee: $35. Electronic applications accepted. *Expenses:* Tuition, state resident: part-time $500 per credit. Tuition, nonresident: part-time $750 per credit. *Required fees:* $115 per credit. One-time fee: $50 part-time. Tuition and fees vary according to degree level. *Financial support:* Career-related internships or fieldwork, Federal Work-Study, scholarships/grants, and unspecified assistantships available. Financial award application deadline: 3/1; financial award applicants required to submit FAFSA. *Unit head:* Dr. Theresa Stahler, Department Chair, 610-683-4259, Fax: 610-683-1338, E-mail: stahler@kutztown.edu. *Application contact:* Dr. Patricia Walsh Coates, Graduate Coordinator, 610-638-4289, Fax: 610-683-1338, E-mail: coates@kutztown.edu.
Website: https://www.kutztown.edu/academcs/graduate-programs/secondary-education.htm

Lake Forest College, Master of Arts in Teaching Program, Lake Forest, IL 60045. Offers elementary education (MAT); K-12 French (MAT); K-12 music (MAT); K-12 Spanish (MAT); K-12 visual art (MAT); secondary biology (MAT); secondary chemistry (MAT); secondary English (MAT); secondary history (MAT); secondary mathematics (MAT). *Degree requirements:* For master's, comprehensive exam, portfolio. *Entrance requirements:* For master's, GRE.

La Salle University, School of Arts and Sciences, Program in Education, Philadelphia, PA 19141-1199. Offers autism spectrum disorders (MA, Certificate); bilingual/bicultural studies (MA); classroom management (MA); dual early childhood and special education (MA); dual middle-level science and math and special education (MA); education (MA); English (MA); English as a second language (Certificate); history (MA); instructional coach (Certificate); instructional leadership (MA); reading specialist (MA, Certificate); secondary education (MA); special education (MA, Certificate). *Program availability:* Part-time, evening/weekend. *Faculty:* 5 full-time (4 women), 8 part-time/adjunct (5 women). *Students:* 2 full-time (1 woman), 110 part-time (81 women); includes 23 minority (11 Black or African American, non-Hispanic/Latino; 1 Asian, non-Hispanic/Latino; 7 Hispanic/Latino; 4 Two or more races, non-Hispanic/Latino). Average age 33. 137 applicants, 70% accepted, 63 enrolled. In 2017, 148 master's awarded. *Degree requirements:* For master's, comprehensive exam. *Entrance requirements:* For master's, MAT or GRE, 2 letters of recommendation; for Certificate, GMAT or GRE, 2 letters of recommendation. Additional exam requirements/recommendations for international students: Required—TOEFL. *Application deadline:* For fall admission, 8/15 priority date for domestic students, 7/15 for international students; for spring admission, 12/15 priority date for domestic students, 11/15 for international students; for summer admission, 4/15 priority date for domestic students, 3/15 for international students. Applications are processed on a rolling basis. Application fee: $35. Electronic applications accepted. Application fee is waived when completed online. *Expenses:* Contact institution. *Financial support:* In 2017–18, 19 students received support. Scholarships/grants available. Support available to part-time students. Financial award application deadline: 8/31; financial award applicants required to submit FAFSA. *Unit head:* Dr. Greer Richardson, Director, 215-951-1806, Fax: 215-951-1843, E-mail: graded@lasalle.edu. *Application contact:* Elizabeth Heenan, Director, Graduate and Adult Enrollment, 215-951-1100, Fax: 215-951-1462, E-mail: heenan@lasalle.edu.
Website: http://www.lasalle.edu/grad-education-programs/

La Salle University, School of Arts and Sciences, Program in History, Philadelphia, PA 19141-1199. Offers American history (Certificate); European history (Certificate); history (MA); history for educators (MA); public history (MA); teaching advanced placement history (Certificate); world history (Certificate). *Program availability:* Part-time. *Faculty:* 4 full-time (1 woman), 2 part-time/adjunct (0 women). *Students:* 2 full-time (0 women), 10 part-time (5 women); includes 1 minority (Asian, non-Hispanic/Latino). Average age 37. 9 applicants, 78% accepted, 2 enrolled. In 2017, 7 master's awarded. *Degree requirements:* For master's, thesis or comprehensive exam. *Entrance requirements:* For master's, GRE or MAT, 18 hours of undergraduate coursework in history or a related discipline with minimum GPA of 3.0; two letters of recommendation; brief personal statement (250 to 500 words); writing sample (preferably from an undergraduate research paper). Additional exam requirements/recommendations for international students: Required—TOEFL. *Application deadline:* For fall admission, 8/15 priority date for domestic students, 7/15 for international students; for spring admission, 12/15 priority date for domestic students, 11/15 for international students; for summer admission, 4/15 priority date for domestic students, 3/15 for international students. Applications are processed on a rolling basis. Application fee: $35. Electronic applications accepted. Application fee is waived when completed online. *Expenses:* Contact institution. *Financial support:* In 2017–18, 1 student received support. Scholarships/grants available. Support available to part-time students. Financial award application deadline: 8/31; financial award applicants required to submit FAFSA. *Unit head:* Dr. George B. Stow, Director, 215-951-1097, E-mail: grahis@lasalle.edu. *Application contact:* Elizabeth Heenan, Director, Graduate and Adult Enrollment, 215-951-1100, Fax: 215-951-1462, E-mail: heenan@lasalle.edu.
Website: http://www.lasalle.edu/master-history/

Social Sciences Education

Lebanon Valley College, Program in Science Education, Annville, PA 17003. Offers integrative STEM education (Certificate); STEM education (MSE). *Program availability:* Part-time-only, evening/weekend, 100% online, blended/hybrid learning. *Faculty:* 14 part-time/adjunct (7 women). *Students:* 3 part-time (all women). Average age 42. 4 applicants, 100% accepted, 3 enrolled. In 2017, 10 master's awarded. *Degree requirements:* For master's, thesis or capstone project. *Entrance requirements:* For master's, baccalaureate degree, minimum GPA of 3.0, teacher certification, 3 letters of recommendation, transcripts, goal statement. Additional exam requirements/recommendations for international students: Required—TOEFL (minimum score 80 iBT). *Application deadline:* Applications are processed on a rolling basis. Application fee: $0. Electronic applications accepted. *Expenses:* $618 per credit hour. *Financial support:* Scholarships/grants available. Financial award application deadline: 3/1; financial award applicants required to submit FAFSA. *Faculty research:* Teacher quality and student achievement, STEM reform, STEM education, effective teaching. *Unit head:* Carrie Coryer, Director of MSE and STEM-based programs, 717-867-6190, Fax: 717-867-6018, E-mail: coryer@lvc.edu.
Website: http://www.lvc.edu/academics/graduate-studies/master-of-science-in-stem-education/

Lee University, Program in Education, Cleveland, TN 37320-3450. Offers art (MAT); curriculum and instruction (M Ed, Ed S); early childhood (MAT); educational leadership (M Ed, Ed S); elementary education (MAT); English and math (MAT); English and science (MAT); English and social studies (MAT); higher education administration (MS); history (MAT); history and economics (MAT); math and science (MAT); math and social studies (MAT); middle grades (MAT); science and social studies (MASW); secondary education (MAT); Spanish (MAT); special education (M Ed, MAT); TESOL (MAT). *Accreditation:* NCATE. *Program availability:* Part-time. *Faculty:* 15 full-time (7 women), 8 part-time/adjunct (3 women). *Students:* 28 full-time (21 women), 77 part-time (48 women); includes 12 minority (7 Black or African American, non-Hispanic/Latino; 2 Hispanic/Latino; 3 Two or more races, non-Hispanic/Latino), 1 international. Average age 31. 35 applicants, 83% accepted, 22 enrolled. In 2017, 54 master's, 4 other advanced degrees awarded. *Degree requirements:* For master's, variable foreign language requirement, thesis optional, internship. *Entrance requirements:* For master's, MAT or GRE General Test, minimum undergraduate GPA of 2.75, 3 letters of recommendation, interview, writing sample, official transcripts, background check; for Ed S, minimum undergraduate and master's GPA of 2.75, official transcripts for undergraduate and master's degrees. Additional exam requirements/recommendations for international students: Required—TOEFL (minimum score 61 iBT). *Application deadline:* For fall admission, 6/1 priority date for domestic and international students; for spring admission, 11/1 priority date for domestic and international students; for summer admission, 4/1 priority date for domestic and international students. Applications are processed on a rolling basis. Application fee: $25. Electronic applications accepted. *Expenses: Tuition:* Full-time $12,780; part-time $710 per credit hour. *Required fees:* $60; $60 per term. Tuition and fees vary according to program. *Financial support:* In 2017–18, 32 students received support. Career-related internships or fieldwork, Federal Work-Study, institutionally sponsored loans, scholarships/grants, and unspecified assistantships available. Financial award application deadline: 3/1; financial award applicants required to submit FAFSA. *Unit head:* Dr. William Kamm, Director, 423-614-8544, E-mail: wkamm@leeuniversity.edu. *Application contact:* Crystal Keeter, Graduate Education Secretary, 423-614-8544, E-mail: ckeeter@leeuniversity.edu.
Website: http://www.leeuniversity.edu/academics/graduate/education

Lehman College of the City University of New York, School of Education, Department of Middle and High School Education, Program in Social Studies 7–12, Bronx, NY 10468-1589. Offers MA. *Accreditation:* NCATE. *Entrance requirements:* For master's, minimum GPA of 3.0 in social sciences, 2.7 overall.

Le Moyne College, Department of Education, Syracuse, NY 13214. Offers adolescent education (MS Ed, MST); adolescent education/special education (MS Ed, MST); adolescent English (MST), including grades 7-12; adolescent English/special education (MST), including grades 7-12; adolescent foreign language (MST), including grades 7-12; adolescent history (MST), including grades 7-12; childhood education (MS Ed); childhood education/special education (MS Ed); elementary education (MS Ed); general education (MS Ed); inclusive childhood education (MST); literacy education (MS Ed), including birth to grade 6, grades 5-12; school building leader (MS Ed); school building leadership (CAS); school district business leader (MS Ed, CAS); school district leader (MS Ed); school district leadership (CAS); secondary education (MS Ed); special education (MS Ed); teaching English to speakers of other languages (MS Ed); urban studies (MS Ed). *Accreditation:* TEAC. *Program availability:* Part-time, evening/weekend. *Faculty:* 7 full-time (5 women), 20 part-time/adjunct (12 women). *Students:* 30 full-time (19 women), 126 part-time (93 women); includes 15 minority (7 Black or African American, non-Hispanic/Latino; 1 American Indian or Alaska Native, non-Hispanic/Latino; 1 Asian, non-Hispanic/Latino; 6 Hispanic/Latino), 4 international. Average age 29. 139 applicants, 65% accepted, 76 enrolled. In 2017, 82 master's, 43 CASs awarded. *Degree requirements:* For master's, thesis. *Entrance requirements:* For master's, bachelor's degree with minimum undergraduate GPA of 3.0, 2 letters of recommendation, transcripts. Additional exam requirements/recommendations for international students: Required—TOEFL (minimum score 550 paper-based; 79 iBT); Recommended—IELTS (minimum score 6.5). *Application deadline:* For fall admission, 4/1 priority date for domestic and international students; for spring admission, 10/1 priority date for domestic and international students; for summer admission, 3/1 priority date for domestic and international students. Applications are processed on a rolling basis. Application fee: $50. Electronic applications accepted. *Expenses:* $700 per credit hour. *Financial support:* In 2017–18, 30 students received support. Career-related internships or fieldwork, scholarships/grants, and health care benefits available. Support available to part-time students. Financial award applicants required to submit FAFSA. *Faculty research:* Minority teachers, special education, multiculturalism, literacy, technology, media literacy learning, autism, school district organization, service-learning, higher level problem solving, teacher leadership. *Unit head:* Dr. Stephen C. Fleury, Chair, Department of Education, 315-445-4376, Fax: 315-445-4744, E-mail: fleurysc@lemoyne.edu. *Application contact:* Kristen P. Richards, Senior Director of Enrollment Management, 315-445-5444, Fax: 315-445-6092, E-mail: trapaskp@lemoyne.edu.
Website: http://www.lemoyne.edu/education

Lewis University, College of Education, Program in Secondary Education, Romeoville, IL 60446. Offers biology (MA); chemistry (MA); English (MA); history (MA); math (MA); physics (MA); psychology and social science (MA). *Program availability:* Part-time. *Students:* 19 full-time (9 women), 22 part-time (12 women); includes 10 minority (2 Black or African American, non-Hispanic/Latino; 1 Asian, non-Hispanic/Latino; 5 Hispanic/Latino; 2 Two or more races, non-Hispanic/Latino). Average age 27. *Degree requirements:* For master's, comprehensive exam, departmental qualifying exam. *Entrance requirements:* For master's, writing exam, Test of Academic Proficiency/Basic Skills Test/ACT/SAT, bachelor's degree, minimum GPA of 2.75, 2 letters of recommendation. Additional exam requirements/recommendations for international students: Required—TOEFL (minimum score 550 paper-based; 79 iBT), IELTS (minimum score 6). *Application deadline:* For fall admission, 5/1 priority date for international students; for spring admission, 11/15 priority date for international students.

Applications are processed on a rolling basis. Application fee: $40. Electronic applications accepted. Tuition and fees vary according to program. *Financial support:* Federal Work-Study, scholarships/grants, and unspecified assistantships available. Financial award application deadline: 5/1; financial award applicants required to submit FAFSA. *Unit head:* Dr. Lauren Rentfro, Program Director, 815-836-5026, E-mail: rentfrla@lewisu.edu. *Application contact:* Kathy Lisak, Graduate Admissions Counselor, 815-836-5610, E-mail: grad@lewisu.edu.

Long Island University–LIU Brooklyn, Richard L. Conolly College of Liberal Arts and Sciences, Brooklyn, NY 11201-8423. Offers biology (MS); chemistry (MS); clinical psychology (PhD); creative writing (MFA); English (MA); media arts (MA, MFA); political science (MA); psychology (MA); social science (MS); United Nations (Advanced Certificate); urban studies (MA); writing and production for television (MFA). *Program availability:* Part-time. *Faculty:* 32 full-time (13 women), 17 part-time/adjunct (6 women). *Students:* 178 full-time (123 women), 143 part-time (96 women); includes 128 minority (65 Black or African American, non-Hispanic/Latino; 22 Asian, non-Hispanic/Latino; 31 Hispanic/Latino; 10 Two or more races, non-Hispanic/Latino), 54 international. Average age 30. 629 applicants, 38% accepted, 74 enrolled. In 2017, 147 master's, 9 doctorates, 8 other advanced degrees awarded. Terminal master's awarded for partial completion of doctoral program. *Degree requirements:* For master's, comprehensive exam (for some programs), thesis (for some programs); for doctorate, thesis/dissertation. *Entrance requirements:* For doctorate, GRE. Additional exam requirements/recommendations for international students: Required—TOEFL (minimum score 550 paper-based, 79 iBT) or IELTS. *Application deadline:* Applications are processed on a rolling basis. Application fee: $50. Electronic applications accepted. *Expenses: Tuition:* Full-time $21,618; part-time $1201 per credit. *Required fees:* $1840; $920 per term. Tuition and fees vary according to course load. *Financial support:* In 2017–18, 214 students received support, including 120 fellowships with full and partial tuition reimbursements available (averaging $915 per year), 5 research assistantships with full and partial tuition reimbursements available (averaging $2,300 per year), 136 teaching assistantships with full and partial tuition reimbursements available (averaging $2,300 per year); career-related internships or fieldwork, Federal Work-Study, institutionally sponsored loans, scholarships/grants, and unspecified assistantships also available. Support available to part-time students. Financial award application deadline: 2/15; financial award applicants required to submit FAFSA. *Faculty research:* Quantum gravity and astrophysics; string theory; pharmaceutical biotechnology with a focus on molecular details of drug susceptibility/resistance mechanisms; entomology, population and community ecology, agroecology, and biodiversity; psychotherapy process-outcome, particularly therapeutic alliance development, the role of common factors, and the study of treatment failures; personality pathology, borderline personality disorder and pathological narcissism. *Unit head:* Dr. Scott Krawczyk, Dean, 718-488-1003, E-mail: scott.krawczyk@liu.edu. *Application contact:* Bayu Sutrisno, Graduate Admissions Counselor, 718-488-1564, Fax: 718-780-6110, E-mail: bayu.sutrisno@liu.edu.

Manhattanville College, School of Education, Jump Start Program, Purchase, NY 10577-2132. Offers childhood education and special education (grades 1-6) (MPS); early childhood education (birth-grade 2) (MAT); education (Advanced Certificate); English and special education (grades 5-12) (MPS); mathematics and special education (grades 5-12) (MPS); science and special education (grades 5-12) (MPS); social studies and special education (grades 5-12) (MPS); Spanish (grades 7-12) (MAT); TESOL (all grades) (MPS). *Program availability:* Part-time, evening/weekend. *Faculty:* 10 full-time (7 women), 39 part-time/adjunct (27 women). *Students:* 3 full-time (2 women), 40 part-time (24 women); includes 11 minority (3 Black or African American, non-Hispanic/Latino; 6 Hispanic/Latino; 1 Native Hawaiian or other Pacific Islander, non-Hispanic/Latino; 1 Two or more races, non-Hispanic/Latino). Average age 33. 25 applicants, 60% accepted, 7 enrolled. In 2017, 17 master's, 2 other advanced degrees awarded. *Degree requirements:* For master's, comprehensive exam (for some programs), thesis (for some programs), student teaching, research seminars, portfolios, internships, writing assessment; for Advanced Certificate, comprehensive exam (for some programs). *Entrance requirements:* For master's, GRE or MAT (for programs leading to certification), minimum GPA of 3.0, 2 letters of recommendation, interview, essay (2-3 page personal statement that describes reasons for choosing teaching or educational leadership as profession and philosophy of education), proof of immunization (for those born after 1957). Additional exam requirements/recommendations for international students: Required—TOEFL (minimum score 600 paper-based; 110 iBT); Recommended—IELTS (minimum score 8). *Application deadline:* Applications are processed on a rolling basis. Application fee: $75. Electronic applications accepted. *Expenses:* $915 per credit. *Financial support:* Teaching assistantships, career-related internships or fieldwork, Federal Work-Study, institutionally sponsored loans, scholarships/grants, and unspecified assistantships available. Financial award application deadline: 3/15; financial award applicants required to submit FAFSA. *Faculty research:* Early childhood and technology, professional development schools and community schools, students with emotional difficulties, literacy and adolescents, mindfulness, changing suburbs institute, and community schools, studying the effects of the environment on special populations, the most difficult cases, students who are presented with multiple challenges: learning, behavioral and ACE experiences who see criminal behavior as a way to cope; working on giving them the tools they need to succeed. *Unit head:* Dr. Shelly Wepner, Dean, 914-323-3153, E-mail: shelly.wepner@mville.edu. *Application contact:* Alissa Wilson, Director, Graduate Admissions, 914-323-3150, Fax: 914-694-1732, E-mail: edschool@mville.edu.
Website: http://www.mville.edu/programs/jump-start

Manhattanville College, School of Education, Program in Middle Childhood/Adolescence Education (Grades 5-12), Purchase, NY 10577-2132. Offers biology (MAT, Advanced Certificate); biology and special education (MPS); chemistry (MAT, Advanced Certificate); chemistry and special education (MPS); earth science (Advanced Certificate); education for sustainability (Advanced Certificate); English (MAT, Advanced Certificate); English and special education (MPS); literacy and special education (MPS); literacy specialist (MPS); math and special education (MPS); mathematics (MAT, Advanced Certificate); physics (MAT, Advanced Certificate); social studies (MAT); social studies and special education (MPS); special education generalist (MPS). *Program availability:* Part-time, evening/weekend. *Faculty:* 2 full-time (both women), 5 part-time/adjunct (1 woman). *Students:* 8 full-time (7 women), 28 part-time (16 women); includes 4 minority (1 Asian, non-Hispanic/Latino; 2 Hispanic/Latino; 1 Two or more races, non-Hispanic/Latino). Average age 31. 7 applicants, 86% accepted, 4 enrolled. In 2017, 13 master's, 1 other advanced degree awarded. *Degree requirements:* For master's, comprehensive exam (for some programs), thesis (for some programs), student teaching, research seminars, portfolios, internships, writing assessment; for Advanced Certificate, comprehensive exam (for some programs). *Entrance requirements:* For master's, GRE or MAT (for programs leading to certification), minimum GPA of 3.0, 2 letters of recommendation, interview, essay (2-3 page personal statement that describes reasons for choosing teaching or educational leadership as profession and philosophy of education), proof of immunization (for those born after 1957). Additional exam requirements/recommendations for international students: Required—TOEFL (minimum score 600 paper-based; 110 iBT); Recommended—IELTS (minimum score 8). *Application deadline:* Applications are processed on a rolling basis. Application fee: $75. Electronic applications accepted. *Expenses:* $915 per credit. *Financial support:*

Teaching assistantships, career-related internships or fieldwork, Federal Work-Study, institutionally sponsored loans, scholarships/grants, and unspecified assistantships available. Financial award application deadline: 3/15; financial award applicants required to submit FAFSA. *Faculty research:* Education for sustainability. *Unit head:* Dr. Shelly Wepner, Dean, 914-323-3153, Fax: 914-323-5493, E-mail: shelly.wepner@mville.edu. *Application contact:* Alissa Wilson, Director, Graduate Admissions, 914-323-3150, Fax: 914-694-1732, E-mail: edschool@mville.edu.
Website: http://www.mville.edu/programs#/search/19

Manhattanville College, School of Education, Program in Special Education, Purchase, NY 10577-2132. Offers childhood (grades 1-6) (MPS); childhood education (grades 1-6) and special education (MPS); early childhood (birth-grade 2) (MPS); early childhood (birth-grade 2) and special education (MPS); early childhood and childhood (birth-grade 6) (MPS); English (5-9 and 7-12) (MPS); grades 7-12 generalist (MPS); literacy (birth-grade 6) and special education childhood (grades 1-6) (MPS); literacy 5-12 (MPS); mathematics (5-9 and 7-12) (MPS); science (biology or chemistry 5-9 and 7-12) (MPS); social studies (5-9 and 7-12) (MPS); special education: childhood (grades 1-6) (Certificate); special education: early childhood (birth-grade 2) and childhood (grades 1-6) (Certificate); special education: early childhood (birth-grade 2) (Certificate); special education: grades 7-12 generalist (Certificate). *Program availability:* Part-time, evening/weekend. *Faculty:* 5 full-time (3 women), 24 part-time/adjunct (16 women). *Students:* 77 full-time (69 women), 154 part-time (132 women); includes 33 minority (9 Black or African American, non-Hispanic/Latino; 2 Asian, non-Hispanic/Latino; 22 Hispanic/Latino), 1 international. Average age 28. 87 applicants, 77% accepted, 57 enrolled. In 2017, 86 master's, 2 Certificates awarded. *Degree requirements:* For master's, comprehensive exam (for some programs), thesis (for some programs), student teaching, research seminars, portfolios, internships, writing assessment; for Certificate, comprehensive exam (for some programs). *Entrance requirements:* For master's, GRE or MAT (for programs leading to certification), minimum GPA of 3.0, 2 letters of recommendation, interview, essay (2-3 page personal statement that describes reasons for choosing teaching or educational leadership as profession and philosophy of education), proof of immunization (for those born after 1957). Additional exam requirements/recommendations for international students: Required—TOEFL (minimum score 600 paper-based; 110 iBT); Recommended—IELTS (minimum score 8). *Application deadline:* Applications are processed on a rolling basis. Application fee: $75. Electronic applications accepted. *Expenses:* $915 per credit. *Financial support:* Teaching assistantships, career-related internships or fieldwork, Federal Work-Study, institutionally sponsored loans, scholarships/grants, and unspecified assistantships available. Financial award application deadline: 3/15; financial award applicants required to submit FAFSA. *Faculty research:* Students with emotional difficulties, literacy and adolescents, mindfulness, studying the effects of the environment on special populations, the most difficult cases, students who are presented with multiple challenges: learning, behavioral and ACE experiences who see criminal behavior as a way to cope; working on giving them the tools they need to succeed emotionally and cognitively despite the odds stacked against them. *Unit head:* Dr. Shelly Wepner, Dean, 914-323-3153, Fax: 914-323-5493, E-mail: shelly.wepner@mville.edu. *Application contact:* Alissa Wilson, Director, Graduate Admissions, 914-323-3150, Fax: 914-694-1732, E-mail: edschool@mville.edu.
Website: http://www.mville.edu/programs/special-education

Michigan State University, The Graduate School, College of Social Science, Department of History, East Lansing, MI 48824. Offers history (MA, PhD); history-secondary school teaching (MA). *Entrance requirements:* Additional exam requirements/recommendations for international students: Required—TOEFL. Electronic applications accepted.

Minnesota State University Mankato, College of Graduate Studies and Research, College of Social and Behavioral Sciences, Department of History, Mankato, MN 56001. Offers history (MA, MS); social studies (MAT). *Degree requirements:* For master's, one foreign language, comprehensive exam, thesis or alternative. *Entrance requirements:* For master's, minimum GPA of 3.0, statement of purpose. Additional exam requirements/recommendations for international students: Required—TOEFL (minimum score 600 paper-based). Electronic applications accepted.

Mississippi College, Graduate School, School of Education, Department of Teacher Education and Leadership, Clinton, MS 39058. Offers art (M Ed); biological science (M Ed); business education (M Ed); computer science (M Ed); dyslexia therapy (M Ed); educational leadership (M Ed, Ed D, Ed S); elementary education (M Ed, Ed S); English (M Ed); higher education administration (MS); mathematics (M Ed); secondary education (M Ed); social studies (history) (M Ed); teaching arts (M Ed). *Program availability:* Part-time, online learning. *Degree requirements:* For master's, comprehensive exam, thesis optional. *Entrance requirements:* For master's, NTE. Additional exam requirements/recommendations for international students: Recommended—TOEFL, IELTS. Electronic applications accepted.

Missouri State University, Graduate College, College of Humanities and Public Affairs, Department of History, Springfield, MO 65897. Offers history (MA); history education (MS Ed); history for teachers (Certificate). *Program availability:* Part-time, 100% online, blended/hybrid learning. *Faculty:* 18 full-time (7 women). *Students:* 10 full-time (5 women), 37 part-time (17 women); includes 1 minority (Asian, non-Hispanic/Latino), 2 international. Average age 33. 31 applicants, 39% accepted, 8 enrolled. In 2017, 16 master's awarded. *Degree requirements:* For master's, comprehensive exam, thesis or alternative. *Entrance requirements:* For master's, minimum GPA of 2.75, 24 hours of undergraduate course work in history (MA), 9-12 teaching certification (MS Ed). Additional exam requirements/recommendations for international students: Required—TOEFL (minimum score 550 paper-based; 79 iBT), IELTS (minimum score 6). *Application deadline:* For fall admission, 7/20 priority date for domestic students, 5/1 for international students; for spring admission, 12/20 priority date for domestic students, 9/1 for international students. Applications are processed on a rolling basis. Application fee: $35 ($50 for international students). Electronic applications accepted. *Expenses:* Tuition, state resident: full-time $2915; part-time $2021 per credit hour. Tuition, nonresident: full-time $5354; part-time $3647 per credit hour. *International tuition:* $11,992 full-time. *Required fees:* $173; $173 per credit hour. Tuition and fees vary according to class time, course level, course load, degree level, campus/location and program. *Financial support:* Federal Work-Study, scholarships/grants, and unspecified assistantships available. Support available to part-time students. Financial award application deadline: 3/31; financial award applicants required to submit FAFSA. *Faculty research:* Early modern France, cultural history of modern Britain, Latin American history, women's history, American Civil War in Missouri. *Unit head:* Dr. Kathleen Kennedy, Department Head, 417-836-5511, Fax: 417-836-5523, E-mail: history@missouristate.edu. *Application contact:* Stephanie Praschan, Director, Graduate Enrollment Management, 417-836-5330, Fax: 417-836-6200, E-mail: stephaniepraschan@missouristate.edu.
Website: http://history.missouristate.edu/

Molloy College, Graduate Education Program, Rockville Centre, NY 11571-5002. Offers adolescent education in biology (MS); adolescent special education (Advanced Certificate); bilingual extension (Advanced Certificate); childhood education (MS); childhood special education (Advanced Certificate); early childhood education (MS); educational technology (MS); English (MS); mathematics (MS); social studies (MS); Spanish (MS); special education on both childhood and adolescent levels (MS);

teaching English to speakers of other languages (TESOL) in grades pre-K to 12 (MS); TESOL (Advanced Certificate). *Accreditation:* NCATE. *Program availability:* Part-time, evening/weekend. *Faculty:* 18 full-time (17 women), 11 part-time/adjunct (9 women). *Students:* 102 full-time (80 women), 217 part-time (167 women); includes 65 minority (16 Black or African American, non-Hispanic/Latino; 7 Asian, non-Hispanic/Latino; 38 Hispanic/Latino; 4 Two or more races, non-Hispanic/Latino), 1 international. Average age 41. 153 applicants, 68% accepted, 85 enrolled. In 2017, 95 master's, 3 other advanced degrees awarded. *Entrance requirements:* Additional exam requirements/recommendations for international students: Required—TOEFL (minimum score 550 paper-based; 79 iBT). *Application deadline:* Applications are processed on a rolling basis. Application fee: $60. Electronic applications accepted. *Expenses:* Tuition: Full-time $19,980; part-time $1110 per credit. *Required fees:* $1040. Tuition and fees vary according to course load and degree level. *Financial support:* Application deadline: 3/1; applicants required to submit FAFSA. *Faculty research:* English Language Learners; social emotional needs of students; gifted education; cultural diversity; collaborative teaching methods. *Unit head:* Joanne O'Brien, Associate Dean and Director of Graduate Education Programs, 516-323-3116, E-mail: jobrien@molloy.edu. *Application contact:* Jaclyn Machowicz, Assistant Director for Admissions, 516-323-4010, E-mail: jmachowicz@molloy.edu.

Morehead State University, Graduate Programs, College of Education, Department of Foundational and Graduate Studies in Education, Morehead, KY 40351. Offers adult and higher education (MA, Ed S); certified professional counselor (Ed S); counseling P-12 (MA); curriculum and instruction (Ed S); educational technology (MA Ed); instructional leadership (Ed S); school administration (MA); school counseling (Ed S); teacher leader business and marketing content (MA Ed); teacher leader business and marketing technology (MA Ed); teacher leader educational technology (MA Ed); teacher leader English (MA Ed); teacher leader gifted education (MA Ed); teacher leader IECE certification (MA Ed); teacher leader interdisciplinary education P-5 (MA Ed); teacher leader middle grades (MA Ed); teacher leader non IECE certification (MA Ed); teacher leader reading/writing - non-certification (MA Ed); teacher leader reading/writing certification (MA Ed); teacher leader school communication - certification (MA Ed); teacher leader school communication - non-certification (MA Ed); teacher leader social studies (MA Ed); teacher leader special education (MA Ed). *Accreditation:* NCATE. *Program availability:* Part-time, evening/weekend. *Degree requirements:* For master's, thesis optional, oral and/or written comprehensive exams; for Ed S, thesis, oral exam. *Entrance requirements:* For master's, GRE General Test, minimum overall undergraduate GPA of 2.5; for Ed S, GRE General Test, interview, master's degree, minimum GPA of 3.5, work experience. Additional exam requirements/recommendations for international students: Required—TOEFL (minimum score 500 paper-based). Electronic applications accepted. *Faculty research:* Character education, school accountability, computer applications for school administrators.

Morehead State University, Graduate Programs, College of Education, Department of Middle Grades and Secondary Education, Morehead, KY 40351. Offers business and marketing education (MAT); English/language arts 5-9 (MAT); French (MAT); health P-12 (MAT); mathematics 5-9 (MAT); physical education P-12 (MAT); science 5-9 (MAT); secondary biology (MAT); secondary chemistry (MAT); secondary earth science (MAT); secondary English (MAT); secondary math (MAT); secondary physics (MAT); secondary social studies (MAT); social studies 5-9 (MAT); Spanish (MAT). *Program availability:* Part-time, evening/weekend. *Degree requirements:* For master's, portfolio. *Entrance requirements:* For master's, GRE or PRAXIS II content exam, minimum overall undergraduate GPA of 2.5. Additional exam requirements/recommendations for international students: Required—TOEFL (minimum score 500 paper-based). Electronic applications accepted.

New York Institute of Technology, School of Interdisciplinary Studies and Education, Department of Teacher Education, Old Westbury, NY 11568-8000. Offers adolescence education (MS), including math (MAT, MS), science; adolescent education (MAT), including biology, chemistry, English, math (MAT, MS), social studies; childhood education (MS); early childhood (MS). *Program availability:* Part-time, evening/weekend, 100% online, blended/hybrid learning. *Faculty:* 2 full-time (both women), 7 part-time/adjunct (3 women). *Students:* 46 full-time (44 women), 30 part-time (22 women); includes 23 minority (8 Black or African American, non-Hispanic/Latino; 6 Asian, non-Hispanic/Latino; 8 Hispanic/Latino; 1 Two or more races, non-Hispanic/Latino), 2 international. Average age 29. 39 applicants, 72% accepted, 15 enrolled. In 2017, 14 master's awarded. *Entrance requirements:* For master's, GRE or MAT, BS or equivalent; minimum cumulative undergraduate GPA of 3.0; NY state provisional or initial certification (for MS in adolescence education); BS with major in biology, chemistry, economics, English, history, life sciences, math, physics, or psychology (for MS in childhood, early childhood education, and MAT); interview; personal statement. Additional exam requirements/recommendations for international students: Required—TOEFL (minimum score 79 iBT), IELTS (minimum score 6). *Application deadline:* Applications are processed on a rolling basis. Application fee: $50. Electronic applications accepted. *Expenses:* $1,285 per credit plus fees. *Financial support:* Career-related internships or fieldwork, Federal Work-Study, scholarships/grants, tuition waivers (full and partial), and unspecified assistantships available. Support available to part-time students. Financial award application deadline: 2/15; financial award applicants required to submit FAFSA. *Faculty research:* Evolving definition of new literacies and its impact on teaching and learning (twenty-first century skills), new literacies practices in teacher education, teachers' professional development, English language and literacy learning through mobile learning, teaching reading to culturally and linguistically diverse children. *Unit head:* Dr. Hui-Yin Hsu, Department Chair, 516-686-1322, Fax: 516-686-7655, E-mail: hhsu02@nyit.edu. *Application contact:* Alice Dolitsky, Director, Graduate Admissions, 516-686-7520, Fax: 516-686-1116, E-mail: nyitgrad@nyit.edu.
Website: http://www.nyit.edu/interdisciplinary/department_teacher_education

New York University, Steinhardt School of Culture, Education, and Human Development, Department of Art and Art Professions, Program in Art Education, New York, NY 10003-5799. Offers art, education, and community practice (MA); teachers of art, all grades (MA); teaching art/social studies 7-12 (MA), including 5-6 extension. *Accreditation:* TEAC. *Program availability:* Part-time. *Students:* Average age 35. 57 applicants, 63% accepted, 22 enrolled. In 2017, 13 master's awarded. *Entrance requirements:* For master's, portfolio. Additional exam requirements/recommendations for international students: Required—TOEFL (minimum score 100 iBT). *Application deadline:* For fall admission, 12/1 priority date for domestic and international students. Applications are processed on a rolling basis. Application fee: $75. Electronic applications accepted. *Expenses:* Tuition: Full-time $41,352; part-time $19,968 per year. *Required fees:* $2496; $1628 per unit. $814 per term. Tuition and fees vary according to course load and program. *Financial support:* Career-related internships or fieldwork, Federal Work-Study, and tuition waivers (partial) available. Support available to part-time students. Financial award application deadline: 2/1; financial award applicants required to submit FAFSA. *Faculty research:* Multicultural aesthetic inquiry, urban art education, feminism, equity and social justice. *Unit head:* Prof. Dipti Desai, Director, 212-998-5700, Fax: 212-995-4320, E-mail: dd25@nyu.edu. *Application contact:* 212-998-5030, Fax: 212-995-4328, E-mail: steinhardt.gradadmissions@nyu.edu.
Website: http://steinhardt.nyu.edu/art/education

Social Sciences Education

New York University, Steinhardt School of Culture, Education, and Human Development, Department of Music and Performing Arts Professions, Program in Educational Theatre, New York, NY 10012. Offers educational theatre and English 7-12 (MA); educational theatre and social studies 7-12 (MA); educational theatre in colleges and communities (MA, Ed D, PhD); educational theatre, all grades (MA). *Program availability:* Part-time. *Students:* Average age 28. 90 applicants, 76% accepted, 37 enrolled. In 2017, 47 master's, 5 doctorates awarded. *Entrance requirements:* For master's, audition; for doctorate, GRE General Test, interview. Additional exam requirements/recommendations for international students: Required—TOEFL (minimum score 100 iBT). *Application deadline:* For fall admission, 12/1 priority date for domestic and international students; for spring admission, 10/1 for domestic and international students. Applications are processed on a rolling basis. Application fee: $75. Electronic applications accepted. *Expenses: Tuition:* Full-time $41,352; part-time $19,968 per year. *Required fees:* $2496; $1628 per unit. $814 per term. Tuition and fees vary according to course load and program. *Financial support:* Teaching assistantships with partial tuition reimbursements, career-related internships or fieldwork, Federal Work-Study, institutionally sponsored loans, and scholarships/grants available. Support available to part-time students. Financial award application deadline: 2/1; financial award applicants required to submit FAFSA. *Faculty research:* Theatre for young audiences, drama in education, applied theatre, arts education assessment, reflective praxis. *Unit head:* Prof. David Montgomery, Director, 212-998-5869, Fax: 212-995-4043, E-mail: dm635@nyu.edu. *Application contact:* 212-998-5030, Fax: 212-995-4328, E-mail: steinhardt.gradadmissions@nyu.edu.
Website: http://steinhardt.nyu.edu/music/edtheatre

New York University, Steinhardt School of Culture, Education, and Human Development, Department of Teaching and Learning, Program in Social Studies Education, New York, NY 10012. Offers teaching art/social studies 7-12 (MA), including 5-6 extension; teaching social studies 7-12 (MA). *Accreditation:* TEAC. *Program availability:* Part-time, evening/weekend. *Students:* Average age 24. 47 applicants, 81% accepted, 11 enrolled. In 2017, 8 master's awarded. *Entrance requirements:* Additional exam requirements/recommendations for international students: Required—TOEFL (minimum score 100 iBT). *Application deadline:* For fall admission, 12/1 priority date for domestic and international students; for spring admission, 10/1 for domestic and international students. Applications are processed on a rolling basis. Application fee: $75. Electronic applications accepted. *Expenses: Tuition:* Full-time $41,352; part-time $19,968 per year. *Required fees:* $2496; $1628 per unit. $814 per term. Tuition and fees vary according to course load and program. *Financial support:* Career-related internships or fieldwork, Federal Work-Study, institutionally sponsored loans, scholarships/grants, and tuition waivers (partial) available. Support available to part-time students. Financial award application deadline: 2/1; financial award applicants required to submit FAFSA. *Faculty research:* Social studies education reform, ethnography and oral history, civic education, labor history and social studies curriculum, material culture. *Unit head:* Dr. Diana Turk, Chairperson, 212-998-5492, Fax: 212-995-4049, E-mail: dt23@nyu.edu. *Application contact:* 212-998-5030, Fax: 212-995-4328, E-mail: steinhardt.gradadmissions@nyu.edu.
Website: http://steinhardt.nyu.edu/teachlearn/social_studies

North Carolina State University, Graduate School, College of Education, Department of Curriculum and Instruction, Program in Social Studies Education, Raleigh, NC 27695. Offers M Ed. *Entrance requirements:* For master's, GRE or MAT, 3 letters of reference, interview, minimum GPA of 3.0.

North Dakota State University, College of Graduate and Interdisciplinary Studies, College of Human Development and Education, School of Education, Fargo, ND 58102. Offers agricultural education (M Ed, MS), including agricultural education; counselor education (M Ed, MS, PhD), including clinical mental health counseling (M Ed, MS), counselor education and supervision (PhD); school counseling (M Ed, MS); curriculum and instruction (M Ed, MS); education (PhD); educational leadership (M Ed, MS, Ed S); family and consumer sciences education (M Ed, MS); history education (M Ed, MS); institutional analysis (Ed D); mathematics education (M Ed, MS); music education (M Ed, MS); occupational and adult education (Ed D); science education (M Ed, MS). *Accreditation:* NCATE. *Program availability:* Part-time, evening/weekend, online learning. *Degree requirements:* For master's, comprehensive exam; for doctorate, thesis/dissertation; for Ed S, thesis. *Entrance requirements:* For degree, GRE General Test, master's degree, minimum GPA of 3.25. Additional exam requirements/recommendations for international students: Required—TOEFL.

Northeastern Illinois University, College of Graduate Studies and Research, Daniel L. Goodwin College of Education, MAT Program in Secondary Education, Chicago, IL 60625. Offers language arts (MAT); mathematics (MAT); science (MAT); social science (MAT). *Expenses:* Tuition, state resident: full-time $7274; part-time $404.11 per credit hour. Tuition, nonresident: full-time $14,548; part-time $808.23 per credit hour. *Required fees:* $1284. *Unit head:* Dr. Brian Schultz, Department Chair, 773-442-5327, E-mail: b-schultz@neiu.edu. *Application contact:* Martha Narvaez, Graduate Admission Representative, 773-442-6006, E-mail: m-narvaez@neiu.edu.

Northwest Missouri State University, Graduate School, College of Arts and Sciences, Maryville, MO 64468-6001. Offers biology (MS); elementary mathematics specialist (MS Ed); English (MA); English education (MS Ed); English pedagogy (MA); geographic information science (MS, Certificate); history (MS Ed); mathematics (MS); mathematics education (MS Ed); teaching: science (MS Ed). *Program availability:* Part-time. *Faculty:* 67 full-time (21 women). *Students:* 11 full-time (5 women), 70 part-time (39 women); includes 9 minority (2 Black or African American, non-Hispanic/Latino; 1 American Indian or Alaska Native, non-Hispanic/Latino; 3 Hispanic/Latino; 3 Two or more races, non-Hispanic/Latino). Average age 34. 33 applicants, 42% accepted, 10 enrolled. In 2017, 19 master's, 7 other advanced degrees awarded. *Degree requirements:* For master's, comprehensive exam. *Entrance requirements:* For master's, GRE General Test, writing sample. Additional exam requirements/recommendations for international students: Required—TOEFL (minimum score 550 paper-based). *Application deadline:* For fall admission, 7/1 for domestic and international students; for spring admission, 11/15 for domestic and international students. Applications are processed on a rolling basis. Application fee: $0 ($50 for international students). Electronic applications accepted. *Expenses:* Tuition, state resident: full-time $4551; part-time $252.86 per credit hour. Tuition, nonresident: full-time $9103; part-time $505.72 per credit hour. *Required fees:* $2453; $136.25 per credit hour. Tuition and fees vary according to course load and program. *Financial support:* Research assistantships with full tuition reimbursements, teaching assistantships with full tuition reimbursements, and administrative assistantships, tutorial assistantships available. Financial award application deadline: 4/1; financial award applicants required to submit FAFSA. *Unit head:* Dr. Michael Steiner, Dean, 660-562-1197.
Website: https://www.nwmissouri.edu/academics/undergraduate/majors/liberal-arts-sciences.htm

Oregon State University, College of Education, Program in Teaching, Corvallis, OR 97331. Offers clinically based elementary education (MAT); elementary education (MAT); language arts (MAT); mathematics (MAT); music education (MAT); science (MAT); social studies (MAT). *Program availability:* Part-time, blended/hybrid learning. *Entrance requirements:* For master's, CBEST. Additional exam requirements/

recommendations for international students: Required—TOEFL (minimum score 575 paper-based). *Application deadline:* For fall admission, 12/1 for domestic students. Application fee: $60. *Expenses:* Contact institution. *Unit head:* Jordon Zardinejad, 541-322-3118, E-mail: jordon.zardinejad@osucascades.edu. *Application contact:* Jordon Zardinejad, 541-322-3118, E-mail: jordon.zardinejad@osucascades.edu.
Website: http://education.oregonstate.edu/mat

Oregon State University, Interdisciplinary/Institutional Programs, Program in Environmental Sciences, Corvallis, OR 97331. Offers biogeochemistry (MA, MS, PSM, PhD); ecology (MA, MS, PSM, PhD); environmental education (MA, MS, MA, PhD); quantitative analysis (PSM); social science (MA, MS, PSM, PhD); water resources (MA, MS, PhD). *Program availability:* Part-time. *Degree requirements:* For master's, variable foreign language requirement, thesis; for doctorate, thesis/dissertation. *Entrance requirements:* For master's and doctorate, GRE. Additional exam requirements/recommendations for international students: Required—TOEFL (minimum score 80 iBT), IELTS (minimum score 6.5). *Application deadline:* For fall admission, 1/15 priority date for domestic and international students. Application fee: $75 ($85 for international students). *Unit head:* Dr. Carolyn Fonyo Boggess, Interim Director, 541-760-4196, E-mail: carolyn.fonyo@oregonstate.edu. *Application contact:* Dr. Carolyn Fonyo Boggess, Interim Director, 541-760-4196, E-mail: carolyn.fonyo@oregonstate.edu.
Website: http://gradschool.oregonstate.edu/environmental-sciences-graduate-program-esgp

Pace University, School of Education, New York, NY 10038. Offers adolescent education (MST), including biology, chemistry, earth science, English, foreign languages, mathematics, physics, social studies; childhood education (MST); early childhood development, learning and intervention (MST); educational technology studies (MS); inclusive adolescent education (MST), including biology, chemistry, earth science, English, foreign languages, mathematics, physics, social studies; integrated instruction for educational technology (Certificate); integrated instruction for literacy and technology (Certificate); literacy (MS Ed); special education (MS Ed). *Accreditation:* NCATE. *Program availability:* Part-time, evening/weekend, 100% online, blended/hybrid learning. *Faculty:* 19 full-time (13 women), 86 part-time/adjunct (49 women). *Students:* 91 full-time (76 women), 548 part-time (401 women); includes 247 minority (112 Black or African American, non-Hispanic/Latino; 2 American Indian or Alaska Native, non-Hispanic/Latino; 31 Asian, non-Hispanic/Latino; 93 Hispanic/Latino; 1 Native Hawaiian or other Pacific Islander, non-Hispanic/Latino; 8 Two or more races, non-Hispanic/Latino), 6 international. Average age 30. 188 applicants, 86% accepted, 114 enrolled. In 2017, 213 master's, 8 other advanced degrees awarded. *Degree requirements:* For master's and Certificate, certification exams. *Entrance requirements:* For master's, GRE (for initial certification programs only), teaching certificate (for MS Ed in literacy and special education programs only). Additional exam requirements/recommendations for international students: Required—TOEFL (minimum score 88 iBT), IELTS or PTE. *Application deadline:* For fall admission, 8/1 priority date for domestic students, 6/1 for international students; for spring admission, 12/1 priority date for domestic students, 10/1 for international students. Applications are processed on a rolling basis. Application fee: $70. Electronic applications accepted. *Expenses:* Contact institution. *Financial support:* In 2017–18, 17 students received support, including 17 research assistantships with partial tuition reimbursements available (averaging $6,020 per year); career-related internships or fieldwork, Federal Work-Study, scholarships/grants, and unspecified assistantships also available. Financial award application deadline: 9/1; financial award applicants required to submit FAFSA. *Faculty research:* STEM education, TESOL, teacher education, special education, language and literary development. *Total annual research expenditures:* $29,706. *Unit head:* Dr. Xiao-Lei Wang, Dean, School of Education, 914-773-3876, E-mail: xwang@pace.edu. *Application contact:* Susan Ford-Goldschein, Director of Graduate Admissions, 212-346-1531, Fax: 212-346-1585, E-mail: graduateadmission@pace.edu.
Website: http://www.pace.edu/school-of-education

Plymouth State University, College of Graduate Studies, Graduate Studies in Education, Program in Heritage Studies, Plymouth, NH 03264-1595. Offers M Ed. *Program availability:* Part-time, evening/weekend. *Degree requirements:* For master's, internship. *Entrance requirements:* For master's, GRE General Test or MAT, minimum GPA of 3.0, resume.

Plymouth State University, College of Graduate Studies, Graduate Studies in Education, Program in Secondary Education, Plymouth, NH 03264-1595. Offers curriculum and instruction (M Ed); language education (M Ed); library media (M Ed); physical education (M Ed); social studies education (M Ed); special education (M Ed). *Program availability:* Part-time, evening/weekend. *Entrance requirements:* For master's, MAT.

Portland State University, Graduate Studies, College of Liberal Arts and Sciences, Interdisciplinary Programs in General Science, General Social Science, and General Arts and Letters, Portland, OR 97207-0751. Offers general arts and letters education (MAT, MST); general science education (MAT, MST); general social science education (MAT, MST). *Program availability:* Part-time, evening/weekend. *Students:* 2 full-time (both women); includes 1 minority (Two or more races, non-Hispanic/Latino). Average age 46. 5 applicants, 80% accepted, 2 enrolled. *Degree requirements:* For master's, variable foreign language requirement, written exam. *Entrance requirements:* For master's, minimum GPA of 3.0 in upper-division course work or 2.75 overall. Additional exam requirements/recommendations for international students: Required—TOEFL (minimum score 550 paper-based; 80 iBT), IELTS (minimum score 6.5). *Application deadline:* For fall admission, 4/1 priority date for domestic students, 3/1 priority date for international students. *Expenses:* Tuition, state resident: full-time $14,436; part-time $401 per credit. Tuition, nonresident: full-time $21,780; part-time $605 per credit. *Required fees:* $1380; $22 per credit. $119 per quarter. One-time fee: $325. Tuition and fees vary according to program. *Financial support:* Federal Work-Study and unspecified assistantships available. Support available to part-time students. Financial award application deadline: 3/1; financial award applicants required to submit FAFSA. *Unit head:* Robert Mercer, Associate Dean, 503-725-5059, Fax: 503-725-3693, E-mail: mercerr@pdx.edu. *Application contact:* CLAS Advising Office, 503-725-3822, E-mail: askclas@pdx.edu.

Purdue University, Graduate School, College of Education, Department of Curriculum and Instruction, West Lafayette, IN 47907. Offers agricultural and extension education (MS, MS Ed, PhD, Ed S); art education (PhD); career and technical education (MS Ed, PhD, Ed S); curriculum studies (MS Ed, PhD, Ed S); educational technology (MS Ed, PhD, Ed S); elementary education (MS Ed); family and consumer sciences education (MS Ed, PhD, Ed S); foreign language education (MS Ed, PhD, Ed S); industrial technology (PhD, Ed S); language arts (MS Ed, PhD, Ed S); literacy (MS Ed, PhD, Ed S); mathematics education (MS, MS Ed, PhD, Ed S); science education (MS, MS Ed, PhD, Ed S); social studies education (MS Ed, PhD, Ed S). *Accreditation:* NCATE. *Program availability:* Part-time, evening/weekend. *Faculty:* 37 full-time (27 women), 1 (woman) part-time/adjunct. *Students:* 78 full-time (50 women), 286 part-time (195 women); includes 68 minority (25 Black or African American, non-Hispanic/Latino; 3 American Indian or Alaska Native, non-Hispanic/Latino; 10 Asian, non-Hispanic/Latino; 22 Hispanic/Latino; 1 Native Hawaiian or other Pacific Islander, non-Hispanic/Latino; 7 Two or more races, non-Hispanic/Latino), 44 international. Average age 36. 150

applicants, 79% accepted, 73 enrolled. In 2017, 107 master's, 20 doctorates, 2 other advanced degrees awarded. *Degree requirements:* For master's, thesis optional; for doctorate, thesis/dissertation, oral and written exams; for Ed S, oral presentation, project. *Entrance requirements:* For master's, GRE General Test (if undergraduate GPA is below 3.0), minimum undergraduate GPA of 3.0 or equivalent; for doctorate, GRE General Test (minimum combined verbal and quantitative score of 1000, 300 for new scoring), minimum undergraduate GPA of 3.0 or equivalent; master's degree with minimum GPA of 3.0 or equivalent; for Ed S, GRE General Test (minimum combined verbal and quantitative score of 1000, 300 for new scoring), minimum undergraduate GPA of 3.0 or equivalent; master's degree. Additional exam requirements/recommendations for international students: Required—TOEFL (minimum score 550 paper-based; 77 iBT). *Application deadline:* For fall admission, 12/15 for domestic students, 3/1 for international students; for spring admission, 9/15 for domestic students, 8/1 for international students. Application fee: $60 ($75 for international students). Electronic applications accepted. *Financial support:* Fellowships with full tuition reimbursements, research assistantships with full tuition reimbursements, teaching assistantships with full tuition reimbursements, career-related internships or fieldwork, and tuition waivers (full) available. Support available to part-time students. Financial award application deadline: 3/1; financial award applicants required to submit FAFSA. *Faculty research:* Literacy acquisition and development, teacher beliefs and knowledge, recruitment and retention of underrepresented students, economic education, literacy discourse. *Unit head:* Janet M. Alsup, Head, 765-494-9667, E-mail: alsupj@purdue.edu. *Application contact:* Heather Brinkman, Graduate Contact, 765-494-2345, E-mail: hbrinkma@purdue.edu.
Website: http://www.edci.purdue.edu/

Queens College of the City University of New York, Division of Education, Department of Secondary Education and Youth Services, Queens, NY 11367-1597. Offers adolescent biology (MAT); art (MS Ed); biology (MS Ed, AC); chemistry (MS Ed, AC); earth sciences (MS Ed, AC); English (MS Ed, AC); French (MS Ed); Italian (MS Ed, AC); literacy education (MS Ed); mathematics (MS Ed, AC); music (MS Ed, AC); physics (MS Ed, AC); social studies (MS Ed, AC); Spanish (MS Ed, AC). *Program availability:* Part-time, evening/weekend. *Students:* 28 full-time (16 women), 349 part-time (202 women); includes 165 minority (18 Black or African American, non-Hispanic/Latino; 56 Asian, non-Hispanic/Latino; 83 Hispanic/Latino; 8 Two or more races, non-Hispanic/Latino), 14 international. Average age 29. *Degree requirements:* For master's, research project. *Entrance requirements:* For master's, minimum GPA of 3.0. Additional exam requirements/recommendations for international students: Required—TOEFL, IELTS. *Application deadline:* For fall admission, 4/1 for domestic students; for spring admission, 11/1 for domestic students. Applications are processed on a rolling basis. Application fee: $125. Electronic applications accepted. *Financial support:* Career-related internships or fieldwork available. Financial award application deadline: 4/1; financial award applicants required to submit FAFSA. *Unit head:* Dr. Eleanor Armour-Thomas, Chairperson, 718-997-5150, E-mail: eleanor.armour-thomas@qc.cuny.edu. *Application contact:* Elizabeth D'Amico-Ramirez, Assistant Director of Graduate Admissions, 718-997-5203, E-mail: elizabeth.damicoramirez@qc.cuny.edu.

Quinnipiac University, School of Education, Program in Secondary Education, Hamden, CT 06518-1940. Offers biology (MAT); English (MAT); history (MAT); mathematics (MAT); Spanish (MAT). *Accreditation:* NCATE. *Faculty:* 8 full-time (5 women), 27 part-time/adjunct (19 women). *Students:* 27 full-time (20 women); includes 5 minority (1 Black or African American, non-Hispanic/Latino; 3 Hispanic/Latino; 1 Two or more races, non-Hispanic/Latino). 43 applicants, 98% accepted, 36 enrolled. In 2017, 34 master's awarded. *Entrance requirements:* For master's, PRAXIS I or PRAXIS Core Academic Skills Exam, minimum GPA of 3.0, interview. *Application deadline:* For fall admission, 5/1 priority date for domestic students. Applications are processed on a rolling basis. Application fee: $45. Electronic applications accepted. *Financial support:* Career-related internships or fieldwork, Federal Work-Study, and unspecified assistantships available. Financial award application deadline: 6/1; financial award applicants required to submit FAFSA. *Faculty research:* Multicultural and urban education/leadership, challenges of teaching diverse learners, scholarship of teaching and learning, technology and teaching, humor and education. *Unit head:* Mordechai Gordon, Program Director, 203-582-8442, E-mail: mordechai.gordon@qu.edu. *Application contact:* Office of Graduate Admissions, 203-582-8672, Fax: 203-582-3443, E-mail: graduate@qu.edu.
Website: http://www.qu.edu/gradeducation

Rhode Island College, School of Graduate Studies, Feinstein School of Education and Human Development, Department of Educational Studies, Providence, RI 02908-1991. Offers advanced studies in teaching and learning (M Ed); English (MAT); French (MAT); history (MAT); math (MAT); secondary education (MAT); Spanish (MAT); teaching English as a second language (M Ed). *Accreditation:* NCATE. *Program availability:* Part-time, evening/weekend. *Faculty:* 2. *Students:* 1 (woman) full-time, 62 part-time (58 women); includes 10 minority (1 Black or African American, non-Hispanic/Latino; 2 Asian, non-Hispanic/Latino; 6 Hispanic/Latino; 1 Two or more races, non-Hispanic/Latino). Average age 37. In 2017, 31 master's awarded. *Degree requirements:* For master's, capstone or comprehensive assessment. *Entrance requirements:* For master's, GRE or MAT (for most programs), minimum undergraduate GPA of 3.0; baccalaureate degree in English, French, history, math or Spanish; 3 letters of recommendation; interview. Additional exam requirements/recommendations for international students: Recommended—TOEFL (minimum score 550 paper-based; 79 iBT). *Application deadline:* For fall admission, 3/1 for domestic students; for spring admission, 11/1 for domestic students. Applications are processed on a rolling basis. Application fee: $50. Electronic applications accepted. *Expenses:* Tuition, state resident: full-time $9768; part-time $407 per credit. Tuition, nonresident: full-time $19,008; part-time $792 per credit. *Required fees:* $696; $29 per credit. One-time fee: $200 full-time; $100 part-time. Tuition and fees vary according to course load. *Financial support:* In 2017–18, 3 teaching assistantships with full tuition reimbursements (averaging $2,500 per year) were awarded; career-related internships or fieldwork, Federal Work-Study, scholarships/grants, health care benefits, and unspecified assistantships also available. Support available to part-time students. Financial award application deadline: 5/15; financial award applicants required to submit FAFSA. *Unit head:* Dr. Leslie Bogad, Chair, 401-456-8170. *Application contact:* Graduate Studies, 401-456-8700.
Website: http://www.ric.edu/educationalStudies/

Rider University, College of Education and Human Services, Teacher Certification Program, Lawrenceville, NJ 08648-3001. Offers bilingual education (Certificate); business education (Certificate); early childhood education (Certificate); elementary education (Certificate); English as a second language (Certificate); English education (Certificate); mathematics education (Certificate); science education (Certificate); secondary education (Certificate); social studies education (Certificate); world languages (Certificate), including French, German, Spanish. *Program availability:* Part-time, online learning. *Degree requirements:* For Certificate, internship, professional portfolio. *Entrance requirements:* For degree, PRAXIS, resume. Additional exam requirements/recommendations for international students: Required—TOEFL (minimum score 550 paper-based). Electronic applications accepted. *Faculty research:* Conceptual

foundations for optimal development of creativity; creative theory, cognitive processes in mathematics learning, teacher collaboration.

Rivier University, School of Graduate Studies, Department of History, Law and Government, Nashua, NH 03060. Offers social studies education (MAT).

Rutgers University–New Brunswick, Graduate School of Education, Department of Educational Theory, Policy and Administration, Program in Social Studies Education, Piscataway, NJ 08854-8097. Offers Ed M, Ed D. *Program availability:* Part-time, evening/weekend. Terminal master's awarded for partial completion of doctoral program. *Degree requirements:* For master's, comprehensive exam; for doctorate, thesis/dissertation, qualifying exam. *Entrance requirements:* For master's and doctorate, GRE General Test. Additional exam requirements/recommendations for international students: Required—TOEFL. Electronic applications accepted. *Faculty research:* Academic freedom, equal educational opportunity, social studies curricula.

St. John Fisher College, Ralph C. Wilson Jr. School of Education, Program in Adolescence Education and Special Education, Rochester, NY 14618-3597. Offers adolescence education: biology with special education (MS Ed); adolescence education: chemistry with special education (MS Ed); adolescence education: English with special education (MS Ed); adolescence education: French with special education (MS Ed); adolescence education: math with special education (MS Ed); adolescence education: physics with special education (MS Ed); adolescence education: social studies with special education (MS Ed); adolescence education: Spanish with special education (MS Ed). *Program availability:* Part-time, evening/weekend. *Faculty:* 5 full-time (4 women), 7 part-time/adjunct (6 women). *Students:* 15 full-time (3 women), 4 part-time (all women); includes 4 minority (2 Black or African American, non-Hispanic/Latino; 1 Hispanic/Latino; 1 Two or more races, non-Hispanic/Latino). Average age 27. 34 applicants, 85% accepted, 12 enrolled. In 2017, 19 master's awarded. *Degree requirements:* For master's, field experiences, student teaching. *Entrance requirements:* For master's, LAST, 2 letters of recommendation, personal statement, current resume. Additional exam requirements/recommendations for international students: Required—TOEFL (minimum score 575 paper-based; 80 iBT). *Application deadline:* Applications are processed on a rolling basis. Application fee: $30. Electronic applications accepted. *Expenses:* Contact institution. *Financial support:* Scholarships/grants available. Financial award applicants required to submit FAFSA. *Faculty research:* Arts and humanities, urban schools, constructivist learning, at-risk students, mentoring. *Unit head:* Dr. Susan Hildenbrand, Program Director, 585-385-7297, E-mail: shildenbrand@sjfc.edu. *Application contact:* Michelle Gosier, Director of Transfer and Graduate Admissions, 585-385-8064, E-mail: mgosier@sjfc.edu.

Slippery Rock University of Pennsylvania, Graduate Studies (Recruitment), College of Education, Department of Secondary Education/Foundations of Education, Slippery Rock, PA 16057-1383. Offers secondary education (M Ed), including English, math/science, social studies. *Accreditation:* NCATE. *Program availability:* Part-time, evening/weekend, 100% online. *Degree requirements:* For master's, comprehensive exam, thesis (for some programs). *Entrance requirements:* For master's, copy of teaching certification and two letters of recommendation (for some programs). Additional exam requirements/recommendations for international students: Required—TOEFL (minimum score 550 paper-based; 80 iBT). Electronic applications accepted. *Expenses:* Contact institution.

Smith College, Graduate and Special Programs, Department of Education and Child Study, Program in Secondary Education, Northampton, MA 01063. Offers secondary education (MAT), including biological sciences education, chemistry education, English education, geology education, government education, history education, mathematics education, physics education. *Program availability:* Part-time. *Students:* 5 full-time (all women), 2 part-time (0 women); includes 3 minority (1 Asian, non-Hispanic/Latino; 2 Hispanic/Latino). Average age 29. 13 applicants, 92% accepted, 5 enrolled. In 2017, 5 master's awarded. *Entrance requirements:* Additional exam requirements/recommendations for international students: Required—TOEFL (minimum score 595 paper-based; 97 iBT), IELTS. *Application deadline:* For fall admission, 4/15 for domestic students, 1/15 priority date for international students; for spring admission, 12/1 for domestic students. Applications are processed on a rolling basis. Application fee: $60. *Expenses:* Contact institution. *Financial support:* In 2017–18, 5 students received support, including 3 fellowships with full tuition reimbursements available; scholarships/grants and human resources employee benefit also available. Support available to part-time students. Financial award application deadline: 4/15; financial award applicants required to submit CSS PROFILE or FAFSA. *Unit head:* Rosetta Cohen, Graduate Student Advisor, 413-585-3266, E-mail: rcohen@smith.edu. *Application contact:* Ruth Morgan, Program Assistant, 413-585-3050, Fax: 413-585-3054, E-mail: gradstdy@smith.edu.
Website: http://www.smith.edu/educ/

Smith College, Graduate and Special Programs, Department of Government, Northampton, MA 01063. Offers secondary education (MAT), including government education. *Program availability:* Part-time. *Students:* 1 (woman) full-time; minority (Hispanic/Latino). Average age 23. 1 applicant, 100% accepted, 1 enrolled. *Entrance requirements:* Additional exam requirements/recommendations for international students: Required—TOEFL (minimum score 595 paper-based; 97 iBT), IELTS. *Application deadline:* For fall admission, 4/15 for domestic students, 1/15 for international students; for spring admission, 12/1 for domestic students. Applications are processed on a rolling basis. Application fee: $60. *Expenses:* Contact institution. *Financial support:* In 2017–18, 1 student received support, including 1 fellowship with full tuition reimbursement available; scholarships/grants also available. Support available to part-time students. Financial award application deadline: 4/15; financial award applicants required to submit CSS PROFILE or FAFSA. *Unit head:* Gregory White, Department Chair, 413-585-3542, E-mail: gwhite@smith.edu. *Application contact:* Ruth Morgan, Program Assistant, 413-585-3050, Fax: 413-585-3054, E-mail: gradstdy@smith.edu.
Website: http://www.smith.edu/gov/

Smith College, Graduate and Special Programs, Department of History, Northampton, MA 01063. Offers secondary education (MAT), including history education. *Program availability:* Part-time. *Students:* 2 full-time (both women), 1 part-time (0 women); includes 1 minority (Hispanic/Latino). Average age 30. 3 applicants, 100% accepted, 1 enrolled. In 2017, 2 master's awarded. *Entrance requirements:* Additional exam requirements/recommendations for international students: Required—TOEFL (minimum score 595 paper-based; 97 iBT), IELTS. *Application deadline:* For fall admission, 4/15 for domestic students, 1/15 for international students; for spring admission, 12/1 for domestic students. Applications are processed on a rolling basis. Application fee: $60. *Expenses:* Contact institution. *Financial support:* In 2017–18, 3 students received support, including 1 fellowship with full tuition reimbursement available; scholarships/grants also available. Support available to part-time students. Financial award application deadline: 4/15; financial award applicants required to submit CSS PROFILE or FAFSA. *Unit head:* Joshua Birk, Graduate Student Adviser, 413-585-3740, E-mail: jbirk@smith.edu. *Application contact:* Ruth Morgan, Program Assistant, 413-585-3050, Fax: 413-585-3054, E-mail: gradstdy@smith.edu.
Website: http://www.smith.edu/history/

Social Sciences Education

South Carolina State University, College of Graduate and Professional Studies, Department of Education, Orangeburg, SC 29117-0001. Offers early childhood education (MAT); education (M Ed); elementary education (M Ed, MAT); English (MAT); general science/biology (MAT); mathematics (MAT); secondary education (M Ed), including biology education, business education, counselor education, English education, home economics education, industrial education, mathematics education, science education, social studies education; special education (M Ed), including emotionally handicapped, learning disabilities, mentally handicapped. *Accreditation:* NCATE. *Program availability:* Part-time, evening/weekend. *Faculty:* 11 full-time (6 women), 4 part-time/adjunct (2 women). *Students:* 26 full-time (18 women), 22 part-time (17 women); includes 41 minority (all Black or African American, non-Hispanic/Latino), 1 international. Average age 33. 25 applicants, 100% accepted, 19 enrolled. In 2017, 6 master's awarded. *Degree requirements:* For master's, thesis optional, departmental qualifying exam. *Entrance requirements:* For master's, GRE General Test, NTE, interview, teaching certificate. *Application deadline:* For fall admission, 6/15 priority date for domestic students, 6/15 for international students; for spring admission, 11/1 for domestic and international students. Application fee: $25. Electronic applications accepted. *Expenses:* Tuition, state resident: full-time $9388; part-time $607 per credit hour. Tuition, nonresident: full-time $19,968; part-time $1194 per credit hour. *Required fees:* $766; $766 per credit hour. *Financial support:* Fellowships, career-related internships or fieldwork, Federal Work-Study, and scholarships/grants available. Financial award application deadline: 6/1. *Unit head:* Dr. Charlie Spell, Interim Chair, Department of Education, 803-536-8963, Fax: 803-516-4568, E-mail: cspell@scsu.edu. *Application contact:* Curtis Foskey, Coordinator of Graduate Studies, 803-536-8419, Fax: 803-536-8812, E-mail: cfoskey@scsu.edu.

Southwestern Oklahoma State University, College of Arts and Sciences, Department of Social Sciences, Weatherford, OK 73096-3098. Offers M Ed. *Degree requirements:* For master's, exam. *Entrance requirements:* For master's, GRE General Test or minimum undergraduate GPA of 3.0. Additional exam requirements/recommendations for international students: Required—TOEFL.

State University of New York at New Paltz, Graduate and Extended Learning School, School of Education, Department of Teaching and Learning, New Paltz, NY 12561. Offers adolescence education: biology (MAT, MS Ed); adolescence education: chemistry (MAT, MS Ed); adolescence education: earth science (MAT, MS Ed); adolescence education: English (MAT, MS Ed); adolescence education: French (MAT, MS Ed); adolescence education: social studies (MAT, MS Ed); adolescence education: Spanish (MAT, MS Ed); second language education (MS Ed, AC), including second language education (MS Ed), teaching English language learners (AC). *Accreditation:* NCATE. *Program availability:* Part-time, evening/weekend. *Faculty:* 6 full-time (5 women), 10 part-time/adjunct (6 women). *Students:* 48 full-time (27 women), 54 part-time (41 women); includes 24 minority (2 Black or African American, non-Hispanic/Latino; 4 Asian, non-Hispanic/Latino; 15 Hispanic/Latino; 3 Two or more races, non-Hispanic/Latino). 33 applicants, 64% accepted, 12 enrolled. In 2017, 49 master's awarded. *Degree requirements:* For master's, comprehensive exam (for some programs), portfolio. *Entrance requirements:* For master's, minimum GPA of 3.0, New York state teaching certificate (MS Ed). Additional exam requirements/recommendations for international students: Required—TOEFL (minimum score 550 paper-based; 80 iBT), IELTS (minimum score 6.5). *Application deadline:* For fall admission, 3/1 priority date for domestic students, 3/1 for international students; for spring admission, 10/1 priority date for domestic students, 10/1 for international students. Application fee: $50. Electronic applications accepted. *Financial support:* Application deadline: 8/1. *Unit head:* Dr. Laura Dull, Chair, 845-257-2849, E-mail: dullj@newpaltz.edu. *Application contact:* Vika Shock, Director of Graduate Admissions, 845-257-3285, Fax: 845-257-3284, E-mail: gradschool@newpaltz.edu.
Website: http://www.newpaltz.edu/secondaryed/

State University of New York at Plattsburgh, School of Education, Health, and Human Services, Program in Teacher Education: Adolescence Education, Plattsburgh, NY 12901-2681. Offers adolescence education (MST); biology 7-12 (MST); chemistry 7-12 (MST); earth science 7-12 (MST); English 7-12 (MST); French 7-12 (MST); mathematics 7-12 (MST); physics 7-12 (MST); social studies 7-12 (MST). *Accreditation:* TEAC. *Program availability:* Part-time, evening/weekend. *Entrance requirements:* For master's, minimum GPA of 2.75. Additional exam requirements/recommendations for international students: Required—TOEFL.

State University of New York College at Geneseo, Graduate Studies, School of Education, Program in Adolescence Education, Geneseo, NY 14454-1401. Offers English 7-12 (MS Ed); French 7-12 (MS Ed); social studies 7-12 (MS Ed); Spanish 7-12 (MS Ed). *Program availability:* Part-time, evening/weekend. *Faculty:* 8 full-time (6 women), 1 (woman) part-time/adjunct. *Students:* 3 full-time (2 women), 2 part-time (1 woman). Average age 27. 9 applicants, 56% accepted, 3 enrolled. In 2017, 6 master's awarded. *Degree requirements:* For master's, 2 foreign languages, comprehensive examination, thesis or research project. *Entrance requirements:* For master's, GRE, MAT, EAS, edTPA, PRAXIS, or another substantially equivalent test, proof of New York State initial certification or equivalent certification from another state. Additional exam requirements/recommendations for international students: Required—TOEFL (minimum score 525 paper-based; 71 iBT), IELTS (minimum score 6.5), PTE, iTEP. *Application deadline:* For fall admission, 4/1 priority date for domestic students; for spring admission, 11/1 priority date for domestic students; for summer admission, 4/1 priority date for domestic students. Applications are processed on a rolling basis. Application fee: $50. Electronic applications accepted. *Expenses:* Contact institution. *Financial support:* In 2017–18, 3 students received support. Fellowships, research assistantships, scholarships/grants, health care benefits, tuition waivers (full and partial), and unspecified assistantships available. Support available to part-time students. Financial award application deadline: 4/1; financial award applicants required to submit FAFSA. *Unit head:* Dr. Anjoo Sikka, Dean of School of Education, 585-245-5151, Fax: 585-245-5220, E-mail: sikka@geneseo.edu. *Application contact:* Michael R. George, Director of Graduate Admissions, 585-245-5148, Fax: 585-245-5550, E-mail: georgem@geneseo.edu.

State University of New York College at Old Westbury, School of Education, Old Westbury, NY 11568-0210. Offers biology (MAT, MS); chemistry (MAT, MS); English language arts (MAT, MS); math (MAT, MS); social studies (MAT, MS); Spanish (MAT, MS). *Program availability:* Part-time, evening/weekend. *Students:* 164 full-time (80 women), 112 part-time (52 women); includes 87 minority (14 Black or African American, non-Hispanic/Latino; 38 Asian, non-Hispanic/Latino; 35 Hispanic/Latino), 2 international. Average age 30. 34 applicants, 82% accepted, 25 enrolled. In 2017, 25 master's awarded. *Entrance requirements:* For master's, Liberal Arts and Sciences Test, undergraduate degree with at least 30 semester hours of appropriate coursework as defined by the respective discipline; minimum cumulative undergraduate GPA of 3.0; two letters of recommendation (one from an academic source); essay. Additional exam requirements/recommendations for international students: Required—TOEFL (minimum score 550 paper-based); Recommended—IELTS. Application fee: $50. *Financial support:* Applicants required to submit FAFSA. *Unit head:* Dr. Nancy Brown, Dean, School of Education, 516-876-3275, E-mail: brownn@oldwestbury.edu. *Application*

contact: Philip D'Angelo, Graduate Admissions Office, 516-876-3073, E-mail: enroll@oldwestbury.edu.

State University of New York College at Potsdam, School of Education and Professional Studies, Program in Secondary Education, Potsdam, NY 13676. Offers English education (MST); mathematics education (MST); science education (MST), including biology, chemistry, earth science, physics; social studies education (MST). *Accreditation:* NCATE. *Degree requirements:* For master's, culminating experience. *Entrance requirements:* For master's, minimum GPA of 2.75 in last 60 hours of course work (3.0 for English program). Additional exam requirements/recommendations for international students: Required—TOEFL (minimum score 550 paper-based; 80 iBT), IELTS (minimum score 6). Electronic applications accepted.

Stony Brook University, State University of New York, School of Professional Development, Stony Brook, NY 11794. Offers biology (MAT); chemistry (MAT); coaching (Graduate Certificate); earth science (MAT); educational computing (Graduate Certificate); educational leadership (Advanced Certificate); English (MAT); environmental management (MPS, Graduate Certificate); French (MAT); German (MAT); higher education administration (MA, Certificate); human resource management (MS, Graduate Certificate); industrial management (Graduate Certificate); information systems management (Graduate Certificate); Italian (MAT); liberal studies (MA); mathematics (MAT); operations research (Graduate Certificate); physics (MAT); school district business leadership (Advanced Certificate); social studies (MAT); Spanish (MAT). *Program availability:* Part-time, evening/weekend, online learning. *Faculty:* 3 full-time (2 women), 101 part-time/adjunct (45 women). *Students:* 190 full-time (126 women), 974 part-time (708 women); includes 255 minority (88 Black or African American, non-Hispanic/Latino; 2 American Indian or Alaska Native, non-Hispanic/Latino; 31 Asian, non-Hispanic/Latino; 113 Hispanic/Latino; 1 Native Hawaiian or other Pacific Islander, non-Hispanic/Latino; 20 Two or more races, non-Hispanic/Latino), 6 international. Average age 33. 411 applicants, 91% accepted, 288 enrolled. In 2017, 333 master's, 180 other advanced degrees awarded. *Entrance requirements:* Additional exam requirements/recommendations for international students: Required—TOEFL (minimum score 85 iBT). *Application deadline:* For fall admission, 1/15 for domestic students, 6/1 for international students; for spring admission, 10/1 for domestic and international students. Applications are processed on a rolling basis. Application fee: $100. *Expenses:* Contact institution. *Financial support:* Fellowships, research assistantships, teaching assistantships, and career-related internships or fieldwork available. Support available to part-time students. *Unit head:* Dr. Ken Lindblom, Dean, 631-632-7049, Fax: 631-632-9046, E-mail: kenneth.lindblom@stonybrook.edu. *Application contact:* Melissa Jordan, Assistant Dean, 631-632-7751, E-mail: melissa.jordan@stonybrook.edu.
Website: http://www.stonybrook.edu/spd/

Syracuse University, School of Education, MS Program in Social Studies Education Preparation (Grades 7-12), Syracuse, NY 13244. Offers MS. *Program availability:* Part-time. *Students:* Average age 24. *Entrance requirements:* For master's, GRE, baccalaureate degree from regionally-accredited college/university, experience working with young people, personal statement, recommendations. Additional exam requirements/recommendations for international students: Required—TOEFL (minimum score 100 iBT). *Application deadline:* For fall admission, 1/15 priority date for domestic and international students; for spring admission, 10/15 priority date for domestic and international students; for summer admission, 4/15 priority date for domestic and international students. Applications are processed on a rolling basis. Application fee: $75. Electronic applications accepted. *Financial support:* Fellowships with full tuition reimbursements, research assistantships, teaching assistantships, career-related internships or fieldwork, and scholarships/grants available. Financial award application deadline: 1/15; financial award applicants required to submit FAFSA. *Faculty research:* Teaching youth with diverse backgrounds and abilities, issues in educating English language learners, social studies and democracy, assessment and data driven instruction, literacy across the curriculum. *Unit head:* Dr. Jeffery Mangram, Program Coordinator/Associate Professor, 315-443-3293, E-mail: jamangra@syr.edu. *Application contact:* Speranza Migliore, Graduate Admissions Recruiter, 315-443-2505, E-mail: gradrcrt@syr.edu.
Website: http://soe.syr.edu/academic/teaching_and_leadership/graduate/masters/social_studies/default.aspx

Teachers College, Columbia University, Department of Arts and Humanities, New York, NY 10027. Offers applied linguistics (MA, Ed D); art and art education (Ed M, MA, Ed D, Ed DCT); arts administration (MA); bilingual and bicultural education (MA); global competence (Certificate); history and education (Ed D, PhD); music and music education (Ed DCT); philosophy and education (MA, Ed D, PhD); social studies education (Ed M, PhD); teaching English to speakers of other languages (Ed M); teaching of English and English education (Ed M, MA, Ed D, PhD), including English education (Ed M, Ed D, PhD), teaching of English (MA); teaching of social studies (MA); TESOL (MA, Ed D). *Program availability:* Part-time, evening/weekend. *Students:* 391 full-time (305 women), 418 part-time (283 women); includes 246 minority (62 Black or African American, non-Hispanic/Latino; 3 American Indian or Alaska Native, non-Hispanic/Latino; 94 Asian, non-Hispanic/Latino; 75 Hispanic/Latino; 12 Two or more races, non-Hispanic/Latino), 209 international. Average age 30. 1,053 applicants, 60% accepted, 334 enrolled. Terminal master's awarded for partial completion of doctoral program. *Financial support:* Fellowships, research assistantships, teaching assistantships, career-related internships or fieldwork, Federal Work-Study, institutionally sponsored loans, tuition waivers (full and partial), and unspecified assistantships available. Support available to part-time students. *Unit head:* Prof. William Gaudelli, Department Chair, E-mail: gaudelli@tc.columbia.edu. *Application contact:* David Estrella, Director of Admissions, 212-678-3305, Fax: 212-678-4171, E-mail: estrella@tc.columbia.edu.

Temple University, College of Education, Department of Teaching and Learning, Philadelphia, PA 19122-6096. Offers career and technical education (Ed M), including business, computing, and information technology, industrial education, marketing education; middle grades education (Ed M), including math and language arts, math and science, science and language arts; secondary education (Ed M), including English, math, social studies; teaching English to speakers of other languages (MS Ed); urban education (Ed M). *Program availability:* Part-time, evening/weekend. *Students:* 218 full-time (144 women), 296 part-time (183 women); includes 128 minority (74 Black or African American, non-Hispanic/Latino; 18 Asian, non-Hispanic/Latino; 25 Hispanic/Latino; 11 Two or more races, non-Hispanic/Latino), 13 international. 254 applicants, 54% accepted, 102 enrolled. In 2017, 128 master's awarded. Terminal master's awarded for partial completion of doctoral program. *Degree requirements:* For master's, thesis or alternative. *Entrance requirements:* Additional exam requirements/recommendations for international students: Required—TOEFL (minimum score 550 paper-based; 79 iBT). *Application deadline:* For fall admission, 4/1 for domestic students, 12/15 for international students; for spring admission, 10/1 for domestic students, 8/1 for international students. Application fee: $60. Electronic applications accepted. *Expenses:* Contact institution. *Financial support:* Fellowships, research assistantships, and teaching assistantships available. Financial award application deadline: 1/15; financial award applicants required to submit FAFSA. *Faculty research:*

Workforce development, vocational education, technical education, industrial education, professional development, literacy, classroom management, school communities, curriculum development, instruction, applied linguistics, cross linguistic influence, bilingual education, oral proficiency, multilingualism. *Unit head:* Dr. Christine Woyshner, Chairperson, 215-204-6387, E-mail: christine.woyshner@temple.edu. *Application contact:* Sarah Stapleton, Assistant Director, Academic Operations, 215-204-8220, E-mail: sarah.stapleton@temple.edu.
Website: http://education.temple.edu/tl

Texas Tech University, Graduate School, Interdisciplinary Programs, Lubbock, TX 79409. Offers arid land studies (MS); biotechnology (MS); heritage and museum sciences (MA); interdisciplinary studies (MA, MS); wind science and engineering (PhD); JD/MS. *Program availability:* Part-time, blended/hybrid learning. *Faculty:* 11 full-time (5 women). *Students:* 106 full-time (56 women), 85 part-time (52 women); includes 65 minority (23 Black or African American, non-Hispanic/Latino; 2 American Indian or Alaska Native, non-Hispanic/Latino; 3 Asian, non-Hispanic/Latino; 32 Hispanic/Latino; 5 Two or more races, non-Hispanic/Latino), 30 international. Average age 30. 116 applicants, 67% accepted, 55 enrolled. In 2017, 52 master's, 1 doctorate awarded. Terminal master's awarded for partial completion of doctoral program. *Degree requirements:* For master's, comprehensive exam (for some programs), thesis (for some programs); for doctorate, comprehensive exam, thesis/dissertation (for some programs). *Entrance requirements:* Additional exam requirements/recommendations for international students: Required—TOEFL (minimum score 550 paper-based; 79 iBT), IELTS (minimum score 6.5), PTE (minimum score 60), Cambridge advanced (B), Cambridge Proficiency (C), ELS English for Academic Purposes (Level 112). *Application deadline:* For fall admission, 6/1 priority date for domestic students, 1/15 priority date for international students; for spring admission, 9/1 priority date for domestic students, 6/15 priority date for international students. Applications are processed on a rolling basis. Application fee: $60. Electronic applications accepted. *Expenses:* Tuition, state resident: full-time $7632; part-time $318 per credit hour. Tuition, nonresident: full-time $17,424; part-time $726 per credit hour. *Required fees:* $2428; $50.50 per credit hour. $608 per semester. Tuition and fees vary according to program. *Financial support:* In 2017–18, 124 students received support, including 106 fellowships (averaging $4,660 per year), 25 research assistantships (averaging $16,239 per year), 16 teaching assistantships (averaging $10,391 per year); scholarships/grants and unspecified assistantships also available. Financial award application deadline: 4/15; financial award applicants required to submit FAFSA. *Total annual research expenditures:* $2.2 million. *Unit head:* Dr. Mark Sheridan, Vice Provost for Graduate and Postdoctoral Affairs/Dean of the Graduate School, 806-742-2787, Fax: 806-742-1746, E-mail: mark.sheridan@ttu.edu. *Application contact:* Claudia Simon, Senior Academic Advisor, 806-834-8290, Fax: 806-742-4038, E-mail: claudia.simon@ttu.edu.
Website: http://www.depts.ttu.edu/gradschool/

Trinity Washington University, School of Education, Washington, DC 20017-1094. Offers clinical mental health counseling (MA); early childhood education (MAT); educating for change (M Ed); educational administration (MSA); elementary education (MAT); reading (M Ed); school counseling (MA); secondary education (MAT), including English, social studies, special education (MAT). *Accreditation:* NCATE. *Program availability:* Part-time, evening/weekend. *Degree requirements:* For master's, thesis (for some programs), capstone project(s). *Entrance requirements:* For master's, PRAXIS I, minimum GPA of 2.8. Additional exam requirements/recommendations for international students: Required—TOEFL (minimum score 550 paper-based). *Faculty research:* Technology, literacy, special education, organizations, inclusion models.

University at Buffalo, the State University of New York, Graduate School, Graduate School of Education, Department of Learning and Instruction, Buffalo, NY 14260. Offers biology education (Ed M, Certificate); chemistry education (Ed M, Certificate); childhood education (Ed M); childhood education with bilingual extension (Ed M); college teaching (Advanced Certificate); curriculum, instruction and the science of learning (PhD); early childhood education (Ed M); early childhood education with bilingual extension (Ed M); earth science education (Ed M, Certificate); education and technology (Ed M); education studies (Ed M); educational technology and new literacies (Certificate); educational technology and new literacies (Advanced Certificate); elementary education (Ed D); English education (Ed M, Certificate); English education studies (Ed M); English for speakers of other languages (Ed M); foreign and second language education (PhD); French education (Ed M, Certificate); German education (Ed M, Certificate); gifted education (Certificate); Latin education (Ed M, Certificate); literacy education studies (Ed M); literacy specialist (Ed M); literacy teaching and learning (Certificate); mathematics education (Ed M, Certificate); music education (Ed M, Certificate); music education studies (Ed M); music learning theory (Advanced Certificate); online education (Advanced Certificate); physics education (Ed M, Certificate); science and the public (Ed M); social studies education (Ed M, Certificate); Spanish education (Ed M, Certificate); special education (PhD); teaching English to speakers of other languages (Ed M). *Program availability:* Part-time, evening/weekend, 100% online. *Faculty:* 26 full-time (19 women), 74 part-time/adjunct (52 women). *Students:* 172 full-time (122 women), 325 part-time (226 women); includes 44 minority (25 Black or African American, non-Hispanic/Latino; 5 American Indian or Alaska Native, non-Hispanic/Latino; 14 Asian, non-Hispanic/Latino), 57 international. Average age 33. 316 applicants, 78% accepted, 174 enrolled. In 2017, 109 master's, 34 doctorates, 15 other advanced degrees awarded. *Degree requirements:* For master's, comprehensive exam; for doctorate, thesis/dissertation, research analysis exam, research experience. *Entrance requirements:* For master's, letters of reference; for doctorate, GRE General Test or MAT, interview, writing sample, letters of recommendation. Additional exam requirements/recommendations for international students: Required—TOEFL (minimum score 600 paper-based; 96 iBT). *Application deadline:* For fall admission, 2/1 priority date for domestic and international students; for spring admission, 11/15 priority date for domestic students, 10/1 for international students. Applications are processed on a rolling basis. Application fee: $50. Electronic applications accepted. *Financial support:* In 2017–18, 42 fellowships (averaging $5,181 per year), 44 research assistantships with tuition reimbursements (averaging $10,908 per year) were awarded; teaching assistantships, career-related internships or fieldwork, Federal Work-Study, institutionally sponsored loans, scholarships/grants, tuition waivers (full and partial), and unspecified assistantships also available. Financial award application deadline: 2/28; financial award applicants required to submit FAFSA. *Faculty research:* Science assessment, foreign language teaching and learning, early learning, new literacies, gender and education. *Total annual research expenditures:* $413,233. *Unit head:* Dr. David Bruce, Chair, 716-645-4069, Fax: 716-645-3161, E-mail: gse-info@buffalo.edu. *Application contact:* Luann Zak, Admissions Assistant, 716-645-2110, Fax: 716-645-7937, E-mail: luannzak@buffalo.edu.
Website: http://gse.buffalo.edu/lai

The University of Akron, Graduate School, College of Education, Department of Curricular and Instructional Studies, Program in Adolescent to Young Adult Education, Akron, OH 44325. Offers chemistry (MS); chemistry and physics (MS); earth science (MS); earth science and chemistry (MS); earth science and physics (MS); integrated language arts (MS); integrated mathematics (MS); integrated social studies (MS); life science (MS); life science and chemistry (MS); life science and earth science (MS); life science and physics (MS); physics (MS). *Accreditation:* NCATE. *Students:* 16 full-time (6 women), 6 part-time (3 women); includes 6 minority (2 Black or African American, non-Hispanic/Latino; 1 Asian, non-Hispanic/Latino; 3 Two or more races, non-Hispanic/Latino). Average age 30. 8 applicants, 100% accepted, 8 enrolled. In 2017, 8 master's awarded. *Degree requirements:* For master's, comprehensive exam. *Entrance requirements:* For master's, minimum GPA of 3.0. Additional exam requirements/recommendations for international students: Required—TOEFL (minimum score 79 iBT), IELTS (minimum score 6.5). *Application deadline:* For fall admission, 3/1 for domestic and international students; for spring admission, 10/1 for domestic and international students. Applications are processed on a rolling basis. Application fee: $45 ($70 for international students). Electronic applications accepted. *Unit head:* Dr. Evonn Welton, Interim Department Chair, 330-972-6742, E-mail: ewelton@uakron.edu. *Application contact:* Kelly Chaff, College Program Specialist, 330-972-7028, E-mail: klchaff@uakron.edu.
Website: http://www.uakron.edu/education/academic-programs/graduate-programs.dot

The University of Alabama in Huntsville, School of Graduate Studies, College of Education, Huntsville, AL 35899. Offers autism spectrum disorders (M Ed, Graduate Certificate); biology (MAT); chemistry (MAT); differentiated instruction in elementary education (M Ed); English language arts (MAT); English speakers of other languages (M Ed, MAT); history (MAT); mathematics (MAT); physics (MAT); reading education (M Ed); secondary education (M Ed).

University of Arkansas at Pine Bluff, School of Education, Pine Bluff, AR 71601-2799. Offers elementary education (M Ed); secondary education (M Ed), including English education, mathematics education, science education, social studies education; teaching (MAT). *Accreditation:* NCATE. *Program availability:* Part-time, evening/weekend. *Degree requirements:* For master's, comprehensive exam. *Entrance requirements:* For master's, GRE, minimum GPA of 2.75, NTE or Standard Arkansas Teaching Certificate. *Faculty research:* Teacher certification, accreditation, assessment, standards, portfolio development, rehabilitation, technology.

The University of British Columbia, Faculty of Education, Department of Curriculum and Pedagogy, Vancouver, BC V6T 1Z4, Canada. Offers art education (M Ed, MA); curriculum studies (M Ed, MA, PhD); home economics education (M Ed, MA); mathematics education (M Ed, MA); media and technology studies education (M Ed, MA); music education (M Ed, MA); physical education (M Ed, MA); science education (M Ed, MA); social studies education (M Ed, MA). *Program availability:* Part-time, online learning. *Degree requirements:* For master's, thesis (MA); for doctorate, comprehensive exam, thesis/dissertation. *Entrance requirements:* Additional exam requirements/recommendations for international students: Required—TOEFL, IELTS. Electronic applications accepted. *Expenses:* Contact institution. *Faculty research:* School subjects, teaching and learning.

University of California, Santa Cruz, Division of Graduate Studies, Division of Social Sciences, Program in Social Documentation, Santa Cruz, CA 95064. Offers MA. *Entrance requirements:* For master's, resume or curriculum vitae, sample of documentary production work. Additional exam requirements/recommendations for international students: Required—TOEFL (minimum score 550 paper-based; 83 iBT); Recommended—IELTS (minimum score 8). Electronic applications accepted. *Faculty research:* Documentation of underrepresented areas of community life.

University of Central Florida, College of Community Innovation and Education, Education Doctoral Programs, Orlando, FL 32816. Offers curriculum and instruction (Ed D); education (PhD), including communication sciences and disorders, counselor education, early childhood education, elementary education, exceptional education, exercise physiology, higher education, instructional design and technology, mathematics education, methodology, measurement and analysis, reading education, science education, social science education, TESOL; educational leadership (Ed D). *Students:* 122 full-time (86 women), 129 part-time (88 women); includes 64 minority (24 Black or African American, non-Hispanic/Latino; 1 American Indian or Alaska Native, non-Hispanic/Latino; 9 Asian, non-Hispanic/Latino; 24 Hispanic/Latino; 6 Two or more races, non-Hispanic/Latino), 26 international. Average age 38. 195 applicants, 47% accepted, 72 enrolled. In 2017, 89 doctorates awarded. *Entrance requirements:* For doctorate, GRE, letters of recommendation, goal statement, resume, writing sample. Application fee: $30. Electronic applications accepted. *Expenses:* Tuition, state resident: part-time $288.16 per credit hour. Tuition, nonresident: part-time $1073.31 per credit hour. Tuition and fees vary according to program. *Financial support:* In 2017–18, 77 students received support, including 28 fellowships with partial tuition reimbursements available (averaging $5,733 per year), 29 research assistantships with partial tuition reimbursements available (averaging $10,230 per year), 54 teaching assistantships with partial tuition reimbursements available (averaging $11,614 per year); health care benefits also available. Financial award application deadline: 3/1; financial award applicants required to submit FAFSA. *Unit head:* Dr. Edward Robinson, Director of Doctoral Programs, 407-823-6106, E-mail: edward.robinson@ucf.edu. *Application contact:* Associate Director, Graduate Admissions, 407-823-2766, Fax: 407-823-6442, E-mail: gradadmissions@ucf.edu.
Website: https://edcollege.ucf.edu/academic-programs/graduate/

University of Central Florida, College of Community Innovation and Education, School of Teacher Education, Program in Teacher Education, Orlando, FL 32816. Offers art education (MAT); English language (MAT); mathematics education (MAT); middle school mathematics (MAT); middle school science (MAT); science education (MAT), including biology, chemistry, physics; social science education (MAT). *Accreditation:* NCATE. *Program availability:* Part-time, evening/weekend. *Students:* 11 full-time (9 women), 28 part-time (23 women); includes 15 minority (5 Black or African American, non-Hispanic/Latino; 2 Asian, non-Hispanic/Latino; 6 Hispanic/Latino; 2 Two or more races, non-Hispanic/Latino), 2 international. Average age 29. In 2017, 6 master's awarded. *Degree requirements:* For master's, thesis or alternative. *Entrance requirements:* For master's, Florida Teacher Certification Examination/General Knowledge Test or GRE General Test. Additional exam requirements/recommendations for international students: Required—TOEFL. *Application deadline:* For spring admission, 12/1 for domestic students; for summer admission, 4/15 for domestic students. Application fee: $30. Electronic applications accepted. *Expenses:* Tuition, state resident: part-time $288.16 per credit hour. Tuition, nonresident: part-time $1073.31 per credit hour. Tuition and fees vary according to program. *Financial support:* Fellowships, research assistantships, teaching assistantships, career-related internships or fieldwork, Federal Work-Study, institutionally sponsored loans, tuition waivers (partial), and unspecified assistantships available. Financial award application deadline: 3/1; financial award applicants required to submit FAFSA. *Unit head:* Dr. Michael Hynes, Director, 407-823-2005, E-mail: mychael.hynes@ucf.edu. *Application contact:* Associate Director, Graduate Admissions, 407-823-2766, Fax: 407-823-6442, E-mail: gradadmissions@ucf.edu.
Website: http://www.graduatecatalog.ucf.edu/programs/program.aspx?id=9727&program=Teacher%20Education%20MAT

University of Connecticut, Graduate School, Neag School of Education, Department of Curriculum and Instruction, Program in History and Social Sciences Education, Storrs, CT 06269. Offers MA, PhD. *Accreditation:* NCATE. Terminal master's awarded for partial completion of doctoral program. *Degree requirements:* For master's, comprehensive exam, thesis or alternative; for doctorate, thesis/dissertation. *Entrance* *requirements:* For doctorate, GRE General Test. Additional exam requirements/recommendations for international students: Required—TOEFL (minimum score 550 paper-based). Electronic applications accepted.

University of Florida, Graduate School, College of Education, School of Teaching and Learning, Gainesville, FL 32611. Offers curriculum and instruction (M Ed, MAE, Ed D, PhD, Ed S); elementary education (M Ed, MAE); English education (M Ed, MAE); mathematics education (M Ed, MAE); reading education (M Ed, MAE); science education (M Ed, MAE); social studies education (M Ed, MAE). *Accreditation:* NCATE. *Program availability:* Part-time, evening/weekend, online learning. Terminal master's awarded for partial completion of doctoral program. *Degree requirements:* For master's, comprehensive exam (for some programs), thesis (for some programs); for doctorate, comprehensive exam (for some programs), thesis/dissertation (for some programs). *Entrance requirements:* For master's and doctorate, GRE General Test, minimum GPA of 3.0; for Ed S, GRE General Test. Additional exam requirements/recommendations for international students: Required—TOEFL (minimum score 550 paper-based; 80 iBT), IELTS (minimum score 6). Electronic applications accepted. *Faculty research:* STEM education; curriculum; teaching and teacher education; languages and literacy; schools, culture, and society; theories and processes of learning.

University of Illinois at Chicago, Program in Learning Sciences, Chicago, IL 60607-7128. Offers PhD.

University of Indianapolis, Graduate Programs, School of Education, Indianapolis, IN 46227-3697. Offers art education (MAT); biology (MAT); chemistry (MAT); curriculum and instruction (MA); earth sciences (MAT); education (MA, MAT); educational leadership (MA); elementary education (MA); English (MAT); French (MAT); math (MAT); physical education (MAT); physics (MAT); secondary education (MA), including art education, education, English education, social studies education; social studies (MAT); Spanish (MAT). *Accreditation:* NCATE. *Program availability:* Part-time, evening/weekend. *Entrance requirements:* For master's, GRE Subject Test, PRAXIS I, minimum GPA of 2.5, 3 letters of recommendation, interview. Additional exam requirements/recommendations for international students: Required—TOEFL (minimum score 550 paper-based). *Faculty research:* Assessment of teacher education, perceptions of prospective teachers by parents.

The University of Iowa, Graduate College, College of Education, Department of Teaching and Learning, Program in Education, Iowa City, IA 52242-1316. Offers art education (MA); developmental reading (MA); elementary education (MA); English education (MA, MAT); foreign and second language education (MAT); foreign language education (MA); foreign language/ESL education (PhD); language, literacy and culture (PhD); mathematics education (MA, MAT, PhD); music education (MM, PhD); science education (MA); secondary education (MA); social studies (MA, PhD). *Degree requirements:* For master's, thesis optional, exam; for doctorate, comprehensive exam, thesis/dissertation. *Entrance requirements:* For master's and doctorate, GRE General Test, minimum GPA of 3.0. Additional exam requirements/recommendations for international students: Required—TOEFL (minimum score 550 paper-based; 81 iBT). Electronic applications accepted.

University of Maine, Graduate School, College of Education and Human Development, School of Learning and Teaching, Orono, ME 04469. Offers counselor education (M Ed, MA, MS, CAS); early childhood teacher (CGS); education (PhD), including counselor education, literacy education, prevention and intervention studies; elementary education (M Ed, CAS); individualized education (M Ed); literacy education (CAS); response to intervention for behavior (CGS); secondary education (M Ed, CAS); social studies education (M Ed); special education (M Ed, CAS). *Program availability:* Part-time. *Faculty:* 21 full-time (12 women), 37 part-time/adjunct (29 women). *Students:* 84 full-time (73 women), 190 part-time (165 women); includes 19 minority (1 Black or African American, non-Hispanic/Latino; 9 American Indian or Alaska Native, non-Hispanic/Latino; 2 Asian, non-Hispanic/Latino; 4 Hispanic/Latino; 3 Two or more races, non-Hispanic/Latino; 4 international. Average age 38. 141 applicants, 94% accepted, 91 enrolled. In 2017, 74 master's, 3 doctorates, 36 other advanced degrees awarded. *Degree requirements:* For master's, thesis (for some programs); for doctorate, comprehensive exam, thesis/dissertation. *Entrance requirements:* For master's, GRE General Test, MAT. Additional exam requirements/recommendations for international students: Required—TOEFL (minimum score 550 paper-based; 80 iBT), IELTS (minimum score 6.5). *Application deadline:* For fall admission, 2/1 priority date for domestic students. Applications are processed on a rolling basis. Application fee: $65. Electronic applications accepted. *Expenses:* Tuition, state resident: full-time $7722; part-time $429 per credit hour. Tuition, nonresident: full-time $25,146; part-time $1397 per credit hour. *Required fees:* $1162; $581 per credit hour. *Financial support:* In 2017–18, 14 students received support, including 11 teaching assistantships (averaging $15,200 per year); Federal Work-Study, scholarships/grants, and unspecified assistantships also available. Financial award application deadline: 3/1. *Faculty research:* Gender and leadership, virtual reality, using writing to improve performance in athletics, digital citizenship, professional development for special and general education. *Total annual research expenditures:* $5 million. *Unit head:* Dr. Jim Artesani, Associate Dean of Accreditation and Graduate Affairs, 207-581-4061. *Application contact:* Scott G. Delcourt, Assistant Vice President for Graduate Studies and Senior Associate Dean, 207-581-3291, Fax: 207-581-3232, E-mail: graduate@maine.edu. Website: http://umaine.edu/edhd/

University of Maryland, Baltimore County, The Graduate School, College of Arts, Humanities and Social Sciences, Department of Education, Program in Teaching, Baltimore, MD 21250. Offers early childhood education (MAT); elementary education (MAT); teaching (MAT), including art, biology, chemistry, choral music, classical foreign language, dance, earth/space science, English, instrumental music, mathematics, modern foreign language, physical science, physics, social studies, theatre. *Program availability:* Part-time, evening/weekend. *Faculty:* 24 full-time (18 women), 25 part-time/adjunct (19 women). *Students:* 41 full-time (34 women), 27 part-time (18 women); includes 26 minority (6 Black or African American, non-Hispanic/Latino; 9 Asian, non-Hispanic/Latino; 7 Hispanic/Latino; 1 Native Hawaiian or other Pacific Islander, non-Hispanic/Latino; 3 Two or more races, non-Hispanic/Latino), 2 international. Average age 30. 54 applicants, 83% accepted, 35 enrolled. In 2017, 50 master's awarded. *Degree requirements:* For master's, comprehensive exam (for some programs), thesis (for some programs). *Entrance requirements:* For master's, PRAXIS Core Examination or GRE (minimum score of 1000), minimum GPA of 3.0. Additional exam requirements/recommendations for international students: Required—TOEFL. *Application deadline:* For fall admission, 6/1 for domestic and international students; for spring admission, 11/1 for domestic and international students. Applications are processed on a rolling basis. Application fee: $50. Electronic applications accepted. *Expenses: Required fees:* $132. *Financial support:* In 2017–18, 8 students received support, including teaching assistantships with tuition reimbursements available (averaging $12,000 per year); career-related internships or fieldwork, Federal Work-Study, scholarships/grants, tuition waivers, and unspecified assistantships also available. Financial award application deadline: 3/15. *Faculty research:* STEM teacher education, culturally sensitive pedagogy, ESOL/bilingual education, early childhood education, language, literacy and culture. *Total annual research expenditures:* $100,000. *Unit head:* Dr. Susan M. Blunck, Graduate Program Director, 410-455-2869, Fax: 410-455-3986, E-mail: blunck@

umbc.edu. *Application contact:* Cheryl Johnson, MAT Program Specialist, 410-455-3388, E-mail: blackwel@umbc.edu.
Website: http://www.umbc.edu/education/

University of Minnesota, Twin Cities Campus, Graduate School, College of Education and Human Development, Department of Curriculum and Instruction, Program in Teaching, Minneapolis, MN 55455-0213. Offers teaching (M Ed), including arts in education, elementary education, English education, mathematics, science, second language education, social studies. *Students:* 251 full-time (180 women), 136 part-time (82 women); includes 68 Black or African American, non-Hispanic/Latino; 15 Asian, non-Hispanic/Latino; 17 Hispanic/Latino; 20 Two or more races, non-Hispanic/Latino), 9 international. Average age 28. 341 applicants, 72% accepted, 229 enrolled. In 2017, 263 master's awarded. Application fee: $75 ($95 for international students). *Unit head:* Dr. Cynthia Lewis, Chair, 612-625-6313, Fax: 612-624-8277, E-mail: lewis@umn.edu. *Application contact:* Dr. Kendall King, Director of Graduate Studies, 612-625-3692, E-mail: roehr013@umn.edu.
Website: http://www.cehd.umn.edu/ci/

University of Missouri, Office of Research and Graduate Studies, College of Education, Department of Learning, Teaching and Curriculum, Columbia, MO 65211. Offers agricultural education (M Ed, PhD, Ed S); art education (M Ed, PhD, Ed S); business and office education (M Ed, PhD, Ed S); early childhood education (M Ed, PhD, Ed S); elementary education (M Ed, PhD, Ed S); English education (M Ed, PhD, Ed S); foreign language education (M Ed, PhD, Ed S); health education and promotion (M Ed, PhD); learning and instruction (M Ed); marketing education (M Ed, PhD, Ed S); mathematics education (M Ed, PhD, Ed S); music education (M Ed, PhD, Ed S); reading education (M Ed, PhD, Ed S); science education (M Ed, PhD, Ed S); social studies education (M Ed, PhD, Ed S); vocational education (M Ed, PhD, Ed S). *Program availability:* Part-time. Terminal master's awarded for partial completion of doctoral program. *Degree requirements:* For doctorate, thesis/dissertation. *Entrance requirements:* For master's and Ed S, GRE General Test or MAT, minimum GPA of 3.0; for doctorate, GRE General Test, minimum GPA of 3.0. Additional exam requirements/recommendations for international students: Required—TOEFL (minimum score 600 paper-based; 100 iBT). Electronic applications accepted.

University of Missouri–St. Louis, College of Arts and Sciences, Department of History, St. Louis, MO 63121. Offers history (MA); history education (Certificate); museum studies (MA, Certificate). *Program availability:* Part-time, evening/weekend. *Faculty:* 12 full-time (4 women), 8 part-time/adjunct (0 women). *Students:* 15 full-time (11 women), 31 part-time (13 women); includes 6 minority (2 Black or African American, non-Hispanic/Latino; 1 American Indian or Alaska Native, non-Hispanic/Latino; 3 Asian, non-Hispanic/Latino). 19 applicants, 89% accepted, 12 enrolled. *Degree requirements:* For master's, thesis (for some programs). *Entrance requirements:* For master's, writing sample; minimum GPA of 2.75 (for history), 3.2 (for museum studies). Additional exam requirements/recommendations for international students: Required—TOEFL (minimum score 550 paper-based; 79 iBT), IELTS (minimum score 6.5). *Application deadline:* For fall admission, 3/15 for domestic and international students; for spring admission, 10/15 for domestic and international students. Applications are processed on a rolling basis. Application fee: $50 ($40 for international students). Electronic applications accepted. *Expenses:* Tuition, state resident: part-time $476.50 per credit hour. Tuition, nonresident: part-time $1169.70 per credit hour. *Financial support:* Research assistantships with tuition reimbursements, teaching assistantships with tuition reimbursements, and career-related internships or fieldwork available. Financial award applicants required to submit FAFSA. *Faculty research:* United States, European, East Asian, Latin American, and African history. *Unit head:* Dr. Laura Westhoff, Chair, 314-516-5692, Fax: 314-516-5781, E-mail: westhoffl@msx.umsl.edu. *Application contact:* 314-516-5458, Fax: 314-516-6996, E-mail: gradadm@umsl.edu.
Website: http://www.umsl.edu/~umslhistory/

The University of North Carolina at Chapel Hill, Graduate School, School of Education, Program in Secondary Education, Chapel Hill, NC 27599. Offers English (Grades 9-12) (MAT); English as a second language (MAT); French (Grades K-12) (MAT); German (Grades K-12) (MAT); Japanese (Grades K-12) (MAT); Latin (Grades 9-12) (MAT); mathematics (Grades 9-12) (MAT); music (Grades K-12) (MAT); science (Grades 9-12) (MAT); social studies (Grades 9-12) (MAT); Spanish (Grades K-12) (MAT). *Accreditation:* NCATE. *Degree requirements:* For master's, comprehensive exam. *Entrance requirements:* For master's, GRE General Test, minimum GPA of 3.0 during last 2 years of undergraduate course work. Additional exam requirements/recommendations for international students: Required—TOEFL (minimum score 550 paper-based). Electronic applications accepted.

The University of North Carolina at Greensboro, Graduate School, School of Education, Department of Teacher Education and Higher Education, Greensboro, NC 27412-5001. Offers college teaching and adult learning (Certificate); curriculum and instruction (M Ed), including chemistry education, elementary education, English as a second language, French education, instructional technology, mathematics education, middle grades education, reading education, science education, social studies education, Spanish education; curriculum and teaching (PhD), including higher education, teacher education and development; English as a second language (Certificate); higher education (M Ed); supervision (M Ed). *Accreditation:* NCATE. *Program availability:* Part-time. *Degree requirements:* For doctorate, thesis/dissertation. *Entrance requirements:* For master's and doctorate, GRE General Test. Additional exam requirements/recommendations for international students: Required—TOEFL. Electronic applications accepted. *Faculty research:* Community college literacy program, middle school mathematics/computer mathematics.

The University of North Carolina at Pembroke, The Graduate School, Department of History, Pembroke, NC 28372-1510. Offers social studies education (MA, MAT). *Program availability:* Part-time, evening/weekend. *Entrance requirements:* For master's, GRE General Test or MAT, minimum GPA of 3.0 in major, 2.5 overall. Additional exam requirements/recommendations for international students: Required—TOEFL. *Application deadline:* For fall admission, 7/15 priority date for domestic and international students; for spring admission, 12/1 priority date for domestic and international students. Applications are processed on a rolling basis. Application fee: $45 ($60 for international students). *Financial support:* Application deadline: 4/15; applicants required to submit FAFSA. *Unit head:* Dr. Serina Cinnamon, Program Director, 618-713-4310, E-mail: serina.cinnamon@uncp.edu. *Application contact:* Dr. Scott C. Billingsley, Associate Provost, 910-521-6807, Fax: 910-775-4026, E-mail: scott.billingsley@uncp.edu.
Website: http://www.uncp.edu/history/

University of North Georgia, Master of Arts in Teaching Program, Dahlonega, GA 30597. Offers physical education (MAT); secondary education - English (MAT); secondary education - history (MAT); secondary education - mathematics (MAT); secondary education - middle grades (MAT). *Students:* 27 part-time (20 women). Average age 29. 12 applicants, 75% accepted, 7 enrolled. In 2017, 15 master's awarded. *Degree requirements:* For master's, internship, capstone. *Entrance requirements:* For master's, GRE or MAT, GACE I and II, GA pre-service application, lawful presence verification, official transcripts, GA Educator Ethics Program entry assessment. Additional exam requirements/recommendations for international students: Required—TOEFL (minimum score 550 paper-based; 79 iBT), IELTS (minimum score

6.5). *Application deadline:* For summer admission, 2/1 for domestic students. Application fee: $40. Electronic applications accepted. *Expenses:* Contact institution. *Financial support:* Application deadline: 3/17; applicants required to submit FAFSA. *Unit head:* Dr. Susan Brandenburg-Ayres, Dean, 706-864-1998, E-mail: susan.ayres@ung.edu. *Application contact:* Melinda Maxwell, Director of Graduate Admissions, 706-867-2077, E-mail: melinda.maxwell@ung.edu.
Website: https://ung.edu/teacher-education/graduate/master-of-arts-teaching.php

University of Oklahoma, Jeannine Rainbolt College of Education, Department of Instructional Leadership and Academic Curriculum, Norman, OK 73019. Offers instructional leadership and academic curriculum (M Ed, PhD), including biomedical education (PhD), early childhood education, elementary education, English education, instructional leadership, mathematics education, reading education, science education, social studies education, world languages education (M Ed); reading specialist (M Ed). *Accreditation:* NCATE. *Program availability:* Part-time. *Faculty:* 19 full-time (15 women), 1 (woman) part-time/adjunct. *Students:* 37 full-time (28 women), 121 part-time (98 women); includes 32 minority (7 Black or African American, non-Hispanic/Latino; 4 American Indian or Alaska Native, non-Hispanic/Latino; 5 Asian, non-Hispanic/Latino; 6 Hispanic/Latino; 1 Native Hawaiian or other Pacific Islander, non-Hispanic/Latino; 9 Two or more races, non-Hispanic/Latino), 12 international. Average age 35. 39 applicants, 77% accepted, 22 enrolled. In 2017, 49 master's, 12 doctorates awarded. Terminal master's awarded for partial completion of doctoral program. *Degree requirements:* For master's, comprehensive exam (for some programs), thesis (for some programs); for doctorate, comprehensive exam (for some programs), thesis/dissertation. *Entrance requirements:* For doctorate, GRE. Additional exam requirements/recommendations for international students: Required—TOEFL (minimum score 79 iBT) or IELTS (minimum score 6.5). Application fee: $50 ($100 for international students). Electronic applications accepted. *Expenses:* Tuition, state resident: full-time $5119; part-time $213.30 per credit hour. Tuition, nonresident: full-time $19,778; part-time $824.10 per credit hour. *Required fees:* $3458; $133.55 per credit hour. $126.50 per semester. *Financial support:* In 2017–18, 90 students received support, including 8 research assistantships (averaging $11,248 per year), 6 teaching assistantships (averaging $12,188 per year); fellowships, scholarships/grants, and unspecified assistantships also available. Financial award application deadline: 6/1; financial award applicants required to submit FAFSA. *Faculty research:* Teacher preparation; instruction; curriculum; learning; constructivist theory. *Total annual research expenditures:* $707,690. *Unit head:* Dr. Stacy Reeder, Chair, 405-325-1498, Fax: 405-325-4061, E-mail: reeder@ou.edu. *Application contact:* Anna Steele, Graduate Programs Officer, 405-325-4525, E-mail: anna.steele@ou.edu.
Website: http://www.ou.edu/education/ilac

University of Pittsburgh, School of Education, Department of Instruction and Learning, Program in Secondary Education, Pittsburgh, PA 15260. Offers English and communications education (M Ed, MAT); foreign language education (M Ed, MAT); language, literacy and culture education (Ed D, PhD); mathematics education (M Ed, MAT, Ed D, PhD); science education (M Ed, MAT, Ed D, PhD); secondary education (PhD); social studies education (M Ed, MAT); STEM education (Ed D). *Program availability:* Part-time, evening/weekend. *Degree requirements:* For master's, thesis; for doctorate, thesis/dissertation. *Entrance requirements:* For master's, PRAXIS I; for doctorate, GRE General Test. Additional exam requirements/recommendations for international students: Required—TOEFL. Electronic applications accepted.

University of Puerto Rico–Río Piedras, College of Education, Program in Curriculum and Teaching, San Juan, PR 00931-3300. Offers biology education (M Ed); chemistry education (M Ed); curriculum and teaching (Ed D); history education (M Ed); mathematics education (M Ed); physics education (M Ed); Spanish education (M Ed). *Program availability:* Part-time. *Degree requirements:* For master's, thesis; for doctorate, thesis/dissertation, internship. *Entrance requirements:* For master's, PAEG or GRE, minimum GPA of 3.0, letter of recommendation; for doctorate, GRE or PAEG, master's degree, minimum GPA of 3.0, letter of recommendation (2), interview. *Faculty research:* Curriculum, math teaching.

University of St. Francis, College of Education, Joliet, IL 60435-6169. Offers educational leadership (MS, Ed D); elementary education (M Ed); reading (MS); secondary education (M Ed), including English education, math education, science education, social studies education, visual arts education; special education (M Ed); teaching and learning (MS); TESOL (Certificate). *Accreditation:* NCATE. *Program availability:* Part-time, evening/weekend, 100% online, blended/hybrid learning. *Faculty:* 11 full-time (8 women), 52 part-time/adjunct (36 women). *Students:* 39 full-time (32 women), 411 part-time (318 women); includes 106 minority (57 Black or African American, non-Hispanic/Latino; 8 Asian, non-Hispanic/Latino; 37 Hispanic/Latino; 4 Two or more races, non-Hispanic/Latino), 4 international. Average age 37. 277 applicants, 55% accepted, 137 enrolled. In 2017, 199 master's, 28 doctorates awarded. *Degree requirements:* For master's, comprehensive exam; for doctorate, thesis/dissertation. *Entrance requirements:* Additional exam requirements/recommendations for international students: Required—TOEFL (minimum score 550 paper-based; 79 iBT), IELTS (minimum score 6). *Application deadline:* Applications are processed on a rolling basis. Application fee: $30. Electronic applications accepted. Application fee is waived when completed online. *Expenses:* $365 to $748 per credit hour. *Financial support:* In 2017–18, 40 students received support. Scholarships/grants and unspecified assistantships available. Support available to part-time students. Financial award applicants required to submit FAFSA. *Unit head:* Dr. John Gambro, Dean, 815-740-3829, Fax: 815-740-2264, E-mail: jgambro@stfrancis.edu. *Application contact:* Sandra Sloka, Director of Admissions for Graduate and Degree Completion Programs, 800-735-7500, Fax: 815-740-3431, E-mail: ssloka@stfrancis.edu.
Website: http://www.stfrancis.edu/academics/college-of-education/

University of South Carolina, The Graduate School, College of Education, Department of Instruction and Teacher Education, Program in Secondary Education, Columbia, SC 29208. Offers art education (IMA, MAT); business education (IMA, MAT); English (MAT); foreign language (MAT); health education (MAT); mathematics (MAT); science (IMA, MAT); secondary (Ed D); secondary education (MT, PhD); social studies (MAT); theatre and speech (MAT). IMA and MT offered jointly with the subject areas. *Accreditation:* NCATE. *Degree requirements:* For master's, comprehensive exam, thesis (for some programs), foreign language (MA); for doctorate, one foreign language, comprehensive exam, thesis/dissertation. *Entrance requirements:* For master's, GRE General Test or MAT, teaching certificate (IMA, M Ed), interview; for doctorate, GRE General Test or MAT, interview. *Faculty research:* Middle school programs, professional development, school collaboration.

University of South Florida, College of Arts and Sciences, Department of Anthropology, Tampa, FL 33620-9951. Offers applied anthropology (MA, PhD), including archaeological and forensic sciences, biocultural medical anthropology, cultural resource management, heritage studies; medical anthropology (Graduate Certificate). *Program availability:* Part-time. *Faculty:* 22 full-time (15 women). *Students:* 73 full-time (50 women), 42 part-time (33 women); includes 30 minority (6 Black or African American, non-Hispanic/Latino; 2 Asian, non-Hispanic/Latino; 18 Hispanic/Latino; 1 Native Hawaiian or other Pacific Islander, non-Hispanic/Latino; 3 Two or more races, non-Hispanic/Latino), 6 international. Average age 32. 117 applicants, 36%

accepted, 26 enrolled. In 2017, 16 master's, 7 doctorates awarded. *Degree requirements:* For master's, one foreign language, comprehensive exam, thesis; for doctorate, one foreign language, comprehensive exam, thesis/dissertation. *Entrance requirements:* For master's and doctorate, GRE, minimum GPA of 3.0, 3 letters of recommendation, statement of purpose, signed research ethics statement, resume or curriculum vitae; for Graduate Certificate, bachelor's degree with minimum GPA of 3.0. Additional exam requirements/recommendations for international students: Required—TOEFL (minimum score 550 paper-based; 79 iBT) or IELTS (minimum score 6.5). *Application deadline:* For fall admission, 12/15 priority date for domestic and international students. Application fee: $30. Electronic applications accepted. *Financial support:* In 2017–18, 19 students received support, including 14 research assistantships with tuition reimbursements available (averaging $14,475 per year), 52 teaching assistantships with partial tuition reimbursements available (averaging $12,540 per year); scholarships/grants and tuition waivers (partial) also available. Financial award application deadline: 1/15; financial award applicants required to submit FAFSA. *Faculty research:* Biocultural medical anthropology; archaeology and culture resource management in the Americas; community identity and heritage; urban community issues; verbal and nonverbal communications in media and education; global dynamics of sustainable resource management and economic development; social and cultural constructions of race, ethnicity, and gender. *Total annual research expenditures:* $1.1 million. *Unit head:* Dr. David Himmelgreen, Professor/Chair, 813-974-5455, E-mail: dhimmelg@usf.edu. *Application contact:* Dr. Rebecca Zarger, Associate Professor and Graduate Director, 813-974-0069, E-mail: rzarger@usf.edu.
Website: http://anthropology.usf.edu/graduate/

The University of Tennessee, Graduate School, College of Education, Health and Human Sciences, Program in Education, Knoxville, TN 37996. Offers art education (MS); counseling education (PhD); cultural studies in education (PhD); curriculum (MS, Ed S); curriculum, educational research and evaluation (Ed D, PhD); early childhood education (PhD); early childhood special education (MS); education of deaf and hard of hearing (MS); educational administration and policy studies (Ed D, PhD); educational administration and supervision (Ed S); educational psychology (Ed D, PhD); elementary education (MS, Ed S); elementary teaching (MS); English education (MS, Ed S); exercise science (PhD); foreign language/ESL education (MS, Ed S); instructional technology (MS, Ed D, PhD, Ed S); literacy, language and ESL education (PhD); literacy, language education, and ESL education (Ed D); mathematics education (MS, Ed S); modified and comprehensive special education (MS); reading education (MS, Ed S); school counseling (Ed S); school psychology (PhD, Ed S); science education (MS, Ed S); secondary teaching (MS); social foundations (MS); social science education (MS, Ed S); socio-cultural foundations of sports and education (PhD); special education (Ed S); teacher education (Ed D, PhD). *Accreditation:* NCATE. *Program availability:* Part-time, evening/weekend. *Degree requirements:* For master's and Ed S, thesis optional; for doctorate, variable foreign language requirement, thesis/dissertation. *Entrance requirements:* For master's, minimum GPA of 2.7; for doctorate and Ed S, GRE General Test, minimum GPA of 2.7. Additional exam requirements/recommendations for international students: Required—TOEFL. Electronic applications accepted.

University of the District of Columbia, College of Arts and Sciences, Program in Teaching, Washington, DC 20008-1175. Offers elementary education (MAT); middle school mathematics (MAT); secondary English language arts (MAT); secondary social studies (MAT).

The University of Toledo, College of Graduate Studies, Judith Herb College of Education, Department of Curriculum and Instruction, Toledo, OH 43606-3390. Offers art education (ME); career and technical education (ME, Ed S); curriculum and instruction (ME, PhD, Ed S); early childhood education (Ed S); education and anthropology (MAE); education and biology (MES); education and chemistry (MES); education and classics (MAE); education and economics (MAE); education and English (MAE); education and French (MAE); education and geology (MES); education and German (MAE); education and history (MAE); education and mathematics (MAE, MES); education and physics (MES); education and political science (MAE); education and sociology (MAE); education and Spanish (MAE); educational media (PhD); educational technology (ME); educational technology: virtual educator (Certificate); elementary education (PhD); English as a second language (MAE); gifted and talented education (PhD); middle childhood education (ME); secondary education (ME, PhD); special education (PhD). *Accreditation:* NCATE. *Program availability:* Part-time, evening/weekend. *Degree requirements:* For master's, comprehensive exam, thesis or alternative; for doctorate, comprehensive exam, thesis/dissertation; for other advanced degree, thesis optional. *Entrance requirements:* For master's, doctorate, and other advanced degree, minimum cumulative GPA of 2.7 for all previous academic work, letters of recommendation. Additional exam requirements/recommendations for international students: Required—TOEFL (minimum score 550 paper-based; 80 iBT). Electronic applications accepted.

University of Victoria, Faculty of Graduate Studies, Faculty of Education, Department of Curriculum and Instruction, Victoria, BC V8W 2Y2, Canada. Offers art education (M Ed, PhD); curriculum studies (M Ed, MA, PhD); early childhood education (M Ed, PhD); educational studies (PhD); language and literacy (M Ed, MA, PhD); mathematics (M Ed, MA, PhD); music education (M Ed, MA, PhD); science (M Ed, MA, PhD); social studies (M Ed, MA); social, cultural and foundational studies (MA, PhD); technology and environmental education (PhD). *Program availability:* Part-time. *Degree requirements:* For master's, thesis, project (M Ed); for doctorate, comprehensive exam, thesis/dissertation. *Entrance requirements:* For master's, minimum B average. Additional exam requirements/recommendations for international students: Required—TOEFL (minimum score 575 paper-based), IELTS (minimum score 7). Electronic applications accepted. *Faculty research:* Elementary and secondary English, language arts, curriculum theory and practice, educational media and technology, educational administration and leadership, history and philosophy of education.

University of Virginia, Curry School of Education, Department of Curriculum, Instruction, and Special Education, Program in Curriculum and Instruction, Charlottesville, VA 22903. Offers curriculum and instruction (M Ed, Ed S); elementary education (M Ed, Ed D); English education (M Ed, Ed D); foreign language education (M Ed); mathematics education (M Ed, Ed D); science education (Ed D); social studies education (M Ed); MBA/M Ed. *Program availability:* 100% online. *Students:* 38 full-time (31 women), 15 part-time (12 women); includes 6 minority (2 Asian, non-Hispanic/Latino; 2 Hispanic/Latino; 2 Two or more races, non-Hispanic/Latino), 2 international. Average age 32. 92 applicants, 64% accepted, 47 enrolled. In 2017, 47 master's, 9 doctorates, 8 other advanced degrees awarded. *Degree requirements:* For master's, comprehensive exam (for some programs); for doctorate, comprehensive exam, thesis/dissertation; for Ed S, comprehensive exam. *Entrance requirements:* For master's, doctorate, and Ed S, GRE General Test, 2 letters of recommendation. Additional exam requirements/recommendations for international students: Required—TOEFL (minimum score 600 paper-based; 90 iBT), IELTS (minimum score 7). *Application deadline:* Applications are processed on a rolling basis. Application fee: $60. Electronic applications accepted. *Financial support:* Fellowships with tuition reimbursements, research assistantships with tuition reimbursements, and teaching assistantships with

tuition reimbursements available. Financial award application deadline: 1/5; financial award applicants required to submit FAFSA. *Unit head:* Susan Mintz, Program Area Director, 434-924-3128, E-mail: slm4r@virginia.edu. *Application contact:* E-mail: curry-admissions@virginia.edu.
Website: http://curry.virginia.edu/academics/areas-of-study/curriculum-teaching-learning

University of Virginia, Curry School of Education, Program in Education, Charlottesville, VA 22903. Offers administration and supervision (PhD); applied developmental science (PhD); counselor education (PhD); curriculum and instruction (PhD); early childhood special education (MT); education evaluation (PhD); educational psychology (PhD); educational research (PhD); elementary education (MT); English education (MT, PhD); foreign language education (MT); higher education (PhD); instructional technology (PhD); kinesiology (MT, PhD); math education (PhD); reading education (PhD); research, statistics and evaluation (PhD); school psychology (PhD); science education (PhD); social studies education (MT, PhD); special education (PhD); world languages education (MT). *Students:* 431 full-time (353 women), 15 part-time (14 women); includes 100 minority (32 Black or African American, non-Hispanic/Latino; 33 Asian, non-Hispanic/Latino; 16 Hispanic/Latino; 19 Two or more races, non-Hispanic/Latino; 14 international. Average age 25. 264 applicants, 49% accepted, 83 enrolled. In 2017, 142 master's, 33 doctorates awarded. *Degree requirements:* For master's, comprehensive exam (for some programs), field project; for doctorate, comprehensive exam, thesis/dissertation. *Entrance requirements:* For doctorate, GRE General Test. Additional exam requirements/recommendations for international students: Required—TOEFL (minimum score 600 paper-based; 90 iBT), IELTS (minimum score 7). *Application deadline:* Applications are processed on a rolling basis. Application fee: $60. Electronic applications accepted. *Financial support:* Fellowships, research assistantships, and teaching assistantships available. Financial award application deadline: 1/5; financial award applicants required to submit FAFSA. *Unit head:* Robert C. Pianta, Dean, 434-924-3334, E-mail: pianta@virginia.edu. *Application contact:* E-mail: curry-admissions@virginia.edu.
Website: http://curry.virginia.edu/teacher-education

University of Washington, Graduate School, College of Education, Seattle, WA 98195. Offers curriculum and instruction (M Ed, Ed D, PhD), including educational technology, general curriculum (Ed D, PhD), language, literacy, and culture, mathematics education, multicultural education, reading and language arts education (Ed D), science education, social studies education, teaching and curriculum (M Ed); educational leadership and policy studies (M Ed, Ed D, PhD), including administration (Ed D), educational policy, organization, and leadership (M Ed, PhD), higher education, leadership for learning (Ed D), social and cultural foundations of education (M Ed, PhD); educational psychology (M Ed, PhD), including educational psychology (PhD), human development and cognition (M Ed), learning sciences, measurement, statistics and research design (M Ed), school psychology (M Ed); instructional leadership (M Ed); intercollegiate athletic leadership (M Ed); special education (M Ed, Ed D, PhD), including early childhood special education (M Ed), emotional and behavioral disabilities (M Ed), learning disabilities (M Ed), low-incidence disabilities (M Ed), severe disabilities (M Ed), special education (Ed D, PhD); teacher education (MIT). *Accreditation:* APA. *Program availability:* Part-time, evening/weekend. *Degree requirements:* For master's, thesis optional; for doctorate, thesis/dissertation. *Entrance requirements:* For master's and doctorate, GRE General Test, minimum GPA of 3.0. Additional exam requirements/recommendations for international students: Required—TOEFL. Electronic applications accepted. *Faculty research:* School restructuring/effective schools, special education interventions, literacy and writing, technology, school partnerships, teacher preparation.

The University of West Alabama, School of Graduate Studies, College of Education, Program in Secondary Education, Livingston, AL 35470. Offers biology (MAT); English language arts (MAT); high school 6-12 (M Ed); history (MAT); mathematics (MAT); science (MAT); social science (MAT). *Program availability:* Part-time, evening/weekend, 100% online. *Faculty:* 21 full-time (7 women), 5 part-time/adjunct (1 woman). *Students:* 259 (183 women); includes 61 minority (51 Black or African American, non-Hispanic/Latino; 2 American Indian or Alaska Native, non-Hispanic/Latino; 3 Asian, non-Hispanic/Latino; 2 Hispanic/Latino; 3 Two or more races, non-Hispanic/Latino). Average age 32. 58 applicants, 93% accepted, 45 enrolled. In 2017, 80 master's awarded. *Degree requirements:* For master's, comprehensive exam, thesis optional. *Entrance requirements:* For master's, GRE, minimum GPA of 2.75, verification of background clearance/fingerprints, valid bachelor's-level Professional Educator Certificate in same teaching field. Additional exam requirements/recommendations for international students: Required—TOEFL (minimum score 500 paper-based; 61 iBT). *Application deadline:* Applications are processed on a rolling basis. Application fee: $40. Electronic applications accepted. *Expenses:* Tuition, state resident: part-time $371 per credit hour. Tuition, nonresident: part-time $742 per credit hour. *Required fees:* $130 per semester. *Financial support:* Teaching assistantships, Federal Work-Study, scholarships/grants, and unspecified assistantships available. Support available to part-time students. Financial award application deadline: 3/1; financial award applicants required to submit FAFSA. *Unit head:* Dr. Jodie Winship, Chair of Teaching and Learning, 205-652-5415, Fax: 205-652-3706, E-mail: jwinship@uwa.edu. *Application contact:* Dr. B. J. Kimbrough, Dean of Graduate Studies, 205-652-3647, Fax: 205-652-3670, E-mail: bkimbrough@uwa.edu.

University of Wisconsin–Milwaukee, Graduate School, School of Education, Department of Curriculum and Instruction, Milwaukee, WI 53201-0413. Offers curriculum and instruction (MS), including cross-curricular focus, early childhood education, English education, mathematics education, middle childhood/early adolescence education, reading education, science education, urban social studies education. *Program availability:* Part-time. *Students:* 17 full-time (13 women), 45 part-time (39 women); includes 13 minority (2 Black or African American, non-Hispanic/Latino; 3 Asian, non-Hispanic/Latino; 1 Hispanic/Latino; 7 Two or more races, non-Hispanic/Latino). Average age 33. 32 applicants, 66% accepted, 16 enrolled. In 2017, 26 master's awarded. *Entrance requirements:* Additional exam requirements/recommendations for international students: Required—TOEFL (minimum score 550 paper-based; 79 iBT), IELTS (minimum score 6.5). *Application deadline:* For fall admission, 1/1 priority date for domestic students; for spring admission, 9/1 for domestic students. Application fee: $56 ($96 for international students). Electronic applications accepted. *Financial support:* Fellowships, research assistantships, teaching assistantships, career-related internships or fieldwork, health care benefits, unspecified assistantships, and project assistantships available. Support available to part-time students. Financial award application deadline: 4/15; financial award applicants required to submit FAFSA. *Application contact:* General Information Contact, 414-229-4721, E-mail: soeinfo@uwm.edu.
Website: http://uwm.edu/education/academics/curriculum-instruction-department/

University of Wisconsin–River Falls, Outreach and Graduate Studies, College of Arts and Science, Department of History and Philosophy, River Falls, WI 54022. Offers social science education (MSE). *Program availability:* Part-time. *Degree requirements:* For master's, thesis. *Entrance requirements:* For master's, minimum GPA of 2.75. Additional exam requirements/recommendations for international students: Required—TOEFL (minimum score 500 paper-based; 65 iBT), IELTS (minimum score

5.5). Electronic applications accepted. *Faculty research:* World War II, Hitler, modern China, women's history, immigration history.

Virginia Polytechnic Institute and State University, Graduate School, College of Liberal Arts and Human Sciences, Blacksburg, VA 24061. Offers career and technical education (MS Ed, Ed S); communication (MA); counselor education (MA); creative writing (MFA); curriculum and instruction (MA Ed, Ed S); educational leadership and policy studies (Ed S); educational research and evaluation (PhD); English (MA); social, political, ethical, and cultural thought (PhD); Ed D/PhD. *Faculty:* 411 full-time (213 women), 3 part-time/adjunct (all women). *Students:* 623 full-time (427 women), 431 part-time (278 women); includes 203 minority (115 Black or African American, non-Hispanic/Latino; 4 American Indian or Alaska Native, non-Hispanic/Latino; 29 Asian, non-Hispanic/Latino; 33 Hispanic/Latino; 2 Native Hawaiian or other Pacific Islander, non-Hispanic/Latino; 20 Two or more races, non-Hispanic/Latino; 87 international. Average age 34. 898 applicants, 50% accepted, 329 enrolled. In 2017, 314 master's, 102 doctorates awarded. *Degree requirements:* For master's, comprehensive exam (for some programs), thesis (for some programs); for doctorate, comprehensive exam (for some programs), thesis/dissertation (for some programs). *Entrance requirements:* For master's and doctorate, GRE/GMAT. Additional exam requirements/recommendations for international students: Required—TOEFL (minimum score 80 iBT). *Application deadline:* For fall admission, 8/1 for domestic students, 4/1 for international students; for spring admission, 1/1 for domestic students, 9/1 for international students. Applications are processed on a rolling basis. Application fee: $75. Electronic applications accepted. *Expenses:* Tuition, state resident: full-time $15,072; part-time $718.50 per credit hour. Tuition, nonresident: full-time $28,810; part-time $1448.25 per credit hour. *Required fees:* $2741; $502 per semester. Tuition and fees vary according to course load, campus/location and program. *Financial support:* In 2017–18, 19 research assistantships with full tuition reimbursements (averaging $19,611 per year), 226 teaching assistantships with full tuition reimbursements (averaging $16,220 per year) were awarded. Financial award application deadline: 3/1; financial award applicants required to submit FAFSA. *Total annual research expenditures:* $7.9 million. *Unit head:* Dr. Rosemary Blieszner, Dean, 540-231-6779, Fax: 540-231-7157, E-mail: rmb@vt.edu. *Application contact:* Chelsea Blanchet, Executive Assistant, 540-231-6779, Fax: 540-231-7157, E-mail: bchels1@vt.edu.
Website: http://www.liberalarts.vt.edu/

Wagner College, Division of Graduate Studies, Education Department, Program in Secondary Education/Students with Disabilities, Staten Island, NY 10301-4495. Offers secondary education 7-12 (MS Ed), including language arts, languages other than English, mathematics and technology, science and technology, social studies. *Program availability:* Evening/weekend. *Faculty:* 2 full-time (1 woman), 7 part-time/adjunct (3 women). *Students:* 17 full-time (14 women), 6 part-time (4 women); includes 2 minority (1 Black or African American, non-Hispanic/Latino; 1 Asian, non-Hispanic/Latino). Average age 24. 15 applicants, 80% accepted, 11 enrolled. In 2017, 8 master's awarded. *Degree requirements:* For master's, thesis (for some programs), completion of state certification exams before student teaching. *Entrance requirements:* For master's, GRE, minimum GPA of 3.0, interview, recommendations. Additional exam requirements/recommendations for international students: Required—TOEFL (minimum score 550 paper-based; 79 iBT), IELTS (minimum score 6.5). *Application deadline:* For fall admission, 12/1 priority date for domestic and international students. Application fee: $60. Electronic applications accepted. *Expenses:* Contact institution. *Financial support:* Unspecified assistantships and alumni fellowship available. Financial award application deadline: 2/15; financial award applicants required to submit FAFSA. *Unit head:* Dr. Jason Fitzgerald, Department Chair, 718-420-4129, Fax: 718-390-3456, E-mail: jason.fitzgerald@wagner.edu. *Application contact:* Patricia Clancy, Assistant Director of Enrollment, 718-420-4464, Fax: 718-390-3105, E-mail: patricia.clancy@wagner.edu.
Website: http://www.wagner.edu/education

Wayland Baptist University, Graduate Programs, Program in Education, Plainview, TX 79072-6998. Offers education administration (M Ed); education diagnostics (M Ed); education literacy (M Ed); elementary certification (M Ed); English (M Ed); English as a second language (M Ed); higher education administration (M Ed); human resources (M Ed); instructional leadership (M Ed); instructional technology (M Ed); leadership training and development (M Ed); science education (M Ed); secondary certification (M Ed); social studies (M Ed); special education (M Ed); sports administration and management (M Ed). *Program availability:* Part-time, evening/weekend, 100% online. *Faculty:* 33 full-time (17 women), 28 part-time/adjunct (17 women). *Students:* 16 full-time (13 women), 221 part-time (143 women); includes 97 minority (26 Black or African American, non-Hispanic/Latino; 1 American Indian or Alaska Native, non-Hispanic/Latino; 5 Asian, non-Hispanic/Latino; 54 Hispanic/Latino; 11 Two or more races, non-Hispanic/Latino), 1 international. Average age 39. 32 applicants, 97% accepted, 23 enrolled. In 2017, 78 master's awarded. *Degree requirements:* For master's, comprehensive exam, capstone course. *Entrance requirements:* For master's, GRE, GMAT or MAT. Additional exam requirements/recommendations for international students: Required—TOEFL (minimum score 500 paper-based; 61 iBT). *Application deadline:* Applications are processed on a rolling basis. Application fee: $50. Electronic applications accepted. *Expenses:* Tuition: Full-time $11,250; part-time $625 per credit hour. *Required fees:* $1200. *Financial support:* Federal Work-Study, institutionally sponsored loans, and scholarships/grants available. Support available to part-time students. Financial award application deadline: 5/1; financial award applicants required to submit FAFSA. *Unit head:* Dr. Gene Whitfill, Dean, 806-291-1047, Fax: 806-291-1951, E-mail: whitfillg@wbu.edu. *Application contact:* Amanda Stanton, Coordinator of Graduate Studies, 806-291-3423, Fax: 806-291-1950, E-mail: stanton@wbu.edu.

Wayne State College, School of Education and Counseling, Department of Educational Foundations and Leadership, Program in Curriculum and Instruction, Wayne, NE 68787. Offers alternative education (MSE); business and information technology education (MSE); communication arts education (MSE); early childhood education (MSE); elementary education (MSE); English as a second language (MSE); English education (MSE); family and consumer sciences education (MSE); industrial technology and vocational education (MSE); learning communities (MSE); mathematics education (MSE); music education (MSE); science education (MSE); social science education (MSE). *Accreditation:* NCATE. *Program availability:* Part-time, evening/weekend. *Degree requirements:* For master's, comprehensive exam, thesis optional. *Entrance requirements:* For master's, GRE General Test. Additional exam requirements/recommendations for international students: Required—TOEFL (minimum score 550 paper-based).

Wayne State University, College of Education, Division of Teacher Education, Detroit, MI 48202. Offers art education (M Ed); bilingual/bicultural education (Certificate); curriculum and instruction (Ed D, PhD, Ed S), including English as a second language (MAT, Ed D, Ed S), K-12 curriculum (PhD); elementary education (MAT), including bilingual/bicultural education (M Ed, MAT), early childhood education (M Ed, MAT), English as a second language (MAT, Ed D, Ed S), foreign language education, science education (M Ed, MAT), special education (M Ed, MAT); elementary mathematics specialist (Certificate); English as a second language (Certificate); reading (M Ed, Ed S); reading, language and literature (Ed D); secondary education (MAT), including bilingual/bicultural education (M Ed, MAT), early childhood education (M Ed, MAT), English as a

second language (MAT, Ed D, Ed S), English education, foreign language education, mathematics education (M Ed, MAT), science education (M Ed, MAT), social studies education (M Ed, MAT); special education (MAT), including career and technical education; teaching and learning (M Ed), including bilingual/bicultural education (M Ed, MAT), early childhood education (M Ed, MAT), elementary education, foreign language, mathematics education (M Ed, MAT), science education (M Ed, MAT), social studies education (M Ed, MAT), special education (M Ed, MAT). *Program availability:* Part-time, blended/hybrid learning. *Faculty:* 22. *Students:* 126 full-time (96 women), 317 part-time (258 women); includes 134 minority (95 Black or African American, non-Hispanic/Latino; 1 American Indian or Alaska Native, non-Hispanic/Latino; 8 Asian, non-Hispanic/Latino; 17 Hispanic/Latino; 1 Native Hawaiian or other Pacific Islander, non-Hispanic/Latino; 12 Two or more races, non-Hispanic/Latino), 13 international. Average age 37. 260 applicants, 33% accepted, 57 enrolled. In 2017, 111 master's, 13 doctorates, 7 other advanced degrees awarded. *Degree requirements:* For master's, essay or project (for some M Ed programs), professional field experience (for MAT programs); for doctorate, thesis/dissertation. *Entrance requirements:* For master's, Michigan Test for Teacher Certification (for most programs), verification of participation in group work with children (for MAT programs), Michigan State Police criminal background check; for doctorate, minimum undergraduate GPA of 3.0, graduate 3.5; interview; curriculum vitae; references; master's degree (for most programs). Additional exam requirements/recommendations for international students: Required—TOEFL (minimum score 550 paper-based; 79 iBT), TWE (minimum score 5.5); Recommended—IELTS (minimum score 6.5). *Application deadline:* For fall admission, 6/1 priority date for domestic students, 5/1 priority date for international students; for winter admission, 10/1 priority date for domestic students, 9/1 priority date for international students; for spring admission, 2/1 priority date for domestic students, 1/1 priority date for international students. Applications are processed on a rolling basis. Application fee: $50. Electronic applications accepted. *Expenses:* Tuition, state resident: full-time $10,224; part-time $638.98 per credit hour. Tuition, nonresident: full-time $22,145; part-time $1384.04 per credit hour. Tuition and fees vary according to course load and program. *Financial support:* In 2017–18, 78 students received support, including 4 fellowships (averaging $13,500 per year), 1 research assistantship with tuition reimbursement available (averaging $16,000 per year); Federal Work-Study, scholarships/grants, and unspecified assistantships also available. Support available to part-time students. Financial award applicants required to submit FAFSA. *Faculty research:* Improving students' skill achievement in mathematics, improving elementary children's understanding of informational text, teachers' use of their pedagogical and mathematical knowledge in the interactive work of teaching, the intersection of identity construction in teaching and learning, identifying effective methods of literacy instruction and assessments for bilingual students in elementary language arts classrooms. *Unit head:* Dr. Thomas Edwards, Interim Associate Dean for Teacher Education, 313-577-3886, E-mail: t.g.edwards@wayne.edu. *Application contact:* 313-577-0902, E-mail: askcoe@wayne.edu.
Website: http://coe.wayne.edu/ted/index.php

Western Governors University, Teachers College, Salt Lake City, UT 84107. Offers curriculum and instruction (MS); educational leadership (MS); educational studies (MA); educational studies (5-12) (MA), including mathematics; elementary education (K-8) (MAT, Postbaccalaureate Certificate); elementary education (PreK-8) (MAT); English language learning (K-12) (MA); instructional design (MAT); learning and technology (M Ed, MA); management and innovation (M Ed); mathematics (5-12) (MAT, Postbaccalaureate Certificate); mathematics (5-9) (MAT, Postbaccalaureate Certificate); mathematics education (5-12) (MA); mathematics education (5-9) (MA); mathematics education (K-6) (MA); measurement and evaluation (M Ed); science (5-12) (Postbaccalaureate Certificate); science (5-9) (MAT, Postbaccalaureate Certificate); science education (5-12) (MA), including biology, chemistry, geology, physics; science education (5-9) (MA); social science (5-12) (MAT, Postbaccalaureate Certificate); special education (MAT, MS). *Accreditation:* NCATE. *Program availability:* Evening/weekend, online learning. *Degree requirements:* For master's, capstone project. *Entrance requirements:* For master's and Postbaccalaureate Certificate, Readiness Assessment, transcripts. Additional exam requirements/recommendations for international students: Required—TOEFL (minimum score 450 paper-based; 80 iBT). Electronic applications accepted. *Expenses:* Contact institution.

Western Oregon University, Graduate Programs, College of Education, Division of Teacher Education, Program in Secondary Education, Monmouth, OR 97361. Offers bilingual education (MS Ed); health (MS Ed); humanities (MAT, MS Ed); initial licensure (MAT); mathematics (MAT, MS Ed); science (MAT, MS Ed); social science (MAT, MS Ed). *Accreditation:* NCATE. *Program availability:* Part-time, evening/weekend. *Degree requirements:* For master's, thesis optional, written exam. *Entrance requirements:* For master's, minimum GPA of 3.0, teaching license. Additional exam requirements/recommendations for international students: Required—TOEFL (minimum score 550 paper-based; 79 iBT), IELTS (minimum score 6.5). *Faculty research:* Literacy, science in primary grades, geography education, retention, teacher burnout.

Westfield State University, College of Graduate and Continuing Education, Department of Education, Westfield, MA 01086. Offers early childhood education (M Ed); elementary education (M Ed); reading specialist (M Ed); secondary education (M Ed), including biology teacher education, chemistry teacher education, general science teacher education, history teacher education, mathematics teacher education, physical education teacher education; special education (M Ed), including moderate disabilities, 5-12, moderate disabilities, preK-8; vocational technical education (M Ed). *Accreditation:* NCATE. *Program availability:* Part-time, evening/weekend. *Faculty:* 6 full-time (all women), 17 part-time/adjunct (13 women). *Students:* 12 full-time (8 women), 137 part-time (110 women); includes 5 minority (1 Black or African American, non-Hispanic/Latino; 1 Asian, non-Hispanic/Latino; 1 Hispanic/Latino; 2 Two or more races, non-Hispanic/Latino). Average age 31. 65 applicants, 98% accepted, 50 enrolled. In 2017, 60 master's awarded. *Degree requirements:* For master's, comprehensive exam, practicum. *Entrance requirements:* For master's, GRE General Test or MAT, minimum undergraduate GPA of 2.8. Additional exam requirements/recommendations for international students: Recommended—TOEFL (minimum score 550 paper-based; 79 iBT). *Application deadline:* For fall admission, 7/1 for domestic students; for spring admission, 11/1 for domestic students; for summer admission, 4/1 for domestic students. Applications are processed on a rolling basis. Application fee: $50. *Expenses:* Tuition, state resident: part-time $332 per credit. Tuition, nonresident: part-time $332 per credit. Required fees: $75 per semester. Tuition and fees vary according to program. *Financial support:* Unspecified assistantships and SOS scholarships (for education

majors only) available. Financial award application deadline: 3/1; financial award applicants required to submit FAFSA. *Faculty research:* Collaborative teacher education, developmental early childhood education. *Unit head:* Dr. Laura Baker, Department Chair, 413-572-5324, E-mail: lbaker@westfield.ma.edu. *Application contact:* Shelly Henrichon, Coordinator of College of Graduate and Continuing Education Admissions, 413-572-8022, Fax: 413-572-5227, E-mail: mhenrichon@westfield.ma.edu.
Website: http://www.westfield.ma.edu/academics/degrees/education-graduate-programs

Westfield State University, College of Graduate and Continuing Education, Department of Education, Programs in Secondary Education, Program in History Teacher Education, Westfield, MA 01086. Offers secondary education-history (M Ed). *Program availability:* Part-time, evening/weekend. *Faculty:* 3 full-time (all women). *Students:* 4 full-time (0 women), 17 part-time (9 women); includes 1 minority (Black or African American, non-Hispanic/Latino). Average age 35. 6 applicants, 100% accepted, 6 enrolled. In 2017, 8 master's awarded. *Degree requirements:* For master's, comprehensive exam, thesis (for some programs). *Entrance requirements:* For master's, GRE General Test or MAT, minimum undergraduate GPA of 2.8. Additional exam requirements/recommendations for international students: Recommended—TOEFL (minimum score 550 paper-based; 79 iBT). *Application deadline:* For fall admission, 7/1 for domestic students; for spring admission, 11/1 for domestic students; for summer admission, 4/1 for domestic students. Applications are processed on a rolling basis. Application fee: $50. *Expenses:* Tuition, state resident: part-time $332 per credit. Tuition, nonresident: part-time $332 per credit. Required fees: $75 per semester. Tuition and fees vary according to program. *Financial support:* Unspecified assistantships and SOS scholarships (for education majors only) available. Financial award application deadline: 3/1; financial award applicants required to submit FAFSA. *Unit head:* Dr. Laura Baker, Department Chair, 413-572-5324, E-mail: lbaker@westfield.ma.edu. *Application contact:* Shelly Henrichon, Coordinator of College of Graduate and Continuing Education Admissions, 413-572-8022, Fax: 413-572-5227, E-mail: mhenrichon@westfield.ma.edu.

Widener University, School of Human Service Professions, Center for Education, Chester, PA 19013-5792. Offers adult education (M Ed); counseling in higher education (M Ed); counselor education (M Ed); early childhood education (M Ed); educational foundations (M Ed); educational leadership (M Ed); educational psychology (M Ed); elementary education (M Ed); English and language arts (M Ed); health education (M Ed); higher education leadership (Ed D); home and school visitor (M Ed); human sexuality (M Ed, PhD); mathematics education (M Ed); middle school education (M Ed); principalship (M Ed); reading and language arts (Ed D); reading education (M Ed); school administration (Ed D); science education (M Ed); social studies education (M Ed); special education (M Ed); technology education (M Ed). *Accreditation:* NCATE. *Program availability:* Part-time, evening/weekend. *Faculty:* 34 full-time (22 women), 37 part-time/adjunct (14 women). *Students:* 131 full-time (112 women), 244 part-time (179 women); includes 94 minority (58 Black or African American, non-Hispanic/Latino; 1 American Indian or Alaska Native, non-Hispanic/Latino; 1 Asian, non-Hispanic/Latino; 22 Hispanic/Latino; 12 Two or more races, non-Hispanic/Latino), 12 international. Average age 37. 140 applicants, 38% accepted, 26 enrolled. In 2017, 45 master's, 21 doctorates awarded. Terminal master's awarded for partial completion of doctoral program. *Degree requirements:* For doctorate, thesis/dissertation. *Entrance requirements:* For master's, minimum GPA of 2.5; for doctorate, GRE or MAT, minimum GPA of 2.0 (undergraduate), 3.5 (graduate). *Application deadline:* Applications are processed on a rolling basis. Application fee: $25 ($300 for international students). Electronic applications accepted. *Expenses:* Contact institution. *Financial support:* Career-related internships or fieldwork, tuition waivers (full and partial), and unspecified assistantships available. Support available to part-time students. Financial award application deadline: 5/1. *Faculty research:* Reading and cognition, adult education, technology education, educational leadership, special education. *Unit head:* Dr. Shawn Fitzgerald, Dean, 610-499-4294, Fax: 610-499-4623, E-mail: smfitzgerald@widener.edu. *Application contact:* Megan Kuft, Director of Graduate Admissions, 610-499-4124, E-mail: gradprograms@widener.edu.
Website: http://www.widener.edu/academics/schools/eics

William Carey University, School of Education, Hattiesburg, MS 39401. Offers art education (M Ed); art of teaching (M Ed); elementary education (M Ed, Ed S); English education (M Ed); gifted education (M Ed); history and social science (M Ed); mild/moderate disabilities (M Ed); secondary education (M Ed). *Accreditation:* NCATE. *Program availability:* Part-time. *Degree requirements:* For master's, comprehensive exam. *Entrance requirements:* For master's, GRE, MAT, minimum GPA of 2.5, Class A teacher's license. Additional exam requirements/recommendations for international students: Required—TOEFL (minimum score 550 paper-based).

Worcester State University, Graduate School, Program in History, Worcester, MA 01602-2597. Offers MA. *Program availability:* Part-time. *Faculty:* 12 full-time, 2 part-time/adjunct. *Students:* 7 full-time (3 women), 13 part-time (9 women); includes 2 minority (1 Black or African American, non-Hispanic/Latino; 1 American Indian or Alaska Native, non-Hispanic/Latino). Average age 39. 17 applicants, 94% accepted, 6 enrolled. In 2017, 12 master's awarded. *Degree requirements:* For master's, comprehensive exam (for some programs), thesis (for some programs), portfolio. *Entrance requirements:* For master's, GRE General Test or MAT, 18 undergraduate credits in history, including U.S. history and Western civilizations. Additional exam requirements/recommendations for international students: Required—TOEFL (minimum score 550 paper-based; 79 iBT). *Application deadline:* For fall admission, 6/15 for domestic and international students; for spring admission, 11/1 for domestic and international students; for summer admission, 4/1 for domestic and international students. Applications are processed on a rolling basis. Application fee: $50. Electronic applications accepted. *Expenses:* Tuition, state resident: full-time $3042; part-time $169 per credit hour. Tuition, nonresident: full-time $3042; part-time $169 per credit hour. Required fees: $2754; $153 per credit hour. *Financial support:* Career-related internships or fieldwork, scholarships/grants, and unspecified assistantships available. Financial award application deadline: 3/1; financial award applicants required to submit FAFSA. *Unit head:* Dr. Erika Briesacher, Coordinator, 508-929-8692, E-mail: ebriesacher@worcester.edu. *Application contact:* Sara Grady, Associate Dean, Graduate Studies and Professional Development, 508-929-8130, Fax: 508-929-8100, E-mail: sara.grady@worcester.edu.

Vocational and Technical Education

Alcorn State University, School of Graduate Studies, Department of Advanced Technologies, Lorman, MS 39096-7500. Offers workforce education leadership (MS).

Alcorn State University, School of Graduate Studies, School of Psychology and Education, Lorman, MS 39096-7500. Offers agricultural education (MS Ed); elementary education (MS Ed, Ed S); guidance and counseling (MS Ed); industrial education (MS Ed); secondary education (MS Ed), including health and physical education; special education (MS Ed). *Accreditation:* NCATE. *Degree requirements:* For master's, thesis optional.

Appalachian State University, Cratis D. Williams Graduate School, Department of Sustainable Technology and the Built Environment, Boone, NC 28608. Offers appropriate technology (MS); renewable energy engineering (MS). *Program availability:* Part-time. *Degree requirements:* For master's, comprehensive exam, thesis optional. *Entrance requirements:* For master's, GRE General Test, 3 letters of recommendation. Additional exam requirements/recommendations for international students: Required—TOEFL (minimum score 550 paper-based; 79 iBT), IELTS (minimum score 6.5). Electronic applications accepted. *Faculty research:* Wind power, biofuels, green construction, solar energy production.

Athens State University, Graduate Programs, Athens, AL 35611. Offers career and technical education (M Ed); global logistics and supply chain management (MS); religious studies (MA). *Students:* 28 full-time (19 women), 119 part-time (55 women). *Expenses:* Tuition, state resident: full-time $3900; part-time $325 per credit hour. Tuition, nonresident: full-time $3900; part-time $325 per credit hour.
Website: http://www.athens.edu/masters/

Bowling Green State University, Graduate College, College of Technology, Program in Career and Technology Education, Bowling Green, OH 43403. Offers career and technology education (M Ed), including technology. *Program availability:* Part-time. *Degree requirements:* For master's, thesis or alternative. *Entrance requirements:* For master's, GRE General Test. Additional exam requirements/recommendations for international students: Required—TOEFL. Electronic applications accepted. *Faculty research:* Curriculum in technology education.

Buffalo State College, State University of New York, The Graduate School, Faculty of Applied Science and Education, Department of Educational Foundations, Program in Career and Technical Education, Buffalo, NY 14222-1095. Offers MS Ed. *Accreditation:* NCATE. *Program availability:* Part-time, evening/weekend. *Degree requirements:* For master's, thesis or project. *Entrance requirements:* For master's, minimum GPA of 2.5 in last 60 hours, New York teaching certificate. Additional exam requirements/recommendations for international students: Required—TOEFL (minimum score 550 paper-based).

Buffalo State College, State University of New York, The Graduate School, Faculty of Applied Science and Education, Department of Technology, Program in Technology Education, Buffalo, NY 14222-1095. Offers MS Ed. *Accreditation:* NCATE. *Degree requirements:* For master's, thesis or project. *Entrance requirements:* For master's, minimum GPA of 2.5 in last 60 hours, New York teaching certificate. Additional exam requirements/recommendations for international students: Required—TOEFL (minimum score 550 paper-based).

California Baptist University, Program in Education, Riverside, CA 92504-3206. Offers educational leadership (MS); educational leadership for faith-based institutions (MS); educational leadership for public institutions (MS); educational technology (MS); instructional computer applications (MS); international education (MS); leadership and adult learning (MS); leadership and organizational studies (MS); online teaching and learning (MS); reading (MS); science education (MA); special education in mild/moderate disabilities (MS); special education in moderate/severe disabilities (MS); teacher leadership (MS); teaching (MS); teaching and learning (MS). *Program availability:* Part-time, evening/weekend, 100% online, blended/hybrid learning. *Faculty:* 19 full-time (11 women), 36 part-time/adjunct (22 women). *Students:* 232 full-time (182 women), 315 part-time (247 women); includes 264 minority (33 Black or African American, non-Hispanic/Latino; 4 American Indian or Alaska Native, non-Hispanic/Latino; 11 Asian, non-Hispanic/Latino; 186 Hispanic/Latino; 7 Native Hawaiian or other Pacific Islander, non-Hispanic/Latino; 23 Two or more races, non-Hispanic/Latino). Average age 31. 217 applicants, 64% accepted, 129 enrolled. In 2017, 196 master's awarded. *Degree requirements:* For master's, comprehensive exam, project, or thesis. *Entrance requirements:* For master's, minimum undergraduate GPA of 2.75; 500-word essay; three letters of recommendation; two prerequisite courses completed with minimum C grade. Additional exam requirements/recommendations for international students: Required—TOEFL (minimum score 80 iBT). *Application deadline:* For fall admission, 8/1 priority date for domestic students, 7/1 for international students; for spring admission, 12/1 priority date for domestic students, 11/1 for international students. Applications are processed on a rolling basis. Application fee: $45. Electronic applications accepted. *Expenses:* Contact institution. *Financial support:* In 2017–18, 162 students received support. Federal Work-Study and scholarships/grants available. Financial award applicants required to submit CSS PROFILE or FAFSA. *Faculty research:* Leadership development, complexity theory, faith and learning, special education, social and philosophical contexts of education. *Unit head:* Dr. John Shoup, Dean, School of Education, 951-343-4516, E-mail: jshoup@calbaptist.edu. *Application contact:* Gavin Andrew, Graduate Admissions Counselor, 951-552-8437, E-mail: gandrew@calbaptist.edu.
Website: http://www.calbaptist.edu/mastersined/

California University of Pennsylvania, School of Graduate Studies and Research, College of Education and Human Services, Program in Technology Education, California, PA 15419-1394. Offers M Ed. *Accreditation:* NCATE. *Program availability:* Part-time, evening/weekend, online only, 100% online. *Degree requirements:* For master's, comprehensive exam, thesis optional. *Entrance requirements:* For master's, MAT, minimum GPA of 3.0, teaching experience in industrial arts. Additional exam requirements/recommendations for international students: Required—TOEFL (minimum score 550 paper-based; 80 iBT). *Application deadline:* For fall admission, 8/1 priority date for domestic and international students; for spring admission, 5/1 priority date for domestic and international students. Applications are processed on a rolling basis. Application fee: $25. Electronic applications accepted. *Financial support:* Applicants required to submit FAFSA. *Faculty research:* Curriculum, trends in technology, standards-based assessment. *Unit head:* Dr. Rene L. Kruse, Global Online Program Coordinator, 724-938-5904, E-mail: kruse@calu.edu. *Application contact:* Suzanne C. Powers, Director of Graduate Admissions and Recruitment, 724-938-4029, Fax: 724-938-5712, E-mail: powers_s@cup.edu.

Capella University, School of Business and Technology, Doctoral Programs in Technology, Minneapolis, MN 55402. Offers general information technology (PhD); global operations and supply chain management (DBA); information assurance and security (PhD); information technology education (PhD); information technology management (DBA, PhD).

Central Connecticut State University, School of Graduate Studies, School of Engineering, Science and Technology, Department of Technology and Engineering Education, New Britain, CT 06050-4010. Offers STEM education (MS). *Program availability:* Part-time, evening/weekend. *Faculty:* 5 full-time (2 women), 1 part-time/adjunct (0 women). *Students:* 7 full-time (2 women), 30 part-time (18 women); includes 2 minority (both Hispanic/Latino). Average age 35. 16 applicants, 81% accepted, 6 enrolled. In 2017, 25 master's awarded. *Degree requirements:* For master's, thesis or alternative, special project. *Entrance requirements:* For master's, minimum undergraduate GPA of 2.7. Additional exam requirements/recommendations for international students: Required—TOEFL (minimum score 550 paper-based; 79 iBT); Recommended—IELTS (minimum score 6.5). *Application deadline:* For fall admission, 8/1 for domestic students, 5/1 for international students; for spring admission, 11/1 for domestic and international students. Applications are processed on a rolling basis. Application fee: $50. Electronic applications accepted. *Expenses: Tuition, area resident:* Full-time $6757. Tuition, state resident: full-time $9750; part-time $374 per credit. Tuition, nonresident: full-time $18,102; part-time $374 per credit. *Required fees:* $4635; $255 per credit. *Financial support:* In 2017–18, 4 students received support. Career-related internships or fieldwork, Federal Work-Study, scholarships/grants, and unspecified assistantships available. Support available to part-time students. Financial award application deadline: 3/1; financial award applicants required to submit FAFSA. *Faculty research:* Instruction, curriculum development, administration, occupational training. *Unit head:* Dr. James DeLaura, Chair, 860-832-1850, E-mail: delaura@ccsu.edu. *Application contact:* Patricia Gardner, Associate Director of Graduate Studies, 860-832-2350, Fax: 860-832-2362.
Website: http://www.ccsu.edu/teched/

Central Washington University, School of Graduate Studies and Research, College of Education and Professional Studies, Department of Family and Consumer Sciences, Ellensburg, WA 98926. Offers career and technical education (MS); family and child life (MS); family and consumer sciences education (MS). *Program availability:* Part-time. *Entrance requirements:* For master's, minimum GPA of 3.0. Additional exam requirements/recommendations for international students: Required—TOEFL (minimum score 550 paper-based; 79 iBT). *Application deadline:* For fall admission, 2/1 priority date for domestic students; for winter admission, 10/1 for domestic students; for spring admission, 1/1 for domestic students. Applications are processed on a rolling basis. Application fee: $50. Electronic applications accepted. *Financial support:* Application deadline: 3/1; applicants required to submit FAFSA. *Unit head:* Dr. Duane Dowd, Department Chair, 509-963-2740, E-mail: duane.dowd@cwu.edu. *Application contact:* Justine Eason, Admissions Program Coordinator, 509-963-3103, Fax: 509-963-1799, E-mail: masters@cwu.edu.
Website: http://www.cwu.edu/~fandcs/

Chicago State University, School of Graduate and Professional Studies, College of Education, Department of Reading, Elementary Education, Library Information and Media Studies, Program in Technology and Performance Improvement Studies, Chicago, IL 60628. Offers MS. *Program availability:* Online learning. *Entrance requirements:* For master's, minimum GPA of 2.75. *Application deadline:* For fall admission, 7/1 for domestic students; for spring admission, 11/10 for domestic students. Application fee: $25. *Unit head:* Dr. Edward Reinhart, Chairperson, 773-995-3807, Fax: 773-995-3868. *Application contact:* Anika Miller, Graduate Studies Office, 773-995-2404, E-mail: g-studies1@csu.edu.
Website: https://www.csu.edu/collegeofeducation/infomediastudies/mstechnology.htm

Clarion University of Pennsylvania, College of Arts, Education and Sciences, Master of Education Program, Clarion, PA 16214. Offers curriculum and instruction (M Ed); early childhood (M Ed); math education (M Ed); reading (M Ed); science education (M Ed); special education (M Ed); technology (M Ed). *Accreditation:* NCATE. *Program availability:* Part-time, evening/weekend, online only, 100% online, blended/hybrid learning. *Faculty:* 6 full-time (3 women). *Students:* 11 full-time (all women), 101 part-time (82 women); includes 4 minority (2 Black or African American, non-Hispanic/Latino; 1 Hispanic/Latino; 1 Two or more races, non-Hispanic/Latino). Average age 30. 80 applicants, 98% accepted, 33 enrolled. In 2017, 52 master's awarded. *Degree requirements:* For master's, comprehensive exam, thesis, or portfolio. *Entrance requirements:* For master's, minimum QPA of 3.0. Additional exam requirements/recommendations for international students: Required—TOEFL (minimum score 550 paper-based, 80 iBT) or IELTS (7). *Application deadline:* For fall admission, 8/15 priority date for domestic students, 7/15 priority date for international students; for winter admission, 11/1 priority date for domestic students; for spring admission, 1/7 priority date for domestic students, 11/15 priority date for international students; for summer admission, 4/1 priority date for domestic students. Applications are processed on a rolling basis. Application fee: $40. Electronic applications accepted. *Expenses:* $655.05 per credit. *Financial support:* Career-related internships or fieldwork and scholarships/grants available. Support available to part-time students. Financial award application deadline: 3/1; financial award applicants required to submit FAFSA. *Unit head:* Dr. John McCullough, Chair, Department of Education, 814-393-2404, Fax: 814-393-2446, E-mail: gradstudies@clarion.edu. *Application contact:* Dana Bearer, Associate Director for Transfer, Adult, and Graduate Programs, 814-393-2337, Fax: 814-393-2722, E-mail: gradstudies@clarion.edu.

Clarkson University, Program in Education, Schenectady, NY 12308. Offers adolescence education 7-12 (MAT); teaching of English to speakers of other languages (MAT); technology education K-12 (MAT). *Accreditation:* TEAC. *Faculty:* 3 full-time (all women), 23 part-time/adjunct (14 women). *Students:* 22 full-time (13 women), 12 part-time (8 women); includes 4 minority (1 Black or African American, non-Hispanic/Latino; 3 Asian, non-Hispanic/Latino), 6 international. 39 applicants, 72% accepted, 21 enrolled. In 2017, 28 master's awarded. *Degree requirements:* For master's, thesis (for some programs), thesis or project. *Entrance requirements:* For master's, GRE, minimum undergraduate GPA of 3.0. Additional exam requirements/recommendations for international students: Required—TOEFL (minimum score 550 paper-based, 80 iBT) or IELTS (6.5). *Application deadline:* Applications are processed on a rolling basis. Application fee: $50. Electronic applications accepted. *Expenses:* Contact institution. *Financial support:* Scholarships/grants available. *Unit head:* Dr. Catherine Snyder, Chair of Education, 518-631-9870, E-mail: csnyder@clarkson.edu. *Application contact:* Dan Capogna, Director of Graduate Admissions, 518-631-9910, E-mail: graduate@clarkson.edu.
Website: https://www.clarkson.edu/academics/graduate

Concordia University, College of Education, Portland, OR 97211-6099. Offers career and technical education (M Ed); curriculum and instruction (M Ed), including adolescent literacy, career and technical education, e-learning/technology education, early childhood education, English for speakers of other languages, English language development, environmental education, mathematics, methods and curriculum, reading, science, teacher leadership, the inclusive classroom; early childhood (MAT); education leadership (Ed D); educational administration (M Ed); elementary education (MAT); secondary education (MAT); special education (M Ed); teacher leadership (Ed D). *Program availability:* Part-time, online learning. *Degree requirements:* For master's, comprehensive exam, work samples/portfolio. *Entrance requirements:* For master's, California Basic Educational Skills Test or PRAXIS I, minimum undergraduate GPA of 2.8, graduate 3.0; 2 letters of recommendation. Additional exam requirements/recommendations for international students: Required—TOEFL (minimum score 525 paper-based). Electronic applications accepted. *Faculty research:* Learner-centered classroom, brain-based learning, future of online learning.

East Carolina University, Graduate School, College of Education, Department of Interdisciplinary Professions, Greenville, NC 27858-4353. Offers adult education (MA Ed); business and marketing education (MA Ed); community college instruction (Certificate); counselor education (MS); education in the healthcare professions (Certificate); library science (MLS); student affairs in higher education (Certificate); vocational education (MS). *Accreditation:* ACA; NCATE. *Program availability:* Part-time, evening/weekend. *Students:* 97 full-time (77 women), 392 part-time (344 women); includes 107 minority (73 Black or African American, non-Hispanic/Latino; 6 American Indian or Alaska Native, non-Hispanic/Latino; 5 Asian, non-Hispanic/Latino; 11 Hispanic/Latino; 12 Two or more races, non-Hispanic/Latino). Average age 36. 148 applicants, 97% accepted, 116 enrolled. In 2017, 148 master's, 23 other advanced degrees awarded. *Degree requirements:* For master's, comprehensive exam, thesis optional. *Entrance requirements:* For master's, GRE General Test or MAT, interview, minimum GPA of 2.5, bachelor's degree in related field, teaching license (MA Ed). Additional exam requirements/recommendations for international students: Required—TOEFL. *Application deadline:* For fall admission, 5/15 priority date for domestic students. Applications are processed on a rolling basis. Application fee: $75. *Expenses:* Tuition, state resident: full-time $4749; part-time $297 per credit hour. Tuition, nonresident: full-time $17,898; part-time $1119 per credit hour. *Required fees:* $2691; $224 per credit hour. Part-time tuition and fees vary according to course load and program. *Financial support:* Research assistantships with partial tuition reimbursements, teaching assistantships with partial tuition reimbursements, and Federal Work-Study available. Support available to part-time students. Financial award application deadline: 6/1. *Unit head:* Dr. Vivian W. Mott, Chair, 252-328-6177, Fax: 252-328-4368, E-mail: mottv@ecu.edu.
Website: http://www.ecu.edu/cs-educ/idp/index.cfm

Eastern Kentucky University, The Graduate School, College of Business and Technology, Department of Technology, Program in Industrial Education, Richmond, KY 40475-3102. Offers occupational training and development (MS); technical administration (MS); technology education (MS). *Accreditation:* NCATE. *Program availability:* Part-time. *Entrance requirements:* For master's, GRE General Test, minimum GPA of 2.5.

Eastern Kentucky University, The Graduate School, College of Education, Department of Curriculum and Instruction, Program in Secondary and Higher Education, Richmond, KY 40475-3102. Offers secondary education (MA Ed), including agricultural education, art education, biological sciences education, business education, English education, geography education, history education, home economics education, industrial education, mathematical sciences education, physical education, school health education. *Accreditation:* NCATE. *Program availability:* Part-time. *Entrance requirements:* For master's, GRE General Test, minimum GPA of 2.5.

Eastern New Mexico University, Graduate School, College of Education and Technology, Department of Curriculum and Instruction, Portales, NM 88130. Offers alternative licensure in elementary education (M Ed); bilingual education (M Ed); career and technical education (M Ed); educational technology (M Ed); elementary education (M Ed); English as a second language (M Ed); pedagogy and learning (M Ed); reading/literacy (M Ed). *Program availability:* Part-time, online learning. *Degree requirements:* For master's, comprehensive exam, thesis optional. *Entrance requirements:* For master's, writing assessment, minimum GPA of 3.0, photocopy of teaching license, letter of recommendation. Additional exam requirements/recommendations for international students: Required—TOEFL (minimum score 550 paper-based; 79 iBT), IELTS (minimum score 6). *Application deadline:* For fall admission, 7/20 priority date for domestic students, 6/20 priority date for international students; for spring admission, 12/15 priority date for domestic students, 11/15 priority date for international students. Applications are processed on a rolling basis. Application fee: $10. Electronic applications accepted. *Financial support:* Applicants required to submit FAFSA. *Unit head:* Dr. Mary Daughrity, Graduate Coordinator, 575-562-2481, Fax: 575-562-2559, E-mail: mary.daughrity@enmu.edu. *Application contact:* Cheryl Reeves, Senior Secretary, 575-562-2443, E-mail: cheryl.reeves@enmu.edu.
Website: http://education.enmu.edu

Fitchburg State University, Division of Graduate and Continuing Education, Program in Occupational Education, Fitchburg, MA 01420-2697. Offers M Ed. *Accreditation:* NCATE. *Program availability:* Part-time, evening/weekend. *Faculty:* 1 full-time (0 women), 12 part-time/adjunct (4 women). *Students:* 1 (woman) full-time, 15 part-time (9 women); includes 2 minority (both Hispanic/Latino). Average age 40. 5 applicants, 100% accepted, 5 enrolled. In 2017, 16 master's awarded. *Entrance requirements:* Additional exam requirements/recommendations for international students: Required—TOEFL (minimum score 550 paper-based; 79 iBT). *Application deadline:* For fall admission, 7/15 for international students; for spring admission, 12/1 for international students. Applications are processed on a rolling basis. Application fee: $50. Electronic applications accepted. *Expenses:* Contact institution. *Financial support:* In 2017–18, research assistantships with partial tuition reimbursements (averaging $5,500 per year) were awarded; Federal Work-Study, scholarships/grants, and unspecified assistantships also available. Support available to part-time students. Financial award application deadline: 3/1; financial award applicants required to submit FAFSA. *Unit head:* James Alicata, Chair, 978-665-3047, Fax: 978-665-3658, E-mail: gce@fitchburgstate.edu. *Application contact:* Jinawa McNeil, Director of Admissions, 978-665-3140, Fax: 978-665-4540, E-mail: admissions@fitchburgstate.edu.
Website: http://www.fitchburgstate.edu

Fitchburg State University, Division of Graduate and Continuing Education, Program in Technology Education, Fitchburg, MA 01420-2697. Offers M Ed. *Accreditation:* NCATE. *Program availability:* Part-time, evening/weekend. *Entrance requirements:* Additional exam requirements/recommendations for international students: Required—TOEFL (minimum score 550 paper-based; 79 iBT). *Application deadline:* For fall admission, 7/15 for international students; for spring admission, 12/1 for international students. Applications are processed on a rolling basis. Application fee: $50. Electronic applications accepted. *Expenses:* Tuition, state resident: part-time $167 per credit. Tuition, nonresident: part-time $167 per credit. *Required fees:* $137 per credit. *Financial support:* In 2017–18, research assistantships with partial tuition reimbursements (averaging $5,500 per year) were awarded; Federal Work-Study, scholarships/grants, and unspecified assistantships also available. Support available to part-time students. Financial award application deadline: 3/1; financial award applicants required to submit FAFSA. *Unit head:* Wayne Whitfield, Chair, 978-665-4807, Fax: 978-665-3658, E-mail: gce@fitchburgstate.edu. *Application contact:* Jinawa McNeil, Director of Admissions, 978-665-3140, Fax: 978-665-4540, E-mail: admissions@fitchburgstate.edu.
Website: http://www.fitchburgstate.edu

Florida Agricultural and Mechanical University, Division of Graduate Studies, Research, and Continuing Education, College of Education, Department of Vocational Education, Tallahassee, FL 32307-3200. Offers business education (MBE); industrial education (MS Ed); technology education (M Ed). *Accreditation:* NCATE. *Degree requirements:* For master's, thesis (for some programs). *Entrance requirements:* For master's, GRE General Test, minimum GPA of 3.0. Additional exam requirements/recommendations for international students: Required—TOEFL.

The George Washington University, Graduate School of Education and Human Development, Department of Counseling and Human Development, Program in Job Development and Placement, Washington, DC 20052. Offers Graduate Certificate. *Program availability:* Online learning. *Students:* 1 applicant, 100% accepted. *Expenses:* Tuition: Full-time $28,800; part-time $1655 per credit hour. *Required fees:* $45; $2.75 per credit hour. *Financial support:* Fellowships available. *Unit head:* Dr. Kenneth C. Hergenrather, Director, 202-994-1334, E-mail: hergenkc@gwu.edu. *Application contact:* Sarah Lang, Director of Graduate Admissions, 202-994-1447, Fax: 202-994-7207, E-mail: slang@gwu.edu.
Website: http://gsehd.gwu.edu/

Indiana State University, College of Graduate and Professional Studies, College of Technology, Department of Human Resource Development and Performance Technologies, Terre Haute, IN 47809. Offers career and technical education (MS); human resource development (MS).

Indiana University of Pennsylvania, School of Graduate Studies and Research, College of Education and Communications, Department of Adult and Community Education, Program in Business/Administrative, Indiana, PA 15705. Offers M Ed. *Program availability:* Part-time. *Faculty:* 2 full-time (both women). *Students:* 2 full-time (both women), 2 part-time (both women). 2 applicants, 100% accepted. *Degree requirements:* For master's, thesis optional. *Entrance requirements:* For master's, GMAT or GRE. Additional exam requirements/recommendations for international students: Required—TOEFL (minimum score 540 paper-based). *Application deadline:* Applications are processed on a rolling basis. Application fee: $50. Electronic applications accepted. *Expenses:* Tuition, state resident: full-time $12,000; part-time $500 per credit. Tuition, nonresident: full-time $18,000; part-time $750 per credit. *Required fees:* $4073; $165.55 per credit. $64 per term. *Financial support:* Career-related internships or fieldwork, Federal Work-Study, scholarships/grants, and unspecified assistantships available. Financial award application deadline: 4/15; financial award applicants required to submit FAFSA. *Unit head:* Prof. Jacqueline McGinty, Coordinator, 724-357-2470, E-mail: jacqueline.mcginty@iup.edu.
Website: http://www.iup.edu/ace/grad/default.aspx

Inter American University of Puerto Rico, Metropolitan Campus, Graduate Programs, Program in Occupational Education, San Juan, PR 00919-1293. Offers MA. *Degree requirements:* For master's, comprehensive exam. *Entrance requirements:* For master's, GRE or EXADEP, interview. Electronic applications accepted.

Iowa State University of Science and Technology, Program in Industrial Agriculture and Technology, Ames, IA 50011. Offers MS, PhD. *Entrance requirements:* For master's and doctorate, GRE General Test. Additional exam requirements/recommendations for international students: Required—TOEFL (minimum score 550 paper-based; 79 iBT), IELTS (minimum score 6.5). Electronic applications accepted. *Faculty research:* Industrial technology, technology education, training and development, technical education.

Jackson State University, Graduate School, College of Science, Engineering and Technology, Department of Civil and Environmental Engineering and Industrial Systems and Technology, Jackson, MS 39217. Offers civil engineering (MS, PhD); coastal engineering (MS, PhD); environmental engineering (MS, PhD); hazardous materials management (MS); technology education (MS Ed). *Program availability:* Part-time, evening/weekend. *Degree requirements:* For master's, comprehensive exam, thesis or alternative. *Entrance requirements:* For master's, GRE General Test. Additional exam requirements/recommendations for international students: Required—TOEFL (minimum score 520 paper-based; 67 iBT).

James Madison University, The Graduate School, College of Education, Program in Adult Education and Human Resource Development, Harrisonburg, VA 22801. Offers higher education (MS Ed); human resource management (MS Ed); individualized (MS Ed); instructional design (MS Ed); leadership and facilitation (MS Ed); program evaluation and measurement (MS Ed). *Accreditation:* NCATE. *Program availability:* Part-time, evening/weekend. *Students:* 11 full-time (7 women), 12 part-time (10 women); includes 7 minority (4 Black or African American, non-Hispanic/Latino; 1 Hispanic/Latino; 2 Two or more races, non-Hispanic/Latino), 1 international. Average age 30. In 2017, 3 master's awarded. Application fee: $55. Electronic applications accepted. *Expenses:* Tuition, state resident: full-time $10,512; part-time $438 per credit hour. Tuition, nonresident: full-time $28,358; part-time $1162 per credit hour. *Required fees:* $1128. *Financial support:* In 2017–18, 10 students received support. Teaching assistantships, Federal Work-Study, and 10 assistantships (averaging $7911) available. Financial award application deadline: 3/1; financial award applicants required to submit FAFSA. *Unit head:* Dr. Jane B. Thall, Department Head, 540-568-5531, E-mail: thalljb@jmu.edu. *Application contact:* Lynette D. Michael, Director of Graduate Admissions, 540-568-6131 Ext. 6395, Fax: 540-568-7860, E-mail: michaeld@jmu.edu.

Kent State University, College of Education, Health and Human Services, School of Teaching, Learning and Curriculum Studies, Program in Career Technical Teacher Education, Kent, OH 44242-0001. Offers M Ed. *Program availability:* Part-time, evening/weekend. *Entrance requirements:* For master's, 2 letters of reference, goals statement. Additional exam requirements/recommendations for international students: Required—TOEFL (minimum score 550 paper-based; 80 iBT). Electronic applications accepted. *Expenses:* Tuition, state resident: full-time $11,310; part-time $515 per credit hour. Tuition, nonresident: full-time $20,396; part-time $928 per credit hour. *International tuition:* $18,544 full-time. *Faculty research:* Workforce education/development, adult education, training and organizational change.

Louisiana State University and Agricultural & Mechanical College, Graduate School, College of Human Sciences and Education, School of Human Resource Education and Workforce Development, Baton Rouge, LA 70803. Offers agriculture and extension education and youth development (MS, PhD); career and technical education (MS, PhD); comprehensive vocational education (MS, PhD); extension and international education (MS, PhD); human resource and leadership development (MS, PhD); industrial education (MS); vocational agriculture education (MS, PhD); vocational business education (MS); vocational home economics education (MS). *Accreditation:* NCATE. *Faculty:* 11 full-time (6 women). *Students:* 102 full-time (71 women), 130 part-time (92 women); includes 89 minority (63 Black or African American, non-Hispanic/

Latino; 3 American Indian or Alaska Native, non-Hispanic/Latino; 8 Asian, non-Hispanic/Latino; 14 Hispanic/Latino; 1 Two or more races, non-Hispanic/Latino), 6 international. Average age 35. 98 applicants, 69% accepted, 52 enrolled. In 2017, 94 master's, 15 doctorates awarded. *Financial support:* In 2017–18, 1 fellowship (averaging $18,238 per year), 16 teaching assistantships (averaging $15,341 per year) were awarded. *Total annual research expenditures:* $1,998.

Middle Tennessee State University, College of Graduate Studies, College of Basic and Applied Sciences, Department of Engineering Technology and Industrial Studies, Murfreesboro, TN 37132. Offers engineering technology (MS). *Program availability:* Part-time, evening/weekend, online learning. *Degree requirements:* For master's, comprehensive exam. *Entrance requirements:* For master's, GRE. Additional exam requirements/recommendations for international students: Required—TOEFL (minimum score 525 paper-based; 71 iBT) or IELTS (minimum score 6). Electronic applications accepted.

Millersville University of Pennsylvania, College of Graduate Studies and Adult Learning, College of Science and Technology, Department of Applied Engineering, Safety, and Technology, Millersville, PA 17551-0302. Offers technology and innovation (M Ed). *Accreditation:* NCATE. *Program availability:* Part-time, evening/weekend. *Faculty:* 2 full-time (0 women), 1 part-time/adjunct (0 women). *Students:* 4 full-time (2 women), 25 part-time (8 women); includes 1 minority (Hispanic/Latino), 12 international. Average age 29. 11 applicants, 100% accepted, 10 enrolled. In 2017, 8 master's awarded. *Degree requirements:* For master's, comprehensive exam (for some programs), thesis optional, graded portfolio (educational foundations). *Entrance requirements:* For master's, GRE or MAT (if undergraduate cumulative GPA is 3.0 or lower). Additional exam requirements/recommendations for international students: Required—TOEFL (minimum score 80 iBT), IELTS (minimum score 6.5), PTE (minimum score 60). *Application deadline:* Applications are processed on a rolling basis. Application fee: $40. Electronic applications accepted. *Expenses:* $500 per credit resident tuition and fees; $750 per credit non-resident tuition and fees; $114.75 per credit general fee (maximum of 12 credits); technology fee $27 per credit (resident), $39 per credit (non-resident). *Financial support:* In 2017–18, 5 students received support. Unspecified assistantships available. Financial award application deadline: 3/15; financial award applicants required to submit FAFSA. *Faculty research:* Professional development schools, engineering design, nanomanufacturing, occupational safety, robotics and artificial vision. *Total annual research expenditures:* $139,356. *Unit head:* Dr. Leonard S. Litowitz, Chairperson, 717-871-7215, Fax: 717-871-7931, E-mail: len.litowitz@millersville.edu. *Application contact:* Dr. Victor S. DeSantis, Dean of College of Graduate Studies and Adult Learning/Associate Provost for Civic and Community Engagement, 717-871-7619, Fax: 717-871-7954, E-mail: victor.desantis@millersville.edu. Website: http://www.millersville.edu/aest/

Mississippi State University, College of Education, Department of Instructional Systems and Workforce Development, Mississippi State, MS 39762. Offers instructional systems and workforce development (MSIT, PhD); technology (MST, Ed S). *Faculty:* 10 full-time (6 women). *Students:* 13 full-time (5 women), 45 part-time (34 women); includes 35 minority (34 Black or African American, non-Hispanic/Latino; 1 Two or more races, non-Hispanic/Latino), 1 international. Average age 37. 28 applicants, 68% accepted, 14 enrolled. In 2017, 4 master's, 6 doctorates, 4 other advanced degrees awarded. *Degree requirements:* For master's, thesis optional, comprehensive oral or written exam; for doctorate, thesis/dissertation, comprehensive oral and written exam; for Ed S, thesis, comprehensive written exam. *Entrance requirements:* For master's, GRE, minimum GPA of 2.75 on undergraduate work, 3.0 graduate; for doctorate, GRE, minimum GPA of 3.4 on graduate work; for Ed S, GRE, minimum GPA of 3.2, master's degree. Additional exam requirements/recommendations for international students: Required—TOEFL (minimum score 550 paper-based; 79 iBT); Recommended—IELTS (minimum score 6.5). *Application deadline:* For fall admission, 7/1 for domestic students, 5/1 for international students; for spring admission, 11/1 for domestic students, 9/1 for international students. Applications are processed on a rolling basis. Application fee: $60 ($80 for international students). Electronic applications accepted. *Expenses:* Tuition, state resident: full-time $8318; part-time $462.12 per credit hour. Tuition, nonresident: full-time $22,358; part-time $1242.12 per credit hour. *Required fees:* $110; $12.24 per credit hour. $6.12 per semester. *Financial support:* In 2017–18, 2 teaching assistantships with full tuition reimbursements (averaging $10,575 per year) were awarded; Federal Work-Study, institutionally sponsored loans, scholarships/grants, and unspecified assistantships also available. Financial award application deadline: 4/1; financial award applicants required to submit FAFSA. *Faculty research:* Computer technology, nontraditional students, interactive video, instructional technology, educational leadership. *Unit head:* Dr. Trey Martindale, Associate Professor and Head, 662-325-7258, Fax: 662-325-7599, E-mail: tmartindale@colled.msstate.edu. *Application contact:* Angie Campbell, Admissions and Enrollment Assistant, 662-325-9514, E-mail: acampbell@grad.msstate.edu. Website: http://www.iswd.msstate.edu

Mississippi State University, College of Education, Educational Leadership Program, Mississippi State, MS 39762. Offers community college education (MAT); community college leadership (PhD); higher education leadership (PhD); P-12 school leadership (PhD); school administration (MS, Ed S); student affairs and higher education (MS); workforce education leadership (MS). MS in workforce education leadership held jointly with Alcorn State University. *Faculty:* 12 full-time (9 women). *Students:* 62 full-time (33 women), 149 part-time (93 women); includes 94 minority (79 Black or African American, non-Hispanic/Latino; 5 American Indian or Alaska Native, non-Hispanic/Latino; 4 Hispanic/Latino; 1 Native Hawaiian or other Pacific Islander, non-Hispanic/Latino; 5 Two or more races, non-Hispanic/Latino). Average age 36. 95 applicants, 79% accepted, 64 enrolled. In 2017, 41 master's, 32 doctorates, 7 other advanced degrees awarded. *Degree requirements:* For master's and Ed S, comprehensive exam, thesis; for doctorate, comprehensive exam, thesis/dissertation. *Entrance requirements:* For master's, GRE, minimum GPA of 2.75 in junior and senior courses; for doctorate, GRE, minimum GPA of 3.4 on previous graduate work; for Ed S, GRE, minimum GPA of 3.2, master's degree. Additional exam requirements/recommendations for international students: Required—TOEFL (minimum score 550 paper-based; 79 iBT); Recommended—IELTS (minimum score 6.5). *Application deadline:* For fall admission, 7/1 for domestic students, 5/1 for international students; for spring admission, 11/1 for domestic students, 9/1 for international students. Application fee: $60 ($80 for international students). Electronic applications accepted. *Expenses:* Tuition, state resident: full-time $8318; part-time $462.12 per credit hour. Tuition, nonresident: full-time $22,358; part-time $1242.12 per credit hour. *Required fees:* $110; $12.24 per credit hour. $6.12 per semester. *Financial support:* In 2017–18, 1 research assistantship with full tuition reimbursement (averaging $10,879 per year) was awarded; Federal Work-Study, institutionally sponsored loans, and unspecified assistantships also available. Financial award application deadline: 4/1; financial award applicants required to submit FAFSA. *Unit head:* Dr. Eric Moyen, Associate Professor and Head, 662-325-0969, Fax: 662-325-0975, E-mail: em1621@msstate.edu. *Application contact:* Nathan Drake, Admissions and Enrollment Assistant, 662-325-3804, E-mail: ndrake@grad.msstate.edu. Website: http://www.educationalleadership.msstate.edu/

Montana State University, The Graduate School, College of Education, Health, and Human Development, Department of Education, Bozeman, MT 59717. Offers adult and higher education (Ed D); curriculum and instruction (M Ed, Ed D), including professional educator (M Ed), technology education (M Ed); education (M Ed), including adult and

higher education, educational leadership, school counseling; educational leadership (Ed D, Ed S). *Accreditation:* TEAC. *Program availability:* Part-time, online learning. *Degree requirements:* For master's, comprehensive exam; for doctorate, comprehensive exam, thesis/dissertation. *Entrance requirements:* For master's, GRE, 3 letters of reference, essays, BA transcripts; for doctorate, GRE, MAT, 3 letters of reference, essay, BA and M Ed transcripts; for Ed S, PRAXIS. Additional exam requirements/recommendations for international students: Required—TOEFL (minimum score 550 paper-based). Electronic applications accepted. *Faculty research:* Critical literacy; standards-based education; school Improvement, organizational change, leadership in rural education, leadership in Indian education; student Learning; multicultural/culturally responsive education for social justice Native American indigenous education, community-centered education teacher preparation.

Morehead State University, Graduate Programs, College of Science and Technology, Department of Industrial and Engineering Technology, Morehead, KY 40351. Offers career and technical education (MS); engineering technology (MS). *Program availability:* Part-time, evening/weekend. *Degree requirements:* For master's, completion and defense of thesis or written and oral comprehensive exit exams. *Entrance requirements:* For master's, GRE, minimum undergraduate GPA of 3.0 in major. Additional exam requirements/recommendations for international students: Required—TOEFL (minimum score 500 paper-based). Electronic applications accepted.

Murray State University, College of Education and Human Services, Department of Adolescent, Career, and Special Education, Murray, KY 42071. Offers career and technical education (MS); middle school teacher leader (MA Ed); secondary teacher leader (MA Ed); special education (MA Ed), including mild learning and behavior disorders, moderate to severe disabilities (P-12), teacher leader in special education learning and behavior disorders; teacher education and professional development (Ed S). *Accreditation:* NCATE. *Program availability:* Part-time. *Faculty:* 10 full-time (9 women). *Students:* 4 full-time (2 women), 78 part-time (56 women); includes 4 minority (2 Black or African American, non-Hispanic/Latino; 1 Asian, non-Hispanic/Latino; 1 Hispanic/Latino), 2 international. Average age 33. 13 applicants, 100% accepted, 8 enrolled. In 2017, 19 master's awarded. *Entrance requirements:* For master's and Ed S, GRE or GMAT, minimum university GPA of 2.75. Additional exam requirements/recommendations for international students: Required—TOEFL (minimum score 527 paper-based; 71 iBT). *Application deadline:* Applications are processed on a rolling basis. Application fee: $40 ($50 for international students). Electronic applications accepted. *Expenses:* Tuition, state resident: full-time $9504. Tuition, nonresident: full-time $26,811. *International tuition:* $14,400 full-time. Tuition and fees vary according to course load, degree level and reciprocity agreements. *Financial support:* Federal Work-Study and unspecified assistantships available. Financial award applicants required to submit FAFSA. *Unit head:* Dr. Barbara Washington, Chair, Department of Adolescent, Career and Special Education, 270-809-2262, Fax: 270-809-2540, E-mail: bwashington@murraystate.edu. *Application contact:* Kaitlyn Burzynski, Interim Assistant Director of Graduate Admission and Records, 270-809-5732, Fax: 270-809-3780, E-mail: msu.graduateadmissions@murraystate.edu. Website: http://www.murraystate.edu/academics/CollegesDepartments/CollegeOfEducationandHumanServices/coehsacademicunits/AdolescentCareerSpecialEd/index.aspx

North Carolina Agricultural and Technical State University, School of Graduate Studies, School of Technology, Department of Graphic Communication Systems and Technological Studies, Greensboro, NC 27411. Offers graphic communication systems (MSTM); technology education (MAT). *Accreditation:* NCATE (one or more programs are accredited). *Program availability:* Part-time, evening/weekend. *Degree requirements:* For master's, comprehensive exam, thesis or alternative, qualifying exam. *Entrance requirements:* For master's, GRE General Test, minimum GPA of 3.0.

North Dakota State University, College of Graduate and Interdisciplinary Studies, College of Human Development and Education, School of Education, Fargo, ND 58102. Offers agricultural education (M Ed, MS), including agricultural education; counselor education (M Ed, MS, PhD), including clinical mental health counseling (M Ed, MS), counselor education and supervision (PhD); school counseling (M Ed, MS); curriculum and instruction (M Ed, MS); education (PhD); educational leadership (M Ed, MS, Ed S); family and consumer sciences education (M Ed, MS); history education (M Ed, MS); institutional analysis (Ed D); mathematics education (M Ed, MS); music education (M Ed, MS); occupational and adult education (Ed D); science education (M Ed, MS). *Accreditation:* NCATE. *Program availability:* Part-time, evening/weekend, online learning. *Degree requirements:* For master's, comprehensive exam; for doctorate, thesis/dissertation; for Ed S, thesis. *Entrance requirements:* For degree, GRE General Test, master's degree, minimum GPA of 3.25. Additional exam requirements/recommendations for international students: Required—TOEFL.

Northern Arizona University, College of Education, Department of Educational Specialties, Flagstaff, AZ 86011. Offers autism spectrum disorders (Certificate); bilingual/multicultural education (M Ed), including bilingual, ESL; career and technical education (M Ed, Certificate); educational technology (M Ed, Certificate); English as a second language (Certificate); positive behavior support (Certificate); special education (M Ed), including early childhood special education, mild/moderate disabilities. *Program availability:* Part-time, 100% online, blended/hybrid learning. *Faculty:* 31 full-time (19 women), 2 part-time/adjunct (1 woman). *Students:* 66 full-time (52 women), 203 part-time (147 women); includes 83 minority (20 Black or African American, non-Hispanic/Latino; 12 American Indian or Alaska Native, non-Hispanic/Latino; 5 Asian, non-Hispanic/Latino; 38 Hispanic/Latino; 3 Native Hawaiian or other Pacific Islander, non-Hispanic/Latino; 5 Two or more races, non-Hispanic/Latino), 6 international. Average age 37. 157 applicants, 94% accepted, 148 enrolled. In 2017, 119 master's, 26 Certificates awarded. *Degree requirements:* For master's, variable foreign language requirement, comprehensive exam (for some programs), thesis (for some programs); for Certificate, comprehensive exam (for some programs). *Entrance requirements:* Additional exam requirements/recommendations for international students: Required—TOEFL (minimum score 80 iBT), IELTS (minimum score 6.5). *Application deadline:* For fall admission, 3/1 for domestic and international students; for spring admission, 10/1 for domestic and international students. Applications are processed on a rolling basis. Application fee: $65. Electronic applications accepted. *Expenses:* Tuition, state resident: full-time $9240; part-time $458 per credit hour. Tuition, nonresident: full-time $21,588; part-time $1199 per credit hour. *Required fees:* $1021; $14 per credit hour. $646 per semester. Tuition and fees vary according to course load, campus/location and program. *Financial support:* In 2017–18, 11 students received support, including 1 fellowship with full and partial tuition reimbursement available (averaging $12,000 per year), 10 teaching assistantships with full and partial tuition reimbursements available (averaging $12,000 per year); Federal Work-Study, institutionally sponsored loans, health care benefits, tuition waivers (full and partial), and unspecified assistantships also available. Financial award application deadline: 2/1; financial award applicants required to submit FAFSA. *Unit head:* Dr. Shadow Armfield, Chair, 928-523-7651, Fax: 928-523-1929, E-mail: laura.sujo-montes@nau.edu. *Application contact:* Tina Sutton, Coordinator, Graduate College, 928-523-4348, Fax: 928-523-8950, E-mail: graduate@nau.edu. Website: https://nau.edu/coe/Ed-Specialties/

Old Dominion University, Darden College of Education, Programs in STEM Education and Professional Studies, Norfolk, VA 23529. Offers community college teaching (MS); human resources training (PhD); technology education (PhD). *Accreditation:* NCATE (one or more programs are accredited). *Program availability:* Part-time, evening/weekend, mix of synchronous and asynchronous study. *Faculty:* 6 full-time (2 women). *Students:* 10 full-time (7 women), 35 part-time (24 women); includes 22 minority (18 Black or African American, non-Hispanic/Latino; 1 American Indian or Alaska Native, non-Hispanic/Latino; 2 Hispanic/Latino; 1 Two or more races, non-Hispanic/Latino), 1 international. Average age 41. 3 applicants, 100% accepted, 3 enrolled. In 2017, 4 master's, 3 doctorates awarded. Terminal master's awarded for partial completion of doctoral program. *Degree requirements:* For master's, comprehensive exam, thesis optional, writing exam, candidacy exam; for doctorate, comprehensive exam, thesis/dissertation, writing exam, candidacy exam. *Entrance requirements:* For master's, GRE General Test or MAT, minimum GPA of 2.8, 2 letters of reference; for doctorate, GRE, minimum GPA of 3.0, 3 letters of reference. Additional exam requirements/recommendations for international students: Required—TOEFL. *Application deadline:* For fall admission, 6/1 priority date for domestic students, 6/1 for international students; for winter admission, 11/1 priority date for domestic students, 11/1 for international students; for spring admission, 3/1 priority date for domestic students, 3/1 for international students. Applications are processed on a rolling basis. Application fee: $50. Electronic applications accepted. *Expenses:* Tuition, state resident: full-time $8928; part-time $496 per credit. Tuition, nonresident: full-time $22,482; part-time $1249 per credit. *Required fees:* $66 per semester. *Financial support:* In 2017–18, 3 students received support, including 2 teaching assistantships with partial tuition reimbursements available (averaging $15,000 per year). Financial award application deadline: 2/15; financial award applicants required to submit FAFSA. *Faculty research:* Training and development, STEM education, visualization, leadership, technology literacy. *Total annual research expenditures:* $1 million. *Unit head:* Dr. Petros Katsioloudis, Department Chair, 757-683-5323, E-mail: pkatsiol@odu.edu. Website: http://education.odu.edu/ots/

Penn State University Park, Graduate School, College of Education, Department of Learning and Performance Systems, University Park, PA 16802. Offers learning, design, and technology (M Ed, MS, PhD, Certificate); lifelong learning and adult education (M Ed, D Ed, PhD, Certificate); workforce education and development (M Ed, MS, PhD). *Unit head:* Dr. David H. Monk, Dean, 814-865-2523, Fax: 814-865-0555. *Application contact:* Lori Hawn, Director, Graduate Student Services, 814-865-1795, Fax: 814-863-4627, E-mail: l-gswww@lists.psu.edu. Website: http://ed.psu.edu/lps/dept-lps

Pittsburg State University, Graduate School, College of Technology, Department of Technology and Workforce Learning, Pittsburg, KS 66762. Offers career and technical education (MS); human resource development (MS); technology (MS), including automotive technology, construction management, graphic design, graphics management, information technology, innovation in technology, personnel development, technology management, workforce learning; workforce development and education (Ed S). *Program availability:* Part-time, evening/weekend, 100% online, blended/hybrid learning. *Students:* 129 (66 women); includes 18 minority (7 Black or African American, non-Hispanic/Latino; 3 American Indian or Alaska Native, non-Hispanic/Latino; 1 Asian, non-Hispanic/Latino; 3 Hispanic/Latino; 4 Two or more races, non-Hispanic/Latino), 29 international. In 2017, 62 master's, 2 other advanced degrees awarded. *Degree requirements:* For master's, thesis or alternative; for Ed S, thesis optional. *Entrance requirements:* Additional exam requirements/recommendations for international students: Required—TOEFL (minimum score 520 paper-based; 68 iBT), IELTS (minimum score 6), PTE (minimum score 47). *Application deadline:* For fall admission, 7/15 for domestic students, 6/1 for international students; for spring admission, 12/15 for domestic students, 10/15 for international students; for summer admission, 5/15 for domestic students, 4/1 for international students. Applications are processed on a rolling basis. Application fee: $35 ($60 for international students). Electronic applications accepted. *Expenses:* Contact institution. *Financial support:* In 2017–18, 8 teaching assistantships with full tuition reimbursements (averaging $5,500 per year) were awarded; career-related internships or fieldwork also available. Financial award application deadline: 2/1; financial award applicants required to submit FAFSA. *Unit head:* Dr. John Iley, Chairperson, 620-235-4373, E-mail: jiley@pittstate.edu. *Application contact:* Lisa Allen, Assistant Director of Graduate and Continuing Studies, 620-235-4218, Fax: 620-235-4219, E-mail: lallen@pittstate.edu.

Purdue University, Graduate School, College of Education, Department of Curriculum and Instruction, West Lafayette, IN 47907. Offers agricultural and extension education (MS, MS Ed, PhD, Ed S); art education (PhD); career and technical education (MS Ed, PhD, Ed S); curriculum studies (MS Ed, PhD, Ed S); educational technology (MS Ed, PhD, Ed S); elementary education (MS Ed); family and consumer sciences education (MS Ed, PhD, Ed S); foreign language education (MS Ed, PhD, Ed S); industrial technology (PhD, Ed S); language arts (MS Ed, PhD, Ed S); literacy (MS Ed, PhD, Ed S); mathematics education (MS, MS Ed, PhD, Ed S); science education (MS, MS Ed, PhD, Ed S); social studies education (MS Ed, PhD, Ed S). *Accreditation:* NCATE. *Program availability:* Part-time, evening/weekend. *Faculty:* 37 full-time (27 women), 1 (woman) part-time/adjunct. *Students:* 78 full-time (50 women), 286 part-time (195 women); includes 68 minority (25 Black or African American, non-Hispanic/Latino; 3 American Indian or Alaska Native, non-Hispanic/Latino; 10 Asian, non-Hispanic/Latino; 22 Hispanic/Latino; 1 Native Hawaiian or other Pacific Islander, non-Hispanic/Latino; 7 Two or more races, non-Hispanic/Latino), 44 international. Average age 36. 150 applicants, 79% accepted, 73 enrolled. In 2017, 107 master's, 20 doctorates, 2 other advanced degrees awarded. *Degree requirements:* For master's, thesis optional; for doctorate, thesis/dissertation, oral and written exams; for Ed S, oral presentation, project. *Entrance requirements:* For master's, GRE General Test (if undergraduate GPA is below 3.0), minimum undergraduate GPA of 3.0 or equivalent; for doctorate, GRE General Test (minimum combined verbal and quantitative score of 1000, 300 for new scoring), minimum undergraduate GPA of 3.0 or equivalent; master's degree with minimum GPA of 3.0 or equivalent; for Ed S, GRE General Test (minimum combined verbal and quantitative score of 1000, 300 for new scoring), minimum undergraduate GPA of 3.0 or equivalent; master's degree. Additional exam requirements/recommendations for international students: Required—TOEFL (minimum score 550 paper-based; 77 iBT). *Application deadline:* For fall admission, 12/15 for domestic students, 3/1 for international students; for spring admission, 9/15 for domestic students, 8/1 for international students. Application fee: $60 ($75 for international students). Electronic applications accepted. *Financial support:* Fellowships with full tuition reimbursements, research assistantships with full tuition reimbursements, teaching assistantships with full tuition reimbursements, career-related internships or fieldwork, and tuition waivers (full) available. Support available to part-time students. Financial award application deadline: 3/1; financial award applicants required to submit FAFSA. *Faculty research:* Literacy acquisition and development, teacher beliefs and knowledge, recruitment and retention of underrepresented students, economic education, literacy discourse. *Unit head:* Janet M. Alsup, Head, 765-494-9667, E-mail: alsupj@purdue.edu. *Application contact:* Heather Brinkman, Graduate Contact, 765-494-2345, E-mail: hbrinkma@purdue.edu. Website: http://www.edci.purdue.edu/

South Carolina State University, College of Graduate and Professional Studies, Department of Education, Orangeburg, SC 29117-0001. Offers early childhood education (MAT); education (M Ed); elementary education (M Ed, MAT); English (MAT); general science/biology (MAT); mathematics (MAT); secondary education (M Ed), including biology education, business education, counselor education, English education, home economics education, industrial education, mathematics education, science education, social studies education; special education (M Ed), including emotionally handicapped, learning disabilities, mentally handicapped. *Accreditation:* NCATE. *Program availability:* Part-time, evening/weekend. *Faculty:* 11 full-time (6 women), 4 part-time/adjunct (2 women). *Students:* 26 full-time (18 women), 22 part-time (17 women); includes 41 minority (all Black or African American, non-Hispanic/Latino), 1 international. Average age 33. 25 applicants, 100% accepted, 19 enrolled. In 2017, 6 master's awarded. *Degree requirements:* For master's, thesis optional, departmental qualifying exam. *Entrance requirements:* For master's, GRE General Test, NTE, interview, teaching certificate. *Application deadline:* For fall admission, 6/15 priority date for domestic students, 6/15 for international students; for spring admission, 11/1 for domestic and international students. Application fee: $25. Electronic applications accepted. *Expenses:* Tuition, state resident: full-time $9388; part-time $607 per credit hour. Tuition, nonresident: full-time $19,968; part-time $1194 per credit hour. *Required fees:* $766; $766 per credit hour. *Financial support:* Fellowships, career-related internships or fieldwork, Federal Work-Study, and scholarships/grants available. Financial award application deadline: 6/1. *Unit head:* Dr. Charlie Spell, Interim Chair, Department of Education, 803-536-8963, Fax: 803-516-4568, E-mail: cspell@scsu.edu. *Application contact:* Curtis Foskey, Coordinator of Graduate Studies, 803-536-8419, Fax: 803-536-8812, E-mail: cfoskey@scsu.edu.

Southern Illinois University Carbondale, Graduate School, College of Education and Human Services, Department of Workforce Education and Development, Carbondale, IL 62901-4701. Offers MS Ed, PhD. *Accreditation:* NCATE. *Program availability:* Part-time. *Degree requirements:* For master's, thesis; for doctorate, thesis/dissertation. *Entrance requirements:* For master's, minimum GPA of 2.7; for doctorate, GRE General Test, minimum GPA of 3.25. Additional exam requirements/recommendations for international students: Required—TOEFL. *Faculty research:* Career education, technical training, curriculum development, competency-based instruction, impact of technology on workplace and workforce.

State University of New York at Oswego, Graduate School, School of Education, Department of Technology, Oswego, NY 13126. Offers MS Ed. *Accreditation:* NCATE. *Program availability:* Part-time. *Degree requirements:* For master's, thesis optional, departmental exam. *Entrance requirements:* For master's, provisional teaching certificate in technology education. Additional exam requirements/recommendations for international students: Required—TOEFL (minimum score 560 paper-based). *Faculty research:* Curriculum development, microcomputer applications.

State University of New York at Oswego, Graduate Studies, School of Education, Department of Vocational Teacher Preparation, Oswego, NY 13126. Offers agriculture (MS Ed); business and marketing (MS Ed); family and consumer sciences (MS Ed); health careers (MS Ed); technical education (MS Ed); trade education (MS Ed). *Accreditation:* NCATE. *Program availability:* Part-time, evening/weekend. *Degree requirements:* For master's, comprehensive exam, thesis or alternative. *Entrance requirements:* Additional exam requirements/recommendations for international students: Required—TOEFL (minimum score 560 paper-based).

Temple University, College of Education, Department of Teaching and Learning, Philadelphia, PA 19122-6096. Offers career and technical education (Ed M), including business, computing, and information technology, industrial education, marketing education; middle grades education (Ed M), including math and language arts, math and science, science and language arts; secondary education (Ed M), including English, math, social studies; teaching English to speakers of other languages (MS Ed); urban education (Ed M). *Program availability:* Part-time, evening/weekend. *Students:* 218 full-time (144 women), 296 part-time (183 women); includes 128 minority (74 Black or African American, non-Hispanic/Latino; 18 Asian, non-Hispanic/Latino; 25 Hispanic/Latino; 11 Two or more races, non-Hispanic/Latino), 13 international. 254 applicants, 54% accepted, 102 enrolled. In 2017, 128 master's awarded. Terminal master's awarded for partial completion of doctoral program. *Degree requirements:* For master's, thesis or alternative. *Entrance requirements:* Additional exam requirements/recommendations for international students: Required—TOEFL (minimum score 550 paper-based; 79 iBT). *Application deadline:* For fall admission, 4/1 for domestic students, 12/15 for international students; for spring admission, 10/1 for domestic students, 8/1 for international students. Application fee: $60. Electronic applications accepted. *Expenses:* Contact institution. *Financial support:* Fellowships, research assistantships, and teaching assistantships available. Financial award application deadline: 1/15; financial award applicants required to submit FAFSA. *Faculty research:* Workforce development, vocational education, technical education, industrial education, professional development, literacy, classroom management, school communities, curriculum development, instruction, applied linguistics, cross linguistic influence, bilingual education, oral proficiency, multilingualism. *Unit head:* Dr. Christine Woyshner, Chairperson, 215-204-6387, E-mail: christine.woyshner@temple.edu. *Application contact:* Sarah Stapleton, Assistant Director, Academic Operations, 215-204-8220, E-mail: sarah.stapleton@temple.edu. Website: http://education.temple.edu/tl

Texas State University, The Graduate College, College of Applied Arts, Interdisciplinary Studies Program in Occupational Education, San Marcos, TX 78666. Offers MAIS, MSIS. *Program availability:* Part-time, evening/weekend, blended/hybrid learning. *Faculty:* 7 full-time (4 women), 6 part-time/adjunct (3 women). *Students:* 19 full-time (9 women), 43 part-time (29 women); includes 31 minority (14 Black or African American, non-Hispanic/Latino; 1 Asian, non-Hispanic/Latino; 15 Hispanic/Latino; 1 Two or more races, non-Hispanic/Latino), 1 international. Average age 36. 42 applicants, 67% accepted, 12 enrolled. In 2017, 23 master's awarded. *Degree requirements:* For master's, comprehensive exam, thesis optional. *Entrance requirements:* For master's, baccalaureate degree from regionally-accredited university; minimum GPA of 2.75 for last 60 hours of undergraduate work or GRE General Test; statement of personal goals. Additional exam requirements/recommendations for international students: Required—TOEFL (minimum score 550 paper-based; 78 iBT), IELTS (minimum score 6.5). *Application deadline:* For fall admission, 2/15 priority date for domestic and international students; for spring admission, 10/15 priority date for domestic students, 10/1 for international students; for summer admission, 4/15 for domestic students, 3/15 for international students. Applications are processed on a rolling basis. Application fee: $40 ($90 for international students). Electronic applications accepted. *Expenses:* Tuition, state resident: full-time $7868; part-time $3934 per semester. Tuition, nonresident: full-time $17,828; part-time $8914 per semester. *Required fees:* $2092; $1435 per semester. Tuition and fees vary according to course load. *Financial support:* In 2017–18, 48 students received support, including 5 research assistantships (averaging $13,059 per year); teaching assistantships, Federal Work-Study, institutionally sponsored loans, scholarships/grants, health care benefits, and unspecified assistantships also available. Support available to part-time students. Financial award application deadline: 3/1; financial award applicants required to submit

FAFSA. *Faculty research:* Reaching under served rural agricultural Latinos and veterans; College Credit for Heroes;. *Total annual research expenditures:* $113,885. *Unit head:* Dr. Mary Jo Garcia Biggs, Chair of Occupational, Workforce, and Leadership Studies Department, 512-245-1680, E-mail: mb56@txstate.edu. *Application contact:* Dr. Andrea Golato, Dean of Graduate School, 512-245-2581, Fax: 512-245-8365, E-mail: gradcollege@txstate.edu.
Website: http://www.OCED.txstate.edu/

Texas State University, The Graduate College, College of Applied Arts, Program in Management of Technical Education, San Marcos, TX 78666. Offers M Ed. *Program availability:* Part-time, evening/weekend. *Faculty:* 7 full-time (4 women), 6 part-time/adjunct (3 women). *Students:* 3 full-time (0 women), 10 part-time (6 women); includes 9 minority (3 Black or African American, non-Hispanic/Latino; 1 American Indian or Alaska Native, non-Hispanic/Latino; 5 Hispanic/Latino). Average age 41. 8 applicants, 75% accepted, 2 enrolled. In 2017, 10 master's awarded. *Degree requirements:* For master's, comprehensive exam. *Entrance requirements:* For master's, baccalaureate degree from regionally-accredited university with minimum GPA of 2.75 in last 60 hours of course work or GRE General Test; statement of purpose. Additional exam requirements/recommendations for international students: Required—TOEFL (minimum score 550 paper-based; 78 iBT), IELTS (minimum score 6.5). *Application deadline:* For fall admission, 2/15 priority date for domestic and international students; for spring admission, 10/15 for domestic students, 10/1 for international students; for summer admission, 4/15 for domestic students, 3/15 for international students. Applications are processed on a rolling basis. Application fee: $40 ($90 for international students). Electronic applications accepted. *Expenses:* Tuition, state resident: full-time $7868; part-time $3934 per semester. Tuition, nonresident: full-time $17,828; part-time $8914 per semester. *Required fees:* $2092; $1435 per semester. Tuition and fees vary according to course load. *Financial support:* In 2017–18, 7 students received support. Research assistantships, teaching assistantships, career-related internships or fieldwork, Federal Work-Study, institutionally sponsored loans, scholarships/grants, and unspecified assistantships available. Support available to part-time students. Financial award application deadline: 3/1; financial award applicants required to submit FAFSA. *Faculty research:* Reaching under served rural agricultural Latinos and veterans; college credit for heroes. *Total annual research expenditures:* $217,098. *Unit head:* Dr. Mary Jo Garcia Biggs, Graduate Advisor, 512-245-2115, E-mail: owlsgradprogram@txstate.edu. *Application contact:* Dr. Andrea Golato, Dean of the Graduate College, 512-245-2581, Fax: 512-245-8365, E-mail: gradcollege@txstate.edu.
Website: http://www.gradcollege.txstate.edu/programs/mtech.html

University of Arkansas, Graduate School, College of Education and Health Professions, Department of Rehabilitation, Human Resources and Communication Disorders, Fayetteville, AR 72701. Offers adult and lifelong learning (M Ed, Ed D); communication disorders (MS); counselor education (MS, PhD); educational statistics and research methods (MS, PhD); higher education (M Ed, Ed D, Ed S); human resource and workforce development education (M Ed, Ed D); rehabilitation (MS, PhD). *Program availability:* Part-time. In 2017, 92 master's, 17 doctorates awarded. *Degree requirements:* For doctorate, thesis/dissertation. *Application deadline:* For fall admission, 8/1 for domestic students, 4/1 for international students; for spring admission, 12/1 for domestic students, 10/1 for international students; for summer admission, 4/15 for domestic students, 3/1 for international students. Applications are processed on a rolling basis. Application fee: $60. Electronic applications accepted. *Expenses:* Tuition, state resident: full-time $3782. Tuition, nonresident: full-time $10,238. *Financial support:* In 2017–18, 55 research assistantships, 3 teaching assistantships were awarded; fellowships with tuition reimbursements, career-related internships or fieldwork, and Federal Work-Study also available. Support available to part-time students. Financial award application deadline: 4/1; financial award applicants required to submit FAFSA. *Unit head:* Dr. Michael Hevel, Interim Department Head, 479-575-4924, Fax: 479-575-3319, E-mail: hevel@uark.edu. *Application contact:* Dr. Brent Williams, Graduate Coordinator, 479-575-4758, E-mail: btwilli@uark.edu.
Website: http://rhrc.uark.edu/

The University of British Columbia, Faculty of Education, Department of Curriculum and Pedagogy, Vancouver, BC V6T 1Z4, Canada. Offers art education (M Ed, MA); curriculum studies (M Ed, MA, PhD); home economics education (M Ed, MA); mathematics education (M Ed, MA); media and technology studies education (M Ed, MA); music education (M Ed, MA); physical education (M Ed, MA); science education (M Ed, MA); social studies education (M Ed, MA). *Program availability:* Part-time, online learning. *Degree requirements:* For master's, thesis (MA); for doctorate, comprehensive exam, thesis/dissertation. *Entrance requirements:* Additional exam requirements/recommendations for international students: Required—TOEFL, IELTS. Electronic applications accepted. *Expenses:* Contact institution. *Faculty research:* School subjects, teaching and learning.

University of Central Florida, College of Arts and Humanities, Department of English, Orlando, FL 32816. Offers creative writing (MFA); English (MA, Certificate); texts and technology (PhD). *Program availability:* Part-time, evening/weekend. *Students:* 72 full-time (53 women), 87 part-time (62 women); includes 36 minority (2 Black or African American, non-Hispanic/Latino; 3 Asian, non-Hispanic/Latino; 27 Hispanic/Latino; 4 Two or more races, non-Hispanic/Latino), 5 international. Average age 33. 117 applicants, 65% accepted, 53 enrolled. In 2017, 37 master's, 6 doctorates, 5 other advanced degrees awarded. *Degree requirements:* For master's, one foreign language, thesis or alternative; for doctorate, thesis/dissertation. *Entrance requirements:* For master's, GRE General Test, letters of recommendation, goal statement. Additional exam requirements/recommendations for international students: Required—TOEFL. *Application deadline:* For fall admission, 3/30 for domestic students; for spring admission, 11/1 for domestic students. Application fee: $30. Electronic applications accepted. *Expenses:* Tuition, state resident: part-time $288.16 per credit hour. Tuition, nonresident: part-time $1073.31 per credit hour. Tuition and fees vary according to program. *Financial support:* In 2017–18, 56 students received support, including 18 fellowships with partial tuition reimbursements available (averaging $6,500 per year), 18 research assistantships with partial tuition reimbursements available (averaging $8,328 per year), 35 teaching assistantships with partial tuition reimbursements available (averaging $10,144 per year); career-related internships or fieldwork, Federal Work-Study, institutionally sponsored loans, tuition waivers (partial), and unspecified assistantships also available. Financial award application deadline: 3/1; financial award applicants required to submit FAFSA. *Unit head:* Dr. Trey Philpotts, Chair, 407-823-1159, E-mail: trey.philpotts@ucf.edu. *Application contact:* Associate Director, Graduate Admissions, 407-823-2766, Fax: 407-823-6442, E-mail: gradadmissions@ucf.edu.
Website: http://www.english.cah.ucf.edu/

University of Central Florida, College of Community Innovation and Education, Department of Educational Leadership and Higher Education, Program in Career and Technical Education, Orlando, FL 32816. Offers MA. *Accreditation:* NCATE. *Program availability:* Part-time, evening/weekend. *Students:* 13 full-time (10 women), 23 part-time (19 women); includes 15 minority (6 Black or African American, non-Hispanic/Latino; 9 Hispanic/Latino). Average age 38. 15 applicants, 73% accepted, 7 enrolled. In 2017, 18 master's awarded. *Degree requirements:* For master's, comprehensive exam. *Entrance requirements:* Additional exam requirements/recommendations for international

students: Required—TOEFL. *Application deadline:* For fall admission, 7/15 for domestic students; for spring admission, 12/1 for domestic students; for summer admission, 4/15 for domestic students. Application fee: $30. Electronic applications accepted. *Expenses:* Tuition, state resident: part-time $288.16 per credit hour. Tuition, nonresident: part-time $1073.31 per credit hour. Tuition and fees vary according to program. *Financial support:* In 2017–18, 2 students received support, including 1 research assistantship (averaging $9,378 per year), 1 teaching assistantship (averaging $9,088 per year); career-related internships or fieldwork, Federal Work-Study, institutionally sponsored loans, and unspecified assistantships also available. Financial award application deadline: 3/1; financial award applicants required to submit FAFSA. *Unit head:* Dr. Jo Ann M. Whiteman, Program Coordinator, 407-823-5303, E-mail: joann.whiteman@ucf.edu. *Application contact:* Associate Director, Graduate Admissions, 407-823-2766, Fax: 407-823-6442, E-mail: gradadmissions@ucf.edu.
Website: http://education.ucf.edu/teched/

University of Central Missouri, The Graduate School, Warrensburg, MO 64093. Offers accountancy (MA); accounting (MBA); applied mathematics (MS); aviation safety (MA); biology (MS); business administration (MBA); career and technical education leadership (MS); college student personnel administration (MS); communication (MA); computer science (MS); counseling (MS); criminal justice (MS); educational leadership (Ed D); educational technology (MS); elementary and early childhood education (MSE); English (MA); environmental studies (MA); finance (MBA); history (MA); human services/educational technology (Ed S); human services/learning resources (Ed S); human services/professional counseling (Ed S); industrial hygiene (MS); industrial management (MS); information systems (MBA); information technology (MS); kinesiology (MS); library science and information services (MS); literacy education (MSE); marketing (MBA); mathematics (MS); music (MA); occupational safety management (MS); psychology (MS); rural family nursing (MS); school administration (MSE); social gerontology (MS); sociology (MA); special education (MSE); speech language pathology (MS); superintendency (Ed S); teaching (MAT); teaching English as a second language (MA); technology (MS); technology management (PhD); theatre (MA). *Program availability:* Part-time, 100% online, blended/hybrid learning. *Faculty:* 337 full-time (145 women), 41 part-time/adjunct (28 women). *Students:* 785 full-time (398 women), 1,633 part-time (1,063 women); includes 231 minority (102 Black or African American, non-Hispanic/Latino; 4 American Indian or Alaska Native, non-Hispanic/Latino; 16 Asian, non-Hispanic/Latino; 52 Hispanic/Latino; 57 Two or more races, non-Hispanic/Latino), 692 international. Average age 30. In 2017, 2,605 master's, 122 other advanced degrees awarded. *Degree requirements:* For master's and Ed S, comprehensive exam (for some programs), thesis (for some programs). *Entrance requirements:* Additional exam requirements/recommendations for international students: Required—TOEFL (minimum score 550 paper-based; 79 iBT). *Application deadline:* For fall admission, 6/1 priority date for domestic and international students; for spring admission, 10/1 priority date for domestic and international students; for summer admission, 4/1 priority date for domestic and international students. Applications are processed on a rolling basis. Application fee: $30 ($75 for international students). Electronic applications accepted. *Expenses:* Tuition, state resident: full-time $8771; part-time $292.35 per credit hour. Tuition, nonresident: full-time $17,541; part-time $584.70 per credit hour. *Required fees:* $372; $24.78 per credit hour. *Financial support:* In 2017–18, 99 students received support. Research assistantships, teaching assistantships, career-related internships or fieldwork, Federal Work-Study, scholarships/grants, and administrative and laboratory assistantships available. Support available to part-time students. Financial award application deadline: 3/1; financial award applicants required to submit FAFSA. *Unit head:* Shellie Hewitt, Director of Graduate and International Student Services, 660-543-4621, Fax: 660-543-4778, E-mail: hewitt@ucmo.edu. *Application contact:* 660-543-4621, E-mail: admit_intl@ucmo.edu.
Website: http://www.ucmo.edu/graduate/

University of Georgia, College of Education, Department of Career and Information Studies, Athens, GA 30602. Offers learning, design, and technology (M Ed, PhD, Ed S), including instructional design and development (M Ed, Ed S); workforce education (MAT, Ed D), including business education (MAT). *Accreditation:* NCATE. *Entrance requirements:* For master's, GRE General Test, MAT; for doctorate, GRE General Test; for Ed S, GRE General Test or MAT. Electronic applications accepted.

University of Idaho, College of Graduate Studies, College of Education, Health and Human Sciences, Department of Curriculum and Instruction, Moscow, ID 83844. Offers career and technology education (M Ed); curriculum and instruction (M Ed, Ed S); special education (M Ed). *Faculty:* 29. *Students:* 25 full-time (19 women), 39 part-time (34 women). Average age 37. In 2017, 33 master's, 2 Ed Ss awarded. *Entrance requirements:* For master's, minimum GPA of 3.0. Additional exam requirements/recommendations for international students: Required—TOEFL (minimum score 79 iBT). *Application deadline:* For fall admission, 8/1 for domestic students; for spring admission, 12/15 for domestic students. Applications are processed on a rolling basis. Application fee: $60. Electronic applications accepted. *Expenses:* Tuition, state resident: full-time $6722; part-time $430 per credit hour. Tuition, nonresident: $23,046; part-time $1337 per credit hour. *Required fees:* $2142; $63 per credit hour. *Financial support:* Research assistantships and teaching assistantships available. Financial award applicants required to submit FAFSA. *Unit head:* Dr. Allen Kitchel, Interim Chair, 208-885-6587, E-mail: teached@uidaho.edu. *Application contact:* Sean Scoggin, Graduate Recruitment Coordinator, 208-885-4001, Fax: 208-885-4406, E-mail: graduateadmissions@uidaho.edu.
Website: http://www.uidaho.edu/ed/ci

University of Maryland Eastern Shore, Graduate Programs, Department of Technology, Princess Anne, MD 21853. Offers career and technology education (M Ed). *Program availability:* Part-time, evening/weekend. *Degree requirements:* For master's, comprehensive exam, seminar paper. *Entrance requirements:* For master's, PRAXIS, writing sample. Additional exam requirements/recommendations for international students: Required—TOEFL (minimum score 80 iBT). Electronic applications accepted. *Faculty research:* Doppler Radar study.

University of Minnesota, Twin Cities Campus, Graduate School, College of Education and Human Development, Department of Organizational Leadership, Policy and Development, Minneapolis, MN 55455-0213. Offers adult literacy (Certificate); comparative and international development education (MA, PhD); disability policy and services (Certificate); education policy and leadership (M Ed, MA, Ed D, PhD), including educational policy and leadership (MA, Ed D, PhD), leadership in education (M Ed); evaluation studies (MA, PhD); higher education (MA, Ed D, PhD), including higher education (MA, PhD), multicultural college teaching and learning (MA); human resource development (M Ed, MA, Ed D, PhD, Certificate); PK-12 administrative licensure (Certificate); private college leadership (Certificate); professional development (Certificate); program evaluation (Certificate); technical education (Certificate); undergraduate multicultural teaching and learning (Certificate). *Faculty:* 32 full-time (14 women). *Students:* 289 full-time (210 women), 251 part-time (157 women); includes 114 minority (41 Black or African American, non-Hispanic/Latino; 4 American Indian or Alaska Native, non-Hispanic/Latino; 27 Asian, non-Hispanic/Latino; 22 Hispanic/Latino; 1 Native Hawaiian or other Pacific Islander, non-Hispanic/Latino; 19 Two or more races, non-Hispanic/Latino), 77 international. Average age 36. 419 applicants, 58% accepted,

204 enrolled. In 2017, 79 master's, 36 doctorates, 49 other advanced degrees awarded. Application fee: $75 ($95 for international students). *Financial support:* In 2017–18, 2 fellowships, 30 research assistantships with full tuition reimbursements (averaging $9,944 per year), 27 teaching assistantships with full tuition reimbursements (averaging $10,036 per year) were awarded; scholarships/grants also available. *Faculty research:* Organizational issues in schools, universities, and other organizations; international education and development; program evaluation and research on applied evaluation methods; international human resource development and change; gender and race/ethnicity in relation to learning and leadership. *Total annual research expenditures:* $930,589. *Unit head:* Dr. Heidi Barajas, Chair, 612-625-4823, Fax: 612-624-3377, E-mail: hbarajas@umn.edu. *Application contact:* Dr. Jeremy J. Hernandez, Coordinator of Graduate Studies, 612-626-9377, E-mail: herna220@umn.edu. Website: http://www.cehd.umn.edu/olpd/

University of Missouri, Office of Research and Graduate Studies, College of Education, Department of Learning, Teaching and Curriculum, Columbia, MO 65211. Offers agricultural education (M Ed, PhD, Ed S); art education (M Ed, PhD, Ed S); business and office education (M Ed, PhD, Ed S); early childhood education (M Ed, PhD, Ed S); elementary education (M Ed, PhD, Ed S); English education (M Ed, PhD, Ed S); foreign language education (M Ed, PhD, Ed S); health education and promotion (M Ed, PhD); learning and instruction (M Ed); marketing education (M Ed, PhD, Ed S); mathematics education (M Ed, PhD, Ed S); music education (M Ed, PhD, Ed S); reading education (M Ed, PhD, Ed S); science education (M Ed, PhD, Ed S); social studies education (M Ed, PhD, Ed S); vocational education (M Ed, PhD, Ed S). *Program availability:* Part-time. Terminal master's awarded for partial completion of doctoral program. *Degree requirements:* For doctorate, thesis/dissertation. *Entrance requirements:* For master's and Ed S, GRE General Test or MAT, minimum GPA of 3.0; for doctorate, GRE General Test, minimum GPA of 3.0. Additional exam requirements/recommendations for international students: Required—TOEFL (minimum score 600 paper-based; 100 iBT). Electronic applications accepted.

University of Nebraska–Lincoln, Graduate College, College of Education and Human Sciences, Department of Teaching, Learning and Teacher Education, Lincoln, NE 68588. Offers adult and continuing education (MA); educational studies (Ed D, PhD), including special education (Ed D); teaching, learning and teacher education (M Ed, MA, MST, Ed D, PhD); vocational and adult education (M Ed, MA). *Accreditation:* NCATE. *Degree requirements:* For master's, thesis optional. *Entrance requirements:* Additional exam requirements/recommendations for international students: Required—TOEFL (minimum score 550 paper-based). Electronic applications accepted. *Faculty research:* Teacher education, instructional leadership, literacy education, technology, improvement of school curriculum.

University of New England, College of Graduate and Professional Studies, Portland, ME 04005-9526. Offers advanced educational leadership (CAGS); applied nutrition (MS); career and technical education (MS Ed); curriculum and instruction (MS Ed); education (CAGS, Post-Master's Certificate); educational leadership (MS Ed, Ed D); generalist (MS Ed); health informatics (MS, Graduate Certificate); inclusion education (MS Ed); literacy K-12 (MS Ed); medical education leadership (MMEL); public health (MPH); public health (Graduate Certificate); reading specialist (MS Ed); social work (MSW). *Program availability:* Part-time, evening/weekend, online only, 100% online. *Faculty:* 125 part-time/adjunct (94 women). *Students:* 1,403 full-time (1,128 women), 594 part-time (475 women); includes 474 minority (332 Black or African American, non-Hispanic/Latino; 13 American Indian or Alaska Native, non-Hispanic/Latino; 83 Asian, non-Hispanic/Latino; 27 Hispanic/Latino; 11 Native Hawaiian or other Pacific Islander, non-Hispanic/Latino; 8 Two or more races, non-Hispanic/Latino). Average age 35. 3,153 applicants, 41% accepted, 990 enrolled. In 2017, 307 master's, 59 doctorates, 124 other advanced degrees awarded. *Application deadline:* Applications are processed on a rolling basis. Electronic applications accepted. Tuition and fees vary according to degree level, program and student level. *Financial support:* Application deadline: 5/1; applicants required to submit FAFSA. *Unit head:* Dr. Martha Wilson, Associate Provost for Online Worldwide Learning/Dean of the College of Graduate and Professional Studies, 207-221-4985, E-mail: mwilson13@une.edu.
Website: http://online.une.edu.

University of Northern Iowa, Graduate College, College of Humanities, Arts and Sciences, Department of Technology, Doctor of Industrial Technology Program, Cedar Falls, IA 50614. Offers DIT.

University of Northern Iowa, Graduate College, College of Humanities, Arts and Sciences, Department of Technology, MS Program in Technology, Cedar Falls, IA 50614. Offers MS.

University of North Texas, Robert B. Toulouse School of Graduate Studies, Denton, TX 76203-5459. Offers accounting (MS); applied anthropology (MA, MS); applied behavior analysis (Certificate); applied geography (MA); applied technology and performance improvement (M Ed, MS); art education (MA); art history (MA); art museum education (Certificate); arts leadership (Certificate); audiology (Au D); behavior analysis (MS); behavioral science (PhD); biochemistry and molecular biology (MS); biology (MA, MS); biomedical engineering (MS); business analysis (MS); chemistry (MS); clinical health psychology (PhD); communication studies (MA, MS); computer engineering (MS); computer science (MS); counseling (M Ed, MS), including clinical mental health counseling (MS), college and university counseling, elementary school counseling, secondary school counseling; creative writing (MA); criminal justice (MS); curriculum and instruction (M Ed); decision sciences (MBA); design (MA, MFA), including fashion design (MFA), innovation studies, interior design (MFA); early childhood studies (MS); economics (MS); educational leadership (M Ed, Ed D); educational psychology (MS, PhD), including family studies (MS), gifted and talented (MS), human development (MS), learning and cognition (MS), research, measurement and evaluation (MS); electrical engineering (MS); emergency management (MPA); engineering technology (MS); English (MA); English as a second language (MA); environmental science (MS); finance (MBA, MS); financial management (MPA); French (MA); health services management (MBA); higher education (M Ed, Ed D); history (MA, MS); hospitality management (MS); human resources management (MPA); information science (MS); information systems (PhD); information technologies (MBA); interdisciplinary studies (MA, MS); international studies (MA); international sustainable tourism (MS); jazz studies (MM); journalism (MA, MJ, Graduate Certificate), including interactive and virtual digital communication (Graduate Certificate), narrative journalism (Graduate Certificate), public relations (Graduate Certificate); kinesiology (MS); linguistics (MA); local government management (MPA); logistics (PhD); logistics and supply chain management (MBA); long-term care, senior housing, and aging services (MA); management (PhD); marketing (MBA); mathematics (MA, MS); mechanical and energy engineering (MS, PhD); music (MA), including ethnomusicology, music theory, musicology, performance; music composition (PhD); music education (MM Ed, PhD); nonprofit management (MPA); operations and supply chain management (MBA); performance (MM, DMA); philosophy (MA); political science (MA); professional and technical communication (MA); radio, television and film (MA, MFA); rehabilitation counseling (Certificate); sociology (MS); Spanish (MA); special education (M Ed); speech-language pathology (MA); strategic management (MBA); studio art (MFA); teaching (M Ed); MBA/MS. *Program availability:* Part-time, evening/weekend, online learning. Terminal master's awarded for partial

completion of doctoral program. *Degree requirements:* For master's, variable foreign language requirement, comprehensive exam (for some programs), thesis (for some programs); for doctorate, variable foreign language requirement, comprehensive exam (for some programs), thesis/dissertation; for other advanced degree, variable foreign language requirement, comprehensive exam (for some programs). *Entrance requirements:* For master's and doctorate, GRE, GMAT. Additional exam requirements/recommendations for international students: Required—TOEFL (minimum score 550 paper-based; 79 iBT). Electronic applications accepted.

University of Phoenix–Phoenix Campus, College of Education, Tempe, AZ 85282-2371. Offers administration and supervision (MA Ed); adult education and training (MA Ed); curriculum and instruction reading (MA Ed); early childhood education (MA Ed); education studies (MA Ed); elementary teacher education (MA Ed); secondary teacher education (MA Ed); special education (MA Ed); teacher leadership (MA Ed). *Program availability:* Evening/weekend, online learning. *Entrance requirements:* Additional exam requirements/recommendations for international students: Required—TOEFL, TOEIC (Test of English as an International Communication), Berlitz Online English Proficiency Exam, PTE, or IELTS. Electronic applications accepted. *Expenses:* Contact institution.

University of South Africa, Institute for Science and Technology Education, Pretoria, South Africa. Offers mathematics, science and technology education (M Sc, D Ed).

University of South Florida, College of Education, Department of Leadership, Counseling, Adult, Career and Higher Education, Tampa, FL 33620-9951. Offers adult education (MA, Ed D, PhD, Ed S); career and technical education (MA); career and workforce education (PhD); higher education/community college teaching (MA, Ed D, PhD); vocational education (Ed S). *Faculty:* 19 full-time (11 women). *Students:* 129 full-time (91 women), 274 part-time (187 women); includes 147 minority (71 Black or African American, non-Hispanic/Latino; 2 American Indian or Alaska Native, non-Hispanic/Latino; 9 Asian, non-Hispanic/Latino; 59 Hispanic/Latino; 6 Two or more races, non-Hispanic/Latino), 15 international. Average age 35. 158 applicants, 67% accepted, 83 enrolled. In 2017, 89 master's, 7 doctorates, 2 other advanced degrees awarded. Application fee: $30. *Total annual research expenditures:* $157,971. *Unit head:* Dr. Judith Ponticell, Chair, 813-974-4897, Fax: 813-974-5423, E-mail: jponticell@usf.edu. Website: http://www.coedu.usf.edu/main/departments/ache/ache.html

The University of Toledo, College of Graduate Studies, Judith Herb College of Education, Department of Curriculum and Instruction, Toledo, OH 43606-3390. Offers art education (ME); career and technical education (ME, Ed S); curriculum and instruction (ME, PhD, Ed S); early childhood education (Ed S); education and anthropology (MAE); education and biology (MES); education and chemistry (MES); education and classics (MAE); education and economics (MAE); education and English (MAE); education and French (MAE); education and geology (MES); education and German (MAE); education and history (MAE); education and mathematics (MAE, MES); education and physics (MES); education and political science (MAE); education and sociology (MAE); education and Spanish (MAE); educational media (PhD); educational technology (ME); educational technology: virtual educator (Certificate); elementary education (PhD); English as a second language (MAE); gifted and talented education (PhD); middle childhood education (ME); secondary education (ME, PhD); special education (PhD). *Accreditation:* NCATE. *Program availability:* Part-time, evening/weekend. *Degree requirements:* For master's, comprehensive exam, thesis or alternative; for doctorate, comprehensive exam, thesis/dissertation; for other advanced degree, thesis optional. *Entrance requirements:* For master's, doctorate, and other advanced degree, minimum cumulative GPA of 2.7 for all previous academic work, letters of recommendation. Additional exam requirements/recommendations for international students: Required—TOEFL (minimum score 550 paper-based; 80 iBT). Electronic applications accepted.

University of Victoria, Faculty of Graduate Studies, Faculty of Education, Department of Curriculum and Instruction, Victoria, BC V8W 2Y2, Canada. Offers art education (M Ed, PhD); curriculum studies (M Ed, MA, PhD); early childhood education (M Ed, PhD); educational studies (PhD); language and literacy (M Ed, MA, PhD); mathematics (M Ed, MA, PhD); music education (M Ed, MA, PhD); science (M Ed, MA, PhD); social studies (M Ed, MA); social, cultural and foundational studies (MA, PhD); technology and environmental education (PhD). *Program availability:* Part-time. *Degree requirements:* For master's, thesis, project (M Ed); for doctorate, comprehensive exam, thesis/dissertation. *Entrance requirements:* For master's, minimum B average. Additional exam requirements/recommendations for international students: Required—TOEFL (minimum score 575 paper-based), IELTS (minimum score 7). Electronic applications accepted. *Faculty research:* Elementary and secondary English, language arts, curriculum theory and practice, educational media and technology, educational administration and leadership, history and philosophy of education.

University of Wisconsin–Stout, Graduate School, College of Education, Health and Human Sciences, School of Education, Program in Career and Technical Education, Menomonie, WI 54751. Offers MS, Ed D, Ed S. *Program availability:* Part-time, online learning. *Degree requirements:* For master's and Ed S, thesis. *Entrance requirements:* For master's, minimum GPA of 2.75; for Ed S, minimum GPA of 3.25. Additional exam requirements/recommendations for international students: Required—TOEFL (minimum score 500 paper-based; 61 iBT). Electronic applications accepted. *Faculty research:* Needs assessment, task analysis, instructional development, learning technologies.

Utah State University, School of Graduate Studies, College of Engineering, Department of Engineering Education, Logan, UT 84322. Offers PhD. *Program availability:* Part-time, evening/weekend. *Entrance requirements:* Additional exam requirements/recommendations for international students: Required—TOEFL. *Faculty research:* Computer-aided design drafting, technology and the public school, materials, electronics, aviation.

Valley City State University, Online Graduate Programs, Valley City, ND 58072. Offers elementary education (M Ed); English education (M Ed); library and information technologies (M Ed); teaching (MAT); teaching and technology (M Ed); teaching English language learners (M Ed); technology education (M Ed). *Accreditation:* NCATE. *Program availability:* Part-time, evening/weekend, online only, 100% online. *Faculty:* 21 full-time (12 women), 15 part-time/adjunct (11 women). *Students:* 12 full-time (9 women), 138 part-time (99 women); includes 5 minority (3 Hispanic/Latino; 2 Two or more races, non-Hispanic/Latino). Average age 36. 13 applicants, 92% accepted, 12 enrolled. In 2017, 45 master's awarded. *Degree requirements:* For master's, action research report, comprehensive portfolio. *Entrance requirements:* For master's, GRE, MAT, PRAXIS II or National Teaching Board for Professional Standards (if GPA is less than 3.0). Additional exam requirements/recommendations for international students: Required—TOEFL (minimum score 525 paper-based; 71 iBT); Recommended—IELTS (minimum score 5.5). *Application deadline:* For fall admission, 7/21 for domestic and international students; for spring admission, 12/8 for domestic and international students; for summer admission, 5/5 for domestic and international students. Applications are processed on a rolling basis. Application fee: $35. Electronic applications accepted. *Expenses:* $384.21 per credit. *Financial support:* In 2017–18, 16 students received support. Scholarships/grants, tuition waivers (full and partial), and unspecified assistantships available. Financial award applicants required to submit

FAFSA. *Faculty research:* Universal accessibility, instructional design and technology, gender communication, STEM education in K-12, English language learners. *Unit head:* Dr. Sheri Okland, Dean, 701-845-7184, E-mail: sheri.l.okland@vcsu.edu. *Application contact:* Misty Lindgren, Graduate Studies, 701-845-7303, Fax: 701-845-7190, E-mail: misty.lindgren@vcsu.edu.
Website: http://www.vcsu.edu/graduate

Virginia Polytechnic Institute and State University, Graduate School, College of Liberal Arts and Human Sciences, Blacksburg, VA 24061. Offers career and technical education (MS Ed, Ed S); communication (MA); counselor education (MA); creative writing (MFA); curriculum and instruction (MA Ed, Ed S); educational leadership and policy studies (Ed S); educational research and evaluation (PhD); English (MA); social, political, ethical, and cultural thought (PhD); Ed D/PhD. *Faculty:* 411 full-time (213 women), 3 part-time/adjunct (all women). *Students:* 623 full-time (427 women), 431 part-time (278 women); includes 203 minority (115 Black or African American, non-Hispanic/Latino; 4 American Indian or Alaska Native, non-Hispanic/Latino; 29 Asian, non-Hispanic/Latino; 33 Hispanic/Latino; 2 Native Hawaiian or other Pacific Islander, non-Hispanic/Latino; 20 Two or more races, non-Hispanic/Latino), 87 international. Average age 34. 898 applicants, 50% accepted, 329 enrolled. In 2017, 314 master's, 102 doctorates awarded. *Degree requirements:* For master's, comprehensive exam (for some programs), thesis (for some programs); for doctorate, comprehensive exam (for some programs), thesis/dissertation (for some programs). *Entrance requirements:* For master's and doctorate, GRE/GMAT. Additional exam requirements/recommendations for international students: Required—TOEFL (minimum score 80 iBT). *Application deadline:* For fall admission, 8/1 for domestic students, 4/1 for international students; for spring admission, 1/1 for domestic students, 9/1 for international students. Applications are processed on a rolling basis. Application fee: $75. Electronic applications accepted. *Expenses:* Tuition, state resident: full-time $15,072; part-time $718.50 per credit hour. Tuition, nonresident: full-time $28,810; part-time $1448.25 per credit hour. *Required fees:* $2741; $502 per semester. Tuition and fees vary according to course load, campus/location and program. *Financial support:* In 2017–18, 19 research assistantships with full tuition reimbursements (averaging $19,611 per year), 226 teaching assistantships with full tuition reimbursements (averaging $16,220 per year) were awarded. Financial award application deadline: 3/1; financial award applicants required to submit FAFSA. *Total annual research expenditures:* $7.9 million. *Unit head:* Dr. Rosemary Blieszner, Dean, 540-231-6779, Fax: 540-231-7157, E-mail: rmb@vt.edu. *Application contact:* Chelsea Blanchet, Executive Assistant, 540-231-6779, Fax: 540-231-7157, E-mail: bchels1@vt.edu.
Website: http://www.liberalarts.vt.edu/

Virginia Polytechnic Institute and State University, VT Online, Blacksburg, VA 24061. Offers advanced transportation systems (Certificate); aerospace engineering (MS); agricultural and life sciences (MSLFS); business information systems (Graduate Certificate); career and technical education (MS); civil engineering (MS); computer engineering (M Eng, MS); decision support systems (Graduate Certificate); eLearning leadership (MA); electrical engineering (M Eng, MS); engineering administration (MEA); environmental engineering (Certificate); environmental politics and policy (Graduate Certificate); environmental sciences and engineering (MS); foundations of political analysis (Graduate Certificate); health product risk management (Graduate Certificate); industrial and systems engineering (MS); information policy and society (Graduate Certificate); information security (Graduate Certificate); information technology (MIT); instructional technology (MA); integrative STEM education (MA Ed); liberal arts (Graduate Certificate); life sciences: health product risk management (MS); natural resources (MNR, Graduate Certificate); networking (Graduate Certificate); nonprofit and nongovernmental organization management (Graduate Certificate); ocean engineering (MS); political science (MA); security studies (Graduate Certificate); software development (Graduate Certificate). *Expenses:* Tuition, state resident: full-time $15,072; part-time $718.50 per credit hour. Tuition, nonresident: full-time $28,810; part-time $1448.25 per credit hour. *Required fees:* $2741; $502 per semester. Tuition and fees vary according to course load, campus/location and program.

Washington State University, College of Education, Department of Teaching and Learning, Pullman, WA 99164-2132. Offers cultural studies and social thought in education (PhD); curriculum and instruction (Ed M, MA); English language learners (Ed M, MA); language, literacy and technology (PhD); literacy education (Ed M, MA); mathematics education (PhD); special education (Ed M, MA, PhD); teacher leadership (Ed D); teaching (MIT), including elementary education, secondary education. Programs offered at the Pullman, Spokane, Tri-cities, Vancouver and Global (online) campuses. *Program availability:* Part-time, online learning. *Degree requirements:* For master's, comprehensive exam, thesis, oral or written exam; for doctorate, comprehensive exam, thesis/dissertation, oral and written exam. *Entrance requirements:* For master's, GRE General Test, minimum GPA of 3.0, 3 letters of recommendation, letter of intent, transcripts, resume/curriculum vitae; for doctorate, GRE General Test, minimum GPA of 3.0, 3 letters of recommendation, letter of intent, transcripts, writing sample, resume/curriculum vitae. Additional exam requirements/recommendations for international students: Required—TOEFL (minimum score 550 paper-based; 80 iBT). Electronic applications accepted. *Faculty research:* Intersection of gender, youth cultures and schooling; examination of ideology of power in children's literature; early childhood special education; analyzing pre-service and in-service teacher development; second language acquisition.

Wayne State College, School of Education and Counseling, Department of Educational Foundations and Leadership, Program in Curriculum and Instruction, Wayne, NE 68787. Offers alternative education (MSE); business and information technology education (MSE); communication arts education (MSE); early childhood education (MSE); elementary education (MSE); English as a second language (MSE); English education (MSE); family and consumer sciences education (MSE); industrial technology and vocational education (MSE); learning communities (MSE); mathematics education (MSE); music education (MSE); science education (MSE); social science education (MSE). *Accreditation:* NCATE. *Program availability:* Part-time, evening/weekend. *Degree requirements:* For master's, comprehensive exam, thesis optional. *Entrance requirements:* For master's, GRE General Test. Additional exam requirements/recommendations for international students: Required—TOEFL (minimum score 550 paper-based).

Western Michigan University, Graduate College, College of Education and Human Development, Department of Family and Consumer Sciences, Kalamazoo, MI 49008. Offers career and technical education (MA); family and consumer sciences (MA).

Westfield State University, College of Graduate and Continuing Education, Department of Education, Program in Vocational Technical Education, Westfield, MA 01086. Offers M Ed. *Accreditation:* NCATE. *Program availability:* Part-time, evening/weekend. *Students:* 8 part-time (5 women). Average age 36. 5 applicants, 100% accepted, 3 enrolled. In 2017, 2 master's awarded. *Degree requirements:* For master's, comprehensive exam. *Entrance requirements:* For master's, GRE General Test or MAT, minimum undergraduate GPA of 2.8. Additional exam requirements/recommendations for international students: Recommended—TOEFL (minimum score 550 paper-based; 79 iBT). *Application deadline:* For fall admission, 7/1 for domestic students; for spring admission, 11/1 for domestic students; for summer admission, 4/1 for domestic students. Applications are processed on a rolling basis. Application fee: $50. *Expenses:* Tuition, state resident: part-time $332 per credit. Tuition, nonresident: part-time $332 per credit. *Required fees:* $75 per semester. Tuition and fees vary according to program. *Financial support:* Unspecified assistantships and SOS scholarships (for education majors only) available. Financial award application deadline: 3/1; financial award applicants required to submit FAFSA. *Unit head:* Dr. Laura Baker, Department Chair, 413-572-5324, E-mail: lbaker@westfield.ma.edu. *Application contact:* Shelly Henrichon, Coordinator of College of Graduate and Continuing Education Admissions, 413-572-8022, Fax: 413-572-5227, E-mail: mhenrichon@westfield.ma.edu.
Website: http://www.westfield.ma.edu/academics/degrees/education-graduate-programs

Wilmington University, College of Education, New Castle, DE 19720-6491. Offers applied technology in education (M Ed); career and technical education (M Ed); educational leadership (Ed D); elementary and secondary school counseling (M Ed); elementary studies (M Ed); ESOL literacy (M Ed); higher education leadership (Ed D); instruction: gifted and talented (M Ed); instruction: teacher of reading (M Ed); instruction: teaching and learning (M Ed); organizational leadership (Ed D); school leadership (M Ed); secondary education (MAT); special education (M Ed). *Accreditation:* NCATE. *Program availability:* Part-time, evening/weekend. *Faculty:* 23 full-time (13 women), 162 part-time/adjunct (99 women). *Students:* 546 full-time (394 women), 960 part-time (732 women); includes 320 minority (241 Black or African American, non-Hispanic/Latino; 12 American Indian or Alaska Native, non-Hispanic/Latino; 11 Asian, non-Hispanic/Latino; 28 Hispanic/Latino; 3 Native Hawaiian or other Pacific Islander, non-Hispanic/Latino; 25 Two or more races, non-Hispanic/Latino), 7 international. Average age 34. 1,068 applicants, 64% accepted, 582 enrolled. In 2017, 430 master's, 59 doctorates awarded. *Entrance requirements:* For master's, 2 letters of recommendation, interview. Additional exam requirements/recommendations for international students: Required—TOEFL (minimum score 500 paper-based). *Application deadline:* For fall admission, 4/30 for domestic students. Applications are processed on a rolling basis. Application fee: $35. Electronic applications accepted. *Expenses:* Tuition: Part-time $466 per credit. *Required fees:* $25 per semester. Tuition and fees vary according to degree level and campus/location. *Financial support:* Applicants required to submit FAFSA. *Unit head:* Dr. John C. Gray, Dean, 302-295-1139. *Application contact:* Laura Morris, Director of Admissions, 877-967-5464, E-mail: infocenter@wilmu.edu.
Website: http://www.wilmu.edu/education/

ACADEMIC AND PROFESSIONAL
PROGRAMS IN LAW

Section 27
Law

This section contains a directory of institutions offering graduate work in law. Additional information about programs listed in the directory may be obtained by writing directly to the dean of a graduate school or chair of a department at the address given in the directory.

For programs offering related work, see also in this book *Business Administration and Management* and *Social Work*. In the other guides in this series:

Graduate Programs in the Humanities, Arts & Social Sciences
See *Criminology and Forensics; Public, Regional, and Industrial Affairs; Economics;* and *Political Science and International Affairs*
Graduate Programs in the Physical Sciences, Mathematics, Agricultural Sciences, the Environment & Natural Resources
See *Environmental Sciences and Management*
Graduate Programs in Engineering & Applied Sciences
See *Management of Engineering and Technology*

CONTENTS

Program Directories

Featured Schools: Displays and Close-Ups

See also:

Environmental Law

Chapman University, Dale E. Fowler School of Law, Orange, CA 92866. Offers advocacy and dispute resolution (JD); business law (LL M, JD); criminal law (JD); entertainment and media law (LL M); entertainment law (JD); environmental, land use, and real estate law (JD); international and comparative law (LL M); international law (JD); law (JD); prosecutorial science (LL M); tax law (JD); taxation (LL M); trial advocacy (LL M); JD/MBA; JD/MFA. *Accreditation:* ABA. *Program availability:* Part-time. *Faculty:* 44 full-time (18 women), 34 part-time/adjunct (9 women). *Students:* 478 full-time (262 women), 37 part-time (24 women); includes 217 minority (9 Black or African American, non-Hispanic/Latino; 1 American Indian or Alaska Native, non-Hispanic/Latino; 69 Asian, non-Hispanic/Latino; 104 Hispanic/Latino; 34 Two or more races, non-Hispanic/Latino), 11 international. Average age 26. 1,499 applicants, 50% accepted, 190 enrolled. In 2017, 17 master's, 149 doctorates awarded. *Entrance requirements:* For doctorate, LSAT. Additional exam requirements/recommendations for international students: Required—TOEFL (minimum score 600 paper-based; 100 iBT). *Application deadline:* For fall admission, 4/17 priority date for domestic students. Applications are processed on a rolling basis. Electronic applications accepted. *Expenses:* Contact institution. *Financial support:* Fellowships, Federal Work-Study, and scholarships/grants available. Financial award applicants required to submit FAFSA. *Unit head:* Matthew J. Parlow, Dean, 714-628-2678, E-mail: parlow@chapman.edu. *Application contact:* Justin Cruz, Assistant Dean of Admissions and Diversity Initiatives, 714-628-2594, E-mail: lawadmission@chapman.edu.
Website: https://www.chapman.edu/law/index.aspx

Florida State University, College of Law, Tallahassee, FL 32306-1601. Offers American law for foreign lawyers (LL M); business law (LL M); environmental law and policy (LL M); financial regulation and compliance (JM); health law compliance (JM); law (JM, JD); legal risk management and HR compliance (JM); JD/MAES; JD/MBA; JD/MPA; JD/MS; JD/MSI; JD/MSP; JD/MSW. *Accreditation:* ABA. *Program availability:* Part-time, 100% online. *Faculty:* 57 full-time (29 women), 36 part-time/adjunct (11 women). *Students:* 520 full-time (268 women), 79 part-time (45 women); includes 184 minority (53 Black or African American, non-Hispanic/Latino; 2 American Indian or Alaska Native, non-Hispanic/Latino; 13 Asian, non-Hispanic/Latino; 71 Hispanic/Latino; 45 Two or more races, non-Hispanic/Latino), 13 international. Average age 26. 1,805 applicants, 36% accepted, 225 enrolled. In 2017, 18 master's, 218 doctorates awarded. Terminal master's awarded for partial completion of doctoral program. *Degree requirements:* For master's, comprehensive exam (for some programs). *Entrance requirements:* For master's, one graduate-level standardized test (for JM), JD or equivalent degree (for LL M); for doctorate, LSAT or GRE (for JD). Additional exam requirements/recommendations for international students: Required—TOEFL (minimum score 600 paper-based; 100 iBT), IELTS (minimum score 7.5). *Application deadline:* For fall admission, 6/30 for domestic and international students; for spring admission, 12/1 for domestic students; for summer admission, 4/15 for domestic students. Applications are processed on a rolling basis. Application fee: $30. Electronic applications accepted. *Expenses:* $20,683. *Financial support:* In 2017–18, 400 students received support, including 2 fellowships with full tuition reimbursements available (averaging $20,683 per year), 30 research assistantships (averaging $1,205 per year), 10 teaching assistantships (averaging $1,354 per year); career-related internships or fieldwork, scholarships/grants, and unspecified assistantships also available. Financial award application deadline: 3/1; financial award applicants required to submit FAFSA. *Faculty research:* Business law; environmental, energy and land use law; international law; criminal law. *Total annual research expenditures:* $99,375. *Unit head:* Erin O'Hara O'Connor, Dean, 850-644-3400, Fax: 850-644-5487, E-mail: eoconnor@law.fsu.edu. *Application contact:* Jennifer L. Kessinger, Director of Admissions and Records, 850-644-3787, Fax: 850-644-7284, E-mail: jkessing@law.fsu.edu.
Website: http://www.law.fsu.edu/

Georgetown University, Law Center, Washington, DC 20001. Offers environmental law (LL M); global health law (LL M); global health law and international institutions (LL M); individualized study (LL M); international business and economic law (LL M); law (JD, SJD); national security law (LL M); securities and financial regulation (LL M); taxation (LL M); JD/LL M; JD/MA; JD/MBA; JD/MPH; JD/PhD. *Accreditation:* ABA. *Program availability:* Part-time, evening/weekend. *Degree requirements:* For master's, thesis; for doctorate, thesis/dissertation (for some programs). *Entrance requirements:* For master's, JD, LL B, or first law degree earned in country of origin; for doctorate, LSAT (for JD). Additional exam requirements/recommendations for international students: Required—TOEFL. *Expenses:* Contact institution. *Faculty research:* Constitutional law, legal history, jurisprudence.

Golden Gate University, School of Law, San Francisco, CA 94105. Offers environmental law (LL M); estate planning (LL M); intellectual property law (LL M); international legal studies (LL M, SJD); law (JD); taxation law (LL M); U.S. legal studies (LL M); JD/MBA. *Accreditation:* ABA. *Program availability:* Part-time, evening/weekend. *Faculty:* 31 full-time (19 women), 160 part-time/adjunct (77 women). *Students:* 286 full-time (184 women), 245 part-time (134 women); includes 242 minority (48 Black or African American, non-Hispanic/Latino; 4 American Indian or Alaska Native, non-Hispanic/Latino; 69 Asian, non-Hispanic/Latino; 95 Hispanic/Latino; 7 Native Hawaiian or other Pacific Islander, non-Hispanic/Latino; 19 Two or more races, non-Hispanic/Latino), 71 international. Average age 31. 1,354 applicants, 66% accepted, 227 enrolled. *Degree requirements:* For doctorate, thesis/dissertation (for some programs). *Entrance requirements:* For doctorate, LSAT (for JD). Additional exam requirements/recommendations for international students: Required—TOEFL (minimum score 600 paper-based). *Application deadline:* For fall admission, 6/30 for domestic students. Applications are processed on a rolling basis. Electronic applications accepted. *Expenses:* Contact institution. *Financial support:* Fellowships, research assistantships, teaching assistantships, career-related internships or fieldwork, Federal Work-Study, institutionally sponsored loans, scholarships/grants, tuition waivers (full and partial), and unspecified assistantships available. Support available to part-time students. Financial award applicants required to submit FAFSA. *Faculty research:* International law, intellectual property law, environmental law, real estate, civil rights. *Unit head:* Anthony Niedwiecki, Dean, 415-442-6601, Fax: 415-442-6609. *Application contact:* Greg Egertson, Associate Dean and Director of Admissions, 415-442-6636, Fax: 415-442-6609, E-mail: lawadmit@ggu.edu.
Website: http://law.ggu.edu/

Lehigh University, College of Arts and Sciences, Environmental Policy Program, Bethlehem, PA 18015. Offers environmental health (Graduate Certificate); environmental justice (Graduate Certificate); environmental policy and law (Graduate Certificate); environmental policy design (MA); sustainable development (Graduate Certificate); urban environmental policy (Graduate Certificate). *Faculty:* 6 full-time (2 women). *Students:* 6 full-time (3 women), 1 (woman) part-time; includes 1 minority (Black or African American, non-Hispanic/Latino). Average age 28. 6 applicants, 83%

accepted, 3 enrolled. In 2017, 3 master's awarded. *Degree requirements:* For master's, thesis or additional course work. *Entrance requirements:* For master's, minimum GPA of 2.75, 3.0 for last two undergraduate semesters; essay; 2 letters of recommendation. Additional exam requirements/recommendations for international students: Required—TOEFL (minimum score 85 iBT), IELTS (minimum score 6.5). *Application deadline:* For fall admission, 1/1 for domestic and international students; for spring admission, 12/1 for domestic and international students. Applications are processed on a rolling basis. Application fee: $75. Electronic applications accepted. *Expenses:* $1,460 per credit. *Financial support:* In 2017–18, 6 students received support. Teaching assistantships and community fellowship and tuition remission available. Financial award application deadline: 1/1. *Faculty research:* Environmental policy, environmental law, urban policy, urban politics, urban environmental policy, sustainability, sustainable development, international environmental law, international environmental policy, environmental justice, social justice. *Unit head:* Dr. Karen B. Pooley, Director, 610-758-1238, E-mail: kbp312@lehigh.edu. *Application contact:* Gary Burgess, Academic Coordinator, 610-758-4281, Fax: 610-758-6232, E-mail: glb215@lehigh.edu.
Website: http://ei.cas2.lehigh.edu/

Lewis & Clark College, Lewis & Clark Law School, Portland, OR 97219. Offers animal law (LL M); environmental, natural resources, and energy law (LL M, MSL); law (JD). *Accreditation:* ABA. *Program availability:* Part-time, evening/weekend. *Entrance requirements:* For doctorate, LSAT. Additional exam requirements/recommendations for international students: Recommended—TOEFL (minimum score 600 paper-based). Electronic applications accepted. Application fee is waived when completed online. *Expenses:* Contact institution.

Montclair State University, The Graduate School, College of Science and Mathematics, Environmental Forensics Certificate Program, Montclair, NJ 07043-1624. Offers Certificate.

Pace University, Elisabeth Haub School of Law, White Plains, NY 10603. Offers comparative legal studies (LL M); environmental law (LL M, SJD), including energy and climate change law (LL M); global environmental law (LL M); law (JD); JD/LL M; JD/MA; JD/MBA; JD/MEM; JD/MPA; JD/MS. JD/MA offered jointly with Sarah Lawrence College; JD/MEM offered jointly with Yale University School of Forestry and Environmental Studies. *Accreditation:* ABA. *Program availability:* Part-time. *Faculty:* 26 full-time (11 women), 52 part-time/adjunct (19 women). *Students:* 548 (301 women); includes 154 minority (31 Black or African American, non-Hispanic/Latino; 3 American Indian or Alaska Native, non-Hispanic/Latino; 20 Asian, non-Hispanic/Latino; 54 Hispanic/Latino; 1 Native Hawaiian or other Pacific Islander, non-Hispanic/Latino; 45 Two or more races, non-Hispanic/Latino), 9 international. Average age 26. 1,443 applicants, 53% accepted, 217 enrolled. In 2017, 20 master's, 170 doctorates awarded. *Degree requirements:* For doctorate, thesis/dissertation (for some programs), extensive thesis proposal (for SJD). *Entrance requirements:* For master's, writing sample; for doctorate, LSAT (for JD). Additional exam requirements/recommendations for international students: Required—TOEFL (minimum score 100 iBT); Recommended—TWE. *Application deadline:* For fall admission, 6/1 priority date for domestic students; for winter admission, 11/15 priority date for domestic students. Applications are processed on a rolling basis. Application fee: $65. Electronic applications accepted. *Expenses:* Contact institution. *Financial support:* In 2017–18, 473 students received support. Fellowships, research assistantships, career-related internships or fieldwork, Federal Work-Study, institutionally sponsored loans, scholarships/grants, and unspecified assistantships available. Support available to part-time students. Financial award application deadline: 2/1; financial award applicants required to submit FAFSA. *Faculty research:* Reform of energy regulations, international law, land use law, prosecutorial misconduct, corporation law. *Unit head:* David Yassky, Dean, 914-422-4407, E-mail: dyassky@law.pace.edu. *Application contact:* Cathy Alexander, Assistant Dean, 914-422-4210, Fax: 914-989-8714, E-mail: calexander@law.pace.edu.
Website: http://www.law.pace.edu/

St. Mary's University, School of Law, Master of Jurisprudence Program, San Antonio, TX 78228. Offers business and entrepreneurship law (MJ); commercial law (MJ); compliance, business law and risk (MJ); criminal justice (MJ); education law (MJ); environmental law (MJ); health law (MJ); healthcare compliance (MJ); international comparative law (MJ); military and national security law (MJ); natural resource law (MJ); tax law (MJ). *Program availability:* Part-time, evening/weekend. *Faculty:* 45 full-time (13 women), 68 part-time/adjunct (22 women). *Students:* 10 full-time (7 women), 26 part-time (18 women); includes 25 minority (2 Black or African American, non-Hispanic/Latino; 1 Asian, non-Hispanic/Latino; 22 Hispanic/Latino). Average age 32. 37 applicants, 92% accepted, 22 enrolled. In 2017, 12 master's awarded. *Degree requirements:* For master's, 30 credits, minimum GPA of 2.0. *Entrance requirements:* For master's, official transcripts, personal statement, resume, 2 letters of recommendation, proof of four-year undergraduate degree from accredited U.S. college/university or foreign institution approved by government or accrediting authority. Additional exam requirements/recommendations for international students: Required—TOEFL (minimum score 550 paper-based; 80 iBT), IELTS (minimum score 6). *Application deadline:* Applications are processed on a rolling basis. Application fee: $0. Electronic applications accepted. *Expenses:* Contact institution. *Financial support:* Fellowships, research assistantships, Federal Work-Study, scholarships/grants, and unspecified assistantships available. Financial award applicants required to submit FAFSA. *Unit head:* Shannon Sevier, Director, Graduate Law Programs, 210-431-4235, E-mail: ssevier@stmarytx.edu. *Application contact:* Shannon Sevier, Director, Graduate Law Programs, 210-431-4235, E-mail: ssevier@stmarytx.edu.
Website: https://law.stmarytx.edu/academics/programs/master-of-jurisprudence/

Stanford University, Law School, Stanford, CA 94305-8610. Offers corporate governance and practice (LL M); environmental law and policy (LL M); international economic law, business and policy (LL M); international legal studies (JSM); law (JD, JSD); law, science and technology (LL M); legal studies (MLS); JD/MA; JD/MBA; JD/MPP; JD/MS; JD/PhD. *Accreditation:* ABA. *Degree requirements:* For doctorate, thesis/dissertation (for some programs). *Entrance requirements:* For doctorate, LSAT (for JD). Electronic applications accepted. *Expenses:* Contact institution.

University at Buffalo, the State University of New York, Graduate School, School of Law, Buffalo, NY 14260-1100. Offers criminal law (LL M); cross-border legal studies (LL M); environmental law (LL M); general law (LL M); law (JD); JD/MA; JD/MBA; JD/MLS; JD/MSW; JD/MUP; JD/PhD; LL M/LL M. *Accreditation:* ABA. *Faculty:* 49 full-time (23 women), 68 part-time/adjunct (25 women). *Students:* 453 full-time (238 women), 2 part-time (both women); includes 85 minority (29 Black or African American, non-Hispanic/Latino; 1 American Indian or Alaska Native, non-Hispanic/Latino; 20 Asian, non-Hispanic/Latino; 22 Hispanic/Latino; 13 Two or more races, non-Hispanic/Latino),

17 international. Average age 27. 903 applicants, 54% accepted, 167 enrolled. In 2017, 2 master's, 151 doctorates awarded. *Entrance requirements:* For master's, JD or LL B; for doctorate, LSAT. Additional exam requirements/recommendations for international students: Required—TOEFL (minimum score 90 iBT), IELTS (minimum score 7). *Application deadline:* Applications are processed on a rolling basis. Application fee: $85. Electronic applications accepted. *Expenses:* $28,016 annual tuition plus fees in-state full-time; $32,106 annual tuition plus fees out-of-state full-time. *Financial support:* In 2017–18, 338 students received support. Federal Work-Study, institutionally sponsored loans, scholarships/grants, tuition waivers (full and partial), and unspecified assistantships available. Financial award application deadline: 3/1; financial award applicants required to submit FAFSA. *Faculty research:* Criminal law, environmental law, international law and human rights, law and finance, cross-border legal studies. *Total annual research expenditures:* $108,173. *Unit head:* Aviva Abramovsky, Dean, 716-645-2052, E-mail: aabramov@buffalo.edu. *Application contact:* Lindsay Gladney, Vice Dean for Admissions, 716-645-2907, Fax: 716-645-6676, E-mail: law-admissions@buffalo.edu.
Website: http://www.law.buffalo.edu/

University of Calgary, Faculty of Graduate Studies, Faculty of Law, Programs in Natural Resources, Energy and Environmental Law, Calgary, AB T2N 1N4, Canada. Offers LL M, Postbaccalaureate Certificate. *Program availability:* Part-time, evening/weekend. *Degree requirements:* For master's, thesis optional. *Entrance requirements:* For master's, JD or LL B. Additional exam requirements/recommendations for international students: Required—TOEFL (minimum score 100 iBT), IELTS (minimum score 7). Electronic applications accepted. *Faculty research:* Natural resources law and regulations; environmental law, ethics and policies; oil and gas and energy law; water and municipal law; Aboriginal law.

University of Colorado Denver, School of Public Affairs, Program in Public Affairs and Administration, Denver, CO 80127. Offers public administration (MPA), including domestic violence, emergency management and homeland security, environmental policy, management and law, homeland security and defense, local government, nonprofit management, public administration; public affairs (PhD). *Accreditation:* NASPAA. *Program availability:* Part-time, evening/weekend, online learning. *Degree requirements:* For master's, thesis or alternative, 36-39 credit hours; for doctorate, comprehensive exam, thesis/dissertation, minimum of 66 semester hours, including at least 30 hours of dissertation. *Entrance requirements:* For master's, GRE, GMAT or LSAT, resume, essay, transcripts, recommendations; for doctorate, GRE, resume, essay, transcripts, recommendations. Additional exam requirements/recommendations for international students: Required—TOEFL (minimum score 550 paper-based; 80 iBT); Recommended—IELTS (minimum score 6.5). Electronic applications accepted. *Expenses:* Contact institution. *Faculty research:* Housing, education and the social and economic issues of vulnerable populations; nonprofit governance and management; education finance, effectiveness and reform; P-20 education initiatives; municipal government accountability.

University of Florida, Levin College of Law, Gainesville, FL 32611. Offers comparative law (LL M), including tropical conservation and development; environmental and land use law (LL M); international taxation (LL M); law (JD); taxation (LL M, SJD). *Accreditation:* ABA. *Entrance requirements:* For doctorate, LSAT (for JD). Electronic applications accepted. *Faculty research:* Environmental and land use law, taxation, dispute resolution, family law, Constitutional law.

University of Houston, University of Houston Law Center, Houston, TX 77204-6060. Offers energy, environment, and natural resources (LL M); health law (LL M); intellectual property and information law (LL M); international law (LL M); law (JD); tax law (LL M); U.S. law (LL M). *Accreditation:* ABA. *Program availability:* Part-time, evening/weekend. *Faculty:* 58 full-time (23 women), 130 part-time/adjunct (36 women). *Students:* 695 full-time (331 women), 120 part-time (55 women); includes 319 minority (62 Black or African American, non-Hispanic/Latino; 10 American Indian or Alaska Native, non-Hispanic/Latino; 73 Asian, non-Hispanic/Latino; 172 Hispanic/Latino; 2 Native Hawaiian or other Pacific Islander, non-Hispanic/Latino), 33 international. Average age 26. 2,751 applicants, 33% accepted, 227 enrolled. In 2017, 75 master's, 231 doctorates awarded. *Degree requirements:* For master's, thesis optional; for doctorate, senior writing requirement. *Entrance requirements:* For doctorate, LSAT. Additional exam requirements/recommendations for international students: Required—TOEFL (minimum score 600 paper-based; 100 iBT). *Application deadline:* For fall admission, 2/15 for domestic and international students. Applications are processed on a rolling basis. Application fee: $0. Electronic applications accepted. *Expenses:* Contact institution. *Financial support:* In 2017–18, 442 students received support, including 20 fellowships (averaging $2,980 per year); research assistantships, career-related internships or fieldwork, Federal Work-Study, scholarships/grants, and tuition waivers also available. Support available to part-time students. Financial award application deadline: 3/15; financial award applicants required to submit FAFSA. *Faculty research:* Health law, international law, tax, environmental law/energy, information law/intellectual property. *Total annual research expenditures:* $472,551. *Unit head:* Leonard M. Baynes, Dean and Professor of Law, 713-743-2100, Fax: 713-743-2122, E-mail: lbaynes@central.uh.edu. *Application contact:* Pilar Mensah, Assistant Dean for Admissions, 713-743-2280, Fax: 713-743-2194, E-mail: lpmensah@central.uh.edu.
Website: http://www.law.uh.edu/

University of Pittsburgh, School of Law, Master of Studies in Law Program, Pittsburgh, PA 15260. Offers biomedical and health services research (MSL); business law (MSL), including commercial law, corporate law, general business law, international business, tax law; Constitutional law (MSL); criminal law and justice (MSL); disability law (MSL); elder and estate planning law (MSL); employment and labor law (MSL); energy law (MSL); environmental and real estate law (MSL); family law (MSL); health law (MSL); intellectual property and technology law (MSL); international and human rights law (MSL); jurisprudence (MSL); regulatory law (MSL); self-designed (MSL). *Program availability:* Part-time. *Faculty:* 47 full-time (22 women), 116 part-time/adjunct (29 women). *Students:* 4 full-time (2 women), 17 part-time (12 women); includes 6 minority (5 Black or African American, non-Hispanic/Latino; 1 Hispanic/Latino). Average age 26. 28 applicants, 75% accepted, 15 enrolled. In 2017, 15 master's awarded. *Entrance requirements:* Additional exam requirements/recommendations for international students: Required—TOEFL (minimum score 600 paper-based; 100 iBT), IELTS (minimum score 7). *Application deadline:* For fall admission, 6/30 for domestic students, 5/1 for international students. Applications are processed on a rolling basis. Application fee: $0. *Faculty research:* Law, health law, business law, contracts, intellectual property, environmental law. *Unit head:* Prof. Alan Meisel, Director, 412-648-1384, Fax: 412-648-2649, E-mail: meisel@pitt.edu. *Application contact:* Beth Ann Pischke, Administrative Coordinator, 412-648-7120, Fax: 412-648-2649, E-mail: pischke@pitt.edu.
Website: http://www.law.pitt.edu/msl

The University of Tulsa, College of Law, Tulsa, OK 74104. Offers American Indian and indigenous law (LL M); American law for foreign lawyers (LL M); energy and natural resources law (LL M); energy law (MJ); health law (Certificate); Indian law (MJ); law (JD); Native American law (Certificate); sustainable energy and resources law (Certificate); JD/MA; JD/MBA; JD/MS. *Accreditation:* ABA. *Program availability:* Part-time, 100% online. *Faculty:* 24 full-time (13 women), 14 part-time/adjunct (7 women). *Students:* 243 full-time (105 women), 29 part-time (12 women); includes 75 minority (12 Black or African American, non-Hispanic/Latino; 17 American Indian or Alaska Native, non-Hispanic/Latino; 1 Asian, non-Hispanic/Latino; 11 Hispanic/Latino; 34 Two or more races, non-Hispanic/Latino), 4 international. Average age 28. 567 applicants, 45% accepted, 94 enrolled. In 2017, 3 master's, 86 doctorates, 26 Certificates awarded. *Degree requirements:* For master's, thesis optional. *Entrance requirements:* For master's, JD from an ABA-approved U.S. law school or a JD equivalent from non-U.S. university; for doctorate, LSAT, BS or BA from 4-year regionally-accredited college/university; for Certificate, BS or BA from 4-year regionally-accredited college/university. Additional exam requirements/recommendations for international students: Required—TOEFL (minimum score 570 paper-based; 90 iBT), IELTS (minimum score 6.5). *Application deadline:* For fall admission, 7/31 priority date for domestic and international students; for spring admission, 12/5 priority date for domestic students, 12/5 for international students; for summer admission, 4/13 for domestic and international students. Applications are processed on a rolling basis. Application fee: $30. Electronic applications accepted. *Expenses:* $24,600 per year tuition; $564 fees. *Financial support:* In 2017–18, 261 students received support. Scholarships/grants available. Support available to part-time students. Financial award application deadline: 8/1; financial award applicants required to submit FAFSA. *Faculty research:* Native American law, criminal law, commercial speech, copyright law, international law. *Unit head:* Prof. Lyn Suzanne Entzeroth, Dean, 918-631-2400, Fax: 918-631-3126, E-mail: lyn-entzeroth@utulsa.edu. *Application contact:* April M. Fox, Associate Dean of Admissions and Financial Aid, 918-631-2406, Fax: 918-631-3630, E-mail: april-fox@utulsa.edu.
Website: http://www.utulsa.edu/law/

Vermont Law School, Graduate and Professional Programs, Master's Programs, South Royalton, VT 05068-0096. Offers American legal studies (LL M); energy law (LL M); energy regulation and law (MERL); environmental law (LL M); environmental law and policy (MELP); food and agriculture law (LL M); food and agriculture law and policy (MFALP); JD/MELP; JD/MERL; JD/MFALP. *Program availability:* Part-time, 100% online, blended/hybrid learning. *Entrance requirements:* Additional exam requirements/recommendations for international students: Required—TOEFL. *Faculty research:* Environment and new economy; takings; international environmental law; interaction among science, law, and environmental policy; climate change and the law.

Western Michigan University Thomas M. Cooley Law School, Graduate Programs, Lansing, MI 48901-3038. Offers administrative law (public law) (JD); business transactions (JD); Canadian law practice (JD); corporate law and finance (LL M); environmental law (public law) (JD); general practice (JD), including solo and small firm; general studies (LL M); homeland and national security law (LL M); insurance law (LL M); intellectual property (JD); intellectual property law (LL M); international law (JD); litigation (JD); taxation (LL M); U.S. legal studies for foreign attorneys (LL M); JD/LL M; JD/MBA; JD/MHA; JD/MPA; JD/MSW. *Program availability:* Part-time, evening/weekend, 100% online, blended/hybrid learning. *Degree requirements:* For master's, thesis (for some programs); for doctorate, minimum of 3 credits of clinical experience. *Entrance requirements:* For master's, JD or LL B; for doctorate, LSAT. Additional exam requirements/recommendations for international students: Required—TOEFL (for U.S. legal studies for foreign attorneys LL M program); Recommended—TOEFL. Electronic applications accepted. *Expenses:* Contact institution. *Faculty research:* Wrongful convictions, civil rights, environmental law, litigation techniques, data mining, intellectual property, practical and skills-based legal education.

Health Law

Boston University, School of Public Health, Health Law, Policy and Management Department, Boston, MA 02215. Offers health law, policy and management (MPH); health services and systems research (MS); health services research (PhD). *Accreditation:* CAHME. *Program availability:* Part-time, evening/weekend. *Degree requirements:* For master's, comprehensive exam (for some programs), thesis (for some programs); for doctorate, comprehensive exam, thesis/dissertation. *Entrance requirements:* For master's, GRE, MCAT, GMAT; for doctorate, GRE. Additional exam requirements/recommendations for international students: Required—TOEFL (minimum score 600 paper-based; 100 iBT), IELTS (minimum score 7). Electronic applications accepted. *Faculty research:* Health policy, health law and ethics, human rights, healthcare management.

Case Western Reserve University, School of Law, Cleveland, OH 44106. Offers financial integrity (MA); health law (SJD); intellectual property (LL M); intellectual property law (ML); international business law (LL M, ML); international criminal law (LL M); law (JD, SJD); patent practice (MA); U.S. and global legal studies (ML); U.S. legal studies (LL M); JD/MA; JD/MBA; JD/MD; JD/MNM; JD/MPH; JD/MS; JD/MSSA. *Accreditation:* ABA. *Faculty:* 37 full-time (13 women), 26 part-time/adjunct (10 women).

Students: 412 full-time (216 women); includes 80 minority (39 Black or African American, non-Hispanic/Latino; 14 Asian, non-Hispanic/Latino; 24 Hispanic/Latino; 3 Two or more races, non-Hispanic/Latino), 36 international. Average age 24. 1,488 applicants, 39% accepted, 131 enrolled. In 2017, 138 master's awarded. *Entrance requirements:* For doctorate, LSAT, LSDAS. Additional exam requirements/recommendations for international students: Required—TOEFL. *Application deadline:* For fall admission, 4/1 priority date for domestic and international students. Applications are processed on a rolling basis. Application fee: $40. Electronic applications accepted. Application fee is waived when completed online. *Expenses:* 50666. *Financial support:* In 2017–18, 395 students received support. Career-related internships or fieldwork, Federal Work-Study, institutionally sponsored loans, and scholarships/grants available. Financial award application deadline: 5/1; financial award applicants required to submit FAFSA. *Unit head:* Jessica Berg, Co-Dean, 216-368-3283. *Application contact:* Kelli Curtis, Associate Dean for Admissions, 216-368-3600, Fax: 216-368-0185, E-mail: lawadmissions@case.edu.
Website: http://law.case.edu/

Health Law

DePaul University, College of Law, Chicago, IL 60604. Offers business law and taxation (MJ); criminal law (MJ); health and intellectual property law (MJ); health care compliance (MJ); health law (LL M, MJ); intellectual property law (LL M); international and comparative law (MJ); international law (LL M); law (JD); public interest law (MJ); taxation (LL M); U.S. legal studies (LL M); JD/LL M; JD/MA; JD/MBA; JD/MS. *Accreditation:* ABA. *Program availability:* Part-time, evening/weekend. *Entrance requirements:* For doctorate, LSAT, LSAC applicant evaluation/letter of recommendation, personal statement, resume. Additional exam requirements/recommendations for international students: Required—TOEFL (minimum score 577 paper-based; 90 iBT), IELTS (minimum score 6.5). *Application deadline:* For fall admission, 3/1 for domestic and international students. Applications are processed on a rolling basis. Electronic applications accepted. *Expenses:* Contact institution. *Financial support:* Application deadline: 3/1; applicants required to submit FAFSA. *Unit head:* Jennifer Rosato Perea, Dean, 312-362-8701, E-mail: jrosato@depaul.edu. *Application contact:* Amanda Noascono, Director of Law Admissions/Assistant Dean, 312-362-8807, Fax: 312-362-5280, E-mail: lawinfo@depaul.edu.
Website: http://law.depaul.edu

Drexel University, Thomas R. Kline School of Law, Philadelphia, PA 19104-2875. Offers business and entrepreneurship law (JD); criminal law (MLS, JD); cybersecurity and information privacy compliance (MLS); entrepreneurship and law (MLS); financial regulatory compliance (MLS); health care compliance (MLS); health law (JD); higher education compliance (MLS); human resources compliance (MLS); intellectual property law (JD); NCAA compliance and sports law (MLS).

Florida State University, College of Law, Tallahassee, FL 32306-1601. Offers American law for foreign lawyers (LL M); business law (LL M); environmental law and policy (LL M); financial regulation and compliance (JM); health law compliance (JM); law (JM, JD); legal risk management and HR compliance (JM); JD/MAES; JD/MBA; JD/MPA; JD/MS; JD/MSI; JD/MSP; JD/MSW. *Accreditation:* ABA. *Program availability:* Part-time, 100% online. *Faculty:* 57 full-time (29 women), 36 part-time/adjunct (11 women). *Students:* 520 full-time (268 women), 79 part-time (45 women); includes 184 minority (53 Black or African American, non-Hispanic/Latino; 2 American Indian or Alaska Native, non-Hispanic/Latino; 13 Asian, non-Hispanic/Latino; 71 Hispanic/Latino; 45 Two or more races, non-Hispanic/Latino), 13 international. Average age 26. 1,805 applicants, 36% accepted, 225 enrolled. In 2017, 18 master's, 218 doctorates awarded. Terminal master's awarded for partial completion of doctoral program. *Degree requirements:* For master's, comprehensive exam (for some programs). *Entrance requirements:* For master's, one graduate-level standardized test (for JM), JD or equivalent degree (for LL M); for doctorate, LSAT or GRE (for JD). Additional exam requirements/recommendations for international students: Required—TOEFL (minimum score 600 paper-based; 100 iBT), IELTS (minimum score 7.5). *Application deadline:* For fall admission, 6/30 for domestic and international students; for spring admission, 12/1 for domestic students; for summer admission, 4/15 for domestic students. Applications are processed on a rolling basis. Application fee: $30. Electronic applications accepted. *Expenses:* $20,683. *Financial support:* In 2017–18, 400 students received support, including 2 fellowships with full tuition reimbursements available (averaging $20,683 per year), 30 research assistantships (averaging $1,205 per year), 10 teaching assistantships (averaging $1,354 per year); career-related internships or fieldwork, scholarships/grants, and unspecified assistantships also available. Financial award application deadline: 3/1; financial award applicants required to submit FAFSA. *Faculty research:* Business law; environmental, energy and land use law; international law; criminal law. *Total annual research expenditures:* $99,375. *Unit head:* Erin O'Hara O'Connor, Dean, 850-644-3400, Fax: 850-644-5487, E-mail: eoconnor@law.fsu.edu. *Application contact:* Jennifer L. Kessinger, Director of Admissions and Records, 850-644-3787, Fax: 850-644-7284, E-mail: jkessing@law.fsu.edu.
Website: http://www.law.fsu.edu/

Georgetown University, Law Center, Washington, DC 20001. Offers environmental law (LL M); global health law (LL M); global health law and international institutions (LL M); individualized study (LL M); international business and economic law (LL M); law (JD, SJD); national security law (LL M); securities and financial regulation (LL M); taxation (LL M); JD/LL M; JD/MA; JD/MBA; JD/MPH; JD/PhD. *Accreditation:* ABA. *Program availability:* Part-time, evening/weekend. *Degree requirements:* For master's, thesis; for doctorate, thesis/dissertation (for some programs). *Entrance requirements:* For master's, JD, LL B, or first law degree earned in country of origin; for doctorate, LSAT (for JD). Additional exam requirements/recommendations for international students: Required—TOEFL. *Expenses:* Contact institution. *Faculty research:* Constitutional law, legal history, jurisprudence.

Hofstra University, Maurice A. Deane School of Law, Hempstead, NY 11549. Offers alternative dispute resolution (JD); American legal studies (LL M); business law honors (JD); clinical bioethics (Certificate); corporate compliance (JD); criminal law and procedure (JD); family law (LL M, JD); health law (JD); health law and policy (LL M, MA); intellectual property law honors (JD); international law honors (JD); JD/MBA; JD/MPH. *Accreditation:* ABA. *Program availability:* Part-time, 100% online. *Faculty:* 41 full-time (23 women), 69 part-time/adjunct (20 women). *Students:* 698 full-time (382 women), 136 part-time (91 women); includes 201 minority (66 Black or African American, non-Hispanic/Latino; 3 American Indian or Alaska Native, non-Hispanic/Latino; 31 Asian, non-Hispanic/Latino; 90 Hispanic/Latino; 8 Native Hawaiian or other Pacific Islander, non-Hispanic/Latino; 3 Two or more races, non-Hispanic/Latino), 28 international. Average age 28. 3,212 applicants, 50% accepted, 317 enrolled. In 2017, 9 master's, 234 doctorates awarded. *Entrance requirements:* For doctorate, LSAT, letter of recommendation, personal statement, undergraduate transcripts; for Certificate, 2 letters of recommendation, JD or LL B, personal statement, law school transcripts. Additional exam requirements/recommendations for international students: Recommended—TOEFL (minimum score 600 paper-based; 100 iBT). *Application deadline:* For fall admission, 4/15 priority date for domestic and international students. Applications are processed on a rolling basis. Application fee: $75. Electronic applications accepted. *Expenses:* $28,397 per term. *Financial support:* In 2017–18, 506 students received support, including 493 fellowships with full and partial tuition reimbursements available (averaging $33,296 per year); research assistantships with full and partial tuition reimbursements available, career-related internships or fieldwork, Federal Work-Study, institutionally sponsored loans, scholarships/grants, tuition waivers (full and partial), and unspecified assistantships also available. Support available to part-time students. Financial award applicants required to submit FAFSA. *Faculty research:* Family law; international law; constitutional law; legal ethics; health law. *Unit head:* Gail Prudenti, Dean, 516-463-4068, E-mail: gail.prudenti@hofstra.edu. *Application contact:* Sunil Samuel, Assistant Vice President of Admissions, 516-463-4723, Fax: 516-463-4664.
Website: http://law.hofstra.edu/

Indiana University–Purdue University Indianapolis, Robert H. McKinney School of Law, Indianapolis, IN 46202. Offers advocacy skills (Certificate); American law for foreign lawyers (LL M); civil and human rights (Certificate); corporate and commercial law (LL M, Certificate); criminal law (Certificate); environmental and natural resources (Certificate); health law (Certificate); health law, policy and bioethics (LL M); intellectual property law (LL M, Certificate); international and comparative law (LL M, Certificate); international human rights law (LL M); law (MJ, JD, SJD); JD/M Phil; JD/MBA; JD/MD; JD/MHA; JD/MLS; JD/MPA; JD/MPH; JD/MSW. *Accreditation:* ABA. *Program availability:* Part-time. *Entrance requirements:* For doctorate, LSAT. Additional exam requirements/recommendations for international students: Required—TOEFL (minimum score 79 iBT), IELTS (minimum score 6.5). Electronic applications accepted. *Expenses:* Contact institution.

Loyola University Chicago, School of Law, Chicago, IL 60611. Offers advocacy (LL M); business and compliance (MJ); business law (LL M); child and family (LL M); child and family law (MJ, Certificate); global competition (LL M, MJ); health law (LL M, MJ, Certificate); international law (LL M); law (JD); public interest law (Certificate); rule of law for development (LL M, MJ); tax (LL M); tax law (Certificate); transactional law (Certificate); trial advocacy (Certificate); JD/MA; JD/MBA; JD/MPP; JD/MSW; MJ/MSW; MS/MJ. *Accreditation:* ABA. *Program availability:* Part-time, evening/weekend, 100% online, blended/hybrid learning. *Faculty:* 69 full-time (36 women), 306 part-time/adjunct (148 women). *Students:* 823 full-time (483 women), 262 part-time (201 women); includes 334 minority (124 Black or African American, non-Hispanic/Latino; 1 American Indian or Alaska Native, non-Hispanic/Latino; 54 Asian, non-Hispanic/Latino; 114 Hispanic/Latino; 1 Native Hawaiian or other Pacific Islander, non-Hispanic/Latino; 40 Two or more races, non-Hispanic/Latino), 42 international. Average age 31. 2,670 applicants, 48% accepted, 372 enrolled. In 2017, 187 master's, 222 doctorates, 104 Certificates awarded. *Degree requirements:* For master's and Certificate, thesis (for some programs); for doctorate, thesis/dissertation (for some programs). *Entrance requirements:* For doctorate, LSAT. Additional exam requirements/recommendations for international students: Required—TOEFL (minimum score 100 iBT); Recommended—IELTS (minimum score 7). *Application deadline:* For fall admission, 4/1 for domestic and international students. Applications are processed on a rolling basis. Application fee: $0. Electronic applications accepted. *Expenses:* $46,460 full-time, $34,860 weekend (for JD). *Financial support:* In 2017–18, 598 students received support, including 67 fellowships; research assistantships, Federal Work-Study, scholarships/grants, and health care benefits also available. Financial award application deadline: 3/1; financial award applicants required to submit FAFSA. *Faculty research:* Constitutional law including hate speech and supreme court advocacy; early childhood education including law policy and pedagogy; hedonic psychology - legal and social determinants of happiness; racial inequality; intersection of law, science, and technology. *Unit head:* James Faught, JD, Associate Dean for Administration, Law School, 312-915-7131, Fax: 312-915-6911, E-mail: law-admissions@luc.edu. *Application contact:* Jill Schur, Director, Graduate Enrollment Management, 312-915-8902, E-mail: gradinfo@luc.edu.
Website: http://www.luc.edu/law/

Nova Southeastern University, Shepard Broad College of Law, Fort Lauderdale, FL 33314. Offers education law (MS), including cybersecurity law, education law advocacy, exceptional education; employment law (MS), including cybersecurity law, employee relations law, human resource managerial law; health law (MS, JD), including clinical research law and regulatory compliance (MS), cybersecurity law (MS), health care administrative law (MS), regulatory compliance (MS), risk management (MS); international law (JD); law and policy (MS), including cybersecurity law; JD/DO; JD/M Acc; JD/M Tax; JD/MBA; JD/MPA; JD/MS; JD/PhD. *Accreditation:* ABA. *Program availability:* Part-time, evening/weekend, 100% online, blended/hybrid learning. *Faculty:* 56 full-time (30 women), 41 part-time/adjunct (14 women). *Students:* 566 full-time (297 women), 138 part-time (84 women); includes 365 minority (62 Black or African American, non-Hispanic/Latino; 3 American Indian or Alaska Native, non-Hispanic/Latino; 23 Asian, non-Hispanic/Latino; 264 Hispanic/Latino; 3 Native Hawaiian or other Pacific Islander, non-Hispanic/Latino; 10 Two or more races, non-Hispanic/Latino), 26 international. Average age 29. 1,070 applicants, 53% accepted, 224 enrolled. In 2017, 45 master's, 225 doctorates awarded. *Degree requirements:* For master's, thesis optional, capstone research project; for doctorate, rigorous upper-level writing fulfilled through faculty-supervised seminar paper, law journal article, workshop, or other research; 6 credits' experiential learning. *Entrance requirements:* For master's, regionally-accredited undergraduate degree; at least 2 years' experience in related field (for employment law and health law); for doctorate, LSAT. Additional exam requirements/recommendations for international students: Recommended—TOEFL (minimum score 600 paper-based; 100 iBT), IELTS (minimum score 7). *Application deadline:* For fall admission, 5/1 priority date for domestic and international students; for winter admission, 12/12 for domestic and international students; for spring admission, 3/31 for domestic and international students; for summer admission, 4/1 for domestic and international students. Applications are processed on a rolling basis. Application fee: $0. Electronic applications accepted. *Expenses:* $40,060 full-time; $30,280 part-time. *Financial support:* In 2017–18, 211 students received support, including 221 fellowships (averaging $12,000 per year); Federal Work-Study, institutionally sponsored loans, scholarships/grants, and unspecified assistantships also available. Support available to part-time students. Financial award application deadline: 4/15; financial award applicants required to submit FAFSA. *Faculty research:* Legal issues in health law, international law, the legal profession, family law, civil rights. *Unit head:* Jon M. Garon, Dean, 954-262-6101, Fax: 954-262-2862, E-mail: garon@nova.edu. *Application contact:* William Daniel Perez, Assistant Dean of Admissions, 954-262-6121, Fax: 954-262-3844, E-mail: wperez1@nova.edu.
Website: http://www.law.nova.edu/

St. Mary's University, School of Law, Master of Jurisprudence Program, San Antonio, TX 78228. Offers business and entrepreneurship law (MJ); commercial law (MJ); compliance, business law and risk (MJ); criminal justice (MJ); education law (MJ); environmental law (MJ); health law (MJ); healthcare compliance (MJ); international comparative law (MJ); military and national security law (MJ); natural resource law (MJ); tax law (MJ). *Program availability:* Part-time, evening/weekend. *Faculty:* 45 full-time (13 women), 68 part-time/adjunct (22 women). *Students:* 10 full-time (7 women), 26 part-time (18 women); includes 25 minority (2 Black or African American, non-Hispanic/Latino; 1 Asian, non-Hispanic/Latino; 22 Hispanic/Latino). Average age 32. 37 applicants, 92% accepted, 22 enrolled. In 2017, 12 master's awarded. *Degree requirements:* For master's, 30 credits, minimum GPA of 2.0. *Entrance requirements:* For master's, official transcripts, personal statement, resume, 2 letters of recommendation, proof of four-year undergraduate degree from accredited U.S. college/university or foreign institution approved by government or accrediting authority. Additional exam requirements/recommendations for international students: Required—TOEFL (minimum score 550 paper-based; 80 iBT), IELTS (minimum score 6). *Application deadline:* Applications are processed on a rolling basis. Application fee: $0. Electronic applications accepted. *Expenses:* Contact institution. *Financial support:* Fellowships, research assistantships, Federal Work-Study, scholarships/grants, and unspecified assistantships available. Financial award applicants required to submit FAFSA. *Unit head:* Shannon Sevier, Director, Graduate Law Programs, 210-431-4235, E-mail: ssevier@stmarytx.edu. *Application contact:* Shannon Sevier, Director, Graduate Law Programs, 210-431-4235, E-mail: ssevier@stmarytx.edu.
Website: https://law.stmarytx.edu/academics/programs/master-of-jurisprudence/

Seattle University, School of Law, Seattle, WA 98122-4340. Offers American legal studies (LL M); business development (MLS); elder law (LL M); health law (MLS); innovation and technology (LL M, MLS); tribal law and governance (LL M, MLS); JD/MATL; JD/MBA; JD/MCJ; JD/MIB; JD/MPA; JD/MSAL; JD/MSF; JD/MSL. *Accreditation:*

ABA. *Program availability:* Part-time, evening/weekend. *Faculty:* 47 full-time (25 women), 48 part-time/adjunct (16 women). *Students:* 500 full-time (265 women), 130 part-time (65 women); includes 268 minority (34 Black or African American, non-Hispanic/Latino; 6 American Indian or Alaska Native, non-Hispanic/Latino; 102 Asian, non-Hispanic/Latino; 69 Hispanic/Latino; 5 Native Hawaiian or other Pacific Islander, non-Hispanic/Latino; 52 Two or more races, non-Hispanic/Latino), 7 international. Average age 27. 1,443 applicants, 67% accepted, 200 enrolled. In 2017, 300 doctorates awarded. *Entrance requirements:* For doctorate, LSAT. Additional exam requirements/recommendations for international students: Required—TOEFL (minimum score 600 paper-based; 100 iBT). *Application deadline:* For fall admission, 3/1 priority date for domestic and international students. Applications are processed on a rolling basis. Application fee: $65. Electronic applications accepted. *Expenses:* Contact institution. *Financial support:* In 2017–18, 500 students received support. Career-related internships or fieldwork, Federal Work-Study, and scholarships/grants available. Support available to part-time students. Financial award application deadline: 2/15; financial award applicants required to submit FAFSA. *Faculty research:* Innovation, technology and cybersecurity; secrecy and democratic decisions; linguistic features of police culture and the coercive impact of police officer swearing in police-citizen interaction; the imprisoned parent: differential power in same-sex families based on legal and cultural understandings of parentage; theology in public reason and legal discourse: a case for the preferential option for the poor. *Unit head:* Annette E. Clark, Dean, 206-398-4300, Fax: 206-398-4310, E-mail: annclark@seattleu.edu. *Application contact:* Gerald Heppler, Director of Admission, 206-398-4205, Fax: 206-398-4058, E-mail: hepplerg@seattleu.edu.
Website: http://www.law.seattleu.edu/

Seton Hall University, School of Law, Newark, NJ 07102-5210. Offers health law (LL M, JD); intellectual property (LL M, JD); law (MSJ); JD/MADIR; JD/MBA; MD/JD; MD/MSJ. MD/JD, MD/MSJ offered jointly with University of Medicine and Dentistry of New Jersey. *Accreditation:* ABA. *Program availability:* Part-time, evening/weekend. *Degree requirements:* For master's, thesis optional. *Entrance requirements:* For master's, professional experience, letters of recommendation; for doctorate, LSAT, active LSDAS registration, letters of recommendation. Additional exam requirements/recommendations for international students: Recommended—TOEFL. Electronic applications accepted. *Expenses:* Contact institution. *Faculty research:* Health law, intellectual property law, science and the law, international law and employment/labor law.

Southern Illinois University Carbondale, School of Law, Program in Legal Studies, Carbondale, IL 62901-4701. Offers general law (MLS); health law and policy (MLS).

Suffolk University, Law School, Boston, MA 02108. Offers business law and financial services (JD); civil litigation (JD); global law and technology (LL M); health and biomedical law (JD); intellectual property law (JD); international law (JD); JD/MBA; JD/MPA; JD/MSCJ; JD/MSF; JD/MSIE. *Accreditation:* ABA. *Program availability:* Part-time, evening/weekend. *Faculty:* 63 full-time (31 women), 54 part-time/adjunct (18 women). *Students:* 663 full-time (358 women), 366 part-time (181 women); includes 181 minority (36 Black or African American, non-Hispanic/Latino; 2 American Indian or Alaska Native, non-Hispanic/Latino; 48 Asian, non-Hispanic/Latino; 73 Hispanic/Latino; 22 Two or more races, non-Hispanic/Latino), 37 international. Average age 27. 1,962 applicants, 66% accepted, 340 enrolled. In 2017, 22 master's, 322 doctorates awarded. *Degree requirements:* For master's, legal writing. *Entrance requirements:* For master's, 2 letters of recommendation, resume, personal statement; for doctorate, LSAT, LSDAS, dean's certification, recommendation. Additional exam requirements/recommendations for international students: Required—TOEFL (minimum score 600 paper-based; 100 iBT). *Application deadline:* For fall admission, 4/1 for domestic and international students. Applications are processed on a rolling basis. Application fee: $60. Electronic applications accepted. *Expenses:* $48,090 per year full-time tuition; $1,603 per credit part-time. *Financial support:* In 2017–18, 663 students received support, including 1 fellowship (averaging $31,390 per year); career-related internships or fieldwork, Federal Work-Study, institutionally sponsored loans, and scholarships/grants also available. Support available to part-time students. Financial award application deadline: 3/1; financial award applicants required to submit FAFSA. *Faculty research:* Civil law, international law, health/biomedical law, business and finance, intellectual property. *Unit head:* Andrew Perlman, Dean, 617-573-8144, Fax: 617-994-6838, E-mail: lawadmin@suffolk.edu. *Application contact:* Matthew Gavin, Assistant Dean for Admissions and Financial Aid, 617-573-8144, Fax: 617-994-6838, E-mail: lawadm@suffolk.edu.
Website: http://www.suffolk.edu/law/

Université de Sherbrooke, Faculty of Law, Sherbrooke, QC J1K 2R1, Canada. Offers alternative dispute resolution (LL M, Diploma); business law (Diploma); common law (JD); criminal and penal law (Diploma); health law (LL M, Diploma); international law (LL M); law (LL D); legal management (Diploma); notarial law (Diploma); transnational law (Diploma). *Program availability:* Part-time, evening/weekend. *Degree requirements:* For master's, thesis; for Diploma, one foreign language. *Entrance requirements:* For master's and Diploma, LL B. Electronic applications accepted.

University of California, San Francisco, Graduate Division, Program in Health Policy and Law, San Francisco, CA 94143. Offers MS. Program offered in conjunction with University of California, Hastings College of the Law and University of California, Berkeley. *Program availability:* Part-time, online learning. *Degree requirements:* For master's, capstone project, comprehensive written and oral final examination.

University of Houston, University of Houston Law Center, Houston, TX 77204-6060. Offers energy, environment, and natural resources (LL M); health law (LL M); intellectual property and information law (LL M); international law (LL M); law (JD); tax law (LL M); U.S. law (LL M). *Accreditation:* ABA. *Program availability:* Part-time, evening/weekend. *Faculty:* 58 full-time (23 women), 130 part-time/adjunct (36 women). *Students:* 695 full-time (331 women), 120 part-time (55 women); includes 319 minority (62 Black or African American, non-Hispanic/Latino; 10 American Indian or Alaska Native, non-Hispanic/Latino; 73 Asian, non-Hispanic/Latino; 172 Hispanic/Latino; 2 Native Hawaiian or other Pacific Islander, non-Hispanic/Latino), 33 international. Average age 26. 2,751 applicants, 33% accepted, 227 enrolled. In 2017, 75 master's, 231 doctorates awarded. *Degree requirements:* For master's, thesis optional; for doctorate, senior writing requirement. *Entrance requirements:* For doctorate, LSAT. Additional exam

requirements/recommendations for international students: Required—TOEFL (minimum score 600 paper-based; 100 iBT). *Application deadline:* For fall admission, 2/15 for domestic and international students. Applications are processed on a rolling basis. Application fee: $0. Electronic applications accepted. *Expenses:* Contact institution. *Financial support:* In 2017–18, 442 students received support, including 20 fellowships (averaging $2,980 per year); research assistantships, career-related internships or fieldwork, Federal Work-Study, scholarships/grants, and tuition waivers also available. Support available to part-time students. Financial award application deadline: 3/15; financial award applicants required to submit FAFSA. *Faculty research:* Health law, international law, tax, environmental law, information law/intellectual property. *Total annual research expenditures:* $472,551. *Unit head:* Leonard M. Baynes, Dean and Professor of Law, 713-743-2100, Fax: 713-743-2122, E-mail: lbaynes@central.uh.edu. *Application contact:* Pilar Mensah, Assistant Dean for Admissions, 713-743-2280, Fax: 713-743-2194, E-mail: lpmensah@central.uh.edu.
Website: http://www.law.uh.edu/

The University of Manchester, School of Law, Manchester, United Kingdom. Offers bioethics and medical jurisprudence (PhD); criminology (M Phil, PhD); law (M Phil, PhD).

University of Pittsburgh, School of Law, Master of Studies in Law Program, Pittsburgh, PA 15260. Offers biomedical and health services research (MSL); business law (MSL), including commercial law, corporate law, general business law, international business, tax law; Constitutional law (MSL); criminal law and justice (MSL); disability law (MSL); elder and estate planning law (MSL); employment and labor law (MSL); energy law (MSL); environmental and real estate law (MSL); family law (MSL); health law (MSL); intellectual property and technology law (MSL); international and human rights law (MSL); jurisprudence (MSL); regulatory law (MSL); self-designed (MSL). *Program availability:* Part-time. *Faculty:* 47 full-time (22 women), 116 part-time/adjunct (29 women). *Students:* 4 full-time (2 women), 17 part-time (12 women); includes 6 minority (5 Black or African American, non-Hispanic/Latino; 1 Hispanic/Latino). Average age 26. 28 applicants, 75% accepted, 15 enrolled. In 2017, 15 master's awarded. *Entrance requirements:* Additional exam requirements/recommendations for international students: Required—TOEFL (minimum score 600 paper-based; 100 iBT), IELTS (minimum score 7). *Application deadline:* For fall admission, 6/30 for domestic students, 5/1 for international students. Applications are processed on a rolling basis. Application fee: $0. *Faculty research:* Law, health law, business law, contracts, intellectual property, environmental law. *Unit head:* Prof. Alan Meisel, Director, 412-648-1384, Fax: 412-648-2649, E-mail: meisel@pitt.edu. *Application contact:* Beth Ann Pischke, Administrative Coordinator, 412-648-7120, Fax: 412-648-2649, E-mail: pischke@pitt.edu.
Website: http://www.law.pitt.edu/msl

The University of Tulsa, College of Law, Tulsa, OK 74104. Offers American Indian and indigenous law (LL M); American law for foreign lawyers (LL M); energy and natural resources law (LL M); energy law (MJ); health law (Certificate); Indian law (MJ); law (JD); Native American law (Certificate); sustainable energy and resources law (Certificate); JD/MA; JD/MBA; JD/MS. *Accreditation:* ABA. *Program availability:* Part-time, 100% online. *Faculty:* 24 full-time (13 women), 14 part-time/adjunct (7 women). *Students:* 243 full-time (105 women), 29 part-time (12 women); includes 75 minority (12 Black or African American, non-Hispanic/Latino; 17 American Indian or Alaska Native, non-Hispanic/Latino; 1 Asian, non-Hispanic/Latino; 11 Hispanic/Latino; 34 Two or more races, non-Hispanic/Latino), 4 international. Average age 28. 567 applicants, 45% accepted, 94 enrolled. In 2017, 3 master's, 86 doctorates, 26 Certificates awarded. *Degree requirements:* For master's, thesis optional. *Entrance requirements:* For master's, JD from an ABA-approved U.S. law school or a JD equivalent from non-U.S. university; for doctorate, LSAT, BS or BA from 4-year regionally-accredited college/university; for Certificate, BS or BA from 4-year regionally-accredited college/university. Additional exam requirements/recommendations for international students: Required—TOEFL (minimum score 570 paper-based; 90 iBT), IELTS (minimum score 6.5). *Application deadline:* For fall admission, 7/31 priority date for domestic and international students; for spring admission, 12/5 priority date for domestic students, 12/5 for international students; for summer admission, 4/13 for domestic and international students. Applications are processed on a rolling basis. Application fee: $30. Electronic applications accepted. *Expenses:* $24,600 per year tuition; $564 fees. *Financial support:* In 2017–18, 261 students received support. Scholarships/grants available. Support available to part-time students. Financial award application deadline: 8/1; financial award applicants required to submit FAFSA. *Faculty research:* Native American law, criminal law, commercial speech, copyright law, international law. *Unit head:* Prof. Lyn Suzanne Entzeroth, Dean, 918-631-2400, Fax: 918-631-3126, E-mail: lyn-entzeroth@utulsa.edu. *Application contact:* April M. Fox, Associate Dean of Admissions and Financial Aid, 918-631-2406, Fax: 918-631-3630, E-mail: april-fox@utulsa.edu.
Website: http://www.utulsa.edu/law/

Widener University, Delaware Law School, Wilmington, DE 19803-0474. Offers corporate and business law (MJ); corporate law and finance (LL M); health law (LL M, MJ, D Law); higher education compliance (MJ); juridical science (SJD); law (JD). *Accreditation:* ABA. *Program availability:* Part-time, 100% online. *Faculty:* 24 full-time (13 women), 42 part-time/adjunct (15 women). *Students:* 530 full-time (269 women), 26 part-time (17 women); includes 136 minority (80 Black or African American, non-Hispanic/Latino; 8 American Indian or Alaska Native, non-Hispanic/Latino; 16 Asian, non-Hispanic/Latino; 27 Hispanic/Latino; 5 Two or more races, non-Hispanic/Latino), 26 international. Average age 29. 942 applicants, 62% accepted, 210 enrolled. *Degree requirements:* For doctorate, thesis/dissertation (for some programs). *Entrance requirements:* For master's, GMAT. *Application deadline:* For fall admission, 5/15 for domestic students; for spring admission, 12/1 for domestic students. Applications are processed on a rolling basis. Application fee: $60. *Financial support:* Career-related internships or fieldwork, Federal Work-Study, institutionally sponsored loans, and scholarships/grants available. Support available to part-time students. Financial award application deadline: 2/15; financial award applicants required to submit FAFSA. *Unit head:* Rod Smolla, Dean, 302-477-2100, Fax: 302-477-2282, E-mail: rasmolla@widener.edu. *Application contact:* Barbara L. Ayars, Assistant Dean of Admissions, 302-477-2210, Fax: 302-477-2224, E-mail: barbara.l.ayars@law.widener.edu.
Website: http://delawarelaw.widener.edu/

Intellectual Property Law

Case Western Reserve University, School of Law, Cleveland, OH 44106. Offers financial integrity (MA); health law (SJD); intellectual property (LL M); intellectual property law (ML); international business law (LL M, ML); international criminal law (LL M); law (JD, SJD); patent practice (MA); U.S. and global legal studies (ML); U.S. legal studies (LL M); JD/MA; JD/MBA; JD/MD; JD/MNM; JD/MPH; JD/MS; JD/MSSA. *Accreditation:* ABA. *Faculty:* 37 full-time (13 women), 26 part-time/adjunct (10 women). *Students:* 412 full-time (216 women); includes 80 minority (39 Black or African American, non-Hispanic/Latino; 14 Asian, non-Hispanic/Latino; 24 Hispanic/Latino; 3 Two or more races, non-Hispanic/Latino; 36 international. Average age 24. 1,488 applicants, 39% accepted, 131 enrolled. In 2017, 138 master's awarded. *Entrance requirements:* For doctorate, LSAT, LSDAS. Additional exam requirements/recommendations for international students: Required—TOEFL. *Application deadline:* For fall admission, 4/1 priority date for domestic and international students. Applications are processed on a rolling basis. Application fee: $40. Electronic applications accepted. Application fee is waived when completed online. *Expenses:* 50666. *Financial support:* In 2017–18, 395 students received support. Career-related internships or fieldwork, Federal Work-Study, institutionally sponsored loans, and scholarships/grants available. Financial award application deadline: 5/1; financial award applicants required to submit FAFSA. *Unit head:* Jessica Berg, Co-Dean, 216-368-3283. *Application contact:* Kelli Curtis, Associate Dean for Admissions, 216-368-3600, Fax: 216-368-0185, E-mail: lawadmissions@case.edu.
Website: http://law.case.edu/

DePaul University, College of Law, Chicago, IL 60604. Offers business law and taxation (MJ); criminal law (MJ); health and intellectual property law (MJ); health care compliance (MJ); health law (LL M, MJ); intellectual property law (LL M); international and comparative law (MJ); international law (LL M); law (JD); public interest law (MJ); taxation (LL M); U.S. legal studies (LL M); JD/LL M; JD/MA; JD/MBA; JD/MS. *Accreditation:* ABA. *Program availability:* Part-time, evening/weekend. *Entrance requirements:* For doctorate, LSAT, LSAC applicant evaluation/letter of recommendation, personal statement, resume. Additional exam requirements/recommendations for international students: Required—TOEFL (minimum score 577 paper-based; 90 iBT), IELTS (minimum score 6.5). *Application deadline:* For fall admission, 3/1 for domestic and international students. Applications are processed on a rolling basis. Electronic applications accepted. *Expenses:* Contact institution. *Financial support:* Application deadline: 3/1; applicants required to submit FAFSA. *Unit head:* Jennifer Rosato Perea, Dean, 312-362-8701, E-mail: jrosato@depaul.edu. *Application contact:* Amanda Noascono, Director of Law Admissions/Assistant Dean, 312-362-8807, Fax: 312-362-5280, E-mail: lawinfo@depaul.edu.
Website: http://law.depaul.edu

Drexel University, Thomas R. Kline School of Law, Philadelphia, PA 19104-2875. Offers business and entrepreneurship law (JD); criminal law (MLS, JD); cybersecurity and information privacy compliance (MLS); entrepreneurship and law (MLS); financial regulatory compliance (MLS); health care compliance (MLS); health law (JD); higher education compliance (MLS); human resources compliance (MLS); intellectual property law (JD); NCAA compliance and sports law (MLS).

Fordham University, School of Law, New York, NY 10023. Offers banking, corporate and finance law (LL M); corporate compliance (MSL); fashion law (MSL); intellectual property and information law (LL M); international business and trade law (LL M); law (JD); JD/MA; JD/MBA; JD/MSW. *Accreditation:* ABA. *Program availability:* Part-time, evening/weekend. *Entrance requirements:* For doctorate, LSAT. Additional exam requirements/recommendations for international students: Required—TOEFL. Electronic applications accepted. *Expenses:* Contact institution. *Faculty research:* Intellectual property, business law, international law.

Golden Gate University, School of Law, San Francisco, CA 94105. Offers environmental law (LL M); estate planning (LL M); intellectual property law (LL M); international legal studies (LL M, SJD); law (JD); taxation law (LL M); U.S. legal studies (LL M); JD/MBA. *Accreditation:* ABA. *Program availability:* Part-time, evening/weekend. *Faculty:* 31 full-time (19 women), 160 part-time/adjunct (77 women). *Students:* 286 full-time (184 women), 245 part-time (134 women); includes 242 minority (48 Black or African American, non-Hispanic/Latino; 4 American Indian or Alaska Native, non-Hispanic/Latino; 69 Asian, non-Hispanic/Latino; 95 Hispanic/Latino; 7 Native Hawaiian or other Pacific Islander, non-Hispanic/Latino; 19 Two or more races, non-Hispanic/Latino; 71 international. Average age 31. 1,354 applicants, 66% accepted, 227 enrolled. *Degree requirements:* For doctorate, thesis/dissertation (for some programs). *Entrance requirements:* For doctorate, LSAT (for JD). Additional exam requirements/recommendations for international students: Required—TOEFL (minimum score 600 paper-based). *Application deadline:* For fall admission, 6/30 for domestic students. Applications are processed on a rolling basis. Electronic applications accepted. *Expenses:* Contact institution. *Financial support:* Fellowships, research assistantships, teaching assistantships, career-related internships or fieldwork, Federal Work-Study, institutionally sponsored loans, scholarships/grants, tuition waivers (full and partial), and unspecified assistantships available. Support available to part-time students. Financial award applicants required to submit FAFSA. *Faculty research:* International law, intellectual property law, environmental law, real estate, civil rights. *Unit head:* Anthony Niedwiecki, Dean, 415-442-6601, Fax: 415-442-6609. *Application contact:* Greg Egertson, Associate Dean and Director of Admissions, 415-442-6636, Fax: 415-442-6609, E-mail: lawadmit@ggu.edu.
Website: http://law.ggu.edu/

Hofstra University, Maurice A. Deane School of Law, Hempstead, NY 11549. Offers alternative dispute resolution (JD); American legal studies (LL M); business law honors (JD); clinical bioethics (Certificate); corporate compliance (JD); criminal law and procedure (JD); family law (LL M, JD); health law (JD); health law and policy (LL M, MA); intellectual property law honors (JD); international law honors (JD); JD/MBA; JD/MPH. *Accreditation:* ABA. *Program availability:* Part-time, 100% online. *Faculty:* 41 full-time (23 women), 69 part-time/adjunct (20 women). *Students:* 698 full-time (382 women), 136 part-time (91 women); includes 201 minority (66 Black or African American, non-Hispanic/Latino; 3 American Indian or Alaska Native, non-Hispanic/Latino; 31 Asian, non-Hispanic/Latino; 90 Hispanic/Latino; 8 Native Hawaiian or other Pacific Islander, non-Hispanic/Latino; 3 Two or more races, non-Hispanic/Latino), 28 international. Average age 28. 3,212 applicants, 50% accepted, 317 enrolled. In 2017, 9 master's, 234 doctorates awarded. *Entrance requirements:* For doctorate, LSAT, letter of recommendation, personal statement, undergraduate transcripts; for Certificate, 2 letters of recommendation, JD or LL B, personal statement, law school transcripts. Additional exam requirements/recommendations for international students: Recommended—TOEFL (minimum score 600 paper-based; 100 iBT). *Application deadline:* For fall admission, 4/15 priority date for domestic and international students. Applications are processed on a rolling basis. Application fee: $75. Electronic

applications accepted. *Expenses:* $28,397 per term. *Financial support:* In 2017–18, 506 students received support, including 493 fellowships with full and partial tuition reimbursements available (averaging $33,296 per year); research assistantships with full and partial tuition reimbursements available, career-related internships or fieldwork, Federal Work-Study, institutionally sponsored loans, scholarships/grants, tuition waivers (full and partial), and unspecified assistantships also available. Support available to part-time students. Financial award applicants required to submit FAFSA. *Faculty research:* Family law; international law; constitutional law; legal ethics; health law. *Unit head:* Gail Prudenti, Dean, 516-463-4068, E-mail: gail.prudenti@hofstra.edu. *Application contact:* Sunil Samuel, Assistant Vice President of Admissions, 516-463-4723, Fax: 516-463-4664.
Website: http://law.hofstra.edu/

Indiana University–Purdue University Indianapolis, Robert H. McKinney School of Law, Indianapolis, IN 46202. Offers advocacy skills (Certificate); American law for foreign lawyers (LL M); civil and human rights (Certificate); corporate and commercial law (LL M, Certificate); criminal law (Certificate); environmental and natural resources (Certificate); health law (Certificate); health law, policy and bioethics (LL M); intellectual property law (LL M, Certificate); international and comparative law (LL M, Certificate); international human rights law (LL M); law (MJ, JD, SJD); JD/M Phil; JD/MBA; JD/MD; JD/MHA; JD/MLS; JD/MPA; JD/MPH; JD/MSW. *Accreditation:* ABA. *Program availability:* Part-time. *Entrance requirements:* For doctorate, LSAT. Additional exam requirements/recommendations for international students: Required—TOEFL (minimum score 79 iBT), IELTS (minimum score 6.5). Electronic applications accepted. *Expenses:* Contact institution.

Michigan State University College of Law, Graduate and Professional Programs, East Lansing, MI 48824-1300. Offers American legal system (LL M, MJ); global food law (LL M, MJ); intellectual property law (LL M, MJ); law (JD); legal studies (MLS). *Accreditation:* ABA. *Program availability:* Part-time. *Faculty:* 55 full-time (23 women), 77 part-time/adjunct (27 women). *Students:* 779 full-time (407 women), 77 part-time (50 women); includes 173 minority (57 Black or African American, non-Hispanic/Latino; 9 American Indian or Alaska Native, non-Hispanic/Latino; 28 Asian, non-Hispanic/Latino; 40 Hispanic/Latino; 2 Native Hawaiian or other Pacific Islander, non-Hispanic/Latino; 37 Two or more races, non-Hispanic/Latino), 91 international. Average age 24. *Entrance requirements:* For doctorate, LSAT. Additional exam requirements/recommendations for international students: Required—TOEFL (minimum score 600 paper-based), IELTS. *Application deadline:* For fall admission, 4/30 priority date for domestic students, 7/1 priority date for international students. Applications are processed on a rolling basis. Application fee: $60. Electronic applications accepted. *Expenses: Tuition:* Full-time $43,400. *Financial support:* Career-related internships or fieldwork, Federal Work-Study, scholarships/grants, and tuition waivers (full and partial) available. Support available to part-time students. Financial award application deadline: 4/1; financial award applicants required to submit FAFSA. *Faculty research:* International, constitutional, health, tax and environmental law; intellectual property, trial practice, corporate law. *Unit head:* Lawrence Ponoroff, Dean/Professor of Law, 517-432-6993, Fax: 517-432-6801, E-mail: lponoroff@law.msu.edu. *Application contact:* Melanie Jacobs, Senior Associate Dean of Admissions and International Programs, 517-432-0222, Fax: 517-432-0098, E-mail: admiss@law.msu.edu.
Website: http://www.law.msu.edu/

Montclair State University, The Graduate School, College of Humanities and Social Sciences, MA Program in Law and Governance, Montclair, NJ 07043-1624. Offers conflict management and peace studies (MA); governance, compliance and regulation (MA); intellectual property (MA); law and governance (MA); legal management (MA). *Program availability:* Part-time, evening/weekend. *Degree requirements:* For master's, thesis or comprehensive exam. *Entrance requirements:* For master's, GRE General Test, minimum cumulative GPA of 2.75 for undergraduate work, 2 letters of recommendation, essay. Additional exam requirements/recommendations for international students: Required—TOEFL (minimum score 83 iBT) or IELTS (minimum score 6.5). Electronic applications accepted.

Santa Clara University, School of Law, Santa Clara, CA 95053. Offers high tech law (Certificate); intellectual property (LL M); international and comparative law (LL M); international law (Certificate); law (JD); public interest and social justice law (Certificate); United States law (LL M); JD/MBA; JD/MSIS. JD/MBA, JD/MSIS offered jointly with Leavey School of Business. *Accreditation:* ABA. *Program availability:* Part-time. *Faculty:* 48 full-time (24 women), 41 part-time/adjunct (23 women). *Students:* 670 full-time (372 women), 57 part-time (23 women); includes 344 minority (30 Black or African American, non-Hispanic/Latino; 138 Asian, non-Hispanic/Latino; 134 Hispanic/Latino; 1 Native Hawaiian or other Pacific Islander, non-Hispanic/Latino; 41 Two or more races, non-Hispanic/Latino), 63 international. Average age 27. 2,092 applicants, 62% accepted, 248 enrolled. In 2017, 30 master's, 134 doctorates awarded. *Entrance requirements:* For master's and doctorate, LSAT, personal statement. *Application deadline:* For fall admission, 3/1 for domestic students. Application fee: $0. Electronic applications accepted. *Expenses:* Contact institution. *Financial support:* In 2017–18, 407 students received support. Fellowships, research assistantships, teaching assistantships, Federal Work-Study, scholarships/grants, health care benefits, and tuition waivers available. Support available to part-time students. Financial award application deadline: 3/1; financial award applicants required to submit FAFSA. *Unit head:* Lisa Kloppenberg, Dean, 408-554-4362, E-mail: lkloppenberg@scu.edu. *Application contact:* Nanette Cannon, Director of Admissions, 408-551-1846, E-mail: ncannon@scu.edu.
Website: http://law.scu.edu/

Suffolk University, Law School, Boston, MA 02108. Offers business law and financial services (JD); civil litigation (JD); global law and technology (LL M); health and biomedical law (JD); intellectual property law (JD); international law (JD); JD/MBA; JD/MPA; JD/MSCJ; JD/MSF; JD/MSIE. *Accreditation:* ABA. *Program availability:* Part-time, evening/weekend. *Faculty:* 63 full-time (31 women), 54 part-time/adjunct (18 women). *Students:* 663 full-time (358 women), 366 part-time (181 women); includes 181 minority (36 Black or African American, non-Hispanic/Latino; 2 American Indian or Alaska Native, non-Hispanic/Latino; 48 Asian, non-Hispanic/Latino; 73 Hispanic/Latino; 22 Two or more races, non-Hispanic/Latino), 37 international. Average age 27. 1,962 applicants, 66% accepted, 340 enrolled. In 2017, 22 master's, 322 doctorates awarded. *Degree requirements:* For master's, legal writing. *Entrance requirements:* For master's, 2 letters of recommendation, resume, personal statement; for doctorate, LSAT, LSDAS, dean's certification, recommendation. Additional exam requirements/recommendations for international students: Required—TOEFL (minimum score 600 paper-based; 100 iBT). *Application deadline:* For fall admission, 4/1 for domestic and international students. Applications are processed on a rolling basis. Application fee: $60. Electronic applications accepted. *Expenses:* $48,090 per year full-time tuition; $1,603 per credit part-time. *Financial support:* In 2017–18, 663 students received support, including 1 fellowship (averaging $31,390 per year); career-related internships or fieldwork, Federal Work-Study, institutionally sponsored loans, and scholarships/grants also available. Support available to part-time students. Financial award application deadline: 3/1; financial award applicants required to submit FAFSA. *Faculty research:* Civil law, international law, health/biomedical law, business and finance, intellectual property. *Unit head:* Andrew Perlman, Dean, 617-573-8144, Fax: 617-994-6838, E-mail: lawadmin@suffolk.edu. *Application contact:* Matthew Gavin, Assistant Dean for Admissions and Financial Aid, 617-573-8144, Fax: 617-994-6838, E-mail: lawadm@suffolk.edu. Website: http://www.suffolk.edu/law/

Texas A&M University, School of Law, College Station, TX 77843. Offers intellectual property (M Jur); jurisprudence (M Jur); law (JD). *Accreditation:* ABA. *Faculty:* 79. *Students:* 404 full-time (206 women), 58 part-time (19 women); includes 120 minority (33 Black or African American, non-Hispanic/Latino; 2 American Indian or Alaska Native, non-Hispanic/Latino; 9 Asian, non-Hispanic/Latino; 73 Hispanic/Latino; 3 Two or more races, non-Hispanic/Latino), 4 international. Average age 29. 541 applicants, 100% accepted, 178 enrolled. *Entrance requirements:* For doctorate, LSAT, personal statement, resume, all post-secondary transcripts, 2-4 letters of recommendation and up to 2 LSAC evaluations, CAS Report. *Application deadline:* For fall admission, 7/1 for domestic students. Applications are processed on a rolling basis. Application fee: $55. *Expenses:* Contact institution. *Financial support:* In 2017–18, 403 students received support, including 6 fellowships with tuition reimbursements available (averaging $29,510 per year); career-related internships or fieldwork, institutionally sponsored loans, scholarships/grants, traineeships, health care benefits, and tuition waivers (full and partial) also available. Support available to part-time students. Financial award applicants required to submit FAFSA. *Unit head:* Dr. Andrew P. Morriss, Dean, 817-212-4139, Fax: 817-212-4139, E-mail: amorriss@law.tamu.edu. *Application contact:* Law School Admissions, 817-212-4040, E-mail: law-admissions@law.tamu.edu. Website: http://law.tamu.edu/

University of Baltimore, School of Law, Baltimore, MD 21201. Offers business law (JD); criminal practice (JD); estate planning (JD); family law (JD); intellectual property (JD); international law (JD); law (JD); law of the United States (LL M); litigation and advocacy (JD); public service (JD); real estate practice (JD); taxation (LL M); JD/LL M; JD/MBA; JD/MPA; JD/MS; JD/PhD. JD/MS offered jointly with Division of Criminology, Criminal Justice, and Social Policy; JD/PhD with University of Maryland, Baltimore. *Accreditation:* ABA. *Program availability:* Part-time, evening/weekend. *Entrance requirements:* For doctorate, LSAT. Additional exam requirements/recommendations for international students: Required—TOEFL (for LL M in law of the United States). Electronic applications accepted. *Expenses:* Contact institution. *Faculty research:* Plain view doctrine, statute of limitations, bankruptcy, family law, international and comparative law, Constitutional law.

University of Houston, University of Houston Law Center, Houston, TX 77204-6060. Offers energy, environment, and natural resources (LL M); health law (LL M); intellectual property and information law (LL M); international law (LL M); law (JD); tax law (LL M); U.S. law (LL M). *Accreditation:* ABA. *Program availability:* Part-time, evening/weekend. *Faculty:* 58 full-time (23 women), 130 part-time/adjunct (36 women). *Students:* 695 full-time (331 women), 120 part-time (55 women); includes 319 minority (62 Black or African American, non-Hispanic/Latino; 10 American Indian or Alaska Native, non-Hispanic/Latino; 73 Asian, non-Hispanic/Latino; 172 Hispanic/Latino; 2 Native Hawaiian or other Pacific Islander, non-Hispanic/Latino), 33 international. Average age 26. 2,751 applicants, 33% accepted, 227 enrolled. In 2017, 75 master's, 231 doctorates awarded. *Degree requirements:* For master's, thesis optional; for doctorate, senior writing requirement. *Entrance requirements:* For doctorate, LSAT. Additional exam requirements/recommendations for international students: Required—TOEFL (minimum score 600 paper-based; 100 iBT). *Application deadline:* For fall admission, 2/15 for domestic and international students. Applications are processed on a rolling basis. Application fee: $0. Electronic applications accepted. *Expenses:* Contact institution. *Financial support:* In 2017–18, 442 students received support, including 20 fellowships (averaging $2,980 per year); research assistantships, career-related internships or fieldwork, Federal Work-Study, scholarships/grants, and tuition waivers also available. Support available to part-time students. Financial award application deadline: 3/15; financial award applicants required to submit FAFSA. *Faculty research:* Health law, international law, tax, environmental law/energy, information law/intellectual property. *Total annual research expenditures:* $472,551. *Unit head:* Leonard M. Baynes, Dean and Professor of Law, 713-743-2100, Fax: 713-743-2122, E-mail: lbaynes@central.uh.edu. *Application contact:* Pilar Mensah, Assistant Dean for Admissions, 713-743-2280, Fax: 713-743-2194, E-mail: lpmensah@central.uh.edu. Website: http://www.law.uh.edu/

University of New Hampshire, School of Law, Concord, NH 03301. Offers business law (JD); commerce and technology (LL M, MCT, Diploma); criminal law (JD); intellectual property (LL M, MIP, JD, Diploma), including patent law (JD), trademarks and copyright (JD); international criminal law and justice (LL M, MICLJ); litigation (JD); public interest and social justice (JD); sports and entertainment law (JD); JD/LL M; JD/MBA; JD/MIP; JD/MPP; JD/MSW. *Accreditation:* ABA. *Program availability:* Part-time, 100% online, limited residential. *Degree requirements:* For doctorate, comprehensive exam. *Entrance requirements:* For doctorate, LSAT. Additional exam requirements/recommendations for international students: Required—TOEFL (minimum score 600 paper-based; 100 iBT), minimum TOEFL iBT score of 80 (for master's programs). Electronic applications accepted. *Expenses:* Contact institution. *Faculty research:*

Intellectual property, health law and policy, sports and entertainment law, patent law, trademarks and copyright.

University of Pittsburgh, School of Law, Master of Studies in Law Program, Pittsburgh, PA 15260. Offers biomedical and health services research (MSL); business law (MSL), including commercial law, corporate law, general business law, international business, tax law; Constitutional law (MSL); criminal law and justice (MSL); disability law (MSL); elder and estate planning law (MSL); employment and labor law (MSL); energy law (MSL); environmental and real estate law (MSL); family law (MSL); health law (MSL); intellectual property and technology law (MSL); international and human rights law (MSL); jurisprudence (MSL); regulatory law (MSL); self-designed (MSL). *Program availability:* Part-time. *Faculty:* 47 full-time (22 women), 116 part-time/adjunct (29 women). *Students:* 4 full-time (2 women), 17 part-time (12 women); includes 6 minority (5 Black or African American, non-Hispanic/Latino; 1 Hispanic/Latino). Average age 26. 28 applicants, 75% accepted, 15 enrolled. In 2017, 15 master's awarded. *Entrance requirements:* Additional exam requirements/recommendations for international students: Required—TOEFL (minimum score 600 paper-based; 100 iBT), IELTS (minimum score 7). *Application deadline:* For fall admission, 6/30 for domestic students, 5/1 for international students. Applications are processed on a rolling basis. Application fee: $0. *Faculty research:* Law, health law, business law, contracts, intellectual property, environmental law. *Unit head:* Prof. Alan Meisel, Director, 412-648-1384, Fax: 412-648-2649, E-mail: meisel@pitt.edu. *Application contact:* Beth Ann Pischke, Administrative Coordinator, 412-648-7120, Fax: 412-648-2649, E-mail: pischke@pitt.edu. Website: http://www.law.pitt.edu/msl

University of San Francisco, School of Law, Master of Law Programs, San Francisco, CA 94117-1080. Offers intellectual property and technology law (LL M); international transactions and comparative law (LL M). *Program availability:* Part-time. *Entrance requirements:* For master's, law degree from U.S. or foreign school (intellectual property and technology law); law degree from foreign school (international transactions and comparative law). Electronic applications accepted.

University of Washington, Graduate School, School of Law, Seattle, WA 98195-3020. Offers Asian law (LL M, PhD); intellectual property law and policy (LL M); law (JD); law of sustainable international development (LL M); taxation (LL M); JD/LL M; JD/MA; JD/MAIS; JD/MBA; JD/MPA; JD/MS; JD/PhD. *Accreditation:* ABA. *Degree requirements:* For master's, thesis; for doctorate, thesis/dissertation (for some programs). *Entrance requirements:* For master's, language proficiency (LL M in Asian law); for doctorate, LSAT (for JD). Additional exam requirements/recommendations for international students: Required—TOEFL. *Expenses:* Contact institution. *Faculty research:* Asian, international and comparative law, intellectual property law, health law, environmental law, taxation.

Western Michigan University Thomas M. Cooley Law School, Graduate Programs, Lansing, MI 48901-3038. Offers administrative law (public law) (JD); business transactions (JD); Canadian law practice (JD); corporate law and finance (LL M); environmental law (public law) (JD); general practice (JD), including solo and small firm; general studies (LL M); homeland and national security law (LL M); insurance law (LL M); intellectual property (JD); intellectual property law (LL M); international law (JD); litigation (JD); taxation (LL M); U.S. legal studies for foreign attorneys (LL M); JD/LL M; JD/MBA; JD/MHA; JD/MPA; JD/MSW. *Program availability:* Part-time, evening/weekend, 100% online, blended/hybrid learning. *Degree requirements:* For master's, thesis (for some programs); for doctorate, minimum of 3 credits of clinical experience. *Entrance requirements:* For master's, JD or LL B; for doctorate, LSAT. Additional exam requirements/recommendations for international students: Required—TOEFL (for U.S. legal studies for foreign attorneys LL M program); Recommended—TOEFL. Electronic applications accepted. *Expenses:* Contact institution. *Faculty research:* Wrongful convictions, civil rights, environmental law, litigation techniques, data mining, intellectual property, practical and skills-based legal education.

Yeshiva University, Benjamin N. Cardozo School of Law, New York, NY 10003-4301. Offers comparative legal thought (LL M); dispute resolution and advocacy (LL M); general studies (LL M); intellectual property law (LL M); law (JD). *Accreditation:* ABA. *Program availability:* Part-time. *Faculty:* 61 full-time (24 women), 92 part-time/adjunct (38 women). *Students:* 994 full-time (530 women), 107 part-time (56 women); includes 218 minority (40 Black or African American, non-Hispanic/Latino; 84 Asian, non-Hispanic/Latino; 74 Hispanic/Latino; 20 Two or more races, non-Hispanic/Latino), 96 international. Average age 25. 2,755 applicants, 52% accepted, 419 enrolled. In 2017, 70 master's, 391 doctorates awarded. *Entrance requirements:* For doctorate, LSAT, 2 letters of recommendation. Additional exam requirements/recommendations for international students: Required—TOEFL (minimum score 100 iBT); Recommended—IELTS (minimum score 7). *Application deadline:* For fall admission, 4/1 priority date for domestic students; for spring admission, 12/1 for domestic students. Applications are processed on a rolling basis. Application fee: $50. Electronic applications accepted. *Expenses:* Contact institution. *Financial support:* In 2017–18, 845 students received support, including 115 research assistantships (averaging $1,429 per year); career-related internships or fieldwork, Federal Work-Study, institutionally sponsored loans, scholarships/grants, health care benefits, and tuition waivers (full and partial) also available. Support available to part-time students. Financial award application deadline: 3/1; financial award applicants required to submit FAFSA. *Faculty research:* Corporate and commercial law, intellectual property law, criminal law and litigation, Constitutional law, legal theory and jurisprudence. *Unit head:* David G. Martinidez, Dean of Admissions, 212-790-0357, Fax: 212-790-0482, E-mail: lawinfo@yu.edu. Website: http://www.cardozo.yu.edu/

Law

Abraham Lincoln University School of Law, Graduate and Professional Programs, Los Angeles, CA 90010. Offers JD.

Albany Law School, Professional Program, Albany, NY 12208-3494. Offers LL M, JD, JD/MBA, JD/MPA, JD/MRP, JD/MS, JD/MSW. JD/MBA offered jointly with The College of Saint Rose, The Sage Colleges, Union Graduate College, and University at Albany, State University of New York; JD/MPA, JD/MRP, and JD/MSW offered jointly with University at Albany, State University of New York. *Accreditation:* ABA. *Program availability:* Part-time. *Entrance requirements:* For master's, GRE or LSAT; for doctorate, LSAT. Additional exam requirements/recommendations for international students: Recommended—TOEFL (minimum score 600 paper-based). *Expenses:* Contact institution. *Faculty research:* Federal tax, Constitutional law, secured transactions, international law, American politics.

Alliant International University–San Francisco, San Francisco Law School, JD Program, San Francisco, CA 94133. Offers JD. *Program availability:* Part-time, evening/weekend. *Entrance requirements:* For doctorate, LSAT, personal statement, interview. Electronic applications accepted.

American University, Washington College of Law, Washington, DC 20016-8181. Offers LL M, JD, SJD, JD/LL M, JD/MA, JD/MBA, JD/MPA, JD/MPP, JD/MS, LL M/MBA, LL M/MIS, LL M/MPA, LL M/MPP. *Accreditation:* ABA. *Program availability:* Part-time, evening/weekend. *Faculty:* 64 full-time (32 women), 134 part-time/adjunct (45 women). *Students:* 1,034 full-time (697 women), 373 part-time (216 women); includes 523 minority (117 Black or African American, non-Hispanic/Latino; 1 American Indian or Alaska Native, non-Hispanic/Latino; 107 Asian, non-Hispanic/Latino; 234 Hispanic/Latino; 1 Native Hawaiian or other Pacific Islander, non-Hispanic/Latino; 63 Two or more races, non-Hispanic/Latino), 122 international. Average age 28. 5,138 applicants, 58% accepted, 550 enrolled. In 2017, 95 master's, 374 doctorates awarded. *Entrance* *requirements:* For master's, statement of purpose, 2 letters of recommendation, transcripts, resume; for doctorate, LSAT, transcript, letters of recommendation. Additional exam requirements/recommendations for international students: Required—TOEFL (minimum score 600 paper-based; 100 iBT). Application fee: $70. Electronic applications accepted. *Expenses:* Contact institution. *Financial support:* Institutionally sponsored loans and scholarships/grants available. Financial award application deadline: 3/1; financial award applicants required to submit FAFSA. *Unit head:* Camille A. Nelson, Dean, 202-274-4004, Fax: 202-274-4005, E-mail: canelson@wcl.american.edu. *Application contact:* Meghan Walter, Associate Director, Graduate Admissions, 202-274-4114, Fax: 202-274-4107, E-mail: mwalter@wcl.american.edu. Website: http://www.wcl.american.edu/

The American University in Cairo, School of Global Affairs and Public Policy, Cairo, Egypt. Offers gender and women's studies (MA); global affairs (MGA); international and comparative law (LL M); international human rights law (MA); journalism and mass communication (MA); Middle East studies (MA); migration and refugee studies (MA, Diploma); public administration (MPA); public policy (MPP); television and digital journalism (MA). *Program availability:* Part-time, evening/weekend. *Faculty:* 26 full-time (11 women), 4 part-time/adjunct (3 women). *Students:* 65 full-time (50 women), 201 part-time (136 women), 39 international. Average age 29. 357 applicants, 51% accepted, 72 enrolled. In 2017, 94 master's awarded. *Degree requirements:* For master's, comprehensive exam (for some programs), thesis (for some programs). *Entrance requirements:* Additional exam requirements/recommendations for international students: Required—TOEFL (minimum score 450 paper-based; 45 iBT), IELTS (minimum score 5). *Application deadline:* For fall admission, 2/1 for domestic and international students; for spring admission, 10/15 for domestic and international students. Applications are processed on a rolling basis. Application fee: $85. Electronic applications accepted. *Expenses:* Contact institution. *Financial support:* Fellowships with partial tuition reimbursements, scholarships/grants, and unspecified assistantships available. Financial award application deadline: 3/10. *Faculty research:* Law, media and journalism; public policy and public administration; gender studies; Middle East Studies; global affairs; refugees studies. *Unit head:* Dr. Nabil Fahmy, Dean, 20-2-2615-2671, E-mail: nfahmy@aucegypt.edu. *Application contact:* Maha Hegazi, Director for Graduate Admissions, 20-2-2615-1462, E-mail: mahahegazi@aucegypt.edu. Website: http://www.aucegypt.edu/GAPP/Pages/default.aspx

American University of Armenia, Graduate Programs, Yerevan, Armenia. Offers business administration (MBA); computer and information science (MS), including business management, design and manufacturing, energy (ME, MS), industrial engineering and systems management; economics (MS); industrial engineering and systems management (ME), including business, computer aided design/manufacturing, energy (ME, MS), information technology; law (LL M); political science and international affairs (MPSIA); public health (MPH); teaching English as a foreign language (MA). *Program availability:* Part-time, evening/weekend. *Degree requirements:* For master's, thesis (for some programs), capstone/project. *Entrance requirements:* For master's, GRE, GMAT, or LSAT. Additional exam requirements/recommendations for international students: Recommended—TOEFL (minimum score 79 iBT), IELTS (minimum score 6.5). *Faculty research:* Microfinance, finance (rural/development, international, corporate), firm life cycle theory, TESOL, language proficiency testing, public policy, administrative law, economic development, cryptography, artificial intelligence, energy efficiency/renewable energy, computer-aided design/manufacturing, health financing, tuberculosis control, mother/child health, preventive ophthalmology, post-earthquake psychopathological investigations, tobacco control, environmental health risk assessments.

The American University of Paris, Graduate Programs, Paris, France. Offers cross-cultural and sustainable business management (MA); cultural translation (MA); global communications (MA); global communications and civil society (MA); international affairs (MA); international affairs, conflict resolution and civil society development (MA); Middle East and Islamic studies (MA); Middle East and Islamic studies and international affairs (MA); public policy and international affairs (MA); public policy and international law (MA). *Degree requirements:* For master's, thesis (for some programs). *Entrance requirements:* For master's, minimum undergraduate GPA of 3.0. Additional exam requirements/recommendations for international students: Recommended—TOEFL, IELTS. Electronic applications accepted.

Appalachian School of Law, Professional Program in Law, Grundy, VA 24614. Offers JD. *Accreditation:* ABA. *Faculty:* 10 full-time (2 women), 10 part-time/adjunct (5 women). *Students:* 128 full-time (63 women). *Entrance requirements:* For doctorate, LSAT, bachelor's degree from accredited institution, personal statement. *Application deadline:* For fall admission, 6/1 for domestic students. Applications are processed on a rolling basis. Application fee: $60. Electronic applications accepted. *Expenses:* $31,700 tuition and fees. *Financial support:* Research assistantships, career-related internships or fieldwork, Federal Work-Study, institutionally sponsored loans, scholarships/grants, and tuition waivers (full and partial) available. Financial award application deadline: 7/1; financial award applicants required to submit FAFSA. *Faculty research:* Natural resources, alternative dispute resolution, Constitutional law, professional ethics, intellectual property. *Unit head:* Sandra Keen McGlothlin, Dean, 276-935-4349 Ext. 1265, Fax: 276-935-8261, E-mail: smcglothlin@asl.edu. *Application contact:* Glenna Owens, Student Services Coordinator, 276-935-4349 Ext. 1281, Fax: 276-935-8496, E-mail: gowens@asl.edu. Website: http://www.asl.edu/jd-curriculum-overview/

Arizona State University at the Tempe campus, Sandra Day O'Connor College of Law, Phoenix, AZ 85287-7906. Offers biotechnology and genomics (LL M); law (JD); legal studies (MLS); patent practice (MLS); sports law and business (MSLB); tribal policy, law and government (LL M); JD/MBA; JD/MD; JD/MSW; JD/PhD. JD/MD offered jointly with Mayo Medical School. *Accreditation:* ABA. *Program availability:* 100% online. *Faculty:* 69 full-time (30 women), 115 part-time/adjunct (29 women). *Students:* 777 full-time (337 women); includes 207 minority (21 Black or African American, non-Hispanic/Latino; 14 American Indian or Alaska Native, non-Hispanic/Latino; 32 Asian, non-Hispanic/Latino; 104 Hispanic/Latino; 3 Native Hawaiian or other Pacific Islander, non-Hispanic/Latino; 33 Two or more races, non-Hispanic/Latino), 15 international. Average age 28. 2,056 applicants, 41% accepted, 215 enrolled. In 2017, 52 master's, 198 doctorates awarded. *Entrance requirements:* For master's, bachelor's degree and JD (for LL M); for doctorate, LSAT, bachelor's degree. Additional exam requirements/recommendations for international students: Required—TOEFL (minimum score 550 paper-based; 80 iBT). *Application deadline:* For fall admission, 3/1 priority date for domestic and international students. Applications are processed on a rolling basis. Electronic applications accepted. *Expenses:* Contact institution. *Financial support:* In 2017–18, 430 students received support. Institutionally sponsored loans and scholarships/grants available. Financial award application deadline: 3/15; financial award applicants required to submit FAFSA. *Faculty research:* Emerging technologies and the law, Indian law, international law, intellectual property, health law, sports law and business. *Total annual research expenditures:* $2.4 million. *Unit head:* Douglas Sylvester, Dean/Professor, 480-965-6188, Fax: 480-965-6521, E-mail: douglas.sylvester@asu.edu. *Application contact:* Chitra Damania, Director, 480-965-1474, Fax: 480-727-7930, E-mail: law.admissions@asu.edu. Website: http://www.law.asu.edu/

Arizona Summit Law School, JD Program, Phoenix, AZ 85004. Offers JD. *Program availability:* Part-time, evening/weekend. *Faculty:* 10 full-time (8 women), 7 part-time/adjunct (4 women). *Students:* 184 full-time (91 women), 202 part-time (113 women); includes 165 minority (68 Black or African American, non-Hispanic/Latino; 11 American Indian or Alaska Native, non-Hispanic/Latino; 20 Asian, non-Hispanic/Latino; 63 Hispanic/Latino; 2 Native Hawaiian or other Pacific Islander, non-Hispanic/Latino; 1 Two or more races, non-Hispanic/Latino), 5 international. Average age 33. In 2017, 221 doctorates awarded. *Expenses:* $45,354 full-time tuition and fees; $36,692 part-time. *Financial support:* Applicants required to submit FAFSA. *Faculty research:* Civil procedure, alternative dispute resolution, indigenous peoples and natural resources, cultural property, American Indian environmental law. *Application contact:* Rick Jackson, Associate Dean of Admissions, 602-682-6817, E-mail: admissions@azsummitlaw.edu.

Atlanta's John Marshall Law School, JD and LL M Programs, Atlanta, GA 30309. Offers American legal studies (LL M); employment law (LL M); law (JD). *Accreditation:* ABA. *Program availability:* Part-time, evening/weekend, online learning. *Entrance requirements:* For master's, JD from accredited law school or bar admission; for doctorate, LSAT, LSDAS report, personal statement, two letters of reference. Additional exam requirements/recommendations for international students: Required—TOEFL. Electronic applications accepted. *Faculty research:* Tort reform, terrorism and the use of the U.S. military, Title VII's referral and deferral scheme, public utilities, eminent domain and land use regulations, recent films and their visions of law in Western society.

Ave Maria School of Law, Professional Program, Naples, FL 34119. Offers law (JD). *Accreditation:* ABA. *Faculty:* 22 full-time (7 women), 18 part-time/adjunct (7 women). *Students:* 241 full-time (132 women); includes 67 minority (13 Black or African American, non-Hispanic/Latino; 1 American Indian or Alaska Native, non-Hispanic/Latino; 1 Asian, non-Hispanic/Latino; 52 Hispanic/Latino), 7 international. Average age 26. 568 applicants, 55% accepted, 97 enrolled. In 2017, 81 doctorates awarded. *Entrance requirements:* For doctorate, LSAT, 2 letters of recommendation, LSDAS, personal statement. Additional exam requirements/recommendations for international students: Required—TOEFL (minimum score 600 paper-based). *Application deadline:* For fall admission, 7/15 priority date for domestic and international students. Applications are processed on a rolling basis. Application fee: $0. Electronic applications accepted. *Expenses:* Contact institution. *Financial support:* In 2017–18, 182 students received support. Research assistantships, career-related internships or fieldwork, Federal Work-Study, and scholarships/grants available. Financial award application deadline: 6/30; financial award applicants required to submit FAFSA. *Faculty research:* International law, immigration, religious freedom, litigation, military law. *Unit head:* Kevin Cieply, President/Dean, 239-687-5300, E-mail: kcieply@avemarialaw.edu. *Application contact:* Claire T. O'Keefe, Associate Dean of Admissions and Student Engagement, 239-687-5423, Fax: 239-352-2890, E-mail: info@avemarialaw.edu. Website: http://www.avemarialaw.edu/

Barry University, Dwayne O. Andreas School of Law, Orlando, FL 32807. Offers JD, JD/MS. *Accreditation:* ABA. *Entrance requirements:* For doctorate, LSAT.

Baylor University, School of Law, Waco, TX 76798-7288. Offers JD, JD/M Div, JD/M Tax, JD/MBA, JD/MPPA. *Accreditation:* ABA. *Faculty:* 28 full-time (9 women), 20 part-time/adjunct (2 women). *Students:* 377 full-time (186 women), 8 part-time (7 women); includes 104 minority (8 Black or African American, non-Hispanic/Latino; 6 American Indian or Alaska Native, non-Hispanic/Latino; 22 Asian, non-Hispanic/Latino; 57 Hispanic/Latino; 2 Native Hawaiian or other Pacific Islander, non-Hispanic/Latino; 9 Two or more races, non-Hispanic/Latino), 1 international. Average age 24. 1,597 applicants, 48% accepted, 86 enrolled. In 2017, 144 doctorates awarded. *Entrance requirements:* For doctorate, LSAT. Additional exam requirements/recommendations for international students: Recommended—TOEFL. *Application deadline:* For fall admission, 7/15 for domestic and international students; for spring admission, 11/15 for domestic and international students; for summer admission, 3/15 for domestic and international students. Applications are processed on a rolling basis. Application fee: $0. Electronic applications accepted. *Expenses:* $60,050. *Financial support:* In 2017–18, 343 students received support. Federal Work-Study and scholarships/grants available. Financial award application deadline: 2/1; financial award applicants required to submit FAFSA. *Unit head:* Bradley J. B. Toben, Dean, 254-710-1911, Fax: 254-710-2316. *Application contact:* Jenny Branson, Assistant Dean of Admissions and Financial Aid, 254-710-1911, Fax: 254-710-2316, E-mail: jenny_branson@baylor.edu. Website: http://www.baylor.edu/law

Belmont University, College of Law, Nashville, TN 37212. Offers JD, JD/Certificate. *Accreditation:* ABA. *Faculty:* 18 full-time (8 women), 9 part-time/adjunct (3 women). *Students:* 276 full-time (146 women); includes 40 minority (12 Black or African American, non-Hispanic/Latino; 4 Asian, non-Hispanic/Latino; 10 Hispanic/Latino; 1 Native Hawaiian or other Pacific Islander, non-Hispanic/Latino; 13 Two or more races, non-Hispanic/Latino). Average age 26. 760 applicants, 47% accepted, 113 enrolled. In 2017, 82 doctorates awarded. *Entrance requirements:* For doctorate, LSAT. Additional exam requirements/recommendations for international students: Required—TOEFL. *Application deadline:* For fall admission, 7/15 priority date for domestic and international students. Applications are processed on a rolling basis. Application fee: $50. Electronic applications accepted. *Expenses:* $20,880 per semester. *Financial support:* In 2017–18, 180 students received support. Career-related internships or fieldwork and scholarships/grants available. Financial award applicants required to submit FAFSA. *Unit head:* Judge Alberto R. Gonzales, Dean, 615-460-8259, E-mail: alberto.gonzales@belmont.edu. *Application contact:* Drew Ford, Recruiting Coordinator, Fax: 615-460-8250, E-mail: drew.ford@belmont.edu. Website: http://www.belmont.edu/law/

Boston College, Law School, Newton, MA 02459. Offers JD, JD/MA, JD/MBA, JD/MSW. *Accreditation:* ABA. *Entrance requirements:* For doctorate, LSAT. Additional exam requirements/recommendations for international students: Required—TOEFL. Electronic applications accepted. *Expenses:* Contact institution. *Faculty research:* Commercial law, labor law, legal history, comparative law, international law, business law, intellectual property law, tax law, environmental law.

Boston University, School of Law, Boston, MA 02215. Offers LL M, JD, JD/LL M, JD/MA, JD/MBA, JD/MPH, JD/MS, MD/JD. MD/JD offered jointly with the School of Medicine. *Accreditation:* ABA. *Program availability:* 100% online, blended/hybrid learning. *Faculty:* 63 full-time (28 women), 138 part-time/adjunct (45 women). *Students:* 923 full-time (528 women), 122 part-time (72 women); includes 201 minority (30 Black or African American, non-Hispanic/Latino; 2 American Indian or Alaska Native, non-Hispanic/Latino; 60 Asian, non-Hispanic/Latino; 84 Hispanic/Latino; 1 Native Hawaiian or other Pacific Islander, non-Hispanic/Latino; 24 Two or more races, non-Hispanic/Latino), 241 international. Average age 26. 5,450 applicants, 29% accepted, 233 enrolled. In 2017, 236 master's, 216 doctorates awarded. *Degree requirements:* For master's, thesis (for some programs); for doctorate, thesis/dissertation, research project resulting in a paper. *Entrance requirements:* For master's, JD; for doctorate, LSAT. Additional exam requirements/recommendations for international students: Required—TOEFL (minimum score 100 iBT), IELTS. *Application deadline:* For fall admission, 4/1 for domestic and international students. Applications are processed on a rolling basis. Application fee: $85. Electronic applications accepted. *Expenses:* $53,236. *Financial support:* In 2017–18, 650 students received support. Career-related internships or fieldwork, Federal Work-Study, institutionally sponsored loans, scholarships/grants, and resident assistantships available. Financial award application deadline: 3/1; financial award applicants required to submit FAFSA. *Faculty research:* Health law, tax, intellectual property, Constitutional law, corporate law, business organizations and financial law, international law, family law. *Total annual research expenditures:* $3.1 million. *Unit head:* Maureen A. O'Rourke, Dean, 617-353-3112, Fax: 617-358-4706, E-mail: lawdean@bu.edu. *Application contact:* Alissa Leonard, Director of Admissions and Financial Aid, 617-353-3100, Fax: 617-353-0578, E-mail: bulawadm@bu.edu. Website: http://www.bu.edu/law/

Brigham Young University, Graduate Studies, J. Reuben Clark Law School, Provo, UT 84602-8000. Offers LL M, JD, JD/M Ed, JD/MBA, JD/MPA. *Accreditation:* ABA. *Students:* 381 full-time (138 women); includes 61 minority (6 Black or African American, non-Hispanic/Latino; 4 American Indian or Alaska Native, non-Hispanic/Latino; 9 Asian, non-Hispanic/Latino; 18 Hispanic/Latino; 4 Native Hawaiian or other Pacific Islander, non-Hispanic/Latino; 20 Two or more races, non-Hispanic/Latino), 2 international. Average age 28. 394 applicants, 44% accepted, 101 enrolled. In 2017, 6 master's, 130 doctorates awarded. *Entrance requirements:* For doctorate, LSAT. Additional exam requirements/recommendations for international students: Recommended—TOEFL (minimum score 590 paper-based), IELTS (minimum score 7). *Application deadline:* For fall admission, 3/1 priority date for domestic students, 3/1 for international students. Applications are processed on a rolling basis. Application fee: $50. Electronic applications accepted. *Expenses:* $12,680 per year for members of the Church of Jesus Christ of Latter-day Saints; $25,360 for those who are not members of the Church. *Financial support:* In 2017–18, 227 students received support, including 12 fellowships (averaging $29,905 per year); career-related internships or fieldwork, institutionally sponsored loans, scholarships/grants, unspecified assistantships, and student employment also available. Financial award application deadline: 6/1; financial award applicants required to submit FAFSA. *Faculty research:* Law, innovation, and entrepreneurship; law and disadvantaged peoples; law and corpus linguistics; law and religion; and international law. *Total annual research expenditures:* $48,826. *Unit head:* D. Gordon Smith, Dean, 801-422-6383, Fax: 801-422-0389, E-mail: smithg@law.byu.edu. *Application contact:* Rebeca Welch, Admissions Coordinator, 801-422-4356, Fax: 801-422-0389, E-mail: welchr@law.byu.edu. Website: http://www.law.byu.edu/

Brooklyn Law School, Graduate and Professional Programs, Brooklyn, NY 11201-3798. Offers LL M, JD, JD/MA, JD/MBA, JD/MS, JD/MUP. JD/MBA offered jointly with Bernard M. Baruch College of the City University of New York; JD/MS with Pratt Institute; JD/MUP with Hunter College of the City University of New York; and JD/MA with Brooklyn College of the City University of New York. *Accreditation:* ABA. *Program availability:* Part-time, evening/weekend. *Entrance requirements:* For doctorate, LSAT, dean's certification, 2 faculty letters of evaluation. Additional exam requirements/recommendations for international students: Required—TOEFL and TWE (required for Foreign Trained Lawyers Program); Recommended—TOEFL (minimum score 600 paper-based; 100 iBT), TWE. Electronic applications accepted. *Faculty research:* Civil procedure, securities regulation, family law, corporate finance, international business and law, health law.

California Western School of Law, Graduate and Professional Programs, San Diego, CA 92101-3090. Offers law (JD); Spanish language in trial advocacy (LL M); JD/MBA; JD/MSW; MCL/LL M. JD/MSW and JD/MBA offered jointly with San Diego State University. *Accreditation:* ABA. *Program availability:* Part-time. *Entrance requirements:* For doctorate, LSAT. Additional exam requirements/recommendations for international students: Required—TOEFL. Electronic applications accepted. *Faculty research:* Biotechnology, health law, international law, labor and employment law, business law.

Campbell University, Graduate and Professional Programs, Norman Adrian Wiggins School of Law, Raleigh, NC 27603. Offers JD, JD/MPA. JD/MPA offered in partnership with North Carolina State University. *Accreditation:* ABA. *Entrance requirements:* For doctorate, LSAT, interview. Additional exam requirements/recommendations for international students: Recommended—TOEFL. Electronic applications accepted. *Expenses:* Contact institution. *Faculty research:* Interdisciplinary approaches to legal problems, management and planning for lawyers, church/state constitutional problems, basic research in substantive legal areas.

Capital University, Law School, Columbus, OH 43215-3200. Offers LL M, MT, JD, JD/LL M, JD/MBA, JD/MSA, JD/MSN, JD/MTS. *Accreditation:* ABA. *Program availability:* Part-time, evening/weekend. *Entrance requirements:* For master's, 24 credit hours of business and accounting courses (including a federal taxation course and business law course); 4-year bachelor's degree from regionally-accredited college or university; for doctorate, LSAT, 4-year bachelor's degree from regionally-accredited college or university. Additional exam requirements/recommendations for international students: Required—TOEFL (minimum score 600 paper-based; 100 iBT); Recommended—IELTS (minimum score 7). Electronic applications accepted. *Expenses:* Contact institution.

Case Western Reserve University, School of Law, Cleveland, OH 44106. Offers financial integrity (MA); health law (SJD); intellectual property (LL M); intellectual property (ML); international business law (LL M, ML); international criminal law (LL M); law (JD, SJD); patent practice (MA); U.S. and global legal studies (ML); U.S. legal studies (LL M); JD/MA; JD/MBA; JD/MD; JD/MNM; JD/MPH; JD/MS; JD/MSSA. *Accreditation:* ABA. *Faculty:* 37 full-time (13 women), 26 part-time/adjunct (10 women). *Students:* 412 full-time (216 women); includes 80 minority (39 Black or African American, 14 Asian, non-Hispanic/Latino; 24 Hispanic/Latino; 3 Two or more races, non-Hispanic/Latino), 36 international. Average age 24. 1,488 applicants, 39% accepted, 131 enrolled. In 2017, 138 master's awarded. *Entrance requirements:* For doctorate, LSAT, LSDAS. Additional exam requirements/recommendations for international students: Required—TOEFL. *Application deadline:* For fall admission, 4/1 priority date for domestic and international students. Applications are processed on a rolling basis. Application fee: $40. Electronic applications accepted. Application fee is waived when completed online. *Expenses:* 50666. *Financial support:* In 2017–18, 395 students received support. Career-related internships or fieldwork, Federal Work-Study, institutionally sponsored loans, and scholarships/grants available. Financial award application deadline: 5/1; financial award applicants required to submit FAFSA. *Unit head:* Jessica Berg, Co-Dean, 216-368-3283. *Application contact:* Kelli Curtis, Associate Dean for Admissions, 216-368-3600, Fax: 216-368-0185, E-mail: lawadmissions@case.edu. Website: http://law.case.edu/

The Catholic University of America, Columbus School of Law, Washington, DC 20064. Offers MLS, JD, JD/JCL, JD/MA, JD/MLS, JD/MSBA, JD/MSW. *Accreditation:* ABA. *Program availability:* Part-time, evening/weekend. *Entrance requirements:* For doctorate, LSAT. Additional exam requirements/recommendations for international students: Required—TOEFL (minimum score 600 paper-based; 100 iBT), IELTS (minimum score 7). Electronic applications accepted. Application fee is waived when completed online. *Expenses:* Contact institution.

Central European University, Department of Legal Studies, Budapest, Hungary. Offers comparative Constitutional law (LL M); human rights (LL M, MA); international business

law (LL M); juridical sciences (SJD). *Faculty:* 10 full-time (5 women), 9 part-time/adjunct (1 woman). *Students:* 90 full-time (52 women). Average age 28. 384 applicants, 33% accepted, 71 enrolled. In 2017, 53 master's, 3 doctorates awarded. Terminal master's awarded for partial completion of doctoral program. *Degree requirements:* For master's, one foreign language, thesis; for doctorate, one foreign language, comprehensive exam, thesis/dissertation. *Entrance requirements:* For master's and doctorate, LSAT. Additional exam requirements/recommendations for international students: Required—TOEFL (minimum score 570 paper-based); Recommended—IELTS (minimum score 6.5). *Application deadline:* For fall admission, 2/4 for domestic and international students. Application fee: $30. Electronic applications accepted. *Expenses:* Contact institution. *Financial support:* Fellowships, career-related internships or fieldwork, institutionally sponsored loans, scholarships/grants, and tuition waivers (full and partial) available. Financial award application deadline: 2/4. *Faculty research:* Institutional, Constitutional and human rights in European Union law; biomedical law and reproductive rights; data protection law; comparative and international business law and the regulation of business environments;. *Unit head:* Dr. Karoly Bard, Head of Department, 36 1 327-3294, Fax: 361-327-3198, E-mail: legalst@ceu.edu. *Application contact:* Zsuzsanna Jaszberenyi, Department Coordinator, 361-327-3272, Fax: 361-327-3198, E-mail: admissions@ceu.edu. Website: http://legal.ceu.edu

Champlain College, Graduate Studies, Burlington, VT 05402-0670. Offers business (MBA); digital forensic science (MS); early childhood education (M Ed); emergent media (MFA, MS); executive leadership (MS); health care administration (MS); information security operations (MS); law (MS); mediation and applied conflict studies (MS). MS in emergent media program held in Shanghai. *Program availability:* Part-time, online learning. *Degree requirements:* For master's, capstone project. *Entrance requirements:* Additional exam requirements/recommendations for international students: Required—TOEFL (minimum score 550 paper-based; 80 iBT). Electronic applications accepted.

Chapman University, Dale E. Fowler School of Law, Orange, CA 92866. Offers advocacy and dispute resolution (JD); business law (LL M, JD); criminal law (JD); entertainment and media law (LL M); entertainment law (JD); environmental, land use, and real estate law (JD); international and comparative law (LL M); international law (JD); law (JD); prosecutorial science (LL M); tax law (JD); taxation (LL M); trial advocacy (LL M); JD/MBA; JD/MFA. *Accreditation:* ABA. *Program availability:* Part-time. *Faculty:* 44 full-time (18 women), 34 part-time/adjunct (9 women). *Students:* 478 full-time (262 women), 37 part-time (24 women); includes 217 minority (9 Black or African American, non-Hispanic/Latino; 1 American Indian or Alaska Native, non-Hispanic/Latino; 69 Asian, non-Hispanic/Latino; 104 Hispanic/Latino; 34 Two or more races, non-Hispanic/Latino), 11 international. Average age 26. 1,499 applicants, 50% accepted, 190 enrolled. In 2017, 17 master's, 149 doctorates awarded. *Entrance requirements:* For doctorate, LSAT. Additional exam requirements/recommendations for international students: Required—TOEFL (minimum score 600 paper-based; 100 iBT). *Application deadline:* For fall admission, 4/17 priority date for domestic students. Applications are processed on a rolling basis. Electronic applications accepted. *Expenses:* Contact institution. *Financial support:* Fellowships, Federal Work-Study, and scholarships/grants available. Financial award applicants required to submit FAFSA. *Unit head:* Matthew J. Parlow, Dean, 714-628-2678, E-mail: parlow@chapman.edu. *Application contact:* Justin Cruz, Assistant Dean of Admissions and Diversity Initiatives, 714-628-2594, E-mail: lawadmission@chapman.edu. Website: https://www.chapman.edu/law/index.aspx

Charleston School of Law, Graduate and Professional Programs, Charleston, SC 29403. Offers law (JD). *Accreditation:* ABA. *Faculty:* 18 full-time (9 women), 58 part-time/adjunct (27 women). *Students:* 514 full-time (275 women), 50 part-time (32 women). *Entrance requirements:* For doctorate, LSAT, two letters of recommendation, personal statement, current resume, official transcripts. *Application deadline:* For fall admission, 6/1 for domestic students; for spring admission, 11/1 for domestic students. Applications are processed on a rolling basis. Electronic applications accepted. *Expenses: Tuition:* Full-time $40,596; part-time $32,618 per year. *Required fees:* $942; $942 per unit. *Financial support:* Scholarships/grants available. *Application contact:* Jacqueline B. Bell, Assistant Dean of Admission, 843-377-2143, Fax: 843-329-4091, E-mail: info@charlestonlaw.edu.

City University of New York School of Law, Professional Program, Long Island City, NY 11101-4356. Offers JD. *Accreditation:* ABA. *Program availability:* Part-time, evening/weekend. *Faculty:* 51 full-time (34 women), 12 part-time/adjunct (2 women). *Students:* 342 full-time (214 women), 138 part-time (79 women); includes 230 minority (68 Black or African American, non-Hispanic/Latino; 1 American Indian or Alaska Native, non-Hispanic/Latino; 49 Asian, non-Hispanic/Latino; 100 Hispanic/Latino; 1 Native Hawaiian or other Pacific Islander, non-Hispanic/Latino; 11 Two or more races, non-Hispanic/Latino), 16 international. Average age 29. 1,427 applicants, 46% accepted, 193 enrolled. In 2017, 94 doctorates awarded. *Entrance requirements:* For doctorate, LSAT, CAS report, bachelor's degree. Additional exam requirements/recommendations for international students: Recommended—TOEFL. *Application deadline:* For fall admission, 6/15 priority date for domestic students. Applications are processed on a rolling basis. Application fee: $60. Electronic applications accepted. *Expenses:* Tuition, state resident: full-time $14,550. Tuition, nonresident: full-time $24,160. *Financial support:* In 2017–18, 148 students received support, including 42 fellowships (averaging $14,813 per year), 18 research assistantships (averaging $839 per year); Federal Work-Study, scholarships/grants, tuition waivers (full and partial), and unspecified assistantships also available. Support available to part-time students. Financial award application deadline: 7/15; financial award applicants required to submit FAFSA. *Faculty research:* Capital punishment, domestic violence, indigenous land rights, cross cultural lawyering, LGBT issues, aging, ecology, international human rights, pedagogy, environmental justice. *Unit head:* Mary Lu Bilek, Dean/Professor of Law, 718-340-4201, Fax: 718-340-4482. *Application contact:* Degna P. Levister, Assistant Dean of Admissions and Enrollment Management, 718-340-4210, Fax: 718-340-4435, E-mail: admissions@law.cuny.edu. Website: http://www.law.cuny.edu/

Cleveland State University, Cleveland-Marshall College of Law, Cleveland, OH 44115. Offers LL M, MLS, JD, Certificate, JD/MAES, JD/MBA, JD/MPA, JD/MSES, JD/MUPDD. *Accreditation:* ABA. *Program availability:* Part-time, evening/weekend. *Faculty:* 34 full-time (17 women), 61 part-time/adjunct (16 women). *Students:* 226 full-time (113 women), 126 part-time (75 women); includes 62 minority (30 Black or African American, non-Hispanic/Latino; 8 Asian, non-Hispanic/Latino; 15 Hispanic/Latino; 9 Two or more races, non-Hispanic/Latino), 5 international. Average age 28. 711 applicants, 44% accepted, 118 enrolled. In 2017, 9 master's, 118 doctorates, 5 Certificates awarded. *Degree requirements:* For master's, thesis for graduates of U.S. law schools (for LL M); 30 credits, 6 in required courses (for MLS); for doctorate, 90 credits (41 in required courses). *Entrance requirements:* For master's, JD or LL B (for LL M); bachelor's degree (for MLS); for doctorate, LSAT, bachelor's degree. Additional exam requirements/recommendations for international students: Required—TOEFL (minimum score 550 paper-based; 78 iBT), TOEFL minimum score 600 paper-based, 100 iBT or IELTS minimum score 7 (for LL M). *Application deadline:* For fall admission, 5/1 for domestic and international students. Applications are processed on a rolling basis. Application

Law

fee: $0. Electronic applications accepted. *Expenses:* Contact institution. *Financial support:* In 2017–18, 198 students received support, including 17 fellowships (averaging $2,500 per year), 34 research assistantships, 7 teaching assistantships with partial tuition reimbursements available (averaging $6,700 per year); career-related internships or fieldwork, Federal Work-Study, scholarships/grants, and unspecified assistantships also available. Support available to part-time students. Financial award application deadline: 5/1; financial award applicants required to submit FAFSA. *Faculty research:* Health law, international law, Constitutional law, criminal law, business law. *Unit head:* Lee Fisher, Dean, 216-687-2300, Fax: 216-687-6881, E-mail: lee.fisher@csuohio.edu. *Application contact:* Christopher Lucak, Assistant Dean for Admission and Financial Aid, 216-687-4692, Fax: 216-687-6881, E-mail: law.admissions@csuohio.edu. Website: http://www.law.csuohio.edu/

The College of William and Mary, William and Mary Law School, Williamsburg, VA 23187-8795. Offers LL M, JD, JD/MA, JD/MBA, JD/MPP. *Accreditation:* ABA. *Faculty:* 47 full-time (20 women), 64 part-time/adjunct (23 women). *Students:* 638 full-time (351 women), 3 part-time (1 woman); includes 113 minority (39 Black or African American, non-Hispanic/Latino; 2 American Indian or Alaska Native, non-Hispanic/Latino; 25 Asian, non-Hispanic/Latino; 30 Hispanic/Latino; 17 Two or more races, non-Hispanic/Latino), 57 international. Average age 23. 4,225 applicants, 38% accepted, 209 enrolled. In 2017, 59 master's, 208 doctorates awarded. *Degree requirements:* For doctorate, major paper. *Entrance requirements:* For master's, LL B; for doctorate, LSAT, baccalaureate degree, references. Additional exam requirements/recommendations for international students: Required—TOEFL (minimum iBT score of 90) or IELTS (6). *Application deadline:* For fall admission, 3/1 priority date for domestic and international students. Application fee: $0. Electronic applications accepted. *Expenses:* $32,964 resident; $41,964 non-resident. *Financial support:* In 2017–18, 560 students received support, including 85 fellowships (averaging $3,858 per year), 224 research assistantships (averaging $1,842 per year), 47 teaching assistantships (averaging $3,957 per year); career-related internships or fieldwork, Federal Work-Study, and scholarships/grants also available. Financial award application deadline: 2/15; financial award applicants required to submit FAFSA. *Faculty research:* Constitutional law, criminal law, corporate law, international law, intellectual property law. *Total annual research expenditures:* $259,440. *Unit head:* Davison M. Douglas, Dean/Professor, 757-221-3790, Fax: 757-221-3261, E-mail: dmdoug@wm.edu. *Application contact:* Faye F. Shealy, Associate Dean for Admission, 757-221-3785, Fax: 757-221-3261, E-mail: ffshea@wm.edu.
Website: http://law.wm.edu/

Columbia University, School of Law, New York, NY 10027. Offers LL M, JD, JSD, JD/M Phil, JD/MA, JD/MBA, JD/MFA, JD/MIA, JD/MPA, JD/MPH, JD/MSW. *Accreditation:* ABA. *Students:* 1,239 full-time (554 women); includes 360 minority (111 Black or African American, non-Hispanic/Latino; 8 American Indian or Alaska Native, non-Hispanic/Latino; 160 Asian, non-Hispanic/Latino; 81 Hispanic/Latino), 124 international. Average age 24. *Entrance requirements:* For doctorate, LSAT or GRE (for JD). *Application deadline:* For fall admission, 2/15 for domestic students. Applications are processed on a rolling basis. Application fee: $85. Electronic applications accepted. *Expenses:* $67,532 tuition. *Financial support:* Fellowships, research assistantships, teaching assistantships, career-related internships or fieldwork, Federal Work-Study, institutionally sponsored loans, scholarships/grants, and tuition waivers (full and partial) available. Financial award application deadline: 3/1; financial award applicants required to submit FAFSA. *Faculty research:* Human rights, law and philosophy, corporate governance, regulation of the workplace, death penalty. *Unit head:* Gillian L. Lester, Dean of Faculty, 212-854-2675, E-mail: glester@law.columbia.edu. *Application contact:* E. Nkonye Iwerebon, Dean of Admissions, 212-854-2674, Fax: 212-854-1109, E-mail: niwere@law.columbia.edu.
Website: http://www.law.columbia.edu/

Concordia University, School of Law, Portland, OR 97211-6099. Offers JD.

Concord Law School, Program in Law, Los Angeles, CA 90024. Offers EJD, JD. *Program availability:* Part-time, evening/weekend, online learning. *Degree requirements:* For doctorate, comprehensive exam. *Entrance requirements:* For doctorate, online admissions test. Additional exam requirements/recommendations for international students: Required—TOEFL (minimum score 520 paper-based). Electronic applications accepted.

Cornell University, Cornell Law School, Ithaca, NY 14853-4901. Offers LL M, JD, JSD, JD/DESS, JD/LL M, JD/MA, JD/MBA, JD/MILR, JD/MLLP, JD/MLP, JD/MPA, JD/MRP, JD/Maitrise en Droit, JD/PhD. JD/MLLP offered jointly with Humboldt University, Berlin; JD/DESS offered jointly with Institut d'etudes Politiques de Paris ("Sciences Po") and Paris I. *Accreditation:* ABA. *Entrance requirements:* For doctorate, LSAT (for JD). Electronic applications accepted. *Expenses:* Contact institution. *Faculty research:* International law, Constitutional law, corporate laws, public interest law, feminist legal theory.

Cornell University, Graduate School, Graduate Field in the Law School, Ithaca, NY 14853. Offers JSD. *Entrance requirements:* For doctorate, JD, LL M, or equivalent; 2 letters of recommendation. Additional exam requirements/recommendations for international students: Required—TOEFL (minimum score 550 paper-based). Electronic applications accepted. *Expenses:* Contact institution. *Faculty research:* International economic integration (World Trade Organization and European Union), international commercial arbitration, feminist jurisprudence, human rights.

Creighton University, School of Law, Omaha, NE 68178-0001. Offers MS, JD, Certificate, JD/MBA, JD/MS. *Accreditation:* ABA. *Program availability:* Part-time. *Entrance requirements:* For doctorate, LSAT, bachelor's degree. Additional exam requirements/recommendations for international students: Recommended—TOEFL. Electronic applications accepted. Application fee is waived when completed online. *Expenses:* Contact institution. *Faculty research:* Conflict of laws, international law, evidence, cyber warfare, Constitutional law.

Dalhousie University, Faculty of Graduate Studies, Dalhousie Law School, Halifax, NS B3H 4H9, Canada. Offers LL M, JSD, LL B/MBA, LL B/MLIS, LL B/MPA. *Program availability:* Part-time. *Degree requirements:* For master's, thesis or alternative; for doctorate, thesis/dissertation. *Entrance requirements:* For master's, LL B; for doctorate, LL M. Additional exam requirements/recommendations for international students: Required—1 of 5 approved tests: TOEFL, IELTS, CANTEST, CAEL, Michigan English Language Assessment Battery. Electronic applications accepted. *Expenses:* Contact institution. *Faculty research:* Marine and environmental law, health law, the family law program.

DePaul University, College of Law, Chicago, IL 60604. Offers business law and taxation (MJ); criminal law (MJ); health and intellectual property law (MJ); health care compliance (MJ); health law (LL M, MJ); intellectual property law (LL M); international and comparative law (MJ); international law (LL M); law (JD); public interest law (MJ); taxation (LL M); U.S. legal studies (LL M); JD/LL M; JD/MA; JD/MBA; JD/MS. *Accreditation:* ABA. *Program availability:* Part-time, evening/weekend. *Entrance requirements:* For doctorate, LSAT, LSAC applicant evaluation/letter of recommendation, personal statement, resume. Additional exam requirements/recommendations for international students: Required—TOEFL (minimum score 577

paper-based; 90 iBT), IELTS (minimum score 6.5). *Application deadline:* For fall admission, 3/1 for domestic and international students. Applications are processed on a rolling basis. Electronic applications accepted. *Expenses:* Contact institution. *Financial support:* Application deadline: 3/1; applicants required to submit FAFSA. *Unit head:* Jennifer Rosato Perea, Dean, 312-362-8701, E-mail: jrosato@depaul.edu. *Application contact:* Amanda Noascono, Director of Law Admissions/Assistant Dean, 312-362-8807, Fax: 312-362-5280, E-mail: lawinfo@depaul.edu.
Website: http://law.depaul.edu

Drake University, Law School, Des Moines, IA 50311. Offers LL M, MJ, JD, JD/LL M, JD/MA, JD/MBA, JD/MHA, JD/MPA, JD/MPH, JD/MS, JD/MSW, JD/Pharm D. *Accreditation:* ABA. *Program availability:* Part-time. *Degree requirements:* For doctorate, 2 internships. *Entrance requirements:* For doctorate, LSAT, LSDAS report. Additional exam requirements/recommendations for international students: Required—TOEFL (minimum score 560 paper-based), TWE. *Application deadline:* For fall admission, 4/1 priority date for domestic and international students. Applications are processed on a rolling basis. Application fee: $40. Electronic applications accepted. *Expenses:* Contact institution. *Financial support:* Research assistantships, teaching assistantships, career-related internships or fieldwork, Federal Work-Study, institutionally sponsored loans, scholarships/grants, and tuition waivers (full and partial) available. Support available to part-time students. Financial award application deadline: 3/1; financial award applicants required to submit FAFSA. *Faculty research:* Constitutional law, environmental law, agricultural law, computers and the law, bioethics and health law. *Unit head:* Jerry Anderson, Dean, 515-271-2658, Fax: 515-271-4118, E-mail: jerry.anderson@drake.edu. *Application contact:* Kara Blanchard, Assistant Dean for Admission and Financial Aid, 515-271-2953, Fax: 515-271-2530, E-mail: kara.blanchard@drake.edu.
Website: http://www.drake.edu/law

Drexel University, Thomas R. Kline School of Law, Philadelphia, PA 19104-2875. Offers business and entrepreneurship law (JD); criminal law (MLS, JD); cybersecurity and information privacy compliance (MLS); entrepreneurship and law (MLS); financial regulatory compliance (MLS); health care compliance (MLS); health law (JD); higher education compliance (MLS); human resources compliance (MLS); intellectual property law (JD); NCAA compliance and sports law (MLS).

Duke University, School of Law, Durham, NC 27708. Offers American law (LL M); judicial studies (MJS); law (JD, SJD); law and entrepreneurship (LL M); JD/LL M; JD/MA; JD/MBA; JD/MEM; JD/MPP; JD/MTS; JD/PhD; MD/JD. *Accreditation:* ABA. *Faculty:* 92 full-time (40 women), 102 part-time/adjunct (30 women). *Students:* 666; includes 161 minority (46 Black or African American, non-Hispanic/Latino; 1 American Indian or Alaska Native, non-Hispanic/Latino; 66 Asian, non-Hispanic/Latino; 43 Hispanic/Latino; 1 Native Hawaiian or other Pacific Islander, non-Hispanic/Latino; 4 Two or more races, non-Hispanic/Latino), 49 international. Average age 24. 4,672 applicants, 23% accepted, 207 enrolled. In 2017, 225 doctorates awarded. *Degree requirements:* For doctorate, thesis/dissertation (for some programs). *Entrance requirements:* For doctorate, LSAT (for JD). Additional exam requirements/recommendations for international students: Required—TOEFL (minimum score 600 paper-based). *Application deadline:* For fall admission, 2/15 for domestic and international students. Applications are processed on a rolling basis. Application fee: $70. Electronic applications accepted. *Expenses:* $62,247. *Financial support:* In 2017–18, 580 students received support. Institutionally sponsored loans, scholarships/grants, and unspecified assistantships available. Financial award application deadline: 3/15; financial award applicants required to submit FAFSA. *Faculty research:* International and comparative law; Constitutional and public law; intellectual property law; science and technology law; business, finance, and corporate law; environmental law and policy; criminal law; health care law and policy. *Unit head:* David F. Levi, Dean/Professor of Law, 919-613-7001, Fax: 919-613-7158. *Application contact:* William J. Hoye, Associate Dean for Admissions and Student Affairs, 919-613-7020, Fax: 919-613-7257, E-mail: hoye@law.duke.edu.
Website: http://www.law.duke.edu/

Dunlap-Stone University, Graduate Law Center, Phoenix, AZ 85024. Offers regulatory trade compliance (M Sc); U.S. regulatory trade law (LL M).

Duquesne University, Bayer School of Natural and Environmental Sciences, Program in Forensic Science and Law, Pittsburgh, PA 15282-0001. Offers MS. *Faculty:* 5 full-time (3 women), 15 part-time/adjunct (9 women). *Students:* 16 full-time (11 women); includes 2 minority (1 Hispanic/Latino; 1 Two or more races, non-Hispanic/Latino), 1 international. Average age 23. In 2017, 21 master's awarded. *Degree requirements:* For master's, comprehensive exam. *Entrance requirements:* For master's, SAT or ACT, recommendation form; minimum total QPA of 3.0, 2.5 in math and science. *Application deadline:* For fall admission, 7/1 for domestic and international students. Applications are processed on a rolling basis. Application fee: $0. Electronic applications accepted. *Expenses:* $1,312 per credit. *Financial support:* In 2017–18, 10 students received support. Career-related internships or fieldwork and scholarships/grants available. Financial award application deadline: 5/1. *Faculty research:* Extraction protocols, mass spectrometry, synthetic fiber analysis, synthetic polymer characterization, trace analysis, amplification of DNA, methods for labeling DNA, construction of a genetic profile, experiential exploration of mitochondrial DNA, the Y-chromosome, amelogenin. *Total annual research expenditures:* $50,419. *Unit head:* Dr. Federick W. Fochtman, Director, 412-396-6373, E-mail: fochtman@duq.edu. *Application contact:* Valerie L. Lijewski, Assistant Director/Academic Advisor, 412-396-1084, E-mail: lijewski@duq.edu.
Website: http://www.duq.edu/academics/schools/natural-and-environmental-sciences/academic-programs/forensic-science-and-law

Duquesne University, School of Law, Pittsburgh, PA 15282-0700. Offers American law for foreign lawyers (LL M); law (JD); JD/M Div; JD/MBA; JD/MS; JD/MSEM. JD/M Div offered jointly with Pittsburgh Theological Seminary. *Accreditation:* ABA. *Program availability:* Part-time, evening/weekend. *Faculty:* 30 full-time (16 women), 35 part-time/adjunct (9 women). *Students:* 404 full-time (214 women); includes 33 minority (7 Black or African American, non-Hispanic/Latino; 2 American Indian or Alaska Native, non-Hispanic/Latino; 6 Asian, non-Hispanic/Latino; 11 Hispanic/Latino; 1 Native Hawaiian or other Pacific Islander, non-Hispanic/Latino; 6 Two or more races, non-Hispanic/Latino), 4 international. Average age 26. 796 applicants, 62% accepted, 149 enrolled. In 2017, 3 master's, 126 doctorates awarded. *Entrance requirements:* For doctorate, LSAT. Additional exam requirements/recommendations for international students: Required—TOEFL (minimum score 85 iBT), IELTS (minimum score 6.5). *Application deadline:* For fall admission, 3/1 priority date for domestic and international students. Applications are processed on a rolling basis. Application fee: $0. Electronic applications accepted. *Expenses:* $16,128 per semester (part-time day and evening JD); $20,987 per semester (day JD); $12,119 per semester (for LL M). *Financial support:* In 2017–18, 338 students received support, including 25 research assistantships with partial tuition reimbursements available (averaging $2,500 per year), 20 teaching assistantships with partial tuition reimbursements available (averaging $2,500 per year); career-related internships or fieldwork, scholarships/grants, tuition waivers (partial), and library assistants also available. Support available to part-time students. Financial award application deadline: 5/1; financial award applicants required to submit FAFSA. *Faculty research:* Constitutional law, law and religion, intellectual property and patents, neuroscience and law, civil and criminal law and procedure, feminist perspective on

environmental law. *Total annual research expenditures:* $100,000. *Unit head:* Maureen Lally-Green, Dean, 412-396-6280, Fax: 412-396-6283, E-mail: lallygreen@duq.edu. *Application contact:* Office of Admissions, 412-396-6296, Fax: 412-396-6659, E-mail: lawadmissions@duq.edu.
Website: https://www.law.duq.edu/

Elon University, Program in Law, Elon, NC 27244-2010. Offers JD. *Accreditation:* ABA. *Faculty:* 36 full-time (16 women), 55 part-time/adjunct (20 women). *Students:* 353 full-time (211 women); includes 81 minority (59 Black or African American, non-Hispanic/Latino; 5 American Indian or Alaska Native, non-Hispanic/Latino; 2 Asian, non-Hispanic/Latino; 15 Hispanic/Latino), 1 international. Average age 25. 819 applicants, 42% accepted, 138 enrolled. In 2017, 91 doctorates awarded. *Entrance requirements:* For doctorate, LSAT, LSDAS. Additional exam requirements/recommendations for international students: Required—TOEFL (minimum score 550 paper-based; 79 iBT). *Application deadline:* For fall admission, 7/30 for domestic students; for spring admission, 4/1 priority date for domestic students. Applications are processed on a rolling basis. Application fee: $50. Electronic applications accepted. *Financial support:* Scholarships/grants available. Financial award applicants required to submit FAFSA. *Faculty research:* Quality of life and job satisfaction, civil procedure, damages, assessment for development of instruments, psychological types. *Unit head:* Dr. Luke Bierman, Dean, 336-279-9201, E-mail: lbierman@elon.edu. *Application contact:* Alan Woodlief, Associate Dean of School of Law/Director of Law School Admissions, 336-279-9203, E-mail: awoodlief@elon.edu.
Website: https://www.elon.edu/law

Emory University, School of Law, Atlanta, GA 30322-2770. Offers LL M, JD, Certificate, JD/Certificate, JD/LL M, JD/M Div, JD/MA, JD/MBA, JD/MPH, JD/MTS, JD/PhD. *Accreditation:* ABA. *Entrance requirements:* For doctorate, LSAT, 2 letters of recommendation. Additional exam requirements/recommendations for international students: Required—TOEFL (minimum score 600 paper-based). Electronic applications accepted. *Expenses:* Contact institution. *Faculty research:* Law and economics, law and religion, international law, human rights, feminism and legal theory.

Empire College, School of Law, Santa Rosa, CA 95403. Offers MLS, JD.

Faulkner University, Thomas Goode Jones School of Law, Montgomery, AL 36109-3398. Offers JD. *Accreditation:* ABA. *Entrance requirements:* For doctorate, LSAT. Additional exam requirements/recommendations for international students: Recommended—TOEFL. Electronic applications accepted. *Expenses: Tuition:* Full-time $9720; part-time $540 per semester hour. *Required fees:* $560; $280 per semester. Tuition and fees vary according to course load, degree level and program.

Florida Agricultural and Mechanical University, College of Law, Tallahassee, FL 32307-3200. Offers JD. *Accreditation:* ABA. *Program availability:* Part-time, evening/weekend. *Entrance requirements:* For doctorate, LSAT, LSDAS, 2 letters of recommendation. Additional exam requirements/recommendations for international students: Required—TOEFL. *Expenses:* Contact institution.

Florida Coastal School of Law, Professional Program, Jacksonville, FL 32256. Offers JD. *Accreditation:* ABA. *Program availability:* Part-time. *Entrance requirements:* For doctorate, LSAT. Additional exam requirements/recommendations for international students: Recommended—TOEFL (minimum score 600 paper-based). Electronic applications accepted. *Expenses:* Contact institution. *Faculty research:* Law and business, law technology and intellectual property, juvenile justice and family law, constitutional law, labor law.

Florida International University, College of Law, Miami, FL 33199. Offers American law for foreign lawyers (LL M); law (JD); JD/MA; JD/MIB. *Accreditation:* ABA. *Program availability:* Part-time, evening/weekend. *Faculty:* 29 full-time (14 women), 48 part-time/adjunct (8 women). *Students:* 484 full-time (269 women), 28 part-time (18 women); includes 315 minority (35 Black or African American, non-Hispanic/Latino; 3 American Indian or Alaska Native, non-Hispanic/Latino; 11 Asian, non-Hispanic/Latino; 261 Hispanic/Latino; 5 Two or more races, non-Hispanic/Latino), 25 international. Average age 27. 1,778 applicants, 32% accepted, 204 enrolled. In 2017, 14 master's, 154 doctorates awarded. *Entrance requirements:* For doctorate, LSAT, 3 letters of recommendation. Additional exam requirements/recommendations for international students: Recommended—TOEFL. *Application deadline:* For fall admission, 5/1 for domestic and international students. Applications are processed on a rolling basis. Application fee: $20. Electronic applications accepted. *Expenses:* Contact institution. *Financial support:* Application deadline: 3/1; applicants required to submit FAFSA. *Unit head:* Tawia B Ansah, Acting Dean, 305-348-1118, Fax: 305-348-1159, E-mail: tawia.ansah@fiu.edu.
Website: http://law.fiu.edu

Florida State University, College of Law, Tallahassee, FL 32306-1601. Offers American law for foreign lawyers (LL M); business law (LL M); environmental law and policy (LL M); financial regulation and compliance (JM); health law compliance (JM); law (JM, JD); legal risk management and HR compliance (JM); JD/MAES; JD/MBA; JD/MPA; JD/MS; JD/MSI; JD/MSP; JD/MSW. *Accreditation:* ABA. *Program availability:* Part-time, 100% online. *Faculty:* 57 full-time (29 women), 36 part-time/adjunct (11 women). *Students:* 520 full-time (268 women), 79 part-time (45 women); includes 184 minority (53 Black or African American, non-Hispanic/Latino; 2 American Indian or Alaska Native, non-Hispanic/Latino; 13 Asian, non-Hispanic/Latino; 71 Hispanic/Latino; 45 Two or more races, non-Hispanic/Latino), 13 international. Average age 26. 1,805 applicants, 36% accepted, 225 enrolled. In 2017, 18 master's, 218 doctorates awarded. Terminal master's awarded for partial completion of doctoral program. *Degree requirements:* For master's, comprehensive exam (for some programs). *Entrance requirements:* For master's, one graduate-level standardized test (for JM), JD or equivalent degree (for LL M); for doctorate, LSAT or GRE (for JD). Additional exam requirements/recommendations for international students: Required—TOEFL (minimum score 600 paper-based; 100 iBT), IELTS (minimum score 7.5). *Application deadline:* For fall admission, 6/30 for domestic and international students; for spring admission, 12/1 for domestic students; for summer admission, 4/15 for domestic students. Applications are processed on a rolling basis. Application fee: $30. Electronic applications accepted. *Expenses:* $20,683. *Financial support:* In 2017–18, 400 students received support, including 2 fellowships with full tuition reimbursements available (averaging $20,683 per year), 30 research assistantships (averaging $1,205 per year), 10 teaching assistantships (averaging $1,354 per year); career-related internships or fieldwork, scholarships/grants, and unspecified assistantships also available. Financial award application deadline: 3/1; financial award applicants required to submit FAFSA. *Faculty research:* Business law; environmental, energy and land use law; international law; criminal law. *Total annual research expenditures:* $99,375. *Unit head:* Erin O'Hara O'Connor, Dean, 850-644-3400, Fax: 850-644-5487, E-mail: eoconnor@law.fsu.edu. *Application contact:* Jennifer L. Kessinger, Director of Admissions and Records, 850-644-3787, Fax: 850-644-7284, E-mail: jkessing@law.fsu.edu.
Website: http://www.law.fsu.edu/

Fordham University, School of Law, New York, NY 10023. Offers banking, corporate and finance law (LL M); corporate compliance (MSL); fashion law (MSL); intellectual property and information law (LL M); international business and trade law (LL M); law (JD); JD/MA; JD/MBA; JD/MSW. *Accreditation:* ABA. *Program availability:* Part-time,

evening/weekend. *Entrance requirements:* For doctorate, LSAT. Additional exam requirements/recommendations for international students: Required—TOEFL. Electronic applications accepted. *Expenses:* Contact institution. *Faculty research:* Intellectual property, business law, international law.

Friends University, Graduate School, Wichita, KS 67213. Offers family therapy (MSFT); global business administration (MBA), including accounting, business law, change management, health care leadership, management information systems, supply chain management and logistics; health care leadership (MHCL); management information systems (MMIS); professional business administration (MBA), including accounting, business law, change management, health care leadership, management information systems, supply chain management and logistics. *Program availability:* Part-time, evening/weekend, online learning. *Degree requirements:* For master's, research project. *Entrance requirements:* For master's, bachelor's degree from accredited institution, official transcripts, interview with program director, letter(s) of recommendation. Additional exam requirements/recommendations for international students: Required—TOEFL (minimum score 560 paper-based). Electronic applications accepted.

George Mason University, Antonin Scalia Law School, Arlington, VA 22201. Offers global antitrust law and economics (LL M); intellectual property (LL M); law (JD); law and economics (LL M); U.S. law (LL M); JD/MA; JD/MPP; JD/PhD. *Accreditation:* ABA. *Program availability:* Part-time, evening/weekend. *Faculty:* 44 full-time (9 women), 157 part-time/adjunct (41 women). *Students:* 401 full-time (199 women), 138 part-time (56 women); includes 115 minority (17 Black or African American, non-Hispanic/Latino; 40 Asian, non-Hispanic/Latino; 38 Hispanic/Latino; 20 Two or more races, non-Hispanic/Latino), 7 international. Average age 26. 2,452 applicants, 25% accepted, 175 enrolled. In 2017, 142 doctorates awarded. *Entrance requirements:* For master's, JD or international equivalent; for doctorate, LSAT or GRE, baccalaureate degree or international equivalent. Additional exam requirements/recommendations for international students: Required—TOEFL or IELTS (for LL M applicants only). *Application deadline:* For fall admission, 6/15 for domestic and international students. Applications are processed on a rolling basis. Application fee: $0. Electronic applications accepted. *Expenses:* Contact institution. *Financial support:* Fellowships, research assistantships, career-related internships or fieldwork, scholarships/grants, and tuition waivers (full and partial) available. Support available to part-time students. Financial award applicants required to submit FAFSA. *Faculty research:* Law and economics; infrastructure protection, including homeland and national security; intellectual property. *Unit head:* Henry N. Butler, Dean, 703-993-8644, Fax: 703-993-8088. *Application contact:* Tiffany J. Williams, Assistant Dean for Admissions and Enrollment Management, 703-993-8010, Fax: 703-993-8088, E-mail: lawadmit@gmu.edu.
Website: http://www.law.gmu.edu

Georgetown University, Law Center, Washington, DC 20001. Offers environmental law (LL M); global health law (LL M); global health law and international institutions (LL M); individualized study (LL M); international business and economic law (LL M); law (JD, SJD); national security law (LL M); securities and financial regulation (LL M); taxation (LL M); JD/LL M; JD/MA; JD/MBA; JD/MPH; JD/PhD. *Accreditation:* ABA. *Program availability:* Part-time, evening/weekend. *Degree requirements:* For master's, thesis; for doctorate, thesis/dissertation (for some programs). *Entrance requirements:* For master's, JD, LL B, or first law degree earned in country of origin; for doctorate, LSAT (for JD). Additional exam requirements/recommendations for international students: Required—TOEFL. *Expenses:* Contact institution. *Faculty research:* Constitutional law, legal history, jurisprudence.

The George Washington University, Law School, Washington, DC 20052. Offers law (SJD); national security and U.S. foreign relations (LL M). *Accreditation:* ABA. *Program availability:* Part-time, evening/weekend. *Faculty:* 84 full-time (33 women), 233 part-time/adjunct (65 women). *Students:* 1,444 full-time (760 women), 249 part-time (118 women); includes 422 minority (157 Black or African American, non-Hispanic/Latino; 11 American Indian or Alaska Native, non-Hispanic/Latino; 198 Asian, non-Hispanic/Latino; 38 Hispanic/Latino; 4 Native Hawaiian or other Pacific Islander, non-Hispanic/Latino; 14 Two or more races, non-Hispanic/Latino), 190 international. Average age 27. 191 applicants, 100% accepted, 128 enrolled. In 2017, 167 master's, 4 doctorates awarded. *Entrance requirements:* For master's, JD or equivalent; for doctorate, LSAT (for JD), LL M or equivalent (for SJD). *Application deadline:* For fall admission, 3/1 for domestic students. Applications are processed on a rolling basis. Application fee: $75. *Expenses:* Contact institution. *Financial support:* Research assistantships, career-related internships or fieldwork, Federal Work-Study, institutionally sponsored loans, scholarships/grants, and tuition waivers (full and partial) available. Support available to part-time students. Financial award application deadline: 3/1; financial award applicants required to submit CSS PROFILE or FAFSA. *Unit head:* Blake D. Morant, Dean, E-mail: bmorant@law.gwu.edu. *Application contact:* Sophia Sim, Assistant Dean of Admissions and Financial Aid, 202-994-7235, Fax: 202-739-0624, E-mail: ssim@law.gwu.edu.
Website: http://www.law.gwu.edu/

Georgia State University, College of Law, Atlanta, GA 30302-4037. Offers JD, JD/MA, JD/MBA, JD/MCRP, JD/MHA, JD/MPA, JD/MSHA. *Accreditation:* ABA. *Program availability:* Part-time, evening/weekend. *Faculty:* 39 full-time (16 women). *Students:* 617 full-time (310 women), 23 part-time (9 women); includes 199 minority (78 Black or African American, non-Hispanic/Latino; 3 American Indian or Alaska Native, non-Hispanic/Latino; 53 Asian, non-Hispanic/Latino; 51 Hispanic/Latino; 14 Two or more races, non-Hispanic/Latino), 17 international. Average age 28. 1,493 applicants, 37% accepted, 204 enrolled. In 2017, 184 doctorates awarded. *Entrance requirements:* For doctorate, LSAT. Additional exam requirements/recommendations for international students: Recommended—TOEFL. *Application deadline:* For fall admission, 3/15 for domestic students, 3/15 priority date for international students. Applications are processed on a rolling basis. Application fee: $50. Electronic applications accepted. *Expenses:* Contact institution. *Financial support:* In 2017–18, research assistantships with tuition reimbursements (averaging $2,500 per year), teaching assistantships (averaging $2,500 per year) were awarded; scholarships/grants, tuition waivers, and unspecified assistantships also available. Financial award application deadline: 4/1; financial award applicants required to submit FAFSA. *Faculty research:* Health law; land use, urban planning and environmental law; intellectual property; criminal law and procedure; Constitutional law. *Unit head:* Dr. Steven J. Kaminshine, Dean, College of Law, 404-413-9035, Fax: 404-413-9227, E-mail: skaminshine@gsu.edu. *Application contact:* Dr. Cheryl Jester-George, Senior Director of Admissions, 404-413-9004, Fax: 404-413-9203, E-mail: cjgeorge@gsu.edu.
Website: http://law.gsu.edu/

Golden Gate University, School of Law, San Francisco, CA 94105. Offers environmental law (LL M); estate planning (LL M); intellectual property law (LL M); international legal studies (LL M); law (JD); taxation law (LL M); U.S. legal studies (LL M); JD/MBA. *Accreditation:* ABA. *Program availability:* Part-time, evening/weekend. *Faculty:* 31 full-time (19 women), 160 part-time/adjunct (77 women). *Students:* 286 full-time (184 women), 245 part-time (134 women); includes 242 minority (48 Black or African American, non-Hispanic/Latino; 4 American Indian or Alaska Native, non-Hispanic/Latino; 69 Asian, non-Hispanic/Latino; 95 Hispanic/Latino; 7 Native Hawaiian or other Pacific Islander, non-Hispanic/Latino; 19 Two or more races, non-Hispanic/

Latino), 71 international. Average age 31. 1,354 applicants, 66% accepted, 227 enrolled. *Degree requirements:* For doctorate, thesis/dissertation (for some programs). *Entrance requirements:* For doctorate, LSAT (for JD). Additional exam requirements/ recommendations for international students: Required—TOEFL (minimum score 600 paper-based). *Application deadline:* For fall admission, 6/30 for domestic students. Applications are processed on a rolling basis. Electronic applications accepted. *Expenses:* Contact institution. *Financial support:* Fellowships, research assistantships, teaching assistantships, career-related internships or fieldwork, Federal Work-Study, institutionally sponsored loans, scholarships/grants, tuition waivers (full and partial), and unspecified assistantships available. Support available to part-time students. Financial award applicants required to submit FAFSA. *Faculty research:* International law, intellectual property law, environmental law, real estate, civil rights. *Unit head:* Anthony Niedwiecki, Dean, 415-442-6601, Fax: 415-442-6609. *Application contact:* Greg Egertson, Associate Dean and Director of Admissions, 415-442-6636, Fax: 415-442-6609, E-mail: lawadmit@ggu.edu.
Website: http://law.ggu.edu/

Gonzaga University, School of Law, Spokane, WA 99220-3528. Offers JD. *Accreditation:* ABA. *Program availability:* Part-time. *Faculty:* 15 full-time (10 women), 19 part-time/adjunct (4 women). *Students:* 312 full-time (146 women), 1 part-time (0 women); includes 48 minority (5 Black or African American, non-Hispanic/Latino; 3 American Indian or Alaska Native, non-Hispanic/Latino; 6 Asian, non-Hispanic/Latino; 20 Hispanic/Latino; 14 Two or more races, non-Hispanic/Latino), 2 international. Average age 26. 905 applicants, 59% accepted, 122 enrolled. In 2017, 105 doctorates awarded. *Degree requirements:* For doctorate, experiential learning, public service. *Entrance requirements:* For doctorate, LSAT, bachelor's degree, all academic transcripts, 2-4 letters of recommendation, resume, personal statement. *Application deadline:* For fall admission, 4/15 priority date for domestic students. Application fee: $50. Electronic applications accepted. *Expenses:* Contact institution. *Financial support:* In 2017–18, 281 students received support. Federal Work-Study and scholarships/ grants available. Support available to part-time students. Financial award applicants required to submit FAFSA. *Faculty research:* Environmental law, business law, public interest law, tax law, international law. *Unit head:* Jane Korn, Dean, 509-313-3700. *Application contact:* Susan Lee, Director of Admissions, 509-313-3734, E-mail: lee@gonzaga.edu.
Website: https://www.gonzaga.edu/school-of-law

Harvard University, Law School, Graduate Programs in Law, Cambridge, MA 02138. Offers LL M, SJD. *Accreditation:* ABA. *Degree requirements:* For master's, thesis optional; for doctorate, thesis/dissertation. *Entrance requirements:* Additional exam requirements/recommendations for international students: Required—TOEFL. *Faculty research:* Corporation finance, national and international law, legal ethics, family law, criminal law, administrative law, constitutional law.

Harvard University, Law School, Professional Programs in Law, Cambridge, MA 02138. Offers international and comparative law (JD); law and business (JD); law and government (JD); law and social change (JD); law, science and technology (JD); JD/ MALD; JD/MBA; JD/MPH; JD/MPP; JD/PhD. *Accreditation:* ABA. *Degree requirements:* For doctorate, 3rd-year paper. *Entrance requirements:* For doctorate, LSAT. *Faculty research:* Constitutional law, voting rights law, cyber law.

Hofstra University, Maurice A. Deane School of Law, Hempstead, NY 11549. Offers alternative dispute resolution (JD); American legal studies (LL M); business law honors (JD); clinical bioethics (Certificate); corporate compliance (JD); criminal law and procedure (JD); family law (LL M, JD); health law (JD); health law and policy (LL M, MA); intellectual property law honors (JD); international law honors (JD); JD/MBA; JD/MPH. *Accreditation:* ABA. *Program availability:* Part-time, 100% online. *Faculty:* 41 full-time (23 women), 69 part-time/adjunct (20 women). *Students:* 698 full-time (382 women), 136 part-time (91 women); includes 201 minority (66 Black or African American, non-Hispanic/Latino; 3 American Indian or Alaska Native, non-Hispanic/Latino; 31 Asian, non-Hispanic/Latino; 90 Hispanic/Latino; 8 Native Hawaiian or other Pacific Islander, non-Hispanic/Latino; 3 Two or more races, non-Hispanic/Latino), 28 international. Average age 28. 3,212 applicants, 50% accepted, 317 enrolled. In 2017, 9 master's, 234 doctorates awarded. *Entrance requirements:* For doctorate, LSAT, letter of recommendation, personal statement, undergraduate transcripts; for Certificate, 2 letters of recommendation, JD or LL B, personal statement, law school transcripts. Additional exam requirements/recommendations for international students: Recommended—TOEFL (minimum score 600 paper-based; 100 iBT). *Application deadline:* For fall admission, 4/15 priority date for domestic and international students. Applications are processed on a rolling basis. Application fee: $75. Electronic applications accepted. *Expenses:* $28,397 per term. *Financial support:* In 2017–18, 506 students received support, including 493 fellowships with full and partial tuition reimbursements available (averaging $33,296 per year); research assistantships with full and partial tuition reimbursements available, career-related internships or fieldwork, Federal Work-Study, institutionally sponsored loans, scholarships/grants, tuition waivers (full and partial), and unspecified assistantships also available. Support available to part-time students. Financial award applicants required to submit FAFSA. *Faculty research:* Family law; international law; constitutional law; legal ethics; health law. *Unit head:* Gail Prudenti, Dean, 516-463-4068, E-mail: gail.prudenti@hofstra.edu. *Application contact:* Sunil Samuel, Assistant Vice President of Admissions, 516-463-4723, Fax: 516-463-4664.
Website: http://law.hofstra.edu/

Howard University, School of Law, Washington, DC 20008. Offers LL M, JD, JD/MBA. *Accreditation:* ABA. *Degree requirements:* For master's, one foreign language, thesis; for doctorate, thesis/dissertation (for some programs). *Entrance requirements:* For doctorate, LSAT. Additional exam requirements/recommendations for international students: Required—TOEFL. Electronic applications accepted. *Expenses:* Contact institution. *Faculty research:* Criminal law, family law, telecommunications, religion, antitrust.

Humphreys University, Drivon School of Law, Stockton, CA 95207-3896. Offers JD. *Program availability:* Part-time, evening/weekend. *Entrance requirements:* For doctorate, LSAT, minimum GPA of 2.5. Electronic applications accepted. Application fee is waived when completed online. *Expenses:* Contact institution.

Illinois Institute of Technology, Chicago-Kent College of Law, Chicago, IL 60661-3691. Offers family law (LL M); financial services law (LL M); international intellectual property law (LL M); law (JD); legal studies (JSD); taxation (LL M); U.S., international, and transnational law (LL M); JD/LL M; JD/MBA; JD/MPA; JD/MPH; JD/MS. *Accreditation:* ABA. *Program availability:* Part-time, evening/weekend. Terminal master's awarded for partial completion of doctoral program. *Entrance requirements:* For master's, 1st degree in law or certified license to practice law; for doctorate, LSAT. Additional exam requirements/recommendations for international students: Required—TOEFL (minimum score 600 paper-based; 100 iBT); Recommended—IELTS (minimum score 7). Electronic applications accepted. *Expenses:* Contact institution. *Faculty research:* Constitutional law, bioethics, environmental law, intellectual property.

Indiana University Bloomington, Maurer School of Law, Bloomington, IN 47405-7000. Offers comparative law (MCL); juridical science (SJD); law (LL M, JD); law and social

sciences (PhD); legal studies (Certificate); JD/MA; JD/MBA; JD/MLS; JD/MPA; JD/MS; JD/MSES. PhD offered through University Graduate School. *Accreditation:* ABA. *Degree requirements:* For master's, thesis or practicum; for doctorate, thesis/dissertation (for some programs), research seminar (for JD). *Entrance requirements:* For master's, LSAT, 3 letters of recommendation, law degree or license to practice; for doctorate, LSAT. Additional exam requirements/recommendations for international students: Required—TOEFL (minimum score 560 paper-based; 80 iBT). Electronic applications accepted. *Faculty research:* Environmental risk assessment and policy analysis, information privacy and security, judicial independence, accountability, ethics.

Indiana University–Purdue University Indianapolis, Robert H. McKinney School of Law, Indianapolis, IN 46202. Offers advocacy skills (Certificate); American law for foreign lawyers (LL M); civil and human rights (Certificate); corporate and commercial law (LL M, Certificate); criminal law (Certificate); environmental and natural resources (Certificate); health law (Certificate); health law, policy and bioethics (LL M); intellectual property law (LL M, Certificate); international and comparative law (LL M, Certificate); international human rights law (LL M); law (MJ, JD, SJD); JD/M Phil; JD/MBA; JD/MD; JD/MHA; JD/MLS; JD/MPA; JD/MPH; JD/MSW. *Accreditation:* ABA. *Program availability:* Part-time. *Entrance requirements:* For doctorate, LSAT. Additional exam requirements/recommendations for international students: Required—TOEFL (minimum score 79 iBT), IELTS (minimum score 6.5). Electronic applications accepted. *Expenses:* Contact institution.

Instituto Tecnológico y de Estudios Superiores de Monterrey, Campus Ciudad de México, School of Humanities and Social Sciences, Ciudad de Mexico, Mexico. Offers LL B. *Program availability:* Part-time, evening/weekend. *Entrance requirements:* For degree, Instituto entrance exam. Additional exam requirements/recommendations for international students: Required—TOEFL. *Faculty research:* Law; politics; international relations.

Inter American University of Puerto Rico School of Law, Professional Program, San Juan, PR 00936-8351. Offers JD. *Accreditation:* ABA. *Program availability:* Part-time, evening/weekend. *Entrance requirements:* For doctorate, LSAT, PAEG, minimum GPA of 2.5. *Expenses:* Contact institution.

John F. Kennedy University, School of Law, Pleasant Hill, CA 94523-4817. Offers JD. *Program availability:* Part-time, evening/weekend. *Entrance requirements:* For doctorate, LSAT, interview. Additional exam requirements/recommendations for international students: Required—TOEFL. *Expenses:* Contact institution.

The John Marshall Law School, Graduate and Professional Programs, Chicago, IL 60604-3968. Offers LL M, MJ, JD, JD/LL M, JD/MA, JD/MBA, JD/MPA. *Accreditation:* ABA. *Program availability:* Part-time, evening/weekend, 100% online, blended/hybrid learning. *Faculty:* 55 full-time (23 women), 202 part-time/adjunct (72 women). *Students:* 688 full-time (364 women), 317 part-time (159 women); includes 379 minority (147 Black or African American, non-Hispanic/Latino; 3 American Indian or Alaska Native, non-Hispanic/Latino; 64 Asian, non-Hispanic/Latino; 140 Hispanic/Latino; 25 Two or more races, non-Hispanic/Latino), 54 international. Average age 28. 1,681 applicants, 69% accepted, 287 enrolled. In 2017, 99 master's, 352 doctorates awarded. *Degree requirements:* For master's, 24 credits; for doctorate, 90 credits. *Entrance requirements:* For doctorate, LSAT, GRE. Additional exam requirements/recommendations for international students: Required—TOEFL (minimum score 90 iBT), IELTS (minimum score 7). *Application deadline:* For fall admission, 4/1 priority date for domestic and international students; for spring admission, 11/15 priority date for domestic and international students. Applications are processed on a rolling basis. Application fee: $0. Electronic applications accepted. *Expenses: Tuition:* Full-time $46,950; part-time $32,865 per year. *Required fees:* $1650; $1650 per unit. *Financial support:* In 2017–18, 538 students received support. Federal Work-Study, scholarships/grants, and tuition waivers (full and partial) available. Support available to part-time students. Financial award application deadline: 4/1; financial award applicants required to submit FAFSA. *Unit head:* Darby Dickerson, Dean, 312-427-2737 Ext. 828, E-mail: ddickerson@jmls.edu. *Application contact:* Chante Spann, Assistant Dean for Admissions, 800-537-4280, Fax: 312-427-5136, E-mail: admissions@jmls.edu.

The Judge Advocate General's School, U.S. Army, Graduate Programs, Charlottesville, VA 22903-1781. Offers LL M. Program available only to active duty military lawyers. *Accreditation:* ABA. *Degree requirements:* For master's, thesis optional. *Entrance requirements:* For master's, active duty military lawyer, international military officer, or DOD civilian attorney; JD or LL B. *Faculty research:* Criminal law, administrative and civil law, contract law, international law, legal research and writing.

Lewis & Clark College, Lewis & Clark Law School, Portland, OR 97219. Offers animal law (LL M); environmental, natural resources, and energy law (LL M, MSL); law (JD). *Accreditation:* ABA. *Program availability:* Part-time, evening/weekend. *Entrance requirements:* For doctorate, LSAT. Additional exam requirements/recommendations for international students: Recommended—TOEFL (minimum score 600 paper-based). Electronic applications accepted. Application fee is waived when completed online. *Expenses:* Contact institution.

Liberty University, School of Law, Lynchburg, VA 24515. Offers American legal studies (JM); international legal studies (JM, LL M). *Program availability:* Online learning. *Students:* 251 full-time (123 women), 116 part-time (57 women); includes 84 minority (46 Black or African American, non-Hispanic/Latino; 4 American Indian or Alaska Native, non-Hispanic/Latino; 7 Asian, non-Hispanic/Latino; 17 Hispanic/Latino; 10 Two or more races, non-Hispanic/Latino), 6 international. Average age 33. 294 applicants, 67% accepted, 136 enrolled. *Entrance requirements:* Additional exam requirements/ recommendations for international students: Required—TOEFL (minimum score 600 paper-based; 100 iBT). *Application deadline:* For fall admission, 6/1 for domestic students. *Expenses:* Contact institution. *Financial support:* Applicants required to submit FAFSA. *Unit head:* B. Keith Faulkner, Dean, 434-592-5300, Fax: 434-592-5400, E-mail: law@liberty.edu. *Application contact:* Joleen Thaxton, Assistant Director of Admissions, 434-592-5300, Fax: 434-592-5400, E-mail: lawadmissions@liberty.edu.

Lincoln Memorial University, Duncan School of Law, Harrogate, TN 37752-1901. Offers JD. *Program availability:* Part-time. *Entrance requirements:* For doctorate, LSAT. Additional exam requirements/recommendations for international students: Required—TOEFL (minimum score 500 paper-based). Electronic applications accepted. *Expenses:* Contact institution.

London Metropolitan University, Graduate Programs, London, United Kingdom. Offers applied psychology (M Sc); architecture (MA); biomedical science (M Sc); blood science (M Sc); cancer pharmacology (M Sc); computer networking and cyber security (M Sc); computing and information systems (M Sc); conference interpreting (MA); counter-terrorism studies (M Sc); creative, digital and professional writing (MA); crime, violence and prevention (M Sc); criminology (M Sc); curating contemporary art (MA); data analytics (MA); digital media (MA); early childhood studies (MA); education (MA, Ed D); financial services law, regulation and compliance (LL M); food science (M Sc); forensic psychology (M Sc); health and social care management and policy (M Sc); human nutrition (M Sc); human resource management (MA); human rights and international conflict (MA); information technology (M Sc); intelligence and security studies (M Sc); international oil, gas and energy law (LL M); international relations (MA); interpreting (MA); learning and teaching in higher education (MA); legal practice (LL M);

media and entertainment law (LL M); organizational and consumer psychology (M Sc); psychological therapy (M Sc); psychology of mental health (M Sc); public health (M Sc); public policy and management (MPA); security studies (M Sc); social work (M Sc); spatial planning and urban design (MA); sports therapy (M Sc); supporting older children and young people with dyslexia (MA); teaching languages (MA), including Arabic, English; translation (MA); woman and child abuse (MA).

Louisiana State University and Agricultural & Mechanical College, Paul M. Hebert Law Center, Baton Rouge, LA 70803. Offers LL M, JD. *Accreditation:* ABA. *Faculty:* 35 full-time (11 women), 20 part-time/adjunct (1 woman). *Students:* 534 full-time (263 women); includes 87 minority (37 Black or African American, non-Hispanic/Latino; 1 American Indian or Alaska Native, non-Hispanic/Latino; 8 Asian, non-Hispanic/Latino; 31 Hispanic/Latino; 10 Two or more races, non-Hispanic/Latino), 11 international. Average age 26. 901 applicants, 58% accepted, 178 enrolled. In 2017, 5 master's awarded. *Degree requirements:* For master's, thesis dissertation. *Entrance requirements:* For doctorate, LSAT. Additional exam requirements/recommendations for international students: Required—TOEFL (minimum score 600 paper-based; 100 iBT). *Application deadline:* For fall admission, 3/1 priority date for domestic and international students. Applications are processed on a rolling basis. Application fee: $50. Electronic applications accepted. Application fee is waived when completed online. *Expenses:* $23,082 in-state, $38,522 out-of-state. *Financial support:* In 2017–18, 522 students received support. Scholarships/grants and tuition waivers (full and partial) available. Financial award application deadline: 7/1; financial award applicants required to submit FAFSA. *Unit head:* Thomas Galligan, Dean, 225-578-8491, Fax: 225-578-8202, E-mail: tgalligan@lsu.edu. *Application contact:* Jake T. Henry, III, Director of Admissions, 225-578-8646, Fax: 225-578-8647, E-mail: jakeh@lsu.edu.
Website: http://www.law.lsu.edu/

Loyola Marymount University, College of Business Administration, MBA/JD Program, Los Angeles, CA 90045-2659. Offers MBA/JD. *Unit head:* Dr. Dennis W. Draper, Dean, College of Business Administration, 310-338-7504, E-mail: ddraper@lmu.edu. *Application contact:* Chake H. Kouyoumjian, Associate Dean of Graduate Studies, 310-338-2721, Fax: 310-338-6086, E-mail: graduateinfo@lmu.edu.
Website: http://lls.edu/admissionaid/degreeprograms/jdprograms/jdmbaprogram

Loyola Marymount University, Loyola Law School Los Angeles, Los Angeles, CA 90015. Offers law (LL M, MLS, JD, JSD); tax (LL M in Tax, MT); JD/LL M; JD/MBA. *Accreditation:* ABA. *Program availability:* Part-time, evening/weekend. *Faculty:* 66 full-time (32 women), 120 part-time/adjunct (42 women). *Students:* 883 full-time (482 women), 182 part-time (92 women); includes 416 minority (47 Black or African American, non-Hispanic/Latino; 1 American Indian or Alaska Native, non-Hispanic/Latino; 123 Asian, non-Hispanic/Latino; 204 Hispanic/Latino; 41 Two or more races, non-Hispanic/Latino), 81 international. Average age 27. 3,744 applicants, 41% accepted, 378 enrolled. In 2017, 44 master's, 297 doctorates awarded. *Degree requirements:* For master's, comprehensive exam; for doctorate, comprehensive exam, defense of dissertation (for JSD). *Entrance requirements:* For master's, JD; for doctorate, LSAT. Additional exam requirements/recommendations for international students: Required—TOEFL (minimum score 600 paper-based; 100 iBT). *Application deadline:* For fall admission, 2/1 priority date for domestic students, 2/1 for international students. Applications are processed on a rolling basis. Application fee: $0. Electronic applications accepted. *Financial support:* In 2017–18, 40 research assistantships (averaging $1,823 per year) were awarded; career-related internships or fieldwork, Federal Work-Study, scholarships/grants, and tuition waivers (partial) also available. Support available to part-time students. Financial award application deadline: 3/15; financial award applicants required to submit FAFSA. *Unit head:* Michael Waterstone, Dean, 213-736-2243, Fax: 213-487-6736, E-mail: michael.waterstone@lls.edu. *Application contact:* Jannell Lundy Roberts, Senior Assistant Dean, Admissions and Enrollment Services, 213-736-1074, Fax: 213-736-6523, E-mail: admissions@lls.edu.
Website: http://www.lls.edu/

Loyola University Chicago, School of Law, Chicago, IL 60611. Offers advocacy (LL M); business and compliance (MJ); business law (LL M); child and family (LL M); child and family law (MJ, Certificate); global competition (LL M, MJ); health law (LL M, MJ, Certificate); international law (LL M); law (JD); public interest law (Certificate); rule of law for development (LL M, MJ); tax (LL M); tax law (Certificate); transactional law (Certificate); trial advocacy (Certificate); JD/MA; JD/MBA; JD/MPP; JD/MSW; MJ/MSW; MS/MJ. *Accreditation:* ABA. *Program availability:* Part-time, evening/weekend, 100% online, blended/hybrid learning. *Faculty:* 69 full-time (36 women), 306 part-time/adjunct (148 women). *Students:* 823 full-time (483 women), 262 part-time (201 women); includes 334 minority (124 Black or African American, non-Hispanic/Latino; 1 American Indian or Alaska Native, non-Hispanic/Latino; 54 Asian, non-Hispanic/Latino; 114 Hispanic/Latino; 1 Native Hawaiian or other Pacific Islander, non-Hispanic/Latino; 40 Two or more races, non-Hispanic/Latino), 42 international. Average age 31. 2,670 applicants, 48% accepted, 372 enrolled. In 2017, 187 master's, 222 doctorates, 104 Certificates awarded. *Degree requirements:* For master's and Certificate, thesis (for some programs); for doctorate, thesis/dissertation (for some programs). *Entrance requirements:* For doctorate, LSAT. Additional exam requirements/recommendations for international students: Required—TOEFL (minimum score 100 iBT); Recommended—IELTS (minimum score 7). *Application deadline:* For fall admission, 4/1 for domestic and international students. Applications are processed on a rolling basis. Application fee: $0. Electronic applications accepted. *Expenses:* $46,460 full-time, $34,860 weekend (for JD). *Financial support:* In 2017–18, 598 students received support, including 67 fellowships; research assistantships, Federal Work-Study, scholarships/grants, and health care benefits also available. Financial award application deadline: 3/1; financial award applicants required to submit FAFSA. *Faculty research:* Constitutional law including hate speech and supreme court advocacy; early childhood education including law policy and pedagogy; hedonic psychology - legal and social determinants of happiness; racial inequality; intersection of law, science, and technology. *Unit head:* James Faught, JD, Associate Dean for Administration, Law School, 312-915-7131, Fax: 312-915-6911, E-mail: law-admissions@luc.edu. *Application contact:* Jill Schur, Director, Graduate Enrollment Management, 312-915-8902, E-mail: gradinfo@luc.edu.
Website: http://www.luc.edu/law/

Loyola University New Orleans, College of Law, New Orleans, LA 70118. Offers LL M, JD, JD/MBA, JD/MPA, JD/MURP. *Accreditation:* ABA. *Program availability:* Part-time, evening/weekend, online learning. *Faculty:* 42 full-time (18 women), 14 part-time/adjunct (2 women). *Students:* 398 full-time (203 women), 96 part-time (49 women); includes 174 minority (77 Black or African American, non-Hispanic/Latino; 12 American Indian or Alaska Native, non-Hispanic/Latino; 16 Asian, non-Hispanic/Latino; 61 Hispanic/Latino; 8 Two or more races, non-Hispanic/Latino), 10 international. Average age 28. 809 applicants, 73% accepted, 177 enrolled. In 2017, 132 doctorates awarded. *Entrance requirements:* For doctorate, LSAT, 2 letters of recommendation, interview, resume, personal statement, bachelor's degree from accredited college/university. Additional exam requirements/recommendations for international students: Required—TOEFL (minimum score 550 paper-based; 89 iBT). *Application deadline:* For fall admission, 8/1 priority date for domestic and international students. Applications are processed on a rolling basis. Application fee: $0. Electronic applications accepted. *Expenses:* $42,840 per academic year full-time tuition; $1,386 per academic year full-time fees; $32,130 per

academic year part-time tuition; $712 per academic year part-time fees. *Financial support:* Fellowships, research assistantships, teaching assistantships, career-related internships or fieldwork, institutionally sponsored loans, scholarships/grants, traineeships, health care benefits, tuition waivers, and unspecified assistantships available. Support available to part-time students. Financial award applicants required to submit FAFSA. *Faculty research:* Louisiana civil code, international law, commercial law, comparative law. *Unit head:* Madeleine Landrieu, Dean, 504-861-5847, Fax: 504-861-5677, E-mail: lmoore@loyno.edu. *Application contact:* Kimberly Jones, Director of Law Admissions, 504-861-5575, Fax: 504-861-5772, E-mail: ladmit@loyno.edu.
Website: http://www.loyno.edu/law/

Marquette University, Law School, Milwaukee, WI 53201-1881. Offers JD, JD/Certificate, JD/MA, JD/MBA. *Accreditation:* ABA. *Program availability:* Part-time, evening/weekend. *Entrance requirements:* For doctorate, LSAT, subscription to LSAC's Credential Assembly Service. Additional exam requirements/recommendations for international students: Required—TOEFL. Electronic applications accepted. *Expenses:* Contact institution. *Faculty research:* Constitutional law, sports law, dispute resolution, intellectual property, legal ethics.

Massachusetts School of Law at Andover, Professional Program, Andover, MA 01810. Offers JD. *Program availability:* Part-time, evening/weekend. *Entrance requirements:* For doctorate, Massachusetts School of Law Aptitude Test (MSLAT), interview. Additional exam requirements/recommendations for international students: Recommended—TOEFL. Electronic applications accepted.

McGill University, Faculty of Graduate and Postdoctoral Studies, Faculty of Law, Department of Law, Montréal, QC H3A 2T5, Canada. Offers LL M, DCL.

McGill University, Faculty of Graduate and Postdoctoral Studies, Faculty of Law, Institute of Air and Space Law, Montréal, QC H3A 2T5, Canada. Offers LL M, DCL, Graduate Certificate.

McGill University, Faculty of Graduate and Postdoctoral Studies, Faculty of Law, Institute of Comparative Law, Montréal, QC H3A 2T5, Canada. Offers LL M, DCL, Graduate Certificate.

Mercer University, Walter F. George School of Law, Macon, GA 31207. Offers JD, JD/MBA offered jointly with Eugene W. Stetson School of Business and Economics. *Accreditation:* ABA. *Faculty:* 29 full-time (11 women), 22 part-time/adjunct (4 women). *Students:* 372 full-time (190 women); includes 83 minority (45 Black or African American, non-Hispanic/Latino; 7 Asian, non-Hispanic/Latino; 26 Hispanic/Latino; 1 Native Hawaiian or other Pacific Islander, non-Hispanic/Latino; 4 Two or more races, non-Hispanic/Latino), 2 international. Average age 25. 788 applicants, 52% accepted, 122 enrolled. In 2017, 124 doctorates awarded. *Entrance requirements:* For doctorate, LSAT. Additional exam requirements/recommendations for international students: Recommended—TOEFL (minimum score 600 paper-based; 100 iBT). *Application deadline:* For fall admission, 3/15 priority date for domestic students. Applications are processed on a rolling basis. Application fee: $0. Electronic applications accepted. *Expenses:* $37,662 tuition, $300 technology fees. *Financial support:* In 2017–18, 325 students received support, including 14 fellowships (averaging $3,714 per year), 35 research assistantships (averaging $277 per year); career-related internships or fieldwork, Federal Work-Study, institutionally sponsored loans, scholarships/grants, and institutional work-study also available. Support available to part-time students. Financial award application deadline: 4/1; financial award applicants required to submit FAFSA. *Faculty research:* Legal ethics, environmental law, employment discrimination, statutory law, legal writing. *Unit head:* Cathy Cox, Dean, 478-301-2602, Fax: 478-301-2101, E-mail: cox_c@law.mercer.edu. *Application contact:* Judie Simpson, Admissions Specialist, 478-301-2605, Fax: 478-301-2989, E-mail: simpson_j@law.mercer.edu.
Website: http://www.mercer.edu/

Michigan State University College of Law, Graduate and Professional Programs, East Lansing, MI 48824-1300. Offers American legal system (LL M, MJ); global food law (LL M, MJ); intellectual property law (LL M, MJ); law (JD); legal studies (MLS). *Accreditation:* ABA. *Program availability:* Part-time. *Faculty:* 55 full-time (23 women), 77 part-time/adjunct (27 women). *Students:* 779 full-time (407 women), 77 part-time (50 women); includes 173 minority (57 Black or African American, non-Hispanic/Latino; 9 American Indian or Alaska Native, non-Hispanic/Latino; 28 Asian, non-Hispanic/Latino; 40 Hispanic/Latino; 2 Native Hawaiian or other Pacific Islander, non-Hispanic/Latino; 37 Two or more races, non-Hispanic/Latino), 91 international. Average age 24. *Entrance requirements:* For doctorate, LSAT. Additional exam requirements/recommendations for international students: Required—TOEFL (minimum score 600 paper-based), IELTS. *Application deadline:* For fall admission, 4/30 priority date for domestic students, 7/1 priority date for international students. Applications are processed on a rolling basis. Application fee: $60. Electronic applications accepted. *Expenses:* Tuition: Full-time $43,400. *Financial support:* Career-related internships or fieldwork, Federal Work-Study, scholarships/grants, and tuition waivers (full and partial) available. Support available to part-time students. Financial award application deadline: 4/1; financial award applicants required to submit FAFSA. *Faculty research:* International, constitutional, health, tax and environmental law; intellectual property, trial practice, corporate law. *Unit head:* Lawrence Ponoroff, Dean/Professor of Law, 517-432-6993, Fax: 517-432-6801, E-mail: lponoroff@law.msu.edu. *Application contact:* Melanie Jacobs, Senior Associate Dean of Admissions and International Programs, 517-432-0222, Fax: 517-432-0098, E-mail: admiss@law.msu.edu.
Website: http://www.law.msu.edu/

Mississippi College, School of Law, Jackson, MS 39201. Offers civil law studies (Certificate); law (JD); JD/MBA. *Accreditation:* ABA. *Degree requirements:* For doctorate, thesis/dissertation. *Entrance requirements:* For doctorate, LSAT, LDAS report. Additional exam requirements/recommendations for international students: Recommended—TOEFL, IELTS. Electronic applications accepted. *Expenses:* Contact institution.

Mitchell Hamline School of Law, Graduate and Professional Programs, Saint Paul, MN 55105-3076. Offers LL M, JD. *Accreditation:* ABA. *Program availability:* Part-time, evening/weekend, blended/hybrid learning. *Entrance requirements:* For master's, any law degree from the U.S. or foreign country; for doctorate, LSAT. Additional exam requirements/recommendations for international students: Required—TOEFL. Electronic applications accepted. *Faculty research:* Child protection, domestic violence, elder law, intellectual property law, preventive detention and post-release civil commitment.

Montclair State University, The Graduate School, College of Humanities and Social Sciences, MA Program in Law and Governance, Montclair, NJ 07043-1624. Offers conflict management and peace studies (MA); governance, compliance and regulation (MA); intellectual property (MA); law and governance (MA); legal management (MA). *Program availability:* Part-time, evening/weekend. *Degree requirements:* For master's, thesis or comprehensive exam. *Entrance requirements:* For master's, GRE General Test, minimum cumulative GPA of 2.75 for undergraduate work, 2 letters of recommendation, essay. Additional exam requirements/recommendations for international students: Required—TOEFL (minimum score 83 iBT) or IELTS (minimum score 6.5). Electronic applications accepted.

Law

New England Law–Boston, Graduate Programs, Boston, MA 02116-5687. Offers American law (LL M); law (JD). *Accreditation:* ABA. *Program availability:* Part-time, evening/weekend. *Faculty:* 42 full-time (16 women), 85 part-time/adjunct (38 women). *Students:* 380 full-time (247 women), 180 part-time (95 women); includes 195 minority (65 Black or African American, non-Hispanic/Latino; 1 American Indian or Alaska Native, non-Hispanic/Latino; 32 Asian, non-Hispanic/Latino; 69 Hispanic/Latino; 28 Two or more races, non-Hispanic/Latino), 15 international. *Entrance requirements:* For doctorate, LSAT, LSDAS. Additional exam requirements/recommendations for international students: Required—TOEFL (minimum score 600 paper-based; 100 iBT). *Application deadline:* For fall admission, 3/15 priority date for domestic and international students. Applications are processed on a rolling basis. Application fee: $65. Electronic applications accepted. *Expenses: Tuition:* Full-time $47,912; part-time $35,912 per year. *Required fees:* $80; $80 per unit. Tuition and fees vary according to class time and course load. *Financial support:* Fellowships, Federal Work-Study, scholarships/grants, and tuition waivers (full and partial) available. Financial award application deadline: 3/18; financial award applicants required to submit FAFSA. *Unit head:* John F. O'Brien, Dean, 617-422-7221, Fax: 617-422-7333. *Application contact:* Michelle L'Etoile, Director of Admissions, 617-422-7210, Fax: 617-422-7201, E-mail: admit@nesl.edu.
Website: https://www.nesl.edu/academics-faculty/programs

New York Law School, Graduate Programs, New York, NY 10013. Offers LL M, JD, JD/MA, JD/MBA. JD/MBA offered jointly with Baruch College of the City University of New York; JD/MA in forensic psychology offered jointly with John Jay College of Criminal Justice of the City University of New York. *Accreditation:* ABA. *Program availability:* Part-time, evening/weekend. *Faculty:* 53 full-time (25 women), 76 part-time/adjunct (28 women). *Students:* 737 full-time (447 women), 258 part-time (135 women); includes 327 minority (62 Black or African American, non-Hispanic/Latino; 1 American Indian or Alaska Native, non-Hispanic/Latino; 71 Asian, non-Hispanic/Latino; 166 Hispanic/Latino; 1 Native Hawaiian or other Pacific Islander, non-Hispanic/Latino; 26 Two or more races, non-Hispanic/Latino), 33 international. Average age 27. 2,752 applicants, 56% accepted, 386 enrolled. In 2017, 12 master's, 241 doctorates awarded. *Entrance requirements:* For master's, JD (for LL M); for doctorate, LSAT, undergraduate degree, letter of recommendation, resume, essay/personal statement. Additional exam requirements/recommendations for international students: Required—TOEFL (minimum score 600 paper-based; 100 iBT). *Application deadline:* For fall admission, 7/1 priority date for domestic and international students; for winter admission, 11/15 priority date for domestic and international students; for spring admission, 12/1 priority date for domestic and international students. Applications are processed on a rolling basis. Application fee: $0. Electronic applications accepted. *Expenses:* $50,717 per year full-time, $39,016 part-time (for JD); $1,500 per credit (for LL M). *Financial support:* In 2017–18, 698 students received support, including 107 fellowships (averaging $4,110 per year), 22 research assistantships (averaging $4,663 per year), 19 teaching assistantships (averaging $4,661 per year); career-related internships or fieldwork, Federal Work-Study, and scholarships/grants also available. Support available to part-time students. Financial award application deadline: 7/1; financial award applicants required to submit FAFSA. *Faculty research:* Immigration law, intellectual property, civil rights, family law, international law. *Unit head:* Anthony W. Crowell, Dean and President, 212-431-2840, Fax: 212-219-3752, E-mail: anthony.crowell@nyls.edu. *Application contact:* Ella Mae Estrada, Associate Dean for Enrollment Management, Financial Aid and Diversity Initiatives, 212-431-2888, Fax: 212-966-1522, E-mail: admissions@nyls.edu.
Website: http://www.nyls.edu

New York University, School of Law, New York, NY 10012-1019. Offers law (LL M, JD, JSD); law and business (Advanced Certificate); taxation (MSL, Advanced Certificate); JD/LL M; JD/MA; JD/MBA; JD/MPA; JD/MPP; JD/MSW; JD/MUP; JD/PhD. *Accreditation:* ABA. *Program availability:* Part-time, blended/hybrid learning. *Faculty:* 158 full-time (51 women), 204 part-time/adjunct (55 women). *Students:* 1,364 full-time (728 women); includes 394 minority (72 Black or African American, non-Hispanic/Latino; 147 Asian, non-Hispanic/Latino; 124 Hispanic/Latino; 51 Two or more races, non-Hispanic/Latino), 127 international. 6,534 applicants, 427 enrolled. In 2017, 516 master's, 484 doctorates awarded. *Entrance requirements:* For doctorate, LSAT (for JD). *Application deadline:* For fall admission, 2/15 for domestic students. Applications are processed on a rolling basis. Application fee: $85. Electronic applications accepted. *Expenses:* Contact institution. *Financial support:* Fellowships, research assistantships, teaching assistantships, career-related internships or fieldwork, Federal Work-Study, scholarships/grants, and loan repayment assistance available. Financial award application deadline: 4/15; financial award applicants required to submit FAFSA. *Faculty research:* International law, environmental law, corporate law, globalization of law, philosophy of law. *Unit head:* Trevor Morrison, Dean, 212-998-6000, Fax: 212-995-3150. *Application contact:* Cassandra Williams, Assistant Dean for Admissions, 212-998-6060, Fax: 212-995-4527.
Website: http://www.law.nyu.edu/

North Carolina Central University, School of Law, Durham, NC 27707. Offers JD, JD/MPA, JD/MPP, MBA/JD. *Accreditation:* ABA. *Program availability:* Part-time, evening/weekend. *Entrance requirements:* For doctorate, LSAT, LSDAS. Additional exam requirements/recommendations for international students: Required—TOEFL. *Application deadline:* For fall admission, 4/15 for domestic students. Application fee: $30. *Expenses:* Contact institution. *Financial support:* Application deadline: 5/1; applicants required to submit FAFSA. *Unit head:* Phyliss Craig-Taylor, Dean, 919-530-6333, E-mail: pcraigtaylor@nccu.edu. *Application contact:* Phyliss Craig-Taylor, Dean, 919-530-6333, E-mail: pcraigtaylor@nccu.edu.
Website: http://www.nccu.edu/law

Northeastern University, School of Law, Boston, MA 02115-5005. Offers LL M, MLS, JD, JD/MA, JD/MBA, JD/MELP, JD/MPH, JD/MS, JD/MSA/MBA, LL M/MA, LL M/MBA. JD/MPH offered jointly with Tufts University; JD/MSA/MBA with Graduate School of Professional Accounting; JD/MS with Program in Law and Public Policy; JD/MELP with Vermont Law School; and JD/MA with Brandeis University. *Accreditation:* ABA. *Program availability:* Online learning. *Faculty:* 48. *Students:* 657. In 2017, 32 master's, 175 doctorates awarded. *Application deadline:* Applications are processed on a rolling basis. Application fee: $75. Electronic applications accepted. *Expenses:* Contact institution. *Financial support:* Scholarships/grants available. Financial award applicants required to submit FAFSA. *Faculty research:* Human rights law, health law, criminal law, corporate/finance law, international law. *Unit head:* Jeremy R. Paul, Dean and Professor of Law, 617-373-3307, Fax: 617-373-8793, E-mail: j.paul@northeastern.edu. *Application contact:* 617-373-2395.
Website: http://www.northeastern.edu/law/

Northern Illinois University, College of Law, De Kalb, IL 60115-2854. Offers JD. *Accreditation:* ABA. *Program availability:* Part-time. *Faculty:* 22 full-time (11 women). *Students:* 227 full-time (96 women), 42 part-time (26 women); includes 67 minority (28 Black or African American, non-Hispanic/Latino; 11 Asian, non-Hispanic/Latino; 24 Hispanic/Latino; 2 Native Hawaiian or other Pacific Islander, non-Hispanic/Latino; 2 Two or more races, non-Hispanic/Latino), 2 international. Average age 28. 626 applicants, 51% accepted, 95 enrolled. In 2017, 70 doctorates awarded. *Entrance requirements:* For doctorate, LSAT. Additional exam requirements/recommendations for international students: Required—TOEFL. *Application deadline:* For fall admission, 4/1 priority date for domestic and international students. Applications are processed on a rolling basis.

Electronic applications accepted. *Expenses:* Contact institution. *Financial support:* In 2017–18, 8 teaching assistantships were awarded; research assistantships, career-related internships or fieldwork, Federal Work-Study, tuition waivers (full and partial), and unspecified assistantships also available. Support available to part-time students. Financial award application deadline: 3/1; financial award applicants required to submit FAFSA. *Faculty research:* Criminal practice, intellectual property, environmental law, taxation. *Unit head:* Mark Cordes, Dean, 815-753-5300, Fax: 815-753-8552, E-mail: edan@niu.edu. *Application contact:* Amanda Noascono, Director of Admissions and Financial Aid, 815-753-8595, Fax: 815-753-5680, E-mail: law-admit@niu.edu.
Website: http://law.niu.edu/

Northern Kentucky University, Chase College of Law, Highland Heights, KY 41099. Offers JD, JD/MBA, JD/MBI. *Accreditation:* ABA. *Program availability:* Part-time, evening/weekend. *Faculty:* 32 full-time (12 women), 38 part-time/adjunct (11 women). *Students:* 329 full-time (168 women), 125 part-time (62 women); includes 65 minority (42 Black or African American, non-Hispanic/Latino; 4 American Indian or Alaska Native, non-Hispanic/Latino; 6 Asian, non-Hispanic/Latino; 12 Hispanic/Latino; 1 Two or more races, non-Hispanic/Latino). Average age 27. 567 applicants, 69% accepted, 145 enrolled. In 2017, 93 doctorates awarded. *Entrance requirements:* For doctorate, LSAT, bachelor's degree. Additional exam requirements/recommendations for international students: Required—TOEFL (minimum score 92 iBT), IELTS (minimum score 6.5). *Application deadline:* For fall admission, 4/1 priority date for domestic and international students; for summer admission, 3/15 priority date for domestic students, 3/15 for international students. Applications are processed on a rolling basis. Application fee: $40. Electronic applications accepted. *Expenses:* Contact institution. *Financial support:* Fellowships, research assistantships, career-related internships or fieldwork, Federal Work-Study, scholarships/grants, and unspecified assistantships available. Support available to part-time students. Financial award application deadline: 3/1; financial award applicants required to submit FAFSA. *Unit head:* Michael Whiteman, Co-Acting Dean, 859-572-5717, E-mail: whiteman@nku.edu. *Application contact:* Ashley Folger Gray, Director of Admissions, 859-572-5841, E-mail: graya4@nku.edu.
Website: http://nku.edu/chaselaw

Northwestern University, Pritzker School of Law, Chicago, IL 60611-3069. Offers international human rights (LL M); law (JD); law and business (LL M); science law (MSL); tax (LL M in Tax); JD/LL M; JD/MBA; JD/PhD; LL M/Certificate. Executive LL M programs offered in Madrid (Spain), Seoul (South Korea), and Tel Aviv (Israel). *Accreditation:* ABA. *Entrance requirements:* For master's, law degree or equivalent, letter of recommendation, resume; for doctorate, LSAT, 1 letter of recommendation, resume. Additional exam requirements/recommendations for international students: Required—TOEFL. Electronic applications accepted. *Expenses:* Contact institution. *Faculty research:* Constitutional law, corporate law, international law, law and social policy, ethical studies.

Nova Southeastern University, Shepard Broad College of Law, Fort Lauderdale, FL 33314. Offers education law (MS), including cybersecurity law, education law advocacy, exceptional education; employment law (MS), including cybersecurity law, employee relations law, human resource managerial law; health law (MS, JD), including clinical research law and regulatory compliance (MS), cybersecurity law (MS), health care administrative law (MS), regulatory compliance (MS), risk management (MS); international law (JD); law and policy (MS), including cybersecurity law; JD/DO; JD/M Acc; JD/M Tax; JD/MBA; JD/MPA; JD/MS; JD/PhD. *Accreditation:* ABA. *Program availability:* Part-time, evening/weekend, 100% online, blended/hybrid learning. *Faculty:* 56 full-time (30 women), 41 part-time/adjunct (14 women). *Students:* 566 full-time (297 women), 138 part-time (84 women); includes 365 minority (62 Black or African American, non-Hispanic/Latino; 3 American Indian or Alaska Native, non-Hispanic/Latino; 23 Asian, non-Hispanic/Latino; 264 Hispanic/Latino; 3 Native Hawaiian or other Pacific Islander, non-Hispanic/Latino; 10 Two or more races, non-Hispanic/Latino), 26 international. Average age 29. 1,070 applicants, 53% accepted, 224 enrolled. In 2017, 45 master's, 225 doctorates awarded. *Degree requirements:* For master's, thesis optional, capstone research project; for doctorate, rigorous upper-level writing fulfilled through faculty-supervised seminar paper, law journal article, workshop, or other research; 6 credits' experiential learning. *Entrance requirements:* For master's, regionally-accredited undergraduate degree; at least 2 years' experience in related field (for employment law and health law); for doctorate, LSAT. Additional exam requirements/recommendations for international students: Recommended—TOEFL (minimum score 600 paper-based; 100 iBT), IELTS (minimum score 7). *Application deadline:* For fall admission, 5/1 priority date for domestic and international students; for winter admission, 12/12 for domestic and international students; for spring admission, 3/31 for domestic and international students; for summer admission, 4/1 for domestic and international students. Applications are processed on a rolling basis. Application fee: $0. Electronic applications accepted. *Expenses:* $40,060 full-time; $30,280 part-time. *Financial support:* In 2017–18, 211 students received support, including 221 fellowships (averaging $12,000 per year); Federal Work-Study, institutionally sponsored loans, scholarships/grants, and unspecified assistantships also available. Support available to part-time students. Financial award application deadline: 4/15; financial award applicants required to submit FAFSA. *Faculty research:* Legal issues in health law, international law, the legal profession, family law, civil rights. *Unit head:* Jon M. Garon, Dean, 954-262-6101, Fax: 954-262-2862, E-mail: garon@nova.edu. *Application contact:* William Daniel Perez, Assistant Dean of Admissions, 954-262-6121, Fax: 954-262-3844, E-mail: wperez1@nova.edu.
Website: http://www.law.nova.edu/

Ohio Northern University, Claude W. Pettit College of Law, Ada, OH 45810-1599. Offers LL M, JD. *Accreditation:* ABA. *Faculty:* 18 full-time (9 women), 3 part-time/adjunct (1 woman). *Students:* 187 full-time (94 women), 1 part-time (0 women); includes 38 minority (17 Black or African American, non-Hispanic/Latino; 2 American Indian or Alaska Native, non-Hispanic/Latino; 6 Asian, non-Hispanic/Latino; 9 Hispanic/Latino; 4 Two or more races, non-Hispanic/Latino), 26 international. Average age 27. 471 applicants, 41% accepted, 55 enrolled. In 2017, 24 master's, 54 doctorates awarded. *Entrance requirements:* For doctorate, LSAT. Additional exam requirements/recommendations for international students: Required—TOEFL. *Application deadline:* Applications are processed on a rolling basis. Electronic applications accepted. *Expenses:* Contact institution. *Financial support:* Career-related internships or fieldwork, Federal Work-Study, institutionally sponsored loans, and scholarships/grants available. Financial award applicants required to submit FAFSA. *Faculty research:* Constitutional law, environmental law, business law and taxation, criminal law, public interest law, death penalty for women and juveniles, international human rights, sports violence. *Unit head:* Dr. David Crago, Dean, 419-772-2205, Fax: 419-772-3051, E-mail: d-crago@onu.edu. *Application contact:* Rachel Frey, Director of Law Admissions, 419-772-2213, Fax: 419-772-2758, E-mail: r-frey@onu.edu.
Website: http://www.law.onu.edu/

The Ohio State University, Moritz College of Law, Columbus, OH 43210. Offers LL M, MSL, JD, JD/MA, JD/MBA, JD/MD, JD/MHA, JD/MPH. *Accreditation:* ABA. *Entrance requirements:* Additional exam requirements/recommendations for international students: Required—TOEFL (minimum score 650 paper-based; 100 iBT). Electronic applications accepted. *Expenses:* Contact institution. *Faculty research:* Alternative dispute resolution, law and policy, criminal law, intellectual property, big data and governance.

Oklahoma City University, School of Law, Oklahoma City, OK 73106-1402. Offers LL M, JD, JD/MBA. *Accreditation:* ABA. *Program availability:* Part-time, evening/weekend. *Faculty:* 16 full-time (5 women), 21 part-time/adjunct (7 women). *Students:* 387 full-time (208 women), 17 part-time (11 women); includes 148 minority (28 Black or African American, non-Hispanic/Latino; 29 American Indian or Alaska Native, non-Hispanic/Latino; 20 Asian, non-Hispanic/Latino; 43 Hispanic/Latino; 1 Native Hawaiian or other Pacific Islander, non-Hispanic/Latino; 27 Two or more races, non-Hispanic/Latino), 6 international. Average age 28. 560 applicants, 71% accepted, 158 enrolled. In 2017, 131 doctorates awarded. *Entrance requirements:* For doctorate, LSAT, bachelor's degree from accredited undergraduate institution (except for OCU students admitted through the Oxford plan). Additional exam requirements/recommendations for international students: Required—TOEFL (minimum score 100 iBT). *Application deadline:* For fall admission, 8/1 for domestic and international students. Application fee: $50. Electronic applications accepted. *Expenses:* $35,630. *Financial support:* In 2017–18, 300 students received support. Career-related internships or fieldwork, Federal Work-Study, institutionally sponsored loans, scholarships/grants, and tuition waivers (full and partial) available. Support available to part-time students. Financial award application deadline: 2/1; financial award applicants required to submit FAFSA. *Faculty research:* Family law, environmental law, consumer law, alternative dispute resolution, criminal law and procedure. *Unit head:* Lee Peoples, Interim Dean, 405-208-5440, Fax: 405-208-6041, E-mail: lpeoples@okcu.edu. *Application contact:* Dr. Laurie W. Jones, Associate Dean of Admissions, Law School, 405-208-5354, Fax: 405-208-5814, E-mail: ljones@okcu.edu.
Website: http://law.okcu.edu/

Pace University, Elisabeth Haub School of Law, White Plains, NY 10603. Offers comparative legal studies (LL M); environmental law (LL M, SJD), including energy and climate change law (LL M), global environmental law (LL M); law (JD); JD/LL M; JD/MA; JD/MBA; JD/MEM; JD/MPA; JD/MS. JD/MA offered jointly with Sarah Lawrence College; JD/MEM offered jointly with Yale University School of Forestry and Environmental Studies. *Accreditation:* ABA. *Program availability:* Part-time. *Faculty:* 26 full-time (11 women), 52 part-time/adjunct (19 women). *Students:* 548 (301 women); includes 154 minority (31 Black or African American, non-Hispanic/Latino; 3 American Indian or Alaska Native, non-Hispanic/Latino; 20 Asian, non-Hispanic/Latino; 54 Hispanic/Latino; 1 Native Hawaiian or other Pacific Islander, non-Hispanic/Latino; 45 Two or more races, non-Hispanic/Latino), 9 international. Average age 26. 1,443 applicants, 53% accepted, 217 enrolled. In 2017, 20 master's, 170 doctorates awarded. *Degree requirements:* For doctorate, thesis/dissertation (for some programs), extensive thesis proposal (for SJD). *Entrance requirements:* For master's, writing sample; for doctorate, LSAT (for JD). Additional exam requirements/recommendations for international students: Required—TOEFL (minimum score 100 iBT); Recommended—TWE. *Application deadline:* For fall admission, 6/1 priority date for domestic students; for winter admission, 11/15 priority date for domestic students. Applications are processed on a rolling basis. Application fee: $65. Electronic applications accepted. *Expenses:* Contact institution. *Financial support:* In 2017–18, 473 students received support. Fellowships, research assistantships, career-related internships or fieldwork, Federal Work-Study, institutionally sponsored loans, scholarships/grants, and unspecified assistantships available. Support available to part-time students. Financial award application deadline: 2/1; financial award applicants required to submit FAFSA. *Faculty research:* Reform of energy regulations, international law, land use law, prosecutorial misconduct, corporation law. *Unit head:* David Yassky, Dean, 914-422-4407, E-mail: dyassky@law.pace.edu. *Application contact:* Cathy Alexander, Assistant Dean, 914-422-4210, Fax: 914-989-8714, E-mail: calexander@law.pace.edu.
Website: http://www.law.pace.edu/

Penn State University–Dickinson Law, Graduate and Professional Programs, Carlisle, PA 17013. Offers LL M, JD. *Accreditation:* ABA. *Faculty:* 21 full-time (12 women), 24 part-time/adjunct (7 women). *Students:* 193 full-time (76 women); includes 37 minority (8 Black or African American, non-Hispanic/Latino; 8 Asian, non-Hispanic/Latino; 15 Hispanic/Latino; 6 Two or more races, non-Hispanic/Latino), 9 international. 671 applicants, 39% accepted, 73 enrolled. In 2017, 61 doctorates awarded. *Entrance requirements:* For doctorate, LSAT. *Application deadline:* Applications are processed on a rolling basis. Application fee: $0. Electronic applications accepted. *Expenses:* Tuition, state resident: full-time $48,000; part-time $2000 per credit hour. Tuition, nonresident: full-time $48,000; part-time $2000 per credit hour. *Required fees:* $686. *Financial support:* Research assistantships, Federal Work-Study, and scholarships/grants available. Financial award application deadline: 4/15; financial award applicants required to submit FAFSA. *Unit head:* Gary S. Gildin, Dean, 717-240-5238, Fax: 717-240-5213, E-mail: gsg2@psu.edu. *Application contact:* Bekah A. Saidman-Krauss, Assistant Dean of Admissions and Financial Aid, 717-240-5207, E-mail: ras1075@psu.edu.
Website: https://dickinsonlaw.psu.edu/

Penn State University Park, Penn State Law, University Park, PA 16802. Offers LL M, JD, SJD. *Accreditation:* ABA. *Faculty:* 45 full-time (21 women), 16 part-time/adjunct (5 women). *Students:* 495 full-time (240 women). 2,023 applicants, 45% accepted, 192 enrolled. *Entrance requirements:* For master's, BA or LL B in law; for doctorate, LSAT. Additional exam requirements/recommendations for international students: Required—TOEFL, IELTS. *Application deadline:* For fall admission, 3/31 for domestic students. Applications are processed on a rolling basis. Application fee: $60. Electronic applications accepted. *Unit head:* Hari M. Osofsky, Dean, 814-863-1521. *Application contact:* Amanda DiPolvere, Assistant Dean, Admissions and Financial Aid, 800-840-1122, E-mail: admissions@pennstatelaw.psu.edu.
Website: https://pennstatelaw.psu.edu/

Pepperdine University, School of Law, Juris Doctor Program, Malibu, CA 90263. Offers JD, JD/M Div, JD/MBA, JD/MDR, JD/MPP. *Accreditation:* ABA. *Students:* 496 full-time (263 women), 5 part-time (2 women); includes 170 minority (30 Black or African American, non-Hispanic/Latino; 3 American Indian or Alaska Native, non-Hispanic/Latino; 42 Asian, non-Hispanic/Latino; 75 Hispanic/Latino; 30 Two or more races, non-Hispanic/Latino), 13 international. Average age 26. 2,077 applicants, 42% accepted, 156 enrolled. In 2017, 220 doctorates awarded. *Entrance requirements:* For doctorate, LSAT, 2 letters of recommendation, resume, personal statement, registration with the Credential Assembly Service (CAS). Additional exam requirements/recommendations for international students: Required—TOEFL. *Application deadline:* For fall admission, 2/1 priority date for domestic students, 6/1 priority date for international students. Applications are processed on a rolling basis. Application fee: $60. *Expenses:* Contact institution. *Financial support:* Federal Work-Study, institutionally sponsored loans, and scholarships/grants available. Financial award application deadline: 4/1; financial award applicants required to submit FAFSA. *Unit head:* Dr. Paul L. Caron, Dean/Professor of Law, 310-506-4676, E-mail: paul.caron@pepperdine.edu. *Application contact:* Shannon Phillips, Assistant Dean, 310-506-4631, Fax: 310-506-4266, E-mail: shannon.phillips@pepperdine.edu.
Website: http://law.pepperdine.edu/degrees-programs/juris-doctor/

Pepperdine University, School of Law, Master of Laws Programs, Malibu, CA 90263. Offers dispute resolution (LL M); entertainment, media, and sports law (LL M); international commercial arbitration (LL M); international commercial law and arbitration (LL M); international commercial law and dispute resolution (LL M); U.S. law and dispute resolution (LL M); United States law (LL M). *Students:* 34 full-time (19 women), 33 part-time (17 women); includes 7 minority (2 Black or African American, non-Hispanic/Latino; 2 Asian, non-Hispanic/Latino; 3 Hispanic/Latino), 42 international. Average age 34. In 2017, 18 master's awarded. *Entrance requirements:* For master's, GRE General Test or LSAT, JD from ABA-accredited institution. Additional exam requirements/recommendations for international students: Required—TOEFL. *Application deadline:* For fall admission, 2/15 for domestic and international students; for spring admission, 8/15 for domestic and international students. Applications are processed on a rolling basis. Application fee: $60. Electronic applications accepted. *Expenses:* Contact institution. *Financial support:* Career-related internships or fieldwork, Federal Work-Study, institutionally sponsored loans, and scholarships/grants available. Support available to part-time students. Financial award application deadline: 4/1; financial award applicants required to submit FAFSA. *Unit head:* Dr. Peter Robinson, Director, Institute for Dispute Resolution, 310-506-4655, Fax: 310-506-4266, E-mail: peter.robinson@pepperdine.edu. *Application contact:* Shellee S. Warnes, Assistant Director, Academic Programs, 310-506-7455, Fax: 310-506-4266, E-mail: shellee.warnes@pepperdine.edu.
Website: https://law.pepperdine.edu/degrees-programs/master-of-laws/

Pontifical Catholic University of Puerto Rico, School of Law, Ponce, PR 00717-0777. Offers JD. *Accreditation:* ABA. *Program availability:* Part-time, evening/weekend. *Entrance requirements:* For doctorate, LSAT, PAEG, 3 letters of recommendation.

Pontificia Universidad Catolica Madre y Maestra, Graduate School, Faculty of Social and Administrative Sciences, Santiago, Dominican Republic. Offers business administration (MBA), including business development, finance, international business, management skills (M Mgmt, MBA), marketing, operations, strategic cost management, strategy, tourist destination planning and management; law (LL M), including civil law, corporate business law, criminal law, international relations, real estate law; management (M Mgmt), including higher financial management, insurance program administration, management skills (M Mgmt, MBA); psychology (MA), including clinical child and adolescent psychology, forensic psychology; strategic human resources (EMBA).

Purdue University Global, School of Criminal Justice, Davenport, IA 52807. Offers corrections (MSCJ); global issues in criminal justice (MSCJ); law (MSCJ); leadership and executive management (MSCJ); policing (MSCJ). *Program availability:* Part-time, evening/weekend, online learning. *Entrance requirements:* Additional exam requirements/recommendations for international students: Required—TOEFL (minimum score 550 paper-based; 80 iBT). Electronic applications accepted.

Queen's University at Kingston, Faculty of Law, Kingston, ON K7L 3N6, Canada. Offers LL M, JD, JD/MBA, JD/MIR, JD/MPA. *Program availability:* Part-time. *Degree requirements:* For master's, thesis. *Entrance requirements:* For doctorate, LSAT, minimum 2 years of college. Additional exam requirements/recommendations for international students: Required—TOEFL, TWE. *Faculty research:* Labor relations law, tax law and policy, criminal law and policy, critical legal theories, international legal relations.

Quinnipiac University, School of Law, Hamden, CT 06518-1940. Offers LL M, JD, JD/MBA, JD/MELP. *Accreditation:* ABA. *Program availability:* Part-time, evening/weekend. *Entrance requirements:* For doctorate, LSAT. Additional exam requirements/recommendations for international students: Recommended—TOEFL. Electronic applications accepted. Application fee is waived when completed online. *Expenses:* Contact institution. *Faculty research:* Sentencing, death penalty, public health law, tax law, legal history.

Regent University, Graduate School, Robertson School of Government, Virginia Beach, VA 23464. Offers government (MA), including American government, healthcare policy and ethics (MA, MPA), international relations, law and public policy, national security studies, political communication, political theory, religion and politics; national security studies (MA), including cybersecurity, homeland security, international security, Middle East politics; public administration (MPA), including emergency management and homeland security, federal government, general public administration, healthcare policy and ethics (MA, MPA), law, nonprofit administration and faith-based organizations, public leadership and management, servant leadership. *Program availability:* Part-time, evening/weekend, 100% online, blended/hybrid learning. *Faculty:* 8 full-time (1 woman), 20 part-time/adjunct (3 women). *Students:* 39 full-time (23 women), 137 part-time (78 women); includes 83 minority (49 Black or African American, non-Hispanic/Latino; 1 American Indian or Alaska Native, non-Hispanic/Latino; 7 Asian, non-Hispanic/Latino; 15 Hispanic/Latino; 11 Two or more races, non-Hispanic/Latino). Average age 35. 345 applicants, 31% accepted, 57 enrolled. In 2017, 38 master's awarded. *Degree requirements:* For master's, thesis optional, internship. *Entrance requirements:* For master's, GRE General Test or LSAT, personal essay, writing sample, resume, college transcripts. Additional exam requirements/recommendations for international students: Required—TOEFL (minimum score 577 paper-based). *Application deadline:* For fall admission, 5/1 priority date for domestic students; for spring admission, 11/1 priority date for domestic students. Applications are processed on a rolling basis. Application fee: $50. Electronic applications accepted. *Expenses:* $650 per credit; $300 technology fee per semester. *Financial support:* In 2017–18, 116 students received support. Career-related internships or fieldwork, scholarships/grants, and unspecified assistantships available. Support available to part-time students. *Faculty research:* International relations and politics, public administration, leadership and ethics, Biblical law, Constitutional law and Supreme Court. *Unit head:* Dr. Eric Patterson, Dean, 757-352-4616, Fax: 757-352-4735, E-mail: epatterson@regent.edu. *Application contact:* Heidi Cece, Assistant Vice President of Enrollment Management, 800-373-5504, Fax: 757-352-4381, E-mail: admissions@regent.edu.
Website: https://www.regent.edu/robertson-school-of-government/

Regent University, Graduate School, School of Law, Virginia Beach, VA 23464. Offers American legal studies (LL M); human rights (LL M); law (MA, JD), including advanced paralegal studies (MA), alternative dispute resolution (MA), business (MA), criminal justice (MA), general legal studies (MA), human resources management (MA), human rights and rule of law (MA), national security (MA), non-profit organizational law (MA), regulatory compliance (MA), wealth management and financial planning (MA); JD/MA; JD/MBA. *Accreditation:* ABA. *Program availability:* Part-time, 100% online, blended/hybrid learning. *Faculty:* 16 full-time (5 women), 76 part-time/adjunct (22 women). *Students:* 313 full-time (181 women), 248 part-time (175 women); includes 240 minority (155 Black or African American, non-Hispanic/Latino; 3 American Indian or Alaska Native, non-Hispanic/Latino; 15 Asian, non-Hispanic/Latino; 45 Hispanic/Latino; 2 Native Hawaiian or other Pacific Islander, non-Hispanic/Latino; 20 Two or more races, non-Hispanic/Latino), 59 international. Average age 35. 923 applicants, 36% accepted, 188 enrolled. In 2017, 138 master's, 80 doctorates awarded. *Entrance requirements:* For master's, college transcripts, resume, personal statement; for doctorate, LSAT, minimum undergraduate GPA of 3.0, official transcripts, 2 letters of recommendation, resume, personal statement. Additional exam requirements/recommendations for international students: Required—TOEFL (minimum score 600 paper-based). *Application deadline:* For fall admission, 3/1 for domestic students. Applications are processed on a rolling basis. Application fee: $50. Electronic applications accepted. *Expenses:* $650 per credit (MA, LL M); $1,140 per credit (JD); $300 per semester

Law

technology fee. *Financial support:* In 2017–18, 459 students received support. Career-related internships or fieldwork, scholarships/grants, and unspecified assistantships available. Support available to part-time students. *Faculty research:* Family law, Constitutional law, law and culture, evidence and practice, intellectual property. *Unit head:* Michael Hernandez, Dean, 757-352-4040, Fax: 757-352-4595, E-mail: michher@regent.edu. *Application contact:* Ernie Walton, Assistant Dean of Admissions, 757-352-4315, E-mail: lawschool@regent.edu.
Website: https://www.regent.edu/school-of-law/

Roger Williams University, School of Law, Bristol, RI 02809-5171. Offers MSL, JD, JD/MLRHR, JD/MMA, JD/MCRP, JD/MPA, JD/MS, JD/MSCJ. JD/MMA and JD/MLRHR offered jointly with University of Rhode Island. *Accreditation:* ABA. *Program availability:* Part-time. *Faculty:* 27 full-time (16 women), 31 part-time/adjunct (14 women). *Students:* 433 full-time (227 women), 7 part-time (4 women); includes 113 minority (39 Black or African American, non-Hispanic/Latino; 1 American Indian or Alaska Native, non-Hispanic/Latino; 12 Asian, non-Hispanic/Latino; 43 Hispanic/Latino; 18 Two or more races, non-Hispanic/Latino), 1 international. Average age 27. 849 applicants, 71% accepted, 161 enrolled. In 2017, 2 master's, 121 doctorates awarded. *Entrance requirements:* For master's, GRE, GMAT; for doctorate, LSAT. Additional exam requirements/recommendations for international students: Required—TOEFL (minimum score 600 paper-based; 100 iBT). *Application deadline:* For fall admission, 4/1 priority date for domestic and international students. Applications are processed on a rolling basis. Application fee: $60. Electronic applications accepted. *Expenses: Tuition:* Full-time $14,936; part-time $9958 per semester. *Required fees:* $258; $258 per degree program. Tuition and fees vary according to program. *Financial support:* In 2017–18, 255 students received support, including 9 fellowships (averaging $1,739 per year), 51 research assistantships (averaging $931 per year); Federal Work-Study also available. Financial award application deadline: 3/15; financial award applicants required to submit FAFSA. *Faculty research:* Civil rights, Constitutional law, contract law, intellectual property, conflicts of law, national security, international law. *Unit head:* Michael Yelnosky, Dean, 401-254-4500, Fax: 401-254-3525, E-mail: myelnosky@rwu.edu. *Application contact:* Michael W. Donnelly-Boylen, Assistant Dean of Admissions, 401-254-4555, Fax: 401-254-4516, E-mail: mdonnelly-boylen@rwu.edu.
Website: http://law.rwu.edu

Rutgers University–Camden, School of Law, Camden, NJ 08102. Offers JD, JD/DO, JD/MA, JD/MBA, JD/MCRP, JD/MD, JD/MPA, JD/MPH, JD/MS, JD/MSW, JD/MCRP, JD/MA, JD/MPA, JD/MSW, JD/MS offered jointly with Rutgers, The State University of New Jersey, New Brunswick; JD/MPA, JD/MD, JD/DO with University of Medicine and Dentistry of New Jersey. *Accreditation:* ABA. *Program availability:* Part-time, evening/weekend. *Entrance requirements:* For doctorate, LSAT. Additional exam requirements/recommendations for international students: Recommended—TOEFL. Electronic applications accepted. *Expenses:* Contact institution. *Faculty research:* International law, commercial law, public law, health law, constitutional law, jurisprudence.

Rutgers University–Newark, School of Law, Newark, NJ 07102-3094. Offers JD, JD/MA, JD/MBA, JD/MCRP, JD/MD, JD/MSW, JD/PhD. JD/MCRP, JD/PhD offered jointly with Rutgers, The State University of New Jersey, New Brunswick. *Accreditation:* ABA. *Program availability:* Part-time, evening/weekend. *Entrance requirements:* For doctorate, LSAT. *Expenses:* Contact institution. *Faculty research:* Civil rights and liberties, women and the law, international human rights and world order, corporate law, employment law.

St. John's University, School of Law, Program in Law, Queens, NY 11439. Offers JD, JD/LL M, MA/JD, MBA/JD. *Accreditation:* ABA. *Program availability:* Part-time, evening/weekend. *Students:* 648 full-time (299 women), 83 part-time (43 women); includes 192 minority (54 Black or African American, non-Hispanic/Latino; 48 Asian, non-Hispanic/Latino; 69 Hispanic/Latino; 21 Two or more races, non-Hispanic/Latino), 20 international. Average age 25. 2,755 applicants, 40% accepted, 251 enrolled. In 2017, 215 doctorates awarded. *Entrance requirements:* For doctorate, LSAT or GRE, bachelor's degree, personal statement, CAS report, 2 letters of recommendation. Additional exam requirements/recommendations for international students: Recommended—TOEFL (minimum score 600 paper-based; 100 iBT), IELTS (minimum score 7). *Application deadline:* For fall admission, 3/15 priority date for domestic and international students. Applications are processed on a rolling basis. Application fee: $0. Electronic applications accepted. *Expenses:* $2,110 per credit tuition, $170 per semester fees; tuition may vary by program. *Financial support:* Research assistantships, teaching assistantships, and scholarships/grants available. Financial award application deadline: 2/1; financial award applicants required to submit FAFSA. *Unit head:* Michael A. Simons, Esq., Dean, 718-990-6602, Fax: 718-990-6694, E-mail: simonsm@stjohns.edu. *Application contact:* Alicia Meehan, Assistant Dean for Admissions and Recruitment, 718-990-6474, E-mail: lawinfo@stjohns.edu.
Website: http://www.stjohns.edu/law/programs-and-majors/juris-doctor

Saint Joseph's University, College of Arts and Sciences, Department of Criminal Justice, Philadelphia, PA 19131-1395. Offers behavior analysis (MS, Post-Master's Certificate); behavior management (MS); criminal justice (MS); federal law enforcement (MS); intelligence and crime analysis (MS). *Program availability:* Part-time, evening/weekend, 100% online, blended/hybrid learning. *Faculty:* 4 full-time (3 women), 33 part-time/adjunct (16 women). *Students:* 18 full-time (13 women), 371 part-time (272 women); includes 105 minority (83 Black or African American, non-Hispanic/Latino; 2 American Indian or Alaska Native, non-Hispanic/Latino; 4 Asian, non-Hispanic/Latino; 16 Hispanic/Latino). Average age 32. 189 applicants, 66% accepted, 94 enrolled. In 2017, 142 master's, 26 other advanced degrees awarded. *Degree requirements:* For master's, thesis optional. *Entrance requirements:* For master's, 2 letters of recommendation, personal statement, resume, official transcripts, minimum GPA of 3.0. Additional exam requirements/recommendations for international students: Required—TOEFL (minimum score 550 paper-based; 80 iBT). *Application deadline:* For fall admission, 7/15 for international students; for spring admission, 11/1 for international students. Applications are processed on a rolling basis. Application fee: $35. Electronic applications accepted. *Expenses:* Contact institution. *Financial support:* In 2017–18, 5 students received support. Federal Work-Study and unspecified assistantships available. Financial award application deadline: 5/1; financial award applicants required to submit FAFSA. *Faculty research:* Ethics in policing, multiculturalism, behavior analysis. *Total annual research expenditures:* $17,309. *Unit head:* Sylvia M. DeSantis, Director, 610-660-3131, E-mail: gradcas@sju.edu. *Application contact:* Lauren Weiss, Graduate Admissions, College of Arts and Sciences, 610-660-3131, E-mail: gradcas@sju.edu.
Website: http://www.sju.edu/majors-programs/graduate-arts-sciences/masters/criminal-justice-ms

Saint Louis University, School of Law, St. Louis, MO 63108. Offers LL M, JD. *Accreditation:* ABA. *Program availability:* Part-time, evening/weekend. *Degree requirements:* For master's, thesis (for some programs). *Entrance requirements:* For master's, JD or equivalent; for doctorate, LSAT, letters of recommendation, resume, personal statement, LSDAS. Additional exam requirements/recommendations for international students: Required—TOEFL (minimum score 590 paper-based). Electronic applications accepted. *Expenses:* Contact institution. *Faculty research:* Health law, employment law, international comparative law, lawyering skills (clinical).

St. Mary's University, School of Law, LL M Program, San Antonio, TX 78228. Offers American legal studies (LL M); international and comparative law (LL M); international criminal law (LL M). *Program availability:* Part-time. *Faculty:* 45 full-time (13 women), 68 part-time/adjunct (22 women). *Students:* 28 full-time (7 women), 3 part-time (2 women); includes 27 minority (5 Black or African American, non-Hispanic/Latino; 9 Asian, non-Hispanic/Latino; 13 Hispanic/Latino). Average age 36. 41 applicants, 45% accepted, 7 enrolled. In 2017, 3 master's awarded. *Degree requirements:* For master's, thesis, 24 hours of academic credit. *Entrance requirements:* For master's, official transcripts, personal statement, resume, 2 letters of recommendation. Additional exam requirements/recommendations for international students: Required—TOEFL (minimum score 550 paper-based; 80 iBT), IELTS (minimum score 6). *Application deadline:* Applications are processed on a rolling basis. Application fee: $0. Electronic applications accepted. *Expenses:* Contact institution. *Unit head:* Shannon Sevier, Director, Graduate Law Programs, 210-431-4235, E-mail: ssevier@stmarytx.edu. *Application contact:* Lupe Valdez, Legal Secretary, 210-431-6878, E-mail: gvaldez@stmarytx.edu.
Website: https://law.stmarytx.edu/academics/programs/ll-m-degrees/

St. Mary's University, School of Law, Master of Jurisprudence Program, San Antonio, TX 78228. Offers business and entrepreneurship law (MJ); commercial law (MJ); compliance, business law and risk (MJ); criminal justice (MJ); education law (MJ); environmental law (MJ); health law (MJ); healthcare compliance (MJ); international comparative law (MJ); military and national security law (MJ); natural resource law (MJ); tax law (MJ). *Program availability:* Part-time, evening/weekend. *Faculty:* 45 full-time (13 women), 68 part-time/adjunct (22 women). *Students:* 10 full-time (7 women), 26 part-time (18 women); includes 25 minority (2 Black or African American, non-Hispanic/Latino; 1 Asian, non-Hispanic/Latino; 22 Hispanic/Latino). Average age 32. 37 applicants, 92% accepted, 22 enrolled. In 2017, 12 master's awarded. *Degree requirements:* For master's, 30 credits, minimum GPA of 2.0. *Entrance requirements:* For master's, official transcripts, personal statement, resume, 2 letters of recommendation, proof of four-year undergraduate degree from accredited U.S. college/university or foreign institution approved by government or accrediting authority. Additional exam requirements/recommendations for international students: Required—TOEFL (minimum score 550 paper-based; 80 iBT), IELTS (minimum score 6). *Application deadline:* Applications are processed on a rolling basis. Application fee: $0. Electronic applications accepted. *Expenses:* Contact institution. *Financial support:* Fellowships, research assistantships, Federal Work-Study, scholarships/grants, and unspecified assistantships available. Financial award applicants required to submit FAFSA. *Unit head:* Shannon Sevier, Director, Graduate Law Programs, 210-431-4235, E-mail: ssevier@stmarytx.edu. *Application contact:* Shannon Sevier, Director, Graduate Law Programs, 210-431-4235, E-mail: ssevier@stmarytx.edu.
Website: https://law.stmarytx.edu/academics/programs/master-of-jurisprudence/

St. Mary's University, School of Law, St. Mary's School of Law, San Antonio, TX 78228. Offers JD. *Accreditation:* ABA. *Program availability:* Part-time, evening/weekend. *Faculty:* 56 full-time (22 women), 68 part-time/adjunct (22 women). *Students:* 606 full-time (301 women), 176 part-time (77 women); includes 437 minority (34 Black or African American, non-Hispanic/Latino; 8 American Indian or Alaska Native, non-Hispanic/Latino; 24 Asian, non-Hispanic/Latino; 370 Hispanic/Latino; 1 Native Hawaiian or other Pacific Islander, non-Hispanic/Latino), 1 international. Average age 28. 1,339 applicants, 63% accepted, 285 enrolled. In 2017, 239 doctorates awarded. *Degree requirements:* For doctorate, 90 credit hours, minimum cumulative GPA of 2.0. *Entrance requirements:* For doctorate, LSAT, explanation of affirmative responses to character and fitness questions, personal statement. Additional exam requirements/recommendations for international students: Required—TOEFL (minimum score 550 paper-based; 80 iBT), IELTS (minimum score 6), LSAT. *Application deadline:* For fall admission, 3/1 priority date for domestic students, 3/1 for international students; for spring admission, 3/1 priority date for domestic students. Application fee: $0. Electronic applications accepted. *Expenses:* $17,775 per semester full-time; $320 per semester student activity fee. *Financial support:* In 2017–18, 380 students received support. Fellowships, research assistantships, teaching assistantships, career-related internships or fieldwork, and scholarships/grants available. Support available to part-time students. Financial award application deadline: 3/1. *Unit head:* Stephen Sheppard, Dean, 210-436-3684, E-mail: sheppard@stmarytx.edu. *Application contact:* Catherine Casiano, Director of Admissions and Recruitment, 210-436-3525, E-mail: ccasiano@stmarytx.edu.
Website: https://law.stmarytx.edu/academics/jd-programs/

St. Thomas University, School of Law, Miami Gardens, FL 33054-6459. Offers international human rights (LL M); international taxation (LL M); law (JD); JD/MBA; JD/MS. *Accreditation:* ABA. *Program availability:* Online learning. *Degree requirements:* For master's, thesis (international taxation). *Entrance requirements:* For doctorate, LSAT. Electronic applications accepted. *Expenses:* Contact institution.

Samford University, Cumberland School of Law, Birmingham, AL 35229. Offers LL M, MCL, MSL, JD, JD/M Acc, JD/M Div, JD/MATS, JD/MBA, JD/MPA, JD/MPH, JD/MS, JD/MSEM. Programs offered jointly with The University of Alabama at Birmingham and Albany Medical School. *Accreditation:* ABA. *Program availability:* Part-time, 100% online, blended/hybrid learning. *Faculty:* 18 full-time (7 women), 19 part-time/adjunct (7 women). *Students:* 447 full-time (232 women), 4 part-time (1 woman); includes 80 minority (46 Black or African American, non-Hispanic/Latino; 6 American Indian or Alaska Native, non-Hispanic/Latino; 4 Asian, non-Hispanic/Latino; 17 Hispanic/Latino; 1 Native Hawaiian or other Pacific Islander, non-Hispanic/Latino; 6 Two or more races, non-Hispanic/Latino), 1 international. Average age 26. 579 applicants, 73% accepted, 150 enrolled. In 2017, 13 master's, 142 doctorates awarded. *Entrance requirements:* For master's, personal statement, professional resume; bachelor's degree with minimum GPA of 3.0 and 2 letters recommendation (for MSL); JD or enrolled as JD student and letter of recommendation (for LL M); for doctorate, LSAT, undergraduate degree. Additional exam requirements/recommendations for international students: Required—TOEFL (minimum score 550 paper-based; 90 iBT). *Application deadline:* For fall admission, 6/1 for domestic students, 6/1 priority date for international students. Applications are processed on a rolling basis. Electronic applications accepted. *Expenses:* $19,224 per fall/spring semester (for JD); $1,262 per credit hour (for LL M); $275 fees. *Financial support:* In 2017–18, 372 students received support. Scholarships/grants available. Financial award application deadline: 2/15; financial award applicants required to submit FAFSA. *Faculty research:* Environmental, criminal, constitutional law, evidence, civil procedure. *Unit head:* Henry C. Strickland, Dean/Professor of Law, 205-726-2704, Fax: 205-726-4457, E-mail: hcstrick@samford.edu. *Application contact:* Whitney Dachelet, Interim Director of Admissions and Student Recruiting, 205-726-2702, Fax: 205-726-2057, E-mail: wdachele@samford.edu.
Website: http://cumberland.samford.edu/

San Joaquin College of Law, Law Program, Clovis, CA 93612-1312. Offers JD. *Program availability:* Part-time, evening/weekend. *Entrance requirements:* For doctorate, LSAT.

The Santa Barbara and Ventura Colleges of Law–Santa Barbara, Graduate and Professional Programs, Santa Barbara, CA 93101. Offers MLS, JD.

The Santa Barbara and Ventura Colleges of Law–Ventura, Graduate and Professional Programs, Ventura, CA 93003. Offers MLS, JD.

Santa Clara University, School of Law, Santa Clara, CA 95053. Offers high tech law (Certificate); intellectual property (LL M); international and comparative law (LL M); international law (Certificate); law (JD); public interest and social justice law (Certificate); United States law (LL M); JD/MBA; JD/MSIS. JD/MBA, JD/MSIS offered jointly with Leavey School of Business. *Accreditation:* ABA. *Program availability:* Part-time. *Faculty:* 48 full-time (24 women), 41 part-time/adjunct (23 women). *Students:* 670 full-time (372 women), 57 part-time (23 women); includes 344 minority (30 Black or African American, non-Hispanic/Latino; 138 Asian, non-Hispanic/Latino; 134 Hispanic/Latino; 1 Native Hawaiian or other Pacific Islander, non-Hispanic/Latino; 41 Two or more races, non-Hispanic/Latino), 63 international. Average age 27. 2,092 applicants, 62% accepted, 248 enrolled. In 2017, 30 master's, 134 doctorates awarded. *Entrance requirements:* For master's and doctorate, LSAT, personal statement. *Application deadline:* For fall admission, 3/1 for domestic students. Application fee: $0. Electronic applications accepted. *Expenses:* Contact institution. *Financial support:* In 2017–18, 407 students received support. Fellowships, research assistantships, teaching assistantships, Federal Work-Study, scholarships/grants, health care benefits, and tuition waivers available. Support available to part-time students. Financial award application deadline: 3/1; financial award applicants required to submit FAFSA. *Unit head:* Lisa Kloppenberg, Dean, 408-554-4362, E-mail: lkloppenberg@scu.edu. *Application contact:* Nanette Cannon, Director of Admissions, 408-551-1846, E-mail: ncannon@scu.edu. Website: http://law.scu.edu/

Savannah Law School, JD Program, Savannah, GA 31401. Offers JD. *Program availability:* Part-time. *Faculty:* 12 full-time (2 women), 7 part-time/adjunct (2 women). *Students:* 76 full-time (49 women), 41 part-time (27 women). *Entrance requirements:* For doctorate, LSAT, 2-3 page personal statement, resume, two letters of recommendation. Electronic applications accepted. *Expenses: Tuition:* Full-time $21,100; part-time $12,660 per semester. Tuition and fees vary according to program. *Financial support:* Fellowships and scholarships/grants available. Financial award application deadline: 6/1; financial award applicants required to submit FAFSA. *Unit head:* Malcolm L. Morris, Dean, 678-916-2603, E-mail: mmorris@savannahlawschool.org. *Application contact:* Jiovanna Bryant, Associate Director of Admissions, 525-912-3913, E-mail: jbryant@savannahlawschool.org.

Seattle University, School of Law, Seattle, WA 98122-4340. Offers American legal studies (LL M); business development (MLS); elder law (LL M); health law (MLS); innovation and technology (LL M, MLS); tribal law and governance (LL M, MLS); JD/MATL; JD/MBA; JD/MCJ; JD/MIB; JD/MPA; JD/MSAL; JD/MSF; JD/MSL. *Accreditation:* ABA. *Program availability:* Part-time, evening/weekend. *Faculty:* 47 full-time (25 women), 48 part-time/adjunct (16 women). *Students:* 500 full-time (265 women), 130 part-time (65 women); includes 268 minority (34 Black or African American, non-Hispanic/Latino; 6 American Indian or Alaska Native, non-Hispanic/Latino; 102 Asian, non-Hispanic/Latino; 69 Hispanic/Latino; 5 Native Hawaiian or other Pacific Islander, non-Hispanic/Latino; 52 Two or more races, non-Hispanic/Latino), 7 international. Average age 27. 1,443 applicants, 67% accepted, 200 enrolled. In 2017, 300 doctorates awarded. *Entrance requirements:* For doctorate, LSAT. Additional exam requirements/recommendations for international students: Required—TOEFL (minimum score 600 paper-based; 100 iBT). *Application deadline:* For fall admission, 3/1 priority date for domestic and international students. Applications are processed on a rolling basis. Application fee: $65. Electronic applications accepted. *Expenses:* Contact institution. *Financial support:* In 2017–18, 500 students received support. Career-related internships or fieldwork, Federal Work-Study, and scholarships/grants available. Support available to part-time students. Financial award application deadline: 2/15; financial award applicants required to submit FAFSA. *Faculty research:* Innovation, technology and cybersecurity; secrecy and democratic decisions; linguistic features of police culture and the coercive impact of police officer swearing in police-citizen interaction; the imprisoned parent: differential power in same-sex families based on legal and cultural understandings of parentage; theology in public reason and legal discourse: a case for the preferential option for the poor. *Unit head:* Annette E. Clark, Dean, 206-398-4300, Fax: 206-398-4310, E-mail: annclark@seattleu.edu. *Application contact:* Gerald Heppler, Director of Admission, 206-398-4205, Fax: 206-398-4058, E-mail: hepplerg@seattleu.edu. Website: http://www.law.seattleu.edu/

Seton Hall University, School of Law, Newark, NJ 07102-5210. Offers health law (LL M, JD); intellectual property (LL M, JD); law (MSJ); JD/MADIR; JD/MBA; MD/JD; MD/MSJ. MD/JD, MD/MSJ offered jointly with University of Medicine and Dentistry of New Jersey. *Accreditation:* ABA. *Program availability:* Part-time, evening/weekend. *Degree requirements:* For master's, thesis optional. *Entrance requirements:* For master's, professional experience, letters of recommendation; for doctorate, LSAT, active LSDAS registration, letters of recommendation. Additional exam requirements/recommendations for international students: Recommended—TOEFL. Electronic applications accepted. *Expenses:* Contact institution. *Faculty research:* Health law, intellectual property law, science and the law, international law and employment/labor law.

Southern Illinois University Carbondale, School of Law, Carbondale, IL 62901-6804. Offers general law (LL M); health law and policy (LL M); law (JD); legal studies (MLS), including general law, health law and policy; JD/M Acc; JD/MBA; JD/MD; JD/MPA; JD/MSW; JD/PhD. *Accreditation:* ABA. *Program availability:* Part-time. *Entrance requirements:* For doctorate, LSAT. Additional exam requirements/recommendations for international students: Required—TOEFL (minimum score 600 paper-based). Electronic applications accepted. *Expenses:* Contact institution. *Faculty research:* Health care, criminal, environmental, and international law; tort reform.

Southern Methodist University, Dedman College of Humanities and Sciences, Department of Economics, Dallas, TX 75205. Offers applied economics (MA); applied economics and predictive analytics (MS); economics (PhD); law and economics (MA). *Program availability:* Part-time, evening/weekend. Terminal master's awarded for partial completion of doctoral program. *Degree requirements:* For master's, thesis, oral qualifying exam; for doctorate, thesis/dissertation, written exams. *Entrance requirements:* For master's, GRE General Test or GMAT, 12 hours of course work in economics, minimum GPA of 3.0, previous course work in calculus and statistics; for doctorate, GRE General Test, minimum GPA of 3.0; 3 semesters of course work in calculus; 1 semester each of course work in statistics and linear algebra. Additional exam requirements/recommendations for international students: Required—TOEFL (minimum score 550 paper-based). Electronic applications accepted. *Faculty research:* Economic theory, game theory, econometrics, international trade, labor.

Southern Methodist University, Dedman School of Law, Dallas, TX 75275-0110. Offers law (JD, SJD); law (for foreign law school graduates) (LL M); law (general) (LL M); taxation (LL M); JD/MA; JD/MBA. *Accreditation:* ABA. *Program availability:* Part-time, evening/weekend. *Degree requirements:* For master's, thesis optional; for doctorate, thesis/dissertation (for some programs), 30 hours of public service (for JD). *Entrance requirements:* For master's, JD; for doctorate, LSAT (for JD). Additional exam requirements/recommendations for international students: Required—TOEFL (minimum score 575 paper-based; 91 iBT). Electronic applications accepted. *Expenses:* Contact institution. *Faculty research:* Corporate law, intellectual property, international law, commercial law, dispute resolution.

Southern University and Agricultural and Mechanical College, Southern University Law Center, Baton Rouge, LA 70813. Offers JD. *Accreditation:* ABA; SACS/CC. *Program*

availability: Part-time, evening/weekend. *Entrance requirements:* For doctorate, LSAT. Additional exam requirements/recommendations for international students: Recommended—TOEFL. Electronic applications accepted. *Expenses:* Contact institution. *Faculty research:* Civil law, comparative law, constitutional law, civil rights law.

South Texas College of Law Houston, Professional Program, Houston, TX 77002-7000. Offers JD. *Accreditation:* ABA. *Program availability:* Part-time, evening/weekend. *Degree requirements:* For doctorate, completion of 90 hours within 7 years of enrollment. *Entrance requirements:* For doctorate, LSAT (taken within last 4 years), degree from accredited 4-year institution. Electronic applications accepted.

★ **Southwestern Law School,** Graduate and Professional Programs, Los Angeles, CA 90010. Offers individualized studies (LL M); law (JD). *Accreditation:* ABA. *Program availability:* Part-time, evening/weekend. *Faculty:* 59 full-time (29 women), 84 part-time/adjunct (32 women). *Students:* 510 full-time (281 women), 255 part-time (159 women); includes 357 minority (51 Black or African American, non-Hispanic/Latino; 77 Asian, non-Hispanic/Latino; 190 Hispanic/Latino; 5 Native Hawaiian or other Pacific Islander, non-Hispanic/Latino; 34 Two or more races, non-Hispanic/Latino), 18 international. Average age 26. 1,749 applicants, 46% accepted, 266 enrolled. In 2017, 25 master's, 287 doctorates awarded. *Degree requirements:* For doctorate, 87 units, minimum cumulative GPA of 2.33. *Entrance requirements:* For master's, JD; for doctorate, LSAT, bachelor's degree from accredited U.S. institution or equivalent with transcript evaluation; personal statement; LSAC Credential Assembly Service Registration (CAS); 1 to 3 letters of recommendation. *Application deadline:* For fall admission, 4/1 priority date for domestic and international students. Applications are processed on a rolling basis. Application fee: $60. Electronic applications accepted. *Expenses:* $51,890 full-time; $34,610 part-time; $200 fees. *Financial support:* In 2017–18, 408 students received support. Federal Work-Study, institutionally sponsored loans, and scholarships/grants available. Support available to part-time students. Financial award application deadline: 6/1; financial award applicants required to submit FAFSA. *Faculty research:* International trade and law, mediation/arbitration, land use and urban planning, antitrust law, entertainment and media law. *Unit head:* Susan Westerberg Prager, Dean, 213-738-6710, Fax: 213-383-1688. *Application contact:* Lisa Gear, Assistant Dean of Admissions, 213-738-6834, Fax: 213-383-1688, E-mail: admissions@swlaw.edu. Website: http://www.swlaw.edu

See Display on the next page and Close-Up on page 1525.

Stanford University, Law School, Stanford, CA 94305-8610. Offers corporate governance and practice (LL M); environmental law and policy (LL M); international economic law, business and policy (LL M); international legal studies (LL M); law (JD, JSD); law, science and technology (LL M); legal studies (MLS); JD/MA; JD/MBA; JD/MPP; JD/MS; JD/PhD. *Accreditation:* ABA. *Degree requirements:* For doctorate, thesis/dissertation (for some programs). *Entrance requirements:* For doctorate, LSAT (for JD). Electronic applications accepted. *Expenses:* Contact institution.

Stetson University, College of Law, Gulfport, FL 33707-3299. Offers advocacy (LL M); elder law (LL M); international law (LL M); law (M Jur, JD); JD/LL M; JD/MBA. *Accreditation:* ABA. *Program availability:* Part-time, evening/weekend, 100% online. *Faculty:* 53 full-time (28 women), 102 part-time/adjunct (36 women). *Students:* 687 full-time (361 women), 170 part-time (85 women); includes 239 minority (56 Black or African American, non-Hispanic/Latino; 4 American Indian or Alaska Native, non-Hispanic/Latino; 23 Asian, non-Hispanic/Latino; 128 Hispanic/Latino; 28 Two or more races, non-Hispanic/Latino), 14 international. Average age 28. 1,967 applicants, 46% accepted, 300 enrolled. In 2017, 40 master's, 265 doctorates awarded. *Entrance requirements:* For doctorate, LSAT. *Application deadline:* For fall admission, 5/15 for domestic and international students. Applications are processed on a rolling basis. Application fee: $55. Electronic applications accepted. *Expenses:* $42,326 per year full-time; $29,244 per year part-time. *Financial support:* In 2017–18, 612 students received support, including 67 research assistantships (averaging $857 per year), 65 teaching assistantships (averaging $664 per year); career-related internships or fieldwork, Federal Work-Study, scholarships/grants, unspecified assistantships, and tuition waivers (for staff and dependents) also available. Support available to part-time students. Financial award application deadline: 8/15; financial award applicants required to submit FAFSA. *Faculty research:* Advocacy and legal communication, law and higher education, elder law, international law including biodiversity and Caribbean law, veterans law and policy. *Total annual research expenditures:* $175,922. *Unit head:* Christopher M. Pietruszkiewicz, Dean/Professor of Law, 727-562-7809, Fax: 727-562-6428, E-mail: cmp@law.stetson.edu. *Application contact:* Darren Kettles, Director of Admissions, 727-562-7802, Fax: 727-343-0136, E-mail: lawadmit@law.stetson.edu. Website: http://www.law.stetson.edu/

Suffolk University, Law School, Boston, MA 02108. Offers business law and financial services (JD); civil litigation (JD); global law and technology (LL M); health and biomedical law (JD); intellectual property law (JD); international law (JD); JD/MBA; JD/MPA; JD/MSCJ; JD/MSF; JD/MSIE. *Accreditation:* ABA. *Program availability:* Part-time, evening/weekend. *Faculty:* 63 full-time (31 women), 54 part-time/adjunct (18 women). *Students:* 663 full-time (358 women), 366 part-time (181 women); includes 181 minority (36 Black or African American, non-Hispanic/Latino; 2 American Indian or Alaska Native, non-Hispanic/Latino; 48 Asian, non-Hispanic/Latino; 73 Hispanic/Latino; 22 Two or more races, non-Hispanic/Latino), 37 international. Average age 27. 1,962 applicants, 66% accepted, 340 enrolled. In 2017, 22 master's, 322 doctorates awarded. *Degree requirements:* For master's, legal writing. *Entrance requirements:* For master's, 2 letters of recommendation, resume, personal statement; for doctorate, LSAT, LSDAS, dean's certification, recommendation. Additional exam requirements/recommendations for international students: Required—TOEFL (minimum score 600 paper-based; 100 iBT). *Application deadline:* For fall admission, 4/1 for domestic and international students. Applications are processed on a rolling basis. Application fee: $60. Electronic applications accepted. *Expenses:* $48,090 per year full-time tuition; $1,603 per credit part-time. *Financial support:* In 2017–18, 663 students received support, including 1 fellowship (averaging $31,390 per year); career-related internships or fieldwork, Federal Work-Study, institutionally sponsored loans, and scholarships/grants also available. Support available to part-time students. Financial award application deadline: 3/1; financial award applicants required to submit FAFSA. *Faculty research:* Civil law, international law, health/biomedical law, business and finance, intellectual property. *Unit head:* Andrew Perlman, Dean, 617-573-8144, Fax: 617-994-6838, E-mail: lawadmin@suffolk.edu. *Application contact:* Matthew Gavin, Assistant Dean for Admissions and Financial Aid, 617-573-8144, Fax: 617-994-6838, E-mail: lawadm@suffolk.edu. Website: http://www.suffolk.edu/law/

Syracuse University, College of Law, JD Program, Syracuse, NY 13244. Offers JD. *Accreditation:* ABA. *Entrance requirements:* For doctorate, LSAT, CAS registration, transcripts of all previous college or university study, 2 letters of recommendation. *Application deadline:* For fall admission, 4/1 priority date for domestic students. *Unit head:* Craig M. Boise, Dean and Professor of Law, 315-443-9580, E-mail: cmboise@law.syr.edu. *Application contact:* Steve Budgar, Director of Admissions, 315-443-1962, Fax: 315-443-9568, E-mail: sbudgar@law.syr.edu. Website: http://law.syr.edu/admissions/jd-admissions

Law

Syracuse University, College of Law, Master of Laws Program in American Law, Syracuse, NY 13207. Offers LL.M. *Entrance requirements:* For master's, first degree in law from foreign institution; interview via Skype. Additional exam requirements/recommendations for international students: Recommended—TOEFL (minimum score 90 iBT), IELTS (minimum score 6). *Application deadline:* For fall admission, 5/15 for international students; for spring admission, 12/15 for international students. *Faculty research:* Human rights and comparative disability law, technology commercialization, corporate law. *Unit head:* Craig M. Boise, Dean and Professor of Law, 315-443-9580, E-mail: cmboise@law.syr.edu. *Application contact:* Steve Budgar, Director of Admissions, 315-443-1962, Fax: 315-443-9568, E-mail: sbudgar@law.syr.edu. Website: http://law.syr.edu/academics/llm-degree

Taft University System, Taft Law School, Denver, CO 80246. Offers American jurisprudence (LL.M); law (JD); taxation (LL.M).

Temple University, Beasley School of Law, JD Program, Philadelphia, PA 19122-6096. Offers JD. *Expenses:* Tuition, state resident: full-time $16,164; part-time $898 per credit hour. Tuition, nonresident: full-time $22,158; part-time $1231 per credit hour. *Required fees:* $890; $445 per semester. Full-time tuition and fees vary according to course load, degree level, campus/location and program.

Temple University, Beasley School of Law, Master's and Certificate Programs, Philadelphia, PA 19122-6096. Offers Asian law (LL.M); business law (Certificate); employee benefits (Certificate); estate planning (Certificate); trial advocacy (LL.M); trial advocacy and litigation (Certificate). *Expenses:* Tuition, state resident: full-time $16,164; part-time $898 per credit hour. Tuition, nonresident: full-time $22,158; part-time $1231 per credit hour. *Required fees:* $890; $445 per semester. Full-time tuition and fees vary according to course load, degree level, campus/location and program.

Texas A&M University, School of Law, College Station, TX 77843. Offers intellectual property (M Jur); jurisprudence (M Jur); law (JD). *Accreditation:* ABA. *Faculty:* 79. *Students:* 404 full-time (206 women), 58 part-time (19 women); includes 120 minority (33 Black or African American, non-Hispanic/Latino; 2 American Indian or Alaska Native, non-Hispanic/Latino; 9 Asian, non-Hispanic/Latino; 73 Hispanic/Latino; 3 Two or more races, non-Hispanic/Latino), 4 international. Average age 29. 541 applicants, 100% accepted, 178 enrolled. *Entrance requirements:* For doctorate, LSAT, personal statement, resume, all post-secondary transcripts, 2-4 letters of recommendation and up to 2 LSAC evaluations, CAS Report. *Application deadline:* For fall admission, 7/1 for domestic students. Applications are processed on a rolling basis. Application fee: $55. *Expenses:* Contact institution. *Financial support:* In 2017–18, 403 students received support, including 6 fellowships with tuition reimbursements available (averaging $29,510 per year); career-related internships or fieldwork, institutionally sponsored loans, scholarships/grants, traineeships, health care benefits, and tuition waivers (full and partial) also available. Support available to part-time students. Financial award applicants required to submit FAFSA. *Unit head:* Dr. Andrew P. Morriss, Dean, 817-212-4139, Fax: 817-212-4139, E-mail: amorriss@law.tamu.edu. *Application contact:* Law School Admissions, 817-212-4040, E-mail: law-admissions@law.tamu.edu. Website: http://law.tamu.edu/

Texas Southern University, Thurgood Marshall School of Law, Houston, TX 77004-4584. Offers JD. *Accreditation:* ABA. *Entrance requirements:* For doctorate, LSAT. Electronic applications accepted. *Expenses:* Contact institution. *Faculty research:* Sports law, civil rights and minors, international economics regulation, contracts principle, standards of judicial review.

Texas Tech University, School of Law, Lubbock, TX 79409-0004. Offers law (JD); United States legal studies (LL.M); JD/M Engr; JD/MBA; JD/MD; JD/MPA; JD/MS; JD/MSA. *Accreditation:* ABA. *Faculty:* 39 full-time (15 women), 8 part-time/adjunct (3 women). *Students:* 434 full-time (183 women), 6 part-time (2 women); includes 113 minority (8 Black or African American, non-Hispanic/Latino; 3 American Indian or Alaska Native, non-Hispanic/Latino; 9 Asian, non-Hispanic/Latino; 68 Hispanic/Latino; 25 Two or more races, non-Hispanic/Latino), 6 international. Average age 26. 1,157 applicants, 45% accepted, 139 enrolled. In 2017, 5 master's, 197 doctorates awarded. *Entrance requirements:* For master's, first/basic degree from a non-U.S. law school; for doctorate, LSAT. Additional exam requirements/recommendations for international students: Required—TOEFL minimum score 600 paper-based; 100 iBT or IELTS minimum score 7 (for LL.M). *Application deadline:* For fall admission, 3/1 priority date for domestic and international students. Applications are processed on a rolling basis. Application fee: $60. Electronic applications accepted. *Expenses:* Contact institution. *Financial support:* In 2017–18, 42 students received support, including 42 teaching assistantships (averaging $1,027 per year); research assistantships, Federal Work-Study, tuition waivers, and tutorships also available. Financial award application deadline: 5/1; financial award applicants required to submit FAFSA. *Faculty research:* Advocacy/practice skills, criminal Law/innocence, energy law, business/estate planning, law and science. *Total annual research expenditures:* $62,697. *Unit head:* Jack Wade Nowlin, Dean/Professor of Law, 806-834-1504, Fax: 806-742-4014, E-mail: jack.nowlin@ttu.edu. *Application contact:* Wendy A. Humphrey, Interim Associate Dean for Admissions and Financial Aid, 806-834-4446, Fax: 806-742-4617, E-mail: admissions.law@ttu.edu. Website: http://www.law.ttu.edu/

Thomas Jefferson School of Law, Graduate and Professional Programs, San Diego, CA 92110-2905. Offers JD. JD/MBA offered in partnership with San Diego State University. *Accreditation:* ABA. *Program availability:* Part-time, evening/weekend. *Entrance requirements:* For doctorate, LSAT. Additional exam requirements/recommendations for international students: Required—TOEFL. Electronic applications accepted. *Faculty research:* Tenant's rights, fetal rights/medical ethics, bilateral treaties/international law, sexual harassment and gender treatment.

Touro College, Jacob D. Fuchsberg Law Center, Central Islip, NY 11743. Offers general law (LL.M); law (JD); U.S. legal studies (LL.M); JD/MBA; JD/MPA; JD/MSW. JD/MBA and JD/MPA offered with Long Island University-LIU Post; JD/MSW offered with Stony Brook University, State University of New York. *Accreditation:* ABA. *Program availability:* Part-time, evening/weekend. *Faculty:* 35 full-time (17 women), 30 part-time/adjunct (7 women). *Students:* 445 full-time (245 women), 22 part-time (15 women); includes 166 minority (47 Black or African American, non-Hispanic/Latino; 2 American Indian or Alaska Native, non-Hispanic/Latino; 41 Asian, non-Hispanic/Latino; 72 Hispanic/Latino; 4 Two or more races, non-Hispanic/Latino), 9 international. Average age 30. *Entrance requirements:* For doctorate, LSAT. *Application deadline:* Applications are processed on a rolling basis. Application fee: $60. *Expenses:* Contact institution. *Financial support:* Fellowships, career-related internships or fieldwork, and Federal Work-Study available. Support available to part-time students. Financial award application deadline: 5/1. *Faculty research:* Business law, civil rights, international law, criminal justice. *Unit head:* Dr. Harry Ballan, Dean, 631-761-7100. *Application contact:* Dr. Susan Thompson, Office of Admissions, 631-761-7010, E-mail: admissions@tourolaw.edu. Website: http://www.tourolaw.edu/

Trinity International University, Trinity Law School, Santa Ana, CA 92705. Offers bioethics (MLS); church and ministry management (MLS); general legal studies (MLS); human resources management (MLS); human rights (MLS); law (JD); nonprofit organizations (MLS). *Program availability:* Part-time, evening/weekend. *Entrance requirements:* For doctorate, LSAT. Additional exam requirements/recommendations for international students: Required—TOEFL (minimum score 580 paper-based). *Expenses:* Contact institution.

Tufts University, The Fletcher School of Law and Diplomacy, Medford, MA 02155. Offers economics and public policy (PhD); international affairs (PhD); international business (MIB); international law (LL M); law and diplomacy (MA, MALD); transatlantic affairs (MA); DVM/MA; JD/MALD; MALD/MA; MALD/MBA; MALD/MS; MD/MA. MA in transatlantic affairs offered jointly with The College of Europe; PhD in economics and public policy with Tufts' Graduate School of Arts and Sciences. *Program availability:* Online learning. *Degree requirements:* For master's, one foreign language, thesis; for doctorate, one foreign language, comprehensive exam, thesis/dissertation, dissertation defense. *Entrance requirements:* For master's and doctorate, GMAT or GRE General Test. Additional exam requirements/recommendations for international students: Required—TOEFL (minimum score 600 paper-based; 100 iBT), IELTS (minimum score 7). Electronic applications accepted. *Expenses:* Contact institution. *Faculty research:* Negotiation and conflict resolution, international organizations, international business and economic law, security studies, development economics.

Tulane University, School of Law, New Orleans, LA 70118. Offers American business law (LL M); international development (MS, PhD), including international development; law (JD, SJD). *Accreditation:* ABA. *Degree requirements:* For doctorate, thesis/dissertation (for some programs). *Entrance requirements:* For doctorate, LSAT (for JD). Additional exam requirements/recommendations for international students: Required—TOEFL (minimum score 575 paper-based). Electronic applications accepted. *Expenses:* Contact institution. *Faculty research:* Civil law.

Universidad Autonoma de Guadalajara, Graduate Programs, Guadalajara, Mexico. Offers administrative law and justice (LL M); advertising and corporate communications (MA); architecture (M Arch); business (MBA); computational science (MCC); education (Ed M, Ed D); English-Spanish translation (MA); entrepreneurship and management (MBA); integrated management of digital animation (MA); international business (MIB); international corporate law (LL M); internet technologies (MS); manufacturing systems (MMS); occupational health (MS); philosophy (MA, PhD); power electronics (MS); quality systems (MQS); renewable energy (MS); social evaluation of projects (MBA); strategic market research (MBA); tax law (MA); teaching mathematics (MA).

Universidad Central del Este, Law School, San Pedro de Macoris, Dominican Republic. Offers JD.

Universidad Iberoamericana, Graduate School, Santo Domingo D.N., Dominican Republic. Offers business administration (MBA, PMBA); constitutional law (LL M); dentistry (DMD); educational management (MA); integrated marketing communication (MA); psychopedagogical intervention (M Ed); real estate law (LL M); strategic management of human talent (MM).

Université de Montréal, Faculty of Law, Montréal, QC H3C 3J7, Canada. Offers business law (DESS); common law (North America) (JD); international law (DESS); law (LL M, LL D, DDN, DESS, LL B); tax law (LL M). *Program availability:* Part-time. *Degree requirements:* For master's, thesis; for doctorate, thesis/dissertation, project; for other advanced degree, thesis (for some programs). Electronic applications accepted. *Faculty research:* Legal theory; constitutional, private, and public law.

Université de Sherbrooke, Faculty of Law, Sherbrooke, QC J1K 2R1, Canada. Offers alternative dispute resolution (LL M, Diploma); business law (Diploma); common law (JD); criminal and penal law (Diploma); health law (LL M, Diploma); international law (LL M); law (LL D); legal management (Diploma); notarial law (Diploma); transnational law (Diploma). *Program availability:* Part-time, evening/weekend. *Degree requirements:* For master's, thesis; for Diploma, one foreign language. *Entrance requirements:* For master's and Diploma, LL B. Electronic applications accepted.

Université du Québec à Montréal, Graduate Programs, Program in Social and Labor Law, Montréal, QC H3C 3P8, Canada. Offers Certificate.

Université Laval, Faculty of Law, Programs in Law, Québec, QC G1K 7P4, Canada. Offers environment, sustainable development and food safety (LL M); international and transnational law (LL M, Diploma); law (LL M, LL D); law of business (LL M, Diploma). *Program availability:* Part-time. Terminal master's awarded for partial completion of doctoral program. *Degree requirements:* For master's, thesis (for some programs); for doctorate, thesis/dissertation. *Entrance requirements:* For master's, doctorate, and Diploma, knowledge of French and English. Electronic applications accepted.

University at Buffalo, the State University of New York, Graduate School, School of Law, Buffalo, NY 14260-1100. Offers criminal law (LL M); cross-border legal studies (LL M); environmental law (LL M); general law (LL M); law (JD); JD/MA; JD/MBA; JD/MLS; JD/MSW; JD/MUP; JD/PhD; LL M/LL M. *Accreditation:* ABA. *Faculty:* 49 full-time (23 women), 68 part-time/adjunct (25 women). *Students:* 453 full-time (238 women), 2 part-time (both women); includes 85 minority (29 Black or African American, non-Hispanic/Latino; 1 American Indian or Alaska Native, non-Hispanic/Latino; 20 Asian, non-Hispanic/Latino; 22 Hispanic/Latino; 13 Two or more races, non-Hispanic/Latino), 17 international. Average age 27. 903 applicants, 54% accepted, 167 enrolled. In 2017, 2 master's, 151 doctorates awarded. *Entrance requirements:* For master's, JD or LL B; for doctorate, LSAT. Additional exam requirements/recommendations for international students: Required—TOEFL (minimum score 90 iBT), IELTS (minimum score 7). *Application deadline:* Applications are processed on a rolling basis. Application fee: $85. Electronic applications accepted. *Expenses:* $28,016 annual tuition plus fees in-state full-time; $32,106 annual tuition plus fees out-of-state full-time. *Financial support:* In 2017–18, 338 students received support. Federal Work-Study, institutionally sponsored loans, scholarships/grants, tuition waivers (full and partial), and unspecified assistantships available. Financial award application deadline: 3/1; financial award applicants required to submit FAFSA. *Faculty research:* Criminal law, environmental law, international law and human rights, law and finance, cross-border legal studies. *Total annual research expenditures:* $108,173. *Unit head:* Aviva Abramovsky, Dean, 716-645-2052, E-mail: aabramov@buffalo.edu. *Application contact:* Lindsay Gladney, Vice Dean for Admissions, 716-645-2907, Fax: 716-645-6676, E-mail: law-admissions@buffalo.edu.
Website: http://www.law.buffalo.edu/

The University of Akron, School of Law, Akron, OH 44325. Offers LL M, JD, JD/LL M, JD/M Tax, JD/MAP, JD/MBA, JD/MPA. *Accreditation:* ABA. *Program availability:* Part-time, evening/weekend. *Faculty:* 38 full-time (16 women), 16 part-time/adjunct (2 women). *Students:* 349 full-time (152 women), 111 part-time (63 women); includes 69 minority (30 Black or African American, non-Hispanic/Latino; 8 Asian, non-Hispanic/Latino; 20 Hispanic/Latino; 11 Two or more races, non-Hispanic/Latino), 7 international. Average age 27. 816 applicants, 56% accepted, 161 enrolled. In 2017, 2 master's, 122 doctorates awarded. *Entrance requirements:* For doctorate, LSAT, LSDAS. Additional exam requirements/recommendations for international students: Required—TOEFL (minimum score 650 paper-based; 115 iBT). *Application deadline:* For fall admission, 3/1 priority date for domestic and international students. Applications are processed on a rolling basis. Application fee: $45 ($70 for international students). Electronic applications accepted. *Expenses:* Contact institution. *Financial support:* In 2017–18, 264 students received support. Career-related internships or fieldwork, scholarships/grants, and tuition waivers (full and partial) available. Support available to part-time students. Financial award applicants required to submit FAFSA. *Faculty research:* Intellectual property; law and science; trust and elder law, including taxation and retirement benefits; professional responsibility and judicial ethics; Constitutional law, theory, and process.

Unit head: Martin H. Belsky, Dean, 330-972-6359, Fax: 330-258-2343, E-mail: belsky@uakron.edu. *Application contact:* Lauri S. File, Assistant Dean of Admission and Financial Aid, 330-972-7331, Fax: 330-258-2343, E-mail: lfile@uakron.edu.
Website: http://www.uakron.edu/law/index.dot

The University of Alabama, School of Law, Tuscaloosa, AL 35487. Offers business transactions (LL M); comparative law (LL M, JSD); law (JD, JSD); taxation (LL M); JD/MBA. *Accreditation:* ABA. *Faculty:* 40 full-time (17 women), 33 part-time/adjunct (7 women). *Students:* 412 full-time (175 women), 56 part-time (17 women); includes 94 minority (53 Black or African American, non-Hispanic/Latino; 4 American Indian or Alaska Native, non-Hispanic/Latino; 9 Asian, non-Hispanic/Latino; 22 Hispanic/Latino; 6 Two or more races, non-Hispanic/Latino), 6 international. Average age 27. 1,532 applicants, 25% accepted, 165 enrolled. In 2017, 45 master's, 132 doctorates awarded. *Degree requirements:* For master's, 24 hours, exams; for doctorate, 90 hours, including 6 hours of experiential learning, 1 seminar, and 34 required hours. *Entrance requirements:* For master's, LSAT, JD (for business transactions and taxation); undergraduate degree in law, letters of recommendation, personal statement, resume, and official transcripts (for comparative law); for doctorate, LSAT (for JD), undergraduate degree, letter of recommendation, resume, personal statement, and CAS report (for JD). Additional exam requirements/recommendations for international students: Required—TOEFL, IELTS. *Application deadline:* Applications are processed on a rolling basis. Application fee: $40. Electronic applications accepted. *Expenses:* Contact institution. *Financial support:* Applicants required to submit FAFSA. *Faculty research:* Public interest law, Constitutional law, civil rights, international law, tax law. *Unit head:* Claude R. Arrington, Associate Dean for Admissions, 205-348-6557, Fax: 205-348-3077, E-mail: carrington@law.ua.edu. *Application contact:* Martha Griffith, Assistant Director for Admissions, 205-348-7945, Fax: 205-348-3917, E-mail: mgriffith@law.ua.edu.
Website: http://www.law.ua.edu/

University of Alberta, Faculty of Law, Edmonton, AB T6G 2E1, Canada. Offers LL M, PhD. *Program availability:* Part-time. *Degree requirements:* For master's, thesis. *Entrance requirements:* For master's, minimum GPA of 3.0, curriculum vitae, 3 letters of recommendation; for doctorate, LSAT. Additional exam requirements/recommendations for international students: Required—TOEFL (minimum score 600 paper-based). Electronic applications accepted. *Faculty research:* Health law, environmental law, native law issues, constitutional law, human rights.

The University of Arizona, James E. Rogers College of Law, Tucson, AZ 85721-0176. Offers indigenous peoples law and policy (LL M); international trade and business law (LL M); law (JD); JD/MA; JD/MBA; JD/MPA; JD/PhD. *Accreditation:* ABA. *Degree requirements:* For doctorate, publishable paper. *Entrance requirements:* For doctorate, LSAT, LSDAS, resume, 2 letters of recommendation. Additional exam requirements/recommendations for international students: Required—TOEFL. Electronic applications accepted. *Expenses:* Contact institution. *Faculty research:* Tax law, employment law, corporate law, torts, trial practice and skills, Constitutional law, Indian law, family law, estates and trusts.

University of Arkansas, School of Law, Fayetteville, AR 72701. Offers agricultural law (LL M); law (JD). *Accreditation:* ABA. In 2017, 104 doctorates awarded. *Entrance requirements:* For doctorate, LSAT. *Application deadline:* For fall admission, 8/1 for domestic students, 4/1 for international students; for spring admission, 12/1 for domestic students, 10/1 for international students; for summer admission, 4/15 for domestic students, 3/1 for international students. Applications are processed on a rolling basis. Application fee: $60. Electronic applications accepted. *Expenses:* Contact institution. *Financial support:* In 2017–18, fellowships with full tuition reimbursements (averaging $6,000 per year), 8 research assistantships (averaging $2,500 per year) were awarded; teaching assistantships, career-related internships or fieldwork, Federal Work-Study, and scholarships/grants also available. Support available to part-time students. Financial award application deadline: 4/1; financial award applicants required to submit FAFSA. *Unit head:* Stacy L. Leeds, Dean, 479-575-5601, Fax: 479-575-3320, E-mail: sleeds@uark.edu.
Website: https://law.uark.edu/

University of Arkansas at Little Rock, William H. Bowen School of Law, Little Rock, AR 72202-5142. Offers JD, JD/MPS. *Accreditation:* ABA. *Program availability:* Part-time, evening/weekend. *Entrance requirements:* For doctorate, LSAT. Electronic applications accepted. *Expenses:* Contact institution. *Faculty research:* Employment discrimination, uniform commercial code, Arkansas legal history, scientific evidence, mediation.

University of Baltimore, School of Law, Baltimore, MD 21201. Offers business law (JD); criminal practice (JD); estate planning (JD); family law (JD); intellectual property (JD); international law (JD); law (JD); law of the United States (LL M); litigation and advocacy (JD); public service (JD); real estate practice (JD); taxation (LL M); LL M; JD/MBA; JD/MPA; JD/MS; JD/PhD. JD/MS offered jointly with Division of Criminology, Criminal Justice, and Social Policy; JD/PhD with University of Maryland, Baltimore. *Accreditation:* ABA. *Program availability:* Part-time, evening/weekend. *Entrance requirements:* For doctorate, LSAT. Additional exam requirements/recommendations for international students: Required—TOEFL (for LL M in law of the United States). Electronic applications accepted. *Expenses:* Contact institution. *Faculty research:* Plain view doctrine, statute of limitations, bankruptcy, family law, international and comparative law, Constitutional law.

The University of British Columbia, Peter A. Allard School of Law, Vancouver, BC V6T 1Z1, Canada. Offers common law (LL M CL); law (LL M, PhD); taxation (LL M). *Program availability:* Part-time. *Degree requirements:* For master's, variable foreign language requirement, thesis, seminar; for doctorate, variable foreign language requirement, comprehensive exam, thesis/dissertation, seminar. *Entrance requirements:* For master's, LL B or JD, thesis proposal, 3 letters of reference; for doctorate, LL B or JD, LL M, thesis proposal, 3 letters of reference. Additional exam requirements/recommendations for international students: Required—TOEFL, IELTS. Electronic applications accepted. *Expenses:* Contact institution. *Faculty research:* Aboriginal rights/native law, Asian legal studies, criminal law, environmental law, international law, corporate, human rights, intellectual property, dispute resolution, entertainment.

University of Calgary, Faculty of Graduate Studies, Faculty of Law, Calgary, AB T2N 1N4, Canada. Offers LL M, JD, Postbaccalaureate Certificate, JD/MBA. *Entrance requirements:* For doctorate, LSAT. Additional exam requirements/recommendations for international students: Required—TOEFL (minimum score 600 paper-based; 100 iBT). *Expenses:* Contact institution.

University of California, Berkeley, Graduate Division, Haas School of Business and School of Law, Concurrent JD/MBA Program, Berkeley, CA 94720-1500. Offers JD/MBA. *Accreditation:* AACSB; ABA. *Students:* 2 full-time (1 woman). Average age 29. *Entrance requirements:* Additional exam requirements/recommendations for international students: Required—TOEFL (minimum score 570 paper-based; 90 iBT). *Application deadline:* For fall admission, 10/1 for domestic and international students; for winter admission, 1/7 for domestic and international students; for spring admission, 3/31 for domestic and international students. Application fee: $200. Electronic applications accepted. *Expenses:* Contact institution. *Financial support:* Fellowships, research

assistantships with partial tuition reimbursements, teaching assistantships with partial tuition reimbursements, career-related internships or fieldwork, institutionally sponsored loans, scholarships/grants, and non-resident tuition waivers for some students, such as veterans available. Financial award applicants required to submit FAFSA. *Faculty research:* Accounting, business and public policy, economic analysis and public policy, entrepreneurship, finance, management of organizations, marketing, operations and information technology management, real estate. *Application contact:* Morgan Bernstein, Executive Director, Full-time MBA Admissions, 510-642-1405, Fax: 510-643-6659, E-mail: mbernstein@haas.berkeley.edu.
Website: http://mba.haas.berkeley.edu/academics/concurrentdegrees.html

University of California, Berkeley, School of Law, Berkeley, CA 94720-7200. Offers jurisprudence and social policy (PhD); law (LL M, JD, JSD); JD/MA; JD/MBA; JD/MCP; JD/MJ; JD/MPP; JD/MSW. *Accreditation:* ABA. Terminal master's awarded for partial completion of doctoral program. *Degree requirements:* For master's, thesis; for doctorate, variable foreign language requirement, thesis/dissertation (for some programs). *Entrance requirements:* For master's and doctorate, letters of recommendation. Additional exam requirements/recommendations for international students: Required—TOEFL. *Expenses:* Contact institution. *Faculty research:* Law and technology; social justice; environmental law; business, law and economics; international/comparative law.

University of California, Davis, School of Law, Davis, CA 95616-5201. Offers LL M, JD, JD/MA, JD/MBA. *Accreditation:* ABA. *Faculty:* 51 full-time (26 women), 60 part-time/adjunct (21 women). *Students:* 500 full-time (267 women); includes 220 minority (15 Black or African American, non-Hispanic/Latino; 1 American Indian or Alaska Native, non-Hispanic/Latino; 75 Asian, non-Hispanic/Latino; 83 Hispanic/Latino; 1 Native Hawaiian or other Pacific Islander, non-Hispanic/Latino; 45 Two or more races, non-Hispanic/Latino), 38 international. Average age 24. 2,988 applicants, 30% accepted, 150 enrolled. In 2017, 167 doctorates awarded. *Degree requirements:* For doctorate, 88 semester units, including skills courses (6 units), Professional Responsibility and upper-division writing requirement. *Entrance requirements:* For doctorate, LSAT. Additional exam requirements/recommendations for international students: Required—TOEFL (minimum score 570 paper-based; 88 iBT). *Application deadline:* For fall admission, 3/15 priority date for domestic students, 3/15 for international students. Applications are processed on a rolling basis. Application fee: $0. Electronic applications accepted. *Expenses:* $47,763 per year resident tuition and fees; $57,014 nonresident. *Financial support:* In 2017–18, 445 students received support, including 35 research assistantships, 27 teaching assistantships with partial tuition reimbursements available; Federal Work-Study, institutionally sponsored loans, scholarships/grants, and health care benefits also available. Financial award application deadline: 3/2; financial award applicants required to submit FAFSA. *Faculty research:* International law, intellectual property, immigration, environmental law, public interest law. *Unit head:* Kevin R. Johnson, Dean, 530-752-0243, Fax: 530-752-7279, E-mail: krjohnson@ucdavis.edu. *Application contact:* Kristen Mercado, JD, Director, Admissions, 530-752-6477, Fax: 530-754-8371, E-mail: admissions@law.ucdavis.edu.
Website: http://www.law.ucdavis.edu/

University of California, Hastings College of the Law, Graduate Programs, San Francisco, CA 94102-4978. Offers LL M, MS, MSL, JD. MSL and MS offered jointly with University of California, San Francisco. *Accreditation:* ABA. *Entrance requirements:* For doctorate, LSAT. Electronic applications accepted.

University of California, Irvine, School of Law, Irvine, CA 92617. Offers JD. *Accreditation:* ABA. *Students:* 417 full-time (232 women); includes 191 minority (18 Black or African American, non-Hispanic/Latino; 1 American Indian or Alaska Native, non-Hispanic/Latino; 90 Asian, non-Hispanic/Latino; 64 Hispanic/Latino; 18 Two or more races, non-Hispanic/Latino), 17 international. 2,314 applicants, 166 enrolled. In 2017, 94 doctorates awarded. *Degree requirements:* For doctorate, project. *Entrance requirements:* For doctorate, LSAT, bachelor's degree, official transcripts, two letters of recommendation, personal statement, current resume. *Application deadline:* For fall admission, 3/1 for domestic students. Application fee: $0. Electronic applications accepted. *Expenses:* Contact institution. *Unit head:* L. Song Richardson, Dean, 949-824-7722, E-mail: srichardson@law.uci.edu. *Application contact:* Estuardo Ponciano, Director of Admissions, 949-824-9926, E-mail: eponciano@law.uci.edu.
Website: http://www.law.uci.edu/

University of California, Los Angeles, School of Law, Los Angeles, CA 90095. Offers LL M, JD, SJD, JD/MA, JD/MBA, JD/MPH, JD/MPP, JD/MSW, JD/MURP, JD/PhD. *Accreditation:* ABA. *Entrance requirements:* For doctorate, LSAT (for JD). Additional exam requirements/recommendations for international students: Required—TOEFL for LL M. Electronic applications accepted. *Expenses:* Contact institution. *Faculty research:* Business law and policy; critical race studies, entertainment; media, and intellectual property law; law and philosophy; public interest law and policy.

University of Chicago, The Law School, Chicago, IL 60637. Offers LL M, MCL, DCL, JD, JSD, JD/AM, JD/MBA, JD/MPP. *Accreditation:* ABA. *Entrance requirements:* For doctorate, LSAT (for JD). Additional exam requirements/recommendations for international students: Required—TOEFL (minimum score 104 iBT). Electronic applications accepted. *Expenses:* Contact institution. *Faculty research:* Law.

University of Cincinnati, College of Law, Cincinnati, OH 45221-0040. Offers LL M, JD, JD/MA, JD/MBA, JD/MCP, JD/MWS. *Accreditation:* ABA. *Entrance requirements:* For master's, Credential evaluation report, diploma for law degree, curriculum vitae, personal statement, two letters of recommendation; for doctorate, LSAT. Additional exam requirements/recommendations for international students: Required—TOEFL (minimum iBT score of 85), IELTS (7), or PTE (65). Electronic applications accepted. *Expenses:* Contact institution. *Faculty research:* Constitutional law; business law; international law; employment law; civil procedure.

University of Colorado Boulder, School of Law, Boulder, CO 80309-0401. Offers JD, JD/MBA, JD/MPA, JD/MS, JD/PhD. *Accreditation:* ABA. *Faculty:* 40 full-time (15 women). *Students:* 553 full-time (277 women), 10 part-time (9 women); includes 124 minority (10 Black or African American, non-Hispanic/Latino; 13 American Indian or Alaska Native, non-Hispanic/Latino; 29 Asian, non-Hispanic/Latino; 67 Hispanic/Latino; 5 Two or more races, non-Hispanic/Latino), 4 international. Average age 27. 1,071 applicants, 100% accepted, 202 enrolled. In 2017, 169 doctorates awarded. *Entrance requirements:* For doctorate, LSAT, minimum undergraduate GPA of 2.75. *Application deadline:* For fall admission, 2/15 for domestic students. Applications are processed on a rolling basis. Application fee: $60 ($80 for international students). Electronic applications accepted. Application fee is waived when completed online. *Expenses:* Contact institution. *Financial support:* In 2017–18, 1,056 students received support, including 768 fellowships (averaging $8,286 per year); institutionally sponsored loans, scholarships/grants, health care benefits, and unspecified assistantships also available. Financial award application deadline: 2/15; financial award applicants required to submit FAFSA. *Faculty research:* Law and society; constitutional law; law; business/corporate law; environmental law. *Total annual research expenditures:* $2.2 million. *Application contact:* E-mail: lawadmin@colorado.edu.
Website: http://www.colorado.edu/law/

University of Connecticut, School of Law, Hartford, CT 06105. Offers JD, JD/LL M, JD/MBA, JD/MLS, JD/MPA, JD/MPH, JD/MSW. *Accreditation:* ABA. *Program availability:* Part-time. *Degree requirements:* For doctorate, extensive research paper. *Entrance requirements:* For doctorate, LSAT, undergraduate degree. Additional exam requirements/recommendations for international students: Required—TOEFL. Electronic applications accepted. *Expenses:* Contact institution. *Faculty research:* International law, intellectual property, human rights, taxation, energy and environmental law.

University of Dayton, School of Law, Dayton, OH 45469-2772. Offers American and transnational law (LL M); criminal law (JD); government contracting and procurement (MSL); intellectual property and technology (MSL). *Accreditation:* ABA. *Program availability:* Part-time, 100% online. *Faculty:* 21 full-time (13 women), 23 part-time/adjunct (6 women). *Students:* 242 full-time (126 women), 27 part-time (13 women); includes 46 minority (29 Black or African American, non-Hispanic/Latino; 1 American Indian or Alaska Native, non-Hispanic/Latino; 5 Asian, non-Hispanic/Latino; 11 Hispanic/Latino), 12 international. Average age 27. 578 applicants, 38% accepted, 118 enrolled. In 2017, 4 master's, 93 doctorates awarded. Terminal master's awarded for partial completion of doctoral program. *Degree requirements:* For master's, variable foreign language requirement, comprehensive exam (for some programs), thesis optional; for doctorate, variable foreign language requirement, comprehensive exam, thesis/dissertation optional. *Entrance requirements:* For master's, GMAT, GRE or waiver from director/dean, bachelor's degree (for MSL); transcripts and law degree (for LL M); for doctorate, LSAT, bachelor's degree, transcripts, letter of recommendation, character and fitness personal statement. Additional exam requirements/recommendations for international students: Required—TOEFL (minimum score 600 paper-based; 100 iBT); Recommended—IELTS (minimum score 7). *Application deadline:* For fall admission, 7/1 priority date for domestic students; for summer admission, 4/15 for domestic students. Application fee: $0. *Expenses:* $1,149 per credit hour, $209 fees per semester. *Financial support:* In 2017–18, 15 fellowships (averaging $1,000 per year), 5 research assistantships (averaging $1,000 per year), 13 teaching assistantships (averaging $400 per year) were awarded; Federal Work-Study, scholarships/grants, tuition waivers (full and partial), and bar course grants also available. Financial award application deadline: 3/1; financial award applicants required to submit FAFSA. *Faculty research:* Trademark and unfair competition law, cyber and cybersecurity law, patent law, trade secret law, copyright law. *Unit head:* Andrew Strauss, Dean, 937-229-3795, Fax: 937-229-2469, E-mail: astrauss1@udayton.edu. *Application contact:* Claire Schrader, Assistant Dean/Executive Director of Enrollment Management and Marketing, 937-229-3555, Fax: 937-229-4194, E-mail: lawinfo@udayton.edu.
Website: http://www.udayton.edu/law

University of Denver, Sturm College of Law, JD Program, Denver, CO 80208. Offers JD. *Accreditation:* ABA. *Program availability:* Part-time, evening/weekend. *Students:* Average age 28. 2,217 applicants, 53% accepted, 260 enrolled. In 2017, 267 doctorates awarded. *Entrance requirements:* For doctorate, LSAT. Additional exam requirements/recommendations for international students: Required—TOEFL (minimum score 587 paper-based; 95 iBT). *Application deadline:* For fall admission, 3/1 for domestic and international students. Applications are processed on a rolling basis. Application fee: $65. Electronic applications accepted. *Expenses:* Contact institution. *Financial support:* In 2017–18, 427 students received support, including 2 teaching assistantships (averaging $8,268 per year); career-related internships or fieldwork, Federal Work-Study, institutionally sponsored loans, scholarships/grants, unspecified assistantships, and tutorships also available. Support available to part-time students. Financial award application deadline: 2/15; financial award applicants required to submit FAFSA. *Faculty research:* Lawyering skills, international and legal studies, natural resources law (domestic and international), transportation law, public interest law, business and commercial law. *Unit head:* Dr. Bruce Smith, Dean, 303-871-6103. *Application contact:* Yvonne Cherena-Pacheco, Associate Director of Admissions, 303-871-6151, Fax: 303-871-6992, E-mail: admissions@law.du.edu.
Website: http://www.law.du.edu

University of Denver, Sturm College of Law, Programs in Environmental and Natural Resources Law and Policy, Denver, CO 80208. Offers environmental and natural resources law and policy (LL M, MLS); natural resources law and policy (Certificate). *Students:* 13 full-time (6 women), 5 part-time (4 women), 6 international. Average age 31. In 2017, 17 master's awarded. *Degree requirements:* For master's, internship. *Entrance requirements:* For master's, bachelor's degree (for MRLS), JD (for LL M), transcripts, two letters of recommendation. Additional exam requirements/recommendations for international students: Required—TOEFL (minimum score 550 paper-based; 80 iBT). *Application deadline:* For fall admission, 7/27 for domestic students, 6/15 for international students; for spring admission, 12/12 for domestic students, 11/7 for international students. Applications are processed on a rolling basis. Application fee: $65. Electronic applications accepted. *Expenses:* $49,022 per year full-time. *Financial support:* In 2017–18, 11 students received support. Federal Work-Study, institutionally sponsored loans, scholarships/grants, and unspecified assistantships available. Support available to part-time students. Financial award application deadline: 2/15; financial award applicants required to submit FAFSA. *Application contact:* E-mail: gradlegalstudies@law.du.edu.
Website: http://www.law.du.edu/index.php/graduate-legal-studies/masters-programs/mls-enrlp

University of Detroit Mercy, School of Law, Detroit, MI 48226. Offers JD, JD/MBA. *Accreditation:* ABA. *Program availability:* Part-time. *Entrance requirements:* For doctorate, LSAT. *Expenses:* Contact institution.

University of Florida, Levin College of Law, Gainesville, FL 32611. Offers comparative law (LL M), including tropical conservation and development; environmental and land use law (LL M); international taxation (LL M); law (JD); taxation (LL M, SJD). *Accreditation:* ABA. *Entrance requirements:* For doctorate, LSAT (for JD). Electronic applications accepted. *Faculty research:* Environmental and land use law, taxation, dispute resolution, family law, Constitutional law.

University of Georgia, School of Law, Athens, GA 30602. Offers LL M, MSL, JD. *Accreditation:* ABA. *Degree requirements:* For master's, thesis. *Entrance requirements:* For doctorate, LSAT. Additional exam requirements/recommendations for international students: Required—TOEFL. Electronic applications accepted. *Expenses:* Contact institution.

University of Hawaii at Manoa, William S. Richardson School of Law, Honolulu, HI 96822-2328. Offers LL M, JD, Graduate Certificate, JD/Certificate, JD/MA, JD/MBA, JD/MLI Sc, JD/MS, JD/MURP, JD/PhD. *Accreditation:* ABA. *Degree requirements:* For doctorate, 6 semesters of full-time residency. *Entrance requirements:* For doctorate, LSAT. Additional exam requirements/recommendations for international students: Required—TOEFL. *Expenses:* Contact institution. *Faculty research:* Law of the sea, Asian and Pacific comparative law, native Hawaiian rights, environmental law.

University of Houston, University of Houston Law Center, Houston, TX 77204-6060. Offers energy, environment, and natural resources (LL M); health law (LL M); intellectual property and information law (LL M); international law (LL M); law (JD); tax law (LL M); U.S. law (LL M). *Accreditation:* ABA. *Program availability:* Part-time, evening/weekend.

Faculty: 58 full-time (23 women), 130 part-time/adjunct (36 women). *Students:* 695 full-time (331 women), 120 part-time (55 women); includes 319 minority (62 Black or African American, non-Hispanic/Latino; 10 American Indian or Alaska Native, non-Hispanic/Latino; 73 Asian, non-Hispanic/Latino; 172 Hispanic/Latino; 2 Native Hawaiian or other Pacific Islander, non-Hispanic/Latino), 33 international. Average age 26. 2,751 applicants, 33% accepted, 227 enrolled. In 2017, 75 master's, 231 doctorates awarded. *Degree requirements:* For master's, thesis optional; for doctorate, senior writing requirement. *Entrance requirements:* For doctorate, LSAT. Additional exam requirements/recommendations for international students: Required—TOEFL (minimum score 600 paper-based; 100 iBT). *Application deadline:* For fall admission, 2/15 for domestic and international students. Applications are processed on a rolling basis. Application fee: $0. Electronic applications accepted. *Expenses:* Contact institution. *Financial support:* In 2017–18, 442 students received support, including 20 fellowships (averaging $2,980 per year), research assistantships, career-related internships or fieldwork, Federal Work-Study, scholarships/grants, and tuition waivers also available. Support available to part-time students. Financial award application deadline: 3/15; financial award applicants required to submit FAFSA. *Faculty research:* Health law, international law, tax, environmental law/energy, international law/intellectual property. *Total annual research expenditures:* $472,551. *Unit head:* Leonard M. Baynes, Dean and Professor of Law, 713-743-2100, Fax: 713-743-2122, E-mail: lbaynes@central.uh.edu. *Application contact:* Pilar Mensah, Assistant Dean for Admissions, 713-743-2280, Fax: 713-743-2194, E-mail: lpmensah@central.uh.edu.
Website: http://www.law.uh.edu/

University of Idaho, College of Law, Moscow, ID 83844-2321. Offers LL M, JD. *Accreditation:* ABA. *Faculty:* 30 full-time, 10 part-time/adjunct. *Students:* 296 full-time (127 women), 12 part-time (7 women). Average age 28. *Entrance requirements:* For doctorate, LSAT, Law School Admission Council Credential Assembly Service (CAS) Report. Additional exam requirements/recommendations for international students: Required—TOEFL. *Application deadline:* For fall admission, 3/15 priority date for domestic students. Applications are processed on a rolling basis. Application fee: $50 ($60 for international students). Electronic applications accepted. *Expenses:* Contact institution. *Financial support:* Career-related internships or fieldwork, Federal Work-Study, and institutionally sponsored loans available. Financial award applicants required to submit FAFSA. *Unit head:* Mark Adams, Dean, 208-885-4977, E-mail: uilaw@uidaho.edu. *Application contact:* Carole Wells, Director of Admissions, 208-885-2300, Fax: 208-885-2252, E-mail: lawadmit@uidaho.edu.
Website: http://www.uidaho.edu/law/

University of Illinois at Urbana–Champaign, College of Law, Champaign, IL 61820. Offers LL M, MCL, JD, JSD, JD/DVM, JD/MBA, JD/MCS, JD/MHRIR, JD/MS, JD/MUP, MAS/JD, MD/JD. *Accreditation:* ABA. *Expenses:* Contact institution.

The University of Iowa, College of Law, Iowa City, IA 52242. Offers LL M, MSL, JD, SJD, JD/MA, JD/MBA, JD/MD, JD/MHA, JD/MPH, JD/MS, JD/PhD. *Accreditation:* ABA. *Faculty:* 44 full-time (20 women), 26 part-time/adjunct (11 women). *Students:* 432 full-time (188 women); includes 96 minority (23 Black or African American, non-Hispanic/Latino; 2 American Indian or Alaska Native, non-Hispanic/Latino; 17 Asian, non-Hispanic/Latino; 41 Hispanic/Latino; 13 Two or more races, non-Hispanic/Latino), 23 international. Average age 24. 1,651 applicants, 41% accepted, 143 enrolled. In 2017, 9 master's, 137 doctorates awarded. *Degree requirements:* For master's, thesis (for some programs); for doctorate, thesis/dissertation. *Entrance requirements:* For doctorate, LSAT. Additional exam requirements/recommendations for international students: Required—TOEFL. *Application deadline:* For fall admission, 5/1 priority date for domestic and international students. Applications are processed on a rolling basis. Application fee: $0. Electronic applications accepted. *Expenses:* $26,456 resident, $45,917 nonresident (for JD); $24,289 resident, $28,811 nonresident (for LL M); $18,281 resident, $21,683 nonresident (for SJD); $15,631 resident, $27,233 nonresident (for MSL). *Financial support:* In 2017–18, 387 students received support, including 387 fellowships with partial tuition reimbursements available (averaging $17,909 per year), 133 research assistantships with partial tuition reimbursements available (averaging $2,175 per year); career-related internships or fieldwork, Federal Work-Study, scholarships/grants, and health care benefits also available. Financial award applicants required to submit FAFSA. *Faculty research:* International and comparative law, business law, intellectual property and property law, criminal law, and Constitutional law. *Total annual research expenditures:* $304,029. *Unit head:* Gail Agrawal, Dean, 319-335-9034, Fax: 319-335-9019, E-mail: gail-agrawal@uiowa.edu. *Application contact:* Collins Byrd, Assistant Dean of Enrollment Management, 319-335-9095, Fax: 319-335-9646, E-mail: law-admissions@uiowa.edu.
Website: https://law.uiowa.edu/

The University of Kansas, School of Law, Lawrence, KS 66045-7608. Offers law (JD); JD/MA; JD/MBA; JD/MHSA; JD/MPA; JD/MS; JD/MSW; JD/MUP. *Accreditation:* ABA. *Faculty:* 30 full-time (16 women), 20 part-time/adjunct (8 women). *Students:* 334 full-time (154 women), 35 part-time (6 women); includes 64 minority (16 Black or African American, non-Hispanic/Latino; 2 American Indian or Alaska Native, non-Hispanic/Latino; 14 Asian, non-Hispanic/Latino; 26 Hispanic/Latino; 6 Two or more races, non-Hispanic/Latino), 27 international. Average age 25. 690 applicants, 54% accepted, 121 enrolled. In 2017, 121 doctorates awarded. *Entrance requirements:* For doctorate, LSAT, 2 letters of recommendation, personal statement, resume, official transcripts. Additional exam requirements/recommendations for international students: Required—TOEFL. *Application deadline:* For fall admission, 4/1 priority date for domestic students, 4/1 for international students. Applications are processed on a rolling basis. Application fee: $55. Electronic applications accepted. *Expenses:* $727 per credit resident, $1,269 per credit nonresident, $916 per year fee; $10,000 per year fee (for SJD). *Financial support:* In 2017–18, 6 fellowships (averaging $1,800 per year), 65 research assistantships (averaging $1,257 per year), 8 teaching assistantships (averaging $1,875 per year) were awarded; career-related internships or fieldwork, Federal Work-Study, institutionally sponsored loans, and scholarships/grants also available. Financial award application deadline: 2/15; financial award applicants required to submit FAFSA. *Faculty research:* International law, business law, criminal law, tribal law, law and public policy. *Unit head:* Stephen W. Mazza, Dean, 785-864-4550, Fax: 785-864-5054. *Application contact:* Steven Freedman, Assistant Dean for Admissions, 866-220-3654, E-mail: admitlaw@ku.edu.
Website: http://www.law.ku.edu/

University of Kentucky, College of Law, Lexington, KY 40506-0048. Offers JD, JD/MA, JD/MBA, JD/MPA. *Accreditation:* ABA. *Entrance requirements:* For doctorate, LSAT, LSDAS. Additional exam requirements/recommendations for international students: Required—TOEFL. Electronic applications accepted. *Expenses:* Contact institution. *Faculty research:* Health law, education law, advocacy, business law, white collar crime, international trade law, corporate mergers, taxation of Internet transactions.

University of La Verne, College of Law, Ontario, CA 91764. Offers JD. *Accreditation:* ABA. *Program availability:* Part-time, evening/weekend. *Entrance requirements:* For doctorate, LSAT. Additional exam requirements/recommendations for international students: Recommended—TOEFL. Electronic applications accepted. *Expenses:* Contact institution.

University of Louisville, Louis D. Brandeis School of Law, Louisville, KY 40208. Offers JD, JD/M Div, JD/MAH, JD/MAPS, JD/MBA, JD/MSSW, JD/MUP. *Accreditation:* ABA. *Program availability:* Part-time. *Degree requirements:* For doctorate, 30 work hours of pro bono service. *Entrance requirements:* For doctorate, LSAT. Additional exam requirements/recommendations for international students: Required—TOEFL (minimum score 550 paper-based). Electronic applications accepted. *Expenses:* Contact institution. *Faculty research:* Intellectual property, environmental law, corporate law, taxation, health law, disability law.

University of Maine, University of Maine School of Law, Portland, ME 04102. Offers JD, JD/MBA, JD/MPH, JD/MPPM. JD/MBA offered in conjunction with the University of Maine and University of Southern Maine; JD/MPH and JD/MPPM offered with the Muskie School of Public Service. *Accreditation:* ABA. *Program availability:* Part-time. *Faculty:* 23 full-time (12 women), 52 part-time/adjunct (21 women). *Students:* 222 full-time (114 women), 15 part-time (11 women); includes 28 minority (7 Black or African American, non-Hispanic/Latino; 5 American Indian or Alaska Native, non-Hispanic/Latino; 4 Asian, non-Hispanic/Latino; 12 Hispanic/Latino), 3 international. Average age 27. 604 applicants, 54% accepted, 82 enrolled. In 2017, 83 doctorates awarded. *Degree requirements:* For doctorate, 90 academic credits. *Entrance requirements:* Additional exam requirements/recommendations for international students: Required—TOEFL (minimum score 550 paper-based, 79 iBT) or IELTS (6.5). *Application deadline:* For fall admission, 7/31 for domestic students, 6/1 for international students; for spring admission, 11/15 for international students. Applications are processed on a rolling basis. Application fee: $0. Electronic applications accepted. *Expenses:* $22,290 per year resident, $33,360 per year non-resident, $30,420 per year New England Regional Program and Canadian citizens; $743 per credit part-time resident, $1,112 per credit part-time non-resident, $1,014 per credit part-time New England Regional Program and Canadian citizens (for JD); $35,000 per year full-time (for LL M). *Financial support:* In 2017–18, 28 fellowships (averaging $3,300 per year), 5 research assistantships (averaging $1,000 per year), 5 teaching assistantships with partial tuition reimbursements (averaging $2,500 per year) were awarded; Federal Work-Study, scholarships/grants, and unspecified assistantships also available. Financial award application deadline: 2/15; financial award applicants required to submit FAFSA. *Faculty research:* Commercial and tax law aspects of intellectual property; domestic violence; race, gender, and law; environmental and land use law; bankruptcy and predatory lending; international investment law; community development law; law governing use and development of the arctic. *Unit head:* Danielle Conway, Dean, 207-780-4344, Fax: 207-780-4239. *Application contact:* Caroline Wilshusen, Director of Admissions, 207-780-4341, Fax: 207-780-4239, E-mail: lawadmissions@maine.edu.
Website: http://mainelaw.maine.edu/

The University of Manchester, School of Law, Manchester, United Kingdom. Offers bioethics and medical jurisprudence (PhD); criminology (M Phil, PhD); law (M Phil, PhD).

University of Manitoba, Faculty of Graduate Studies, Faculty of Law, Winnipeg, MB R3T 2N2, Canada. Offers LL M. *Degree requirements:* For master's, thesis. *Entrance requirements:* For master's, LL B, minimum GPA of 3.0. Additional exam requirements/recommendations for international students: Required—TOEFL (minimum score 600 paper-based). Electronic applications accepted. *Faculty research:* Constitutional law, alternative dispute resolution, human rights law, international trade law, corporate law.

University of Maryland, Baltimore, Francis King Carey School of Law, Baltimore, MD 21201. Offers LL M, JD, JD/MA, JD/MBA, JD/MCP, JD/MPH, JD/MPM, JD/MPP, JD/MS, JD/MSN, JD/MSW, JD/PhD, JD/Pharm D. *Accreditation:* ABA. *Program availability:* Part-time, evening/weekend, 100% online. *Faculty:* 47 full-time (24 women), 70 part-time/adjunct (26 women). *Students:* 547 full-time (292 women), 224 part-time (125 women); includes 278 minority (126 Black or African American, non-Hispanic/Latino; 2 American Indian or Alaska Native, non-Hispanic/Latino; 73 Asian, non-Hispanic/Latino; 53 Hispanic/Latino; 24 Two or more races, non-Hispanic/Latino), 28 international. Average age 27. 2,135 applicants, 53% accepted, 291 enrolled. In 2017, 45 master's, 187 doctorates awarded. *Degree requirements:* For master's, thesis optional. *Entrance requirements:* For doctorate, LSAT, CAS registration (transcripts, transcript analysis, letters of recommendation). Additional exam requirements/recommendations for international students: Required—TOEFL (minimum score 600 paper-based; 90 iBT), IELTS (minimum score 7). *Application deadline:* For fall admission, 4/1 priority date for domestic and international students. Applications are processed on a rolling basis. Application fee: $70. Electronic applications accepted. *Expenses:* $32,492 resident, $47,036 non-resident (first-year), $1,433 per credit hour resident, $1,982 per credit hour non-resident (second and third year); $28,261 (for LL M); $838 per credit $838 (for MSL). *Financial support:* In 2017–18, 664 students received support, including 23 fellowships (averaging $4,000 per year); Federal Work-Study, institutionally sponsored loans, and scholarships/grants also available. Support available to part-time students. Financial award application deadline: 3/1; financial award applicants required to submit FAFSA. *Faculty research:* Environmental regulation, health care policy, information privacy, race and criminal justice, international and comparative law. *Total annual research expenditures:* $4.6 million. *Unit head:* Donald B. Tobin, Dean/Professor, 410-706-7214, Fax: 410-706-4403, E-mail: dtobin@law.umaryland.edu. *Application contact:* Susan Krinsky, Associate Dean for Student Affairs and Communications, 410-706-3492, Fax: 410-706-1793, E-mail: admissions@law.umaryland.edu.
Website: http://www.law.umaryland.edu/

University of Maryland, College Park, Academic Affairs, Robert H. Smith School of Business, Program in Business Management/Law, College Park, MD 20742. Offers JD/MBA. *Accreditation:* AACSB. *Entrance requirements:* Additional exam requirements/recommendations for international students: Required—TOEFL.

University of Maryland, College Park, Academic Affairs, School of Public Policy, Joint Program in Public Policy/Law, College Park, MD 20742. Offers JD/MPM. Electronic applications accepted.

University of Massachusetts Dartmouth, Graduate School, University of Massachusetts School of Law –Dartmouth, Dartmouth, MA 02747. Offers JD. *Accreditation:* ABA. *Program availability:* Part-time, evening/weekend. *Faculty:* 15 full-time (8 women), 15 part-time/adjunct (3 women). *Students:* 154 full-time (77 women), 48 part-time (27 women); includes 59 minority (19 Black or African American, non-Hispanic/Latino; 9 Asian, non-Hispanic/Latino; 24 Hispanic/Latino; 1 Native Hawaiian or other Pacific Islander, non-Hispanic/Latino; 6 Two or more races, non-Hispanic/Latino), 2 international. Average age 30. 793 applicants, 64% accepted, 82 enrolled. In 2017, 50 doctorates awarded. *Degree requirements:* For doctorate, comprehensive exam, bar exam. *Entrance requirements:* For doctorate, LSAT, LSAC report, 2 letters of recommendation, resume, personal statement (minimum 2-3 pages), official transcripts. Additional exam requirements/recommendations for international students: Recommended—TOEFL. *Application deadline:* For fall admission, 6/30 priority date for domestic students, 5/30 priority date for international students. Application fee: $60. Electronic applications accepted. *Expenses:* Contact institution. *Financial support:* Fellowships, institutionally sponsored loans, and scholarships/grants available. Support available to part-time students. Financial award application deadline: 3/1; financial award applicants required to submit FAFSA. *Faculty research:* Gender violence, ethics, feminist jurisprudence, legal history, legal philosophy, criminal law, criminal procedure

Law

issues, law and inequality, legal education and methodology, liberalism, procedural due process, copyright law, legal writing and rhetoric. *Unit head:* Daniel Fitzpatrick, Assistant Dean, University of Massachusetts School of Law - Dartmouth, 508-985-1110, Fax: 508-985-1175, E-mail: lawadmissions@umassd.edu. *Application contact:* Nancy Fitzsimmons-Hebert, Assistant Director of Marketing and Recruitment, 508-985-1110, Fax: 508-985-1175, E-mail: lawadmissions@umassd.edu.
Website: http://www.umassd.edu/law

University of Memphis, Cecil C. Humphreys School of Law, Memphis, TN 38103-2189. Offers JD, JD/MA, JD/MBA, JD/MPH. *Accreditation:* ABA. *Program availability:* Part-time. *Faculty:* 25 full-time (11 women), 23 part-time/adjunct (7 women). *Students:* 297 full-time (128 women), 14 part-time (10 women); includes 79 minority (60 Black or African American, non-Hispanic/Latino; 5 American Indian or Alaska Native, non-Hispanic/Latino; 5 Asian, non-Hispanic/Latino; 9 Hispanic/Latino). Average age 26. 647 applicants, 52% accepted, 107 enrolled. In 2017, 1 doctorate awarded. *Entrance requirements:* For doctorate, LSAT, CAS report, letters of recommendation, or evaluations. Additional exam requirements/recommendations for international students: Required—TOEFL. *Application deadline:* For fall admission, 3/15 priority date for domestic and international students. Applications are processed on a rolling basis. Application fee: $0 ($40 for international students). Electronic applications accepted. *Expenses:* $191,97 full-time resident tuition and fees, $26,402 full-time non-resident. *Financial support:* In 2017–18, 138 students received support, including 26 fellowships (averaging $12,118 per year), 20 research assistantships (averaging $5,000 per year); teaching assistantships, career-related internships or fieldwork, Federal Work-Study, scholarships/grants, and tuition waivers (partial) also available. Support available to part-time students. Financial award application deadline: 5/1; financial award applicants required to submit FAFSA. *Faculty research:* Tort law, gun violence, mass incarceration, evidence law, employment law. *Total annual research expenditures:* $37,000. *Unit head:* Peter V. Letsou, Dean, 901-678-2421, Fax: 901-678-5210, E-mail: pvletsou@memphis.edu. *Application contact:* Dr. Sue Ann McClellan, Assistant Dean for Law Admissions, Recruiting and Scholarships, 901-678-5403, Fax: 901-678-0741, E-mail: smcclell@memphis.edu.
Website: http://www.memphis.edu/law/

University of Miami, Graduate School, University of Miami School of Law, Coral Gables, FL 33146. Offers entertainment, arts, and sports law (LL M); estate planning (LL M); intensive English (LL M); international arbitration (LL M); international law (LL M), including general international law, inter-American law; law (JD); maritime law (LL M); real estate/property development (LL M); taxation (LL M); taxation of cross-border investment (LL M); the business of innovation, law and technology (BILT) (JD); U.S. and transnational law for foreign-trained lawyers (LL M); JD/LL M; JD/MA; JD/MBA; JD/MBA/LL M; JD/MD; JD/MM; JD/MPA; JD/MPH; JD/MPS; JD/MS Ed; JD/PhD. *Accreditation:* ABA. *Program availability:* Part-time. *Faculty:* 89 full-time (45 women), 115 part-time/adjunct (27 women). *Students:* 1,099 full-time (534 women), 93 part-time (48 women); includes 455 minority (63 Black or African American, non-Hispanic/Latino; 3 American Indian or Alaska Native, non-Hispanic/Latino; 25 Asian, non-Hispanic/Latino; 330 Hispanic/Latino; 1 Native Hawaiian or other Pacific Islander, non-Hispanic/Latino; 33 Two or more races, non-Hispanic/Latino), 53 international. 2,356 applicants, 59% accepted, 316 enrolled. *Entrance requirements:* For doctorate, LSAT, 2 letters of recommendation. Additional exam requirements/recommendations for international students: Required—TOEFL (minimum score 580 paper-based; 92 iBT), IELTS (minimum score 7). *Application deadline:* For fall admission, 7/31 for domestic and international students. Applications are processed on a rolling basis. Application fee: $60. Electronic applications accepted. *Expenses:* Contact institution. *Financial support:* Fellowships, research assistantships, career-related internships or fieldwork, Federal Work-Study, institutionally sponsored loans, scholarships/grants, and unspecified

assistantships available. Financial award application deadline: 3/1; financial award applicants required to submit FAFSA. *Faculty research:* Energy/climate change, international finance, Internet law/law of electronic commerce, race/social justice, art law/cultural heritage law. *Unit head:* Michael Goodnight, Associate Dean of Admissions and Enrollment Management, 305-284-2527, Fax: 305-284-3084, E-mail: mgoodnig@law.miami.edu. *Application contact:* Therese Lambert, Director of Student Recruitment, 305-284-6746, Fax: 305-284-3084, E-mail: tlambert@law.miami.edu.
Website: http://www.law.miami.edu.

See Display below and Close-Up on page 1527.

University of Michigan, Law School, Ann Arbor, MI 48109-1215. Offers comparative law (MCL); international tax (LL M); law (LL M, JD, SJD); JD/MA; JD/MBA; JD/MHSA; JD/MPH; JD/MPP; JD/MS; JD/MSI; JD/MSW; JD/MUP; JD/PhD. *Accreditation:* ABA. *Faculty:* 113 full-time (40 women), 33 part-time/adjunct (7 women). *Students:* 931 full-time (435 women); includes 194 minority (36 Black or African American, non-Hispanic/Latino; 7 American Indian or Alaska Native, non-Hispanic/Latino; 65 Asian, non-Hispanic/Latino; 44 Hispanic/Latino; 42 Two or more races, non-Hispanic/Latino), 52 international. 5,284 applicants, 22% accepted, 320 enrolled. In 2017, 41 master's, 331 doctorates awarded. *Entrance requirements:* For doctorate, LSAT. *Application deadline:* For fall admission, 2/15 for domestic students. Applications are processed on a rolling basis. Application fee: $75. Electronic applications accepted. *Expenses:* Contact institution. *Financial support:* In 2017–18, 777 students received support. Career-related internships or fieldwork, Federal Work-Study, institutionally sponsored loans, and scholarships/grants available. Financial award applicants required to submit FAFSA. *Unit head:* Mark D. West, Dean, 734-764-1358. *Application contact:* Sarah C. Zearfoss, Assistant Dean and Director of Admissions, 734-764-0537, Fax: 734-647-3218, E-mail: law.jd.admissions@umich.edu.
Website: http://www.law.umich.edu/

University of Minnesota, Twin Cities Campus, Law School, Minneapolis, MN 55455. Offers LL M, MS, JD, SJD, JD/MA, JD/MBA, JD/MBS, JD/MD, JD/MHA, JD/MPA, JD/MPH, JD/MPP, JD/MS, JD/MSST, JD/MURP, JD/PhD. *Accreditation:* ABA. *Faculty:* 74 full-time (30 women), 138 part-time/adjunct (44 women). *Students:* 566 full-time (268 women); includes 87 minority (8 Black or African American, non-Hispanic/Latino; 3 American Indian or Alaska Native, non-Hispanic/Latino; 35 Asian, non-Hispanic/Latino; 22 Hispanic/Latino; 19 Two or more races, non-Hispanic/Latino), 58 international. 1,808 applicants, 47% accepted, 191 enrolled. In 2017, 206 doctorates awarded. *Entrance requirements:* For doctorate, LSAT. Additional exam requirements/recommendations for international students: Recommended—TOEFL, IELTS. *Application deadline:* For fall admission, 7/15 for domestic students. Applications are processed on a rolling basis. Application fee: $60. Electronic applications accepted. *Expenses:* Contact institution. *Financial support:* In 2017–18, 577 students received support. Fellowships, research assistantships, career-related internships or fieldwork, Federal Work-Study, institutionally sponsored loans, and scholarships/grants available. Financial award application deadline: 7/1; financial award applicants required to submit FAFSA. *Faculty research:* International and comparative law; law, science, and technology; criminal justice; environmental and energy law; business law. *Unit head:* Garry W. Jenkins, Dean, 612-625-4841. *Application contact:* Robin Ingli, Director of Admissions, 612-625-3487, Fax: 612-625-2011, E-mail: jdadmissions@umn.edu.
Website: http://www.law.umn.edu/

University of Mississippi, School of Law, University, MS 38677. Offers LL M, JD, JD/MBA. *Accreditation:* ABA. *Faculty:* 32 full-time (14 women), 9 part-time/adjunct (3 women). *Students:* 358 full-time (161 women), 3 part-time (0 women); includes 86 minority (46 Black or African American, non-Hispanic/Latino; 5 Asian, non-Hispanic/Latino; 21 Hispanic/Latino; 14 Two or more races, non-Hispanic/Latino). Average age

25. In 2017, 179 doctorates awarded. *Entrance requirements:* For doctorate, LSAT, LSDAS. Additional exam requirements/recommendations for international students: Required—TOEFL. *Application deadline:* For fall admission, 4/1 for domestic students. Application fee: $50. *Expenses:* Contact institution. *Financial support:* Fellowships, research assistantships, teaching assistantships, career-related internships or fieldwork, Federal Work-Study, institutionally sponsored loans, and scholarships/grants available. Support available to part-time students. Financial award application deadline: 3/1; financial award applicants required to submit FAFSA. *Unit head:* Dr. Susan Duncan, Dean, 662-915-6900, Fax: 662-915-6895, E-mail: lawadmin@olemiss.edu. *Application contact:* Macey Edmondson, Assistant Dean for Admissions and Scholarships, 662-915-6819, Fax: 662-915-7577, E-mail: clee@olemiss.edu.

University of Missouri, School of Law, Columbia, MO 65211. Offers dispute resolution (LL M); law (JD); JD/MA; JD/MBA; JD/MPA. *Accreditation:* ABA. *Entrance requirements:* For doctorate, LSAT. Additional exam requirements/recommendations for international students: Required—TOEFL (minimum score 600 paper-based; 100 iBT), IELTS (minimum score 7). *Expenses:* Contact institution.

University of Missouri–Kansas City, School of Law, Kansas City, MO 64110-2499. Offers LL M, JD, JD/LL M, JD/MBA, JD/MPA, LL M/MPA. *Accreditation:* ABA. *Program availability:* Part-time. *Degree requirements:* For master's, thesis (for general). *Entrance requirements:* For master's, LSAT, minimum GPA of 3.0 (for general), 2.7 (for taxation); for doctorate, LSAT. Additional exam requirements/recommendations for international students: Required—TOEFL (minimum score 550 paper-based; 80 iBT). Electronic applications accepted. *Expenses:* Contact institution. *Faculty research:* Family and children's issues, litigation, estate planning, urban law, business, tax entrepreneurial law.

University of Montana, Alexander Blewett III School of Law, Missoula, MT 59812. Offers JD, JD/MBA, JD/MPA. *Accreditation:* ABA. *Degree requirements:* For doctorate, oral presentation, paper. *Entrance requirements:* For doctorate, LSAT. *Expenses:* Contact institution. *Faculty research:* Legal education curriculum, business and probate law reform, rules of civil procedure reform, tribal courts, women's issues.

University of Nebraska–Lincoln, College of Law, Lincoln, NE 68583-0902. Offers law (JD); legal studies (MLS); space and telecommunications law (LL M); JD/MA; JD/MBA; JD/MCRP; JD/MPA; JD/PhD. *Accreditation:* ABA. *Entrance requirements:* For doctorate, LSAT. Electronic applications accepted. *Expenses:* Contact institution. *Faculty research:* Law and medicine, constitutional law, criminal procedure, international trade.

University of Nevada, Las Vegas, William S. Boyd School of Law, Las Vegas, NV 89154-1003. Offers gaming law and regulation (LL M); law (JD); JD/MBA; JD/MSW; JD/PhD. *Accreditation:* ABA. *Program availability:* Part-time, evening/weekend. *Faculty:* 38 full-time (24 women), 20 part-time/adjunct (4 women). *Students:* 315 full-time (157 women), 63 part-time (29 women); includes 140 minority (28 Black or African American, non-Hispanic/Latino; 21 Asian, non-Hispanic/Latino; 71 Hispanic/Latino; 1 Native Hawaiian or other Pacific Islander, non-Hispanic/Latino; 19 Two or more races, non-Hispanic/Latino), 4 international. Average age 30. 643 applicants, 34% accepted, 124 enrolled. In 2017, 12 master's, 126 doctorates awarded. *Degree requirements:* For doctorate, 89 credits with minimum cumulative GPA of 2.3, community service, professional skills/experiential learning, capstone writing. *Entrance requirements:* For doctorate, LSAT. Additional exam requirements/recommendations for international students: Recommended—TOEFL (minimum score 61 iBT), IELTS (minimum score 6), TSE (minimum score 44). *Application deadline:* For fall admission, 3/15 for domestic students. Applications are processed on a rolling basis. Application fee: $50. Electronic applications accepted. *Expenses:* $25,900 in-state; $37,500 out-of-state. *Financial support:* In 2017–18, 252 students received support, including 18 fellowships with partial tuition reimbursements available (averaging $17,950 per year), 26 research assistantships (averaging $503 per year); career-related internships or fieldwork, scholarships/grants, and tuition waivers (full and partial) also available. Support available to part-time students. Financial award application deadline: 5/1; financial award applicants required to submit FAFSA. *Faculty research:* Civil procedure; constitutional law; professional responsibility; health law; intellectual property. *Unit head:* Daniel W. Hamilton, Dean, 702-895-3671, Fax: 702-895-1095, E-mail: christine.smith@unlv.edu. *Application contact:* Lindsey Baker, Administrative Assistant IV, 702-895-2424, Fax: 702-895-2414, E-mail: lindsey.baker@unlv.edu.
Website: http://law.unlv.edu

University of New Hampshire, School of Law, Concord, NH 03301. Offers business law (JD); commerce and technology (LL M, MCT, Diploma); criminal law (JD); intellectual property (LL M, MIP, JD, Diploma), including patent law (JD), trademarks and copyright (JD); international criminal law and justice (LL M, MICLJ); litigation (JD); public interest and social justice (JD); sports and entertainment law (JD); JD/LL M; JD/MBA; JD/MIP; JD/MPP; JD/MSW. *Accreditation:* ABA. *Program availability:* Part-time, 100% online, limited residential. *Degree requirements:* For doctorate, comprehensive exam. *Entrance requirements:* For doctorate, LSAT. Additional exam requirements/recommendations for international students: Required—TOEFL (minimum score 600 paper-based; 100 iBT), minimum TOEFL iBT score of 80 (for master's programs). Electronic applications accepted. *Expenses:* Contact institution. *Faculty research:* Intellectual property, health law and policy, sports and entertainment law, patent law, trademarks and copyright.

University of New Mexico, School of Law, Albuquerque, NM 87131-0001. Offers JD, JD/M Acct, JD/MA, JD/MBA, JD/MPA. *Degree requirements:* For doctorate, ethics class, 2 writing classes, clinic. *Entrance requirements:* For doctorate, LSAT, bachelor's degree. Additional exam requirements/recommendations for international students: Required—TOEFL (minimum score 600 paper-based; 100 iBT). Electronic applications accepted. *Expenses:* Contact institution. *Faculty research:* Clinical legal education, international law, Indian law, natural resources and environmental law, Constitutional law, business and tax law, legal writing.

University of North Alabama, College of Arts and Sciences, Department of Politics, Justice, and Law, Florence, AL 35632-0001. Offers criminal justice (MSCJ). *Program availability:* Part-time, 100% online. *Faculty:* 4 full-time (0 women), 3 part-time/adjunct (1 woman). *Students:* 5 full-time (4 women), 17 part-time (11 women); includes 9 minority (6 Black or African American, non-Hispanic/Latino; 3 Hispanic/Latino). Average age 30. 18 applicants, 94% accepted, 9 enrolled. In 2017, 6 master's awarded. *Degree requirements:* For master's, comprehensive exam (for some programs), thesis optional. *Entrance requirements:* For master's, GRE General Test, MAT, three letters of recommendation; essay. Additional exam requirements/recommendations for international students: Required—TOEFL (minimum score 79 iBT), IELTS (minimum score 6), PTE (minimum score 54). *Application deadline:* Applications are processed on a rolling basis. Application fee: $50 ($100 for international students). Electronic applications accepted. *Expenses:* Tuition, state resident: full-time $7824; part-time $5943 per year. Tuition, nonresident: full-time $15,648; part-time $11,736 per year. *Required fees:* $3064; $2298 per unit. Tuition and fees vary according to course load and reciprocity agreements. *Financial support:* Federal Work-Study, scholarships/grants, and unspecified assistantships available. Financial award application deadline: 2/1; financial award applicants required to submit FAFSA. *Unit head:* Dr. Tim Collins, Chair, 256-765-5045, Fax: 256-765-5045, E-mail: jtcollins@una.edu. *Application contact:* Hillary N. Coats, Graduate Admissions Coordinator, 256-765-4447, E-mail: graduate@una.edu.
Website: http://www.una.edu/criminaljustice/

The University of North Carolina at Chapel Hill, School of Law, Chapel Hill, NC 27599-3380. Offers LL M, JD, JD/MAMC, JD/MBA, JD/MPA, JD/MPH, JD/MPP, JD/MRP, JD/MSA, JD/MSIS, JD/MSLS, JD/MSW, JD/PhD. *Accreditation:* ABA. *Entrance requirements:* For doctorate, LSAT, bachelor's degree from accredited college or university, two letters of recommendation, essays, resume. Additional exam requirements/recommendations for international students: Required—TOEFL (minimum score 650 paper-based; 100 iBT). Electronic applications accepted. *Expenses:* Contact institution. *Faculty research:* Corporate and banking law, environmental policy, state and U.S. Constitutional law, health law policy, immigration law and civil rights.

University of North Dakota, School of Law, Grand Forks, ND 58202. Offers JD. *Accreditation:* ABA. *Entrance requirements:* For doctorate, LSAT. *Expenses:* Contact institution.

University of North Texas at Dallas, College of Law, Dallas, TX 75241. Offers JD.

University of Notre Dame, Law School, Notre Dame, IN 46556-0780. Offers human rights (LL M, JSD); international and comparative law (LL M); law (JD). *Accreditation:* ABA. *Degree requirements:* For master's, thesis, 1-year residency; for doctorate, thesis/dissertation, 2-year residency (for JSD). *Entrance requirements:* For doctorate, LSAT (for JD), LL M (for JSD). Additional exam requirements/recommendations for international students: Required—TOEFL. Electronic applications accepted. *Expenses:* Contact institution. *Faculty research:* Constitutional structure; international law (public and private); law and religion; land, energy, and environmental law; intellectual property, including patent, copyright, and trademark law.

University of Oklahoma, College of Law, Norman, OK 73019. Offers LL M, JD, JD/MA, JD/MBA, JD/MPH, JD/MS. *Accreditation:* ABA. *Program availability:* Part-time, 100% online, blended/hybrid learning. *Faculty:* 31 full-time (14 women), 21 part-time/adjunct (7 women). *Students:* 518 full-time (223 women), 237 part-time (165 women); includes 243 minority (36 Black or African American, non-Hispanic/Latino; 112 American Indian or Alaska Native, non-Hispanic/Latino; 14 Asian, non-Hispanic/Latino; 30 Hispanic/Latino; 51 Two or more races, non-Hispanic/Latino), 10 international. Average age 28. 960 applicants, 40% accepted, 159 enrolled. In 2017, 24 master's, 156 doctorates awarded. *Entrance requirements:* For master's, JD or equivalent; for doctorate, LSAT. Additional exam requirements/recommendations for international students: Required—TOEFL minimum score 550 paper-based, 79 iBT (for LL M); 600 paper-based, 100 iBT (for JD). *Application deadline:* For fall admission, 3/15 for domestic and international students. Applications are processed on a rolling basis. Application fee: $50. Electronic applications accepted. *Expenses:* Contact institution. *Financial support:* In 2017–18, 471 students received support. Career-related internships or fieldwork, Federal Work-Study, scholarships/grants, and tuition waivers (full and partial) available. Financial award application deadline: 6/1; financial award applicants required to submit FAFSA. *Faculty research:* Energy and natural resources; indigenous peoples law; business and commercial; litigation and procedure; tax, pensions and retirement. *Unit head:* Joseph Harroz, Jr., Dean, 405-325-4884, Fax: 405-325-7712, E-mail: jharroz@ou.edu. *Application contact:* Vicki Ferguson, Admissions Coordinator, 405-325-4728, Fax: 405-325-0502, E-mail: admissions@law.ou.edu.
Website: http://www.law.ou.edu/

University of Oregon, School of Law, Eugene, OR 97403. Offers MA, MS, JD, JD/MBA, JD/MS. *Accreditation:* ABA. *Entrance requirements:* For doctorate, LSAT. *Expenses:* Contact institution.

University of Ottawa, Faculty of Graduate and Postdoctoral Studies, Faculty of Law, Ottawa, ON K1N 6N5, Canada. Offers LL M, LL D. *Program availability:* Part-time, evening/weekend. *Degree requirements:* For master's, thesis or alternative; for doctorate, thesis/dissertation. *Entrance requirements:* For master's, minimum B average, LL B; for doctorate, LL M, minimum B+ average. Electronic applications accepted. *Faculty research:* International law, human rights law, family law.

University of Pennsylvania, Law School, Philadelphia, PA 19104. Offers LL CM, LL M, ML, JD, SJD, JD/DMD, JD/Ed D, JD/LL M, JD/MA, JD/MBA, JD/MBE, JD/MCIT, JD/MCP, JD/MD, JD/MES, JD/MPA, JD/MPH, JD/MS, JD/MS Ed, JD/MSE, JD/MSSP, JD/MSW, JD/PhD. JD/LL M offered jointly with Hong Kong University. *Accreditation:* ABA. *Faculty:* 100 full-time (36 women), 146 part-time/adjunct (52 women). *Students:* 736 full-time (351 women); includes 208 minority (49 Black or African American, non-Hispanic/Latino; 2 American Indian or Alaska Native, non-Hispanic/Latino; 78 Asian, non-Hispanic/Latino; 48 Hispanic/Latino; 31 Two or more races, non-Hispanic/Latino), 47 international. Average age 27. 5,601 applicants, 18% accepted, 234 enrolled. In 2017, 256 doctorates awarded. *Degree requirements:* For doctorate, thesis/dissertation. *Entrance requirements:* For doctorate, LSAT (for JD). Additional exam requirements/recommendations for international students: Recommended—TOEFL, IELTS. *Application deadline:* For fall admission, 3/1 for domestic and international students. Applications are processed on a rolling basis. Application fee: $80. Electronic applications accepted. *Expenses:* Contact institution. *Financial support:* In 2017–18, 366 students received support, including 172 research assistantships (averaging $3,112 per year), 4 teaching assistantships (averaging $1,250 per year); fellowships, career-related internships or fieldwork, Federal Work-Study, institutionally sponsored loans, and scholarships/grants also available. Financial award application deadline: 3/1; financial award applicants required to submit CSS PROFILE or FAFSA. *Faculty research:* Administrative law and regulation, business and corporate law, civil procedure, Constitutional law, criminal law, environmental law, health law, intellectual property and technology law, international and comparative law, law and economics, legal history, philosophy, tax law and policy. *Total annual research expenditures:* $649,303. *Unit head:* Theodore W. Ruger, Dean, 215-898-7463, Fax: 215-573-2025. *Application contact:* Renee Post, Associate Dean of Admissions and Financial Aid, 215-898-7400, Fax: 215-898-9606, E-mail: contactadmissions@law.upenn.edu.
Website: http://www.law.upenn.edu/

University of Pittsburgh, Katz Graduate School of Business, MBA/Juris Doctor Program, Pittsburgh, PA 15260. Offers MBA/JD. *Faculty:* 91 full-time (30 women), 14 part-time/adjunct (4 women). *Students:* 10 full-time (4 women); includes 2 minority (1 Black or African American, non-Hispanic/Latino; 1 Two or more races, non-Hispanic/Latino), 1 international. Average age 27. 7 applicants, 71% accepted, 4 enrolled. *Entrance requirements:* Additional exam requirements/recommendations for international students: Required—TOEFL (minimum score 100 iBT) or IELTS (minimum score 7.0). *Application deadline:* For fall admission, 4/1 priority date for domestic students, 2/1 priority date for international students. Application fee: $50. Electronic applications accepted. *Financial support:* Scholarships/grants available. Financial award application deadline: 6/1; financial award applicants required to submit FAFSA. *Faculty research:* Accounting systems/financial reporting, corporate finance, shopper marketing/consumer behavior, management information systems, organizational behavior and entrepreneurship. *Total annual research expenditures:* $475,077. *Unit head:* Dr. Arjang A. Assad, Dean, 412-648-1556, Fax: 412-648-1552, E-mail: aassad@katz.pitt.edu. *Application contact:* Thomas Keller, Director of MBA Admissions, 412-648-1700, Fax: 412-648-1659, E-mail: mba@katz.pitt.edu.
Website: http://www.katz.business.pitt.edu/mba/joint-and-dual/juris-doc

See Display on page 158 and Close-Up on page 187.

Law

University of Pittsburgh, School of Law, LL M Program for Foreign-Trained Lawyers, Pittsburgh, PA 15260. Offers LL M. Program offered to international students only. *Accreditation:* ABA. *Program availability:* Part-time. *Faculty:* 47 full-time (22 women), 116 part-time/adjunct (29 women). *Students:* 26 full-time (15 women), 3 part-time (1 woman); includes 5 minority (3 Black or African American, non-Hispanic/Latino; 1 Asian, non-Hispanic/Latino; 1 Hispanic/Latino), 11 international. Average age 25. 44 applicants, 73% accepted, 19 enrolled. In 2017, 23 master's awarded. *Entrance requirements:* For master's, law degree from foreign university. Additional exam requirements/recommendations for international students: Required—TOEFL (minimum score 577 paper-based; 90 iBT), IELTS (minimum score 6.5). *Application deadline:* Applications are processed on a rolling basis. Application fee: $0 ($55 for international students). Electronic applications accepted. *Expenses:* $38,500 tuition; $890 fees. *Financial support:* In 2017–18, 13 students received support, including 13 fellowships with partial tuition reimbursements available (averaging $14,000 per year); research assistantships, teaching assistantships, and tuition waivers also available. *Faculty research:* International arbitration, private international law, Islamic law, environmental criminal and comparative law. *Unit head:* Prof. Ronald A. Brand, Academic Director, 412-648-1307, Fax: 412-648-2648, E-mail: rbrand@pitt.edu. *Application contact:* Austin A. Lebo, Program Administrator, 412-648-7023, Fax: 412-648-2648, E-mail: aal37@pitt.edu.
Website: http://www.law.pitt.edu/llm

University of Puerto Rico–Río Piedras, School of Law, San Juan, PR 00931-3349. Offers LL M, JD. *Accreditation:* ABA. *Program availability:* Part-time, evening/weekend. *Entrance requirements:* For master's, LSAT, minimum GPA of 3.0, letter of recommendation; for doctorate, GMAT, GRE, LSAT, EXADEP, minimum GPA of 3.0. Additional exam requirements/recommendations for international students: Required—TOEFL. *Faculty research:* Civil code; Puerto Rico constitutional law; professional behavior, rules and regulations; international law; expert testimony.

University of Richmond, School of Law, University of Richmond, VA 23173. Offers JD, JD/MA, JD/MBA, JD/MHA, JD/MPA, JD/MS, JD/MSW, JD/MURP. JD/MHA, JD/MPA offered jointly with Virginia Commonwealth University; JD/MURP with Virginia Commonwealth University; JD/MA with Department of History; JD/MS with Department of Biology. *Accreditation:* ABA. *Entrance requirements:* For doctorate, LSAT. Electronic applications accepted. *Expenses:* Contact institution.

University of St. Thomas, School of Law, Minneapolis, MN 55403-2015. Offers law (JD); organizational ethics and compliance (LL M, MSL); U.S. law (LL M); JD/LL M; JD/MA; JD/MBA; JD/MSW. *Accreditation:* ABA. *Program availability:* 100% online. *Faculty:* 29 full-time (8 women), 68 part-time/adjunct (26 women). *Students:* 387 full-time (207 women); includes 65 minority (21 Black or African American, non-Hispanic/Latino; 1 American Indian or Alaska Native, non-Hispanic/Latino; 13 Asian, non-Hispanic/Latino; 20 Hispanic/Latino; 10 Two or more races, non-Hispanic/Latino), 9 international. Average age 25. 545 applicants, 64% accepted, 145 enrolled. In 2017, 5 master's, 122 doctorates awarded. *Degree requirements:* For doctorate, mentor externship, public service. *Entrance requirements:* For doctorate, LSAT, 2 letters of recommendation, personal statement. Additional exam requirements/recommendations for international students: Recommended—TOEFL (minimum score 80 iBT). *Application deadline:* For fall admission, 8/1 priority date for domestic and international students. Applications are processed on a rolling basis. Application fee: $0. Electronic applications accepted. *Expenses:* $40,247 per academic year. *Financial support:* In 2017–18, 364 students received support. Scholarships/grants available. Financial award application deadline: 7/1; financial award applicants required to submit FAFSA. *Faculty research:* Constitutional law (executive powers and First Amendment); banking, securities, and financial markets; law, religion, and jurisprudence; international law, development and dispute resolution; formation of professional identity, values, and skills. *Unit head:* Robert K. Vischer, Dean, 651-962-4838, Fax: 651-962-4881, E-mail: rkvischer@stthomas.edu. *Application contact:* Cari Haaland, Assistant Dean for Admissions, 651-962-4872, Fax: 651-962-4876, E-mail: lawschool@stthomas.edu.
Website: http://www.stthomas.edu/law/

University of San Diego, School of Law, San Diego, CA 92110. Offers business and corporate law (LL M); comparative law (LL M); general studies (LL M); international law (LL M); law (JD); taxation (LL M, Diploma); JD/IMBA; JD/MA; JD/MBA. *Accreditation:* ABA. *Program availability:* Part-time, evening/weekend. *Faculty:* 45 full-time (13 women), 46 part-time/adjunct (13 women). *Students:* 693 full-time (371 women), 96 part-time (40 women); includes 265 minority (31 Black or African American, non-Hispanic/Latino; 15 American Indian or Alaska Native, non-Hispanic/Latino; 97 Asian, non-Hispanic/Latino; 107 Hispanic/Latino; 4 Native Hawaiian or other Pacific Islander, non-Hispanic/Latino; 11 Two or more races, non-Hispanic/Latino), 28 international. Average age 27. 3,260 applicants, 238 enrolled. In 2017, 57 master's, 206 doctorates awarded. *Entrance requirements:* For master's, JD, LL B or equivalent from an ABA-accredited law school; for doctorate, LSAT (less than 5 years old), bachelor's degree, registration with the Credential Assemble Service (CAS). Additional exam requirements/recommendations for international students: Required—TOEFL (minimum score 600 paper-based; 100 iBT). *Application deadline:* For fall admission, 2/1 priority date for domestic students. Applications are processed on a rolling basis. Electronic applications accepted. *Expenses:* Contact institution. *Financial support:* In 2017–18, 617 students received support. Career-related internships or fieldwork, Federal Work-Study, institutionally sponsored loans, and scholarships/grants available. Support available to part-time students. Financial award application deadline: 3/1; financial award applicants required to submit FAFSA. *Faculty research:* Corporate law, children's advocacy, Constitutional and criminal law, international and comparative law, public interest law, intellectual property and tax law. *Unit head:* Dr. Stephen C. Ferruolo, Dean, 619-260-4527, E-mail: lawdean@sandiego.edu. *Application contact:* Jorge Garcia, Assistant Dean, JD Admissions, 619-260-4528, Fax: 619-260-2218, E-mail: jdinfo@sandiego.edu.
Website: http://www.sandiego.edu/law/

University of San Francisco, School of Law, JD Program, San Francisco, CA 94117-1080. Offers JD. *Accreditation:* ABA. *Program availability:* Part-time.

University of Saskatchewan, College of Graduate Studies and Research, College of Law, Saskatoon, SK S7N 5A2, Canada. Offers LL M, JD. *Program availability:* Part-time. *Degree requirements:* For master's, thesis. *Entrance requirements:* For master's, LL B; for doctorate, LSAT. Additional exam requirements/recommendations for international students: Required—TOEFL. *Faculty research:* Cooperative, native/aboriginal, constitutional, commercial, consumer, and natural resource law; criminal justice; human rights.

University of South Africa, College of Law, Pretoria, South Africa. Offers correctional services management (M Tech); criminology (MA, PhD); law (LL M, LL D); penology (MA, PhD); police science (MA, PhD); policing (M Tech); security risk management (M Tech); social science in criminology (MA).

University of South Carolina, School of Law, Columbia, SC 29208. Offers JD, JD/IMBA, JD/M Acc, JD/MCJ, JD/MEERM, JD/MHA, JD/MHR, JD/MIBS, JD/MPA, JD/MSEL, JD/MSW. *Accreditation:* ABA. *Degree requirements:* For doctorate, thesis/dissertation. *Entrance requirements:* For doctorate, LSAT. *Expenses:* Contact institution.

University of South Dakota, Graduate School, School of Law, Vermillion, SD 57069-2390. Offers JD, JD/MA, JD/MBA, JD/MP Acc, JD/MPA, JD/MS. *Accreditation:* ABA.

Program availability: Part-time. *Entrance requirements:* For doctorate, LSAT. Additional exam requirements/recommendations for international students: Required—TOEFL (minimum score 600 paper-based). *Application deadline:* For fall admission, 3/1 priority date for domestic students. Applications are processed on a rolling basis. Application fee: $35. Electronic applications accepted. *Expenses:* Contact institution. *Financial support:* Research assistantships with partial tuition reimbursements, career-related internships or fieldwork, Federal Work-Study, scholarships/grants, and unspecified assistantships available. Financial award application deadline: 4/1; financial award applicants required to submit FAFSA. *Faculty research:* Indian law, skills training, international law, family law, evidence. *Application contact:* Admissions Officer/Registrar, 605-677-5444, E-mail: jean.henriques@usd.edu.
Website: http://www.usd.edu/law

University of Southern California, Graduate School, Gould School of Law, Los Angeles, CA 90089. Offers comparative law for foreign attorneys (MCL); law (JD); law for foreign-educated attorneys (LL M); JD/MA; JD/MBA; JD/MBT; JD/MPA; JD/MPP; JD/MRED; JD/MS; JD/MSW; JD/PhD; JD/Pharm D. *Accreditation:* ABA. *Entrance requirements:* For doctorate, LSAT. Additional exam requirements/recommendations for international students: Required—TOEFL. *Faculty research:* Intellectual property law, tax law, criminal law, law and philosophy, law and history.

The University of Tennessee, College of Law, Knoxville, TN 37996-1810. Offers business transactions (JD); law (JD); trial advocacy and dispute resolution (JD); JD/MA; JD/MBA; JD/MPH; JD/MPPA. *Accreditation:* ABA. *Entrance requirements:* For doctorate, LSAT. Additional exam requirements/recommendations for international students: Recommended—TOEFL. Electronic applications accepted. Application fee is waived when completed online. *Expenses:* Contact institution. *Faculty research:* Legal expert systems, medical malpractice remedies, professional ethics, insanity defense.

The University of Texas at Austin, Graduate School, College of Liberal Arts, Teresa Lozano Long Institute of Latin American Studies, Austin, TX 78712-1111. Offers cultural politics of Afro-Latin and indigenous peoples (MA); development studies (MA); environmental studies (MA); human rights (MA); Latin American and international law (LL M); JD/MA; MA/MA; MBA/MA; MP Aff/MA; MSCRP/MA. LL M offered jointly with The University of Texas School of Law. *Entrance requirements:* For master's, GRE General Test.

The University of Texas at Austin, School of Law, Austin, TX 78705-3224. Offers LL M, JD, JD/MA, JD/MBA, JD/MGPS, JD/MP Aff, JD/MSCRP. *Accreditation:* ABA. *Entrance requirements:* For doctorate, LSAT, minimum GPA of 2.2. Electronic applications accepted. *Expenses:* Contact institution. *Faculty research:* Constitutional law, corporate law, environmental law, employment and labor law, intellectual property law.

The University of Texas at Dallas, School of Economic, Political and Policy Sciences, Program in Political Science, Richardson, TX 75080. Offers Constitutional law (MA); legislative studies (MA); political science (MA, PhD). *Program availability:* Part-time, evening/weekend. *Faculty:* 11 full-time (2 women), 1 part-time/adjunct (0 women). *Students:* 29 full-time (7 women), 18 part-time (8 women); includes 10 minority (5 Black or African American, non-Hispanic/Latino; 1 Asian, non-Hispanic/Latino; 4 Hispanic/Latino), 10 international. Average age 34. 34 applicants, 53% accepted, 12 enrolled. In 2017, 7 master's, 3 doctorates awarded. Terminal master's awarded for partial completion of doctoral program. *Degree requirements:* For master's, thesis optional, independent study; for doctorate, thesis/dissertation, practicum research. *Entrance requirements:* For master's, GRE (minimum combined verbal and quantitative score of 1100), minimum undergraduate GPA of 3.0; for doctorate, GRE (minimum combined verbal and quantitative score of 1200, writing 4.5), minimum undergraduate GPA of 3.2. Additional exam requirements/recommendations for international students: Required—TOEFL (minimum score 550 paper-based). *Application deadline:* For fall admission, 7/15 for domestic students, 5/1 priority date for international students; for spring admission, 11/15 for domestic students, 9/1 priority date for international students. Applications are processed on a rolling basis. Application fee: $50 ($100 for international students). Electronic applications accepted. *Expenses:* Tuition, state resident: full-time $12,916; part-time $718 per credit hour. Tuition, nonresident: full-time $25,252; part-time $1403 per credit hour. *Financial support:* In 2017–18, 28 students received support, including 1 research assistantship with partial tuition reimbursement available (averaging $17,466 per year), 15 teaching assistantships with partial tuition reimbursements available (averaging $13,100 per year); career-related internships or fieldwork, Federal Work-Study, institutionally sponsored loans, and scholarships/grants also available. Support available to part-time students. Financial award application deadline: 4/30; financial award applicants required to submit FAFSA. *Faculty research:* Terrorism and democratic stability, redistricting and representation, trust and social exchange, how economic ideas impact political thought and public policy. *Unit head:* Dr. Jennifer Holmes, Program Head, 972-883-6843, Fax: 972-883-2735, E-mail: jholmes@utdallas.edu. *Application contact:* Victoria Diesing, Graduate Program Administrator, 972-883-2932, Fax: 972-883-2735, E-mail: psci@utdallas.edu.
Website: http://www.utdallas.edu/epps/political-science/

University of the District of Columbia, David A. Clarke School of Law, Washington, DC 20008. Offers clinical teaching and social justice (LL M); law (JD). *Accreditation:* ABA. *Program availability:* Part-time, evening/weekend. *Degree requirements:* For doctorate, 90 credits, advanced legal writing. *Entrance requirements:* For doctorate, LSAT. Additional exam requirements/recommendations for international students: Recommended—TOEFL. Electronic applications accepted. *Expenses:* Contact institution. *Faculty research:* HIV law, juvenile law, legislative law, community development, small business, immigration and human rights.

University of the Pacific, McGeorge School of Law, Sacramento, CA 95817. Offers advocacy (JD); international water resources law (JSD); public policy and law (LL M); JD/MBA; JD/MPPA. *Accreditation:* ABA. *Program availability:* Part-time, evening/weekend. *Faculty:* 39 full-time (18 women), 38 part-time/adjunct (14 women). *Students:* 376 full-time (200 women), 219 part-time (126 women); includes 199 minority (22 Black or African American, non-Hispanic/Latino; 4 American Indian or Alaska Native, non-Hispanic/Latino; 40 Asian, non-Hispanic/Latino; 119 Hispanic/Latino; 2 Native Hawaiian or other Pacific Islander, non-Hispanic/Latino; 12 Two or more races, non-Hispanic/Latino), 181 international. Average age 29. 1,063 applicants, 61% accepted, 201 enrolled. In 2017, 26 master's, 135 doctorates awarded. *Degree requirements:* For master's, thesis (for some programs); for doctorate, thesis/dissertation (for some programs). *Entrance requirements:* For master's, JD; for doctorate, LSAT (for JD), LL M (for JSD). Additional exam requirements/recommendations for international students: Required—TOEFL (minimum score 600 paper-based; 100 iBT). *Application deadline:* For fall admission, 3/15 priority date for domestic students. Applications are processed on a rolling basis. Application fee: $50. Electronic applications accepted. *Expenses:* Contact institution. *Financial support:* Fellowships, research assistantships, teaching assistantships, career-related internships or fieldwork, Federal Work-Study, institutionally sponsored loans, and scholarships/grants available. Support available to part-time students. Financial award applicants required to submit FAFSA. *Faculty research:* International legal studies, public policy and law, advocacy, intellectual property law, taxation, criminal law. *Unit head:* Michael Schwartz, Dean, 916-739-7151, E-mail: jmootz@pacific.edu. *Application contact:* 916-739-7105, Fax: 916-739-7301, E-mail: mcgeorge@pacific.edu.
Website: http://www.mcgeorge.edu/

The University of Toledo, College of Law, Toledo, OH 43606. Offers compliance (Certificate); health care compliance (Certificate); higher education compliance (Certificate); law (MLW, JD); JD/MACJ; JD/MBA; JD/MD; JD/MPH; JD/MSE. *Accreditation:* ABA. *Program availability:* Part-time, evening/weekend, 100% online. *Faculty:* 24 full-time (10 women), 12 part-time/adjunct (4 women). *Students:* 194 full-time (87 women), 73 part-time (45 women); includes 42 minority (21 Black or African American, non-Hispanic/Latino; 1 American Indian or Alaska Native, non-Hispanic/Latino; 4 Asian, non-Hispanic/Latino; 13 Hispanic/Latino; 1 Native Hawaiian or other Pacific Islander, non-Hispanic/Latino; 2 Two or more races, non-Hispanic/Latino). Average age 28. 524 applicants, 55% accepted, 92 enrolled. In 2017, 3 master's, 80 doctorates awarded. *Degree requirements:* For master's, thesis or alternative, 30 credits (mix of required and elective courses); for doctorate, 89 credits (mix of required and elective courses); for Certificate, 16-17 credits. *Entrance requirements:* For doctorate, LSAT, bachelor's degree. Additional exam requirements/recommendations for international students: Recommended—TOEFL (minimum score 600 paper-based; 100 iBT). *Application deadline:* For fall admission, 8/1 priority date for domestic students, 7/31 for international students; for winter admission, 11/15 for domestic students. Application fee: $0. Electronic applications accepted. *Expenses:* $19,974 full-time resident, $31,522 full-time non-resident; $14,984 part-time resident, $23,645 part-time non-resident. *Financial support:* In 2017–18, 214 students received support, including 9 teaching assistantships; research assistantships, career-related internships or fieldwork, Federal Work-Study, and scholarships/grants also available. Support available to part-time students. Financial award application deadline: 8/1; financial award applicants required to submit FAFSA. *Faculty research:* Feminist legal theory; housing rights; methods of statutory interpretation; interlocutory appeals in federal court; theories of corporation; health law federalism and methods used by states to reform their health care systems using waivers of federal law. *Total annual research expenditures:* $96,000. *Unit head:* D. Benjamin Barros, Dean, 419-530-2379, Fax: 419-530-4526, E-mail: ben.barros@utoledo.edu. *Application contact:* Jessica Mehl, Assistant Dean of Law Admissions, 419-530-4131, Fax: 419-530-4345, E-mail: law.admissions@utoledo.edu. Website: http://www.utoledo.edu/law/

University of Toronto, School of Graduate Studies, Faculty of Law and School of Graduate Studies, Graduate Programs in Law, Toronto, ON M5S 1A1, Canada. Offers LL M, MSL, SJD. *Degree requirements:* For master's, thesis (for some programs); for doctorate, thesis/dissertation. *Entrance requirements:* Additional exam requirements/recommendations for international students: Required—TOEFL (minimum score 600 paper-based; 100 iBT), TWE (minimum score 5). Electronic applications accepted.

University of Toronto, School of Graduate Studies, Faculty of Law, Professional Program in Law, Toronto, ON M5S 1A1, Canada. Offers JD, JD/Certificate, JD/MA, JD/MBA, JD/MI, JD/MSW, JD/PhD. *Entrance requirements:* For doctorate, LSAT. *Expenses:* Contact institution.

The University of Tulsa, College of Law, Tulsa, OK 74104. Offers American Indian and indigenous law (LL M); American law for foreign lawyers (LL M); energy and natural resources law (LL M); energy law (MJ); health law (Certificate); Indian law (MJ); law (JD); Native American law (Certificate); sustainable energy and resources law (Certificate); JD/MA; JD/MBA; JD/MS. *Accreditation:* ABA. *Program availability:* Part-time, 100% online. *Faculty:* 24 full-time (13 women), 14 part-time/adjunct (7 women). *Students:* 243 full-time (105 women), 29 part-time (12 women); includes 75 minority (12 Black or African American, non-Hispanic/Latino; 17 American Indian or Alaska Native, non-Hispanic/Latino; 1 Asian, non-Hispanic/Latino; 11 Hispanic/Latino; 34 Two or more races, non-Hispanic/Latino), 4 international. Average age 28. 567 applicants, 45% accepted, 94 enrolled. In 2017, 3 master's, 86 doctorates, 26 Certificates awarded. *Degree requirements:* For master's, thesis optional. *Entrance requirements:* For master's, JD from an ABA-approved U.S. law school or a JD equivalent from non-U.S. university; for doctorate, LSAT, BS or BA from 4-year regionally-accredited college/university; for Certificate, BS or BA from 4-year regionally-accredited college/university. Additional exam requirements/recommendations for international students: Required—TOEFL (minimum score 570 paper-based; 90 iBT), IELTS (minimum score 6.5). *Application deadline:* For fall admission, 7/31 priority date for domestic and international students; for spring admission, 12/5 priority date for domestic students, 12/5 for international students; for summer admission, 4/13 for domestic and international students. Applications are processed on a rolling basis. Application fee: $30. Electronic applications accepted. *Expenses:* $24,600 per year tuition; $564 fees. *Financial support:* In 2017–18, 261 students received support. Scholarships/grants available. Support available to part-time students. Financial award application deadline: 8/1; financial award applicants required to submit FAFSA. *Faculty research:* Native American law, criminal law, commercial speech, copyright law, international law. *Unit head:* Prof. Lyn Suzanne Entzeroth, Dean, 918-631-2400, Fax: 918-631-3126, E-mail: lyn-entzeroth@utulsa.edu. *Application contact:* April M. Fox, Associate Dean of Admissions and Financial Aid, 918-631-2406, Fax: 918-631-3630, E-mail: april-fox@utulsa.edu. Website: http://www.utulsa.edu/law/

University of Utah, S. J. Quinney College of Law, Salt Lake City, UT 84112. Offers LL M, MLS, JD, JD/MBA, JD/MCMP, JD/MPA, JD/MPP, JD/MRED, JD/MSW. *Accreditation:* ABA. *Students:* 271 full-time (125 women), 4 part-time (1 woman); includes 28 minority (1 Black or African American, non-Hispanic/Latino; 2 American Indian or Alaska Native, non-Hispanic/Latino; 4 Asian, non-Hispanic/Latino; 18 Hispanic/Latino; 1 Native Hawaiian or other Pacific Islander, non-Hispanic/Latino; 2 Two or more races, non-Hispanic/Latino), 3 international. Average age 28. In 2017, 116 doctorates awarded. *Entrance requirements:* For doctorate, LSAT, bachelor's degree from college or university whose accreditation is recognized by the U.S. Department of Education. Additional exam requirements/recommendations for international students: Required—TOEFL (minimum score 100 iBT). *Application deadline:* For fall admission, 1/15 priority date for domestic students, 2/15 priority date for international students. Applications are processed on a rolling basis. Application fee: $60. Electronic applications accepted. *Expenses:* Contact institution. *Financial support:* Fellowships with partial tuition reimbursements, research assistantships with partial tuition reimbursements, career-related internships or fieldwork, Federal Work-Study, institutionally sponsored loans, scholarships/grants, and unspecified assistantships available. Financial award application deadline: 4/7; financial award applicants required to submit FAFSA. *Faculty research:* Environmental law, intellectual property, international law, criminal law, business law. *Unit head:* Robert Adler, Dean, 801-581-6571, Fax: 801-581-6897, E-mail: robert.adler@law.utah.edu. *Application contact:* Susan Baca, Program Manager for Admissions and Financial Aid, 801-581-7479, Fax: 801-581-6897, E-mail: susan.baca@law.utah.edu. Website: http://www.law.utah.edu

University of Victoria, Faculty of Law, Victoria, BC V8W 2Y2, Canada. Offers LL M, JD, PhD, MBA/JD, MPA/JD. *Program availability:* Part-time. *Degree requirements:* For master's, thesis; for doctorate, thesis/dissertation (for some programs), major research paper (for JD). *Entrance requirements:* For master's, LL B or JD; for doctorate, LSAT (for JD), LL B or JD (for PhD); minimum 3 years of full-time study or part-time equivalent leading toward a bachelor's degree (for JD). Additional exam requirements/recommendations for international students: Required—TOEFL (minimum score 600 paper-based; 100 iBT). Electronic applications accepted. *Expenses:* Contact institution.

Faculty research: Environmental law and policy, international law, alternative dispute resolution, intellectual property law, Aboriginal law.

University of Virginia, School of Law, Charlottesville, VA 22903-1789. Offers LL M, JD, SJD, JD/MA, JD/MBA, JD/MP, JD/MPH, JD/MS, JD/MUEP. JD/MA in international relations offered jointly with The Johns Hopkins University. *Accreditation:* ABA. *Faculty:* 86 full-time (24 women), 3 part-time/adjunct (2 women). *Students:* 972 full-time (447 women), 2 part-time (0 women); includes 202 minority (50 Black or African American, non-Hispanic/Latino; 60 Asian, non-Hispanic/Latino; 45 Hispanic/Latino; 1 Native Hawaiian or other Pacific Islander, non-Hispanic/Latino; 46 Two or more races, non-Hispanic/Latino), 53 international. Average age 25. 5,642 applicants, 19% accepted, 363 enrolled. In 2017, 36 master's, 297 doctorates awarded. *Degree requirements:* For doctorate, thesis/dissertation (for some programs), oral exam (for SJD). *Entrance requirements:* For master's, 2 letters of recommendation; personal statement; for doctorate, LSAT (for JD). Additional exam requirements/recommendations for international students: Required—TOEFL. *Application deadline:* For fall admission, 3/1 priority date for domestic students, 3/2 for international students. Applications are processed on a rolling basis. Application fee: $75. Electronic applications accepted. *Expenses:* Contact institution. *Financial support:* Fellowships, career-related internships or fieldwork, Federal Work-Study, and institutionally sponsored loans available. Financial award application deadline: 3/1; financial award applicants required to submit FAFSA. *Unit head:* Risa Goluboff, Dean, 434-924-7343, Fax: 434-982-2128, E-mail: goluboff@virginia.edu. *Application contact:* Grace Applefeld Cleveland, Director of Admissions, 434-243-1456, Fax: 434-982-2128, E-mail: lawadmit@virginia.edu. Website: http://www.law.virginia.edu/

University of Washington, Graduate School, School of Law, Seattle, WA 98195-3020. Offers Asian law (LL M, PhD); intellectual property law and policy (LL M); law (JD); law of sustainable international development (LL M); taxation (LL M); JD/LL M; JD/MA; JD/MAIS; JD/MBA; JD/MPA; JD/MS; JD/PhD. *Accreditation:* ABA. *Degree requirements:* For master's, thesis; for doctorate, thesis/dissertation (for some programs). *Entrance requirements:* For master's, language proficiency (LL M in Asian law); for doctorate, LSAT (for JD). Additional exam requirements/recommendations for international students: Required—TOEFL. *Expenses:* Contact institution. *Faculty research:* Asian, international and comparative law, intellectual property law, health law, environmental law, taxation.

The University of Western Ontario, Faculty of Law, London, ON N6A 5B8, Canada. Offers LL M, MLS, JD, Diploma. *Entrance requirements:* For master's, B+ average in BA, sample of legal academic writing; for doctorate, LSAT. Additional exam requirements/recommendations for international students: Required—TOEFL. *Expenses:* Contact institution. *Faculty research:* Taxation, administrative law, torts, drug and alcohol law and policy, property.

University of Wisconsin–Madison, Law School, Madison, WI 53706-1399. Offers LL M, JD, SJD. *Accreditation:* ABA. *Program availability:* Part-time, evening/weekend. *Faculty:* 67 full-time (40 women), 67 part-time/adjunct (22 women). *Students:* 525 full-time (249 women), 31 part-time (19 women); includes 113 minority (33 Black or African American, non-Hispanic/Latino; 3 American Indian or Alaska Native, non-Hispanic/Latino; 14 Asian, non-Hispanic/Latino; 51 Hispanic/Latino; 12 Two or more races, non-Hispanic/Latino), 54 international. Average age 26. 1,375 applicants, 42% accepted, 148 enrolled. In 2017, 41 master's, 166 doctorates awarded. *Degree requirements:* For master's, thesis (for some programs); for doctorate, comprehensive exam (for some programs), thesis/dissertation (for some programs). *Entrance requirements:* For doctorate, LSAT (for JD). Additional exam requirements/recommendations for international students: Required—TOEFL. *Application deadline:* For fall admission, 4/1 for domestic and international students. Applications are processed on a rolling basis. Application fee: $60. Electronic applications accepted. *Expenses:* $22,496 resident full-time; $41,192 non-resident full-time. *Financial support:* In 2017–18, 398 students received support. Fellowships, research assistantships, teaching assistantships, career-related internships or fieldwork, Federal Work-Study, scholarships/grants, health care benefits, tuition waivers (full and partial), and unspecified assistantships available. Support available to part-time students. Financial award application deadline: 4/1; financial award applicants required to submit FAFSA. *Unit head:* Margaret Raymond, Dean, 608-262-0618, Fax: 608-890-0134. *Application contact:* Rebecca L. Scheller, Assistant Dean for Admissions and Financial Aid, 608-262-5914, Fax: 608-263-3190, E-mail: admissions@law.wisc.edu. Website: https://www.law.wisc.edu/

University of Wyoming, College of Law, Laramie, WY 82071. Offers JD, JD/MPA. *Accreditation:* ABA. *Entrance requirements:* For doctorate, LSAT. Additional exam requirements/recommendations for international students: Required—TOEFL. Electronic applications accepted. *Expenses:* Contact institution. *Faculty research:* Environmental, public land, constitutional, securities law, criminal law.

Valparaiso University, Law School, Valparaiso, IN 46383-4945. Offers LL M, JD, JD/MA, JD/MALS, JD/MBA, JD/MS, JD/MSSA. *Accreditation:* ABA. *Program availability:* Part-time. *Faculty:* 30 full-time (11 women), 26 part-time/adjunct (11 women). *Students:* 219 full-time (110 women), 15 part-time (9 women); includes 67 minority (24 Black or African American, non-Hispanic/Latino; 2 American Indian or Alaska Native, non-Hispanic/Latino; 6 Asian, non-Hispanic/Latino; 29 Hispanic/Latino; 2 Native Hawaiian or other Pacific Islander, non-Hispanic/Latino; 4 Two or more races, non-Hispanic/Latino). Average age 29. 471 applicants, 38% accepted, 28 enrolled. In 2017, 125 doctorates awarded. *Degree requirements:* For doctorate, 60 hours of pro bono service. *Entrance requirements:* For doctorate, LSAT. Additional exam requirements/recommendations for international students: Required—TOEFL (minimum score 600 paper-based; 95 iBT), IELTS (minimum score 7), or LSAT. *Application deadline:* For fall admission, 6/15 priority date for domestic students. Applications are processed on a rolling basis. Application fee: $0. Electronic applications accepted. *Expenses:* Contact institution. *Financial support:* Fellowships, research assistantships, teaching assistantships, career-related internships or fieldwork, Federal Work-Study, institutionally sponsored loans, scholarships/grants, and tuition waivers (partial) available. Support available to part-time students. Financial award application deadline: 3/1; financial award applicants required to submit FAFSA. *Faculty research:* Animal law, food law, national security law, immigration law, tax law. *Unit head:* David R. Cleveland, Interim Dean/Professor of Law, 219-465-7834, Fax: 219-465-7872, E-mail: david.cleveland@valpo.edu. *Application contact:* Anne Brandt, Director of Marketing and Admissions, 219-465-7821, Fax: 219-465-7975, E-mail: law.admissions@valpo.edu. Website: http://www.valpo.edu/law/

Vanderbilt University, Vanderbilt Law School, Nashville, TN 37203. Offers law (LL M, JD); law and economics (PhD); JD/M Div; JD/MA; JD/MBA; JD/MD; JD/MPP; JD/MTS; JD/PhD; LL M/MA. *Accreditation:* ABA. *Degree requirements:* For doctorate, comprehensive exam (for some programs), thesis/dissertation (for some programs), 72 hours of coursework and research (for PhD). *Entrance requirements:* For master's, foreign law degree; for doctorate, GRE (for PhD), LSAT, advanced undergraduate economics (for PhD). Additional exam requirements/recommendations for international students: Required—TOEFL. Electronic applications accepted. *Expenses:* Contact institution.

Law

Vermont Law School, Graduate and Professional Programs, Professional Program, South Royalton, VT 05068-0096. Offers JD, JD/LL M, JD/MELP, JD/MERL, JD/MFALP. *Accreditation:* ABA. *Entrance requirements:* For doctorate, LSAT, LSDAS/registration, resume. Additional exam requirements/recommendations for international students: Required—TOEFL (minimum score 600 paper-based). Electronic applications accepted. *Expenses:* Contact institution. *Faculty research:* Environmental law, energy regulation and law, food and agriculture law, international law, water and justice.

Villanova University, Charles Widger School of Law, Program in Law, Villanova, PA 19085. Offers JD, JD/LL M, JD/MBA. *Accreditation:* ABA. *Entrance requirements:* For doctorate, LSAT. Electronic applications accepted. *Expenses:* Contact institution. *Faculty research:* Business law; international law (public and private); tax law; criminal law, procedure, and sentencing; law and religion.

Wake Forest University, School of Law, Winston-Salem, NC 27109. Offers LL M, MSL, JD, SJD, JD/M Div, JD/MA, JD/MBA. LL M program is designed for foreign law graduates in American law. *Accreditation:* ABA. *Entrance requirements:* For doctorate, LSAT (for JD). Additional exam requirements/recommendations for international students: Required—TOEFL (minimum score 600 paper-based, 100 iBT) or IELTS (minimum score 7). Electronic applications accepted. *Expenses:* Contact institution. *Faculty research:* Constitutional law, family law, land use planning, torts, taxation.

Walden University, Graduate Programs, School of Public Policy and Administration, Minneapolis, MN 55401. Offers criminal justice (MPA, MPP, MS, Graduate Certificate), including emergency management (MS, PhD), general program (MS), global leadership (MS, PhD), homeland security and policy coordination (MS, PhD), law and public policy (MS, PhD), policy analysis (MS, PhD), public management and leadership (MS, PhD), self-designed (MS), terrorism, mediation, and peace (MS, PhD); criminal justice and executive management (MS), including global leadership (MS, PhD); criminal justice leadership and executive management (MS), including emergency management (MS, PhD), general program, homeland security and policy coordination (MS, PhD), law and public policy (MS, PhD), policy analysis (MS, PhD), public management and leadership (MS, PhD), self-designed, terrorism, mediation, and peace (MS, PhD); emergency management (MPA, MPP, MS), including criminal justice (MS, PhD), general program (MS), homeland security (MS), public management and leadership (MS, PhD), terrorism and emergency management (MS); general program (MPA, MPP); global leadership (MPA, MPP); government management (Graduate Certificate); health policy (MPA, MPP); homeland security (Graduate Certificate); homeland security and policy coordination (MPA, MPP); international nongovernmental organizations (MPA, MPP); law and public policy (MPA, MPP); local government management for sustainable communities (MPA, MPP); nonprofit management (Graduate Certificate); nonprofit management and leadership (MPA, MPP, MS), including global leadership (MS, PhD), international nongovernmental organization (MS), local government for sustainable communities (MS), self designed (MS); online teaching in higher education (Post-Master's Certificate); policy analysis (MPA); public management and leadership (MPA, MPP, Graduate Certificate); public policy (Graduate Certificate); public policy and administration (PhD), including criminal justice (MS, PhD), emergency management (MS, PhD), global leadership (MS, PhD), health policy, homeland security and policy coordination (MS, PhD), international nongovernmental organizations, law and public policy (MS, PhD), local government management for sustainable communities, nonprofit management and leadership, policy analysis (MS, PhD), public management and leadership (MS, PhD), terrorism, mediation, and peace (MS, PhD); strategic planning and public policy (Graduate Certificate); terrorism, mediation, and peace (MPA, MPP). *Program availability:* Part-time, evening/weekend, online only, 100% online. *Degree requirements:* For doctorate, thesis/dissertation, residency. *Entrance requirements:* For master's, bachelor's degree or higher; minimum GPA of 2.5; official transcripts; goal statement (for some programs); access to computer and Internet; for doctorate, master's degree or higher; three years of related professional or academic experience (preferred); minimum GPA of 3.0; goal statement and current resume (for select programs); official transcripts; access to computer and Internet; for other advanced degree, relevant work experience; access to computer and Internet. Additional exam requirements/recommendations for international students: Required—TOEFL (minimum score 550 paper-based, 79 iBT), IELTS (minimum score 6.5), Michigan English Language Assessment Battery (minimum score 82), or PTE (minimum score 53). Electronic applications accepted.

Washburn University, School of Law, Topeka, KS 66621. Offers global legal studies (LL M); law (MSL, JD). *Accreditation:* ABA. *Entrance requirements:* For doctorate, LSAT. Additional exam requirements/recommendations for international students: Recommended—TOEFL (minimum score 550 paper-based). Electronic applications accepted. Application fee is waived when completed online. *Expenses:* Contact institution. *Faculty research:* Constitutional law, family law, energy law, banking and securities law, oil and gas.

Washington and Lee University, School of Law, Lexington, VA 24450. Offers law (JD). *Accreditation:* ABA. *Entrance requirements:* For doctorate, LSAT. Electronic applications accepted. *Expenses:* Contact institution. *Faculty research:* Criminal law, corporate law, experiential education, international and comparative law, public interest law.

Washington University in St. Louis, School of Law, St. Louis, MO 63130-4899. Offers LL M, MJS, JD, JSD, JD/MA, JD/MBA, JD/MHA, JD/MS, JD/MSW, JD/PhD. *Accreditation:* ABA. *Entrance requirements:* For doctorate, LSAT or GRE. Electronic applications accepted. *Expenses:* Contact institution. *Faculty research:* International law, environmental law, employment discrimination, reproductive rights, bankruptcy and white-collar crime.

Wayne State University, Law School, Detroit, MI 48202. Offers corporate and finance law (LL M); labor and employment law (LL M); law (JD); taxation (LL M); United States law (LL M); JD/MA; JD/MADR; JD/MBA; JD/MS. *Accreditation:* ABA. *Program availability:* Part-time, evening/weekend. *Faculty:* 43 full-time (18 women), 17 part-time/adjunct (9 women). *Students:* 409 full-time (184 women), 46 part-time (22 women); includes 61 minority (33 Black or African American, non-Hispanic/Latino; 1 American Indian or Alaska Native, non-Hispanic/Latino; 14 Asian, non-Hispanic/Latino; 3 Hispanic/Latino; 10 Two or more races, non-Hispanic/Latino), 11 international. Average age 26. 811 applicants, 54% accepted, 146 enrolled. In 2017, 4 master's, 113 doctorates awarded. *Degree requirements:* For master's, thesis (for some programs). *Entrance requirements:* For master's, JD or LL B from ABA-accredited institution and member institution of the AALS; for doctorate, LSAT, LDAS report, bachelor's degree from accredited institution, personal statement, transcripts from all U.S. undergraduate schools attended and an analysis and summary of the transcripts; letter of recommendation (up to two are accepted). Additional exam requirements/recommendations for international students: Required—TOEFL, Michigan English Language Assessment Battery (minimum score 85); Recommended—IELTS. *Application deadline:* For fall admission, 7/1 for domestic students, 5/1 priority date for international students. Applications are processed on a rolling basis. Application fee: $0. Electronic applications accepted. *Expenses:* Contact institution. *Financial support:* In 2017–18, 386 students received support. Fellowships, Federal Work-Study, and scholarships/grants available. Support available to part-time students. Financial award application deadline: 6/30; financial award applicants required to submit FAFSA. *Unit*

head: Richard A. Bierschbach, Dean and Professor of Law, 313-577-3933, E-mail: rbierschbach@wayne.edu. *Application contact:* Kathy Fox, Assistant Dean of Admissions, 313-577-3937, Fax: 313-993-8129, E-mail: lawinquire@wayne.edu. Website: http://law.wayne.edu/

Western Michigan University Thomas M. Cooley Law School, Graduate Programs, Lansing, MI 48901-3038. Offers administrative law (public law) (JD); business transactions (JD); Canadian law practice (JD); corporate law and finance (LL M); environmental law (public law) (JD); general practice (JD), including solo and small firm; general studies (LL M); homeland and national security law (LL M); insurance law (LL M); intellectual property (JD); intellectual property law (LL M); international law (JD); litigation (JD); taxation (LL M); U.S. legal studies for foreign attorneys (LL M); JD/LL M; JD/MBA; JD/MHA; JD/MPA; JD/MSW. *Program availability:* Part-time, evening/weekend, 100% online, blended/hybrid learning. *Degree requirements:* For master's, thesis (for some programs); for doctorate, minimum of 3 credits of clinical experience. *Entrance requirements:* For master's, JD or LL B; for doctorate, LSAT. Additional exam requirements/recommendations for international students: Required—TOEFL (for U.S. legal studies for foreign attorneys LL M program); Recommended—TOEFL. Electronic applications accepted. *Expenses:* Contact institution. *Faculty research:* Wrongful convictions, civil rights, environmental law, litigation techniques, data mining, intellectual property, practical and skills-based legal education.

Western New England University, School of Law, Springfield, MA 01119. Offers estate planning and elder law (LL M, MS); law (MS, JD); JD/MBA; JD/MRP; JD/MS; JD/MSW. *Accreditation:* ABA. *Program availability:* Part-time, evening/weekend. *Faculty:* 24 full-time (13 women), 25 part-time/adjunct (8 women). *Students:* 171 full-time (96 women), 110 part-time (65 women); includes 78 minority (35 Black or African American, non-Hispanic/Latino; 2 American Indian or Alaska Native, non-Hispanic/Latino; 16 Asian, non-Hispanic/Latino; 25 Hispanic/Latino). Average age 30. 606 applicants, 58% accepted, 100 enrolled. In 2017, 21 master's, 101 doctorates awarded. *Entrance requirements:* For master's, official law school transcript, resume; for doctorate, LSAT, two letters of recommendation, personal statement. *Application deadline:* For fall admission, 3/15 priority date for domestic students. Applications are processed on a rolling basis. Application fee: $0. Electronic applications accepted. *Expenses:* Contact institution. *Financial support:* Career-related internships or fieldwork, Federal Work-Study, and scholarships/grants available. Support available to part-time students. Financial award application deadline: 4/15; financial award applicants required to submit FAFSA. *Unit head:* Eric Gouvin, Dean/Professor, 413-796-2031, E-mail: eric.gouvin@law.wne.edu. *Application contact:* Anthony Orlando, Director of Law Admissions, 413-782-1281, Fax: 413-796-2067, E-mail: admissions@law.wne.edu. Website: http://www.law.wne.edu/

Western State College of Law at Argosy University, Professional Program, Irvine, CA 92618-3601. Offers JD. *Accreditation:* ABA. *Program availability:* Part-time, evening/weekend. *Entrance requirements:* For doctorate, LSAT, 2 letters of recommendation. Additional exam requirements/recommendations for international students: Required—TOEFL (minimum score 550 paper-based; 80 iBT). Electronic applications accepted. *Faculty research:* Criminal law and practice, entrepreneurship, teaching effectiveness and student success, learning theory and legal education.

West Virginia University, College of Law, Morgantown, WV 26506-6130. Offers energy law and sustainable development (LL M); forensic justice (LL M); law (JD); white collar forensic justice (LL M). *Accreditation:* ABA. *Program availability:* Part-time. *Students:* 306 full-time (138 women), 1 part-time (0 women); includes 33 minority (10 Black or African American, non-Hispanic/Latino; 4 Asian, non-Hispanic/Latino; 11 Hispanic/Latino; 8 Two or more races, non-Hispanic/Latino), 1 international. *Entrance requirements:* For doctorate, LSAT. Additional exam requirements/recommendations for international students: Required—TOEFL (minimum score 600 paper-based; 100 iBT). *Application deadline:* For fall admission, 2/1 for domestic and international students. Applications are processed on a rolling basis. Application fee: $60. Electronic applications accepted. *Expenses:* Contact institution. *Financial support:* Fellowships, research assistantships, teaching assistantships, career-related internships or fieldwork, Federal Work-Study, institutionally sponsored loans, scholarships/grants, health care benefits, tuition waivers (full), unspecified assistantships, and administrative assistantships, resident assistantships available. Support available to part-time students. Financial award application deadline: 3/1; financial award applicants required to submit FAFSA. *Faculty research:* Constitutional law, public interest law, corporate law, environment and natural resources innocence project, professional skills, leadership, intellectual property, entrepreneurship, labor, sustainable development, family law, IR human rights, immigration. *Unit head:* Beth Pierpont, Assistant Dean for Admissions and Student Financial Support, 304-293-7320, E-mail: beth.pierpont@mail.wvu.edu. Website: https://law.wvu.edu

Widener University, Commonwealth Law School, Harrisburg, PA 17106-9381. Offers JD. *Accreditation:* ABA. *Program availability:* Part-time. *Faculty:* 17 full-time (8 women), 18 part-time/adjunct (6 women). *Students:* 272 full-time (138 women), 4 part-time (3 women); includes 60 minority (30 Black or African American, non-Hispanic/Latino; 2 American Indian or Alaska Native, non-Hispanic/Latino; 8 Asian, non-Hispanic/Latino; 19 Hispanic/Latino; 1 Two or more races, non-Hispanic/Latino), 2 international. Average age 27. 601 applicants, 62% accepted, 129 enrolled. *Entrance requirements:* For doctorate, LSAT. *Application deadline:* For fall admission, 5/15 for domestic students. Applications are processed on a rolling basis. Application fee: $60. Electronic applications accepted. *Expenses:* Contact institution. *Financial support:* Fellowships, research assistantships, career-related internships or fieldwork, Federal Work-Study, institutionally sponsored loans, and scholarships/grants available. Support available to part-time students. Financial award application deadline: 2/15; financial award applicants required to submit FAFSA. *Faculty research:* Health law, toxic torts, Constitutional law, intellectual property, corporate law. *Unit head:* Christian Johnson, Dean, 302-477-2100, Fax: 302-477-2282, E-mail: cajohnson2@widener.edu. *Application contact:* John Benfield, Associate Dean for Admissions and Administration, 302-477-2210, Fax: 302-477-2224, E-mail: jsbenfield@widener.edu. Website: http://www.law.widener.edu/

Widener University, Delaware Law School, Wilmington, DE 19803-0474. Offers corporate and business law (MJ); corporate law and finance (LL M); health law (LL M, MJ, D Law); higher education compliance (MJ); juridical science (SJD); law (JD). *Accreditation:* ABA. *Program availability:* Part-time, 100% online. *Faculty:* 24 full-time (13 women), 42 part-time/adjunct (15 women). *Students:* 530 full-time (269 women), 26 part-time (17 women); includes 136 minority (80 Black or African American, non-Hispanic/Latino; 8 American Indian or Alaska Native, non-Hispanic/Latino; 16 Asian, non-Hispanic/Latino; 27 Hispanic/Latino; 5 Two or more races, non-Hispanic/Latino), 26 international. Average age 29. 942 applicants, 62% accepted, 210 enrolled. *Degree requirements:* For doctorate, thesis/dissertation (for some programs). *Entrance requirements:* For master's, GMAT. *Application deadline:* For fall admission, 5/15 for domestic students; for spring admission, 12/1 for domestic students. Applications are processed on a rolling basis. Application fee: $60. *Financial support:* Career-related internships or fieldwork, Federal Work-Study, institutionally sponsored loans, and scholarships/grants available. Support available to part-time students. Financial award

application deadline: 2/15; financial award applicants required to submit FAFSA. *Unit head:* Rod Smolla, Dean, 302-477-2100, Fax: 302-477-2282, E-mail: rasmolla@widener.edu. *Application contact:* Barbara L. Ayars, Assistant Dean of Admissions, 302-477-2210, Fax: 302-477-2224, E-mail: barbara.l.ayars@law.widener.edu.
Website: http://delawarelaw.widener.edu/

Widener University, School of Human Service Professions, Institute for Graduate Clinical Psychology, Law-Psychology Program, Chester, PA 19013-5792. Offers JD/Psy D. *Faculty:* 15 full-time (6 women), 18 part-time/adjunct (10 women). *Students:* 2 full-time (both women). Average age 28. 21 applicants, 19% accepted. *Application deadline:* For fall admission, 2/1 for domestic students. Applications are processed on a rolling basis. Application fee: $60. Electronic applications accepted. *Financial support:* Research assistantships, career-related internships or fieldwork, Federal Work-Study, institutionally sponsored loans, and scholarships/grants available. Financial award application deadline: 5/31.

Willamette University, College of Law, Salem, OR 97301-3922. Offers dispute resolution (LL M); law (MLS, JD); transnational law (LL M); JD/MBA. *Accreditation:* ABA. *Program availability:* Part-time. *Degree requirements:* For master's, thesis, 25 credit hours (for LL M); 26 credit hours (for MLS); for doctorate, thesis/dissertation, 90 credit hours. *Entrance requirements:* For master's, bachelor's degree (for MLS); domestic or foreign JD (for LL M); for doctorate, LSAT. Additional exam requirements/recommendations for international students: Required—TOEFL (minimum score 480 paper-based; 45 iBT); Recommended—IELTS (minimum score 5). Electronic applications accepted. Application fee is waived when completed online. *Expenses:* Contact institution. *Faculty research:* Dispute resolution, international law, business law, law and government, sustainability.

Yale University, Yale Law School, New Haven, CT 06520-8215. Offers LL M, MSL, JD, JSD, PhD, JD/MA, JD/MAR, JD/MBA, JD/MD, JD/MES, JD/PhD. *Accreditation:* ABA. *Faculty:* 64 full-time, 113 part-time/adjunct. *Students:* 625 full-time (299 women). Average age 26. 2,862 applicants, 8% accepted, 205 enrolled. *Entrance requirements:* For doctorate, LSAT (for JD). Additional exam requirements/recommendations for international students: Required—TOEFL (minimum score 600 paper-based). *Application deadline:* For fall admission, 2/28 for domestic students. Applications are processed on a rolling basis. Application fee: $60. Electronic applications accepted. *Expenses:* Contact institution. *Financial support:* Application deadline: 3/15; applicants required to submit FAFSA. *Unit head:* Heather Gerken, Dean, 203-432-1660.

Application contact: Craig Janecek, Director of Admissions, 203-432-4995, E-mail: admissions.law@yale.edu.
Website: http://www.law.yale.edu/

Yeshiva University, Benjamin N. Cardozo School of Law, New York, NY 10003-4301. Offers comparative legal thought (LL M); dispute resolution and advocacy (LL M); general studies (LL M); intellectual property law (LL M); law (JD). *Accreditation:* ABA. *Program availability:* Part-time. *Faculty:* 61 full-time (24 women), 92 part-time/adjunct (38 women). *Students:* 994 full-time (530 women), 107 part-time (56 women); includes 218 minority (40 Black or African American, non-Hispanic/Latino; 84 Asian, non-Hispanic/Latino; 74 Hispanic/Latino; 20 Two or more races, non-Hispanic/Latino), 96 international. Average age 25. 2,755 applicants, 52% accepted, 419 enrolled. In 2017, 70 master's, 391 doctorates awarded. *Entrance requirements:* For doctorate, LSAT, 2 letters of recommendation. Additional exam requirements/recommendations for international students: Required—TOEFL (minimum score 100 iBT); Recommended—IELTS (minimum score 7). *Application deadline:* For fall admission, 4/1 priority date for domestic students; for spring admission, 12/1 for domestic students. Applications are processed on a rolling basis. Application fee: $50. Electronic applications accepted. *Expenses:* Contact institution. *Financial support:* In 2017–18, 845 students received support, including 115 research assistantships (averaging $1,429 per year); career-related internships or fieldwork, Federal Work-Study, institutionally sponsored loans, scholarships/grants, health care benefits, and tuition waivers (full and partial) also available. Support available to part-time students. Financial award application deadline: 3/1; financial award applicants required to submit FAFSA. *Faculty research:* Corporate and commercial law, intellectual property law, criminal law and litigation, Constitutional law, legal theory and jurisprudence. *Unit head:* David G. Martinidez, Dean of Admissions, 212-790-0357, Fax: 212-790-0482, E-mail: lawinfo@yu.edu.
Website: http://www.cardozo.yu.edu/

York University, Faculty of Graduate Studies, Faculty of Liberal Arts and Professional Studies, Program in Public Policy, Administration and Law, Toronto, ON M3J 1P3, Canada. Offers MPPAL.

York University, Faculty of Graduate Studies, Osgoode Hall Law School, Toronto, ON M3J 1P3, Canada. Offers LL M, JD, PhD. *Program availability:* Part-time, evening/weekend. *Degree requirements:* For master's, thesis; for doctorate, comprehensive exam, thesis/dissertation. *Entrance requirements:* For doctorate, LSAT. Electronic applications accepted.

Legal and Justice Studies

Arizona State University at the Tempe campus, College of Liberal Arts and Sciences, School of Social Transformation, Tempe, AZ 85287-4902. Offers African studies (Graduate Certificate); gender studies (PhD, Graduate Certificate); justice studies (MS, PhD); social and cultural pedagogy (MA); socio-economic justice (Graduate Certificate); PhD/JD. *Program availability:* Part-time. Terminal master's awarded for partial completion of doctoral program. *Degree requirements:* For master's, thesis or alternative, interactive Program of Study (iPOS) submitted before completing 50 percent of required credit hours; for doctorate, comprehensive exam, thesis/dissertation, interactive Program of Study (iPOS) submitted before completing 50 percent of required credit hours. *Entrance requirements:* For master's, GRE or LSAT, minimum GPA of 3.0, or equivalent in last 2 years of work leading to bachelor's degree; for doctorate, GRE or LSAT (for justice studies program), minimum GPA of 3.0 or equivalent in last 2 years of work leading to bachelor's degree. Additional exam requirements/recommendations for international students: Required—TOEFL, IELTS, or PTE. Electronic applications accepted.

Arizona State University at the Tempe campus, New College of Interdisciplinary Arts and Sciences, Program in Social Justice and Human Rights, Phoenix, AZ 85069-7100. Offers MA. Fall admission only. *Program availability:* Part-time, evening/weekend. *Degree requirements:* For master's, thesis or applied project, interactive Program of Study (iPOS) submitted before completing 50 percent of required credit hours. *Entrance requirements:* For master's, GRE, minimum GPA of 3.0 or equivalent in last 2 years of work leading to bachelor's degree, 2 letters of recommendation, official transcripts, writing sample, personal statement, resume. Additional exam requirements/recommendations for international students: Required—TOEFL, IELTS, or PTE. Electronic applications accepted. *Faculty research:* Social movements, violence against women, globalization, innovative uses of human rights law, environmental ethics, social justice and art, women and international development, slavery, genocide, metropolitan studies, urban culture and social space, fair trade, citizenship; immigration.

Arizona State University at the Tempe campus, Sandra Day O'Connor College of Law, Phoenix, AZ 85287-7906. Offers biotechnology and genomics (LL M); law (JD); legal studies (MLS); patent practice (MLS); sports law and business (MSLB); tribal policy, law and government (LL M); JD/MBA; JD/MD; JD/MSW; JD/PhD. JD/MD offered jointly with Mayo Medical School. *Accreditation:* ABA. *Program availability:* 100% online. *Faculty:* 69 full-time (30 women), 115 part-time/adjunct (29 women). *Students:* 777 full-time (337 women); includes 207 minority (21 Black or African American, non-Hispanic/Latino; 14 American Indian or Alaska Native, non-Hispanic/Latino; 32 Asian, non-Hispanic/Latino; 104 Hispanic/Latino; 3 Native Hawaiian or other Pacific Islander, non-Hispanic/Latino; 33 Two or more races, non-Hispanic/Latino), 15 international. Average age 28. 2,056 applicants, 41% accepted, 215 enrolled. In 2017, 52 master's, 198 doctorates awarded. *Entrance requirements:* For master's, bachelor's degree and JD (for LL M); for doctorate, LSAT, bachelor's degree. Additional exam requirements/recommendations for international students: Required—TOEFL (minimum score 550 paper-based; 80 iBT). *Application deadline:* For fall admission, 3/1 priority date for domestic and international students. Applications are processed on a rolling basis. Electronic applications accepted. *Expenses:* Contact institution. *Financial support:* In 2017–18, 430 students received support. Institutionally sponsored loans and scholarships/grants available. Financial award application deadline: 3/15; financial award applicants required to submit FAFSA. *Faculty research:* Emerging technologies and the law, Indian law, international law, intellectual property, health law, sports law and business. *Total annual research expenditures:* $2.4 million. *Unit head:* Douglas Sylvester, Dean/Professor, 480-965-6188, Fax: 480-965-6521, E-mail: douglas.sylvester@asu.edu. *Application contact:* Chitra Damania, Director, 480-965-1474, Fax: 480-727-7930, E-mail: law.admissions@asu.edu.
Website: http://www.law.asu.edu/

Auburn University at Montgomery, College of Public Policy and Justice, Department of Justice and Public Safety, Montgomery, AL 36124-4023. Offers criminal studies (MSJPS); homeland security (MSJPS); homeland security and emergency management (MS); legal studies (MSJPS); organizational leadership (MSJPS). *Program availability:*

Part-time, evening/weekend. *Faculty:* 5 full-time (2 women). *Students:* 9 full-time (3 women), 33 part-time (20 women); includes 23 minority (22 Black or African American, non-Hispanic/Latino; 1 Asian, non-Hispanic/Latino). Average age 30. 24 applicants, 75% accepted, 9 enrolled. In 2017, 23 master's awarded. *Degree requirements:* For master's, comprehensive exam, thesis optional. *Entrance requirements:* For master's, GRE General Test or MAT. Additional exam requirements/recommendations for international students: Recommended—TOEFL (minimum score 500 paper-based; 61 iBT), IELTS (minimum score 5.5), TSE (minimum score 44). *Application deadline:* For fall admission, 7/15 for international students; for spring admission, 11/15 for international students; for summer admission, 4/15 for international students. Applications are processed on a rolling basis. Application fee: $25. Electronic applications accepted. *Expenses:* Tuition, state resident: full-time $6930; part-time $385 per credit hour. Tuition, nonresident: full-time $15,588; part-time $866 per credit hour. *Required fees:* $640. *Financial support:* Career-related internships or fieldwork and scholarships/grants available. Support available to part-time students. Financial award application deadline: 3/1; financial award applicants required to submit FAFSA. *Faculty research:* Law enforcement, corrections, juvenile justice. *Unit head:* Dr. Ralph Ioimo, Head, 334-244-3691, Fax: 334-244-3244, E-mail: rioimo@aum.edu.
Website: http://cppj.aum.edu/departments/justice-and-public-safety

Binghamton University, State University of New York, Graduate School, Harpur College of Arts and Sciences, Program in Social, Political, Ethical and Legal Philosophy, Binghamton, NY 13902-6000. Offers MA, PhD. *Program availability:* Part-time. *Faculty:* 14 full-time (6 women), 2 part-time/adjunct (0 women). *Students:* 13 full-time (4 women), 23 part-time (9 women); includes 5 minority (1 Black or African American, non-Hispanic/Latino; 1 Asian, non-Hispanic/Latino; 3 Hispanic/Latino), 6 international. Average age 32. 38 applicants, 47% accepted, 4 enrolled. In 2017, 2 master's, 4 doctorates awarded. Terminal master's awarded for partial completion of doctoral program. *Degree requirements:* For master's, comprehensive exam, thesis or alternative; for doctorate, one foreign language, thesis/dissertation. *Entrance requirements:* For master's and doctorate, GRE General Test, writing sample. Additional exam requirements/recommendations for international students: Required—TOEFL (minimum score 550 paper-based; 80 iBT). *Application deadline:* For fall admission, 2/1 for domestic and international students; for spring admission, 10/15 for domestic and international students. Application fee: $75. Electronic applications accepted. *Financial support:* In 2017–18, 23 students received support, including 23 teaching assistantships with full tuition reimbursements available (averaging $15,000 per year); career-related internships or fieldwork, Federal Work-Study, institutionally sponsored loans, scholarships/grants, health care benefits, tuition waivers (full and partial), and unspecified assistantships also available. Financial award applicants required to submit FAFSA. *Unit head:* Dr. Christopher M. Knapp, Chairperson, 607-777-4163, E-mail: c.morgan-knapp@binghamton.edu. *Application contact:* Ben Balkaya, Assistant Dean and Director, 607-777-2151, Fax: 607-777-2501, E-mail: balkaya@binghamton.edu.
Website: http://philosophy.binghamton.edu

Brock University, Faculty of Graduate Studies, Faculty of Social Sciences, Program in Social Justice and Equity Studies, St. Catharines, ON L2S 3A1, Canada. Offers MA. *Program availability:* Part-time. *Degree requirements:* For master's, thesis optional. *Entrance requirements:* For master's, honors degree. Additional exam requirements/recommendations for international students: Required—TOEFL (minimum score 550 paper-based; 80 iBT), IELTS (minimum score 6.5), TWE (minimum score 4). Electronic applications accepted. *Faculty research:* Social inequality, social movements, gender, racism, environmental justice.

California University of Pennsylvania, School of Graduate Studies and Research, College of Liberal Arts, Department of History, Politics, Society and Law, California, PA 15419-1394. Offers legal studies (MS), including criminal justice, homeland security, law and public policy. *Program availability:* Part-time, evening/weekend, online learning. *Faculty:* 2 part-time/adjunct (both women). *Degree requirements:* For master's, thesis optional. *Entrance requirements:* For master's, interview, minimum GPA of 3.0. Additional exam requirements/recommendations for international students: Required—

TOEFL (minimum score 550 paper-based; 80 iBT). *Application deadline:* For fall admission, 8/1 priority date for domestic and international students; for winter admission, 12/1 priority date for domestic and international students; for spring admission, 5/1 priority date for domestic and international students. Applications are processed on a rolling basis. Application fee: $25. Electronic applications accepted. *Financial support:* Career-related internships or fieldwork, scholarships/grants, traineeships, and unspecified assistantships available. Financial award applicants required to submit FAFSA. *Faculty research:* Ethics in political practice, ethics and law, law and morality, St. Thomas Aquinas and crime, police policy. *Unit head:* Dr. Christina A. Toras, Chair, 724-938-4761, E-mail: toras@calu.edu. *Application contact:* Suzanne C. Powers, Director of Graduate Admissions and Recruitment, 724-938-4029, Fax: 724-938-5712, E-mail: powers_s@cup.edu.

Campbellsville University, College of Arts and Sciences, Campbellsville, KY 42718-2799. Offers justice studies (MS); sport management (MA). *Program availability:* Part-time, evening/weekend, 100% online, blended/hybrid learning. *Faculty:* 12 full-time (4 women), 2 part-time/adjunct (1 woman). *Students:* 6 full-time (3 women), 28 part-time (12 women); includes 9 minority (all Black or African American, non-Hispanic/Latino), 1 international. Average age 29. 38 applicants, 66% accepted, 25 enrolled. In 2017, 5 master's awarded. *Degree requirements:* For master's, comprehensive exam, thesis optional. *Entrance requirements:* For master's, GRE General Test, minimum GPA of 2.9, letters of recommendation, college transcripts. Additional exam requirements/recommendations for international students: Recommended—TOEFL, IELTS. *Application deadline:* Applications are processed on a rolling basis. Application fee: $25. Electronic applications accepted. Application fee is waived when completed online. *Expenses:* $399 per credit hour. *Financial support:* In 2017–18, 2 students received support. Unspecified assistantships and employee tuition waivers available. Financial award application deadline: 6/1; financial award applicants required to submit FAFSA. *Unit head:* Dr. Mike Page, Dean, 270-789-5394. *Application contact:* Monica Bamwine, Assistant Director of Graduate Admissions, 270-789-5221, Fax: 270-789-5071, E-mail: mkbamwine@campbellsville.edu.
Website: http://www.campbellsville.edu/

Capital University, School of Nursing, Columbus, OH 43209-2394. Offers administration (MSN); legal studies (MSN); theological studies (MSN); JD/MSN; MBA/MSN; MSN/MTS. *Accreditation:* AACN. *Program availability:* Part-time, evening/weekend. *Degree requirements:* For master's, thesis or alternative. *Entrance requirements:* For master's, BSN, current RN license, minimum GPA of 3.0, undergraduate courses in statistics and research. Additional exam requirements/recommendations for international students: Required—TOEFL (minimum score 550 paper-based). *Expenses:* Contact institution. *Faculty research:* Bereavement, wellness/health promotion, emergency cardiac care, critical thinking, complementary and alternative healthcare.

Carleton University, Faculty of Graduate Studies, Faculty of Public Affairs and Management, Department of Law, Ottawa, ON K1S 5B6, Canada. Offers conflict resolution (Certificate); legal studies (MA). *Degree requirements:* For master's, thesis. *Entrance requirements:* For master's, honors degree. Additional exam requirements/recommendations for international students: Required—TOEFL. *Faculty research:* Legal and social theory; women, law, and gender relations; law, crime, and social order; political economy of law; international law.

Case Western Reserve University, School of Law, Cleveland, OH 44106. Offers financial integrity (MA); health law (SJD); intellectual property (LL M); intellectual property law (ML); international business law (LL M, ML); international criminal law (LL M); law (JD, SJD); patent practice (MA); U.S. and global legal studies (ML); U.S. legal studies (LL M); JD/MA; JD/MBA; JD/MD; JD/MNM; JD/MPH; JD/MS; JD/MSSA. *Accreditation:* ABA. *Faculty:* 37 full-time (13 women), 26 part-time/adjunct (10 women). *Students:* 412 full-time (216 women); includes 80 minority (39 Black or African American, non-Hispanic/Latino; 14 Asian, non-Hispanic/Latino; 24 Hispanic/Latino; 3 Two or more races, non-Hispanic/Latino), 36 international. Average age 24. 1,488 applicants, 39% accepted, 131 enrolled. In 2017, 138 master's awarded. *Entrance requirements:* For doctorate, LSAT, LSDAS. Additional exam requirements/recommendations for international students: Required—TOEFL. *Application deadline:* For fall admission, 4/1 priority date for domestic and international students. Applications are processed on a rolling basis. Application fee: $40. Electronic applications accepted. Application fee is waived when completed online. *Expenses:* 50666. *Financial support:* In 2017–18, 395 students received support. Career-related internships or fieldwork, Federal Work-Study, institutionally sponsored loans, and scholarships/grants available. Financial award application deadline: 5/1; financial award applicants required to submit FAFSA. *Unit head:* Jessica Berg, Co-Dean, 216-368-3283. *Application contact:* Kelli Curtis, Associate Dean for Admissions, 216-368-3600, Fax: 216-368-0185, E-mail: lawadmissions@case.edu.
Website: http://law.case.edu/

The Catholic University of America, School of Canon Law, Washington, DC 20064. Offers Canon law (JCD, JCL); church administration (MCA); JD/JCL. JD/JCL offered jointly with Columbus School of Law. *Program availability:* Part-time. *Faculty:* 7 full-time (1 woman), 2 part-time/adjunct (0 women). *Students:* 32 full-time (6 women), 49 part-time (6 women); includes 9 minority (2 Black or African American, non-Hispanic/Latino; 3 Asian, non-Hispanic/Latino; 2 Hispanic/Latino; 2 Two or more races, non-Hispanic/Latino), 13 international. Average age 38. 36 applicants, 89% accepted, 27 enrolled. In 2017, 10 master's, 3 doctorates awarded. *Degree requirements:* For master's, one foreign language, comprehensive exam, thesis, fluency in canonical Latin; for doctorate, 2 foreign languages, thesis/dissertation, fluency in canonical Latin. *Entrance requirements:* For master's, GRE General Test, statement of purpose, official copies of academic transcripts, two letters of recommendation; for doctorate, GRE General Test, minimum A- average, JCL. Additional exam requirements/recommendations for international students: Required—TOEFL (minimum score 550 paper-based; 80 iBT). *Application deadline:* For fall admission, 7/15 priority date for domestic students, 7/1 for international students; for spring admission, 11/15 priority date for domestic students, 11/1 for international students. Applications are processed on a rolling basis. Application fee: $55. Electronic applications accepted. *Expenses:* Contact institution. *Financial support:* Fellowships, research assistantships, teaching assistantships, Federal Work-Study, scholarships/grants, tuition waivers (full and partial), and unspecified assistantships available. Financial award application deadline: 2/1; financial award applicants required to submit FAFSA. *Faculty research:* Ecclesiology and the Sacrament of Orders, procedural law, temporal goods, matrimonial jurisprudence, sacramental and liturgical law. *Unit head:* Msgr. Ronny Jenkins, Dean, 202-319-5492, Fax: 202-319-4187, E-mail: cua-canonlaw@cua.edu. *Application contact:* Dr. Steven Brown, Director of Graduate Admissions, 202-319-5057, Fax: 202-319-6533, E-mail: cua-admissions@cua.edu.
Website: https://canonlaw.catholic.edu/

Central European University, Department of Legal Studies, Budapest, Hungary. Offers comparative Constitutional law (LL M); human rights (LL M, MA); international business law (LL M); juridical sciences (SJD). *Faculty:* 10 full-time (5 women), 9 part-time/adjunct (1 woman). *Students:* 90 full-time (52 women). Average age 28. 384 applicants, 33% accepted, 71 enrolled. In 2017, 53 master's, 3 doctorates awarded. Terminal master's

awarded for partial completion of doctoral program. *Degree requirements:* For master's, one foreign language, thesis; for doctorate, one foreign language, comprehensive exam, thesis/dissertation. *Entrance requirements:* For master's and doctorate, LSAT. Additional exam requirements/recommendations for international students: Required—TOEFL (minimum score 570 paper-based); Recommended—IELTS (minimum score 6.5). *Application deadline:* For fall admission, 2/4 for domestic and international students. Application fee: $30. Electronic applications accepted. *Expenses:* Contact institution. *Financial support:* Fellowships, career-related internships or fieldwork, institutionally sponsored loans, scholarships/grants, and tuition waivers (full and partial) available. Financial award application deadline: 2/4. *Faculty research:* Institutional, Constitutional and human rights in European Union law; biomedical law and reproductive rights; data protection law; comparative and international business law and the regulation of business environments; *Unit head:* Dr. Karoly Bard, Head of Department, 36 1 327-3294, Fax: 361-327-3198, E-mail: legalst@ceu.edu. *Application contact:* Zsuzsanna Jaszberenyi, Department Coordinator, 361-327-3272, Fax: 361-327-3198, E-mail: admissions@ceu.edu.
Website: http://legal.ceu.edu

Columbia University, Graduate School of Arts and Sciences, New York, NY 10027. Offers African-American studies (MA); American studies (MA); anthropology (MA, PhD); art history and archaeology (MA, PhD); astronomy (PhD); biological sciences (PhD); biotechnology (MA); chemical physics (PhD); chemistry (PhD); classical studies (MA, PhD); classics (MA, PhD); climate and society (MA); conservation biology (MA); earth and environmental sciences (PhD); East Asia: regional studies (MA); East Asian languages and cultures (MA, PhD); ecology, evolution and environmental biology (MA), including conservation biology; ecology, evolution, and environmental biology (PhD), including ecology and evolutionary biology, evolutionary primatology; economics (MA, PhD); English and comparative literature (MA, PhD); French and Romance philology (MA, PhD); Germanic languages (MA, PhD); global French studies (MA); global thought (MA); Hispanic cultural studies (MA); history (PhD); history and literature (MA); human rights studies (MA); Islamic studies (MA); Italian (MA, PhD); Japanese pedagogy (MA); Jewish studies (MA); Latin America and the Caribbean: regional studies (MA); Latin American and Iberian cultures (PhD); mathematics (MA, PhD), including finance (MA); medieval and Renaissance studies (MA); Middle Eastern, South Asian, and African studies (MA, PhD); modern art: critical and curatorial studies (MA); modern European studies (MA); museum anthropology (MA); music (DMA, PhD); oral history (MA); philosophical foundations of physics (MA); philosophy (MA, PhD); physics (PhD); political science (MA, PhD); psychology (PhD); quantitative methods in the social sciences (MA); religion (MA, PhD); Russia, Eurasia and East Europe: regional studies (MA); Russian translation (MA); Slavic cultures (MA); Slavic languages (MA, PhD); sociology (MA, PhD); South Asian studies (MA, PhD); statistics (MA, PhD); theatre (PhD). Dual-degree programs require admission to both Graduate School of Arts and Sciences and another Columbia school. *Program availability:* Part-time. Terminal master's awarded for partial completion of doctoral program. *Degree requirements:* For master's, variable foreign language requirement, comprehensive exam (for some programs), thesis (for some programs); for doctorate, variable foreign language requirement, comprehensive exam (for some programs), thesis/dissertation. *Entrance requirements:* For master's and doctorate, GRE General Test, GRE Subject Test (for some programs). Additional exam requirements/recommendations for international students: Required—TOEFL, IELTS. Electronic applications accepted. *Expenses: Tuition:* Full-time $44,864; part-time $1704 per credit. *Required fees:* $2370 per semester. One-time fee: $105.

The George Washington University, College of Professional Studies, Paralegal Studies Programs, Washington, DC 20052. Offers MPS, Graduate Certificate. *Students:* 24 full-time (16 women), 89 part-time (76 women); includes 52 minority (35 Black or African American, non-Hispanic/Latino; 3 Asian, non-Hispanic/Latino; 12 Hispanic/Latino; 2 Two or more races, non-Hispanic/Latino), 2 international. Average age 38. 120 applicants, 75% accepted, 63 enrolled. In 2017, 60 master's, 18 other advanced degrees awarded. *Application deadline:* For fall admission, 7/15 for domestic and international students; for spring admission, 10/1 for domestic and international students. Electronic applications accepted. *Expenses: Tuition:* Full-time $28,800; part-time $1655 per credit hour. *Required fees:* $45; $2.75 per credit hour. *Unit head:* Toni Marsh, Director, 202-994-2844, E-mail: marsht01@gwu.edu. *Application contact:* Analisa Encinas, Paralegal Studies Program Representative, 703-248-6011, E-mail: aencinas@gwu.edu.
Website: http://nearyou.gwu.edu/plx/

The George Washington University, College of Professional Studies, Program in Law Firm Management, Washington, DC 20052. Offers MPS, Graduate Certificate. Program offered in partnership with The Hildebrandt Institute and held in Alexandria, VA. *Program availability:* Online learning. *Students:* 19 part-time (12 women); includes 4 minority (2 Black or African American, non-Hispanic/Latino; 1 Asian, non-Hispanic/Latino; 1 Hispanic/Latino), 1 international. Average age 42. 19 applicants, 100% accepted, 13 enrolled. In 2017, 6 master's awarded. *Entrance requirements:* For master's, resume, 2 references. Additional exam requirements/recommendations for international students: Required—TOEFL. *Application deadline:* For fall admission, 4/1 for domestic and international students. Electronic applications accepted. *Expenses: Tuition:* Full-time $28,800; part-time $1655 per credit hour. *Required fees:* $45; $2.75 per credit hour. *Unit head:* Kathleen M. Burke, Dean, 202-994-9711. *Application contact:* Kristin Williams, Assistant Vice President for Graduate and Special Enrollment Management, 202-994-0467, Fax: 202-994-0371, E-mail: ksw@gwu.edu.
Website: http://nearyou.gwu.edu/lawfirm/

The George Washington University, Columbian College of Arts and Sciences, Department of Political Science, Washington, DC 20052. Offers legal institutions and theory (MA); political science (MA). *Program availability:* Part-time, evening/weekend. *Faculty:* 33 full-time (9 women), 35 part-time/adjunct (9 women). *Students:* 40 full-time (19 women), 47 part-time (16 women); includes 12 minority (3 Black or African American, non-Hispanic/Latino; 3 Asian, non-Hispanic/Latino; 5 Hispanic/Latino; 1 Two or more races, non-Hispanic/Latino), 17 international. Average age 30. 378 applicants, 16% accepted, 21 enrolled. In 2017, 13 master's, 14 doctorates awarded. Terminal master's awarded for partial completion of doctoral program. *Degree requirements:* For master's, one foreign language, comprehensive exam, thesis or alternative; for doctorate, 2 foreign languages, thesis/dissertation, general exam. *Entrance requirements:* For master's and doctorate, GRE General Test, minimum GPA of 3.0. Additional exam requirements/recommendations for international students: Required—TOEFL (minimum score 550 paper-based; 80 iBT). *Application deadline:* For fall admission, 1/15 priority date for domestic students; for spring admission, 10/1 priority date for domestic students. Applications are processed on a rolling basis. Application fee: $75. Electronic applications accepted. *Expenses: Tuition:* Full-time $28,800; part-time $1655 per credit hour. *Required fees:* $45; $2.75 per credit hour. *Financial support:* In 2017–18, 43 students received support. Fellowships with tuition reimbursements available, teaching assistantships with tuition reimbursements available, Federal Work-Study, and tuition waivers available. *Unit head:* Christopher J. Deering, Chair, 202-994-6564, E-mail: rocket@gwu.edu. *Application contact:* 202-994-6290, Fax: 202-994-6213, E-mail: askccas@gwu.edu.
Website: http://politicalscience.columbian.gwu.edu/

Georgian Court University, School of Arts and Sciences, Lakewood, NJ 08701-2697. Offers applied behavior analysis (MA); autism spectrum disorders (Certificate); clinical mental health counseling (MA); criminal justice and human rights (MS); holistic health studies (MA, Certificate); homeland security (Certificate); instructional technology (CPC); mercy spirituality (Certificate); parish business management (Certificate); professional counselor (Certificate); school psychology (MA, Certificate); theology (MA, Certificate). *Program availability:* Part-time, evening/weekend. *Faculty:* 18 full-time (11 women), 8 part-time/adjunct (4 women). *Students:* 100 full-time (86 women), 92 part-time (67 women); includes 34 minority (9 Black or African American, non-Hispanic/Latino; 1 Asian, non-Hispanic/Latino; 20 Hispanic/Latino; 4 Two or more races, non-Hispanic/Latino), 2 international. Average age 34. 187 applicants, 56% accepted, 78 enrolled. In 2017, 58 master's, 20 other advanced degrees awarded. *Degree requirements:* For master's, comprehensive exam (for some programs), thesis (for some programs). *Entrance requirements:* For master's, GRE, GMAT, or NTE/PRAXIS, 3 letters of recommendation. Additional exam requirements/recommendations for international students: Required—TOEFL (minimum score 550 paper-based). *Application deadline:* For fall admission, 8/15 for domestic students, 5/1 for international students; for spring admission, 1/15 for domestic students, 10/1 for international students. Applications are processed on a rolling basis. Application fee: $40. Electronic applications accepted. *Expenses:* Tuition: Part-time $839 per credit. *Required fees:* $248 per semester. Tuition and fees vary according to campus/location and program. *Financial support:* Scholarships/grants, health care benefits, and unspecified assistantships available. Financial award application deadline: 4/15; financial award applicants required to submit FAFSA. *Unit head:* Dr. Mary Chinery, Dean, 732-987-2493, Fax: 732-987-2007, E-mail: mchinery@georgian.edu. *Application contact:* Patrick Givens, Director of Graduate and Professional Studies Admissions, 732-987-2736, Fax: 732-987-2000, E-mail: gps@georgian.edu.
Website: https://georgian.edu/academics/school-of-arts-sciences/

Golden Gate University, School of Law, San Francisco, CA 94105. Offers environmental law (LL M); estate planning (LL M); intellectual property law (LL M); international legal studies (LL M, SJD); law (JD); taxation law (LL M); U.S. legal studies (LL M); JD/MBA. *Accreditation:* ABA. *Program availability:* Part-time, evening/weekend. *Faculty:* 31 full-time (19 women), 160 part-time/adjunct (77 women). *Students:* 286 full-time (184 women), 245 part-time (134 women); includes 242 minority (48 Black or African American, non-Hispanic/Latino; 4 American Indian or Alaska Native, non-Hispanic/Latino; 69 Asian, non-Hispanic/Latino; 95 Hispanic/Latino; 7 Native Hawaiian or other Pacific Islander, non-Hispanic/Latino; 19 Two or more races, non-Hispanic/Latino), 71 international. Average age 31. 1,354 applicants, 66% accepted, 227 enrolled. *Degree requirements:* For doctorate, thesis/dissertation (for some programs). *Entrance requirements:* For doctorate, LSAT (for JD). Additional exam requirements/recommendations for international students: Required—TOEFL (minimum score 600 paper-based). *Application deadline:* For fall admission, 6/30 for domestic students. Applications are processed on a rolling basis. Electronic applications accepted. *Expenses:* Contact institution. *Financial support:* Fellowships, research assistantships, teaching assistantships, career-related internships or fieldwork, Federal Work-Study, institutionally sponsored loans, scholarships/grants, tuition waivers (full and partial), and unspecified assistantships available. Support available to part-time students. Financial award applicants required to submit FAFSA. *Faculty research:* International law, intellectual property law, environmental law, real estate, civil rights. *Unit head:* Anthony Niedwiecki, Dean, 415-442-6601, Fax: 415-442-6609. *Application contact:* Greg Egertson, Associate Dean and Director of Admissions, 415-442-6636, Fax: 415-442-6609, E-mail: lawadmit@ggu.edu.
Website: http://law.ggu.edu/

Governors State University, College of Arts and Sciences, Program in Political and Justice Studies, University Park, IL 60484. Offers MA. *Program availability:* Part-time. *Faculty:* 60 full-time (34 women), 115 part-time/adjunct (58 women). *Students:* 3 full-time (1 woman), 26 part-time (12 women); includes 16 minority (all Black or African American, non-Hispanic/Latino), 1 international. Average age 37. 2 applicants, 50% accepted. In 2017, 5 master's awarded. *Application deadline:* For fall admission, 4/1 for domestic students. Applications are processed on a rolling basis. Application fee: $50. Electronic applications accepted. *Expenses:* Tuition, state resident: full-time $8472; part-time $353 per credit hour. Tuition, nonresident: full-time $16,944; part-time $706 per credit hour. *Required fees:* $1824; $76 per credit hour. $38 per term. Tuition and fees vary according to course load, degree level and program. *Financial support:* Application deadline: 5/1; applicants required to submit FAFSA. *Unit head:* Lori Montalbano, Chair, Division of Arts and Letters, 708-534-5000 Ext. 2802, E-mail: lmontalbano@govst.edu.

Harrison Middleton University, Graduate Program, Tempe, AZ 85282. Offers education (MA, Ed D); humanities (MA); imaginative literature (MA); interdisciplinary studies (DA); jurisprudence (MA); natural science (MA); philosophy and religion (MA); social science (MA). *Program availability:* Part-time, evening/weekend, online learning. *Degree requirements:* For master's and doctorate, capstone project. *Entrance requirements:* For master's, interview; for doctorate, 2 academic letters of reference, interview, essay. Additional exam requirements/recommendations for international students: Required—TOEFL (minimum score 550 paper-based; 80 iBT). Electronic applications accepted. *Faculty research:* Japanese animation, educational leadership, war art, John Muir's wilderness.

Harvard University, Law School, Professional Programs in Law, Cambridge, MA 02138. Offers international and comparative law (JD); law and business (JD); law and government (JD); law and social change (JD); law, science and technology (JD); JD/MALD; JD/MBA; JD/MPH; JD/MPP; JD/PhD. *Accreditation:* ABA. *Degree requirements:* For doctorate, 3rd-year paper. *Entrance requirements:* For doctorate, LSAT. *Faculty research:* Constitutional law, voting rights law, cyber law.

Hodges University, Graduate Programs, Naples, FL 34119. Offers accounting (M Acc); business administration (MBA); clinical mental health counseling (MS); health services administration (MS); information systems management (MIS); legal studies (MS); management (MSM). *Program availability:* Part-time, evening/weekend, 100% online, blended/hybrid learning. *Degree requirements:* For master's, comprehensive exam (for some programs), thesis (for some programs). *Entrance requirements:* For master's, essay. Additional exam requirements/recommendations for international students: Recommended—TOEFL. Electronic applications accepted.

Hofstra University, Maurice A. Deane School of Law, Hempstead, NY 11549. Offers alternative dispute resolution (JD); American legal studies (LL M); business law honors (JD); clinical bioethics (Certificate); corporate compliance (JD); criminal law and procedure (JD); family law (LL M, JD); health law (JD); health law and policy (LL M, MA); intellectual property law honors (JD); international law honors (JD); JD/MBA; JD/MPH. *Accreditation:* ABA. *Program availability:* Part-time, 100% online. *Faculty:* 41 full-time (23 women), 69 part-time/adjunct (20 women). *Students:* 698 full-time (382 women), 136 part-time (91 women); includes 201 minority (66 Black or African American, non-Hispanic/Latino; 3 American Indian or Alaska Native, non-Hispanic/Latino; 31 Asian, non-Hispanic/Latino; 90 Hispanic/Latino; 8 Native Hawaiian or other Pacific Islander, non-Hispanic/Latino; 3 Two or more races, non-Hispanic/Latino), 28 international. Average age 28. 3,212 applicants, 50% accepted, 317 enrolled. In 2017, 9 master's, 234

doctorates awarded. *Entrance requirements:* For doctorate, LSAT, letter of recommendation, personal statement, undergraduate transcripts; for Certificate, 2 letters of recommendation, JD or LL B, personal statement, law school transcripts. Additional exam requirements/recommendations for international students: Recommended—TOEFL (minimum score 600 paper-based; 100 iBT). *Application deadline:* For fall admission, 4/15 priority date for domestic and international students. Applications are processed on a rolling basis. Application fee: $75. Electronic applications accepted. *Expenses:* $28,397 per term. *Financial support:* In 2017–18, 506 students received support, including 493 fellowships with full and partial tuition reimbursements available (averaging $33,296 per year); research assistantships with full and partial tuition reimbursements available, career-related internships or fieldwork, Federal Work-Study, institutionally sponsored loans, scholarships/grants, tuition waivers (full and partial), and unspecified assistantships also available. Support available to part-time students. Financial award applicants required to submit FAFSA. *Faculty research:* Family law; international law; constitutional law; legal ethics; health law. *Unit head:* Gail Prudenti, Dean, 516-463-4068, E-mail: gail.prudenti@hofstra.edu. *Application contact:* Sunil Samuel, Assistant Vice President of Admissions, 516-463-4723, Fax: 516-463-4664.
Website: http://law.hofstra.edu/

Illinois Institute of Technology, Chicago-Kent College of Law, Chicago, IL 60661-3691. Offers family law (LL M); financial services law (LL M); international intellectual property law (LL M); law (JD); legal studies (JSD); taxation (LL M); U.S., international, and transnational law (LL M); JD/LL M; JD/MBA; JD/MPA; JD/MPH; JD/MS. *Accreditation:* ABA. *Program availability:* Part-time, evening/weekend. Terminal master's awarded for partial completion of doctoral program. *Entrance requirements:* For master's, 1st degree in law or certified license to practice law; for doctorate, LSAT. Additional exam requirements/recommendations for international students: Required—TOEFL (minimum score 600 paper-based; 100 iBT); Recommended—IELTS (minimum score 7). Electronic applications accepted. *Expenses:* Contact institution. *Faculty research:* Constitutional law, bioethics, environmental law, intellectual property.

Indiana University South Bend, College of Liberal Arts and Sciences, South Bend, IN 46615. Offers advanced computer programming (Graduate Certificate); applied informatics (Graduate Certificate); applied mathematics and computer science (MS); behavior modification (Graduate Certificate); computer applications (Graduate Certificate); computer programming (Graduate Certificate); correctional management and supervision (Graduate Certificate); English (MA); health systems management (Graduate Certificate); international studies (Graduate Certificate); liberal studies (MLS); nonprofit management (Graduate Certificate); paralegal studies (Graduate Certificate); professional writing (Graduate Certificate); public affairs (MPA); public management (Graduate Certificate); social and cultural diversity (Graduate Certificate); strategic sustainability leadership (Graduate Certificate); technology for administration (Graduate Certificate). *Program availability:* Part-time, evening/weekend. *Degree requirements:* For master's, variable foreign language requirement, thesis (for some programs). *Entrance requirements:* For master's, minimum GPA of 3.0. Additional exam requirements/recommendations for international students: Required—TOEFL (minimum score 550 paper-based; 80 iBT). *Expenses:* Contact institution. *Faculty research:* Artificial intelligence, bioinformatics, English language and literature, creative writing, computer networks.

John Jay College of Criminal Justice of the City University of New York, Graduate Studies, Programs in Criminal Justice, New York, NY 10019. Offers criminal justice (MA, PhD); criminology and deviance (PhD); forensic psychology (PhD); forensic science (PhD); international crime and justice (MA); law and philosophy (PhD); organizational behavior (PhD); public policy (PhD). *Program availability:* Part-time, evening/weekend. Terminal master's awarded for partial completion of doctoral program. *Degree requirements:* For master's, thesis or alternative; for doctorate, one foreign language, thesis/dissertation. *Entrance requirements:* For master's, GRE General Test, minimum B average; for doctorate, GRE General Test. Additional exam requirements/recommendations for international students: Required—TOEFL (minimum score 500 paper-based).

Liberty University, School of Law, Lynchburg, VA 24515. Offers American legal studies (JM); international legal studies (JM, LL M). *Program availability:* Online learning. *Students:* 251 full-time (123 women), 116 part-time (57 women); includes 84 minority (46 Black or African American, non-Hispanic/Latino; 4 American Indian or Alaska Native, non-Hispanic/Latino; 7 Asian, non-Hispanic/Latino; 17 Hispanic/Latino; 10 Two or more races, non-Hispanic/Latino), 6 international. Average age 33. 294 applicants, 67% accepted, 136 enrolled. *Entrance requirements:* Additional exam requirements/recommendations for international students: Required—TOEFL (minimum score 600 paper-based; 100 iBT). *Application deadline:* For fall admission, 6/1 for domestic students. *Expenses:* Contact institution. *Financial support:* Applicants required to submit FAFSA. *Unit head:* B. Keith Faulkner, Dean, 434-592-5300, Fax: 434-592-5400, E-mail: law@liberty.edu. *Application contact:* Joleen Thaxton, Assistant Director of Admissions, 434-592-5300, Fax: 434-592-5400, E-mail: lawadmissions@liberty.edu.

Loyola University Chicago, Institute of Pastoral Studies, Chicago, IL 60611. Offers Christian spirituality (MA), including spiritual direction; church management (Certificate); counseling for ministry (MA); divinity (M Div); health care ministry leadership (Certificate); health care mission leadership (MA); pastoral counseling (MA, Certificate); pastoral studies (MA); religious education (Certificate); social justice (MA, Certificate); spiritual direction (Certificate); M Div/MA; M Div/MSW; MSW/MA. MSW/MA offered with School of Social Work. *Accreditation:* ACIPE. *Program availability:* Part-time, evening/weekend, 100% online, blended/hybrid learning. *Faculty:* 11 full-time (5 women), 20 part-time/adjunct (9 women). *Students:* 80 full-time (51 women), 150 part-time (107 women); includes 58 minority (24 Black or African American, non-Hispanic/Latino; 7 Asian, non-Hispanic/Latino; 27 Hispanic/Latino), 29 international. Average age 45. 128 applicants, 79% accepted, 72 enrolled. In 2017, 53 master's, 5 other advanced degrees awarded. *Degree requirements:* For master's, thesis optional, project. *Entrance requirements:* Additional exam requirements/recommendations for international students: Required—TOEFL (minimum score 550 paper-based; 79 iBT), IELTS (minimum score 6.5). *Application deadline:* Applications are processed on a rolling basis. Application fee: $50. Electronic applications accepted. Application fee is waived when completed online. *Expenses:* Contact institution. *Financial support:* In 2017–18, 111 students received support. Career-related internships or fieldwork, Federal Work-Study, scholarships/grants, and unspecified assistantships available. Support available to part-time students. Financial award application deadline: 3/15. *Faculty research:* Catholic theology, skills of religious ministry, family ministries, spirituality and divorced men. *Unit head:* Dr. Brian J. Schmisek, Dean, 312-915-7400, Fax: 312-915-7410, E-mail: bschmisek@luc.edu. *Application contact:* Dr. M. Therese Lysaught, Associate Dean, 312-915-7485, Fax: 312-915-7410, E-mail: mlysaught@luc.edu.
Website: http://www.luc.edu/ips/

Marlboro College, Graduate and Professional Studies, Program in Teaching for Social Justice, Marlboro, VT 05344. Offers MAT. *Program availability:* Evening/weekend. *Degree requirements:* For master's, 36 credits including teaching internship and portfolio. *Entrance requirements:* For master's, statement of intent, 2 letters of recommendation, transcripts, interview. Additional exam requirements/

recommendations for international students: Required—TOEFL (minimum score of 577 paper-based, 90 iBT) or IELTS (minimum score of 7). *Application deadline:* For fall admission, 7/1 priority date for domestic and international students; for winter admission, 11/1 priority date for domestic and international students. Applications are processed on a rolling basis. Electronic applications accepted. *Expenses:* Contact institution. *Financial support:* Scholarships/grants available. Financial award application deadline: 8/5; financial award applicants required to submit FAFSA. *Unit head:* Janaki Natarajan, Director, 802-451-7506, Fax: 802-258-9201. *Application contact:* Amanda Mehegan, Assistant Director of Graduate Admissions, 802-451-7505, Fax: 802-258-9201, E-mail: graduateadmissions@marlboro.edu.
Website: https://www.marlboro.edu/academics/graduate/teach

Marygrove College, Graduate Studies, Detroit, MI 48221-2599. Offers autism spectrum disorders (M Ed, Certificate); curriculum instruction and assessment (MAT); educational leadership (MA); educational technology (M Ed); effective teaching in the 21st century-classroom focus (MAT); effective teaching in the 21st century-technology focus (MAT); human resource management (MA, Certificate); mathematics 6-8 (MAT); mathematics K-5 (MAT); reading and literacy K-6 (MAT); reading specialist (M Ed); school administrator (Certificate); social justice (MA); special education (MAT); special education - learning disabilities (M Ed); teaching - pre-elementary education (M Ed); teaching - pre-secondary education (M Ed). *Program availability:* Part-time, evening/weekend, 100% online, blended/hybrid learning. *Students:* 163 full-time (123 women), 264 part-time (186 women). Average age 34. *Entrance requirements:* For master's, all official bachelor's transcripts. Additional exam requirements/recommendations for international students: Required—TOEFL (minimum score 550 paper-based; 80 iBT). *Application deadline:* Applications are processed on a rolling basis. Electronic applications accepted. *Expenses: Tuition:* Part-time $590 per credit hour. *Required fees:* $120 per semester. One-time fee: $25 part-time. *Financial support:* Applicants required to submit FAFSA. *Unit head:* Marygrove College Admissions, 313-927-1240, E-mail: info@marygrove.edu. *Application contact:* Marygrove College Admissions, 313-927-1240, E-mail: info@marygrove.edu.

Michigan State University College of Law, Graduate and Professional Programs, East Lansing, MI 48824-1300. Offers American legal system (LL M, MJ); global food law (LL M, MJ); intellectual property law (LL M, MJ); law (JD); legal studies (MLS). *Accreditation:* ABA. *Program availability:* Part-time. *Faculty:* 55 full-time (23 women), 77 part-time/adjunct (27 women). *Students:* 779 full-time (407 women), 77 part-time (50 women); includes 173 minority (57 Black or African American, non-Hispanic/Latino; 9 American Indian or Alaska Native, non-Hispanic/Latino; 28 Asian, non-Hispanic/Latino; 40 Hispanic/Latino; 2 Native Hawaiian or other Pacific Islander, non-Hispanic/Latino; 37 Two or more races, non-Hispanic/Latino), 91 international. Average age 24. *Entrance requirements:* For doctorate, LSAT. Additional exam requirements/recommendations for international students: Required—TOEFL (minimum score 600 paper-based), IELTS. *Application deadline:* For fall admission, 4/30 priority date for domestic students, 7/1 priority date for international students. Applications are processed on a rolling basis. Application fee: $60. Electronic applications accepted. *Expenses: Tuition:* Full-time $43,400. *Financial support:* Career-related internships or fieldwork, Federal Work-Study, scholarships/grants, and tuition waivers (full and partial) available. Support available to part-time students. Financial award application deadline: 4/1; financial award applicants required to submit FAFSA. *Faculty research:* International, constitutional, health, tax and environmental law; intellectual property, trial practice, corporate law. *Unit head:* Lawrence Ponoroff, Dean/Professor of Law, 517-432-6993, Fax: 517-432-6801, E-mail: lponoroff@law.msu.edu. *Application contact:* Melanie Jacobs, Senior Associate Dean of Admissions and International Programs, 517-432-0222, Fax: 517-432-0098, E-mail: admiss@law.msu.edu.
Website: http://www.law.msu.edu/

Mississippi College, Graduate School, College of Arts and Sciences, School of Humanities and Social Sciences, Department of History, Political Science, Administration of Justice, and Paralegal Studies, Clinton, MS 39058. Offers administration of justice (MSS); history (M Ed, MA, MSS); paralegal studies (Certificate); political science (MSS); social sciences (M Ed, MSS). *Program availability:* Part-time. *Degree requirements:* For master's, one foreign language, comprehensive exam, thesis (for some programs). *Entrance requirements:* For master's, GRE or NTE, minimum GPA of 2.5. Additional exam requirements/recommendations for international students: Recommended—TOEFL, IELTS. Electronic applications accepted.

Montclair State University, The Graduate School, College of Humanities and Social Sciences, Paralegal Studies Certificate Program, Montclair, NJ 07043-1624. Offers Certificate. *Program availability:* Part-time, evening/weekend. *Entrance requirements:* For degree, 2 letters of recommendation, essay. Additional exam requirements/recommendations for international students: Required—TOEFL (minimum score 83 iBT) or IELTS. Electronic applications accepted.

National Paralegal College, Graduate Programs, Phoenix, AZ 85014. Offers compliance law (MS); legal studies (MS); taxation (MS). *Program availability:* Part-time. Electronic applications accepted.

National University, Academic Affairs, School of Professional Studies, La Jolla, CA 92037-1011. Offers criminal justice (MCJ); digital cinema production (MFA); digital journalism (MA); homeland security and emergency management (MS); juvenile justice (MS); professional screenwriting (MFA); public administration (MPA), including human resource management, organizational leadership. *Program availability:* Part-time, evening/weekend, 100% online, blended/hybrid learning. *Degree requirements:* For master's, thesis (for some programs). *Entrance requirements:* For master's, interview, minimum GPA of 2.5. Additional exam requirements/recommendations for international students: Required—TOEFL (minimum score 550 paper-based; 79 iBT), IELTS (minimum score 6). *Application deadline:* Applications are processed on a rolling basis. Application fee: $60 ($65 for international students). Electronic applications accepted. *Expenses: Tuition:* Part-time $430 per quarter hour. *Financial support:* Career-related internships or fieldwork, institutionally sponsored loans, scholarships/grants, and tuition waivers (partial) available. Support available to part-time students. Financial award application deadline: 6/30; financial award applicants required to submit FAFSA. *Unit head:* Dr. Daniel Donaldson, Dean, 858-642-8480, E-mail: sops@nu.edu. *Application contact:* Brandon Jouganatos, Vice President for Enrollment Services, 800-628-8648, E-mail: advisor@nu.edu.
Website: http://www.nu.edu/OurPrograms/School-of-Professional-Studies.html

New York University, Graduate School of Arts and Science and School of Law, Institute for Law and Society, New York, NY 10012-1019. Offers MA, PhD, JD/MA, JD/PhD. *Students:* Average age 36. In 2017, 2 doctorates awarded. *Degree requirements:* For doctorate, one foreign language, thesis/dissertation. *Entrance requirements:* Additional exam requirements/recommendations for international students: Required—TOEFL. Application fee: $100. *Expenses: Tuition:* Full-time $41,352; part-time $19,968 per year. *Required fees:* $2496; $1628 per unit. $814 per term. Tuition and fees vary according to course load and program. *Financial support:* Fellowships, teaching assistantships, career-related internships or fieldwork, Federal Work-Study, institutionally sponsored loans, scholarships/grants, health care benefits, and unspecified assistantships available. Financial award applicants required to submit FAFSA. *Faculty research:* Politics of law, law and social policy, law in comparative

global perspective, rights and social movements. *Unit head:* Jo Dixon, Director of Graduate Studies, 212-998-8040, Fax: 212-995-4557, E-mail: gsas.admissions@nyu.edu. *Application contact:* Carly Vignogna, Graduate Administrator, 212-998-8040, Fax: 212-995-4557, E-mail: gsas.admissions@nyu.edu.

Northeastern University, College of Social Sciences and Humanities, Boston, MA 02115. Offers criminology and criminal justice (MSCJ); criminology and justice policy (PhD); economics (MA, PhD); English (MA, PhD); international affairs (MA); law and public policy (PhD); political science (MA, PhD); public administration (MPA); public policy (MPP); security and resilience studies (MS); sociology (MA, PhD); urban and regional policy (MS); urban informatics (MS); world history (MA, PhD). *Program availability:* Online learning. *Faculty:* 242. *Students:* 491. In 2017, 143 master's, 38 doctorates awarded. *Degree requirements:* For doctorate, variable foreign language requirement, comprehensive exam, thesis/dissertation. *Entrance requirements:* For master's and doctorate, GRE. Additional exam requirements/recommendations for international students: Required—TOEFL, IELTS. Application fee: $75. Electronic applications accepted. *Expenses:* Contact institution. *Financial support:* Teaching assistantships, career-related internships or fieldwork, scholarships/grants, health care benefits, tuition waivers (full and partial), and unspecified assistantships available. Support available to part-time students. Financial award applicants required to submit FAFSA. *Unit head:* Dr. Uta Poiger, Dean, 617-373-5173, E-mail: college_of_social_sciences_and_humanities@neu.edu. *Application contact:* 617-373-5990, E-mail: gradcssh@northeastern.edu.
Website: http://www.northeastern.edu/cssh/

Nova Southeastern University, Shepard Broad College of Law, Fort Lauderdale, FL 33314. Offers education law (MS), including cybersecurity law, education law advocacy, exceptional education; employment law (MS), including cybersecurity law, employee relations law, human resource managerial law; health law (MS, JD), including clinical research law and regulatory compliance (MS), cybersecurity law (MS), health care administrative law (MS), regulatory compliance (MS), risk management (MS); international law (JD); law and policy (MS), including cybersecurity law; JD/DO; JD/M Acc; JD/M Tax; JD/MBA; JD/MPA; JD/MS; JD/PhD. *Accreditation:* ABA. *Program availability:* Part-time, evening/weekend, 100% online, blended/hybrid learning. *Faculty:* 56 full-time (30 women), 41 part-time/adjunct (14 women). *Students:* 566 full-time (297 women), 138 part-time (84 women); includes 365 minority (62 Black or African American, non-Hispanic/Latino; 3 American Indian or Alaska Native, non-Hispanic/Latino; 23 Asian, non-Hispanic/Latino; 264 Hispanic/Latino; 3 Native Hawaiian or other Pacific Islander, non-Hispanic/Latino; 10 Two or more races, non-Hispanic/Latino), 26 international. Average age 29. 1,070 applicants, 53% accepted, 224 enrolled. In 2017, 45 master's, 225 doctorates awarded. *Degree requirements:* For master's, thesis optional, capstone research project; for doctorate, rigorous upper-level writing fulfilled through faculty-supervised seminar paper, law journal article, workshop, or other research; 6 credits' experiential learning. *Entrance requirements:* For master's, regionally-accredited undergraduate degree; at least 2 years' experience in related field (for employment law and health law); for doctorate, LSAT. Additional exam requirements/recommendations for international students: Recommended—TOEFL (minimum score 600 paper-based; 100 iBT), IELTS (minimum score 7). *Application deadline:* For fall admission, 5/1 priority date for domestic and international students; for winter admission, 12/12 for domestic and international students; for spring admission, 3/31 for domestic and international students; for summer admission, 4/1 for domestic and international students. Applications are processed on a rolling basis. Application fee: $0. Electronic applications accepted. *Expenses:* $40,060 full-time; $30,280 part-time. *Financial support:* In 2017–18, 211 students received support, including 221 fellowships (averaging $12,000 per year); Federal Work-Study, institutionally sponsored loans, scholarships/grants, and unspecified assistantships also available. Support available to part-time students. Financial award application deadline: 4/15; financial award applicants required to submit FAFSA. *Faculty research:* Legal issues in health law, international law, the legal profession, family law, civil rights. *Unit head:* Jon M. Garon, Dean, 954-262-6101, Fax: 954-262-2862, E-mail: garon@nova.edu. *Application contact:* William Daniel Perez, Assistant Dean of Admissions, 954-262-6121, Fax: 954-262-3844, E-mail: wperez1@nova.edu.
Website: http://www.law.nova.edu/

Pace University, Elisabeth Haub School of Law, White Plains, NY 10603. Offers comparative legal studies (LL M); environmental law (LL M, SJD), including energy and climate change law (LL M); global environmental law (LL M); law (JD); JD/LL M; JD/MA; JD/MBA; JD/MEM; JD/MPA; JD/MS. JD/MA offered jointly with Sarah Lawrence College; JD/MEM offered jointly with Yale University School of Forestry and Environmental Studies. *Accreditation:* ABA. *Program availability:* Part-time. *Faculty:* 26 full-time (11 women), 52 part-time/adjunct (19 women). *Students:* 548 (301 women); includes 154 minority (31 Black or African American, non-Hispanic/Latino; 3 American Indian or Alaska Native, non-Hispanic/Latino; 20 Asian, non-Hispanic/Latino; 54 Hispanic/Latino; 1 Native Hawaiian or other Pacific Islander, non-Hispanic/Latino; 45 Two or more races, non-Hispanic/Latino), 9 international. Average age 26. 1,443 applicants, 53% accepted, 217 enrolled. In 2017, 20 master's, 170 doctorates awarded. *Degree requirements:* For doctorate, thesis/dissertation (for some programs), extensive thesis proposal (for SJD). *Entrance requirements:* For master's, writing sample; for doctorate, LSAT (for JD). Additional exam requirements/recommendations for international students: Required—TOEFL (minimum score 100 iBT); Recommended—TWE. *Application deadline:* For fall admission, 6/1 priority date for domestic students; for winter admission, 11/15 priority date for domestic students. Applications are processed on a rolling basis. Application fee: $65. Electronic applications accepted. *Expenses:* Contact institution. *Financial support:* In 2017–18, 473 students received support. Fellowships, research assistantships, career-related internships or fieldwork, Federal Work-Study, institutionally sponsored loans, scholarships/grants, and unspecified assistantships available. Support available to part-time students. Financial award application deadline: 2/1; financial award applicants required to submit FAFSA. *Faculty research:* Reform of energy regulations, international law, land use law, prosecutorial misconduct, corporation law. *Unit head:* David Yassky, Dean, 914-422-4407, E-mail: dyassky@law.pace.edu. *Application contact:* Cathy Alexander, Assistant Dean, 914-422-4210, Fax: 914-989-8714, E-mail: calexander@law.pace.edu.
Website: http://www.law.pace.edu/

Prairie View A&M University, College of Juvenile Justice and Psychology, Prairie View, TX 77446. Offers clinical adolescent psychology (PhD); juvenile forensic psychology (MSJFP); juvenile justice (MSJJ, PhD). *Program availability:* Part-time, evening/weekend, online only, 100% online. *Faculty:* 7 full-time (5 women), 3 part-time/adjunct (1 woman). *Students:* 23 full-time (18 women), 30 part-time (25 women); includes 50 minority (41 Black or African American, non-Hispanic/Latino; 8 Hispanic/Latino; 1 Two or more races, non-Hispanic/Latino), 2 international. Average age 31. 39 applicants, 82% accepted, 24 enrolled. In 2017, 19 master's, 3 doctorates awarded. *Degree requirements:* For master's, comprehensive exam; for doctorate, thesis/dissertation. *Entrance requirements:* For master's, GRE, minimum GPA of 2.75; for doctorate, GRE, previous course work in clinical adolescent psychology, minimum GPA of 3.5. Additional exam requirements/recommendations for international students: Required—TOEFL (minimum score 550 paper-based; 79 iBT). *Application deadline:* For fall admission, 5/1 priority date for domestic and international students; for spring admission, 10/1 priority date for domestic students, 9/1 priority date for international students; for summer admission, 3/1 priority date for domestic students, 2/1 priority date for international students. Applications are processed on a rolling basis. Application fee: $50. Electronic applications accepted. *Expenses:* Tuition, state resident: part-time $242 per credit. Tuition, nonresident: part-time $695 per credit. *Required fees:* $149 per credit. *Financial support:* Research assistantships, teaching assistantships, scholarships/grants, and unspecified assistantships available. Financial award application deadline: 4/1; financial award applicants required to submit FAFSA. *Faculty research:* Juvenile justice, community policing, adolescent substance use, reducing mental illness stigma and promoting positive psychological well-being in diverse communities, promoting prosocial behavior among at-risk youth. *Unit head:* Dr. Tamara L. Brown, Dean, 936-261-5206, Fax: 936-261-5253, E-mail: tlbrown@pvamu.edu. *Application contact:* Pauline Walker, Executive Secretary, Graduate Program, 936-261-3521, Fax: 936-261-3529, E-mail: gradadmissions@pvamu.edu.

Prescott College, Graduate Programs, Program in Arts and Humanities, Prescott, AZ 86301. Offers humanities (MA); social justice and human rights (MA); student-directed independent study (MA). *Program availability:* Part-time, online learning. *Degree requirements:* For master's, thesis, fieldwork or internship, practicum. *Entrance requirements:* For master's, 2 letters of recommendation, resume, essay. Additional exam requirements/recommendations for international students: Required—TOEFL (minimum score 500 paper-based). Electronic applications accepted.

Purdue University Global, School of Legal Studies, Davenport, IA 52807. Offers health care delivery (MS); pathway to paralegal (Postbaccalaureate Certificate); state and local government (MS). *Program availability:* Part-time, evening/weekend, online learning. *Entrance requirements:* Additional exam requirements/recommendations for international students: Required—TOEFL (minimum score 550 paper-based; 80 iBT).

Queen's University at Kingston, School of Graduate Studies, Faculty of Arts and Sciences, Department of Sociology, Kingston, ON K7L 3N6, Canada. Offers communication and Information technology (MA, PhD); feminist sociology (MA, PhD); socio-legal studies (MA, PhD); sociological theory (MA, PhD). *Program availability:* Part-time. *Degree requirements:* For master's, thesis; for doctorate, comprehensive exam, thesis/dissertation. *Entrance requirements:* For master's, honors bachelors degree in sociology; for doctorate, honors bachelors degree, masters degree in sociology. Additional exam requirements/recommendations for international students: Required—TOEFL. *Faculty research:* Social change and modernization, social control, deviance and criminology, surveillance.

Regent University, Graduate School, School of Law, Virginia Beach, VA 23464. Offers American legal studies (LL M); human rights (LL M); law (MA, JD), including advanced paralegal studies (MA), alternative dispute resolution (MA), business (MA), criminal justice (MA), general legal studies (MA), human resources management (MA), human rights and rule of law (MA), national security (MA), non-profit organizational law (MA), regulatory compliance (MA), wealth management and financial planning (MA); JD/MA; JD/MBA. *Accreditation:* ABA. *Program availability:* Part-time, 100% online, blended/hybrid learning. *Faculty:* 16 full-time (5 women), 76 part-time/adjunct (22 women). *Students:* 313 full-time (181 women), 248 part-time (175 women); includes 240 minority (155 Black or African American, non-Hispanic/Latino; 3 American Indian or Alaska Native, non-Hispanic/Latino; 15 Asian, non-Hispanic/Latino; 45 Hispanic/Latino; 2 Native Hawaiian or other Pacific Islander, non-Hispanic/Latino; 20 Two or more races, non-Hispanic/Latino), 59 international. Average age 35. 923 applicants, 36% accepted, 188 enrolled. In 2017, 138 master's, 80 doctorates awarded. *Entrance requirements:* For master's, college transcripts, resume, personal statement; for doctorate, LSAT, minimum undergraduate GPA of 3.0, official transcripts, 2 letters of recommendation, resume, personal statement. Additional exam requirements/recommendations for international students: Required—TOEFL (minimum score 600 paper-based). *Application deadline:* For fall admission, 3/1 for domestic students. Applications are processed on a rolling basis. Application fee: $50. Electronic applications accepted. *Expenses:* $650 per credit (MA, LL M); $1,140 per credit (JD); $300 per semester technology fee. *Financial support:* In 2017–18, 459 students received support. Career-related internships or fieldwork, scholarships/grants, and unspecified assistantships available. Support available to part-time students. *Faculty research:* Family law, Constitutional law, law and culture, evidence and practice, intellectual property. *Unit head:* Michael Hernandez, Dean, 757-352-4040, Fax: 757-352-4595, E-mail: michher@regent.edu. *Application contact:* Ernie Walton, Assistant Dean of Admissions, 757-352-4315, E-mail: lawschool@regent.edu.
Website: https://www.regent.edu/school-of-law/

Rhode Island College, School of Graduate Studies, Faculty of Arts and Sciences, Department of Sociology, Providence, RI 02908-1991. Offers justice studies (MA). *Program availability:* Part-time. *Students:* 1 part-time (0 women). Average age 26. *Entrance requirements:* Additional exam requirements/recommendations for international students: Recommended—TOEFL (minimum score 550 paper-based; 79 iBT). Application fee: $50. *Expenses:* Tuition, state resident: full-time $9768; part-time $407 per credit. Tuition, nonresident: full-time $19,008; part-time $792 per credit. *Required fees:* $696; $29 per credit. One-time fee: $200 full-time; $100 part-time. Tuition and fees vary according to course load. *Financial support:* Application deadline: 5/15; applicants required to submit FAFSA. *Unit head:* Mikaila Arthur, Chair, 401-456-8026, Fax: 401-456-8665. *Application contact:* Graduate Studies, 401-456-8700.
Website: http://www.ric.edu/sociology/

Royal Roads University, Graduate Studies, Peace and Conflict Studies Program, Victoria, BC V9B 5Y2, Canada. Offers conflict analysis (G Dip); conflict analysis and management (MA); disaster and emergency management (MA, G Dip); human security and peacebuilding (MA, G Dip); justice studies (G Dip); peace and conflict studies (MAIS). *Program availability:* Blended/hybrid learning. *Degree requirements:* For master's, thesis. *Entrance requirements:* For master's, 5-7 years of related work experience. Additional exam requirements/recommendations for international students: Required—TOEFL (minimum score 570 paper-based) or IELTS (7) recommended. *Application deadline:* Applications are processed on a rolling basis. Application fee: $120 ($240 for international students). Electronic applications accepted. *Financial support:* Federal Work-Study, institutionally sponsored loans, and scholarships/grants available. Support available to part-time students. *Faculty research:* Conflict analysis, ethno-political conflict reconciliation, international relations, displaced persons, resiliency. *Unit head:* Dr. Brigitte Harris, Dean, 250-391-2511, E-mail: admissions@royalroads.ca. *Application contact:* E-mail: admissions@royalroads.ca.
Website: http://www.royalroads.ca/

Rutgers University–New Brunswick, Graduate School-New Brunswick, Department of Political Science, Piscataway, NJ 08854-8097. Offers American politics (PhD); comparative politics (PhD); international relations (PhD); political theory (PhD); public law (PhD); United Nations and global policy studies (MA); women and politics (PhD). *Degree requirements:* For doctorate, one foreign language, comprehensive exam, thesis/dissertation. *Entrance requirements:* For master's, bachelor's degree from accredited U.S. college or university or a comparable institution in another country; for doctorate, GRE General Test. Additional exam requirements/recommendations for international students: Required—TOEFL.

St. John's University, St. John's College of Liberal Arts and Sciences, Program in Global Development and Social Justice, Queens, NY 11439. Offers MA. *Program availability:* Blended/hybrid learning, Program is 90% Online. *Students:* 33 part-time (17 women); includes 8 minority (4 Black or African American, non-Hispanic/Latino; 1 Asian, non-Hispanic/Latino; 3 Hispanic/Latino), 3 international. Average age 32. In 2017, 15 master's awarded. *Degree requirements:* For master's, thesis or alternative, capstone research paper. *Entrance requirements:* For master's, letters of recommendation, transcripts, resume, personal statement. Additional exam requirements/recommendations for international students: Required—TOEFL (minimum score 80 iBT), IELTS (minimum score 6.5). *Application deadline:* For spring admission, 3/1 for domestic students. Applications are processed on a rolling basis. Application fee: $0. Electronic applications accepted. *Expenses: Tuition:* Full-time $44,280; part-time $1230 per credit. *Required fees:* $340; $340 per credit. Tuition and fees vary according to course load, degree level and program. *Financial support:* Fellowships, research assistantships, teaching assistantships, scholarships/grants, tuition waivers, and unspecified assistantships available. Support available to part-time students. Financial award application deadline: 2/1; financial award applicants required to submit FAFSA. *Faculty research:* Global development; sustainability, social justice, migration, peace-building. *Unit head:* Barrett P. Brenton, PhD, Director of the Center for Global Development, 718-990-5662, Fax: 718-990-5878, E-mail: brentonb@stjohns.edu. *Application contact:* Robert Medrano, Director of Graduate Admissions, 718-990-1601, Fax: 718-990-5686, E-mail: gradhelp@stjohns.edu.
Website: https://www.stjohns.edu/academics/schools-and-colleges/st-johns-college-liberal-arts-and-sciences/programs-and-majors/global-development-and-social-ju

St. John's University, School of Law, Program in Bankruptcy, Queens, NY 11439. Offers LL M. *Program availability:* Part-time, evening/weekend. *Students:* 3 full-time (0 women), 3 part-time (1 woman); includes 1 minority (Hispanic/Latino). Average age 37. In 2017, 6 master's awarded. *Degree requirements:* For master's, 24 credits. *Entrance requirements:* For master's, LSAT, bachelor's degree, two letters of recommendation, personal statement, resume, official transcripts from law school (including class rank) and undergraduate schools attended. Additional exam requirements/recommendations for international students: Recommended—TOEFL (minimum score 600 paper-based; 100 iBT), IELTS (minimum score 7). *Application deadline:* For fall admission, 5/15 priority date for domestic and international students; for spring admission, 10/15 priority date for domestic and international students. Applications are processed on a rolling basis. Application fee: $100. Electronic applications accepted. *Expenses:* $1,969 per credit tuition, $170 per semester fees; tuition may vary by program. *Financial support:* Research assistantships, teaching assistantships, and scholarships/grants available. Financial award application deadline: 2/1; financial award applicants required to submit FAFSA. *Faculty research:* Bankruptcy, commercial law and consumer law, international insolvency, creditor's rights, corporate reorganization and insolvency. *Unit head:* Sarah Jean Kelly, Assistant Dean for Graduate Studies, 718-990-8358. *Application contact:* Yvette Gutierrez, Director of Graduate Admissions and Bankruptcy Programs, 718-990-1923, E-mail: llm@stjohns.edu.
Website: http://www.stjohns.edu/law/programs-and-majors/bankruptcy-llm

St. John's University, School of Law, Program in Transnational Legal Practice, Queens, NY 11439. Offers LL M. *Program availability:* Part-time. *Students:* 53 full-time (27 women), 7 part-time (6 women), 59 international. Average age 25. In 2017, 39 master's awarded. *Degree requirements:* For master's, 24 credits. *Entrance requirements:* For master's, LSAT, bachelor's degree, two letters of recommendation, personal statement, resume, official transcripts from law school (including class rank) and undergraduate schools attended. Additional exam requirements/recommendations for international students: Recommended—TOEFL (minimum score 600 paper-based; 100 iBT), IELTS (minimum score 7). *Application deadline:* For fall admission, 5/15 priority date for domestic and international students; for spring admission, 10/15 priority date for domestic and international students. Applications are processed on a rolling basis. Application fee: $100. Electronic applications accepted. *Expenses:* $2,461 per credit tuition, $170 per semester fees; tuition may vary by program. *Financial support:* Research assistantships, teaching assistantships, and scholarships/grants available. Financial award application deadline: 2/1; financial award applicants required to submit FAFSA. *Faculty research:* Public and private international law, international human rights law, international security and the resolution of armed conflict, the role and influence of international law in the United States, international finance. *Unit head:* Sarah Jean Kelly, Assistant Dean for Graduate Studies, 718-990-8538, E-mail: kellys@stjohns.edu. *Application contact:* Yvette Gutierrez, Assistant Dean of Graduate Admissions and Bankruptcy Programs, 718-990-1923, Fax: 718-990-8095, E-mail: llm@stjohns.edu.
Website: http://www.stjohns.edu/academics/graduate/law/academics/llm/tlp

St. John's University, School of Law, Program in U.S. Legal Studies for Foreign Law School Graduates, Queens, NY 11439. Offers LL M. *Program availability:* Part-time. *Students:* 15 full-time (10 women), 3 part-time (1 woman); includes 6 minority (all Asian, non-Hispanic/Latino), 5 international. Average age 34. In 2017, 7 master's awarded. *Degree requirements:* For master's, 24 credits. *Entrance requirements:* For master's, LSAT, law degree from non-U.S. law school, bachelor's degree, two letters of recommendation, personal statement, resume, official transcripts from law school (including class rank) and undergraduate schools attended. Additional exam requirements/recommendations for international students: Recommended—TOEFL (minimum score 600 paper-based; 100 iBT), IELTS (minimum score 7). *Application deadline:* For fall admission, 5/1 priority date for domestic students, 5/15 priority date for international students; for spring admission, 10/15 priority date for domestic and international students. Applications are processed on a rolling basis. Application fee: $100. Electronic applications accepted. *Expenses:* $2,461 per credit tuition, $170 per semester fees; tuition may vary by program. *Financial support:* Research assistantships, teaching assistantships, and scholarships/grants available. Financial award application deadline: 2/1; financial award applicants required to submit FAFSA. *Unit head:* Sarah Jean Kelly, Assistant Dean for Graduate Studies, 718-990-8538, E-mail: kellys@stjohns.edu. *Application contact:* Yvette Gutierrez, Director of Graduate Admissions and Bankruptcy Programs, 718-990-1923, Fax: 718-990-8095, E-mail: llm@stjohns.edu.
Website: http://www.stjohns.edu/academics/graduate/law/academics/llm/usls

Saint Leo University, Graduate Studies in Public Safety Administration, Saint Leo, FL 33574-6665. Offers criminal justice (MS), including behavioral studies, corrections, criminal investigation, criminal justice, emergency and disaster management, forensic science, legal studies; emergency and disaster management (MS), including emergency and disaster management, fire science. *Program availability:* Part-time, evening/weekend, 100% online, blended/hybrid learning. *Faculty:* 8 full-time (3 women), 32 part-time/adjunct (7 women). *Students:* 7 full-time (6 women), 617 part-time (385 women); includes 313 minority (235 Black or African American, non-Hispanic/Latino; 5 American Indian or Alaska Native, non-Hispanic/Latino; 3 Asian, non-Hispanic/Latino; 54 Hispanic/Latino; 1 Native Hawaiian or other Pacific Islander, non-Hispanic/Latino; 15 Two or more races, non-Hispanic/Latino). Average age 36. 336 applicants, 63% accepted, 197 enrolled. In 2017, 267 master's awarded. *Degree requirements:* For master's, comprehensive project. *Entrance requirements:* For master's, official transcripts, bachelor's degree from regionally-accredited university with minimum GPA of 3.0.

Additional exam requirements/recommendations for international students: Required—TOEFL (minimum score 550 paper-based; 78 iBT). *Application deadline:* For fall admission, 7/1 priority date for domestic and international students; for spring admission, 11/1 priority date for domestic and international students. Applications are processed on a rolling basis. Application fee: $80. Electronic applications accepted. *Expenses:* $555 per credit hour. *Financial support:* In 2017–18, 21 students received support. Scholarships/grants, health care benefits, unspecified assistantships, and tuition remission for Saint Leo employees and their dependents available. Financial award application deadline: 3/1; financial award applicants required to submit FAFSA. *Faculty research:* Emergency management, fire science, community policing. *Unit head:* Dr. Robert Diemer, Director of Graduate Studies in Safety Administration, 352-588-8974, Fax: 352-588-8289, E-mail: graduatepublicsafety@saintleo.edu. *Application contact:* Mark Russum, Assistant Vice President, Enrollment, 800-707-8846, Fax: 352-588-7873, E-mail: grad.admissions@saintleo.edu.
Website: https://www.saintleo.edu/criminal-justice-master-degree

St. Mary's University, School of Law, LL M Program, San Antonio, TX 78228. Offers American legal studies (LL M); international and comparative law (LL M); international criminal law (LL M). *Program availability:* Part-time. *Faculty:* 45 full-time (13 women), 68 part-time/adjunct (22 women). *Students:* 28 full-time (7 women), 3 part-time (2 women); includes 27 minority (5 Black or African American, non-Hispanic/Latino; 9 Asian, non-Hispanic/Latino; 13 Hispanic/Latino). Average age 36. 41 applicants, 63% accepted, 7 enrolled. In 2017, 3 master's awarded. *Degree requirements:* For master's, thesis, 24 hours of academic credit. *Entrance requirements:* For master's, official transcripts, personal statement, resume, 2 letters of recommendation. Additional exam requirements/recommendations for international students: Required—TOEFL (minimum score 550 paper-based; 80 iBT), IELTS (minimum score 6). *Application deadline:* Applications are processed on a rolling basis. Application fee: $0. Electronic applications accepted. *Expenses:* Contact institution. *Unit head:* Shannon Sevier, Director, Graduate Law Programs, 210-431-4235, E-mail: ssevier@stmarytx.edu. *Application contact:* Lupe Valdez, Legal Secretary, 210-431-6878, E-mail: gvaldez@stmarytx.edu.
Website: https://law.stmarytx.edu/academics/programs/ll-m-degrees/

San Francisco State University, Division of Graduate Studies, College of Education, Department of Equity, Leadership Studies, and Instructional Technologies, Program in Equity and Social Justice, San Francisco, CA 94132-1722. Offers MA. *Unit head:* Dr. Doris Flowers, Chair, 415-338-2614, Fax: 415-338-0568, E-mail: dflowers@sfsu.edu. *Application contact:* Dr. Ming Yeh Lee, Graduate Coordinator, 415-338-1061, Fax: 415-338-0568, E-mail: mylee@sfsu.edu.
Website: http://elsit.sfsu.edu/

San Jose State University, Graduate Studies and Research, College of Health and Human Sciences, San Jose, CA 95192-0049. Offers criminology (MS), including global criminology, law and justice; justice studies (MS); kinesiology (MA), including athletic training, exercise physiology, interdisciplinary, sport studies, sports management; library and information science (MLIS); mass communications (MS); nursing (MS), including family nurse practitioner; nutritional science (MS); occupational therapy (MS); public health (MPH); social work (MSW); MD/M Div. *Program availability:* Part-time, 100% online, blended/hybrid learning. *Faculty:* 15 full-time (7 women), 6 part-time/adjunct (3 women). *Students:* 517 full-time (407 women), 405 part-time (302 women); includes 523 minority (39 Black or African American, non-Hispanic/Latino; 2 American Indian or Alaska Native, non-Hispanic/Latino; 141 Asian, non-Hispanic/Latino; 226 Hispanic/Latino; 2 Native Hawaiian or other Pacific Islander, non-Hispanic/Latino; 113 Two or more races, non-Hispanic/Latino), 14 international. Average age 32. 1,250 applicants, 45% accepted, 375 enrolled. In 2017, 808 master's awarded. *Degree requirements:* For master's, thesis (for some programs), graduate writing assessment. *Entrance requirements:* Additional exam requirements/recommendations for international students: Required—TOEFL (minimum score 550 paper-based; 80 iBT), IELTS (minimum score 6.5), PTE (minimum score 53). *Application deadline:* For fall admission, 2/1 for domestic and international students. Applications are processed on a rolling basis. Application fee: $55. Electronic applications accepted. *Expenses:* Tuition, state resident: full-time $7176. Tuition, nonresident: full-time $16,680. Tuition and fees vary according to course load and program. *Financial support:* Fellowships, research assistantships, teaching assistantships, career-related internships or fieldwork, Federal Work-Study, scholarships/grants, and tuition waivers (full and partial) available. Support available to part-time students. Financial award application deadline: 4/24; financial award applicants required to submit FAFSA. *Unit head:* Dr. Mary Schutten, Dean, College of Health and Human Sciences, 408-924-2900, Fax: 408-924-2901, E-mail: mary.schutten@sjsu.edu.
Website: http://www.sjsu.edu/casa/

The Santa Barbara and Ventura Colleges of Law–Santa Barbara, Graduate and Professional Programs, Santa Barbara, CA 93101. Offers MLS, JD.

The Santa Barbara and Ventura Colleges of Law–Ventura, Graduate and Professional Programs, Ventura, CA 93003. Offers MLS, JD.

Simon Fraser University, Office of Graduate Studies and Postdoctoral Fellows, Faculty of Arts and Social Sciences, School of Criminology, Burnaby, BC V5A 1S6, Canada. Offers applied legal studies (MA); criminology (MA, PhD). *Degree requirements:* For master's, thesis or alternative, practicum; for doctorate, thesis/dissertation. *Entrance requirements:* For master's, minimum GPA of 3.0 (on scale of 4.33) or 3.33 based on last 60 credits of undergraduate courses; for doctorate, minimum GPA of 3.5 (on scale of 4.33). Additional exam requirements/recommendations for international students: Recommended—TOEFL (minimum score 580 paper-based; 93 iBT), IELTS (minimum score 7), TWE (minimum score 5). Electronic applications accepted. *Faculty research:* Media and crime, feminist jurisprudence, policy evaluation, forensic entomology, restorative justice.

Southern Illinois University Carbondale, School of Law, Program in Legal Studies, Carbondale, IL 62901-4701. Offers general law (MLS); health law and policy (MLS).

Southern New Hampshire University, School of Business, Manchester, NH 03106-1045. Offers accounting (MBA, Graduate Certificate); accounting finance (MS); accounting/auditing (MS); accounting/forensic accounting (MS); accounting/management accounting (MS); accounting/taxation (MS); applied economics (MS); athletic administration (MBA, Graduate Certificate); business administration (IMBA, Certificate), including business information systems (Certificate), human resource management (Certificate); business analytics (MBA); business intelligence (MBA); communication (MA), including new media and marketing, public relations; community economic development (MBA); criminal justice (MBA); data analytics (MS); economics (MBA); engineering management (MBA); entrepreneurship (MBA); finance (MBA, MS, Graduate Certificate); finance/corporate finance (MS); finance/investments (MS); forensic accounting (MBA); forensic accounting and fraud examination (Graduate Certificate); healthcare informatics (MBA); healthcare management (MBA); human resource management (MS); human resources (MBA); information technology (MS); information technology management (MBA); international business (PhD); Internet marketing (MBA); leadership (MBA); leadership of nonprofit organizations (Graduate Certificate); management (MS); marketing (MBA, MS, Graduate Certificate); music business (MBA); operations and project management (MS); operations and supply chain management (MBA, Graduate Certificate); organizational leadership (MS); project management (MBA, Graduate Certificate); public administration (MBA, Graduate Certificate); quantitative analysis (MBA); Six Sigma (Graduate Certificate); Six Sigma quality (MBA); social media marketing (MBA, Graduate Certificate); sport management (MBA, MS, Graduate Certificate); sustainability and environmental compliance (MBA); MBA/Certificate. *Accreditation:* ACBSP. *Program availability:* Part-time, evening/weekend, online learning. Terminal master's awarded for partial completion of doctoral program. *Degree requirements:* For master's, one foreign language, comprehensive exam (for some programs), thesis or alternative; for doctorate, one foreign language, comprehensive exam, thesis/dissertation. *Entrance requirements:* For master's, minimum GPA of 2.5; for doctorate, GMAT. Additional exam requirements/recommendations for international students: Required—TOEFL (minimum score 500 paper-based). *Application deadline:* Applications are processed on a rolling basis. Application fee: $40. Electronic applications accepted. *Expenses:* Tuition: Part-time $627 per credit hour. Part-time tuition and fees vary according to campus/location and program. *Financial support:* Career-related internships or fieldwork, Federal Work-Study, institutionally sponsored loans, scholarships/grants, tuition waivers (partial), and unspecified assistantships available. Support available to part-time students. Financial award applicants required to submit FAFSA. *Unit head:* Dr. Bill Lightfoot, Dean, 603-644-3102, Fax: 603-644-3144. *Application contact:* Office of Graduate Admission, 888-327-SNHU, Fax: 603-644-3144, E-mail: enroll@snhu.edu.

Stanford University, Law School, Stanford, CA 94305-8610. Offers corporate governance and practice (LL M); environmental law and policy (LL M); international economic law, business and policy (LL M); international legal studies (JSM); law (JD, JSD); law, science and technology (LL M); legal studies (MLS); JD/MA; JD/MBA; JD/MPP; JD/MS; JD/PhD. *Accreditation:* ABA. *Degree requirements:* For doctorate, thesis/dissertation (for some programs). *Entrance requirements:* For doctorate, LSAT (for JD). Electronic applications accepted. *Application contact:* Contact institution.

Taft University System, Taft Law School, Denver, CO 80246. Offers American jurisprudence (LL M); law (JD); taxation (LL M).

Temple University, Beasley School of Law, Philadelphia, PA 19122. Offers Asian law (LL M); law (JD); legal education (SJD); taxation (LL M); transnational law (LL M); trial advocacy (LL M); JD/LL M; JD/MBA; JD/MPH. *Accreditation:* ABA. *Program availability:* Part-time, evening/weekend. *Faculty:* 66 full-time (33 women), 136 part-time/adjunct (51 women). *Students:* 541 full-time (288 women), 147 part-time (62 women); includes 197 minority (65 Black or African American, non-Hispanic/Latino; 2 American Indian or Alaska Native, non-Hispanic/Latino; 52 Asian, non-Hispanic/Latino; 73 Hispanic/Latino; 5 Two or more races, non-Hispanic/Latino), 11 international. Average age 27. 2,096 applicants, 41% accepted, 223 enrolled. In 2017, 218 doctorates awarded. *Entrance requirements:* For doctorate, LSAT (for JD). Additional exam requirements/recommendations for international students: Recommended—TOEFL. *Application deadline:* For fall admission, 3/1 for domestic and international students. Applications are processed on a rolling basis. Application fee: $65. Electronic applications accepted. *Expenses:* $26,103 resident full-time, $21,107 resident part-time; $39,793 nonresident full-time, $32,065 nonresident part-time. *Financial support:* In 2017–18, 506 students received support, including research assistantships (averaging $5,500 per year), teaching assistantships (averaging $5,500 per year); Federal Work-Study, scholarships/grants, tuition waivers (full and partial), and unspecified assistantships also available. Support available to part-time students. Financial award application deadline: 3/1; financial award applicants required to submit FAFSA. *Faculty research:* Cybersecurity, gender issues, health care law, immigration law, intellectual property law. *Unit head:* Gregory N. Mandel, Dean, 215-204-7863, Fax: 215-204-1185, E-mail: law@temple.edu. *Application contact:* Johanne L. Johnston, Assistant Dean for Admissions and Financial Aid, 800-560-1428, Fax: 215-204-9319, E-mail: lawadmis@temple.edu.
Website: http://www.law.temple.edu

Texas State University, The Graduate College, College of Liberal Arts, Program in Legal Studies, San Marcos, TX 78666. Offers MA. *Program availability:* Part-time. *Faculty:* 5 full-time (2 women), 6 part-time/adjunct (2 women). *Students:* 46 full-time (38 women), 35 part-time (26 women); includes 44 minority (13 Black or African American, non-Hispanic/Latino; 1 Asian, non-Hispanic/Latino; 27 Hispanic/Latino; 3 Two or more races, non-Hispanic/Latino), 1 international. Average age 29. 65 applicants, 88% accepted, 21 enrolled. In 2017, 19 master's awarded. *Degree requirements:* For master's, comprehensive exam. *Entrance requirements:* For master's, baccalaureate degree from regionally-accredited university with minimum GPA of 3.0 on last 60 undergraduate semester hours, interview with legal studies graduate advisor, personal statement, 2 letters of recommendation. Additional exam requirements/recommendations for international students: Required—TOEFL (minimum score 550 paper-based; 78 iBT), IELTS (minimum score 6.5). *Application deadline:* For fall admission, 2/15 priority date for domestic and international students; for spring admission, 10/15 for domestic students, 10/1 for international students; for summer admission, 4/15 for domestic students, 3/15 for international students. Applications are processed on a rolling basis. Application fee: $90 ($140 for international students). Electronic applications accepted. *Expenses:* Tuition, state resident: full-time $7868; part-time $3934 per semester. Tuition, nonresident: full-time $17,828; part-time $8914 per semester. *Required fees:* $2092; $1435 per semester. Tuition and fees vary according to course load. *Financial support:* In 2017–18, 50 students received support, including 1 research assistantship (averaging $13,896 per year), 8 teaching assistantships (averaging $12,067 per year); Federal Work-Study, institutionally sponsored loans, scholarships/grants, health care benefits, and unspecified assistantships also available. Financial award application deadline: 3/1; financial award applicants required to submit FAFSA. *Unit head:* Dr. Lynn Crossett, Graduate Advisor, 512-245-2233, Fax: 512-245-7815, E-mail: lc25@txstate.edu. *Application contact:* Dr. Andrea Golato, Dean of Graduate School, 512-245-2581, Fax: 512-245-8365, E-mail: gradcollege@txstate.edu.
Website: http://mals.polisci.txstate.edu/

Texas Tech University, School of Law, Lubbock, TX 79409-0004. Offers law (JD); United States legal studies (LL M); JD/M Engr; JD/MBA; JD/MD; JD/MPA; JD/MS; JD/MSA. *Accreditation:* ABA. *Faculty:* 39 full-time (15 women), 8 part-time/adjunct (3 women). *Students:* 434 full-time (183 women), 6 part-time (2 women); includes 113 minority (8 Black or African American, non-Hispanic/Latino; 3 American Indian or Alaska Native, non-Hispanic/Latino; 9 Asian, non-Hispanic/Latino; 68 Hispanic/Latino; 25 Two or more races, non-Hispanic/Latino), 6 international. Average age 26. 1,157 applicants, 45% accepted, 139 enrolled. In 2017, 5 master's, 197 doctorates awarded. *Entrance requirements:* For master's, first/basic degree from a non-U.S. law school; for doctorate, LSAT. Additional exam requirements/recommendations for international students: Required—TOEFL minimum score 600 paper-based; 100 iBT or IELTS minimum score 7 (for LL M). *Application deadline:* For fall admission, 3/1 priority date for domestic and international students. Applications are processed on a rolling basis. Application fee: $60. Electronic applications accepted. *Expenses:* Contact institution. *Financial support:* In 2017–18, 42 students received support, including 42 teaching assistantships (averaging $1,027 per year); research assistantships, Federal Work-Study, tuition waivers, and tutorships also available. Financial award application deadline: 5/1; financial award applicants required to submit FAFSA. *Faculty research:* Advocacy/

practice skills, criminal Law/innocence, energy law, business/estate planning, law and science. *Total annual research expenditures:* $62,697. *Unit head:* Jack Wade Nowlin, Dean/Professor of Law, 806-834-1504, Fax: 806-742-4014, E-mail: jack.nowlin@ ttu.edu. *Application contact:* Wendy A. Humphrey, Interim Associate Dean for Admissions and Financial Aid, 806-834-4446, Fax: 806-742-4617, E-mail: admissions.law@ttu.edu.
Website: http://www.law.ttu.edu/

Touro College, Jacob D. Fuchsberg Law Center, Central Islip, NY 11743. Offers general law (LL M); law (JD); U.S. legal studies (LL M); JD/MBA; JD/MPA; JD/MSW. JD/ MBA and JD/MPA offered with Long Island University-LIU Post; JD/MSW offered with Stony Brook University, State University of New York. *Accreditation:* ABA. *Program availability:* Part-time, evening/weekend. *Faculty:* 35 full-time (17 women), 30 part-time/ adjunct (7 women). *Students:* 445 full-time (245 women), 22 part-time (15 women); includes 166 minority (47 Black or African American, non-Hispanic/Latino; 2 American Indian or Alaska Native, non-Hispanic/Latino; 41 Asian, non-Hispanic/Latino; 72 Hispanic/Latino; 4 Two or more races, non-Hispanic/Latino), 9 international. Average age 30. *Entrance requirements:* For doctorate, LSAT. *Application deadline:* Applications are processed on a rolling basis. Application fee: $60. *Expenses:* Contact institution. *Financial support:* Fellowships, career-related internships or fieldwork, and Federal Work-Study available. Support available to part-time students. Financial award application deadline: 5/1. *Faculty research:* Business law, civil rights, international law, criminal justice. *Unit head:* Dr. Harry Ballan, Dean, 631-761-7100. *Application contact:* Dr. Susan Thompson, Office of Admissions, 631-761-7010, E-mail: admissions@ tourolaw.edu.
Website: http://www.tourolaw.edu/

Trident University International, College of Health Sciences, Program in Health Sciences, Cypress, CA 90630. Offers clinical research administration (MS, Certificate); emergency and disaster management (MS, Certificate); environmental health science (Certificate); health care administration (PhD); health care management (MS), including health informatics (MS, Certificate); health informatics (Certificate); health sciences (PhD); international health (MS); international health: educator or researcher option (PhD); international health: practitioner option (PhD); law and expert witness studies (MS, Certificate); public health (MS); quality assurance (Certificate). *Program availability:* Part-time, evening/weekend, online learning. *Degree requirements:* For doctorate, comprehensive exam, thesis/dissertation, defense of dissertation. *Entrance requirements:* For master's, minimum GPA of 2.5 (students with GPA 3.0 or greater may transfer up to 30% of graduate level credits); for doctorate, minimum GPA of 3.4, curriculum vitae, course work in research methods or statistics. Additional exam requirements/recommendations for international students: Required—TOEFL. Electronic applications accepted.

Universidad Autonoma de Guadalajara, Graduate Programs, Guadalajara, Mexico. Offers administrative law and justice (LL M); advertising and corporate communications (MA); architecture (M Arch); business (MBA); computational science (MCC); education (Ed M, Ed D); English-Spanish translation (MA); entrepreneurship and management (MBA); integrated management of digital animation (MA); international business (MIB); international corporate law (LL M); internet technologies (MS); manufacturing systems (MMS); occupational health (MS); philosophy (MA, PhD); power electronics (MS); quality systems (MQS); renewable energy (MS); social evaluation of projects (MBA); strategic market research (MBA); tax law (MA); teaching mathematics (MA).

Université Laval, Faculty of Law, Program in Notarial Law, Québec, QC G1K 7P4, Canada. Offers Diploma. *Program availability:* Part-time. *Entrance requirements:* For degree, knowledge of French. Electronic applications accepted.

University at Buffalo, the State University of New York, Graduate School, School of Law, Buffalo, NY 14260-1100. Offers criminal law (LL M); cross-border legal studies (LL M); environmental law (LL M); general law (LL M); law (JD); JD/MA; JD/MBA; JD/ MLS; JD/MSW; JD/MUP; JD/PhD; LL M/LL M. *Accreditation:* ABA. *Faculty:* 49 full-time (23 women), 68 part-time/adjunct (25 women). *Students:* 453 full-time (238 women), 2 part-time (both women); includes 85 minority (29 Black or African American, non-Hispanic/Latino; 1 American Indian or Alaska Native, non-Hispanic/Latino; 20 Asian, non-Hispanic/Latino; 22 Hispanic/Latino; 13 Two or more races, non-Hispanic/Latino), 17 international. Average age 27. 903 applicants, 54% accepted, 167 enrolled. In 2017, 2 master's, 151 doctorates awarded. *Entrance requirements:* For master's, JD or LL B; for doctorate, LSAT. Additional exam requirements/recommendations for international students: Required—TOEFL (minimum score 90 iBT), IELTS (minimum score 7). *Application deadline:* Applications are processed on a rolling basis. Application fee: $85. Electronic applications accepted. *Expenses:* $28,016 annual tuition plus fees in-state full-time; $32,106 annual tuition plus fees out-of-state full-time. *Financial support:* In 2017–18, 338 students received support. Federal Work-Study, institutionally sponsored loans, scholarships/grants, tuition waivers (full and partial), and unspecified assistantships available. Financial award application deadline: 3/1; financial award applicants required to submit FAFSA. *Faculty research:* Criminal law, environmental law, international law and human rights, law and finance, cross-border legal studies. *Total annual research expenditures:* $108,173. *Unit head:* Aviva Abramovsky, Dean, 716-645-2052, E-mail: aabramov@buffalo.edu. *Application contact:* Lindsay Gladney, Vice Dean for Admissions, 716-645-2907, Fax: 716-645-6676, E-mail: law-admissions@ buffalo.edu.
Website: http://www.law.buffalo.edu/

University of Baltimore, Graduate School, Yale Gordon College of Arts and Sciences, Program in Legal and Ethical Studies, Baltimore, MD 21201-5779. Offers MA. *Program availability:* Part-time, evening/weekend. *Degree requirements:* For master's, thesis optional. *Entrance requirements:* For master's, minimum GPA of 3.0. Additional exam requirements/recommendations for international students: Required—TOEFL (minimum score 550 paper-based). Electronic applications accepted. *Faculty research:* Morality in law and economics, religion in lawmaking, comparative legal history, law and social change, critical issues in Constitutional law, theories of justice.

University of Calgary, Faculty of Graduate Studies, Faculty of Law, Programs in Natural Resources, Energy and Environmental Law, Calgary, AB T2N 1N4, Canada. Offers LL M, Postbaccalaureate Certificate. *Program availability:* Part-time, evening/ weekend. *Degree requirements:* For master's, thesis optional. *Entrance requirements:* For master's, JD or LL B. Additional exam requirements/recommendations for international students: Required—TOEFL (minimum score 100 iBT), IELTS (minimum score 7). Electronic applications accepted. *Faculty research:* Natural resources law and regulations; environmental law, ethics and policies; oil and gas and energy law; water and municipal law; Aboriginal law.

University of California, Berkeley, School of Law, Program in Jurisprudence and Social Policy, Berkeley, CA 94720-1500. Offers PhD. *Degree requirements:* For doctorate, one foreign language, thesis/dissertation, oral qualifying exam. *Entrance requirements:* For doctorate, GRE General Test, sample of written work, letters of recommendation. Electronic applications accepted. *Expenses:* Contact institution. *Faculty research:* Law and philosophy, legal history, law and economics, law and political science, law and sociology.

University of Charleston, Master of Forensic Accounting Program, Charleston, WV 25304-1099. Offers EMFA. *Program availability:* Part-time, blended/hybrid learning. *Entrance requirements:* Additional exam requirements/recommendations for international students: Required—TOEFL. Electronic applications accepted.

University of Denver, Sturm College of Law, Program in Legal Administration, Denver, CO 80208. Offers MSLA, Certificate. *Program availability:* Part-time, evening/weekend. *Students:* Average age 36. 9 applicants, 100% accepted, 3 enrolled. In 2017, 8 master's awarded. *Entrance requirements:* For master's, GRE General Test, GMAT, or LSAT. Additional exam requirements/recommendations for international students: Required— TOEFL (minimum score 570 paper-based; 88 iBT). *Application deadline:* For fall admission, 8/15 priority date for domestic and international students; for spring admission, 1/11 priority date for domestic and international students; for summer admission, 5/31 priority date for domestic and international students. Applications are processed on a rolling basis. Application fee: $65. Electronic applications accepted. *Expenses:* Contact institution. *Financial support:* In 2017–18, 7 students received support. Career-related internships or fieldwork, Federal Work-Study, scholarships/ grants, and unspecified assistantships available. Support available to part-time students. Financial award application deadline: 2/15; financial award applicants required to submit FAFSA. *Unit head:* Carol Larkin, Interim Director, 303-871-6249, E-mail: gradlegalstudies@law.du.edu. *Application contact:* E-mail: gradlegalstudies@ law.du.edu.
Website: http://www.law.du.edu/index.php/msla

University of Illinois at Springfield, Graduate Programs, College of Public Affairs and Administration, Program in Legal Studies, Springfield, IL 62703-5407. Offers MA. *Program availability:* Part-time, evening/weekend, 100% online. *Faculty:* 5 full-time (3 women). *Students:* 7 full-time (4 women), 47 part-time (34 women); includes 16 minority (7 Black or African American, non-Hispanic/Latino; 3 Asian, non-Hispanic/Latino; 4 Hispanic/Latino; 2 Two or more races, non-Hispanic/Latino), 1 international. Average age 39. 45 applicants, 29% accepted, 13 enrolled. In 2017, 11 master's awarded. *Degree requirements:* For master's, thesis or seminar. *Entrance requirements:* For master's, minimum undergraduate GPA of 3.0; demonstration of writing ability. Additional exam requirements/recommendations for international students: Required— TOEFL (minimum score 570 paper-based; 100 iBT). *Application deadline:* Applications are processed on a rolling basis. Application fee: $60 ($75 for international students). Electronic applications accepted. *Expenses:* Tuition, state resident: full-time $7896; part-time $329 per credit hour. Tuition, nonresident: full-time $16,200; part-time $675 per credit hour. Tuition and fees vary according to program. *Financial support:* In 2017– 18, research assistantships with full tuition reimbursements (averaging $10,249 per year), teaching assistantships with full tuition reimbursements (averaging $10,303 per year) were awarded; fellowships, career-related internships or fieldwork, Federal Work-Study, scholarships/grants, health care benefits, and unspecified assistantships also available. Support available to part-time students. Financial award application deadline: 11/15; financial award applicants required to submit FAFSA. *Unit head:* Dr. Gwen Jordan, Program Administrator, 217-206-8520, Fax: 217-206-7807, E-mail: gjorda2@ uis.edu.
Website: http://www.uis.edu/legalstudies/

University of Massachusetts Lowell, College of Fine Arts, Humanities and Social Sciences, School of Criminology and Justice Studies, Lowell, MA 01854. Offers criminal justice (MA). *Program availability:* Part-time, evening/weekend. *Degree requirements:* For master's, thesis optional. *Entrance requirements:* For master's, GRE General Test or MAT. Electronic applications accepted. *Faculty research:* Family violence, criminal justice management, corrections, policing, delinquency.

University of Montana, Graduate School, College of Humanities and Sciences, Department of Sociology, Missoula, MT 59812. Offers criminology (MA); inequality and social justice (MA); rural and environmental change (MA); sociology (MA). *Entrance requirements:* For master's, GRE General Test. Additional exam requirements/ recommendations for international students: Required—TOEFL. *Faculty research:* Housing, homelessness, hunger, infant mortality, work safety.

University of Nebraska–Lincoln, College of Law, Program in Legal Studies, Lincoln, NE 68588. Offers MLS. *Entrance requirements:* For master's, GRE or LSAT. Additional exam requirements/recommendations for international students: Required—TOEFL (minimum score 600 paper-based). Electronic applications accepted.

University of Nevada, Reno, Graduate School, College of Liberal Arts, School of Social Research and Justice Studies, Program in Judicial Studies, Reno, NV 89557. Offers MJS, PhD. Offered jointly with the National Judicial College and the National Council of Juvenile and Family Court Judges. *Program availability:* Part-time. Terminal master's awarded for partial completion of doctoral program. *Degree requirements:* For master's, thesis; for doctorate, thesis/dissertation. *Entrance requirements:* For master's and doctorate, sitting judge, law degree from an accredited school. Additional exam requirements/recommendations for international students: Required—TOEFL (minimum score 500 paper-based; 61 iBT), IELTS (minimum score 6). Electronic applications accepted. *Expenses:* Contact institution. *Faculty research:* Jury research, capital punishment, expert testimony, environmental law, medical issues.

University of New Hampshire, Graduate School, College of Liberal Arts, Program in Justice Studies, Durham, NH 03824. Offers MA. Program offered in summer only. *Program availability:* Part-time. *Students:* 4 full-time (3 women). Average age 22. 2 applicants, 50% accepted. In 2017, 9 master's awarded. *Entrance requirements:* For master's, GRE. Additional exam requirements/recommendations for international students: Required—TOEFL (minimum score 550 paper-based; 80 iBT); Recommended—TWE. *Application deadline:* For summer admission, 3/15 priority date for domestic students. Application fee: $65. Electronic applications accepted. *Financial support:* In 2017–18, 3 students received support, including 3 teaching assistantships; fellowships, research assistantships, career-related internships or fieldwork, Federal Work-Study, scholarships/grants, and tuition waivers (full and partial) also available. Support available to part-time students. Financial award application deadline: 2/15. *Unit head:* Todd DeMitchell, Chair, 603-862-5043. *Application contact:* Deborah Briand, Administrative Assistant, 603-862-1716, E-mail: justice.studies@unh.edu.
Website: http://www.cola.unh.edu/justice-studies

University of New Hampshire, School of Law, Concord, NH 03301. Offers business law (JD); commerce and technology (LL M, MCT, Diploma); criminal law (JD); intellectual property (LL M, MIP, JD, Diploma), including patent law (JD), trademarks and copyright (JD); international criminal law and justice (LL M, MICLJ); litigation (JD); public interest and social justice (JD); sports and entertainment law (JD); JD/LL M; JD/ MBA; JD/MIP; JD/MPP; JD/MSW. *Accreditation:* ABA. *Program availability:* Part-time, 100% online, limited residential. *Degree requirements:* For doctorate, comprehensive exam. *Entrance requirements:* For doctorate, LSAT. Additional exam requirements/ recommendations for international students: Required—TOEFL (minimum score 600 paper-based; 100 iBT), minimum TOEFL iBT score of 80 (for master's programs). Electronic applications accepted. *Expenses:* Contact institution. *Faculty research:* Intellectual property, health law and policy, sports and entertainment law, patent law, trademarks and copyright.

Legal and Justice Studies

University of Pennsylvania, Wharton School, Legal Studies and Business Ethics Department, Philadelphia, PA 19104. Offers MBA, PhD.

University of Pittsburgh, School of Law, Master of Studies in Law Program, Pittsburgh, PA 15260. Offers biomedical and health services research (MSL); business law (MSL), including commercial law, corporate law, general business law, international business, tax law; Constitutional law (MSL); criminal law and justice (MSL); disability law (MSL); elder and estate planning law (MSL); employment and labor law (MSL); energy law (MSL); environmental and real estate law (MSL); family law (MSL); health law (MSL); intellectual property and technology law (MSL); international and human rights law (MSL); jurisprudence (MSL); regulatory law (MSL); self-designed (MSL). *Program availability:* Part-time. *Faculty:* 47 full-time (22 women), 116 part-time/adjunct (29 women). *Students:* 4 full-time (2 women), 17 part-time (12 women); includes 6 minority (5 Black or African American, non-Hispanic/Latino; 1 Hispanic/Latino). Average age 26. 28 applicants, 75% accepted, 15 enrolled. In 2017, 15 master's awarded. *Entrance requirements:* Additional exam requirements/recommendations for international students: Required—TOEFL (minimum score 600 paper-based; 100 iBT), IELTS (minimum score 7). *Application deadline:* For fall admission, 6/30 for domestic students, 5/1 for international students. Applications are processed on a rolling basis. Application fee: $0. *Faculty research:* Law, health law, business law, contracts, intellectual property, environmental law. *Unit head:* Prof. Alan Meisel, Director, 412-648-1384, Fax: 412-648-2649, E-mail: meisel@pitt.edu. *Application contact:* Beth Ann Pischke, Administrative Coordinator, 412-648-7120, Fax: 412-648-2649, E-mail: pischke@pitt.edu. Website: http://www.law.pitt.edu/msl

University of San Diego, School of Law, San Diego, CA 92110. Offers business and corporate law (LL M); comparative law (LL M); general studies (LL M); international law (LL M); law (JD); taxation (LL M, Diploma); JD/IMBA; JD/MA; JD/MBA. *Accreditation:* ABA. *Program availability:* Part-time, evening/weekend. *Faculty:* 45 full-time (13 women), 46 part-time/adjunct (13 women). *Students:* 693 full-time (371 women), 96 part-time (40 women); includes 265 minority (31 Black or African American, non-Hispanic/Latino; 15 American Indian or Alaska Native, non-Hispanic/Latino; 97 Asian, non-Hispanic/Latino; 107 Hispanic/Latino; 4 Native Hawaiian or other Pacific Islander, non-Hispanic/Latino; 11 Two or more races, non-Hispanic/Latino), 28 international. Average age 27. 3,260 applicants, 238 enrolled. In 2017, 57 master's, 206 doctorates awarded. *Entrance requirements:* For master's, JD, LL B or equivalent from an ABA-accredited law school; for doctorate, LSAT (less than 5 years old); bachelor's degree, registration with the Credential Assemble Service (CAS). Additional exam requirements/recommendations for international students: Required—TOEFL (minimum score 600 paper-based; 100 iBT). *Application deadline:* For fall admission, 2/1 priority date for domestic students. Applications are processed on a rolling basis. Electronic applications accepted. *Expenses:* Contact institution. *Financial support:* In 2017–18, 617 students received support. Career-related internships or fieldwork, Federal Work-Study, institutionally sponsored loans, and scholarships/grants available. Support available to part-time students. Financial award application deadline: 3/1; financial award applicants required to submit FAFSA. *Faculty research:* Corporate law, children's advocacy, Constitutional and criminal law, international and comparative law, public interest law, intellectual property and tax law. *Unit head:* Dr. Stephen C. Ferruolo, Dean, 619-260-4527, E-mail: lawdean@sandiego.edu. *Application contact:* Jorge Garcia, Assistant Dean, JD Admissions, 619-260-4528, Fax: 619-260-2218, E-mail: jdinfo@sandiego.edu. Website: http://www.sandiego.edu/law/

University of South Florida, Innovative Education, Tampa, FL 33620-9951. Offers adult, career and higher education (Graduate Certificate), including college teaching, leadership in developing human resources, leadership in higher education; Africana studies (Graduate Certificate), including diasporas and health disparities, genocide and human rights; aging studies (Graduate Certificate), including gerontology; art research (Graduate Certificate), including museum studies; business foundations (Graduate Certificate); chemical and biomedical engineering (Graduate Certificate), including materials science and engineering, water, health and sustainability; child and family studies (Graduate Certificate), including positive behavior support; civil and industrial engineering (Graduate Certificate), including transportation systems analysis; community and family health (Graduate Certificate), including maternal and child health, social marketing and public health, violence and injury: prevention and intervention, women's health; criminology (Graduate Certificate), including criminal justice administration; data science for public administration (Graduate Certificate); digital humanities (Graduate Certificate); educational measurement and research (Graduate Certificate), including evaluation; English (Graduate Certificate), including comparative literary studies, creative writing, professional and technical communication; entrepreneurship (Graduate Certificate); environmental health (Graduate Certificate), including safety management; epidemiology and biostatistics (Graduate Certificate), including applied biostatistics, biostatistics, concepts and tools of epidemiology, epidemiology, epidemiology of infectious diseases; geography, environment and planning (Graduate Certificate), including community development, environmental policy and management, geographical information systems; geology (Graduate Certificate), including hydrogeology; global health (Graduate Certificate), including disaster management, global health and Latin American and Caribbean studies, global health practice, humanitarian assistance, infection control; government and international affairs (Graduate Certificate), including Cuban studies, globalization studies; health policy and management (Graduate Certificate), including health management and leadership, public health policy and programs; hearing specialist: early intervention (Graduate Certificate); industrial and management systems engineering (Graduate Certificate), including systems engineering, technology management; information studies (Graduate Certificate), including school library media specialist; information systems/decision sciences (Graduate Certificate), including analytics and business intelligence; instructional technology (Graduate Certificate), including distance education, Florida digital/virtual educator, instructional design, multimedia design, Web design; internal medicine, bioethics and medical humanities (Graduate Certificate), including biomedical ethics; Latin American and Caribbean studies (Graduate Certificate); leadership for coastal resiliency planning (Graduate Certificate); mass communications (Graduate Certificate), including multimedia journalism; mathematics and statistics (Graduate Certificate), including mathematics; medicine (Graduate Certificate), including aging and neuroscience, bioinformatics, biotechnology, brain fitness and memory management, clinical investigation, hand and upper limb rehabilitation, health informatics, health sciences, integrative weight management, intellectual property, medicine and gender, metabolic and nutritional medicine, metabolic cardiology, pharmacy sciences; national and competitive intelligence (Graduate Certificate); nursing (Graduate Certificate), including simulation based academic fellowship in advanced pain management; psychological and social foundations (Graduate Certificate), including career counseling, college teaching, diversity in education, mental health counseling, school counseling; public affairs (Graduate Certificate), including nonprofit management, public management, research administration; public health (Graduate Certificate), including assessing chemical toxicity and public health risks, health equity, pharmacoepidemiology, public health generalist, toxicology, translational research in adolescent behavioral health; public health practices (Graduate Certificate), including planning for healthy communities; rehabilitation and mental health counseling (Graduate Certificate), including integrative mental health care, marriage and family therapy,

rehabilitation technology; secondary education (Graduate Certificate), including ESOL, foreign language education: culture and content, foreign language education: professional; social work (Graduate Certificate), including geriatric social work/clinical gerontology; special education (Graduate Certificate), including autism spectrum disorder, disabilities education: severe/profound; world languages (Graduate Certificate), including teaching English as a second language (TESL) or foreign language. *Unit head:* Dr. Cynthia DeLuca, Associate Vice President and Assistant Vice Provost, 813-974-3077, Fax: 813-974-7061, E-mail: deluca@usf.edu. *Application contact:* Owen Hooper, Director, Summer and Alternative Calendar Programs, 813-974-6917, E-mail: hooper@usf.edu. Website: http://www.usf.edu/innovative-education/

University of the District of Columbia, David A. Clarke School of Law, Washington, DC 20008. Offers clinical teaching and social justice (LL M); law (JD). *Accreditation:* ABA. *Program availability:* Part-time, evening/weekend. *Degree requirements:* For doctorate, 90 credits, advanced legal writing. *Entrance requirements:* For doctorate, LSAT. Additional exam requirements/recommendations for international students: Recommended—TOEFL. Electronic applications accepted. *Expenses:* Contact institution. *Faculty research:* HIV law, juvenile law, legislative law, community development, small business, immigration and human rights.

University of the Sacred Heart, Graduate Programs, Program in Systems of Justice, San Juan, PR 00914-0383. Offers human rights and anti-discriminatory processes (MASJ); mediation and transformation of conflicts (MASJ).

University of Washington, Graduate School, School of Law, Seattle, WA 98195-3020. Offers Asian law (LL M, PhD); intellectual property law and policy (LL M); law (JD); law of sustainable international development (LL M); taxation (LL M); JD/LL M; JD/MA; JD/MAIS; JD/MBA; JD/MPA; JD/MS; JD/PhD. *Accreditation:* ABA. *Degree requirements:* For master's, thesis; for doctorate, thesis/dissertation (for some programs). *Entrance requirements:* For master's, language proficiency (LL M in Asian law); for doctorate, LSAT (for JD). Additional exam requirements/recommendations for international students: Required—TOEFL. *Expenses:* Contact institution. *Faculty research:* Asian, international and comparative law, intellectual property law, health law, environmental law, taxation.

University of Windsor, Faculty of Graduate Studies, Faculty of Arts and Social Sciences, Department of Communication Studies, Windsor, ON N9B 3P4, Canada. Offers communication and social justice (MA). *Degree requirements:* For master's, thesis. *Entrance requirements:* For master's, writing sample/media production or multimedia portfolio. Additional exam requirements/recommendations for international students: Required—TOEFL (minimum score 600 paper-based). Electronic applications accepted. *Faculty research:* Sociology of news, media ownership and control, communication networks and social movements, issues of media representation.

Vermont Law School, Graduate and Professional Programs, Master's Programs, South Royalton, VT 05068-0096. Offers American legal studies (LL M); energy law (LL M); energy regulation and law (MERL); environmental law (LL M); environmental law and policy (MELP); food and agriculture law (LL M); food and agriculture law and policy (MFALP); JD/MELP; JD/MERL; JD/MFALP. *Program availability:* Part-time, 100% online, blended/hybrid learning. *Entrance requirements:* Additional exam requirements/recommendations for international students: Required—TOEFL. *Faculty research:* Environment and new economy; takings; international environmental law; interaction among science, law, and environmental policy; climate change and the environment.

Washburn University, School of Law, Topeka, KS 66621. Offers global legal studies (LL M); law (MSL, JD). *Accreditation:* ABA. *Entrance requirements:* For doctorate, LSAT. Additional exam requirements/recommendations for international students: Recommended—TOEFL (minimum score 550 paper-based). Electronic applications accepted. Application fee is waived when completed online. *Expenses:* Contact institution. *Faculty research:* Constitutional law, family law, energy law, banking and securities law, oil and gas.

Weber State University, College of Social and Behavioral Sciences, Program in Criminal Justice, Ogden, UT 84408-1001. Offers MCJ. *Program availability:* Part-time, evening/weekend, 100% online. *Faculty:* 6 full-time (0 women), 1 part-time/adjunct (0 women). *Students:* 5 full-time (2 women), 23 part-time (9 women); includes 7 minority (3 Black or African American, non-Hispanic/Latino; 1 American Indian or Alaska Native, non-Hispanic/Latino; 2 Hispanic/Latino; 1 Two or more races, non-Hispanic/Latino). Average age 35. In 2017, 12 master's awarded. *Entrance requirements:* Additional exam requirements/recommendations for international students: Required—TOEFL (minimum score 550 paper-based). *Application deadline:* For fall admission, 7/29 for domestic students; for spring admission, 12/11 for domestic students; for summer admission, 4/1 for domestic students. Application fee: $60 ($90 for international students). Electronic applications accepted. *Expenses:* Contact institution. *Financial support:* In 2017–18, 7 students received support. Scholarships/grants available. Financial award application deadline: 2/1; financial award applicants required to submit FAFSA. *Unit head:* Dr. Bruce Bayley, Graduate Director/Associate Professor, 801-626-8134, Fax: 801-626-6145, E-mail: bbayley@weber.edu. *Application contact:* Faye Medd, Secretary, 801-626-6146, Fax: 801-626-6146, E-mail: fmedd@weber.edu. Website: http://www.weber.edu/cj/CJMastersDegree/CJMastersDegree.html

Webster University, College of Arts and Sciences, Department of Legal Studies, St. Louis, MO 63119-3194. Offers MA, Graduate Certificate. *Program availability:* Part-time, evening/weekend. *Degree requirements:* For master's, thesis optional. *Entrance requirements:* Additional exam requirements/recommendations for international students: Required—TOEFL. *Faculty research:* Intellectual property rights, emerging torts, death penalty, juvenile justice, confidentiality issues in banking.

Western Michigan University Thomas M. Cooley Law School, Graduate Programs, Lansing, MI 48901-3038. Offers administrative law (public law) (JD); business transactions (JD); Canadian law practice (JD); corporate law and finance (LL M); environmental law (public law) (JD); general practice (JD), including solo and small firm; general studies (LL M); homeland and national security law (LL M); insurance law (LL M); intellectual property (JD); intellectual property law (LL M); international law (JD); litigation (JD); taxation (LL M); U.S. legal studies for foreign attorneys (LL M); JD/LL M; JD/MBA; JD/MHA; JD/MPA; JD/MSW. *Program availability:* Part-time, evening/weekend, 100% online, blended/hybrid learning. *Degree requirements:* For master's, thesis (for some programs); for doctorate, minimum of 3 credits of clinical experience. *Entrance requirements:* For master's, JD or LL B; for doctorate, LSAT. Additional exam requirements/recommendations for international students: Required—TOEFL (for U.S. legal studies for foreign attorneys LL M program); Recommended—TOEFL. Electronic applications accepted. *Expenses:* Contact institution. *Faculty research:* Wrongful convictions, civil rights, environmental law, litigation techniques, data mining, intellectual property, practical and skills-based legal education.

West Virginia University, College of Law, Morgantown, WV 26506-6130. Offers energy law and sustainable development (LL M); forensic justice (LL M); law (JD); white collar forensic justice (LL M). *Accreditation:* ABA. *Program availability:* Part-time. *Students:* 306 full-time (138 women), 1 part-time (0 women); includes 33 minority (10 Black or African American, non-Hispanic/Latino; 4 Asian, non-Hispanic/Latino; 11 Hispanic/Latino; 8 Two or more races, non-Hispanic/Latino), 1 international. *Entrance*

requirements: For doctorate, LSAT. Additional exam requirements/recommendations for international students: Required—TOEFL (minimum score 600 paper-based; 100 iBT). *Application deadline:* For fall admission, 2/1 for domestic and international students. Applications are processed on a rolling basis. Application fee: $60. Electronic applications accepted. *Expenses:* Contact institution. *Financial support:* Fellowships, research assistantships, teaching assistantships, career-related internships or fieldwork, Federal Work-Study, institutionally sponsored loans, scholarships/grants, health care benefits, tuition waivers (full), unspecified assistantships, and administrative assistantships, resident assistantships available. Support available to part-time students. Financial award application deadline: 3/1; financial award applicants required to submit FAFSA. *Faculty research:* Constitutional law, public interest law, corporate law, environment and natural resources innocence project, professional skills, leadership, intellectual property, entrepreneurship, labor, sustainable development, family law, IR human rights, immigration. *Unit head:* Beth Pierpont, Assistant Dean for Admissions and Student Financial Support, 304-293-7320, E-mail: beth.pierpont@mail.wvu.edu.
Website: https://law.wvu.edu

West Virginia University, Eberly College of Arts and Sciences, Morgantown, WV 26506. Offers biology (MS, PhD); chemistry (MS, PhD); communication studies (MA, PhD); computational statistics (PhD); creative writing (MFA); English (MA, PhD); forensic and investigative science (MS); forensic science (PhD); geography (MA); geology (MA, PhD); history (MA, PhD); legal studies (MLS); math (MS); physics (MS, PhD); political science (MA, PhD); professional writing and editing (MA); psychology (MA); public administration (MPA); social work (MSW); sociology (MA, PhD); statistics (MS). *Program availability:* Part-time, evening/weekend, online learning. *Students:* 831 full-time (437 women), 236 part-time (142 women); includes 112 minority (35 Black or African American, non-Hispanic/Latino; 15 Asian, non-Hispanic/Latino; 29 Hispanic/Latino; 33 Two or more races, non-Hispanic/Latino), 235 international. Terminal master's awarded for partial completion of doctoral program. *Degree requirements:* For master's, thesis (for some programs); for doctorate, comprehensive exam, thesis/dissertation. *Entrance requirements:* For master's and doctorate, GRE. Additional exam

requirements/recommendations for international students: Required—TOEFL (minimum score 600 paper-based); Recommended—TWE. *Application deadline:* For spring admission, 2/15 priority date for domestic and international students. Applications are processed on a rolling basis. Application fee: $45. Electronic applications accepted. *Expenses:* Tuition, state resident: full-time $9450. Tuition, nonresident: full-time $24,390. *Financial support:* Fellowships with full tuition reimbursements, research assistantships with full tuition reimbursements, teaching assistantships with full tuition reimbursements, career-related internships or fieldwork, Federal Work-Study, institutionally sponsored loans, scholarships/grants, health care benefits, tuition waivers (full and partial), unspecified assistantships, and administrative assistantships available. Financial award application deadline: 2/1; financial award applicants required to submit FAFSA. *Faculty research:* Humanities, social sciences, life science, physical sciences, mathematics. *Unit head:* Dr. Mary Ellen Mazey, Dean, 304-293-4611, Fax: 304-293-6858, E-mail: mary.mazey@mail.wvu.edu. *Application contact:* Dr. Fred L. King, Associate Dean for Graduate Studies, 304-293-4611 Ext. 5205, Fax: 304-293-6858, E-mail: fred.king@mail.wvu.edu.
Website: http://www.as.wvu.edu/

Wilfrid Laurier University, Faculty of Graduate and Postdoctoral Studies, School of International Policy and Governance, Global Governance Program, Waterloo, ON N2L 3C5, Canada. Offers conflict and security (PhD); global environment (PhD); global justice and human rights (PhD); global political economy (PhD); global social governance (PhD); multilateral institutions and diplomacy (PhD). Offered jointly with University of Waterloo. *Degree requirements:* For doctorate, thesis/dissertation. *Entrance requirements:* For doctorate, MA in political science, history, economics, international development studies, international peace studies, globalization studies, environmental studies or related field with minimum A-. Additional exam requirements/recommendations for international students: Required—TOEFL (minimum score 89 iBT). Electronic applications accepted. *Faculty research:* Global political economy, global environment, conflict and security, global justice and human rights, multilateral institutions and diplomacy.

Sports and Entertainment Law

Arizona State University at the Tempe campus, Sandra Day O'Connor College of Law, Phoenix, AZ 85287-7906. Offers biotechnology and genomics (LL M); law (JD); legal studies (MLS); patent practice (MLS); sports law and business (MSLB); tribal policy, law and government (LL M); JD/MBA; JD/MD; JD/MSW; JD/PhD. JD/MD offered jointly with Mayo Medical School. *Accreditation:* ABA. *Program availability:* 100% online. *Faculty:* 69 full-time (30 women), 115 part-time/adjunct (29 women). *Students:* 777 full-time (337 women); includes 207 minority (21 Black or African American, non-Hispanic/Latino; 14 American Indian or Alaska Native, non-Hispanic/Latino; 32 Asian, non-Hispanic/Latino; 104 Hispanic/Latino; 3 Native Hawaiian or other Pacific Islander, non-Hispanic/Latino; 33 Two or more races, non-Hispanic/Latino), 15 international. Average age 28. 2,056 applicants, 41% accepted, 215 enrolled. In 2017, 52 master's, 198 doctorates awarded. *Entrance requirements:* For master's, bachelor's degree and JD (for LL M); for doctorate, LSAT, bachelor's degree. Additional exam requirements/recommendations for international students: Required—TOEFL (minimum score 550 paper-based; 80 iBT). *Application deadline:* For fall admission, 3/1 priority date for domestic and international students. Applications are processed on a rolling basis. Electronic applications accepted. *Expenses:* Contact institution. *Financial support:* In 2017–18, 430 students received support. Institutionally sponsored loans and scholarships/grants available. Financial award application deadline: 3/15; financial award applicants required to submit FAFSA. *Faculty research:* Emerging technologies and the law, Indian law, international law, intellectual property, health law, sports law and business. Total annual research expenditures: $2.4 million. *Unit head:* Douglas Sylvester, Dean/Professor, 480-965-6188, Fax: 480-965-6521, E-mail: douglas.sylvester@asu.edu. *Application contact:* Chitra Damania, Director, 480-965-1474, Fax: 480-727-7930, E-mail: law.admissions@asu.edu.
Website: http://www.law.asu.edu/

Chapman University, Dale E. Fowler School of Law, Orange, CA 92866. Offers advocacy and dispute resolution (JD); business law (LL M, JD); criminal law (JD); entertainment and media law (LL M); entertainment law (JD); environmental, land use, and real estate law (JD); international and comparative law (LL M); international law (JD); law (JD); prosecutorial science (LL M); tax law (JD); taxation (LL M); trial advocacy (LL M); JD/MBA; JD/MFA. *Accreditation:* ABA. *Program availability:* Part-time. *Faculty:* 44 full-time (18 women), 34 part-time/adjunct (9 women). *Students:* 478 full-time (262 women), 37 part-time (24 women); includes 217 minority (9 Black or African American, non-Hispanic/Latino; 1 American Indian or Alaska Native, non-Hispanic/Latino; 69 Asian, non-Hispanic/Latino; 104 Hispanic/Latino; 34 Two or more races, non-Hispanic/Latino), 11 international. Average age 26. 1,499 applicants, 50% accepted, 190 enrolled. In 2017, 17 master's, 149 doctorates awarded. *Entrance requirements:* For doctorate, LSAT. Additional exam requirements/recommendations for international students: Required—TOEFL (minimum score 600 paper-based; 100 iBT). *Application deadline:* For fall admission, 4/17 priority date for domestic students. Applications are processed on a rolling basis. Electronic applications accepted. *Expenses:* Contact institution. *Financial support:* Fellowships, Federal Work-Study, and scholarships/grants available. Financial award applicants required to submit FAFSA. *Unit head:* Matthew J. Parlow, Dean, 714-628-2678, E-mail: parlow@chapman.edu. *Application contact:* Justin Cruz, Assistant Dean of Admissions and Diversity Initiatives, 714-628-2594, E-mail: lawadmission@chapman.edu.
Website: https://www.chapman.edu/law/index.aspx

Drexel University, Thomas R. Kline School of Law, Philadelphia, PA 19104-2875. Offers business and entrepreneurship law (JD); criminal law (MLS, JD); cybersecurity and information privacy compliance (MLS); entrepreneurship and law (MLS); financial regulatory compliance (MLS); health care compliance (MLS); health law (JD); higher education compliance (MLS); human resources compliance (MLS); intellectual property law (JD); NCAA compliance and sports law (MLS).

London Metropolitan University, Graduate Programs, London, United Kingdom. Offers applied psychology (M Sc); architecture (MA); biomedical science (M Sc); blood science (M Sc); cancer pharmacology (M Sc); computer networking and cyber security (M Sc); computing and information systems (M Sc); conference interpreting (MA); counter-terrorism studies (M Sc); creative, digital and professional writing (MA); crime, violence and prevention (M Sc); criminology (M Sc); curating contemporary art (MA); data analytics (M Sc); digital media (MA); early childhood studies (MA); education (MA, Ed D); financial services law, regulation and compliance (LL M); food science (M Sc);

forensic psychology (M Sc); health and social care management and policy (M Sc); human nutrition (M Sc); human resource management (MA); human rights and international conflict (MA); information technology (M Sc); intelligence and security studies (M Sc); international oil, gas and energy law (LL M); international relations (MA); interpreting (MA); learning and teaching in higher education (MA); legal practice (LL M); media and entertainment law (LL M); organizational and consumer psychology (M Sc); psychological therapy (M Sc); psychology of mental health (M Sc); public health (M Sc); public policy and management (MPA); security studies (M Sc); social work (M Sc); spatial planning and urban design (MA); sports therapy (M Sc); supporting older children and young people with dyslexia (MA); teaching languages (MA), including Arabic, English; translation (MA); woman and child abuse (MA).

New York University, School of Professional Studies, Preston Robert Tisch Institute for Global Sport, New York, NY 10012-1019. Offers sports business (MS), including global sports media, professional and collegiate sports operations, sports law, sports marketing and sales. *Program availability:* Part-time, evening/weekend. *Students:* 70 full-time (21 women), 38 part-time (13 women); includes 21 minority (6 Black or African American, non-Hispanic/Latino; 7 Asian, non-Hispanic/Latino; 5 Hispanic/Latino; 1 Native Hawaiian or other Pacific Islander, non-Hispanic/Latino; 2 Two or more races, non-Hispanic/Latino), 52 international. Average age 26. 145 applicants, 67% accepted, 46 enrolled. In 2017, 78 master's awarded. *Degree requirements:* For master's, thesis. *Entrance requirements:* For master's, GRE or GMAT (only upon request), bachelor's degree, resume with relevant professional work, internship or volunteer experience, two letters of recommendation, statement of purpose. Additional exam requirements/recommendations for international students: Required—TOEFL (minimum score 600 paper-based; 100 iBT), IELTS (minimum score 7). *Application deadline:* For fall admission, 2/1 priority date for domestic and international students; for spring admission, 10/15 priority date for domestic students, 8/15 priority date for international students. Applications are processed on a rolling basis. Application fee: $150. Electronic applications accepted. *Expenses:* $20,244 per term. *Financial support:* Fellowships, career-related internships or fieldwork, Federal Work-Study, scholarships/grants, and health care benefits available. Support available to part-time students. Financial award application deadline: 6/30; financial award applicants required to submit FAFSA. *Unit head:* Vince Gennaro, Associate Dean/Clinical Associate Professor, 212-995-4676. *Application contact:* Admissions Office, 212-998-7100, E-mail: sps.gradadmissions@nyu.edu.
Website: http://www.sps.nyu.edu/content/scps/academics/departments/tisch-institute.html

Pepperdine University, School of Law, Master of Laws Programs, Malibu, CA 90263. Offers dispute resolution (LL M); entertainment, media, and sports law (LL M); international commercial arbitration (LL M); international commercial law and arbitration (LL M); international commercial law and dispute resolution (LL M); U.S. law and dispute resolution (LL M); United States law (LL M). *Students:* 34 full-time (19 women), 33 part-time (17 women); includes 7 minority (2 Black or African American, non-Hispanic/Latino; 2 Asian, non-Hispanic/Latino; 3 Hispanic/Latino), 42 international. Average age 34. In 2017, 18 master's awarded. *Entrance requirements:* For master's, GRE General Test or LSAT, JD from ABA-accredited institution. Additional exam requirements/recommendations for international students: Required—TOEFL. *Application deadline:* For fall admission, 2/15 for domestic and international students; for spring admission, 8/15 for domestic and international students. Applications are processed on a rolling basis. Application fee: $60. Electronic applications accepted. *Expenses:* Contact institution. *Financial support:* Career-related internships or fieldwork, Federal Work-Study, institutionally sponsored loans, and scholarships/grants available. Support available to part-time students. Financial award application deadline: 4/1; financial award applicants required to submit FAFSA. *Unit head:* Dr. Peter Robinson, Director, Institute for Dispute Resolution, 310-506-4655, Fax: 310-506-4266, E-mail: peter.robinson@pepperdine.edu. *Application contact:* Shellee S. Warnes, Assistant Director, Academic Programs, 310-506-7455, Fax: 310-506-4266, E-mail: shellee.warnes@pepperdine.edu.
Website: https://law.pepperdine.edu/degrees-programs/master-of-laws/

University of Miami, Graduate School, University of Miami School of Law, Coral Gables, FL 33146. Offers entertainment, arts, and sports law (LL M); estate planning (LL M); intensive English (LL M); international arbitration (LL M); international law

(LL M), including general international law, inter-American law; law (JD); maritime law (LL M); real estate/property development (LL M); taxation (LL M); taxation of cross-border investment (LL M); the business of innovation, law and technology (BILT) (JD); U.S. and transnational law for foreign-trained lawyers (LL M); JD/LL M; JD/MA; JD/MBA; JD/MBA/LL M; JD/MD; JD/MM; JD/MPA; JD/MPH; JD/MPS; JD/MS Ed; JD/PhD. *Accreditation:* ABA. *Program availability:* Part-time. *Faculty:* 89 full-time (45 women), 115 part-time/adjunct (27 women). *Students:* 1,099 full-time (534 women), 93 part-time (48 women); includes 455 minority (63 Black or African American, non-Hispanic/Latino; 3 American Indian or Alaska Native, non-Hispanic/Latino; 25 Asian, non-Hispanic/Latino; 330 Hispanic/Latino; 1 Native Hawaiian or other Pacific Islander, non-Hispanic/Latino; 33 Two or more races, non-Hispanic/Latino), 53 international. 2,356 applicants, 59% accepted, 316 enrolled. *Entrance requirements:* For doctorate, LSAT, 2 letters of recommendation. Additional exam requirements/recommendations for international students: Required—TOEFL (minimum score 580 paper-based; 92 iBT), IELTS (minimum score 7). *Application deadline:* For fall admission, 7/31 for domestic and international students. Applications are processed on a rolling basis. Application fee: $60. Electronic applications accepted. *Expenses:* Contact institution. *Financial support:* Fellowships, research assistantships, career-related internships or fieldwork, Federal Work-Study, institutionally sponsored loans, scholarships/grants, and unspecified assistantships available. Financial award application deadline: 3/1; financial award applicants required to submit FAFSA. *Faculty research:* Energy/climate change, international finance, Internet law/law of electronic commerce, race/social justice, art law/cultural heritage law. *Unit head:* Michael Goodnight, Associate Dean of Admissions and Enrollment Management, 305-284-2527, Fax: 305-284-3084, E-mail: mgoodnig@law.miami.edu. *Application contact:* Therese Lambert, Director of Student Recruitment, 305-284-6746, Fax: 305-284-3084, E-mail: tlambert@law.miami.edu. Website: http://www.law.miami.edu/

See Display on page 1510 and Close-Up on page 1527.

University of New Hampshire, School of Law, Concord, NH 03301. Offers business law (JD); commerce and technology (LL M, MCT, Diploma); criminal law (JD); intellectual property (LL M, MIP, JD, Diploma), including patent law (JD), trademarks and copyright (JD); international criminal law and justice (LL M, MICLJ); litigation (JD); public interest and social justice (JD); sports and entertainment law (JD); JD/LL M; JD/MBA; JD/MIP; JD/MPP; JD/MSW. *Accreditation:* ABA. *Program availability:* Part-time, 100% online, limited residential. *Degree requirements:* For doctorate, comprehensive exam. *Entrance requirements:* For doctorate, LSAT. Additional exam requirements/recommendations for international students: Required—TOEFL (minimum score 600 paper-based; 100 iBT), minimum TOEFL iBT score of 80 (for master's programs). Electronic applications accepted. *Expenses:* Contact institution. *Faculty research:* Intellectual property, health law and policy, sports and entertainment law, patent law, trademarks and copyright.

SOUTHWESTERN LAW SCHOOL

 For more information, visit http://petersons.to/swlawschool

SOUTHWESTERN LAW SCHOOL
Los Angeles, California • www.swlaw.edu

Programs of Study

Founded more than 100 years ago, Southwestern Law School has developed a reputation for graduating lawyers who are well-rounded, entrepreneurial, and prepared to succeed. Southwestern offers a history of community, innovative teachers, brilliant scholars, and trailblazing alumni. An innovative curriculum and experiential learning opportunities challenge students, while the vibrant Los Angeles campus provides the ideal setting for the study of law, fostering an emphasis on community, diversity, and public service.

J.D. Programs: Southwestern is the only American Bar Association–approved law school offering four programs of study leading to a J.D. degree that differ in scheduling and instructional approach. In addition to traditional full-time day and part-time evening programs, Southwestern has developed two innovative options: PLEAS, one of the only part-time day programs in the country designed to meet the needs of students with child- or elder-care responsibilities, and SCALE®, a unique accelerated two-year J.D. course of instruction. SCALE is the first ABA-approved program of its kind in the U.S., featuring small classes, practical skills training, and real-world experience since 1975.

Southwestern's J.D. offerings enable students to follow either a broad-based or a personalized curriculum focusing on a particular area of law while earning the 87 units required for the degree. Southwestern offers more than 200 elective courses and numerous experiential opportunities to design an individualized program of study.

Concurrent J.D. Programs: Southwestern offers concurrent J.D./M.B.A. and J.D./E.M.B.A. degree programs with The Drucker Graduate School of Management.

Southwestern also offers two other concurrent degree programs: a J.D./M.A. in Negotiation, Conflict Resolution, and Peacebuilding in conjunction with California State University, Dominguez Hills, and a 3+3 B.A./J.D. with California State University, Northridge.

LL.M Programs: For law graduates who wish to pursue a post-J.D. degree, Southwestern offers two Master of Laws programs: a General (Individualized Studies) LL.M. and an Entertainment and Media Law LL.M., under the auspices of the Donald E. Biederman Entertainment and Media Law Institute.

J.D. Concentrations: Southwestern offers five concentrations (similar to an undergraduate major): Civil Litigation and Advocacy, Criminal Law and Advocacy, Entertainment and Media Law, Public Interest Law, and Technology Law and Entrepreneurship.

Upon meeting the curricular requirements of a concentration, students receive a designation on their transcript. Students earning a concentration GPA of 3.33 or higher in the designated courses receive an honors designation.

Summer Entertainment and Media Law Programs: Summer programs are open to Southwestern students, transfer students, and visiting students.

In Los Angeles, Southwestern has hosted an annual summer entertainment and media law program for many years. The Los Angeles program features specialized entertainment, fashion, media, and sports law courses taught by renowned industry attorneys; and a variety of summer legal externships at television/film studios, record labels and music publishing companies, talent agencies, unions and guilds, fashion houses, sports organizations, and other entertainment industry and industry-related settings. Southwestern also hosts a summer-abroad program in London, the first program wholly dedicated to international entertainment and media law. This five-week program is designed to provide a novel and inspiring educational and international networking experience for law school students from the United States and abroad. The program features excursions to the UK Supreme Court, the Royal Courts of Justice, Chelsea Stadium, and other legal, entertainment, media and cultural institutions in London.

Student Success from Pre-Law to Bar Preparation

Southwestern dedicates a wide range of resources to help students succeed academically while enhancing the overall law-school experience. There are more than 30 student organizations offering opportunities to socialize, develop networking skills, and connect with students, professors, and alumni.

Peer Mentors / Dean's Fellows act as student guides to help students navigate and succeed in a new environment. The Academic Excellence Academy is a noncredit pre-law summer program providing a comprehensive introduction to the study of law and the Writing Center provides individualized assistance and specialized workshops. Additionally, Southwestern provides special bar prep programming designed to assist students in stress management. Southwestern's campus includes a counseling center, wellness programs including relaxation therapy and a no-cost 10,000 square-foot fitness center.

Experiential Learning

While classroom learning is important, the most rewarding hours in law school are those students spend applying what they have learned in class to the real-world environment. Southwestern offers valuable and practical hands-on experiences through an abundant variety of clinics, externships, practicums, and public interest opportunities.

Southwestern's externship program, one of the largest in the country, provides students with an opportunity to directly experience the attorney's role through a variety of structured on-site placements. Southwestern students participate in approximately 350 to 400 externships annually. About three-quarters of students complete at least one externship, and more than one-quarter complete two externships as part of their J.D. curriculum.

Southwestern also operates eight clinics in which students work on real cases for academic credit under the close supervision and guidance of faculty who are practicing attorneys. Students take on substantial responsibility for strategizing and executing on an array of legal matters and are often involved in cases from beginning to end. Southwestern clinics: Appellate Litigation Clinic, Children's Rights Clinic, Community Lawyering Clinic, Entertainment & the Arts Legal Clinic, Family Law Clinic, Immigration Law Clinic, Street Law Clinic, and the Youth Offender Parole Hearing Clinic.

Financial Aid

Southwestern University offers a comprehensive program of loans, federal work study, and scholarship assistance. Future students should submit the Free Application for Federal Student Aid (FAFSA) at www.FAFSA.ed.gov. Southwestern's Title IV FAFSA code is G01295.

Southwestern Law School is an approved institution for veterans' benefits and active duty, vets, spouses and dependents who have eligible educational benefits by the U.S. Department of Veterans Affairs. Southwestern Law School proudly participates in the Veteran Affairs' Yellow Ribbon program and agrees to contribute $10,000 per year to eligible veterans pursuing their J.D. degree. Southwestern will offer this scholarship to a maximum of 10 veterans per academic year on a first-come, first-served basis.

Cost of Study

For the 2018–19 academic year, J.D. tuition is $53,966 for the full-time program and $35,994 for the part-time program. Tuition for the SCALE program is $75,816. The most comprehensive and up-to-date tuition and fee information can be found online at www.swlaw.edu/tuition.

Living and Housing

There is a wide variety of living choices for students within a 30-minute drive from campus. The Residences at 7th, Southwestern's award-winning on-campus student housing, accommodates about 152 students. The units are priced below comparably appointed apartments in the area. Entering students are given priority for a large percentage of these units on a first-come, first-served basis.

Diversity and Student Groups

Southwestern students have a strong sense of community. They come from virtually every state, more than a dozen countries, and represent over 200 undergraduate institutions. In the most recent entering class, women represent 53 percent, while minorities make up 49 percent, and students report fluency in over 20 foreign languages. The average age is 27, with a range from 21 to over 50. Recently, Southwestern was ranked the 8th best ABA law school for diversity and was ranked in the top tier for Asian, African-American and

Latino students. The Student Bar Association sponsors award-winning student welfare and community outreach programs and oversees over 50 student organizations, including legal fraternities; minority, cultural, political, and religious groups; and societies focused on specific areas of law.

Location

Southwestern has created a welcoming student-centered oasis close to the vibrant city center of Los Angeles.

The campus is strategically located in a thriving and diverse metropolis offering a distinctively Californian lifestyle and a wealth of opportunities for students. The school is close to courthouses, studios, silicon beach, and companies/firms of all sizes. The Wilshire/Vermont METRO Station is about a block from campus and provides convenient access to mid-Wilshire, Downtown Los Angeles (DTLA), Santa Monica, Hollywood, Long Beach, Pasadena, Studio City, and more.

The School

Southwestern is a leader in curricular innovation and expertise, particularly in the areas of entertainment and media law, international law, criminal law, and trial advocacy/litigation. It is also the only law school to offer four J.D. programs that differ in both scheduling and instructional approach. The required curriculum is enriched by approximately 200 electives, 150 externship placements, 8 clinics, and 4 practicums. Upper-division enhancements include over 50 professional skills courses, a January intersession, capstone courses, and special mini-term courses taught by international legal experts. Students at Southwestern devote well over 20,000 hours each year to pro bono service in the community.

Southwestern was the first law school to establish an institution for entertainment and media law. The internationally recognized Biederman Entertainment and Media Law Institute helps prepare students for the practice of law in creative industries such as film, television, and music.

Ten months after graduation, 80 percent of the 2017 graduating class reported being employed. Of those, 133 were employed in law firms, 61 in business/industry, 18 by the government, 10 in public interest, 3 in education, and 2 had judicial clerkships. One-hundred percent of 2017 graduates who passed the bar exam reported being employed within ten months of graduation.

Faculty

Southwestern's entire community is invested in student success. The faculty is talented and devoted; the staff is knowledgeable and helpful; the student body fosters a supportive (instead of overly-competitive) environment.

Applying

Admission to Southwestern's J.D. programs is based on a number of factors which may be predictive of an applicant's success in the study of law. Applicants are required to have completed an undergraduate degree from an accredited institution prior to enrollment.

Applications for the first-year entering class are accepted for the fall semester only. Every applicant must register with the Law School Admission Council (LSAC) which will provides Southwestern with the applicant's Law School Admissions Test (LSAT) scores and a summary of all undergraduate academic work. In addition to the information provided by the LSAC, each applicant must complete an Application File as outlined online at https://www.swlaw.edu/admissions-financial-aid/admissions-jd/application-process-requirements.

Applications for Southwestern's J.D. Program are reviewed as they are completed. Students are therefore strongly advised to apply as early as possible. Files submitted after the application deadline will be considered on an individual basis. Applicants should be aware, however, that waiting lists are often established as early as March, and eligibility for certain forms of financial aid most preferred by students (e.g., scholarship programs) may be reduced substantially after April 1.

Correspondence Information

Southwestern Law School
3050 Wilshire Boulevard
Los Angeles, California 90010
United States
Phone: 213-738-6834
E-mail: Admissions@SWLaw.edu
Website: www.swlaw.edu

Southwestern Law School was founded in 1911 on the principles of innovation and inclusion. The award-winning Bullocks Wilshire building functions as the heart of Southwestern's vibrant urban-campus.

We are DIVERSITY! Student quote: "Southwestern's diversity really defines the law school. When you are living and working in a place as eclectic as L.A., you have to be capable of understanding the worldviews of the people around you. Everyone at Southwestern offers something different, and it makes for a balanced and transformative legal education."

UNIVERSITY OF MIAMI
School of Law

Programs of Study

The University of Miami School of Law (Miami Law) provides a solid foundation in all the traditional subjects basic to understanding and practicing the law. In addition, the school is regularly expanding its offerings to ensure they reflect the opportunities of the changing world. The school offers more than 300 courses, clinics, skills workshops, and seminars, including renowned course offerings in inter-american, international, arbitration, and transnational law. Students ordinarily complete the J.D. degree in three years of full-time study.

Litigation and Lawyering Skills: Miami Law offers one of the most comprehensive and sophisticated litigation skills training programs in the nation, integrating trial, pre-trial, litigation, and clinical experiences. In addition, students who graduate from the course are placed in an externship program in which they are certified by the Florida Supreme Court to engage in the supervised practice of law. Miami's two-semester Legal Communication and Research Skills Program uses simulated client cases to produce practice-ready students. Students learn to write an array of legal documents, including memoranda, motions, briefs, emails, and correspondence.

Dual Degrees and Concentrations: Miami Law offers students more than 20 options in joint degrees and concentrations to focus their study. Joint degrees are offered in cooperation with the University of Miami's renowned graduate schools.

Joint J.D./Master's programs are offered in public administration, business, public health, music business, communications, entertainment management, Latin American studies, social change, and marine affairs.

Miami Law's Joint J.D./LL.M. degrees are for students interested in exploring specific fields of the law. LL.M. options include: Entertainment, Arts, and Sports Law; International Arbitration; Estate Planning; Taxation; Real Estate/Property Development; Maritime Law; International Law; and U.S. and Transnational Law for Foreign-Trained Lawyers LL.M.

Optional concentrations and areas of focus include, Social Justice and Public Interest Concentration; the Business of Innovation, Law, and Technology (BILT Concentration); Litigation and Dispute Resolution Concentration; and Immigration, Asylum, and Citizenship Law Area of Focus.

Experiential Learning and International Opportunities

The school provides practical training opportunities in courts, corporations, and clinics. Miami Law's award-winning clinics serve as training grounds and give students the unparalleled opportunity to work with clients and acquire valuable legal skills while helping underrepresented individuals and groups in Miami, across the nation, and around the globe. Clinics include: Bankruptcy Assistance, Children and Youth Law, Environmental Justice, Federal Appellate, Health Rights, Human Rights, Immigration, Innocence, Investor Rights, and Tenants' Rights.

The Law School offers practicum experiences in the areas of entrepreneurial startup law, civil rights, the death penalty, affordable housing, criminal justice reform, and cyber rights.

Miami Law's Externship Program offers students an opportunity to gain practical legal experience by working with local, national, and international organizations, and the judiciary for academic credit. The 12-credit Washington, D.C., Semester in Practice provides students the opportunity to combine an externship in a DC-based government agency, nonprofit, or advocacy organization with coursework. The Florida Supreme Court Internship Program allows exceptional law students to serve as clerks to one of seven Florida Supreme Court justices.

HOPE (Helping Others Through Pro Bono Efforts) is the law school's public interest resource center. This center provides guidance and training to law students dedicated to community service and advocacy. It also runs the Miami Scholars Public Interest Program—a prestigious full-tuition scholarship program for incoming students with exceptional academic and public interest achievements.

The Center for Ethics and Public Service is an interdisciplinary project teaching the values of ethical judgment, professional responsibility, and public service. The center includes the Historic Black Church Program, and the Environmental Justice Clinic.

The Professional Responsibility and Ethics Program (PREP) develops continuing legal education (CLE) ethics training for the legal community.

Miami Law also conducts the nationally known STREET Law program in which law students empower youth at local high schools through interactive education about law, democracy, and human rights.

Miami Law also offers opportunities for study abroad and international travel, with 25 foreign study and exchange programs. Students can focus on specific interests, such as international law, arbitration of international business disputes, comparative law issues in international business, foreign legal systems, and human rights in Argentina, Belgium, Brazil, China, Colombia, France, Germany, India, Ireland, Israel, Spain, or Switzerland.

The school has an International Moot Court Program. Students take a workshop and participate around the globe in international competitions, some of which are conducted in Spanish. Students argue in mock court on topics in international law.

Miami Law's groundbreaking LawWithoutWalls Program brings together students, faculty, practitioners, and entrepreneurs from around the country and the world to explore innovation in legal education and practice.

Research Facilities

With over 630,000 volumes and volume equivalents and a wide array of electronic resources, Miami Law's library is one of the most comprehensive resources for legal research in the Southeast. The Law Library has liberal hours, energetic and experienced reference librarians, and seating for individual and group study.

Financial Aid

Scholarship aid available through the school does not exceed the cost of tuition. Most scholarships are merit based, although need is sometimes considered. Admitted applicants are automatically considered for most scholarship awards. Applicants who wish to be considered for a merit scholarship should complete their admission files prior to January 9. Most scholarships are awarded on a rolling basis. Those admitted by February 1 are considered for the prestigious Harvey T. Reid and Soia Mentschikoff scholarships. In addition, admitted students are eligible to apply for the Miami Scholars Public Interest Program—a prestigious full-tuition scholarship program for incoming students with exceptional academic and public interest achievements, which requires a separate application with a deadline of April 1.

The law school assists and encourages all students to apply for federal aid (loans) prior to considering private educational loans. Federal loans may be applied for by first completing the FAFSA online by the priority deadline of March 1.

Cost of Study

Tuition and any additional financial aid information can be found on the University's website at www.law.miami.edu/iml/financial-aid

Housing

The law school does not provide on-campus housing but Miami is a large, metropolitan city full of diverse housing options and locations in which to live within a convenient distance of campus. The University is situated in the heart of Coral Gables and surrounded by an abundance of housing options to meet students' needs and budgets within walking and commuting distance of the law school.

Student Organizations

Miami Law's student activities include more than 55 diverse student organizations that provide members with personal, academic, and career support. All encourage student leadership and assist in recruiting, networking, and career opportunities with alumni and other members of the legal community.

Some of the organizations include: diversity/affinity groups (Black, Hispanic and Asian/Pacific American law student organizations; OUTLaw; Miami Law Women); legal thought/political groups (Federalist Society, Democratic Law Students Association, Republican Law Student Association); legal practice area groups (International Law Society, Entertainment and Sports Law Society, Intellectual Property Law Society); and advocacy groups (Student Advocates for Veterans, Child Advocacy Family Law).

The school's law journals include University of Miami Law Review, University of Miami Inter-American Law Review, University of Miami International and Comparative Law Review, Race and Social Justice Law Review, and Business Law Review.

The Mindfulness in Law Program has an academic component and also coordinates special wellness programs to help students achieve a better balance between work and life.

Location

The University of Miami School of Law is located on the 260-acre main campus of one of the largest private research universities in the United States. The law school is situated in Coral Gables, known as one of Florida's most desirable areas, where students receive all the benefits of large-city living while in a suburban setting. Next door is Miami, a burgeoning international center for trade and finance. Miami and its region—South Florida—stand at the crossroads of the Americas, a location that lends students at University of Miami School of Law an international perspective.

The Law School

University of Miami School of Law is at the forefront in training legal professionals for this rapidly changing world. Miami Law is accredited by the ABA, is a member of the AALS, and has a chapter of the prestigious scholastic society, the Order of the Coif.

Graduates of this law school are among the best in the profession. More than 20,000 alumni practice throughout the United States and in nearly 91 countries around the world. They work for both small and large firms as well as in private practice, in government service, and as sole practitioners.

The Career Development Office (CDO), composed of nine attorneys, provides extraordinary professional and career development to students and alumni. The CDO offers a wide range of job-related programming and recruiting opportunities, individual career counseling, professional connections with attorneys in varied practices, and online access to a resource library and national job postings.

Faculty

Miami Law faculty are graduates of the world's top universities and law schools, have completed prestigious judicial clerkships, and have significant work experience in private practice and government. They are leading scholars in their fields and are renowned for combining their scholarly distinction and real-world experience with an enthusiastic approach to teaching. Their areas of expertise are especially strong in international and foreign law, arbitration, taxation, criminal law, securities regulation, immigration, human rights, the Internet, legal theory, evidence, and ethics.

Applying

Admission is competitive. Undergraduate and graduate grade-point averages are used in the review process. While all LSAT scores are considered, the highest score is given the greatest weight. Two letters of recommendation or two evaluations (or a combination thereof) are required, and a personal statement is strongly encouraged. Work experience, extracurricular activities, special skills, and background are also considered. First-year students are admitted only in the fall semester. Applicants are urged to apply as early as possible after September 1. Applications received after February 1 will be considered on a space-available basis until July 31.

Correspondence and Information

University of Miami School of Law
Office of Admissions & Student Recruitment
P.O. Box 248087
Coral Gables, Florida 33124-8087
Phone: 305-284-2523
E-mail: admissions@law.miami.edu
Website: www.law.miami.edu

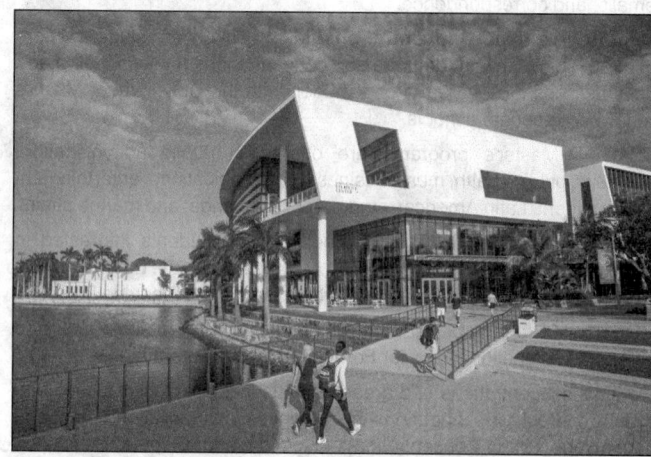

The law school resides on the main University of Miami campus and is across the street from the central student center, pictured.

The central courtyard of University of Miami Law is where students meet and study throughout the year, including winter.

ACADEMIC AND PROFESSIONAL PROGRAMS IN LIBRARY AND INFORMATION STUDIES

Section 28
Library and Information Studies

This section contains a directory of institutions offering graduate work in library and information studies, followed by in-depth entries submitted by institutions that chose to prepare detailed program descriptions. Additional information about programs listed in the directory but not augmented by an in-depth entry may be obtained by writing directly to the dean of a graduate school or chair of a department at the address given in the directory.

For programs offering related work, see also in this book *Education*. In another guide in this series:

Graduate Programs in Engineering & Applied Sciences
See *Computer Science and Information Technology*

CONTENTS

Program Directories

Featured Schools: Displays and Close-Ups

Archives/Archival Administration

Claremont Graduate University, Graduate Programs, School of Arts and Humanities, Department of History, Claremont, CA 91711-6160. Offers Africana history (Certificate); American studies and U.S. history (MA, PhD); archival studies (MA); early modern studies (MA, PhD); European studies (MA, PhD); oral history (MA, PhD); MBA/MA; MBA/PhD. Terminal master's awarded for partial completion of doctoral program. *Entrance requirements:* For master's and doctorate, GRE General Test. Additional exam requirements/recommendations for international students: Required—TOEFL (minimum score 75 iBT). Electronic applications accepted. *Faculty research:* Intellectual and social history, cultural studies, gender studies, Western history, Chicano history.

Clayton State University, School of Graduate Studies, College of Information and Mathematical Sciences, Program in Archival Studies, Morrow, GA 30260-0285. Offers MAS. *Program availability:* Online learning. *Entrance requirements:* For master's, GRE, 2 official transcripts; 3 letters of recommendation; statement of purpose; essay. Additional exam requirements/recommendations for international students: Required—TOEFL (minimum score 550 paper-based). Electronic applications accepted.

Columbia University, School of Professional Studies, Program in Information and Archive Management, New York, NY 10027. Offers MS. *Program availability:* Part-time. *Entrance requirements:* For master's, minimum undergraduate GPA of 3.0. Additional exam requirements/recommendations for international students: Required—American Language Program placement test. Electronic applications accepted. *Expenses: Tuition:* Full-time $44,864; part-time $1704 per credit. *Required fees:* $2370 per semester. One-time fee: $105. *Faculty research:* Library science technology, information systems.

Drexel University, Westphal College of Media Arts and Design, Program in Museum Leadership, Philadelphia, PA 19104-2875. Offers MS. Offered in partnership with the Academy of Natural Sciences of Drexel University. *Program availability:* Part-time, online learning. *Degree requirements:* For master's, practicum.

East Tennessee State University, School of Graduate Studies, School of Continuing Studies and Academic Outreach, Johnson City, TN 37614. Offers archival studies (Postbaccalaureate Certificate); liberal studies (MALS); reinforcing education through artistic learning (Postbaccalaureate Certificate); strategic leadership (MPS); training and development (MPS). *Program availability:* Part-time, online learning. In 2017, 9 master's, 1 other advanced degree awarded. *Degree requirements:* For master's, comprehensive exam, thesis (for some programs), professional project. *Entrance requirements:* For master's, GRE General Test, minimum GPA of 2.75, professional portfolio, three letters of recommendation, interview, writing sample; for Postbaccalaureate Certificate, minimum GPA of 2.5, three letters of recommendation, interview. Additional exam requirements/recommendations for international students: Required—TOEFL (minimum score 550 paper-based; 79 iBT). *Application deadline:* For fall admission, 6/1 for domestic students, 4/29 for international students; for spring admission, 11/1 for domestic students, 9/29 for international students. Application fee: $55 ($65 for international students). Electronic applications accepted. *Financial support:* Research assistantships with full tuition reimbursements, teaching assistantships with full tuition reimbursements, institutionally sponsored loans, scholarships/grants, tuition waivers, and unspecified assistantships available. Financial award application deadline: 7/1; financial award applicants required to submit FAFSA. *Faculty research:* Appalachian studies, women's and gender studies, interdisciplinary theory, regional and Southern cultures. *Unit head:* Dr. Rick E. Osborn, Dean, 423-439-4223, Fax: 423-439-7091, E-mail: osbornr@etsu.edu. *Application contact:* Dr. Rick E. Osborn, Dean, 423-439-4223, Fax: 423-439-7091, E-mail: osbornr@etsu.edu.
Website: http://www.etsu.edu/academicaffairs/scs/

Middle Tennessee State University, College of Graduate Studies, College of Liberal Arts, Department of History, Murfreesboro, TN 37132. Offers archival management (Graduate Certificate); history (MA); public history (PhD). *Program availability:* Part-time, evening/weekend, online learning. *Degree requirements:* For master's, one foreign language, comprehensive exam, thesis optional; for doctorate, one foreign language, comprehensive exam, thesis/dissertation. *Entrance requirements:* For master's and doctorate, GRE. Additional exam requirements/recommendations for international students: Required—TOEFL (minimum score 525 paper-based; 71 iBT) or IELTS (minimum score 6). Electronic applications accepted.

Montclair State University, The Graduate School, College of the Arts, Program in Fine Art, Montclair, NJ 07043-1624. Offers museum management (MA); studio (MA). *Accreditation:* NASAD. *Program availability:* Part-time, evening/weekend. *Degree requirements:* For master's, project. *Entrance requirements:* For master's, GRE or MAT, 2 letters of recommendation, essay. Electronic applications accepted.

New York University, Graduate School of Arts and Science, Department of History, New York, NY 10012-1019. Offers African diaspora (PhD); African history (PhD); archival management (Advanced Certificate); Atlantic history (PhD); French studies/history (PhD); Hebrew and Judaic studies/history (PhD); history (MA, PhD), including Europe (PhD), Latin America and the Caribbean (PhD), United States (PhD), women's history (MA); Middle Eastern history (MA); Middle Eastern studies/history (PhD); public history (Advanced Certificate); world history (MA); JD/MA; MA/Advanced Certificate. *Program availability:* Part-time. *Students:* Average age 29. 401 applicants, 31% accepted, 38 enrolled. In 2017, 24 master's, 16 doctorates awarded. Terminal master's awarded for partial completion of doctoral program. *Degree requirements:* For master's, seminar paper; for doctorate, one foreign language, thesis/dissertation, oral and written exams; for Advanced Certificate, internship. *Entrance requirements:* For master's, GRE General Test, minimum GPA of 3.0, writing sample; for doctorate, GRE. Additional exam requirements/recommendations for international students: Required—TOEFL. *Application deadline:* For fall admission, 12/18 for domestic and international students. Application fee: $100. *Expenses: Tuition:* Full-time $41,352; part-time $19,968 per year. *Required fees:* $2496; $1628 per unit. $814 per term. Tuition and fees vary according to course load and program. *Financial support:* Fellowships, research assistantships, teaching assistantships, career-related internships or fieldwork, Federal Work-Study, institutionally sponsored loans, scholarships/grants, health care benefits, and unspecified assistantships available. Financial award application deadline: 12/18; financial award applicants required to submit FAFSA. *Faculty research:* African, East Asian, medieval, early modern, and modern European history; U.S. history; African and African diaspora; Latin American history; Atlantic world. *Unit head:* Barbara Weinstein, Chair, 212-998-8600, Fax: 212-995-4017, E-mail: history.admissions@nyu.edu. *Application contact:* Stepfanos Geroulanos, Director of Graduate Studies, 212-998-8600, Fax: 212-995-4017, E-mail: history.admissions@nyu.edu.
Website: http://history.as.nyu.edu/

New York University, Tisch School of the Arts and Graduate School of Arts and Science, Department of Cinema Studies, New York, NY 10012-1019. Offers cinema studies (MA, PhD); moving image archiving and preservation (MA). *Faculty:* 15 full-time, 9 part-time/adjunct. *Students:* 80 full-time (53 women); includes 11 minority (5 Black or African American, non-Hispanic/Latino; 1 Asian, non-Hispanic/Latino; 4 Hispanic/Latino; 1 Two or more races, non-Hispanic/Latino), 45 international. Average age 31. 233 applicants, 42% accepted, 49 enrolled. In 2017, 36 master's, 9 doctorates awarded. *Degree requirements:* For master's, comprehensive exam; for doctorate, one foreign language, thesis/dissertation, 3 comprehensive exams. *Entrance requirements:* For master's, GRE, sample of written work; for doctorate, GRE, master's degree, writing sample. Additional exam requirements/recommendations for international students: Required—TOEFL or IELTS. *Application deadline:* For fall admission, 12/1 for domestic and international students. Application fee: $60. Electronic applications accepted. *Expenses:* Contact institution. *Financial support:* In 2017–18, 59 students received support, including 45 fellowships with full and partial tuition reimbursements available, 10 research assistantships, 4 teaching assistantships; Federal Work-Study, institutionally sponsored loans, tuition waivers (full and partial), and unspecified assistantships also available. Support available to part-time students. Financial award application deadline: 2/15; financial award applicants required to submit FAFSA. *Faculty research:* History and aesthetics of American, European, and Third World cinemas; theory of film and the moving image; cultural studies; gay and lesbian media. *Unit head:* Dr. Richard Allen, Chair, 212-998-1600. *Application contact:* Dan Sandford, Director of Graduate Admissions, 212-998-1918, Fax: 212-995-4060, E-mail: tisch.gradadmissions@nyu.edu.
Website: http://www.cinema.tisch.nyu.edu/

New York University, Tisch School of the Arts, Program in Moving Image Archiving and Preservation, New York, NY 10012-1019. Offers MA. *Faculty:* 2 full-time, 4 part-time/adjunct. *Students:* 20 full-time (12 women); includes 4 minority (3 Hispanic/Latino; 1 Two or more races, non-Hispanic/Latino), 2 international. Average age 28. 36 applicants, 50% accepted, 10 enrolled. In 2017, 12 master's awarded. *Entrance requirements:* For master's, GRE. Application fee: $60. Electronic applications accepted. *Expenses: Tuition:* Full-time $41,352; part-time $19,968 per year. *Required fees:* $2496; $1628 per unit. $814 per term. Tuition and fees vary according to course load and program. *Financial support:* In 2017–18, 11 students received support. Fellowships and tuition waivers (partial) available. Financial award application deadline: 2/15. *Unit head:* Richard Allen, Head, 212-998-1618. *Application contact:* Dan Sandford, Director of Graduate Admissions, 212-998-1918, Fax: 212-995-4060, E-mail: tisch.gradadmissions@nyu.edu.
Website: http://www.cinema.tisch.nyu.edu/

Queens College of the City University of New York, Division of Social Sciences, Graduate School of Library and Information Studies, Queens, NY 11367-1597. Offers archives and preservation of cultural materials (AC); children's and young adult services in the public library (AC); librarianship (AC); library science (MLS); school library media specialist (MLS). *Accreditation:* ALA (one or more programs are accredited). *Program availability:* Part-time, evening/weekend. *Students:* 28 full-time (20 women), 289 part-time (205 women); includes 116 minority (37 Black or African American, non-Hispanic/Latino; 17 Asian, non-Hispanic/Latino; 53 Hispanic/Latino; 9 Two or more races, non-Hispanic/Latino), 4 international. Average age 33. *Degree requirements:* For master's, thesis; for AC, thesis optional. *Entrance requirements:* For master's, minimum GPA of 3.0; for AC, master's degree or equivalent. Additional exam requirements/recommendations for international students: Required—TOEFL, IELTS. *Application deadline:* For fall admission, 4/1 for domestic students; for spring admission, 11/1 for domestic students. Applications are processed on a rolling basis. Application fee: $125. Electronic applications accepted. *Financial support:* Career-related internships or fieldwork and unspecified assistantships available. Financial award application deadline: 4/1; financial award applicants required to submit FAFSA. *Unit head:* Colleen Cool, Director/Chair, 718-997-3790, E-mail: colleen.cool@qc.cuny.edu. *Application contact:* Elizabeth D'Amico-Ramirez, Assistant Director of Graduate Admissions, 718-997-5203, E-mail: elizabeth.damicoramirez@qc.cuny.edu.

The University of British Columbia, Faculty of Arts, School of Library, Archival and Information Studies, Master of Archival Studies Program, Vancouver, BC V6T 1Z1, Canada. Offers MAS. *Degree requirements:* For master's, thesis optional. *Entrance requirements:* For master's, minimum B+ average or minimum GPA of 3.3 in undergraduate upper-division courses. Additional exam requirements/recommendations for international students: Required—TOEFL. Electronic applications accepted. *Expenses:* Contact institution. *Faculty research:* Diplomatic, electronic record, appraisal, descriptive standards, preservation.

The University of British Columbia, Faculty of Arts, School of Library, Archival and Information Studies, PhD Program in Library, Archival and Information Studies, Vancouver, BC V6T 1Z1, Canada. Offers PhD. *Degree requirements:* For doctorate, thesis/dissertation. *Entrance requirements:* For doctorate, GRE, minimum GPA of 3.3 in MAS or MLIS. Additional exam requirements/recommendations for international students: Required—TOEFL. Electronic applications accepted. *Expenses:* Contact institution. *Faculty research:* Computer systems/database design; library and archival management; archival description and organization; children's literature and youth services; interactive information retrieval.

University of California, Los Angeles, Graduate Division, Graduate School of Education and Information Studies, Department of Information Studies, Los Angeles, CA 90095-1521. Offers archival studies (MLIS); informatics (MLIS); information studies (PhD); library and information science (Certificate); library studies (MLIS); moving image archive studies (MA); rare books, print and visual culture (MLIS); MBA/MLIS; MLIS/MA. *Accreditation:* ALA (one or more programs are accredited). Terminal master's awarded for partial completion of doctoral program. *Degree requirements:* For master's, thesis or alternative, professional portfolio; for doctorate, thesis/dissertation, oral and written qualifying exams. *Entrance requirements:* For master's, GRE General Test, previous course work in statistics; for doctorate, GRE General Test, previous course work in statistics, 2 samples of research writing in English. Additional exam requirements/recommendations for international students: Required—TOEFL (minimum score 560 paper-based; 87 iBT), IELTS (minimum score 7). Electronic applications accepted. *Faculty research:* Digital libraries, archives and electronic records, interface design, cultural informatics, preservation/conservation, access.

University of California, Los Angeles, Graduate Division, School of Theater, Film and Television, Interdepartmental Program in Moving Image Archive Studies, Los Angeles, CA 90095. Offers MA. *Degree requirements:* For master's, comprehensive exam, thesis. *Entrance requirements:* For master's, bachelor's degree; minimum undergraduate GPA of 3.0 (or its equivalent if letter grade system not used); writing sample. Additional exam requirements/recommendations for international students: Required—TOEFL. Electronic applications accepted.

University of California, Riverside, Graduate Division, Department of History, Riverside, CA 92521-0102. Offers archival management (MA); history (PhD). *Program* availability: Part-time. Terminal master's awarded for partial completion of doctoral program. *Degree requirements:* For master's, one foreign language, comprehensive exam, internship report and oral exams, or thesis; for doctorate, 2 foreign languages, thesis/dissertation, qualifying exams. *Entrance requirements:* For master's and doctorate, GRE General Test, minimum GPA of 3.2. Additional exam requirements/recommendations for international students: Required—TOEFL (minimum score 550 paper-based; 80 iBT). Electronic applications accepted. *Expenses:* Tuition, state resident: full-time $5746. Tuition, nonresident: full-time $10,780. Tuition and fees vary according to campus/location and program. *Faculty research:* Native American history, United States, public history, Europe, Latin America.

University of Manitoba, Faculty of Graduate Studies, Faculty of Arts, Department of History, Winnipeg, MB R3T 2N2, Canada. Offers archival studies (MA); history (MA, PhD). MA offered jointly with The University of Winnipeg. *Degree requirements:* For master's, thesis; for doctorate, one foreign language, thesis/dissertation.

University of Massachusetts Boston, College of Liberal Arts, Program in History, Boston, MA 02125-3393. Offers archival methods (MA). *Program availability:* Part-time, evening/weekend. *Faculty:* 18 full-time (11 women), 9 part-time/adjunct (5 women). *Students:* 16 full-time (9 women), 58 part-time (33 women); includes 8 minority (3 Black or African American, non-Hispanic/Latino; 1 Asian, non-Hispanic/Latino; 4 Hispanic/Latino). Average age 34. 55 applicants, 85% accepted, 22 enrolled. In 2017, 22 master's awarded. *Entrance requirements:* For master's, minimum GPA of 2.75. *Application deadline:* For fall admission, 3/1 for domestic students; for spring admission, 11/1 for domestic students. *Expenses:* Tuition, state resident: full-time $17,375. Tuition, nonresident: full-time $33,915. *Required fees:* $355. *Financial support:* Research assistantships, teaching assistantships, career-related internships or fieldwork, Federal Work-Study, and unspecified assistantships available. Support available to part-time students. Financial award application deadline: 3/1; financial award applicants required to submit FAFSA. *Faculty research:* European intellectual history, American labor and social history in nineteenth century, colonial American Revolution, Afro-American Cold War. *Unit head:* Dr. Spencer DiScala, Director, 617-287-6860, E-mail: spencer.discala@umb.edu. *Application contact:* Graduate Admissions Coordinator, 617-287-6400, Fax: 617-287-6236, E-mail: bos.gadm@dpc.umassp.edu.

University of Oklahoma, College of Arts and Sciences, School of Library and Information Studies, Norman, OK 73019. Offers archival studies (Graduate Certificate); digital humanities (Graduate Certificate); information studies (PhD); library and information studies (MLIS); M Ed/MLIS; MBA/MLIS. *Accreditation:* ALA (one or more programs are accredited). *Program availability:* Part-time, evening/weekend, 100% online, blended/hybrid learning. *Faculty:* 11 full-time (8 women), 1 (woman) part-time/adjunct. *Students:* 64 full-time (53 women), 117 part-time (95 women); includes 40 minority (6 Black or African American, non-Hispanic/Latino; 6 American Indian or Alaska Native, non-Hispanic/Latino; 3 Asian, non-Hispanic/Latino; 14 Hispanic/Latino; 1 Native Hawaiian or other Pacific Islander, non-Hispanic/Latino; 10 Two or more races, non-Hispanic/Latino). Average age 32. 58 applicants, 93% accepted, 48 enrolled. In 2017, 53 master's awarded. Terminal master's awarded for partial completion of doctoral program. *Degree requirements:* For master's, comprehensive exam (for some programs), thesis optional; for doctorate, comprehensive exam, thesis/dissertation. *Entrance requirements:* For master's, three letters of recommendation, personal statement, resume, transcript; for doctorate, GRE, three letters of recommendation, personal statement, resume, writing sample; for Graduate Certificate, transcripts, personal statement (for some certificates), letter of recommendation (for some certificates). Additional exam requirements/recommendations for international students: Required—TOEFL (minimum score 79 iBT) or IELTS (minimum score 6.5). *Application deadline:* Applications are processed on a rolling basis. Application fee: $50 ($100 for international students). Electronic applications accepted. *Expenses:* Tuition, state resident: full-time $5119; part-time $213.30 per credit hour. Tuition, nonresident: full-time $19,778; part-time $824.10 per credit hour. *Required fees:* $3458; $133.55 per credit hour. $126.50 per semester. *Financial support:* In 2017–18, 82 students received support, including 3 research assistantships with full tuition reimbursements available (averaging $10,579 per year), 3 teaching assistantships with full tuition reimbursements available (averaging $10,579 per year); scholarships/grants, health care benefits, and unspecified assistantships also available. Financial award application deadline: 6/1; financial award applicants required to submit FAFSA. *Faculty research:* Family and youth technology in libraries, consumer health information, text mining, big data analytics. *Total annual research expenditures:* $107,620. *Unit head:* Dr. Susan K. Burke, Director, 405-325-3921, E-mail: sburke@ou.edu. *Application contact:* Sarah Connelly, Admissions and Student Services Coordinator, 405-325-3921, E-mail: sarahee@ou.edu.
Website: http://slis.ou.edu

University of Rochester, School of Arts and Sciences, Program in Photographic Preservation and Collections Management, Rochester, NY 14627. Offers MA. Program offered jointly with George Eastman Museum. *Students:* 9 full-time (6 women), 1 (woman) part-time; includes 1 minority (Black or African American, non-Hispanic/Latino). Average age 28. 14 applicants, 86% accepted, 4 enrolled. In 2017, 9 master's awarded. *Degree requirements:* For master's, essay (counts as qualifying exam). *Entrance requirements:* For master's, writing sample, transcripts, three letters of recommendation, one- to two-page statement of purpose. Additional exam requirements/recommendations for international students: Required—TOEFL. *Application deadline:* For fall admission, 1/15 for domestic and international students. Application fee: $60. Electronic applications accepted. *Expenses:* $1,596 per credit hour. *Financial support:* In 2017–18, 4 students received support. Tuition waivers (partial) available. Financial award application deadline: 1/15. *Unit head:* Jacob Lewis, Associate Academic Director, 585-275-4287, E-mail: joan.saab@rochester.edu. *Application contact:* Martin Collier, Administrator, 585-275-7451, E-mail: marty.collier@rochester.edu.
Website: https://www.sas.rochester.edu/ppc/

University of South Carolina, The Graduate School, College of Arts and Sciences, Department of History, Program in Public History, Columbia, SC 29208. Offers archive management (MA); historic preservation (MA); museum administration (MA); museum management (Certificate); MLIS/MA. *Degree requirements:* For master's, one foreign language, thesis, internship. *Entrance requirements:* For master's, GRE General Test, writing sample. Additional exam requirements/recommendations for international students: Required—TOEFL. Electronic applications accepted. *Faculty research:* Museum studies, historic preservation, archives administration.

Wayne State University, School of Information Sciences, Detroit, MI 48202. Offers archival administration (Graduate Certificate); information management (MS, Graduate Certificate); library and information science (MLIS, Graduate Certificate, Spec); public library services to children and young adults (Graduate Certificate); MLIS/MA. *Accreditation:* ALA (one or more programs are accredited). *Program availability:* Part-time, evening/weekend, 100% online, blended/hybrid learning. *Faculty:* 12 full-time (9 women), 17 part-time/adjunct (12 women). *Students:* 100 full-time (80 women), 359 part-time (290 women); includes 77 minority (42 Black or African American, non-Hispanic/Latino; 2 American Indian or Alaska Native, non-Hispanic/Latino; 3 Asian, non-Hispanic/Latino; 19 Hispanic/Latino; 1 Native Hawaiian or other Pacific Islander, non-Hispanic/Latino; 10 Two or more races, non-Hispanic/Latino), 1 international. Average age 33. 258 applicants, 60% accepted, 100 enrolled. In 2017, 149 master's, 34 other advanced degrees awarded. *Degree requirements:* For master's and other advanced degree, e-portfolio. *Entrance requirements:* For master's, GRE or MAT (if undergraduate GPA is between 2.5 and 2.99), minimum undergraduate GPA of 3.0 or graduate degree, personal statement, resume or curriculum vitae; for other advanced degree, GRE or MAT (if undergraduate GPA is between 2.5 and 2.99), minimum undergraduate GPA of 3.0 or graduate degree, personal statement, resume or curriculum vitae, MLIS (for specialist certificate). Additional exam requirements/recommendations for international students: Required—TOEFL (minimum score 550 paper-based; 79 iBT); Recommended—IELTS (minimum score 6.5), TWE (minimum score 5.5). *Application deadline:* For fall admission, 7/1 for domestic students, 5/1 priority date for international students; for winter admission, 10/1 priority date for domestic students, 9/1 priority date for international students; for spring admission, 2/1 priority date for domestic students, 1/1 priority date for international students. Applications are processed on a rolling basis. Application fee: $50. Electronic applications accepted. *Financial support:* In 2017–18, 133 students received support. Fellowships with tuition reimbursements available, scholarships/grants, health care benefits, and unspecified assistantships available. Support available to part-time students. Financial award applicants required to submit FAFSA. *Faculty research:* Library services, information management issues, digital content management, library/community engagement, archives and preservation. *Unit head:* Dr. Jon Cawthorne, Dean, 313-577-4020, E-mail: jon.cawthorne@wayne.edu. *Application contact:* Academic Services Officer II, 313-577-1825, E-mail: asklis@wayne.edu.
Website: http://slis.wayne.edu/

Information Studies

The Catholic University of America, School of Arts and Sciences, Department of Library and Information Science, Washington, DC 20064. Offers MSLS, Certificate, JD/MSLS, MSLS/MA, MSLS/MS. *Accreditation:* ALA (one or more programs are accredited). *Program availability:* Part-time. *Faculty:* 7 full-time (6 women), 1 (woman) part-time/adjunct. *Students:* 14 full-time (13 women), 70 part-time (49 women); includes 24 minority (10 Black or African American, non-Hispanic/Latino; 2 Asian, non-Hispanic/Latino; 4 Hispanic/Latino; 8 Two or more races, non-Hispanic/Latino), 1 international. Average age 32. 48 applicants, 90% accepted, 26 enrolled. In 2017, 37 master's, 1 Certificate awarded. *Degree requirements:* For master's, comprehensive exam. *Entrance requirements:* For master's, statement of purpose, official copies of academic transcripts, three letters of recommendation, interview. Additional exam requirements/recommendations for international students: Required—TOEFL (minimum score 550 paper-based; 80 iBT). *Application deadline:* For fall admission, 7/15 priority date for domestic students, 7/1 for international students; for spring admission, 11/15 priority date for domestic students, 11/1 for international students. Applications are processed on a rolling basis. Application fee: $55. Electronic applications accepted. *Expenses:* Contact institution. *Financial support:* Fellowships, research assistantships, teaching assistantships, Federal Work-Study, scholarships/grants, tuition waivers (full and partial), and unspecified assistantships available. Financial award application deadline: 2/1; financial award applicants required to submit FAFSA. *Faculty research:* Digital collections, library and information science education, information design and architecture, information system design and evaluation. *Unit head:* Dr. Youngok Choi, Chair, 202-319-5877, E-mail: choiy@cua.edu. *Application contact:* Dr. Steven Brown, Director of Graduate Admissions, 202-319-5057, Fax: 202-319-6533, E-mail: cua-admissions@cua.edu.
Website: http://lis.cua.edu/

Central Connecticut State University, School of Graduate Studies, College of Liberal Arts and Social Sciences, Department of Design, New Britain, CT 06050-4010. Offers information design (MA). *Program availability:* Part-time, evening/weekend. *Faculty:* 1 full-time (0 women), 1 (woman) part-time/adjunct. *Students:* 10 full-time (5 women), 6 part-time (5 women); includes 2 minority (1 Black or African American, non-Hispanic/Latino; 1 Two or more races, non-Hispanic/Latino). Average age 28. 15 applicants, 87% accepted, 11 enrolled. In 2017, 6 master's awarded. *Degree requirements:* For master's, thesis or alternative, research project. *Entrance requirements:* For master's, portfolio, minimum undergraduate GPA of 3.0, essay. Additional exam requirements/recommendations for international students: Required—TOEFL (minimum score 550 paper-based; 79 iBT); Recommended—IELTS (minimum score 6.5). *Application deadline:* For fall admission, 8/1 for domestic students, 5/1 for international students; for spring admission, 11/1 for domestic and international students. Applications are processed on a rolling basis. Application fee: $50. Electronic applications accepted. *Expenses:* Tuition, area resident: Full-time $6757. Tuition, state resident: full-time $9750; part-time $374 per credit. Tuition, nonresident: full-time $18,102; part-time $374 per credit. *Required fees:* $4635; $255 per credit. *Financial support:* In 2017–18, 7 students received support. Career-related internships or fieldwork, Federal Work-Study, scholarships/grants, and unspecified assistantships available. Support available to part-time students. Financial award application deadline: 3/1; financial award applicants required to submit FAFSA. *Unit head:* Dr. Eleanor Thornton, Chair, 860-832-2564, E-mail: thorntone@ccsu.edu. *Application contact:* Patricia Gardner, Associate Director of Graduate Studies, 860-832-2350, Fax: 860-832-2362.
Website: http://www.design.ccsu.edu/

Columbia University, School of Professional Studies, Program in Information and Archive Management, New York, NY 10027. Offers MS. *Program availability:* Part-time. *Entrance requirements:* For master's, minimum undergraduate GPA of 3.0. Additional exam requirements/recommendations for international students: Required—American Language Program placement test. Electronic applications accepted. *Expenses:* Tuition: Full-time $44,864; part-time $1704 per credit. *Required fees:* $2370 per semester. One-time fee: $105. *Faculty research:* Library science technology, information systems.

Information Studies

Cornell University, Graduate School, Graduate Fields of Arts and Sciences, Field of Information Science, Ithaca, NY 14853. Offers cognition (PhD); human computer interaction (PhD); information science (PhD); information systems (PhD); social aspects of information (PhD). *Degree requirements:* For doctorate, comprehensive exam, thesis/dissertation. *Entrance requirements:* For doctorate, GRE General Test, 3 letters of recommendation. Additional exam requirements/recommendations for international students: Required—TOEFL (minimum score 550 paper-based; 77 iBT). Electronic applications accepted. *Faculty research:* Digital libraries, game theory, data mining, human-computer interaction, computational linguistics.

Dalhousie University, Faculty of Management, School of Information Management, Halifax, NS B3H 3J5, Canada. Offers MIM, MLIS, LL B/MLIS, MBA/MLIS, MLIS/MPA, MLIS/MREM. *Accreditation:* ALA (one or more programs are accredited). *Program availability:* Part-time. *Degree requirements:* For master's, one foreign language, thesis optional. *Entrance requirements:* For master's, resume, interview. Additional exam requirements/recommendations for international students: Required—TOEFL, IELTS, CANTEST, CAEL, or Michigan English Language Assessment Battery. Electronic applications accepted. *Faculty research:* Information-seeking behavior, electronic text design, browsing in digital environments, information diffusion among scientists.

Dominican University, School of Information Studies, River Forest, IL 60305-1099. Offers information management (MSIM); knowledge management (Certificate); library and information science (MLIS, MPS, PhD); special studies (CSS); MBA/MLIS; MLIS/MA. MLIS/M Div offered jointly with McCormick Theological Seminary, MLIS/MA with Loyola University Chicago, MLIS/MM with Northwestern University. *Accreditation:* ALA (one or more programs are accredited). *Program availability:* Part-time, evening/weekend, 100% online, blended/hybrid learning. *Faculty:* 11 full-time (7 women), 16 part-time/adjunct (10 women). *Students:* 58 full-time (49 women), 184 part-time (145 women); includes 53 minority (29 Black or African American, non-Hispanic/Latino; 2 Asian, non-Hispanic/Latino; 21 Hispanic/Latino; 1 Two or more races, non-Hispanic/Latino), 5 international. Average age 34. 84 applicants, 94% accepted, 52 enrolled. In 2017, 86 master's awarded. *Degree requirements:* For doctorate, thesis/dissertation. *Entrance requirements:* For master's, minimum GPA of 3.0, GRE General Test, or MAT; for doctorate, MLIS or related MA, minimum GPA of 3.0, GRE General Test, or MAT. Additional exam requirements/recommendations for international students: Required—TOEFL. *Application deadline:* For fall admission, 6/1 priority date for domestic students; for winter admission, 3/1 priority date for domestic students; for spring admission, 10/1 priority date for domestic students. Applications are processed on a rolling basis. Application fee: $25. *Expenses:* Contact institution. *Financial support:* Fellowships, research assistantships, career-related internships or fieldwork, scholarships/grants, and unspecified assistantships available. Support available to part-time students. Financial award application deadline: 4/15; financial award applicants required to submit FAFSA. *Faculty research:* Productivity and the information environment, bibliometrics, library history, subject access, library materials and services for children. *Unit head:* Dr. Kate Marek, Director, 708-524-6648, Fax: 708-524-6657, E-mail: kmarek@dom.edu. *Application contact:* Catherine Galarza-Espino, Coordinator of Graduate Marketing and Recruiting, 708-524-6983, E-mail: cgalarza@dom.edu.
Website: http://sois.dom.edu/

Florida State University, The Graduate School, College of Communication and Information, School of Information, Tallahassee, FL 32306-2100. Offers information (MA, MS, PhD, Specialist); information technology (MS). *Accreditation:* ALA (one or more programs are accredited). *Program availability:* Part-time, evening/weekend, 100% online, blended/hybrid learning. *Faculty:* 27 full-time (14 women), 4 part-time/adjunct (2 women). *Students:* 45 full-time (26 women), 264 part-time (197 women); includes 102 minority (31 Black or African American, non-Hispanic/Latino; 13 Asian, non-Hispanic/Latino; 46 Hispanic/Latino; 12 Two or more races, non-Hispanic/Latino), 16 international. Average age 34. 168 applicants, 62% accepted, 83 enrolled. In 2017, 108 master's, 7 doctorates, 2 other advanced degrees awarded. Terminal master's awarded for partial completion of doctoral program. *Degree requirements:* For master's, thesis optional, minimum GPA of 3.0, 36 hours (MSI); 32 hours (MSIT); for doctorate, comprehensive exam, thesis/dissertation, dissertation defense, manuscript clearance, minimum GPA of 3.0; for Specialist, minimum GPA of 3.0; 30 hours. *Entrance requirements:* For master's, GRE (recommended minimum percentile of 50 on each of the verbal and quantitative portions and writing score of 4.0), minimum GPA of 3.0 on last 2 years of baccalaureate degree, resume, statement of goals, two letters of recommendation, official transcripts from every college-level institution attended; for doctorate, GRE (recommended minimum percentile of 50 on each of the verbal and quantitative portions and writing score of 4.0), minimum GPA of 3.0 on last degree program, resume, 3 letters of recommendation, personal/goals statement, writing sample, brief digital video, official transcripts from all college-level institutions attended; for Specialist, GRE (recommended minimum percentile of 50 on each of the verbal and quantitative portions and writing score of 4.0), minimum graduate GPA of 3.2, resume, statement of goals, 2 letters of recommendation, writing sample, official transcripts from every college-level institution attended. Additional exam requirements/recommendations for international students: Required—TOEFL (minimum score 585 paper-based; 94 iBT), IELTS (minimum score 6.5). *Application deadline:* For fall admission, 7/1 for domestic and international students; for spring admission, 11/1 for domestic and international students. Applications are processed on a rolling basis. Application fee: $30. Electronic applications accepted. *Expenses:* Contact institution. *Financial support:* In 2017–18, 115 students received support, including 2 research assistantships with full tuition reimbursements available (averaging $18,310 per year), 24 teaching assistantships with full tuition reimbursements available (averaging $18,310 per year); career-related internships or fieldwork, Federal Work-Study, health care benefits, tuition waivers (full), and 4 assistantships (averaging $18,310) also available. Financial award application deadline: 3/1; financial award applicants required to submit FAFSA. *Faculty research:* Information technology, social informatics, health information, human information behavior, youth services. *Total annual research expenditures:* $296,509. *Unit head:* Dr. Lorri Mon, Director/Associate Professor, 850-644-5776, Fax: 850-644-9763, E-mail: lmon@fsu.edu. *Application contact:* Student Services, 850-645-3280, Fax: 850-644-9763, E-mail: ischooladvising@admin.fsu.edu.
Website: http://ischool.cci.fsu.edu

Lock Haven University of Pennsylvania, The Stephen Poorman College of Business, Information Systems, and Human Services, Lock Haven, PA 17745-2390. Offers clinical mental health counseling (MS); sport science (MS). *Program availability:* Online learning. *Degree requirements:* For master's, thesis. *Entrance requirements:* For master's, minimum undergraduate GPA of 3.0. Additional exam requirements/recommendations for international students: Required—TOEFL. Electronic applications accepted.

Louisiana State University and Agricultural & Mechanical College, Graduate School, College of Human Sciences and Education, School of Library and Information Science, Baton Rouge, LA 70803. Offers MLIS. *Accreditation:* ALA. *Faculty:* 8 full-time (3 women). *Students:* 67 full-time (59 women), 129 part-time (110 women); includes 45 minority (32 Black or African American, non-Hispanic/Latino; 10 Hispanic/Latino; 3 Two or more races, non-Hispanic/Latino). Average age 33. 96 applicants, 83% accepted, 63 enrolled. In 2017, 37 master's awarded. *Financial support:* In 2017–18, 1 research

assistantship (averaging $14,198 per year), 10 teaching assistantships (averaging $14,266 per year) were awarded. *Total annual research expenditures:* $345.

Mansfield University of Pennsylvania, Graduate Studies, Program in School Library and Information Technologies, Mansfield, PA 16933. Offers library science (M Ed). *Program availability:* Part-time, evening/weekend, online learning. *Degree requirements:* For master's, comprehensive exam, thesis optional. *Entrance requirements:* For master's, minimum GPA of 3.0. Additional exam requirements/recommendations for international students: Required—TOEFL (minimum score 550 paper-based). Electronic applications accepted. *Expenses:* Contact institution.

McGill University, Faculty of Graduate and Postdoctoral Studies, Faculty of Education, School of Information Studies, Montréal, QC H3A 2T5, Canada. Offers MLIS, PhD, Certificate, Diploma. *Accreditation:* ALA (one or more programs are accredited).

Metropolitan State University, College of Management, St. Paul, MN 55106-5000. Offers business administration (MBA, DBA); business analytics (Graduate Certificate); database administration (Graduate Certificate); global supply chain management (Graduate Certificate); information assurance security (Graduate Certificate); management information systems (MMIS); MIS generalist (Graduate Certificate); MIS systems analysis and design (Graduate Certificate); project management (Graduate Certificate). *Program availability:* Part-time, evening/weekend. *Degree requirements:* For master's, thesis optional, computer language (MMIS). *Entrance requirements:* For master's, GMAT (for MBA), resume. Additional exam requirements/recommendations for international students: Required—TOEFL (minimum score 550 paper-based). *Application deadline:* For fall admission, 7/15 for international students; for winter admission, 11/15 for international students; for spring admission, 3/15 for international students. Applications are processed on a rolling basis. Application fee: $20. Electronic applications accepted. *Expenses:* Tuition, state resident: part-time $388.55 per credit. Tuition, nonresident: part-time $777.11 per credit. *Required fees:* $35.11 per credit. Part-time tuition and fees vary according to campus/location and program. *Financial support:* Research assistantships with partial tuition reimbursements, career-related internships or fieldwork, and Federal Work-Study available. Support available to part-time students. Financial award applicants required to submit FAFSA. *Faculty research:* Yugoslav economic system, workers' cooperatives, participative management and job enrichment, global business systems. *Unit head:* Allen Bellas, Interim Dean, 612-659-7272, Fax: 612-659-7268, E-mail: allen.bellas@metrostate.edu. *Application contact:* Allen Bellas, Interim Dean, 612-659-7272, Fax: 612-659-7268, E-mail: allen.bellas@metrostate.edu.
Website: https://www.metrostate.edu/academics/management

Missouri Western State University, Program in Information Management, St. Joseph, MO 64507-2294. Offers enterprise resource planning (MIM). *Program availability:* Part-time. *Students:* 9 full-time (6 women), 9 part-time (3 women); includes 1 minority (Black or African American, non-Hispanic/Latino), 9 international. Average age 32. 7 applicants, 100% accepted, 3 enrolled. In 2017, 33 master's awarded. *Entrance requirements:* Additional exam requirements/recommendations for international students: Recommended—TOEFL (minimum score 79 iBT), IELTS (minimum score 6). *Application deadline:* For fall admission, 7/15 for domestic and international students; for spring admission, 10/1 for domestic and international students; for summer admission, 3/15 for domestic students. Applications are processed on a rolling basis. Application fee: $45 ($50 for international students). Electronic applications accepted. *Expenses:* Tuition, state resident: full-time $6391; part-time $336 per credit hour. Tuition, nonresident: full-time $11,483; part-time $604 per credit hour. *Required fees:* $542; $99 per credit hour. $176 per semester. One-time fee: $45. Tuition and fees vary according to course load and program. *Financial support:* Scholarships/grants and unspecified assistantships available. Support available to part-time students. *Unit head:* Dr. Logan Jones, Assistant Professor, 816-271-4351, E-mail: jones@missouriwestern.edu. *Application contact:* Dr. Benjamin D. Caldwell, Dean of the Graduate School, 816-271-4394, Fax: 816-271-4525, E-mail: graduate@missouriwestern.edu.
Website: https://www.missouriwestern.edu/mim/

Monmouth University, Graduate Studies, Program in Computer Science, West Long Branch, NJ 07764-1898. Offers MS. *Program availability:* Part-time, evening/weekend. *Faculty:* 5 full-time (3 women), 7 part-time/adjunct (0 women). *Students:* 28 full-time (9 women), 23 part-time (6 women); includes 7 minority (2 Black or African American, non-Hispanic/Latino; 4 Asian, non-Hispanic/Latino; 1 Hispanic/Latino), 25 international. Average age 29. In 2017, 48 master's awarded. *Degree requirements:* For master's, thesis (for some programs), practicum. *Entrance requirements:* For master's, minimum GPA of 3.0 in major, 2.75 overall; two letters of recommendation; calculus I and II with minimum C grade; two semesters of computer programming within past five years with minimum B grade; undergraduate degree in major that requires substantial component of software development and/or business administration. Additional exam requirements/recommendations for international students: Required—TOEFL (minimum score 550 paper-based, 79 iBT), IELTS (minimum score 6), Michigan English Language Assessment Battery (minimum score 77) or Certificate of Advanced English (minimum score 160). *Application deadline:* For fall admission, 7/15 priority date for domestic students, 6/1 for international students; for spring admission, 12/1 priority date for domestic students, 11/1 for international students; for summer admission, 5/1 for domestic students. Applications are processed on a rolling basis. Application fee: $50. Electronic applications accepted. *Expenses:* Tuition: Full-time $21,366; part-time $7122 per credit. *Required fees:* $700; $175 per term. *Financial support:* In 2017–18, 26 students received support. Institutionally sponsored loans, scholarships/grants, and unspecified assistantships available. Support available to part-time students. Financial award applicants required to submit FAFSA. *Faculty research:* Databases, natural language processing, protocols, performance analysis, communications networks (systems), cybersecurity. *Unit head:* Dr. Jiacun Wang, Director, 732-571-7501, Fax: 732-263-5202, E-mail: jwang@monmouth.edu. *Application contact:* Andrea Thompson, Graduate Admission Counselor, 732-571-3452, Fax: 732-263-5123, E-mail: gradadm@monmouth.edu.
Website: https://www.monmouth.edu/graduate/ms-computer-science/

North Carolina Central University, School of Library and Information Sciences, Durham, NC 27707-3129. Offers MIS, MLS. *Accreditation:* ALA (one or more programs are accredited). *Program availability:* Part-time, evening/weekend. *Degree requirements:* For master's, one foreign language, thesis, research paper, or project. *Entrance requirements:* For master's, GRE, 90 hours in liberal arts. Additional exam requirements/recommendations for international students: Required—TOEFL. *Application deadline:* For fall admission, 8/1 for domestic students. Application fee: $30. *Expenses:* Tuition, state resident: full-time $2770; part-time $692.50 per credit hour. Tuition, nonresident: full-time $9247; part-time $2311.75 per credit hour. *Financial support:* Application deadline: 5/1; applicants required to submit FAFSA. *Unit head:* Dr. Jon P. Gant, Dean, 919-530-6402, Fax: 919-530-6402, E-mail: slis-dean@nccu.edu. *Application contact:* Dr. Jon P. Gant, Dean, 919-530-6402, Fax: 919-530-6402, E-mail: slis-dean@nccu.edu.
Website: http://www.nccuslis.org/

Pratt Institute, School of Information, New York, NY 10011. Offers MS, Adv C, JD/MS, MS/MFA. *Accreditation:* ALA. *Program availability:* Part-time. *Students:* 134 full-time (109 women), 52 part-time (43 women); includes 44 minority (10 Black or African

American, non-Hispanic/Latino; 10 Asian, non-Hispanic/Latino; 19 Hispanic/Latino; 5 Two or more races, non-Hispanic/Latino), 31 international. Average age 30. 303 applicants, 75% accepted, 67 enrolled. In 2017, 59 master's, 1 other advanced degree awarded. *Degree requirements:* For master's, thesis. *Entrance requirements:* For degree, master's degree in library and information science. Additional exam requirements/recommendations for international students: Required—TOEFL (minimum score 600 paper-based; 100 iBT). *Application deadline:* For fall admission, 1/5 for domestic and international students; for spring admission, 10/1 for domestic and international students. Applications are processed on a rolling basis. Application fee: $50 ($90 for international students). Electronic applications accepted. *Expenses:* $24,768 tuition full-time; $1,974 fees. *Financial support:* Career-related internships or fieldwork, Federal Work-Study, institutionally sponsored loans, scholarships/grants, health care benefits, and unspecified assistantships available. Support available to part-time students. Financial award application deadline: 2/1; financial award applicants required to submit FAFSA. *Faculty research:* Development of urban libraries and information centers, medical and law librarianship, information management. *Unit head:* Anthony Cocciolo, Interim Dean, 212-647-7702, Fax: 212-367-2492, E-mail: acocciol@pratt.edu. *Application contact:* Natalie Capannelli, Director of Graduate Admissions, 718-636-3551, Fax: 718-399-4242, E-mail: ncapanne@pratt.edu. Website: https://www.pratt.edu/academics/information/

See Display on this page and Close-Up on page 1547.

Queens College of the City University of New York, Division of Social Sciences, Graduate School of Library and Information Studies, Queens, NY 11367-1597. Offers archives and preservation of cultural materials (AC); children's and young adult services in the public library (AC); librarianship (AC); library science (MLS); school library media specialist (MLS). *Accreditation:* ALA (one or more programs are accredited). *Program availability:* Part-time, evening/weekend. *Students:* 28 full-time (20 women), 289 part-time (205 women); includes 116 minority (37 Black or African American, non-Hispanic/Latino; 17 Asian, non-Hispanic/Latino; 53 Hispanic/Latino; 9 Two or more races, non-Hispanic/Latino), 4 international. Average age 33. *Degree requirements:* For master's, thesis; for AC, thesis optional. *Entrance requirements:* For master's, minimum GPA of 3.0; for AC, master's degree or equivalent. Additional exam requirements/recommendations for international students: Required—TOEFL, IELTS. *Application deadline:* For fall admission, 4/1 for domestic students; for spring admission, 11/1 for domestic students. Applications are processed on a rolling basis. Application fee: $125. Electronic applications accepted. *Financial support:* Career-related internships or fieldwork and unspecified assistantships available. Financial award application deadline: 4/1; financial award applicants required to submit FAFSA. *Unit head:* Colleen Cool, Director/Chair, 718-997-3790, E-mail: colleen.cool@qc.cuny.edu. *Application contact:* Elizabeth D'Amico-Ramirez, Assistant Director of Graduate Admissions, 718-997-5203, E-mail: elizabeth.damicoramirez@qc.cuny.edu.

Queen's University at Kingston, School of Graduate Studies, Faculty of Arts and Sciences, Department of Sociology, Kingston, ON K7L 3N6, Canada. Offers communication and Information technology (MA, PhD); feminist sociology (MA, PhD); socio-legal studies (MA, PhD); sociological theory (MA, PhD). *Program availability:* Part-time. *Degree requirements:* For master's, thesis; for doctorate, comprehensive exam, thesis/dissertation. *Entrance requirements:* For master's, honors bachelors degree in sociology; for doctorate, honors bachelors degree, masters degree in sociology. Additional exam requirements/recommendations for international students: Required—TOEFL. *Faculty research:* Social change and modernization, social control, deviance and criminology, surveillance.

Rutgers University–New Brunswick, School of Communication and Information, Program in Communication and Information Studies, Piscataway, NJ 08854-8097. Offers MCIS. *Program availability:* Part-time. *Entrance requirements:* For master's, GRE General Test. Additional exam requirements/recommendations for international students: Required—TOEFL. Electronic applications accepted. *Faculty research:* Communication processes and systems, information process and systems, human information and communication behavior.

Rutgers University–New Brunswick, School of Communication and Information, Program in Communication, Information and Library Studies, Piscataway, NJ 08854-8097. Offers PhD. *Program availability:* Part-time. *Degree requirements:* For doctorate, comprehensive exam, thesis/dissertation, qualifying exams. *Entrance requirements:* For doctorate, GRE General Test, proficiency in statistics. Additional exam requirements/recommendations for international students: Required—TOEFL (minimum score 600 paper-based). Electronic applications accepted. *Faculty research:* Information science, media studies.

St. Catherine University, Graduate Programs, Program in Library and Information Science, St. Paul, MN 55105. Offers MLIS. *Accreditation:* ALA. *Program availability:* Part-time, evening/weekend. *Degree requirements:* For master's, microcomputer competency. *Entrance requirements:* For master's, GRE or MAT, minimum GPA of 3.2 or GRE. Additional exam requirements/recommendations for international students: Required—Michigan English Language Assessment Battery or TOEFL (minimum score 600 paper-based; 100 iBT). *Application deadline:* For fall admission, 3/1 for domestic students; for winter admission, 10/1 for domestic students. Application fee: $35. *Expenses:* Contact institution. *Financial support:* Institutionally sponsored loans available. Support available to part-time students. Financial award application deadline: 4/1; financial award applicants required to submit FAFSA. *Unit head:* Anthony Molaro, Director, 651-690-6626. *Application contact:* Kristina Sande, Director of Graduate Admissions, 651-690-6507, Fax: 651-690-6064. Website: https://www.stkate.edu/academics/graduate-degrees/academic-programs/mlis

St. John's University, St. John's College of Liberal Arts and Sciences, Division of Library and Information Science, Queens, NY 11439. Offers library science (MS); management for information professionals (Adv C); MA/MS. *Accreditation:* ALA (one or more programs are accredited). *Program availability:* Part-time, online only, 100% online. *Faculty:* 5 full-time (2 women), 1 (woman) part-time/adjunct. *Students:* 25 full-time (22 women), 39 part-time (33 women); includes 19 minority (7 Black or African American, non-Hispanic/Latino; 1 American Indian or Alaska Native, non-Hispanic/Latino; 4 Asian, non-Hispanic/Latino; 6 Hispanic/Latino; 1 Two or more races, non-Hispanic/Latino). Average age 33. 63 applicants, 63% accepted, 21 enrolled. In 2017, 30 master's awarded. *Degree requirements:* For master's, e-portfolio end-of-program assessment; for Adv C, 15 credits (five courses) including capstone course. *Entrance requirements:* For master's, letters of recommendation, transcripts, resume, personal statement. Additional exam requirements/recommendations for international students: Required—TOEFL (minimum score 80 iBT), IELTS (minimum score 6.5). *Application deadline:* For fall admission, 5/1 for domestic students; for spring admission, 11/1 for domestic students. Applications are processed on a rolling basis. Application fee: $70. Electronic applications accepted. *Expenses:* $23,724 per year. *Financial support:* Fellowships, research assistantships, teaching assistantships, scholarships/grants, tuition waivers, and unspecified assistantships available. Support available to part-time students. Financial award application deadline: 2/1; financial award applicants required to submit FAFSA. *Faculty research:* Social justice in the information professions, teen spaces in public libraries, information organization, management, marketing and

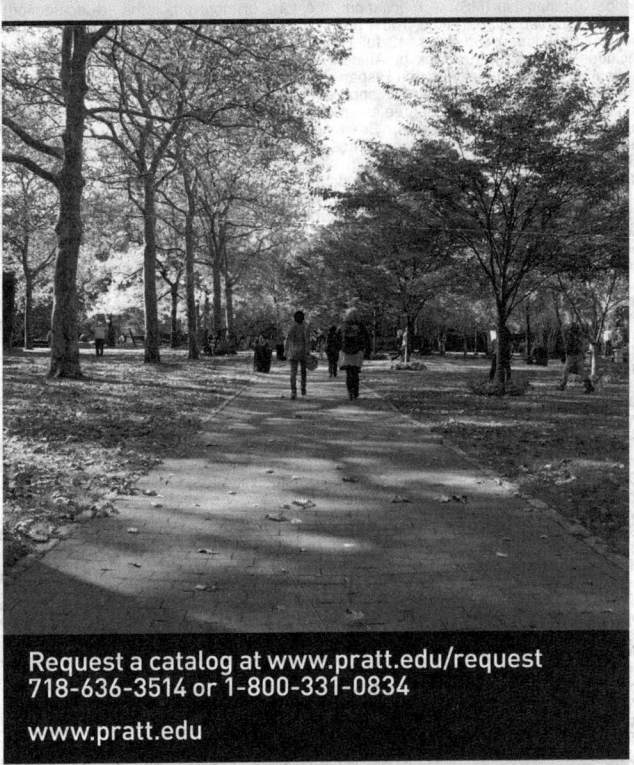

Information Studies

advocacy in information organizations, digital libraries. *Total annual research expenditures:* $24,163. *Unit head:* Dr. James Vorbach, Director, 718-990-1834, Fax: 718-990-2071, E-mail: vorbachj@stjohns.edu. *Application contact:* Robert Medrano, Director of Graduate Admissions, 718-990-1601, Fax: 718-990-5686, E-mail: gradhelp@stjohns.edu.
Website: https://www.stjohns.edu/academics/schools-and-colleges/st-johns-college-liberal-arts-and-sciences/library-and-information-science

Southern Connecticut State University, School of Graduate Studies, School of Education, Department of Information and Library Science, New Haven, CT 06515-1355. Offers information studies (Diploma); library science (MLS). *Program availability:* Part-time, evening/weekend. *Degree requirements:* For master's and Diploma, thesis or alternative. *Entrance requirements:* For master's, GRE General Test, interview, minimum QPA of 2.7, introductory computer science course; for Diploma, master's degree in library science or information science. Electronic applications accepted.

Syracuse University, School of Information Studies, MS Program in Information Management, Syracuse, NY 13244. Offers MS. *Program availability:* Part-time, evening/weekend, online learning. *Entrance requirements:* For master's, GRE General Test, personal statement, two letters of recommendation, resume. Additional exam requirements/recommendations for international students: Required—TOEFL (minimum score 100 iBT). *Application deadline:* For fall admission, 2/1 priority date for domestic and international students; for spring admission, 10/15 priority date for domestic and international students. Applications are processed on a rolling basis. Application fee: $75. Electronic applications accepted. *Financial support:* Fellowships with full tuition reimbursements, research assistantships with partial tuition reimbursements, teaching assistantships with partial tuition reimbursements, and scholarships/grants available. Financial award application deadline: 1/1; financial award applicants required to submit FAFSA. *Faculty research:* Increasing the effectiveness of managers and executives who work with information resources, designing and managing mission-critical information technologies within organizations, developing corporate and government policies to maximize the benefits resulting from the widespread use of these technologies. *Unit head:* Carsten Oesterlund, Program Director, 315-443-2911, Fax: 315-443-6886, E-mail: igrad@syr.edu. *Application contact:* Susan Corieri, Assistant Dean for Enrollment Management, 315-443-2575, E-mail: igrad@syr.edu.
Website: https://ischool.syr.edu/academics/graduate/masters-degrees/ms-in-information-management/

Universidad del Turabo, Graduate Programs, Programs in Education, Program in Library Service and Information Technology, Gurabo, PR 00778-3030. Offers M Ed. *Program availability:* Part-time, evening/weekend. *Entrance requirements:* For master's, GRE, EXADEP, GMAT, interview, official transcript, essay, recommendation letters. Electronic applications accepted.

Université de Montréal, Faculty of Arts and Sciences, School of Library and Information Sciences, Montréal, QC H3C 3J7, Canada. Offers information sciences (MIS, PhD). *Accreditation:* ALA (one or more programs are accredited). *Degree requirements:* For master's, thesis optional. *Entrance requirements:* For master's, interview, master's degree in library and information science or equivalent. Electronic applications accepted.

University at Buffalo, the State University of New York, Graduate School, Graduate School of Education, Department of Library and Information Studies, Buffalo, NY 14260. Offers information and library science (MS); library and information studies (Certificate); school librarianship (MS). *Accreditation:* ALA (one or more programs are accredited). *Program availability:* Part-time, 100% online. *Faculty:* 9 full-time (6 women), 8 part-time/adjunct (6 women). *Students:* 42 full-time (32 women), 162 part-time (131 women); includes 11 minority (5 Black or African American, non-Hispanic/Latino; 2 American Indian or Alaska Native, non-Hispanic/Latino; 4 Asian, non-Hispanic/Latino); 2 international. Average age 34. 117 applicants, 91% accepted, 73 enrolled. In 2017, 62 master's, 1 other advanced degree awarded. *Degree requirements:* For master's, thesis optional; for Certificate, thesis. *Entrance requirements:* For master's, letters of recommendation. Additional exam requirements/recommendations for international students: Required—TOEFL (minimum score 550 paper-based; 79 iBT). *Application deadline:* For fall admission, 4/1 priority date for domestic and international students; for spring admission, 10/15 priority date for domestic students, 10/15 for international students. Applications are processed on a rolling basis. Application fee: $50. Electronic applications accepted. *Financial support:* In 2017–18, 16 fellowships (averaging $2,345 per year), 6 research assistantships with tuition reimbursements (averaging $10,222 per year) were awarded; teaching assistantships, Federal Work-Study, scholarships/grants, tuition waivers (full and partial), and unspecified assistantships also available. Support available to part-time students. Financial award application deadline: 3/1; financial award applicants required to submit FAFSA. *Faculty research:* Information-seeking behavior, thesauri, impact of technology, questioning behaviors, educational informatics. *Total annual research expenditures:* $56,553. *Unit head:* Dr. Heidi Julien, Chair, 716-645-1474, Fax: 716-645-3775, E-mail: heidijul@buffalo.edu. *Application contact:* Pat Glinski, Admissions Assistant, 716-645-2110, Fax: 716-645-7937, E-mail: gse-info@buffalo.edu.
Website: http://www.gse.buffalo.edu/lis/

The University of Alabama, Graduate School, College of Communication and Information Sciences, School of Library and Information Studies, Tuscaloosa, AL 35487. Offers book arts (MFA); library and information studies (MLIS, PhD). *Accreditation:* ALA (one or more programs are accredited). *Program availability:* Part-time, evening/weekend, online learning. *Faculty:* 12 full-time (5 women), 1 (woman) part-time/adjunct. *Students:* 55 full-time (42 women), 174 part-time (145 women); includes 27 minority (13 Black or African American, non-Hispanic/Latino; 2 Asian, non-Hispanic/Latino; 6 Hispanic/Latino; 6 Two or more races, non-Hispanic/Latino), 4 international. Average age 33. 135 applicants, 81% accepted, 85 enrolled. In 2017, 73 master's awarded. *Degree requirements:* For master's, comprehensive exam (for some programs), thesis optional; for doctorate, comprehensive exam, thesis/dissertation. *Entrance requirements:* For master's, GRE General Test or MAT, minimum GPA of 3.0; for doctorate, GRE. Additional exam requirements/recommendations for international students: Required—TOEFL. *Application deadline:* For fall admission, 7/1 priority date for domestic and international students; for spring admission, 11/1 priority date for domestic and international students. Applications are processed on a rolling basis. Application fee: $50 ($60 for international students). Electronic applications accepted. *Financial support:* In 2017–18, 18 students received support, including fellowships with full tuition reimbursements available (averaging $15,000 per year), research assistantships with tuition reimbursements available (averaging $6,183 per year), teaching assistantships with tuition reimbursements available (averaging $6,183 per year); career-related internships or fieldwork, scholarships/grants, health care benefits, tuition waivers (full), unspecified assistantships, and 15 grant-funded fellowships also available. Support available to part-time students. Financial award application deadline: 3/15. *Faculty research:* Library administration, user services, digital libraries, book arts, evaluation. *Unit head:* Dr. Ann Ethelynd Prentice, Director and Professor, 205-348-4610, Fax: 205-348-3746, E-mail: aeprentice@ua.edu. *Application contact:* Dr. Ann Bourne, Assistant Director, 205-348-1524, Fax: 205-348-3746, E-mail: abourne@ua.edu.
Website: http://www.slis.ua.edu/

University of Alberta, Faculty of Graduate Studies and Research, School of Library and Information Studies, Edmonton, AB T6G 2E1, Canada. Offers MLIS. *Accreditation:* ALA. *Entrance requirements:* Additional exam requirements/recommendations for international students: Required—TOEFL, Canadian Academic English Language Assessment. Electronic applications accepted. *Faculty research:* Intellectual freedom, materials for children and young adults, library classification, multi-media literacy.

The University of Arizona, College of Social and Behavioral Sciences, School of Information Resources and Library Science, Tucson, AZ 85721. Offers MA, PhD. *Accreditation:* ALA (one or more programs are accredited). *Program availability:* Part-time. *Degree requirements:* For master's, proficiency in disk operating system (DOS); for doctorate, thesis/dissertation. *Entrance requirements:* For master's and doctorate, GRE General Test, 3 letters of recommendation, resume. Additional exam requirements/recommendations for international students: Required—TOEFL (minimum score 550 paper-based; 79 iBT). Electronic applications accepted. *Faculty research:* Microcomputer applications; quantitative methods systems; information transfer, planning, evaluation, and technology.

The University of British Columbia, Faculty of Arts, School of Library, Archival and Information Studies, Dual Master of Archival Studies/Master of Library and Information Studies Program, Vancouver, BC V6T 1Z1, Canada. Offers MLIS/MAS. *Entrance requirements:* Additional exam requirements/recommendations for international students: Required—TOEFL. Electronic applications accepted. *Expenses:* Contact institution. *Faculty research:* Computer systems/database design, information-seeking behavior, archives and records management, children's literature and services, digital libraries and archives.

The University of British Columbia, Faculty of Arts, School of Library, Archival and Information Studies, Master of Library and Information Studies Program, Vancouver, BC V6T 1Z1, Canada. Offers MLIS. *Accreditation:* ALA. *Program availability:* Part-time. *Degree requirements:* For master's, thesis optional. *Entrance requirements:* For master's, minimum GPA of 3.3 in undergraduate upper-division courses. Additional exam requirements/recommendations for international students: Required—TOEFL. Electronic applications accepted. *Expenses:* Contact institution. *Faculty research:* Computer systems/database design; digital libraries; metadata/classification; human-computer interaction; children's literature and services.

The University of British Columbia, Faculty of Arts, School of Library, Archival and Information Studies, PhD Program in Library, Archival and Information Studies, Vancouver, BC V6T 1Z1, Canada. Offers PhD. *Degree requirements:* For doctorate, thesis/dissertation. *Entrance requirements:* For doctorate, GRE, minimum GPA of 3.3 in MAS or MLIS. Additional exam requirements/recommendations for international students: Required—TOEFL. Electronic applications accepted. *Expenses:* Contact institution. *Faculty research:* Computer systems/database design; library and archival management; archival description and organization; children's literature and youth services; interactive information retrieval.

University of California, Berkeley, Graduate Division, School of Information, Berkeley, CA 94720-1500. Offers MIDS, MIMS, PhD. *Degree requirements:* For doctorate, thesis/dissertation, qualifying exam. *Entrance requirements:* For master's, GRE General Test, minimum GPA of 3.0, previous course work in java or C programming, 3 letters of recommendation; for doctorate, GRE General Test, minimum GPA of 3.0. Additional exam requirements/recommendations for international students: Required—TOEFL. Electronic applications accepted. *Faculty research:* Information retrieval research, design and evaluation of information systems, work practice-based design of information systems, economics of information, intellectual property law.

University of California, Los Angeles, Graduate Division, Graduate School of Education and Information Studies, Department of Information Studies, Los Angeles, CA 90095-1521. Offers archival studies (MLIS); informatics (MLIS); information studies (PhD); library and information science (Certificate); library studies (MLIS); moving image archive studies (MA); rare books, print and visual culture (MLIS); MBA/MLIS; MLIS/MA. *Accreditation:* ALA (one or more programs are accredited). Terminal master's awarded for partial completion of doctoral program. *Degree requirements:* For master's, thesis or alternative, professional portfolio; for doctorate, thesis/dissertation, oral and written qualifying exams. *Entrance requirements:* For master's, GRE General Test, previous course work in statistics; for doctorate, GRE General Test, previous course work in statistics, 2 samples of research writing in English. Additional exam requirements/recommendations for international students: Required—TOEFL (minimum score 560 paper-based; 87 iBT), IELTS (minimum score 7). Electronic applications accepted. *Faculty research:* Digital libraries, archives and electronic records, interface design, cultural informatics, preservation/conservation, access.

University of Hawaii at Manoa, Office of Graduate Education, College of Natural Sciences, Department of Information and Computer Sciences, Library and Information Science Program, Honolulu, HI 96822-2233. Offers advanced library and information science (Graduate Certificate); library and information science (MLI Sc). *Accreditation:* ALA (one or more programs are accredited). *Program availability:* Part-time. *Degree requirements:* For master's, comprehensive exam, thesis optional. *Entrance requirements:* For master's, GRE General Test. Additional exam requirements/recommendations for international students: Required—TOEFL (minimum score 600 paper-based). Electronic applications accepted. *Faculty research:* Information behavior, evaluation of electronic information sources, online learning, history of libraries, information literacy.

University of Illinois at Urbana–Champaign, Graduate College, School of Information Sciences, Champaign, IL 61820. Offers bioinformatics (MS); digital libraries (CAS); information management (MS); library and information science (MS, PhD, CAS). *Accreditation:* ALA (one or more programs are accredited). *Program availability:* Part-time, online learning. *Entrance requirements:* For degree, master's degree in library and information science or related field with minimum GPA of 3.0.

The University of Iowa, Graduate College, School of Library and Information Science, Iowa City, IA 52242-1316. Offers MA, PhD, MA/Certificate, PhD/Certificate. *Accreditation:* ALA (one or more programs are accredited). *Degree requirements:* For master's, thesis optional, exam, portfolio. *Entrance requirements:* For master's, GRE General Test, minimum GPA of 3.0. Additional exam requirements/recommendations for international students: Required—TOEFL (minimum score 550 paper-based; 81 iBT). Electronic applications accepted.

University of Maryland, College Park, Academic Affairs, College of Information Studies, College Park, MD 20742. Offers MIM, MLS, PhD, MA/MLS. *Accreditation:* ALA (one or more programs are accredited). *Program availability:* Part-time, evening/weekend. Terminal master's awarded for partial completion of doctoral program. *Degree requirements:* For master's, thesis optional; for doctorate, comprehensive exam, thesis/dissertation, 1-year residency. *Entrance requirements:* For master's and doctorate, GRE General Test, minimum GPA of 3.0, 3 letters of recommendation. Additional exam requirements/recommendations for international students: Required—TOEFL. Electronic applications accepted.

University of Michigan, Rackham Graduate School, School of Information, Ann Arbor, MI 48109-1285. Offers health informatics (MHI); information (MSI, PhD). *Accreditation:*

ALA (one or more programs are accredited). *Program availability:* Part-time. Terminal master's awarded for partial completion of doctoral program. *Degree requirements:* For master's, thesis optional, internship; for doctorate, thesis/dissertation. *Entrance requirements:* For master's and doctorate, GRE General Test. Additional exam requirements/recommendations for international students: Required—TOEFL (minimum score 100 iBT). Electronic applications accepted. *Expenses:* Contact institution.

University of Missouri, Office of Research and Graduate Studies, College of Education, School of Information Science and Learning Technologies, Columbia, MO 65211. Offers educational technology (M Ed, Ed S); information science and learning technology (PhD, Certificate); library science (MA). *Accreditation:* ALA (one or more programs are accredited). *Program availability:* Part-time, evening/weekend. *Entrance requirements:* For master's, GRE General Test or MAT, minimum GPA of 3.0. Additional exam requirements/recommendations for international students: Required—TOEFL (minimum score 540 paper-based; 76 iBT). Electronic applications accepted.

The University of North Carolina at Chapel Hill, Graduate School, School of Information and Library Science, Chapel Hill, NC 27599. Offers data curation (PMC); digital curation (PSM); information and library science (PhD); information science (MSIS); library science (MSLS). *Accreditation:* ALA (one or more programs are accredited). *Program availability:* Part-time. *Faculty:* 24 full-time (8 women), 46 part-time/adjunct (23 women). *Students:* 228 full-time (169 women), 27 part-time (20 women); includes 36 minority (7 Black or African American, non-Hispanic/Latino; 10 Asian, non-Hispanic/Latino; 4 Hispanic/Latino; 15 Two or more races, non-Hispanic/Latino), 55 international. Average age 28. 304 applicants, 75% accepted, 100 enrolled. In 2017, 67 master's, 10 doctorates awarded. Terminal master's awarded for partial completion of doctoral program. *Degree requirements:* For master's, comprehensive exam, paper or project; for doctorate, comprehensive exam, thesis/dissertation. *Entrance requirements:* For master's and doctorate, GRE General Test. Additional exam requirements/recommendations for international students: Required—TOEFL (minimum score 90 iBT). *Application deadline:* For fall admission, 12/12 priority date for domestic and international students; for spring admission, 10/10 for domestic and international students. Applications are processed on a rolling basis. Application fee: $88. Electronic applications accepted. *Expenses:* $7,464 in-state full-time per semester, $16,070 out-of-state(for MSLS/MSIS); $5,964 in-state full-time per semester, $14,570 out-of-state(for PhD); $7,266 in-state full-time per semester$14,862 out-of-state (for PMC); $8,220 in-state, $16,266 out-of-state (for PMS). *Financial support:* In 2017–18, 59 fellowships with full tuition reimbursements (averaging $2,565 per year), 46 research assistantships with full tuition reimbursements (averaging $3,528 per year), 7 teaching assistantships with full tuition reimbursements (averaging $22,917 per year) were awarded; career-related internships or fieldwork, Federal Work-Study, scholarships/grants, health care benefits, and unspecified assistantships also available. Financial award application deadline: 12/12. *Faculty research:* Information retrieval and management, digital libraries, management of information resources, archives and records management, health informatics. *Unit head:* Dr. Gary Marchionini, Dean, 919-962-8363, Fax: 919-962-8071, E-mail: gary@ils.unc.edu. *Application contact:* Lara Bailey, Student Services Coordinator, 919-962-7601, Fax: 919-962-8071, E-mail: bailey@email.unc.edu. Website: http://sils.unc.edu

The University of North Carolina at Greensboro, Graduate School, School of Education, Department of Library and Information Studies, Greensboro, NC 27412-5001. Offers MLIS. *Accreditation:* ALA. *Program availability:* Part-time, evening/weekend, online learning. *Degree requirements:* For master's, portfolio. *Entrance requirements:* For master's, GRE General Test. Additional exam requirements/recommendations for international students: Required—TOEFL (minimum score 550 paper-based), IELTS (minimum score 6.5). Electronic applications accepted. *Faculty research:* Library history, gender studies, children's literature, web design, homeless, technical services.

University of Oklahoma, College of Arts and Sciences, School of Library and Information Studies, Norman, OK 73019. Offers archival studies (Graduate Certificate); digital humanities (Graduate Certificate); information studies (PhD); library and information studies (MLIS); M Ed/MLIS; MBA/MLIS. *Accreditation:* ALA (one or more programs are accredited). *Program availability:* Part-time, evening/weekend, 100% online, blended/hybrid learning. *Faculty:* 11 full-time (8 women), 1 (woman) part-time/adjunct. *Students:* 64 full-time (53 women), 117 part-time (95 women); includes 40 minority (6 Black or African American, non-Hispanic/Latino; 6 American Indian or Alaska Native, non-Hispanic/Latino; 3 Asian, non-Hispanic/Latino; 14 Hispanic/Latino; 1 Native Hawaiian or other Pacific Islander, non-Hispanic/Latino; 10 Two or more races, non-Hispanic/Latino). Average age 32. 58 applicants, 93% accepted, 48 enrolled. In 2017, 53 master's awarded. Terminal master's awarded for partial completion of doctoral program. *Degree requirements:* For master's, comprehensive exam (for some programs), thesis optional; for doctorate, comprehensive exam, thesis/dissertation. *Entrance requirements:* For master's, three letters of recommendation, personal statement, resume, transcript; for doctorate, GRE, three letters of recommendation, personal statement, resume, writing sample; for Graduate Certificate, transcripts, personal statement (for some certificates), letter of recommendation (for some certificates). Additional exam requirements/recommendations for international students: Required—TOEFL (minimum score 79 iBT) or IELTS (minimum score 6.5). *Application deadline:* Applications are processed on a rolling basis. Application fee: $50 ($100 for international students). Electronic applications accepted. *Expenses:* Tuition, state resident: full-time $5119; part-time $213.30 per credit hour. Tuition, nonresident: full-time $19,778; part-time $824.10 per credit hour. *Required fees:* $3458; $133.55 per credit hour. $126.50 per semester. *Financial support:* In 2017–18, 82 students received support, including 3 research assistantships with full tuition reimbursements available (averaging $10,579 per year), 3 teaching assistantships with full tuition reimbursements available (averaging $10,579 per year); scholarships/grants, health care benefits, and unspecified assistantships also available. Financial award application deadline: 6/1; financial award applicants required to submit FAFSA. *Faculty research:* Family and youth technology in libraries, consumer health information, text mining, big data analytics. *Total annual research expenditures:* $107,620. *Unit head:* Dr. Susan K. Burke, Director, 405-325-3921, E-mail: sburke@ou.edu. *Application contact:* Sarah Connelly, Admissions and Student Services Coordinator, 405-325-3921, E-mail: sarahee@ou.edu. Website: http://slis.ou.edu

University of Puerto Rico–Río Piedras, Graduate School of Information Sciences and Technologies, San Juan, PR 00931-3300. Offers administration of academic libraries (PMC); administration of public libraries (PMC); administration of special libraries (PMC); consultant in information services (PMC); documents and files administration (Post-Graduate Certificate); electronic information resources analyst (Post-Graduate Certificate); information science (MIS); librarianship and information services (MLS); school librarian (Post-Graduate Certificate); school librarian distance education mode (Post-Graduate Certificate); specialist in legal information (PMC). *Accreditation:* ALA. *Program availability:* Part-time. *Degree requirements:* For master's, comprehensive exam, thesis, portfolio. *Entrance requirements:* For master's, PAEG, GRE, interview, minimum GPA of 3.0, 3 letters of recommendation; for other advanced degree, PAEG,

GRE, minimum GPA of 3.0, IST master's degree. *Faculty research:* Investigating the users needs and preferences for a specialized environmental library.

University of Rhode Island, Graduate School, College of Arts and Sciences, Graduate School of Library and Information Studies, Kingston, RI 02881. Offers libraries, leadership and transforming communities (MLIS); organization of digital media (MLIS); school library media (MLIS); MLIS/MA; MLIS/MPA. *Accreditation:* ALA (one or more programs are accredited). *Program availability:* Part-time. *Faculty:* 4 full-time (all women). *Students:* 17 full-time (12 women), 85 part-time (74 women); includes 13 minority (2 Black or African American, non-Hispanic/Latino; 3 Asian, non-Hispanic/Latino; 3 Hispanic/Latino; 1 Native Hawaiian or other Pacific Islander, non-Hispanic/Latino; 4 Two or more races, non-Hispanic/Latino). 47 applicants, 89% accepted, 26 enrolled. In 2017, 41 master's awarded. *Entrance requirements:* For master's, GRE or MAT if undergraduate GPA below 3.3, 2 letters of recommendation. Additional exam requirements/recommendations for international students: Required—TOEFL. *Application deadline:* For fall admission, 6/15 for domestic students, 2/1 for international students; for spring admission, 10/15 for domestic students, 7/15 for international students; for summer admission, 3/15 for domestic students. Application fee: $65. Electronic applications accepted. *Expenses:* Tuition, state resident: full-time $12,706; part-time $786 per credit. Tuition, nonresident: full-time $25,216; part-time $1401 per credit. *Required fees:* $1598; $45 per credit. One-time fee: $30 part-time. *Financial support:* Research assistantships and teaching assistantships available. Financial award application deadline: 1/15; financial award applicants required to submit FAFSA. *Unit head:* Dr. Valerie Karno, Director, Graduate School of Library and Information Studies, 401-874-4682, Fax: 401-874-4127, E-mail: karno@uri.edu. Website: http://www.uri.edu/artsci/lsc/

University of South Carolina, The Graduate School, College of Mass Communications and Information Studies, School of Library and Information Science, Columbia, SC 29208. Offers MLIS, PhD, Certificate, Specialist, MLIS/MA. *Accreditation:* ALA (one or more programs are accredited). *Program availability:* Part-time, online learning. *Degree requirements:* For master's, end of program portfolio; for doctorate, comprehensive exam, thesis/dissertation. *Entrance requirements:* For master's and other advanced degree, GRE General Test or MAT; for doctorate, GTE, writing sample. Additional exam requirements/recommendations for international students: Required—TOEFL (minimum score 570 paper-based; 75 iBT). Electronic applications accepted. *Faculty research:* Information technology management, distance education, library services for children and young adults, special libraries.

University of South Florida, College of Arts and Sciences, School of Information, Tampa, FL 33620-9951. Offers intelligence studies (MS), including cyber intelligence, strategic intelligence; library and information science (MA). *Accreditation:* ALA (one or more programs are accredited). *Program availability:* Part-time, evening/weekend, online learning. *Faculty:* 16 full-time (9 women). *Students:* 120 full-time (87 women), 187 part-time (141 women); includes 89 minority (26 Black or African American, non-Hispanic/Latino; 9 Asian, non-Hispanic/Latino; 47 Hispanic/Latino; 7 Two or more races, non-Hispanic/Latino), 1 international. Average age 32. 180 applicants, 86% accepted, 98 enrolled. In 2017, 90 master's awarded. *Degree requirements:* For master's, comprehensive exam, thesis (for some programs). *Entrance requirements:* For master's, GRE General Test (for some programs). Additional exam requirements/recommendations for international students: Required—TOEFL (minimum score 550 paper-based; 79 iBT) or IELTS (minimum score 6.5). *Application deadline:* For fall admission, 6/1 priority date for domestic students, 5/1 for international students; for spring admission, 10/15 priority date for domestic students, 9/15 for international students. Applications are processed on a rolling basis. Application fee: $30. Electronic applications accepted. *Financial support:* In 2017–18, 25 students received support. Unspecified assistantships available. Financial award application deadline: 6/30. *Faculty research:* Youth services in libraries, community engagement and libraries, information architecture, biomedical informatics, health informatics. *Total annual research expenditures:* $168,525. *Unit head:* Dr. Jim Andrews, Director and Associate Professor, 813-974-2108, Fax: 813-974-6840, E-mail: jimandrews@usf.edu. *Application contact:* Dr. Randy Borum, Graduate Program Director, 813-974-3520, Fax: 813-974-6840, E-mail: wborum@usf.edu. Website: http://si.usf.edu/

University of South Florida, Innovative Education, Tampa, FL 33620-9951. Offers adult, career and higher education (Graduate Certificate), including college teaching, leadership in developing human resources, leadership in higher education; Africana studies (Graduate Certificate), including diasporas and health disparities, genocide and human rights; aging studies (Graduate Certificate), including gerontology; art research (Graduate Certificate), including museum studies; business foundations (Graduate Certificate); chemical and biomedical engineering (Graduate Certificate), including materials science and engineering, water, health and sustainability; child and family studies (Graduate Certificate), including positive behavior support; civil and industrial engineering (Graduate Certificate), including transportation systems analysis; community and family health (Graduate Certificate), including maternal and child health, social marketing and public health, violence and injury: prevention and intervention, women's health; criminology (Graduate Certificate), including criminal justice administration; data science for public administration (Graduate Certificate); digital humanities (Graduate Certificate); educational measurement and research (Graduate Certificate), including evaluation; English (Graduate Certificate), including comparative literary studies, creative writing, professional and technical communication; entrepreneurship (Graduate Certificate); environmental health (Graduate Certificate), including safety management; epidemiology and biostatistics (Graduate Certificate), including applied biostatistics, biostatistics, concepts and tools of epidemiology, epidemiology, epidemiology of infectious diseases; geography, environment and planning (Graduate Certificate), including community development, environmental policy and management, geographical information systems; geology (Graduate Certificate), including hydrogeology; global health (Graduate Certificate), including disaster management, global health and Latin American and Caribbean studies, global health practice, humanitarian assistance, infection control; government and international affairs (Graduate Certificate), including Cuban studies, globalization studies; health policy and management (Graduate Certificate), including health management and leadership, public health policy and programs; hearing specialist: early intervention (Graduate Certificate); industrial and management systems engineering (Graduate Certificate), including systems engineering, technology management; information studies (Graduate Certificate), including school library media specialist; information systems/decision sciences (Graduate Certificate), including analytics and business intelligence; instructional technology (Graduate Certificate), including distance education, Florida digital/virtual educator, instructional design, multimedia design, Web design; internal medicine, bioethics and medical humanities (Graduate Certificate), including biomedical ethics; Latin American and Caribbean studies (Graduate Certificate); leadership for coastal resiliency planning (Graduate Certificate); mass communications (Graduate Certificate), including multimedia journalism; mathematics and statistics (Graduate Certificate), including mathematics; medicine (Graduate Certificate), including aging and neuroscience, bioinformatics, biotechnology, brain fitness and memory management, clinical investigation, hand and upper limb rehabilitation, health informatics, health sciences, integrative weight management, intellectual property, medicine and gender,

metabolic and nutritional medicine, metabolic cardiology, pharmacy sciences; national and competitive intelligence (Graduate Certificate); nursing (Graduate Certificate), including simulation based academic fellowship in advanced pain management; psychological and social foundations (Graduate Certificate), including career counseling, college teaching, diversity in education, mental health counseling, school counseling; public affairs (Graduate Certificate), including nonprofit management, public management, research administration; public health (Graduate Certificate), including assessing chemical toxicity and public health risks, health equity, pharmacoepidemiology, public health generalist, toxicology, translational research in adolescent behavioral health; public health practices (Graduate Certificate), including planning for healthy communities; rehabilitation and mental health counseling (Graduate Certificate), including integrative mental health care, marriage and family therapy, rehabilitation technology; secondary education (Graduate Certificate), including ESOL, foreign language education: culture and content, foreign language education: professional; social work (Graduate Certificate), including geriatric social work/clinical gerontology; special education (Graduate Certificate), including autism spectrum disorder, disabilities education: severe/profound; world languages (Graduate Certificate), including teaching English as a second language (TESL) or foreign language. *Unit head:* Dr. Cynthia DeLuca, Associate Vice President and Assistant Vice Provost, 813-974-3077, Fax: 813-974-7061, E-mail: deluca@usf.edu. *Application contact:* Owen Hooper, Director, Summer and Alternative Calendar Programs, 813-974-6917, E-mail: hooper@usf.edu.
Website: http://www.usf.edu/innovative-education/

The University of Texas at Austin, Graduate School, School of Information, Austin, TX 78712-1111. Offers identity management and security (MSIMS); information (PhD); information studies (MSIS). MSIS/MA. MSIMS program offered in conjunction with the Center for Identity. *Accreditation:* ALA (one or more programs are accredited). *Program availability:* Part-time. *Degree requirements:* For doctorate, 2 foreign languages, thesis/dissertation. *Entrance requirements:* For master's and doctorate, GRE General Test. Electronic applications accepted. *Faculty research:* Information retrieval and artificial intelligence, library history and administration, classification and cataloguing.

University of Toronto, School of Graduate Studies, Faculty of Information, Toronto, ON M5S 1A1, Canada. Offers information (MI, PhD); museum studies (MM St); JD/MI. *Accreditation:* ALA (one or more programs are accredited). *Program availability:* Part-time. *Degree requirements:* For master's, thesis optional; for doctorate, thesis/dissertation, oral exam/thesis defense. *Entrance requirements:* For master's, 2 letters of reference; for doctorate, 3 letters of reference, minimum B+ average. Additional exam requirements/recommendations for international students: Required—TOEFL (minimum score 600 paper-based; 100 iBT), IELTS (minimum score 8), TWE (minimum score 5.5), or Michigan English Language Assessment Battery (minimum score 95). Electronic applications accepted. *Expenses:* Contact institution.

The University of Western Ontario, Faculty of Graduate Studies, Faculty of Information and Media Studies, Programs in Library and Information Science, London, ON N6A 5B8, Canada. Offers MLIS, PhD. Program conducted on a trimester basis. *Accreditation:* ALA (one or more programs are accredited). *Program availability:* Part-time, evening/weekend. *Degree requirements:* For doctorate, comprehensive exam, thesis/dissertation. *Entrance requirements:* For master's, honors degree, minimum B average during previous 2 years of course work; for doctorate, MLIS or equivalent. Additional exam requirements/recommendations for international students: Required—TOEFL (minimum score 625 paper-based), TWE (minimum score 5). Electronic applications accepted. *Faculty research:* Information, individuals, and society; information systems, policy, power, and institutions.

University of Wisconsin–Madison, Graduate School, College of Letters and Science, School of Library and Information Studies, Madison, WI 53706-1380. Offers MA, PhD. *Accreditation:* ALA (one or more programs are accredited). *Program availability:* Part-time. *Degree requirements:* For doctorate, comprehensive exam, thesis/dissertation. Electronic applications accepted. *Faculty research:* Intellectual freedom, children's literature, print culture history, information systems design and evaluation, school library media centers.

University of Wisconsin–Milwaukee, Graduate School, School of Information Studies, Milwaukee, WI 53201-0413. Offers MLIS, MS, PhD, CAS. *Accreditation:* ALA (one or more programs are accredited). *Program availability:* Part-time. *Students:* 120 full-time (81 women), 243 part-time (181 women); includes 52 minority (13 Black or African American, non-Hispanic/Latino; 11 Asian, non-Hispanic/Latino; 4 Hispanic/Latino; 24 Two or more races, non-Hispanic/Latino), 16 international. Average age 34. 276 applicants, 64% accepted, 122 enrolled. In 2017, 169 master's, 4 doctorates, 1 other

advanced degree awarded. *Entrance requirements:* For master's, GRE General Test or MAT; for doctorate, GRE. Additional exam requirements/recommendations for international students: Required—TOEFL (minimum score 550 paper-based), IELTS (minimum score 6.5). *Application deadline:* For fall admission, 1/1 priority date for domestic students; for spring admission, 9/1 for domestic students. Application fee: $56 ($96 for international students). Electronic applications accepted. *Financial support:* Fellowships, research assistantships, teaching assistantships, career-related internships or fieldwork, Federal Work-Study, health care benefits, unspecified assistantships, and project assistantships available. Support available to part-time students. Financial award application deadline: 4/15; financial award applicants required to submit FAFSA. *Unit head:* Tomas A. Lipinski, Dean/Professor, 414-229-4707, E-mail: tlipinsk@uwm.edu. *Application contact:* Linda Barajas, Admissions Coordinator, 414-229-3316, E-mail: barajas@uwm.edu.
Website: http://uwm.edu/informationstudies

Valdosta State University, Program in Library and Information Science, Valdosta, GA 31698. Offers MLIS. *Accreditation:* ALA. *Program availability:* 100% online. *Degree requirements:* For master's, comprehensive exam. *Entrance requirements:* For master's, two essays, resume, three recommendations. Additional exam requirements/recommendations for international students: Required—TOEFL (minimum score 523 paper-based); Recommended—IELTS. *Application deadline:* For fall admission, 4/15 for domestic and international students. Application fee: $45. *Expenses:* Contact institution. *Financial support:* Research assistantships with full tuition reimbursements, institutionally sponsored loans, scholarships/grants, and unspecified assistantships available. Support available to part-time students. Financial award application deadline: 7/1; financial award applicants required to submit FAFSA. *Unit head:* Dr. Linda Most, Director, 229-333-5966, Fax: 229-333-5862, E-mail: lrmost@valdosta.edu. *Application contact:* Jessica Powers, Admission Specialist, 229-333-5694, Fax: 229-245-3853, E-mail: jldevane@valdosta.edu.
Website: http://www.valdosta.edu/academics/graduate-school/our-programs/library-and-information-science.php

Wayne State University, School of Information Sciences, Detroit, MI 48202. Offers archival administration (Graduate Certificate); information management (MS, Graduate Certificate); library and information science (MLIS, Graduate Certificate, Spec); public library services to children and young adults (Graduate Certificate); MLIS/MA. *Accreditation:* ALA (one or more programs are accredited). *Program availability:* Part-time, evening/weekend, 100% online, blended/hybrid learning. *Faculty:* 12 full-time (9 women), 17 part-time/adjunct (12 women). *Students:* 100 full-time (80 women), 359 part-time (290 women); includes 77 minority (42 Black or African American, non-Hispanic/Latino; 2 American Indian or Alaska Native, non-Hispanic/Latino; 3 Asian, non-Hispanic/Latino; 19 Hispanic/Latino; 1 Native Hawaiian or other Pacific Islander, non-Hispanic/Latino; 10 Two or more races, non-Hispanic/Latino), 1 international. Average age 33. 258 applicants, 60% accepted, 100 enrolled. In 2017, 149 master's, 34 other advanced degrees awarded. *Degree requirements:* For master's and other advanced degree, e-portfolio. *Entrance requirements:* For master's, GRE or MAT (if undergraduate GPA is between 2.5 and 2.99), minimum undergraduate GPA of 3.0 or graduate degree, personal statement, resume or curriculum vitae; for other advanced degree, GRE or MAT (if undergraduate GPA is between 2.5 and 2.99), minimum undergraduate GPA of 3.0 or graduate degree, personal statement, resume or curriculum vitae, MLIS (for specialist certificate). Additional exam requirements/recommendations for international students: Required—TOEFL (minimum score 550 paper-based; 79 iBT); Recommended—IELTS (minimum score 6.5), TWE (minimum score 5.5). *Application deadline:* For fall admission, 7/1 for domestic students, 5/1 priority date for international students; for winter admission, 10/1 priority date for domestic students, 9/1 priority date for international students; for spring admission, 2/1 priority date for domestic students, 1/1 priority date for international students. Applications are processed on a rolling basis. Application fee: $50. Electronic applications accepted. *Expenses:* Contact institution. *Financial support:* In 2017–18, 133 students received support. Fellowships with tuition reimbursements available, scholarships/grants, health care benefits, and unspecified assistantships available. Support available to part-time students. Financial award applicants required to submit FAFSA. *Faculty research:* Library services, information management issues, digital content management, library/community engagement, archives and preservation. *Unit head:* Dr. Jon Cawthorne, Dean, 313-577-4020, E-mail: jon.cawthorne@wayne.edu. *Application contact:* Academic Services Officer II, 313-577-1825, E-mail: asklis@wayne.edu.
Website: http://slis.wayne.edu/

Library Science

Appalachian State University, Cratis D. Williams Graduate School, Department of Leadership and Educational Studies, Boone, NC 28608. Offers educational administration (Ed S); educational media (MA); higher education (MA, Ed S); library science (MLS); school administration (MSA). *Program availability:* Part-time, evening/weekend, online learning. *Degree requirements:* For master's and Ed S, comprehensive exam, thesis optional. *Entrance requirements:* For master's and Ed S, GRE or MAT, 3 letters of recommendation. Additional exam requirements/recommendations for international students: Required—TOEFL (minimum score 570 paper-based; 79 iBT), IELTS (minimum score 6.5). Electronic applications accepted. *Faculty research:* Brain, learning and meditation; leadership of teaching and learning.

The Catholic University of America, School of Arts and Sciences, Department of Library and Information Science, Washington, DC 20064. Offers MSLS, Certificate, JD/MSLS, MSLS/MA, MSLS/MS. *Accreditation:* ALA (one or more programs are accredited). *Program availability:* Part-time. *Faculty:* 7 full-time (6 women), 1 (woman) part-time/adjunct. *Students:* 14 full-time (13 women), 70 part-time (49 women); includes 24 minority (10 Black or African American, non-Hispanic/Latino; 2 Asian, non-Hispanic/Latino; 4 Hispanic/Latino; 8 Two or more races, non-Hispanic/Latino), 1 international. Average age 32. 48 applicants, 90% accepted, 26 enrolled. In 2017, 37 master's, 1 Certificate awarded. *Degree requirements:* For master's, comprehensive exam. *Entrance requirements:* For master's, statement of purpose, official copies of academic transcripts, three letters of recommendation, interview. Additional exam requirements/recommendations for international students: Required—TOEFL (minimum score 550 paper-based; 80 iBT). *Application deadline:* For fall admission, 7/15 priority date for domestic students, 7/1 for international students; for spring admission, 11/15 priority date for domestic students, 11/1 for international students. Applications are processed on a rolling basis. Application fee: $55. Electronic applications accepted. *Expenses:* Contact institution. *Financial support:* Fellowships, research assistantships, teaching

assistantships, Federal Work-Study, scholarships/grants, tuition waivers (full and partial), and unspecified assistantships available. Financial award application deadline: 2/1; financial award applicants required to submit FAFSA. *Faculty research:* Digital collections, library and information science education, information design and architecture, information system design and evaluation. *Unit head:* Dr. Youngok Choi, Chair, 202-319-5877, E-mail: choiy@cua.edu. *Application contact:* Dr. Steven Brown, Director of Graduate Admissions, 202-319-5057, Fax: 202-319-6533, E-mail: cua-admissions@cua.edu.
Website: http://lis.cua.edu/

Chicago State University, School of Graduate and Professional Studies, College of Education, Department of Reading, Elementary Education, Library Information and Media Studies, Program in Library Science, Chicago, IL 60628. Offers MS. *Entrance requirements:* For master's, minimum GPA of 2.75. *Application deadline:* For fall admission, 7/1 for domestic students; for spring admission, 11/10 for domestic students. Application fee: $25. *Unit head:* Dr. Kimberly Black, Chairperson, 773-995-2598, Fax: 773-821-2441, E-mail: kblack21@csu.edu. *Application contact:* Anika Miller, Graduate Studies Office, 773-995-2404, E-mail: g-studies1@csu.edu.

Clarion University of Pennsylvania, College of Business Administration and Information Sciences, Certificate Program in Library Science, Clarion, PA 16214. Offers Certificate. *Program availability:* Part-time, evening/weekend, online only, 100% online. *Faculty:* 8 full-time (5 women), 6 part-time/adjunct (3 women). In 2017, 1 Certificate awarded. *Entrance requirements:* For degree, written statement of goals, completion of program from ALA-accredited school. Additional exam requirements/recommendations for international students: Required—TOEFL (minimum score 550 paper-based, 80 iBT) or IELTS (7). *Application deadline:* For fall admission, 8/15 priority date for domestic students, 7/15 priority date for international students; for winter admission, 11/1 priority date for domestic students; for spring admission, 1/17 priority date for domestic students, 11/15 priority date for international students; for summer admission, 4/1 priority date for domestic students. Applications are processed on a rolling basis. Application fee: $40. Electronic applications accepted. *Expenses:* $655.05 per credit. *Financial support:* Career-related internships or fieldwork available. Support available to part-time students. Financial award application deadline: 3/1; financial award applicants required to submit FAFSA. *Unit head:* Linda Lillard, Department Chair, 814-393-2383, E-mail: llillard@clarion.edu. *Application contact:* Dana Bearer, Associate Director for Transfer, Adult and Graduate Admissions, 814-393-2337, Fax: 814-393-2772, E-mail: gradstudies@clarion.edu.

Clarion University of Pennsylvania, College of Business Administration and Information Sciences, MSLS Program in Information and Library Science, Clarion, PA 16214. Offers information and library science (MSLS); school library media (MSLS). *Program availability:* Part-time, evening/weekend, online only, 100% online. *Faculty:* 8 full-time (5 women), 6 part-time/adjunct (3 women). *Students:* 84 full-time (68 women), 253 part-time (212 women); includes 47 minority (20 Black or African American, non-Hispanic/Latino; 4 Asian, non-Hispanic/Latino; 16 Hispanic/Latino; 7 Two or more races, non-Hispanic/Latino), 1 international. Average age 33. 249 applicants, 87% accepted, 110 enrolled. In 2017, 139 master's awarded. *Entrance requirements:* For master's, minimum undergraduate QPA of 3.0. Additional exam requirements/recommendations for international students: Required—TOEFL (minimum score 550 paper-based, 80 iBT) or IELTS (7). *Application deadline:* For fall admission, 8/15 priority date for domestic students, 7/15 priority date for international students; for winter admission, 11/1 priority date for domestic students; for spring admission, 1/7 priority date for domestic students, 11/15 priority date for international students; for summer admission, 4/1 priority date for domestic students. Applications are processed on a rolling basis. Application fee: $40. Electronic applications accepted. *Expenses:* $655.05 per credit. *Financial support:* Career-related internships or fieldwork, scholarships/grants, and unspecified assistantships available. Support available to part-time students. Financial award application deadline: 3/1; financial award applicants required to submit FAFSA. *Unit head:* Linda Lillard, Department Chair, 814-393-2383, E-mail: llillard@clarion.edu. *Application contact:* Dana Bearer, Associate Director, Transfer, Adult, and Graduate Programs, 814-393-2337, Fax: 814-393-2772, E-mail: gradstudies@clarion.edu. Website: http://www.clarion.edu/academics/colleges-and-schools/college-of-business-administration-and-information-sciences/library-science/

Dalhousie University, Faculty of Management, School of Information Management, Halifax, NS B3H 3J5, Canada. Offers MIM, MLIS, LL B/MLIS, MBA/MLIS, MLIS/MPA, MLIS/MREM. *Accreditation:* ALA (one or more programs are accredited). *Program availability:* Part-time. *Degree requirements:* For master's, one foreign language, thesis optional. *Entrance requirements:* For master's, resume, interview. Additional exam requirements/recommendations for international students: Required—TOEFL, IELTS, CANTEST, CAEL, or Michigan English Language Assessment Battery. Electronic applications accepted. *Faculty research:* Information-seeking behavior, electronic text design, browsing in digital environments, information diffusion among scientists.

Drexel University, College of Computing and Informatics, Philadelphia, PA 19104-2875. Offers MS, PhD, Post-Master's Certificate, Postbaccalaureate Certificate. *Accreditation:* ALA (one or more programs are accredited). *Program availability:* Part-time, evening/weekend, 100% online. *Faculty:* 40 full-time (16 women), 15 part-time/adjunct (7 women). *Students:* 228 full-time (112 women), 280 part-time (160 women); includes 92 minority (35 Black or African American, non-Hispanic/Latino; 21 Asian, non-Hispanic/Latino; 26 Hispanic/Latino; 10 Two or more races, non-Hispanic/Latino), 118 international. Average age 32. 609 applicants, 63% accepted, 157 enrolled. In 2017, 210 master's, 8 doctorates, 17 other advanced degrees awarded. *Degree requirements:* For doctorate, thesis/dissertation. *Entrance requirements:* For master's and doctorate, GRE General Test. Additional exam requirements/recommendations for international students: Required—TOEFL (minimum score 90 iBT), IELTS (minimum score 6.5). *Application deadline:* For fall admission, 8/15 for domestic students, 7/15 for international students; for spring admission, 3/1 for domestic students, 2/1 for international students. Applications are processed on a rolling basis. Application fee: $65. Electronic applications accepted. *Financial support:* In 2017–18, 122 students received support, including 3 fellowships with full tuition reimbursements available (averaging $33,111 per year), 42 research assistantships with full tuition reimbursements available (averaging $27,342 per year), 14 teaching assistantships with full tuition reimbursements available (averaging $27,500 per year); career-related internships or fieldwork, institutionally sponsored loans, scholarships/grants, health care benefits, and tuition waivers (partial) also available. Support available to part-time students. Financial award application deadline: 3/1; financial award applicants required to submit FAFSA. *Faculty research:* Computer science: theory of algorithms, graph theory, combinatorial optimization, computer vision; human-centered computing: social computing, human-computer interaction, computer-supported cooperative work, computer-supported collaborative learning, information literacy; systems and software engineering: formal software design modeling and analysis, software economics, software evolution and modularity. *Total annual research expenditures:* $4.1 million. *Unit head:* Dr. Yi Deng, Dean/Professor, 215-895-2475, Fax: 215-895-2494, E-mail: yd362@drexel.edu. *Application contact:* Matthew Lechtenberg, Director, Recruitment, 215-895-2474, Fax: 215-895-2303, E-mail: cciinfo@drexel.edu. Website: http://cci.drexel.edu/

East Carolina University, Graduate School, College of Education, Department of Interdisciplinary Professions, Greenville, NC 27858-4353. Offers adult education (MA Ed); business and marketing education (MA Ed); community college instruction (Certificate); counselor education (MS); education in the healthcare professions (Certificate); library science (MLS); student affairs in higher education (Certificate); vocational education (MS). *Accreditation:* ACA; NCATE. *Program availability:* Part-time, evening/weekend. *Students:* 97 full-time (77 women), 392 part-time (344 women); includes 107 minority (73 Black or African American, non-Hispanic/Latino; 6 American Indian or Alaska Native, non-Hispanic/Latino; 5 Asian, non-Hispanic/Latino; 11 Hispanic/Latino; 12 Two or more races, non-Hispanic/Latino). Average age 36. 148 applicants, 97% accepted, 116 enrolled. In 2017, 148 master's, 23 other advanced degrees awarded. *Degree requirements:* For master's, comprehensive exam, thesis optional. *Entrance requirements:* For master's, GRE General Test or MAT, interview, minimum GPA of 2.5, bachelor's degree in related field, teaching license (MA Ed). Additional exam requirements/recommendations for international students: Required—TOEFL. *Application deadline:* For fall admission, 5/15 priority date for domestic students. Applications are processed on a rolling basis. Application fee: $75. *Expenses:* Tuition, state resident: full-time $4749; part-time $297 per credit hour. Tuition, nonresident: full-time $17,898; part-time $1119 per credit hour. *Required fees:* $2691; $224 per credit hour. Part-time tuition and fees vary according to course load and program. *Financial support:* Research assistantships with partial tuition reimbursements, teaching assistantships with partial tuition reimbursements, and Federal Work-Study available. Support available to part-time students. Financial award application deadline: 6/1. *Unit head:* Dr. Vivian W. Mott, Chair, 252-328-6177, Fax: 252-328-4368, E-mail: mottv@ecu.edu. Website: http://www.ecu.edu/cs-educ/idp/index.cfm

Eastern Kentucky University, The Graduate School, College of Education, Department of Curriculum and Instruction, Richmond, KY 40475-3102. Offers elementary education (MA Ed), including early elementary education, reading; library science (MA Ed); music education (MA Ed); secondary and higher education (MA Ed), including secondary education; teaching (MAT). *Accreditation:* NCATE. *Program availability:* Part-time. *Degree requirements:* For master's, portfolio is part of exam. *Entrance requirements:* For master's, GRE General Test, PRAXIS II (KY), minimum GPA of 2.5. *Faculty research:* Technology in education, reading instruction, e-portfolios, induction to teacher education, dispositions of teachers.

East Tennessee State University, School of Graduate Studies, College of Education, Department of Curriculum and Instruction, Johnson City, TN 37614. Offers advanced studies in teaching and learning (M Ed), including childhood literacy; educational technology (M Ed), including educational communications and technology, school library media; elementary education (M Ed); reading (M Ed, MA), including reading education (MA), storytelling (MA); response to intervention (Post-Master's Certificate); school library professional (Post-Master's Certificate); secondary education (M Ed); STEAM K-12 education (Postbaccalaureate Certificate); storytelling (Postbaccalaureate Certificate); teacher education (MAT), including elementary education K-5, middle grades education 4-8, middle grades education 6-8, secondary education 6-12 and preK-12, secondary education K-12. *Accreditation:* NCATE. *Program availability:* Part-time, evening/weekend, online learning. *Degree requirements:* For master's, comprehensive exam, thesis optional, student teaching, practicum; for other advanced degree, field work (school library); culminating experience (storytelling). *Entrance requirements:* For master's, GRE, SAT, ACT, PRAXIS, minimum GPA of 3.0, interview, 3 letters of recommendation, background check; for other advanced degree, master's degree, TN teaching license. Additional exam requirements/recommendations for international students: Required—TOEFL (minimum score 550 paper-based; 79 iBT). *Application deadline:* For fall admission, 6/1 for domestic students, 4/29 for international students; for spring admission, 11/1 for domestic students, 4/29 for international students. Application fee: $55 ($65 for international students). Electronic applications accepted. *Financial support:* Research assistantships with full tuition reimbursements, teaching assistantships with tuition reimbursements, career-related internships or fieldwork, institutionally sponsored loans, scholarships/grants, and unspecified assistantships available. Financial award application deadline: 7/1; financial award applicants required to submit FAFSA. *Faculty research:* Critical thinking; curriculum development in reading, math, and science education; cultural diversity; cognitive processes; effective teaching strategies. *Unit head:* Dr. Karin Keith, Chair, 423-439-7598, Fax: 423-439-8362, E-mail: keithkj@etsu.edu. *Application contact:* Dr. Aimee Govett, Graduate Coordinator, 423-439-7804, Fax: 423-439-5624, E-mail: govett@etsu.edu. Website: http://www.etsu.edu/coe/cuai/

Emporia State University, School of Library and Information Management, Emporia, KS 66801-5415. Offers archives studies (Certificate); information technology and science literacy (Certificate); library and information management (MLS, PhD). *Accreditation:* ALA (one or more programs are accredited). *Program availability:* Part-time, evening/weekend, online learning. *Faculty:* 9 full-time (5 women), 1 (woman) part-time/adjunct. *Students:* 23 full-time (17 women), 310 part-time (250 women); includes 14 minority (2 Black or African American, non-Hispanic/Latino; 10 Hispanic/Latino; 2 Two or more races, non-Hispanic/Latino), 4 international. 137 applicants, 76% accepted, 85 enrolled. In 2017, 145 master's, 1 doctorate, 27 other advanced degrees awarded. *Degree requirements:* For master's, comprehensive exam, thesis optional; for doctorate, thesis/dissertation. *Entrance requirements:* For master's, GRE General Test, interview, minimum undergraduate GPA of 3.0, letters of recommendation; for doctorate, GRE General Test, interview, minimum graduate GPA of 3.5. Additional exam requirements/recommendations for international students: Required—TOEFL (minimum score 520 paper-based; 68 iBT). *Application deadline:* For fall admission, 8/15 priority date for domestic students. Applications are processed on a rolling basis. Application fee: $30 ($75 for international students). Electronic applications accepted. *Expenses:* Tuition, state resident: full-time $6084; part-time $253.50 per credit hour. Tuition, nonresident: full-time $18,924; part-time $788.50 per credit hour. *Required fees:* $1943; $80.95 per credit hour. Tuition and fees vary according to campus/location. *Financial support:* Federal Work-Study, institutionally sponsored loans, and unspecified assistantships available. Financial award application deadline: 3/15; financial award applicants required to submit FAFSA. *Unit head:* Dr. Wooseob Jeong, Dean, 620-341-5203, Fax: 620-341-5203, E-mail: wjeong1@emporia.edu. *Application contact:* Candace Boardman, Director, Kansas MLS Program, 620-341-6159, E-mail: cboardma@emporia.edu. Website: http://www.emporia.edu/slim/

Florida State University, The Graduate School, College of Communication and Information, School of Information, Tallahassee, FL 32306-2100. Offers information (MA, MS, PhD, Specialist); information technology (MS). *Accreditation:* ALA (one or more programs are accredited). *Program availability:* Part-time, evening/weekend, 100% online, blended/hybrid learning. *Faculty:* 27 full-time (14 women), 4 part-time/adjunct (2 women). *Students:* 45 full-time (26 women), 264 part-time (197 women); includes 102 minority (31 Black or African American, non-Hispanic/Latino; 13 Asian, non-Hispanic/Latino; 46 Hispanic/Latino; 12 Two or more races, non-Hispanic/Latino), 16 international. Average age 34. 168 applicants, 62% accepted, 83 enrolled. In 2017, 108 master's, 7 doctorates, 2 other advanced degrees awarded. Terminal master's awarded for partial completion of doctoral program. *Degree requirements:* For master's, thesis optional, minimum GPA of 3.0, 36 hours (MSI); 32 hours (MSIT); for doctorate, comprehensive exam, thesis/dissertation, dissertation defense, manuscript clearance, minimum GPA of 3.0; for Specialist, minimum GPA of 3.0; 30 hours. *Entrance requirements:* For master's, GRE (recommended minimum percentile of 50 on each of the verbal and quantitative portions and writing score of 4.0), minimum GPA of 3.0 on last 2 years of baccalaureate degree, resume, statement of goals, two letters of recommendation, official transcripts from every college-level institution attended; for doctorate, GRE (recommended minimum percentile of 50 on each of the verbal and quantitative portions and writing score of 4.0), minimum GPA of 3.0 on last degree program, resume, 3 letters of recommendation, personal/goals statement, writing sample, brief digital video, official transcripts from all college-level institutions attended; for Specialist, GRE (recommended minimum percentile of 50 on each of the verbal and quantitative portions and writing score of 4.0), minimum graduate GPA of 3.2, resume, statement of goals, 2 letters of recommendation, writing sample, official transcripts from every college-level institution attended. Additional exam requirements/recommendations for international students: Required—TOEFL (minimum score 585 paper-based; 94 iBT), IELTS (minimum score 6.5). *Application deadline:* For fall admission, 7/1 for domestic and international students; for spring admission, 11/1 for domestic and international students. Applications are processed on a rolling basis. Application fee: $30. Electronic applications accepted. *Expenses:* Contact institution. *Financial support:* In 2017–18, 115 students received support, including 2 research assistantships with full tuition reimbursements available (averaging $18,310 per year), 24 teaching assistantships with full tuition reimbursements available (averaging $18,310 per year); career-related internships or fieldwork, Federal Work-Study, health care benefits, tuition waivers (full), and 4 assistantships (averaging $18,310) also available. Financial award application deadline: 3/1; financial award applicants required to submit FAFSA. *Faculty research:*

Library Science

Information technology, social informatics, health information, human information behavior, youth services. *Total annual research expenditures:* $296,509. *Unit head:* Dr. Lorri Mon, Director/Associate Professor, 850-644-5776, Fax: 850-644-9763, E-mail: lmon@fsu.edu. *Application contact:* Student Services, 850-645-3280, Fax: 850-644-9763, E-mail: ischooladvising@admin.fsu.edu.
Website: http://ischool.cci.fsu.edu

Indiana University Bloomington, School of Informatics and Computing, Department of Information and Library Science, Bloomington, IN 47405-3907. Offers information architecture (Graduate Certificate); information science (MIS, PhD); library and information science (Sp LIS); library science (MLS); JD/MLS; MIS/MA; MLS/MA; MPA/MIS; MPA/MLS. *Accreditation:* ALA (one or more programs are accredited). *Program availability:* Part-time. Terminal master's awarded for partial completion of doctoral program. *Degree requirements:* For master's, internship; for doctorate, comprehensive exam, thesis/dissertation. *Entrance requirements:* For master's, GRE General Test (for applicants whose previous undergraduate degree GPA was below 3.0 or previous graduate degree GPA was below 3.2), 3 letters of reference, resume, personal statement (500 words minimum), transcripts; for doctorate, GRE General Test, resume, personal statement (800-1000 words), writing sample, transcripts, 3 letters of reference. Additional exam requirements/recommendations for international students: Required—TOEFL (minimum score 600 paper-based; 100 iBT), IELTS. Electronic applications accepted. *Expenses:* Contact institution. *Faculty research:* Scholarly communication, interface design, library and management policy, computer-mediated communication, information retrieval, documentation, web analysis, e-business, information architecture, social informatics, virtual groups and online communities, online deviant behaviors, knowledge sharing, indexing, philosophy of information, information policy, resource management, research methods digital humanities, digital libraries, semantic web, digital preservation, natural language processing.

Indiana University–Purdue University Indianapolis, School of Informatics and Computing, Department of Library and Information Science, Indianapolis, IN 46202. Offers MLS. *Program availability:* Part-time, evening/weekend, 100% online. *Entrance requirements:* For master's, GRE General Test. Additional exam requirements/recommendations for international students: Required—TOEFL (minimum score 600 paper-based).

Indiana University–Purdue University Indianapolis, School of Public and Environmental Affairs, Indianapolis, IN 46202. Offers criminal justice and public safety (MS); homeland security and emergency management (Graduate Certificate); library management (Graduate Certificate); nonprofit management (Graduate Certificate); public affairs (MPA); public management (Graduate Certificate); social entrepreneurship: nonprofit and public benefit organizations (Graduate Certificate); JD/MPA; MLS/NMC; MLS/PMC; MPA/MA. *Accreditation:* CAHME (one or more programs are accredited); NASPAA. *Program availability:* Part-time, evening/weekend, online learning. *Entrance requirements:* For master's, GRE General Test, GMAT or LSAT, minimum GPA of 3.0 (preferred). Additional exam requirements/recommendations for international students: Required—TOEFL (minimum score 93 iBT), IELTS (minimum score 6.5). Electronic applications accepted. *Faculty research:* Nonprofit and public management, public policy, urban policy, sustainability policy, disaster preparedness and recovery, vehicular safety, homicide, offender rehabilitation and re-entry.

Instituto Tecnológico y de Estudios Superiores de Monterrey, Campus Irapuato, Graduate Programs, Irapuato, Mexico. Offers administration (MBA); administration of information technology (MAIT); administration of telecommunications (MAT); architecture (M Arch); computer science (MCS); education (M Ed); educational administration (MEA); educational innovation and technology (DEIT); educational technology (MET); electronic commerce (MBA); environmental administration and planning (MEAP); environmental systems (MES); finances (MBA); humanistic studies (MHS); international management for Latin American executives (MIMLAE); library and information science (MLIS); manufacturing quality management (MMQM); marketing research (MBA).

Inter American University of Puerto Rico, Barranquitas Campus, Program in Education, Barranquitas, PR 00794. Offers curriculum and teaching (M Ed), including biology, English as a second language, history, Spanish; educational leadership and management (MA); elementary education (M Ed); information and library service technology (M Ed); special education (MA). *Accreditation:* TEAC. *Program availability:* Part-time, evening/weekend. *Faculty:* 1 full-time (0 women), 3 part-time/adjunct (2 women). *Students:* 17 full-time (16 women), 2 part-time (both women); all minorities (all Hispanic/Latino). Average age 34. 9 applicants, 89% accepted, 8 enrolled. In 2017, 5 master's awarded. *Degree requirements:* For master's, 2 foreign languages, comprehensive exam, thesis (for some programs). *Entrance requirements:* For master's, GRE or EXADEP, bachelor's degree or its equivalent from accredited institution, official academic transcript from institution that conferred bachelor's degree, minimum GPA of 2.5, two recommendation letters, interview (for some programs), essay (for some programs). *Application deadline:* Applications are processed on a rolling basis. Application fee: $31. Electronic applications accepted. *Expenses:* $3,392 full-time tuition plus $652 fees. *Financial support:* Applicants required to submit FAFSA. *Unit head:* Juan A. Negron-Berrios, PhD, Chancellor, 787-857-3600 Ext. 2002, Fax: 787-857-2125, E-mail: janegron@br.inter.edu. *Application contact:* Aramilda Cartagena-Santiago, Dean of Students, 787-857-3600 Ext. 2009, Fax: 787-857-2125, E-mail: aramildacartagena@br.inter.edu.

Inter American University of Puerto Rico, San Germán Campus, Graduate Studies Center, Program in Library Sciences, San Germán, PR 00683-5008. Offers MLS. *Program availability:* Part-time, evening/weekend. *Degree requirements:* For master's, comprehensive exam. *Entrance requirements:* For master's, GRE General Test or EXADEP, minimum GPA of 3.0.

Kent State University, College of Communication and Information, School of Information, Kent, OH 44242-0001. Offers health informatics (MS), including health informatics, knowledge management, user experience design; library and information science (MLIS), including K-12 school library media; M Ed/MLIS; MBA/MLIS; MLIS/MS. *Accreditation:* ALA (one or more programs are accredited). *Program availability:* Part-time, online learning. *Faculty:* 20 full-time (16 women), 30 part-time/adjunct (19 women). *Students:* 162 full-time (132 women), 561 part-time (422 women); includes 93 minority (41 Black or African American, non-Hispanic/Latino; 1 American Indian or Alaska Native, non-Hispanic/Latino; 10 Asian, non-Hispanic/Latino; 28 Hispanic/Latino; 1 Native Hawaiian or other Pacific Islander, non-Hispanic/Latino; 12 Two or more races, non-Hispanic/Latino), 7 international. Average age 33. 212 applicants, 98% accepted, 162 enrolled. In 2017, 321 master's awarded. *Degree requirements:* For master's, portfolio (MLIS); internship, project, paper, or thesis. *Entrance requirements:* For master's, GRE if total GPA is below 3.0 in highest completed degree, minimum GPA of 3.0, statement of purpose, 3 letters of recommendation, curriculum vitae/resume, transcripts, writing sample, personal interview. Additional exam requirements/recommendations for international students: Required—TOEFL (minimum score 587 paper-based, 94 iBT), Michigan English Language Assessment Battery (minimum score 82), IELTS (minimum score 7.0) or PTE (minimum score 65). *Application deadline:* For fall admission, 3/15 for domestic and international students; for spring admission, 9/15 for domestic and international students; for summer admission, 1/15 for domestic and international

students. Applications are processed on a rolling basis. Application fee: $45 ($70 for international students). Electronic applications accepted. *Expenses:* Tuition, state resident: full-time $11,310; part-time $515 per credit hour. Tuition, nonresident: full-time $20,396; part-time $928 per credit hour. *International tuition:* $18,544 full-time. *Financial support:* Fellowships with full tuition reimbursements, research assistantships with full tuition reimbursements, teaching assistantships with full tuition reimbursements, scholarships/grants, and unspecified assistantships available. Financial award application deadline: 3/1. *Unit head:* Dr. Kendra Albright, Director and Professor, 330-672-8535, E-mail: kalbrig7@kent.edu. *Application contact:* Dr. Karen Gracy, Graduate Co-Coordinator/Associate Professor, 330-672-2782, E-mail: kgracy@kent.edu.
Website: https://www.kent.edu/iSchool

Kutztown University of Pennsylvania, College of Education, Program in Library Science, Kutztown, PA 19530-0730. Offers MLS. *Program availability:* Part-time, evening/weekend, 100% online, blended/hybrid learning. *Faculty:* 2 full-time (both women). *Students:* 2 full-time (both women), 21 part-time (18 women); includes 1 minority (Black or African American, non-Hispanic/Latino). Average age 45. 22 applicants, 100% accepted, 11 enrolled. In 2017, 6 master's awarded. *Degree requirements:* For master's, comprehensive exam. *Entrance requirements:* For master's, GRE General Test or valid PA teaching certificate, 3 letters of recommendation. Additional exam requirements/recommendations for international students: Required—TOEFL (minimum score 550 paper-based, 79 iBT), IELTS (minimum score 6.5), or PTE (minimum score 53). *Application deadline:* For fall admission, 8/1 for domestic and international students; for spring admission, 12/1 for domestic and international students. Application fee: $35. Electronic applications accepted. *Expenses:* Tuition, state resident: part-time $500 per credit. Tuition, nonresident: part-time $750 per credit. *Required fees:* $115 per credit. One-time fee: $50 part-time. Tuition and fees vary according to degree level. *Financial support:* Career-related internships or fieldwork, Federal Work-Study, and unspecified assistantships available. Financial award application deadline: 3/1; financial award applicants required to submit FAFSA. *Unit head:* Dr. Andrea Harmer, Professor, 610-683-4301, Fax: 610-683-1326, E-mail: harmer@kutztown.edu.
Website: https://www.kutztown.edu/academics/graduate-programs/library-science.htm

Long Island University–Brentwood Campus, Graduate Programs, Brentwood, NY 11717. Offers childhood education (MS), including grades 1-6; childhood education/literacy B-6 (MS); childhood education/special education (grades 1-6) (MS); clinical mental health counseling (MS, Advanced Certificate); criminal justice (MS); early childhood education (MS); educational leadership (MS Ed); family nurse practitioner (MS, Advanced Certificate); health administration (MPA); library and information science (MS); literacy (B-6) (MS Ed); school counselor (MS, Advanced Certificate); social work (MSW); special education (MS Ed); students with disabilities generalist (grades 7-12) (Advanced Certificate). *Program availability:* Part-time. *Faculty:* 14 full-time (9 women), 22 part-time/adjunct (11 women). *Students:* 111 full-time (89 women), 47 part-time (34 women); includes 35 minority (8 Black or African American, non-Hispanic/Latino; 1 American Indian or Alaska Native, non-Hispanic/Latino; 3 Asian, non-Hispanic/Latino; 22 Hispanic/Latino; 1 Two or more races, non-Hispanic/Latino), 1 international. Average age 30. 110 applicants, 82% accepted, 63 enrolled. In 2017, 58 master's, 5 other advanced degrees awarded. *Entrance requirements:* For master's and Advanced Certificate, GRE. Additional exam requirements/recommendations for international students: Required—TOEFL or IELTS. *Application deadline:* Applications are processed on a rolling basis. Application fee: $50. Electronic applications accepted. *Expenses:* Tuition: Full-time $21,168; part-time $1201 per credit. *Required fees:* $1840; $920 per term. Tuition and fees vary according to course load. *Financial support:* In 2017–18, 121 students received support. Scholarships/grants available. Support available to part-time students. Financial award application deadline: 2/15; financial award applicants required to submit FAFSA. *Unit head:* Dr. Abby Van Vlerah, Dean and Chief Operating Officer, 631-299-3831, E-mail: abagail.vanvlerah@liu.edu. *Application contact:* Scott Aug, Associate Director of Enrollment Management, 631-287-8506, E-mail: scott.aug@liu.edu.
Website: http://liu.edu/brentwood

Long Island University–LIU Post, College of Education, Information and Technology, Brookville, NY 11548-1300. Offers adolescence education (MS); adolescence education 7-12 (MS); archives and records management (AC); art education (MS); childhood education (MS); childhood education/literacy B-6 (MS); childhood education/special education (MS); clinical mental health counseling (MS, AC); early childhood education (MS); early childhood education/childhood education (MS); educational leadership (AC); educational technology (MS); information studies (PhD); interdisciplinary educational studies (Ed D); middle childhood education (MS); music education (MS); public library administration (AC); school counselor (MS); special education (MS Ed); speech-language pathology (MA); students with disabilities, 7-12 generalist (AC); TESOL (MA). *Accreditation:* TEAC. *Program availability:* Part-time, 100% online, blended/hybrid learning. *Faculty:* 40 full-time (26 women), 73 part-time/adjunct (38 women). *Students:* 472 full-time (400 women), 696 part-time (543 women); includes 254 minority (93 Black or African American, non-Hispanic/Latino; 46 Asian, non-Hispanic/Latino; 105 Hispanic/Latino; 10 Two or more races, non-Hispanic/Latino), 33 international. Average age 33. 917 applicants, 82% accepted, 357 enrolled. In 2017, 408 master's, 31 other advanced degrees awarded. Terminal master's awarded for partial completion of doctoral program. *Degree requirements:* For master's, variable foreign language requirement, comprehensive exam (for some programs), thesis optional; for doctorate, comprehensive exam, thesis/dissertation. *Entrance requirements:* For master's and AC, GRE (for some programs). Additional exam requirements/recommendations for international students: Required—TOEFL (minimum score 550 paper-based, 75 iBT), IELTS, or PTE. *Application deadline:* Applications are processed on a rolling basis. Application fee: $50. Electronic applications accepted. *Expenses:* Tuition: Full-time $21,618; part-time $1201 per credit. *Required fees:* $1840; $920 per term. Tuition and fees vary according to course load. *Financial support:* In 2017–18, 376 students received support. Career-related internships or fieldwork, Federal Work-Study, institutionally sponsored loans, scholarships/grants, tuition waivers (partial), and unspecified assistantships available. Support available to part-time students. Financial award application deadline: 2/15; financial award applicants required to submit FAFSA. *Faculty research:* Sleep; use of technology to develop executive function by students with disabilities; early childhood literacy development through play; social justice through education; using a structured protocol to discuss Bad News. *Unit head:* Dr. Albert Inserra, Dean, 516-299-2210, E-mail: albert.inserra@liu.edu. *Application contact:* Rita Langdon, Graduate Admissions, 516-299-2900, Fax: 516-299-2137, E-mail: post-enroll@liu.edu.
Website: http://liu.edu/CWPost/Academics/College-of-Education-Information-and-Technology

Louisiana State University and Agricultural & Mechanical College, Graduate School, College of Human Sciences and Education, School of Library and Information Science, Baton Rouge, LA 70803. Offers MLIS. *Accreditation:* ALA. *Faculty:* 8 full-time (3 women). *Students:* 67 full-time (59 women), 129 part-time (110 women); includes 45 minority (32 Black or African American, non-Hispanic/Latino; 10 Hispanic/Latino; 3 Two or more races, non-Hispanic/Latino). Average age 33. 96 applicants, 83% accepted, 63 enrolled. In 2017, 37 master's awarded. *Financial support:* In 2017–18, 1 research assistantship (averaging $14,198 per year), 10 teaching assistantships (averaging $14,266 per year) were awarded. *Total annual research expenditures:* $345.

Mansfield University of Pennsylvania, Graduate Studies, Program in School Library and Information Technologies, Mansfield, PA 16933. Offers library science (M Ed). *Program availability:* Part-time, evening/weekend, online learning. *Degree requirements:* For master's, comprehensive exam, thesis optional. *Entrance requirements:* For master's, minimum GPA of 3.0. Additional exam requirements/recommendations for international students: Required—TOEFL (minimum score 550 paper-based). Electronic applications accepted. *Expenses:* Contact institution.

McDaniel College, Graduate and Professional Studies, Program in School Librarianship, Westminster, MD 21157-4390. Offers MS. *Program availability:* Part-time, evening/weekend, online only, 100% online. *Faculty:* 1 (woman) full-time, 5 part-time/adjunct (all women). *Students:* 3 full-time (all women), 66 part-time (60 women); includes 3 minority (1 Black or African American, non-Hispanic/Latino; 2 Asian, non-Hispanic/Latino), 1 international. Average age 38. 10 applicants, 100% accepted, 9 enrolled. In 2017, 8 master's awarded. *Degree requirements:* For master's, comprehensive exam, thesis optional. *Entrance requirements:* For master's, PRAXIS, 3 recommendations, essay. Additional exam requirements/recommendations for international students: Required—TOEFL (minimum score 79 iBT), IELTS (minimum score 6). *Application deadline:* For fall admission, 6/1 priority date for domestic students; for spring admission, 11/1 priority date for domestic students; for summer admission, 3/1 priority date for domestic students. Applications are processed on a rolling basis. Application fee: $75. Electronic applications accepted. *Expenses: Tuition:* Full-time $11,760; part-time $490 per credit hour. Tuition and fees vary according to course load and program. *Financial support:* Career-related internships or fieldwork available. Financial award application deadline: 3/1; financial award applicants required to submit FAFSA. *Unit head:* Fax: 410-857-2515, E-mail: gradadms@mcdaniel.edu. *Application contact:* Crystal L. Perry, Assistant Director, Graduate Enrollment Management, 410-857-2516, Fax: 410-857-2515, E-mail: cperry@mcdaniel.edu.

McGill University, Faculty of Graduate and Postdoctoral Studies, Faculty of Education, School of Information Studies, Montréal, QC H3A 2T5, Canada. Offers MLIS, PhD, Certificate, Diploma. *Accreditation:* ALA (one or more programs are accredited).

McNeese State University, Doré School of Graduate Studies, Burton College of Education, Department of Education Professions, Program in School Librarian, Lake Charles, LA 70609. Offers Postbaccalaureate Certificate. *Entrance requirements:* For degree, PRAXIS, 2 letters of recommendation, autobiography. *Application deadline:* For fall admission, 5/15 priority date for domestic and international students; for spring admission, 10/15 priority date for domestic and international students. Applications are processed on a rolling basis. Application fee: $20 ($30 for international students). *Financial support:* Application deadline: 5/1. *Unit head:* Dr. Veronica Faye White, Head, 337-475-5400, Fax: 337-475-5272, E-mail: vfwhite@mcneese.edu. *Application contact:* Dr. Dustin M. Hebert, Director of Doré' School of Graduate Studies, 337-475-5396, Fax: 337-475-5397, E-mail: admissions@mcneese.edu.

North Carolina Central University, School of Library and Information Sciences, Durham, NC 27707-3129. Offers MIS, MLS. *Accreditation:* ALA (one or more programs are accredited). *Program availability:* Part-time, evening/weekend. *Degree requirements:* For master's, one foreign language, thesis, research paper, or project. *Entrance requirements:* For master's, GRE, 90 hours in liberal arts. Additional exam requirements/recommendations for international students: Required—TOEFL. *Application deadline:* For fall admission, 8/1 for domestic students. Application fee: $30. *Expenses:* Tuition, state resident: full-time $2770; part-time $692.50 per credit hour. Tuition, nonresident: full-time $9247; part-time $2311.75 per credit hour. *Financial support:* Application deadline: 5/1; applicants required to submit FAFSA. *Unit head:* Dr. Jon P. Gant, Dean, 919-530-6402, Fax: 919-530-6402, E-mail: slis-dean@nccu.edu. *Application contact:* Dr. Jon P. Gant, Dean, 919-530-6402, Fax: 919-530-6402, E-mail: slis-dean@nccu.edu. Website: http://www.nccuslis.org/

Old Dominion University, Darden College of Education, Program in Elementary/Middle Education, Norfolk, VA 23529. Offers elementary education (Postbaccalaureate Certificate); instructional technology (MS Ed); library science (MS Ed). *Accreditation:* NCATE. *Program availability:* Part-time, evening/weekend, 100% online, blended/hybrid learning. *Faculty:* 21 full-time (19 women), 24 part-time/adjunct (22 women). *Students:* 134 full-time (127 women), 123 part-time (108 women); includes 60 minority (34 Black or African American, non-Hispanic/Latino; 1 American Indian or Alaska Native, non-Hispanic/Latino; 2 Asian, non-Hispanic/Latino; 15 Hispanic/Latino; 8 Two or more races, non-Hispanic/Latino). Average age 32. 213 applicants, 88% accepted, 172 enrolled. In 2017, 121 master's awarded. *Degree requirements:* For master's, comprehensive exam. *Entrance requirements:* For master's, GRE General Test or MAT; PRAXIS I, SAT or ACT, minimum GPA of 2.8. Additional exam requirements/recommendations for international students: Required—TOEFL (minimum score 600 paper-based). *Application deadline:* For fall admission, 6/1 priority date for domestic students; for winter admission, 11/1 priority date for domestic students; for spring admission, 3/1 priority date for domestic students. Applications are processed on a rolling basis. Application fee: $50. Electronic applications accepted. *Expenses:* Contact institution. *Financial support:* In 2017–18, 180 students received support. Unspecified assistantships available. Financial award application deadline: 2/15; financial award applicants required to submit FAFSA. *Faculty research:* Education pre-K to 6, school librarianship, reading, TESOL, literacy. *Unit head:* Dr. KaaVonia Hinton, Chair, Department of Teaching and Learning, 757-683-3284, Fax: 757-683-5862, E-mail: khintonj@odu.edu. *Application contact:* William Heffelfinger, Director of Graduate Admissions, 757-683-5554, Fax: 757-683-3255, E-mail: gradadmit@odu.edu. Website: http://education.odu.edu/eci/

Olivet Nazarene University, Graduate School, Division of Education, Program in Library Information Specialist, Bourbonnais, IL 60914. Offers MAE.

Pratt Institute, School of Information, New York, NY 10011. Offers MS, Adv C, JD/MS, MS/MFA. *Accreditation:* ALA. *Program availability:* Part-time. *Students:* 134 full-time (109 women), 52 part-time (43 women); includes 44 minority (10 Black or African American, non-Hispanic/Latino; 10 Asian, non-Hispanic/Latino; 19 Hispanic/Latino; 5 Two or more races, non-Hispanic/Latino), 31 international. Average age 30. 303 applicants, 75% accepted, 67 enrolled. In 2017, 59 master's, 1 other advanced degree awarded. *Degree requirements:* For master's, thesis. *Entrance requirements:* For degree, master's degree in library and information science. Additional exam requirements/recommendations for international students: Required—TOEFL (minimum score 600 paper-based; 100 iBT). *Application deadline:* For fall admission, 1/5 for domestic and international students; for spring admission, 10/1 for domestic and international students. Applications are processed on a rolling basis. Application fee: $50 ($90 for international students). Electronic applications accepted. *Expenses:* $24,768 tuition full-time; $1,974 fees. *Financial support:* Career-related internships or fieldwork, Federal Work-Study, institutionally sponsored loans, scholarships/grants, health care benefits, and unspecified assistantships available. Support available to part-time students. Financial award application deadline: 2/1; financial award applicants required to submit FAFSA. *Faculty research:* Development of urban libraries and information centers, medical and law librarianship, information management. *Unit head:* Anthony Cocciolo, Interim Dean, 212-647-7702, Fax: 212-367-2492, E-mail: acocciol@pratt.edu. *Application contact:* Natalie Capannelli, Director of Graduate Admissions, 718-636-3551, Fax: 718-399-4242, E-mail: ncapanne@pratt.edu. Website: https://www.pratt.edu/academics/information/

See Display on page 1535 and Close-Up on page 1547.

Queens College of the City University of New York, Division of Social Sciences, Graduate School of Library and Information Studies, Queens, NY 11367-1597. Offers archives and preservation of cultural materials (AC); children's and young adult services in the public library (AC); librarianship (AC); library science (MLS); school library media specialist (MLS). *Accreditation:* ALA (one or more programs are accredited). *Program availability:* Part-time, evening/weekend. *Students:* 28 full-time (20 women), 289 part-time (205 women); includes 116 minority (37 Black or African American, non-Hispanic/Latino; 17 Asian, non-Hispanic/Latino; 53 Hispanic/Latino; 9 Two or more races, non-Hispanic/Latino), 4 international. Average age 33. *Degree requirements:* For master's, thesis; for AC, thesis optional. *Entrance requirements:* For master's, minimum GPA of 3.0; for AC, master's degree or equivalent. Additional exam requirements/recommendations for international students: Required—TOEFL, IELTS. *Application deadline:* For fall admission, 4/1 for domestic students; for spring admission, 11/1 for domestic students. Applications are processed on a rolling basis. Application fee: $125. Electronic applications accepted. *Financial support:* Career-related internships or fieldwork and unspecified assistantships available. Financial award application deadline: 4/1; financial award applicants required to submit FAFSA. *Unit head:* Colleen Cool, Director/Chair, 718-997-3790, E-mail: colleen.cool@qc.cuny.edu. *Application contact:* Elizabeth D'Amico-Ramirez, Assistant Director of Graduate Admissions, 718-997-5203, E-mail: elizabeth.damicoramirez@qc.cuny.edu.

Rowan University, Graduate School, College of Education, Department of Educational Services and Leadership, Glassboro, NJ 08028-1701. Offers counseling in educational settings (MA); educational leadership (Ed D, CAGS); higher education administration (MA); principal preparation (CAGS); school administration (MA); school and public librarianship (MA); school nursing (Postbaccalaureate Certificate); school psychology (MA, Ed S); supervisor (CAGS). *Accreditation:* NCATE. *Program availability:* Part-time, evening/weekend. *Degree requirements:* For master's, comprehensive exam, thesis; for other advanced degree, thesis or alternative. *Entrance requirements:* For master's and other advanced degree, GRE General Test. Additional exam requirements/recommendations for international students: Required—TOEFL. Electronic applications accepted. *Expenses:* Tuition, state resident: full-time $15,020; part-time $751 per semester hour. Tuition, nonresident: full-time $15,020; part-time $751 per semester hour. *Required fees:* $3158; $157.90 per semester hour. Tuition and fees vary according to course load, campus/location and program.

Rutgers University–New Brunswick, School of Communication and Information, Program in Communication, Information and Library Studies, Piscataway, NJ 08854-8097. Offers PhD. *Program availability:* Part-time. *Degree requirements:* For doctorate, comprehensive exam, thesis/dissertation, qualifying exams. *Entrance requirements:* For doctorate, GRE General Test, proficiency in statistics. Additional exam requirements/recommendations for international students: Required—TOEFL (minimum score 600 paper-based). Electronic applications accepted. *Faculty research:* Information science, media studies.

St. Catherine University, Graduate Programs, Program in Library and Information Science, St. Paul, MN 55105. Offers MLIS. *Accreditation:* ALA. *Program availability:* Part-time, evening/weekend. *Degree requirements:* For master's, microcomputer competency. *Entrance requirements:* For master's, GRE or MAT, minimum GPA of 3.2 or GRE. Additional exam requirements/recommendations for international students: Required—Michigan English Language Assessment Battery or TOEFL (minimum score 600 paper-based; 100 iBT). *Application deadline:* For fall admission, 3/1 for domestic students; for winter admission, 10/1 for domestic students. Application fee: $35. *Expenses:* Contact institution. *Financial support:* Institutionally sponsored loans available. Support available to part-time students. Financial award application deadline: 4/1; financial award applicants required to submit FAFSA. *Unit head:* Anthony Molaro, Director, 651-690-6626. *Application contact:* Kristina Sande, Director of Graduate Admissions, 651-690-6507, Fax: 651-690-6064. Website: https://www.stkate.edu/academics/graduate-degrees/academic-programs/mlis

St. John's University, St. John's College of Liberal Arts and Sciences, Department of Government and Politics and Division of Library and Information Science, Program in Government and Library and Information Science, Queens, NY 11439. Offers MA/MS. *Program availability:* Part-time, evening/weekend. *Students:* 1 applicant, 100% accepted. *Entrance requirements:* Additional exam requirements/recommendations for international students: Required—TOEFL (minimum score 80 iBT), IELTS (minimum score 6.5). *Application deadline:* For fall admission, 5/1 for domestic students; for spring admission, 11/1 for domestic students. Applications are processed on a rolling basis. Application fee: $70. Electronic applications accepted. *Expenses: Tuition:* Full-time $44,280; part-time $1230 per credit. *Required fees:* $340; $340 per credit. Tuition and fees vary according to course load, degree level and program. *Financial support:* Fellowships, research assistantships, teaching assistantships, scholarships/grants, tuition waivers, and unspecified assistantships available. Support available to part-time students. Financial award application deadline: 2/1; financial award applicants required to submit FAFSA. *Faculty research:* Presidential leadership, morality and politics, U.S. foreign policy, U.S. national security policy, NY state and local government and politics, state building and social policy, public opinion, campaigns and elections, education politics, North African politics, energy and European Union politics. *Unit head:* Dr. Fred Pompeo Cocozzelli, Chair, 718-990-5267, E-mail: cocozzef@stjohns.edu. *Application contact:* Robert Medrano, Director of Graduate Admission, 718-990-1601, Fax: 718-990-5686, E-mail: gradhelp@stjohns.edu.

St. John's University, St. John's College of Liberal Arts and Sciences, Division of Library and Information Science, Queens, NY 11439. Offers library science (MS); management for information professionals (Adv C); MA/MS. *Accreditation:* ALA (one or more programs are accredited). *Program availability:* Part-time, online only, 100% online. *Faculty:* 5 full-time (2 women), 1 (woman) part-time/adjunct. *Students:* 25 full-time (22 women), 39 part-time (33 women); includes 19 minority (7 Black or African American, non-Hispanic/Latino; 1 American Indian or Alaska Native, non-Hispanic/Latino; 4 Asian, non-Hispanic/Latino; 6 Hispanic/Latino; 1 Two or more races, non-Hispanic/Latino). Average age 33. 63 applicants, 63% accepted, 21 enrolled. In 2017, 30 master's awarded. *Degree requirements:* For master's, e-portfolio end-of-program assessment; for Adv C, 15 credits (five courses) including capstone course. *Entrance requirements:* For master's, letters of recommendation, transcripts, resume, personal statement. Additional exam requirements/recommendations for international students: Required—TOEFL (minimum score 80 iBT), IELTS (minimum score 6.5). *Application deadline:* For fall admission, 5/1 for domestic students; for spring admission, 11/1 for domestic students. Applications are processed on a rolling basis. Application fee: $70. Electronic applications accepted. *Expenses:* $23,724 per year. *Financial support:* Fellowships, research assistantships, teaching assistantships, scholarships/grants, tuition waivers, and unspecified assistantships available. Support available to part-time students. Financial award application deadline: 2/1; financial award applicants required to submit FAFSA. *Faculty research:* Social justice in the information professions, teen spaces in public libraries, information organization, management, marketing and advocacy in information organizations, digital libraries. *Total annual research expenditures:* $24,163. *Unit head:* Dr. James Vorbach, Director, 718-990-1834, Fax: 718-990-2071, E-mail: vorbachj@stjohns.edu. *Application contact:* Robert Medrano, Director of Graduate Admissions, 718-990-1601, Fax: 718-990-5686, E-mail: gradhelp@stjohns.edu. Website: https://www.stjohns.edu/academics/schools-and-colleges/st-johns-college-liberal-arts-and-sciences/library-and-information-science

Library Science

Sam Houston State University, College of Education, Department of Library Science, Huntsville, TX 77341. Offers MLS. *Program availability:* Part-time, evening/weekend. *Degree requirements:* For master's, portfolio, intership. *Entrance requirements:* For master's, GRE General Test. Additional exam requirements/recommendations for international students: Required—TOEFL (minimum score 550 paper-based; 79 iBT), IELTS (minimum score 6.5). Electronic applications accepted.

San Jose State University, Graduate Studies and Research, College of Health and Human Sciences, San Jose, CA 95192-0049. Offers criminology (MS), including global criminology, law and justice; justice studies (MS); kinesiology (MA), including athletic training, exercise physiology, interdisciplinary, sport studies, sports management; library and information science (MLIS); mass communications (MS); nursing (MS), including family nurse practitioner; nutritional science (MS); occupational therapy (MS); public health (MPH); social work (MSW); MD/M Div. *Program availability:* Part-time, 100% online, blended/hybrid learning. *Faculty:* 15 full-time (7 women), 6 part-time/adjunct (3 women). *Students:* 517 full-time (407 women), 405 part-time (302 women); includes 523 minority (39 Black or African American, non-Hispanic/Latino; 2 American Indian or Alaska Native, non-Hispanic/Latino; 141 Asian, non-Hispanic/Latino; 226 Hispanic/Latino; 2 Native Hawaiian or other Pacific Islander, non-Hispanic/Latino; 113 Two or more races, non-Hispanic/Latino), 14 international. Average age 32. 1,250 applicants, 45% accepted, 375 enrolled. In 2017, 808 master's awarded. *Degree requirements:* For master's, thesis (for some programs), graduate writing assessment. *Entrance requirements:* Additional exam requirements/recommendations for international students: Required—TOEFL (minimum score 550 paper-based; 80 iBT), IELTS (minimum score 6.5), PTE (minimum score 53). *Application deadline:* For fall admission, 2/1 for domestic and international students. Applications are processed on a rolling basis. Application fee: $55. Electronic applications accepted. *Expenses:* Tuition, state resident: full-time $7176. Tuition, nonresident: full-time $16,680. Tuition and fees vary according to course load and program. *Financial support:* Fellowships, research assistantships, teaching assistantships, career-related internships or fieldwork, Federal Work-Study, scholarships/grants, and tuition waivers (full and partial) available. Support available to part-time students. Financial award application deadline: 4/24; financial award applicants required to submit FAFSA. *Unit head:* Dr. Mary Schutten, Dean, College of Health and Human Sciences, 408-924-2900, Fax: 408-924-2901, E-mail: mary.schutten@sjsu.edu.
Website: http://www.sjsu.edu/casa/

Simmons College, School of Library and Information Science, Boston, MA 02115. Offers children's literature (MA); library and information science (MS, PhD, Certificate), including archives management (MS), cultural heritage (MS), information science and technology (MS); school library teacher (MS); writing for children (MFA); MA/MA; MA/MAT; MA/MFA; MS/MA. *Accreditation:* ALA (one or more programs are accredited). *Program availability:* Part-time, evening/weekend, 100% online, blended/hybrid learning. *Faculty:* 28 full-time (21 women), 34 part-time/adjunct (25 women). *Students:* 339 full-time (287 women), 509 part-time (415 women); includes 91 minority (15 Black or African American, non-Hispanic/Latino; 18 Asian, non-Hispanic/Latino; 35 Hispanic/Latino; 23 Two or more races, non-Hispanic/Latino), 12 international. Average age 30. 533 applicants, 98% accepted, 268 enrolled. In 2017, 300 master's, 10 doctorates, 5 other advanced degrees awarded. *Degree requirements:* For master's, thesis optional, capstone project experience; for doctorate, comprehensive exam, thesis/dissertation, 36 credit hours. *Entrance requirements:* For master's, GRE when applicants' GPA is below 3.0 for all degrees, statement of purpose, current resume or curriculum vitae, college transcripts, three letters of recommendation; for doctorate, GRE or MTEL, transcripts, personal statement, resume, recommendations, master's degree. Additional exam requirements/recommendations for international students: Required—TOEFL (minimum score 550 paper-based; 79 iBT), IELTS (minimum score 7). *Application deadline:* For fall admission, 3/1 for domestic and international students; for spring admission, 9/1 for domestic and international students; for summer admission, 2/1 for domestic and international students. Applications are processed on a rolling basis. Application fee: $65. Electronic applications accepted. *Expenses:* $1,135 per credit, $3,405 per course, $55 activity fee per semester. *Financial support:* In 2017–18, 10 fellowships with partial tuition reimbursements were awarded; scholarships/grants and unspecified assistantships also available. Support available to part-time students. Financial award application deadline: 6/1; financial award applicants required to submit FAFSA. *Faculty research:* Archives and social justice, information-seeking behavior, information retrieval, organization of information, cultural heritage informatics. *Unit head:* Dr. Eileen G. Abels, Dean, 617-521-2869. *Application contact:* Kate Benson, Director, SLIS Admission, 617-521-2801, Fax: 617-521-3192, E-mail: slisadm@simmons.edu.
Website: http://www.simmons.edu/slis/

Southern Arkansas University–Magnolia, School of Graduate Studies, Magnolia, AR 71753. Offers agriculture (MS); business administration (MBA), including agribusiness, social entrepreneurship, supply chain management; clinical and mental health counseling (MS); computer and information sciences (MS), including cyber security and privacy, data science, information technology; gifted and talented (M Ed), including curriculum and instruction, educational administration and supervision, gifted and talented P-8/7-12, instructional specialist P-4; higher, adult and lifelong education (M Ed); kinesiology (M Ed), including coaching; library media and information specialist (M Ed); public administration (MPA); school counseling K-12 (M Ed); student affairs and college counseling (M Ed); teaching (MAT). *Accreditation:* NCATE. *Program availability:* Part-time, 100% online, blended/hybrid learning. *Faculty:* 36 full-time (20 women), 31 part-time/adjunct (12 women). *Students:* 242 full-time (89 women), 889 part-time (459 women); includes 167 minority (143 Black or African American, non-Hispanic/Latino; 7 American Indian or Alaska Native, non-Hispanic/Latino; 7 Asian, non-Hispanic/Latino; 3 Hispanic/Latino; 7 Two or more races, non-Hispanic/Latino), 562 international. Average age 28. 400 applicants, 100% accepted, 239 enrolled. In 2017, 875 master's awarded. *Degree requirements:* For master's, comprehensive exam (for some programs), thesis optional. *Entrance requirements:* For master's, GRE, MAT or GMAT, minimum GPA of 2.5. Additional exam requirements/recommendations for international students: Required—TOEFL (minimum score 550 paper-based), IELTS (minimum score 6). *Application deadline:* For fall admission, 7/20 for domestic students, 7/10 for international students; for spring admission, 12/1 for domestic students, 11/15 for international students; for summer admission, 4/1 for domestic students, 5/1 for international students. Applications are processed on a rolling basis. Application fee: $25 ($50 for international students). Electronic applications accepted. *Expenses:* Tuition, state resident: full-time $6038. Tuition, nonresident: full-time $8558. *Required fees:* $804. One-time fee: $110 full-time. Tuition and fees vary according to course load. *Financial support:* Career-related internships or fieldwork, Federal Work-Study, scholarships/grants, tuition waivers (full), and unspecified assistantships available. Financial award applicants required to submit FAFSA. *Faculty research:* Alternative certification for teachers, supervision of instruction, instructional leadership, counseling. *Unit head:* Dr. Kim Bloss, Dean, School of Graduate Studies, 870-235-4150, Fax: 870-235-5227, E-mail: kkbloss@saumag.edu. *Application contact:* Shrijana Malakar, Admissions Specialist, 870-235-4150, Fax: 870-235-5227, E-mail: smalakar@saumag.edu.
Website: http://www.saumag.edu/graduate

Southern Connecticut State University, School of Graduate Studies, School of Education, Department of Information and Library Science, New Haven, CT 06515-1355. Offers information studies (Diploma); library science (MLS). *Program availability:* Part-time, evening/weekend. *Degree requirements:* For master's and Diploma, thesis or alternative. *Entrance requirements:* For master's, GRE General Test, interview, minimum QPA of 2.7, introductory computer science course; for Diploma, master's degree in library science or information science. Electronic applications accepted.

Syracuse University, School of Information Studies, MS Program in Library and Information Science, Syracuse, NY 13244. Offers MS. *Accreditation:* ALA. *Program availability:* Part-time, evening/weekend, online learning. *Students:* Average age 30. *Entrance requirements:* For master's, GRE General Test, two letters of recommendation, personal statement, resume. Additional exam requirements/recommendations for international students: Required—TOEFL (minimum score 100 iBT). *Application deadline:* For fall admission, 2/1 priority date for domestic and international students; for spring admission, 10/15 priority date for domestic and international students. Applications are processed on a rolling basis. Application fee: $75. Electronic applications accepted. *Financial support:* Fellowships with full tuition reimbursements and teaching assistantships available. Financial award application deadline: 1/1; financial award applicants required to submit FAFSA. *Faculty research:* Information environments, library planning and marketing, management principles, information policy. *Unit head:* Prof. Caroline Haythornthwaite, Program Director, 315-443-2911, E-mail: igrad@syr.edu. *Application contact:* Susan Corieri, Director of Enrollment Management, 315-443-1070, E-mail: ischool@syr.edu.
Website: https://ischool.syr.edu/academics/graduate/masters-degrees/ms-library-and-information-science/

See Display on the next page and Close-Up on page 1549.

Tennessee Technological University, College of Graduate Studies, College of Education, Department of Curriculum and Instruction, Program in Library Science, Cookeville, TN 38505. Offers MA, Ed S. *Program availability:* Part-time, evening/weekend. *Students:* 7 full-time (all women), 7 part-time (all women). 7 applicants, 100% accepted, 4 enrolled. In 2017, 1 master's, 1 other advanced degree awarded. *Degree requirements:* For master's, comprehensive exam, thesis or alternative. *Entrance requirements:* For master's, MAT or GRE. Additional exam requirements/recommendations for international students: Required—TOEFL (minimum score 527 paper-based; 71 iBT), IELTS (minimum score 5.5), PTE (minimum score 48), or TOEIC (Test of English as an International Communication). *Application deadline:* For fall admission, 8/1 for domestic students, 5/1 for international students; for spring admission, 12/1 for domestic students, 10/1 for international students; for summer admission, 5/1 for domestic students, 2/1 for international students. Applications are processed on a rolling basis. Application fee: $35 ($40 for international students). Electronic applications accepted. *Expenses:* Tuition, state resident: full-time $9925; part-time $565 per credit hour. Tuition, nonresident: full-time $22,993; part-time $1291 per credit hour. *Financial support:* Research assistantships and teaching assistantships available. Financial award application deadline: 4/1. *Unit head:* Dr. Jeremy Wendt, Interim Chairperson, 931-372-3181, Fax: 931-372-6270, E-mail: jwendt@tntech.edu. *Application contact:* Shelia K. Kendrick, Coordinator of Graduate Studies, 931-372-3808, Fax: 931-372-3497, E-mail: skendrick@tntech.edu.

Texas A&M University–Commerce, College of Education and Human Services, Commerce, TX 75429. Offers counseling (M Ed, MS, PhD); early childhood education (M Ed, MS); educational administration (M Ed, MS, Ed D); educational psychology (PhD); educational technology leadership (M Ed, MS); educational technology library science (M Ed, MS); elementary education (M Ed); health, kinesiology and sports studies (MS); higher education (MS, Ed D); psychology (MS); reading (M Ed, MS); secondary education (M Ed, MS); social work (MSW); special education (M Ed, MS); supervision, curriculum and instruction-elementary education (Ed D); training and development (MS). *Program availability:* Part-time, evening/weekend, 100% online, blended/hybrid learning. *Faculty:* 91 full-time (51 women), 38 part-time/adjunct (31 women). *Students:* 400 full-time (310 women), 1,400 part-time (1,117 women); includes 724 minority (412 Black or African American, non-Hispanic/Latino; 8 American Indian or Alaska Native, non-Hispanic/Latino; 24 Asian, non-Hispanic/Latino; 220 Hispanic/Latino; 60 Two or more races, non-Hispanic/Latino), 18 international. Average age 37. 951 applicants, 46% accepted, 331 enrolled. In 2017, 564 master's, 24 doctorates awarded. *Degree requirements:* For master's, comprehensive exam, thesis optional, departmental qualifying exams (for some programs); for doctorate, comprehensive exam, thesis/dissertation, departmental qualifying exam; for SSP, comprehensive exam, thesis optional. *Entrance requirements:* For master's and doctorate, GRE General Test. Additional exam requirements/recommendations for international students: Required—TOEFL (minimum score 550 paper-based; 79 iBT), IELTS (minimum score 6). *Application deadline:* For fall admission, 6/1 priority date for international students; for spring admission, 10/15 priority date for international students; for summer admission, 3/15 priority date for international students. Applications are processed on a rolling basis. Application fee: $50. Electronic applications accepted. *Expenses:* Tuition, state resident: full-time $3630. Tuition, nonresident: full-time $11,100. *Required fees:* $2564. Tuition and fees vary according to course load, degree level and program. *Financial support:* In 2017–18, 84 students received support, including 40 research assistantships with partial tuition reimbursements available (averaging $10,800 per year), 12 teaching assistantships with partial tuition reimbursements available (averaging $13,000 per year); career-related internships or fieldwork, Federal Work-Study, institutionally sponsored loans, scholarships/grants, health care benefits, and unspecified assistantships also available. Financial award application deadline: 6/15; financial award applicants required to submit FAFSA. *Faculty research:* Cognitive and bilingual education, positive behavioral intervention, literacy, math readiness. *Total annual research expenditures:* $1.1 million. *Unit head:* Dr. Timothy Letzring, Dean, 903-886-5181, Fax: 903-886-5905, E-mail: tim.letzring@tamuc.edu. *Application contact:* Vicky Turner, Doctoral Degree and Special Programs Coordinator, 903-886-5167, E-mail: vicky.turner@tamuc.edu.
Website: http://www.tamuc.edu/academics/graduateSchool/programs/education/default.aspx

Texas Woman's University, Graduate School, College of Professional Education, School of Library and Information Studies, Denton, TX 76204. Offers library science (MA, MLS). *Accreditation:* ALA (one or more programs are accredited). *Program availability:* Part-time, evening/weekend, online only, 100% online. *Faculty:* 12 full-time (9 women), 16 part-time/adjunct (10 women). *Students:* 120 full-time (115 women), 420 part-time (405 women); includes 171 minority (34 Black or African American, non-Hispanic/Latino; 1 American Indian or Alaska Native, non-Hispanic/Latino; 10 Asian, non-Hispanic/Latino; 120 Hispanic/Latino; 6 Two or more races, non-Hispanic/Latino), 1 international. Average age 36. 160 applicants, 78% accepted, 99 enrolled. In 2017, 134 master's awarded. *Degree requirements:* For master's, comprehensive exam, practicum (for MLS); thesis (for MA). *Entrance requirements:* For master's, GRE (preferred), GMAT, MCAT, MAT, 3 letters of recommendation, 2-page statement of intent, resume. Additional exam requirements/recommendations for international students: Required—TOEFL (minimum score 550 paper-based; 79 iBT); Recommended—IELTS (minimum score 6.5), TSE (minimum score 53). *Application deadline:* For fall admission, 3/1 priority date for domestic and international students. Applications are processed on a

rolling basis. Application fee: $50 ($75 for international students). Electronic applications accepted. *Expenses:* $7,700 per year full-time in-state; $17,000 per year full-time out-of-state. *Financial support:* In 2017–18, 103 students received support, including 2 research assistantships (averaging $14,671 per year); career-related internships or fieldwork, Federal Work-Study, institutionally sponsored loans, scholarships/grants, traineeships, health care benefits, and unspecified assistantships also available. Support available to part-time students. Financial award application deadline: 3/1; financial award applicants required to submit FAFSA. *Faculty research:* Information needs analysis, school library leadership, library management and assessment, informatics, information retrieval. *Unit head:* Dr. Ling Hwey Jeng, Director, 940-898-2602, Fax: 940-898-2611, E-mail: slis@twu.edu. *Application contact:* Korie Hawkins, Associate Director of Admissions, Graduate Recruitment, 940-898-3188, Fax: 940-898-3081, E-mail: admissions@twu.edu.
Website: http://www.twu.edu/slis/

Trevecca Nazarene University, Graduate Education Program, Nashville, TN 37210-2877. Offers accountability and instructional leadership (Ed S); curriculum and instruction for Christian school educators (M Ed); curriculum and instruction K-12 (M Ed); educational leadership (M Ed); English second language (M Ed); library and information science (MLI Sc); special education: visual impairments (M Ed); teaching (MAT), including teaching 6-12, teaching K-5. *Accreditation:* NCATE. *Program availability:* Part-time, evening/weekend, online learning. *Faculty:* 8 full-time (6 women), 22 part-time/adjunct (18 women). *Students:* 150 full-time (114 women), 3 part-time (1 woman); includes 54 minority (49 Black or African American, non-Hispanic/Latino; 4 Hispanic/Latino; 1 Two or more races, non-Hispanic/Latino). Average age 36. In 2017, 57 master's, 4 other advanced degrees awarded. *Degree requirements:* For master's, comprehensive exam, exit assessment/e-portfolio. *Entrance requirements:* For master's, GRE or MAT; PRAXIS (for MAT), minimum GPA of 3.0, official transcript from regionally-accredited institution, references, interview, writing sample, at least 3 years' successful teaching experience (for M Ed in educational leadership); for Ed S, GRE or MAT, master's degree with minimum GPA of 3.0, official transcript from regionally accredited institution, at least 3 years' successful teaching experience, interview, writing sample, background and fingerprinting check, recommendations. Additional exam requirements/recommendations for international students: Required—TOEFL (minimum score 550 paper-based). *Application deadline:* Applications are processed on a rolling basis. Electronic applications accepted. *Expenses:* Contact institution. *Financial support:* Applicants required to submit FAFSA. *Unit head:* Dr. Suzie Harris, Dean, School of Education, 615-248-1201, Fax: 615-248-1597, E-mail: admissions_ged@trevecca.edu. *Application contact:* 844-TNU-GRAD, E-mail: sgcsadmissions@trevecca.edu.
Website: http://www.trevecca.edu/soe

Universidad del Turabo, Graduate Programs, Programs in Education, Program in Library Service and Information Technology, Gurabo, PR 00778-3030. Offers M Ed. *Program availability:* Part-time, evening/weekend. *Entrance requirements:* For master's, GRE, EXADEP, GMAT, interview, official transcript, essay, recommendation letters. Electronic applications accepted.

Université de Montréal, Faculty of Arts and Sciences, School of Library and Information Sciences, Montréal, QC H3C 3J7, Canada. Offers information sciences (MIS, PhD). *Accreditation:* ALA (one or more programs are accredited). *Degree requirements:* For master's, thesis optional. *Entrance requirements:* For master's, interview, master's degree in library and information science or equivalent. Electronic applications accepted.

University at Buffalo, the State University of New York, Graduate School, Graduate School of Education, Department of Library and Information Studies, Buffalo, NY 14260. Offers information and library science (MS); library and information studies (Certificate);

school librarianship (MS). *Accreditation:* ALA (one or more programs are accredited). *Program availability:* Part-time, 100% online. *Faculty:* 9 full-time (6 women), 8 part-time/adjunct (6 women). *Students:* 42 full-time (32 women), 162 part-time (131 women); includes 11 minority (5 Black or African American, non-Hispanic/Latino; 2 American Indian or Alaska Native, non-Hispanic/Latino; 4 Asian, non-Hispanic/Latino), 2 international. Average age 34. 117 applicants, 91% accepted, 73 enrolled. In 2017, 62 master's, 1 other advanced degree awarded. *Degree requirements:* For master's, thesis optional; for Certificate, thesis. *Entrance requirements:* For master's, letters of recommendation. Additional exam requirements/recommendations for international students: Required—TOEFL (minimum score 550 paper-based; 79 iBT). *Application deadline:* For fall admission, 4/1 priority date for domestic and international students; for spring admission, 10/15 priority date for domestic students, 10/15 for international students. Applications are processed on a rolling basis. Application fee: $50. Electronic applications accepted. *Financial support:* In 2017–18, 16 fellowships (averaging $2,345 per year), 6 research assistantships with tuition reimbursements (averaging $10,222 per year) were awarded; teaching assistantships, Federal Work-Study, scholarships/grants, tuition waivers (full and partial), and unspecified assistantships also available. Support available to part-time students. Financial award application deadline: 3/1; financial award applicants required to submit FAFSA. *Faculty research:* Information-seeking behavior, thesauri, impact of technology, questioning behaviors, educational informatics. *Total annual research expenditures:* $56,553. *Unit head:* Dr. Heidi Julien, Chair, 716-645-1474, Fax: 716-645-3775, E-mail: heidijul@buffalo.edu. *Application contact:* Pat Glinski, Admissions Assistant, 716-645-2110, Fax: 716-645-7937, E-mail: gse-info@buffalo.edu.
Website: http://www.gse.buffalo.edu/lis/

The University of Alabama, Graduate School, College of Communication and Information Sciences, School of Library and Information Studies, Tuscaloosa, AL 35487. Offers book arts (MFA); library and information studies (MLIS, PhD). *Accreditation:* ALA (one or more programs are accredited). *Program availability:* Part-time, evening/weekend, online learning. *Faculty:* 12 full-time (5 women), 1 (woman) part-time/adjunct. *Students:* 55 full-time (42 women), 174 part-time (145 women); includes 27 minority (13 Black or African American, non-Hispanic/Latino; 2 Asian, non-Hispanic/Latino; 6 Hispanic/Latino; 6 Two or more races, non-Hispanic/Latino), 4 international. Average age 33. 135 applicants, 81% accepted, 85 enrolled. In 2017, 73 master's awarded. *Degree requirements:* For master's, comprehensive exam (for some programs), thesis optional; for doctorate, comprehensive exam, thesis/dissertation. *Entrance requirements:* For master's, GRE General Test or MAT, minimum GPA of 3.0; for doctorate, GRE. Additional exam requirements/recommendations for international students: Required—TOEFL. *Application deadline:* For fall admission, 7/1 priority date for domestic and international students; for spring admission, 11/1 priority date for domestic and international students. Applications are processed on a rolling basis. Application fee: $50 ($60 for international students). Electronic applications accepted. *Financial support:* In 2017–18, 18 students received support, including fellowships with full tuition reimbursements available (averaging $15,000 per year), research assistantships with tuition reimbursements available (averaging $6,183 per year), teaching assistantships with tuition reimbursements available (averaging $6,183 per year); career-related internships or fieldwork, scholarships/grants, health care benefits, tuition waivers (full), unspecified assistantships, and 15 grant-funded fellowships also available. Support available to part-time students. Financial award application deadline: 3/15. *Faculty research:* Library administration, user services, digital libraries, book arts, evaluation. *Unit head:* Dr. Ann Ethelynd Prentice, Director and Professor, 205-348-4610, Fax: 205-348-3746, E-mail: aeprentice@ua.edu. *Application contact:* Dr. Ann Bourne, Assistant Director, 205-348-1524, Fax: 205-348-3746, E-mail: abourne@ua.edu.
Website: http://www.slis.ua.edu/

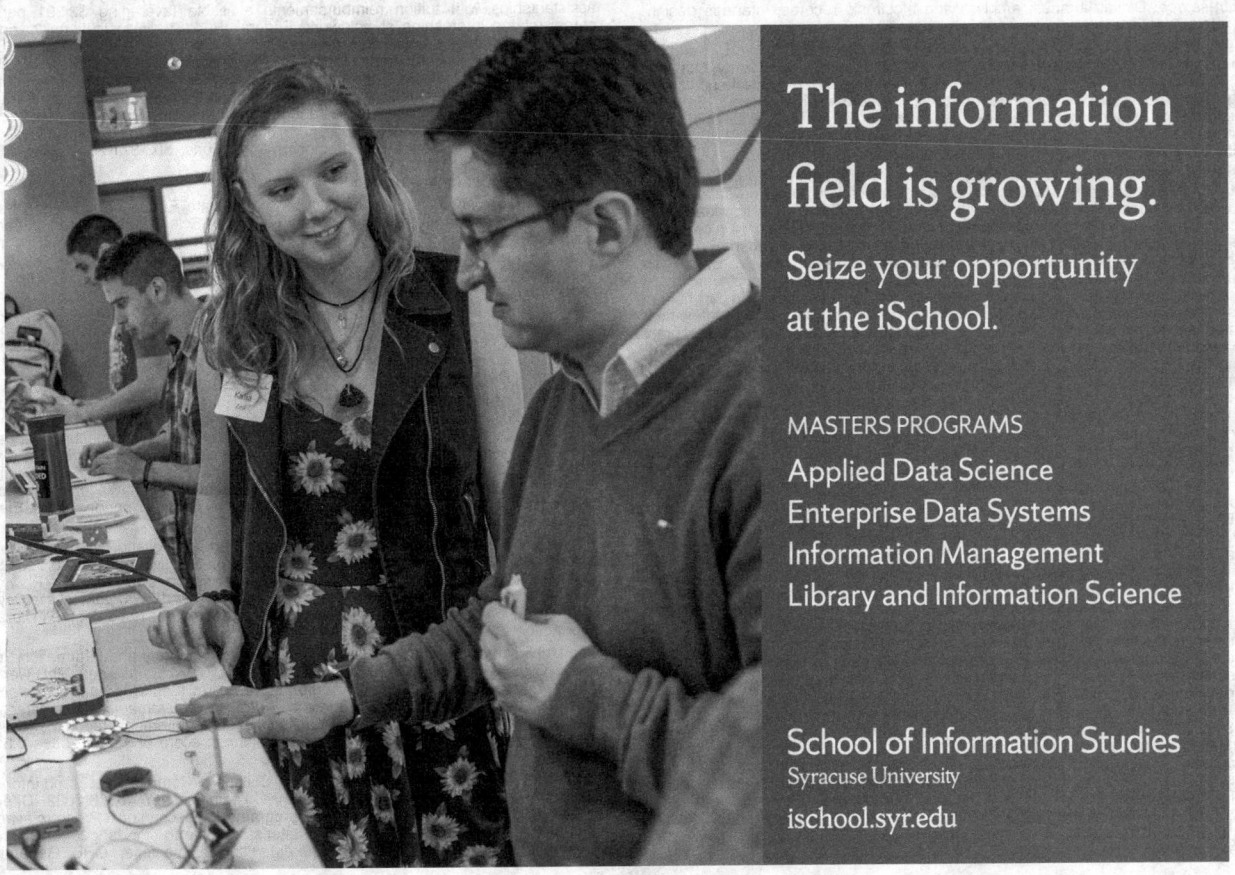

Library Science

University of Alberta, Faculty of Graduate Studies and Research, School of Library and Information Studies, Edmonton, AB T6G 2E1, Canada. Offers MLIS. *Accreditation:* ALA. *Entrance requirements:* Additional exam requirements/recommendations for international students: Required—TOEFL, Canadian Academic English Language Assessment. Electronic applications accepted. *Faculty research:* Intellectual freedom, materials for children and young adults, library classification, multi-media literacy.

The University of Arizona, College of Social and Behavioral Sciences, School of Information Resources and Library Science, Tucson, AZ 85721. Offers MA, PhD. *Accreditation:* ALA (one or more programs are accredited). *Program availability:* Part-time. *Degree requirements:* For master's, proficiency in disk operating system (DOS); for doctorate, thesis/dissertation. *Entrance requirements:* For master's and doctorate, GRE General Test, 3 letters of recommendation, resume. Additional exam requirements/recommendations for international students: Required—TOEFL (minimum score 550 paper-based; 79 iBT). Electronic applications accepted. *Faculty research:* Microcomputer applications; quantitative methods systems; information transfer, planning, evaluation, and technology.

The University of British Columbia, Faculty of Arts, School of Library, Archival and Information Studies, Dual Master of Archival Studies/Master of Library and Information Studies Program, Vancouver, BC V6T 1Z1, Canada. Offers MLIS/MAS. *Entrance requirements:* Additional exam requirements/recommendations for international students: Required—TOEFL. Electronic applications accepted. *Expenses:* Contact institution. *Faculty research:* Computer systems/database design, information-seeking behavior, archives and records management, children's literature and services, digital libraries and archives.

The University of British Columbia, Faculty of Arts, School of Library, Archival and Information Studies, Master of Library and Information Studies Program, Vancouver, BC V6T 1Z1, Canada. Offers MLIS. *Accreditation:* ALA. *Program availability:* Part-time. *Degree requirements:* For master's, thesis optional. *Entrance requirements:* For master's, minimum GPA of 3.3 in undergraduate upper-division courses. Additional exam requirements/recommendations for international students: Required—TOEFL. Electronic applications accepted. *Expenses:* Contact institution. *Faculty research:* Computer systems/database design; digital libraries; metadata/classification; human-computer interaction; children's literature and services.

The University of British Columbia, Faculty of Arts, School of Library, Archival and Information Studies, PhD Program in Library, Archival and Information Studies, Vancouver, BC V6T 1Z1, Canada. Offers PhD. *Degree requirements:* For doctorate, thesis/dissertation. *Entrance requirements:* For doctorate, GRE, minimum GPA of 3.3 in MAS or MLIS. Additional exam requirements/recommendations for international students: Required—TOEFL. Electronic applications accepted. *Expenses:* Contact institution. *Faculty research:* Computer systems/database design; library and archival management; archival description and organization; children's literature and youth services; interactive information retrieval.

University of California, Los Angeles, Graduate Division, Graduate School of Education and Information Studies, Department of Information Studies, Los Angeles, CA 90095-1521. Offers archival studies (MLIS); informatics (MLIS); information studies (PhD); library and information science (Certificate); library studies (MLIS); moving image archive studies (MA); rare books, print and visual culture (MLIS); MBA/MLIS; MLIS/MA. *Accreditation:* ALA (one or more programs are accredited). Terminal master's awarded for partial completion of doctoral program. *Degree requirements:* For master's, thesis or alternative, professional portfolio; for doctorate, thesis/dissertation, oral and written qualifying exams. *Entrance requirements:* For master's, GRE General Test, previous course work in statistics; for doctorate, GRE General Test, previous course work in statistics, 2 samples of research writing in English. Additional exam requirements/recommendations for international students: Required—TOEFL (minimum score 560 paper-based; 87 iBT), IELTS (minimum score 7). Electronic applications accepted. *Faculty research:* Digital libraries, archives and electronic records, interface design, cultural informatics, preservation/conservation, access.

University of Central Arkansas, Graduate School, College of Education, Department of Leadership Studies, Program in Library Media and Information Technology, Conway, AR 72035-0001. Offers MS. *Program availability:* Part-time, evening/weekend, online learning. *Degree requirements:* For master's, comprehensive exam. *Entrance requirements:* For master's, GRE General Test, minimum GPA of 2.7. Additional exam requirements/recommendations for international students: Required—TOEFL (minimum score 550 paper-based). Electronic applications accepted.

University of Central Missouri, The Graduate School, Warrensburg, MO 64093. Offers accountancy (MA); accounting (MBA); applied mathematics (MS); aviation safety (MA); biology (MS); business administration (MBA); career and technical education leadership (MS); college student personnel administration (MS); communication (MA); computer science (MS); counseling (MS); criminal justice (MS); educational leadership (Ed D); educational technology (MS); elementary and early childhood education (MSE); English (MA); environmental studies (MA); finance (MBA); history (MA); human services/educational technology (Ed S); human services/learning resources (Ed S); human services/professional counseling (Ed S); industrial hygiene (MS); industrial management (MS); information systems (MBA); information technology (MS); kinesiology (MS); library science and information services (MS); literacy education (MSE); marketing (MBA); mathematics (MS); music (MA); occupational safety management (MS); psychology (MS); rural family nursing (MS); school administration (MSE); social gerontology (MS); sociology (MA); special education (MSE); speech language pathology (MS); superintendency (Ed S); teaching (MAT); teaching English as a second language (MA); technology (MS); technology management (PhD); theatre (MA). *Program availability:* Part-time, 100% online, blended/hybrid learning. *Faculty:* 337 full-time (145 women), 41 part-time/adjunct (28 women). *Students:* 785 full-time (398 women), 1,633 part-time (1,063 women); includes 231 minority (102 Black or African American, non-Hispanic/Latino; 4 American Indian or Alaska Native, non-Hispanic/Latino; 16 Asian, non-Hispanic/Latino; 52 Hispanic/Latino; 57 Two or more races, non-Hispanic/Latino), 692 international. Average age 30. In 2017, 2,605 master's, 122 other advanced degrees awarded. *Degree requirements:* For master's and Ed S, comprehensive exam (for some programs), thesis (for some programs). *Entrance requirements:* Additional exam requirements/recommendations for international students: Required—TOEFL (minimum score 550 paper-based; 79 iBT). *Application deadline:* For fall admission, 6/1 priority date for domestic and international students; for spring admission, 10/1 priority date for domestic and international students; for summer admission, 4/1 priority date for domestic and international students. Applications are processed on a rolling basis. Application fee: $30 ($75 for international students). Electronic applications accepted. *Expenses:* Tuition, state resident: full-time $8771; part-time $292.35 per credit hour. Tuition, nonresident: full-time $17,541; part-time $584.70 per credit hour. *Required fees:* $372; $24.78 per credit hour. *Financial support:* In 2017–18, 99 students received support. Research assistantships, teaching assistantships, career-related internships or fieldwork, Federal Work-Study, scholarships/grants, and administrative and laboratory assistantships available. Support available to part-time students. Financial award application deadline: 3/1; financial award applicants required to submit FAFSA. *Unit head:* Shellie Hewitt, Director of Graduate and International Student Services, 660-543-4621, Fax: 660-543-4778, E-mail: hewitt@ucmo.edu. *Application contact:* 660-543-4621, E-mail: admit_intl@ucmo.edu. Website: http://www.ucmo.edu/graduate/

University of Central Oklahoma, The Jackson College of Graduate Studies, College of Education and Professional Studies, Donna Nigh Department of Advanced Professional and Special Services, Edmond, OK 73034-5209. Offers educational leadership (M Ed); library media education (M Ed); reading (M Ed); school counseling (M Ed); special education (M Ed), including mild/moderate disabilities, severe-profound/multiple disabilities; speech-language pathology (MS). *Accreditation:* ASHA. *Program availability:* Part-time. *Faculty:* 17 full-time (12 women), 8 part-time/adjunct (4 women). *Students:* 73 full-time (65 women), 286 part-time (239 women); includes 91 minority (41 Black or African American, non-Hispanic/Latino; 8 American Indian or Alaska Native, non-Hispanic/Latino; 5 Asian, non-Hispanic/Latino; 20 Hispanic/Latino; 17 Two or more races, non-Hispanic/Latino), 3 international. Average age 35. 146 applicants, 83% accepted, 91 enrolled. In 2017, 128 master's awarded. *Degree requirements:* For master's, comprehensive exam (for some programs), thesis (for some programs). *Entrance requirements:* Additional exam requirements/recommendations for international students: Required—TOEFL (minimum score 550 paper-based; 79 iBT), IELTS (minimum score 6.5). *Application deadline:* For fall admission, 7/15 for international students; for spring admission, 11/15 for international students; for summer admission, 1/31 for domestic students. Applications are processed on a rolling basis. Application fee: $60. Electronic applications accepted. *Expenses:* Tuition, state resident: full-time $5375; part-time $268.75 per credit hour. Tuition, nonresident: full-time $13,295; part-time $664.75 per credit hour. *Required fees:* $626; $31.30 per credit hour. One-time fee: $50. Tuition and fees vary according to program. *Financial support:* In 2017–18, 74 students received support, including 1 research assistantship with partial tuition reimbursement available (averaging $2,958 per year), 1 teaching assistantship with partial tuition reimbursement available (averaging $5,915 per year); career-related internships or fieldwork, scholarships/grants, tuition waivers (partial), and unspecified assistantships also available. Financial award application deadline: 3/31; financial award applicants required to submit FAFSA. *Unit head:* Dr. Cheryl Evans, Chair, 405-974-5437, Fax: 405-974-3857. *Application contact:* Carlie Wellington, Assistant Director, CEPS Graduate Enrollment, 405-974-5105, Fax: 405-974-3851, E-mail: gradcoll@uco.edu.
Website: http://sites.uco.edu/ceps/dept/Education-Programs/apss/index.asp

University of Denver, Morgridge College of Education, Denver, CO 80208. Offers child, family and school psychology (MA, PhD, Ed S); counseling psychology (MA, PhD); curriculum and instruction (MA, Ed D, PhD); curriculum instruction and teaching (Certificate); early childhood special education (MA, Certificate); educational leadership and policy studies (MA, Ed D, PhD, Certificate); higher education (Ed D, PhD); library and information science (MLIS); research methods and statistics (MA, PhD). *Accreditation:* ALA; APA (one or more programs are accredited). *Program availability:* Part-time, evening/weekend, online learning. *Faculty:* 39 full-time (29 women), 60 part-time/adjunct (42 women). *Students:* 502 full-time (406 women), 361 part-time (267 women); includes 233 minority (54 Black or African American, non-Hispanic/Latino; 6 American Indian or Alaska Native, non-Hispanic/Latino; 25 Asian, non-Hispanic/Latino; 113 Hispanic/Latino; 35 Two or more races, non-Hispanic/Latino), 52 international. Average age 31. 1,167 applicants, 64% accepted, 415 enrolled. In 2017, 285 master's, 51 doctorates, 157 other advanced degrees awarded. Terminal master's awarded for partial completion of doctoral program. *Degree requirements:* For master's, comprehensive exam; for doctorate, 2 foreign languages, comprehensive exam, thesis/dissertation. *Entrance requirements:* For master's and doctorate, GRE General Test or GMAT. Additional exam requirements/recommendations for international students: Required—TOEFL (minimum score 550 paper-based; 80 iBT). *Application deadline:* Applications are processed on a rolling basis. Application fee: $65. Electronic applications accepted. *Expenses:* $31,935 per year full-time. *Financial support:* In 2017–18, 765 students received support, including 26 research assistantships with tuition reimbursements available (averaging $10,957 per year), 38 teaching assistantships with tuition reimbursements available (averaging $3,391 per year); career-related internships or fieldwork, Federal Work-Study, institutionally sponsored loans, scholarships/grants, and unspecified assistantships also available. Support available to part-time students. Financial award application deadline: 2/15; financial award applicants required to submit FAFSA. *Faculty research:* Early childhood education, educational leadership, access and opportunity to postsecondary education, marriage and family therapy, data management and archival research. *Unit head:* Dr. Karen Riley, Dean, 303-871-3665, Fax: 303-871-4456, E-mail: karen.riley@du.edu. *Application contact:* Jodi Dye, Director of Admissions, 303-871-2510, Fax: 303-871-4456, E-mail: jodi.dye@du.edu.
Website: http://morgridge.du.edu

University of Hawaii at Manoa, Office of Graduate Education, College of Natural Sciences, Department of Information and Computer Sciences, Library and Information Science Program, Honolulu, HI 96822-2233. Offers advanced library and information science (Graduate Certificate); library and information science (MLI Sc). *Accreditation:* ALA (one or more programs are accredited). *Program availability:* Part-time. *Degree requirements:* For master's, comprehensive exam, thesis optional. *Entrance requirements:* For master's, GRE General Test. Additional exam requirements/recommendations for international students: Required—TOEFL (minimum score 600 paper-based). Electronic applications accepted. *Faculty research:* Information behavior, evaluation of electronic information sources, online learning, history of libraries, information literacy.

University of Houston–Clear Lake, School of Education, Program in Curriculum and Instruction, Houston, TX 77058-1002. Offers curriculum and instruction (MS); early childhood education (MS); reading (MS); school library and information science (MS). *Program availability:* Part-time, evening/weekend. *Degree requirements:* For master's, thesis (for some programs). *Entrance requirements:* For master's, GRE or minimum GPA of 3.0 in last 60 hours. Additional exam requirements/recommendations for international students: Required—TOEFL (minimum score 550 paper-based). Electronic applications accepted.

University of Illinois at Urbana–Champaign, Graduate College, School of Information Sciences, Champaign, IL 61820. Offers bioinformatics (MS); digital libraries (CAS); information management (MS); library and information science (MS, PhD, CAS). *Accreditation:* ALA (one or more programs are accredited). *Program availability:* Part-time, online learning. *Entrance requirements:* For degree, master's degree in library and information science or related field with minimum GPA of 3.0.

The University of Iowa, Graduate College, School of Library and Information Science, Iowa City, IA 52242-1316. Offers MA, PhD, MA/Certificate, PhD/Certificate. *Accreditation:* ALA (one or more programs are accredited). *Degree requirements:* For master's, thesis optional, exam, portfolio. *Entrance requirements:* For master's, GRE General Test, minimum GPA of 3.0. Additional exam requirements/recommendations for international students: Required—TOEFL (minimum score 550 paper-based; 81 iBT). Electronic applications accepted.

University of Kentucky, Graduate School, College of Communication and Information, Program in Library and Information Science, Lexington, KY 40506-0032. Offers MA, MSLS. *Accreditation:* ALA (one or more programs are accredited). *Program availability:* Part-time. *Degree requirements:* For master's, variable foreign language requirement, comprehensive exam. *Entrance requirements:* For master's, GRE General Test, minimum undergraduate GPA of 2.75. Additional exam requirements/recommendations for international students: Required—TOEFL (minimum score 550 paper-based). *Faculty research:* Information retrieval systems, information-seeking behavior, organizational behavior, computer cataloging, library resource sharing.

University of Maryland, College Park, Academic Affairs, Program in History, Library, and Information Services, College Park, MD 20742. Offers MA/MLS. *Entrance requirements:* Additional exam requirements/recommendations for international students: Required—TOEFL. Electronic applications accepted.

University of Missouri, Office of Research and Graduate Studies, College of Education, School of Information Science and Learning Technologies, Columbia, MO 65211. Offers educational technology (M Ed, Ed S); information science and learning technology (PhD, Certificate); library science (MA). *Accreditation:* ALA (one or more programs are accredited). *Program availability:* Part-time, evening/weekend. *Entrance requirements:* For master's, GRE General Test or MAT, minimum GPA of 3.0. Additional exam requirements/recommendations for international students: Required—TOEFL (minimum score 540 paper-based; 76 iBT). Electronic applications accepted.

University of Nebraska at Kearney, College of Education, Department of Teacher Education, Kearney, NE 68849-0001. Offers curriculum and instruction (MA Ed), including early childhood education, elementary education, English as a second language, instructional effectiveness, reading/special education, secondary education; instructional technology (MS Ed), including information technology, instructional technology, school librarian; reading PK-12 (MA Ed); special education (MA Ed), including advanced practitioner: assistive technology specialist, advanced practitioner: behavioral interventionist, advanced practitioner: inclusive collaboration specialist, gifted, teacher education. *Program availability:* Part-time, evening/weekend, online only, 100% online. *Degree requirements:* For master's, comprehensive exam, thesis optional. *Entrance requirements:* For master's, portfolio or GRE. Additional exam requirements/recommendations for international students: Recommended—TOEFL (minimum score 550 paper-based; 79 iBT), IELTS (minimum score 6.5). Electronic applications accepted. *Expenses:* Contact institution.

The University of North Carolina at Chapel Hill, Graduate School, School of Information and Library Science, Chapel Hill, NC 27599. Offers data curation (PMC); digital curation (PSM); information and library science (PhD); information science (MSIS); library science (MSLS). *Accreditation:* ALA (one or more programs are accredited). *Program availability:* Part-time. *Faculty:* 24 full-time (8 women), 46 part-time/adjunct (23 women). *Students:* 228 full-time (169 women), 27 part-time (20 women); includes 36 minority (7 Black or African American, non-Hispanic/Latino; 10 Asian, non-Hispanic/Latino; 4 Hispanic/Latino; 15 Two or more races, non-Hispanic/Latino), 55 international. Average age 28. 304 applicants, 75% accepted, 100 enrolled. In 2017, 67 master's, 10 doctorates awarded. Terminal master's awarded for partial completion of doctoral program. *Degree requirements:* For master's, comprehensive exam, paper or project; for doctorate, comprehensive exam, thesis/dissertation. *Entrance requirements:* For master's and doctorate, GRE General Test. Additional exam requirements/recommendations for international students: Required—TOEFL (minimum score 90 iBT). *Application deadline:* For fall admission, 12/12 priority date for domestic and international students; for spring admission, 10/10 for domestic and international students. Applications are processed on a rolling basis. Application fee: $88. Electronic applications accepted. *Expenses:* $7,464 in-state full-time per semester, $16,070 out-of-state(for MSLS/MSIS); $5,964 in-state full-time per semester, $14,570 out-of-state(for PhD); $7,266 in-state full-time per semester$14,862 out-of-state (for PMC); $8,220 in-state, $16,266 out-of-state (for PMS). *Financial support:* In 2017–18, 59 fellowships with full tuition reimbursements (averaging $2,565 per year), 46 research assistantships with full tuition reimbursements (averaging $3,528 per year), 7 teaching assistantships with full tuition reimbursements (averaging $22,917 per year) were awarded; career-related internships or fieldwork, Federal Work-Study, scholarships/grants, health care benefits, and unspecified assistantships also available. Financial award application deadline: 12/12. *Faculty research:* Information retrieval and management, digital libraries, management of information resources, archives and records management, health informatics. *Unit head:* Dr. Gary Marchionini, Dean, 919-962-8363, Fax: 919-962-8071, E-mail: gary@ils.unc.edu. *Application contact:* Lara Bailey, Student Services Coordinator, 919-962-7601, Fax: 919-962-8071, E-mail: bailey@email.unc.edu. Website: http://sils.unc.edu

The University of North Carolina at Greensboro, Graduate School, School of Education, Department of Library and Information Studies, Greensboro, NC 27412-5001. Offers MLIS. *Accreditation:* ALA. *Program availability:* Part-time, evening/weekend, online learning. *Degree requirements:* For master's, portfolio. *Entrance requirements:* For master's, GRE General Test. Additional exam requirements/recommendations for international students: Required—TOEFL (minimum score 550 paper-based), IELTS (minimum score 6.5). Electronic applications accepted. *Faculty research:* Library history, gender studies, children's literature, web design, homeless, technical services.

University of Oklahoma, College of Arts and Sciences, School of Library and Information Studies, Norman, OK 73019. Offers archival studies (Graduate Certificate); digital humanities (Graduate Certificate); information studies (PhD); library and information studies (MLIS); M Ed/MLIS; MBA/MLIS. *Accreditation:* ALA (one or more programs are accredited). *Program availability:* Part-time, evening/weekend, 100% online, blended/hybrid learning. *Faculty:* 11 full-time (8 women), 1 (woman) part-time/adjunct. *Students:* 64 full-time (53 women), 117 part-time (95 women); includes 40 minority (6 Black or African American, non-Hispanic/Latino; 6 American Indian or Alaska Native, non-Hispanic/Latino; 3 Asian, non-Hispanic/Latino; 14 Hispanic/Latino; 1 Native Hawaiian or other Pacific Islander, non-Hispanic/Latino; 10 Two or more races, non-Hispanic/Latino). Average age 32. 58 applicants, 93% accepted, 48 enrolled. In 2017, 53 master's awarded. Terminal master's awarded for partial completion of doctoral program. *Degree requirements:* For master's, comprehensive exam (for some programs), thesis optional; for doctorate, comprehensive exam, thesis/dissertation. *Entrance requirements:* For master's, three letters of recommendation, personal statement, resume, transcript; for doctorate, GRE, three letters of recommendation, personal statement, resume, writing sample; for Graduate Certificate, transcripts, personal statement (for some certificates), letter of recommendation (for some certificates). Additional exam requirements/recommendations for international students: Required—TOEFL (minimum score 79 iBT) or IELTS (minimum score 6.5). *Application deadline:* Applications are processed on a rolling basis. Application fee: $50 ($100 for international students). Electronic applications accepted. *Expenses:* Tuition, state resident: full-time $5119; part-time $213.30 per credit hour. Tuition, nonresident: full-time $19,778; part-time $824.10 per credit hour. *Required fees:* $3458; $133.55 per credit hour. $126.50 per semester. *Financial support:* In 2017–18, 82 students received support, including 3 research assistantships with full tuition reimbursements available (averaging $10,579 per year), 3 teaching assistantships with full tuition reimbursements available (averaging $10,579 per year); scholarships/grants, health care benefits, and unspecified assistantships also available. Financial award application deadline: 6/1; financial award applicants required to submit FAFSA. *Faculty research:* Family and youth technology in libraries, consumer health information, text mining, big data analytics. *Total annual research expenditures:* $107,620. *Unit head:* Dr. Susan K. Burke,

Director, 405-325-3921, E-mail: sburke@ou.edu. *Application contact:* Sarah Connelly, Admissions and Student Services Coordinator, 405-325-3921, E-mail: sarahee@ou.edu.
Website: http://slis.ou.edu

University of Pittsburgh, School of Computing and Information, Department of Information Culture and Data Stewardship, Pittsburgh, PA 15260. Offers library and information science (MLIS, PhD). *Program availability:* Part-time, evening/weekend, 100% online. *Faculty:* 14 full-time (9 women), 3 part-time/adjunct (all women). *Students:* 50 full-time (42 women), 47 part-time (38 women); includes 10 minority (3 Black or African American, non-Hispanic/Latino; 2 Asian, non-Hispanic/Latino; 4 Hispanic/Latino; 1 Two or more races, non-Hispanic/Latino), 12 international. Average age 32. 122 applicants, 89% accepted, 59 enrolled. In 2017, 54 master's, 3 doctorates awarded. *Degree requirements:* For master's, thesis optional; for doctorate, comprehensive exam, thesis/dissertation. *Entrance requirements:* For master's, GRE General Test, GMAT, MAT, MCAT, LSAT, bachelor's degree with minimum GPA of 3.0; for doctorate, GRE General Test, GMAT, MAT, MCAT, LSAT, master's degree with minimum GPA of 3.5. Additional exam requirements/recommendations for international students: Required—TOEFL (minimum score 550 paper-based; 80 iBT), IELTS (minimum score 6.5). *Application deadline:* For fall admission, 1/15 priority date for domestic and international students. Applications are processed on a rolling basis. Application fee: $50. Electronic applications accepted. *Expenses:* $23,438 in-state tuition, $38,886 out-of-state, $850 mandatory fees (fall and spring); $954 per credit in-state, $1,599 out-of-state (summer). *Financial support:* Fellowships with full and partial tuition reimbursements, research assistantships with full and partial tuition reimbursements, teaching assistantships with full and partial tuition reimbursements, career-related internships or fieldwork, institutionally sponsored loans, scholarships/grants, health care benefits, and unspecified assistantships available. Financial award application deadline: 1/15; financial award applicants required to submit FAFSA. *Faculty research:* Data and information, archives and data preservation, information and society, children and youth services, research data management. *Unit head:* Dr. Bruce R. Childers, Chair, 412-624-8414, Fax: 421-624-5231, E-mail: childers@cs.pitt.edu. *Application contact:* Shabana Reza, Enrollment Manager, 412-624-3988, Fax: 412-624-5231, E-mail: shabana.reza@pitt.edu.
Website: http://www.icds.pitt.edu/

University of Puerto Rico–Río Piedras, Graduate School of Information Sciences and Technologies, San Juan, PR 00931-3300. Offers administration of academic libraries (PMC); administration of public libraries (PMC); administration of special libraries (PMC); consultant in information services (PMC); documents and files administration (Post-Graduate Certificate); electronic information resources analyst (Post-Graduate Certificate); information science (MIS); librarianship and information services (MLS); school librarian (Post-Graduate Certificate); school librarian distance education mode (Post-Graduate Certificate); specialist in legal information (PMC). *Accreditation:* ALA. *Program availability:* Part-time. *Degree requirements:* For master's, comprehensive exam, thesis, portfolio. *Entrance requirements:* For master's, PAEG, GRE, interview, minimum GPA of 3.0, 3 letters of recommendation; for other advanced degree, PAEG, GRE, minimum GPA of 3.0, IST master's degree. *Faculty research:* Investigating the users needs and preferences for a specialized environmental library.

University of Rhode Island, Graduate School, College of Arts and Sciences, Graduate School of Library and Information Studies, Kingston, RI 02881. Offers libraries, leadership and transforming communities (MLIS); organization of digital media (MLIS); school library media (MLIS); MLIS/MA; MLIS/MPA. *Accreditation:* ALA (one or more programs are accredited). *Program availability:* Part-time. *Faculty:* 4 full-time (all women). *Students:* 17 full-time (12 women), 85 part-time (74 women); includes 13 minority (2 Black or African American, non-Hispanic/Latino; 3 Asian, non-Hispanic/Latino; 3 Hispanic/Latino; 1 Native Hawaiian or other Pacific Islander, non-Hispanic/Latino; 4 Two or more races, non-Hispanic/Latino). 47 applicants, 89% accepted, 26 enrolled. In 2017, 41 master's awarded. *Entrance requirements:* For master's, GRE or MAT if undergraduate GPA below 3.3, 2 letters of recommendation. Additional exam requirements/recommendations for international students: Required—TOEFL. *Application deadline:* For fall admission, 6/15 for domestic students, 2/1 for international students; for spring admission, 10/15 for domestic students, 7/15 for international students; for summer admission, 3/15 for domestic students. Application fee: $65. Electronic applications accepted. *Expenses:* Tuition, state resident: full-time $12,706; part-time $786 per credit. Tuition, nonresident: full-time $25,216; part-time $1401 per credit. *Required fees:* $1598; $45 per credit. One-time fee: $30 part-time. *Financial support:* Research assistantships and teaching assistantships available. Financial award application deadline: 1/15; financial award applicants required to submit FAFSA. *Unit head:* Dr. Valerie Karno, Director, Graduate School of Library and Information Studies, 401-874-4682, Fax: 401-874-4127, E-mail: karno@uri.edu.
Website: http://www.uri.edu/artsci/lsc/

University of South Carolina, The Graduate School, College of Mass Communications and Information Studies, School of Library and Information Science, Columbia, SC 29208. Offers MLIS, PhD, Certificate, Specialist, MLIS/MA. *Accreditation:* ALA (one or more programs are accredited). *Program availability:* Part-time, online learning. *Degree requirements:* For master's, end of program portfolio; for doctorate, comprehensive exam, thesis/dissertation. *Entrance requirements:* For master's and other advanced degree, GRE General Test or MAT; for doctorate, GTE, writing sample. Additional exam requirements/recommendations for international students: Required—TOEFL (minimum score 570 paper-based; 75 iBT). Electronic applications accepted. *Faculty research:* Information technology management, distance education, library services for children and young adults, special libraries.

University of Southern Mississippi, College of Education and Psychology, School of Library and Information Science, Hattiesburg, MS 39406-0001. Offers library and information science (MLIS); youth services and literature (Graduate Certificate). *Accreditation:* ALA (one or more programs are accredited). *Program availability:* Part-time, evening/weekend, online learning. *Students:* 17 full-time (12 women), 8 part-time (all women). 35 applicants, 100% accepted, 25 enrolled. *Degree requirements:* For master's, comprehensive exam, thesis. *Entrance requirements:* For master's, GRE General Test, minimum GPA of 3.0. Additional exam requirements/recommendations for international students: Required—TOEFL, IELTS. *Application deadline:* For fall admission, 3/15 priority date for domestic students, 3/15 for international students; for spring admission, 1/10 priority date for domestic and international students. Applications are processed on a rolling basis. Application fee: $60. Electronic applications accepted. *Expenses:* Tuition, state resident: full-time $3830. *Financial support:* Fellowships with tuition reimbursements, research assistantships with full tuition reimbursements, teaching assistantships with full tuition reimbursements, career-related internships or fieldwork, Federal Work-Study, institutionally sponsored loans, scholarships/grants, health care benefits, and unspecified assistantships available. Financial award application deadline: 3/15; financial award applicants required to submit FAFSA. *Faculty research:* Printing, library history, children's literature, telecommunications, management. *Unit head:* Dr. Theresa Welsh, Director, 601-266-4236, Fax: 601-266-5774.
Website: https://www.usm.edu/library-information-science

Library Science

University of South Florida, College of Arts and Sciences, School of Information, Tampa, FL 33620-9951. Offers intelligence studies (MS), including cyber intelligence, strategic intelligence; library and information science (MA). *Accreditation:* ALA (one or more programs are accredited). *Program availability:* Part-time, evening/weekend, online learning. *Faculty:* 16 full-time (9 women). *Students:* 120 full-time (87 women), 187 part-time (141 women); includes 89 minority (26 Black or African American, non-Hispanic/Latino; 9 Asian, non-Hispanic/Latino; 47 Hispanic/Latino; 7 Two or more races, non-Hispanic/Latino), 1 international. Average age 32. 180 applicants, 86% accepted, 98 enrolled. In 2017, 90 master's awarded. *Degree requirements:* For master's, comprehensive exam, thesis (for some programs). *Entrance requirements:* For master's, GRE General Test (for some programs). Additional exam requirements/recommendations for international students: Required—TOEFL (minimum score 550 paper-based; 79 iBT) or IELTS (minimum score 6.5). *Application deadline:* For fall admission, 6/1 priority date for domestic students, 5/1 for international students; for spring admission, 10/15 priority date for domestic students, 9/15 for international students. Applications are processed on a rolling basis. Application fee: $30. Electronic applications accepted. *Financial support:* In 2017–18, 25 students received support. Unspecified assistantships available. Financial award application deadline: 6/30. *Faculty research:* Youth services in libraries, community engagement and libraries, information architecture, biomedical informatics, health informatics. *Total annual research expenditures:* $168,525. *Unit head:* Dr. Jim Andrews, Director and Associate Professor, 813-974-2108, Fax: 813-974-6840, E-mail: jimandrews@usf.edu. *Application contact:* Dr. Randy Borum, Graduate Program Director, 813-974-3520, Fax: 813-974-6840, E-mail: wborum@usf.edu.
Website: http://si.usf.edu/

University of Washington, Graduate School, Information School, Seattle, WA 98195. Offers information management (MSIM), including business intelligence, data science, information architecture, information consulting, information security, user experience; information science (PhD); library and information science (MLIS). *Accreditation:* ALA (one or more programs are accredited). *Program availability:* Part-time, 100% online coursework with required attendance at on-campus orientation at start of program. *Faculty:* 49 full-time (21 women), 36 part-time/adjunct (15 women). *Students:* 353 full-time (222 women), 252 part-time (187 women); includes 144 minority (19 Black or African American, non-Hispanic/Latino; 11 American Indian or Alaska Native, non-Hispanic/Latino; 64 Asian, non-Hispanic/Latino; 48 Hispanic/Latino; 2 Native Hawaiian or other Pacific Islander, non-Hispanic/Latino), 143 international. Average age 30. 1,194 applicants, 44% accepted, 259 enrolled. In 2017, 231 master's, 10 doctorates awarded. Terminal master's awarded for partial completion of doctoral program. *Degree requirements:* For master's, comprehensive exam (for some programs), thesis or alternative, capstone project; for doctorate, comprehensive exam, thesis/dissertation. *Entrance requirements:* For master's, GRE General Test, GMAT; for doctorate, GRE General Test. Additional exam requirements/recommendations for international students: Required—TOEFL (minimum score 590 paper-based; 100 iBT). *Application deadline:* For fall admission, 12/1 priority date for domestic and international students. Application fee: $85. Electronic applications accepted. *Expenses:* Contact institution. *Financial support:* In 2017–18, 70 students received support. Fellowships with full tuition reimbursements available, research assistantships with full tuition reimbursements available, teaching assistantships with full tuition reimbursements available, Federal Work-Study, institutionally sponsored loans, scholarships/grants, health care benefits, tuition waivers (full and partial), and unspecified assistantships available. Support available to part-time students. Financial award application deadline: 10/1; financial award applicants required to submit FAFSA. *Faculty research:* Human/computer interaction, information policy and ethics, knowledge organization, information literacy and access, data science, information assurance and cyber security, digital youth, information architecture, project management, systems analyst, user experience, user design. *Total annual research expenditures:* $5.1 million. *Unit head:* Dr. Anind Dey, Dean, E-mail: anind@uw.edu. *Application contact:* Kari Brothers, Admissions Counselor, 206-616-5541, Fax: 206-616-3152, E-mail: kari683@uw.edu.
Website: http://ischool.uw.edu/

The University of Western Ontario, Faculty of Graduate Studies, Faculty of Information and Media Studies, Programs in Library and Information Science, London, ON N6A 5B8, Canada. Offers MLIS, PhD. Program conducted on a trimester basis. *Accreditation:* ALA (one or more programs are accredited). *Program availability:* Part-time, evening/weekend. *Degree requirements:* For doctorate, comprehensive exam, thesis/dissertation. *Entrance requirements:* For master's, honors degree, minimum B average during previous 2 years of course work; for doctorate, MLIS or equivalent. Additional exam requirements/recommendations for international students: Required—TOEFL (minimum score 625 paper-based), TWE (minimum score 5). Electronic applications accepted. *Faculty research:* Information, individuals, and society; information systems, policy, power, and institutions.

University of Wisconsin–Eau Claire, College of Education and Human Sciences, Program in Secondary Education, Eau Claire, WI 54702-4004. Offers professional development (ME-PD), including library science, professional development. *Program availability:* Part-time, online learning. *Degree requirements:* For master's, comprehensive exam, thesis, research paper, portfolio or written exam; oral exam. *Entrance requirements:* For master's, certification to teach, minimum GPA of 2.75. Additional exam requirements/recommendations for international students: Required—TOEFL (minimum score 79 iBT).

University of Wisconsin–Madison, Graduate School, College of Letters and Science, School of Library and Information Studies, Madison, WI 53706-1380. Offers MA, PhD. *Accreditation:* ALA (one or more programs are accredited). *Program availability:* Part-time. *Degree requirements:* For doctorate, comprehensive exam, thesis/dissertation. Electronic applications accepted. *Faculty research:* Intellectual freedom, children's literature, print culture history, information systems design and evaluation, school library media centers.

University of Wisconsin–Milwaukee, Graduate School, School of Information Studies, Milwaukee, WI 53201-0413. Offers MLIS, MS, PhD, CAS. *Accreditation:* ALA (one or more programs are accredited). *Program availability:* Part-time. *Students:* 120 full-time (81 women), 243 part-time (181 women); includes 52 minority (13 Black or African American, non-Hispanic/Latino; 11 Asian, non-Hispanic/Latino; 4 Hispanic/Latino; 24 Two or more races, non-Hispanic/Latino), 16 international. Average age 34. 276 applicants, 64% accepted, 122 enrolled. In 2017, 169 master's, 4 doctorates, 1 other advanced degree awarded. *Entrance requirements:* For master's, GRE General Test or MAT; for doctorate, GRE. Additional exam requirements/recommendations for international students: Required—TOEFL (minimum score 550 paper-based); IELTS (minimum score 6.5). *Application deadline:* For fall admission, 1/1 priority date for domestic students; for spring admission, 9/1 for domestic students. Application fee: $56 ($96 for international students). Electronic applications accepted. *Financial support:* Fellowships, research assistantships, teaching assistantships, career-related internships or fieldwork, Federal Work-Study, health care benefits, unspecified assistantships, and project assistantships available. Support available to part-time students. Financial award application deadline: 4/15; financial award applicants required to submit FAFSA. *Unit head:* Tomas A. Lipinski, Dean/Professor, 414-229-4707, E-mail: tlipinsk@uwm.edu. *Application contact:* Linda Barajas, Admissions Coordinator, 414-229-3316, E-mail: barajas@uwm.edu.
Website: http://uwm.edu/informationstudies

Valdosta State University, Program in Library and Information Science, Valdosta, GA 31698. Offers MLIS. *Accreditation:* ALA. *Program availability:* 100% online. *Degree requirements:* For master's, comprehensive exam. *Entrance requirements:* For master's, two essays, resume, three recommendations. Additional exam requirements/recommendations for international students: Required—TOEFL (minimum score 523 paper-based); Recommended—IELTS. *Application deadline:* For fall admission, 4/15 for domestic and international students. Application fee: $45. *Expenses:* Contact institution. *Financial support:* Research assistantships with full tuition reimbursements, institutionally sponsored loans, scholarships/grants, and unspecified assistantships available. Support available to part-time students. Financial award application deadline: 7/1; financial award applicants required to submit FAFSA. *Unit head:* Dr. Linda Most, Director, 229-333-5966, Fax: 229-333-5862, E-mail: lrmost@valdosta.edu. *Application contact:* Jessica Powers, Admission Specialist, 229-333-5694, Fax: 229-245-3853, E-mail: jldevane@valdosta.edu.
Website: http://www.valdosta.edu/academics/graduate-school/our-programs/library-and-information-science.php

Valley City State University, Online Graduate Programs, Valley City, ND 58072. Offers elementary education (M Ed); English education (M Ed); library and information technologies (M Ed); teaching (MAT); teaching and technology (M Ed); teaching English language learners (M Ed); technology education (M Ed). *Accreditation:* NCATE. *Program availability:* Part-time, evening/weekend, online only, 100% online. *Faculty:* 21 full-time (12 women), 15 part-time/adjunct (11 women). *Students:* 12 full-time (9 women), 138 part-time (99 women); includes 5 minority (3 Hispanic/Latino; 2 Two or more races, non-Hispanic/Latino). Average age 36. 13 applicants, 92% accepted, 12 enrolled. In 2017, 45 master's awarded. *Degree requirements:* For master's, action research report, comprehensive portfolio. *Entrance requirements:* For master's, GRE, MAT, PRAXIS II or National Teaching Board for Professional Standards (if GPA is less than 3.0). Additional exam requirements/recommendations for international students: Required—TOEFL (minimum score 525 paper-based; 71 iBT); Recommended—IELTS (minimum score 5.5). *Application deadline:* For fall admission, 7/21 for domestic and international students; for spring admission, 12/8 for domestic and international students; for summer admission, 5/5 for domestic and international students. Applications are processed on a rolling basis. Application fee: $35. Electronic applications accepted. *Expenses:* $384.21 per credit. *Financial support:* In 2017–18, 16 students received support. Scholarships/grants, tuition waivers (full and partial), and unspecified assistantships available. Financial award applicants required to submit FAFSA. *Faculty research:* Universal accessibility, instructional design and technology, gender communication, STEM education in K-12, English language learners. *Unit head:* Dr. Sheri Okland, Dean, 701-845-7184, E-mail: sheri.l.okland@vcsu.edu. *Application contact:* Misty Lindgren, Graduate Studies, 701-845-7303, Fax: 701-845-7190, E-mail: misty.lindgren@vcsu.edu.
Website: http://www.vcsu.edu/graduate

Wayne State University, School of Information Sciences, Detroit, MI 48202. Offers archival administration (Graduate Certificate); information management (MS, Graduate Certificate); library and information science (MLIS, Graduate Certificate, Spec); public library services to children and young adults (Graduate Certificate); MLIS/MA. *Accreditation:* ALA (one or more programs are accredited). *Program availability:* Part-time, evening/weekend, 100% online, blended/hybrid learning. *Faculty:* 12 full-time (9 women), 17 part-time/adjunct (12 women). *Students:* 100 full-time (80 women), 359 part-time (290 women); includes 77 minority (42 Black or African American, non-Hispanic/Latino; 2 American Indian or Alaska Native, non-Hispanic/Latino; 3 Asian, non-Hispanic/Latino; 19 Hispanic/Latino; 1 Native Hawaiian or other Pacific Islander, non-Hispanic/Latino; 10 Two or more races, non-Hispanic/Latino), 1 international. Average age 33. 258 applicants, 60% accepted, 100 enrolled. In 2017, 149 master's, 34 other advanced degrees awarded. *Degree requirements:* For master's and other advanced degree, e-portfolio. *Entrance requirements:* For master's, GRE or MAT (if undergraduate GPA is between 2.5 and 2.99), minimum undergraduate GPA of 3.0 or graduate degree, personal statement, resume or curriculum vitae; for other advanced degree, GRE or MAT (if undergraduate GPA is between 2.5 and 2.99), minimum undergraduate GPA of 3.0 or graduate degree, personal statement, resume or curriculum vitae, MLIS (for specialist certificate). Additional exam requirements/recommendations for international students: Required—TOEFL (minimum score 550 paper-based; 79 iBT); Recommended—IELTS (minimum score 6.5), TWE (minimum score 5.5). *Application deadline:* For fall admission, 7/1 for domestic students, 5/1 priority date for international students; for winter admission, 10/1 priority date for domestic students, 9/1 priority date for international students; for spring admission, 2/1 priority date for domestic students, 1/1 priority date for international students. Applications are processed on a rolling basis. Application fee: $50. Electronic applications accepted. *Expenses:* Contact institution. *Financial support:* In 2017–18, 133 students received support. Fellowships with tuition reimbursements available, scholarships/grants, health care benefits, and unspecified assistantships available. Support available to part-time students. Financial award applicants required to submit FAFSA. *Faculty research:* Library services, information management issues, digital content management, library/community engagement, archives and preservation. *Unit head:* Dr. Jon Cawthorne, Dean, 313-577-2020, E-mail: jon.cawthorne@wayne.edu. *Application contact:* Academic Services Officer II, 313-577-1825, E-mail: asklis@wayne.edu.
Website: http://slis.wayne.edu/

PRATT INSTITUTE
School of Information

 For more information, visit http://petersons.to/prattlibraryscience

Programs of Study

Distinguished as the only ALA-accredited graduate library and information science (LIS) program based in Manhattan and the oldest library and information science school in North America, Pratt's School of Information, established in 1890 and renamed in 2015, has been continuously accredited since 1923, when accreditation was first introduced to the field. The Archives program was ranked 11th in the country by *U.S. News & World Report*.

Building upon Pratt's national reputation as a leading school in art and design, Pratt brings creativity and innovation to library science education to offer students exciting and cutting-edge programs and courses from archives and digital libraries, to special libraries and school library media.

Pratt's School of Information offers five 36-credit Master of Science degrees: M.S. in Library and Information Science (M.S.L.I.S.), M.S. in Museums and Digital Culture, M.S. in Data Analytics and Visualization, and M.S. in Information Experience Design. Pratt offers two joint-degree programs, one with Pratt's History of Art Department (M.S.L.I.S./M.A. in history of art, 60 credits), and one with Pratt's Digital Arts M.F.A. (M.S.L.I.S./M.F.A. in digital arts, 75 credits). The School of Information also offers advanced certificate programs in Archives, Conservation and Digital Curation, Digital Humanities, Library and Information Studies, Museum Libraries, and User Experience (UX).

The School of Information prepares students for leadership positions in the information professions, including special opportunities in arts and humanities librarianship for students pursuing careers in academic and research libraries, art and museum libraries, and archives and special collections. The program combines a core curriculum (information professions, information services and sources, information technologies, and knowledge organization) with elective courses, such as advanced Web design, digital libraries, human information behavior, information architecture, information policy, and projects in digital archives. Some courses are taught on location in museums and libraries, such as the New York Public Library, the Watson Library, and the Metropolitan Museum of Art. Other courses are held on the Brooklyn Campus in the Pratt Library, and students in the library and media specialist (LMS) studies program take courses in the Art and Design Education Department. The School of Information maintains a dean's office in North Hall. Students carry out practicum internships at many of New York's leading cultural institutions. Students may choose from a number of program concentrations, depending on their interests and career goals, including business, cultural informatics, digital technology and knowledge organization, legal and health information, library media specialist studies, management and leadership, public urban libraries, and reference and information literacy.

The master's program may be completed in as little as two semesters and one summer and must be completed within four years of enrollment. Courses are offered in the evening, during the day, and on Saturday and Sunday to accommodate students who work.

Research Facilities

The program's teaching and research facilities occupy the entire sixth floor of a seven-story facility in its home at 144 West 14th Street, Manhattan, in a beautifully restored landmark building, designated the Pratt Manhattan Center (PMC). Here, students find faculty and staff offices, smart classrooms, large computer labs, an elegant conference room, and the student cyber place. The fifth-floor computer lab adds to the School of Information's resources, and a separate scanning lab supports digital library projects. The fourth floor is home to the PMC library, containing extensive LIS collections of books, journals, and full-text online databases. Special School of Information events and lectures are held in a 150-person lecture hall adjoining the second-floor gallery space. This rich complex of facilities, all with wireless access and convenient to students

and faculty members, adds greatly to effective operations and enhances the learning environment.

Financial Aid

Financial aid awards are offered through a variety of institutional, state, and federally funded programs. These include Graduate Scholarships awarded to incoming students on the basis of merit, endowed and restricted scholarships for continuing students, and student employment. Assistantships are awarded on a competitive basis to continuing students in all departments. Special alumni-sponsored fellowships are also available.

Cost of Study

In 2018–19, tuition is $1,428 per credit for the M.S.L.I.S. degree, and student fees are approximately $1,980 per year. The cost of books and supplies varies widely among the different programs.

Living and Housing Costs

Limited graduate housing is available for single students on the Brooklyn Campus. The cost averages $19,550 (room and board $23,310) per year. The Office of Residential Life maintains extensive listings of off-campus housing to help students find suitable accommodations.

Student Group

Graduate students at Pratt are drawn from all parts of the United States (42 states) and fifty-three other countries. The SILS graduate program average age is 31, with most students working full-time while taking M.S.L.I.S. courses. The employment outlook for Pratt graduates is bright. At present, more than 95 percent of the graduates obtain positions in a broad range of work environments from academic libraries and museums, to special libraries, including those in the corporate, business, and medical fields. The growth potential of the job market is seemingly unlimited. Job opportunities have been increasing for graduates of the information and library science program.

Location

Pratt's School of Information is headquartered in the heart of Manhattan. Here, most School of Information courses are offered at times convenient to those students who wish to work as well as those who wish to pursue full-time study. The main campus of Pratt Institute is located in the Clinton Hill section of Brooklyn. Some courses are offered there to support programs such as program courses in urban librarianship at Brooklyn Public Library. In Manhattan, courses are taught at Cornell Medical Center for health sciences specialization and the New York Public Library/Research Libraries for special collections.

School of Information students enjoy the advantages of New York's position as a world center for the information professions. Students also benefit from the wealth of professional experience and expertise that complements their formal study. A vast variety of cultural and recreational activities are available in the neighborhood, in Brooklyn, in the city, and in the region. Pratt has a park-like campus in a quiet neighborhood of Victorian buildings set in the midst of one of the most vibrant cities in the world.

The Institute

A private, nonsectarian institute of higher education, Pratt was founded in 1887 by industrialist and philanthropist Charles Pratt. Changing with the requirements of the professions for which it educates, Pratt today prepares a student body of more than 4,800 undergraduate and graduate students for a wide range of careers in architecture and planning, design and fine arts, and information science.

Applying

The deadline for applications and all supporting materials, including portfolio, is January 5. Applicants should complete the application process online. Early submission of applications with all necessary credentials is highly desirable. Applications received after these dates are considered if openings exist in a particular program. For applicants who intend to file for financial aid, the FAFSA should be filed by March 1 for fall entrance and by October 1 for spring entrance

Correspondence and Information

Graduate Admissions Office
Pratt Institute
200 Willoughby Avenue
Brooklyn, New York 11205
Phone: 718-636-3514
        800-331-0834 (toll-free)
Fax: 718-399-4242
Website: http://www.pratt.edu/admissions

School of Information
Pratt Institute
144 West 14th Street, 6th Floor
New York, New York 10011
Phone: 212-647-7682
E-mail: infosils@pratt.edu
Website: http://www.pratt.edu/academics/information

THE FACULTY

Anthony Cocciolo, Chair, Associate Professor; Ed.D., Columbia.
Johanna Bauman, Visiting Assistant Professor; M.L.S., CUNY, Queens.
Jason Baumann, Visiting Assistant Professor; M.L.S., CUNY, Queens.
Amber Billey, Visiting Instructor; M.S.L.I.S., Pratt.
Jeremiah Christensen, Visiting Assistant Professor, M.L.S., LIU.
Carl Collins, Visiting Assistant Professor, M.L.S., LIU.
Anthony M. Cucchiara, Visiting Assistant Professor; M.L.S., Pratt.
Sara Devine, Visiting Assistant Professor; M.A., George Washington.
Deirdre Donohue, Visiting Assistant Professor; M.L.S., Pratt.
Emily Drabinski, Visiting Assistant Professor; M.L.S., Syracuse.
Barbara Genco, Visiting Associate Professor; M.L.S., Pratt.
Tula Giannini, Professor; Ph.D., Bryn Mawr.
Joshua Hadro, Visiting Instructor; M.L.S., Pratt.
Alexis Hagadorn, Visiting Assistant Professor; M.L.S., Columbia.
Emily Holmes, Visiting Assistant Professor; M.L.S., Simmons.
Jennifer Hubert-Swan, Visiting Assistant Professor; M.L.S., Wayne State (Michigan).
Ian Kerrigan, Visiting Assistant Professor, M.A., George Washington.
Nickolas Krabbenhoeft, Visiting Assistant Professor, M.S., University of Michigan.
Irene Lopatovska, Associate Professor; Ph.D., Rutgers.
Craig MacDonald, Associate Professor; Ph.D., Information Studies, Drexel.
Monica Maceli, Assistant Professor; Ph.D., Drexel.
Susan L. Malbin, Visiting Assistant Professor; Ph.D., Brandeis.
Bree Midavaine, Visiting Assistant Professor, M.S., Pratt.
Matthew Miller, Visiting Assistant Professor; M.S.L.I.S., Pratt.
Monica Montgomery, Visiting Assistant Professor, M.A., LaSalle University
Cristina Pattuelli, Associate Professor; Ph.D., North Carolina at Chapel Hill.
Pamela Pavliscak Ellis, Visiting Assistant Professor, M.S.I.S., University of Michigan.
Slava Polishchuk, Visiting Assistant Professor; M.F.A., CUNY, Brooklyn.
Debbie Rabina, Professor; Ph.D., Rutgers.
Ellie Ransom, Visiting Assistant Professor, M.S.L.I.S., Pratt.
Lisa Rosenblum, Visiting Assistant Professor, M.S.L.I.S., Pratt.
Charles Rubenstein, Professor; Ph.D., Polytechnic of NYU.

Margaret Smith, Visiting Assistant Professor, M.S.L.I.S., Syracuse University.
Kenneth Soehner, Visiting Associate Professor, M.L.S., Columbia.
Chris Alen Sula, Associate Professor; Ph.D., CUNY Graduate Center.
Cynthia Tobar, Visiting Assistant Professor; M.S.L.I.S., Pratt.
Erik Trainer, Visiting Assistant Professor, Ph.D., U.C., Irvine.
Kyle Triplett, Visiting Instructor; M.S.L.I.S., Pratt.
Elena Villaespesa Cantalapiedra, Assistant Professor, Ph.D., University of Leicester.
Farris Wahbeh, Visiting Professor, M.A., Art Institute of Chicago.
William Ying, Visiting Associate Professor; Ph.D., Columbia.

© 2017 Bob Handelman

© 2017 Bob Handelman

SYRACUSE UNIVERSITY

School of Information Studies
Master of Science in Applied Data Science
Master of Science in Enterprise Data Systems
Master of Science in Information Management
Master of Science in Library and Information Science

Programs of Study

The Syracuse University School of Information Studies (iSchool), ranked number two in Information Systems in Library and Information Studies by U.S. News & World Report, offers M.S. degree programs to prepare students for a growing number of dynamic careers that involve the management and use of information. Master's students in the iSchool obtain specialized skills in areas such as cloud management, digital enterprises, data science, global enterprise technologies, library science, virtual environments, databases, information security, IT governance, information and communication technologies, school media librarianship, wireless networks, and mobile and web applications. Students can earn M.S. degrees on campus or online with limited residency requirements. Note: The Enterprise Data Systems program is offered only on campus.

The M.S. in applied data science (ADS) prepares students with the practical analytical and technical skills to apply analytical concepts to gain insight from small and large datasets. The program requires completion of 36 credit hours and the curriculum combines a primary core, analytics application core, and electives to give students a strong data science and analytics foundation with a secondary focus of their choosing. The M.S. in ADS is a fully interdisciplinary degree and is offered in collaboration with Syracuse University's Whitman School of Management.

The M.S. in enterprise data systems (EDS) requires completion of 36 credit hours and is designed for students who want to prepare professionally to manage, design, support and optimize the infrastructure that supports the digital enterprise. The EDS curriculum is built around the core concepts and procedures required to understand the technical, security, policy, and management principles of current and future information network infrastructures and systems. Students can choose from focus areas that include cloud and virtualized information systems, and infrastructure and applications related to data science, enterprise IT infrastructure management, information security, and mobile services and applications.

The iSchool's M.S. in information management (IM) requires the completion of 42 credit hours. Each student completes course work in management approaches and strategies, user information needs, technological infrastructures, and elective subjects to prepare for a wide range of positions in the information field. The program's interdisciplinary philosophy means that students from any academic or professional background have the opportunity to thrive in the program. Many IM students concurrently pursue a Certificate of Advanced Study in information security management or data science graduates have become consultants and analysts, worked for technology giants and the U.S. government, and worked for startup companies—or founded their own. The iSchool also offers a reduction of credits for significant experience or executive status (30-credit executive option) for the M.S. in information management, which aids midcareer professionals to advance their organizations and their job prospects. The program can be completed part-time or full-time and is available online or on campus.

Accredited by the American Library Association (ALA), the M.S. in library and information science (LIS) program requires the completion of 36 credit hours. The program is dedicated to educating students to become leaders in the evolution of the library and information profession. LIS students work with interdisciplinary faculty advisers to plan their programs of study, which may include course work in other academic areas. The program offers a specialization in school media (ranked fourth in the 2018 U.S. News & World Report rankings) and certificates of advanced study in digital libraries and school media, as well as a certificate in cultural heritage preservation and data science.

All four degree programs focus on employing technology and digital tools to find, evaluate, organize, and use information for the betterment of people. Graduates of the iSchool at Syracuse work in a broad range of managerial and technical positions in business, government, education, health care, and other fields.

The iSchool also offers a research-oriented Ph.D. in information science and technology for those individuals interested in becoming researchers, professors, and consultants.

The iSchool's Certificates of Advanced Study have broad appeal and attract students across disciplines. Options include information security management, e-government management and leadership, school media, and data science. These certificates can be earned on campus or online, and provide a valuable development opportunity both for emerging and experienced professionals in the information field.

Research Facilities

Research at the iSchool is characterized by the faculty's diverse interests in information, its uses by people, and the increasing opportunities and issues provided by digital and computational resources. iSchool researchers are trained in a range of disciplines and pursue independent and collaborative work with colleagues across campus and across the world.

Many of the faculty conduct their research individually and in small, flexible, interdisciplinary teams. For certain specialized areas and cross-unit collaborations, however, research centers and laboratories provide a venue that supports long-term commitment to a particular research area. These research and development centers, which have achieved national and international distinction, allow students to apply classroom lessons to authentic problems, sometimes using technologies that have not yet made it to market. These centers include the Behavior, Information, Technology, and Society Lab; the Center for Computational and Data Sciences; the Center for Convergence and Emerging Network Technologies; the Center for Digital Literacy; the Smart Grid Project Center; and the Social Computing Systems Lab.

The University's library system includes collections of 3.1 million volumes, more than 24,000 online and print journals, and extensive collections of microforms, maps, images, music scores, videos, rare books, and manuscripts. Many of these resources can be accessed from academic and residence hall computer clusters. Among its special collections is the Belfer Audio Laboratory and Archive, which contains more than 340,000 historical sound recordings in all formats, including a collection of 22,000 cylinder records, the largest held by any private institution in North America.

Financial Aid

All master's students are reviewed at admission for merit awards and scholarships. Typically, awards do not require an additional application but offerings are altered from year to year. For up-to-date details: https://ischool.syr.edu/admissions/merit-based-awards. Most master's awards are 25- 50% of program tuition and are selectively awarded to both domestic and international students. Fellowships, scholarships, and assistantships are available to full-time doctoral students on campus. The most prestigious and competitive are Syracuse University graduate fellowships, which include a scholarship and a stipend for the academic year. University scholarships provide 24 credit hours of tuition, and graduate assistantships provide tuition and a stipend for the academic year. Syracuse also offers fellowships through the McNair Scholars program and Syracuse University participates in the Yellow Ribbon Campaign for our military and veterans.

Loans are available through the University financial aid office. Financial aid is awarded according to federal financial need guidelines.

Cost of Study

Tuition for 2018–19 is $1,559 per graduate credit hour.

Living and Housing Costs

Academic-year living expenses are about $14,000 for single students (housing and meals only). The University has residence hall rooms and on-campus apartments for single and married graduate students. Many graduate students choose to live off campus.

Student Group

Syracuse University has about 20,000 students, including about 5,000 graduate students. Approximately 1,280 graduate students are enrolled in the School of Information Studies. Fifty percent are international students, with the remainder coming from all parts of the United States. Students have diverse backgrounds, with undergraduate majors in the liberal arts, natural sciences, fine arts, business administration, computer science, and engineering. They participate in more than 300 student groups and extracurricular activities, including Women in Information Technology, Information Studies Graduate Organization, Black and Latino Information Studies Support, the Association for Computing Machinery, and chapters of national information and library associations.

Student Outcomes

Career opportunities for graduates of the programs are excellent. Graduates of the iSchool's master's programs find lucrative professional positions in a wide variety of organizations, with responsibilities ranging from cloud architecture, information systems analysis, information security, and database design to risk assessment and systems management. Library and information science graduates not only work in library settings, but they also hold professional positions in corporations, media and communications outlets, museums, government agencies, and universities. Placements rates are 95 percent from 2014–17. (Placement rates do not apply to the ADS and EDS degrees, which are new in 2017.)

Location

The Syracuse metropolitan area is home to more than a half million people and is the commercial, industrial, medical, and cultural center of central New York State. The 200-acre Main Campus is spacious and attractive, and new University facilities extend the campus into the heart of downtown Syracuse, which is only a 20-minute walk from the University. Winters are snowy and summers are pleasant. Lake Ontario, the Finger Lakes, and the Adirondack and Catskill Mountains are nearby. Boston, Toronto, New York, and Philadelphia are within a 5-hour drive.

The School

The School of Information Studies is a leading center for innovative graduate programs in information fields. The school's focus on information users and understanding user information needs sets it apart from other institutions that offer computer science, management, and related programs. The interdisciplinary faculty combines expertise in information science, telecommunications, public administration, education, school media, business management and management information systems, social science, design, linguistics, computer science, library science, and communications. The iSchool also offers an undergraduate degree program in information management and technology.

Applying

Applicants for the master's degree programs must have a bachelor's degree from an accredited undergraduate institution and an academic record that is satisfactory for admission to the graduate school. Two letters of recommendation, a resume, and an essay on academic plans and professional goals are also required. Applicants for the master's degree and doctoral programs are required to submit scores from the Graduate Record Examinations (GRE). International students should plan to take the Test of English as a Foreign Language (TOEFL); a score of at least 90 on the internet-based test is expected. Doctoral students interested in University fellowships must apply by January 3. Fall master's applicants' priority date is Feb 1; and the deadline is June 1. Spring master's applicants' priority date is October 15 and deadline December 15.

For additional information, please visit the School of Information Studies website, http://ischool.syr.edu or e-mail iGrad@syr.edu. Follow the School on Facebook or Twitter at http://facebook.com/su.ischool and http://twitter.com/ischoolsu. Videos about the School can be found at http://www.youtube.com/user/syracuseischool.

Correspondence and Information

School of Information Studies
343 Hinds Hall
Syracuse University
Syracuse, New York 13244-4100
United States
Phone: 315-443-2911
E-mail: iGrad@syr.edu
Websites: http://ischool.syr.edu
      http://facebook.com/su.ischool (Facebook)
      http://twitter.com/ischoolsu (Twitter)

THE FACULTY AND THEIR RESEARCH

Daniel E. Acuna, Assistant Professor; Ph.D. (computer science), Minnesota, Twin Cities. Scientific innovation, artificial intelligence, machine learning.

Marilyn Arnone, Research Associate Professor; Ph.D. (instructional design, development, and evaluation), Syracuse. Information literacy education, children's learning and curiosity in interactive multimedia environments.

Carlos E. Caicedo, Assistant Professor; Ph.D. (telecommunications), Pittsburgh. Security in future data environments, spectrum trading markets and technology, security management, telecommunication and network systems management.

Kevin Crowston, Professor; Ph.D. (information technologies), MIT. Organizational implications of technology, free/libre open source software development, coordination in distributed teams, ICT in real estate.

Rachel Ivy Clarke, Assistant Professor; Ph.D. (information sciences), Washington. Application of design methodologies and epistemologies to librarianship.

Jason Dedrick, Associate Professor; Ph.D. (management information systems), California, Irvine. Globalization of information technology, national technology policy, offshoring of knowledge work, personal computing industry, green information technologies.

Ingrid Erickson, Assistant Professor; Ph.D. (management science and engineering), Stanford. Work and technology, organizational studies, human-centered computing.

Michael Fudge, Assistant Professor of Practice; M.S. (information management), Syracuse. Database management systems; systems analysis and design; programming, scripting, and web/mobile development; big data; data lakes; warehousing and business intelligence; cloud services and technologies.

Paul Gandel, Professor; Ph.D. (information studies), Syracuse. Digital libraries; digital services; information organization and retrieval; information technology and development; information, organizations, and society knowledge.

Martha A. Garcia-Murillo, Associate Professor; Ph.D. (international political economy and telecommunications), USC. Digital divide, economics of the information industry, information and communications policy and regulations.

Caroline Haythornthwaite, Professor; Ph.D. (information science), Toronto. ICT support of work, learning and social interaction.

Jeff Hemsley, Assistant Professor; Ph.D. (information sciences), Washington. Power as it relates to information asymmetries, computer-mediated social networks in the context of politics or social movements.

Yun Huang, Assistant Professor; Ph.D. (information and computer science), California, Irvine. Crowdsourcing systems, mobile applications, human-computer interaction, social media.

Jill Hurst-Wahl, Assistant Professor of Practice; M.L.S., Maryland. Digitization, digital libraries, copyright, online social networking, web 2.0, virtual worlds.

Michelle Lynn Kaarst-Brown, Associate Professor; Ph.D. (organizational theory and management information systems), York. Information technology culture, strategic alignment of information technology with business strategy, perceptions of risk and opportunity in IT adoption, influences on IT governance, Internet-based business.

Bruce Kingma, Professor of Entrepreneurship; Ph.D. (economics), Rochester. Economics of online education, digital libraries, scholarly publishing, library and nonprofit management.

Elizabeth D. Liddy, Dean and Trustee Professor; Ph.D. (information transfer), Syracuse. Indexing, data mining, natural-language processing, information retrieval.

Ian MacInnes, Associate Dean for Academic Affairs; Ph.D. (political economy and public policy), USC. Electronic commerce, competition policy, information technology and globalization, public policy, standardization, network economics, microeconomics.

Nancy McCracken, Research Associate Professor; Ph.D. (computer and information science), Syracuse. Computational linguistics, natural language processing, data mining, information extraction and retrieval, question answering, knowledge representation.

Lee McKnight, Associate Professor; Ph.D. (political science, communication, and international relations), MIT. Wireless grids, nomadicity, social networking of devices, Internet economics and policy, national and international technology policy.

David Molta, Assistant Dean, Technology Integration; M.P.A., North Texas. Mobile and wireless information systems; interoperability and performance testing; impact of mobile communications technologies on individuals, organizations, and society.

Deborah Nosky, Assistant Professor of Practice; M.S., Syracuse. Technology, project and time management, presentation delivery.

Megan Oakleaf, Assistant Professor; Ph.D. (information and library science), North Carolina at Chapel Hill. Evolution and assessment of information services, outcomes-based assessment, evidence-based decision making, digital reference, digital libraries, information services.

Carsten Osterlund, Associate Professor; Ph.D. (organization studies and behavioral policy science), MIT. Medical informatics, documenting work, distributed work, organizational implications of information technology, indoor tracking systems, qualitative research techniques.

Beth Patin, Assistant Professor; Ph.D. (information science), Washington. Equity of information in two areas: crisis informatics and building cultural competence.

Joon S. Park, Professor; Ph.D. (information technology and information security), George Mason. Information and systems security; security policies, models, mechanisms, evaluation, survivability, and applications.

Jian Qin, Associate Professor; Ph.D. (library and information science), Illinois at Urbana-Champaign. Knowledge organization, information organization, information technology applications in managing knowledge and information.

Jeffrey Rubin, Assistant Professor of Practice; M.S. (telecommunications and network management), Syracuse. Managing websites, e-business, content management systems, information architecture, designing Internet services, web analytics.

Jeff Saltz, Associate Professor; Ph.D. (information systems), NJIT. Analyzing and visualizing large datasets, experiential learning and teaching, investigating startup ecosystems.

Steven B. Sawyer, Associate Professor; D.B.A. (management information systems), Boston. Social informatics, design and development of information systems, project management, role of information and communication technologies relative to organizational and social change.

Carl Schramm, Professor; Ph.D. (labor economics and industrial relations), Wisconsin. Entrepreneurship, innovation and economic growth.

Bryan Semaan, Assistant Professor; Ph.D. (information and computer science), California, Irvine. How people appropriate and are shaped by interactive and collaborative technologies.

Ruth V. Small, Meredith Professor; Ph.D. (instructional design, development, and evaluation), Syracuse. Motivational aspects of information literacy, design and use of information and information technologies in education, role of school media specialist, information components of inventive thinking.

Marcene Sonneborn, Assistant Professor of Practice; M.B.A., Syracuse. Strategic planning, business development, organizational leadership, entrepreneurship.

Jeffrey Stanton, Associate Provost, Professor; Ph.D. (information studies), Connecticut. Organizational psychology and data collection; behavioral information security; statistical models to predict attitudes, motivation, and behavior; interactions between people and technology.

Jennifer Stromer-Galley, Professor, Ph.D. (communication), Pennsylvania. Social media, presidential campaigns, online political participation, social dynamics in online groups.

Arthur Thomas, Assistant Professor of Practice; Ph.D. (research and evaluation/instructional systems design and management), SUNY at Buffalo. Performance improvement, project management, data networking engineering, instructional design, information systems management.

Murali Venkatesh, Associate Professor; Ph.D. (management), Indiana. Civic network design, group-based decision support systems, sociological analyses of administrative documents, human-computer interaction, telecommunications.

Stephen Wallace, Professor of Practice; D.P.S. (computing), Pace University. Theory, practice, and adoption of data science and data mining in organizations.

Jun Wang, Assistant Research Professor; Ph.D. (library and information science), Illinois at Urbana-Champaign. Human computation, machine learning, computational neuroscience, computational language evolution.

Yang Wang, Assistant Professor; Ph.D. (information and computer science), California, Irvine. Privacy and security, social media, crowdsourcing, online communities, persuasive computing.

Lu Xiao, Assistant Professor; Ph.D. (information science and technology), Pennsylvania State University. Collaborative and social computing, digital humanities, and community informatics.

Bei Yu, Assistant Professor; Ph.D. (library and information science), Illinois at Urbana-Champaign. Text classification and analysis, natural language processing, political linguistics, language and social behavior, automated language extraction and classification development.

Ping Zhang, Professor; Ph.D. (information systems), Texas at Austin. Human computer interaction, information management, intellectual development of information-related fields.

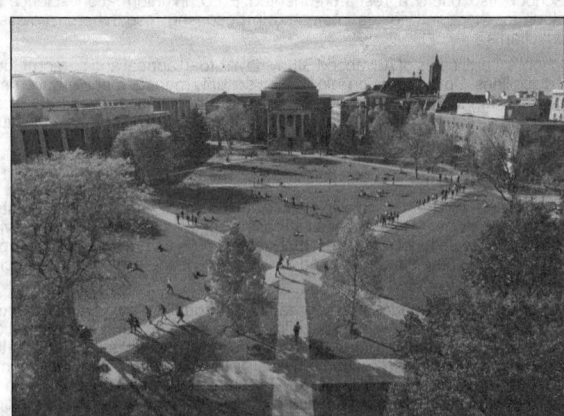

The iSchool is located on the Main Campus Quad in the heart of the Syracuse University campus.

ACADEMIC AND PROFESSIONAL PROGRAMS IN PHYSICAL EDUCATION, SPORTS, AND RECREATION

Section 29
Leisure Studies and Recreation

This section contains a directory of institutions offering graduate work in leisure studies and recreation. Additional information about programs listed in the directory may be obtained by writing directly to the dean of a graduate school or chair of a department at the address given in the directory.

In the other guides in this series:

Graduate Programs in the Humanities, Arts & Social Sciences
See *Performing Arts*

Graduate Programs in the Physical Sciences, Mathematics, Agricultural Sciences, the Environment & Natural Resources

See *Natural Resources*

CONTENTS

Program Directories

Leisure Studies

Bowling Green State University, Graduate College, College of Education and Human Development, School of Human Movement, Sport, and Leisure Studies, Bowling Green, OH 43403. Offers developmental kinesiology (M Ed); recreation and leisure (M Ed); sport administration (M Ed). *Program availability:* Part-time. *Degree requirements:* For master's, thesis or alternative. *Entrance requirements:* For master's, GRE General Test, minimum GPA of 2.7. Additional exam requirements/recommendations for international students: Required—TOEFL. Electronic applications accepted. *Faculty research:* Teacher-learning process, travel and tourism, sport marketing and management, exercise physiology and sport psychology, life-span motor development.

California State University, Long Beach, Graduate Studies, College of Health and Human Services, Department of Recreation and Leisure Studies, Long Beach, CA 90840. Offers recreation administration (MS). *Program availability:* Part-time. *Degree requirements:* For master's, comprehensive exam or thesis. *Entrance requirements:* For master's, GRE General Test. Electronic applications accepted.

Dalhousie University, Faculty of Health Professions, School of Health and Human Performance, Program in Leisure Studies, Halifax, NS B3H 1T8, Canada. Offers MA. *Program availability:* Part-time. *Degree requirements:* For master's, thesis. *Entrance requirements:* For master's, minimum GPA of 3.3. Additional exam requirements/recommendations for international students: Required—TOEFL, IELTS, CANTEST, CAEL, or Michigan English Language Assessment Battery. Electronic applications accepted. *Faculty research:* Leisure and lifestyles of social groups such as older adults, women, and persons with health problems or disabilities; historical analysis of leisure; sport and leisure administration.

East Carolina University, Graduate School, College of Health and Human Performance, Department of Recreation and Leisure Studies, Greenville, NC 27858-4353. Offers aquatic therapy (Certificate); biofeedback (Certificate); recreation services and interventions (MS), including generalist. *Program availability:* Part-time, evening/weekend, online learning. *Students:* 24 full-time (13 women), 11 part-time (8 women); includes 8 minority (3 Black or African American, non-Hispanic/Latino; 2 Hispanic/Latino; 3 Two or more races, non-Hispanic/Latino). Average age 28. 15 applicants, 93% accepted, 8 enrolled. In 2017, 2 master's, 5 other advanced degrees awarded. *Degree requirements:* For master's, comprehensive exam, thesis optional. *Entrance requirements:* For master's, GRE General Test or MAT. Additional exam requirements/recommendations for international students: Recommended—TOEFL (minimum score 78 iBT), IELTS (minimum score 6.5), TWE. *Application deadline:* For fall admission, 6/1 priority date for domestic students. Applications are processed on a rolling basis. Application fee: $75. *Expenses:* Tuition, state resident: full-time $4749; part-time $297 per credit hour. Tuition, nonresident: full-time $17,898; part-time $1119 per credit hour. *Required fees:* $2691; $224 per credit hour. Part-time tuition and fees vary according to course load and program. *Financial support:* Research assistantships and teaching assistantships with partial tuition reimbursements available. Financial award application deadline: 6/1. *Faculty research:* Therapeutic recreation, stress and coping behavior, medicine carrying capacity, choice behavior, tourism preferences. *Unit head:* Dr. Matthew Mahar, Interim Chair, 252-328-0008, E-mail: maharm@ecu.edu.
Website: https://hhp.ecu.edu/rcls/

Howard University, Graduate School, Department of Health, Human Performance and Leisure Studies, Washington, DC 20059-0002. Offers exercise physiology (MS); health education (MS); sports studies (MS), including sociology of sports, sports management; urban recreation (MS), including leisure studies. *Program availability:* Part-time, evening/weekend. *Degree requirements:* For master's, comprehensive exam, thesis. *Entrance requirements:* For master's, BS in human performance or related field. Additional exam requirements/recommendations for international students: Recommended—TOEFL. Electronic applications accepted. *Faculty research:* Health promotion, cardiovascular hypertension, physical activity, sport and human rights issues.

Indiana University Bloomington, School of Public Health, Department of Recreation, Park, and Tourism Studies, Bloomington, IN 47405-7000. Offers leisure behavior (PhD); outdoor recreation (MS); park and public lands management (MS); recreation administration (MS); recreational sports administration (MS); recreational therapy (MS); tourism management (MS). Terminal master's awarded for partial completion of doctoral program. *Degree requirements:* For master's, thesis optional; for doctorate, comprehensive exam, thesis/dissertation. *Entrance requirements:* For master's, GRE General Test, minimum GPA of 2.8; for doctorate, GRE General Test, minimum GPA of 3.0 (undergraduate), 3.5 (graduate). Additional exam requirements/recommendations for international students: Required—TOEFL (minimum score 550 paper-based; 80 iBT). Electronic applications accepted. *Faculty research:* Leisure counseling, gerontology, special populations, planning and development.

Penn State University Park, Graduate School, College of Health and Human Development, Department of Recreation, Park and Tourism Management, University Park, PA 16802. Offers MS, PhD. *Unit head:* Dr. Ann C. Crouter, Dean, 814-865-1420, Fax: 814-865-3282. *Application contact:* Lori Hawn, Director, Graduate Student Services, 814-865-1795, Fax: 814-863-4627, E-mail: l-gswww@lists.psu.edu.
Website: http://hhd.psu.edu/rptm

Prescott College, Graduate Programs, Program in Adventure Education, Prescott, AZ 86301. Offers adventure education (MA); adventure-based environmental education (MA); student-directed concentration (MA). *Program availability:* Part-time, online learning. *Degree requirements:* For master's, thesis, fieldwork or internship, practicum. *Entrance requirements:* For master's, 2 letters of recommendation, resume. Additional exam requirements/recommendations for international students: Required—TOEFL (minimum score 500 paper-based). Electronic applications accepted.

San Francisco State University, Division of Graduate Studies, College of Health and Social Sciences, Department of Recreation, Parks, and Tourism, San Francisco, CA 94132-1722. Offers MS. *Program availability:* Part-time. *Application deadline:* Applications are processed on a rolling basis. *Financial support:* Career-related internships or fieldwork available. *Unit head:* Dr. Erik Rosegard, Chair, 415-338-7529, Fax: 415-338-0543, E-mail: rosegard@sfsu.edu. *Application contact:* Dr. Jackson Wilson, Graduate Coordinator, 415-338-1487, Fax: 415-338-0543, E-mail: wilsonj@sfsu.edu.
Website: http://recdept.sfsu.edu/graduate

Southeast Missouri State University, School of Graduate Studies, Department of Health, Human Performance and Recreation, Cape Girardeau, MO 63701-4799. Offers MS. *Program availability:* Part-time. *Faculty:* 8 full-time (2 women), 2 part-time/adjunct (1 woman). *Students:* 19 full-time (12 women), 7 part-time (6 women); includes 1 minority (Hispanic/Latino), 9 international. Average age 25. 39 applicants, 82% accepted, 14 enrolled. In 2017, 10 master's awarded. *Degree requirements:* For master's,

comprehensive exam, thesis optional. *Entrance requirements:* For master's, GRE General Test (minimum combined score of 950). Additional exam requirements/recommendations for international students: Required—TOEFL (minimum score 550 paper-based; 79 iBT), IELTS (minimum score 6), PTE (minimum score 53). *Application deadline:* For fall admission, 8/1 for domestic students, 5/1 for international students; for spring admission, 11/21 for domestic students, 10/1 for international students; for summer admission, 5/15 for domestic students. Applications are processed on a rolling basis. Application fee: $30 ($40 for international students). Electronic applications accepted. *Expenses:* $270.35 per credit hour in-state tuition, $33.40 per credit hour fees. *Financial support:* In 2017–18, 11 students received support. Teaching assistantships with full tuition reimbursements available, career-related internships or fieldwork, Federal Work-Study, scholarships/grants, traineeships, tuition waivers (full), and unspecified assistantships available. Financial award application deadline: 6/30; financial award applicants required to submit FAFSA. *Faculty research:* Body composition assessment techniques, serum lipid adaptations with physical activity in smokers, professional attitudes of pre-service teachers, high intensity training with clinical populations. *Unit head:* Dr. Joe Pujol, Professor and Chairperson, 573-651-2664, Fax: 573-651-5150, E-mail: jpujol@semo.edu. *Application contact:* Dr. Jeremy Barnes, Professor/Graduate Coordinator, 573-651-2197, Fax: 573-651-5150, E-mail: jbarnes@semo.edu.
Website: http://www.semo.edu/health/

Southern Connecticut State University, School of Graduate Studies, School of Health and Human Services, Department of Recreation and Leisure Studies, New Haven, CT 06515-1355. Offers MS. *Program availability:* Part-time, evening/weekend. *Degree requirements:* For master's, thesis or alternative. *Entrance requirements:* For master's, interview, minimum undergraduate QPA of 3.0 in graduate major field or 2.5 overall. Electronic applications accepted.

Texas State University, The Graduate College, College of Education, Program in Recreation Management, San Marcos, TX 78666. Offers recreation management (MSRLS). *Program availability:* Part-time. *Faculty:* 7 full-time (3 women), 1 (woman) part-time/adjunct. *Students:* 15 full-time (4 women), 6 part-time (2 women); includes 9 minority (5 Black or African American, non-Hispanic/Latino; 4 Hispanic/Latino). Average age 28. 22 applicants, 59% accepted, 6 enrolled. In 2017, 1 master's awarded. *Degree requirements:* For master's, comprehensive exam, thesis optional. *Entrance requirements:* For master's, baccalaureate degree from regionally-accredited institution with minimum GPA of 2.75 in last 60 hours of course work, background course work in marketing and management, statement of purpose. Additional exam requirements/recommendations for international students: Required—TOEFL (minimum score 550 paper-based; 78 iBT), IELTS (minimum score 6.5). *Application deadline:* For fall admission, 2/15 priority date for domestic students, 2/15 for international students; for spring admission, 10/15 priority date for domestic students, 10/1 for international students; for summer admission, 4/15 for domestic students, 3/15 for international students. Applications are processed on a rolling basis. Application fee: $40 ($90 for international students). Electronic applications accepted. *Expenses:* Tuition, state resident: full-time $7868; part-time $3934 per semester. Tuition, nonresident: full-time $17,828; part-time $8914 per semester. *Required fees:* $2092; $1435 per semester. Tuition and fees vary according to course load. *Financial support:* In 2017–18, 12 students received support, including 2 teaching assistantships (averaging $12,152 per year); research assistantships, scholarships/grants, and unspecified assistantships also available. Financial award application deadline: 3/1; financial award applicants required to submit FAFSA. *Faculty research:* Effects of neuromuscular electrical stimulation frequency on metabolic markers, effects of focal knee join cooling on different modes of the quadriceps strength. *Total annual research expenditures:* $5,229. *Unit head:* Dr. Jan Hodges, Graduate Advisor, 512-245-7482, Fax: 512-245-8678, E-mail: jh223@txstate.edu. *Application contact:* Dr. Andrea Golato, Dean of the Graduate College, 512-245-2581, Fax: 512-245-8365, E-mail: gradcollege@txstate.edu.
Website: http://www.gradcollege.txstate.edu/programs/msrls-mgmt.html

Universidad Metropolitana, School of Education, Program in Managing Recreation and Sports Services, San Juan, PR 00928-1150. Offers M Ed. *Program availability:* Part-time. *Degree requirements:* For master's, thesis or alternative. *Entrance requirements:* For master's, EXADEP, interview. Electronic applications accepted.

Université du Québec à Trois-Rivières, Graduate Programs, Program in Leisure, Culture and Tourism Sciences, Trois-Rivières, QC G9A 5H7, Canada. Offers MA, DESS. *Program availability:* Part-time. *Degree requirements:* For master's, thesis optional. *Entrance requirements:* For master's, appropriate bachelor's degree, proficiency in French.

University of Illinois at Urbana–Champaign, Graduate College, College of Applied Health Sciences, Department of Recreation, Sport and Tourism, Champaign, IL 61820. Offers MS, PhD. *Program availability:* Part-time, online learning.

The University of Iowa, Graduate College, College of Liberal Arts and Sciences, Department of Health and Human Physiology, Iowa City, IA 52242-1316. Offers athletic training (MS); clinical exercise physiology (MS); health and human physiology (PhD); leisure studies (MA, PhD), including recreational sport management (PhD); therapeutic recreation (MA). *Degree requirements:* For master's, thesis optional, exam; for doctorate, comprehensive exam, thesis/dissertation. *Entrance requirements:* For master's and doctorate, GRE General Test, minimum GPA of 3.0. Additional exam requirements/recommendations for international students: Required—TOEFL (minimum score 600 paper-based; 100 iBT). Electronic applications accepted.

University of Nebraska at Kearney, College of Education, Kinesiology and Sport Sciences Department, Kearney, NE 68849-0001. Offers general physical education (MA Ed), including recreation and leisure, sports administration; physical education exercise science (MA Ed); physical education master teacher (MA Ed), including pedagogy, special populations. *Program availability:* Part-time, evening/weekend, 100% online. *Degree requirements:* For master's, comprehensive exam, thesis optional. *Entrance requirements:* For master's, GRE General Test (for some programs), personal statement. Additional exam requirements/recommendations for international students: Recommended—TOEFL (minimum score 550 paper-based; 79 iBT), IELTS (minimum score 6.5). Electronic applications accepted. *Faculty research:* Ergonomic aids, nutrition, motor development, sports pedagogy, applied behavior analysis, physical activity and wellness, athletic training, therapeutic Interventions, exercise physiology, endocrinology and metabolism.

The University of Tennessee, Graduate School, College of Education, Health and Human Sciences, Department of Exercise, Sport, and Leisure Studies, Knoxville, TN 37996. Offers exercise science (MS, PhD), including biomechanics/sports medicine, exercise physiology; recreation and leisure studies (MS); sport management (MS); sport studies (MS, PhD); therapeutic recreation (MS). *Program availability:* Part-time, evening/

weekend. *Degree requirements:* For master's, thesis optional. *Entrance requirements:* For master's, minimum GPA of 2.7. Additional exam requirements/recommendations for international students: Required—TOEFL. Electronic applications accepted.

The University of Toledo, College of Graduate Studies, College of Health and Human Services, School of Exercise and Rehabilitation Sciences, Toledo, OH 43606-3390. Offers athletic training (MSES); exercise physiology (MSES); exercise science (PhD); occupational therapy (OTD); physical therapy (DPT); recreation and leisure studies (MA), including recreation administration, recreation therapy. *Degree requirements:* For master's, comprehensive exam, thesis; for doctorate, thesis/dissertation or alternative. *Entrance requirements:* For master's, GRE, minimum cumulative GPA of 2.7 for all previous academic work, letters of recommendation; for doctorate, GRE, minimum cumulative GPA of 3.0 for all previous academic work, letters of recommendation; OTCAS or PTCAS application and UT supplemental application (for OTD and DPT). Additional exam requirements/recommendations for international students: Required—TOEFL (minimum score 550 paper-based; 80 iBT). Electronic applications accepted.

University of Utah, Graduate School, College of Health, Department of Health, Kinesiology, and Recreation, Salt Lake City, UT 84112. Offers kinesiology (MS, PhD); parks, recreation, and tourism (MS, PhD). *Program availability:* Part-time. *Faculty:* 7 full-time (4 women), 4 part-time/adjunct (0 women). *Students:* 92 full-time (58 women), 44 part-time (23 women); includes 21 minority (1 Black or African American, non-Hispanic/Latino; 1 American Indian or Alaska Native, non-Hispanic/Latino; 5 Asian, non-Hispanic/Latino; 10 Hispanic/Latino; 2 Native Hawaiian or other Pacific Islander, non-Hispanic/Latino; 2 Two or more races, non-Hispanic/Latino), 10 international. Average age 24. 24 applicants, 58% accepted, 8 enrolled. In 2017, 34 master's, 4 doctorates awarded. Terminal master's awarded for partial completion of doctoral program. *Degree requirements:* For master's, comprehensive exam, thesis or alternative; for doctorate, comprehensive exam, thesis/dissertation. *Entrance requirements:* For master's and doctorate, GRE General Test, minimum GPA of 3.0. Additional exam requirements/recommendations for international students: Required—TOEFL (minimum score 500 paper-based). *Application deadline:* For fall admission, 1/15 priority date for domestic and international students. Application fee: $55 ($65 for international students). Electronic applications accepted. *Expenses:* Contact institution. *Financial support:* In 2017–18, 13 students received support, including 3 research assistantships with full tuition reimbursements available, 8 teaching assistantships with full tuition reimbursements available; career-related internships or fieldwork, scholarships/grants, health care benefits, and unspecified assistantships also available. Financial award application deadline: 1/15; financial award applicants required to submit FAFSA. *Faculty research:* Community and sport, outdoor recreation, protected area management,

sustainable tourism and youth development. *Total annual research expenditures:* $300,000. *Unit head:* Dr. Kelly S. Bricker, Program Director, 801-585-6503, E-mail: kelly.bricker@health.utah.edu. *Application contact:* Dr. Jim Sibthorp, Director of Graduate Studies, 801-581-5940, Fax: 801-581-4930, E-mail: jim.sibthorp@health.utah.edu.
Website: http://www.health.utah.edu/prt/

University of Victoria, Faculty of Graduate Studies, Faculty of Education, School of Exercise Science, Physical, and Health Education, Victoria, BC V8W 2Y2, Canada. Offers coaching studies (co-operative education) (M Ed); kinesiology (M Sc, MA); leisure service administration (MA); physical education (MA). *Program availability:* Part-time. *Degree requirements:* For master's, comprehensive exam (for some programs), thesis (for some programs). *Entrance requirements:* For master's, minimum B average. Additional exam requirements/recommendations for international students: Required—TOEFL (minimum score 575 paper-based), IELTS (minimum score 7). Electronic applications accepted. *Faculty research:* Children and exercise, mental skills in sports, teaching effectiveness, neural control of human movement, physical performance and health.

University of Waterloo, Graduate Studies, Faculty of Applied Health Sciences, Department of Recreation and Leisure Studies, Waterloo, ON N2L 3G1, Canada. Offers MA, PhD. *Program availability:* Part-time. *Degree requirements:* For master's, thesis; for doctorate, comprehensive exam, thesis/dissertation. *Entrance requirements:* For master's, honors degree, minimum B average, writing sample, resume; for doctorate, GRE (recommended), master's degree, minimum B average, writing sample, resume. Additional exam requirements/recommendations for international students: Required—TOEFL, IELTS, PTE. Electronic applications accepted. *Faculty research:* Tourism, leisure behavior, special populations, leisure service management, outdoor resources, aging, health and well-being, work and health.

University of West Florida, Usha Kundu, MD College of Health, Department of Exercise Science and Community Health, Pensacola, FL 32514-5750. Offers health promotion (MS); health, leisure, and exercise science (MS), including exercise science, physical education. *Program availability:* Part-time, evening/weekend. *Degree requirements:* For master's, thesis or alternative. *Entrance requirements:* For master's, GRE or MAT, official transcripts; minimum GPA of 3.0; letter of intent; three personal references; work experience as reflected in resume. Additional exam requirements/recommendations for international students: Required—TOEFL (minimum score 550 paper-based).

Recreation and Park Management

Acadia University, Faculty of Professional Studies, School of Recreation Management and Community Development, Wolfville, NS B4P 2R6, Canada. Offers recreation management (MR). *Entrance requirements:* Additional exam requirements/recommendations for international students: Required—TOEFL (minimum score 630 paper-based; 93 iBT), IELTS (minimum score 6.5). *Application deadline:* For fall admission, 2/1 priority date for domestic and international students. Applications are processed on a rolling basis. Application fee: $50. *Financial support:* Application deadline: 2/1. *Unit head:* Dr. Glyn Bissix, Program Head, 902-585-1123, Fax: 902-585-1702, E-mail: glyn.bissix@acadiau.ca. *Application contact:* Rosie Hare, Administrative Assistant, 902-585-1597, Fax: 902-585-1086, E-mail: rosie.hare@acadiau.ca.
Website: http://rec.acadiau.ca/

Bowling Green State University, Graduate College, College of Education and Human Development, School of Human Movement, Sport, and Leisure Studies, Bowling Green, OH 43403. Offers developmental kinesiology (M Ed); recreation and leisure (M Ed); sport administration (M Ed). *Program availability:* Part-time. *Degree requirements:* For master's, thesis or alternative. *Entrance requirements:* For master's, GRE General Test, minimum GPA of 2.7. Additional exam requirements/recommendations for international students: Required—TOEFL. Electronic applications accepted. *Faculty research:* Teacher-learning process, travel and tourism, sport marketing and management, exercise physiology and sport psychology, life-span motor development.

California State University, Chico, Office of Graduate Studies, College of Communication and Education, Recreation, Hospitality and Parks Management Department, Chico, CA 95929-0722. Offers recreation, parks, and tourism (MS). *Program availability:* Part-time. *Degree requirements:* For master's, thesis or project. *Entrance requirements:* For master's, GRE General Test, 3 letters of recommendation, statement of purpose, resume. Additional exam requirements/recommendations for international students: Required—TOEFL (minimum score 550 paper-based; 80 iBT), IELTS (minimum score 6.5), PTE. Electronic applications accepted.

California State University, East Bay, Office of Graduate Studies, College of Education and Allied Studies, Department of Hospitality, Recreation and Tourism, Hayward, CA 94542-3000. Offers recreation and tourism (MS). *Program availability:* Part-time, evening/weekend, online learning. *Faculty:* 11 full-time (6 women), 16 part-time/adjunct (9 women). *Students:* 20 full-time (13 women), 9 part-time (7 women); includes 20 minority (8 Black or African American, non-Hispanic/Latino; 6 Asian, non-Hispanic/Latino; 4 Hispanic/Latino; 2 Two or more races, non-Hispanic/Latino). Average age 35. 23 applicants, 48% accepted, 7 enrolled. In 2017, 17 master's awarded. *Degree requirements:* For master's, thesis optional. *Entrance requirements:* For master's, minimum GPA of 2.75; 2 years' related work experience; 3 letters of recommendation; resume; baccalaureate degree. Additional exam requirements/recommendations for international students: Required—TOEFL (minimum score 550 paper-based). *Application deadline:* For fall admission, 6/1 for domestic and international students. Applications are processed on a rolling basis. Application fee: $55. Electronic applications accepted. *Financial support:* Federal Work-Study, institutionally sponsored loans, and scholarships/grants available. Support available to part-time students. Financial award application deadline: 3/2; financial award applicants required to submit FAFSA. *Faculty research:* Leisure, online vs. face-to-face (F2F) learning, risk management, leadership, tourism consumer behavior. *Unit head:* Dr. Chris Chamberlain, Chair, 510-885-2101, E-mail: chris.chamberlain@csueastbay.edu. *Application contact:* Philip Cole-Regis, Administrative Support Coordinator, 510-885-3716, Fax: 510-885-4777, E-mail: philip.coleregis@csueastbay.edu.

California State University, Long Beach, Graduate Studies, College of Health and Human Services, Department of Recreation and Leisure Studies, Long Beach, CA 90840. Offers recreation administration (MS). *Program availability:* Part-time. *Degree requirements:* For master's, comprehensive exam or thesis. *Entrance requirements:* For master's, GRE General Test. Electronic applications accepted.

California State University, Northridge, Graduate Studies, College of Health and Human Development, Department of Recreation and Tourism Management, Northridge, CA 91330. Offers hospitality and tourism (MS); recreational sport management/campus recreation (MS). *Students:* 19 full-time (6 women), 12 part-time (10 women); includes 12 minority (9 Hispanic/Latino; 1 Native Hawaiian or other Pacific Islander, non-Hispanic/Latino; 2 Two or more races, non-Hispanic/Latino), 7 international. Average age 29. 36 applicants, 67% accepted, 12 enrolled. In 2017, 17 master's awarded. *Degree requirements:* For master's, thesis (for some programs). *Entrance requirements:* For master's, GRE (if cumulative undergraduate GPA less than 3.0). Additional exam requirements/recommendations for international students: Required—TOEFL. *Application deadline:* For fall admission, 11/30 for domestic students. Application fee: $55. *Financial support:* Application deadline: 3/1. *Unit head:* Dr. Mechelle Best, Chair, 818-677-3202.
Website: http://www.csun.edu/hhd/rtm/

California State University, Northridge, Graduate Studies, Tseng College, Northridge, CA 91330. Offers business administration (Graduate Certificate); health administration (MPA); health education (MPH); knowledge management (MKM); music industry administration (MA); nonprofit-sector management (Graduate Certificate); public administration (MPA); public sector management and leadership (MPA); social work (MSW); taxation (MS); tourism, hospitality and recreation management (MS). *Students:* 4 part-time (all women); includes 1 minority (Black or African American, non-Hispanic/Latino). Average age 37. In 2017, 2 master's awarded. *Entrance requirements:* For master's, GRE (if cumulative undergraduate GPA less than 3.0). *Unit head:* Joyce Feucht-Haviar, Dean, 866-873-6439.

California State University, Sacramento, College of Health and Human Services, Department of Recreation, Parks and Tourism Administration, Sacramento, CA 95819. Offers MS. *Program availability:* Part-time. *Students:* 5 full-time (3 women), 15 part-time (13 women); includes 4 minority (2 Black or African American, non-Hispanic/Latino; 2 Hispanic/Latino), 1 international. Average age 30. 16 applicants, 81% accepted, 10 enrolled. In 2017, 3 master's awarded. *Degree requirements:* For master's, thesis or project; writing proficiency exam. *Entrance requirements:* For master's, minimum overall GPA of 2.75, 3.0 in the major. Additional exam requirements/recommendations for international students: Required—TOEFL (minimum score 550 paper-based; 80 iBT); Recommended—IELTS, TSE. *Application deadline:* For fall admission, 3/1 for domestic and international students; for spring admission, 9/15 for domestic students, 9/30 for international students. Applications are processed on a rolling basis. Application fee: $55. Electronic applications accepted. *Expenses:* Contact institution. *Financial support:* Teaching assistantships, career-related internships or fieldwork, Federal Work-Study, and scholarships/grants available. Support available to part-time students. Financial award application deadline: 3/1; financial award applicants required to submit FAFSA. *Unit head:* Dr. Greg Shaw, Chair, 916-278-6752, E-mail: shaw@csus.edu. *Application contact:* Jose Martinez, Graduate Admissions Supervisor, 916-278-7871, E-mail: martinj@skymail.csus.edu.
Website: http://www.csus.edu/hhs/rpta

Central Michigan University, Central Michigan University Global Campus, Program in Administration, Mount Pleasant, MI 48859. Offers acquisitions administration (MSA, Certificate); engineering management administration (MSA, Certificate); general administration (MSA, Certificate); health services administration (MSA, Certificate); human resources administration (MSA, Certificate); information resource management (MSA); information resource management administration (Certificate); international administration (MSA, Certificate); leadership (MSA, Certificate); philanthropy and fundraising administration (MSA, Certificate); public administration (MSA, Certificate); recreation and park administration (MSA); research administration (MSA, Certificate). *Program availability:* Part-time, evening/weekend, online learning. *Entrance requirements:* For master's, minimum GPA of 2.7 in major. Electronic applications accepted.

Recreation and Park Management

Clemson University, Graduate School, College of Behavioral, Social and Health Sciences, Department of Parks, Recreation, and Tourism Management, Clemson, SC 29634. Offers international parks and tourism (Certificate); parks, recreation and tourism management (MS, PhD), including recreational therapy (PhD); public administration (MPA, Certificate); recreational therapy (MS); youth development leadership (MS, Certificate). *Program availability:* Part-time, evening/weekend, 100% online. *Faculty:* 31 full-time (10 women), 3 part-time/adjunct (0 women). *Students:* 90 full-time (62 women), 193 part-time (114 women); includes 57 minority (44 Black or African American, non-Hispanic/Latino; 1 American Indian or Alaska Native, non-Hispanic/Latino; 1 Asian, non-Hispanic/Latino; 8 Hispanic/Latino; 3 Two or more races, non-Hispanic/Latino), 14 international. Average age 32. 245 applicants, 80% accepted, 129 enrolled. In 2017, 37 master's, 5 doctorates, 38 other advanced degrees awarded. *Degree requirements:* For master's, comprehensive exam (for some programs), thesis (for some programs); for doctorate, comprehensive exam, thesis/dissertation; for Certificate, portfolio. *Entrance requirements:* For master's and doctorate, GRE General Test, unofficial transcripts, letter of intent, letters of reference; for Certificate, letter of recommendation, unofficial transcripts, personal statement, resume. Additional exam requirements/recommendations for international students: Required—TOEFL (minimum score 610 paper-based; 80 iBT), IELTS (minimum score 6.5), PTE (minimum score 54). *Application deadline:* For fall admission, 1/15 priority date for domestic and international students; for spring admission, 11/15 priority date for domestic and international students. Applications are processed on a rolling basis. Application fee: $80 ($90 for international students). Electronic applications accepted. *Expenses:* $5,767 per semester full-time resident, $10,918 per semester full-time non-resident, $656 per credit hour part-time resident, $1,310 per credit hour part-time non-resident, $915 per credit hour online; $5,174 per semester full-time resident, $9,714 per semester full-time non-resident, $511 per credit hour part-time resident, $1,017 per credit hour part-time non-resident, $741 per credit hour online (for online non-thesis ms and doctoral programs); $613 per credit hour (for online youth development leadership); other fees may apply per session. *Financial support:* In 2017–18, 68 students received support, including 4 fellowships with partial tuition reimbursements available (averaging $5,250 per year), 7 research assistantships with partial tuition reimbursements available (averaging $11,653 per year), 52 teaching assistantships with partial tuition reimbursements available (averaging $8,517 per year); career-related internships or fieldwork and unspecified assistantships also available. Financial award application deadline: 1/15. *Faculty research:* Human behavior, land use, recreational therapy, sustainability, tourism. *Total annual research expenditures:* $400,772. *Unit head:* Dr. Fran McGuire, Interim Chair, 864-656-3036, E-mail: lefty@clemson.edu. *Application contact:* Dr. Jeff Hallo, Graduate Coordinator, 864-656-3237, E-mail: jhallo@clemson.edu.
Website: http://www.clemson.edu/hehd/departments/prtm/

Colorado State University, Warner College of Natural Resources, Department of Human Dimensions of Natural Resources, Fort Collins, CO 80523-1480. Offers human dimensions of natural resources (MS, PhD); tourism management (MTM). *Program availability:* Part-time, evening/weekend, 100% online. *Faculty:* 15 full-time (6 women). *Students:* 49 full-time (32 women), 132 part-time (67 women); includes 23 minority (6 Black or African American, non-Hispanic/Latino; 1 American Indian or Alaska Native, non-Hispanic/Latino; 1 Asian, non-Hispanic/Latino; 9 Hispanic/Latino; 6 Two or more races, non-Hispanic/Latino), 14 international. Average age 29. 159 applicants, 77% accepted, 84 enrolled. In 2017, 58 master's awarded. Terminal master's awarded for partial completion of doctoral program. *Degree requirements:* For master's, thesis (for some programs); for doctorate, comprehensive exam, thesis/dissertation. *Entrance requirements:* For master's, GRE General Test, minimum GPA of 3.0, 3 letters of recommendation, statement of interest, official transcripts; for doctorate, GRE General Test, minimum GPA of 3.0, 3 letters of recommendation, copy of master's thesis or professional paper, statement of interest, official transcripts. *Application deadline:* For fall admission, 2/15 for domestic and international students. Applications are processed on a rolling basis. Application fee: $60 ($70 for international students). Electronic applications accepted. *Expenses:* $749 per credit hour (for online MTM); $1,200 per semester (for MS in conservation leadership and on-campus MTM). *Financial support:* In 2017–18, 8 research assistantships with full and partial tuition reimbursements (averaging $21,923 per year), 9 teaching assistantships with full and partial tuition reimbursements (averaging $14,256 per year) were awarded; scholarships/grants and unspecified assistantships also available. Financial award application deadline: 2/15. *Faculty research:* Biocultural approaches to conservation; conservation governance; dimensions of wildlife management; marine conservation; park recreation and management. *Total annual research expenditures:* $1.4 million. *Unit head:* Dr. Michael J. Manfredo, Professor and Department Head, 970-491-6591, Fax: 970-491-2255, E-mail: michael.manfredo@colostate.edu. *Application contact:* Jesse Striegel, Administrative Assistant, 970-491-6591, Fax: 970-491-2255, E-mail: jessie.striegel@colostate.edu.
Website: http://warnercnr.colostate.edu/hdnr-home

Delta State University, Graduate Programs, College of Education, Division of Health, Physical Education, and Recreation, Cleveland, MS 38733-0001. Offers health, physical education, and recreation (M Ed); sport and human performance (MS). *Program availability:* Part-time, evening/weekend. *Degree requirements:* For master's, thesis optional. *Entrance requirements:* For master's, GRE General Test or MAT, Class A teaching certificate. *Faculty research:* Blood pressure, body fat, power and reaction time, learning disorders of athletes, effects of walking.

East Carolina University, Graduate School, College of Health and Human Performance, Department of Recreation and Leisure Studies, Greenville, NC 27858-4353. Offers aquatic therapy (Certificate); biofeedback (Certificate); recreation services and interventions (MS), including generalist. *Program availability:* Part-time, evening/weekend, online learning. *Students:* 24 full-time (13 women), 11 part-time (8 women); includes 8 minority (3 Black or African American, non-Hispanic/Latino; 2 Hispanic/Latino; 3 Two or more races, non-Hispanic/Latino). Average age 28. 15 applicants, 93% accepted, 8 enrolled. In 2017, 2 master's, 5 other advanced degrees awarded. *Degree requirements:* For master's, comprehensive exam, thesis optional. *Entrance requirements:* For master's, GRE General Test or MAT. Additional exam requirements/recommendations for international students: Recommended—TOEFL (minimum score 78 iBT), IELTS (minimum score 6.5), TWE. *Application deadline:* For fall admission, 6/1 priority date for domestic students. Applications are processed on a rolling basis. Application fee: $75. *Expenses:* Tuition, state resident: full-time $4749; part-time $297 per credit hour. Tuition, nonresident: full-time $17,898; part-time $1119 per credit hour. *Required fees:* $2691; $224 per credit hour. Part-time tuition and fees vary according to course load and program. *Financial support:* Research assistantships and teaching assistantships with partial tuition reimbursements available. Financial award application deadline: 6/1. *Faculty research:* Therapeutic recreation, stress and coping behavior, medicine carrying capacity, choice behavior, tourism preferences. *Unit head:* Dr. Matthew Mahar, Interim Chair, 252-328-0008, E-mail: maharm@ecu.edu.
Website: https://hhp.ecu.edu/rcls/

Eastern Kentucky University, The Graduate School, College of Health Sciences, Department of Recreation and Park Administration, Richmond, KY 40475-3102. Offers MS. *Program availability:* Part-time. *Degree requirements:* For master's, comprehensive exam, thesis optional. *Entrance requirements:* For master's, GRE General Test, MAT, minimum GPA of 2.5. *Faculty research:* Marketing, at risk youth, outdoor education, event planning, TR in schools.

Eastern Washington University, Graduate Studies, College of Arts, Letters and Education, Department of Physical Education, Health and Recreation, Cheney, WA 99004-2431. Offers exercise science (MS); sports and recreation administration (MS). *Faculty:* 7. *Students:* 15 full-time (6 women), 2 part-time (1 woman); includes 1 minority (Black or African American, non-Hispanic/Latino), 1 international. Average age 28. 34 applicants, 26% accepted, 8 enrolled. In 2017, 5 master's awarded. *Degree requirements:* For master's, comprehensive exam, thesis or alternative. *Entrance requirements:* For master's, minimum GPA of 3.0. Additional exam requirements/recommendations for international students: Required—TOEFL (minimum score 580 paper-based; 92 iBT), IELTS (minimum score 7), PTE (minimum score 63). *Application deadline:* For fall admission, 4/1 priority date for domestic students; for spring admission, 1/15 for domestic students. Applications are processed on a rolling basis. Application fee: $50. Electronic applications accepted. *Expenses:* Tuition, state resident: full-time $11,191; part-time $373.06 per credit. Tuition, nonresident: full-time $25,995; part-time $866.52 per credit. *Financial support:* Teaching assistantships with partial tuition reimbursements, career-related internships or fieldwork, Federal Work-Study, institutionally sponsored loans, and scholarships/grants available. Support available to part-time students. Financial award application deadline: 2/1; financial award applicants required to submit FAFSA. *Unit head:* Dr. Chadron Hazelbaker, Graduate Program Director, 509-359-2486, Fax: 509-359-4833, E-mail: chazelbaker@ewu.edu.

Florida International University, College of Arts, Sciences, and Education, Department of Leadership and Professional Studies, Miami, FL 33199. Offers adult education and human resource development (MS, Ed D); counseling (MS), including rehabilitation counseling, school counseling; counselor education (MS), including clinical mental health counseling; educational administration and supervision (Ed D); educational leadership (MS, Certificate, Ed S); higher education (Ed D); higher education administration (MS); international and comparative education (MS); recreation and sport management (MS), including recreation and sport management, recreational therapy; school psychology (Ed S); urban education (MS), including instruction in urban settings, learning technologies, multicultural/bilingual, multicultural/TESOL, urban education. *Program availability:* Part-time, evening/weekend. *Faculty:* 60 full-time (41 women), 112 part-time/adjunct (77 women). *Students:* 221 full-time (162 women), 301 part-time (239 women); includes 418 minority (127 Black or African American, non-Hispanic/Latino; 9 Asian, non-Hispanic/Latino; 271 Hispanic/Latino; 11 Two or more races, non-Hispanic/Latino), 10 international. Average age 31. 330 applicants, 55% accepted, 100 enrolled. In 2017, 181 master's, 6 doctorates awarded. *Degree requirements:* For doctorate, thesis/dissertation. *Entrance requirements:* For master's, minimum GPA of 3.0; for doctorate and other advanced degree, GRE General Test. Additional exam requirements/recommendations for international students: Required—TOEFL (minimum score 550 paper-based; 80 iBT), IELTS (minimum score 6.3). *Application deadline:* For fall admission, 6/1 priority date for domestic students, 4/1 for international students; for winter admission, 10/1 priority date for domestic students, 9/1 for international students; for spring admission, 3/1 priority date for domestic students, 2/1 for international students. Applications are processed on a rolling basis. Application fee: $30. Electronic applications accepted. *Expenses:* Tuition, state resident: full-time $8912; part-time $446 per credit hour. Tuition, nonresident: full-time $21,393; part-time $992 per credit hour. *Required fees:* $390; $195 per semester. *Financial support:* Fellowships, research assistantships with tuition reimbursements, teaching assistantships with tuition reimbursements, Federal Work-Study, and tuition waivers (full and partial) available. Support available to part-time students. Financial award applicants required to submit FAFSA. *Unit head:* Dr. Benjamin Baez, Chair, 305-348-3214, Fax: 305-348-1515, E-mail: benjamin.baez@fiu.edu. *Application contact:* Nanett Rojas, Assistant Director, Graduate Admissions, 305-348-7464, Fax: 305-348-7441, E-mail: gradadm@fiu.edu.
Website: http://education.fiu.edu

Frostburg State University, College of Education, Program in Parks and Recreational Management, Frostburg, MD 21532. Offers MS. *Program availability:* Part-time, evening/weekend. *Faculty:* 7 full-time (4 women), 3 part-time/adjunct (all women). *Students:* 1 (woman) full-time, 26 part-time (15 women); includes 5 minority (3 Black or African American, non-Hispanic/Latino; 2 Hispanic/Latino). Average age 32. 17 applicants, 71% accepted, 11 enrolled. In 2017, 9 master's awarded. *Degree requirements:* For master's, thesis. *Entrance requirements:* For master's, resume. Additional exam requirements/recommendations for international students: Required—TOEFL. *Application deadline:* For fall admission, 7/15 priority date for domestic students. Applications are processed on a rolling basis. Application fee: $45. Electronic applications accepted. *Expenses:* Tuition, state resident: part-time $433 per credit hour. Tuition, nonresident: part-time $557 per credit hour. *Required fees:* $121 per credit hour. $27 per term. *Financial support:* In 2017–18, 1 research assistantship with full tuition reimbursement (averaging $5,000 per year) was awarded; career-related internships or fieldwork and Federal Work-Study also available. Financial award application deadline: 4/1; financial award applicants required to submit FAFSA. *Unit head:* Dr. Natalia Buta, Coordinator, 301-687-4458, E-mail: nbuta@frostburg.edu. *Application contact:* Vickie Mazer, Director, Graduate Services, 301-687-7053, Fax: 301-687-4597, E-mail: vmmazer@frostburg.edu.

Hardin-Simmons University, Graduate School, Irvin School of Education, Kinesiology, Sport, and Recreation Program, Abilene, TX 79698-0001. Offers kinesiology, sport, and recreation (M Ed). *Program availability:* Part-time. *Faculty:* 5 full-time (2 women). *Students:* 10 full-time (6 women), 28 part-time (8 women); includes 16 minority (7 Black or African American, non-Hispanic/Latino; 7 Hispanic/Latino; 2 Two or more races, non-Hispanic/Latino), 1 international. Average age 25. 26 applicants, 96% accepted, 20 enrolled. In 2017, 14 master's awarded. *Degree requirements:* For master's, comprehensive exam, professional project. *Entrance requirements:* For master's, minimum undergraduate GPA of 3.0 in major, 2.7 overall; writing sample; letters of recommendation; resume; personal interview. Additional exam requirements/recommendations for international students: Required—TOEFL (minimum score 550 paper-based; 79 iBT). *Application deadline:* For fall admission, 8/15 priority date for domestic students, 4/1 for international students; for spring admission, 1/5 priority date for domestic students, 9/1 for international students. Applications are processed on a rolling basis. Application fee: $50 ($150 for international students). Electronic applications accepted. *Expenses:* Tuition: Full-time $13,500; part-time $750 per semester hour. *Required fees:* $220 per term. One-time fee: $50. Tuition and fees vary according to course load, campus/location and program. *Financial support:* In 2017–18, 6 students received support. Fellowships, career-related internships or fieldwork, scholarships/grants, and unspecified assistantships available. Support available to part-time students. Financial award application deadline: 6/30; financial award applicants required to submit FAFSA. *Unit head:* Dr. Lindsay Edwards, Program Director, 325-670-5893, Fax: 325-670-1572, E-mail: ledwards@hsutx.edu. *Application contact:* Dr. Nancy Kucinski, Dean of Graduate Studies, 325-670-1298, Fax: 325-670-1564, E-mail: gradoff@hsutx.edu.
Website: http://www.hsutx.edu/academics/irvin/graduate/kinesiology

Peterson's Graduate Programs in Business, Education, Information Studies, Law & Social Work 2019

Indiana State University, College of Graduate and Professional Studies, College of Health and Human Services, Department of Kinesiology, Recreation, and Sport, Terre Haute, IN 47809. Offers physical education (MS); recreation and sport management (MS); sport management (PhD). *Degree requirements:* For master's, comprehensive exam (for some programs), thesis (for some programs). *Entrance requirements:* For master's, GRE General Test, undergraduate major in related field. Electronic applications accepted.

Indiana University Bloomington, School of Public Health, Department of Recreation, Park, and Tourism Studies, Bloomington, IN 47405-7000. Offers leisure behavior (PhD); outdoor recreation (MS); park and public lands management (MS); recreation administration (MS); recreational sports administration (MS); recreational therapy (MS); tourism management (MS). Terminal master's awarded for partial completion of doctoral program. *Degree requirements:* For master's, thesis optional; for doctorate, comprehensive exam, thesis/dissertation. *Entrance requirements:* For master's, GRE General Test, minimum GPA of 2.8; for doctorate, GRE General Test, minimum GPA of 3.0 (undergraduate), 3.5 (graduate). Additional exam requirements/recommendations for international students: Required—TOEFL (minimum score 550 paper-based; 80 iBT). Electronic applications accepted. *Faculty research:* Leisure counseling, gerontology, special populations, planning and development.

Iona College, School of Business, Department of Marketing and International Business, New Rochelle, NY 10801-1890. Offers international business (AC, PMC); marketing (MBA); sports and entertainment management (AC). *Program availability:* Part-time, evening/weekend. *Faculty:* 3 full-time (1 woman), 1 (woman) part-time/adjunct. *Students:* 13 full-time (8 women), 16 part-time (6 women); includes 10 minority (5 Black or African American, non-Hispanic/Latino; 1 Asian, non-Hispanic/Latino; 4 Hispanic/Latino), 2 international. Average age 24. 15 applicants, 100% accepted, 9 enrolled. In 2017, 21 master's, 65 other advanced degrees awarded. *Entrance requirements:* For master's, GMAT, 2 letters of recommendation, minimum GPA of 3.0; for other advanced degree, GMAT, minimum GPA of 3.0. Additional exam requirements/recommendations for international students: Required—TOEFL (minimum score 550 paper-based; 80 iBT), IELTS (minimum score 6.5). *Application deadline:* For fall admission, 8/15 priority date for domestic students, 8/1 priority date for international students; for winter admission, 11/15 priority date for domestic students, 11/1 priority date for international students; for spring admission, 2/15 priority date for domestic students, 2/1 priority date for international students; for summer admission, 5/15 for domestic students, 5/1 priority date for international students. Applications are processed on a rolling basis. Application fee: $50. Electronic applications accepted. *Expenses:* Contact institution. *Financial support:* In 2017–18, 7 students received support. Scholarships/grants, tuition waivers (partial), and unspecified assistantships available. Support available to part-time students. Financial award application deadline: 4/15; financial award applicants required to submit FAFSA. *Faculty research:* Business ethics, international retailing, mega-marketing, consumer behavior and consumer confidence. *Unit head:* Dr. Susan G. Rozensher, Department Chair, 914-637-2748, E-mail: srozensher@iona.edu. *Application contact:* Katelyn Brunck, Director of MBA Admissions, 914-633-2451, Fax: 914-633-2277, E-mail: kbrunck@iona.edu.
Website: http://www.iona.edu/Academics/Hagan-School-of-Business/Departments/Marketing/Graduate-Programs.aspx

Kent State University, College of Education, Health and Human Services, School of Foundations, Leadership and Administration, Sports Recreation and Management Program, Kent, OH 44242-0001. Offers sport and recreation management (MA); sports studies (MA). *Degree requirements:* For master's, thesis optional. *Entrance requirements:* For master's, GRE if undergraduate GPA below 3.0, goals statement, 2 letters of recommendation. Additional exam requirements/recommendations for international students: Required—TOEFL (minimum score 550 paper-based; 80 iBT). *Expenses:* Tuition, state resident: full-time $11,310; part-time $515 per credit hour. Tuition, nonresident: full-time $20,396; part-time $928 per credit hour. *International tuition:* $18,544 full-time.

Lasell College, Graduate and Professional Studies in Sport Management, Newton, MA 02466-2709. Offers athletic administration (MS); parks and recreation (MS); sport leadership (MS, Graduate Certificate); sport tourism and hospitality (MS). *Program availability:* Part-time, evening/weekend, online only, 100% online. *Faculty:* 5 full-time (1 woman), 2 part-time/adjunct (1 woman). *Students:* 10 full-time (6 women), 25 part-time (8 women); includes 12 minority (9 Black or African American, non-Hispanic/Latino; 3 Hispanic/Latino). Average age 29. 35 applicants, 46% accepted, 11 enrolled. In 2017, 26 master's awarded. *Degree requirements:* For master's, minimum GPA of 3.0; internship or thesis. *Entrance requirements:* For master's, one-page personal statement, 2 letters of recommendation, resume, bachelor's degree transcript; for Graduate Certificate, bachelor's degree transcript, 2 letters of recommendation, 1-page personal statement, resume. Additional exam requirements/recommendations for international students: Required—TOEFL (minimum score 550 paper-based, 79 iBT) or IELTS (minimum score 6). *Application deadline:* For fall admission, 8/31 priority date for domestic students, 6/30 priority date for international students; for spring admission, 12/31 priority date for domestic students, 10/31 priority date for international students. Applications are processed on a rolling basis. Electronic applications accepted. *Expenses:* $600 per credit. *Financial support:* Federal Work-Study, scholarships/grants, and tuition discounts available. Support available to part-time students. Financial award application deadline: 8/31; financial award applicants required to submit FAFSA. *Faculty research:* How do fans attribute team failure; investigating cross-cultural difference in attribution; sense of ownership as a key predictor of fan loyalty; fans' normative beliefs about sponsorship and sponsors; investigation of new attitudinal variables in sponsorship. *Unit head:* Eric Turner, Vice President of Graduate and Professional Studies, 617-243-2071, Fax: 617-243-2450, E-mail: gradinfo@lasell.edu. *Application contact:* Adrienne Franciosi, Director of Graduate Enrollment, 617-243-2214, Fax: 617-243-2450, E-mail: gradinfo@lasell.edu.
Website: http://www.lasell.edu/academics/graduate-and-professional-studies/programs-of-study/master-of-science-in-sport-management.html

Lehman College of the City University of New York, School of Health Sciences, Human Services and Nursing, Department of Health Sciences, Program in Recreation, Bronx, NY 10468-1589. Offers recreation education (MA, MS Ed). *Program availability:* Part-time, evening/weekend. *Degree requirements:* For master's, comprehensive exam, thesis or alternative. *Entrance requirements:* For master's, minimum GPA of 2.7. *Faculty research:* Therapeutic recreation philosophy, curriculum, current approaches to treatment, impact of societal trends, ethical issues.

Loyola Marymount University, Bellarmine College of Liberal Arts, Program in Yoga Studies, Los Angeles, CA 90045-2659. Offers MA. *Unit head:* Dr. Christopher Key Chapple, Director, Master of Arts in Yoga Studies, 310-338-2846, E-mail: christopher.chapple@lmu.edu. *Application contact:* Chake H. Kouyoumjian, Associate Dean of Graduate Studies, 310-338-2721, Fax: 310-338-6086, E-mail: graduateinfo@lmu.edu.
Website: http://bellarmine.lmu.edu/yoga/

Michigan State University, The Graduate School, College of Agriculture and Natural Resources, Department of Community, Agriculture, Recreation, and Resource Studies, East Lansing, MI 48824. Offers MS, PhD. *Entrance requirements:* Additional exam

requirements/recommendations for international students: Required—TOEFL. Electronic applications accepted.

Middle Tennessee State University, College of Graduate Studies, College of Behavioral and Health Sciences, Department of Health and Human Performance, Program in Health, Physical Education and Recreation, Murfreesboro, TN 37132. Offers health and human performance (MS); leisure and sport management (MS). *Program availability:* Part-time, evening/weekend, online learning. *Degree requirements:* For master's, comprehensive exam, thesis optional. *Entrance requirements:* For master's, GRE. Additional exam requirements/recommendations for international students: Required—TOEFL (minimum score 525 paper-based; 71 iBT) or IELTS (minimum score 6). *Faculty research:* Kinesiometrics, leisure behavior, health, lifestyles.

Naropa University, Graduate Programs, Program in Clinical Mental Health Counseling, Concentration in Transpersonal Wilderness Therapy, Boulder, CO 80302-6697. Offers MA. *Faculty:* 10 full-time (7 women), 24 part-time/adjunct (17 women). *Students:* 35 full-time (29 women), 12 part-time (10 women); includes 9 minority (2 Black or African American, non-Hispanic/Latino; 5 Hispanic/Latino; 2 Two or more races, non-Hispanic/Latino), 2 international. Average age 28. 41 applicants, 66% accepted, 18 enrolled. In 2017, 13 master's awarded. *Degree requirements:* For master's, internship, counseling practicum. *Entrance requirements:* For master's, interview; 2 letters of recommendation; transcripts; curriculum vitae/resume with pertinent academic, employment and volunteer activities; statement of interest essay; 10 consecutive days of wilderness experience in the backcountry; wilderness/outdoor skills. Additional exam requirements/recommendations for international students: Required—TOEFL (minimum score 550 paper-based; 80 iBT). *Application deadline:* For fall admission, 1/15 priority date for domestic and international students. Applications are processed on a rolling basis. Application fee: $60. Electronic applications accepted. *Expenses:* $995 per credit. *Financial support:* In 2017–18, 30 students received support. Career-related internships or fieldwork, Federal Work-Study, scholarships/grants, tuition waivers (partial), and unspecified assistantships available. Support available to part-time students. Financial award application deadline: 3/1; financial award applicants required to submit FAFSA. *Unit head:* Dr. Kathleen Gregory, Dean, Graduate School of Counseling and Psychology, 303-546-3559, E-mail: kgregory@naropa.edu. *Application contact:* Office of Admissions, 303-546-3572, Fax: 303-546-3583, E-mail: admissions@naropa.edu. Website: http://www.naropa.edu/academics/masters/clinical-mental-health-counseling/wilderness-therapy/index.php

New England College, Program in Sports and Recreation Management: Coaching, Henniker, NH 03242-3293. Offers MS. *Entrance requirements:* For master's, resume, 2 letters of reference.

North Carolina Central University, College of Behavioral and Social Sciences, Department of Physical Education and Recreation, Durham, NC 27707-3129. Offers general physical education (MS); recreation administration (MS). *Program availability:* Part-time, evening/weekend. *Degree requirements:* For master's, one foreign language, comprehensive exam, thesis. *Entrance requirements:* For master's, GRE, minimum GPA of 3.0 in major, 2.5 overall. Additional exam requirements/recommendations for international students: Required—TOEFL. *Application deadline:* For fall admission, 8/1 for domestic students. Application fee: $30. *Expenses:* Tuition, state resident: full-time $2770; part-time $692.50 per credit hour. Tuition, nonresident: full-time $9247; part-time $2311.75 per credit hour. *Financial support:* Application deadline: 5/1; applicants required to submit FAFSA. *Unit head:* Virginia Politano, Chair, 919-530-6186, Fax: 919-530-6156, E-mail: politano@nccu.edu. *Application contact:* Virginia Politano, Chair, 919-530-6186, Fax: 919-530-6156, E-mail: politano@nccu.edu.

North Carolina State University, Graduate School, College of Natural Resources, Department of Parks, Recreation and Tourism Management, Raleigh, NC 27695. Offers natural resource management (MPRTM, MS); park and recreation management (MPRTM, MS); parks, recreation and tourism management (PhD); recreational sport management (MPRTM, MS); spatial information science (MPRTM, MS); tourism policy and development (MPRTM, MS). *Degree requirements:* For master's, thesis (for some programs); for doctorate, thesis/dissertation. *Entrance requirements:* For master's and doctorate, GRE General Test. Additional exam requirements/recommendations for international students: Required—TOEFL. Electronic applications accepted. *Faculty research:* Tourism policy and development, spatial information systems, natural resource management, recreational sports management, park and recreation management.

Northern Arizona University, College of Social and Behavioral Sciences, Department of Geography, Planning, and Recreation, Flagstaff, AZ 86011. Offers applied geospatial sciences (MS); community planning (Certificate); geographic information systems (Certificate); parks and recreation management (MS). *Program availability:* Part-time, 100% online, blended/hybrid learning. *Faculty:* 18 full-time (9 women), 1 part-time/adjunct (0 women). *Students:* 22 full-time (16 women), 25 part-time (11 women); includes 7 minority (3 Black or African American, non-Hispanic/Latino; 2 Hispanic/Latino; 2 Two or more races, non-Hispanic/Latino), 2 international. Average age 33. 42 applicants, 86% accepted, 35 enrolled. In 2017, 14 master's, 7 other advanced degrees awarded. *Degree requirements:* For master's, variable foreign language requirement, comprehensive exam (for some programs), thesis (for some programs); for Certificate, comprehensive exam (for some programs). *Entrance requirements:* Additional exam requirements/recommendations for international students: Required—TOEFL (minimum score 80 iBT), IELTS (minimum score 6.5). *Application deadline:* For fall admission, 3/1 for domestic and international students; for spring admission, 10/1 for domestic and international students. Applications are processed on a rolling basis. Application fee: $65. Electronic applications accepted. *Expenses:* Tuition, state resident: full-time $9240; part-time $458 per credit hour. Tuition, nonresident: full-time $21,588; part-time $1199 per credit hour. *Required fees:* $1021; $14 per credit hour. $646 per semester. Tuition and fees vary according to course load, campus/location and program. *Financial support:* In 2017–18, 5 students received support, including 5 teaching assistantships with partial tuition reimbursements available (averaging $9,000 per year); institutionally sponsored loans, health care benefits, tuition waivers (partial), and unspecified assistantships also available. Financial award application deadline: 2/1; financial award applicants required to submit FAFSA. *Unit head:* Dr. Alan Lew, Chair, 928-523-6567, Fax: 928-523-2275. *Application contact:* Dana Mandino, Administrative Associate, 928-523-7988, Fax: 928-523-2275, E-mail: geog@nau.edu.
Website: https://nau.edu/SBS/GPR/

Northwest Missouri State University, Graduate School, School of Health Science and Wellness, Maryville, MO 64468-6001. Offers applied health and sport sciences (MS); guidance and counseling (MS Ed); health and physical education (MS Ed); recreation (MS); sport and exercise psychology (MS). *Accreditation:* NCATE. *Program availability:* Part-time. *Faculty:* 23 full-time (11 women). *Students:* 68 full-time (43 women), 41 part-time (29 women); includes 9 minority (3 Black or African American, non-Hispanic/Latino; 4 Hispanic/Latino; 2 Two or more races, non-Hispanic/Latino), 5 international. Average age 27. 49 applicants, 47% accepted, 16 enrolled. In 2017, 34 master's awarded. *Degree requirements:* For master's, comprehensive exam. *Entrance requirements:* For master's, GRE General Test, minimum undergraduate GPA of 2.75, teaching certificate, writing sample. Additional exam requirements/recommendations for international students: Required—TOEFL (minimum score 550 paper-based). *Application deadline:*

Recreation and Park Management

For fall admission, 7/1 for domestic and international students; for spring admission, 11/15 for domestic and international students. Applications are processed on a rolling basis. Application fee: $0 ($50 for international students). *Expenses:* Tuition, state resident: full-time $4551; part-time $252.86 per credit hour. Tuition, nonresident: full-time $9103; part-time $505.72 per credit hour. *Required fees:* $2453; $136.25 per credit hour. Tuition and fees vary according to course load and program. *Financial support:* Teaching assistantships with full tuition reimbursements and unspecified assistantships available. Financial award application deadline: 4/1; financial award applicants required to submit FAFSA. *Unit head:* Dr. Terry Long, Director, School of Health Science and Wellness, 660-562-1706, Fax: 660-562-1483, E-mail: tlong@nwmissouri.edu. *Application contact:* Gina Smith, Secretary, 660-562-1297, Fax: 660-562-1963, E-mail: smigina@nwmissouri.edu.
Website: http://www.nwmissouri.edu/health/

Ohio University, Graduate College, Gladys W. and David H. Patton College of Education and Human Services, Department of Recreation and Sport Pedagogy, Program in Recreation Studies, Athens, OH 45701-2979. Offers MS. *Program availability:* Part-time. *Degree requirements:* For master's, thesis or alternative. *Entrance requirements:* For master's, GRE. Additional exam requirements/recommendations for international students: Required—TOEFL (minimum score 550 paper-based; 80 iBT) or IELTS (minimum score 6.5). Electronic applications accepted. *Faculty research:* Recreation, leisure studies, physical education, national parks.

Penn State University Park, Graduate School, College of Health and Human Development, Department of Recreation, Park and Tourism Management, University Park, PA 16802. Offers MS, PhD. *Unit head:* Dr. Ann C. Crouter, Dean, 814-865-1420, Fax: 814-865-3282. *Application contact:* Lori Hawn, Director, Graduate Student Services, 814-865-1795, Fax: 814-863-4627, E-mail: l-gswww@lists.psu.edu.
Website: http://hhd.psu.edu/rptm

Purdue University, Graduate School, College of Health and Human Sciences, Department of Health and Kinesiology, West Lafayette, IN 47907. Offers athletic training education administration (MS, PhD); biomechanics (MS, PhD); exercise physiology (MS, PhD); health education (MS, PhD); history/philosophy of sport (MS, PhD); motor control and development (MS, PhD); physical education pedagogy (PhD); physical education teacher education (MS); recreation and sport management (MS, PhD); sport and exercise psychology (MS, PhD). *Program availability:* Part-time. *Faculty:* 19 full-time (7 women). *Students:* 30 full-time (13 women), 10 part-time (5 women); includes 2 minority (1 Asian, non-Hispanic/Latino; 1 Two or more races, non-Hispanic/Latino), 6 international. Average age 26. 77 applicants, 29% accepted, 18 enrolled. In 2017, 18 master's, 9 doctorates awarded. *Degree requirements:* For master's, thesis optional; for doctorate, comprehensive exam, thesis/dissertation, qualifying examination, preliminary examination. *Entrance requirements:* For master's, GRE General Test (minimum score 1000 combined verbal and quantitative), minimum undergraduate GPA of 3.0 or equivalent; for doctorate, GRE General Test (minimum score 1100 combined verbal and quantitative), minimum undergraduate GPA of 3.0 or equivalent; master's degree with minimum GPA of 3.25 (recommended). Additional exam requirements/recommendations for international students: Required—TOEFL (minimum score 77 iBT); Recommended—TWE. *Application deadline:* For fall admission, 4/30 for domestic and international students; for spring admission, 10/15 for domestic and international students. Applications are processed on a rolling basis. Application fee: $60 ($75 for international students). Electronic applications accepted. *Financial support:* Fellowships with partial tuition reimbursements, research assistantships with partial tuition reimbursements, teaching assistantships with partial tuition reimbursements, and Federal Work-Study available. Support available to part-time students. Financial award applicants required to submit FAFSA. *Faculty research:* Wellness, motivation, teaching effectiveness, learning and development. *Unit head:* Dr. Timothy P. Gavin, Head of the Graduate Program, 765-494-3178, Fax: 765-494-1239, E-mail: gavin1@purdue.edu. *Application contact:* David B. Klenosky, Graduate Contact, 765-494-0865, E-mail: klenosky@purdue.edu.
Website: http://www.purdue.edu/hhs/hk/

San Francisco State University, Division of Graduate Studies, College of Health and Social Sciences, Department of Recreation, Parks, and Tourism, San Francisco, CA 94132-1722. Offers MS. *Program availability:* Part-time. *Application deadline:* Applications are processed on a rolling basis. *Financial support:* Career-related internships or fieldwork available. *Unit head:* Dr. Erik Rosegard, Chair, 415-338-7529, Fax: 415-338-0543, E-mail: rosegard@sfsu.edu. *Application contact:* Dr. Jackson Wilson, Graduate Coordinator, 415-338-1487, Fax: 415-338-0543, E-mail: wilsonj@sfsu.edu.
Website: http://recdept.sfsu.edu/graduate

Slippery Rock University of Pennsylvania, Graduate Studies (Recruitment), College of Health, Environment, and Science, Department of Parks and Recreation, Slippery Rock, PA 16057-1383. Offers environmental education (M Ed); park and resource management (MS). *Program availability:* Part-time, evening/weekend, online only, 100% online. *Degree requirements:* For master's, comprehensive exam (for some programs), thesis (for some programs), internship. *Entrance requirements:* For master's, official transcripts, minimum GPA of 2.75, personal statement. Additional exam requirements/recommendations for international students: Required—TOEFL (minimum score 550 paper-based; 80 iBT). Electronic applications accepted. *Expenses:* Contact institution.

South Dakota State University, Graduate School, College of Education and Human Sciences, Department of Health and Nutritional Sciences, Brookings, SD 57007. Offers athletic training (MS); dietetics (MS); nutrition and exercise sciences (MS, PhD); sport and recreation studies (MS). *Program availability:* Part-time. *Degree requirements:* For master's, comprehensive exam (for some programs), thesis (for some programs), oral exam. *Entrance requirements:* Additional exam requirements/recommendations for international students: Required—TOEFL (minimum score 525 paper-based). *Faculty research:* Food chemistry, bone density, functional food, nutrition education, nutrition biochemistry.

Southern Connecticut State University, School of Graduate Studies, School of Health and Human Services, Department of Recreation and Leisure Studies, New Haven, CT 06515-1355. Offers MS. *Program availability:* Part-time, evening/weekend. *Degree requirements:* For master's, thesis or alternative. *Entrance requirements:* For master's, interview, minimum undergraduate QPA of 3.0 in graduate major field or 2.5 overall. Electronic applications accepted.

Southern Illinois University Carbondale, Graduate School, College of Education and Human Services, Department of Health Education and Recreation, Program in Recreation, Carbondale, IL 62901-4701. Offers MS Ed. *Program availability:* Part-time. *Degree requirements:* For master's, thesis. *Entrance requirements:* For master's, minimum GPA of 2.7. Additional exam requirements/recommendations for international students: Required—TOEFL. *Faculty research:* Leisure across the life span, outdoor recreation, recreation therapy, leisure service administration.

Southern University and Agricultural and Mechanical College, College of Nursing and Allied Health, Department of Therapeutic Recreation and Leisure Studies, Baton Rouge, LA 70813. Offers therapeutic recreation (MS). *Degree requirements:* For master's, comprehensive exam, thesis optional. *Entrance requirements:* For master's,

GMAT or GRE General Test. Additional exam requirements/recommendations for international students: Required—TOEFL (minimum score 525 paper-based).

Southwestern Oklahoma State University, College of Professional and Graduate Studies, School of Behavioral Sciences and Education, Specialization in Parks and Recreation Management, Weatherford, OK 73096-3098. Offers M Ed.

Springfield College, Graduate Programs, Programs in Sport Management and Recreation, Springfield, MA 01109-3797. Offers recreation management (M Ed, MS); sport management (M Ed, MS); therapeutic recreation management (M Ed, MS). *Program availability:* Part-time. *Students:* 43 applicants, 49% accepted, 10 enrolled. In 2017, 13 master's awarded. *Degree requirements:* For master's, comprehensive exam, research project. *Entrance requirements:* Additional exam requirements/recommendations for international students: Required—TOEFL (minimum score 550 paper-based); Recommended—IELTS (minimum score 7). *Application deadline:* For fall admission, 1/15 for domestic and international students; for winter admission, 11/1 for international students; for spring admission, 11/1 for domestic and international students. Applications are processed on a rolling basis. Application fee: $50. Electronic applications accepted. *Financial support:* Fellowships with partial tuition reimbursements, teaching assistantships with partial tuition reimbursements, career-related internships or fieldwork, Federal Work-Study, institutionally sponsored loans, scholarships/grants, and unspecified assistantships available. Financial award application deadline: 3/1; financial award applicants required to submit FAFSA. *Unit head:* Dr. Kevin McAllister, Coordinator, 413-748-3476, Fax: 413-748-3685, E-mail: kmcallis@springfield.edu. *Application contact:* Anne Griffin, Director of Graduate Admissions, 413-748-3225, Fax: 413-748-3694, E-mail: agriffin2@springfield.edu.
Website: http://springfield.edu/programs

State University of New York College at Cortland, Graduate Studies, School of Professional Studies, Department of Recreation, Parks and Leisure Studies, Cortland, NY 13045. Offers outdoor education (MS, MS Ed); recreation management (MS, MS Ed); therapeutic recreation (MS, MS Ed). *Program availability:* Part-time, evening/weekend. *Degree requirements:* For master's, comprehensive exam, thesis (for some programs). *Entrance requirements:* Additional exam requirements/recommendations for international students: Required—TOEFL.

Temple University, College of Public Health, Department of Rehabilitation Sciences, Philadelphia, PA 19122. Offers occupational therapy (MOT, DOT); therapeutic recreation (MS), including recreation therapy. *Accreditation:* AOTA. *Program availability:* Part-time. *Faculty:* 17 full-time (16 women), 3 part-time/adjunct (2 women). *Students:* 117 full-time (108 women), 24 part-time (22 women); includes 24 minority (5 Black or African American, non-Hispanic/Latino; 6 Asian, non-Hispanic/Latino; 7 Hispanic/Latino; 6 Two or more races, non-Hispanic/Latino). 12 applicants, 100% accepted, 10 enrolled. In 2017, 49 master's, 7 doctorates awarded. *Degree requirements:* For doctorate, comprehensive exam (for some programs), thesis/dissertation (for some programs). *Entrance requirements:* For master's and doctorate, GRE General Test, minimum GPA of 3.0. Additional exam requirements/recommendations for international students: Required—TOEFL (minimum score 550 paper-based; 79 iBT). *Application deadline:* For fall admission, 2/1 for domestic students, 1/1 for international students; for spring admission, 11/1 for domestic students, 10/1 for international students. Applications are processed on a rolling basis. Application fee: $60. Electronic applications accepted. *Expenses:* Contact institution. *Financial support:* Career-related internships or fieldwork and Federal Work-Study available. *Faculty research:* Participation, community inclusion, disability issues, leisure/recreation, occupation, quality of life, adaptive equipment and technology. *Unit head:* Dr. Mark Salzer, Chair, 215-204-7879, E-mail: mark.salzer@temple.edu.
Website: http://cph.temple.edu/rs/home

Texas A&M University, College of Agriculture and Life Sciences, Department of Recreation, Park and Tourism Sciences, College Station, TX 77843. Offers recreation and resources development (MRRD); recreation, park, and tourism sciences (MS, PhD). *Faculty:* 20. *Students:* 53 full-time (23 women), 23 part-time (10 women); includes 19 minority (6 Black or African American, non-Hispanic/Latino; 4 Asian, non-Hispanic/Latino; 6 Hispanic/Latino; 3 Two or more races, non-Hispanic/Latino), 21 international. Average age 32. 20 applicants, 85% accepted, 16 enrolled. In 2017, 17 master's, 12 doctorates awarded. *Degree requirements:* For master's, thesis (for some programs), internship and professional paper (M Agr); for doctorate, thesis/dissertation. *Entrance requirements:* For master's and doctorate, GRE General Test. Additional exam requirements/recommendations for international students: Required—TOEFL (minimum score 550 paper-based; 80 iBT), IELTS (minimum score 6), PTE (minimum score 53). *Application deadline:* For fall admission, 3/1 for domestic and international students; for spring admission, 8/1 for domestic and international students; for summer admission, 11/1 for domestic and international students. Applications are processed on a rolling basis. Application fee: $50 ($90 for international students). Electronic applications accepted. *Expenses:* Contact institution. *Financial support:* In 2017–18, 60 students received support, including 3 fellowships with tuition reimbursements available (averaging $12,667 per year), 9 research assistantships with tuition reimbursements available (averaging $8,269 per year), 29 teaching assistantships with tuition reimbursements available (averaging $9,844 per year); career-related internships or fieldwork, institutionally sponsored loans, scholarships/grants, traineeships, health care benefits, tuition waivers (full and partial), and unspecified assistantships also available. Support available to part-time students. Financial award application deadline: 3/15; financial award applicants required to submit FAFSA. *Faculty research:* Administration and tourism, outdoor recreation, commercial recreation, environmental law, system planning. *Unit head:* Dr. Gary Ellis, Department Head, 979-845-7324, E-mail: gellis@ag.tamu.edu. *Application contact:* Irina Shatruk, Graduate Program Coordinator, 979-845-5412, E-mail: jshatruk@tamu.edu.
Website: http://rpts.tamu.edu/

Texas State University, The Graduate College, College of Education, Program in Recreation Management, San Marcos, TX 78666. Offers recreation management (MSRLS). *Program availability:* Part-time. *Faculty:* 7 full-time (3 women), 1 (woman) part-time/adjunct. *Students:* 15 full-time (4 women), 6 part-time (2 women); includes 9 minority (5 Black or African American, non-Hispanic/Latino; 4 Hispanic/Latino). Average age 28. 22 applicants, 59% accepted, 6 enrolled. In 2017, 1 master's awarded. *Degree requirements:* For master's, comprehensive exam, thesis optional. *Entrance requirements:* For master's, baccalaureate degree from regionally-accredited institution with minimum GPA of 2.75 in last 60 hours of course work, background course work in marketing and management, statement of purpose. Additional exam requirements/recommendations for international students: Required—TOEFL (minimum score 550 paper-based; 78 iBT), IELTS (minimum score 6.5). *Application deadline:* For fall admission, 2/15 priority date for domestic students, 2/15 for international students; for spring admission, 10/15 priority date for domestic students, 10/1 for international students; for summer admission, 4/15 for domestic students, 3/15 for international students. Applications are processed on a rolling basis. Application fee: $40 ($90 for international students). Electronic applications accepted. *Expenses:* Tuition, state resident: full-time $7868; part-time $3934 per semester. Tuition, nonresident: full-time $17,828; part-time $8914 per semester. *Required fees:* $2092; $1435 per semester. Tuition and fees vary according to course load. *Financial support:* In 2017–18, 12 students received support, including 2 teaching assistantships (averaging $12,152 per year); research assistantships, scholarships/grants, and unspecified assistantships also available. Financial award application deadline: 3/1; financial award applicants required to submit FAFSA. *Faculty research:* Effects of neuromuscular electrical stimulation frequency on metabolic markers, effects of focal knee join cooling on different modes of the quadriceps strength. *Total annual research expenditures:* $5,229. *Unit head:* Dr. Jan Hodges, Graduate Advisor, 512-245-7482, Fax: 512-245-8678, E-mail: jh223@txstate.edu. *Application contact:* Dr. Andrea Golato, Dean of the Graduate College, 512-245-2581, Fax: 512-245-8365, E-mail: gradcollege@txstate.edu. Website: http://www.gradcollege.txstate.edu/programs/msrls-mgmt.html

United States Sports Academy, Graduate Programs, Program in Recreation Management, Daphne, AL 36526-7055. Offers MSS. *Program availability:* Part-time, 100% online. *Degree requirements:* For master's, comprehensive exam, thesis optional. *Entrance requirements:* For master's, GRE General Test, GMAT, or MAT, minimum GPA of 2.5, 3 letters of recommendation, personal statement. Additional exam requirements/recommendations for international students: Required—TOEFL (minimum score 550 paper-based; 79 iBT). *Application deadline:* Applications are processed on a rolling basis. Application fee: $50 ($125 for international students). Electronic applications accepted. *Expenses:* $640 per credit hour. *Financial support:* Career-related internships or fieldwork, Federal Work-Study, and scholarships/grants available. Support available to part-time students. Financial award application deadline: 8/15; financial award applicants required to submit FAFSA. *Faculty research:* Psychiatric aspects of injury rehabilitation, geriatric exercises and mobility. *Unit head:* Dr. Rodney J. Blackman, Chair, 251-626-3303 Ext. 7155, Fax: 251-626-1149, E-mail: rblackman@ussa.edu. *Application contact:* Dr. Taffy Sithole, Student Services Coordinator, 251-626-3303 Ext. 7147, Fax: 251-625-1035, E-mail: tsithole@ussa.edu.

Universidad Metropolitana, School of Education, Program in Managing Recreation and Sports Services, San Juan, PR 00928-1150. Offers M Ed. *Program availability:* Part-time. *Degree requirements:* For master's, thesis or alternative. *Entrance requirements:* For master's, EXADEP, interview. Electronic applications accepted.

University of Alberta, Faculty of Graduate Studies and Research, Department of Physical Education and Recreation, Edmonton, AB T6G 2E1, Canada. Offers physical education (M Sc); recreation and physical education (MA, PhD). *Program availability:* Part-time. Terminal master's awarded for partial completion of doctoral program. *Degree requirements:* For master's, thesis (for some programs); for doctorate, thesis/dissertation. *Entrance requirements:* For master's, bachelor's degree in related field; for doctorate, master's degree in related field with thesis. Additional exam requirements/recommendations for international students: Required—TOEFL. *Faculty research:* Motivation and adherence to physical ability, performance enhancement, adapted physical activity, exercise physiology, sport administration, tourism.

University of Arkansas, Graduate School, College of Education and Health Professions, Department of Health, Human Performance and Recreation, Program in Recreation and Sports Management, Fayetteville, AR 72701. Offers M Ed, Ed D. In 2017, 31 master's, 2 doctorates awarded. *Degree requirements:* For master's, thesis optional; for doctorate, thesis/dissertation. *Entrance requirements:* For doctorate, GRE General Test. *Application deadline:* For fall admission, 8/1 for domestic students, 4/1 for international students; for spring admission, 12/1 for domestic students, 10/1 for international students; for summer admission, 4/15 for domestic students, 3/1 for international students. Applications are processed on a rolling basis. Application fee: $60. Electronic applications accepted. *Expenses:* Tuition, state resident: full-time $3782. Tuition, nonresident: full-time $10,238. *Financial support:* In 2017–18, 8 research assistantships, 10 teaching assistantships were awarded; fellowships with tuition reimbursements, career-related internships or fieldwork, and Federal Work-Study also available. Support available to part-time students. Financial award application deadline: 4/1; financial award applicants required to submit FAFSA. *Unit head:* Dr. Matthew Stueck Ganio, Department Head, 479-575-2956, Fax: 479-575-5728, E-mail: msganio@uark.edu. *Application contact:* Dr. Stephen Dittmore, Coordinator of Graduate Studies, 479-575-6625, E-mail: dittmore@uark.edu.
Website: https://hhpr.uark.edu

University of Florida, Graduate School, College of Health and Human Performance, Department of Tourism, Recreation and Sport Management, Gainesville, FL 32611. Offers health and human performance (PhD), including historic preservation (MS, PhD), recreation, parks and tourism (MS, PhD), sport management; recreation, parks and tourism (MS), including historic preservation (MS, PhD), natural resource recreation, recreation, parks and tourism (MS, PhD), therapeutic recreation, tourism, tropical conservation and development; sport management (MS), including historic preservation (MS, PhD), tropical conservation and development; JD/MS; MSM/MS. *Degree requirements:* For master's, comprehensive exam (for some programs), thesis (for some programs); for doctorate, comprehensive exam, thesis/dissertation. *Entrance requirements:* For master's and doctorate, GRE General Test, minimum GPA of 3.0. Additional exam requirements/recommendations for international students: Required—TOEFL (minimum score 550 paper-based; 80 iBT), IELTS (minimum score 6). Electronic applications accepted. *Faculty research:* Hospitality, natural resource management, sport management, tourism.

The University of Iowa, Graduate College, College of Liberal Arts and Sciences, Department of Health and Human Physiology, Iowa City, IA 52242-1316. Offers athletic training (MS); clinical exercise physiology (MS); health and human physiology (PhD); leisure studies (MA, PhD), including recreational sport management (PhD), therapeutic recreation (MA). *Degree requirements:* For master's, thesis optional, exam; for doctorate, comprehensive exam, thesis/dissertation. *Entrance requirements:* For master's and doctorate, GRE General Test, minimum GPA of 3.0. Additional exam requirements/recommendations for international students: Required—TOEFL (minimum score 600 paper-based; 100 iBT). Electronic applications accepted.

University of Louisiana at Monroe, Graduate School, College of Health and Pharmaceutical Sciences, Department of Kinesiology, Monroe, LA 71209-0001. Offers applied exercise science (MS); clinical exercise physiology (MS); sports, fitness and recreation management (MS). *Program availability:* Part-time, evening/weekend, online learning. *Faculty:* 6 full-time (2 women), 1 part-time/adjunct (0 women). *Students:* 28 full-time (15 women), 13 part-time (5 women); includes 12 minority (8 Black or African American, non-Hispanic/Latino; 4 Hispanic/Latino), 3 international. Average age 24. 27 applicants, 52% accepted, 11 enrolled. In 2017, 27 master's awarded. *Degree requirements:* For master's, comprehensive exam, thesis, 6-hour internship. *Entrance requirements:* For master's, GRE General Test. Additional exam requirements/recommendations for international students: Required—TOEFL (minimum score 500 paper-based; 61 iBT). *Application deadline:* For fall admission, 8/24 priority date for domestic students, 7/1 for international students; for winter admission, 12/14 priority date for domestic students; for spring admission, 1/19 for domestic students, 11/1 for international students. Applications are processed on a rolling basis. Application fee: $20 ($30 for international students). Electronic applications accepted. *Expenses:* Tuition, state resident: full-time $6489; part-time $479 per hour. Tuition, nonresident: full-time $12,100; part-time $479 per hour. *Required fees:* $8860; $802 per hour. $3273 per semester. *Financial support:* In 2017–18, 12 students received support. Research assistantships, career-related internships or fieldwork, Federal Work-Study, and

unspecified assistantships available. Financial award application deadline: 4/1; financial award applicants required to submit FAFSA. *Faculty research:* Cardiovascular disease risk factors; exercise and immunological system; attitude, exercise, and the aged. *Unit head:* Dr. Ken Alford, Director, 318-342-1306, E-mail: alford@ulm.edu. *Application contact:* Dr. Tommie Church, Director of Graduate Studies, 318-342-1321, E-mail: church@ulm.edu.
Website: http://www.ulm.edu/kinesiology/

University of Manitoba, Faculty of Graduate Studies, Faculty of Kinesiology and Recreation Management, Winnipeg, MB R3T 2N2, Canada. Offers kinesiology and recreation (M Sc, MA).

University of Mississippi, Graduate School, School of Applied Sciences, University, MS 38677. Offers communicative disorders (MS); criminal justice (MCJ); exercise science (MS); food and nutrition services (MS); health and kinesiology (PhD); health promotion (MS); nutrition and hospitality management (PhD); park and recreation management (MA); social welfare (PhD); social work (MSW). *Faculty:* 66 full-time (38 women), 33 part-time/adjunct (18 women). *Students:* 182 full-time (139 women), 41 part-time (27 women); includes 49 minority (41 Black or African American, non-Hispanic/Latino; 1 American Indian or Alaska Native, non-Hispanic/Latino; 3 Asian, non-Hispanic/Latino; 3 Hispanic/Latino; 1 Two or more races, non-Hispanic/Latino), 13 international. Average age 26. *Entrance requirements:* For master's, GRE General Test, minimum GPA of 3.0. Additional exam requirements/recommendations for international students: Required—TOEFL. *Application deadline:* For fall admission, 4/1 for domestic students; for spring admission, 10/1 for domestic students. Applications are processed on a rolling basis. Application fee: $50. Electronic applications accepted. *Financial support:* Scholarships/grants available. Financial award application deadline: 3/1; financial award applicants required to submit FAFSA. *Unit head:* Dr. Teresa C. Carithers, Dean, 662-915-1081, Fax: 662-915-5717, E-mail: applsci@olemiss.edu.

University of Montana, Graduate School, College of Forestry and Conservation, Missoula, MT 59812. Offers fish and wildlife biology (PhD); forest and conservation sciences (PhD); forestry (MS); recreation management (MS); resource conservation (MS); systems ecology (MS, PhD); wildlife biology (MS). *Degree requirements:* For doctorate, thesis/dissertation. *Entrance requirements:* For master's and doctorate, GRE General Test. Additional exam requirements/recommendations for international students: Required—TOEFL (minimum score 575 paper-based).

University of Nebraska at Kearney, College of Education, Kinesiology and Sport Sciences Department, Kearney, NE 68849-0001. Offers general physical education (MA Ed), including recreation and leisure, sports administration; physical education exercise science (MA Ed); physical education master teacher (MA Ed), including pedagogy, special populations. *Program availability:* Part-time, evening/weekend, 100% online. *Degree requirements:* For master's, comprehensive exam, thesis optional. *Entrance requirements:* For master's, GRE General Test (for some programs), personal statement. Additional exam requirements/recommendations for international students: Recommended—TOEFL (minimum score 550 paper-based; 79 iBT), IELTS (minimum score 6.5). Electronic applications accepted. *Faculty research:* Ergonomic aids, nutrition, motor development, sports pedagogy, applied behavior analysis, physical activity and wellness, athletic training, therapeutic interventions, exercise physiology, endocrinology and metabolism.

University of New Brunswick Fredericton, School of Graduate Studies, Faculty of Kinesiology, Fredericton, NB E3B 5A3, Canada. Offers exercise and sport science (M Sc); sport and recreation management (MBA); sport and recreation studies (MA). *Program availability:* Part-time. *Degree requirements:* For master's, thesis (for some programs). *Entrance requirements:* For master's, GMAT (minimum score of 550 for sport and recreation management program), minimum GPA of 3.0, written statement of research goals and interests. Additional exam requirements/recommendations for international students: Required—TOEFL (minimum score 92 iBT), IELTS (minimum score 7). Electronic applications accepted.

University of New Hampshire, Graduate School, College of Health and Human Services, Department of Recreation Management and Policy, Durham, NH 03824. Offers adaptive sports (MS); recreation administration (MS); therapeutic recreation administration (MS). *Program availability:* Part-time. *Students:* 8 full-time (6 women), 4 part-time (2 women); includes 1 minority (Hispanic/Latino), 1 international. Average age 27. 8 applicants, 88% accepted, 3 enrolled. In 2017, 5 master's awarded. *Entrance requirements:* Additional exam requirements/recommendations for international students: Required—TOEFL (minimum score 550 paper-based; 80 iBT); Recommended—TWE. *Application deadline:* For fall admission, 7/1 for domestic students, 3/1 for international students; for spring admission, 11/1 for domestic students. Application fee: $65. Electronic applications accepted. *Financial support:* In 2017–18, 7 students received support, including 7 teaching assistantships; fellowships and research assistantships also available. Financial award application deadline: 2/15. *Unit head:* Dr. Bob Barcelona, Chair, 603-862-5345. *Application contact:* Tracy Phillips, Administrative Assistant, 603-862-2391, E-mail: rmp.graduate@unh.edu.
Website: http://chhs.unh.edu/rmp

The University of North Carolina at Greensboro, Graduate School, School of Health and Human Sciences, Department of Community and Therapeutic Recreation, Greensboro, NC 27412-5001. Offers community recreation management (MS); therapeutic recreation (MS). *Degree requirements:* For master's, thesis. *Entrance requirements:* For master's, GRE General Test. Additional exam requirements/recommendations for international students: Required—TOEFL. Electronic applications accepted.

University of Rhode Island, Graduate School, College of Health Sciences, Department of Kinesiology, Kingston, RI 02881. Offers cultural studies of sport and physical culture (MS); exercise science (MS); psychosocial/behavioral aspects of physical activity (MS). *Accreditation:* NCATE. *Program availability:* Part-time. *Faculty:* 14 full-time (9 women). *Students:* 10 full-time (4 women), 3 part-time (1 woman), 1 international. 8 applicants, 100% accepted, 6 enrolled. In 2017, 7 master's awarded. *Entrance requirements:* Additional exam requirements/recommendations for international students: Required—TOEFL. *Application deadline:* For fall admission, 7/15 for domestic students, 2/1 for international students; for spring admission, 11/15 for domestic students, 7/15 for international students. Application fee: $65. Electronic applications accepted. *Expenses:* Tuition, state resident: full-time $12,706; part-time $786 per credit. Tuition, nonresident: full-time $25,216; part-time $1401 per credit. *Required fees:* $1598; $45 per credit. One-time fee: $30 part-time. *Financial support:* In 2017–18, 5 teaching assistantships with tuition reimbursements (averaging $11,078 per year) were awarded. Financial award application deadline: 2/1; financial award applicants required to submit FAFSA. *Unit head:* Dr. Disa Hatfield, Interim Chair, 401-874-5183, E-mail: doch@uri.edu. *Application contact:* Dr. Matthew Delmonico, Graduate Program Director, 401-874-5440, E-mail: delmonico@uri.edu.
Website: http://web.uri.edu/kinesiology/

The University of Tennessee, Graduate School, College of Education, Health and Human Sciences, Department of Exercise, Sport, and Leisure Studies, Knoxville, TN 37996. Offers exercise science (MS, PhD), including biomechanics/sports medicine, exercise physiology; recreation and leisure studies (MS); sport management (MS); sport studies (MS, PhD); therapeutic recreation (MS). *Program availability:* Part-time, evening/weekend. *Degree requirements:* For master's, thesis optional. *Entrance requirements:* For master's, minimum GPA of 2.7. Additional exam requirements/recommendations for international students: Required—TOEFL. Electronic applications accepted.

The University of Toledo, College of Graduate Studies, College of Health and Human Services, School of Exercise and Rehabilitation Sciences, Toledo, OH 43606-3390. Offers athletic training (MSES); exercise physiology (MSES); exercise science (PhD); occupational therapy (OTD); physical therapy (DPT); recreation and leisure studies (MA), including recreation administration, recreation therapy. *Degree requirements:* For master's, comprehensive exam, thesis; for doctorate, thesis/dissertation or alternative. *Entrance requirements:* For master's, GRE, minimum cumulative GPA of 2.7 for all previous academic work, letters of recommendation; for doctorate, GRE, minimum cumulative GPA of 3.0 for all previous academic work, letters of recommendation; OTCAS or PTCAS application and UT supplemental application (for OTD and DPT). Additional exam requirements/recommendations for international students: Required—TOEFL (minimum score 550 paper-based; 80 iBT). Electronic applications accepted.

University of Utah, Graduate School, College of Health, Department of Health, Kinesiology, and Recreation, Salt Lake City, UT 84112. Offers kinesiology (MS, PhD); parks, recreation, and tourism (MS, PhD). *Program availability:* Part-time. *Faculty:* 7 full-time (4 women), 4 part-time/adjunct (0 women). *Students:* 92 full-time (58 women), 44 part-time (23 women); includes 21 minority (1 Black or African American, non-Hispanic/Latino; 1 American Indian or Alaska Native, non-Hispanic/Latino; 5 Asian, non-Hispanic/Latino; 10 Hispanic/Latino; 2 Native Hawaiian or other Pacific Islander, non-Hispanic/Latino; 2 Two or more races, non-Hispanic/Latino), 10 international. Average age 24. 24 applicants, 58% accepted, 8 enrolled. In 2017, 34 master's, 4 doctorates awarded. Terminal master's awarded for partial completion of doctoral program. *Degree requirements:* For master's, comprehensive exam, thesis or alternative; for doctorate, comprehensive exam, thesis/dissertation. *Entrance requirements:* For master's and doctorate, GRE General Test, minimum GPA of 3.0. Additional exam requirements/recommendations for international students: Required—TOEFL (minimum score 500 paper-based). *Application deadline:* For fall admission, 1/15 priority date for domestic and international students. Application fee: $55 ($65 for international students). Electronic applications accepted. *Expenses:* Contact institution. *Financial support:* In 2017–18, 13 students received support, including 3 research assistantships with full tuition reimbursements available, 8 teaching assistantships with full tuition reimbursements available; career-related internships or fieldwork, scholarships/grants, health care benefits, and unspecified assistantships also available. Financial award application deadline: 1/15; financial award applicants required to submit FAFSA. *Faculty research:* Community and sport, outdoor recreation, protected area management, sustainable tourism and youth development. *Total annual research expenditures:* $300,000. *Unit head:* Dr. Kelly S. Bricker, Program Director, 801-585-6503, E-mail: kelly.bricker@health.utah.edu. *Application contact:* Dr. Jim Sibthorp, Director of Graduate Studies, 801-581-5940, Fax: 801-581-4930, E-mail: jim.sibthorp@health.utah.edu.
Website: http://www.health.utah.edu/prt/

University of Utah, Graduate School, College of Health, Department of Occupational and Recreational Therapies, Salt Lake City, UT 84108. Offers MOT, OTD. *Accreditation:* AOTA. *Program availability:* Part-time, evening/weekend, 100% online. *Faculty:* 5 full-time (all women), 9 part-time/adjunct (7 women). *Students:* 100 full-time (82 women), 19 part-time (16 women); includes 18 minority (1 Black or African American, non-Hispanic/Latino; 4 Asian, non-Hispanic/Latino; 8 Hispanic/Latino; 5 Two or more races, non-Hispanic/Latino), 1 international. Average age 28. 200 applicants, 23% accepted, 34 enrolled. In 2017, 34 master's, 5 doctorates awarded. *Entrance requirements:* For master's, GRE General Test. Additional exam requirements/recommendations for international students: Required—TOEFL (minimum score 575 paper-based). *Application deadline:* For fall admission, 11/20 for domestic and international students. Application fee: $125. Electronic applications accepted. *Expenses:* Contact institution. *Financial support:* In 2017–18, 10 students received support. Career-related internships or fieldwork, Federal Work-Study, institutionally sponsored loans, scholarships/grants, and unspecified assistantships available. Financial award application deadline: 2/15; financial award applicants required to submit FAFSA. *Faculty research:* Community-based practice, occupational science, refugees, resilience, executive function, traumatic brain injury, pediatrics. *Total annual research expenditures:* $13,409. *Unit head:* Dr. Lorie Richards, Chairperson, 801-585-1069, Fax: 801-585-1001, E-mail: lorie.richards@hsc.utah.edu. *Application contact:* Kelly C. Brown, Academic Advisor, 801-585-0555, Fax: 801-585-1001, E-mail: kelly.brown@hsc.utah.edu.
Website: http://health.utah.edu/occupational-recreational-therapies/

University of Waterloo, Graduate Studies, Faculty of Applied Health Sciences, Department of Recreation and Leisure Studies, Waterloo, ON N2L 3G1, Canada. Offers MA, PhD. *Program availability:* Part-time. *Degree requirements:* For master's, thesis; for doctorate, comprehensive exam, thesis/dissertation. *Entrance requirements:* For master's, honors degree, minimum B average, writing sample, resume; for doctorate, GRE (recommended), master's degree, minimum B average, writing sample, resume. Additional exam requirements/recommendations for international students: Required—TOEFL, IELTS, PTE. Electronic applications accepted. *Faculty research:* Tourism, leisure behavior, special populations, leisure service management, outdoor resources, aging, health and well-being, work and health.

University of Wisconsin–La Crosse, College of Science and Health, Department of Recreation Management and Therapeutic Recreation, La Crosse, WI 54601-3742. Offers recreation management (MS); therapeutic recreation (MS). *Program availability:* Part-time. *Students:* 21 full-time (16 women), 5 part-time (1 woman); includes 3 minority (1 American Indian or Alaska Native, non-Hispanic/Latino; 1 Asian, non-Hispanic/Latino; 1 Hispanic/Latino), 1 international. Average age 26. 36 applicants, 100% accepted, 13 enrolled. In 2017, 10 master's awarded. *Degree requirements:* For master's, thesis or alternative, project or internship. *Entrance requirements:* Additional exam requirements/recommendations for international students: Required—TOEFL (minimum score 550 paper-based; 79 iBT). *Application deadline:* For fall admission, 3/15 priority date for domestic students. Applications are processed on a rolling basis. Electronic applications accepted. *Financial support:* Research assistantships with partial tuition reimbursements, Federal Work-Study, scholarships/grants, health care benefits, and tuition waivers (partial) available. Support available to part-time students. Financial award application deadline: 3/15; financial award applicants required to submit FAFSA. *Unit head:* Dr. Gretchen Newhouse, Chairperson, Department Chair, 608-785-8207, E-mail: gnewhouse@uwlax.edu. *Application contact:* Brandon Schaller, Senior Graduate Student Status Examiner, 608-785-8941, E-mail: admissions@uwlax.edu.
Website: http://www.uwlax.edu/sah/rmtr/

University of Wisconsin–Milwaukee, Graduate School, College of Health Sciences, Department of Occupational Science and Technology, Milwaukee, WI 53201-0413. Offers assistive technology and design (MS); disability and occupation (MS); ergonomics (MS); therapeutic recreation (MS). *Accreditation:* AOTA. *Students:* 86 full-time (74 women), 1 (woman) part-time; includes 6 minority (3 Asian, non-Hispanic/Latino; 1 Hispanic/Latino; 2 Two or more races, non-Hispanic/Latino), 1 international. Average age 27. 115 applicants, 30% accepted, 32 enrolled. In 2017, 22 master's awarded. *Degree requirements:* For master's, thesis or alternative. *Entrance requirements:* Additional exam requirements/recommendations for international students: Required—TOEFL (minimum score 550 paper-based; 79 iBT), IELTS (minimum score 6.5). *Application deadline:* For fall admission, 1/1 priority date for domestic students; for spring admission, 9/1 for domestic students. Applications are processed on a rolling basis. Application fee: $56 ($75 for international students). *Financial support:* Fellowships, research assistantships, teaching assistantships, and unspecified assistantships available. Support available to part-time students. Financial award application deadline: 4/15. *Unit head:* Jay Kapellusch, PhD, Department Chair, 414-229-5292, Fax: 414-229-2619, E-mail: kap@uwm.edu. *Application contact:* Bhagwant S. Sindhu, PhD, Graduate Program Coordinator, 414-229-1180, Fax: 414-229-5100, E-mail: sindhu@uwm.edu.
Website: http://uwm.edu/healthsciences/academics/occupational-science-technology/

Utah State University, School of Graduate Studies, S.J. and Jessie E. Quinney College of Natural Resources, Department of Environment and Society, Logan, UT 84322. Offers bioregional planning (MS); geography (MA, MS); human dimensions of ecosystem science and management (MS, PhD); recreation resource management (MS, PhD). *Degree requirements:* For master's, comprehensive exam, thesis (for some programs). *Entrance requirements:* For master's and doctorate, GRE General Test, minimum GPA of 3.0. Additional exam requirements/recommendations for international students: Required—TOEFL. Electronic applications accepted. *Faculty research:* Geographic information systems/geographic and environmental education, bioregional planning, natural resource and environmental policy, outdoor recreation and tourism, natural resource and environmental management.

Virginia Commonwealth University, Graduate School, School of Education, Program in Sport Leadership, Richmond, VA 23284-9005. Offers M Ed. *Entrance requirements:* For master's, GRE General Test or MAT. Additional exam requirements/recommendations for international students: Required—TOEFL (minimum score 600 paper-based; 100 iBT). Electronic applications accepted.

Western Illinois University, School of Graduate Studies, College of Education and Human Services, Department of Recreation, Park, and Tourism Administration, Macomb, IL 61455-1390. Offers MS. *Program availability:* Part-time. *Degree requirements:* For master's, thesis or alternative. *Entrance requirements:* Additional exam requirements/recommendations for international students: Required—TOEFL (minimum score 550 paper-based; 80 iBT). *Application deadline:* Applications are processed on a rolling basis. Application fee: $30. Electronic applications accepted. *Financial support:* Unspecified assistantships available. Financial award applicants required to submit FAFSA. *Unit head:* Dr. Dan Yoder, Chairperson, 309-298-1584. *Application contact:* Dr. Nancy Parsons, Assistant Director of Graduate Studies, 309-298-1806, Fax: 309-298-2345, E-mail: grad-office@wiu.edu.
Website: http://www.wiu.edu/rpta

Western Kentucky University, Graduate Studies, College of Health and Human Services, Department of Kinesiology, Recreation and Sport, Bowling Green, KY 42101. Offers athletic administration and coaching (MS); physical education (MS); recreation and sport administration (MS). *Program availability:* Part-time, evening/weekend, online learning. *Degree requirements:* For master's, comprehensive exam, thesis optional. *Entrance requirements:* For master's, GRE General Test, minimum GPA of 2.75. Additional exam requirements/recommendations for international students: Required—TOEFL (minimum score 555 paper-based; 79 iBT). *Faculty research:* Orthopedic rehabilitation, fitness center coordination, heat acclimation, biomechanical and physiological parameters.

West Virginia University, Davis College of Agriculture, Forestry and Consumer Sciences, Morgantown, WV 26506. Offers agricultural and extension education (MS, PhD); agriculture and resource management (MS); agriculture, natural resources and design (M Agr); agronomy (MS); animal and food science (PhD); animal physiology (MS); applied and environmental microbiology (MS); design and merchandising (MS); entomology (MS); forest resource science (PhD); forestry (MSF); genetics and developmental biology (MS, PhD); horticulture (MS); human and community development (PhD); landscape architecture (MLA); natural resource economics (PhD); nutritional and food science (MS); plant and soil science (PhD); plant pathology (MS); recreation, parks and tourism resources (MS, PhD); reproductive physiology (MS, PhD); wildlife and fisheries resources (PhD). *Program availability:* Part-time. *Students:* 200 full-time (97 women), 53 part-time (32 women); includes 27 minority (6 Black or African American, non-Hispanic/Latino; 1 American Indian or Alaska Native, non-Hispanic/Latino; 4 Asian, non-Hispanic/Latino; 11 Hispanic/Latino; 5 Two or more races, non-Hispanic/Latino), 67 international. *Degree requirements:* For master's, thesis; for doctorate, thesis/dissertation. *Entrance requirements:* Additional exam requirements/recommendations for international students: Required—TOEFL (minimum score 550 paper-based). *Application deadline:* For fall admission, 6/1 priority date for domestic students, 6/1 for international students; for spring admission, 1/5 for domestic and international students. Applications are processed on a rolling basis. Application fee: $60. Electronic applications accepted. *Expenses:* Tuition, state resident: full-time $9450. Tuition, nonresident: full-time $24,390. *Financial support:* Fellowships, research assistantships, teaching assistantships, career-related internships or fieldwork, Federal Work-Study, institutionally sponsored loans, tuition waivers (full and partial), and unspecified assistantships available. Financial award application deadline: 2/1; financial award applicants required to submit FAFSA. *Faculty research:* Reproductive physiology, soil and water quality, human nutrition, aquaculture, wildlife management. *Unit head:* Dr. Dan J. Robison, Dean, 304-293-2395, Fax: 304-293-3740, E-mail: dan.robison@mail.wvu.edu. *Application contact:* Dr. Dennis K. Smith, Associate Dean, 304-293-2275, Fax: 304-293-3740, E-mail: denny.smith@mail.wvu.edu.
Website: https://www.davis.wvu.edu

Section 30
Physical Education and Kinesiology

This section contains a directory of institutions offering graduate work in physical education and kinesiology. Additional information about programs listed in the directory may be obtained by writing directly to the dean of a graduate school or chair of a department at the address given in the directory.

For programs offering related work, see also in this book *Business Administration and Management, Education,* and *Sports Management.* In another guide in this series:

Graduate Programs in the Humanities, Arts & Social Sciences
See *Performing Arts*

CONTENTS

Program Directories

Athletic Training and Sports Medicine

Adrian College, Graduate Programs, Adrian, MI 49221-2575. Offers accounting (MS); athletic training (MS); criminal justice (MA). *Degree requirements:* For master's, comprehensive exam (for some programs), thesis (for some programs), thesis, internship or practicum with corresponding in-depth paper and/or presentation. *Entrance requirements:* For master's, appropriate undergraduate degree, minimum cumulative and major GPA of 3.0, personal statement.

A.T. Still University, Arizona School of Health Sciences, Mesa, AZ 85206. Offers advanced occupational therapy (MS); advanced physician assistant studies (MS); athletic training (MS, DAT); audiology (Au D); clinical decision making in athletic training (Graduate Certificate); occupational therapy (MS, OTD); orthopedic rehabilitation (Graduate Certificate); physical therapy (DPT); physician assistant studies (MS); transitional audiology (Au D); transitional physical therapy (DPT). *Accreditation:* AOTA (one or more programs are accredited); ASHA. *Program availability:* Part-time, 100% online. *Faculty:* 59 full-time (39 women), 221 part-time/adjunct (155 women). *Students:* 608 full-time (405 women), 431 part-time (310 women); includes 247 minority (54 Black or African American, non-Hispanic/Latino; 13 American Indian or Alaska Native, non-Hispanic/Latino; 151 Asian, non-Hispanic/Latino; 2 Hispanic/Latino; 1 Native Hawaiian or other Pacific Islander, non-Hispanic/Latino; 26 Two or more races, non-Hispanic/Latino), 1 international. Average age 33. 4,882 applicants, 9% accepted, 278 enrolled. In 2017, 132 master's, 270 doctorates awarded. *Degree requirements:* For master's, thesis (for some programs); for doctorate, thesis/dissertation (for some programs). *Entrance requirements:* For master's, GRE General Test; for doctorate, GRE, Physical Therapist Evaluation Tool (for DPT), current state licensure. Additional exam requirements/recommendations for international students: Required—TOEFL (minimum score 80 iBT). *Application deadline:* For fall admission, 7/7 for domestic and international students; for winter admission, 10/3 for domestic and international students; for spring admission, 1/16 for domestic and international students; for summer admission, 4/17 for domestic and international students. Applications are processed on a rolling basis. Application fee: $70. Electronic applications accepted. Application fee is waived when completed online. *Financial support:* In 2017–18, 161 students received support. Federal Work-Study and scholarships/grants available. Financial award application deadline: 6/1; financial award applicants required to submit FAFSA. *Faculty research:* Pediatric sport-related concussion, adolescent athlete health-related quality of life; geriatric and pediatric well-being, pain management for participation, practice-based research network, BMI and dental caries. *Total annual research expenditures:* $63,003. *Unit head:* Dr. Randy Danielsen, Dean, 480-219-6009, Fax: 480-219-6110, E-mail: rdanielsen@atsu.edu. *Application contact:* Donna Sparks, Director, Admissions Processing, 660-626-2117, Fax: 660-626-2969, E-mail: admissions@atsu.edu. Website: http://www.atsu.edu/ashs

Azusa Pacific University, School of Behavioral and Applied Sciences, Department of Kinesiology, Azusa, CA 91702-7000. Offers athletic training (MS); physical education (MA, MS).

Barry University, School of Human Performance and Leisure Sciences, Programs in Movement Science, Specialization in Athletic Training, Miami Shores, FL 33161-6695. Offers MS. *Program availability:* Part-time, evening/weekend. *Degree requirements:* For master's, comprehensive exam, project or thesis. *Entrance requirements:* For master's, GRE General Test, minimum GPA of 3.0. Electronic applications accepted. *Faculty research:* Pain management, prevention and injury analysis, low energy static magnetic field therapy, upper extremity biomechanics.

Baylor University, Graduate School, Robbins College of Health and Human Sciences, Department of Health, Human Performance and Recreation, Waco, TX 76798. Offers athletic training (MS); community health (MPH); exercise physiology (MS); kinesiology, exercise nutrition, and health promotion (PhD); sport pedagogy (MS). *Accreditation:* NCATE. *Program availability:* Part-time. *Faculty:* 24 full-time (11 women). *Students:* 86 full-time (52 women), 9 part-time (6 women); includes 24 minority (7 Black or African American, non-Hispanic/Latino; 3 Asian, non-Hispanic/Latino; 10 Hispanic/Latino; 1 Native Hawaiian or other Pacific Islander, non-Hispanic/Latino; 3 Two or more races, non-Hispanic/Latino), 8 international. 109 applicants, 59% accepted, 44 enrolled. In 2017, 30 master's, 3 doctorates awarded. *Degree requirements:* For master's, comprehensive exam, thesis optional; for doctorate, comprehensive exam, thesis/dissertation. *Entrance requirements:* For master's and doctorate, GRE General Test. Additional exam requirements/recommendations for international students: Required—TOEFL (minimum score 550 paper-based; 80 iBT). *Application deadline:* For fall admission, 2/1 priority date for domestic students, 2/1 for international students; for spring admission, 10/1 for domestic and international students. Applications are processed on a rolling basis. Application fee: $25. Electronic applications accepted. *Financial support:* In 2017–18, 60 students received support, including 1 research assistantship with full tuition reimbursement available (averaging $12,700 per year), 33 teaching assistantships with full tuition reimbursements available (averaging $7,650 per year); career-related internships or fieldwork, Federal Work-Study, institutionally sponsored loans, scholarships/grants, tuition waivers (full), and unspecified assistantships also available. Financial award application deadline: 2/1. *Faculty research:* Exercise testing, cardio-metabolic health, resistance exercise and training, nutritional intervention, population health, health promotion, global health epidemiology, coaching, natural resource management, stimulant misuse, diet, microbiome and colon cancer etiology. *Total annual research expenditures:* $250,118. *Unit head:* Dr. Jaeho Shim, Graduate Program Director, 254-710-4009, Fax: 254-710-3527, E-mail: joe_shim@baylor.edu. *Application contact:* Deepa Morris, Graduate Program Coordinator, 254-710-3526, Fax: 254-710-3527, E-mail: deepa_morris@baylor.edu. Website: http://www.baylor.edu/HHPR

Bellarmine University, College of Health Professions, School of Movement and Rehabilitation Sciences, Louisville, KY 40205. Offers athletic training (MSAT); physical therapy (DPT). *Program availability:* Part-time. *Faculty:* 22 full-time (15 women), 27 part-time/adjunct (17 women). *Students:* 212 full-time (136 women), 2 part-time (both women); includes 18 minority (2 Black or African American, non-Hispanic/Latino; 4 Asian, non-Hispanic/Latino; 2 Hispanic/Latino; 10 Two or more races, non-Hispanic/Latino), 1 international. Average age 25. In 2017, 62 doctorates awarded. *Degree requirements:* For master's and doctorate, comprehensive exam. *Entrance requirements:* For master's, minimum undergraduate GPA of 2.75 or GRE, 3.0 in prerequisite courses; grade of C or better in all prerequisites; for doctorate, GRE, minimum undergraduate GPA of 2.75, 3.0 in prerequisite courses; grade of C or better in all prerequisites; documented work/volunteer hours in PT setting; physical ability to perform tasks required of a physical therapist. Additional exam requirements/recommendations for international students: Required—TOEFL (minimum iBT score of 83, 26 on speaking test), IELTS (minimum score 7, speaking band score of 8). *Application deadline:* Applications are processed on a rolling basis. Application fee: $40. Electronic applications accepted. Tuition and fees vary according to program. *Financial support:* Applicants required to submit FAFSA. *Unit head:* Dr. Tony Brosky, Dean, 502-272-8375, E-mail: jbrosky@bellarmine.edu. *Application contact:* Dr. Sara Pettingill, Dean of Graduate Admission, 502-272-8401, Fax: 502-272-8002, E-mail: spettingill@bellarmine.edu. Website: https://www.bellarmine.edu/movement/

Bloomsburg University of Pennsylvania, School of Graduate Studies, College of Science and Technology, Department of Exercise Science and Athletics, Bloomsburg, PA 17815-1301. Offers clinical athletic training (MS); exercise science (MS). *Degree requirements:* For master's, thesis optional, practical clinical experience. *Entrance requirements:* For master's, GRE, minimum QPA of 3.0, related undergraduate coursework, interview. Additional exam requirements/recommendations for international students: Required—TOEFL (minimum score 550 paper-based; 79 iBT), IELTS. Electronic applications accepted. *Expenses:* Tuition, state resident: full-time $10,000; part-time $500 per credit hour. Tuition, nonresident: full-time $15,000; part-time $750 per credit hour. *Required fees:* $2484; $110.75 per credit hour. $75 per term. Tuition and fees vary according to program.

Boston University, College of Health and Rehabilitation Sciences: Sargent College, Department of Physical Therapy and Athletic Training, Boston, MA 02215. Offers athletic training (MS); physical therapy (DPT); rehabilitation sciences (PhD). *Accreditation:* APTA (one or more programs are accredited). *Faculty:* 13 full-time (10 women), 26 part-time/adjunct (12 women). *Students:* 187 full-time (138 women), 4 part-time (2 women); includes 27 minority (1 Black or African American, non-Hispanic/Latino; 14 Asian, non-Hispanic/Latino; 6 Hispanic/Latino; 6 Two or more races, non-Hispanic/Latino), 9 international. Average age 25. 812 applicants, 16% accepted, 41 enrolled. In 2017, 66 doctorates awarded. *Degree requirements:* For doctorate, comprehensive exam and thesis (for PhD). *Entrance requirements:* For master's, GRE General Test, bachelor's degree; for doctorate, GRE General Test, bachelor's degree (for DPT), master's degree (for PhD). Additional exam requirements/recommendations for international students: Required—TOEFL (minimum score 550 paper-based; 84 iBT). *Application deadline:* For fall admission, 12/15 priority date for domestic and international students. Applications are processed on a rolling basis. Application fee: $145. Electronic applications accepted. *Financial support:* In 2017–18, 120 students received support, including 16 research assistantships with full tuition reimbursements available (averaging $22,000 per year), 6 teaching assistantships (averaging $2,500 per year); fellowships, career-related internships or fieldwork, Federal Work-Study, institutionally sponsored loans, scholarships/grants, and tuition waivers (full and partial) also available. Financial award application deadline: 12/15; financial award applicants required to submit FAFSA. *Faculty research:* Gait, balance, motor control, dynamic systems analysis, spinal cord injury. *Total annual research expenditures:* $1.5 million. *Unit head:* Dr. LaDora Thompson, Department Chair, 617-353-2724, E-mail: pt@bu.edu. *Application contact:* Sharon Sankey, Assistant Dean, Student Services, 617-353-2713, Fax: 617-353-7500, E-mail: ssankey@bu.edu.

Bridgewater College, Program in Athletic Training, Bridgewater, VA 22812-1599. Offers MS. Electronic applications accepted.

Brigham Young University, Graduate Studies, College of Life Sciences, Department of Exercise Sciences, Provo, UT 84602. Offers athletic training (MS); exercise physiology (MS, PhD); exercise sciences (MS); health promotion (MS, PhD); physical medicine and rehabilitation (PhD). *Faculty:* 21 full-time (2 women). *Students:* 12 full-time (4 women), 18 part-time (11 women); includes 4 minority (3 Asian, non-Hispanic/Latino; 1 Hispanic/Latino). Average age 32. 21 applicants, 48% accepted, 6 enrolled. In 2017, 7 master's awarded. *Degree requirements:* For master's, thesis, oral defense; for doctorate, comprehensive exam, thesis/dissertation, oral defense, oral and written exams. *Entrance requirements:* For master's, GRE General Test (minimum score of 300, 4.0 on analytic writing portion), minimum GPA of 3.2 in last 60 hours of course work; for doctorate, GRE General Test (minimum score of 300, 4.0 on analytic writing portion), minimum GPA of 3.5 in last 60 hours of course work. Additional exam requirements/recommendations for international students: Required—TOEFL (minimum score 580 paper-based; 85 iBT), IELTS (minimum score 7). *Application deadline:* For fall admission, 2/1 for domestic and international students. Application fee: $50. Electronic applications accepted. *Expenses:* $5,160 per year. *Financial support:* In 2017–18, 40 students received support, including 19 research assistantships (averaging $69,400 per year), 21 teaching assistantships (averaging $38,500 per year); career-related internships or fieldwork, scholarships/grants, unspecified assistantships, and 8 PhD full-tuition scholarships also available. Financial award application deadline: 4/15. *Faculty research:* Injury prevention and rehabilitation, human skeletal muscle adaptation, cardiovascular health and fitness, lifestyle modification and health promotion. *Total annual research expenditures:* $107,348. *Unit head:* Dr. Allen Parcell, Chair, 801-422-4450, Fax: 801-422-0555, E-mail: allenparcell@gmail.com. *Application contact:* Dr. J. Ty Hopkins, Graduate Coordinator, 801-422-1573, Fax: 801-422-0555, E-mail: tyhopkins@byu.edu. Website: http://exsc.byu.edu/

California Baptist University, Program in Athletic Training, Riverside, CA 92504-3206. Offers MS. *Program availability:* Part-time. *Faculty:* 4 full-time (3 women). *Students:* 36 full-time (20 women); includes 21 minority (2 Black or African American, non-Hispanic/Latino; 3 Asian, non-Hispanic/Latino; 16 Hispanic/Latino). Average age 25. 2 applicants. In 2017, 19 master's awarded. *Degree requirements:* For master's, 53-56 units of core courses; at least 900 cumulative hours of athletic training clinical education courses. *Entrance requirements:* For master's, minimum GPA of 2.75; three recommendations; comprehensive essay; current resume; CPR Professional Rescuer Certification; 150 hours of clinical observation; interview. Additional exam requirements/recommendations for international students: Required—TOEFL (minimum score 80 iBT). *Application deadline:* For fall admission, 8/1 priority date for domestic students, 7/1 for international students; for spring admission, 12/1 priority date for domestic students, 11/1 for international students. Applications are processed on a rolling basis. Application fee: $45. Electronic applications accepted. *Expenses:* Contact institution. *Financial support:* In 2017–18, 3 students received support. Research assistantships, Federal Work-Study, and scholarships/grants available. Financial award applicants required to submit CSS PROFILE or FAFSA. *Faculty research:* Nutrition, weight management, public health, stress, athletic training. *Unit head:* Dr. David Pearson, Dean of the College of Health Science, 951-343-4298, E-mail: dpearson@calbaptist.edu. *Application contact:* Dr. Nicole MacDonald, Director, Athletic Training Program, 951-343-4379, E-mail: nmacdona@calbaptist.edu. Website: http://www.calbaptist.edu/at/

California State University, Long Beach, Graduate Studies, College of Health and Human Services, Department of Kinesiology, Long Beach, CA 90840. Offers adapted physical education (MA); coaching and student athlete development (MA); exercise physiology and nutrition (MS); exercise science (MS); individualized studies (MA); kinesiology (MA); pedagogical studies (MA); sport and exercise psychology (MS); sport management (MA); sports medicine and injury studies (MS). *Program availability:* Part-time. *Degree requirements:* For master's, oral and written comprehensive exams or thesis. *Entrance requirements:* For master's, GRE General Test, minimum GPA of 2.75 during previous 2 years of course work. Electronic applications accepted. *Faculty research:* Pulmonary functioning, feedback and practice structure, strength training, history and politics of sports, special population research issues.

California University of Pennsylvania, School of Graduate Studies and Research, College of Education and Human Services, Department of Health Science, California, PA 15419-1394. Offers athletic training (MS). *Degree requirements:* For master's, comprehensive exam, thesis. *Entrance requirements:* For master's, minimum GPA of 3.0. Additional exam requirements/recommendations for international students: Required—TOEFL (minimum score 550 paper-based; 80 iBT). *Application deadline:* For summer admission, 4/1 for domestic and international students. Applications are processed on a rolling basis. Application fee: $25. *Financial support:* Applicants required to submit FAFSA. *Faculty research:* Exercise physiology, pedagogy, athletic training, biomechanical engineering, case studies in injury and athletic medicine. *Unit head:* Dr. Shelly Fetchen DiCesaro, Program Director, 724-938-5831, E-mail: dicesaro@calu.edu. *Application contact:* Suzanne C. Powers, Director of Graduate Admissions and Recruitment, 724-938-4029, Fax: 724-938-5712, E-mail: powers_s@cup.edu.
Website: http://www.calu.edu/academics/colleges/education/health-science/

Chapman University, Crean College of Health and Behavioral Sciences, Athletic Training Program, Orange, CA 92866. Offers MS. *Faculty:* 4 full-time (2 women). *Students:* 15 full-time (10 women), 18 part-time (14 women); includes 14 minority (1 Black or African American, non-Hispanic/Latino; 2 Asian, non-Hispanic/Latino; 8 Hispanic/Latino; 3 Two or more races, non-Hispanic/Latino). Average age 23. In 2017, 7 master's awarded. *Degree requirements:* For master's, 1200 hours of clinical fieldwork. *Entrance requirements:* For master's, GRE. *Application deadline:* For summer admission, 12/1 priority date for domestic students. Application fee: $60. Electronic applications accepted. *Expenses:* Contact institution. *Financial support:* Fellowships, scholarships/grants, and unspecified assistantships available. Financial award applicants required to submit FAFSA. *Unit head:* Dr. Jason Bennett, Director, 714-997-6567, E-mail: jbennett@chapman.edu.

The College of St. Scholastica, Graduate Studies, Department of Athletic Training, Duluth, MN 55811-4199. Offers MS. *Program availability:* Part-time, online learning. *Entrance requirements:* Additional exam requirements/recommendations for international students: Required—TOEFL. Electronic applications accepted.

Drake University, College of Pharmacy and Health Sciences, Des Moines, IA 50311-4516. Offers athletic training (MAT); occupational therapy (OTD); pharmacy (Pharm D); Pharm D/JD; Pharm D/MBA; Pharm D/MPA. *Accreditation:* ACPE. *Degree requirements:* For doctorate, rotations. *Entrance requirements:* For doctorate, PCAT, interview. Additional exam requirements/recommendations for international students: Required—TOEFL. *Application deadline:* For fall admission, 2/1 priority date for domestic students. Application fee: $135. Electronic applications accepted. *Expenses:* Contact institution. *Financial support:* Teaching assistantships, career-related internships or fieldwork, Federal Work-Study, institutionally sponsored loans, and scholarships/grants available. Support available to part-time students. Financial award application deadline: 3/1; financial award applicants required to submit FAFSA. *Faculty research:* Cost-benefit and cost-analysis of pharmaceutical products and services, patient satisfaction, community health planning and development, nutrition, ambulatory care. *Unit head:* Dr. Renae Chesnut, Dean, 515-271-3018, Fax: 515-271-4171, E-mail: renae.chesnut@drake.edu.
Website: http://www.drake.edu/cphs/

Eastern Michigan University, Graduate School, College of Health and Human Services, School of Health Promotion and Human Performance, Programs in Exercise Physiology, Ypsilanti, MI 48197. Offers exercise physiology (MS); sports medicine-biomechanics (MS); sports medicine-corporate adult fitness (MS); sports medicine-exercise physiology (MS). *Program availability:* Part-time, evening/weekend. *Students:* 9 full-time (3 women), 13 part-time (5 women); includes 5 minority (2 Black or African American, non-Hispanic/Latino; 1 Asian, non-Hispanic/Latino; 1 Hispanic/Latino; 1 Two or more races, non-Hispanic/Latino), 1 international. Average age 29. 43 applicants, 56% accepted, 7 enrolled. In 2017, 13 master's awarded. *Degree requirements:* For master's, comprehensive exam, thesis or 450-hour internship. *Entrance requirements:* Additional exam requirements/recommendations for international students: Required—TOEFL. *Application deadline:* For fall admission, 8/1 for domestic students, 5/1 for international students; for winter admission, 12/1 for domestic students, 10/1 for international students; for spring admission, 3/15 for domestic students, 3/1 for international students. Application fee: $45. *Application contact:* Dr. Becca Moore, Program Coordinator, 734-487-2824, Fax: 734-487-2024, E-mail: rmoore41@emich.edu.

Eastern Michigan University, Graduate School, College of Health and Human Services, School of Health Promotion and Human Performance, Programs in Orthotics and Prosthetics, Ypsilanti, MI 48197. Offers MS, Graduate Certificate. *Students:* 42 full-time (27 women); includes 3 minority (1 Asian, non-Hispanic/Latino; 2 Two or more races, non-Hispanic/Latino). Average age 25. 112 applicants, 27% accepted, 22 enrolled. In 2017, 17 master's awarded. *Degree requirements:* For master's, comprehensive exam, thesis or project, 500 hours of clinicals. *Entrance requirements:* For master's, MAT. Additional exam requirements/recommendations for international students: Required—TOEFL. Application deadline: For fall admission, 5/1 for domestic students. Applications are processed on a rolling basis. Application fee: $45. *Financial support:* Fellowships, research assistantships with full tuition reimbursements, teaching assistantships with full tuition reimbursements, career-related internships or fieldwork, Federal Work-Study, institutionally sponsored loans, scholarships/grants, tuition waivers (partial), and unspecified assistantships available. Support available to part-time students. Financial award applicants required to submit FAFSA. *Application contact:* Wendy Beattie, Clinical and Program Director, 734-487-2814, Fax: 734-487-2024, E-mail: wbeattie@emich.edu.

East Stroudsburg University of Pennsylvania, Graduate and Extended Studies, College of Health Sciences, Department of Athletic Training, East Stroudsburg, PA 18301-2999. Offers MS. *Program availability:* Part-time, evening/weekend, online learning. *Faculty:* 2 full-time (0 women), 3 part-time/adjunct (2 women). *Students:* 38 full-time (19 women), 2 part-time (0 women); includes 8 minority (1 Black or African American, non-Hispanic/Latino; 5 Hispanic/Latino; 2 Two or more races, non-Hispanic/Latino), 1 international. Average age 24. 31 applicants, 48% accepted. In 2017, 39 master's awarded. *Entrance requirements:* For master's, GRE. Additional exam requirements/recommendations for international students: Recommended—TOEFL (minimum score 560 paper-based; 83 iBT), IELTS. *Application deadline:* For fall admission, 7/31 for domestic students, 6/30 for international students; for spring admission, 10/30 for domestic students, 10/31 for international students. Applications are processed on a rolling basis. Application fee: $50. Electronic applications accepted. *Expenses:* Tuition, state resident: full-time $4500; part-time $3000 per credit. Tuition,

nonresident: full-time $6750; part-time $4500 per credit. *Required fees:* $2642; $1756 per credit. $878 per semester. Tuition and fees vary according to course load, campus/location and program. *Financial support:* Research assistantships with tuition reimbursements, career-related internships or fieldwork, Federal Work-Study, and unspecified assistantships available. Support available to part-time students. Financial award application deadline: 3/1; financial award applicants required to submit FAFSA. *Unit head:* Keith Vanic, Graduate Coordinator, 570-422-3314, E-mail: kvanic@esu.edu. *Application contact:* Kevin Quintero, Associate Director, Graduate and Extended Studies, 570-422-3890, Fax: 570-422-2711, E-mail: kquintero@esu.edu.

Florida International University, Nicole Wertheim College of Nursing and Health Sciences, Department of Athletic Training, Miami, FL 33199. Offers MS. *Faculty:* 5 full-time (4 women), 7 part-time/adjunct (3 women). *Students:* 41 full-time (31 women), 2 part-time (both women); includes 34 minority (14 Black or African American, non-Hispanic/Latino; 19 Hispanic/Latino; 1 Two or more races, non-Hispanic/Latino), 1 international. Average age 24. 5 applicants, 20% accepted. In 2017, 21 master's awarded. *Degree requirements:* For master's, 800 clinical education hours. *Entrance requirements:* For master's, bachelor's degree from accredited institution; minimum GPA of 3.0 overall and in last 60 credits of upper-division courses of the bachelor's degree; three letters of recommendation; resume; personal statement of professional/educational goals. Additional exam requirements/recommendations for international students: Required—TOEFL (minimum score 550 paper-based; 80 iBT). *Application deadline:* For fall admission, 2/15 for domestic and international students. Application fee: $30. Electronic applications accepted. *Expenses:* Contact institution. *Financial support:* Institutionally sponsored loans and scholarships/grants available. Financial award application deadline: 3/1; financial award applicants required to submit FAFSA. *Faculty research:* Continuing professional education, leadership styles and outcomes, professionalism and professional image. *Unit head:* Dr. Gabriel M. Casanova, Director, 305-348-1072, Fax: 305-348-3673, E-mail: gabe.casanova@fiu.edu. *Application contact:* Nanett Rojas, Manager, Admissions Operations, 305-348-7464, Fax: 305-348-7441, E-mail: gradadm@fiu.edu.

Franklin College, Program in Athletic Training, Franklin, IN 46131. Offers MSAT.

Gannon University, School of Graduate Studies, Morosky College of Health Professions and Sciences, School of Health Professions, Program in Athletic Training, Erie, PA 16541-0001. Offers MAT. *Program availability:* Part-time, evening/weekend. *Entrance requirements:* For master's, undergraduate degree in exercise science, kinesiology, human performance, sports medicine or related field; minimum GPA of 2.75; 3 letters of recommendation. Additional exam requirements/recommendations for international students: Required—TOEFL (minimum score 79 iBT). Electronic applications accepted. Application fee is waived when completed online.

George Mason University, College of Education and Human Development, School of Recreation, Health and Tourism, Manassas, VA 20110. Offers athletic training (MS); exercise, fitness, and health promotion (MS), including advanced practitioner, wellness practitioner; international sport management (Certificate); recreation, health and tourism (Certificate); sport management (MS), including sport and recreation studies. *Program availability:* Part-time, evening/weekend. *Faculty:* 29 full-time (13 women), 87 part-time/adjunct (48 women). *Students:* 62 full-time (24 women), 23 part-time (11 women); includes 27 minority (20 Black or African American, non-Hispanic/Latino; 1 Asian, non-Hispanic/Latino; 3 Hispanic/Latino; 1 Native Hawaiian or other Pacific Islander, non-Hispanic/Latino; 2 Two or more races, non-Hispanic/Latino), 8 international. Average age 26. 74 applicants, 93% accepted, 46 enrolled. In 2017, 20 master's awarded. *Degree requirements:* For master's, thesis optional. *Entrance requirements:* For master's, 3 letters of recommendation; official transcripts; expanded goals statement; undergraduate course in statistics and minimum GPA of 3.0 in last 60 credit hours and overall (for MS in sport and recreation studies); baccalaureate degree related to kinesiology, exercise science or athletic training (for MS in exercise, fitness and health promotion). Additional exam requirements/recommendations for international students: Required—TOEFL (minimum score 575 paper-based; 88 iBT), IELTS (minimum score 6.5), PTE (minimum score 59). *Application deadline:* For fall admission, 4/2 priority date for domestic and international students; for spring admission, 11/1 for domestic and international students. Application fee: $75 ($80 for international students). Electronic applications accepted. *Expenses:* Tuition, state resident: full-time $11,228; part-time $459.50 per credit. Tuition, nonresident: full-time $30,932; part-time $1280.50 per credit. *Required fees:* $3252; $135.50 per credit. Part-time tuition and fees vary according to course load and program. *Financial support:* In 2017–18, 1 student received support, including 1 research assistantship with tuition reimbursement available; career-related internships or fieldwork, Federal Work-Study, scholarships/grants, unspecified assistantships, and health care benefits (for full-time research or teaching assistantship recipients) also available. Support available to part-time students. Financial award application deadline: 3/1; financial award applicants required to submit FAFSA. *Faculty research:* Sport for development and peace, sport analytics, leadership and coaching, diversity and inclusion in sport, sport communication. *Total annual research expenditures:* $826,386. *Unit head:* Martin Ford, Senior Associate Dean, 703-993-2004, E-mail: mford@gmu.edu. *Application contact:* Lindsey Olson, Office Assistant, 703-993-2098, Fax: 703-993-2025, E-mail: lolson7@gmu.edu.
Website: http://rht.gmu.edu/

Georgia Southern University–Armstrong Campus, College of Graduate Studies, Program in Sports Medicine, Savannah, GA 31419-1997. Offers sports medicine (MSSM); strength and conditioning (MSSM). *Program availability:* Part-time. *Faculty:* 4 full-time (0 women). *Students:* 16 full-time (7 women), 2 part-time (0 women); includes 7 minority (6 Black or African American, non-Hispanic/Latino; 1 Asian, non-Hispanic/Latino). Average age 25. 49 applicants, 24% accepted, 5 enrolled. In 2017, 10 master's awarded. *Degree requirements:* For master's, comprehensive exam, thesis optional, project. *Entrance requirements:* For master's, GRE General Test, MAT, GMAT, minimum GPA of 2.7, letter of intent. Additional exam requirements/recommendations for international students: Required—TOEFL (minimum score 523 paper-based; 70 iBT). *Application deadline:* For fall admission, 6/1 priority date for domestic students, 5/1 priority date for international students; for spring admission, 11/15 priority date for domestic students, 9/15 priority date for international students; for summer admission, 4/15 for domestic students, 9/15 for international students. Applications are processed on a rolling basis. Application fee: $30. Electronic applications accepted. *Expenses:* Tuition, state resident: part-time $211 per credit hour. Tuition, nonresident: part-time $782 per credit hour. *Required fees:* $737 per semester. Tuition and fees vary according to course load, degree level, campus/location and program. *Financial support:* In 2017–18, research assistantships with full tuition reimbursements (averaging $5,000 per year) were awarded; scholarships/grants, tuition waivers (full), and unspecified assistantships also available. Financial award application deadline: 3/15; financial award applicants required to submit FAFSA. *Unit head:* Dr. Robert LeFavi, Department Head, 912-921-3208, Fax: 912-344-3490, E-mail: robert.lefavi@armstrong.edu. *Application contact:* McKenzie Peterman, Graduate Admissions Specialist, 912-478-5678, Fax: 912-478-0740, E-mail: mpeterman@georgiasouthern.edu.
Website: http://www.armstrong.edu/Majors/degree/sports_medicine1

Georgia State University, College of Education and Human Development, Department of Kinesiology and Health, Program in Sports Medicine, Atlanta, GA 30302-3083. Offers

Athletic Training and Sports Medicine

MS. *Entrance requirements:* For master's, GRE General Test, minimum GPA of 2.5. Application fee: $50. *Expenses:* Tuition, state resident: full-time $7020. Tuition, nonresident: full-time $22,518. *Required fees:* $2128. Tuition and fees vary according to degree level and program. *Financial support:* Research assistantships available. *Faculty research:* Athletic training. *Unit head:* Dr. Jacalyn Lea Lund, Chair, 404-413-8051, E-mail: jlund@gsu.edu. *Application contact:* Dr. Shelley Linens, Program Coordinator, 404-413-8366, E-mail: slinens@gsu.edu.
Website: http://education.gsu.edu/KIN/kh_sportsMed_MS.html

Grand View University, Graduate Studies, Des Moines, IA 50316-1599. Offers athletic training (MS); clinical nurse leader (MSN, Post Master's Certificate); nursing education (MSN, Post Master's Certificate); organizational leadership (MS); sport management (MS); teacher leadership (M Ed); urban education (M Ed). *Program availability:* Part-time, evening/weekend. *Degree requirements:* For master's, completion of all required coursework in common core and selected track with minimum cumulative GPA of 3.0 and no more than two grades of C. *Entrance requirements:* For master's, GRE, GMAT, or essay, minimum undergraduate GPA of 3.0, professional resume, 3 letters of recommendation, interview. Additional exam requirements/recommendations for international students: Required—TOEFL (minimum score 550 paper-based). Electronic applications accepted.

High Point University, Norcross Graduate School, High Point, NC 27268. Offers athletic training (MSAT); business administration (MBA); educational leadership (M Ed, Ed D); elementary education (M Ed, MAT); pharmacy (Pharm D); physical therapy (DPT); physician assistant studies (MPAS); secondary mathematics (M Ed, MAT); special education (M Ed); strategic communication (MA). *Accreditation:* NCATE. *Program availability:* Part-time, evening/weekend. *Degree requirements:* For master's, comprehensive exam (for some programs), thesis (for some programs). *Entrance requirements:* For master's, GMAT (MBA), GRE, MAT, minimum GPA of 3.0. Additional exam requirements/recommendations for international students: Required—TOEFL (minimum score 550 paper-based). Electronic applications accepted.

Idaho State University, Office of Graduate Studies, College of Education, Department of Sport Science and Physical Education, Pocatello, ID 83209-8105. Offers athletic administration (MPE); athletic training (MSAT). *Program availability:* Part-time. *Degree requirements:* For master's, comprehensive exam (for some programs), thesis optional, internship, oral defense of dissertation, or written exams. *Entrance requirements:* For master's, MAT or GRE General Test, minimum GPA of 3.0 in upper division classes. Additional exam requirements/recommendations for international students: Required—TOEFL (minimum score 550 paper-based; 80 iBT). Electronic applications accepted. *Faculty research:* Gender and diversity; concussion awareness/sports medicine; legal aspects of athletic health care; sports psychology; exercise physiology; sports management and leadership; adapted activities; fitness, wellness, and nutrition; coaching perspectives; critical features of athletic activities.

Indiana State University, College of Graduate and Professional Studies, College of Health and Human Services, Department of Applied Medicine and Rehabilitation, Terre Haute, IN 47809. Offers athletic training (MS, DAT); occupational therapy (MS); physical therapy (DPT); physician assistant (MS). *Degree requirements:* For master's, thesis or alternative. *Entrance requirements:* For master's, GRE General Test. Electronic applications accepted.

Indiana University Bloomington, School of Public Health, Department of Kinesiology, Bloomington, IN 47405. Offers applied sport science (MS); athletic administration/sport management (MS); athletic training (MS); biomechanics (MS); ergonomics (MS); exercise physiology (MS); human performance (PhD), including biomechanics, exercise physiology, motor learning/control, sport management; motor learning/control (MS); physical activity (MPH); physical activity, fitness and wellness (MS). *Program availability:* Part-time. Terminal master's awarded for partial completion of doctoral program. *Degree requirements:* For master's, thesis optional; for doctorate, variable foreign language requirement, comprehensive exam, thesis/dissertation. *Entrance requirements:* For master's, GRE General Test, minimum GPA of 2.8; for doctorate, GRE General Test, minimum graduate GPA of 3.5, undergraduate 3.0. Additional exam requirements/recommendations for international students: Required—TOEFL (minimum score 80 iBT). *Faculty research:* Exercise physiology and biochemistry, sports biomechanics, human motor control, adaptation of fitness and exercise to special populations.

Inter American University of Puerto Rico, Metropolitan Campus, Graduate Programs, Program in Physical Education, San Juan, PR 00919-1293. Offers teaching of physical education (MA); training and sport performance (MA). *Degree requirements:* For master's, comprehensive exam. *Entrance requirements:* For master's, GRE or EXADEP, interview. Electronic applications accepted.

Kent State University, College of Education, Health and Human Services, School of Health Sciences, Program in Exercise Physiology, Kent, OH 44242-0001. Offers athletic training (MS); exercise physiology (PhD). *Degree requirements:* For doctorate, comprehensive exam, thesis/dissertation. *Entrance requirements:* For master's, GRE, 2 letters of reference, goals statement; for doctorate, GRE, 2 letters of reference, goals statement, minimum master's-level GPA of 3.0. Additional exam requirements/recommendations for international students: Required—TOEFL (minimum score 550 paper-based; 80 iBT). *Expenses:* Tuition, state resident: full-time $11,310; part-time $515 per credit hour. Tuition, nonresident: full-time $20,396; part-time $928 per credit hour. *International tuition:* $18,544 full-time.

Lebanon Valley College, Program in Athletic Training, Annville, PA 17003-1400. Offers MAT. *Faculty:* 4 full-time (2 women), 4 part-time/adjunct (2 women). *Students:* 103 applicants, 54% accepted, 20 enrolled. *Degree requirements:* For master's, research project. *Entrance requirements:* For master's, GRE, BS. Additional exam requirements/recommendations for international students: Required—TOEFL (minimum score 80 iBT). *Application deadline:* For fall admission, 3/1 priority date for domestic and international students. Applications are processed on a rolling basis. Electronic applications accepted. *Expenses:* Contact institution. *Financial support:* Federal Work-Study and scholarships/grants available. Financial award applicants required to submit FAFSA. *Faculty research:* Epidemiology, clinical education, clinical decision making. *Unit head:* Dr. Joseph M. Murphy, Assistant Professor/Director, 717-867-6845, Fax: 717-867-6849, E-mail: jmurphy@lvc.edu.
Website: http://www.lvc.edu/academics/programs-of-study/athletic-training

Lenoir-Rhyne University, Graduate Programs, School of Health, Exercise and Sport Science, Program in Athletic Training, Hickory, NC 28601. Offers MS. *Program availability:* Part-time. *Entrance requirements:* For master's, GRE or MAT, official transcripts, 75 observational hours with certified athletic trainer, essay, resume. Additional exam requirements/recommendations for international students: Required—TOEFL (minimum score 600 paper-based). Electronic applications accepted. *Expenses:* Contact institution.

Life University, College of Graduate and Undergraduate Studies, Marietta, GA 30060-2903. Offers athletic training (MAT); chiropractic sport science (MS); nutrition and sport science (MS), including chiropractic sport science; positive psychology (MS), including life coaching psychology; sport coaching (MS), including exercise sport science; sport injury management (MS), including nutrition and sport science; sports health science

(MS), including sports injury management. *Program availability:* Part-time, 100% online, blended/hybrid learning. *Faculty:* 11 full-time (6 women), 12 part-time/adjunct (10 women). *Students:* 82 full-time (58 women), 131 part-time (86 women); includes 116 minority (85 Black or African American, non-Hispanic/Latino; 2 American Indian or Alaska Native, non-Hispanic/Latino; 3 Asian, non-Hispanic/Latino; 26 Hispanic/Latino), 25 international. Average age 30. In 2017, 53 master's awarded. *Degree requirements:* For master's, comprehensive exam (for some programs), thesis optional. *Entrance requirements:* For master's, GRE General Test, minimum GPA of 3.0, 3 letters of recommendation, curriculum vitae. Additional exam requirements/recommendations for international students: Required—TOEFL (minimum score 500 paper-based). *Application deadline:* For fall admission, 4/1 priority date for domestic and international students; for winter admission, 12/1 priority date for domestic and international students; for spring admission, 3/1 priority date for domestic and international students. Applications are processed on a rolling basis. Application fee: $50. Electronic applications accepted. *Expenses:* Contact institution. *Financial support:* Career-related internships or fieldwork, Federal Work-Study, and tuition waivers (full and partial) available. Support available to part-time students. Financial award application deadline: 9/1; financial award applicants required to submit FAFSA. *Faculty research:* Nutrient metabolism, organizational effectiveness, injury prevention, athlete development, recovery modalities and treatment, sport nutrition, functional neurology, peace and conflict studies. *Unit head:* Dr. Jana Holwick, Dean of Graduate and Undergraduate Studies, 678-331-4407, Fax: 770-426-2699, E-mail: jana.holwick@life.edu. *Application contact:* Robyn Stanley, Director of Enrollment, 770-426-2889, E-mail: robin.stanley@life.edu.
Website: http://www.life.edu/enrollment/admissions/graduate-admissions

Lock Haven University of Pennsylvania, College of Natural, Behavioral and Health Sciences, Lock Haven, PA 17745-2390. Offers actuarial science (PSM); athletic training (MS); health promotion/education (MHS); healthcare management (MHS); physician assistant (MHS). Program also offered at the Clearfield, Coudersport, and Harrisburg campuses. *Accreditation:* ARC-PA. *Entrance requirements:* For master's, minimum undergraduate GPA of 3.0. Additional exam requirements/recommendations for international students: Required—TOEFL. Electronic applications accepted.

London Metropolitan University, Graduate Programs, London, United Kingdom. Offers applied psychology (M Sc); architecture (MA); biomedical science (M Sc); blood science (M Sc); cancer pharmacology (M Sc); computer networking and cyber security (M Sc); computing and information systems (M Sc); conference interpreting (MA); counter-terrorism studies (M Sc); creative, digital and professional writing (MA); crime, violence and prevention (M Sc); criminology (M Sc); curating contemporary art (MA); data analytics (MA); digital media (MA); early childhood studies (MA); education (MA, Ed D); financial services law, regulation and compliance (LL M); food science (M Sc); forensic psychology (M Sc); health and social care management and policy (M Sc); human nutrition (M Sc); human resource management (MA); human rights and international conflict (MA); information technology (M Sc); intelligence and security studies (M Sc); international oil, gas and energy law (LL M); international relations (MA); interpreting (MA); learning and teaching in higher education (MA); legal practice (LL M); media and entertainment law (LL M); organizational and consumer psychology (M Sc); psychological therapy (M Sc); psychology of mental health (M Sc); public health (M Sc); public policy and management (MPA); security studies (M Sc); social work (M Sc); spatial planning and urban design (MA); supporting older children and young people with dyslexia (MA); teaching languages (MA), including Arabic, English; translation (MA); woman and child abuse (MA).

Long Island University–LIU Brooklyn, School of Health Professions, Brooklyn, NY 11201-8423. Offers athletic training and sport sciences (MS); community health (MS Ed); exercise science (MS); forensic social work (Advanced Certificate); occupational therapy (MS); physical therapy (DPT); physician assistant (MS); public health (MPH); social work (MSW); speech-language pathology (MS). *Faculty:* 33 full-time (23 women), 82 part-time/adjunct (55 women). *Students:* 690 full-time (508 women), 86 part-time (74 women); includes 259 minority (120 Black or African American, non-Hispanic/Latino; 1 American Indian or Alaska Native, non-Hispanic/Latino; 52 Asian, non-Hispanic/Latino; 76 Hispanic/Latino; 10 Two or more races, non-Hispanic/Latino), 65 international. Average age 27. 1,241 applicants, 45% accepted, 255 enrolled. In 2017, 249 master's, 42 doctorates, 8 other advanced degrees awarded. *Degree requirements:* For master's, comprehensive exam (for some programs), thesis (for some programs); for doctorate, comprehensive exam (for some programs). *Entrance requirements:* For master's and doctorate, GRE. Additional exam requirements/recommendations for international students: Required—TOEFL (minimum score 550 paper-based; 79 iBT). *Application deadline:* Applications are processed on a rolling basis. Application fee: $50. Electronic applications accepted. *Expenses:* Tuition: Full-time $21,618; part-time $1201 per credit. *Required fees:* $1840; $920 per term. Tuition and fees vary according to course load. *Financial support:* In 2017–18, 187 students received support. Research assistantships, teaching assistantships, career-related internships or fieldwork, Federal Work-Study, scholarships/grants, and unspecified assistantships available. Support available to part-time students. Financial award application deadline: 2/15; financial award applicants required to submit FAFSA. *Faculty research:* Pediatric physical therapy, complementary and alternative medicine, global health and human rights, sport leadership and entrepreneurship, feminist sport psychology. *Unit head:* Dr. Barry S. Eckert, Dean, 718-780-6578, Fax: 718-780-4561, E-mail: barry.eckert@liu.edu. *Application contact:* Dr. Dominick Fortugno, Associate Dean, 718-488-1496, Fax: 718-780-4561, E-mail: dominick.fortugno@liu.edu.
Website: http://liu.edu/brooklyn/academics/school-of-health-professions

Manchester University, Master of Athletic Training Program, North Manchester, IN 46962-1225. Offers MAT. *Faculty:* 6 full-time (2 women), 1 part-time/adjunct (0 women). *Students:* 21 full-time (16 women); includes 4 minority (3 Black or African American, non-Hispanic/Latino; 1 Hispanic/Latino). Average age 23. 31 applicants, 74% accepted, 15 enrolled. In 2017, 7 master's awarded. *Degree requirements:* For master's, 51 semester hours; minimum cumulative GPA of 3.0, 2.0 in each required course; completion of all required didactic and clinical courses. *Entrance requirements:* For master's, baccalaureate degree from regionally-accredited institution; minimum cumulative undergraduate GPA of 3.0; certification in first aid and CPR; letters of recommendation. Additional exam requirements/recommendations for international students: Required—TOEFL (minimum score 550 paper-based; 79 iBT). *Application deadline:* For fall admission, 1/1 priority date for domestic students. Applications are processed on a rolling basis. Application fee: $60. Electronic applications accepted. *Expenses:* $24,050. *Financial support:* In 2017–18, 21 students received support, including 21 fellowships (averaging $7,850 per year). Financial award application deadline: 5/1; financial award applicants required to submit FAFSA. *Unit head:* Mark Huntington, Program Director, Graduate Athletic Training Education, 260-982-5033, E-mail: mwhuntington@manchester.edu.
Website: https://www.manchester.edu/academics/colleges/college-of-pharmacy-natural-health-sciences/academic-programs/exercise-science-athletic-training/exercis

Marshall University, Academic Affairs Division, College of Health Professions, School of Kinesiology, Program in Athletic Training, Huntington, WV 25755. Offers MS. *Students:* 8 full-time (6 women); includes 1 minority (Black or African American, non-

Hispanic/Latino). Average age 23. In 2017, 5 master's awarded. *Entrance requirements:* For master's, GRE. *Unit head:* Dr. Gary McIlvain, Interim Chair, 304-696-2930, E-mail: mcilvain@marshall.edu. *Application contact:* Information Contact, 304-746-1900, Fax: 304-746-1902, E-mail: services@marshall.edu.

Mercer University, Graduate Studies, Cecil B. Day Campus, College of Health Professions, Atlanta, GA 30341. Offers athletic training (MAT); clinical medical psychology (Psy D); physical therapy (DPT); physician assistant studies (MM Sc); public health (MPH); DPT/MBA; DPT/MPH; MM Sc/MPH; Pharm D/MPH. *Faculty:* 23 full-time (14 women), 10 part-time/adjunct (7 women). *Students:* 345 full-time (261 women), 67 part-time (55 women); includes 167 minority (116 Black or African American, non-Hispanic/Latino; 28 Asian, non-Hispanic/Latino; 21 Hispanic/Latino; 2 Two or more races, non-Hispanic/Latino), 2 international. Average age 26. In 2017, 83 master's, 37 doctorates awarded. *Expenses:* Contact institution. *Financial support:* Federal Work-Study, traineeships, and unspecified assistantships available. *Faculty research:* Scholarship of teaching and learning, health disparities, clinical outcomes, health promotion. *Unit head:* Dr. Lisa Lundquist, Dean/Clinical Professor, 678-547-6308, E-mail: lundquist_lm@mercer.edu. *Application contact:* Laura Ellison, Director of Admissions and Student Affairs, 678-547-6391, E-mail: ellison_la@mercer.edu.
Website: http://chp.mercer.edu/

Merrimack College, School of Health Sciences, North Andover, MA 01845-5800. Offers athletic training (MS); community health education (MS); exercise and sport science (MS); health and wellness management (MS). *Program availability:* Part-time, evening/weekend. *Faculty:* 8 full-time, 6 part-time/adjunct. *Students:* 87 full-time (58 women), 4 part-time (all women); includes 10 minority (2 Black or African American, non-Hispanic/Latino; 7 Hispanic/Latino; 1 Two or more races, non-Hispanic/Latino), 3 international. Average age 25. 147 applicants, 90% accepted, 83 enrolled. In 2017, 47 master's awarded. *Degree requirements:* For master's, capstone (for community health education, exercise and sport science, and health and wellness management). *Entrance requirements:* For master's, resume, official college transcripts, personal statement, 2 recommendations. Additional exam requirements/recommendations for international students: Required—TOEFL (minimum score 84 iBT), IELTS (minimum score 6.5), PTE (minimum score 56). *Application deadline:* For fall admission, 8/24 for domestic students, 7/30 for international students; for summer admission, 5/10 for domestic students, 4/10 for international students. Applications are processed on a rolling basis. Electronic applications accepted. *Expenses:* $865 per credit hour tuition; $670 per credit hour (for MAT); comprehensive fees are $165 per semester for 1-8 credit hours and $320 per semester for 9+ credit hours. *Financial support:* Fellowships with partial tuition reimbursements, career-related internships or fieldwork, scholarships/grants, and health care benefits available. Support available to part-time students. Financial award application deadline: 5/1; financial award applicants required to submit FAFSA. *Unit head:* Kyle McInnis, Dean, 978-837-3590, E-mail: mcinnisk@merrimack.edu. *Application contact:* Allison Pena, Office of Graduate Studies, 978-837-3563, E-mail: graduate@merrimack.edu.
Website: http://www.merrimack.edu/academics/health-sciences/

Missouri State University, Graduate College, College of Health and Human Services, Department of Sports Medicine and Athletic Training, Springfield, MO 65897. Offers athletic training (MS); occupational therapy (MOT). *Program availability:* Part-time. *Faculty:* 7 full-time (4 women), 5 part-time/adjunct (3 women). *Students:* 21 full-time (11 women), 4 part-time (2 women); includes 1 minority (Two or more races, non-Hispanic/Latino). Average age 23. 28 applicants, 43% accepted, 11 enrolled. In 2017, 12 master's awarded. *Degree requirements:* For master's, comprehensive exam, thesis or alternative. *Entrance requirements:* For master's, GRE, current Professional Rescuer and AED certification, BOC certification, licensure as an athletic trainer, minimum undergraduate GPA of 3.0 (for MS); OTCAS application (for MOT). Additional exam requirements/recommendations for international students: Required—TOEFL (minimum score 550 paper-based; 79 iBT), IELTS (minimum score 6). *Application deadline:* For fall admission, 1/15 for domestic and international students. Application fee: $35 ($50 for international students). Electronic applications accepted. *Expenses:* Tuition, state resident: full-time $2915; part-time $2021 per credit hour. Tuition, nonresident: full-time $5354; part-time $3647 per credit hour. *International tuition:* $11,992 full-time. *Required fees:* $173; $173 per credit hour. Tuition and fees vary according to class time, course level, course load, degree level, campus/location and program. *Financial support:* In 2017–18, 5 teaching assistantships with partial tuition reimbursements (averaging $8,772 per year) were awarded; Federal Work-Study, institutionally sponsored loans, and unspecified assistantships also available. Financial award application deadline: 3/31; financial award applicants required to submit FAFSA. *Unit head:* Dr. Tona Hetzler, Head, 417-836-8924, Fax: 417-836-8554, E-mail: tonahetzler@missouristate.edu. *Application contact:* Stephanie Praschan, Director, Graduate Enrollment Management, 417-836-5330, Fax: 417-836-6200, E-mail: stephaniepraschan@missouristate.edu.
Website: http://sportsmed.missouristate.edu/

Montana State University Billings, College of Allied Health Professions, Program in Athletic Training, Billings, MT 59101. Offers MS. *Program availability:* Part-time. *Degree requirements:* For master's, thesis optional. *Entrance requirements:* For master's, GRE, minimum GPA of 3.0, letters of recommendation, letter of intent. Additional exam requirements/recommendations for international students: Required—TOEFL (minimum score 79 iBT), IELTS (minimum score 6.5). *Application deadline:* For summer admission, 5/28 for domestic students. Applications are processed on a rolling basis. Electronic applications accepted. *Expenses:* Tuition, state resident: full-time $11,740; part-time $7880 per year. Tuition, nonresident: full-time $32,200; part-time $24,140 per year. *Financial support:* Research assistantships with partial tuition reimbursements, teaching assistantships with partial tuition reimbursements, institutionally sponsored loans, scholarships/grants, and unspecified assistantships available. Support available to part-time students. Financial award application deadline: 5/1; financial award applicants required to submit FAFSA. *Unit head:* Dr. Suzette Nynas, Director, 406-657-2351, E-mail: snynas@msubillings.edu. *Application contact:* Dr. Suzette Nynas, Director, 406-657-2351, E-mail: snynas@msubillings.edu.
Website: http://www.msubillings.edu/cahp/athletic_training/

Moravian College, Graduate and Continuing Studies, Rehabilitation Science Programs, Bethlehem, PA 18018-6650. Offers athletic training (MS, DAT). *Faculty:* 3 full-time (1 woman), 1 (woman) part-time/adjunct. *Students:* 20 full-time (12 women); includes 3 minority (1 Asian, non-Hispanic/Latino; 2 Hispanic/Latino). Average age 24. 24 applicants, 54% accepted, 11 enrolled. *Degree requirements:* For master's, completion of clinical rotation. *Entrance requirements:* For master's, GRE, official transcripts, bachelor's degree from accredited institution, minimum undergraduate GPA of 3.0, documentation of clinical observation with supervision of certified/licensed athletic trainer, interview, essay. Additional exam requirements/recommendations for international students: Required—TOEFL (minimum score 577 paper-based; 90 iBT), IELTS (minimum score 6.5). *Application deadline:* For summer admission, 5/1 priority date for domestic and international students. Applications are processed on a rolling basis. Electronic applications accepted. *Expenses:* Contact institution. *Financial support:* In 2017–18, 1 teaching assistantship with full tuition reimbursement was awarded. Financial award applicants required to submit FAFSA. *Faculty research:* Shortwave diathermy, cryotherapy, iontophoresis, immersion clinical education,

sacroiliac joint. *Unit head:* Dr. James Scifers, Chair, 610-625-7210, E-mail: scifersj@moravian.edu. *Application contact:* Kristina Sullivan, Director of Student Recruitment Operations, 610-861-1400, Fax: 610-861-1466, E-mail: graduate@moravian.edu.

North Dakota State University, College of Graduate and Interdisciplinary Studies, College of Human Development and Education, Department of Health, Nutrition, and Exercise Sciences, Fargo, ND 58102. Offers athletic training (MAT, MS); dietetics (MS); exercise science and nutrition (PhD); exercise/nutrition science (MS); health promotion (MPH); leadership in physical education and sport (MS). *Program availability:* Part-time, evening/weekend, online learning. *Degree requirements:* For master's, thesis (for some programs). *Entrance requirements:* For master's, minimum GPA of 3.0. Additional exam requirements/recommendations for international students: Required—TOEFL (minimum score 525 paper-based; 71 iBT). Electronic applications accepted. *Faculty research:* Biomechanics, sport specialization, recreation, nutrition, athletic training.

Ohio University, Graduate College, College of Health Sciences and Professions, School of Applied Health Sciences and Wellness, Program in Athletic Training, Athens, OH 45701-2979. Offers MS. *Entrance requirements:* For master's, GRE. Additional exam requirements/recommendations for international students: Required—TOEFL (minimum score 550 paper-based; 80 iBT) or IELTS (minimum score 7.5). *Faculty research:* Athletic training, heart, injuries, health, muscles, exercise, sport.

Old Dominion University, College of Health Sciences, School of Physical Therapy and Athletic Training, Program in Athletic Training, Norfolk, VA 23529. Offers MSAT. *Faculty:* 4 full-time (3 women). *Students:* 17 full-time (10 women); includes 2 minority (1 Hispanic/Latino; 1 Two or more races, non-Hispanic/Latino), 1 international. Average age 23. 40 applicants, 18% accepted, 7 enrolled. In 2017, 8 master's awarded. *Degree requirements:* For master's, variable foreign language requirement, comprehensive exam, thesis or alternative. *Entrance requirements:* For master's, GRE, bachelor's degree, minimum undergraduate GPA of 3.0 overall and in all science/athletic training prerequisite course work, three letters of recommendation, two-page statement of career goals, current copy of resume, transcripts. Additional exam requirements/recommendations for international students: Required—TOEFL (minimum score 550 paper-based; 79 iBT). *Application deadline:* For fall admission, 1/1 for domestic students. Applications are processed on a rolling basis. Application fee: $50. Electronic applications accepted. *Expenses:* $20,336 resident full-time, $51,209 nonresident full-time. *Financial support:* In 2017–18, 15 students received support, including 15 research assistantships with partial tuition reimbursements available (averaging $15,000 per year). Financial award application deadline: 4/15. *Faculty research:* Patient outcomes, chronic ankle instability, standardized patients, student learning outcomes, lower extremity injuries. *Total annual research expenditures:* $11,040. *Unit head:* Dr. Bonnie Van Lunen, Director, 757-683-4519, Fax: 757-683-4410, E-mail: bvanlune@odu.edu. *Application contact:* William Heffelfinger, Director of Graduate Admissions, 757-683-5554, Fax: 757-683-3255, E-mail: gradadmit@odu.edu.
Website: http://www.odu.edu/ptat

Oregon State University, College of Public Health and Human Sciences, Program in Athletic Training, Corvallis, OR 97331. Offers MATRN. *Entrance requirements:* For master's, GRE, baccalaureate degree; two letters of recommendation; personal statement; minimum of 50 hours of work, volunteering and/or observation under a certified athletic trainer. *Application deadline:* For fall admission, 1/1 priority date for domestic and international students. Application fee: $75 ($85 for international students). Electronic applications accepted. *Unit head:* Kim Hannigan, Program Director, 541-737-5314, E-mail: kim.hannigan-downs@oregonstate.edu. *Application contact:* Kim Hannigan, Program Director, 541-737-5314, E-mail: kim.hannigan-downs@oregonstate.edu.
Website: http://health.oregonstate.edu/degrees/athletic-training

Pacific University, School of Physical Therapy, Forest Grove, OR 97116-1797. Offers athletic training (MSAT); physical therapy (DPT). *Accreditation:* APTA. *Degree requirements:* For doctorate, evidence-based capstone project thesis. *Entrance requirements:* For doctorate, 100 hours of volunteer/observational hours, minimum cumulative GPA of 3.0, prerequisite courses with a C grade or better, minimum GPA of 2.5 in science/statistics. Additional exam requirements/recommendations for international students: Required—TOEFL (minimum score 600 paper-based). Electronic applications accepted. *Expenses:* Contact institution. *Faculty research:* Balance disorders, geriatrics, orthopedic treatment outcomes, obesity, women's health.

Plymouth State University, College of Graduate Studies, Graduate Studies in Education, Program in Athletic Training, Plymouth, NH 03264-1595. Offers MS. *Program availability:* Part-time, evening/weekend. *Entrance requirements:* For master's, MAT, GRE General Test.

Saint Louis University, Graduate Programs, Doisy College of Health Sciences, Department of Physical Therapy, St. Louis, MO 63103. Offers athletic training (MAT); physical therapy (DPT). *Accreditation:* APTA. *Program availability:* Part-time. *Entrance requirements:* Additional exam requirements/recommendations for international students: Required—TOEFL (minimum score 525 paper-based; 55 iBT). Electronic applications accepted. *Faculty research:* Patellofemoral pain and associated risk factors; prevalence of disordered eating in physical therapy students; effects of selected interventions for children with cerebral palsy on gait and posture; hippotherapy, ankle strengthening, supported treadmill training, spirituality in physical therapy/patient care, risk factors for exercise-related leg pain in running athletes.

Salisbury University, Program in Athletic Training, Salisbury, MD 21801-6837. Offers MSAT. *Faculty:* 3 full-time (all women). *Students:* 5 full-time (2 women), 3 part-time (all women); includes 4 minority (2 Black or African American, non-Hispanic/Latino; 2 Hispanic/Latino). Average age 24. 10 applicants, 50% accepted, 5 enrolled. *Entrance requirements:* For master's, two letters of recommendation; official transcripts from all colleges and universities attended; essay; verification of current BLS certification; verification of First Aid certification; minimum GPA of 3.0. Additional exam requirements/recommendations for international students: Required—TOEFL (minimum score 550 paper-based; 79 iBT), IELTS (minimum score 6.5). *Application deadline:* For summer admission, 3/1 priority date for domestic and international students. Applications are processed on a rolling basis. Application fee: $65. Electronic applications accepted. *Expenses:* $600 per credit hour resident; $750 per credit hour non-resident; $92 per credit hour fees. *Financial support:* In 2017–18, 1 student received support. Career-related internships or fieldwork and scholarships/grants available. Support available to part-time students. Financial award application deadline: 3/1; financial award applicants required to submit FAFSA. *Faculty research:* Concussion management protocols; interprofessional education; implementing outcomes-based research in the clinical setting; assessing student learning and disposition. *Unit head:* Dr. Kelly Fiala, Graduate Program Director, Athletic Training, 410-543-6335, E-mail: kafiala@salisbury.edu. *Application contact:* Dr. Kelly Fiala, Graduate Program Director, Athletic Training, 410-543-6335, E-mail: kafiala@salisbury.edu.
Website: http://www.salisbury.edu/gsr/gradstudies/MSATpage.html

Samford University, School of Health Professions, Birmingham, AL 35229. Offers athletic training (MAT); physical therapy (DPT); respiratory care (MS); speech language pathology (MS). *Faculty:* 20 full-time (12 women), 1 part-time/adjunct (0 women). *Students:* 140 full-time (105 women), 2 part-time (both women); includes 14 minority (3 Black or African American, non-Hispanic/Latino; 1 Asian, non-Hispanic/Latino; 4 Hispanic/Latino; 6 Two or more races, non-Hispanic/Latino). Average age 24. 191

applicants, 60% accepted, 5 enrolled. In 2017, 17 master's awarded. *Degree requirements:* For master's and doctorate, capstone course. *Entrance requirements:* For master's and doctorate, GRE, recommendations, resume, on-campus interview, personal statement, shadowing hours. Additional exam requirements/recommendations for international students: Required—TOEFL (minimum score 550 paper-based). *Application deadline:* For fall admission, 10/1 for domestic students; for spring admission, 5/1 for domestic students. Application fee: $120. Electronic applications accepted. *Expenses:* $813 per credit hour. *Financial support:* In 2017–18, 36 students received support. Scholarships/grants available. Financial award application deadline: 2/15; financial award applicants required to submit FAFSA. *Faculty research:* Physical disabilities related to Parkinson's disease, neurogenic communication disorders, skeletal muscle physiology, spinal cord injuries, medical ventilation and tobacco treatment and prevention. *Unit head:* Dr. Alan Jung, Dean of the School of Health Professions, 205-726-2716, E-mail: apjung@samford.edu. *Application contact:* Dr. Marian Carter, Assistant Dean of Enrollment Management and Student Services, 205-726-2611, E-mail: mwcarter@samford.edu.
Website: http://www.samford.edu/healthprofessions

San Jose State University, Graduate Studies and Research, College of Health and Human Sciences, San Jose, CA 95192-0049. Offers criminology (MS), including global criminology, law and justice; justice studies (MS); kinesiology (MA), including athletic training, exercise physiology, interdisciplinary, sport studies, sports management; library and information science (MLIS); mass communications (MS); nursing (MS), including family nurse practitioner; nutritional science (MS); occupational therapy (MS); public health (MPH); social work (MSW); MD/M Div. *Program availability:* Part-time, 100% online, blended/hybrid learning. *Faculty:* 15 full-time (7 women), 6 part-time/adjunct (3 women). *Students:* 517 full-time (407 women), 405 part-time (302 women); includes 523 minority (39 Black or African American, non-Hispanic/Latino; 2 American Indian or Alaska Native, non-Hispanic/Latino; 141 Asian, non-Hispanic/Latino; 226 Hispanic/Latino; 2 Native Hawaiian or other Pacific Islander, non-Hispanic/Latino; 113 Two or more races, non-Hispanic/Latino), 14 international. Average age 32. 1,250 applicants, 45% accepted, 375 enrolled. In 2017, 808 master's awarded. *Degree requirements:* For master's, thesis (for some programs), graduate writing assessment. *Entrance requirements:* Additional exam requirements/recommendations for international students: Required—TOEFL (minimum score 550 paper-based; 80 iBT), IELTS (minimum score 6.5), PTE (minimum score 53). *Application deadline:* For fall admission, 2/1 for domestic and international students. Applications are processed on a rolling basis. Application fee: $55. Electronic applications accepted. *Expenses:* Tuition, state resident: full-time $7176. Tuition, nonresident: full-time $16,680. Tuition and fees vary according to course load and program. *Financial support:* Fellowships, research assistantships, teaching assistantships, career-related internships or fieldwork, Federal Work-Study, scholarships/grants, and tuition waivers (full and partial) available. Support available to part-time students. Financial award application deadline: 4/24; financial award applicants required to submit FAFSA. *Unit head:* Dr. Mary Schutten, Dean, College of Health and Human Sciences, 408-924-2900, Fax: 408-924-2901, E-mail: mary.schutten@sjsu.edu.
Website: http://www.sjsu.edu/casa/

Seton Hall University, School of Health and Medical Sciences, Program in Athletic Training, South Orange, NJ 07079-2697. Offers MS. *Degree requirements:* For master's, research project. *Entrance requirements:* Additional exam requirements/recommendations for international students: Required—TOEFL. Electronic applications accepted. *Faculty research:* Electrotherapy.

Shenandoah University, School of Health Professions, Winchester, VA 22601. Offers athletic training (MSAT); non-traditional physical therapy (MS); occupational training (MS); performing arts medicine (Certificate); physician assistant studies (MS); public health (MPH, Certificate); transitional physical therapy (DPT). *Program availability:* Part-time, all online except for two on-site weekend sessions (for DPT). *Faculty:* 35 full-time (27 women), 18 part-time/adjunct (13 women). *Students:* 446 full-time (355 women), 134 part-time (112 women); includes 78 minority (14 Black or African American, non-Hispanic/Latino; 28 Asian, non-Hispanic/Latino; 25 Hispanic/Latino; 11 Two or more races, non-Hispanic/Latino), 22 international. Average age 28. 839 applicants, 31% accepted, 166 enrolled. In 2017, 100 master's, 75 doctorates, 4 other advanced degrees awarded. *Degree requirements:* For master's and Certificate, thesis; for doctorate, comprehensive exam. *Entrance requirements:* For master's, GRE; for doctorate, GRE, minimum cumulative and prerequisite GPA of 2.8. Additional exam requirements/recommendations for international students: Required—TOEFL (minimum score 558 paper-based; 83 iBT). *Application deadline:* For fall admission, 10/1 for domestic and international students; for summer admission, 4/1 for domestic and international students. Application fee: $30. Electronic applications accepted. *Expenses:* Contact institution. *Financial support:* In 2017–18, 53 students received support. Scholarships/grants and unspecified assistantships available. Financial award applicants required to submit FAFSA. *Faculty research:* 3D motion analysis of running mechanics; quality improvement in clinical practice; functional movement screen to predict injury in professional athletes and dancers; sensory integration for children with autism; chronic ankle instability. *Total annual research expenditures:* $15,000. *Unit head:* Dr. Karen Elizabeth Abraham, Dean of School of Health Professions, 540-545-6209, Fax: 540-665-5530, E-mail: kabraham@su.edu. *Application contact:* Jon Brannon, Graduate Admissions Specialist, Office of Admissions, 540-545-7394, Fax: 540-665-4627, E-mail: jbannon09@su.edu.
Website: http://www.health.su.edu

South Dakota State University, Graduate School, College of Education and Human Sciences, Department of Health and Nutritional Sciences, Brookings, SD 57007. Offers athletic training (MS); dietetics (MS); nutrition and exercise sciences (MS, PhD); sport and recreation studies (MS). *Program availability:* Part-time. *Degree requirements:* For master's, comprehensive exam (for some programs), thesis (for some programs), oral exam. *Entrance requirements:* Additional exam requirements/recommendations for international students: Required—TOEFL (minimum score 525 paper-based). *Faculty research:* Food chemistry, bone density, functional food, nutrition education, nutrition biochemistry.

Spalding University, Graduate Studies, Kosair College of Health and Natural Sciences, Program in Athletic Training, Louisville, KY 40203-2188. Offers MS. *Entrance requirements:* For master's, transcripts, letter of recommendation, 20 observation hours, interview, writing sample. Additional exam requirements/recommendations for international students: Required—TOEFL (minimum score 535 paper-based). Application fee is waived when completed online.

Springfield College, Graduate Programs, Programs in Exercise Science and Sport Studies, Springfield, MA 01109-3797. Offers athletic training (MS); clinical exercise physiology (MS); exercise physiology (MS); sport and exercise psychology (MS); strength and conditioning (MS). *Program availability:* Part-time. *Students:* 121 applicants, 60% accepted, 36 enrolled. In 2017, 19 master's awarded. Terminal master's awarded for partial completion of doctoral program. *Degree requirements:* For master's, comprehensive exam, research project or thesis. *Entrance requirements:* For master's, GRE General Test. Additional exam requirements/recommendations for international students: Required—TOEFL (minimum score 550 paper-based); Recommended—

IELTS (minimum score 7). *Application deadline:* For fall admission, 1/15 for domestic and international students; for winter admission, 11/1 for domestic and international students; for spring admission, 11/1 for domestic and international students. Application fee: $50. Electronic applications accepted. *Financial support:* Fellowships with partial tuition reimbursements, teaching assistantships with partial tuition reimbursements, career-related internships or fieldwork, Federal Work-Study, institutionally sponsored loans, scholarships/grants, and unspecified assistantships available. Financial award application deadline: 3/1; financial award applicants required to submit FAFSA. *Unit head:* Dr. Sue Guyer, Chair, 413-748-3404, E-mail: mguyer@springfield.edu. *Application contact:* Anne Griffin, Director of Graduate Admissions, 413-748-3225, Fax: 413-748-3694, E-mail: agriffin2@springfield.edu.
Website: http://springfield.edu/gradesss

Stephen F. Austin State University, Graduate School, College of Education, Department of Kinesiology and Health Science, Nacogdoches, TX 75962. Offers athletic training (MS); kinesiology (M Ed). *Degree requirements:* For master's, comprehensive exam. *Entrance requirements:* For master's, GRE General Test. Additional exam requirements/recommendations for international students: Required—TOEFL.

Tarleton State University, College of Graduate Studies, College of Education, Department of Kinesiology, Stephenville, TX 76402. Offers athletic training (MS); kinesiology (MS). *Program availability:* Part-time, evening/weekend. *Faculty:* 10 full-time (4 women), 1 (woman) part-time/adjunct. *Students:* 45 full-time (25 women), 36 part-time (15 women); includes 25 minority (13 Black or African American, non-Hispanic/Latino; 1 Asian, non-Hispanic/Latino; 9 Hispanic/Latino; 2 Two or more races, non-Hispanic/Latino), 2 international. Average age 25. 21 applicants, 81% accepted, 17 enrolled. In 2017, 48 master's awarded. *Degree requirements:* For master's, comprehensive exam, thesis optional. *Entrance requirements:* For master's, GRE General Test, minimum GPA of 3.0. Additional exam requirements/recommendations for international students: Required—TOEFL (minimum score 550 paper-based; 80 iBT), IELTS (minimum score 6). *Application deadline:* For fall admission, 8/15 priority date for domestic students; for spring admission, 1/7 for domestic students. Applications are processed on a rolling basis. Application fee: $45 ($145 for international students). Electronic applications accepted. *Expenses:* Contact institution. *Financial support:* Research assistantships, teaching assistantships with partial tuition reimbursements, career-related internships or fieldwork, Federal Work-Study, and institutionally sponsored loans available. Support available to part-time students. Financial award application deadline: 5/1; financial award applicants required to submit FAFSA. *Unit head:* Dr. Kayla Peak, Department Head, 254-968-9824, E-mail: peak@tarleton.edu. *Application contact:* Information Contact, 254-968-9104, Fax: 254-968-9670, E-mail: gradoffice@tarleton.edu.
Website: http://www.tarleton.edu/kinesiology/

Temple University, College of Public Health, Department of Kinesiology, Philadelphia, PA 19122. Offers athletic training (MSAT, DAT); kinesiology (MS, PhD); neuromotor science (MS, PhD). *Program availability:* Part-time. *Faculty:* 17 full-time (8 women), 6 part-time/adjunct (3 women). *Students:* 52 full-time (21 women), 39 part-time (22 women); includes 25 minority (11 Black or African American, non-Hispanic/Latino; 1 Asian, non-Hispanic/Latino; 8 Hispanic/Latino; 5 Two or more races, non-Hispanic/Latino), 5 international. 78 applicants, 72% accepted, 37 enrolled. In 2017, 15 master's, 3 doctorates awarded. Terminal master's awarded for partial completion of doctoral program. *Degree requirements:* For master's, thesis, final project; for doctorate, comprehensive exam, thesis/dissertation. *Entrance requirements:* For master's, GRE General Test or MAT, minimum undergraduate GPA of 3.0, 3 letters of reference, statement of goals, interview, resume; for doctorate, GRE General Test, minimum undergraduate GPA of 3.0, 3 letters of reference, statement of goals, interview, resume. Additional exam requirements/recommendations for international students: Required—TOEFL (minimum score 550 paper-based; 79 iBT). *Application deadline:* For fall admission, 1/15 for domestic students, 12/15 for international students; for spring admission, 10/1 for domestic students, 8/1 for international students. Applications are processed on a rolling basis. Application fee: $60. Electronic applications accepted. *Expenses:* Contact institution. *Financial support:* Fellowships, research assistantships with tuition reimbursements, teaching assistantships with tuition reimbursements, career-related internships or fieldwork, Federal Work-Study, scholarships/grants, tuition waivers, and unspecified assistantships available. Financial award application deadline: 1/15. *Faculty research:* Exercise physiology, athletic training, motor neuroscience, exercise and sports psychology. *Unit head:* John Jeka, Chair, 214-204-4405, Fax: 215-204-4414, E-mail: jjeka@temple.edu. *Application contact:* Rosalind Robinson, Department Coordinator, 215-204-8707, E-mail: rosalind.robinson@temple.edu.
Website: http://cph.temple.edu/kinesiology/home

Texas A&M University, College of Education and Human Development, Department of Health and Kinesiology, College Station, TX 77843. Offers athletic training (MS); health education (MS, PhD); kinesiology (MS, PhD); sports management (MS). *Program availability:* Part-time. *Faculty:* 53. *Students:* 223 full-time (120 women), 94 part-time (53 women); includes 106 minority (42 Black or African American, non-Hispanic/Latino; 2 American Indian or Alaska Native, non-Hispanic/Latino; 5 Asian, non-Hispanic/Latino; 50 Hispanic/Latino; 7 Two or more races, non-Hispanic/Latino), 27 international. Average age 29. 161 applicants, 79% accepted, 81 enrolled. In 2017, 126 master's, 13 doctorates awarded. *Degree requirements:* For master's, thesis (for some programs); for doctorate, comprehensive exam, thesis/dissertation. *Entrance requirements:* For master's and doctorate, GRE General Test. Additional exam requirements/recommendations for international students: Required—TOEFL (minimum score 550 paper-based; 80 iBT), IELTS (minimum score 6), PTE (minimum score 53). *Application deadline:* For fall admission, 1/15 for domestic students; for spring admission, 10/1 for domestic students. Applications are processed on a rolling basis. Application fee: $50 ($90 for international students). Electronic applications accepted. *Expenses:* Contact institution. *Financial support:* In 2017–18, 204 students received support, including 2 fellowships with tuition reimbursements available (averaging $43,805 per year), 33 research assistantships with tuition reimbursements available (averaging $10,102 per year), 59 teaching assistantships with tuition reimbursements available (averaging $9,712 per year); career-related internships or fieldwork, institutionally sponsored loans, scholarships/grants, traineeships, health care benefits, tuition waivers (full and partial), and unspecified assistantships also available. Support available to part-time students. Financial award application deadline: 3/15; financial award applicants required to submit FAFSA. *Unit head:* Dr. Richard Kreider, Head, 979-845-1333, Fax: 979-847-8987, E-mail: rkreider@hlkn.tamu.edu. *Application contact:* Jenny Bilski, Academic Advisor, 979-862-4052, E-mail: jenny.bilski@tamu.edu.
Website: http://hlknweb.tamu.edu/

Texas State University, The Graduate College, College of Education, Program in Athletic Training, San Marcos, TX 78666. Offers MS. *Faculty:* 6 full-time (4 women), 1 part-time/adjunct (0 women). *Students:* 34 full-time (19 women); includes 17 minority (6 Black or African American, non-Hispanic/Latino; 2 Asian, non-Hispanic/Latino; 9 Hispanic/Latino). Average age 24. 163 applicants, 47% accepted, 20 enrolled. In 2017, 16 master's awarded. *Degree requirements:* For master's, comprehensive exam, thesis optional. *Entrance requirements:* For master's, baccalaureate degree from regionally-accredited institution with minimum GPA of 3.0 in last 60 hours of undergraduate work, statement of purpose, resume, Athletic Trainer Certification or eligible to sit for the exam,

3 recommendation forms. Additional exam requirements/recommendations for international students: Required—TOEFL (minimum score 550 paper-based; 78 iBT), IELTS (minimum score 6.5). *Application deadline:* For fall admission, 1/15 priority date for domestic and international students. Applications are processed on a rolling basis. Application fee: $40 ($90 for international students). Electronic applications accepted. *Expenses:* Tuition, state resident: full-time $7868; part-time $3934 per semester. Tuition, nonresident: full-time $17,828; part-time $8914 per semester. *Required fees:* $2092; $1435 per semester. Tuition and fees vary according to course load. *Financial support:* In 2017–18, 9 students received support, including 9 teaching assistantships (averaging $13,289 per year); research assistantships, Federal Work-Study, scholarships/grants, and unspecified assistantships also available. Financial award application deadline: 3/1; financial award applicants required to submit FAFSA. *Faculty research:* Ethnic diversity enhancement; teacher quality partnerships; the effects of different blue light photo-bio-modulation therapy. *Total annual research expenditures:* $205,438. *Unit head:* Dr. Rod Harter, Graduate Advisor, 512-245-2972, E-mail: rh56@txstate.edu. *Application contact:* Dr. Andrea Golato, Dean of the Graduate College, 512-245-2581, Fax: 512-245-8365, E-mail: gradcollege@txstate.edu.
Website: http://www.gradcollege.txstate.edu/programs/athletic-training.html

Texas Tech University Health Sciences Center, School of Health Professions, Program in Athletic Training, Lubbock, TX 79430. Offers MAT. *Faculty:* 3 full-time (1 woman). *Students:* 43 full-time (26 women), 1 (woman) part-time; includes 24 minority (8 Black or African American, non-Hispanic/Latino; 7 Asian, non-Hispanic/Latino; 9 Hispanic/Latino). Average age 25. 78 applicants, 56% accepted, 27 enrolled. In 2017, 21 master's awarded. *Entrance requirements:* Additional exam requirements/recommendations for international students: Required—TOEFL (minimum score 550 paper-based; 79 iBT). *Application deadline:* For summer admission, 2/1 for domestic students. Applications are processed on a rolling basis. Application fee: $75. Electronic applications accepted. *Financial support:* Career-related internships or fieldwork, institutionally sponsored loans, and scholarships/grants available. Financial award application deadline: 9/1; financial award applicants required to submit FAFSA. *Unit head:* Dr. LesLee Taylor, Program Director, 806-743-1032, Fax: 806-743-2189, E-mail: leslee.taylor@ttuhsc.edu. *Application contact:* Lindsay Johnson, Associate Dean for Admissions and Student Affairs, 806-743-3220, Fax: 806-743-2994, E-mail: lindsay.johnson@ttuhsc.edu.
Website: http://www.ttuhsc.edu/health-professions/master-athletic-training/

Thomas Jefferson University, College of Science, Health and the Liberal Arts, Program in Athletic Training, Philadelphia, PA 19107. Offers MS.

Trinity International University, Trinity Graduate School, Deerfield, IL 60015-1284. Offers athletic training (MA); bioethics (MA); counseling psychology (MA); diverse learning (M Ed); leadership (MA); teaching (MA). *Program availability:* Part-time, evening/weekend, online learning. *Degree requirements:* For master's, comprehensive exam. *Entrance requirements:* For master's, GRE General Test or MAT, minimum undergraduate GPA of 3.0. Additional exam requirements/recommendations for international students: Required—TOEFL (minimum score 580 paper-based), TWE (minimum score 4). Electronic applications accepted.

Universidad del Turabo, Graduate Programs, Programs in Education, Program in Athletic Therapeutic, Gurabo, PR 00778-3030. Offers MPHE. *Program availability:* Part-time, evening/weekend. *Entrance requirements:* For master's, GRE, EXADEP, GMAT, interview, official transcript, essay, recommendation letters. Electronic applications accepted.

University of Arkansas, Graduate School, College of Education and Health Professions, Department of Health, Human Performance and Recreation, Program in Athletic Training, Fayetteville, AR 72701. Offers MAT. In 2017, 15 master's awarded. *Application deadline:* For fall admission, 8/1 for domestic students, 4/1 for international students; for spring admission, 12/1 for domestic students, 10/1 for international students; for summer admission, 4/15 for domestic students, 3/1 for international students. Applications are processed on a rolling basis. Application fee: $60. Electronic applications accepted. *Expenses:* Tuition, state resident: full-time $3782. Tuition, nonresident: full-time $10,238. *Financial support:* In 2017–18, 2 research assistantships were awarded; teaching assistantships also available. *Unit head:* Dr. Bart Hammig, Department Head, 479-575-2858, Fax: 479-575-5778, E-mail: bhammig@uark.edu. *Application contact:* Dr. Stephen Dittmore, Coordinator of Graduate Studies, 479-575-6625, Fax: 479-575-5778, E-mail: dittmore@uark.edu.
Website: http://kins.uark.edu

University of Central Oklahoma, The Jackson College of Graduate Studies, College of Education and Professional Studies, Department of Kinesiology and Health Studies, Edmond, OK 73034-5209. Offers athletic training (MS); wellness management (MS), including exercise science, health promotion. *Faculty:* 7 full-time (4 women), 1 (woman) part-time/adjunct. *Students:* 31 full-time (20 women), 32 part-time (18 women); includes 19 minority (8 Black or African American, non-Hispanic/Latino; 2 American Indian or Alaska Native, non-Hispanic/Latino; 6 Hispanic/Latino; 3 Two or more races, non-Hispanic/Latino), 5 international. Average age 29. 41 applicants, 71% accepted, 13 enrolled. In 2017, 19 master's awarded. *Degree requirements:* For master's, comprehensive exam (for some programs), thesis (for some programs). *Entrance requirements:* Additional exam requirements/recommendations for international students: Required—TOEFL (minimum score 550 paper-based; 79 iBT), IELTS (minimum score 6.5). *Application deadline:* For fall admission, 12/15 priority date for domestic students, 7/15 for international students; for spring admission, 11/15 for international students; for summer admission, 3/1 for domestic and international students. Application fee: $60. Electronic applications accepted. *Expenses:* Tuition, state resident: full-time $5375; part-time $268.75 per credit hour. Tuition, nonresident: full-time $13,295; part-time $664.75 per credit hour. *Required fees:* $626; $31.30 per credit hour. One-time fee: $50. Tuition and fees vary according to program. *Financial support:* In 2017–18, 15 students received support, including 2 research assistantships with partial tuition reimbursements available (averaging $4,436 per year), 1 teaching assistantship with partial tuition reimbursement available (averaging $2,958 per year); career-related internships or fieldwork, scholarships/grants, tuition waivers (partial), and unspecified assistantships also available. Financial award application deadline: 3/31; financial award applicants required to submit FAFSA. *Unit head:* Dr. Debra Traywick, Chair, 405-974-5230, Fax: 405-974-3805. *Application contact:* Carlie Wellington, Assistant Director, CEPS Graduate Enrollment, 405-974-5105, Fax: 405-974-3851, E-mail: gradcoll@uco.edu.
Website: http://sites.uco.edu/ceps/dept/Professional-Studies-Programs/khs/index.asp

University of Evansville, College of Education and Health Sciences, School of Health Sciences, Evansville, IN 47722. Offers athletic training (MSAT); health policy (MPH); health services administration (MS). *Program availability:* Part-time, evening/weekend. *Entrance requirements:* Additional exam requirements/recommendations for international students: Required—TOEFL, IELTS (minimum score 6.5). *Expenses:* Contact institution.

The University of Findlay, Office of Graduate Admissions, Findlay, OH 45840. Offers applied security and analytics (MSAS); athletic training (MAT); business (MBA), including certified management accountant, certified public accountant, health care management, hospitality management; education (MA Ed, Ed D), including children's literature (MA Ed), curriculum and teaching (MA Ed), education (MA Ed), educational administration (MA Ed), human resource development (MA Ed), mathematics (MA Ed), reading (MA Ed), science education (MA Ed), superintendent (Ed D), teaching (Ed D), technology (MA Ed); environmental, safety, and health management (MSEM); health informatics (MS); occupational therapy (MOT); pharmacy (Pharm D); physical therapy (DPT); physician assistant (MPA); rhetoric and writing (MA); teaching English to speakers of other languages (TESOL) and applied linguistics (MA). *Program availability:* Part-time, evening/weekend, 100% online, blended/hybrid learning. *Students:* 688 full-time (430 women), 553 part-time (308 women), 170 international. Average age 28. In 2017, 366 master's, 137 doctorates awarded. *Degree requirements:* For master's, comprehensive exam (for some programs), thesis (for some programs), cumulative project, capstone project; for doctorate, thesis/dissertation (for some programs). *Entrance requirements:* For master's, bachelor's degree from accredited institution, minimum undergraduate GPA of 2.5 in last 64 hours of course work; for doctorate, GRE, MAT, minimum cumulative GPA of 3.0. Additional exam requirements/recommendations for international students: Required—TOEFL (minimum score 79 iBT), IELTS (minimum score 7), PTE (minimum score 61). *Application deadline:* Applications are processed on a rolling basis. Electronic applications accepted. *Financial support:* In 2017–18, 10 research assistantships with partial tuition reimbursements (averaging $7,200 per year), 35 teaching assistantships with partial tuition reimbursements (averaging $7,200 per year) were awarded; Federal Work-Study, institutionally sponsored loans, and unspecified assistantships also available. Financial award applicants required to submit FAFSA. *Unit head:* Christopher M. Harris, Director of Admissions, 419-434-4347, E-mail: harrisc1@findlay.edu. *Application contact:* Madeline Fauser Brennan, Graduate Admissions Counselor, 419-434-4636, Fax: 419-434-4898, E-mail: fauserbrennan@findlay.edu.
Website: http://www.findlay.edu/admissions/graduate/Pages/default.aspx

University of Florida, Graduate School, College of Health and Human Performance, Department of Applied Physiology and Kinesiology, Gainesville, FL 32611. Offers applied physiology and kinesiology (MS); athletic training/sports medicine (MS); biobehavioral science (MS); clinical exercise physiology (MS); exercise physiology (MS); health and human performance (PhD), including applied physiology and kinesiology, biobehavioral science, exercise physiology; human performance (MS). *Degree requirements:* For master's, comprehensive exam, thesis (for some programs); for doctorate, comprehensive exam, thesis/dissertation. *Entrance requirements:* For master's and doctorate, GRE General Test, minimum GPA of 3.0. Additional exam requirements/recommendations for international students: Required—TOEFL (minimum score 550 paper-based; 80 iBT), IELTS (minimum score 6). Electronic applications accepted. *Faculty research:* Cardiovascular disease; basic mechanisms that underlie exercise-induced changes in the body at the organ, tissue, cellular and molecular level; development of rehabilitation techniques for regaining motor control after stroke or as a consequence of Parkinson's disease; maintaining optimal health and delaying age-related declines in physiological function; psychomotor mechanisms impacting health and performance across the life span.

University of Idaho, College of Graduate Studies, College of Education, Health and Human Sciences, Department of Movement Sciences, Moscow, ID 83844. Offers athletic training (MSAT, DAT); exercise science and health (MS); physical education teacher education (M Ed, MS); recreation, sport, and tourism management (MS). *Faculty:* 22. *Students:* 89 full-time (41 women), 18 part-time (7 women). Average age 28. In 2017, 24 master's awarded. *Degree requirements:* For doctorate, thesis/dissertation. *Entrance requirements:* For master's and doctorate, minimum GPA of 3.0. Additional exam requirements/recommendations for international students: Required—TOEFL. *Application deadline:* For fall admission, 8/1 for domestic students; for spring admission, 12/15 for domestic students. Applications are processed on a rolling basis. Application fee: $60. Electronic applications accepted. *Expenses:* Tuition, state resident: full-time $6722; part-time $430 per credit hour. Tuition, nonresident: full-time $23,046; part-time $1337 per credit hour. *Required fees:* $2142; $63 per credit hour. *Financial support:* Research assistantships and teaching assistantships available. Financial award applicants required to submit FAFSA. *Unit head:* Dr. Philip W. Scruggs, Chair, 208-885-7921, E-mail: movementsciences@uidaho.edu. *Application contact:* Sean Scoggin, Graduate Recruitment Coordinator, 208-885-4001, Fax: 208-885-4406, E-mail: graduateadmissions@uidaho.edu.
Website: https://www.uidaho.edu/ed/mvsc

The University of Iowa, Graduate College, College of Liberal Arts and Sciences, Department of Health and Human Physiology, Iowa City, IA 52242-1316. Offers athletic training (MS); clinical exercise physiology (MS); health and human physiology (PhD); leisure studies (MA, PhD), including recreational sport management (PhD), therapeutic recreation (MA). *Degree requirements:* For master's, thesis optional, exam; for doctorate, comprehensive exam, thesis/dissertation. *Entrance requirements:* For master's and doctorate, GRE General Test, minimum GPA of 3.0. Additional exam requirements/recommendations for international students: Required—TOEFL (minimum score 600 paper-based; 100 iBT). Electronic applications accepted.

University of Kentucky, Graduate School, College of Health Sciences, Division of Athletic Training, Lexington, KY 40506-0032. Offers MS.

University of Lynchburg, Graduate Studies, MS Program in Athletic Training, Lynchburg, VA 24501-3199. Offers MS. *Faculty:* 8 full-time (5 women). *Students:* 18 full-time (9 women); includes 10 minority (5 Black or African American, non-Hispanic/Latino; 1 Asian, non-Hispanic/Latino; 1 Hispanic/Latino; 3 Two or more races, non-Hispanic/Latino). Average age 24. 19 applicants, 100% accepted, 18 enrolled. *Degree requirements:* For master's, thesis. *Entrance requirements:* Additional exam requirements/recommendations for international students: Required—TOEFL (minimum score 550 paper-based), IELTS (minimum score 6). *Application deadline:* For fall admission, 7/31 for domestic students; for summer admission, 5/1 for domestic students. Applications are processed on a rolling basis. Application fee: $30. Electronic applications accepted. Application fee is waived when completed online. *Expenses:* $645 per credit tuition. *Financial support:* Fellowships, teaching assistantships, scholarships/grants, and unspecified assistantships available. Financial award applicants required to submit FAFSA. *Unit head:* Dr. Debbie Bradney, Director of Athletic Training Programs, 434-544-8522, E-mail: bradney@lynchburg.edu. *Application contact:* Ellen Thompson, Graduate Admissions Counselor, 434-544-8841, E-mail: gradstudies@lynchburg.edu.
Website: https://www.lynchburg.edu/graduate/master-of-science-in-athletic-training/

University of Miami, Graduate School, School of Education and Human Development, Department of Kinesiology and Sport Sciences, Program in Exercise Physiology, Coral Gables, FL 33124. Offers exercise physiology (MS Ed, PhD); strength and conditioning (MS Ed). *Program availability:* Part-time, evening/weekend. Terminal master's awarded for partial completion of doctoral program. *Degree requirements:* For master's, comprehensive exam (for some programs), thesis optional, special project; for doctorate, thesis/dissertation, qualifying exam. *Entrance requirements:* For master's and doctorate, GRE General Test. Additional exam requirements/recommendations for international students: Required—TOEFL (minimum score 550 paper-based; 80 iBT); Recommended—IELTS (minimum score 6.5). Electronic applications accepted. *Faculty research:* Women's health, cardiovascular health, aging, metabolism, obesity.

Athletic Training and Sports Medicine

University of Miami, Graduate School, School of Education and Human Development, Department of Kinesiology and Sport Sciences, Program in Sports Medicine, Coral Gables, FL 33124. Offers athletic training (MS Ed). *Program availability:* Part-time, evening/weekend. *Degree requirements:* For master's, comprehensive exam, thesis optional, special project. *Entrance requirements:* For master's, GRE General Test. Additional exam requirements/recommendations for international students: Required—TOEFL (minimum score 550 paper-based; 80 iBT); Recommended—IELTS (minimum score 6.5). Electronic applications accepted. *Faculty research:* Care, prevention, and treatment of athletic injuries.

University of Nebraska at Omaha, Graduate Studies, College of Education, School of Health and Kinesiology, Omaha, NE 68182. Offers athletic training (MA); exercise science (PhD); health, physical education, and recreation (MA, MS). *Program availability:* Part-time, evening/weekend. *Degree requirements:* For master's, comprehensive exam, thesis (for some programs). *Entrance requirements:* For master's, GRE; entrance exam, minimum GPA of 3.0, official transcripts, statement of purpose, 2 letters of recommendation; for doctorate, GRE, minimum GPA of 3.2, official transcripts, statement of purpose, 3 letters of recommendation, resume, writing sample. Additional exam requirements/recommendations for international students: Required—TOEFL, IELTS, PTE. Electronic applications accepted.

The University of North Carolina at Chapel Hill, Graduate School, College of Arts and Sciences, Department of Exercise and Sport Science, Chapel Hill, NC 27599. Offers athletic training (MA); exercise physiology (MA); sport administration (MA). *Degree requirements:* For master's, comprehensive exam, thesis. *Entrance requirements:* For master's, GRE General Test, minimum GPA of 3.0. Additional exam requirements/recommendations for international students: Required—TOEFL (minimum score 550 paper-based). Electronic applications accepted. *Faculty research:* Mild head injury in sport, endocrine system's response to exercise, obesity and children, effect of aerobic exercise on cerebral bloodflow in elderly population.

The University of North Carolina at Greensboro, Graduate School, School of Health and Human Sciences, Department of Kinesiology, Greensboro, NC 27412-5001. Offers athletic training (MSAT); kinesiology (MS, Ed D, PhD). *Program availability:* Online learning. *Degree requirements:* For master's, thesis (for some programs); for doctorate, thesis/dissertation. *Entrance requirements:* For master's and doctorate, GRE General Test. Additional exam requirements/recommendations for international students: Required—TOEFL. Electronic applications accepted.

University of Northern Iowa, Graduate College, College of Education, School of Kinesiology, Allied Health and Human Services, MS Program in Athletic Training, Cedar Falls, IA 50614. Offers MS. *Program availability:* Part-time, evening/weekend. *Degree requirements:* For master's, comprehensive exam. *Entrance requirements:* Additional exam requirements/recommendations for international students: Required—TOEFL (minimum score 550 paper-based; 79 iBT). Electronic applications accepted.

University of North Georgia, Program in Athletic Training, Dahlonega, GA 30597. Offers MS. *Faculty:* 15 full-time (6 women), 3 part-time/adjunct (all women). *Students:* 44 part-time (25 women); includes 5 minority (3 Black or African American, non-Hispanic/Latino; 1 Hispanic/Latino; 1 Two or more races, non-Hispanic/Latino). Average age 26. 45 applicants, 82% accepted, 35 enrolled. In 2017, 32 master's awarded. *Degree requirements:* For master's, seminar, capstone experience. *Entrance requirements:* For master's, GRE General Test (minimum combined score of 280 on verbal and quantitative sections taken on or after August 1, 2011, 3.5 on analytical writing section), letter of intent, resume, 2 letters of recommendation, proof of minimum of 50 observation hours with a certified athletic trainer, proof of CPR certification, background check, physical and immunization forms, technical standards form signed by a physician, prerequisite courses with minimum grade of C. Additional exam requirements/recommendations for international students: Required—TOEFL (minimum score 550 paper-based; 79 iBT), IELTS (minimum score 6.5). *Application deadline:* For fall admission, 5/10 for domestic students; for summer admission, 4/1 priority date for domestic students. Application fee: $40. Electronic applications accepted. *Expenses:* Contact institution. *Financial support:* Application deadline: 3/17; applicants required to submit FAFSA. *Unit head:* Dr. Susan Brandenburg-Ayres, Dean, 706-864-1998, E-mail: susan.ayres@ung.edu. *Application contact:* Melinda Maxwell, Director of Graduate Admissions, 706-864-1543, E-mail: melinda.maxwell@ung.edu. Website: https://ung.edu/kinesiology/masters/ms-athletic-training.php

University of Pittsburgh, School of Health and Rehabilitation Sciences, Department of Sports Medicine and Nutrition, Pittsburgh, PA 15260. Offers health and rehabilitation sciences (MS), including sports medicine, wellness and human performance; nutrition and dietetics (MS). *Program availability:* Online learning. *Faculty:* 15 full-time (8 women), 3 part-time/adjunct (all women). *Students:* 55 full-time (48 women), 8 part-time (7 women); includes 8 minority (1 Black or African American, non-Hispanic/Latino; 1 American Indian or Alaska Native, non-Hispanic/Latino; 2 Hispanic/Latino; 4 Two or more races, non-Hispanic/Latino), 4 international. Average age 26. 128 applicants, 65% accepted, 28 enrolled. In 2017, 29 master's awarded. *Degree requirements:* For master's, comprehensive exam (for some programs). *Entrance requirements:* Additional exam requirements/recommendations for international students: Required—TOEFL (minimum score 550 paper-based; 80 iBT), IELTS (minimum score 6.5). *Application deadline:* For fall admission, 3/15 for domestic and international students. Application fee: $50. Electronic applications accepted. *Financial support:* In 2017–18, 6 fellowships (averaging $15,060 per year), 7 research assistantships (averaging $27,400 per year) were awarded; career-related internships or fieldwork, Federal Work-Study, scholarships/grants, traineeships, and unspecified assistantships also available. *Faculty research:* Nutrition and fitness; movement science; injury prevention and human performance; molecular transducers of physical activity; characterization of psychological resilience and readiness. *Total annual research expenditures:* $2.4 million. *Unit head:* Dr. Kevin Conley, Chair/Associate Professor, 412-383-6737, Fax: 412-383-6636, E-mail: kconley@pitt.edu. *Application contact:* Jessica Maguire, Director of Admissions, 412-383-6557, Fax: 412-383-6535, E-mail: maguire@pitt.edu. Website: http://www.shrs.pitt.edu/smn

University of St. Augustine for Health Sciences, Graduate Programs, Master of Health Science Program, San Marcos, CA 92069. Offers athletic training (MHS); executive leadership (MHS); informatics (MHS); teaching and learning (MHS). *Program availability:* Online learning. *Degree requirements:* For master's, comprehensive project.

University of South Florida, Morsani College of Medicine and College of Graduate Studies, Graduate Programs in Medical Sciences, Tampa, FL 33620-9951. Offers advanced athletic training (MS); athletic training (MS); bioinformatics and computational biology (MSBCB); biotechnology (MSB); health informatics (MSHI); medical sciences (MSMS, PhD), including aging and neuroscience (MSMS), allergy, immunology and infectious disease (PhD), anatomy, biochemistry and molecular biology, clinical and translational research, health science (MSMS), interdisciplinary medical sciences (MSMS), medical microbiology and immunology (MSMS), metabolic and nutritional medicine (MSMS), microbiology and immunology (PhD), molecular medicine, molecular pharmacology and physiology (PhD), neuroscience (PhD), pathology and cell biology (PhD), women's health (MSMS). *Students:* 372 full-time (212 women), 216 part-time (142 women); includes 257 minority (78 Black or African American, non-Hispanic/Latino;

1 American Indian or Alaska Native, non-Hispanic/Latino; 79 Asian, non-Hispanic/Latino; 84 Hispanic/Latino; 15 Two or more races, non-Hispanic/Latino), 62 international. Average age 28. 1,048 applicants, 46% accepted, 309 enrolled. In 2017, 351 master's, 56 doctorates awarded. Terminal master's awarded for partial completion of doctoral program. *Degree requirements:* For master's, comprehensive exam, thesis; for doctorate, comprehensive exam, thesis/dissertation. *Entrance requirements:* For master's, GRE General Test or GMAT, bachelor's degree or equivalent from regionally-accredited university with minimum GPA of 3.0 in upper-division sciences coursework; prerequisites in general biology, general chemistry, general physics, organic chemistry, quantitative analysis, and integral and differential calculus; for doctorate, GRE General Test, bachelor's degree from regionally-accredited university with minimum GPA of 3.0 in upper-division sciences coursework; 3 letters of recommendation; personal interview; 1-2 page personal statement; prerequisites in biology, chemistry, physics, organic chemistry, quantitative analysis, and integral/differential calculus. Additional exam requirements/recommendations for international students: Required—TOEFL (minimum score 550 paper-based; 79 iBT) or IELTS (minimum score 6.5). *Application deadline:* For fall admission, 2/1 priority date for domestic students, 2/1 for international students. Application fee: $30. Electronic applications accepted. *Expenses:* Contact institution. *Financial support:* In 2017–18, 109 students received support. *Faculty research:* Anatomy, biochemistry, cancer biology, cardiovascular disease, cell biology, immunology, microbiology, molecular biology, neuroscience, pharmacology, physiology. *Total annual research expenditures:* $45.3 million. *Unit head:* Dr. Michael Barber, Professor/Associate Dean for Graduate and Postdoctoral Affairs, 813-974-9908, Fax: 813-974-4317, E-mail: mbarber@health.usf.edu. *Application contact:* Dr. Eric Bennett, Graduate Director, PhD Program in Medical Sciences, 813-974-1545, Fax: 813-974-4317, E-mail: esbennet@health.usf.edu. Website: http://health.usf.edu/nocms/medicine/graduatestudies/

The University of Tennessee, Graduate School, College of Education, Health and Human Sciences, Department of Exercise, Sport, and Leisure Studies, Program in Exercise Science, Knoxville, TN 37996. Offers biomechanics/sports medicine (MS, PhD); exercise physiology (MS, PhD). *Accreditation:* CEPH (one or more programs are accredited). *Program availability:* Part-time. *Degree requirements:* For master's, thesis optional. *Entrance requirements:* For master's, minimum GPA of 2.7. Additional exam requirements/recommendations for international students: Required—TOEFL. Electronic applications accepted.

The University of Tennessee at Chattanooga, Department of Health and Human Performance, Chattanooga, TN 37403. Offers athletic training (MSAT); health and human performance (MS). *Students:* 42 full-time (30 women); includes 7 minority (2 Black or African American, non-Hispanic/Latino; 3 Hispanic/Latino; 2 Two or more races, non-Hispanic/Latino). Average age 23. 24 applicants, 100% accepted, 22 enrolled. In 2017, 21 master's awarded. *Degree requirements:* For master's, thesis or alternative, clinical rotations. *Entrance requirements:* For master's, GRE General Test, minimum GPA of 2.75 overall or 3.0 in last 60 hours; CPR and First Aid certification. Additional exam requirements/recommendations for international students: Required—TOEFL (minimum score 550 paper-based; 79 iBT), IELTS (minimum score 6). *Application deadline:* For fall admission, 6/15 priority date for domestic students, 7/1 for international students; for spring admission, 11/1 priority date for domestic students, 11/1 for international students. Applications are processed on a rolling basis. Application fee: $35 ($40 for international students). Electronic applications accepted. *Expenses:* Contact institution. *Financial support:* Research assistantships with tuition reimbursements, teaching assistantships with tuition reimbursements, career-related internships or fieldwork, scholarships/grants, and unspecified assistantships available. Support available to part-time students. Financial award application deadline: 7/1; financial award applicants required to submit FAFSA. *Faculty research:* Therapeutic exercise, lumbar spine biomechanics, physical activity epidemiology, functional rehabilitation outcomes, metabolic health. *Total annual research expenditures:* $16,000. *Unit head:* Dr. Marisa Colston, Department Head, 423-425-4743, E-mail: marisa-colston@utc.edu. *Application contact:* Dr. Joanne Romagni, Dean of the Graduate School, 423-425-4478, Fax: 423-425-5223, E-mail: joanne-romagni@utc.edu. Website: https://www.utc.edu/health-human-performance/

The University of Texas at Arlington, Graduate School, College of Nursing and Health Innovation, Arlington, TX 76019. Offers athletic training (MS); exercise science (MS); kinesiology (PhD); nurse practitioner (MSN); nursing (PhD); nursing administration (MSN); nursing education (MSN); nursing practice (DNP). *Accreditation:* AACN. *Program availability:* Part-time, evening/weekend, online learning. *Degree requirements:* For master's, practicum course; for doctorate, comprehensive exam (for some programs), thesis/dissertation (for some programs), proposal defense dissertation (for PhD); scholarship project (for DNP). *Entrance requirements:* For master's, GRE General Test if GPA less than 3.0, minimum GPA of 3.0, Texas nursing license, minimum C grade in undergraduate statistics course; for doctorate, GRE General Test (waived for MSN-to-PhD applicants), minimum undergraduate, graduate and statistics GPA of 3.0; Texas RN license; interview; written statement of goals. Additional exam requirements/recommendations for international students: Required—TOEFL (minimum score 550 paper-based), IELTS (minimum score 7). *Faculty research:* Simulation in clinical education and practice, cultural diversity, vulnerable populations, substance abuse.

The University of Toledo, College of Graduate Studies, College of Health and Human Services, School of Exercise and Rehabilitation Sciences, Toledo, OH 43606-3390. Offers athletic training (MSES); exercise physiology (MSES); exercise science (PhD); occupational therapy (OTD); physical therapy (DPT); recreation and leisure studies (MA), including recreation administration, recreation therapy. *Degree requirements:* For master's, comprehensive exam, thesis; for doctorate, thesis/dissertation or alternative. *Entrance requirements:* For master's, GRE, minimum cumulative GPA of 2.7 for all previous academic work, letters of recommendation; for doctorate, GRE, minimum cumulative GPA of 3.0 for all previous academic work, letters of recommendation; OTCAS or PTCAS application and UT supplemental application (for OTD and DPT). Additional exam requirements/recommendations for international students: Required—TOEFL (minimum score 550 paper-based; 80 iBT). Electronic applications accepted.

University of Wisconsin–La Crosse, College of Science and Health, Department of Exercise and Sport Science, Program in Human Performance, La Crosse, WI 54601-3742. Offers exercise sport science: human performance (MS), including applied sport science, strength and conditioning. *Program availability:* Part-time. *Students:* 16 full-time (7 women), 6 part-time (0 women); includes 1 minority (Hispanic/Latino). Average age 25. 37 applicants, 57% accepted, 13 enrolled. In 2017, 8 master's awarded. *Degree requirements:* For master's, comprehensive exam (for some programs), thesis optional. *Entrance requirements:* For master's, GRE, course work in anatomy, physiology, biomechanics, and exercise physiology. Additional exam requirements/recommendations for international students: Required—TOEFL (minimum score 550 paper-based; 79 iBT). *Application deadline:* For fall admission, 2/1 priority date for domestic and international students. Electronic applications accepted. *Financial support:* Federal Work-Study, scholarships/grants, health care benefits, and tuition waivers (partial) available. Support available to part-time students. Financial award application deadline: 3/15; financial award applicants required to submit FAFSA. *Faculty research:* Anaerobic metabolism, power development, strength training, biomechanics, athletic performance. *Unit head:* Dr. Glenn Wright, Director, 608-785-8689, Fax: 608-785-8172, E-mail: wright.glen@uwlax.edu. *Application contact:* Brandon Schaller, Senior Graduate Student Status Examiner, 608-785-8941, E-mail: admissions@uwlax.edu. Website: https://www.uwlax.edu/human-performance-ms/

University of Wisconsin–Milwaukee, Graduate School, College of Health Sciences, Department of Kinesiology, Milwaukee, WI 53201-0413. Offers athletic training (MS); kinesiology (MS, PhD), including exercise and nutrition in health and disease (MS), integrative human performance (MS), neuromechanics (MS); physical therapy (DPT). *Program availability:* Part-time. *Students:* 100 full-time (60 women), 16 part-time (9 women); includes 11 minority (1 Black or African American, non-Hispanic/Latino; 1 American Indian or Alaska Native, non-Hispanic/Latino; 9 Two or more races, non-Hispanic/Latino), 3 international. Average age 27. 36 applicants, 42% accepted, 5 enrolled. In 2017, 2 master's awarded. *Degree requirements:* For master's, comprehensive exam, thesis optional. *Entrance requirements:* For master's, GRE General Test. Additional exam requirements/recommendations for international students: Required—TOEFL (minimum score 550 paper-based; 79 iBT), IELTS (minimum score 6.5). *Application deadline:* For fall admission, 1/1 priority date for domestic students; for spring admission, 9/1 for domestic students. Applications are processed on a rolling basis. Application fee: $56 ($96 for international students). *Financial support:* Fellowships, research assistantships, teaching assistantships, career-related internships or fieldwork, unspecified assistantships, and project assistantships available. Support available to part-time students. Financial award application deadline: 4/15. *Unit head:* Dr. Kyle T. Ebersole, Department Chair, 414-229-6717, Fax: 414-229-3366, E-mail: ebersole@uwm.edu. *Application contact:* Stephen C. Cobb, Graduate Program Coordinator, 414-229-3369, Fax: 414-229-3366, E-mail: cobbsc@uwm.edu. Website: http://uwm.edu/healthsciences/academics/kinesiology/

Wayne State University, College of Education, Division of Kinesiology, Health and Sports Studies, Detroit, MI 48202. Offers athletic training (MSAT); health education (M Ed); kinesiology (M Ed, PhD), including exercise and sport science (PhD), physical education and physical activity leadership (PhD); sports administration (MA). *Program availability:* Part-time, 100% online. *Faculty:* 9. *Students:* 65 full-time (33 women), 109 part-time (56 women); includes 70 minority (59 Black or African American, non-Hispanic/Latino; 3 Hispanic/Latino; 8 Two or more races, non-Hispanic/Latino), 8 international. Average age 30. 182 applicants, 53% accepted, 56 enrolled. In 2017, 62 master's, 3 doctorates awarded. *Degree requirements:* For master's, thesis (for some programs); for doctorate, thesis/dissertation. *Entrance requirements:* For master's, minimum undergraduate GPA of 3.0; undergraduate degree directly relating to the field of specialization being applied for or one accompanied by extensive educational background in closely-related field; teaching certificates in specific areas (for some programs); for doctorate, minimum undergraduate GPA of 3.0; undergraduate degree directly relating to the field of specialization being applied for or one accompanied by extensive educational background in closely-related field. Additional exam requirements/recommendations for international students: Required—TOEFL (minimum score 79 iBT), TWE (minimum score 5.5); Recommended—IELTS (minimum score 6.5). *Application deadline:* For fall admission, 6/1 priority date for domestic students, 5/1 priority date for international students; for winter admission, 10/1 priority date for domestic students, 9/1 priority date for international students; for spring admission, 2/1 priority date for domestic students, 1/1 priority date for international students. Application fee: $50. Electronic applications accepted. *Expenses:* Contact institution. *Financial support:* In 2017–18, 47 students received support, including 6 research assistantships with tuition reimbursements available (averaging $18,534 per year), 5 teaching assistantships with tuition reimbursements available (averaging $18,534 per year); fellowships with tuition reimbursements available, scholarships/grants, health care benefits, and unspecified assistantships also available. Support available to part-time students. Financial award applicants required to submit FAFSA. *Faculty research:* Exercise and sport science, nutrition and physical activity interventions, school and community health, obesity prevention. *Unit head:* Dr. Nate McCaughtry, Assistant Dean, Division of Kinesiology, Health and Sport Studies/Director, Center for School Health, 313-577-0014, Fax: 313-577-5002, E-mail: aj4391@wayne.edu. *Application contact:* 313-577-4249, E-mail: askcoe@wayne.edu. Website: http://coe.wayne.edu/kinesiology/index.php

Weber State University, Jerry and Vickie Moyes College of Education, Program in Athletic Training, Ogden, UT 84408-1001. Offers MSAT. *Program availability:* Part-time. *Faculty:* 7 full-time (1 woman), 1 part-time/adjunct (0 women). *Students:* 30 full-time (18 women); includes 1 minority (Asian, non-Hispanic/Latino), 4 international. Average age 25. In 2017, 17 master's awarded. *Degree requirements:* For master's, thesis. *Entrance requirements:* For master's, GRE (if GPA less than 3.0), physical, immunizations. Additional exam requirements/recommendations for international students: Required—TOEFL (minimum score 525 paper-based). *Application deadline:* For fall admission, 1/15 priority date for domestic and international students. Application fee: $60 ($90 for international students). Electronic applications accepted. *Expenses:* Tuition, state resident: full-time $7283. Tuition, nonresident: full-time $17,166. *Required fees:* $898. Tuition and fees vary according to program. *Financial support:* In 2017–18, 24 students received support. Scholarships/grants available. Financial award application deadline: 4/1; financial award applicants required to submit FAFSA. *Unit head:* Dr. Valerie W. Herzog, Program Director, 801-626-7675, Fax: 801-626-6228, E-mail: valerieherzog@weber.edu. Website: http://www.weber.edu/athletictraining/graduateprograms.html

West Chester University of Pennsylvania, College of Health Sciences, Department of Kinesiology, West Chester, PA 19383. Offers adapted physical education (Certificate); exercise and sport physiology (MS), including athletic training; sport management and athletics (MPA), including administration. *Program availability:* Part-time, evening/weekend, blended/hybrid learning. *Students:* 44 full-time (24 women), 12 part-time (3

women); includes 5 minority (2 Black or African American, non-Hispanic/Latino; 2 Hispanic/Latino; 1 Two or more races, non-Hispanic/Latino), 1 international. Average age 25. 68 applicants, 87% accepted, 29 enrolled. In 2017, 13 master's, 14 other advanced degrees awarded. *Degree requirements:* For master's, thesis or research report (for MS); two internships and capstone course that includes a research project or thesis (for MPA); for Certificate, six courses of study. *Entrance requirements:* For master's, GRE (for MS), 2 letters of recommendation, statement of professional goals; transcripts (for MS); two letters of reference, career goals, resume (for MPA); for Certificate, two letters of recommendation, transcript. Additional exam requirements/recommendations for international students: Required—TOEFL or IELTS. *Application deadline:* For fall admission, 5/15 for international students; for spring admission, 10/15 for international students. Applications are processed on a rolling basis. Application fee: $50. Electronic applications accepted. *Expenses:* Tuition, state resident: full-time $9000; part-time $500 per credit. Tuition, nonresident: full-time $13,500; part-time $750 per credit. *Required fees:* $2959; $149.79 per credit. *Financial support:* Scholarships/grants and unspecified assistantships available. Financial award application deadline: 2/15; financial award applicants required to submit FAFSA. *Faculty research:* Metabolism during exercise, biomechanics, rating of perceived exertion, motor learning, environmental physiology. *Unit head:* Dr. W. Craig Stevens, Chair, 610-436-2610, Fax: 610-436-2860, E-mail: cstevens@wcpua.edu. *Application contact:* Office of Graduate Studies and Extended Education, 610-436-2943, Fax: 610-436-2763, E-mail: gradstudy@wcupa.edu. Website: http://www.wcupa.edu/healthsciences/kinesiology/

West Chester University of Pennsylvania, College of Health Sciences, Department of Sports Medicine, West Chester, PA 19383. Offers athletic training (MS). *Students:* 12 full-time (6 women); includes 2 minority (1 Black or African American, non-Hispanic/Latino; 1 Asian, non-Hispanic/Latino). Average age 24. 28 applicants, 86% accepted, 12 enrolled. *Entrance requirements:* For master's, ATCAS application, personal statement, three letters of reference, official transcripts, CPR certification. Additional exam requirements/recommendations for international students: Required—TOEFL or IELTS. *Application deadline:* For fall admission, 5/15 for international students; for spring admission, 10/15 for international students. Applications are processed on a rolling basis. Application fee: $50. Electronic applications accepted. *Expenses:* Tuition, state resident: full-time $9000; part-time $500 per credit. Tuition, nonresident: full-time $13,500; part-time $750 per credit. *Required fees:* $2959; $149.79 per credit. *Financial support:* Scholarships/grants and unspecified assistantships available. Financial award application deadline: 2/15; financial award applicants required to submit FAFSA. *Faculty research:* Heat illness, osteoarthritis, patient centered care, mental health, clinical education, manual therapy. *Unit head:* Dr. Katherine Morrison, Interim Chairperson, 610-436-3293, E-mail: kmorrison@wcupa.edu. *Application contact:* Office of Graduate Studies, 610-436-2943, Fax: 610-436-2763, E-mail: gradstudy@wcupa.edu. Website: https://www.wcupa.edu/healthsciences/sportsmed/

Western Michigan University, Graduate College, College of Education and Human Development, Department of Health, Physical Education and Recreation, Kalamazoo, MI 49008. Offers athletic training (MS), including exercise physiology; sport management (MA), including pedagogy, special physical education.

West Virginia University, College of Physical Activity and Sport Sciences, Morgantown, WV 26506. Offers athletic training (MS); coaching and sport education (MS); coaching and teaching studies (Ed D, PhD), including curriculum and instruction (PhD); physical education/teacher education (MS); sport and exercise psychology (MS); sport coaching (MS); sport management (MS). *Students:* 104 full-time (37 women), 75 part-time (28 women); includes 30 minority (12 Black or African American, non-Hispanic/Latino; 2 Asian, non-Hispanic/Latino; 9 Hispanic/Latino; 7 Two or more races, non-Hispanic/Latino), 12 international. *Degree requirements:* For doctorate, comprehensive exam, thesis/dissertation, oral exam. *Entrance requirements:* For master's, GRE or MAT, minimum GPA of 3.0; for doctorate, GRE General Test or MAT, minimum GPA of 3.5. Additional exam requirements/recommendations for international students: Required—TOEFL (minimum score 550 paper-based). *Application deadline:* For fall admission, 12/15 for domestic students, 10/1 for international students. Application fee: $60. Electronic applications accepted. *Expenses:* Tuition, state resident: full-time $9450. Tuition, nonresident: full-time $24,390. *Financial support:* Research assistantships, teaching assistantships, career-related internships or fieldwork, Federal Work-Study, institutionally sponsored loans, health care benefits, tuition waivers (full and partial), and administrative assistantships available. Support available to part-time students. Financial award application deadline: 2/1; financial award applicants required to submit FAFSA. *Faculty research:* Sport psych sociology, teacher education, exercise psychology, counseling. *Unit head:* Sean Bulger, Online Program Coordinator, 304-293-0845, Fax: 304-293-4641, E-mail: sean.bulger@mail.wvu.edu. Website: http://www.cpass.wvu.edu

West Virginia Wesleyan College, Department of Exercise Science, Buckhannon, WV 26201. Offers athletic training (MS).

Xavier University, College of Social Sciences, Health and Education, Department of Sports Studies, Cincinnati, OH 45207. Offers coaching education and athlete development (M Ed); sport administration (M Ed). *Program availability:* Part-time, evening/weekend, online learning. *Degree requirements:* For master's, thesis optional, internship or research project. *Entrance requirements:* For master's, GRE or MAT, official transcript; resume; one-page statement of career goals; 2 letters of recommendation. Additional exam requirements/recommendations for international students: Required—TOEFL (minimum score 550 paper-based; 79 iBT). Electronic applications accepted. Application fee is waived when completed online. *Expenses:* Contact institution. *Faculty research:* Coaching education, brand equity, strategic management, economic impact, place marketing.

Exercise and Sports Science

Adams State University, Office of Graduate Studies, Department of Human Performance and Physical Education, Alamosa, CO 81101. Offers human performance and physical education (MA, MS), including applied sport psychology, coaching (MA), exercise science (MA), sport management (MA). *Program availability:* Part-time. *Entrance requirements:* For master's, GRE General Test or MAT, minimum undergraduate GPA of 2.75. *Application deadline:* For fall admission, 5/15 priority date for domestic students; for spring admission, 10/15 for domestic students. Applications are processed on a rolling basis. Application fee: $30. *Expenses:* Tuition, state resident: full-time $4800; part-time $2400 per credit. Tuition, nonresident: full-time $7100; part-time $3550 per credit. *Required fees:* $213; $106 per credit. One-time fee: $100. Tuition

and fees vary according to campus/location and program. *Financial support:* In 2017–18, fellowships with partial tuition reimbursements (averaging $4,000 per year), teaching assistantships with partial tuition reimbursements (averaging $4,000 per year) were awarded; career-related internships or fieldwork, Federal Work-Study, institutionally sponsored loans, and unspecified assistantships also available. Support available to part-time students. Financial award application deadline: 4/15; financial award applicants required to submit FAFSA. *Unit head:* Dr. Marty Jones, Interim Chair, 719-587-7271, E-mail: hppe@adams.edu. *Application contact:* Caryn Chavez, Administrative Assistant III, 719-587-7208, Fax: 719-587-8230, E-mail: hppe@adams.edu. Website: http://hppe.adams.edu

Exercise and Sports Science

American International College, School of Health Sciences, Springfield, MA 01109-3189. Offers exercise science (MS); family nurse practitioner (MSN, Post-Master's Certificate); nursing administrator (MSN); nursing educator (MSN); occupational therapy (MSOT, OTD); physical therapy (DPT). *Program availability:* Part-time, 100% online. *Faculty:* 14 full-time (13 women), 10 part-time/adjunct (all women). *Students:* 286 full-time (220 women), 11 part-time (9 women); includes 75 minority (30 Black or African American, non-Hispanic/Latino; 21 Asian, non-Hispanic/Latino; 19 Hispanic/Latino; 5 Two or more races, non-Hispanic/Latino), 2 international. Average age 27. 652 applicants, 49% accepted, 109 enrolled. In 2017, 48 master's, 28 doctorates, 2 other advanced degrees awarded. *Degree requirements:* For master's, practicum; for doctorate, thesis/dissertation, practicum. *Entrance requirements:* For master's, 3 letters of recommendation, personal goal statement; minimum GPA of 3.2, interview, BS or BA, and 2 clinical PT observations (for DPT); minimum GPA of 3.0, MSOT, OT licensen, and 2 clinical OT observations (for OTD); for doctorate, personal goal statement, 2 letters of recommendation; minimum GPA of 3.0, BS or BA, 2 clinical OT observations (for MSOT); RN license and minimum GPA of 3.0 (for MSN). Additional exam requirements/recommendations for international students: Required—TOEFL (minimum score 577 paper-based; 91 iBT). *Application deadline:* For fall admission, 12/1 priority date for domestic and international students; for spring admission, 11/15 priority date for domestic and international students. Application fee: $50. Electronic applications accepted. *Expenses:* Contact institution. *Faculty research:* Teaching simulation, ergonomics, orthopedics, use of social media in health care. *Unit head:* Dr. Cesarina Thompson, Dean, 413-205-3056, Fax: 413-654-1430, E-mail: cesarina.thompson@aic.edu. *Application contact:* Kerry Barnes, Director of Graduate Admissions, 413-205-3703, Fax: 413-205-3051, E-mail: kerry.barnes@aic.edu.
Website: http://www.aic.edu/academics/hs

Appalachian State University, Cratis D. Williams Graduate School, Department of Health and Exercise Science, Boone, NC 28608. Offers exercise science (MS), including clinical exercise physiology, strength and conditioning. *Degree requirements:* For master's, comprehensive exam, thesis optional. *Entrance requirements:* For master's, GRE General Test, 3 letters of recommendation. Additional exam requirements/recommendations for international students: Required—TOEFL (minimum score 570 paper-based; 79 iBT), IELTS (minimum score 6.5). Electronic applications accepted. *Faculty research:* Exercise immunology, biomechanics, exercise and chronic disease, muscle damage, strength and conditioning.

Arizona State University at the Tempe campus, College of Health Solutions, School of Nutrition and Health Promotion, Tempe, AZ 85287. Offers clinical exercise physiology (MS); exercise and wellness (MS); nutrition (MS), including dietetics, human nutrition; obesity prevention and management (MS); physical activity, nutrition and wellness (PhD).

Arkansas State University, Graduate School, College of Education and Behavioral Science, Department of Health, Physical Education, and Sport Sciences, State University, AR 72467. Offers exercise science (MS); physical education (MSE, SCCT); sports administration (MS). *Program availability:* Part-time. *Degree requirements:* For master's, comprehensive exam, thesis or alternative; for SCCT, comprehensive exam. *Entrance requirements:* For master's, GRE General Test or MAT, appropriate bachelor's degree, official transcripts, immunization records, statement of goals, letters of recommendation; for SCCT, GRE General Test or MAT, interview, master's degree, official transcript, immunization records. Additional exam requirements/recommendations for international students: Required—TOEFL (minimum score 550 paper-based; 79 iBT), IELTS (minimum score 6), PTE (minimum score 56). Electronic applications accepted.

Ashland University, Dwight Schar College of Nursing and Health Sciences, Department of Health Sciences, Ashland, OH 44805-3702. Offers applied exercise science (MS). *Program availability:* Part-time. *Degree requirements:* For master's, practicum, inquiry seminar, thesis, or internship. *Entrance requirements:* For master's, teaching certificate or license, bachelor's degree, minimum cumulative GPA of 2.75. Additional exam requirements/recommendations for international students: Recommended—TOEFL, IELTS, TSE. *Application deadline:* Applications are processed on a rolling basis. Application fee: $30. Electronic applications accepted. *Expenses:* Tuition: Full-time $9621; part-time $4707 per credit hour. *Required fees:* $15 per semester. *Financial support:* Teaching assistantships, institutionally sponsored loans, and scholarships/grants available. Financial award application deadline: 4/15; financial award applicants required to submit FAFSA. *Faculty research:* Coaching, legal issues, strength and conditioning, sport management rating of perceived exertion, youth fitness, geriatric exercise science. *Unit head:* Dr. Randall F. Gearhart, Chair, 419-289-6198, E-mail: rgearhar@ashland.edu. *Application contact:* Bernie Bannin, Director, Graduate, Online, and Adult Admissions, 419-289-5291, E-mail: grad-admissions@ashland.edu.

Auburn University, Graduate School, College of Education, Department of Kinesiology, Auburn University, AL 36849. Offers exercise science (M Ed). *Accreditation:* NCATE. *Program availability:* Part-time. *Faculty:* 21 full-time (10 women), 2 part-time/adjunct (0 women). *Students:* 94 full-time (45 women), 31 part-time (16 women); includes 30 minority (17 Black or African American, non-Hispanic/Latino; 1 Asian, non-Hispanic/Latino; 8 Hispanic/Latino; 4 Two or more races, non-Hispanic/Latino), 8 international. Average age 26. 132 applicants, 68% accepted, 59 enrolled. In 2017, 53 master's, 8 doctorates awarded. *Degree requirements:* For master's, thesis (for some programs); for doctorate, thesis/dissertation; for Ed S, exam, field project. *Entrance requirements:* For master's, GRE General Test; for doctorate and Ed S, GRE General Test, interview, master's degree. *Application deadline:* Applications are processed on a rolling basis. Application fee: $50 ($60 for international students). Electronic applications accepted. *Expenses:* Tuition, state resident: full-time $10,974; part-time $519 per credit hour. Tuition, nonresident: full-time $29,658; part-time $1557 per credit hour. *Required fees:* $816 per semester. Tuition and fees vary according to degree level and program. *Financial support:* Research assistantships, teaching assistantships, and Federal Work-Study available. Support available to part-time students. Financial award application deadline: 3/15; financial award applicants required to submit FAFSA. *Faculty research:* Biomechanics, exercise physiology, motor skill learning, school health, curriculum development. *Unit head:* Dr. Mary E. Rudisill, Director, 334-844-1458. *Application contact:* Dr. George Flowers, Dean of the Graduate School, 334-844-2125.

Auburn University at Montgomery, College of Education, Department of Kinesiology, Montgomery, AL 36124-4023. Offers exercise science (M Ed); physical education (Ed S); sport management (M Ed). *Program availability:* Online learning. *Faculty:* 7 full-time (3 women), 1 (woman) part-time/adjunct. *Students:* 12 full-time (9 women), 18 part-time (11 women); includes 12 minority (11 Black or African American, non-Hispanic/Latino; 1 Hispanic/Latino). Average age 29. 23 applicants, 74% accepted, 10 enrolled. In 2017, 18 master's awarded. *Entrance requirements:* For master's, GRE or MAT. Additional exam requirements/recommendations for international students: Recommended—TOEFL (minimum score 500 paper-based; 61 iBT), IELTS (minimum score 5.5), TSE (minimum score 44). *Application deadline:* For fall admission, 7/15 for international students; for spring admission, 11/15 for international students; for summer admission, 4/15 for international students. Applications are processed on a rolling basis. Application fee: $25. Electronic applications accepted. *Expenses:* Tuition, state resident: full-time $6930; part-time $385 per credit hour. Tuition, nonresident: full-time $15,588; part-time $866 per credit hour. *Required fees:* $640. *Financial support:*

Teaching assistantships available. Financial award application deadline: 3/1; financial award applicants required to submit FAFSA. *Unit head:* Dr. George Schaefer, Head, 334-244-3887, Fax: 334-244-3835, E-mail: gschaefe@aum.edu. *Application contact:* Janis Bigelow, Graduate Advisor, 334-244-3135, E-mail: jbigelo1@aum.edu.
Website: http://www.education.aum.edu/academic-programs/academic-programs/kinesiology

Austin Peay State University, College of Graduate Studies, College of Behavioral and Health Sciences, Department of Health and Human Performance, Clarksville, TN 37044. Offers public health education (MS); sports and wellness leadership (MS). *Program availability:* Part-time, evening/weekend, online learning. *Faculty:* 8 full-time (4 women). *Students:* 14 full-time (7 women), 38 part-time (27 women); includes 15 minority (10 Black or African American, non-Hispanic/Latino; 1 Asian, non-Hispanic/Latino; 2 Hispanic/Latino; 2 Two or more races, non-Hispanic/Latino), 1 international. Average age 29. 66 applicants, 67% accepted, 33 enrolled. In 2017, 34 master's awarded. *Degree requirements:* For master's, comprehensive exam, thesis optional. *Entrance requirements:* For master's, GRE General Test, 3 letters of recommendation, minimum undergraduate GPA of 2.5. Additional exam requirements/recommendations for international students: Required—TOEFL (minimum score 500 paper-based). *Application deadline:* For fall admission, 8/8 priority date for domestic students. Applications are processed on a rolling basis. Application fee: $45 ($55 for international students). Electronic applications accepted. *Expenses:* Tuition, state resident: full-time $7686; part-time $427 per credit hour. Tuition, nonresident: full-time $20,268; part-time $1126 per credit hour. *Required fees:* $1529; $76.45 per credit hour. *Financial support:* Research assistantships with full tuition reimbursements, career-related internships or fieldwork, Federal Work-Study, institutionally sponsored loans, scholarships/grants, and unspecified assistantships available. Support available to part-time students. Financial award application deadline: 4/1; financial award applicants required to submit FAFSA. *Unit head:* Dr. Marcy Maurer, Chair, 931-221-6105, Fax: 931-221-7040, E-mail: maurerm@apsu.edu. *Application contact:* Megan Mitchell, Coordinator of Graduate Admissions, 931-221-6189, Fax: 931-221-7641, E-mail: mitchellm@apsu.edu.
Website: http://www.apsu.edu/hhp/index.php

Ball State University, Graduate School, College of Health, School of Kinesiology, Program in Exercise Science, Muncie, IN 47306. Offers exercise science (MA, MS), including biomechanics (MS), clinical exercise physiology, exercise physiology (MS), sports performance. *Program availability:* Part-time. *Students:* 18 full-time (9 women), 24 part-time (9 women); includes 4 minority (2 Asian, non-Hispanic/Latino; 2 Two or more races, non-Hispanic/Latino), 3 international. Average age 24. 58 applicants, 40% accepted, 18 enrolled. In 2017, 14 master's awarded. *Entrance requirements:* For master's, GRE General Test, minimum baccalaureate GPA of 2.75 or 3.0 in latter half of baccalaureate, curriculum vitae, three letters of recommendation, transcripts of all prior course work; campus visit to meet faculty and see facilities (strongly encouraged). Additional exam requirements/recommendations for international students: Required—TOEFL (minimum score 550 paper-based; 79 iBT), IELTS (minimum score 6.5). *Application deadline:* For fall admission, 1/15 for domestic students. Applications are processed on a rolling basis. Application fee: $60. Electronic applications accepted. *Financial support:* Research assistantships with partial tuition reimbursements available. Financial award application deadline: 3/1; financial award applicants required to submit FAFSA. *Unit head:* Dr. Tom Weidner, Chairperson, 765-285-5039, Fax: 765-285-8746, E-mail: tweidner@bsu.edu.

Ball State University, Graduate School, College of Health, School of Kinesiology, Program in Human Bioenergetics, Muncie, IN 47306. Offers PhD. *Program availability:* Part-time. *Students:* 1 full-time (0 women), 4 part-time (1 woman). Average age 27. 4 applicants. In 2017, 3 doctorates awarded. *Degree requirements:* For doctorate, comprehensive exam, thesis/dissertation. *Entrance requirements:* For doctorate, GRE General Test, curriculum vitae, three letters of recommendation, electronic transcripts of all prior college work, minimum graduate GPA of 3.2, approval of Human Performance Lab selection committee; campus visit to meet faculty and see facilities (strongly encouraged). Additional exam requirements/recommendations for international students: Required—TOEFL (minimum score 550 paper-based; 79 iBT), IELTS (minimum score 6.5). *Application deadline:* For fall admission, 1/15 for domestic students. Applications are processed on a rolling basis. Application fee: $60. Electronic applications accepted. *Financial support:* Research assistantships with partial tuition reimbursements available. Financial award application deadline: 3/1; financial award applicants required to submit FAFSA. *Unit head:* Dr. Scott Trappe, Director, 765-285-1145, Fax: 765-285-8596, E-mail: strappe@bsu.edu.
Website: http://cms.bsu.edu/academics/centersandinstitutes/hpl/graduateprograms/humanbioenergetics

Barry University, School of Human Performance and Leisure Sciences, Programs in Movement Science, Specialization in Exercise Science, Miami Shores, FL 33161-6695. Offers MS. *Degree requirements:* For master's, comprehensive exam, thesis. *Entrance requirements:* For master's, GRE, minimum GPA of 3.0. Electronic applications accepted. *Faculty research:* Physiological adaptations to exercise.

Baylor University, Graduate School, Robbins College of Health and Human Sciences, Department of Health, Human Performance and Recreation, Waco, TX 76798. Offers athletic training (MS); community health (MPH); exercise physiology (MS); kinesiology, exercise nutrition, and health promotion (PhD); sport pedagogy (MS). *Accreditation:* NCATE. *Program availability:* Part-time. *Faculty:* 24 full-time (11 women). *Students:* 86 full-time (52 women), 9 part-time (6 women); includes 24 minority (7 Black or African American, non-Hispanic/Latino; 3 Asian, non-Hispanic/Latino; 10 Hispanic/Latino; 1 Native Hawaiian or other Pacific Islander, non-Hispanic/Latino; 3 Two or more races, non-Hispanic/Latino), 8 international. 109 applicants, 59% accepted, 44 enrolled. In 2017, 30 master's, 3 doctorates awarded. *Degree requirements:* For master's, comprehensive exam, thesis optional; for doctorate, comprehensive exam, thesis/dissertation. *Entrance requirements:* For master's and doctorate, GRE General Test. Additional exam requirements/recommendations for international students: Required—TOEFL (minimum score 550 paper-based; 80 iBT). *Application deadline:* For fall admission, 2/1 priority date for domestic students, 2/1 for international students; for spring admission, 10/1 for domestic and international students. Applications are processed on a rolling basis. Application fee: $25. Electronic applications accepted. *Financial support:* In 2017–18, 60 students received support, including 1 research assistantship with full tuition reimbursement available (averaging $12,700 per year), 33 teaching assistantships with full tuition reimbursements available (averaging $7,650 per year); career-related internships or fieldwork, Federal Work-Study, institutionally sponsored loans, scholarships/grants, tuition waivers (full), and unspecified assistantships also available. Financial award application deadline: 2/1. *Faculty research:* Exercise testing, cardio-metabolic health, resistance exercise and training, nutritional intervention, population health, health promotion, global health epidemiology, coaching, natural resource management, stimulant misuse, diet, microbiome and colon cancer etiology. *Total annual research expenditures:* $250,118. *Unit head:* Dr. Jaeho Shim, Graduate Program Director, 254-710-4009, Fax: 254-710-3527, E-mail: joe_shim@baylor.edu. *Application contact:* Deepa Morris, Graduate Program Coordinator, 254-710-3526, Fax: 254-710-3527, E-mail: deepa_morris@baylor.edu.
Website: http://www.baylor.edu/HHPR/

Benedictine University, Graduate Programs, Program in Clinical Exercise Physiology, Lisle, IL 60532. Offers MS. *Program availability:* Part-time. *Entrance requirements:* Additional exam requirements/recommendations for international students: Required—TOEFL (minimum score 550 paper-based). Electronic applications accepted. *Faculty research:* Protein synthesis cell signaling control, aging.

Bloomsburg University of Pennsylvania, School of Graduate Studies, College of Science and Technology, Department of Exercise Science and Athletics, Bloomsburg, PA 17815-1301. Offers clinical athletic training (MS); exercise science (MS). *Degree requirements:* For master's, thesis optional, practical clinical experience. *Entrance requirements:* For master's, GRE, minimum QPA of 3.0, related undergraduate coursework, interview. Additional exam requirements/recommendations for international students: Required—TOEFL (minimum score 550 paper-based; 79 iBT), IELTS. Electronic applications accepted. *Expenses:* Tuition, state resident: full-time $10,000; part-time $500 per credit hour. Tuition, nonresident: full-time $15,000; part-time $750 per credit hour. *Required fees:* $2484; $110.75 per credit hour. $75 per term. Tuition and fees vary according to program.

Brigham Young University, Graduate Studies, College of Life Sciences, Department of Exercise Sciences, Provo, UT 84602. Offers athletic training (MS); exercise physiology (MS, PhD); exercise sciences (MS); health promotion (MS, PhD); physical medicine and rehabilitation (PhD). *Faculty:* 21 full-time (2 women). *Students:* 12 full-time (4 women), 18 part-time (11 women); includes 4 minority (3 Asian, non-Hispanic/Latino; 1 Hispanic/Latino). Average age 32. 21 applicants, 48% accepted, 6 enrolled. In 2017, 7 master's awarded. *Degree requirements:* For master's, thesis, oral defense; for doctorate, comprehensive exam, thesis/dissertation, oral defense, oral and written exams. *Entrance requirements:* For master's, GRE General Test (minimum score of 300, 4.0 on analytic writing portion), minimum GPA of 3.2 in last 60 hours of course work; for doctorate, GRE General Test (minimum score of 300, 4.0 on analytic writing portion), minimum GPA of 3.5 in last 60 hours of course work. Additional exam requirements/recommendations for international students: Required—TOEFL (minimum score 580 paper-based; 85 iBT), IELTS (minimum score 7). *Application deadline:* For fall admission, 2/1 for domestic and international students. Application fee: $50. Electronic applications accepted. *Expenses:* $5,160 per year. *Financial support:* In 2017–18, 40 students received support, including 19 research assistantships (averaging $69,400 per year), 21 teaching assistantships (averaging $38,500 per year); career-related internships or fieldwork, scholarships/grants, unspecified assistantships, and 8 PhD full-tuition scholarships also available. Financial award application deadline: 4/15. *Faculty research:* Injury prevention and rehabilitation, human skeletal muscle adaptation, cardiovascular health and fitness, lifestyle modification and health promotion. *Total annual research expenditures:* $107,348. *Unit head:* Dr. Allen Parcell, Chair, 801-422-4450, Fax: 801-422-0555, E-mail: allenparcell@gmail.com. *Application contact:* Dr. J. Ty Hopkins, Graduate Coordinator, 801-422-1573, Fax: 801-422-0555, E-mail: tyhopkins@byu.edu.
Website: http://www.exsc.byu.edu/

Brooklyn College of the City University of New York, School of Natural and Behavioral Sciences, Department of Kinesiology, Brooklyn, NY 11210-2889. Offers exercise and sports science (MS); physical education teacher (MS); sport management (MS). *Program availability:* Part-time. *Degree requirements:* For master's, comprehensive exam or thesis. *Entrance requirements:* For master's, previous course work in physical education and education, minimum GPA of 3.0, 2 letters of recommendation, essay. Additional exam requirements/recommendations for international students: Required—TOEFL (minimum score 500 paper-based; 61 iBT). Electronic applications accepted. *Faculty research:* Exercise physiology, motor learning, sports psychology, women in athletics.

California Baptist University, Program in Kinesiology, Riverside, CA 92504-3206. Offers exercise science (MS); physical education (MS); sport management (MS). *Program availability:* Part-time, 100% online, blended/hybrid learning. *Faculty:* 11 full-time (6 women), 5 part-time/adjunct (0 women). *Students:* 86 full-time (43 women), 45 part-time (21 women); includes 63 minority (20 Black or African American, non-Hispanic/Latino; 5 Asian, non-Hispanic/Latino; 35 Hispanic/Latino; 3 Two or more races, non-Hispanic/Latino), 20 international. Average age 28. 47 applicants, 62% accepted, 24 enrolled. In 2017, 55 master's awarded. *Degree requirements:* For master's, comprehensive exam or research thesis. *Entrance requirements:* For master's, minimum undergraduate GPA of 2.75; completion of course prerequisites with minimum C grade; three recommendations; 500-word essay; resume; interview. Additional exam requirements/recommendations for international students: Required—TOEFL (minimum score 80 iBT). *Application deadline:* For fall admission, 8/1 priority date for domestic students, 7/1 for international students; for spring admission, 12/1 priority date for domestic students, 11/1 for international students. Applications are processed on a rolling basis. Application fee: $45. Electronic applications accepted. *Expenses:* Contact institution. *Financial support:* In 2017–18, 11 students received support. Federal Work-Study, scholarships/grants, and unspecified assistantships available. Financial award applicants required to submit CSS PROFILE or FAFSA. *Faculty research:* Physical education pedagogy, exercise management and prevention of cardiovascular and metabolic diseases, sport management, immune function, carbohydrate oxidation. *Unit head:* Dr. David Pearson, Dean, College of Allied Health, 951-343-4298, E-mail: dpearson@calbaptist.edu. *Application contact:* Dr. Sean Sullivan, Chair, Department of Kinesiology, 951-343-4528, Fax: 951-343-5095, E-mail: ssullivan@calbaptist.edu.
Website: http://www.calbaptist.edu/mskin/

California State University, Fresno, Division of Research and Graduate Studies, College of Health and Human Services, Department of Kinesiology, Fresno, CA 93740-8027. Offers exercise science (MA); general kinesiology (MA); sport administration (MA); sport psychology (MA). *Program availability:* Part-time, evening/weekend. *Degree requirements:* For master's, thesis or alternative. *Entrance requirements:* For master's, GRE General Test, minimum GPA of 2.7. Additional exam requirements/recommendations for international students: Required—TOEFL. Electronic applications accepted. *Faculty research:* Refugee education, homeless, geriatrics, fitness.

California State University, Long Beach, Graduate Studies, College of Health and Human Services, Department of Kinesiology, Long Beach, CA 90840. Offers adapted physical education (MA); coaching and student athlete development (MA); exercise physiology and nutrition (MS); exercise science (MA); individualized studies (MA); kinesiology (MA); pedagogical studies (MA); sport and exercise psychology (MS); sport management (MA); sports medicine and injury studies (MS). *Program availability:* Part-time. *Degree requirements:* For master's, oral and written comprehensive exams or thesis. *Entrance requirements:* For master's, GRE General Test, minimum GPA of 2.75 during previous 2 years of course work. Electronic applications accepted. *Faculty research:* Pulmonary functioning, feedback and practice structure, strength training, history and politics of sports, special population research issues.

California State University, Sacramento, College of Health and Human Services, Department of Kinesiology and Health Science, Sacramento, CA 95819. Offers exercise science (MS); movement studies (MS). *Accreditation:* APTA. *Program availability:* Part-time, evening/weekend. *Students:* 14 full-time (8 women), 18 part-time (11 women); includes 11 minority (3 Black or African American, non-Hispanic/Latino; 4 Asian, non-Hispanic/Latino; 4 Hispanic/Latino), 1 international. Average age 29. 33 applicants, 67%

accepted, 14 enrolled. In 2017, 8 master's awarded. *Degree requirements:* For master's, thesis or project; writing proficiency exam. *Entrance requirements:* For master's, minimum overall GPA of 2.8, 3.0 in last 60 semester units; upper-division statistics course. Additional exam requirements/recommendations for international students: Required—TOEFL (minimum score 550 paper-based; 80 iBT); Recommended—IELTS, TSE. *Application deadline:* For fall admission, 1/28 for domestic students, 3/1 for international students; for spring admission, 9/30 for international students. Applications are processed on a rolling basis. Application fee: $55. Electronic applications accepted. *Expenses:* Contact institution. *Financial support:* Teaching assistantships, career-related internships or fieldwork, Federal Work-Study, and scholarships/grants available. Support available to part-time students. Financial award application deadline: 3/1; financial award applicants required to submit FAFSA. *Unit head:* Katherine Jamieson, Chair, 916-278-6441, E-mail: katherine.jamieson@csus.edu. *Application contact:* Jose Martinez, Graduate Admissions Supervisor, 916-278-7871, E-mail: martinj@skymail.csus.edu.
Website: http://www.csus.edu/hhs/khs

California University of Pennsylvania, School of Graduate Studies and Research, College of Education and Human Services, Department of Exercise Science and Sport Studies, California, PA 15419-1394. Offers applied sport science (MS); exercise science (MS), including group fitness leadership, nutrition, performance enhancement and injury prevention, rehabilitation science; group fitness leadership (MS); nutrition (MS); wellness coaching (MS). *Program availability:* Part-time, evening/weekend, online learning. *Degree requirements:* For master's, comprehensive exam, thesis optional. *Entrance requirements:* For master's, minimum GPA of 3.0. Additional exam requirements/recommendations for international students: Required—TOEFL (minimum score 550 paper-based; 80 iBT). *Application deadline:* For winter admission, 12/1 priority date for domestic and international students. Applications are processed on a rolling basis. Application fee: $25. Electronic applications accepted. *Expenses:* Contact institution. *Financial support:* Applicants required to submit FAFSA. *Faculty research:* Reducing obesity in children, sport performance, creating unique biomechanical assessment techniques, web-based training for fitness professionals, webcams. *Unit head:* Dr. William B. Biddington, Interim Dean, 724-938-4356, E-mail: biddington_w@calu.edu. *Application contact:* Suzanne C. Powers, Director of Graduate Admissions and Recruitment, 724-938-4029, Fax: 724-938-5712, E-mail: powers_s@cup.edu.

Carroll University, Program in Exercise Physiology, Waukesha, WI 53186-5593. Offers MS.

Central Connecticut State University, School of Graduate Studies, School of Education and Professional Studies, Department of Physical Education and Human Performance, New Britain, CT 06050-4010. Offers physical education (MS). *Program availability:* Part-time, evening/weekend. *Faculty:* 7 full-time (3 women). *Students:* 22 full-time (7 women), 30 part-time (10 women); includes 7 minority (2 Black or African American, non-Hispanic/Latino; 3 Hispanic/Latino; 2 Two or more races, non-Hispanic/Latino), 1 international. Average age 28. 29 applicants, 86% accepted, 15 enrolled. In 2017, 12 master's, 3 other advanced degrees awarded. *Degree requirements:* For master's, comprehensive exam, thesis or alternative; for Certificate, qualifying exam. *Entrance requirements:* For master's, minimum GPA of 2.7, bachelor's degree in physical education (preferred), essay, interview, letters of recommendation. Additional exam requirements/recommendations for international students: Required—TOEFL (minimum score 550 paper-based; 79 iBT); Recommended—IELTS (minimum score 6.5). *Application deadline:* For fall admission, 5/1 for domestic and international students; for spring admission, 11/1 for domestic and international students; for summer admission, 3/1 for domestic and international students. Applications are processed on a rolling basis. Application fee: $50. Electronic applications accepted. *Expenses:* Tuition, area resident: Full-time $6757. Tuition, state resident: full-time $9750; part-time $374 per credit. Tuition, nonresident: full-time $18,102; part-time $374 per credit. *Required fees:* $4635; $255 per credit. *Financial support:* In 2017–18, 11 students received support. Career-related internships or fieldwork, Federal Work-Study, scholarships/grants, and unspecified assistantships available. Support available to part-time students. Financial award application deadline: 3/1; financial award applicants required to submit FAFSA. *Faculty research:* Exercise science, athletic training, preparation of physical education for schools. *Unit head:* Dr. Carol Ciotto, Interim Chair, 860-832-2177, E-mail: ciottocaj@ccsu.edu. *Application contact:* Patricia Gardner, Associate Director of Graduate Studies, 860-832-2350, Fax: 860-832-2362.
Website: http://www.ccsu.edu/pehp/

Central Michigan University, College of Graduate Studies, The Herbert H. and Grace A. Dow College of Health Professions, School of Health Sciences, Mount Pleasant, MI 48859. Offers exercise science (MA); health administration (DHA). *Program availability:* Part-time, evening/weekend, online learning. *Degree requirements:* For doctorate, comprehensive exam, thesis/dissertation. *Entrance requirements:* For doctorate, accredited master's or doctoral degree, 5 years of related work experience. Electronic applications accepted. *Faculty research:* Exercise science.

The Citadel, The Military College of South Carolina, Citadel Graduate College, School of Science and Mathematics, Department of Health, Exercise, and Sport Science, Charleston, SC 29409. Offers health, exercise, and sport science (MS); sport management (MA, Graduate Certificate). *Accreditation:* NCATE. *Program availability:* Part-time, evening/weekend. *Degree requirements:* For master's, comprehensive exam (for some programs), internship and professional portfolio (for some programs). *Entrance requirements:* For master's, GRE (minimum combined verbal and quantitative score 290) or MAT (minimum score 396), official transcript reflecting highest degree earned from regionally-accredited college or university, minimum undergraduate GPA of 2.5, 3 letters of recommendation, resume detailing previous work experience. Additional exam requirements/recommendations for international students: Required—TOEFL (minimum score 550 paper-based; 79 iBT). Electronic applications accepted. *Expenses:* Tuition, state resident: part-time $587 per credit hour. Tuition, nonresident: part-time $988 per credit hour. *Required fees:* $90 per term.

The College of St. Scholastica, Graduate Studies, Department of Exercise Physiology, Duluth, MN 55811-4199. Offers MA. *Program availability:* Part-time. *Degree requirements:* For master's, thesis (for some programs). *Entrance requirements:* Additional exam requirements/recommendations for international students: Required—TOEFL (minimum score 550 paper-based; 79 iBT). Electronic applications accepted. *Faculty research:* Cardiovascular and metabolic responses, cardiorespiratory effects, orthostatic intolerance, lower extremity asymmetry.

Colorado State University, College of Health and Human Sciences, Department of Food Science and Human Nutrition, Fort Collins, CO 80523-1571. Offers dietetics (MS); food science and human nutrition (PhD); food science and nutrition (MS); nutrition and exercise science (MS). *Accreditation:* AND. *Program availability:* Part-time, 100% online, blended/hybrid learning. *Faculty:* 15 full-time (11 women), 2 part-time/adjunct (1 woman). *Students:* 51 full-time (42 women), 85 part-time (46 women); includes 8 minority (6 Hispanic/Latino; 2 Two or more races, non-Hispanic/Latino), 3 international. Average age 31. 114 applicants, 35% accepted, 22 enrolled. In 2017, 20 master's, 1 doctorate awarded. Terminal master's awarded for partial completion of doctoral program. *Degree requirements:* For master's, thesis; for doctorate, thesis/dissertation. *Entrance requirements:* For master's and doctorate, GRE (minimum 50th percentile), minimum GPA of 3.0; statement of purpose; resume; letters of recommendation; transcript. Additional exam requirements/recommendations for international students: Required—TOEFL (minimum score 550 paper-based; 80 iBT), IELTS (minimum score 6.5). *Application deadline:* For fall admission, 2/1 priority date for domestic and international students. Application fee: $60 ($70 for international students). Electronic applications accepted. *Expenses:* $580 per credit hour. *Financial support:* In 2017–18, 12 research assistantships (averaging $13,851 per year), 15 teaching assistantships (averaging $8,316 per year) were awarded; fellowships, scholarships/grants, and unspecified assistantships also available. Financial award application deadline: 2/1. *Faculty research:* Community-based interventions on public health outcomes; consumer food handling behavior; adult learning and assessment; food and culture issues; role of microbes in ecosystem functioning. *Total annual research expenditures:* $2.2 million. *Unit head:* Dr. Michael Pagliassotti, Department Head, 970-491-1390, E-mail: michael.pagliassotti@colostate.edu. *Application contact:* Paula Coleman, Administrative Assistant, 970-491-3819, Fax: 970-491-3875, E-mail: paula.coleman@colostate.edu. Website: http://www.fshn.chhs.colostate.edu/

Colorado State University, College of Health and Human Sciences, Department of Health and Exercise Science, Fort Collins, CO 80523-1582. Offers exercise science and nutrition (MS); human bioenergetics (PhD). *Faculty:* 9 full-time (5 women), 1 (woman) part-time/adjunct. *Students:* 25 full-time (9 women), 9 part-time (2 women); includes 5 minority (3 Hispanic/Latino; 2 Two or more races, non-Hispanic/Latino), 3 international. Average age 28. 57 applicants, 23% accepted, 7 enrolled. In 2017, 8 master's, 1 doctorate awarded. Terminal master's awarded for partial completion of doctoral program. *Degree requirements:* For master's, thesis or alternative; for doctorate, comprehensive exam, thesis/dissertation. *Entrance requirements:* For master's, minimum GPA of 3.0; personal statement; identification of faculty mentor; for doctorate, minimum GPA of 3.0; personal statement; funding plan with PhD mentor for all 4 years; bachelor's or master's degree. Additional exam requirements/recommendations for international students: Recommended—TOEFL. *Application deadline:* For fall admission, 1/1 for domestic and international students; for spring admission, 5/1 for domestic and international students. Application fee: $60 ($70 for international students). Electronic applications accepted. *Expenses:* Tuition, state resident: full-time $9917. Tuition, nonresident: full-time $24,312. *Required fees:* $2284. Tuition and fees vary according to course load and program. *Financial support:* In 2017–18, 28 students received support, including 1 fellowship with full tuition reimbursement available (averaging $19,637 per year), 8 research assistantships with full tuition reimbursements available (averaging $17,906 per year), 14 teaching assistantships with full tuition reimbursements available (averaging $16,422 per year); scholarships/grants, health care benefits, and unspecified assistantships also available. *Faculty research:* Age-related disease and disability, cardiovascular physiology, rehabilitation, neurophysiology, human performance. *Total annual research expenditures:* $1.3 million. *Unit head:* Dr. Barry Braun, Professor and Department Head, 970-491-7875, Fax: 970-491-0445, E-mail: barry.braun@colostate.edu. *Application contact:* Dr. Matt Hickey, Professor, 970-491-5727, Fax: 970-491-0445, E-mail: matthew.hickey@colostate.edu. Website: http://www.hes.chhs.colostate.edu/

Columbus State University, Graduate Studies, College of Education and Health Professions, Department of Health, Physical Education and Exercise Science, Columbus, GA 31907-5645. Offers exercise science (MS); health and physical education (M Ed, MAT). *Program availability:* Part-time, evening/weekend. *Faculty:* 6 full-time (4 women). *Students:* 19 full-time (8 women), 9 part-time (3 women); includes 13 minority (8 Black or African American, non-Hispanic/Latino; 1 Asian, non-Hispanic/Latino; 3 Hispanic/Latino; 1 Two or more races, non-Hispanic/Latino). Average age 28. 20 applicants, 65% accepted, 9 enrolled. In 2017, 14 master's awarded. *Degree requirements:* For master's, thesis optional. *Entrance requirements:* For master's, GRE, minimum undergraduate GPA of 2.75. Additional exam requirements/recommendations for international students: Required—TOEFL (minimum score 550 paper-based; 79 iBT). *Application deadline:* For fall admission, 5/1 for domestic students, 4/1 for international students; for spring admission, 11/1 for domestic and international students; for summer admission, 2/1 for domestic students, 3/1 for international students. Applications are processed on a rolling basis. Application fee: $50. Electronic applications accepted. *Expenses:* Tuition, state resident: full-time $3708; part-time $2472 per year. Tuition, nonresident: full-time $14,418; part-time $9612 per year. *International tuition:* $19,218 full-time. *Required fees:* $1605. Tuition and fees vary according to program. *Financial support:* In 2017–18, 2 students received support, including 6 research assistantships (averaging $3,000 per year). Financial award application deadline: 5/15; financial award applicants required to submit FAFSA. *Unit head:* Dr. Tara Underwood, Chair, 706-568-2485, E-mail: underwood_tara@columbusstate.edu. *Application contact:* Catrina Smith-Edmond, Assistant Director for Graduate and Global Admission, 706-507-8824, Fax: 706-568-5091, E-mail: smithedmond_catrina@columbusstate.edu. Website: http://hpex.columbusstate.edu/

Concordia University, School of Graduate Studies, Faculty of Arts and Science, Department of Exercise Science, Montréal, QC H3G 1M8, Canada. Offers M Sc.

Concordia University Chicago, College of Graduate and Innovative Programs, Program in Human Services, River Forest, IL 60305-1499. Offers human services (MA), including administration, exercise science. *Program availability:* Part-time, evening/weekend. *Degree requirements:* For master's, comprehensive exam, thesis. *Entrance requirements:* For master's, minimum GPA of 2.9. Additional exam requirements/recommendations for international students: Required—TOEFL (minimum score 550 paper-based). Electronic applications accepted.

Concordia University, St. Paul, College of Health and Science, St. Paul, MN 55104-5494. Offers exercise science (MS); orthotics and prosthetics (MS); physical therapy (DPT); sports management (MA). *Program availability:* Part-time, evening/weekend, 100% online, blended/hybrid learning. *Faculty:* 14 full-time (8 women), 22 part-time/adjunct (8 women). *Students:* 260 full-time (127 women), 20 part-time (9 women); includes 48 minority (24 Black or African American, non-Hispanic/Latino; 5 Asian, non-Hispanic/Latino; 11 Hispanic/Latino; 1 Native Hawaiian or other Pacific Islander, non-Hispanic/Latino; 7 Two or more races, non-Hispanic/Latino), 4 international. Average age 28. 218 applicants, 43% accepted, 84 enrolled. In 2017, 57 master's, 26 doctorates awarded. *Degree requirements:* For master's, comprehensive exam (for some programs), thesis (for some programs); for doctorate, at least one 8-12 week clinical rotation outside the St. Paul area. *Entrance requirements:* For master's, official transcripts from regionally-accredited institution stating the conferral of a bachelor's degree with minimum cumulative GPA of 3.0; personal statement; resume; for doctorate, GRE, official transcript from regionally-accredited institution showing bachelor's degree and minimum coursework GPA of 3.0; 100 physical therapy observation hours; two letters of professional recommendation. Additional exam requirements/recommendations for international students: Recommended—TOEFL (minimum score 547 paper-based; 78 iBT), IELTS (minimum score 6), TSE (minimum score 52). *Application deadline:* For fall admission, 4/1 for domestic students. Applications are processed on a rolling basis. Application fee: $0. Electronic applications accepted. *Expenses:* $475 per credit (for MA and MS); $810 per credit (for DPT). *Financial support:* In 2017–18, 60 students received support. Scholarships/grants and unspecified assistantships available. Financial award applicants required to submit FAFSA. *Faculty research:* Developmental screening in early childhood, cardiovascular responses to aerobic exercise. *Unit head:* Dr. Katie Fischer, Dean, 651-641-8735, E-mail: fischer@csp.edu. *Application contact:* Amber Faletti, Director of Enrollment Management, 651-641-8838, Fax: 651-603-6320, E-mail: faletti@csp.edu.

Delaware State University, Graduate Programs, College of Education, Health and Public Policy, Department of Sport Sciences, Dover, DE 19901-2277. Offers sport administration (MS). *Entrance requirements:* Additional exam requirements/recommendations for international students: Required—TOEFL (minimum score 550 paper-based). Electronic applications accepted.

Delta State University, Graduate Programs, College of Education, Division of Health, Physical Education, and Recreation, Cleveland, MS 38733-0001. Offers health, physical education, and recreation (M Ed); sport and human performance (MS). *Program availability:* Part-time, evening/weekend. *Degree requirements:* For master's, thesis optional. *Entrance requirements:* For master's, GRE General Test or MAT, Class A teaching certificate. *Faculty research:* Blood pressure, body fat, power and reaction time, learning disorders of athletes, effects of walking.

East Carolina University, Graduate School, College of Health and Human Performance, Department of Kinesiology, Greenville, NC 27858-4353. Offers adapted physical education (MS); bioenergetics and exercise science (PhD); biomechanics and motor control (MS); exercise physiology (MS); physical activity promotion (MS); physical education (MA Ed, MAT); physical education clinical supervision (Certificate); physical education pedagogy (MS); sport and exercise psychology (MS); sport management (MS, Certificate). *Students:* 72 full-time (30 women), 25 part-time (10 women); includes 21 minority (10 Black or African American, non-Hispanic/Latino; 1 American Indian or Alaska Native, non-Hispanic/Latino; 3 Asian, non-Hispanic/Latino; 4 Hispanic/Latino; 3 Two or more races, non-Hispanic/Latino), 3 international. Average age 27. 88 applicants, 68% accepted, 40 enrolled. In 2017, 35 master's, 5 doctorates, 4 other advanced degrees awarded. *Degree requirements:* For master's, comprehensive exam, thesis optional; for doctorate, comprehensive exam, thesis/dissertation. *Entrance requirements:* For master's, GRE General Test or MAT; for doctorate, GRE. Additional exam requirements/recommendations for international students: Recommended—TOEFL (minimum score 78 iBT), IELTS. *Application deadline:* For fall admission, 2/1 priority date for domestic students, 2/1 for international students. Applications are processed on a rolling basis. Application fee: $75. *Expenses:* Tuition, state resident: full-time $4749; part-time $297 per credit hour. Tuition, nonresident: full-time $17,898; part-time $1119 per credit hour. *Required fees:* $2691; $224 per credit hour. Part-time tuition and fees vary according to course load and program. *Financial support:* Research assistantships with tuition reimbursements and teaching assistantships available. Support available to part-time students. Financial award application deadline: 2/1. *Faculty research:* Diabetes metabolism, pediatric obesity, biomechanics of arthritis, physical activity measurement. *Unit head:* Dr. Stacey Altman, Chair, 252-328-2973, E-mail: altmans@ecu.edu.
Website: https://hhp.ecu.edu/kine/

Eastern Illinois University, Graduate School, College of Health and Human Services, Department of Kinesiology and Sports Studies, Charleston, IL 61920. Offers MS. *Program availability:* Part-time, evening/weekend. *Degree requirements:* For master's, comprehensive exam (for some programs), thesis (for some programs). *Entrance requirements:* For master's, minimum GPA of 3.0 with kinesiology focus, three letters of recommendation, resume, personal statement. Additional exam requirements/recommendations for international students: Required—TOEFL (minimum score 500 paper-based; 61 iBT), IELTS (minimum score 6). *Application deadline:* For fall admission, 5/15 for domestic and international students; for spring admission, 10/15 for domestic and international students. Applications are processed on a rolling basis. Application fee: $30. Electronic applications accepted. *Financial support:* Teaching assistantships with full tuition reimbursements, career-related internships or fieldwork, Federal Work-Study, and unspecified assistantships available. Support available to part-time students. Financial award application deadline: 3/1; financial award applicants required to submit FAFSA. *Unit head:* Dr. Scott Ronspies, Graduate Coordinator, 217-581-7594, Fax: 217-581-7973, E-mail: sronspies@eiu.edu. *Application contact:* Dr. Scott Ronspies, Graduate Coordinator, 217-581-7594, Fax: 217-581-7973, E-mail: sronspies@eiu.edu.
Website: http://www.eiu.edu/kssgrad/

Eastern Kentucky University, The Graduate School, College of Health Sciences, Department of Exercise and Sport Science, Richmond, KY 40475-3102. Offers exercise and sport science (MS); exercise and wellness (MS); sports administration (MS). *Program availability:* Part-time. *Entrance requirements:* For master's, GRE General Test (minimum score 700 verbal and quantitative), minimum GPA of 2.5 (for most), minimum GPA of 3.0 (analytical writing). *Faculty research:* Nutrition and exercise.

Eastern Michigan University, Graduate School, College of Health and Human Services, School of Health Promotion and Human Performance, Programs in Exercise Physiology, Ypsilanti, MI 48197. Offers exercise physiology (MS); sports medicine-biomechanics (MS); sports medicine-corporate adult fitness (MS); sports medicine-exercise physiology (MS). *Program availability:* Part-time, evening/weekend. *Students:* 9 full-time (3 women), 13 part-time (5 women); includes 5 minority (2 Black or African American, non-Hispanic/Latino; 1 Asian, non-Hispanic/Latino; 1 Hispanic/Latino; 1 Two or more races, non-Hispanic/Latino), 1 international. Average age 29. 43 applicants, 56% accepted, 7 enrolled. In 2017, 13 master's awarded. *Degree requirements:* For master's, comprehensive exam, thesis or 450-hour internship. *Entrance requirements:* Additional exam requirements/recommendations for international students: Required—TOEFL. *Application deadline:* For fall admission, 8/1 for domestic students, 5/1 for international students; for winter admission, 12/1 for domestic students, 10/1 for international students; for spring admission, 3/15 for domestic students, 3/1 for international students. Application fee: $45. *Application contact:* Dr. Becca Moore, Program Coordinator, 734-487-2824, Fax: 734-487-2024, E-mail: rmoore41@emich.edu.

Eastern New Mexico University, Graduate School, College of Education and Technology, Department of Health and Physical Education, Portales, NM 88130. Offers sport administration (MS), including coaching, sport science. *Program availability:* Part-time. *Degree requirements:* For master's, comprehensive exam, thesis optional. *Entrance requirements:* For master's, minimum GPA of 3.0, 15 hours of leveling courses without bachelor's degree in physical education, two references. Additional exam requirements/recommendations for international students: Required—TOEFL (minimum score 550 paper-based; 79 iBT), IELTS (minimum score 6). *Application deadline:* For fall admission, 7/20 priority date for domestic students, 6/20 priority date for international students; for spring admission, 12/15 priority date for domestic students, 11/15 priority date for international students. Applications are processed on a rolling basis. Application fee: $10. Electronic applications accepted. *Financial support:* Applicants required to submit FAFSA. *Unit head:* Dr. Beth Birky, Graduate Coordinator, 575-562-2683, E-mail: beth.birky@enmu.edu. *Application contact:* Cheryl Reeves, Senior Secretary, 575-562-2443, Fax: 575-562-2559, E-mail: cheryl.reeves@enmu.edu.
Website: http://education.enmu.edu

Eastern Washington University, Graduate Studies, College of Arts, Letters and Education, Department of Physical Education, Health and Recreation, Cheney, WA 99004-2431. Offers exercise science (MS); sports and recreation administration (MS). *Faculty:* 7. *Students:* 15 full-time (6 women), 2 part-time (1 woman); includes 1 minority (Black or African American, non-Hispanic/Latino), 1 international. Average age 28. 34 applicants, 26% accepted, 8 enrolled. In 2017, 5 master's awarded. *Degree requirements:* For master's, comprehensive exam, thesis or alternative. *Entrance requirements:* For master's, minimum GPA of 3.0. Additional exam requirements/recommendations for international students: Required—TOEFL (minimum score 580 paper-based; 92 iBT), IELTS (minimum score 7), PTE (minimum score 63). *Application deadline:* For fall admission, 4/1 priority date for domestic students; for spring admission, 1/15 for domestic students. Applications are processed on a rolling basis. Application fee: $50. Electronic applications accepted. *Expenses:* Tuition, state resident: full-time $11,191; part-time $373.06 per credit. Tuition, nonresident: full-time $25,995; part-time $866.52 per credit. *Financial support:* Teaching assistantships with partial tuition reimbursements, career-related internships or fieldwork, Federal Work-Study, institutionally sponsored loans, and scholarships/grants available. Support available to part-time students. Financial award application deadline: 2/1; financial award applicants required to submit FAFSA. *Unit head:* Dr. Chadron Hazelbaker, Graduate Program Director, 509-359-2486, Fax: 509-359-4833, E-mail: chazelbaker@ewu.edu.

East Tennessee State University, School of Graduate Studies, College of Education, Department of Sport, Exercise, Recreation, and Kinesiology, Johnson City, TN 37614-1701. Offers sport management (MA); sport physiology and performance (PhD), including sport performance, sport physiology; sport science and coach education (MS), including applied sport science, strength and conditioning. *Program availability:* Part-time, evening/weekend. Terminal master's awarded for partial completion of doctoral program. *Degree requirements:* For master's, comprehensive exam, thesis or internship; for doctorate, comprehensive exam, thesis/dissertation, 2-semester residency. *Entrance requirements:* For master's, GRE General Test or GMAT, undergraduate degree in related field; minimum GPA of 3.0; resume; three references; essay explaining goals and reasons for pursuing degree; for doctorate, GRE, resume; 4 letters of recommendation; master's or bachelor's degree in related field; minimum GPA of 3.4 overall with master's, 3.0 with bachelor's; interview. Additional exam requirements/recommendations for international students: Required—TOEFL (minimum score 550 paper-based; 79 iBT). *Application deadline:* For fall admission, 6/1 for domestic students, 4/29 for international students; for spring admission, 11/1 for domestic students, 9/29 for international students. Application fee: $55 ($65 for international students). Electronic applications accepted. *Financial support:* Fellowships, research assistantships with full tuition reimbursements, teaching assistantships with full tuition reimbursements, career-related internships or fieldwork, institutionally sponsored loans, scholarships/grants, and unspecified assistantships available. Financial award application deadline: 7/1; financial award applicants required to submit FAFSA. *Faculty research:* Methods of training for individual and team sports, enhancing acute sport performance, fatigue management in athletes, risk management, facilities management, motorsport. *Unit head:* Dr. Mike Ramsey, Chair, 423-439-4375, Fax: 423-439-7560, E-mail: ramseym@etsu.edu. *Application contact:* Dr. Mike Stone, Graduate Program Coordinator, 423-439-5796, Fax: 423-439-5624, E-mail: stonem@etsu.edu. Website: http://www.etsu.edu/coe/serk/

Fairmont State University, Programs in Education, Fairmont, WV 26554. Offers digital media, new literacies and learning (M Ed); education (MAT); exercise science, fitness and wellness (M Ed); professional studies (M Ed); reading (M Ed); special education (M Ed). *Accreditation:* NCATE. *Program availability:* Part-time, evening/weekend, 100% online. *Entrance requirements:* For master's, GRE. Additional exam requirements/recommendations for international students: Required—TOEFL (minimum score 80 iBT), IELTS (minimum score 6.5). Electronic applications accepted.

Florida Atlantic University, College of Education, Department of Exercise Science and Health Promotion, Boca Raton, FL 33431-0991. Offers MS. *Program availability:* Part-time, evening/weekend. *Faculty:* 6 full-time (2 women). *Students:* 40 full-time (16 women), 10 part-time (6 women); includes 13 minority (5 Black or African American, non-Hispanic/Latino; 7 Hispanic/Latino; 1 Two or more races, non-Hispanic/Latino), 2 international. Average age 26. 73 applicants, 52% accepted, 20 enrolled. In 2017, 29 master's awarded. *Degree requirements:* For master's, comprehensive exam, thesis optional. *Entrance requirements:* For master's, GRE General Test, minimum GPA of 3.0 during last 60 hours of course work. Additional exam requirements/recommendations for international students: Required—TOEFL (minimum score 500 paper-based; 61 iBT), IELTS (minimum score 6). *Application deadline:* For fall admission, 7/1 priority date for domestic students, 2/15 for international students; for spring admission, 11/1 priority date for domestic students, 7/15 for international students. Applications are processed on a rolling basis. Application fee: $30. *Expenses:* Tuition, state resident: full-time $7400; part-time $369.82 per credit. Tuition, nonresident: full-time $20,496; part-time $1042.81 per credit. *Financial support:* Research assistantships with partial tuition reimbursements, teaching assistantships with partial tuition reimbursements, and career-related internships or fieldwork available. *Faculty research:* Pulmonary limitations during exercise, metabolism regulation, determinants of performance, age-related change in functional mobility and geriatric exercise, behavioral change aimed at promoting active lifestyles. *Unit head:* Dr. Michael Whitehurst, 561-297-2938, E-mail: eshpinfo@fau.edu. Website: http://www.coe.fau.edu/academicdepartments/eshp/

Florida State University, The Graduate School, College of Human Sciences, Department of Nutrition, Food and Exercise Sciences, Tallahassee, FL 32306-1493. Offers exercise physiology (MS, PhD); nutrition and food science (MS, PhD), including clinical nutrition (MS), food science, human nutrition (PhD), nutrition education and health promotion (MS), nutrition science (MS); sports nutrition (MS); sports sciences (MS). *Program availability:* Part-time. *Faculty:* 21 full-time (8 women). *Students:* 86 full-time (56 women), 5 part-time (2 women); includes 13 minority (1 Black or African American, non-Hispanic/Latino; 1 Asian, non-Hispanic/Latino; 2 Hispanic/Latino; 9 Two or more races, non-Hispanic/Latino), 17 international. 116 applicants, 57% accepted, 29 enrolled. In 2017, 23 master's, 9 doctorates awarded. *Degree requirements:* For master's, thesis optional; for doctorate, thesis/dissertation, preliminary examination, minimum of 24 credit hours dissertation, dissertation defense. *Entrance requirements:* For master's and doctorate, GRE General Test, minimum upper-division GPA of 3.0. Additional exam requirements/recommendations for international students: Required—TOEFL (minimum score 550 paper-based; 80 iBT). *Application deadline:* For fall admission, 4/1 for domestic and international students; for spring admission, 10/1 for domestic and international students. Applications are processed on a rolling basis. Application fee: $30. Electronic applications accepted. *Expenses:* $480 per credit hour in-state; $1,111 per credit hour out-of-state. *Financial support:* In 2017–18, 53 students received support, including 22 research assistantships with full tuition reimbursements available (averaging $9,446 per year), 36 teaching assistantships with full tuition reimbursements available (averaging $14,725 per year); career-related internships or fieldwork, Federal Work-Study, institutionally sponsored loans, scholarships/grants, and unspecified assistantships also available. Financial award application deadline: 2/1; financial award applicants required to submit FAFSA. *Faculty research:* Body

composition, functional food, chronic disease and aging response; food safety, food allergy, and safety/quality detection methods; sports nutrition, energy and human performance; strength training, functional performance, cardiovascular physiology, sarcopenia. *Total annual research expenditures:* $613,329. *Unit head:* Dr. Chester Ray, Department Chair, 850-644-1850, Fax: 850-645-5000, E-mail: caray@fsu.edu. *Application contact:* Mary-Sue McLemore, Academic Support Assistant, 850-644-1117, E-mail: mmclemore@fsu.edu. Website: https://humansciences.fsu.edu/nutrition-food-exercise-sciences/students/graduate-programs/

Gannon University, School of Graduate Studies, Morosky College of Health Professions and Sciences, School of Health Professions, Program in Sport and Exercise Science, Erie, PA 16541-0001. Offers human performance (MS). *Program availability:* Part-time, evening/weekend. *Degree requirements:* For master's, thesis (for some programs), internship (for some programs). *Entrance requirements:* For master's, undergraduate degree in exercise science, kinesiology, human performance, sports medicine, or related field with minimum GPA of 2.75; 3 letters of recommendation. Additional exam requirements/recommendations for international students: Required—TOEFL (minimum score 79 iBT). Electronic applications accepted. Application fee is waived when completed online.

Gardner-Webb University, Graduate School, Department of Physical Education, Wellness, and Sport Studies, Boiling Springs, NC 28017. Offers sport science and pedagogy (MA). *Program availability:* Part-time, evening/weekend. *Faculty:* 2 full-time (1 woman). *Students:* 1 (woman) full-time, 9 part-time (2 women); includes 1 minority (Asian, non-Hispanic/Latino). Average age 24. 27 applicants, 48% accepted, 7 enrolled. In 2017, 5 master's awarded. *Degree requirements:* For master's, comprehensive exam. *Entrance requirements:* For master's, GRE General Test or NTE, PRAXIS, minimum GPA of 2.5. *Application deadline:* For fall admission, 8/1 priority date for domestic students. Applications are processed on a rolling basis. Application fee: $0. Electronic applications accepted. *Expenses:* Contact institution. *Financial support:* Unspecified assistantships available. *Unit head:* Dr. Ken Baker, Chair, 704-406-4481, Fax: 704-406-4739. *Application contact:* Office of Graduate Admissions, 877-498-4723, Fax: 704-406-3895, E-mail: gradinfo@gardner-webb.edu.

George Mason University, College of Education and Human Development, School of Recreation, Health and Tourism, Manassas, VA 20110. Offers athletic training (MS); exercise, fitness, and health promotion (MS), including advanced practitioner, wellness practitioner; international sport management (Certificate); recreation, health and tourism (Certificate); sport management (MS), including sport and recreation studies. *Program availability:* Part-time, evening/weekend. *Faculty:* 29 full-time (13 women), 87 part-time/adjunct (48 women). *Students:* 62 full-time (24 women), 23 part-time (11 women); includes 27 minority (20 Black or African American, non-Hispanic/Latino; 1 Asian, non-Hispanic/Latino; 3 Hispanic/Latino; 1 Native Hawaiian or other Pacific Islander, non-Hispanic/Latino; 2 Two or more races, non-Hispanic/Latino), 8 international. Average age 26. 74 applicants, 93% accepted, 46 enrolled. In 2017, 20 master's awarded. *Degree requirements:* For master's, thesis optional. *Entrance requirements:* For master's, 3 letters of recommendation; official transcripts; expanded goals statement; undergraduate course in statistics and minimum GPA of 3.0 in last 60 credit hours and overall (for MS in sport and recreation studies); baccalaureate degree related to kinesiology, exercise science or athletic training (for MS in exercise, fitness and health promotion). Additional exam requirements/recommendations for international students: Required—TOEFL (minimum score 575 paper-based; 88 iBT), IELTS (minimum score 6.5), PTE (minimum score 59). *Application deadline:* For fall admission, 4/2 priority date for domestic and international students; for spring admission, 11/1 for domestic and international students. Application fee: $75 ($80 for international students). Electronic applications accepted. *Expenses:* Tuition, state resident: full-time $11,228; part-time $459.50 per credit. Tuition, nonresident: full-time $30,932; part-time $1280.50 per credit. *Required fees:* $3252; $135.50 per credit. Part-time tuition and fees vary according to course load and program. *Financial support:* In 2017–18, 1 student received support, including 1 research assistantship with tuition reimbursement available; career-related internships or fieldwork, Federal Work-Study, scholarships/grants, unspecified assistantships, and health care benefits (for full-time research or teaching assistantship recipients) also available. Support available to part-time students. Financial award application deadline: 3/1; financial award applicants required to submit FAFSA. *Faculty research:* Sport for development and peace, sport analytics, leadership and coaching, diversity and inclusion in sport, sport communication. *Total annual research expenditures:* $826,386. *Unit head:* Martin Ford, Senior Associate Dean, 703-993-2004, E-mail: mford@gmu.edu. *Application contact:* Lindsey Olson, Office Assistant, 703-993-2098, Fax: 703-993-2025, E-mail: lolson7@gmu.edu. Website: http://rht.gmu.edu/

The George Washington University, Milken Institute School of Public Health, Department of Exercise and Nutrition Sciences, Washington, DC 20052. Offers MS. *Students:* 7 full-time (3 women), 6 part-time (2 women); includes 2 minority (1 Black or African American, non-Hispanic/Latino; 1 Two or more races, non-Hispanic/Latino). Average age 28. 17 applicants, 76% accepted, 9 enrolled. In 2017, 7 master's awarded. *Degree requirements:* For master's, comprehensive exam, thesis. *Entrance requirements:* For master's, GRE General Test or MAT. Additional exam requirements/recommendations for international students: Required—TOEFL. *Application deadline:* For fall admission, 4/15 priority date for domestic students, 4/15 for international students; for spring admission, 11/1 for domestic and international students. Applications are processed on a rolling basis. Application fee: $75. *Expenses: Tuition:* Full-time $28,800; part-time $1655 per credit hour. *Required fees:* $45; $2.75 per credit hour. *Financial support:* In 2017–18, 12 students received support. Tuition waivers available. Financial award application deadline: 2/15. *Faculty research:* Fitness and cardiac rehabilitation, exercise testing, women in exercise. *Unit head:* Dr. Loretta DiPietro, Chair, 202-994-4910, Fax: 202-994-1420, E-mail: ldp1@gwu.edu. *Application contact:* Jane Smith, Director of Admissions, 202-994-0248, Fax: 202-994-1860, E-mail: sphhsinfo@gwumc.edu.

Georgia College & State University, Graduate School, College of Health Sciences, School of Health and Human Performance, Milledgeville, GA 31061. Offers health and human performance (MS), including health performance, health promotion; kinesiology/health education (MAT). *Accreditation:* NCATE (one or more programs are accredited). *Program availability:* Part-time, 100% online. *Faculty:* 19 full-time (9 women). *Students:* 35 full-time (20 women), 17 part-time (10 women); includes 9 minority (3 Black or African American, non-Hispanic/Latino; 5 Hispanic/Latino; 1 Two or more races, non-Hispanic/Latino), 2 international. Average age 27. 21 applicants, 100% accepted, 19 enrolled. In 2017, 21 master's awarded. *Degree requirements:* For master's, thesis (for some programs), completed in 6 years with minimum GPA of 3.0 (for MS); minimum GPA of 3.0 and electronic teaching portfolio (for MAT). *Entrance requirements:* For master's, GRE with minimum score of 297 or MAT with minimum score of 385 (for MS); GRE with minimum score of 297, MAT 385, SAT 1000, ACT 43, or GACE with 250 on each section (for MAT), resume, 3 professional references; minimum GPA of 2.75 in upper-level undergraduate courses and undergraduate statistics course (for MS); minimum GPA of 2.75 on upper-division major courses (for MAT). *Application deadline:* For fall admission, 7/15 priority date for domestic students, 4/1 for international students; for spring

Exercise and Sports Science

admission, 11/15 priority date for domestic students, 9/1 for international students; for summer admission, 4/15 priority date for domestic students. Applications are processed on a rolling basis. Application fee: $40. Electronic applications accepted. *Expenses:* Contact institution. *Financial support:* In 2017–18, 22 students received support. Unspecified assistantships available. Support available to part-time students. Financial award application deadline: 3/1; financial award applicants required to submit FAFSA. *Unit head:* Dr. Lisa Griffin, Director, School of Health and Human Performance, 478-445-4072, Fax: 478-445-4074, E-mail: lisa.griffin@gcsu.edu.
Website: http://www.gcsu.edu/health/shhp

Georgia Southern University–Armstrong Campus, College of Graduate Studies, Program in Sports Medicine, Savannah, GA 31419-1997. Offers sports medicine (MSSM); strength and conditioning (Certificate). *Program availability:* Part-time. *Faculty:* 4 full-time (0 women). *Students:* 16 full-time (7 women), 2 part-time (0 women); includes 7 minority (6 Black or African American, non-Hispanic/Latino; 1 Asian, non-Hispanic/Latino). Average age 25. 49 applicants, 24% accepted, 5 enrolled. In 2017, 10 master's awarded. *Degree requirements:* For master's, comprehensive exam, thesis optional, project. *Entrance requirements:* For master's, GRE General Test, GMAT, minimum GPA of 2.7, letter of intent. Additional exam requirements/recommendations for international students: Required—TOEFL (minimum score 523 paper-based; 70 iBT). *Application deadline:* For fall admission, 6/1 priority date for domestic students, 5/1 priority date for international students; for spring admission, 11/15 priority date for domestic students, 9/15 priority date for international students; for summer admission, 4/15 for domestic students, 9/15 for international students. Applications are processed on a rolling basis. Application fee: $30. Electronic applications accepted. *Expenses:* Tuition, state resident: part-time $211 per credit hour. Tuition, nonresident: part-time $782 per credit hour. *Required fees:* $737 per semester. Tuition and fees vary according to course load, degree level, campus/location and program. *Financial support:* In 2017–18, research assistantships with full tuition reimbursements (averaging $5,000 per year) were awarded; scholarships/grants, tuition waivers (full), and unspecified assistantships also available. Financial award application deadline: 3/15; financial award applicants required to submit FAFSA. *Unit head:* Dr. Robert LeFavi, Department Head, 912-921-3208, Fax: 912-344-3490, E-mail: robert.lefavi@armstrong.edu. *Application contact:* McKenzie Peterman, Graduate Admissions Specialist, 912-478-5678, Fax: 912-478-0740, E-mail: mpeterman@georgiasouthern.edu.
Website: http://www.armstrong.edu/Majors/degree/sports_medicine1

Georgia State University, College of Education and Human Development, Department of Kinesiology and Health, Program in Exercise Science, Atlanta, GA 30302-3083. Offers MS. *Entrance requirements:* For master's, GRE General Test, minimum GPA of 2.5. Application fee: $50. *Expenses:* Tuition, state resident: full-time $7020. Tuition, nonresident: full-time $22,518. *Required fees:* $2128. Tuition and fees vary according to degree level and program. *Financial support:* Research assistantships available. *Faculty research:* Aging, exercise metabolism, biomechanics and ergonomics, blood pressure regulation, exercise performance. *Unit head:* Dr. Jacalyn Lea Lund, Chair, 404-413-8051, E-mail: jlund@gsu.edu. *Application contact:* Dr. Christopher Ingalls, Program Coordinator, 404-413-8377, E-mail: cingalls@gsu.edu.
Website: http://kh.education.gsu.edu/academics-admissions/exercise-science/exercise-science-b-s/

Hofstra University, School of Health Professions and Human Services, Programs in Health, Hempstead, NY 11549. Offers foundations of public health (Advanced Certificate); health administration (MHA); health informatics (MS); occupational therapy (MS); public health (MPH); security and privacy in health information systems (Advanced Certificate); sports science (MS), including exercise physiology, strength and conditioning; teacher of students with speech-language disabilities (Advanced Certificate). *Program availability:* Part-time, evening/weekend. *Students:* 257 full-time (176 women), 128 part-time (95 women); includes 197 minority (76 Black or African American, non-Hispanic/Latino; 2 American Indian or Alaska Native, non-Hispanic/Latino; 70 Asian, non-Hispanic/Latino; 42 Hispanic/Latino; 6 Native Hawaiian or other Pacific Islander, non-Hispanic/Latino; 1 Two or more races, non-Hispanic/Latino), 25 international. Average age 28. 620 applicants, 50% accepted, 151 enrolled. In 2017, 87 master's awarded. *Degree requirements:* For master's, internship, minimum GPA of 3.0. *Entrance requirements:* For master's, interview, 2 letters of recommendation, essay, resume. Additional exam requirements/recommendations for international students: Required—TOEFL (minimum score 550 paper-based; 80 iBT). *Application deadline:* Applications are processed on a rolling basis. Application fee: $75. Electronic applications accepted. *Expenses:* Tuition: Full-time $1292. *Required fees:* $970. Tuition and fees vary according to program. *Financial support:* In 2017–18, 148 students received support, including 88 fellowships with full and partial tuition reimbursements available (averaging $3,026 per year), 4 research assistantships with full and partial tuition reimbursements available (averaging $5,619 per year); career-related internships or fieldwork, Federal Work-Study, institutionally sponsored loans, scholarships/grants, traineeships, tuition waivers (full and partial), and unspecified assistantships also available. Support available to part-time students. Financial award applicants required to submit FAFSA. *Faculty research:* Hand and upper extremity rehabilitation; orthotic fabrication; palliative care; neurorehabilitation; public health and health inequities, particularly in the American suburbs and minority communities; obesity; physical activity; social justice in physical education pedagogy. *Unit head:* Dr. Corinne Kyriacou, Chairperson, 516-463-4553, E-mail: corinne.m.kyriacou@hofstra.edu. *Application contact:* Sunil Samuel, Assistant Vice President of Admissions, 516-463-4723, Fax: 516-463-4664, E-mail: graduateadmission@hofstra.edu.
Website: http://www.hofstra.edu/academics/colleges/healthscienceshumanservices/

Howard University, Graduate School, Department of Health, Human Performance and Leisure Studies, Washington, DC 20059-0002. Offers exercise physiology (MS); health education (MS); sports studies (MS), including sociology of sports, sports management; urban recreation (MS), including leisure studies. *Program availability:* Part-time, evening/weekend. *Degree requirements:* For master's, comprehensive exam, thesis. *Entrance requirements:* For master's, BS in human performance or related field. Additional exam requirements/recommendations for international students: Recommended—TOEFL. Electronic applications accepted. *Faculty research:* Health promotion, cardiovascular hypertension, physical activity, sport and human rights issues.

Indiana University Bloomington, School of Public Health, Department of Kinesiology, Bloomington, IN 47405. Offers applied sport science (MS); athletic administration/sport management (MS); athletic training (MS); biomechanics (MS); ergonomics (MS); exercise physiology (MS); human performance (PhD), including biomechanics, exercise physiology, motor learning/control, sport management; motor learning/control (MS); physical activity (MPH); physical activity, fitness and wellness (MS). *Program availability:* Part-time. Terminal master's awarded for partial completion of doctoral program. *Degree requirements:* For master's, thesis optional; for doctorate, variable foreign language requirement, comprehensive exam, thesis/dissertation. *Entrance requirements:* For master's, GRE General Test, minimum GPA of 2.8; for doctorate, GRE General Test, minimum graduate GPA of 3.5, undergraduate 3.0. Additional exam requirements/recommendations for international students: Required—TOEFL (minimum score 80 iBT). *Faculty research:* Exercise physiology and biochemistry, sports biomechanics, human motor control, adaptation of fitness and exercise to special populations.

Indiana University of Pennsylvania, School of Graduate Studies and Research, College of Health and Human Services, Department of Kinesiology, Health, and Sport Science, MS Program in Sport Science/Exercise Science, Indiana, PA 15705. Offers MS. *Program availability:* Part-time. *Faculty:* 10 full-time (3 women). *Students:* 14 full-time (5 women), 1 part-time (0 women); includes 2 minority (1 Black or African American, non-Hispanic/Latino; 1 Hispanic/Latino). Average age 23. 29 applicants, 79% accepted, 10 enrolled. In 2017, 8 master's awarded. *Degree requirements:* For master's, thesis optional. *Entrance requirements:* For master's, 2 letters of recommendation. Additional exam requirements/recommendations for international students: Required—TOEFL (minimum score 540 paper-based). *Application deadline:* Applications are processed on a rolling basis. Application fee: $50. Electronic applications accepted. *Expenses:* Tuition, state resident: full-time $12,000; part-time $500 per credit. Tuition, nonresident: full-time $18,000; part-time $750 per credit. *Required fees:* $4073; $165.55 per credit. $64 per term. *Financial support:* In 2017–18, 5 research assistantships with tuition reimbursements (averaging $4,208 per year) were awarded; fellowships with partial tuition reimbursements, career-related internships or fieldwork, scholarships/grants, and unspecified assistantships also available. Support available to part-time students. Financial award application deadline: 4/15; financial award applicants required to submit FAFSA. *Unit head:* Dr. Madeline Bayles, Coordinator, 724-357-7835, E-mail: mpbayles@iup.edu.
Website: http://www.iup.edu/kines/grad/sport-science-exercise-science-ms/default.aspx

Indiana University of Pennsylvania, School of Graduate Studies and Research, College of Health and Human Services, Department of Kinesiology, Health, and Sport Science, Program in Sport Science/Sport Studies, Indiana, PA 15705. Offers MS. *Program availability:* Part-time. *Faculty:* 10 full-time (3 women). *Students:* 5 full-time (4 women), 1 part-time (0 women); includes 2 minority (1 Black or African American, non-Hispanic/Latino; 1 Hispanic/Latino). Average age 23. 6 applicants, 100% accepted, 2 enrolled. In 2017, 6 master's awarded. *Degree requirements:* For master's, thesis optional. *Entrance requirements:* Additional exam requirements/recommendations for international students: Required—TOEFL (minimum score 540 paper-based). *Application deadline:* Applications are processed on a rolling basis. Application fee: $50. Electronic applications accepted. *Expenses:* Contact institution. *Financial support:* In 2017–18, 2 research assistantships with tuition reimbursements (averaging $2,720 per year) were awarded; career-related internships or fieldwork, Federal Work-Study, scholarships/grants, and unspecified assistantships also available. Support available to part-time students. Financial award application deadline: 4/15; financial award applicants required to submit FAFSA. *Unit head:* Dr. Robert Kostelnik, Graduate Coordinator, 724-357-7645, E-mail: bkostel@iup.edu.
Website: http://www.iup.edu/grad/sportscience/default.aspx

Inter American University of Puerto Rico, Metropolitan Campus, Graduate Programs, Program in Physical Education, San Juan, PR 00919-1293. Offers teaching of physical education (MA); training and sport performance (MA). *Degree requirements:* For master's, comprehensive exam. *Entrance requirements:* For master's, GRE or EXADEP, interview. Electronic applications accepted.

Iowa State University of Science and Technology, Program in Diet and Exercise, Ames, IA 50011. Offers MS. *Entrance requirements:* For master's, GRE, minimum GPA of 3.5, 3 letters of recommendation. Additional exam requirements/recommendations for international students: Required—TOEFL (minimum score 550 paper-based; 79 iBT), IELTS (minimum score 6.5). Electronic applications accepted.

Ithaca College, School of Health Sciences and Human Performance, Program in Exercise and Sport Sciences, Ithaca, NY 14850. Offers MS. *Program availability:* Part-time. *Faculty:* 11 full-time (3 women). *Students:* 29 full-time (14 women), 13 part-time (6 women); includes 5 minority (3 Black or African American, non-Hispanic/Latino; 2 Hispanic/Latino), 3 international. Average age 24. 123 applicants, 66% accepted, 26 enrolled. In 2017, 17 master's awarded. *Degree requirements:* For master's, thesis optional. *Entrance requirements:* For master's, GRE General Test. Additional exam requirements/recommendations for international students: Required—TOEFL (minimum score 550 paper-based; 80 iBT). *Application deadline:* For fall admission, 3/1 for domestic and international students. Applications are processed on a rolling basis. Application fee: $40. Electronic applications accepted. *Expenses:* Contact institution. *Financial support:* In 2017–18, 28 students received support, including 28 research assistantships (averaging $13,299 per year); career-related internships or fieldwork, Federal Work-Study, scholarships/grants, and unspecified assistantships also available. Support available to part-time students. Financial award application deadline: 3/1; financial award applicants required to submit FAFSA. *Unit head:* Dr. Jeff Ives, Chair, 607-274-1751, Fax: 607-274-1263, E-mail: jives@ithaca.edu. *Application contact:* Nicole Eversley Bradwell, Director, Office of Admission, 607-274-3124, Fax: 607-274-1263, E-mail: admission@ithaca.edu.
Website: http://www.ithaca.edu/gradprograms/ess

James Madison University, The Graduate School, College of Health and Behavioral Studies, Program in Kinesiology, Harrisonburg, VA 22801. Offers clinical exercise physiology (MS); exercise physiology (MS); kinesiology (MAT, MS); nutrition and exercise (MS); physical and health education (MAT); sport and recreation leadership (MS). *Program availability:* Part-time, evening/weekend. *Students:* 43 full-time (22 women), 3 part-time (2 women); includes 10 minority (4 Black or African American, non-Hispanic/Latino; 1 Asian, non-Hispanic/Latino; 4 Hispanic/Latino; 1 Two or more races, non-Hispanic/Latino). Average age 30. In 2017, 46 master's awarded. Application fee: $55. Electronic applications accepted. *Expenses:* Tuition, state resident: full-time $10,512; part-time $438 per credit hour. Tuition, nonresident: full-time $28,358; part-time $1162 per credit hour. *Required fees:* $1128. *Financial support:* In 2017–18, 32 students received support, including 13 teaching assistantships with full tuition reimbursements available (averaging $8,837 per year); Federal Work-Study and 19 assistantships (averaging $7911), 20 athletic assistantships (averaging $9284) also available. Financial award application deadline: 3/1; financial award applicants required to submit FAFSA. *Unit head:* Dr. Christopher J. Womack, Department Head, 540-568-6145, E-mail: womackcx@jmu.edu. *Application contact:* Lynette D. Michael, Director of Graduate Admissions, 540-568-6131 Ext. 6395, Fax: 540-568-7860, E-mail: michaeld@jmu.edu.
Website: http://www.jmu.edu/kinesiology/

Kean University, College of Education, Program in Exercise Science, Union, NJ 07083. Offers MS. *Program availability:* Part-time. *Faculty:* 16 full-time (9 women). *Students:* 14 full-time (4 women), 5 part-time (3 women); includes 7 minority (2 Black or African American, non-Hispanic/Latino; 5 Hispanic/Latino). Average age 25. 12 applicants, 100% accepted, 6 enrolled. In 2017, 3 master's awarded. *Degree requirements:* For master's, comprehensive exam, thesis, research component. *Entrance requirements:* For master's, GRE General Test, minimum B average in undergraduate prerequisites; minimum cumulative GPA of 3.0; official transcripts from all institutions attended; two letters of recommendation; personal statement; professional resume/curriculum vitae. Additional exam requirements/recommendations for international students: Required—TOEFL (minimum score 550 paper-based; 79 iBT), IELTS (minimum score 6.5). *Application deadline:* For fall admission, 6/30 for domestic and international students; for spring admission, 12/1 for domestic and international students. Applications are processed on a rolling basis. Application fee: $75. Electronic applications accepted.

Expenses: Tuition, state resident: full-time $13,419; part-time $653 per credit. Tuition, nonresident: full-time $18,188; part-time $801 per credit. *Required fees:* $3382; $154 per credit. Tuition and fees vary according to course level, course load, degree level and program. *Financial support:* Scholarships/grants and unspecified assistantships available. Financial award applicants required to submit FAFSA. *Unit head:* Dr. Walter D. Andzel, Program Coordinator, 908-737-0662, E-mail: wandzel@kean.edu. *Application contact:* Brittany Gerstenhaber, Admissions Counselor, 908-737-7100, E-mail: grad-adm@kean.edu.
Website: http://grad.kean.edu/masters-programs/exercise-science

Kennesaw State University, WellStar College of Health and Human Services, Program in Applied Exercise and Health Science, Kennesaw, GA 30144. Offers MS. *Program availability:* Part-time, evening/weekend. *Entrance requirements:* For master's, GRE, resume. Additional exam requirements/recommendations for international students: Required—TOEFL (minimum score 550 paper-based; 80 iBT), IELTS (minimum score 6.5). Electronic applications accepted.

Kent State University, College of Education, Health and Human Services, School of Foundations, Leadership and Administration, Sports Recreation and Management Program, Kent, OH 44242-0001. Offers sport and recreation management (MA); sports studies (MA). *Degree requirements:* For master's, thesis optional. *Entrance requirements:* For master's, GRE if undergrad GPA below 3.0, goals statement, 2 letters of recommendation. Additional exam requirements/recommendations for international students: Required—TOEFL (minimum score 550 paper-based; 80 iBT). *Expenses:* Tuition, state resident: full-time $11,310; part-time $515 per credit hour. Tuition, nonresident: full-time $20,396; part-time $928 per credit hour. *International tuition:* $18,544 full-time.

Kent State University, College of Education, Health and Human Services, School of Health Sciences, Program in Exercise Physiology, Kent, OH 44242-0001. Offers athletic training (MS); exercise physiology (PhD). *Degree requirements:* For doctorate, comprehensive exam, thesis/dissertation. *Entrance requirements:* For master's, GRE, 2 letters of reference, goals statement; for doctorate, GRE, 2 letters of reference, goals statement, minimum master's-level GPA of 3.0. Additional exam requirements/ recommendations for international students: Required—TOEFL (minimum score 550 paper-based; 80 iBT). *Expenses:* Tuition, state resident: full-time $11,310; part-time $515 per credit hour. Tuition, nonresident: full-time $20,396; part-time $928 per credit hour. *International tuition:* $18,544 full-time.

Lakehead University, Graduate Studies, School of Kinesiology, Thunder Bay, ON P7B 5E1, Canada. Offers kinesiology (M Sc); kinesiology and gerontology (M Sc). *Program availability:* Part-time. *Degree requirements:* For master's, thesis. *Entrance requirements:* For master's, minimum B average. Additional exam requirements/ recommendations for international students: Required—TOEFL. *Faculty research:* Social psychology and physical education, sport history, sports medicine, exercise physiology, gerontology.

Liberty University, School of Health Sciences, Lynchburg, VA 24515. Offers anatomy and cell biology (PhD); biomedical sciences (MS); epidemiology (MPH); exercise science (MS), including clinical, community physical activity, human performance, nutrition; global health (MPH); health promotion (MPH); medical sciences (MA), including biopsychology, business management, health informatics, molecular medicine, public health; nutrition (MPH). *Program availability:* Part-time, online learning. *Students:* 542 full-time (394 women), 696 part-time (541 women); includes 402 minority (286 Black or African American, non-Hispanic/Latino; 10 American Indian or Alaska Native, non-Hispanic/Latino; 34 Asian, non-Hispanic/Latino; 46 Hispanic/Latino; 1 Native Hawaiian or other Pacific Islander, non-Hispanic/Latino; 25 Two or more races, non-Hispanic/Latino), 59 international. Average age 32. 1,592 applicants, 40% accepted, 297 enrolled. In 2017, 204 master's awarded. *Degree requirements:* For master's, thesis (for some programs); for doctorate, thesis/dissertation. *Entrance requirements:* For doctorate, MAT or GRE, minimum GPA of 3.25 in master's program, 2-3 recommendations, writing samples (for some programs), letter of intent, professional vitae. Additional exam requirements/recommendations for international students: Required—TOEFL (minimum score 600 paper-based; 100 iBT). Application fee: $50. *Financial support:* Applicants required to submit FAFSA. *Unit head:* Dr. Ralph Linstra, Dean. *Application contact:* Jay Bridge, Director of Admissions, 800-424-9595, Fax: 800-628-7977, E-mail: gradadmissions@liberty.edu.

Life University, College of Graduate and Undergraduate Studies, Marietta, GA 30060-2903. Offers athletic training (MAT); chiropractic sport science (MS); nutrition and sport science (MS), including chiropractic sport science; positive psychology (MS), including life coaching psychology; sport coaching (MS), including exercise sport science; sport injury management (MS), including nutrition and sport science; sports health science (MS), including sports injury management. *Program availability:* Part-time, 100% online, blended/hybrid learning. *Faculty:* 11 full-time (6 women), 12 part-time/adjunct (10 women). *Students:* 82 full-time (58 women), 131 part-time (86 women); includes 116 minority (85 Black or African American, non-Hispanic/Latino; 2 American Indian or Alaska Native, non-Hispanic/Latino; 3 Asian, non-Hispanic/Latino; 26 Hispanic/Latino), 25 international. Average age 30. In 2017, 53 master's awarded. *Degree requirements:* For master's, comprehensive exam (for some programs), thesis optional. *Entrance requirements:* For master's, GRE General Test, minimum GPA of 3.0, 3 letters of recommendation, curriculum vitae. Additional exam requirements/recommendations for international students: Required—TOEFL (minimum score 500 paper-based). *Application deadline:* For fall admission, 4/1 priority date for domestic and international students; for winter admission, 12/1 priority date for domestic and international students; for spring admission, 3/1 priority date for domestic and international students. Applications are processed on a rolling basis. Application fee: $50. Electronic applications accepted. *Expenses:* Contact institution. *Financial support:* Career-related internships or fieldwork, Federal Work-Study, and tuition waivers (full and partial) available. Support available to part-time students. Financial award application deadline: 9/1; financial award applicants required to submit FAFSA. *Faculty research:* Nutrient metabolism, organizational effectiveness, injury prevention, athlete development, recovery modalities and treatment, sport nutrition, functional neurology, peace and conflict studies. *Unit head:* Dr. Jana Holwick, Dean of Graduate and Undergraduate Studies, 678-331-4407, Fax: 770-426-2699, E-mail: jana.holwick@life.edu. *Application contact:* Robyn Stanley, Director of Enrollment, 770-426-2889, E-mail: robin.stanley@life.edu.
Website: http://www.life.edu/enrollment/admissions/graduate-admissions

Lipscomb University, Program in Exercise and Nutrition Science, Nashville, TN 37204-3951. Offers MS. *Program availability:* Part-time, evening/weekend. *Faculty:* 6 full-time (3 women). *Students:* 40 full-time (33 women), 20 part-time (15 women); includes 12 minority (4 Black or African American, non-Hispanic/Latino; 2 Asian, non-Hispanic/Latino; 5 Hispanic/Latino; 1 Two or more races, non-Hispanic/Latino), 1 international. Average age 25. 59 applicants, 44% accepted, 12 enrolled. In 2017, 14 master's awarded. *Degree requirements:* For master's, comprehensive exam (for some programs), thesis optional. *Entrance requirements:* For master's, GRE (minimum score of 800), minimum GPA of 2.75 on all undergraduate work; 2 letters of recommendation; resume. Additional exam requirements/recommendations for international students: Required—TOEFL (minimum score 570 paper-based; 80 iBT). *Application deadline:* For fall admission, 6/1 for domestic students; for spring admission, 12/1 for domestic

students. Applications are processed on a rolling basis. Application fee: $50 ($75 for international students). Electronic applications accepted. *Expenses:* Contact institution. *Financial support:* Unspecified assistantships available. Financial award applicants required to submit FAFSA. *Unit head:* Dr. Karen Robichaud, Director, 615-966-5602, E-mail: karen.robichaud@lipscomb.edu. *Application contact:* Julie Lillicrap, Administrative Assistant, 615-966-5700, E-mail: julie.lillicrap@lipscomb.edu.
Website: http://www.lipscomb.edu/kinesiology/graduate-programs

Logan University, College of Health Sciences, Chesterfield, MO 63017. Offers health informatics (MS); health professionals education (DHPE); nutrition and human performance (MS); sports science and rehabilitation (MS). *Program availability:* Part-time, online only, 100% online. *Faculty:* 4 full-time (1 woman), 25 part-time/adjunct (13 women). *Students:* 84 full-time (63 women), 417 part-time (314 women); includes 75 minority (36 Black or African American, non-Hispanic/Latino; 3 American Indian or Alaska Native, non-Hispanic/Latino; 15 Asian, non-Hispanic/Latino; 17 Hispanic/Latino; 4 Two or more races, non-Hispanic/Latino), 1 international. Average age 36. 238 applicants, 72% accepted, 134 enrolled. In 2017, 61 master's awarded. *Entrance requirements:* For master's, minimum GPA of 2.5; 6 hours of biology and physical science; bachelor's degree and 9 hours of business health administration (for health informatics). Additional exam requirements/ recommendations for international students: Required—TOEFL (minimum score 500 paper-based; 79 iBT); Recommended—IELTS (minimum score 6.5). *Application deadline:* Applications are processed on a rolling basis. Application fee: $50. Electronic applications accepted. *Expenses:* $450 per credit hour (for MS), $650 per credit hour (for DHPE), $80 fee per trimester. *Financial support:* In 2017–18, 4 students received support. Federal Work-Study available. Support available to part-time students. Financial award applicants required to submit FAFSA. *Faculty research:* Ankle injury prevention in high school athletes, low back pain in college football players, short arc banding and low back pain, the effects of enzymes on inflammatory blood markers, gait analysis in high school and college athletes. *Unit head:* Dr. Sherri Cole, Dean, College of Health Sciences, 636-227-2100 Ext. 2702, Fax: 636-207-2418, E-mail: sherri.cole@logan.edu. *Application contact:* Natacha Douglas, Executive Director of Admissions, 636-227-2100 Ext. 1718, Fax: 636-207-2425, E-mail: admissions@logan.edu.

Long Island University–LIU Brooklyn, School of Health Professions, Brooklyn, NY 11201-8423. Offers athletic training and sport sciences (MS); community health (MS Ed); exercise science (MS); forensic social work (Advanced Certificate); occupational therapy (MS); physical therapy (DPT); physician assistant (MS); public health (MPH); social work (MSW); speech-language pathology (MS). *Faculty:* 33 full-time (23 women), 82 part-time/adjunct (55 women). *Students:* 690 full-time (508 women), 86 part-time (74 women); includes 259 minority (120 Black or African American, non-Hispanic/Latino; 1 American Indian or Alaska Native, non-Hispanic/Latino; 52 Asian, non-Hispanic/Latino; 76 Hispanic/Latino; 10 Two or more races, non-Hispanic/Latino), 65 international. Average age 27. 1,241 applicants, 45% accepted, 255 enrolled. In 2017, 249 master's, 42 doctorates, 8 other advanced degrees awarded. *Degree requirements:* For master's, comprehensive exam (for some programs), thesis (for some programs); for doctorate, comprehensive exam (for some programs). *Entrance requirements:* For master's and doctorate, GRE. Additional exam requirements/recommendations for international students: Required—TOEFL (minimum score 550 paper-based; 79 iBT). *Application deadline:* Applications are processed on a rolling basis. Application fee: $50. Electronic applications accepted. *Expenses:* Tuition: Full-time $21,618; part-time $1201 per credit. *Required fees:* $1840; $920 per term. Tuition and fees vary according to course load. *Financial support:* In 2017–18, 187 students received support. Research assistantships, teaching assistantships, career-related internships or fieldwork, Federal Work-Study, scholarships/grants, and unspecified assistantships available. Support available to part-time students. Financial award application deadline: 2/15; financial award applicants required to submit FAFSA. *Faculty research:* Pediatric physical therapy, complementary and alternative medicine, global health and human rights, sport leadership and entrepreneurship, feminist sport psychology. *Unit head:* Dr. Barry S. Eckert, Dean, 718-780-6578, Fax: 718-780-4561, E-mail: barry.eckert@liu.edu. *Application contact:* Dr. Dominick Fortugno, Associate Dean, 718-488-1496, Fax: 718-780-4561, E-mail: dominick.fortugno@liu.edu.
Website: http://liu.edu/brooklyn/academics/school-of-health-professions

Manhattanville College, School of Education, Program in Physical Education and Sports Pedagogy, Purchase, NY 10577-2132. Offers health and wellness specialist (Advanced Certificate); physical education and sport pedagogy (MAT). *Program availability:* Part-time, evening/weekend. *Faculty:* 3 full-time (2 women), 7 part-time/ adjunct (2 women). *Students:* 39 full-time (10 women), 45 part-time (10 women); includes 15 minority (4 Black or African American, non-Hispanic/Latino; 11 Hispanic/ Latino). Average age 28. 9 applicants, 89% accepted, 8 enrolled. In 2017, 42 master's awarded. *Degree requirements:* For master's, comprehensive exam (for some programs), thesis (for some programs), student teaching, research seminars, portfolios, internships, writing assessment; for Advanced Certificate, comprehensive exam (for some programs). *Entrance requirements:* For master's, GRE or MAT (for programs leading to certification), minimum GPA of 3.0, 2 letters of recommendation, interview, essay (2-3 page personal statement that describes reasons for choosing teaching or educational leadership as profession and philosophy of education), proof of immunization (for those born after 1957). Additional exam requirements/ recommendations for international students: Required—TOEFL (minimum score 600 paper-based; 110 iBT); Recommended—IELTS (minimum score 8). *Application deadline:* Applications are processed on a rolling basis. Application fee: $75. Electronic applications accepted. *Expenses:* $915 per credit. *Financial support:* Teaching assistantships, career-related internships or fieldwork, Federal Work-Study, institutionally sponsored loans, scholarships/grants, and unspecified assistantships available. Financial award application deadline: 3/15; financial award applicants required to submit FAFSA. *Faculty research:* Early childhood and physical education. *Unit head:* Dr. Shelly Wepner, Dean, 914-323-3153, Fax: 914-323-5493, E-mail: shelly.wepner@ mville.edu. *Application contact:* Alissa Wilson, Director, Graduate Admissions, 914-323-3150, Fax: 914-694-1732, E-mail: edschool@mville.edu.
Website: http://www.mville.edu/programs/physical-education-and-sports-pedagogy

Marshall University, Academic Affairs Division, College of Health Professions, School of Kinesiology, Program in Biomechanics, Huntington, WV 25755. Offers MS. *Students:* 5 full-time (0 women); includes 1 minority (Black or African American, non-Hispanic/ Latino). Average age 26. *Unit head:* Dr. Gary McIlvain, Interim Chair, 304-696-2930, E-mail: mcilvain@marshall.edu. *Application contact:* Information Contact, 304-746-1900, Fax: 304-746-1902, E-mail: services@marshall.edu.
Website: http://www.marshall.edu/biomechanics/master-of-science/

Marshall University, Academic Affairs Division, College of Health Professions, School of Kinesiology, Program in Exercise Science, Huntington, WV 25755. Offers MS. *Students:* 25 full-time (16 women), 4 part-time (2 women); includes 7 minority (4 Black or African American, non-Hispanic/Latino; 1 Hispanic/Latino; 2 Two or more races, non-Hispanic/Latino). Average age 25. In 2017, 12 master's awarded. *Degree requirements:* For master's, thesis optional, comprehensive assessment. *Entrance requirements:* For master's, GRE General Test. Application fee: $40. *Unit head:* Dr. Gary McIlvain, Chair, 304-696-2930, E-mail: mcilvain2@marshall.edu. *Application contact:* Information Contact, 304-746-1900, Fax: 304-746-1902, E-mail: services@marshall.edu.

Exercise and Sports Science

Marywood University, Academic Affairs, College of Health and Human Services, Department of Nutrition and Dietetics, Program in Sports Nutrition and Exercise Science, Scranton, PA 18509-1598. Offers MS. *Program availability:* Part-time. Electronic applications accepted.

McNeese State University, Doré School of Graduate Studies, Burton College of Education, Department of Health and Human Performance, Lake Charles, LA 70609. Offers exercise physiology (MS); health promotion (MS); nutrition and wellness (MS). *Accreditation:* NCATE. *Program availability:* Evening/weekend. *Entrance requirements:* For master's, GRE, undergraduate major or minor in health and human performance or related field of study. *Application deadline:* For fall admission, 5/15 priority date for domestic and international students; for spring admission, 10/15 priority date for domestic and international students. Applications are processed on a rolling basis. Application fee: $20 ($30 for international students). *Financial support:* Application deadline: 5/1. *Unit head:* Dr. Michael Soileau, Department Head, 337-475-5274, Fax: 337-475-5947, E-mail: msoileau@mcneese.edu. *Application contact:* Dr. Dustin M. Hebert, Director of Dore' School of Graduate Studies, 337-475-5396, Fax: 337-475-5397, E-mail: admissions@mcneese.edu.

Memorial University of Newfoundland, School of Graduate Studies, School of Human Kinetics and Recreation, St. John's, NL A1C 5S7, Canada. Offers administration, curriculum and supervision (MPE); biomechanics/ergonomics (MS Kin); exercise and work physiology (MS Kin); psychology of sport, exercise and recreation (MS Kin); socio-cultural studies of physical activity and health (MS Kin). *Program availability:* Part-time. *Degree requirements:* For master's, thesis optional, seminars, thesis presentations. *Entrance requirements:* For master's, bachelor's degree in a related field, minimum B average. Electronic applications accepted. *Faculty research:* Administration, sociology of sports, kinesiology, physiology/recreation.

Merrimack College, School of Health Sciences, North Andover, MA 01845-5800. Offers athletic training (MS); community health education (MS); exercise and sport science (MS); health and wellness management (MS). *Program availability:* Part-time, evening/weekend. *Faculty:* 8 full-time, 6 part-time/adjunct. *Students:* 87 full-time (58 women), 4 part-time (all women); includes 10 minority (2 Black or African American, non-Hispanic/Latino; 7 Hispanic/Latino; 1 Two or more races, non-Hispanic/Latino), 3 international. Average age 25. 147 applicants, 90% accepted, 83 enrolled. In 2017, 47 master's awarded. *Degree requirements:* For master's, capstone (for community health education, exercise and sport science, and health and wellness management). *Entrance requirements:* For master's, resume, official college transcripts, personal statement, 2 recommendations. Additional exam requirements/recommendations for international students: Required—TOEFL (minimum score 84 iBT), IELTS (minimum score 6.5), PTE (minimum score 56). *Application deadline:* For fall admission, 8/24 for domestic students, 7/30 for international students; for summer admission, 5/10 for domestic students, 4/10 for international students. Applications are processed on a rolling basis. Electronic applications accepted. *Expenses:* $865 per credit hour tuition; $670 per credit hour (for MAT); comprehensive fees are $165 per semester for 1-8 credit hours and $320 per semester for 9+ credit hours. *Financial support:* Fellowships with partial tuition reimbursements, career-related internships or fieldwork, scholarships/grants, and health care benefits available. Support available to part-time students. Financial award application deadline: 5/1; financial award applicants required to submit FAFSA. *Unit head:* Kyle McInnis, Dean, 978-837-3590, E-mail: mcinnisk@merrimack.edu. *Application contact:* Allison Pena, Office of Graduate Studies, 978-837-3563, E-mail: graduate@merrimack.edu.
Website: http://www.merrimack.edu/academics/health-sciences/

Miami University, College of Education, Health and Society, Department of Kinesiology and Health, Oxford, OH 45056. Offers MS. *Students:* 70 full-time (35 women), 12 part-time (8 women); includes 13 minority (3 Black or African American, non-Hispanic/Latino; 1 American Indian or Alaska Native, non-Hispanic/Latino; 3 Asian, non-Hispanic/Latino; 3 Hispanic/Latino; 3 Two or more races, non-Hispanic/Latino), 5 international. Average age 24. In 2017, 24 master's awarded. *Expenses:* Tuition, state resident: full-time $13,812; part-time $575 per credit hour. Tuition, nonresident: full-time $30,860; part-time $1286 per credit hour. *Unit head:* Dr. Helaine Alessio, Professor and Chair, 513-529-2700, E-mail: alessih@miamioh.edu. *Application contact:* 513-529-2700, E-mail: knhdept@miamioh.edu.
Website: http://www.MiamiOH.edu/KNH

Middle Tennessee State University, College of Graduate Studies, College of Behavioral and Health Sciences, Department of Health and Human Performance, Program in Exercise Science, Murfreesboro, TN 37132. Offers MS. *Program availability:* Part-time, evening/weekend, online learning. *Degree requirements:* For master's, comprehensive exam, thesis optional. *Entrance requirements:* For master's, GRE. Additional exam requirements/recommendations for international students: Required—TOEFL (minimum score 525 paper-based; 71 iBT) or IELTS (minimum score 6). *Faculty research:* Kinesiometrics, leisure behavior, health, lifestyles.

Middle Tennessee State University, College of Graduate Studies, College of Behavioral and Health Sciences, Department of Health and Human Performance, Program in Human Performance, Murfreesboro, TN 37132. Offers PhD. *Program availability:* Part-time, evening/weekend, online learning. *Degree requirements:* For doctorate, comprehensive exam, thesis/dissertation. *Entrance requirements:* For doctorate, GRE. Additional exam requirements/recommendations for international students: Required—TOEFL (minimum score 525 paper-based; 71 iBT) or IELTS (minimum score 6). *Faculty research:* Kinesiometrics, leisure behavior, health/lifestyles.

Midwestern State University, Billie Doris McAda Graduate School, Robert D. and Carol Gunn College of Health Sciences and Human Services, Department of Athletic Training and Exercise Physiology, Wichita Falls, TX 76308. Offers exercise physiology (MS). *Program availability:* Part-time. *Degree requirements:* For master's, comprehensive exam, thesis optional. *Entrance requirements:* For master's, GRE General Test or MAT. Additional exam requirements/recommendations for international students: Required—TOEFL (minimum score 550 paper-based). Electronic applications accepted. *Faculty research:* Exercise adherence, muscular tissue remodeling during hypertrophy, student engagement and success, operational paradigms of the exercise sciences.

Mississippi State University, College of Education, Department of Kinesiology, Mississippi State, MS 39762. Offers disability studies (MS); exercise physiology (MS); exercise science (PhD); sport administration (MS); sport pedagogy (MS); sport studies (PhD). *Program availability:* Part-time, blended/hybrid learning. *Faculty:* 16 full-time (3 women). *Students:* 64 full-time (20 women), 8 part-time (3 women); includes 13 minority (2 Black or African American, non-Hispanic/Latino; 4 Asian, non-Hispanic/Latino; 4 Hispanic/Latino; 3 Two or more races, non-Hispanic/Latino), 10 international. Average age 26. 66 applicants, 59% accepted, 31 enrolled. In 2017, 23 master's awarded. *Degree requirements:* For master's, comprehensive exam, thesis optional; for doctorate, comprehensive exam. *Entrance requirements:* For master's, GRE General Test, minimum GPA of 2.75 on undergraduate work from four-year accredited institution, 3.0 graduate; for doctorate, GRE, minimum GPA of 3.4 on previous graduate degree(s) earned from accredited institutions. Additional exam requirements/recommendations for international students: Required—TOEFL (minimum score 550 paper-based; 79 iBT);

Recommended—IELTS (minimum score 6.5). *Application deadline:* For fall admission, 7/1 for domestic students, 5/1 for international students; for spring admission, 11/1 for domestic students, 9/1 for international students. Applications are processed on a rolling basis. Application fee: $60 ($80 for international students). Electronic applications accepted. *Expenses:* Tuition, state resident: full-time $8318; part-time $462.12 per credit hour. Tuition, nonresident: full-time $22,358; part-time $1242.12 per credit hour. *Required fees:* $110; $12.24 per credit hour. $6.12 per semester. *Financial support:* In 2017–18, 13 teaching assistantships with partial tuition reimbursements (averaging $10,510 per year) were awarded; career-related internships or fieldwork, Federal Work-Study, institutionally sponsored loans, and unspecified assistantships also available. Financial award application deadline: 4/1; financial award applicants required to submit FAFSA. *Faculty research:* Static balance and stepping performance of older adults, organizational justice, public health, strength training and recovery drinks, high risk drinking perceptions and behaviors. *Unit head:* Dr. Stanley P. Brown, Professor and Head, 662-325-7229, Fax: 662-325-4525, E-mail: spb107@msstate.edu. *Application contact:* Marina Hung, Admissions and Enrollment Assistant, 662-325-5188, E-mail: lbonner@grad.msstate.edu.
Website: http://www.kinesiology.msstate.edu/

Montclair State University, The Graduate School, College of Education and Human Services, Nutrition and Exercise Science Certificate Program, Montclair, NJ 07043-1624. Offers Certificate. Electronic applications accepted.

Montclair State University, The Graduate School, College of Education and Human Services, Program in Exercise Science and Physical Education, Montclair, NJ 07043-1624. Offers exercise science (MA); sports administration and coaching (MA); teaching and supervision in physical education (MA). *Program availability:* Part-time, evening/weekend. *Degree requirements:* For master's, comprehensive exam, thesis or alternative. *Entrance requirements:* For master's, GRE General Test, essay, 2 letters of recommendation. Additional exam requirements/recommendations for international students: Required—TOEFL (minimum score 83 iBT), IELTS (minimum score 6.5). Electronic applications accepted.

Morehead State University, Graduate Programs, College of Science and Technology, Department of Health, Wellness and Human Performance, Morehead, KY 40351. Offers health/physical education (MA). *Accreditation:* NCATE. *Program availability:* Part-time, evening/weekend. *Degree requirements:* For master's, comprehensive exam, thesis, oral exam, written core exam. *Entrance requirements:* For master's, GRE General Test or MAT, minimum GPA of 2.5; undergraduate major/minor in health, physical education, or recreation. Additional exam requirements/recommendations for international students: Required—TOEFL (minimum score 500 paper-based). Electronic applications accepted. *Faculty research:* Child growth and performance, instructional strategies, outdoor leadership qualities, exercise science, athletic training.

New Mexico Highlands University, Graduate Studies, College of Arts and Sciences, Department of Exercise and Sport Sciences, Las Vegas, NM 87701. Offers human performance and sport (MA), including human performance and sport sciences, sports administration, teacher education. *Program availability:* Part-time. *Degree requirements:* For master's, comprehensive exam, thesis or alternative. *Entrance requirements:* For master's, minimum undergraduate GPA of 3.0. Additional exam requirements/recommendations for international students: Required—TOEFL (minimum score 540 paper-based). *Faculty research:* Child obesity and physical inactivity, body composition and fitness assessment, motor development, sport marketing, sport finance.

North Dakota State University, College of Graduate and Interdisciplinary Studies, College of Human Development and Education, Department of Health, Nutrition, and Exercise Sciences, Fargo, ND 58102. Offers athletic training (MAT, MS); dietetics (MS); exercise science and nutrition (PhD); exercise/nutrition science (MS); health promotion (MPH); leadership in physical education and sport (MS). *Program availability:* Part-time, evening/weekend, online learning. *Degree requirements:* For master's, thesis (for some programs). *Entrance requirements:* For master's, minimum GPA of 3.0. Additional exam requirements/recommendations for international students: Required—TOEFL (minimum score 525 paper-based; 71 iBT). Electronic applications accepted. *Faculty research:* Biomechanics, sport specialization, recreation, nutrition, athletic training.

Northeastern Illinois University, College of Graduate Studies and Research, Daniel L. Goodwin College of Education, Program in Exercise Science, Chicago, IL 60625. Offers MS. *Degree requirements:* For master's, thesis optional, internship. *Entrance requirements:* For master's, 21 hours of undergraduate course work in science, minimum GPA of 2.75. *Application deadline:* For fall admission, 4/1 priority date for domestic students; for spring admission, 8/15 for domestic students. Applications are processed on a rolling basis. Application fee: $25. *Expenses:* Tuition, state resident: full-time $7274; part-time $404.11 per credit hour. Tuition, nonresident: full-time $14,548; part-time $808.23 per credit hour. *Required fees:* $1284. *Unit head:* Dr. Moira Stuart, Department Chair, 773-442-5546, E-mail: m-stuart@neiu.edu. *Application contact:* Martha Narvaez, Graduate Admission Representative, 773-442-6006.

Northeastern University, Bouvé College of Health Sciences, Boston, MA 02115-5096. Offers applied behavior analysis (MS); audiology (Au D); counseling psychology (MS, PhD, CAGS); exercise science (MS); nursing (MS, PhD, CAGS), including administration (MS), adult-gerontology acute care nurse practitioner (MS, CAGS), adult-gerontology primary care nurse practitioner (MS, CAGS), anesthesia (MS), family nurse practitioner (MS, CAGS), neonatal nurse practitioner (MS, CAGS), pediatric nurse practitioner (MS, CAGS), psychiatric mental health nurse practitioner (MS, CAGS); nursing practice (DNP); pharmaceutical sciences (MS, PhD), including interdisciplinary concentration, pharmaceutics and drug delivery systems; pharmacology (MS); pharmacy (Pharm D); school psychology (PhD); speech-language pathology (MS); urban health (MPH); MS/MBA. *Accreditation:* ACPE (one or more programs are accredited). *Program availability:* Part-time, evening/weekend, online learning. *Faculty:* 192 full-time. *Students:* 1,685. In 2017, 352 master's, 312 doctorates, 25 other advanced degrees awarded. *Degree requirements:* For doctorate, thesis/dissertation (for some programs); for CAGS, comprehensive exam. Application fee: $75. Electronic applications accepted. *Expenses:* Contact institution. *Financial support:* Fellowships, research assistantships, teaching assistantships, career-related internships or fieldwork, scholarships/grants, health care benefits, tuition waivers, and unspecified assistantships available. Support available to part-time students. Financial award applicants required to submit FAFSA. *Unit head:* Susan L. Parish, Dean, Bouve College of Health Sciences, 617-373-3321, Fax: 617-373-3030, E-mail: s.parish@northeastern.edu. *Application contact:* 617-373-2708, Fax: 617-373-4701, E-mail: bouvegrad@northeastern.edu.
Website: https://www.northeastern.edu/bouve/

Northern Michigan University, Office of Graduate Education and Research, College of Health Sciences and Professional Studies, School of Health and Human Performance, Marquette, MI 49855-5301. Offers exercise science (MS). *Program availability:* Part-time. *Degree requirements:* For master's, thesis (for some programs), two scholarly papers or thesis. *Entrance requirements:* For master's, minimum GPA of 3.0 plus relevant major or 9 semester hours of course work in human anatomy/physiology, exercise physiology, physics, biomechanics, kinesiology. Additional exam requirements/recommendations for international students: Required—TOEFL (minimum score 550 paper-based; 79 iBT), IELTS (minimum score 6.6). *Application deadline:* For fall

admission, 7/1 priority date for domestic students, 2/15 for international students; for winter admission, 11/15 for domestic students; for spring admission, 3/17 for domestic students. Applications are processed on a rolling basis. Application fee: $50. Electronic applications accepted. *Expenses:* Tuition, state resident: full-time $9417; part-time $542 per credit hour. Tuition, nonresident: full-time $12,873; part-time $758 per credit hour. Tuition and fees vary according to course load, degree level and program. *Financial support:* Teaching assistantships with full tuition reimbursements, career-related internships or fieldwork, Federal Work-Study, institutionally sponsored loans, and unspecified assistantships available. Support available to part-time students. Financial award application deadline: 3/1; financial award applicants required to submit FAFSA. *Faculty research:* Physiology of rock climbing and cross country ski racing, physical activity behaviors of children, exercise training and cancer treatment, normobaric hypoxia, concussion. *Unit head:* Elizabeth Wuorinen, Associate Dean/Director, 906-227-2528, E-mail: ewuorine@nmu.edu. *Application contact:* Dr. Randall L. Jensen, Coordinator, 906-227-1184, E-mail: rajensen@nmu.edu.
Website: http://www.nmu.edu/hhp/

Northwest Missouri State University, Graduate School, School of Health Science and Wellness, Maryville, MO 64468-6001. Offers applied health and sport sciences (MS); guidance and counseling (MS Ed); health and physical education (MS Ed); recreation (MS); sport and exercise psychology (MS). *Accreditation:* NCATE. *Program availability:* Part-time. *Faculty:* 23 full-time (11 women). *Students:* 68 full-time (43 women), 41 part-time (29 women); includes 9 minority (3 Black or African American, non-Hispanic/Latino; 4 Hispanic/Latino; 2 Two or more races, non-Hispanic/Latino), 5 international. Average age 27. 49 applicants, 47% accepted, 16 enrolled. In 2017, 34 master's awarded. *Degree requirements:* For master's, comprehensive exam. *Entrance requirements:* For master's, GRE General Test, minimum undergraduate GPA of 2.75, teaching certificate, writing sample. Additional exam requirements/recommendations for international students: Required—TOEFL (minimum score 550 paper-based). *Application deadline:* For fall admission, 7/1 for domestic and international students; for spring admission, 11/15 for domestic and international students. Applications are processed on a rolling basis. Application fee: $0 ($50 for international students). *Expenses:* Tuition, state resident: full-time $4551; part-time $252.86 per credit hour. Tuition, nonresident: full-time $9103; part-time $505.72 per credit hour. *Required fees:* $2453; $136.25 per credit hour. Tuition and fees vary according to course load and program. *Financial support:* Teaching assistantships with full tuition reimbursements and unspecified assistantships available. Financial award application deadline: 4/1; financial award applicants required to submit FAFSA. *Unit head:* Dr. Terry Long, Director, School of Health Science and Wellness, 660-562-1706, Fax: 660-562-1483, E-mail: tlong@nwmissouri.edu. *Application contact:* Gina Smith, Secretary, 660-562-1297, Fax: 660-562-1963, E-mail: smigina@nwmissouri.edu.
Website: http://www.nwmissouri.edu/health/

Oakland University, Graduate Study and Lifelong Learning, School of Health Sciences, Program in Exercise Science, Rochester, MI 48309-4401. Offers MS, Graduate Certificate. *Degree requirements:* For master's, thesis (for some programs). *Entrance requirements:* For master's, minimum GPA of 3.0. Additional exam requirements/recommendations for international students: Required—TOEFL (minimum score 550 paper-based). Electronic applications accepted. *Expenses:* Contact institution.

Oakland University, Graduate Study and Lifelong Learning, School of Health Sciences, Program in Physical Therapy, Rochester, MI 48309-4401. Offers clinical exercise science (Dr Sc PT); complementary medicine and wellness (Dr Sc PT); corporate worksite wellness (Dr Sc PT); exercise science (Dr Sc PT); neurological rehabilitation (Dr Sc PT, TDPT); orthopedic manual physical therapy (Dr Sc PT, TDPT, Graduate Certificate); orthopedic physical therapy (Graduate Certificate); orthopedics (Dr Sc PT, TDPT); pediatric rehabilitation (Dr Sc PT, TDPT); physical therapy (DPT); teaching and learning for rehabilitation professionals (Dr Sc PT, TDPT). *Accreditation:* APTA. *Entrance requirements:* For doctorate, GRE General Test. Additional exam requirements/recommendations for international students: Required—TOEFL (minimum score 550 paper-based). *Expenses:* Contact institution.

Ohio University, Graduate College, College of Arts and Sciences, Department of Biological Sciences, Athens, OH 45701-2979. Offers biological sciences (MS, PhD); cell biology and physiology (MS, PhD); ecology and evolutionary biology (MS, PhD); exercise physiology and muscle biology (MS, PhD); microbiology (MS, PhD); neuroscience (MS, PhD). Terminal master's awarded for partial completion of doctoral program. *Degree requirements:* For master's, comprehensive exam, thesis, 1 quarter of teaching experience; for doctorate, comprehensive exam, thesis/dissertation, 2 quarters of teaching experience. *Entrance requirements:* For master's, GRE General Test, names of three faculty members whose research interests most closely match the applicant's interest; for doctorate, GRE General Test, essay concerning prior training, research interest and career goals, plus names of three faculty members whose research interests most closely match the applicant's interest. Additional exam requirements/recommendations for international students: Required—TOEFL (minimum score 620 paper-based; 105 iBT) or IELTS (minimum score 7.5). Electronic applications accepted. *Faculty research:* Ecology and evolutionary biology, exercise physiology and muscle biology, neurobiology, cell biology, physiology.

Ohio University, Graduate College, College of Health Sciences and Professions, School of Applied Health Sciences and Wellness, Program in Physiology of Exercise, Athens, OH 45701-2979. Offers MS. *Degree requirements:* For master's, thesis or alternative. *Entrance requirements:* For master's, GRE, minimum GPA of 3.0. Additional exam requirements/recommendations for international students: Required—TOEFL (minimum score 550 paper-based; 80 iBT) or IELTS (minimum score 6.5). Electronic applications accepted. *Faculty research:* Blood pressure, heart rate, health skeleton, muscles, training.

Old Dominion University, Darden College of Education, Program in Physical Education, Exercise Science and Wellness Emphasis, Norfolk, VA 23529. Offers physical education (MS Ed), including exercise science and wellness. *Program availability:* Part-time, evening/weekend. *Faculty:* 7 full-time (3 women). *Students:* 14 full-time (9 women), 3 part-time (1 woman); includes 6 minority (3 Black or African American, non-Hispanic/Latino; 1 Asian, non-Hispanic/Latino; 1 Hispanic/Latino; 1 Two or more races, non-Hispanic/Latino). Average age 26. 16 applicants, 88% accepted, 8 enrolled. In 2017, 9 master's awarded. *Degree requirements:* For master's, comprehensive exam, thesis or alternative, internship, research project. *Entrance requirements:* For master's, GRE (minimum score of 291 for combined verbal and quantitative), minimum GPA of 2.8 overall, 3.0 in major. Additional exam requirements/recommendations for international students: Required—TOEFL (minimum score 550 paper-based; 79 iBT). *Application deadline:* For fall admission, 3/1 for domestic and international students. Applications are processed on a rolling basis. Application fee: $50. Electronic applications accepted. *Expenses:* Tuition, state resident: full-time $8928; part-time $496 per credit. Tuition, nonresident: full-time $22,482; part-time $1249 per credit. *Required fees:* $66 per semester. *Financial support:* In 2017–18, 7 students received support, including 4 research assistantships (averaging $10,000 per year), 3 teaching assistantships (averaging $10,000 per year); unspecified assistantships also available. Financial award application deadline: 3/1. *Faculty research:* Cardiovascular response to exercise, exercise prescription, nutrition, lower

extremity biomechanics, metabolic responses in special populations. *Total annual research expenditures:* $104,000. *Unit head:* Dr. Lynn Ridinger, Chair, 757-683-4353, E-mail: lridinge@odu.edu. *Application contact:* William Heffelfinger, Director of Graduate Admissions, 757-683-5554, Fax: 757-683-3255, E-mail: gradadmit@odu.edu.
Website: http://www.odu.edu/hms/academics/exercise/graduate#.Wr0u402otrQ

Pittsburg State University, Graduate School, College of Education, Department of Health, Physical Education and Recreation, Pittsburg, KS 66762. Offers health, human performance, and recreation (MS), including human performance and wellness, sport and leisure service management. *Program availability:* Part-time, online only, 100% online. *Students:* 66 (25 women); includes 17 minority (5 Black or African American, non-Hispanic/Latino; 2 American Indian or Alaska Native, non-Hispanic/Latino; 4 Hispanic/Latino; 6 Two or more races, non-Hispanic/Latino). In 2017, 33 master's awarded. *Degree requirements:* For master's, thesis or alternative. *Entrance requirements:* For master's, letter of intent. Additional exam requirements/recommendations for international students: Required—TOEFL (minimum score 520 paper-based; 68 iBT), IELTS (minimum score 6), PTE (minimum score 47). *Application deadline:* For fall admission, 6/1 for international students; for spring admission, 10/15 for international students; for summer admission, 4/1 for international students. Applications are processed on a rolling basis. Application fee: $35 ($60 for international students). Electronic applications accepted. *Expenses:* Contact institution. *Financial support:* In 2017–18, 9 teaching assistantships with full tuition reimbursements (averaging $5,500 per year) were awarded; career-related internships or fieldwork, Federal Work-Study, and unspecified assistantships also available. Financial award application deadline: 2/1; financial award applicants required to submit FAFSA. *Faculty research:* Personality of athletes, fitness activities for children, aerobic conditioning, fitness evaluation. *Unit head:* Dr. John Oppliger, Chairperson, 620-235-4668, E-mail: joppliger@pittstate.edu. *Application contact:* Lisa Allen, Assistant Director of Graduate and Continuing Studies, 620-235-4223, Fax: 620-235-4219, E-mail: lallen@pittstate.edu.

Point Loma Nazarene University, Department of Kinesiology, San Diego, CA 92106-2899. Offers exercise science (MS); sport performance (MS), including exercise science, sport management, sport performance. *Program availability:* Part-time, online learning. *Faculty:* 5 full-time (2 women), 8 part-time/adjunct (2 women). *Students:* 55 full-time (26 women), 3 part-time (2 women); includes 20 minority (2 Black or African American, non-Hispanic/Latino; 3 Asian, non-Hispanic/Latino; 12 Hispanic/Latino; 1 Native Hawaiian or other Pacific Islander, non-Hispanic/Latino; 2 Two or more races, non-Hispanic/Latino), 3 international. Average age 29. 92 applicants, 92% accepted, 55 enrolled. In 2017, 30 master's awarded. *Entrance requirements:* For master's, baccalaureate degree, minimum undergraduate cumulative GPA of 3.0. Application fee: $50. *Expenses:* Contact institution. *Financial support:* Teaching assistantships, scholarships/grants, and unspecified assistantships available. *Unit head:* Jeff Sullivan, Chair, 619-849-2629, E-mail: jeffsullivan@pointloma.edu. *Application contact:* Joanie Joy, Senior Director of Enrollment Management, 619-329-6785, E-mail: gradinfo@pointloma.edu.
Website: https://www.pointloma.edu/graduate-studies/programs/kinesiology-ms

Purdue University, Graduate School, College of Health and Human Sciences, Department of Health and Kinesiology, West Lafayette, IN 47907. Offers athletic training education administration (MS, PhD); biomechanics (MS, PhD); exercise physiology (MS, PhD); health education (MS, PhD); history/philosophy of sport (MS, PhD); motor control and development (MS, PhD); physical education pedagogy (PhD); physical education teacher education (MS); recreation and sport management (MS, PhD); sport and exercise psychology (MS, PhD). *Program availability:* Part-time. *Faculty:* 19 full-time (7 women). *Students:* 30 full-time (13 women), 10 part-time (5 women); includes 2 minority (1 Asian, non-Hispanic/Latino; 1 Two or more races, non-Hispanic/Latino), 6 international. Average age 26. 77 applicants, 29% accepted, 18 enrolled. In 2017, 18 master's, 9 doctorates awarded. *Degree requirements:* For master's, thesis optional; for doctorate, comprehensive exam, thesis/dissertation, qualifying examination, preliminary examination. *Entrance requirements:* For master's, GRE General Test (minimum score 1000 combined verbal and quantitative), minimum undergraduate GPA of 3.0 or equivalent; for doctorate, GRE General Test (minimum score 1100 combined verbal and quantitative), minimum undergraduate GPA of 3.0 or equivalent; master's degree with minimum GPA of 3.25 (recommended). Additional exam requirements/recommendations for international students: Required—TOEFL (minimum score 77 iBT); Recommended—TWE. *Application deadline:* For fall admission, 4/30 for domestic and international students; for spring admission, 10/15 for domestic and international students. Applications are processed on a rolling basis. Application fee: $60 ($75 for international students). Electronic applications accepted. *Financial support:* Fellowships with partial tuition reimbursements, research assistantships with partial tuition reimbursements, teaching assistantships with partial tuition reimbursements, and Federal Work-Study available. Support available to part-time students. Financial award applicants required to submit FAFSA. *Faculty research:* Wellness, motivation, teaching effectiveness, learning and development. *Unit head:* Dr. Timothy P. Gavin, Head of the Graduate Program, 765-494-3178, Fax: 765-494-1239, E-mail: gavin1@purdue.edu. *Application contact:* David B. Klenosky, Graduate Contact, 765-494-0865, E-mail: klenosky@purdue.edu.
Website: http://www.purdue.edu/hhs/hk/

Queens College of the City University of New York, Mathematics and Natural Sciences Division, Department of Family, Nutrition and Exercise Sciences, Queens, NY 11367-1597. Offers exercise science specialist (MS); family and consumer science (K-12) (AC); family and consumer science/teaching curriculum (K-12) (MS Ed); nutrition and exercise science (MS); nutrition specialist (MS); physical education (K-12) (AC); physical education/teaching curriculum (pre K-12) (MS Ed). *Program availability:* Part-time, evening/weekend. *Faculty:* 13 full-time (11 women), 7 part-time/adjunct (4 women). *Students:* 15 full-time (7 women), 136 part-time (75 women); includes 67 minority (19 Black or African American, non-Hispanic/Latino; 1 American Indian or Alaska Native, non-Hispanic/Latino; 21 Asian, non-Hispanic/Latino; 25 Hispanic/Latino; 1 Two or more races, non-Hispanic/Latino), 3 international. Average age 30. 95 applicants, 76% accepted, 45 enrolled. In 2017, 34 master's, 12 other advanced degrees awarded. *Degree requirements:* For master's, research project. *Entrance requirements:* For master's, minimum GPA of 3.0. Additional exam requirements/recommendations for international students: Required—TOEFL (minimum paper-based score of 600) or IELTS (for program in nutrition). *Application deadline:* For fall admission, 4/1 for domestic students; for spring admission, 11/1 for domestic students. Applications are processed on a rolling basis. Application fee: $125. Electronic applications accepted. *Financial support:* Career-related internships or fieldwork and unspecified assistantships available. Financial award application deadline: 4/1; financial award applicants required to submit FAFSA. *Faculty research:* Health disparities; correlates of taste acuity, structuring and implementation of competition and competitive activities in physical education; exercise and metabolic risk in people living with HIV/AIDS; biomechanics, motor learning and motor control. *Unit head:* Dr. Ashima K. Kant, Chair, 718-997-4156 Ext. 4475, Fax: 718-997-4163, E-mail: ashima.kant@qc.cuny.edu. *Application contact:* Elizabeth D'Amico-Ramirez, Assistant Director of Graduate Admissions, 718-997-5203, E-mail: elizabeth.damicoramirez@qc.cuny.edu.

Exercise and Sports Science

Queen's University at Kingston, School of Graduate Studies, School of Kinesiology and Health Studies, Kingston, ON K7L 3N6, Canada. Offers applied exercise science (PhD); biomechanics/ergonomics (M Sc); exercise physiology (M Sc); social psychology of sport and exercise rehabilitation (MA); sociology of sport (MA). *Program availability:* Part-time. *Degree requirements:* For master's, thesis (for some programs); for doctorate, comprehensive exam, thesis/dissertation. *Entrance requirements:* For master's and doctorate, minimum B+ average. Additional exam requirements/recommendations for international students: Required—TOEFL. Electronic applications accepted. *Faculty research:* Expert performance ergonomics, obesity research, pregnancy and exercise, gender and sport participation.

Rowan University, Graduate School, School of Biomedical Science and Health Professions, Department of Health and Exercise Science, Glassboro, NJ 08028-1701. Offers wellness and lifestyle management (MA). *Degree requirements:* For master's, comprehensive exam, thesis. *Entrance requirements:* For master's, GRE General Test, GRE Subject Test, interview, minimum GPA of 2.8. Additional exam requirements/recommendations for international students: Required—TOEFL. Electronic applications accepted. *Expenses:* Tuition, state resident: full-time $15,020; part-time $751 per semester hour. Tuition, nonresident: full-time $15,020; part-time $751 per semester hour. *Required fees:* $3158; $157.90 per semester hour. Tuition and fees vary according to course load, campus/location and program.

Sacred Heart University, Graduate Programs, College of Health Professions, Department of Exercise Science, Fairfield, CT 06825. Offers exercise science and nutrition (MS). *Program availability:* Part-time, evening/weekend. *Faculty:* 8 full-time (2 women). *Students:* 31 full-time (14 women), 1 part-time (0 women); includes 5 minority (2 Black or African American, non-Hispanic/Latino; 1 American Indian or Alaska Native, non-Hispanic/Latino; 1 Asian, non-Hispanic/Latino; 1 Hispanic/Latino). Average age 24. 42 applicants, 79% accepted, 16 enrolled. In 2017, 9 master's awarded. *Degree requirements:* For master's, thesis. *Entrance requirements:* For master's, bachelor's degree in related major, minimum GPA of 3.0, anatomy and physiology (with labs), exercise physiology, nutrition, statistics or health/exercise-specific research methods course, kinesiology (preferred). Additional exam requirements/recommendations for international students: Required—TOEFL (minimum score 570 paper-based, 80 iBT), TWE, or IELTS (6.5). *Application deadline:* Applications are processed on a rolling basis. Application fee: $75. Electronic applications accepted. *Expenses:* Contact institution. *Financial support:* Unspecified assistantships available. Financial award applicants required to submit FAFSA. *Unit head:* Beau Greer, Director of Graduate Exercise Science and Nutrition, 203-396-8064, E-mail: greerb@sacredheart.edu. *Application contact:* Tara Chudy, Executive Director of Graduate Admissions, 203-365-4735, E-mail: chudyt@sacredheart.edu.
Website: http://www.sacredheart.edu/academics/collegeofhealthprofessions/academicprograms/exercisescience/masterofscienceinexercisesciencenutrition/

St. Ambrose University, College of Health and Human Services, Program in Exercise Physiology, Davenport, IA 52803-2898. Offers MS.

St. Cloud State University, School of Graduate Studies, School of Health and Human Services, Department of Kinesiology, St. Cloud, MN 56301-4498. Offers exercise science (MS); sports management (MS). *Degree requirements:* For master's, thesis or alternative. *Entrance requirements:* For master's, GRE General Test, minimum overall GPA of 2.75 in previous undergraduate and graduate records or in last half of undergraduate work. Additional exam requirements/recommendations for international students: Required—Michigan English Language Assessment Battery; Recommended—TOEFL (minimum score 550 paper-based; 79 iBT), IELTS (minimum score 6.5). Electronic applications accepted.

Saint Mary's College of California, School of Liberal Arts, Department of Kinesiology, Moraga, CA 94575. Offers fitness management (MA); sport management (MA); sport studies (MA). *Program availability:* Part-time. *Degree requirements:* For master's, thesis or special project. *Entrance requirements:* For master's, minimum GPA of 2.75, BA in physical education or related field, or professional experience. Electronic applications accepted. *Expenses:* Contact institution. *Faculty research:* Moral development in sport, applied motor learning, achievement motivation, sport history.

San Diego State University, Graduate and Research Affairs, College of Health and Human Services, School of Exercise and Nutritional Sciences, Program in Exercise Physiology, San Diego, CA 92182. Offers MS, MS/MS. *Degree requirements:* For master's, thesis. *Entrance requirements:* For master's, GRE General Test, 2 letters of reference. Additional exam requirements/recommendations for international students: Required—TOEFL. Electronic applications accepted.

San Jose State University, Graduate Studies and Research, College of Health and Human Sciences, San Jose, CA 95192-0049. Offers criminology (MS), including global criminology, law and justice; justice studies (MS); kinesiology (MA), including athletic training, exercise physiology, interdisciplinary, sport studies, sports management; library and information science (MLIS); mass communications (MS); nursing (MS), including family nurse practitioner; nutritional science (MS); occupational therapy (MS); public health (MPH); social work (MSW); MD/M Div. *Program availability:* Part-time, 100% online, blended/hybrid learning. *Faculty:* 15 full-time (7 women), 6 part-time/adjunct (3 women). *Students:* 517 full-time (407 women), 405 part-time (302 women); includes 523 minority (39 Black or African American, non-Hispanic/Latino; 2 American Indian or Alaska Native, non-Hispanic/Latino; 141 Asian, non-Hispanic/Latino; 226 Hispanic/Latino; 2 Native Hawaiian or other Pacific Islander, non-Hispanic/Latino; 113 Two or more races, non-Hispanic/Latino), 14 international. Average age 32. 1,250 applicants, 45% accepted, 375 enrolled. In 2017, 808 master's awarded. *Degree requirements:* For master's, thesis (for some programs), graduate writing assessment. *Entrance requirements:* Additional exam requirements/recommendations for international students: Required—TOEFL (minimum score 550 paper-based; 80 iBT), IELTS (minimum score 6.5), PTE (minimum score 53). *Application deadline:* For fall admission, 2/1 for domestic and international students. Applications are processed on a rolling basis. Application fee: $55. Electronic applications accepted. *Expenses:* Tuition, state resident: full-time $7176. Tuition, nonresident: full-time $16,680. Tuition and fees vary according to course load and program. *Financial support:* Fellowships, research assistantships, teaching assistantships, career-related internships or fieldwork, Federal Work-Study, scholarships/grants, and tuition waivers (full and partial) available. Support available to part-time students. Financial award application deadline: 4/24; financial award applicants required to submit FAFSA. *Unit head:* Dr. Mary Schutten, Dean, College of Health and Human Sciences, 408-924-2900, Fax: 408-924-2901, E-mail: mary.schutten@sjsu.edu.
Website: http://www.sjsu.edu/casa/

Smith College, Graduate and Special Programs, Department of Exercise and Sport Studies, Northampton, MA 01063. Offers MS. *Program availability:* Part-time. *Students:* 24 full-time (20 women), 2 part-time (both women); includes 3 minority (1 Asian, non-Hispanic/Latino; 2 Hispanic/Latino). Average age 25. 51 applicants, 43% accepted, 14 enrolled. In 2017, 7 master's awarded. *Entrance requirements:* Additional exam requirements/recommendations for international students: Required—TOEFL (minimum score 595 paper-based; 97 iBT), IELTS. *Application deadline:* For fall admission, 1/15 for domestic and international students; for spring admission, 12/1 for domestic

students. Application fee: $60. *Expenses: Tuition:* Full-time $37,440; part-time $1560 per credit. Tuition and fees vary according to course load and program. *Financial support:* In 2017–18, 26 students received support, including 2 fellowships with full tuition reimbursements available (averaging $14,000 per year), 4 teaching assistantships with full tuition reimbursements available (averaging $14,000 per year); scholarships/grants and human resources employee benefit also available. Support available to part-time students. Financial award application deadline: 1/15; financial award applicants required to submit CSS PROFILE or FAFSA. *Faculty research:* Women in sport, perceived exertion, motor programming, race in sport, stress management. *Unit head:* Lynn Oberbillig, Graduate Student Adviser, 413-585-2701, E-mail: loberbil@smith.edu. *Application contact:* Ruth Morgan, Program Assistant, 413-585-3050, Fax: 413-585-3054, E-mail: rmorgan@smith.edu.
Website: http://www.smith.edu/ess/

Sonoma State University, School of Science and Technology, Department of Kinesiology, Rohnert Park, CA 94928. Offers exercise science/pre-physical therapy (MA); interdisciplinary (MA); interdisciplinary pre-occupational therapy (MA); lifetime physical activity (MA), including coach education, fitness and wellness. *Program availability:* Part-time. *Degree requirements:* For master's, thesis, oral exam. *Entrance requirements:* For master's, minimum GPA of 2.8. Additional exam requirements/recommendations for international students: Required—TOEFL (minimum score 500 paper-based). *Application deadline:* For fall admission, 11/30 for domestic students; for spring admission, 9/1 for domestic students. Applications are processed on a rolling basis. Application fee: $55. *Financial support:* Career-related internships or fieldwork available. Financial award application deadline: 3/2; financial award applicants required to submit FAFSA. *Unit head:* Dr. Steven Winter, Chair, 707-664-2188, E-mail: steven.winter@sonoma.edu. *Application contact:* Dr. Bulent Sokmen, Graduate Coordinator, 707-664-2789, E-mail: sokmen@sonoma.edu.
Website: http://www.sonoma.edu/kinesiology/

South Dakota State University, Graduate School, College of Education and Human Sciences, Department of Health and Nutritional Sciences, Brookings, SD 57007. Offers athletic training (MS); dietetics (MS); nutrition and exercise sciences (MS, PhD); sport and recreation studies (MS). *Program availability:* Part-time. *Degree requirements:* For master's, comprehensive exam (for some programs), thesis (for some programs), oral exam. *Entrance requirements:* Additional exam requirements/recommendations for international students: Required—TOEFL (minimum score 525 paper-based). *Faculty research:* Food chemistry, bone density, functional food, nutrition education, nutrition biochemistry.

Southeast Missouri State University, School of Graduate Studies, Department of Health, Human Performance and Recreation, Cape Girardeau, MO 63701-4799. Offers MS. *Program availability:* Part-time. *Faculty:* 8 full-time (2 women), 2 part-time/adjunct (1 woman). *Students:* 19 full-time (12 women), 7 part-time (6 women); includes 1 minority (Hispanic/Latino), 9 international. Average age 25. 39 applicants, 82% accepted, 14 enrolled. In 2017, 10 master's awarded. *Degree requirements:* For master's, comprehensive exam, thesis optional. *Entrance requirements:* For master's, GRE General Test (minimum combined score of 950). Additional exam requirements/recommendations for international students: Required—TOEFL (minimum score 550 paper-based; 79 iBT), IELTS (minimum score 6), PTE (minimum score 53). *Application deadline:* For fall admission, 8/1 for domestic students, 5/1 for international students; for spring admission, 11/21 for domestic students, 10/1 for international students; for summer admission, 5/15 for domestic students. Applications are processed on a rolling basis. Application fee: $30 ($40 for international students). Electronic applications accepted. *Expenses:* $270.35 per credit hour in-state tuition, $33.40 per credit hour fees. *Financial support:* In 2017–18, 11 students received support. Teaching assistantships with full tuition reimbursements available, career-related internships or fieldwork, Federal Work-Study, scholarships/grants, traineeships, tuition waivers (full), and unspecified assistantships available. Financial award application deadline: 6/30; financial award applicants required to submit FAFSA. *Faculty research:* Body composition assessment techniques, serum lipid adaptations with physical activity in smokers, professional attitudes of pre-service teachers, high intensity training with clinical populations. *Unit head:* Dr. Joe Pujol, Professor and Chairperson, 573-651-2664, Fax: 573-651-5150, E-mail: jpujol@semo.edu. *Application contact:* Dr. Jeremy Barnes, Professor/Graduate Coordinator, 573-651-2197, Fax: 573-651-5150, E-mail: jbarnes@semo.edu.
Website: http://www.semo.edu/health/

Southern Connecticut State University, School of Graduate Studies, School of Health and Human Services, Department of Exercise Science, New Haven, CT 06515-1355. Offers human performance (MS); physical education (MS); school health education (MS). *Program availability:* Part-time, evening/weekend. *Degree requirements:* For master's, thesis or alternative. *Entrance requirements:* For master's, interview. Electronic applications accepted.

Southern Illinois University Edwardsville, Graduate School, School of Education, Health, and Human Behavior, Department of Kinesiology and Health Education, Program in Exercise Physiology, Edwardsville, IL 62026. Offers MS. *Program availability:* Part-time, evening/weekend. *Degree requirements:* For master's, thesis (for some programs), internship. *Entrance requirements:* Additional exam requirements/recommendations for international students: Required—TOEFL (minimum score 550 paper-based, 79 iBT), IELTS (minimum score 6.5), Michigan Test of English Language Proficiency or PTE. Electronic applications accepted.

Southern Utah University, Program in Sports Conditioning and Performance, Cedar City, UT 84720-2498. Offers MS. *Program availability:* Part-time, online only, three intensive summer courses/clinical workshops on campus for 1-2 weeks. *Faculty:* 6 full-time (3 women). *Students:* 17 full-time (8 women), 37 part-time (15 women); includes 6 minority (1 Black or African American, non-Hispanic/Latino; 1 American Indian or Alaska Native, non-Hispanic/Latino; 3 Asian, non-Hispanic/Latino; 1 Native Hawaiian or other Pacific Islander, non-Hispanic/Latino), 1 international. Average age 27. 25 applicants, 92% accepted, 17 enrolled. In 2017, 14 master's awarded. *Entrance requirements:* For master's, GRE or MAT (if GPA is lower than 3.25). Additional exam requirements/recommendations for international students: Required—TOEFL (minimum score 550 paper-based; 79 iBT), IELTS (minimum score 6). *Application deadline:* For fall admission, 7/15 for domestic and international students; for spring admission, 10/15 for domestic and international students; for summer admission, 2/15 for domestic and international students. Applications are processed on a rolling basis. Application fee: $60 ($65 for international students). Electronic applications accepted. *Expenses:* Contact institution. *Unit head:* Dr. Camille Thomas, Department Chair, 435-586-7815, Fax: 435-865-8057, E-mail: camillethomas1@suu.edu. *Application contact:* Joan Anderson, Administrative Assistant, 435-586-7816, Fax: 435-865-8057, E-mail: stephanie-smith@leavitt.com.
Website: https://www.suu.edu/ed/pe/master.html

Springfield College, Graduate Programs, Programs in Exercise Science and Sport Studies, Springfield, MA 01109-3797. Offers athletic training (MS); clinical exercise physiology (MS); exercise physiology (MS); sport and exercise psychology (MS); strength and conditioning (MS). *Program availability:* Part-time. *Students:* 121 applicants, 60% accepted, 36 enrolled. In 2017, 19 master's awarded. Terminal master's

awarded for partial completion of doctoral program. *Degree requirements:* For master's, comprehensive exam, research project or thesis. *Entrance requirements:* For master's, GRE General Test. Additional exam requirements/recommendations for international students: Required—TOEFL (minimum score 550 paper-based); Recommended—IELTS (minimum score 7). *Application deadline:* For fall admission, 1/15 for domestic and international students; for winter admission, 11/1 for domestic and international students; for spring admission, 11/1 for domestic and international students. Application fee: $50. Electronic applications accepted. *Financial support:* Fellowships with partial tuition reimbursements, teaching assistantships with partial tuition reimbursements, career-related internships or fieldwork, Federal Work-Study, institutionally sponsored loans, scholarships/grants, and unspecified assistantships available. Financial award application deadline: 3/1; financial award applicants required to submit FAFSA. *Unit head:* Dr. Sue Guyer, Chair, 413-748-3404, E-mail: mguyer@springfield.edu. *Application contact:* Anne Griffin, Director of Graduate Admissions, 413-748-3225, Fax: 413-748-3694, E-mail: agriffin2@springfield.edu.
Website: http://springfield.edu/gradesss

Springfield College, Graduate Programs, Programs in Physical Education, Springfield, MA 01109-3797. Offers adapted physical education (MS); advanced-level coaching (M Ed); athletic administration (MS); exercise physiology (PhD); health promotion and disease prevention (MS); physical education initial licensure (CAGS); sport and exercise psychology (PhD); teaching and administration (PhD). *Program availability:* Part-time. *Students:* 82 applicants, 73% accepted, 37 enrolled. *Degree requirements:* For master's, comprehensive exam, thesis (for some programs). *Entrance requirements:* For master's and doctorate, GRE General Test. Additional exam requirements/recommendations for international students: Required—TOEFL (minimum score 550 paper-based); Recommended—IELTS (minimum score 7). *Application deadline:* For fall admission, 1/15 priority date for domestic students, 1/15 for international students; for winter admission, 11/1 for domestic and international students; for spring admission, 11/1 for domestic and international students. Applications are processed on a rolling basis. Application fee: $50. Electronic applications accepted. *Financial support:* Fellowships with partial tuition reimbursements, teaching assistantships with partial tuition reimbursements, career-related internships or fieldwork, Federal Work-Study, institutionally sponsored loans, scholarships/grants, and unspecified assistantships available. Financial award application deadline: 3/1; financial award applicants required to submit FAFSA. *Unit head:* Dr. Michelle Moosbrugger, Graduate Coordinator, 413-748-3486, E-mail: mmoosbrugger@springfield.edu. *Application contact:* Anne Griffin, Director of Graduate Admissions, 413-748-3225, Fax: 413-748-3694, E-mail: agriffin2@springfield.edu.
Website: http://springfield.edu/gradpe

Syracuse University, School of Education, MS Program in Exercise Science, Syracuse, NY 13244. Offers MS. *Program availability:* Part-time. *Entrance requirements:* For master's, GRE, baccalaureate degree from regionally-accredited college/university; 8 hours each in general biology and human anatomy and physiology; 6 hours of exercise science (including physiology of exercise and general science); three letters of recommendation; personal statement; resume; transcripts. Additional exam requirements/recommendations for international students: Required—TOEFL. *Application deadline:* For fall admission, 1/15 priority date for domestic and international students; for spring admission, 10/15 priority date for domestic and international students; for summer admission, 1/15 priority date for domestic and international students. Applications are processed on a rolling basis. Application fee: $75. Electronic applications accepted. *Financial support:* Fellowships, research assistantships, teaching assistantships, career-related internships or fieldwork, and scholarships/grants available. Financial award application deadline: 1/15. *Faculty research:* Bone density, obesity in females, cardiovascular functioning, attitudes toward physical education, sports management and psychology. *Unit head:* Dr. Tom Brutsaert, Chair, 315-443-9697, E-mail: tdbrutsa@syr.edu. *Application contact:* Speranza Migliore, Graduate Admissions Recruiter, 315-443-2505, E-mail: gradrcrt@syr.edu.
Website: http://soe.syr.edu/academic/exercise_science/graduate/masters/default.aspx

Tennessee State University, The School of Graduate Studies and Research, College of Health Sciences, Department of Human Performance and Sports Sciences, Nashville, TN 37209-1561. Offers exercise science (MA Ed); sports administration (MA Ed). *Degree requirements:* For master's, thesis optional. *Entrance requirements:* For master's, GRE General Test or MAT.

Texas A&M University–Commerce, College of Education and Human Services, Commerce, TX 75429. Offers counseling (M Ed, MS, PhD); early childhood education (M Ed, MS); educational administration (M Ed, MS, Ed D); educational psychology (PhD); educational technology leadership (M Ed, MS); educational technology library science (M Ed, MS); elementary education (M Ed); health, kinesiology and sports studies (MS); higher education (MS, Ed D); psychology (MS); reading (M Ed, MS); secondary education (M Ed, MS); social work (MSW); special education (M Ed, MS); supervision, curriculum and instruction-elementary education (Ed D); training and development (MS). *Program availability:* Part-time, evening/weekend, 100% online, blended/hybrid learning. *Faculty:* 91 full-time (51 women), 38 part-time/adjunct (31 women). *Students:* 400 full-time (310 women), 1,400 part-time (1,117 women); includes 724 minority (412 Black or African American, non-Hispanic/Latino; 8 American Indian or Alaska Native, non-Hispanic/Latino; 24 Asian, non-Hispanic/Latino; 220 Hispanic/Latino; 60 Two or more races, non-Hispanic/Latino), 18 international. Average age 37. 951 applicants, 46% accepted, 331 enrolled. In 2017, 564 master's, 24 doctorates awarded. *Degree requirements:* For master's, comprehensive exam, thesis optional, departmental qualifying exams (for some programs); for doctorate, comprehensive exam, thesis/dissertation, departmental qualifying exam; for SSP, comprehensive exam, thesis optional. *Entrance requirements:* For master's and doctorate, GRE General Test. Additional exam requirements/recommendations for international students: Required—TOEFL (minimum score 550 paper-based; 79 iBT), IELTS (minimum score 6). *Application deadline:* For fall admission, 6/1 priority date for international students; for spring admission, 10/15 priority date for international students; for summer admission, 3/15 priority date for international students. Applications are processed on a rolling basis. Application fee: $50. Electronic applications accepted. *Expenses:* Tuition, state resident: full-time $3630. Tuition, nonresident: full-time $11,100. *Required fees:* $2564. Tuition and fees vary according to course load, degree level and program. *Financial support:* In 2017–18, 84 students received support, including 40 research assistantships with partial tuition reimbursements available (averaging $10,800 per year), 12 teaching assistantships with partial tuition reimbursements available (averaging $13,000 per year); career-related internships or fieldwork, Federal Work-Study, institutionally sponsored loans, scholarships/grants, health care benefits, and unspecified assistantships also available. Financial award application deadline: 6/15; financial award applicants required to submit FAFSA. *Faculty research:* Cognitive and bilingual education, positive behavioral intervention, literacy, math readiness. *Total annual research expenditures:* $1.1 million. *Unit head:* Dr. Timothy Letzring, Dean, 903-886-5181, Fax: 903-886-5905, E-mail: tim.letzring@tamuc.edu. *Application contact:* Vicky Turner, Doctoral Degree and Special Programs Coordinator, 903-886-5167, E-mail: vicky.turner@tamuc.edu.
Website: http://www.tamuc.edu/academics/graduateSchool/programs/education/default.aspx

Texas Tech University, Graduate School, College of Arts and Sciences, Department of Kinesiology and Sport Management, Lubbock, TX 79409. Offers kinesiology (MS); sport management (MS). *Program availability:* Part-time. *Faculty:* 21 full-time (9 women), 9 part-time/adjunct (5 women). *Students:* 65 full-time (32 women), 7 part-time (1 woman); includes 28 minority (8 Black or African American, non-Hispanic/Latino; 3 Asian, non-Hispanic/Latino; 15 Hispanic/Latino; 2 Two or more races, non-Hispanic/Latino), 11 international. Average age 24. 96 applicants, 48% accepted, 38 enrolled. In 2017, 38 master's awarded. *Degree requirements:* For master's, comprehensive exam (for some programs), thesis (for some programs). *Entrance requirements:* For master's, GRE or minimum GPA of 3.5 on last 60 hours of undergraduate coursework (only for kinesiology), letter of intent, 3 letters of recommendation (preferably from academic professors), minimum GPA of 2.8 in the last 60 hours. Additional exam requirements/recommendations for international students: Required—TOEFL (minimum score 550 paper-based; 79 iBT). *Application deadline:* For fall admission, 6/1 priority date for domestic students, 1/15 priority date for international students; for spring admission, 9/1 priority date for domestic students, 6/15 priority date for international students. Applications are processed on a rolling basis. Application fee: $60. Electronic applications accepted. *Expenses:* Contact institution. *Financial support:* In 2017–18, 51 students received support, including 49 fellowships (averaging $4,508 per year), 35 teaching assistantships (averaging $12,637 per year); research assistantships, career-related internships or fieldwork, scholarships/grants, health care benefits, and unspecified assistantships also available. Financial award application deadline: 8/1; financial award applicants required to submit FAFSA. *Faculty research:* Sport management, exercise physiology, human performance, motor behavior, exercise and sport psychology. *Total annual research expenditures:* $144,825. *Unit head:* Dr. Angela Lumpkin, Professor/Department Chair, 806-834-6935, Fax: 806-742-1688, E-mail: angela.lumpkin@ttu.edu. *Application contact:* Donna Torres, Graduate Admissions Coordinator, 806-834-7968, Fax: 806-742-1688, E-mail: donna.torres@ttu.edu.
Website: http://www.depts.ttu.edu/ksm/

Texas Woman's University, Graduate School, College of Health Sciences, Department of Kinesiology, Denton, TX 76204. Offers kinesiology (MS, PhD), including adapted physical activity, biomechanics, coaching (MS), exercise physiology, sport management. *Program availability:* Part-time, evening/weekend. *Faculty:* 11 full-time (3 women), 2 part-time/adjunct (both women). *Students:* 48 full-time (36 women), 65 part-time (39 women); includes 40 minority (19 Black or African American, non-Hispanic/Latino; 2 Asian, non-Hispanic/Latino; 17 Hispanic/Latino; 2 Two or more races, non-Hispanic/Latino), 14 international. Average age 30. 63 applicants, 81% accepted, 37 enrolled. In 2017, 32 master's, 9 doctorates awarded. Terminal master's awarded for partial completion of doctoral program. *Degree requirements:* For master's, comprehensive exam, thesis (for some programs), thesis or professional paper; for doctorate, comprehensive exam, thesis/dissertation, qualifying exam. *Entrance requirements:* For master's, GRE General Test (biomechanics emphasis only), 2 letters of reference, curriculum vitae; for doctorate, GRE General Test (biomechanics emphasis only), interview, 3 letters of reference, curriculum vitae, letter of intent. Additional exam requirements/recommendations for international students: Required—TOEFL (minimum score 550 paper-based; 79 iBT); Recommended—IELTS (minimum score 6.5), TSE (minimum score 53). *Application deadline:* For fall admission, 7/15 for domestic students, 3/1 priority date for international students; for spring admission, 11/1 for domestic students, 7/1 priority date for international students; for summer admission, 4/1 for domestic students, 2/1 priority date for international students. Applications are processed on a rolling basis. Application fee: $50 ($75 for international students). Electronic applications accepted. *Expenses:* $7,520 per year full-time in-state; $16,829 per year full-time out-of-state. *Financial support:* In 2017–18, 36 students received support, including 1 research assistantship (averaging $11,926 per year), 15 teaching assistantships (averaging $20,354 per year); career-related internships or fieldwork, Federal Work-Study, institutionally sponsored loans, scholarships/grants, traineeships, health care benefits, and unspecified assistantships also available. Support available to part-time students. Financial award application deadline: 3/1; financial award applicants required to submit FAFSA. *Faculty research:* Exercise and Type 2 diabetes risk, bone mineral density and exercise in special populations, obesity in children, factors influencing sport consumer behavior and loyalty, roles and responsibilities of Para educators in adapted physical education. *Unit head:* Dr. George King, Chair, 940-898-2575, Fax: 940-898-2581. *Application contact:* Korie Hawkins, Associate Director of Admissions, Graduate Recruitment, 940-898-3188, Fax: 940-898-3081, E-mail: admissions@twu.edu.
Website: http://www.twu.edu/kinesiology

Texas Woman's University, Graduate School, College of Health Sciences, Department of Nutrition and Food Sciences, Denton, TX 76204. Offers exercise and sports nutrition (MS); food science and flavor chemistry (MS); food systems administration (MS); nutrition (MS, PhD). *Program availability:* Part-time, evening/weekend. *Faculty:* 15 full-time (12 women), 1 (woman) part-time/adjunct. *Students:* 92 full-time (83 women), 109 part-time (100 women); includes 58 minority (10 Black or African American, non-Hispanic/Latino; 17 Asian, non-Hispanic/Latino; 24 Hispanic/Latino; 7 Two or more races, non-Hispanic/Latino), 10 international. Average age 29. 102 applicants, 84% accepted, 54 enrolled. In 2017, 71 master's, 1 doctorate awarded. *Degree requirements:* For master's, thesis or alternative, thesis (for food and flavor chemistry); thesis or coursework (for exercise and sports nutrition, nutrition); for doctorate, comprehensive exam, thesis/dissertation, qualifying exam, 50% of all required hours must be earned at TWU. *Entrance requirements:* For master's, GRE General Test (preferred minimum score 143 [350 old version] Verbal, 141 [450 old version] Quantitative, minimum GPA of 3.25, resume, personal statement of interest (food science and flavor chemistry only); for doctorate, GRE General Test (preferred minimum score 150 [450 old version] Verbal, 146 [550 old version] Quantitative), minimum GPA of 3.5 on last 60 undergraduate hours and graduate course work, 2 letters of reference, resume, statement of purpose. Additional exam requirements/recommendations for international students: Required—TOEFL (minimum score 550 paper-based; 79 iBT); Recommended—IELTS (minimum score 6.5), TSE (minimum score 53). *Application deadline:* For fall admission, 3/1 priority date for domestic and international students; for spring admission, 11/1 priority date for domestic students, 7/1 priority date for international students; for summer admission, 5/1 priority date for domestic students, 2/1 priority date for international students. Applications are processed on a rolling basis. Application fee: $50 ($75 for international students). Electronic applications accepted. *Expenses:* $7,520 per year full-time in-state; $16,829 per year full-time out-of-state. *Financial support:* In 2017–18, 66 students received support, including 5 research assistantships (averaging $19,791 per year), 4 teaching assistantships (averaging $19,586 per year); career-related internships or fieldwork, Federal Work-Study, institutionally sponsored loans, scholarships/grants, traineeships, health care benefits, and unspecified assistantships also available. Support available to part-time students. Financial award application deadline: 3/1; financial award applicants required to submit FAFSA. *Faculty research:* Bioactive food components and cancer, nutraceuticals and functional foods in diabetes, obesity and bone health, food safety, obesity prevention in children. *Total annual research expenditures:* $186,045. *Unit head:* Dr. K. Shane Broughton, Chair, 940-898-2636, Fax: 940-898-2634, E-mail: nutrfdsci@twu.edu. *Application contact:* Korie Hawkins, Associate Director of Admissions, Graduate Recruitment, 940-898-3188, Fax: 940-898-3081, E-mail: admissions@twu.edu.
Website: http://www.twu.edu/nutrition-food-sciences/

Exercise and Sports Science

United States Sports Academy, Graduate Programs, Program in Sports Health and Fitness, Daphne, AL 36526-7055. Offers MSS. *Program availability:* Part-time, 100% online. *Degree requirements:* For master's, comprehensive exam, thesis optional. *Entrance requirements:* For master's, GRE General Test, GMAT, or MAT, minimum GPA of 2.5, 3 letters of recommendation, personal statement. Additional exam requirements/recommendations for international students: Required—TOEFL (minimum score 550 paper-based; 79 iBT). *Application deadline:* Applications are processed on a rolling basis. Application fee: $50 ($125 for international students). Electronic applications accepted. *Expenses:* $640 per credit hour. *Financial support:* Application deadline: 8/15; applicants required to submit FAFSA. *Faculty research:* Exercise physiology, conditioning. *Unit head:* Dr. Brian Wallace, Chair of Sports Exercise Science, 251-626-3303 Ext. 7156, Fax: 251-625-1035, E-mail: bwallace@ussa.edu. *Application contact:* Dr. Taffy Sithole, Student Services Coordinator, 251-626-3303 Ext. 7147, Fax: 251-625-1035, E-mail: tsithole@ussa.edu.

United States Sports Academy, Graduate Programs, Program in Sports Studies, Daphne, AL 36526-7055. Offers MSS. *Program availability:* Part-time, 100% online. *Degree requirements:* For master's, comprehensive exam, thesis optional. *Entrance requirements:* For master's, GRE General Test, GMAT, or MAT, minimum GPA of 2.5, 3 letters of recommendation, personal statement. Additional exam requirements/recommendations for international students: Required—TOEFL (minimum score 550 paper-based; 79 iBT). *Application deadline:* Applications are processed on a rolling basis. Application fee: $50 ($125 for international students). Electronic applications accepted. *Expenses:* $640 per credit hour. *Unit head:* Dr. Sandra Geringer, Director, 251-626-3303 Ext. 7151, Fax: 251-625-1035, E-mail: sgeringer@ussa.edu. *Application contact:* Dr. Taffy Sithole, Student Services Coordinator, 251-626-3303 Ext. 7147, Fax: 251-625-1035, E-mail: tsithole@ussa.edu.

University at Buffalo, the State University of New York, Graduate School, School of Public Health and Health Professions, Department of Exercise and Nutrition Sciences, Buffalo, NY 14260. Offers exercise science (MS, PhD); nutrition (MS, Advanced Certificate). *Program availability:* Part-time. *Faculty:* 18 full-time (8 women), 8 part-time/adjunct (4 women). *Students:* 74 full-time (62 women), 3 part-time (2 women); includes 5 minority (2 Black or African American, non-Hispanic/Latino; 3 Asian, non-Hispanic/Latino), 18 international. Average age 24. 109 applicants, 52% accepted, 50 enrolled. In 2017, 30 master's, 1 doctorate, 19 other advanced degrees awarded. *Entrance requirements:* For master's, doctorate, and Advanced Certificate, GRE General Test, minimum GPA of 3.0. Additional exam requirements/recommendations for international students: Required—TOEFL (minimum score 550 paper-based; 79 iBT), IELTS (minimum score 6.5). *Application deadline:* For fall admission, 4/1 for domestic students, 3/1 for international students; for spring admission, 8/15 for international students. Applications are processed on a rolling basis. Application fee: $50. Electronic applications accepted. *Financial support:* In 2017–18, 14 students received support, including 1 research assistantship with full tuition reimbursement available (averaging $15,000 per year), 11 teaching assistantships with tuition reimbursements available (averaging $6,980 per year); tuition waivers (full) and Fulbright scholarship also available. Financial award application deadline: 3/15; financial award applicants required to submit FAFSA. *Faculty research:* Cardiovascular disease-diet and exercise, respiratory control and muscle function, plasticity of connective and neural tissue, exercise nutrition, diet and cancer. *Total annual research expenditures:* $891,096. *Unit head:* Dr. David Hostler, Chair, 716-829-6756, Fax: 716-829-2428, E-mail: dhostler@buffalo.edu. *Application contact:* Dr. Jennifer Temple, Director of Graduate Studies, 716-829-5593, Fax: 716-829-2428, E-mail: jltemple@buffalo.edu.
Website: http://sphhp.buffalo.edu/exercise-and-nutrition-sciences.html

The University of Akron, Graduate School, College of Health Professions, School of Sport Science and Wellness Education, Program in Exercise Physiology/Adult Fitness, Akron, OH 44325. Offers MA, MS. *Students:* 29 full-time (21 women), 12 part-time (5 women); includes 10 minority (2 Black or African American, non-Hispanic/Latino; 3 Asian, non-Hispanic/Latino; 3 Hispanic/Latino; 2 Two or more races, non-Hispanic/Latino), 2 international. Average age 25. 16 applicants, 100% accepted, 11 enrolled. In 2017, 36 master's awarded. *Degree requirements:* For master's, comprehensive exam, thesis optional. *Entrance requirements:* For master's, minimum GPA of 2.75, three letters of recommendation, statement of purpose. Additional exam requirements/recommendations for international students: Required—TOEFL (minimum score 79 iBT), IELTS (minimum score 6.5). *Application deadline:* Applications are processed on a rolling basis. Application fee: $45 ($70 for international students). Electronic applications accepted. *Unit head:* Dr. Victor Pinheiro, Department Chair, 330-972-6055, E-mail: victor@uakron.edu. *Application contact:* Dr. Ron Otterstetter, Program Contact, 330-972-7738.
Website: http://www.uakron.edu/sswe/

The University of Akron, Graduate School, College of Health Professions, School of Sport Science and Wellness Education, Program in Sport Science/Coaching, Akron, OH 44325. Offers MA, MS. *Students:* 35 full-time (11 women), 16 part-time (6 women); includes 14 minority (12 Black or African American, non-Hispanic/Latino; 1 Asian, non-Hispanic/Latino; 1 Hispanic/Latino), 3 international. Average age 26. 30 applicants, 100% accepted, 26 enrolled. In 2017, 38 master's awarded. *Degree requirements:* For master's, comprehensive exam, thesis optional. *Entrance requirements:* For master's, minimum GPA of 2.75, three letters of recommendation, statement of purpose. Additional exam requirements/recommendations for international students: Required—TOEFL (minimum score 79 iBT), IELTS (minimum score 6.5). *Application deadline:* Applications are processed on a rolling basis. Application fee: $45 ($70 for international students). Electronic applications accepted. *Unit head:* Dr. Victor Pinheiro, Department Chair, 330-972-6055, E-mail: victor@uakron.edu. *Application contact:* Dr. Alan Kornspan, Program Contact, 330-972-8145.
Website: http://www.uakron.edu/sswe/programs/sport-science-coaching/index.dot

The University of Alabama, Graduate School, College of Education, Department of Kinesiology, Tuscaloosa, AL 35487. Offers alternative sport pedagogy (MA); exercise science (PhD). *Program availability:* Part-time. *Faculty:* 12 full-time (2 women). *Students:* 51 full-time (21 women), 20 part-time (9 women); includes 17 minority (12 Black or African American, non-Hispanic/Latino; 3 Hispanic/Latino; 2 Two or more races, non-Hispanic/Latino), 7 international. Average age 27. 58 applicants, 60% accepted, 18 enrolled. In 2017, 35 master's, 8 doctorates awarded. *Degree requirements:* For master's, comprehensive exam, thesis optional; for doctorate, comprehensive exam, thesis/dissertation. *Entrance requirements:* For master's and doctorate, GRE, minimum GPA of 3.0. Additional exam requirements/recommendations for international students: Required—TOEFL. *Application deadline:* Applications are processed on a rolling basis. Electronic applications accepted. *Financial support:* In 2017–18, 18 students received support. Application deadline: 3/1. *Total annual research expenditures:* $50,518. *Unit head:* Dr. Jonathan Wingo, Associate Professor and Head, 205-348-4699, Fax: 205-348-0867, E-mail: jwingo@ua.edu. *Application contact:* Dr. Kathy S. Wetzel, Associate Dean for Student Services and Certification, 205-348-1154, E-mail: kwetzel@bamaed.ua.edu.
Website: http://education.ua.edu/academics/kine/

University of Alberta, Faculty of Graduate Studies and Research, Department of Physical Education and Recreation, Edmonton, AB T6G 2E1, Canada. Offers physical education (M Sc); recreation and physical education (MA, PhD). *Program availability:* Part-time. Terminal master's awarded for partial completion of doctoral program. *Degree requirements:* For master's, thesis (for some programs); for doctorate, thesis/dissertation. *Entrance requirements:* For master's, bachelor's degree in related field; for doctorate, master's degree in related field with thesis. Additional exam requirements/recommendations for international students: Required—TOEFL. *Faculty research:* Motivation and adherence to physical ability, performance enhancement, adapted physical activity, exercise physiology, sport administration, tourism.

University of Arkansas at Little Rock, Graduate School, College of Education and Health Professions, Department of Health, Human Performance and Sport Management, Little Rock, AR 72204-1099. Offers exercise science (MS); health education and promotion (MS); sport management (MS). *Program availability:* Part-time, evening/weekend. *Degree requirements:* For master's, directed study or residency. *Entrance requirements:* For master's, GRE General Test, minimum GPA of 3.0, 3 reference letters.

University of California, Davis, Graduate Studies, Graduate Group in Exercise Science, Davis, CA 95616. Offers MS. *Degree requirements:* For master's, thesis. *Entrance requirements:* For master's, GRE, minimum GPA of 3.25. Additional exam requirements/recommendations for international students: Required—TOEFL (minimum score 550 paper-based). Electronic applications accepted.

University of Central Florida, College of Community Innovation and Education, Department of Learning Sciences and Educational Research, Program in Sport and Exercise Science, Orlando, FL 32816. Offers applied exercise physiology (MS). *Program availability:* Part-time, evening/weekend. *Students:* 51 full-time (23 women), 16 part-time (7 women); includes 18 minority (4 Black or African American, non-Hispanic/Latino; 1 American Indian or Alaska Native, non-Hispanic/Latino; 2 Asian, non-Hispanic/Latino; 10 Hispanic/Latino; 1 Two or more races, non-Hispanic/Latino), 5 international. Average age 26. 95 applicants, 66% accepted, 39 enrolled. In 2017, 41 master's awarded. *Degree requirements:* For master's, thesis or alternative. *Entrance requirements:* For master's, GRE General Test, letters of recommendation, resume. Additional exam requirements/recommendations for international students: Required—TOEFL. *Application deadline:* For fall admission, 7/15 for domestic students; for spring admission, 12/1 for domestic students; for summer admission, 4/15 for domestic students. Application fee: $30. Electronic applications accepted. *Expenses:* Tuition, state resident: part-time $288.16 per credit hour. Tuition, nonresident: part-time $1073.31 per credit hour. Tuition and fees vary according to program. *Financial support:* In 2017–18, 6 students received support, including 6 research assistantships with partial tuition reimbursements available (averaging $7,380 per year), 2 teaching assistantships with partial tuition reimbursements available (averaging $8,406 per year); fellowships, career-related internships or fieldwork, Federal Work-Study, institutionally sponsored loans, tuition waivers (partial), and unspecified assistantships also available. Financial award application deadline: 3/1; financial award applicants required to submit FAFSA. *Unit head:* Dr. David Fukuda, Program Coordinator, 407-823-0442, E-mail: david.fukuda@ucf.edu. *Application contact:* Associate Director, Graduate Admissions, 407-823-2766, Fax: 407-823-6442, E-mail: gradadmissions@ucf.edu.
Website: http://education.ucf.edu/sportexscience/

University of Central Florida, College of Community Innovation and Education, Education Doctoral Programs, Orlando, FL 32816. Offers curriculum and instruction (Ed D); education (PhD), including communication sciences and disorders, counselor education, early childhood education, elementary education, exceptional education, exercise physiology, higher education, instructional design and technology, mathematics education, methodology, measurement and analysis, reading education, science education, social science education, TESOL; educational leadership (Ed D). *Students:* 122 full-time (86 women), 129 part-time (88 women); includes 64 minority (24 Black or African American, non-Hispanic/Latino; 1 American Indian or Alaska Native, non-Hispanic/Latino; 9 Asian, non-Hispanic/Latino; 24 Hispanic/Latino; 6 Two or more races, non-Hispanic/Latino), 26 international. Average age 38. 195 applicants, 47% accepted, 72 enrolled. In 2017, 89 doctorates awarded. *Entrance requirements:* For doctorate, GRE, letters of recommendation, goal statement, resume, writing sample. Application fee: $30. Electronic applications accepted. *Expenses:* Tuition, state resident: part-time $288.16 per credit hour. Tuition, nonresident: part-time $1073.31 per credit hour. Tuition and fees vary according to program. *Financial support:* In 2017–18, 77 students received support, including 28 fellowships with partial tuition reimbursements available (averaging $5,733 per year), 29 research assistantships with partial tuition reimbursements available (averaging $10,230 per year), 54 teaching assistantships with partial tuition reimbursements available (averaging $11,614 per year); health care benefits also available. Financial award application deadline: 3/1; financial award applicants required to submit FAFSA. *Unit head:* Dr. Edward Robinson, Director of Doctoral Programs, 407-823-6106, E-mail: edward.robinson@ucf.edu. *Application contact:* Associate Director, Graduate Admissions, 407-823-2766, Fax: 407-823-6442, E-mail: gradadmissions@ucf.edu.
Website: https://edcollege.ucf.edu/academic-programs/graduate/

University of Central Oklahoma, The Jackson College of Graduate Studies, College of Education and Professional Studies, Department of Kinesiology and Health Studies, Edmond, OK 73034-5209. Offers athletic training (MS); wellness management (MS), including exercise science, health promotion. *Faculty:* 7 full-time (4 women), 1 (woman) part-time/adjunct. *Students:* 31 full-time (20 women), 32 part-time (18 women); includes 19 minority (8 Black or African American, non-Hispanic/Latino; 2 American Indian or Alaska Native, non-Hispanic/Latino; 6 Hispanic/Latino; 3 Two or more races, non-Hispanic/Latino), 5 international. Average age 29. 41 applicants, 71% accepted, 13 enrolled. In 2017, 19 master's awarded. *Degree requirements:* For master's, comprehensive exam (for some programs), thesis (for some programs). *Entrance requirements:* Additional exam requirements/recommendations for international students: Required—TOEFL (minimum score 550 paper-based; 79 iBT), IELTS (minimum score 6.5). *Application deadline:* For fall admission, 12/15 priority date for domestic students, 7/15 for international students; for spring admission, 11/15 for international students; for summer admission, 3/1 for domestic and international students. Application fee: $60. Electronic applications accepted. *Expenses:* Tuition, state resident: full-time $5375; part-time $268.75 per credit hour. Tuition, nonresident: full-time $13,295; part-time $664.75 per credit hour. *Required fees:* $626; $31.30 per credit hour. One-time fee: $50. Tuition and fees vary according to program. *Financial support:* In 2017–18, 15 students received support, including 2 research assistantships with partial tuition reimbursements available (averaging $4,436 per year), 1 teaching assistantship with partial tuition reimbursement available (averaging $2,958 per year); career-related internships or fieldwork, scholarships/grants, tuition waivers (partial), and unspecified assistantships also available. Financial award application deadline: 3/31; financial award applicants required to submit FAFSA. *Unit head:* Dr. Debra Traywick, Chair, 405-974-5230, Fax: 405-974-3805. *Application contact:* Carlie Wellington, Assistant Director, CEPS Graduate Enrollment, 405-974-5105, Fax: 405-974-3851, E-mail: gradcoll@uco.edu.
Website: http://sites.uco.edu/ceps/dept/Professional-Studies-Programs/khs/index.asp

University of Connecticut, Graduate School, College of Agriculture, Health and Natural Resources, Department of Kinesiology, Program in Exercise Science, Storrs, CT

06269. Offers MS, PhD. Terminal master's awarded for partial completion of doctoral program. *Degree requirements:* For master's, comprehensive exam, thesis or alternative; for doctorate, thesis/dissertation. *Entrance requirements:* For doctorate, GRE General Test. Additional exam requirements/recommendations for international students: Required—TOEFL (minimum score 550 paper-based). Electronic applications accepted.

University of Dayton, Department of Health and Sport Science, Dayton, OH 45469. Offers exercise science (MS Ed). *Program availability:* Part-time, 100% online. *Faculty:* 10 full-time (5 women), 23 part-time/adjunct (16 women). *Students:* 7 full-time (4 women), 2 part-time (1 woman); includes 3 minority (2 Black or African American, non-Hispanic/Latino; 1 Hispanic/Latino), 3 international. Average age 24. 37 applicants, 30% accepted. In 2017, 7 master's awarded. *Degree requirements:* For master's, thesis. *Entrance requirements:* For master's, GRE General Test or MAT if undergraduate GPA was 2.75 or below, minimum GPA of 2.75; official academic records of all previously-attended colleges or universities; three letters of recommendation from professors or employers; personal statement or resume. Additional exam requirements/recommendations for international students: Required—TOEFL (minimum score 550 paper-based; 80 iBT). *Application deadline:* Applications are processed on a rolling basis. Application fee: $0 ($50 for international students). Electronic applications accepted. *Expenses:* Contact institution. *Financial support:* In 2017–18, 4 research assistantships with partial tuition reimbursements (averaging $9,640 per year) were awarded; career-related internships or fieldwork, institutionally sponsored loans, and unspecified assistantships also available. Financial award application deadline: 3/1; financial award applicants required to submit FAFSA. *Faculty research:* Exercise science, physiology, nutrition, sport management. *Unit head:* Dr. Corinne Daprano, Chair, 937-229-4240, Fax: 937-229-4244, E-mail: cdaprano1@udayton.edu. *Application contact:* Laura Greger, Administrative Assistant, 937-229-4225, E-mail: lgreger1@udayton.edu.
Website: https://www.udayton.edu/education/departments_and_programs/hss

University of Florida, Graduate School, College of Health and Human Performance, Department of Applied Physiology and Kinesiology, Gainesville, FL 32611. Offers applied physiology and kinesiology (MS); athletic training/sports medicine (MS); biobehavioral science (MS); clinical exercise physiology (MS); exercise physiology (MS); health and human performance (PhD), including applied physiology and kinesiology, biobehavioral science, exercise physiology; human performance (MS). *Degree requirements:* For master's, comprehensive exam, thesis (for some programs); for doctorate, comprehensive exam, thesis/dissertation. *Entrance requirements:* For master's and doctorate, GRE General Test, minimum GPA of 3.0. Additional exam requirements/recommendations for international students: Required—TOEFL (minimum score 550 paper-based; 80 iBT), IELTS (minimum score 6). Electronic applications accepted. *Faculty research:* Cardiovascular disease; basic mechanisms that underlie exercise-induced changes in the body at the organ, tissue, cellular and molecular level; development of rehabilitation techniques for regaining motor control after stroke or as a consequence of Parkinson's disease; maintaining optimal health and delaying age-related declines in physiological function; psychomotor mechanisms impacting health and performance across the life span.

University of Houston, College of Liberal Arts and Social Sciences, Department of Health and Human Performance, Houston, TX 77204. Offers exercise science (MS); human nutrition (MS); human space exploration sciences (MS); kinesiology (PhD); physical education (M Ed). *Accreditation:* NCATE (one or more programs are accredited). *Program availability:* Part-time, evening/weekend. *Degree requirements:* For master's, comprehensive exam (for some programs), thesis (for some programs); for doctorate, comprehensive exam, thesis/dissertation, qualifying exam, candidacy paper. *Entrance requirements:* For master's, GRE (minimum 35th percentile on each section), minimum cumulative GPA of 3.0; for doctorate, GRE (minimum 35th percentile on each section), minimum cumulative GPA of 3.3. Additional exam requirements/recommendations for international students: Required—TOEFL (minimum score 550 paper-based; 79 iBT). Electronic applications accepted. *Faculty research:* Biomechanics, exercise physiology, obesity, nutrition, space exploration science.

University of Houston–Clear Lake, School of Human Sciences and Humanities, Programs in Human Sciences, Houston, TX 77058-1002. Offers behavioral sciences (MA), including criminology, cross cultural studies, general psychology, sociology; clinical psychology (MA); criminology (MA); cross cultural studies (MA); family therapy (MA); fitness and human performance (MA); school psychology (MA). *Accreditation:* AAMFT/COAMFTE. *Program availability:* Part-time, evening/weekend, online learning. *Degree requirements:* For master's, thesis or alternative. *Entrance requirements:* For master's, GRE General Test. Additional exam requirements/recommendations for international students: Required—TOEFL (minimum score 550 paper-based). Electronic applications accepted. *Faculty research:* Smoking cessation, adolescent sexuality, white collar crime, serial murder, human factors/human computer interaction.

University of Idaho, College of Graduate Studies, College of Education, Health and Human Sciences, Department of Movement Sciences, Moscow, ID 83844. Offers athletic training (MSAT, DAT); exercise science and health (MS); physical education teacher education (M Ed, MS); recreation, sport, and tourism management (MS). *Faculty:* 22. *Students:* 89 full-time (41 women), 18 part-time (7 women). Average age 28. In 2017, 24 master's awarded. *Degree requirements:* For doctorate, thesis/dissertation. *Entrance requirements:* For master's and doctorate, minimum GPA of 3.0. Additional exam requirements/recommendations for international students: Required—TOEFL. *Application deadline:* For fall admission, 8/1 for domestic students; for spring admission, 12/15 for domestic students. Applications are processed on a rolling basis. Application fee: $60. Electronic applications accepted. *Expenses:* Tuition, state resident: full-time $6722; part-time $430 per credit hour. Tuition, nonresident: full-time $23,046; part-time $1337 per credit hour. *Required fees:* $2142; $63 per credit hour. *Financial support:* Research assistantships and teaching assistantships available. Financial award applicants required to submit FAFSA. *Unit head:* Dr. Philip W. Scruggs, Chair, 208-885-7921, E-mail: movementsciences@uidaho.edu. *Application contact:* Sean Scoggin, Graduate Recruitment Coordinator, 208-885-4001, Fax: 208-885-4406, E-mail: graduateadmissions@uidaho.edu.
Website: https://www.uidaho.edu/ed/mvsc

The University of Iowa, Graduate College, College of Liberal Arts and Sciences, Department of Health and Human Physiology, Iowa City, IA 52242-1316. Offers athletic training (MS); clinical exercise physiology (MS); health and human physiology (PhD); leisure studies (MA, PhD), including recreational sport management (PhD), therapeutic recreation (MA). *Degree requirements:* For master's, thesis optional, exam; for doctorate, comprehensive exam, thesis/dissertation. *Entrance requirements:* For master's and doctorate, GRE General Test, minimum GPA of 3.0. Additional exam requirements/recommendations for international students: Required—TOEFL (minimum score 600 paper-based; 100 iBT). Electronic applications accepted.

The University of Kansas, Graduate Studies, School of Education, Department of Health, Sport, and Exercise Sciences, Lawrence, KS 66045. Offers exercise science (MS Ed); health, sport, and exercise sciences (PhD); sport management (MS Ed). *Accreditation:* NCATE. *Program availability:* Part-time, evening/weekend. *Students:* 56 full-time (23 women), 11 part-time (5 women); includes 8 minority (2 Black or African American, non-Hispanic/Latino; 1 American Indian or Alaska Native, non-Hispanic/Latino; 2 Hispanic/Latino; 3 Two or more races, non-Hispanic/Latino), 4 international. Average age 26. 70 applicants, 63% accepted, 23 enrolled. In 2017, 19 master's, 6 doctorates awarded. *Entrance requirements:* For master's, GRE General Test (minimum score 1000, 450 verbal, 450 quantitative, 4.0 analytical), minimum GPA 3.0, three letters of recommendation, personal statement, resume, writing sample; for doctorate, GRE General Test (minimum score 1100, verbal 500, quantitative 500, analytical 4.5), minimum graduate GPA of 3.5, undergraduate 3.0; three letters of recommendation; personal statement; resume; writing sample; interview with an advisor. *Application deadline:* For fall admission, 3/15 for domestic and international students; for spring admission, 10/1 for domestic and international students; for summer admission, 3/15 for domestic and international students. Application fee: $65 ($85 for international students). Electronic applications accepted. *Financial support:* Research assistantships, teaching assistantships, Federal Work-Study, scholarships/grants, and unspecified assistantships available. Financial award application deadline: 2/21. *Faculty research:* Exercise and sport psychology, obesity prevention, sexuality health, sport ethics, skeletal muscle cell signaling and performance. *Unit head:* Dr. Joseph Weir, Chair, 785-864-0784, E-mail: joseph.weir@ku.edu. *Application contact:* Sarah Clopton, Graduate Admissions Coordinator, 785-864-7268, E-mail: sclopton@ku.edu.
Website: http://hses.soe.ku.edu

University of Kentucky, Graduate School, College of Education, Program in Kinesiology and Health Promotion, Lexington, KY 40506-0032. Offers biomechanics (MS); exercise physiology (MS, PhD); exercise science (PhD); health promotion (MS, Ed D); physical education training (Ed D); sport leadership (MS); teaching and coaching (MS). Terminal master's awarded for partial completion of doctoral program. *Degree requirements:* For master's, comprehensive exam, thesis optional; for doctorate, comprehensive exam, thesis/dissertation. *Entrance requirements:* For master's, GRE General Test, minimum undergraduate GPA of 2.75; for doctorate, GRE General Test, minimum graduate GPA of 3.0. Additional exam requirements/recommendations for international students: Required—TOEFL (minimum score 550 paper-based). Electronic applications accepted.

University of Lethbridge, School of Graduate Studies, Lethbridge, AB T1K 3M4, Canada. Offers addictions counseling (M Sc); agricultural biotechnology (M Sc); agricultural studies (M Sc, MA); anthropology (MA); archaeology (M Sc, MA); art (MA, MFA); biochemistry (M Sc); biological sciences (M Sc); biomolecular science (PhD); biosystems and biodiversity (PhD); Canadian studies (MA); chemistry (M Sc); computer science (M Sc); computer science and geographical information science (M Sc); counseling (MC); counseling psychology (M Ed); dramatic arts (MA); earth, space, and physical science (PhD); economics (MA); education (MA, PhD); educational leadership (M Ed); English (MA); environmental science (M Sc); evolution and behavior (PhD); exercise science (M Sc); French (MA); French/German (MA); French/Spanish (MA); general education (M Ed); geography (M Sc, MA); German (MA); health sciences (M Sc); individualized multidisciplinary (M Sc, MA); kinesiology (M Sc, MA); management (M Sc), including accounting, finance, human resource management and labor relations, information systems, international management, marketing, policy and strategy; mathematics (M Sc); music (M Mus, MA); Native American studies (MA); neuroscience (M Sc, PhD); new media (MA, MFA); nursing (M Sc, MN); philosophy (MA); physics (M Sc); political science (MA); psychology (M Sc, MA); religious studies (MA); sociology (MA); theatre and dramatic arts (MFA); theoretical and computational science (PhD); urban and regional studies (MA); women and gender studies (MA). *Program availability:* Part-time, evening/weekend. *Degree requirements:* For master's, thesis (for some programs); for doctorate, comprehensive exam, thesis/dissertation. *Entrance requirements:* For master's, GMAT (for M Sc in management); bachelor's degree in related field, minimum GPA of 3.0 during previous 20 graded semester courses, 2 years' teaching or related experience (M Ed); for doctorate, master's degree, minimum graduate GPA of 3.5. Additional exam requirements/recommendations for international students: Required—TOEFL (minimum score 580 paper-based; 93 iBT). Electronic applications accepted. *Faculty research:* Movement and brain plasticity, gibberellin physiology, photosynthesis, carbon cycling, molecular properties of main-group ring components.

University of Louisiana at Monroe, Graduate School, College of Health and Pharmaceutical Sciences, Department of Kinesiology, Monroe, LA 71209-0001. Offers applied exercise science (MS); clinical exercise physiology (MS); sports, fitness and recreation management (MS). *Program availability:* Part-time, evening/weekend, online learning. *Faculty:* 6 full-time (2 women), 1 part-time/adjunct (0 women). *Students:* 28 full-time (15 women), 13 part-time (5 women); includes 12 minority (8 Black or African American, non-Hispanic/Latino; 4 Hispanic/Latino), 3 international. Average age 24. 27 applicants, 52% accepted, 11 enrolled. In 2017, 27 master's awarded. *Degree requirements:* For master's, comprehensive exam, thesis, 6-hour internship. *Entrance requirements:* For master's, GRE General Test. Additional exam requirements/recommendations for international students: Required—TOEFL (minimum score 500 paper-based; 61 iBT). *Application deadline:* For fall admission, 8/24 priority date for domestic students, 7/1 for international students; for winter admission, 12/14 priority date for domestic students; for spring admission, 1/19 for domestic students, 11/1 for international students. Applications are processed on a rolling basis. Application fee: $20 ($30 for international students). Electronic applications accepted. *Expenses:* Tuition, state resident: full-time $6489; part-time $479 per hour. Tuition, nonresident: full-time $12,100; part-time $479 per hour. *Required fees:* $8860; $802 per hour. $3273 per semester. *Financial support:* In 2017–18, 12 students received support. Research assistantships, career-related internships or fieldwork, Federal Work-Study, and unspecified assistantships available. Financial award application deadline: 4/1; financial award applicants required to submit FAFSA. *Faculty research:* Cardiovascular disease risk factors; exercise and immunological system; attitude, exercise, and the aged. *Unit head:* Dr. Ken Alford, Director, 318-342-1306, E-mail: alford@ulm.edu. *Application contact:* Dr. Tommie Church, Director of Graduate Studies, 318-342-1321, E-mail: church@ulm.edu.
Website: http://www.ulm.edu/kinesiology/

University of Louisville, Graduate School, College of Education and Human Development, Department of Health and Sport Sciences, Louisville, KY 40292-0001. Offers community health education (M Ed); exercise physiology (MS), including health and sport sciences, strength and conditioning; health and physical education (MAT); sport administration (MS). *Program availability:* Part-time, evening/weekend. *Students:* 35 full-time (11 women), 6 part-time (4 women); includes 10 minority (5 Black or African American, non-Hispanic/Latino; 4 Hispanic/Latino; 1 Two or more races, non-Hispanic/Latino), 1 international. Average age 28. 46 applicants, 67% accepted, 20 enrolled. In 2017, 21 master's awarded. Application fee: $65. *Expenses:* Tuition, state resident: full-time $12,246; part-time $681 per credit hour. Tuition, nonresident: full-time $25,486; part-time $1417 per credit hour. *Required fees:* $196. Tuition and fees vary according to course load, program and reciprocity agreements. *Financial support:* Applicants required to submit FAFSA. *Faculty research:* Sport administration, exercise physiology, exercise science, physical education, health education. *Total annual research expenditures:* $91,688. *Unit head:* Dr. Margaret Hancock, Interim Chair/Assistant Professor, 502-852-6645, E-mail: meg.hancock@louisville.edu. *Application contact:* Betty Hampton, Director of Graduate Student Services, 502-852-5597, Fax: 502-852-1465, E-mail: edadvise@louisville.edu.
Website: http://www.louisville.edu/education/departments/hss

Exercise and Sports Science

University of Louisville, Graduate School, College of Education and Human Development, Departments of Early Childhood and Elementary Education, Middle and Secondary Education, and Special Education, Louisville, KY 40292-0001. Offers art education (MAT); autism and applied behavior analysis (Certificate); curriculum and instruction (PhD); early elementary education (MAT); exercise physiology (MS); health and physical education (MAT); health professions education (Certificate); higher education (MA); human resources and organization development (MS); instructional technology (M Ed); interdisciplinary early childhood education (MAT); middle school education (MAT); music education (MAT); secondary education (MAT); special education (MAT); sport administration (MS); teacher leadership (M Ed). *Program availability:* Part-time, evening/weekend. *Students:* 114 full-time (73 women), 173 part-time (114 women); includes 49 minority (19 Black or African American, non-Hispanic/Latino; 5 Asian, non-Hispanic/Latino; 13 Hispanic/Latino; 12 Two or more races, non-Hispanic/Latino), 7 international. Average age 29. 132 applicants, 73% accepted, 57 enrolled. In 2017, 70 master's, 2 doctorates, 2 other advanced degrees awarded. *Application deadline:* For spring admission, 1/1 priority date for international students. Application fee: $65. *Expenses:* Tuition, state resident: full-time $12,246; part-time $681 per credit hour. Tuition, nonresident: full-time $25,486; part-time $1417 per credit hour. *Required fees:* $196. Tuition and fees vary according to course load, program and reciprocity agreements. *Financial support:* Application deadline: 6/1; applicants required to submit FAFSA. *Faculty research:* STEM teaching and learning; content literacy for English language learners; social justice in teacher education; adolescent literacy; mathematics teacher development. *Total annual research expenditures:* $1.7 million. *Unit head:* Dr. Ann E. Larson, Dean, College of Education and Human Development, 502-852-6411, Fax: 502-852-1464, E-mail: ann@louisville.edu. *Application contact:* Betty Hampton, Director of Graduate Student Services, 502-852-5597, Fax: 502-852-1465, E-mail: edadvise@louisville.edu.
Website: http://louisville.edu/delphi

University of Maine, Graduate School, College of Education and Human Development, School of Kinesiology, Physical Education and Athletic Training, Orono, ME 04469. Offers classroom technology integrationist (CGS); education data specialist (CGS); educational technology coordinator (CGS); kinesiology and physical education (M Ed, MS); science education (M Ed, MS); STEM education (PhD). *Program availability:* Part-time, evening/weekend. *Faculty:* 3 full-time (0 women). *Students:* 10 full-time (3 women), 1 part-time (0 women); includes 2 minority (1 Black or African American, non-Hispanic/Latino; 1 Asian, non-Hispanic/Latino). Average age 24. 8 applicants, 100% accepted, 5 enrolled. In 2017, 6 master's awarded. *Degree requirements:* For master's, thesis (for some programs); for doctorate, comprehensive exam, thesis/dissertation. *Entrance requirements:* For master's, GRE General Test, MAT; for doctorate, GRE General Test. Additional exam requirements/recommendations for international students: Required—TOEFL. *Application deadline:* For fall admission, 1/15 for domestic students. Applications are processed on a rolling basis. Application fee: $65. Electronic applications accepted. *Expenses:* Tuition, state resident: full-time $7722; part-time $429 per credit hour. Tuition, nonresident: full-time $25,146; part-time $1397 per credit hour. *Required fees:* $1162; $581 per credit hour. *Financial support:* In 2017–18, 7 students received support, including 6 teaching assistantships with full tuition reimbursements available (averaging $15,200 per year); Federal Work-Study, scholarships/grants, and unspecified assistantships also available. Financial award application deadline: 3/1. *Faculty research:* Geriatric equilibrium, physical activity and technology, muscle cell metabolism, hormonal response to exercise. *Unit head:* Dr. Jim Artesani, Associate Dean of Accreditation and Graduate Affairs, 207-581-4061, Fax: 207-581-2423. *Application contact:* Scott G. Delcourt, Assistant Vice President for Graduate Studies and Senior Associate Dean, 207-581-3291, Fax: 207-581-3232, E-mail: graduate@maine.edu.
Website: http://umaine.edu/edhd/

University of Mary, School of Health Sciences, Program in Clinical Exercise Physiology, Bismarck, ND 58504-9652. Offers MS. *Program availability:* Online learning.

University of Mary Hardin-Baylor, Graduate Studies in Exercise Physiology, Belton, TX 76513. Offers exercise physiology (MS Ed); sport administration (MS Ed). *Program availability:* Part-time, 100% online. *Faculty:* 6 full-time (2 women). *Students:* 18 full-time (5 women), 30 part-time (11 women); includes 21 minority (5 Black or African American, non-Hispanic/Latino; 14 Hispanic/Latino; 2 Two or more races, non-Hispanic/Latino). Average age 26. 30 applicants, 90% accepted, 19 enrolled. In 2017, 19 master's awarded. *Degree requirements:* For master's, comprehensive exam, thesis optional. *Entrance requirements:* For master's, bachelor's degree in exercise science or related field; minimum GPA of 3.0; interview with program director. Additional exam requirements/recommendations for international students: Required—TOEFL (minimum score 60 iBT), IELTS (minimum score 4.5). *Application deadline:* For fall admission, 6/1 for domestic students, 4/30 priority date for international students; for spring admission, 11/1 for domestic students, 9/30 priority date for international students. Applications are processed on a rolling basis. Application fee: $35 ($135 for international students). Electronic applications accepted. *Expenses: Tuition:* Full-time $15,570; part-time $10,380 per credit hour. *Required fees:* $1350; $75 per credit hour. $50 per term. Tuition and fees vary according to course load and degree level. *Financial support:* In 2017–18, 37 students received support. Federal Work-Study, unspecified assistantships, and scholarships for some active duty military personnel available. Support available to part-time students. Financial award application deadline: 6/1; financial award applicants required to submit FAFSA. *Faculty research:* Evaluation of the efficacy and safety of Fenugreek extract ingestion on markers of muscle damage and inflammation on healthy non-resistance trained subjects; genetic influences on sport performance and athlete health; examination of biomarkers of sub-concussive impacts in men and women's Division III soccer players; The Acute Response of nutritive vs. non-nutritive sweeteners in soft drinks of blood glucose and insulin in regular soft drink consumers. *Unit head:* Dr. Lem Taylor, Director, MS Ed in Exercise Physiology Program, 254-295-4895, E-mail: ltaylor@umhb.edu. *Application contact:* Sharon Aguilera, Assistant Director, Graduate Admissions, 254-295-4835, E-mail: saguilera@umhb.edu.
Website: https://go.umhb.edu/graduate/exercise-physiology/home

University of Massachusetts Boston, College of Nursing and Health Sciences, Program in Exercise and Health Sciences, Boston, MA 02125-3393. Offers MS, PhD. *Faculty:* 15 full-time (9 women), 2 part-time/adjunct (0 women). *Students:* 20 full-time (13 women), 5 part-time (4 women); includes 6 minority (3 Black or African American, non-Hispanic/Latino; 1 Asian, non-Hispanic/Latino; 1 Hispanic/Latino; 1 Two or more races, non-Hispanic/Latino), 2 international. Average age 29. 35 applicants, 63% accepted, 12 enrolled. In 2017, 9 master's awarded. *Expenses:* Tuition, state resident: full-time $17,375. Tuition, nonresident: full-time $33,915. *Required fees:* $355. *Unit head:* Dr. Linda Thompson, 617-287-6876, E-mail: linda.thompson@umb.edu. *Application contact:* Graduate Admissions Coordinator, 617-287-6400, Fax: 617-287-6236, E-mail: bos.gadm@dpc.umassp.edu.

University of Memphis, Graduate School, School of Health Studies, Memphis, TN 38152. Offers faith and health (Graduate Certificate); health studies (MS), including exercise, sport and movement sciences, health promotion, physical education teacher education; nutrition (MS), including clinical nutrition, environmental nutrition, nutrition science; sport nutrition and dietary supplementation (Graduate Certificate). *Program availability:* 100% online. *Faculty:* 19 full-time (10 women), 2 part-time/adjunct (both women). In 2017, 42 master's awarded. *Degree requirements:* For master's, comprehensive exam, thesis or alternative, culminating experience; for Graduate Certificate, practicum. *Entrance requirements:* For master's, GRE or PRAXIS II, letters of recommendation, statement of goals, minimum undergraduate GPA of 2.5; for Graduate Certificate, minimum undergraduate GPA of 2.5. Additional exam requirements/recommendations for international students: Required—TOEFL (minimum score 550 paper-based; 79 iBT). *Application deadline:* For fall admission, 4/15 priority date for domestic students; for spring admission, 10/15 priority date for domestic students; for summer admission, 4/15 priority date for domestic students. Application fee: $35 ($60 for international students). *Expenses:* Contact institution. *Financial support:* In 2017–18, 33 research assistantships (averaging $11,930 per year), 4 teaching assistantships (averaging $10,000 per year) were awarded; career-related internships or fieldwork, Federal Work-Study, scholarships/grants, and unspecified assistantships also available. Financial award application deadline: 2/1; financial award applicants required to submit FAFSA. *Unit head:* Dr. Richard J. Bloomer, Director, 901-678-4316, Fax: 901-678-3591, E-mail: rbloomer@memphis.edu. *Application contact:* Dr. Lawrence Weiss, Director of Graduate Programs, 901-678-5037, E-mail: lweiss@memphis.edu.
Website: http://www.memphis.edu/shs/

University of Miami, Graduate School, School of Education and Human Development, Department of Kinesiology and Sport Sciences, Program in Exercise Physiology, Coral Gables, FL 33124. Offers exercise physiology (MS Ed, PhD); strength and conditioning (MS Ed). *Program availability:* Part-time, evening/weekend. Terminal master's awarded for partial completion of doctoral program. *Degree requirements:* For master's, comprehensive exam (for some programs), thesis optional, special project; for doctorate, thesis/dissertation, qualifying exam. *Entrance requirements:* For master's and doctorate, GRE General Test. Additional exam requirements/recommendations for international students: Required—TOEFL (minimum score 550 paper-based; 80 iBT); Recommended—IELTS (minimum score 6.5). Electronic applications accepted. *Faculty research:* Women's health, cardiovascular health, aging, metabolism, obesity.

University of Minnesota, Twin Cities Campus, Graduate School, College of Education and Human Development, School of Kinesiology, Minneapolis, MN 55455-0213. Offers kinesiology (MS, PhD), including behavioral aspects of physical activity, biomechanics and neuromotor control, exercise physiology, perceptual-motor control and learning, sport and exercise psychology, sport management (PhD), sport sociology; sport and exercise science (M Ed); sport management (M Ed, MA). *Program availability:* Part-time. *Faculty:* 16 full-time (7 women). *Students:* 111 full-time (52 women), 22 part-time (8 women); includes 21 minority (7 Black or African American, non-Hispanic/Latino; 1 American Indian or Alaska Native, non-Hispanic/Latino; 4 Asian, non-Hispanic/Latino; 7 Hispanic/Latino; 2 Two or more races, non-Hispanic/Latino), 15 international. Average age 27. 120 applicants, 25% accepted, 30 enrolled. In 2017, 41 master's, 9 doctorates awarded. Terminal master's awarded for partial completion of doctoral program. *Degree requirements:* For master's, final oral exam; for doctorate, thesis/dissertation, preliminary written/oral exam, final oral exam. *Entrance requirements:* For master's, GRE or MAT, minimum GPA of 3.0; for doctorate, GRE or MAT, minimum GPA of 3.0, writing sample. Application fee: $75 ($95 for international students). *Financial support:* In 2017–18, 2 fellowships, 9 research assistantships with full tuition reimbursements (averaging $6,651 per year), 41 teaching assistantships with full tuition reimbursements (averaging $14,060 per year) were awarded; career-related internships or fieldwork, Federal Work-Study, institutionally sponsored loans, and tuition waivers (full and partial) also available. Support available to part-time students. *Faculty research:* Role of physical activity in preventing health related problems; mechanism of age-related disorders, diseases and mental problems, and the ways to ameliorate them; role of sports in society and social justice; sports among populations with low income and racial diversity; fundamental functions of the body and the mechanism controlling the mechanisms; psychological issues related to physical activity and sports. *Total annual research expenditures:* $948,746. *Unit head:* Dr. Li Li Ji, Director, 612-624-9809, E-mail: llji@umn.edu. *Application contact:* Dr. Michael Wade, Director of Graduate Studies, 612-626-2094, E-mail: mwade@umn.edu.
Website: http://www.cehd.umn.edu/kin/

University of Mississippi, Graduate School, School of Applied Sciences, University, MS 38677. Offers communicative disorders (MS); criminal justice (MCJ); exercise science (MS); food and nutrition services (MS); health and kinesiology (PhD); health promotion (MS); nutrition and hospitality management (PhD); park and recreation management (MA); social welfare (PhD); social work (MSW). *Faculty:* 66 full-time (38 women), 33 part-time/adjunct (14 women). *Students:* 182 full-time (139 women), 41 part-time (27 women); includes 49 minority (41 Black or African American, non-Hispanic/Latino; 1 American Indian or Alaska Native, non-Hispanic/Latino; 3 Asian, non-Hispanic/Latino; 3 Hispanic/Latino; 1 Two or more races, non-Hispanic/Latino), 13 international. Average age 26. *Entrance requirements:* For master's, GRE General Test, minimum GPA of 3.0. Additional exam requirements/recommendations for international students: Required—TOEFL. *Application deadline:* For fall admission, 4/1 for domestic students; for spring admission, 10/1 for domestic students. Applications are processed on a rolling basis. Application fee: $50. Electronic applications accepted. *Financial support:* Scholarships/grants available. Financial award application deadline: 3/1; financial award applicants required to submit FAFSA. *Unit head:* Dr. Teresa C. Carithers, Dean, 662-915-1081, Fax: 662-915-5717, E-mail: applsci@olemiss.edu.

University of Montana, Graduate School, Phyllis J. Washington College of Education and Human Sciences, Department of Health and Human Performance, Missoula, MT 59812. Offers community health (MS); exercise science (MS); health and human performance generalist (MS). *Program availability:* Part-time. *Entrance requirements:* For master's, GRE General Test. Additional exam requirements/recommendations for international students: Required—TOEFL. *Faculty research:* Exercise physiology, performance psychology, nutrition, pre-employment physical screening, program evaluation.

University of Nebraska at Kearney, College of Education, Kinesiology and Sport Sciences Department, Kearney, NE 68849-0001. Offers general physical education (MA Ed), including recreation and leisure, sports administration; physical education exercise science (MA Ed); physical education master teacher (MA Ed), including pedagogy, special populations. *Program availability:* Part-time, evening/weekend, 100% online. *Degree requirements:* For master's, comprehensive exam, thesis optional. *Entrance requirements:* For master's, GRE General Test (for some programs), personal statement. Additional exam requirements/recommendations for international students: Recommended—TOEFL (minimum score 550 paper-based; 79 iBT), IELTS (minimum score 6.5). Electronic applications accepted. *Faculty research:* Ergonomic aids, nutrition, motor development, sports pedagogy, applied behavior analysis, physical activity and wellness, athletic training, therapeutic interventions, exercise physiology, endocrinology and metabolism.

University of Nebraska at Omaha, Graduate Studies, College of Education, School of Health and Kinesiology, Omaha, NE 68182. Offers athletic training (MA); exercise science (PhD); health, physical education, and recreation (MA, MS). *Program availability:* Part-time, evening/weekend. *Degree requirements:* For master's, comprehensive exam, thesis (for some programs). *Entrance requirements:* For master's, GRE; entrance exam, minimum GPA of 3.0, official transcripts, statement of purpose, 2 letters of recommendation; for doctorate, GRE, minimum GPA of 3.2, official transcripts, statement of purpose, 3 letters of recommendation, resume, writing sample. Additional exam requirements/recommendations for international students: Required—TOEFL, IELTS, PTE. Electronic applications accepted.

University of Nebraska–Lincoln, Graduate College, College of Education and Human Sciences, Department of Nutrition and Health Sciences, Lincoln, NE 68588. Offers community nutrition (MS); nutrition (MS, PhD); nutrition and health promotion (MS); nutrition and exercise (MS); nutrition and health sciences (MS, PhD). *Degree requirements:* For master's, thesis optional. *Entrance requirements:* For master's, GRE General Test. Additional exam requirements/recommendations for international students: Required—TOEFL (minimum score 550 paper-based). Electronic applications accepted. *Faculty research:* Foods/food service administration, community nutrition science, diet-health relationships.

University of Nevada, Las Vegas, Graduate College, School of Allied Health Sciences, Department of Kinesiology and Nutrition Sciences, Las Vegas, NV 89154-3034. Offers exercise physiology (MS); kinesiology (PhD); nutrition sciences (MS). *Program availability:* Part-time. *Faculty:* 10 full-time (5 women), 2 part-time/adjunct (1 woman). *Students:* 34 full-time (19 women), 11 part-time (4 women); includes 10 minority (2 Black or African American, non-Hispanic/Latino; 1 American Indian or Alaska Native, non-Hispanic/Latino; 2 Asian, non-Hispanic/Latino; 4 Hispanic/Latino; 1 Two or more races, non-Hispanic/Latino), 2 international. Average age 27. 54 applicants, 52% accepted, 17 enrolled. In 2017, 15 master's awarded. *Degree requirements:* For master's, thesis (for some programs), professional paper; for doctorate, comprehensive exam, thesis/dissertation. *Entrance requirements:* For master's, GRE General Test, bachelor's degree; statement of purpose; 2 letters of recommendation; for doctorate, GRE General Test (minimum 70th percentile on the Verbal section), master's degree/bachelor's degree with minimum GPA of 3.25; 3 letters of recommendation; statement of purpose; personal interview. Additional exam requirements/recommendations for international students: Required—TOEFL (minimum score 550 paper-based; 80 iBT), IELTS (minimum score 7). *Application deadline:* For fall admission, 6/15 for domestic and international students; for spring admission, 11/15 for domestic and international students. Application fee: $60 ($95 for international students). Electronic applications accepted. *Expenses:* $275 per credit, $850 per course, $7,969 per year resident, $22,157 per year non-resident, $7,094 non-resident fee (7 credits or more), $1,307 annual health insurance fee. *Financial support:* In 2017–18, 12 students received support, including 12 research assistantships with full and partial tuition reimbursements available (averaging $14,396 per year), 10 teaching assistantships with full and partial tuition reimbursements available (averaging $12,350 per year); institutionally sponsored loans, scholarships/grants, health care benefits, and unspecified assistantships also available. Financial award application deadline: 3/15; financial award applicants required to submit FAFSA. *Faculty research:* Biomechanics of gait, factors in motor skill acquisition and performance, nutritional supplements and performance, lipoprotein biochemistry, transcranial direct current stimulation. *Total annual research expenditures:* $49,804. *Unit head:* Dr. Brian Schilling, Chair/Professor, 702-895-1130, Fax: 702-895-1500, E-mail: brian.schilling@unlv.edu. *Application contact:* Dr. James Navalta, Graduate Coordinator, 702-895-2344, E-mail: james.navalta@unlv.edu.

University of New Brunswick Fredericton, School of Graduate Studies, Faculty of Kinesiology, Fredericton, NB E3B 5A3, Canada. Offers exercise and sport science (M Sc); sport and recreation management (MBA); sport and recreation studies (MA). *Program availability:* Part-time. *Degree requirements:* For master's, thesis (for some programs). *Entrance requirements:* For master's, GMAT (minimum score of 550 for sport and recreation management program), minimum GPA of 3.0, written statement of research goals and interests. Additional exam requirements/recommendations for international students: Required—TOEFL (minimum score 92 iBT), IELTS (minimum score 7). Electronic applications accepted.

University of New Mexico, Graduate Studies, College of Education, Program in Physical Education, Sports and Exercise Science, Albuquerque, NM 87131-2039. Offers curriculum and instruction (PhD); exercise science (PhD); sports administration (PhD). *Program availability:* Part-time. *Students:* Average age 30. 67 applicants, 75% accepted, 35 enrolled. In 2017, 13 doctorates awarded. *Degree requirements:* For doctorate, comprehensive exam, thesis/dissertation, inquiry skills, 24 credits in supporting area. *Entrance requirements:* For doctorate, GRE, letter of intent, 3 letters of reference, minimum cumulative GPA of 3.0 in last 2 years of bachelor's degree. Additional exam requirements/recommendations for international students: Required—TOEFL (minimum score 550 paper-based). *Application deadline:* For fall admission, 3/1 priority date for domestic students; for spring admission, 11/1 priority date for domestic students. Application fee: $50. Electronic applications accepted. *Financial support:* Fellowships, teaching assistantships with full tuition reimbursements, career-related internships or fieldwork, Federal Work-Study, institutionally sponsored loans, scholarships/grants, health care benefits, tuition waivers, and unspecified assistantships available. Financial award application deadline: 3/1; financial award applicants required to submit FAFSA. *Faculty research:* Facility risk management, physical education pedagogy practices, physiological adaptations to exercise, physiological adaptations to heat, sport leadership. *Unit head:* Dr. Todd Seidler, Chair, 505-277-2783, Fax: 505-277-6227, E-mail: tseidler@unm.edu. *Application contact:* Monica Lopez, Program Office, 505-277-5151, Fax: 505-277-6227, E-mail: mllopez@unm.edu. Website: https://coe.unm.edu/departments-programs/hess/physical-education/physical-education-phd/index.html

University of North Alabama, College of Education, Department of Health, Physical Education, and Recreation, Florence, AL 35632-0001. Offers health and human performance (MS), including exercise science, kinesiology, wellness and health promotion. *Program availability:* Part-time. *Faculty:* 7 full-time (2 women), 1 part-time/adjunct (0 women). *Students:* 14 full-time (10 women), 14 part-time (6 women); includes 4 minority (all Black or African American, non-Hispanic/Latino), 3 international. Average age 25. 22 applicants, 82% accepted, 9 enrolled. In 2017, 7 master's awarded. *Degree requirements:* For master's, comprehensive exam (for some programs), thesis optional. *Entrance requirements:* For master's, MAT or GRE, 3 letters of recommendation, essay. Additional exam requirements/recommendations for international students: Required—TOEFL (minimum score 79 iBT), IELTS (minimum score 6), PTE (minimum score 54). *Application deadline:* Applications are processed on a rolling basis. Application fee: $50 ($100 for international students). Electronic applications accepted. *Expenses:* Tuition, state resident: full-time $7824; part-time $5943 per year. Tuition, nonresident: full-time $15,648; part-time $11,736 per year. *Required fees:* $3064; $2298 per unit. Tuition and fees vary according to course load and reciprocity agreements. *Financial support:* In 2017–18, 19 students received support. Federal Work-Study, scholarships/grants, and unspecified assistantships available. Financial award application deadline: 2/1; financial award applicants required to submit FAFSA. *Total annual research expenditures:* $13,976. *Unit head:* Dr. Thomas E. Coates, Chair, 256-765-4377. *Application contact:* Hillary N. Coats, Graduate Admissions Coordinator, 256-765-4447, E-mail: graduate@una.edu. Website: https://www.una.edu/hper/index.html

The University of North Carolina at Chapel Hill, Graduate School, College of Arts and Sciences, Department of Exercise and Sport Science, Chapel Hill, NC 27599. Offers athletic training (MA); exercise physiology (MA); sport administration (MA). *Degree requirements:* For master's, comprehensive exam, thesis. *Entrance requirements:* For master's, GRE General Test, minimum GPA of 3.0. Additional exam requirements/recommendations for international students: Required—TOEFL (minimum score 550 paper-based). Electronic applications accepted. *Faculty research:* Mild head injury in sport, endocrine system's response to exercise, obesity and children, effect of aerobic exercise on cerebral bloodflow in elderly population.

The University of North Carolina at Pembroke, The Graduate School, School of Education, Department of Health and Human Performance, Pembroke, NC 28372-1510. Offers health/physical education (MAT); physical education (MA), including exercise/sports administration, physical education advanced licensure. *Program availability:* Part-time, evening/weekend. *Degree requirements:* For master's, comprehensive exam, thesis optional. *Entrance requirements:* For master's, MAT or GRE, minimum GPA of 3.0 in major, 2.5 overall. Additional exam requirements/recommendations for international students: Required—TOEFL. *Application deadline:* For fall admission, 7/15 priority date for domestic and international students; for spring admission, 12/1 priority date for domestic and international students. Applications are processed on a rolling basis. Application fee: $45 ($60 for international students). *Financial support:* Application deadline: 4/15; applicants required to submit FAFSA. *Unit head:* Dr. Leah Fiorentino, Program Director, 910-775-4354, E-mail: leah.fiorentino@uncp.edu. Website: https://www.uncp.edu/departments/health-and-human-performance

University of Northern Colorado, Graduate School, College of Natural and Health Sciences, School of Sport and Exercise Science, Greeley, CO 80639. Offers exercise science (MS, PhD); physical education and physical activity leadership (MAT); sport administration (MS, PhD); sport pedagogy (MS, PhD); sports coaching (MA). *Program availability:* Part-time, evening/weekend. *Degree requirements:* For master's, comprehensive exam; for doctorate, comprehensive exam, thesis/dissertation. *Entrance requirements:* For master's, 2 letters of recommendation, resume; for doctorate, GRE General Test, 3 letters of recommendation, resume. Electronic applications accepted.

University of North Florida, Brooks College of Health, Department of Clinical and Applied Movement Sciences, Jacksonville, FL 32224. Offers MSH, DPT. *Accreditation:* APTA. *Program availability:* Part-time, evening/weekend. *Entrance requirements:* For master's, GRE General Test, minimum GPA of 3.0 in last 60 hours, volunteer/observation experience. Additional exam requirements/recommendations for international students: Required—TOEFL (minimum score 500 paper-based). Electronic applications accepted. *Faculty research:* Clinical outcomes related to orthopedic physical therapy interventions, instructional multimedia in physical therapy education, effect of functional electrical stimulation orthostatic hypotension in acute complete spinal cord injury individuals.

University of Oklahoma, College of Arts and Sciences, Department of Health and Exercise Science, Norman, OK 73019. Offers exercise physiology (MS, PhD); health and exercise science (MS); health promotion (MS, PhD). *Faculty:* 10 full-time (5 women), 1 part-time/adjunct (0 women). *Students:* 36 full-time (13 women), 16 part-time (8 women); includes 15 minority (2 Black or African American, non-Hispanic/Latino; 2 Asian, non-Hispanic/Latino; 5 Hispanic/Latino; 1 Native Hawaiian or other Pacific Islander, non-Hispanic/Latino; 5 Two or more races, non-Hispanic/Latino), 7 international. Average age 26. 28 applicants, 50% accepted, 14 enrolled. In 2017, 12 master's, 4 doctorates awarded. *Degree requirements:* For master's, comprehensive exam (for some programs), thesis; for doctorate, comprehensive exam, thesis/dissertation. *Entrance requirements:* For master's and doctorate, GRE. Additional exam requirements/recommendations for international students: Required—TOEFL (minimum score 79 iBT) or IELTS (minimum score 6.5). *Application deadline:* For fall admission, 2/1 priority date for domestic and international students. Applications are processed on a rolling basis. Application fee: $50 ($100 for international students). Electronic applications accepted. *Expenses:* Tuition, state resident: full-time $5119; part-time $213.30 per credit hour. Tuition, nonresident: full-time $19,778; part-time $824.10 per credit hour. *Required fees:* $3458; $133.55 per credit hour. $126.50 per semester. *Financial support:* In 2017–18, 51 students received support, including 46 teaching assistantships with full tuition reimbursements available (averaging $12,396 per year); health care benefits, tuition waivers (full), and unspecified assistantships also available. Financial award application deadline: 6/1; financial award applicants required to submit FAFSA. *Faculty research:* Health promotion, neuromuscular exercise physiology, aging, endocrine and bone metabolism, behavioral science. *Unit head:* Dr. Michael G. Bemben, Professor/Chair, 405-325-2717, Fax: 405-325-0594, E-mail: mgbemben@ou.edu. *Application contact:* Dr. Marshall Cheney, Assistant Professor/Graduate Liaison, 405-325-6322, Fax: 405-325-0594, E-mail: marshall@ou.edu. Website: http://www.ou.edu/cas/hes

University of Pittsburgh, School of Education, Department of Health and Physical Activity, Program in Developmental Movement, Pittsburgh, PA 15260. Offers MS. *Degree requirements:* For master's, thesis. *Entrance requirements:* Additional exam requirements/recommendations for international students: Required—TOEFL. Electronic applications accepted.

University of Pittsburgh, School of Education, Department of Health and Physical Activity, Program in Exercise Physiology, Pittsburgh, PA 15260. Offers MS, PhD. *Entrance requirements:* Additional exam requirements/recommendations for international students: Required—TOEFL (minimum score 550 paper-based; 80 iBT). Electronic applications accepted.

University of Puerto Rico–Mayagüez, Graduate Studies, College of Arts and Sciences, Department of Kinesiology, Mayagüez, PR 00681-9000. Offers kinesiology (MA), including biomechanics, education, exercise physiology, sports training. *Program availability:* Part-time. *Degree requirements:* For master's, thesis. *Entrance requirements:* For master's, EXADEP or GRE, minimum GPA of 2.5. Electronic applications accepted.

University of Puerto Rico–Río Piedras, College of Education, Program in Exercise Sciences, San Juan, PR 00931-3300. Offers MS. *Entrance requirements:* For master's, PAEG or GRE, minimum GPA of 3.0.

University of Rhode Island, Graduate School, College of Health Sciences, Department of Kinesiology, Kingston, RI 02881. Offers cultural studies of sport and physical culture (MS); exercise science (MS); psychosocial/behavioral aspects of physical activity (MS). *Accreditation:* NCATE. *Program availability:* Part-time. *Faculty:* 14 full-time (9 women). *Students:* 10 full-time (4 women), 3 part-time (1 woman), 1 international. 8 applicants, 100% accepted, 6 enrolled. In 2017, 7 master's awarded. *Entrance requirements:* Additional exam requirements/recommendations for international students: Required—TOEFL. *Application deadline:* For fall admission, 7/15 for domestic students, 2/1 for international students; for spring admission, 11/15 for domestic students, 7/15 for international students. Application fee: $65. Electronic applications accepted. *Expenses:* Tuition, state resident: full-time $12,706; part-time $786 per credit. Tuition, nonresident: full-time $25,216; part-time $1401 per credit. *Required fees:* $1598; $45 per credit. One-time fee: $30 part-time. *Financial support:* In 2017–18, 5 teaching assistantships with tuition reimbursements (averaging $11,078 per year) were awarded. Financial award

Exercise and Sports Science

application deadline: 2/1; financial award applicants required to submit FAFSA. *Unit head:* Dr. Disa Hatfield, Interim Chair, 401-874-5183, E-mail: doch@uri.edu. *Application contact:* Dr. Matthew Delmonico, Graduate Program Director, 401-874-5440, E-mail: delmonico@uri.edu.
Website: http://web.uri.edu/kinesiology/

University of South Alabama, College of Education and Professional Studies, Department of Health, Kinesiology, and Sport, Mobile, AL 36688. Offers exercise science (MS); health education (M Ed, MS); physical education (M Ed); sport management (MS). *Accreditation:* NCATE (one or more programs are accredited). *Program availability:* Part-time. *Faculty:* 7 full-time (2 women). *Students:* 47 full-time (15 women), 7 part-time (3 women); includes 23 minority (19 Black or African American, non-Hispanic/Latino; 1 American Indian or Alaska Native, non-Hispanic/Latino; 2 Asian, non-Hispanic/Latino; 1 Hispanic/Latino), 4 international. Average age 25. 48 applicants, 54% accepted, 19 enrolled. In 2017, 23 master's awarded. *Degree requirements:* For master's, comprehensive exam, thesis optional. *Entrance requirements:* For master's, GRE General Test or MAT, Alabama Class B certificate or the equivalent (for students seeking the master's-level/Class A certification). Additional exam requirements/recommendations for international students: Required—TOEFL. *Application deadline:* For fall admission, 7/1 priority date for domestic students, 6/15 priority date for international students; for spring admission, 11/15 priority date for domestic students, 11/1 priority date for international students; for summer admission, 4/15 for domestic students, 4/1 for international students. Applications are processed on a rolling basis. Application fee: $35. Electronic applications accepted. *Expenses:* Tuition, state resident: full-time $10,104; part-time $421 per semester hour. Tuition, nonresident: full-time $20,208; part-time $842 per semester hour. *Financial support:* Fellowships, research assistantships, teaching assistantships with partial tuition reimbursements, career-related internships or fieldwork, Federal Work-Study, institutionally sponsored loans, scholarships/grants, and unspecified assistantships available. Support available to part-time students. Financial award application deadline: 3/31; financial award applicants required to submit FAFSA. *Unit head:* Dr. John Kovaleski, Department Chair, 251-461-1622, Fax: 251-460-7252, E-mail: jkovales@southalabama.edu. *Application contact:* Dr. Susan Santoli, Director of Graduate Studies, 251-380-2836, Fax: 251-380-2748, E-mail: ssantoli@southalabama.edu.
Website: http://www.southalabama.edu/colleges/ceps/hks/index.html

University of South Carolina, The Graduate School, Arnold School of Public Health, Department of Exercise Science, Columbia, SC 29208. Offers MS, DPT, PhD. *Program availability:* Part-time. *Degree requirements:* For master's, comprehensive exam, thesis (for some programs), project; for doctorate, comprehensive exam, thesis/dissertation. *Entrance requirements:* For master's and doctorate, GRE General Test. Additional exam requirements/recommendations for international students: Required—TOEFL (minimum score 570 paper-based). Electronic applications accepted. *Faculty research:* Effects of acute and chronic exercise on human function and health, motor control.

University of South Dakota, Graduate School, School of Education, Division of Kinesiology and Sport Management, Vermillion, SD 57069. Offers exercise science (MA); sport management (MA). *Accreditation:* NCATE. *Program availability:* Part-time. *Degree requirements:* For master's, comprehensive exam, thesis or alternative. *Entrance requirements:* For master's, GRE General Test, MAT, minimum GPA of 3.0. Additional exam requirements/recommendations for international students: Required—TOEFL (minimum score 550 paper-based; 79 iBT). *Application deadline:* Applications are processed on a rolling basis. Application fee: $35. Electronic applications accepted. *Financial support:* Research assistantships with partial tuition reimbursements, teaching assistantships with partial tuition reimbursements, Federal Work-Study, and unspecified assistantships available. Financial award applicants required to submit FAFSA. *Application contact:* Graduate School, 605-658-6140, Fax: 605-677-6118, E-mail: grad@usd.edu.
Website: http://www.usd.edu/ksm

The University of Tampa, Program in Exercise and Nutrition Science, Tampa, FL 33606-1490. Offers MS. *Program availability:* Part-time, evening/weekend. *Faculty:* 3 full-time (1 woman), 1 (woman) part-time/adjunct. *Students:* 37 full-time (20 women), 7 part-time (6 women); includes 7 minority (4 Black or African American, non-Hispanic/Latino; 1 Asian, non-Hispanic/Latino; 2 Two or more races, non-Hispanic/Latino), 3 international. Average age 26. 207 applicants, 52% accepted, 33 enrolled. In 2017, 44 master's awarded. *Degree requirements:* For master's, comprehensive exam, practicum. *Entrance requirements:* For master's, GMAT or GRE, official transcripts from all colleges and/or universities previously attended, resume, personal statement, letters of recommendation, bachelor's degree in related field. Additional exam requirements/recommendations for international students: Required—TOEFL (minimum score 577 paper-based; 90 iBT), IELTS (minimum score 7.5). *Application deadline:* Applications are processed on a rolling basis. Application fee: $40. Electronic applications accepted. *Expenses:* Contact institution. *Financial support:* In 2017–18, 1 student received support. Career-related internships or fieldwork, scholarships/grants, and unspecified assistantships available. Financial award applicants required to submit FAFSA. *Unit head:* Dr. Ronda C. Sturgill, Associate Professor, Health Sciences and Human Performance, 813-257-3445, E-mail: rsturgill@ut.edu. *Application contact:* Chanelle Cox, Staff Assistant, Admissions for Graduate and Continuing Studies, 813-253-6249, E-mail: ccox@ut.edu.
Website: http://www.ut.edu/msexercisenutrition/

The University of Tennessee, Graduate School, College of Education, Health and Human Sciences, Department of Exercise, Sport, and Leisure Studies, Program in Exercise Science, Knoxville, TN 37996. Offers biomechanics/sports medicine (MS, PhD); exercise physiology (MS, PhD). *Accreditation:* CEPH (one or more programs are accredited). *Program availability:* Part-time. *Degree requirements:* For master's, thesis optional. *Entrance requirements:* For master's, minimum GPA of 2.7. Additional exam requirements/recommendations for international students: Required—TOEFL. Electronic applications accepted.

The University of Tennessee, Graduate School, College of Education, Health and Human Sciences, Program in Education, Knoxville, TN 37996. Offers art education (MS); counseling education (PhD); cultural studies in education (PhD); curriculum (MS, Ed S); curriculum, educational research and evaluation (Ed D, PhD); early childhood education (PhD); early childhood special education (MS); education of deaf and hard of hearing (MS); educational administration and policy studies (Ed D, PhD); educational administration and supervision (Ed S); educational psychology (Ed D, PhD); elementary education (MS, Ed S); elementary teaching (MS); English education (MS, Ed S); exercise science (PhD); foreign language/ESL education (MS, Ed S); instructional technology (MS, Ed D, PhD, Ed S); literacy, language and ESL education (PhD); literacy, language education, and ESL education (Ed D); mathematics education (MS, Ed S); modified and comprehensive special education (MS); reading education (MS, Ed S); school counseling (Ed S); school psychology (PhD, Ed S); science education (MS, Ed S); secondary teaching (MS); social foundations (MS); social science education (MS, Ed S); socio-cultural foundations of sports and education (PhD); special education (Ed S); teacher education (Ed D, PhD). *Accreditation:* NCATE. *Program availability:* Part-time, evening/weekend. *Degree requirements:* For master's and Ed S, thesis optional; for doctorate, variable foreign language requirement, thesis/dissertation.

Entrance requirements: For master's, minimum GPA of 2.7; for doctorate and Ed S, GRE General Test, minimum GPA of 2.7. Additional exam requirements/recommendations for international students: Required—TOEFL. Electronic applications accepted.

The University of Texas at Arlington, Graduate School, College of Nursing and Health Innovation, Arlington, TX 76019. Offers athletic training (MS); exercise science (MS); kinesiology (PhD); nurse practitioner (MSN); nursing (PhD); nursing administration (MSN); nursing education (MSN); nursing practice (DNP). *Accreditation:* AACN. *Program availability:* Part-time, evening/weekend, online learning. *Degree requirements:* For master's, practicum course; for doctorate, comprehensive exam (for some programs), thesis/dissertation (for some programs), proposal defense dissertation (for PhD); scholarship project (for DNP). *Entrance requirements:* For master's, GRE General Test if GPA less than 3.0, minimum GPA of 3.0, Texas nursing license, minimum C grade in undergraduate statistics course; for doctorate, GRE General Test (waived for MSN-to-PhD applicants), minimum undergraduate, graduate and statistics GPA of 3.0; Texas RN license; interview; written statement of goals. Additional exam requirements/recommendations for international students: Required—TOEFL (minimum score 550 paper-based), IELTS (minimum score 7). *Faculty research:* Simulation in clinical education and practice, cultural diversity, vulnerable populations, substance abuse.

The University of Texas at Austin, Graduate School, College of Education, Department of Kinesiology and Health Education, Austin, TX 78712-1111. Offers behavioral health (PhD); exercise and sport psychology (M Ed, MA); exercise science (M Ed, MS, PhD); health education (M Ed, MS, Ed D, PhD). *Program availability:* Part-time. Terminal master's awarded for partial completion of doctoral program. *Degree requirements:* For master's, thesis (for some programs); for doctorate, thesis/dissertation. *Entrance requirements:* For master's and doctorate, GRE General Test. Additional exam requirements/recommendations for international students: Required—TOEFL. Electronic applications accepted. *Faculty research:* Health promotion, human performance and exercise biochemistry, motor behavior and biomechanics, sport management, aging and pediatric development.

The University of Texas Rio Grande Valley, College of Health Affairs, Department of Health and Human Performance, Edinburg, TX 78539. Offers exercise science (MS); kinesiology (MS). *Program availability:* Part-time-only, evening/weekend, 100% online. *Faculty:* 13 full-time (5 women), 2 part-time/adjunct (0 women). *Students:* 8 full-time (4 women), 32 part-time (10 women); includes 33 minority (1 Black or African American, non-Hispanic/Latino; 32 Hispanic/Latino), 2 international. Average age 25. 27 applicants, 96% accepted, 25 enrolled. In 2017, 18 master's awarded. *Degree requirements:* For master's, comprehensive exam, thesis optional. *Entrance requirements:* For master's, GRE, minimum GPA of 3.0 in last 60 hours. Additional exam requirements/recommendations for international students: Required—TOEFL (minimum score 550 paper-based; 79 iBT), IELTS (minimum score 6.5). *Application deadline:* For fall admission, 7/17 for domestic students; for spring admission, 11/16 for domestic students. Applications are processed on a rolling basis. Application fee: $50. Electronic applications accepted. *Expenses:* Tuition, state resident: full-time $5550; part-time $417 per credit hour. Tuition, nonresident: full-time $13,020; part-time $832 per credit hour. *Required fees:* $1169. *Financial support:* In 2017–18, 8 students received support, including 6 research assistantships (averaging $5,000 per year); unspecified assistantships also available. Financial award application deadline: 4/15; financial award applicants required to submit FAFSA. *Faculty research:* Physiology of exercise, fitness levels, Mexican American children, nutrition, diabetes prevention. *Unit head:* Dr. Zelma D. Mata, Chair, 956-665-3501, Fax: 956-665-3502, E-mail: zelma.mata@utrgv.edu. *Application contact:* Dr. Murat Karabulut, Associate Professor and Graduate Program Coordinator, 956-882-8290, E-mail: murat.karabulut@utrgv.edu.
Website: http://www.utrgv.edu/hhp/

University of the Pacific, College of the Pacific, Department of Health, Exercise and Sport Science, Stockton, CA 95211-0197. Offers MA. *Faculty:* 1 full-time (0 women), 4 part-time/adjunct (2 women). *Students:* 1 (woman) full-time, 20 part-time (8 women); includes 7 minority (1 Black or African American, non-Hispanic/Latino; 3 Asian, non-Hispanic/Latino; 2 Hispanic/Latino; 1 Two or more races, non-Hispanic/Latino), 1 international. Average age 24. 36 applicants, 72% accepted, 14 enrolled. In 2017, 12 master's awarded. *Degree requirements:* For master's, comprehensive exam (for some programs), thesis (for some programs). *Entrance requirements:* For master's, GRE General Test. Additional exam requirements/recommendations for international students: Required—TOEFL. *Application deadline:* For fall admission, 3/1 priority date for domestic students; for spring admission, 10/1 for domestic students. Applications are processed on a rolling basis. Application fee: $75. *Financial support:* Teaching assistantships and institutionally sponsored loans available. Support available to part-time students. Financial award application deadline: 3/1; financial award applicants required to submit FAFSA. *Unit head:* Dr. Margaret J. Ciccolella, Chairperson, 209-946-2473, E-mail: mciccolella@pacific.edu. *Application contact:* Miguel Medrano, Information Contact, 209-946-2209, E-mail: mmedrano@pacific.edu.
Website: http://www.pacific.edu/Documents/school-graduate/acrobat/Pacific-MA-Healthy,%20Excercise,%20Sport%20Science-Fact-Sheet-17-18.pdf

The University of Toledo, College of Graduate Studies, College of Health and Human Services, School of Exercise and Rehabilitation Sciences, Toledo, OH 43606-3390. Offers athletic training (MSES); exercise physiology (MSES); exercise science (PhD); occupational therapy (OTD); physical therapy (DPT); recreation and leisure studies (MA), including recreation administration, recreation therapy. *Degree requirements:* For master's, comprehensive exam, thesis; for doctorate, thesis/dissertation or alternative. *Entrance requirements:* For master's, GRE, minimum cumulative GPA of 2.7 for all previous academic work, letters of recommendation; for doctorate, GRE, minimum cumulative GPA of 3.0 for all previous academic work, letters of recommendation; OTCAS or PTCAS application and UT supplemental application (for OTD and DPT). Additional exam requirements/recommendations for international students: Required—TOEFL (minimum score 550 paper-based; 80 iBT). Electronic applications accepted.

University of West Florida, Usha Kundu, MD College of Health, Department of Exercise Science and Community Health, Pensacola, FL 32514-5750. Offers health promotion (MS); health, leisure, and exercise science (MS), including exercise science, physical education. *Program availability:* Part-time, evening/weekend. *Degree requirements:* For master's, thesis or alternative. *Entrance requirements:* For master's, GRE or MAT, official transcripts; minimum GPA of 3.0; letter of intent; three personal references; work experience as reflected in resume. Additional exam requirements/recommendations for international students: Required—TOEFL (minimum score 550 paper-based).

University of Wisconsin–La Crosse, College of Science and Health, Department of Exercise and Sport Science, Program in Clinical Exercise Physiology, La Crosse, WI 54601-3742. Offers MS. *Students:* 15 full-time (8 women), 2 part-time (both women), 2 international. Average age 24. 28 applicants, 54% accepted, 15 enrolled. In 2017, 15 master's awarded. *Degree requirements:* For master's, thesis optional. *Entrance requirements:* Additional exam requirements/recommendations for international students: Required—TOEFL (minimum score 550 paper-based; 79 iBT). *Application deadline:* For fall admission, 2/1 priority date for domestic and international students. Electronic applications accepted. *Financial support:* Federal Work-Study, scholarships/grants,

health care benefits, and tuition waivers (partial) available. Support available to part-time students. Financial award application deadline: 3/15; financial award applicants required to submit FAFSA. *Unit head:* Dr. John Porcari, Director, 608-785-8684, Fax: 608-785-8686, E-mail: porcari.john@uwlax.edu. *Application contact:* Brandon Schaller, Senior Graduate Student Status Examiner, 608-785-8941, E-mail: admissions@uwlax.edu.
Website: http://www.uwlax.edu/sah/ess/cep/

University of Wisconsin–La Crosse, College of Science and Health, Department of Exercise and Sport Science, Program in Human Performance, La Crosse, WI 54601-3742. Offers exercise sport science: human performance (MS), including applied sport science, strength and conditioning. *Program availability:* Part-time. *Students:* 16 full-time (7 women), 6 part-time (0 women); includes 1 minority (Hispanic/Latino). Average age 25. 37 applicants, 57% accepted, 13 enrolled. In 2017, 8 master's awarded. *Degree requirements:* For master's, comprehensive exam (for some programs), thesis optional. *Entrance requirements:* For master's, GRE, course work in anatomy, physiology, biomechanics, and exercise physiology. Additional exam requirements/recommendations for international students: Required—TOEFL (minimum score 550 paper-based; 79 iBT). *Application deadline:* For fall admission, 2/1 priority date for domestic and international students. Electronic applications accepted. *Financial support:* Federal Work-Study, scholarships/grants, health care benefits, and tuition waivers (partial) available. Support available to part-time students. Financial award application deadline: 3/15; financial award applicants required to submit FAFSA. *Faculty research:* Anaerobic metabolism, power development, strength training, biomechanics, athletic performance. *Unit head:* Dr. Glenn Wright, Director, 608-785-8689, Fax: 608-785-8172, E-mail: wright.glen@uwlax.edu. *Application contact:* Brandon Schaller, Senior Graduate Student Status Examiner, 608-785-8941, E-mail: admissions@uwlax.edu.
Website: https://www.uwlax.edu/human-performance-ms/

University of Wisconsin–Milwaukee, Graduate School, College of Health Sciences, Department of Kinesiology, Milwaukee, WI 53201-0413. Offers athletic training (MS); kinesiology (MS, PhD), including exercise and nutrition in health and disease (MS), integrative human performance (MS), neuromechanics (MS); physical therapy (DPT). *Program availability:* Part-time. *Students:* 100 full-time (60 women), 16 part-time (9 women); includes 11 minority (1 Black or African American, non-Hispanic/Latino; 1 American Indian or Alaska Native, non-Hispanic/Latino; 9 Two or more races, non-Hispanic/Latino), 3 international. Average age 27. 36 applicants, 42% accepted, 5 enrolled. In 2017, 2 master's awarded. *Degree requirements:* For master's, comprehensive exam, thesis optional. *Entrance requirements:* For master's, GRE General Test. Additional exam requirements/recommendations for international students: Required—TOEFL (minimum score 550 paper-based; 79 iBT), IELTS (minimum score 6.5). *Application deadline:* For fall admission, 1/1 priority date for domestic students; for spring admission, 9/1 for domestic students. Applications are processed on a rolling basis. Application fee: $56 ($96 for international students). *Financial support:* Fellowships, research assistantships, teaching assistantships, career-related internships or fieldwork, unspecified assistantships, and project assistantships available. Support available to part-time students. Financial award application deadline: 4/15. *Unit head:* Dr. Kyle T. Ebersole, Department Chair, 414-229-6717, Fax: 414-229-3366, E-mail: ebersole@uwm.edu. *Application contact:* Stephen C. Cobb, Graduate Program Coordinator, 414-229-3369, Fax: 414-229-3366, E-mail: cobbsc@uwm.edu.
Website: http://uwm.edu/healthsciences/academics/kinesiology/

University of Wyoming, College of Health Sciences, Division of Kinesiology and Health, Laramie, WY 82071. Offers MS. *Accreditation:* NCATE. *Program availability:* Part-time, online learning. *Degree requirements:* For master's, comprehensive exam (for some programs), thesis (for some programs). *Entrance requirements:* For master's, GRE General Test, minimum GPA of 3.0. Additional exam requirements/recommendations for international students: Required—TOEFL. Electronic applications accepted. *Faculty research:* Teacher effectiveness, effects of exercising on heart function, physiological responses of overtraining, psychological benefits of physical activity, health behavior.

Valdosta State University, College of Nursing and Health Sciences, Valdosta, GA 31698. Offers adult gerontology nurse practitioner (MSN); exercise physiology (MS); family nurse practitioner (MSN); family psychiatric mental health nurse practitioner (MSN). *Accreditation:* AACN. *Program availability:* Part-time, online learning. *Degree requirements:* For master's, thesis (for some programs), comprehensive written and/or oral exams. *Entrance requirements:* For master's, minimum GPA of 2.8. Additional exam requirements/recommendations for international students: Required—TOEFL (minimum score 523 paper-based). *Application deadline:* For fall admission, 7/1 for domestic and international students; for spring admission, 11/15 for domestic and international students. Applications are processed on a rolling basis. Application fee: $45. Electronic applications accepted. *Financial support:* Research assistantships with full tuition reimbursements, institutionally sponsored loans, scholarships/grants, and unspecified assistantships available. Support available to part-time students. Financial award application deadline: 7/1; financial award applicants required to submit FAFSA. *Faculty research:* Nutrition, children's health beliefs, alternative treatment modalities, job satisfaction, leadership. *Unit head:* Sheri Noviello, Dean, 229-333-5959, E-mail: srnoviello@valdosta.edu. *Application contact:* Sheri Noviello, Dean, 229-333-5959, E-mail: srnoviello@valdosta.edu.
Website: https://www.valdosta.edu/colleges/nursing-and-health-sciences/

Virginia Commonwealth University, Graduate School, College of Humanities and Sciences, Department of Kinesiology and Health Sciences, Program in Health and Movement Sciences, Richmond, VA 23284-9005. Offers MS. *Entrance requirements:* For master's, GRE or MAT. Additional exam requirements/recommendations for international students: Required—TOEFL (minimum score 600 paper-based; 100 iBT). Electronic applications accepted.

Virginia Polytechnic Institute and State University, Graduate School, College of Agriculture and Life Sciences, Blacksburg, VA 24061. Offers agricultural and applied economics (MS, PhD); agricultural and life sciences (MS); agriculture, leadership, and community education (MS, PhD); animal and poultry science (MS, PhD); biochemistry (MS, PhD); crop and soil environmental sciences (MS, PhD); dairy science (MS, PhD); entomology (MS, PhD); food science and technology (MS, PhD); horticulture (PhD); human nutrition, foods and exercise (MS, PhD); plant pathology, physiology, and weed science (MS, PhD). *Faculty:* 241 full-time (73 women), 1 (woman) part-time/adjunct. *Students:* 379 full-time (221 women), 126 part-time (75 women); includes 64 minority (21 Black or African American, non-Hispanic/Latino; 15 Asian, non-Hispanic/Latino; 14 Hispanic/Latino; 14 Two or more races, non-Hispanic/Latino), 119 international. Average age 29. 357 applicants, 46% accepted, 118 enrolled. In 2017, 105 master's, 54 doctorates awarded. *Degree requirements:* For master's, comprehensive exam (for some programs), thesis (for some programs); for doctorate, comprehensive exam (for some programs), thesis/dissertation (for some programs). *Entrance requirements:* For master's and doctorate, GRE/GMAT. Additional exam requirements/recommendations for international students: Required—TOEFL (minimum score 80 iBT). *Application deadline:* For fall admission, 8/1 for domestic students, 4/1 for international students; for spring admission, 1/1 for domestic students, 9/1 for international students. Applications are processed on a rolling basis. Application fee: $75. Electronic applications accepted. *Expenses:* Tuition, state resident: full-time $15,072; part-time $718.50 per credit hour.

Tuition, nonresident: full-time $28,810; part-time $1448.25 per credit hour. *Required fees:* $2741; $502 per semester. Tuition and fees vary according to course load, campus/location and program. *Financial support:* In 2017–18, 232 research assistantships with full tuition reimbursements (averaging $21,852 per year), 94 teaching assistantships with full tuition reimbursements (averaging $21,643 per year) were awarded. Financial award application deadline: 3/1; financial award applicants required to submit FAFSA. *Total annual research expenditures:* $44.3 million. *Unit head:* Dr. Alan L. Grant, Dean, 540-231-4152, Fax: 540-231-4163, E-mail: algrant@vt.edu. *Application contact:* Crystal Tawney, Administrative Assistant, 540-231-4152, Fax: 540-231-4163, E-mail: cdtawney@vt.edu.
Website: http://www.cals.vt.edu/

Wake Forest University, Graduate School of Arts and Sciences, Department of Health and Exercise Science, Winston-Salem, NC 27109. Offers MS. *Degree requirements:* For master's, one foreign language, thesis. *Entrance requirements:* For master's, GRE General Test, resume. Additional exam requirements/recommendations for international students: Required—TOEFL (minimum score 79 iBT). Electronic applications accepted. *Faculty research:* Cardiac rehabilitation, biomechanics, health psychology, exercise physiology.

Washington State University, College of Pharmacy, Nutrition and Exercise Physiology Program, Pullman, WA 99164. Offers MS. Programs offered at the Spokane campus. *Degree requirements:* For master's, internship. *Entrance requirements:* For master's, BS in nutrition and exercise physiology, exercise science, human nutrition, or related degree; interview.

Wayne State College, Department of Health, Human Performance and Sport, Wayne, NE 68787. Offers exercise science (MSE); organizational management (MS), including sport management. *Program availability:* Part-time, evening/weekend. *Degree requirements:* For master's, comprehensive exam, thesis optional. *Entrance requirements:* For master's, GRE General Test, minimum GPA of 3.0. Additional exam requirements/recommendations for international students: Required—TOEFL (minimum score 550 paper-based). Electronic applications accepted.

Wayne State University, College of Education, Division of Kinesiology, Health and Sports Studies, Detroit, MI 48202. Offers athletic training (MSAT); health education (M Ed); kinesiology (M Ed, PhD), including exercise and sport science (PhD), physical education and physical activity leadership (PhD); sports administration (MA). *Program availability:* Part-time, 100% online. *Faculty:* 9. *Students:* 65 full-time (33 women), 109 part-time (56 women); includes 70 minority (59 Black or African American, non-Hispanic/Latino; 3 Hispanic/Latino; 8 Two or more races, non-Hispanic/Latino), 8 international. Average age 30. 182 applicants, 53% accepted, 56 enrolled. In 2017, 62 master's, 3 doctorates awarded. *Degree requirements:* For master's, thesis (for some programs); for doctorate, thesis/dissertation. *Entrance requirements:* For master's, minimum undergraduate GPA of 3.0; undergraduate degree directly relating to the field of specialization being applied for or one accompanied by extensive educational background in closely-related field; teaching certificates in specific areas (for some programs); for doctorate, minimum undergraduate GPA of 3.0; undergraduate degree directly relating to the field of specialization being applied for or one accompanied by extensive educational background in closely-related field. Additional exam requirements/recommendations for international students: Required—TOEFL (minimum score 79 iBT), TWE (minimum score 5.5); Recommended—IELTS (minimum score 6.5). *Application deadline:* For fall admission, 6/1 priority date for domestic students, 5/1 priority date for international students; for winter admission, 10/1 priority date for domestic students, 9/1 priority date for international students; for spring admission, 2/1 priority date for domestic students, 1/1 priority date for international students. Application fee: $50. Electronic applications accepted. *Expenses:* Contact institution. *Financial support:* In 2017–18, 47 students received support, including 6 research assistantships with tuition reimbursements available (averaging $18,534 per year), 5 teaching assistantships with tuition reimbursements available (averaging $18,534 per year); fellowships with tuition reimbursements available, scholarships/grants, health care benefits, and unspecified assistantships also available. Support available to part-time students. Financial award applicants required to submit FAFSA. *Faculty research:* Exercise and sport science, nutrition and physical activity interventions, school and community health, obesity prevention. *Unit head:* Dr. Nate McCaughtry, Assistant Dean, Division of Kinesiology, Health and Sport Studies/Director, Center for School Health, 313-577-0014, Fax: 313-577-5002, E-mail: aj4391@wayne.edu. *Application contact:* 313-577-4249, E-mail: askcoe@wayne.edu.
Website: http://coe.wayne.edu/kinesiology/index.php

West Chester University of Pennsylvania, College of Health Sciences, Department of Kinesiology, West Chester, PA 19383. Offers adapted physical education (Certificate); exercise and sport physiology (MS), including athletic training; sport management and athletics (MPA), including administration. *Program availability:* Part-time, evening/weekend, blended/hybrid learning. *Students:* 44 full-time (24 women), 12 part-time (3 women); includes 5 minority (2 Black or African American, non-Hispanic/Latino; 2 Hispanic/Latino; 1 Two or more races, non-Hispanic/Latino), 1 international. Average age 25. 68 applicants, 87% accepted, 29 enrolled. In 2017, 13 master's, 14 other advanced degrees awarded. *Degree requirements:* For master's, thesis or research report (for MS); two internships and capstone course that includes a research project or thesis (for MPA); for Certificate, six courses of study. *Entrance requirements:* For master's, GRE (for MS), 2 letters of recommendation, statement of professional goals; transcripts (for MS); two letters of reference, career goals, resume (for MPA); for Certificate, two letters of recommendation, transcript. Additional exam requirements/recommendations for international students: Required—TOEFL or IELTS. *Application deadline:* For fall admission, 5/15 for international students; for spring admission, 10/15 for international students. Applications are processed on a rolling basis. Application fee: $50. Electronic applications accepted. *Expenses:* Tuition, state resident: full-time $9000; part-time $500 per credit. Tuition, nonresident: full-time $13,500; part-time $750 per credit. *Required fees:* $2959; $149.79 per credit. *Financial support:* Scholarships/grants and unspecified assistantships available. Financial award application deadline: 2/15; financial award applicants required to submit FAFSA. *Faculty research:* Metabolism during exercise, biomechanics, rating of perceived exertion, motor learning, environmental physiology. *Unit head:* Dr. W. Craig Stevens, Chair, 610-436-2610, Fax: 610-436-2860, E-mail: cstevens@wcpua.edu. *Application contact:* Office of Graduate Studies and Extended Education, 610-436-2943, Fax: 610-436-2763, E-mail: gradstudy@wcpua.edu.
Website: http://www.wcupa.edu/healthsciences/kinesiology/

Western Michigan University, Graduate College, College of Education and Human Development, Department of Health, Physical Education and Recreation, Kalamazoo, MI 49008. Offers athletic training (MS), including exercise physiology; sport management (MA), including pedagogy, special physical education.

Western Washington University, Graduate School, College of Humanities and Social Sciences, Department of Physical Education, Health, and Recreation, Bellingham, WA 98225-5996. Offers exercise science (MS); sport psychology (MS). *Program availability:* Part-time. *Degree requirements:* For master's, thesis. *Entrance requirements:* For master's, GRE General Test, minimum GPA of 3.0 in last 60 semester hours or last 90 quarter hours. Additional exam requirements/recommendations for international students: Required—TOEFL (minimum score 567 paper-based). Electronic applications accepted. *Faculty research:* Spinal motor control, biomechanics/kinesiology, biomechanics of aging, mobility of older adults, fall prevention, exercise interventions and function, magnesium and inspiratory muscle training (IMT).

West Texas A&M University, College of Nursing and Health Sciences, Department of Sports and Exercise Sciences, Canyon, TX 79015. Offers sport management (MS); sports and exercise sciences (MS). *Program availability:* Part-time, evening/weekend. *Degree requirements:* For master's, comprehensive exam, thesis optional. *Entrance requirements:* For master's, GRE General Test. Additional exam requirements/recommendations for international students: Required—TOEFL. Electronic applications accepted.

West Virginia University, School of Medicine, Morgantown, WV 26506-9600. Offers biochemistry and molecular biology (PhD); biomedical science (MS); cancer cell biology (PhD); cellular and integrative physiology (PhD); exercise physiology (MS, PhD); health sciences (MS); immunology (PhD); medicine (MD); occupational therapy (MOT); pathologists assistant (MHS); physical therapy (DPT). *Program availability:* Part-time, evening/weekend. *Students:* 781 full-time (440 women), 25 part-time (13 women); includes 140 minority (15 Black or African American, non-Hispanic/Latino; 1 American Indian or Alaska Native, non-Hispanic/Latino; 68 Asian, non-Hispanic/Latino; 37 Hispanic/Latino; 1 Native Hawaiian or other Pacific Islander, non-Hispanic/Latino; 18 Two or more races, non-Hispanic/Latino), 19 international. *Entrance requirements:* Additional exam requirements/recommendations for international students: Required—TOEFL. *Application deadline:* Applications are processed on a rolling basis. Application fee: $60. Electronic applications accepted. *Expenses:* Contact institution. *Financial support:* Fellowships, research assistantships, teaching assistantships, career-related internships or fieldwork, Federal Work-Study, institutionally sponsored loans, health care benefits, tuition waivers (full and partial), and administrative assistantships available. Financial award applicants required to submit FAFSA. *Unit head:* Dr. Clay Marsh, Executive Dean, 304-293-6607, Fax: 304-293-6627, E-mail: clay.marsh@hsc.wvu.edu. *Application contact:* Lisa M. Salati, Assistant Vice President, Graduate Education, 304-293-7759, Fax: 304-293-3080, E-mail: lsalati@hsc.wvu.edu.
Website: https://medicine.hsc.wvu.edu

Wichita State University, Graduate School, College of Education, Department of Human Performance Studies, Wichita, KS 67260. Offers exercise science (M Ed). *Program availability:* Part-time. *Unit head:* Dr. Michael Rogers, Chairperson, 316-978-3340, Fax: 316-978-3302, E-mail: michael.rogers@wichita.edu. *Application contact:* Jordan Oleson, Admissions Coordinator, 316-978-3095, Fax: 316-978-3253, E-mail: jordan.oleson@wichita.edu.
Website: http://www.wichita.edu/hps

William Paterson University of New Jersey, College of Science and Health, Wayne, NJ 07470-8420. Offers adult gerontology nurse practitioner (Certificate); biology (MS); biotechnology (MS); communication disorders (MS); exercise and sport studies (MS); materials chemistry (MS); nurse practitioner (Certificate); nursing (MSN); nursing education (Certificate); nursing practice (DNP); school nurse (Certificate). *Program availability:* Part-time (15 women), 25 part-time/adjunct (24 women). *Students:* 66 full-time (56 women), 197 part-time (163 women); includes 104 minority (15 Black or African American, non-Hispanic/Latino; 45 Asian, non-Hispanic/Latino; 38 Hispanic/Latino; 6 Two or more races, non-Hispanic/Latino), 3 international. Average age 33. 387 applicants, 34% accepted, 77 enrolled. In 2017, 87 master's, 5 doctorates awarded. *Degree requirements:* For master's, comprehensive exam (for some programs), thesis (for some programs), non-thesis internship/practicum (for some programs). *Entrance requirements:* For master's, GRE/MAT, minimum GPA of 3.0; 2-3 letters of recommendation; personal statement; work experience (for some programs); for doctorate, GRE/MAT, minimum GPA of 3.3; work experience; 3 letters of recommendation; interview; master's degree in nursing. Additional exam requirements/recommendations for international students: Required—TOEFL (minimum score 550 paper-based; 79 iBT), IELTS (minimum score 6). *Application deadline:* For fall admission, 6/1 for domestic students, 3/1 for international students; for spring admission, 11/1 for domestic students, 10/1 for international students. Applications are processed on a rolling basis. Application fee: $50. Electronic applications accepted. *Expenses:* Tuition, state resident: full-time $13,920; part-time $6264 per year. Tuition, nonresident: full-time $21,700; part-time $9765 per year. *Required fees:* $80; $36 per year. Tuition and fees vary according to course load, degree level and program. *Financial support:* In 2017–18, 9,800 students received support. Career-related internships or fieldwork, Federal Work-Study, scholarships/grants, and unspecified assistantships available. Support available to part-time students. Financial award application deadline: 3/15; financial award applicants required to submit FAFSA. *Faculty research:* Behaviors of American long-eared bats, postpartum fatigue, methodologies for coating carbon nano-tubes, paleoclimatology, and pre-linguistic gestures in children with language disorders. *Total annual research expenditures:* $291,600. *Unit head:* Dr. Venkat Sharma, Dean, 973-720-2194, Fax: 973-720-3414, E-mail: sharmav@wpunj.edu. *Application contact:* Christina Aiello, Assistant Director, Graduate Admissions, 973-720-2506, Fax: 973-720-2035, E-mail: aielloc@wpunj.edu.
Website: http://www.wpunj.edu/cosh

Kinesiology and Movement Studies

Alabama Agricultural and Mechanical University, School of Graduate Studies, College of Education, Humanities, and Behavioral Sciences, Department of Health Sciences, Human Performance, and Communicative Disorders, Huntsville, AL 35811. Offers kinesiology (MS); physical education (MS); speech-language pathology (MS). *Program availability:* Part-time, evening/weekend. *Degree requirements:* For master's, comprehensive exam. *Entrance requirements:* For master's, GRE General Test. Additional exam requirements/recommendations for international students: Required—TOEFL (minimum score 500 paper-based; 61 iBT). Electronic applications accepted. *Faculty research:* Cardiorespiratory assessment.

A.T. Still University, College of Graduate Health Studies, Kirksville, MO 63501. Offers dental public health (MPH); exercise and sport psychology (Certificate); fundamentals of education (Certificate); geriatric exercise science (Certificate); global health (Certificate); health administration (MHA, DHA); health professions (Ed D); health sciences (DH Sc); kinesiology (MS); leadership and organizational behavior (Certificate); public health (MPH); sports conditioning (Certificate). *Program availability:* Part-time, evening/weekend, online only, 100% online, blended/hybrid learning. *Faculty:* 28 full-time (18 women), 83 part-time/adjunct (43 women). *Students:* 537 full-time (334 women), 516 part-time (316 women); includes 397 minority (171 Black or African American, non-Hispanic/Latino; 14 American Indian or Alaska Native, non-Hispanic/Latino; 84 Asian, non-Hispanic/Latino; 106 Hispanic/Latino; 1 Native Hawaiian or other Pacific Islander, non-Hispanic/Latino; 21 Two or more races, non-Hispanic/Latino), 43 international. Average age 36. 392 applicants, 84% accepted, 270 enrolled. In 2017, 138 master's, 102 doctorates, 116 other advanced degrees awarded. *Degree requirements:* For master's, thesis, integrated terminal project, practicum; for doctorate, thesis/dissertation. *Entrance requirements:* For master's, minimum GPA of 2.5, bachelor's degree or equivalent, essay, resume, English proficiency; for doctorate, minimum GPA of 2.5, master's or terminal degree, essay, past experience in relevant field, resume, English proficiency. Additional exam requirements/recommendations for international students: Required—TOEFL (minimum score 550 paper-based; 80 iBT). *Application deadline:* For fall admission, 6/26 for domestic students, 5/20 for international students; for winter admission, 9/11 for domestic students, 9/12 for international students; for spring admission, 12/11 for domestic students, 12/12 for international students; for summer admission, 3/5 for domestic students, 3/6 for international students. Applications are processed on a rolling basis. Application fee: $70. Electronic applications accepted. *Financial support:* In 2017–18, 18 students received support. Scholarships/grants available. Financial award applicants required to submit FAFSA. *Faculty research:* Public health: influence of availability of comprehensive wellness resources online, student wellness, oral health care needs assessment of community, oral health knowledge and behaviors of Medicaid-eligible pregnant women and mothers of young children in relations to early childhood caries and tooth decay, alcohol use and alcohol related problems among college students. *Unit head:* Dr. Donald Altman, Dean, 480-219-6008, Fax: 660-626-2826, E-mail: daltman@atsu.edu. *Application contact:* Amie Waldemer, Associate Director, Online Admissions, 480-219-6146, E-mail: awaldemer@atsu.edu.
Website: http://www.atsu.edu/college-of-graduate-health-studies

Azusa Pacific University, School of Behavioral and Applied Sciences, Department of Kinesiology, Azusa, CA 91702-7000. Offers athletic training (MS); physical education (MA, MS).

Ball State University, Graduate School, College of Health, School of Kinesiology, Muncie, IN 47306. Offers athletic coaching education (Certificate); exercise science (MA, MS), including exercise science; human bioenergetics (PhD), including human bioenergetics; physical education (MS); physical education and sport (MA, MS), including physical education and sport; wellness management (MA, MS). *Program availability:* Part-time, 100% online. *Faculty:* 16 full-time (4 women), 3 part-time/adjunct (2 women). *Students:* 39 full-time (15 women), 97 part-time (32 women); includes 10 minority (2 Black or African American, non-Hispanic/Latino; 2 Asian, non-Hispanic/Latino; 4 Hispanic/Latino; 2 Two or more races, non-Hispanic/Latino), 5 international. Average age 26. 140 applicants, 37% accepted, 45 enrolled. In 2017, 55 master's, 3 doctorates, 1 other advanced degree awarded. *Degree requirements:* For doctorate,

thesis/dissertation. *Entrance requirements:* For master's, minimum baccalaureate GPA of 2.75 or 3.0 in latter half of baccalaureate; for doctorate, GRE General Test, minimum graduate GPA of 3.2. Additional exam requirements/recommendations for international students: Required—TOEFL (minimum score 550 paper-based; 79 iBT), IELTS (minimum score 6.5). *Application deadline:* Applications are processed on a rolling basis. Application fee: $60. Electronic applications accepted. *Financial support:* In 2017–18, 21 students received support, including 21 research assistantships with partial tuition reimbursements available (averaging $11,674 per year); teaching assistantships with partial tuition reimbursements available and unspecified assistantships also available. Financial award application deadline: 3/1; financial award applicants required to submit FAFSA. *Unit head:* Dr. Tom Weidner, Chairperson, 765-285-5039, Fax: 765-285-8254, E-mail: tweidner@bsu.edu. *Application contact:* Dr. David Pearson, Graduate Programs Coordinator, 765-285-1143, Fax: 765-285-8254, E-mail: dpearson@bsu.edu.
Website: http://www.bsu.edu/kinesiology

Barry University, School of Human Performance and Leisure Sciences, Programs in Movement Science, General Movement Science Program, Miami Shores, FL 33161-6695. Offers MS.

Barry University, School of Human Performance and Leisure Sciences, Programs in Movement Science, Specialization in Biomechanics, Miami Shores, FL 33161-6695. Offers MS. *Entrance requirements:* For master's, GRE General Test, minimum GPA of 3.0. Electronic applications accepted. *Faculty research:* Upper extremity biomechanics, orthopedic biomechanics.

Baylor University, Graduate School, Robbins College of Health and Human Sciences, Department of Health, Human Performance and Recreation, Waco, TX 76798. Offers athletic training (MS); community health (MPH); exercise physiology (MS); kinesiology, exercise nutrition, and health promotion (PhD); sport pedagogy (MS). *Accreditation:* NCATE. *Program availability:* Part-time. *Faculty:* 24 full-time (11 women). *Students:* 86 full-time (52 women), 9 part-time (6 women); includes 24 minority (7 Black or African American, non-Hispanic/Latino; 3 Asian, non-Hispanic/Latino; 10 Hispanic/Latino; 1 Native Hawaiian or other Pacific Islander, non-Hispanic/Latino; 3 Two or more races, non-Hispanic/Latino), 8 international. 109 applicants, 59% accepted, 44 enrolled. In 2017, 30 master's, 3 doctorates awarded. *Degree requirements:* For master's, comprehensive exam, thesis optional; for doctorate, comprehensive exam, thesis/dissertation. *Entrance requirements:* For master's and doctorate, GRE General Test. Additional exam requirements/recommendations for international students: Required—TOEFL (minimum score 550 paper-based; 80 iBT). *Application deadline:* For fall admission, 2/1 priority date for domestic students, 2/1 for international students; for spring admission, 10/1 for domestic and international students. Applications are processed on a rolling basis. Application fee: $25. Electronic applications accepted. *Financial support:* In 2017–18, 60 students received support, including 1 research assistantship with full tuition reimbursement available (averaging $12,700 per year), 33 teaching assistantships with full tuition reimbursements available (averaging $7,650 per year); career-related internships or fieldwork, Federal Work-Study, institutionally sponsored loans, scholarships/grants, tuition waivers (full), and unspecified assistantships also available. Financial award application deadline: 2/1. *Faculty research:* Exercise testing, cardio-metabolic health, resistance exercise and training, nutritional intervention, population health, health promotion, global health epidemiology, coaching, natural resource management, stimulant misuse, diet, microbiome and colon cancer etiology. *Total annual research expenditures:* $250,118. *Unit head:* Dr. Jaeho Shim, Graduate Program Director, 254-710-4009, Fax: 254-710-3527, E-mail: joe_shim@baylor.edu. *Application contact:* Deepa Morris, Graduate Program Coordinator, 254-710-3526, Fax: 254-710-3527, E-mail: deepa_morris@baylor.edu.
Website: http://www.baylor.edu/HHPR/

Boise State University, College of Health Sciences, Department of Kinesiology, Boise, ID 83725-0399. Offers athletic leadership (MAL); kinesiology (MK, MS). *Program availability:* Part-time. *Faculty:* 11. *Students:* 23 full-time (9 women), 31 part-time (10

women); includes 11 minority (4 Black or African American, non-Hispanic/Latino; 6 Hispanic/Latino; 1 Two or more races, non-Hispanic/Latino). Average age 25. 37 applicants, 65% accepted, 15 enrolled. In 2017, 22 master's awarded. *Degree requirements:* For master's, thesis (for some programs). *Entrance requirements:* For master's, minimum GPA of 3.0. Additional exam requirements/recommendations for international students: Required—TOEFL (minimum score 550 paper-based; 80 iBT), IELTS (minimum score 6). *Application deadline:* For fall admission, 5/1 for domestic and international students. Application fee: $65 ($95 for international students). Electronic applications accepted. *Expenses:* Tuition, state resident: full-time $6471; part-time $390 per credit. Tuition, nonresident: full-time $21,787; part-time $685 per credit. *Required fees:* $2283; $100 per term. Part-time tuition and fees vary according to course load and program. *Financial support:* Scholarships/grants and unspecified assistantships available. Financial award application deadline: 1/15; financial award applicants required to submit FAFSA. *Unit head:* Dr. John McChesney, Department Chair, 208-426-4270, E-mail: johnmcchesney@boisestate.edu. *Application contact:* Dr. Shelley Lucas, Program Coordinator, 208-426-2446, E-mail: smlucas@boisestate.edu.
Website: https://hs.boisestate.edu/kinesiology/

Bowling Green State University, Graduate College, College of Education and Human Development, School of Human Movement, Sport, and Leisure Studies, Bowling Green, OH 43403. Offers developmental kinesiology (M Ed); recreation and leisure (M Ed); sport administration (M Ed). *Program availability:* Part-time. *Degree requirements:* For master's, thesis and/or alternative. *Entrance requirements:* For master's, GRE General Test, minimum GPA of 2.7. Additional exam requirements/recommendations for international students: Required—TOEFL. Electronic applications accepted. *Faculty research:* Teacher-learning process, travel and tourism, sport marketing and management, exercise physiology and sport psychology, life-span motor development.

Brooklyn College of the City University of New York, School of Natural and Behavioral Sciences, Department of Kinesiology, Brooklyn, NY 11210-2889. Offers exercise and sports science (MS); physical education teacher (MS); sport management (MS). *Program availability:* Part-time. *Degree requirements:* For master's, comprehensive exam or thesis. *Entrance requirements:* For master's, previous course work in physical education and education, minimum GPA of 3.0, 2 letters of recommendation, essay. Additional exam requirements/recommendations for international students: Required—TOEFL (minimum score 500 paper-based; 61 iBT). Electronic applications accepted. *Faculty research:* Exercise physiology, motor learning, sports psychology, women in athletics.

California State Polytechnic University, Pomona, Program in Kinesiology, Pomona, CA 91768-2557. Offers MS. *Program availability:* Part-time, evening/weekend. *Students:* 6 full-time (3 women), 7 part-time (4 women); includes 8 minority (4 Asian, non-Hispanic/Latino; 2 Hispanic/Latino; 2 Two or more races, non-Hispanic/Latino). Average age 27. 20 applicants, 60% accepted, 7 enrolled. In 2017, 12 master's awarded. *Degree requirements:* For master's, thesis or alternative. *Entrance requirements:* Additional exam requirements/recommendations for international students: Required—TOEFL (minimum score 550 paper-based). *Application deadline:* Applications are processed on a rolling basis. Application fee: $55. Electronic applications accepted. *Expenses:* Contact institution. *Financial support:* Application deadline: 3/2; applicants required to submit FAFSA. *Unit head:* Ken Hansen, Professor/Graduate Coordinator, 909-869-4638, Fax: 909-869-4797, E-mail: kahansen@cpp.edu. *Application contact:* Deborah L. Brandon, Executive Director of Admissions and Enrollment Planning, 909-869-3427, Fax: 909-869-5315, E-mail: dlbrandon@cpp.edu.
Website: http://www.cpp.edu/~sci/kinesiology-health-promotion/academic-programs/graduate-program.shtml

California State University, Chico, Office of Graduate Studies, College of Communication and Education, Department of Kinesiology, Chico, CA 95929-0722. Offers MA. *Program availability:* Part-time. *Degree requirements:* For master's, thesis, project, or comprehensive examination. *Entrance requirements:* For master's, GRE General Test, 2 letters of recommendation, statement of purpose. Additional exam requirements/recommendations for international students: Required—TOEFL (minimum score 550 paper-based; 80 iBT), IELTS (minimum score 6.5), PTE (minimum score 59). Electronic applications accepted.

California State University, Fresno, Division of Research and Graduate Studies, College of Health and Human Services, Department of Kinesiology, Fresno, CA 93740-8027. Offers exercise science (MA); general kinesiology (MA); sport administration (MA); sport psychology (MA). *Program availability:* Part-time, evening/weekend. *Degree requirements:* For master's, thesis or alternative. *Entrance requirements:* For master's, GRE General Test, minimum GPA of 2.7. Additional exam requirements/recommendations for international students: Required—TOEFL. Electronic applications accepted. *Faculty research:* Refugee education, homeless, geriatrics, fitness.

California State University, Long Beach, Graduate Studies, College of Health and Human Services, Department of Kinesiology, Long Beach, CA 90840. Offers adapted physical education (MA); coaching and student athlete development (MA); exercise physiology and nutrition (MS); exercise science (MS); individualized studies (MA); kinesiology (MA); pedagogical studies (MA); sport and exercise psychology (MS); sport management (MA); sports medicine and injury studies (MS). *Program availability:* Part-time. *Degree requirements:* For master's, oral and written comprehensive exams or thesis. *Entrance requirements:* For master's, GRE General Test, minimum GPA of 2.75 during previous 2 years of course work. Electronic applications accepted. *Faculty research:* Pulmonary functioning, feedback and practice structure, strength training, history and politics of sports, special population research issues.

California State University, Los Angeles, Graduate Studies, College of Health and Human Services, Department of Kinesiology and Nutritional Sciences, Los Angeles, CA 90032-8530. Offers nutritional science (MS); physical education and kinesiology (MA). *Accreditation:* AND. *Program availability:* Part-time, evening/weekend. *Degree requirements:* For master's, comprehensive exam, project or thesis. *Entrance requirements:* For master's, minimum GPA of 2.75. Additional exam requirements/recommendations for international students: Required—TOEFL (minimum score 500 paper-based).

California State University, Northridge, Graduate Studies, College of Health and Human Development, Department of Kinesiology, Northridge, CA 91330. Offers MS. *Program availability:* Part-time, evening/weekend. *Students:* 28 full-time (10 women), 41 part-time (21 women); includes 42 minority (1 Black or African American, non-Hispanic/Latino; 1 American Indian or Alaska Native, non-Hispanic/Latino; 9 Asian, non-Hispanic/Latino; 22 Hispanic/Latino; 9 Two or more races, non-Hispanic/Latino), 4 international. Average age 28. 67 applicants, 42% accepted, 19 enrolled. In 2017, 23 master's awarded. *Degree requirements:* For master's, thesis or alternative. *Entrance requirements:* For master's, GRE General Test or minimum GPA of 3.0, 3 letters of recommendation. Additional exam requirements/recommendations for international students: Required—TOEFL. *Application deadline:* For fall admission, 11/30 for domestic students. Application fee: $55. *Financial support:* Teaching assistantships and unspecified assistantships available. Financial award application deadline: 3/1. *Unit head:* Dr. K. Dino Vrongistinos, Chair, 818-677-3205.
Website: http://www.csun.edu/hhd/kin/

Canisius College, Graduate Division, School of Education and Human Services, Department of Kinesiology, Buffalo, NY 14208-1098. Offers physical education (MS Ed); physical education birth - 12 (MS Ed). *Program availability:* Part-time, evening/weekend, 100% online, blended/hybrid learning. *Faculty:* 6 full-time (1 woman), 9 part-time/adjunct (2 women). *Students:* 90 full-time (29 women), 87 part-time (31 women); includes 33 minority (23 Black or African American, non-Hispanic/Latino; 1 Asian, non-Hispanic/Latino; 7 Hispanic/Latino; 2 Two or more races, non-Hispanic/Latino), 5 international. Average age 29. 62 applicants, 95% accepted, 54 enrolled. In 2017, 91 master's awarded. *Degree requirements:* For master's, research project. *Entrance requirements:* For master's, official college and/or university transcript(s) showing completion of bachelor's degree from accredited institution with evidence of teaching certification (not for initial certification candidates); two letters of recommendation; minimum cumulative undergraduate GPA of 2.7. Additional exam requirements/recommendations for international students: Required—TOEFL (minimum score 550 paper-based, 79 iBT), IELTS (minimum score 6.5), or CAEL (minimum score 70). *Application deadline:* Applications are processed on a rolling basis. Application fee: $0. Electronic applications accepted. *Expenses:* Contact institution. *Financial support:* Career-related internships or fieldwork, Federal Work-Study, scholarships/grants, tuition waivers (partial), and unspecified assistantships available. Support available to part-time students. Financial award application deadline: 4/30; financial award applicants required to submit FAFSA. *Faculty research:* Culturally congruent pedagogy in physical education, information processing and perceptual styles of athletes, qualities of effective coaches. *Unit head:* Dr. Nicolas Lorgnier, Chair/Professor of Kinesiology, 716-888-3733, Fax: 716-888-8445, E-mail: lorgnien@canisius.edu. *Application contact:* Fax: 716-888-3195, E-mail: daviskb@canisius.edu.
Website: http://www.canisius.edu/graduate/

Columbia University, College of Physicians and Surgeons, Programs in Occupational Therapy, New York, NY 10032. Offers movement science (Ed D), including occupational therapy; occupational therapy (MS); occupational therapy and cognition (OTD); MPH/MS. EdD offered in tandem with Teachers College, Columbia University. *Accreditation:* AOTA. *Degree requirements:* For master's, project, 6 months of fieldwork, thesis (for post-professional students); for doctorate, comprehensive exam, thesis/dissertation. *Entrance requirements:* For master's, undergraduate course work in anatomy, physiology, statistics, psychology, social sciences, humanities, and English composition; for doctorate, master's degree in occupational therapy (for OTD). Additional exam requirements/recommendations for international students: Required—TOEFL (minimum score 100 iBT) or IELTS (minimum score 8). Electronic applications accepted. *Expenses:* Contact institution. *Faculty research:* Community mental health, motor learning, cognition, literacy, LGBTQ.

Dalhousie University, Faculty of Health Professions, School of Health and Human Performance, Program in Kinesiology, Halifax, NS B3H 3J5, Canada. Offers M Sc. *Program availability:* Part-time. *Degree requirements:* For master's, thesis. *Entrance requirements:* Additional exam requirements/recommendations for international students: Required—TOEFL, IELTS, CANTEST, CAEL, or Michigan English Language Assessment Battery. Electronic applications accepted. *Faculty research:* Sport science, fitness, neuromuscular physiology, biomechanics, ergonomics, sport psychology.

Dallas Baptist University, Dorothy M. Bush College of Education, Program in Kinesiology, Dallas, TX 75211-9299. Offers M Ed. *Program availability:* Part-time, evening/weekend, online learning. *Application deadline:* Applications are processed on a rolling basis. Application fee: $25. Electronic applications accepted. Application fee is waived when completed online. *Expenses: Tuition:* Full-time $16,308; part-time $906 per credit hour. *Required fees:* $900; $450 per semester. Tuition and fees vary according to course load and degree level. *Unit head:* Dr. Neil Dugger, Dean, 214-333-5202, E-mail: neil@dbu.edu. *Application contact:* Dr. Ray Galloway, Program Director, 214-333-5253, E-mail: rayg@dbu.edu.
Website: http://www3.dbu.edu/graduate/kinesiology.asp

East Carolina University, Graduate School, College of Health and Human Performance, Department of Kinesiology, Greenville, NC 27858-4353. Offers adapted physical education (MS); bioenergetics and exercise science (PhD); biomechanics and motor control (MS); exercise physiology (MS); physical activity promotion (MS); physical education (MA Ed, MAT); physical education clinical supervision (Certificate); physical education pedagogy (MS); sport and exercise psychology (MS); sport management (MS, Certificate). *Students:* 72 full-time (30 women), 25 part-time (10 women); includes 21 minority (10 Black or African American, non-Hispanic/Latino; 1 American Indian or Alaska Native, non-Hispanic/Latino; 3 Asian, non-Hispanic/Latino; 4 Hispanic/Latino; 3 Two or more races, non-Hispanic/Latino), 3 international. Average age 27. 88 applicants, 68% accepted, 40 enrolled. In 2017, 35 master's, 5 doctorates, 4 other advanced degrees awarded. *Degree requirements:* For master's, comprehensive exam, thesis optional; for doctorate, comprehensive exam, thesis/dissertation. *Entrance requirements:* For master's, GRE General Test or MAT; for doctorate, GRE. Additional exam requirements/recommendations for international students: Recommended—TOEFL (minimum score 78 iBT), IELTS. *Application deadline:* For fall admission, 2/1 priority date for domestic students, 2/1 for international students. Applications are processed on a rolling basis. Application fee: $75. *Expenses:* Tuition, state resident: full-time $4749; part-time $297 per credit hour. Tuition, nonresident: full-time $17,898; part-time $1119 per credit hour. *Required fees:* $2691; $224 per credit hour. Part-time tuition and fees vary according to course load and program. *Financial support:* Research assistantships with tuition reimbursements and teaching assistantships available. Support available to part-time students. Financial award application deadline: 2/1. *Faculty research:* Diabetes metabolism, pediatric obesity, biomechanics of arthritis, physical activity measurement. *Unit head:* Dr. Stacey Altman, Chair, 252-328-2973, E-mail: altmans@ecu.edu.
Website: https://hhp.ecu.edu/kine/

Eastern Illinois University, Graduate School, College of Health and Human Services, Department of Kinesiology and Sports Studies, Charleston, IL 61920. Offers MS. *Program availability:* Part-time, evening/weekend. *Degree requirements:* For master's, comprehensive exam (for some programs), thesis (for some programs). *Entrance requirements:* For master's, minimum GPA of 3.0 with kinesiology focus, three letters of recommendation, resume, personal statement. Additional exam requirements/recommendations for international students: Required—TOEFL (minimum score 500 paper-based; 61 iBT), IELTS (minimum score 6). *Application deadline:* For fall admission, 5/15 for domestic and international students; for spring admission, 10/15 for domestic and international students. Applications are processed on a rolling basis. Application fee: $30. Electronic applications accepted. *Financial support:* Teaching assistantships with full tuition reimbursements, career-related internships or fieldwork, Federal Work-Study, and unspecified assistantships available. Support available to part-time students. Financial award application deadline: 3/1; financial award applicants required to submit FAFSA. *Unit head:* Dr. Scott Ronspies, Graduate Coordinator, 217-581-7594, Fax: 217-581-7973, E-mail: sronspies@eiu.edu. *Application contact:* Dr. Scott Ronspies, Graduate Coordinator, 217-581-7594, Fax: 217-581-7973, E-mail: sronspies@eiu.edu.
Website: http://www.eiu.edu/kssgrad/

Eastern Michigan University, Graduate School, College of Health and Human Services, School of Health Promotion and Human Performance, Programs in Exercise Physiology, Ypsilanti, MI 48197. Offers exercise physiology (MS); sports medicine-biomechanics (MS); sports medicine-corporate adult fitness (MS); sports medicine-exercise physiology (MS). *Program availability:* Part-time, evening/weekend. *Students:* 9 full-time (3 women), 13 part-time (5 women); includes 5 minority (2 Black or African American, non-Hispanic/Latino; 1 Asian, non-Hispanic/Latino; 1 Hispanic/Latino; 1 Two or more races, non-Hispanic/Latino), 1 international. Average age 29. 43 applicants, 56% accepted, 7 enrolled. In 2017, 13 master's awarded. *Degree requirements:* For master's, comprehensive exam, thesis or 450-hour internship. *Entrance requirements:* Additional exam requirements/recommendations for international students: Required—TOEFL. *Application deadline:* For fall admission, 8/1 for domestic students, 5/1 for international students; for winter admission, 12/1 for domestic students, 10/1 for international students; for spring admission, 3/15 for domestic students, 3/1 for international students. Application fee: $45. *Application contact:* Dr. Becca Moore, Program Coordinator, 734-487-2824, Fax: 734-487-2024, E-mail: rmoore41@emich.edu.

East Tennessee State University, School of Graduate Studies, College of Education, Department of Sport, Exercise, Recreation, and Kinesiology, Johnson City, TN 37614-1701. Offers sport management (MA); sport physiology and performance (PhD), including sport performance, sport physiology; sport science and coach education (MS), including applied sport science, strength and conditioning. *Program availability:* Part-time, evening/weekend. Terminal master's awarded for partial completion of doctoral program. *Degree requirements:* For master's, comprehensive exam, thesis or internship; for doctorate, comprehensive exam, thesis/dissertation, 2-semester residency. *Entrance requirements:* For master's, GRE General Test or GMAT, undergraduate degree in related field; minimum GPA of 3.0; resume; three references; essay explaining goals and reasons for pursuing degree; for doctorate, GRE, resume; 4 letters of recommendation; master's or bachelor's degree in related field; minimum GPA of 3.4 overall with master's, 3.0 with bachelor's; interview. Additional exam requirements/recommendations for international students: Required—TOEFL (minimum score 550 paper-based; 79 iBT). *Application deadline:* For fall admission, 6/1 for domestic students, 4/29 for international students; for spring admission, 11/1 for domestic students, 9/29 for international students. Application fee: $55 ($65 for international students). Electronic applications accepted. *Financial support:* Fellowships, research assistantships with full tuition reimbursements, teaching assistantships with full tuition reimbursements, career-related internships or fieldwork, institutionally sponsored loans, scholarships/grants, and unspecified assistantships available. Financial award application deadline: 7/1; financial award applicants required to submit FAFSA. *Faculty research:* Methods of training for individual and team sports, enhancing acute sport performance, fatigue management in athletes, risk management, facilities management, motorsport. *Unit head:* Dr. Mike Ramsey, Chair, 423-439-4375, Fax: 423-439-7560, E-mail: ramseym@etsu.edu. *Application contact:* Dr. Mike Stone, Graduate Program Coordinator, 423-439-5796, Fax: 423-439-5624, E-mail: stonem@etsu.edu. Website: http://www.etsu.edu/coe/serk/

East Texas Baptist University, Master of Science in Kinesiology Program, Marshall, TX 75670-1498. Offers MS. *Program availability:* Part-time, evening/weekend. *Faculty:* 2 full-time (0 women). *Students:* 6 part-time (2 women); includes 3 minority (1 Black or African American, non-Hispanic/Latino; 1 Hispanic/Latino; 1 Two or more races, non-Hispanic/Latino). Average age 24. 9 applicants, 56% accepted, 5 enrolled. *Entrance requirements:* Additional exam requirements/recommendations for international students: Recommended—TOEFL (minimum score 550 paper-based; 79 iBT). *Application deadline:* For fall admission, 8/13 for domestic students; for spring admission, 1/7 for domestic students; for summer admission, 5/10 for domestic students. Applications are processed on a rolling basis. Application fee: $50. Electronic applications accepted. *Expenses:* $700 per credit hour tuition, $150 per semester fees ($75 per semester if less than 6 hours). *Financial support:* In 2017–18, 3 students received support. Federal Work-Study, scholarships/grants, unspecified assistantships, and staff grants available. Financial award applicants required to submit FAFSA. *Unit head:* Dr. Joseph D. Brown, Dean, Frank S. Groner School of Professional Studies, 903-923-2270, Fax: 903-935-4318, E-mail: jbrown@etbu.edu. *Application contact:* Den Murley, Director of Graduate Admissions, 903-923-2079, Fax: 903-934-8115, E-mail: gradadmissions@etbu.edu.
Website: https://www.etbu.edu/school-professional-studies/kinesiology/ms-kinesiology/

Fresno Pacific University, Graduate Programs, Program in Kinesiology, Fresno, CA 93702-4709. Offers MA. *Entrance requirements:* Additional exam requirements/recommendations for international students: Required—TOEFL (minimum score 550 paper-based).

Georgia College & State University, Graduate School, College of Health Sciences, School of Health and Human Performance, Milledgeville, GA 31061. Offers health and human performance (MS), including health performance, health promotion; kinesiology/health education (MAT). *Accreditation:* NCATE (one or more programs are accredited). *Program availability:* Part-time, 100% online. *Faculty:* 19 full-time (9 women). *Students:* 35 full-time (20 women), 17 part-time (10 women); includes 9 minority (3 Black or African American, non-Hispanic/Latino; 5 Hispanic/Latino; 1 Two or more races, non-Hispanic/Latino), 2 international. Average age 27. 21 applicants, 100% accepted, 19 enrolled. In 2017, 21 master's awarded. *Degree requirements:* For master's, thesis (for some programs), completed in 6 years with minimum GPA of 3.0 (for MS); minimum GPA of 3.0 and electronic teaching portfolio (for MAT). *Entrance requirements:* For master's, GRE with minimum score of 297 or MAT with minimum score of 385 (for MS); GRE with minimum score of 297, MAT 385, SAT 1000, ACT 43, or GACE with 250 on each section (for MAT), resume, 3 professional references; minimum GPA of 2.75 in upper-level undergraduate courses and undergraduate statistics course (for MS); minimum GPA of 2.75 on upper-division major courses (for MAT). *Application deadline:* For fall admission, 7/15 priority date for domestic students, 4/1 for international students; for spring admission, 11/15 priority date for domestic students, 9/1 for international students; for summer admission, 4/15 priority date for domestic students. Applications are processed on a rolling basis. Application fee: $40. Electronic applications accepted. *Expenses:* Contact institution. *Financial support:* In 2017–18, 22 students received support. Unspecified assistantships available. Support available to part-time students. Financial award application deadline: 3/1; financial award applicants required to submit FAFSA. *Unit head:* Dr. Lisa Griffin, Director, School of Health and Human Performance, 478-445-4072, Fax: 478-445-4074, E-mail: lisa.griffin@gcsu.edu.
Website: http://www.gcsu.edu/health/shhp

Georgia Southern University, Jack N. Averitt College of Graduate Studies, College of Health and Human Sciences, School of Health and Kinesiology, Program in Kinesiology, Statesboro, GA 30458. Offers MS. *Program availability:* Part-time. *Faculty:* 78 full-time (54 women), 6 part-time/adjunct (4 women). *Students:* 59 full-time (35 women), 44 part-time (11 women); includes 28 minority (19 Black or African American, non-Hispanic/Latino; 1 Asian, non-Hispanic/Latino; 6 Hispanic/Latino; 2 Two or more races, non-Hispanic/Latino), 4 international. Average age 25. 123 applicants, 37% accepted, 21 enrolled. In 2017, 63 master's awarded. *Entrance requirements:* For master's, minimum GPA of 2.75. Additional exam requirements/recommendations for international students:

Required—TOEFL (minimum score 550 paper-based; 80 iBT), IELTS (minimum score 6). *Application deadline:* For fall admission, 2/1 for domestic students. Application fee: $50. Electronic applications accepted. *Expenses:* Contact institution. *Financial support:* In 2017–18, 67 students received support, including 12 fellowships with full tuition reimbursements available (averaging $7,750 per year), 1 research assistantship with full tuition reimbursement available (averaging $7,750 per year), 33 teaching assistantships with full tuition reimbursements available (averaging $7,750 per year). Financial award application deadline: 4/20; financial award applicants required to submit FAFSA. *Faculty research:* Athletic training, coaching, exercise science, nutrition and food science, sport psychology, sport management, physical education. *Unit head:* Dr. Stephen Rossi, Interim Chair, 912-478-0200, Fax: 912-478-0381, E-mail: srossi@georgiasouthern.edu.

Georgia State University, College of Education and Human Development, Department of Kinesiology and Health, Program in Kinesiology, Atlanta, GA 30302-3083. Offers PhD. *Entrance requirements:* For doctorate, GRE General Test or MAT, minimum GPA of 3.3. Application fee: $50. *Expenses:* Tuition, state resident: full-time $7020. Tuition, nonresident: full-time $22,518. *Required fees:* $2128. Tuition and fees vary according to degree level and program. *Financial support:* Research assistantships and teaching assistantships available. *Faculty research:* Aging, exercise metabolism, biomechanics and ergonomics, blood pressure regulation, exercise performance. *Unit head:* Dr. Jacalyn Lea Lund, Chair, 404-413-8051, E-mail: jlund@gsu.edu. *Application contact:* Dr. Christopher Ingalls, Program Coordinator, 404-413-8377, E-mail: cingalls@gsu.edu.
Website: http://kh.education.gsu.edu/

Hardin-Simmons University, Graduate School, Irvin School of Education, Kinesiology, Sport, and Recreation Program, Abilene, TX 79698-0001. Offers kinesiology, sport, and recreation (M Ed). *Program availability:* Part-time. *Faculty:* 5 full-time (2 women). *Students:* 10 full-time (6 women), 28 part-time (8 women); includes 16 minority (7 Black or African American, non-Hispanic/Latino; 7 Hispanic/Latino; 2 Two or more races, non-Hispanic/Latino), 1 international. Average age 25. 26 applicants, 96% accepted, 20 enrolled. In 2017, 14 master's awarded. *Degree requirements:* For master's, comprehensive exam, professional project. *Entrance requirements:* For master's, minimum undergraduate GPA of 3.0 in major, 2.7 overall; writing sample; letters of recommendation; resume; personal interview. Additional exam requirements/recommendations for international students: Required—TOEFL (minimum score 550 paper-based; 79 iBT). *Application deadline:* For fall admission, 8/15 priority date for domestic students, 4/1 for international students; for spring admission, 1/5 priority date for domestic students, 9/1 for international students. Applications are processed on a rolling basis. Application fee: $50 ($150 for international students). Electronic applications accepted. *Expenses:* Tuition: Full-time $13,500; part-time $750 per semester hour. *Required fees:* $220 per term. One-time fee: $50. Tuition and fees vary according to course load, campus/location and program. *Financial support:* In 2017–18, 6 students received support. Fellowships, career-related internships or fieldwork, scholarships/grants, and unspecified assistantships available. Support available to part-time students. Financial award application deadline: 6/30; financial award applicants required to submit FAFSA. *Unit head:* Dr. Lindsay Edwards, Program Director, 325-670-5893, Fax: 325-670-1572, E-mail: ledwards@hsutx.edu. *Application contact:* Dr. Nancy Kucinski, Dean of Graduate Studies, 325-670-1298, Fax: 325-670-1564, E-mail: gradoff@hsutx.edu.
Website: http://www.hsutx.edu/academics/irvin/graduate/kinesiology

Houston Baptist University, School of Nursing and Allied Health, Program in Kinesiology - Sport Management, Houston, TX 77074-3298. Offers sport management (MSK). *Program availability:* Online only, 100% online. *Students:* 9 full-time (7 women); includes 4 minority (1 Black or African American, non-Hispanic/Latino; 3 Hispanic/Latino). Average age 23. 43 applicants, 23% accepted, 9 enrolled. *Degree requirements:* For master's, internship or thesis. *Entrance requirements:* For master's, GRE, bachelor's degree conferred transcript, personal statement/essay, resume. Additional exam requirements/recommendations for international students: Required—TOEFL (minimum score 80 iBT), IELTS (minimum score 6.5). *Application deadline:* For fall admission, 8/1 for domestic students, 6/1 for international students; for spring admission, 1/1 for domestic students, 11/1 for international students. Applications are processed on a rolling basis. Application fee: $0 ($100 for international students). Electronic applications accepted. Application fee is waived when completed online. *Expenses:* $20,350 tuition; $1,000 fees (general, technology). *Financial support:* In 2017–18, 8 students received support. *Unit head:* Dr. Kylee Studer O'Daniel, Chair, Department of Kinesiology, 281-649-3128, E-mail: kstuder@hbu.edu. *Application contact:* Allyson Cates, Director of Admissions, Graduate School, 281-649-3099, Fax: 281-649-3390, E-mail: acates@hbu.edu.

Humboldt State University, Academic Programs, College of Professional Studies, Department of Kinesiology and Recreation Administration, Arcata, CA 95521-8299. Offers kinesiology (MS). *Degree requirements:* For master's, thesis or alternative. *Entrance requirements:* For master's, GMAT, minimum GPA of 2.5. Additional exam requirements/recommendations for international students: Required—TOEFL. *Faculty research:* Human performance, adapted physical education, physical therapy.

Indiana University Bloomington, School of Public Health, Department of Kinesiology, Bloomington, IN 47405. Offers applied sport science (MS); athletic administration/sport management (MS); athletic training (MS); biomechanics (MS); ergonomics (MS); exercise physiology (MS); human performance (PhD), including biomechanics, exercise physiology, motor learning/control, sport management; motor learning/control (MS); physical activity (MPH); physical activity, fitness and wellness (MS). *Program availability:* Part-time. Terminal master's awarded for partial completion of doctoral program. *Degree requirements:* For master's, thesis optional; for doctorate, variable foreign language requirement, comprehensive exam, thesis/dissertation. *Entrance requirements:* For master's, GRE General Test, minimum GPA of 2.8; for doctorate, GRE General Test, minimum graduate GPA of 3.5, undergraduate 3.0. Additional exam requirements/recommendations for international students: Required—TOEFL (minimum score 80 iBT). *Faculty research:* Exercise physiology and biochemistry, sports biomechanics, human motor control, adaptation of fitness and exercise to special populations.

Indiana University–Purdue University Indianapolis, School of Physical Education and Tourism Management, Indianapolis, IN 46202-5193. Offers event tourism (MS), including sport event tourism; kinesiology (MS), including clinical exercise science; public health (Graduate Certificate). *Degree requirements:* For master's, comprehensive exam (for some programs), thesis (for some programs). *Entrance requirements:* For master's, GRE. Additional exam requirements/recommendations for international students: Required—TOEFL. Electronic applications accepted. *Expenses:* Contact institution. *Faculty research:* Physical activity, exercise and diseases; human movement science; sport performance; sport event tourism; destination marketing and event management.

Inter American University of Puerto Rico, San Germán Campus, Graduate Studies Center, Program in Health and Physical Education, San Germán, PR 00683-5008. Offers MA. *Program availability:* Part-time, evening/weekend. *Degree requirements:* For master's, comprehensive exam. *Entrance requirements:* For master's, GRE General Test or EXADEP, minimum GPA of 3.0.

Iowa State University of Science and Technology, Department of Kinesiology, Ames, IA 50011. Offers MS, PhD. *Entrance requirements:* For master's and doctorate, GRE General Test. Additional exam requirements/recommendations for international students: Required—TOEFL (minimum score 560 paper-based; 79 iBT), IELTS (minimum score 6.5). Electronic applications accepted.

Jacksonville University, Brooks Rehabilitation College of Healthcare Sciences, School of Applied Health Sciences, Program in Kinesiological Sciences, Jacksonville, FL 32211. Offers MS. *Program availability:* Part-time, blended/hybrid learning. *Faculty:* 5 full-time (1 woman), 4 part-time/adjunct (2 women). *Students:* 18 full-time (9 women), 10 part-time (5 women); includes 8 minority (6 Black or African American, non-Hispanic/Latino; 2 Hispanic/Latino), 2 international. Average age 25. 20 applicants, 100% accepted, 16 enrolled. In 2017, 5 master's awarded. *Degree requirements:* For master's, thesis, internship. *Entrance requirements:* For master's, GRE (priority given to students who achieve minimum combined score of 300 on current scale (1080 prior scale) for verbal and quantitative sections), baccalaureate degree from accredited college or university with minimum GPA of 3.0; official transcripts; essay on personal professional goals (minimum 1000 words); resume (education, work experience); 3 letters of recommendation; interview; prerequisites in anatomy, physiology, chemistry, physics, psychology, and statistics. Additional exam requirements/recommendations for international students: Required—TOEFL (minimum score 650 paper-based; 114 iBT), IELTS (minimum score 8). *Application deadline:* For fall admission, 2/1 for domestic and international students. Applications are processed on a rolling basis. Application fee: $50. Electronic applications accepted. *Expenses:* $780 per credit hour. *Financial support:* Federal Work-Study, institutionally sponsored loans, scholarships/grants, and health care benefits available. Support available to part-time students. Financial award application deadline: 3/15; financial award applicants required to submit FAFSA. *Unit head:* Dr. Heather Hausenblas, Associate Dean, School of Applied Health Sciences/Professor of Kinesiology, 904-256-7975, E-mail: hhausen@ju.edu. *Application contact:* Ashlea Rieser, Assistant Director of Enrollment and Advising, 904-256-8934, E-mail: arieser0@ju.edu.
Website: https://www.ju.edu/kinesiology/

James Madison University, The Graduate School, College of Health and Behavioral Studies, Program in Health Sciences, Harrisonburg, VA 22801. Offers nutrition and physical activity (MS). *Program availability:* Part-time. *Students:* 3 full-time (all women), 1 part-time (0 women); includes 1 minority (Black or African American, non-Hispanic/Latino). Average age 30. In 2017, 4 master's awarded. Application fee: $55. Electronic applications accepted. *Expenses:* Tuition, state resident: full-time $10,512; part-time $438 per credit hour. Tuition, nonresident: full-time $28,358; part-time $1162 per credit hour. *Required fees:* $1128. *Financial support:* In 2017–18, 2 students received support. Federal Work-Study and 2 assistantships (averaging $7911) available. Financial award application deadline: 3/1; financial award applicants required to submit FAFSA. *Unit head:* Dr. Allen Lewis, Department Head, 540-568-6510, E-mail: amatohk@jmu.edu. *Application contact:* Lynette D. Michael, Director of Graduate Admissions and Student Records, 540-568-6131 Ext. 6395, Fax: 540-568-7860, E-mail: michaeld@jmu.edu.
Website: http://www.healthsci.jmu.edu/index.html

James Madison University, The Graduate School, College of Health and Behavioral Studies, Program in Kinesiology, Harrisonburg, VA 22801. Offers clinical exercise physiology (MS); exercise physiology (MS); kinesiology (MAT, MS); nutrition and exercise (MS); physical and health education (MAT); sport and recreation leadership (MS). *Program availability:* Part-time, evening/weekend. *Students:* 43 full-time (22 women), 3 part-time (2 women); includes 10 minority (4 Black or African American, non-Hispanic/Latino; 1 Asian, non-Hispanic/Latino; 4 Hispanic/Latino; 1 Two or more races, non-Hispanic/Latino). Average age 30. In 2017, 46 master's awarded. Application fee: $55. Electronic applications accepted. *Expenses:* Tuition, state resident: full-time $10,512; part-time $438 per credit hour. Tuition, nonresident: full-time $28,358; part-time $1162 per credit hour. *Required fees:* $1128. *Financial support:* In 2017–18, 32 students received support, including 13 teaching assistantships with full tuition reimbursements available (averaging $8,837 per year); Federal Work-Study and 19 assistantships (averaging $7911), 20 athletic assistantships (averaging $9284) also available. Financial award application deadline: 3/1; financial award applicants required to submit FAFSA. *Unit head:* Dr. Christopher J. Womack, Department Head, 540-568-6145, E-mail: womackcx@jmu.edu. *Application contact:* Lynette D. Michael, Director of Graduate Admissions, 540-568-6131 Ext. 6395, Fax: 540-568-7860, E-mail: michaeld@jmu.edu.
Website: http://www.jmu.edu/kinesiology/

Kansas State University, Graduate School, College of Human Ecology, Department of Food, Nutrition, Dietetics and Health, Manhattan, KS 66506. Offers dietetics (MS); human nutrition (PhD); nutrition, dietetics and sensory sciences (MS); nutritional sciences (PhD); public health nutrition (PhD); public health physical activity (PhD); sensory analysis and consumer behavior (PhD). *Program availability:* Part-time. *Degree requirements:* For master's, thesis or alternative, residency; for doctorate, thesis/dissertation, residency. *Entrance requirements:* For master's, GRE General Test, minimum undergraduate GPA of 3.0; for doctorate, GRE General Test, minimum graduate GPA of 3.0. Additional exam requirements/recommendations for international students: Required—TOEFL (minimum score 550 paper-based; 79 iBT), IELTS (minimum score 6.5). Electronic applications accepted. *Faculty research:* Cancer and immunology, obesity, sensory analysis and consumer behavior, nutrient metabolism, clinical and community interventions.

Kansas State University, Graduate School, College of Human Ecology, Department of Kinesiology, Manhattan, KS 66506. Offers MS, PhD. *Program availability:* Part-time. *Degree requirements:* For master's, thesis or final comprehensive exam; for doctorate, comprehensive exam, thesis/dissertation. *Entrance requirements:* For master's, GRE General Test, bachelor's degree in kinesiology or exercise science, minimum GPA of 3.0; for doctorate, GRE General Test. Additional exam requirements/recommendations for international students: Required—TOEFL. Electronic applications accepted. *Expenses:* Contact institution. *Faculty research:* Exercise physiology, vascular function, cardiorespiratory disease, microgravity, cancer, physical inactivity, exercise adherence and compliance, public health/physical activity.

Kansas State University, Graduate School, College of Human Ecology, Doctorate in Human Ecology Program, Manhattan, KS 66506-1407. Offers apparel and textiles (PhD); applied family sciences (PhD); couple and family therapy (PhD); hospitality administration (PhD); kinesiology (PhD); life-span human development (PhD). *Program availability:* Part-time. *Degree requirements:* For doctorate, thesis/dissertation. *Entrance requirements:* Additional exam requirements/recommendations for international students: Required—TOEFL. Electronic applications accepted.

Lakehead University, Graduate Studies, School of Kinesiology, Thunder Bay, ON P7B 5E1, Canada. Offers kinesiology (M Sc); kinesiology and gerontology (M Sc). *Program availability:* Part-time. *Degree requirements:* For master's, thesis. *Entrance requirements:* For master's, minimum B average. Additional exam requirements/recommendations for international students: Required—TOEFL. *Faculty research:* Social psychology and physical education, sport history, sports medicine, exercise physiology, gerontology.

Lamar University, College of Graduate Studies, College of Education and Human Development, Department of Health and Kinesiology, Beaumont, TX 77701. Offers public health (MS); science of kinesiology promotion (MS). *Faculty:* 16 full-time (7 women), 5 part-time/adjunct (3 women). *Students:* 26 full-time (8 women), 42 part-time (35 women); includes 36 minority (29 Black or African American, non-Hispanic/Latino; 1 Asian, non-Hispanic/Latino; 5 Hispanic/Latino; 1 Two or more races, non-Hispanic/Latino), 4 international. Average age 29. 55 applicants, 100% accepted, 23 enrolled. In 2017, 23 master's awarded. *Degree requirements:* For master's, comprehensive exam (for some programs), thesis optional. *Entrance requirements:* For master's, GRE General Test, minimum GPA of 2.5. Additional exam requirements/recommendations for international students: Required—TOEFL (minimum score 550 paper-based; 79 iBT), IELTS (minimum score 6.5). *Application deadline:* For fall admission, 8/10 for domestic students, 7/1 for international students; for spring admission, 1/5 for domestic students, 12/1 for international students. Applications are processed on a rolling basis. Application fee: $25. Electronic applications accepted. *Expenses:* Contact institution. *Financial support:* In 2017–18, 4 teaching assistantships (averaging $7,500 per year) were awarded. Financial award application deadline: 4/1; financial award applicants required to submit FAFSA. *Faculty research:* Motor learning, exercise physiology, pedagogy. *Unit head:* Dr. Bill Holmes, Interim Chair, 409-880-8724, Fax: 409-880-1761. *Application contact:* Deidre Mayer, Interim Director, Admissions and Academic Services, 409-880-8888, Fax: 409-880-7419, E-mail: gradmissions@lamar.edu.
Website: http://education.lamar.edu/health-and-kinesiology

Louisiana State University and Agricultural & Mechanical College, Graduate School, College of Human Sciences and Education, Department of Kinesiology, Baton Rouge, LA 70803. Offers MS, PhD. *Faculty:* 24 full-time (5 women). *Students:* 89 full-time (40 women), 38 part-time (12 women); includes 30 minority (22 Black or African American, non-Hispanic/Latino; 3 Hispanic/Latino; 5 Two or more races, non-Hispanic/Latino), 12 international. Average age 29. 126 applicants, 63% accepted, 37 enrolled. In 2017, 50 master's, 5 doctorates awarded. *Financial support:* In 2017–18, 3 research assistantships (averaging $14,959 per year), 26 teaching assistantships (averaging $16,978 per year) were awarded. *Total annual research expenditures:* $68,665.

Louisiana Tech University, Graduate School, College of Education, Ruston, LA 71272. Offers counseling and guidance (MA), including clinical mental health counseling, human services, orientation and mobility; counseling psychology (PhD); curriculum and instruction (M Ed); cyber education (Graduate Certificate); dynamics of domestic and family violence (Graduate Certificate); early childhood education - PreK-3 (MAT); educational leadership (M Ed, Ed D); elementary education and special education mild/moderate grades 1-5 (MAT); higher education administration (Graduate Certificate); industrial/organizational psychology (MA, PhD); kinesiology (MS); middle school education (MAT), including mathematics; orientation and mobility (Graduate Certificate); rehabilitation teaching for the blind (Graduate Certificate); secondary education (MAT), including agriculture, biology, business, chemistry, English; special education: visually impaired (MAT); teacher leader education (Graduate Certificate); visual impairments - blind education (Graduate Certificate). *Accreditation:* NCATE. *Program availability:* Part-time. *Faculty:* 28 full-time (16 women), 23 part-time/adjunct (22 women). *Students:* 269 full-time (192 women), 194 part-time (150 women); includes 127 minority (94 Black or African American, non-Hispanic/Latino; 2 American Indian or Alaska Native, non-Hispanic/Latino; 6 Asian, non-Hispanic/Latino; 16 Hispanic/Latino; 1 Native Hawaiian or other Pacific Islander, non-Hispanic/Latino; 8 Two or more races, non-Hispanic/Latino), 8 international. Average age 34. 226 applicants, 74% accepted, 60 enrolled. In 2017, 5 master's, 2 doctorates, 1 other advanced degree awarded. *Degree requirements:* For master's, thesis; for doctorate, thesis/dissertation. *Entrance requirements:* For master's and doctorate, GRE General Test. Additional exam requirements/recommendations for international students: Required—TOEFL (minimum score 550 paper-based; 80 iBT), IELTS (minimum score 6.5). *Application deadline:* For fall admission, 9/1 priority date for domestic students, 6/1 for international students; for winter admission, 11/1 priority date for domestic students, 9/1 for international students; for spring admission, 2/1 priority date for domestic students, 12/1 for international students; for summer admission, 5/1 priority date for domestic students, 3/1 for international students. Application fee: $40. Electronic applications accepted. *Expenses:* Tuition, state resident: full-time $5146. Tuition, nonresident: full-time $10,147. *International tuition:* $10,267 full-time. *Required fees:* $2273. *Financial support:* In 2017–18, 40 students received support, including 23 research assistantships (averaging $10,346 per year), 15 teaching assistantships (averaging $6,887 per year); fellowships and career-related internships or fieldwork also available. Financial award application deadline: 2/1. *Faculty research:* Blindness and the best methods for increasing independence for individuals who are blind or visually impaired; educating and investigating factors contributing to improvements in human performance across the lifespan and a reduction in injury rates during training. *Total annual research expenditures:* $2.1 million. *Unit head:* Dr. Don Schillinger, Dean, 318-257-3712, E-mail: dschill@latech.edu. *Application contact:* Dr. Dawn Basinger, Associate Dean of Academic Affairs, 318-257-2977, Fax: 318-257-2379, E-mail: dbasing@latech.edu.
Website: http://education.latech.edu/

McDaniel College, Graduate and Professional Studies, Program in Kinesiology, Westminster, MD 21157-4390. Offers MS. *Program availability:* Part-time, evening/weekend. *Faculty:* 2 full-time (both women), 5 part-time/adjunct (1 woman). *Students:* 14 full-time (4 women), 23 part-time (9 women); includes 6 minority (5 Black or African American, non-Hispanic/Latino; 1 Two or more races, non-Hispanic/Latino), 1 international. Average age 26. 20 applicants, 100% accepted, 16 enrolled. In 2017, 22 master's awarded. *Degree requirements:* For master's, comprehensive exam, thesis optional. *Entrance requirements:* For master's, 3 references. Additional exam requirements/recommendations for international students: Required—TOEFL (minimum score 79 iBT), IELTS (minimum score 6). *Application deadline:* For fall admission, 6/1 priority date for domestic students; for spring admission, 11/1 priority date for domestic students; for summer admission, 3/1 priority date for domestic students. Applications are processed on a rolling basis. Application fee: $75. Electronic applications accepted. *Expenses: Tuition:* Full-time $11,760; part-time $490 per credit hour. Tuition and fees vary according to course load and program. *Financial support:* Unspecified assistantships available. Financial award application deadline: 3/1; financial award applicants required to submit FAFSA. *Unit head:* Fax: 410-857-2515, E-mail: gradadms@mcdaniel.edu. *Application contact:* Penny Pfeiffer, Senior Graduate Enrollment Management Specialist, 410-857-2516, Fax: 410-857-2515, E-mail: cperry@mcdaniel.edu.

McGill University, Faculty of Graduate and Postdoctoral Studies, Faculty of Education, Department of Kinesiology and Physical Education, Montréal, QC H3A 2T5, Canada. Offers M Sc, MA, PhD, Certificate, Diploma.

McMaster University, School of Graduate Studies, Faculty of Social Sciences, Department of Kinesiology, Hamilton, ON L8S 4M2, Canada. Offers human biodynamics (M Sc, PhD). *Degree requirements:* For master's, thesis. *Entrance requirements:* For master's, minimum B+ average in undergraduate course work. Additional exam requirements/recommendations for international students: Required—TOEFL (minimum score 580 paper-based). *Faculty research:* Motor learning and control, neuromuscular physiology, exercise rehabilitation, cellular responses to exercise, management.

Memorial University of Newfoundland, School of Graduate Studies, School of Human Kinetics and Recreation, St. John's, NL A1C 5S7, Canada. Offers administration, curriculum and supervision (MPE); biomechanics/ergonomics (MS Kin); exercise and work physiology (MS Kin); psychology of sport, exercise and recreation (MS Kin); socio-cultural studies of physical activity and health (MS Kin). *Program availability:* Part-time. *Degree requirements:* For master's, thesis optional, seminars, thesis presentations. *Entrance requirements:* For master's, bachelor's degree in a related field, minimum B average. Electronic applications accepted. *Faculty research:* Administration, sociology of sports, kinesiology, physiology/recreation.

Michigan State University, The Graduate School, College of Education, Department of Kinesiology, East Lansing, MI 48824. Offers MS, PhD. *Entrance requirements:* Additional exam requirements/recommendations for international students: Required—TOEFL. Electronic applications accepted.

Michigan Technological University, Graduate School, College of Sciences and Arts, Department of Kinesiology and Integrative Physiology, Houghton, MI 49931. Offers integrative physiology (PhD); kinesiology (MS). *Program availability:* Part-time. *Faculty:* 10 full-time, 5 part-time/adjunct. *Students:* 5 full-time, 4 part-time. Average age 25. 14 applicants, 43% accepted, 4 enrolled. In 2017, 4 master's awarded. *Degree requirements:* For master's, thesis (for some programs). *Entrance requirements:* For master's, GRE (Michigan Tech students with a GPA of 3.5 or above exempt), statement of purpose, personal statement, official transcripts, 2-3 letters of recommendation, resume/curriculum vitae. Additional exam requirements/recommendations for international students: Required—TOEFL (recommended minimum score 85 iBT) or IELTS (minimum score 6.5). *Application deadline:* Applications are processed on a rolling basis. Electronic applications accepted. *Expenses:* Tuition, state resident: full-time $17,100; part-time $950 per credit. Tuition, nonresident: full-time $17,100; part-time $950 per credit. *Required fees:* $248; $124 per term. Tuition and fees vary according to course load and program. *Financial support:* In 2017–18, 6 students received support, including fellowships (averaging $15,790 per year), 2 research assistantships (averaging $15,790 per year), teaching assistantships (averaging $15,790 per year); career-related internships or fieldwork, Federal Work-Study, health care benefits, and unspecified assistantships also available. Financial award applicants required to submit FAFSA. *Faculty research:* Electrophysiology and hypertension, neural control of circulation, molecular physiology and hypertension, human aeromechanics, musculoskeletal control of movement. *Total annual research expenditures:* $360,258. *Unit head:* Dr. Jason R. Carter, Chair, 906-487-2994, Fax: 906-487-0985, E-mail: jcarter@mtu.edu. *Application contact:* Carol T. Wingerson, Administrative Aide, 906-487-2328, Fax: 906-487-2284, E-mail: gradadms@mtu.edu.
Website: http://www.mtu.edu/kip/

Mississippi College, Graduate School, School of Education, Department of Kinesiology, Clinton, MS 39058. Offers athletic administration (MS). *Degree requirements:* For master's, comprehensive exam, thesis optional. *Entrance requirements:* For master's, GRE, GMAT, or PRAXIS, minimum GPA of 2.5. Additional exam requirements/recommendations for international students: Recommended—TOEFL, IELTS. Electronic applications accepted.

Mississippi State University, College of Education, Department of Kinesiology, Mississippi State, MS 39762. Offers disability studies (MS); exercise physiology (MS); exercise science (PhD); sport administration (MS); sport pedagogy (MS); sport studies (PhD). *Program availability:* Part-time, blended/hybrid learning. *Faculty:* 16 full-time (3 women). *Students:* 64 full-time (20 women), 8 part-time (3 women); includes 13 minority (2 Black or African American, non-Hispanic/Latino; 4 Asian, non-Hispanic/Latino; 4 Hispanic/Latino; 3 Two or more races, non-Hispanic/Latino), 10 international. Average age 26. 66 applicants, 59% accepted, 31 enrolled. In 2017, 23 master's awarded. *Degree requirements:* For master's, comprehensive exam, thesis optional; for doctorate, comprehensive exam. *Entrance requirements:* For master's, GRE General Test, minimum GPA of 2.75 on undergraduate work from four-year accredited institution, 3.0 graduate; for doctorate, GRE, minimum GPA of 3.4 on previous graduate degree(s) earned from accredited institutions. Additional exam requirements/recommendations for international students: Required—TOEFL (minimum score 550 paper-based; 79 iBT); Recommended—IELTS (minimum score 6.5). *Application deadline:* For fall admission, 7/1 for domestic students, 5/1 for international students; for spring admission, 11/1 for domestic students, 9/1 for international students. Applications are processed on a rolling basis. Application fee: $60 ($80 for international students). Electronic applications accepted. *Expenses:* Tuition, state resident: full-time $8318; part-time $462.12 per credit hour. Tuition, nonresident: full-time $22,358; part-time $1242.12 per credit hour. *Required fees:* $110; $12.24 per credit hour. $6.12 per semester. *Financial support:* In 2017–18, 13 teaching assistantships with partial tuition reimbursements (averaging $10,510 per year) were awarded; career-related internships or fieldwork, Federal Work-Study, institutionally sponsored loans, and unspecified assistantships also available. Financial award application deadline: 4/1; financial award applicants required to submit FAFSA. *Faculty research:* Static balance and stepping performance of older adults, organizational justice, public health, strength training and recovery drinks, high risk drinking perceptions and behaviors. *Unit head:* Dr. Stanley P. Brown, Professor and Head, 662-325-7229, Fax: 662-325-4525, E-mail: spb107@msstate.edu. *Application contact:* Marina Hung, Admissions and Enrollment Assistant, 662-325-5188, E-mail: lbonner@grad.msstate.edu.
Website: http://www.kinesiology.msstate.edu/

Missouri State University, Graduate College, College of Health and Human Services, Department of Kinesiology, Springfield, MO 65897. Offers health promotion and wellness management (MS); secondary education (MS Ed), including physical education. *Program availability:* Part-time. *Faculty:* 14 full-time (6 women). *Students:* 21 full-time (11 women), 11 part-time (4 women); includes 4 minority (1 Black or African American, non-Hispanic/Latino; 1 Asian, non-Hispanic/Latino; 1 Hispanic/Latino; 1 Two or more races, non-Hispanic/Latino), 2 international. Average age 24. 23 applicants, 48% accepted, 11 enrolled. In 2017, 8 master's awarded. *Degree requirements:* For master's, comprehensive exam, thesis or alternative. *Entrance requirements:* For master's, GRE (for MS), minimum GPA of 2.8 (MS); 9-12 teaching certification (MS Ed). Additional exam requirements/recommendations for international students: Required—TOEFL (minimum score 550 paper-based; 79 iBT), IELTS (minimum score 6). *Application deadline:* For fall admission, 7/20 priority date for domestic students, 5/1 for international students; for spring admission, 12/20 priority date for domestic students, 9/1 for international students. Applications are processed on a rolling basis. Application fee: $35 ($50 for international students). Electronic applications accepted. *Expenses:* Tuition, state resident: full-time $2915; part-time $2021 per credit hour. Tuition, nonresident: full-time $5354; part-time $3647 per credit hour. *International tuition:* $11,992 full-time. *Required fees:* $173; $173 per credit hour. Tuition and fees vary according to class time, course level, course load, degree level, campus/location and program. *Financial support:* In 2017–18, 7 teaching assistantships with partial tuition reimbursements (averaging $8,772 per year) were awarded; Federal Work-Study, institutionally sponsored loans, scholarships/grants, and unspecified assistantships also available. Financial award application deadline: 3/31; financial award applicants required to submit FAFSA. *Unit head:* Dr. Sarah McCallister, Head, 417-836-6582, Fax: 417-836-5371, E-mail: sarahmccallister@missouristate.edu. *Application contact:* Stephanie Praschan, Director, Graduate Enrollment Management, 417-836-5330, Fax: 417-836-6200, E-mail: stephaniepraschan@missouristate.edu.
Website: http://www.missouristate.edu/kinesiology/

New Mexico State University, College of Education, Department of Kinesiology and Dance, Las Cruces, NM 88003. Offers kinesiology (PhD). *Program availability:* Part-time. *Faculty:* 10 full-time (2 women). *Students:* 4 full-time (1 woman), 1 (woman) part-time; includes 2 minority (1 Hispanic/Latino; 1 Two or more races, non-Hispanic/Latino), 1 international. Average age 31. 10 applicants, 10% accepted, 1 enrolled. *Entrance requirements:* For doctorate, GRE General Test, bachelor's and master's degrees in related field; minimum cumulative GPA of 3.0; 3 letters of recommendation; curriculum vitae or resume. Additional exam requirements/recommendations for international students: Required—TOEFL (minimum score 550 paper-based; 79 iBT), IELTS (minimum score 6.5). *Application deadline:* For fall admission, 1/15 for domestic and international students. Application fee: $40 ($50 for international students). Electronic applications accepted. *Expenses:* Tuition, state resident: full-time $4390. Tuition, nonresident: full-time $15,309. *Required fees:* $853. *Financial support:* In 2017–18, 4 students received support, including 3 research assistantships (averaging $16,608 per year), 6 teaching assistantships (averaging $14,238 per year); career-related internships or fieldwork, Federal Work-Study, scholarships/grants, traineeships, health care benefits, and unspecified assistantships also available. Support available to part-time students. Financial award application deadline: 3/1. *Faculty research:* Biomechanics of muscle injury; fighting youth inactivity and obesity; aging and falls prevention. *Total annual research expenditures:* $93,294. *Unit head:* Dr. Michael Johnson, Interim Department Head, 575-646-1729, Fax: 575-646-4065, E-mail: johnson@nmsu.edu. *Application contact:* 575-646-4067, Fax: 575-646-4065.
Website: http://kind.nmsu.edu

New York University, Steinhardt School of Culture, Education, and Human Development, Department of Physical Therapy, New York, NY 10010-5615. Offers orthopedic physical therapy (Advanced Certificate); physical therapy (MA, DPT, PhD), including pathokinesiology (MA). *Accreditation:* APTA (one or more programs are accredited). *Program availability:* Part-time. *Students:* Average age 29. 49 applicants, 23% accepted, 51 enrolled. In 2017, 5 master's, 36 doctorates, 6 other advanced degrees awarded. *Entrance requirements:* For master's, physical therapy certificate; for doctorate, GRE General Test, interview, physical therapy certificate. Additional exam requirements/recommendations for international students: Required—TOEFL (minimum score 100 iBT). *Application deadline:* For fall admission, 12/1 priority date for domestic and international students; for spring admission, 10/1 for domestic and international students. Applications are processed on a rolling basis. Application fee: $75. Electronic applications accepted. *Expenses:* Tuition: full-time $41,352; part-time $19,968 per year. *Required fees:* $2496; $1628 per unit. $814 per term. Tuition and fees vary according to course load and program. *Financial support:* Fellowships with full and partial tuition reimbursements, research assistantships with full and partial tuition reimbursements, career-related internships or fieldwork, Federal Work-Study, scholarships/grants, tuition waivers (partial), and unspecified assistantships available. Support available to part-time students. Financial award application deadline: 2/1; financial award applicants required to submit FAFSA. *Faculty research:* Motor learning and control, neuromuscular disorders, biomechanics and ergonomics, movement analysis, pathomechanics. *Unit head:* Prof. Mitchell Batavia, Chairperson, 212-998-9400, Fax: 212-995-4190, E-mail: mitchell.batavia@nyu.edu. *Application contact:* 212-998-5030, Fax: 212-995-4328, E-mail: steinhardt.gradadmissions@nyu.edu.
Website: http://steinhardt.nyu.edu/pt

Northeastern State University, College of Education, Department of Health and Kinesiology, Tahlequah, OK 74464-2399. Offers MS. *Program availability:* Part-time, evening/weekend. *Faculty:* 3 full-time (1 woman). *Students:* 13 full-time (5 women), 25 part-time (16 women); includes 17 minority (2 Black or African American, non-Hispanic/Latino; 7 American Indian or Alaska Native, non-Hispanic/Latino; 2 Hispanic/Latino; 6 Two or more races, non-Hispanic/Latino), 3 international. Average age 26. In 2017, 10 master's awarded. *Entrance requirements:* For master's, MAT or GRE, minimum GPA of 2.5. Additional exam requirements/recommendations for international students: Required—TOEFL. *Application deadline:* For fall admission, 6/1 for domestic and international students; for winter admission, 11/1 for domestic and international students; for spring admission, 3/1 for domestic students, 2/1 for international students. Applications are processed on a rolling basis. Application fee: $25. Electronic applications accepted. *Expenses:* Tuition, state resident: part-time $222 per credit hour. Tuition, nonresident: part-time $501.75 per credit hour. *Required fees:* $37.40 per credit hour. Tuition and fees vary according to degree level. *Unit head:* Dee Gerlach, Department Chair, 918-444-3929, E-mail: gerlach@nsuok.edu. *Application contact:* Josh McCollum, Graduate Coordinator, 918-444-2093, E-mail: mccolluj@nsuok.edu.
Website: http://academics.nsuok.edu/education/DegreePrograms/GraduatePrograms/HealthandKinesiology.aspx

Northwestern University, Feinberg School of Medicine, Department of Physical Therapy and Human Movement Sciences, Chicago, IL 60611-2814. Offers neuroscience (PhD), including movement and rehabilitation science; physical therapy (DPT); DPT/MPH; DPT/PhD. *Accreditation:* APTA. *Degree requirements:* For doctorate, research project. *Entrance requirements:* For doctorate, GRE General Test (for DPT), baccalaureate degree with minimum GPA of 3.0 in required course work (DPT). Additional exam requirements/recommendations for international students: Required—TOEFL (minimum score 100 iBT). *Application deadline:* For fall admission, 10/1 for domestic and international students. Applications are processed on a rolling basis. Electronic applications accepted. *Expenses:* Contact institution. *Financial support:* Institutionally sponsored loans and scholarships/grants available. Financial award application deadline: 3/1; financial award applicants required to submit FAFSA. *Unit head:* Dr. Julius P. A. Dewald, Professor and Chair, 312-908-8160, Fax: 312-908-0741. *Application contact:* Dr. Jane Sullivan, Professor/Assistant Chair for Recruitment and Admissions, 312-908-8160, Fax: 312-908-0741, E-mail: dpt-admissions@northwestern.edu.
Website: http://www.feinberg.northwestern.edu/sites/pthms/

The Ohio State University, Graduate School, College of Education and Human Ecology, Department of Human Sciences, Columbus, OH 43210. Offers consumer sciences (MS, PhD); human development and family science (PhD); human nutrition (MS, PhD); kinesiology (MA, Ed D, PhD). *Program availability:* Part-time. *Faculty:* 55. *Students:* 127 full-time (71 women), 14 part-time (12 women). Average age 27. In 2017, 31 master's, 14 doctorates awarded. *Degree requirements:* For master's, thesis optional; for doctorate, thesis/dissertation. *Entrance requirements:* For master's and doctorate, GRE. Additional exam requirements/recommendations for international students: Required—TOEFL (minimum score 550 paper-based; 79 iBT), Michigan English Language Assessment Battery (minimum score 82); Recommended—IELTS (minimum score 7). *Application deadline:* For fall admission, 12/1 priority date for domestic and international students. Applications are processed on a rolling basis. Application fee: $60 ($70 for international students). Electronic applications accepted. *Financial support:* Fellowships with tuition reimbursements, research assistantships with tuition reimbursements, teaching assistantships with tuition reimbursements, Federal Work-Study, and institutionally sponsored loans available. Support available to

part-time students. *Unit head:* Dr. Brian Focht, Associate Chair and Professor, E-mail: focht.10@osu.edu. *Application contact:* Graduate and Professional Admissions, 614-292-9444, Fax: 614-292-3895, E-mail: gpadmissions@osu.edu.
Website: http://ehe.osu.edu/human-sciences/

Old Dominion University, College of Health Sciences, School of Physical Therapy and Athletic Training, Doctor of Kinesiology and Rehabilitation Program, Norfolk, VA 23529. Offers PhD. *Faculty:* 3 full-time (1 woman), 7 part-time/adjunct (3 women). *Students:* 9 full-time (6 women), 2 part-time (both women); includes 2 minority (1 Hispanic/Latino; 1 Two or more races, non-Hispanic/Latino). Average age 30. 11 applicants, 82% accepted, 9 enrolled. *Degree requirements:* For doctorate, comprehensive exam, thesis/dissertation. *Entrance requirements:* For doctorate, master's degree or higher in an associated area of basic science, such as kinesiology, exercise science, or biomechanics, or in a health profession such as athletic training, nursing, occupational therapy, physical therapy, or speech/language pathology. Additional exam requirements/recommendations for international students: Recommended—TOEFL (minimum score 550 paper-based; 79 iBT), IELTS (minimum score 6.5). *Application deadline:* For fall admission, 2/1 for domestic and international students. Application fee: $50. Electronic applications accepted. *Expenses:* $496 per credit. *Financial support:* In 2017–18, 5 students received support, including 5 research assistantships with full tuition reimbursements available (averaging $15,000 per year); unspecified assistantships also available. *Faculty research:* Balance and falls, gait, perceptual information in action and virtual reality, sensorimotor compromise following joint injury, evidence-based practice and patient-centered care. *Unit head:* Daniel Russell, Director, 757-683-6016, E-mail: dmrussel@odu.edu. *Application contact:* William Heffelfinger, Director of Graduate Admissions, 757-683-5554, Fax: 757-683-3255, E-mail: gradadmit@odu.edu.
Website: http://www.odu.edu/ptat/phd-kinesiology-rehabilitation

Old Dominion University, Darden College of Education, Program in Human Movement Science, Norfolk, VA 23529. Offers PhD. *Faculty:* 14 full-time (5 women). *Students:* 4 full-time (3 women), 4 part-time (1 woman); includes 2 minority (1 Black or African American, non-Hispanic/Latino; 1 Two or more races, non-Hispanic/Latino). Average age 37. 3 applicants, 67% accepted. In 2017, 1 doctorate awarded. *Degree requirements:* For doctorate, comprehensive exam, thesis/dissertation. *Entrance requirements:* For doctorate, GRE (minimum combined score for verbal and quantitative of 297, 4.5 for analytical writing), minimum GPA of 3.5. Additional exam requirements/recommendations for international students: Required—TOEFL (minimum score 550 paper-based; 79 iBT). *Application deadline:* For fall admission, 1/15 for domestic students. Application fee: $50. Electronic applications accepted. *Expenses:* Tuition, state resident: full-time $8928; part-time $496 per credit. Tuition, nonresident: full-time $22,482; part-time $1249 per credit. *Required fees:* $66 per semester. *Financial support:* In 2017–18, 4 students received support, including 4 teaching assistantships with full tuition reimbursements available (averaging $15,000 per year); unspecified assistantships also available. Financial award application deadline: 5/1. *Faculty research:* Exercise science, sport management, recreation management, health and physical education. *Total annual research expenditures:* $104,000. *Unit head:* Dr. Lynn Ridinger, Chair, 757-683-4353, Fax: 757-683-4270, E-mail: lridinge@odu.edu. *Application contact:* William Heffelfinger, Director of Graduate Admissions, 757-683-5554, Fax: 757-683-3255, E-mail: gradadmit@odu.edu.
Website: http://www.odu.edu/hms/academics/hms

Old Dominion University, Darden College of Education, Program in Physical Education, Curriculum and Instruction Emphasis, Norfolk, VA 23529. Offers human movement sciences (PhD), including health and sport pedagogy; physical education (MS Ed), including adapted physical education, coaching education, curriculum and instruction. *Program availability:* Part-time, evening/weekend. *Faculty:* 3 full-time (1 woman). *Students:* 2 full-time (1 woman), 5 part-time (1 woman); includes 2 minority (1 Black or African American, non-Hispanic/Latino; 1 Two or more races, non-Hispanic/Latino). Average age 29. 2 applicants, 50% accepted. In 2017, 2 master's awarded. *Degree requirements:* For master's, comprehensive exam (for some programs), thesis or alternative, internship, research project. *Entrance requirements:* For master's, GRE, PRAXIS tests (for licensure only), minimum GPA of 2.8 overall, 3.0 in major. Additional exam requirements/recommendations for international students: Required—TOEFL (minimum score 500 paper-based; 97 iBT). *Application deadline:* For fall admission, 3/1 priority date for domestic students; for spring admission, 11/1 for domestic students. Applications are processed on a rolling basis. Application fee: $50. Electronic applications accepted. *Expenses:* Tuition, state resident: full-time $8928; part-time $496 per credit. Tuition, nonresident: full-time $22,482; part-time $1249 per credit. *Required fees:* $66 per semester. *Financial support:* Unspecified assistantships available. Financial award application deadline: 4/15. *Faculty research:* Motor development, physical activity and fitness, motivation and learning in physical education, curriculum and instruction, adapted physical education. *Total annual research expenditures:* $104,000. *Unit head:* Dr. Lynn Ridinger, Chair, 757-683-4995, E-mail: lridinge@odu.edu. *Application contact:* William Heffelfinger, Director of Graduate Admissions, 757-683-5554, Fax: 757-683-3255, E-mail: gradadmit@odu.edu.
Website: https://www.odu.edu/hms/academics/hpe/graduate

Oregon State University, College of Public Health and Human Sciences, Program in Kinesiology, Corvallis, OR 97331. Offers biophysical kinesiology (MS, PhD); psychosocial kinesiology (MS, PhD). *Program availability:* Part-time. Terminal master's awarded for partial completion of doctoral program. *Entrance requirements:* For master's and doctorate, GRE, minimum GPA of 3.0 in last 90 hours. Additional exam requirements/recommendations for international students: Required—TOEFL (minimum score 80 iBT), IELTS (minimum score 6.5). *Application deadline:* For fall admission, 12/1 for domestic and international students. Electronic applications accepted. *Financial support:* Application deadline: 12/1. *Faculty research:* Motor control, sports medicine, exercise physiology, sport psychology, biomechanics. *Unit head:* Debi Rothermund, Advisor, 541-737-3324, E-mail: debi.rothermund@oregonstate.edu. *Application contact:* Debi Rothermund, Administrative Program Specialist, 541-737-3324, E-mail: debi.rothermund@oregonstate.edu.
Website: http://health.oregonstate.edu/degrees/graduate/kinesiology

Penn State University Park, Graduate School, College of Health and Human Development, Department of Kinesiology, University Park, PA 16802. Offers MS, PhD, Certificate. *Unit head:* Dr. Ann C. Crouter, Dean, 814-865-1420, Fax: 814-865-3282. *Application contact:* Lori Hawn, Director, Graduate Student Services, 814-865-1795, Fax: 814-863-4627, E-mail: l-gswww@lists.psu.edu.
Website: http://hhd.psu.edu/kines

Point Loma Nazarene University, Department of Kinesiology, San Diego, CA 92106-2899. Offers exercise science (MS); sport performance (MS), including exercise science, sport management, sport performance. *Program availability:* Part-time, online learning. *Faculty:* 5 full-time (2 women), 8 part-time/adjunct (2 women). *Students:* 55 full-time (26 women), 3 part-time (2 women); includes 20 minority (2 Black or African American, non-Hispanic/Latino; 3 Asian, non-Hispanic/Latino; 12 Hispanic/Latino; 1 Native Hawaiian or other Pacific Islander, non-Hispanic/Latino; 2 Two or more races, non-Hispanic/Latino), 3 international. Average age 29. 92 applicants, 92% accepted, 55 enrolled. In 2017, 30 master's awarded. *Entrance requirements:* For master's,

baccalaureate degree, minimum undergraduate cumulative GPA of 3.0. Application fee: $50. *Expenses:* Contact institution. *Financial support:* Teaching assistantships, scholarships/grants, and unspecified assistantships available. *Unit head:* Jeff Sullivan, Chair, 619-849-2629, E-mail: jeffsullivan@pointloma.edu. *Application contact:* Joanie Joy, Senior Director of Enrollment Management, 619-329-6785, E-mail: gradinfo@pointloma.edu.
Website: https://www.pointloma.edu/graduate-studies/programs/kinesiology-ms

Prairie View A&M University, College of Education, Department of Health and Kinesiology, Prairie View, TX 77446. Offers M Ed, MS. *Accreditation:* NCATE. *Program availability:* Part-time, evening/weekend. *Faculty:* 4 full-time (all women). *Students:* 26 full-time (18 women), 4 part-time (1 woman); all minorities (27 Black or African American, non-Hispanic/Latino; 1 Hispanic/Latino; 1 Native Hawaiian or other Pacific Islander, non-Hispanic/Latino; 1 Two or more races, non-Hispanic/Latino). Average age 26. 18 applicants, 100% accepted, 14 enrolled. In 2017, 13 master's awarded. *Degree requirements:* For master's, thesis. *Entrance requirements:* For master's, GRE General Test. Additional exam requirements/recommendations for international students: Required—TOEFL (minimum score 550 paper-based; 79 iBT). *Application deadline:* For fall admission, 5/1 priority date for domestic and international students; for spring admission, 10/1 priority date for domestic students, 9/1 priority date for international students; for summer admission, 3/1 priority date for domestic students, 2/1 priority date for international students. Applications are processed on a rolling basis. Application fee: $50. Electronic applications accepted. *Expenses:* Tuition, state resident: part-time $242 per credit. Tuition, nonresident: part-time $695 per credit. *Required fees:* $149 per credit. *Financial support:* Career-related internships or fieldwork available. Support available to part-time students. Financial award application deadline: 4/1; financial award applicants required to submit FAFSA. *Unit head:* Dr. Angela Branch-Vital, Department Head, 936-261-3900, Fax: 936-261-3905, E-mail: abranch-vital@pvamu.edu. *Application contact:* Pauline Walker, Administrative Assistant II, Research and Graduate Studies, 936-261-3521, Fax: 936-261-3529, E-mail: gradadmissions@pvamu.edu.

Purdue University, Graduate School, College of Health and Human Sciences, Department of Health and Kinesiology, West Lafayette, IN 47907. Offers athletic training education administration (MS, PhD); biomechanics (MS, PhD); exercise physiology (MS, PhD); health education (MS, PhD); history/philosophy of sport (MS, PhD); motor control and development (MS, PhD); physical education pedagogy (PhD); physical education teacher education (MS); recreation and sport management (MS, PhD); sport and exercise psychology (MS, PhD). *Program availability:* Part-time. *Faculty:* 19 full-time (7 women). *Students:* 30 full-time (13 women), 10 part-time (5 women); includes 2 minority (1 Asian, non-Hispanic/Latino; 1 Two or more races, non-Hispanic/Latino), 6 international. Average age 26. 77 applicants, 29% accepted, 18 enrolled. In 2017, 18 master's, 9 doctorates awarded. *Degree requirements:* For master's, thesis optional; for doctorate, comprehensive exam, thesis/dissertation, qualifying examination, preliminary examination. *Entrance requirements:* For master's, GRE General Test (minimum score 1000 combined verbal and quantitative), minimum undergraduate GPA of 3.0 or equivalent; for doctorate, GRE General Test (minimum score 1100 combined verbal and quantitative), minimum undergraduate GPA of 3.0 or equivalent; master's degree with minimum GPA of 3.25 (recommended). Additional exam requirements/recommendations for international students: Required—TOEFL (minimum score 77 iBT); Recommended—TWE. *Application deadline:* For fall admission, 4/30 for domestic and international students; for spring admission, 10/15 for domestic and international students. Applications are processed on a rolling basis. Application fee: $60 ($75 for international students). Electronic applications accepted. *Financial support:* Fellowships with partial tuition reimbursements, research assistantships with partial tuition reimbursements, teaching assistantships with partial tuition reimbursements, and Federal Work-Study available. Support available to part-time students. Financial award applicants required to submit FAFSA. *Faculty research:* Wellness, motivation, teaching effectiveness, learning and development. *Unit head:* Dr. Timothy P. Gavin, Head of the Graduate Program, 765-494-3178, Fax: 765-494-1239, E-mail: gavin1@purdue.edu. *Application contact:* David B. Klenosky, Graduate Contact, 765-494-0865, E-mail: klenosky@purdue.edu.
Website: http://www.purdue.edu/hhs/hk/

Saint Mary's College of California, School of Liberal Arts, Department of Kinesiology, Moraga, CA 94575. Offers fitness management (MA); sport management (MA); sport studies (MA). *Program availability:* Part-time. *Degree requirements:* For master's, thesis or special project. *Entrance requirements:* For master's, minimum GPA of 2.75, BA in physical education or related field, or professional experience. Electronic applications accepted. *Expenses:* Contact institution. *Faculty research:* Moral development in sport, applied motor learning, achievement motivation, sport history.

Sam Houston State University, College of Health Sciences, Department of Kinesiology, Huntsville, TX 77341. Offers sport and human performance (MA); sport management (MA). *Program availability:* Part-time. *Degree requirements:* For master's, comprehensive exam, thesis optional. *Entrance requirements:* For master's, GRE, letters of recommendation, statement of interest/intent. Additional exam requirements/recommendations for international students: Required—TOEFL (minimum score 550 paper-based; 79 iBT), IELTS (minimum score 6.5). Electronic applications accepted.

San Diego State University, Graduate and Research Affairs, College of Health and Human Services, School of Exercise and Nutritional Sciences, Program in Kinesiology, San Diego, CA 92182. Offers MA. *Degree requirements:* For master's, thesis. *Entrance requirements:* For master's, GRE General Test, 2 letters of reference. Additional exam requirements/recommendations for international students: Required—TOEFL. Electronic applications accepted.

San Francisco State University, Division of Graduate Studies, College of Health and Social Sciences, Department of Kinesiology, San Francisco, CA 94132-1722. Offers MS. *Application deadline:* Applications are processed on a rolling basis. *Unit head:* Dr. Marialice Kern, Chair, 415-338-2244, Fax: 415-338-7566, E-mail: mkern@sfsu.edu. *Application contact:* Prof. Kate Hamel, Graduate Coordinator, 415-338-2186, Fax: 415-338-7566, E-mail: hamelk@sfsu.edu.
Website: http://kin.sfsu.edu/

San Jose State University, Graduate Studies and Research, College of Health and Human Sciences, San Jose, CA 95192-0049. Offers criminology (MS), including global criminology, law and justice; justice studies (MS); kinesiology (MA), including athletic training, exercise physiology, interdisciplinary, sport studies, sports management; library and information science (MLIS); mass communications (MS); nursing (MS), including family nurse practitioner; nutritional science (MS); occupational therapy (MS); public health (MPH); social work (MSW); MD/M Div. *Program availability:* Part-time, 100% online, blended/hybrid learning. *Faculty:* 15 full-time (7 women), 6 part-time/adjunct (3 women). *Students:* 517 full-time (407 women), 405 part-time (302 women); includes 523 minority (39 Black or African American, non-Hispanic/Latino; 2 American Indian or Alaska Native, non-Hispanic/Latino; 141 Asian, non-Hispanic/Latino; 226 Hispanic/Latino; 2 Native Hawaiian or other Pacific Islander, non-Hispanic/Latino; 113 Two or more races, non-Hispanic/Latino), 14 international. Average age 32. 1,250 applicants, 45% accepted, 375 enrolled. In 2017, 808 master's awarded. *Degree requirements:* For master's, thesis (for some programs), graduate writing assessment. *Entrance*

Kinesiology and Movement Studies

requirements: Additional exam requirements/recommendations for international students: Required—TOEFL (minimum score 550 paper-based; 80 iBT), IELTS (minimum score 6.5), PTE (minimum score 53). *Application deadline:* For fall admission, 2/1 for domestic and international students. Applications are processed on a rolling basis. Application fee: $55. Electronic applications accepted. *Expenses:* Tuition, state resident: full-time $7176. Tuition, nonresident: full-time $16,680. Tuition and fees vary according to course load and program. *Financial support:* Fellowships, research assistantships, teaching assistantships, career-related internships or fieldwork, Federal Work-Study, scholarships/grants, and tuition waivers (full and partial) available. Support available to part-time students. Financial award application deadline: 4/24; financial award applicants required to submit FAFSA. *Unit head:* Dr. Mary Schutten, Dean, College of Health and Human Sciences, 408-924-2900, Fax: 408-924-2901, E-mail: mary.schutten@sjsu.edu.
Website: http://www.sjsu.edu/casa/

Sarah Lawrence College, Graduate Studies, Program in Dance/Movement Therapy, Bronxville, NY 10708-5999. Offers MS. *Degree requirements:* For master's, thesis, practicum.

Simon Fraser University, Office of Graduate Studies and Postdoctoral Fellows, Faculty of Science, Department of Biomedical Physiology and Kinesiology, Burnaby, BC V5A 1S6, Canada. Offers M Sc, PhD. *Degree requirements:* For master's, thesis, thesis proposal; for doctorate, comprehensive exam, thesis/dissertation, dissertation proposal, seminar presentations. *Entrance requirements:* For master's, minimum GPA of 3.0 (on scale of 4.33) or 3.33 based on last 60 credits of undergraduate courses; for doctorate, minimum GPA of 3.5 (on scale of 4.33). Additional exam requirements/recommendations for international students: Recommended—TOEFL (minimum score 580 paper-based; 93 iBT), IELTS (minimum score 7), TWE (minimum score 5). Electronic applications accepted. *Faculty research:* Cardiovascular physiology, chronic disease, environmental physiology, neuromechanics, neuroscience.

Sonoma State University, School of Science and Technology, Department of Kinesiology, Rohnert Park, CA 94928. Offers exercise science/pre-physical therapy (MA); interdisciplinary (MA); interdisciplinary pre-occupational therapy (MA); lifetime physical activity (MA), including coach education, fitness and wellness. *Program availability:* Part-time. *Degree requirements:* For master's, thesis, oral exam. *Entrance requirements:* For master's, minimum GPA of 2.8. Additional exam requirements/recommendations for international students: Required—TOEFL (minimum score 500 paper-based). *Application deadline:* For fall admission, 11/30 for domestic students; for spring admission, 9/1 for domestic students. Applications are processed on a rolling basis. Application fee: $55. *Financial support:* Career-related internships or fieldwork available. Financial award application deadline: 3/2; financial award applicants required to submit FAFSA. *Unit head:* Dr. Steven Winter, Chair, 707-664-2188, E-mail: steven.winter@sonoma.edu. *Application contact:* Dr. Bulent Sokmen, Graduate Coordinator, 707-664-2789, E-mail: sokmen@sonoma.edu.
Website: http://www.sonoma.edu/kinesiology/

Southeastern Louisiana University, College of Nursing and Health Sciences, Department of Kinesiology and Health Studies, Hammond, LA 70402. Offers MS. *Accreditation:* NCATE. *Program availability:* Part-time. *Faculty:* 6 full-time (2 women), 1 part-time/adjunct (0 women). *Students:* 26 full-time (14 women), 16 part-time (7 women); includes 19 minority (10 Black or African American, non-Hispanic/Latino; 4 Hispanic/Latino; 1 Native Hawaiian or other Pacific Islander, non-Hispanic/Latino; 4 Two or more races, non-Hispanic/Latino), 1 international. Average age 26. 28 applicants, 57% accepted, 11 enrolled. In 2017, 11 master's awarded. *Degree requirements:* For master's, comprehensive exam (for some programs), thesis (for some programs). *Entrance requirements:* For master's, GRE (minimum combined Verbal and Quantitative score of 286), undergraduate human anatomy and physiology course. Additional exam requirements/recommendations for international students: Required—TOEFL (minimum score 500 paper-based; 61 iBT). *Application deadline:* For fall admission, 7/15 priority date for domestic students, 6/1 priority date for international students; for spring admission, 12/1 priority date for domestic students, 10/1 priority date for international students. Applications are processed on a rolling basis. Application fee: $20 ($30 for international students). Electronic applications accepted. *Expenses:* Tuition, state resident: full-time $6684. Tuition, nonresident: full-time $19,162. *Required fees:* $2088. *Financial support:* In 2017–18, 16 students received support, including 7 research assistantships (averaging $9,275 per year), 4 teaching assistantships (averaging $9,550 per year); career-related internships or fieldwork, Federal Work-Study, institutionally sponsored loans, scholarships/grants, and unspecified assistantships also available. Support available to part-time students. Financial award application deadline: 5/1; financial award applicants required to submit FAFSA. *Faculty research:* Exercise physiology, motor learning, sport and exercise psychology, school health, health and aging. *Unit head:* Dr. Eddie Hebert, Department Head, 985-549-2129, Fax: 985-549-5119, E-mail: ehebert@southeastern.edu. *Application contact:* Amanda Harper, Graduate Admissions Analyst, 985-549-5620, Fax: 985-549-5632, E-mail: admissions@southeastern.edu.
Website: http://www.southeastern.edu/acad_research/depts/kin_hs/index.html

Southeastern University, College of Education, Lakeland, FL 33801-6099. Offers curriculum and instruction (Ed D); educational leadership (M Ed); elementary education (M Ed); exceptional student education (M Ed); exceptional student education/educational therapy (M Ed); kinesiology (M Ed); organizational leadership (Ed D); reading education (M Ed); teaching English to speakers of other languages (M Ed). *Faculty:* 8 full-time (5 women), 12 part-time/adjunct (7 women). *Students:* 139 full-time (109 women), 225 part-time (172 women); includes 107 minority (57 Black or African American, non-Hispanic/Latino; 2 Asian, non-Hispanic/Latino; 48 Hispanic/Latino), 4 international. Average age 40. Application fee: $50. Electronic applications accepted. *Unit head:* James A. Anderson, Dean, 863-667-5366, E-mail: jaanderson2@seu.edu.
Website: http://www.seu.edu/education/

Southern Arkansas University–Magnolia, School of Graduate Studies, Magnolia, AR 71753. Offers agriculture (MS); business administration (MBA), including agribusiness, social entrepreneurship, supply chain management; clinical and mental health counseling (MS); computer and information sciences (MS), including cyber security and privacy, data science, information technology; gifted and talented (M Ed), including curriculum and instruction, educational administration and supervision, gifted and talented P-8/7-12, instructional specialist P-4; higher, adult and lifelong education (M Ed); kinesiology (M Ed), including coaching; library media and information specialist (M Ed); public administration (MPA); school counseling K-12 (M Ed); student affairs and college counseling (M Ed); teaching (MAT). *Accreditation:* NCATE. *Program availability:* Part-time, 100% online, blended/hybrid learning. *Faculty:* 36 full-time (20 women), 31 part-time/adjunct (12 women). *Students:* 242 full-time (89 women), 889 part-time (459 women); includes 167 minority (143 Black or African American, non-Hispanic/Latino; 7 American Indian or Alaska Native, non-Hispanic/Latino; 7 Asian, non-Hispanic/Latino; 3 Hispanic/Latino; 7 Two or more races, non-Hispanic/Latino), 562 international. Average age 28. 400 applicants, 100% accepted, 239 enrolled. In 2017, 875 master's awarded. *Degree requirements:* For master's, comprehensive exam (for some programs), thesis optional. *Entrance requirements:* For master's, GRE, MAT or GMAT, minimum GPA of 2.5. Additional exam requirements/recommendations for international students:

Required—TOEFL (minimum score 550 paper-based), IELTS (minimum score 6). *Application deadline:* For fall admission, 7/20 for domestic students, 7/10 for international students; for spring admission, 12/1 for domestic students, 11/15 for international students; for summer admission, 4/1 for domestic students, 5/1 for international students. Applications are processed on a rolling basis. Application fee: $25 ($50 for international students). Electronic applications accepted. *Expenses:* Tuition, state resident: full-time $6038. Tuition, nonresident: full-time $8558. *Required fees:* $804. One-time fee: $110 full-time. Tuition and fees vary according to course load. *Financial support:* Career-related internships or fieldwork, Federal Work-Study, scholarships/grants, tuition waivers (full), and unspecified assistantships available. Financial award applicants required to submit FAFSA. *Faculty research:* Alternative certification for teachers, supervision of instruction, instructional leadership, counseling. *Unit head:* Dr. Kim Bloss, Dean, School of Graduate Studies, 870-235-4150, Fax: 870-235-5227, E-mail: kkbloss@saumag.edu. *Application contact:* Shrijana Malakar, Admissions Specialist, 870-235-4150, Fax: 870-235-5227, E-mail: smalakar@saumag.edu.
Website: http://www.saumag.edu/graduate

Southern Illinois University Carbondale, Graduate School, College of Education and Human Services, Department of Kinesiology, Carbondale, IL 62901-4701. Offers MS Ed. *Program availability:* Part-time. *Degree requirements:* For master's, thesis. *Entrance requirements:* For master's, GRE, minimum GPA of 2.7. Additional exam requirements/recommendations for international students: Required—TOEFL. *Faculty research:* Caffeine and exercise effects, ground reaction forces in walking and running, social psychology of sports.

Southern Illinois University Edwardsville, Graduate School, School of Education, Health, and Human Behavior, Department of Kinesiology and Health Education, Program in Physical Education and Coaching Pedagogy, Edwardsville, IL 62026. Offers MS Ed. *Program availability:* Part-time, evening/weekend. *Degree requirements:* For master's, comprehensive exam (for some programs), thesis (for some programs). *Entrance requirements:* Additional exam requirements/recommendations for international students: Required—TOEFL (minimum score 550 paper-based, 79 iBT), IELTS (minimum score 6.5), Michigan Test of English Language Proficiency or PTE. Electronic applications accepted.

Southwestern Oklahoma State University, College of Professional and Graduate Studies, School of Behavioral Sciences and Education, Specialization in Kinesiology, Weatherford, OK 73096-3098. Offers M Ed. *Program availability:* Part-time. *Degree requirements:* For master's, exam. *Entrance requirements:* For master's, GRE General Test or minimum undergraduate GPA of 3.0. Additional exam requirements/recommendations for international students: Required—TOEFL.

Stephen F. Austin State University, Graduate School, College of Education, Department of Kinesiology and Health Science, Nacogdoches, TX 75962. Offers athletic training (MS); kinesiology (M Ed). *Degree requirements:* For master's, comprehensive exam. *Entrance requirements:* For master's, GRE General Test. Additional exam requirements/recommendations for international students: Required—TOEFL.

Syracuse University, David B. Falk College of Sport and Human Dynamics, Syracuse, NY 13244. Offers MA, MS, MSW, PhD, CAS, MSW/MA. *Accreditation:* AAMFT/COAMFTE (one or more programs are accredited). *Program availability:* Part-time, evening/weekend. *Faculty:* 70 full-time (40 women), 28 part-time/adjunct (21 women). *Students:* 222 full-time (187 women), 93 part-time (75 women); includes 77 minority (39 Black or African American, non-Hispanic/Latino; 3 American Indian or Alaska Native, non-Hispanic/Latino; 7 Asian, non-Hispanic/Latino; 18 Hispanic/Latino; 10 Two or more races, non-Hispanic/Latino), 30 international. Average age 29. 452 applicants, 72% accepted, 165 enrolled. In 2017, 145 master's, 6 doctorates, 38 other advanced degrees awarded. *Degree requirements:* For master's, comprehensive exam (for some programs), thesis (for some programs); for doctorate, comprehensive exam, thesis/dissertation. *Entrance requirements:* For master's, GRE (for most programs), resume, official transcripts, personal statement, three letters of recommendation; for doctorate, GRE, resume, official transcripts, personal statement, three letters of recommendation. Additional exam requirements/recommendations for international students: Required—TOEFL. *Application deadline:* For fall admission, 2/15 priority date for domestic and international students; for spring admission, 11/15 priority date for domestic students, 11/15 for international students; for summer admission, 3/15 priority date for domestic students, 3/15 for international students. Applications are processed on a rolling basis. Application fee: $75. Electronic applications accepted. *Financial support:* Fellowships with full tuition reimbursements, research assistantships with tuition reimbursements, teaching assistantships with tuition reimbursements, and tuition waivers available. Financial award application deadline: 1/1; financial award applicants required to submit FAFSA. *Faculty research:* Child and family studies, marriage and family therapy, public health, food studies and nutrition, social work, sport management. *Unit head:* Dr. Diane Lyden Murphy, Dean, 315-443-5582, Fax: 315-443-2562. *Application contact:* Felicia Otero, Director of College Admissions, 315-443-5555, Fax: 315-443-2562, E-mail: falk@syr.edu.
Website: http://falk.syr.edu/

Tarleton State University, College of Graduate Studies, College of Education, Department of Kinesiology, Stephenville, TX 76402. Offers athletic training (MS); kinesiology (MS). *Program availability:* Part-time, evening/weekend. *Faculty:* 10 full-time (4 women), 1 (woman) part-time/adjunct. *Students:* 45 full-time (25 women), 36 part-time (15 women); includes 25 minority (13 Black or African American, non-Hispanic/Latino; 1 Asian, non-Hispanic/Latino; 9 Hispanic/Latino; 2 Two or more races, non-Hispanic/Latino), 2 international. Average age 25. 21 applicants, 81% accepted, 17 enrolled. In 2017, 48 master's awarded. *Degree requirements:* For master's, comprehensive exam, thesis optional. *Entrance requirements:* For master's, GRE General Test, minimum GPA of 3.0. Additional exam requirements/recommendations for international students: Required—TOEFL (minimum score 550 paper-based; 80 iBT), IELTS (minimum score 6). *Application deadline:* For fall admission, 8/15 priority date for domestic students; for spring admission, 1/7 for domestic students. Applications are processed on a rolling basis. Application fee: $45 ($145 for international students). Electronic applications accepted. *Expenses:* Contact institution. *Financial support:* Research assistantships, teaching assistantships with partial tuition reimbursements, career-related internships or fieldwork, Federal Work-Study, and institutionally sponsored loans available. Support available to part-time students. Financial award application deadline: 5/1; financial award applicants required to submit FAFSA. *Unit head:* Dr. Kayla Peak, Department Head, 254-968-9824, E-mail: peak@tarleton.edu. *Application contact:* Information Contact, 254-968-9104, Fax: 254-968-9670, E-mail: gradoffice@tarleton.edu.
Website: http://www.tarleton.edu/kinesiology/

Teachers College, Columbia University, Department of Biobehavioral Sciences, New York, NY 10027-6696. Offers applied exercise physiology (Ed M, MA, Ed D); communication sciences and disorders (MS, Ed D, PhD); kinesiology (PhD); motor learning and control (Ed M, MA); motor learning/movement science (Ed D); neuroscience and education (MS); physical education (MA, Ed D). *Accreditation:* ASHA. *Program availability:* Part-time, evening/weekend. *Students:* 180 full-time (160 women), 176 part-time (141 women); includes 149 minority (17 Black or African American, non-Hispanic/Latino; 40 Asian, non-Hispanic/Latino; 83 Hispanic/Latino; 9 Two or more

races, non-Hispanic/Latino), 30 international. Average age 29. 738 applicants, 41% accepted, 164 enrolled. *Financial support:* Fellowships, teaching assistantships, career-related internships or fieldwork, Federal Work-Study, institutionally sponsored loans, traineeships, and tuition waivers (full and partial) available. Support available to part-time students. *Unit head:* Prof. Carol Garber, Chair, 212-678-3891, E-mail: garber@tc.columbia.edu. *Application contact:* David Estrella, Director of Admissions, 212-678-3305, E-mail: estrella@tc.columbia.edu.
Website: http://www.tc.columbia.edu/biobehavioral-sciences/

Temple University, College of Public Health, Department of Kinesiology, Philadelphia, PA 19122. Offers athletic training (MSAT, DAT); kinesiology (MS, PhD); neuromotor science (MS, PhD). *Program availability:* Part-time. *Faculty:* 17 full-time (8 women), 6 part-time/adjunct (3 women). *Students:* 52 full-time (21 women), 39 part-time (22 women); includes 25 minority (11 Black or African American, non-Hispanic/Latino; 1 Asian, non-Hispanic/Latino; 8 Hispanic/Latino; 5 Two or more races, non-Hispanic/Latino), 5 international. 78 applicants, 72% accepted, 37 enrolled. In 2017, 15 master's, 3 doctorates awarded. Terminal master's awarded for partial completion of doctoral program. *Degree requirements:* For master's, thesis, final project; for doctorate, comprehensive exam, thesis/dissertation. *Entrance requirements:* For master's, GRE General Test or MAT, minimum undergraduate GPA of 3.0, 3 letters of reference, statement of goals, interview, resume; for doctorate, GRE General Test, minimum undergraduate GPA of 3.0, 3 letters of reference, statement of goals, interview, resume. Additional exam requirements/recommendations for international students: Required—TOEFL (minimum score 550 paper-based; 79 iBT). *Application deadline:* For fall admission, 1/15 for domestic students, 12/15 for international students; for spring admission, 10/1 for domestic students, 8/1 for international students. Applications are processed on a rolling basis. Application fee: $60. Electronic applications accepted. *Expenses:* Contact institution. *Financial support:* Fellowships, research assistantships with tuition reimbursements, teaching assistantships with tuition reimbursements, career-related internships or fieldwork, Federal Work-Study, scholarships/grants, tuition waivers, and unspecified assistantships available. Financial award application deadline: 1/15. *Faculty research:* Exercise physiology, athletic training, motor neuroscience, exercise and sports psychology. *Unit head:* John Jeka, Chair, 214-204-4405, Fax: 215-204-4414, E-mail: jjeka@temple.edu. *Application contact:* Rosalind Robinson, Department Coordinator, 215-204-8707, E-mail: rosalind.robinson@temple.edu.
Website: http://cph.temple.edu/kinesiology/home

Tennessee Technological University, College of Graduate Studies, College of Education, Department of Exercise Science, Physical Education and Wellness, Cookeville, TN 38505. Offers adapted physical education (MA); elementary/middle school physical education (MA); lifetime wellness (MA); sport management (MA). *Accreditation:* NCATE. *Program availability:* Part-time, online learning. *Faculty:* 7 full-time (0 women). *Students:* 17 full-time (8 women), 34 part-time (14 women); includes 10 minority (5 Black or African American, non-Hispanic/Latino; 1 Asian, non-Hispanic/Latino; 2 Hispanic/Latino; 2 Two or more races, non-Hispanic/Latino). 35 applicants, 71% accepted, 23 enrolled. In 2017, 28 master's awarded. *Degree requirements:* For master's, comprehensive exam, thesis or alternative. *Entrance requirements:* For master's, MAT or GRE. Additional exam requirements/recommendations for international students: Required—TOEFL (minimum score 527 paper-based; 71 iBT), IELTS (minimum score 5.5), PTE (minimum score 48), or TOEIC (Test of English as an International Communication). *Application deadline:* For fall admission, 8/1 for domestic students, 5/1 for international students; for spring admission, 12/1 for domestic students, 10/1 for international students; for summer admission, 5/1 for domestic students, 2/1 for international students. Applications are processed on a rolling basis. Application fee: $35 ($40 for international students). Electronic applications accepted. *Expenses:* Tuition, state resident: full-time $9925; part-time $565 per credit hour. Tuition, nonresident: full-time $22,993; part-time $1291 per credit hour. *Financial support:* Fellowships, research assistantships, teaching assistantships, and career-related internships or fieldwork available. Financial award application deadline: 4/1. *Unit head:* Dr. Christy Killman, Chairperson, 931-372-3467, Fax: 931-372-6319, E-mail: ckillman@tntech.edu. *Application contact:* Shelia K. Kendrick, Coordinator of Graduate Studies, 931-372-3808, Fax: 931-372-3497, E-mail: skendrick@tntech.edu.

Texas A&M University, College of Education and Human Development, Department of Health and Kinesiology, College Station, TX 77843. Offers athletic training (MS); health education (MS, PhD); kinesiology (MS, PhD); sports management (MS). *Program availability:* Part-time. *Faculty:* 53. *Students:* 223 full-time (120 women), 94 part-time (53 women); includes 106 minority (42 Black or African American, non-Hispanic/Latino; 2 American Indian or Alaska Native, non-Hispanic/Latino; 5 Asian, non-Hispanic/Latino; 50 Hispanic/Latino; 7 Two or more races, non-Hispanic/Latino), 27 international. Average age 29. 161 applicants, 79% accepted, 81 enrolled. In 2017, 126 master's, 13 doctorates awarded. *Degree requirements:* For master's, thesis (for some programs); for doctorate, comprehensive exam, thesis/dissertation. *Entrance requirements:* For master's and doctorate, GRE General Test. Additional exam requirements/recommendations for international students: Required—TOEFL (minimum score 550 paper-based; 80 iBT), IELTS (minimum score 6), PTE (minimum score 53). *Application deadline:* For fall admission, 1/15 for domestic students; for spring admission, 10/1 for domestic students. Applications are processed on a rolling basis. Application fee: $50 ($90 for international students). Electronic applications accepted. *Expenses:* Contact institution. *Financial support:* In 2017–18, 204 students received support, including 2 fellowships with tuition reimbursements available (averaging $43,805 per year), 33 research assistantships with tuition reimbursements available (averaging $10,102 per year), 59 teaching assistantships with tuition reimbursements available (averaging $9,712 per year); career-related internships or fieldwork, institutionally sponsored loans, scholarships/grants, traineeships, health care benefits, tuition waivers (full and partial), and unspecified assistantships also available. Support available to part-time students. Financial award application deadline: 3/15; financial award applicants required to submit FAFSA. *Unit head:* Dr. Richard Kreider, Head, 979-845-1333, Fax: 979-847-8987, E-mail: rkreider@hlkn.tamu.edu. *Application contact:* Jenny Bilski, Academic Advisor, 979-862-4052, E-mail: jenny.bilski@tamu.edu.
Website: http://hlknweb.tamu.edu/

Texas A&M University–Commerce, College of Education and Human Services, Commerce, TX 75429. Offers counseling (M Ed, MS, PhD); early childhood education (M Ed, MS); educational administration (M Ed, MS, Ed D); educational psychology (PhD); educational technology leadership (M Ed, MS); educational technology library science (M Ed, MS); elementary education (M Ed); health, kinesiology and sports studies (MS); higher education (MS, Ed D); psychology (MS); reading (M Ed, MS); secondary education (M Ed, MS); social work (MSW); special education (M Ed, MS); supervision, curriculum and instruction-elementary education (Ed D); training and development (MS). *Program availability:* Part-time, evening/weekend, 100% online, blended/hybrid learning. *Faculty:* 91 full-time (51 women), 38 part-time/adjunct (31 women). *Students:* 400 full-time (310 women), 1,400 part-time (1,117 women); includes 724 minority (412 Black or African American, non-Hispanic/Latino; 8 American Indian or Alaska Native, non-Hispanic/Latino; 24 Asian, non-Hispanic/Latino; 220 Hispanic/Latino; 60 Two or more races, non-Hispanic/Latino), 18 international. Average age 37. 951 applicants, 46% accepted, 331 enrolled. In 2017, 564 master's, 24 doctorates awarded. *Degree requirements:* For master's, comprehensive exam, thesis optional, departmental

qualifying exams (for some programs); for doctorate, comprehensive exam, thesis/dissertation, departmental qualifying exam; for SSP, comprehensive exam, thesis optional. *Entrance requirements:* For master's and doctorate, GRE General Test. Additional exam requirements/recommendations for international students: Required—TOEFL (minimum score 550 paper-based; 79 iBT), IELTS (minimum score 6). *Application deadline:* For fall admission, 6/1 priority date for international students; for spring admission, 10/15 priority date for international students; for summer admission, 3/15 priority date for international students. Applications are processed on a rolling basis. Application fee: $50. Electronic applications accepted. *Expenses:* Tuition, state resident: full-time $3630. Tuition, nonresident: full-time $11,100. *Required fees:* $2564. Tuition and fees vary according to course load, degree level and program. *Financial support:* In 2017–18, 84 students received support, including 40 research assistantships with partial tuition reimbursements available (averaging $10,800 per year), 12 teaching assistantships with partial tuition reimbursements available (averaging $13,000 per year); career-related internships or fieldwork, Federal Work-Study, institutionally sponsored loans, scholarships/grants, health care benefits, and unspecified assistantships also available. Financial award application deadline: 6/15; financial award applicants required to submit FAFSA. *Faculty research:* Cognitive and bilingual education, positive behavioral intervention, literacy, math readiness. *Total annual research expenditures:* $1.1 million. *Unit head:* Dr. Timothy Letzring, Dean, 903-886-5181, Fax: 903-886-5905, E-mail: tim.letzring@tamuc.edu. *Application contact:* Vicky Turner, Doctoral Degree and Special Programs Coordinator, 903-886-5167, E-mail: vicky.turner@tamuc.edu.
Website: http://www.tamuc.edu/academics/graduateSchool/programs/education/default.aspx

Texas A&M University–Corpus Christi, College of Graduate Studies, College of Education and Human Development, Corpus Christi, TX 78412. Offers counseling (MS), including counseling; counselor education (PhD); curriculum and instruction (MS, PhD); early childhood education (MS); educational administration (MS); educational leadership (Ed D); elementary education (MS); instructional design and educational technology (MS); kinesiology (MS); reading (MS); secondary education (MS); special education (MS). *Program availability:* Part-time, evening/weekend, blended/hybrid learning. *Faculty:* 50 full-time (29 women), 29 part-time/adjunct (18 women). *Students:* 160 full-time (127 women), 366 part-time (293 women); includes 279 minority (40 Black or African American, non-Hispanic/Latino; 3 Asian, non-Hispanic/Latino; 228 Hispanic/Latino; 8 Two or more races, non-Hispanic/Latino), 18 international. Average age 35. 296 applicants, 65% accepted, 155 enrolled. In 2017, 103 master's, 27 doctorates awarded. *Degree requirements:* For master's, comprehensive exam, capstone; for doctorate, thesis/dissertation. *Entrance requirements:* For master's, GRE General Test, essay (300 words); for doctorate, GRE, essay, resume, 3-4 reference forms. *Application deadline:* For fall admission, 7/15 priority date for domestic students, 5/1 priority date for international students; for spring admission, 11/15 priority date for domestic students, 9/1 priority date for international students. Applications are processed on a rolling basis. Application fee: $50 ($70 for international students). Electronic applications accepted. *Expenses:* Tuition, state resident: full-time $3568; part-time $198.24 per credit hour. Tuition, nonresident: full-time $11,038; part-time $613.24 per credit hour. *Required fees:* $2129; $1422.58 per semester. Tuition and fees vary according to program. *Financial support:* Research assistantships, teaching assistantships, career-related internships or fieldwork, Federal Work-Study, institutionally sponsored loans, scholarships/grants, health care benefits, and unspecified assistantships available. Support available to part-time students. Financial award application deadline: 3/15; financial award applicants required to submit FAFSA. *Unit head:* Dr. David Scott, Dean, 361-825-2660, E-mail: david.scott@tamucc.edu. *Application contact:* Graduate Admissions Coordinator, 361-825-2177, Fax: 361-825-2755, E-mail: gradweb@tamucc.edu.
Website: http://education.tamucc.edu/

Texas A&M University–Kingsville, College of Graduate Studies, College of Education and Human Performance, Department of Health and Kinesiology, Kingsville, TX 78363. Offers MA, MS. *Degree requirements:* For master's, variable foreign language requirement, comprehensive exam, thesis (for some programs). *Entrance requirements:* For master's, GRE, MAT, GMAT, essay. Additional exam requirements/recommendations for international students: Required—TOEFL (minimum score 550 paper-based; 79 iBT). Electronic applications accepted.

Texas A&M University–San Antonio, Department of Counseling, Health and Kinesiology, San Antonio, TX 78224. Offers clinical mental health counseling (MA); counseling and guidance (MA); kinesiology (MS); marriage and family counseling (MA). *Program availability:* Part-time, evening/weekend, online learning. *Faculty:* 12 full-time (5 women), 6 part-time/adjunct (4 women). *Students:* 48 full-time (35 women), 146 part-time (118 women); includes 135 minority (24 Black or African American, non-Hispanic/Latino; 3 Asian, non-Hispanic/Latino; 103 Hispanic/Latino; 5 Two or more races, non-Hispanic/Latino), 2 international. Average age 34. 201 applicants, 56% accepted, 62 enrolled. In 2017, 68 master's awarded. *Degree requirements:* For master's, comprehensive exam, thesis or alternative. *Entrance requirements:* For master's, MAT or GRE (composite quantitative and verbal). Additional exam requirements/recommendations for international students: Required—TOEFL (minimum score 550 paper-based; 79 iBT), IELTS (minimum score 6). *Application deadline:* For fall admission, 3/15 priority date for domestic and international students; for spring admission, 11/1 priority date for domestic and international students; for summer admission, 4/1 priority date for domestic and international students. Applications are processed on a rolling basis. Application fee: $35 ($50 for international students). Electronic applications accepted. *Expenses:* Tuition, state resident: full-time $3475; part-time $1930 per semester. Tuition, nonresident: full-time $10,945; part-time $6080 per semester. *Required fees:* $2148; $1412 per year. $706 per semester. Tuition and fees vary according to course load. *Financial support:* In 2017–18, 10 students received support. Federal Work-Study, scholarships/grants, and tuition waivers available. Financial award application deadline: 3/15; financial award applicants required to submit FAFSA. *Unit head:* Dr. Suzanne Mudge, Department Chair. *Application contact:* Caitie Garza, Graduate Admissions Coordinator, 210-784-1300, E-mail: beajaguar@tamusa.edu.
Website: http://www.tamusa.edu/collegeofeducationandhumandevelopment/counselinghealthkinesiology/index.html

Texas Christian University, Harris College of Nursing and Health Sciences, Department of Kinesiology, Fort Worth, TX 76129. Offers MS. *Program availability:* Part-time. *Faculty:* 7 full-time (5 women), 1 part-time/adjunct (0 women). *Students:* 23 full-time (17 women); includes 5 minority (1 Asian, non-Hispanic/Latino; 4 Hispanic/Latino), 2 international. Average age 24. 39 applicants, 46% accepted, 11 enrolled. In 2017, 8 master's awarded. *Degree requirements:* For master's, thesis. *Entrance requirements:* For master's, GRE General Test. Additional exam requirements/recommendations for international students: Recommended—TOEFL (minimum score 600 paper-based; 100 iBT). *Application deadline:* For fall admission, 3/1 for domestic and international students; for spring admission, 12/1 for domestic and international students. Applications are processed on a rolling basis. Application fee: $50. Electronic applications accepted. *Financial support:* In 2017–18, 16 students received support, including 16 research assistantships with full and partial tuition reimbursements available (averaging $6,300 per year); tuition waivers (full and partial) also available.

Kinesiology and Movement Studies

Financial award application deadline: 3/1. *Faculty research:* Meal composition and gut hormones, exercise and reduction of inflammation, mental toughness, risk factors for disease in special populations, eating behavior and caloric intake, concussion risk in impact sports, physical activity in elementary school children. *Total annual research expenditures:* $150,000. *Unit head:* Dr. Joel Mitchell, Professor/Chair, 817-257-7665, Fax: 817-257-7702, E-mail: j.mitchell@tcu.edu. *Application contact:* Adam C. King, PhD, Graduate Program Director, 817-257-7665, E-mail: a.king@tcu.edu.
Website: http://www.kinesiology.tcu.edu

Texas Tech University, Graduate School, College of Arts and Sciences, Department of Kinesiology and Sport Management, Lubbock, TX 79409. Offers kinesiology (MS); sport management (MS). *Program availability:* Part-time. *Faculty:* 21 full-time (9 women), 9 part-time/adjunct (5 women). *Students:* 65 full-time (32 women), 7 part-time (1 woman); includes 28 minority (8 Black or African American, non-Hispanic/Latino; 3 Asian, non-Hispanic/Latino; 15 Hispanic/Latino; 2 Two or more races, non-Hispanic/Latino), 11 international. Average age 24. 96 applicants, 48% accepted, 38 enrolled. In 2017, 38 master's awarded. *Degree requirements:* For master's, comprehensive exam (for some programs), thesis (for some programs). *Entrance requirements:* For master's, GRE or minimum GPA of 3.5 on last 60 hours of undergraduate coursework (only for kinesiology), letter of intent, 3 letters of recommendation (preferably from academic professors), minimum GPA of 2.8 in the last 60 hours. Additional exam requirements/recommendations for international students: Required—TOEFL (minimum score 550 paper-based; 79 iBT). *Application deadline:* For fall admission, 6/1 priority date for domestic students, 1/15 priority date for international students; for spring admission, 9/1 priority date for domestic students, 6/15 priority date for international students. Applications are processed on a rolling basis. Application fee: $60. Electronic applications accepted. *Expenses:* Contact institution. *Financial support:* In 2017–18, 51 students received support, including 49 fellowships (averaging $4,508 per year), 35 teaching assistantships (averaging $12,637 per year); research assistantships, career-related internships or fieldwork, scholarships/grants, health care benefits, and unspecified assistantships also available. Financial award application deadline: 8/1; financial award applicants required to submit FAFSA. *Faculty research:* Sport management, exercise physiology, human performance, motor behavior, exercise and sport psychology. *Total annual research expenditures:* $144,825. *Unit head:* Dr. Angela Lumpkin, Professor/Department Chair, 806-834-6935, Fax: 806-742-1688, E-mail: angela.lumpkin@ttu.edu. *Application contact:* Donna Torres, Graduate Admissions Coordinator, 806-834-7968, Fax: 806-742-1688, E-mail: donna.torres@ttu.edu.
Website: http://www.depts.ttu.edu/ksm/

Texas Woman's University, Graduate School, College of Health Sciences, Department of Kinesiology, Denton, TX 76204. Offers kinesiology (MS, PhD), including adapted physical activity, biomechanics, coaching (MS), exercise physiology, sport management. *Program availability:* Part-time, evening/weekend. *Faculty:* 11 full-time (3 women), 2 part-time/adjunct (both women). *Students:* 48 full-time (36 women), 65 part-time (39 women); includes 40 minority (19 Black or African American, non-Hispanic/Latino; 2 Asian, non-Hispanic/Latino; 17 Hispanic/Latino; 2 Two or more races, non-Hispanic/Latino), 14 international. Average age 30. 63 applicants, 81% accepted, 37 enrolled. In 2017, 32 master's, 9 doctorates awarded. Terminal master's awarded for partial completion of doctoral program. *Degree requirements:* For master's, comprehensive exam, thesis (for some programs), thesis or professional paper; for doctorate, comprehensive exam, thesis/dissertation, qualifying exam. *Entrance requirements:* For master's, GRE General Test (biomechanics emphasis only), 2 letters of reference, curriculum vitae; for doctorate, GRE General Test (biomechanics emphasis only), interview, 3 letters of reference, curriculum vitae, letter of intent. Additional exam requirements/recommendations for international students: Required—TOEFL (minimum score 550 paper-based; 79 iBT). Recommended—IELTS (minimum score 6.5), TSE (minimum score 53). *Application deadline:* For fall admission, 7/15 for domestic students, 3/1 priority date for international students; for spring admission, 11/1 for domestic students, 7/1 priority date for international students; for summer admission, 4/1 for domestic students, 2/1 priority date for international students. Applications are processed on a rolling basis. Application fee: $50 ($75 for international students). Electronic applications accepted. *Expenses:* $7,520 per year full-time in-state; $16,829 per year full-time out-of-state. *Financial support:* In 2017–18, 36 students received support, including 1 research assistantship (averaging $11,926 per year), 15 teaching assistantships (averaging $20,354 per year); career-related internships or fieldwork, Federal Work-Study, institutionally sponsored loans, scholarships/grants, traineeships, health care benefits, and unspecified assistantships also available. Support available to part-time students. Financial award application deadline: 3/1; financial award applicants required to submit FAFSA. *Faculty research:* Exercise and Type 2 diabetes risk, bone mineral density and exercise in special populations, obesity in children, factors influencing sport consumer behavior and loyalty, roles and responsibilities of Para educators in adapted physical education. *Unit head:* Dr. George King, Chair, 940-898-2575, Fax: 940-898-2581. *Application contact:* Korie Hawkins, Associate Director of Admissions, Graduate Recruitment, 940-898-3188, Fax: 940-898-3081, E-mail: admissions@twu.edu.
Website: http://www.twu.edu/kinesiology/

Université de Montréal, Department of Kinesiology, Montréal, QC H3C 3J7, Canada. Offers kinesiology (M Sc, DESS); physical activity (M Sc, PhD). *Degree requirements:* For master's, one foreign language, thesis (for some programs); for doctorate, one foreign language, thesis/dissertation, general exam. Electronic applications accepted. *Faculty research:* Physiology of exercise, psychology of sports, biomechanics, dance, sociology of sports.

Université de Sherbrooke, Faculty of Physical Education and Sports, Program in Physical Education, Sherbrooke, QC J1K 2R1, Canada. Offers kinanthropology (M Sc); physical activity (Diploma). *Degree requirements:* For master's, thesis. *Entrance requirements:* For master's, minimum GPA of 2.7; for Diploma, bachelor's degree in physical education. *Faculty research:* Physical fitness, nutrition, human factors, sociology, teaching.

Université du Québec à Montréal, Graduate Programs, Program in Human Movement Studies, Montréal, QC H3C 3P8, Canada. Offers M Sc. *Program availability:* Part-time. *Degree requirements:* For master's, thesis optional. *Entrance requirements:* For master's, appropriate bachelor's degree or equivalent and proficiency in French.

Université Laval, Faculty of Medicine, Graduate Programs in Medicine, Programs in Kinesiology, Québec, QC G1K 7P4, Canada. Offers M Sc, PhD. Terminal master's awarded for partial completion of doctoral program. *Degree requirements:* For master's, thesis; for doctorate, comprehensive exam, thesis/dissertation. *Entrance requirements:* For master's and doctorate, French exam, knowledge of French, comprehension of written English. Electronic applications accepted.

The University of Alabama, Graduate School, College of Education, Department of Kinesiology, Tuscaloosa, AL 35487. Offers alternative sport pedagogy (MA); exercise science (PhD). *Program availability:* Part-time. *Faculty:* 12 full-time (2 women). *Students:* 51 full-time (21 women), 20 part-time (9 women); includes 17 minority (12 Black or African American, non-Hispanic/Latino; 3 Hispanic/Latino; 2 Two or more races, non-Hispanic/Latino), 7 international. Average age 27. 58 applicants, 60% accepted, 18 enrolled. In 2017, 35 master's, 8 doctorates awarded. *Degree requirements:* For

master's, comprehensive exam, thesis optional; for doctorate, comprehensive exam, thesis/dissertation. *Entrance requirements:* For master's and doctorate, GRE, minimum GPA of 3.0. Additional exam requirements/recommendations for international students: Required—TOEFL. *Application deadline:* Applications are processed on a rolling basis. Electronic applications accepted. *Financial support:* In 2017–18, 18 students received support. Application deadline: 3/1. *Total annual research expenditures:* $50,518. *Unit head:* Dr. Jonathan Wingo, Associate Professor and Head, 205-348-4699, Fax: 205-348-0867, E-mail: jwingo@ua.edu. *Application contact:* Dr. Kathy S. Wetzel, Associate Dean for Student Services and Certification, 205-348-1154, E-mail: kwetzel@bamaed.ua.edu.
Website: http://education.ua.edu/academics/kine

University of Arkansas, Graduate School, College of Education and Health Professions, Department of Health, Human Performance and Recreation, Program in Kinesiology, Fayetteville, AR 72701. Offers MS, PhD. In 2017, 20 master's, 1 doctorate awarded. *Degree requirements:* For doctorate, thesis/dissertation. *Entrance requirements:* For doctorate, GRE General Test. *Application deadline:* For fall admission, 8/1 for domestic students, 4/1 for international students; for spring admission, 12/1 for domestic students, 10/1 for international students; for summer admission, 4/15 for domestic students, 3/1 for international students. Applications are processed on a rolling basis. Application fee: $60. Electronic applications accepted. *Expenses:* Tuition, state resident: full-time $3782. Tuition, nonresident: full-time $10,238. *Financial support:* Fellowships with tuition reimbursements, research assistantships, teaching assistantships, career-related internships or fieldwork, and Federal Work-Study available. Support available to part-time students. Financial award application deadline: 4/1; financial award applicants required to submit FAFSA. *Unit head:* Dr. Matthew Stueck Ganio, Department Head, 479-575-2956, Fax: 479-575-5778, E-mail: msganio@uark.edu. *Application contact:* Dr. Stephen Dittmore, Coordinator of Graduate Studies, 479-575-6625, E-mail: dittmore@uark.edu.
Website: https://hhpr.uark.edu

The University of British Columbia, Faculty of Education, School of Kinesiology, Vancouver, BC V6T 1Z1, Canada. Offers high performance coaching and technical leadership (MHPCTL); kinesiology (M Kin, M Sc, MA, PhD). *Program availability:* Part-time. *Degree requirements:* For master's, thesis (for some programs); for doctorate, comprehensive exam, thesis/dissertation. *Entrance requirements:* For doctorate, thesis-based master's degree. Additional exam requirements/recommendations for international students: Required—TOEFL, IELTS. Electronic applications accepted. *Expenses:* Contact institution. *Faculty research:* Exercise physiology, biomechanics, motor learning, natural sciences, socio-managerial.

University of Calgary, Faculty of Graduate Studies, Faculty of Kinesiology, Calgary, AB T2N 1N4, Canada. Offers M Kin, M Sc, PhD. *Degree requirements:* For master's, thesis (M Sc); for doctorate, thesis/dissertation. *Entrance requirements:* Additional exam requirements/recommendations for international students: Required—TOEFL. Electronic applications accepted. *Faculty research:* Load acting on the human body, muscle mechanics and physiology, optimizing high performance athlete performance, eye movement in sports, analysis of body composition.

University of Central Arkansas, Graduate School, College of Health and Behavioral Sciences, Department of Kinesiology, Conway, AR 72035-0001. Offers MS. *Program availability:* Part-time. *Degree requirements:* For master's, comprehensive exam, thesis optional. *Entrance requirements:* For master's, GRE General Test, minimum GPA of 2.7. Additional exam requirements/recommendations for international students: Required—TOEFL (minimum score 550 paper-based; 80 iBT). Electronic applications accepted.

University of Central Missouri, The Graduate School, Warrensburg, MO 64093. Offers accountancy (MA); accounting (MBA); applied mathematics (MS); aviation safety (MA); biology (MS); business administration (MBA); career and technical education leadership (MS); college student personnel administration (MS); communication (MA); computer science (MS); counseling (MS); criminal justice (MS); educational leadership (Ed D); educational technology (MS); elementary and early childhood education (MSE); English (MA); environmental studies (MA); finance (MBA); history (MA); human services/educational technology (Ed S); human services/learning resources (Ed S); human services/professional counseling (Ed S); industrial hygiene (MS); industrial management (MS); information systems (MBA); information technology (MS); kinesiology (MS); library science and information services (MS); literacy education (MSE); marketing (MBA); mathematics (MS); music (MA); occupational safety management (MS); psychology (MS); rural family nursing (MS); school administration (MSE); social gerontology (MS); sociology (MA); special education (MSE); speech language pathology (MS); superintendency (Ed S); teaching (MAT); teaching English as a second language (MA); technology (MS); technology management (PhD); theatre (MA). *Program availability:* Part-time, 100% online, blended/hybrid learning. *Faculty:* 337 full-time (145 women), 41 part-time/adjunct (28 women). *Students:* 785 full-time (398 women), 1,633 part-time (1,063 women); includes 231 minority (102 Black or African American, non-Hispanic/Latino; 4 American Indian or Alaska Native, non-Hispanic/Latino; 16 Asian, non-Hispanic/Latino; 52 Hispanic/Latino; 57 Two or more races, non-Hispanic/Latino), 692 international. Average age 30. In 2017, 2,605 master's, 122 other advanced degrees awarded. *Degree requirements:* For master's and Ed S, comprehensive exam (for some programs), thesis (for some programs). *Entrance requirements:* Additional exam requirements/recommendations for international students: Required—TOEFL (minimum score 550 paper-based; 79 iBT). *Application deadline:* For fall admission, 6/1 priority date for domestic and international students; for spring admission, 10/1 priority date for domestic and international students; for summer admission, 4/1 priority date for domestic and international students. Applications are processed on a rolling basis. Application fee: $30 ($75 for international students). Electronic applications accepted. *Expenses:* Tuition, state resident: full-time $8771; part-time $292.35 per credit hour. Tuition, nonresident: full-time $17,541; part-time $584.70 per credit hour. *Required fees:* $372; $24.78 per credit hour. *Financial support:* In 2017–18, 99 students received support. Research assistantships, teaching assistantships, career-related internships or fieldwork, Federal Work-Study, scholarships/grants, and administrative and laboratory assistantships available. Support available to part-time students. Financial award application deadline: 3/1; financial award applicants required to submit FAFSA. *Unit head:* Shellie Hewitt, Director of Graduate and International Student Services, 660-543-4621, Fax: 660-543-4778, E-mail: hewitt@ucmo.edu. *Application contact:* 660-543-4621, E-mail: admit_intl@ucmo.edu.
Website: http://www.ucmo.edu/graduate/

University of Colorado Boulder, Graduate School, College of Arts and Sciences, Department of Integrative Physiology, Boulder, CO 80309. Offers MS, PhD. *Faculty:* 23 full-time (7 women). *Students:* 62 full-time (29 women); includes 10 minority (1 Black or African American, non-Hispanic/Latino; 3 Asian, non-Hispanic/Latino; 5 Hispanic/Latino; 1 Two or more races, non-Hispanic/Latino), 3 international. Average age 27. 78 applicants, 19% accepted, 14 enrolled. In 2017, 15 master's, 8 doctorates awarded. Terminal master's awarded for partial completion of doctoral program. *Degree requirements:* For master's, comprehensive exam, thesis or alternative; for doctorate, thesis/dissertation. *Entrance requirements:* For master's, GRE General Test, minimum undergraduate GPA of 2.75. *Application deadline:* For fall admission, 1/10 for domestic students; for spring admission, 12/1 for domestic students. Applications are processed

on a rolling basis. Application fee: $60 ($80 for international students). Electronic applications accepted. Application fee is waived when completed online. *Financial support:* In 2017–18, 183 students received support, including 52 fellowships (averaging $5,252 per year), 22 research assistantships with full and partial tuition reimbursements available (averaging $23,500 per year), 44 teaching assistantships with full and partial tuition reimbursements available (averaging $35,806 per year); institutionally sponsored loans, scholarships/grants, health care benefits, and unspecified assistantships also available. Financial award application deadline: 2/15; financial award applicants required to submit FAFSA. *Faculty research:* Aging/gerontology; nervous system; neurophysiology; neuroscience; physiological controls and systems. *Total annual research expenditures:* $8.2 million. *Application contact:* E-mail: iphygrad@colorado.edu.
Website: http://www.colorado.edu/intphys/

University of Delaware, College of Arts and Sciences, Interdisciplinary Program in Biomechanics and Movement Science, Newark, DE 19716. Offers MS, PhD. *Program availability:* Part-time. Terminal master's awarded for partial completion of doctoral program. *Degree requirements:* For master's, thesis; for doctorate, thesis/dissertation. *Entrance requirements:* For master's and doctorate, GRE General Test, minimum undergraduate GPA of 3.0. Additional exam requirements/recommendations for international students: Required—TOEFL (minimum score 550 paper-based). Electronic applications accepted. *Faculty research:* Muscle modeling, gait, motor control, human movement.

University of Delaware, College of Health Sciences, Department of Kinesiology and Applied Physiology, Newark, DE 19716. Offers MS, PhD.

University of Florida, Graduate School, College of Health and Human Performance, Department of Applied Physiology and Kinesiology, Gainesville, FL 32611. Offers applied physiology and kinesiology (MS); athletic training/sports medicine (MS); biobehavioral science (MS); clinical exercise physiology (MS); exercise physiology (MS); health and human performance (PhD), including applied physiology and kinesiology, biobehavioral science, exercise physiology; human performance (MS). *Degree requirements:* For master's, comprehensive exam, thesis (for some programs); for doctorate, comprehensive exam, thesis/dissertation. *Entrance requirements:* For master's and doctorate, GRE General Test, minimum GPA of 3.0. Additional exam requirements/recommendations for international students: Required—TOEFL (minimum score 550 paper-based; 80 iBT), IELTS (minimum score 6). Electronic applications accepted. *Faculty research:* Cardiovascular disease; basic mechanisms that underlie exercise-induced changes in the body at the organ, tissue, cellular and molecular level; development of rehabilitation techniques for regaining motor control after stroke or as a consequence of Parkinson's disease; maintaining optimal health and delaying age-related declines in physiological function; psychomotor mechanisms impacting health and performance across the life span.

University of Georgia, College of Education, Department of Kinesiology, Athens, GA 30602. Offers MS, PhD. *Entrance requirements:* For master's, GRE General Test or MAT; for doctorate, GRE General Test. Additional exam requirements/recommendations for international students: Required—TOEFL. Electronic applications accepted.

University of Hawaii at Manoa, Office of Graduate Education, College of Education, Department of Kinesiology and Rehabilitation Science, Honolulu, HI 96822. Offers kinesiology (MS). *Program availability:* Part-time. *Degree requirements:* For master's, thesis optional. *Entrance requirements:* For master's, GRE General Test. Additional exam requirements/recommendations for international students: Required—TOEFL (minimum score 540 paper-based; 76 iBT), IELTS (minimum score 5).

University of Hawaii at Manoa, Office of Graduate Education, College of Education, PhD in Education Program, Honolulu, HI 96822. Offers curriculum and instruction (PhD); educational administration (PhD); educational foundations (PhD); educational policy studies (PhD); educational psychology (PhD); exceptionalities (PhD); kinesiology (PhD); learning design and technology (PhD). *Program availability:* Part-time, evening/weekend. *Degree requirements:* For doctorate, thesis/dissertation. *Entrance requirements:* For doctorate, GRE General Test, sample of written work. Additional exam requirements/recommendations for international students: Required—TOEFL (minimum score 600 paper-based; 100 iBT), IELTS (minimum score 7).

University of Houston, College of Liberal Arts and Social Sciences, Department of Health and Human Performance, Houston, TX 77204. Offers exercise science (MS); human nutrition (MS); human space exploration sciences (MS); kinesiology (PhD); physical education (M Ed). *Accreditation:* NCATE (one or more programs are accredited). *Program availability:* Part-time, evening/weekend. *Degree requirements:* For master's, comprehensive exam (for some programs), thesis (for some programs); for doctorate, comprehensive exam, thesis/dissertation, qualifying exam, candidacy paper. *Entrance requirements:* For master's, GRE (minimum 35th percentile on each section), minimum cumulative GPA of 3.0; for doctorate, GRE (minimum 35th percentile on each section), minimum cumulative GPA of 3.3. Additional exam requirements/recommendations for international students: Required—TOEFL (minimum score 550 paper-based; 79 iBT). Electronic applications accepted. *Faculty research:* Biomechanics, exercise physiology, obesity, nutrition, space exploration science.

University of Idaho, College of Graduate Studies, College of Education, Health and Human Sciences, Department of Movement Sciences, Moscow, ID 83844. Offers athletic training (MSAT, DAT); exercise science and health (MS); physical education teacher education (M Ed, MS); recreation, sport, and tourism management (MS). *Faculty:* 22. *Students:* 89 full-time (41 women), 18 part-time (7 women). Average age 28. In 2017, 24 master's awarded. *Degree requirements:* For doctorate, thesis/dissertation. *Entrance requirements:* For master's and doctorate, minimum GPA of 3.0. Additional exam requirements/recommendations for international students: Required—TOEFL. *Application deadline:* For fall admission, 8/1 for domestic students; for spring admission, 12/15 for domestic students. Applications are processed on a rolling basis. Application fee: $60. Electronic applications accepted. *Expenses:* Tuition, state resident: full-time $6722; part-time $430 per credit hour. Tuition, nonresident: full-time $23,046; part-time $1337 per credit hour. *Required fees:* $2142; $63 per credit hour. *Financial support:* Research assistantships and teaching assistantships available. Financial award applicants required to submit FAFSA. *Unit head:* Dr. Philip W. Scruggs, Chair, 208-885-7921, E-mail: movementsciences@uidaho.edu. *Application contact:* Sean Scoggin, Graduate Recruitment Coordinator, 208-885-4001, Fax: 208-885-4406, E-mail: graduateadmissions@uidaho.edu.
Website: https://www.uidaho.edu/ed/mvsc

University of Illinois at Chicago, College of Applied Health Sciences, Program in Kinesiology, Chicago, IL 60607-7128. Offers MS, PhD. *Program availability:* Part-time. *Degree requirements:* For master's, thesis. *Entrance requirements:* For master's, GRE General Test, minimum GPA of 2.75. Additional exam requirements/recommendations for international students: Required—TOEFL. Electronic applications accepted. *Expenses:* Contact institution. *Faculty research:* Mitochondrial biogenesis, glucocorticoid lipid metabolism, at-risk youth, motor control.

University of Illinois at Urbana–Champaign, Graduate College, College of Applied Health Sciences, Department of Kinesiology and Community Health, Champaign, IL

61820. Offers community health (MS, MSPH, PhD); kinesiology (MS, PhD); public health (MPH); rehabilitation (MS); PhD/MPH.

University of Kentucky, Graduate School, College of Education, Program in Kinesiology and Health Promotion, Lexington, KY 40506-0032. Offers biomechanics (MS); exercise physiology (MS, PhD); exercise science (PhD); health promotion (MS, Ed D); physical education training (Ed D); sport leadership (MS); teaching and coaching (MS). Terminal master's awarded for partial completion of doctoral program. *Degree requirements:* For master's, comprehensive exam, thesis optional; for doctorate, comprehensive exam, thesis/dissertation. *Entrance requirements:* For master's, GRE General Test, minimum undergraduate GPA of 2.75; for doctorate, GRE General Test, minimum graduate GPA of 3.0. Additional exam requirements/recommendations for international students: Required—TOEFL (minimum score 550 paper-based). Electronic applications accepted.

University of Lethbridge, School of Graduate Studies, Lethbridge, AB T1K 3M4, Canada. Offers addictions counseling (M Sc); agricultural biotechnology (M Sc); agricultural studies (M Sc, MA); anthropology (MA); archaeology (M Sc, MA); art (MA, MFA); biochemistry (M Sc); biological sciences (M Sc); biomolecular science (PhD); biosystems and biodiversity (PhD); Canadian studies (MA); chemistry (M Sc); computer science (M Sc); computer science and geographical information science (M Sc); counseling (MC); counseling psychology (M Ed); dramatic arts (MA); earth, space, and physical science (PhD); economics (MA); education (MA, PhD); educational leadership (M Ed); English (MA); environmental science (M Sc); evolution and behavior (PhD); exercise science (M Sc); French (MA); French/German (MA); French/Spanish (MA); general education (M Ed); geography (M Sc, MA); German (MA); health sciences (M Sc); individualized multidisciplinary (M Sc, MA); kinesiology (M Sc, MA); management (M Sc), including accounting, finance, human resource management and labor relations, information systems, international management, marketing, policy and strategy; mathematics (M Sc); music (M Mus, MA); Native American studies (MA); neuroscience (M Sc, PhD); new media (MA, MFA); nursing (M Sc, MN); philosophy (MA); physics (M Sc); political science (MA); psychology (M Sc, MA); religious studies (MA); sociology (MA); theatre and dramatic arts (MFA); theoretical and computational science (PhD); urban and regional studies (MA); women and gender studies (MA). *Program availability:* Part-time, evening/weekend. *Degree requirements:* For master's, thesis (for some programs); for doctorate, comprehensive exam, thesis/dissertation. *Entrance requirements:* For master's, GMAT (for M Sc in management), bachelor's degree in related field, minimum GPA of 3.0 during previous 20 graded semester courses, 2 years' teaching or related experience (M Ed); for doctorate, master's degree, minimum graduate GPA of 3.5. Additional exam requirements/recommendations for international students: Required—TOEFL (minimum score 580 paper-based; 93 iBT). Electronic applications accepted. *Faculty research:* Movement and brain plasticity, gibberellin physiology, photosynthesis, carbon cycling, molecular properties of main-group ring components.

University of Maine, Graduate School, College of Education and Human Development, School of Kinesiology, Physical Education and Athletic Training, Orono, ME 04469. Offers classroom technology integrationist (CGS); education data specialist (CGS); educational technology coordinator (CGS); kinesiology and physical education (M Ed, MS); science education (M Ed, MS); STEM education (PhD). *Program availability:* Part-time, evening/weekend. *Faculty:* 3 full-time (0 women). *Students:* 10 full-time (3 women), 1 part-time (0 women); includes 2 minority (1 Black or African American, non-Hispanic/Latino; 1 Asian, non-Hispanic/Latino). Average age 24. 8 applicants, 100% accepted, 5 enrolled. In 2017, 6 master's awarded. *Degree requirements:* For master's, thesis (for some programs); for doctorate, comprehensive exam, thesis/dissertation. *Entrance requirements:* For master's, GRE General Test, MAT; for doctorate, GRE General Test. Additional exam requirements/recommendations for international students: Required—TOEFL. *Application deadline:* For fall admission, 1/15 for domestic students. Applications are processed on a rolling basis. Application fee: $65. Electronic applications accepted. *Expenses:* Tuition, state resident: full-time $7722; part-time $429 per credit hour. Tuition, nonresident: full-time $25,146; part-time $1397 per credit hour. *Required fees:* $1162; $581 per credit hour. *Financial support:* In 2017–18, 7 students received support, including 6 teaching assistantships with full tuition reimbursements available (averaging $15,200 per year); Federal Work-Study, scholarships/grants, and unspecified assistantships also available. Financial award application deadline: 3/1. *Faculty research:* Geriatric equilibrium, physical activity and technology, muscle cell metabolism, hormonal response to exercise. *Unit head:* Dr. Jim Artesani, Associate Dean of Accreditation and Graduate Affairs, 207-581-4061, Fax: 207-581-2423. *Application contact:* Scott G. Delcourt, Assistant Vice President for Graduate Studies and Senior Associate Dean, 207-581-3291, Fax: 207-581-3232, E-mail: graduate@maine.edu.
Website: http://umaine.edu/edhd/

University of Manitoba, Faculty of Graduate Studies, Faculty of Kinesiology and Recreation Management, Winnipeg, MB R3T 2N2, Canada. Offers kinesiology and recreation (M Sc, MA).

University of Mary, School of Health Sciences, Program in Kinesiology, Bismarck, ND 58504-9652. Offers MS. *Program availability:* Part-time, online learning.

University of Maryland, College Park, Academic Affairs, School of Public Health, Department of Kinesiology, College Park, MD 20742. Offers MA, PhD. *Program availability:* Part-time, evening/weekend. *Degree requirements:* For master's, thesis optional; for doctorate, thesis/dissertation. *Entrance requirements:* For master's, GRE General Test, minimum GPA of 3.0, 3 letters of recommendation; for doctorate, GRE General Test, minimum GPA of 3.5, 3 letters of recommendation. Electronic applications accepted. *Faculty research:* Sports, biophysical and professional studies, cognitive motor behavior, exercise physiology.

University of Massachusetts Amherst, Graduate School, School of Public Health and Health Sciences, Department of Kinesiology, Amherst, MA 01003. Offers MS, PhD. *Program availability:* Part-time. Terminal master's awarded for partial completion of doctoral program. *Degree requirements:* For master's, comprehensive exam (for some programs), thesis optional; for doctorate, comprehensive exam, thesis/dissertation. *Entrance requirements:* For master's and doctorate, GRE General Test. Additional exam requirements/recommendations for international students: Required—TOEFL (minimum score 550 paper-based; 80 iBT), IELTS (minimum score 6.5). Electronic applications accepted.

University of Michigan, Rackham Graduate School, School of Kinesiology, Ann Arbor, MI 48109. Offers movement science (MS, PhD); sport management (MS, PhD). *Faculty:* 31 full-time (16 women). *Students:* 94 full-time (40 women); includes 22 minority (6 Black or African American, non-Hispanic/Latino; 5 Asian, non-Hispanic/Latino; 7 Hispanic/Latino; 4 Two or more races, non-Hispanic/Latino). Average age 26. 230 applicants, 48% accepted, 52 enrolled. In 2017, 25 master's, 7 doctorates awarded. Terminal master's awarded for partial completion of doctoral program. *Degree requirements:* For master's, thesis optional; for doctorate, comprehensive exam, thesis/dissertation, oral defense of dissertation. *Entrance requirements:* For master's and doctorate, GRE General Test. Additional exam requirements/recommendations for international students: Required—TOEFL (minimum score 84 iBT). *Application deadline:*

Kinesiology and Movement Studies

For fall admission, 12/1 priority date for domestic students, 12/1 for international students. Applications are processed on a rolling basis. Application fee: $75 ($90 for international students). Electronic applications accepted. *Expenses:* Tuition, state resident: full-time $22,368; part-time $1201 per credit hour. Tuition, nonresident: full-time $45,156; part-time $2467 per credit hour. *Required fees:* $376 per term. Tuition and fees vary according to course load, degree level and program. *Financial support:* In 2017–18, 34 students received support, including 11 fellowships with full tuition reimbursements available, 12 research assistantships with full tuition reimbursements available, 11 teaching assistantships with full tuition reimbursements available; Federal Work-Study, scholarships/grants, traineeships, health care benefits, and unspecified assistantships also available. Financial award application deadline: 12/1. *Faculty research:* Motor development, exercise physiology, biomechanics, sport medicine, sport management. *Unit head:* Dr. Ketra L. Armstrong, Associate Dean for Graduate Programs, 734-647-3027, Fax: 734-647-2808, E-mail: ketra@umich.edu. *Application contact:* Charlene F. Ruloff, Graduate Program Coordinator, 734-764-1343, Fax: 734-647-2808, E-mail: cruloff@umich.edu.
Website: http://www.kines.umich.edu/

University of Minnesota, Twin Cities Campus, Graduate School, College of Education and Human Development, School of Kinesiology, Minneapolis, MN 55455-0213. Offers kinesiology (MS, PhD), including behavioral aspects of physical activity, biomechanics and neuromotor control, exercise physiology, perceptual-motor control and learning, sport and exercise psychology, sport management (PhD), sport sociology; sport and exercise science (M Ed); sport management (M Ed, MA). *Program availability:* Part-time. *Faculty:* 16 full-time (7 women). *Students:* 111 full-time (52 women), 22 part-time (8 women); includes 21 minority (7 Black or African American, non-Hispanic/Latino; 1 American Indian or Alaska Native, non-Hispanic/Latino; 4 Asian, non-Hispanic/Latino; 7 Hispanic/Latino; 2 Two or more races, non-Hispanic/Latino), 15 international. Average age 27. 120 applicants, 25% accepted, 30 enrolled. In 2017, 41 master's, 9 doctorates awarded. Terminal master's awarded for partial completion of doctoral program. *Degree requirements:* For master's, final oral exam; for doctorate, thesis/dissertation, preliminary written/oral exam, final oral exam. *Entrance requirements:* For master's, GRE or MAT, minimum GPA of 3.0; for doctorate, GRE or MAT, minimum GPA of 3.0, writing sample. Application fee: $75 ($95 for international students). *Financial support:* In 2017–18, 2 fellowships, 9 research assistantships with full tuition reimbursements (averaging $6,651 per year), 41 teaching assistantships with full tuition reimbursements (averaging $14,060 per year) were awarded; career-related internships or fieldwork, Federal Work-Study, institutionally sponsored loans, and tuition waivers (full and partial) also available. Support available to part-time students. *Faculty research:* Role of physical activity in preventing health related problems; mechanism of age-related disorders, diseases and mental problems, and the ways to ameliorate them; role of sports in society and social justice; sports among populations with low income and racial diversity; fundamental functions of the body and the mechanism controlling the mechanisms; psychological issues related to physical activity and sports. *Total annual research expenditures:* $948,746. *Unit head:* Dr. Li Li Ji, Director, 612-624-9809, E-mail: llji@umn.edu. *Application contact:* Dr. Michael Wade, Director of Graduate Studies, 612-626-2094, E-mail: mwade@umn.edu.
Website: http://www.cehd.umn.edu/kin/

University of Mississippi, Graduate School, School of Applied Sciences, University, MS 38677. Offers communicative disorders (MS); criminal justice (MCJ); exercise science (MS); food and nutrition services (MS); health and kinesiology (PhD); health promotion (MS); nutrition and hospitality management (PhD); park and recreation management (MA); social welfare (PhD); social work (MSW). *Faculty:* 66 full-time (38 women), 33 part-time/adjunct (14 women). *Students:* 182 full-time (139 women), 41 part-time (27 women); includes 49 minority (41 Black or African American, non-Hispanic/Latino; 1 American Indian or Alaska Native, non-Hispanic/Latino; 3 Asian, non-Hispanic/Latino; 3 Hispanic/Latino; 1 Two or more races, non-Hispanic/Latino), 13 international. Average age 26. *Entrance requirements:* For master's, GRE General Test, minimum GPA of 3.0. Additional exam requirements/recommendations for international students: Required—TOEFL. *Application deadline:* For fall admission, 4/1 for domestic students; for spring admission, 10/1 for domestic students. Applications are processed on a rolling basis. Application fee: $50. Electronic applications accepted. *Financial support:* Scholarships/grants available. Financial award application deadline: 3/1; financial award applicants required to submit FAFSA. *Unit head:* Dr. Teresa C. Carithers, Dean, 662-915-1081, Fax: 662-915-5717, E-mail: applsci@olemiss.edu.

University of Nebraska at Omaha, Graduate Studies, College of Education, School of Health and Kinesiology, Omaha, NE 68182. Offers athletic training (MA); exercise science (PhD); health, physical education, and recreation (MA, MS). *Program availability:* Part-time, evening/weekend. *Degree requirements:* For master's, comprehensive exam, thesis (for some programs). *Entrance requirements:* For master's, GRE; entrance exam, minimum GPA of 3.0, official transcripts, statement of purpose, 2 letters of recommendation; for doctorate, GRE, minimum GPA of 3.2, official transcripts, statement of purpose, 3 letters of recommendation, resume, writing sample. Additional exam requirements/recommendations for international students: Required—TOEFL, IELTS, PTE. Electronic applications accepted.

University of Nevada, Las Vegas, Graduate College, School of Allied Health Sciences, Department of Kinesiology and Nutrition Sciences, Las Vegas, NV 89154-3034. Offers exercise physiology (MS); kinesiology (PhD); nutrition sciences (MS). *Program availability:* Part-time. *Faculty:* 10 full-time (5 women), 2 part-time/adjunct (1 woman). *Students:* 34 full-time (19 women), 11 part-time (4 women); includes 10 minority (2 Black or African American, non-Hispanic/Latino; 1 American Indian or Alaska Native, non-Hispanic/Latino; 2 Asian, non-Hispanic/Latino; 4 Hispanic/Latino; 1 Two or more races, non-Hispanic/Latino), 2 international. Average age 27. 54 applicants, 52% accepted, 17 enrolled. In 2017, 15 master's awarded. *Degree requirements:* For master's, thesis (for some programs), professional paper; for doctorate, comprehensive exam, thesis/dissertation. *Entrance requirements:* For master's, GRE General Test, bachelor's degree; statement of purpose; 2 letters of recommendation; for doctorate, GRE General Test (minimum 70th percentile on the Verbal section), master's degree/bachelor's degree with minimum GPA of 3.25; 3 letters of recommendation; statement of purpose; personal interview. Additional exam requirements/recommendations for international students: Required—TOEFL (minimum score 550 paper-based; 80 iBT), IELTS (minimum score 7). *Application deadline:* For fall admission, 6/15 for domestic and international students; for spring admission, 11/15 for domestic and international students. Application fee: $60 ($95 for international students). Electronic applications accepted. *Expenses:* $275 per credit, $850 per course, $7,969 per year resident, $22,157 per year non-resident, $7,094 non-resident fee (7 credits or more), $1,307 annual health insurance fee. *Financial support:* In 2017–18, 12 students received support, including 12 research assistantships with full and partial tuition reimbursements available (averaging $14,396 per year), 10 teaching assistantships with full and partial tuition reimbursements available (averaging $12,350 per year); institutionally sponsored loans, scholarships/grants, health care benefits, and unspecified assistantships also available. Financial award application deadline: 3/15; financial award applicants required to submit FAFSA. *Faculty research:* Biomechanics of gait, factors in motor skill acquisition and performance, nutritional supplements and performance, lipoprotein biochemistry, transcranial direct current stimulation. *Total annual research expenditures:*

$49,804. *Unit head:* Dr. Brian Schilling, Chair/Professor, 702-895-1130, Fax: 702-895-1500, E-mail: brian.schilling@unlv.edu. *Application contact:* Dr. James Navalta, Graduate Coordinator, 702-895-2344, E-mail: james.navalta@unlv.edu.

University of New Hampshire, Graduate School, College of Health and Human Services, Department of Kinesiology, Durham, NH 03824. Offers adapted physical education (Postbaccalaureate Certificate); kinesiology (MS); kinesiology and social work (MS). *Program availability:* Part-time. *Students:* 5 full-time (1 woman), 5 part-time (2 women), 1 international. Average age 28. 16 applicants, 56% accepted, 4 enrolled. In 2017, 10 master's awarded. *Entrance requirements:* For master's, GRE General Test. Additional exam requirements/recommendations for international students: Required—TOEFL (minimum score 550 paper-based; 80 iBT). *Application deadline:* For fall admission, 4/1 priority date for domestic students, 4/1 for international students; for spring admission, 12/1 for domestic students. Application fee: $65. Electronic applications accepted. *Financial support:* In 2017–18, 5 students received support, including 3 teaching assistantships; fellowships, research assistantships, career-related internships or fieldwork, Federal Work-Study, scholarships/grants, and tuition waivers (full and partial) also available. Support available to part-time students. Financial award application deadline: 2/15. *Unit head:* Karen Collins, Chair, 603-862-0361. *Application contact:* Jayson Seaman, Administrative Assistant, 603-862-1162, E-mail: kinesiology.dept@unh.edu.
Website: http://chhs.unh.edu/kin

University of North Alabama, College of Education, Department of Health, Physical Education, and Recreation, Florence, AL 35632-0001. Offers health and human performance (MS), including exercise science, kinesiology, wellness and health promotion. *Program availability:* Part-time. *Faculty:* 7 full-time (2 women), 1 part-time/adjunct (0 women). *Students:* 14 full-time (10 women), 14 part-time (6 women); includes 4 minority (all Black or African American, non-Hispanic/Latino), 3 international. Average age 25. 22 applicants, 82% accepted, 9 enrolled. In 2017, 7 master's awarded. *Degree requirements:* For master's, comprehensive exam (for some programs), thesis optional. *Entrance requirements:* For master's, MAT or GRE, 3 letters of recommendation, essay. Additional exam requirements/recommendations for international students: Required—TOEFL (minimum score 79 iBT), IELTS (minimum score 6), PTE (minimum score 54). *Application deadline:* Applications are processed on a rolling basis. Application fee: $50 ($100 for international students). Electronic applications accepted. *Expenses:* Tuition, state resident: full-time $7824; part-time $5943 per year. Tuition, nonresident: full-time $15,648; part-time $11,736 per year. *Required fees:* $3064; $2298 per unit. Tuition and fees vary according to course load and reciprocity agreements. *Financial support:* In 2017–18, 19 students received support. Federal Work-Study, scholarships/grants, and unspecified assistantships available. Financial award application deadline: 2/1; financial award applicants required to submit FAFSA. *Total annual research expenditures:* $13,976. *Unit head:* Dr. Thomas E. Coates, Chair, 256-765-4377. *Application contact:* Hillary N. Coats, Graduate Admissions Coordinator, 256-765-4447, E-mail: graduate@una.edu.
Website: https://www.una.edu/hper/index.html

The University of North Carolina at Chapel Hill, School of Medicine and Graduate School, Graduate Programs in Medicine, Department of Allied Health Sciences, Program in Human Movement Science, Chapel Hill, NC 27599. Offers PhD. *Entrance requirements:* Additional exam requirements/recommendations for international students: Required—TOEFL (minimum score 550 paper-based). Electronic applications accepted.

The University of North Carolina at Charlotte, College of Health and Human Services, Department of Kinesiology, Charlotte, NC 28223-0001. Offers kinesiology (MS); respiratory care (MS). *Program availability:* Part-time. *Faculty:* 14 full-time (7 women). *Students:* 31 full-time (19 women), 25 part-time (17 women); includes 12 minority (6 Black or African American, non-Hispanic/Latino; 5 Hispanic/Latino; 1 Two or more races, non-Hispanic/Latino), 2 international. Average age 26. 52 applicants, 85% accepted, 37 enrolled. In 2017, 19 master's awarded. *Degree requirements:* For master's, comprehensive exam, thesis (for some programs), thesis or practicum. *Entrance requirements:* For master's, GRE, minimum overall cumulative GPA of 3.0 in all college coursework, upper-division 3.25; demonstrated evidence of sufficient interest, ability, and preparation to adequately profit from graduate study. Additional exam requirements/recommendations for international students: Required—TOEFL (minimum score 523 paper-based, 70 iBT) or IELTS (6.5). *Application deadline:* For fall admission, 2/1 priority date for domestic and international students; for spring admission, 10/1 priority date for domestic and international students; for summer admission, 2/1 priority date for domestic and international students. Applications are processed on a rolling basis. Application fee: $75. Electronic applications accepted. *Expenses:* Tuition, state resident: full-time $4337. Tuition, nonresident: full-time $17,771. *Required fees:* $3211. Tuition and fees vary according to course load and program. *Financial support:* In 2017–18, 29 students received support, including 10 research assistantships (averaging $7,977 per year), 19 teaching assistantships (averaging $12,105 per year); career-related internships or fieldwork, institutionally sponsored loans, scholarships/grants, traineeships, and unspecified assistantships also available. Support available to part-time students. Financial award application deadline: 3/1; financial award applicants required to submit FAFSA. *Total annual research expenditures:* $169,220. *Unit head:* Dr. Vivian B. Lord, Interim Chair, 704-687-0752, E-mail: vblord@uncc.edu. *Application contact:* Kathy B. Giddings, Director of Graduate Admissions, 704-687-5503, Fax: 704-687-1668, E-mail: gradadm@uncc.edu.
Website: http://kinesiology.uncc.edu

The University of North Carolina at Greensboro, Graduate School, School of Health and Human Sciences, Department of Kinesiology, Greensboro, NC 27412-5001. Offers athletic training (MSAT); kinesiology (MS, Ed D, PhD). *Program availability:* Online learning. *Degree requirements:* For master's, thesis (for some programs); for doctorate, thesis/dissertation. *Entrance requirements:* For master's and doctorate, GRE General Test. Additional exam requirements/recommendations for international students: Required—TOEFL. Electronic applications accepted.

University of North Dakota, Graduate School, College of Education and Human Development, Department of Kinesiology and Public Health Education, Grand Forks, ND 58202. Offers kinesiology (MS). *Program availability:* Part-time. *Degree requirements:* For master's, thesis or alternative, final or comprehensive examination. *Entrance requirements:* For master's, GRE General Test, minimum GPA of 3.0. Additional exam requirements/recommendations for international students: Required—TOEFL (minimum score 550 paper-based; 79 iBT), IELTS (minimum score 6.5). Electronic applications accepted. *Faculty research:* Exercise physiology, exercise biomechanics, anatomy and physiology, exercise psychology.

University of Northern Iowa, Graduate College, College of Education, School of Kinesiology, Allied Health and Human Services, MA Program in Physical Education, Cedar Falls, IA 50614. Offers kinesiology (MA); teaching/coaching (MA). *Program availability:* Part-time, evening/weekend. *Degree requirements:* For master's, comprehensive exam, thesis or alternative. *Entrance requirements:* For master's, minimum GPA of 3.0. Additional exam requirements/recommendations for international students: Required—TOEFL (minimum score 500 paper-based; 61 iBT). Electronic applications accepted.

University of North Georgia, Program in Kinesiology, Dahlonega, GA 30597. Offers MS. *Program availability:* Part-time, evening/weekend, online only, 100% online. *Students:* 1 full-time (0 women), 33 part-time (19 women); includes 8 minority (6 Black or African American, non-Hispanic/Latino; 1 Asian, non-Hispanic/Latino; 1 Hispanic/Latino). Average age 26. *Degree requirements:* For master's, capstone course. *Entrance requirements:* For master's, GRE (minimum score of 301) or MAT (minimum score of 391), minimum baccalaureate GPA of 2.75, official transcripts, verification of lawful presence. Additional exam requirements/recommendations for international students: Required—TOEFL (minimum score 550 paper-based; 79 iBT), IELTS (minimum score 6.5). *Application deadline:* For summer admission, 5/20 priority date for domestic students. Application fee: $40. Electronic applications accepted. *Expenses:* Contact institution. *Financial support:* Application deadline: 3/17; applicants required to submit FAFSA. *Unit head:* Dr. Mitchum Parker, Coordinator, 706-864-1600, E-mail: coegrads@ung.edu. *Application contact:* Melinda Maxwell, Director of Graduate Admissions, 706-867-2077, E-mail: melinda.maxwell@ung.edu. Website: https://ung.edu/teacher-education/graduate/master-science-physical-education.php

University of North Texas, Robert B. Toulouse School of Graduate Studies, Denton, TX 76203-5459. Offers accounting (MS); applied anthropology (MA, MS); applied behavior analysis (Certificate); applied geography (MA); applied technology and performance improvement (M Ed, MS); art education (MA); art history (MA); art museum education (Certificate); arts leadership (Certificate); audiology (Au D); behavior analysis (MS); behavioral science (PhD); biochemistry and molecular biology (MS); biology (MA, MS); biomedical engineering (MS); business analysis (MS); chemistry (MS); clinical health psychology (PhD); communication studies (MA, MS); computer engineering (MS); computer science (MS); counseling (M Ed, MS), including clinical mental health counseling (MS), college and university counseling, elementary school counseling, secondary school counseling; creative writing (MA); criminal justice (MS); curriculum and instruction (M Ed); decision sciences (MBA); design (MA, MFA), including fashion design (MFA), innovation studies, interior design (MFA); early childhood studies (MS); economics (MS); educational leadership (M Ed, Ed D); educational psychology (MS, PhD), including family studies (MS), gifted and talented (MS), human development (MS), learning and cognition (MS), research, measurement and evaluation (MS); electrical engineering (MS); emergency management (MPA); engineering technology (MS); English (MA); English as a second language (MA); environmental science (MS); finance (MBA, MS); financial management (MPA); French (MA); health services management (MBA); higher education (M Ed, Ed D); history (MA, MS); hospitality management (MS); human resources management (MPA); information science (MS); information systems (PhD); information technologies (MBA); interdisciplinary studies (MA, MS); international studies (MA); international sustainable tourism (MS); jazz studies (MM); journalism (MA, MJ, Graduate Certificate), including interactive and virtual digital communication (Graduate Certificate), narrative journalism (Graduate Certificate), public relations (Graduate Certificate); kinesiology (MS); linguistics (MA); local government management (MPA); logistics (PhD); logistics and supply chain management (MBA); long-term care, senior housing, and aging services (MA); management (PhD); marketing (MBA); mathematics (MA, MS); mechanical and energy engineering (MS, PhD); music (MA), including ethnomusicology, music theory, musicology, performance; music composition (PhD); music education (MM Ed, PhD); nonprofit management (MPA); operations and supply chain management (MBA); performance (MM, DMA); philosophy (MA); political science (MA); professional and technical communication (MA); radio, television and film (MA, MFA); rehabilitation counseling (Certificate); sociology (MA); Spanish (MA); special education (M Ed); speech-language pathology (MA); strategic management (MBA); studio art (MFA); teaching (M Ed); MBA/MS. *Program availability:* Part-time, evening/weekend, online learning. Terminal master's awarded for partial completion of doctoral program. *Degree requirements:* For master's, variable foreign language requirement, comprehensive exam (for some programs), thesis (for some programs); for doctorate, variable foreign language requirement, comprehensive exam (for some programs), thesis/dissertation; for other advanced degree, variable foreign language requirement, comprehensive exam (for some programs). *Entrance requirements:* For master's and doctorate, GRE, GMAT. Additional exam requirements/recommendations for international students: Required—TOEFL (minimum score 550 paper-based; 79 iBT). Electronic applications accepted.

University of Ottawa, Faculty of Graduate and Postdoctoral Studies, Faculty of Health Sciences, School of Human Kinetics, Ottawa, ON K1N 6N5, Canada. Offers MA. *Degree requirements:* For master's, thesis or alternative. *Entrance requirements:* For master's, honors degree or equivalent, minimum B average. Electronic applications accepted. *Faculty research:* Psychosocial sciences, physical and health administration of sport and physical activity, intervention and consultation in sport, physical activity and health.

University of Puerto Rico–Mayagüez, Graduate Studies, College of Arts and Sciences, Department of Kinesiology, Mayagüez, PR 00681-9000. Offers kinesiology (MA), including biomechanics, education, exercise physiology, sports training. *Program availability:* Part-time. *Degree requirements:* For master's, thesis. *Entrance requirements:* For master's, EXADEP or GRE, minimum GPA of 2.5. Electronic applications accepted.

University of Regina, Faculty of Graduate Studies and Research, Faculty of Kinesiology and Health Studies, Regina, SK S4S 0A2, Canada. Offers M Sc, PhD. *Faculty:* 17 full-time (8 women), 29 part-time/adjunct (15 women). *Students:* 41 full-time (18 women), 15 part-time (8 women). 30 applicants, 53% accepted. In 2017, 3 master's, 2 doctorates awarded. *Degree requirements:* For master's, thesis; for doctorate, thesis/dissertation. *Entrance requirements:* For doctorate, writing sample. Additional exam requirements/recommendations for international students: Required—TOEFL (minimum score 580 paper-based; 80 iBT), IELTS (minimum score 6.5), PTE (minimum score 59). *Application deadline:* Applications are processed on a rolling basis. Application fee: $100. Electronic applications accepted. *Expenses:* CAD$10,681 per year (for M Sc); CAD$9,930 per year (for PhD). *Financial support:* In 2017–18, fellowships (averaging $6,750 per year), teaching assistantships (averaging $2,562 per year) were awarded; research assistantships and scholarships/grants also available. Financial award application deadline: 6/15. *Faculty research:* Social psychology of physical activity and health, social science of physical activity and recreation, recreation and leisure, sport management, exercise science. *Unit head:* Dr. Harold Riemer, Dean, 306-585-4131, Fax: 306-585-4854, E-mail: khs.dean@uregina.ca. *Application contact:* Dr. Darren Candow, Associate Dean, Graduate Studies and Research, 306-585-4906, Fax: 306-585-4854, E-mail: darren.candow@uregina.ca. Website: http://www.uregina.ca/kinesiology/

University of Saskatchewan, College of Graduate Studies and Research, College of Kinesiology, Saskatoon, SK S7N 5A2, Canada. Offers M Sc, PhD, Diploma. *Degree requirements:* For master's, thesis; for doctorate, thesis/dissertation. *Entrance requirements:* Additional exam requirements/recommendations for international students: Required—TOEFL.

University of South Alabama, College of Education and Professional Studies, Department of Health, Kinesiology, and Sport, Mobile, AL 36688. Offers exercise science (MS); health education (M Ed, MS); physical education (M Ed); sport management (MS). *Accreditation:* NCATE (one or more programs are accredited).

Program availability: Part-time. *Faculty:* 7 full-time (2 women). *Students:* 47 full-time (15 women), 7 part-time (3 women); includes 23 minority (19 Black or African American, non-Hispanic/Latino; 1 American Indian or Alaska Native, non-Hispanic/Latino; 2 Asian, non-Hispanic/Latino; 1 Hispanic/Latino), 4 international. Average age 25. 48 applicants, 54% accepted, 19 enrolled. In 2017, 23 master's awarded. *Degree requirements:* For master's, comprehensive exam, thesis optional. *Entrance requirements:* For master's, GRE General Test or MAT, Alabama Class B certificate or the equivalent (for students seeking the master's-level/Class A certification). Additional exam requirements/recommendations for international students: Required—TOEFL. *Application deadline:* For fall admission, 7/1 priority date for domestic students, 6/15 priority date for international students; for spring admission, 11/15 priority date for domestic students, 11/1 priority date for international students; for summer admission, 4/15 for domestic students, 4/1 for international students. Applications are processed on a rolling basis. Application fee: $35. Electronic applications accepted. *Expenses:* Tuition, state resident: full-time $10,104; part-time $421 per semester hour. Tuition, nonresident: full-time $20,208; part-time $842 per semester hour. *Financial support:* Fellowships, research assistantships, teaching assistantships with partial tuition reimbursements, career-related internships or fieldwork, Federal Work-Study, institutionally sponsored loans, scholarships/grants, and unspecified assistantships available. Support available to part-time students. Financial award application deadline: 3/31; financial award applicants required to submit FAFSA. *Unit head:* Dr. John Kovaleski, Department Chair, 251-461-1622, Fax: 251-460-7252, E-mail: jkovales@southalabama.edu. *Application contact:* Dr. Susan Santoli, Director of Graduate Studies, 251-380-2836, Fax: 251-380-2748, E-mail: ssantoli@southalabama.edu. Website: http://www.southalabama.edu/colleges/ceps/hks/index.html

University of South Dakota, Graduate School, School of Education, Division of Kinesiology and Sport Management, Vermillion, SD 57069. Offers exercise science (MA); sport management (MA). *Accreditation:* NCATE. *Program availability:* Part-time. *Degree requirements:* For master's, comprehensive exam, thesis or alternative. *Entrance requirements:* For master's, GRE General Test, MAT, minimum GPA of 3.0. Additional exam requirements/recommendations for international students: Required—TOEFL (minimum score 550 paper-based; 79 iBT). *Application deadline:* Applications are processed on a rolling basis. Application fee: $35. Electronic applications accepted. *Financial support:* Research assistantships with partial tuition reimbursements, teaching assistantships with partial tuition reimbursements, Federal Work-Study, and unspecified assistantships available. Financial award applicants required to submit FAFSA. *Application contact:* Graduate School, 605-658-6140, Fax: 605-677-6118, E-mail: grad@usd.edu. Website: http://www.usd.edu/ksm

University of Southern California, Graduate School, Herman Ostrow School of Dentistry, Division of Biokinesiology and Physical Therapy, Los Angeles, CA 90089. Offers biokinesiology (MS, PhD); physical therapy (DPT). *Accreditation:* APTA (one or more programs are accredited). *Degree requirements:* For master's, comprehensive exam; for doctorate, thesis/dissertation. *Entrance requirements:* For master's and doctorate, GRE (minimum combined score 1200, verbal 600, quantitative 600). Additional exam requirements/recommendations for international students: Required—TOEFL. Electronic applications accepted. *Expenses:* Contact institution. *Faculty research:* Exercise and aging biomechanics, musculoskeletal biomechanics, exercise and hormones related to muscle wasting, computational neurorehabilitation, motor behavior and neurorehabilitation, motor development, infant motor performance.

The University of Tennessee, Graduate School, College of Education, Health and Human Sciences, Department of Exercise, Sport, and Leisure Studies, Program in Exercise Science, Knoxville, TN 37996. Offers biomechanics/sports medicine (MS, PhD); exercise physiology (MS, PhD). *Accreditation:* CEPH (one or more programs are accredited). *Program availability:* Part-time. *Degree requirements:* For master's, thesis optional. *Entrance requirements:* For master's, minimum GPA of 2.7. Additional exam requirements/recommendations for international students: Required—TOEFL. Electronic applications accepted.

The University of Texas at Arlington, Graduate School, College of Nursing and Health Innovation, Arlington, TX 76019. Offers athletic training (MS); exercise science (MS); kinesiology (PhD); nurse practitioner (MSN); nursing (PhD); nursing administration (MSN); nursing education (MSN); nursing practice (DNP). *Accreditation:* AACN. *Program availability:* Part-time, evening/weekend, online learning. *Degree requirements:* For master's, practicum course; for doctorate, comprehensive exam (for some programs), thesis/dissertation (for some programs), proposal defense dissertation (for PhD); scholarship project (for DNP). *Entrance requirements:* For master's, GRE General Test if GPA less than 3.0, minimum GPA of 3.0, Texas nursing license, minimum C grade in undergraduate statistics course; for doctorate, GRE General Test (waived for MSN-to-PhD applicants), minimum undergraduate, graduate and statistics GPA of 3.0; Texas RN license; interview; written statement of goals. Additional exam requirements/recommendations for international students: Required—TOEFL (minimum score 550 paper-based), IELTS (minimum score 7). *Faculty research:* Simulation in clinical education and practice, cultural diversity, vulnerable populations, substance abuse.

The University of Texas at Austin, Graduate School, College of Education, Department of Kinesiology and Health Education, Austin, TX 78712-1111. Offers behavioral health (PhD); exercise and sport psychology (M Ed, MA); exercise science (M Ed, MS, PhD); health education (M Ed, MS, Ed D, PhD). *Program availability:* Part-time. Terminal master's awarded for partial completion of doctoral program. *Degree requirements:* For master's, thesis (for some programs); for doctorate, thesis/dissertation. *Entrance requirements:* For master's and doctorate, GRE General Test. Additional exam requirements/recommendations for international students: Required—TOEFL. Electronic applications accepted. *Faculty research:* Health promotion, human performance and exercise biochemistry, motor behavior and biomechanics, sport management, aging and pediatric development.

The University of Texas at El Paso, Graduate School, College of Health Sciences, Department of Kinesiology, El Paso, TX 79968-0001. Offers MS. *Program availability:* Part-time, evening/weekend, online learning. *Degree requirements:* For master's, thesis optional. *Entrance requirements:* For master's, GRE. Additional exam requirements/recommendations for international students: Required—TOEFL; Recommended—IELTS. Electronic applications accepted.

The University of Texas at San Antonio, College of Education and Human Development, Department of Kinesiology, Health, and Nutrition, San Antonio, TX 78249-0617. Offers health and kinesiology (MS). *Program availability:* Part-time, evening/weekend. *Faculty:* 10 full-time (4 women), 1 (woman) part-time/adjunct. *Students:* 68 full-time (41 women), 42 part-time (22 women); includes 76 minority (11 Black or African American, non-Hispanic/Latino; 7 Asian, non-Hispanic/Latino; 56 Hispanic/Latino; 2 Two or more races, non-Hispanic/Latino), 1 international. Average age 27. 67 applicants, 78% accepted, 25 enrolled. In 2017, 56 master's awarded. *Degree requirements:* For master's, comprehensive exam, thesis optional. *Entrance requirements:* For master's, bachelor's degree with minimum GPA of 3.0 in last 60 hours of coursework; resume; statement of purpose; two letters of recommendation. Additional exam requirements/recommendations for international students: Required—TOEFL (minimum score 550 paper-based; 79 iBT), IELTS (minimum score 6.5). *Application deadline:* For fall

Kinesiology and Movement Studies

admission, 6/15 for domestic students, 3/1 for international students; for spring admission, 10/15 for domestic students, 9/15 for international students; for summer admission, 4/15 for domestic students, 2/15 for international students. Applications are processed on a rolling basis. Application fee: $50 ($90 for international students). Electronic applications accepted. *Expenses:* Contact institution. *Financial support:* Unspecified assistantships available. Financial award applicants required to submit FAFSA. *Faculty research:* Childhood obesity, health disparities, community health, exercise physiology, sport psychology. *Total annual research expenditures:* $767,220. *Unit head:* Dr. Sara Oswalt, Chair, 210-458-6227, E-mail: sara.oswalt@utsa.edu. Website: http://education.utsa.edu/health_and_kinesiology

The University of Texas at Tyler, College of Nursing and Health Sciences, Department of Health and Kinesiology, Tyler, TX 75799-0001. Offers health and kinesiology (M Ed, MA); health sciences (MS); kinesiology (MS). *Accreditation:* TEAC. *Program availability:* Part-time, online learning. *Degree requirements:* For master's, comprehensive exam (for some programs), thesis (for some programs). *Entrance requirements:* Additional exam requirements/recommendations for international students: Required—TOEFL. Electronic applications accepted. *Faculty research:* Osteoporosis, muscle soreness, economy of locomotion, adoption of rehabilitation programs, effect of inactivity and aging on muscle blood vessels, territoriality.

The University of Texas of the Permian Basin, Office of Graduate Studies, College of Arts and Sciences, Department of Kinesiology, Odessa, TX 79762-0001. Offers MS. *Program availability:* Part-time, evening/weekend, online learning. *Degree requirements:* For master's, comprehensive exam (for some programs), thesis (for some programs). *Entrance requirements:* For master's, GRE General Test, minimum GPA of 2.5. Additional exam requirements/recommendations for international students: Required—TOEFL (minimum score 550 paper-based).

The University of Texas Rio Grande Valley, College of Health Affairs, Department of Health and Human Performance, Edinburg, TX 78539. Offers exercise science (MS); kinesiology (MS). *Program availability:* Part-time-only, evening/weekend, 100% online. *Faculty:* 13 full-time (5 women), 2 part-time/adjunct (0 women). *Students:* 8 full-time (4 women), 32 part-time (10 women); includes 33 minority (1 Black or African American, non-Hispanic/Latino; 32 Hispanic/Latino), 3 international. Average age 25. 27 applicants, 96% accepted, 25 enrolled. In 2017, 18 master's awarded. *Degree requirements:* For master's, comprehensive exam, thesis optional. *Entrance requirements:* For master's, GRE, minimum GPA of 3.0 in last 60 hours. Additional exam requirements/recommendations for international students: Required—TOEFL (minimum score 550 paper-based; 79 iBT), IELTS (minimum score 6.5). *Application deadline:* For fall admission, 7/17 for domestic students; for spring admission, 11/16 for domestic students. Applications are processed on a rolling basis. Application fee: $50. Electronic applications accepted. *Expenses:* Tuition, state resident: full-time $5550; part-time $417 per credit hour. Tuition, nonresident: full-time $13,020; part-time $832 per credit hour. *Required fees:* $1169. *Financial support:* In 2017–18, 8 students received support, including 6 research assistantships (averaging $5,000 per year); unspecified assistantships also available. Financial award application deadline: 4/15; financial award applicants required to submit FAFSA. *Faculty research:* Physiology of exercise, fitness levels, Mexican American children, nutrition, diabetes prevention. *Unit head:* Dr. Zelma D. Mata, Chair, 956-665-3501, Fax: 956-665-3502, E-mail: zelma.mata@utrgv.edu. *Application contact:* Dr. Murat Karabulut, Associate Professor and Graduate Program Coordinator, 956-882-8290, E-mail: murat.karabulut@utrgv.edu. Website: http://www.utrgv.edu/hhp/

University of the Incarnate Word, Ila Faye Miller School of Nursing and Health Professions, San Antonio, TX 78209-6397. Offers kinesiology (MS); nursing (MSN, DNP); sport management (MS). *Program availability:* Part-time, evening/weekend. *Faculty:* 18 full-time (14 women). *Students:* 48 full-time (26 women), 75 part-time (62 women); includes 86 minority (22 Black or African American, non-Hispanic/Latino; 1 American Indian or Alaska Native, non-Hispanic/Latino; 8 Asian, non-Hispanic/Latino; 53 Hispanic/Latino; 2 Two or more races, non-Hispanic/Latino), 3 international. In 2017, 31 master's, 10 doctorates awarded. *Degree requirements:* For master's, comprehensive exam (for some programs), thesis or alternative, capstone. *Entrance requirements:* For master's, GRE General Test, MAT, baccalaureate degree in ACEN- or CCNE-accredited nursing program with health assessment and statistics; minimum cumulative GPA of 2.5 (3.0 in upper-division courses); three professional references; Texas State license or multi-state compact. Additional exam requirements/recommendations for international students: Required—TOEFL (minimum score 560 paper-based; 83 iBT). *Application deadline:* Applications are processed on a rolling basis. Application fee: $20. Electronic applications accepted. *Expenses:* $905 per credit hour (for DNP); $915 per credit hour (for master's-level prograrns). *Financial support:* Research assistantships, Federal Work-Study, scholarships/grants, tuition waivers (partial), and unspecified assistantships available. Financial award applicants required to submit FAFSA. *Faculty research:* Pediatric oncology, military pregnancy and the family, diabetes prevention, substance abuse and addictions, nursing of vulnerable populations. *Unit head:* Dr. Mary Hoke, Dean, 210-829-3982, Fax: 210-829-3174, E-mail: mhoke@uiwtx.edu. *Application contact:* Johnny Garcia, Graduate Admissions Counselor, 210-805-3554, Fax: 210-829-3921, E-mail: admis@uiwtx.edu. Website: http://uiw.edu/snhp/

University of Toronto, School of Graduate Studies, Faculty of Kinesiology and Physical Education, Toronto, ON M5S 1A1, Canada. Offers M Sc, PhD. *Degree requirements:* For master's, thesis, oral defense of thesis; for doctorate, comprehensive exam, defense of thesis. *Entrance requirements:* For master's, background in physical education and health, minimum B+ average in final year of undergraduate study, 2 letters of reference, resume, 2 writing samples; for doctorate, master's degree with successful defense of thesis, background in exercise sciences, minimum A- average, 2 letters of reference. Additional exam requirements/recommendations for international students: Required—TOEFL (minimum score 580 paper-based; 93 iBT), TWE (minimum score 5). Electronic applications accepted.

The University of Tulsa, Graduate School, Oxley College of Health Sciences, Department of Kinesiology and Rehabilitative Sciences, Tulsa, OK 74104-3189. Offers MAT. Summer enrollment only. *Faculty:* 10 full-time (4 women), 7 part-time/adjunct (2 women). *Students:* 5 full-time (2 women), 2 part-time (1 woman), 4 international. Average age 24. 1 applicant, 100% accepted, 1 enrolled. *Entrance requirements:* For master's, GRE General Test. Additional exam requirements/recommendations for international students: Required—TOEFL (minimum score 577 paper-based; 90 iBT), IELTS (minimum score 6.5). Application fee: $55. *Expenses:* $800 per credit hour tuition. *Financial support:* Applicants required to submit FAFSA. *Unit head:* Robin Ploeger, Interim Dean, 918-631-3170, E-mail: robin-ploeger@utulsa.edu. *Application contact:* Dr. Rachel Hildebrand, Program Advisor, 918-631-3204, Fax: 918-631-2156, E-mail: rachel-hildebrand@utulsa.edu. Website: https://healthsciences.utulsa.edu/departments-schools/athletic-training/graduate-program/

University of Utah, Graduate School, College of Health, Department of Health, Kinesiology, and Recreation, Salt Lake City, UT 84112. Offers kinesiology (MS, PhD); parks, recreation, and tourism (MS, PhD). *Program availability:* Part-time. *Faculty:* 7 full-time (4 women), 4 part-time/adjunct (0 women). *Students:* 92 full-time (58 women), 44 part-time (23 women); includes 21 minority (1 Black or African American, non-Hispanic/Latino; 1 American Indian or Alaska Native, non-Hispanic/Latino; 5 Asian, non-Hispanic/Latino; 10 Hispanic/Latino; 2 Native Hawaiian or other Pacific Islander, non-Hispanic/Latino; 2 Two or more races, non-Hispanic/Latino), 10 international. Average age 24. 24 applicants, 58% accepted, 8 enrolled. In 2017, 34 master's, 4 doctorates awarded. Terminal master's awarded for partial completion of doctoral program. *Degree requirements:* For master's, comprehensive exam, thesis or alternative; for doctorate, comprehensive exam, thesis/dissertation. *Entrance requirements:* For master's and doctorate, GRE General Test, minimum GPA of 3.0. Additional exam requirements/recommendations for international students: Required—TOEFL (minimum score 500 paper-based). *Application deadline:* For fall admission, 1/15 priority date for domestic and international students. Application fee: $55 ($65 for international students). Electronic applications accepted. *Expenses:* Contact institution. *Financial support:* In 2017–18, 13 students received support, including 3 research assistantships with full tuition reimbursements available, 8 teaching assistantships with full tuition reimbursements available; career-related internships or fieldwork, scholarships/grants, health care benefits, and unspecified assistantships also available. Financial award application deadline: 1/15; financial award applicants required to submit FAFSA. *Faculty research:* Community and sport, outdoor recreation, protected area management, sustainable tourism and youth development. *Total annual research expenditures:* $300,000. *Unit head:* Dr. Kelly S. Bricker, Program Director, 801-585-6503, E-mail: kelly.bricker@health.utah.edu. *Application contact:* Dr. Jim Sibthorp, Director of Graduate Studies, 801-581-5940, Fax: 801-581-4930, E-mail: jim.sibthorp@health.utah.edu. Website: http://www.health.utah.edu/prt/

University of Victoria, Faculty of Graduate Studies, Faculty of Education, School of Exercise Science, Physical, and Health Education, Victoria, BC V8W 2Y2, Canada. Offers coaching studies (co-operative education) (M Ed); kinesiology (M Sc, MA); leisure service administration (MA); physical education (MA). *Program availability:* Part-time. *Degree requirements:* For master's, comprehensive exam (for some programs), thesis (for some programs). *Entrance requirements:* For master's, minimum B average. Additional exam requirements/recommendations for international students: Required—TOEFL (minimum score 575 paper-based), IELTS (minimum score 7). Electronic applications accepted. *Faculty research:* Children and exercise, mental skills in sports, teaching effectiveness, neural control of human movement, physical performance and health.

University of Virginia, Curry School of Education, Department of Kinesiology, Charlottesville, VA 22903. Offers M Ed, MS, PhD. *Faculty:* 13 full-time (4 women). *Students:* 48 full-time (27 women), 6 part-time (4 women); includes 10 minority (3 Black or African American, non-Hispanic/Latino; 2 Asian, non-Hispanic/Latino; 3 Hispanic/Latino; 2 Two or more races, non-Hispanic/Latino), 2 international. Average age 25. 26 applicants, 81% accepted, 15 enrolled. In 2017, 46 master's awarded. *Entrance requirements:* For master's and doctorate, GRE General Test, 2 letters of recommendation. Additional exam requirements/recommendations for international students: Required—TOEFL (minimum score 600 paper-based; 90 iBT), IELTS (minimum score 7). *Application deadline:* Applications are processed on a rolling basis. Application fee: $60. Electronic applications accepted. *Financial support:* Applicants required to submit FAFSA. *Unit head:* Arthur L. Weltman, Chair, Kinesiology, 434-924-6191, E-mail: alw2v@virginia.edu. *Application contact:* E-mail: curry-admissions@virginia.edu. Website: http://curry.virginia.edu/academics/department/kinesiology

University of Virginia, Curry School of Education, Program in Education, Charlottesville, VA 22903. Offers administration and supervision (PhD); applied developmental science (PhD); counselor education (PhD); curriculum and instruction (PhD); early childhood special education (MT); education evaluation (PhD); educational psychology (PhD); educational research (PhD); elementary education (MT); English education (MT, PhD); foreign language education (MT); higher education (PhD); instructional technology (PhD); kinesiology (MT, PhD); math education (PhD); reading education (PhD); research, statistics and evaluation (PhD); school psychology (PhD); science education (PhD); social studies education (MT, PhD); special education (PhD); world languages education (MT). *Students:* 431 full-time (353 women), 15 part-time (14 women); includes 100 minority (32 Black or African American, non-Hispanic/Latino; 33 Asian, non-Hispanic/Latino; 16 Hispanic/Latino; 19 Two or more races, non-Hispanic/Latino), 14 international. Average age 25. 264 applicants, 49% accepted, 83 enrolled. In 2017, 142 master's, 33 doctorates awarded. *Degree requirements:* For master's, comprehensive exam (for some programs), field project; for doctorate, comprehensive exam, thesis/dissertation. *Entrance requirements:* For doctorate, GRE General Test. Additional exam requirements/recommendations for international students: Required—TOEFL (minimum score 600 paper-based; 90 iBT), IELTS (minimum score 7). *Application deadline:* Applications are processed on a rolling basis. Application fee: $60. Electronic applications accepted. *Financial support:* Fellowships, research assistantships, and teaching assistantships available. Financial award application deadline: 1/5; financial award applicants required to submit FAFSA. *Unit head:* Robert C. Pianta, Dean, 434-924-3334, E-mail: pianta@virginia.edu. *Application contact:* E-mail: curry-admissions@virginia.edu. Website: http://curry.virginia.edu/teacher-education

University of Waterloo, Graduate Studies, Faculty of Applied Health Sciences, Department of Kinesiology, Waterloo, ON N2L 3G1, Canada. Offers M Sc, PhD. *Program availability:* Part-time. *Degree requirements:* For master's, thesis; for doctorate, comprehensive exam, thesis/dissertation. *Entrance requirements:* For master's, honors degree, minimum B average, writing sample; for doctorate, GRE (recommended), master's degree, minimum B average, writing sample. Additional exam requirements/recommendations for international students: Required—TOEFL, IELTS, PTE. Electronic applications accepted. *Faculty research:* Work physiology, biomechanics and neural control of human movement, psychomotor learning and performance, aging, health and well-being, work and health.

The University of Western Ontario, Faculty of Graduate Studies, Health Sciences Division, School of Kinesiology, London, ON N6A 5B8, Canada. Offers M Sc, MA, PhD. *Degree requirements:* For master's, thesis optional; for doctorate, comprehensive exam, thesis/dissertation. *Entrance requirements:* For doctorate, MA in physical education or kinesiology. Additional exam requirements/recommendations for international students: Required—Michigan English Language Assessment Battery, TOEFL or IELTS. *Faculty research:* Exercise physiology/biochemistry, sports injuries, sport psychology, sport history, sport philosophy.

University of Windsor, Faculty of Graduate Studies, Faculty of Human Kinetics, Windsor, ON N9B 3P4, Canada. Offers MHK. *Program availability:* Part-time. *Degree requirements:* For master's, thesis optional. *Entrance requirements:* For master's, minimum B average. Additional exam requirements/recommendations for international students: Required—TOEFL (minimum score 600 paper-based). Electronic applications accepted. *Faculty research:* Movement sciences, sport and lifestyle management, historical and sociological studies of sport.

University of Wisconsin–Madison, Graduate School, School of Education, Department of Kinesiology, Madison, WI 53706-1380. Offers kinesiology (MS, PhD);

occupational therapy (MS, PhD). *Accreditation:* AOTA. *Degree requirements:* For doctorate, thesis/dissertation. *Entrance requirements:* For master's and doctorate, GRE General Test. Electronic applications accepted.

University of Wisconsin–Milwaukee, Graduate School, College of Health Sciences, Department of Kinesiology, Milwaukee, WI 53201-0413. Offers athletic training (MS); kinesiology (MS, PhD), including exercise and nutrition in health and disease (MS), integrative human performance (MS), neuromechanics (MS); physical therapy (DPT). *Program availability:* Part-time. *Students:* 100 full-time (60 women), 16 part-time (9 women); includes 11 minority (1 Black or African American, non-Hispanic/Latino; 1 American Indian or Alaska Native, non-Hispanic/Latino; 9 Two or more races, non-Hispanic/Latino), 3 international. Average age 27. 36 applicants, 42% accepted, 5 enrolled. In 2017, 2 master's awarded. *Degree requirements:* For master's, comprehensive exam, thesis optional. *Entrance requirements:* For master's, GRE General Test. Additional exam requirements/recommendations for international students: Required—TOEFL (minimum score 550 paper-based; 79 iBT), IELTS (minimum score 6.5). *Application deadline:* For fall admission, 1/1 priority date for domestic students; for spring admission, 9/1 for domestic students. Applications are processed on a rolling basis. Application fee: $56 ($96 for international students). *Financial support:* Fellowships, research assistantships, teaching assistantships, career-related internships or fieldwork, unspecified assistantships, and project assistantships available. Support available to part-time students. Financial award application deadline: 4/15. *Unit head:* Dr. Kyle T. Ebersole, Department Chair, 414-229-6717, Fax: 414-229-3366, E-mail: ebersole@uwm.edu. *Application contact:* Stephen C. Cobb, Graduate Program Coordinator, 414-229-3369, Fax: 414-229-3366, E-mail: cobbsc@uwm.edu.
Website: http://uwm.edu/healthsciences/academics/kinesiology/

University of Wisconsin–Milwaukee, Graduate School, College of Health Sciences, Program in Health Sciences, Milwaukee, WI 53201-0413. Offers health sciences (PhD), including diagnostic and biomedical sciences, disability and rehabilitation, health administration and policy, human movement sciences, population health. *Students:* 17 full-time (10 women), 7 part-time (4 women); includes 6 minority (1 Black or African American, non-Hispanic/Latino; 3 Asian, non-Hispanic/Latino; 2 Two or more races, non-Hispanic/Latino), 11 international. Average age 33. 7 applicants, 43% accepted, 3 enrolled. In 2017, 1 doctorate awarded. *Degree requirements:* For doctorate, comprehensive exam, thesis/dissertation. *Entrance requirements:* For doctorate, GRE. Additional exam requirements/recommendations for international students: Required—TOEFL (minimum score 600 paper-based), IELTS (minimum score 6.5). Application fee: $56 ($96 for international students). *Financial support:* Fellowships, research assistantships, teaching assistantships, and project assistantships available. *Application contact:* Susan Cashin, PhD, Assistant Dean, 414-229-3303, E-mail: scashin@uwm.edu.
Website: http://uwm.edu/healthsciences/academics/phd-health-sciences/

University of Wyoming, College of Health Sciences, Division of Kinesiology and Health, Laramie, WY 82071. Offers MS. *Accreditation:* NCATE. *Program availability:* Part-time, online learning. *Degree requirements:* For master's, comprehensive exam (for some programs), thesis (for some programs). *Entrance requirements:* For master's, GRE General Test, minimum GPA of 3.0. Additional exam requirements/recommendations for international students: Required—TOEFL. Electronic applications accepted. *Faculty research:* Teacher effectiveness, effects of exercising on heart function, physiological responses of overtraining, psychological benefits of physical activity, health behavior.

Utah State University, School of Graduate Studies, Emma Eccles Jones College of Education and Human Services, Department of Kinesiology and Health Science, Logan, UT 84322. Offers fitness promotion (MS); health and human movement (MS); pathokinesiology (PhD); physical and sport eductaion (M Ed); public health (MPH). *Program availability:* Part-time, evening/weekend, online learning. *Degree requirements:* For master's, thesis (for some programs). *Entrance requirements:* For master's, GRE General Test or MAT, minimum GPA of 3.0. Additional exam requirements/recommendations for international students: Required—TOEFL. *Faculty research:* Sport psychology intervention, motor learning biomechanics, pedagogy, physiology.

Washington University in St. Louis, School of Medicine, Interdisciplinary Program in Movement Science, St. Louis, MO 63130-4899. Offers PhD. *Degree requirements:* For doctorate, thesis/dissertation. *Entrance requirements:* For doctorate, GRE General Test. Electronic applications accepted.

Wayne State University, College of Education, Division of Kinesiology, Health and Sports Studies, Detroit, MI 48202. Offers athletic training (MSAT); health education (M Ed); kinesiology (M Ed, PhD), including exercise and sport science (PhD), physical education and physical activity leadership (PhD); sports administration (MA). *Program availability:* Part-time, 100% online. *Faculty:* 9. *Students:* 65 full-time (33 women), 109 part-time (56 women); includes 70 minority (59 Black or African American, non-Hispanic/Latino; 3 Hispanic/Latino; 8 Two or more races, non-Hispanic/Latino), 8 international. Average age 30. 182 applicants, 53% accepted, 56 enrolled. In 2017, 62 master's, 3 doctorates awarded. *Degree requirements:* For master's, thesis (for some programs); for doctorate, thesis/dissertation. *Entrance requirements:* For master's, minimum undergraduate GPA of 3.0; undergraduate degree directly relating to the field of specialization being applied for or one accompanied by extensive educational background in closely-related field; teaching certificates in specific areas (for some

programs); for doctorate, minimum undergraduate GPA of 3.0; undergraduate degree directly relating to the field of specialization being applied for or one accompanied by extensive educational background in closely-related field. Additional exam requirements/recommendations for international students: Required—TOEFL (minimum score 79 iBT), TWE (minimum score 5.5); Recommended—IELTS (minimum score 6.5). *Application deadline:* For fall admission, 6/1 priority date for domestic students, 5/1 priority date for international students; for winter admission, 10/1 priority date for domestic students, 9/1 priority date for international students; for spring admission, 2/1 priority date for domestic students, 1/1 priority date for international students. Application fee: $50. Electronic applications accepted. *Expenses:* Contact institution. *Financial support:* In 2017–18, 47 students received support, including 6 research assistantships with tuition reimbursements available (averaging $18,534 per year), 5 teaching assistantships with tuition reimbursements available (averaging $18,534 per year); fellowships with tuition reimbursements available, scholarships/grants, health care benefits, and unspecified assistantships also available. Support available to part-time students. Financial award applicants required to submit FAFSA. *Faculty research:* Exercise and sport science, nutrition and physical activity interventions, school and community health, obesity prevention. *Unit head:* Dr. Nate McCaughtry, Assistant Dean, Division of Kinesiology, Health and Sport Studies/Director, Center for School Health, 313-577-0014, Fax: 313-577-5002, E-mail: aj4391@wayne.edu. *Application contact:* 313-577-4249, E-mail: askcoe@wayne.edu.
Website: http://coe.wayne.edu/kinesiology/index.php

West Chester University of Pennsylvania, College of Health Sciences, Department of Kinesiology, West Chester, PA 19383. Offers adapted physical education (Certificate); exercise and sport physiology (MS), including athletic training; sport management and athletics (MPA), including administration. *Program availability:* Part-time, evening/weekend, blended/hybrid learning. *Students:* 44 full-time (24 women), 12 part-time (3 women); includes 5 minority (2 Black or African American, non-Hispanic/Latino; 2 Hispanic/Latino; 1 Two or more races, non-Hispanic/Latino), 1 international. Average age 25. 68 applicants, 87% accepted, 29 enrolled. In 2017, 13 master's, 14 other advanced degrees awarded. *Degree requirements:* For master's, thesis or research report (for MS); two internships and capstone course that includes a research project or thesis (for MPA); for Certificate, six courses of study. *Entrance requirements:* For master's, GRE (for MS), 2 letters of recommendation, statement of professional goals; transcripts (for MS); two letters of reference, career goals, resume (for MPA); for Certificate, two letters of recommendation, transcript. Additional exam requirements/recommendations for international students: Required—TOEFL or IELTS. *Application deadline:* For fall admission, 5/15 for international students; for spring admission, 10/15 for international students. Applications are processed on a rolling basis. Application fee: $50. Electronic applications accepted. *Expenses:* Tuition, state resident: full-time $9000; part-time $500 per credit. Tuition, nonresident: full-time $13,500; part-time $750 per credit. *Required fees:* $2959; $149.79 per credit. *Financial support:* Scholarships/grants and unspecified assistantships available. Financial award application deadline: 2/15; financial award applicants required to submit FAFSA. *Faculty research:* Metabolism during exercise, biomechanics, rating of perceived exertion, motor learning, environmental physiology. *Unit head:* Dr. W. Craig Stevens, Chair, 610-436-2610, Fax: 610-436-2860, E-mail: cstevens@wcpua.edu. *Application contact:* Office of Graduate Studies and Extended Education, 610-436-2943, Fax: 610-436-2763, E-mail: gradstudy@wcupa.edu.
Website: http://www.wcupa.edu/healthsciences/kinesiology/

Western Illinois University, School of Graduate Studies, College of Education and Human Services, Department of Kinesiology, Program in Kinesiology, Macomb, IL 61455-1390. Offers MS. *Program availability:* Part-time. *Entrance requirements:* For master's, minimum GPA of 3.0. Additional exam requirements/recommendations for international students: Required—TOEFL (minimum score 550 paper-based; 80 iBT). *Application deadline:* Applications are processed on a rolling basis. Application fee: $30. Electronic applications accepted. *Financial support:* Teaching assistantships with full tuition reimbursements and unspecified assistantships available. Financial award applicants required to submit FAFSA. *Unit head:* Coordinator, 309-298-1981, E-mail: c-piletic@wiu.edu. *Application contact:* Dr. Nancy Parsons, Associate Provost and Director of Graduate Studies, 309-298-1806, Fax: 309-298-2345, E-mail: grad-office@wiu.edu.
Website: http://www.wiu.edu/coehs/kinesiology/graduate_programs/kin/

Wilfrid Laurier University, Faculty of Graduate and Postdoctoral Studies, Faculty of Science, Department of Kinesiology and Physical Education, Waterloo, ON N2L 3C5, Canada. Offers physical activity and health (M Sc). *Degree requirements:* For master's, thesis. *Entrance requirements:* For master's, honours degree in kinesiology, health, physical education with a minimum B+ in kinesiology and health-related courses. Additional exam requirements/recommendations for international students: Required—TOEFL (minimum score 89 iBT). Electronic applications accepted. *Faculty research:* Biomechanics, health, exercise physiology, motor control, sport psychology.

York University, Faculty of Graduate Studies, Faculty of Health, Program in Kinesiology and Health Science, Toronto, ON M3J 1P3, Canada. Offers M Sc, MA, PhD. *Program availability:* Part-time. *Degree requirements:* For master's, thesis or alternative; for doctorate, comprehensive exam, thesis/dissertation. Electronic applications accepted.

Physical Education

Adams State University, Office of Graduate Studies, Department of Human Performance and Physical Education, Alamosa, CO 81101. Offers human performance and physical education (MA, MS), including applied sport psychology, coaching (MA), exercise science (MA), sport management (MA). *Program availability:* Part-time. *Entrance requirements:* For master's, GRE General Test or MAT, minimum undergraduate GPA of 2.75. *Application deadline:* For fall admission, 5/15 priority date for domestic students; for spring admission, 10/15 for domestic students. Applications are processed on a rolling basis. Application fee: $30. *Expenses:* Tuition, state resident: full-time $4800; part-time $2400 per credit. Tuition, nonresident: full-time $7100; part-time $3550 per credit. *Required fees:* $213; $106 per credit. One-time fee: $100. Tuition and fees vary according to campus/location and program. *Financial support:* In 2017–18, fellowships with partial tuition reimbursements (averaging $4,000 per year), teaching assistantships with partial tuition reimbursements (averaging $4,000 per year) were awarded; career-related internships or fieldwork, Federal Work-Study, institutionally sponsored loans, and unspecified assistantships also available. Support available to part-time students. Financial award application deadline: 4/15; financial award

applicants required to submit FAFSA. *Unit head:* Dr. Marty Jones, Interim Chair, 719-587-7271, E-mail: hppe@adams.edu. *Application contact:* Caryn Chavez, Administrative Assistant III, 719-587-7208, Fax: 719-587-8230, E-mail: hppe@adams.edu.
Website: http://hppe.adams.edu

Adelphi University, Ruth S. Ammon School of Education, Program in Physical Education and Human Performance Science, Garden City, NY 11530-0701. Offers aging (Certificate); physical/educational human performance science (MA). *Program availability:* Part-time, evening/weekend. *Students:* 84 full-time (32 women), 78 part-time (30 women); includes 56 minority (26 Black or African American, non-Hispanic/Latino; 1 American Indian or Alaska Native, non-Hispanic/Latino; 1 Asian, non-Hispanic/Latino; 25 Hispanic/Latino; 3 Two or more races, non-Hispanic/Latino), 8 international. Average age 27. 131 applicants, 69% accepted, 59 enrolled. In 2017, 45 master's awarded. *Degree requirements:* For master's, internship. *Entrance requirements:* For master's, 3 letters of recommendation, resume. Additional exam requirements/recommendations for international students: Required—TOEFL (minimum score 550 paper-based; 80 iBT),

Physical Education

IELTS (minimum score 6.5). *Application deadline:* For fall admission, 4/1 for international students; for spring admission, 11/1 for international students. Applications are processed on a rolling basis. Application fee: $50. Electronic applications accepted. *Expenses:* Contact institution. *Financial support:* Research assistantships, teaching assistantships, career-related internships or fieldwork, institutionally sponsored loans, scholarships/grants, traineeships, and unspecified assistantships available. Support available to part-time students. Financial award application deadline: 2/15; financial award applicants required to submit FAFSA. *Faculty research:* Physical education for the handicapped, sport sociology, sport pedagogy. *Unit head:* Dr. Ronald Feingold, Chair, 516-877-4764, E-mail: feingold@adelphi.edu. *Application contact:* E-mail: graduateadmissions@adelphi.edu.

Alabama Agricultural and Mechanical University, School of Graduate Studies, College of Education, Humanities, and Behavioral Sciences, Department of Health Sciences, Human Performance, and Communicative Disorders, Huntsville, AL 35811. Offers kinesiology (MS); physical education (MS); speech-language pathology (MS). *Program availability:* Part-time, evening/weekend. *Degree requirements:* For master's, comprehensive exam. *Entrance requirements:* For master's, GRE General Test. Additional exam requirements/recommendations for international students: Required—TOEFL (minimum score 500 paper-based; 61 iBT). Electronic applications accepted. *Faculty research:* Cardiorespiratory assessment.

Alabama State University, College of Education, Department of Health, Physical Education, and Recreation, Montgomery, AL 36101-0271. Offers health education (M Ed); physical education (M Ed). *Program availability:* Part-time. *Students:* 4 full-time (2 women), 6 part-time (2 women); includes 8 minority (all Black or African American, non-Hispanic/Latino), 1 international. Average age 29. 2 applicants, 100% accepted, 2 enrolled. In 2017, 5 master's awarded. *Degree requirements:* For master's, comprehensive exam. *Entrance requirements:* For master's, GRE General Test, MAT, writing competency test, bachelor's degree or its equivalent from accredited college or university with minimum GPA of 2.5. Additional exam requirements/recommendations for international students: Required—TOEFL (minimum score 500 paper-based). *Application deadline:* For fall admission, 4/15 for domestic and international students; for spring admission, 11/15 for domestic and international students; for summer admission, 3/15 for domestic and international students. Applications are processed on a rolling basis. Application fee: $25. Electronic applications accepted. *Expenses:* Contact institution. *Financial support:* Research assistantships available. Financial award application deadline: 6/30; financial award applicants required to submit FAFSA. *Faculty research:* Risk factors for heart disease in the college-age population, cardiovascular reactivity for the Cold Pressor Test. *Unit head:* Dr. Charlie Gibbons, Interim Chair, 334-229-4504, Fax: 334-229-4928, E-mail: cgibbons@alasu.edu. *Application contact:* Dr. William Person, Dean of Graduate Studies, 334-229-4274, Fax: 334-229-4928, E-mail: wperson@alasu.edu.
Website: http://www.alasu.edu/academics/colleges—departments/college-of-education/health-physical-education—recreation/index.aspx

Albany State University, College of Education, Albany, GA 31705-2717. Offers early childhood education (M Ed); educational leadership (Ed S); health and physical education (M Ed); middle grades education (M Ed); school counseling (M Ed); special education (M Ed). *Accreditation:* NCATE. *Program availability:* Part-time, evening/weekend, online learning. *Degree requirements:* For master's, comprehensive exam, internship, GACE Content Exam. *Entrance requirements:* For master's, GRE or MAT. Electronic applications accepted. *Faculty research:* GACE preparation, STEM (science, technology, engineering, and mathematics), technology education, special education, professional teacher development, health implications liberation philosophy, NET-Q, learning community, disabled or at-risk students.

Alcorn State University, School of Graduate Studies, School of Psychology and Education, Lorman, MS 39096-7500. Offers agricultural education (MS Ed); elementary education (MS Ed, Ed S); guidance and counseling (MS Ed); industrial education (MS Ed); secondary education (MS Ed), including health and physical education; special education (MS Ed). *Accreditation:* NCATE. *Degree requirements:* For master's, thesis optional.

American University of Puerto Rico, Program in Education, Bayamon, PR 00960-2037. Offers art education (M Ed); elementary education 4-6 (M Ed); elementary education K-3 (M Ed); general science education (M Ed); physical education (M Ed); special education (M Ed). *Program availability:* Part-time, evening/weekend. *Faculty:* 17 part-time/adjunct (7 women). *Students:* 22 full-time (18 women), 54 part-time (42 women); all minorities (all Hispanic/Latino). Average age 33. 22 applicants, 86% accepted, 19 enrolled. In 2017, 53 master's awarded. *Entrance requirements:* For master's, EXADEP, GRE, or MAT, 2 letters of recommendation, minimum GPA of 2.5. *Application deadline:* For fall admission, 8/1 for domestic students; for winter admission, 10/18 for domestic students; for spring admission, 3/15 for domestic students. Applications are processed on a rolling basis. Application fee: $25. Tuition and fees vary according to course load and degree level. *Financial support:* In 2017–18, 79 students received support, including 76 fellowships (averaging $400 per year), 55 teaching assistantships (averaging $1,741 per year). Financial award applicants required to submit FAFSA. *Unit head:* Prof. Bolivar Ramirez-Carlo, III, Dean of Faculty, 787-620-2040 Ext. 2010, Fax: 787-620-2958, E-mail: bramirez@aupr.edu. *Application contact:* Keren I. Llanos-Figueroa, Information Contact, 787-620-2040 Ext. 2021, Fax: 787-785-7377, E-mail: oficnaadmisiones@aupr.edu.

Arizona State University at the Tempe campus, Mary Lou Fulton Teachers College, Program in Curriculum and Instruction, Phoenix, AZ 85069. Offers curriculum and instruction (M Ed, MA); elementary education (M Ed); physical education (MPE); secondary education (M Ed). *Program availability:* Part-time, evening/weekend, online learning. Terminal master's awarded for partial completion of doctoral program. *Degree requirements:* For master's, thesis or alternative, applied project, interactive Program of Study (iPOS) submitted before completing 50 percent of required credit hours. *Entrance requirements:* For master's, GRE or GMAT (for some programs), minimum GPA of 3.0 or equivalent in last 2 years of work leading to bachelor's degree, 3 letters of recommendation, personal statement describing research and career goals, curriculum vitae or resume, IVP fingerprint clearance card (for those seeking Arizona certification). Additional exam requirements/recommendations for international students: Required—TOEFL, IELTS, or PTE. Electronic applications accepted. *Expenses:* Contact institution. *Faculty research:* Early childhood, media and computers, elementary education, secondary education, English education, bilingual education, language and literacy, science education, engineering education, exercise and wellness education.

Arkansas State University, Graduate School, College of Education and Behavioral Science, Department of Health, Physical Education, and Sport Sciences, State University, AR 72467. Offers exercise science (MS); physical education (MSE, SCCT); sports administration (MS). *Program availability:* Part-time. *Degree requirements:* For master's, comprehensive exam, thesis or alternative; for SCCT, comprehensive exam. *Entrance requirements:* For master's, GRE General Test or MAT, appropriate bachelor's degree, official transcripts, immunization records, statement of goals, letters of recommendation; for SCCT, GRE General Test or MAT, interview, master's degree, official transcript, immunization records. Additional exam requirements/recommendations for international students: Required—TOEFL (minimum score 550

paper-based; 79 iBT), IELTS (minimum score 6), PTE (minimum score 56). Electronic applications accepted.

Auburn University, Graduate School, College of Education, Department of Kinesiology, Auburn University, AL 36849. Offers exercise science (M Ed). *Accreditation:* NCATE. *Program availability:* Part-time. *Faculty:* 21 full-time (10 women), 2 part-time/adjunct (0 women). *Students:* 94 full-time (45 women), 31 part-time (16 women); includes 30 minority (17 Black or African American, non-Hispanic/Latino; 1 Asian, non-Hispanic/Latino; 8 Hispanic/Latino; 4 Two or more races, non-Hispanic/Latino), 8 international. Average age 26. 132 applicants, 68% accepted, 59 enrolled. In 2017, 53 master's, 8 doctorates awarded. *Degree requirements:* For master's, thesis (for some programs); for doctorate, thesis/dissertation; for Ed S, exam, field project. *Entrance requirements:* For master's, GRE General Test; for doctorate and Ed S, GRE General Test, interview, master's degree. *Application deadline:* Applications are processed on a rolling basis. Application fee: $50 ($60 for international students). Electronic applications accepted. *Expenses:* Tuition, state resident: full-time $10,974; part-time $519 per credit hour. Tuition, nonresident: full-time $29,658; part-time $1557 per credit hour. *Required fees:* $816 per semester. Tuition and fees vary according to degree level and program. *Financial support:* Research assistantships, teaching assistantships, and Federal Work-Study available. Support available to part-time students. Financial award application deadline: 3/15; financial award applicants required to submit FAFSA. *Faculty research:* Biomechanics, exercise physiology, motor skill learning, school health, curriculum development. *Unit head:* Dr. Mary E. Rudisill, Director, 334-844-1458. *Application contact:* Dr. George Flowers, Dean of the Graduate School, 334-844-2125.

Auburn University at Montgomery, College of Education, Department of Kinesiology, Montgomery, AL 36124-4023. Offers exercise science (M Ed); physical education (Ed S); sport management (M Ed). *Program availability:* Online learning. *Faculty:* 7 full-time (3 women), 1 (woman) part-time/adjunct. *Students:* 12 full-time (9 women), 18 part-time (11 women); includes 12 minority (11 Black or African American, non-Hispanic/Latino; 1 Hispanic/Latino). Average age 29. 23 applicants, 74% accepted, 10 enrolled. In 2017, 18 master's awarded. *Entrance requirements:* For master's, GRE or MAT. Additional exam requirements/recommendations for international students: Recommended—TOEFL (minimum score 500 paper-based; 61 iBT), IELTS (minimum score 5.5), TSE (minimum score 44). *Application deadline:* For fall admission, 7/15 for international students; for spring admission, 11/15 for international students; for summer admission, 4/15 for international students. Applications are processed on a rolling basis. Application fee: $25. Electronic applications accepted. *Expenses:* Tuition, state resident: full-time $6930; part-time $385 per credit hour. Tuition, nonresident: full-time $15,588; part-time $866 per credit hour. *Required fees:* $640. *Financial support:* Teaching assistantships available. Financial award application deadline: 3/1; financial award applicants required to submit FAFSA. *Unit head:* Dr. George Schaefer, Head, 334-244-3887, Fax: 334-244-3835, E-mail: gschaefe@aum.edu. *Application contact:* Janis Bigelow, Graduate Advisor, 334-244-3135, E-mail: jbigelo1@aum.edu.
Website: http://www.education.aum.edu/academic-programs/academic-programs/kinesiology

Avila University, School of Education, Kansas City, MO 64145-1698. Offers advanced classroom management (MA); art K-12 (Teaching Certificate); educational technology (MA, Certificate); elementary education (Teaching Certificate); English as a second language (MA); English language learners (Advanced Certificate); middle school (Teaching Certificate); physical education K-12 (Teaching Certificate); secondary education (Teaching Certificate); special education (Teaching Certificate); special reading (Advanced Certificate); teaching and learning (MA). *Program availability:* Part-time, evening/weekend, online learning. *Faculty:* 6 full-time (5 women), 9 part-time/adjunct (8 women). *Students:* 81 full-time (63 women), 20 part-time (11 women); includes 14 minority (8 Black or African American, non-Hispanic/Latino; 2 Asian, non-Hispanic/Latino; 3 Hispanic/Latino; 1 Two or more races, non-Hispanic/Latino), 4 international. Average age 35. 92 applicants, 62% accepted, 40 enrolled. In 2017, 24 master's awarded. *Entrance requirements:* For master's, minimum GPA of 3.0, writing sample, recommendation, interview; for other advanced degree, foreign language. Additional exam requirements/recommendations for international students: Required—TOEFL (minimum score 580 paper-based; 92 iBT). *Application deadline:* Applications are processed on a rolling basis. Electronic applications accepted. *Expenses:* Contact institution. *Financial support:* In 2017–18, 14 students received support. Unspecified assistantships available. Financial award applicants required to submit FAFSA. *Unit head:* Dr. Stacy Keith, Director of Graduate Education, 816-501-2446, Fax: 816-501-2915, E-mail: stacy.keith@avila.edu. *Application contact:* Cory Roup, Graduate Education Enrollment and Academic Advisor, 816-501-2464, E-mail: cory.roup@avila.edu.
Website: https://www.avila.edu/academics/graduate-studies/grad-education

Ball State University, Graduate School, College of Health, School of Kinesiology, Program in Physical Education and Sport, Muncie, IN 47306. Offers physical education and sport (MA, MS), including athletic coaching education, sport administration, sport and exercise psychology. *Program availability:* Part-time, 100% online. *Students:* 19 full-time (5 women), 69 part-time (25 women); includes 6 minority (2 Black or African American, non-Hispanic/Latino; 4 Hispanic/Latino), 1 international. Average age 26. 83 applicants, 35% accepted, 27 enrolled. In 2017, 32 master's awarded. *Entrance requirements:* For master's, GRE General Test, minimum baccalaureate GPA of 2.75 or 3.0 in latter half of baccalaureate, curriculum vitae, three letters of recommendation; campus visit to meet faculty and see facilities (strongly encouraged). Additional exam requirements/recommendations for international students: Required—TOEFL (minimum score 550 paper-based; 79 iBT), IELTS (minimum score 6.5). *Application deadline:* For fall admission, 1/15 for domestic students. Applications are processed on a rolling basis. Application fee: $60. Electronic applications accepted. *Financial support:* Research assistantships with partial tuition reimbursements and unspecified assistantships available. Financial award application deadline: 3/1; financial award applicants required to submit FAFSA. *Unit head:* Dr. Tom Weidner, Chairperson, 765-285-5039, Fax: 765-285-8254, E-mail: tweidner@bsu.edu.

Baylor University, Graduate School, Robbins College of Health and Human Sciences, Department of Health, Human Performance and Recreation, Waco, TX 76798. Offers athletic training (MS); community health (MPH); exercise physiology (MS); kinesiology, exercise nutrition, and health promotion (PhD); sport pedagogy (MS). *Accreditation:* NCATE. *Program availability:* Part-time. *Faculty:* 24 full-time (11 women). *Students:* 86 full-time (52 women), 9 part-time (6 women); includes 24 minority (7 Black or African American, non-Hispanic/Latino; 3 Asian, non-Hispanic/Latino; 10 Hispanic/Latino; 1 Native Hawaiian or other Pacific Islander, non-Hispanic/Latino; 3 Two or more races, non-Hispanic/Latino), 8 international. 109 applicants, 59% accepted, 44 enrolled. In 2017, 30 master's, 3 doctorates awarded. *Degree requirements:* For master's, comprehensive exam, thesis optional; for doctorate, comprehensive exam, thesis/dissertation. *Entrance requirements:* For master's and doctorate, GRE General Test. Additional exam requirements/recommendations for international students: Required—TOEFL (minimum score 550 paper-based; 80 iBT). *Application deadline:* For fall admission, 2/1 priority date for domestic students, 2/1 for international students; for spring admission, 10/1 for domestic and international students. Applications are processed on a rolling basis. Application fee: $25. Electronic applications accepted.

Financial support: In 2017–18, 60 students received support, including 1 research assistantship with full tuition reimbursement available (averaging $12,700 per year), 33 teaching assistantships with full tuition reimbursements available (averaging $7,650 per year); career-related internships or fieldwork, Federal Work-Study, institutionally sponsored loans, scholarships/grants, tuition waivers (full), and unspecified assistantships also available. Financial award application deadline: 2/1. *Faculty research:* Exercise testing, cardio-metabolic health, resistance exercise and training, nutritional intervention, population health, health promotion, global health epidemiology, coaching, natural resource management, stimulant misuse, diet, microbiome and colon cancer etiology. *Total annual research expenditures:* $250,118. *Unit head:* Dr. Jaeho Shim, Graduate Program Director, 254-710-4009, Fax: 254-710-3527, E-mail: joe_shim@baylor.edu. *Application contact:* Deepa Morris, Graduate Program Coordinator, 254-710-3526, Fax: 254-710-3527, E-mail: deepa_morris@baylor.edu. Website: http://www.baylor.edu/HHPR/

Bridgewater State University, College of Graduate Studies, College of Education and Allied Studies, Department of Movement Arts, Health Promotion, and Leisure Studies, Program in Physical Education, Bridgewater, MA 02325. Offers MS. *Program availability:* Part-time, evening/weekend. *Degree requirements:* For master's, thesis or alternative. *Entrance requirements:* For master's, GRE General Test.

Brooklyn College of the City University of New York, School of Natural and Behavioral Sciences, Department of Kinesiology, Brooklyn, NY 11210-2889. Offers exercise and sports science (MS); physical education teacher (MS); sport management (MS). *Program availability:* Part-time. *Degree requirements:* For master's, comprehensive exam or thesis. *Entrance requirements:* For master's, previous course work in physical education and education, minimum GPA of 3.0, 2 letters of recommendation, essay. Additional exam requirements/recommendations for international students: Required—TOEFL (minimum score 500 paper-based; 61 iBT). Electronic applications accepted. *Faculty research:* Exercise physiology, motor learning, sports psychology, women in athletics.

California Baptist University, Program in Kinesiology, Riverside, CA 92504-3206. Offers exercise science (MS); physical education (MS); sport management (MS). *Program availability:* Part-time, 100% online, blended/hybrid learning. *Faculty:* 11 full-time (6 women), 5 part-time/adjunct (0 women). *Students:* 86 full-time (43 women), 45 part-time (21 women); includes 63 minority (20 Black or African American, non-Hispanic/Latino; 5 Asian, non-Hispanic/Latino; 35 Hispanic/Latino; 3 Two or more races, non-Hispanic/Latino), 20 international. Average age 28. 47 applicants, 62% accepted, 24 enrolled. In 2017, 55 master's awarded. *Degree requirements:* For master's, comprehensive exam or research thesis. *Entrance requirements:* For master's, minimum undergraduate GPA of 2.75; completion of course prerequisites with minimum C grade; three recommendations; 500-word essay; resume; interview. Additional exam requirements/recommendations for international students: Required—TOEFL (minimum score 80 iBT). *Application deadline:* For fall admission, 8/1 priority date for domestic students, 7/1 for international students; for spring admission, 12/1 priority date for domestic students, 11/1 for international students. Applications are processed on a rolling basis. Application fee: $45. Electronic applications accepted. *Expenses:* Contact institution. *Financial support:* In 2017–18, 11 students received support. Federal Work-Study, scholarships/grants, and unspecified assistantships available. Financial award applicants required to submit CSS PROFILE or FAFSA. *Faculty research:* Physical education pedagogy, exercise management and prevention of cardiovascular and metabolic diseases, sport management, immune function, carbohydrate oxidation. *Unit head:* Dr. David Pearson, Dean, College of Allied Health, 951-343-4298, E-mail: dpearson@calbaptist.edu. *Application contact:* Dr. Sean Sullivan, Chair, Department of Kinesiology, 951-343-4528, Fax: 951-343-5095, E-mail: ssullivan@calbaptist.edu. Website: http://www.calbaptist.edu/mskin/

California State University, East Bay, Office of Graduate Studies, College of Education and Allied Studies, Department of Kinesiology, Hayward, CA 94542-3000. Offers MS. *Faculty:* 16 full-time (9 women), 21 part-time/adjunct (13 women). *Students:* 3 full-time (1 woman), 19 part-time (4 women); includes 13 minority (2 Black or African American, non-Hispanic/Latino; 2 Asian, non-Hispanic/Latino; 5 Hispanic/Latino; 4 Two or more races, non-Hispanic/Latino), 3 international. Average age 31. 23 applicants, 48% accepted, 7 enrolled. In 2017, 15 master's awarded. *Degree requirements:* For master's, exam or thesis. *Entrance requirements:* For master's, BA in kinesiology or related discipline, minimum major course work GPA of 3.0. Additional exam requirements/recommendations for international students: Required—TOEFL (minimum score 550 paper-based). *Application deadline:* For fall admission, 6/1 for domestic and international students. Applications are processed on a rolling basis. Application fee: $55. Electronic applications accepted. *Financial support:* Fellowships, Federal Work-Study, institutionally sponsored loans, and scholarships/grants available. Support available to part-time students. Financial award application deadline: 3/2; financial award applicants required to submit FAFSA. *Faculty research:* Physiology, psychology of sport/movement, skill acquisition, cultural influence on physical activity. *Unit head:* Dr. Paul Carpenter, Chair, 510-885-3061, E-mail: paul.carpenter@csueastbay.edu. *Application contact:* Prof. Cathy Inouye, Kinesiology Graduate Advisor, 510-885-3048, Fax: 510-885-2423, E-mail: cathy.inouye@csueastbay.edu. Website: http://www20.csueastbay.edu/ecat/graduate-chapters/g-kin.html

California State University, Fullerton, Graduate Studies, College of Health and Human Development, Department of Kinesiology, Fullerton, CA 92831-3599. Offers MS. *Program availability:* Part-time. *Faculty:* 14 full-time (6 women). *Students:* 34 full-time (18 women), 44 part-time (19 women); includes 39 minority (7 Black or African American, non-Hispanic/Latino; 6 Asian, non-Hispanic/Latino; 19 Hispanic/Latino; 7 Two or more races, non-Hispanic/Latino), 1 international. Average age 26. 102 applicants, 43% accepted, 25 enrolled. *Entrance requirements:* For master's, minimum GPA of 3.0 in field, 2.5 overall. Application fee: $55. *Financial support:* Career-related internships or fieldwork, Federal Work-Study, institutionally sponsored loans, and scholarships/grants available. Support available to part-time students. Financial award application deadline: 3/1; financial award applicants required to submit FAFSA. *Unit head:* Dr. Stephen Walk, Head, 657-278-3320. *Application contact:* Admissions/Applications, 657-278-2371.

California State University, Long Beach, Graduate Studies, College of Health and Human Services, Department of Kinesiology, Long Beach, CA 90840. Offers adapted physical education (MA); coaching and student athlete development (MA); exercise physiology and nutrition (MS); exercise science (MS); individualized studies (MA); kinesiology (MA); pedagogical studies (MA); sport and exercise psychology (MS); sport management (MA); sports medicine and injury studies (MS). *Program availability:* Part-time. *Degree requirements:* For master's, oral and written comprehensive exams or thesis. *Entrance requirements:* For master's, GRE General Test, minimum GPA of 2.75 during previous 2 years of course work. Electronic applications accepted. *Faculty research:* Pulmonary functioning, feedback and practice structure, strength training, history and politics of sports, special population research issues.

California State University, Los Angeles, Graduate Studies, College of Health and Human Services, Department of Kinesiology and Nutritional Sciences, Los Angeles, CA 90032-8530. Offers nutritional science (MS); physical education and kinesiology (MA). *Accreditation:* AND. *Program availability:* Part-time, evening/weekend. *Degree requirements:* For master's, comprehensive exam, project or thesis. *Entrance*

requirements: For master's, minimum GPA of 2.75. Additional exam requirements/recommendations for international students: Required—TOEFL (minimum score 500 paper-based).

California State University, Sacramento, College of Health and Human Services, Department of Kinesiology and Health Science, Sacramento, CA 95819. Offers exercise science (MS); movement studies (MS). *Accreditation:* APTA. *Program availability:* Part-time, evening/weekend. *Students:* 14 full-time (8 women), 18 part-time (11 women); includes 11 minority (3 Black or African American, non-Hispanic/Latino; 4 Asian, non-Hispanic/Latino), 1 international. Average age 29. 33 applicants, 67% accepted, 14 enrolled. In 2017, 8 master's awarded. *Degree requirements:* For master's, thesis or project; writing proficiency exam. *Entrance requirements:* For master's, minimum overall GPA of 2.8, 3.0 in last 60 semester units; upper-division statistics course. Additional exam requirements/recommendations for international students: Required—TOEFL (minimum score 550 paper-based; 80 iBT); Recommended—IELTS, TSE. *Application deadline:* For fall admission, 1/28 for domestic students, 3/1 for international students; for spring admission, 9/30 for international students. Applications are processed on a rolling basis. Application fee: $55. Electronic applications accepted. *Expenses:* Contact institution. *Financial support:* Teaching assistantships, career-related internships or fieldwork, Federal Work-Study, and scholarships/grants available. Support available to part-time students. Financial award application deadline: 3/1; financial award applicants required to submit FAFSA. *Unit head:* Katherine Jamieson, Chair, 916-278-6441, E-mail: katherine.jamieson@csus.edu. *Application contact:* Jose Martinez, Graduate Admissions Supervisor, 916-278-7871, E-mail: martinj@skymail.csus.edu. Website: http://www.csus.edu/hhs/khs

California State University, Stanislaus, College of Education, Kinesiology and Social Work, MA Program in Education, Turlock, CA 95382. Offers curriculum and instruction (MA), including education technology, elementary education, multilingual education, physical education, reading, secondary education, special education; school administration (MA); school counseling (MA). *Program availability:* Part-time, evening/weekend. *Degree requirements:* For master's, comprehensive exam (for some programs), thesis (for some programs). *Entrance requirements:* For master's, MAT, GRE, or CBEST (varies by concentration), 3 letters of recommendation, personal statement. Additional exam requirements/recommendations for international students: Required—TOEFL (minimum score 550 paper-based). Electronic applications accepted. *Faculty research:* Children's perspectives on historical events, method elementary schools dual language education, K-12 reading programs.

Campbell University, Graduate and Professional Programs, School of Education, Buies Creek, NC 27506. Offers elementary education (M Ed); interdisciplinary studies (M Ed); middle grades education (M Ed); physical education (M Ed); school administration (MSA); school counseling (M Ed); secondary education (M Ed). *Accreditation:* NCATE. *Program availability:* Part-time, evening/weekend. *Degree requirements:* For master's, comprehensive exam. *Entrance requirements:* For master's, GRE General Test, minimum GPA of 2.7. *Faculty research:* Spiritual values and wellness issues in counseling, stress and professional burnout among counselors, thinking strategies, leadership, adaptive technology.

Canisius College, Graduate Division, School of Education and Human Services, Department of Kinesiology, Buffalo, NY 14208-1098. Offers physical education (MS Ed); physical education birth - 12 (MS Ed). *Program availability:* Part-time, evening/weekend, 100% online, blended/hybrid learning. *Faculty:* 6 full-time (1 woman), 9 part-time/adjunct (2 women). *Students:* 90 full-time (29 women), 87 part-time (31 women); includes 33 minority (23 Black or African American, non-Hispanic/Latino; 1 Asian, non-Hispanic/Latino; 7 Hispanic/Latino; 2 Two or more races, non-Hispanic/Latino), 5 international. Average age 29. 62 applicants, 95% accepted, 54 enrolled. In 2017, 91 master's awarded. *Degree requirements:* For master's, research project. *Entrance requirements:* For master's, official college and/or university transcript(s) showing completion of bachelor's degree from accredited institution with evidence of teaching certification (not for initial certification candidates); two letters of recommendation; minimum cumulative undergraduate GPA of 2.7. Additional exam requirements/recommendations for international students: Required—TOEFL (minimum score 550 paper-based, 79 iBT), IELTS (minimum score 6.5), or CAEL (minimum score 70). *Application deadline:* Applications are processed on a rolling basis. Application fee: $0. Electronic applications accepted. *Expenses:* Contact institution. *Financial support:* Career-related internships or fieldwork, Federal Work-Study, scholarships/grants, tuition waivers (partial), and unspecified assistantships available. Support available to part-time students. Financial award application deadline: 4/30; financial award applicants required to submit FAFSA. *Faculty research:* Culturally congruent pedagogy in physical education, information processing and perceptual styles of athletes, qualities of effective coaches. *Unit head:* Dr. Nicolas Lorgnier, Chair/Professor of Kinesiology, 716-888-3733, Fax: 716-888-8445, E-mail: lorgnien@canisius.edu. *Application contact:* Fax: 716-888-3195, E-mail: daviskb@canisius.edu. Website: http://www.canisius.edu/graduate/

Caribbean University, Graduate School, Bayamón, PR 00960-0493. Offers administration and supervision (MA Ed); criminal justice (MA); curriculum and instruction (MA Ed, PhD), including elementary education (MA Ed), English education (MA Ed), history education (MA Ed), mathematics education (MA Ed), primary education (MA Ed), science education (MA Ed), Spanish education (MA Ed); educational technology in instructional systems (MA Ed); gerontology (MSN); human resources (MBA); museology, archiving and art history (MA Ed); neonatal pediatrics (MSN); physical education (MA Ed); special education (MA Ed). *Entrance requirements:* For master's, interview, minimum GPA of 2.5.

Central Connecticut State University, School of Graduate Studies, School of Education and Professional Studies, Department of Physical Education and Human Performance, New Britain, CT 06050-4010. Offers physical education (MS). *Program availability:* Part-time, evening/weekend. *Faculty:* 7 full-time (3 women). *Students:* 22 full-time (7 women), 30 part-time (10 women); includes 7 minority (2 Black or African American, non-Hispanic/Latino; 3 Hispanic/Latino; 2 Two or more races, non-Hispanic/Latino), 1 international. Average age 28. 29 applicants, 86% accepted, 15 enrolled. In 2017, 12 master's, 3 other advanced degrees awarded. *Degree requirements:* For master's, comprehensive exam, thesis or alternative; for Certificate, qualifying exam. *Entrance requirements:* For master's, minimum GPA of 2.7, bachelor's degree in physical education (preferred), essay, interview, letters of recommendation. Additional exam requirements/recommendations for international students: Required—TOEFL (minimum score 550 paper-based; 79 iBT); Recommended—IELTS (minimum score 6.5). *Application deadline:* For fall admission, 5/1 for domestic and international students; for spring admission, 11/1 for domestic and international students; for summer admission, 3/1 for domestic and international students. Applications are processed on a rolling basis. Application fee: $50. Electronic applications accepted. *Expenses:* Tuition, area resident: Full-time $6757. Tuition, state resident: full-time $9750; part-time $374 per credit. Tuition, nonresident: full-time $18,102; part-time $374 per credit. *Required fees:* $4635; $255 per credit. *Financial support:* In 2017–18, 11 students received support. Career-related internships or fieldwork, Federal Work-Study, scholarships/grants, and unspecified assistantships available. Support available to part-time students.

Physical Education

Financial award application deadline: 3/1; financial award applicants required to submit FAFSA. *Faculty research:* Exercise science, athletic training, preparation of physical education for schools. *Unit head:* Dr. Carol Ciotto, Interim Chair, 860-832-2177, E-mail: ciottocaj@ccsu.edu. *Application contact:* Patricia Gardner, Associate Director of Graduate Studies, 860-832-2350, Fax: 860-832-2362.
Website: http://www.ccsu.edu/pehp/

Central Washington University, School of Graduate Studies and Research, College of Education and Professional Studies, Department of Physical Education, School Health and Movement Studies, Ellensburg, WA 98926. Offers athletic administration (MS); health and physical education (MS). *Program availability:* Part-time. *Degree requirements:* For master's, comprehensive exam, thesis or alternative. *Entrance requirements:* For master's, minimum GPA of 3.0. Additional exam requirements/recommendations for international students: Required—TOEFL (minimum score 550 paper-based; 79 iBT), IELTS. *Application deadline:* For fall admission, 2/1 priority date for domestic students; for winter admission, 10/1 for domestic students; for spring admission, 1/1 for domestic students. Applications are processed on a rolling basis. Application fee: $50. Electronic applications accepted. *Financial support:* Applicants required to submit FAFSA. *Unit head:* Dr. Heidi Henschel Pellett, Chair, 509-963-1483, E-mail: heidi.henschelpellett@cwu.edu. *Application contact:* Justine Eason, Admissions Program Coordinator, 509-963-3103, Fax: 509-963-1799, E-mail: masters@cwu.edu.
Website: http://www.cwu.edu/~pesph/

Chicago State University, School of Graduate and Professional Studies, College of Education, Department of Health, Physical Education and Recreation, Chicago, IL 60628. Offers physical education (MS Ed). *Program availability:* Part-time, evening/weekend, online learning. *Entrance requirements:* For master's, minimum GPA of 2.75. *Application deadline:* For fall admission, 7/1 for domestic students; for spring admission, 11/10 for domestic students. Application fee: $25. *Faculty research:* Sports psychology, recreation and leisure studies administration. *Unit head:* Dr. Lisa Raymond-Pesavento, Chairperson, 773-995-2290, E-mail: lc-pesavento@csu.edu. *Application contact:* Dr. John Fitzpatrick, Graduate Adviser, 773-995-3649, Fax: 773-995-3644, E-mail: j-fitzpatrick@csu.edu.

The Citadel, The Military College of South Carolina, Citadel Graduate College, School of Science and Mathematics; Department of Health, Exercise, and Sport Science, Charleston, SC 29409. Offers health, exercise, and sport science (MS); sport management (MA, Graduate Certificate). *Accreditation:* NCATE. *Program availability:* Part-time, evening/weekend. *Degree requirements:* For master's, comprehensive exam (for some programs), internship and professional portfolio (for some programs). *Entrance requirements:* For master's, GRE (minimum combined verbal and quantitative score 290) or MAT (minimum score 396), official transcript reflecting highest degree earned from regionally-accredited college or university, minimum undergraduate GPA of 2.5, 3 letters of recommendation, resume detailing previous work experience. Additional exam requirements/recommendations for international students: Required—TOEFL (minimum score 550 paper-based; 79 iBT). Electronic applications accepted. *Expenses:* Tuition, state resident: part-time $587 per credit hour. Tuition, nonresident: part-time $988 per credit hour. *Required fees:* $90 per term.

The Citadel, The Military College of South Carolina, Citadel Graduate College, Zucker Family School of Education, Charleston, SC 29409. Offers elementary/secondary school administration and supervision (M Ed); elementary/secondary school counseling (M Ed); interdisciplinary STEM education (M Ed); literacy education (M Ed, Graduate Certificate); middle grades (MAT), including English, mathematics, science, social studies; physical education (grades K-12) (MAT); school superintendency (Ed S); secondary education (MAT), including biology, English, mathematics, social studies; student affairs (Graduate Certificate); student affairs and college counseling (M Ed). *Accreditation:* NCATE. *Program availability:* Part-time, evening/weekend, 100% online, blended/hybrid learning. *Degree requirements:* For master's, comprehensive exam (for some programs). *Entrance requirements:* For master's, GRE (minimum combined verbal and quantitative score of 290) or MAT (minimum score 396). Additional exam requirements/recommendations for international students: Required—TOEFL (minimum score 550 paper-based; 79 iBT). Electronic applications accepted. *Expenses:* Tuition, state resident: part-time $587 per credit hour. Tuition, nonresident: part-time $988 per credit hour. *Required fees:* $90 per term.

Cleveland State University, College of Graduate Studies, College of Education and Human Services, Department of Health and Human Performance, Cleveland, OH 44115. Offers physical education pedagogy (M Ed); public health (MPH). *Program availability:* Part-time. *Faculty:* 7 full-time (4 women), 3 part-time/adjunct (2 women). *Students:* 30 full-time (16 women), 60 part-time (36 women); includes 43 minority (33 Black or African American, non-Hispanic/Latino; 4 Asian, non-Hispanic/Latino; 2 Hispanic/Latino; 1 Native Hawaiian or other Pacific Islander, non-Hispanic/Latino; 3 Two or more races, non-Hispanic/Latino), 5 international. Average age 29. 103 applicants, 72% accepted, 43 enrolled. In 2017, 44 master's awarded. *Degree requirements:* For master's, comprehensive exam, thesis optional. *Entrance requirements:* For master's, GRE General Test or MAT (if undergraduate GPA less than 2.75), minimum undergraduate GPA of 2.75. Additional exam requirements/recommendations for international students: Required—TOEFL (minimum score 550 paper-based; 78 iBT), IELTS (minimum score 6). *Application deadline:* For fall admission, 7/15 priority date for domestic students; for spring admission, 12/15 priority date for domestic students. Applications are processed on a rolling basis. Application fee: $30. Electronic applications accepted. *Financial support:* In 2017–18, 6 research assistantships with tuition reimbursements (averaging $3,480 per year), 1 teaching assistantship with tuition reimbursement (averaging $3,480 per year) were awarded; career-related internships or fieldwork, tuition waivers (full), and unspecified assistantships also available. Financial award application deadline: 3/15; financial award applicants required to submit FAFSA. *Faculty research:* Bone density, marketing fitness centers, motor development of disabled, online learning and survey research. *Unit head:* Dr. Mike Loovis, Associate Professor/Department Chairperson, 216-687-3665, Fax: 216-687-5410, E-mail: e.loovis@csuohio.edu. *Application contact:* David Easler, Director, Graduate Recruitment, 216-687-5047, Fax: 216-687-5400, E-mail: d.easler@csuohio.edu.
Website: http://www.csuohio.edu/cehs/departments/HPERD/hperd_dept.html

The College at Brockport, State University of New York, School of Education, Health, and Human Services, Department of Kinesiology, Sports Studies and Physical Education, Brockport, NY 14420-2997. Offers adapted physical education (AGC); physical education (MS Ed), including adapted physical education, athletic administration, physical education/pedagogy. *Program availability:* Part-time. *Faculty:* 11 full-time (4 women), 1 part-time/adjunct (0 women). *Students:* 33 full-time (15 women), 28 part-time (11 women); includes 12 minority (3 Black or African American, non-Hispanic/Latino; 3 Asian, non-Hispanic/Latino; 4 Hispanic/Latino; 2 Two or more races, non-Hispanic/Latino), 1 international. 43 applicants, 81% accepted, 27 enrolled. In 2017, 37 master's awarded. *Degree requirements:* For master's, thesis or alternative. *Entrance requirements:* For master's, minimum GPA of 3.0; statement of objectives. Additional exam requirements/recommendations for international students: Required—TOEFL (minimum score 550 paper-based; 79 iBT), IELTS (minimum score 6.5). *Application deadline:* For fall admission, 4/15 priority date for domestic and international students; for spring admission, 11/15 priority date for domestic and international

students; for summer admission, 4/15 priority date for domestic students, 4/15 for international students. Application fee: $80. Electronic applications accepted. *Expenses:* Tuition, state resident: full-time $10,870; part-time $453 per credit hour. Tuition, nonresident: full-time $22,210. *Required fees:* $988; $246 per semester. *Financial support:* In 2017–18, 11 teaching assistantships with full tuition reimbursements (averaging $7,000 per year) were awarded; Federal Work-Study, scholarships/grants, and unspecified assistantships also available. Support available to part-time students. Financial award application deadline: 3/15; financial award applicants required to submit FAFSA. *Faculty research:* Athletic administration, adapted physical education, physical education curriculum, physical education teaching/coaching, children's physical activity. *Unit head:* Dr. Cathy Houston-Wilson, Chairperson, 585-395-5352, Fax: 585-395-2771, E-mail: chouston@brockport.edu. *Application contact:* Dr. Melanie Perreault, Graduate Program Director, 585-395-5299, Fax: 585-395-2771, E-mail: mperreault@brockport.edu.
Website: https://www.brockport.edu/academics/kinesiology/

Colorado State University–Pueblo, College of Education, Engineering and Professional Studies, Education Program, Pueblo, CO 81001-4901. Offers art education (M Ed); foreign language education (M Ed); health and physical education (M Ed); instructional technology (M Ed); linguistically diverse education (M Ed); music education (M Ed); special education (M Ed). *Accreditation:* TEAC. *Program availability:* Part-time. *Degree requirements:* For master's, portfolio. *Entrance requirements:* For master's, 3 recommendations, teaching license. Additional exam requirements/recommendations for international students: Required—TOEFL (minimum score 500 paper-based). Electronic applications accepted. *Faculty research:* Portfolio assessment, math education, science education.

Columbus State University, Graduate Studies, College of Education and Health Professions, Department of Health, Physical Education and Exercise Science, Columbus, GA 31907-5645. Offers exercise science (MS); health and physical education (M Ed, MAT). *Program availability:* Part-time, evening/weekend. *Faculty:* 6 full-time (4 women). *Students:* 19 full-time (8 women), 9 part-time (3 women); includes 13 minority (8 Black or African American, non-Hispanic/Latino; 1 Asian, non-Hispanic/Latino; 3 Hispanic/Latino; 1 Two or more races, non-Hispanic/Latino). Average age 28. 20 applicants, 65% accepted, 9 enrolled. In 2017, 14 master's awarded. *Degree requirements:* For master's, thesis optional. *Entrance requirements:* For master's, GRE, minimum undergraduate GPA of 2.75. Additional exam requirements/recommendations for international students: Required—TOEFL (minimum score 550 paper-based; 79 iBT). *Application deadline:* For fall admission, 5/1 for domestic students, 4/1 for international students; for spring admission, 11/1 for domestic and international students; for summer admission, 2/1 for domestic students, 3/1 for international students. Applications are processed on a rolling basis. Application fee: $50. Electronic applications accepted. *Expenses:* Tuition, state resident: full-time $3708; part-time $2472 per year. Tuition, nonresident: full-time $14,418; part-time $9612 per year. *International tuition:* $19,218 full-time. *Required fees:* $1605. Tuition and fees vary according to program. *Financial support:* In 2017–18, 2 students received support, including 6 research assistantships (averaging $3,000 per year). Financial award application deadline: 5/15; financial award applicants required to submit FAFSA. *Unit head:* Dr. Tara Underwood, Chair, 706-568-2485, E-mail: underwood_tara@columbusstate.edu. *Application contact:* Catrina Smith-Edmond, Assistant Director for Graduate and Global Admission, 706-507-8824, Fax: 706-568-5091, E-mail: smithedmond_catrina@columbusstate.edu.
Website: http://hpex.columbusstate.edu/

Concordia University Irvine, School of Arts and Sciences, Irvine, CA 92612-3299. Offers coaching and athletic administration (MA). *Program availability:* Part-time, evening/weekend, online learning. *Degree requirements:* For master's, culminating project. *Entrance requirements:* For master's, official college/university transcript(s); signed statement of intent. Additional exam requirements/recommendations for international students: Required—TOEFL (minimum score 550 paper-based; 79 iBT). Electronic applications accepted. *Expenses:* Contact institution.

Delta State University, Graduate Programs, College of Education, Division of Health, Physical Education, and Recreation, Cleveland, MS 38733-0001. Offers health, physical education, and recreation (M Ed); sport and human performance (MS). *Program availability:* Part-time, evening/weekend. *Degree requirements:* For master's, thesis optional. *Entrance requirements:* For master's, GRE General Test or MAT, Class A teaching certificate. *Faculty research:* Blood pressure, body fat, power and reaction time, learning disorders of athletes, effects of walking.

DePaul University, College of Education, Chicago, IL 60614. Offers bilingual-bicultural education (M Ed, MA); counseling (M Ed, MA), including clinical mental health counseling, college student development, school counseling; curriculum studies (M Ed, MA, Ed D); early childhood education (M Ed, MA, Ed D); educational leadership (M Ed, MA, Ed D), including Catholic leadership (M Ed, MA), general (M Ed, MA), higher education (M Ed, MA), physical education (M Ed, MA), principal preparation (M Ed); teacher preparation (M Ed); elementary education (M Ed, MA); middle grades education (M Ed); middle school mathematics education (MS); reading specialist (M Ed, MA); secondary education (M Ed, MA); social and cultural foundations in education (M Ed, MA); special education (M Ed); sport, fitness and recreation leadership (MS); value-creating education for global citizenship (M Ed); world languages education (M Ed, MA). *Program availability:* Part-time, evening/weekend, online learning. *Degree requirements:* For doctorate, thesis/dissertation. *Application deadline:* Applications are processed on a rolling basis. Application fee: $40. Electronic applications accepted. *Financial support:* Application deadline: 12/31; applicants required to submit FAFSA. *Unit head:* Dr. Paul Zionts, Dean, 773-325-7581, Fax: 773-325-7713, E-mail: pzionts@depaul.edu. *Application contact:* Dr. Paul Zionts, Dean, 773-325-7581, Fax: 773-325-7713, E-mail: pzionts@depaul.edu.
Website: http://education.depaul.edu

East Carolina University, Graduate School, College of Health and Human Performance, Department of Kinesiology, Greenville, NC 27858-4353. Offers adapted physical education (MS); bioenergetics and exercise science (PhD); biomechanics and motor control (MS); exercise physiology (MS); physical activity promotion (MS); physical education (MA Ed, MAT); physical education clinical supervision (Certificate); physical education pedagogy (MS); sport and exercise psychology (MS); sport management (MS, Certificate). *Students:* 72 full-time (30 women), 25 part-time (10 women); includes 21 minority (10 Black or African American, non-Hispanic/Latino; 1 American Indian or Alaska Native, non-Hispanic/Latino; 3 Asian, non-Hispanic/Latino; 4 Hispanic/Latino; 3 Two or more races, non-Hispanic/Latino), 3 international. Average age 27. 88 applicants, 68% accepted, 40 enrolled. In 2017, 35 master's, 5 doctorates, 4 other advanced degrees awarded. *Degree requirements:* For master's, comprehensive exam, thesis optional; for doctorate, comprehensive exam, thesis/dissertation. *Entrance requirements:* For master's, GRE General Test or MAT; for doctorate, GRE. Additional exam requirements/recommendations for international students: Recommended—TOEFL (minimum score 78 iBT), IELTS. *Application deadline:* For fall admission, 2/1 priority date for domestic students, 2/1 for international students. Applications are processed on a rolling basis. Application fee: $75. *Expenses:* Tuition, state resident: full-time $4749; part-time $297 per credit hour. Tuition, nonresident: full-time $17,898; part-time $1119 per credit hour. *Required fees:* $2691; $224 per credit hour. Part-time

tuition and fees vary according to course load and program. *Financial support:* Research assistantships with tuition reimbursements and teaching assistantships available. Support available to part-time students. Financial award application deadline: 2/1. *Faculty research:* Diabetes metabolism, pediatric obesity, biomechanics of arthritis, physical activity measurement. *Unit head:* Dr. Stacey Altman, Chair, 252-328-2973, E-mail: altmans@ecu.edu.
Website: https://hhp.ecu.edu/kine/

Eastern Kentucky University, The Graduate School, College of Education, Department of Curriculum and Instruction, Program in Secondary and Higher Education, Richmond, KY 40475-3102. Offers secondary education (MA Ed), including agricultural education, art education, biological sciences education, business education, English education, geography education, history education, home economics education, industrial education, mathematical sciences education, physical education, school health education. *Accreditation:* NCATE. *Program availability:* Part-time. *Entrance requirements:* For master's, GRE General Test, minimum GPA of 2.5.

Eastern Michigan University, Graduate School, College of Health and Human Services, School of Health Promotion and Human Performance, Programs in Physical Education Pedagogy, Ypsilanti, MI 48197. Offers adapted physical education (MS); physical education pedagogy (MS). *Program availability:* Part-time, evening/weekend, online learning. *Students:* 2 part-time (1 woman). Average age 30. *Degree requirements:* For master's, thesis or independent study project and comprehensive exams. *Entrance requirements:* Additional exam requirements/recommendations for international students: Required—TOEFL. *Application deadline:* For fall admission, 8/1 for domestic students, 5/1 for international students; for winter admission, 12/1 for domestic students, 10/1 for international students; for spring admission, 4/15 for domestic students, 3/1 for international students. Applications are processed on a rolling basis. Application fee: $45. *Financial support:* Fellowships, research assistantships with full tuition reimbursements, teaching assistantships with full tuition reimbursements, career-related internships or fieldwork, Federal Work-Study, institutionally sponsored loans, scholarships/grants, tuition waivers (partial), and unspecified assistantships available. Support available to part-time students. Financial award applicants required to submit FAFSA. *Application contact:* Dr. Roberta Faust, Program Coordinator, 734-487-7120 Ext. 2745, Fax: 734-487-2024, E-mail: rfaust@emich.edu.

Eastern New Mexico University, Graduate School, College of Education and Technology, Department of Health and Physical Education, Portales, NM 88130. Offers sport administration (MS), including coaching, sport science. *Program availability:* Part-time. *Degree requirements:* For master's, comprehensive exam, thesis optional. *Entrance requirements:* For master's, minimum GPA of 3.0, 15 hours of leveling courses without bachelor's degree in physical education, two references. Additional exam requirements/recommendations for international students: Required—TOEFL (minimum score 550 paper-based; 79 iBT), IELTS (minimum score 6). *Application deadline:* For fall admission, 7/20 priority date for domestic students, 6/20 priority date for international students; for spring admission, 12/15 priority date for domestic students, 11/15 priority date for international students. Applications are processed on a rolling basis. Application fee: $10. Electronic applications accepted. *Financial support:* Applicants required to submit FAFSA. *Unit head:* Dr. Beth Birky, Graduate Coordinator, 575-562-2683, E-mail: beth.birky@enmu.edu. *Application contact:* Cheryl Reeves, Senior Secretary, 575-562-2443, Fax: 575-562-2559, E-mail: cheryl.reeves@enmu.edu.
Website: http://education.enmu.edu

Eastern University, Graduate Education Programs, St. Davids, PA 19087-3696. Offers ESL program specialist (K-12) (Certificate); general supervisor (PreK-12) (Certificate); health and physical education (K-12) (Certificate); middle level (4-8) (Certificate); multicultural education (M Ed); music (K-12) (Certificate); Pre K-4 (Certificate); Pre K-4 with special education (Certificate); reading (M Ed); reading specialist (K-12) (Certificate); reading supervisor (K-12) (Certificate); school counseling (MA, CAGS); school principalship (preK-12) (Certificate); school psychology (MS, CAGS); secondary biology education (7-12) (Certificate); secondary chemistry education (7-12) (Certificate); secondary communication education (7-12) (Certificate); secondary English education (7-12) (Certificate); secondary math education (7-12) (Certificate); secondary social studies education (7-12) (Certificate); special education (M Ed); special education (7-12) (Certificate); special education (Pre K-8) (Certificate); special education supervisor (K-12) (Certificate); TESOL (M Ed); world language (Certificate), including Spanish. *Program availability:* Part-time, evening/weekend, online learning. *Students:* 46 full-time (40 women), 115 part-time (93 women); includes 65 minority (42 Black or African American, non-Hispanic/Latino; 3 Asian, non-Hispanic/Latino; 14 Hispanic/Latino; 6 Two or more races, non-Hispanic/Latino), 1 international. Average age 32. In 2017, 72 master's awarded. *Entrance requirements:* Additional exam requirements/recommendations for international students: Required—TOEFL. *Application deadline:* Applications are processed on a rolling basis. Application fee: $35. Electronic applications accepted. Application fee is waived when completed online. *Expenses:* Contact institution. *Unit head:* Michael Dziedziak, Executive Director of Enrollment, 800-452-0996, E-mail: gpsadmissions@eastern.edu.
Website: https://www.eastern.edu/academics/programs/education-department-graduate-programs/graduate-programs

Eastern Washington University, Graduate Studies, College of Arts, Letters and Education, Department of Physical Education, Health and Recreation, Cheney, WA 99004-2431. Offers exercise science (MS); sports and recreation administration (MS). *Faculty:* 7. *Students:* 15 full-time (6 women), 2 part-time (1 woman); includes 1 minority (Black or African American, non-Hispanic/Latino), 1 international. Average age 28. 34 applicants, 26% accepted, 8 enrolled. In 2017, 5 master's awarded. *Degree requirements:* For master's, comprehensive exam, thesis or alternative. *Entrance requirements:* For master's, minimum GPA of 3.0. Additional exam requirements/recommendations for international students: Required—TOEFL (minimum score 580 paper-based; 92 iBT), IELTS (minimum score 7), PTE (minimum score 63). *Application deadline:* For fall admission, 4/1 priority date for domestic students; for spring admission, 1/15 for domestic students. Applications are processed on a rolling basis. Application fee: $50. Electronic applications accepted. *Expenses:* Tuition, state resident: full-time $11,191; part-time $373.06 per credit. Tuition, nonresident: full-time $25,995; part-time $866.52 per credit. *Financial support:* Teaching assistantships with partial tuition reimbursements, career-related internships or fieldwork, Federal Work-Study, institutionally sponsored loans, and scholarships/grants available. Support available to part-time students. Financial award application deadline: 2/1; financial award applicants required to submit FAFSA. *Unit head:* Dr. Chadron Hazelbaker, Graduate Program Director, 509-359-2486, Fax: 509-359-4833, E-mail: chazelbaker@ewu.edu.

East Stroudsburg University of Pennsylvania, Graduate and Extended Studies, College of Health Sciences, Department of Exercise Science, East Stroudsburg, PA 18301-2999. Offers MS. *Program availability:* Part-time, evening/weekend, online learning. *Faculty:* 8 full-time (2 women). *Students:* 59 full-time (22 women), 4 part-time (2 women); includes 16 minority (8 Black or African American, non-Hispanic/Latino; 1 Asian, non-Hispanic/Latino; 4 Hispanic/Latino; 3 Two or more races, non-Hispanic/Latino), 2 international. Average age 25. 19 applicants, 47% accepted, 8 enrolled. In 2017, 40 master's awarded. *Degree requirements:* For master's, comprehensive exam, thesis or alternative, computer literacy. *Entrance requirements:* Additional exam

requirements/recommendations for international students: Recommended—TOEFL (minimum score 560 paper-based; 83 iBT), IELTS. *Application deadline:* For fall admission, 3/1 priority date for domestic and international students; for spring admission, 11/30 for domestic students, 10/31 for international students. Applications are processed on a rolling basis. Application fee: $50. Electronic applications accepted. *Expenses:* Tuition, state resident: full-time $4500; part-time $3000 per credit. Tuition, nonresident: full-time $6750; part-time $4500 per credit. *Required fees:* $2642; $1756 per credit. $878 per semester. Tuition and fees vary according to course load, campus/location and program. *Financial support:* Research assistantships with tuition reimbursements, Federal Work-Study, and unspecified assistantships available. Support available to part-time students. Financial award application deadline: 3/1; financial award applicants required to submit FAFSA. *Unit head:* Dr. Chad Witmer, Graduate Coordinator, 570-422-3362, E-mail: cwitmer@esu.edu. *Application contact:* Kevin Quintero, Associate Director, Graduate and Extended Studies, 570-422-3890, Fax: 570-422-2711, E-mail: kquintero@esu.edu.

Emporia State University, Department of Health, Physical Education and Recreation, Emporia, KS 66801-5415. Offers MS. *Program availability:* Part-time, 100% online. *Faculty:* 16 full-time (8 women), 2 part-time/adjunct (both women). *Students:* 37 full-time (14 women), 157 part-time (74 women); includes 13 minority (5 Black or African American, non-Hispanic/Latino; 1 American Indian or Alaska Native, non-Hispanic/Latino; 3 Hispanic/Latino; 4 Two or more races, non-Hispanic/Latino). 49 applicants, 67% accepted, 31 enrolled. In 2017, 90 master's awarded. *Degree requirements:* For master's, comprehensive exam or thesis. *Entrance requirements:* For master's, bachelor's degree in physical education, health, and recreation; letters of recommendation. Additional exam requirements/recommendations for international students: Required—TOEFL (minimum score 520 paper-based; 68 iBT). *Application deadline:* For fall admission, 8/15 priority date for domestic students. Applications are processed on a rolling basis. Application fee: $30 ($75 for international students). Electronic applications accepted. *Expenses:* Tuition, state resident: full-time $6084; part-time $253.50 per credit hour. Tuition, nonresident: full-time $18,924; part-time $788.50 per credit hour. *Required fees:* $1943; $80.95 per credit hour. Tuition and fees vary according to campus/location. *Financial support:* In 2017–18, 5 teaching assistantships with full tuition reimbursements (averaging $6,610 per year) were awarded; research assistantships with full tuition reimbursements, career-related internships or fieldwork, Federal Work-Study, institutionally sponsored loans, health care benefits, and unspecified assistantships also available. Financial award application deadline: 3/15; financial award applicants required to submit FAFSA. *Unit head:* Dr. Paul Luebbers, Chair, 620-341-5653, E-mail: pluebber@emporia.edu. *Application contact:* Mary Sewell, Admissions Coordinator, 800-950-GRAD, Fax: 620-341-5909, E-mail: msewell@emporia.edu.
Website: http://www.emporia.edu/hper/

Florida Agricultural and Mechanical University, Division of Graduate Studies, Research, and Continuing Education, College of Education, Department of Health, Physical Education, and Recreation, Tallahassee, FL 32307-3200. Offers sport management (MS). *Accreditation:* NCATE. *Program availability:* Part-time, evening/weekend. *Degree requirements:* For master's, thesis optional. *Entrance requirements:* For master's, GRE General Test, minimum GPA of 3.0. Additional exam requirements/recommendations for international students: Required—TOEFL. *Faculty research:* Administration/curriculum, work behavior, psychology.

Florida International University, College of Arts, Sciences, and Education, Department of Teaching and Learning, Miami, FL 33199. Offers art education (MA, MS); curriculum and instruction (MS, Ed D, PhD, Ed S), including curriculum development (MS), elementary education (MS), English education (MS), learning technologies (MS), mathematics education (MS), modern language education (MS), physical education (MS), science education (MS), social studies education (MS), special education (MS); early childhood education (MS); exceptional student education (Ed D); foreign language education (MS), including foreign language education, teaching English to speakers of other languages (TESOL); language, literacy and culture (PhD); mathematics, science, and learning technologies (PhD); physical education (MS), including sport and fitness; reading education (MS). *Program availability:* Part-time, evening/weekend. *Faculty:* 60 full-time (41 women), 112 part-time/adjunct (77 women). *Students:* 165 full-time (139 women), 191 part-time (148 women); includes 270 minority (56 Black or African American, non-Hispanic/Latino; 12 Asian, non-Hispanic/Latino; 191 Hispanic/Latino; 11 Two or more races, non-Hispanic/Latino), 13 international. Average age 34. 238 applicants, 68% accepted, 107 enrolled. In 2017, 184 master's, 15 doctorates awarded. *Degree requirements:* For doctorate, comprehensive exam, thesis/dissertation. *Entrance requirements:* For master's, GRE General Test, Florida General Knowledge Test or Florida College Level Academic Skills Test; for doctorate and Ed S, GRE General Test. Additional exam requirements/recommendations for international students: Required—TOEFL (minimum score 550 paper-based; 80 iBT), IELTS (minimum score 6.3). *Application deadline:* For fall admission, 6/1 priority date for domestic students, 4/1 for international students; for winter admission, 10/1 priority date for domestic students, 9/1 for international students; for spring admission, 3/1 priority date for domestic students, 2/1 for international students. Applications are processed on a rolling basis. Application fee: $30. Electronic applications accepted. *Expenses:* Tuition, state resident: full-time $8912; part-time $446 per credit hour. Tuition, nonresident: full-time $21,393; part-time $992 per credit hour. *Required fees:* $390; $195 per semester. *Financial support:* Research assistantships with tuition reimbursements and teaching assistantships with tuition reimbursements available. *Unit head:* Dr. Lynn Miller, Chair, 305-348-2005, Fax: 305-348-2086, E-mail: lynne.miller@fiu.edu. *Application contact:* Nanett Rojas, Assistant Director, Graduate Admissions, 305-348-7464, Fax: 305-348-7441, E-mail: gradadm@fiu.edu.
Website: https://tl.fiu.edu/

Fort Hays State University, Graduate School, College of Health and Life Sciences, Department of Health and Human Performance, Hays, KS 67601-4099. Offers MS. *Program availability:* Part-time. *Degree requirements:* For master's, comprehensive exam, thesis optional. *Entrance requirements:* For master's, GRE General Test or MAT. Additional exam requirements/recommendations for international students: Required—TOEFL (minimum score 550 paper-based). Electronic applications accepted. *Faculty research:* Isoproterenol hydrochloride and exercise, dehydrogenase and high-density lipoprotein levels in athletics, venous blood parameters to adipose fat.

Gardner-Webb University, Graduate School, Department of Physical Education, Wellness, and Sport Studies, Boiling Springs, NC 28017. Offers sport science and pedagogy (MA). *Program availability:* Part-time, evening/weekend. *Faculty:* 2 full-time (1 woman). *Students:* 1 (woman) full-time, 9 part-time (2 women); includes 1 minority (Asian, non-Hispanic/Latino). Average age 24. 27 applicants, 48% accepted, 7 enrolled. In 2017, 5 master's awarded. *Degree requirements:* For master's, comprehensive exam. *Entrance requirements:* For master's, GRE General Test or NTE, PRAXIS, minimum GPA of 2.5. *Application deadline:* For fall admission, 8/1 priority date for domestic students. Applications are processed on a rolling basis. Application fee: $0. Electronic applications accepted. *Expenses:* Contact institution. *Financial support:* Unspecified assistantships available. *Unit head:* Dr. Ken Baker, Chair, 704-406-4481, Fax: 704-406-4739. *Application contact:* Office of Graduate Admissions, 877-498-4723, Fax: 704-406-3895, E-mail: gradinfo@gardner-webb.edu.

Physical Education

George Mason University, College of Education and Human Development, Programs in Curriculum and Instruction, Fairfax, VA 22030. Offers advanced international baccalaureate (M Ed); assistive technology (M Ed); designing digital learning in schools (M Ed); early childhood education (M Ed); early childhood education for diverse learners (M Ed); elementary education (M Ed); English as a second language (M Ed); gifted child education (M Ed); history (M Ed); literacy (M Ed), including PK-12 classroom teachers, reading specialist; literacy leadership for diverse schools (M Ed), including K-12 reading; physical education (M Ed); science K-12 (M Ed); secondary education (M Ed), including biology, chemistry, earth science, English, history/social science, math, physics; special education (M Ed); teacher leadership (M Ed); teaching culturally, linguistically diverse and exceptional learners (M Ed); transformative teaching (M Ed). *Program availability:* Part-time, evening/weekend, 100% online, blended/hybrid learning. *Faculty:* 41 full-time (36 women), 45 part-time/adjunct (37 women). *Students:* 173 full-time (151 women), 729 part-time (611 women); includes 271 minority (65 Black or African American, non-Hispanic/Latino; 5 American Indian or Alaska Native, non-Hispanic/Latino; 88 Asian, non-Hispanic/Latino; 94 Hispanic/Latino; 1 Native Hawaiian or other Pacific Islander, non-Hispanic/Latino; 18 Two or more races, non-Hispanic/Latino), 28 international. Average age 32. 426 applicants, 91% accepted, 289 enrolled. In 2017, 349 master's awarded. *Degree requirements:* For master's, thesis. *Entrance requirements:* For master's, PRAXIS Core (for some programs), 2 letters of recommendation, interview, program goals statement; 9 hours of complete licensure endorsement requirements (for elementary education); minimum GPA of 3.0 in applicant's last 60 hours of undergraduate coursework (for secondary education); at least 1 year of teaching experience (for literacy). Additional exam requirements/recommendations for international students: Required—TOEFL (minimum score 575 paper-based; 88 iBT), IELTS (minimum score 6.5), PTE (minimum score 59). *Application deadline:* For fall admission, 4/2 priority date for domestic and international students; for spring admission, 11/1 for domestic and international students. Application fee: $75 ($80 for international students). Electronic applications accepted. *Expenses:* Tuition, state resident: full-time $11,228; part-time $459.50 per credit. Tuition, nonresident: full-time $30,932; part-time $1280.50 per credit. *Required fees:* $3252; $135.50 per credit. Part-time tuition and fees vary according to course load and program. *Financial support:* In 2017–18, 2 students received support, including 2 teaching assistantships; career-related internships or fieldwork, Federal Work-Study, scholarships/grants, unspecified assistantships, and health care benefits (for full-time research or teaching assistantship recipients) also available. Support available to part-time students. Financial award application deadline: 3/1; financial award applicants required to submit FAFSA. *Faculty research:* Teacher preparation and professional development; adaptive teaching; wonder in science teacher preparation; literacy (digital, adolescent); site based course instruction. *Unit head:* Rebecca Fox, Professor and Academic Program Coordinator, 703-993-4123, E-mail: rfox@gmu.edu.
Website: http://gse.gmu.edu/programs/gsemasters

Georgia College & State University, Graduate School, College of Health Sciences, School of Health and Human Performance, Milledgeville, GA 31061. Offers health and human performance (MS), including health performance, health promotion; kinesiology/health education (MAT). *Accreditation:* NCATE (one or more programs are accredited). *Program availability:* Part-time, 100% online. *Faculty:* 19 full-time (9 women). *Students:* 35 full-time (20 women), 17 part-time (10 women); includes 9 minority (3 Black or African American, non-Hispanic/Latino; 5 Hispanic/Latino; 1 Two or more races, non-Hispanic/Latino), 2 international. Average age 27. 21 applicants, 100% accepted, 19 enrolled. In 2017, 21 master's awarded. *Degree requirements:* For master's, thesis (for some programs), completed in 6 years with minimum GPA of 3.0 (for MS); minimum GPA of 3.0 and electronic teaching portfolio (for MAT). *Entrance requirements:* For master's, GRE with minimum score of 297 or MAT with minimum score of 385 (for MS); GRE with minimum score of 297, MAT 385, SAT 1000, ACT 43, or GACE with 250 on each section (for MAT), resume, 3 professional references; minimum GPA of 2.75 in upper-level undergraduate courses and undergraduate statistics course (for MS); minimum GPA of 2.75 on upper-division major courses (for MAT). *Application deadline:* For fall admission, 7/15 priority date for domestic students, 4/1 for international students; for spring admission, 11/15 priority date for domestic students, 9/1 for international students; for summer admission, 4/15 priority date for domestic students. Applications are processed on a rolling basis. Application fee: $40. Electronic applications accepted. *Expenses:* Contact institution. *Financial support:* In 2017–18, 22 students received support. Unspecified assistantships available. Support available to part-time students. Financial award application deadline: 3/1; financial award applicants required to submit FAFSA. *Unit head:* Dr. Lisa Griffin, Director, School of Health and Human Performance, 478-445-4072, Fax: 478-445-4074, E-mail: lisa.griffin@gcsu.edu.
Website: http://www.gcsu.edu/health/shhp

Georgia Southern University–Armstrong Campus, College of Graduate Studies, Department of Secondary, Adult, and Physical Education, Savannah, GA 31419-1997. Offers adolescent and adult education (Certificate); adult education and community leadership (M Ed); curriculum and instruction (M Ed); secondary education (MAT). *Program availability:* Part-time, evening/weekend, online learning. *Faculty:* 8 full-time (all women), 4 part-time/adjunct (3 women). *Students:* 19 full-time (16 women), 106 part-time (60 women); includes 41 minority (31 Black or African American, non-Hispanic/Latino; 1 Asian, non-Hispanic/Latino; 3 Hispanic/Latino; 6 Two or more races, non-Hispanic/Latino), 1 international. Average age 33. 83 applicants, 48% accepted, 40 enrolled. In 2017, 43 master's, 1 other advanced degree awarded. *Degree requirements:* For master's, comprehensive exam (for some programs), thesis (for some programs), capstone project (for M Ed). *Entrance requirements:* For master's, edTPA (for MAT). Additional exam requirements/recommendations for international students: Required—TOEFL (minimum score 523 paper-based). *Application deadline:* For fall admission, 6/30 priority date for domestic students, 5/1 priority date for international students; for spring admission, 11/15 priority date for domestic students, 9/15 priority date for international students; for summer admission, 4/15 priority date for domestic students, 9/15 for international students. Applications are processed on a rolling basis. Application fee: $30. Electronic applications accepted. *Expenses:* Tuition, state resident: part-time $211 per credit hour. Tuition, nonresident: part-time $782 per credit hour. *Required fees:* $737 per semester. Tuition and fees vary according to course load, degree level, campus/location and program. *Financial support:* In 2017–18, research assistantships with full tuition reimbursements (averaging $5,000 per year) were awarded; career-related internships or fieldwork, Federal Work-Study, scholarships/grants, and unspecified assistantships also available. Support available to part-time students. Financial award application deadline: 3/15; financial award applicants required to submit FAFSA. *Faculty research:* Quality of teacher leadership, classroom management and first year teachers; edTPA preparation and success of candidates; social justice issues related to educational preparation; recruitment of STEM teachers. *Unit head:* Dr. Amelia Adkins, Department Head, 912-344-2562, E-mail: amee.adkins@armstrong.edu. *Application contact:* McKenzie Peterman, Graduate Admissions Specialist, 912-478-5678, Fax: 912-478-0740, E-mail: mpeterman@georgiasouthern.edu.
Website: http://www.armstrong.edu/Education/adolescent_adult_education2/aaed_welcome

Georgia State University, College of Education and Human Development, Department of Kinesiology and Health, Program in Health and Physical Education, Atlanta, GA 30302-3083. Offers M Ed. *Program availability:* Part-time, evening/weekend. *Entrance requirements:* For master's, GRE General Test, minimum GPA of 2.5. Application fee: $50. *Expenses:* Tuition, state resident: full-time $7020. Tuition, nonresident: full-time $22,518. *Required fees:* $2128. Tuition and fees vary according to degree level and program. *Financial support:* Teaching assistantships and career-related internships or fieldwork available. *Faculty research:* Exercise science, teacher behavior. *Unit head:* Dr. Jacalyn Lea Lund, Chair, 404-413-8051, E-mail: jlund@gsu.edu. *Application contact:* Dr. Rachel Gurvitch, Program Coordinator, 404-413-8374, E-mail: rgurvitch@gsu.edu.
Website: http://education.gsu.edu/KIN/kh_programs.htm

Goucher College, Graduate Programs in Education, Baltimore, MD 21204-2794. Offers at-risk and diverse learners (M Ed, Certificate); athletic program leadership and administration (M Ed, Certificate); elementary education (MAT); literacy strategies for content learning (M Ed); middle school (M Ed, Certificate); Montessori studies (M Ed); reading instruction (M Ed, Certificate); reducing student, classroom, and school disruption (M Ed); school improvement leadership (M Ed); secondary education (MAT); special education (MAT), including elementary education; special education for certified elementary and secondary teachers (M Ed); teacher as leader in technology (M Ed). *Program availability:* Part-time, evening/weekend. *Degree requirements:* For master's, thesis (M Ed), final presentation (MAT). *Entrance requirements:* For master's, minimum GPA of 3.0. Additional exam requirements/recommendations for international students: Required—TOEFL (minimum score 550 paper-based; 80 iBT), IELTS (minimum score 7). *Application deadline:* For fall admission, 9/1 for domestic students; for spring admission, 1/15 for domestic students. Applications are processed on a rolling basis. Application fee: $75. Electronic applications accepted. *Expenses:* Contact institution. *Financial support:* Career-related internships or fieldwork and unspecified assistantships available. Support available to part-time students. Financial award application deadline: 4/15; financial award applicants required to submit FAFSA. *Faculty research:* Urban education, middle school, school improvement, teacher behavior, at-risk student achievement. *Unit head:* Dr. Phyllis Sunshine, Assistant Provost, 410-337-6047, Fax: 410-337-6394, E-mail: psunshin@goucher.edu. *Application contact:* Carlton E. Surbeck, III, Director of Admissions, 410-337-6100, Fax: 410-337-6085, E-mail: admissions@goucher.edu.
Website: http://www.goucher.edu/graduate-programs/graduate-programs-in-education

Henderson State University, Graduate Studies, Teachers College, Department of Health, Physical Education, Recreation and Athletic Training, Arkadelphia, AR 71999-0001. Offers sports administration (MS). *Program availability:* Part-time. *Entrance requirements:* For master's, GRE General Test or MAT, minimum GPA of 2.7 as an undergraduate student. Additional exam requirements/recommendations for international students: Required—TOEFL (minimum score 600 paper-based); Recommended—IELTS (minimum score 6.5).

Hofstra University, School of Education, Programs in Teacher Education, Hempstead, NY 11549. Offers bilingual education (MA); bilingual extension (Advanced Certificate), including education/speech language pathology, intensive teacher institute; business education (MS Ed); curriculum studies (MS Ed); early childhood and childhood education (MS Ed); early childhood education (MA, MS Ed); educational technology (Advanced Certificate); elementary education (MA, MS Ed), including science, technology, engineering, and mathematics (STEM) (MA); English education (MS Ed); family and consumer science (MS Ed); fine arts and music education (Advanced Certificate); fine arts education (MS Ed); foreign language and TESOL (MS Ed); foreign language education (MA, MS Ed), including Arabic (MS Ed), biology, chemistry, Chinese (MS Ed), earth science, French, German, Italian (MS Ed), Mandarin (MS Ed), physics, Russian, Spanish; foundations of education (Advanced Certificate), including grades 5-6, grades 7-9; languages other than English and teaching English as a second language (MA); learning and teaching (Ed D), including applied linguistics, art education, arts and humanities, early childhood education, English education, human development, math education, math, science, and technology, multicultural education, physical education, science education, social studies education, special education; mathematics education (MA, MS Ed); music education (MA, MS Ed); science education (MA), including biology (MA, MS Ed), chemistry (MA, MS Ed), earth science (MA, MS Ed), physics (MA, MS Ed); secondary education (Advanced Certificate); social studies education (MA, MS Ed); teaching languages other than English and TESOL (MS Ed); technology for learning (MA); TESOL (MS Ed, Advanced Certificate); TESOL with specialization in STEM (MA); work based learning extension (Advanced Certificate). *Program availability:* Part-time, evening/weekend, blended/hybrid learning. *Students:* 119 full-time (83 women), 124 part-time (90 women); includes 54 minority (15 Black or African American, non-Hispanic/Latino; 9 Asian, non-Hispanic/Latino; 29 Hispanic/Latino; 1 Native Hawaiian or other Pacific Islander, non-Hispanic/Latino), 12 international. Average age 29. 205 applicants, 88% accepted, 93 enrolled. In 2017, 103 master's, 4 doctorates, 32 other advanced degrees awarded. *Degree requirements:* For master's, comprehensive exam, thesis (for some programs), exit project, student teaching, fieldwork, electronic portfolio, curriculum project, minimum GPA of 3.0; for doctorate, thesis/dissertation; for Advanced Certificate, 3 foreign languages, comprehensive exam (for some programs), thesis project. *Entrance requirements:* For master's, GRE, 2 letters of recommendation, portfolio, teacher certification (MA), interview, essay; for doctorate, GMAT, GRE, LSAT, or MAT; for Advanced Certificate, 2 letters of recommendation, essay, interview and/or portfolio, teaching certificate. Additional exam requirements/recommendations for international students: Required—TOEFL (minimum score 550 paper-based; 80 iBT). *Application deadline:* Applications are processed on a rolling basis. Application fee: $75. Electronic applications accepted. *Expenses:* Tuition: Full-time $1292. *Required fees:* $970. Tuition and fees vary according to program. *Financial support:* In 2017–18, 112 students received support, including 56 fellowships with full and partial tuition reimbursements available (averaging $4,998 per year), 2 research assistantships with full and partial tuition reimbursements available (averaging $8,753 per year); career-related internships or fieldwork, Federal Work-Study, institutionally sponsored loans, scholarships/grants, traineeships, tuition waivers (full and partial), and unspecified assistantships also available. Support available to part-time students. Financial award applicants required to submit FAFSA. *Faculty research:* Educational interventions that foster critical-thinking skills; teachers' attitudes about professional development; threats to teacher quality. *Unit head:* Dr. Eustace Thompson, Chairperson, 516-463-5749, Fax: 516-463-6275, E-mail: eustace.g.thompson@hofstra.edu. *Application contact:* Sunil Samuel, Assistant Vice President of Admissions, 516-463-4723, Fax: 516-463-4664, E-mail: graduateadmission@hofstra.edu.
Website: http://www.hofstra.edu/education/

Hofstra University, School of Education, Specialized Programs in Education, Hempstead, NY 11549. Offers applied behavior analysis (Advanced Certificate); childhood special education (MS Ed); early childhood special education (MS Ed, Advanced Certificate); educational and policy leadership (Ed D); educational leadership (Advanced Certificate), including school building leader/school district business leader; educational leadership and policy studies (MS Ed), including K-12; elementary special education (MS Ed); gifted education (Advanced Certificate), including school building leader/school district business leader; health education (MS); health professions pedagogy and leadership (MS); higher education leadership and policy studies (MS Ed);

inclusive early childhood special education (MS Ed); inclusive elementary special education (MS Ed); inclusive secondary special education (MS Ed); literacy studies (MA, MS Ed, Ed D, Advanced Certificate), including birth-grade 6 (MS Ed, Advanced Certificate), grades 5-12 (MS Ed, Advanced Certificate), literacy studies (Ed D); pedagogy for health professions (Advanced Certificate); physical education (MS); school district business leader (Advanced Certificate); secondary education generalist - students with disabilities 7-12 (MS Ed), including students with disabilities 7-12; secondary special education generalist (MS Ed), including extension in secondary education; special education (MS Ed, Advanced Certificate); special education assessment and diagnosis (Advanced Certificate); special education early childhood intervention (MS Ed); special education: international perspectives (MS Ed); teaching students with severe or multiple disabilities (Advanced Certificate). *Program availability:* Part-time, evening/weekend, blended/hybrid learning. *Students:* 148 full-time (110 women), 249 part-time (188 women); includes 105 minority (54 Black or African American, non-Hispanic/Latino; 1 American Indian or Alaska Native, non-Hispanic/Latino; 13 Asian, non-Hispanic/Latino; 35 Hispanic/Latino; 1 Native Hawaiian or other Pacific Islander, non-Hispanic/Latino; 1 Two or more races, non-Hispanic/Latino), 1 international. Average age 32. 228 applicants, 93% accepted, 132 enrolled. In 2017, 97 master's, 22 doctorates, 31 other advanced degrees awarded. *Degree requirements:* For master's, one foreign language, comprehensive exam (for some programs), thesis (for some programs), electronic portfolio, capstone course, internship, practicum, student teaching, seminars, minimum GPA of 3.0; for doctorate, one foreign language, comprehensive exam, thesis/dissertation, qualifying hearing. *Entrance requirements:* For master's, GRE, interview, letters of recommendation, portfolio, essay, certification; for doctorate, GRE or MAT, interview, resume, essay, master's degree, 3 letters of recommendation, writing sample; for Advanced Certificate, GRE, interview, letters of recommendation, essay, professional experience, resume, master's degree. Additional exam requirements/recommendations for international students: Required—TOEFL (minimum score 550 paper-based; 80 iBT). *Application deadline:* Applications are processed on a rolling basis. Application fee: $75. Electronic applications accepted. *Expenses: Tuition:* Full-time $1292. *Required fees:* $970. Tuition and fees vary according to program. *Financial support:* In 2017–18, 225 students received support, including 118 fellowships with full and partial tuition reimbursements available (averaging $3,887 per year), 12 research assistantships with full and partial tuition reimbursements available (averaging $7,215 per year); career-related internships or fieldwork, Federal Work-Study, institutionally sponsored loans, scholarships/grants, traineeships, tuition waivers (full and partial), and unspecified assistantships also available. Support available to part-time students. Financial award applicants required to submit FAFSA. *Faculty research:* Collaborative teaching and learning; language and culture; new media literacies; applied behavior analysis; K-12 leadership development. *Unit head:* Dr. Elfreda Blue, Chairperson, 516-463-5762, Fax: 516-463-6184, E-mail: elfreda.blue@hofstra.edu. *Application contact:* Sunil Samuel, Assistant Vice President of Admissions, 516-463-4723, Fax: 516-463-4664, E-mail: graduateadmission@hofstra.edu.
Website: http://www.hofstra.edu/education/

Howard University, Graduate School, Department of Health, Human Performance and Leisure Studies, Washington, DC 20059-0002. Offers exercise physiology (MS); health education (MS); sports studies (MS), including sociology of sports, sports management; urban recreation (MS), including leisure studies. *Program availability:* Part-time, evening/weekend. *Degree requirements:* For master's, comprehensive exam, thesis. *Entrance requirements:* For master's, BS in human performance or related field. Additional exam requirements/recommendations for international students: Recommended—TOEFL. Electronic applications accepted. *Faculty research:* Health promotion, cardiovascular hypertension, physical activity, sport and human rights issues.

Idaho State University, Office of Graduate Studies, College of Education, Department of Sport Science and Physical Education, Pocatello, ID 83209-8105. Offers athletic administration (MPE); athletic training (MSAT). *Program availability:* Part-time. *Degree requirements:* For master's, comprehensive exam (for some programs), thesis optional, internship, oral defense of dissertation, or written exams. *Entrance requirements:* For master's, MAT or GRE General Test, minimum GPA of 3.0 in upper division classes. Additional exam requirements/recommendations for international students: Required—TOEFL (minimum score 550 paper-based; 80 iBT). Electronic applications accepted. *Faculty research:* Gender and diversity; concussion awareness/sports medicine; legal aspects of athletic health care; sports psychology; exercise physiology; sports management and leadership; adapted activities; fitness, wellness, and nutrition; coaching perspectives; critical features of athletic activities.

Illinois State University, Graduate School, College of Applied Science and Technology, School of Kinesiology and Recreation, Normal, IL 61790. Offers health education (MS). *Degree requirements:* For master's, thesis or alternative. *Entrance requirements:* For master's, GRE General Test, minimum GPA of 2.6 in last 60 hours of course work. *Faculty research:* Influences on positive youth development through sport, country-wide health fitness project, graduate practicum in athletic training, perceived exertion and self-selected intensity during resistance exercise in younger and older.

Indiana State University, College of Graduate and Professional Studies, College of Health and Human Services, Department of Kinesiology, Recreation, and Sport, Terre Haute, IN 47809. Offers physical education (MS); recreation and sport management (MS); sport management (PhD). *Degree requirements:* For master's, comprehensive exam (for some programs), thesis (for some programs). *Entrance requirements:* For master's, GRE General Test, undergraduate major in related field. Electronic applications accepted.

Indiana University Bloomington, School of Public Health, Department of Kinesiology, Bloomington, IN 47405. Offers applied sport science (MS); athletic administration/sport management (MS); athletic training (MS); biomechanics (MS); ergonomics (MS); exercise physiology (MS); human performance (PhD), including biomechanics, exercise physiology, motor learning/control, sport management; motor learning/control (MS); physical activity (MPH); physical activity, fitness and wellness (MS). *Program availability:* Part-time. Terminal master's awarded for partial completion of doctoral program. *Degree requirements:* For master's, thesis optional; for doctorate, variable foreign language requirement, comprehensive exam, thesis/dissertation. *Entrance requirements:* For master's, GRE General Test, minimum GPA of 2.8; for doctorate, GRE General Test, minimum graduate GPA of 3.5, undergraduate 3.0. Additional exam requirements/recommendations for international students: Required—TOEFL (minimum score 80 iBT). *Faculty research:* Exercise physiology and biochemistry, sports biomechanics, human motor control, adaptation of fitness and exercise to special populations.

Indiana University of Pennsylvania, School of Graduate Studies and Research, College of Health and Human Services, Department of Kinesiology, Health, and Sport Science, Program in Health and Physical Education, Indiana, PA 15705. Offers M Ed. *Program availability:* Part-time. *Faculty:* 10 full-time (3 women). *Students:* 34 full-time (17 women), 11 part-time (9 women); includes 4 minority (3 Black or African American, non-Hispanic/Latino; 1 Two or more races, non-Hispanic/Latino). Average age 25. 35 applicants, 89% accepted, 21 enrolled. In 2017, 11 master's awarded. *Entrance*

requirements: Additional exam requirements/recommendations for international students: Required—TOEFL (minimum score 540 paper-based). *Application deadline:* Applications are processed on a rolling basis. Application fee: $50. Electronic applications accepted. *Expenses:* Tuition, state resident: full-time $12,000; part-time $500 per credit. Tuition, nonresident: full-time $18,000; part-time $750 per credit. *Required fees:* $4073; $165.55 per credit. $64 per term. *Financial support:* In 2017–18, 7 research assistantships with tuition reimbursements (averaging $3,303 per year) were awarded; career-related internships or fieldwork, Federal Work-Study, scholarships/grants, and unspecified assistantships also available. Support available to part-time students. Financial award application deadline: 4/15; financial award applicants required to submit FAFSA. *Unit head:* Dr. Keri Kulik, Coordinator, 724-357-5656, E-mail: kskulik@iup.edu.
Website: http://www.iup.edu/grad/healthphysed/default.aspx

Indiana University–Purdue University Indianapolis, School of Physical Education and Tourism Management, Indianapolis, IN 46202-5193. Offers event tourism (MS), including sport event tourism; kinesiology (MS), including clinical exercise science; public health (Graduate Certificate). *Degree requirements:* For master's, comprehensive exam (for some programs), thesis (for some programs). *Entrance requirements:* For master's, GRE. Additional exam requirements/recommendations for international students: Required—TOEFL. Electronic applications accepted. *Expenses:* Contact institution. *Faculty research:* Physical activity, exercise and diseases; human movement science; sport performance; sport event tourism; destination marketing and event management.

Inter American University of Puerto Rico, Metropolitan Campus, Graduate Programs, Program in Physical Education, San Juan, PR 00919-1293. Offers teaching of physical education (MA); training and sport performance (MA). *Degree requirements:* For master's, comprehensive exam. *Entrance requirements:* For master's, GRE or EXADEP, interview. Electronic applications accepted.

Inter American University of Puerto Rico, San Germán Campus, Graduate Studies Center, Program in Health and Physical Education, San Germán, PR 00683-5008. Offers MA. *Program availability:* Part-time, evening/weekend. *Degree requirements:* For master's, comprehensive exam. *Entrance requirements:* For master's, GRE General Test or EXADEP, minimum GPA of 3.0.

Ithaca College, School of Health Sciences and Human Performance, Program in Physical Education, Ithaca, NY 14850. Offers MS. *Program availability:* Part-time. *Faculty:* 3 full-time (2 women). *Degree requirements:* For master's, thesis optional, fieldwork. *Entrance requirements:* Additional exam requirements/recommendations for international students: Required—TOEFL (minimum score 550 paper-based; 80 iBT). *Application deadline:* For fall admission, 3/1 for domestic and international students; for spring admission, 12/1 for domestic and international students. Applications are processed on a rolling basis. Application fee: $40. Electronic applications accepted. *Expenses:* Contact institution. *Financial support:* Research assistantships, career-related internships or fieldwork, Federal Work-Study, scholarships/grants, and unspecified assistantships available. Support available to part-time students. Financial award application deadline: 3/1; financial award applicants required to submit FAFSA. *Unit head:* Dr. Stewart Auyash, Chair, 607-274-1312, E-mail: auyash@ithaca.edu. *Application contact:* Nicole Eversley Bradwell, Director, Office of Admission, 607-274-3124, Fax: 607-274-1263, E-mail: admission@ithaca.edu.
Website: http://www.ithaca.edu/gradprograms/hppe/programs/physed

Jackson State University, Graduate School, College of Education and Human Development, Department of Health, Physical Education and Recreation, Jackson, MS 39217. Offers physical education (MS Ed); sport science (MS). *Accreditation:* NCATE. *Program availability:* Part-time, evening/weekend, 100% online, blended/hybrid learning. *Degree requirements:* For master's, comprehensive exam, thesis or alternative. *Entrance requirements:* For master's, GRE General Test. Additional exam requirements/recommendations for international students: Required—TOEFL (minimum score 520 paper-based; 67 iBT). Electronic applications accepted. *Expenses:* Contact institution.

Jacksonville State University, College of Graduate Studies and Continuing Education, College of Education and Professional Studies, Program in Physical Education, Jacksonville, AL 36265-1602. Offers MS Ed and Ed S. *Accreditation:* NCATE. *Program availability:* Part-time, evening/weekend. *Degree requirements:* For master's, comprehensive exam, thesis (for some programs). *Entrance requirements:* For master's, GRE General Test or MAT. Additional exam requirements/recommendations for international students: Required—TOEFL (minimum score 500 paper-based; 61 iBT). Electronic applications accepted.

James Madison University, The Graduate School, College of Health and Behavioral Studies, Program in Kinesiology, Harrisonburg, VA 22801. Offers clinical exercise physiology (MS); exercise physiology (MS); kinesiology (MAT, MS); nutrition and exercise (MS); physical and health education (MAT); sport and recreation leadership (MS). *Program availability:* Part-time, evening/weekend. *Students:* 43 full-time (22 women), 3 part-time (2 women); includes 10 minority (4 Black or African American, non-Hispanic/Latino; 1 Asian, non-Hispanic/Latino; 4 Hispanic/Latino; 1 Two or more races, non-Hispanic/Latino). Average age 30. In 2017, 46 master's awarded. Application fee: $55. Electronic applications accepted. *Expenses:* Tuition, state resident: full-time $10,512; part-time $438 per credit hour. Tuition, nonresident: full-time $28,358; part-time $1162 per credit hour. *Required fees:* $1128. *Financial support:* In 2017–18, 32 students received support, including 13 teaching assistantships with full tuition reimbursements available (averaging $8,837 per year); Federal Work-Study and 19 assistantships (averaging $7911), 20 athletic assistantships (averaging $9284) also available. Financial award application deadline: 3/1; financial award applicants required to submit FAFSA. *Unit head:* Dr. Christopher J. Womack, Department Head, 540-568-6145, E-mail: womackcx@jmu.edu. *Application contact:* Lynette D. Michael, Director of Graduate Admissions, 540-568-6131 Ext. 6395, Fax: 540-568-7860, E-mail: michaeld@jmu.edu.
Website: http://www.jmu.edu/kinesiology/

Longwood University, College of Graduate and Professional Studies, College of Education and Human Services, Farmville, VA 23909. Offers education (MS), including algebra and middle school mathematics, counselor education, elementary and middle school mathematics, elementary education, elementary education initial licensure, health and physical education, special education general curriculum, special education initial licensure; reading, literacy and learning (M Ed); school librarianship (M Ed); social work and communication sciences and disorders (MS), including communication sciences and disorders. *Accreditation:* NCATE. *Program availability:* Part-time, evening/weekend. *Degree requirements:* For master's, comprehensive exam (for some programs), thesis optional, professional portfolio, internship, clinical experience, or practicum. *Entrance requirements:* For master's, PRAXIS I (for initial teaching licensure programs); GRE (for some programs), bachelor's degree from regionally-accredited institution, 2 recommendations (3 for some programs), minimum 500-word personal essay, official transcripts, minimum GPA of 2.75, valid teaching license (for some programs). Additional exam requirements/recommendations for international students: Required—TOEFL (minimum score 570 paper-based), IELTS (minimum score 6.5). Electronic applications accepted. *Expenses:* Contact institution.

Physical Education

Massachusetts College of Liberal Arts, Graduate Programs, North Adams, MA 01247-4100. Offers business (MBA); educational administration (M Ed); educational leadership (CAGS); instruction and curriculum (M Ed); instructional technology (M Ed); physical education and health (M Ed); reading (M Ed); special education (M Ed). *Program availability:* Part-time, evening/weekend. *Degree requirements:* For master's, thesis. *Entrance requirements:* For master's, writing sample.

McGill University, Faculty of Graduate and Postdoctoral Studies, Faculty of Education, Department of Kinesiology and Physical Education, Montréal, QC H3A 2T5, Canada. Offers M Sc, MA, PhD, Certificate, Diploma.

McNeese State University, Doré School of Graduate Studies, Burton College of Education, Department of Education Professions, Program in Multiple Levels Grades K-12, Lake Charles, LA 70609. Offers multiple levels grades K-12 (Postbaccalaureate Certificate), including art, health and physical education, music - instrumental, music - vocal. *Entrance requirements:* For degree, PRAXIS, 2 letters of recommendation, autobiography. *Application deadline:* For fall admission, 5/15 priority date for domestic and international students; for spring admission, 10/15 priority date for domestic and international students. Applications are processed on a rolling basis. Application fee: $20 ($30 for international students). *Financial support:* Application deadline: 5/1. *Unit head:* Dr. Veronica Faye White, Head, 337-475-5400, Fax: 337-475-5272, E-mail: vfwhite@mcneese.edu. *Application contact:* Dr. Dustin M. Hebert, Director of Dore' School of Graduate Studies, 337-475-5396, Fax: 337-475-5397, E-mail: admissions@mcneese.edu.

Memorial University of Newfoundland, School of Graduate Studies, School of Human Kinetics and Recreation, St. John's, NL A1C 5S7, Canada. Offers administration, curriculum and supervision (MPE); biomechanics/ergonomics (MS Kin); exercise and work physiology (MS Kin); psychology of sport, exercise and recreation (MS Kin); socio-cultural studies of physical activity and health (MS Kin). *Program availability:* Part-time. *Degree requirements:* For master's, thesis optional, seminars, thesis presentations. *Entrance requirements:* For master's, bachelor's degree in a related field, minimum B average. Electronic applications accepted. *Faculty research:* Administration, sociology of sports, kinesiology, physiology/recreation.

Meredith College, School of Education, Health and Human Sciences, Raleigh, NC 27607-5298. Offers academically and intellectually gifted (M Ed); elementary education (M Ed, MAT); English as a second language (M Ed, MAT); health and physical education (MAT); nutrition, health and human performance (MS, Postbaccalaureate Certificate), including dietetic internship (Postbaccalaureate Certificate), nutrition (MS); psychology (MA), including industrial/organizational psychology; reading (M Ed); special education (MAT); special education (general curriculum) (M Ed). *Accreditation:* NCATE. *Program availability:* Part-time, evening/weekend. *Students:* 25 full-time (24 women), 22 part-time (all women); includes 13 minority (8 Black or African American, non-Hispanic/Latino; 1 American Indian or Alaska Native, non-Hispanic/Latino; 1 Asian, non-Hispanic/Latino; 3 Hispanic/Latino). Average age 31. 57 applicants, 54% accepted, 31 enrolled. In 2017, 14 master's awarded. *Degree requirements:* For master's, thesis optional. *Entrance requirements:* For master's, GRE General Test or MAT, minimum GPA of 2.5, teaching license, recommendations. Additional exam requirements/recommendations for international students: Required—TOEFL. *Application deadline:* For fall admission, 7/1 priority date for domestic students; for spring admission, 11/1 priority date for domestic students. Applications are processed on a rolling basis. Application fee: $50. Electronic applications accepted. *Expenses:* Contact institution. *Financial support:* Career-related internships or fieldwork, institutionally sponsored loans, and tuition waivers (partial) available. Support available to part-time students. Financial award application deadline: 2/15; financial award applicants required to submit FAFSA. *Unit head:* Dr. Monica McKinney, Graduate Program Manager, 919-760-8056, Fax: 919-760-2303, E-mail: mckinneym@meredith.edu.
Website: https://www.meredith.edu/school-of-education-health-and-human-sciences

Middle Tennessee State University, College of Graduate Studies, College of Behavioral and Health Sciences, Department of Health and Human Performance, Program in Health, Physical Education and Recreation, Murfreesboro, TN 37132. Offers health and human performance (MS); leisure and sport management (MS). *Program availability:* Part-time, evening/weekend, online learning. *Degree requirements:* For master's, comprehensive exam, thesis optional. *Entrance requirements:* For master's, GRE. Additional exam requirements/recommendations for international students: Required—TOEFL (minimum score 525 paper-based; 71 iBT) or IELTS (minimum score 6). *Faculty research:* Kinesiometrics, leisure behavior, health, lifestyles.

Millersville University of Pennsylvania, College of Graduate Studies and Adult Learning, College of Education and Human Services, Department of Wellness and Sport Sciences, Program in Sport Management: Athletic Coaching Option, Millersville, PA 17551-0302. Offers coaching education (Post-Master's Certificate); sport management (M Ed), including athletic coaching. *Program availability:* Part-time, evening/weekend. *Faculty:* 6 full-time (3 women). *Students:* 1 full-time (0 women), 4 part-time (0 women); includes 2 minority (1 Black or African American, non-Hispanic/Latino; 1 Asian, non-Hispanic/Latino), 1 international. Average age 26. 4 applicants, 75% accepted, 2 enrolled. In 2017, 6 master's awarded. *Degree requirements:* For master's, thesis optional, internship. *Entrance requirements:* For master's, GRE, MAT, GMAT, or interview with writing assignment if undergraduate cumulative GPA lower than 3.0, all transcripts, at least 1 academic reference, sport management goal statement. Additional exam requirements/recommendations for international students: Required—TOEFL (minimum score 80 iBT), IELTS (minimum score 6.5), PTE (minimum score 60). *Application deadline:* Applications are processed on a rolling basis. Application fee: $40. Electronic applications accepted. *Expenses:* $500 per credit resident tuition and fees; $750 per credit non-resident tuition and fees; $114.75 per credit general fee (maximum of 12 credits); technology fee $27 per credit (resident), $39 per credit (non-resident). *Financial support:* In 2017–18, 2 students received support. Unspecified assistantships available. Financial award application deadline: 3/15; financial award applicants required to submit FAFSA. *Faculty research:* Applied sport management; leadership and sport; marketing and sport; gender and sport; leadership development; ADR, restorative justice and hazing; legal issues applied to sport management; women and fitness/sport. *Unit head:* Dr. Rebecca J. Mowrey, Coordinator, 717-871-4214, Fax: 717-871-7987, E-mail: rebecca.mowrey@millersville.edu. *Application contact:* Dr. Victor S. DeSantis, Dean of College of Graduate Studies and Adult Learning/Associate Provost for Civic and Community Engagement, 717-871-7619, Fax: 717-871-7954, E-mail: victor.desantis@millersville.edu.
Website: http://www.millersville.edu/wssd/graduate/index.php

Minnesota State University Mankato, College of Graduate Studies and Research, College of Allied Health and Nursing, Department of Human Performance, Mankato, MN 56001. Offers physical education (MA, MS). *Program availability:* Part-time. *Degree requirements:* For master's, comprehensive exam, thesis. *Entrance requirements:* For master's, minimum GPA of 3.0 during previous 2 years. Additional exam requirements/recommendations for international students: Required—TOEFL.

Mississippi State University, College of Education, Department of Kinesiology, Mississippi State, MS 39762. Offers disability studies (MS); exercise physiology (MS); exercise science (PhD); sport administration (MS); sport pedagogy (MS); sport studies

(PhD). *Program availability:* Part-time, blended/hybrid learning. *Faculty:* 16 full-time (3 women). *Students:* 64 full-time (20 women), 8 part-time (3 women); includes 13 minority (2 Black or African American, non-Hispanic/Latino; 4 Asian, non-Hispanic/Latino; 4 Hispanic/Latino; 3 Two or more races, non-Hispanic/Latino), 10 international. Average age 26. 66 applicants, 59% accepted, 31 enrolled. In 2017, 23 master's awarded. *Degree requirements:* For master's, comprehensive exam, thesis optional; for doctorate, comprehensive exam. *Entrance requirements:* For master's, GRE General Test, minimum GPA of 2.75 on undergraduate work from four-year accredited institution, 3.0 graduate; for doctorate, GRE, minimum GPA of 3.4 on previous graduate degree(s) earned from accredited institutions. Additional exam requirements/recommendations for international students: Required—TOEFL (minimum score 550 paper-based; 79 iBT); Recommended—IELTS (minimum score 6.5). *Application deadline:* For fall admission, 7/1 for domestic students, 5/1 for international students; for spring admission, 11/1 for domestic students, 9/1 for international students. Applications are processed on a rolling basis. Application fee: $60 ($80 for international students). Electronic applications accepted. *Expenses:* Tuition: state resident: full-time $8318; part-time $462.12 per credit hour. Tuition, nonresident: full-time $22,358; part-time $1242.12 per credit hour. *Required fees:* $110; $12.24 per credit hour. $6.12 per semester. *Financial support:* In 2017–18, 13 teaching assistantships with partial tuition reimbursements (averaging $10,510 per year) were awarded; career-related internships or fieldwork, Federal Work-Study, institutionally sponsored loans, and unspecified assistantships also available. Financial award application deadline: 4/1; financial award applicants required to submit FAFSA. *Faculty research:* Static balance and stepping performance of older adults, organizational justice, public health, strength training and recovery drinks, high risk drinking perceptions and behaviors. *Unit head:* Dr. Stanley P. Brown, Professor and Head, 662-325-7229, Fax: 662-325-4525, E-mail: spb107@msstate.edu. *Application contact:* Marina Hung, Admissions and Enrollment Assistant, 662-325-5188, E-mail: lbonner@grad.msstate.edu.
Website: http://www.kinesiology.msstate.edu/

Missouri State University, Graduate College, College of Health and Human Services, Department of Kinesiology, Springfield, MO 65897. Offers health promotion and wellness management (MS); secondary education (MS Ed), including physical education. *Program availability:* Part-time. *Faculty:* 14 full-time (6 women). *Students:* 21 full-time (11 women), 11 part-time (4 women); includes 4 minority (1 Black or African American, non-Hispanic/Latino; 1 Asian, non-Hispanic/Latino; 1 Hispanic/Latino; 1 Two or more races, non-Hispanic/Latino), 2 international. Average age 24. 23 applicants, 48% accepted, 11 enrolled. In 2017, 8 master's awarded. *Degree requirements:* For master's, comprehensive exam, thesis or alternative. *Entrance requirements:* For master's, GRE (for MS), minimum GPA of 2.8 (MS); 9-12 teaching certification (MS Ed). Additional exam requirements/recommendations for international students: Required—TOEFL (minimum score 550 paper-based; 79 iBT), IELTS (minimum score 6). *Application deadline:* For fall admission, 7/20 priority date for domestic students, 5/1 for international students; for spring admission, 12/20 priority date for domestic students, 9/1 for international students. Applications are processed on a rolling basis. Application fee: $35 ($50 for international students). Electronic applications accepted. *Expenses:* Tuition, state resident: full-time $2915; part-time $2021 per credit hour. Tuition, nonresident: full-time $5354; part-time $3647 per credit hour. *International tuition:* $11,992 full-time. *Required fees:* $173; $173 per credit hour. Tuition and fees vary according to class time, course level, course load, degree level, campus/location and program. *Financial support:* In 2017–18, 7 teaching assistantships with partial tuition reimbursements (averaging $8,772 per year) were awarded; Federal Work-Study, institutionally sponsored loans, scholarships/grants, and unspecified assistantships also available. Financial award application deadline: 3/31; financial award applicants required to submit FAFSA. *Unit head:* Dr. Sarah McCallister, Head, 417-836-6582, Fax: 417-836-5371, E-mail: sarahmccallister@missouristate.edu. *Application contact:* Stephanie Praschan, Director, Graduate Enrollment Management, 417-836-5330, Fax: 417-836-6200, E-mail: stephaniepraschan@missouristate.edu.
Website: http://www.missouristate.edu/kinesiology/

Montclair State University, The Graduate School, College of Education and Human Services, MAT Program in Teaching, Montclair, NJ 07043-1624. Offers art (MAT); biology (MAT); chemistry (MAT); earth science (MAT); English (MAT); French (MAT); health and physical education (MAT); health education (MAT); mathematics (MAT); music (MAT); physical education (MAT); physical science (MAT); social studies (MAT); Spanish (MAT); teacher of English as a second language (MAT). *Degree requirements:* For master's, comprehensive exam, thesis or alternative. *Entrance requirements:* For master's, interview, 2 letters of recommendation. Additional exam requirements/recommendations for international students: Required—TOEFL (minimum score 83 iBT), IELTS (minimum score 6.5). Electronic applications accepted.

Montclair State University, The Graduate School, College of Education and Human Services, Program in Exercise Science and Physical Education, Montclair, NJ 07043-1624. Offers exercise science (MA); sports administration and coaching (MA); teaching and supervision in physical education (MA). *Program availability:* Part-time, evening/weekend. *Degree requirements:* For master's, comprehensive exam, thesis or alternative. *Entrance requirements:* For master's, GRE General Test, essay, 2 letters of recommendation. Additional exam requirements/recommendations for international students: Required—TOEFL (minimum score 83 iBT), IELTS (minimum score 6.5). Electronic applications accepted.

Montclair State University, The Graduate School, College of Science and Mathematics, Program in Teaching Physical Education, Montclair, NJ 07043-1624. Offers MAT. *Degree requirements:* For master's, comprehensive exam. *Entrance requirements:* For master's, GRE General Test, interview, 2 letters of recommendation, essay. Additional exam requirements/recommendations for international students: Required—TOEFL (minimum score 83 iBT), IELTS (minimum score 6.5). Electronic applications accepted. *Faculty research:* Teaching physics.

Morehead State University, Graduate Programs, College of Education, Department of Middle Grades and Secondary Education, Morehead, KY 40351. Offers business and marketing education (MAT); English/language arts 5-9 (MAT); French (MAT); health P-12 (MAT); mathematics 5-9 (MAT); physical education P-12 (MAT); science 5-9 (MAT); secondary biology (MAT); secondary chemistry (MAT); secondary earth science (MAT); secondary English (MAT); secondary math (MAT); secondary physics (MAT); secondary social studies (MAT); social studies 5-9 (MAT); Spanish (MAT). *Program availability:* Part-time, evening/weekend. *Degree requirements:* For master's, portfolio. *Entrance requirements:* For master's, GRE or PRAXIS II content exam, minimum overall undergraduate GPA of 2.5. Additional exam requirements/recommendations for international students: Required—TOEFL (minimum score 500 paper-based). Electronic applications accepted.

Morehead State University, Graduate Programs, College of Science and Technology, Department of Health, Wellness and Human Performance, Morehead, KY 40351. Offers health/physical education (MA). *Accreditation:* NCATE. *Program availability:* Part-time, evening/weekend. *Degree requirements:* For master's, comprehensive exam, thesis, oral exam, written core exam. *Entrance requirements:* For master's, GRE General Test or MAT, minimum GPA of 2.5; undergraduate major/minor in health, physical education, or recreation. Additional exam requirements/recommendations for international students: Required—TOEFL (minimum score 500 paper-based). Electronic applications accepted. *Faculty research:* Child growth and performance, instructional strategies, outdoor leadership qualities, exercise science, athletic training.

North Carolina Agricultural and Technical State University, School of Graduate Studies, School of Education, Department of Human Performance and Leisure Studies, Greensboro, NC 27411. Offers physical education (MAT, MS). *Accreditation:* NCATE. *Program availability:* Part-time, evening/weekend. *Degree requirements:* For master's, comprehensive exam, thesis or alternative, qualifying exam. *Entrance requirements:* For master's, GRE General Test or MAT.

North Carolina Central University, College of Behavioral and Social Sciences, Department of Physical Education and Recreation, Durham, NC 27707-3129. Offers general physical education (MS); recreation administration (MS). *Program availability:* Part-time, evening/weekend. *Degree requirements:* For master's, one foreign language, comprehensive exam, thesis. *Entrance requirements:* For master's, GRE, minimum GPA of 3.0 in major, 2.5 overall. Additional exam requirements/recommendations for international students: Required—TOEFL. *Application deadline:* For fall admission, 8/1 for domestic students. Application fee: $30. *Expenses:* Tuition, state resident: full-time $2770; part-time $692.50 per credit hour. Tuition, nonresident: full-time $9247; part-time $2311.75 per credit hour. *Financial support:* Application deadline: 5/1; applicants required to submit FAFSA. *Unit head:* Virginia Politano, Chair, 919-530-6186, Fax: 919-530-6156, E-mail: politano@nccu.edu. *Application contact:* Virginia Politano, Chair, 919-530-6186, Fax: 919-530-6156, E-mail: politano@nccu.edu.

Northern Illinois University, Graduate School, College of Education, Department of Kinesiology and Physical Education, De Kalb, IL 60115-2854. Offers MS, MS Ed. *Program availability:* Part-time, evening/weekend. *Faculty:* 21 full-time (12 women). *Students:* 84 full-time (32 women), 40 part-time (17 women); includes 31 minority (16 Black or African American, non-Hispanic/Latino; 2 Asian, non-Hispanic/Latino; 7 Hispanic/Latino; 6 Two or more races, non-Hispanic/Latino), 1 international. Average age 25. 88 applicants, 80% accepted, 48 enrolled. In 2017, 56 master's awarded. *Degree requirements:* For master's, comprehensive exam, thesis optional. *Entrance requirements:* For master's, GRE General Test, minimum GPA of 2.75, undergraduate major in related area. Additional exam requirements/recommendations for international students: Required—TOEFL (minimum score 550 paper-based). *Application deadline:* For fall admission, 6/1 for domestic students, 5/1 for international students; for spring admission, 11/1 for domestic students, 10/1 for international students. Applications are processed on a rolling basis. Application fee: $40. Electronic applications accepted. *Financial support:* In 2017–18, 2 research assistantships with full tuition reimbursements, 31 teaching assistantships with full tuition reimbursements were awarded; fellowships with full tuition reimbursements, career-related internships or fieldwork, Federal Work-Study, scholarships/grants, tuition waivers (full), and unspecified assistantships also available. Support available to part-time students. Financial award applicants required to submit FAFSA. *Faculty research:* Leadership in athletic training, motor development, dance education, gait analysis, fat phobia. *Unit head:* Dr. Chad D. McEvoy, Chair, 815-753-8284, Fax: 815-753-1413, E-mail: knpe@niu.edu. *Application contact:* Dr. Laurie Zittel, Director, Graduate Studies, 815-753-1425, E-mail: lzape@niu.edu.
Website: http://cedu.niu.edu/knpe/

Northwest Missouri State University, Graduate School, School of Health Science and Wellness, Maryville, MO 64468-6001. Offers applied health and sport sciences (MS); guidance and counseling (MS Ed); health and physical education (MS Ed); recreation (MS); sport and exercise psychology (MS). *Accreditation:* NCATE. *Program availability:* Part-time. *Faculty:* 23 full-time (11 women). *Students:* 68 full-time (43 women), 41 part-time (29 women); includes 9 minority (3 Black or African American, non-Hispanic/Latino; 4 Hispanic/Latino; 2 Two or more races, non-Hispanic/Latino), 5 international. Average age 27. 49 applicants, 47% accepted, 16 enrolled. In 2017, 34 master's awarded. *Degree requirements:* For master's, comprehensive exam. *Entrance requirements:* For master's, GRE General Test, minimum undergraduate GPA of 2.75, teaching certificate, writing sample. Additional exam requirements/recommendations for international students: Required—TOEFL (minimum score 550 paper-based). *Application deadline:* For fall admission, 7/1 for domestic and international students; for spring admission, 11/15 for domestic and international students. Applications are processed on a rolling basis. Application fee: $0 ($50 for international students). *Expenses:* Tuition, state resident: full-time $4551; part-time $252.86 per credit hour. Tuition, nonresident: full-time $9103; part-time $505.72 per credit hour. *Required fees:* $2453; $136.25 per credit hour. Tuition and fees vary according to course load and program. *Financial support:* Teaching assistantships with full tuition reimbursements and unspecified assistantships available. Financial award application deadline: 4/1; financial award applicants required to submit FAFSA. *Unit head:* Dr. Terry Long, Director, School of Health Science and Wellness, 660-562-1706, Fax: 660-562-1483, E-mail: tlong@nwmissouri.edu. *Application contact:* Gina Smith, Secretary, 660-562-1297, Fax: 660-562-1963, E-mail: smigina@nwmissouri.edu.
Website: http://www.nwmissouri.edu/health/

The Ohio State University, Graduate School, College of Education and Human Ecology, Department of Human Sciences, Columbus, OH 43210. Offers consumer sciences (MS, PhD); human development and family science (PhD); human nutrition (MS, PhD); kinesiology (MA, Ed D, PhD). *Program availability:* Part-time. *Faculty:* 55. *Students:* 127 full-time (71 women), 14 part-time (12 women). Average age 27. In 2017, 31 master's, 14 doctorates awarded. *Degree requirements:* For master's, thesis optional; for doctorate, thesis/dissertation. *Entrance requirements:* For master's and doctorate, GRE. Additional exam requirements/recommendations for international students: Required—TOEFL (minimum score 550 paper-based; 79 iBT), Michigan English Language Assessment Battery (minimum score 82); Recommended—IELTS (minimum score 7). *Application deadline:* For fall admission, 12/1 priority date for domestic and international students. Applications are processed on a rolling basis. Application fee: $60 ($70 for international students). Electronic applications accepted. *Financial support:* Fellowships with tuition reimbursements, research assistantships with tuition reimbursements, teaching assistantships with tuition reimbursements, Federal Work-Study, and institutionally sponsored loans available. Support available to part-time students. *Unit head:* Dr. Brian Focht, Associate Chair and Professor, E-mail: focht.10@osu.edu. *Application contact:* Graduate and Professional Admissions, 614-292-9444, Fax: 614-292-3895, E-mail: gpadmissions@osu.edu.
Website: http://ehe.osu.edu/human-sciences/

Ohio University, Graduate College, Gladys W. and David H. Patton College of Education and Human Services, Department of Recreation and Sport Pedagogy, Program in Coaching Education, Athens, OH 45701-2979. Offers MS. *Entrance requirements:* For master's, GRE. Additional exam requirements/recommendations for international students: Required—TOEFL (minimum score 550 paper-based; 80 iBT) or IELTS (minimum score 6.5). Electronic applications accepted. *Faculty research:* Sports, physical activity, athletes.

Old Dominion University, Darden College of Education, Program in Physical Education, Adapted Physical Education Emphasis, Norfolk, VA 23529. Offers MS Ed. *Program availability:* Part-time. *Faculty:* 2 full-time (0 women). *Students:* 2 full-time (both women), 2 part-time (both women); includes 1 minority (Black or African American, non-

Hispanic/Latino). Average age 30. 1 applicant, 100% accepted, 1 enrolled. *Degree requirements:* For master's, comprehensive exam (for some programs), thesis (for some programs). *Entrance requirements:* Additional exam requirements/recommendations for international students: Required—TOEFL (minimum score 550 paper-based; 79 iBT). *Application deadline:* Applications are processed on a rolling basis. Application fee: $50. Electronic applications accepted. *Expenses:* Tuition, state resident: full-time $8928; part-time $496 per credit. Tuition, nonresident: full-time $22,482; part-time $1249 per credit. *Required fees:* $66 per semester. *Financial support:* Unspecified assistantships available. Financial award application deadline: 3/1; financial award applicants required to submit FAFSA. *Faculty research:* Adapted physical education/activity, inclusion, individuals with disabilities, assessment and evaluation. *Total annual research expenditures:* $104,000. *Unit head:* Dr. Lynn Ridinger, Chair, 757-683-3351. *Application contact:* Justin Haegele, Coordinator, 757-683-4353, E-mail: jhaegele@odu.edu.
Website: https://www.odu.edu/hms/academics/hpe/graduate

Old Dominion University, Darden College of Education, Program in Physical Education, Coaching Science Emphasis, Norfolk, VA 23529. Offers MS Ed. *Program availability:* Part-time. *Faculty:* 2 full-time (0 women). *Students:* 5 full-time (1 woman), 3 part-time (1 woman); includes 5 minority (4 Black or African American, non-Hispanic/Latino; 1 Two or more races, non-Hispanic/Latino). Average age 26. 6 applicants, 83% accepted, 4 enrolled. In 2017, 2 master's awarded. *Degree requirements:* For master's, comprehensive exam, internship, research project, or thesis. *Entrance requirements:* For master's, GRE, bachelor's degree with minimum cumulative undergraduate GPA of 2.8, 3.0 in undergraduate major courses. Additional exam requirements/recommendations for international students: Required—TOEFL (minimum score 550 paper-based; 79 iBT). *Application deadline:* Applications are processed on a rolling basis. Application fee: $50. Electronic applications accepted. *Expenses:* Tuition, state resident: full-time $8928; part-time $496 per credit. Tuition, nonresident: full-time $22,482; part-time $1249 per credit. *Required fees:* $66 per semester. *Financial support:* Unspecified assistantships available. Financial award application deadline: 3/1. *Faculty research:* Curriculum development, learning and coaching theory, planning and administration in physical education and sports, adapted physical education. *Total annual research expenditures:* $104,000. *Unit head:* Dr. Lynn Ridinger, Chair, 757-683-4995. *Application contact:* Dr. Xihe Zhu, Coordinator, 757-683-3545.
Website: https://www.odu.edu/hms/academics/hpe/graduate

Old Dominion University, Darden College of Education, Program in Physical Education, Curriculum and Instruction Emphasis, Norfolk, VA 23529. Offers human movement sciences (PhD), including health and sport pedagogy; physical education (MS Ed), including adapted physical education, coaching education, curriculum and instruction. *Program availability:* Part-time, evening/weekend. *Faculty:* 3 full-time (1 woman). *Students:* 2 full-time (1 woman), 5 part-time (1 woman); includes 2 minority (1 Black or African American, non-Hispanic/Latino; 1 Two or more races, non-Hispanic/Latino). Average age 29. 2 applicants, 50% accepted. In 2017, 2 master's awarded. *Degree requirements:* For master's, comprehensive exam (for some programs), thesis or alternative, internship, research project. *Entrance requirements:* For master's, GRE, PRAXIS tests (for licensure only), minimum GPA of 2.8 overall, 3.0 in major. Additional exam requirements/recommendations for international students: Required—TOEFL (minimum score 500 paper-based; 97 iBT). *Application deadline:* For fall admission, 3/1 priority date for domestic students; for spring admission, 11/1 for domestic students. Applications are processed on a rolling basis. Application fee: $50. Electronic applications accepted. *Expenses:* Tuition, state resident: full-time $8928; part-time $496 per credit. Tuition, nonresident: full-time $22,482; part-time $1249 per credit. *Required fees:* $66 per semester. *Financial support:* Unspecified assistantships available. Financial award application deadline: 4/15. *Faculty research:* Motor development, physical activity and fitness, motivation and learning in physical education, curriculum and instruction, adapted physical education. *Total annual research expenditures:* $104,000. *Unit head:* Dr. Lynn Ridinger, Chair, 757-683-4995, E-mail: lridinge@odu.edu. *Application contact:* William Heffelfinger, Director of Graduate Admissions, 757-683-5554, Fax: 757-683-3255, E-mail: gradadmit@odu.edu.
Website: https://www.odu.edu/hms/academics/hpe/graduate

Old Dominion University, Darden College of Education, Program in Physical Education, Exercise Science and Wellness Emphasis, Norfolk, VA 23529. Offers physical education (MS Ed), including exercise science and wellness. *Program availability:* Part-time, evening/weekend. *Faculty:* 7 full-time (3 women). *Students:* 14 full-time (9 women), 3 part-time (1 woman); includes 6 minority (3 Black or African American, non-Hispanic/Latino; 1 Asian, non-Hispanic/Latino; 1 Hispanic/Latino; 1 Two or more races, non-Hispanic/Latino). Average age 26. 16 applicants, 88% accepted, 8 enrolled. In 2017, 9 master's awarded. *Degree requirements:* For master's, comprehensive exam, thesis or alternative, internship, research project. *Entrance requirements:* For master's, GRE (minimum score of 291 for combined verbal and quantitative), minimum GPA of 2.8 overall, 3.0 in major. Additional exam requirements/recommendations for international students: Required—TOEFL (minimum score 550 paper-based; 79 iBT). *Application deadline:* For fall admission, 3/1 for domestic and international students. Applications are processed on a rolling basis. Application fee: $50. Electronic applications accepted. *Expenses:* Tuition, state resident: full-time $8928; part-time $496 per credit. Tuition, nonresident: full-time $22,482; part-time $1249 per credit. *Required fees:* $66 per semester. *Financial support:* In 2017–18, 7 students received support, including 4 research assistantships (averaging $10,000 per year), 3 teaching assistantships (averaging $10,000 per year); unspecified assistantships also available. Financial award application deadline: 3/1. *Faculty research:* Cardiovascular response to exercise, exercise prescription, nutrition, lower extremity biomechanics, metabolic responses in special populations. *Total annual research expenditures:* $104,000. *Unit head:* Dr. Lynn Ridinger, Chair, 757-683-4353, E-mail: lridinge@odu.edu. *Application contact:* William Heffelfinger, Director of Graduate Admissions, 757-683-5554, Fax: 757-683-3255, E-mail: gradadmit@odu.edu.
Website: http://www.odu.edu/hms/academics/exercise/graduate#.Wr0u402otrQ

Pittsburg State University, Graduate School, College of Education, Department of Health, Physical Education and Recreation, Pittsburg, KS 66762. Offers health, human performance, and recreation (MS), including human performance and wellness, sport and leisure service management. *Program availability:* Part-time, online only, 100% online. *Students:* 66 (25 women); includes 17 minority (5 Black or African American, non-Hispanic/Latino; 2 American Indian or Alaska Native, non-Hispanic/Latino; 4 Hispanic/Latino; 6 Two or more races, non-Hispanic/Latino). In 2017, 33 master's awarded. *Degree requirements:* For master's, thesis or alternative. *Entrance requirements:* For master's, letter of intent. Additional exam requirements/recommendations for international students: Required—TOEFL (minimum score 520 paper-based; 68 iBT), IELTS (minimum score 6), PTE (minimum score 47). *Application deadline:* For fall admission, 6/1 for international students; for spring admission, 10/15 for international students; for summer admission, 4/1 for international students. Applications are processed on a rolling basis. Application fee: $35 ($60 for international students). Electronic applications accepted. *Expenses:* Contact institution. *Financial support:* In 2017–18, 9 teaching assistantships with full tuition reimbursements (averaging $5,500 per year) were awarded; career-related internships or fieldwork, Federal Work-Study, and unspecified assistantships also available. Financial award application deadline: 2/1; financial award applicants required to submit FAFSA. *Faculty*

Physical Education

research: Personality of athletes, fitness activities for children, aerobic conditioning, fitness evaluation. *Unit head:* Dr. John Oppliger, Chairperson, 620-235-4668, E-mail: joppliger@pittstate.edu. *Application contact:* Lisa Allen, Assistant Director of Graduate and Continuing Studies, 620-235-4223, Fax: 620-235-4219, E-mail: lallen@pittstate.edu.

Plymouth State University, College of Graduate Studies, Graduate Studies in Education, Program in Secondary Education, Plymouth, NH 03264-1595. Offers curriculum and instruction (M Ed); language education (M Ed); library media (M Ed); physical education (M Ed); social studies education (M Ed); special education (M Ed). *Program availability:* Part-time, evening/weekend. *Entrance requirements:* For master's, MAT.

Purdue University, Graduate School, College of Health and Human Sciences, Department of Health and Kinesiology, West Lafayette, IN 47907. Offers athletic training education administration (MS, PhD); biomechanics (MS, PhD); exercise physiology (MS, PhD); health education (MS, PhD); history/philosophy of sport (MS, PhD); motor control and development (MS, PhD); physical education pedagogy (PhD); physical education teacher education (MS); recreation and sport management (MS, PhD); sport and exercise psychology (MS, PhD). *Program availability:* Part-time. *Faculty:* 19 full-time (7 women). *Students:* 30 full-time (13 women), 10 part-time (5 women); includes 2 minority (1 Asian, non-Hispanic/Latino; 1 Two or more races, non-Hispanic/Latino), 6 international. Average age 26. 77 applicants, 29% accepted, 18 enrolled. In 2017, 18 master's, 9 doctorates awarded. *Degree requirements:* For master's, thesis optional; for doctorate, comprehensive exam, thesis/dissertation, qualifying examination, preliminary examination. *Entrance requirements:* For master's, GRE General Test (minimum score 1000 combined verbal and quantitative), minimum undergraduate GPA of 3.0 or equivalent; for doctorate, GRE General Test (minimum score 1100 combined verbal and quantitative), minimum undergraduate GPA of 3.0 or equivalent; master's degree with minimum GPA of 3.25 (recommended). Additional exam requirements/recommendations for international students: Required—TOEFL (minimum score 77 iBT); Recommended—TWE. *Application deadline:* For fall admission, 4/30 for domestic and international students; for spring admission, 10/15 for domestic and international students. Applications are processed on a rolling basis. Application fee: $60 ($75 for international students). Electronic applications accepted. *Financial support:* Fellowships with partial tuition reimbursements, research assistantships with partial tuition reimbursements, teaching assistantships with partial tuition reimbursements, and Federal Work-Study available. Support available to part-time students. Financial award applicants required to submit FAFSA. *Faculty research:* Wellness, motivation, teaching effectiveness, learning and development. *Unit head:* Dr. Timothy P. Gavin, Head of the Graduate Program, 765-494-3178, Fax: 765-494-1239, E-mail: gavin1@purdue.edu. *Application contact:* David B. Klenosky, Graduate Contact, 765-494-0865, E-mail: klenosky@purdue.edu.
Website: http://www.purdue.edu/hhs/hk/

Queens College of the City University of New York, Mathematics and Natural Sciences Division, Department of Family, Nutrition and Exercise Sciences, Queens, NY 11367-1597. Offers exercise science specialist (MS); family and consumer science (K-12) (AC); family and consumer science/teaching curriculum (K-12) (MS Ed); nutrition and exercise science (MS); nutrition specialist (MS); physical education (K-12) (AC); physical education/teaching curriculum (pre K-12) (MS Ed). *Program availability:* Part-time, evening/weekend. *Faculty:* 13 full-time (11 women), 7 part-time/adjunct (4 women). *Students:* 15 full-time (7 women), 136 part-time (75 women); includes 67 minority (19 Black or African American, non-Hispanic/Latino; 1 American Indian or Alaska Native, non-Hispanic/Latino; 21 Asian, non-Hispanic/Latino; 25 Hispanic/Latino; 1 Two or more races, non-Hispanic/Latino), 3 international. Average age 30. 95 applicants, 76% accepted, 45 enrolled. In 2017, 34 master's, 12 other advanced degrees awarded. *Degree requirements:* For master's, research project. *Entrance requirements:* For master's, minimum GPA of 3.0. Additional exam requirements/recommendations for international students: Required—TOEFL (minimum paper-based score of 600) or IELTS (for program in nutrition). *Application deadline:* For fall admission, 4/1 for domestic students; for spring admission, 11/1 for domestic students. Applications are processed on a rolling basis. Application fee: $125. Electronic applications accepted. *Financial support:* Career-related internships or fieldwork and unspecified assistantships available. Financial award application deadline: 4/1; financial award applicants required to submit FAFSA. *Faculty research:* Health disparities; correlates of taste acuity, structuring and implementation of competition and competitive activities in physical education; exercise and metabolic risk in people living with HIV/AIDS; biomechanics, motor learning and motor control. *Unit head:* Dr. Ashima K. Kant, Chair, 718-997-4156 Ext. 4475, Fax: 718-997-4163, E-mail: ashima.kant@qc.cuny.edu. *Application contact:* Elizabeth D'Amico-Ramirez, Assistant Director of Graduate Admissions, 718-997-5203, E-mail: elizabeth.damicoramirez@qc.cuny.edu.

Rhode Island College, School of Graduate Studies, Feinstein School of Education and Human Development, Department of Health and Physical Education, Providence, RI 02908-1991. Offers health education (M Ed); physical education (CGS). *Accreditation:* NCATE. *Program availability:* Part-time, evening/weekend. *Faculty:* 1. *Students:* 3 part-time (all women); includes 1 minority (Hispanic/Latino). Average age 38. In 2017, 4 master's awarded. *Degree requirements:* For master's, comprehensive assessment. *Entrance requirements:* For master's, GRE General Test or MAT, undergraduate transcripts; minimum undergraduate GPA of 3.0; 3 letters of recommendation; for CGS, GRE or MAT (for most programs), undergraduate transcripts; minimum undergraduate GPA of 3.0; 3 letters of recommendation. Additional exam requirements/recommendations for international students: Recommended—TOEFL (minimum score 550 paper-based; 79 iBT). *Application deadline:* For fall admission, 3/1 for domestic students; for spring admission, 11/1 for domestic students. Applications are processed on a rolling basis. Application fee: $50. Electronic applications accepted. *Expenses:* Tuition, state resident: full-time $9768; part-time $407 per credit. Tuition, nonresident: full-time $19,008; part-time $792 per credit. *Required fees:* $696; $29 per credit. One-time fee: $200 full-time; $100 part-time. Tuition and fees vary according to course load. *Financial support:* In 2017–18, 1 teaching assistantship with full tuition reimbursement (averaging $2,250 per year) was awarded; Federal Work-Study, scholarships/grants, health care benefits, and unspecified assistantships also available. Support available to part-time students. Financial award application deadline: 5/15; financial award applicants required to submit FAFSA. *Unit head:* Dr. Robin Kirkwood Auld, Chair, 401-456-8046. *Application contact:* Graduate Studies, 401-456-8700.
Website: http://www.ric.edu/healthPhysicalEducation/

Salem State University, School of Graduate Studies, Program in Physical Education, Salem, MA 01970-5353. Offers M Ed. *Program availability:* Part-time, evening/weekend. *Entrance requirements:* For master's, GRE or MAT. Additional exam requirements/recommendations for international students: Required—TOEFL (minimum score 550 paper-based; 80 iBT) or IELTS (minimum score 5.5).

Shenandoah University, School of Education and Leadership, Winchester, VA 22601. Offers administration and supervision (Certificate); administrative leadership (D Ed); early childhood literacy (MS); educational administration (MSE); elementary school teacher education (Certificate); emphasis in teaching (MSE); health and physical education (Certificate); individualized focus (MS, MSE); literacy education (MS); middle

school teacher education (Certificate); organizational leadership (MS, D Prof); reading licensure (MS, Certificate); reading non-licensure (MS); secondary school teacher education (Certificate); special education (MSE); writing (MS). *Accreditation:* TEAC. *Program availability:* Part-time, evening/weekend. *Faculty:* 8 full-time (7 women), 22 part-time/adjunct (16 women). *Students:* 16 full-time (14 women), 221 part-time (167 women); includes 32 minority (17 Black or African American, non-Hispanic/Latino; 1 American Indian or Alaska Native, non-Hispanic/Latino; 6 Asian, non-Hispanic/Latino; 5 Hispanic/Latino; 1 Native Hawaiian or other Pacific Islander, non-Hispanic/Latino; 2 Two or more races, non-Hispanic/Latino), 3 international. Average age 38. 81 applicants, 99% accepted, 63 enrolled. In 2017, 53 master's, 11 doctorates, 49 other advanced degrees awarded. *Degree requirements:* For master's, comprehensive exam (for some programs), thesis (for some programs); for doctorate, comprehensive exam, thesis/dissertation. *Entrance requirements:* For degree, PRAXIS Academic Core, SAT/ACT, PRAXIS Academic Core Math, or VCLA, three letters of recommendation, writing sample, undergraduate degree. Additional exam requirements/recommendations for international students: Required—TOEFL (minimum score 550 paper-based, 79 iBT) or IELTS (6.5). *Application deadline:* For fall admission, 5/1 priority date for domestic students, 5/1 for international students; for spring admission, 10/15 priority date for domestic students, 10/15 for international students; for summer admission, 3/15 priority date for domestic students, 3/15 for international students. Application fee: $30. Electronic applications accepted. *Expenses:* $15,600 tuition plus $1,296 fees (technology and student services). *Financial support:* In 2017–18, 26 students received support. Scholarships/grants and unspecified assistantships available. Financial award applicants required to submit FAFSA. *Faculty research:* Mentoring, behavior support for students, teacher change agency, educational technology in pedagogy, literacy education. *Unit head:* Jill Lindsey, PhD, Director, 540-535-7324, Fax: 540-665-4726, E-mail: jlindsey@su.edu. *Application contact:* Andrew Woodall, Executive Director of Recruitment and Admissions, 540-665-4581, Fax: 540-665-4627, E-mail: admit@su.edu.
Website: http://www.su.edu/education/

Slippery Rock University of Pennsylvania, Graduate Studies (Recruitment), College of Education, Department of Physical and Health Education, Slippery Rock, PA 16057-1383. Offers adapted physical activity (MS). *Degree requirements:* For master's, internship. *Entrance requirements:* For master's, official transcripts, minimum GPA of 2.75, two letters of recommendation, essay. Additional exam requirements/recommendations for international students: Required—TOEFL (minimum score 550 paper-based; 80 iBT). Electronic applications accepted. *Expenses:* Contact institution.

Southern Connecticut State University, School of Graduate Studies, School of Health and Human Services, Department of Exercise Science, New Haven, CT 06515-1355. Offers human performance (MS); physical education (MS); school health education (MS). *Program availability:* Part-time, evening/weekend. *Degree requirements:* For master's, thesis or alternative. *Entrance requirements:* For master's, interview. Electronic applications accepted.

Southern Illinois University Carbondale, Graduate School, College of Education and Human Services, Department of Kinesiology, Carbondale, IL 62901-4701. Offers MS Ed. *Program availability:* Part-time. *Degree requirements:* For master's, thesis. *Entrance requirements:* For master's, GRE, minimum GPA of 2.7. Additional exam requirements/recommendations for international students: Required—TOEFL. *Faculty research:* Caffeine and exercise effects, ground reaction forces in walking and running, social psychology of sports.

Southern Illinois University Edwardsville, Graduate School, School of Education, Health, and Human Behavior, Department of Kinesiology and Health Education, Program in Physical Education and Coaching Pedagogy, Edwardsville, IL 62026. Offers MS Ed. *Program availability:* Part-time, evening/weekend. *Degree requirements:* For master's, comprehensive exam (for some programs), thesis (for some programs). *Entrance requirements:* Additional exam requirements/recommendations for international students: Required—TOEFL (minimum score 550 paper-based, 79 iBT), IELTS (minimum score 6.5), Michigan Test of English Language Proficiency or PTE. Electronic applications accepted.

Springfield College, Graduate Programs, Programs in Physical Education, Springfield, MA 01109-3797. Offers adapted physical education (MS); advanced-level coaching (M Ed); athletic administration (MS); exercise physiology (PhD); health promotion and disease prevention (MS); physical education initial licensure (CAGS); sport and exercise psychology (PhD); teaching and administration (PhD). *Program availability:* Part-time. *Students:* 82 applicants, 73% accepted, 37 enrolled. *Degree requirements:* For master's, comprehensive exam, thesis (for some programs). *Entrance requirements:* For master's and doctorate, GRE General Test. Additional exam requirements/recommendations for international students: Required—TOEFL (minimum score 550 paper-based); Recommended—IELTS (minimum score 7). *Application deadline:* For fall admission, 1/15 priority date for domestic students, 1/15 for international students; for winter admission, 11/1 for domestic and international students; for spring admission, 11/1 for domestic and international students. Applications are processed on a rolling basis. Application fee: $50. Electronic applications accepted. *Financial support:* Fellowships with partial tuition reimbursements, teaching assistantships with partial tuition reimbursements, career-related internships or fieldwork, Federal Work-Study, institutionally sponsored loans, scholarships/grants, and unspecified assistantships available. Financial award application deadline: 3/1; financial award applicants required to submit FAFSA. *Unit head:* Dr. Michelle Moosbrugger, Graduate Coordinator, 413-748-3486, E-mail: mmoosbrugger@springfield.edu. *Application contact:* Anne Griffin, Director of Graduate Admissions, 413-748-3225, Fax: 413-748-3694, E-mail: agriffin2@springfield.edu.
Website: http://springfield.edu/gradpe

State University of New York College at Cortland, Graduate Studies, School of Professional Studies, Department of Physical Education, Cortland, NY 13045. Offers adapted physical education (MS Ed); coaching pedagogy (MS Ed); physical education leadership (MS Ed). *Program availability:* Part-time, evening/weekend. *Entrance requirements:* Additional exam requirements/recommendations for international students: Required—TOEFL.

Stony Brook University, State University of New York, School of Professional Development, Stony Brook, NY 11794. Offers biology (MAT); chemistry (MAT); coaching (Graduate Certificate); earth science (MAT); educational computing (Graduate Certificate); educational leadership (Advanced Certificate); English (MAT); environmental management (MPS, Graduate Certificate); French (MAT); German (MAT); higher education administration (MA, Certificate); human resource management (MS, Graduate Certificate); industrial management (Graduate Certificate); information systems management (Graduate Certificate); Italian (MAT); liberal studies (MA); mathematics (MAT); operations research (Graduate Certificate); physics (MAT); school district business leadership (Advanced Certificate); social studies (MAT); Spanish (MAT). *Program availability:* Part-time, evening/weekend, online learning. *Faculty:* 1 full-time (2 women), 101 part-time/adjunct (45 women). *Students:* 190 full-time (126 women), 974 part-time (708 women); includes 255 minority (88 Black or African American, non-Hispanic/Latino; 2 American Indian or Alaska Native, non-Hispanic/Latino; 31 Asian, non-Hispanic/Latino; 113 Hispanic/Latino; 1 Native Hawaiian or other

Pacific Islander, non-Hispanic/Latino; 20 Two or more races, non-Hispanic/Latino), 6 international. Average age 33. 411 applicants, 91% accepted, 288 enrolled. In 2017, 333 master's, 180 other advanced degrees awarded. *Entrance requirements:* Additional exam requirements/recommendations for international students: Required—TOEFL (minimum score 85 iBT). *Application deadline:* For fall admission, 1/15 for domestic students, 6/1 for international students; for spring admission, 10/1 for domestic and international students. Applications are processed on a rolling basis. Application fee: $100. *Expenses:* Contact institution. *Financial support:* Fellowships, research assistantships, teaching assistantships, and career-related internships or fieldwork available. Support available to part-time students. *Unit head:* Dr. Ken Lindblom, Dean, 631-632-7049, Fax: 631-632-9046, E-mail: kenneth.lindblom@stonybrook.edu. *Application contact:* Melissa Jordan, Assistant Dean, 631-632-7751, E-mail: melissa.jordan@stonybrook.edu.
Website: http://www.stonybrook.edu/spd/

Sul Ross State University, College of Professional Studies, Department of Physical Education, Alpine, TX 79832. Offers M Ed. *Program availability:* Part-time. *Entrance requirements:* For master's, GMAT or GRE General Test, minimum GPA of 2.5 in last 60 hours of undergraduate work.

Teachers College, Columbia University, Department of Biobehavioral Sciences, New York, NY 10027-6696. Offers applied exercise physiology (Ed M, MA, Ed D); communication sciences and disorders (MS, Ed D, PhD); kinesiology (PhD); motor learning and control (Ed M, MA); motor learning/movement science (Ed D); neuroscience and education (MS); physical education (MA, Ed D). *Accreditation:* ASHA. *Program availability:* Part-time, evening/weekend. *Students:* 180 full-time (160 women), 176 part-time (141 women); includes 149 minority (17 Black or African American, non-Hispanic/Latino; 40 Asian, non-Hispanic/Latino; 83 Hispanic/Latino; 9 Two or more races, non-Hispanic/Latino), 30 international. Average age 29. 738 applicants, 41% accepted, 164 enrolled. *Financial support:* Fellowships, teaching assistantships, career-related internships or fieldwork, Federal Work-Study, institutionally sponsored loans, traineeships, and tuition waivers (full and partial) available. Support available to part-time students. *Unit head:* Prof. Carol Garber, Chair, 212-678-3891, E-mail: garber@tc.columbia.edu. *Application contact:* David Estrella, Director of Admissions, 212-678-3305, E-mail: estrella@tc.columbia.edu.
Website: http://www.tc.columbia.edu/biobehavioral-sciences/

Temple University, College of Public Health, Department of Kinesiology, Philadelphia, PA 19122. Offers athletic training (MSAT, DAT); kinesiology (MS, PhD); neuromotor science (MS, PhD). *Program availability:* Part-time. *Faculty:* 17 full-time (8 women), 6 part-time/adjunct (3 women). *Students:* 52 full-time (21 women), 39 part-time (22 women); includes 25 minority (11 Black or African American, non-Hispanic/Latino; 1 Asian, non-Hispanic/Latino; 8 Hispanic/Latino; 5 Two or more races, non-Hispanic/Latino), 5 international. 78 applicants, 72% accepted, 37 enrolled. In 2017, 15 master's, 3 doctorates awarded. Terminal master's awarded for partial completion of doctoral program. *Degree requirements:* For master's, thesis, final project; for doctorate, comprehensive exam, thesis/dissertation. *Entrance requirements:* For master's, GRE General Test or MAT, minimum undergraduate GPA of 3.0, 3 letters of reference, statement of goals, interview, resume; for doctorate, GRE General Test, minimum undergraduate GPA of 3.0, 3 letters of reference, statement of goals, interview, resume. Additional exam requirements/recommendations for international students: Required—TOEFL (minimum score 550 paper-based; 79 iBT). *Application deadline:* For fall admission, 1/15 for domestic students, 12/15 for international students; for spring admission, 10/1 for domestic students, 8/1 for international students. Applications are processed on a rolling basis. Application fee: $60. Electronic applications accepted. *Expenses:* Contact institution. *Financial support:* Fellowships, research assistantships with tuition reimbursements, teaching assistantships with tuition reimbursements, career-related internships or fieldwork, Federal Work-Study, scholarships/grants, tuition waivers, and unspecified assistantships available. Financial award application deadline: 1/15. *Faculty research:* Exercise physiology, athletic training, motor neuroscience, exercise and sports psychology. *Unit head:* John Jeka, Chair, 214-204-4405, Fax: 215-204-4414, E-mail: jjeka@temple.edu. *Application contact:* Rosalind Robinson, Department Coordinator, 215-204-8707, E-mail: rosalind.robinson@temple.edu.
Website: http://cph.temple.edu/kinesiology/home

Tennessee State University, The School of Graduate Studies and Research, College of Health Sciences, Department of Human Performance and Sports Sciences, Nashville, TN 37209-1561. Offers exercise science (MA Ed); sports administration (MA Ed). *Degree requirements:* For master's, thesis optional. *Entrance requirements:* For master's, GRE General Test or MAT.

Tennessee Technological University, College of Graduate Studies, College of Education, Department of Exercise Science, Physical Education and Wellness, Cookeville, TN 38505. Offers adapted physical education (MA); elementary/middle school physical education (MA); lifetime wellness (MA); sport management (MA). *Accreditation:* NCATE. *Program availability:* Part-time, online learning. *Faculty:* 7 full-time (0 women). *Students:* 17 full-time (8 women), 34 part-time (14 women); includes 10 minority (5 Black or African American, non-Hispanic/Latino; 1 Asian, non-Hispanic/Latino; 2 Hispanic/Latino; 2 Two or more races, non-Hispanic/Latino). 35 applicants, 71% accepted, 23 enrolled. In 2017, 28 master's awarded. *Degree requirements:* For master's, comprehensive exam, thesis or alternative. *Entrance requirements:* For master's, MAT or GRE. Additional exam requirements/recommendations for international students: Required—TOEFL (minimum score 527 paper-based; 71 iBT), IELTS (minimum score 5.5), PTE (minimum score 48), or TOEIC (Test of English as an International Communication). *Application deadline:* For fall admission, 8/1 for domestic students, 5/1 for international students; for spring admission, 12/1 for domestic students, 10/1 for international students; for summer admission, 5/1 for domestic students, 2/1 for international students. Applications are processed on a rolling basis. Application fee: $35 ($40 for international students). Electronic applications accepted. *Expenses:* Tuition, state resident: full-time $9925; part-time $565 per credit hour. Tuition, nonresident: full-time $22,993; part-time $1291 per credit hour. *Financial support:* Fellowships, research assistantships, teaching assistantships, and career-related internships or fieldwork available. Financial award application deadline: 4/1. *Unit head:* Dr. Christy Killman, Chairperson, 931-372-3467, Fax: 931-372-6319, E-mail: ckillman@tntech.edu. *Application contact:* Shelia K. Kendrick, Coordinator of Graduate Studies, 931-372-3808, Fax: 931-372-3497, E-mail: skendrick@tntech.edu.

Texas Southern University, College of Education, Department of Health and Kinesiology, Houston, TX 77004-4584. Offers health education (MS); human performance (MS). *Program availability:* Part-time, evening/weekend. *Degree requirements:* For master's, comprehensive exam, thesis optional. *Entrance requirements:* For master's, GRE General Test, minimum GPA of 2.5. Additional exam requirements/recommendations for international students: Required—TOEFL. Electronic applications accepted.

Texas State University, The Graduate College, College of Education, Program in Physical Education, San Marcos, TX 78666. Offers M Ed. *Program availability:* Part-time, evening/weekend. *Faculty:* 14 full-time (7 women), 1 (woman) part-time/adjunct. *Students:* 9 full-time (3 women), 2 part-time (both women); includes 6 minority (2 Black or African American, non-Hispanic/Latino; 1 Asian, non-Hispanic/Latino; 3 Hispanic/

Latino). Average age 25. 12 applicants, 50% accepted, 4 enrolled. In 2017, 4 master's awarded. *Degree requirements:* For master's, comprehensive exam, thesis optional. *Entrance requirements:* For master's, GRE General Test or minimum GPA of 3.0 in last 60 hours, baccalaureate degree from regionally-accredited institution with minimum GPA of 3.0 in last 60 hours of course work; background course work in physical education; 3 letters of recommendation; resume; statement of aspiration addressing professional goals, motivation, strengths and weaknesses to be evaluated for content, style and quality. Additional exam requirements/recommendations for international students: Required—TOEFL (minimum iBT scores: 22 listening, 22 reading, 24 speaking, 21 writing). *Application deadline:* For fall admission, 3/1 priority date for domestic and international students; for spring admission, 11/1 for domestic students, 10/1 for international students; for summer admission, 1/15 for domestic and international students. Applications are processed on a rolling basis. Application fee: $40 ($90 for international students). Electronic applications accepted. *Expenses:* Tuition, state resident: full-time $7868; part-time $3934 per semester. Tuition, nonresident: full-time $17,828; part-time $8914 per semester. *Required fees:* $2092; $1435 per semester. Tuition and fees vary according to course load. *Financial support:* In 2017–18, 8 students received support, including 5 teaching assistantships (averaging $12,152 per year); research assistantships, career-related internships or fieldwork, Federal Work-Study, institutionally sponsored loans, and scholarships/grants also available. Support available to part-time students. Financial award application deadline: 3/1; financial award applicants required to submit FAFSA. *Faculty research:* Employee wellness, isometric strength evaluation, overpowering osteoarthritis, cycling for fitness and for life, effects of neuromuscular electrical stimulation. *Total annual research expenditures:* $110,579. *Unit head:* Dr. Karen Meaney, Graduate Advisor, 512-245-2952, Fax: 512-245-8678, E-mail: km66@txstate.edu. *Application contact:* Dr. Andrea Golato, Head, 512-245-2581, Fax: 512-245-8365, E-mail: gradcollege@txstate.edu.
Website: http://www.gradcollege.txstate.edu/programs/physical-ed.html

Texas Woman's University, Graduate School, College of Health Sciences, Department of Kinesiology, Denton, TX 76204. Offers kinesiology (MS, PhD), including adapted physical activity, biomechanics, coaching (MS), exercise physiology, sport management. *Program availability:* Part-time, evening/weekend. *Faculty:* 11 full-time (3 women), 2 part-time/adjunct (both women). *Students:* 48 full-time (36 women), 65 part-time (39 women); includes 40 minority (19 Black or African American, non-Hispanic/Latino; 2 Asian, non-Hispanic/Latino; 17 Hispanic/Latino; 2 Two or more races, non-Hispanic/Latino), 14 international. Average age 30. 63 applicants, 81% accepted, 37 enrolled. In 2017, 32 master's, 9 doctorates awarded. Terminal master's awarded for partial completion of doctoral program. *Degree requirements:* For master's, comprehensive exam, thesis (for some programs), thesis or professional paper; for doctorate, comprehensive exam, thesis/dissertation, qualifying exam. *Entrance requirements:* For master's, GRE General Test (biomechanics emphasis only), 2 letters of reference, curriculum vitae; for doctorate, GRE General Test (biomechanics emphasis only), interview, 3 letters of reference, curriculum vitae, letter of intent. Additional exam requirements/recommendations for international students: Required—TOEFL (minimum score 550 paper-based; 79 iBT). Recommended—IELTS (minimum score 6.5), TSE (minimum score 53). *Application deadline:* For fall admission, 7/15 for domestic students, 3/1 priority date for international students; for spring admission, 11/1 for domestic students, 7/1 priority date for international students; for summer admission, 4/1 for domestic students, 2/1 priority date for international students. Applications are processed on a rolling basis. Application fee: $50 ($75 for international students). Electronic applications accepted. *Expenses:* $7,520 per year full-time in-state; $16,829 per year full-time out-of-state. *Financial support:* In 2017–18, 36 students received support, including 1 research assistantship (averaging $11,926 per year), 15 teaching assistantships (averaging $20,354 per year); career-related internships or fieldwork, Federal Work-Study, institutionally sponsored loans, scholarships/grants, traineeships, health care benefits, and unspecified assistantships also available. Support available to part-time students. Financial award application deadline: 3/1; financial award applicants required to submit FAFSA. *Faculty research:* Exercise and Type 2 diabetes risk, bone mineral density and exercise in special populations, obesity in children, factors influencing sport consumer behavior and loyalty, roles and responsibilities of Para educators in adapted physical education. *Unit head:* Dr. George King, Chair, 940-898-2575, Fax: 940-898-2581. *Application contact:* Korie Hawkins, Associate Director of Admissions, Graduate Recruitment, 940-898-3188, Fax: 940-898-3081, E-mail: admissions@twu.edu.
Website: http://www.twu.edu/kinesiology/

Union College, Graduate Programs, Department of Education, Barbourville, KY 40906-1499. Offers elementary education (MA); health and physical education (MA); middle grades (MA); music education (MA); principalship (MA); reading specialist (MA); secondary education (MA); special education (MA). *Degree requirements:* For master's, thesis optional. *Entrance requirements:* For master's, GRE General Test, NTE.

United States Sports Academy, Graduate Programs, Program in Sports Coaching, Daphne, AL 36526-7055. Offers MSS. *Program availability:* Part-time, 100% online. *Degree requirements:* For master's, comprehensive exam, thesis optional. *Entrance requirements:* For master's, GRE General Test, GMAT, or MAT, minimum GPA of 2.5, 3 letters of recommendation, personal statement. Additional exam requirements/recommendations for international students: Required—TOEFL (minimum score 550 paper-based; 79 iBT). *Application deadline:* Applications are processed on a rolling basis. Application fee: $50 ($125 for international students). Electronic applications accepted. *Expenses:* $640 per credit hour. *Financial support:* Career-related internships or fieldwork, Federal Work-Study, scholarships/grants, and service assistantships available. Support available to part-time students. Financial award application deadline: 8/15; financial award applicants required to submit FAFSA. *Faculty research:* Effect of attentional skill on sports performance, survey of coaching qualifications, coaching certification. *Unit head:* Chair, 251-626-3303 Ext. 7139, Fax: 251-626-1149. *Application contact:* Dr. Taffy Sithole, Student Services Coordinator, 251-626-3303 Ext. 7147, Fax: 251-625-1035, E-mail: tsithole@ussa.edu.

Universidad del Turabo, Graduate Programs, Programs in Education, Program in Coaching, Gurabo, PR 00778-3030. Offers MPHE. *Entrance requirements:* For master's, GRE, EXADEP, GMAT, interview, official transcript, essay, recommendation letters. Electronic applications accepted.

Universidad Metropolitana, School of Education, Program in Teaching of Physical Education, San Juan, PR 00928-1150. Offers teaching of adult physical education (M Ed); teaching of elementary physical education (M Ed); teaching of secondary physical education (M Ed). *Degree requirements:* For master's, thesis or alternative. *Entrance requirements:* For master's, EXADEP, interview. Electronic applications accepted.

Université de Montréal, Department of Kinesiology, Montréal, QC H3C 3J7, Canada. Offers kinesiology (M Sc, DESS); physical activity (M Sc, PhD). *Degree requirements:* For master's, one foreign language, thesis (for some programs); for doctorate, one foreign language, thesis/dissertation, general exam. Electronic applications accepted. *Faculty research:* Physiology of exercise, psychology of sports, biomechanics, dance, sociology of sports.

Physical Education

Université de Sherbrooke, Faculty of Physical Education and Sports, Program in Physical Education, Sherbrooke, QC J1K 2R1, Canada. Offers kinanthropology (M Sc); physical activity (Diploma). *Degree requirements:* For master's, thesis. *Entrance requirements:* For master's, minimum GPA of 2.7; for Diploma, bachelor's degree in physical education. *Faculty research:* Physical fitness, nutrition, human factors, sociology, teaching.

Université du Québec à Trois-Rivières, Graduate Programs, Program in Physical Education, Trois-Rivières, QC G9A 5H7, Canada. Offers M Sc. *Program availability:* Part-time. *Degree requirements:* For master's, thesis. *Entrance requirements:* For master's, appropriate bachelor's degree, proficiency in French.

The University of Akron, Graduate School, College of Health Professions, School of Sport Science and Wellness Education, Program in Sport Science/Coaching, Akron, OH 44325. Offers MA, MS. *Students:* 35 full-time (11 women), 16 part-time (6 women); includes 14 minority (12 Black or African American, non-Hispanic/Latino; 1 Asian, non-Hispanic/Latino; 1 Hispanic/Latino), 3 international. Average age 26. 30 applicants, 100% accepted, 26 enrolled. In 2017, 38 master's awarded. *Degree requirements:* For master's, comprehensive exam, thesis optional. *Entrance requirements:* For master's, minimum GPA of 2.75, three letters of recommendation, statement of purpose. Additional exam requirements/recommendations for international students: Required—TOEFL (minimum score 79 iBT), IELTS (minimum score 6.5). *Application deadline:* Applications are processed on a rolling basis. Application fee: $45 ($70 for international students). Electronic applications accepted. *Unit head:* Dr. Victor Pinheiro, Department Chair, 330-972-6055, E-mail: victor@uakron.edu. *Application contact:* Dr. Alan Kornspan, Program Contact, 330-972-8145.
Website: http://www.uakron.edu/sswe/programs/sport-science-coaching/index.dot

The University of Alabama, Graduate School, College of Education, Department of Kinesiology, Tuscaloosa, AL 35487. Offers alternative sport pedagogy (MA); exercise science (PhD). *Program availability:* Part-time. *Faculty:* 12 full-time (2 women). *Students:* 51 full-time (21 women), 20 part-time (9 women); includes 17 minority (12 Black or African American, non-Hispanic/Latino; 3 Hispanic/Latino; 2 Two or more races, non-Hispanic/Latino), 7 international. Average age 27. 58 applicants, 60% accepted, 18 enrolled. In 2017, 35 master's, 8 doctorates awarded. *Degree requirements:* For master's, comprehensive exam, thesis optional; for doctorate, comprehensive exam, thesis/dissertation. *Entrance requirements:* For master's and doctorate, GRE, minimum GPA of 3.0. Additional exam requirements/recommendations for international students: Required—TOEFL. *Application deadline:* Applications are processed on a rolling basis. Electronic applications accepted. *Financial support:* In 2017–18, 18 students received support. Application deadline: 3/1. *Total annual research expenditures:* $50,518. *Unit head:* Dr. Jonathan Wingo, Associate Professor and Head, 205-348-4699, Fax: 205-348-0867, E-mail: jwingo@ua.edu. *Application contact:* Dr. Kathy S. Wetzel, Associate Dean for Student Services and Certification, 205-348-1154, E-mail: kwetzel@bamaed.ua.edu.
Website: http://education.ua.edu/academics/kine/

University of Alberta, Faculty of Graduate Studies and Research, Department of Physical Education and Recreation, Edmonton, AB T6G 2E1, Canada. Offers physical education (M Sc); recreation and physical education (MA, PhD). *Program availability:* Part-time. Terminal master's awarded for partial completion of doctoral program. *Degree requirements:* For master's, thesis (for some programs); for doctorate, thesis/dissertation. *Entrance requirements:* For master's, bachelor's degree in related field; for doctorate, master's degree in related field with thesis. Additional exam requirements/recommendations for international students: Required—TOEFL. *Faculty research:* Motivation and adherence to physical ability, performance enhancement, adapted physical activity, exercise physiology, sport administration, tourism.

University of Arkansas, Graduate School, College of Education and Health Professions, Department of Health, Human Performance and Recreation, Program in Physical Education, Fayetteville, AR 72701. Offers M Ed, MAT. In 2017, 9 master's awarded. *Degree requirements:* For master's, thesis optional. *Application deadline:* For fall admission, 8/1 for domestic students, 4/1 for international students; for spring admission, 12/1 for domestic students, 10/1 for international students; for summer admission, 4/15 for domestic students, 3/1 for international students. Applications are processed on a rolling basis. Application fee: $60. Electronic applications accepted. *Expenses:* Tuition, state resident: full-time $3782. Tuition, nonresident: full-time $10,238. *Financial support:* Fellowships with tuition reimbursements, research assistantships, teaching assistantships, career-related internships or fieldwork, and Federal Work-Study available. Support available to part-time students. Financial award application deadline: 4/1; financial award applicants required to submit FAFSA. *Unit head:* Dr. Bart Hammig, Department Chairperson, 479-575-2890, Fax: 479-575-5778, E-mail: bhammig@uark.edu. *Application contact:* Dr. Stephen Dittmore, Coordinator of Graduate Studies, 479-575-6625, E-mail: dittmore@uark.edu.
Website: http://hkrd.uark.edu/

The University of British Columbia, Faculty of Education, Department of Curriculum and Pedagogy, Vancouver, BC V6T 1Z4, Canada. Offers art education (M Ed, MA); curriculum studies (M Ed, MA, PhD); home economics education (M Ed, MA); mathematics education (M Ed, MA); media and technology studies education (M Ed, MA); music education (M Ed, MA); physical education (M Ed, MA); science education (M Ed, MA); social studies education (M Ed, MA). *Program availability:* Part-time, online learning. *Degree requirements:* For master's, thesis (MA); for doctorate, comprehensive exam, thesis/dissertation. *Entrance requirements:* Additional exam requirements/recommendations for international students: Required—TOEFL, IELTS. Electronic applications accepted. *Expenses:* Contact institution. *Faculty research:* School subjects, teaching and learning.

University of Dayton, Department of Health and Sport Science, Dayton, OH 45469. Offers exercise science (MS Ed). *Program availability:* Part-time, 100% online. *Faculty:* 10 full-time (5 women), 23 part-time/adjunct (16 women). *Students:* 7 full-time (4 women), 2 part-time (1 woman); includes 3 minority (2 Black or African American, non-Hispanic/Latino; 1 Hispanic/Latino), 3 international. Average age 24. 37 applicants, 30% accepted. In 2017, 7 master's awarded. *Degree requirements:* For master's, thesis. *Entrance requirements:* For master's, GRE General Test or MAT if undergraduate GPA was 2.75 or below, minimum GPA of 2.75; official academic records of all previously-attended colleges or universities; three letters of recommendation from professors or employers; personal statement or resume. Additional exam requirements/recommendations for international students: Required—TOEFL (minimum score 550 paper-based; 80 iBT). *Application deadline:* Applications are processed on a rolling basis. Application fee: $0 ($50 for international students). Electronic applications accepted. *Expenses:* Contact institution. *Financial support:* In 2017–18, 4 research assistantships with partial tuition reimbursements (averaging $9,640 per year) were awarded; career-related internships or fieldwork, institutionally sponsored loans, and unspecified assistantships also available. Financial award application deadline: 3/1; financial award applicants required to submit FAFSA. *Faculty research:* Exercise science, physiology, nutrition, sport management. *Unit head:* Dr. Corinne Daprano, Chair, 937-229-4240, Fax: 937-229-4244, E-mail: cdaprano1@udayton.edu. *Application contact:* Laura Greger, Administrative Assistant, 937-229-4225, E-mail: lgreger1@udayton.edu.
Website: https://www.udayton.edu/education/departments_and_programs/hss

University of Florida, Graduate School, College of Health and Human Performance, Department of Applied Physiology and Kinesiology, Gainesville, FL 32611. Offers applied physiology and kinesiology (MS); athletic training/sports medicine (MS); biobehavioral science (MS); clinical exercise physiology (MS); exercise physiology (MS); health and human performance (PhD), including applied physiology and kinesiology, biobehavioral science, exercise physiology; human performance (MS). *Degree requirements:* For master's, comprehensive exam, thesis (for some programs); for doctorate, comprehensive exam, thesis/dissertation. *Entrance requirements:* For master's and doctorate, GRE General Test, minimum GPA of 3.0. Additional exam requirements/recommendations for international students: Required—TOEFL (minimum score 550 paper-based; 80 iBT), IELTS (minimum score 6). Electronic applications accepted. *Faculty research:* Cardiovascular disease; basic mechanisms that underlie exercise-induced changes in the body at the organ, tissue, cellular and molecular level; development of rehabilitation techniques for regaining motor control after stroke or as a consequence of Parkinson's disease; maintaining optimal health and delaying age-related declines in physiological function; psychomotor mechanisms impacting health and performance across the life span.

University of Georgia, College of Education, Department of Kinesiology, Athens, GA 30602. Offers MS, PhD. *Entrance requirements:* For master's, GRE General Test or MAT; for doctorate, GRE General Test. Additional exam requirements/recommendations for international students: Required—TOEFL. Electronic applications accepted.

University of Houston, College of Liberal Arts and Social Sciences, Department of Health and Human Performance, Houston, TX 77204. Offers exercise science (MS); human nutrition (MS); human space exploration sciences (MS); kinesiology (PhD); physical education (M Ed). *Accreditation:* NCATE (one or more programs are accredited). *Program availability:* Part-time, evening/weekend. *Degree requirements:* For master's, comprehensive exam (for some programs), thesis (for some programs); for doctorate, comprehensive exam, thesis/dissertation, qualifying exam, candidacy paper. *Entrance requirements:* For master's, GRE (minimum 35th percentile on each section), minimum cumulative GPA of 3.0; for doctorate, GRE (minimum 35th percentile on each section), minimum cumulative GPA of 3.3. Additional exam requirements/recommendations for international students: Required—TOEFL (minimum score 550 paper-based; 79 iBT). Electronic applications accepted. *Faculty research:* Biomechanics, exercise physiology, obesity, nutrition, space exploration science.

University of Idaho, College of Graduate Studies, College of Education, Health and Human Sciences, Department of Movement Sciences, Moscow, ID 83844. Offers athletic training (MSAT, DAT); exercise science and health (MS); physical education teacher education (M Ed, MS); recreation, sport, and tourism management (MS). *Faculty:* 22. *Students:* 89 full-time (41 women), 18 part-time (7 women). Average age 28. In 2017, 24 master's awarded. *Degree requirements:* For doctorate, thesis/dissertation. *Entrance requirements:* For master's and doctorate, minimum GPA of 3.0. Additional exam requirements/recommendations for international students: Required—TOEFL. *Application deadline:* For fall admission, 8/1 for domestic students; for spring admission, 12/15 for domestic students. Applications are processed on a rolling basis. Application fee: $60. Electronic applications accepted. *Expenses:* Tuition, state resident: full-time $6722; part-time $430 per credit hour. Tuition, nonresident: full-time $23,046; part-time $1337 per credit hour. *Required fees:* $2142; $63 per credit hour. *Financial support:* Research assistantships and teaching assistantships available. Financial award applicants required to submit FAFSA. *Unit head:* Dr. Philip W. Scruggs, Chair, 208-885-7921, E-mail: movementsciences@uidaho.edu. *Application contact:* Sean Scoggin, Graduate Recruitment Coordinator, 208-885-4001, Fax: 208-885-4406, E-mail: graduateadmissions@uidaho.edu.
Website: https://www.uidaho.edu/ed/mvsc

University of Indianapolis, Graduate Programs, School of Education, Indianapolis, IN 46227-3697. Offers art education (MAT); biology (MAT); chemistry (MAT); curriculum and instruction (MA); earth sciences (MAT); education (MA, MAT); educational leadership (MA); elementary education (MA); English (MAT); French (MAT); math (MAT); physical education (MAT); physics (MAT); secondary education (MA), including art education, education, English education, social studies education; social studies (MAT); Spanish (MAT). *Accreditation:* NCATE. *Program availability:* Part-time, evening/weekend. *Entrance requirements:* For master's, GRE Subject Test, PRAXIS I, minimum GPA of 2.5, 3 letters of recommendation, interview. Additional exam requirements/recommendations for international students: Required—TOEFL (minimum score 550 paper-based). *Faculty research:* Assessment of teacher education, perceptions of prospective teachers by parents.

The University of Kansas, Graduate Studies, School of Education, Department of Health, Sport, and Exercise Sciences, Lawrence, KS 66045. Offers exercise science (MS Ed); health, sport, and exercise sciences (PhD); sport management (MS Ed). *Accreditation:* NCATE. *Program availability:* Part-time, evening/weekend. *Students:* 56 full-time (23 women), 11 part-time (5 women); includes 8 minority (2 Black or African American, non-Hispanic/Latino; 1 American Indian or Alaska Native, non-Hispanic/Latino; 2 Hispanic/Latino; 3 Two or more races, non-Hispanic/Latino), 4 international. Average age 26. 70 applicants, 63% accepted, 23 enrolled. In 2017, 19 master's, 6 doctorates awarded. *Entrance requirements:* For master's, GRE General Test (minimum score 1000, 450 verbal, 450 quantitative, 4.0 analytical), minimum GPA of 3.0, three letters of recommendation, personal statement, resume, writing sample; for doctorate, GRE General Test (minimum score 1100, verbal 500, quantitative 500, analytical 4.5), minimum graduate GPA of 3.5, undergraduate 3.0; three letters of recommendation; personal statement; resume; writing sample; interview with an advisor. *Application deadline:* For fall admission, 3/15 for domestic and international students; for spring admission, 10/1 for domestic and international students; for summer admission, 3/15 for domestic and international students. Application fee: $65 ($85 for international students). Electronic applications accepted. *Financial support:* Research assistantships, teaching assistantships, Federal Work-Study, scholarships/grants, and unspecified assistantships available. Financial award application deadline: 2/21. *Faculty research:* Exercise and sport psychology, obesity prevention, sexuality health, sport ethics, skeletal muscle cell signaling and performance. *Unit head:* Dr. Joseph Weir, Chair, 785-864-0784, E-mail: joseph.weir@ku.edu. *Application contact:* Sarah Clopton, Graduate Admissions Coordinator, 785-864-7268, E-mail: sclopton@ku.edu.
Website: http://hses.soe.ku.edu/

University of Kentucky, Graduate School, College of Education, Program in Kinesiology and Health Promotion, Lexington, KY 40506-0032. Offers biomechanics (MS); exercise physiology (MS, PhD); exercise science (PhD); health promotion (MS, Ed D); physical education training (Ed D); sport leadership (MS); teaching and coaching (MS). Terminal master's awarded for partial completion of doctoral program. *Degree requirements:* For master's, comprehensive exam, thesis optional; for doctorate, comprehensive exam, thesis/dissertation. *Entrance requirements:* For master's, GRE General Test, minimum undergraduate GPA of 2.75; for doctorate, GRE General Test, minimum graduate GPA of 3.0. Additional exam requirements/recommendations for international students: Required—TOEFL (minimum score 550 paper-based). Electronic applications accepted.

University of Louisville, Graduate School, College of Education and Human Development, Department of Health and Sport Sciences, Louisville, KY 40292-0001. Offers community health education (M Ed); exercise physiology (MS), including health and sport sciences, strength and conditioning; health and physical education (MAT); sport administration (MS). *Program availability:* Part-time, evening/weekend. *Students:* 35 full-time (11 women), 6 part-time (4 women); includes 10 minority (5 Black or African American, non-Hispanic/Latino; 4 Hispanic/Latino; 1 Two or more races, non-Hispanic/Latino), 1 international. Average age 28. 46 applicants, 67% accepted, 20 enrolled. In 2017, 21 master's awarded. Application fee: $65. *Expenses:* Tuition, state resident: full-time $12,246; part-time $681 per credit hour. Tuition, nonresident: full-time $25,486; part-time $1417 per credit hour. *Required fees:* $196. Tuition and fees vary according to course load, program and reciprocity agreements. *Financial support:* Applicants required to submit FAFSA. *Faculty research:* Sport administration, exercise physiology, exercise science, physical education, health education. *Total annual research expenditures:* $91,688. *Unit head:* Dr. Margaret Hancock, Interim Chair/Assistant Professor, 502-852-6645, E-mail: meg.hancock@louisville.edu. *Application contact:* Betty Hampton, Director of Graduate Student Services, 502-852-5597, Fax: 502-852-1465, E-mail: edadvise@louisville.edu.
Website: http://www.louisville.edu/education/departments/hss

University of Louisville, Graduate School, College of Education and Human Development, Departments of Early Childhood and Elementary Education, Middle and Secondary Education, and Special Education, Louisville, KY 40292-0001. Offers art education (MAT); autism and applied behavior analysis (Certificate); curriculum and instruction (PhD); early elementary education (MAT); exercise physiology (MS); health and physical education (MAT); health professions education (Certificate); higher education (MA); human resources and organization development (MS); instructional technology (M Ed); interdisciplinary early childhood education (MAT); middle school education (MAT); music education (MAT); secondary education (MAT); special education (MAT); sport administration (MS); teacher leadership (M Ed). *Program availability:* Part-time, evening/weekend. *Students:* 114 full-time (73 women), 173 part-time (114 women); includes 49 minority (19 Black or African American, non-Hispanic/Latino; 5 Asian, non-Hispanic/Latino; 13 Hispanic/Latino; 12 Two or more races, non-Hispanic/Latino), 7 international. Average age 29. 132 applicants, 73% accepted, 57 enrolled. In 2017, 70 master's, 2 doctorates, 2 other advanced degrees awarded. *Application deadline:* For spring admission, 1/1 priority date for international students. Application fee: $65. *Expenses:* Tuition, state resident: full-time $12,246; part-time $681 per credit hour. Tuition, nonresident: full-time $25,486; part-time $1417 per credit hour. *Required fees:* $196. Tuition and fees vary according to course load, program and reciprocity agreements. *Financial support:* Application deadline: 6/1; applicants required to submit FAFSA. *Faculty research:* STEM teaching and learning; content literacy for English language learners; social justice in teacher education; adolescent literacy; mathematics teacher development. *Total annual research expenditures:* $1.7 million. *Unit head:* Dr. Ann E. Larson, Dean, College of Education and Human Development, 502-852-6411, Fax: 502-852-1464, E-mail: ann@louisville.edu. *Application contact:* Betty Hampton, Director of Graduate Student Services, 502-852-5597, Fax: 502-852-1465, E-mail: edadvise@louisville.edu.
Website: http://louisville.edu/delphi

University of Maine, Graduate School, College of Education and Human Development, School of Kinesiology, Physical Education and Athletic Training, Orono, ME 04469. Offers classroom technology integrationist (CGS); education data specialist (CGS); educational technology coordinator (CGS); kinesiology and physical education (M Ed, MS); science education (M Ed, MS); STEM education (PhD). *Program availability:* Part-time, evening/weekend. *Faculty:* 3 full-time (0 women). *Students:* 10 full-time (3 women), 1 part-time (0 women); includes 2 minority (1 Black or African American, non-Hispanic/Latino; 1 Asian, non-Hispanic/Latino). Average age 24. 8 applicants, 100% accepted, 5 enrolled. In 2017, 6 master's awarded. *Degree requirements:* For master's, thesis (for some programs). For doctorate, comprehensive exam, thesis/dissertation. *Entrance requirements:* For master's, GRE General Test, MAT; for doctorate, GRE General Test. Additional exam requirements/recommendations for international students: Required—TOEFL. *Application deadline:* For fall admission, 1/15 for domestic students. Applications are processed on a rolling basis. Application fee: $65. Electronic applications accepted. *Expenses:* Tuition, state resident: full-time $7722; part-time $429 per credit hour. Tuition, nonresident: full-time $25,146; part-time $1397 per credit hour. *Required fees:* $1162; $581 per credit hour. *Financial support:* In 2017–18, 7 students received support, including 6 teaching assistantships with full tuition reimbursements available (averaging $15,200 per year); Federal Work-Study, scholarships/grants, and unspecified assistantships also available. Financial award application deadline: 3/1. *Faculty research:* Geriatric equilibrium, physical activity and technology, muscle cell metabolism, hormonal response to exercise. *Unit head:* Dr. Jim Artesani, Associate Dean of Accreditation and Graduate Affairs, 207-581-4061, Fax: 207-581-2423. *Application contact:* Scott G. Delcourt, Assistant Vice President for Graduate Studies and Senior Associate Dean, 207-581-3291, Fax: 207-581-3232, E-mail: graduate@maine.edu.
Website: http://umaine.edu/edhd/

University of Manitoba, Faculty of Graduate Studies, Faculty of Kinesiology and Recreation Management, Winnipeg, MB R3T 2N2, Canada. Offers kinesiology and recreation (M Sc, MA).

University of Mary, School of Health Sciences, Program in Sports and Physical Education Administration, Bismarck, ND 58504-9652. Offers MS. *Program availability:* Online learning. *Entrance requirements:* For master's, bachelorsdegreeinathletictraining,exercisescience,physicaleducation,orarelatedfield;minimumundergraduateGPAof2.5.'

University of Memphis, Graduate School, School of Health Studies, Memphis, TN 38152. Offers faith and health (Graduate Certificate); health studies (MS), including exercise, sport and movement sciences, health promotion, physical education teacher education; nutrition (MS), including clinical nutrition, environmental nutrition, nutrition science; sport nutrition and dietary supplementation (Graduate Certificate). *Program availability:* 100% online. *Faculty:* 19 full-time (10 women), 2 part-time/adjunct (both women). In 2017, 42 master's awarded. *Degree requirements:* For master's, comprehensive exam, thesis or alternative, culminating experience; for Graduate Certificate, practicum. *Entrance requirements:* For master's, GRE or PRAXIS II, letters of recommendation, statement of goals, minimum undergraduate GPA of 2.5; for Graduate Certificate, minimum undergraduate GPA of 2.5. Additional exam requirements/recommendations for international students: Required—TOEFL (minimum score 550 paper-based; 79 iBT). *Application deadline:* For fall admission, 4/15 priority date for domestic students; for spring admission, 10/15 priority date for domestic students; for summer admission, 4/15 priority date for domestic students. Application fee: $35 ($60 for international students). *Expenses:* Contact institution. *Financial support:* In 2017–18, 33 research assistantships (averaging $11,930 per year), 4 teaching assistantships (averaging $10,000 per year) were awarded; career-related internships or fieldwork, Federal Work-Study, scholarships/grants, and unspecified assistantships also available. Financial award application deadline: 2/1; financial award applicants required to submit FAFSA. *Unit head:* Dr. Richard J. Bloomer, Director, 901-

678-4316, Fax: 901-678-3591, E-mail: rbloomer@memphis.edu. *Application contact:* Dr. Lawrence Weiss, Director of Graduate Programs, 901-678-5037, E-mail: lweiss@memphis.edu.
Website: http://www.memphis.edu/shs/

University of Montana, Graduate School, Phyllis J. Washington College of Education and Human Sciences, Department of Health and Human Performance, Missoula, MT 59812. Offers community health (MS); exercise science (MS); health and human performance generalist (MS). *Program availability:* Part-time. *Entrance requirements:* For master's, GRE General Test. Additional exam requirements/recommendations for international students: Required—TOEFL. *Faculty research:* Exercise physiology, performance psychology, nutrition, pre-employment physical screening, program evaluation.

University of Nebraska at Kearney, College of Education, Kinesiology and Sport Sciences Department, Kearney, NE 68849-0001. Offers general physical education (MA Ed), including recreation and leisure, sports administration; physical education exercise science (MA Ed); physical education master teacher (MA Ed), including pedagogy, special populations. *Program availability:* Part-time, evening/weekend, 100% online. *Degree requirements:* For master's, comprehensive exam, thesis optional. *Entrance requirements:* For master's, GRE General Test (for some programs), personal statement. Additional exam requirements/recommendations for international students: Recommended—TOEFL (minimum score 550 paper-based; 79 iBT), IELTS (minimum score 6.5). Electronic applications accepted. *Faculty research:* Ergonomic aids, nutrition, motor development, sports pedagogy, applied behavior analysis, physical activity and wellness, athletic training, therapeutic Interventions, exercise physiology, endocrinology and metabolism.

University of New Brunswick Fredericton, School of Graduate Studies, Faculty of Kinesiology, Fredericton, NB E3B 5A3, Canada. Offers exercise and sport science (M Sc); sport and recreation management (MBA); sport and recreation studies (MA). *Program availability:* Part-time. *Degree requirements:* For master's, thesis (for some programs). *Entrance requirements:* For master's, GMAT (minimum score of 550 for sport and recreation management program), minimum GPA of 3.0, written statement of research goals and interests. Additional exam requirements/recommendations for international students: Required—TOEFL (minimum score 92 iBT), IELTS (minimum score 7). Electronic applications accepted.

University of New Hampshire, Graduate School, College of Health and Human Services, Department of Kinesiology, Durham, NH 03824. Offers adapted physical education (Postbaccalaureate Certificate); kinesiology (MS); kinesiology and social work (MS). *Program availability:* Part-time. *Students:* 5 full-time (1 woman), 5 part-time (2 women), 1 international. Average age 28. 16 applicants, 56% accepted, 4 enrolled. In 2017, 10 master's awarded. *Entrance requirements:* For master's, GRE General Test. Additional exam requirements/recommendations for international students: Required—TOEFL (minimum score 550 paper-based; 80 iBT). *Application deadline:* For fall admission, 4/1 priority date for domestic students, 4/1 for international students; for spring admission, 12/1 for domestic students. Application fee: $65. Electronic applications accepted. *Financial support:* In 2017–18, 5 students received support, including 3 teaching assistantships; fellowships, research assistantships, career-related internships or fieldwork, Federal Work-Study, scholarships/grants, and tuition waivers (full and partial) also available. Support available to part-time students. Financial award application deadline: 2/15. *Unit head:* Karen Collins, Chair, 603-862-0361. *Application contact:* Jayson Seaman, Administrative Assistant, 603-862-1162, E-mail: kinesiology.dept@unh.edu.
Website: http://chhs.unh.edu/kin

University of New Mexico, Graduate Studies, College of Education, Program in Physical Education, Sports and Exercise Science, Albuquerque, NM 87131-2039. Offers curriculum and instruction (PhD); exercise science (PhD); sports administration (PhD). *Program availability:* Part-time. *Students:* Average age 30. 67 applicants, 75% accepted, 35 enrolled. In 2017, 13 doctorates awarded. *Degree requirements:* For doctorate, comprehensive exam, thesis/dissertation, inquiry skills, 24 credits in supporting area. *Entrance requirements:* For doctorate, GRE, letter of intent, 3 letters of reference, minimum cumulative GPA of 3.0 in last 2 years of bachelor's degree. Additional exam requirements/recommendations for international students: Required—TOEFL (minimum score 550 paper-based). *Application deadline:* For fall admission, 3/1 priority date for domestic students; for spring admission, 11/1 priority date for domestic students. Application fee: $50. Electronic applications accepted. *Financial support:* Fellowships, teaching assistantships with full tuition reimbursements, career-related internships or fieldwork, Federal Work-Study, institutionally sponsored loans, scholarships/grants, health care benefits, tuition waivers, and unspecified assistantships available. Financial award application deadline: 3/1; financial award applicants required to submit FAFSA. *Faculty research:* Facility risk management, physical education pedagogy practices, physiological adaptations to exercise, physiological adaptations to heat, sport leadership. *Unit head:* Dr. Todd Seidler, Chair, 505-277-2783, Fax: 505-277-6227, E-mail: tseidler@unm.edu. *Application contact:* Monica Lopez, Program Office, 505-277-5151, Fax: 505-277-6227, E-mail: mllopez@unm.edu.
Website: https://coe.unm.edu/departments-programs/hess/physical-education/physical-education-phd/index.html

University of North Alabama, College of Education, Department of Health, Physical Education, and Recreation, Florence, AL 35632-0001. Offers health and human performance (MS), including exercise science, kinesiology, wellness and health promotion. *Program availability:* Part-time. *Faculty:* 7 full-time (2 women), 1 part-time/adjunct (0 women). *Students:* 14 full-time (10 women), 14 part-time (6 women); includes 4 minority (all Black or African American, non-Hispanic/Latino), 3 international. Average age 25. 22 applicants, 82% accepted, 9 enrolled. In 2017, 7 master's awarded. *Degree requirements:* For master's, comprehensive exam (for some programs), thesis optional. *Entrance requirements:* For master's, MAT or GRE, 3 letters of recommendation, essay. Additional exam requirements/recommendations for international students: Required—TOEFL (minimum score 79 iBT), IELTS (minimum score 6), PTE (minimum score 54). *Application deadline:* Applications are processed on a rolling basis. Application fee: $50 ($100 for international students). Electronic applications accepted. *Expenses:* Tuition, state resident: full-time $7824; part-time $5943 per year. Tuition, nonresident: full-time $15,648; part-time $11,736 per year. *Required fees:* $3064; $2298 per unit. Tuition and fees vary according to course load and reciprocity agreements. *Financial support:* In 2017–18, 19 students received support. Federal Work-Study, scholarships/grants, and unspecified assistantships available. Financial award application deadline: 2/1; financial award applicants required to submit FAFSA. *Total annual research expenditures:* $13,976. *Unit head:* Dr. Thomas E. Coates, Chair, 256-765-4377. *Application contact:* Hillary N. Coats, Graduate Admissions Coordinator, 256-765-4447, E-mail: graduate@una.edu.
Website: https://www.una.edu/hper/index.html

The University of North Carolina at Chapel Hill, Graduate School, College of Arts and Sciences, Department of Exercise and Sport Science, Chapel Hill, NC 27599. Offers athletic training (MA); exercise physiology (MA); sport administration (MA). *Degree requirements:* For master's, comprehensive exam, thesis. *Entrance requirements:* For master's, GRE General Test, minimum GPA of 3.0. Additional exam requirements/

Physical Education

recommendations for international students: Required—TOEFL (minimum score 550 paper-based). Electronic applications accepted. *Faculty research:* Mild head injury in sport, endocrine system's response to exercise, obesity and children, effect of aerobic exercise on cerebral bloodflow in elderly population.

The University of North Carolina at Pembroke, The Graduate School, School of Education, Department of Health and Human Performance, Pembroke, NC 28372-1510. Offers health/physical education (MAT); physical education (MA), including exercise/sports administration, physical education advanced licensure. *Program availability:* Part-time, evening/weekend. *Degree requirements:* For master's, comprehensive exam, thesis optional. *Entrance requirements:* For master's, MAT or GRE, minimum GPA of 3.0 in major, 2.5 overall. Additional exam requirements/recommendations for international students: Required—TOEFL. *Application deadline:* For fall admission, 7/15 priority date for domestic and international students; for spring admission, 12/1 priority date for domestic and international students. Applications are processed on a rolling basis. Application fee: $45 ($60 for international students). *Financial support:* Application deadline: 4/15; applicants required to submit FAFSA. *Unit head:* Dr. Leah Fiorentino, Program Director, 910-775-4354, E-mail: leah.fiorentino@uncp.edu. Website: https://www.uncp.edu/departments/health-and-human-performance

University of Northern Colorado, Graduate School, College of Natural and Health Sciences, School of Sport and Exercise Science, Greeley, CO 80639. Offers exercise science (MS, PhD); physical education and physical activity leadership (MAT); sport administration (MS, PhD); sport pedagogy (MS, PhD); sports coaching (MA). *Program availability:* Part-time, evening/weekend. *Degree requirements:* For master's, comprehensive exam; for doctorate, comprehensive exam, thesis/dissertation. *Entrance requirements:* For master's, 2 letters of recommendation, resume; for doctorate, GRE General Test, 3 letters of recommendation, resume. Electronic applications accepted.

University of Northern Iowa, Graduate College, College of Education, School of Kinesiology, Allied Health and Human Services, MA Program in Physical Education, Cedar Falls, IA 50614. Offers kinesiology (MA); teaching/coaching (MA). *Program availability:* Part-time, evening/weekend. *Degree requirements:* For master's, comprehensive exam, thesis or alternative. *Entrance requirements:* For master's, minimum GPA of 3.0. Additional exam requirements/recommendations for international students: Required—TOEFL (minimum score 500 paper-based; 61 iBT). Electronic applications accepted.

University of North Georgia, Master of Arts in Teaching Program, Dahlonega, GA 30597. Offers physical education (MAT); secondary education - English (MAT); secondary education - history (MAT); secondary education - mathematics (MAT); secondary education - middle grades (MAT). *Students:* 27 part-time (20 women). Average age 29. 12 applicants, 75% accepted, 7 enrolled. In 2017, 15 master's awarded. *Degree requirements:* For master's, internship, capstone. *Entrance requirements:* For master's, GRE or MAT, GACE I and II, GA pre-service application, lawful presence verification, official transcripts, GA Educator Ethics Program entry assessment. Additional exam requirements/recommendations for international students: Required—TOEFL (minimum score 550 paper-based; 79 iBT), IELTS (minimum score 6.5). *Application deadline:* For summer admission, 2/1 for domestic students. Application fee: $40. Electronic applications accepted. *Expenses:* Contact institution. *Financial support:* Application deadline: 3/17; applicants required to submit FAFSA. *Unit head:* Dr. Susan Brandenburg-Ayres, Dean, 706-864-1998, E-mail: susan.ayres@ung.edu. *Application contact:* Melinda Maxwell, Director of Graduate Admissions, 706-867-2077, E-mail: melinda.maxwell@ung.edu.
Website: https://ung.edu/teacher-education/graduate/master-of-arts-teaching.php

University of Rhode Island, Graduate School, College of Health Sciences, Department of Kinesiology, Kingston, RI 02881. Offers cultural studies of sport and physical culture (MS); exercise science (MS); psychosocial/behavioral aspects of physical activity (MS). *Accreditation:* NCATE. *Program availability:* Part-time. *Faculty:* 14 full-time (9 women). *Students:* 10 full-time (4 women), 3 part-time (1 woman), 1 international. 8 applicants, 100% accepted, 6 enrolled. In 2017, 7 master's awarded. *Entrance requirements:* Additional exam requirements/recommendations for international students: Required—TOEFL. *Application deadline:* For fall admission, 7/15 for domestic students, 2/1 for international students; for spring admission, 11/15 for domestic students, 7/15 for international students. Application fee: $65. Electronic applications accepted. *Expenses:* Tuition, state resident: full-time $12,706; part-time $786 per credit. Tuition, nonresident: full-time $25,216; part-time $1401 per credit. *Required fees:* $1598; $45 per credit. One-time fee: $30 part-time. *Financial support:* In 2017–18, 5 teaching assistantships with tuition reimbursements (averaging $11,078 per year) were awarded. Financial award application deadline: 2/1; financial award applicants required to submit FAFSA. *Unit head:* Dr. Disa Hatfield, Interim Chair, 401-874-5183, E-mail: doch@uri.edu. *Application contact:* Dr. Matthew Delmonico, Graduate Program Director, 401-874-5440, E-mail: delmonico@uri.edu.
Website: http://web.uri.edu/kinesiology/

University of Rio Grande, Graduate School, Rio Grande, OH 45674. Offers athletic coaching leadership (M Ed); educational leadership (M Ed); integrated arts (M Ed); intervention specialist in early childhood (M Ed); intervention specialist in mild/moderate (M Ed). *Accreditation:* NCATE. *Program availability:* Part-time. *Degree requirements:* For master's, final research project, portfolio. *Entrance requirements:* For master's, minimum GPA of 2.7 in major, 2.5 overall. Additional exam requirements/recommendations for international students: Required—TOEFL. *Faculty research:* Interagency collaboration, reading and mathematics, learning styles, college access, literacy.

University of South Alabama, College of Education and Professional Studies, Department of Health, Kinesiology, and Sport, Mobile, AL 36688. Offers exercise science (MS); health education (M Ed, MS); physical education (M Ed); sport management (MS). *Accreditation:* NCATE (one or more programs are accredited). *Program availability:* Part-time. *Faculty:* 7 full-time (2 women). *Students:* 47 full-time (15 women), 7 part-time (3 women); includes 23 minority (19 Black or African American, non-Hispanic/Latino; 1 American Indian or Alaska Native, non-Hispanic/Latino; 2 Asian, non-Hispanic/Latino; 1 Hispanic/Latino), 4 international. Average age 25. 48 applicants, 54% accepted, 19 enrolled. In 2017, 23 master's awarded. *Degree requirements:* For master's, comprehensive exam, thesis optional. *Entrance requirements:* For master's, GRE General Test or MAT, Alabama Class B certificate or the equivalent (for students seeking the master's-level/Class A certification). Additional exam requirements/recommendations for international students: Required—TOEFL. *Application deadline:* For fall admission, 7/1 priority date for domestic students, 6/15 priority date for international students; for spring admission, 11/15 priority date for domestic students, 11/1 priority date for international students; for summer admission, 4/15 for domestic students, 4/1 for international students. Applications are processed on a rolling basis. Application fee: $35. Electronic applications accepted. *Expenses:* Tuition, state resident: full-time $10,104; part-time $421 per semester hour. Tuition, nonresident: full-time $20,208; part-time $842 per semester hour. *Financial support:* Fellowships, research assistantships, teaching assistantships with partial tuition reimbursements, career-related internships or fieldwork, Federal Work-Study, institutionally sponsored loans, scholarships/grants, and unspecified assistantships available. Support available to part-time students. Financial award application deadline: 3/31; financial award

applicants required to submit FAFSA. *Unit head:* Dr. John Kovaleski, Department Chair, 251-461-1622, Fax: 251-460-7252, E-mail: jkovales@southalabama.edu. *Application contact:* Dr. Susan Santoli, Director of Graduate Studies, 251-380-2836, Fax: 251-380-2748, E-mail: ssantoli@southalabama.edu.
Website: http://www.southalabama.edu/colleges/ceps/hks/index.html

University of South Carolina, The Graduate School, College of Education, Department of Physical Education, Columbia, SC 29208. Offers IMA, MAT, MS, PhD. *Program availability:* Part-time. *Degree requirements:* For master's, comprehensive exam, thesis (for some programs); for doctorate, comprehensive exam, thesis/dissertation. *Entrance requirements:* For master's, GRE General Test, or Miller Analogies Test, writing sample, letter of intent, letters of recommendation; for doctorate, GRE General Test or Miller Analogies Test, writing sample, interview, letter of intent, letters of recommendation. *Faculty research:* Teaching/learning processes, anthropometric measurement, growth and development, motor development.

University of Southern Mississippi, College of Health, School of Kinesiology, Hattiesburg, MS 39406-0001. Offers MS, PhD. *Program availability:* Part-time, evening/weekend. *Students:* 17 full-time (12 women), 1 (woman) part-time. 34 applicants, 74% accepted, 18 enrolled. In 2017, 3 doctorates awarded. *Degree requirements:* For master's, comprehensive exam, thesis optional; for doctorate, comprehensive exam, thesis/dissertation. *Entrance requirements:* For master's, GRE General Test, minimum GPA of 2.75 in last 60 hours; for doctorate, GRE General Test, minimum GPA of 3.5. Additional exam requirements/recommendations for international students: Required—TOEFL, IELTS. *Application deadline:* For fall admission, 3/1 priority date for domestic students, 3/1 for international students; for spring admission, 1/10 priority date for domestic and international students. Applications are processed on a rolling basis. Application fee: $60. Electronic applications accepted. *Expenses:* Tuition, state resident: full-time $3830. *Financial support:* Fellowships, research assistantships with full tuition reimbursements, teaching assistantships with full tuition reimbursements, career-related internships or fieldwork, Federal Work-Study, institutionally sponsored loans, scholarships/grants, health care benefits, and unspecified assistantships available. Financial award application deadline: 3/15; financial award applicants required to submit FAFSA. *Faculty research:* Exercise physiology, health behaviors, resource management, activity interaction, site development. *Unit head:* Dr. Scott Piland, Director, 601-266-5386, Fax: 601-266-4445, E-mail: scott.piland@usm.edu. *Application contact:* Dr. Trenton Gould, Dean, College of Health, 601-266-6339, Fax: 601-266-4445.
Website: https://www.usm.edu/kinesiology

The University of Tennessee at Chattanooga, Department of Health and Human Performance, Chattanooga, TN 37403. Offers athletic training (MSAT); health and human performance (MS). *Students:* 42 full-time (30 women); includes 7 minority (2 Black or African American, non-Hispanic/Latino; 3 Hispanic/Latino; 2 Two or more races, non-Hispanic/Latino). Average age 23. 24 applicants, 100% accepted, 22 enrolled. In 2017, 21 master's awarded. *Degree requirements:* For master's, thesis or alternative, clinical rotations. *Entrance requirements:* For master's, GRE General Test, minimum GPA of 2.75 overall or 3.0 in last 60 hours; CPR and First Aid certification. Additional exam requirements/recommendations for international students: Required—TOEFL (minimum score 550 paper-based; 79 iBT), IELTS (minimum score 6). *Application deadline:* For fall admission, 6/15 priority date for domestic students, 7/1 for international students; for spring admission, 11/1 priority date for domestic students, 11/1 for international students. Applications are processed on a rolling basis. Application fee: $35 ($40 for international students). Electronic applications accepted. *Expenses:* Contact institution. *Financial support:* Research assistantships with tuition reimbursements, teaching assistantships with tuition reimbursements, career-related internships or fieldwork, scholarships/grants, and unspecified assistantships available. Support available to part-time students. Financial award application deadline: 7/1; financial award applicants required to submit FAFSA. *Faculty research:* Therapeutic exercise, lumbar spine biomechanics, physical activity epidemiology, functional rehabilitation outcomes, metabolic health. *Total annual research expenditures:* $16,000. *Unit head:* Dr. Marisa Colston, Department Head, 423-425-4743, E-mail: marisa-colston@utc.edu. *Application contact:* Dr. Joanne Romagni, Dean of the Graduate School, 423-425-4478, Fax: 423-425-5223, E-mail: joanne-romagni@utc.edu.
Website: https://www.utc.edu/health-human-performance/

The University of Tennessee at Martin, Graduate Programs, College of Education, Health and Behavioral Sciences, Program in Teaching, Martin, TN 38238. Offers curriculum and instruction (MS Ed), including 7-12, K-6; initial licensure (MS Ed), including elementary education, secondary education; initial licensure K-12 (MS Ed), including physical education, special education; interdisciplinary (MS Ed). *Program availability:* Part-time, online only, 100% online. *Students:* 20 full-time (17 women), 92 part-time (66 women); includes 20 minority (14 Black or African American, non-Hispanic/Latino; 2 Hispanic/Latino; 4 Two or more races, non-Hispanic/Latino). Average age 32. 79 applicants, 70% accepted, 38 enrolled. In 2017, 14 master's awarded. *Entrance requirements:* Additional exam requirements/recommendations for international students: Required—TOEFL (minimum score 525 paper-based; 71 iBT). *Application deadline:* For fall admission, 7/27 for domestic and international students; for spring admission, 12/17 for domestic and international students; for summer admission, 5/10 for domestic and international students. Applications are processed on a rolling basis. Electronic applications accepted. *Expenses:* Tuition, state resident: full-time $8658; part-time $481 per credit hour. Tuition, nonresident: full-time $14,418; part-time $801 per credit hour. *International tuition:* $22,602 full-time. *Required fees:* $1404; $79 per credit hour. Part-time tuition and fees vary according to course load. *Financial support:* In 2017–18, 26 students received support, including 1 research assistantship with full tuition reimbursement available (averaging $6,283 per year), 5 teaching assistantships with full tuition reimbursements available (averaging $7,001 per year); scholarships/grants and tuition waivers also available. Financial award applicants required to submit FAFSA. *Faculty research:* Special education, science/math/technology, school reform, reading. *Unit head:* Cynthia West, Dean, 731-881-7125, Fax: 731-881-7975, E-mail: cwest@utm.edu. *Application contact:* Jolene L. Cunningham, Student Services Specialist, 731-881-7012, Fax: 731-881-7499, E-mail: jcunningham@utm.edu.

The University of Texas at Austin, Graduate School, College of Education, Department of Curriculum and Instruction, Austin, TX 78712-1111. Offers bilingual/bicultural education (M Ed, MA, PhD); cultural studies in education (M Ed, MA, PhD); early childhood education (M Ed, MA, PhD); language and literacy studies (M Ed, MA, PhD); learning technologies (M Ed, MA, PhD); physical education (M Ed, MA, PhD). Terminal master's awarded for partial completion of doctoral program. *Degree requirements:* For doctorate, thesis/dissertation. *Entrance requirements:* For master's and doctorate, GRE General Test. Electronic applications accepted.

The University of Toledo, College of Graduate Studies, Judith Herb College of Education, Department of Early Childhood, Physical and Special Education, Toledo, OH 43606-3390. Offers early childhood education (ME); physical education (ME); special education (ME). *Program availability:* Part-time. *Degree requirements:* For master's, thesis. *Entrance requirements:* For master's, minimum cumulative GPA of 2.7 for all previous academic work, letters of recommendation. Additional exam requirements/recommendations for international students: Required—TOEFL (minimum score 550 paper-based; 80 iBT). Electronic applications accepted.

University of Toronto, School of Graduate Studies, Faculty of Kinesiology and Physical Education, Toronto, ON M5S 1A1, Canada. Offers M Sc, PhD. *Degree requirements:* For master's, thesis, oral defense of thesis; for doctorate, comprehensive exam, defense of thesis. *Entrance requirements:* For master's, background in physical education and health, minimum B+ average in final year of undergraduate study, 2 letters of reference, resume, 2 writing samples; for doctorate, master's degree with successful defense of thesis, background in exercise sciences, minimum A- average, 2 letters of reference. Additional exam requirements/recommendations for international students: Required—TOEFL (minimum score 580 paper-based; 93 iBT), TWE (minimum score 5). Electronic applications accepted.

University of Victoria, Faculty of Graduate Studies, Faculty of Education, School of Exercise Science, Physical, and Health Education, Victoria, BC V8W 2Y2, Canada. Offers coaching studies (co-operative education) (M Ed); kinesiology (M Sc, MA); leisure service administration (MA); physical education (MA). *Program availability:* Part-time. *Degree requirements:* For master's, comprehensive exam (for some programs), thesis (for some programs). *Entrance requirements:* For master's, minimum B average. Additional exam requirements/recommendations for international students: Required—TOEFL (minimum score 575 paper-based), IELTS (minimum score 7). Electronic applications accepted. *Faculty research:* Children and exercise, mental skills in sports, teaching effectiveness, neural control of human movement, physical performance and health.

University of Virginia, Curry School of Education, Department of Kinesiology, Charlottesville, VA 22903. Offers M Ed, MS, PhD. *Faculty:* 13 full-time (4 women). *Students:* 48 full-time (27 women), 6 part-time (4 women); includes 10 minority (3 Black or African American, non-Hispanic/Latino; 2 Asian, non-Hispanic/Latino; 3 Hispanic/Latino; 2 Two or more races, non-Hispanic/Latino), 2 international. Average age 25. 26 applicants, 81% accepted, 15 enrolled. In 2017, 46 master's awarded. *Entrance requirements:* For master's and doctorate, GRE General Test, 2 letters of recommendation. Additional exam requirements/recommendations for international students: Required—TOEFL (minimum score 600 paper-based; 90 iBT), IELTS (minimum score 7). *Application deadline:* Applications are processed on a rolling basis. Application fee: $60. Electronic applications accepted. *Financial support:* Applicants required to submit FAFSA. *Unit head:* Arthur L. Weltman, Chair, Kinesiology, 434-924-6191, E-mail: alw2v@virginia.edu. *Application contact:* E-mail: curry-admissions@virginia.edu.
Website: http://curry.virginia.edu/academics/department/kinesiology

University of Washington, Graduate School, College of Education, Seattle, WA 98195. Offers curriculum and instruction (M Ed, Ed D, PhD), including educational technology, general curriculum (Ed D, PhD), language, literacy, and culture, mathematics education, multicultural education, reading and language arts education (Ed D), science education, social studies education, teaching and curriculum (M Ed); educational leadership and policy studies (M Ed, Ed D, PhD), including administration (Ed D), educational policy, organization, and leadership (M Ed, PhD), higher education, leadership for learning (Ed D), social and cultural foundations of education (M Ed, PhD); educational psychology (M Ed, PhD), including educational psychology (PhD), human development and cognition (M Ed), learning sciences, measurement, statistics and research design (M Ed); school psychology (M Ed); instructional leadership (M Ed); intercollegiate athletic leadership (M Ed); special education (M Ed, Ed D, PhD), including early childhood special education (M Ed), emotional and behavioral disabilities (M Ed), learning disabilities (M Ed), low-incidence disabilities (M Ed), severe disabilities (M Ed), special education (Ed D, PhD); teacher education (MIT). *Accreditation:* APA. *Program availability:* Part-time, evening/weekend. *Degree requirements:* For master's, thesis optional; for doctorate, thesis/dissertation. *Entrance requirements:* For master's and doctorate, GRE General Test, minimum GPA of 3.0. Additional exam requirements/recommendations for international students: Required—TOEFL. Electronic applications accepted. *Faculty research:* School restructuring/effective schools, special education interventions, literacy and writing, technology, school partnerships, teacher preparation.

The University of West Alabama, School of Graduate Studies, College of Natural Sciences and Mathematics, Program in Physical Education, Livingston, AL 35470. Offers M Ed, MAT, MS. *Program availability:* Part-time, evening/weekend, 100% online. *Faculty:* 3 full-time (0 women), 3 part-time/adjunct (1 woman). *Students:* 119 (32 women); includes 41 minority (39 Black or African American, non-Hispanic/Latino; 1 American Indian or Alaska Native, non-Hispanic/Latino; 1 Hispanic/Latino). Average age 31. 42 applicants, 100% accepted, 37 enrolled. In 2017, 29 master's awarded. *Degree requirements:* For master's, comprehensive exam, thesis optional, field experience, internship. *Entrance requirements:* For master's, GRE, minimum GPA of 2.75. Additional exam requirements/recommendations for international students: Required—TOEFL (minimum score 500 paper-based; 61 iBT). *Application deadline:* Applications are processed on a rolling basis. Application fee: $40. Electronic applications accepted. *Expenses:* Tuition, state resident: part-time $371 per credit hour. Tuition, nonresident: part-time $742 per credit hour. *Required fees:* $130 per semester. *Financial support:* In 2017–18, 3 teaching assistantships (averaging $7,344 per year) were awarded; Federal Work-Study, scholarships/grants, and unspecified assistantships also available. Support available to part-time students. Financial award application deadline: 3/1; financial award applicants required to submit FAFSA. *Unit head:* Dr. R. T. Floyd, Assistant Dean of College of Natural Sciences and Mathematics, 205-652-3714, E-mail: rtf@uwa.edu. *Application contact:* Dr. John McCall, Dean of College of Natural Sciences and Mathematics, 205-652-3414, Fax: 205-652-3831, E-mail: jmccall@uwa.edu.
Website: http://www.uwa.edu/academics/collegeofnaturalsciencesandmathematics

University of West Florida, College of Education and Professional Studies, Ed D Programs, Specialization in Physical Education and Health, Pensacola, FL 32514-5750. Offers Ed D. *Program availability:* Part-time, evening/weekend. *Degree requirements:* For doctorate, comprehensive exam, thesis/dissertation. *Entrance requirements:* For doctorate, GRE, MAT, or GMAT, letter of intent; writing sample; three letters of recommendation; two completed disposition assessment forms; written statement of goals; interview with admissions committee. Additional exam requirements/recommendations for international students: Required—TOEFL (minimum score 550 paper-based).

University of West Florida, Usha Kundu, MD College of Health, Department of Exercise Science and Community Health, Pensacola, FL 32514-5750. Offers health promotion (MS); health, leisure, and exercise science (MS), including exercise science, physical education. *Program availability:* Part-time, evening/weekend. *Degree requirements:* For master's, thesis or alternative. *Entrance requirements:* For master's, GRE or MAT, official transcripts; minimum GPA of 3.0; letter of intent; three personal references; work experience as reflected in resume. Additional exam requirements/recommendations for international students: Required—TOEFL (minimum score 550 paper-based).

University of Wisconsin–La Crosse, College of Science and Health, Department of Exercise and Sport Science, Program in Physical Education Teaching, La Crosse, WI 54601-3742. Offers exercise sport science: physical education teaching (MS), including adapted physical education, adventure education. *Program availability:* Part-time, evening/weekend. *Students:* 12 full-time (6 women), 1 part-time (0 women), 2 international. Average age 25. 21 applicants, 95% accepted, 12 enrolled. In 2017, 8

master's awarded. *Degree requirements:* For master's, thesis optional. *Entrance requirements:* For master's, minimum GPA of 3.0 during previous 2 years, 2.85 overall; BA in physical education. Additional exam requirements/recommendations for international students: Required—TOEFL (minimum score 550 paper-based; 79 iBT). *Application deadline:* Applications are processed on a rolling basis. Electronic applications accepted. *Financial support:* Federal Work-Study, scholarships/grants, health care benefits, and tuition waivers (partial) available. Support available to part-time students. Financial award application deadline: 3/15; financial award applicants required to submit FAFSA. *Unit head:* Dr. Jooyeon Jin, Program Director, 608-785-8182, E-mail: jjin@uwlax.edu. *Application contact:* Brandon Schaller, Senior Graduate Student Status Examiner, 608-785-8941, E-mail: admissions@uwlax.edu.
Website: https://www.uwlax.edu/grad/physical-education-teaching

University of Wyoming, College of Health Sciences, Division of Kinesiology and Health, Laramie, WY 82071. Offers MS. *Accreditation:* NCATE. *Program availability:* Part-time, online learning. *Degree requirements:* For master's, comprehensive exam (for some programs), thesis (for some programs). *Entrance requirements:* For master's, GRE General Test, minimum GPA of 3.0. Additional exam requirements/recommendations for international students: Required—TOEFL. Electronic applications accepted. *Faculty research:* Teacher effectiveness, effects of exercising on heart function, physiological responses of overtraining, psychological benefits of physical activity, health behavior.

Utah State University, School of Graduate Studies, Emma Eccles Jones College of Education and Human Services, Department of Kinesiology and Health Science, Logan, UT 84322. Offers fitness promotion (MS); health and human movement (MS); pathokinesiology (PhD); physical and sport eductaion (M Ed); public health (MPH). *Program availability:* Part-time, evening/weekend, online learning. *Degree requirements:* For master's, thesis (for some programs). *Entrance requirements:* For master's, GRE General Test or MAT, minimum GPA of 3.0. Additional exam requirements/recommendations for international students: Required—TOEFL. *Faculty research:* Sport psychology intervention, motor learning biomechanics, pedagogy, physiology.

Wayne State College, Department of Health, Human Performance and Sport, Wayne, NE 68787. Offers exercise science (MSE); organizational management (MS), including sport management. *Program availability:* Part-time, evening/weekend. *Degree requirements:* For master's, comprehensive exam, thesis optional. *Entrance requirements:* For master's, GRE General Test, minimum GPA of 3.0. Additional exam requirements/recommendations for international students: Required—TOEFL (minimum score 550 paper-based). Electronic applications accepted.

Wayne State University, College of Education, Division of Kinesiology, Health and Sports Studies, Detroit, MI 48202. Offers athletic training (MSAT); health education (M Ed); kinesiology (M Ed, PhD), including exercise and sport science (PhD), physical education and physical activity leadership (PhD); sports administration (MA). *Program availability:* Part-time, 100% online. *Faculty:* 9. *Students:* 65 full-time (33 women), 109 part-time (56 women); includes 70 minority (59 Black or African American, non-Hispanic/Latino; 3 Hispanic/Latino; 8 Two or more races, non-Hispanic/Latino), 8 international. Average age 30. 182 applicants, 53% accepted, 56 enrolled. In 2017, 62 master's, 3 doctorates awarded. *Degree requirements:* For master's, thesis (for some programs); for doctorate, thesis/dissertation. *Entrance requirements:* For master's, minimum undergraduate GPA of 3.0; undergraduate degree directly relating to the field of specialization being applied for or one accompanied by extensive educational background in closely-related field; teaching certificates in specific areas (for some programs); for doctorate, minimum undergraduate GPA of 3.0; undergraduate degree directly relating to the field of specialization being applied for or one accompanied by extensive educational background in closely-related field. Additional exam requirements/recommendations for international students: Required—TOEFL (minimum score 79 iBT), TWE (minimum score 5.5); Recommended—IELTS (minimum score 6.5). *Application deadline:* For fall admission, 6/1 priority date for domestic students, 5/1 priority date for international students; for winter admission, 10/1 priority date for domestic students, 9/1 priority date for international students; for spring admission, 2/1 priority date for domestic students, 1/1 priority date for international students. Application fee: $50. Electronic applications accepted. *Expenses:* Contact institution. *Financial support:* In 2017–18, 47 students received support, including 6 research assistantships with tuition reimbursements available (averaging $18,534 per year), 5 teaching assistantships with tuition reimbursements available (averaging $18,534 per year); fellowships with tuition reimbursements available, scholarships/grants, health care benefits, and unspecified assistantships also available. Support available to part-time students. Financial award applicants required to submit FAFSA. *Faculty research:* Exercise and sport science, nutrition and physical activity interventions, school and community health, obesity prevention. *Unit head:* Dr. Nate McCaughtry, Assistant Dean, Division of Kinesiology, Health and Sport Studies/Director, Center for School Health, 313-577-0014, Fax: 313-577-5002, E-mail: aj4391@wayne.edu. *Application contact:* 313-577-4249, E-mail: askcoe@wayne.edu.
Website: http://coe.wayne.edu/kinesiology/index.php

West Chester University of Pennsylvania, College of Health Sciences, Department of Kinesiology, West Chester, PA 19383. Offers adapted physical education (Certificate); exercise and sport physiology (MS), including athletic training; sport management and athletics (MPA), including administration. *Program availability:* Part-time, evening/weekend, blended/hybrid learning. *Students:* 44 full-time (24 women), 12 part-time (3 women); includes 5 minority (2 Black or African American, non-Hispanic/Latino; 2 Hispanic/Latino; 1 Two or more races, non-Hispanic/Latino), 1 international. Average age 25. 68 applicants, 87% accepted, 29 enrolled. In 2017, 13 master's, 14 other advanced degrees awarded. *Degree requirements:* For master's, thesis or research report (for MS); two internships and capstone course that includes a research project or thesis (for MPA); for Certificate, six courses of study. *Entrance requirements:* For master's, GRE (for MS), 2 letters of recommendation, statement of professional goals; transcripts (for MS); two letters of reference, career goals, resume (for MPA); for Certificate, two letters of recommendation, transcript. Additional exam requirements/recommendations for international students: Required—TOEFL or IELTS. *Application deadline:* For fall admission, 5/15 for international students; for spring admission, 10/15 for international students. Applications are processed on a rolling basis. Application fee: $50. Electronic applications accepted. *Expenses:* Tuition, state resident: full-time $9000; part-time $500 per credit. Tuition, nonresident: full-time $13,500; part-time $750 per credit. *Required fees:* $2959; $149.79 per credit. *Financial support:* Scholarships/grants and unspecified assistantships available. Financial award application deadline: 2/15; financial award applicants required to submit FAFSA. *Faculty research:* Metabolism during exercise, biomechanics, rating of perceived exertion, motor learning, environmental physiology. *Unit head:* Dr. W. Craig Stevens, Chair, 610-436-2610, Fax: 610-436-2860, E-mail: cstevens@wcpua.edu. *Application contact:* Office of Graduate Studies and Extended Education, 610-436-2943, Fax: 610-436-2763, E-mail: gradstudy@wcupa.edu.
Website: http://www.wcupa.edu/healthsciences/kinesiology/

Western Kentucky University, Graduate Studies, College of Health and Human Services, Department of Kinesiology, Recreation and Sport, Bowling Green, KY 42101. Offers athletic administration and coaching (MS); physical education (MS); recreation

Physical Education

and sport administration (MS). *Program availability:* Part-time, evening/weekend, online learning. *Degree requirements:* For master's, comprehensive exam, thesis optional. *Entrance requirements:* For master's, GRE General Test, minimum GPA of 2.75. Additional exam requirements/recommendations for international students: Required—TOEFL (minimum score 555 paper-based; 79 iBT). *Faculty research:* Orthopedic rehabilitation, fitness center coordination, heat acclimation, biomechanical and physiological parameters.

Western Michigan University, Graduate College, College of Education and Human Development, Department of Health, Physical Education and Recreation, Kalamazoo, MI 49008. Offers athletic training (MS), including exercise physiology; sport management (MA), including pedagogy, special physical education.

Western Washington University, Graduate School, College of Humanities and Social Sciences, Department of Physical Education, Health, and Recreation, Bellingham, WA 98225-5996. Offers exercise science (MS); sport psychology (MS). *Program availability:* Part-time. *Degree requirements:* For master's, thesis. *Entrance requirements:* For master's, GRE General Test, minimum GPA of 3.0 in last 60 semester hours or last 90 quarter hours. Additional exam requirements/recommendations for international students: Required—TOEFL (minimum score 567 paper-based). Electronic applications accepted. *Faculty research:* Spinal motor control, biomechanics/kinesiology, biomechanics of aging, mobility of older adults, fall prevention, exercise interventions and function, magnesium and inspiratory muscle training (IMT).

Westfield State University, College of Graduate and Continuing Education, Department of Education, Westfield, MA 01086. Offers early childhood education (M Ed); elementary education (M Ed); reading specialist (M Ed); secondary education (M Ed), including biology teacher education, chemistry teacher education, general science teacher education, history teacher education, mathematics teacher education, physical education teacher education; special education (M Ed), including moderate disabilities, 5-12, moderate disabilities, preK-8; vocational technical education (M Ed). *Accreditation:* NCATE. *Program availability:* Part-time, evening/weekend. *Faculty:* 6 full-time (all women), 17 part-time/adjunct (13 women). *Students:* 12 full-time (8 women), 137 part-time (110 women); includes 5 minority (1 Black or African American, non-Hispanic/Latino; 1 Asian, non-Hispanic/Latino; 1 Hispanic/Latino; 2 Two or more races, non-Hispanic/Latino). Average age 31. 65 applicants, 98% accepted, 50 enrolled. In 2017, 60 master's awarded. *Degree requirements:* For master's, comprehensive exam, practicum. *Entrance requirements:* For master's, GRE General Test or MAT, minimum undergraduate GPA of 2.8. Additional exam requirements/recommendations for international students: Recommended—TOEFL (minimum score 550 paper-based; 79 iBT). *Application deadline:* For fall admission, 7/1 for domestic students; for spring admission, 11/1 for domestic students; for summer admission, 4/1 for domestic students. Applications are processed on a rolling basis. Application fee: $50. *Expenses:* Tuition, state resident: part-time $332 per credit. Tuition, nonresident: part-time $332 per credit. *Required fees:* $75 per semester. Tuition and fees vary according to program. *Financial support:* Unspecified assistantships and SOS scholarships (for education majors only) available. Financial award application deadline: 3/1; financial award applicants required to submit FAFSA. *Faculty research:* Collaborative teacher education, developmental early childhood education. *Unit head:* Dr. Laura Baker, Department Chair, 413-572-5324, E-mail: lbaker@westfield.ma.edu. *Application contact:* Shelly Henrichon, Coordinator of College of Graduate and Continuing Education Admissions, 413-572-8022, Fax: 413-572-5227, E-mail: mhenrichon@westfield.ma.edu.
Website: http://www.westfield.ma.edu/academics/degrees/education-graduate-programs

Westfield State University, College of Graduate and Continuing Education, Department of Education, Programs in Secondary Education, Program in Physical Education Teacher Education, Westfield, MA 01086. Offers secondary education-physical education (M Ed). *Program availability:* Part-time, evening/weekend. *Faculty:* 1 (woman) full-time, 1 (woman) part-time/adjunct. *Students:* 11 part-time (7 women); includes 1 minority (Two or more races, non-Hispanic/Latino). Average age 32. 4 applicants, 75% accepted, 3 enrolled. In 2017, 4 master's awarded. *Degree requirements:* For master's, comprehensive exam, thesis (for some programs) *Entrance requirements:* For master's, GRE General Test or MAT, minimum undergraduate GPA of 2.8. Additional exam requirements/recommendations for international students: Recommended—TOEFL (minimum score 550 paper-based; 79 iBT). *Application deadline:* For fall admission, 7/1 for domestic students; for spring admission, 11/1 for domestic students; for summer admission, 4/1 for domestic students. Applications are processed on a rolling basis. Application fee: $50. *Expenses:* Tuition, state resident: part-time $332 per credit. Tuition, nonresident: part-time $332 per credit. *Required fees:* $75 per semester. Tuition and fees vary according to program. *Financial support:* Unspecified assistantships and SOS scholarships (for education majors only) available. Financial award application deadline: 3/1; financial award applicants required to submit FAFSA. *Unit head:* Dr. Laura Baker, Chair, 413-572-5324, E-mail: lbaker@westfield.ma.edu. *Application contact:* Shelly Henrichon, Coordinator of College of Graduate and Continuing Education Admissions, 413-572-8022, Fax: 413-572-5227, E-mail: mhenrichon@westfield.ma.edu.

West Liberty University, College of Education and Human Performance, West Liberty, WV 26074. Offers community education research and leadership (MA Ed); innovative instruction (MA Ed); leadership in disability services (MA Ed); leadership studies (MA Ed); multi-categorical special education (MA Ed); reading specialist (MA Ed); sports leadership and coaching (MA Ed). *Accreditation:* NCATE. *Program availability:* Part-time, evening/weekend. *Students:* 18 full-time (12 women), 74 part-time (60 women); includes 2 minority (1 Black or African American, non-Hispanic/Latino; 1 Native Hawaiian or other Pacific Islander, non-Hispanic/Latino). Average age 32. *Degree requirements:* For master's, capstone experience. *Entrance requirements:* For master's, minimum GPA of 2.5 or 3.0 (depending on track). Additional exam requirements/recommendations for international students: Required—TOEFL. *Application deadline:* Applications are processed on a rolling basis. Application fee: $0. Electronic applications accepted. Tuition and fees vary according to course load and program. *Financial support:* Teaching assistantships and unspecified assistantships available. *Unit head:* Dr. Catherine Monteroso, Interim Dean, 304-336-8247, E-mail: cmonteroso@westliberty.edu. *Application contact:* Sara Sweeney, Director, Office of Graduate Studies, 304-336-8545, E-mail: sara.sweeney@westliberty.edu.
Website: http://westliberty.edu/education/

West Virginia University, College of Physical Activity and Sport Sciences, Morgantown, WV 26506. Offers athletic training (MS); coaching and sport education (MS); coaching and teaching studies (Ed D, PhD), including curriculum and instruction (PhD); physical education/teacher education (MS); sport and exercise psychology (MS); sport coaching (MS); sport management (MS). *Students:* 104 full-time (37 women), 75 part-time (28 women); includes 30 minority (12 Black or African American, non-Hispanic/Latino; 2 Asian, non-Hispanic/Latino; 9 Hispanic/Latino; 7 Two or more races, non-Hispanic/Latino), 12 international. *Degree requirements:* For doctorate, comprehensive exam, thesis/dissertation, oral exam. *Entrance requirements:* For master's, GRE or MAT, minimum GPA of 3.0; for doctorate, GRE General Test or MAT, minimum GPA of 3.5. Additional exam requirements/recommendations for international students: Required—TOEFL (minimum score 550 paper-based). *Application deadline:* For fall admission, 12/15 for domestic students, 10/1 for international students. Application fee: $60. Electronic applications accepted. *Expenses:* Tuition, state resident: full-time $9450. Tuition, nonresident: full-time $24,390. *Financial support:* Research assistantships, teaching assistantships, career-related internships or fieldwork, Federal Work-Study, institutionally sponsored loans, health care benefits, tuition waivers (full and partial), and administrative assistantships available. Support available to part-time students. Financial award application deadline: 2/1; financial award applicants required to submit FAFSA. *Faculty research:* Sport psych sociology, teacher education, exercise psychology, counseling. *Unit head:* Sean Bulger, Online Program Coordinator, 304-293-0845, Fax: 304-293-4641, E-mail: sean.bulger@mail.wvu.edu.
Website: http://www.cpass.wvu.edu

Wilfrid Laurier University, Faculty of Graduate and Postdoctoral Studies, Faculty of Science, Department of Kinesiology and Physical Education, Waterloo, ON N2L 3C5, Canada. Offers physical activity and health (M Sc). *Degree requirements:* For master's, thesis. *Entrance requirements:* For master's, honours degree in kinesiology, health, physical education with a minimum B+ in kinesiology and health-related courses. Additional exam requirements/recommendations for international students: Required—TOEFL (minimum score 89 iBT). Electronic applications accepted. *Faculty research:* Biomechanics, health, exercise physiology, motor control, sport psychology.

William Woods University, Graduate and Adult Studies, Fulton, MO 65251-1098. Offers administration (M Ed, Ed S); athletic/activities administration (M Ed); curriculum and instruction (M Ed, Ed S); educational leadership (Ed D); equestrian education (M Ed); health management (MBA); human resources (MBA); leadership (MBA); marketing, advertising, and public relations (MBA); teaching and technology (M Ed). *Program availability:* Part-time, evening/weekend. *Degree requirements:* For master's, capstone course (MBA), action research (M Ed); for Ed S, field experience. *Entrance requirements:* Additional exam requirements/recommendations for international students: Required—TOEFL (minimum score 550 paper-based). Electronic applications accepted. *Expenses:* Contact institution.

Winthrop University, College of Education, Program in Physical Education, Rock Hill, SC 29733. Offers MAT. *Program availability:* Part-time. *Students:* 21 full-time (11 women), 3 part-time (0 women); includes 10 minority (all Black or African American, non-Hispanic/Latino). Average age 26. *Degree requirements:* For master's, comprehensive exam, thesis optional. *Entrance requirements:* For master's, GRE General Test or PRAXIS. Additional exam requirements/recommendations for international students: Required—TOEFL (minimum score 550 paper-based; 79 iBT), IELTS (minimum score 6). *Application deadline:* For fall admission, 7/15 priority date for domestic students; for spring admission, 12/1 for domestic students. Applications are processed on a rolling basis. Application fee: $50. Electronic applications accepted. *Financial support:* Research assistantships with full tuition reimbursements, career-related internships or fieldwork, Federal Work-Study, scholarships/grants, and unspecified assistantships available. Support available to part-time students. Financial award application deadline: 2/1; financial award applicants required to submit FAFSA. *Unit head:* Dan Drane, Graduate Program Advisor, 803-323-2588, E-mail: draned@winthrop.edu. *Application contact:* 800-411-7041, Fax: 803-323-2292, E-mail: graduatestu@winthrop.edu.
Website: http://www.winthrop.edu/graduateschool

Section 31
Sports Management

This section contains a directory of institutions offering graduate work in sports management. Additional information about programs listed in the directory may be obtained by writing directly to the dean of a graduate school or chair of a department at the address given in the directory.

For programs offering related work, see also in this book *Business Administration and Management, Education,* and *Physical Education and Kinesiology.*

CONTENTS

Sports Management

Adams State University, Office of Graduate Studies, Department of Human Performance and Physical Education, Alamosa, CO 81101. Offers human performance and physical education (MA, MS), including applied sport psychology, coaching (MA), exercise science (MA), sport management (MA). *Program availability:* Part-time. *Entrance requirements:* For master's, GRE General Test or MAT, minimum undergraduate GPA of 2.75. *Application deadline:* For fall admission, 5/15 priority date for domestic students; for spring admission, 10/15 for domestic students. Applications are processed on a rolling basis. Application fee: $30. *Expenses:* Tuition, state resident: full-time $4800; part-time $2400 per credit. Tuition, nonresident: full-time $7100; part-time $3550 per credit. *Required fees:* $213; $106 per credit. One-time fee: $100. Tuition and fees vary according to campus/location and program. *Financial support:* In 2017–18, fellowships with partial tuition reimbursements (averaging $4,000 per year), teaching assistantships with partial tuition reimbursements (averaging $4,000 per year) were awarded; career-related internships or fieldwork, Federal Work-Study, institutionally sponsored loans, and unspecified assistantships also available. Support available to part-time students. Financial award application deadline: 4/15; financial award applicants required to submit FAFSA. *Unit head:* Dr. Marty Jones, Interim Chair, 719-587-7271, E-mail: hppe@adams.edu. *Application contact:* Caryn Chavez, Administrative Assistant III, 719-587-7208, Fax: 719-587-8230, E-mail: hppe@adams.edu. Website: http://hppe.adams.edu

Adelphi University, Robert B. Willumstad School of Business, MBA Program, Garden City, NY 11530-0701. Offers accounting (MBA); finance (MBA); health services administration (MBA); human resource management (MBA); management (MBA); management information systems (MBA); marketing (MBA); sport management (MBA). *Accreditation:* AACSB. *Program availability:* Part-time, evening/weekend. *Students:* 257 full-time (110 women), 78 part-time (38 women); includes 56 minority (18 Black or African American, non-Hispanic/Latino; 16 Asian, non-Hispanic/Latino; 19 Hispanic/Latino; 3 Two or more races, non-Hispanic/Latino), 181 international. Average age 28. 435 applicants, 61% accepted, 205 enrolled. In 2017, 130 master's awarded. *Degree requirements:* For master's, capstone course. *Entrance requirements:* For master's, GMAT, 2 letters of recommendation. Additional exam requirements/recommendations for international students: Required—TOEFL (minimum score 550 paper-based; 80 iBT), IELTS (minimum score 6.5). *Application deadline:* For fall admission, 4/1 for international students; for spring admission, 11/1 for international students. Applications are processed on a rolling basis. Application fee: $50. Electronic applications accepted. *Expenses:* Contact institution. *Financial support:* Research assistantships with partial tuition reimbursements, career-related internships or fieldwork, Federal Work-Study, institutionally sponsored loans, scholarships/grants, tuition waivers (partial), and unspecified assistantships available. Financial award application deadline: 3/1; financial award applicants required to submit FAFSA. *Faculty research:* Supply chain management, distribution channels, productivity benchmark analysis, data envelopment analysis, financial portfolio analysis. *Unit head:* Dr. Rakesh Gupta, Associate Dean, 516-877-4629. *Application contact:* E-mail: graduateadmissions@adelphi.edu. Website: http://business.adelphi.edu/degree-programs/graduate-degree-programs/m-b-a/

American Public University System, AMU/APU Graduate Programs, Charles Town, WV 25414. Offers accounting (MS); applied business analytics (MS); business administration (MBA); criminal justice (MA); cybersecurity studies (MS); educational leadership (M Ed); environmental policy and management (MS); global security (DGS); health information management (MS); history (MA), including American military history, American Revolution, civil war, war since 1945, World War II; information technology (MS); international relations and conflict resolution (MA), including American politics and government, comparative government and development, general, international relations, public policy; national security studies (MA); nursing (MSN); political science (MA); public policy (MPP); reverse logistics management (MA), including comparative and security issues, conflict resolution, international and transnational security issues, peacekeeping; space studies (MS); sports management (MS); strategic intelligence (DSI); teaching (M Ed), including secondary social studies; transportation and logistics management (MA). *Program availability:* Part-time, evening/weekend, online only, 100% online. *Students:* 455 full-time (227 women), 7,939 part-time (3,353 women); includes 2,793 minority (1,429 Black or African American, non-Hispanic/Latino; 48 American Indian or Alaska Native, non-Hispanic/Latino; 205 Asian, non-Hispanic/Latino; 766 Hispanic/Latino; 62 Native Hawaiian or other Pacific Islander, non-Hispanic/Latino; 283 Two or more races, non-Hispanic/Latino), 101 international. Average age 37. In 2017, 2,977 master's awarded. *Degree requirements:* For master's, comprehensive exam or practicum. *Entrance requirements:* For master's, official transcript showing earned bachelor's degree from institution accredited by recognized accrediting body. Additional exam requirements/recommendations for international students: Required—TOEFL (minimum score 550 paper-based), IELTS (minimum score 6.5). *Application deadline:* Applications are processed on a rolling basis. Application fee: $0. Electronic applications accepted. *Expenses:* Tuition: Full-time $6300; part-time $350 per credit. *Required fees:* $300; $50 per course. *Financial support:* Scholarships/grants available. Financial award applicants required to submit FAFSA. *Unit head:* Dr. Wallace Boston, President, 877-468-6268, Fax: 304-728-2348, E-mail: president@apus.edu. *Application contact:* Yoci Deal, Associate Vice President, Graduate and International Admissions, 877-468-6268, Fax: 304-724-3764, E-mail: info@apus.edu. Website: http://www.apus.edu

American University, School of Professional and Extended Studies, Washington, DC 20016-8030. Offers agile project management (MS); healthcare management (MS, Graduate Certificate); human resource analytics and management (MS, Graduate Certificate); instructional design and learning analytics (MS); measurement and evaluation (MS); project monitoring and evaluation (Graduate Certificate); sports analytics and management (MS, Graduate Certificate). *Program availability:* Part-time, evening/weekend, 100% online. *Faculty:* 27 full-time (13 women), 21 part-time/adjunct (10 women). *Students:* 17 full-time (8 women), 59 part-time (34 women); includes 9 minority (5 Black or African American, non-Hispanic/Latino; 2 Asian, non-Hispanic/Latino; 1 Hispanic/Latino; 1 Two or more races, non-Hispanic/Latino), 5 international. Average age 31. 55 applicants, 89% accepted, 38 enrolled. In 2017, 8 other advanced degrees awarded. *Entrance requirements:* For master's, official transcript(s), resume. Additional exam requirements/recommendations for international students: Required—TOEFL (minimum score 600 paper-based; 100 iBT). *Application deadline:* Applications are processed on a rolling basis. Application fee: $55. Electronic applications accepted. *Expenses:* Contact institution. *Financial support:* Applicants required to submit FAFSA. *Unit head:* Carola Weil, Dean, 202-885-5990, Fax: 202-895-4960, E-mail: weil@american.edu. *Application contact:* Emily Aronoff, Assistant Director for Recruitment and Admission, 202-895-4953, E-mail: aronoff@american.edu. Website: http://www.american.edu/spexs/

Angelo State University, College of Graduate Studies and Research, Archer College of Health and Human Services, Department of Kinesiology, San Angelo, TX 76909. Offers M Ed. *Program availability:* Part-time, evening/weekend. *Students:* 8 full-time (3 women), 38 part-time (22 women); includes 17 minority (6 Black or African American, non-Hispanic/Latino; 11 Hispanic/Latino), 2 international. Average age 25. *Degree requirements:* For master's, comprehensive exam. *Entrance requirements:* Additional exam requirements/recommendations for international students: Required—TOEFL or IELTS. *Application deadline:* For fall admission, 7/15 priority date for domestic students, 6/10 for international students; for spring admission, 12/1 priority date for domestic students, 11/1 for international students. Applications are processed on a rolling basis. Application fee: $40 ($50 for international students). Electronic applications accepted. *Expenses:* Tuition, state resident: full-time $3856. Tuition, nonresident: full-time $11,324. *Required fees:* $2650. *Financial support:* Career-related internships or fieldwork, Federal Work-Study, scholarships/grants, and unspecified assistantships available. Support available to part-time students. Financial award application deadline: 3/1; financial award applicants required to submit FAFSA. *Unit head:* Dr. Steven Snowden, Chair, 325-486-6178, Fax: 325-942-2129, E-mail: steven.snowden@angelo.edu. *Application contact:* Dr. Warren Simpson, Graduate Advisor, 325-942-2173 Ext. 224, Fax: 325-942-2129, E-mail: warren.simpson@angelo.edu. Website: http://www.angelo.edu/dept/kinesiology/

Arkansas State University, Graduate School, College of Education and Behavioral Science, Department of Health, Physical Education, and Sport Sciences, State University, AR 72467. Offers exercise science (MS); physical education (MSE, SCCT); sports administration (MS). *Program availability:* Part-time. *Degree requirements:* For master's, comprehensive exam, thesis or alternative; for SCCT, comprehensive exam. *Entrance requirements:* For master's, GRE General Test or MAT, appropriate bachelor's degree, official transcripts, immunization records, statement of goals, letters of recommendation; for SCCT, GRE General Test or MAT, interview, master's degree, official transcript, immunization records. Additional exam requirements/recommendations for international students: Required—TOEFL (minimum score 550 paper-based; 79 iBT), IELTS (minimum score 6), PTE (minimum score 56). Electronic applications accepted.

Ashland University, Dauch College of Business and Economics, Ashland, OH 44805-3702. Offers accounting (MBA); business analytics (MBA); entrepreneurship (MBA); financial management (MBA); global management (MBA); health care management and leadership (MBA); human resource management (MBA); human resources (MBA); management information systems (MBA); project management (MBA); sport management (MBA); supply chain management (MBA). *Accreditation:* ACBSP. *Program availability:* Part-time, evening/weekend, 100% online, blended/hybrid learning. *Faculty:* 20 full-time (8 women), 13 part-time/adjunct (2 women). *Students:* 458 full-time (210 women), 144 part-time (52 women); includes 88 minority (63 Black or African American, non-Hispanic/Latino; 1 American Indian or Alaska Native, non-Hispanic/Latino; 10 Asian, non-Hispanic/Latino; 14 Hispanic/Latino), 202 international. Average age 31. 216 applicants, 74% accepted, 115 enrolled. In 2017, 184 master's awarded. Terminal master's awarded for partial completion of doctoral program. *Degree requirements:* For master's, thesis optional, capstone course. *Entrance requirements:* For master's, 2 years of full-time work experience. Additional exam requirements/recommendations for international students: Required—TOEFL (minimum score 550 paper-based; 78 iBT). *Application deadline:* For fall admission, 8/1 priority date for domestic students; for spring admission, 12/1 priority date for domestic students. Applications are processed on a rolling basis. Application fee: $30. Electronic applications accepted. *Expenses:* $815 per credit hour, $15 technology fee for online sections. *Financial support:* Scholarships/grants, tuition waivers (partial), and unspecified assistantships available. Financial award application deadline: 4/15; financial award applicants required to submit FAFSA. *Faculty research:* Relationship marketing strategy, executive compensation and company performance, online marketplaces in electronic commerce, diversity training in campus recreation departments, entrepreneurship in developing and emerging economies. *Unit head:* Dr. Elad Granot, Dean, 419-289-5932, E-mail: egranot@ashland.edu. *Application contact:* Stephen W. Krispinsky, Executive Director of MBA Program, 419-289-5236, Fax: 419-289-5910, E-mail: skrispin@ashland.edu. Website: http://www.mba.ashland.edu

Auburn University at Montgomery, College of Education, Department of Kinesiology, Montgomery, AL 36124-4023. Offers exercise science (M Ed); physical education (Ed S); sport management (M Ed). *Program availability:* Online learning. *Faculty:* 7 full-time (3 women), 1 (woman) part-time/adjunct. *Students:* 12 full-time (9 women), 18 part-time (11 women); includes 12 minority (11 Black or African American, non-Hispanic/Latino; 1 Hispanic/Latino). Average age 29. 23 applicants, 74% accepted, 10 enrolled. In 2017, 18 master's awarded. *Entrance requirements:* For master's, GRE or MAT. Additional exam requirements/recommendations for international students: Recommended—TOEFL (minimum score 500 paper-based; 61 iBT), IELTS (minimum score 5.5), TSE (minimum score 44). *Application deadline:* For fall admission, 7/15 for international students; for spring admission, 11/15 for international students; for summer admission, 4/15 for international students. Applications are processed on a rolling basis. Application fee: $25. Electronic applications accepted. *Expenses:* Tuition, state resident: full-time $6930; part-time $385 per credit hour. Tuition, nonresident: full-time $15,588; part-time $866 per credit hour. *Required fees:* $640. *Financial support:* Teaching assistantships available. Financial award application deadline: 3/1; financial award applicants required to submit FAFSA. *Unit head:* Dr. George Schaefer, Head, 334-244-3887, Fax: 334-244-3835, E-mail: gschaefe@aum.edu. *Application contact:* Janis Bigelow, Graduate Advisor, 334-244-3135, E-mail: jbigelo1@aum.edu. Website: http://www.education.aum.edu/academic-programs/academic-programs/kinesiology

Augustana University, Sports Administration and Leadership Program, Sioux Falls, SD 57197. Offers MA. *Program availability:* Part-time. *Faculty:* 2 full-time (0 women), 4 part-time/adjunct (1 woman). *Students:* 3 full-time (0 women), 17 part-time (4 women); includes 1 minority (Black or African American, non-Hispanic/Latino). Average age 25. 9 applicants, 100% accepted, 8 enrolled. In 2017, 5 master's awarded. *Degree requirements:* For master's, thesis or alternative. *Entrance requirements:* For master's, GMAT or GRE, minimum cumulative undergraduate GPA of 3.0 for last 60 semester hours; appropriate bachelor's degree; 2-3 page essay discussing academic interests, education goals, and plans for graduate study. Additional exam requirements/recommendations for international students: Required—TOEFL (minimum score 550 paper-based). *Application deadline:* For fall admission, 4/1 priority date for domestic students, 6/1 priority date for international students. Applications are processed on a rolling basis. Application fee: $60. Electronic applications accepted. *Expenses:* Contact institution. *Financial support:* Unspecified assistantships available. Financial award application deadline: 3/1; financial award applicants required to submit FAFSA. *Unit*

head: Shelly Gardner, Program Coordinator, 605-274-5318, E-mail: shelly.gardner@augie.edu. *Application contact:* Julia Paulich, Graduate Education Assistant, 605-274-4043, Fax: 605-274-4450, E-mail: graduate@augie.edu.
Website: http://www.augie.edu/academics/graduate-education/sal

Austin Peay State University, College of Graduate Studies, College of Behavioral and Health Sciences, Department of Health and Human Performance, Clarksville, TN 37044. Offers public health education (MS); sports and wellness leadership (MS). *Program availability:* Part-time, evening/weekend, online learning. *Faculty:* 8 full-time (4 women). *Students:* 14 full-time (7 women), 38 part-time (27 women); includes 15 minority (10 Black or African American, non-Hispanic/Latino; 1 Asian, non-Hispanic/Latino; 2 Hispanic/Latino; 2 Two or more races, non-Hispanic/Latino), 1 international. Average age 29. 66 applicants, 67% accepted, 33 enrolled. In 2017, 34 master's awarded. *Degree requirements:* For master's, comprehensive exam, thesis optional. *Entrance requirements:* For master's, GRE General Test, 3 letters of recommendation, minimum undergraduate GPA of 2.5. Additional exam requirements/recommendations for international students: Required—TOEFL (minimum score 500 paper-based). *Application deadline:* For fall admission, 8/8 priority date for domestic students. Applications are processed on a rolling basis. Application fee: $45 ($55 for international students). Electronic applications accepted. *Expenses:* Tuition, state resident: full-time $7686; part-time $427 per credit hour. Tuition, nonresident: full-time $20,268; part-time $1126 per credit hour. *Required fees:* $1529; $76.45 per credit hour. *Financial support:* Research assistantships with full tuition reimbursements, career-related internships or fieldwork, Federal Work-Study, institutionally sponsored loans, scholarships/grants, and unspecified assistantships available. Support available to part-time students. Financial award application deadline: 4/1; financial award applicants required to submit FAFSA. *Unit head:* Dr. Marcy Maurer, Chair, 931-221-6105, Fax: 931-221-7040, E-mail: maurerm@apsu.edu. *Application contact:* Megan Mitchell, Coordinator of Graduate Admissions, 931-221-6189, Fax: 931-221-7641, E-mail: mitchellm@apsu.edu.
Website: http://www.apsu.edu/hhp/index.php

Azusa Pacific University, School of Behavioral and Applied Sciences, Department of Leadership and Organizational Psychology, Program in Leadership, Azusa, CA 91702-7000. Offers executive leadership (MA); leadership development (MA); leadership studies (MA); sport management (MA). *Expenses:* Contact institution.

Azusa Pacific University, School of Business and Management, Azusa, CA 91702-7000. Offers accounting (MBA); business administration (MBA); entrepreneurship (MBA); finance (MBA); international business (MBA); marketing (MBA); organizational science (MBA); professional accountancy (M Acc); sport management (MBA). *Program availability:* Part-time, evening/weekend. *Degree requirements:* For master's, thesis (for some programs), final project. *Entrance requirements:* For master's, GMAT, minimum GPA of 3.0. Additional exam requirements/recommendations for international students: Required—TOEFL (minimum score 600 paper-based). *Expenses:* Contact institution. *Faculty research:* Gender issues, financial risk, leadership and ethics, marketing strategy.

Ball State University, Graduate School, College of Health, School of Kinesiology, Program in Physical Education and Sport, Muncie, IN 47306. Offers physical education and sport (MA, MS), including athletic coaching education, sport administration, sport and exercise psychology. *Program availability:* Part-time, 100% online. *Students:* 19 full-time (5 women), 69 part-time (25 women); includes 6 minority (2 Black or African American, non-Hispanic/Latino; 4 Hispanic/Latino), 1 international. Average age 26. 83 applicants, 35% accepted, 27 enrolled. In 2017, 32 master's awarded. *Entrance requirements:* For master's, GRE General Test, minimum baccalaureate GPA of 2.75 or 3.0 in latter half of baccalaureate, curriculum vitae, three letters of recommendation; campus visit to meet faculty and see facilities (strongly encouraged). Additional exam requirements/recommendations for international students: Required—TOEFL (minimum score 550 paper-based; 79 iBT), IELTS (minimum score 6.5). *Application deadline:* For fall admission, 1/15 for domestic students. Applications are processed on a rolling basis. Application fee: $60. Electronic applications accepted. *Financial support:* Research assistantships with partial tuition reimbursements and unspecified assistantships available. Financial award application deadline: 3/1; financial award applicants required to submit FAFSA. *Unit head:* Dr. Tom Weidner, Chairperson, 765-285-5039, Fax: 765-285-8254, E-mail: tweidner@bsu.edu.

Barry University, School of Human Performance and Leisure Sciences, Program in Sport Management, Miami Shores, FL 33161-6695. Offers MS. *Program availability:* Part-time, evening/weekend. *Degree requirements:* For master's, comprehensive exam, project or thesis. *Entrance requirements:* For master's, GMAT or GRE General Test, minimum GPA of 3.0. Electronic applications accepted. *Faculty research:* Economic impact of professional sports, sport marketing.

Barry University, School of Human Performance and Leisure Sciences and Andreas School of Business, Program in Sport Management and Business Administration, Miami Shores, FL 33161-6695. Offers MS/MBA. *Program availability:* Part-time, evening/weekend. Electronic applications accepted. *Faculty research:* Economic impact of professional sports, sport marketing.

Belhaven University, School of Business, Jackson, MS 39202-1789. Offers business administration (MBA); health administration (MBA, MHA); human resources (MBA, MSL); leadership (MBA); public administration (MPA); sports administration (MBA, MSA). *Program availability:* Part-time, evening/weekend, 100% online. *Faculty:* 11 full-time (4 women), 93 part-time/adjunct (39 women). *Students:* 20 full-time (12 women), 1,441 part-time (1,061 women); includes 1,168 minority (1,100 Black or African American, non-Hispanic/Latino; 22 American Indian or Alaska Native, non-Hispanic/Latino; 2 Asian, non-Hispanic/Latino; 23 Hispanic/Latino; 1 Native Hawaiian or other Pacific Islander, non-Hispanic/Latino; 20 Two or more races, non-Hispanic/Latino), 21 international. Average age 35. 501 applicants, 74% accepted, 261 enrolled. In 2017, 326 master's awarded. *Degree requirements:* For master's, comprehensive exam (for some programs), thesis or alternative. *Entrance requirements:* For master's, minimum GPA of 2.8 (for MBA and MHA), 2.5 (for MSL, MPA and MSA). *Application deadline:* Applications are processed on a rolling basis. Application fee: $25. Electronic applications accepted. *Expenses:* Contact institution. *Financial support:* Applicants required to submit FAFSA. *Unit head:* Dr. Ralph Mason, Dean, 601-968-8949, Fax: 601-968-8951, E-mail: cmason@belhaven.edu. *Application contact:* Dr. Audrey Kelleher, Vice President of Adult and Graduate Marketing and Development, 407-804-1424, Fax: 407-620-5210, E-mail: akelleher@belhaven.edu.
Website: http://www.belhaven.edu/campuses/index.htm

Boise State University, College of Health Sciences, Department of Kinesiology, Boise, ID 83725-0399. Offers athletic leadership (MAL); kinesiology (MK, MS). *Program availability:* Part-time. *Faculty:* 11. *Students:* 23 full-time (9 women), 31 part-time (10 women); includes 11 minority (4 Black or African American, non-Hispanic/Latino; 6 Hispanic/Latino; 1 Two or more races, non-Hispanic/Latino). Average age 25. 37 applicants, 65% accepted, 15 enrolled. In 2017, 22 master's awarded. *Degree requirements:* For master's, thesis (for some programs). *Entrance requirements:* For master's, minimum GPA of 3.0. Additional exam requirements/recommendations for international students: Required—TOEFL (minimum score 550 paper-based; 80 iBT), IELTS (minimum score 6). *Application deadline:* For fall admission, 5/1 for domestic and international students. Application fee: $65 ($95 for international students). Electronic

applications accepted. *Expenses:* Tuition, state resident: full-time $6471; part-time $390 per credit. Tuition, nonresident: full-time $21,787; part-time $685 per credit. *Required fees:* $2283; $100 per term. Part-time tuition and fees vary according to course load and program. *Financial support:* Scholarships/grants and unspecified assistantships available. Financial award application deadline: 1/15; financial award applicants required to submit FAFSA. *Unit head:* Dr. John McChesney, Department Chair, 208-426-4270, E-mail: johnmcchesney@boisestate.edu. *Application contact:* Dr. Shelley Lucas, Program Coordinator, 208-426-2446, E-mail: smlucas@boisestate.edu.
Website: https://hs.boisestate.edu/kinesiology/

Bowling Green State University, Graduate College, College of Education and Human Development, School of Human Movement, Sport, and Leisure Studies, Bowling Green, OH 43403. Offers developmental kinesiology (M Ed); recreation and leisure (M Ed); sport administration (M Ed). *Program availability:* Part-time. *Degree requirements:* For master's, thesis. *Entrance requirements:* For master's, GRE General Test, minimum GPA of 2.7. Additional exam requirements/recommendations for international students: Required—TOEFL. Electronic applications accepted. *Faculty research:* Teacher-learning process, travel and tourism, sport marketing and management, exercise physiology and sport psychology, life-span motor development.

Brooklyn College of the City University of New York, School of Natural and Behavioral Sciences, Department of Kinesiology, Brooklyn, NY 11210-2889. Offers exercise and sports science (MS); physical education teacher (MS); sport management (MS). *Program availability:* Part-time. *Degree requirements:* For master's, comprehensive exam or thesis. *Entrance requirements:* For master's, previous course work in physical education and education, minimum GPA of 3.0, 2 letters of recommendation, essay. Additional exam requirements/recommendations for international students: Required—TOEFL (minimum score 500 paper-based; 61 iBT). Electronic applications accepted. *Faculty research:* Exercise physiology, motor learning, sports psychology, women in athletics.

Bryan College, MBA Program, Dayton, TN 37321. Offers business administration (MBA); healthcare administration (MBA); human resources (MBA); marketing (MBA); ministry (MBA); sports management (MBA). *Program availability:* Online only, 100% online. *Entrance requirements:* For master's, resume, 2 letters of recommendation. Additional exam requirements/recommendations for international students: Required—TOEFL. *Application deadline:* For fall admission, 7/1 for domestic and international students; for winter admission, 11/15 for domestic and international students; for spring admission, 12/1 for domestic and international students; for summer admission, 5/1 for domestic and international students. Applications are processed on a rolling basis. Application fee: $50. Electronic applications accepted. *Expenses:* Contact institution. *Financial support:* Scholarships/grants available. Financial award applicants required to submit FAFSA. *Unit head:* Dr. Adina Scruggs, Dean of Adult and Graduate Studies, 423-634-2057, E-mail: adina.scruggs@bryan.edu. *Application contact:* Mandi K Sullivan, Director of Academic Programs, 423-634-9880, E-mail: mandi.sullivan@bryan.edu.
Website: http://www.bryan.edu/academics/adult-education/graduate/online-mba/

Butler University, College of Education, Indianapolis, IN 46208-3485. Offers applied educational neuroscience (Certificate); educational administration (MS); effective teaching and leadership (MS); licensed mental health counselor (Certificate); school counseling (MS); wellness and sport leadership (Certificate). *Accreditation:* ACA; NCATE. *Program availability:* Part-time. *Faculty:* 12 full-time (8 women), 10 part-time/adjunct (7 women). *Students:* 3 full-time (2 women), 131 part-time (102 women); includes 13 minority (7 Black or African American, non-Hispanic/Latino; 2 Asian, non-Hispanic/Latino; 2 Hispanic/Latino; 2 Two or more races, non-Hispanic/Latino). Average age 31. 65 applicants, 75% accepted, 41 enrolled. In 2017, 45 master's, 10 other advanced degrees awarded. *Degree requirements:* For master's, thesis. *Entrance requirements:* For master's, GRE (minimum score 291) or MAT (minimum score 396) unless undergraduate GPA is a 3.0 or higher, two letters of recommendation, transcripts, interview, professional resume. Additional exam requirements/recommendations for international students: Required—TOEFL (minimum score 550 paper-based; 79 iBT), IELTS (minimum score 6). *Application deadline:* For fall admission, 2/1 for domestic and international students; for spring admission, 11/1 for domestic and international students; for summer admission, 4/1 for domestic and international students. Applications are processed on a rolling basis. Application fee: $0. Electronic applications accepted. *Expenses:* $560 per credit. *Financial support:* In 2017–18, 64 students received support. Scholarships/grants, tuition waivers (full and partial), and unspecified assistantships available. Financial award application deadline: 7/15; financial award applicants required to submit FAFSA. *Faculty research:* Principals role in school improvement, leadership and school climate, retention of teachers in special education, the neuro-diversity brain, school counseling intervention. *Unit head:* Dr. Ena Shelley, Dean, 317-940-9752, Fax: 317-940-6481. *Application contact:* Diane Dubord, Graduate Student Services Specialist, 317-940-8100, Fax: 317-940-8250, E-mail: ddubord@butler.edu.
Website: https://www.butler.edu/coe/graduate-programs

California Baptist University, Program in Kinesiology, Riverside, CA 92504-3206. Offers exercise science (MS); physical education (MS); sport management (MS). *Program availability:* Part-time, 100% online, blended/hybrid learning. *Faculty:* 11 full-time (6 women), 5 part-time/adjunct (0 women). *Students:* 86 full-time (43 women), 45 part-time (21 women); includes 63 minority (20 Black or African American, non-Hispanic/Latino; 5 Asian, non-Hispanic/Latino; 35 Hispanic/Latino; 3 Two or more races, non-Hispanic/Latino), 20 international. Average age 28. 47 applicants, 62% accepted, 24 enrolled. In 2017, 55 master's awarded. *Degree requirements:* For master's, comprehensive exam or research thesis. *Entrance requirements:* For master's, minimum undergraduate GPA of 2.75; completion of course prerequisites with minimum C grade; three recommendations; 500-word essay; resume; interview. Additional exam requirements/recommendations for international students: Required—TOEFL (minimum score 80 iBT). *Application deadline:* For fall admission, 8/1 priority date for domestic students, 7/1 for international students; for spring admission, 12/1 priority date for domestic students, 11/1 for international students. Applications are processed on a rolling basis. Application fee: $45. Electronic applications accepted. *Expenses:* Contact institution. *Financial support:* In 2017–18, 11 students received support. Federal Work-Study, scholarships/grants, and unspecified assistantships available. Financial award applicants required to submit CSS PROFILE or FAFSA. *Faculty research:* Physical education pedagogy, exercise management and prevention of cardiovascular and metabolic diseases, sport management, immune function, carbohydrate oxidation. *Unit head:* Dr. David Pearson, Dean, College of Allied Health, 951-343-4298, E-mail: dpearson@calbaptist.edu. *Application contact:* Dr. Sean Sullivan, Chair, Department of Kinesiology, 951-343-4528, Fax: 951-343-5095, E-mail: ssullivan@calbaptist.edu.
Website: http://www.calbaptist.edu/mskin/

California State University, Fresno, Division of Research and Graduate Studies, College of Health and Human Services, Department of Kinesiology, Fresno, CA 93740-8027. Offers exercise science (MA); general kinesiology (MA); sport administration (MA); sport psychology (MA). *Program availability:* Part-time, evening/weekend. *Degree requirements:* For master's, thesis or alternative. *Entrance requirements:* For master's, GRE General Test, minimum GPA of 2.7. Additional exam requirements/recommendations for international students: Required—TOEFL. Electronic applications accepted. *Faculty research:* Refugee education, homeless, geriatrics, fitness.

Sports Management

California State University, Long Beach, Graduate Studies, College of Health and Human Services, Department of Kinesiology, Long Beach, CA 90840. Offers adapted physical education (MA); coaching and student athlete development (MA); exercise physiology and nutrition (MS); exercise science (MS); individualized studies (MA); kinesiology (MA); pedagogical studies (MA); sport and exercise psychology (MS); sport management (MA); sports medicine and injury studies (MS). *Program availability:* Part-time. *Degree requirements:* For master's, oral and written comprehensive exams or thesis. *Entrance requirements:* For master's, GRE General Test, minimum GPA of 2.75 during previous 2 years of course work. Electronic applications accepted. *Faculty research:* Pulmonary functioning, feedback and practice structure, strength training, history and politics of sports, special population research issues.

California University of Management and Sciences, Graduate Programs, Anaheim, CA 92801. Offers business administration (MBA, DBA); computer information systems (MS); economics (MS); international business (MS); sports management (MS).

California University of Pennsylvania, School of Graduate Studies and Research, College of Education and Human Services, Program in Sport Management Studies, California, PA 15419-1394. Offers sport management studies (MS), including intercollegiate athletic administration, sport management; strategic sport analysis (MS). *Program availability:* Part-time, 100% online. *Unit head:* Laura Miller, Program Director, 724-938-5032, E-mail: miller_la@calu.edu. *Application contact:* Suzanne C. Powers, Director of Graduate Admissions and Recruitment, 724-938-4029, Fax: 724-938-5712, E-mail: powers_s@cup.edu.

Campbellsville University, College of Arts and Sciences, Campbellsville, KY 42718-2799. Offers justice studies (MS); sport management (MA). *Program availability:* Part-time, evening/weekend, 100% online, blended/hybrid learning. *Faculty:* 12 full-time (4 women), 2 part-time/adjunct (1 woman). *Students:* 6 full-time (3 women), 28 part-time (12 women); includes 9 minority (all Black or African American, non-Hispanic/Latino), 1 international. Average age 29. 38 applicants, 66% accepted, 25 enrolled. In 2017, 5 master's awarded. *Degree requirements:* For master's, comprehensive exam, thesis optional. *Entrance requirements:* For master's, GRE General Test, minimum GPA of 2.9, letters of recommendation, college transcripts. Additional exam requirements/recommendations for international students: Recommended—TOEFL, IELTS. *Application deadline:* Applications are processed on a rolling basis. Application fee: $25. Electronic applications accepted. Application fee is waived when completed online. *Expenses:* $399 per credit hour. *Financial support:* In 2017–18, 2 students received support. Unspecified assistantships and employee tuition waivers available. Financial award application deadline: 6/1; financial award applicants required to submit FAFSA. *Unit head:* Dr. Mike Page, Dean, 270-789-5394. *Application contact:* Monica Bamwine, Assistant Director of Graduate Admissions, 270-789-5221, Fax: 270-789-5071, E-mail: mkbamwine@campbellsville.edu.
Website: http://www.campbellsville.edu/

Canisius College, Graduate Division, School of Education and Human Services, Program in Sport Administration, Buffalo, NY 14208-1098. Offers MSA. *Program availability:* Part-time, evening/weekend, 100% online. *Faculty:* 2 full-time (0 women), 9 part-time/adjunct (1 woman). *Students:* 57 full-time (18 women), 49 part-time (18 women); includes 27 minority (19 Black or African American, non-Hispanic/Latino; 1 Asian, non-Hispanic/Latino; 5 Hispanic/Latino; 2 Two or more races, non-Hispanic/Latino), 3 international. Average age 28. 70 applicants, 93% accepted, 40 enrolled. In 2017, 65 master's awarded. *Entrance requirements:* For master's, transcripts, essay, minimum GPA of 2.7, resume, BA. Additional exam requirements/recommendations for international students: Required—TOEFL (minimum score 550 paper-based, 79 iBT), IELTS (minimum score 6.5), or CAEL (minimum score 70). *Application deadline:* Applications are processed on a rolling basis. Application fee: $0. Electronic applications accepted. *Expenses: Tuition:* Full-time $22,860; part-time $820 per credit. *Required fees:* $720; $25 per credit. $65 per semester. One-time fee: $425. *Financial support:* Career-related internships or fieldwork, Federal Work-Study, scholarships/grants, tuition waivers (partial), and unspecified assistantships available. Support available to part-time students. Financial award application deadline: 4/30; financial award applicants required to submit FAFSA. *Unit head:* Dr. Shawn O'Rourke, Associate Dean, 716-888-3179, E-mail: orourke1@canisius.edu.
Website: http://www.canisius.edu/graduate/

Cardinal Stritch University, College of Arts and Sciences, Department of Sport Science and Management, Milwaukee, WI 53217-3985. Offers sport management (MS). *Program availability:* Part-time, evening/weekend. *Students:* 11 part-time (4 women); includes 3 minority (all Black or African American, non-Hispanic/Latino), 1 international. Average age 26. In 2017, 18 master's awarded. *Entrance requirements:* Additional exam requirements/recommendations for international students: Required—TOEFL (minimum score 79 iBT), IELTS (minimum score 6.5). *Application deadline:* Applications are processed on a rolling basis. Electronic applications accepted. *Expenses:* $782 per credit. *Financial support:* Career-related internships or fieldwork, Federal Work-Study, scholarships/grants, and unspecified assistantships available. Financial award applicants required to submit FAFSA. *Unit head:* Alexandra Fairchild, Chair, 414-410-4494, E-mail: anfairchild1@stritch.edu. *Application contact:* Graduate Admissions, 800-347-8822 Ext. 4042, E-mail: admissions@stritch.edu.

Central Michigan University, College of Graduate Studies, The Herbert H. and Grace A. Dow College of Health Professions, Department of Physical Education and Sport, Mount Pleasant, MI 48859. Offers sport administration (MA). *Program availability:* Part-time, evening/weekend. *Degree requirements:* For master's, thesis or alternative. *Entrance requirements:* For master's, GRE (recommended). Electronic applications accepted. *Faculty research:* Athletic administration and sport management, performance enhancing substance use in sport, computer applications for sport managers, mental skill development for ultimate performance, teaching methods.

Central Michigan University, College of Graduate Studies, Interdisciplinary Administration Programs, Mount Pleasant, MI 48859. Offers acquisitions administration (MSA, Graduate Certificate); general administration (MSA, Graduate Certificate); health services administration (MSA, Graduate Certificate); human resource administration (Graduate Certificate); human resources administration (MSA); information resource management (MSA, Graduate Certificate); international administration (MSA, Graduate Certificate); leadership (MSA, Graduate Certificate); public administration (MSA, Graduate Certificate); research administration (Graduate Certificate); sport administration (MSA). *Accreditation:* AACSB. *Program availability:* Part-time, evening/weekend, online learning. *Degree requirements:* For master's, thesis or alternative. *Entrance requirements:* For master's, bachelor's degree with minimum GPA of 2.7. Electronic applications accepted. *Faculty research:* Interdisciplinary studies in acquisitions administration, health services administration, sport administration, recreation and park administration, and international administration.

Central Washington University, School of Graduate Studies and Research, College of Education and Professional Studies, Department of Physical Education, School Health and Movement Studies, Ellensburg, WA 98926. Offers athletic administration (MS); health and physical education (MS). *Program availability:* Part-time. *Degree requirements:* For master's, comprehensive exam, thesis or alternative. *Entrance requirements:* For master's, minimum GPA of 3.0. Additional exam requirements/

recommendations for international students: Required—TOEFL (minimum score 550 paper-based; 79 iBT), IELTS. *Application deadline:* For fall admission, 2/1 priority date for domestic students; for winter admission, 10/1 for domestic students; for spring admission, 1/1 for domestic students. Applications are processed on a rolling basis. Application fee: $50. Electronic applications accepted. *Financial support:* Applicants required to submit FAFSA. *Unit head:* Dr. Heidi Henschel Pellett, Chair, 509-963-1483, E-mail: heidi.henschelpellett@cwu.edu. *Application contact:* Justine Eason, Admissions Program Coordinator, 509-963-3103, Fax: 509-963-1799, E-mail: masters@cwu.edu. Website: http://www.cwu.edu/~pesph/

The Citadel, The Military College of South Carolina, Citadel Graduate College, School of Science and Mathematics, Department of Health, Exercise, and Sport Science, Charleston, SC 29409. Offers health, exercise, and sport science (MS); sport management (MA, Graduate Certificate). *Accreditation:* NCATE. *Program availability:* Part-time, evening/weekend. *Degree requirements:* For master's, comprehensive exam (for some programs), internship and professional portfolio (for some programs). *Entrance requirements:* For master's, GRE (minimum combined verbal and quantitative score 290) or MAT (minimum score 396), official transcript reflecting highest degree earned from regionally-accredited college or university, minimum undergraduate GPA of 2.5, 3 letters of recommendation, resume detailing previous work experience. Additional exam requirements/recommendations for international students: Required—TOEFL (minimum score 550 paper-based; 79 iBT). Electronic applications accepted. *Expenses:* Tuition, state resident: part-time $587 per credit hour. Tuition, nonresident: part-time $988 per credit hour. *Required fees:* $90 per term.

Clayton State University, School of Graduate Studies, College of Business, Program in Business Administration, Morrow, GA 30260-0285. Offers accounting (MBA); human resource leadership (MBA); international business (MBA); sports and entertainment management (MBA); supply chain management (MBA). *Accreditation:* AACSB. *Program availability:* Part-time, evening/weekend. *Degree requirements:* For master's, thesis. *Entrance requirements:* For master's, GMAT, 3 letters of recommendation; statement of purpose; 2 official transcripts. Additional exam requirements/recommendations for international students: Required—TOEFL (minimum score 550 paper-based; 80 iBT). Electronic applications accepted. *Expenses:* Contact institution.

Clemson University, Graduate School, College of Education, Department of Educational and Organizational Leadership Development, Clemson, SC 29634. Offers administration and supervision (M Ed, Ed S); athletic leadership (MS, Certificate); education systems improvement science (Ed D); educational leadership (PhD), including higher education, P-12; human resource development (MHRD), including human resource development; leadership (Certificate); student affairs (M Ed). *Program availability:* Part-time, evening/weekend, 100% online. *Faculty:* 21 full-time (14 women), 1 part-time/adjunct (0 women). *Students:* 55 full-time (32 women), 285 part-time (169 women); includes 89 minority (71 Black or African American, non-Hispanic/Latino; 1 American Indian or Alaska Native, non-Hispanic/Latino; 1 Asian, non-Hispanic/Latino; 13 Hispanic/Latino; 3 Two or more races, non-Hispanic/Latino), 2 international. Average age 35. 216 applicants, 69% accepted, 100 enrolled. In 2017, 58 master's, 16 doctorates, 20 other advanced degrees awarded. *Degree requirements:* For master's, thesis (for some programs); for doctorate, comprehensive exam, thesis/dissertation. *Entrance requirements:* For master's, doctorate, and other advanced degree, GRE General Test, unofficial transcripts, letters of recommendation. Additional exam requirements/recommendations for international students: Required—TOEFL (minimum score 80 iBT), IELTS (minimum score 7), PTE (minimum score 54). *Application deadline:* For fall admission, 3/1 priority date for domestic and international students; for spring admission, 10/1 priority date for domestic and international students. Applications are processed on a rolling basis. Application fee: $80 ($90 for international students). Electronic applications accepted. *Expenses:* $5,174 per semester full-time resident, $9,714 per semester full-time non-resident, $511 per credit hour part-time resident, $1,017 per credit hour part-time non-resident; $741 per credit hour online; other fees may apply per session. *Financial support:* In 2017–18, 20 students received support, including 4 fellowships with partial tuition reimbursements available (averaging $8,750 per year), 1 research assistantship with partial tuition reimbursement available (averaging $9,378 per year); career-related internships or fieldwork and unspecified assistantships also available. Financial award application deadline: 3/1. *Total annual research expenditures:* $31,201. *Unit head:* Dr. Roy Jones, Interim Department Chair, 864-656-7915, E-mail: royj@clemson.edu. *Application contact:* Alison Search, Student Services Program Coordinator, 864-250-8880, E-mail: alisonp@clemson.edu. Website: http://www.clemson.edu/education/departments/educational-organizational-leadership-development/index.html

Coastal Carolina University, College of Science, Conway, SC 29528-6054. Offers applied computing and information systems (Certificate); coastal marine and wetland studies (MS); information systems technology (MS); marine science (PhD); sports management (MS). *Program availability:* Part-time, evening/weekend, 100% online. *Faculty:* 29 full-time (7 women), 2 part-time/adjunct (1 woman). *Students:* 58 full-time (19 women), 38 part-time (19 women); includes 19 minority (14 Black or African American, non-Hispanic/Latino; 1 American Indian or Alaska Native, non-Hispanic/Latino; 2 Hispanic/Latino; 2 Two or more races, non-Hispanic/Latino), 8 international. Average age 27. 104 applicants, 62% accepted, 42 enrolled. In 2017, 9 master's awarded. *Degree requirements:* For master's, thesis or internship; for doctorate, comprehensive exam, thesis/dissertation. *Entrance requirements:* For master's, GRE, 3 letters of recommendation, resume, official transcripts, written statement of educational and career goals, baccalaureate degree; for doctorate, GRE, official transcripts; baccalaureate or master's degree; minimum GPA of 3.0 for all collegiate coursework; successful completion of at least two semesters of college-level calculus, physics, and chemistry; 3 letters of recommendation; written statement of educational and career goals; resume; for Certificate, 2 letters of reference, official transcripts, minimum GPA of 3.0 in all computing and information systems courses, documentation of graduation from accredited four-year college or university. Additional exam requirements/recommendations for international students: Required—TOEFL (minimum score 550 paper-based; 79 iBT), IELTS (minimum score 6.5). *Application deadline:* For fall admission, 1/15 priority date for domestic and international students; for spring admission, 11/1 priority date for domestic and international students. Applications are processed on a rolling basis. Application fee: $45. Electronic applications accepted. *Expenses:* Tuition, state resident: full-time $5184; part-time $576 per credit hour. Tuition, nonresident: full-time $9369; part-time $1041 per credit hour. *Required fees:* $90; $5 per credit hour. *Financial support:* Fellowships, research assistantships, teaching assistantships, and tuition waivers available. Financial award application deadline: 3/1; financial award applicants required to submit FAFSA. *Unit head:* Dr. Michael H. Roberts, Dean/Vice President for Research and Emerging Initiatives, 843-349-2282, Fax: 843-349-2545, E-mail: mroberts@coastal.edu. *Application contact:* Dr. James O. Luken, Associate Provost for Graduate Program/Vice-Dean of the Coastal Environment, 843-349-2235, Fax: 843-349-6444, E-mail: joluken@coastal.edu. Website: https://www.coastal.edu/science/

Coker College, Graduate Programs, Hartsville, SC 29550. Offers college athletic administration (MS); criminal and social justice policy (MS); curriculum and instructional technology (M Ed); literacy studies (M Ed); management and leadership (MS). *Program*

availability: Part-time, 100% online. *Faculty:* 9 full-time (4 women), 3 part-time/adjunct (2 women). *Students:* 77 full-time (47 women), 9 part-time (4 women); includes 21 minority (15 Black or African American, non-Hispanic/Latino; 1 American Indian or Alaska Native, non-Hispanic/Latino; 1 Hispanic/Latino; 4 Two or more races, non-Hispanic/Latino), 1 international. Average age 30. *Degree requirements:* For master's, comprehensive exam, portfolio. *Entrance requirements:* For master's, GRE or GMAT, minimum overall GPA of 2.85 in bachelor's program, official transcripts, resume, three letters of recommendation, teacher licensure. *Application deadline:* Applications are processed on a rolling basis. Application fee: $25. Electronic applications accepted. *Expenses:* Tuition: Full-time $14,424; part-time $601 per credit hour. *Required fees:* $176; $176 per credit hour. Tuition and fees vary according to course load and program. *Financial support:* Unspecified assistantships available. Financial award application deadline: 6/30; financial award applicants required to submit FAFSA. *Application contact:* Lacey Rice-Serafin, Director of Graduate Programs, 843-857-4128, E-mail: lriceserafin@coker.edu.

The College at Brockport, State University of New York, School of Education, Health, and Human Services, Department of Kinesiology, Sports Studies and Physical Education, Brockport, NY 14420-2997. Offers adapted physical education (AGC); physical education (MS Ed), including adapted physical education, athletic administration, physical education/pedagogy. *Program availability:* Part-time. *Faculty:* 11 full-time (4 women), 1 part-time/adjunct (0 women). *Students:* 33 full-time (15 women), 28 part-time (11 women); includes 12 minority (3 Black or African American, non-Hispanic/Latino; 3 Asian, non-Hispanic/Latino; 4 Hispanic/Latino; 2 Two or more races, non-Hispanic/Latino), 1 international. 43 applicants, 81% accepted, 27 enrolled. In 2017, 37 master's awarded. *Degree requirements:* For master's, thesis or alternative. *Entrance requirements:* For master's, minimum GPA of 3.0; statement of objectives. Additional exam requirements/recommendations for international students: Required—TOEFL (minimum score 550 paper-based; 79 iBT), IELTS (minimum score 6.5). *Application deadline:* For fall admission, 4/15 priority date for domestic and international students; for spring admission, 11/15 priority date for domestic and international students; for summer admission, 4/15 priority date for domestic students, 4/15 for international students. Application fee: $80. Electronic applications accepted. *Expenses:* Tuition, state resident: full-time $10,870; part-time $453 per credit hour. Tuition, nonresident: full-time $22,210. *Required fees:* $988; $246 per semester. *Financial support:* In 2017–18, 11 teaching assistantships with full tuition reimbursements (averaging $7,000 per year) were awarded; Federal Work-Study, scholarships/grants, and unspecified assistantships also available. Support available to part-time students. Financial award application deadline: 3/15; financial award applicants required to submit FAFSA. *Faculty research:* Athletic administration, adapted physical education, physical education curriculum, physical education teaching/coaching, children's physical activity. *Unit head:* Dr. Cathy Houston-Wilson, Chairperson, 585-395-5352, Fax: 585-395-2771, E-mail: chouston@brockport.edu. *Application contact:* Dr. Melanie Perreault, Graduate Program Director, 585-395-5299, Fax: 585-395-2771, E-mail: mperreault@brockport.edu.
Website: https://www.brockport.edu/academics/kinesiology/

Columbia University, School of Professional Studies, Program in Global Sports Law and Sports Management, New York, NY 10027. Offers MS/MGSL. Program offered in collaboration with Instituto Superior de Derecho y Economia (ISDE) in Madrid. *Expenses:* Tuition: Full-time $44,864; part-time $1704 per credit. *Required fees:* $2370 per semester. One-time fee: $105.

Columbia University, School of Professional Studies, Program in Sports Management, New York, NY 10027. Offers MS. *Program availability:* Part-time. *Entrance requirements:* For master's, minimum GPA of 3.0, 2 letters of recommendation, professional resume. Electronic applications accepted. *Expenses:* Tuition: Full-time $44,864; part-time $1704 per credit. *Required fees:* $2370 per semester. One-time fee: $105.

Concordia University Irvine, School of Arts and Sciences, Irvine, CA 92612-3299. Offers coaching and athletic administration (MA). *Program availability:* Part-time, evening/weekend, online learning. *Degree requirements:* For master's, culminating project. *Entrance requirements:* For master's, official college/university transcript(s); signed statement of intent. Additional exam requirements/recommendations for international students: Required—TOEFL (minimum score 550 paper-based; 79 iBT). Electronic applications accepted. *Expenses:* Contact institution.

Concordia University, St. Paul, College of Health and Science, St. Paul, MN 55104-5494. Offers exercise science (MS); orthotics and prosthetics (MS); physical therapy (DPT); sports management (MA). *Program availability:* Part-time, evening/weekend, 100% online, blended/hybrid learning. *Faculty:* 14 full-time (8 women), 22 part-time/adjunct (8 women). *Students:* 260 full-time (127 women), 20 part-time (6 women); includes 48 minority (24 Black or African American, non-Hispanic/Latino; 5 Asian, non-Hispanic/Latino; 11 Hispanic/Latino; 1 Native Hawaiian or other Pacific Islander, non-Hispanic/Latino; 7 Two or more races, non-Hispanic/Latino), 4 international. Average age 28. 218 applicants, 43% accepted, 84 enrolled. In 2017, 57 master's, 26 doctorates awarded. *Degree requirements:* For master's, comprehensive exam (for some programs), thesis (for some programs); for doctorate, at least one 8-12 week clinical rotation outside the St. Paul area. *Entrance requirements:* For master's, official transcripts from regionally-accredited institution stating the conferral of a bachelor's degree with minimum cumulative GPA of 3.0; personal statement; resume; for doctorate, GRE, official transcript from regionally-accredited institution showing bachelor's degree and minimum coursework GPA of 3.0; 100 physical therapy observation hours; two letters of professional recommendation. Additional exam requirements/recommendations for international students: Recommended—TOEFL (minimum score 547 paper-based; 78 iBT), IELTS (minimum score 6), TSE (minimum score 52). *Application deadline:* For fall admission, 4/1 for domestic students. Applications are processed on a rolling basis. Application fee: $0. Electronic applications accepted. *Expenses:* $475 per credit (for MA and MS); $810 per credit (for DPT). *Financial support:* In 2017–18, 60 students received support. Scholarships/grants and unspecified assistantships available. Financial award applicants required to submit FAFSA. *Faculty research:* Developmental screening in early childhood, cardiovascular responses to aerobic exercise. *Unit head:* Dr. Katie Fischer, Dean, 651-641-8735, E-mail: fischer@csp.edu. *Application contact:* Amber Faletti, Director of Enrollment Management, 651-641-8838, Fax: 651-603-6320, E-mail: faletti@csp.edu.

Dallas Baptist University, Dorothy M. Bush College of Education, Sport Management Program, Dallas, TX 75211-9299. Offers MA. *Program availability:* Part-time, evening/weekend. *Application deadline:* Applications are processed on a rolling basis. Application fee: $25. Electronic applications accepted. Application fee is waived when completed online. *Expenses:* Tuition: Full-time $16,308; part-time $906 per credit hour. *Required fees:* $900; $450 per semester. Tuition and fees vary according to course load and degree level. *Unit head:* Dr. Neil Dugger, Dean, 214-333-5202, E-mail: neil@dbu.edu. *Application contact:* Dr. Jim Tennison, Program Director, 214-333-5643, E-mail: jimt@dbu.edu.
Website: http://www3.dbu.edu/graduate/sport_management.asp

Drexel University, Goodwin College of Professional Studies, School of Technology and Professional Studies, Philadelphia, PA 19104-2875. Offers construction management

(MS); creativity and innovation (MS); engineering technology (MS); food science (MS); hospitality management (MS); professional studies: creativity studies (MS); professional studies: e-learning leadership (MS); professional studies: homeland security management (MS); project management (MS); property management (MS); sport management (MS). *Program availability:* Part-time, evening/weekend. *Entrance requirements:* Additional exam requirements/recommendations for international students: Required—TOEFL, IELTS. Electronic applications accepted. Application fee is waived when completed online.

Duquesne University, Palumbo-Donahue School of Business, Pittsburgh, PA 15282-0001. Offers accounting (M Acc); finance (MBA); information systems management (MSISM); management (MBA, MS); marketing (MBA); sports business (MS); supply chain management (MS); sustainability (MBA); JD/MBA; MBA/M Acc; MBA/MA; MBA/MES; MBA/MHMS; MSISM/MBA; Pharm D/MBA. *Accreditation:* AACSB. *Program availability:* Part-time, evening/weekend, minimal on-campus study. *Faculty:* 59 full-time (23 women), 25 part-time/adjunct (6 women). *Students:* 232 full-time (83 women), 46 part-time (18 women); includes 28 minority (14 Black or African American, non-Hispanic/Latino; 8 Asian, non-Hispanic/Latino; 4 Hispanic/Latino; 2 Two or more races, non-Hispanic/Latino), 24 international. Average age 29. 220 applicants, 83% accepted, 121 enrolled. In 2017, 113 master's awarded. *Entrance requirements:* For master's, GMAT or GRE, undergraduate transcripts, 2 letters of recommendation, current resume, personal statement. Additional exam requirements/recommendations for international students: Required—TOEFL (minimum score 577 paper-based; 90 iBT), IELTS (minimum score 7). *Application deadline:* For fall admission, 7/1 priority date for domestic and international students; for spring admission, 12/1 for domestic and international students; for summer admission, 4/1 for domestic and international students. Applications are processed on a rolling basis. Application fee: $0. Electronic applications accepted. *Expenses:* $934 per credit (MS in management, sports business); $1,259 per credit (MBA, MS in accountancy, information systems management). *Financial support:* In 2017–18, 211 students received support, including 12 fellowships with partial tuition reimbursements available (averaging $14,200 per year), 20 research assistantships with partial tuition reimbursements available (averaging $22,662 per year); career-related internships or fieldwork, scholarships/grants, and unspecified assistantships also available. Support available to part-time students. Financial award application deadline: 7/1; financial award applicants required to submit FAFSA. *Faculty research:* Investment management, business ethics, technology management, supply chain management, entrepreneurship. *Unit head:* Dr. Karen Donovan, Associate Dean of Graduate Programs and Executive Education, 412-396-6276, Fax: 412-396-1726, E-mail: donovan6@duq.edu. *Application contact:* Jeff Jewett, Director of Admissions and Enrollment Management, 412-396-6244, Fax: 412-396-1726, E-mail: decrostam@duq.edu.
Website: http://www.duq.edu/business/grad

East Carolina University, Graduate School, College of Health and Human Performance, Department of Kinesiology, Greenville, NC 27858-4353. Offers adapted physical education (MS); bioenergetics and exercise science (PhD); biomechanics and motor control (MS); exercise physiology (MS); physical activity promotion (MS); physical education (MA Ed, MAT); physical education clinical supervision (Certificate); physical education pedagogy (MS); sport and exercise psychology (MS); sport management (MS, Certificate). *Students:* 72 full-time (30 women), 25 part-time (10 women); includes 21 minority (10 Black or African American, non-Hispanic/Latino; 1 American Indian or Alaska Native, non-Hispanic/Latino; 3 Asian, non-Hispanic/Latino; 4 Hispanic/Latino; 3 Two or more races, non-Hispanic/Latino), 3 international. Average age 27. 88 applicants, 68% accepted, 40 enrolled. In 2017, 35 master's, 5 doctorates, 4 other advanced degrees awarded. *Degree requirements:* For master's, comprehensive exam, thesis optional; for doctorate, comprehensive exam, thesis/dissertation. *Entrance requirements:* For master's, GRE General Test or MAT; for doctorate, GRE. Additional exam requirements/recommendations for international students: Recommended—TOEFL (minimum score 78 iBT), IELTS. *Application deadline:* For fall admission, 2/1 priority date for domestic students, 2/1 for international students. Applications are processed on a rolling basis. Application fee: $75. *Expenses:* Tuition, state resident: full-time $4749; part-time $297 per credit hour. Tuition, nonresident: full-time $17,898; part-time $1119 per credit hour. *Required fees:* $2691; $224 per credit hour. Part-time tuition and fees vary according to course load and program. *Financial support:* Research assistantships with tuition reimbursements and teaching assistantships available. Support available to part-time students. Financial award application deadline: 2/1. *Faculty research:* Diabetes metabolism, pediatric obesity, biomechanics of arthritis, physical activity measurement. *Unit head:* Dr. Stacey Altman, Chair, 252-328-2973, E-mail: altmans@ecu.edu.
Website: https://hhp.ecu.edu/kine/

Eastern Kentucky University, The Graduate School, College of Health Sciences, Department of Exercise and Sport Science, Richmond, KY 40475-3102. Offers exercise and sport science (MS); exercise and wellness (MS); sports administration (MS). *Program availability:* Part-time. *Entrance requirements:* For master's, GRE General Test (minimum score 700 verbal and quantitative), minimum GPA of 2.5 (for most), minimum GPA of 3.0 (analytical writing). *Faculty research:* Nutrition and exercise.

Eastern Michigan University, Graduate School, College of Health and Human Services, School of Health Promotion and Human Performance, Program in Sports Management, Ypsilanti, MI 48197. Offers MS. *Program availability:* Part-time, evening/weekend. *Students:* 21 full-time (11 women), 17 part-time (7 women); includes 5 minority (2 Black or African American, non-Hispanic/Latino; 1 Asian, non-Hispanic/Latino; 1 Hispanic/Latino; 1 Two or more races, non-Hispanic/Latino), 1 international. Average age 25. 46 applicants, 70% accepted, 13 enrolled. In 2017, 24 master's awarded. *Degree requirements:* For master's, comprehensive exams or thesis. *Entrance requirements:* For master's, minimum GPA of 2.75. Additional exam requirements/recommendations for international students: Required—TOEFL. *Application deadline:* For fall admission, 8/1 for domestic students, 5/1 for international students; for winter admission, 12/1 for domestic students, 10/1 for international students; for spring admission, 4/15 for domestic students, 3/1 for international students. Applications are processed on a rolling basis. Application fee: $45. *Financial support:* Fellowships, research assistantships with full tuition reimbursements, teaching assistantships with full tuition reimbursements, career-related internships or fieldwork, Federal Work-Study, institutionally sponsored loans, scholarships/grants, tuition waivers (partial), and unspecified assistantships available. Support available to part-time students. Financial award applicants required to submit FAFSA. *Application contact:* Dr. Brenda Riemer, Advisor, 734-487-0090 Ext. 2745, Fax: 734-487-2024, E-mail: briemer@emich.edu.

Eastern New Mexico University, Graduate School, College of Education and Technology, Department of Health and Physical Education, Portales, NM 88130. Offers sport administration (MS), including coaching, sport science. *Program availability:* Part-time. *Degree requirements:* For master's, comprehensive exam, thesis optional. *Entrance requirements:* For master's, minimum GPA of 3.0, 15 hours of leveling courses without bachelor's degree in physical education, two references. Additional exam requirements/recommendations for international students: Required—TOEFL (minimum score 550 paper-based; 79 iBT), IELTS (minimum score 6). *Application deadline:* For fall admission, 7/20 priority date for domestic students, 6/20 priority date for international

Sports Management

students; for spring admission, 12/15 priority date for domestic students, 11/15 priority date for international students. Applications are processed on a rolling basis. Application fee: $10. Electronic applications accepted. *Financial support:* Applicants required to submit FAFSA. *Unit head:* Dr. Beth Birky, Graduate Coordinator, 575-562-2683, E-mail: beth.birky@enmu.edu. *Application contact:* Cheryl Reeves, Senior Secretary, 575-562-2443, Fax: 575-562-2559, E-mail: cheryl.reeves@enmu.edu. Website: http://education.enmu.edu

Eastern Washington University, Graduate Studies, College of Arts, Letters and Education, Department of Physical Education, Health and Recreation, Cheney, WA 99004-2431. Offers exercise science (MS); sports and recreation administration (MS). *Faculty:* 7. *Students:* 15 full-time (6 women), 2 part-time (1 woman); includes 1 minority (Black or African American, non-Hispanic/Latino), 1 international. Average age 28. 34 applicants, 26% accepted, 8 enrolled. In 2017, 5 master's awarded. *Degree requirements:* For master's, comprehensive exam, thesis or alternative. *Entrance requirements:* For master's, minimum GPA of 3.0. Additional exam requirements/recommendations for international students: Required—TOEFL (minimum score 580 paper-based; 92 iBT), IELTS (minimum score 7), PTE (minimum score 63). *Application deadline:* For fall admission, 4/1 priority date for domestic students; for spring admission, 1/15 for domestic students. Applications are processed on a rolling basis. Application fee: $50. Electronic applications accepted. *Expenses:* Tuition, state resident: full-time $11,191; part-time $373.06 per credit. Tuition, nonresident: full-time $25,995; part-time $866.52 per credit. *Financial support:* Teaching assistantships with partial tuition reimbursements, career-related internships or fieldwork, Federal Work-Study, institutionally sponsored loans, and scholarships/grants available. Support available to part-time students. Financial award application deadline: 2/1; financial award applicants required to submit FAFSA. *Unit head:* Dr. Chadron Hazelbaker, Graduate Program Director, 509-359-2486, Fax: 509-359-4833, E-mail: chazelbaker@ewu.edu.

East Stroudsburg University of Pennsylvania, Graduate and Extended Studies, College of Business and Management, Department of Sport Management, East Stroudsburg, PA 18301-2999. Offers MS. *Program availability:* Part-time, evening/weekend, online learning. *Faculty:* 5 full-time (2 women), 1 part-time/adjunct (0 women). *Students:* 14 full-time (5 women), 9 part-time (3 women); includes 6 minority (all Black or African American, non-Hispanic/Latino), 4 international. Average age 25. 26 applicants, 85% accepted, 15 enrolled. In 2017, 10 master's awarded. *Degree requirements:* For master's, comprehensive exam. *Entrance requirements:* For master's, GRE and/or GMAT. Additional exam requirements/recommendations for international students: Recommended—TOEFL (minimum score 560 paper-based; 83 iBT), IELTS. *Application deadline:* For fall admission, 7/31 priority date for domestic students, 6/30 priority date for international students; for spring admission, 11/30 for domestic students, 10/31 for international students. Applications are processed on a rolling basis. Application fee: $50. Electronic applications accepted. *Expenses:* Tuition, state resident: full-time $4500; part-time $3000 per credit. Tuition, nonresident: full-time $6750; part-time $4500 per credit. *Required fees:* $2642; $1756 per credit. $878 per semester. Tuition and fees vary according to course load, campus/location and program. *Financial support:* Research assistantships, Federal Work-Study, and unspecified assistantships available. Support available to part-time students. Financial award application deadline: 3/1; financial award applicants required to submit FAFSA. *Unit head:* Dr. Jaedock Lee, Chair, 570-422-3340, Fax: 570-422-3824, E-mail: jaedeock@esu.edu. *Application contact:* Kevin Quintero, Associate Director, Graduate and Extended Studies, 570-422-3890, Fax: 570-422-2711, E-mail: kquintero@esu.edu.

East Tennessee State University, School of Graduate Studies, College of Education, Department of Sport, Exercise, Recreation, and Kinesiology, Johnson City, TN 37614-1701. Offers sport management (MA); sport physiology and performance (PhD), including sport performance, sport physiology; sport science and coach education (MS), including applied sport science, strength and conditioning. *Program availability:* Part-time, evening/weekend. Terminal master's awarded for partial completion of doctoral program. *Degree requirements:* For master's, comprehensive exam, thesis or internship; for doctorate, comprehensive exam, thesis/dissertation, 2-semester residency. *Entrance requirements:* For master's, GRE General Test or GMAT, undergraduate degree in related field; minimum GPA of 3.0; resume; three references; essay explaining goals and reasons for pursuing degree; for doctorate, GRE, resume; 4 letters of recommendation; master's or bachelor's degree in related field; minimum GPA of 3.4 overall with master's, 3.0 with bachelor's; interview. Additional exam requirements/recommendations for international students: Required—TOEFL (minimum score 550 paper-based; 79 iBT). *Application deadline:* For fall admission, 6/1 for domestic students, 4/29 for international students; for spring admission, 11/1 for domestic students, 9/29 for international students). Electronic applications accepted. *Financial support:* Fellowships, research assistantships with full tuition reimbursements, teaching assistantships with full tuition reimbursements, career-related internships or fieldwork, institutionally sponsored loans, scholarships/grants, and unspecified assistantships available. Financial award application deadline: 7/1; financial award applicants required to submit FAFSA. *Faculty research:* Methods of training for individual and team sports, enhancing acute sport performance, fatigue management in athletes, risk management, facilities management, motorsport. *Unit head:* Dr. Mike Ramsey, Chair, 423-439-4375, Fax: 423-439-7560, E-mail: ramseym@etsu.edu. *Application contact:* Dr. Mike Stone, Graduate Program Coordinator, 423-439-5796, Fax: 423-439-5624, E-mail: stonem@etsu.edu. Website: http://www.etsu.edu/coe/serk/

East Tennessee State University, School of Graduate Studies, Program in Global Sport Leadership, Johnson City, TN 37614. Offers Ed D.

Endicott College, Van Loan School of Graduate and Professional Studies, Program in Athletic Administration, Beverly, MA 01915-2096. Offers M Ed. *Program availability:* Part-time, evening/weekend. *Faculty:* 2 full-time (1 woman), 10 part-time/adjunct (3 women). *Students:* 20 full-time (9 women), 43 part-time (11 women); includes 6 minority (2 Black or African American, non-Hispanic/Latino; 4 Two or more races, non-Hispanic/Latino). Average age 30. 24 applicants, 100% accepted, 19 enrolled. In 2017, 30 master's awarded. *Degree requirements:* For master's, thesis, practicum. *Entrance requirements:* For master's, GRE or MAT, undergraduate transcript, personal statement, interview, two letters of recommendation. Additional exam requirements/recommendations for international students: Required—TOEFL. *Application deadline:* Applications are processed on a rolling basis. Application fee: $50. Electronic applications accepted. *Expenses:* Contact institution. *Financial support:* Scholarships/grants available. Financial award applicants required to submit FAFSA. *Unit head:* Anthony D'Onofrio, Associate Director, Graduate Athletic Administration, 978-998-7791, Fax: 978-232-3000, E-mail: adonofrio@endicott.edu. *Application contact:* Ian Menchini, Director, Graduate Enrollment and Advising, 978-232-2744, Fax: 978-232-5292, E-mail: imenchin@endicott.edu. Website: http://www.endicott.edu/VanLoan/Graduate-Studies/Master-Education/Athletic-Administration.aspx

Fairleigh Dickinson University, Florham Campus, Anthony J. Petrocelli College of Continuing Studies, Program in Sports Administration, Madison, NJ 07940-1099. Offers MSA.

Fairleigh Dickinson University, Metropolitan Campus, Anthony J. Petrocelli College of Continuing Studies, Department of Sports Administration, Program in Sports Administration, Teaneck, NJ 07666-1914. Offers MSA.

Florida Agricultural and Mechanical University, Division of Graduate Studies, Research, and Continuing Education, College of Education, Department of Health, Physical Education, and Recreation, Tallahassee, FL 32307-3200. Offers sport management (MS). *Accreditation:* NCATE. *Program availability:* Part-time, evening/weekend. *Degree requirements:* For master's, thesis optional. *Entrance requirements:* For master's, GRE General Test, minimum GPA of 3.0. Additional exam requirements/recommendations for international students: Required—TOEFL. *Faculty research:* Administration/curriculum, work behavior, psychology.

Florida Atlantic University, College of Business, Department of Management, Boca Raton, FL 33431-0991. Offers business administration (MBA); entrepreneurship (MBA); health administration (MBA); international business (MBA); sport management (MBA). *Faculty:* 4 full-time (1 woman). *Students:* 122 full-time (86 women), 81 part-time (67 women); includes 117 minority (61 Black or African American, non-Hispanic/Latino; 12 Asian, non-Hispanic/Latino; 44 Hispanic/Latino), 3 international. Average age 35. 124 applicants, 73% accepted, 75 enrolled. In 2017, 70 master's awarded. *Entrance requirements:* For master's, GMAT or GRE General Test, minimum GPA of 3.0 in last 60 hours of course work. Additional exam requirements/recommendations for international students: Required—TOEFL (minimum score 600 paper-based; 61 iBT), IELTS (minimum score 6). *Application deadline:* For fall admission, 7/25 for domestic students, 2/15 for international students; for spring admission, 12/10 for domestic students, 7/15 for international students. Applications are processed on a rolling basis. Application fee: $30. Electronic applications accepted. *Expenses:* Tuition, state resident: full-time $7400; part-time $369.82 per credit. Tuition, nonresident: full-time $20,496; part-time $1042.81 per credit. *Financial support:* Research assistantships with full tuition reimbursements, career-related internships or fieldwork, tuition waivers (partial), and unspecified assistantships available. *Faculty research:* Sports administration, healthcare, policy, finance, real estate, senior living. *Unit head:* Dr. Roland Kidwell, Chair, 561-297-5634, E-mail: kidwellr@fau.edu. Website: http://business.fau.edu/departments/management/index.aspx

Florida International University, College of Arts, Sciences, and Education, Department of Leadership and Professional Studies, Miami, FL 33199. Offers adult education and human resource development (MS, Ed D); counseling (MS), including rehabilitation counseling, school counseling; counselor education (MS), including clinical mental health counseling; educational administration and supervision (Ed D); educational leadership (MS, Certificate, Ed S); higher education (Ed D); higher education administration (MS); international and comparative education (MS); recreation and sport management (MS), including recreation and sport management, recreational therapy; school psychology (Ed S); urban education (MS), including instruction in urban settings, learning technologies, multicultural/bilingual, multicultural/TESOL, urban education. *Program availability:* Part-time, evening/weekend. *Faculty:* 60 full-time (41 women), 112 part-time/adjunct (77 women). *Students:* 221 full-time (162 women), 301 part-time (239 women); includes 418 minority (127 Black or African American, non-Hispanic/Latino; 9 Asian, non-Hispanic/Latino; 271 Hispanic/Latino; 11 Two or more races, non-Hispanic/Latino), 10 international. Average age 31. 330 applicants, 55% accepted, 100 enrolled. In 2017, 181 master's, 6 doctorates awarded. *Degree requirements:* For doctorate, thesis/dissertation. *Entrance requirements:* For master's, minimum GPA of 3.0; for doctorate and other advanced degree, GRE General Test. Additional exam requirements/recommendations for international students: Required—TOEFL (minimum score 550 paper-based; 80 iBT), IELTS (minimum score 6.3). *Application deadline:* For fall admission, 6/1 priority date for domestic students, 4/1 for international students; for winter admission, 10/1 priority date for domestic students, 9/1 for international students; for spring admission, 3/1 priority date for domestic students, 2/1 for international students. Applications are processed on a rolling basis. Application fee: $30. Electronic applications accepted. *Expenses:* Tuition, state resident: full-time $8912; part-time $446 per credit hour. Tuition, nonresident: full-time $21,393; part-time $992 per credit hour. *Required fees:* $390; $195 per semester. *Financial support:* Fellowships, research assistantships with tuition reimbursements, teaching assistantships with tuition reimbursements, Federal Work-Study, and tuition waivers (full and partial) available. Support available to part-time students. Financial award applicants required to submit FAFSA. *Unit head:* Dr. Benjamin Baez, Chair, 305-348-3214, Fax: 305-348-1515, E-mail: benjamin.baez@fiu.edu. *Application contact:* Nanett Rojas, Assistant Director, Graduate Admissions, 305-348-7464, Fax: 305-348-7441, E-mail: gradadm@fiu.edu. Website: http://education.fiu.edu

Florida State University, The Graduate School, College of Education, Department of Sport Management, Tallahassee, FL 32306. Offers MS, PhD. *Program availability:* Part-time, evening/weekend, 100% online, blended/hybrid learning, asynchronous, minimal on-campus study. *Faculty:* 9 full-time (3 women), 3 part-time/adjunct (2 women). *Students:* 83 full-time (34 women), 22 part-time (11 women); includes 23 minority (13 Black or African American, non-Hispanic/Latino; 1 American Indian or Alaska Native, non-Hispanic/Latino; 6 Hispanic/Latino; 3 Two or more races, non-Hispanic/Latino), 20 international. Average age 27. 143 applicants, 45% accepted, 38 enrolled. In 2017, 59 master's, 6 doctorates awarded. Terminal master's awarded for partial completion of doctoral program. *Degree requirements:* For master's, comprehensive exam, thesis optional; for doctorate, comprehensive exam, thesis/dissertation, diagnostic exam, preliminary exam, prospectus defense, dissertation defense. *Entrance requirements:* For master's and doctorate, GRE General Test, minimum upper-division GPA of 3.0. Additional exam requirements/recommendations for international students: Required—TOEFL (minimum score 550 paper-based, 80 iBT), IELTS (minimum score 6.5), Michigan English Language Assessment Battery (minimum score 77), or PTE (minimum score 55). Application fee: $30. Electronic applications accepted. *Financial support:* Fellowships, research assistantships, teaching assistantships, scholarships/grants, tuition waivers (full and partial), and unspecified assistantships available. Financial award application deadline: 1/15; financial award applicants required to submit FAFSA. *Faculty research:* Sociology of sport; media and culture studies in sport; sport marketing and sport consumer behavior; legal and policy studies in sport; sports gambling; sport management; social network analysis. *Unit head:* Dr. Jeffrey D. James, Professor/Department Chair, 850-644-6885, Fax: 850-644-2725, E-mail: jdjames@fsu.edu. *Application contact:* Jeffrey Hoh, Academic Program Specialist, 850-644-0577, Fax: 850-644-7903, E-mail: jhoh@admin.fsu.edu.

Franklin Pierce University, Graduate and Professional Studies, Rindge, NH 03461-0060. Offers curriculum and instruction (M Ed); elementary education (MS Ed); emerging network technologies (Graduate Certificate); energy and sustainability studies (MBA, Graduate Certificate); health administration (MBA, Graduate Certificate); human resource management (MBA, Graduate Certificate); information technology (MBA); leadership (MBA); nursing education (MS); nursing leadership (MS); physical therapy (DPT); physician assistant studies (MPAS); special education (M Ed); sports management (MBA). *Accreditation:* APTA. *Program availability:* Part-time, 100% online, blended/hybrid learning. *Degree requirements:* For master's, concentrated original research projects; student teaching; fieldwork and/or internship; leadership project;

PRAXIS I and II (for M Ed); for doctorate, concentrated original research projects, clinical fieldwork and/or internship, leadership project. *Entrance requirements:* For master's, minimum GPA of 2.5, 3 letters of recommendation; competencies in accounting, economics, statistics, and computer skills through life experience or undergraduate coursework (for MBA); certification/e-portfolio, minimum C grade in all education courses (for M Ed); license to practice as RN (for MS); for doctorate, GRE, 80 hours of observation/work in PT settings; completion of anatomy, chemistry, physics, and statistics; minimum GPA of 3.0. Additional exam requirements/recommendations for international students: Required—TOEFL (minimum score 550 paper-based; 61 iBT). Electronic applications accepted. *Faculty research:* Evidence-based practice in sports physical therapy, human resource management in economic crisis, leadership in nursing, innovation in sports facility management, differentiated learning and understanding by design.

George Mason University, College of Education and Human Development, School of Recreation, Health and Tourism, Manassas, VA 20110. Offers athletic training (MS); exercise, fitness, and health promotion (MS), including advanced practitioner, wellness practitioner; international sport management (Certificate); recreation, health and tourism (Certificate); sport management (MS), including sport and recreation studies. *Program availability:* Part-time, evening/weekend. *Faculty:* 29 full-time (13 women), 87 part-time/adjunct (48 women). *Students:* 62 full-time (24 women), 23 part-time (11 women); includes 27 minority (20 Black or African American, non-Hispanic/Latino; 1 Asian, non-Hispanic/Latino; 3 Hispanic/Latino; 1 Native Hawaiian or other Pacific Islander, non-Hispanic/Latino; 2 Two or more races, non-Hispanic/Latino), 8 international. Average age 26. 74 applicants, 93% accepted, 46 enrolled. In 2017, 20 master's awarded. *Degree requirements:* For master's, thesis option. *Entrance requirements:* For master's, 3 letters of recommendation; official transcripts; expanded goals statement; undergraduate course in statistics and minimum GPA of 3.0 in last 60 credit hours and overall (for MS in sport and recreation studies); baccalaureate degree related to kinesiology, exercise science or athletic training (for MS in exercise, fitness and health promotion). Additional exam requirements/recommendations for international students: Required—TOEFL (minimum score 575 paper-based; 88 iBT), IELTS (minimum score 6.5), PTE (minimum score 59). *Application deadline:* For fall admission, 4/2 priority date for domestic and international students; for spring admission, 11/1 for domestic and international students. Application fee: $75 ($80 for international students). Electronic applications accepted. *Expenses:* Tuition, state resident: full-time $11,228; part-time $459.50 per credit. Tuition, nonresident: full-time $30,932; part-time $1280.50 per credit. *Required fees:* $3252; $135.50 per credit. Part-time tuition and fees vary according to course load and program. *Financial support:* In 2017–18, 1 student received support, including 1 research assistantship with tuition reimbursement available; career-related internships or fieldwork, Federal Work-Study, scholarships/grants, unspecified assistantships, and health care benefits (for full-time research or teaching assistantship recipients) also available. Support available to part-time students. Financial award application deadline: 3/1; financial award applicants required to submit FAFSA. *Faculty research:* Sport for development and peace, sport analytics, leadership and coaching, diversity and inclusion in sport, sport communication. *Total annual research expenditures:* $826,386. *Unit head:* Martin Ford, Senior Associate Dean, 703-993-2004, E-mail: mford@gmu.edu. *Application contact:* Lindsey Olson, Office Assistant, 703-993-2098, Fax: 703-993-2025, E-mail: lolson7@gmu.edu.
Website: http://rht.gmu.edu/

Georgetown University, Graduate School of Arts and Sciences, School of Continuing Studies, Washington, DC 20057. Offers American studies (MALS); applied intelligence (MPS); Catholic studies (MALS); classical civilizations (MALS); emergency and disaster management (MPS); ethics and the professions (MPS); global strategic communications (MPS); hospitality management (MPS); human resources management (MPS); humanities (MALS); individualized study (MALS); integrated marketing communications (MPS); international affairs (MALS); Islam and Muslim-Christian relations (MALS); journalism (MPS); liberal studies (DLS); literature and society (MALS); medieval and early modern European studies (MALS); public relations and corporate communications (MPS); real estate (MPS); religious studies (MALS); social and public policy (MALS); sports industry management (MPS); systems engineering management (MPS); technology management (MPS); the theory and practice of American democracy (MALS); urban and regional planning (MPS); visual culture (MALS). MPS in systems engineering management offered jointly with Stevens Institute of Technology. *Entrance requirements:* Additional exam requirements/recommendations for international students: Required—TOEFL.

The George Washington University, School of Business, Department of Tourism and Hospitality Management, Washington, DC 20052. Offers destination management (Professional Certificate); event and meeting management (MTA); event management (Professional Certificate); hospitality management (MTA); individualized studies (MTA); sport management (MTA); sustainable tourism destination management (MTA); tourism and hospitality management (MBA). *Program availability:* Part-time, online learning. *Students:* 69 full-time (46 women), 51 part-time (36 women); includes 35 minority (23 Black or African American, non-Hispanic/Latino; 3 Asian, non-Hispanic/Latino; 6 Hispanic/Latino; 3 Two or more races, non-Hispanic/Latino), 46 international. Average age 28. 185 applicants, 74% accepted, 53 enrolled. In 2017, 51 master's awarded. *Degree requirements:* For master's, comprehensive exam, thesis. *Entrance requirements:* For master's, GRE General Test. Additional exam requirements/recommendations for international students: Required—TOEFL. *Application deadline:* For fall admission, 4/1 priority date for domestic students; for spring admission, 10/1 for domestic students. Applications are processed on a rolling basis. Application fee: $75. *Expenses:* Tuition: Full-time $28,800; part-time $1655 per credit hour. *Required fees:* $45; $2.75 per credit hour. *Financial support:* In 2017–18, 32 students received support. Fellowships, teaching assistantships, career-related internships or fieldwork, Federal Work-Study, institutionally sponsored loans, and tuition waivers (partial) available. Financial award application deadline: 4/1. *Faculty research:* Tourism policy, tourism impact forecasting, geotourism. *Unit head:* Prof. Lisa Delpy Neirotti, Faculty Director, 202-994-6623, E-mail: delpy@gwu.edu. *Application contact:* Christopher Storer, Executive Director, Graduate Admissions, 202-994-1212, E-mail: gwmba@gwu.edu.
Website: http://business.gwu.edu/tourism/

Georgia Southern University, Jack N. Averitt College of Graduate Studies, College of Health and Human Sciences, School of Health and Kinesiology, Program in Sport Management, Statesboro, GA 30460. Offers MS. *Program availability:* Part-time. *Students:* 9 full-time (1 woman), 24 part-time (12 women); includes 10 minority (8 Black or African American, non-Hispanic/Latino; 1 Hispanic/Latino; 1 Two or more races, non-Hispanic/Latino), 1 international. Average age 26. 36 applicants, 67% accepted, 16 enrolled. In 2017, 12 master's awarded. *Degree requirements:* For master's, terminal exam. *Entrance requirements:* For master's, GMAT, GRE, resume. Additional exam requirements/recommendations for international students: Required—TOEFL (minimum score 550 paper-based; 80 iBT), IELTS (minimum score 6). *Application deadline:* For fall admission, 3/1 priority date for domestic and international students; for spring admission, 10/15 priority date for domestic students, 10/15 for international students. Applications are processed on a rolling basis. Application fee: $50. Electronic applications accepted. *Expenses:* Tuition, state resident: full-time $4986; part-time $3324 per year. Tuition, nonresident: full-time $21,982; part-time $15,352 per year.

Required fees: $2092; $1802 per credit hour. $901 per semester. Tuition and fees vary according to course load, campus/location and program. *Financial support:* In 2017–18, 12 students received support, including 12 fellowships with full tuition reimbursements available (averaging $7,750 per year), 9 research assistantships with full tuition reimbursements available (averaging $7,750 per year), 33 teaching assistantships with full tuition reimbursements available (averaging $7,750 per year); career-related internships or fieldwork, Federal Work-Study, scholarships/grants, and tuition waivers (full) also available. Support available to part-time students. Financial award application deadline: 4/15; financial award applicants required to submit FAFSA. *Faculty research:* Outsourcing sport marketing, international integration of North American sports, sport law, sport financing, sport economics. *Unit head:* Dr. Stephen Rossi, Associate Dean, 912-478-0200, Fax: 912-478-0386, E-mail: srossi@georgiasouthern.edu.

Georgia State University, College of Education and Human Development, Department of Kinesiology and Health, Program in Sports Administration, Atlanta, GA 30302-3083. Offers MS. *Entrance requirements:* For master's, GRE General Test, minimum GPA of 2.5. Application fee: $50. *Expenses:* Tuition, state resident: full-time $7020. Tuition, nonresident: full-time $22,518. *Required fees:* $2128. Tuition and fees vary according to degree level and program. *Financial support:* Research assistantships available. *Faculty research:* Sports marketing. *Unit head:* Dr. Jacalyn Lea Lund, Chair, 404-413-8051, E-mail: jlund@gsu.edu. *Application contact:* Kaila Muecke, Academic Ambassador, 404-413-8360, E-mail: khambassador@gsu.edu.
Website: http://kh.education.gsu.edu/academics-admissions/sports-administration/

Gonzaga University, School of Education, Spokane, WA 99258. Offers clinical mental health counseling (MA); educational leadership (M Ed, Ed D); elementary education (MIT); marriage and family counseling (MA); school counseling (MA); secondary education (MIT); special education (M Ed, MIT); sport and athletic administration (MA). *Accreditation:* NCATE. *Program availability:* Part-time, evening/weekend, 100% online, blended/hybrid learning. *Faculty:* 16 full-time (11 women), 31 part-time/adjunct (19 women). *Students:* 108 full-time (90 women), 225 part-time (140 women); includes 34 minority (4 Black or African American, non-Hispanic/Latino; 2 American Indian or Alaska Native, non-Hispanic/Latino; 5 Asian, non-Hispanic/Latino; 18 Hispanic/Latino; 5 Two or more races, non-Hispanic/Latino), 114 international. Average age 31. 367 applicants, 74% accepted, 160 enrolled. In 2017, 175 master's awarded. *Degree requirements:* For master's, comprehensive exam. *Entrance requirements:* For master's, GRE, MAT, and/or Washington Educator Skills Test-Basic (WEST-B), Washington Educator Skills Test-Endorsements (WEST-E), official transcripts from all colleges or universities attended, interview, two letters of recommendation, resume, essay, minimum GPA of 3.0. Additional exam requirements/recommendations for international students: Required—TOEFL (minimum score 580 paper-based, 88 iBT) or IELTS (minimum score 6.5). *Application deadline:* Applications are processed on a rolling basis. Application fee: $50. Electronic applications accepted. *Expenses:* $990 per credit. *Financial support:* In 2017–18, 51 students received support. Scholarships/grants and unspecified assistantships available. Support available to part-time students. Financial award applicants required to submit FAFSA. *Unit head:* Dr. Vincent Alfonso, Dean, 509-313-3594, Fax: 509-313-5821, E-mail: alfonso@gonzaga.edu. *Application contact:* Meg Martens, Graduate Admissions Program Specialist, 509-313-4314, E-mail: martens@gonzaga.edu.
Website: https://www.gonzaga.edu/school-of-education

Grambling State University, School of Graduate Studies and Research, College of Education, Department of Kinesiology, Sport and Leisure Studies, Grambling, LA 71245. Offers sports administration (MS). *Program availability:* Part-time. *Degree requirements:* For master's, comprehensive exam. *Entrance requirements:* For master's, GRE General Test, minimum GPA of 2.5 on last degree. Additional exam requirements/recommendations for international students: Required—TOEFL (minimum score 500 paper-based; 62 iBT). Electronic applications accepted. *Faculty research:* Administrative relations and organization, measuring human performance, sport history from ancient times through current date, learning dynamics of personality and sports selection.

Grand Canyon University, Colangelo College of Business, Phoenix, AZ 85017-1097. Offers accounting (MBA, MS); business analytics (MS); disaster preparedness and executive fire service leadership (MBA); finance (MBA); general management (MBA); health systems management (MBA); information technology management (MS); leadership (MBA, MS); marketing (MBA); organizational leadership and entrepreneurship (MS); project management (MBA); sports business (MBA); strategic human resource management (MBA). *Accreditation:* ACBSP. *Program availability:* Part-time, evening/weekend, online learning. *Entrance requirements:* For master's, equivalent of two years' full-time professional work experience. Additional exam requirements/recommendations for international students: Required—TOEFL (minimum score 575 paper-based; 90 iBT), IELTS (minimum score 7). Electronic applications accepted.

Grand View University, Graduate Studies, Des Moines, IA 50316-1599. Offers athletic training (MS); clinical nurse leader (MSN, Post Master's Certificate); nursing education (MSN, Post Master's Certificate); organizational leadership (MS); sport management (MS); teacher leadership (M Ed); urban education (M Ed). *Program availability:* Part-time, evening/weekend. *Degree requirements:* For master's, completion of all required coursework in common core and selected track with minimum cumulative GPA of 3.0 and no more than two grades of C. *Entrance requirements:* For master's, GRE, GMAT, or essay, minimum undergraduate GPA of 3.0, professional resume, 3 letters of recommendation, interview. Additional exam requirements/recommendations for international students: Required—TOEFL (minimum score 550 paper-based). Electronic applications accepted.

Hampton University, School of Liberal Arts and Education, Program in Sport Administration, Hampton, VA 23668. Offers intercollegiate athletics (MS); international sports (MS); organizational behavior and sport business leadership (MS). *Program availability:* Part-time, evening/weekend. *Students:* 29 full-time (6 women), 21 part-time (7 women); includes 46 minority (all Black or African American, non-Hispanic/Latino). Average age 26. 34 applicants, 53% accepted, 1 enrolled. In 2017, 14 master's awarded. *Degree requirements:* For master's, thesis (for some programs). *Entrance requirements:* For master's, GRE. Additional exam requirements/recommendations for international students: Required—TOEFL (minimum score 525 paper-based) or IELTS (6.5). *Application deadline:* For fall admission, 6/1 priority date for domestic students, 4/1 priority date for international students; for spring admission, 11/1 priority date for domestic students, 9/1 priority date for international students; for summer admission, 4/1 priority date for domestic students, 2/1 priority date for international students. Applications are processed on a rolling basis. Application fee: $35. Electronic applications accepted. *Expenses:* Contact institution. *Financial support:* Fellowships, research assistantships, teaching assistantships, and career-related internships or fieldwork available. Financial award application deadline: 6/30; financial award applicants required to submit FAFSA. *Faculty research:* International sport, intercollegiate sport, sport leadership, professional sport, event management. *Unit head:* Dr. Aaron Livingston, Program Coordinator, 757-637-2278, E-mail: aaron.livingston@hamptonu.edu.

Hardin-Simmons University, Graduate School, Kelley College of Business, Abilene, TX 79698-0001. Offers business administration (MBA); information science (MS); sports

management (MBA). *Accreditation:* ACBSP. *Program availability:* Part-time. *Faculty:* 6 full-time (3 women). *Students:* 17 full-time (7 women), 14 part-time (5 women); includes 5 minority (1 Black or African American, non-Hispanic/Latino; 4 Hispanic/Latino), 2 international. Average age 26. 25 applicants, 100% accepted, 15 enrolled. In 2017, 14 master's awarded. *Degree requirements:* For master's, thesis or alternative. *Entrance requirements:* For master's, GMAT, minimum GPA of 3.0 in upper-level course work, resume, interview. Additional exam requirements/recommendations for international students: Required—TOEFL (minimum score 550 paper-based; 75 iBT). *Application deadline:* For fall admission, 8/15 priority date for domestic students, 4/1 for international students; for spring admission, 1/5 priority date for domestic students, 9/1 for international students. Applications are processed on a rolling basis. Application fee: $50. Electronic applications accepted. *Expenses:* Tuition: Full-time $13,500; part-time $750 per semester hour. *Required fees:* $220 per term. One-time fee: $50. Tuition and fees vary according to course load, campus/location and program. *Financial support:* In 2017–18, 22 students received support. Fellowships and scholarships/grants available. Support available to part-time students. Financial award application deadline: 6/30; financial award applicants required to submit FAFSA. *Unit head:* Dr. Jennifer Plantier, Program Director, 325-671-2166, Fax: 325-670-1523, E-mail: jplantier@hsutx.edu. *Application contact:* Dr. Nancy Kucinski, Dean of Graduate Studies, 325-670-1298, Fax: 325-670-1564, E-mail: gradoff@hsutx.edu.
Website: http://www.hsutx.edu/academics/kelley/graduate/

Henderson State University, Graduate Studies, Teachers College, Department of Health, Physical Education, Recreation and Athletic Training, Arkadelphia, AR 71999-0001. Offers sports administration (MS). *Program availability:* Part-time. *Entrance requirements:* For master's, GRE General Test or MAT, minimum GPA of 2.7 as an undergraduate student. Additional exam requirements/recommendations for international students: Required—TOEFL (minimum score 600 paper-based); Recommended—IELTS (minimum score 6.5).

Hofstra University, Frank G. Zarb School of Business, Programs in Management and General Business, Hempstead, NY 11549. Offers business administration (MBA), including health services management, management, sports and entertainment management, strategic business management, strategic healthcare management; general management (Advanced Certificate); human resource management (MS, Advanced Certificate). *Program availability:* Part-time, evening/weekend, blended/hybrid learning. *Students:* 131 full-time (58 women), 145 part-time (65 women); includes 102 minority (23 Black or African American, non-Hispanic/Latino; 39 Asian, non-Hispanic/Latino; 37 Hispanic/Latino; 3 Two or more races, non-Hispanic/Latino), 25 international. Average age 33. 327 applicants, 72% accepted, 104 enrolled. In 2017, 116 master's awarded. *Degree requirements:* For master's, thesis optional, capstone course (for MBA), thesis (for MS), minimum GPA of 3.0. *Entrance requirements:* For master's, GMAT/GRE, 2 letters of recommendation, resume, essay. Additional exam requirements/recommendations for international students: Required—TOEFL (minimum score 550 paper-based; 80 iBT); Recommended—IELTS (minimum score 6). *Application deadline:* Applications are processed on a rolling basis. Application fee: $75. Electronic applications accepted. *Expenses:* $1,322 per credit. *Financial support:* In 2017–18, 78 students received support, including 75 fellowships with full and partial tuition reimbursements available (averaging $4,785 per year); research assistantships with full and partial tuition reimbursements available, career-related internships or fieldwork, Federal Work-Study, institutionally sponsored loans, scholarships/grants, tuition waivers (full and partial), and unspecified assistantships also available. Support available to part-time students. Financial award applicants required to submit FAFSA. *Faculty research:* Organizational change; sustainability; entrepreneurial spawning; family business; global supply chain strategies. *Unit head:* Dr. Kaushik Sengupta, Chairperson, 516-463-7825, Fax: 516-463-4834, E-mail: kaushik.sengupta@hofstra.edu. *Application contact:* Sunil Samuel, Assistant Vice President of Admissions, 516-463-4723, Fax: 516-463-4664, E-mail: graduateadmission@hofstra.edu.
Website: http://www.hofstra.edu/business/

Houston Baptist University, School of Nursing and Allied Health, Program in Kinesiology - Sport Management, Houston, TX 77074-3298. Offers sport management (MSK). *Program availability:* Online only, 100% online. *Students:* 9 full-time (7 women); includes 4 minority (1 Black or African American, non-Hispanic/Latino; 3 Hispanic/Latino). Average age 23. 43 applicants, 23% accepted, 9 enrolled. *Degree requirements:* For master's, internship or thesis. *Entrance requirements:* For master's, GRE, bachelor's degree conferred transcript, personal statement/essay, resume. Additional exam requirements/recommendations for international students: Required—TOEFL (minimum score 80 iBT), IELTS (minimum score 6.5). *Application deadline:* For fall admission, 8/1 for domestic students, 6/1 for international students; for spring admission, 1/1 for domestic students, 11/1 for international students. Applications are processed on a rolling basis. Application fee: $0 ($100 for international students). Electronic applications accepted. Application fee is waived when completed online. *Expenses:* $20,350 tuition; $1,000 fees (general, technology). *Financial support:* In 2017–18, 8 students received support. *Unit head:* Dr. Kylee Studer O'Daniel, Chair, Department of Kinesiology, 281-649-3128, E-mail: kstuder@hbu.edu. *Application contact:* Allyson Cates, Director of Admissions, Graduate School, 281-649-3099, Fax: 281-649-3390, E-mail: acates@hbu.edu.

Howard Payne University, Program in Sport and Wellness Leadership, Brownwood, TX 76801-2715. Offers M Ed. *Program availability:* Part-time. *Entrance requirements:* For master's, baccalaureate degree and major or minor in exercise and sport science, kinesiology, sport administration, wellness or a related field; minimum undergraduate GPA of 3.0; official transcripts; 500-word statement of professional goals; two letters of recommendation. Additional exam requirements/recommendations for international students: Required—TOEFL. Electronic applications accepted.

Howard University, Graduate School, Department of Health, Human Performance and Leisure Studies, Washington, DC 20059-0002. Offers exercise physiology (MS); health education (MS); sports studies (MS), including sociology of sports, sports management; urban recreation (MS), including leisure studies. *Program availability:* Part-time, evening/weekend. *Degree requirements:* For master's, comprehensive exam, thesis. *Entrance requirements:* For master's, BS in human performance or related field. Additional exam requirements/recommendations for international students: Recommended—TOEFL. Electronic applications accepted. *Faculty research:* Health promotion, cardiovascular hypertension, physical activity, sport and human rights issues.

Husson University, Master of Business Administration Program, Bangor, ME 04401-2999. Offers athletic administration (MBA); biotechnology and innovation (MBA); general business administration (MBA); healthcare management (MBA); hospitality and tourism management (MBA); organizational management (MBA); risk management (MBA). *Program availability:* Part-time, evening/weekend, 100% online, blended/hybrid learning. *Faculty:* 11 full-time (5 women), 2 part-time/adjunct (4 women). *Students:* 83 full-time (44 women), 287 part-time (176 women); includes 25 minority (7 Black or African American, non-Hispanic/Latino; 11 Asian, non-Hispanic/Latino; 4 Hispanic/Latino; 3 Two or more races, non-Hispanic/Latino), 16 international. Average age 35. 158 applicants, 77% accepted, 49 enrolled. In 2017, 120 master's awarded. *Degree requirements:* For master's, comprehensive exam (for some programs), thesis optional. *Entrance*

requirements: For master's, minimum GPA of 3.0, letter of recommendation. Additional exam requirements/recommendations for international students: Required—TOEFL (minimum score 550 paper-based; 80 iBT), IELTS (minimum score 6.5). *Application deadline:* Applications are processed on a rolling basis. Application fee: $50. Electronic applications accepted. *Expenses:* $464 per credit. *Financial support:* In 2017–18, 13 students received support. Career-related internships or fieldwork, Federal Work-Study, scholarships/grants, and unspecified assistantships available. Financial award application deadline: 4/15; financial award applicants required to submit FAFSA. *Unit head:* Prof. Stephanie Shayne, Director, Graduate and Online Programs, 207-404-5632, Fax: 207-992-4987, E-mail: shaynes@husson.edu. *Application contact:* Kristen Card, Director of Graduate Admissions, 207-404-5660, Fax: 207-941-7935, E-mail: cardk@husson.edu.
Website: http://www.husson.edu/college-of-business/school-of-business-and-management/master-of-business-administration-mba/

Idaho State University, Office of Graduate Studies, College of Education, Department of Sport Science and Physical Education, Pocatello, ID 83209-8105. Offers athletic administration (MPE); athletic training (MSAT). *Program availability:* Part-time. *Degree requirements:* For master's, comprehensive exam (for some programs), thesis optional, internship, oral defense of dissertation, or written exams. *Entrance requirements:* For master's, MAT or GRE General Test, minimum GPA of 3.0 in upper division classes. Additional exam requirements/recommendations for international students: Required—TOEFL (minimum score 550 paper-based; 80 iBT). Electronic applications accepted. *Faculty research:* Gender and diversity; concussion awareness/sports medicine; legal aspects of athletic health care; sports psychology; exercise physiology; sports management and leadership; adapted activities; fitness, wellness, and nutrition; coaching perspectives; critical features of athletic activities.

Indiana State University, College of Graduate and Professional Studies, College of Health and Human Services, Department of Kinesiology, Recreation, and Sport, Terre Haute, IN 47809. Offers physical education (MS); recreation and sport management (MS); sport management (PhD). *Degree requirements:* For master's, comprehensive exam (for some programs), thesis (for some programs). *Entrance requirements:* For master's, GRE General Test, undergraduate major in related field. Electronic applications accepted.

Indiana University Bloomington, School of Public Health, Department of Kinesiology, Bloomington, IN 47405. Offers applied sport science (MS); athletic administration/sport management (MS); athletic training (MS); biomechanics (MS); ergonomics (MS); exercise physiology (MS); human performance (PhD), including biomechanics, exercise physiology, motor learning/control, sport management; motor learning/control (MS); physical activity (MPH); physical activity, fitness and wellness (MS). *Program availability:* Part-time. Terminal master's awarded for partial completion of doctoral program. *Degree requirements:* For master's, thesis optional; for doctorate, variable foreign language requirement, comprehensive exam, thesis/dissertation. *Entrance requirements:* For master's, GRE General Test, minimum GPA 2.8; for doctorate, GRE General Test, minimum graduate GPA of 3.5, undergraduate 3.0. Additional exam requirements/recommendations for international students: Required—TOEFL (minimum score 80 iBT). *Faculty research:* Exercise physiology and biochemistry, sports biomechanics, human motor control, adaptation of fitness and exercise to special populations.

Indiana University Bloomington, School of Public Health, Department of Recreation, Park, and Tourism Studies, Bloomington, IN 47405-7000. Offers leisure behavior (PhD); outdoor recreation (MS); park and public lands management (MS); recreation administration (MS); recreational sports administration (MS); recreational therapy (MS); tourism management (MS). Terminal master's awarded for partial completion of doctoral program. *Degree requirements:* For master's, thesis optional; for doctorate, comprehensive exam, thesis/dissertation. *Entrance requirements:* For master's, GRE General Test, minimum GPA of 2.8; for doctorate, GRE General Test, minimum GPA of 3.0 (undergraduate), 3.5 (graduate). Additional exam requirements/recommendations for international students: Required—TOEFL (minimum score 550 paper-based; 80 iBT). Electronic applications accepted. *Faculty research:* Leisure counseling, gerontology, special populations, planning and development.

Indiana University of Pennsylvania, School of Graduate Studies and Research, College of Health and Human Services, Department of Kinesiology, Health, and Sport Science, Program in Sport Science/Sport Management, Indiana, PA 15705. Offers MS. *Faculty:* 10 full-time (3 women). *Students:* 14 full-time (8 women), 6 part-time (9 women); includes 1 minority (Black or African American, non-Hispanic/Latino), 1 international. Average age 25. 21 applicants, 90% accepted, 10 enrolled. In 2017, 12 master's awarded. *Degree requirements:* For master's, thesis or internship. *Entrance requirements:* Additional exam requirements/recommendations for international students: Required—TOEFL (minimum score 540 paper-based). Application fee: $50. *Expenses:* Contact institution. *Financial support:* In 2017–18, 7 research assistantships with tuition reimbursements (averaging $4,417 per year) were awarded. Financial award application deadline: 4/15; financial award applicants required to submit FAFSA. *Unit head:* Dr. Richard Hsaio, Graduate Coordinator, 724-357-0123, E-mail: hsaio@iup.edu.
Website: http://www.iup.edu/grad/sportscience/default.aspx

Iona College, School of Business, Department of Marketing and International Business, New Rochelle, NY 10801-1890. Offers international business (AC, PMC); marketing (MBA); sports and entertainment management (AC). *Program availability:* Part-time, evening/weekend. *Faculty:* 3 full-time (1 woman), 1 (woman) part-time/adjunct. *Students:* 13 full-time (8 women), 16 part-time (6 women); includes 10 minority (5 Black or African American, non-Hispanic/Latino; 1 Asian, non-Hispanic/Latino; 4 Hispanic/Latino), 2 international. Average age 24. 15 applicants, 100% accepted, 9 enrolled. In 2017, 21 master's, 65 other advanced degrees awarded. *Entrance requirements:* For master's, GMAT, 2 letters of recommendation, minimum GPA of 3.0; for other advanced degree, GMAT, minimum GPA of 3.0. Additional exam requirements/recommendations for international students: Required—TOEFL (minimum score 550 paper-based; 80 iBT), IELTS (minimum score 6.5). *Application deadline:* For fall admission, 8/15 priority date for domestic students, 8/1 priority date for international students; for winter admission, 11/15 priority date for domestic students, 11/1 priority date for international students; for spring admission, 2/15 priority date for domestic students, 2/1 priority date for international students; for summer admission, 5/15 for domestic students, 5/1 priority date for international students. Applications are processed on a rolling basis. Application fee: $50. Electronic applications accepted. *Expenses:* Contact institution. *Financial support:* In 2017–18, 7 students received support. Scholarships/grants, tuition waivers (partial), and unspecified assistantships available. Support available to part-time students. Financial award application deadline: 4/15; financial award applicants required to submit FAFSA. *Faculty research:* Business ethics, international retailing, mega-marketing, consumer behavior and consumer confidence. *Unit head:* Dr. Susan G. Rozensher, Department Chair, 914-637-2748, E-mail: srozensher@iona.edu. *Application contact:* Katelyn Brunck, Director of MBA Admissions, 914-633-2451, Fax: 914-633-2277, E-mail: kbrunck@iona.edu.
Website: http://www.iona.edu/Academics/Hagan-School-of-Business/Departments/Marketing/Graduate-Programs.aspx

Ithaca College, School of Business, Program in Business Administration, Ithaca, NY 14850. Offers sport management (MBA). *Accreditation:* AACSB. *Program availability:* Part-time. *Faculty:* 6 full-time (4 women). *Students:* 8 full-time (2 women), 2 part-time (1 woman). Average age 24. 18 applicants, 56% accepted, 8 enrolled. In 2017, 12 master's awarded. *Entrance requirements:* For master's, GMAT. Additional exam requirements/recommendations for international students: Required—TOEFL (minimum score 550 paper-based; 80 iBT). *Application deadline:* For fall admission, 5/15 for domestic and international students; for spring admission, 11/1 for domestic and international students. Applications are processed on a rolling basis. Application fee: $40. Electronic applications accepted. *Expenses:* Contact institution. *Financial support:* In 2017–18, 7 students received support, including 5 fellowships (averaging $7,600 per year); career-related internships or fieldwork, Federal Work-Study, and scholarships/grants also available. Support available to part-time students. Financial award application deadline: 3/1; financial award applicants required to submit FAFSA. *Unit head:* Dr. Rasoul Rezvanian, Associate Dean and Director, MBA Programs, 607-274-1762, Fax: 607-274-1263, E-mail: rrezvanian@ithaca.edu. *Application contact:* Nicole Eversley Bradwell, Director, Office of Admission, 607-274-3124, Fax: 607-274-1263, E-mail: admission@ithaca.edu.
Website: http://www.ithaca.edu/business/programs/busadmin

Jackson State University, Graduate School, College of Education and Human Development, Department of Health, Physical Education and Recreation, Jackson, MS 39217. Offers physical education (MS Ed); sport science (MS). *Accreditation:* NCATE. *Program availability:* Part-time, evening/weekend, 100% online, blended/hybrid learning. *Degree requirements:* For master's, comprehensive exam, thesis or alternative. *Entrance requirements:* For master's, GRE General Test. Additional exam requirements/recommendations for international students: Required—TOEFL (minimum score 520 paper-based; 67 iBT). Electronic applications accepted. *Expenses:* Contact institution.

Jacksonville University, Brooks Rehabilitation College of Healthcare Sciences, School of Applied Health Sciences, Program in Sport Management, Jacksonville, FL 32211. Offers MS. Program offered in conjunction with the Davis College of Business. *Program availability:* Part-time, online only, 100% online. *Faculty:* 3 full-time (1 woman), 1 (woman) part-time/adjunct. *Students:* 11 full-time (4 women), 19 part-time (11 women); includes 16 minority (11 Black or African American, non-Hispanic/Latino; 3 Hispanic/Latino; 2 Two or more races, non-Hispanic/Latino). Average age 26. 27 applicants, 100% accepted, 16 enrolled. *Entrance requirements:* For master's, GRE (minimum total score of 290), baccalaureate degree from accredited college or university with minimum GPA of 3.0; official transcripts; essay on personal professional goals (minimum 1000 words); resume (education, work experience); 3 letters of recommendation; interview. Additional exam requirements/recommendations for international students: Required—TOEFL (minimum score 650 paper-based; 114 iBT), IELTS (minimum score 8). *Application deadline:* For fall admission, 2/1 priority date for domestic students, 2/1 for international students. Applications are processed on a rolling basis. Application fee: $50. Electronic applications accepted. *Expenses:* $630 per credit hour. *Financial support:* Federal Work-Study, institutionally sponsored loans, scholarships/grants, and health care benefits available. Support available to part-time students. Financial award application deadline: 3/15; financial award applicants required to submit FAFSA. *Unit head:* Dr. Carol Dole, Department Chair, Sport Business/Professor of Economics, 904-256-7003, E-mail: cdole@ju.edu. *Application contact:* Ashlea Rieser, Assistant Director of Enrollment and Advising, 904-256-8934, E-mail: arieser0@ju.edu.
Website: http://www.ju.edu/chs/ahs/sportmanagement/

Johnson & Wales University, Graduate Studies, MBA Program, Providence, RI 02903-3703. Offers accounting (MBA); business administration (MBA); finance (MBA); global fashion merchandising and management (MBA); hospitality (MBA); human resource management (MBA); information security/assurance (MBA); information technology (MBA); nonprofit management (MBA); operations and supply chain management (MBA); organizational leadership (MBA); organizational psychology (MBA); sport leadership (MBA). Program also offered on Denver campus. *Program availability:* Part-time, online learning. *Entrance requirements:* For master's, minimum GPA of 2.75. Additional exam requirements/recommendations for international students: Required—TOEFL (minimum score 550 paper-based); Recommended—IELTS, TWE. *Application deadline:* For fall admission, 8/15 priority date for domestic students, 6/28 priority date for international students; for winter admission, 11/10 priority date for domestic students, 9/20 priority date for international students; for spring admission, 2/5 priority date for domestic students, 12/20 priority date for international students. Applications are processed on a rolling basis. *Expenses:* Tuition: Full-time $12,636; part-time $702 per credit hour. *Financial support:* Tuition waivers (partial) and unspecified assistantships available. Support available to part-time students. Financial award application deadline: 5/1. *Faculty research:* International banking, global economy, international trade, cultural differences. *Unit head:* Dr. Karen Silva, Director, 401-598-2849, Fax: 401-598-1125. *Application contact:* Graduate School Admissions, 401-598-1015, Fax: 401-598-1286, E-mail: gradadm@jwu.edu.

Johnson & Wales University, Graduate Studies, MS Program in Sport Leadership, Providence, RI 02903-3703. Offers MS. *Expenses:* Tuition: Full-time $12,636; part-time $702 per credit hour. *Unit head:* Louis A. Pullano, Director, 401-598-1358, E-mail: louis.pullano@jwu.edu. *Application contact:* Graduate School Admissions, 401-598-1015, Fax: 401-598-1286, E-mail: pvdgrad@admissions.jwu.edu.
Website: https://www.jwu.edu/academics/programs-by-campus/providence-programs/sport-leadership-ms.html

Kansas Wesleyan University, Program in Business Administration, Salina, KS 67401-6196. Offers business administration (MBA); sports management (MBA). *Program availability:* Part-time, evening/weekend. *Entrance requirements:* For master's, GMAT, minimum graduate GPA of 3.0 or undergraduate GPA of 3.25.

Kent State University, College of Education, Health and Human Services, School of Foundations, Leadership and Administration, Sports Recreation and Management Program, Kent, OH 44242-0001. Offers sport and recreation management (MA); sports studies (MA). *Degree requirements:* For master's, thesis optional. *Entrance requirements:* For master's, GRE if undergraduate GPA below 3.0, goals statement, 2 letters of recommendation. Additional exam requirements/recommendations for international students: Required—TOEFL (minimum score 550 paper-based; 80 iBT). *Expenses:* Tuition, state resident: full-time $11,310; part-time $515 per credit hour. Tuition, nonresident: full-time $20,396; part-time $928 per credit hour. International tuition: $18,544 full-time.

Keystone College, Program in Sport Leadership and Management, La Plume, PA 18440. Offers MS. *Program availability:* Part-time, online only, 100% online. *Faculty:* 2 full-time (0 women). *Students:* 5 full-time (4 women), 1 part-time (0 women). 2 applicants, 100% accepted, 1 enrolled. In 2017, 9 master's awarded. *Degree requirements:* For master's, internship or research project. *Entrance requirements:* For master's, college transcripts, resume or curriculum vitae. Additional exam requirements/recommendations for international students: Required—TOEFL (minimum score 80 iBT) or IELTS (minimum score 6.5). *Application deadline:* For fall admission, 8/1 for domestic students; for spring admission, 12/1 for domestic students; for summer admission, 5/1 for domestic students. Applications are processed on a rolling basis. Application fee: $0. Electronic applications accepted. *Expenses:* $650 per credit. *Financial support:* In

2017–18, 1 student received support. Unspecified assistantships available. Financial award application deadline: 5/1; financial award applicants required to submit FAFSA. *Application contact:* Jennifer Sekol, Director of Admissions, 570-945-8117, Fax: 570-945-7916, E-mail: jennifer.sekol@keystone.edu.

Lasell College, Graduate and Professional Studies in Sport Management, Newton, MA 02466-2709. Offers athletic administration (MS); parks and recreation (MS); sport leadership (MS, Graduate Certificate); sport tourism and hospitality (MS). *Program availability:* Part-time, evening/weekend, online only, 100% online. *Faculty:* 5 full-time (1 woman), 2 part-time/adjunct (1 woman). *Students:* 10 full-time (6 women), 25 part-time (8 women); includes 12 minority (9 Black or African American, non-Hispanic/Latino; 3 Hispanic/Latino). Average age 29. 35 applicants, 46% accepted, 11 enrolled. In 2017, 26 master's awarded. *Degree requirements:* For master's, minimum GPA of 3.0; internship or thesis. *Entrance requirements:* For master's, one-page personal statement, 2 letters of recommendation, resume, bachelor's degree transcript; for Graduate Certificate, bachelor's degree transcript, 2 letters of recommendation, 1-page personal statement, resume. Additional exam requirements/recommendations for international students: Required—TOEFL (minimum score 550 paper-based, 79 iBT) or IELTS (minimum score 6). *Application deadline:* For fall admission, 8/31 priority date for domestic students, 6/30 priority date for international students; for spring admission, 12/31 priority date for domestic students, 10/31 priority date for international students. Applications are processed on a rolling basis. Electronic applications accepted. *Expenses:* $600 per credit. *Financial support:* Federal Work-Study, scholarships/grants, and tuition discounts available. Support available to part-time students. Financial award application deadline: 8/31; financial award applicants required to submit FAFSA. *Faculty research:* How do fans attribute team failure; investigating cross-cultural difference in attribution; sense of ownership as a key predictor of fan loyalty; fans' normative beliefs about sponsorship and sponsors; investigation of new attitudinal variables in sponsorship. *Unit head:* Eric Turner, Vice President of Graduate and Professional Studies, 617-243-2071, Fax: 617-243-2450, E-mail: gradinfo@lasell.edu. *Application contact:* Adrienne Franciosi, Director of Graduate Enrollment, 617-243-2214, Fax: 617-243-2450, E-mail: gradinfo@lasell.edu.
Website: http://www.lasell.edu/academics/graduate-and-professional-studies/programs-of-study/master-of-science-in-sport-management.html

Lewis University, College of Arts and Sciences, Program in Organizational Leadership, Romeoville, IL 60446. Offers higher education/student services (MA); non-profit management (MA); organizational and leadership coaching (MA); organizational management (MA); training and development (MA). *Program availability:* Part-time, evening/weekend, 100% online, blended/hybrid learning. *Students:* 16 full-time (11 women), 154 part-time (115 women); includes 49 minority (27 Black or African American, non-Hispanic/Latino; 1 American Indian or Alaska Native, non-Hispanic/Latino; 4 Asian, non-Hispanic/Latino; 12 Hispanic/Latino; 5 Two or more races, non-Hispanic/Latino), 4 international. Average age 37. *Entrance requirements:* For master's, bachelor's degree, personal statement, minimum GPA of 3.0, letters of recommendation. Additional exam requirements/recommendations for international students: Required—TOEFL (minimum score 550 paper-based; 79 iBT), IELTS (minimum score 6). *Application deadline:* For fall admission, 5/1 priority date for international students; for spring admission, 11/15 priority date for international students. Applications are processed on a rolling basis. Application fee: $40. Electronic applications accepted. Tuition and fees vary according to program. *Financial support:* Federal Work-Study, tuition waivers, and unspecified assistantships available. Financial award application deadline: 5/1; financial award applicants required to submit FAFSA. *Unit head:* Dr. Lesley Page, Chair of Organizational Leadership, 815-838-0500, E-mail: pagele@lewisu.edu. *Application contact:* Kathy Lisak, Graduate Admission Counselor, 815-836-5610, E-mail: grad@lewisu.edu.

Liberty University, School of Education, Lynchburg, VA 24515. Offers curriculum and instruction (Ed D, Ed S), including elementary education, middle grades education, secondary education, special education; educational leadership (Ed D); gifted education (Certificate); math specialist (M Ed); middle grades (MAT, Certificate); reading specialist (M Ed); school leadership (Certificate); secondary education (MAT); sport management (MS), including coaching and athletic administration, outdoor adventure sport, sport administration, tourism. *Accreditation:* NCATE. *Program availability:* Part-time, online learning. *Students:* 1,966 full-time (1,428 women), 3,484 part-time (2,528 women); includes 1,323 minority (1,026 Black or African American, non-Hispanic/Latino; 29 American Indian or Alaska Native, non-Hispanic/Latino; 49 Asian, non-Hispanic/Latino; 100 Hispanic/Latino; 9 Native Hawaiian or other Pacific Islander, non-Hispanic/Latino; 110 Two or more races, non-Hispanic/Latino), 58 international. Average age 37. 3,748 applicants, 58% accepted, 1167 enrolled. In 2017, 656 master's, 110 doctorates, 316 other advanced degrees awarded. *Degree requirements:* For doctorate, comprehensive exam, thesis/dissertation. *Entrance requirements:* For master's, GRE General Test or MAT (if taken in or before 1999), 2 letters of recommendation, minimum undergraduate GPA of 3.0, curriculum vitae; for doctorate and other advanced degree, GRE General Test or MAT (if taken before 1999), minimum master's GPA of 3.0, 3 years of teaching experience. Additional exam requirements/recommendations for international students: Required—TOEFL (minimum score 600 paper-based; 100 iBT). *Application deadline:* For fall admission, 6/1 for domestic students; for spring admission, 11/1 for domestic students. Applications are processed on a rolling basis. Application fee: $50. Electronic applications accepted. *Expenses:* Contact institution. *Financial support:* Federal Work-Study and tuition waivers (partial) available. *Faculty research:* Self-determination, character education, bibliotherapy, learning styles, distance education. *Unit head:* Dr. Heather Schoffstall, Dean, 434-582-2445, Fax: 434-582-2468, E-mail: awgunter@liberty.edu. *Application contact:* Jay Bridge, Director of Graduate Admissions, 800-424-9595, Fax: 800-628-7977, E-mail: gradadmissions@liberty.edu.
Website: http://www.liberty.edu/academics/education/graduate/

Lindenwood University, Graduate Programs, Plaster School of Business and Entrepreneurship, St. Charles, MO 63301-1695. Offers accountancy (M Acc); accounting (MBA); business administration (MBA); entrepreneurial studies (MBA); finance (MBA, MS); human resource management (MBA); international business (MBA); leadership (MA); management (MBA); marketing (MBA, MS); nonprofit administration (MA); public administration (MBA); sport management (MBA); supply chain management (MBA). *Accreditation:* ACBSP. *Program availability:* Part-time, evening/weekend, 100% online. *Faculty:* 15 full-time (8 women), 26 part-time/adjunct (9 women). *Students:* 201 full-time (116 women), 253 part-time (153 women); includes 102 minority (80 Black or African American, non-Hispanic/Latino; 2 American Indian or Alaska Native, non-Hispanic/Latino; 6 Asian, non-Hispanic/Latino; 7 Hispanic/Latino; 7 Two or more races, non-Hispanic/Latino), 61 international. Average age 32. 370 applicants, 42% accepted, 134 enrolled. In 2017, 178 master's awarded. *Degree requirements:* For master's, comprehensive exam (for some programs), thesis (for some programs), minimum GPA of 3.0. *Entrance requirements:* For master's, interview, minimum undergraduate cumulative GPA of 3.0, letter of recommendation. Additional exam requirements/recommendations for international students: Required—TOEFL (minimum score 550 paper-based; 80 iBT); Recommended—IELTS (minimum score 6.5). *Application deadline:* For fall admission, 8/27 priority date for domestic and international students; for winter admission, 1/14 priority date for domestic and international students; for spring admission, 3/18 for domestic students, 3/18 priority date for international students; for

Sports Management

summer admission, 6/3 priority date for domestic and international students. Applications are processed on a rolling basis. Application fee: $30 ($100 for international students). Electronic applications accepted. *Expenses:* Contact institution. *Financial support:* In 2017–18, 439 students received support. Career-related internships or fieldwork, Federal Work-Study, institutionally sponsored loans, scholarships/grants, tuition waivers (partial), and unspecified assistantships available. Financial award application deadline: 6/30; financial award applicants required to submit FAFSA. *Unit head:* Roger Ellis, Dean, School of Business and Entrepreneurship, 636-949-4839, E-mail: rellis@lindenwood.edu. *Application contact:* Kara Schilli, Director, Evening and Graduate Admissions, 636-949-4349, Fax: 636-949-4109, E-mail: adultadmissions@lindenwood.edu.
Website: http://www.lindenwood.edu/academics/academic-schools/robert-w-plaster-school-of-business-entrepreneurship/

Lock Haven University of Pennsylvania, The Stephen Poorman College of Business, Information Systems, and Human Services, Lock Haven, PA 17745-2390. Offers clinical mental health counseling (MS); sport science (MS). *Program availability:* Online learning. *Degree requirements:* For master's, thesis. *Entrance requirements:* For master's, minimum undergraduate GPA of 3.0. Additional exam requirements/recommendations for international students: Required—TOEFL. Electronic applications accepted.

Lynn University, College of Business and Management, Boca Raton, FL 33431-5598. Offers business administration (MBA), including aviation management, entrepreneurial management, financial valuation and investment management, hospitality management, human resource management, international business management, marketing, media management, social innovation management, sports management, Web development. *Program availability:* Part-time, evening/weekend, 100% online, blended/hybrid learning. *Faculty:* 29 full-time (11 women), 19 part-time/adjunct (7 women). *Students:* 287 full-time (124 women), 195 part-time (105 women); includes 110 minority (44 Black or African American, non-Hispanic/Latino; 2 American Indian or Alaska Native, non-Hispanic/Latino; 11 Asian, non-Hispanic/Latino; 47 Hispanic/Latino; 6 Two or more races, non-Hispanic/Latino), 135 international. Average age 28. 293 applicants, 94% accepted, 192 enrolled. In 2017, 236 master's awarded. *Degree requirements:* For master's, thesis, minimum GPA of 3.0, strategic management seminar, written presentation reflecting the integration and application of theory to practice. *Entrance requirements:* For master's, bachelor's degree from accredited institution, minimum undergraduate GPA of 2.5, official undergraduate transcripts, resume, personal statement, letter of recommendation from academic or professional sources, writing sample demonstrating capacity to perform at graduate level. Additional exam requirements/recommendations for international students: Required—TOEFL (minimum score 550 paper-based; 80 iBT), IELTS (minimum score 6.5). *Application deadline:* For fall admission, 8/18 for domestic students, 8/4 for international students; for spring admission, 12/15 for domestic students, 12/1 for international students; for summer admission, 4/17 for domestic students, 4/3 for international students. Applications are processed on a rolling basis. Application fee: $45. Electronic applications accepted. *Expenses:* $740 per credit. *Financial support:* Career-related internships or fieldwork, Federal Work-Study, scholarships/grants, tuition waivers (full and partial), and unspecified assistantships available. Support available to part-time students. Financial award application deadline: 3/1; financial award applicants required to submit FAFSA. *Faculty research:* Knowledge economy, urban economy, U.S. manufacturing industries, leadership personality, stock market reactions to terrorism, personality psychology, industrial/organizational psychology. *Unit head:* Dr. RT Good, Dean of the College of Business and Management, 561-237-7458, E-mail: rgood@lynn.edu. *Application contact:* Steven Pruitt, Director of Graduate and Undergraduate Evening Admission, 561-237-7834, Fax: 561-237-7100, E-mail: spruitt@lynn.edu.
Website: http://www.lynn.edu/academics/colleges/business-and-management

Manhattanville College, School of Business, Master of Science in Sport Business and Entertainment Management Program, Purchase, NY 10577-2132. Offers sport business and entertainment management (MS, Advanced Certificate), including entertainment management (MS), sport business (MS). *Program availability:* Part-time, evening/weekend. *Faculty:* 9 part-time/adjunct (0 women). *Students:* 36 full-time (11 women), 4 part-time (1 woman); includes 12 minority (2 Black or African American, non-Hispanic/Latino; 1 American Indian or Alaska Native, non-Hispanic/Latino; 9 Hispanic/Latino), 7 international. Average age 27. 35 applicants, 51% accepted, 12 enrolled. In 2017, 25 master's awarded. *Degree requirements:* For master's, thesis (for some programs), internship, portfolio. *Entrance requirements:* For master's, personal essay, transcripts, 2 letters of recommendation (academic or professional), resume, health form with proof of immunization (for those born after 1957). Additional exam requirements/recommendations for international students: Required—TOEFL (minimum score 563 paper-based, 85 iBT), IELTS (7), or iTEP (B2). *Application deadline:* Applications are processed on a rolling basis. Application fee: $75. Electronic applications accepted. *Expenses:* $915 per credit. *Financial support:* Federal Work-Study, institutionally sponsored loans, scholarships/grants, and unspecified assistantships available. Financial award application deadline: 3/15; financial award applicants required to submit FAFSA. *Unit head:* David Torromeo, Program Director, 914-323-5301, Fax: 914-694-3488, E-mail: david.torromeo@mville.edu. *Application contact:* Monika Pottgen, Assistant Director, Recruitment and Admissions, 914-323-5150, E-mail: business@mville.edu.
Website: https://www.mville.edu/programs/ms-sport-business-and-entertainment-management

Marquette University, Graduate School of Management, Executive MBA Program, Milwaukee, WI 53201-1881. Offers economics (MBA); finance (MBA); human resources (MBA); international business (MBA); management information systems (MBA); marketing (MBA); operations and supply chain management (MBA); sports business (MBA). *Accreditation:* AACSB. *Degree requirements:* For master's, international trip. *Entrance requirements:* For master's, GMAT or GRE, two letters of recommendation, official transcripts from current and previous colleges/universities. Additional exam requirements/recommendations for international students: Required—TOEFL (minimum score 550 paper-based; 88 iBT), IELTS (minimum score 6.5), PTE. Electronic applications accepted. *Expenses:* Contact institution. *Faculty research:* International trade and finance, customer relationship management, consumer satisfaction, customer service.

Marquette University, Graduate School of Management, Program in Business Administration, Milwaukee, WI 53201-1881. Offers business administration (MBA); economics (MBA); entrepreneurship (Certificate); finance (MBA); human resources (MBA); international business (MBA); management information systems (MBA); marketing (MBA); operations and supply chain management (MBA); sports business (MBA); JD/MBA; MBA/MA; MBA/MSN. *Accreditation:* AACSB. *Program availability:* Part-time, evening/weekend. *Degree requirements:* For Certificate, business plan. *Entrance requirements:* For master's, GMAT or GRE, letters of recommendation. Additional exam requirements/recommendations for international students: Required—TOEFL (minimum score 550 paper-based; 88 iBT), IELTS (minimum score 6.5), PTE. Electronic applications accepted. *Faculty research:* Ethics in the professions, services marketing, technology impact on decision-making, mentoring.

Marshall University, Academic Affairs Division, College of Health Professions, School of Kinesiology, Program in Sport Administration, Huntington, WV 25755. Offers MS. *Students:* 14 full-time (3 women), 3 part-time (all women); includes 3 minority (1 Black or African American, non-Hispanic/Latino; 2 Native Hawaiian or other Pacific Islander, non-Hispanic/Latino). Average age 24. In 2017, 6 master's awarded. *Degree requirements:* For master's, thesis optional, comprehensive assessment. *Entrance requirements:* For master's, GRE General Test. Application fee: $40. *Unit head:* Dr. Jennifer Mak, Director, 304-696-2927, E-mail: mak@marshall.edu. *Application contact:* Information Contact, 304-746-1900, Fax: 304-746-1902, E-mail: services@marshall.edu.

Maryville University of Saint Louis, The John E. Simon School of Business, St. Louis, MO 63141-7299. Offers accounting (MBA, MS, Certificate); business studies (Certificate); cybersecurity (MBA, MS, Certificate); financial services (MBA, Certificate); healthcare practice management (MBA, Certificate); human resource management (MBA, Certificate); information technology (MBA, Certificate); management (MBA, Certificate); management and leadership (MA); marketing (MBA, Certificate); project management (MBA, Certificate); sport business management (MBA); supply chain management (Certificate); supply chain management/logistics (MBA). *Accreditation:* ACBSP. *Program availability:* Part-time, 100% online, blended/hybrid learning. *Faculty:* 5 full-time (3 women), 51 part-time/adjunct (16 women). *Students:* 222 full-time (96 women), 498 part-time (222 women); includes 185 minority (104 Black or African American, non-Hispanic/Latino; 5 American Indian or Alaska Native, non-Hispanic/Latino; 30 Asian, non-Hispanic/Latino; 37 Hispanic/Latino; 9 Two or more races, non-Hispanic/Latino), 26 international. Average age 33. In 2017, 106 master's awarded. *Degree requirements:* For master's, capstone course (for MBA). *Entrance requirements:* Additional exam requirements/recommendations for international students: Required—TOEFL (minimum score 563 paper-based; 85 iBT). *Application deadline:* Applications are processed on a rolling basis. Electronic applications accepted. *Expenses:* Contact institution. *Financial support:* Career-related internships or fieldwork, Federal Work-Study, tuition waivers (partial), and campus employment available. Financial award application deadline: 4/1; financial award applicants required to submit FAFSA. *Unit head:* Pam Horwitz, Interim Dean, 314-529-9680, Fax: 314-529-9975. *Application contact:* Dustin Loeffler, Director for Graduate Studies in Business, 314-529-9571, Fax: 314-529-9975, E-mail: dloeffler@maryville.edu.
Website: http://www.maryville.edu/bu/business-administration-masters/

Mercyhurst University, Graduate Studies, Program in Organizational Leadership, Erie, PA 16546. Offers accounting (MS); higher education administration (MS); human resources (MS); organizational leadership (MS, Certificate); sports leadership (MS); strategy and innovation (MS). *Program availability:* Part-time, evening/weekend. *Degree requirements:* For master's, thesis. *Entrance requirements:* For master's, GRE General Test or MAT, interview, resume, essay, three professional references, transcripts. Additional exam requirements/recommendations for international students: Required—TOEFL (minimum score 80 iBT), IELTS (minimum score 6.5). Electronic applications accepted. *Faculty research:* Leadership training, organizational communication, leadership pedagogy.

Messiah College, Program in Higher Education, Mechanicsburg, PA 17055. Offers college athletics management (MA); self-designed concentration (MA); student affairs (MA). *Program availability:* Part-time. Electronic applications accepted. *Faculty research:* College athletics management, assessment and student learning outcomes, the life and legacy of Ernest L. Boyer, common learning, student affairs practice.

Midwestern State University, Billie Doris McAda Graduate School, West College of Education, Program in Sport Administration, Wichita Falls, TX 76308. Offers M Ed.

Millersville University of Pennsylvania, College of Graduate Studies and Adult Learning, College of Education and Human Services, Department of Wellness and Sport Sciences, Program in Sport Management: Athletic Coaching Option, Millersville, PA 17551-0302. Offers coaching education (Post-Master's Certificate); sport management (M Ed), including athletic coaching. *Program availability:* Part-time, evening/weekend. *Faculty:* 6 full-time (3 women). *Students:* 1 full-time (0 women), 4 part-time (0 women); includes 2 minority (1 Black or African American, non-Hispanic/Latino; 1 Asian, non-Hispanic/Latino), 1 international. Average age 26. 4 applicants, 75% accepted, 2 enrolled. In 2017, 6 master's awarded. *Degree requirements:* For master's, thesis optional, internship. *Entrance requirements:* For master's, GRE, MAT, GMAT, or interview with writing assignment if undergraduate cumulative GPA lower than 3.0, all transcripts, at least 1 academic reference, sport management goal statement. Additional exam requirements/recommendations for international students: Required—TOEFL (minimum score 80 iBT), IELTS (minimum score 6.5), PTE (minimum score 60). *Application deadline:* Applications are processed on a rolling basis. Application fee: $40. Electronic applications accepted. *Expenses:* $500 per credit resident tuition and fees; $750 per credit non-resident tuition and fees; $114.75 per credit general fee (maximum of 12 credits); technology fee $27 per credit (resident), $39 per credit (non-resident). *Financial support:* In 2017–18, 2 students received support. Unspecified assistantships available. Financial award application deadline: 3/15; financial award applicants required to submit FAFSA. *Faculty research:* Applied sport management; leadership and sport; marketing and sport; gender and sport; leadership development; ADR, restorative justice and hazing; legal issues applied to sport management; women and fitness/sport. *Unit head:* Dr. Rebecca J. Mowrey, Coordinator, 717-871-4214, Fax: 717-871-7987, E-mail: rebecca.mowrey@millersville.edu. *Application contact:* Dr. Victor S. DeSantis, Dean of College of Graduate Studies and Adult Learning/Associate Provost for Civic and Community Engagement, 717-871-7619, Fax: 717-871-7954, E-mail: victor.desantis@millersville.edu.
Website: http://www.millersville.edu/wssd/graduate/index.php

Millersville University of Pennsylvania, College of Graduate Studies and Adult Learning, College of Education and Human Services, Department of Wellness and Sport Sciences, Program in Sport Management: Athletic Management Option, Millersville, PA 17551-0302. Offers M Ed. *Program availability:* Part-time. *Faculty:* 6 full-time (3 women). *Students:* 14 full-time (7 women), 14 part-time (6 women); includes 9 minority (5 Black or African American, non-Hispanic/Latino; 3 Hispanic/Latino; 1 Two or more races, non-Hispanic/Latino). Average age 26. 28 applicants, 89% accepted, 13 enrolled. In 2017, 11 master's awarded. *Degree requirements:* For master's, thesis optional, internship. *Entrance requirements:* For master's, GRE, MAT, GMAT, or interview with writing assignment if undergraduate cumulative GPA lower than 3.0, all transcripts, at least 1 academic reference, sport management goal statement. Additional exam requirements/recommendations for international students: Required—TOEFL (minimum score 80 iBT), IELTS (minimum score 6.5), PTE (minimum score 60). *Application deadline:* Applications are processed on a rolling basis. Application fee: $40. Electronic applications accepted. *Expenses:* $500 per credit resident tuition and fees; $750 per credit non-resident tuition and fees; $114.75 per credit general fee (maximum of 12 credits); technology fee $27 per credit (resident), $39 per credit (non-resident). *Financial support:* In 2017–18, 11 students received support. Unspecified assistantships available. Financial award application deadline: 3/15; financial award applicants required to submit FAFSA. *Faculty research:* Applied sport management; leadership and sport; marketing and sport; gender and sport; leadership development; ADR, restorative justice and hazing; legal issues applied to sport management; women and fitness/sport; growth and physical activity. *Unit head:* Dr. Rebecca J. Mowrey, Coordinator, 717-871-

4214, Fax: 717-871-7987, E-mail: rebecca.mowrey@millersville.edu. *Application contact:* Dr. Victor S. DeSantis, Dean of College of Graduate Studies and Adult Learning/Associate Provost for Civic and Community Engagement, 717-871-7619, Fax: 717-871-7954, E-mail: victor.desantis@millersville.edu.
Website: http://www.millersville.edu/wssd/graduate/index.php

Misericordia University, College of Business, Master of Business Administration Program, Dallas, PA 18612-1098. Offers accounting (MBA); healthcare management (MBA); human resource management (MBA); management (MBA); sport management (MBA). *Program availability:* Part-time, evening/weekend, online learning. *Entrance requirements:* For master's, GMAT, MAT, GRE (50th percentile or higher), or minimum undergraduate GPA of 3.0, interview. Additional exam requirements/recommendations for international students: Required—TOEFL. Electronic applications accepted. Application fee is waived when completed online. *Expenses:* Contact institution.

Mississippi State University, College of Education, Department of Kinesiology, Mississippi State, MS 39762. Offers disability studies (MS); exercise physiology (MS); exercise science (PhD); sport administration (MS); sport pedagogy (MS); sport studies (PhD). *Program availability:* Part-time, blended/hybrid learning. *Faculty:* 16 full-time (3 women). *Students:* 64 full-time (20 women), 8 part-time (3 women); includes 13 minority (2 Black or African American, non-Hispanic/Latino; 4 Asian, non-Hispanic/Latino; 4 Hispanic/Latino; 3 Two or more races, non-Hispanic/Latino), 10 international. Average age 26. 66 applicants, 59% accepted, 31 enrolled. In 2017, 23 master's awarded. *Degree requirements:* For master's, comprehensive exam, thesis optional; for doctorate, comprehensive exam. *Entrance requirements:* For master's, GRE General Test, minimum GPA of 2.75 on undergraduate work from four-year accredited institution, 3.0 graduate; for doctorate, GRE, minimum GPA of 3.4 on previous graduate degree(s) earned from accredited institutions. Additional exam requirements/recommendations for international students: Required—TOEFL (minimum score 550 paper-based; 79 iBT); Recommended—IELTS (minimum score 6.5). *Application deadline:* For fall admission, 7/1 for domestic students, 5/1 for international students; for spring admission, 11/1 for domestic students, 9/1 for international students. Applications are processed on a rolling basis. Application fee: $60 ($80 for international students). Electronic applications accepted. *Expenses:* Tuition, state resident: full-time $8318; part-time $462.12 per credit hour. Tuition, nonresident: full-time $22,358; part-time $1242.12 per credit hour. *Required fees:* $110; $12.24 per credit hour. $6.12 per semester. *Financial support:* In 2017–18, 13 teaching assistantships with partial tuition reimbursements (averaging $10,510 per year) were awarded; career-related internships or fieldwork, Federal Work-Study, institutionally sponsored loans, and unspecified assistantships also available. Financial award application deadline: 4/1; financial award applicants required to submit FAFSA. *Faculty research:* Static balance and stepping performance of older adults, organizational justice, public health, strength training and recovery drinks, high risk drinking perceptions and behaviors. *Unit head:* Dr. Stanley P. Brown, Professor and Head, 662-325-7229, Fax: 662-325-4525, E-mail: spb107@msstate.edu. *Application contact:* Marina Hung, Admissions and Enrollment Assistant, 662-325-5188, E-mail: lbonner@grad.msstate.edu.
Website: http://www.kinesiology.msstate.edu/

Missouri State University, Graduate College, Interdisciplinary Program in Professional Studies, Springfield, MO 65897. Offers administrative studies (Certificate); applied communication (MS); criminal justice (MS); environmental management (MS); homeland security (MS); individualized (MS); professional studies (MS); screenwriting and producing (MS); sports management (MS). *Program availability:* Part-time, evening/weekend, 100% online, blended/hybrid learning. *Students:* 51 full-time (33 women), 95 part-time (41 women); includes 21 minority (8 Black or African American, non-Hispanic/Latino; 1 Asian, non-Hispanic/Latino; 7 Hispanic/Latino; 5 Two or more races, non-Hispanic/Latino), 37 international. Average age 24. 71 applicants, 69% accepted, 35 enrolled. In 2017, 50 master's awarded. *Degree requirements:* For master's, comprehensive exam, thesis or alternative. *Entrance requirements:* For master's, GRE, GMAT (if GPA less than 3.0). Additional exam requirements/recommendations for international students: Required—TOEFL (minimum score 550 paper-based; 79 iBT), IELTS (minimum score 6). *Application deadline:* For fall admission, 7/15 priority date for domestic students; for spring admission, 12/1 priority date for domestic students; for summer admission, 5/1 for domestic students. Applications are processed on a rolling basis. Application fee: $35 ($50 for international students). Electronic applications accepted. *Expenses:* Tuition, state resident: full-time $2915; part-time $2021 per credit hour. Tuition, nonresident: full-time $5354; part-time $3647 per credit hour. *International tuition:* $11,992 full-time. *Required fees:* $173; $173 per credit hour. Tuition and fees vary according to class time, course level, course load, degree level, campus/location and program. *Financial support:* Career-related internships or fieldwork, Federal Work-Study, institutionally sponsored loans, scholarships/grants, and unspecified assistantships available. Support available to part-time students. Financial award application deadline: 3/31; financial award applicants required to submit FAFSA. *Unit head:* Dr. Gerald Masterson, Program Director, 417-836-5251, Fax: 417-836-6888, E-mail: mps@missouristate.edu. *Application contact:* Stephanie Praschan, Director, Graduate Enrollment Management, 417-836-5330, Fax: 417-836-6200, E-mail: stephaniepraschan@missouristate.edu.
Website: http://mps.missouristate.edu

Missouri Western State University, Program in Applied Science, St. Joseph, MO 64507-2294. Offers chemistry (MAS); engineering technology management (MAS); industrial life science (MAS); sport and fitness management (MAS). *Accreditation:* AACSB. *Program availability:* Part-time. *Students:* 37 full-time (16 women), 20 part-time (9 women); includes 8 minority (6 Black or African American, non-Hispanic/Latino; 1 Asian, non-Hispanic/Latino; 1 Two or more races, non-Hispanic/Latino), 10 international. Average age 27. 28 applicants, 86% accepted, 16 enrolled. In 2017, 32 master's awarded. *Entrance requirements:* Additional exam requirements/recommendations for international students: Recommended—TOEFL (minimum score 79 iBT), IELTS (minimum score 6). *Application deadline:* For fall admission, 7/15 for domestic and international students; for spring admission, 10/1 for domestic and international students; for summer admission, 3/15 for domestic students. Applications are processed on a rolling basis. Application fee: $45 ($50 for international students). Electronic applications accepted. *Expenses:* Tuition, state resident: full-time $6391; part-time $336 per credit hour. Tuition, nonresident: full-time $11,483; part-time $604 per credit hour. *Required fees:* $542; $99 per credit hour. $176 per semester. One-time fee: $45. Tuition and fees vary according to course load and program. *Financial support:* Scholarships/grants and unspecified assistantships available. Support available to part-time students. *Unit head:* Dr. Benjamin D. Caldwell, Dean of the Graduate School, 816-271-4394, Fax: 816-271-4525, E-mail: graduate@missouriwestern.edu.

Montclair State University, The Graduate School, College of Education and Human Services, Program in Exercise Science and Physical Education, Montclair, NJ 07043-1624. Offers exercise science (MA); sports administration and coaching (MA); teaching and supervision in physical education (MA). *Program availability:* Part-time, evening/weekend. *Degree requirements:* For master's, comprehensive exam, thesis or alternative. *Entrance requirements:* For master's, GRE General Test, essay, 2 letters of recommendation. Additional exam requirements/recommendations for international students: Required—TOEFL (minimum score 83 iBT), IELTS (minimum score 6.5). Electronic applications accepted.

Morehead State University, Graduate Programs, College of Business and Public Affairs, School of Business Administration, Morehead, KY 40351. Offers business administration (MBA); information systems (MSIS); sport management (MA). *Program availability:* Part-time, evening/weekend. *Entrance requirements:* For master's, GRE or GMAT. Additional exam requirements/recommendations for international students: Required—TOEFL (minimum score 500 paper-based). Electronic applications accepted.

Mount St. Mary's University, Program in Sport Management, Emmitsburg, MD 21727-7799. Offers MS. *Program availability:* Part-time, evening/weekend. *Degree requirements:* For master's, project or internship. *Entrance requirements:* For master's, personal essay; baccalaureate degree; minimum undergraduate GPA of 2.75, two full years of relevant work experience with resume, or GMAT. Additional exam requirements/recommendations for international students: Required—TOEFL (minimum score 550 paper-based; 83 iBT). Electronic applications accepted. *Expenses:* Contact institution.

Neumann University, Graduate Programs in Business and Information Management, Aston, PA 19014-1298. Offers accounting (MS), including forensic and fraud detection; sport business (MS). *Program availability:* Part-time, evening/weekend. *Faculty:* 2 full-time (both women), 4 part-time/adjunct (1 woman). *Students:* 7 full-time (1 woman), 29 part-time (14 women); includes 12 minority (10 Black or African American, non-Hispanic/Latino; 1 Asian, non-Hispanic/Latino; 1 Hispanic/Latino). Average age 30. 35 applicants, 37% accepted, 7 enrolled. In 2017, 16 master's awarded. *Degree requirements:* For master's, thesis (for some programs). *Entrance requirements:* For master's, official transcripts from all institutions attended, resume, letter of intent, 2-3 letters of recommendation. Additional exam requirements/recommendations for international students: Required—TOEFL (minimum score 70 iBT). *Application deadline:* Applications are processed on a rolling basis. Application fee: $0. Electronic applications accepted. *Expenses:* $600 per credit hour (for accounting program); $495 per credit hour (for sport business program). *Financial support:* Scholarships/grants and health care benefits available. Support available to part-time students. Financial award application deadline: 3/15; financial award applicants required to submit FAFSA. *Unit head:* Dr. Eric R. Wellington, Dean of Business and Information Management, 610-558-5596, Fax: 610-558-5574, E-mail: wellinge@neumann.edu. *Application contact:* Dr. Erika K. Davis, Director of Adult and Graduate Admissions, 800-9-NEUMANN Ext. 5208, Fax: 610-361-2548, E-mail: gradadultadmiss@neumann.edu.

New England College, Program in Sports and Recreation Management: Coaching, Henniker, NH 03242-3293. Offers MS. *Entrance requirements:* For master's, resume, 2 letters of reference.

New Mexico Highlands University, Graduate Studies, College of Arts and Sciences, Department of Exercise and Sport Sciences, Las Vegas, NM 87701. Offers human performance and sport (MA), including human performance and sport sciences, sports administration, teacher education. *Program availability:* Part-time. *Degree requirements:* For master's, comprehensive exam, thesis or alternative. *Entrance requirements:* For master's, minimum undergraduate GPA of 3.0. Additional exam requirements/recommendations for international students: Required—TOEFL (minimum score 540 paper-based). *Faculty research:* Child obesity and physical inactivity, body composition and fitness assessment, motor development, sport marketing, sport finance.

North Carolina State University, Graduate School, College of Natural Resources, Department of Parks, Recreation and Tourism Management, Raleigh, NC 27695. Offers natural resource management (MPRTM, MS); park and recreation management (MPRTM, MS); parks, recreation and tourism management (PhD); recreational sport management (MPRTM, MS); spatial information science (MPRTM, MS); tourism policy and development (MPRTM, MS). *Degree requirements:* For master's, thesis (for some programs); for doctorate, thesis/dissertation. *Entrance requirements:* For master's and doctorate, GRE General Test. Additional exam requirements/recommendations for international students: Required—TOEFL. Electronic applications accepted. *Faculty research:* Tourism policy and development, spatial information systems, natural resource management, recreational sports management, park and recreation management.

Northeastern University, College of Professional Studies, Boston, MA 02115-5096. Offers applied nutrition (MS); college athletics administration (MSL); commerce and economic development (MS); corporate and organizational communication (MS); criminal justice (MS); digital media (MPS); elearning and instructional design (M Ed); elementary education (MAT); geographic information technology (MPS); global studies and international relations (MS); higher education administration (M Ed); homeland security (MA); human services (MS); informatics (MPS); leadership (MS); learning analytics (M Ed); learning and instruction (M Ed); nonprofit management (MS); professional sports administration (MSL); project management (MS); regulatory affairs for drugs, biologics, and medical devices (MS); respiratory care leadership (MS); special education (M Ed); technical communication (MS). *Program availability:* Part-time, evening/weekend, 100% online, blended/hybrid learning. *Faculty:* 82 full-time (51 women), 853 part-time/adjunct (366 women). *Students:* 5,278 part-time (3,230 women). In 2017, 1,586 master's awarded. *Application deadline:* Applications are processed on a rolling basis. Application fee: $0. Electronic applications accepted. *Expenses:* Contact institution. *Financial support:* Applicants required to submit FAFSA. *Unit head:* Dr. Mary Loeffelholz, Dean of the College of Professional Studies. *Application contact:* E-mail: cpsadmissions@northeastern.edu.
Website: https://cps.northeastern.edu/

Northern State University, MS Ed Program in Sport Performance and Leadership, Aberdeen, SD 57401-7198. Offers MS Ed. *Program availability:* Part-time. *Degree requirements:* For master's, comprehensive exam, thesis optional. *Entrance requirements:* For master's, minimum GPA of 2.75. Additional exam requirements/recommendations for international students: Required—TOEFL (minimum score 550 paper-based; 78 iBT), IELTS (minimum score 6). Electronic applications accepted.

Northwestern University, School of Professional Studies, Program in Sports Administration, Evanston, IL 60208. Offers MA. *Program availability:* Part-time, evening/weekend.
Website: https://sps.northwestern.edu/masters/sports-administration/index.php

Ohio Dominican University, Division of Business, Program in Business Administration, Columbus, OH 43219-2099. Offers accounting (MBA); data analytics (MBA); finance (MBA); leadership (MBA); risk management (MBA); sport management (MBA). *Program availability:* Part-time, evening/weekend, 100% online, blended/hybrid learning. *Faculty:* 7 full-time (4 women), 9 part-time/adjunct (2 women). *Students:* 53 full-time (21 women), 112 part-time (49 women); includes 37 minority (20 Black or African American, non-Hispanic/Latino; 1 American Indian or Alaska Native, non-Hispanic/Latino; 6 Asian, non-Hispanic/Latino; 5 Hispanic/Latino; 5 Two or more races, non-Hispanic/Latino), 5 international. Average age 31. 110 applicants, 45% accepted, 40 enrolled. In 2017, 93 master's awarded. *Entrance requirements:* For master's, minimum overall GPA of 3.0 in undergraduate degree from regionally-accredited institution or 2.75 in last 60 semester hours of bachelor's degree. Additional exam requirements/recommendations for international students: Required—TOEFL (minimum score 550 paper-based), IELTS (minimum score 6.5). *Application deadline:* For fall admission, 8/15 for domestic students, 6/10 for international students; for spring admission, 1/4 for domestic students,

Sports Management

11/2 for international students; for summer admission, 5/30 for domestic students. Applications are processed on a rolling basis. Application fee: $25. Electronic applications accepted. *Expenses:* $600 per credit hour, $175 per semester technology fee, $50 per semester activity fee. *Financial support:* Applicants required to submit FAFSA. *Unit head:* Dr. Steve Vickner, Director of Master of Business Administration Program, 614-251-4569, E-mail: vickners@ohiodominican.edu. *Application contact:* John W. Naughton, Associate Vice President for Enrollment Management, 614-251-4721, Fax: 614-251-6654, E-mail: grad@ohiodominican.edu.
Website: http://www.ohiodominican.edu/academics/graduate/mba

Ohio Dominican University, Division of Business, Program in Sport Management, Columbus, OH 43219-2099. Offers MS. *Program availability:* Part-time, evening/weekend. *Faculty:* 1 full-time (0 women), 3 part-time/adjunct (2 women). *Students:* 6 full-time (1 woman), 7 part-time (1 woman); includes 2 minority (1 Black or African American, non-Hispanic/Latino; 1 Hispanic/Latino). Average age 25. 21 applicants, 48% accepted, 7 enrolled. In 2017, 8 master's awarded. *Degree requirements:* For master's, thesis or alternative. *Entrance requirements:* For master's, GRE, bachelor's degree from regionally-accredited institution; minimum undergraduate cumulative GPA of 3.0. Additional exam requirements/recommendations for international students: Required—TOEFL (minimum score 550 paper-based), IELTS (minimum score 6.5). *Application deadline:* For fall admission, 8/15 for domestic students, 6/10 for international students; for spring admission, 1/4 for domestic students, 11/2 for international students; for summer admission, 5/30 for domestic students. Applications are processed on a rolling basis. Application fee: $25. Electronic applications accepted. *Expenses:* $600 per credit hour, $175 per semester technology fee, $50 per semester activity fee. *Financial support:* Applicants required to submit FAFSA. *Unit head:* Dr. James Strode, Dean of Graduate Studies, 614-251-4669, E-mail: strodej@ohiodominican.edu. *Application contact:* John W. Naughton, Associate Vice President for Enrollment Management, 614-251-4721, Fax: 614-251-6654, E-mail: grad@ohiodominican.edu.
Website: http://www.ohiodominican.edu/academics/graduate/mssm

Ohio University, Graduate College, College of Business, Department of Sports Administration, Athens, OH 45701-2979. Offers athletic administration (MS). *Program availability:* Part-time, evening/weekend, online learning. *Degree requirements:* For master's, 11-week internship. *Entrance requirements:* For master's, interview. Additional exam requirements/recommendations for international students: Required—TOEFL (minimum score 600 paper-based; 100 iBT) or IELTS (minimum score 7.5). Electronic applications accepted. *Faculty research:* Sport management, sport marketing, sports and technology, career development.

Old Dominion University, Darden College of Education, Program in Sport Management, Norfolk, VA 23529. Offers MS. *Program availability:* Part-time, evening/weekend, 100% online, blended/hybrid learning. *Faculty:* 5 full-time (2 women), 8 part-time/adjunct (4 women). *Students:* 18 full-time (6 women), 17 part-time (9 women); includes 15 minority (11 Black or African American, non-Hispanic/Latino; 2 Hispanic/Latino; 2 Two or more races, non-Hispanic/Latino). Average age 27. 31 applicants, 55% accepted, 12 enrolled. In 2017, 18 master's awarded. *Degree requirements:* For master's, comprehensive exam, thesis or alternative, internship, research project. *Entrance requirements:* For master's, GRE, GMAT or MAT, minimum GPA of 2.8 overall, 3.0 in major. Additional exam requirements/recommendations for international students: Required—TOEFL (minimum score 550 paper-based; 79 iBT); Recommended—IELTS (minimum score 6.5). *Application deadline:* For fall admission, 3/1 for domestic students. Application fee: $50. Electronic applications accepted. *Expenses:* Tuition, state resident: full-time $8928; part-time $496 per credit. Tuition, nonresident: full-time $22,482; part-time $1249 per credit. *Required fees:* $66 per semester. *Financial support:* In 2017–18, 3 students received support. Unspecified assistantships available. Financial award application deadline: 6/1; financial award applicants required to submit FAFSA. *Faculty research:* Leadership, consumer behavior in sport, sport finance, sport marketing, sport involvement. *Total annual research expenditures:* $104,000. *Unit head:* Dr. Lynn Ridinger, Chair, 757-683-4353, Fax: 757-683-4270, E-mail: lridinge@odu.edu. *Application contact:* William Heffelfinger, Director of Graduate Admissions, 757-683-5554, Fax: 757-683-3255, E-mail: gradadmit@odu.edu.
Website: https://www.odu.edu/hms/academics/sport

Pittsburg State University, Graduate School, College of Education, Department of Health, Physical Education and Recreation, Pittsburg, KS 66762. Offers health, human performance, and recreation (MS), including human performance and wellness, sport and leisure service management. *Program availability:* Part-time, online only, 100% online. *Students:* 66 (25 women); includes 17 minority (5 Black or African American, non-Hispanic/Latino; 2 American Indian or Alaska Native, non-Hispanic/Latino; 4 Hispanic/Latino; 6 Two or more races, non-Hispanic/Latino). In 2017, 33 master's awarded. *Degree requirements:* For master's, thesis or alternative. *Entrance requirements:* For master's, letter of intent. Additional exam requirements/recommendations for international students: Required—TOEFL (minimum score 520 paper-based; 68 iBT), IELTS (minimum score 6), PTE (minimum score 47). *Application deadline:* For fall admission, 6/1 for international students; for spring admission, 10/15 for international students; for summer admission, 4/1 for international students. Applications are processed on a rolling basis. Application fee: $35 ($60 for international students). Electronic applications accepted. *Expenses:* Contact institution. *Financial support:* In 2017–18, 9 teaching assistantships with full tuition reimbursements (averaging $5,500 per year) were awarded; career-related internships or fieldwork, Federal Work-Study, and unspecified assistantships also available. Financial award application deadline: 2/1; financial award applicants required to submit FAFSA. *Faculty research:* Personality of athletes, fitness activities for children, aerobic conditioning, fitness evaluation. *Unit head:* Dr. John Oppliger, Chairperson, 620-235-4668, E-mail: joppliger@pittstate.edu. *Application contact:* Lisa Allen, Assistant Director of Graduate and Continuing Studies, 620-235-4223, Fax: 620-235-4219, E-mail: lallen@pittstate.edu.

Point Loma Nazarene University, Department of Kinesiology, San Diego, CA 92106-2899. Offers exercise science (MS); sport performance (MS), including exercise science, sport management, sport performance. *Program availability:* Part-time, online learning. *Faculty:* 5 full-time (2 women), 8 part-time/adjunct (2 women). *Students:* 55 full-time (26 women), 3 part-time (2 women); includes 20 minority (2 Black or African American, non-Hispanic/Latino; 3 Asian, non-Hispanic/Latino; 12 Hispanic/Latino; 1 Native Hawaiian or other Pacific Islander, non-Hispanic/Latino; 2 Two or more races, non-Hispanic/Latino), 3 international. Average age 29. 92 applicants, 92% accepted, 56 enrolled. In 2017, 30 master's awarded. *Entrance requirements:* For master's, baccalaureate degree, minimum undergraduate cumulative GPA of 3.0. Application fee: $50. *Expenses:* Contact institution. *Financial support:* Teaching assistantships, scholarships/grants, and unspecified assistantships available. *Unit head:* Jeff Sullivan, Chair, 619-849-2629, E-mail: jeffsullivan@pointloma.edu. *Application contact:* Joanie Joy, Senior Director of Enrollment Management, 619-329-6785, E-mail: gradinfo@pointloma.edu.
Website: https://www.pointloma.edu/graduate-studies/programs/kinesiology-ms

Point Park University, Rowland School of Business, Program in Business Administration, Pittsburgh, PA 15222-1984. Offers business analytics (MBA); global

management and administration (MBA); health systems management (MBA); international business (MBA); management (MBA); management information systems (MBA); sports, arts and entertainment management (MBA). *Program availability:* Evening/weekend, 100% online.

Purdue University, Graduate School, College of Health and Human Sciences, Department of Health and Kinesiology, West Lafayette, IN 47907. Offers athletic training education administration (MS, PhD); biomechanics (MS, PhD); exercise physiology (MS, PhD); health education (MS, PhD); history/philosophy of sport (MS, PhD); motor control and development (MS, PhD); physical education pedagogy (PhD); physical education teacher education (MS); recreation and sport management (MS, PhD); sport and exercise psychology (MS, PhD). *Program availability:* Part-time. *Faculty:* 19 full-time (7 women). *Students:* 30 full-time (13 women), 10 part-time (5 women); includes 2 minority (1 Asian, non-Hispanic/Latino; 1 Two or more races, non-Hispanic/Latino), 6 international. Average age 26. 77 applicants, 29% accepted, 18 enrolled. In 2017, 18 master's, 9 doctorates awarded. *Degree requirements:* For master's, thesis optional; for doctorate, comprehensive exam, thesis/dissertation, qualifying examination, preliminary examination. *Entrance requirements:* For master's, GRE General Test (minimum score 1000 combined verbal and quantitative), minimum undergraduate GPA of 3.0 or equivalent; for doctorate, GRE General Test (minimum score 1100 combined verbal and quantitative), minimum undergraduate GPA of 3.0 or equivalent; master's degree with minimum GPA of 3.25 (recommended). Additional exam requirements/recommendations for international students: Required—TOEFL (minimum score 77 iBT); Recommended—TWE. *Application deadline:* For fall admission, 4/30 for domestic and international students; for spring admission, 10/15 for domestic and international students. Applications are processed on a rolling basis. Application fee: $60 ($75 for international students). Electronic applications accepted. *Financial support:* Fellowships with partial tuition reimbursements, research assistantships with partial tuition reimbursements, teaching assistantships with partial tuition reimbursements, and Federal Work-Study available. Support available to part-time students. Financial award applicants required to submit FAFSA. *Faculty research:* Wellness, motivation, teaching effectiveness, learning and development. *Unit head:* Dr. Timothy P. Gavin, Head of the Graduate Program, 765-494-3178, Fax: 765-494-1239, E-mail: gavin1@purdue.edu. *Application contact:* David B. Klenosky, Graduate Contact, 765-494-0865, E-mail: klenosky@purdue.edu.
Website: http://www.purdue.edu/hhs/hk/

Robert Morris University Illinois, Morris Graduate School of Management, Chicago, IL 60605. Offers accounting (MBA); accounting/finance (MBA); business analytics (MIS); health care administration (MM); higher education administration (MM); human performance (MS); human resource management (MBA); information security (MIS); information systems management (MIS); law enforcement administration (MM); management (MBA); management/finance (MBA); management/human resource management (MBA); sports administration (MM). *Program availability:* Part-time, evening/weekend. *Faculty:* 2 full-time (0 women), 26 part-time/adjunct (8 women). *Students:* 186 full-time (108 women), 114 part-time (57 women); includes 167 minority (88 Black or African American, non-Hispanic/Latino; 15 Asian, non-Hispanic/Latino; 62 Hispanic/Latino; 1 Native Hawaiian or other Pacific Islander, non-Hispanic/Latino; 1 Two or more races, non-Hispanic/Latino), 18 international. Average age 32. 157 applicants, 78% accepted, 72 enrolled. In 2017, 191 master's awarded. *Entrance requirements:* For master's, official transcripts and letters of recommendation (for some programs); written personal statement. Additional exam requirements/recommendations for international students: Required—TOEFL (minimum score 550 paper-based). *Application deadline:* Applications are processed on a rolling basis. Application fee: $20 ($100 for international students). Electronic applications accepted. *Expenses:* Tuition: Full-time $17,100; part-time $2850 per course. *Financial support:* In 2017–18, 381 students received support. Federal Work-Study, scholarships/grants, and unspecified assistantships available. Support available to part-time students. Financial award applicants required to submit FAFSA. *Unit head:* Kayed Akkawi, Dean, 312-935-6050, Fax: 312-935-6020, E-mail: kakkawi@robertmorris.edu. *Application contact:* Mark Daugherty, Director of Admissions, 312-935-4814, Fax: 312-935-6020, E-mail: mdaugherty@robertmorris.edu.

St. Cloud State University, School of Graduate Studies, School of Health and Human Services, Department of Kinesiology, St. Cloud, MN 56301-4498. Offers exercise science (MS); sports management (MS). *Degree requirements:* For master's, thesis or alternative. *Entrance requirements:* For master's, GRE General Test, minimum overall GPA of 2.75 in previous undergraduate and graduate records or in last half of undergraduate work. Additional exam requirements/recommendations for international students: Required—Michigan English Language Assessment Battery; Recommended—TOEFL (minimum score 550 paper-based; 79 iBT), IELTS (minimum score 6.5). Electronic applications accepted.

St. John's University, College of Professional Studies, Department of Sport Management, Queens, NY 11439. Offers MPS. *Faculty:* 8 full-time (3 women), 17 part-time/adjunct (16 women). *Students:* 63 full-time (27 women), 16 part-time (7 women); includes 30 minority (18 Black or African American, non-Hispanic/Latino; 1 Asian, non-Hispanic/Latino; 6 Hispanic/Latino; 1 Native Hawaiian or other Pacific Islander, non-Hispanic/Latino; 4 Two or more races, non-Hispanic/Latino), 12 international. Average age 26. 99 applicants, 68% accepted, 26 enrolled. In 2017, 28 master's awarded. *Entrance requirements:* For master's, letters of recommendation, transcripts, resume, personal statement. Additional exam requirements/recommendations for international students: Required—TOEFL (minimum score 90 iBT), IELTS (minimum score 7). *Application deadline:* For fall admission, 5/1 for domestic students; for spring admission, 11/1 for domestic students. Applications are processed on a rolling basis. Application fee: $70. Electronic applications accepted. *Expenses:* Tuition: Full-time $44,280; part-time $1230 per credit. *Required fees:* $340; $340 per credit. Tuition and fees vary according to course load, degree level and program. *Financial support:* Research assistantships, teaching assistantships, scholarships/grants, and unspecified assistantships available. Financial award application deadline: 2/1; financial award applicants required to submit FAFSA. *Unit head:* Dr. Emese Ivan, Chair, 718-990-2038, E-mail: ivane@stjohns.edu. *Application contact:* Robert Medrano, Director of Graduate Admissions, 718-990-1601, Fax: 718-990-5686, E-mail: gradhelp@stjohns.edu.
Website: https://www.stjohns.edu/academics/schools-and-colleges/college-professional-studies/sport-management

Saint Mary's College of California, School of Liberal Arts, Department of Kinesiology, Moraga, CA 94575. Offers fitness management (MA); sport management (MA); sport studies (MA). *Program availability:* Part-time. *Degree requirements:* For master's, thesis or special project. *Entrance requirements:* For master's, minimum GPA of 2.75, BA in physical education or related field, or professional experience. Electronic applications accepted. *Expenses:* Contact institution. *Faculty research:* Moral development in sport, applied motor learning, achievement motivation, sport history.

St. Thomas University, School of Business, Department of Management, Miami Gardens, FL 33054-6459. Offers accounting (MBA); general management (MSM, Certificate); health management (MBA, MSM, Certificate); human resource management (MBA, MSM, Certificate); international business (MBA, MIB, MSM, Certificate); justice administration (MSM, Certificate); management accounting (MSM, Certificate); public management (MSM, Certificate); sports administration (MS).

Program availability: Part-time, evening/weekend. *Degree requirements:* For master's, comprehensive exam. *Entrance requirements:* For master's, interview, minimum GPA of 3.0 or GMAT. Additional exam requirements/recommendations for international students: Required—TOEFL (minimum score 550 paper-based; 79 iBT). Electronic applications accepted.

Sam Houston State University, College of Health Sciences, Department of Kinesiology, Huntsville, TX 77341. Offers sport and human performance (MA); sport management (MA). *Program availability:* Part-time. *Degree requirements:* For master's, comprehensive exam, thesis optional. *Entrance requirements:* For master's, GRE, letters of recommendation, statement of interest/intent. Additional exam requirements/recommendations for international students: Required—TOEFL (minimum score 550 paper-based; 79 iBT), IELTS (minimum score 6.5). Electronic applications accepted.

San Diego State University, Graduate and Research Affairs, College of Business Administration, Sports Business Management Program, San Diego, CA 92182. Offers MBA.

San Jose State University, Graduate Studies and Research, College of Health and Human Sciences, San Jose, CA 95192-0049. Offers criminology (MS), including global criminology, law and justice; justice studies (MS); kinesiology (MA), including athletic training, exercise physiology, interdisciplinary, sport studies, sports management; library and information science (MLIS); mass communications (MS); nursing (MS), including family nurse practitioner; nutritional science (MS); occupational therapy (MS); public health (MPH); social work (MSW); MD/M Div. *Program availability:* Part-time, 100% online, blended/hybrid learning. *Faculty:* 15 full-time (7 women), 6 part-time/adjunct (3 women). *Students:* 517 full-time (407 women), 405 part-time (302 women); includes 523 minority (39 Black or African American, non-Hispanic/Latino; 2 American Indian or Alaska Native, non-Hispanic/Latino; 141 Asian, non-Hispanic/Latino; 226 Hispanic/Latino; 2 Native Hawaiian or other Pacific Islander, non-Hispanic/Latino; 113 Two or more races, non-Hispanic/Latino), 14 international. Average age 32. 1,250 applicants, 45% accepted, 375 enrolled. In 2017, 808 master's awarded. *Degree requirements:* For master's, thesis (for some programs), graduate writing assessment. *Entrance requirements:* Additional exam requirements/recommendations for international students: Required—TOEFL (minimum score 550 paper-based; 80 iBT), IELTS (minimum score 6.5), PTE (minimum score 53). *Application deadline:* For fall admission, 2/1 for domestic and international students. Applications are processed on a rolling basis. Application fee: $55. Electronic applications accepted. *Expenses:* Tuition, state resident: full-time $7176. Tuition, nonresident: full-time $16,680. Tuition and fees vary according to course load and program. *Financial support:* Fellowships, research assistantships, teaching assistantships, career-related internships or fieldwork, Federal Work-Study, scholarships/grants, and tuition waivers (full and partial) available. Support available to part-time students. Financial award application deadline: 4/24; financial award applicants required to submit FAFSA. *Unit head:* Dr. Mary Schutten, Dean, College of Health and Human Sciences, 408-924-2900, Fax: 408-924-2901, E-mail: mary.schutten@sjsu.edu.
Website: http://www.sjsu.edu/casa/

Seattle University, College of Arts and Sciences, Center for the Study of Sport and Exercise, Seattle, WA 98122-1090. Offers MSAL, JD/MSAL. *Program availability:* Part-time, evening/weekend. *Faculty:* 3 full-time (1 woman). *Students:* 8 full-time (2 women), 31 part-time (11 women); includes 6 minority (1 Black or African American, non-Hispanic/Latino; 5 Asian, non-Hispanic/Latino), 5 international. Average age 26. 1 applicant, 100% accepted, 1 enrolled. In 2017, 22 master's awarded. *Degree requirements:* For master's, thesis or applied inquiry. *Entrance requirements:* For master's, GRE (Verbal, Quantitative, and Analytical), minimum GPA of 3.0, three letters of recommendation, essay, resume. Additional exam requirements/recommendations for international students: Required—TOEFL, IELTS. *Application deadline:* For fall admission, 2/15 for domestic and international students. Application fee: $55. Electronic applications accepted. *Expenses:* Tuition: Full-time $12,960. Required fees: $570. Tuition and fees vary according to program. *Financial support:* In 2017–18, 20 students received support. Research assistantships and scholarships/grants available. Financial award applicants required to submit FAFSA. *Faculty research:* Sport consumer behavior, strategic management of sport organizations, leadership in sport, organizational behavior, lifestyle sports. *Unit head:* Dr. Dan Tripps, Director, 206-398-4605, E-mail: trippsd@seattleu.edu. *Application contact:* Janet Shandley, Associate Dean of Graduate Admissions, 206-296-5900, Fax: 206-298-5656, E-mail: grad_admissions@seattleu.edu.
Website: https://www.seattleu.edu/artsci/departments/sport-exercise/

Seton Hall University, Stillman School of Business, Programs in Business Administration, South Orange, NJ 07079-2697. Offers accounting (MBA); entrepreneurial studies (Certificate); finance (MBA); financial decision making (Certificate); information technology management (MBA); international business (MBA); management (MBA); marketing (MBA); sport management (MBA); supply chain management (MBA, Certificate). *Program availability:* Part-time, evening/weekend. *Faculty:* 29 full-time (4 women), 18 part-time/adjunct (0 women). *Students:* 140 full-time (58 women), 154 part-time (49 women); includes 66 minority (25 Black or African American, non-Hispanic/Latino; 14 Asian, non-Hispanic/Latino; 23 Hispanic/Latino; 4 Two or more races, non-Hispanic/Latino), 88 international. Average age 32. 406 applicants, 75% accepted, 100 enrolled. In 2017, 132 master's awarded. *Degree requirements:* For master's, 20 hours of community service (Social Responsibility Project). *Entrance requirements:* For master's, GMAT or CPA, GRE (waived based on work experience or advanced degree from AACSB institution), MS in business discipline, professional degree or designation (MD, JD, PhD, DVM, DDS, CPA, etc.), minimum undergraduate GPA of 3.0. Additional exam requirements/recommendations for international students: Required—TOEFL (minimum score 607 paper-based; 80 iBT), IELTS (minimum score 6), PTE. *Application deadline:* For fall admission, 5/31 priority date for domestic students, 4/30 priority date for international students; for spring admission, 10/31 priority date for domestic students, 9/30 priority date for international students; for summer admission, 3/31 priority date for domestic students. Applications are processed on a rolling basis. Application fee: $75. Electronic applications accepted. *Expenses:* $1,305 per credit; $126 fees (fall and spring semester), $51 (summer semester). *Financial support:* In 2017–18, 41 students received support, including 25 research assistantships with full tuition reimbursements available (averaging $3,644 per year); career-related internships or fieldwork, scholarships/grants, and unspecified assistantships also available. Financial award application deadline: 6/30; financial award applicants required to submit FAFSA. *Faculty research:* Sport, hedge funds, executive compensation, social media, legal studies. *Unit head:* Dr. Joyce Strawser, Dean, 973-761-9013, Fax: 973-761-9217, E-mail: joyce.strawser@shu.edu. *Application contact:* Alfred Ayoub, Director of Graduate Admissions, 973-761-9262, Fax: 973-761-9208, E-mail: alfred.ayoub@shu.edu.
Website: http://www.shu.edu/business/mba-programs.cfm

Sonoma State University, School of Science and Technology, Department of Kinesiology, Rohnert Park, CA 94928. Offers exercise science/pre-physical therapy (MA); interdisciplinary (MA); interdisciplinary pre-occupational therapy (MA); lifetime physical activity (MA), including coach education, fitness and wellness. *Program availability:* Part-time. *Degree requirements:* For master's, thesis, oral exam. *Entrance*

requirements: For master's, minimum GPA of 2.8. Additional exam requirements/recommendations for international students: Required—TOEFL (minimum score 500 paper-based). *Application deadline:* For fall admission, 11/30 for domestic students; for spring admission, 9/1 for domestic students. Applications are processed on a rolling basis. Application fee: $55. *Financial support:* Career-related internships or fieldwork available. Financial award application deadline: 3/2; financial award applicants required to submit FAFSA. *Unit head:* Dr. Steven Winter, Chair, 707-664-2188, E-mail: steven.winter@sonoma.edu. *Application contact:* Dr. Bulent Sokmen, Graduate Coordinator, 707-664-2789, E-mail: sokmen@sonoma.edu.
Website: http://www.sonoma.edu/kinesiology/

Southeastern University, Jannetides College of Business and Entrepreneurial Leadership, Lakeland, FL 33801-6099. Offers executive leadership (MBA); global business administration (MBA); healthcare administration (MBA); missional leadership (MBA); organizational leadership (PhD); sport management (MBA); strategic leadership (DSL). *Accreditation:* ACBSP. *Program availability:* Evening/weekend, online learning. *Faculty:* 10 full-time (2 women), 8 part-time/adjunct (1 woman). *Students:* 80 full-time (38 women), 110 part-time (54 women); includes 51 minority (18 Black or African American, non-Hispanic/Latino; 5 Asian, non-Hispanic/Latino; 28 Hispanic/Latino), 7 international. Average age 31. *Entrance requirements:* For master's, GMAT, minimum cumulative GPA of 3.0, writing sample. Application fee: $50. Electronic applications accepted. *Unit head:* Lyle L. Bowlin, Dean, 863-667-5118, E-mail: llbowlin@seu.edu.
Website: http://www.seu.edu/business/

Southeast Missouri State University, School of Graduate Studies, Harrison College of Business, Cape Girardeau, MO 63701-4799. Offers accounting (MBA); entrepreneurship (MBA); financial management (MBA); sport management (MBA). *Accreditation:* AACSB. *Program availability:* Part-time, evening/weekend, 100% online. *Faculty:* 27 full-time (7 women), 1 (woman) part-time/adjunct. *Students:* 71 full-time (38 women), 68 part-time (31 women); includes 13 minority (7 Black or African American, non-Hispanic/Latino; 4 Asian, non-Hispanic/Latino; 2 Two or more races, non-Hispanic/Latino), 47 international. Average age 30. 51 applicants, 100% accepted, 51 enrolled. In 2017, 95 master's awarded. *Degree requirements:* For master's, variable foreign language requirement, comprehensive exam (for some programs), thesis or alternative. *Entrance requirements:* For master's, GMAT or GRE, minimum undergraduate GPA of 2.5, minimum grade of C in prerequisite courses. Additional exam requirements/recommendations for international students: Required—TOEFL (minimum score 550 paper-based; 79 iBT), IELTS (minimum score 6), PTE (minimum score 53). *Application deadline:* For fall admission, 8/1 for domestic students, 6/1 for international students; for spring admission, 11/21 for domestic students, 10/1 for international students; for summer admission, 5/15 for domestic students. Applications are processed on a rolling basis. Application fee: $30 ($40 for international students). Electronic applications accepted. *Expenses:* $270.35 per credit hour in-state tuition, $33.40 per credit hour fees. *Financial support:* In 2017–18, 26 students received support. Career-related internships or fieldwork, Federal Work-Study, scholarships/grants, traineeships, tuition waivers (full), and unspecified assistantships available. Financial award application deadline: 6/30; financial award applicants required to submit FAFSA. *Faculty research:* Organizational justice, ethics, leadership, corporate finance, generational differences. *Unit head:* Dr. Judy A. Wiles, Interim Dean, Harrison College of Business, 573-651-2913, Fax: 573-651-5032, E-mail: jwiles@semo.edu.
Website: http://www.semo.edu/mba

Southern Methodist University, Annette Caldwell Simmons School of Education and Human Development, Department of Allied Physiology and Wellness, Dallas, TX 75275. Offers sport management (MS). Program offered jointly with Cox School of Business. *Entrance requirements:* For master's, GMAT, resume, essays, transcripts from all colleges and universities attended, two references. Additional exam requirements/recommendations for international students: Required—TOEFL or PTE.

Southern Nazarene University, College of Professional and Graduate Studies, School of Kinesiology, Bethany, OK 73008. Offers sports management and administration (MA). *Entrance requirements:* For master's, baccalaureate degree from regionally-accredited college or university, official transcripts from each institution attended, three letters of recommendation, essay.

Southern New Hampshire University, School of Business, Manchester, NH 03106-1045. Offers accounting (MBA, Graduate Certificate); accounting finance (MS); accounting/auditing (MS); accounting/forensic accounting (MS); accounting/management accounting (MS); accounting/taxation (MS); applied economics (MS); athletic administration (MBA, Graduate Certificate); business administration (IMBA, Certificate), including business information systems (Certificate), human resource management (Certificate); business analytics (MBA); business intelligence (MBA); communication (MA), including new media and marketing, public relations; community economic development (MBA); criminal justice (MBA); data analytics (MS); economics (MBA); engineering management (MBA); entrepreneurship (MBA); finance (MBA, MS, Graduate Certificate); finance/corporate finance (MS); finance/investments (MS); forensic accounting (MBA); forensic accounting and fraud examination (Graduate Certificate); healthcare informatics (MBA); healthcare management (MBA); human resource management (MS); human resources (MBA); information technology (MS); information technology management (MBA); international business (PhD); Internet marketing (MBA); leadership (MBA); leadership of nonprofit organizations (Graduate Certificate); management (MS); marketing (MBA, MS, Graduate Certificate); music business (MBA); operations and project management (MS); operations and supply chain management (MBA, Graduate Certificate); organizational leadership (MS); project management (MBA, Graduate Certificate); public administration (MBA, Graduate Certificate); quantitative analysis (MBA); Six Sigma (Graduate Certificate); Six Sigma quality (MBA); social media marketing (MBA, Graduate Certificate); sport management (MBA, MS, Graduate Certificate); sustainability and environmental compliance (MBA); MBA/Certificate. *Accreditation:* ACBSP. *Program availability:* Part-time, evening/weekend, online learning. Terminal master's awarded for partial completion of doctoral program. *Degree requirements:* For master's, one foreign language, comprehensive exam (for some programs), thesis or alternative; for doctorate, one foreign language, comprehensive exam, thesis/dissertation. *Entrance requirements:* For master's, minimum GPA of 2.5; for doctorate, GMAT. Additional exam requirements/recommendations for international students: Required—TOEFL (minimum score 500 paper-based). *Application deadline:* Applications are processed on a rolling basis. Application fee: $40. Electronic applications accepted. *Expenses:* Tuition: Part-time $627 per credit hour. Part-time tuition and fees vary according to campus/location and program. *Financial support:* Career-related internships or fieldwork, Federal Work-Study, institutionally sponsored loans, scholarships/grants, tuition waivers (partial), and unspecified assistantships available. Support available to part-time students. Financial award applicants required to submit FAFSA. *Unit head:* Dr. Bill Lightfoot, Dean, 603-644-3102, Fax: 603-644-3144. *Application contact:* Office of Graduate Admission, 888-327-SNHU, Fax: 603-644-3144, E-mail: enroll@snhu.edu.

Springfield College, Graduate Programs, Programs in Physical Education, Springfield, MA 01109-3797. Offers adapted physical education (MS); advanced-level coaching (M Ed); athletic administration (MS); exercise physiology (PhD); health promotion and disease prevention (MS); physical education initial licensure (CAGS); sport and exercise

Sports Management

psychology (PhD); teaching and administration (PhD). *Program availability:* Part-time. *Students:* 82 applicants, 73% accepted, 37 enrolled. *Degree requirements:* For master's, comprehensive exam, thesis (for some programs). *Entrance requirements:* For master's and doctorate, GRE General Test. Additional exam requirements/recommendations for international students: Required—TOEFL (minimum score 550 paper-based); Recommended—IELTS (minimum score 7). *Application deadline:* For fall admission, 1/15 priority date for domestic students, 1/15 for international students; for winter admission, 11/1 for domestic and international students; for spring admission, 11/1 for domestic and international students. Applications are processed on a rolling basis. Application fee: $50. Electronic applications accepted. *Financial support:* Fellowships with partial tuition reimbursements, teaching assistantships with partial tuition reimbursements, career-related internships or fieldwork, Federal Work-Study, institutionally sponsored loans, scholarships/grants, and unspecified assistantships available. Financial award application deadline: 3/1; financial award applicants required to submit FAFSA. *Unit head:* Dr. Michelle Moosbrugger, Graduate Coordinator, 413-748-3486, E-mail: mmoosbrugger@springfield.edu. *Application contact:* Anne Griffin, Director of Graduate Admissions, 413-748-3225, Fax: 413-748-3694, E-mail: agriffin2@springfield.edu.
Website: http://springfield.edu/gradpe

Springfield College, Graduate Programs, Programs in Sport Management and Recreation, Springfield, MA 01109-3797. Offers recreation management (M Ed, MS); sport management (M Ed, MS); therapeutic recreation management (M Ed, MS). *Program availability:* Part-time. *Students:* 43 applicants, 49% accepted, 10 enrolled. In 2017, 13 master's awarded. *Degree requirements:* For master's, comprehensive exam, research project. *Entrance requirements:* Additional exam requirements/recommendations for international students: Required—TOEFL (minimum score 550 paper-based); Recommended—IELTS (minimum score 7). *Application deadline:* For fall admission, 1/15 for domestic and international students; for winter admission, 11/1 for international students; for spring admission, 11/1 for domestic and international students. Applications are processed on a rolling basis. Application fee: $50. Electronic applications accepted. *Financial support:* Fellowships with partial tuition reimbursements, teaching assistantships with partial tuition reimbursements, career-related internships or fieldwork, Federal Work-Study, institutionally sponsored loans, scholarships/grants, and unspecified assistantships available. Financial award application deadline: 3/1; financial award applicants required to submit FAFSA. *Unit head:* Dr. Kevin McAllister, Coordinator, 413-748-3476, Fax: 413-748-3685, E-mail: kmcallis@springfield.edu. *Application contact:* Anne Griffin, Director of Graduate Admissions, 413-748-3225, Fax: 413-748-3694, E-mail: agriffin2@springfield.edu.
Website: http://springfield.edu/programs

State University of New York College at Cortland, Graduate Studies, School of Professional Studies, Department of Sport Management, Cortland, NY 13045. Offers international sport management (MS); sport management (MS). *Entrance requirements:* For master's, GMAT or GRE, 2 letters of recommendation.

Syracuse University, David B. Falk College of Sport and Human Dynamics, MS Program in Sport Venue and Event Management, Syracuse, NY 13244. Offers MS. *Entrance requirements:* For master's, GRE, undergraduate transcripts, three recommendations, resume, personal statement. Additional exam requirements/recommendations for international students: Required—TOEFL (minimum score 100 iBT). *Application deadline:* For fall admission, 2/15 for domestic students; for spring admission, 11/1 priority date for domestic and international students. Application fee: $75. Electronic applications accepted. *Financial support:* Fellowships, research assistantships, teaching assistantships, and career-related internships or fieldwork available. Financial award application deadline: 1/1; financial award applicants required to submit FAFSA. *Faculty research:* Managing and operating sport and entertainment facilities and events, sociology of sport, psychological and social issues in sport. *Unit head:* Jeff Pauline, Graduate Program Director, 315-443-0364, Fax: 315-443-9811, E-mail: jspaulin@syr.edu. *Application contact:* Felicia Otero, Director of Admissions, 315-443-5555, E-mail: falk@syr.edu.
Website: https://falk.syr.edu/sport-management/academic-programs/#mssvem

Temple University, Fox School of Business, Doctoral Programs in Business, Philadelphia, PA 19122-6096. Offers accounting (PhD); entrepreneurship (PhD); finance (PhD); international business (PhD); management information systems (PhD); marketing (PhD); risk management and insurance (PhD); statistics (PhD); strategic management (PhD); tourism and sport (PhD). *Accreditation:* AACSB. *Degree requirements:* For doctorate, thesis/dissertation. *Entrance requirements:* For doctorate, GRE General Test, GMAT, minimum GPA of 3.0, master's degree. Additional exam requirements/recommendations for international students: Required—TOEFL (minimum score 600 paper-based; 100 iBT), IELTS (minimum score 7.5). Electronic applications accepted. *Expenses:* Tuition, state resident: full-time $16,164; part-time $898 per credit hour. Tuition, nonresident: full-time $22,158; part-time $1231 per credit hour. *Required fees:* $890; $445 per semester. Full-time tuition and fees vary according to course load, degree level, campus/location and program.

Temple University, School of Sport, Tourism and Hospitality Management, Philadelphia, PA 19122-6096. Offers sport business (MS); tourism and hospitality management (MTHM); tourism and sport (PhD); travel and tourism (MS). *Program availability:* Part-time, evening/weekend. *Faculty:* 28 full-time (9 women), 9 part-time/adjunct (2 women). *Students:* 158 full-time (72 women), 32 part-time (19 women); includes 46 minority (29 Black or African American, non-Hispanic/Latino; 4 Asian, non-Hispanic/Latino; 11 Hispanic/Latino; 2 Two or more races, non-Hispanic/Latino), 31 international. 235 applicants, 74% accepted, 96 enrolled. In 2017, 37 master's awarded. *Entrance requirements:* For master's, GRE General Test, GMAT, or MAT, bachelor's degree or equivalent with minimum GPA of 3.0, 500-word essay, 2 letters of recommendation, resume; for doctorate, GMAT or GRE. Additional exam requirements/recommendations for international students: Required—TOEFL (minimum score 550 paper-based; 79 iBT), IELTS (minimum score 6.5). *Application deadline:* For fall admission, 3/1 priority date for domestic students, 1/15 priority date for international students; for spring admission, 8/15 priority date for domestic students, 6/30 priority date for international students. Applications are processed on a rolling basis. Application fee: $60. Electronic applications accepted. *Expenses:* Contact institution. *Financial support:* Fellowships, research assistantships, and teaching assistantships available. Financial award application deadline: 3/1; financial award applicants required to submit FAFSA. *Unit head:* Dr. M. Moshe Porat, Dean, 215-204-1836, Fax: 215-204-8705, E-mail: porat@temple.edu. *Application contact:* James Alton, Manager of Graduate Student Services, 215-204-7140, Fax: 215-204-8705, E-mail: jim.alton@temple.edu.
Website: http://sthm.temple.edu/

Tennessee State University, The School of Graduate Studies and Research, College of Health Sciences, Department of Human Performance and Sports Sciences, Nashville, TN 37209-1561. Offers exercise science (MA Ed); sports administration (MA Ed). *Degree requirements:* For master's, thesis optional. *Entrance requirements:* For master's, GRE General Test or MAT.

Tennessee Technological University, College of Graduate Studies, College of Education, Department of Exercise Science, Physical Education and Wellness, Cookeville, TN 38505. Offers adapted physical education (MA); elementary/middle school physical education (MA); lifetime wellness (MA); sport management (MA). *Accreditation:* NCATE. *Program availability:* Part-time, online learning. *Faculty:* 7 full-time (0 women). *Students:* 17 full-time (8 women), 34 part-time (14 women); includes 10 minority (5 Black or African American, non-Hispanic/Latino; 1 Asian, non-Hispanic/Latino; 2 Hispanic/Latino; 2 Two or more races, non-Hispanic/Latino). 35 applicants, 71% accepted, 23 enrolled. In 2017, 28 master's awarded. *Degree requirements:* For master's, comprehensive exam, thesis or alternative. *Entrance requirements:* For master's, MAT or GRE. Additional exam requirements/recommendations for international students: Required—TOEFL (minimum score 527 paper-based; 71 iBT), IELTS (minimum score 5.5), PTE (minimum score 48), or TOEIC (Test of English as an International Communication). *Application deadline:* For fall admission, 8/1 for domestic students, 5/1 for international students; for spring admission, 12/1 for domestic students, 10/1 for international students; for summer admission, 5/1 for domestic students, 2/1 for international students. Applications are processed on a rolling basis. Application fee: $35 ($40 for international students). Electronic applications accepted. *Expenses:* Tuition, state resident: full-time $9925; part-time $565 per credit hour. Tuition, nonresident: full-time $22,993; part-time $1291 per credit hour. *Financial support:* Fellowships, research assistantships, teaching assistantships, and career-related internships or fieldwork available. Financial award application deadline: 4/1. *Unit head:* Dr. Christy Killman, Chairperson, 931-372-3467, Fax: 931-372-6319, E-mail: ckillman@tntech.edu. *Application contact:* Shelia K. Kendrick, Coordinator of Graduate Studies, 931-372-3808, Fax: 931-372-3497, E-mail: skendrick@tntech.edu.

Texas A&M University, College of Education and Human Development, Department of Health and Kinesiology, College Station, TX 77843. Offers athletic training (MS); health education (MS, PhD); kinesiology (MS, PhD); sports management (MS). *Program availability:* Part-time. *Faculty:* 53. *Students:* 223 full-time (120 women), 94 part-time (53 women); includes 106 minority (42 Black or African American, non-Hispanic/Latino; 2 American Indian or Alaska Native, non-Hispanic/Latino; 5 Asian, non-Hispanic/Latino; 50 Hispanic/Latino; 7 Two or more races, non-Hispanic/Latino), 27 international. Average age 29. 161 applicants, 79% accepted, 81 enrolled. In 2017, 126 master's, 13 doctorates awarded. *Degree requirements:* For master's, thesis (for some programs); for doctorate, comprehensive exam, thesis/dissertation. *Entrance requirements:* For master's and doctorate, GRE General Test. Additional exam requirements/recommendations for international students: Required—TOEFL (minimum score 550 paper-based; 80 iBT), IELTS (minimum score 6), PTE (minimum score 53). *Application deadline:* For fall admission, 1/15 for domestic students; for spring admission, 10/1 for domestic students. Applications are processed on a rolling basis. Application fee: $50 ($90 for international students). Electronic applications accepted. *Expenses:* Contact institution. *Financial support:* In 2017–18, 204 students received support, including 2 fellowships with tuition reimbursements available (averaging $43,805 per year), 33 research assistantships with tuition reimbursements available (averaging $10,102 per year), 59 teaching assistantships with tuition reimbursements available (averaging $9,712 per year); career-related internships or fieldwork, institutionally sponsored loans, scholarships/grants, traineeships, health care benefits, tuition waivers (full and partial), and unspecified assistantships also available. Support available to part-time students. Financial award application deadline: 3/15; financial award applicants required to submit FAFSA. *Unit head:* Dr. Richard Kreider, Head, 979-845-1333, Fax: 979-847-8987, E-mail: rkreider@hlkn.tamu.edu. *Application contact:* Jenny Bilski, Academic Advisor, 979-862-4052, E-mail: jenny.bilski@tamu.edu.
Website: http://hlknweb.tamu.edu/

Texas Tech University, Graduate School, College of Arts and Sciences, Department of Kinesiology and Sport Management, Lubbock, TX 79409. Offers kinesiology (MS); sport management (MS). *Program availability:* Part-time. *Faculty:* 21 full-time (9 women), 9 part-time/adjunct (5 women). *Students:* 65 full-time (32 women), 7 part-time (1 woman); includes 28 minority (8 Black or African American, non-Hispanic/Latino; 3 Asian, non-Hispanic/Latino; 15 Hispanic/Latino; 2 Two or more races, non-Hispanic/Latino), 11 international. Average age 24. 96 applicants, 48% accepted, 38 enrolled. In 2017, 38 master's awarded. *Degree requirements:* For master's, comprehensive exam (for some programs), thesis (for some programs). *Entrance requirements:* For master's, GRE or minimum GPA of 3.5 on last 60 hours of undergraduate coursework (only for kinesiology), letter of intent, 3 letters of recommendation (preferably from academic professors), minimum GPA of 2.8 in the last 60 hours. Additional exam requirements/recommendations for international students: Required—TOEFL (minimum score 550 paper-based; 79 iBT). *Application deadline:* For fall admission, 6/1 priority date for domestic students, 1/15 priority date for international students; for spring admission, 9/1 priority date for domestic students, 6/15 priority date for international students. Applications are processed on a rolling basis. Application fee: $60. Electronic applications accepted. *Expenses:* Contact institution. *Financial support:* In 2017–18, 51 students received support, including 49 fellowships (averaging $4,508 per year), 35 teaching assistantships (averaging $12,637 per year); research assistantships, career-related internships or fieldwork, scholarships/grants, health care benefits, and unspecified assistantships also available. Financial award application deadline: 8/1; financial award applicants required to submit FAFSA. *Faculty research:* Sport management, exercise physiology, human performance, motor behavior, exercise and sport psychology. *Total annual research expenditures:* $144,825. *Unit head:* Dr. Angela Lumpkin, Professor/Department Chair, 806-834-6935, Fax: 806-742-1688, E-mail: angela.lumpkin@ttu.edu. *Application contact:* Donna Torres, Graduate Admissions Coordinator, 806-834-7968, Fax: 806-742-1688, E-mail: donna.torres@ttu.edu.
Website: http://www.depts.ttu.edu/ksm/

Texas Woman's University, Graduate School, College of Health Sciences, Department of Kinesiology, Denton, TX 76204. Offers kinesiology (MS, PhD), including adapted physical activity, biomechanics, coaching (MS), exercise physiology, sport management. *Program availability:* Part-time, evening/weekend. *Faculty:* 11 full-time (3 women), 2 part-time/adjunct (both women). *Students:* 48 full-time (36 women), 65 part-time (39 women); includes 40 minority (19 Black or African American, non-Hispanic/Latino; 2 Asian, non-Hispanic/Latino; 17 Hispanic/Latino; 2 Two or more races, non-Hispanic/Latino), 14 international. Average age 30. 63 applicants, 81% accepted, 37 enrolled. In 2017, 32 master's, 9 doctorates awarded. Terminal master's awarded for partial completion of doctoral program. *Degree requirements:* For master's, comprehensive exam, thesis (for some programs), thesis or professional paper; for doctorate, comprehensive exam, thesis/dissertation, qualifying exam. *Entrance requirements:* For master's, GRE General Test (biomechanics emphasis only), 2 letters of reference, curriculum vitae; for doctorate, GRE General Test (biomechanics emphasis only), interview, 3 letters of reference, curriculum vitae, letter of intent. Additional exam requirements/recommendations for international students: Required—TOEFL (minimum score 550 paper-based; 79 iBT); Recommended—IELTS (minimum score 6.5), TSE (minimum score 53). *Application deadline:* For fall admission, 7/15 for domestic students, 3/1 priority date for international students; for spring admission, 11/1 for domestic students, 7/1 priority date for international students; for summer admission, 4/1 for domestic students, 2/1 priority date for international students. Applications are processed on a rolling basis. Application fee: $50 ($75 for international students). Electronic applications accepted. *Expenses:* $7,520 per year full-time in-state; $16,829 per year full-time out-of-state. *Financial support:* In 2017–18, 36 students received support, including 1 research assistantship (averaging $11,926 per year), 15 teaching

assistantships (averaging $20,354 per year); career-related internships or fieldwork, Federal Work-Study, institutionally sponsored loans, scholarships/grants, traineeships, health care benefits, and unspecified assistantships also available. Support available to part-time students. Financial award application deadline: 3/1; financial award applicants required to submit FAFSA. *Faculty research:* Exercise and Type 2 diabetes risk, bone mineral density and exercise in special populations, obesity in children, factors influencing sport consumer behavior and loyalty, roles and responsibilities of Para educators in adapted physical education. *Unit head:* Dr. George King, Chair, 940-898-2575, Fax: 940-898-2581. *Application contact:* Korie Hawkins, Associate Director of Admissions, Graduate Recruitment, 940-898-3188, Fax: 940-898-3081, E-mail: admissions@twu.edu.
Website: http://www.twu.edu/kinesiology/

Tiffin University, Program in Business Administration, Tiffin, OH 44883-2161. Offers finance (MBA); general management (MBA); healthcare administration (MBA); human resource management (MBA); international business (MBA); leadership (MBA); marketing (MBA); non-profit management (MBA); sports management (MBA). *Accreditation:* ACBSP. *Program availability:* Part-time, evening/weekend, online learning. *Entrance requirements:* For master's, minimum undergraduate GPA of 2.5, work experience. Additional exam requirements/recommendations for international students: Required—TOEFL (minimum score 550 paper-based; 79 iBT), IELTS. Electronic applications accepted. Application fee is waived when completed online. *Faculty research:* Small business, executive development operations, research and statistical analysis, market research, management information systems.

Troy University, Graduate School, College of Health and Human Services, Program in Sport and Fitness Management, Troy, AL 36082. Offers MS, DPH. *Program availability:* Part-time, evening/weekend. *Faculty:* 10 full-time (1 woman), 1 part-time/adjunct (0 women). *Students:* 57 full-time (23 women), 85 part-time (34 women); includes 30 minority (24 Black or African American, non-Hispanic/Latino; 2 Asian, non-Hispanic/Latino; 1 Hispanic/Latino; 3 Two or more races, non-Hispanic/Latino). Average age 28. 83 applicants, 77% accepted, 41 enrolled. In 2017, 35 master's awarded. *Degree requirements:* For master's, comprehensive exam, minimum GPA of 3.0, candidacy, research course. *Entrance requirements:* For master's, GRE (minimum score of 850 on old exam or 290 on new exam), GMAT (minimum score of 380), or MAT (minimum score of 385), bachelor's degree; minimum undergraduate GPA of 2.5 or 3.0 on last 30 semester hours, letter of recommendation; for doctorate, GRE (minimum score 1000 on old exam or 297 on new exam), bachelor's or master's degree, minimum GPA of 3.0, 2 letters of recommendation. Additional exam requirements/recommendations for international students: Required—TOEFL (minimum score 523 paper-based; 70 iBT), IELTS (minimum score 6). *Application deadline:* Applications are processed on a rolling basis. Application fee: $50. Electronic applications accepted. *Expenses:* Tuition, state resident: part-time $417 per credit hour. Tuition, nonresident: part-time $834 per credit hour. *Required fees:* $42 per credit hour. $50 per semester. Tuition and fees vary according to campus/location. *Financial support:* Fellowships, career-related internships or fieldwork, scholarships/grants, and unspecified assistantships available. Support available to part-time students. *Faculty research:* Sport marketing, fitness, sport law. *Unit head:* Dr. Gi-Yon Koo, Coordinator, 334-670-5763, Fax: 334-670-3743, E-mail: johnm@troy.edu. *Application contact:* Jessica A. Kimbro, Director of Graduate Admissions, 334-670-3178, E-mail: jacord@troy.edu.

United States Sports Academy, Graduate Programs, Program in Sports Management, Daphne, AL 36526-7055. Offers MSS, Ed D. *Program availability:* Part-time, 100% online. *Degree requirements:* For master's, comprehensive exam, thesis optional; for doctorate, comprehensive exam, thesis/dissertation. *Entrance requirements:* For master's, GRE General Test, GMAT, or MAT, minimum GPA of 2.5, 3 letters of recommendation, resume; for doctorate, GRE General Test, GMAT, or MAT, master's degree, 3 letters of recommendation, resume. Additional exam requirements/recommendations for international students: Required—TOEFL (minimum score 500 paper-based). *Application deadline:* Applications are processed on a rolling basis. Application fee: $100. Electronic applications accepted. *Expenses:* $640 per credit hour (for MSS) $747 per credit hour (for Ed D). *Financial support:* Research assistantships with full tuition reimbursements, career-related internships or fieldwork, Federal Work-Study, scholarships/grants, and service assistantships available. Support available to part-time students. Financial award application deadline: 8/15; financial award applicants required to submit FAFSA. *Faculty research:* Sport law, leadership behavior, personnel evaluation. *Unit head:* Dr. Fred Cromartie, Director of Doctoral Studies, 251-626-3303 Ext. 7140, Fax: 251-625-1035, E-mail: cromarti@ussa.edu. *Application contact:* Dr. Taffy Sithole, Student Services Coordinator, 251-626-3303 Ext. 7147, Fax: 251-625-1035, E-mail: tsithole@ussa.edu.

The University of Alabama, Graduate School, College of Human Environmental Sciences, Program in Human Environmental Science, Tuscaloosa, AL 35487. Offers interactive technology (MS); quality management (MS); restaurant and meeting management (MS); rural community health (MS); sport management (MS). *Program availability:* Part-time, evening/weekend, online learning. *Students:* 90 full-time (44 women), 158 part-time (86 women); includes 60 minority (42 Black or African American, non-Hispanic/Latino; 1 American Indian or Alaska Native, non-Hispanic/Latino; 2 Asian, non-Hispanic/Latino; 7 Hispanic/Latino; 3 Native Hawaiian or other Pacific Islander, non-Hispanic/Latino; 5 Two or more races, non-Hispanic/Latino). Average age 34. 147 applicants, 84% accepted, 110 enrolled. In 2017, 108 master's awarded. *Degree requirements:* For master's, comprehensive exam. *Entrance requirements:* For master's, GRE (for some specializations), minimum GPA of 3.0. Additional exam requirements/recommendations for international students: Required—TOEFL. *Application deadline:* For fall admission, 7/1 for domestic students; for spring admission, 11/1 for domestic students; for summer admission, 4/15 for domestic students. Applications are processed on a rolling basis. Application fee: $50 ($60 for international students). Electronic applications accepted. *Financial support:* Teaching assistantships with full tuition reimbursements available. Financial award application deadline: 7/1. *Faculty research:* Rural health, hospitality management, sport management, interactive technology, consumer quality management, environmental health and safety. *Unit head:* Dr. Milla D. Boschung, Dean, 205-348-6250, Fax: 205-348-1786, E-mail: mboschun@ches.ua.edu. *Application contact:* Dr. Stuart Usdan, Associate Dean, 205-348-6150, Fax: 205-348-3789, E-mail: susdan@ches.ua.edu.
Website: http://www.ches.ua.edu/programs-of-study.html

University of Alberta, Faculty of Graduate Studies and Research, Program in Business Administration, Edmonton, AB T6G 2E1, Canada. Offers international business (MBA); leisure and sport management (MBA); natural resources and energy (MBA); technology commercialization (MBA); MBA/LL B; MBA/M Ag; MBA/M Eng; MBA/MF; MBA/PhD. *Accreditation:* AACSB. *Program availability:* Part-time, evening/weekend. *Degree requirements:* For master's, thesis or alternative. *Entrance requirements:* For master's, GMAT. Additional exam requirements/recommendations for international students: Required—TOEFL (minimum score 600 paper-based). Electronic applications accepted. *Faculty research:* Natural resources and energy/management and policy/family enterprise/international business/healthcare research management.

University of Arkansas, Graduate School, College of Education and Health Professions, Department of Health, Human Performance and Recreation, Program in Recreation and Sports Management, Fayetteville, AR 72701. Offers M Ed, Ed D. In 2017, 31 master's, 2 doctorates awarded. *Degree requirements:* For master's, thesis optional; for doctorate, thesis/dissertation. *Entrance requirements:* For doctorate, GRE General Test. *Application deadline:* For fall admission, 8/1 for domestic students, 4/1 for international students; for spring admission, 12/1 for domestic students, 10/1 for international students; for summer admission, 4/15 for domestic students, 3/1 for international students. Applications are processed on a rolling basis. Application fee: $60. Electronic applications accepted. *Expenses:* Tuition, state resident: full-time $3782. Tuition, nonresident: full-time $10,238. *Financial support:* In 2017–18, 8 research assistantships, 10 teaching assistantships were awarded; fellowships with tuition reimbursements, career-related internships or fieldwork, and Federal Work-Study also available. Support available to part-time students. Financial award application deadline: 4/1; financial award applicants required to submit FAFSA. *Unit head:* Dr. Matthew Stueck Ganio, Department Head, 479-575-2956, Fax: 479-575-5728, E-mail: msganio@uark.edu. *Application contact:* Dr. Stephen Dittmore, Coordinator of Graduate Studies, 479-575-6625, E-mail: dittmore@uark.edu.
Website: https://hhp.uark.edu

University of Arkansas at Little Rock, Graduate School, College of Education and Health Professions, Department of Health, Human Performance and Sport Management, Little Rock, AR 72204-1099. Offers exercise science (MS); health education and promotion (MS); sport management (MS). *Program availability:* Part-time, evening/weekend. *Degree requirements:* For master's, directed study or residency. *Entrance requirements:* For master's, GRE General Test, minimum GPA of 3.0, 3 reference letters.

University of Central Florida, College of Business Administration, DeVos Sport Business Management Program, Orlando, FL 32816. Offers MSBM. *Students:* 65 full-time (31 women), 2 part-time (both women); includes 21 minority (12 Black or African American, non-Hispanic/Latino; 1 Asian, non-Hispanic/Latino; 8 Hispanic/Latino), 8 international. Average age 25. 79 applicants, 48% accepted, 31 enrolled. In 2017, 32 master's awarded. *Degree requirements:* For master's, thesis or alternative, internship. *Entrance requirements:* For master's, GMAT, minimum GPA of 3.0, letters of recommendation, essay, resume. Additional exam requirements/recommendations for international students: Required—TOEFL. *Application deadline:* For fall admission, 1/15 for domestic students. Application fee: $30. Electronic applications accepted. *Expenses:* Tuition, state resident: part-time $288.16 per credit hour. Tuition, nonresident: part-time $1073.31 per credit hour. Tuition and fees vary according to program. *Financial support:* In 2017–18, 51 students received support, including 49 research assistantships with partial tuition reimbursements available (averaging $7,837 per year), 3 teaching assistantships with partial tuition reimbursements available (averaging $9,088 per year); fellowships also available. Financial award application deadline: 11/1; financial award applicants required to submit FAFSA. *Unit head:* Dr. Richard Lapchick, Director and Chair, 407-823-4886, E-mail: rlapchick@ucf.edu. *Application contact:* Associate Director, Graduate Admissions, 407-823-2766, Fax: 407-823-6442, E-mail: gradadmissions@ucf.edu.
Website: http://business.ucf.edu/devos/

University of Cincinnati, Graduate School, College of Education, Criminal Justice, and Human Services, School of Human Services, Program in Sport Administration, Cincinnati, OH 45221. Offers MS. *Program availability:* 100% online. *Degree requirements:* For master's, thesis or alternative, capstone internship. *Entrance requirements:* Additional exam requirements/recommendations for international students: Required—TOEFL. Electronic applications accepted. *Expenses: Tuition, area resident:* Full-time $14,468. Tuition, state resident: full-time $14,968; part-time $754 per credit hour. Tuition, nonresident: full-time $24,210; part-time $1311 per credit hour. *International tuition:* $26,460 full-time. *Required fees:* $3958; $84 per credit hour. One-time fee: $85 full-time. Tuition and fees vary according to course load, degree level and program.

University of Colorado Denver, Business School, Master of Business Administration Program, Denver, CO 80217. Offers bioinnovation and entrepreneurship (MBA); business intelligence (MBA); business strategy (MBA); business to business marketing (MBA); business to consumer marketing (MBA); change management (MBA); corporate financial management (MBA); enterprise technology management (MBA); entrepreneurship (MBA); health administration (MBA), including financial management, health administration, health information technologies, international health management and policy; human resources management (MBA); international business (MBA); investment management (MBA); managing for sustainability (MBA); sports and entertainment management (MBA). *Accreditation:* AACSB. *Program availability:* Part-time, evening/weekend, 100% online, blended/hybrid learning. *Degree requirements:* For master's, 48 semester hours, including 30 of core courses, 3 in international business, and 15 in electives from over 50 other business courses. *Entrance requirements:* For master's, GMAT, resume, official transcripts, essay, two letters of recommendation, financial statements (for international applicants). Additional exam requirements/recommendations for international students: Required—TOEFL (minimum score 560 paper-based; 83 iBT); Recommended—IELTS (minimum score 6.5). Electronic applications accepted. *Expenses:* Contact institution. *Faculty research:* Marketing, management, entrepreneurship, finance, health administration.

University of Colorado Denver, Business School, Program in Management and Organization, Denver, CO 80217. Offers business strategy (MS); change and innovation (MS); enterprise technology management (MS); entrepreneurship and innovation (MS); global management (MS); leadership (MS); managing for sustainability (MS); managing human resources (MS); sports and entertainment management (MS). *Accreditation:* AACSB. *Program availability:* Part-time, evening/weekend, online learning. *Degree requirements:* For master's, 30 semester hours (12 of required courses, 12 of management electives, and 6 of free electives). *Entrance requirements:* For master's, GMAT, resume, two letters of recommendation, essay, financial statements (for international applicants). Additional exam requirements/recommendations for international students: Required—TOEFL (minimum score 525 paper-based; 71 iBT); Recommended—IELTS (minimum score 6.5). Electronic applications accepted. *Expenses:* Contact institution. *Faculty research:* Human resource management, management of catastrophe, turnaround strategies.

University of Connecticut, Graduate School, College of Agriculture, Health and Natural Resources, Department of Kinesiology, Sport Management Program, Storrs, CT 06269. Offers MS. Terminal master's awarded for partial completion of doctoral program. *Degree requirements:* For master's, comprehensive exam, thesis or alternative. *Entrance requirements:* Additional exam requirements/recommendations for international students: Required—TOEFL (minimum score 550 paper-based). Electronic applications accepted.

University of Dallas, Satish and Yasmin Gupta College of Business, Irving, TX 75062-4736. Offers accounting (MBA, MS); business administration (DBA); business analytics (MS); business management (MBA); corporate finance (MBA); cybersecurity (MS); finance (MS); financial services (MBA); global business (MBA, MS); health services management (MBA); human resource management (MBA); information and technology management (MS); information assurance (MBA); information technology (MBA); information technology service management (MBA); marketing management (MBA);

Sports Management

organization development (MBA); project management (MBA); sports and entertainment management (MBA); strategic leadership (MBA); supply chain management (MBA). *Accreditation:* AACSB. *Program availability:* Part-time, evening/weekend, online learning. *Entrance requirements:* Additional exam requirements/recommendations for international students: Required—TOEFL. *Application deadline:* Applications are processed on a rolling basis. *Application fee:* $50. Electronic applications accepted. *Expenses:* Contact institution. *Financial support:* Application deadline: 2/15; applicants required to submit FAFSA. *Unit head:* Brett J.L. Landry, Dean, 972-721-5356, E-mail: blandry@udallas.edu. *Application contact:* Dr. David Sweet, Dean, Braniff Graduate School, 972-721-5288, Fax: 972-721-5280, E-mail: dsweet@udallas.edu.
Website: http://www.udallas.edu/cob/

University of Florida, Graduate School, College of Health and Human Performance, Department of Tourism, Recreation and Sport Management, Gainesville, FL 32611. Offers health and human performance (PhD), including historic preservation (MS, PhD), recreation, parks and tourism (MS, PhD), sport management; recreation, parks and tourism (MS), including historic preservation (MS, PhD), natural resource recreation, recreation, parks and tourism (MS, PhD), therapeutic recreation, tourism, tropical conservation and development; sport management (MS), including historic preservation (MS, PhD), tropical conservation and development; JD/MS; MSM/MS. *Degree requirements:* For master's, comprehensive exam (for some programs), thesis (for some programs); for doctorate, comprehensive exam, thesis/dissertation. *Entrance requirements:* For master's and doctorate, GRE General Test, minimum GPA of 3.0. Additional exam requirements/recommendations for international students: Required—TOEFL (minimum score 550 paper-based; 80 iBT), IELTS (minimum score 6). Electronic applications accepted. *Faculty research:* Hospitality, natural resource management, sport management, tourism.

University of Idaho, College of Graduate Studies, College of Education, Health and Human Sciences, Department of Movement Sciences, Moscow, ID 83844. Offers athletic training (MSAT, DAT); exercise science and health (MS); physical education teacher education (M Ed, MS); recreation, sport, and tourism management (MS). *Faculty:* 22. *Students:* 89 full-time (41 women), 18 part-time (7 women). Average age 28. In 2017, 24 master's awarded. *Degree requirements:* For doctorate, thesis/dissertation. *Entrance requirements:* For master's and doctorate, minimum GPA of 3.0. Additional exam requirements/recommendations for international students: Required—TOEFL. *Application deadline:* For fall admission, 8/1 for domestic students; for spring admission, 12/15 for domestic students. Applications are processed on a rolling basis. Application fee: $60. Electronic applications accepted. *Expenses:* Tuition, state resident: full-time $6722; part-time $430 per credit hour. Tuition, nonresident: full-time $23,046; part-time $1337 per credit hour. *Required fees:* $2142; $63 per credit hour. *Financial support:* Research assistantships and teaching assistantships available. Financial award applicants required to submit FAFSA. *Unit head:* Dr. Philip W. Scruggs, Chair, 208-885-7921, E-mail: movementsciences@uidaho.edu. *Application contact:* Sean Scoggin, Graduate Recruitment Coordinator, 208-885-4001, Fax: 208-885-4406, E-mail: graduateadmissions@uidaho.edu.
Website: https://www.uidaho.edu/ed/mvsc

University of Indianapolis, Graduate Programs, College of Health Sciences, Department of Kinesiology, Indianapolis, IN 46227-3697. Offers sport management (MS). *Program availability:* Evening/weekend.

The University of Iowa, Graduate College, College of Liberal Arts and Sciences, Department of Health and Human Physiology, Iowa City, IA 52242-1316. Offers athletic training (MS); clinical exercise physiology (MS); health and human physiology (PhD); leisure studies (MA, PhD), including recreational sport management (PhD), therapeutic recreation (MA). *Degree requirements:* For master's, thesis optional, exam; for doctorate, comprehensive exam, thesis/dissertation. *Entrance requirements:* For master's and doctorate, GRE General Test, minimum GPA of 3.0. Additional exam requirements/recommendations for international students: Required—TOEFL (minimum score 600 paper-based; 100 iBT). Electronic applications accepted.

The University of Kansas, Graduate Studies, School of Education, Department of Health, Sport, and Exercise Sciences, Lawrence, KS 66045. Offers exercise science (MS Ed); health, sport, and exercise sciences (PhD); sport management (MS Ed). *Accreditation:* NCATE. *Program availability:* Part-time, evening/weekend. *Students:* 56 full-time (23 women), 11 part-time (5 women); includes 8 minority (2 Black or African American, non-Hispanic/Latino; 1 American Indian or Alaska Native, non-Hispanic/Latino; 2 Hispanic/Latino; 3 Two or more races, non-Hispanic/Latino), 4 international. Average age 26. 70 applicants, 63% accepted, 23 enrolled. In 2017, 19 master's, 6 doctorates awarded. *Entrance requirements:* For master's, GRE General Test (minimum score 1000, 450 verbal, 450 quantitative, 4.0 analytical), minimum GPA of 3.0, three letters of recommendation, personal statement, resume, writing sample; for doctorate, GRE General Test (minimum score 1100, verbal 500, quantitative 500, analytical 4.5), minimum graduate GPA of 3.5, undergraduate 3.0; three letters of recommendation; personal statement; resume; writing sample; interview with an advisor. *Application deadline:* For fall admission, 3/15 for domestic and international students; for spring admission, 10/1 for domestic and international students; for summer admission, 3/15 for domestic and international students. Application fee: $65 ($85 for international students). Electronic applications accepted. *Financial support:* Research assistantships, teaching assistantships, Federal Work-Study, scholarships/grants, and unspecified assistantships available. Financial award application deadline: 2/21. *Faculty research:* Exercise and sport psychology, obesity prevention, sexuality health, sport ethics, skeletal muscle cell signaling and performance. *Unit head:* Dr. Joseph Weir, Chair, 785-864-0784, E-mail: joseph.weir@ku.edu. *Application contact:* Sarah Clopton, Graduate Admissions Coordinator, 785-864-7268, E-mail: sclopton@ku.edu.
Website: http://hses.soe.ku.edu/

University of Louisiana at Monroe, Graduate School, College of Health and Pharmaceutical Sciences, Department of Kinesiology, Monroe, LA 71209-0001. Offers applied exercise science (MS); clinical exercise physiology (MS); sports, fitness and recreation management (MS). *Program availability:* Part-time, evening/weekend, online learning. *Faculty:* 6 full-time (2 women), 1 part-time/adjunct (0 women). *Students:* 28 full-time (15 women), 13 part-time (5 women); includes 12 minority (8 Black or African American, non-Hispanic/Latino; 4 Hispanic/Latino), 3 international. Average age 24. 27 applicants, 52% accepted, 11 enrolled. In 2017, 27 master's awarded. *Degree requirements:* For master's, comprehensive exam, thesis, 6-hour internship. *Entrance requirements:* For master's, GRE General Test. Additional exam requirements/recommendations for international students: Required—TOEFL (minimum score 500 paper-based; 61 iBT). *Application deadline:* For fall admission, 8/24 priority date for domestic students, 7/1 for international students; for winter admission, 12/14 priority date for domestic students; for spring admission, 1/19 for domestic students, 11/1 for international students. Applications are processed on a rolling basis. Application fee: $20 ($30 for international students). Electronic applications accepted. *Expenses:* Tuition, state resident: full-time $6489; part-time $479 per hour. Tuition, nonresident: full-time $12,100; part-time $479 per hour. *Required fees:* $8860; $802 per hour. $3273 per semester. *Financial support:* In 2017–18, 12 students received support. Research assistantships, career-related internships or fieldwork, Federal Work-Study, and unspecified assistantships available. Financial award application deadline: 4/1; financial

award applicants required to submit FAFSA. *Faculty research:* Cardiovascular disease risk factors; exercise and immunological system; attitude, exercise, and the aged. *Unit head:* Dr. Ken Alford, Director, 318-342-1306, E-mail: alford@ulm.edu. *Application contact:* Dr. Tommie Church, Director of Graduate Studies, 318-342-1321, E-mail: church@ulm.edu.
Website: http://www.ulm.edu/kinesiology/

University of Louisville, Graduate School, College of Education and Human Development, Department of Health and Sport Sciences, Louisville, KY 40292-0001. Offers community health education (M Ed); exercise physiology (MS), including health and sport sciences, strength and conditioning; health and physical education (MAT); sport administration (MS). *Program availability:* Part-time, evening/weekend. *Students:* 35 full-time (11 women), 6 part-time (4 women); includes 10 minority (5 Black or African American, non-Hispanic/Latino; 4 Hispanic/Latino; 1 Two or more races, non-Hispanic/Latino), 1 international. Average age 28. 46 applicants, 67% accepted, 20 enrolled. In 2017, 21 master's awarded. Application fee: $65. *Expenses:* Tuition, state resident: full-time $12,246; part-time $681 per credit hour. Tuition, nonresident: full-time $25,486; part-time $1417 per credit hour. *Required fees:* $196. Tuition and fees vary according to course load, program and reciprocity agreements. *Financial support:* Applicants required to submit FAFSA. *Faculty research:* Sport administration, exercise physiology, exercise science, physical education, health education. *Total annual research expenditures:* $91,688. *Unit head:* Dr. Margaret Hancock, Interim Chair/Assistant Professor, 502-852-6645, E-mail: meg.hancock@louisville.edu. *Application contact:* Betty Hampton, Director of Graduate Student Services, 502-852-5597, Fax: 502-852-1465, E-mail: edadvise@louisville.edu.
Website: http://www.louisville.edu/education/departments/hss

University of Louisville, Graduate School, College of Education and Human Development, Departments of Early Childhood and Elementary Education, Middle and Secondary Education, and Special Education, Louisville, KY 40292-0001. Offers art education (MAT); autism and applied behavior analysis (Certificate); curriculum and instruction (PhD); early elementary education (MAT); exercise physiology (MS); health and physical education (MAT); health professions education (Certificate); higher education (MA); human resources and organization development (MS); instructional technology (M Ed); interdisciplinary early childhood education (MAT); middle school education (MAT); music education (MAT); secondary education (MAT); special education (MAT); sport administration (MS); teacher leadership (M Ed). *Program availability:* Part-time, evening/weekend. *Students:* 114 full-time (73 women), 173 part-time (114 women); includes 49 minority (19 Black or African American, non-Hispanic/Latino; 5 Asian, non-Hispanic/Latino; 13 Hispanic/Latino; 12 Two or more races, non-Hispanic/Latino), 7 international. Average age 29. 132 applicants, 73% accepted, 57 enrolled. In 2017, 70 master's, 2 doctorates, 2 other advanced degrees awarded. *Application deadline:* For spring admission, 1/1 priority date for international students. Application fee: $65. *Expenses:* Tuition, state resident: full-time $12,246; part-time $681 per credit hour. Tuition, nonresident: full-time $25,486; part-time $1417 per credit hour. *Required fees:* $196. Tuition and fees vary according to course load, program and reciprocity agreements. *Financial support:* Application deadline: 6/1; applicants required to submit FAFSA. *Faculty research:* STEM teaching and learning; content literacy for English language learners; social justice in teacher education; adolescent literacy; mathematics teacher development. *Total annual research expenditures:* $1.7 million. *Unit head:* Dr. Ann E. Larson, Dean, College of Education and Human Development, 502-852-6411, Fax: 502-852-1464, E-mail: ann@louisville.edu. *Application contact:* Betty Hampton, Director of Graduate Student Services, 502-852-5597, Fax: 502-852-1465, E-mail: edadvise@louisville.edu.
Website: http://louisville.edu/delphi

University of Mary, School of Health Sciences, Program in Sports and Physical Education Administration, Bismarck, ND 58504-9652. Offers MS. *Program availability:* Online learning. *Entrance requirements:* For master's, bachelor's degree in athletic training, exercise science, physical education, or a related field; minimum undergraduate GPA of 2.5.

University of Mary Hardin-Baylor, Graduate Studies in Exercise Physiology, Belton, TX 76513. Offers exercise physiology (MS Ed); sport administration (MS Ed). *Program availability:* Part-time, 100% online. *Faculty:* 6 full-time (2 women). *Students:* 18 full-time (5 women), 30 part-time (11 women); includes 21 minority (5 Black or African American, non-Hispanic/Latino; 14 Hispanic/Latino; 2 Two or more races, non-Hispanic/Latino). Average age 26. 30 applicants, 90% accepted, 19 enrolled. In 2017, 19 master's awarded. *Degree requirements:* For master's, comprehensive exam, thesis optional. *Entrance requirements:* For master's, bachelor's degree in exercise science or related field; minimum GPA of 3.0; interview with program director. Additional exam requirements/recommendations for international students: Required—TOEFL (minimum score 60 iBT), IELTS (minimum score 4.5). *Application deadline:* For fall admission, 6/1 for domestic students, 4/30 priority date for international students; for spring admission, 11/1 for domestic students, 9/30 priority date for international students. Applications are processed on a rolling basis. Application fee: $35 ($135 for international students). Electronic applications accepted. *Expenses:* Tuition: Full-time $15,570; part-time $10,380 per credit hour. *Required fees:* $1350; $75 per credit hour. $50 per term. Tuition and fees vary according to course load and degree level. *Financial support:* In 2017–18, 37 students received support. Federal Work-Study, unspecified assistantships, and scholarships for some active duty military personnel available. Support available to part-time students. Financial award application deadline: 6/1; financial award applicants required to submit FAFSA. *Faculty research:* Evaluation of the efficacy and safety of Fenugreek extract ingestion on markers of muscle damage and inflammation on healthy non-resistance trained subjects; genetic influences on sport performance and athlete health; examination of biomarkers of sub-concussive impacts in men and women's Division III soccer players; The Acute Response of nutritive vs. non-nutritive sweeteners in soft drinks of blood glucose and insulin in regular soft drink consumers. *Unit head:* Dr. Lem Taylor, Director, MS Ed in Exercise Physiology Program, 254-295-4895, E-mail: ltaylor@umhb.edu. *Application contact:* Sharon Aguilera, Assistant Director, Graduate Admissions, 254-295-4835, E-mail: saguilera@umhb.edu.
Website: https://go.umhb.edu/graduate/exercise-physiology/home

University of Massachusetts Amherst, Graduate School, Interdisciplinary Programs, Dual Degree Program in Management and Sport Management, Amherst, MA 01003. Offers MBA/MS. *Program availability:* Part-time. *Entrance requirements:* Additional exam requirements/recommendations for international students: Required—TOEFL (minimum score 600 paper-based; 100 iBT), IELTS (minimum score 7). Electronic applications accepted.

University of Massachusetts Amherst, Graduate School, Isenberg School of Management, Department of Sport Management, Amherst, MA 01003. Offers MBA, MS, MBA/MS. *Program availability:* Part-time. Terminal master's awarded for partial completion of doctoral program. *Degree requirements:* For master's, thesis or alternative. *Entrance requirements:* For master's, GMAT or GRE General Test. Additional exam requirements/recommendations for international students: Required—TOEFL (minimum score 550 paper-based; 80 iBT), IELTS (minimum score 6.5). Electronic applications accepted.

University of Massachusetts Amherst, Graduate School, Isenberg School of Management, Program in Management, Amherst, MA 01003. Offers accounting (PhD); business administration (MBA); entrepreneurship (MBA); finance (MBA, PhD); healthcare administration (MBA); hospitality and tourism management (PhD); management science (PhD); marketing (MBA, PhD); organization studies (PhD); sport management (PhD); strategic management (MBA); MBA/MS. *Accreditation:* AACSB. *Program availability:* Part-time, evening/weekend, online learning. Terminal master's awarded for partial completion of doctoral program. *Degree requirements:* For doctorate, comprehensive exam, thesis/dissertation. *Entrance requirements:* For master's and doctorate, GMAT or GRE General Test. Additional exam requirements/recommendations for international students: Required—TOEFL (minimum score 550 paper-based; 80 iBT), IELTS (minimum score 6.5). Electronic applications accepted.

University of Miami, Graduate School, School of Education and Human Development, Department of Kinesiology and Sport Sciences, Program in Sport Administration, Coral Gables, FL 33124. Offers MS Ed. *Program availability:* Part-time, evening/weekend, 100% online. *Degree requirements:* For master's, thesis optional, special project. *Entrance requirements:* For master's, GRE General Test. Additional exam requirements/recommendations for international students: Required—TOEFL (minimum score 550 paper-based; 80 iBT); Recommended—IELTS (minimum score 6.5). Electronic applications accepted. *Faculty research:* Constitutional procedural due process, legal liability, tort law, moral development in sports administration, ethics intervention.

University of Michigan, Rackham Graduate School, School of Kinesiology, Ann Arbor, MI 48109. Offers movement science (MS, PhD); sport management (MS, PhD). *Faculty:* 31 full-time (16 women). *Students:* 94 full-time (40 women); includes 22 minority (6 Black or African American, non-Hispanic/Latino; 5 Asian, non-Hispanic/Latino; 7 Hispanic/Latino; 4 Two or more races, non-Hispanic/Latino). Average age 26. 230 applicants, 48% accepted, 52 enrolled. In 2017, 25 master's, 7 doctorates awarded. Terminal master's awarded for partial completion of doctoral program. *Degree requirements:* For master's, thesis optional; for doctorate, comprehensive exam, thesis/dissertation, oral defense of dissertation. *Entrance requirements:* For master's and doctorate, GRE General Test. Additional exam requirements/recommendations for international students: Required—TOEFL (minimum score 84 iBT). *Application deadline:* For fall admission, 12/1 priority date for domestic students, 12/1 for international students. Applications are processed on a rolling basis. Application fee: $75 ($90 for international students). Electronic applications accepted. *Expenses:* Tuition, state resident: full-time $22,368; part-time $1201 per credit hour. Tuition, nonresident: full-time $45,156; part-time $2467 per credit hour. *Required fees:* $376 per term. Tuition and fees vary according to course load, degree level and program. *Financial support:* In 2017–18, 34 students received support, including 11 fellowships with full tuition reimbursements available, 12 research assistantships with full tuition reimbursements available, 11 teaching assistantships with full tuition reimbursements available; Federal Work-Study, scholarships/grants, traineeships, health care benefits, and unspecified assistantships also available. Financial award application deadline: 12/1. *Faculty research:* Motor development, exercise physiology, biomechanics, sport medicine, sport management. *Unit head:* Dr. Ketra L. Armstrong, Associate Dean for Graduate Programs, 734-647-3027, Fax: 734-647-2808, E-mail: ketra@umich.edu. *Application contact:* Charlene F. Ruloff, Graduate Program Coordinator, 734-764-1343, Fax: 734-647-2808, E-mail: cruloff@umich.edu.
Website: http://www.kines.umich.edu/

University of Minnesota, Twin Cities Campus, Graduate School, College of Education and Human Development, School of Kinesiology, Minneapolis, MN 55455-0213. Offers kinesiology (MS, PhD), including behavioral aspects of physical activity, biomechanics and neuromotor control, exercise physiology, perceptual-motor control and learning, sport and exercise psychology, sport management (PhD), sport sociology; sport and exercise science (M Ed); sport management (M Ed, MA). *Program availability:* Part-time. *Faculty:* 16 full-time (7 women). *Students:* 111 full-time (52 women), 22 part-time (8 women); includes 21 minority (7 Black or African American, non-Hispanic/Latino; 1 American Indian or Alaska Native, non-Hispanic/Latino; 4 Asian, non-Hispanic/Latino; 7 Hispanic/Latino; 2 Two or more races, non-Hispanic/Latino), 15 international. Average age 27. 120 applicants, 25% accepted, 30 enrolled. In 2017, 41 master's, 9 doctorates awarded. Terminal master's awarded for partial completion of doctoral program. *Degree requirements:* For master's, final oral exam; for doctorate, thesis/dissertation, preliminary written/oral exam, final oral exam. *Entrance requirements:* For master's, GRE or MAT, minimum GPA of 3.0; for doctorate, GRE or MAT, minimum GPA of 3.0, writing sample. Application fee: $75 ($95 for international students). *Financial support:* In 2017–18, 2 fellowships, 9 research assistantships with full tuition reimbursements (averaging $6,651 per year), 41 teaching assistantships with full tuition reimbursements (averaging $14,060 per year) were awarded; career-related internships or fieldwork, Federal Work-Study, institutionally sponsored loans, and tuition waivers (full and partial) also available. Support available to part-time students. *Faculty research:* Role of physical activity in preventing health related problems; mechanism of age-related disorders, diseases and mental problems, and the ways to ameliorate them; role of sports in society and social justice; sports among populations with low income and racial diversity; fundamental functions of the body and the mechanism controlling the mechanisms; psychological issues related to physical activity and sports. *Total annual research expenditures:* $948,746. *Unit head:* Dr. Li Li Ji, Director, 612-624-9809, E-mail: llji@umn.edu. *Application contact:* Dr. Michael Wade, Director of Graduate Studies, 612-626-2094, E-mail: mwade@umn.edu.
Website: http://www.cehd.umn.edu/kin/

University of Nebraska at Kearney, College of Education, Kinesiology and Sport Sciences Department, Kearney, NE 68849-0001. Offers general physical education (MA Ed), including recreation and leisure, sports administration; physical education exercise science (MA Ed); physical education master teacher (MA Ed), including pedagogy, special populations. *Program availability:* Part-time, evening/weekend, 100% online. *Degree requirements:* For master's, comprehensive exam, thesis optional. *Entrance requirements:* For master's, GRE General Test (for some programs), personal statement. Additional exam requirements/recommendations for international students: Recommended—TOEFL (minimum score 550 paper-based; 79 iBT), IELTS (minimum score 6.5). Electronic applications accepted. *Faculty research:* Ergonomic aids, nutrition, motor development, sports pedagogy, applied behavior analysis, physical activity and wellness, athletic training, therapeutic Interventions, exercise physiology, endocrinology and metabolism.

University of New Brunswick Fredericton, School of Graduate Studies, Faculty of Business Administration, Fredericton, NB E3B 5A3, Canada. Offers business administration (MBA); engineering management (MBA); entrepreneurship (MBA); sports and recreation management (MBA); MBA/LL B. *Program availability:* Part-time. *Degree requirements:* For master's, thesis optional. *Entrance requirements:* For master's, GMAT (minimum score 550), minimum GPA of 3.0; 3-5 years of work experience; 3 letters of reference with at least one academic reference. Additional exam requirements/recommendations for international students: Required—TOEFL (minimum score 580 paper-based; 92 iBT) or IELTS (minimum score 7). Electronic applications accepted. *Faculty research:* Entrepreneurship, finance, law, sport and recreation management, engineering management.

University of New Brunswick Fredericton, School of Graduate Studies, Faculty of Kinesiology, Fredericton, NB E3B 5A3, Canada. Offers exercise and sport science (M Sc); sport and recreation management (MBA); sport and recreation studies (MA). *Program availability:* Part-time. *Degree requirements:* For master's, thesis (for some programs). *Entrance requirements:* For master's, GMAT (minimum score of 550 for sport and recreation management program), minimum GPA of 3.0, written statement of research goals and interests. Additional exam requirements/recommendations for international students: Required—TOEFL (minimum score 92 iBT), IELTS (minimum score 7). Electronic applications accepted.

University of New Haven, Graduate School, College of Business, Program in Business Administration, West Haven, CT 06516. Offers accounting (MBA); business administration (MBA); business intelligence (MBA); business policy and strategic leadership (MBA); finance (MBA), including chartered financial analyst; global marketing (MBA); human resources management (MBA); sport management (MBA). *Accreditation:* AACSB. *Program availability:* Part-time, evening/weekend. *Students:* 123 full-time (56 women), 67 part-time (28 women); includes 53 minority (27 Black or African American, non-Hispanic/Latino; 11 Asian, non-Hispanic/Latino; 12 Hispanic/Latino; 3 Two or more races, non-Hispanic/Latino), 50 international. Average age 28. 148 applicants, 89% accepted, 67 enrolled. In 2017, 106 master's awarded. *Entrance requirements:* For master's, GMAT. Additional exam requirements/recommendations for international students: Required—TOEFL (minimum score 80 iBT), IELTS, PTE. *Application deadline:* Applications are processed on a rolling basis. Application fee: $50. Electronic applications accepted. Application fee is waived when completed online. *Expenses:* Tuition: Full-time $16,020; part-time $890 per credit hour. *Required fees:* $220; $90 per term. *Financial support:* Research assistantships with partial tuition reimbursements, teaching assistantships with partial tuition reimbursements, career-related internships or fieldwork, Federal Work-Study, scholarships/grants, and unspecified assistantships available. Support available to part-time students. Financial award applicants required to submit FAFSA. *Unit head:* Darell Singleterry, Director, 203-932-1085, E-mail: dsingleterry@newhaven.edu. *Application contact:* Michelle Mason, Director of Graduate Enrollment, 203-932-7067, E-mail: mmason@newhaven.edu.
Website: http://www.newhaven.edu/business/graduate-programs/mba/index.php
See Display on page 154 and Close-Up on page 185.

University of New Haven, Graduate School, College of Business, Program in Sport Management, West Haven, CT 06516. Offers collegiate athletic administration (MS); facility management (MS); sport analytics (MS); sport management (Graduate Certificate). *Program availability:* Part-time, evening/weekend. *Students:* 16 full-time (4 women), 7 part-time (5 women); includes 5 minority (4 Black or African American, non-Hispanic/Latino; 1 Native Hawaiian or other Pacific Islander, non-Hispanic/Latino), 3 international. Average age 26. 34 applicants, 88% accepted, 12 enrolled. In 2017, 15 master's awarded. *Entrance requirements:* For master's, GMAT. Additional exam requirements/recommendations for international students: Required—TOEFL (minimum score 80 iBT), IELTS, PTE. *Application deadline:* Applications are processed on a rolling basis. Application fee: $50. Electronic applications accepted. Application fee is waived when completed online. *Expenses:* Tuition: Full-time $16,020; part-time $890 per credit hour. *Required fees:* $220; $90 per term. *Financial support:* Research assistantships with partial tuition reimbursements, teaching assistantships with partial tuition reimbursements, Federal Work-Study, scholarships/grants, and unspecified assistantships available. Support available to part-time students. Financial award applicants required to submit FAFSA. *Unit head:* Gil B. Fried, Professor, 203-932-7081, E-mail: gfried@newhaven.edu.
Website: http://www.newhaven.edu/6851/
See Display on page 154 and Close-Up on page 185.

University of New Mexico, Graduate Studies, College of Education, Program in Physical Education, Sports and Exercise Science, Albuquerque, NM 87131-2039. Offers curriculum and instruction (PhD); exercise science (PhD); sports administration (PhD). *Program availability:* Part-time. *Students:* Average age 30. 67 applicants, 75% accepted, 35 enrolled. In 2017, 13 doctorates awarded. *Degree requirements:* For doctorate, comprehensive exam, thesis/dissertation, inquiry skills, 24 credits in supporting area. *Entrance requirements:* For doctorate, GRE, letter of intent, 3 letters of reference, minimum cumulative GPA of 3.0 in last 2 years of bachelor's degree. Additional exam requirements/recommendations for international students: Required—TOEFL (minimum score 550 paper-based). *Application deadline:* For fall admission, 3/1 priority date for domestic students; for spring admission, 11/1 priority date for domestic students. Application fee: $50. Electronic applications accepted. *Financial support:* Fellowships, teaching assistantships with full tuition reimbursements, career-related internships or fieldwork, Federal Work-Study, institutionally sponsored loans, scholarships/grants, health care benefits, tuition waivers, and unspecified assistantships available. Financial award application deadline: 3/1; financial award applicants required to submit FAFSA. *Faculty research:* Facility risk management, physical education pedagogy practices, physiological adaptations to exercise, physiological adaptations to heat, sport leadership. *Unit head:* Dr. Todd Seidler, Chair, 505-277-2783, Fax: 505-277-6227, E-mail: tseidler@unm.edu. *Application contact:* Monica Lopez, Program Office, 505-277-5151, Fax: 505-277-6227, E-mail: mllopez@unm.edu.
Website: https://coe.unm.edu/departments-programs/hess/physical-education/physical-education-phd/index.html

The University of North Carolina at Chapel Hill, Graduate School, College of Arts and Sciences, Department of Exercise and Sport Science, Chapel Hill, NC 27599. Offers athletic training (MA); exercise physiology (MA); sport administration (MA). *Degree requirements:* For master's, comprehensive exam, thesis. *Entrance requirements:* For master's, GRE General Test, minimum GPA of 3.0. Additional exam requirements/recommendations for international students: Required—TOEFL (minimum score 550 paper-based). Electronic applications accepted. *Faculty research:* Mild head injury in sport, endocrine system's response to exercise, obesity and children, effect of aerobic exercise on cerebral bloodflow in elderly population.

The University of North Carolina at Pembroke, The Graduate School, School of Education, Department of Health and Human Performance, Pembroke, NC 28372-1510. Offers health/physical education (MAT); physical education (MA), including exercise/sports administration, physical education advanced licensure. *Program availability:* Part-time, evening/weekend. *Degree requirements:* For master's, comprehensive exam, thesis optional. *Entrance requirements:* For master's, MAT or GRE, minimum GPA of 3.0 in major, 2.5 overall. Additional exam requirements/recommendations for international students: Required—TOEFL. *Application deadline:* For fall admission, 7/15 priority date for domestic and international students; for spring admission, 12/1 priority date for domestic and international students. Applications are processed on a rolling basis. Application fee: $45 ($60 for international students). *Financial support:* Application deadline: 4/15; applicants required to submit FAFSA. *Unit head:* Dr. Leah Fiorentino, Program Director, 910-775-4354, E-mail: leah.fiorentino@uncp.edu.
Website: https://www.uncp.edu/departments/health-and-human-performance

University of Northern Colorado, Graduate School, College of Natural and Health Sciences, School of Sport and Exercise Science, Greeley, CO 80639. Offers exercise science (MS, PhD); physical education and physical activity leadership (MAT); sport

Sports Management

administration (MS, PhD); sport pedagogy (MS, PhD); sports coaching (MA). *Program availability:* Part-time, evening/weekend. *Degree requirements:* For master's, comprehensive exam; for doctorate, comprehensive exam, thesis/dissertation. *Entrance requirements:* For master's, 2 letters of recommendation, resume; for doctorate. GRE General Test, 3 letters of recommendation, resume. Electronic applications accepted.

University of Northern Iowa, Graduate College, College of Education, School of Kinesiology, Allied Health and Human Services, MA Program in Physical Education, Cedar Falls, IA 50614. Offers kinesiology (MA); teaching/coaching (MA). *Program availability:* Part-time, evening/weekend. *Degree requirements:* For master's, comprehensive exam, thesis or alternative. *Entrance requirements:* For master's, minimum GPA of 3.0. Additional exam requirements/recommendations for international students: Required—TOEFL (minimum score 500 paper-based; 61 iBT). Electronic applications accepted.

University of North Florida, College of Education and Human Services, Department of Leadership, School Counseling and Sport Management, Jacksonville, FL 32224. Offers counselor education (M Ed), including school counseling; educational leadership (M Ed, Ed D), including athletic administration (M Ed), educational leadership, educational technology (M Ed), instructional leadership (M Ed). *Program availability:* Part-time, evening/weekend. *Degree requirements:* For doctorate, thesis/dissertation. *Entrance requirements:* For master's, GRE General Test, minimum GPA of 3.0 in last 60 hours, interview, 3 letters of recommendation; for doctorate, GRE General Test, master's degree, interview, 3 letters of recommendation, writing sample. Additional exam requirements/recommendations for international students: Required—TOEFL (minimum score 500 paper-based). Electronic applications accepted. *Faculty research:* Counseling: ethics; lesbian, bisexual and transgender issues; educational leadership: school culture and climate; educational assessment and accountability; school safety and student discipline.

University of Oregon, Graduate School, Charles H. Lundquist College of Business, Program in Sports Product Management, Portland, OR 97209. Offers MS.

University of San Francisco, College of Arts and Sciences, Sport Management Program, San Francisco, CA 94117-1080. Offers MA. *Program availability:* Evening/weekend. *Degree requirements:* For master's, thesis or alternative. *Entrance requirements:* For master's, interview, minimum GPA of 2.75. Additional exam requirements/recommendations for international students: Required—TOEFL, IELTS, PTE. *Faculty research:* Media and sports, sports marketing, sports law, management and organization.

University of South Alabama, College of Education and Professional Studies, Department of Health, Kinesiology, and Sport, Mobile, AL 36688. Offers exercise science (MS); health education (M Ed, MS); physical education (M Ed); sport management (MS). *Accreditation:* NCATE (one or more programs are accredited). *Program availability:* Part-time. *Faculty:* 7 full-time (2 women). *Students:* 47 full-time (15 women), 7 part-time (3 women); includes 23 minority (19 Black or African American, non-Hispanic/Latino; 1 American Indian or Alaska Native, non-Hispanic/Latino; 2 Asian, non-Hispanic/Latino; 1 Hispanic/Latino), 4 international. Average age 25. 48 applicants, 54% accepted, 19 enrolled. In 2017, 23 master's awarded. *Degree requirements:* For master's, comprehensive exam, thesis optional. *Entrance requirements:* For master's, GRE General Test or MAT, Alabama Class B certificate or the equivalent (for students seeking the master's-level/Class A certification). Additional exam requirements/recommendations for international students: Required—TOEFL. *Application deadline:* For fall admission, 7/1 priority date for domestic students, 6/15 priority date for international students; for spring admission, 11/15 priority date for domestic students, 11/1 priority date for international students; for summer admission, 4/15 for domestic students, 4/1 for international students. Applications are processed on a rolling basis. Application fee: $35. Electronic applications accepted. *Expenses:* Tuition, state resident: full-time $10,104; part-time $421 per semester hour. Tuition, nonresident: full-time $20,208; part-time $842 per semester hour. *Financial support:* Fellowships, research assistantships, teaching assistantships with partial tuition reimbursements, career-related internships or fieldwork, Federal Work-Study, institutionally sponsored loans, scholarships/grants, and unspecified assistantships available. Support available to part-time students. Financial award application deadline: 3/31; financial award applicants required to submit FAFSA. *Unit head:* Dr. John Kovaleski, Department Chair, 251-461-1622, Fax: 251-460-7252, E-mail: jkovales@southalabama.edu. *Application contact:* Dr. Susan Santoli, Director of Graduate Studies, 251-380-2836, Fax: 251-380-2748, E-mail: ssantoli@southalabama.edu.
Website: http://www.southalabama.edu/colleges/ceps/hks/index.html

University of South Carolina, The Graduate School, College of Hospitality, Retail, and Sport Management, Department of Sport and Entertainment Management, Columbia, SC 29208. Offers live sport and entertainment events (MS); public assembly facilities management (MS). *Program availability:* Part-time. *Degree requirements:* For master's, comprehensive exam, thesis optional. *Entrance requirements:* For master's, GRE General Test or GMAT (preferred), minimum GPA of 3.0. Additional exam requirements/recommendations for international students: Required—TOEFL (minimum score 570 paper-based; 70 iBT). Electronic applications accepted. *Expenses:* Contact institution. *Faculty research:* Public assembly marketing, operations, box office, booking and scheduling, law/economic impacts.

University of Southern Indiana, Graduate Studies, Pott College of Science, Engineering, and Education, Program in Sport Management, Evansville, IN 47712-3590. Offers MSSM. *Program availability:* Part-time, evening/weekend. *Faculty:* 3 full-time (2 women), 1 (woman) part-time/adjunct. *Students:* 27 full-time (6 women), 6 part-time (2 women); includes 6 minority (2 Black or African American, non-Hispanic/Latino; 3 Hispanic/Latino; 1 Two or more races, non-Hispanic/Latino), 3 international. Average age 25. In 2017, 3 master's awarded. *Entrance requirements:* For master's, personal statement, three letters of recommendation. Additional exam requirements/recommendations for international students: Required—TOEFL (minimum score 550 paper-based; 79 iBT), IELTS (minimum score 6). *Application deadline:* Applications are processed on a rolling basis. Application fee: $40. Electronic applications accepted. *Expenses:* Tuition, state resident: full-time $9394. Tuition, nonresident: full-time $17,917. *Required fees:* $510. *Financial support:* In 2017–18, 10 students received support. Federal Work-Study, scholarships/grants, tuition waivers (full and partial), and unspecified assistantships available. Financial award application deadline: 3/1; financial award applicants required to submit FAFSA. *Unit head:* Dr. Glenna G. Bower, Department Chair, 812-464-1709, E-mail: gbower@usi.edu. *Application contact:* Dr. Mayola Rowser, Director, Graduate Studies, 812-465-7015, Fax: 812-464-1956, E-mail: mrowser@usi.edu.
Website: https://www.usi.edu/science/kinesiology-and-sport/programs/master-of-science-in-sport-management

University of South Florida, Muma College of Business, Department of Marketing, Tampa, FL 33620-9951. Offers business administration (PhD), including marketing; marketing (MSM); sport and entertainment management (MS). *Program availability:* Part-time, evening/weekend. *Faculty:* 15 full-time (3 women). *Students:* 55 full-time (23 women), 17 part-time (10 women); includes 5 minority (1 Asian, non-Hispanic/Latino; 3 Hispanic/Latino; 1 Two or more races, non-Hispanic/Latino), 44 international. Average

age 25. 89 applicants, 66% accepted, 39 enrolled. In 2017, 41 master's, 3 doctorates awarded. Terminal master's awarded for partial completion of doctoral program. *Degree requirements:* For master's, comprehensive exam, thesis or alternative; for doctorate, comprehensive exam, thesis/dissertation. *Entrance requirements:* For master's, GMAT or GRE, minimum GPA of 3.0 in upper-division undergraduate and marketing coursework, two letters of recommendation; for doctorate, GMAT or GRE, personal statement, recommendations, interview. Additional exam requirements/recommendations for international students: Required—TOEFL (minimum score 550 paper-based; 79 iBT) or IELTS (minimum score 6.5). *Application deadline:* For fall admission, 1/2 for domestic and international students; for spring admission, 10/15 for domestic students, 7/1 for international students. Applications are processed on a rolling basis. Application fee: $30. Electronic applications accepted. *Financial support:* In 2017–18, 6 students received support, including 5 research assistantships (averaging $14,943 per year), 6 teaching assistantships (averaging $11,972 per year); health care benefits and unspecified assistantships also available. *Faculty research:* Branding; consumer behavior; marketing communications' effectiveness; customer satisfaction; customer delight; consumer reactions to new technology, products and services; consumer emotions; brand strategies; communications; advertising effectiveness; green alliances; strategic marketing; international business; international marketing; consumer research; customer service branding; focus group research; market surveys; market research; promotion; services marketing; strategic planning. *Total annual research expenditures:* $17,504. *Unit head:* Dr. Anand Kumar, Interim Department Chair/Associate Professor, 813-974-6205, Fax: 813-974-6175, E-mail: akumar@usf.edu. *Application contact:* Stacee Bender, 813-974-4516, Fax: 813-974-6175, E-mail: staceebender@usf.edu.
Website: http://business.usf.edu/departments/marketing/

The University of Tennessee, Graduate School, College of Education, Health and Human Sciences, Department of Exercise, Sport, and Leisure Studies, Knoxville, TN 37996. Offers exercise science (MS, PhD), including biomechanics/sports medicine, exercise physiology; recreation and leisure studies (MS); sport management (MS); sport studies (MS, PhD); therapeutic recreation (MS). *Program availability:* Part-time, evening/weekend. *Degree requirements:* For master's, thesis optional. *Entrance requirements:* For master's, minimum GPA of 2.7. Additional exam requirements/recommendations for international students: Required—TOEFL. Electronic applications accepted.

University of the Incarnate Word, Ila Faye Miller School of Nursing and Health Professions, San Antonio, TX 78209-6397. Offers kinesiology (MS); nursing (MSN, DNP); sport management (MS). *Program availability:* Part-time, evening/weekend. *Faculty:* 18 full-time (14 women). *Students:* 48 full-time (26 women), 75 part-time (62 women); includes 86 minority (22 Black or African American, non-Hispanic/Latino; 1 American Indian or Alaska Native, non-Hispanic/Latino; 8 Asian, non-Hispanic/Latino; 53 Hispanic/Latino; 2 Two or more races, non-Hispanic/Latino), 3 international. In 2017, 31 master's, 10 doctorates awarded. *Degree requirements:* For master's, comprehensive exam (for some programs), thesis or alternative, capstone. *Entrance requirements:* For master's, GRE General Test, MAT, baccalaureate degree in ACEN- or CCNE-accredited nursing program with health assessment and statistics; minimum cumulative GPA of 2.5 (3.0 in upper-division courses); three professional references; Texas State license or multi-state compact. Additional exam requirements/recommendations for international students: Required—TOEFL (minimum score 560 paper-based; 83 iBT). *Application deadline:* Applications are processed on a rolling basis. Application fee: $20. Electronic applications accepted. *Expenses:* $905 per credit hour (for DNP); $915 per credit hour (for master's-level prorgams). *Financial support:* Research assistantships, Federal Work-Study, scholarships/grants, tuition waivers (partial), and unspecified assistantships available. Financial award applicants required to submit FAFSA. *Faculty research:* Pediatric oncology, military pregnancy and the family, diabetes prevention, substance abuse and addictions, nursing of vulnerable populations. *Unit head:* Dr. Mary Hoke, Dean, 210-829-3982, Fax: 210-829-3174, E-mail: mhoke@uiwtx.edu. *Application contact:* Johnny Garcia, Graduate Admissions Counselor, 210-805-3554, Fax: 210-829-3921, E-mail: admis@uiwtx.edu.
Website: http://uiw.edu/snhp/

University of the Southwest, Graduate Programs, Hobbs, NM 88240-9129. Offers business administration (MBA); curriculum and instruction (MSE); curriculum and instruction: bilingual (MSE); curriculum and instruction: TESOL (MSE); early childhood education (MSE); educational administration (MSE); mental health counseling (MSE); school counseling (MSE); special education (MSE); sports management (MBA). *Program availability:* Part-time, evening/weekend, online learning. *Degree requirements:* For master's, comprehensive exam, thesis (for some programs). *Entrance requirements:* Additional exam requirements/recommendations for international students: Recommended—TOEFL. Electronic applications accepted.

University of Wisconsin–Parkside, College of Natural and Health Sciences, Program in Sport Management, Kenosha, WI 53141-2000. Offers MS. *Degree requirements:* For master's, thesis optional. *Entrance requirements:* For master's, official transcripts, at least three letters of recommendation. Additional exam requirements/recommendations for international students: Required—TOEFL (minimum score 525 paper-based; 71 iBT). Electronic applications accepted.

Upper Iowa University, Online Master's Programs, Fayette, IA 52142-1857. Offers accounting (MBA); corporate financial management (MBA); emergency management and homeland security (MPA); general management (MBA); general studies (MPA); government administration (MPA); health and human services (MPA); human resources management (MBA); nonprofit organizational management (MPA); organizational development (MBA); public management (MPA); sport administration (MSA). MBA also available at Madison, WI campus. *Program availability:* Part-time, online learning. *Degree requirements:* For master's, research project. *Entrance requirements:* For master's, GMAT, GRE, or minimum GPA of 2.7 during last 60 hours. Additional exam requirements/recommendations for international students: Required—TOEFL (minimum score 570 paper-based). Electronic applications accepted. *Faculty research:* Total quality management, teams, organization culture and climate, management.

Valparaiso University, Graduate School and Continuing Education, Program in Sports Administration, Valparaiso, IN 46383. Offers MS, JD/MS. *Program availability:* Part-time, evening/weekend. *Entrance requirements:* For master's, minimum GPA of 3.0. Additional exam requirements/recommendations for international students: Required—TOEFL (minimum score 550 paper-based; 80 iBT), IELTS (minimum score 6). Electronic applications accepted. *Expenses: Tuition:* Full-time $11,340; part-time $630 per credit hour. *Required fees:* $520; $250 per year. $125 per semester. Tuition and fees vary according to program and reciprocity agreements.

Waldorf University, Program in Organizational Leadership, Forest City, IA 50436. Offers criminal justice leadership (MA); emergency management leadership (MA); fire/rescue executive leadership (MA); human resource development (MA); public administration (MA); sport management (MA); teacher leader (MA).

Washington State University, College of Education, Department of Educational Leadership, Sports Studies, and Educational/Counseling Psychology, Pullman, WA 99164-2136. Offers counseling psychology (PhD); educational leadership (Ed M, MA, Ed D, PhD); educational psychology (MA, PhD); sport management (MA). Programs also offered at the Spokane, Tri-Cities, Vancouver and Global (online) campuses. *Program availability:* Part-time, online learning. *Degree requirements:* For master's, comprehensive exam (for some programs), thesis (for some programs), oral or written exam; for doctorate, comprehensive exam, thesis/dissertation, oral and written exam, internship. *Entrance requirements:* For master's and doctorate, GRE General Test, minimum GPA of 3.0, 3 letters of recommendation, transcripts showing all college or university course work, statement of professional objectives, current curriculum vitae/ resume. Additional exam requirements/recommendations for international students: Required—TOEFL (minimum score 550 paper-based; 80 iBT). Electronic applications accepted. *Faculty research:* Multicultural counseling and career development, educational and psychological measurement issues, business decision-making process and power relationships, leadership practices and processes as suffused with and constituted by emotion work.

Wayland Baptist University, Graduate Programs, Program in Education, Plainview, TX 79072-6998. Offers education administration (M Ed); education diagnostics (M Ed); education literacy (M Ed); elementary certification (M Ed); English (M Ed); English as a second language (M Ed); higher education administration (M Ed); human resources (M Ed); instructional leadership (M Ed); instructional technology (M Ed); leadership training and development (M Ed); science education (M Ed); secondary certification (M Ed); social studies (M Ed); special education (M Ed); sports administration and management (M Ed). *Program availability:* Part-time, evening/weekend, 100% online. *Faculty:* 33 full-time (17 women), 28 part-time/adjunct (17 women). *Students:* 16 full-time (13 women), 221 part-time (143 women); includes 97 minority (26 Black or African American, non-Hispanic/Latino; 1 American Indian or Alaska Native, non-Hispanic/ Latino; 5 Asian, non-Hispanic/Latino; 54 Hispanic/Latino; 11 Two or more races, non-Hispanic/Latino), 1 international. Average age 39. 32 applicants, 97% accepted, 23 enrolled. In 2017, 78 master's awarded. *Degree requirements:* For master's, comprehensive exam, capstone course. *Entrance requirements:* For master's, GRE, GMAT or MAT. Additional exam requirements/recommendations for international students: Required—TOEFL (minimum score 500 paper-based; 61 iBT). *Application deadline:* Applications are processed on a rolling basis. Application fee: $50. Electronic applications accepted. *Expenses: Tuition:* Full-time $11,250; part-time $625 per credit hour. *Required fees:* $1200. *Financial support:* Federal Work-Study, institutionally sponsored loans, and scholarships/grants available. Support available to part-time students. Financial award application deadline: 5/1; financial award applicants required to submit FAFSA. *Unit head:* Dr. Gene Whitfill, Dean, 806-291-1047, Fax: 806-291-1951, E-mail: whitfillg@wbu.edu. *Application contact:* Amanda Stanton, Coordinator of Graduate Studies, 806-291-3423, Fax: 806-291-1950, E-mail: stanton@wbu.edu.

Wayne State College, Department of Health, Human Performance and Sport, Wayne, NE 68787. Offers exercise science (MSE); organizational management (MS), including sport management. *Program availability:* Part-time, evening/weekend. *Degree requirements:* For master's, comprehensive exam, thesis optional. *Entrance requirements:* For master's, GRE General Test, minimum GPA of 3.0. Additional exam requirements/recommendations for international students: Required—TOEFL (minimum score 550 paper-based). Electronic applications accepted.

Wayne State University, College of Education, Division of Kinesiology, Health and Sports Studies, Detroit, MI 48202. Offers athletic training (MSAT); health education (M Ed); kinesiology (M Ed, PhD), including exercise and sport science (PhD), physical education and physical activity leadership (PhD); sports administration (MA). *Program availability:* Part-time, 100% online. *Faculty:* 9. *Students:* 65 full-time (33 women), 109 part-time (56 women); includes 70 minority (59 Black or African American, non-Hispanic/ Latino; 3 Hispanic/Latino; 8 Two or more races, non-Hispanic/Latino), 8 international. Average age 30. 182 applicants, 53% accepted, 56 enrolled. In 2017, 62 master's, 3 doctorates awarded. *Degree requirements:* For master's, thesis (for some programs); for doctorate, thesis/dissertation. *Entrance requirements:* For master's, minimum undergraduate GPA of 3.0; undergraduate degree directly relating to the field of specialization being applied for or one accompanied by extensive educational background in closely-related field; teaching certificates in specific areas (for some programs); for doctorate, minimum undergraduate GPA of 3.0; undergraduate degree directly relating to the field of specialization being applied for or one accompanied by extensive educational background in closely-related field. Additional exam requirements/recommendations for international students: Required—TOEFL (minimum score 79 iBT), TWE (minimum score 5.5); Recommended—IELTS (minimum score 6.5). *Application deadline:* For fall admission, 6/1 priority date for domestic students, 5/1 priority date for international students; for winter admission, 10/1 priority date for domestic students, 9/1 priority date for international students; for spring admission, 2/1 priority date for domestic students, 1/1 priority date for international students. Application fee: $50. Electronic applications accepted. *Expenses:* Contact institution. *Financial support:* In 2017–18, 47 students received support, including 6 research assistantships with tuition reimbursements available (averaging $18,534 per year), 5 teaching assistantships with tuition reimbursements available (averaging $18,534 per year); fellowships with tuition reimbursements available, scholarships/grants, health care benefits, and unspecified assistantships also available. Support available to part-time students. Financial award applicants required to submit FAFSA. *Faculty research:* Exercise and sport science, nutrition and physical activity interventions, school and community health, obesity prevention. *Unit head:* Dr. Nate McCaughtry, Assistant Dean, Division of Kinesiology, Health and Sport Studies/Director, Center for School Health, 313-577-0014, Fax: 313-577-5002, E-mail: aj4391@wayne.edu. *Application contact:* 313-577-4249, E-mail: askcoe@wayne.edu.
Website: http://coe.wayne.edu/kinesiology/index.php

Webber International University, Graduate School of Business, Babson Park, FL 33827-0096. Offers accounting (MBA); business (MBA); criminal justice management (MBA); international business (MBA); sport business management (MBA). *Program availability:* Part-time, evening/weekend, 100% online. *Faculty:* 10 full-time (4 women), 1 part-time/adjunct (0 women). *Students:* 50 full-time (29 women), 6 part-time (2 women); includes 19 minority (12 Black or African American, non-Hispanic/Latino; 6 Hispanic/ Latino; 1 Two or more races, non-Hispanic/Latino), 6 international. Average age 24. 64 applicants, 61% accepted, 32 enrolled. In 2017, 29 master's awarded. *Degree requirements:* For master's, class trip (for international business); practicum (for criminal justice management). *Entrance requirements:* For master's, three recommendation letters, résumé, essay, official transcripts from all colleges and universities attended. Additional exam requirements/recommendations for international students: Recommended—TOEFL (minimum score 500 paper-based; 61 iBT), IELTS (minimum score 6). *Application deadline:* For fall admission, 7/1 for international students. Applications are processed on a rolling basis. Application fee: $50 ($75 for international students). Electronic applications accepted. *Expenses: Tuition:* Part-time $688 per hour. *Financial support:* In 2017–18, 11 students received support. Scholarships/grants and unspecified assistantships available. Financial award application deadline: 8/1; financial award applicants required to submit FAFSA. *Unit head:* Dr. Nikos Orphanoudakis, Dean, 863-638-2910, Fax: 863-638-1591, E-mail: orphanoudakisn@webber.edu. *Application contact:* Lacy Edwards, Admissions Counselor and MBA Coordinator, 863-638-2910, Fax: 863-638-1591, E-mail: admissions@webber.edu.

West Chester University of Pennsylvania, College of Health Sciences, Department of Kinesiology, West Chester, PA 19383. Offers adapted physical education (Certificate); exercise and sport physiology (MS), including athletic training; sport management and athletics (MPA), including administration. *Program availability:* Part-time, evening/ weekend, blended/hybrid learning. *Students:* 44 full-time (24 women), 12 part-time (3 women); includes 5 minority (2 Black or African American, non-Hispanic/Latino; 2 Hispanic/Latino; 1 Two or more races, non-Hispanic/Latino), 1 international. Average age 25. 68 applicants, 87% accepted, 29 enrolled. In 2017, 13 master's, 14 other advanced degrees awarded. *Degree requirements:* For master's, thesis or research report (for MS); two internships and capstone course that includes a research project or thesis (for MPA); for Certificate, six courses of study. *Entrance requirements:* For master's, GRE (for MS), 2 letters of recommendation, statement of professional goals; transcripts (for MS); two letters of reference, career goals, resume (for MPA); for Certificate, two letters of recommendation, transcript. Additional exam requirements/ recommendations for international students: Required—TOEFL or IELTS. *Application deadline:* For fall admission, 5/15 for international students; for spring admission, 10/15 for international students. Applications are processed on a rolling basis. Application fee: $50. Electronic applications accepted. *Expenses:* Tuition, state resident: full-time $9000; part-time $500 per credit. Tuition, nonresident: full-time $13,500; part-time $750 per credit. *Required fees:* $2959; $149.79 per credit. *Financial support:* Scholarships/ grants and unspecified assistantships available. Financial award application deadline: 2/ 15; financial award applicants required to submit FAFSA. *Faculty research:* Metabolism during exercise, biomechanics, rating of perceived exertion, motor learning, environmental physiology. *Unit head:* Dr. W. Craig Stevens, Chair, 610-436-2610, Fax: 610-436-2860, E-mail: cstevens@wcpua.edu. *Application contact:* Office of Graduate Studies and Extended Education, 610-436-2943, Fax: 610-436-2763, E-mail: gradstudy@wcupa.edu.
Website: http://www.wcupa.edu/healthsciences/kinesiology/

Western Illinois University, School of Graduate Studies, College of Education and Human Services, Department of Kinesiology, Program in Sport Management, Macomb, IL 61455-1390. Offers MS. *Program availability:* Part-time. *Entrance requirements:* For master's, minimum GPA of 3.0. Additional exam requirements/recommendations for international students: Required—TOEFL (minimum score 550 paper-based; 80 iBT). *Application deadline:* Applications are processed on a rolling basis. Application fee: $30. Electronic applications accepted. *Financial support:* Unspecified assistantships available. *Application contact:* Dr. Nancy Parsons, Associate Provost and Director of Graduate Studies, 309-298-1806, Fax: 309-298-2345, E-mail: grad-office@wiu.edu.
Website: http://www.wiu.edu/coehs/kinesiology/graduate_programs/sm/

Western Kentucky University, Graduate Studies, College of Health and Human Services, Department of Kinesiology, Recreation and Sport, Bowling Green, KY 42101. Offers athletic administration and coaching (MS); physical education (MS); recreation and sport administration (MS). *Program availability:* Part-time, evening/weekend, online learning. *Degree requirements:* For master's, comprehensive exam, thesis optional. *Entrance requirements:* For master's, GRE General Test, minimum GPA of 2.75. Additional exam requirements/recommendations for international students: Required— TOEFL (minimum score 555 paper-based; 79 iBT). *Faculty research:* Orthopedic rehabilitation, fitness center coordination, heat acclimation, biomechanical and physiological parameters.

Western Michigan University, Graduate College, College of Education and Human Development, Department of Health, Physical Education and Recreation, Kalamazoo, MI 49008. Offers athletic training (MS), including exercise physiology; sport management (MA), including pedagogy, special physical education.

Western New England University, College of Business, Program in Business Administration, Springfield, MA 01119. Offers general business (MBA); sport management (MBA); JD/MBA; MS/MBA; Pharm D/MBA. *Accreditation:* AACSB. *Program availability:* Part-time, evening/weekend, online learning. *Faculty:* 8 full-time (6 women). *Students:* 74 part-time (34 women); includes 7 minority (2 Black or African American, non-Hispanic/Latino; 2 Asian, non-Hispanic/Latino; 2 Hispanic/Latino; 1 Two or more races, non-Hispanic/Latino), 1 international. Average age 32. 79 applicants, 66% accepted, 47 enrolled. In 2017, 48 master's awarded. *Entrance requirements:* For master's, GMAT or GRE, official transcript, two letters of recommendation, essay, resume. Additional exam requirements/recommendations for international students: Required—TOEFL (minimum score 79 iBT). *Application deadline:* Applications are processed on a rolling basis. Application fee: $30. Electronic applications accepted. *Expenses:* Contact institution. *Financial support:* Application deadline: 4/15; applicants required to submit FAFSA. *Unit head:* Dr. Rob Kleine, Dean, 413-782-1395, E-mail: rob.kleine@wne.edu. *Application contact:* Matthew Fox, Director of Admissions for Graduate Students and Adult Learners, 413-782-1410, Fax: 413-782-1777, E-mail: study@wne.edu.
Website: http://www1.wne.edu/academics/graduate/mba.cfm

Western New England University, College of Business, Program in Sport Leadership and Coaching, Springfield, MA 01119. Offers MS. *Faculty:* 5 full-time (1 woman). *Students:* 5 part-time (0 women); includes 1 minority (Asian, non-Hispanic/Latino). Average age 26. *Entrance requirements:* For master's, GMAT or GRE, official transcript, two recommendations, personal statement, résumé or curriculum vitae. Additional exam requirements/recommendations for international students: Required—TOEFL (minimum score 79 iBT). *Application deadline:* Applications are processed on a rolling basis. Application fee: $30. Electronic applications accepted. *Expenses:* Contact institution. *Financial support:* Application deadline: 4/15; applicants required to submit FAFSA. *Unit head:* Dr. Rob Kleine, Dean, 413-782-1395, Fax: 413-796-2068, E-mail: rob.kleine@ wne.edu. *Application contact:* Matthew Fox, Director of Admissions for Graduate Students and Adult Learners, 413-782-1410, Fax: 413-782-1777, E-mail: study@ wne.edu.
Website: http://www1.wne.edu/academics/graduate/ms-sport.cfm

West Liberty University, College of Education and Human Performance, West Liberty, WV 26074. Offers community education research and leadership (MA Ed); innovative instruction (MA Ed); leadership in disability services (MA Ed); leadership studies (MA Ed); multi-categorical special education (MA Ed); reading specialist (MA Ed); sports leadership and coaching (MA Ed). *Accreditation:* NCATE. *Program availability:* Part-time, evening/weekend. *Students:* 18 full-time (12 women), 74 part-time (60 women); includes 2 minority (1 Black or African American, non-Hispanic/Latino; 1 Native Hawaiian or other Pacific Islander, non-Hispanic/Latino). Average age 32. *Degree requirements:* For master's, capstone experience. *Entrance requirements:* For master's, minimum GPA of 2.5 or 3.0 (depending on track). Additional exam requirements/ recommendations for international students: Required—TOEFL. *Application deadline:* Applications are processed on a rolling basis. Application fee: $0. Electronic applications accepted. Tuition and fees vary according to course load and program. *Financial support:* Teaching assistantships and unspecified assistantships available. *Unit head:* Dr. Catherine Monteroso, Interim Dean, 304-336-8247, E-mail: cmonteroso@ westliberty.edu. *Application contact:* Sara Sweeney, Director, Office of Graduate Studies, 304-336-8545, E-mail: sara.sweeney@westliberty.edu.
Website: http://westliberty.edu/education/

Sports Management

West Texas A&M University, College of Nursing and Health Sciences, Department of Sports and Exercise Sciences, Canyon, TX 79015. Offers sport management (MS); sports and exercise sciences (MS). *Program availability:* Part-time, evening/weekend. *Degree requirements:* For master's, comprehensive exam, thesis optional. *Entrance requirements:* For master's, GRE General Test. Additional exam requirements/recommendations for international students: Required—TOEFL. Electronic applications accepted.

West Virginia University, College of Physical Activity and Sport Sciences, Morgantown, WV 26506. Offers athletic training (MS); coaching and sport education (MS); coaching and teaching studies (Ed D, PhD), including curriculum and instruction (PhD); physical education/teacher education (MS); sport and exercise psychology (MS); sport coaching (MS); sport management (MS). *Students:* 104 full-time (37 women), 75 part-time (28 women); includes 30 minority (12 Black or African American, non-Hispanic/Latino; 2 Asian, non-Hispanic/Latino; 9 Hispanic/Latino; 7 Two or more races, non-Hispanic/Latino), 12 international. *Degree requirements:* For doctorate, comprehensive exam, thesis/dissertation, oral exam. *Entrance requirements:* For master's, GRE or MAT, minimum GPA of 3.0; for doctorate, GRE General Test or MAT, minimum GPA of 3.5. Additional exam requirements/recommendations for international students: Required—TOEFL (minimum score 550 paper-based). *Application deadline:* For fall admission, 12/15 for domestic students, 10/1 for international students. Application fee: $60. Electronic applications accepted. *Expenses:* Tuition, state resident: full-time $9450. Tuition, nonresident: full-time $24,390. *Financial support:* Research assistantships, teaching assistantships, career-related internships or fieldwork, Federal Work-Study, institutionally sponsored loans, health care benefits, tuition waivers (full and partial), and administrative assistantships available. Support available to part-time students. Financial award application deadline: 2/1; financial award applicants required to submit FAFSA. *Faculty research:* Sport psych sociology, teacher education, exercise psychology, counseling. *Unit head:* Sean Bulger, Online Program Coordinator, 304-293-0845, Fax: 304-293-4641, E-mail: sean.bulger@mail.wvu.edu. Website: http://www.cpass.wvu.edu

Wichita State University, Graduate School, College of Education, Department of Sport Management, Wichita, KS 67260. Offers M Ed. *Unit head:* Dr. Mark Vermillion, Chair, 316-978-5444, Fax: 316-978-5451, E-mail: mark.vermillion@wichita.edu. *Application contact:* Jordan Oleson, Admissions Coordinator, 316-978-3095, Fax: 316-978-3253, E-mail: jordan.oleson@wichita.edu.
Website: http://www.wichita.edu/sportmanagement

Wingate University, School of Sport Sciences, Wingate, NC 28174. Offers sport management (MA). *Entrance requirements:* For master's, MAT, GRE, or GMAT, bachelor's degree, minimum GPA of 2.75, two recommendation forms, official transcripts. Electronic applications accepted.

Winona State University, College of Education, Department of Leadership Education, Winona, MN 55987. Offers education leadership (MS, Ed S), including k-12 principal (Ed S), superintendent (Ed S); organizational leadership (MS); professional leadership (MS); sport management (MS). MS in sport management offered in cooperation with Department of Physical Education and Sport Science. *Accreditation:* NCATE. *Program availability:* Part-time, evening/weekend. *Degree requirements:* For master's, comprehensive exam, thesis optional; for Ed S, thesis optional.

Xavier University, College of Social Sciences, Health and Education, Department of Sports Studies, Cincinnati, OH 45207. Offers coaching education and athlete development (M Ed); sport administration (M Ed). *Program availability:* Part-time, evening/weekend, online learning. *Degree requirements:* For master's, thesis optional, internship or research project. *Entrance requirements:* For master's, GRE or MAT, official transcript; resume; one-page statement of career goals; 2 letters of recommendation. Additional exam requirements/recommendations for international students: Required—TOEFL (minimum score 550 paper-based; 79 iBT). Electronic applications accepted. Application fee is waived when completed online. *Expenses:* Contact institution. *Faculty research:* Coaching education, brand equity, strategic management, economic impact, place marketing.

ACADEMIC AND PROFESSIONAL
PROGRAMS IN SOCIAL WORK

Section 32
Social Work

This section contains a directory of institutions offering graduate work in social work, followed by in-depth entries submitted by institutions that chose to prepare detailed program descriptions. Additional information about programs listed in the directory but not augmented by an in-depth entry may be obtained by writing directly to the dean of a graduate school or chair of a department at the address given in the directory.

For programs offering related work, see also in this book *Allied Health* and *Education.* In another guide in this series:
Graduate Programs in the Humanities, Arts & Social Sciences

See *Criminology and Forensics, Family and Consumer Sciences, Psychology and Counseling,* and *Sociology, Anthropology, and Archaeology*

CONTENTS

Program Directories

Human Services

Abilene Christian University, Graduate Programs, College of Education and Human Services, Abilene, TX 79699. Offers M Ed, MS, MSSW, Certificate. *Accreditation:* TEAC. *Faculty:* 4 full-time (3 women), 32 part-time/adjunct (23 women). *Students:* 177 full-time (165 women), 40 part-time (38 women); includes 36 minority (13 Black or African American, non-Hispanic/Latino; 1 American Indian or Alaska Native, non-Hispanic/Latino; 5 Asian, non-Hispanic/Latino; 17 Hispanic/Latino), 3 international. 600 applicants, 41% accepted, 141 enrolled. In 2017, 72 master's awarded. *Degree requirements:* For master's, comprehensive exam (for some programs), thesis (for some programs), practicum. *Entrance requirements:* For master's, GRE. Additional exam requirements/recommendations for international students: Required—TOEFL (minimum score 80 iBT), IELTS (minimum score 6), PTE. *Application deadline:* For fall admission, 8/15 priority date for domestic students; for winter admission, 10/1 priority date for domestic students; for spring admission, 12/15 priority date for domestic students; for summer admission, 4/15 for domestic students. Applications are processed on a rolling basis. Application fee: $50. Electronic applications accepted. *Expenses: Tuition:* Full-time $20,664; part-time $1148 per contact hour. *Financial support:* In 2017–18, 110 students received support. Career-related internships or fieldwork and scholarships/grants available. Financial award application deadline: 4/1; financial award applicants required to submit FAFSA. *Unit head:* Dr. Jennifer Shewmaker, Dean, 325-674-2700, Fax: 325-674-3707, E-mail: cehs@acu.edu. *Application contact:* Graduate Admission, 325-674-6911, Fax: 325-674-6717, E-mail: gradinfo@acu.edu.
Website: http://www.acu.edu/graduate/academics/education-and-human-services.html

Albertus Magnus College, Master of Science in Human Services Program, New Haven, CT 06511-1189. Offers MS. *Program availability:* Part-time, evening/weekend, blended/hybrid learning. *Degree requirements:* For master's, thesis, internship, capstone thesis, minimum GPA of 3.0. *Entrance requirements:* For master's, minimum GPA of 2.8; 2 letters of recommendation; official transcripts; minimum of 15 credits in psychology, human services, and/or social work. Additional exam requirements/recommendations for international students: Required—TOEFL (minimum score 550 paper-based; 80 iBT). *Application deadline:* For fall admission, 8/15 for domestic students; for spring admission, 1/15 for domestic students. Applications are processed on a rolling basis. Application fee: $50. Electronic applications accepted. *Expenses:* Contact institution. *Financial support:* Federal Work-Study and unspecified assistantships available. Support available to part-time students. Financial award applicants required to submit FAFSA. *Unit head:* Ragaa Mazen, Director, 203-773-8574, E-mail: rmazen@albertus.edu. *Application contact:* Anthony Reich, Director of Admission, Division of Professional and Graduate Studies, 203-773-5032, E-mail: arreich@albertus.edu.
Website: http://www.albertus.edu/human-services/ms/

Amridge University, Graduate and Professional Programs, Montgomery, AL 36117. Offers Biblical studies (MA, PhD); Christian ministry (MS); family therapy (D Min); human services (MS); leadership and management (MS); marriage and family therapy (M Div, MA, PhD); ministerial leadership (M Div, MS); New Testament studies (MA); Old Testament studies (MA); professional counseling (M Div, MA, PhD); theology (M Div, D Min). *Program availability:* Part-time, evening/weekend, online learning. *Faculty:* 23 full-time (3 women), 9 part-time/adjunct (5 women). *Students:* 105 full-time (55 women), 250 part-time (152 women); includes 217 minority (167 Black or African American, non-Hispanic/Latino; 4 Asian, non-Hispanic/Latino; 42 Hispanic/Latino; 4 Native Hawaiian or other Pacific Islander, non-Hispanic/Latino). Average age 42. 160 applicants, 100% accepted, 110 enrolled. *Degree requirements:* For master's, one foreign language, comprehensive exam (for some programs), thesis (for some programs); for doctorate, one foreign language, comprehensive exam (for some programs), thesis/dissertation (for some programs). *Entrance requirements:* For master's, official transcript showing an earned 4-year BA or BS from regionally- or nationally-accredited institution; for doctorate, official transcript showing earned graduate degree from regionally- or nationally-accredited institution; writing sample (e.g. career monograph, published journal article, term paper from master's degree or doctoral dissertation); interview. Additional exam requirements/recommendations for international students: Required—TOEFL (minimum score 79 iBT). *Application deadline:* Applications are processed on a rolling basis. Application fee: $50. Electronic applications accepted. *Financial support:* In 2017–18, 33 students received support. Federal Work-Study and scholarships/grants available. Support available to part-time students. Financial award applicants required to submit FAFSA. *Faculty research:* Technology and mental healthcare, resilience in black families, theology and congregational ministry. *Unit head:* Laina Costanza, Vice President, Student Affairs, 888-790-8080 Ext. 1, Fax: 334-387-3878, E-mail: cc@amridgeuniversity.edu. *Application contact:* Brooks Housley, Student Affairs Coordinator, 888-790-8080 Ext. 1, Fax: 334-387-3878, E-mail: admissions@amridgeuniversity.edu.

Bellevue University, Graduate School, College of Arts and Sciences, Bellevue, NE 68005-3098. Offers clinical counseling (MS); healthcare administration (MHA); human services (MA); international security and intelligence studies (MS); managerial communication (MA). *Program availability:* Online learning.

Boricua College, Program in Human Services, New York, NY 10032-1560. Offers MS. Program offered in Brooklyn and Manhattan. *Program availability:* Evening/weekend. *Degree requirements:* For master's, thesis. *Entrance requirements:* For master's, interview by the faculty.

Brandeis University, The Heller School for Social Policy and Management, Program in Nonprofit Management, Waltham, MA 02454-9110. Offers child, youth, and family management (MBA); health care management (MBA); social impact management (MBA); social policy and management (MBA); sustainable development (MBA); MBA/MA; MBA/MD. MBA/MD program offered in conjunction with Tufts University School of Medicine. *Accreditation:* AACSB. *Program availability:* Part-time. *Degree requirements:* For master's, team consulting project. *Entrance requirements:* For master's, GMAT (preferred) or GRE, 2 letters of recommendation, problem statement analysis, 3-5 years of professional experience. Additional exam requirements/recommendations for international students: Required—TOEFL (minimum score 600 paper-based; 100 iBT). Electronic applications accepted. *Expenses:* Contact institution. *Faculty research:* Health care; children and families; elder and disabled services; social impact management; organizations in the non-profit, for-profit, or public sector.

California State University, Sacramento, College of Health and Human Services, Division of Social Work, Sacramento, CA 95819. Offers family and children's services (MSW). *Accreditation:* CSWE. *Program availability:* Part-time, evening/weekend. *Students:* 230 full-time (202 women), 14 part-time (10 women); includes 125 minority (24 Black or African American, non-Hispanic/Latino; 3 American Indian or Alaska Native, non-Hispanic/Latino; 28 Asian, non-Hispanic/Latino; 69 Hispanic/Latino; 1 Native Hawaiian or other Pacific Islander, non-Hispanic/Latino). Average age 31. 306

applicants, 41% accepted, 109 enrolled. In 2017, 107 master's awarded. *Degree requirements:* For master's, thesis, project; writing proficiency exam. *Entrance requirements:* For master's, GRE, minimum GPA of 2.8 during previous 2 years of course work. Additional exam requirements/recommendations for international students: Required—TOEFL (minimum score 550 paper-based; 80 iBT); Recommended—IELTS, TSE. *Application deadline:* For fall admission, 1/18 for domestic and international students. Applications are processed on a rolling basis. Application fee: $55. Electronic applications accepted. *Expenses:* Contact institution. *Financial support:* Career-related internships or fieldwork, Federal Work-Study, and scholarships/grants available. Support available to part-time students. Financial award application deadline: 3/1; financial award applicants required to submit FAFSA. *Unit head:* Dr. Dale Russell, Chair, 916-278-6943, E-mail: drussell@csus.edu. *Application contact:* Jose Martinez, Graduate Admissions Supervisor, 916-278-7871, E-mail: martinj@skymail.csus.edu.
Website: http://www.csus.edu/hhs/sw

Capella University, School of Public Service Leadership, Doctoral Programs in Healthcare, Minneapolis, MN 55402. Offers criminal justice (PhD); emergency management (PhD); epidemiology (Dr PH); general health administration (DHA); general public administration (DPA); health advocacy and leadership (Dr PH); health care administration (PhD); health care leadership (DHA); health policy advocacy (DHA); multidisciplinary human services (PhD); nonprofit management and leadership (PhD); public safety leadership (PhD); social and community services (PhD).

Capella University, School of Public Service Leadership, Master's Programs in Healthcare, Minneapolis, MN 55402. Offers criminal justice (MS); emergency management (MS); general public health (MPH); gerontology (MS); health administration (MHA); health care operations (MHA); health management policy (MPH); health policy (MHA); homeland security (MS); multidisciplinary human services (MS); public administration (MPA); public safety leadership (MS); social and community services (MS); social behavioral sciences (MPH); MS/MPA.

Carlos Albizu University, Miami Campus, Graduate Programs, Miami, FL 33172-2209. Offers clinical psychology (PhD, Psy D); entrepreneurship (MBA); exceptional student education (MS); human services (PhD); industrial/organizational psychology (MS); marriage and family therapy (MS); mental health counseling (MS); nonprofit management (MBA); organizational management (MBA); psychology (MS); speech and language pathology (MS); teaching English for speakers of other languages (MS). *Accreditation:* APA. *Program availability:* Part-time, evening/weekend, 100% online, blended/hybrid learning. *Faculty:* 32 full-time (24 women), 27 part-time/adjunct (15 women). *Students:* 411 full-time (345 women), 248 part-time (215 women); includes 562 minority (53 Black or African American, non-Hispanic/Latino; 4 Asian, non-Hispanic/Latino; 498 Hispanic/Latino; 7 Two or more races, non-Hispanic/Latino), 23 international. Average age 34. 391 applicants, 42% accepted, 154 enrolled. In 2017, 96 master's, 54 doctorates awarded. Terminal master's awarded for partial completion of doctoral program. *Degree requirements:* For master's, comprehensive exam (for some programs), integrative project (for MBA); research project (for exceptional student education, teaching English as a second language); for doctorate, comprehensive examinations, internship, project/dissertation. *Entrance requirements:* For master's, GRE/EXADEP, bachelor's degree from accredited institution, minimum GPA of 3.0, 3 letters of recommendation, interview, resume, statement of purpose, official transcripts; for doctorate, GRE (for Psy D), 3 letters of recommendation, resume, interview, statement of purpose, official transcripts; bachelor's degree and minimum GPA of 3.25 (for Psy D); master's degree and minimum GPA of 3.0 (for PhD). Additional exam requirements/recommendations for international students: Required—Michigan Test of English Language Proficiency. *Application deadline:* For fall admission, 4/1 priority date for domestic students, 5/1 priority date for international students; for spring admission, 11/1 priority date for domestic students, 9/1 priority date for international students. Applications are processed on a rolling basis. Application fee: $50. Electronic applications accepted. Application fee is waived when completed online. *Expenses:* Contact institution. *Financial support:* In 2017–18, 145 students received support. Federal Work-Study, scholarships/grants, unspecified assistantships, and tuition discounts available. Financial award application deadline: 6/1; financial award applicants required to submit FAFSA. *Faculty research:* Psychotherapy, forensic psychology, neuropsychology, special education, speech-language pathology, criminal justice. *Unit head:* Dr. Etiony Aldarondo, Provost, 305-593-1223 Ext. 3138, Fax: 305-592-7930, E-mail: ealdarondo@albizu.edu. *Application contact:* Sonia Feliciano, Institutional Director of Student Recruitment, 305-593-1223 Ext. 3108, Fax: 305-477-8983, E-mail: sfeliciano@albizu.edu.

Chestnut Hill College, School of Graduate Studies, Program in Administration of Human Services, Philadelphia, PA 19118-2693. Offers administration of human services (MS, CAS), including adult and aging services (CAS), leadership development (CAS). *Program availability:* Part-time, evening/weekend. *Degree requirements:* For master's, special projects or internship. *Entrance requirements:* For master's, GRE General Test or MAT, 100 volunteer hours or 1 year of work-related human services experience, statement of professional goals, writing sample, letters of recommendation. Additional exam requirements/recommendations for international students: Required—TOEFL (minimum score 500 paper-based), IELTS (minimum score 6.0), or TWE (minimum score 22). Electronic applications accepted. *Expenses:* Contact institution. *Faculty research:* Best practices and trends in adult education degree programs, middle and late adulthood development, quality of living issues for older persons.

Concordia University Chicago, College of Graduate and Innovative Programs, Program in Human Services, River Forest, IL 60305-1499. Offers human services (MA), including administration, exercise science. *Program availability:* Part-time, evening/weekend. *Degree requirements:* For master's, comprehensive exam, thesis. *Entrance requirements:* For master's, minimum GPA of 2.9. Additional exam requirements/recommendations for international students: Required—TOEFL (minimum score 550 paper-based). Electronic applications accepted.

Coppin State University, Division of Graduate Studies, Division of Arts and Sciences, Department of Social Sciences, Baltimore, MD 21216-3698. Offers human services administration (MS). *Program availability:* Part-time, evening/weekend. *Entrance requirements:* For master's, resume, references, interview.

Eastern Illinois University, Graduate School, College of Health and Human Services, Program in Human Services Program Development, Charleston, IL 61920. Offers MHS. *Program availability:* Part-time, evening/weekend, online learning. *Degree requirements:* For master's, comprehensive exam (for some programs), thesis (for some programs). *Entrance requirements:* For master's, GMAT or GRE. Additional exam requirements/recommendations for international students: Required—TOEFL (minimum score 500 paper-based; 61 iBT), IELTS (minimum score 6). *Application deadline:* For fall admission, 5/15 for domestic and international students; for spring admission, 10/15 for domestic and international students. Applications are processed on a rolling basis. Application fee: $30. Electronic applications accepted. *Financial support:* Research assistantships with full tuition reimbursements, teaching assistantships with full tuition reimbursements, career-related internships or fieldwork, Federal Work-Study, and unspecified assistantships available. Support available to part-time students. Financial award application deadline: 3/1; financial award applicants required to submit FAFSA. *Unit head:* Linda Simpson, Coordinator, 217-581-2315, Fax: 217-581-6090, E-mail: ldsimpson@eiu.edu. *Application contact:* Linda Simpson, Coordinator, 217-581-2315, Fax: 217-581-6090, E-mail: ldsimpson@eiu.edu. Website: https://www.eiu.edu/mhs/

Eastern Michigan University, Graduate School, College of Health and Human Services, Interdisciplinary Program in Health and Human Services, Ypsilanti, MI 48197. Offers Graduate Certificate. *Program availability:* Part-time, evening/weekend. In 2017, 2 Graduate Certificates awarded. *Entrance requirements:* Additional exam requirements/recommendations for international students: Required—TOEFL. Application fee: $45. *Unit head:* Dr. Marcia Bombyk, Program Coordinator, 734-487-0393, Fax: 734-487-8536, E-mail: mbombyk@emich.edu. *Application contact:* Graduate Admissions, 734-487-2400, Fax: 734-487-6559, E-mail: graduate.admissions@emich.edu.

East Tennessee State University, School of Graduate Studies, College of Education, Department of Counseling and Human Services, Johnson City, TN 37614. Offers clinical mental health counseling (MA); college counseling/student affairs higher education (MA); couples and family therapy (MA); human services (MS); school counseling (MA). *Accreditation:* ACA; NCATE. *Program availability:* Part-time. *Degree requirements:* For master's, comprehensive exam, thesis optional, internship, student teaching, culminating experience. *Entrance requirements:* For master's, GRE General Test, minimum GPA of 3.0, three letters of recommendation, interview, 2-3 page essay detailing experiences that have shaped pursuit of degree, resume. Additional exam requirements/recommendations for international students: Required—TOEFL (minimum score 550 paper-based; 79 iBT). *Application deadline:* For fall admission, 1/31 priority date for domestic and international students. Application fee: $55 ($65 for international students). Electronic applications accepted. *Financial support:* Research assistantships with full tuition reimbursements, teaching assistantships with full tuition reimbursements, career-related internships or fieldwork, institutionally sponsored loans, scholarships/grants, traineeships, and unspecified assistantships available. Financial award application deadline: 7/1; financial award applicants required to submit FAFSA. *Faculty research:* Intervention and assistance with at-risk and under-served youth and high conflict families; service and social justice; women and girls' issues in counseling; counseling competence with LGBTQ individuals; counselor education and supervision. *Unit head:* Dr. Janna Scarborough, Chair, 423-439-4191, Fax: 423-439-7790, E-mail: scarboro@etsu.edu. *Application contact:* Dr. Janna Scarborough, Chair, 423-439-4191, Fax: 423-439-7790, E-mail: scarboro@etsu.edu. Website: http://www.etsu.edu/coe/chs/

Ferris State University, College of Education and Human Services, Big Rapids, MI 49307. Offers M Ed, MS, MSCJ, MSCTE. *Program availability:* Part-time, evening/weekend, blended/hybrid learning. *Faculty:* 15 full-time (6 women), 9 part-time/adjunct (6 women). *Students:* 10 full-time (6 women), 72 part-time (41 women); includes 21 minority (12 Black or African American, non-Hispanic/Latino; 4 Hispanic/Latino; 5 Two or more races, non-Hispanic/Latino), 4 international. Average age 35. 36 applicants, 97% accepted, 24 enrolled. In 2017, 63 master's awarded. *Degree requirements:* For master's, comprehensive exam or thesis/dissertation, research paper or project. *Entrance requirements:* For master's, minimum GPA of 3.0. Additional exam requirements/recommendations for international students: Required—TOEFL (minimum score 500 paper-based, 79 iBT) or IELTS (minimum score 6.5). *Application deadline:* For fall admission, 7/1 priority date for domestic and international students; for winter admission, 12/15 priority date for domestic and international students; for spring admission, 11/1 priority date for domestic and international students; for summer admission, 3/1 priority date for domestic and international students. Applications are processed on a rolling basis. Application fee: $30. Electronic applications accepted. Application fee is waived when completed online. *Financial support:* In 2017–18, 1 research assistantship (averaging $4,850 per year) was awarded; career-related internships or fieldwork, Federal Work-Study, scholarships/grants, and unspecified assistantships also available. Support available to part-time students. Financial award applicants required to submit FAFSA. *Faculty research:* Competency testing, teaching methodologies, assessment of teaching effectiveness, suicide prevention, women in education, special needs. *Unit head:* Arrick L. Jackson, Dean, 231-591-2702, Fax: 231-592-3792, E-mail: arrickjackson@ferris.edu. *Application contact:* Dr. Kristen Salomonson, Dean, Enrollment Services/Director, Admissions and Records, 231-591-2100, Fax: 231-591-3944, E-mail: admissions@ferris.edu.

Georgia State University, Andrew Young School of Policy Studies, School of Social Work, Atlanta, GA 30294. Offers child welfare leadership (Certificate); community partnerships (MSW); forensic social work (Certificate). *Accreditation:* CSWE. *Program availability:* Part-time. *Faculty:* 17 full-time (12 women). *Students:* 117 full-time (107 women), 8 part-time (6 women); includes 77 minority (63 Black or African American, non-Hispanic/Latino; 2 Asian, non-Hispanic/Latino; 7 Hispanic/Latino; 5 Two or more races, non-Hispanic/Latino), 1 international. Average age 30. 168 applicants, 42% accepted, 47 enrolled. In 2017, 59 master's awarded. *Entrance requirements:* For master's and Certificate, GRE. Additional exam requirements/recommendations for international students: Required—TOEFL (minimum score 550 paper-based; 100 iBT) or IELTS (minimum score 7). *Application deadline:* For fall admission, 2/1 priority date for domestic and international students. Application fee: $50. Electronic applications accepted. *Expenses:* Tuition, state resident: full-time $7020. Tuition, nonresident: full-time $22,518. *Required fees:* $2128. Tuition and fees vary according to degree level and program. *Financial support:* In 2017–18, research assistantships with tuition reimbursements (averaging $4,000 per year), teaching assistantships with tuition reimbursements (averaging $4,000 per year) were awarded; career-related internships or fieldwork, institutionally sponsored loans, scholarships/grants, tuition waivers, and unspecified assistantships also available. Financial award application deadline: 2/1; financial award applicants required to submit FAFSA. *Faculty research:* Community partnership, non-profit organizations, child welfare practice and policy, gerontological practice and policy, restorative justice. *Unit head:* Brian Bride, Director of School of Social Work, 404-413-1052, Fax: 404-413-1075, E-mail: bbride@gsu.edu. Website: http://aysps.gsu.edu/socialwork

Governors State University, College of Health and Human Services, University Park, IL 60484. Offers MHA, MHS, MOT, MSN, MSW, DPT. *Accreditation:* CAHME; CSWE. *Program availability:* Part-time. *Faculty:* 54 full-time (47 women), 85 part-time/adjunct (63 women). *Students:* 406 full-time (317 women), 356 part-time (311 women); includes 404 minority (270 Black or African American, non-Hispanic/Latino; 1 American Indian or Alaska Native, non-Hispanic/Latino; 27 Asian, non-Hispanic/Latino; 98 Hispanic/Latino; 1 Native Hawaiian or other Pacific Islander, non-Hispanic/Latino; 7 Two or more races, non-Hispanic/Latino), 9 international. Average age 33. 399 applicants, 54% accepted, 160 enrolled. In 2017, 203 master's, 57 doctorates awarded. *Entrance requirements:* For master's, GMAT/GRE. Additional exam requirements/recommendations for international

students: Required—TOEFL (minimum score 550 paper-based; 80 iBT), IELTS. *Application deadline:* For fall admission, 4/1 for domestic students. Applications are processed on a rolling basis. Application fee: $50. Electronic applications accepted. *Expenses:* Contact institution. *Financial support:* Federal Work-Study and unspecified assistantships available. Financial award application deadline: 5/1; financial award applicants required to submit FAFSA. *Unit head:* Catherine Balthazar, Interim Dean, College of Health and Human Services, 708-534-5000 Ext. 4592, E-mail: cbalthazar@govst.edu. *Application contact:* Paul McGuinness, Executive Director, Enrollment Management/Director, Admissions, 708-534-5000 Ext. 7308, E-mail: pmcguinness@govst.edu. Website: https://www.govst.edu/chhs/

Judson University, Master of Arts in Human Services Administration Program, Elgin, IL 60123-1498. Offers MA. *Program availability:* Evening/weekend. *Faculty:* 6 full-time (3 women), 6 part-time/adjunct (3 women). *Students:* 10 full-time (9 women), 12 part-time (9 women); includes 13 minority (10 Black or African American, non-Hispanic/Latino; 3 Hispanic/Latino). Average age 41. 9 applicants, 89% accepted, 7 enrolled. *Entrance requirements:* For master's, bachelor's degree; two years of work experience; professional resume; minimum GPA of 2.5; official transcripts of all college and graduate work; two letters of reference; essay. *Application deadline:* Applications are processed on a rolling basis. Application fee: $35. Electronic applications accepted. Tuition and fees vary according to course load, degree level and program. *Financial support:* Unspecified assistantships available. *Faculty research:* Dementia and community services, spirituality and counseling. *Unit head:* Dr. Susan Wesner, 847-628-1544, E-mail: susan.wesner@judsonu.edu. *Application contact:* Maria Aguirre, Student Academic Advisor, 847-628-1160, E-mail: maguirre@judsonu.edu.

Kansas State University, Graduate School, College of Human Ecology, School of Family Studies and Human Services, Manhattan, KS 66506-1403. Offers applied family sciences (MS); communication sciences and disorders (MS); conflict resolution (Graduate Certificate); couple and family therapy (MS); early childhood education (MS); family and community service (MS); life-span human development (MS); personal financial planning (MS, PhD, Graduate Certificate); youth development (MS, Graduate Certificate). *Accreditation:* AAMFT/COAMFTE; ASHA. *Program availability:* Part-time, online learning. *Degree requirements:* For master's, comprehensive exam (for some programs), thesis optional. *Entrance requirements:* For master's, GRE, minimum GPA of 3.0 in last 2 years (60 semester hours) of undergraduate study; for doctorate, GRE. Additional exam requirements/recommendations for international students: Required—TOEFL (minimum score 600 paper-based). Electronic applications accepted. *Faculty research:* Health and security of military families, training in and evaluation of professional human services (marriage and couple therapy, family life education, treatment of speech and swallowing disorders, financial therapy), disorders of communication and swallowing, family and relationship development and health, financial decision-making.

Kent State University, College of Education, Health and Human Services, Kent, OH 44242-0001. Offers M Ed, MA, MAT, MS, Au D, PhD, Ed S. *Accreditation:* NCATE. *Program availability:* Part-time, evening/weekend, online learning. *Degree requirements:* For master's, thesis (for some programs); for doctorate, comprehensive exam, thesis/dissertation. *Entrance requirements:* For doctorate and Ed S, GRE General Test. Additional exam requirements/recommendations for international students: Required—TOEFL (minimum score 550 paper-based; 80 iBT). Electronic applications accepted. *Expenses:* Tuition, state resident: full-time $11,310; part-time $515 per credit hour. Tuition, nonresident: full-time $20,396; part-time $928 per credit hour. *International tuition:* $18,544 full-time.

Lehigh University, College of Education, Program in Counseling Psychology, Bethlehem, PA 18015. Offers counseling and human services (M Ed); counseling psychology (PhD); international counseling (M Ed, Certificate); school counseling (M Ed). *Accreditation:* APA (one or more programs are accredited). *Faculty:* 7 full-time (5 women), 10 part-time/adjunct (8 women). *Students:* 69 full-time (62 women), 28 part-time (22 women); includes 22 minority (6 Black or African American, non-Hispanic/Latino; 6 Asian, non-Hispanic/Latino; 10 Hispanic/Latino), 13 international. Average age 29. 181 applicants, 30% accepted, 22 enrolled. In 2017, 27 master's, 4 doctorates awarded. *Degree requirements:* For master's, thesis (for some programs); for doctorate, comprehensive exam, thesis/dissertation. *Entrance requirements:* For master's, minimum GPA of 3.0, 2 letters of recommendation, essay, transcript; for doctorate, GRE General Test, 2 letters of recommendation, transcript, essay; for Certificate, minimum GPA of 3.0 (undergraduate), 3.5 (graduate). Additional exam requirements/recommendations for international students: Required—TOEFL (minimum score 600 paper-based, 93 iBT) or IELTS. *Application deadline:* For fall admission, 2/1 for domestic and international students. Application fee: $65. Electronic applications accepted. *Financial support:* In 2017–18, 31 students received support, including 7 research assistantships with full and partial tuition reimbursements available (averaging $15,249 per year); fellowships and unspecified assistantships also available. Financial award application deadline: 2/15. *Faculty research:* Maternal/infant attachment, multicultural training and counseling, career development and health interventions, intersection of identities, community based participatory research, cognitive development, gerontology, multicultural competence, south Asian-Asian American concerns, sexual assault prevention, LGBTQ, intimate partner violence, feminist theory and therapy, sexual and reproductive health, women's health, culture and health, prevention, minority student development, educational access an. *Total annual research expenditures:* $423,020. *Unit head:* Dr. Christopher Liang, Director, 610-758-3253, Fax: 610-758-3227, E-mail: ctl212@lehigh.edu. *Application contact:* Kristi Ball, Coordinator, Counseling Psychology, 610-758-3250, Fax: 610-758-6223, E-mail: kmb618@lehigh.edu. Website: https://ed.lehigh.edu/academics/programs/counseling-psychology

Lenoir-Rhyne University, Graduate Programs, School of Counseling and Human Services, Hickory, NC 28601. Offers MA. *Program availability:* Part-time, evening/weekend. *Degree requirements:* For master's, comprehensive exam, thesis optional. *Entrance requirements:* Additional exam requirements/recommendations for international students: Required—TOEFL. Electronic applications accepted. *Expenses:* Contact institution.

Lenoir-Rhyne University, Graduate Programs, School of Education, Program in Human Services, Hickory, NC 28601. Offers management (MA); substance abuse (MA); vocational strategies (MA). *Program availability:* Part-time, online only, 100% online. *Degree requirements:* For master's, comprehensive exam. *Entrance requirements:* For master's, GRE General Test or MAT, essay; minimum GPA of 2.7 undergraduate, 3.0 graduate. Additional exam requirements/recommendations for international students: Required—TOEFL (minimum score 600 paper-based). Electronic applications accepted. *Expenses:* Contact institution.

Liberty University, School of Behavioral Sciences, Lynchburg, VA 24515. Offers applied psychology (MA), including developmental psychology (MA, MS), industrial/organizational psychology (MA, MS); clinical mental health counseling (MA); community care and counseling (Ed D), including marriage and family counseling, pastoral care and counseling, traumatology; counselor education and supervision (PhD); human services counseling (MA), including addictions and recovery, business, child and family law,

Christian ministries, criminal justice, crisis response and trauma, executive leadership, health and wellness, life coaching, marriage and family, military resilience; marriage and family counseling (MA); marriage and family therapy (MA); military resilience (Certificate); pastoral counseling (MA), including addictions and recovery, community chaplaincy, crisis response and trauma, discipleship and church ministry, leadership, life coaching, marriage and family, marriage and family studies, military resilience, parenting and child/adolescent, pastoral counseling, theology; professional counseling (MA); psychology (MS), including developmental psychology (MA, MS), industrial/organizational psychology (MA, MS); school counseling (M Ed). *Program availability:* Part-time, online learning. *Students:* 2,649 full-time (2,085 women), 5,086 part-time (4,015 women); includes 2,275 minority (1,784 Black or African American, non-Hispanic/Latino; 44 American Indian or Alaska Native, non-Hispanic/Latino; 67 Asian, non-Hispanic/Latino; 200 Hispanic/Latino; 11 Native Hawaiian or other Pacific Islander, non-Hispanic/Latino; 169 Two or more races, non-Hispanic/Latino), 145 international. Average age 39. 5,839 applicants, 51% accepted, 1710 enrolled. In 2017, 1,626 master's, 7 doctorates, 61 other advanced degrees awarded. *Application deadline:* Applications are processed on a rolling basis. Application fee: $50. Electronic applications accepted. *Financial support:* Applicants required to submit FAFSA. *Unit head:* Dr. Ronald Hawkins, Founding Dean, School of Behavioral Sciences. *Application contact:* Jay Bridge, Director of Admissions, 800-424-9595, Fax: 800-628-7977, E-mail: gradadmissions@liberty.edu.

Lincoln University, Graduate Programs, Philadelphia, PA 19104. Offers counseling (MSC); early childhood education (M Ed), including PreK-4; early childhood education and special education (M Ed); educational leadership (M Ed), including principal certification; finance (MBA); human resources management (MBA); human services delivery (MAHS). *Program availability:* Part-time, evening/weekend. *Faculty:* 9 full-time (3 women), 25 part-time/adjunct (15 women). *Students:* 196 full-time (138 women), 68 part-time (46 women); includes 236 minority (227 Black or African American, non-Hispanic/Latino; 1 American Indian or Alaska Native, non-Hispanic/Latino; 7 Hispanic/Latino; 1 Two or more races, non-Hispanic/Latino), 3 international. Average age 34. 120 applicants, 100% accepted, 95 enrolled. In 2017, 126 master's awarded. *Degree requirements:* For master's, comprehensive exam, thesis or alternative, capstone, grant proposal. *Entrance requirements:* For master's, official academic transcript(s), letters of recommendation, personal statement, resume, supervisor's evaluation form. Additional exam requirements/recommendations for international students: Recommended—TOEFL (minimum score 500 paper-based; 71 iBT), IELTS. *Application deadline:* For fall admission, 8/1 priority date for domestic students, 7/1 priority date for international students; for spring admission, 12/1 priority date for domestic students, 10/1 for international students. Applications are processed on a rolling basis. Application fee: $50. Electronic applications accepted. *Expenses:* Contact institution. *Financial support:* Scholarships/grants available. Financial award application deadline: 6/30; financial award applicants required to submit FAFSA. *Unit head:* Dr. Patricia Pierce Ramsey, Provost, 484-365-7437, Fax: 484-365-8108, E-mail: provost@lincoln.edu. *Application contact:* Jernice Lea, Director, University City Student Services and Admissions, 215-590-8231, Fax: 215-387-3859, E-mail: jlea@lincoln.edu.
Website: http://www.lincoln.edu/admissions/graduate-admissions

Lock Haven University of Pennsylvania, The Stephen Poorman College of Business, Information Systems, and Human Services, Lock Haven, PA 17745-2390. Offers clinical mental health counseling (MS); sport science (MS). *Program availability:* Online learning. *Degree requirements:* For master's, thesis. *Entrance requirements:* For master's, minimum undergraduate GPA of 3.0. Additional exam requirements/recommendations for international students: Required—TOEFL. Electronic applications accepted.

Louisiana Tech University, Graduate School, College of Education, Ruston, LA 71272. Offers counseling and guidance (MA), including clinical mental health counseling, human services, orientation and mobility; counseling psychology (PhD); curriculum and instruction (M Ed); cyber education (Graduate Certificate); dynamics of domestic and family violence (Graduate Certificate); early childhood education - PreK-3 (MAT); educational leadership (M Ed, Ed D); elementary education and special education mild/moderate grades 1-5 (MAT); higher education administration (Graduate Certificate); industrial/organizational psychology (MA, PhD); kinesiology (MS); middle school education (MAT), including mathematics; orientation and mobility (Graduate Certificate); rehabilitation teaching for the blind (Graduate Certificate); secondary education (MAT), including agriculture, biology, business, chemistry, English; special education: visually impaired (MAT); teacher leader education (Graduate Certificate); visual impairments - blind education (Graduate Certificate). *Accreditation:* NCATE. *Program availability:* Part-time. *Faculty:* 28 full-time (16 women), 23 part-time/adjunct (22 women). *Students:* 269 full-time (192 women), 194 part-time (150 women); includes 127 minority (94 Black or African American, non-Hispanic/Latino; 2 American Indian or Alaska Native, non-Hispanic/Latino; 6 Asian, non-Hispanic/Latino; 16 Hispanic/Latino; 1 Native Hawaiian or other Pacific Islander, non-Hispanic/Latino; 8 Two or more races, non-Hispanic/Latino), 8 international. Average age 34. 226 applicants, 74% accepted, 60 enrolled. In 2017, 5 master's, 2 doctorates, 1 other advanced degree awarded. *Degree requirements:* For master's, thesis; for doctorate, thesis/dissertation. *Entrance requirements:* For master's and doctorate, GRE General Test. Additional exam requirements/recommendations for international students: Required—TOEFL (minimum score 550 paper-based; 80 iBT), IELTS (minimum score 6.5). *Application deadline:* For fall admission, 9/1 priority date for domestic students, 6/1 for international students; for winter admission, 11/1 priority date for domestic students, 9/1 for international students; for spring admission, 2/1 priority date for domestic students, 12/1 for international students; for summer admission, 5/1 priority date for domestic students, 3/1 for international students. Application fee: $40. Electronic applications accepted. *Expenses:* Tuition, state resident: full-time $5146. Tuition, nonresident: full-time $10,147. *International tuition:* $10,267 full-time. *Required fees:* $2273. *Financial support:* In 2017–18, 40 students received support, including 23 research assistantships (averaging $10,346 per year), 15 teaching assistantships (averaging $6,887 per year); fellowships and career-related internships or fieldwork also available. Financial award application deadline: 2/1. *Faculty research:* Blindness and the best methods for increasing independence for individuals who are blind or visually impaired; educating and investigating factors contributing to improvements in human performance across the lifespan and a reduction in injury rates during training. *Total annual research expenditures:* $2.1 million. *Unit head:* Dr. Don Schillinger, Dean, 318-257-3712, E-mail: dschill@latech.edu. *Application contact:* Dr. Dawn Basinger, Associate Dean of Academic Affairs, 318-257-2977, Fax: 318-257-2379, E-mail: dbasing@latech.edu.
Website: http://education.latech.edu/

McDaniel College, Graduate and Professional Studies, Program in Human Services Management, Westminster, MD 21157-4390. Offers MS. *Accreditation:* NCATE. *Program availability:* Evening/weekend. *Faculty:* 1 full-time (0 women), 2 part-time/adjunct (1 woman). *Students:* 17 full-time (16 women), 2 part-time (both women); includes 5 minority (all Black or African American, non-Hispanic/Latino), 1 international. Average age 25. 2 applicants, 50% accepted. In 2017, 9 master's awarded. *Degree requirements:* For master's, internship. *Entrance requirements:* For master's, 3 recommendations; successful employment interview with Target Community and Educational Services, Inc. Additional exam requirements/recommendations for

international students: Required—TOEFL (minimum score 79 iBT), IELTS (minimum score 6). *Application deadline:* Applications are processed on a rolling basis. Application fee: $75. Electronic applications accepted. *Expenses:* Tuition: Full-time $11,760; part-time $490 per credit hour. Tuition and fees vary according to course load and program. *Financial support:* Application deadline: 3/1; applicants required to submit FAFSA. *Unit head:* E-mail: gradadms@mcdaniel.edu. *Application contact:* Crystal L. Perry, Assistant Director, Graduate Enrollment Management, 410-857-2516, Fax: 410-857-2515, E-mail: cperry@mcdaniel.edu.

Mercer University, Graduate Studies, Cecil B. Day Campus, Penfield College, Atlanta, GA 30341. Offers certified rehabilitation counseling (MS); clinical mental health (MS); counselor education and supervision (PhD); criminal justice and public safety leadership (MS); health informatics (MS); human services (MS), including child and adolescent services, gerontology services; organizational leadership (MS), including leadership for the health care professional, leadership for the nonprofit organization, organizational development and change; school counseling (MS). *Program availability:* Part-time, evening/weekend, 100% online, blended/hybrid learning. *Faculty:* 17 full-time (10 women), 27 part-time/adjunct (24 women). *Students:* 199 full-time (165 women), 266 part-time (218 women); includes 268 minority (226 Black or African American, non-Hispanic/Latino; 1 American Indian or Alaska Native, non-Hispanic/Latino; 19 Asian, non-Hispanic/Latino; 19 Hispanic/Latino; 3 Two or more races, non-Hispanic/Latino). Average age 32. 300 applicants, 45% accepted, 114 enrolled. In 2017, 101 master's, 5 doctorates awarded. *Degree requirements:* For master's, comprehensive exam (for some programs), thesis (for some programs); for doctorate, thesis/dissertation. *Entrance requirements:* For master's, GRE or MAT, Georgia Professional Standards Commission (GPSC) Certification at the SC-5 level; for doctorate, GRE or MAT. Additional exam requirements/recommendations for international students: Recommended—TOEFL (minimum score 550 paper-based; 80 iBT), IELTS (minimum score 6.5). *Application deadline:* For fall admission, 7/1 priority date for domestic and international students; for spring admission, 11/1 priority date for domestic and international students; for summer admission, 4/1 priority date for domestic and international students. Application fee: $35. Electronic applications accepted. Application fee is waived when completed online. *Expenses:* $637 per credit. *Financial support:* In 2017–18, 32 students received support. Federal Work-Study, scholarships/grants, and unspecified assistantships available. Financial award applicants required to submit FAFSA. *Faculty research:* Marriage and families issues, leadership and ethics, cyber-bullying, trauma, narrative counseling and theory. *Total annual research expenditures:* $85,000. *Unit head:* Dr. Priscilla R. Danheiser, Dean, 678-547-6028, Fax: 678-547-6008, E-mail: danheiser_p@mercer.edu. *Application contact:* Dr. Melissa McCants Cruz, Director of Graduate Admissions, 678-547-6024, E-mail: penfield.admissions@mercer.edu.
Website: http://penfield.mercer.edu/programs/graduate-professional

Minnesota State University Mankato, College of Graduate Studies and Research, College of Social and Behavioral Sciences, Department of Sociology and Corrections, Mankato, MN 56001. Offers sociology (MA); sociology: college teaching (MA); sociology: corrections (MS); sociology: human services planning and administration (MS). *Program availability:* Part-time. *Degree requirements:* For master's, comprehensive exam, thesis or alternative. *Entrance requirements:* For master's, minimum GPA of 3.0 during previous 2 years, 3 letters of reference, resume. Additional exam requirements/recommendations for international students: Required—TOEFL. Electronic applications accepted.

Murray State University, College of Education and Human Services, Department of Educational Studies, Leadership and Counseling, Murray, KY 42071. Offers college advising (Certificate); education administration (MA Ed); human development and leadership (MS, Certificate); library media (MA Ed); middle school teacher leader (MA Ed); P-20 and community leadership (Ed D); postsecondary education administration (MA Ed); school counseling (MA Ed); school guidance and counseling (Ed S); secondary teacher leader (MA Ed). *Program availability:* Part-time, evening/weekend, 100% online, blended/hybrid learning. *Faculty:* 38 full-time (16 women), 3 part-time/adjunct (1 woman). *Students:* 45 full-time (22 women), 190 part-time (140 women); includes 33 minority (25 Black or African American, non-Hispanic/Latino; 4 Asian, non-Hispanic/Latino; 3 Hispanic/Latino; 1 Two or more races, non-Hispanic/Latino), 6 international. Average age 35. 87 applicants, 77% accepted, 51 enrolled. In 2017, 21 master's, 16 doctorates, 12 other advanced degrees awarded. *Entrance requirements:* For master's and other advanced degree, GRE or GMAT, minimum university GPA of 2.75. Additional exam requirements/recommendations for international students: Required—TOEFL (minimum score 527 paper-based; 71 iBT). *Application deadline:* Applications are processed on a rolling basis. Application fee: $40 ($50 for international students). Electronic applications accepted. *Expenses:* Tuition, state resident: full-time $9504. Tuition, nonresident: full-time $26,811. *International tuition:* $14,400 full-time. Tuition and fees vary according to course load, degree level and reciprocity agreements. *Financial support:* Federal Work-Study and unspecified assistantships available. Financial award applicants required to submit FAFSA. *Unit head:* Dr. Susana Bloomdahl, Chair, Department of Educational Studies, Leadership, and Counseling, 270-809-6471, Fax: 270-809-3799, E-mail: sbloomdahl@murraystate.edu. *Application contact:* Kaitlyn Burzynski, Interim Assistant Director for Graduate Admission and Records, 270-809-5732, Fax: 270-809-3780, E-mail: msu.graduateadmissions@murraystate.edu.
Website: http://www.murraystate.edu/academics/CollegesDepartments/CollegeOfEducationandHumanServices/coehsacademicunits/EducationalStudiesLeadershipandCounseli

National Louis University, College of Arts and Sciences, Chicago, IL 60603. Offers adult education (Ed D); counseling and human services (MS); language and academic development (M Ed, Certificate); psychology (MA, PhD, Certificate); public policy (MA); written communication (MS, Certificate). *Program availability:* Part-time, evening/weekend, online learning. *Degree requirements:* For master's and Certificate, comprehensive exam (for some programs), thesis (for some programs); for doctorate, thesis/dissertation. *Entrance requirements:* For master's, GRE or MAT, 3 professional or academic references, interview, minimum GPA of 3.0; for doctorate, GRE General Test, MAT, or Watson-Glaser Critical Thinking Appraisal, three professional or academic references, statement of academic and professional goals, 3 years of experience in field, interview, master's degree, resume, writing sample; for Certificate, GRE, MAT, or Watson-Glaser Critical Thinking Appraisal, three professional or academic references, statement of academic and professional goals, interview, minimum GPA of 3.0. Additional exam requirements/recommendations for international students: Required—Department of Language Studies Assessment or TOEFL (minimum score 550 paper-based; 79 iBT). Electronic applications accepted.

New England College, Program in Community Mental Health Counseling, Henniker, NH 03242-3293. Offers human services (MS); mental health counseling (MS). *Program availability:* Part-time, evening/weekend. *Degree requirements:* For master's, internship.

Northeastern University, College of Professional Studies, Boston, MA 02115-5096. Offers applied nutrition (MS); college athletics administration (MSL); commerce and economic development (MS); corporate and organizational communication (MS); criminal justice (MS); digital media (MPS); elearning and instructional design (M Ed); elementary education (MAT); geographic information technology (MPS); global studies

and international relations (MS); higher education administration (M Ed); homeland security (MA); human services (MS); informatics (MPS); leadership (MS); learning analytics (M Ed); learning and instruction (M Ed); nonprofit management (MS); professional sports administration (MSL); project management (MS); regulatory affairs for drugs, biologics, and medical devices (MS); respiratory care leadership (MS); special education (M Ed); technical communication (MS). *Program availability:* Part-time, evening/weekend, 100% online, blended/hybrid learning. *Faculty:* 82 full-time (51 women), 853 part-time/adjunct (366 women). *Students:* 5,278 part-time (3,230 women). In 2017, 1,586 master's awarded. *Application deadline:* Applications are processed on a rolling basis. Application fee: $0. Electronic applications accepted. *Expenses:* Contact institution. *Financial support:* Applicants required to submit FAFSA. *Unit head:* Dr. Mary Loeffelholz, Dean of the College of Professional Studies. *Application contact:* E-mail: cpsadmissions@northeastern.edu.
Website: https://cps.northeastern.edu/

Pontifical Catholic University of Puerto Rico, College of Graduate Studies in Behavioral Science and Community Affairs, Ponce, PR 00717-0777. Offers clinical psychology (PhD, Psy D); clinical social work (MSW); criminology (MA); industrial psychology (PhD); psychology (PhD); public administration (MSS); rehabilitation counseling (MA). *Program availability:* Part-time, evening/weekend. *Degree requirements:* For master's, thesis; for doctorate, comprehensive exam, thesis/dissertation. *Entrance requirements:* For master's, EXADEP, GRE General Test, 3 letters of recommendation, interview, minimum GPA of 2.75.

Post University, Program in Counseling and Human Services, Waterbury, CT 06723-2540. Offers counseling and human services (MS); counseling and human services/alcohol and drug counseling (MS); counseling and human services/clinical mental health counseling (MS); counseling and human services/forensic mental health counseling (MS); counseling and human services/non-profit management (MS). *Program availability:* Part-time, evening/weekend, online learning. *Entrance requirements:* For master's, resume. *Expenses:* Tuition: Part-time $730 per credit hour. Part-time tuition and fees vary according to degree level and program. *Application contact:* Veronica Montalvo, Vice President, Online Education Enrollment Management and Admissions, 203-596-6164, E-mail: vmontalvo@post.edu.
Website: https://post.edu/academics/online-master-of-science-in-counseling-and-human-services

Purdue University Northwest, Graduate Studies Office, School of Education, Program in Counseling, Hammond, IN 46323-2094. Offers human services (MS Ed); mental health counseling (MS Ed); school counseling (MS Ed). *Accreditation:* ACA. *Entrance requirements:* Additional exam requirements/recommendations for international students: Required—TOEFL.

Regent University, Graduate School, School of Psychology and Counseling, Virginia Beach, VA 23464-9800. Offers clinical mental health counseling (MA); clinical psychology (Psy D); counseling and psychological studies - clinical (PhD); counseling and psychological studies - research (PhD); counseling studies (CAGS); counselor education and supervision (PhD); general psychology (MS); human services (MA), including addictions counseling, Biblical counseling, Christian counseling, conflict and mediation ministry, criminal justice and ministry, grief counseling, human services counseling, human services for student affairs, life coaching, marriage and family ministry, trauma and crisis counseling; marriage, couple, and family counseling (MA); pastoral counseling (MA); school counseling (MA); M Div/MA; M Ed/MA; MBA/MA. *Accreditation:* ACA; APA (one or more programs are accredited). *Program availability:* Part-time, evening/weekend, 100% online, blended/hybrid learning. *Faculty:* 28 full-time (16 women), 51 part-time/adjunct (30 women). *Students:* 294 full-time (236 women), 404 part-time (317 women); includes 286 minority (218 Black or African American, non-Hispanic/Latino; 4 American Indian or Alaska Native, non-Hispanic/Latino; 17 Asian, non-Hispanic/Latino; 30 Hispanic/Latino; 17 Two or more races, non-Hispanic/Latino), 13 international. Average age 37. 2,109 applicants, 18% accepted, 233 enrolled. In 2017, 158 master's, 28 doctorates awarded. *Degree requirements:* For master's, thesis or alternative, internship, practicum, written competency exam; for doctorate, thesis/dissertation or alternative. *Entrance requirements:* For master's, GRE General Test (including writing exam) or MAT, minimum undergraduate GPA of 3.0, resume, transcripts, writing sample, personal goals statement; for doctorate, GRE General Test (including writing exam), minimum undergraduate GPA of 3.0, graduate 3.5; writing sample; 3 recommendations; resume; college transcripts; personal goals statement. Additional exam requirements/recommendations for international students: Required—TOEFL (minimum score 577 paper-based). *Application deadline:* For fall admission, 4/1 priority date for domestic students; for spring admission, 11/1 priority date for domestic students. Applications are processed on a rolling basis. Application fee: $50. Electronic applications accepted. *Expenses:* Contact institution. *Financial support:* In 2017–18, 557 students received support, including 5 fellowships (averaging $10,000 per year), 11 research assistantships (averaging $3,200 per year); career-related internships or fieldwork, scholarships/grants, and unspecified assistantships also available. Support available to part-time students. *Faculty research:* Marriage enrichment, clinical psychology, troubled youth, faith and learning, trauma. *Unit head:* Dr. William Hathaway, Dean, 757-352-4294, Fax: 757-352-4282, E-mail: willhat@regent.edu. *Application contact:* Heidi Cece, Assistant Vice President of Enrollment Management, 800-373-5504, Fax: 757-352-4381, E-mail: admissions@regent.edu.
Website: https://www.regent.edu/school-of-psychology-and-counseling/

Roberts Wesleyan College, Department of Social Work, Rochester, NY 14624-1997. Offers child and family practice (MSW); mental health practice (MSW). *Accreditation:* CSWE. *Entrance requirements:* For master's, minimum GPA of 2.75. *Faculty research:* Religion and social work, family studies, values and ethics.

Rosemont College, Schools of Graduate and Professional Studies, Counseling Psychology Program, Rosemont, PA 19010-1699. Offers human services (MA); school counseling (MA). *Program availability:* Part-time, evening/weekend. *Degree requirements:* For master's, thesis or alternative, practicum. *Entrance requirements:* For master's, minimum undergraduate GPA of 3.0, 3 letters of recommendation. Additional exam requirements/recommendations for international students: Required—TOEFL. Electronic applications accepted. Application fee is waived when completed online. *Expenses:* Contact institution. *Faculty research:* Addictions counseling.

St. Joseph's College, Long Island Campus, Programs in Management, Field in Human Services Leadership, Patchogue, NY 11772-2399. Offers MS. *Program availability:* Part-time, evening/weekend, 100% online, blended/hybrid learning. *Faculty:* 15 full-time (7 women), 22 part-time/adjunct (7 women). *Students:* 1 (woman) full-time, 21 part-time (16 women); includes 8 minority (4 Black or African American, non-Hispanic/Latino; 2 Hispanic/Latino; 2 Two or more races, non-Hispanic/Latino). Average age 39. 24 applicants, 58% accepted, 11 enrolled. In 2017, 17 master's awarded. Application fee: $25. *Expenses:* Tuition: Full-time $17,550; part-time $975 per credit. *Required fees:* $362. *Financial support:* In 2017–18, 4 students received support. *Unit head:* Dr. Jo Anne Durovich, Chair, 631-687-5193, E-mail: jdurovich@sjcny.edu.

St. Joseph's College, New York, Programs in Management, Field in Human Services Management and Leadership, Brooklyn, NY 11205-3688. Offers MS. *Program availability:* Part-time, evening/weekend, 100% online, blended/hybrid learning. *Faculty:* 1 full-time (0 women), 6 part-time/adjunct (4 women). *Students:* 13 part-time (9 women); includes 11 minority (9 Black or African American, non-Hispanic/Latino; 1 Asian, non-Hispanic/Latino; 1 Hispanic/Latino). Average age 40. 18 applicants, 61% accepted, 10 enrolled. In 2017, 5 master's awarded. *Entrance requirements:* For master's, official transcripts, resume, two letters of reference, verification of employment. Additional exam requirements/recommendations for international students: Required—TOEFL (minimum score 80 iBT). *Application deadline:* Applications are processed on a rolling basis. Application fee: $25. Electronic applications accepted. *Expenses:* Tuition: $17,550; part-time $975 per credit. *Required fees:* $362. *Financial support:* In 2017–18, 1 student received support. *Unit head:* Sharon Didier, Assistant Chair/Co-Director of Graduate Management Studies/Associate Professor, 718-940-5790, E-mail: sdidier@sjcny.edu.
Website: http://www.sjcny.edu

Saint Leo University, Graduate Studies in Human Services, Saint Leo, FL 33574-6665. Offers MS. *Program availability:* Part-time, evening/weekend, 100% online. *Faculty:* 4 full-time (all women), 2 part-time/adjunct (both women). *Students:* 70 part-time (66 women); includes 52 minority (50 Black or African American, non-Hispanic/Latino; 2 Hispanic/Latino). Average age 40. 77 applicants, 65% accepted, 47 enrolled. In 2017, 7 master's awarded. *Degree requirements:* For master's, project, field placement. *Entrance requirements:* For master's, official transcripts, bachelor's degree from regionally-accredited university with minimum GPA of 3.0, current resumé, 3 professional recommendations, statement of professional goals. Additional exam requirements/recommendations for international students: Required—TOEFL (minimum score 550 paper-based; 78 iBT). *Application deadline:* For fall admission, 7/1 for domestic and international students; for spring admission, 11/1 for domestic and international students. Applications are processed on a rolling basis. Application fee: $80. Electronic applications accepted. *Expenses:* $520 per credit hour. *Financial support:* In 2017–18, 4 students received support. Career-related internships or fieldwork, scholarships/grants, health care benefits, and tuition remission for Saint Leo employees and their dependents available. Financial award application deadline: 3/1; financial award applicants required to submit FAFSA. *Faculty research:* Grantsmanship, animal-assisted therapy, interdisciplinary education, leadership, creation of human services agencies, child welfare services. *Unit head:* Dr. Susan Kinsella, Dean, School of Education and Social Services, 352-588-8272, Fax: 352-588-8289, E-mail: susan.kinsella@saintleo.edu. *Application contact:* Mary Martinez-Drovie, Graduate Enrollment Counselor, 352-588-5802, Fax: 352-588-8289, E-mail: mary.martinez-drovie@saintleo.edu.
Website: https://www.saintleo.edu/human-services-administration-master-degree

South Carolina State University, College of Graduate and Professional Studies, Department of Human Services, Orangeburg, SC 29117-0001. Offers counselor education (M Ed); rehabilitation counseling (MA). *Accreditation:* CORE. *Program availability:* Part-time, evening/weekend. *Faculty:* 8 full-time (6 women), 3 part-time/adjunct (all women). *Students:* 87 full-time (74 women), 25 part-time (17 women); includes 106 minority (all Black or African American, non-Hispanic/Latino). Average age 32. 60 applicants, 93% accepted, 51 enrolled. In 2017, 38 master's awarded. *Degree requirements:* For master's, comprehensive exam (for some programs), departmental qualifying exam, internship. *Entrance requirements:* For master's, GRE, MAT, minimum GPA of 2.7. *Application deadline:* For fall admission, 6/15 priority date for domestic students, 6/15 for international students; for spring admission, 11/1 for domestic and international students. Application fee: $25. Electronic applications accepted. *Expenses:* Tuition, state resident: full-time $9388; part-time $607 per credit hour. Tuition, nonresident: full-time $19,968; part-time $1194 per credit hour. *Required fees:* $766; $766 per credit hour. *Financial support:* Fellowships, career-related internships or fieldwork, scholarships/grants, and unspecified assistantships available. Financial award application deadline: 6/1. *Unit head:* Dr. Michelle Maultsby-Priester, Interim Chair, Department of Human Services, 803-536-7075, Fax: 803-533-3636, E-mail: mmaultsb@scsu.edu. *Application contact:* Curtis Foskey, Coordinator of Graduate Admissions, 803-536-8419, Fax: 803-536-8812, E-mail: cfoskey@scsu.edu.

Southeastern University, College of Behavioral and Social Sciences, Lakeland, FL 33801-6099. Offers human services (MA); international community development (MA); marriage and family counseling (MS); professional counseling (MS); school counseling (MS); social work (MSW). *Program availability:* Evening/weekend. *Faculty:* 9 full-time (6 women), 7 part-time/adjunct (4 women). *Students:* 72 full-time (60 women), 9 part-time (all women); includes 28 minority (12 Black or African American, non-Hispanic/Latino; 2 Asian, non-Hispanic/Latino; 13 Hispanic/Latino; 1 Native Hawaiian or other Pacific Islander, non-Hispanic/Latino), 1 international. Average age 29. Application fee: $50. Electronic applications accepted. *Unit head:* Erica H. Sirrine, Dean, 863-667-5341, E-mail: ehsirrine@seu.edu.
Website: http://www.seu.edu/behavior/

Springfield College, Graduate Programs, Program in Human Services, Springfield, MA 01109-3797. Offers mental health counseling (MS); organizational management and leadership (MS). *Program availability:* Part-time, evening/weekend, blended/hybrid learning. *Degree requirements:* For master's, comprehensive exam, thesis (for some programs), Community Action Research Project. *Entrance requirements:* Additional exam requirements/recommendations for international students: Required—TOEFL (minimum score 550 paper-based). *Application deadline:* For fall admission, 8/31 for domestic and international students; for winter admission, 11/1 for domestic and international students; for spring admission, 12/31 for domestic and international students; for summer admission, 4/30 for domestic and international students. Applications are processed on a rolling basis. Application fee: $40. Electronic applications accepted. *Expenses:* Contact institution. *Financial support:* Application deadline: 3/1; applicants required to submit FAFSA. *Unit head:* Dr. John Eisler, Dean, 413-748-3982, E-mail: jeisler@springfieldcollege.edu. *Application contact:* Marisol Guevara, Assistant Director of Recruitment and Outreach, 413-748-3624, E-mail: mguevara@springfieldcollege.edu.
Website: https://springfield.edu/school-of-professional-and-continuing-studies/degrees-and-programs/master-of-science

Texas Southern University, College of Liberal Arts and Behavioral Sciences, Department of Human Services and Consumer Sciences, Houston, TX 77004-4584. Offers MS. *Program availability:* Part-time, evening/weekend. *Degree requirements:* For master's, comprehensive exam, thesis (for some programs). *Entrance requirements:* For master's, GRE General Test, minimum GPA of 2.5. Additional exam requirements/recommendations for international students: Required—TOEFL. Electronic applications accepted. *Faculty research:* Food radiation/food for space travel, adolescent parenting, gerontology/grandparenting.

Thomas University, Department of Human Services, Thomasville, GA 31792-7499. Offers community counseling (MSCC); rehabilitation counseling (MRC). *Accreditation:* CORE. *Program availability:* Part-time. *Entrance requirements:* For master's, resume, 3 academic/professional references. Additional exam requirements/recommendations for international students: Required—TOEFL (minimum score 600 paper-based). Electronic applications accepted.

Universidad del Turabo, Graduate Programs, School of Social Sciences and Humanities, Programs in Public Affairs, Program in Human Services Administration, Gurabo, PR 00778-3030. Offers MPA. *Entrance requirements:* For master's, GRE, EXADEP or GMAT, interview, essay, official transcript, recommendation letters. Electronic applications accepted.

Université de Montréal, Faculty of Arts and Sciences, Programs in Applied Human Sciences, Montréal, QC H3C 3J7, Canada. Offers PhD. *Degree requirements:* For doctorate, thesis/dissertation, general exam. Electronic applications accepted.

University of Baltimore, Graduate School, College of Public Affairs, Program in Human Services Administration, Baltimore, MD 21201-5779. Offers MS. *Program availability:* Part-time, evening/weekend. *Entrance requirements:* For master's, interview. Additional exam requirements/recommendations for international students: Required—TOEFL (minimum score 550 paper-based). Electronic applications accepted.

University of Bridgeport, School of Arts and Sciences, Department of Counseling, Bridgeport, CT 06604. Offers clinical mental health counseling (MS); college student personnel (MS); community counseling (MS); human resource development (MS); human service (MS). *Program availability:* Part-time, evening/weekend. *Degree requirements:* For master's, thesis, project. *Entrance requirements:* Additional exam requirements/recommendations for international students: Recommended—TOEFL (minimum score 550 paper-based; 80 iBT), IELTS (minimum score 6.5). Electronic applications accepted. *Expenses:* Contact institution.

University of Central Missouri, The Graduate School, Warrensburg, MO 64093. Offers accountancy (MA); accounting (MBA); applied mathematics (MS); aviation safety (MA); biology (MS); business administration (MBA); career and technical education leadership (MS); college student personnel administration (MS); communication (MA); computer science (MS); counseling (MS); criminal justice (MS); educational leadership (Ed D); educational technology (MS); elementary and early childhood education (MSE); English (MA); environmental studies (MA); finance (MBA); history (MA); human services/educational technology (Ed S); human services/learning resources (Ed S); human services/professional counseling (Ed S); industrial hygiene (MS); industrial management (MS); information systems (MBA); information technology (MS); kinesiology (MS); library science and information services (MS); literacy education (MSE); marketing (MBA); mathematics (MS); music (MA); occupational safety management (MS); psychology (MS); rural family nursing (MS); school administration (MSE); social gerontology (MS); sociology (MA); special education (MSE); speech language pathology (MS); superintendency (Ed S); teaching (MAT); teaching English as a second language (MA); technology (MS); technology management (PhD); theatre (MA). *Program availability:* Part-time, 100% online, blended/hybrid learning. *Faculty:* 337 full-time (145 women), 41 part-time/adjunct (28 women). *Students:* 785 full-time (398 women), 1,633 part-time (1,063 women); includes 231 minority (102 Black or African American, non-Hispanic/Latino; 4 American Indian or Alaska Native, non-Hispanic/Latino; 16 Asian, non-Hispanic/Latino; 52 Hispanic/Latino; 57 Two or more races, non-Hispanic/Latino), 692 international. Average age 30. In 2017, 2,605 master's, 122 other advanced degrees awarded. *Degree requirements:* For master's and Ed S, comprehensive exam (for some programs), thesis (for some programs). *Entrance requirements:* Additional exam requirements/recommendations for international students: Required—TOEFL (minimum score 550 paper-based; 79 iBT). *Application deadline:* For fall admission, 6/1 priority date for domestic and international students; for spring admission, 10/1 priority date for domestic and international students; for summer admission, 4/1 priority date for domestic and international students. Applications are processed on a rolling basis. Application fee: $30 ($75 for international students). Electronic applications accepted. *Expenses:* Tuition, state resident: full-time $8771; part-time $292.35 per credit hour. Tuition, nonresident: full-time $17,541; part-time $584.70 per credit hour. *Required fees:* $372; $24.78 per credit hour. *Financial support:* In 2017–18, 99 students received support. Research assistantships, teaching assistantships, career-related internships or fieldwork, Federal Work-Study, scholarships/grants, and administrative and laboratory assistantships available. Support available to part-time students. Financial award application deadline: 3/1; financial award applicants required to submit FAFSA. *Unit head:* Shellie Hewitt, Director of Graduate and International Student Services, 660-543-4621, Fax: 660-543-4778, E-mail: hewitt@ucmo.edu. *Application contact:* 660-543-4621, E-mail: admit_intl@ucmo.edu.
Website: http://www.ucmo.edu/graduate/

University of Colorado Colorado Springs, College of Education, Colorado Springs, CO 80918. Offers counseling and human services (MA); curriculum and instruction (MA); educational leadership (MA); educational leadership, research and policy (PhD); special education (MA); teaching English to speakers of other languages (MA). *Accreditation:* ACA; NCATE. *Program availability:* Part-time, evening/weekend, 100% online, blended/hybrid learning. *Faculty:* 30 full-time (21 women), 61 part-time/adjunct (38 women). *Students:* 190 full-time (132 women), 286 part-time (202 women); includes 117 minority (20 Black or African American, non-Hispanic/Latino; 2 American Indian or Alaska Native, non-Hispanic/Latino; 12 Asian, non-Hispanic/Latino; 59 Hispanic/Latino; 24 Two or more races, non-Hispanic/Latino), 6 international. Average age 36. 169 applicants, 85% accepted, 113 enrolled. In 2017, 160 master's, 16 doctorates awarded. *Degree requirements:* For master's, comprehensive exam, thesis or alternative, microcomputer proficiency; for doctorate, comprehensive exam, thesis/dissertation, research lab. *Entrance requirements:* For master's and doctorate, GRE General Test. Additional exam requirements/recommendations for international students: Recommended—TOEFL (minimum score 550 paper-based; 80 iBT), IELTS (minimum score 6). *Application deadline:* For fall admission, 1/28 priority date for domestic and international students; for spring admission, 11/1 priority date for domestic and international students. Applications are processed on a rolling basis. Application fee: $60 ($100 for international students). Electronic applications accepted. *Expenses:* $10,350 per year resident tuition, $20,935 nonresident, $11,961 nonresidential online; annual costs vary depending on program, course-load, and residency status. *Financial support:* In 2017–18, 81 students received support. Career-related internships or fieldwork, Federal Work-Study, scholarships/grants, and unspecified assistantships available. Support available to part-time students. Financial award application deadline: 3/1; financial award applicants required to submit FAFSA. *Faculty research:* Linguistically diverse education (LDE), educational policy, evidence-based reading and writing instruction, relational and social aggression, positive behavior supports, inclusive schooling, K-12 education policy. *Total annual research expenditures:* $607,967. *Unit head:* Dr. Valerie Martin Conley, Dean, 719-255-4133, E-mail: vmconley@uccs.edu. *Application contact:* The College of Education Student Resource Office, 719-255-4996, E-mail: education@uccs.edu.
Website: http://www.uccs.edu/coe

University of Idaho, College of Graduate Studies, College of Education, Health and Human Sciences, Department of Leadership and Counseling, Boise, ID 83844-2282. Offers adult/organizational learning and leadership (Ed S); educational leadership (Ed S); rehabilitation counseling and human services (M Ed); school counseling (M Ed, MS). *Faculty:* 14 full-time, 6 part-time/adjunct. *Students:* 29 full-time (20 women), 147 part-time (78 women). Average age 38. In 2017, 62 master's, 32 other advanced degrees awarded. *Entrance requirements:* For master's, minimum GPA of 3.0, writing sample. Additional exam requirements/recommendations for international students: Required—TOEFL (minimum score 79 iBT). *Application deadline:* Applications are processed on a rolling basis. Application fee: $60. Electronic applications accepted. *Expenses:* Tuition, state resident: full-time $6722; part-time $430 per credit hour. Tuition, nonresident: full-time $23,046; part-time $1337 per credit hour. *Required fees:* $2142; $63 per credit hour. *Financial support:* Applicants required to submit FAFSA.

Unit head: Dr. Kathy Canfield-Davis, Chair, 208-364-4047, E-mail: lead@uidaho.edu. *Application contact:* Sean Scoggin, Graduate Recruitment Coordinator, 208-885-4723, Fax: 208-885-4406, E-mail: graduateadmissions@uidaho.edu.
Website: https://www.uidaho.edu/ed/lc

University of Illinois at Springfield, Graduate Programs, College of Education and Human Services, Program in Human Services, Springfield, IL 62703-5407. Offers alcohol and substance abuse (Graduate Certificate); alcoholism and substance abuse (MA); child and family services (MA); gerontology (MA); social services administration (MA). *Program availability:* Part-time, evening/weekend, 100% online, blended/hybrid learning. *Faculty:* 5 full-time (all women). *Students:* 8 full-time (7 women), 72 part-time (63 women); includes 38 minority (26 Black or African American, non-Hispanic/Latino; 9 Hispanic/Latino; 3 Two or more races, non-Hispanic/Latino). Average age 33. 49 applicants, 47% accepted, 20 enrolled. In 2017, 21 master's, 1 other advanced degree awarded. *Degree requirements:* For master's, internship; capstone project. *Entrance requirements:* For master's, minimum undergraduate GPA of 3.0, 2 letters of recommendation from professional or academic sources, statement of intent, interview. Additional exam requirements/recommendations for international students: Required—TOEFL (minimum score 500 paper-based; 61 iBT). *Application deadline:* Applications are processed on a rolling basis. Application fee: $60 ($75 for international students). Electronic applications accepted. *Expenses:* Tuition, state resident: full-time $7896; part-time $329 per credit hour. Tuition, nonresident: full-time $16,200; part-time $675 per credit hour. Tuition and fees vary according to program. *Financial support:* In 2017–18, research assistantships with full tuition reimbursements (averaging $10,249 per year), teaching assistantships with full tuition reimbursements (averaging $10,303 per year) were awarded; fellowships, career-related internships or fieldwork, Federal Work-Study, scholarships/grants, health care benefits, and unspecified assistantships also available. Support available to part-time students. Financial award application deadline: 11/15; financial award applicants required to submit FAFSA. *Unit head:* Dr. Carolyn Peck, Program Administrator, 217-206-7577, Fax: 217-206-6775, E-mail: peck.carolyn@uis.edu.
Website: http://www.uis.edu/humanservices

University of Illinois at Urbana–Champaign, Graduate College, School of Social Work, Champaign, IL 61820. Offers advocacy, leadership, and social change (MSW); children, youth and family services (MSW); health care (MSW); mental health (MSW); school social work (MSW); social work (PhD). *Accreditation:* CSWE (one or more programs are accredited). *Entrance requirements:* For master's and doctorate, minimum GPA of 3.0.

University of Maryland, Baltimore County, The Graduate School, College of Arts, Humanities and Social Sciences, Department of Psychology, Program in Human Services Psychology, Baltimore, MD 21250. Offers applied behavioral analysis (MA); human services psychology (PhD), including behavioral medicine, clinical psychology, community psychology. *Faculty:* 17 full-time (9 women), 11 part-time/adjunct (4 women). *Students:* 82 full-time (65 women), 1 (woman) part-time; includes 26 minority (10 Black or African American, non-Hispanic/Latino; 6 Asian, non-Hispanic/Latino; 9 Hispanic/Latino; 1 Two or more races, non-Hispanic/Latino). Average age 25. 136 applicants, 21% accepted, 18 enrolled. In 2017, 25 master's, 7 doctorates awarded. *Degree requirements:* For master's, thesis; for doctorate, comprehensive exam, thesis/dissertation. *Entrance requirements:* For master's, GRE General Test, minimum GPA of 3.0; for doctorate, GRE General Test, GRE Subject Test, minimum GPA of 3.0. Additional exam requirements/recommendations for international students: Required—TOEFL. *Application deadline:* For fall admission, 12/1 for domestic and international students. Application fee: $50. Electronic applications accepted. *Expenses:* Contact institution. *Financial support:* In 2017–18, 43 students received support, including 3 fellowships with full tuition reimbursements available (averaging $26,000 per year), 27 research assistantships with full tuition reimbursements available (averaging $20,400 per year), 8 teaching assistantships with full tuition reimbursements available (averaging $17,250 per year); career-related internships or fieldwork, Federal Work-Study, scholarships/grants, health care benefits, tuition waivers, and unspecified assistantships also available. Financial award application deadline: 3/1; financial award applicants required to submit FAFSA. *Faculty research:* Addictive behaviors, cardiovascular and cerebrovascular disease, family violence, pediatric psychology, community prevention. *Unit head:* Dr. Lynnda Dahlquist, Director, 410-455-2567, Fax: 410-455-1055, E-mail: dahlquis@umbc.edu. *Application contact:* Beverly McDougall, Program Management Specialist, 410-455-2567, Fax: 410-455-1055, E-mail: psycdept@umbc.edu.
Website: http://psychology.umbc.edu/

University of Massachusetts Boston, College of Public and Community Service, Program in Human Services, Boston, MA 02125-3393. Offers MS. *Program availability:* Part-time, evening/weekend. *Faculty:* 1 (woman) full-time. *Students:* 2 full-time (both women), 9 part-time (6 women); includes 7 minority (2 Black or African American, non-Hispanic/Latino; 1 Asian, non-Hispanic/Latino; 3 Hispanic/Latino; 1 Two or more races, non-Hispanic/Latino). Average age 37. 14 applicants, 79% accepted. In 2017, 11 master's awarded. *Entrance requirements:* For master's, MAT, GRE, minimum GPA of 2.75. Additional exam requirements/recommendations for international students: Recommended—TOEFL. *Expenses:* Tuition, state resident: full-time $17,375. Tuition, nonresident: full-time $33,915. *Required fees:* $355. *Financial support:* Research assistantships, teaching assistantships, career-related internships or fieldwork, Federal Work-Study, and unspecified assistantships available. Support available to part-time students. Financial award application deadline: 3/1; financial award applicants required to submit FAFSA. *Faculty research:* Institutional and policy context of human services, ethics and social policy, public law and human services, social welfare, politics and human services. *Application contact:* Graduate Admissions Coordinator, 617-287-6400, Fax: 617-287-6236, E-mail: bos.gadm@dpc.umassp.edu.

University of Nebraska at Kearney, College of Business and Technology, Department of Business, Kearney, NE 68849-0001. Offers accounting (MBA); generalist (MBA); human resources (MBA); human services (MBA); marketing (MBA). *Accreditation:* AACSB. *Program availability:* Part-time, evening/weekend. *Degree requirements:* For master's, thesis optional, capstone course. *Entrance requirements:* For master's, GRE or GMAT (if no significant managerial experience), letters of recommendation, essay, resume. Additional exam requirements/recommendations for international students: Recommended—TOEFL (minimum score 550 paper-based; 79 iBT), IELTS (minimum score 6.5). Electronic applications accepted. *Faculty research:* Small business financial management, employment law, expert systems, international trade and marketing, environmental economics.

University of Northern Iowa, Graduate College, College of Education, School of Kinesiology, Allied Health and Human Services, MA Program in Leisure, Youth and Human Services, Cedar Falls, IA 50614. Offers MA. *Degree requirements:* For master's, comprehensive exam, thesis or alternative. *Entrance requirements:* For master's, minimum GPA of 3.0. Additional exam requirements/recommendations for international students: Required—TOEFL (minimum score 500 paper-based; 61 iBT). Electronic applications accepted.

University of North Georgia, Program in Human Services and Delivery Administration, Dahlonega, GA 30597. Offers MS. *Program availability:* Evening/weekend. *Faculty:* 4 full-time (3 women). *Students:* 1 full-time (1 woman), 4 part-time (all women); includes 1

minority (Black or African American, non-Hispanic/Latino), 1 international. Average age 27. 12 applicants, 75% accepted, 6 enrolled. *Degree requirements:* For master's, service learning. *Entrance requirements:* For master's, GRE or MAT, written statement of goals, 3 UNG recommendation forms, professional resume. Additional exam requirements/recommendations for international students: Required—TOEFL (minimum score 550 paper-based; 79 iBT), IELTS (minimum score 6.5). *Application deadline:* For fall admission, 4/1 for domestic students. Application fee: $40. Electronic applications accepted. *Expenses:* Contact institution. *Financial support:* Application deadline: 3/17; applicants required to submit FAFSA. *Unit head:* Sara Mason, Head, Department of Sociology and Human Services, 678-717-3878, E-mail: sara.mason@ung.edu. *Application contact:* Melinda Maxwell, Director of Graduate Admissions, 706-864-1543, E-mail: melinda.maxwell@ung.edu.
Website: https://ung.edu/graduate-admissions/programs/master-of-science-with-a-major-in-human-services-delivery-admin.php

University of Northwestern–St. Paul, Master of Arts in Human Services Program, St. Paul, MN 55113-1598. Offers MAHS. *Program availability:* Part-time, evening/weekend, online learning. *Application deadline:* Applications are processed on a rolling basis. Electronic applications accepted. *Application contact:* Graduate Studies Admissions, 651-631-5200, E-mail: gradstudies@unwsp.edu.
Website: https://www.unwsp.edu/web/graduate-studies/master-of-arts-in-human-services

University of Oklahoma, College of Arts and Sciences, Department of Human Relations, Norman, OK 73019. Offers clinical mental health (MHR); helping skills in human relations (Graduate Certificate); human relations (MHR); human resource diversity and development (Graduate Certificate); human resources (MHR); licensed professional counselor (MHR). *Program availability:* Part-time, evening/weekend. *Faculty:* 20 full-time (12 women), 9 part-time/adjunct (4 women). *Students:* 297 full-time (221 women), 335 part-time (227 women); includes 316 minority (159 Black or African American, non-Hispanic/Latino; 25 American Indian or Alaska Native, non-Hispanic/Latino; 21 Asian, non-Hispanic/Latino; 68 Hispanic/Latino; 3 Native Hawaiian or other Pacific Islander, non-Hispanic/Latino; 40 Two or more races, non-Hispanic/Latino), 13 international. Average age 35. 152 applicants, 89% accepted, 97 enrolled. In 2017, 255 master's, 95 other advanced degrees awarded. *Degree requirements:* For master's, comprehensive exam or thesis. *Entrance requirements:* For degree, minimum GPA of 3.0. Additional exam requirements/recommendations for international students: Required—TOEFL (minimum score 79 iBT) or IELTS (minimum score 6.5). *Application deadline:* For fall admission, 8/21 for domestic and international students; for spring admission, 1/23 for domestic and international students; for summer admission, 6/5 for domestic and international students. Application fee: $50 ($100 for international students). Electronic applications accepted. *Expenses:* Tuition, state resident: full-time $5119; part-time $213.30 per credit hour. Tuition, nonresident: full-time $19,778; part-time $824.10 per credit hour. *Required fees:* $3458; $133.55 per credit hour. $126.50 per semester. *Financial support:* In 2017–18, 101 students received support, including 6 research assistantships with full tuition reimbursements available (averaging $11,124 per year), 4 teaching assistantships with full tuition reimbursements available (averaging $12,468 per year); scholarships/grants also available. Financial award application deadline: 6/1; financial award applicants required to submit FAFSA. *Faculty research:* At-risk youth, strength model, women's health, adolescent addiction and recovery, group psychotherapy. *Unit head:* Dr. Wesley Long, Chair of Department of Human Relations, 405-325-1756, Fax: 405-325-4402, E-mail: wlong@ou.edu. *Application contact:* Lawana Miller, Admissions Coordinator, 405-325-1756, Fax: 405-325-4402, E-mail: lmiller@ou.edu.
Website: http://www.ou.edu/cas/humanrelations

University of Oklahoma, College of Professional and Continuing Studies, Norman, OK 73019. Offers administrative leadership (MA, Graduate Certificate), including government and military leadership (MA), organizational leadership (MA), volunteer and non-profit leadership (MA); corrections management (Graduate Certificate); criminal justice (MS); integrated studies (MA), including human and health services administration, integrated studies, museum studies (MA); prevention science (MPS); restorative justice administration (Graduate Certificate). *Program availability:* Part-time, 100% online, blended/hybrid learning. *Faculty:* 16 full-time (8 women). *Students:* 64 full-time (39 women), 558 part-time (278 women); includes 191 minority (42 Black or African American, non-Hispanic/Latino; 42 American Indian or Alaska Native, non-Hispanic/Latino; 16 Asian, non-Hispanic/Latino; 46 Hispanic/Latino; 1 Native Hawaiian or other Pacific Islander, non-Hispanic/Latino; 44 Two or more races, non-Hispanic/Latino), 4 international. Average age 35. 151 applicants, 95% accepted, 97 enrolled. In 2017, 202 master's, 11 other advanced degrees awarded. *Degree requirements:* For master's, comprehensive exam, thesis optional, 33 credit hours; project/internship (for museum studies program only); for Graduate Certificate, 12 graduate credit hours (for Graduate Certificate). *Entrance requirements:* For master's and Graduate Certificate, minimum GPA of 3.0 in last 60 undergraduate hours; statement of goals; resume. Additional exam requirements/recommendations for international students: Required—TOEFL (minimum score 79 iBT) or IELTS (minimum score 6.5). *Application deadline:* For fall admission, 7/15 for domestic and international students; for winter admission, 12/1 for domestic and international students; for spring admission, 5/1 for domestic and international students. Applications are processed on a rolling basis. Application fee: $50 ($100 for international students). Electronic applications accepted. *Expenses:* Tuition, state resident: full-time $5119; part-time $213.30 per credit hour. Tuition, nonresident: full-time $19,778; part-time $824.10 per credit hour. *Required fees:* $3458; $133.55 per credit hour. $126.50 per semester. *Financial support:* In 2017–18, 92 students received support. Career-related internships or fieldwork, institutionally sponsored loans, scholarships/grants, health care benefits, and tuition waivers available. Support available to part-time students. Financial award application deadline: 6/1; financial award applicants required to submit FAFSA. *Faculty research:* Change management and leadership; policing and corrections management; neuro-psychology of addiction; disproportionate minority contact; ethnic identity and nationalism. *Unit head:* Dr. Martha L. Banz, Associate Provost for Continuing Education/Interim Dean, College of Professional and Continuing Studies, 405-325-4414, Fax: 405-325-7132, E-mail: mlbanz@ou.edu. *Application contact:* Lindsey Gunderson, Graduate Academic Advisor, 405-325-5827, Fax: 405-325-7132, E-mail: lindsey.gunderson@ou.edu.
Website: https://pacs.ou.edu/

University of Providence, Graduate Studies, Program in Organization Management, Great Falls, MT 59405. Offers human development (MSM); management (MSM). *Program availability:* Part-time, evening/weekend, online learning. *Degree requirements:* For master's, thesis optional. *Entrance requirements:* For master's, GRE General Test or MAT, 3 letters of recommendation. Additional exam requirements/recommendations for international students: Required—TOEFL (minimum score 500 paper-based). Electronic applications accepted.

Upper Iowa University, Online Master's Programs, Fayette, IA 52142-1857. Offers accounting (MBA); corporate financial management (MBA); emergency management and homeland security (MPA); general management (MBA); general studies (MPA); government administration (MPA); health and human services (MPA); human resources management (MBA); nonprofit organizational management (MPA); organizational

development (MBA); public management (MPA); sport administration (MSA). MBA also available at Madison, WI campus. *Program availability:* Part-time, online learning. *Degree requirements:* For master's, research project. *Entrance requirements:* For master's, GMAT, GRE, or minimum GPA of 2.7 during last 60 hours. Additional exam requirements/recommendations for international students: Required—TOEFL (minimum score 570 paper-based). Electronic applications accepted. *Faculty research:* Total quality management, teams, organization culture and climate, management.

Walden University, Graduate Programs, School of Social Work and Human Services, Minneapolis, MN 55401. Offers addictions and social work (DSW); advanced clinical practice (MSW); clinical expertise (DSW); criminal justice (DSW); disaster, crisis, and intervention (DSW); family studies and interventions (DSW); human and social services (PhD), including advanced research, community and social services, community intervention and leadership, conflict management, criminal justice, disaster crisis and intervention, family studies and intervention, gerontology, global social services, higher education, human services and nonprofit administration, mental health facilitation; medical social work (DSW); military social work (MSW); policy practice (DSW); social work (PhD), including addictions and social work, clinical expertise, criminal justice, disaster, crisis and intervention, family studies and interventions, medical social work, policy practice, social work administration; social work administration (DSW); social work in healthcare (MSW); social work with children and families (MSW). *Accreditation:* CSWE. *Program availability:* Part-time, evening/weekend, online only, 100% online. *Degree requirements:* For master's, residency (for some programs); for doctorate, thesis/dissertation, residency. *Entrance requirements:* For master's, bachelor's degree or higher; minimum GPA of 2.5; official transcripts; goal statement (for some programs); access to computer and Internet; for doctorate, master's degree or higher; three years of related professional or academic experience (preferred); minimum GPA of 3.0; goal statement and current resume (for select programs); official transcripts; access to computer and Internet. Additional exam requirements/recommendations for international students: Required—TOEFL (minimum score 550 paper-based, 79 iBT), IELTS (minimum score 6.5), Michigan English Language Assessment Battery (minimum score 82), or PTE (minimum score 53). Electronic applications accepted.

Warner Pacific University, Graduate Programs, Portland, OR 97215-4099. Offers human services (MA); not-for-profit leadership (MS); organizational leadership (MS); teaching (MAT). *Program availability:* Part-time, evening/weekend. *Degree requirements:* For master's, thesis or alternative, presentation of defense. *Entrance requirements:* For master's, interview, minimum GPA of 2.5, letters of recommendation. *Faculty research:* New Testament studies, nineteenth-century Wesleyan theology, preaching and church growth, Christian ethics.

Washburn University, School of Applied Studies, Department of Human Services, Topeka, KS 66621. Offers addiction counseling (MA). *Program availability:* Evening/weekend. *Entrance requirements:* For master's, minimum GPA of 3.0 in last 60 hours of coursework. Additional exam requirements/recommendations for international students: Required—TOEFL (minimum score 80 iBT). *Faculty research:* Professional identity development in students, expressive therapeutic writing, prevention, community mental health, agency professional development, behavioral analysis, group living among the elderly, ethical identity development, higher education pedagogy, Morita therapy/anxiety disorders, ecological/contextual healing, post-trauma.

Webster University, College of Arts and Sciences, Department of Anthropology and Sociology, St. Louis, MO 63119-3194. Offers human services (MA).

Western Michigan University, Graduate College, College of Health and Human Services, Department of Interdisciplinary Health and Human Services, Kalamazoo, MI 49008. Offers interdisciplinary health services (PhD).

West Virginia University, College of Education and Human Services, Morgantown, WV 26506. Offers audiology (Au D); autism spectrum disorder (MA); clinical rehabilitation and mental health counseling (MS); communication science and disorders (PhD); counseling (MA); counseling psychology (PhD); curriculum and instruction (Ed D); early childhood education (MA); early intervention (MA); education (PhD); educational leadership (MA, Ed D); educational leadership/public school administration (MA); educational psychology (MA, Ed D); elementary education (MA); gifted education (MA); higher education administration (MA, Ed D); higher education curriculum and teaching (MA); instructional design and technology (MA); instructional design and technology (Ed D); literacy education (MA); secondary education (MA); secondary education/English (MA); special education (Ed D); speech pathology (MS). *Accreditation:* NCATE. *Program availability:* Part-time, evening/weekend, online learning. *Students:* 423 full-time (347 women), 367 part-time (316 women); includes 57 minority (14 Black or African American, non-Hispanic/Latino; 7 Asian, non-Hispanic/Latino; 20 Hispanic/Latino; 16 Two or more races, non-Hispanic/Latino), 13 international. *Degree requirements:* For master's, content exams; for doctorate, comprehensive exam, thesis/dissertation. *Entrance requirements:* Additional exam requirements/recommendations for international students: Required—TOEFL (minimum score 500 paper-based; 61 iBT). *Application deadline:* For fall admission, 8/1 for domestic students; for spring admission, 1/1 for domestic students; for summer admission, 5/1 for domestic students. Application fee: $60. Electronic applications accepted. *Expenses:* Tuition, state resident: full-time $9450. Tuition, nonresident: full-time $24,390. *Financial support:* Fellowships, research assistantships, teaching assistantships, career-related internships or fieldwork, Federal Work-Study, institutionally sponsored loans, health care benefits, tuition waivers (full and partial), and administrative assistantships available. Financial award applicants required to submit FAFSA. *Faculty research:* Internet training and integration for teachers, rural education, teacher preparation, organization of schools, evaluation of personnel. *Unit head:* Dr. Gypsy Denzine, Dean, 304-293-5703, Fax: 304-293-7565, E-mail: gypsy.denzine@mail.wvu.edu. *Application contact:* Dr. M. Cecil Smith, Associate Dean for Research and Graduate Education, 304-293-2174, Fax: 304-293-3802, E-mail: mcecil.smith@mail.wvu.edu.
Website: http://cehs.wvu.edu/

West Virginia University, Eberly College of Arts and Sciences, School of Social Work, Morgantown, WV 26506. Offers aging and health care (MSW); children and families (MSW); community mental health (MSW); community organization and social administration (MSW); direct (clinical) social work practice (MSW). *Accreditation:* CSWE. *Program availability:* Part-time. *Degree requirements:* For master's, fieldwork. *Entrance requirements:* For master's, GRE, minimum GPA of 2.75, 2 letters of reference. Additional exam requirements/recommendations for international students: Required—TOEFL. *Expenses:* Tuition, state resident: full-time $9450. Tuition, nonresident: full-time $24,390. *Faculty research:* Rural and small town social work practice, gerontology, health and mental health, welfare reform, child welfare.

Wichita State University, Graduate School, Fairmount College of Liberal Arts and Sciences, School of Community Affairs, Wichita, KS 67260. Offers criminal justice (MA). *Program availability:* Part-time, 100% online, blended/hybrid learning. *Unit head:* Dr. Andra Bannister, Interim Director, 316-978-7200, Fax: 316-978-3626, E-mail: andra.bannister@wichita.edu. *Application contact:* Jordan Oleson, Admissions Coordinator, 316-978-3095, Fax: 316-978-3253, E-mail: jordan.oleson@wichita.edu.
Website: http://www.wichita.edu/cj

Human Services

Wilmington University, College of Social and Behavioral Sciences, New Castle, DE 19720-6491. Offers administration of human services (MS); administration of justice (MS); clinical mental health counseling (MS); homeland security (MS). *Accreditation:* ACA. *Program availability:* Part-time, evening/weekend. *Faculty:* 11 full-time (6 women), 74 part-time/adjunct (34 women). *Students:* 174 full-time (132 women), 428 part-time (334 women); includes 269 minority (229 Black or African American, non-Hispanic/Latino; 5 American Indian or Alaska Native, non-Hispanic/Latino; 7 Asian, non-Hispanic/Latino; 17 Hispanic/Latino; 11 Two or more races, non-Hispanic/Latino), 11 international. Average age 35. 541 applicants, 81% accepted, 292 enrolled. In 2017, 271 master's awarded. *Entrance requirements:* Additional exam requirements/recommendations for international students: Required—TOEFL (minimum score 500 paper-based). *Application deadline:* Applications are processed on a rolling basis. Application fee: $35. Electronic applications accepted. *Expenses: Tuition:* Part-time $466 per credit. *Required fees:* $25 per semester. Tuition and fees vary according to degree level and campus/location. *Financial support:* Applicants required to submit FAFSA. *Unit head:* Dr. Edward L. Guthrie, Dean, 302-356-6870. *Application contact:* Laura Morris, Director of Admissions, 877-967-5464, E-mail: inquire@wilmcoll.edu. Website: http://www.wilmu.edu/behavioralscience/

Winona State University, College of Education, Department of Counselor Education, Winona, MN 55987. Offers addiction counseling (Certificate); clinical mental health counseling (MS); human services (MS); school counseling (MS). *Accreditation:* ACA (one or more programs are accredited); NCATE. *Program availability:* Part-time, evening/weekend. *Degree requirements:* For master's, thesis or alternative. *Entrance requirements:* For master's, letters of reference, interview, group activity, on-site writing. Electronic applications accepted.

Youngstown State University, Graduate School, Bitonte College of Health and Human Services, Department of Health Professions, Youngstown, OH 44555-0001. Offers health and human services (MHHS); public health (MPH). *Accreditation:* NAACLS. *Program availability:* Part-time, evening/weekend. *Degree requirements:* For master's, thesis optional. *Entrance requirements:* For master's, GRE General Test, minimum GPA of 3.0. Additional exam requirements/recommendations for international students: Required—TOEFL. *Faculty research:* Drug prevention, multiskilling in health care, organizational behavior, health care management, health behaviors, research management.

Social Work

Abilene Christian University, Graduate Programs, College of Education and Human Services, School of Social Work, Abilene, TX 79699. Offers MSSW. *Accreditation:* CSWE. *Program availability:* Part-time. *Faculty:* 7 part-time/adjunct (3 women). *Students:* 31 full-time (27 women), 7 part-time (5 women); includes 13 minority (8 Black or African American, non-Hispanic/Latino; 5 Hispanic/Latino), 3 international. 46 applicants, 57% accepted, 19 enrolled. In 2017, 15 master's awarded. *Degree requirements:* For master's, thesis. *Entrance requirements:* For master's, GRE (if undergraduate GPA less than 3.0) or MAT. Additional exam requirements/recommendations for international students: Required—TOEFL (minimum score 80 iBT), IELTS (minimum score 6), PTE. *Application deadline:* For fall admission, 2/16 priority date for domestic students; for spring admission, 11/1 for domestic students. Applications are processed on a rolling basis. Application fee: $50. Electronic applications accepted. *Expenses:* $1,148 per hour. *Financial support:* In 2017–18, 23 students received support, including 2 research assistantships with partial tuition reimbursements available (averaging $5,800 per year); career-related internships or fieldwork, Federal Work-Study, scholarships/grants, and tuition waivers (partial) also available. Financial award application deadline: 4/1; financial award applicants required to submit FAFSA. *Unit head:* Dr. Thomas Winter, Director, 325-674-2072, Fax: 325-674-6525, E-mail: socialwork@acu.edu. *Application contact:* Graduate Admissions, 325-674-6911, Fax: 325-674-6717, E-mail: gradinfo@acu.edu.
Website: http://www.acu.edu/undergraduate/academics/education-and-human-services/social-work.html

Adelphi University, School of Social Work, MSW Program, Garden City, NY 11530-0701. Offers MSW. *Accreditation:* CSWE. *Program availability:* Part-time. *Students:* 386 full-time (342 women), 183 part-time (152 women); includes 300 minority (164 Black or African American, non-Hispanic/Latino; 22 Asian, non-Hispanic/Latino; 105 Hispanic/Latino; 9 Two or more races, non-Hispanic/Latino), 5 international. Average age 32. 562 applicants, 70% accepted, 227 enrolled. In 2017, 268 master's awarded. *Entrance requirements:* For master's, baccalaureate degree, minimum undergraduate cumulative GPA of 3.0, paid or volunteer experience in human services (preferred), interview, two reference letters, official transcripts, personal statement. Additional exam requirements/recommendations for international students: Required—TOEFL (minimum score 585 paper-based; 80 iBT), IELTS (minimum score 6.5). *Application deadline:* Applications are processed on a rolling basis. Application fee: $50. *Financial support:* Research assistantships, teaching assistantships, career-related internships or fieldwork, institutionally sponsored loans, scholarships/grants, traineeships, and unspecified assistantships available. Support available to part-time students. *Unit head:* Dr. Andrew Safyer, Dean, 516-877-4300, E-mail: asafyer@adelphi.edu. *Application contact:* E-mail: graduateadmissions@adelphi.edu.

Adelphi University, School of Social Work, PhD in Social Work Program, Garden City, NY 11530-0701. Offers PhD. *Program availability:* Part-time. *Students:* 1 (woman) full-time, 57 part-time (41 women); includes 32 minority (14 Black or African American, non-Hispanic/Latino; 2 Asian, non-Hispanic/Latino; 12 Hispanic/Latino; 4 Two or more races, non-Hispanic/Latino), 1 international. Average age 41. 29 applicants, 52% accepted, 12 enrolled. In 2017, 1 doctorate awarded. *Degree requirements:* For doctorate, thesis/dissertation. *Entrance requirements:* For doctorate, four-page essay or personal statement, three letters of recommendation, curriculum vitae, writing sample, official transcripts. Additional exam requirements/recommendations for international students: Required—TOEFL (minimum iBT score of 80) or IELTS (minimum score of 6.5). *Application deadline:* For fall admission, 4/15 for domestic students. *Unit head:* Dr. Subadra Panchanadeswaran, Director, 516-877-4310, Fax: 516-877-4392. *Application contact:* Tracy A. Nilsen, Director of Admissions, 516-877-3050, Fax: 516-877-3039, E-mail: graduateadmissions@adelphi.edu.
Website: http://socialwork.adelphi.edu/academics/ph-d-program/

Alabama Agricultural and Mechanical University, School of Graduate Studies, College of Education, Humanities, and Behavioral Sciences, Department of Social Work, Psychology and Counseling, Huntsville, AL 35811. Offers psychology and counseling (MS, Ed S), including clinical psychology (MS), counseling psychology (MS), guidance and counseling, rehabilitation counseling (MS), school counseling (MS), school psychology (MS), school psychometry (MS); social work (MSW). *Accreditation:* CORE; NCATE. *Program availability:* Part-time, evening/weekend. *Degree requirements:* For master's, comprehensive exam. *Entrance requirements:* For master's, GRE General Test. Additional exam requirements/recommendations for international students: Required—TOEFL (minimum score 500 paper-based; 61 iBT). *Faculty research:* Increasing numbers of minorities in special education and speech-language pathology.

Alabama State University, College of Liberal Arts and Social Sciences, Department of Social Work, Montgomery, AL 36101-0271. Offers MSW. *Accreditation:* CSWE. *Faculty:* 5 full-time (4 women). *Students:* 36 full-time (31 women); all minorities (all Black or African American, non-Hispanic/Latino). Average age 22. 15 applicants, 100% accepted, 8 enrolled. In 2017, 7 master's awarded. *Degree requirements:* For master's, comprehensive exam. *Entrance requirements:* For master's, bachelor's degree or its equivalent from accredited college or university with minimum GPA of 2.5. Additional exam requirements/recommendations for international students: Required—TOEFL (minimum score 500 paper-based). *Application deadline:* For fall admission, 4/15 priority

date for domestic and international students; for spring admission, 11/15 priority date for domestic students, 9/15 priority date for international students; for summer admission, 3/15 priority date for domestic and international students. Application fee: $25. Electronic applications accepted. *Expenses:* Tuition, state resident: part-time $412 per credit hour. Tuition, nonresident: part-time $824 per credit hour. *Required fees:* $685 per semester. *Financial support:* Fellowships, Federal Work-Study, and tuition waivers (full and partial) available. Support available to part-time students. Financial award applicants required to submit FAFSA. *Unit head:* Dr. Turenza Smith, Chair, 334-229-6957, E-mail: tsmith@alasu.edu. *Application contact:* Dr. William Person, Dean of Graduate Studies, 334-229-4274, Fax: 334-229-4928, E-mail: wperson@alasu.edu.

Albany State University, College of Arts and Humanities, Albany, GA 31705-2717. Offers criminal justice (MS); English education (M Ed); public administration (MPA), including community and economic development, criminal justice administration, health administration and policy, human resources management, public management, public policy, water resources management and policy; social work (MSW). *Accreditation:* NASPAA. *Program availability:* Part-time. *Degree requirements:* For master's, comprehensive exam, professional portfolio (for MPA), internship, capstone report. *Entrance requirements:* For master's, GRE, MAT, minimum GPA of 3.0, official transcript, pre-medical record/certificate of immunization, letters of reference. Electronic applications accepted. *Faculty research:* HIV prevention for minority students.

American Jewish University, Graduate School of Nonprofit Management, Program in Jewish Communal Studies, Bel Air, CA 90077-1599. Offers MAJCS. *Degree requirements:* For master's, thesis. *Entrance requirements:* For master's, GMAT or GRE General Test, interview.

Andrews University, School of Graduate Studies, College of Arts and Sciences, Department of Social Work, Berrien Springs, MI 49104. Offers MSW. *Accreditation:* CSWE. *Faculty:* 7 full-time (6 women). *Students:* 30 full-time (26 women), 24 part-time (18 women); includes 34 minority (22 Black or African American, non-Hispanic/Latino; 1 Asian, non-Hispanic/Latino; 9 Hispanic/Latino; 2 Two or more races, non-Hispanic/Latino), 10 international. Average age 33. 51 applicants, 76% accepted, 23 enrolled. In 2017, 28 master's awarded. *Entrance requirements:* For master's, GRE. Additional exam requirements/recommendations for international students: Required—TOEFL (minimum score 550 paper-based). *Application deadline:* Applications are processed on a rolling basis. Application fee: $40. *Unit head:* Dr. Curtis VanderWaal, Chair, 269-471-6196. *Application contact:* Justina Clayburn, Supervisor of Graduate Admission, 800-253-2874, Fax: 269-471-6321, E-mail: graduate@andrews.edu.

Anna Maria College, Graduate Division, Program in Social Work, Paxton, MA 01612. Offers MSW. *Program availability:* Part-time.

Appalachian State University, Cratis D. Williams Graduate School, Department of Social Work, Boone, NC 28608. Offers MSW. *Accreditation:* CSWE. *Program availability:* Part-time, evening/weekend, online learning. *Degree requirements:* For master's, comprehensive exam. *Entrance requirements:* For master's, GRE General Test, 3 letters of recommendation. Additional exam requirements/recommendations for international students: Required—TOEFL (minimum score 550 paper-based; 79 iBT), IELTS (minimum score 6.5). Electronic applications accepted. *Faculty research:* Community and organizational practice, individual and family.

Arizona State University at the Tempe campus, College of Public Programs, School of Social Work, Phoenix, AZ 85004-0689. Offers advanced direct practice (MSW); assessment of integrative health modalities (Graduate Certificate); gerontology (Graduate Certificate); Latino cultural competency (Graduate Certificate); planning, administration and community practice (MSW); social work (PhD); trauma and bereavement (Graduate Certificate); MPA/MSW. *Accreditation:* CSWE (one or more programs are accredited). *Program availability:* Part-time. Terminal master's awarded for partial completion of doctoral program. *Degree requirements:* For master's, thesis or alternative, capstone project, interactive Program of Study (iPOS) submitted before completing 50 percent of required credit hours; for doctorate, comprehensive exam, thesis/dissertation, interactive Program of Study (iPOS) submitted before completing 50 percent of required credit hours. *Entrance requirements:* For master's, GRE or MAT, minimum GPA of 3.2 or equivalent in last 2 years of work leading to bachelor's degree; for doctorate, GRE, minimum GPA of 3.0 or equivalent in last 2 years of work leading to bachelor's degree, 3 letters of recommendation, resume, samples of professional writing, personal statement. Additional exam requirements/recommendations for international students: Required—TOEFL, IELTS, or PTE. Electronic applications accepted. *Expenses:* Contact institution.

Arkansas State University, Graduate School, College of Nursing and Health Professions, Department of Social Work, State University, AR 72467. Offers addiction studies (Graduate Certificate); social work (MSW). *Accreditation:* CSWE. *Program availability:* Part-time. *Degree requirements:* For master's and Graduate Certificate, comprehensive exam, thesis (for some programs). *Entrance requirements:* For master's and Graduate Certificate, GRE or MAT, appropriate bachelor's degree, letters of reference, personal statement, resume, official transcript, immunization records. Additional exam requirements/recommendations for international students: Required—TOEFL (minimum score 550 paper-based; 79 iBT), IELTS (minimum score 6), PTE (minimum score 56). Electronic applications accepted. *Expenses:* Contact institution.

Asbury University, School of Graduate and Professional Studies, Master of Social Work Program, Wilmore, KY 40390-1198. Offers child and family services (MSW). *Accreditation:* CSWE. *Degree requirements:* For master's, comprehensive exam, 954 practicum hours completed in agency. *Entrance requirements:* For master's, prerequisite courses in psychology, sociology, and statistics. Additional exam requirements/recommendations for international students: Required—TOEFL. Electronic applications accepted. *Expenses:* Contact institution. *Faculty research:* Integration of faith and practice, survivors of family violence, program evaluation, cross-cultural counseling.

Augsburg University, Program in Social Work, Minneapolis, MN 55454-1351. Offers MSW. *Accreditation:* CSWE. *Program availability:* Part-time, evening/weekend. *Degree requirements:* For master's, thesis optional. *Entrance requirements:* For master's, previous course work in human biology and statistics.

Aurora University, School of Social Work, Aurora, IL 60506-4892. Offers MSW, DSW. *Accreditation:* CSWE. *Program availability:* Part-time, evening/weekend, 100% online. *Faculty:* 17 full-time (10 women), 72 part-time/adjunct (65 women). *Students:* 862 full-time (764 women), 80 part-time (63 women); includes 316 minority (147 Black or African American, non-Hispanic/Latino; 1 American Indian or Alaska Native, non-Hispanic/Latino; 18 Asian, non-Hispanic/Latino; 125 Hispanic/Latino; 25 Two or more races, non-Hispanic/Latino), 1 international. Average age 31. 602 applicants, 98% accepted, 227 enrolled. In 2017, 379 master's, 7 doctorates awarded. *Degree requirements:* For master's, thesis optional, field instruction; for doctorate, comprehensive exam, thesis/dissertation. *Entrance requirements:* For master's, minimum GPA of 3.0; for doctorate, GRE, MSW from CSWE-accredited school; minimum GPA of 3.0; at least 3 years of post-MSW social work experience; 3 letters of recommendation; writing sample in the area of clinical social work; personal interview. Additional exam requirements/recommendations for international students: Required—TOEFL (minimum score 550 paper-based; 79 iBT). *Application deadline:* For fall admission, 6/1 for international students; for spring admission, 10/1 for international students. Applications are processed on a rolling basis. Application fee: $0. Electronic applications accepted. *Expenses:* Contact institution. *Financial support:* In 2017–18, 521 students received support. Federal Work-Study, scholarships/grants, and unspecified assistantships available. Support available to part-time students. Financial award applicants required to submit FAFSA. *Unit head:* Dr. Brenda Barnwell, Dean, School of Social Work, 630-947-8933, E-mail: mckenzie@aurora.edu. *Application contact:* Luke Kerber, Director of Graduate Recruitment, 630-947-8904, E-mail: lkerber@aurora.edu.
Website: http://www.aurora.edu/socialwork

Austin Peay State University, College of Graduate Studies, College of Behavioral and Health Sciences, Department of Social Work, Clarksville, TN 37044. Offers MSW. *Program availability:* Part-time, evening/weekend. *Faculty:* 5 full-time (2 women), 1 (woman) part-time/adjunct. *Students:* 29 full-time (24 women), 14 part-time (13 women); includes 20 minority (14 Black or African American, non-Hispanic/Latino; 1 Asian, non-Hispanic/Latino; 3 Hispanic/Latino; 2 Two or more races, non-Hispanic/Latino). Average age 31. 40 applicants, 80% accepted, 30 enrolled. In 2017, 32 master's awarded. *Degree requirements:* For master's, internship of 400-500 hours. *Entrance requirements:* For master's, GRE General Test, 3 letters of recommendation, minimum GPA of 2.75. Additional exam requirements/recommendations for international students: Required—TOEFL (minimum score 500 paper-based). *Application deadline:* For fall admission, 8/8 priority date for domestic students. Applications are processed on a rolling basis. Application fee: $45 ($55 for international students). Electronic applications accepted. *Expenses:* Tuition, state resident: full-time $7686; part-time $427 per credit hour. Tuition, nonresident: full-time $20,268; part-time $1126 per credit hour. *Required fees:* $1529; $76.45 per credit hour. *Financial support:* Research assistantships with full tuition reimbursements, career-related internships or fieldwork, Federal Work-Study, institutionally sponsored loans, scholarships/grants, and unspecified assistantships available. Support available to part-time students. Financial award application deadline: 4/1; financial award applicants required to submit FAFSA. *Unit head:* Mary Fran Davis, Interim Chair, 931-221-7717, Fax: 931-221-6440, E-mail: davism@apsu.edu. *Application contact:* Megan Mitchell, Coordinator of Graduate Admissions, 800-859-4723, Fax: 931-221-7641, E-mail: gradadmissions@apsu.edu.
Website: http://www.apsu.edu/socialwork/

Azusa Pacific University, School of Behavioral and Applied Sciences, Department of Social Work, Azusa, CA 91702-7000. Offers MSW. *Accreditation:* CSWE.

Barry University, Ellen Whiteside McDonnell School of Social Work, Doctoral Program in Social Work, Miami Shores, FL 33161-6695. Offers PhD. *Program availability:* Part-time, evening/weekend. *Degree requirements:* For doctorate, thesis/dissertation. *Entrance requirements:* For doctorate, GRE, MSW from an accredited school of social work, 2 years of professional experience. Electronic applications accepted. *Faculty research:* Family and children services, homelessness, gerontology, school social work.

Barry University, Ellen Whiteside McDonnell School of Social Work, Master's Program in Social Work, Miami Shores, FL 33161-6695. Offers MSW. *Accreditation:* CSWE. *Program availability:* Part-time, evening/weekend. *Degree requirements:* For master's, fieldwork. *Entrance requirements:* For master's, minimum GPA of 3.0, minimum of 30 liberal arts credits. Additional exam requirements/recommendations for international students: Required—TOEFL (minimum score 550 paper-based). Electronic applications accepted. *Faculty research:* Family and children services, homelessness, gerontology, school social work.

Baylor University, Diana R. Garland School of Social Work, Waco, TX 76798-7320. Offers MSW, PhD, M Div/MSW, MSW/MBA, MTS/MSW. *Accreditation:* CSWE. *Program availability:* Part-time, blended/hybrid learning. *Faculty:* 11 full-time (5 women), 13 part-time/adjunct (7 women). *Students:* 121 full-time (112 women), 20 part-time (17 women); includes 47 minority (16 Black or African American, non-Hispanic/Latino; 6 Asian, non-Hispanic/Latino; 18 Hispanic/Latino; 7 Two or more races, non-Hispanic/Latino), 6 international. Average age 29. 190 applicants, 72% accepted, 71 enrolled. In 2017, 69 master's awarded. *Degree requirements:* For master's, research project; for doctorate, comprehensive exam, thesis/dissertation. *Entrance requirements:* For master's, writing sample; for doctorate, GRE, writing sample. Additional exam requirements/recommendations for international students: Required—TOEFL (minimum score 550 paper-based; 80 iBT), IELTS (minimum score 6.5). *Application deadline:* For spring admission, 3/15 for domestic and international students. Applications are processed on a rolling basis. Application fee: $45. Electronic applications accepted. *Financial support:* In 2017–18, 138 students received support, including 12 research assistantships with tuition reimbursements available (averaging $6,800 per year); career-related internships or fieldwork, Federal Work-Study, institutionally sponsored loans, scholarships/grants, traineeships, tuition waivers (full and partial), and unspecified assistantships also available. Support available to part-time students. Financial award application deadline: 6/1; financial award applicants required to submit FAFSA. *Faculty research:* Healthy marriage, family literacy, Alzheimer's and grief, spirituality, congregational community service, clergy sexual abuse, older volunteers, military family support. *Total annual research expenditures:* $533,412. *Unit head:* Dr. David Pooler, Associate Dean for Academic Affairs, 254-710-3884, Fax: 254-710-7412, E-mail: david_pooler@baylor.edu. *Application contact:* Dr. Crystal Diaz-Espinoza, Director of Recruitment and Career Services, 254-710-4479, Fax: 254-710-6455, E-mail: crystal_diaz-espinoza@baylor.edu.
Website: http://www.baylor.edu/social_work/?_buref-661-48570

Binghamton University, State University of New York, Graduate School, College of Community and Public Affairs, Department of Social Work, Binghamton, NY 13902-6000. Offers MSW. *Accreditation:* CSWE. *Program availability:* Part-time. *Faculty:* 16 full-time (13 women). *Students:* 111 full-time (92 women), 67 part-time (58 women); includes 41 minority (13 Black or African American, non-Hispanic/Latino; 3 Asian, non-Hispanic/Latino; 17 Hispanic/Latino; 1 Native Hawaiian or other Pacific Islander, non-Hispanic/Latino; 7 Two or more races, non-Hispanic/Latino), 1 international. Average age 29. 144 applicants, 78% accepted, 74 enrolled. In 2017, 66 master's awarded. *Degree requirements:* For master's, thesis. *Entrance requirements:* Additional exam requirements/recommendations for international students: Required—TOEFL (minimum score 550 paper-based; 80 iBT). *Application deadline:* For fall admission, 2/1 priority date for domestic and international students. Application fee: $75. Electronic applications accepted. *Expenses:* Contact institution. *Financial support:* In 2017–18, 39 students received support. Fellowships, career-related internships or fieldwork, Federal Work-Study, institutionally sponsored loans, scholarships/grants, health care benefits, and unspecified assistantships available. Financial award applicants required to submit FAFSA. *Unit head:* Dr. Victoria M. Rizzo, Chairperson, 607-777-9179, Fax: 607-777-5683, E-mail: vrizzo@binghamton.edu. *Application contact:* Ben Balkaya, Assistant Dean and Director, 607-777-2151, Fax: 607-777-2501, E-mail: balkaya@binghamton.edu.

Boise State University, College of Health Sciences, School of Social Work, Boise, ID 83725-0399. Offers MSW. *Accreditation:* CSWE. *Program availability:* Part-time, 100% online. *Faculty:* 33. *Students:* 177 full-time (146 women), 23 part-time (22 women); includes 13 minority (2 Black or African American, non-Hispanic/Latino; 10 Hispanic/Latino; 1 Two or more races, non-Hispanic/Latino). Average age 34. 139 applicants, 46% accepted, 47 enrolled. In 2017, 104 master's awarded. *Entrance requirements:* For master's, GRE General Test, minimum GPA of 3.0. Additional exam requirements/recommendations for international students: Required—TOEFL (minimum score 550 paper-based; 80 iBT), IELTS (minimum score 6). *Application deadline:* For fall admission, 1/10 for domestic and international students. Application fee: $65 ($95 for international students). Electronic applications accepted. *Expenses:* Tuition, state resident: full-time $6471; part-time $390 per credit. Tuition, nonresident: full-time $21,787; part-time $685 per credit. *Required fees:* $2283; $100 per term. Part-time tuition and fees vary according to course load and program. *Financial support:* Research assistantships, scholarships/grants, and unspecified assistantships available. Financial award applicants required to submit FAFSA. *Unit head:* Dr. Randy Magen, Director, 208-426-1789, E-mail: randymagen@boisestate.edu. *Application contact:* Dr. Cynthia Sanders, Program Coordinator, 208-426-1780, E-mail: cynthiasanders@boisestate.edu.
Website: http://hs.boisestate.edu/socialwork/graduate/

Boston College, School of Social Work, Chestnut Hill, MA 02467-3800. Offers MSW, PhD, JD/MSW, MSW/MA, MSW/MBA. *Accreditation:* CSWE (one or more programs are accredited). *Program availability:* Part-time. *Degree requirements:* For master's, 2 internships; for doctorate, comprehensive exam, thesis/dissertation. *Entrance requirements:* For doctorate, GRE, master's degree. Additional exam requirements/recommendations for international students: Required—TOEFL (minimum score 550 paper-based; 80 iBT). Electronic applications accepted. *Expenses:* Contact institution. *Faculty research:* Well-being of children and families, health and mental health issues, aging and work, consumer-directed services, international social work practice.

Boston University, School of Social Work, Boston, MA 02215. Offers MSW, PhD, D Min/MSW, M Div/MSW, MSW/Ed D, MSW/Ed M, MSW/MPH, MSW/MTS. *Accreditation:* CSWE (one or more programs are accredited). *Program availability:* Part-time, evening/weekend, 100% online. *Faculty:* 29 full-time (18 women), 39 part-time/adjunct (31 women). *Students:* 197 full-time (178 women), 587 part-time (528 women); includes 229 minority (73 Black or African American, non-Hispanic/Latino; 2 American Indian or Alaska Native, non-Hispanic/Latino; 26 Asian, non-Hispanic/Latino; 111 Hispanic/Latino; 2 Native Hawaiian or other Pacific Islander, non-Hispanic/Latino; 15 Two or more races, non-Hispanic/Latino), 7 international. Average age 30. 988 applicants, 75% accepted, 254 enrolled. In 2017, 204 master's awarded. *Degree requirements:* For doctorate, one foreign language, thesis/dissertation, critical essay. *Entrance requirements:* For doctorate, GRE General Test or MAT, writing sample. Additional exam requirements/recommendations for international students: Required—TOEFL (minimum score 577 paper-based; 100 iBT), IELTS (minimum score 7). *Application deadline:* For fall admission, 2/15 for domestic students, 1/15 for international students. Application fee: $95. Electronic applications accepted. *Expenses:* Contact institution. *Financial support:* In 2017–18, 165 students received support. Career-related internships or fieldwork, Federal Work-Study, scholarships/grants, and stipends available. Support available to part-time students. Financial award application deadline: 3/1; financial award applicants required to submit FAFSA. *Faculty research:* Aging, children and families, substance abuse and HIV, trauma and mental health, public health social work. *Total annual research expenditures:* $2.6 million. *Unit head:* Dr. Jorge Delva, Dean, 617-353-3760, Fax: 617-353-5612. *Application contact:* Julie Billings, Admissions and Financial Aid Coordinator, 617-353-3750, Fax: 617-353-5612, E-mail: busswad@bu.edu.
Website: http://www.bu.edu/ssw/

Brandman University, School of Arts and Sciences, Irvine, CA 92618. Offers psychology (MA), including counseling, marriage and family therapy, professional clinical counseling; social work (MSW). *Expenses: Tuition:* Part-time $640 per credit hour. Tuition and fees vary according to degree level and program. *Unit head:* Dr. Jeremy Korr, Dean, 949-341-9831. *Application contact:* Dr. Jeremy Korr, Dean, 949-341-9831.
Website: https://www.brandman.edu/academic-programs/arts-and-sciences

Brescia University, Program in Social Work, Owensboro, KY 42301-3023. Offers MSW. *Program availability:* Online learning. *Entrance requirements:* For master's, bachelor's degree, minimum GPA of 3.0 for last 60 hours earned, personal statement. Electronic applications accepted.

Bridgewater State University, College of Graduate Studies, College of Humanities and Social Sciences, School of Social Work, Bridgewater, MA 02325. Offers MSW. *Accreditation:* CSWE.

Brigham Young University, Graduate Studies, College of Family, Home, and Social Sciences, School of Social Work, Provo, UT 84602. Offers social work (MSW), including clinical practice, research. *Accreditation:* CSWE. *Faculty:* 8 full-time (4 women), 5 part-time/adjunct (3 women). *Students:* 80 full-time (61 women); includes 11 minority (2 Black or African American, non-Hispanic/Latino; 1 American Indian or Alaska Native, non-Hispanic/Latino; 1 Asian, non-Hispanic/Latino; 5 Hispanic/Latino; 2 Two or more races, non-Hispanic/Latino). Average age 28. 104 applicants, 43% accepted, 40 enrolled. In 2017, 41 master's awarded. *Degree requirements:* For master's, thesis optional. *Entrance requirements:* For master's, minimum prerequisite courses grade of B- within past 7 years. Additional exam requirements/recommendations for international students: Required—TOEFL (minimum score 580 paper-based; 85 iBT), IELTS (minimum score 7). *Application deadline:* For fall admission, 1/15 for domestic and international students. Application fee: $50. Electronic applications accepted. *Expenses:* $3,440 per semester tuition. *Financial support:* In 2017–18, 60 students received

Social Work

support, including 60 fellowships with tuition reimbursements available (averaging $3,249 per year), 16 research assistantships (averaging $2,240 per year), 4 teaching assistantships (averaging $5,760 per year); career-related internships or fieldwork, scholarships/grants, and tuition waivers (partial) also available. Financial award application deadline: 1/15. *Faculty research:* Poverty, adoptions, depression, spirituality, child welfare, marriage and family, American Indian child welfare, health care, mental health, mood disorders, substance abuse, refugees, military. *Total annual research expenditures:* $100,000. *Unit head:* Dr. Gordon E. Limb, Director, 801-422-3282, Fax: 801-422-0624, E-mail: socialwork@byu.edu. *Application contact:* Nanci Shumpert, Program Manager, 801-422-5681, Fax: 801-422-0624, E-mail: msw@byu.edu. Website: https://socialwork.byu.edu/Pages/Home.aspx

Bryn Mawr College, Graduate School of Social Work and Social Research, Bryn Mawr, PA 19010. Offers MSS, PhD. *Accreditation:* CSWE (one or more programs are accredited). *Program availability:* Part-time, evening/weekend. *Faculty:* 14 full-time (8 women), 7 part-time/adjunct (5 women). *Students:* 134 full-time (111 women), 27 part-time (26 women); includes 30 minority (16 Black or African American, non-Hispanic/Latino; 3 Asian, non-Hispanic/Latino; 4 Hispanic/Latino; 7 Two or more races, non-Hispanic/Latino). Average age 33. 128 applicants, 77% accepted, 74 enrolled. In 2017, 68 master's, 6 doctorates awarded. *Degree requirements:* For master's, fieldwork; for doctorate, comprehensive exam, thesis/dissertation. *Entrance requirements:* For master's, bachelor's degree, personal statement, 3 letters of recommendation, official transcripts, interview; for doctorate, GRE General Test (minimum scores 500 on the verbal and quantitative sections and 5.0 on analytic writing test), master's degree; minimum undergraduate GPA of 3.0, graduate 3.5; 2 years of post-MSW work experience (recommended); personal statement; 3 letters of recommendation (2 from academic references); official transcripts. *Application deadline:* For fall admission, 4/15 for domestic and international students. Applications are processed on a rolling basis. Application fee: $50. Electronic applications accepted. *Expenses:* Contact institution. *Financial support:* In 2017–18, 131 students received support. Fellowships, research assistantships, teaching assistantships, career-related internships or fieldwork, Federal Work-Study, institutionally sponsored loans, scholarships/grants, tuition waivers, and dissertation awards (for PhD) available. Support available to part-time students. Financial award application deadline: 4/15; financial award applicants required to submit FAFSA. *Unit head:* Dr. Darlyne Bailey, Dean, 610-520-2610, Fax: 610-520-2613, E-mail: dbailey01@brynmawr.edu. *Application contact:* Sheila Gillin, Director of Graduate Admissions, 610-520-7533, E-mail: sgillin@brynmawr.edu.
Website: http://www.brynmawr.edu/socialwork

California Baptist University, Program in Social Work, Riverside, CA 92504-3206. Offers clinical social work (MSW); community social work practice (MSW). *Program availability:* Part-time. *Faculty:* 5 full-time (4 women). *Students:* 68 full-time (60 women); includes 54 minority (14 Black or African American, non-Hispanic/Latino; 1 Asian, non-Hispanic/Latino; 33 Hispanic/Latino; 6 Two or more races, non-Hispanic/Latino). Average age 30. 136 applicants, 71% accepted, 72 enrolled. *Entrance requirements:* For master's, bachelor's degree, minimum GPA of 2.75, official transcripts, three recommendations, statistics, essay, interview. Additional exam requirements/recommendations for international students: Required—TOEFL (minimum score 80 iBT). *Application deadline:* For fall admission, 8/1 priority date for domestic students, 7/1 for international students; for spring admission, 12/1 priority date for domestic students, 11/1 for international students. Applications are processed on a rolling basis. Application fee: $45. Electronic applications accepted. *Expenses:* Contact institution. *Financial support:* Federal Work-Study and scholarships/grants available. *Faculty research:* Urban/marginalized communities, healthy marriages and families, community organization/engagement, health disparities, global social work. *Unit head:* Dr. Satara Armstrong, Director, Social Work Program, 951-552-8442, E-mail: sarmstrong@calbaptist.edu. *Application contact:* Debbie Passalacqua, Associate Director of Graduate Admissions, 951-343-4527, Fax: 877-228-8877, E-mail: dpassala@calbaptist.edu.

California State University, Bakersfield, Division of Graduate Studies, School of Social Sciences and Education, Program in Social Work, Bakersfield, CA 93311. Offers MSW. *Accreditation:* CSWE. *Faculty:* 8 full-time (1 woman), 4 part-time/adjunct (3 women). *Students:* 155 full-time (127 women), 5 part-time (all women); includes 125 minority (18 Black or African American, non-Hispanic/Latino; 1 American Indian or Alaska Native, non-Hispanic/Latino; 12 Asian, non-Hispanic/Latino; 92 Hispanic/Latino; 2 Two or more races, non-Hispanic/Latino, 5 international. Average age 28. 167 applicants, 65% accepted, 79 enrolled. In 2017, 66 master's awarded. *Application deadline:* For fall admission, 2/1 for domestic students. Applications are processed on a rolling basis. Application fee: $55. *Expenses:* Tuition, state resident: full-time $7176; part-time $4164 per year. *Financial support:* In 2017–18, fellowships (averaging $1,850 per year) were awarded; Federal Work-Study, scholarships/grants, and tuition waivers (full and partial) also available. Financial award application deadline: 3/2; financial award applicants required to submit FAFSA. *Unit head:* Dr. Jong Choi, Graduate Coordinator, 661-654-2308, Fax: 661-665-6928, E-mail: jchoi6@csub.edu. *Application contact:* Luz Roldan, Admissions Specialist, 661-664-2107, Fax: 661-654-6928, E-mail: lroldan@csub.edu.
Website: https://www.csub.edu/socialwork/index.html

California State University, Chico, Office of Graduate Studies, College of Behavioral and Social Sciences, School of Social Work, Chico, CA 95929-0722. Offers MSW. *Accreditation:* CSWE. *Program availability:* Evening/weekend. *Degree requirements:* For master's, thesis, project, or comprehensive exam. *Entrance requirements:* For master's, 3 letters of recommendation on departmental form, statement of purpose, prerequisites/liberal arts worksheet. Additional exam requirements/recommendations for international students: Required—TOEFL (minimum score 550 paper-based; 80 iBT), IELTS (minimum score 6.5), PTE (minimum score 59). Electronic applications accepted.

California State University, Dominguez Hills, College of Health, Human Services and Nursing, Program in Social Work, Carson, CA 90747-0001. Offers MSW. *Accreditation:* CSWE. *Program availability:* Part-time, evening/weekend. *Degree requirements:* For master's, thesis. *Entrance requirements:* For master's, minimum GPA of 2.75 in last 60 units; 3 courses in behavioral science, 2 in humanities, 1 each in English composition, elementary statistics, and human biology. *Faculty research:* HIV/AIDS, community capacity, program evaluation.

California State University, East Bay, Office of Graduate Studies, College of Letters, Arts, and Social Sciences, Department of Social Work, Hayward, CA 94542-3000. Offers children, youth, and family services (MSW); community mental health services (MSW). *Accreditation:* CSWE. *Faculty:* 8 full-time (7 women), 10 part-time/adjunct (9 women). *Students:* 137 full-time (108 women), 1 (woman) part-time; includes 118 minority (34 Black or African American, non-Hispanic/Latino; 19 Asian, non-Hispanic/Latino; 58 Hispanic/Latino; 1 Native Hawaiian or other Pacific Islander, non-Hispanic/Latino; 6 Two or more races, non-Hispanic/Latino), 5 international. Average age 32. 334 applicants, 26% accepted, 71 enrolled. In 2017, 90 master's awarded. *Degree requirements:* For master's, comprehensive exam. *Entrance requirements:* For master's, minimum GPA of 2.8; courses in statistics and either human biology, physiology, or anatomy; liberal arts or social science baccalaureate degree; 3 letters of recommendation; personal statement; criminal background check; student professional

liability insurance. Additional exam requirements/recommendations for international students: Required—TOEFL (minimum score 550 paper-based). *Application deadline:* For fall admission, 12/1 for domestic and international students. Applications are processed on a rolling basis. Application fee: $55. Electronic applications accepted. *Financial support:* Fellowships, career-related internships or fieldwork, Federal Work-Study, institutionally sponsored loans, and scholarships/grants available. Support available to part-time students. Financial award application deadline: 3/2; financial award applicants required to submit FAFSA. *Unit head:* Dr. Holly Vugia, Interim Chair, 510-885-2121, E-mail: holly.vugia@csueastbay.edu. *Application contact:* Philip Cole-Regis, Administrative Support Coordinator, 510-885-3286, E-mail: philip.coleregis@csueastbay.edu.
Website: http://www20.csueastbay.edu/class/departments/socialwork/

California State University, Fresno, Division of Research and Graduate Studies, College of Health and Human Services, Department of Social Work Education, Fresno, CA 93740-8027. Offers MSW. *Accreditation:* CSWE. *Program availability:* Part-time, evening/weekend. *Degree requirements:* For master's, thesis or alternative. *Entrance requirements:* For master's, GRE General Test, minimum GPA of 2.5. Additional exam requirements/recommendations for international students: Required—TOEFL. Electronic applications accepted. *Faculty research:* Children at risk, international cooperation, child welfare training, nutrition.

California State University, Fullerton, Graduate Studies, College of Health and Human Development, Department of Social Work, Fullerton, CA 92831-3599. Offers aging (MSW); child welfare (MSW); community mental health (MSW). *Accreditation:* CSWE. *Program availability:* Part-time. *Faculty:* 15 full-time (10 women), 8 part-time/adjunct (7 women). *Students:* 167 full-time (145 women), 3 part-time (2 women); includes 118 minority (5 Black or African American, non-Hispanic/Latino; 1 American Indian or Alaska Native, non-Hispanic/Latino; 25 Asian, non-Hispanic/Latino; 81 Hispanic/Latino; 6 Two or more races, non-Hispanic/Latino), 3 international. Average age 27. 571 applicants, 23% accepted, 84 enrolled. *Entrance requirements:* For master's, minimum GPA of 3.0 for last 60 semester or 90 quarter units. Application fee: $55. *Financial support:* Career-related internships or fieldwork, Federal Work-Study, institutionally sponsored loans, and scholarships/grants available. Support available to part-time students. Financial award application deadline: 3/1; financial award applicants required to submit FAFSA. *Unit head:* Dr. David Chenot, Chair, 657-278-8452, E-mail: dchenot@fullerton.edu. *Application contact:* Admissions/Applications, 657-278-2371.
Website: http://hhd.fullerton.edu/msw

California State University, Long Beach, Graduate Studies, College of Health and Human Services, School of Social Work, Long Beach, CA 90840. Offers MSW. *Accreditation:* CSWE. *Program availability:* Part-time, evening/weekend, online learning. *Degree requirements:* For master's, thesis. Electronic applications accepted.

California State University, Los Angeles, Graduate Studies, College of Health and Human Services, School of Social Work, Los Angeles, CA 90032-8530. Offers MSW. *Accreditation:* CSWE. *Entrance requirements:* Additional exam requirements/recommendations for international students: Required—TOEFL (minimum score 500 paper-based).

California State University, Monterey Bay, College of Health Sciences and Human Services, Seaside, CA 93955-8001. Offers social work (MSW). *Accreditation:* CSWE. *Program availability:* Part-time. *Degree requirements:* For master's, internship. *Entrance requirements:* For master's, GRE, curriculum vitae, recommendations. Additional exam requirements/recommendations for international students: Required—TOEFL (minimum score 525 paper-based; 71 iBT). Electronic applications accepted. *Faculty research:* Social policy, health policy, politics and government.

California State University, Northridge, Graduate Studies, College of Social and Behavioral Sciences, Department of Social Work, Northridge, CA 91330. Offers MSW. *Accreditation:* CSWE. *Students:* 215 full-time (181 women), 45 part-time (38 women); includes 186 minority (23 Black or African American, non-Hispanic/Latino; 1 American Indian or Alaska Native, non-Hispanic/Latino; 5 Asian, non-Hispanic/Latino; 146 Hispanic/Latino; 11 Two or more races, non-Hispanic/Latino), 9 international. Average age 30. 713 applicants, 29% accepted, 141 enrolled. In 2017, 178 master's awarded. *Unit head:* Dr. Eli Bartle, Chair, 818-677-7630, E-mail: msw@csun.edu.

California State University, Northridge, Graduate Studies, Tseng College, Northridge, CA 91330. Offers business administration (Graduate Certificate); health administration (MPA); health education (MPH); knowledge management (MKM); music industry administration (MA); nonprofit-sector management (Graduate Certificate); public administration (MPA); public sector management and leadership (MPA); social work (MSW); taxation (MS); tourism, hospitality and recreation management (MS). *Students:* 4 part-time (all women); includes 1 minority (Black or African American, non-Hispanic/Latino). Average age 37. In 2017, 2 master's awarded. *Entrance requirements:* For master's, GRE (if cumulative undergraduate GPA less than 3.0). *Unit head:* Joyce Feucht-Haviar, Dean, 866-873-6439.

California State University, Sacramento, College of Health and Human Services, Division of Social Work, Sacramento, CA 95819. Offers family and children's services (MSW). *Accreditation:* CSWE. *Program availability:* Part-time, evening/weekend. *Students:* 230 full-time (202 women), 14 part-time (10 women); includes 125 minority (24 Black or African American, non-Hispanic/Latino; 3 American Indian or Alaska Native, non-Hispanic/Latino; 28 Asian, non-Hispanic/Latino; 69 Hispanic/Latino; 1 Native Hawaiian or other Pacific Islander, non-Hispanic/Latino). Average age 31. 306 applicants, 41% accepted, 109 enrolled. In 2017, 107 master's awarded. *Degree requirements:* For master's, thesis, project; writing proficiency exam. *Entrance requirements:* For master's, GRE, minimum GPA of 2.8 during previous 2 years of course work. Additional exam requirements/recommendations for international students: Required—TOEFL (minimum score 550 paper-based; 80 iBT); Recommended—IELTS, TSE. *Application deadline:* For fall admission, 1/18 for domestic and international students. Applications are processed on a rolling basis. Application fee: $55. Electronic applications accepted. *Expenses:* Contact institution. *Financial support:* Career-related internships or fieldwork, Federal Work-Study, and scholarships/grants available. Support available to part-time students. Financial award application deadline: 3/1; financial award applicants required to submit FAFSA. *Unit head:* Dr. Dale Russell, Chair, 916-278-6943, E-mail: drussell@csus.edu. *Application contact:* Jose Martinez, Graduate Admissions Supervisor, 916-278-7871, E-mail: martinj@skymail.csus.edu.
Website: http://www.csus.edu/hhs/sw

California State University, San Bernardino, Graduate Studies, College of Social and Behavioral Sciences, Program in Social Work, San Bernardino, CA 92407. Offers MSW. *Accreditation:* CSWE. *Program availability:* Part-time, evening/weekend. *Faculty:* 8 full-time (4 women), 13 part-time/adjunct (11 women). *Students:* 162 full-time (133 women), 25 part-time (24 women); includes 127 minority (19 Black or African American, non-Hispanic/Latino; 2 American Indian or Alaska Native, non-Hispanic/Latino; 103 Hispanic/Latino; 3 Two or more races, non-Hispanic/Latino), 2 international. Average age 29. 302 applicants, 38% accepted, 80 enrolled. In 2017, 105 master's awarded. *Entrance requirements:* Additional exam requirements/recommendations for international students: Required—TOEFL. *Application deadline:* For fall admission, 7/16 for domestic students. Application fee: $55. *Financial support:* Institutionally sponsored loans available. Financial award application deadline: 5/1. *Faculty research:* Addiction, computers in social work practice, minority issues, gerontology. *Unit head:* Laurie Smith, Director/Associate Professor/Graduate Coordinator, 909-537-3837, Fax: 909-537-7029, E-mail: lasmith@csusb.edu. *Application contact:* Dr. Dorota Huizinga, Dean of Graduate Studies, 909-537-3064, E-mail: dorota.huizinga@csusb.edu.

California State University, San Marcos, College of Education, Health and Human Services, Department of Social Work, San Marcos, CA 92096-0001. Offers behavioral health (MSW); children, youth and families (MSW). *Accreditation:* CSWE. *Degree requirements:* For master's, thesis, capstone project. *Expenses:* Contact institution. *Unit head:* Dr. Blake Beecher, Chair, 760-750-7373.
Website: http://www.csusm.edu/socialwork/

California State University, Stanislaus, College of Education, Kinesiology and Social Work, Master of Social Work Program, Turlock, CA 95382. Offers MSW. *Accreditation:* CSWE. *Degree requirements:* For master's, thesis. *Entrance requirements:* For master's, minimum GPA of 3.0, 3 letters of reference, personal statement. Electronic applications accepted. *Faculty research:* Mental health supervision, health issues on adulthood and aging, geriatric social work, effects of violence on children, rural mental health.

California University of Pennsylvania, School of Graduate Studies and Research, College of Education and Human Services, Department of Social Work, California, PA 15419-1394. Offers MSW. *Accreditation:* CSWE. *Program availability:* Part-time. *Degree requirements:* For master's, comprehensive exam. *Entrance requirements:* For master's, GRE, letters of reference. Additional exam requirements/recommendations for international students: Required—TOEFL. *Application deadline:* For fall admission, 8/1 priority date for domestic and international students. Applications are processed on a rolling basis. Application fee: $25. Electronic applications accepted. *Financial support:* Applicants required to submit FAFSA. *Faculty research:* Social welfare and policy, housing and community development, health and mental health, Black Appalachian, aging. *Unit head:* Molly Kenkinds, Program Coordinator, 724-938-4168, E-mail: jenkins_m@calu.edu.
Website: http://www.calu.edu/academics/colleges/education/social-work/

Campbellsville University, Carver School of Social Work, Campbellsville, KY 42718-2799. Offers MSW. *Accreditation:* CSWE. *Program availability:* Part-time, evening/weekend, 100% online, blended/hybrid learning. *Faculty:* 15 full-time (14 women), 25 part-time/adjunct (23 women). *Students:* 80 full-time (76 women), 243 part-time (223 women); includes 44 minority (39 Black or African American, non-Hispanic/Latino; 1 American Indian or Alaska Native, non-Hispanic/Latino; 1 Asian, non-Hispanic/Latino; 2 Hispanic/Latino; 1 Two or more races, non-Hispanic/Latino), 3 international. Average age 33. 328 applicants, 68% accepted, 170 enrolled. In 2017, 71 master's awarded. *Degree requirements:* For master's, variable foreign language requirement, comprehensive exam, thesis (for some programs). *Entrance requirements:* For master's, GRE, college transcripts, 3 letters of recommendation. Additional exam requirements/recommendations for international students: Recommended—TOEFL (minimum score 550 paper-based; 79 iBT), IELTS (minimum score 6). *Application deadline:* Applications are processed on a rolling basis. Application fee: $25. Electronic applications accepted. Application fee is waived when completed online. *Expenses:* $559 per credit hour (online); $479 per credit hour (on-campus); $75 per term fees. *Financial support:* Unspecified assistantships available. Financial award applicants required to submit FAFSA. *Unit head:* Dr. Helen K. Mudd, Program Director, 270-789-5045, Fax: 270-789-5542, E-mail: hkmudd@campbellsville.edu. *Application contact:* Monica Bamwine, Assistant Director of Graduate Admissions, 270-789-5221, Fax: 270-789-5071, E-mail: mkbamwine@campbellsville.edu.
Website: http://www.campbellsville.edu/carver-school

Capella University, Harold Abel School of Social and Behavioral Science, Doctoral Programs in Counseling, Minneapolis, MN 55402. Offers general counselor education and supervision (PhD); general social work (DSW). *Accreditation:* ACA.

Carleton University, Faculty of Graduate Studies, Faculty of Public Affairs and Management, School of Social Work, Ottawa, ON K1S 5B6, Canada. Offers MSW. *Program availability:* Part-time. *Degree requirements:* For master's, thesis optional. *Entrance requirements:* For master's, basic research methods course. Additional exam requirements/recommendations for international students: Required—TOEFL. *Faculty research:* Social administration, program evaluation, history of Canadian social welfare, women's issues, education in social work.

Carlow University, College of Leadership and Social Change, Program in Social Work, Pittsburgh, PA 15213-3165. Offers MSW. *Program availability:* Part-time, evening/weekend. *Entrance requirements:* For master's, personal essay; resume or curriculum vitae; three recommendations; official transcripts; interview; minimum undergraduate GPA of 3.0. Additional exam requirements/recommendations for international students: Required—TOEFL (minimum score 550 paper-based). *Application deadline:* Applications are processed on a rolling basis. *Expenses:* Tuition: Full-time $12,103; part-time $825 per credit hour. Tuition and fees vary according to program. *Financial support:* Application deadline: 4/1; applicants required to submit FAFSA. *Unit head:* Dr. Allyson M. Lowe, Dean, 412-578-6663, Fax: 412-578-6357, E-mail: amlowe@carlow.edu. *Application contact:* 412-578-6059, Fax: 412-578-6321, E-mail: gradstudies@carlow.edu.
Website: http://www.carlow.edu/masters_of_social_work.aspx

Case Western Reserve University, Jack, Joseph and Morton Mandel School of Applied Social Sciences, Cleveland, OH 44087. Offers nonprofit management (MNO); social welfare (PhD); social work (MSSA); JD/MSSA; MSSA/MA; MSSA/MBA; MSSA/MNO. *Accreditation:* CSWE (one or more programs are accredited). *Program availability:* Part-time, evening/weekend, 100% online. *Students:* 630 full-time (544 women), 61 part-time (54 women); includes 253 minority (187 Black or African American, non-Hispanic/Latino; 2 American Indian or Alaska Native, non-Hispanic/Latino; 10 Asian, non-Hispanic/Latino; 34 Hispanic/Latino; 1 Native Hawaiian or other Pacific Islander, non-Hispanic/Latino; 19 Two or more races, non-Hispanic/Latino), 34 international. Average age 32. 848 applicants, 78% accepted, 320 enrolled. In 2017, 184 master's, 3 doctorates awarded. *Degree requirements:* For master's, fieldwork; for doctorate, thesis/dissertation. *Entrance requirements:* For master's, minimum undergraduate GPA of 2.7 or GRE/MAT; for doctorate, GRE General Test. Additional exam requirements/recommendations for international students: Required—TOEFL (minimum score 557 paper-based, 90 iBT) or IELTS (minimum score 7). *Application deadline:* For fall admission, 4/15 for domestic and international students; for spring admission, 11/2 for domestic students; for summer admission, 3/1 for domestic students. Applications are processed on a rolling basis. Application fee: $0. Electronic applications accepted. *Expenses:* Contact institution. *Financial support:* In 2017–18, 650 students received support, including 650 fellowships with full tuition reimbursements available (averaging $10,000 per year); career-related internships or fieldwork, Federal Work-Study, institutionally sponsored loans, scholarships/grants, tuition waivers (partial), and paid field placements (for MSSA students) also available. Support available to part-time students. Financial award application deadline: 4/15; financial award applicants required to submit FAFSA. *Faculty research:* Urban poverty, community social development, substance abuse, health, child welfare, aging, mental

health, behavioral health, policy, mixed income communities, trauma, school social work, adoption. *Total annual research expenditures:* $9.1 million. *Unit head:* Dr. Grover Cleveland Gilmore, Dean, 216-368-2256, E-mail: msassdean@case.edu. *Application contact:* Richard Sigg, Director of Recruitment and Enrollment, 216-368-1655, E-mail: richard.sigg@case.edu.
Website: http://msass.case.edu/

The Catholic University of America, National Catholic School of Social Service, Washington, DC 20064. Offers clinical (MSW), including clinical health care, clinical military, veterans, and families; combined (clinical and social change) (MSW), including clinical and macro practice; social change (MSW); social work (PhD); MSW/JD. MSW/JD offered with Columbus School of Law. *Accreditation:* CSWE (one or more programs are accredited). *Program availability:* Part-time, 100% online. *Faculty:* 16 full-time (13 women), 38 part-time/adjunct (32 women). *Students:* 126 full-time (102 women), 447 part-time (385 women); includes 273 minority (161 Black or African American, non-Hispanic/Latino; 14 Asian, non-Hispanic/Latino; 53 Hispanic/Latino; 1 Native Hawaiian or other Pacific Islander, non-Hispanic/Latino; 44 Two or more races, non-Hispanic/Latino), 7 international. Average age 36. 301 applicants, 78% accepted, 141 enrolled. In 2017, 76 master's, 3 doctorates awarded. *Degree requirements:* For master's, thesis; for doctorate, comprehensive exam, thesis/dissertation, minimum GPA of 3.0. *Entrance requirements:* For master's, GRE or MAT (if undergraduate GPA less than 3.0), statement of purpose, official copies of academic transcripts, three letters of recommendation, resume; for doctorate, GRE General Test, statement of purpose, official copies of academic transcripts, three letters of recommendation, resume, writing sample. Additional exam requirements/recommendations for international students: Required—TOEFL (minimum score 600 paper-based; 92 iBT). *Application deadline:* For fall admission, 7/15 priority date for domestic students, 7/1 for international students; for spring admission, 11/15 priority date for domestic students, 11/1 for international students. Applications are processed on a rolling basis. Application fee: $60. Electronic applications accepted. *Expenses:* Contact institution. *Financial support:* Fellowships, research assistantships, teaching assistantships, Federal Work-Study, scholarships/grants, tuition waivers (full and partial), and unspecified assistantships available. Financial award application deadline: 3/15; financial award applicants required to submit FAFSA. *Faculty research:* International social development; advancement of children, youth, and families; global aging; community development and social justice; promotion of health and mental health well-being. *Total annual research expenditures:* $388,329. *Unit head:* Dr. Will Rainford, Dean, 202-319-5454, Fax: 202-319-5093, E-mail: rainford@cua.edu. *Application contact:* Dr. Steven Brown, Director of Graduate Admissions, 202-319-5057, Fax: 202-319-6533, E-mail: cua-admissions@cua.edu.
Website: https://ncsss.catholic.edu/

Chicago State University, School of Graduate and Professional Studies, College of Arts and Sciences, Program in Social Work, Chicago, IL 60628. Offers MSW. *Accreditation:* CSWE. *Application deadline:* For fall admission, 3/15 for domestic students. Application fee: $30. Electronic applications accepted. *Unit head:* Dr. Sherri Seyfried, Program Director, 773-995-2415, E-mail: sseyfrie@csu.edu. *Application contact:* Anika Miller, Graduate Studies Office, 773-995-2404, E-mail: g-studies1@csu.edu.
Website: http://www.csu.edu/cas/socialwork/

Clark Atlanta University, School of Social Work, Atlanta, GA 30314. Offers MSW, PhD. *Accreditation:* CSWE (one or more programs are accredited). *Program availability:* Part-time. *Faculty:* 18 full-time (10 women), 3 part-time/adjunct (all women). *Students:* 169 full-time (146 women), 26 part-time (23 women); includes 150 minority (148 Black or African American, non-Hispanic/Latino; 1 American Indian or Alaska Native, non-Hispanic/Latino; 1 Hispanic/Latino), 21 international. Average age 31. 75 applicants, 87% accepted, 37 enrolled. In 2017, 89 master's, 3 doctorates awarded. Terminal master's awarded for partial completion of doctoral program. *Degree requirements:* For master's, one foreign language; for doctorate, one foreign language, comprehensive exam, thesis/dissertation. *Entrance requirements:* For master's, GRE General Test, minimum undergraduate GPA of 3.0; for doctorate, GRE General Test. Additional exam requirements/recommendations for international students: Required—TOEFL (minimum score 500 paper-based; 61 iBT). *Application deadline:* For fall admission, 4/1 for domestic and international students; for spring admission, 11/1 for domestic and international students. Applications are processed on a rolling basis. Application fee: $40 ($55 for international students). Electronic applications accepted. *Financial support:* Career-related internships or fieldwork, Federal Work-Study, scholarships/grants, and unspecified assistantships available. Support available to part-time students. Financial award application deadline: 4/30; financial award applicants required to submit FAFSA. *Unit head:* Dr. Jenny Jones, Dean, 404-880-8549, E-mail: jjones@cau.edu.

Clarke University, Department of Social Work, Dubuque, IA 52001-3198. Offers MSW. *Program availability:* Part-time, evening/weekend. *Faculty:* 7 full-time (all women). *Students:* 30 full-time (25 women), 2 part-time (both women); includes 3 minority (2 Hispanic/Latino; 1 Two or more races, non-Hispanic/Latino). Average age 28. 61 applicants, 38% accepted, 20 enrolled. In 2017, 4 master's awarded. *Entrance requirements:* For master's, prerequisite courses in statistics, biology, psychology, and sociology; minimum major GPA of 3.0; interview. Additional exam requirements/recommendations for international students: Required—TOEFL (minimum score 550 paper-based; 80 iBT), IELTS (minimum score 6.5). *Application deadline:* For fall admission, 2/1 priority date for domestic students. Application fee: $35. Electronic applications accepted. *Expenses:* $650 per credit. *Financial support:* Applicants required to submit FAFSA. *Unit head:* Regina Boarman, Chair, 888-825-2753 Ext. 6583, E-mail: regina.boarman@clarke.edu. *Application contact:* Kimberly Roush, Director of Admission, Graduate and Adult Programs, 563-588-6539, Fax: 563-552-7994, E-mail: graduate@clarke.edu.

Cleveland State University, College of Graduate Studies, College of Liberal Arts and Social Sciences, School of Social Work, Cleveland, OH 44115. Offers MSW. Program offered jointly with The University of Akron. *Accreditation:* CSWE. *Program availability:* Part-time, evening/weekend, online learning. *Faculty:* 10 full-time (2 women), 8 part-time/adjunct (5 women). *Students:* 124 full-time (108 women), 52 part-time (45 women); includes 70 minority (60 Black or African American, non-Hispanic/Latino; 1 Asian, non-Hispanic/Latino; 4 Hispanic/Latino; 5 Two or more races, non-Hispanic/Latino), 1 international. Average age 34. 82 applicants, 78% accepted, 63 enrolled. In 2017, 108 master's awarded. *Entrance requirements:* For master's, 3 letters of reference. Additional exam requirements/recommendations for international students: Required—TOEFL (minimum score 550 paper-based; 78 iBT); Recommended—IELTS (minimum score 6). Application fee: $40. Electronic applications accepted. *Expenses:* Contact institution. *Financial support:* In 2017–18, 15 students received support. Research assistantships and tuition waivers (full) available. Financial award applicants required to submit FAFSA. *Faculty research:* Mental health, aging. *Total annual research expenditures:* $1.2 million. *Unit head:* Dr. Maggie Jackson, Director, 216-687-4599, Fax: 216-687-5590, E-mail: m.jackson@csuohio.edu. *Application contact:* Deborah L. Brown, Interim Assistant Director, Graduate Admissions, 216-523-7572, Fax: 216-687-5400, E-mail: d.l.brown@csuohio.edu.
Website: http://www.csuohio.edu/class/social-work/social-work

Social Work

The College at Brockport, State University of New York, School of Education, Health, and Human Services, Greater Rochester Collaborative Master of Social Work Program, Brockport, NY 14420-2997. Offers family and community practice (MSW); gerontology (AGC); interdisciplinary health practice (MSW). Program offered jointly with Nazareth College of Rochester. *Accreditation:* CSWE. *Program availability:* Part-time. *Faculty:* 6 full-time (4 women), 6 part-time/adjunct (4 women). *Students:* 54 full-time (47 women), 144 part-time (128 women); includes 35 minority (19 Black or African American, non-Hispanic/Latino; 1 American Indian or Alaska Native, non-Hispanic/Latino; 2 Asian, non-Hispanic/Latino; 6 Hispanic/Latino; 1 Native Hawaiian or other Pacific Islander, non-Hispanic/Latino; 6 Two or more races, non-Hispanic/Latino). 143 applicants, 78% accepted, 78 enrolled. In 2017, 72 master's, 9 other advanced degrees awarded. *Degree requirements:* For master's, thesis or alternative. *Entrance requirements:* For master's, minimum GPA of 3.0, letters of recommendation, statement of objectives. Additional exam requirements/recommendations for international students: Required—TOEFL (minimum score 550 paper-based; 79 iBT), IELTS (minimum score 6.5). *Application deadline:* For fall admission, 1/15 priority date for domestic and international students; for summer admission, 1/15 priority date for domestic and international students. Application fee: $50. Electronic applications accepted. *Expenses:* Tuition, state resident: full-time $10,870; part-time $453 per credit hour. Tuition, nonresident: full-time $22,210. *Required fees:* $988; $246 per semester. *Financial support:* Federal Work-Study, scholarships/grants, and unspecified assistantships available. Support available to part-time students. Financial award application deadline: 3/15; financial award applicants required to submit FAFSA. *Faculty research:* Care giving, child welfare, gerontological social work, home-school-community partnerships, domestic violence. *Unit head:* Debra Fromm Faria, Co-Director, 585-395-8455, Fax: 585-395-8603, E-mail: grcmsw@brockport.edu. *Application contact:* Brad Snyder, Coordinator of Admissions, 585-395-3845, Fax: 585-395-8603, E-mail: bsynder@brockport.edu.
Website: https://www.brockport.edu/academics/social_work/graduate/masters.html

The College of Saint Rose, Graduate Studies, School of Mathematics and Sciences, Program in Social Work, Albany, NY 12203-1419. Offers MSSW. *Program availability:* Part-time, evening/weekend. *Students:* 13 full-time (all women), 6 part-time (all women); includes 6 minority (3 Black or African American, non-Hispanic/Latino; 3 Two or more races, non-Hispanic/Latino). Average age 27. 26 applicants, 96% accepted, 18 enrolled. *Entrance requirements:* Additional exam requirements/recommendations for international students: Required—TOEFL (minimum score 550 paper-based; 80 iBT), IELTS (minimum score 6), PTE (minimum score 56). *Application deadline:* For fall admission, 4/1 priority date for domestic and international students; for spring admission, 10/15 priority date for domestic and international students; for summer admission, 3/15 priority date for domestic and international students. Applications are processed on a rolling basis. Application fee: $40. Electronic applications accepted. *Expenses: Tuition:* Full-time $7191; part-time $799 per credit hour. *Required fees:* $924; $462 per credit hour. Tuition and fees vary according to course load. *Financial support:* Career-related internships or fieldwork, scholarships/grants, tuition waivers (partial), and unspecified assistantships available. Support available to part-time students. Financial award application deadline: 4/15. *Unit head:* Maureen Rotondi, Department Chair, 518-454-2003, E-mail: rotondim@strose.edu. *Application contact:* Cris Murray, Assistant Vice President for Graduate Recruitment and Enrollment, 518-485-3390, Fax: 518-458-5479, E-mail: grad@strose.edu.

The College of St. Scholastica, Graduate Studies, Department of Social Work, Duluth, MN 55811-4199. Offers MSW. *Accreditation:* CSWE. *Program availability:* Part-time.

College of Staten Island of the City University of New York, Graduate Programs, School of Health Sciences, Program in Social Work, Staten Island, NY 10314-6600. Offers MSW. *Program availability:* Part-time, evening/weekend. *Faculty:* 6 full-time, 7 part-time/adjunct. *Students:* 72. 126 applicants, 45% accepted, 30 enrolled. In 2017, 27 master's awarded. *Degree requirements:* For master's, 16 required courses, 4 internships, 3 integrative seminars, and 1 social work elective. *Entrance requirements:* For master's, bachelor's degree from regionally-accredited college, statistics course, 3 letters of recommendation, personal statement, résumé. Additional exam requirements/recommendations for international students: Required—TOEFL (minimum score 600 paper-based; 100 iBT), IELTS (minimum score 7). *Application deadline:* For fall admission, 2/15 priority date for domestic and international students. Applications are processed on a rolling basis. Application fee: $125. Electronic applications accepted. *Expenses:* Contact institution. *Faculty research:* Children and adults with disabilities, social work theories and methods, alcohol and drug problems, restorative approaches with justice-involved populations and critical multiculturalism, gender and sexuality studies. *Unit head:* Dr. Barbra Teater, 718-982-2166, E-mail: barbra.teater@csi.cuny.edu. *Application contact:* Sasha Spence, Associate Director for Graduate Admissions, 718-982-2019, Fax: 718-982-2500, E-mail: sasha.spence@csi.cuny.edu.
Website: http://www.csi.cuny.edu/departments/socialwork/MSW_welcome.html

Colorado State University, College of Health and Human Sciences, School of Social Work, Fort Collins, CO 80523-1586. Offers MSW, PhD, MSW/MPH. *Accreditation:* CSWE. *Program availability:* Part-time, evening/weekend, 100% online, blended/hybrid learning. *Faculty:* 8 full-time (7 women), 10 part-time/adjunct (9 women). *Students:* 69 full-time (62 women), 113 part-time (98 women); includes 42 minority (12 Black or African American, non-Hispanic/Latino; 3 American Indian or Alaska Native, non-Hispanic/Latino; 26 Hispanic/Latino; 1 Two or more races, non-Hispanic/Latino), 2 international. Average age 34. 108 applicants, 41% accepted, 21 enrolled. In 2017, 57 master's, 3 doctorates awarded. *Degree requirements:* For master's, thesis (for some programs), thesis or program evaluation; for doctorate, comprehensive exam, thesis/dissertation. *Entrance requirements:* For master's, minimum GPA of 3.0; statement of purpose; experience summary; references; degree from accredited university; 400 hours' human service/volunteer work; three letters of recommendation; transcripts; for doctorate, letter of intent; resume; transcripts; 3 letters of recommendation; personal statement; interview; MSW. Additional exam requirements/recommendations for international students: Required—TOEFL (minimum score 550 paper-based), IELTS (minimum score 6.5). *Application deadline:* For fall admission, 1/2 for domestic and international students; for spring admission, 5/31 for domestic and international students; for summer admission, 1/2 for domestic and international students. Application fee: $60 ($70 for international students). Electronic applications accepted. *Expenses:* $689 per credit hour (for online MSW). *Financial support:* In 2017–18, 7 students received support, including 3 fellowships (averaging $7,128 per year), 3 research assistantships (averaging $9,504 per year), 1 teaching assistantship (averaging $9,001 per year); scholarships/grants and unspecified assistantships also available. Financial award applicants required to submit FAFSA. *Faculty research:* Aging and palliative care, alternative treatment to psychopharmacology for mental health issues, healthy cognitive aging and worker engagement, harm reduction for cannabis use among older adolescents, child welfare intervention science. *Total annual research expenditures:* $1.3 million. *Unit head:* Dr. Audrey Shillington, Director, 970-491-2378, Fax: 970-491-7280, E-mail: audrey.shillington@colostate.edu. *Application contact:* Timothy Frank, Graduate Program Coordinator, 970-491-2536, Fax: 970-491-7280, E-mail: timothy.frank@colostate.edu.
Website: http://www.ssw.chhs.colostate.edu/index.aspx

Columbia University, Columbia School of Social Work, New York, NY 10027. Offers advanced clinical practice (MSSW); advanced generalist practice and programming (MSSW); policy practice (MSSW); social enterprise administration (MSSW); JD/MS; MBA/MS; MPA/MS; MPH/MS; MS/M Div; MS/MA; MS/MS; MS/MS Ed. *Accreditation:* CSWE (one or more programs are accredited). *Program availability:* 100% online, blended/hybrid learning. *Faculty:* 40 full-time (28 women), 116 part-time/adjunct (88 women). *Students:* 992 full-time (855 women), 124 part-time (107 women); includes 432 minority (123 Black or African American, non-Hispanic/Latino; 1 American Indian or Alaska Native, non-Hispanic/Latino; 108 Asian, non-Hispanic/Latino; 163 Hispanic/Latino; 2 Native Hawaiian or other Pacific Islander, non-Hispanic/Latino; 35 Two or more races, non-Hispanic/Latino), 118 international. Average age 26. 1,683 applicants. In 2017, 454 master's, 2 doctorates awarded. *Entrance requirements:* Additional exam requirements/recommendations for international students: Required—TOEFL (minimum score 98 iBT). Recommended—IELTS (minimum score 7). *Application deadline:* For fall admission, 2/1 for domestic and international students; for spring admission, 10/15 for domestic and international students. Application fee: $75. Electronic applications accepted. *Expenses: Tuition:* Full-time $44,864; part-time $1704 per credit. *Required fees:* $2370 per semester. One-time fee: $105. *Financial support:* Teaching assistantships, Federal Work-Study, scholarships/grants, and unspecified assistantships available. Financial award application deadline: 2/15; financial award applicants required to submit FAFSA. *Faculty research:* Addiction; HIV; gender-based violence and migration in the U.S. and globally; low-income children and families in NYC, the U.S. and other developed countries; dialectical behavior therapy (DBT); bereavement and complicated grief and trauma; responsible fatherhood; social determinants of health and mental health care; racism and health disparities; community violence and social media. *Unit head:* Michael Lovaglio, Assistant Dean, Enrollment and Student Services, 212-851-2359, E-mail: ml3992@columbia.edu. *Application contact:* Andrew Rapin, Director of Admissions, 212-851-2400, E-mail: cssw-admit@columbia.edu.
Website: http://www.socialwork.columbia.edu

Concord University, Graduate Studies, Athens, WV 24712-1000. Offers educational leadership and supervision (M Ed); health promotion (MA); reading specialist (M Ed); social work (MSW); special education (M Ed); teaching (MAT). *Program availability:* Part-time, evening/weekend, 100% online. *Faculty:* 16 full-time (10 women), 7 part-time/adjunct (4 women). *Students:* 146 full-time (117 women), 195 part-time (161 women); includes 26 minority (15 Black or African American, non-Hispanic/Latino; 1 American Indian or Alaska Native, non-Hispanic/Latino; 4 Asian, non-Hispanic/Latino; 1 Hispanic/Latino; 5 Two or more races, non-Hispanic/Latino). Average age 34. 591 applicants, 99% accepted, 144 enrolled. In 2017, 114 master's awarded. *Degree requirements:* For master's, thesis (for some programs). *Entrance requirements:* For master's, GRE or MAT, baccalaureate degree with minimum GPA of 2.5 from regionally-accredited institution; teaching license; 2 letters of recommendation; completed disposition assessment form. *Application deadline:* Applications are processed on a rolling basis. Application fee: $30. Electronic applications accepted. *Expenses:* Tuition, state resident: full-time $8132; part-time $453 per semester hour. Tuition, nonresident: full-time $14,180; part-time $788 per semester hour. *Financial support:* Tuition waivers and unspecified assistantships available. Financial award applicants required to submit FAFSA. *Unit head:* Dr. Cheryl Barnes, Director, 304-384-6306, E-mail: cbarnes@concord.edu. *Application contact:* Debra Moore, Special Events Assistant, 304-384-5113, E-mail: dlm@concord.edu.
Website: http://www.concord.edu/graduate

Cornell University, Graduate School, Graduate Fields of Human Ecology, Field of Policy Analysis and Management, Ithaca, NY 14853. Offers consumer policy (PhD); family and social welfare policy (PhD); health administration (MHA); health management and policy (PhD); public policy (PhD). *Degree requirements:* For master's, thesis; for doctorate, thesis/dissertation. *Entrance requirements:* For master's, GRE General Test or GMAT, 2 letters of recommendation; for doctorate, GRE General Test, 2 letters of recommendation. Additional exam requirements/recommendations for international students: Required—TOEFL (minimum score 550 paper-based; 77 iBT). Electronic applications accepted. *Faculty research:* Health policy, family policy, social welfare policy, program evaluation, consumer policy.

Daemen College, Program in Social Work, Amherst, NY 14226-3592. Offers MSW.

Dalhousie University, Faculty of Health Professions, School of Social Work, Halifax, NS B3H3J5, Canada. Offers MSW. *Program availability:* Part-time, online learning. *Degree requirements:* For master's, thesis optional, field placement. *Entrance requirements:* For master's, bachelor's degree in social work, 2 years work experience in social work, minimum GPA of 3.0. Additional exam requirements/recommendations for international students: Required—TOEFL, IELTS, CANTEST, CAEL, or Michigan English Language Assessment Battery. Electronic applications accepted. *Expenses:* Contact institution. *Faculty research:* Family and child welfare, physical and mental health, public policy, elder abuse, violence against women, community practice.

Delaware State University, Graduate Programs, College of Education, Health and Public Policy, Department of Social Work, Program in Social Work, Dover, DE 19901-2277. Offers MSW. *Accreditation:* CSWE. *Program availability:* Evening/weekend. *Entrance requirements:* For master's, GRE, minimum GPA of 3.0 in major, 2.75 overall. Additional exam requirements/recommendations for international students: Required—TOEFL. Electronic applications accepted. *Faculty research:* Gerontology, human behavior, corrections, child welfare, adolescent behavior policy.

DePaul University, College of Liberal Arts and Social Sciences, Chicago, IL 60614. Offers Arabic (MA); Chinese (MA); critical ethnic studies (MA); English (MA); French (MA); German (MA); history (MA); interdisciplinary studies (MA, MS); international public service (MS); international studies (MA); Italian (MA); Japanese (MA); liberal studies (MA); nonprofit management (MNM); public administration (MPA); public health (MPH); public policy (MPP); public service management (MS); refugee and forced migration studies (MS); social work (MSW); sociology (MA); Spanish (MA); sustainable urban development (MA); women's and gender studies (MA); writing and publishing (MA); writing, rhetoric and discourse (MA); MA/PhD. *Program availability:* Part-time, evening/weekend, online learning. Terminal master's awarded for partial completion of doctoral program. *Degree requirements:* For master's, variable foreign language requirement, comprehensive exam (for some programs), thesis (for some programs). *Application deadline:* Applications are processed on a rolling basis. Application fee: $40. Electronic applications accepted. *Financial support:* Applicants required to submit FAFSA. *Unit head:* Dr. Guillermo Vasquez de Velasco, Dean, 773-325-7305. *Application contact:* Ann Spittle, Director of Graduate Admission, 773-325-8369, Fax: 312-476-3244, E-mail: graddepaul@depaul.edu.
Website: http://las.depaul.edu/

Dominican University, School of Social Work, River Forest, IL 60305. Offers MSW, MSW/MBA. *Accreditation:* CSWE. *Program availability:* Part-time. *Faculty:* 7 full-time (4 women), 18 part-time/adjunct (15 women). *Students:* 126 full-time (112 women), 80 part-time (72 women); includes 92 minority (36 Black or African American, non-Hispanic/Latino; 4 Asian, non-Hispanic/Latino; 46 Hispanic/Latino; 2 Native Hawaiian or other Pacific Islander, non-Hispanic/Latino; 4 Two or more races, non-Hispanic/Latino), 4 international. Average age 33. 134 applicants, 81% accepted, 72 enrolled. In 2017, 115

master's awarded. *Entrance requirements:* For master's, minimum GPA of 2.75. Additional exam requirements/recommendations for international students: Required—TOEFL (minimum score 83 iBT); Recommended—IELTS (minimum score 7). *Application deadline:* For fall admission, 7/1 for domestic and international students; for spring admission, 11/1 for domestic and international students. Applications are processed on a rolling basis. Application fee: $25. Electronic applications accepted. *Expenses:* Contact institution. *Financial support:* Research assistantships with partial tuition reimbursements, Federal Work-Study, scholarships/grants, and unspecified assistantships available. Financial award applicants required to submit FAFSA. *Faculty research:* Human trafficking, domestic violence, gerontology, school social work, child welfare. *Unit head:* Dr. Julie Bach, Executive Director, School of Social Work, 708-714-9102, E-mail: jbach@dom.edu. *Application contact:* Catherine Galarza-Espino, Coordinator of Graduate Marketing and Recruiting, 708-524-6983, E-mail: cgalarza@dom.edu.
Website: http://socialwork.dom.edu/

East Carolina University, Graduate School, College of Health and Human Performance, School of Social Work, Greenville, NC 27858-4353. Offers gerontology (Certificate); social work (MSW); substance abuse (Certificate). *Accreditation:* CSWE. *Program availability:* Online learning. *Students:* 103 full-time (95 women), 23 part-time (22 women); includes 65 minority (52 Black or African American, non-Hispanic/Latino; 1 American Indian or Alaska Native, non-Hispanic/Latino; 3 Asian, non-Hispanic/Latino; 7 Hispanic/Latino; 2 Two or more races, non-Hispanic/Latino), 1 international. Average age 30. 107 applicants, 87% accepted, 62 enrolled. In 2017, 69 master's, 30 other advanced degrees awarded. *Degree requirements:* For master's, comprehensive exam. *Entrance requirements:* For master's, GRE or MAT. Additional exam requirements/recommendations for international students: Recommended—TOEFL (minimum score 78 iBT), IELTS (minimum score 6.5). *Application deadline:* For fall admission, 2/1 priority date for domestic and international students. Application fee: $75. *Expenses:* Tuition, state resident: full-time $4749; part-time $297 per credit hour. Tuition, nonresident: full-time $17,898; part-time $1119 per credit hour. *Required fees:* $2691; $224 per credit hour. Part-time tuition and fees vary according to course load and program. *Financial support:* Fellowships and research assistantships available. Financial award application deadline: 6/1. *Faculty research:* Social research, gerontology, women's issues, social services in schools, human behavior. *Unit head:* Dr. Shelia Bunch, Director, 252-328-4202, E-mail: bunchs@ecu.edu.
Website: https://hhp.ecu.edu/socw/

Eastern Michigan University, Graduate School, College of Health and Human Services, School of Social Work, Ypsilanti, MI 48197. Offers MSW. *Accreditation:* CSWE. *Program availability:* Part-time, evening/weekend. *Faculty:* 29 full-time (26 women). *Students:* 8 full-time (all women), 196 part-time (160 women); includes 82 minority (55 Black or African American, non-Hispanic/Latino; 1 American Indian or Alaska Native, non-Hispanic/Latino; 4 Asian, non-Hispanic/Latino; 16 Hispanic/Latino; 1 Native Hawaiian or other Pacific Islander, non-Hispanic/Latino; 5 Two or more races, non-Hispanic/Latino). Average age 33. 192 applicants, 48% accepted, 59 enrolled. In 2017, 83 master's awarded. *Entrance requirements:* Additional exam requirements/recommendations for international students: Required—TOEFL. *Application deadline:* For fall admission, 1/15 priority date for domestic students. Applications are processed on a rolling basis. Application fee: $45. *Financial support:* Fellowships, research assistantships with full tuition reimbursements, teaching assistantships with full tuition reimbursements, career-related internships or fieldwork, Federal Work-Study, institutionally sponsored loans, scholarships/grants, tuition waivers (partial), and unspecified assistantships available. Support available to part-time students. Financial award applicants required to submit FAFSA. *Unit head:* Dr. Lynn Nybell, Director, 734-487-0393, Fax: 734-487-6832, E-mail: lnybell@emich.edu. *Application contact:* Julie Harkema, Admissions Coordinator, 734-487-0393, Fax: 734-487-6832, E-mail: jharkema@emich.edu.
Website: http://www.emich.edu/sw

Eastern Washington University, Graduate Studies, College of Social Sciences, School of Social Work, Cheney, WA 99004-2431. Offers MSW, MPA/MSW. *Accreditation:* CSWE. *Program availability:* Part-time. *Students:* 111 full-time (93 women), 119 part-time (107 women); includes 18 minority (3 Black or African American, non-Hispanic/Latino; 6 American Indian or Alaska Native, non-Hispanic/Latino; 9 Hispanic/Latino). Average age 32. 91 applicants, 52% accepted, 43 enrolled. *Degree requirements:* For master's, comprehensive exam. *Entrance requirements:* For master's, minimum GPA of 3.0. Additional exam requirements/recommendations for international students: Required—TOEFL (minimum score 580 paper-based), IELTS (minimum score 7), PTE (minimum score 63). *Application deadline:* Applications are processed on a rolling basis. Application fee: $75. Electronic applications accepted. *Expenses:* Tuition, state resident: full-time $11,191; part-time $373.06 per credit. Tuition, nonresident: full-time $25,995; part-time $866.52 per credit. *Financial support:* Teaching assistantships with partial tuition reimbursements, career-related internships or fieldwork, Federal Work-Study, institutionally sponsored loans, scholarships/grants, health care benefits, tuition waivers (partial), and unspecified assistantships available. Support available to part-time students. Financial award application deadline: 2/1; financial award applicants required to submit FAFSA. *Unit head:* Diane Somerday, 509-359-6482.
Website: http://www.ewu.edu/csbssw/programs/social-work/social-work-degrees/msw.xml

East Tennessee State University, School of Graduate Studies, College of Clinical and Rehabilitative Health Sciences, Department of Social Work, Johnson City, TN 37614. Offers MSW. *Accreditation:* CSWE. *Degree requirements:* For master's, comprehensive exam, field practicum. *Entrance requirements:* For master's, bachelor's degree; minimum GPA of 2.75, 3.0 for last 60 hours; three letters of recommendation; resume; autobiographical statement. Additional exam requirements/recommendations for international students: Required—TOEFL (minimum score 550 paper-based; 79 iBT). *Application deadline:* For fall admission, 2/1 for domestic and international students. Application fee: $55 ($65 for international students). Electronic applications accepted. *Financial support:* Research assistantships with tuition reimbursements, career-related internships or fieldwork, institutionally sponsored loans, scholarships/grants, and unspecified assistantships available. Financial award application deadline: 7/1; financial award applicants required to submit FAFSA. *Faculty research:* Social work education, domestic violence, factors that contribute to a quality therapeutic relationship, mental illness stigma. *Unit head:* Dr. Michael Smith, Chair, 423-439-6013, Fax: 423-439-6010, E-mail: smithml1@etsu.edu. *Application contact:* E. Philip Stork, MSW Executive Assistant, 423-439-6013, E-mail: storke@etsu.edu.
Website: http://www.etsu.edu/cas/socialwork/

Edinboro University of Pennsylvania, Department of Social Work, Edinboro, PA 16444. Offers MSW. *Accreditation:* CSWE. *Program availability:* Evening/weekend. *Degree requirements:* For master's, competency exam. Electronic applications accepted.

Fayetteville State University, Graduate School, Program in Social Work, Fayetteville, NC 28301-4298. Offers MSW. *Accreditation:* CSWE. *Program availability:* Part-time, evening/weekend. *Faculty:* 10 full-time (5 women), 15 part-time/adjunct (11 women). *Students:* 158 full-time (125 women), 11 part-time (10 women); includes 119 minority (98 Black or African American, non-Hispanic/Latino; 2 American Indian or Alaska Native, non-

Hispanic/Latino; 8 Asian, non-Hispanic/Latino; 7 Hispanic/Latino; 4 Native Hawaiian or other Pacific Islander, non-Hispanic/Latino). Average age 35. 68 applicants, 100% accepted, 68 enrolled. In 2017, 65 master's awarded. *Entrance requirements:* For master's, GRE. Additional exam requirements/recommendations for international students: Required—TOEFL. *Application deadline:* For fall admission, 1/15 for domestic students. Application fee: $40. *Expenses:* Tuition, state resident: full-time $8604. Tuition, nonresident: full-time $19,669. *Financial support:* Application deadline: 3/1; applicants required to submit FAFSA. *Unit head:* Dr. Terri Moore-Brown, Interim Dean of School of Social Work, 910-672-1853, Fax: 910-672-1755, E-mail: tmbrown@uncfsu.edu. *Application contact:* Gregory Perkins, Assistant Department Chair and Graduate Coordinator, 910-672-1021, Fax: 910-672-1755, E-mail: gperkins@uncfsu.edu.

Ferris State University, College of Arts and Sciences, Big Rapids, MI 49307. Offers social work (MSW). *Program availability:* Part-time, evening/weekend. *Faculty:* 7 full-time (all women), 5 part-time/adjunct (4 women). *Students:* 32 full-time (29 women), 30 part-time (28 women); includes 7 minority (3 Black or African American, non-Hispanic/Latino; 1 American Indian or Alaska Native, non-Hispanic/Latino; 2 Hispanic/Latino; 1 Two or more races, non-Hispanic/Latino), 1 international. Average age 32. 60 applicants, 77% accepted, 38 enrolled. In 2017, 43 master's awarded. *Degree requirements:* For master's, capstone project. *Entrance requirements:* For master's, minimum GPA of 3.0. *Application deadline:* For fall admission, 3/1 for domestic students. Electronic applications accepted. *Expenses:* $610 per credit. *Financial support:* Federal Work-Study available. Financial award application deadline: 4/15; financial award applicants required to submit FAFSA. *Unit head:* Dr. Wendy Samuels, Director of Social Work Program, 231-591-5896, E-mail: wendysamuels@ferris.edu. *Application contact:* Dr. Janet Vizina-Roubal, MSW Coordinator, 231-357-2816, E-mail: janetvizinaroubal@ferris.edu.
Website: https://ferris.edu/arts-sciences/index.htm

Florida Agricultural and Mechanical University, Division of Graduate Studies, Research, and Continuing Education, College of Social Sciences, Arts and Humanities, Department of History and Political Science, Program in Social Work, Tallahassee, FL 32307-3200. Offers MSW. *Accreditation:* CSWE. *Entrance requirements:* For master's, GRE General Test, minimum GPA of 3.0, 3 letters of recommendation. Additional exam requirements/recommendations for international students: Required—TOEFL.

Florida Atlantic University, College for Design and Social Inquiry, Phyllis and Harvey Sandler School of Social Work, Boca Raton, FL 33431-0991. Offers MSW, DSW. *Accreditation:* CSWE. *Program availability:* Part-time, evening/weekend. *Faculty:* 12 full-time (7 women), 1 (woman) part-time/adjunct. *Students:* 137 full-time (105 women), 120 part-time (103 women); includes 106 minority (49 Black or African American, non-Hispanic/Latino; 5 Asian, non-Hispanic/Latino; 39 Hispanic/Latino; 13 Two or more races, non-Hispanic/Latino), 1 international. Average age 32. 371 applicants, 49% accepted, 140 enrolled. In 2017, 130 master's awarded. *Entrance requirements:* Additional exam requirements/recommendations for international students: Required—TOEFL (minimum score 500 paper-based; 61 iBT), IELTS (minimum score 6). *Application deadline:* For fall admission, 5/1 priority date for domestic students, 2/15 for international students. Applications are processed on a rolling basis. Application fee: $30. *Expenses:* Tuition, state resident: full-time $7400; part-time $369.82 per credit. Tuition, nonresident: full-time $20,496; part-time $1042.81 per credit. *Financial support:* Fellowships with tuition reimbursements, research assistantships with tuition reimbursements, career-related internships or fieldwork, Federal Work-Study, institutionally sponsored loans, and tuition waivers (partial) available. Financial award application deadline: 4/1. *Faculty research:* Child welfare, social work education. *Unit head:* Joy McClellan, Program Coordinator, 561-297-3234, E-mail: jmcclel2@fau.edu.
Website: http://cdsi.fau.edu/ssw/

Florida Gulf Coast University, Elaine Nicpon Marieb College of Health and Human Services, Program in Social Work, Fort Myers, FL 33965-6565. Offers MSW. *Accreditation:* CSWE. *Program availability:* Part-time, evening/weekend. *Faculty:* 71 full-time (49 women), 49 part-time/adjunct (32 women). *Students:* 30 full-time (29 women), 20 part-time (13 women); includes 22 minority (12 Black or African American, non-Hispanic/Latino; 2 Asian, non-Hispanic/Latino; 7 Hispanic/Latino; 1 Two or more races, non-Hispanic/Latino), 1 international. Average age 30. 55 applicants, 75% accepted, 33 enrolled. In 2017, 17 master's awarded. *Entrance requirements:* For master's, GRE General Test, MAT, minimum GPA of 3.0. Additional exam requirements/recommendations for international students: Required—TOEFL (minimum score 550 paper-based). *Application deadline:* For summer admission, 2/15 priority date for domestic students. Applications are processed on a rolling basis. Application fee: $30. Electronic applications accepted. *Expenses:* Tuition, state resident: part-time $290 per credit hour. Tuition, nonresident: part-time $1173 per credit hour. *Required fees:* $127 per credit hour. Tuition and fees vary according to course load. *Financial support:* In 2017–18, 9 students received support. Research assistantships, career-related internships or fieldwork, health care benefits, and tuition waivers (partial) available. Support available to part-time students. Financial award application deadline: 6/30; financial award applicants required to submit FAFSA. *Faculty research:* Gerontology, clinical case management, domestic violence, homelessness, migrant workers. *Unit head:* Dr. Thomas Felke, Program Director/Interim Chair, 239-590-7841, E-mail: tfelke@fgcu.edu. *Application contact:* Amanda Evans, 239-590-7829, Fax: 239-590-7843, E-mail: aevans@fgcu.edu.

Florida International University, Robert Stempel College of Public Health and Social Work, School of Social Work, Miami, FL 33199. Offers social welfare (PhD); social work (MSW). *Accreditation:* CSWE (one or more programs are accredited). *Program availability:* Part-time, evening/weekend. *Faculty:* 17 full-time (12 women), 14 part-time/adjunct (10 women). *Students:* 139 full-time (117 women), 70 part-time (59 women); includes 176 minority (51 Black or African American, non-Hispanic/Latino; 1 Asian, non-Hispanic/Latino; 117 Hispanic/Latino; 7 Two or more races, non-Hispanic/Latino), 5 international. Average age 31. 143 applicants, 48% accepted, 55 enrolled. In 2017, 85 master's, 1 doctorate awarded. *Degree requirements:* For doctorate, comprehensive exam, thesis/dissertation. *Entrance requirements:* For master's, minimum undergraduate GPA of 3.0 in upper-level coursework; letters of recommendation; undergraduate courses in biology (including human biology), statistics, and social/behavioral science (12 credits); BSW from accredited program; for doctorate, GRE, minimum graduate GPA of 3.5, 3 letters of recommendation, resume, writing samples, 2 examples of scholarly work. Additional exam requirements/recommendations for international students: Required—TOEFL (minimum score 550 paper-based; 80 iBT). *Application deadline:* For fall admission, 6/1 for domestic students, 4/1 for international students; for spring admission, 10/1 for domestic students, 9/1 for international students. Applications are processed on a rolling basis. Application fee: $30. Electronic applications accepted. *Expenses:* Tuition, state resident: full-time $8912; part-time $446 per credit hour. Tuition, nonresident: full-time $21,393; part-time $992 per credit hour. *Required fees:* $390; $195 per semester. *Financial support:* Institutionally sponsored loans and scholarships/grants available. Financial award application deadline: 3/1; financial award applicants required to submit FAFSA. *Unit head:* Dr. Mary Helen Hayden, Director, 305-348-1208, E-mail: haydenm@fiu.edu. *Application contact:* Gladys Ramos, Program Assistant, 305-348-5887, E-mail: gladys.ramos@fiu.edu.
Website: http://ssph.fiu.edu/

Social Work

Florida State University, The Graduate School, College of Social Work, Tallahassee, FL 32306. Offers clinical social work (MSW); social leadership (MSW); social work (PhD); JD/MSW; MPA/MSW; MS/MSW; MSW/MBA. *Accreditation:* CSWE (one or more programs are accredited). *Program availability:* Part-time, evening/weekend, 100% online coursework with face to face internship requirements. *Faculty:* 34 full-time (24 women), 8 part-time/adjunct (4 women). *Students:* 224 full-time (191 women), 300 part-time (263 women); includes 205 minority (112 Black or African American, non-Hispanic/Latino; 2 American Indian or Alaska Native, non-Hispanic/Latino; 10 Asian, non-Hispanic/Latino; 57 Hispanic/Latino; 24 Two or more races, non-Hispanic/Latino). Average age 31. 324 applicants, 70% accepted, 197 enrolled. In 2017, 270 master's, 3 doctorates awarded. *Degree requirements:* For master's, thesis optional; for doctorate, comprehensive exam, thesis/dissertation. *Entrance requirements:* For master's and doctorate, GRE General Test, minimum upper-division GPA of 3.0. Additional exam requirements/recommendations for international students: Required—TOEFL (minimum score 80 iBT). *Application deadline:* For fall admission, 6/1 for domestic and international students; for spring admission, 10/1 for domestic and international students; for summer admission, 3/1 for domestic and international students. Applications are processed on a rolling basis. Application fee: $30. Electronic applications accepted. *Expenses:* Contact institution. *Financial support:* In 2017–18, 77 students received support, including 26 research assistantships with full tuition reimbursements available, 6 teaching assistantships with full tuition reimbursements available; fellowships with full tuition reimbursements available, career-related internships or fieldwork, scholarships/grants, health care benefits, tuition waivers (full and partial), and unspecified assistantships also available. Financial award application deadline: 5/1; financial award applicants required to submit FAFSA. *Faculty research:* Family violence, AIDS/HIV, aging, family therapy, child welfare, criminal justice, mental health, suicide prevention. *Unit head:* Dr. James Clark, Dean, 850-644-4752, Fax: 850-644-9750, E-mail: jclark5@fsu.edu. *Application contact:* Dana DeBoer, Coordinator of MSW Admissions, 800-378-9550, Fax: 850-644-9591, E-mail: ddeboer2@admin.fsu.edu.
Website: http://csw.fsu.edu/

Fordham University, Graduate School of Social Service, New York, NY 10023. Offers nonprofit leadership (MS); social work (MSW, PhD); JD/MSW; MSW/MPH. MS program jointly sponsored with Graduate School of Business and conducted through the Fordham Center for Nonprofit Leaders; MSW/MPH offered with Ichan School of Public Health at Mount Sinai. *Accreditation:* CSWE (one or more programs are accredited). *Program availability:* Part-time, evening/weekend, 100% online, blended/hybrid learning. *Faculty:* 37 full-time (25 women), 106 part-time/adjunct (29 women). *Students:* 1,026 full-time (891 women), 636 part-time (560 women); includes 881 minority (377 Black or African American, non-Hispanic/Latino; 3 American Indian or Alaska Native, non-Hispanic/Latino; 52 Asian, non-Hispanic/Latino; 411 Hispanic/Latino; 7 Native Hawaiian or other Pacific Islander, non-Hispanic/Latino; 31 Two or more races, non-Hispanic/Latino), 24 international. Average age 32. In 2017, 697 master's, 5 doctorates awarded. *Degree requirements:* For master's, 1200 hours of field placement; for doctorate, comprehensive exam, thesis/dissertation. *Entrance requirements:* For master's, BA in liberal arts; for doctorate, GRE, master's degree in social work or related field. Additional exam requirements/recommendations for international students: Required—TOEFL (minimum score 600 paper-based; 100 iBT), IELTS. *Application deadline:* For fall admission, 2/1 priority date for domestic students; for spring admission, 11/1 priority date for domestic students. Applications are processed on a rolling basis. Application fee: $60. Electronic applications accepted. *Expenses:* Contact institution. *Financial support:* In 2017–18, 838 students received support, including 39 research assistantships with partial tuition reimbursements available (averaging $1,980 per year); fellowships with partial tuition reimbursements available, career-related internships or fieldwork, Federal Work-Study, scholarships/grants, tuition waivers (partial), and unspecified assistantships also available. Support available to part-time students. Financial award application deadline: 2/1. *Faculty research:* Aging, children and family, healthcare, domestic violence, substance abuse. *Unit head:* Dr. Debra McPhee, Dean, 212-636-6616, E-mail: dmcphee1@fordham.edu. *Application contact:* Melba Remice, Assistant Dean of Admissions, 212-636-6600, Fax: 212-636-6613, E-mail: gssadmission@fordham.edu.
Website: http://www.fordham.edu/gss/

Gallaudet University, The Graduate School, Washington, DC 20002-3625. Offers American Sign Language/English bilingual early childhood deaf education: birth to 5 (Certificate); audiology (Au D); clinical psychology (PhD); deaf and hard of hearing infants, toddlers, and their families (Certificate); deaf education (MA, Ed S); deaf history (Certificate); deaf studies (Certificate); educating deaf students with disabilities (Certificate); education: teacher preparation (MA), including deaf education, early childhood education and deaf education, elementary education and deaf education, secondary education and deaf education; educational neuroscience (PhD); hearing, speech and language sciences (MS, PhD); international development (MA); interpretation (MA, PhD), including combined interpreting practice and research (MA), interpreting research (MA); linguistics (MA, PhD); mental health counseling (MA); peer mentoring (Certificate); public administration (MPA); school counseling (MA); school psychology (Psy S); sign language teaching (MA); social work (MSW); speech-language pathology (MS). *Program availability:* Part-time. Terminal master's awarded for partial completion of doctoral program. *Degree requirements:* For master's, comprehensive exam (for some programs), thesis optional; for doctorate, comprehensive exam, thesis/dissertation. *Entrance requirements:* For master's and doctorate, GRE General Test or MAT, letters of recommendation, interviews, goals statement, American Sign Language proficiency interview, written English competency. Additional exam requirements/recommendations for international students: Required—TOEFL. Electronic applications accepted. *Faculty research:* Signing math dictionaries, telecommunications access, cancer genetics, linguistics, visual language and visual learning, integrated quantum materials, deaf legal discourse, advance recruitment and retention in geosciences.

George Fox University, School of Social Work, Newberg, OR 97132-2697. Offers MSW.

George Mason University, College of Health and Human Services, Department of Social Work, Fairfax, VA 22030. Offers MSW. *Accreditation:* CSWE. *Program availability:* Part-time. *Faculty:* 15 full-time (11 women), 41 part-time/adjunct (34 women). *Students:* 178 full-time (157 women), 37 part-time (33 women); includes 96 minority (43 Black or African American, non-Hispanic/Latino; 12 Asian, non-Hispanic/Latino; 37 Hispanic/Latino; 4 Two or more races, non-Hispanic/Latino), 2 international. Average age 29. 295 applicants, 83% accepted, 114 enrolled. In 2017, 54 master's awarded. *Degree requirements:* For master's, 1,050 hours of field practicum. *Entrance requirements:* For master's, minimum GPA of 3.0; personal statement; resume; references/recommendations; experience in human services; prerequisites in statistics, history/government, social sciences, and English composition. Additional exam requirements/recommendations for international students: Required—TOEFL (minimum score 570 paper-based; 88 iBT), IELTS (minimum score 6.5), PTE (minimum score 59). *Application deadline:* For fall admission, 1/15 for domestic and international students. Application fee: $75 ($80 for international students). Electronic applications accepted. *Expenses:* Contact institution. *Financial support:* In 2017–18, 23 students received support, including 8 fellowships (averaging $10,000 per year), 14 research

assistantships with tuition reimbursements available (averaging $9,000 per year), 1 teaching assistantship; career-related internships or fieldwork, Federal Work-Study, scholarships/grants, unspecified assistantships, and health care benefits (for full-time research or teaching assistantship recipients) also available. Financial award application deadline: 3/1; financial award applicants required to submit FAFSA. *Faculty research:* Behavioral health; older adults/gerontology; child welfare; immigration; human rights. *Total annual research expenditures:* $104,084. *Unit head:* Michael Wolf-Branigin, Chair, 703-993-4229, Fax: 703-994-2193, E-mail: mwolfbra@gmu.edu. *Application contact:* Vannary Khov, Administrative Program Specialist, 703-993-2030, Fax: 703-993-2193, E-mail: vkhov@gmu.edu.
Website: http://chhs.gmu.edu/socialwork/

Georgia State University, Andrew Young School of Policy Studies, School of Social Work, Atlanta, GA 30294. Offers child welfare leadership (Certificate); community partnerships (MSW); forensic social work (Certificate). *Accreditation:* CSWE. *Program availability:* Part-time. *Faculty:* 17 full-time (12 women). *Students:* 117 full-time (107 women), 8 part-time (6 women); includes 77 minority (63 Black or African American, non-Hispanic/Latino; 2 Asian, non-Hispanic/Latino; 7 Hispanic/Latino; 5 Two or more races, non-Hispanic/Latino), 1 international. Average age 30. 168 applicants, 42% accepted, 47 enrolled. In 2017, 59 master's awarded. *Entrance requirements:* For master's and Certificate, GRE. Additional exam requirements/recommendations for international students: Required—TOEFL (minimum score 550 paper-based; 100 iBT) or IELTS (minimum score 7). *Application deadline:* For fall admission, 2/1 priority date for domestic and international students. Application fee: $50. Electronic applications accepted. *Expenses:* Tuition, state resident: full-time $7020. Tuition, nonresident: full-time $22,518. *Required fees:* $2128. Tuition and fees vary according to degree level and program. *Financial support:* In 2017–18, research assistantships with tuition reimbursements (averaging $4,000 per year), teaching assistantships with tuition reimbursements (averaging $4,000 per year) were awarded; career-related internships or fieldwork, institutionally sponsored loans, scholarships/grants, tuition waivers, and unspecified assistantships also available. Financial award application deadline: 2/1; financial award applicants required to submit FAFSA. *Faculty research:* Community partnership, non-profit organizations, child welfare practice and policy, gerontological practice and policy, restorative justice. *Unit head:* Brian Bride, Director of School of Social Work, 404-413-1052, Fax: 404-413-1075, E-mail: bbride@gsu.edu.
Website: http://aysps.gsu.edu/socialwork

Governors State University, College of Health and Human Services, Program in Social Work, University Park, IL 60484. Offers MSW. *Accreditation:* CSWE. *Program availability:* Part-time. *Faculty:* 12 full-time (all women), 14 part-time/adjunct (11 women). *Students:* 97 full-time (85 women), 49 part-time (44 women); includes 85 minority (73 Black or African American, non-Hispanic/Latino; 11 Hispanic/Latino; 1 Two or more races, non-Hispanic/Latino), 2 international. Average age 33. 147 applicants, 52% accepted, 67 enrolled. In 2017, 53 master's awarded. *Application deadline:* For fall admission, 4/1 for domestic students. Applications are processed on a rolling basis. Application fee: $50. Electronic applications accepted. *Expenses:* Tuition, state resident: full-time $8472; part-time $353 per credit hour. Tuition, nonresident: full-time $16,944; part-time $706 per credit hour. *Required fees:* $1824; $76 per credit hour. $38 per term. Tuition and fees vary according to course load, degree level and program. *Financial support:* Application deadline: 5/1; applicants required to submit FAFSA. *Unit head:* Gerri Outlaw, Chair, Department of Social Work, 708-534-5000 Ext. 2178, E-mail: goutlaw@govst.edu.

The Graduate Center, City University of New York, Graduate Studies, Program in Social Welfare, New York, NY 10016-4039. Offers DSW, PhD. *Faculty:* 17 full-time (7 women). *Students:* 65 full-time (41 women), 1 part-time (0 women); includes 30 minority (19 Black or African American, non-Hispanic/Latino; 2 Asian, non-Hispanic/Latino; 8 Hispanic/Latino; 1 Two or more races, non-Hispanic/Latino), 3 international. Average age 43. 58 applicants, 21% accepted, 9 enrolled. In 2017, 4 doctorates awarded. *Degree requirements:* For doctorate, thesis/dissertation, project, qualifying exam. *Entrance requirements:* For doctorate, MSW or equivalent, 3 years of post-master's work experience. Additional exam requirements/recommendations for international students: Required—TOEFL. *Application deadline:* For fall admission, 3/1 for domestic students. Application fee: $125. Electronic applications accepted. *Financial support:* In 2017–18, 52 students received support, including 36 fellowships, 1 teaching assistantship; research assistantships, career-related internships or fieldwork, Federal Work-Study, institutionally sponsored loans, and tuition waivers (full and partial) also available. Financial award application deadline: 2/1; financial award applicants required to submit FAFSA. *Unit head:* Dr. Harriet Goodman, Executive Officer, 212-452-7023, Fax: 212-452-7440. *Application contact:* Les Gribben, Director of Admissions, 212-817-7470, Fax: 212-817-1624, E-mail: lgribben@gc.cuny.edu.

Grambling State University, School of Graduate Studies and Research, College of Professional Studies, School of Social Work, Grambling, LA 71245. Offers MSW. *Accreditation:* CSWE. *Program availability:* Part-time. *Degree requirements:* For master's, comprehensive exam, research project or thesis. *Entrance requirements:* For master's, GRE, minimum GPA of 3.0 on last degree, 36 hours in liberal arts, autobiography, interview. Additional exam requirements/recommendations for international students: Required—TOEFL (minimum score 500 paper-based; 62 iBT). Electronic applications accepted.

Grand Valley State University, College of Community and Public Service, School of Social Work, Allendale, MI 49401-9403. Offers MSW. *Accreditation:* CSWE. *Program availability:* Part-time. *Faculty:* 14 full-time (9 women), 18 part-time/adjunct (13 women). *Students:* 175 full-time (146 women), 122 part-time (111 women); includes 66 minority (32 Black or African American, non-Hispanic/Latino; 3 American Indian or Alaska Native, non-Hispanic/Latino; 2 Asian, non-Hispanic/Latino; 18 Hispanic/Latino; 11 Two or more races, non-Hispanic/Latino), 2 international. Average age 28. 158 applicants, 90% accepted, 83 enrolled. In 2017, 153 master's awarded. *Degree requirements:* For master's, field education. *Entrance requirements:* For master's, three letters of recommendation, current resume, 2- to 3-page essay about life experiences that have led to interest in administrative practice in social agency, 2-page essay on how pursuing MSW will help achieve educational and professional career goals. Additional exam requirements/recommendations for international students: Required—TOEFL (minimum iBT score of 80), IELTS (6.5), or Michigan English Language Assessment Battery (77). *Application deadline:* For fall admission, 5/1 priority date for domestic students; for winter admission, 10/1 priority date for domestic students; for spring admission, 3/15 priority date for domestic students. Applications are processed on a rolling basis. Application fee: $30. Electronic applications accepted. *Expenses:* $627 per credit hour. *Financial support:* In 2017–18, 46 students received support, including 29 fellowships, 18 research assistantships with full and partial tuition reimbursements available (averaging $4,000 per year); career-related internships or fieldwork, Federal Work-Study, institutionally sponsored loans, and unspecified assistantships also available. *Faculty research:* Drug addiction, aging, management, effectiveness of therapy. *Unit head:* Dr. Scott Berlin, Chair, 616-331-6550, Fax: 616-331-6570, E-mail: berlins@gvsu.edu. *Application contact:* Dr. Cray Mulder, Graduate Program Director/Recruiting Contact, 616-331-6596, Fax: 616-331-6570, E-mail: muldercra@gvsu.edu.

Gratz College, Graduate Programs, Program in Jewish Communal Service, Melrose Park, PA 19027. Offers MA, Certificate, MA/MSW. MA/MSW offered jointly with University of Pennsylvania. *Program availability:* Part-time, evening/weekend, online learning. *Degree requirements:* For master's, one foreign language, internship.

Hawai'i Pacific University, College of Health and Society, Program in Social Work, Honolulu, HI 96813. Offers MSW. *Accreditation:* CSWE. *Program availability:* Part-time, evening/weekend. *Faculty:* 3 full-time (2 women), 1 part-time/adjunct (0 women). *Students:* 40 full-time (24 women), 8 part-time (6 women); includes 32 minority (3 Black or African American, non-Hispanic/Latino; 8 Asian, non-Hispanic/Latino; 5 Hispanic/Latino; 16 Two or more races, non-Hispanic/Latino), 2 international. Average age 33. 35 applicants, 86% accepted, 18 enrolled. In 2017, 32 master's awarded. *Entrance requirements:* Additional exam requirements/recommendations for international students: Recommended—TOEFL (minimum score 550 paper-based; 80 iBT), IELTS (minimum score 6), TWE (minimum score 5). *Application deadline:* For fall admission, 1/15 priority date for domestic students. Applications are processed on a rolling basis. Application fee: $50. Electronic applications accepted. *Expenses: Tuition:* Full-time $18,000; part-time $1000 per credit. *Required fees:* $200; $26 per credit. Tuition and fees vary according to course load and program. *Financial support:* In 2017–18, 8 students received support. Career-related internships or fieldwork, Federal Work-Study, scholarships/grants, tuition waivers (partial), and unspecified assistantships available. Financial award application deadline: 3/1; financial award applicants required to submit FAFSA. *Unit head:* Dr. Peter Mataira, Program Director, 808-544-1487, E-mail: pmataira@hpu.edu. *Application contact:* Danny Lam, Assistant Director of Graduate Admissions, 808-544-1135, E-mail: graduate@hpu.edu.
Website: https://www.hpu.edu/chs/social-work/ma-sw/index.html

Howard University, School of Social Work, Washington, DC 20059. Offers MSW, PhD. *Accreditation:* CSWE (one or more programs are accredited). *Program availability:* Part-time. *Degree requirements:* For doctorate, comprehensive exam, thesis/dissertation, qualifying exam. *Entrance requirements:* For master's, minimum GPA of 2.5; for doctorate, GRE General Test, minimum GPA of 3.3, MSW or master's in related field. Additional exam requirements/recommendations for international students: Required—TOEFL. Electronic applications accepted. *Faculty research:* Infant mortality, child and family services, displaced populations, social work practice, domestic violence, Black males, mental health.

Humboldt State University, Academic Programs, College of Professional Studies, Department of Social Work, Arcata, CA 95521-8299. Offers MSW. *Accreditation:* CSWE. *Entrance requirements:* For master's, 3 letters of recommendation. Additional exam requirements/recommendations for international students: Required—TOEFL (minimum score 500 paper-based).

Hunter College of the City University of New York, Graduate School, Silberman School of Social Work, New York, NY 10065-5085. Offers MSW. *Accreditation:* CSWE. *Degree requirements:* For master's, major paper. *Entrance requirements:* Additional exam requirements/recommendations for international students: Required—TOEFL. *Faculty research:* Child welfare, AIDS, homeless, aging, mental health.

Illinois State University, Graduate School, College of Arts and Sciences, School of Social Work, Normal, IL 61790. Offers MSW. *Accreditation:* CSWE. *Faculty research:* Developing professional careers in child welfare, research and policy work for the Evan B. Donaldson Adoption Institute, evidence-based practice training pilot evaluation.

Indiana State University, College of Graduate and Professional Studies, College of Health and Human Services, Department of Social Work, Terre Haute, IN 47809. Offers MSW. *Accreditation:* CSWE.

Indiana University East, School of Social Work, Richmond, IN 47374-1289. Offers MSW.

Indiana University Northwest, School of Social Work, Gary, IN 46408-1197. Offers health (MSW); mental health and addictions (MSW). *Program availability:* Part-time, evening/weekend. *Degree requirements:* For master's, practicum. *Entrance requirements:* For master's, minimum GPA of 3.0; bachelor's degree from accredited university including the successful completion of 6 courses in social or behavioral sciences and 1 course in statistics; 3 professional references. Electronic applications accepted. *Expenses:* Contact institution. *Faculty research:* Educational outcomes, generalist practice, homelessness.

Indiana University–Purdue University Indianapolis, School of Social Work, Indianapolis, IN 46202. Offers MSW, PhD, Certificate. *Accreditation:* CSWE (one or more programs are accredited). *Program availability:* Part-time, evening/weekend. Terminal master's awarded for partial completion of doctoral program. *Degree requirements:* For master's, field practicum; for doctorate, thesis/dissertation, residential internship. *Entrance requirements:* For master's, minimum GPA of 2.5; course work in social behavior, statistics, research methodology, and human biology; for doctorate, GRE General Test. Additional exam requirements/recommendations for international students: Required—TOEFL. *Expenses:* Contact institution. *Faculty research:* Social justice, institutional child welfare, mental health, aging, AIDS/HIV.

Indiana University South Bend, School of Social Work, South Bend, IN 46615. Offers MSW. *Program availability:* Part-time, evening/weekend. *Expenses:* Contact institution.

Institute for Clinical Social Work, Graduate Programs, Chicago, IL 60601. Offers PhD. *Program availability:* Part-time. *Degree requirements:* For doctorate, thesis/dissertation, supervised practicum. *Entrance requirements:* For doctorate, 2 years of experience. *Faculty research:* Impact of AIDS on partners, effects of learning disabilities on children and families, clinical social work issues.

Inter American University of Puerto Rico, Metropolitan Campus, Graduate Programs, Program in Social Work, San Juan, PR 00919-1293. Offers advanced clinical services (MSW); advanced social work administration (MSW); clinical services (MSW); social work administration (MSW). *Program availability:* Evening/weekend. *Degree requirements:* For master's, comprehensive exam. *Entrance requirements:* For master's, GRE or EXADEP, interview. Electronic applications accepted.

Jackson State University, Graduate School, College of Public Service, School of Social Work, Jackson, MS 39217. Offers MSW, PhD. *Accreditation:* CSWE (one or more programs are accredited). *Program availability:* Evening/weekend. *Degree requirements:* For master's, comprehensive exam; for doctorate, comprehensive exam, thesis/dissertation. *Entrance requirements:* For master's, GRE General Test; for doctorate, MAT. Additional exam requirements/recommendations for international students: Required—TOEFL (minimum score 520 paper-based; 67 iBT).

Johnson C. Smith University, Program in Social Work, Charlotte, NC 28216-5398. Offers MSW. *Accreditation:* CSWE. *Program availability:* Part-time, evening/weekend. *Degree requirements:* For master's, 60 credit hours (39 for advanced standing) and 900 clock hours of field (500 for advanced standing). *Entrance requirements:* For master's, official transcripts for all colleges attended; 3 references on forms provided; personal statement. Additional exam requirements/recommendations for international students: Required—TOEFL.

Kean University, Nathan Weiss Graduate College, Program in Social Work, Union, NJ 07083. Offers MSW. *Accreditation:* CSWE. *Program availability:* Part-time. *Faculty:* 8 full-time (5 women). *Students:* 161 full-time (133 women), 6 part-time (4 women); includes 119 minority (70 Black or African American, non-Hispanic/Latino; 2 Asian, non-Hispanic/Latino; 44 Hispanic/Latino; 3 Two or more races, non-Hispanic/Latino), 1 international. Average age 31. 191 applicants, 62% accepted, 67 enrolled. In 2017, 42 master's awarded. *Degree requirements:* For master's, field work. *Entrance requirements:* For master's, baccalaureate degree, official transcripts, three letters of recommendation, professional resume/curriculum vitae, personal statement. Additional exam requirements/recommendations for international students: Required—TOEFL (minimum score 550 paper-based; 79 iBT), IELTS (minimum score 6.5). *Application deadline:* For fall admission, 3/1 priority date for domestic and international students. Applications are processed on a rolling basis. Application fee: $75. Electronic applications accepted. *Expenses:* Contact institution. *Financial support:* Scholarships/grants and unspecified assistantships available. Financial award applicants required to submit FAFSA. *Unit head:* Dr. Telvis Rich, Program Coordinator, 908-737-4033, E-mail: terich@kean.edu. *Application contact:* Brittany Gerstenhaber, Admissions Counselor, 908-737-7100, E-mail: grad-adm@kean.edu.
Website: http://grad.kean.edu/msw

Kennesaw State University, WellStar College of Health and Human Services, Program in Social Work, Kennesaw, GA 30144. Offers MSW. *Accreditation:* CSWE. *Entrance requirements:* For master's, GRE, criminal history check, minimum GPA of 2.75, 3 letters of recommendation, resume. Additional exam requirements/recommendations for international students: Required—TOEFL (minimum score 550 paper-based; 80 iBT), IELTS (minimum score 6.5). Electronic applications accepted.

Keuka College, Program in Social Work, Keuka Park, NY 14478. Offers MSW. *Degree requirements:* For master's, field practicum. *Entrance requirements:* For master's, BS in social work. Additional exam requirements/recommendations for international students: Required—TOEFL (minimum score 550 paper-based). Electronic applications accepted. *Expenses:* Contact institution. *Faculty research:* Foster care; maternal health; trauma; family.

Kutztown University of Pennsylvania, College of Liberal Arts and Sciences, Program in Social Work, Kutztown, PA 19530-0730. Offers MSW, DSW. *Accreditation:* CSWE. *Program availability:* Part-time, evening/weekend. *Faculty:* 17 full-time (11 women). *Students:* 64 full-time (56 women), 47 part-time (37 women); includes 27 minority (12 Black or African American, non-Hispanic/Latino; 1 American Indian or Alaska Native, non-Hispanic/Latino; 1 Asian, non-Hispanic/Latino; 10 Hispanic/Latino; 3 Two or more races, non-Hispanic/Latino). Average age 31. 100 applicants, 91% accepted, 56 enrolled. In 2017, 25 master's awarded. *Degree requirements:* For master's, comprehensive exam; for doctorate, thesis/dissertation. *Entrance requirements:* For master's, GRE (except for BSW and other master's degree holders), 3 letters of recommendation, personal and social issues essay (waived for Kutztown University BSW holders); for doctorate, MSW from CSWE-accredited program, 3 letters of recommendation, knowledge statement, personal statement. Additional exam requirements/recommendations for international students: Required—TOEFL (minimum score 550 paper-based, 79 iBT), IELTS (minimum score 6.5), or PTE (minimum score 53). *Application deadline:* For fall admission, 8/1 for domestic and international students; for spring admission, 12/1 for domestic and international students. Application fee: $35. Electronic applications accepted. *Expenses:* Tuition, state resident: part-time $500 per credit. Tuition, nonresident: part-time $750 per credit. *Required fees:* $115 per credit. One-time fee: $50 part-time. Tuition and fees vary according to degree level. *Financial support:* Career-related internships or fieldwork, Federal Work-Study, and unspecified assistantships available. Financial award application deadline: 3/1; financial award applicants required to submit FAFSA. *Unit head:* Dr. John Vafeas, Department Chair, 610-683-4235, E-mail: vafeas@kutztown.edu. *Application contact:* Andrea Snyder, Academic Department Secretary, 610-683-4235, E-mail: asnyder@kutztown.edu.
Website: https://www.kutztown.edu/socialwork

Lakehead University, Graduate Studies, Gerontology Collaborative Program-Northern Educational Center for Aging and Health, Thunder Bay, ON P7B 5E1, Canada. Offers gerontology (M Ed, M Sc, MA, MSW). *Program availability:* Part-time. *Degree requirements:* For master's, thesis (for some programs). *Entrance requirements:* Additional exam requirements/recommendations for international students: Required—TOEFL. *Faculty research:* Integrated health information systems.

Lakehead University, Graduate Studies, School of Social Work, Thunder Bay, ON P7B 5E1, Canada. Offers gerontology (MSW); social work (MSW); women's studies (MSW). *Program availability:* Part-time. *Degree requirements:* For master's, thesis or project. *Entrance requirements:* For master's, minimum B average. Additional exam requirements/recommendations for international students: Required—TOEFL. *Faculty research:* Clinical psychology, social work and practice theory, long-term care, health care for frail elderly, women's studies.

Laurentian University, School of Graduate Studies and Research, School of Social Work, Sudbury, ON P3E 2C6, Canada. Offers MSW. Open only to French-speaking students. *Program availability:* Part-time. *Degree requirements:* For master's, thesis. *Faculty research:* Income security, poverty, violence against women, child poverty, effects of economic crisis on families.

Lewis University, College of Arts and Sciences, Program in Social Work, Romeoville, IL 60446. Offers MSW. *Program availability:* Part-time. *Students:* 7 full-time (all women), 3 part-time (all women); includes 5 minority (2 Black or African American, non-Hispanic/Latino; 3 Hispanic/Latino). Average age 27. *Degree requirements:* For master's, two field placements, capstone paper. *Entrance requirements:* For master's, bachelor's degree, minimum undergraduate GPA of 3.0, two letters of recommendation, personal statement. Additional exam requirements/recommendations for international students: Required—TOEFL (minimum score 550 paper-based; 79 iBT), IELTS (minimum score 6). *Application deadline:* For fall admission, 5/1 priority date for international students; for spring admission, 11/15 priority date for international students. Application fee: $40. Electronic applications accepted. Tuition and fees vary according to program. *Financial support:* Federal Work-Study, health care benefits, and unspecified assistantships available. Financial award application deadline: 5/1; financial award applicants required to submit FAFSA. *Unit head:* Dr. Ellen Thursby, Director, 815-836-5162, E-mail: thursbel@lewisu.edu. *Application contact:* Linda Campbell, Graduate Admissions Counselor, 815-836-5610, E-mail: grad@lewisu.edu.
Website: http://www.lewisu.edu/academics/mssocialwork/index.htm

Loma Linda University, School of Behavioral Health, Department of Social Work and Social Ecology, Loma Linda, CA 92350. Offers criminal justice (MS); gerontology (MS); social policy and social research (PhD); social work (MSW). *Accreditation:* CSWE. *Degree requirements:* For master's, comprehensive exam, thesis optional; for doctorate, comprehensive exam, thesis/dissertation. *Entrance requirements:* For master's and doctorate, GRE General Test. Additional exam requirements/recommendations for international students: Required—TOEFL, Michigan English Language Assessment Battery. Electronic applications accepted.

London Metropolitan University, Graduate Programs, London, United Kingdom. Offers applied psychology (M Sc); architecture (MA); biomedical science (M Sc); blood science (M Sc); cancer pharmacology (M Sc); computer networking and cyber security (M Sc); computing and information systems (M Sc); conference interpreting (MA);

Social Work

counter-terrorism studies (M Sc); creative, digital and professional writing (MA); crime, violence and prevention (M Sc); criminology (M Sc); curating contemporary art (MA); data analytics (M Sc); digital media (MA); early childhood studies (MA); education (MA, Ed D); financial services law, regulation and compliance (LL M); food science (M Sc); forensic psychology (M Sc); health and social care management and policy (M Sc); human nutrition (M Sc); human resource management (MA); human rights and international conflict (MA); information technology (M Sc); intelligence and security studies (MA); international oil, gas and energy law (LL M); international relations (MA); interpreting (MA); learning and teaching in higher education (MA); legal practice (LL M); media and entertainment law (LL M); organizational and consumer psychology (M Sc); psychological therapy (M Sc); psychology of mental health (M Sc); public health (M Sc); public policy and management (MPA); security studies (M Sc); social work (M Sc); spatial planning and urban design (MA); sports therapy (M Sc); supporting older children and young people with dyslexia (MA); teaching languages (MA), including Arabic, English; translation (MA); woman and child abuse (MA).

Long Island University–Brentwood Campus, Graduate Programs, Brentwood, NY 11717. Offers childhood education (MS), including grades 1-6; childhood education/literacy B-6 (MS); childhood education/special education (grades 1-6) (MS); clinical mental health counseling (MS, Advanced Certificate); criminal justice (MS); early childhood education (MS); educational leadership (MS Ed); family nurse practitioner (MS, Advanced Certificate); health administration (MPA); library and information science (MS); literacy (B-6) (MS Ed); school counselor (MS, Advanced Certificate); social work (MSW); special education (MS Ed); students with disabilities generalist (grades 7-12) (Advanced Certificate). *Program availability:* Part-time. *Faculty:* 14 full-time (9 women), 22 part-time/adjunct (11 women). *Students:* 111 full-time (89 women), 47 part-time (34 women); includes 35 minority (8 Black or African American, non-Hispanic/Latino; 1 American Indian or Alaska Native, non-Hispanic/Latino; 3 Asian, non-Hispanic/Latino; 22 Hispanic/Latino; 1 Two or more races, non-Hispanic/Latino), 1 international. Average age 30. 110 applicants, 82% accepted, 63 enrolled. In 2017, 58 master's, 5 other advanced degrees awarded. *Entrance requirements:* For master's and Advanced Certificate, GRE. Additional exam requirements/recommendations for international students: Required—TOEFL or IELTS. *Application deadline:* Applications are processed on a rolling basis. Application fee: $50. Electronic applications accepted. *Expenses: Tuition:* Full-time $21,168; part-time $1201 per credit. *Required fees:* $1840; $920 per term. Tuition and fees vary according to course load. *Financial support:* In 2017–18, 121 students received support. Scholarships/grants available. Support available to part-time students. Financial award application deadline: 2/15; financial award applicants required to submit FAFSA. *Unit head:* Dr. Abby Van Vlerah, Dean and Chief Operating Officer, 631-299-3831, E-mail: abagail.vanvlerah@liu.edu. *Application contact:* Scott Aug, Associate Director of Enrollment Management, 631-287-8506, E-mail: scott.aug@liu.edu.
Website: http://liu.edu/brentwood

Long Island University–LIU Brooklyn, School of Health Professions, Brooklyn, NY 11201-8423. Offers athletic training and sport sciences (MS); community health (MS Ed); exercise science (MS); forensic social work (Advanced Certificate); occupational therapy (MS); physical therapy (DPT); physician assistant (MS); public health (MPH); social work (MSW); speech-language pathology (MS). *Faculty:* 33 full-time (23 women), 82 part-time/adjunct (55 women). *Students:* 690 full-time (508 women), 86 part-time (74 women); includes 259 minority (120 Black or African American, non-Hispanic/Latino; 1 American Indian or Alaska Native, non-Hispanic/Latino; 52 Asian, non-Hispanic/Latino; 76 Hispanic/Latino; 10 Two or more races, non-Hispanic/Latino), 65 international. Average age 27. 1,241 applicants, 45% accepted, 255 enrolled. In 2017, 249 master's, 42 doctorates, 8 other advanced degrees awarded. *Degree requirements:* For master's, comprehensive exam (for some programs), thesis (for some programs); for doctorate, comprehensive exam (for some programs). *Entrance requirements:* For master's and doctorate, GRE. Additional exam requirements/recommendations for international students: Required—TOEFL (minimum score 550 paper-based; 79 iBT). *Application deadline:* Applications are processed on a rolling basis. Application fee: $50. Electronic applications accepted. *Expenses: Tuition:* Full-time $21,618; part-time $1201 per credit. *Required fees:* $1840; $920 per term. Tuition and fees vary according to course load. *Financial support:* In 2017–18, 187 students received support. Research assistantships, teaching assistantships, career-related internships or fieldwork, Federal Work-Study, scholarships/grants, and unspecified assistantships available. Support available to part-time students. Financial award application deadline: 2/15; financial award applicants required to submit FAFSA. *Faculty research:* Pediatric physical therapy, complementary and alternative medicine, global health and human rights, sport leadership and entrepreneurship, feminist sport psychology. *Unit head:* Dr. Barry S. Eckert, Dean, 718-780-6578, Fax: 718-780-4561, E-mail: barry.eckert@liu.edu. *Application contact:* Dr. Dominick Fortugno, Associate Dean, 718-488-1496, Fax: 718-780-4561, E-mail: dominick.fortugno@liu.edu.
Website: http://liu.edu/brooklyn/academics/school-of-health-professions

Long Island University–LIU Post, School of Health Professions and Nursing, Brookville, NY 11548-1300. Offers biomedical science (MS); cardiovascular perfusion (MS); clinical lab sciences (MS); clinical laboratory management (MS); dietetic internship (Advanced Certificate); family nurse practitioner (MS, Advanced Certificate); forensic social work (Advanced Certificate); gerontology (Advanced Certificate); health administration (MPA); non-profit management (Advanced Certificate); nursing education (MS); nutrition (MS); public administration (MPA); social work (MSW). *Program availability:* Part-time, blended/hybrid learning. *Faculty:* 23 full-time (17 women), 33 part-time/adjunct (19 women). *Students:* 228 full-time (174 women), 227 part-time (185 women); includes 172 minority (76 Black or African American, non-Hispanic/Latino; 1 American Indian or Alaska Native, non-Hispanic/Latino; 44 Asian, non-Hispanic/Latino; 48 Hispanic/Latino; 3 Two or more races, non-Hispanic/Latino), 60 international. Average age 31. 392 applicants, 67% accepted, 138 enrolled. In 2017, 180 master's, 26 other advanced degrees awarded. *Degree requirements:* For master's, comprehensive exam (for some programs), thesis (for some programs). *Entrance requirements:* Additional exam requirements/recommendations for international students: Required—TOEFL (minimum score 85 iBT) or IELTS (7.5). *Application deadline:* Applications are processed on a rolling basis. Application fee: $50. Electronic applications accepted. *Expenses: Tuition:* Full-time $21,618; part-time $1201 per credit. *Required fees:* $1840; $920 per term. Tuition and fees vary according to course load. *Financial support:* In 2017–18, 102 students received support. Research assistantships, teaching assistantships, career-related internships or fieldwork, Federal Work-Study, scholarships/grants, and unspecified assistantships available. Support available to part-time students. Financial award application deadline: 2/15; financial award applicants required to submit FAFSA. *Faculty research:* Antibiotic resistance, evidence-based practice, family care, interprofessional learning, simulation learning. *Unit head:* Dr. Stacy Gropack, Dean, 516-299-2485, Fax: 516-299-2527, E-mail: post-shpn@liu.edu. *Application contact:* Kathy Riley, Associate Director of Graduate Admissions, 516-299-2900, Fax: 516-299-2137, E-mail: post-enroll@liu.edu.
Website: http://liu.edu/post/health

Louisiana State University and Agricultural & Mechanical College, Graduate School, College of Human Sciences and Education, School of Social Work, Baton Rouge, LA 70803. Offers MSW, PhD. *Accreditation:* CSWE (one or more programs are accredited). *Faculty:* 15 full-time (11 women). *Students:* 296 full-time (260 women), 107 part-time (97 women); includes 157 minority (122 Black or African American, non-Hispanic/Latino; 4 American Indian or Alaska Native, non-Hispanic/Latino; 3 Asian, non-Hispanic/Latino; 19 Hispanic/Latino; 9 Two or more races, non-Hispanic/Latino), 2 international. Average age 30. 407 applicants, 54% accepted, 167 enrolled. In 2017, 97 master's, 4 doctorates awarded. *Financial support:* In 2017–18, 2 fellowships (averaging $18,238 per year), 8 research assistantships (averaging $22,132 per year), 10 teaching assistantships (averaging $19,332 per year) were awarded. *Total annual research expenditures:* $18,412.

Loyola University Chicago, School of Social Work, Chicago, IL 60660. Offers MSW, PhD, PGC, JD/MSW, M Div/MSW, MJ/MSW, MSW/MA. *Accreditation:* CSWE (one or more programs are accredited). *Program availability:* Part-time. *Degree requirements:* For doctorate, comprehensive exam, thesis/dissertation. *Entrance requirements:* For master's, GRE; for doctorate, GRE or MAT. Additional exam requirements/recommendations for international students: Required—TOEFL (minimum score 550 paper-based; 79 iBT). Tuition and fees vary according to course load, degree level and program. *Faculty research:* Aging, trauma, migration, poverty, substance abuse.

Marshall University, Academic Affairs Division, College of Health Professions, Department of Social Work, Huntington, WV 25755. Offers MSW. *Program availability:* Part-time, online learning. *Students:* 96 full-time (79 women), 3 part-time (2 women); includes 17 minority (13 Black or African American, non-Hispanic/Latino; 4 Two or more races, non-Hispanic/Latino). Average age 33. *Application contact:* Information Contact, 304-746-1900, Fax: 304-746-1902, E-mail: services@marshall.edu.
Website: http://www.marshall.edu/social-work/

Marywood University, Academic Affairs, Center for Interdisciplinary Studies, Scranton, PA 18509-1598. Offers human development (PhD), including educational administration, health promotion, higher education administration, instructional leadership, social work. *Program availability:* Part-time. Electronic applications accepted. *Expenses:* Contact institution.

Marywood University, Academic Affairs, College of Health and Human Services, School of Social Work, Program in Social Work, Scranton, PA 18509-1598. Offers MSW. *Accreditation:* CSWE. *Program availability:* Part-time. *Entrance requirements:* For master's, minimum GPA of 3.0. Electronic applications accepted.

McGill University, Faculty of Graduate and Postdoctoral Studies, Faculty of Arts, School of Social Work, Montréal, QC H3A 2T5, Canada. Offers MSW, PhD, Diploma, MSW/LL B. PhD offered jointly with Université de Montréal.

McMaster University, School of Graduate Studies, Faculty of Social Sciences, School of Social Work, Hamilton, ON L8S 4M2, Canada. Offers analysis of social welfare policy (MSW); analysis of social work practice (MSW). *Program availability:* Part-time. *Entrance requirements:* For master's, minimum B+ average in final year, BSW from accredited program, half course each in introductory statistics and introductory social research methods. Additional exam requirements/recommendations for international students: Required—TOEFL (minimum score 580 paper-based). *Faculty research:* Health policy, income maintenance, child welfare, native issues, immigration policies, racism.

Memorial University of Newfoundland, School of Graduate Studies, School of Social Work, St. John's, NL A1C 5S7, Canada. Offers MSW, PhD. *Degree requirements:* For master's, thesis optional, internship; for doctorate, comprehensive exam, thesis/dissertation, internship, oral thesis defense. *Entrance requirements:* For master's, BSW with a minimum of 2nd-class standing or equivalent; for doctorate, MSW or equivalent, 3 years of post-BSW practice experience. Electronic applications accepted. *Faculty research:* Violence, child abuse, sexual abuse, social policy, gerontology.

Metropolitan State University of Denver, College of Letters, Arts and Sciences, Denver, CO 80204. Offers individual and families (MSW); macro practice (MSW); social work (MSW). *Accreditation:* CSWE. *Degree requirements:* For master's, field work. *Expenses:* Contact institution.

Michigan State University, The Graduate School, College of Social Science, School of Social Work, East Lansing, MI 48824. Offers clinical social work (MSW); organizational and community practice (MSW); social work (PhD). *Accreditation:* CSWE. *Program availability:* Part-time, online learning. *Entrance requirements:* Additional exam requirements/recommendations for international students: Required—TOEFL. Electronic applications accepted.

Middle Tennessee State University, College of Graduate Studies, College of Behavioral and Health Sciences, Department of Social Work, Murfreesboro, TN 37132. Offers MSW. *Accreditation:* CSWE. *Entrance requirements:* Additional exam requirements/recommendations for international students: Required—TOEFL (minimum score 525 paper-based; 71 iBT), IELTS (minimum score 6). Electronic applications accepted.

Millersville University of Pennsylvania, College of Graduate Studies and Adult Learning, College of Education and Human Services, School of Social Work, Doctor of Social Work Program, Millersville, PA 17551-0302. Offers DSW. *Program availability:* Part-time-only, evening/weekend, coursework completed primarily online, with a weekend residency once a semester. *Faculty:* 12 full-time (10 women), 4 part-time/adjunct (all women). *Students:* 23 part-time (19 women); includes 5 minority (2 Black or African American, non-Hispanic/Latino; 2 Asian, non-Hispanic/Latino; 1 Hispanic/Latino). Average age 43. 9 applicants, 100% accepted, 7 enrolled. *Degree requirements:* For doctorate, thesis/dissertation, weekend residency. *Entrance requirements:* For doctorate, resume; writing sample; MSW. Additional exam requirements/recommendations for international students: Required—TOEFL (minimum score 80 iBT), IELTS (minimum score 6.5), PTE (minimum score 60). *Application deadline:* Applications are processed on a rolling basis. Application fee: $40. Electronic applications accepted. *Expenses:* $650 per credit resident tuition, $975 per credit non-resident tuition. *Financial support:* Unspecified assistantships available. Financial award application deadline: 3/15; financial award applicants required to submit FAFSA. *Faculty research:* Food insecurity of college students; enhancing compassion and social justice advocacy through inter-group dialogue; bridging the gap through social empathy skills; understanding students' sense of belonging on college campuses. *Unit head:* Dr. Karen M. Rice, Chair, 717-871-5279, Fax: 717-871-7941, E-mail: karen.rice@millersville.edu. *Application contact:* Dr. Victor S. DeSantis, Dean of College of Graduate Studies and Adult Learning/Associate Provost for Civic and Community Engagement, 717-871-7619, Fax: 717-871-7954, E-mail: victor.desantis@millersville.edu.
Website: http://www.millersville.edu/socialwork/dsw/index.php

Millersville University of Pennsylvania, College of Graduate Studies and Adult Learning, College of Education and Human Services, School of Social Work, Master of Social Work Program, Millersville, PA 17551-0302. Offers MSW. *Accreditation:* CSWE. *Program availability:* Part-time, evening/weekend. *Faculty:* 12 full-time (10 women), 4 part-time/adjunct (all women). *Students:* 56 full-time (50 women), 74 part-time (66 women); includes 30 minority (11 Black or African American, non-Hispanic/Latino; 2 American Indian or Alaska Native, non-Hispanic/Latino; 1 Asian, non-Hispanic/Latino; 16 Hispanic/Latino). Average age 29. 102 applicants, 92% accepted, 63 enrolled. In 2017, 66 master's awarded. *Degree requirements:* For master's, field practicum.

Entrance requirements: For master's, GRE or MAT if GPA from all coursework is lower than 2.8, resume, all transcripts, at least 1 academic and 1 supervisory reference (specialized recommendation form). Additional exam requirements/recommendations for international students: Required—TOEFL (minimum score 80 iBT), IELTS (minimum score 6.5), PTE (minimum score 60). *Application deadline:* For summer admission, 2/1 for domestic students. Application fee: $40. Electronic applications accepted. *Expenses:* $500 per credit resident tuition and fees; $750 per credit non-resident tuition and fees; $114.75 per credit general fee (maximum of 12 credits); technology fee $27 per credit (resident), $39 per credit (non-resident). *Financial support:* In 2017–18, 21 students received support. Unspecified assistantships available. Financial award application deadline: 3/15; financial award applicants required to submit FAFSA. *Faculty research:* Food insecurity of college students; enhancing compassion and social justice advocacy through intergroup dialogue; bridging the gap through social empathy skills; understanding students' sense of belonging on college campuses. *Unit head:* Dr. Karen M. Rice, Chair, 717-871-5279, Fax: 717-871-7941, E-mail: karen.rice@millersville.edu. *Application contact:* Dr. Victor S. DeSantis, Dean of College of Graduate Studies and Adult Learning/Associate Provost for Civic and Community Engagement, 717-871-7619, Fax: 717-871-7954, E-mail: victor.desantis@millersville.edu.
Website: http://www.millersville.edu/socialwork/msw/index.php

Minnesota State University Mankato, College of Graduate Studies and Research, College of Social and Behavioral Sciences, Department of Social Work, Mankato, MN 56001. Offers MSW. *Accreditation:* CSWE. *Entrance requirements:* Additional exam requirements/recommendations for international students: Required—TOEFL.

Missouri State University, Graduate College, College of Health and Human Services, School of Social Work, Springfield, MO 65897. Offers MSW. *Accreditation:* CSWE. *Program availability:* Part-time. *Faculty:* 10 full-time (9 women), 10 part-time/adjunct (7 women). *Students:* 19 full-time (16 women), 44 part-time (36 women); includes 7 minority (3 Black or African American, non-Hispanic/Latino; 1 Asian, non-Hispanic/Latino; 3 Two or more races, non-Hispanic/Latino). Average age 31. 54 applicants, 37% accepted, 19 enrolled. In 2017, 31 master's awarded. *Degree requirements:* For master's, comprehensive exam, thesis or alternative. *Entrance requirements:* For master's, GRE, minimum GPA of 3.0. Additional exam requirements/recommendations for international students: Required—TOEFL (minimum score 550 paper-based; 79 iBT), IELTS (minimum score 6). *Application deadline:* For fall admission, 1/31 priority date for domestic and international students. Application fee: $35 ($50 for international students). Electronic applications accepted. *Expenses:* Tuition, state resident: full-time $2915; part-time $2021 per credit hour. Tuition, nonresident: full-time $5354; part-time $3647 per credit hour. *International tuition:* $11,992 full-time. *Required fees:* $173; $173 per credit hour. Tuition and fees vary according to class time, course level, course load, degree level, campus/location and program. *Financial support:* Federal Work-Study, institutionally sponsored loans, scholarships/grants, and unspecified assistantships available. Financial award application deadline: 3/31; financial award applicants required to submit FAFSA. *Faculty research:* Child and family therapy, rural social work, adolescent social issues, domestic violence. *Unit head:* Michele Day, Department Head, 417-836-6967, Fax: 417-836-7688, E-mail: swk@missouristate.edu. *Application contact:* Stephanie Praschan, Director, Graduate Enrollment Management, 417-836-5330, Fax: 417-836-6200, E-mail: stephaniepraschan@missouristate.edu.
Website: http://www.missouristate.edu/swk/

Monmouth University, Graduate Studies, School of Social Work, West Long Branch, NJ 07764-1898. Offers clinical practice with families and children (MSW); international and community development (MSW); play therapy (Certificate). *Accreditation:* CSWE. *Program availability:* Part-time, evening/weekend. *Faculty:* 12 full-time (8 women), 22 part-time/adjunct (18 women). *Students:* 102 full-time (97 women), 100 part-time (77 women); includes 73 minority (34 Black or African American, non-Hispanic/Latino; 1 American Indian or Alaska Native, non-Hispanic/Latino; 3 Asian, non-Hispanic/Latino; 28 Hispanic/Latino; 7 Two or more races, non-Hispanic/Latino). Average age 30. In 2017, 119 master's awarded. *Degree requirements:* For master's, thesis, internship. *Entrance requirements:* For master's, minimum GPA of 3.0 in major, 2.75 overall with college course each in English, math, biology, and psychology (preferred additional work in history, sociology, political science, anthropology, and economics); three recommendation forms; autobiographical statement form; for Certificate, master's degree in medical or mental health discipline and eligibility for licensure in that discipline. Additional exam requirements/recommendations for international students: Required—TOEFL (minimum score 550 paper-based, 79 iBT), IELTS (minimum score 6), Michigan English Language Assessment Battery (minimum score 77) or Certificate of Advanced English (minimum score 160). *Application deadline:* For fall admission, 3/15 for domestic and international students. Applications are processed on a rolling basis. Application fee: $50. Electronic applications accepted. *Expenses:* Tuition: Full-time $21,366; part-time $7122 per credit. *Required fees:* $700; $175 per term. *Financial support:* In 2017–18, 75 students received support. Institutionally sponsored loans, scholarships/grants, and unspecified assistantships available. Support available to part-time students. Financial award applicants required to submit FAFSA. *Faculty research:* Child welfare citizen participation, cultural diversity, diversity issues, employee help. *Unit head:* Dr. Carolyn Bradley, Program Director, 732-263-5477, Fax: 732-263-5217, E-mail: cbradley@monmouth.edu. *Application contact:* Lucia Fedele, Graduate Admission Counselor, 732-571-3452, Fax: 732-263-5123, E-mail: gradm@monmouth.edu.
Website: https://www.monmouth.edu/graduate/msw-social-work/

Morgan State University, School of Graduate Studies, School of Social Work, Baltimore, MD 21251. Offers MSW. *Accreditation:* CSWE. *Application deadline:* Applications are processed on a rolling basis. Application fee: $0. *Expenses:* Tuition, state resident: part-time $433 per credit. Tuition, nonresident: part-time $851 per credit. *Required fees:* $81.50 per credit. *Unit head:* Dr. Melissa Littlefield, Chairperson, 443-885-4300, E-mail: melissa.littlefield@morgan.edu. *Application contact:* Dr. Dean Campbell, Graduate Recruitment Specialist, 443-885-3185, Fax: 443-885-8226, E-mail: dean.campbell@morgan.edu.

Nazareth College of Rochester, Graduate Studies, Department of Social Work, Rochester, NY 14618. Offers MSW. Program offered jointly with The College at Brockport, State University of New York. *Program availability:* Part-time, evening/weekend. *Entrance requirements:* For master's, minimum GPA of 3.0. Additional exam requirements/recommendations for international students: Required—TOEFL (minimum score 550 paper-based, 79 iBT) or IELTS (6.5). Electronic applications accepted. *Expenses:* Contact institution.

Newman University, School of Social Work, Wichita, KS 67213-2097. Offers MSW. *Accreditation:* CSWE. *Program availability:* Online learning. *Degree requirements:* For master's, comprehensive exam (for some programs), thesis optional, fieldwork. *Entrance requirements:* For master's, minimum GPA of 3.0, 3 letters of reference. Additional exam requirements/recommendations for international students: Required—TOEFL (minimum score 600 paper-based; 100 iBT). *Expenses:* Contact institution.

New Mexico Highlands University, Graduate Studies, Facundo Valdez School of Social Work, Las Vegas, NM 87701. Offers bilingual/bicultural clinical practice (MSW); clinical practice (MSW). *Accreditation:* CSWE. *Program availability:* Part-time. *Degree requirements:* For master's, comprehensive exam, thesis or alternative. *Entrance requirements:* For master's, minimum undergraduate GPA of 3.0. Additional exam

requirements/recommendations for international students: Required—TOEFL (minimum score 540 paper-based). *Faculty research:* Treatment attrition among domestic violence batterers, children's health and mental health, Dejando Huellas: meeting the bilingual/bicultural needs of the Latino mental health patient, impact of culture on the therapeutic process, effects of generational gang involvement on adolescents' future.

New Mexico State University, College of Health and Social Services, School of Social Work, Las Cruces, NM 88003. Offers MSW. *Accreditation:* CSWE. *Program availability:* Part-time, online learning. *Faculty:* 10 full-time (8 women), 9 part-time/adjunct (6 women). *Students:* 96 full-time (81 women), 8 part-time (all women); includes 76 minority (3 Black or African American, non-Hispanic/Latino; 2 American Indian or Alaska Native, non-Hispanic/Latino; 1 Asian, non-Hispanic/Latino; 67 Hispanic/Latino; 3 Two or more races, non-Hispanic/Latino). Average age 32. 79 applicants, 70% accepted, 36 enrolled. In 2017, 68 master's awarded. *Entrance requirements:* For master's, minimum cumulative GPA of 3.0. Additional exam requirements/recommendations for international students: Required—TOEFL (minimum score 550 paper-based; 79 iBT), IELTS (minimum score 6.5). *Application deadline:* For fall admission, 1/16 priority date for domestic students, 2/16 priority date for international students. Applications are processed on a rolling basis. Application fee: $40 ($50 for international students). Electronic applications accepted. *Expenses:* Tuition, state resident: full-time $4390. Tuition, nonresident: full-time $15,309. *Required fees:* $853. *Financial support:* In 2017–18, 46 students received support, including 7 research assistantships (averaging $8,482 per year), 1 teaching assistantship (averaging $8,482 per year); career-related internships or fieldwork, Federal Work-Study, scholarships/grants, traineeships, health care benefits, and unspecified assistantships also available. Support available to part-time students. Financial award application deadline: 3/1. *Faculty research:* Mental health, gerontology, community-based social work, domestic violence, immigration, child welfare. *Total annual research expenditures:* $18,234. *Unit head:* Dr. Ivan de la Rosa, Interim Director, 575-646-2143, Fax: 575-646-4116, E-mail: lilo@nmsu.edu. *Application contact:* Dr. Wanda Whittlesey-Jerome, Program Coordinator, 575-646-0322, Fax: 575-646-4116, E-mail: wkjerome@nmsu.edu.
Website: http://socialwork.nmsu.edu/

New York University, Silver School of Social Work, New York, NY 10003. Offers MSW, PhD, MSW/JD, MSW/MA, MSW/MPA, MSW/MPH. *Accreditation:* CSWE (one or more programs are accredited). *Program availability:* Part-time, evening/weekend. *Students:* 772 full-time (668 women), 333 part-time (279 women); includes 369 minority (123 Black or African American, non-Hispanic/Latino; 1 American Indian or Alaska Native, non-Hispanic/Latino; 65 Asian, non-Hispanic/Latino; 160 Hispanic/Latino; 1 Native Hawaiian or other Pacific Islander, non-Hispanic/Latino; 19 Two or more races, non-Hispanic/Latino), 86 international. Average age 30. 1,568 applicants, 89% accepted, 498 enrolled. In 2017, 526 master's, 1 doctorate awarded. *Degree requirements:* For doctorate, comprehensive exam, thesis/dissertation. *Entrance requirements:* For master's, bachelor's degree; for doctorate, GRE, MSW. Additional exam requirements/recommendations for international students: Required—TOEFL, IELTS, TWE. *Application deadline:* For fall admission, 1/9 priority date for domestic and international students; for spring admission, 10/3 priority date for domestic and international students. Applications are processed on a rolling basis. Application fee: $60. Electronic applications accepted. *Expenses:* Contact institution. *Financial support:* In 2017–18, 995 students received support. Career-related internships or fieldwork, Federal Work-Study, scholarships/grants, health care benefits, tuition waivers (partial), and unspecified assistantships available. Support available to part-time students. Financial award application deadline: 3/1; financial award applicants required to submit FAFSA. *Faculty research:* Social welfare policies, public health, aging, mental health, substance abuse. *Unit head:* Dr. Lynn Videka, Dean, 212-998-5959, Fax: 212-995-4172. *Application contact:* Robert W. Sommo, Jr., Assistant Dean for Enrollment Services, 212-998-5910, Fax: 212-995-4171, E-mail: ssw.admissions@nyu.edu.
Website: http://www.socialwork.nyu.edu/

Norfolk State University, School of Graduate Studies, Ethelyn R. Strong School of Social Work, Norfolk, VA 23504. Offers MSW, PhD. *Accreditation:* CSWE (one or more programs are accredited). *Program availability:* Part-time. *Degree requirements:* For doctorate, thesis/dissertation. *Entrance requirements:* For master's, minimum GPA of 2.7. Additional exam requirements/recommendations for international students: Required—TOEFL.

North Carolina Agricultural and Technical State University, School of Graduate Studies, College of Arts and Sciences, Department of Sociology and Social Work, Greensboro, NC 27411. Offers MSW. Joint program with The University of North Carolina at Greensboro. *Accreditation:* CSWE. *Program availability:* Part-time, evening/weekend. *Degree requirements:* For master's, comprehensive exam, qualifying exam. *Entrance requirements:* For master's, GRE General Test.

North Carolina State University, Graduate School, College of Humanities and Social Sciences, Department of Social Work, Raleigh, NC 27695. Offers MSW. *Accreditation:* CSWE.

Northern Kentucky University, Office of Graduate Programs, College of Education and Human Services, Program in Social Work, Highland Heights, KY 41099. Offers MSW. *Accreditation:* CSWE. *Program availability:* Part-time, evening/weekend. *Entrance requirements:* For master's, GRE (minimum score of 1000), minimum GPA of 3.0; undergraduate courses in psychology, sociology, and statistics with minimum C average; 3 letters of recommendation; essay; letter of intent; resume; interview. Additional exam requirements/recommendations for international students: Required—TOEFL (minimum score 79 iBT); Recommended—IELTS (minimum score 6.5). Electronic applications accepted. *Faculty research:* Children and families experiencing homelessness, team-based learning and diversity, impact of mentoring, photovoice and barriers to college, family directed structural therapy.

Northwest Nazarene University, Program in Social Work, Nampa, ID 83686-5897. Offers clinical mental health and addictions practice (MSW). *Accreditation:* CSWE. *Program availability:* Part-time-only, evening/weekend. *Students:* Average age 27. 152 applicants, 54% accepted, 73 enrolled. In 2017, 54 master's awarded. *Degree requirements:* For master's, comprehensive exam, thesis or alternative. *Entrance requirements:* For master's, interview, letters of reference, degree from regionally-accredited college/university, written personal statement. *Application deadline:* Applications are processed on a rolling basis. Application fee: $50. Electronic applications accepted. *Faculty research:* Test anxiety, trauma, statistics. *Unit head:* Dr. Lawanna Lancaster, Director/Department Chair, 208-467-8372, Fax: 208-467-8879, E-mail: mswinfo@nnu.edu. *Application contact:* Jodie Rodriguez-Engel, Program Coordinator, 208-467-8679, Fax: 208-467-8879, E-mail: jrodriguez-engel@nnu.edu.
Website: http://msw.nnu.edu

Nyack College, School of Social Work, Nyack, NY 10960. Offers clinical social work practice (MSW); leadership in organizations and communities (MSW). *Program availability:* Part-time, evening/weekend. *Students:* 58 full-time (50 women), 27 part-time (21 women); includes 79 minority (50 Black or African American, non-Hispanic/Latino; 5 Asian, non-Hispanic/Latino; 21 Hispanic/Latino; 1 Two or more races, non-Hispanic/Latino), 3 international. Average age 36. In 2017, 15 master's awarded. *Degree requirements:* For master's, field work. *Entrance requirements:* For master's, official

Social Work

transcripts, academic and professional references, personal statement, essay or case reflection. Additional exam requirements/recommendations for international students: Required—TOEFL (minimum score 550 paper-based; 80 iBT). *Application deadline:* Applications are processed on a rolling basis. Application fee: $45. Electronic applications accepted. *Expenses:* $800 per credit. *Financial support:* Scholarships/ grants available. Financial award applicants required to submit FAFSA. *Unit head:* Dr. Janet Furness, Director of MSW Program, 646-378-6169. *Application contact:* DeLissa Dixon, Admissions Associate, 646-378-6105, E-mail: admissions.grad@nyack.edu. Website: https://www.nyack.edu/msw

The Ohio State University, Graduate School, College of Social Work, Columbus, OH 43210. Offers MSW, PhD. *Accreditation:* CSWE (one or more programs are accredited). *Program availability:* Part-time. *Faculty:* 29. *Students:* 471 full-time (395 women), 117 part-time (100 women); includes 108 minority (61 Black or African American, non-Hispanic/Latino; 7 Asian, non-Hispanic/Latino; 19 Hispanic/Latino; 21 Two or more races, non-Hispanic/Latino), 16 international. Average age 28. In 2017, 242 master's, 6 doctorates awarded. *Degree requirements:* For master's, thesis optional; for doctorate, thesis/dissertation. *Entrance requirements:* For master's and doctorate, GRE. Additional exam requirements/recommendations for international students: Required—TOEFL (minimum score 550 paper-based; 79 iBT), Michigan English Language Assessment Battery (minimum score 82); Recommended—IELTS (minimum score 7). *Application deadline:* For fall admission, 12/13 priority date for domestic students, 11/30 priority date for international students; for summer admission, 4/1 for domestic students, 3/1 for international students. Applications are processed on a rolling basis. Application fee: $60 ($70 for international students). Electronic applications accepted. *Financial support:* Fellowships, research assistantships, teaching assistantships, Federal Work-Study, institutionally sponsored loans, and unspecified assistantships available. Support available to part-time students. *Unit head:* Dr. Tom Gregoire, Dean, 614-292-9426, E-mail: gregoire.5@osu.edu. *Application contact:* Graduate and Professional Admissions, 614-292-6031, Fax: 614-292-3656, E-mail: gpadmissions@osu.edu. Website: http://csw.osu.edu

The Ohio State University at Lima, Graduate Programs, Lima, OH 45804. Offers social work (MSW). *Program availability:* Part-time. *Faculty:* 33. *Students:* 4 (3 women). Terminal master's awarded for partial completion of doctoral program. *Degree requirements:* For master's, comprehensive exam (for some programs), thesis (for some programs). *Entrance requirements:* For master's, GRE (in some cases), minimum GPA of 3.0. Additional exam requirements/recommendations for international students: Required—TOEFL (minimum score 550 paper-based, 79 iBT), IELTS (minimum score 7), or Michigan English Language Assessment Battery (minimum score 82). *Application deadline:* For fall admission, 4/1 for domestic students, 3/1 for international students; for spring admission, 10/15 for domestic and international students; for summer admission, 4/10 for domestic students, 3/1 for international students. Applications are processed on a rolling basis. Application fee: $60 ($70 for international students). Electronic applications accepted. *Financial support:* Application deadline: 2/15. *Unit head:* Dr. Joseph Brandesky, Dean and Director, 419-995-8600, E-mail: brandesky.1@osu.edu. *Application contact:* Graduate and Professional Admissions, 614-292-9444, Fax: 614-292-3895, E-mail: gpadmissions@osu.edu.

The Ohio State University at Mansfield, Graduate Programs, Mansfield, OH 44906-1599. Offers education (MA); social work (MSW). *Program availability:* Part-time. *Faculty:* 39. *Students:* 1. *Degree requirements:* For master's, comprehensive exam (for some programs), thesis (for some programs). *Entrance requirements:* For master's, GRE, minimum GPA of 3.0. Additional exam requirements/recommendations for international students: Required—TOEFL (minimum 550 paper-based, 79 iBT), IELTS (minimum score 7) or Michigan English Language Assessment Battery (minimum score 82). *Application deadline:* For fall admission, 4/1 for domestic students, 3/1 for international students; for spring admission, 10/15 for domestic and international students. Applications are processed on a rolling basis. Application fee: $60 ($70 for international students). Electronic applications accepted. *Financial support:* Teaching assistantships with full tuition reimbursements, Federal Work-Study, and scholarships/ grants available. Support available to part-time students. Financial award application deadline: 2/15; financial award applicants required to submit FAFSA. *Unit head:* Dr. Norman W. Jones, Interim Dean and Director, E-mail: jones.2376@osu.edu. *Application contact:* Graduate and Professional Admissions, 614-292-9444, Fax: 614-292-3895, E-mail: gpadmissions@osu.edu.

The Ohio State University at Newark, Graduate Programs, Newark, OH 43055-1797. Offers education - teaching and learning (MA); social work (MSW). *Program availability:* Part-time. *Faculty:* 49. *Students:* 13 (12 women). Average age 33. Terminal master's awarded for partial completion of doctoral program. *Degree requirements:* For master's, comprehensive exam (for some programs), thesis (for some programs). *Entrance requirements:* For master's, GRE, minimum GPA of 3.0. Additional exam requirements/ recommendations for international students: Required—TOEFL (minimum score 550 paper-based; 79 iBT), IELTS (minimum score 7), or Michigan English Language Assessment Battery (minimum score 82). *Application deadline:* For fall admission, 3/1 for domestic and international students. Applications are processed on a rolling basis. Application fee: $60 ($70 for international students). Electronic applications accepted. *Financial support:* Application deadline: 2/15. *Unit head:* Dr. William L. MacDonald, Dean and Director, 740-366-9333 Ext. 330, E-mail: macdonald.24@osu.edu. *Application contact:* Graduate and Professional Admissions, 614-292-9444, Fax: 614-292-3985, E-mail: gpadmissions@osu.edu.

Ohio University, Graduate College, College of Health Sciences and Professions, Department of Social and Public Health, Program in Social Work, Athens, OH 45701-2979. Offers MSW. *Accreditation:* CSWE. *Program availability:* Part-time. *Degree requirements:* For master's, fieldwork. *Entrance requirements:* For master's, GRE General Test or minimum GPA of 3.0, liberal arts background with coursework in human biology, statistics, and three social science areas; paid or volunteer work in human services. Additional exam requirements/recommendations for international students: Required—TOEFL (minimum score 620 paper-based; 105 iBT) or IELTS (minimum score 7.5). Electronic applications accepted. *Faculty research:* Violence, families, rural life.

Our Lady of the Lake University, Worden School of Social Service, San Antonio, TX 78207-4689. Offers social work (MSW). *Accreditation:* CSWE. *Program availability:* Part-time, evening/weekend, 100% online, blended/hybrid learning. *Faculty:* 3 full-time (all women), 92 part-time/adjunct (77 women). *Students:* 775 full-time (702 women), 131 part-time (122 women); includes 557 minority (274 Black or African American, non-Hispanic/Latino; 283 Hispanic/Latino). Average age 35. 296 applicants, 90% accepted, 188 enrolled. In 2017, 339 master's awarded. *Entrance requirements:* For master's, official transcripts demonstrating minimum cumulative GPA of 2.5, 3 letters of recommendation, personal statement, current resume. Additional exam requirements/ recommendations for international students: Required—TOEFL. *Application deadline:* For fall admission, 6/15 for domestic and international students; for spring admission, 11/15 for domestic and international students; for summer admission, 4/15 for domestic and international students. Applications are processed on a rolling basis. Application fee: $40 ($50 for international students). Electronic applications accepted. *Expenses:* Tuition: Full-time $10,668; part-time $5334 per year. *Required fees:* $816; $816 per

year. $408 per semester. *Financial support:* In 2017–18, 35 students received support, including 1 research assistantship (averaging $15,300 per year); teaching assistantships, Federal Work-Study, scholarships/grants, unspecified assistantships, and tuition discounts also available. Support available to part-time students. Financial award application deadline: 5/1; financial award applicants required to submit FAFSA. *Faculty research:* Acculturation, mindfulness, pedagogy, spirituality, child welfare. *Unit head:* Rebecca Gomez, Program Director, 210-434-6711 Ext. 5578, E-mail: rjgomez@ ollusa.edu. *Application contact:* Office of Graduate Admissions, 210-431-3995, Fax: 210-431-3945, E-mail: gradadm@lake.ollusa.edu. Website: http://www.ollusa.edu/s/1190/hybrid/default-hybrid-ollu.aspx?sid-1190&gid-1&pgid-7916

Pacific University, Program in Social Work, Forest Grove, OR 97116-1797. Offers MSW.

Park University, School of Graduate and Professional Studies, Kansas City, MO 54105. Offers adult education (M Ed); business and government leadership (Graduate Certificate); business, government, and global society (MPA); communication and leadership (MA); creative and life writing (Graduate Certificate); disaster and emergency management (MPA, Graduate Certificate); educational leadership (M Ed); finance (MBA, Graduate Certificate); general business (MBA); global business (Graduate Certificate); healthcare administration (MHA); healthcare services management and leadership (Graduate Certificate); international business (MBA); language and literacy (M Ed), including English for speakers of other languages, special reading teacher/ literacy coach; leadership of international healthcare organizations (Graduate Certificate); management information systems (MBA, Graduate Certificate); music performance (ADP, Graduate Certificate), including cello (MM, ADP), piano (MM, ADP), viola (MM, ADP), violin (MM, ADP); nonprofit and community services management (MPA); nonprofit leadership (Graduate Certificate); performance (MM), including cello (MM, ADP), piano (MM, ADP), viola (MM, ADP), violin (MM, ADP); public management (MPA); social work (MSW); teacher leadership (M Ed), including curriculum and assessment, instructional leader. *Program availability:* Part-time, evening/weekend, online learning. *Degree requirements:* For master's, comprehensive exam (for some programs), thesis (for some programs), internship (for some programs); exam (for some programs). *Entrance requirements:* For master's, GRE or GMAT (for some programs), teacher certification (for some M Ed programs), letters of recommendation, essay, resume (for some programs). Additional exam requirements/recommendations for international students: Required—TOEFL (minimum score 550 paper-based; 79 iBT), IELTS (minimum score 6). Electronic applications accepted.

Phillips Theological Seminary, Programs in Theology, Tulsa, OK 74116. Offers administration of church agencies (M Div); campus ministry (M Div); church-related social work (M Div); college and seminary teaching (M Div); global mission work (M Div); institutional chaplaincy (M Div); ministerial vocations in Christian education (M Div); ministry (D Min), including parish ministry, pastoral counseling, practices of ministry; ministry and culture (MAMC), including Christian education, congregational leadership, history and practice of Christian spirituality, theology, ethics, and culture; ministry of music (M Div); pastoral care and counseling (M Div); pastoral ministry (M Div); theological studies (MTS). *Accreditation:* ATS. *Program availability:* Part-time, online learning. *Degree requirements:* For master's, thesis (for some programs); for doctorate, thesis/dissertation. *Entrance requirements:* For master's, minimum GPA of 2.5; for doctorate, M Div, minimum GPA of 3.0. *Faculty research:* Biblical studies, historical studies, theology and culture, practical theology, theology and film.

Pontifical Catholic University of Puerto Rico, College of Graduate Studies in Behavioral Science and Community Affairs, Program in Clinical Social Work, Ponce, PR 00717-0777. Offers MSW. *Accreditation:* CSWE. *Program availability:* Part-time, evening/weekend. *Entrance requirements:* For master's, EXADEP, 3 letters of recommendation, interview, minimum GPA of 2.75.

Portland State University, Graduate Studies, School of Social Work, Portland, OR 97207-0751. Offers social work (MSW); social work and social research (PhD). *Accreditation:* CSWE (one or more programs are accredited). *Program availability:* Part-time. *Faculty:* 33 full-time (26 women), 46 part-time/adjunct (33 women). *Students:* 382 full-time (304 women), 232 part-time (197 women); includes 160 minority (29 Black or African American, non-Hispanic/Latino; 14 American Indian or Alaska Native, non-Hispanic/Latino; 23 Asian, non-Hispanic/Latino; 64 Hispanic/Latino; 1 Native Hawaiian or other Pacific Islander, non-Hispanic/Latino; 29 Two or more races, non-Hispanic/ Latino), 4 international. Average age 34. 624 applicants, 42% accepted, 195 enrolled. In 2017, 205 master's, 4 doctorates awarded. *Degree requirements:* For master's, two 500-hour field placements; for doctorate, comprehensive exam, thesis/dissertation, residency. *Entrance requirements:* For master's, minimum GPA of 3.0 in upper-division course work or 2.75 overall, resume, 3 letters of reference, 3-4 page statement of purpose; for doctorate, GRE General Test, 4 references. Additional exam requirements/ recommendations for international students: Required—TOEFL (minimum score 550 paper-based; 80 iBT). *Application deadline:* For fall admission, 2/1 for domestic and international students. Application fee: $65. *Expenses:* Contact institution. *Financial support:* In 2017–18, 88 students received support, including 12 research assistantships with full and partial tuition reimbursements available (averaging $11,761 per year), 3 teaching assistantships with full and partial tuition reimbursements available (averaging $12,720 per year); career-related internships or fieldwork, Federal Work-Study, scholarships/grants, tuition waivers (full and partial), and unspecified assistantships also available. Support available to part-time students. Financial award application deadline: 3/1; financial award applicants required to submit FAFSA. *Faculty research:* Child welfare; child mental health; social welfare policies and services; work, family, and dependent care; adult mental health. *Total annual research expenditures:* $18 million. *Unit head:* Dr. Laura B. Nissen, Dean, 503-725-3997, Fax: 503-725-5545, E-mail: nissen@pdx.edu. *Application contact:* William Donlan, Director of MSW Program, 503-725-8977, E-mail: donlan@pdx.edu. Website: https://www.pdx.edu/ssw/

Quinnipiac University, School of Health Sciences, Program in Social Work, Hamden, CT 06518-1940. Offers MSW. *Accreditation:* CSWE. *Faculty:* 5 full-time (all women), 4 part-time/adjunct (3 women). *Students:* 51 full-time (38 women), 14 part-time (13 women); includes 15 minority (9 Black or African American, non-Hispanic/Latino; 1 Asian, non-Hispanic/Latino; 5 Hispanic/Latino). 72 applicants, 90% accepted, 25 enrolled. In 2017, 31 master's awarded. *Entrance requirements:* For master's, bachelor's degree with at least 20 semester credits in liberal arts and a course in statistics with minimum C grade; minimum GPA of 3.0. *Application deadline:* For fall admission, 3/15 for domestic students; for spring admission, 11/15 for domestic students. Applications are processed on a rolling basis. Application fee: $45. Electronic applications accepted. *Financial support:* Federal Work-Study, scholarships/grants, and unspecified assistantships available. Financial award application deadline: 6/1; financial award applicants required to submit FAFSA. *Faculty research:* Older adult sexuality, social work practice in health settings, gerontology and social work, adolescent sexuality, prevention programs in social work practice, international social work, evidence-based treatments for children and families, organizational practice, inter-professional education, curriculum development in social work education and inter-professional practice, stress reduction approaches in clinical practice and professional

education. *Unit head:* Deborah Rejent, MSW Program Director, 203-582-6433, E-mail: graduate@qu.edu. *Application contact:* Office of Graduate Admissions, 800-462-1944, Fax: 203-582-3443, E-mail: graduate@qu.edu.
Website: http://www.qu.edu/msw

Radford University, College of Graduate Studies and Research, Program in Social Work, Radford, VA 24142. Offers MSW. *Accreditation:* CSWE. *Program availability:* Part-time. *Faculty:* 9 full-time (7 women), 10 part-time/adjunct (9 women). *Students:* 48 full-time (39 women), 66 part-time (55 women); includes 32 minority (24 Black or African American, non-Hispanic/Latino; 1 Asian, non-Hispanic/Latino; 4 Hispanic/Latino; 3 Two or more races, non-Hispanic/Latino). Average age 30. 90 applicants, 77% accepted, 51 enrolled. In 2017, 34 master's awarded. *Degree requirements:* For master's, comprehensive exam. *Entrance requirements:* For master's, minimum GPA of 2.75, 3.0 in last 60 hours of upper-division coursework; 3 letters of reference; personal essay; case study; previous experience in the field of human services; legal/military history form; resume; official transcripts. Additional exam requirements/recommendations for international students: Required—TOEFL (minimum score 550 paper-based; 79 iBT), IELTS (minimum score 6.5). *Application deadline:* For fall admission, 2/15 priority date for domestic students, 12/1 for international students; for spring admission, 7/1 for international students. Applications are processed on a rolling basis. Application fee: $50. Electronic applications accepted. *Expenses:* Tuition, state resident: full-time $8336; part-time $347 per credit hour. Tuition, nonresident: full-time $16,862; part-time $702 per credit hour. *Required fees:* $3220; $135 per credit hour. Tuition and fees vary according to course load and program. *Financial support:* In 2017–18, 7 students received support, including 1 research assistantship (averaging $5,000 per year), 3 teaching assistantships (averaging $7,000 per year); career-related internships or fieldwork, scholarships/grants, and unspecified assistantships also available. Support available to part-time students. Financial award application deadline: 3/1; financial award applicants required to submit FAFSA. *Unit head:* Deneen Evans, MSW Program Coordinator, 540-831-7681, E-mail: devans18@radford.edu.
Website: http://www.radford.edu/content/grad/home/academics/graduate-programs/msw.html

Ramapo College of New Jersey, Master of Social Work Program, Mahwah, NJ 07430-1680. Offers MSW. *Program availability:* Part-time. *Faculty:* 6 full-time (4 women), 7 part-time/adjunct (all women). *Students:* 79 full-time (66 women), 19 part-time (17 women); includes 27 minority (10 Black or African American, non-Hispanic/Latino; 2 Asian, non-Hispanic/Latino; 14 Hispanic/Latino; 1 Two or more races, non-Hispanic/Latino), 1 international. Average age 32. 205 applicants, 48% accepted, 58 enrolled. In 2017, 37 master's awarded. *Entrance requirements:* For master's, official transcript of baccalaureate degree from accredited institution with minimum recommended GPA of 3.0; personal statement; 2 letters of recommendation; resume; 3-5 page narrative highlighting personal and professional accomplishments, values, and strengths. Additional exam requirements/recommendations for international students: Required—TOEFL (minimum score 550 paper-based; 79 iBT); Recommended—IELTS (minimum score 6). *Application deadline:* For fall admission, 3/1 for domestic and international students. Applications are processed on a rolling basis. Application fee: $65. Electronic applications accepted. *Expenses:* $690.60 per credit tuition, $56.95 per credit fees. *Financial support:* Scholarships/grants available. Financial award application deadline: 3/1; financial award applicants required to submit FAFSA. *Faculty research:* Substance abuse, narrative therapy, military families, child welfare. *Unit head:* Ann Marie Moreno, Assistant Dean/Director, 201-684-7191, E-mail: amoreno@ramapo.edu.
Website: http://www.ramapo.edu/msw/

Rhode Island College, School of Graduate Studies, School of Social Work, Providence, RI 02908-1991. Offers MSW. *Accreditation:* CSWE. *Program availability:* Part-time. *Students:* 92 full-time (79 women), 138 part-time (112 women); includes 65 minority (14 Black or African American, non-Hispanic/Latino; 1 American Indian or Alaska Native, non-Hispanic/Latino; 1 Asian, non-Hispanic/Latino; 46 Hispanic/Latino; 3 Two or more races, non-Hispanic/Latino). Average age 31. In 2017, 84 master's awarded. *Entrance requirements:* For master's, official transcripts, personal statement, 3 letters of recommendation. Additional exam requirements/recommendations for international students: Recommended—TOEFL (minimum score 550 paper-based; 79 iBT). *Application deadline:* For fall admission, 2/1 for domestic students. Applications are processed on a rolling basis. Application fee: $50. Electronic applications accepted. *Expenses:* Contact institution. *Financial support:* Career-related internships or fieldwork, Federal Work-Study, scholarships/grants, health care benefits, and unspecified assistantships available. Support available to part-time students. Financial award application deadline: 5/15; financial award applicants required to submit FAFSA. *Unit head:* Dr. Jayashree Nimmagadda, Interim Dean, 401-456-8042.
Website: http://www.ric.edu/socialWork/

Roberts Wesleyan College, Department of Social Work, Rochester, NY 14624-1997. Offers child and family practice (MSW); mental health practice (MSW). *Accreditation:* CSWE. *Entrance requirements:* For master's, minimum GPA of 2.75. *Faculty research:* Religion and social work, family studies, values and ethics.

Rutgers University–New Brunswick, School of Social Work, New Brunswick, NJ 08901. Offers MSW, PhD, JD/MSW, M Div/MSW. *Accreditation:* CSWE (one or more programs are accredited). *Program availability:* Part-time. *Degree requirements:* For doctorate, comprehensive exam, thesis/dissertation. *Entrance requirements:* For doctorate, GRE General Test. Additional exam requirements/recommendations for international students: Required—TOEFL. Electronic applications accepted. *Faculty research:* Family theory, adolescent development, child and adolescent mental health delivery systems, poverty and employment policy.

Sacred Heart University, Graduate Programs, College of Arts and Sciences, Department of Social Work, Fairfield, CT 06825. Offers MSW. *Faculty:* 6 full-time (5 women), 3 part-time/adjunct (all women). *Students:* 26 full-time (20 women), 54 part-time (48 women); includes 29 minority (11 Black or African American, non-Hispanic/Latino; 1 American Indian or Alaska Native, non-Hispanic/Latino; 1 Asian, non-Hispanic/Latino; 15 Hispanic/Latino; 1 Two or more races, non-Hispanic/Latino). Average age 31. 74 applicants, 69% accepted, 32 enrolled. *Entrance requirements:* Additional exam requirements/recommendations for international students: Required—TOEFL (minimum iBT score of 80), TWE, or IELTS (6.5). Application fee: $75. *Expenses: Tuition:* Full-time $28,114; part-time $739 per credit. *Unit head:* Dr. Bronwyn Cross-Denny, Chair, 203-371-7941, Fax: 203-365-4892, E-mail: cross-dennyb@sacredheart.edu. *Application contact:* Pam Pillo, Executive Director of Graduate Admissions, 203-365-7619, E-mail: gradstudies@sacredheart.edu.

Saginaw Valley State University, College of Health and Human Services, Program in Social Work, University Center, MI 48710. Offers MSW. *Program availability:* Part-time. *Students:* 19 full-time (13 women), 5 part-time (3 women); includes 5 minority (3 Black or African American, non-Hispanic/Latino; 1 Asian, non-Hispanic/Latino; 1 Two or more races, non-Hispanic/Latino). Average age 28. 37 applicants, 81% accepted, 24 enrolled. *Entrance requirements:* For master's, minimum preferred GPA of 3.0 in most recent 60 credits. Additional exam requirements/recommendations for international students: Required—TOEFL (minimum score 79 iBT), IELTS (minimum score 6.5). *Application deadline:* For fall admission, 7/1 for international students; for winter admission, 11/1 for international students. Applications are processed on a rolling basis. Application fee:

$30 ($90 for international students). Electronic applications accepted. *Expenses:* Tuition, state resident: full-time $10,156; part-time $564.20 per credit hour. Tuition, nonresident: full-time $19,336; part-time $1074.20 per credit hour. *Required fees:* $263; $14.60 per credit hour. Tuition and fees vary according to degree level and program. *Financial support:* Career-related internships or fieldwork, Federal Work-Study, and scholarships/grants available. Support available to part-time students. Financial award application deadline: 4/1; financial award applicants required to submit FAFSA. *Unit head:* Lucy Mercier, Director, 989-964-4077, E-mail: mercier@svsu.edu. *Application contact:* Jenna Briggs, Director, Graduate and International Admissions, 989-964-6096, Fax: 989-964-2788, E-mail: gradadm@svsu.edu.
Website: http://svsu.edu/socialworkmsw/

St. Ambrose University, College of Health and Human Services, Program in Social Work, Davenport, IA 52803-2898. Offers MSW. *Accreditation:* CSWE. *Program availability:* Part-time, evening/weekend. *Degree requirements:* For master's, comprehensive exam (for some programs), thesis or alternative, integration projects. *Entrance requirements:* For master's, minimum GPA of 3.0, course work in statistics, bachelor's degree in liberal arts. Additional exam requirements/recommendations for international students: Required—TOEFL. Electronic applications accepted. *Faculty research:* Social work practice, cults/sects, family therapy, developmental disabilities.

St. Catherine University, Graduate Programs, Program in Social Work, St. Paul, MN 55105. Offers MSW, DSW. Program offered jointly with University of St. Thomas. *Accreditation:* CSWE. *Program availability:* Part-time, evening/weekend. *Degree requirements:* For master's, clinical research paper. *Entrance requirements:* For master's, minimum GPA of 3.0. Additional exam requirements/recommendations for international students: Required—Michigan English Language Assessment Battery or TOEFL (minimum score 600 paper-based; 100 iBT). *Application deadline:* For fall admission, 1/10 for domestic students. Application fee: $35. *Expenses:* Contact institution. *Financial support:* Career-related internships or fieldwork and institutionally sponsored loans available. Support available to part-time students. Financial award application deadline: 4/1; financial award applicants required to submit FAFSA. *Unit head:* Lisa M. Richardson, Director, 651-690-6825, Fax: 651-690-6024.
Website: https://www.stkate.edu/academics/graduate-degrees/academic-programs/msw

St. Cloud State University, School of Graduate Studies, School of Health and Human Services, Department of Social Work, St. Cloud, MN 56301-4498. Offers MSW. *Accreditation:* CSWE. *Program availability:* Part-time. *Entrance requirements:* For master's, minimum GPA of 3.0.

Saint Leo University, Graduate Studies in Social Work, Saint Leo, FL 33574-6665. Offers advanced clinical practice (MSW). *Accreditation:* CSWE. *Program availability:* Online only, blended/hybrid learning. *Faculty:* 10 full-time (8 women), 17 part-time/adjunct (15 women). *Students:* 127 full-time (110 women), 80 part-time (68 women); includes 100 minority (78 Black or African American, non-Hispanic/Latino; 1 Asian, non-Hispanic/Latino; 18 Hispanic/Latino; 3 Two or more races, non-Hispanic/Latino). Average age 36. 257 applicants, 49% accepted, 111 enrolled. In 2017, 95 master's awarded. *Entrance requirements:* For master's, official transcripts, current resumé, 3 professional recommendations, personal statement. Additional exam requirements/recommendations for international students: Required—TOEFL (minimum score 550 paper-based; 78 iBT). *Application deadline:* For fall admission, 6/1 for domestic and international students. Application fee: $80. Electronic applications accepted. *Expenses:* $480 per credit hour. *Financial support:* In 2017–18, 4 students received support. Career-related internships or fieldwork, Federal Work-Study, health care benefits, and tuition remission for Saint Leo employees and their dependents available. Financial award application deadline: 3/1. *Faculty research:* Juvenile crime and violence, trauma, distance education, animal-assisted therapy, sibling caregivers of families with persons with developmental disabilities, trauma informed care, animal assisted therapy, art therapy, veterans services, aging services. *Unit head:* Dr. Cindy Lee, Director of Graduate Studies in Social Work, 352-588-8869, Fax: 352-588-8289, E-mail: cindy.lee@saintleo.edu. *Application contact:* Mark Russum, Assistant Vice President, Enrollment, 800-707-8846, Fax: 352-588-7873, E-mail: grad.admissions@saintleo.edu.
Website: https://www.saintleo.edu/social-work-master-three-year-program-degree

Saint Louis University, Graduate Programs, College for Public Health and Social Justice, School of Social Work, St. Louis, MO 63103. Offers applied behavior analysis (MS); social work (MSW, PhD). *Accreditation:* CSWE. *Program availability:* Part-time. *Entrance requirements:* For master's, minimum GPA of 3.0, letters of recommendation. Additional exam requirements/recommendations for international students: Required—TOEFL (minimum score 550 paper-based). *Expenses:* Contact institution. *Faculty research:* Gerontology, mental health issues, child welfare (especially abuse and neglect), social justice, and peace making, homelessness.

Salem State University, School of Graduate Studies, Program in Social Work, Salem, MA 01970-5353. Offers MSW. *Accreditation:* CSWE. *Program availability:* Part-time, evening/weekend. *Entrance requirements:* For master's, GRE, MAT. Additional exam requirements/recommendations for international students: Required—TOEFL (minimum score 550 paper-based; 80 iBT) or IELTS (minimum score 5.5).

Salisbury University, Department of Social Work, Salisbury, MD 21801-6837. Offers MSW. *Accreditation:* CSWE. *Program availability:* Part-time, 100% online, blended/hybrid learning. *Faculty:* 22 full-time (18 women), 47 part-time/adjunct (37 women). *Students:* 295 full-time (263 women), 82 part-time (78 women); includes 66 minority (50 Black or African American, non-Hispanic/Latino; 6 Hispanic/Latino; 2 Native Hawaiian or other Pacific Islander, non-Hispanic/Latino; 8 Two or more races, non-Hispanic/Latino). Average age 32. 270 applicants, 59% accepted, 160 enrolled. In 2017, 126 master's awarded. *Entrance requirements:* For master's, letters of recommendation; transcripts from colleges and universities attended; essay; resume. Additional exam requirements/recommendations for international students: Required—TOEFL (minimum score 550 paper-based; 79 iBT), IELTS (minimum score 6.5). *Application deadline:* For fall admission, 2/3 for domestic and international students; for spring admission, 11/15 for domestic and international students. Application fee: $65. Electronic applications accepted. *Expenses:* $392 per credit hour resident; $703 per credit hour non-resident; $92 per credit hour fees; $594 per credit hour (Hagerstown); $750 per credit hour (online, no fees charge). *Financial support:* In 2017–18, 22 students received support, including 6 teaching assistantships with full tuition reimbursements available (averaging $8,160 per year); career-related internships or fieldwork and scholarships/grants also available. Support available to part-time students. Financial award application deadline: 3/1; financial award applicants required to submit FAFSA. *Faculty research:* Aging; mass incarceration; professional identity development. *Unit head:* Dr. Vicki Root, Graduate Program Director, Social Work, 410-543-6307, E-mail: vbroot@salisbury.edu. *Application contact:* Susan Mareski, Administrative Assistant, 410-677-5363, E-mail: smmareski@salisbury.edu.
Website: http://www.salisbury.edu/gsr/gradstudies/MSWpage.html

Samford University, School of Public Health, Birmingham, AL 35229. Offers health informatics (MSHI); healthcare administration (MHA); nutrition (MS); public health (MPH); social work (MSW). *Program availability:* Part-time, 100% online. *Faculty:* 17 full-time (12 women), 4 part-time/adjunct (2 women). *Students:* 93 full-time (87 women), 5

Social Work

part-time (all women); includes 20 minority (14 Black or African American, non-Hispanic/Latino; 2 Asian, non-Hispanic/Latino; 2 Hispanic/Latino; 2 Two or more races, non-Hispanic/Latino), 1 international. Average age 27. 90 applicants, 44% accepted, 32 enrolled. In 2017, 34 master's awarded. *Degree requirements:* For master's, capstone course. *Entrance requirements:* For master's, GRE, MAT, recommendations, resume, personal statement. Additional exam requirements/recommendations for international students: Required—TOEFL (minimum score 550 paper-based); Recommended—IELTS. *Application deadline:* For fall admission, 10/1 for domestic students; for spring admission, 5/1 for domestic students. Application fee: $75. Electronic applications accepted. *Expenses:* $813 per credit hour. *Financial support:* In 2017–18, 32 students received support. Scholarships/grants available. Financial award application deadline: 2/15; financial award applicants required to submit FAFSA. *Faculty research:* Chronic kidney disease, disasters and vulnerable populations, children's health, obesity, metabolism and diabetes, health policy and health care delivery. *Unit head:* Dr. Keith Elder, Dean, School of Public Health, 205-726-4655, E-mail: kelder@samford.edu. *Application contact:* Dr. Marian Carter, Assistant Dean of Enrollment Management and Student Services, 205-726-2611, E-mail: mwcarter@samford.edu.
Website: http://www.samford.edu/publichealth/

San Diego State University, Graduate and Research Affairs, College of Health and Human Services, School of Social Work, San Diego, CA 92182. Offers MSW, JD/MSW, MSW/MPH. JD/MSW offered jointly with California Western School of Law. *Accreditation:* CSWE. *Program availability:* Part-time. *Degree requirements:* For master's, comprehensive exam, thesis optional. *Entrance requirements:* For master's, GRE General Test. Additional exam requirements/recommendations for international students: Required—TOEFL. Electronic applications accepted. *Faculty research:* Child maltreatment, substance abuse, neighborhood studies, child welfare.

San Francisco State University, Division of Graduate Studies, College of Health and Social Sciences, School of Social Work, San Francisco, CA 94132-1722. Offers MSW. *Accreditation:* CSWE. *Program availability:* Part-time. *Degree requirements:* For master's, thesis optional. *Application deadline:* Applications are processed on a rolling basis. *Financial support:* Career-related internships or fieldwork and Federal Work-Study available. *Unit head:* Dr. Susanna Jones, Director, 415-405-4084, Fax: 415-338-0591, E-mail: susjones@sfsu.edu. *Application contact:* Victoria Lee, Office Manager, 415-338-7538, Fax: 415-338-0591, E-mail: victorialee@sfsu.edu.
Website: http://socwork.sfsu.edu/

San Jose State University, Graduate Studies and Research, College of Health and Human Sciences, San Jose, CA 95192-0049. Offers criminology (MS), including global criminology, law and justice; justice studies (MS); kinesiology (MA), including athletic training, exercise physiology, interdisciplinary, sport studies, sports management; library and information science (MLIS); mass communications (MS); nursing (MS), including family nurse practitioner; nutritional science (MS); occupational therapy (MS); public health (MPH); social work (MSW); MD/M Div. *Program availability:* Part-time, 100% online, blended/hybrid learning. *Faculty:* 15 full-time (7 women), 6 part-time/adjunct (3 women). *Students:* 517 full-time (407 women), 405 part-time (302 women); includes 523 minority (39 Black or African American, non-Hispanic/Latino; 2 American Indian or Alaska Native, non-Hispanic/Latino; 141 Asian, non-Hispanic/Latino; 226 Hispanic/Latino; 2 Native Hawaiian or other Pacific Islander, non-Hispanic/Latino; 113 Two or more races, non-Hispanic/Latino), 14 international. Average age 32. 1,250 applicants, 45% accepted, 375 enrolled. In 2017, 808 master's awarded. *Degree requirements:* For master's, thesis (for some programs), graduate writing assessment. *Entrance requirements:* Additional exam requirements/recommendations for international students: Required—TOEFL (minimum score 550 paper-based; 80 iBT), IELTS (minimum score 6.5), PTE (minimum score 53). *Application deadline:* For fall admission, 2/1 for domestic and international students. Applications are processed on a rolling basis. Application fee: $55. Electronic applications accepted. *Expenses:* Tuition, state resident: full-time $7176. Tuition, nonresident: full-time $16,680. Tuition and fees vary according to course load and program. *Financial support:* Fellowships, research assistantships, teaching assistantships, career-related internships or fieldwork, Federal Work-Study, scholarships/grants, and tuition waivers (full and partial) available. Support available to part-time students. Financial award application deadline: 4/24; financial award applicants required to submit FAFSA. *Unit head:* Dr. Mary Schutten, Dean, College of Health and Human Sciences, 408-924-2900, Fax: 408-924-2901, E-mail: mary.schutten@sjsu.edu.
Website: http://www.sjsu.edu/casa/

Savannah State University, Master of Social Work Program, Savannah, GA 31404. Offers MSW. *Accreditation:* CSWE. *Degree requirements:* For master's, 1000-hour field practicum, seminar course for each semester in field placement. *Entrance requirements:* For master's, GRE General Test (minimum score of 3.0 in analytical writing portion), minimum GPA of 2.8, degree from accredited institution with liberal arts courses, official transcripts, directed essay, 3 letters of recommendation. Additional exam requirements/recommendations for international students: Required—TOEFL. *Expenses:* Contact institution. *Faculty research:* Clinical and administrative social work.

Seattle University, College of Arts and Sciences, Program in Social Work, Seattle, WA 98122-1090. Offers MSW. *Faculty:* 8 full-time (6 women), 2 part-time/adjunct (both women). *Students:* 51 full-time (40 women), 1 (woman) part-time; includes 17 minority (4 Black or African American, non-Hispanic/Latino; 4 Asian, non-Hispanic/Latino; 3 Hispanic/Latino; 1 Native Hawaiian or other Pacific Islander, non-Hispanic/Latino; 5 Two or more races, non-Hispanic/Latino). Average age 28. 87 applicants, 62% accepted, 24 enrolled. *Application deadline:* For fall admission, 1/20 priority date for domestic students. *Expenses:* Tuition: Full-time $12,960. *Required fees:* $570. Tuition and fees vary according to program. *Financial support:* In 2017–18, 39 students received support. *Unit head:* Dr. Hye-Kyung Kang, Director, 206-296-5558, E-mail: kangh@seattleu.edu. *Application contact:* Janet Shandley, Director of Graduate Admissions, 206-296-5900, Fax: 206-298-5656, E-mail: grad_admissions@seattleu.edu.
Website: http://www.seattleu.edu/artsci/msw/

Seton Hall University, College of Arts and Sciences, Department of Sociology, Anthropology and Social Work, South Orange, NJ 07079-2697. Offers social work (MSW).

Shippensburg University of Pennsylvania, School of Graduate Studies, College of Education and Human Services, Department of Social Work and Gerontology, Shippensburg, PA 17257-2299. Offers social work (MSW). *Program availability:* Part-time, evening/weekend, blended/hybrid learning. *Faculty:* 9 full-time (7 women), 5 part-time/adjunct (3 women). *Students:* 31 full-time (26 women), 35 part-time (28 women); includes 11 minority (6 Black or African American, non-Hispanic/Latino; 3 Hispanic/Latino; 2 Two or more races, non-Hispanic/Latino), 1 international. Average age 29. 67 applicants, 69% accepted, 36 enrolled. In 2017, 36 master's awarded. *Degree requirements:* For master's, thesis, field practicum. *Entrance requirements:* For master's, GRE or MAT (if GPA is below 2.8), 3 professional references with minimum of one from faculty and one from current or recent agency employer or supervisor; current resume; written personal statement; course work in human biology, economics, government/political science, psychology, sociology/anthropology and statistics. Additional exam requirements/recommendations for international students: Required—TOEFL (minimum score 550 paper-based, 68 iBT) or IELTS (minimum score 6).

Application deadline: For fall admission, 4/30 for international students; for spring admission, 9/30 for international students. Applications are processed on a rolling basis. Application fee: $45. Electronic applications accepted. *Expenses:* Tuition, state resident: part-time $500 per credit. Tuition, nonresident: part-time $750 per credit. *Required fees:* $145 per credit. *Financial support:* In 2017–18, 11 students received support. Career-related internships or fieldwork, scholarships/grants, unspecified assistantships, and resident hall director and student payroll positions available. Support available to part-time students. Financial award application deadline: 3/1; financial award applicants required to submit FAFSA. *Unit head:* Dr. Deborah F. Jacobs, Co-Director, MU-SU Master of Social Work Program, 717-477-1276, Fax: 717-477-4051, E-mail: dfjaco@ship.edu. *Application contact:* Maya T. Mapp, Director of Admissions, 717-477-1231, Fax: 717-477-4016, E-mail: mtmapp@ship.edu.
Website: http://www.ship.edu/social_work/

Simmons College, School of Social Work, Boston, MA 02115. Offers behavior analysis (MS, PhD, Ed S); education (MS Ed); social work (MSW, PhD); special education (MS Ed), including moderate and severe disabilities; teaching (MAT), including elementary education; MSW/MBA. *Accreditation:* CSWE (one or more programs are accredited). *Program availability:* Part-time, 100% online, blended/hybrid learning. *Faculty:* 57 full-time (47 women), 48 part-time/adjunct (36 women). *Students:* 878 full-time (757 women), 979 part-time (869 women); includes 468 minority (213 Black or African American, non-Hispanic/Latino; 1 American Indian or Alaska Native, non-Hispanic/Latino; 45 Asian, non-Hispanic/Latino; 152 Hispanic/Latino; 3 Native Hawaiian or other Pacific Islander, non-Hispanic/Latino; 54 Two or more races, non-Hispanic/Latino), 12 international. Average age 30. 1,521 applicants, 74% accepted, 545 enrolled. In 2017, 611 master's, 7 doctorates, 1 other advanced degree awarded. Terminal master's awarded for partial completion of doctoral program. *Degree requirements:* For master's, thesis (for some programs); for doctorate, comprehensive exam (for some programs), thesis/dissertation (for some programs). *Entrance requirements:* For master's, GRE, MAT, Massachusetts Tests for Education Licensure (for different programs), minimum grade of B in introductory statistics course within five years prior to entering program, resume, transcripts, three letters of recommendation, personal statement; for doctorate, GRE, BCBA Analyst Exam. Additional exam requirements/recommendations for international students: Required—TOEFL (minimum score 600 paper-based; 100 iBT). *Application deadline:* For fall admission, 8/1 for domestic students; for spring admission, 12/15 for domestic students; for summer admission, 5/1 for domestic students. Applications are processed on a rolling basis. Application fee: $35. Electronic applications accepted. *Expenses:* $1,001 per credit hour, $3,003 per course, $55 activity fee per semester. *Financial support:* In 2017–18, 12 fellowships with partial tuition reimbursements were awarded; scholarships/grants and unspecified assistantships also available. Support available to part-time students. Financial award applicants required to submit FAFSA. *Unit head:* Dr. Cheryl Parks, Dean, 617-521-3293, E-mail: cheryl.parks@simmons.edu. *Application contact:* Carlos D. Frontado, Director of Admissions, 617-521-3920, Fax: 617-521-3980, E-mail: ssw@simmons.edu.
Website: http://www.simmons.edu/ssw/

Smith College, School for Social Work, Northampton, MA 01063. Offers clinical social work (MSW, PhD). *Accreditation:* CSWE (one or more programs are accredited). *Faculty:* 36 full-time (26 women), 223 part-time/adjunct (178 women). *Students:* 272 full-time (236 women), 53 part-time (43 women); includes 85 minority (26 Black or African American, non-Hispanic/Latino; 3 American Indian or Alaska Native, non-Hispanic/Latino; 21 Asian, non-Hispanic/Latino; 28 Hispanic/Latino; 7 Two or more races, non-Hispanic/Latino), 9 international. Average age 32. 400 applicants, 64% accepted, 128 enrolled. In 2017, 101 master's, 6 doctorates awarded. *Degree requirements:* For doctorate, thesis/dissertation. *Entrance requirements:* For doctorate, MAT. Additional exam requirements/recommendations for international students: Required—TOEFL (minimum score 94 IBT) or IELTS (7.0). *Application deadline:* For fall admission, 2/21 for domestic students, 2/15 for international students. Applications are processed on a rolling basis. Application fee: $60. Electronic applications accepted. *Expenses:* $26,020 tuition and activity fee (for MSW); $30,075 tuition and activity fee (for PhD). *Financial support:* In 2017–18, 265 students received support. Career-related internships or fieldwork and scholarships/grants available. Financial award application deadline: 3/1; financial award applicants required to submit FAFSA. *Faculty research:* Social work practice, social work research, prevention and intervention for communities experiencing trauma, human behavior in the social environment, increasing resilient contexts. *Unit head:* Dr. Marianne Yoshioka, Dean/Professor, 413-585-7977, E-mail: myoshioka@smith.edu. *Application contact:* Irene Rodriguez Martin, Associate Dean, Graduate Enrollment and Student Services, 413-585-7960, Fax: 413-585-7994, E-mail: imartin@smith.edu.
Website: http://www.smith.edu/ssw/

Southeastern University, College of Behavioral and Social Sciences, Lakeland, FL 33801-6099. Offers human services (MA); international community development (MA); marriage and family counseling (MS); professional counseling (MS); school counseling (MS); social work (MSW). *Program availability:* Evening/weekend. *Faculty:* 9 full-time (6 women), 7 part-time/adjunct (4 women). *Students:* 72 full-time (60 women), 9 part-time (all women); includes 28 minority (12 Black or African American, non-Hispanic/Latino; 2 Asian, non-Hispanic/Latino; 13 Hispanic/Latino; 1 Native Hawaiian or other Pacific Islander, non-Hispanic/Latino), 1 international. Average age 29. Application fee: $50. Electronic applications accepted. *Unit head:* Erica H. Sirrine, Dean, 863-667-5341, E-mail: ehsirrine@seu.edu.
Website: http://www.seu.edu/behavior/

Southern Adventist University, School of Social Work, Collegedale, TN 37315-0370. Offers MSW. *Accreditation:* CSWE. *Program availability:* Online learning. Application fee: $40. *Expenses:* Tuition: Full-time $11,430; part-time $635 per credit hour. Tuition and fees vary according to degree level and program. *Unit head:* Kristie Wilder, JD, Dean, 423-236-2206, E-mail: kwilder@southern.edu. *Application contact:* Laurie Gauthier, Director of Graduate Marketing and Enrollment Management, 423-236-2585, Fax: 423-236-1694, E-mail: graduatestudies@southern.edu.
Website: https://www.southern.edu/academics/socialwork.html

Southern Connecticut State University, School of Graduate Studies, School of Health and Human Services, Department of Social Work, New Haven, CT 06515-1355. Offers MSW. *Accreditation:* CSWE. *Program availability:* Part-time, evening/weekend. *Degree requirements:* For master's, thesis. *Entrance requirements:* For master's, minimum undergraduate QPA of 3.0 in graduate major field, interview. Electronic applications accepted. *Faculty research:* Social work practice; social service development; services for women, the aging, children, and families in educational and health care systems.

Southern Illinois University Carbondale, Graduate School, College of Education and Human Services, School of Social Work, Carbondale, IL 62901-4701. Offers MSW, JD/MSW. *Accreditation:* CSWE. *Entrance requirements:* For master's, GRE General Test, minimum GPA of 2.7. Additional exam requirements/recommendations for international students: Required—TOEFL. *Faculty research:* Service delivery systems, comparative race relations, advocacy research, gerontology, child welfare and health.

Southern Illinois University Edwardsville, Graduate School, College of Arts and Sciences, Department of Social Work, Edwardsville, IL 62026. Offers school social work (MSW); social work (MSW). *Accreditation:* CSWE. *Program availability:* Part-time, evening/weekend. *Degree requirements:* For master's, final exam, capstone course. *Entrance requirements:* Additional exam requirements/recommendations for international students: Required—TOEFL (minimum score 550 paper-based; 79 iBT), IELTS (minimum score 6.5). Electronic applications accepted.

Southern University at New Orleans, School of Graduate Studies, New Orleans, LA 70126-1009. Offers criminal justice (MA); management information systems (MS); museum studies (MA); social work (MSW). *Accreditation:* CSWE. *Program availability:* Part-time, evening/weekend. *Degree requirements:* For master's, thesis. *Entrance requirements:* For master's, GRE/GMAT. Additional exam requirements/recommendations for international students: Required—TOEFL.

Spalding University, Graduate Studies, Kosair College of Health and Natural Sciences, School of Social Work, Louisville, KY 40203-2188. Offers MSW. *Accreditation:* CSWE. *Program availability:* Evening/weekend. *Degree requirements:* For master's, thesis or alternative. *Entrance requirements:* For master's, transcripts, letters of recommendation, personal essay, personal interview. Additional exam requirements/recommendations for international students: Required—TOEFL (minimum score 535 paper-based). Electronic applications accepted. *Faculty research:* Addictions, spirituality, feminist studies, mental retardation, action research.

Springfield College, Graduate Programs, School of Social Work, Springfield, MA 01108. Offers advanced practice with children and adolescents (Post-Master's Certificate); social work (MSW); JD/MSW. *Accreditation:* CSWE. *Program availability:* Part-time, evening/weekend. *Faculty:* 14 full-time (5 women), 28 part-time/adjunct (20 women). *Students:* 252 full-time (214 women), 98 part-time (84 women); includes 150 minority (89 Black or African American, non-Hispanic/Latino; 5 Asian, non-Hispanic/Latino; 47 Hispanic/Latino; 9 Two or more races, non-Hispanic/Latino). 223 applicants, 69% accepted, 102 enrolled. In 2017, 151 master's awarded. *Degree requirements:* For master's, comprehensive exam. *Entrance requirements:* Additional exam requirements/recommendations for international students: Required—TOEFL (minimum score 550 paper-based); Recommended—IELTS (minimum score 7). *Application deadline:* For fall admission, 5/1 for domestic and international students; for summer admission, 3/1 for domestic and international students. Applications are processed on a rolling basis. Application fee: $50. Electronic applications accepted. *Financial support:* Fellowships with partial tuition reimbursements, research assistantships, career-related internships or fieldwork, Federal Work-Study, institutionally sponsored loans, scholarships/grants, and unspecified assistantships available. Support available to part-time students. Financial award application deadline: 3/1; financial award applicants required to submit FAFSA. *Faculty research:* Children and families, health and mental health, school social work, gerontology, international social work. *Unit head:* Dr. Francine Vecchiola, Dean, 413-748-3065. *Application contact:* Franklin Kirshner, Admissions Coordinator, 413-748-3060, Fax: 413-748-3069, E-mail: fkirschner@springfield.edu.
Website: http://springfield.edu/ssw

Stephen F. Austin State University, Graduate School, College of Applied Arts and Science, School of Social Work, Nacogdoches, TX 75962. Offers MSW. *Accreditation:* CSWE. *Degree requirements:* For master's, comprehensive exam, thesis optional. *Entrance requirements:* For master's, GRE General Test, interview. Additional exam requirements/recommendations for international students: Required—TOEFL (minimum score 550 paper-based).

Stockton University, Office of Graduate Studies, Program in Social Work, Galloway, NJ 08205-9441. Offers MSW. *Accreditation:* CSWE. *Program availability:* Evening/weekend. *Faculty:* 8 full-time (6 women), 7 part-time/adjunct (6 women). *Students:* 80 full-time (76 women), 13 part-time (10 women); includes 39 minority (17 Black or African American, non-Hispanic/Latino; 3 Asian, non-Hispanic/Latino; 18 Hispanic/Latino; 1 Two or more races, non-Hispanic/Latino). Average age 32. 162 applicants, 73% accepted, 64 enrolled. In 2017, 61 master's awarded. *Entrance requirements:* Additional exam requirements/recommendations for international students: Required—TOEFL. *Application deadline:* For fall admission, 2/1 for domestic and international students. Applications are processed on a rolling basis. Application fee: $50. Electronic applications accepted. *Expenses:* Contact institution. *Financial support:* Fellowships, research assistantships, career-related internships or fieldwork, Federal Work-Study, scholarships/grants, and unspecified assistantships available. Financial award application deadline: 3/1; financial award applicants required to submit FAFSA. *Unit head:* Dr. Diane Falk, Program Director, 609-626-3640, E-mail: gradschool@stockton.edu. *Application contact:* Tara Williams, Assistant Director of Graduate Enrollment Management, 609-626-3640, Fax: 609-626-6050, E-mail: gradschool@stockton.edu.
Website: http://www.stockton.edu/grad

Stony Brook University, State University of New York, Stony Brook Medicine, School of Social Welfare, Doctoral Program in Social Welfare, Stony Brook, NY 11794. Offers PhD. *Faculty:* 19 full-time (13 women), 44 part-time/adjunct (29 women). *Students:* 15 full-time (12 women), 6 part-time (5 women); includes 5 minority (4 Black or African American, non-Hispanic/Latino; 1 Asian, non-Hispanic/Latino). Average age 29. In 2017, 2 doctorates awarded. *Degree requirements:* For doctorate, thesis/dissertation. *Entrance requirements:* For doctorate, GRE, three letters of reference, personal statement, writing sample. Additional exam requirements/recommendations for international students: Required—TOEFL. *Application deadline:* For fall admission, 1/15 for domestic students; for spring admission, 10/1 for domestic students. Application fee: $100. *Expenses:* Contact institution. *Financial support:* Fellowships and teaching assistantships available. Financial award application deadline: 2/1. *Faculty research:* Social welfare, social work, rape or sexual abuse, child welfare, social justice. *Unit head:* Dr. Jacqueline B. Mondros, Dean and Assistant Vice President for Social Determinants of Health, 631-444-2139, E-mail: jacqueline.mondros@stonybrook.edu. *Application contact:* Jamie Weissbach, Staff Assistant, 631-444-3146, Fax: 631-444-7565, E-mail: jamie.weissbach@stonybrook.edu.
Website: http://socialwelfare.stonybrookmedicine.edu/

Stony Brook University, State University of New York, Stony Brook Medicine, School of Social Welfare, Master's Program in Social Work, Stony Brook, NY 11794. Offers MSW. *Accreditation:* CSWE. *Faculty:* 19 full-time (13 women), 44 part-time/adjunct (29 women). *Students:* 481 full-time (409 women), 16 part-time (13 women); includes 186 minority (80 Black or African American, non-Hispanic/Latino; 1 American Indian or Alaska Native, non-Hispanic/Latino; 15 Asian, non-Hispanic/Latino; 83 Hispanic/Latino; 7 Two or more races, non-Hispanic/Latino), 1 international. Average age 31. 500 applicants, 82% accepted, 283 enrolled. In 2017, 214 master's awarded. *Degree requirements:* For master's, project or thesis. *Entrance requirements:* For master's, interview, minimum cumulative GPA of 2.5. Additional exam requirements/recommendations for international students: Required—TOEFL. *Application deadline:* For fall admission, 3/1 for domestic students. Application fee: $100. *Expenses:* Contact institution. *Financial support:* Teaching assistantships available. Financial award application deadline: 3/1. *Faculty research:* Social welfare, social work, rape or sexual abuse, child welfare, social justice. *Unit head:* Dr. Jacqueline B. Mondros, Dean and Assistant Vice President for Social Determinants of Health, 631-444-2139, E-mail: jacqueline.mondros@stonybrook.edu. *Application contact:* Dr. Sunday F. Coward, Assistant Dean for Academic Services, 631-444-3154, Fax: 631-444-7565, E-mail: sunday.coward@stonybrook.edu.
Website: http://socialwelfare.stonybrookmedicine.edu/

Syracuse University, David B. Falk College of Sport and Human Dynamics, Dual Master's Program in Social Work and Marriage and Family Therapy (MSW/MA), Syracuse, NY 13244. Offers MSW/MA. *Accreditation:* AAMFT/COAMFTE. *Entrance requirements:* Additional exam requirements/recommendations for international students: Required—TOEFL or IELTS. *Application deadline:* For fall admission, 2/15 priority date for domestic and international students; for summer admission, 1/15 priority date for domestic students, 1/15 for international students. Application fee: $75. Electronic applications accepted. *Financial support:* Fellowships, research assistantships, teaching assistantships, career-related internships or fieldwork, and scholarships/grants available. Financial award application deadline: 1/1. *Faculty research:* Human diversity in social context, foundations of social work practice, policy and services in child welfare, child and family policy, social welfare policy and services. *Unit head:* Prof. Keith Alford, Director, School of Social Work, 315-443-5562, Fax: 315-443-2562, E-mail: kalford@syr.edu. *Application contact:* Felicia Otero, Director of College Admissions, 315-443-5555, Fax: 315-443-2562, E-mail: falk@syr.edu.
Website: https://falk.syr.edu/marriage-family-therapy/academic-programs/#mswmft

Syracuse University, David B. Falk College of Sport and Human Dynamics, MSW Program in Social Work, Syracuse, NY 13244. Offers MSW. *Accreditation:* CSWE. *Program availability:* Part-time, evening/weekend. *Degree requirements:* For master's, thesis or alternative, field placement. *Entrance requirements:* For master's, personal statement, official transcripts, three letters of recommendation, resume. Additional exam requirements/recommendations for international students: Required—TOEFL (minimum score 100 iBT). *Application deadline:* For fall admission, 2/15 priority date for domestic and international students; for spring admission, 11/1 for domestic students, 11/1 priority date for international students. Applications are processed on a rolling basis. Application fee: $75. Electronic applications accepted. *Financial support:* Fellowships with full tuition reimbursements, research assistantships with tuition reimbursements, teaching assistantships with tuition reimbursements, career-related internships or fieldwork, and tuition waivers available. Financial award application deadline: 1/1; financial award applicants required to submit FAFSA. *Faculty research:* Child welfare, substance abuse counseling, health care, public policy, industry and business, school social work, gerontology, mental health services. *Unit head:* Prof. Keith Alford, Director, School of Social Work, 315-443-5562, E-mail: kalford@syr.edu. *Application contact:* Felicia Otero, Director of College Admissions, 315-443-5555, E-mail: falk@syr.edu.
Website: http://falk.syr.edu/SocialWork/Default.aspx

Tarleton State University, College of Graduate Studies, College of Health Sciences and Human Services, Master of Social Work Program, Stephenville, TX 76402. Offers MSW. *Program availability:* Part-time, evening/weekend. *Faculty:* 8 full-time (7 women), 4 part-time/adjunct (all women). *Students:* 39 full-time (35 women), 15 part-time (all women); includes 34 minority (18 Black or African American, non-Hispanic/Latino; 13 Hispanic/Latino; 3 Two or more races, non-Hispanic/Latino). Average age 33. 76 applicants, 93% accepted, 51 enrolled. In 2017, 13 master's awarded. *Degree requirements:* For master's, comprehensive exam, thesis (for some programs). *Entrance requirements:* For master's, GRE, minimum GPA of 3.0. Additional exam requirements/recommendations for international students: Required—TOEFL (minimum score 550 paper-based; 80 iBT), IELTS (minimum score 6). *Application deadline:* For fall admission, 8/15 for domestic students; for spring admission, 1/5 for domestic students. Applications are processed on a rolling basis. Application fee: $45 ($145 for international students). Electronic applications accepted. *Expenses:* Contact institution. *Financial support:* Applicants required to submit FAFSA. *Unit head:* Dr. Melody Loya, Department Head, 254-968-1696, E-mail: loya@tarleton.edu. *Application contact:* Information Contact, 254-968-9104, Fax: 254-968-9670, E-mail: gradoffice@tarleton.edu.

Temple University, College of Public Health, School of Social Work, Philadelphia, PA 19122. Offers MSW. *Accreditation:* CSWE. *Program availability:* Part-time, evening/weekend. *Faculty:* 27 full-time (17 women), 6 part-time/adjunct (4 women). *Students:* 213 full-time (189 women), 136 part-time (114 women); includes 154 minority (98 Black or African American, non-Hispanic/Latino; 1 American Indian or Alaska Native, non-Hispanic/Latino; 6 Asian, non-Hispanic/Latino; 33 Hispanic/Latino; 16 Two or more races, non-Hispanic/Latino). 318 applicants, 67% accepted, 86 enrolled. In 2017, 189 master's awarded. *Degree requirements:* For master's, internship, field practicum. *Entrance requirements:* For master's, minimum GPA of 3.0, 3 letters of recommendation, statement of goals, resume. Additional exam requirements/recommendations for international students: Required—TOEFL (minimum score 550 paper-based; 79 iBT). *Application deadline:* For fall admission, 3/15 priority date for domestic students, 2/15 for international students; for spring admission, 11/1 priority date for domestic students, 10/15 for international students; for summer admission, 3/15 for domestic students, 2/15 for international students. Applications are processed on a rolling basis. Application fee: $60. Electronic applications accepted. *Expenses:* Contact institution. *Financial support:* Research assistantships with tuition reimbursements, career-related internships or fieldwork, Federal Work-Study, scholarships/grants, traineeships, tuition waivers (partial), unspecified assistantships, and field assistantships available. Support available to part-time students. Financial award application deadline: 1/1. *Faculty research:* Child welfare, alcoholism, social work practice, developmental disabilities, human sexuality, mental health services, health and corrections. *Unit head:* Bernie Newman, Chairperson, 215-204-1205, Fax: 215-204-9606, E-mail: bernie.newman@temple.edu. *Application contact:* Cheryl A. Hyde, Associate Professor/MSW Program Director, 215-204-7112, E-mail: chyde@temple.edu.
Website: https://cph.temple.edu/ssa

Tennessee State University, The School of Graduate Studies and Research, College of Public Service, Nashville, TN 37209-1561. Offers human resource management (MPS); public administration (MPA, PhD); social work (MSW); strategic leadership (MPS); training and development (MPS). *Accreditation:* NASPAA (one or more programs are accredited). *Program availability:* Part-time, evening/weekend. *Degree requirements:* For master's, comprehensive exam, thesis optional; for doctorate, comprehensive exam, thesis/dissertation. *Entrance requirements:* For master's, GRE General Test, minimum GPA of 2.5, writing sample; for doctorate, GRE General Test, minimum GPA of 3.25, writing sample. *Faculty research:* Total quality management and process improvement, national health care policy and administration, starting non-profit ventures, public service ethics, state education financing across the U.S. public.

Texas A&M University–Commerce, College of Education and Human Services, Commerce, TX 75429. Offers counseling (M Ed, MS, PhD); early childhood education (M Ed, MS); educational administration (M Ed, MS, Ed D); educational psychology (PhD); educational technology leadership (M Ed, MS); educational technology library science (M Ed, MS); elementary education (M Ed); health, kinesiology and sports studies (MS); higher education (MS, Ed D); psychology (MS); reading (M Ed, MS); secondary education (M Ed, MS); social work (MSW); special education (M Ed, MS); supervision, curriculum and instruction-elementary education (Ed D); training and development (M Ed, MS). *Program availability:* Part-time, evening/weekend, 100% online, blended/hybrid learning. *Faculty:* 91 full-time (51 women), 38 part-time/adjunct (31 women). *Students:* 400 full-time (310 women), 1,400 part-time (1,117 women); includes 724 minority (412 Black or African American, non-Hispanic/Latino; 8 American Indian or Alaska Native, non-Hispanic/Latino; 24 Asian, non-Hispanic/Latino; 220 Hispanic/Latino; 60 Two or more races, non-Hispanic/Latino), 18 international. Average age 37. 951

Social Work

applicants, 46% accepted, 331 enrolled. In 2017, 564 master's, 24 doctorates awarded. *Degree requirements:* For master's, comprehensive exam, thesis optional, departmental qualifying exams (for some programs); for doctorate, comprehensive exam, thesis/dissertation, departmental qualifying exam; for SSP, comprehensive exam, thesis optional. *Entrance requirements:* For master's and doctorate, GRE General Test. Additional exam requirements/recommendations for international students: Required—TOEFL (minimum score 550 paper-based; 79 iBT), IELTS (minimum score 6). *Application deadline:* For fall admission, 6/1 priority date for international students; for spring admission, 10/15 priority date for international students; for summer admission, 3/15 priority date for international students. Applications are processed on a rolling basis. Application fee: $50. Electronic applications accepted. *Expenses:* Tuition, state resident: full-time $3630. Tuition, nonresident: full-time $11,100. *Required fees:* $2564. Tuition and fees vary according to course load, degree level and program. *Financial support:* In 2017–18, 84 students received support, including 40 research assistantships with partial tuition reimbursements available (averaging $10,800 per year), 12 teaching assistantships with partial tuition reimbursements available (averaging $13,000 per year); career-related internships or fieldwork, Federal Work-Study, institutionally sponsored loans, scholarships/grants, health care benefits, and unspecified assistantships also available. Financial award application deadline: 6/15; financial award applicants required to submit FAFSA. *Faculty research:* Cognitive and bilingual education, positive behavioral intervention, literacy, math readiness. *Total annual research expenditures:* $1.1 million. *Unit head:* Dr. Timothy Letzring, Dean, 903-886-5181, Fax: 903-886-5905, E-mail: tim.letzring@tamuc.edu. *Application contact:* Vicky Turner, Doctoral Degree and Special Programs Coordinator, 903-886-5167, E-mail: vicky.turner@tamuc.edu.
Website: http://www.tamuc.edu/academics/graduateSchool/programs/education/default.aspx

Texas Christian University, Harris College of Nursing and Health Sciences, Department of Social Work, Fort Worth, TX 76129. Offers MSW. *Accreditation:* CSWE. *Faculty:* 5 full-time (3 women), 3 part-time/adjunct (1 woman). *Students:* 32 full-time (29 women); includes 13 minority (6 Black or African American, non-Hispanic/Latino; 2 Asian, non-Hispanic/Latino; 3 Hispanic/Latino; 2 Two or more races, non-Hispanic/Latino), 3 international. Average age 27. 40 applicants, 78% accepted, 22 enrolled. In 2017, 27 master's awarded. *Degree requirements:* For master's, research project in field agency. *Entrance requirements:* Additional exam requirements/recommendations for international students: Recommended—TOEFL (minimum score 550 paper-based; 80 iBT), IELTS (minimum score 6.5). *Application deadline:* For fall admission, 4/2 for domestic and international students. Application fee: $60. Electronic applications accepted. *Expenses:* $930 per credit hour. *Financial support:* In 2017–18, 39 students received support. Tuition waivers (partial) available. Financial award application deadline: 4/2. *Faculty research:* Homelessness, sexual violence prevention, developmental disabilities, gendered organizations, social identity transitioning. *Total annual research expenditures:* $325,000. *Unit head:* Dr. James Petrovich, Chair, 817-257-6157, Fax: 817-257-7665, E-mail: j.petrovich@tcu.edu. *Application contact:* Catherine Tanner, Academic Program Specialist, 817-257-7612, Fax: 817-257-5784, E-mail: c.tanner@tcu.edu.
Website: https://harriscollege.tcu.edu/social-work/

Texas State University, The Graduate College, College of Applied Arts, Program in Social Work, San Marcos, TX 78666. Offers MSW. *Accreditation:* CSWE. *Program availability:* Part-time, evening/weekend, 100% online, blended/hybrid learning. *Faculty:* 28 full-time (16 women), 14 part-time/adjunct (13 women). *Students:* 171 full-time (154 women), 181 part-time (166 women); includes 190 minority (60 Black or African American, non-Hispanic/Latino; 4 Asian, non-Hispanic/Latino; 115 Hispanic/Latino; 11 Two or more races, non-Hispanic/Latino). Average age 31. 431 applicants, 42% accepted, 110 enrolled. In 2017, 145 master's awarded. *Degree requirements:* For master's, comprehensive exam, field practicum/internship under the supervision of a licensed master social worker within a social service agency. *Entrance requirements:* For master's, baccalaureate degree from regionally-accredited institution with minimum GPA of 3.0 in last 60 hours of course work, in last two full academic years, and in all undergraduate social work courses; resume; statement of purpose. Additional exam requirements/recommendations for international students: Required—TOEFL (minimum score 550 paper-based; 78 iBT), IELTS (minimum score 6.5). *Application deadline:* For fall admission, 3/15 for domestic and international students. Applications are processed on a rolling basis. Application fee: $40 ($90 for international students). Electronic applications accepted. *Expenses:* Tuition, state resident: full-time $7868; part-time $3934 per semester. Tuition, nonresident: full-time $17,828; part-time $8914 per semester. *Required fees:* $2092; $1435 per semester. Tuition and fees vary according to course load. *Financial support:* In 2017–18, 228 students received support, including 7 research assistantships (averaging $10,953 per year), 3 teaching assistantships (averaging $12,152 per year); career-related internships or fieldwork, Federal Work-Study, institutionally sponsored loans, scholarships/grants, and unspecified assistantships also available. Support available to part-time students. Financial award application deadline: 3/1; financial award applicants required to submit FAFSA. *Faculty research:* Community-based HIV education research program for diverse racial and ethnic groups. *Unit head:* Dr. Angela Ausbrooks, Graduate Advisor, 512-245-9067, E-mail: aa16@txstate.edu. *Application contact:* Dr. Andrea Golato, Dean of the Graduate College, 512-245-2581, Fax: 512-245-8365, E-mail: gradcollege@txstate.edu.
Website: http://www.gradcollege.txstate.edu/programs/msw.html

Texas Tech University, Graduate School, College of Arts and Sciences, Department of Sociology, Anthropology and Social Work, Lubbock, TX 79409. Offers anthropology (MA); social work (MSW); sociology (MA). *Program availability:* Part-time. *Faculty:* 28 full-time (17 women), 5 part-time/adjunct (3 women). *Students:* 46 full-time (32 women), 7 part-time (all women); includes 19 minority (3 Black or African American, non-Hispanic/Latino; 14 Hispanic/Latino; 2 Two or more races, non-Hispanic/Latino), 2 international. Average age 28. 52 applicants, 44% accepted, 19 enrolled. In 2017, 22 master's awarded. *Degree requirements:* For master's, one foreign language, comprehensive exam (for some programs), thesis (for some programs). *Entrance requirements:* For master's, GRE (for MA in anthropology), two letters of recommendation, statement of purpose, writing sample, curriculum vitae; minimum GPA of 3.0 and coursework in sociology or closely-related fields (for MA in sociology); coursework in anthropology (for MA in anthropology). Additional exam requirements/recommendations for international students: Required—TOEFL (minimum score 550 paper-based; 79 iBT). *Application deadline:* For fall admission, 6/1 priority date for domestic students, 1/15 priority date for international students; for spring admission, 9/1 priority date for domestic students, 6/15 priority date for international students. Applications are processed on a rolling basis. Application fee: $60. Electronic applications accepted. *Financial support:* In 2017–18, 43 students received support, including 35 fellowships (averaging $4,324 per year), 28 teaching assistantships (averaging $13,091 per year); research assistantships, Federal Work-Study, scholarships/grants, tuition waivers (partial), and unspecified assistantships also available. Financial award application deadline: 2/1; financial award applicants required to submit FAFSA. *Faculty research:* Sociology of criminology/deviance, population/migration, forensic anthropology, archaeology, social work (advanced generalist). *Total annual research expenditures:* $153,180. *Unit head:* Dr.

Brett A. Houk, Chair and Associate Professor, 806-834-8107, Fax: 806-742-1088, E-mail: brett.houk@ttu.edu. *Application contact:* Dr. Martha Smithey, Associate Professor/Sociology Graduate Program Director, 806-834-1995, E-mail: martha.smithey@ttu.edu.
Website: http://www.depts.ttu.edu/sasw/

Thompson Rivers University, Program in Social Work, Kamloops, BC V2C 0C8, Canada. Offers MSW.

Touro College, Graduate School of Social Work, New York, NY 10010. Offers MSW. *Accreditation:* CSWE. *Faculty:* 9 full-time (6 women), 54 part-time/adjunct (32 women). *Students:* 442 full-time (281 women), 86 part-time (56 women); includes 227 minority (134 Black or African American, non-Hispanic/Latino; 1 American Indian or Alaska Native, non-Hispanic/Latino; 6 Asian, non-Hispanic/Latino; 73 Hispanic/Latino; 13 Two or more races, non-Hispanic/Latino), 12 international. Average age 34. *Entrance requirements:* Additional exam requirements/recommendations for international students: Required—TOEFL (minimum score 83 iBT), IELTS (minimum score 6.5), PTE (minimum score 58). *Financial support:* Scholarships/grants available. *Unit head:* Dr. Steven Huberman, Dean, 212-463-0400 Ext. 5269, E-mail: msw@touro.edu. *Application contact:* Peter Stewart, Director of Recruitment, Admissions and Enrollment Management, 212-463-0400 Ext. 5630, Fax: 212-627-3693, E-mail: peter.stewart@touro.edu.
Website: http://gssw.touro.edu/

Troy University, Graduate School, College of Health and Human Services, Program in Social Work, Troy, AL 36082. Offers MSW. *Program availability:* Part-time, evening/weekend. *Faculty:* 7 full-time (4 women), 5 part-time/adjunct (4 women). *Students:* 162 full-time (149 women), 25 part-time (24 women); includes 95 minority (89 Black or African American, non-Hispanic/Latino; 3 Hispanic/Latino; 3 Two or more races, non-Hispanic/Latino). Average age 31. 155 applicants, 95% accepted, 103 enrolled. In 2017, 99 master's awarded. *Degree requirements:* For master's, practicum. *Entrance requirements:* For master's, GRE (minimum score of 850 on old exam or 290 on new exam), GMAT (minimum score of 380) or MAT (minimum score of 385), minimum GPA of 2.5 on last 30 semester hours taken, criminal background check. Additional exam requirements/recommendations for international students: Required—TOEFL (minimum score 523 paper-based; 70 iBT), IELTS (minimum score 6). *Application deadline:* Applications are processed on a rolling basis. Application fee: $50. Electronic applications accepted. *Expenses:* Tuition, state resident: part-time $417 per credit hour. Tuition, nonresident: part-time $834 per credit hour. *Required fees:* $42 per credit hour. $50 per semester. Tuition and fees vary according to campus/location. *Financial support:* Fellowships, career-related internships or fieldwork, and scholarships/grants available. Support available to part-time students. *Unit head:* Dr. Denise Green, Chairman, 334-670-5767, E-mail: dmgreen@troy.edu. *Application contact:* Jessica A. Kimbro, Director of Graduate Admissions, 334-670-3178, Fax: 334-670-3733, E-mail: jacord@troy.edu.

Tulane University, School of Social Work, New Orleans, LA 70118-5669. Offers city, culture and community (PhD); disaster resilience leadership (MS); social work (MSW, DSW). *Accreditation:* CSWE (one or more programs are accredited). *Program availability:* Part-time. *Degree requirements:* For master's, thesis. *Entrance requirements:* Additional exam requirements/recommendations for international students: Required—TOEFL. Electronic applications accepted. *Expenses:* Tuition: Full-time $50,920; part-time $2829 per credit hour. *Required fees:* $2040; $44.50 per credit hour. $580 per term. Tuition and fees vary according to course load, degree level and program.

Union University, School of Social Work, Jackson, TN 38305-3697. Offers MSW. *Accreditation:* CSWE.

Universidad del Este, Graduate School, Carolina, PR 00984. Offers accounting (MBA); adult education (M Ed); agribusiness (MBA); criminal justice and criminology (MA); curriculum and instruction - early education (M Ed); curriculum and instruction - elementary (M Ed); curriculum and instruction - English (M Ed); curriculum and instruction - Spanish (M Ed); human resources (MBA); information security management (MBA); information technology and Web business development (MBA); management (MBA); public policy (MPA); social work (MA), including clinical social work; special education (M Ed); strategic leadership (MBA).

Université de Moncton, Faculty of Arts and Social Sciences, School of Social Work, Moncton, NB E1A 3E9, Canada. Offers MSW. *Degree requirements:* For master's, one foreign language, major paper. *Entrance requirements:* For master's, minimum GPA of 3.0. *Faculty research:* Burnout and education, mental health (institutionalization), unemployment's effect on youth, women and health services.

Université de Montréal, Faculty of Arts and Sciences, School of Social Service, Program in Social Administration, Montréal, QC H3C 3J7, Canada. Offers DESS. Electronic applications accepted.

Université de Sherbrooke, Faculty of Letters and Human Sciences, Department of Social Service, Sherbrooke, QC J1K 2R1, Canada. Offers MSS.

Université du Québec à Montréal, Graduate Programs, Program in Social Intervention, Montréal, QC H3C 3P8, Canada. Offers MA. *Program availability:* Part-time. *Degree requirements:* For master's, thesis. *Entrance requirements:* For master's, appropriate bachelor's degree or equivalent, proficiency in French.

Université du Québec en Abitibi-Témiscamingue, Graduate Programs, Program in Social Work, Rouyn-Noranda, QC J9X 5E4, Canada. Offers MSW.

Université du Québec en Outaouais, Graduate Programs, Program in Social Work, Gatineau, QC J8X 3X7, Canada. Offers MA. *Degree requirements:* For master's, thesis (for some programs).

Université Laval, Faculty of Social Sciences, School of Social Work, Programs in Social Work, Québec, QC G1K 7P4, Canada. Offers M Serv Soc, PhD. Terminal master's awarded for partial completion of doctoral program. *Degree requirements:* For master's, thesis (for some programs); for doctorate, comprehensive exam, thesis/dissertation. *Entrance requirements:* For master's and doctorate, knowledge of French, comprehension of written English. Electronic applications accepted.

University at Albany, State University of New York, School of Social Welfare, Albany, NY 12222-0001. Offers MSW, PhD, MSW/MA. *Accreditation:* CSWE (one or more programs are accredited). *Program availability:* Part-time, evening/weekend. *Faculty:* 30 full-time (23 women), 37 part-time/adjunct (31 women). *Students:* 281 full-time (235 women), 110 part-time (93 women); includes 102 minority (43 Black or African American, non-Hispanic/Latino; 1 American Indian or Alaska Native, non-Hispanic/Latino; 8 Asian, non-Hispanic/Latino; 42 Hispanic/Latino; 8 Two or more races, non-Hispanic/Latino), 13 international. 435 applicants, 63% accepted, 192 enrolled. In 2017, 144 master's, 7 doctorates awarded. *Degree requirements:* For doctorate, thesis/dissertation. *Entrance requirements:* For doctorate, GRE General Test. Additional exam requirements/recommendations for international students: Required—TOEFL (minimum score 550 paper-based). *Application deadline:* For fall admission, 2/15 for domestic and international students. Application fee: $75. Electronic applications accepted. *Expenses:* $14,866 per year in-state; $24,126 out-of-state. *Financial support:* Fellowships, career-related internships or fieldwork, and Federal Work-Study available. Financial award application deadline: 2/15. *Faculty research:* Welfare reform, homelessness, children and families, mental health, substance abuse. *Unit head:* Lynn Warner, Dean, 518-442-5324, E-mail: lwarner@albany.edu.

University at Buffalo, the State University of New York, Graduate School, School of Social Work, Buffalo, NY 14260. Offers social welfare (PhD); social work (MSW); JD/MSW; MBA/MSW; MPH/MSW; MSW/PhD. *Accreditation:* CSWE (one or more programs are accredited). *Program availability:* Part-time, 100% online, blended/hybrid learning. *Faculty:* 32 full-time (24 women), 53 part-time/adjunct (42 women). *Students:* 272 full-time (265 women), 228 part-time (163 women); includes 81 minority (51 Black or African American, non-Hispanic/Latino; 3 American Indian or Alaska Native, non-Hispanic/Latino; 17 Asian, non-Hispanic/Latino; 10 Hispanic/Latino). Average age 30. 445 applicants, 74% accepted, 222 enrolled. In 2017, 240 master's, 1 doctorate awarded. *Degree requirements:* For master's, 900 hours of field work; for doctorate, comprehensive exam, thesis/dissertation. *Entrance requirements:* For master's, 24 credits of course work in liberal arts; for doctorate, GRE General Test, MSW or equivalent. Additional exam requirements/recommendations for international students: Required—TOEFL (minimum score 600 paper-based; 100 iBT). *Application deadline:* For fall admission, 3/1 priority date for domestic and international students; for spring admission, 9/15 for domestic and international students; for summer admission, 2/1 for domestic and international students. Application fee: $75. Electronic applications accepted. *Expenses:* Contact institution. *Financial support:* In 2017–18, 10 fellowships with full tuition reimbursements (averaging $10,800 per year), 2 research assistantships with full tuition reimbursements (averaging $16,500 per year), 13 teaching assistantships with full tuition reimbursements (averaging $5,000 per year) were awarded; Federal Work-Study, scholarships/grants, health care benefits, tuition waivers (full and partial), unspecified assistantships, and instructorships and research grants (for PhD students) also available. Financial award application deadline: 4/30; financial award applicants required to submit FAFSA. *Faculty research:* Violence and victimization; trauma and trauma-informed care; health, behavioral health and addictions; children and adolescents; aging. *Total annual research expenditures:* $963,430. *Unit head:* Dr. Nancy J. Smyth, Dean, 716-645-3381, Fax: 716-645-3883, E-mail: sw-dean@buffalo.edu. *Application contact:* Maria Carey, Admissions Processor, 716-645-3381, Fax: 716-645-3456, E-mail: sw-info@buffalo.edu.
Website: http://www.socialwork.buffalo.edu

The University of Akron, Graduate School, College of Health Professions, School of Social Work, Akron, OH 44325. Offers MSW. *Accreditation:* CSWE. *Faculty:* 7 full-time (3 women), 17 part-time/adjunct (14 women). *Students:* 110 full-time (89 women), 32 part-time (24 women); includes 38 minority (26 Black or African American, non-Hispanic/Latino; 3 Hispanic/Latino; 9 Two or more races, non-Hispanic/Latino), 1 international. Average age 31. 81 applicants, 89% accepted, 72 enrolled. In 2017, 70 master's awarded. *Entrance requirements:* For master's, undergraduate major in social work or related field, three letters of recommendation, essay, resume. Additional exam requirements/recommendations for international students: Required—TOEFL (minimum score 79 iBT), IELTS (minimum score 6.5). *Application deadline:* For fall admission, 2/15 for domestic and international students. Application fee: $45 ($70 for international students). Electronic applications accepted. *Financial support:* In 2017–18, 2 teaching assistantships with full tuition reimbursements were awarded. *Faculty research:* Spirituality and alternative healing, child welfare education and training, ethics and social work practice, evidence-based social work practice, social work continuing education. *Total annual research expenditures:* $45,599. *Unit head:* Dr. Timothy McCarragher, Director, 330-972-5976, E-mail: mccarra@uakron.edu.
Website: http://www.uakron.edu/socialwork/

The University of Alabama, Graduate School, School of Social Work, Tuscaloosa, AL 35487-0314. Offers MSW, PhD. *Accreditation:* CSWE (one or more programs are accredited). *Program availability:* Part-time, blended/hybrid learning. *Faculty:* 27 full-time (21 women), 18 part-time/adjunct (15 women). *Students:* 344 full-time (295 women), 66 part-time (55 women); includes 130 minority (111 Black or African American, non-Hispanic/Latino; 1 Asian, non-Hispanic/Latino; 9 Hispanic/Latino; 1 Native Hawaiian or other Pacific Islander, non-Hispanic/Latino; 8 Two or more races, non-Hispanic/Latino), 13 international. Average age 31. 450 applicants, 55% accepted, 186 enrolled. In 2017, 190 master's, 3 doctorates awarded. *Degree requirements:* For master's, professional internship; for doctorate, comprehensive exam, thesis/dissertation. *Entrance requirements:* For master's, GRE or MAT (if GPA less than 3.0), minimum GPA of 2.5; for doctorate, GRE, minimum GPA of 3.0. Additional exam requirements/recommendations for international students: Required—TOEFL (minimum score 79 iBT), IELTS, PTE. *Application deadline:* For fall admission, 2/1 priority date for domestic and international students; for spring admission, 9/1 priority date for domestic and international students; for summer admission, 2/1 priority date for domestic and international students. Application fee: $50 ($60 for international students). Electronic applications accepted. *Financial support:* In 2017–18, 21 students received support, including research assistantships with full tuition reimbursements available (averaging $12,744 per year), teaching assistantships with full tuition reimbursements available (averaging $12,744 per year); career-related internships or fieldwork, scholarships/grants, traineeships, health care benefits, and unspecified assistantships also available. Financial award application deadline: 2/1; financial award applicants required to submit FAFSA. *Faculty research:* Children and adolescents at risk, trauma, gerontology, child welfare policy, health. *Total annual research expenditures:* $863,942. *Unit head:* Dr. Vikki L. Vandiver, Professor and Dean, 205-348-3924, Fax: 205-348-9419, E-mail: vlvandiver@sw.ua.edu. *Application contact:* Amanda Moore, Coordinator of Student Services, 205-348-5272, Fax: 205-348-9419, E-mail: almoore2@ua.edu.
Website: http://www.socialwork.ua.edu/

University of Alaska Anchorage, College of Health, School of Social Work, Anchorage, AK 99508. Offers clinical social work practice (Certificate); social work (MSW); social work management (Certificate). *Accreditation:* CSWE. *Program availability:* Part-time, evening/weekend, online learning. *Degree requirements:* For master's, comprehensive exam (for some programs), thesis or alternative, research project. *Entrance requirements:* For master's, GRE General Test, writing sample. Additional exam requirements/recommendations for international students: Required—TOEFL (minimum score 550 paper-based). Electronic applications accepted. *Expenses:* Contact institution.

University of Arkansas, Graduate School, J. William Fulbright College of Arts and Sciences, School of Social Work, Fayetteville, AR 72701. Offers MSW. *Accreditation:* CSWE. In 2017, 22 master's awarded. *Entrance requirements:* For master's, GRE General Test. *Application deadline:* For fall admission, 8/1 for domestic students, 4/1 for international students; for spring admission, 12/1 for domestic students, 10/1 for international students; for summer admission, 4/15 for domestic students, 3/1 for international students. Applications are processed on a rolling basis. Application fee: $60. Electronic applications accepted. *Expenses:* Tuition, state resident: full-time $3782. Tuition, nonresident: full-time $10,238. *Financial support:* In 2017–18, 4 research assistantships were awarded; fellowships with tuition reimbursements and teaching assistantships also available. *Unit head:* Dr. Alishia Ferguson, Director, 479-575-5039, Fax: 479-575-4145, E-mail: ajfergus@uark.edu. *Application contact:* Dr.

Glenda House, Graduate Coordinator, 479-575-3783, E-mail: ghouse@uark.edu.
Website: https://fulbright.uark.edu/departments/social-work/

University of Arkansas at Little Rock, Graduate School, College of Education and Health Professions, School of Social Work, Program in Social Work, Little Rock, AR 72204-1099. Offers clinical social work (MSW); management and community practice (MSW). *Accreditation:* CSWE. *Entrance requirements:* For master's, GRE General Test or MAT, three letters of reference.

The University of British Columbia, Faculty of Arts and Faculty of Graduate Studies, School of Social Work, Vancouver, BC V6T 1Z2, Canada. Offers MSW, PhD. *Degree requirements:* For master's, thesis or essay; for doctorate, comprehensive exam, thesis/dissertation. *Entrance requirements:* For master's, BSW; for doctorate, MSW. Additional exam requirements/recommendations for international students: Required—TOEFL. Electronic applications accepted. *Expenses:* Contact institution. *Faculty research:* Gerontology, family resources, diversity, social inequality.

University of Calgary, Faculty of Graduate Studies, Faculty of Social Work, Calgary, AB T2N 1N4, Canada. Offers MSW, PhD, Postgraduate Diploma. *Degree requirements:* For master's, thesis (for some programs); for doctorate, thesis/dissertation, candidacy exam. *Entrance requirements:* For master's, BSW, minimum undergraduate GPA of 3.4 (1 year program), minimum GPA of 3.5 (2 year program); for doctorate, minimum graduate GPA of 3.5, MSW (preferred); for Postgraduate Diploma, MSW, minimum graduate GPA of 3.5. Additional exam requirements/recommendations for international students: Required—TOEFL (paper-based 550) or IELTS (7). Electronic applications accepted. *Faculty research:* Family violence, direct practice, gerontology, child welfare, community development.

University of California, Berkeley, Graduate Division, School of Social Welfare, Berkeley, CA 94720-1500. Offers MSW, PhD, MSW/PhD. *Accreditation:* CSWE (one or more programs are accredited). Terminal master's awarded for partial completion of doctoral program. *Degree requirements:* For master's, thesis optional; for doctorate, thesis/dissertation, qualifying exam. *Entrance requirements:* For master's and doctorate, GRE General Test, minimum GPA of 3.0, 3 letters of recommendation. Additional exam requirements/recommendations for international students: Required—TOEFL (minimum score 570 paper-based; 90 iBT), TWE. Electronic applications accepted. *Faculty research:* Child welfare, law and social welfare, minority mental health, social welfare policy analysis, health services.

University of California, Los Angeles, Graduate Division, Luskin School of Public Affairs, Program in Social Welfare, Los Angeles, CA 90095. Offers MSW, PhD, JD/MSW. *Accreditation:* CSWE (one or more programs are accredited). *Degree requirements:* For master's, comprehensive exam, research project; for doctorate, thesis/dissertation, oral and written qualifying exams. *Entrance requirements:* For master's, GRE General Test, minimum GPA of 3.0; for doctorate, GRE General Test, minimum undergraduate GPA of 3.0. Additional exam requirements/recommendations for international students: Required—TOEFL. Electronic applications accepted.

University of Central Florida, College of Health Professions and Sciences, School of Social Work, Orlando, FL 32816. Offers military social work (Certificate); social work (MSW). *Accreditation:* CSWE. *Program availability:* Part-time, evening/weekend. *Students:* 215 full-time (190 women), 267 part-time (236 women); includes 241 minority (106 Black or African American, non-Hispanic/Latino; 2 American Indian or Alaska Native, non-Hispanic/Latino; 7 Asian, non-Hispanic/Latino; 113 Hispanic/Latino; 2 Native Hawaiian or other Pacific Islander, non-Hispanic/Latino; 11 Two or more races, non-Hispanic/Latino), 1 international. Average age 31. 336 applicants, 53% accepted, 135 enrolled. In 2017, 131 master's, 17 other advanced degrees awarded. *Degree requirements:* For master's, thesis or alternative, field education. *Entrance requirements:* For master's, letters of recommendation, resume, professional statement, academic writing sample. Additional exam requirements/recommendations for international students: Required—TOEFL. *Application deadline:* For fall admission, 4/1 for domestic students. Application fee: $30. Electronic applications accepted. *Expenses:* Tuition, state resident: part-time $288.16 per credit hour. Tuition, nonresident: part-time $1073.31 per credit hour. Tuition and fees vary according to program. *Financial support:* In 2017–18, 2 students received support, including 2 research assistantships with partial tuition reimbursements available (averaging $5,068 per year); fellowships, career-related internships or fieldwork, institutionally sponsored loans, and unspecified assistantships also available. Financial award application deadline: 3/1; financial award applicants required to submit FAFSA. *Unit head:* Dr. Bonnie Yegidis, Director, 407-823-2114, E-mail: bonnie.yegidis@ucf.edu. *Application contact:* Associate Director, Graduate Admissions, 407-823-2766, Fax: 407-823-6442, E-mail: gradadmissions@ucf.edu.
Website: https://www.cohpa.ucf.edu/socialwork/

University of Chicago, School of Social Service Administration, Doctoral Program, Chicago, IL 60637. Offers PhD, AM/PhD. *Students:* 54 full-time (35 women); includes 20 minority (11 Black or African American, non-Hispanic/Latino; 6 Asian, non-Hispanic/Latino; 3 Hispanic/Latino), 10 international. Average age 33. 62 applicants, 18% accepted, 7 enrolled. In 2017, 7 doctorates awarded. *Degree requirements:* For doctorate, comprehensive exam, thesis/dissertation. *Entrance requirements:* For doctorate, GRE General Test, prior master's degree in social work; 4 letters of recommendation; transcripts; curriculum vitae or resume; writing sample. Additional exam requirements/recommendations for international students: Required—TOEFL (minimum score 600 paper-based; 104 iBT), IELTS (minimum score 7). *Application deadline:* For fall admission, 12/15 for domestic and international students. Application fee: $75. Electronic applications accepted. *Financial support:* In 2017–18, 10 research assistantships with full tuition reimbursements (averaging $27,000 per year) were awarded; fellowships, teaching assistantships, Federal Work-Study, scholarships/grants, and health care benefits also available. Financial award application deadline: 12/15. *Faculty research:* Health administration, youth violence prevention, family well-being, social policy, crime, college success, urban education. *Unit head:* Dr. Deborah Gorman-Smith, Interim Dean/Professor, 773-702-1250, E-mail: admissions@ssa.uchicago.edu. *Application contact:* Ronald Martin, Director of Admissions, 773-702-1250, E-mail: admissions@ssa.uchicago.edu.
Website: http://www.ssa.uchicago.edu/doctoral-program

University of Chicago, School of Social Service Administration, Master's Program, Chicago, IL 60637. Offers MA, AM/M Div, MBA/AM, MPP/AM. *Accreditation:* CSWE. *Program availability:* Part-time, evening/weekend. *Students:* 360 full-time (309 women), 61 part-time (53 women); includes 147 minority (42 Black or African American, non-Hispanic/Latino; 33 Asian, non-Hispanic/Latino; 61 Hispanic/Latino; 1 Native Hawaiian or other Pacific Islander, non-Hispanic/Latino; 10 Two or more races, non-Hispanic/Latino), 29 international. Average age 27. 675 applicants, 62% accepted, 207 enrolled. In 2017, 205 master's awarded. *Degree requirements:* For master's, field education. *Entrance requirements:* For master's, transcripts, statement of purpose, 3 letters of recommendation. Additional exam requirements/recommendations for international students: Required—TOEFL (minimum score 600 paper-based; 104 iBT), IELTS (minimum score 7). *Application deadline:* For fall admission, 4/1 for domestic students, 1/15 priority date for international students; for spring admission, 10/15 for domestic students. Application fee: $75. Electronic applications accepted. *Financial support:* In

Social Work

2017–18, 13 research assistantships (averaging $5,000 per year) were awarded; Federal Work-Study, institutionally sponsored loans, scholarships/grants, and tuition waivers (partial) also available. Financial award application deadline: 4/1; financial award applicants required to submit FAFSA. *Application contact:* Ronald Martin, Director of Admissions, 773-702-1250, E-mail: admissions@ssa.uchicago.edu.
Website: http://www.ssa.uchicago.edu/masters-program

University of Cincinnati, Graduate School, College of Allied Health Sciences, School of Social Work, Cincinnati, OH 45221. Offers MSW. *Accreditation:* CSWE. *Program availability:* Part-time. *Entrance requirements:* Additional exam requirements/recommendations for international students: Required—TOEFL. Electronic applications accepted. *Expenses: Tuition, area resident:* Full-time $14,468. Tuition, state resident: full-time $14,968; part-time $754 per credit hour. Tuition, nonresident: full-time $24,210; part-time $1311 per credit hour. *International tuition:* $26,460 full-time. *Required fees:* $3958; $84 per credit hour. One-time fee: $85 full-time. Tuition and fees vary according to course load, degree level and program. *Faculty research:* Fatherhood, mediation, mental illness, child welfare, elderly.

University of Connecticut, Graduate School, School of Social Work, Storrs, CT 06269. Offers MSW, PhD. *Accreditation:* CSWE. *Degree requirements:* For master's, comprehensive exam; for doctorate, thesis/dissertation. *Entrance requirements:* Additional exam requirements/recommendations for international students: Required—TOEFL (minimum score 550 paper-based). Electronic applications accepted.

University of Denver, Graduate School of Social Work, Denver, CO 80208. Offers animal-assisted social work (Certificate); couples and family therapy (Certificate); social work (MSW, PhD); social work with Latinos/as (Certificate). *Accreditation:* CSWE (one or more programs are accredited). *Program availability:* Part-time, evening/weekend. *Faculty:* 40 full-time (27 women), 103 part-time/adjunct (88 women). *Students:* 511 full-time (457 women), 11 part-time (10 women); includes 117 minority (19 Black or African American, non-Hispanic/Latino; 7 American Indian or Alaska Native, non-Hispanic/Latino; 14 Asian, non-Hispanic/Latino; 58 Hispanic/Latino; 19 Two or more races, non-Hispanic/Latino), 1 international. Average age 28. 919 applicants, 79% accepted, 302 enrolled. In 2017, 278 master's, 7 doctorates, 55 other advanced degrees awarded. *Degree requirements:* For doctorate, comprehensive exam, thesis/dissertation. *Entrance requirements:* For master's, 20 undergraduate semester hours in the arts and humanities, social/behavioral sciences, and biological sciences; for doctorate, master's degree in social work or in one of the social sciences with substantial professional experience in the social work field; two years of post-master's practice experience (preferred). Additional exam requirements/recommendations for international students: Required—TOEFL (minimum score 587 paper-based; 95 iBT). *Application deadline:* For fall admission, 1/15 priority date for domestic and international students. Applications are processed on a rolling basis. Application fee: $65. Electronic applications accepted. *Expenses:* $47,823 per year on-campus full-time. *Financial support:* In 2017–18, 492 students received support, including 1 teaching assistantship with tuition reimbursement available (averaging $16,000 per year); Federal Work-Study, scholarships/grants, and unspecified assistantships also available. Support available to part-time students. Financial award application deadline: 2/15; financial award applicants required to submit FAFSA. *Faculty research:* Aging, youth, community, mental health, families. *Unit head:* Dr. Amanda Moore McBride, Dean, 303-871-2203, Fax: 303-871-2845. *Application contact:* Roberto Garcia, Director of Enrollment Management, 303-871-2602, E-mail: gssw-admission@du.edu.
Website: http://www.du.edu/socialwork

University of Georgia, School of Social Work, Athens, GA 30602. Offers MA, MSW, PhD, Certificate, MSW/JD. *Accreditation:* CSWE (one or more programs are accredited). *Program availability:* Part-time, evening/weekend. *Degree requirements:* For master's, thesis or alternative; for doctorate, one foreign language, thesis/dissertation. *Entrance requirements:* For master's and doctorate, GRE General Test. Electronic applications accepted. *Faculty research:* Juvenile justice, substance abuse, civil rights and social justice, gerontology, social policy.

University of Guam, Office of Graduate Studies, College of Natural and Applied Sciences, Program in Social Work, Mangilao, GU 96923. Offers MSW.

University of Hawaii at Manoa, Office of Graduate Education, School of Social Work, Honolulu, HI 96822. Offers social welfare (PhD); social work (MSW). *Accreditation:* CSWE (one or more programs are accredited). *Program availability:* Part-time. *Degree requirements:* For doctorate, comprehensive exam, thesis/dissertation. *Entrance requirements:* For doctorate, master's degree (MSW preferred), minimum GPA of 3.0. Additional exam requirements/recommendations for international students: Required—TOEFL (minimum score 560 paper-based; 83 iBT); IELTS (minimum score 5). *Faculty research:* Health, mental health, AIDS, substance abuse, rural health, community-based research, social policy.

University of Houston, Graduate College of Social Work, Houston, TX 77204. Offers MSW, PhD. *Accreditation:* CSWE (one or more programs are accredited). *Program availability:* Part-time. *Degree requirements:* For master's, 900 clock hours of field experience, integrative paper. *Entrance requirements:* For master's, GRE, minimum GPA of 3.0 in last 60 hours, bachelor's degree. Additional exam requirements/recommendations for international students: Required—TOEFL (minimum score 550 paper-based; 79 iBT). *Faculty research:* Health care, gerontology, political social work, mental health, children and families.

University of Houston–Downtown, College of Public Service, Department of Criminal Justice and Social Work, Houston, TX 77002. Offers MS. *Program availability:* Part-time, evening/weekend, 100% online. *Faculty:* 13 full-time (8 women). *Students:* 19 full-time (13 women), 43 part-time (32 women); includes 45 minority (20 Black or African American, non-Hispanic/Latino; 3 Asian, non-Hispanic/Latino; 22 Hispanic/Latino), 1 international. Average age 32. 29 applicants, 59% accepted, 15 enrolled. In 2017, 19 master's awarded. *Degree requirements:* For master's, thesis or project. *Entrance requirements:* For master's, personal statement, 3 letters of recommendation, minimum GPA of 3.0 on last 60 hours. Additional exam requirements/recommendations for international students: Required—TOEFL (minimum score 550 paper-based; 50 iBT). *Application deadline:* For fall admission, 7/15 for domestic and international students; for spring admission, 11/15 for domestic and international students. Application fee: $35 ($60 for international students). Electronic applications accepted. *Expenses:* $335 per credit resident; $700 per credit non-resident. *Financial support:* Federal Work-Study and scholarships/grants available. Financial award application deadline: 4/1; financial award applicants required to submit FAFSA. *Faculty research:* Policing issues, issues in security, community supervision, legal and other issues in prisons, juvenile justice. *Unit head:* Dr. Ashley Blackburn, Chair, 713-222-5326, Fax: 713-221-2726, E-mail: blackburna@uhd.edu. *Application contact:* Ceshia Love, Director of Admissions, 713-221-8093, Fax: 713-223-7408, E-mail: gradadmissions@uhd.edu.
Website: http://www.uhd.edu/mscj

University of Illinois at Chicago, Jane Addams College of Social Work, Chicago, IL 60607-7128. Offers MSW, PhD, Certificate. *Accreditation:* CSWE (one or more programs are accredited). *Program availability:* Part-time. Terminal master's awarded for partial completion of doctoral program. *Degree requirements:* For doctorate, thesis/dissertation. *Entrance requirements:* For master's, GMAT, minimum GPA of 2.75; for

doctorate, GRE General Test or MAT, minimum GPA of 2.75. Additional exam requirements/recommendations for international students: Required—TOEFL. Electronic applications accepted. *Expenses:* Contact institution. *Faculty research:* Children, youth, and family; criminal justice; health; gerontology; international.

University of Illinois at Urbana–Champaign, Graduate College, School of Social Work, Champaign, IL 61820. Offers advocacy, leadership, and social change (MSW); children, youth and family services (MSW); health care (MSW); mental health (MSW); school social work (MSW); social work (PhD). *Accreditation:* CSWE (one or more programs are accredited). *Entrance requirements:* For master's and doctorate, minimum GPA of 3.0.

The University of Iowa, Graduate College, College of Liberal Arts and Sciences, School of Social Work, Iowa City, IA 52242-1316. Offers MSW, PhD, JD/MSW, MSW/MA, MSW/MS, MSW/PhD. *Accreditation:* CSWE. *Degree requirements:* For master's, thesis optional; for doctorate, comprehensive exam, thesis/dissertation. *Entrance requirements:* For master's, minimum GPA of 3.0; for doctorate, GRE General Test, minimum GPA of 3.0. Additional exam requirements/recommendations for international students: Required—TOEFL (minimum score 600 paper-based; 100 iBT). Electronic applications accepted.

The University of Kansas, Graduate Studies, School of Social Welfare, Lawrence, KS 66045. Offers MSW, PhD, JD/MSW. *Accreditation:* CSWE (one or more programs are accredited). *Program availability:* Part-time, online learning. *Students:* 330 full-time (290 women), 56 part-time (49 women); includes 87 minority (34 Black or African American, non-Hispanic/Latino; 7 American Indian or Alaska Native, non-Hispanic/Latino; 3 Asian, non-Hispanic/Latino; 17 Hispanic/Latino; 21 Two or more races, non-Hispanic/Latino), 5 international. Average age 30. 315 applicants, 82% accepted, 185 enrolled. In 2017, 180 master's, 4 doctorates awarded. *Entrance requirements:* For master's, minimum GPA of 3.0, social work related experience, 3 letters of recommendation, student-issued transcripts from all previously attended schools regardless of degree status; for doctorate, GRE (Quantitative and Verbal), master's degree in social work or related field, minimum GPA of 3.5, personal statement, 3 letters of recommendation, completion of a statistics course with minimum B grade. Additional exam requirements/recommendations for international students: Required—TOEFL. *Application deadline:* For fall admission, 1/17 for domestic and international students. Application fee: $65 ($85 for international students). Electronic applications accepted. *Financial support:* Fellowships, research assistantships, teaching assistantships, Federal Work-Study, scholarships/grants, and tuition waivers (partial) available. Support available to part-time students. Financial award application deadline: 1/17; financial award applicants required to submit FAFSA. *Faculty research:* Poverty, child welfare, children's mental health, aging and long-term care, families and connections. *Unit head:* Steve Kapp, Interim Dean, 785-864-2269, E-mail: stevek@ku.edu. *Application contact:* Becky Hofer, Director of Graduate Admissions, 785-864-8956, E-mail: bhofer@ku.edu.
Website: http://socwel.ku.edu/

University of Kentucky, Graduate School, College of Social Work, Lexington, KY 40506-0032. Offers MSW, PhD. *Accreditation:* CSWE. *Degree requirements:* For master's, comprehensive exam; for doctorate, comprehensive exam, thesis/dissertation. *Entrance requirements:* For master's, GRE General Test, minimum undergraduate GPA of 2.75; for doctorate, GRE General Test, minimum undergraduate GPA of 3.0. Additional exam requirements/recommendations for international students: Required—TOEFL (minimum score 550 paper-based). Electronic applications accepted.

University of Louisville, Graduate School, Kent School of Social Work, Louisville, KY 40292-0001. Offers marriage and family therapy (PMC), including mental health; social work (MSSW, PhD), including alcohol and drug counseling (MSSW), gerontology (MSSW), marriage and family (PhD), school social work (MSSW). *Accreditation:* AAMFT/COAMFTE; CSWE (one or more programs are accredited). *Program availability:* Part-time, evening/weekend, 100% online, blended/hybrid learning. *Faculty:* 31 full-time (22 women), 44 part-time/adjunct (35 women). *Students:* 402 full-time (357 women), 103 part-time (88 women); includes 119 minority (68 Black or African American, non-Hispanic/Latino; 1 American Indian or Alaska Native, non-Hispanic/Latino; 8 Asian, non-Hispanic/Latino; 16 Hispanic/Latino; 26 Two or more races, non-Hispanic/Latino), 5 international. Average age 31. 396 applicants, 78% accepted, 228 enrolled. In 2017, 179 master's awarded. *Degree requirements:* For doctorate, comprehensive exam, thesis/dissertation. *Entrance requirements:* For master's, GRE or minimum GPA of 2.75; for doctorate, GRE General Test, interview, writing sample. Additional exam requirements/recommendations for international students: Required—TOEFL (minimum score 550 paper-based; 79 iBT), IELTS (minimum score 6.5). *Application deadline:* For fall admission, 5/30 for domestic and international students; for spring admission, 9/30 for domestic and international students; for summer admission, 2/28 for domestic and international students. Applications are processed on a rolling basis. Application fee: $65. Electronic applications accepted. *Expenses:* Contact institution. *Financial support:* In 2017–18, 11 research assistantships with full tuition reimbursements (averaging $21,500 per year), 1 teaching assistantship with full tuition reimbursement (averaging $19,000 per year) were awarded; scholarships/grants, health care benefits, and unspecified assistantships also available. Financial award application deadline: 5/15; financial award applicants required to submit FAFSA. *Faculty research:* Equipping young children with skills, assisting abused or neglected children, helping juveniles with sexual behavioral problems, illuminating the contributions that men and women make to their families, managing chronic conditions, enhancing trauma-informed services, addressing social and health issues of older adults, palliative and end-of-life care. *Total annual research expenditures:* $6.1 million. *Unit head:* Dr. David Jenkins, Dean, 502-852-3944, Fax: 502-852-0422, E-mail: dajenk03@exchange.louisville.edu. *Application contact:* Misty Kupka, Program Manager for Admissions and Recruitment, 502-852-0414, Fax: 502-852-0422, E-mail: misty.kupka@louisville.edu.
Website: http://www.louisville.edu/kent

University of Maine, Graduate School, College of Natural Sciences, Forestry, and Agriculture, School of Social Work, Orono, ME 04469. Offers MSW, CGS. *Accreditation:* CSWE. *Program availability:* Part-time, evening/weekend. *Faculty:* 12 full-time (10 women), 16 part-time/adjunct (10 women). *Students:* 116 full-time (101 women), 10 part-time (9 women); includes 9 minority (3 Black or African American, non-Hispanic/Latino; 2 American Indian or Alaska Native, non-Hispanic/Latino; 1 Asian, non-Hispanic/Latino; 1 Hispanic/Latino; 2 Two or more races, non-Hispanic/Latino), 2 international. Average age 34. 123 applicants, 71% accepted, 58 enrolled. In 2017, 37 master's, 7 other advanced degrees awarded. *Entrance requirements:* For master's, GRE General Test, MAT. Additional exam requirements/recommendations for international students: Required—TOEFL (minimum score 577 paper-based; 77 iBT), IELTS (minimum score 6). *Application deadline:* For fall admission, 2/1 priority date for domestic and international students; for summer admission, 2/1 for domestic and international students. Applications are processed on a rolling basis. Application fee: $65. Electronic applications accepted. *Expenses:* Tuition, state resident: full-time $7722; part-time $429 per credit hour. Tuition, nonresident: full-time $25,146; part-time $1397 per credit hour. *Required fees:* $1162; $581 per credit hour. *Financial support:* In 2017–18, 14 students received support, including 1 research assistantship with full tuition reimbursement available (averaging $15,200 per year), 1 teaching assistantship with full tuition reimbursement available (averaging $15,200 per year); Federal Work-Study, scholarships/grants, health care benefits, and unspecified assistantships also available. Financial award application deadline: 3/1. *Faculty research:* Intimate partner violence; substance abuse; long-term care workforce; aging and isolation; services and design in assistive technologies. *Total annual research expenditures:* $170,742. *Unit head:* Dr. Gail Werrbach, Director, 207-581-2397, Fax: 207-581-2396. *Application contact:* Scott G. Delcourt, Assistant Vice President for Graduate Studies and Senior Associate Dean, 207-581-3291, Fax: 207-581-3232, E-mail: graduate@maine.edu. Website: https://www.umaine.edu/socialwork/

The University of Manchester, School of Nursing, Midwifery and Social Work, Manchester, United Kingdom. Offers nursing (M Phil, PhD); social work (M Phil, PhD).

University of Manitoba, Faculty of Graduate Studies, Faculty of Social Work, Winnipeg, MB R3T 2N2, Canada. Offers MSW, PhD. *Degree requirements:* For master's, thesis or alternative.

University of Maryland, Baltimore, Graduate School, School of Social Work, Doctoral Program in Social Work, Baltimore, MD 21201. Offers PhD. *Program availability:* Part-time. *Degree requirements:* For doctorate, thesis/dissertation. *Entrance requirements:* For doctorate, GRE General Test, minimum GPA of 3.5, MSW. *Expenses:* Tuition, state resident: full-time $13,990; part-time $661 per credit. Tuition, nonresident: full-time $30,484; part-time $1310 per credit. *Required fees:* $1894; $94 per credit. $415 per semester. Part-time tuition and fees vary according to course load, degree level and program. *Faculty research:* Social work research, social work teaching.

University of Maryland, Baltimore, Graduate School, School of Social Work, Master's Program in Social Work, Baltimore, MD 21201. Offers MSW, MBA/MSW, MSW/JD, MSW/MA, MSW/MPH. MSW/MA offered jointly with Baltimore Hebrew University; MBA/MSU with University of Maryland, College Park; MSW/MPH with The Johns Hopkins University. *Accreditation:* CSWE. *Entrance requirements:* For master's, minimum GPA of 3.0. Additional exam requirements/recommendations for international students: Required—TOEFL. Electronic applications accepted. *Expenses:* Tuition, state resident: full-time $13,990; part-time $661 per credit. Tuition, nonresident: full-time $30,484; part-time $1310 per credit. *Required fees:* $1894; $94 per credit. $415 per semester. Part-time tuition and fees vary according to course load, degree level and program. *Faculty research:* Aging, families and children, health, mental health, social action and community development.

University of Maryland, College Park, Academic Affairs, Robert H. Smith School of Business, Combined MSW/MBA Program, College Park, MD 20742. Offers MSW/MBA. *Accreditation:* AACSB. *Entrance requirements:* Additional exam requirements/recommendations for international students: Required—TOEFL.

University of Memphis, Graduate School, College of Arts and Sciences, Department of Social Work, Memphis, TN 38152. Offers adults and families (MSW); children, youth, and families (MSW). *Program availability:* Part-time, online learning. *Faculty:* 7 full-time (5 women), 14 part-time/adjunct (12 women). *Students:* 93 full-time (12 women), 41 part-time (3 women); includes 88 minority (85 Black or African American, non-Hispanic/Latino; 1 Hispanic/Latino; 2 Two or more races, non-Hispanic/Latino), 1 international. Average age 34. 60 applicants, 87% accepted, 38 enrolled. In 2017, 53 master's awarded. *Financial support:* In 2017–18, 4 research assistantships (averaging $8,500 per year) were awarded. *Unit head:* Dr. Susan Neely-Barnes, Chair, 901-678-3438, Fax: 901-678-2981, E-mail: snlybrns@memphis.edu. Website: http://www.memphis.edu/socialwork/

University of Michigan, School of Social Work, Master of Social Work Program, Ann Arbor, MI 48109. Offers MSW, MSW/JD, MSW/MBA, MSW/MPH, MSW/MPP, MSW/MSI, MSW/MUP. PhD offered through the Rackham Graduate School. *Faculty:* 57 full-time (36 women), 56 part-time/adjunct (42 women). *Students:* 755 full-time (635 women); includes 229 minority (78 Black or African American, non-Hispanic/Latino; 2 American Indian or Alaska Native, non-Hispanic/Latino; 34 Asian, non-Hispanic/Latino; 85 Hispanic/Latino; 1 Native Hawaiian or other Pacific Islander, non-Hispanic/Latino; 29 Two or more races, non-Hispanic/Latino), 30 international. Average age 23. 1,249 applicants, 74% accepted, 417 enrolled. In 2017, 376 master's awarded. *Entrance requirements:* For master's, minimum of 20 academic semester credits total in at least three of the following disciplines: psychology, sociology, anthropology, economics, history, political science, government, and/or languages. Additional exam requirements/recommendations for international students: Required—TOEFL (minimum score 600 paper-based; 100 iBT), IELTS (minimum score 7), Michigan English Language Assessment Battery (minimum score 85). *Application deadline:* For fall admission, 3/1 priority date for domestic students, 2/1 priority date for international students. Applications are processed on a rolling basis. *Application fee:* $75. Electronic applications accepted. *Expenses:* $13,583 resident full-time per semester, $21,663 nonresident full-time per semester. *Financial support:* In 2017–18, 663 students received support. Career-related internships or fieldwork, Federal Work-Study, scholarships/grants, traineeships, and unspecified assistantships available. Financial award application deadline: 3/15; financial award applicants required to submit FAFSA. *Faculty research:* Children and families, aging, community organization, health and mental health, policy and evaluation. *Total annual research expenditures:* $4.1 million. *Unit head:* Lynn Videka, Dean, 734-764-5347, Fax: 734-615-5403, E-mail: lvideka@umich.edu. *Application contact:* Timothy Colenback, Assistant Dean for Student Services, 734-936-0961, Fax: 734-936-1961, E-mail: timot@umich.edu. Website: https://ssw.umich.edu/programs/msw

University of Minnesota, Duluth, Graduate School, College of Education and Human Service Professions, Department of Social Work, Duluth, MN 55812-2496. Offers MSW. *Accreditation:* CSWE. *Program availability:* Part-time, evening/weekend, online learning. *Entrance requirements:* For master's, minimum GPA of 3.0. Additional exam requirements/recommendations for international students: Required—TOEFL (minimum score 550 paper-based). *Faculty research:* Domestic abuse, substance abuse, minority health, child welfare, gerontology.

University of Minnesota, Twin Cities Campus, Graduate School, College of Education and Human Development, School of Social Work, Minneapolis, MN 55455-0213. Offers social work (MSW, PhD); youth development leadership (M Ed). *Accreditation:* CSWE (one or more programs are accredited). *Program availability:* Part-time, evening/weekend, online learning. *Faculty:* 20 full-time (12 women). *Students:* 283 full-time (236 women), 41 part-time (28 women); includes 108 minority (37 Black or African American, non-Hispanic/Latino; 7 American Indian or Alaska Native, non-Hispanic/Latino; 20 Asian, non-Hispanic/Latino; 22 Hispanic/Latino; 1 Native Hawaiian or other Pacific Islander, non-Hispanic/Latino; 21 Two or more races, non-Hispanic/Latino), 8 international. Average age 30. 323 applicants, 48% accepted, 150 enrolled. In 2017, 157 master's, 5 doctorates awarded. *Degree requirements:* For doctorate, thesis/dissertation. *Entrance requirements:* For master's, minimum GPA of 3.0, 1 year of work experience; for doctorate, GRE, minimum GPA of 3.0, MSW. *Application deadline:* For fall admission, 1/15 for domestic students. *Application fee:* $75 ($95 for international students). *Financial support:* In 2017–18, 142 students received support, including 9 fellowships, 39 research assistantships (averaging $13,053 per year), 1 teaching assistantship (averaging $7,391 per year); career-related internships or fieldwork, Federal Work-Study, institutionally sponsored loans, and tuition waivers (full and partial) also available. Support available to part-time students. Financial award applicants

required to submit FAFSA. *Faculty research:* Behavioral health, clinical mental health, aging and disability, work with youth, family and community violence prevention, new American and immigrant populations, child welfare, youth leadership, community engagement, mediation and restitution, social justice. *Total annual research expenditures:* $4.7 million. *Unit head:* Dr. James Reinardy, Director, 612-624-3673, E-mail: jreinard@umn.edu. *Application contact:* Dr. Joseph Merighi, Director of Graduate Studies, 612-625-1220, E-mail: jmerighi@umn.edu. Website: http://www.cehd.umn.edu/ssw/

University of Mississippi, Graduate School, School of Applied Sciences, University, MS 38677. Offers communicative disorders (MS); criminal justice (MCJ); exercise science (MS); food and nutrition services (MS); health and kinesiology (PhD); health promotion (MS); nutrition and hospitality management (PhD); park and recreation management (MA); social welfare (PhD); social work (MSW). *Faculty:* 66 full-time (38 women), 33 part-time/adjunct (14 women). *Students:* 182 full-time (139 women), 41 part-time (27 women); includes 49 minority (41 Black or African American, non-Hispanic/Latino; 1 American Indian or Alaska Native, non-Hispanic/Latino; 3 Asian, non-Hispanic/Latino; 3 Hispanic/Latino; 1 Two or more races, non-Hispanic/Latino), 13 international. Average age 26. *Entrance requirements:* For master's, GRE General Test, minimum GPA of 3.0. Additional exam requirements/recommendations for international students: Required—TOEFL. *Application deadline:* For fall admission, 4/1 for domestic students; for spring admission, 10/1 for domestic students. Applications are processed on a rolling basis. *Application fee:* $50. Electronic applications accepted. *Financial support:* Scholarships/grants available. Financial award application deadline: 3/1; financial award applicants required to submit FAFSA. *Unit head:* Dr. Teresa C. Carithers, Dean, 662-915-1081, Fax: 662-915-5717, E-mail: applsci@olemiss.edu.

University of Missouri, Office of Research and Graduate Studies, School of Social Work, Columbia, MO 65211. Offers gerontological social work (Certificate); military social work (Certificate); social work (MSW, PhD). *Accreditation:* CSWE. *Program availability:* Part-time. *Entrance requirements:* For master's, GRE General Test, minimum GPA of 3.0. Additional exam requirements/recommendations for international students: Required—TOEFL (minimum score 90 iBT), IELTS (minimum score 7). Electronic applications accepted.

University of Missouri–Kansas City, College of Arts and Sciences, School of Social Work, Kansas City, MO 64110-2499. Offers MSW. *Accreditation:* CSWE. *Program availability:* Part-time, evening/weekend. *Entrance requirements:* For master's, minimum GPA of 3.0, 3 letters of reference. Additional exam requirements/recommendations for international students: Recommended—TOEFL (minimum score 550 paper-based; 80 iBT). *Faculty research:* Social justice, LGBT issues, deinstitutionalization, community collaboration and partnerships, evaluation of strengths model with addiction model.

University of Missouri–St. Louis, School of Social Work, St. Louis, MO 63121. Offers MSW. *Accreditation:* CSWE. *Program availability:* Part-time. *Faculty:* 13 full-time (8 women), 3 part-time/adjunct (2 women). *Students:* 90 full-time (78 women), 65 part-time (51 women); includes 36 minority (27 Black or African American, non-Hispanic/Latino; 1 Asian, non-Hispanic/Latino; 4 Hispanic/Latino; 1 Native Hawaiian or other Pacific Islander, non-Hispanic/Latino; 3 Two or more races, non-Hispanic/Latino), 1 international. 118 applicants, 68% accepted, 62 enrolled. *Entrance requirements:* For master's, 3 letters of recommendation, minimum GPA of 2.75. Additional exam requirements/recommendations for international students: Required—TOEFL (minimum score 550 paper-based; 79 iBT), IELTS (minimum score 6.5). *Application deadline:* For fall admission, 3/1 for domestic and international students; for spring admission, 10/15 for domestic and international students. *Application fee:* $50 ($40 for international students). Electronic applications accepted. *Expenses:* Tuition, state resident: part-time $476.50 per credit hour. Tuition, nonresident: part-time $1169.70 per credit hour. *Financial support:* Research assistantships with tuition reimbursements, teaching assistantships with tuition reimbursements, and scholarships/grants available. Financial award applicants required to submit FAFSA. *Faculty research:* Family violence, child abuse/neglect, immigration, community economic development. *Unit head:* Sharon Johnson, Dean, 314-516-6385, Fax: 314-516-5816, E-mail: socialwork@umsl.edu. *Application contact:* 314-516-5458, Fax: 314-516-6996, E-mail: gradadm@umsl.edu. Website: http://www.umsl.edu/~socialwk/

University of Montana, Graduate School, College of Health Professions and Biomedical Sciences, School of Social Work, Missoula, MT 59812. Offers MSW. *Accreditation:* CSWE.

University of Nebraska at Omaha, Graduate Studies, College of Public Affairs and Community Service, Grace Abbott School of Social Work, Omaha, NE 68182. Offers social work (MSW). *Accreditation:* CSWE. *Degree requirements:* For master's, comprehensive exam, thesis (for some programs). *Entrance requirements:* For master's, minimum GPA of 3.0, 3 letters of recommendation, resume, statement of purpose. Additional exam requirements/recommendations for international students: Required—TOEFL (minimum score 550 paper-based; 61 iBT), IELTS (minimum score 5.5), PTE (minimum score 44). Electronic applications accepted.

University of Nevada, Las Vegas, Graduate College, Greenspun College of Urban Affairs, School of Social Work, Las Vegas, NV 89154-5032. Offers MSW, MSW/JD. *Accreditation:* CSWE. *Faculty:* 9 full-time (7 women), 7 part-time/adjunct (5 women). *Students:* 157 full-time (131 women), 46 part-time (41 women); includes 118 minority (37 Black or African American, non-Hispanic/Latino; 1 American Indian or Alaska Native, non-Hispanic/Latino; 7 Asian, non-Hispanic/Latino; 57 Hispanic/Latino; 16 Two or more races, non-Hispanic/Latino), 2 international. Average age 33. 135 applicants, 73% accepted, 76 enrolled. In 2017, 72 master's awarded. *Degree requirements:* For master's, thesis (for some programs). *Entrance requirements:* For master's, bachelor's degree with minimum GPA 2.75; 3 letters of recommendation; completion of some liberal arts courses. Additional exam requirements/recommendations for international students: Required—TOEFL (minimum score 550 paper-based; 80 iBT), IELTS (minimum score 7). *Application deadline:* For fall admission, 11/1 for domestic students; for summer admission, 11/1 for domestic students. *Application fee:* $60 ($95 for international students). Electronic applications accepted. *Expenses:* $275 per credit, $850 per course, $7,969 per year resident, $22,157 per year non-resident, $7,094 non-resident fee (7 credits or more), $1,307 annual health insurance fee. *Financial support:* In 2017–18, 19 students received support, including 10 research assistantships with full and partial tuition reimbursements available (averaging $11,455 per year), 9 teaching assistantships with full and partial tuition reimbursements available (averaging $11,111 per year); institutionally sponsored loans, scholarships/grants, health care benefits, and unspecified assistantships also available. Financial award application deadline: 3/15; financial award applicants required to submit FAFSA. *Faculty research:* Child welfare and juvenile justice, health and mental health, poverty and social justice, substance abuse, public policy. *Total annual research expenditures:* $806,812. *Unit head:* Dr. Carlton Craig, Director/Professor, 702-895-0521, Fax: 702-895-4079, E-mail: carlton.craig@unlv.edu. *Application contact:* Dr. Maryann Overcamp-Martini, Graduate Coordinator, 702-895-4603, Fax: 702-895-4079, E-mail: mao.martini@unlv.edu. Website: http://socialwork.unlv.edu/

University of Nevada, Reno, Graduate School, Division of Health Sciences, School of Social Work, Reno, NV 89557. Offers MSW. *Accreditation:* CSWE. *Degree*

Social Work

requirements: For master's, thesis optional. *Entrance requirements:* For master's, GRE General Test, minimum GPA of 2.75, statistics course. Additional exam requirements/recommendations for international students: Required—TOEFL (minimum score 500 paper-based; 61 iBT), IELTS (minimum score 6). Electronic applications accepted. *Faculty research:* Policy practice, poverty, women's issues, race and diversity, vulnerable family, social justice, social change, diversity.

University of New England, College of Graduate and Professional Studies, Portland, ME 04005-9526. Offers advanced educational leadership (CAGS); applied nutrition (MS); career and technical education (MS Ed); curriculum and instruction (MS Ed); education (CAGS, Post-Master's Certificate); educational leadership (MS Ed, Ed D); generalist (MS Ed); health informatics (MS, Graduate Certificate); inclusion education (MS Ed); literacy K-12 (MS Ed); medical education leadership (MMEL); public health (MPH); public health (Graduate Certificate); reading specialist (MS Ed); social work (MSW). *Program availability:* Part-time, evening/weekend, online only, 100% online. *Faculty:* 125 part-time/adjunct (94 women). *Students:* 1,403 full-time (1,128 women), 594 part-time (475 women); includes 474 minority (332 Black or African American, non-Hispanic/Latino; 13 American Indian or Alaska Native, non-Hispanic/Latino; 83 Asian, non-Hispanic/Latino; 27 Hispanic/Latino; 11 Native Hawaiian or other Pacific Islander, non-Hispanic/Latino; 8 Two or more races, non-Hispanic/Latino). Average age 35. 3,153 applicants, 41% accepted, 990 enrolled. In 2017, 307 master's, 59 doctorates, 124 other advanced degrees awarded. *Application deadline:* Applications are processed on a rolling basis. Electronic applications accepted. Tuition and fees vary according to degree level, program and student level. *Financial support:* Application deadline: 5/1; applicants required to submit FAFSA. *Unit head:* Dr. Martha Wilson, Associate Provost for Online Worldwide Learning/Dean of the College of Graduate and Professional Studies, 207-221-4985, E-mail: mwilson13@une.edu.
Website: http://online.une.edu

University of New England, Westbrook College of Health Professions, Biddeford, ME 04005-9526. Offers nurse anesthesia (MSNA); occupational therapy (MS); physical therapy (DPT); physician assistant (MS); social work (MSW). *Program availability:* Part-time. *Faculty:* 43 full-time (30 women), 26 part-time/adjunct (19 women). *Students:* 527 full-time (401 women), 5 part-time (4 women); includes 50 minority (11 Black or African American, non-Hispanic/Latino; 1 American Indian or Alaska Native, non-Hispanic/Latino; 24 Asian, non-Hispanic/Latino; 5 Hispanic/Latino; 1 Native Hawaiian or other Pacific Islander, non-Hispanic/Latino; 8 Two or more races, non-Hispanic/Latino), 1 international. Average age 27. 2,499 applicants, 18% accepted, 226 enrolled. In 2017, 440 master's, 71 doctorates awarded. *Application deadline:* Applications are processed on a rolling basis. Electronic applications accepted. Tuition and fees vary according to degree level, program and student level. *Financial support:* Application deadline: 5/1; applicants required to submit FAFSA. *Unit head:* Dr. Elizabeth Francis- Connolly, Dean, Westbrook College of Health Professions, 207-221-4523, E-mail: efrancisconnolly@une.edu. *Application contact:* Scott Steinberg, Dean of University Admission, 207-221-4225, Fax: 207-523-1925, E-mail: ssteinberg@une.edu.
Website: http://www.une.edu/wchp/index.cfm

University of New Hampshire, Graduate School, College of Health and Human Services, Department of Kinesiology, Durham, NH 03824. Offers adapted physical education (Postbaccalaureate Certificate); kinesiology (MS); kinesiology and social work (MS). *Program availability:* Part-time. *Students:* 5 full-time (1 woman), 5 part-time (2 women), 1 international. Average age 28. 16 applicants, 56% accepted, 4 enrolled. In 2017, 10 master's awarded. *Entrance requirements:* For master's, GRE General Test. Additional exam requirements/recommendations for international students: Required—TOEFL (minimum score 550 paper-based; 80 iBT). *Application deadline:* For fall admission, 4/1 priority date for domestic students, 4/1 for international students; for spring admission, 12/1 for domestic students. Application fee: $65. Electronic applications accepted. *Financial support:* In 2017–18, 5 students received support, including 3 teaching assistantships; fellowships, research assistantships, career-related internships or fieldwork, Federal Work-Study, scholarships/grants, and tuition waivers (full and partial) also available. Support available to part-time students. Financial award application deadline: 2/15. *Unit head:* Karen Collins, Chair, 603-862-0361. *Application contact:* Jayson Seaman, Administrative Assistant, 603-862-1162, E-mail: kinesiology.dept@unh.edu.
Website: http://chhs.unh.edu/kin

University of New Hampshire, Graduate School, College of Health and Human Services, Department of Social Work, Durham, NH 03824. Offers child welfare (Postbaccalaureate Certificate); intellectual and development disabilities (Postbaccalaureate Certificate); social work (MSW); substance use disorders (Postbaccalaureate Certificate); MSW/JD; MSW/MS. *Accreditation:* CSWE. *Program availability:* Part-time, online learning. *Students:* 186 full-time (155 women), 36 part-time (31 women); includes 23 minority (3 Black or African American, non-Hispanic/Latino; 15 Hispanic/Latino; 5 Two or more races, non-Hispanic/Latino), 1 international. Average age 31. 182 applicants, 67% accepted, 72 enrolled. In 2017, 71 master's, 2 other advanced degrees awarded. *Entrance requirements:* Additional exam requirements/recommendations for international students: Required—TOEFL (minimum score 550 paper-based; 80 iBT). *Application deadline:* For fall admission, 2/1 for domestic and international students. Application fee: $65. Electronic applications accepted. *Financial support:* In 2017–18, 20 students received support, including 8 teaching assistantships; fellowships, research assistantships, career-related internships or fieldwork, Federal Work-Study, and scholarships/grants also available. Support available to part-time students. Financial award application deadline: 2/15. *Unit head:* Vernon Carter, Chair, 603-862-0199. *Application contact:* Emilie Cilley, Administrative Assistant, 603-862-0215, E-mail: emilie.cilley@unh.edu.
Website: https://chhs.unh.edu/sw/master-social-work-msw

University of New Hampshire, Graduate School Manchester Campus, Manchester, NH 03101. Offers business administration (MBA); cybersecurity policy and risk management (MS); educational administration and supervision (Ed S); educational studies (M Ed); elementary education (M Ed); information technology (MS); public administration (MPA); public health (MPH, Certificate); secondary education (M Ed, MAT); social work (MSW); substance use disorders (Certificate). *Program availability:* Part-time, evening/weekend. *Students:* 13 full-time (6 women), 17 part-time (0 women); includes 7 minority (1 Black or African American, non-Hispanic/Latino; 4 Asian, non-Hispanic/Latino; 1 Hispanic/Latino; 1 Two or more races, non-Hispanic/Latino), 10 international. Average age 33. 42 applicants, 71% accepted, 8 enrolled. In 2017, 4 master's awarded. *Entrance requirements:* Additional exam requirements/recommendations for international students: Required—TOEFL (minimum score 550 paper-based; 80 iBT). *Application deadline:* For fall admission, 6/1 for domestic students, 4/1 for international students; for spring admission, 12/1 for domestic students. Application fee: $65. Electronic applications accepted. *Financial support:* Fellowships, research assistantships, teaching assistantships, Federal Work-Study, scholarships/grants, health care benefits, and unspecified assistantships available. Support available to part-time students. Financial award application deadline: 2/15; financial award applicants required to submit FAFSA. *Unit head:* Candice Morey, Educational Programs Coordinator, 603-641-4313, E-mail: unhm.gradcenter@unh.edu.
Website: http://www.gradschool.unh.edu/manchester/

The University of North Carolina at Chapel Hill, Graduate School, School of Social Work, Chapel Hill, NC 27599. Offers MSW, PhD, JD/MSW, MHA/MCRP, MPA/MSW, MSPH/MSW. *Accreditation:* CSWE (one or more programs are accredited). *Program availability:* Part-time. Terminal master's awarded for partial completion of doctoral program. *Degree requirements:* For doctorate, thesis/dissertation, qualifying exam. *Entrance requirements:* For master's and doctorate, GRE General Test, minimum GPA of 3.0. Electronic applications accepted. *Faculty research:* School success, risk and resiliency, welfare reform, aging, substance abuse.

The University of North Carolina at Charlotte, College of Health and Human Services, School of Social Work, Charlotte, NC 28223-0001. Offers MSW. *Accreditation:* CSWE. *Program availability:* Part-time. *Faculty:* 14 full-time (11 women), 11 part-time/adjunct (10 women). *Students:* 168 full-time (153 women); includes 80 minority (50 Black or African American, non-Hispanic/Latino; 9 Asian, non-Hispanic/Latino; 15 Hispanic/Latino; 6 Two or more races, non-Hispanic/Latino), 4 international. Average age 28. 295 applicants, 49% accepted, 96 enrolled. In 2017, 73 master's awarded. *Degree requirements:* For master's, thesis or alternative, capstone. *Entrance requirements:* For master's, GRE, minimum GPA of 3.0, statement of purpose, liberal arts foundation, resume, 3 letters of recommendation, interview, relevant volunteer or paid experience. Additional exam requirements/recommendations for international students: Required—TOEFL (minimum score 523 paper-based, 70 iBT) or IELTS (6.5). *Application deadline:* For fall admission, 2/1 for domestic and international students. Applications are processed on a rolling basis. Application fee: $75. Electronic applications accepted. *Expenses:* Tuition, state resident: full-time $4337. Tuition, nonresident: full-time $17,771. *Required fees:* $3211. Tuition and fees vary according to course load and program. *Financial support:* In 2017–18, 16 students received support, including 16 research assistantships (averaging $4,029 per year); career-related internships or fieldwork, Federal Work-Study, institutionally sponsored loans, scholarships/grants, unspecified assistantships, and administrative assistantship also available. Support available to part-time students. Financial award application deadline: 3/1; financial award applicants required to submit FAFSA. *Total annual research expenditures:* $569,906. *Unit head:* Dr. Diana Rowan, Associate Professor and MSW Director, 704-687-7934, E-mail: drowan@uncc.edu. *Application contact:* Kathy B. Giddings, Director of Graduate Admissions, 704-687-5503, Fax: 704-687-1668, E-mail: gradadm@uncc.edu.
Website: http://socialwork.uncc.edu/

The University of North Carolina at Greensboro, Graduate School, School of Health and Human Sciences, Department of Social Work, Greensboro, NC 27412-5001. Offers MSW. Program offered jointly with North Carolina Agricultural and Technical State University. *Entrance requirements:* For master's, GRE General Test. Additional exam requirements/recommendations for international students: Required—TOEFL. Electronic applications accepted.

The University of North Carolina at Pembroke, The Graduate School, Department of Social Work, Pembroke, NC 28372-1510. Offers MSW. *Accreditation:* CSWE. *Program availability:* Part-time. Application fee: $45 ($60 for international students). *Unit head:* Dr. Summer Gainey Woodside, Program Director, 910-775-4085, E-mail: summer.woodside@uncp.edu.
Website: http://www.uncp.edu/sw/

The University of North Carolina Wilmington, School of Social Work, Wilmington, NC 28403-3297. Offers MSW. *Accreditation:* CSWE. *Program availability:* Part-time. *Faculty:* 13 full-time (8 women). *Students:* 69 full-time (64 women), 36 part-time (33 women); includes 19 minority (7 Black or African American, non-Hispanic/Latino; 1 Asian, non-Hispanic/Latino; 8 Hispanic/Latino; 3 Two or more races, non-Hispanic/Latino). Average age 29. 101 applicants, 52% accepted, 46 enrolled. In 2017, 41 master's awarded. *Degree requirements:* For master's, comprehensive exam, thesis or alternative, field experience. *Entrance requirements:* For master's, GRE General Test, 3 letters of recommendation; resume; statement of interest; completion of introduction to sociology, introduction to psychology, basic statistics and either human biology or human development courses at the undergraduate level. Additional exam requirements/recommendations for international students: Required—TOEFL (minimum score 550 paper-based; 79 iBT), IELTS (minimum score 6.5). *Application deadline:* For fall admission, 2/1 for domestic students. Applications are processed on a rolling basis. Application fee: $75. Electronic applications accepted. *Expenses:* Tuition, state resident: full-time $4626; part-time $226.76 per credit hour. Tuition, nonresident: full-time $17,834; part-time $874.22 per credit hour. *Required fees:* $2124. Tuition and fees vary according to program. *Financial support:* Teaching assistantships and scholarships/grants available. Financial award application deadline: 1/1; financial award applicants required to submit FAFSA. *Unit head:* Dr. Stacey Kolomer, Director, 910-962-2853, Fax: 910-962-7283, E-mail: kolomers@uncw.edu. *Application contact:* Dr. Kristin Bolton, Interim Graduate Coordinator, 910-962-2308, Fax: 910-962-7283, E-mail: boltonk@uncw.edu.
Website: http://www.uncw.edu/swk/

University of North Dakota, Graduate School, College of Nursing and Professional Disciplines, Department of Social Work, Grand Forks, ND 58202. Offers MSW. *Accreditation:* CSWE. *Degree requirements:* For master's, comprehensive exam, thesis or alternative. *Entrance requirements:* For master's, minimum GPA of 3.0. Additional exam requirements/recommendations for international students: Required—TOEFL (minimum score 550 paper-based; 79 iBT), IELTS (minimum score 6.5). Electronic applications accepted. *Faculty research:* Mental health, gerontology, chemical abuse, children and families.

University of Northern British Columbia, Office of Graduate Studies, Prince George, BC V2N 4Z9, Canada. Offers business administration (Diploma); community health science (M Sc); disability management (MA); education (M Ed); first nations studies (MA); gender studies (MA); history (MA); interdisciplinary studies (MA); international studies (MA); mathematical, computer and physical sciences (M Sc); natural resources and environmental studies (M Sc, MA, MNRES, PhD); political science (MA); psychology (M Sc, PhD); social work (MSW). *Program availability:* Part-time, evening/weekend, online learning. *Degree requirements:* For master's, thesis; for doctorate, thesis/dissertation. *Entrance requirements:* For master's, GRE, minimum B average in undergraduate course work; for doctorate, candidacy exam, minimum A average in graduate course work.

University of Northern Iowa, Graduate College, College of Social and Behavioral Sciences, Department of Social Work, Cedar Falls, IA 50614. Offers MSW. *Accreditation:* CSWE. *Entrance requirements:* For master's, minimum GPA of 3.0; 3 letters of recommendation; personal autobiographical statement. Additional exam requirements/recommendations for international students: Required—TOEFL (minimum score 500 paper-based; 61 iBT). Electronic applications accepted.

University of Oklahoma, College of Arts and Sciences, Anne and Henry Zarrow School of Social Work, Norman, OK 73019. Offers direct practice (MSW), including administrative and community practice. *Accreditation:* CSWE. *Program availability:* Part-time, evening/weekend. *Faculty:* 30 full-time (21 women), 12 part-time/adjunct (9 women). *Students:* 212 full-time (177 women), 194 part-time (163 women); includes 169 minority (56 Black or African American, non-Hispanic/Latino; 40 American Indian or

Alaska Native, non-Hispanic/Latino; 6 Asian, non-Hispanic/Latino; 27 Hispanic/Latino; 40 Two or more races, non-Hispanic/Latino). Average age 32. 187 applicants, 74% accepted, 116 enrolled. In 2017, 153 master's awarded. *Degree requirements:* For master's, comprehensive exam, thesis or alternative. *Entrance requirements:* Additional exam requirements/recommendations for international students: Required—TOEFL (minimum score 79 iBT) or IELTS (minimum score 6.5). *Application deadline:* For fall admission, 2/1 priority date for domestic and international students; for summer admission, 2/1 priority date for domestic and international students. Application fee: $50 ($100 for international students). Electronic applications accepted. *Expenses:* Tuition, state resident: full-time $5119; part-time $213.30 per credit hour. Tuition, nonresident: full-time $19,778; part-time $824.10 per credit hour. *Required fees:* $3458; $133.55 per credit hour. $126.50 per semester. *Financial support:* In 2017–18, 132 students received support, including 20 research assistantships with tuition reimbursements available (averaging $10,372 per year), 1 teaching assistantship (averaging $12,750 per year); career-related internships or fieldwork, scholarships/grants, traineeships, health care benefits, tuition waivers, and unspecified assistantships also available. Support available to part-time students. Financial award application deadline: 6/1; financial award applicants required to submit FAFSA. *Faculty research:* Poverty, health, child welfare, mental health, interpersonal violence, community development. *Total annual research expenditures:* $124,333. *Unit head:* Dr. Julie Miller-Cribbs, Director, 918-660-3378, Fax: 918-660-3383, E-mail: jmcribbs@ou.edu. *Application contact:* Amy Ann Arnold, Admissions and Enrollment Coordinator, 918-660-3385, Fax: 918-660-3383, E-mail: aarnold@ou.edu.
Website: http://socialwork.ou.edu

University of Ottawa, Faculty of Graduate and Postdoctoral Studies, Faculty of Social Sciences, School of Social Work, Ottawa, ON K1N 6N5, Canada. Offers MSS. Program offered in French. *Degree requirements:* For master's, thesis or alternative. *Entrance requirements:* For master's, honors bachelor's degree or equivalent, minimum B average. Electronic applications accepted. *Faculty research:* Family-children, health.

University of Pennsylvania, School of Social Policy and Practice, Graduate Group on Social Welfare, Philadelphia, PA 19104. Offers PhD. *Degree requirements:* For doctorate, thesis/dissertation. *Entrance requirements:* For doctorate, GRE General Test, MSW or master's degree in related field. Additional exam requirements/recommendations for international students: Required—TOEFL (minimum score 600 paper-based; 100 iBT). Electronic applications accepted. *Faculty research:* Mental health, child welfare, organizational behavior, urban poverty, comparative social welfare.

University of Pennsylvania, School of Social Policy and Practice, Program in Social Work, Philadelphia, PA 19104. Offers MNPL, MSSP, MSW, DSW, JD/MSW, MSW/Certificate, MSW/MBA, MSW/MBE, MSW/MCP, MSW/MGA, MSW/MPH, MSW/MS Ed, MSW/MSC, MSW/PhD. *Accreditation:* CSWE. *Program availability:* Part-time. Terminal master's awarded for partial completion of doctoral program. *Degree requirements:* For master's, fieldwork; for doctorate, thesis/dissertation. *Entrance requirements:* For master's, GRE, GMAT, or LSAT (for MSSP or MNPL); for doctorate, GRE, MSW or master's degree in related field. Additional exam requirements/recommendations for international students: Required—TOEFL (minimum score 600 paper-based; 100 iBT). Electronic applications accepted. *Faculty research:* Homelessness, juvenile justice, mental health/children's mental health, child welfare, domestic and family violence.

University of Pittsburgh, School of Social Work, Pittsburgh, PA 15260. Offers MSW, PhD, Certificate, M Div/MSW, MPA/MSW, MPH/PhD, MPIA/MSW, MSW/JD, MSW/MBA, MSW/MPH. *Accreditation:* CSWE (one or more programs are accredited). *Program availability:* Part-time. *Faculty:* 24 full-time (14 women), 37 part-time/adjunct (27 women). *Students:* 419 full-time (357 women), 54 part-time (46 women); includes 88 minority (58 Black or African American, non-Hispanic/Latino; 20 Hispanic/Latino; 10 Two or more races, non-Hispanic/Latino). Average age 28. 568 applicants, 80% accepted, 207 enrolled. *Degree requirements:* For master's, practicum; for doctorate, comprehensive exam, thesis/dissertation. *Entrance requirements:* For master's, minimum GPA of 3.0, course work in statistics; for doctorate, GRE, MSW or related degree, course work in statistics. Additional exam requirements/recommendations for international students: Required—TOEFL (minimum score 600 paper-based; 100 iBT). *Application deadline:* For fall admission, 12/31 priority date for domestic and international students. Applications are processed on a rolling basis. Application fee: $40 ($50 for international students). Electronic applications accepted. *Expenses:* $22,290 full-time resident tuition per year, $30,540 non-resident, $850 full-time fees; $898 part-time resident tuition per credit, $1,247 non-resident, $270 part-time fees per term. *Financial support:* In 2017–18, 40 fellowships (averaging $10,000 per year), 8 teaching assistantships with full tuition reimbursements (averaging $18,450 per year) were awarded; research assistantships with full tuition reimbursements, career-related internships or fieldwork, institutionally sponsored loans, scholarships/grants, traineeships, tuition waivers (full), and unspecified assistantships also available. Financial award application deadline: 3/31; financial award applicants required to submit FAFSA. *Faculty research:* Mental health services research, child abuse and neglect, geriatrics, criminal justice, race issues. *Unit head:* Dr. Larry E. Davis, Dean, 412-624-6304, Fax: 412-624-6323, E-mail: ledavis@pitt.edu. *Application contact:* Philip Mack, Director of Admissions, 412-624-6346, Fax: 412-624-6323, E-mail: psm8@pitt.edu.
Website: http://www.socialwork.pitt.edu

University of Puerto Rico–Río Piedras, College of Social Sciences, Graduate School of Social Work, San Juan, PR 00931-3300. Offers MSW, PhD. *Accreditation:* CSWE. *Program availability:* Part-time. *Degree requirements:* For master's, comprehensive exam, thesis; for doctorate, comprehensive exam, thesis/dissertation. *Entrance requirements:* For master's, PAEG or GRE, interview, minimum GPA of 3.0, letter of recommendation; for doctorate, PAEG or GRE, interview, minimum GPA of 3.0, 3 letters of recommendation, social work experience. *Faculty research:* Social work in Puerto Rico, Cuba, and the Dominican Republic; migration; poverty in Puerto Rico.

University of Regina, Faculty of Graduate Studies and Research, Faculty of Social Work, Regina, SK S4S 0A2, Canada. Offers indigenous social work (MISW); social work (MSW, PhD). PhD offered as a special case program. *Program availability:* Part-time. *Faculty:* 24 full-time (17 women), 11 part-time/adjunct (5 women). *Students:* 24 full-time (20 women), 83 part-time (73 women). 68 applicants, 38% accepted. In 2017, 25 master's awarded. *Degree requirements:* For master's, thesis (for some programs); internship (for MISW); thesis, research practicum, or field practicum (for MSW); for doctorate, thesis/dissertation. *Entrance requirements:* For master's, BSW. Additional exam requirements/recommendations for international students: Required—TOEFL (minimum score 580 paper-based; 80 iBT), IELTS (minimum score 6.5), PTE (minimum score 59). *Application deadline:* For fall admission, 1/31 for domestic and international students. Application fee: $100. Electronic applications accepted. *Expenses:* CAD$8,783 per year (for MSW, MISW); CAD$9,930 per year (for PhD). *Financial support:* In 2017–18, fellowships (averaging $6,000 per year), teaching assistantships (averaging $2,562 per year) were awarded; research assistantships, career-related internships or fieldwork, and scholarships/grants also available. Financial award application deadline: 6/15. *Faculty research:* Social policy analysis; social justice, human rights, and social work; family and child policies and programs; aging, society, and human service work; work, welfare, and social justice. *Unit head:* Dr. Judy White, Dean, 306-585-4037, Fax: 306-585-5691, E-mail: sw.dean@uregina.ca. *Application*

contact: Dr. Nuelle Novik, Graduate Program Coordinator, 306-585-4573, Fax: 306-585-4872, E-mail: nuelle.novik@uregina.ca.
Website: http://www.uregina.ca/socialwork/

University of St. Francis, College of Arts and Sciences, Joliet, IL 60435-6169. Offers forensic social work (Post-Master's Certificate); physician assistant practice (MS); social work (MSW). *Program availability:* Part-time. *Faculty:* 7 full-time (5 women), 5 part-time/adjunct (4 women). *Students:* 107 full-time (82 women), 24 part-time (22 women); includes 40 minority (13 Black or African American, non-Hispanic/Latino; 3 Asian, non-Hispanic/Latino; 20 Hispanic/Latino; 2 Native Hawaiian or other Pacific Islander, non-Hispanic/Latino; 2 Two or more races, non-Hispanic/Latino), 6 international. Average age 28. 69 applicants, 48% accepted, 26 enrolled. In 2017, 64 master's awarded. *Entrance requirements:* For master's, GRE (for MS). Additional exam requirements/recommendations for international students: Required—TOEFL (minimum score 550 paper-based; 79 iBT), IELTS (minimum score 6). *Application deadline:* Applications are processed on a rolling basis. Application fee: $30. Electronic applications accepted. Application fee is waived when completed online. *Expenses:* $748 per credit. *Financial support:* In 2017–18, 10 students received support. Scholarships/grants and unspecified assistantships available. Support available to part-time students. Financial award applicants required to submit FAFSA. *Unit head:* Dr. Robert Kase, Dean, 815-740-3367, Fax: 815-740-6366. *Application contact:* Sandra Sloka, Director of Admissions for Graduate and Degree Completion Programs, 800-735-7500, Fax: 815-740-3431, E-mail: ssloka@stfrancis.edu.
Website: http://www.stfrancis.edu/academics/cas

University of St. Thomas, School of Social Work, St. Paul, MN 55116. Offers MSW. Programs offered in collaboration with St. Catherine University. *Accreditation:* CSWE. *Program availability:* Part-time, evening/weekend, blended/hybrid learning. *Students:* 79 full-time (75 women), 226 part-time (202 women); includes 55 minority (16 Black or African American, non-Hispanic/Latino; 1 American Indian or Alaska Native, non-Hispanic/Latino; 13 Asian, non-Hispanic/Latino; 10 Hispanic/Latino; 15 Two or more races, non-Hispanic/Latino). Average age 28. In 2017, 142 master's awarded. *Degree requirements:* For master's, thesis optional, fieldwork. *Entrance requirements:* For master's, previous course work in lifespan developmental psychology, human biology, and statistics or research methods. Additional exam requirements/recommendations for international students: Required—TOEFL (minimum score 80 iBT). *Application deadline:* For fall admission, 1/10 for domestic and international students. Application fee: $0. Electronic applications accepted. *Expenses:* Contact institution. *Financial support:* Fellowships, research assistantships, career-related internships or fieldwork, Federal Work-Study, institutionally sponsored loans, scholarships/grants, and unspecified assistantships available. Support available to part-time students. Financial award application deadline: 7/1; financial award applicants required to submit FAFSA. *Faculty research:* Clinical supervision and practice, group work, child welfare and social work. *Unit head:* Dr. Corrine Carvalho, Interim Dean and Professor, 651-962-6031, Fax: 651-962-6031, E-mail: clcarvalho@stthomas.edu. *Application contact:* Mary Palin, Graduate Admissions Counselor, 651-690-6185, Fax: 651-690-6549, E-mail: mbpalin@stkate.edu.
Website: http://www.stthomas.edu/socialwork

University of South Africa, College of Human Sciences, Pretoria, South Africa. Offers adult education (M Ed); African languages (MA, PhD); African politics (MA, PhD); Afrikaans (MA, PhD); ancient history (MA, PhD); ancient Near Eastern studies (MA, PhD); anthropology (MA, PhD); applied linguistics (MA); Arabic (MA, PhD); archaeology (MA); art history (MA); Biblical archaeology (MA); Biblical studies (M Th, D Th, PhD); Christian spirituality (M Th, D Th); church history (M Th, D Th); classical studies (MA, PhD); clinical psychology (MA); communication (MA, PhD); comparative education (M Ed, Ed D); consulting psychology (D Admin, D Com, PhD); curriculum studies (M Ed, Ed D); development studies (M Admin, MA, D Admin, PhD); didactics (M Ed, Ed D); education (M Tech); education management (M Ed, Ed D); educational psychology (M Ed); English (MA); environmental education (M Ed); French (MA, PhD); German (MA, PhD); Greek (MA); guidance and counseling (M Ed); health studies (MA, PhD), including health sciences education (MA), health services management (MA), medical and surgical nursing science (critical care general) (MA), midwifery and neonatal nursing science (MA), trauma and emergency care (MA); history (MA, PhD); history of education (Ed D); inclusive education (M Ed, Ed D); information and communications technology policy and regulation (MA); information science (MA, MIS, PhD); international politics (MA, PhD); Islamic studies (MA, PhD); Italian (MA, PhD); Judaica (MA, PhD); linguistics (MA, PhD); mathematical education (M Ed); mathematics education (MA); missiology (M Th, D Th); modern Hebrew (MA, PhD); musicology (MA, MMus, D Mus, PhD); natural science education (M Ed); New Testament (M Th, D Th); Old Testament (D Th); pastoral therapy (M Th, D Th); philosophy (MA); philosophy of education (M Ed, Ed D); politics (MA, PhD); Portuguese (MA, PhD); practical theology (M Th, D Th); psychology (MA, MS, PhD); psychology of education (M Ed, Ed D); public health (MA); religious studies (MA, D Th, PhD); Romance languages (MA); Russian (MA, PhD); Semitic languages (MA, PhD); social behavior studies in HIV/AIDS (MA); social science (mental health) (MA); social science in development studies (MA); social science in psychology (MA); social science in social work (MA); social science in sociology (MA); social work (MSW, DSW, PhD); socio-education (M Ed, Ed D); sociolinguistics (MA); sociology (MA, PhD); Spanish (MA, PhD); systematic theology (M Th, D Th); TESOL (teaching English to speakers of other languages) (MA); theological ethics (M Th, D Th); theory of literature (MA, PhD); urban ministries (D Th); urban ministry (M Th).

University of South Carolina, The Graduate School, College of Social Work, Columbia, SC 29208. Offers MSW, PhD, JD/MSW, MSW/MPA, MSW/MPH. *Accreditation:* CSWE (one or more programs are accredited). *Program availability:* Part-time. *Degree requirements:* For master's, comprehensive exam; for doctorate, thesis/dissertation. *Entrance requirements:* For master's, GRE (minimum combined score 800), minimum undergraduate GPA of 3.0. Additional exam requirements/recommendations for international students: Required—TOEFL (minimum score 570 paper-based). Electronic applications accepted. *Expenses:* Contact institution. *Faculty research:* Victimization, child abuse and neglect, families.

University of South Dakota, Graduate School, School of Health Sciences, Department of Social Work, Vermillion, SD 57069. Offers MSW. *Program availability:* Part-time, 100% online. *Entrance requirements:* For master's, baccalaureate degree, minimum cumulative undergraduate GPA of 3.0. Additional exam requirements/recommendations for international students: Required—TOEFL (minimum score 550 paper-based; 79 iBT), IELTS (minimum score 6). *Application deadline:* For fall admission, 12/1 for domestic students; for summer admission, 12/1 for domestic students. Application fee: $35. *Financial support:* Applicants required to submit FAFSA. *Application contact:* Graduate School, 605-658-6140, Fax: 605-677-6118, E-mail: grad@usd.edu.
Website: http://www.usd.edu/socialwork

University of Southern California, Graduate School, School of Social Work, Los Angeles, CA 90089. Offers community organization, planning and administration (MSW); families and children (MSW); health (MSW); mental health (MSW); military social work and veterans services (MSW); older adults (MSW); public child welfare (MSW); school settings (MSW); social work (MSW, PhD); systems of mental illness recovery (MSW); work and life (MSW); JD/MSW; M PI/MSW; MPA/MSW; MSW/MBA;

Social Work

MSW/MJCS; MSW/MS. *Accreditation:* CSWE (one or more programs are accredited). *Degree requirements:* For doctorate, comprehensive exam, thesis/dissertation, qualifying exam/publishable paper. *Entrance requirements:* For doctorate, GRE General Test. Additional exam requirements/recommendations for international students: Required—TOEFL (minimum score 600 paper-based; 100 iBT), ESL exam. Electronic applications accepted. *Faculty research:* Department of Defense Educational Activity, detection/treatment of depression among older adults, health/aging, psychosocial adaptation to extreme environments/man made disasters; mental health needs of older adults.

University of Southern Indiana, Graduate Studies, College of Liberal Arts, Program in Social Work, Evansville, IN 47712-3590. Offers MSW. *Accreditation:* CSWE. *Faculty:* 10 full-time (6 women), 2 part-time/adjunct (1 woman). *Students:* 96 full-time (88 women); includes 12 minority (5 Black or African American, non-Hispanic/Latino; 4 Hispanic/Latino; 3 Two or more races, non-Hispanic/Latino). Average age 27. In 2017, 64 master's awarded. *Entrance requirements:* For master's, minimum GPA of 3.0, evidence of writing skills, personal interview or video, minimum of 24 hours of social/behavioral science. Additional exam requirements/recommendations for international students: Required—TOEFL (minimum score 550 paper-based; 79 iBT), IELTS (minimum score 6). *Application deadline:* For fall admission, 2/1 for domestic and international students. Application fee: $40. Electronic applications accepted. *Expenses:* Tuition, state resident: full-time $9394. Tuition, nonresident: full-time $17,917. *Required fees:* $510. *Financial support:* In 2017–18, 13 students received support. Federal Work-Study, scholarships/grants, tuition waivers (full and partial), and unspecified assistantships available. Financial award application deadline: 3/1; financial award applicants required to submit FAFSA. *Unit head:* Dr. James G. Dickerson, Program Director, 812-461-5243, E-mail: jgdickerso1@usi.edu. *Application contact:* Dr. Mayola Rowser, Director, Graduate Studies, 812-465-7015, Fax: 812-464-1956, E-mail: mrowser@usi.edu. Website: http://www.usi.edu/liberal-arts/master-of-social-work

University of Southern Maine, College of Management and Human Service, School of Social Work, Portland, ME 04103. Offers MSW. *Accreditation:* CSWE. *Program availability:* Part-time, evening/weekend. *Entrance requirements:* For master's, GRE or MAT. Electronic applications accepted. *Faculty research:* Poverty and discrimination, aging, interpersonal violence, evaluation of interventions and effectiveness, child and adult mental health, social welfare history, diversity issues.

University of Southern Mississippi, College of Health, School of Social Work, Hattiesburg, MS 39406-0001. Offers MSW. *Accreditation:* CSWE. *Program availability:* Part-time. *Students:* 40 full-time (32 women), 2 part-time (both women). 92 applicants, 79% accepted, 42 enrolled. In 2017, 1 master's awarded. *Degree requirements:* For master's, comprehensive exam, thesis or alternative, practicum. *Entrance requirements:* For master's, GRE General Test, minimum GPA of 2.75 in last 60 hours. Additional exam requirements/recommendations for international students: Required—TOEFL, IELTS. *Application deadline:* For fall admission, 4/1 priority date for domestic and international students; for spring admission, 1/10 priority date for domestic and international students. Applications are processed on a rolling basis. Application fee: $60. Electronic applications accepted. *Expenses:* Tuition, state resident: full-time $3830. *Financial support:* Research assistantships with tuition reimbursements, teaching assistantships with tuition reimbursements, career-related internships or fieldwork, Federal Work-Study, scholarships/grants, health care benefits, and unspecified assistantships available. Financial award application deadline: 3/15; financial award applicants required to submit FAFSA. *Faculty research:* Delinquency prevention, risk and resiliency in youth, successful aging, women in social service management, social work and the law. *Unit head:* Dr. Tim Rehner, Director, 601-266-4171, Fax: 601-266-4165, E-mail: tim.rehner@usm.edu. Website: https://www.usm.edu/social-work

University of South Florida, College of Behavioral and Community Sciences, School of Social Work, Tampa, FL 33620. Offers MSW, PhD, MSW/MPH. *Accreditation:* CSWE. *Program availability:* Part-time, evening/weekend. *Faculty:* 13 full-time (12 women). *Students:* 179 full-time (161 women), 41 part-time (34 women); includes 89 minority (42 Black or African American, non-Hispanic/Latino; 1 American Indian or Alaska Native, non-Hispanic/Latino; 4 Asian, non-Hispanic/Latino; 38 Hispanic/Latino; 1 Native Hawaiian or other Pacific Islander, non-Hispanic/Latino; 3 Two or more races, non-Hispanic/Latino), 1 international. Average age 30. 228 applicants, 51% accepted, 76 enrolled. In 2017, 127 master's, 4 doctorates awarded. *Degree requirements:* For master's, comprehensive exam, thesis; for doctorate, comprehensive exam, thesis/dissertation. *Entrance requirements:* For master's, GRE General Test, three letters of recommendation; 750-word biographical sketch; interview; field experience (preferred); for doctorate, GRE General Test, minimum GPA of 3.0 in last two years of undergraduate work; master's degree in social work program with minimum GPA of 3.5; three letters of recommendation; statement of purpose, career goals and research interests; professional/academic writing sample; interview. Additional exam requirements/recommendations for international students: Required—TOEFL (minimum score 550 paper-based; 79 iBT). *Application deadline:* For fall admission, 2/15 priority date for domestic students, 2/15 for international students; for spring admission, 10/15 for domestic students, 9/15 for international students; for summer admission, 2/15 for domestic students, 1/15 for international students. Applications are processed on a rolling basis. Application fee: $30. Electronic applications accepted. *Financial support:* In 2017–18, 29 students received support, including 1 research assistantship with tuition reimbursement available (averaging $9,001 per year); unspecified assistantships also available. Financial award application deadline: 3/15; financial award applicants required to submit FAFSA. *Faculty research:* Kinship care, child trauma, juvenile delinquency, end-of-life issues, aging issues, child welfare, health and mental health disparities among various populations, HIV/AIDS and sexual violence in Haiti, integrated behavioral health care, international social work practice. *Total annual research expenditures:* $620,613. *Unit head:* Dr. Nan Sook Park, PhD Program Chair/Assistant Professor, 813-974-4194, Fax: 813-974-4675, E-mail: nanpark@usf.edu. *Application contact:* Dr. Marion Becker, MSW Chair/Professor, 813-974-7188, Fax: 813-974-4675, E-mail: mbecker2@usf.edu. Website: http://www.cas.usf.edu/social_work/

University of South Florida, Innovative Education, Tampa, FL 33620-9951. Offers adult, career and higher education (Graduate Certificate), including college teaching, leadership in developing human resources, leadership in higher education; Africana studies (Graduate Certificate), including diasporas and health disparities, genocide and human rights; aging studies (Graduate Certificate), including gerontology; art research (Graduate Certificate), including museum studies; business foundations (Graduate Certificate); chemical and biomedical engineering (Graduate Certificate), including materials science and engineering, water, health and sustainability; child and family studies (Graduate Certificate), including positive behavior support; civil and industrial engineering (Graduate Certificate), including transportation systems analysis; community and family health (Graduate Certificate), including maternal and child health, social marketing and public health, violence and injury: prevention and intervention, women's health; criminology (Graduate Certificate), including criminal justice administration; data science for public administration (Graduate Certificate); digital humanities (Graduate Certificate); educational measurement and research (Graduate

Certificate), including evaluation; English (Graduate Certificate), including comparative literary studies, creative writing, professional and technical communication; entrepreneurship (Graduate Certificate); environmental health (Graduate Certificate), including safety management; epidemiology and biostatistics (Graduate Certificate), including applied biostatistics, biostatistics, concepts and tools of epidemiology, epidemiology, epidemiology of infectious diseases; geography, environment and planning (Graduate Certificate), including community development, environmental policy and management, geographical information systems; geology (Graduate Certificate), including hydrogeology; global health (Graduate Certificate), including disaster management, global health and Latin American and Caribbean studies, global health practice, humanitarian assistance, infection control; government and international affairs (Graduate Certificate), including Cuban studies, globalization studies; health policy and management (Graduate Certificate), including health management and leadership, public health policy and programs; hearing specialist: early intervention (Graduate Certificate); industrial and management systems engineering (Graduate Certificate), including systems engineering, technology management; information studies (Graduate Certificate), including school library media specialist; information systems/decision sciences (Graduate Certificate), including analytics and business intelligence; instructional technology (Graduate Certificate), including distance education, Florida digital/virtual educator, instructional design, multimedia design, Web design; internal medicine, bioethics and medical humanities (Graduate Certificate), including biomedical ethics; Latin American and Caribbean studies (Graduate Certificate); leadership for coastal resiliency planning (Graduate Certificate); mass communications (Graduate Certificate), including multimedia journalism; mathematics and statistics (Graduate Certificate), including mathematics; medicine (Graduate Certificate), including aging and neuroscience, bioinformatics, biotechnology, brain fitness and memory management, clinical investigation, hand and upper limb rehabilitation, health informatics, health sciences, integrative weight management, intellectual property, medicine and gender, metabolic and nutritional medicine, metabolic cardiology, pharmacy sciences; national and competitive intelligence (Graduate Certificate); nursing (Graduate Certificate), including simulation based academic fellowship in advanced pain management; psychological and social foundations (Graduate Certificate), including career counseling, college teaching, diversity in education, mental health counseling, school counseling; public affairs (Graduate Certificate), including nonprofit management, public management, research administration; public health (Graduate Certificate), including assessing chemical toxicity and public health risks, health equity, pharmacoepidemiology, public health generalist, toxicology, translational research in adolescent behavioral health; public health practices (Graduate Certificate), including planning for healthy communities; rehabilitation and mental health counseling (Graduate Certificate), including integrative mental health care, marriage and family therapy, rehabilitation technology; secondary education (Graduate Certificate), including ESOL, foreign language education: culture and content, foreign language education: professional; social work (Graduate Certificate), including geriatric social work/clinical gerontology; special education (Graduate Certificate), including autism spectrum disorder, disabilities education: severe/profound; world languages (Graduate Certificate), including teaching English as a second language (TESL) or foreign language. *Unit head:* Dr. Cynthia DeLuca, Associate Vice President and Assistant Vice Provost, 813-974-3077, Fax: 813-974-7061, E-mail: deluca@usf.edu. *Application contact:* Owen Hooper, Director, Summer and Alternative Calendar Programs, 813-974-6917, E-mail: hooper@usf.edu. Website: http://www.usf.edu/innovative-education/

University of South Florida Sarasota-Manatee, College of Liberal Arts and Social Sciences, Sarasota, FL 34243. Offers criminal justice (MA); education (MA); educational leadership (M Ed), including curriculum leadership, K-12 public school leadership, non-public/charter school leadership; elementary education (MAT); English education (MA); social work (MSW). *Program availability:* Part-time, 100% online, blended/hybrid learning. *Faculty:* 15 full-time (12 women), 8 part-time/adjunct (6 women). *Students:* 11 full-time (10 women), 43 part-time (37 women); includes 17 minority (7 Black or African American, non-Hispanic/Latino; 2 Asian, non-Hispanic/Latino; 8 Hispanic/Latino), 1 international. Average age 35. 62 applicants, 27% accepted, 14 enrolled. In 2017, 32 master's awarded. *Degree requirements:* For master's, comprehensive exam (for some programs). *Entrance requirements:* For master's, GRE. Additional exam requirements/recommendations for international students: Required—TOEFL (minimum score 550 paper-based; 79 iBT), IELTS (minimum score 6.5). *Application deadline:* For fall admission, 3/1 priority date for domestic students, 3/1 for international students; for spring admission, 10/1 priority date for domestic students, 10/1 for international students. Applications are processed on a rolling basis. Application fee: $30. Electronic applications accepted. *Expenses:* Tuition, state resident: full-time $8350; part-time $418 per credit hour. Tuition, nonresident: full-time $19,047; part-time $863 per credit hour. *Required fees:* $1689. Tuition and fees vary according to degree level and program. *Financial support:* In 2017–18, 1 student received support. Career-related internships or fieldwork, institutionally sponsored loans, scholarships/grants, health care benefits, and unspecified assistantships available. Support available to part-time students. Financial award application deadline: 3/1; financial award applicants required to submit FAFSA. *Faculty research:* Educational leadership, secondary education, elementary education, criminal justice, social work. *Total annual research expenditures:* $72,000. *Unit head:* Dr. Jane Rose, Dean, 941-359-4469, Fax: 941-359-4778, E-mail: jane.rose@sar.usf.edu. *Application contact:* Brandon Avery, Assistant Director, Admissions, 941-359-4331, E-mail: bavery@sar.usf.edu.

The University of Tennessee, Graduate School, College of Social Work, Doctor of Social Work Program, Knoxville, TN 37996. Offers clinical practice and leadership (DSW).

The University of Tennessee, Graduate School, College of Social Work, Master of Science in Social Work Program, Knoxville, TN 37996. Offers evidenced-based interpersonal practice (MSSW); management leadership and community practice (MSSW). *Accreditation:* CSWE. *Program availability:* Part-time, online learning.

The University of Tennessee, Graduate School, College of Social Work, PhD in Social Work Program, Knoxville, TN 37996. Offers PhD.

The University of Tennessee at Chattanooga, Program in Social Work, Chattanooga, TN 37403. Offers MSW. *Students:* 39 full-time (30 women), 2 part-time (1 woman); includes 10 minority (5 Black or African American, non-Hispanic/Latino; 4 Hispanic/Latino; 1 Two or more races, non-Hispanic/Latino). Average age 28. 41 applicants, 73% accepted, 28 enrolled. *Degree requirements:* For master's, portfolio, field practicum. *Entrance requirements:* For master's, GRE, 2 letters of reference, criminal background check. Additional exam requirements/recommendations for international students: Required—TOEFL (minimum score 550 paper-based; 79 iBT), IELTS (minimum score 6). *Application deadline:* For fall admission, 6/15 priority date for domestic students, 7/1 for international students; for spring admission, 11/1 priority date for domestic students, 11/1 for international students. Applications are processed on a rolling basis. Application fee: $35 ($40 for international students). Electronic applications accepted. *Expenses:* Tuition, state resident: full-time $8244; part-time $458 per credit hour. Tuition, nonresident: full-time $24,362; part-time $1353 per credit hour. *Required fees:* $1776; $487 per semester. Tuition and fees vary according to course load. *Financial support:*

Career-related internships or fieldwork, scholarships/grants, and unspecified assistantships available. Support available to part-time students. Financial award application deadline: 7/1; financial award applicants required to submit FAFSA. *Faculty research:* Dementia care, foster parenting, juvenile justice system. *Unit head:* Dr. Amy Doolittle, Coordinator, 423-425-5563, E-mail: amy-doolittle@utc.edu. *Application contact:* Dr. Joanne Romagni, Dean of the Graduate School, 423-425-4478, Fax: 423-425-5223, E-mail: joanne-romagni@utc.edu.
Website: https://www.utc.edu/social-work/

The University of Texas at Arlington, Graduate School, School of Social Work, Arlington, TX 76019. Offers MSW, PhD. *Accreditation:* CSWE (one or more programs are accredited). *Program availability:* Part-time, evening/weekend, online learning. *Degree requirements:* For master's, thesis optional; for doctorate, comprehensive exam, thesis/dissertation. *Entrance requirements:* For master's, GRE General Test (if GPA less than 3.0), 3 letters of recommendation; for doctorate, GRE General Test (if GPA is below 3.4), minimum graduate GPA of 3.4. Additional exam requirements/recommendations for international students: Required—TOEFL (minimum score 550 paper-based). Electronic applications accepted. *Faculty research:* Community practice, administrative practice, mental health and children and families.

The University of Texas at Austin, Graduate School, School of Social Work, Austin, TX 78712-1111. Offers MSSW, PhD. *Accreditation:* CSWE (one or more programs are accredited). *Program availability:* Part-time. *Degree requirements:* For doctorate, thesis/dissertation. *Entrance requirements:* For master's and doctorate, GRE General Test. Additional exam requirements/recommendations for international students: Required—TOEFL. *Faculty research:* Substance abuse, child welfare, gerontology, mental health, public policy.

The University of Texas at El Paso, Graduate School, College of Health Sciences, Social Work Program, El Paso, TX 79968-0001. Offers social work in the border region (MSW). *Accreditation:* CSWE. *Program availability:* Part-time. *Entrance requirements:* For master's, statistics and biology, undergraduate degree from accredited university. Additional exam requirements/recommendations for international students: Required—TOEFL (minimum score 550 paper-based; 80 iBT). Electronic applications accepted. *Faculty research:* Immigration, trauma, health, farm workers, child welfare, mental health.

The University of Texas at San Antonio, College of Public Policy, Department of Social Work, San Antonio, TX 78249-0617. Offers MSW. *Accreditation:* CSWE. *Faculty:* 10 full-time (7 women), 11 part-time/adjunct (7 women). *Students:* 99 full-time (90 women), 138 part-time (113 women); includes 163 minority (42 Black or African American, non-Hispanic/Latino; 5 Asian, non-Hispanic/Latino; 111 Hispanic/Latino; 5 Two or more races, non-Hispanic/Latino), 1 international. Average age 33. 81 applicants, 77% accepted, 49 enrolled. In 2017, 49 master's awarded. *Entrance requirements:* For master's, GRE, bachelor's degree, three letters of recommendation, statement of purpose. Additional exam requirements/recommendations for international students: Required—TOEFL (minimum score 550 paper-based; 79 iBT), IELTS (minimum score 6.5). *Application deadline:* For fall admission, 6/15 for domestic students, 3/1 for international students; for spring admission, 10/15 for domestic students, 9/15 for international students. Application fee: $50 ($90 for international students). Electronic applications accepted. *Expenses:* Tuition, state resident: full-time $5495. Tuition, nonresident: full-time $21,938. *Required fees:* $1915. Tuition and fees vary according to program. *Unit head:* Dr. Amy Chanmugam, Department Chair, 210-458-2938, E-mail: amy.chanmugam@utsa.edu. *Application contact:* Derek Plantenga, Graduate Advisor of Record, 210-458-2026, E-mail: derek.plantenga@utsa.edu.
Website: http://copp.utsa.edu/social-work/

The University of Texas Rio Grande Valley, College of Health Affairs, Department of Social Work, Edinburg, TX 78539. Offers community practice and administration (MSSW); direct practice (MSSW). *Accreditation:* CSWE. *Program availability:* Part-time. *Faculty:* 11 full-time (7 women), 9 part-time/adjunct (5 women). *Students:* 70 full-time (63 women), 45 part-time (42 women); includes 108 minority (all Hispanic/Latino). Average age 31. 37 applicants, 59% accepted, 22 enrolled. In 2017, 48 master's awarded. *Degree requirements:* For master's, field practicum. *Entrance requirements:* For master's, minimum GPA of 3.0, basic statistics course, three letters of reference, personal statement. Additional exam requirements/recommendations for international students: Required—TOEFL (minimum score 550 paper-based). *Application deadline:* For fall admission, 4/15 priority date for domestic and international students. Applications are processed on a rolling basis. Application fee: $50. *Financial support:* In 2017–18, 3 research assistantships (averaging $5,000 per year) were awarded; unspecified assistantships also available. Financial award application deadline: 3/15; financial award applicants required to submit FAFSA. *Faculty research:* Child welfare, family violence, social justice, community development, aging, health disparities, mental health, teen pregnancy, environmental justice, cultural competency. *Unit head:* Dr. John Gonzalez, Interim Chair, 956-665-3575, Fax: 956-665-3516, E-mail: john.gonzalez@utrgv.edu.
Website: http://www.utrgv.edu/socialwork/index.htm

University of the Fraser Valley, Graduate Studies, Abbotsford, BC V2S 7M8, Canada. Offers criminal justice (MA); social work (MSW). *Program availability:* Evening/weekend. *Faculty:* 23 full-time (13 women). *Students:* 41 full-time (24 women), 4 part-time (2 women); includes 4 minority (all American Indian or Alaska Native, non-Hispanic/Latino). Average age 36. 42 applicants, 31% accepted, 13 enrolled. In 2017, 15 master's awarded. *Degree requirements:* For master's, thesis optional, major research paper. *Entrance requirements:* For master's, bachelor's degree, work experience in related field. Additional exam requirements/recommendations for international students: Recommended—TOEFL (minimum score 570 paper-based; 88 iBT), IELTS (minimum score 6.5), TWE (minimum score 4.5), TSE (minimum score 61). *Application deadline:* For fall admission, 1/31 priority date for domestic students, 4/1 priority date for international students; for winter admission, 8/31 priority date for domestic students; for spring admission, 12/31 priority date for domestic students. Application fee: $75 ($250 for international students). Electronic applications accepted. *Expenses:* Contact institution. *Financial support:* Research assistantships, scholarships/grants, health care benefits, and bursaries available. Financial award application deadline: 5/10. *Faculty research:* Criminal justice, criminology, social work, child welfare. *Unit head:* Dr. Adrienne Chan, Associate Vice President for Research, Engagement and Graduate Studies, 604-504-4074, Fax: 778-880-0356, E-mail: adrienne.chan@ufv.ca. *Application contact:* Educational Advisors, 604-854-4528, Fax: 604-855-7614, E-mail: advising@ufv.ca.
Website: http://www.ufv.ca/Graduate_Studies.htm

The University of Toledo, College of Graduate Studies, College of Health and Human Services, School of Social Justice, Toledo, OH 43606-3390. Offers criminal justice (MA); social work (MSW).

The University of Toledo, College of Graduate Studies, College of Social Justice and Human Service, Department of Criminal Justice and Social Work, Toledo, OH 43606-3390. Offers child advocacy (Certificate); criminal justice (MA); elder law (Certificate); juvenile justice (Certificate); patient advocacy (Certificate); social work (MSW); JD/MA. *Accreditation:* CSWE. *Program availability:* Part-time. *Degree requirements:* For master's, comprehensive exam, thesis. *Entrance requirements:* For master's and

Certificate, minimum cumulative GPA of 2.7 for all previous academic work, letters of recommendation. Additional exam requirements/recommendations for international students: Required—TOEFL (minimum score 550 paper-based; 80 iBT). Electronic applications accepted.

University of Toronto, School of Graduate Studies, Faculty of Social Work, Toronto, ON M5S 1A1, Canada. Offers MSW, PhD, MH Sc/MSW. *Program availability:* Part-time. *Degree requirements:* For doctorate, thesis/dissertation, oral exam/thesis defense. *Entrance requirements:* For master's, minimum mid-B average in final year of full-time study, 3 full courses in social sciences, experience in social services (recommended), 3 letters of reference, resume; for doctorate, MSW or equivalent, minimum B+ average, competency in basic statistical methods. Additional exam requirements/recommendations for international students: Required—TOEFL (minimum score 580 paper-based; 93 iBT), IELTS (minimum score 7), TWE (minimum score 5), or Michigan English Language Assessment Battery (minimum score 85). Electronic applications accepted. *Expenses:* Contact institution.

University of Utah, Graduate School, College of Social Work, Salt Lake City, UT 84112. Offers MSW, PhD, MSW/JD, MSW/MPA, MSW/MPH. *Accreditation:* CSWE (one or more programs are accredited). *Program availability:* Part-time, evening/weekend. *Students:* 294 full-time (227 women), 43 part-time (36 women); includes 77 minority (11 Black or African American, non-Hispanic/Latino; 6 American Indian or Alaska Native, non-Hispanic/Latino; 6 Asian, non-Hispanic/Latino; 39 Hispanic/Latino; 1 Native Hawaiian or other Pacific Islander, non-Hispanic/Latino; 14 Two or more races, non-Hispanic/Latino), 4 international. Average age 30. In 2017, 171 master's, 4 doctorates awarded. *Degree requirements:* For master's, thesis or alternative; for doctorate, comprehensive exam, thesis/dissertation. *Entrance requirements:* For master's, GRE General Test or MAT (if cumulative GPA is below 3.0), minimum GPA of 3.0; for doctorate, GRE General Test. Additional exam requirements/recommendations for international students: Required—TOEFL (minimum score 600 paper-based; 100 iBT). *Application deadline:* For fall admission, 11/1 for domestic and international students. Application fee: $55 ($65 for international students). Electronic applications accepted. *Expenses:* Contact institution. *Financial support:* Fellowships with tuition reimbursements, research assistantships with tuition reimbursements, teaching assistantships with partial tuition reimbursements, career-related internships or fieldwork, scholarships/grants, and unspecified assistantships available. Financial award application deadline: 3/15; financial award applicants required to submit FAFSA. *Faculty research:* Health, mental health, gerontology, child welfare, forensic social work, instructional social work. *Unit head:* Dr. Martell L. Teasley, Dean, 801-581-6194, Fax: 801-585-3219, E-mail: martell.teasley@utah.edu. *Application contact:* Dr. Mary Jane Taylor, Associate Dean for Academic Affairs, 801-581-8828, Fax: 801-585-3219, E-mail: maryjane.taylor@socwk.utah.edu.
Website: https://socialwork.utah.edu/

University of Vermont, Graduate College, College of Education and Social Services, Department of Social Work, Burlington, VT 05405. Offers MSW. *Accreditation:* CSWE. *Students:* 62 (50 women). 86 applicants, 78% accepted, 31 enrolled. In 2017, 29 master's awarded. *Entrance requirements:* For master's, resume. Additional exam requirements/recommendations for international students: Required—TOEFL (minimum score 550 paper-based, 90 iBT) or IELTS (6.5). *Application deadline:* For fall admission, 2/1 priority date for domestic and international students. Applications are processed on a rolling basis. Application fee: $65. Electronic applications accepted. *Expenses:* Tuition, state resident: full-time $11,628; part-time $646 per credit. Tuition, nonresident: full-time $29,340; part-time $1630 per credit. *Required fees:* $1994; $10 per credit. Tuition and fees vary according to course load and program. *Financial support:* In 2017–18, 18 students received support, including 6 teaching assistantships with partial tuition reimbursements available (averaging $8,000 per year); scholarships/grants and health care benefits also available. Financial award application deadline: 2/1. *Application contact:* Kenneth Bechtel, Academic Support, 802-656-8800, E-mail: kbechtel@uvm.edu.
Website: https://www.uvm.edu/cess/socialwork/msw

University of Victoria, Faculty of Graduate Studies, Faculty of Human and Social Development, School of Social Work, Victoria, BC V8W 2Y2, Canada. Offers MSW. *Entrance requirements:* For master's, BSW. Additional exam requirements/recommendations for international students: Required—TOEFL (minimum score 575 paper-based), IELTS (minimum score 7). Electronic applications accepted. *Faculty research:* Women's issues, public policy formation and implementation, child welfare, First Nations, community development.

University of Victoria, Faculty of Graduate Studies, Faculty of Human and Social Development, Studies in Policy and Practice Program, Victoria, BC V8W 2Y2, Canada. Offers MA. *Program availability:* Part-time. *Degree requirements:* For master's, thesis. *Entrance requirements:* For master's, resume. Additional exam requirements/recommendations for international students: Required—TOEFL (minimum score 575 paper-based), IELTS (minimum score 7). Electronic applications accepted. *Faculty research:* Women's issues, public policy formation and implementation, health promotion and education, children, youth and families.

University of Washington, Graduate School, School of Social Work, Seattle, WA 98195. Offers MSW, PhD, MPH/MSW. *Accreditation:* CSWE (one or more programs are accredited). *Program availability:* Evening/weekend, online learning. *Degree requirements:* For master's, thesis optional; for doctorate, thesis/dissertation. *Entrance requirements:* For master's, GRE General Test, minimum GPA of 3.0; for doctorate, master's degree, sample of scholarly work, minimum GPA of 3.0. Additional exam requirements/recommendations for international students: Required—TOEFL. *Faculty research:* Health and mental health; children, youth, and families; multicultural issues; reducing risk and enhancing protective factors in children; etrology of substance use.

University of Washington, Tacoma, Graduate Programs, Program in Social Work, Tacoma, WA 98402-3100. Offers advanced integrative practice (MSW); social work (MSW). *Program availability:* Part-time, evening/weekend. *Degree requirements:* For master's, completion of all 75 required credits with minimum cumulative GPA of 3.0, 2.7 in each course; degree completion within 6 years. *Entrance requirements:* For master's, baccalaureate degree from regionally-accredited institution, minimum GPA of 3.0 on most recent 90 quarter credit hours or 60 semester hours, resume, social service experience form, two essay question responses, criminal/conviction history and background check clearance, three letters of reference. Additional exam requirements/recommendations for international students: Required—TOEFL (minimum score 580 paper-based; 70 iBT). Electronic applications accepted. *Faculty research:* Domestic violence and prevention, LGBT issues, gerontological social work, transnational social work, child welfare-mental health.

University of West Florida, College of Education and Professional Studies, Department of Social Work, Pensacola, FL 32514-5750. Offers MSW. *Accreditation:* CSWE. *Program availability:* Part-time, evening/weekend. *Entrance requirements:* For master's, GRE or MAT, official transcripts; minimum undergraduate cumulative GPA of 3.0; academic preparation as demonstrated by quality and relevance of undergraduate degree major; letter of intent; 3 letters of recommendation; work experience as documented on the Social Work Supplemental Application. Additional exam requirements/recommendations for international students: Required—TOEFL (minimum score 550 paper-based). Electronic applications accepted.

Social Work

University of Windsor, Faculty of Graduate Studies, Faculty of Arts and Social Sciences, School of Social Work, Windsor, ON N9B 3P4, Canada. Offers MSW. *Program availability:* Part-time. *Degree requirements:* For master's, thesis or alternative. *Entrance requirements:* For master's, minimum B+ average in last year of undergraduate study. Additional exam requirements/recommendations for international students: Required—TOEFL (minimum score 600 paper-based). Electronic applications accepted. *Faculty research:* Addiction, social policy analysis, gerontology and health care.

University of Wisconsin–Green Bay, Graduate Studies, Program in Social Work, Green Bay, WI 54311-7001. Offers MSW. *Accreditation:* CSWE. *Program availability:* Part-time. *Degree requirements:* For master's, thesis or alternative. *Entrance requirements:* For master's, GRE, minimum GPA of 2.75. Electronic applications accepted. *Faculty research:* Child welfare.

University of Wisconsin–Madison, Graduate School, College of Letters and Science, School of Social Work, Madison, WI 53706-1380. Offers social welfare (PhD); social work (MSW). *Accreditation:* CSWE (one or more programs are accredited). Terminal master's awarded for partial completion of doctoral program. *Degree requirements:* For doctorate, thesis/dissertation. *Entrance requirements:* For master's, minimum GPA of 3.0 on last 60 credits; for doctorate, GRE General Test, minimum GPA of 3.0 on last 60 credits. Electronic applications accepted. *Expenses:* Contact institution. *Faculty research:* Poverty, caregiving, child welfare, developmental disabilities, mental health, severe mental illnesses, adolescence, family, social policy, child support.

University of Wisconsin–Milwaukee, Graduate School, Helen Bader School of Social Welfare, Department of Social Work, Milwaukee, WI 53201-0413. Offers applied gerontology (Graduate Certificate); nonprofit management (Graduate Certificate); social welfare (PhD); social work (MSW, PhD). *Accreditation:* CSWE. *Program availability:* Part-time. *Students:* 194 full-time (169 women), 111 part-time (97 women); includes 83 minority (36 Black or African American, non-Hispanic/Latino; 1 American Indian or Alaska Native, non-Hispanic/Latino; 9 Asian, non-Hispanic/Latino; 1 Hispanic/Latino; 36 Two or more races, non-Hispanic/Latino), 3 international. Average age 31. 361 applicants, 61% accepted, 128 enrolled. In 2017, 156 master's, 68 other advanced degrees awarded. *Entrance requirements:* For doctorate, GRE, bachelor's degree. Additional exam requirements/recommendations for international students: Required—TOEFL (minimum score 550 paper-based; 79 iBT), IELTS (minimum score 6.5). *Application deadline:* For fall admission, 1/1 priority date for domestic students; for spring admission, 9/1 for domestic students. Application fee: $56 ($96 for international students). Electronic applications accepted. *Financial support:* Fellowships, research assistantships, teaching assistantships, career-related internships or fieldwork, health care benefits, unspecified assistantships, and project assistantships available. Support available to part-time students. Financial award application deadline: 4/15; financial award applicants required to submit FAFSA. *Application contact:* Deb Padgett, Associate Professor, Social Work, 414-229-6452, E-mail: dpadgett@uwm.edu. Website: http://uwm.edu/socialwelfare/academics/

University of Wisconsin–Oshkosh, Graduate Studies, Department of Social Work, Oshkosh, WI 54901. Offers MSW. Program offered jointly with University of Wisconsin–Green Bay. *Accreditation:* CSWE. *Program availability:* Part-time. *Entrance requirements:* For master's, GRE, letters of recommendation, previous courses in statistics and human biology, work experience. Additional exam requirements/recommendations for international students: Required—TOEFL (minimum score 550 paper-based; 79 iBT).

University of Wyoming, College of Health Sciences, Division of Social Work, Laramie, WY 82071. Offers MSW. *Accreditation:* CSWE. *Degree requirements:* For master's, comprehensive exam, thesis or alternative. *Entrance requirements:* For master's, minimum GPA of 3.0. Additional exam requirements/recommendations for international students: Required—TOEFL. *Expenses:* Contact institution. *Faculty research:* Social work education, child welfare, mental health, diversity, school social work.

Utah State University, School of Graduate Studies, College of Humanities and Social Sciences, Department of Sociology, Social Work, and Anthropology, Logan, UT 84322. Offers anthropology (MS); social work (MSW); sociology (MS, PhD). *Degree requirements:* For master's, thesis; for doctorate, comprehensive exam, thesis/dissertation. *Entrance requirements:* For master's, GRE General Test, minimum GPA of 3.0, recommendation letters; for doctorate, GRE General Test, minimum GPA of 3.0, recommendation letters, transcripts, personal statement, MS degree. Additional exam requirements/recommendations for international students: Required—TOEFL; Recommended—TWE. *Faculty research:* Demography, environmental/natural resource sociology, rural community change, international development, health studies.

Valdosta State University, Department of Social Work, Valdosta, GA 31698. Offers MSW. *Accreditation:* CSWE. *Program availability:* Part-time, evening/weekend, online learning. *Degree requirements:* For master's, comprehensive exam, 5 practica. *Entrance requirements:* For master's, GRE General Test, MAT, minimum GPA of 3.0 in last 2 years of course work. Additional exam requirements/recommendations for international students: Required—TOEFL (minimum score 523 paper-based); Recommended—IELTS. *Application deadline:* For fall admission, 3/15 for domestic and international students. Applications are processed on a rolling basis. Application fee: $45. *Expenses:* Contact institution. *Financial support:* Research assistantships with full tuition reimbursements, career-related internships or fieldwork, institutionally sponsored loans, scholarships/grants, and unspecified assistantships available. Financial award application deadline: 7/1; financial award applicants required to submit FAFSA. *Unit head:* Dr. Mizanur Miah, Head, 229-249-4893, Fax: 229-245-4341, E-mail: mrmiah@valdosta.edu. *Application contact:* Rebecca Powers, Admission Specialist, 229-333-5694, Fax: 229-245-3853, E-mail: rlwaters@valdosta.edu. Website: http://www.valdosta.edu/colleges/education/social-work/

Virginia Commonwealth University, Graduate School, School of Social Work, Doctoral Program in Social Work, Richmond, VA 23284-9005. Offers PhD. *Degree requirements:* For doctorate, comprehensive exam, thesis/dissertation. *Entrance requirements:* For doctorate, GRE General Test, MSW or related degree. Additional exam requirements/recommendations for international students: Required—TOEFL (minimum score 600 paper-based; 100 iBT). Electronic applications accepted.

Virginia Commonwealth University, Graduate School, School of Social Work, Master's Program in Social Work, Richmond, VA 23284-9005. Offers MSW, JD/MSW, MSW/M Div, MSW/MPH. *Accreditation:* CSWE. *Entrance requirements:* Additional exam requirements/recommendations for international students: Required—TOEFL (minimum score 600 paper-based; 100 iBT). Electronic applications accepted.

Walden University, Graduate Programs, School of Social Work and Human Services, Minneapolis, MN 55401. Offers addictions and social work (DSW); advanced clinical practice (MSW); clinical expertise (DSW); criminal justice (DSW); disaster, crisis and intervention (DSW); family studies and interventions (DSW); human and social services (PhD), including advanced research, community and social services, community intervention and leadership, conflict management, criminal justice, disaster crisis and intervention, family studies and intervention, gerontology, global social services, higher education, human services and nonprofit administration, mental health facilitation; medical social work (DSW); military social work (MSW); policy practice (DSW); social work (PhD), including addictions and social work, clinical expertise, criminal justice, disaster, crisis and intervention, family studies and interventions, medical social work, policy practice, social work administration; social work administration (DSW); social work in healthcare (MSW); social work with children and families (MSW). *Accreditation:* CSWE. *Program availability:* Part-time, evening/weekend, online only, 100% online. *Degree requirements:* For master's, residency (for some programs); for doctorate, thesis/dissertation, residency. *Entrance requirements:* For master's, bachelor's degree or higher; minimum GPA of 2.5; official transcripts; goal statement (for some programs); access to computer and Internet; for doctorate, master's degree or higher; three years of related professional or academic experience (preferred); minimum GPA of 3.0; goal statement and current resume (for select programs); official transcripts; access to computer and Internet. Additional exam requirements/recommendations for international students: Required—TOEFL (minimum score 550 paper-based, 79 iBT), IELTS (minimum score 6.5), Michigan English Language Assessment Battery (minimum score 82), or PTE (minimum score 53). Electronic applications accepted.

Walla Walla University, Graduate Studies, Wilma Hepker School of Social Work and Sociology, College Place, WA 99324. Offers social work (MSW). *Accreditation:* CSWE. *Program availability:* Part-time. *Entrance requirements:* For master's, minimum GPA of 2.75, essay. Additional exam requirements/recommendations for international students: Required—TOEFL (minimum score 550 paper-based; 79 iBT). *Application deadline:* For fall admission, 7/15 priority date for domestic students. Applications are processed on a rolling basis. Application fee: $50. Electronic applications accepted. *Financial support:* Career-related internships or fieldwork, Federal Work-Study, and scholarships/grants available. Support available to part-time students. Financial award application deadline: 4/30; financial award applicants required to submit FAFSA. *Unit head:* Dr. Susan B. Smith, Dean, 509-527-2443, Fax: 509-527-2270, E-mail: susan.smith@wallawalla.edu. *Application contact:* Dr. Heather Vonderfecht, Program Director, 509-527-2584, Fax: 509-527-2237, E-mail: heather.vonderfecht@wallawalla.edu. Website: https://wallawalla.edu/academics/areas-of-study/undergraduate-programs/school-of-social-work-and-sociology/

Washburn University, School of Applied Studies, Department of Social Work, Topeka, KS 66621. Offers clinical social work (MSW); JD/MSW. *Accreditation:* CSWE. *Program availability:* Part-time, evening/weekend. *Degree requirements:* For master's, practicum. *Entrance requirements:* For master's, coursework in human biology and cultural anthropology, multiculturalism, or human diversity. Additional exam requirements/recommendations for international students: Required—TOEFL (minimum score 80 iBT). *Faculty research:* Trauma, multicultural issues, school social work, emotional intelligence, animal-assisted therapy.

Washington University in St. Louis, Brown School, St. Louis, MO 63110. Offers American Indian/Alaska native (MSW); children, youth and families (MSW); epidemiology/biostatistics (MPH); generalist (MPH); global health (MPH); health (MSW); health policy analysis (MPH); individualized (MSW), including health; mental health (MSW); older adults and aging societies (MSW); public health sciences (PhD); social and economic development (MSW), including domestic, international; social work (PhD); urban design (MPH); violence and injury prevention (MSW); JD/MSW; M Arch/MSW; MPH/MBA; MSW/M Div; MSW/M Ed; MSW/MAPS; MSW/MBA; MSW/MPH; MUD/MSW. MSW/M Div and MSW/MAPS offered in partnership with Eden Theological Seminary. *Accreditation:* CSWE (one or more programs are accredited). *Faculty:* 54 full-time (31 women), 87 part-time/adjunct (61 women). *Students:* 294 full-time (254 women); includes 114 minority (56 Black or African American, non-Hispanic/Latino; 8 American Indian or Alaska Native, non-Hispanic/Latino; 17 Asian, non-Hispanic/Latino; 10 Hispanic/Latino; 1 Native Hawaiian or other Pacific Islander, non-Hispanic/Latino; 22 Two or more races, non-Hispanic/Latino), 246 international. Average age 26. *Degree requirements:* For master's, 60 credit hours (for MSW); 52 credit hours (for MPH); practicum; for doctorate, comprehensive exam, thesis/dissertation. *Entrance requirements:* For master's, GRE (preferred), GMAT, LSAT, MCAT, PCAT, or United States Medical Licensing Exam (for MPH); for doctorate, GRE. Additional exam requirements/recommendations for international students: Required—TOEFL (minimum score 100 iBT), IELTS (minimum score 7). *Application deadline:* For fall admission, 12/15 priority date for domestic and international students; for winter admission, 3/1 priority date for domestic and international students. Applications are processed on a rolling basis. Electronic applications accepted. *Expenses:* Contact institution. *Financial support:* In 2017–18, 30 fellowships, 60 research assistantships were awarded; career-related internships or fieldwork, Federal Work-Study, scholarships/grants, and unspecified assistantships also available. Support available to part-time students. Financial award applicants required to submit FAFSA. *Faculty research:* Mental health, social policy, health policy, epidemiology, social and economic development. *Total annual research expenditures:* $14.5 million. *Unit head:* Jamie L. Adkisson-Hennessey, Director of Admissions and Recruitment, 314-935-3524, Fax: 314-935-4859, E-mail: jadkisson@wustl.edu. *Application contact:* Office of Admissions and Recruitment, 314-935-6676, Fax: 314-935-4859, E-mail: brownadmissions@wustl.edu. Website: http://brownschool.wustl.edu

Wayne State University, College of Liberal Arts and Sciences, Department of Anthropology, Detroit, MI 48202. Offers anthropology (MA, PhD); social work (PhD). Doctoral program admits for fall only. *Program availability:* Part-time. *Faculty:* 13. *Students:* 31 full-time (25 women), 25 part-time (16 women); includes 9 minority (4 Black or African American, non-Hispanic/Latino; 2 Hispanic/Latino; 3 Two or more races, non-Hispanic/Latino), 3 international. Average age 33. 30 applicants, 33% accepted, 8 enrolled. In 2017, 9 master's, 3 doctorates awarded. *Degree requirements:* For master's, thesis (for some programs); for doctorate, one foreign language, thesis/dissertation. *Entrance requirements:* For master's, three letters of recommendation, completion of introduction to anthropology, letter of intent, writing sample, minimum undergraduate GPA of 3.2; for doctorate, GRE, bachelor's degree in anthropology or a related field, three letters of recommendation, completion of introduction to anthropology, letter of intent, writing sample, minimum undergraduate GPA of 3.2. Additional exam requirements/recommendations for international students: Required—TOEFL (minimum score 550 paper-based; 79 iBT), TWE (minimum score 5.5), Michigan English Language Assessment Battery (minimum score 85); Recommended—IELTS (minimum score 6.5). *Application deadline:* For fall admission, 1/10 for domestic and international students; for winter admission, 10/1 for domestic and international students. Application fee: $50. Electronic applications accepted. *Expenses:* Tuition, state resident: full-time $10,224; part-time $638.98 per credit hour. Tuition, nonresident: full-time $22,145; part-time $1384.04 per credit hour. Tuition and fees vary according to course load and program. *Financial support:* In 2017–18, 28 students received support, including 1 fellowship with tuition reimbursement available (averaging $16,000 per year), 1 research assistantship with tuition reimbursement available (averaging $18,885 per year), 6 teaching assistantships with tuition reimbursements available (averaging $18,534 per year); scholarships/grants and unspecified assistantships also available. Financial award applicants required to submit FAFSA. *Faculty research:* Anthropology of Detroit, archaeology, business and organizational anthropology, linguistic anthropology, cultural anthropology, medical anthropology, biological anthropology. *Unit head:* Dr. Andrea Sankar, Professor and Chair, 313-577-6961, E-mail: asankar@wayne.edu. *Application contact:* Dr. Stephen Chrisomalis, Director of Graduate Studies, 313-577-9922, E-mail: chrisomalis@wayne.edu. Website: http://clas.wayne.edu/anthropology/

Wayne State University, School of Social Work, Detroit, MI 48202. Offers gerontology (Certificate); social work (MSW, PhD). Application deadlines: April 1 for MSW, December 19 for PhD. *Accreditation:* CSWE (one or more programs are accredited). *Program availability:* Part-time, evening/weekend. *Degree requirements:* For master's, filed work; for doctorate, variable foreign language requirement, comprehensive exam, thesis/dissertation. *Entrance requirements:* For master's, personal interest statement, resume, 3 references; for doctorate, GRE (minimum combined score of 1000 on Verbal and Quantitative components), minimum undergraduate GPA of 3.5, MSW from CSWE-accredited institution (or working towards one), resume, three letters of reference, personal statement, summary of relevant research and professional experience, writing sample, interview; for Certificate, MSW or actively enrolled in advanced portion of MSW program. Additional exam requirements/recommendations for international students: Required—TOEFL (minimum score 550 paper-based; 79 iBT), TWE (minimum score 5.5), Michigan English Language Assessment Battery (minimum score 85); Recommended—IELTS (minimum score 6.5). *Application deadline:* Applications are processed on a rolling basis. Application fee: $50. Electronic applications accepted. *Expenses:* Contact institution. *Financial support:* Fellowships with tuition reimbursements, research assistantships with tuition reimbursements, teaching assistantships with tuition reimbursements, scholarships/grants, and unspecified assistantships available. Financial award applicants required to submit FAFSA. *Faculty research:* Aging, child welfare, health and behavioral health, interpersonal violence, community development, policy and program development. *Unit head:* Dr. Jerrold Brandell, Interim Dean, 313-577-4409, E-mail: aa4537@wayne.edu. *Application contact:* Shantalea Johns, Interim Director of Admissions, 313-577-4409, E-mail: shantalea@wayne.edu.
Website: http://socialwork.wayne.edu/

West Chester University of Pennsylvania, College of Education and Social Work, Department of Social Work, West Chester, PA 19383. Offers gerontology (Certificate); social work (MSW). *Accreditation:* CSWE. *Program availability:* Part-time, evening/weekend. *Students:* 190 full-time (165 women), 100 part-time (83 women); includes 143 minority (111 Black or African American, non-Hispanic/Latino; 3 Asian, non-Hispanic/Latino; 17 Hispanic/Latino; 12 Two or more races, non-Hispanic/Latino). Average age 30. 275 applicants, 77% accepted, 137 enrolled. In 2017, 80 master's, 3 other advanced degrees awarded. *Degree requirements:* For master's, completion of foundation courses and field practicums. *Entrance requirements:* For master's, minimum GPA of 3.0, personal statement of 3 to 5 pages clearly articulating professional goals, two letters of recommendation. Additional exam requirements/recommendations for international students: Required—TOEFL or IELTS. *Application deadline:* For fall admission, 5/15 for international students; for spring admission, 10/15 for international students. Applications are processed on a rolling basis. Application fee: $50. Electronic applications accepted. *Expenses:* Tuition, state resident: full-time $9000; part-time $500 per credit. Tuition, nonresident: full-time $13,500; part-time $750 per credit. *Required fees:* $2959; $149.79 per credit. *Financial support:* Scholarships/grants and unspecified assistantships available. Financial award application deadline: 2/15; financial award applicants required to submit FAFSA. *Faculty research:* Recovery in mental health and substance abuse disorders, integrated health and interprofessional education, trauma and disaster intervention, multicultural resources, human rights including LGBTQA rights. *Unit head:* Dr. Christina M. Chiarelli-Helminiak, Chairperson, 610-436-3615, E-mail: cchiarelli-helminiak@wcupa.edu. *Application contact:* Dr. Stacie Metz, Graduate Coordinator, 610-436-2101, Fax: 610-436-2763, E-mail: smetz@wcupa.edu.
Website: http://www.wcupa.edu/education-socialWork/gradSocialWork/

Western Carolina University, Graduate School, College of Health and Human Sciences, Department of Social Work, Cullowhee, NC 28723. Offers MSW. *Accreditation:* CSWE. *Program availability:* Part-time. *Entrance requirements:* For master's, appropriate undergraduate major with minimum GPA of 3.0, 3 recommendations, resume. Additional exam requirements/recommendations for international students: Required—TOEFL (minimum score 550 paper-based; 79 iBT). *Expenses:* Tuition, state resident: full-time $4436. Tuition, nonresident: full-time $14,842. *Required fees:* $2926.

Western Illinois University, School of Graduate Studies, College of Education and Human Services, Department of Health Sciences and Social Work, Macomb, IL 61455-1390. Offers health sciences (MS), including public health, school health. *Accreditation:* NCATE. *Program availability:* Part-time. *Degree requirements:* For master's, comprehensive exam, thesis or alternative. *Entrance requirements:* Additional exam requirements/recommendations for international students: Required—TOEFL (minimum score 550 paper-based; 80 iBT). *Application deadline:* Applications are processed on a rolling basis. Application fee: $30. Electronic applications accepted. *Financial support:* Unspecified assistantships available. Financial award applicants required to submit FAFSA. *Unit head:* Dr. Lorette Oden, Chairperson, 309-298-1076. *Application contact:* Dr. Nancy Parsons, Associate Provost and Director of Graduate Studies, 309-298-1806, Fax: 309-298-2345, E-mail: grad-office@wiu.edu.
Website: http://www.wiu.edu/coehs/health_sciences/

Western Kentucky University, Graduate Studies, College of Health and Human Services, Department of Social Work, Bowling Green, KY 42101. Offers MSW. *Accreditation:* CSWE. *Entrance requirements:* Additional exam requirements/recommendations for international students: Required—TOEFL (minimum score 555 paper-based; 79 iBT).

Western Michigan University, Graduate College, College of Health and Human Services, School of Social Work, Kalamazoo, MI 49008. Offers MSW. *Accreditation:* CSWE. *Program availability:* Part-time.

Western New Mexico University, Graduate Division, Department of Social Work, Silver City, NM 88062-0680. Offers MSW. *Accreditation:* CSWE. *Program availability:* Part-time, evening/weekend, online learning. Electronic applications accepted.

Westfield State University, College of Graduate and Continuing Education, Department of Social Work, Westfield, MA 01086. Offers MSW. *Accreditation:* CSWE. *Program availability:* Part-time, evening/weekend. *Faculty:* 10 full-time (5 women), 13 part-time/adjunct (10 women). *Students:* 180 full-time (141 women), 38 part-time (30 women); includes 63 minority (16 Black or African American, non-Hispanic/Latino; 4 Asian, non-Hispanic/Latino; 39 Hispanic/Latino; 4 Two or more races, non-Hispanic/Latino). Average age 32. 175 applicants, 64% accepted, 81 enrolled. In 2017, 64

master's awarded. *Degree requirements:* For master's, comprehensive exam, thesis (for some programs). *Entrance requirements:* For master's, GRE General Test or MAT, minimum undergraduate GPA of 2.8. Additional exam requirements/recommendations for international students: Recommended—TOEFL (minimum score 550 paper-based; 79 iBT). *Application deadline:* For fall admission, 2/1 for domestic students. Applications are processed on a rolling basis. Application fee: $50. *Expenses:* Contact institution. *Financial support:* Unspecified assistantships available. Financial award application deadline: 3/1; financial award applicants required to submit FAFSA. *Unit head:* Dr. Robert Kersting, Chair, 413-572-5536, Fax: 413-579-3122, E-mail: rkersting@westfield.ma.edu. *Application contact:* Shelly Henrichon, Admissions Coordinator, 413-572-8022, Fax: 413-572-5227, E-mail: mhenrichon@westfield.ma.edu.

West Texas A&M University, College of Education and Social Sciences, Department of Psychology, Sociology and Social Work, Canyon, TX 79015. Offers psychology (MA); social work (MS). *Program availability:* Part-time, evening/weekend. *Degree requirements:* For master's, comprehensive exam, thesis optional. *Entrance requirements:* For master's, GRE General Test, 3 letters of recommendation; interview; minimum GPA of 3.25 in psychology, 3.0 overall. Additional exam requirements/recommendations for international students: Required—TOEFL. Electronic applications accepted.

West Virginia University, Eberly College of Arts and Sciences, School of Social Work, Morgantown, WV 26506. Offers aging and health care (MSW); children and families (MSW); community mental health (MSW); community organization and social administration (MSW); direct (clinical) social work practice (MSW). *Accreditation:* CSWE. *Program availability:* Part-time. *Degree requirements:* For master's, fieldwork. *Entrance requirements:* For master's, GRE, minimum GPA of 2.75, 2 letters of reference. Additional exam requirements/recommendations for international students: Required—TOEFL. *Expenses:* Tuition, state resident: full-time $9450. Tuition, nonresident: full-time $24,390. *Faculty research:* Rural and small town social work practice, gerontology, health and mental health, welfare reform, child welfare.

Wichita State University, Graduate School, Fairmount College of Liberal Arts and Sciences, School of Social Work, Wichita, KS 67260. Offers MSW. *Accreditation:* CSWE. *Unit head:* Dr. Brien Bolin, Director, 316-978-7250, Fax: 316-978-3328, E-mail: brien.bolin@wichita.edu. *Application contact:* Jordan Oleson, Admissions Coordinator, 316-978-3095, Fax: 316-978-3253, E-mail: jordan.oleson@wichita.edu.
Website: http://www.wichita.edu/sw

Widener University, School of Human Service Professions, Center for Social Work Education, Chester, PA 19013-5792. Offers MSW, PhD. *Accreditation:* CSWE. *Students:* 63 full-time (54 women), 893 part-time (803 women); includes 451 minority (318 Black or African American, non-Hispanic/Latino; 1 American Indian or Alaska Native, non-Hispanic/Latino; 13 Asian, non-Hispanic/Latino; 78 Hispanic/Latino; 1 Native Hawaiian or other Pacific Islander, non-Hispanic/Latino; 40 Two or more races, non-Hispanic/Latino), 5 international. Average age 34. 442 applicants, 59% accepted, 183 enrolled. *Unit head:* Dr. Beth Berol, Associate Dean, 610-499-1152, E-mail: bibarol@widener.edu.

Wilfrid Laurier University, Faculty of Graduate and Postdoctoral Studies, Lyle S. Hallman Faculty of Social Work, Waterloo, ON N2L 3C5, Canada. Offers Aboriginal studies (MSW); community, policy, planning and organizations (MSW); critical social policy and organizational studies (PhD); individuals, families and groups (MSW); social work practice (individuals, families, groups and communities) (PhD); social work practice: individuals, families, groups and communities (PhD). *Program availability:* Part-time. *Degree requirements:* For master's, thesis optional; for doctorate, thesis/dissertation. *Entrance requirements:* For master's, course work in social science, research methodology, and statistics; honors BA with a minimum B average; for doctorate, master's degree in social work, minimum A- average. Additional exam requirements/recommendations for international students: Required—TOEFL (minimum score 89 iBT). Electronic applications accepted. *Expenses:* Contact institution.

Winthrop University, College of Arts and Sciences, Program in Social Work, Rock Hill, SC 29733. Offers MSW. *Accreditation:* CSWE. *Students:* 108 full-time (100 women), 13 part-time (11 women); includes 51 minority (40 Black or African American, non-Hispanic/Latino; 1 Asian, non-Hispanic/Latino; 7 Hispanic/Latino; 3 Two or more races, non-Hispanic/Latino), 1 international. Average age 39. In 2017, 53 master's awarded. *Entrance requirements:* For master's, GRE or MAT, minimum GPA of 3.0, 3 letters of recommendation, resume. Additional exam requirements/recommendations for international students: Required—TOEFL (minimum score 550 paper-based; 79 iBT), IELTS (minimum score 6). *Application deadline:* For fall admission, 7/15 priority date for domestic students; for spring admission, 12/1 for domestic students. Applications are processed on a rolling basis. Application fee: $50. Electronic applications accepted. *Financial support:* Research assistantships with full tuition reimbursements available. *Faculty research:* Field study placement opportunities. *Unit head:* Dr. Kori Bloomquist, Graduate Program Director, 803-323-2647, E-mail: bloomquistk@winthrop.edu. *Application contact:* 800-411-7041, Fax: 803-323-2292, E-mail: gradschool@winthrop.edu.
Website: http://www.winthrop.edu/cas/socialwork/msw

Yeshiva University, Wurzweiler School of Social Work, New York, NY 10033-3201. Offers MSW, PhD, MSW/Certificate. *Accreditation:* CSWE (one or more programs are accredited). *Program availability:* Part-time, evening/weekend. Terminal master's awarded for partial completion of doctoral program. *Degree requirements:* For master's, thesis, integrative essay; for doctorate, comprehensive exam, thesis/dissertation. *Entrance requirements:* For master's, interview, minimum GPA of 3.0, letters of reference; for doctorate, GRE, interview, letters of reference, writing sample, MSW, minimum of 2 years of professional social work experience. Additional exam requirements/recommendations for international students: Required—TOEFL (minimum score 577 paper-based). *Expenses:* Contact institution. *Faculty research:* Child abuse, AIDS, day care, non profits, gerontology.

York University, Faculty of Graduate Studies, Faculty of Liberal Arts and Professional Studies, Program in Social Work, Toronto, ON M3J 1P3, Canada. Offers MSW, PhD. *Program availability:* Part-time, evening/weekend. *Degree requirements:* For master's, thesis or alternative. Electronic applications accepted.

APPENDIXES

APPENDIXES

Institutional Changes
Since the 2018 Edition

Following is an alphabetical listing of institutions that have recently closed, merged with other institutions, or changed their names or status. In the case of a name change, the former name appears first, followed by the new name.

Argosy University, Dallas (Farmers Branch, TX): *closed.*

Argosy University, Denver (Denver, CO): *closed.*

Argosy University, Inland Empire (Ontario, CA): *closed.*

Argosy University, Nashville (Nashville, TN): *closed.*

Argosy University, Salt Lake City (Draper, UT): *closed.*

Argosy University, San Diego (San Diego, CA): *closed.*

Argosy University, San Francisco Bay Area (Alameda, CA): *closed.*

Argosy University, Sarasota (Sarasota, FL): *closed.*

Argosy University, Schaumburg (Schaumburg, IL): *closed.*

Arlington Baptist College (Arlington, TX): *name changed to Arlington Baptist University.*

Armstrong State University (Savannah, GA): *name changed to Georgia Southern University-Armstrong Campus.*

Art Center College of Design (Pasadena, CA): *name changed to ArtCenter College of Design.*

The Art Institute of California-San Francisco, a campus of Argosy University (San Francisco, CA): *closed.*

Augsburg College (Minneapolis, MN): *name changed to Augsburg University.*

Bristol University (Anaheim, CA): *closed.*

Claremont McKenna College (Claremont, CA): *no longer profiled by request from the institution. Graduate program is for students attending the Claremont Colleges.*

Coleman University (San Diego, CA): *closed.*

Digital Media Arts College (Boca Raton, FL): *merged into Lynn University (Boca Raton, FL).*

Episcopal Divinity School (Cambridge, MA): *merged into Union Theological Seminary in the City of New York (New York, NY).*

Everest University (Tampa, FL): *name changed to Altierus Career College and no longer offers graduate degrees.*

Fairleigh Dickinson University, College at Florham (Madison, NJ): *name changed to Fairleigh Dickinson University, Florham Campus.*

Faith Evangelical College & Seminary (Tacoma, WA): *name changed to Faith International University.*

Frank Lloyd Wright School of Architecture (Scottsdale, AZ): *name changed to School of Architecture at Taliesin.*

Future Generations Graduate School (Franklin, WV): *name changed to Future Generations University.*

Grace University (Omaha, NE): *closed.*

Greenville College (Greenville, IL): *name changed to Greenville University.*

Hazelden Graduate School of Addiction Studies (Center City, MN): *name changed to Hazelden Betty Ford Graduate School of Addiction Studies.*

Henley-Putnam University (San Jose, CA): *name changed to Henley-Putnam School of Strategic Security.*

Huntington College of Health Sciences (Knoxville, TN): *name changed to Huntington University of Health Sciences.*

The Institute for the Psychological Sciences (Arlington, VA): *name changed to Divine Mercy University.*

International College of the Cayman Islands (Newlands, Cayman Islands): *no longer accredited by agency recognized by USDE or CHEA.*

Johnson State College (Johnson, VT): *name changed to Northern Vermont University-Johnson.*

John Wesley University (High Point, NC): *closed.*

Kaplan University, Davenport Campus (Davenport, IA): *name changed to Purdue University Global.*

Knowledge Systems Institute (Skokie, IL): *no longer degree granting.*

Long Island University-Hudson at Westchester (Purchase, NY): *name changed to Long Island University-Hudson.*

Lutheran Theological Seminary at Gettysburg (Gettysburg, PA): *name changed to United Lutheran Seminary.*

The Lutheran Theological Seminary at Philadelphia (Philadelphia, PA): *name changed to United Lutheran Seminary.*

Lynchburg College (Lynchburg, VA): *name changed to University of Lynchburg.*

Lyndon State College (Lyndonville, VT): *name changed to Northern Vermont University-Lyndon.*

Marylhurst University (Marylhurst, OR): *closed.*

McNally Smith College of Music (Saint Paul, MN): *closed.*

Memphis College of Art (Memphis, TN): *closed.*

Mirrer Yeshiva (Brooklyn, NY): *name changed to Mirrer Yeshiva Central Institute.*

Mount Ida College (Newton, MA): *merged into University of Massachusetts Amherst (Amherst, MA).*

National American University (Rapid City, SD): *graduate programs now listed under National American University (Austin, TX).*

The Ohio State University-Mansfield Campus (Mansfield, OH): *name changed to The Ohio State University at Mansfield.*

The Ohio State University-Newark Campus (Newark, OH): *name changed to The Ohio State University at Newark.*

Our Lady of the Lake College (Baton Rouge, LA): *name changed to Franciscan Missionaries of Our Lady University.*

Philadelphia University (Philadelphia, PA): *merged into Thomas Jefferson University (Philadelphia, PA).*

Sacred Heart School of Theology (Hales Corners, WI): *name changed to Sacred Heart Seminary and School of Theology.*

Sewanee: The University of the South (Sewanee, TN): *name changed to The University of the South.*

Shepherd University (Los Angeles, CA): *closed.*

Silicon Valley University (San Jose, CA): *closed.*

South University (Novi, MI): *closed.*

South University (High Point, NC): *closed.*

South University (Cleveland, OH): *closed.*

University of Great Falls (Great Falls, MT): *name changed to University of Providence.*

University of Phoenix-Atlanta Campus (Sandy Springs, GA): *closed.*

University of Phoenix-Augusta Campus (Augusta, GA): *closed.*

University of Phoenix-Central Florida Campus (Orlando, FL): *closed.*

University of Phoenix-Charlotte Campus (Charlotte, NC): *closed.*

University of Phoenix-Colorado Campus (Lone Tree, CO): *closed.*

University of Phoenix-Colorado Springs Downtown Campus (Colorado Springs, CO): *closed.*

University of Phoenix-Columbus Georgia Campus (Columbus, GA): *closed.*

University of Phoenix-Jersey City Campus (Jersey City, NJ): *closed.*

University of Phoenix-New Mexico Campus (Albuquerque, NM): *closed.*

University of Phoenix-North Florida Campus (Jacksonville, FL): *closed.*

University of Phoenix-Southern Arizona Campus (Tucson, AZ): *closed.*

University of Phoenix-Southern California Campus (Costa Mesa, CA): *closed.*

University of Phoenix-South Florida Campus (Miramar, FL): *closed.*

University of Phoenix-Utah Campus (Salt Lake City, UT): *closed.*

University of Phoenix-Washington D.C. Campus (Washington, DC): *closed.*

University of Phoenix-Western Washington Campus (Tukwila, WA): *closed.*

University of Puerto Rico, Mayagüez Campus (Mayagüez, PR): *name changed to University of Puerto Rico-Mayagüez.*

University of Puerto Rico, Medical Sciences Campus (San Juan, PR): *name changed to University of Puerto Rico-Medical Sciences Campus.*

University of Puerto Rico, Río Piedras Campus (San Juan, PR): *name changed to University of Puerto Rico-Río Piedras.*

The University of South Dakota (Vermillion, SD): *name changed to University of South Dakota.*

Urbana University (Urbana, OH): *name changed to Urbana University-A Branch Campus of Franklin University.*

Virginia College in Birmingham (Birmingham, AL): *no longer offers graduate degrees.*

Warner Pacific College (Portland, OR): *name changed to Warner Pacific University.*

Wheelock College (Boston, MA): *merged with Boston University's School of Education.*

Wright Institute (Berkeley, CA): *name changed to The Wright Institute.*

Yeshiva Karlin Stolin Rabbinical Institute (Brooklyn, NY): *name changed to Yeshiva Karlin Stolin.*

Abbreviations Used in the Guides

The following list includes abbreviations of degree names used in the profiles in the 2019 edition of the guides. Because some degrees (e.g., Doctor of Education) can be abbreviated in more than one way (e.g., D.Ed. or Ed.D.), and because the abbreviations used in the guides reflect the preferences of the individual colleges and universities, the list may include two or more abbreviations for a single degree.

DEGREES

A Mus D	Doctor of Musical Arts
AC	Advanced Certificate
AD	Artist's Diploma
	Doctor of Arts
ADP	Artist's Diploma
Adv C	Advanced Certificate
AGC	Advanced Graduate Certificate
AGSC	Advanced Graduate Specialist Certificate
ALM	Master of Liberal Arts
AM	Master of Arts
AMBA	Accelerated Master of Business Administration
APC	Advanced Professional Certificate
APMPH	Advanced Professional Master of Public Health
App Sc	Applied Scientist
App Sc D	Doctor of Applied Science
AstE	Astronautical Engineer
ATC	Advanced Training Certificate
Au D	Doctor of Audiology
B Th	Bachelor of Theology
BN	Bachelor of Naturopathy
CAES	Certificate of Advanced Educational Specialization
CAGS	Certificate of Advanced Graduate Studies
CAL	Certificate in Applied Linguistics
CAPS	Certificate of Advanced Professional Studies
CAS	Certificate of Advanced Studies
CATS	Certificate of Achievement in Theological Studies
CE	Civil Engineer
CEM	Certificate of Environmental Management
CET	Certificate in Educational Technologies
CGS	Certificate of Graduate Studies
Ch E	Chemical Engineer
Clin Sc D	Doctor of Clinical Science
CM	Certificate in Management
CMH	Certificate in Medical Humanities
CMM	Master of Church Ministries
CMS	Certificate in Ministerial Studies
CNM	Certificate in Nonprofit Management
CPC	Certificate in Publication and Communication
CPH	Certificate in Public Health
CPS	Certificate of Professional Studies
CScD	Doctor of Clinical Science
CSD	Certificate in Spiritual Direction
CSS	Certificate of Special Studies
CTS	Certificate of Theological Studies
D Ac	Doctor of Acupuncture
D Admin	Doctor of Administration
D Arch	Doctor of Architecture
D Be	Doctor in Bioethics
D Com	Doctor of Commerce
D Couns	Doctor of Counseling
D Des	Doctorate of Design
D Div	Doctor of Divinity
D Ed	Doctor of Education
D Ed Min	Doctor of Educational Ministry
D Eng	Doctor of Engineering
D Engr	Doctor of Engineering
D Ent	Doctor of Enterprise
D Env	Doctor of Environment
D Law	Doctor of Law
D Litt	Doctor of Letters
D Med Sc	Doctor of Medical Science
D Mgt	Doctor of Management
D Min	Doctor of Ministry
D Miss	Doctor of Missiology
D Mus	Doctor of Music
D Mus A	Doctor of Musical Arts
D Phil	Doctor of Philosophy
D Prof	Doctor of Professional Studies
D Ps	Doctor of Psychology
D Sc	Doctor of Science
D Sc D	Doctor of Science in Dentistry
D Sc IS	Doctor of Science in Information Systems
D Sc PA	Doctor of Science in Physician Assistant Studies
D Th	Doctor of Theology
D Th P	Doctor of Practical Theology
DA	Doctor of Accounting
	Doctor of Arts
DACM	Doctor of Acupuncture and Chinese Medicine
DAIS	Doctor of Applied Intercultural Studies
DAOM	Doctorate in Acupuncture and Oriental Medicine
DAT	Doctorate of Athletic Training
	Professional Doctor of Art Therapy
DBA	Doctor of Business Administration
DBH	Doctor of Behavioral Health
DBL	Doctor of Business Leadership
DC	Doctor of Chiropractic
DCC	Doctor of Computer Science
DCD	Doctor of Communications Design
DCE	Doctor of Computer Engineering
DCL	Doctor of Civil Law
	Doctor of Comparative Law
DCM	Doctor of Church Music
DCN	Doctor of Clinical Nutrition
DCS	Doctor of Computer Science
DDN	Diplôme du Droit Notarial
DDS	Doctor of Dental Surgery
DE	Doctor of Education
	Doctor of Engineering
DED	Doctor of Economic Development
DEIT	Doctor of Educational Innovation and Technology
DEL	Doctor of Executive Leadership
DEM	Doctor of Educational Ministry
DEPD	Diplôme Études Spécialisées
DES	Doctor of Engineering Science
DESS	Diplôme Études Supérieures Spécialisées
DET	Doctor of Educational Technology
DFA	Doctor of Fine Arts
DGP	Diploma in Graduate and Professional Studies
DGS	Doctor of Global Security
DH Sc	Doctor of Health Sciences
DHA	Doctor of Health Administration
DHCE	Doctor of Health Care Ethics
DHL	Doctor of Hebrew Letters
DHPE	Doctorate of Health Professionals Education
DHS	Doctor of Health Science
DHSc	Doctor of Health Science
DIT	Doctor of Industrial Technology

	Doctor of Information Technology
DJS	Doctor of Jewish Studies
DLS	Doctor of Liberal Studies
DM	Doctor of Management
	Doctor of Music
DMA	Doctor of Musical Arts
DMD	Doctor of Dental Medicine
DME	Doctor of Manufacturing Management
	Doctor of Music Education
DMFT	Doctor of Marital and Family Therapy
DMH	Doctor of Medical Humanities
DML	Doctor of Modern Languages
DMP	Doctorate in Medical Physics
DMPNA	Doctor of Management Practice in Nurse Anesthesia
DN Sc	Doctor of Nursing Science
DNAP	Doctor of Nurse Anesthesia Practice
DNP	Doctor of Nursing Practice
DNP-A	Doctor of Nursing Practice - Anesthesia
DNS	Doctor of Nursing Science
DO	Doctor of Osteopathy
DOL	Doctorate of Organizational Leadership
DOM	Doctor of Oriental Medicine
DOT	Doctor of Occupational Therapy
DPA	Diploma in Public Administration
	Doctor of Public Administration
DPDS	Doctor of Planning and Development Studies
DPH	Doctor of Public Health
DPM	Doctor of Plant Medicine
	Doctor of Podiatric Medicine
DPPD	Doctor of Policy, Planning, and Development
DPS	Doctor of Professional Studies
DPT	Doctor of Physical Therapy
DPTSc	Doctor of Physical Therapy Science
Dr DES	Doctor of Design
Dr NP	Doctor of Nursing Practice
Dr OT	Doctor of Occupational Therapy
Dr PH	Doctor of Public Health
Dr Sc PT	Doctor of Science in Physical Therapy
DRSc	Doctor of Regulatory Science
DS	Doctor of Science
DS Sc	Doctor of Social Science
DScPT	Doctor of Science in Physical Therapy
DSI	Doctor of Strategic Intelligence
DSJS	Doctor of Science in Jewish Studies
DSL	Doctor of Strategic Leadership
DSS	Doctor of Strategic Security
DSW	Doctor of Social Work
DTL	Doctor of Talmudic Law
	Doctor of Transformational Leadership
DV Sc	Doctor of Veterinary Science
DVM	Doctor of Veterinary Medicine
DWS	Doctor of Worship Studies
EAA	Engineer in Aeronautics and Astronautics
EASPh D	Engineering and Applied Science Doctor of Philosophy
ECS	Engineer in Computer Science
Ed D	Doctor of Education
Ed DCT	Doctor of Education in College Teaching
Ed L D	Doctor of Education Leadership
Ed M	Master of Education
Ed S	Specialist in Education
Ed Sp	Specialist in Education
EDB	Executive Doctorate in Business
EDM	Executive Doctorate in Management
EE	Electrical Engineer
EJD	Executive Juris Doctor
EMBA	Executive Master of Business Administration
EMFA	Executive Master of Forensic Accounting

EMHA	Executive Master of Health Administration
EMHCL	Executive Master in Healthcare Leadership
EMIB	Executive Master of International Business
EMIR	Executive Master in International Relations
EML	Executive Master of Leadership
EMPA	Executive Master of Public Administration
EMPL	Executive Master in Policy Leadership
	Executive Master in Public Leadership
EMS	Executive Master of Science
EMTM	Executive Master of Technology Management
Eng	Engineer
Eng Sc D	Doctor of Engineering Science
Engr	Engineer
Exec MHA	Executive Master of Health Administration
Exec Ed D	Executive Doctor of Education
Exec MBA	Executive Master of Business Administration
Exec MPA	Executive Master of Public Administration
Exec MPH	Executive Master of Public Health
Exec MS	Executive Master of Science
G Dip	Graduate Diploma
GBC	Graduate Business Certificate
GDM	Graduate Diploma in Management
GDPA	Graduate Diploma in Public Administration
GEMBA	Global Executive Master of Business Administration
GM Acc	Graduate Master of Accountancy
GMBA	Global Master of Business Administration
GP LL M	Global Professional Master of Laws
GPD	Graduate Performance Diploma
GSS	Graduate Special Certificate for Students in Special Situations
IEMBA	International Executive Master of Business Administration
IMA	Interdisciplinary Master of Arts
IMBA	International Master of Business Administration
IMES	International Master's in Environmental Studies
Ingeniero	Engineer
JCD	Doctor of Canon Law
JCL	Licentiate in Canon Law
JD	Juris Doctor
JM	Juris Master
JSD	Doctor of Juridical Science
	Doctor of Jurisprudence
	Doctor of the Science of Law
JSM	Master of the Science of Law
L Th	Licenciate in Theology
LL B	Bachelor of Laws
LL CM	Master of Comparative Law
LL D	Doctor of Laws
LL M	Master of Laws
LL M in Tax	Master of Laws in Taxation
LL M CL	Master of Laws in Common Law
M Ac	Master of Accountancy
	Master of Accounting
	Master of Acupuncture
M Ac OM	Master of Acupuncture and Oriental Medicine
M Acc	Master of Accountancy
	Master of Accounting
M Acct	Master of Accountancy
	Master of Accounting
M Accy	Master of Accountancy
M Actg	Master of Accounting
M Acy	Master of Accountancy
M Ad	Master of Administration
M Ad Ed	Master of Adult Education
M Adm	Master of Administration
M Adm Mgt	Master of Administrative Management
M Admin	Master of Administration

M ADU	Master of Architectural Design and Urbanism
M Adv	Master of Advertising
M AEST	Master of Applied Environmental Science and Technology
M Ag	Master of Agriculture
M Ag Ed	Master of Agricultural Education
M Agr	Master of Agriculture
M App Comp Sc	Master of Applied Computer Science
M App St	Master of Applied Statistics
M Appl Stat	Master of Applied Statistics
M Aq	Master of Aquaculture
M Ar	Master of Architecture
M Arc	Master of Architecture
M Arch	Master of Architecture
M Arch I	Master of Architecture I
M Arch II	Master of Architecture II
M Arch E	Master of Architectural Engineering
M Arch H	Master of Architectural History
M Bioethics	Master in Bioethics
M Biomath	Master of Biomathematics
M Cat	Master of Catechesis
M Ch E	Master of Chemical Engineering
M Cl D	Master of Clinical Dentistry
M Cl Sc	Master of Clinical Science
M Comm	Master of Communication
M Comp	Master of Computing
M Comp Sc	Master of Computer Science
M Coun	Master of Counseling
M Dent	Master of Dentistry
M Dent Sc	Master of Dental Sciences
M Des	Master of Design
M Des S	Master of Design Studies
M Div	Master of Divinity
M E Sci	Master of Earth Science
M Ec	Master of Economics
M Econ	Master of Economics
M Ed	Master of Education
M Ed T	Master of Education in Teaching
M En	Master of Engineering
M En S	Master of Environmental Sciences
M Eng	Master of Engineering
M Eng Mgt	Master of Engineering Management
M Engr	Master of Engineering
M Ent	Master of Enterprise
M Env	Master of Environment
M Env Des	Master of Environmental Design
M Env E	Master of Environmental Engineering
M Env Sc	Master of Environmental Science
M Ext Ed	Master of Extension Education
M Fin	Master of Finance
M Geo E	Master of Geological Engineering
M Geoenv E	Master of Geoenvironmental Engineering
M Geog	Master of Geography
M Hum	Master of Humanities
M IDST	Master's in Interdisciplinary Studies
M Jur	Master of Jurisprudence
M Kin	Master of Kinesiology
M Land Arch	Master of Landscape Architecture
M Litt	Master of Letters
M Mark	Master of Marketing
M Mat SE	Master of Material Science and Engineering
M Math	Master of Mathematics
M Mech E	Master of Mechanical Engineering
M Med Sc	Master of Medical Science
M Mgmt	Master of Management
M Mgt	Master of Management
M Min	Master of Ministries
M Mtl E	Master of Materials Engineering
M Mu	Master of Music
M Mus	Master of Music
M Mus Ed	Master of Music Education
M Music	Master of Music
M Pet E	Master of Petroleum Engineering
M Pharm	Master of Pharmacy
M Phil	Master of Philosophy
M Phil F	Master of Philosophical Foundations
M Pl	Master of Planning
M Plan	Master of Planning
M Pol	Master of Political Science
M Pr Met	Master of Professional Meteorology
M Prob S	Master of Probability and Statistics
M Psych	Master of Psychology
M Pub	Master of Publishing
M Rel	Master of Religion
M Sc	Master of Science
M Sc A	Master of Science (Applied)
M Sc AC	Master of Science in Applied Computing
M Sc AHN	Master of Science in Applied Human Nutrition
M Sc BMC	Master of Science in Biomedical Communications
M Sc CS	Master of Science in Computer Science
M Sc E	Master of Science in Engineering
M Sc Eng	Master of Science in Engineering
M Sc Engr	Master of Science in Engineering
M Sc F	Master of Science in Forestry
M Sc FE	Master of Science in Forest Engineering
M Sc Geogr	Master of Science in Geography
M Sc N	Master of Science in Nursing
M Sc OT	Master of Science in Occupational Therapy
M Sc P	Master of Science in Planning
M Sc Pl	Master of Science in Planning
M Sc PT	Master of Science in Physical Therapy
M Sc T	Master of Science in Teaching
M SEM	Master of Sustainable Environmental Management
M Serv Soc	Master of Social Service
M Soc	Master of Sociology
M Sp Ed	Master of Special Education
M Stat	Master of Statistics
M Sys E	Master of Systems Engineering
M Sys Sc	Master of Systems Science
M Tax	Master of Taxation
M Tech	Master of Technology
M Th	Master of Theology
M Tox	Master of Toxicology
M Trans E	Master of Transportation Engineering
M U Ed	Master of Urban Education
M Urb	Master of Urban Planning
M Vet Sc	Master of Veterinary Science
MA	Master of Accounting
	Master of Administration
	Master of Arts
MA Comm	Master of Arts in Communication
MA Ed	Master of Arts in Education
MA Ed/HD	Master of Arts in Education and Human Development
MA Ext	Master of Agricultural Extension
MA Islamic	Master of Arts in Islamic Studies
MA Min	Master of Arts in Ministry
MA Miss	Master of Arts in Missiology
MA Past St	Master of Arts in Pastoral Studies
MA Ph	Master of Arts in Philosophy
MA Psych	Master of Arts in Psychology
MA Sc	Master of Applied Science
MA Sp	Master of Arts (Spirituality)
MA Th	Master of Arts in Theology
MA-R	Master of Arts (Research)

MAA	Master of Applied Anthropology
	Master of Applied Arts
	Master of Arts in Administration
MAAA	Master of Arts in Arts Administration
MAAAP	Master of Arts Administration and Policy
MAAD	Master of Advanced Architectural Design
MAAE	Master of Arts in Art Education
MAAPPS	Master of Arts in Asia Pacific Policy Studies
MAAS	Master of Arts in Aging and Spirituality
MAASJ	Master of Arts in Applied Social Justice
MAAT	Master of Arts in Applied Theology
	Master of Arts in Art Therapy
MAB	Master of Agribusiness
	Master of Applied Bioengineering
MABA	Master's in Applied Behavior Analysis
MABC	Master of Arts in Biblical Counseling
MABE	Master of Arts in Bible Exposition
MABL	Master of Arts in Biblical Languages
MABM	Master of Agribusiness Management
MABS	Master of Arts in Biblical Studies
MABT	Master of Arts in Bible Teaching
MAC	Master of Accountancy
	Master of Accounting
	Master of Arts in Communication
	Master of Arts in Counseling
MACC	Master of Arts in Christian Counseling
MACCT	Master of Accounting
MACD	Master of Arts in Christian Doctrine
MACE	Master of Arts in Christian Education
MACH	Master of Arts in Church History
MACI	Master of Arts in Curriculum and Instruction
MACIS	Master of Accounting and Information Systems
MACJ	Master of Arts in Criminal Justice
MACL	Master of Arts in Christian Leadership
	Master of Arts in Community Leadership
MACM	Master of Arts in Christian Ministries
	Master of Arts in Christian Ministry
	Master of Arts in Church Music
	Master of Arts in Counseling Ministries
MACML	Master of Arts in Christian Ministry and Leadership
MACN	Master of Arts in Counseling
MACO	Master of Arts in Counseling
MAcOM	Master of Acupuncture and Oriental Medicine
MACP	Master of Arts in Christian Practice
	Master of Arts in Church Planting
	Master of Arts in Counseling Psychology
MACS	Master of Applied Computer Science
	Master of Arts in Catholic Studies
	Master of Arts in Christian Studies
MACSE	Master of Arts in Christian School Education
MACT	Master of Arts in Communications and Technology
MAD	Master in Educational Institution Administration
	Master of Applied Design
	Master of Art and Design
MADR	Master of Arts in Dispute Resolution
MADS	Master of Applied Disability Studies
MAE	Master of Aerospace Engineering
	Master of Agricultural Economics
	Master of Agricultural Education
	Master of Applied Economics
	Master of Architectural Engineering
	Master of Art Education
	Master of Arts in Education
	Master of Arts in English
MAEd	Master of Arts Education
MAEE	Master of Agricultural and Extension Education

MAEL	Master of Arts in Educational Leadership
MAEM	Master of Arts in Educational Ministries
MAEP	Master of Arts in Economic Policy
	Master of Arts in Educational Psychology
MAES	Master of Arts in Environmental Sciences
MAET	Master of Arts in English Teaching
MAF	Master of Arts in Finance
MAFE	Master of Arts in Financial Economics
MAFM	Master of Accounting and Financial Management
MAFS	Master of Arts in Family Studies
MAG	Master of Applied Geography
MAGU	Master of Urban Analysis and Management
MAH	Master of Arts in Humanities
MAHA	Master of Arts in Humanitarian Assistance
MAHCM	Master of Arts in Health Care Mission
MAHG	Master of American History and Government
MAHL	Master of Arts in Hebrew Letters
MAHN	Master of Applied Human Nutrition
MAHR	Master of Applied Historical Research
MAHS	Master of Arts in Human Services
MAHSR	Master in Applied Health Services Research
MAIA	Master of Arts in International Administration
	Master of Arts in International Affairs
MAICS	Master of Arts in Intercultural Studies
MAIDM	Master of Arts in Interior Design and Merchandising
MAIH	Master of Arts in Interdisciplinary Humanities
MAIOP	Master of Applied Industrial/Organizational Psychology
MAIS	Master of Arts in Intercultural Studies
	Master of Arts in Interdisciplinary Studies
	Master of Arts in International Studies
MAIT	Master of Administration in Information Technology
MAJ	Master of Arts in Journalism
MAJCS	Master of Arts in Jewish Communal Service
MAJPS	Master of Arts in Jewish Professional Studies
MAJS	Master of Arts in Jewish Studies
MAL	Master of Athletic Leadership
MALA	Master of Arts in Liberal Arts
MALCM	Master in Arts Leadership and Cultural Management
MALD	Master of Arts in Law and Diplomacy
MALER	Master of Arts in Labor and Employment Relations
MALL	Master of Arts in Language Learning
MALLT	Master of Arts in Language, Literature, and Translation
MALP	Master of Arts in Language Pedagogy
MALS	Master of Arts in Liberal Studies
MAM	Master of Acquisition Management
	Master of Agriculture and Management
	Master of Applied Mathematics
	Master of Arts in Management
	Master of Arts in Ministry
	Master of Arts Management
	Master of Aviation Management
MAMC	Master of Arts in Mass Communication
	Master of Arts in Ministry and Culture
	Master of Arts in Ministry for a Multicultural Church
MAME	Master of Arts in Missions/Evangelism
MAMFC	Master of Arts in Marriage and Family Counseling
MAMFT	Master of Arts in Marriage and Family Therapy
MAMHC	Master of Arts in Mental Health Counseling
MAMS	Master of Applied Mathematical Sciences
	Master of Arts in Ministerial Studies
	Master of Arts in Ministry and Spirituality

MAMT	Master of Arts in Mathematics Teaching
MAN	Master of Applied Nutrition
MANT	Master of Arts in New Testament
MAOL	Master of Arts in Organizational Leadership
MAOM	Master of Acupuncture and Oriental Medicine
	Master of Arts in Organizational Management
MAOT	Master of Arts in Old Testament
MAP	Master of Applied Politics
	Master of Applied Psychology
	Master of Arts in Planning
	Master of Psychology
	Master of Public Administration
MAP Min	Master of Arts in Pastoral Ministry
MAPA	Master of Arts in Public Administration
MAPC	Master of Arts in Pastoral Counseling
MAPE	Master of Arts in Physics Education
MAPM	Master of Arts in Pastoral Ministry
	Master of Arts in Pastoral Music
	Master of Arts in Practical Ministry
MAPP	Master of Arts in Public Policy
MAPS	Master of Applied Psychological Sciences
	Master of Arts in Pastoral Studies
	Master of Arts in Public Service
MAPW	Master of Arts in Professional Writing
MAQRM	Master's of Actuarial and Quantitative Risk Management
MAR	Master of Arts in Reading
	Master of Arts in Religion
Mar Eng	Marine Engineer
MARC	Master of Arts in Rehabilitation Counseling
MARE	Master of Arts in Religious Education
MARL	Master of Arts in Religious Leadership
MARS	Master of Arts in Religious Studies
MAS	Master of Accounting Science
	Master of Actuarial Science
	Master of Administrative Science
	Master of Advanced Study
	Master of American Studies
	Master of Animal Science
	Master of Applied Science
	Master of Applied Statistics
	Master of Archival Studies
MASA	Master of Advanced Studies in Architecture
MASC	Master of Arts in School Counseling
MASD	Master of Arts in Spiritual Direction
MASE	Master of Arts in Special Education
MASF	Master of Arts in Spiritual Formation
MASJ	Master of Arts in Systems of Justice
MASLA	Master of Advanced Studies in Landscape Architecture
MASM	Master of Aging Services Management
	Master of Arts in Specialized Ministries
MASP	Master of Arts in School Psychology
MASS	Master of Applied Social Science
MASW	Master of Aboriginal Social Work
MAT	Master of Arts in Teaching
	Master of Arts in Theology
	Master of Athletic Training
	Master's in Administration of Telecommunications
Mat E	Materials Engineer
MATCM	Master of Acupuncture and Traditional Chinese Medicine
MATDE	Master of Arts in Theology, Development, and Evangelism
MATDR	Master of Territorial Management and Regional Development
MATE	Master of Arts for the Teaching of English
MATESL	Master of Arts in Teaching English as a Second Language

MATESOL	Master of Arts in Teaching English to Speakers of Other Languages
MATF	Master of Arts in Teaching English as a Foreign Language/Intercultural Studies
MATFL	Master of Arts in Teaching Foreign Language
MATH	Master of Arts in Therapy
MATI	Master of Administration of Information Technology
MATL	Master of Arts in Teaching of Languages
	Master of Arts in Transformational Leadership
MATM	Master of Arts in Teaching of Mathematics
MATRN	Master of Athletic Training
MATS	Master of Arts in Theological Studies
	Master of Arts in Transforming Spirituality
MAUA	Master of Arts in Urban Affairs
MAUD	Master of Arts in Urban Design
MAURP	Master of Arts in Urban and Regional Planning
MAW	Master of Arts in Worship
MAWSHP	Master of Arts in Worship
MAYM	Master of Arts in Youth Ministry
MB	Master of Bioinformatics
MBA	Master of Business Administration
MBA-AM	Master of Business Administration in Aviation Management
MBA-EP	Master of Business Administration–Experienced Professionals
MBAA	Master of Business Administration in Aviation
MBAE	Master of Biological and Agricultural Engineering
	Master of Biosystems and Agricultural Engineering
MBAH	Master of Business Administration in Health
MBAi	Master of Business Administration–International
MBAICT	Master of Business Administration in Information and Communication Technology
MBC	Master of Building Construction
MBE	Master of Bilingual Education
	Master of Bioengineering
	Master of Bioethics
	Master of Biomedical Engineering
	Master of Business Economics
	Master of Business Education
MBEE	Master in Biotechnology Enterprise and Entrepreneurship
MBET	Master of Business, Entrepreneurship and Technology
MBI	Master in Business Informatics
MBIOT	Master of Biotechnology
MBiotech	Master of Biotechnology
MBL	Master of Business Leadership
MBLE	Master in Business Logistics Engineering
MBME	Master's in Biomedical Engineering
MBMSE	Master of Business Management and Software Engineering
MBOE	Master of Business Operational Excellence
MBS	Master of Biblical Studies
	Master of Biological Science
	Master of Biomedical Sciences
	Master of Bioscience
	Master of Building Science
	Master of Business and Science
	Master of Business Statistics
MBST	Master of Biostatistics
MBT	Master of Biomedical Technology
	Master of Biotechnology
	Master of Business Taxation
MBV	Master of Business for Veterans
MC	Master of Classics
	Master of Communication
	Master of Counseling

MC Ed	Master of Continuing Education
MC Sc	Master of Computer Science
MCA	Master of Commercial Aviation
	Master of Communication Arts
	Master of Criminology (Applied)
MCAM	Master of Computational and Applied Mathematics
MCC	Master of Computer Science
MCD	Master of Communications Disorders
	Master of Community Development
MCE	Master in Electronic Commerce
	Master of Chemistry Education
	Master of Christian Education
	Master of Civil Engineering
	Master of Control Engineering
MCEM	Master of Construction Engineering Management
MCEPA	Master of Chinese Economic and Political Affairs
MCHE	Master of Chemical Engineering
MCIS	Master of Communication and Information Studies
	Master of Computer and Information Science
	Master of Computer Information Systems
MCIT	Master of Computer and Information Technology
MCJ	Master of Criminal Justice
MCL	Master in Communication Leadership
	Master of Canon Law
	Master of Christian Leadership
	Master of Comparative Law
MCM	Master of Christian Ministry
	Master of Church Ministry
	Master of Church Music
	Master of Communication Management
	Master of Community Medicine
	Master of Construction Management
	Master of Contract Management
MCMin	Master of Christian Ministry
MCMM	Master in Communications and Media Management
MCMP	Master of City and Metropolitan Planning
MCMS	Master of Clinical Medical Science
MCN	Master of Clinical Nutrition
MCOL	Master of Arts in Community and Organizational Leadership
MCP	Master of City Planning
	Master of Community Planning
	Master of Counseling Psychology
	Master of Cytopathology Practice
	Master of Science in Quality Systems and Productivity
MCPD	Master of Community Planning and Development
MCR	Master in Clinical Research
MCRP	Master of City and Regional Planning
	Master of Community and Regional Planning
MCRS	Master of City and Regional Studies
MCS	Master of Chemical Sciences
	Master of Christian Studies
	Master of Clinical Science
	Master of Combined Sciences
	Master of Communication Studies
	Master of Computer Science
	Master of Consumer Science
MCSE	Master of Computer Science and Engineering
MCSL	Master of Catholic School Leadership
MCSM	Master of Construction Science and Management
MCT	Master of Commerce and Technology

MCTM	Master of Clinical Translation Management
MCTP	Master of Communication Technology and Policy
MCTS	Master of Clinical and Translational Science
MCVS	Master of Cardiovascular Science
MD	Doctor of Medicine
MDA	Master of Dietetic Administration
MDB	Master of Design-Build
MDE	Master in Design Engineering
	Master of Developmental Economics
	Master of Distance Education
	Master of the Education of the Deaf
MDH	Master of Dental Hygiene
MDI	Master of Disruptive Innovation
MDM	Master of Design Methods
	Master of Digital Media
MDP	Master in Sustainable Development Practice
	Master of Development Practice
MDR	Master of Dispute Resolution
MDS	Master in Data Science
	Master of Dental Surgery
	Master of Design Studies
	Master of Digital Sciences
MDSPP	Master in Data Science for Public Policy
ME	Master of Education
	Master of Engineering
	Master of Entrepreneurship
ME Sc	Master of Engineering Science
ME-PD	Master of Education–Professional Development
MEA	Master of Educational Administration
	Master of Engineering Administration
MEAE	Master of Entertainment Arts and Engineering
MEAP	Master of Environmental Administration and Planning
MEB	Master of Energy Business
MEBD	Master in Environmental Building Design
MEBT	Master in Electronic Business Technologies
MEC	Master of Electronic Commerce
Mech E	Mechanical Engineer
MEDS	Master of Environmental Design Studies
MEE	Master in Education
	Master of Electrical Engineering
	Master of Energy Engineering
	Master of Environmental Engineering
MEECON	Master of Energy Economics
MEEM	Master of Environmental Engineering and Management
MEENE	Master of Engineering in Environmental Engineering
MEEP	Master of Environmental and Energy Policy
MEERM	Master of Earth and Environmental Resource Management
MEH	Master in Humanistic Studies
	Master of Environmental Health
	Master of Environmental Horticulture
MEHS	Master of Environmental Health and Safety
MEIM	Master of Entertainment Industry Management
	Master of Equine Industry Management
MEL	Master of Educational Leadership
	Master of Engineering Leadership
	Master of English Literature
MELP	Master of Environmental Law and Policy
MEM	Master of Engineering Management
	Master of Environmental Management
	Master of Marketing
MEME	Master of Engineering in Manufacturing Engineering
	Master of Engineering in Mechanical Engineering
MENR	Master of Environment and Natural Resources

MENVEGR	Master of Environmental Engineering
MEP	Master of Engineering Physics
MEPC	Master of Environmental Pollution Control
MEPD	Master of Environmental Planning and Design
MER	Master of Employment Relations
MERE	Master of Entrepreneurial Real Estate
MERL	Master of Energy Regulation and Law
MES	Master of Education and Science
	Master of Engineering Science
	Master of Environment and Sustainability
	Master of Environmental Science
	Master of Environmental Studies
	Master of Environmental Systems
MESM	Master of Environmental Science and Management
MET	Master of Educational Technology
	Master of Engineering Technology
	Master of Entertainment Technology
	Master of Environmental Toxicology
METM	Master of Engineering and Technology Management
MEVE	Master of Environmental Engineering
MF	Master of Finance
	Master of Forestry
MFA	Master of Financial Administration
	Master of Fine Arts
MFALP	Master of Food and Agriculture Law and Policy
MFAS	Master of Fisheries and Aquatic Science
MFC	Master of Forest Conservation
MFCS	Master of Family and Consumer Sciences
MFE	Master of Financial Economics
	Master of Financial Engineering
	Master of Forest Engineering
MFES	Master of Fire and Emergency Services
MFG	Master of Functional Genomics
MFHD	Master of Family and Human Development
MFM	Master of Financial Management
	Master of Financial Mathematics
MFPE	Master of Food Process Engineering
MFR	Master of Forest Resources
MFRC	Master of Forest Resources and Conservation
MFRE	Master of Food and Resource Economics
MFS	Master of Food Science
	Master of Forensic Sciences
	Master of Forest Science
	Master of Forest Studies
	Master of French Studies
MFST	Master of Food Safety and Technology
MFT	Master of Family Therapy
MFWCB	Master of Fish, Wildlife and Conservation Biology
MFWS	Master of Fisheries and Wildlife Sciences
MFYCS	Master of Family, Youth and Community Sciences
MG	Master of Genetics
MGA	Master of Global Affairs
	Master of Government Administration
	Master of Governmental Administration
MGBA	Master of Global Business Administration
MGC	Master of Genetic Counseling
MGCS	Master of Genetic Counselor Studies
MGD	Master of Graphic Design
MGE	Master of Geotechnical Engineering
MGEM	Master of Geomatics for Environmental Management
	Master of Global Entrepreneurship and Management
MGIS	Master of Geographic Information Science
	Master of Geographic Information Systems

MGM	Master of Global Management
MGMA	Master of Greenhouse Gas Management and Accounting
MGP	Master of Gestion de Projet
MGPS	Master of Global Policy Studies
MGREM	Master of Global Real Estate Management
MGS	Master of Gender Studies
	Master of Gerontological Studies
	Master of Global Studies
MH	Master of Humanities
MH Sc	Master of Health Sciences
MHA	Master of Health Administration
	Master of Healthcare Administration
	Master of Hospital Administration
	Master of Hospitality Administration
MHB	Master of Human Behavior
MHC	Master of Mental Health Counseling
MHCA	Master of Health Care Administration
MHCD	Master of Health Care Design
MHCI	Master of Human-Computer Interaction
MHCL	Master of Health Care Leadership
MHCM	Master of Health Care Management
MHE	Master of Health Education
	Master of Human Ecology
MHE Ed	Master of Home Economics Education
MHEA	Master of Higher Education Administration
MHHS	Master of Health and Human Services
MHI	Master of Health Informatics
	Master of Healthcare Innovation
MHID	Master of Healthcare Interior Design
MHIHIM	Master of Health Informatics and Health Information Management
MHIIM	Master of Health Informatics and Information Management
MHK	Master of Human Kinetics
MHM	Master of Healthcare Management
MHMS	Master of Health Management Systems
MHP	Master of Health Physics
	Master of Heritage Preservation
	Master of Historic Preservation
MHPA	Master of Heath Policy and Administration
MHPCTL	Master of High Performance Coaching and Technical Leadership
MHPE	Master of Health Professions Education
MHR	Master of Human Resources
MHRD	Master in Human Resource Development
MHRIR	Master of Human Resources and Industrial Relations
MHRLR	Master of Human Resources and Labor Relations
MHRM	Master of Human Resources Management
MHS	Master of Health Science
	Master of Health Sciences
	Master of Health Studies
	Master of Hispanic Studies
	Master of Human Services
	Master of Humanistic Studies
MHSA	Master of Health Services Administration
MHSM	Master of Health Systems Management
MI	Master of Information
	Master of Instruction
MI Arch	Master of Interior Architecture
MIA	Master of Interior Architecture
	Master of International Affairs
MIAA	Master of International Affairs and Administration
MIAM	Master of International Agribusiness Management
MIAPD	Master of Interior Architecture and Product Design

MIB	Master of International Business
MIBS	Master of International Business Studies
MICLJ	Master of International Criminal Law and Justice
MICM	Master of International Construction Management
MID	Master of Industrial Design
	Master of Industrial Distribution
	Master of Innovation Design
	Master of Interior Design
	Master of International Development
MIDA	Master of International Development Administration
MIDP	Master of International Development Policy
MIDS	Master of Information and Data Science
MIE	Master of Industrial Engineering
MIF	Master of International Forestry
MIHTM	Master of International Hospitality and Tourism Management
MIJ	Master of International Journalism
MILR	Master of Industrial and Labor Relations
MIM	Master in Ministry
	Master of Information Management
	Master of International Management
	Master of International Marketing
MIMFA	Master of Investment Management and Financial Analysis
MIMLAE	Master of International Management for Latin American Executives
MIMS	Master of Information Management and Systems
	Master of Integrated Manufacturing Systems
MIP	Master of Infrastructure Planning
	Master of Intellectual Property
	Master of International Policy
MIPA	Master of International Public Affairs
MIPD	Master of Integrated Product Design
MIPER	Master of International Political Economy of Resources
MIPM	Master of International Policy Management
MIPP	Master of International Policy and Practice
	Master of International Public Policy
MIPS	Master of International Planning Studies
MIR	Master of Industrial Relations
	Master of International Relations
MIRD	Master of International Relations and Diplomacy
MIRHR	Master of Industrial Relations and Human Resources
MIS	Master of Imaging Science
	Master of Industrial Statistics
	Master of Information Science
	Master of Information Systems
	Master of Integrated Science
	Master of Interdisciplinary Studies
	Master of International Service
	Master of International Studies
MISE	Master of Industrial and Systems Engineering
MISKM	Master of Information Sciences and Knowledge Management
MISM	Master of Information Systems Management
MISW	Master of Indigenous Social Work
MIT	Master in Teaching
	Master of Industrial Technology
	Master of Information Technology
	Master of Initial Teaching
	Master of International Trade
MITA	Master of Information Technology Administration
MITM	Master of Information Technology and Management

MJ	Master of Journalism
	Master of Jurisprudence
MJ Ed	Master of Jewish Education
MJA	Master of Justice Administration
MJM	Master of Justice Management
MJS	Master of Judaic Studies
	Master of Judicial Studies
	Master of Juridical Studies
MK	Master of Kinesiology
MKM	Master of Knowledge Management
ML	Master of Latin
	Master's in Law
ML Arch	Master of Landscape Architecture
MLA	Master of Landscape Architecture
	Master of Liberal Arts
MLAS	Master of Laboratory Animal Science
	Master of Liberal Arts and Sciences
MLAUD	Master of Landscape Architecture in Urban Development
MLD	Master of Leadership Development
	Master of Leadership Studies
MLE	Master of Applied Linguistics and Exegesis
MLER	Master of Labor and Employment Relations
MLI Sc	Master of Library and Information Science
MLIS	Master of Library and Information Science
	Master of Library and Information Studies
MLM	Master of Leadership in Ministry
MLPD	Master of Land and Property Development
MLRHR	Master of Labor Relations and Human Resources
MLS	Master of Leadership Studies
	Master of Legal Studies
	Master of Liberal Studies
	Master of Library Science
	Master of Life Sciences
	Master of Medical Laboratory Sciences
MLSCM	Master of Logistics and Supply Chain Management
MLT	Master of Language Technologies
MLTCA	Master of Long Term Care Administration
MLW	Master of Studies in Law
MLWS	Master of Land and Water Systems
MM	Master of Management
	Master of Mediation
	Master of Ministry
	Master of Music
MM Ed	Master of Music Education
MM Sc	Master of Medical Science
MM St	Master of Museum Studies
MMA	Master of Marine Affairs
	Master of Media Arts
	Master of Ministry Administration
	Master of Musical Arts
MMAL	Master of Maritime Administration and Logistics
MMAS	Master of Military Art and Science
MMB	Master of Microbial Biotechnology
MMC	Master of Manufacturing Competitiveness
	Master of Mass Communications
MMCM	Master of Music in Church Music
MMCSS	Master of Mathematical Computational and Statistical Sciences
MME	Master of Management in Energy
	Master of Manufacturing Engineering
	Master of Mathematics for Educators
	Master of Mechanical Engineering
	Master of Mining Engineering
	Master of Music Education
MMEL	Master's in Medical Education Leadership

MMF	Master of Mathematical Finance	
MMFC/T	Master of Marriage and Family Counseling/ Therapy	
MMFT	Master of Marriage and Family Therapy	
MMG	Master of Management	
MMH	Master of Management in Hospitality	
	Master of Medical Humanities	
MMI	Master of Management of Innovation	
MMIS	Master of Management Information Systems	
MML	Master of Managerial Logistics	
MMM	Master of Manufacturing Management	
	Master of Marine Management	
	Master of Medical Management	
MMP	Master of Marine Policy	
	Master of Medical Physics	
	Master of Music Performance	
MMPA	Master of Management and Professional Accounting	
MMQM	Master of Manufacturing Quality Management	
MMR	Master of Marketing Research	
MMRM	Master of Marine Resources Management	
MMS	Master in Migration Studies	
	Master of Management Science	
	Master of Management Studies	
	Master of Manufacturing Systems	
	Master of Marine Studies	
	Master of Materials Science	
	Master of Mathematical Sciences	
	Master of Medical Science	
	Master of Medieval Studies	
MMSE	Master of Manufacturing Systems Engineering	
MMSM	Master of Music in Sacred Music	
MMT	Master in Marketing	
	Master of Math for Teaching	
	Master of Music Therapy	
	Master's in Marketing Technology	
MMus	Master of Music	
MN	Master of Nursing	
	Master of Nutrition	
MN NP	Master of Nursing in Nurse Practitioner	
MNA	Master of Nonprofit Administration	
	Master of Nurse Anesthesia	
MNAL	Master of Nonprofit Administration and Leadership	
MNAS	Master of Natural and Applied Science	
MNCL	Master of Nonprofit and Civic Leadership	
MNCM	Master of Network and Communications Management	
MNE	Master of Nuclear Engineering	
MNL	Master in International Business for Latin America	
MNM	Master of Nonprofit Management	
MNO	Master of Nonprofit Organization	
MNPL	Master of Not-for-Profit Leadership	
MNpS	Master of Nonprofit Studies	
MNR	Master of Natural Resources	
MNRD	Master of Natural Resources Development	
MNRES	Master of Natural Resources and Environmental Studies	
MNRM	Master of Natural Resource Management	
MNRMG	Master of Natural Resource Management and Geography	
MNRS	Master of Natural Resource Stewardship	
MNS	Master of Natural Science	
MNSE	Master of Natural Sciences Education	
MO	Master of Oceanography	
MOD	Master of Organizational Development	
MOGS	Master of Oil and Gas Studies	
MOL	Master of Organizational Leadership	
MOM	Master of Organizational Management	

	Master of Oriental Medicine
MOR	Master of Operations Research
MOT	Master of Occupational Therapy
MP	Master of Physiology
	Master of Planning
MP Ac	Master of Professional Accountancy
MP Acc	Master of Professional Accountancy
	Master of Professional Accounting
	Master of Public Accounting
MP Aff	Master of Public Affairs
MP Th	Master of Pastoral Theology
MPA	Master of Performing Arts
	Master of Physician Assistant
	Master of Professional Accountancy
	Master of Professional Accounting
	Master of Public Administration
	Master of Public Affairs
MPAC	Master of Professional Accounting
MPAID	Master of Public Administration and International Development
MPAP	Master of Physician Assistant Practice
	Master of Public Administration and Policy
	Master of Public Affairs and Politics
MPAS	Master of Physician Assistant Science
	Master of Physician Assistant Studies
MPC	Master of Professional Communication
MPD	Master of Product Development
	Master of Public Diplomacy
MPDS	Master of Planning and Development Studies
MPE	Master of Physical Education
MPEM	Master of Project Engineering and Management
MPFM	Master of Public Financial Management
MPH	Master of Public Health
MPHE	Master of Public Health Education
MPHM	Master in Plant Health Management
MPHS	Master of Population Health Sciences
MPHTM	Master of Public Health and Tropical Medicine
MPIA	Master of Public and International Affairs
MPL	Master of Pastoral Leadership
MPM	Master of Pastoral Ministry
	Master of Pest Management
	Master of Policy Management
	Master of Practical Ministries
	Master of Professional Management
	Master of Project Management
	Master of Public Management
MPNA	Master of Public and Nonprofit Administration
MPNL	Master of Philanthropy and Nonprofit Leadership
MPO	Master of Prosthetics and Orthotics
MPOD	Master of Positive Organizational Development
MPP	Master of Public Policy
MPPA	Master of Public Policy Administration
	Master of Public Policy and Administration
MPPAL	Master of Public Policy, Administration and Law
MPPGA	Master of Public Policy and Global Affairs
MPPM	Master of Public Policy and Management
MPRTM	Master of Parks, Recreation, and Tourism Management
MPS	Master of Pastoral Studies
	Master of Perfusion Science
	Master of Planning Studies
	Master of Political Science
	Master of Preservation Studies
	Master of Prevention Science
	Master of Professional Studies
	Master of Public Service
MPSA	Master of Public Service Administration

MPSG	Master of Population and Social Gerontology
MPSIA	Master of Political Science and International Affairs
MPSL	Master of Public Safety Leadership
MPT	Master of Pastoral Theology
	Master of Physical Therapy
	Master of Practical Theology
MPVM	Master of Preventive Veterinary Medicine
MPW	Master of Professional Writing
	Master of Public Works
MQF	Master of Quantitative Finance
MQM	Master of Quality Management
	Master of Quantitative Management
MQS	Master of Quality Systems
MR	Master of Recreation
	Master of Retailing
MRA	Master in Research Administration
	Master of Regulatory Affairs
MRC	Master of Rehabilitation Counseling
MRCP	Master of Regional and City Planning
	Master of Regional and Community Planning
MRD	Master of Rural Development
MRE	Master of Real Estate
	Master of Religious Education
MRED	Master of Real Estate Development
MREM	Master of Resource and Environmental Management
MRLS	Master of Resources Law Studies
MRM	Master of Resources Management
MRP	Master of Regional Planning
MRRD	Master in Recreation Resource Development
MRS	Master of Religious Studies
MRSc	Master of Rehabilitation Science
MRUD	Master of Resilient Design
MS	Master of Science
MS Cmp E	Master of Science in Computer Engineering
MS Kin	Master of Science in Kinesiology
MS Acct	Master of Science in Accounting
MS Accy	Master of Science in Accountancy
MS Aero E	Master of Science in Aerospace Engineering
MS Ag	Master of Science in Agriculture
MS Arch	Master of Science in Architecture
MS Arch St	Master of Science in Architectural Studies
MS Bio E	Master of Science in Bioengineering
MS Bm E	Master of Science in Biomedical Engineering
MS Ch E	Master of Science in Chemical Engineering
MS Cp E	Master of Science in Computer Engineering
MS Eco	Master of Science in Economics
MS Econ	Master of Science in Economics
MS Ed	Master of Science in Education
MS Ed Admin	Master of Science in Educational Administration
MS El	Master of Science in Educational Leadership and Administration
MS En E	Master of Science in Environmental Engineering
MS Eng	Master of Science in Engineering
MS Engr	Master of Science in Engineering
MS Env E	Master of Science in Environmental Engineering
MS Exp Surg	Master of Science in Experimental Surgery
MS Mat SE	Master of Science in Material Science and Engineering
MS Met E	Master of Science in Metallurgical Engineering
MS Mgt	Master of Science in Management
MS Min	Master of Science in Mining
MS Min E	Master of Science in Mining Engineering
MS Mt E	Master of Science in Materials Engineering
MS Otol	Master of Science in Otolaryngology
MS Pet E	Master of Science in Petroleum Engineering

MS Sc	Master of Social Science
MS Sp Ed	Master of Science in Special Education
MS Stat	Master of Science in Statistics
MS Surg	Master of Science in Surgery
MS Tax	Master of Science in Taxation
MS Tc E	Master of Science in Telecommunications Engineering
MS-R	Master of Science (Research)
MSA	Master of School Administration
	Master of Science in Accountancy
	Master of Science in Accounting
	Master of Science in Administration
	Master of Science in Aeronautics
	Master of Science in Agriculture
	Master of Science in Analytics
	Master of Science in Anesthesia
	Master of Science in Architecture
	Master of Science in Aviation
	Master of Sports Administration
	Master of Surgical Assisting
MSAA	Master of Science in Astronautics and Aeronautics
MSABE	Master of Science in Agricultural and Biological Engineering
MSAC	Master of Science in Acupuncture
MSACC	Master of Science in Accounting
MSACS	Master of Science in Applied Computer Science
MSAE	Master of Science in Aeronautical Engineering
	Master of Science in Aerospace Engineering
	Master of Science in Applied Economics
	Master of Science in Applied Engineering
	Master of Science in Architectural Engineering
MSAEM	Master of Science in Aerospace Engineering and Mechanics
MSAF	Master of Science in Aviation Finance
MSAG	Master of Science in Applied Geosciences
MSAH	Master of Science in Allied Health
MSAL	Master of Sport Administration and Leadership
MSAM	Master of Science in Applied Mathematics
MSANR	Master of Science in Agriculture and Natural Resources
MSAS	Master of Science in Administrative Studies
	Master of Science in Applied Statistics
	Master of Science in Architectural Studies
MSAT	Master of Science in Accounting and Taxation
	Master of Science in Advanced Technology
	Master of Science in Athletic Training
MSB	Master of Science in Biotechnology
MSBA	Master of Science in Business Administration
	Master of Science in Business Analysis
MSBAE	Master of Science in Biological and Agricultural Engineering
	Master of Science in Biosystems and Agricultural Engineering
MSBCB	Master's in Bioinformatics and Computational Biology
MSBE	Master of Science in Biological Engineering
	Master of Science in Biomedical Engineering
MSBENG	Master of Science in Bioengineering
MSBH	Master of Science in Behavioral Health
MSBM	Master of Sport Business Management
MSBME	Master of Science in Biomedical Engineering
MSBMS	Master of Science in Basic Medical Science
MSBS	Master of Science in Biomedical Sciences
MSBTM	Master of Science in Biotechnology and Management
MSC	Master of Science in Commerce
	Master of Science in Communication
	Master of Science in Counseling
	Master of Science in Criminology

	Master of Strategic Communication
MSCC	Master of Science in Community Counseling
MSCD	Master of Science in Communication Disorders
	Master of Science in Community Development
MSCE	Master of Science in Chemistry Education
	Master of Science in Civil Engineering
	Master of Science in Clinical Epidemiology
	Master of Science in Computer Engineering
	Master of Science in Continuing Education
MSCEE	Master of Science in Civil and Environmental Engineering
MSCF	Master of Science in Computational Finance
MSCH	Master of Science in Chemical Engineering
MSChE	Master of Science in Chemical Engineering
MSCI	Master of Science in Clinical Investigation
MSCID	Master of Science in Community and International Development
MSCIS	Master of Science in Computer and Information Science
	Master of Science in Computer and Information Systems
	Master of Science in Computer Information Science
	Master of Science in Computer Information Systems
MSCIT	Master of Science in Computer Information Technology
MSCJ	Master of Science in Criminal Justice
MSCJA	Master of Science in Criminal Justice Administration
MSCJS	Master of Science in Crime and Justice Studies
MSCLS	Master of Science in Clinical Laboratory Studies
MSCM	Master of Science in Church Management
	Master of Science in Conflict Management
	Master of Science in Construction Management
	Master of Supply Chain Management
MSCMP	Master of Science in Cybersecurity Management and Policy
MSCNU	Master of Science in Clinical Nutrition
MSCP	Master of Science in Clinical Psychology
	Master of Science in Community Psychology
	Master of Science in Computer Engineering
	Master of Science in Counseling Psychology
MSCPE	Master of Science in Computer Engineering
MSCPharm	Master of Science in Pharmacy
MSCR	Master of Science in Clinical Research
MSCRP	Master of Science in City and Regional Planning
	Master of Science in Community and Regional Planning
MSCS	Master of Science in Clinical Science
	Master of Science in Computer Science
	Master of Science in Cyber Security
MSCSD	Master of Science in Communication Sciences and Disorders
MSCSE	Master of Science in Computer Science and Engineering
MSCTE	Master of Science in Career and Technical Education
MSD	Master of Science in Dentistry
	Master of Science in Design
	Master of Science in Dietetics
MSDM	Master of Security and Disaster Management
MSE	Master of Science Education
	Master of Science in Education
	Master of Science in Engineering
	Master of Science in Engineering Management
	Master of Software Engineering
	Master of Special Education
	Master of Structural Engineering
MSECE	Master of Science in Electrical and Computer Engineering
MSED	Master of Sustainable Economic Development
MSEE	Master of Science in Electrical Engineering
	Master of Science in Environmental Engineering
MSEH	Master of Science in Environmental Health
MSEL	Master of Science in Educational Leadership
MSEM	Master of Science in Engineering and Management
	Master of Science in Engineering Management
	Master of Science in Engineering Mechanics
	Master of Science in Environmental Management
MSENE	Master of Science in Environmental Engineering
MSEO	Master of Science in Electro-Optics
MSES	Master of Science in Embedded Software Engineering
	Master of Science in Engineering Science
	Master of Science in Environmental Science
	Master of Science in Environmental Studies
	Master of Science in Exercise Science
MSESE	Master of Science in Energy Systems Engineering
MSET	Master of Science in Educational Technology
	Master of Science in Engineering Technology
MSEV	Master of Science in Environmental Engineering
MSF	Master of Science in Finance
	Master of Science in Forestry
MSFA	Master of Science in Financial Analysis
MSFCS	Master of Science in Family and Consumer Science
MSFE	Master of Science in Financial Engineering
MSFM	Master of Sustainable Forest Management
MSFOR	Master of Science in Forestry
MSFP	Master of Science in Financial Planning
MSFS	Master of Science in Financial Sciences
	Master of Science in Forensic Science
MSFSB	Master of Science in Financial Services and Banking
MSFT	Master of Science in Family Therapy
MSGC	Master of Science in Genetic Counseling
MSH	Master of Science in Health
	Master of Science in Hospice
MSHA	Master of Science in Health Administration
MSHCA	Master of Science in Health Care Administration
MSHCPM	Master of Science in Health Care Policy and Management
MSHE	Master of Science in Health Education
MSHES	Master of Science in Human Environmental Sciences
MSHFID	Master of Science in Human Factors in Information Design
MSHFS	Master of Science in Human Factors and Systems
MSHI	Master of Science in Health Informatics
MSHP	Master of Science in Health Professions
	Master of Science in Health Promotion
MSHR	Master of Science in Human Resources
MSHRL	Master of Science in Human Resource Leadership
MSHRM	Master of Science in Human Resource Management
MSHROD	Master of Science in Human Resources and Organizational Development
MSHS	Master of Science in Health Science
	Master of Science in Health Services
	Master of Science in Homeland Security

MSHSR	Master of Science in Human Security and Resilience
MSI	Master of Science in Information
	Master of Science in Instruction
	Master of System Integration
MSIA	Master of Science in Industrial Administration
	Master of Science in Information Assurance
MSIB	Master of Science in International Business
MSIDM	Master of Science in Interior Design and Merchandising
MSIE	Master of Science in Industrial Engineering
MSIEM	Master of Science in Information Engineering and Management
MSIM	Master of Science in Industrial Management
	Master of Science in Information Management
	Master of Science in International Management
MSIMC	Master of Science in Integrated Marketing Communications
MSIMS	Master of Science in Identity Management and Security
MSIS	Master of Science in Information Science
	Master of Science in Information Studies
	Master of Science in Information Systems
	Master of Science in Interdisciplinary Studies
MSISE	Master of Science in Infrastructure Systems Engineering
MSISM	Master of Science in Information Systems Management
MSISPM	Master of Science in Information Security Policy and Management
MSIST	Master of Science in Information Systems Technology
MSIT	Master of Science in Industrial Technology
	Master of Science in Information Technology
	Master of Science in Instructional Technology
MSITM	Master of Science in Information Technology Management
MSJ	Master of Science in Journalism
	Master of Science in Jurisprudence
MSJC	Master of Social Justice and Criminology
MSJFP	Master of Science in Juvenile Forensic Psychology
MSJJ	Master of Science in Juvenile Justice
MSJPS	Master of Science in Justice and Public Safety
MSK	Master of Science in Kinesiology
MSL	Master in the Study of Law
	Master of School Leadership
	Master of Science in Leadership
	Master of Science in Limnology
	Master of Sports Leadership
	Master of Strategic Leadership
	Master of Studies in Law
MSLA	Master of Science in Legal Administration
MSLB	Master of Sports Law and Business
MSLFS	Master of Science in Life Sciences
MSLP	Master of Speech-Language Pathology
MSLS	Master of Science in Library Science
MSLSCM	Master of Science in Logistics and Supply Chain Management
MSLT	Master of Second Language Teaching
MSM	Master of Sacred Ministry
	Master of Sacred Music
	Master of School Mathematics
	Master of Science in Management
	Master of Science in Medicine
	Master of Science in Organization Management
	Master of Security Management
	Master of Strategic Ministry
	Master of Supply Management
MSMA	Master of Science in Marketing Analysis
MSMAE	Master of Science in Materials Engineering

MSMC	Master of Science in Management and Communications
	Master of Science in Mass Communications
MSME	Master of Science in Mathematics Education
	Master of Science in Mechanical Engineering
	Master of Science in Medical Ethics
MSMHC	Master of Science in Mental Health Counseling
MSMIT	Master of Science in Management and Information Technology
MSMLS	Master of Science in Medical Laboratory Science
MSMOT	Master of Science in Management of Technology
MSMP	Master of Science in Medical Physics
	Master of Science in Molecular Pathology
MSMS	Master of Science in Management Science
	Master of Science in Marine Science
	Master of Science in Medical Sciences
MSMSE	Master of Science in Manufacturing Systems Engineering
	Master of Science in Material Science and Engineering
	Master of Science in Material Science Engineering
	Master of Science in Mathematics and Science Education
MSMus	Master of Sacred Music
MSN	Master of Science in Nursing
MSNA	Master of Science in Nurse Anesthesia
MSNE	Master of Science in Nuclear Engineering
MSNS	Master of Science in Natural Science
	Master of Science in Nutritional Science
MSOD	Master of Science in Organization Development
	Master of Science in Organizational Development
MSOEE	Master of Science in Outdoor and Environmental Education
MSOES	Master of Science in Occupational Ergonomics and Safety
MSOH	Master of Science in Occupational Health
MSOL	Master of Science in Organizational Leadership
MSOM	Master of Science in Oriental Medicine
MSOR	Master of Science in Operations Research
MSOT	Master of Science in Occupational Technology
	Master of Science in Occupational Therapy
MSP	Master of Science in Pharmacy
	Master of Science in Planning
	Master of Speech Pathology
	Master of Sustainable Peacebuilding
MSPA	Master of Science in Physician Assistant
MSPAS	Master of Science in Physician Assistant Studies
MSPC	Master of Science in Professional Communications
MSPE	Master of Science in Petroleum Engineering
MSPH	Master of Science in Public Health
MSPHR	Master of Science in Pharmacy
MSPM	Master of Science in Professional Management
	Master of Science in Project Management
MSPNGE	Master of Science in Petroleum and Natural Gas Engineering
MSPPM	Master of Science in Public Policy and Management
MSPS	Master of Science in Pharmaceutical Science
	Master of Science in Political Science
	Master of Science in Psychological Services
MSPT	Master of Science in Physical Therapy
MSpVM	Master of Specialized Veterinary Medicine
MSRA	Master of Science in Recreation Administration
MSRE	Master of Science in Real Estate
	Master of Science in Religious Education

MSRED	Master of Science in Real Estate Development		Master of Teaching Arts
	Master of Sustainable Real Estate Development		Master of Tourism Administration
MSRLS	Master of Science in Recreation and Leisure Studies	MTC	Master of Technical Communications
		MTCM	Master of Traditional Chinese Medicine
MSRM	Master of Science in Risk Management	MTD	Master of Training and Development
MSRMP	Master of Science in Radiological Medical Physics	MTE	Master in Educational Technology
			Master of Technological Entrepreneurship
MSRS	Master of Science in Radiological Sciences	MTESOL	Master in Teaching English to Speakers of Other Languages
	Master of Science in Rehabilitation Science		
MSS	Master of Security Studies	MTHM	Master of Tourism and Hospitality Management
	Master of Social Science	MTI	Master of Information Technology
	Master of Social Services	MTID	Master of Tangible Interaction Design
	Master of Sports Science	MTL	Master of Talmudic Law
	Master of Strategic Studies	MTM	Master of Technology Management
	Master's in Statistical Science		Master of Telecommunications Management
MSSA	Master of Science in Social Administration		Master of the Teaching of Mathematics
MSSCM	Master of Science in Supply Chain Management		Master of Transformative Ministry
MSSD	Master of Arts in Software Driven Systems Design		Master of Translational Medicine
		MTMH	Master of Tropical Medicine and Hygiene
	Master of Science in Sustainable Design	MTMS	Master in Teaching Mathematics and Science
MSSE	Master of Science in Software Engineering	MTOM	Master of Traditional Oriental Medicine
	Master of Science in Special Education	MTPC	Master of Technical and Professional Communication
MSSEM	Master of Science in Systems and Engineering Management		
		MTR	Master of Translational Research
MSSI	Master of Science in Security Informatics	MTS	Master of Theatre Studies
	Master of Science in Strategic Intelligence		Master of Theological Studies
MSSIS	Master of Science in Security and Intelligence Studies	MTW	Master of Teaching Writing
		MTWM	Master of Trust and Wealth Management
MSSL	Master of Science in School Leadership	MUA	Master of Urban Affairs
MSSLP	Master of Science in Speech-Language Pathology	MUAP	Master's of Urban Affairs and Policy
		MUCD	Master of Urban and Community Design
MSSM	Master of Science in Sports Medicine	MUD	Master of Urban Design
	Master of Science in Systems Management	MUDS	Master of Urban Design Studies
MSSP	Master of Science in Social Policy	MUEP	Master of Urban and Environmental Planning
MSSS	Master of Science in Safety Science	MUP	Master of Urban Planning
	Master of Science in Systems Science	MUPD	Master of Urban Planning and Development
MSST	Master of Science in Security Technologies	MUPP	Master of Urban Planning and Policy
MSSW	Master of Science in Social Work	MUPRED	Master of Urban Planning and Real Estate Development
MSSWE	Master of Science in Software Engineering		
MST	Master of Science and Technology	MURP	Master of Urban and Regional Planning
	Master of Science in Taxation		Master of Urban and Rural Planning
	Master of Science in Teaching	MURPL	Master of Urban and Regional Planning
	Master of Science in Technology	MUS	Master of Urban Studies
	Master of Science in Telecommunications	Mus M	Master of Music
	Master of Science Teaching	MUSA	Master of Urban Spatial Analytics
MSTC	Master of Science in Technical Communication	MVP	Master of Voice Pedagogy
	Master of Science in Telecommunications	MVPH	Master of Veterinary Public Health
MSTCM	Master of Science in Traditional Chinese Medicine	MVS	Master of Visual Studies
		MWBS	Master of Won Buddhist Studies
MSTE	Master of Science in Telecommunications Engineering	MWC	Master of Wildlife Conservation
		MWPS	Master of Wood and Paper Science
	Master of Science in Transportation Engineering	MWR	Master of Water Resources
		MWS	Master of Women's Studies
MSTL	Master of Science in Teacher Leadership		Master of Worship Studies
MSTM	Master of Science in Technology Management	MWSc	Master of Wildlife Science
	Master of Science in Transfusion Medicine	MZS	Master of Zoological Science
MSTOM	Master of Science in Traditional Oriental Medicine	Nav Arch	Naval Architecture
		Naval E	Naval Engineer
MSUASE	Master of Science in Unmanned and Autonomous Systems Engineering	ND	Doctor of Naturopathic Medicine
			Doctor of Nursing
MSUD	Master of Science in Urban Design	NE	Nuclear Engineer
MSUS	Master of Science in Urban Studies	Nuc E	Nuclear Engineer
MSW	Master of Social Work	OD	Doctor of Optometry
MSWE	Master of Software Engineering		Doctor of Occupational Therapy
MSWREE	Master of Science in Water Resources and Environmental Engineering	OTD	Doctor of Occupational Therapy
		PBME	Professional Master of Biomedical Engineering
MT	Master of Taxation	PC	Performer's Certificate
	Master of Teaching	PD	Professional Diploma
	Master of Technology	PGC	Post-Graduate Certificate
	Master of Textiles	PGD	Postgraduate Diploma
MTA	Master of Tax Accounting		

Ph L	Licentiate of Philosophy
Pharm D	Doctor of Pharmacy
PhD	Doctor of Philosophy
PhD Otol	Doctor of Philosophy in Otolaryngology
PhD Surg	Doctor of Philosophy in Surgery
PhDEE	Doctor of Philosophy in Electrical Engineering
PMBA	Professional Master of Business Administration
PMC	Post Master Certificate
PMD	Post-Master's Diploma
PMS	Professional Master of Science
	Professional Master's
Post-Doctoral MS	Post-Doctoral Master of Science
Post-MSN Certificate	Post-Master of Science in Nursing Certificate
PPDPT	Postprofessional Doctor of Physical Therapy
Pro-MS	Professional Science Master's
Professional MA	Professional Master of Arts
Professional MBA	Professional Master of Business Administration
Professional MS	Professional Master of Science
PSM	Professional Master of Science
	Professional Science Master's
Psy D	Doctor of Psychology
Psy M	Master of Psychology
Psy S	Specialist in Psychology
Psya D	Doctor of Psychoanalysis
S Psy S	Specialist in Psychological Services
Sc D	Doctor of Science
Sc M	Master of Science
SCCT	Specialist in Community College Teaching
ScDPT	Doctor of Physical Therapy Science

SD	Specialist Degree
SJD	Doctor of Juridical Sciences
SLPD	Doctor of Speech-Language Pathology
SM	Master of Science
SM Arch S	Master of Science in Architectural Studies
SMACT	Master of Science in Art, Culture and Technology
SMBT	Master of Science in Building Technology
SP	Specialist Degree
Sp Ed	Specialist in Education
Sp LIS	Specialist in Library and Information Science
SPA	Specialist in Arts
Spec	Specialist's Certificate
Spec M	Specialist in Music
Spt	Specialist Degree
SSP	Specialist in School Psychology
STB	Bachelor of Sacred Theology
STD	Doctor of Sacred Theology
STL	Licentiate of Sacred Theology
STM	Master of Sacred Theology
tDACM	Transitional Doctor of Acupuncture and Chinese Medicine
TDPT	Transitional Doctor of Physical Therapy
Th D	Doctor of Theology
Th M	Master of Theology
TOTD	Transitional Doctor of Occupational Therapy
VMD	Doctor of Veterinary Medicine
WEMBA	Weekend Executive Master of Business Administration
XMA	Executive Master of Arts

INDEXES

Displays and Close-Ups

Directories and Subject Areas

Following is an alphabetical listing of directories and subject areas. Also listed are cross-references for subject area names not used in the directory structure of the guides, for example, "City and Regional Planning (see Urban and Regional Planning)"

Graduate Programs in the Humanities, Arts & Social Sciences

Addictions/Substance Abuse Counseling
Administration (see Arts Administration; Public Administration)
African-American Studies
African Languages and Literatures (see African Studies)
African Studies
Agribusiness (see Agricultural Economics and Agribusiness)
Agricultural Economics and Agribusiness
Alcohol Abuse Counseling (see Addictions/Substance Abuse Counseling)
American Indian/Native American Studies
American Studies
Anthropology
Applied Arts and Design—General
Applied Behavior Analysis
Applied Economics
Applied History (see Public History)
Applied Psychology
Applied Social Research
Arabic (see Near and Middle Eastern Languages)
Arab Studies (see Near and Middle Eastern Studies)
Archaeology
Architectural History
Architecture
Archives Administration (see Public History)
Area and Cultural Studies (see African-American Studies; African Studies; American Indian/Native American Studies; American Studies; Asian-American Studies; Asian Studies; Canadian Studies; Cultural Studies; East European and Russian Studies; Ethnic Studies; Folklore; Gender Studies; Hispanic Studies; Holocaust Studies; Jewish Studies; Latin American Studies; Near and Middle Eastern Studies; Northern Studies; Pacific Area/Pacific Rim Studies; Western European Studies; Women's Studies)
Art/Fine Arts
Art History
Arts Administration
Arts Journalism
Art Therapy
Asian-American Studies
Asian Languages
Asian Studies
Behavioral Sciences (see Psychology)
Bible Studies (see Religion; Theology)
Biological Anthropology
Black Studies (see African-American Studies)
Broadcasting (see Communication; Film, Television, and Video Production)
Broadcast Journalism
Building Science
Canadian Studies
Celtic Languages
Ceramics (see Art/Fine Arts)
Child and Family Studies
Child Development
Chinese
Chinese Studies (see Asian Languages; Asian Studies)
Christian Studies (see Missions and Missiology; Religion; Theology)
Cinema (see Film, Television, and Video Production)
City and Regional Planning (see Urban and Regional Planning)
Classical Languages and Literatures (see Classics)

Classics
Clinical Psychology
Clothing and Textiles
Cognitive Psychology (see Psychology—General; Cognitive Sciences)
Cognitive Sciences
Communication—General
Community Affairs (see Urban and Regional Planning; Urban Studies)
Community Planning (see Architecture; Environmental Design; Urban and Regional Planning; Urban Design; Urban Studies)
Community Psychology (see Social Psychology)
Comparative and Interdisciplinary Arts
Comparative Literature
Composition (see Music)
Computer Art and Design
Conflict Resolution and Mediation/Peace Studies
Consumer Economics
Corporate and Organizational Communication
Corrections (see Criminal Justice and Criminology)
Counseling (see Counseling Psychology; Pastoral Ministry and Counseling)
Counseling Psychology
Crafts (see Art/Fine Arts)
Creative Arts Therapies (see Art Therapy; Therapies—Dance, Drama, and Music)
Criminal Justice and Criminology
Cultural Anthropology
Cultural Studies
Dance
Decorative Arts
Demography and Population Studies
Design (see Applied Arts and Design; Architecture; Art/Fine Arts; Environmental Design; Graphic Design; Industrial Design; Interior Design; Textile Design; Urban Design)
Developmental Psychology
Diplomacy (see International Affairs)
Disability Studies
Drama Therapy (see Therapies—Dance, Drama, and Music)
Dramatic Arts (see Theater)
Drawing (see Art/Fine Arts)
Drug Abuse Counseling (see Addictions/Substance Abuse Counseling)
Drug and Alcohol Abuse Counseling (see Addictions/Substance Abuse Counseling)
East Asian Studies (see Asian Studies)
East European and Russian Studies
Economic Development
Economics
Educational Theater (see Theater; Therapies—Dance, Drama, and Music)
Emergency Management
English
Environmental Design
Ethics
Ethnic Studies
Ethnomusicology (see Music)
Experimental Psychology
Family and Consumer Sciences—General
Family Studies (see Child and Family Studies)
Family Therapy (see Child and Family Studies; Clinical Psychology; Counseling Psychology; Marriage and Family Therapy)
Filmmaking (see Film, Television, and Video Production)
Film Studies (see Film, Television, and Video Production)
Film, Television, and Video Production
Film, Television, and Video Theory and Criticism
Fine Arts (see Art/Fine Arts)
Folklore
Foreign Languages (see specific language)
Foreign Service (see International Affairs; International Development)
Forensic Psychology
Forensic Sciences
Forensics (see Speech and Interpersonal Communication)

French
Gender Studies
General Studies (*see* Liberal Studies)
Genetic Counseling
Geographic Information Systems
Geography
German
Gerontology
Graphic Design
Greek (*see* Classics)
Health Communication
Health Psychology
Hebrew (*see* Near and Middle Eastern Languages)
Hebrew Studies (*see* Jewish Studies)
Hispanic and Latin American Languages
Hispanic Studies
Historic Preservation
History
History of Art (*see* Art History)
History of Medicine
History of Science and Technology
Holocaust and Genocide Studies
Home Economics (*see* Family and Consumer Sciences—General)
Homeland Security
Household Economics, Sciences, and Management (*see* Family and Consumer Sciences—General)
Human Development
Humanities
Illustration
Industrial and Labor Relations
Industrial and Organizational Psychology
Industrial Design
Interdisciplinary Studies
Interior Design
International Affairs
International Development
International Economics
International Service (*see* International Affairs; International Development)
International Trade Policy
Internet and Interactive Multimedia
Interpersonal Communication (*see* Speech and Interpersonal Communication)
Interpretation (*see* Translation and Interpretation)
Islamic Studies (*see* Near and Middle Eastern Studies; Religion)
Italian
Japanese
Japanese Studies (*see* Asian Languages; Asian Studies; Japanese)
Jewelry (*see* Art/Fine Arts)
Jewish Studies
Journalism
Judaic Studies (*see* Jewish Studies; Religion)
Labor Relations (*see* Industrial and Labor Relations)
Landscape Architecture
Latin American Studies
Latin (*see* Classics)
Law Enforcement (*see* Criminal Justice and Criminology)
Liberal Studies
Lighting Design
Linguistics
Literature (*see* Classics; Comparative Literature; specific language)
Marriage and Family Therapy
Mass Communication
Media Studies
Medical Illustration
Medieval and Renaissance Studies
Metalsmithing (*see* Art/Fine Arts)
Middle Eastern Studies (*see* Near and Middle Eastern Studies)
Military and Defense Studies
Mineral Economics
Ministry (*see* Pastoral Ministry and Counseling; Theology)
Missions and Missiology
Motion Pictures (*see* Film, Television, and Video Production)
Museum Studies
Music
Musicology (*see* Music)

Music Therapy (*see* Therapies—Dance, Drama, and Music)
National Security
Native American Studies (*see* American Indian/Native American Studies)
Near and Middle Eastern Languages
Near and Middle Eastern Studies
Northern Studies
Organizational Psychology (*see* Industrial and Organizational Psychology)
Oriental Languages (*see* Asian Languages)
Oriental Studies (*see* Asian Studies)
Pacific Area/Pacific Rim Studies
Painting (*see* Art/Fine Arts)
Pastoral Ministry and Counseling
Philanthropic Studies
Philosophy
Photography
Playwriting (*see* Theater; Writing)
Policy Studies (*see* Public Policy)
Political Science
Population Studies (*see* Demography and Population Studies)
Portuguese
Printmaking (*see* Art/Fine Arts)
Product Design (*see* Industrial Design)
Psychoanalysis and Psychotherapy
Psychology—General
Public Administration
Public Affairs
Public History
Public Policy
Public Speaking (*see* Mass Communication; Rhetoric; Speech and Interpersonal Communication)
Publishing
Regional Planning (*see* Architecture; Urban and Regional Planning; Urban Design; Urban Studies)
Rehabilitation Counseling
Religion
Renaissance Studies (*see* Medieval and Renaissance Studies)
Rhetoric
Romance Languages
Romance Literatures (*see* Romance Languages)
Rural Planning and Studies
Rural Sociology
Russian
Scandinavian Languages
School Psychology
Sculpture (*see* Art/Fine Arts)
Security Administration (*see* Criminal Justice and Criminology)
Slavic Languages
Slavic Studies (*see* East European and Russian Studies; Slavic Languages)
Social Psychology
Social Sciences
Sociology
Southeast Asian Studies (*see* Asian Studies)
Soviet Studies (*see* East European and Russian Studies; Russian)
Spanish
Speech and Interpersonal Communication
Sport Psychology
Studio Art (*see* Art/Fine Arts)
Substance Abuse Counseling (*see* Addictions/Substance Abuse Counseling)
Survey Methodology
Sustainable Development
Technical Communication
Technical Writing
Telecommunications (*see* Film, Television, and Video Production)
Television (*see* Film, Television, and Video Production)
Textile Design
Textiles (*see* Clothing and Textiles; Textile Design)
Thanatology
Theater
Theater Arts (*see* Theater)
Theology
Therapies—Dance, Drama, and Music
Translation and Interpretation

Transpersonal and Humanistic Psychology
Urban and Regional Planning
Urban Design
Urban Planning (*see* Architecture; Urban and Regional Planning; Urban Design; Urban Studies)
Urban Studies
Video (*see* Film, Television, and Video Production)
Visual Arts (*see* Applied Arts and Design; Art/Fine Arts; Film, Television, and Video Production; Graphic Design; Illustration; Photography)
Western European Studies
Women's Studies
World Wide Web (*see* Internet and Interactive Multimedia)
Writing

Graduate Programs in the Biological/ Biomedical Sciences & Health-Related Medical Professions

Acupuncture and Oriental Medicine
Acute Care/Critical Care Nursing Administration (*see* Health Services Management and Hospital Administration; Nursing and Healthcare Administration; Pharmaceutical Administration)
Adult Nursing
Advanced Practice Nursing (*see* Family Nurse Practitioner Studies)
Allied Health—General
Allied Health Professions (*see* Clinical Laboratory Sciences/Medical Technology; Clinical Research; Communication Disorders; Dental Hygiene; Emergency Medical Services; Occupational Therapy; Physical Therapy; Physician Assistant Studies; Rehabilitation Sciences)
Allopathic Medicine
Anatomy
Anesthesiologist Assistant Studies
Animal Behavior
Bacteriology
Behavioral Sciences (*see* Biopsychology; Neuroscience; Zoology)
Biochemistry
Bioethics
Biological and Biomedical Sciences—General Biological Chemistry (*see* Biochemistry)
Biological Oceanography (*see* Marine Biology)
Biophysics
Biopsychology
Botany
Breeding (*see* Botany; Plant Biology; Genetics)
Cancer Biology/Oncology
Cardiovascular Sciences
Cell Biology
Cellular Physiology (*see* Cell Biology; Physiology)
Child-Care Nursing (*see* Maternal and Child/Neonatal Nursing)
Chiropractic
Clinical Laboratory Sciences/Medical Technology
Clinical Research
Community Health
Community Health Nursing
Computational Biology
Conservation (*see* Conservation Biology; Environmental Biology)
Conservation Biology
Crop Sciences (*see* Botany; Plant Biology)
Cytology (*see* Cell Biology)
Dental and Oral Surgery (*see* Oral and Dental Sciences)
Dental Assistant Studies (*see* Dental Hygiene)
Dental Hygiene
Dental Services (*see* Dental Hygiene)
Dentistry
Developmental Biology Dietetics (*see* Nutrition)
Ecology
Embryology (*see* Developmental Biology)
Emergency Medical Services
Endocrinology (*see* Physiology)
Entomology

Environmental Biology
Environmental and Occupational Health
Epidemiology
Evolutionary Biology
Family Nurse Practitioner Studies
Foods (*see* Nutrition)
Forensic Nursing
Genetics
Genomic Sciences
Gerontological Nursing
Health Physics/Radiological Health
Health Promotion
Health-Related Professions (*see* individual allied health professions)
Health Services Management and Hospital Administration
Health Services Research
Histology (*see* Anatomy; Cell Biology)
HIV/AIDS Nursing
Hospice Nursing
Hospital Administration (*see* Health Services Management and Hospital Administration)
Human Genetics
Immunology
Industrial Hygiene
Infectious Diseases
International Health
Laboratory Medicine (*see* Clinical Laboratory Sciences/Medical Technology; Immunology; Microbiology; Pathology)
Life Sciences (*see* Biological and Biomedical Sciences)
Marine Biology
Maternal and Child Health
Maternal and Child/Neonatal Nursing
Medical Imaging
Medical Microbiology
Medical Nursing (*see* Medical/Surgical Nursing)
Medical Physics
Medical/Surgical Nursing
Medical Technology (*see* Clinical Laboratory Sciences/Medical Technology)
Medical Sciences (*see* Biological and Biomedical Sciences)
Medical Science Training Programs (*see* Biological and Biomedical Sciences)
Medicinal and Pharmaceutical Chemistry
Medicinal Chemistry (*see* Medicinal and Pharmaceutical Chemistry)
Medicine (*see* Allopathic Medicine; Naturopathic Medicine; Osteopathic Medicine; Podiatric Medicine)
Microbiology
Midwifery (*see* Nurse Midwifery)
Molecular Biology
Molecular Biophysics
Molecular Genetics
Molecular Medicine
Molecular Pathogenesis
Molecular Pathology
Molecular Pharmacology
Molecular Physiology
Molecular Toxicology
Naturopathic Medicine
Neural Sciences (*see* Biopsychology; Neurobiology; Neuroscience)
Neurobiology
Neuroendocrinology (*see* Biopsychology; Neurobiology; Neuroscience; Physiology)
Neuropharmacology (*see* Biopsychology; Neurobiology; Neuroscience; Pharmacology)
Neurophysiology (*see* Biopsychology; Neurobiology; Neuroscience; Physiology)
Neuroscience
Nuclear Medical Technology (*see* Clinical Laboratory Sciences/Medical Technology)
Nurse Anesthesia
Nurse Midwifery
Nurse Practitioner Studies (*see* Family Nurse Practitioner Studies)
Nursing Administration (*see* Nursing and Healthcare Administration)
Nursing and Healthcare Administration
Nursing Education
Nursing—General
Nursing Informatics

Nutrition
Occupational Health (*see* Environmental and Occupational Health; Occupational Health Nursing)
Occupational Health Nursing
Occupational Therapy
Oncology (*see* Cancer Biology/Oncology)
Oncology Nursing
Optometry
Oral and Dental Sciences
Oral Biology (*see* Oral and Dental Sciences)
Oral Pathology (*see* Oral and Dental Sciences)
Organismal Biology (*see* Biological and Biomedical Sciences; Zoology)
Oriental Medicine and Acupuncture (*see* Acupuncture and Oriental Medicine)
Orthodontics (*see* Oral and Dental Sciences)
Osteopathic Medicine
Parasitology
Pathobiology
Pathology
Pediatric Nursing
Pedontics (*see* Oral and Dental Sciences)
Perfusion
Pharmaceutical Administration
Pharmaceutical Chemistry (*see* Medicinal and Pharmaceutical Chemistry)
Pharmaceutical Sciences
Pharmacology
Pharmacy
Photobiology of Cells and Organelles (*see* Botany; Cell Biology; Plant Biology)
Physical Therapy
Physician Assistant Studies
Physiological Optics (*see* Vision Sciences)
Podiatric Medicine
Preventive Medicine (*see* Community Health and Public Health)
Physiological Optics (*see* Physiology)
Physiology
Plant Biology
Plant Molecular Biology
Plant Pathology
Plant Physiology
Pomology (*see* Botany; Plant Biology)
Psychiatric Nursing
Public Health—General
Public Health Nursing (*see* Community Health Nursing)
Psychiatric Nursing
Psychobiology (*see* Biopsychology)
Psychopharmacology (*see* Biopsychology; Neuroscience; Pharmacology)
Radiation Biology
Radiological Health (*see* Health Physics/Radiological Health)
Rehabilitation Nursing
Rehabilitation Sciences
Rehabilitation Therapy (*see* Physical Therapy)
Reproductive Biology
School Nursing
Sociobiology (*see* Evolutionary Biology)
Structural Biology
Surgical Nursing (*see* Medical/Surgical Nursing)
Systems Biology
Teratology
Therapeutics
Theoretical Biology (*see* Biological and Biomedical Sciences)
Therapeutics (*see* Pharmaceutical Sciences; Pharmacology; Pharmacy)
Toxicology
Transcultural Nursing
Translational Biology
Tropical Medicine (*see* Parasitology)
Veterinary Medicine
Veterinary Sciences
Virology
Vision Sciences
Wildlife Biology (*see* Zoology)
Women's Health Nursing
Zoology

Graduate Programs in the Physical Sciences, Mathematics, Agricultural Sciences, the Environment & Natural Resources

Acoustics
Agricultural Sciences
Agronomy and Soil Sciences
Analytical Chemistry
Animal Sciences
Applied Mathematics
Applied Physics
Applied Statistics
Aquaculture
Astronomy
Astrophysical Sciences (*see* Astrophysics; Atmospheric Sciences; Meteorology; Planetary and Space Sciences)
Astrophysics
Atmospheric Sciences
Biological Oceanography (*see* Marine Affairs; Marine Sciences; Oceanography)
Biomathematics
Biometry
Biostatistics
Chemical Physics
Chemistry
Computational Sciences
Condensed Matter Physics
Dairy Science (*see* Animal Sciences)
Earth Sciences (*see* Geosciences)
Environmental Management and Policy
Environmental Sciences
Environmental Studies (*see* Environmental Management and Policy)
Experimental Statistics (*see* Statistics)
Fish, Game, and Wildlife Management
Food Science and Technology
Forestry
General Science (*see* specific topics)
Geochemistry
Geodetic Sciences
Geological Engineering (*see* Geology)
Geological Sciences (*see* Geology)
Geology
Geophysical Fluid Dynamics (*see* Geophysics)
Geophysics
Geosciences
Horticulture
Hydrogeology
Hydrology
Inorganic Chemistry
Limnology
Marine Affairs
Marine Geology
Marine Sciences
Marine Studies (*see* Marine Affairs; Marine Geology; Marine Sciences; Oceanography)
Mathematical and Computational Finance
Mathematical Physics
Mathematical Statistics (*see* Applied Statistics; Statistics)
Mathematics
Meteorology
Mineralogy
Natural Resource Management (*see* Environmental Management and Policy; Natural Resources)
Natural Resources
Nuclear Physics (*see* Physics)
Ocean Engineering (*see* Marine Affairs; Marine Geology; Marine Sciences; Oceanography)
Oceanography
Optical Sciences
Optical Technologies (*see* Optical Sciences)
Optics (*see* Applied Physics; Optical Sciences; Physics)
Organic Chemistry

Paleontology
Paper Chemistry (*see* Chemistry)
Photonics
Physical Chemistry
Physics
Planetary and Space Sciences
Plant Sciences
Plasma Physics
Poultry Science (*see* Animal Sciences)
Radiological Physics (*see* Physics)
Range Management (*see* Range Science)
Range Science
Resource Management (*see* Environmental Management and Policy; Natural Resources)
Solid-Earth Sciences (*see* Geosciences)
Space Sciences (*see* Planetary and Space Sciences)
Statistics
Theoretical Chemistry
Theoretical Physics
Viticulture and Enology
Water Resources

Graduate Programs in Engineering & Applied Sciences

Aeronautical Engineering (*see* Aerospace/Aeronautical Engineering)
Aerospace/Aeronautical Engineering
Aerospace Studies (*see* Aerospace/Aeronautical Engineering)
Agricultural Engineering
Applied Mechanics (*see* Mechanics)
Applied Science and Technology
Architectural Engineering
Artificial Intelligence/Robotics
Astronautical Engineering (*see* Aerospace/Aeronautical Engineering)
Automotive Engineering
Aviation
Biochemical Engineering
Bioengineering
Bioinformatics
Biological Engineering (*see* Bioengineering)
Biomedical Engineering
Biosystems Engineering
Biotechnology
Ceramic Engineering (*see* Ceramic Sciences and Engineering)
Ceramic Sciences and Engineering
Ceramics (*see* Ceramic Sciences and Engineering)
Chemical Engineering
Civil Engineering
Computer and Information Systems Security
Computer Engineering
Computer Science
Computing Technology (*see* Computer Science)
Construction Engineering
Construction Management
Database Systems
Electrical Engineering
Electronic Materials
Electronics Engineering (*see* Electrical Engineering)
Energy and Power Engineering
Energy Management and Policy
Engineering and Applied Sciences
Engineering and Public Affairs (*see* Technology and Public Policy)
Engineering and Public Policy (*see* Energy Management and Policy; Technology and Public Policy)
Engineering Design
Engineering Management
Engineering Mechanics (*see* Mechanics)
Engineering Metallurgy (*see* Metallurgical Engineering and Metallurgy)
Engineering Physics
Environmental Design (*see* Environmental Engineering)
Environmental Engineering
Ergonomics and Human Factors
Financial Engineering

Fire Protection Engineering
Food Engineering (*see* Agricultural Engineering)
Game Design and Development
Gas Engineering (*see* Petroleum Engineering)
Geological Engineering
Geophysics Engineering (*see* Geological Engineering)
Geotechnical Engineering
Hazardous Materials Management
Health Informatics
Health Systems (*see* Safety Engineering; Systems Engineering)
Highway Engineering (*see* Transportation and Highway Engineering)
Human-Computer Interaction
Human Factors (*see* Ergonomics and Human Factors)
Hydraulics
Hydrology (*see* Water Resources Engineering)
Industrial Engineering (*see* Industrial/Management Engineering)
Industrial/Management Engineering
Information Science
Internet Engineering
Macromolecular Science (*see* Polymer Science and Engineering)
Management Engineering (*see* Engineering Management; Industrial/Management Engineering)
Management of Technology
Manufacturing Engineering
Marine Engineering (*see* Civil Engineering)
Materials Engineering
Materials Sciences
Mechanical Engineering
Mechanics
Medical Informatics
Metallurgical Engineering and Metallurgy
Metallurgy (*see* Metallurgical Engineering and Metallurgy)
Mineral/Mining Engineering
Modeling and Simulation
Nanotechnology
Nuclear Engineering
Ocean Engineering
Operations Research
Paper and Pulp Engineering
Petroleum Engineering
Pharmaceutical Engineering
Plastics Engineering (*see* Polymer Science and Engineering)
Polymer Science and Engineering
Public Policy (*see* Energy Management and Policy; Technology and Public Policy)
Reliability Engineering
Robotics (*see* Artificial Intelligence/Robotics)
Safety Engineering
Software Engineering
Solid-State Sciences (*see* Materials Sciences)
Structural Engineering
Surveying Science and Engineering
Systems Analysis (*see* Systems Engineering)
Systems Engineering
Systems Science
Technology and Public Policy
Telecommunications
Telecommunications Management
Textile Sciences and Engineering
Textiles (*see* Textile Sciences and Engineering)
Transportation and Highway Engineering
Urban Systems Engineering (*see* Systems Engineering)
Waste Management (*see* Hazardous Materials Management)
Water Resources Engineering

Graduate Programs in Business, Education, Information Studies, Law & Social Work

Accounting
Actuarial Science
Adult Education
Advertising and Public Relations
Agricultural Education
Alcohol Abuse Counseling (*see* Counselor Education)
Archival Management and Studies
Art Education
Athletics Administration (*see* Kinesiology and Movement Studies)
Athletic Training and Sports Medicine
Audiology (*see* Communication Disorders)
Aviation Management
Banking (*see* Finance and Banking)
Business Administration and Management—General
Business Education
Communication Disorders
Community College Education
Computer Education
Continuing Education (*see* Adult Education)
Counseling (*see* Counselor Education)
Counselor Education
Curriculum and Instruction
Developmental Education
Distance Education Development
Drug Abuse Counseling (*see* Counselor Education)
Early Childhood Education
Educational Leadership and Administration
Educational Measurement and Evaluation
Educational Media/Instructional Technology
Educational Policy
Educational Psychology
Education—General
Education of the Blind (*see* Special Education)
Education of the Deaf (*see* Special Education)
Education of the Gifted
Education of the Hearing Impaired (*see* Special Education)
Education of the Learning Disabled (*see* Special Education)
Education of the Mentally Retarded (*see* Special Education)
Education of the Physically Handicapped (*see* Special Education)
Education of Students with Severe/Multiple Disabilities
Education of the Visually Handicapped (*see* Special Education)
Electronic Commerce
Elementary Education
English as a Second Language
English Education
Entertainment Management
Entrepreneurship
Environmental Education
Environmental Law
Exercise and Sports Science
Exercise Physiology (*see* Kinesiology and Movement Studies)
Facilities and Entertainment Management
Finance and Banking
Food Services Management (*see* Hospitality Management)
Foreign Languages Education
Foundations and Philosophy of Education
Guidance and Counseling (*see* Counselor Education)
Health Education
Health Law
Hearing Sciences (*see* Communication Disorders)
Higher Education
Home Economics Education
Hospitality Management
Hotel Management (*see* Travel and Tourism)
Human Resources Development
Human Resources Management
Human Services
Industrial Administration (*see* Industrial and Manufacturing Management)
Industrial and Manufacturing Management

Industrial Education (*see* Vocational and Technical Education)
Information Studies
Instructional Technology (*see* Educational Media/Instructional Technology)
Insurance
Intellectual Property Law
International and Comparative Education
International Business
International Commerce (*see* International Business)
International Economics (*see* International Business)
International Trade (*see* International Business)
Investment and Securities (*see* Business Administration and Management; Finance and Banking; Investment Management)
Investment Management
Junior College Education (*see* Community College Education)
Kinesiology and Movement Studies
Law
Legal and Justice Studies
Leisure Services (*see* Recreation and Park Management)
Leisure Studies
Library Science
Logistics
Management (*see* Business Administration and Management)
Management Information Systems
Management Strategy and Policy
Marketing
Marketing Research
Mathematics Education
Middle School Education
Movement Studies (*see* Kinesiology and Movement Studies)
Multilingual and Multicultural Education
Museum Education
Music Education
Nonprofit Management
Nursery School Education (*see* Early Childhood Education)
Occupational Education (*see* Vocational and Technical Education)
Organizational Behavior
Organizational Management
Parks Administration (*see* Recreation and Park Management)
Personnel (*see* Human Resources Development; Human Resources Management; Organizational Behavior; Organizational Management; Student Affairs)
Philosophy of Education (*see* Foundations and Philosophy of Education)
Physical Education
Project Management
Public Relations (*see* Advertising and Public Relations)
Quality Management
Quantitative Analysis
Reading Education
Real Estate
Recreation and Park Management
Recreation Therapy (*see* Recreation and Park Management)
Religious Education
Remedial Education (*see* Special Education)
Restaurant Administration (*see* Hospitality Management)
Science Education
Secondary Education
Social Sciences Education
Social Studies Education (*see* Social Sciences Education)
Social Work
Special Education
Speech-Language Pathology and Audiology (*see* Communication Disorders)
Sports Management
Sports Medicine (*see* Athletic Training and Sports Medicine)
Sports Psychology and Sociology (*see* Kinesiology and Movement Studies)
Student Affairs
Substance Abuse Counseling (*see* Counselor Education)
Supply Chain Management
Sustainability Management
Systems Management (*see* Management Information Systems)
Taxation
Teacher Education (*see* specific subject areas)

Teaching English as a Second Language (*see* English as a Second Language)
Technical Education (*see* Vocational and Technical Education)
Transportation Management
Travel and Tourism
Urban Education
Vocational and Technical Education
Vocational Counseling (*see* Counselor Education)

Directories and Subject Areas in This Book

NOTES

NOTES

NOTES

NOTES

JAN - - 2019